Make Sure Your VOICE IS HEARD!

Bring your product, service, or message to the attention of the **17,000** lawyers, lobbyists, foreign agents, and government affairs representatives listed in this directory.

ORDER A Washington Representatives MAILING LIST

SAMPLE LABEL

Officer's Name *Correct Title*

Samuel Craig
President
CB Representatives
1825 Connecticut Ave., N.W.
Washington, DC 20009

Business/Organization

Complete Mailing Address

We have the **MOST COMPLETE AND ACCURATE LISTS AVAILABLE** of the firms and individuals who make up Washington's advocacy community and the associations, businesses, governments, and special interests they represent. Because our lists are derived from information in this directory, our staff is correcting and updating them *all through the year!*

Order our complete lists —

OR

Request customized lists.

Contact information, including name, title, organization and address is available on your choice of diskette or pressure sensitive labels.

SEE REVERSE FOR ORDERING INSTRUCTIONS.

Washington Representatives Directory

MAIL LIST ORDER FORM

CHOOSE FROM:

- [ ] **INDIVIDUALS** — Includes both in-house and contract lobbyists and government relations personnel (Approximate Count: 17,000)
- [ ] **ORGANIZATIONS REPRESENTED** — Includes the organizations with DC offices who retain federal government representation here in the nation's capital. (Approximate Count: 3,400)
- [ ] **FIRMS** — Includes the DC law and lobbying firms who have been hired to represent the interests of their clients before the federal government. (Approximate Count: 1,500)
- [ ] **FEDERAL GOVERNMENT LEGISLATIVE AFFAIRS PERSONNEL** — Includes the individuals doing legislative and congressional affairs work for each of the Executive Branch departments and regulatory agencies. (Approximate Count: 500)
- [ ] **CUSTOMIZED LISTS** — Sort by issue area or industry — call (202) 464-1662 ext. 22 for details.

____

____

____

____

PRICES:

$100 per thousand ($200 minimum). Charges for selects apply.
Multiple use license also available ($200/thousand, $300 minimum).

ADDITIONAL OPTIONS:

- [ ] **PHONE/FAX** — $100/thousand
- [ ] **EMAIL/WEB** — $100/thousand

For industry/issue area breakdowns and exact counts call Columbia Books at (202) 464-1662, ext. 22

LIST FORMAT (Check One)

- [ ] Pressure Sensitive Labels (add $10/M)
- [ ] 3 1/2" Diskette (add $10 disk fee)

NOTE: Check, money order, or credit card information MUST accompany initial orders.

SEND TO: Columbia Books, Inc.,
1825 Connecticut Ave, NW, Suite 625
Washington, DC 20009
PHONE: (202) 464-1662, ext 22
FAX: (202) 464-1775
E-MAIL: info@columbiabooks.com

NAME: ______________________________

TITLE: ______________________________

ORGANIZATION: ______________________________

ADDRESS: ______________________________

CITY/STATE/ZIP CODE: ______________________________

TELEPHONE (required): ______________________________

FAX: ______________________________

- [ ] **Check enclosed**
- [ ] **Charge to credit card #**

[ ] Visa [ ] M/C [ ] AMEX **Exp. Date:** ____________

SIGNATURE (required): ______________________________

DATE: ______________________________

Washington Representatives 2001

A compilation of Washington representatives of the major national associations, labor unions, and U. S. companies; registered foreign agents; lobbyists; lawyers; law firms; and special interest groups, together with their clients and areas of legislative and regulatory concern.

Columbia Books, Inc.
Publishers
Washington, DC

Senior Editor: Valerie S. Sheridan
Associate Editors: Mark D. Francis
Natacha Leonard
Assistant Editor: Diane R. Murphy
Editorial Assistant: Jonathan A. Cook

Twenty-fifth Annual Edition – 2001

ISBN 1-880873-45-1
ISSN 0192-060X

Columbia Books, Inc.

Debra Mayberry, President
Gino DiAngelo, Business Manager

Editorial Office

1825 Connecticut Ave., N.W.
Suite 625
Washington, DC 20009
Phone: (202) 464-1662
E-mail: info@columbiabooks.com
Web Site: www.columbiabooks.com

Customer Service

P.O. Box 251
Annapolis Junction, MD 20701-0251
Toll-free: (888) 265-0600
Fax: (240) 646-7020

Washington Representatives 2001

Table Of Contents

Organization and Use of This Directory

This book is basically a list of people — the individuals in Washington who work in government affairs or public relations for American trade associations, professional societies, labor unions, corporations and a great variety of special interest and public interest groups. Some, but by no means all, are registered as lobbyists on Capitol Hill. Others represent foreign governmental interests and are registered at the Department of Justice as foreign agents. Another element consists of employees of the Executive Branch of the federal government who are charged with legislative affairs and Congressional liaison responsibilities and are, therefore, also part of the lobbying community of Washington. All serve as advocates for the interests of their employers and/or clients here in the nation's capital.

The information in this volume comes from a variety of sources including federal lobby registrations filed with the Clerk of the House and Secretary of the Senate; FARA registrations at the Department of Justice; press releases; and responses to annual questionnaires from the firms and organizations listed.

All of this information has been organized into four main sections. The first section, titled The Firms, is comprised of an alphabetical list of the law, lobbying, and public relations firms which make up Washington's advocacy community and identifies the organizations they represent in a government relations capacity. Notations have been made whenever a firm is registered to lobby under LDA (Lobbying Disclosure Act) or FARA (Foreign Agents Registration Act).

The Clients section provides the reader with an alphabetical list of the companies, associations, interest groups and government entities which currently retain government representation here in the nation's capital and indicates the individuals and/or firms who work for them. Whenever possible, information is provided regarding the specific legislative issues on which each client lobbies. In some cases, the clients represent themselves on these issues, while in other cases, they have retained outside counsel to lobby on their behalf. It should be noted that legislative issues information was not always made available to Columbia Books. The absence of this information is not meant to imply that a client is inactive in these areas. A key to the three-letter legislative issues codes has been provided in the appendix at the back of this volume.

As in the preceding section, organizations who are currently registered to lobby at Congress under the LDA or who are registered as foreign agents at the Department of Justice under FARA have this fact noted in their listings. PACs that are affiliated with the organizations listed in this section appear within the listing of the sponsoring organization. Freestanding PACs, or those who have no sponsoring organization, maintain their own listings here.

The next section, Executive Branch Legislative Offices, lists the congressional and legislative affairs offices within the various departments and agencies in the Executive Branch of our federal government.

The People is a compilation of all of the individuals who work for the firms, organizations, and offices listed in the previous three sections. In cases where an individual acts as the sole proprietor of a law or lobbying firm or consultancy, a separate listing for the firm can also be found in The Firms section. Indications have also been made when an individual is named on LDA and/or FARA registrations. Each individual's experience as a full-time, paid employee of the federal government is mentioned in his or her personal listing in this section. Although many of the individuals listed in this directory have valuable and noteworthy experience in the private sector, space constraints have prevented listing that fact here. The absence of a background note is in no way meant to reflect an individual's lack of related experience.

In addition to these main sections, four indices have also been included in this volume to aid the user in locating listed organizations or firms. The first three indices aid the researcher in locating organizations listed in The Clients section. The Client Index by Industry identifies companies and organizations within a given industry or principal subject of concern. The PAC Index provides assistance in locating both sponsored and freestanding PACs. The Foreign Client Index by Country is a country-by-country listing of organizations and foreign governments with representation in Washington. A fourth index, the Legislative Issues Index, enables the researcher to identify and locate both clients *and* firms according to the specific legislative areas in which they lobby. More detailed information on the organization and use of these four reference tools is given at the beginning of each index.

It should be noted that the information contained in this directory is transitory in nature. Firm/client relationships fluctuate, people move from job to job, and registration status under LDA and FARA changes on a daily basis. Every attempt has been made to present an accurate picture of Washington's advocacy community as it existed at the time this edition was published.

Further information regarding lobby registration requirements and procedures may be obtained from:

Senate Office of Public Records
232 Hart Senate Office Bldg.
Washington, DC 20510
(202) 224-0758

House Legislative Resource Center
1036 Longworth House Office Bldg.
Washington, DC 20515
(202) 225-1300

Information on requirements and procedures for registering under FARA may be obtained from:

Foreign Agent Registration Unit
Department of Justice
Bond Building
1400 New York Ave., N.W., Suite 9500
Washington, DC 20530
(202) 514-1216

Lobbying: A Sacred Trust

By James J. Albertine
President, American League of Lobbyists

Government officials are continuously making public policy decisions that affect the vital interests of individuals, corporations, labor unions, religious groups, charitable institutions and other entities. In order to make informed policy judgments, they need to receive factual information from affected interests and to know the views of such parties. In exercising their constitutional right to influence public policy, interests often employ professional representatives to monitor developments and advocate their positions, or they use lobbyists through their memberships in trade associations and other organizations. Tens of thousands of men and women are now professional lobbyists and represent virtually every type of interest.

It is imperative in a free and open democratic society that citizens both understand and have confidence in their democratic institutions. In order to preserve that most important and sacred trust, professional lobbyists have a strong obligation to always act in the highest ethical and moral manner in their dealings with all parties. They also have a duty to advance public understanding of the lobbying profession. To that end, The American League of Lobbyists (ALL) has adopted a strong "Code of Ethics" to provide the basic guidelines and standards for lobbyists' conduct and to encourage all lobbyists to act in the highest ethical and moral manner. The Code of Ethics has been made public on ALL's website at www.alldc.org/ethicscode.htm

One very important aspect of this code is to provide full disclosure on all activities related to the professional representation of interests in Washington, DC before the U.S. Federal Government. Lobbyists collect and distribute millions of dollars in political contributions to candidates for elected office every year. Therefore, they are subject to total and full disclosure and must be prepared for this scrutiny and for the myriad of questions that follow. That is part of our role and critical to the democratic system.

The 2001 edition of *Washington Representatives* is vital to the disclosure effort. This book lists, for all to read, approximately 17,000 people involved in the business of professional lobbying and describes in detail the special interests represented and those who represent them. In an era of "campaign reform", it is imperative that the public have access to the names of both the lobbyists and the interests they represent.

Lobbying is a constitutionally-guaranteed right and an integral part of our nation's democratic process in which lobbyists involve millions of Americans every day. Americans must have faith in their institutions and so they must begin by knowing who is representing the special interests before their government. This book helps that process immeasurably.

2001 Washington Representatives

The Firms

The following section comprises the firms that advocate on behalf of various companies, labor unions, associations, government entities, and special interest groups who have dealings with the federal government of the United States. Although some of this material has been provided directly by the firms listed below and/or their clients, much of it has been compiled from public records. It is necessarily transitory, as firm/client relationships may cease once a point of view has been presented and a proposed measure is passed or voted down. This directory serves as a mere snapshot of the firm/client relationships as they existed at the time the records were consulted. Columbia Books has made every effort to ensure the accuracy of the information contained within, but accepts no responsibility for any errors.

AB Management Associates, Inc.

6123 Lundy Pl.
Burke, VA 22015
Tel: (703)455-2332
Fax: (703)455-4894
Registered: LDA

DC-Area Employees Representing Listed Clients
BARNETT, Larry P., President

Clients

AAAE-ACI
Issues: AVI
Rep By: Larry P. Barnett

Diversified Internat'l Sciences Corp.
Issues: AVI
Rep By: Larry P. Barnett

Megapulse, Inc.
Issues: AVI
Rep By: Larry P. Barnett

Pegasus Management
Issues: AVI
Rep By: Larry P. Barnett

U.S. Contract Tower Ass'n
Rep By: Larry P. Barnett

Vero Beach, Florida, City of
Issues: AVI
Rep By: Larry P. Barnett

Ablondi, Foster, Sobin & Davidow, P.C.

1150 18th St. NW
Ninth Floor
Washington, DC 20036
Tel: (202)296-3355
Fax: (202)296-3922
Registered: LDA, FARA
Web: www.ablondifoster.com
E-mail: afsd@ablondifoster.com
A law firm specializing in international trade regulation (including customs and export control), antitrust, unfair competition, international transactions, and intellectual property licensing and litigation.

DC-Area Employees Representing Listed Clients
ABBEY, Richard H., Partner
ABLONDI, Italo H., Senior Partner
BURNS, Robert, Partner
CHIU, Johnny C., Associate
COOPERMAN, Leonard, Associate
EHRENHAFT, Peter D., Partner
FOSTER, F. David, Partner
KOENIG, Peter J., Partner
LEONARD, Will E., Partner
NAPPI, Sarah, Associate
ROGERS, Joel W., Partner
SMITH, Kristen, Associate
TAYLOR, Jr., James, Partner

Clients

California Department of Education

China, Board of Foreign Trade of the Republic of

The Stanley Works
Issues: TRD
Rep By: Richard H. Abbey

United States Beet Sugar Ass'n
Rep By: F. David Foster

The Accord Group

1225 I St. NW
Suite 810
Washington, DC 20005
Tel: (202)289-9800
Fax: (202)289-3588
Registered: LDA

Political Action Committee
The Accord Political Action Committee
1225 I St. NW
Suite 810
Washington, DC 20005
Contact: Philip T. Cummings
Tel: (202)289-9800
Fax: (202)289-3588

DC-Area Employees Representing Listed Clients
CUMMINGS, Philip T., Principal and PAC Contact
HURLEY, Robert F., Principal
MORE, Jeffery T., Principal
QUINN, Patrick H., Principal

Clients

American Forest & Paper Ass'n
Issues: CAW ENV NAT
Rep By: Robert F. Hurley

Ass'n of American Railroads
Issues: CAW ENV TAX TRA
Rep By: Robert F. Hurley

Ciba Specialty Chemicals Corp.
Issues: CHM ENV TRD
Rep By: Robert F. Hurley

The Clark Estates, Inc.
Issues: RES SPO
Rep By: Jeffery T. More

Clean Water Act Reauthorization Coalition
Issues: CAW ENV NAT
Rep By: Philip T. Cummings

Ducks Unlimited Inc.
Issues: ENV
Rep By: Jeffery T. More

DuPont
Issues: AUT
Rep By: Robert F. Hurley

Energy and Environment Coalition
Issues: DIS ENG ENV UTI
Rep By: Patrick H. Quinn

General Electric Co.
Issues: BUD CAW ENV NAT WAS
Rep By: Philip T. Cummings

Innovation Reform Group
Issues: CHM ENV
Rep By: Patrick H. Quinn

Internat'l Paint Inc.
Issues: CAW ENV MAR
Rep By: Patrick H. Quinn

Natural Gas Vehicle Coalition
Issues: FUE
Rep By: Patrick H. Quinn

Novartis Corp.
Issues: CAW ENV FOO
Rep By: Robert F. Hurley

Water Infrastructure Network
Issues: CAW
Rep By: Robert F. Hurley, Jeffery T. More

Zurich Financial Services Group
Rep By: Jeffery T. More

Zurich U.S. Specialties
Issues: AGR ENV INS RES WAS
Rep By: Jeffery T. More

ADA Consulting Services

25461 Carberry Dr.
South Riding, VA 20152
Tel: (703)327-0598
Fax: (703)327-9477
Registered: LDA
E-mail: aduganstar@aol.com
A government relations and strategic planning consulting firm.

DC-Area Employees Representing Listed Clients
DUGAN, Alicia A., President

Clients

Air Quality Standards Coalition
Issues: CAW ENV SCI
Rep By: Alicia A. Dugan

Edison Electric Institute
Issues: CAW ENG ENV

General Motors Corp.
Issues: CAW ENV

Superfund Action Alliance
Issues: ENV SCI WAS
Rep By: Alicia A. Dugan

Adams and Reese LLP

409 Ninth St. NW
Suite 610 South
Washington, DC 20004
Tel: (202)737-3234
Fax: (202)737-0264
Registered: LDA
Web: www.arlaw.com

E-mail: info@arlaw.com
A full service law firm with offices in New Orleans and Baton Rouge, LA; Jackson, MS; Mobile, AL; and Houston, TX.

Political Action Committee
ARPAC
409 Ninth St. NW
Suite 610 South
Washington, DC 20004
Tel: (202)737-3234
Fax: (202)737-0264

DC-Area Employees Representing Listed Clients
BROOKS, B. Jeffrey, Partner-in-Charge, Washington Office
COLLINS, Charlotte, Legislative Assistant
FORSGREN, D. Lee, Special Counsel
HAYES, Hon. James A. "Jimmy", Special Counsel
JONES, Beverly E., Special Counsel
WILKINSON, Andrea, Government Relations Director

Clients

AHL Shipping Co.
Issues: FUE TRA
Rep By: D. Lee Forsgren, Hon. James A. "Jimmy" Hayes

Baton Rouge, Louisiana, City of
Issues: CAW ECN TRA
Rep By: B. Jeffrey Brooks, Charlotte Collins, D. Lee Forsgren, Hon. James A. "Jimmy" Hayes, Andrea Wilkinson

Coastal Impact Assistance & Reinvestment
Issues: BUD FUE NAT ROD
Rep By: B. Jeffrey Brooks, Hon. James A. "Jimmy" Hayes

Coweta County (Georgia) School Board
Issues: EDU
Rep By: B. Jeffrey Brooks

Dominion Resources, Inc.
Issues: FUE TAX
Rep By: Beverly E. Jones

First American Aircraft Title
Issues: MAR
Rep By: D. Lee Forsgren, Hon. James A. "Jimmy" Hayes

First American Title Aircraft
Issues: INS MAR
Rep By: D. Lee Forsgren, Hon. James A. "Jimmy" Hayes

GE Capital Corp.
Issues: WAS
Rep By: B. Jeffrey Brooks, D. Lee Forsgren

Iberville Parish
Issues: BUD ENV NAT TRA
Rep By: B. Jeffrey Brooks, Andrea Wilkinson

Interregional Associates
Issues: ECN TRD
Rep By: B. Jeffrey Brooks

Jefferson Parish Council
Issues: BUD DEF ENG ENV LBR TRA URB
Rep By: B. Jeffrey Brooks

Lafayette Airport Commission
Issues: AVI BUD
Rep By: B. Jeffrey Brooks, Hon. James A. "Jimmy" Hayes

Lehtinen O'Donnell
Issues: ENV GOV NAT
Rep By: D. Lee Forsgren, Hon. James A. "Jimmy" Hayes

Louisiana Credit Union Ass'n
Issues: BAN
Rep By: B. Jeffrey Brooks, Hon. James A. "Jimmy" Hayes, Andrea Wilkinson

Louisiana Internat'l Group
Issues: BUD DIS
Rep By: B. Jeffrey Brooks

Louisiana State University
Issues: BUD EDU ENG FIN NAT TRA
Rep By: B. Jeffrey Brooks, Hon. James A. "Jimmy" Hayes, Andrea Wilkinson

Loyola University
Issues: BUD DEF EDU ENG ENV LAW
Rep By: B. Jeffrey Brooks

Miccosukee Indians
Issues: ENV IND
Rep By: D. Lee Forsgren, Hon. James A. "Jimmy" Hayes

New Orleans, Louisiana, Regional Transit Authority of
Issues: BUD TRA
Rep By: B. Jeffrey Brooks, Hon. James A. "Jimmy" Hayes, Andrea Wilkinson

NiSource Inc.
Issues: FUE TAX
Rep By: Hon. James A. "Jimmy" Hayes

Pennington BioMedical Research Center
Issues: AGR BUD DEF EDU ENG FIN NAT TRA
Rep By: B. Jeffrey Brooks

Plaquemine, Louisiana, City of
Issues: ECN
Rep By: B. Jeffrey Brooks, Charlotte Collins

Project ACTA
Issues: MAR
Rep By: D. Lee Forsgren

Q-ZAB Coalition
Issues: ECN EDU
Rep By: B. Jeffrey Brooks

Regional Transit Authority
Issues: BUD TRA
Rep By: B. Jeffrey Brooks

South Louisiana, Port of
Issues: BUD
Rep By: B. Jeffrey Brooks, Hon. James A. "Jimmy" Hayes, Andrea Wilkinson

Southeastern Louisiana University
Issues: BUD
Rep By: B. Jeffrey Brooks

Technology Integration Group
Issues: GOV
Rep By: Hon. James A. "Jimmy" Hayes, Beverly E. Jones

Unisys Corp.
Issues: DEF MED
Rep By: B. Jeffrey Brooks, Andrea Wilkinson

Z-Tel Communications Inc.
Issues: TEC
Rep By: Hon. James A. "Jimmy" Hayes

Zachery Taylor Parkway Commission
Issues: TAX TRA
Rep By: B. Jeffrey Brooks, Hon. James A. "Jimmy" Hayes

John Adams Associates Inc.

655 National Press Bldg.
Washington, DC 20045
Tel: (202)737-8400
Fax: (202)737-8406
Registered: FARA

E-mail: jadams@johnadams.com
A research and consulting firm specializing in environmental and health issues.

DC-Area Employees Representing Listed Clients
ADAMS, A. John, President
CRAMPTON, Ann F., V. President and Director, Administration
ESCOBEDO, Esperanza
HEINZE, Ph.D., John E., Senior V. President and Senior Science Advisor
KLOSE, Christopher, Principal and Senior Partner
MCCARTHY, Elizabeth, Senior V. President
SEKLEMIAN, Caroline, Senior V. President

Clients

Alliance for Chemical Awareness
Rep By: Elizabeth McCarthy

Council for LAB/LAS Environmental Research (CLER)
Rep By: A. John Adams

Environmental Industry Council
Rep By: A. John Adams

GlobalNet Holdings Corp.
Rep By: Esperanza Escobedo

King Communications Corp.
Rep By: A. John Adams

Styrene Information and Research Center
Rep By: A. John Adams

Michael W. Adcock

4215 Wynnwood Dr.
Annandale, VA 22003
Tel: (202)638-1950
Fax: (202)638-7714
Registered: LDA

E-mail: madcock@vsadc.com
A government relations consultant.

Clients

Cooper Green Hospital
Issues: BUD HCR
Rep By: Michael W. Adcock

Intergraph Corp. Federal Systems Division
Issues: DEF
Rep By: Michael W. Adcock

Jefferson State Community College
Issues: BUD EDU
Rep By: Michael W. Adcock

PEI Electronics
Issues: DEF
Rep By: Michael W. Adcock

University of Alabama System
Rep By: Michael W. Adcock

Uwohali, Inc.
Issues: DEF
Rep By: Michael W. Adcock

Van Scoyoc Associates, Inc.
Issues: BUD EDU FOR MED MMM SCI TRA
Rep By: Michael W. Adcock

Adduci, Mastriani & Schaumberg, L.L.P.

1200 17th St. NW
Fifth Floor
Washington, DC 20036
Tel: (202)467-6300
Fax: (202)466-2006
Registered: LDA

Web: www.adduci.com
E-mail: ams@adduci.com

DC-Area Employees Representing Listed Clients
ADDUCI, II, V. James, Partner
BERDUT, Caridad
BROWNE, Maureen, Associate
DOANE, Michael L., Associate
SCHAUMBERG, Tom M., Partner

Clients

Rubie's Costume Co., Inc.
Issues: TRD
Rep By: V. James Adduci, II, Michael L. Doane

Advantage Associates, Inc.

908 Pennsylvania Ave. SE
Washington, DC 20003
Tel: (202)544-5666
Fax: (202)544-4647
Registered: LDA

Web: www.advantage-dc.com
E-mail: bsarpalius@advantage-dc.com
A closely-held corporation staffed principally by former Members of Congress who specialize in helping clients with government, politics, and international affairs.

DC-Area Employees Representing Listed Clients
ALEXANDER, Jr., Hon. William V. "Bill", Associate
DICKINSON, Hon. Bill, Partner
GONZALEZ, USA (Ret.), Lt. Col. Roberto, Professional Staff
GRANT, Hon. James William "Bill", Partner
HANRAHAN, Hon. Robert P., Partner
MCEWEN, Hon. Robert D., Partner
ORTON, Hon. Bill, Partner
PATTERSON, Hon. Jerry M., Partner
POLLOCK, Hon. Howard, Partner
SARPALIUS, Hon. Bill, President and Chief Exec. Officer
SCHULZE, Hon. Richard T., Senior Legislative Director
TALLON, Hon. Robin, Partner
WORKS, George, Professional Staff

Clients

Christus Health
Issues: HCR TRA
Rep By: Hon. Bill Sarpalius

Sisters of Charity of the Incarnate Word
Issues: DEF
Rep By: Hon. Bill Sarpalius

TCOM, L.P.
Issues: AER AVI DEF
Rep By: Hon. Bill Sarpalius, Hon. Robin Tallon

Uniformed Services Dental Alliance
Issues: DEF HCR
Rep By: Hon. Robert D. McEwen, Hon. Bill Sarpalius, Hon. Robin Tallon

The Advocacy Group

1350 I St. NW
Suite 680
Washington, DC 20005-3305
Tel: (202)393-4841
Fax: (202)393-5596
Registered: LDA

Web: www.advocacy.com
E-mail: info@advocacy.com

DC-Area Employees Representing Listed Clients
BOISCLAIR, Jon L.
DOTCHIN, Robert J.
MILLS, Robert E.
NUGENT, Jr., John M.
RAMONAS, George A.
SMITH, Anne V.

Clients

American Institute for Foreign Studies
Issues: FOR
Rep By: Robert J. Dotchin

Arizona Science Center
Issues: EDU SCI
Rep By: George A. Ramonas

Ass'n of Chiropractic Colleges
Issues: EDU
Rep By: Robert E. Mills

Atlantic Corridor USA
Issues: FOR
Rep By: Robert E. Mills

Authentica Inc.
Issues: CPI
Rep By: George A. Ramonas

BitWise Designs Inc.
Issues: CPI
Rep By: Robert E. Mills, George A. Ramonas

Buffalo Sewer Authority
Issues: ENV
Rep By: Robert E. Mills

Buffalo, New York, City of
Issues: ECN
Rep By: Robert E. Mills

Consumer Electronics Ass'n
Issues: COM MAN TAX TEC
Rep By: Jon L. Boisclair, Robert J. Dotchin

Daemen College
Issues: EDU HCR SCI
Rep By: Robert E. Mills

Detroit Internat'l Bridge Co./The Ambassador Bridge
Issues: TRD
Rep By: Jon L. Boisclair, Robert E. Mills

Digital Descriptor Services, Inc.
Issues: CPI DEF LAW
Rep By: Robert E. Mills

Dowling College
Issues: EDU
Rep By: Robert E. Mills

First American Real Estate Solutions LLC
Issues: BAN RES
Rep By: George A. Ramonas

Florida Atlantic University
Issues: EDU
Rep By: Robert E. Mills, George A. Ramonas

Florida State University
Issues: EDU
Rep By: Robert E. Mills, George A. Ramonas

Fluor Corp.
Issues: ENG
Rep By: George A. Ramonas

Fuels Management Inc.
Issues: ENG
Rep By: John M. Nugent, Jr.

Greater Cleveland Regional Transit Authority
Issues: TRA
Rep By: George A. Ramonas

Harbor Branch Institute
Issues: EDU MED SCI
Rep By: Robert E. Mills

Internat'l Research and Exchanges Board (IREX)
Issues: EDU FOR
Rep By: George A. Ramonas, Anne V. Smith

Logan College of Chiropractic
Issues: EDU MED
Rep By: Robert E. Mills

Long Island University
Issues: EDU
Rep By: Robert J. Dotchin, George A. Ramonas

Minnesota Life Insurance Co.
Issues: BAN INS TAX
Rep By: Jon L. Boisclair

Nat'l Ass'n of Small Business Investment Companies
Issues: SMB
Rep By: Robert J. Dotchin

Nuclear Energy Institute
Issues: BUD WAS
Rep By: John M. Nugent, Jr., George A. Ramonas

Palmer Chiropractic University
Issues: EDU
Rep By: Robert E. Mills

Rineco Chemical Industries
Issues: CHM ENG
Rep By: John M. Nugent, Jr., George A. Ramonas

Sam Houston University
Issues: EDU
Rep By: Robert E. Mills

Silicon Graphics/SGI
Issues: CPI
Rep By: George A. Ramonas

Siscorp
Issues: EDU ENV MED SCI
Rep By: Robert E. Mills

Southwest Texas State University
Issues: EDU
Rep By: Robert E. Mills

TCF Financial Corp.
Issues: BAN BNK
Rep By: Jon L. Boisclair

Tempe, Arizona, City of
Issues: ECN
Rep By: George A. Ramonas

Texas Chiropractic College
Issues: EDU MED
Rep By: Robert E. Mills

TRW Inc.
Issues: ENV
Rep By: John M. Nugent, Jr., George A. Ramonas

Tyco Internat'l (US), Inc.
Issues: MED
Rep By: Robert J. Dotchin

University of Central Florida
Rep By: Robert E. Mills

University of Houston
Issues: EDU
Rep By: Robert J. Dotchin, George A. Ramonas

UST Public Affairs, Inc.
Issues: BEV TAX TOB
Rep By: Robert J. Dotchin

Westinghouse Government Services Group
Rep By: John M. Nugent, Jr.

The Aegis Group, Ltd.

2472 Belmont Rd. NW
Washington, DC 20008
Tel: (202)518-9590
Fax: (202)518-9592
Registered: LDA, FARA

Consultants in international trade development and government and public relations.

DC-Area Employees Representing Listed Clients
CASTILLO, A. Mario, President

Clients

Dairy Trade Advisory Council
Issues: AGR
Rep By: A. Mario Castillo

The Dairy Trade Coalition
Issues: AGR
Rep By: A. Mario Castillo

Pump Service and Supply Co.
Rep By: A. Mario Castillo

U.S.-Canadian Caucus of Mayors
Issues: TOU TRD
Rep By: A. Mario Castillo

World Duty Free Americas, Inc.
Issues: TOU TRD
Rep By: A. Mario Castillo

AESOP Enterprises, Ltd.

236 Massachusetts Ave. NE
Suite 400
Washington, DC 20002
E-mail: aesop@aesop-ent.com
Tel: (202)675-4511
Fax: (202)675-4512
Registered: LDA

DC-Area Employees Representing Listed Clients
NADDAF, May, V. President
NIPP, Terry, President

Clients

Internat'l Committee on Organization & Policy
Issues: AGR
Rep By: Terry Nipp

Africa Global Partners

1050 17th St. NW
Suite 600
Washington, DC 20036
Tel: (202)496-1285
Fax: (202)496-9620
Registered: LDA, FARA

DC-Area Employees Representing Listed Clients
NEDELCOVYCH, Mimi, Partner

Clients

Equatorial Guinea, Republic of
Issues: FOR
Rep By: Mimi Nedelcovych

Swaziland, Kingdom of
Issues: ECN
Rep By: Mimi Nedelcovych

Afridi & Angell LLP

1025 Connecticut Ave. NW
Suite 904
Washington, DC 20036
Tel: (202)518-8900
Fax: (202)518-8903
Registered: FARA

Clients

Egypt, Government of the Arab Republic of

Japan External Trade Organization (JETRO)

Tunisian Agency for External Communication

Agri/Washington

1629 K St. NW
Suite 1100
Washington, DC 20006
Web: www.agriwashington.org
E-mail: agriwash@aol.com
Tel: (202)785-6710
Fax: (202)331-4212

Public affairs, association management, public relations, and legislative representation.

DC-Area Employees Representing Listed Clients
BALL, Andrea, Accounts Director
MOORE, Jon, Legislative Representative
SAWYER, Jeffrey
WELLER, Jr., Paul S., President

Clients

Agricultural Biotechnology Forum
Issues: AGR
Rep By: Paul S. Weller, Jr.

American Ass'n of Grain Inspection and Weighing Agencies
Issues: AGR
Rep By: Andrea Ball, Jon Moore, Paul S. Weller, Jr.

American Grain Inspection Institute
Issues: AGR
Rep By: Jon Moore, Paul S. Weller, Jr.

Apple Processors Ass'n
Issues: AGR
Rep By: Andrea Ball, Jon Moore, Paul S. Weller, Jr.

Canadian-American Business Council
Rep By: Andrea Ball, Paul S. Weller, Jr.

Financial Executives International
Issues: FIN
Rep By: Jeffrey Sawyer

Maryland Dairy Industry Ass'n
Issues: AGR
Rep By: Jon Moore, Paul S. Weller, Jr.

Ainslie Associates

3812 N. Sixth Rd.
Arlington, VA 22203
E-mail: vainslie@aol.com
Tel: (703)527-5404
Fax: (703)243-9251
Registered: LDA

DC-Area Employees Representing Listed Clients
AINSLIE, Virginia J., President

Clients

Cleveland Advanced Manufacturing Program
Issues: DEF MAN
Rep By: Virginia J. Ainslie

Cleveland Clinic Foundation
Issues: BUD DEF MED SCI
Rep By: Virginia J. Ainslie

Cleveland State University - College of Urban Affairs
Issues: BUD ECN EDU URB
Rep By: Virginia J. Ainslie

Northeast Ohio Areawide Coordination Agency (NOACA)
Issues: BUD CAW ENV GOV ROD TRA
Rep By: Virginia J. Ainslie

Northeast Ohio Regional Sewer District
Issues: CAW
Rep By: Virginia J. Ainslie

Youngstown-Warren Regional Chamber
Issues: BUD CAW ENV ROD TRD
Rep By: Virginia J. Ainslie

Aitken, Irvin, Lewin, Berlin, Vrooman & Cohn

666 11th St. NW
Suite 315
Washington, DC 20001
E-mail: 75031.241@compuserve.com
Tel: (202)331-8045
Fax: (202)331-8191
Registered: LDA, FARA

DC-Area Employees Representing Listed Clients
AITKEN, Bruce, Partner
APATOFF, Adam S., Associate
LEWIN, Martin J., Partner
SHARPE, Kieran, Associate

Clients

American Import Shippers Ass'n
Rep By: Martin J. Lewin

Colgate Palmolive
Issues: TRD
Rep By: Bruce Aitken, Adam S. Apatoff, Martin J. Lewin, Kieran Sharpe

Hyundai Motor Co.
Rep By: Bruce Aitken

Pro Trade Group
Rep By: Bruce Aitken

Ukraine, Ministries of Industy, Foreign Economic Relations, and Foreign Affairs of the Government of

The Aker Partners Inc.

2000 K St. NW
Suite 801
Washington, DC 20006
Web: www.akerpartners.com
E-mail: aker@akerpartners.com
Tel: (202)789-2424
Fax: (202)789-1818
Registered: LDA

A communications consulting firm with a significant public affairs and issue management practice.

DC-Area Employees Representing Listed Clients
AKER, G. Colburn, Managing Partner
AMBERSON, Michele, Associate Partner
PRICE, Richard, Senior Associate

Clients

Ass'n of Clinical Research Professionals
Issues: HCR
Rep By: G. Colburn Aker

Ephedra Education Council
Issues: FOO
Rep By: G. Colburn Aker

Moore Medical Corp.
Issues: HCR
Rep By: G. Colburn Aker

Newspaper Ass'n of America
Issues: POS
Rep By: G. Colburn Aker

Akin, Gump, Strauss, Hauer & Feld, L.L.P.

1333 New Hampshire Ave. NW
Suite 400
Washington, DC 20036
Tel: (202)887-4000
Fax: (202)887-4288
Registered: LDA, FARA
Web: www.akingump.com
Washington office of a Dallas law firm.

Political Action Committee
Akin, Gump, Strauss, Hauer & Feld Civic Action Committee
1333 New Hampshire Ave. NW
Suite 400
Washington, DC 20036
Tel: (202)887-4000
Fax: (202)887-4288
Contact: Joel Jankowsky

DC-Area Employees Representing Listed Clients
ALDERFER, Kenneth, Senior Counsel
ALEXANDER, Donald C., Partner
BLINKEN, Alan J., Senior Advisor
BOYD, Janet C., Partner
BRANDON, Barry W., Senior Counsel
BRODIE, Katherine D.
BURNS, Thaddeus
CALLETT, David P., Partner
CARLIN, J. David, Partner
CATANIA, David A., Associate
COHEN, Jay Gordon, Partner
COLUCCI, Marlene M., Senior Counsel
CONNELLY, Warren E., Partner
CORNELISON, Joseph, Senior Counsel
CORSO, Anthony R., Senior Advisor
CRAVEN, Donald B., Partner
CRUM, Janis, Associate
CUTLER, Eliot R., Partner
D'ARCY, Sean G., Partner
DAVIS, Smith W., Partner
DE LEON, Sylvia A., Partner
DOBRIANSKY, Larisa
DONATELLI, Frank J., Partner
DONOHOE, David A., Partner
DOWD, John W., Partner
EISENSTAT, David H., Partner
FALVEY, Cheryl, Partner
FARAH, William J., Senior Counsel
FOTI, Anthony
GATI, Toby T.
GEANACOPOULOS, David, Partner
GLICKMAN, Hon. Daniel R., Partner
GOLDBERG, Avrum M., Partner
GOLDMEIER GREEN, Karen E., Associate
GRIFFITH, Spencer S., Partner
HAGERUP, Stefan A., Associate
HAQUE, Bradley O., Associate
HEIMBERG, Gary A., Counsel
HESSE, Christine
HOFFMAN, Laurence J., Partner
HYMAN, Elizabeth, Associate
JANKOWSKY, Joel, Partner
JOHNSON, IV, Charles W., Counsel
JOHNSON, Owen M., Partner
JOYCE, Jonathan R.
KAYE, D. Michael, Partner
KIM, Sukhan, Partner
LANGDON, Jr., James C., Partner
LASSMAN, Malcolm, Partner
LEARY, James, Exec. Director
LECHTMAN, Vladimir
LENT, Susan H., Senior Counsel
LEVIEN, Lawrence D., Partner
LIVINGSTON, Donald R., Partner
LOPEZ, Jr., Jorge J., Partner
MACHIDA, Ado A.
MADIGAN, Michael J., Partner
MANDEL, Michael S., Partner
MARCUS, Michael S., Partner
MCLEAN, R. Bruce, Chairman
MCLISH, Thomas, Partner
MENDELSOHN, Bruce S., Partner
MUELLER, Michael, Partner
NUSCHLER, Robin M., Partner
PALMER, David B.
PARK, Jaemin, Partner
PAXON, Hon. William L., Senior Advisor
PIERCE, Anthony, Partner
PONGRACE, Donald R., Partner
QUIGLEY, David
ROSS, Steven R., Partner
RUBIN, Richard, Partner
RUBINOFF, Edward L., Partner
SALEM, George R., Partner
SELF, Richard B.
SINGISER, Dana E.
SKLADANY, Jr., Barney J., Partner
SLATER, Valerie A., Partner
SPIEGEL, Daniel L., Partner
STRAUSS, Robert S., Partner
TERHUNE, Henry A., Partner
TOLIVER, Karen Bland, Counsel
TUCKER, Jr., James R.
TUITE, James, Partner
TURNER, Leslie M., Partner
TURZI, Joseph A., Partner
VILLARREAL, Jose H., Partner
WEILER, Steven A., Counsel
WEISMAN, Robin
WILSON, S. Bruce, Partner
WOLFF, Samuel, Of Counsel
WYATT, Jr., Richard, Partner
ZENSKY, David, Partner

Clients

Ad Hoc Nitrogen Committee
Issues: TRD
Rep By: Valerie A. Slater, S. Bruce Wilson

ADM Milling Co.

Air Transport Ass'n of America
Rep By: Donald C. Alexander

Ajinomoto U.S.A., Inc.

Albertson's Inc.
Issues: LBR
Rep By: Barney J. Skladany, Jr.

Allegheny River Mining Co.

Alliance for Quality Nursing Home Care
Issues: MMM
Rep By: Karen E. Goldmeier Green, Joel Jankowsky, Dana E. Singiser, Jose H. Villarreal

Alliance of American Insurers
Issues: ENV HCR INS
Rep By: Donald C. Alexander, Sean G. D'Arcy

American Airlines
Issues: AVI FIN RET TAX
Rep By: Janet C. Boyd, Sean G. D'Arcy, Smith W. Davis, Sylvia A. de Leon, Barney J. Skladany, Jr.

American Amateur Karate Federation
Issues: SPO
Rep By: Marlene M. Colucci, Henry A. Terhune

American Consulting Engineers Council
Issues: GOV SMB TAX TRA WAS
Rep By: Marlene M. Colucci, Barney J. Skladany, Jr.

American Express Co.
Issues: BAN BUD FIN TOU
Rep By: Smith W. Davis, Sylvia A. de Leon, Joel Jankowsky, Barney J. Skladany, Jr.

American Financial Group
Issues: ENV INS TAX
Rep By: Donald C. Alexander

American Home Products Corp.
Issues: CPT HCR PHA
Rep By: Elizabeth Hyman, Daniel L. Spiegel, S. Bruce Wilson

American Legion
Issues: CON
Rep By: Marlene M. Colucci, Frank J. Donatelli, Joel Jankowsky, Charles W. Johnson, IV, Steven R. Ross

American Mutual Share Insurance Corp.

Americans for Affordable Electricity
Issues: ENG FUE UTI
Rep By: Anthony Foti, Hon. William L. Paxon, James R. Tucker, Jr.

AOL Time Warner
Issues: COM TAX
Rep By: Janet C. Boyd, Joel Jankowsky, George R. Salem, Barney J. Skladany, Jr., Daniel L. Spiegel, Robin Weisman, S. Bruce Wilson

APKINDO
Issues: FOR TRD
Rep By: Sean G. D'Arcy, David Geanacopoulos, Barney J. Skladany, Jr.

Arab American Institute

Archer Daniels Midland Co.

Asosiasi Panel Kayu Indonesia

ASSE Internat'l Student Exchange Program

AT&T
Issues: TEC
Rep By: Marlene M. Colucci, Joel Jankowsky, Barney J. Skladany, Jr., Daniel L. Spiegel, Jose H. Villarreal, Robin Weisman

Avax Technologies, Inc.
Issues: HCR MED
Rep By: Karen E. Goldmeier Green

Bankers Trust Co.
Rep By: Joel Jankowsky

Barrick Goldstrike Mines, Inc.
Issues: ENG FOR GOV TAX
Rep By: Janet C. Boyd, William J. Farah, Henry A. Terhune, S. Bruce Wilson

Base Ten Systems, Inc.
Issues: PHA
Rep By: Karen E. Goldmeier Green, Barney J. Skladany, Jr.

Bear, Stearns and Co.
Rep By: Donald C. Alexander, Janet C. Boyd, Sean G. D'Arcy, Frank J. Donatelli, Joel Jankowsky

Bechtel Group, Inc.
Issues: TAX
Rep By: Donald C. Alexander, Sean G. D'Arcy

Belridge Water Storage District

The Boeing Co.
Issues: TRD
Rep By: Sean G. D'Arcy, Barney J. Skladany, Jr., S. Bruce Wilson

Bolivia, Government of the Republic of
Rep By: David Geanacopoulos, Barney J. Skladany, Jr.

Bolt, Beranek and Newman, Inc.

Bombardier, Inc.
Issues: AVI
Rep By: Marlene M. Colucci, David Geanacopoulos, Charles W. Johnson, IV, Jonathan R. Joyce, Barney J. Skladany, Jr.

Boston Stock Exchange

Bridgestone/Firestone, Inc.
Issues: AUT CSP TRA
Rep By: J. David Carlin, David Geanacopoulos, Charles W. Johnson, IV, Susan H. Lent, Hon. William L. Paxon, Barney J. Skladany, Jr., Daniel L. Spiegel, Robin Weisman

British Columbia, Canada, Government of the Province of
Rep By: Frank J. Donatelli, David Geanacopoulos, Spencer S. Griffith

Broadwave USA Inc.
Issues: TEC
Rep By: Barney J. Skladany, Jr., James R. Tucker, Jr.

Brunswick Corp.
Issues: TRD
Rep By: William J. Farah, Valerie A. Slater, Daniel L. Spiegel

Capital Gaming Internat'l, Inc.
Issues: GAM
Rep By: Charles W. Johnson, IV, Henry A. Terhune, Leslie M. Turner

Cargill, Inc.
Issues: TRD
Rep By: Valerie A. Slater, Karen Bland Toliver, S. Bruce Wilson

The Carlyle Group
Issues: TAX
Rep By: Janet C. Boyd

Celanese Government Relations Office

Chilean Exporters Ass'n

Chiquita Brands Internat'l, Inc.

Citizen's Educational Foundation
Rep By: Marlene M. Colucci, Sean G. D'Arcy, Gary A. Heimberg, Steven R. Ross, Barney J. Skladany, Jr., Jose H. Villarreal

Collagen Corp.
Issues: HCR
Rep By: Gary A. Heimberg, Steven R. Ross, Barney J. Skladany, Jr.

College Football Bowl Ass'n

Colombia Flower Council

Colombia, Government of the Republic of
Rep By: David Geanacopoulos, Barney J. Skladany, Jr.

Commerce Clause Coalition
Rep By: Barney J. Skladany, Jr.

Committee for Fair Ammonium Nitrate Trade
Issues: TRD
Rep By: Valerie A. Slater, S. Bruce Wilson

Competitive Broadband Coalition
Rep By: Hon. William L. Paxon

Competitive Consumer Lending Coalition
Issues: HOU
Rep By: J. David Carlin, Smith W. Davis, Joel Jankowsky

Construction Industry Round Table, Inc.
Issues: ENV GOV WAS
Rep By: Marlene M. Colucci

Corrections Corp. of America
Issues: GOV LAW
Rep By: Michael J. Madigan, Steven R. Ross, Barney J. Skladany, Jr., James R. Tucker, Jr.

Cummins Engine Co.
Issues: LBR RET TAX
Rep By: Donald C. Alexander, Janet C. Boyd, Henry A. Terhune

Donohue Industries Inc.
Issues: ENV

Dow Jones & Co., Inc.
Issues: CPT TRD
Rep By: Katherine D. Brodie, Smith W. Davis, Donald R. Pongrace

Edison Internat'l

Educational Foundation for Citizenship and Statehood Project
Rep By: Marlene M. Colucci, Sean G. D'Arcy, Gary A. Heimberg, Steven R. Ross, Barney J. Skladany, Jr.

EMC Corp.
Issues: FIN TAX
Rep By: Donald C. Alexander, Sean G. D'Arcy, Smith W. Davis, Christine Hesse, Barney J. Skladany, Jr.

Environmental Industry Ass'ns

Ethiopia, Government of

European-American Phytomedicine Coalition

Executive Life Insurance Co.

Exxon Mobil Corp.
Issues: ENG ENV FOR FUE NAT TAX
Rep By: David P. Callett, Smith W. Davis, David Geanacopoulos, Barney J. Skladany, Jr., Henry A. Terhune, Robin Weisman

Farm Credit Bank of Texas
Issues: AGR
Rep By: J. David Carlin

Feld Entertainment Inc.
Issues: TRD

First Nationwide Bank
Rep By: Janet C. Boyd, Marlene M. Colucci, Michael S. Mandel

FirstEnergy Co.
Issues: LBR
Rep By: Barney J. Skladany, Jr.

FM Watch

Fontana Union Water Co.
Issues: NAT
Rep By: J. David Carlin, Joel Jankowsky

Food Lion, Inc.
Rep By: Thomas McLish, Michael Mueller, Richard Wyatt, Jr.

Fremont Group, Inc.
Issues: TAX
Rep By: Kenneth Alderfer, Sean G. D'Arcy

Fujitsu Limited
Rep By: Warren E. Connelly

Gila River Indian Community
Issues: BUD GAM IND ROD TAX
Rep By: Katherine D. Brodie, Smith W. Davis, Susan H. Lent, Ado A. Machida, Donald R. Pongrace, Barney J. Skladany, Jr.

Gordon Investment Corp.

Granite Broadcasting Co.
Issues: COM
Rep By: Marlene M. Colucci, Smith W. Davis, Karen E. Goldmeier Green, Joel Jankowsky, Charles W. Johnson, IV

GTECH Corp.

Harris, Beach & Wilcox
Issues: BUD TRA
Rep By: Susan H. Lent

Frederic R. Harris, Inc.
Issues: ROD TRA
Rep By: Sylvia A. de Leon, Elizabeth Hyman, Susan H. Lent

Harris, Texas, Metropolitan Transit Authority of
Issues: BUD TRA
Rep By: Sylvia A. de Leon, Susan H. Lent, Barney J. Skladany, Jr.

Heard Goggan Blair & Williams
Issues: BNK GOV
Rep By: Sean G. D'Arcy, Karen E. Goldmeier Green

Home Office Ass'n of America

Honey Users Council of America

Howland Hook Container Terminal Inc.
Issues: BUD MAR TRA
Rep By: Anthony Foti, Susan H. Lent, Ado A. Machida, Hon. William L. Paxon, Henry A. Terhune

Human Genome Sciences Inc.
Issues: CPT
Rep By: Thaddeus Burns, Barney J. Skladany, Jr., Daniel L. Spiegel, Robin Weisman

Hyundai Pipe Co.

Internat'l Karate Federation
Rep By: Henry A. Terhune

Internat'l Republican Institute

Johnson & Johnson, Inc.
Issues: HCR TAX
Rep By: Donald C. Alexander, Gary A. Heimberg, Jorge J. Lopez, Jr., Barney J. Skladany, Jr.

Joint Corporate Committee on Cuban Claims
Issues: FOR
Rep By: Barney J. Skladany, Jr.

Susan G. Komen Breast Cancer Foundation
Issues: HCR MED MMM
Rep By: Marlene M. Colucci, Karen E. Goldmeier Green

Korea Internat'l Trade Ass'n

L.L. Capital Partners, Inc.
Issues: TOB
Rep By: Smith W. Davis, Frank J. Donatelli

Liberty Mutual Insurance Group
Issues: ENV HCR
Rep By: Sean G. D'Arcy, Barney J. Skladany, Jr.

Loral Space and Communications, Ltd.

Lucent Technologies
Issues: TRD
Rep By: Daniel L. Spiegel, S. Bruce Wilson

Manufactured Housing Institute
Rep By: Joel Jankowsky, Jose H. Villarreal

MCA Inc.

The Medical Protective Co.

Memorial Sloan-Kettering Cancer Center
Issues: HCR MED MMM
Rep By: Jorge J. Lopez, Jr., Barney J. Skladany, Jr.

Mesa Inc.

Miller Brewing Co.

Mitsubishi Corp.
Issues: ENV FOR MAR
Rep By: Larisa Dobriansky, Elizabeth Hyman, Ado A. Machida, David Quigley, Daniel L. Spiegel, S. Bruce Wilson

The Robert Mondavi Winery
Issues: BEV TAX
Rep By: David Geanacopoulos, Henry A. Terhune

Mortgage Insurance Companies of America
Issues: BAN HOU INS
Rep By: Smith W. Davis, Christine Hesse, Joel Jankowsky, Barney J. Skladany, Jr.

Motion Picture Ass'n of America
Issues: CPT
Rep By: Smith W. Davis, William J. Farah, Joel Jankowsky, Barney J. Skladany, Jr., Robin Weisman

Municipal Financial Consultants Inc.
Issues: TAX
Rep By: Donald C. Alexander

Naples Community Hospital

Nat'l Ass'n of Chain Drug Stores
Rep By: Barney J. Skladany, Jr.

Nat'l Ass'n of Securities Dealers, Inc. (NASD)

Nat'l Basketball Ass'n
Issues: IMM SPO
Rep By: Frank J. Donatelli

Nat'l Deposit Insurance Corp.

Nat'l Hockey League
Issues: IMM SPO
Rep By: Frank J. Donatelli

Nat'l Medical Enterprises, Inc.

Nationwide Mutual Insurance Co.
Issues: ENV HCR INS TAX
Rep By: Donald C. Alexander, Sean G. D'Arcy

Naucalpan, Mexico, County of

Nehemiah Progressive Housing Development Corp.
Issues: HOU
Rep By: J. David Carlin, Smith W. Davis, Frank J. Donatelli, Anthony Foti

New California Life Holding, Inc.

New York Public Library
Issues: EDU
Rep By: Marlene M. Colucci, Smith W. Davis, Barney J. Skladany, Jr.

New York State Health Facilities Ass'n
Issues: MMM
Rep By: Smith W. Davis, Karen E. Goldmeier Green, Barney J. Skladany, Jr.

Niagara Frontier Transportation Authority
Issues: AVI BUD ROD TRA
Rep By: Anthony Foti, Susan H. Lent, Hon. William L. Paxon

NiSource Inc.
Issues: ENG
Rep By: Barney J. Skladany, Jr., Henry A. Terhune

Northpoint Technology, Ltd.
Issues: TEC
Rep By: Barney J. Skladany, Jr., James R. Tucker, Jr.

OMNIPLEX World Services Corp.
Issues: GOV LBR SMB
Rep By: David Geanacopoulos, Charles W. Johnson, IV, Barney J. Skladany, Jr.

Panama Trans-Shipment Consortium

PARC Limited

Pegasus Capital Advisors, L.P.
Issues: AER FOR
Rep By: Frank J. Donatelli, Elizabeth Hyman, S. Bruce Wilson

PerkinElmer Detection Systems
Issues: AVI LAW
Rep By: Sean G. D'Arcy, Smith W. Davis, Barney J. Skladany, Jr., Jose H. Villarreal

Pfizer, Inc.
Issues: TRA TRD
Rep By: Charles W. Johnson, IV, Susan H. Lent, Henry A. Terhune

PG&E Corp.
Issues: ENG TAX UTI
Rep By: Joel Jankowsky, Robin M. Nuschler, Barney J. Skladany, Jr., Henry A. Terhune, Jose H. Villarreal

PG&E Gas Transmission Northwest
Rep By: Janet C. Boyd, Joel Jankowsky

Phillips Foods, Inc.
Issues: TRD
Rep By: Warren E. Connelly, Barney J. Skladany, Jr., S. Bruce Wilson

Policy Group
Rep By: Malcolm Lassman

The Project Leadership Committee, Lincoln Center for the Performing Arts
Issues: BUD TAX
Rep By: Donald C. Alexander, Katherine D. Brodie, Smith W. Davis, Joel Jankowsky, Donald R. Pongrace

Quad Dimension
Issues: CPT
Rep By: J. David Carlin, Elizabeth Hyman, Barney J. Skladany, Jr.

Christopher Reeve Paralysis Foundation

Riggs Bank, N.A.
Issues: BAN
Rep By: Smith W. Davis, Ado A. Machida

RJR Nabisco Holdings Co.

Ryder System, Inc.
Issues: CSP HCR TAX
Rep By: Smith W. Davis, Barney J. Skladany, Jr.

Samsung Corp.
Issues: TRD
Rep By: Frank J. Donatelli

San Antonio, Texas, City of
Issues: BUD DEF TRD
Rep By: Jose H. Villarreal

San Gabriel Basin Water Quality Authority
Issues: CAW ENV
Rep By: Susan H. Lent, David Quigley

Saudi Arabia, Government of
Rep By: Richard B. Self, S. Bruce Wilson

Saudi Arabia, Ministry of Commerce

Schooner Capital Internat'l

Sequoia Ventures
Issues: TAX

Serono Laboratories, Inc.
Issues: HCR MED
Rep By: Karen E. Goldmeier Green, Gary A. Heimberg, Barney J. Skladany, Jr., Daniel L. Spiegel, S. Bruce Wilson

St. Barnabas Healthcare System
Issues: MMM
Rep By: Anthony Foti, Gary A. Heimberg, Jorge J. Lopez, Jr., David B. Palmer, Hon. William L. Paxon, Barney J. Skladany, Jr.

St. Bernard's Hospital
Issues: HCR IMM INS MED MMM
Rep By: James R. Tucker, Jr.

A. E. Staley Manufacturing Co.

Stamps.com
Issues: POS
Rep By: David Geanacopoulos, Daniel L. Spiegel, Robin Weisman

State University of New York at Albany

Svenska Petroleum Exploration AB
Issues: FOR FUE TRD
Rep By: Steven R. Ross, Edward L. Rubinoff

Texas Manufactured Housing Ass'n
Issues: HOU
Rep By: Marlene M. Colucci, Smith W. Davis, Joel Jankowsky, Michael S. Mandel, Barney J. Skladany, Jr., Jose H. Villarreal

The Texas Medical Center
Rep By: Sylvia A. de Leon

Transamerica Financial Services Co.
Rep By: Janet C. Boyd, Joel Jankowsky, Michael S. Mandel, Steven R. Ross

Transamerica Occidental Life Insurance Co.
Rep By: Marlene M. Colucci, Smith W. Davis, Steven R. Ross

Uniden Corp.
Issues: TEC
Rep By: Marlene M. Colucci, David Geanacopoulos, Barney J. Skladany, Jr.

Volkswagen, AG
Issues: AUT CAW CSP ENV TRA TRD
Rep By: David Geanacopoulos, Daniel L. Spiegel, S. Bruce Wilson

Walker Digital Corp.

Arthur T. Walker

Wartsila Diesel, Inc.
Rep By: Gary A. Heimberg, Charles W. Johnson, IV, Barney J. Skladany, Jr.

Wausau Insurance Cos.
Issues: ENV HCR INS TAX
Rep By: Donald C. Alexander, Sean G. D'Arcy

Westar Group, Inc.
Issues: TRD
Rep By: Smith W. Davis, William J. Farah, Barney J. Skladany, Jr., S. Bruce Wilson

Westfield Companies

Wheelabrator Environmental Systems, Inc.

Woodmont Corporation
Issues: CAW ENV GOV RES
Rep By: David Geanacopoulos, Charles W. Johnson, IV

Albers & Co.

1911 N. Ft. Myer Dr.
Suite 707
Arlington, VA 22209
Tel: (703)358-9100
Fax: (703)358-9106
Registered: LDA

A government relations firm specializing in state legislative issues.

DC-Area Employees Representing Listed Clients

ALBERS, William E., President
BEARDSLEY, Daniel B., Managing Partner
ROHLING, M. Guy, Regional Manager - South

Clients

Infiltrator Systems, Inc.
Issues: CAW ENV UTI
Rep By: William E. Albers, Daniel B. Beardsley, M. Guy Rohling

Eli Lilly and Co.
Issues: PHA
Rep By: William E. Albers, Daniel B. Beardsley, M. Guy Rohling

May Department Stores Co.
Issues: BNK
Rep By: William E. Albers, M. Guy Rohling

Profit Recovery Group Internat'l
Issues: BUD DEF
Rep By: William E. Albers, Daniel B. Beardsley, M. Guy Rohling

Albertine Enterprises, Inc.

1156 15th St. NW
Suite 505
Washington, DC 20005
Tel: (202)659-2979
Fax: (202)659-3020
Registered: LDA
Web: www.albertine.com
E-mail: jalbert729@aol.com

DC-Area Employees Representing Listed Clients

ALBERTINE, James J., Partner
ALBERTINE, Dr. John M., Chairman
KING, Aubrey C., Principal

Clients

American Ass'n of Entrepreneurs
Issues: SMB
Rep By: James J. Albertine, Dr. John M. Albertine, Aubrey C. King

Ass'n of School Business Officials Internat'l
Issues: ECN
Rep By: James J. Albertine

Carlson Cos.
Issues: TAX
Rep By: Aubrey C. King

Coleman Aerospace Co.
Issues: SCI
Rep By: James J. Albertine, Dr. John M. Albertine

Employers Council on Flexible Compensation
Issues: TAX
Rep By: James J. Albertine

Energy Absorption Systems, Inc.
Issues: TRA
Rep By: James J. Albertine, Dr. John M. Albertine, Aubrey C. King

Greater Washington Soc. of Ass'n Executives
Issues: TAX
Rep By: James J. Albertine

Health Data Exchange Corp.
Rep By: James J. Albertine

Internat'l Snowmobile Manufacturers Ass'n
Issues: NAT SPO TOU
Rep By: James J. Albertine, Dr. John M. Albertine, Aubrey C. King

Jam Shoe Concepts, Inc.
Issues: TAX TRD
Rep By: Dr. John M. Albertine

Micell Technologies, Inc.

Nat'l Ass'n of RV Parks and Campgrounds
Issues: TOU
Rep By: Aubrey C. King

Nevada, Washington Office of the State of
Issues: TOU
Rep By: James J. Albertine

Polaris Industries
Issues: CSP MAN
Rep By: James J. Albertine, Dr. John M. Albertine

Powerware
Issues: AVI GOV TEC
Rep By: James J. Albertine, Dr. John M. Albertine

SMS Corp.
Issues: HCR VET
Rep By: James J. Albertine

TASC, Inc.
Rep By: James J. Albertine, Dr. John M. Albertine

UNIFI, Inc.
Issues: CAW TAX
Rep By: James J. Albertine, Dr. John M. Albertine

Western States Tourism Policy Council
Issues: TOU
Rep By: Aubrey C. King

Word Chiropractic Alliance
Rep By: James J. Albertine

Sally L. Albright

507 G St. SW
Washington, DC 20024
Tel: (202)421-4555
Fax: (202)546-0506
Registered: LDA

Clients

Gallery Watch
Issues: ADV MIA
Rep By: Sally L. Albright

Stillman College
Issues: EDU HCR TEC URB
Rep By: Sally L. Albright

U.S. Internet Council
Issues: TAX TEC
Rep By: Sally L. Albright

Alcalde & Fay

2111 Wilson Blvd.
Eighth Floor
Arlington, VA 22201-3058
Tel: (703)841-0626
Fax: (703)243-2874
Registered: LDA
Web: www.alcalde-fay.com

A government and public affairs consulting firm.

DC-Area Employees Representing Listed Clients

ALCALDE, Hector, Founder/Senior Partner
AUSTIN, Joe, Partner
BAFALIS, Hon. Louis A. "Skip", Partner
BILBRAY, Hon. James H., Partner
BROWN, Shantrel
CANTUS, H. Hollister, Partner, Aerospace and Technology
COLEMAN, Rodney A., Partner
COLENDA, Cynthia
CORTINA, Thomas A., Partner
CRYE, J. Michael, Partner
DAVENPORT, Jim, Associate
FAY, Kevin J., President
FOWLER, Mary Litton, Associate
HANCOCK, J. B., Partner
HATHAWAY, Kris, Associate
HIRSHBERG, Jennefer A., Partner
ISEMAN, Vicki L., Partner
LEE, Jason, Associate
MCBETH, Danielle, Partner
MOORE, Lois, Partner
MUNOZ, Kathy Jurado, Partner
PATTERSON, Julie, Associate
PLOTT, Angela, Partner
PROWITT, Nancy Gibson, Partner
SCHLESINGER, Paul, Partner
STIRPE, David J., Partner
STROUD, Tim, Associate
SULLIVAN, Bill, Partner
TURNER, Christopher L., Associate
WALKER, Liz, Senior Associate
WEINSTEIN, Alana, Associate
ZORTHIAN, Barry, Partner

Clients

Alliance for Responsible Atmospheric Policy
Issues: ENV
Rep By: Kevin J. Fay, David J. Stirpe

American Maglev Technology Inc.
Rep By: Hector Alcalde, Vicki L. Iseman, Christopher L. Turner

American Magline Group
Issues: TRA
Rep By: Hon. James H. Bilbray, Paul Schlesinger, Christopher L. Turner

AMFM, Inc.
Issues: COM TEC
Rep By: Hector Alcalde, Jim Davenport, Vicki L. Iseman, Julie Patterson

Arcata Associates, Inc.
Issues: DEF
Rep By: Hon. James H. Bilbray, Rodney A. Coleman

Bay County, Florida
Issues: ENV GOV TRA
Rep By: Hector Alcalde, Hon. Louis A. "Skip" Bafalis, Jim Davenport

Boca Raton, Florida, City of
Issues: NAT
Rep By: Hon. Louis A. "Skip" Bafalis, Jim Davenport

Cargill, Inc.
Issues: TRA
Rep By: Hector Alcalde, Lois Moore

Carnival Foundation
Issues: TAX
Rep By: Hector Alcalde, Vicki L. Iseman

Christian Network, Inc.
Issues: COM REL
Rep By: Jim Davenport, Vicki L. Iseman, Julie Patterson

Clearwater, Florida, City of
Issues: BUD ECN GOV HOU ROD TRA URB WEL
Rep By: Hector Alcalde, Danielle McBeth, Lois Moore

CNF Transportation, Inc.
Issues: LBR POS ROD TAX TRA TRU
Rep By: Hector Alcalde, Paul Schlesinger, Tim Stroud

Computer Sciences Corp.
Issues: CPI
Rep By: Hector Alcalde, Jim Davenport, Vicki L. Iseman, Lois Moore, Julie Patterson

CORFAC, Internat'l
Rep By: J. B. Hancock

Cruise Industry Charitable Foundation
Rep By: Hector Alcalde, Cynthia Colenda, Danielle McBeth, Lois Moore, Christopher L. Turner

Dallas, Texas, City of
Issues: BUD CAW NAT RES ROD URB
Rep By: Hector Alcalde, Paul Schlesinger, Tim Stroud

Deerfield Beach, Florida, City of
Issues: ENV TRA TRD
Rep By: Hon. Louis A. "Skip" Bafalis, Shantrel Brown, Jim Davenport, Angela Plott

E.ssociation
Rep By: J. B. Hancock

Earthshell Container Corp.
Issues: ENV
Rep By: Thomas A. Cortina, Kevin J. Fay, Kris Hathaway, Kathy Jurado Munoz

EC-MAC
Rep By: Paul Schlesinger, Tim Stroud

Fairfax County Water Authority
Issues: CAW
Rep By: Kevin J. Fay, Mary Litton Fowler, Nancy Gibson Prowitt

Future Leaders of America
Issues: EDU
Rep By: Lois Moore

Glencairn, Ltd.
Rep By: Hector Alcalde, Jim Davenport, Vicki L. Iseman, Julie Patterson

Golden Gate Bridge Highway and Transportation District
Issues: NAT ROD RRR
Rep By: Jason Lee, Paul Schlesinger

Grand Valley State University
Rep By: Jennefer A. Hirshberg, Tim Stroud, Christopher L. Turner

Great Lakes Chemical Corp.
Rep By: Thomas A. Cortina

Halon Alternatives Research Corp.
Rep By: Thomas A. Cortina

Hillsborough, Florida, County of
Issues: ECN NAT TAX TRA WAS WEL
Rep By: Hector Alcalde, Rodney A. Coleman, Lois Moore

Hispanic Broadcasting Inc.
Issues: COM CPT TEC
Rep By: Hector Alcalde, Jim Davenport, Vicki L. Iseman, Tim Stroud

Houston Independent School District
Issues: EDU
Rep By: Danielle McBeth, Lois Moore, Kathy Jurado Munoz, Tim Stroud

Intel Corp.
Rep By: Thomas A. Cortina, Kevin J. Fay

Internat'l Climate Change Partnership
Issues: ENV
Rep By: Thomas A. Cortina, Kevin J. Fay, Kris Hathaway, David J. Stirpe

Internat'l Council of Cruise Lines
Issues: MAR TAX
Rep By: Hector Alcalde, Hon. Louis A. "Skip" Bafalis, J. Michael Crye, Lois Moore, Nancy Gibson Prowitt, Alana Weinstein, Barry Zorthian

Jacksonville Chamber of Commerce
Issues: EDU
Rep By: Lois Moore

Jacksonville, Florida, Port Authority of the City of
Issues: TRA
Rep By: Hector Alcalde, Lois Moore

Jovan Broadcasting
Issues: COM
Rep By: Hector Alcalde, Shantrel Brown, Jim Davenport, Vicki L. Iseman, Julie Patterson, Christopher L. Turner

Lake, California, County of
Issues: BUD POS RES ROD TRA URB
Rep By: Paul Schlesinger, Tim Stroud

Las Vegas Convention and Visitors Authority
Issues: TOU
Rep By: Hon. James H. Bilbray, Julie Patterson, Christopher L. Turner

Marin, California, County of
Issues: DEF HOU LAW NAT TRA
Rep By: Paul Schlesinger

Metromedia Co.
Rep By: Jennefer A. Hirshberg

Miami Heat
Rep By: Cynthia Colenda, Nancy Gibson Prowitt, Christopher L. Turner, Alana Weinstein

Miami-Dade County Public Schools
Rep By: Danielle McBeth, Lois Moore, Kathy Jurado Munoz, Tim Stroud

Miami-Dade, Florida, County of
Rep By: Hector Alcalde, Danielle McBeth, Lois Moore, Christopher L. Turner

Mitretek Systems
Issues: LAW
Rep By: Hector Alcalde, Hon. Louis A. "Skip" Bafalis, Rodney A. Coleman, Jim Davenport

Nat'l Ass'n of Gas Chlorinators
Issues: TRA
Rep By: Paul Schlesinger, Tim Stroud

Nat'l Peace Foundation
Rep By: Jennefer A. Hirshberg

NEDA
Rep By: Kevin J. Fay

North American Sports Management, Inc.
Issues: IND
Rep By: Hon. Louis A. "Skip" Bafalis, Jim Davenport

North Miami Beach, Florida, City of
Issues: HOU TRA
Rep By: Hector Alcalde, Danielle McBeth

Norwegian Cruise Line
Issues: GAM MAR
Rep By: Hector Alcalde, Cynthia Colenda

Office of Naval Research
Rep By: J. B. Hancock

Osceola, Florida, County of
Issues: ENV TRA
Rep By: Hon. Louis A. "Skip" Bafalis, Jim Davenport

Palm Beach, Florida, Port of
Issues: ENV TRA
Rep By: Hon. Louis A. "Skip" Bafalis, Angela Plott

Palm Springs, California, City of
Issues: AVI IND RRR
Rep By: Mary Litton Fowler, Nancy Gibson Prowitt

Panama, Government of the Republic of
Rep By: Hector Alcalde, Cynthia Colenda, Alana Weinstein

Paxson Communications Corp.
Issues: COM TEC
Rep By: Hector Alcalde, Jim Davenport, Vicki L. Iseman, Julie Patterson

PetrolRem, Inc.
Issues: ENV MAR SCI
Rep By: Hon. Louis A. "Skip" Bafalis, J. Michael Crye, Jim Davenport

Riviera Beach, Florida, City of
Issues: ENV TRA
Rep By: Hon. Louis A. "Skip" Bafalis, Shantrel Brown, Jim Davenport, Danielle McBeth

Section 877 Coalition
Issues: TAX
Rep By: Hector Alcalde, Hon. Louis A. "Skip" Bafalis

Sonoma County Water Agency
Issues: ENV
Rep By: Jason Lee, Paul Schlesinger

Sonoma, California, County of
Issues: ECN TRA
Rep By: Jason Lee, Paul Schlesinger

Stevens Institute of Technology
Issues: DEF ECN
Rep By: Hon. Louis A. "Skip" Bafalis, Jim Davenport

Tampa Port Authority
Issues: TRA
Rep By: Hector Alcalde, J. Michael Crye, Lois Moore

Tampa, Florida, City of
Issues: HOU TRA
Rep By: Hector Alcalde, Kathy Jurado Munoz

Tulare, California, County of
Issues: ECN LAW ROD
Rep By: Paul Schlesinger, Tim Stroud

University of Nevada - Las Vegas
Issues: EDU
Rep By: Hon. James H. Bilbray, Kathy Jurado Munoz

Virginia Beach, Virginia, City of
Issues: ENV TRA TRD
Rep By: Mary Litton Fowler, Angela Plott, Nancy Gibson Prowitt

Washington Workshops
Issues: EDU
Rep By: Danielle McBeth, Lois Moore

World Wide Technology
Rep By: Rodney A. Coleman

Alexander Strategy Group

P.O. Box 5711
Arlington, VA 22205
Tel: (202)543-5136
Fax: (202)543-5266
Registered: LDA

DC-Area Employees Representing Listed Clients
BUCKHAM, Edwin A.
ELLIS, James W., V. President

Clients

Enron Corp.
Issues: ENG UTI
Rep By: Edwin A. Buckham

Nat'l Religious Broadcasters, Music License Committee
Issues: COM

Nuclear Energy Institute
Issues: ENG WAS
Rep By: Edwin A. Buckham

Pharmaceutical Research and Manufacturers of America
Issues: MMM PHA TRD
Rep By: Edwin A. Buckham

Salem Communications Corp.
Issues: COM

The Alexandria Group

526 King St.
Alexandria, VA 22314
Tel: (703)706-9580
Fax: (703)706-9583
Web: www.alexandriagroup.com
E-mail: alexgrp@alexandriagroup.com

DC-Area Employees Representing Listed Clients
KOLAR, CAE, Mary Jane, President and Chief Exec. Officer
MITCHEL, M. Lynn, Managing Partner

Clients

Nat'l Ass'n of Government Communicators

Nat'l Cargo Security Council

Alford & Associates

3207 Chichester Lane
Fairfax, VA 22301
Tel: (703)204-2867
Fax: (703)204-2867
Registered: LDA

DC-Area Employees Representing Listed Clients
ALFORD, Marty
ALFORD, Ralph, President

Clients

Aeromet, Inc.
Issues: DEF
Rep By: Marty Alford

Air Cruisers, Inc.
Issues: DEF
Rep By: Marty Alford

Go! Systems, Inc.
Issues: DEF
Rep By: Marty Alford

W. L. Gore & Associates
Issues: DEF
Rep By: Marty Alford

Lockheed Martin Aeronautical Systems Co.
Issues: DEF
Rep By: Marty Alford

Newport News Shipbuilding Inc.
Issues: DEF
Rep By: Marty Alford

Sparton Electronics, Florida, Inc.
Issues: DEF
Rep By: Marty Alford

Harry C. Alford & Associates, Inc.

1350 Connecticut Ave. NW
Suite 825
Washington, DC 20036
Tel: (202)466-6888
Fax: (202)466-4918
Registered: LDA

DC-Area Employees Representing Listed Clients
ALFORD, Jr., Harry C.
THOMAS, Kermit R.

Clients

James E. Schneider, LLM Inc.
Issues: BAN CAW CIV ECN ENV FIN LBR SMB TAX
Rep By: Harry C. Alford, Jr., Kermit R. Thomas

Alpine Group, Inc.

660 Pennsylvania Ave. SE
Suite 201
Washington, DC 20003
Tel: (202)547-1831
Fax: (202)547-4658
Registered: LDA
Web: www.alpinegroup.com
E-mail: alpine@alpinegroup.com
A government relations consulting firm.

DC-Area Employees Representing Listed Clients
BROUILLETTE, Dan, Partner
MASSIE, James D., Partner
MEANS, James Gregory, Partner
SHAW, Rhod M., Partner
SKOPEC, Monica, Associate
WHITE, Richard C., Partner
WHITE, Sam, Partner

Clients

American Cable Ass'n
Issues: COM CPT GOV SMB TEC
Rep By: James Gregory Means, Rhod M. Shaw, Monica Skopec

American Crop Protection Ass'n
Issues: AGR ENV FOO
Rep By: James D. Massie, Sam White

Arthur Andersen LLP
Issues: ACC
Rep By: Dan Brouillette, James Gregory Means, Rhod M. Shaw

AT&T

BP Amoco Corp.
Issues: ENG TAX
Rep By: Dan Brouillette, James D. Massie, James Gregory Means

Bracco Diagnostics
Issues: HCR MMM
Rep By: James D. Massie, Richard C. White

Business Software Alliance
Issues: COM CPI CPT
Rep By: Dan Brouillette, Rhod M. Shaw

Cinergy Corp.
Issues: ENV
Rep By: James D. Massie

Council on Radionuclides and Radiopharmaceuticals (CORAR)
Issues: BUD ENG HCR MMM TRA
Rep By: James D. Massie, Richard C. White

Dow AgroSciences
Issues: TRD
Rep By: James D. Massie, Richard C. White

The DuPont Pharmaceutical Co.
Issues: HCR TRD
Rep By: Richard C. White

Dynegy, Inc.
Issues: ENG UTI
Rep By: Rhod M. Shaw

El Paso Corporation
Issues: ENG ENV FUE NAT TAX
Rep By: James D. Massie, Rhod M. Shaw

Jackson Nat'l Life Insurance
Issues: BAN FIN LAW TAX TEC
Rep By: James D. Massie, Richard C. White

Lafarge Corp.
Issues: BUD CAW ENV TRA TRD WAS
Rep By: James Gregory Means

Lockheed Martin Global Telecommunications
Issues: TEC
Rep By: Dan Brouillette

Medical Imaging Contrast Agent Ass'ns
Issues: HCR MMM
Rep By: James D. Massie, Monica Skopec, Richard C. White

Nat'l Ass'n of Insurance and Financial Advisors
Issues: COM INS TAX
Rep By: James D. Massie, Rhod M. Shaw, Richard C. White

Nat'l Corn Growers Ass'n
Issues: CAW
Rep By: James D. Massie

Pharmacia Corp.
Issues: CPT HCR MED MMM PHA
Rep By: Dan Brouillette, James D. Massie, James Gregory Means, Rhod M. Shaw, Richard C. White, Sam White

Recording Industry Ass'n of America
Issues: CPI CPT LAW
Rep By: Dan Brouillette, Rhod M. Shaw

Seneca Resources Corporation
Issues: BUD NAT
Rep By: Rhod M. Shaw, Monica Skopec

Southwire, Inc.
Issues: BUD ENV TAX TRD
Rep By: James D. Massie

Swedish Match
Issues: FOO HCR TOB
Rep By: Dan Brouillette, James Gregory Means

Syngenta

Toyota Motor North America, U.S.A., Inc.
Issues: AUT ENV FUE
Rep By: Rhod M. Shaw, Monica Skopec

TVA Watch
Issues: BUD ENG UTI
Rep By: James Gregory Means

U.S. Filter
Issues: CAW ENV URB
Rep By: Dan Brouillette, James D. Massie, James Gregory Means

Alston & Bird LLP

601 Pennsylvania Ave. NW
11th Floor, North Bldg.
Washington, DC 20004-2601
Tel: (202)756-3300
Fax: (202)756-3333
Registered: LDA
Web: www.alston.com
E-mail: info@alston.com
Maintains offices in Atlanta, GA, Washington, DC, Charlotte, NC, and the Research Triangle in Raleigh, NC.

DC-Area Employees Representing Listed Clients
BIRNKRANT, Henry J., Partner
BOYD, Thomas M., Partner
COLE, Robert T., Partner
CONNER, III, Frank M.
CROCKER, Thomas E., Partner
DOUGLAS, John L., Partner
JOYCE, Frederick, Partner
KONTIO, Peter
LOVETT, A.E.
MCLAUGHLIN, Christine, Counsel
PARSONS, Oscar N., Partner
QUIRK, Jr., Ronald, Senior Associate
SCHALL, John A.
SMITH, III, Dwight C., Counsel
TALCOTT, Jonathan H.
WHEELER, Charles
WINER, Jonathan

Clients

Advanced Glassfiber Yarns
Issues: MAN
Rep By: Thomas M. Boyd

AFLAC, Inc.
Issues: INS
Rep By: Thomas M. Boyd, Dwight C. Smith, III

The Assurant Group
Issues: BAN FIN
Rep By: Thomas M. Boyd, Dwight C. Smith, III

CarsDirect.com
Issues: AUT TEC
Rep By: Thomas M. Boyd, Jonathan Winer

Employers Council on Flexible Compensation

General Electric Co.
Issues: CSP MAN
Rep By: Thomas M. Boyd, Thomas E. Crocker, Jonathan Winer

GTE Mobilnet
Rep By: Peter Kontio

Matsushita Electric Corp. of America
Issues: TAX
Rep By: Henry J. Birnkrant, Robert T. Cole

Morgan Stanley Dean Witter & Co.
Issues: FIN
Rep By: Thomas M. Boyd

Nat'l Coalition on E-Commerce and Privacy
Issues: CSP TEC
Rep By: Thomas M. Boyd, A.E. Lovett, John A. Schall, Dwight C. Smith, III, Jonathan Winer

Nat'l Foreign Trade Council, Inc.
Issues: TRD
Rep By: Robert T. Cole, Charles Wheeler

Regions Financial Corp.
Rep By: Frank M. Conner, III, Jonathan H. Talcott

Alvarado & Gerken

300 Third St. NE
Suite 204
Washington, DC 20002
Tel: (202)544-0003
Fax: (202)544-6635
Registered: LDA
A firm providing government consulting services.

DC-Area Employees Representing Listed Clients
ALVARADO, Susan E., Partner
GERKEN, David A., Partner

Clients

Grumman Olson
Issues: GOV TRA
Rep By: Susan E. Alvarado

Mas-Hamilton Group
Issues: DEF
Rep By: Susan E. Alvarado, David A. Gerken

MCI WorldCom Corp.
Issues: COM TEC
Rep By: Susan E. Alvarado, David A. Gerken

Puerto Rico Senate
Issues: AVI TAX TEC
Rep By: David A. Gerken

SAT
Issues: DEF
Rep By: Susan E. Alvarado

TransNat'l Business Development Corp.
Issues: MAR
Rep By: Susan E. Alvarado, David A. Gerken

American Continental Group, Inc.

2099 Pennsylvania Ave. NW
Suite 850
Washington, DC 20006
Tel: (202)419-2500
Fax: (202)419-2510
Registered: LDA, FARA
Web: www.acgrep.com
E-mail: info@acgrep.com
Political consultants.

DC-Area Employees Representing Listed Clients
CLINE, John A., Consultant, Government Relations
COLOVAS, Steve, Director
METZNER, David A., Managing Director
SMEALLIE, Shawn H., Managing Director
STROM, Thaddeus E., Managing Director
TERPELUK, Jr., Peter, Managing Director

Clients

American Standard Cos. Inc.
Rep By: David A. Metzner, Shawn H. Smeallie

Americans Against Unfair Family Taxation

Ass'n of American Railroads
Issues: TRA
Rep By: John A. Cline, Shawn H. Smeallie, Peter Terpeluk, Jr.

Campaign for Tobacco-Free Kids
Issues: TOB
Rep By: Shawn H. Smeallie, Peter Terpeluk, Jr.

Central European Media Enterprises
Issues: FOR
Rep By: Shawn H. Smeallie

Coalition for Travel Industry Parity
Issues: TOU
Rep By: John A. Cline, Steve Colovas, Shawn H. Smeallie

Colorado Intermountain Fixed Guideway Authority
Issues: TRA
Rep By: John A. Cline, Shawn H. Smeallie

EEI
Rep By: Steve Colovas, Shawn H. Smeallie, Peter Terpeluk, Jr.

Ernst & Young LLP
Issues: BAN
Rep By: David A. Metzner, Shawn H. Smeallie, Thaddeus E. Strom, Peter Terpeluk, Jr.

Fisher Imaging
Issues: HCR
Rep By: Steve Colovas, David A. Metzner

Healthnow
Rep By: David A. Metzner, Shawn H. Smeallie

IMAX Corp.
Issues: ART
Rep By: Peter Terpeluk, Jr.

Los Angeles County Metropolitan Transportation Authority
Issues: TRA
Rep By: John A. Cline, Shawn H. Smeallie

Martin Color-Fi
Issues: TRD
Rep By: John A. Cline, Thaddeus E. Strom

Northpoint Technology, Ltd.
Issues: COM
Rep By: Steve Colovas, Shawn H. Smeallie, Peter Terpeluk, Jr.

OSI Systems, Inc.
Issues: LAW
Rep By: John A. Cline, David A. Metzner, Shawn H. Smeallie

Pennsylvania Higher Education Assistance Agency
Issues: EDU
Rep By: Shawn H. Smeallie, Peter Terpeluk, Jr.

PepsiCo, Inc.
Issues: BEV
Rep By: Steve Colovas, Shawn H. Smeallie, Peter Terpeluk, Jr.

Plasma-Therm, Inc.
Issues: DEF MAN SCI
Rep By: Steve Colovas, David A. Metzner

Prudential Insurance Co. of America
Rep By: David A. Metzner, Shawn H. Smeallie, Peter Terpeluk, Jr.

Public Financial Management
Issues: FIN
Rep By: Peter Terpeluk, Jr.

Recording Industry Ass'n of America
Issues: CPT TEC
Rep By: Thaddeus E. Strom

Scholastic, Inc.
Issues: EDU GOV
Rep By: Shawn H. Smeallie

Securify
Rep By: Steve Colovas, David A. Metzner

Siemens Corp.
Rep By: David A. Metzner, Shawn H. Smeallie, Peter Terpeluk, Jr.

Southeastern Pennsylvania Transit Authority
Issues: TRA
Rep By: John A. Cline, Peter Terpeluk, Jr.

Stony Brook Foundation
Issues: EDU HCR
Rep By: Steve Colovas, David A. Metzner, Shawn H. Smeallie

Tri-County Commuter Rail Authority
Issues: TRA
Rep By: John A. Cline, Shawn H. Smeallie

Trifinery, Inc.
Issues: FUE
Rep By: John A. Cline, David A. Metzner, Shawn H. Smeallie

Vanguard Research, Inc.
Issues: ENV
Rep By: David A. Metzner

Verizon Communications
Issues: TEC
Rep By: Thaddeus E. Strom

American Defense Internat'l, Inc.

1800 K St. NW
Suite 1010
Washington, DC 20006
Tel: (202)296-5030
Fax: (202)296-4750
Registered: LDA, FARA
E-mail: amerdefint@aol.com
A consulting firm specializing in government affairs, business development, and public relations.

DC-Area Employees Representing Listed Clients
DAFFRON, Thomas
HERSON, Michael, President
HIPP, Jr., Van D., Chairman
MARCINIK, Dr. Ed
PHILLIPS, George
SHINDELMAN, Bonnie
WILBERDING, Dave, V. President, Government Affairs

Clients

3D Metrics Inc.
Issues: DEF
Rep By: Van D. Hipp, Jr., Dave Wilberding

ANSAR Inc.
Issues: DEF
Rep By: Van D. Hipp, Jr., Dave Wilberding

Barber Colman Co.
Issues: DEF
Rep By: Michael Herson, Van D. Hipp, Jr., Dave Wilberding

Beretta U.S.A. Corp.
Issues: DEF
Rep By: Michael Herson, Van D. Hipp, Jr., Dave Wilberding

Bofors Defence AB
Issues: DEF
Rep By: Michael Herson, Van D. Hipp, Jr., George Phillips, Dave Wilberding

Dialogic Communications Corp.
Issues: DEF
Rep By: Michael Herson, Van D. Hipp, Jr.

Drexel University
Issues: DEF
Rep By: Michael Herson, Van D. Hipp, Jr., Dave Wilberding

East/West Industries
Issues: DEF
Rep By: Michael Herson, Van D. Hipp, Jr., Bonnie Shindelman, Dave Wilberding

Eickhorn-Solingen
Issues: DEF
Rep By: Van D. Hipp, Jr., Dave Wilberding

Ensign-Bickford Co.
Issues: DEF
Rep By: Michael Herson, Van D. Hipp, Jr., Dave Wilberding

EWA Land Information Group, Inc.
Issues: DEF
Rep By: Michael Herson, Van D. Hipp, Jr., Dave Wilberding

Fibernet LLC
Rep By: Michael Herson, Van D. Hipp, Jr., Dave Wilberding

Friction Free Technologies Inc.
Issues: DEF
Rep By: Michael Herson, Van D. Hipp, Jr., Bonnie Shindelman, Dave Wilberding

Ganaden Biotech Inc.
Issues: DEF
Rep By: Michael Herson, Van D. Hipp, Jr., Dave Wilberding

Gentex Corp.
Issues: DEF
Rep By: Van D. Hipp, Jr., Dave Wilberding

GIAT Industries
Issues: DEF
Rep By: Michael Herson, Van D. Hipp, Jr., Dave Wilberding

Hagglunds Moelv AS
Issues: DEF
Rep By: Michael Herson, Van D. Hipp, Jr., Dave Wilberding

InformaTech, Inc.
Issues: DEF
Rep By: Michael Herson, Van D. Hipp, Jr., Dave Wilberding

InvenCom LLC
Rep By: Michael Herson, Van D. Hipp, Jr., Dave Wilberding

Koable Co., Ltd.
Issues: DEF
Rep By: Michael Herson, Van D. Hipp, Jr., Dave Wilberding

Large Scale Biology
Issues: DEF
Rep By: Michael Herson, Van D. Hipp, Jr., Dr. Ed Marcinik, Dave Wilberding

Le Meilleur Co., Ltd.
Issues: DEF
Rep By: Michael Herson, Van D. Hipp, Jr., Dave Wilberding

Longworth Industries Inc.
Issues: DEF
Rep By: Michael Herson, Van D. Hipp, Jr., Dave Wilberding

Marine Desalination Systems LLC
Issues: DEF
Rep By: Thomas Daffron, Michael Herson, Van D. Hipp, Jr., Dave Wilberding

MEGAXESS, Inc.
Issues: GOV
Rep By: Michael Herson, Van D. Hipp, Jr., Dave Wilberding

Ordnance Development and Engineering Co. of Singapore
Issues: DEF
Rep By: Michael Herson, Van D. Hipp, Jr., Dave Wilberding

Pacific Consolidated Industries
Issues: DEF
Rep By: Michael Herson, Van D. Hipp, Jr., Dave Wilberding

PDI Ground Support Systems, Inc.
Issues: DEF
Rep By: Michael Herson, Van D. Hipp, Jr., Dave Wilberding

Raytheon Missile Systems
Issues: DEF
Rep By: Michael Herson, Van D. Hipp, Jr., Dave Wilberding

Saab AB
Issues: DEF
Rep By: Michael Herson, Van D. Hipp, Jr., Dave Wilberding

Sarnoff Corp.
Rep By: Michael Herson, Van D. Hipp, Jr., Dave Wilberding

SINTEF Telecom and Informatics
Issues: DEF
Rep By: Michael Herson, Van D. Hipp, Jr., Dave Wilberding

Smiths Industries Aerospace and Defense Systems
Issues: DEF
Rep By: Michael Herson, Van D. Hipp, Jr., Dave Wilberding

Stidd Systems, Inc.
Issues: DEF
Rep By: Michael Herson, Van D. Hipp, Jr., Bonnie Shindelman, Dave Wilberding

Stratus Systems Inc.
Issues: DEF
Rep By: Michael Herson, Van D. Hipp, Jr., Dave Wilberding

Swiss Munition Enterprise
Issues: DEF
Rep By: Van D. Hipp, Jr., Dave Wilberding

Syntroleum Corp.
Issues: DEF
Rep By: Michael Herson, Van D. Hipp, Jr., Dave Wilberding

Time Domain Corp.
Issues: DEF
Rep By: Michael Herson, Van D. Hipp, Jr., Dave Wilberding

Virtual Drug Development
Issues: DEF
Rep By: Michael Herson, Van D. Hipp, Jr., Dave Wilberding

Virtual Impact Productions
Issues: DEF
Rep By: Michael Herson, Van D. Hipp, Jr., Dave Wilberding

VISICU
Issues: DEF
Rep By: Michael Herson, Van D. Hipp, Jr., Dave Wilberding

ViTel Net
Issues: DEF
Rep By: Michael Herson, Van D. Hipp, Jr., Dave Wilberding

Xeta Internat'l Corp.
Issues: DEF
Rep By: Michael Herson, Van D. Hipp, Jr., Dave Wilberding

Youyang
Issues: DEF
Rep By: Michael Herson, Van D. Hipp, Jr., Dave Wilberding

American Strategies, Inc.

1300 Connecticut Ave. NW
Suite 600
Washington, DC 20036
Tel: (202)293-0231
Fax: (202)223-0358
Registered: LDA
E-mail: strategies@cais.com
A grassroots lobbying firm.

DC-Area Employees Representing Listed Clients
KOWALCZUK, Paula, President

Clients

The Business Roundtable

Education First Alliance

American Systems Internat'l Corp.

2800 Shirlington Rd.
Suite 401
Arlington, VA 22206
Tel: (703)824-0300
Fax: (703)824-0320
Registered: LDA
Web: www.asic-dc.com

DC-Area Employees Representing Listed Clients
KHARE, Joe, Consultant
MCVEY, Robert D., Chief Exec. Officer
SKIPPER, Jr., William H., President
TESNOW, David, Consultant

Clients

Battelle Memorial Institute
Issues: DEF MAN
Rep By: Robert D. McVey, William H. Skipper, Jr.

Battelle Memorial Labs
Issues: DEF MAN
Rep By: Robert D. McVey, William H. Skipper, Jr.

Elbet Forth Worth
Issues: DEF MAN
Rep By: Joe Khare, Robert D. McVey, William H. Skipper, Jr.

FN Herstal, USA
Issues: DEF MAN
Rep By: Robert D. McVey, William H. Skipper, Jr.

Israel Aircraft Industries, Ltd.
Rep By: Robert D. McVey, William H. Skipper, Jr.

Lockheed Martin Corp.
Rep By: Robert D. McVey, William H. Skipper, Jr.

Logis-Tech, Inc.
Issues: DEF MAN
Rep By: Robert D. McVey, William H. Skipper, Jr.

Media Fusion L.L.C.

Northrop Grumman Corp.
Issues: DEF MAN
Rep By: Robert D. McVey, William H. Skipper, Jr.

Pennsylvania Nat'l Guard Ass'n
Issues: DEF MAN
Rep By: Robert D. McVey, William H. Skipper, Jr.

Precision Lift
Issues: DEF MAN
Rep By: Robert D. McVey, William H. Skipper, Jr.

PulseTech Products Corp.
Issues: DEF MAN
Rep By: William H. Skipper, Jr.

Raytheon Co.
Issues: DEF MAN
Rep By: Robert D. McVey, William H. Skipper, Jr.

Safety Storage Inc.
Rep By: Robert D. McVey, William H. Skipper, Jr.

South Carolina Nat'l Guard Ass'n
Issues: DEF MAN

Vision Systems Internat'l
Rep By: Robert D. McVey, William H. Skipper, Jr.

American Trade and Professional Ass'n Management

P.O. Box 59811
Potomac, MD 20859-9811
Tel: (301)365-2521
Fax: (301)365-7705
Registered: LDA, FARA
E-mail: russbarker@mindspring.com, atpam@mindspring.com
A trade and professional association management company.

DC-Area Employees Representing Listed Clients
BARKER, Russell E., President

Clients

Peanut and Tree Nut Processors Ass'n
Rep By: Russell E. Barker

Morris J. Amitay, P.C.

444 N. Capitol St. NW
Suite 712
Washington, DC 20001
Tel: (202)347-6613
Fax: (202)393-7006
Registered: LDA
E-mail: mjapc@erols.com
A law and lobbying firm. .

DC-Area Employees Representing Listed Clients
AMITAY, Morris J., President
AMITAY, Stephen D., Of Counsel

Clients

Advantage Healthplan Inc.
Issues: MMM
Rep By: Morris J. Amitay, Stephen D. Amitay

Israel Aircraft Industries, Ltd.
Issues: DEF
Rep By: Morris J. Amitay

Lau Technologies
Issues: SCI
Rep By: Morris J. Amitay

Northrop Grumman Corp.
Issues: DEF
Rep By: Morris J. Amitay

TRW Space and Electronics Group
Issues: DEF
Rep By: Morris J. Amitay

Washington Political Action Committee
Rep By: Morris J. Amitay

Jeffrey M. Anders

1615 L St. NW
Suite 650
Washington, DC 20036
Tel: (202)659-0979
Fax: (202)659-3010
Registered: LDA
A self-employed government relations consultant.

Clients

Cephalon, Inc.
Rep By: Jeffrey M. Anders

UniServe Inc.
Issues: TRA
Rep By: Jeffrey M. Anders

Anderson and Corrie

12600 Fair Lakes Circle
Suite 220
Fairfax, VA 22033
Tel: (703)222-2200
Fax: (703)222-0321

DC-Area Employees Representing Listed Clients
CORRIE, Quentin R., Partner

Clients

AAA MidAtlantic
Rep By: Quentin R. Corrie

Anderson and Pendleton, C.A.

206 N. Washington St.
Suite 330
Alexandria, VA 22304
Tel: (703)683-4420
Fax: (703)683-4538
Registered: LDA, FARA
E-mail: francis_mckenna@hotmail.com

DC-Area Employees Representing Listed Clients

MCKENNA, Francis G., President

Clients

Tourist Railroad Ass'n, Inc.
Rep By: Francis G. McKenna

West Virginia State Rail Authority
Rep By: Francis G. McKenna

Andreae, Vick & Associates, L.L.C.

1250 I St. NW
Suite 1105
Washington, DC 20005
Tel: (202)682-5151
Fax: (202)682-2185
Registered: LDA

An international corporate and government relations firm.

DC-Area Employees Representing Listed Clients

ANDREAE, III, Charles N., Partner
BURLEW, William
HAYS, F. Wallace, Senior Associate
SZYMANSKI, Tauna M., Senior Research Associate
VICK, M. Christine, Partner

Clients

Pharmaceutical Research and Manufacturers of America
Issues: TRD
Rep By: M. Christine Vick

U.S. Colombia Business Partnership
Issues: FOR
Rep By: Charles N. Andreae, III, William Burlew

Andrews and Kurth, L.L.P.

1701 Pennsylvania Ave. NW
Suite 300
Washington, DC 20006
Tel: (202)662-2700
Fax: (202)662-2739
Registered: LDA
E-mail: webmaster@andrew-kurth.com

DC-Area Employees Representing Listed Clients

FARRIS, Elaine
RYAN, Kevin, Associate

Clients

Bank of New England Holding Company Trustee

El Paso Natural Gas Co.

IPALCO Enterprises, Inc./Indianapolis Power & Light Co.

Andrews Associates, Inc.

2550 M St. NW
Suite 250
Washington, DC 20037
Tel: (202)457-5671
Fax: (202)785-0480
Registered: LDA

A governmental affairs consulting firm.

DC-Area Employees Representing Listed Clients

ANDREWS, Hon. Mark, Chairman
BALK-TUSA, Dr. Jacqueline, President

Clients

Mars, Inc.
Rep By: Hon. Mark Andrews, Dr. Jacqueline Balk-Tusa

Nat'l Trailer Dealers Ass'n
Rep By: Hon. Mark Andrews, Dr. Jacqueline Balk-Tusa

Patton Boggs, LLP
Issues: AGR EDU TAX
Rep By: Hon. Mark Andrews, Dr. Jacqueline Balk-Tusa

Safeguard America's Family Enterprises
Issues: TAX
Rep By: Hon. Mark Andrews, Dr. Jacqueline Balk-Tusa

APCO Worldwide

1615 L St. NW
Suite 900
Washington, DC 20036
Tel: (202)778-1000
Fax: (202)466-6002
Registered: LDA, FARA
Web: www.apcoworldwide.com
E-mail: info@apcoworldwide.com

A global public affairs firm offering a wide range of services in public affairs, grassroots coalition building, corporate philanthropy, government relations, legislative tracking and media/technology consulting. Serves public and private sector clients, governments and corporations, as well as non-profits and trade associations. Also maintains offices in Sacramento and Los Angeles, CA; Seattle, WA; Beijing, Shanghai, Hong Kong, and Shenzhen, China; Brussels, Belgium; Geneva, Switzerland; Hanoi and Ho Chi Minh City, Vietnam; London, England; Moscow, Russia; Ottawa and Toronto, Canada; Paris, France; and Rome, Italy.

DC-Area Employees Representing Listed Clients

ALLNUT, Bob, Senior Counselor
BERLS, Tatiana G., V. President and Managing Director, Russia/CIS Services
BISSEN, Robert, V. President, Government Relations
BONKER, Hon. Don L., Exec. V. President
COHEN, Neal M., Exec. V. President and Managing Director, APCO US
COOPER, B. Jay, Senior V. President
FANCHER, Marilyn, V. President and Creative Director
FARR, Stephen, V. President, Corporate Community Strategies
FITZPATRICK, Maggie, V. President and Director, Internet Positioning
GOELZ, Peter
HARTMAN, Arthur A., Senior Consultant
HAUSRATH, Jan E., Senior V. President and Director, Strategic Communications
JARRELL, Kent, Senior V. President, PA Practice
JUDD, Terry W., V. President
KESSER, Sheri, V. President, Global Services
KRAUS, Margery, President and Chief Exec. Officer
KRAUSE, Charles, Senior V. President, Global Services
LABUDA, Laurie, V. President, Public Affairs
LOUISON, Deborah L., Senior V. President and Director, Global Services
MIGNONI, Ellen, Senior V. President and Director, Corporate Community Strategies
PINES, Wayne L., President, Healthcare and Director, Crisis Communications
RINGWOOD, Danielle, Junior Associate
SCHOOLING, Robert, Senior V. President and Director, Public Affairs
SCHUMACHER, Barry J., Senior V. President and Director, International Policy
SOLARZ, Hon. Stephen J., Senior Counselor
THISTLE, Kirsten, V. President, Public Affairs

Clients

Alaska Airlines
Issues: AVI DIS
Rep By: Peter Goelz

American Camping Ass'n
Issues: AGR CSP EDU IMM IRA NAT TAX
Rep By: Danielle Ringwood

COSCO Americas Inc.
Issues: MAR
Rep By: Hon. Don L. Bonker, Barry J. Schumacher

Creme de la Creme, Inc.
Issues: ANI FOR TRD
Rep By: Barry J. Schumacher, Hon. Stephen J. Solarz

Formosan Ass'n for Public Affairs
Rep By: Hon. Stephen J. Solarz

Holy Land Trust
Issues: FOR TOU
Rep By: Hon. Don L. Bonker, Barry J. Schumacher

India, Government of the Republic of
Issues: FOR
Rep By: Hon. Don L. Bonker, Barry J. Schumacher

Most Group Limited
Issues: FOR MIA
Rep By: Hon. Don L. Bonker

Orcon Corp.
Issues: AVI
Rep By: Hon. Don L. Bonker

Singapore, Government of the Republic of

Ukraine, Government of
Issues: FOR
Rep By: Hon. Don L. Bonker, Deborah L. Louison

Arent Fox Kintner Plotkin & Kahn, PLLC

1050 Connecticut Ave. NW
Washington, DC 20036-5339
Tel: (202)857-6000
Fax: (202)857-6395
Registered: LDA, FARA
Web: www.arentfox.com
E-mail: infolaw@arentfox.com

A law firm.

Political Action Committee

Arent Fox Civic Participation Fund
1050 Connecticut Ave. NW
Washington, DC 20036-5339
Tel: (202)857-6000
Fax: (202)857-6395
Contact: Elliott I. Portnoy

DC-Area Employees Representing Listed Clients

ABRAMSON, Stanley H., Member
AKMAN, Jerome P., Member
APPLEGATE, Bill, Government Relations Director
BAILEY, Melissa, Associate
BARDIN, David J., Of-Counsel
BUMPERS, Hon. Dale L., Member
CAMPBELL, Bonnie, Counsel
CHARYK, William R., Member
CLARKE, Katie, Government Relations Director
CULVER, Hon. John C., Member
DAVIS, Mary Hope, Government Relations Director
DIMOND, Kendra, Member
ENGLE, Craig, Counsel
ESTRADA, Lisa, Associate
FISHEL, Alan, Member
FLEISCHAKER, Marc L., Member
GOODRICH, Jr., William W., Member
GRYCE, David, Member
GURLEY, John, Member
HALPERN, Ilisa, Government Relations Director
HAMBRICK, Edith, Associate
HARBISON, Stacy, Government Relations Director
HENNEBERGER, Lawrence F., Member
HUEY, Robert H., Member
HUTCHERSON, Carolyn, Healthcare Specialist
JAFFE, Michael Evan, Member
KAMINSKI, Jim, Associate
KATRICHIS, Harry, Counsel
KAYSER, Susan, Member
KING, Craig S., Member
KOCHES, Paul A., Member
KURMAN, Michael J., Member
KUTLER, Alison, Associate
LARSON, Dave, Government Relations Director
LUPO, Anthony V., Member
MASSEY, Eugene A., Member
MATELSKI, Wayne H., Member
MCCONKEY, Matthew J., Associate
MCCORMACK, Douglas, Associate
MCNAMARA, Michael T., Associate
MEIGHER, Eugene J., Member
OTTAVIANO, Deanne M., Member
PETERS, Jeff, Associate
PORTNOY, Elliott I., Member
RAFFA, Connie A., Member
RANDALL, Deborah A., Member
RAVITZ, Georgia C., Member
REDFERN, Ed, Government Relations Director
REICHS, Kerry, Associate
REIDER, Alan E., Member
RICE, Paul Jackson, Member
SARRAILLE, William A., Member
SHORT, Larri A., Associate
SHUREN, Allison, Associate
SINCLAIR, Van H., Member
SMITH, Christopher, Member
SPENCER, Anna, Associate
STEVENS, Michael L., Member
TALENT, Hon. James, Counsel
TEPPER, Gary C., Member
VALENSTEIN, Carl A., Member
VAN HOLLEN, Christopher, Member
VIDAL-CORDERO, David, Member
WAHL, Barbara S., Member
WASSERMAN, Ivan J., Associate
WATERS, Robert J., Member
WEISS, Todd, Government Relations Director
WERTZBERGER, Marsha C., Member
WILLCOX, Breckinridge L., Member
WISOR, Jr., Ronald L., Associate
WOODBURY, Jennifer S., Associate
YAMPOLSKY, Harvey A., Member

Clients

Acxiom Corp.
Issues: CSP
Rep By: Hon. Dale L. Bumpers, Michael T. McNamara

Alaska Rainforest Campaign
Issues: ENG ENV
Rep By: Alison Kutler, Michael T. McNamara, Elliott I. Portnoy, Todd Weiss

American Academy of Orthotists and Prosthetists
Issues: BUD HCR
Rep By: Katie Clarke, Douglas McCormack, Robert J. Waters

American Airlines
Issues: AVI
Rep By: Hon. Dale L. Bumpers, Michael T. McNamara

American Amusement Machine Ass'n
Issues: ART CPT MON
Rep By: Alison Kutler, Michael T. McNamara, Elliott I. Portnoy, Todd Weiss

American Ass'n of Bioanalysts
Issues: MED MMM
Rep By: Bill Applegate, Stacy Harbison, Robert J. Waters

American Ass'n of Occupational Health Nurses
Issues: HCR LBR
Rep By: Bill Applegate, Douglas McCormack, Larri A. Short, Allison Shuren, Robert J. Waters

American Ass'n of Physician Specialists
Issues: VET
Rep By: Edith Hambrick, Robert J. Waters, Todd Weiss

American College of Nurse Practitioners
Issues: HCR MMM
Rep By: Bill Applegate, Stacy Harbison, Allison Shuren, Robert J. Waters

American Hospital Ass'n
Issues: HCR
Rep By: Stacy Harbison, William A. Sarraille

American Plywood Ass'n
Issues: HOU
Rep By: Marc L. Fleischaker, Michael T. McNamara

American Public Power Ass'n
Issues: UTI
Rep By: Hon. Dale L. Bumpers, Mary Hope Davis, Michael T. McNamara

American Soc. of Transplantation
Issues: HCR
Rep By: Bill Applegate, Robert J. Waters

Amputee Coalition
Issues: BUD HCR
Rep By: Katie Clarke, Stacy Harbison, Douglas McCormack

Amusement and Music Operators Ass'n
Issues: ART COM CON CPT GAM MON
Rep By: Alison Kutler, Michael T. McNamara, Elliott I. Portnoy, Todd Weiss

Arthritis Foundation
Issues: BUD
Rep By: Katie Clarke, Stacy Harbison, Alison Kutler, Douglas McCormack

Ass'n of Pain Management Anesthesiologist
Issues: MMM
Rep By: Bill Applegate, Stacy Harbison, Alison Kutler, Jeff Peters, William A. Sarraille, Allison Shuren

Assisted Living Federation of America
Issues: MMM
Rep By: Bill Applegate, Susan Kayser, Robert J. Waters

Bassett Healthcare
Issues: BUD HCR
Rep By: Katie Clarke, Douglas McCormack

Bergen Community College
Issues: BUD HCR
Rep By: Douglas McCormack, William A. Sarraille

Biomedical Research Institute
Issues: BUD HCR
Rep By: Hon. John C. Culver, Douglas McCormack, Todd Weiss

Biotechnology Industry Organization
Issues: FOO
Rep By: Stanley H. Abramson

Bombardier, Inc.
Issues: TRA
Rep By: Paul Jackson Rice

Building Service Contractors Ass'n Internat'l
Issues: CSP ENV INS LBR SMB TAX
Rep By: Michael T. McNamara, Elliott I. Portnoy

Children and Adults with Attention Deficit Disorders (CHADD)
Issues: BUD DEF EDU HCR
Rep By: Elliott I. Portnoy

CIS Global
Issues: CPI
Rep By: Michael T. McNamara, Todd Weiss

Coalition for a Procompetitive Stark Law
Issues: HCR MMM
Rep By: William A. Sarraille, Allison Shuren

Dartmouth-Hitchcock Medical Center
Issues: BUD
Rep By: Douglas McCormack, William A. Sarraille

Datahr Rehabilitation Institute
Issues: HCR
Rep By: Stacy Harbison, Douglas McCormack, Connie A. Raffa

Diamond Manufacturing, Inc.
Issues: BUD DEF TRD
Rep By: Douglas McCormack

Eastman Kodak Co.
Issues: HCR MMM TEC
Rep By: Bill Applegate, Robert J. Waters

Economic Development Alliance of Jefferson County, Arkansas
Issues: TRA
Rep By: Todd Weiss

Education and Training Resources
Issues: BUD LBR
Rep By: Katie Clarke, Douglas McCormack

Epilepsy Foundation of America
Issues: BUD HCR
Rep By: Stacy Harbison, Douglas McCormack

Exeter Architectural Products
Issues: DIS
Rep By: Stacy Harbison, Alison Kutler, Douglas McCormack, Michael T. McNamara, Todd Weiss

Federated Ambulatory Surgery Ass'n
Issues: HCR MMM
Rep By: Robert J. Waters, Ronald L. Wisor, Jr.

France Telecom America do Sul Ltda.
Issues: TEC
Rep By: Bill Applegate, Alan Fishel, David Vidal-Cordero, Todd Weiss

Fresno Community Hospital and Medical Center
Issues: BUD HCR
Rep By: Douglas McCormack, William A. Sarraille

Fresno Metropolitan Museum
Issues: BUD
Rep By: Douglas McCormack

George Washington University Medical Center
Rep By: Douglas McCormack, William A. Sarraille

Global Associates
Issues: LBR
Rep By: Alison Kutler, Douglas McCormack

Guardian Angel Holdings, Inc.
Issues: ALC BUD
Rep By: Alison Kutler, Michael T. McNamara, Todd Weiss

Inoveon Corp.
Issues: BUD HCR
Rep By: Douglas McCormack, Robert J. Waters

Interactive Amusement and Tournament Video Game Coalition
Issues: ART GAM
Rep By: Michael T. McNamara, Elliott I. Portnoy, Todd Weiss

Internat'l Soc. of Refractive Surgery
Issues: HCR
Rep By: Jeff Peters, Alan E. Reider

Iowa Department of Public Health
Issues: HCR
Rep By: Douglas McCormack, Robert J. Waters

Johns Hopkins University Hospital, School of Hygiene and Public Health
Issues: BUD
Rep By: Douglas McCormack

S.C. Johnson and Son, Inc.
Issues: AGR ENV FOR TRD
Rep By: Alison Kutler, Michael T. McNamara, Todd Weiss

Kellogg Co.
Issues: AGR FOO MAN
Rep By: Michael T. McNamara

Lakeland Regional Medical Center
Issues: BUD HCR
Rep By: Stacy Harbison, Douglas McCormack

Landmine Survivors
Issues: BUD
Rep By: Stacy Harbison, Douglas McCormack

Magnitude Information Systems
Issues: CPI GOV HCR
Rep By: Katie Clarke, Douglas McCormack

Medix Pharmaceuticals
Issues: HCR
Rep By: Stacy Harbison, Douglas McCormack

Mercy Hospital of Des Moines, Iowa
Issues: ALC BUD EDU HCR MMM
Rep By: Bill Applegate, Lisa Estrada, Douglas McCormack, Elliott I. Portnoy, Allison Shuren, Robert J. Waters

Middlesex Hospital Home Care
Issues: HCR
Rep By: Stacy Harbison, Douglas McCormack, Connie A. Raffa

Molina Medical Centers
Issues: GOV IMM MMM
Rep By: Bill Applegate, Michael T. McNamara, William A. Sarraille

Motor and Equipment Manufacturers Ass'n
Issues: ENV TRD
Rep By: Marc L. Fleischaker, Lawrence F. Henneberger, Matthew J. McConkey, Michael T. McNamara, Deanne M. Ottaviano, Todd Weiss

Nat'l Ass'n of College Stores
Issues: TAX
Rep By: Marc L. Fleischaker, Michael T. McNamara

Nat'l Ass'n of Pediatric Nurse Associates and Practitioners
Issues: HCR
Rep By: Stacy Harbison, Allison Shuren

Nat'l Ass'n of Retail Collection Attorneys
Issues: CSP
Rep By: Michael T. McNamara, Deanne M. Ottaviano, Kerry Reichs

Nat'l Ass'n of School Nurses
Issues: EDU HCR
Rep By: Stacy Harbison, Michael T. McNamara, Elliott I. Portnoy, Allison Shuren, Robert J. Waters

Nat'l Council of State Boards of Nursing
Issues: HCR
Rep By: Allison Shuren, Robert J. Waters

Nat'l Grain and Feed Ass'n
Issues: AGR
Rep By: Marc L. Fleischaker

Navajo Nation
Issues: AGR BUD EDU IND LAW TAX
Rep By: Michael J. Kurman, Elliott I. Portnoy

New Orleans, Louisiana, City of
Issues: BUD DIS ECN ENV URB
Rep By: Alison Kutler, Michael T. McNamara, Elliott I. Portnoy

Ovarian Cancer Nat'l Alliance
Issues: BUD
Rep By: Katie Clarke, Douglas McCormack

Parker Hannifin Corp.
Issues: TRA
Rep By: Lawrence F. Henneberger, Michael T. McNamara

Pedorthic Footwear Ass'n
Issues: HCR MMM
Rep By: Bill Applegate, Robert J. Waters

Phoenix Cardiovascular, Inc.
Issues: BUD HCR
Rep By: Douglas McCormack, William A. Sarraille

Prevent Blindness America
Issues: BUD HCR
Rep By: Katie Clarke, Stacy Harbison, Douglas McCormack

Priority Care
Issues: HCR
Rep By: Stacy Harbison, Douglas McCormack, Connie A. Raffa

Raytheon Co.
Issues: AVI BUD DEF LBR TAX TRD
Rep By: Hon. Dale L. Bumpers, Hon. John C. Culver, Craig S. King, Michael T. McNamara, Todd Weiss

Recreation Vehicle Ass'n
Issues: AUT MAN TRA
Rep By: Todd Weiss

Christopher Reeve Paralysis Foundation
Issues: BUD HCR
Rep By: Hon. Dale L. Bumpers, Katie Clarke, Douglas McCormack, Robert J. Waters

Renewable Resources LLC
Issues: FIN NAT
Rep By: Hon. John C. Culver, Alison Kutler, Michael T. McNamara

Research 2 Prevention
Issues: BUD
Rep By: Douglas McCormack, Robert J. Waters

Sabolich Research & Development
Issues: BUD
Rep By: Kendra Dimond, Stacy Harbison, Douglas McCormack

Salton, Inc.
Issues: CSP
Rep By: Georgia C. Ravitz, Ivan J. Wasserman

Soc. for Excellence in Eyecare
Issues: HCR
Rep By: Jeff Peters, Alan E. Reider, Allison Shuren

Soc. for Vascular Surgery
Issues: HCR MMM
Rep By: Stacy Harbison, William A. Sarraille, Allison Shuren

Soc. of Diagnostic Medical Sonographers
Issues: HCR MMM
Rep By: Stacy Harbison, William A. Sarraille, Allison Shuren

Soc. of Vascular Technology
Issues: HCR MMM
Rep By: Stacy Harbison, William A. Sarraille, Allison Shuren

State University of New York (SUNY)
Issues: BUD
Rep By: Stacy Harbison, Douglas McCormack

TECHHEALTH.COM
Issues: BUD DEF HCR
Rep By: Douglas McCormack, Robert J. Waters

Tyson Foods, Inc.
Issues: ENV FOO
Rep By: Hon. Dale L. Bumpers, Mary Hope Davis, Michael T. McNamara, Todd Weiss

UniGroup, Inc.
Issues: BAN

University of Medicine and Dentistry of New Jersey - School of Health Related Professionals
Issues: BUD HCR
Rep By: Douglas McCormack, William A. Sarraille

webwasher.com
Issues: CPI
Rep By: Alison Kutler, Michael T. McNamara

Argo Public Enterprise

2819 Winchester Way
Falls Church, VA 22042

Tel: (703)532-4256
Fax: (703)532-4976
Registered: LDA

DC-Area Employees Representing Listed Clients
BEASHER, Mark, Beasher

Clients

Diversified Collection Services, Inc.
Issues: GOV
Rep By: Mark Beasher

The Argus Group, L.L.C.

333 N. Fairfax St.
Suite 302
Alexandria, VA 22314
Tel: (703)548-5868
Fax: (703)548-5869
Registered: LDA

Provides law, advocacy, government affairs and economic services at the federal level and in developing states. Specializes in legislative, regulatory, tax, environmental and technology issues.

DC-Area Employees Representing Listed Clients
BURTON, David R., Partner
GRAY, Tom, Of Counsel
MASTROMARCO, Dan R., Partner

Clients

America Outdoors
Issues: TAX
Rep By: David R. Burton, Dan R. Mastromarco

American Soc. of Travel Agents
Issues: TAX TOU
Rep By: David R. Burton, Dan R. Mastromarco

Americans for Fair Taxation
Issues: TAX
Rep By: David R. Burton, Dan R. Mastromarco

Nat'l Park Hospitality Ass'n
Issues: TAX
Rep By: David R. Burton, Dan R. Mastromarco

Nat'l Tour Ass'n
Issues: TAX TOU
Rep By: David R. Burton, Dan R. Mastromarco

Small Business Regulatory Council
Issues: ECN SMB TAX

Travel Council for Fair Competition
Issues: TAX
Rep By: David R. Burton, Dan R. Mastromarco

United Motorcoach Ass'n
Issues: TAX TOU
Rep By: David R. Burton, Dan R. Mastromarco

Armstrong Associates, Inc.

1225 I St. NW
Suite 500
Washington, DC 20005-3914
Tel: (202)682-4778
Fax: (301)770-2416
Web: www.armstrongassociates.com
E-mail: jmarmstro@aol.com

DC-Area Employees Representing Listed Clients
ARMSTRONG, Jan M., President

Clients

Avis, Inc.
Rep By: Jan M. Armstrong

HealthFEST of Maryland, Inc.
Rep By: Jan M. Armstrong

Thomas K. Arnold

6043 Shaffer Dr.
Alexandria, VA 22310
Tel: (703)660-6311
Fax: (703)660-6577
Registered: LDA
E-mail: tarnold@brokerpower.com
A lobbying consultant.

Clients

American Network of Community Options and Resources (ANCOR)
Issues: TAX
Rep By: Thomas K. Arnold

Arnold & Porter

555 12th St. NW
Washington, DC 20004-1206
Tel: (202)942-5000
Fax: (202)942-5999
Registered: LDA, FARA
Web: www.arnoldporter.com

Political Action Committee
Arnold & Porter Political Action Committee
555 12th St. NW
Washington, DC 20004-1206
Tel: (202)942-5228
Fax: (202)942-5999
Contact: Martha L. Cochran

DC-Area Employees Representing Listed Clients
ARONOW, Geoffrey, Partner
BAER, William J., Partner
BAGLEY, Grant, Partner
BEERS, Donald O., Partner
BENNETT, Alexander E., Partner
BERGER, Paul S., Partner
BERNSTEIN, Michael L., Partner
BORN, Brooksley, Partner
BROMME, Jeffrey S., Partner
CASSIDY, Susan Booth, Partner
COCHRAN, Martha L., Partner
CULLEEN, Lawrence E., Special Counsel
DANEKER, Michael, Partner
DEBEVOISE, II, Eli Whitney, Partner
DEWITT, Timothy, Partner
ENGLUND, Steven R., Partner
EWING, Richard S., Partner
FITZPATRICK, James F., Partner
FLAX, Samuel A., Partner
FOIS, Sonia P., Partner
FRANK, Theodore, Partner
FREEMAN, Jr., David F., Partner
FRESHOUR, Paul, Partner
GARRETT, Robert A., Partner
GRANT, Patrick J., Partner
GROSSI, Jr., Peter T., Partner
HARKER, Drew A., Partner
HUBBARD, Richard L., Partner
HURLEY, Judith, Exec. Dir. and Chief Financial Officer
JOHNSON, Richard A., Partner
JONES, Robert J., Partner
KAHN, Sarah E., Partner
KAPLAN, Steven L., Partner
KENTOFF, David R., Partner
KOTLER, Sarah B., Associate
KRASH, Abe, Partner
LEDERMAN, Gordon N., Associate
LEE, Susan G., Partner
LETZLER, Kenneth A., Partner
LEVINE, Arthur N., Partner
LYONS, Dennis G., Partner
NATHAN, Irvin B., Partner
NICKEL, Leslie A., Associate
OTT, Robert B., Partner
PATTERSON, Donna E., Partner
PERKINS, Nancy L., Partner
READE, Claire E., Partner
RICHMAN, Jeffrey W., Associate
ROCKLER, Walter J., Partner
ROGERS, William D., Partner
ROSENBAUM, Robert D., Partner
ROSS, Stanford G., Partner
RUBEL, Eric A., Partner
RUBIN, Blake D., Partner
SACKS, Stephen M., Partner
SANDMAN, James, Managing Partner
SCHMIDT, K. Peter
SCHNEIDER, Lawrence A., Partner
SHOR, Michael T., Partner
SINEL, Norman M., Partner
SISSON, Edward, Partner
SMITH, Jeffrey H., Partner
SOHN, Michael N., Partner
VIETH, G. Duane, Partner
VODRA, William W., Partner
WALDMAN, Daniel, Partner
ZENNER, Jr., Walter F., Partner

Clients

Argentina, Government of

Asociacion de Productores de Salon y Truncha de Chile

Ass'n of Floral Importers of Florida

Beverly Hills Federal Savings Bank

Bruce Vladek
Issues: GOV
Rep By: Martha L. Cochran, James F. Fitzpatrick

Cellular Telecommunications and Internet Ass'n
Issues: TAX TEC

Children's Hospice Internat'l

Chilean Salmon Farmers Ass'n

Consolidated Administration and Security Services, Inc.
Rep By: Martha L. Cochran

The Continental Corp.

Democratic Nat'l Committee

ECI Telecom Ltd.

Employee Benefit Research Institute

First Savings Bank, F.S.B.
Rep By: Martha L. Cochran

Greenwich Capital Markets, Inc.
Rep By: Martha L. Cochran

Health Services of Kansas and Mid Missouri
Issues: FAM HCR
Rep By: James F. Fitzpatrick, Jeffrey W. Richman

Hopi Indian Tribe

Israel, Economic Mission of the Government of the State of
Rep By: Paul S. Berger

Israel, Embassy of the State of

Israel, Goverment of the State of

Israel, Ministry of Finance of the State of

Johns Hopkins Center for Civilian Biodefense Studies
Issues: AGR BUD DEF DIS HCR LAW SCI
Rep By: Jeffrey W. Richman, Jeffrey H. Smith

Kazakhstan, Government of the Republic of

Kosovo, Government of the Republic of

London Futures and Options Exchange

Major League Baseball, Office of the Commissioner of

Mentor Corp.
Issues: MMM
Rep By: Grant Bagley

Metropolitan Mortgage and Securities, Inc.
Rep By: Martha L. Cochran, David F. Freeman, Jr.

Michigan Nat'l Corp.

Miller Brewing Co.

Monsanto Co.

Moscow Interbank Currency Exchange (MICEX)

Motorola, Inc.

Nat'l Ass'n of Dealers in Ancient, Oriental and Primitive Art
Issues: FOR GOV
Rep By: James F. Fitzpatrick

New York City Board of Estimate
Rep By: Norman M. Sinel

Nilit America Corp.

Nilit Ltd.

Novartis Corp.
Issues: MMM
Rep By: Grant Bagley

Novell, Inc.

PaineWebber Group, Inc.
Issues: FIN
Rep By: Martha L. Cochran

Panama, Foreign Minister of the Republic of

Panama, Government of the Republic of

Planned Parenthood of America

Quebecor World (USA) Inc.
Issues: ECN
Rep By: Martha L. Cochran

Reading, Pennsylvania, City of

RoTech Medical Corp.
Issues: MMM
Rep By: Grant Bagley

Roxanne Laboratories, Inc.
Issues: MMM
Rep By: Grant Bagley, Martha L. Cochran

Scripps Research Institute

State Farm Insurance Cos.
Issues: AUT CSP DIS FIN HCR INS
Rep By: Martha L. Cochran, James F. Fitzpatrick, Nancy L. Perkins, Stanford G. Ross

Tambrands, Inc.

Turkey, Government of the Republic of

U.S. Investigations Services
Issues: BUD
Rep By: Martha L. Cochran

Venezuela, Bolivarian Republic of

Vestal Group of Companies
Issues: APP
Rep By: Nancy L. Perkins

Waste Control Specialists, Inc.
Issues: WAS
Rep By: Martha L. Cochran

Wyeth-Ayerst Pharmaceuticals
Issues: MMM
Rep By: Grant Bagley

Wayne Arny & Assoc.

975 Main St.
P.O. Box 290
Galesville, MD 20765
Tel: (301)261-5430
Fax: (301)261-5430
Registered: LDA

DC-Area Employees Representing Listed Clients
ARNY, Wayne, President
O'BRIEN, David D., Partner

Clients

American Logistics Infrastructure Improvement Consortium
Issues: DEF
Rep By: Wayne Arny

John Crane-LIPS, Inc.
Issues: DEF GOV TRD
Rep By: Wayne Arny, David D. O'Brien

Cruising America Coalition
Issues: TOU
Rep By: Wayne Arny, David D. O'Brien

DRS Technologies, Inc.
Issues: DEF TRD
Rep By: Wayne Arny, David D. O'Brien

The Environmental Co., Inc.
Rep By: Wayne Arny

Guam Internat'l Airport Authority
Issues: AER AVI TRA
Rep By: Wayne Arny

Jered Industries, Inc.
Rep By: Wayne Arny, David D. O'Brien

The Kinetics Group
Issues: CHM CPI ENV MAN
Rep By: Wayne Arny, David D. O'Brien

MacGregor
Issues: DEF TRD
Rep By: Wayne Arny, David D. O'Brien

Robbins-Gioia, Inc.
Issues: DEF
Rep By: Wayne Arny, David D. O'Brien

San Francisco Wholesale Produce Ass'n
Issues: DEF
Rep By: Wayne Arny, David D. O'Brien

Arter & Hadden

1801 K St. NW
Washington, DC 20006
Tel: (202)775-7100
Fax: (202)857-0172
Registered: LDA, FARA
Web: www.arterhadden.com

DC-Area Employees Representing Listed Clients

BIERMAN, Everett E., Consultant
COHEN, Daniel L., Principal
DABAGHI, William K., Partner
JONAS, III, W. James, Partner
KEANE, William K., Partner
LOEFFLER, Hon. Thomas G., Partner
PLEBANI, Jon W., Principal
POLLACK, Michael J., Partner
TROUP, Jamie U., Partner

Clients

Academy of Radiology Research
Issues: HCR MED
Rep By: Hon. Thomas G. Loeffler, Jon W. Plebani

American Electric Power Co.
Issues: UTI

American Gaming Ass'n
Issues: GAM

American Koyo Corp.
Rep By: Daniel L. Cohen

Americans for Fair Taxation
Issues: TAX
Rep By: Daniel L. Cohen, Hon. Thomas G. Loeffler, Jon W. Plebani

Ass'n for Responsible Thermal Treatment
Rep By: Daniel L. Cohen, Jon W. Plebani

Atlas Iron Processing, Inc.

Billing Concepts, Inc.
Issues: TEC
Rep By: Daniel L. Cohen, Hon. Thomas G. Loeffler

BKK Corp.
Rep By: Daniel L. Cohen, Hon. Thomas G. Loeffler

Bristol-Myers Squibb Co.
Rep By: Hon. Thomas G. Loeffler, Jon W. Plebani

CAI Wireless

Canadian Broiler Hatching Egg Marketing Agency
Rep By: William K. Dabaghi

Canadian Chicken Marketing Agency
Rep By: William K. Dabaghi

Canadian Egg Marketing Agency
Rep By: William K. Dabaghi

Canadian Turkey Marketing Agency
Rep By: William K. Dabaghi

Cellular Telecommunications and Internet Ass'n
Issues: TEC
Rep By: Daniel L. Cohen

Centerior Energy Corp.
Rep By: Daniel L. Cohen, Hon. Thomas G. Loeffler

Christus Santa Rosa Hospital

Circus Circus Enterprises, Inc.
Rep By: Daniel L. Cohen, Hon. Thomas G. Loeffler, Jon W. Plebani

Citigroup
Issues: BAN
Rep By: Daniel L. Cohen, Hon. Thomas G. Loeffler, Jon W. Plebani

Edison Electric Institute
Issues: UTI
Rep By: Daniel L. Cohen

ELGARD Corp.

Envirocare of Utah, Inc.
Issues: WAS
Rep By: Daniel L. Cohen

Fairchild Aircraft, Inc.
Rep By: Hon. Thomas G. Loeffler, Jon W. Plebani

Federated Investors, Inc.
Rep By: Daniel L. Cohen

Financial Guaranty Insurance Corp.
Rep By: Jon W. Plebani

Fort James Corp.
Issues: ENV

HCA Healthcare Corp.
Rep By: Daniel L. Cohen, Hon. Thomas G. Loeffler, Jon W. Plebani

Hicks, Muse, Tate & Furst
Issues: BAN COM ENV TEC
Rep By: Daniel L. Cohen, Hon. Thomas G. Loeffler, Jon W. Plebani

Hong Kong Economic and Trade Office

Hong Kong, Government of

Houston Clearing House Ass'n
Rep By: William K. Dabaghi

Houston, Texas, Port Authority of the City of
Issues: TRA
Rep By: Hon. Thomas G. Loeffler, Jon W. Plebani

Hunt Valve Co., Inc.

Investment Co. Institute
Issues: TAX

Koyo Corp. of U.S.A.
Rep By: Jon W. Plebani

LCOR, Inc.
Issues: RES
Rep By: Daniel L. Cohen

Malrite Communications Group, Inc.

Manufacturers Radio Frequency Advisory Committee, Inc.
Issues: COM
Rep By: William K. Keane

Metabolife
Issues: HCR
Rep By: Daniel L. Cohen, Hon. Thomas G. Loeffler

Monsanto Co.

Mount Carmel Health

Nintendo of America, Inc.

OnCare, Inc.
Rep By: Daniel L. Cohen, Hon. Thomas G. Loeffler

Pinpoint Communications
Rep By: Hon. Thomas G. Loeffler

Prince George's, Maryland, County of

Reusable Pallet and Container Coalition
Issues: ENV TAX

Sammons Enterprises, Inc.
Rep By: Daniel L. Cohen, Hon. Thomas G. Loeffler, Jon W. Plebani

San Antonio, Texas, City of
Issues: GOV
Rep By: Hon. Thomas G. Loeffler, Jon W. Plebani

Sand Creek Descendants Trust
Issues: IND

SBC Communications Inc.
Rep By: Daniel L. Cohen, Hon. Thomas G. Loeffler, Jon W. Plebani

South West Florida Enterprises, Inc.
Rep By: W. James Jonas, III, Hon. Thomas G. Loeffler

Taxicab, Limousine and Paratransit Ass'n
Issues: COM
Rep By: William K. Keane

Tesoro Petroleum Corp.
Rep By: W. James Jonas, III, Hon. Thomas G. Loeffler

Thunderbird, The American Graduate School of Internat'l Management
Issues: BUD
Rep By: Daniel L. Cohen

Tribal Alliance of Northern California
Rep By: Hon. Thomas G. Loeffler

United Parcel Service

USAA - United Services Automobile Ass'n

USPCI, Inc.

Whirlpool Corp.
Rep By: Hon. Thomas G. Loeffler

H. B. Zachry
Rep By: Daniel L. Cohen, Hon. Thomas G. Loeffler, Jon W. Plebani

Arthur Andersen LLP

1666 K St. NW
Suite 800
Washington, DC 20006
Tel: (202)481-7000
Fax: (202)862-7098
Registered: LDA
Web: www.arthurandersen.com

Political Action Committee

Arthur Andersen Political Action Committee
1666 K St. NW
Suite 800
Washington, DC 20006
Tel: (202)481-7000
Fax: (202)862-7098
Contact: Jeffrey J. Peck

DC-Area Employees Representing Listed Clients

BECCHI, Rosemary D., Manager
BERNSTEIN, Rachelle, Tax Partner, Office of Federal Tax Services
CARLSON, George N., Partner, Office of Federal Tax Services
CARRINGTON, Glenn, Partner
COHEN, Harrison J., National Director
COLLINS, Bryan, Partner
COULAM, Weston J., Manager
CRYAN, Thomas M., Principal
DANCE, Glenn E., Partner
FARB, Warren, Manager
FOGARASI, Andre P., Managing Director, Office of Federal Tax Services
FULLER, Thomas D., Principal
GORDON, Richard A., Partner
GRAFMEYER, Richard, Partner
HEETER, Charles P., Partner, Officer of Government Affairs
KLEIN, Carol Doran, Partner
KULISH, Carol, Principal
LAWSON, Peter H., Director, Government Affairs
MACNEIL, C. Ellen, Partner
MULLET, Melinda R., Congressional Specialist
PECK, Jeffrey J., Managing Partner, Office of Government Affairs
PETERSON, Mark
PROUDFIT, Elizabeth M., Congressional Specialist
TUERFF, T. Timothy, Partner

Clients

AutoNation, Inc.
Issues: TAX
Rep By: Rachelle Bernstein, Glenn Carrington, Bryan Collins

Benchmark Communications Radio LP

Branch Banking and Trust Co.

Coalition for Job Growth and Internat'l Competitiveness Through AMT Reform
Rep By: Carol Kulish

Coalition for the Fair Taxation of Business Transactions
Issues: TAX
Rep By: Rachelle Bernstein, Weston J. Coulam

Coalition on Royalties Taxation
Rep By: Rachelle Bernstein, Richard A. Gordon, T. Timothy Tuerff

Coalition to Preserve Employee Ownership of S Corporation
Issues: TAX
Rep By: Weston J. Coulam, Carol Kulish

Eagle-Picher Personal Injury Settlement Trust
Issues: TAX
Rep By: Rosemary D. Becchi, Rachelle Bernstein, Glenn Carrington, Weston J. Coulam, Warren Farb

Hybrid Branch Coalition
Issues: TAX
Rep By: Rachelle Bernstein, Weston J. Coulam, Thomas D. Fuller, Richard A. Gordon, T. Timothy Tuerff

Microsoft Corp.
Issues: TAX
Rep By: Rachelle Bernstein, Richard A. Gordon

Nat'l Ass'n of Investors Corporation (NAIC)
Issues: TAX
Rep By: Rachelle Bernstein, Weston J. Coulam, Glenn E. Dance, Carol Kulish

Nat'l Retail Federation
Issues: TAX
Rep By: Rachelle Bernstein

Oracle Corp.
Issues: TAX
Rep By: Rachelle Bernstein, Richard A. Gordon

UtiliCorp United, Inc.
Issues: TAX
Rep By: Rachelle Bernstein, Harrison J. Cohen, Weston J. Coulam, Richard A. Gordon, Carol Doran Klein

Verizon Communications

Ashby and Associates

1350 I St. NW
Suite 1240
Washington, DC 20005
Tel: (202)296-3840
Fax: (202)682-0146
Web: www.pengroup.com/affiliate/ashby
E-mail: rbashby@aol.com

Specialists in marketing, international trade development, facility security, strategic alliance formation, market research, and technology transfer and assessment for industrial client interests in high technology applied to national needs.

DC-Area Employees Representing Listed Clients

ASHBY, R. Barry, President
MCLAUGHLIN, P.E., Frank R., Associate
MONTANO, William B., Associate
YOUNTS, George R., Technical Director

Clients

American Security Resources, Inc.
Rep By: William B. Montano

Business News Publishing Co.
Rep By: R. Barry Ashby

Composite Innovations, Inc.
Rep By: R. Barry Ashby

Imaging Technologies Inc.
Rep By: R. Barry Ashby

Intelligent Optical Systems, Inc.
Rep By: R. Barry Ashby

The Lared Group
Rep By: R. Barry Ashby

Time Domain Corp.
Rep By: R. Barry Ashby

Tracer ES&T Inc.
Rep By: R. Barry Ashby

The Ventura Group
Rep By: R. Barry Ashby

Waveband, Inc.
Rep By: R. Barry Ashby

James Nicholas Ashmore & Associates

1156 15th St. NW
Suite 315
Washington, DC 20005-1704
Tel: (202)452-1003
Fax: (202)452-1311
Registered: LDA
E-mail: jnashmore@erols.com
A government affairs consulting firm.

DC-Area Employees Representing Listed Clients
ASHMORE, James Nicholas, President

Clients

American Crop Protection Ass'n
Issues: ENV GOV TRD
Rep By: James Nicholas Ashmore

Battelle
Rep By: James Nicholas Ashmore

Battelle Memorial Institute
Issues: AER AGR BUD CAW CHM ENV FOO MAN SCI TRA
Rep By: James Nicholas Ashmore

The Boeing Co.
Issues: DEF MAN TRD
Rep By: James Nicholas Ashmore

Gardena Alfalfa Growers Ass'n
Issues: AGR BNK
Rep By: James Nicholas Ashmore

Nat'l Rural Telecom Ass'n
Issues: AGR
Rep By: James Nicholas Ashmore

Northwest Horticultural Council
Issues: AGR TRD
Rep By: James Nicholas Ashmore

Oneonta Trading Corp.
Issues: AGR BUD FOR TRD
Rep By: James Nicholas Ashmore

Western Ag Resources Inc.
Issues: AGR TRD
Rep By: James Nicholas Ashmore

Ass'n and Government Relations Management, Inc.

4900-B S. 31st St.
Arlington, VA 22206
Tel: (703)820-7400
Fax: (703)931-4520

DC-Area Employees Representing Listed Clients
BOMAR, Ernest, V. President
FISE, Thomas F., Principal

Clients

American College of Gastroenterology
Rep By: Thomas F. Fise

American Dental Trade Ass'n
Rep By: Thomas F. Fise

Ass'n and Soc. Management Internat'l Inc.

111 Park Place
Falls Church, VA 22046-4513
Tel: (703)533-0251
Fax: (703)241-5603
Web: www.asmii.com
E-mail: info@asmii.com

DC-Area Employees Representing Listed Clients
ARMSTRONG, CAE, Elizabeth B., Senior V. President
BUZZERD, Jr., CAE, Harry W., President
DENSTON, Susan, Account Executive
STARCHVILLE, Amy
STEWART, Michael, Account Executive
TYERYAR, CAE, Clay D., Senior V. President

Clients

American Paper Machinery Ass'n
Issues: MAN
Rep By: Elizabeth B. Armstrong, CAE

American Pipe Fittings Ass'n
Rep By: Clay D. Tyeryar, CAE

Ass'n of State and Territorial Chronic Disease Program Directors
Rep By: Michael Stewart

Capital Goods Standards Coalition

Internat'l Ass'n of Emergency Managers
Issues: DIS
Rep By: Elizabeth B. Armstrong, CAE, Amy Starchville

Meat Industry Suppliers Ass'n
Rep By: Clay D. Tyeryar, CAE

Nat'l Ass'n of State EMS Directors
Rep By: Elizabeth B. Armstrong, CAE

Process Equipment Manufacturers' Ass'n

Product Liability Prevention and Defense Group
Rep By: Harry W. Buzzerd, Jr., CAE, Clay D. Tyeryar, CAE

Ass'n Growth Enterprises

1101 Mercantile Ln.
Suite 100
Springdale, MD 20774
Tel: (301)925-1420
Fax: (301)925-1429
Registered: LDA
Web: www.age.org

DC-Area Employees Representing Listed Clients
MAY, John Paul, President and Chief Exec. Officer
PACINO, Thomas L., V. President

Clients

American Military Soc.
Issues: HCR INS RET VET
Rep By: John Paul May, Thomas L. Pacino

Nat'l Ass'n for Uniformed Services
Rep By: John Paul May, Thomas L. Pacino

Ass'n Innovation and Management, Inc.

1767 Business Center Dr.
Suite 302
Reston, VA 20190
Tel: (703)438-3101
Fax: (703)438-3113
A multiple association management firm.

DC-Area Employees Representing Listed Clients
LAMB, Shawn D., President
MASSON, Tonia, Senior Account Executive
RUSSELL-WILSON, Clarissa, Senior Account Executive

Clients

Soc. of Toxicology
Rep By: Shawn D. Lamb

The Teratology Soc.
Rep By: Tonia Masson

Ass'n Management Bureau

1595 Spring Hill Rd.
Suite 330
Vienna, VA 22182
Tel: (703)506-3260
Fax: (703)506-3266
Web: www.amb.org
E-mail: info@ambnet.org

DC-Area Employees Representing Listed Clients
BEATY, Elizabeth
BRENNAN, Maria E.
DUNCAN, Jacci
GIBSON, Thomas C., President/Chief Exec. Officer
SKOFF, Laura, V. President

Clients

American Soc. of Women Accountants (ACC)
Rep By: Laura Skoff

American Women in Radio and Television

Ass'n of Female Exhibit Contractors and Event Organizers
Rep By: Maria E. Brennan

Emergency Department Practice Management Ass'n (EDPMA)
Rep By: Thomas C. Gibson

Nat'l Ass'n of Telecommunications Officers and Advisors
Rep By: Elizabeth Beaty

Soc. of Nat'l Ass'n Publications
Rep By: Laura Skoff

Ass'n Management Group

8201 Greensboro Dr.
Suite 300
McLean, VA 22102
Tel: (703)610-9000
Fax: (703)610-9005
Web: www.amg-inc.com
E-mail: crumbarger@amg-inc.com

DC-Area Employees Representing Listed Clients
ALLISON, Kathy
AVILA, Pilar
BIANCHI, Maria
BOYNTON, Rex
DARROW, Diane L.
GAVILAN, Horacio
LINDSEY, Elise
NIERO, Christine
NIZANKIEWICZ, Mike
NORMANDY, Joseph
RUGH, Timothy R.
RUMBARGER, Charles D., Chairman
SILBERMAN, Karen
WARDLE, Bruce, President

Clients

Ass'n of Hispanic Advertising Agencies
Rep By: Horacio Gavilan

Ass'n of Legal Administrators, Capital Chapter

Ass'n of Water Technologies
Rep By: Elise Lindsey

Consulting Engineers Council of Metropolitan Washington
Rep By: Karen Silberman

Federal Physicians Ass'n

Internat'l Cast Polymer Ass'n
Rep By: Timothy R. Rugh

Nat'l Ass'n of Independent Life Brokerage Agency
Rep By: Joseph Normandy

Nat'l Ass'n of Mortgage Brokers
Issues: BAN BNK FIN HOU RES
Rep By: Mike Nizankiewicz

Nat'l Ass'n of Naturopathic Physicians
Rep By: Maria Bianchi

Nat'l Ass'n of Retail Collection Attorneys
Rep By: Kathy Allison, Diane L. Darrow

Nat'l Certification Board for Therapeutic Massage and Bodywork
Rep By: Christine Niero

New America Alliance
Rep By: Pilar Avila

North American Technician Excellence
Rep By: Rex Boynton

Associated Child Care Consultants, Ltd.

3612 Bent Branch Ct.
Falls Church, VA 22041
Tel: (703)941-4329
Fax: (703)941-4329
Registered: LDA

DC-Area Employees Representing Listed Clients
TOBIN, Dr. William J., President

Clients

American Ass'n of Early Childhood Educators

Child Care Institute of America, Inc.

Nat'l Accreditation Council for Early Childhood Professional Personnel and Programs

Nat'l Childcare Parents Ass'n

Astra Solutions, LLC

1717 Pennsylvania Ave. NW
Suite 1300
Washington, DC 20006
Tel: (202)452-6925
Fax: (202)452-6190

DC-Area Employees Representing Listed Clients
HOFFMEIER, Donna L.

Clients

Spectrum Health Care Resources, Inc.
Issues: BUD DEF HCR
Rep By: Donna L. Hoffmeier

United Concordia Companies, Inc.
Issues: DEF HCR INS
Rep By: Donna L. Hoffmeier

Ross Atkins

216 Justice Ct. NE
Suite A
Washington, DC 20006
Tel: (202)547-7721
Fax: (202)547-7835
E-mail: ratkins@ix.netcom.com

Clients

Connectcuba
Rep By: Ross Atkins

Monroe, Louisiana, Chamber of Commerce of the City of
Issues: AVI BUD ECN ROD SMB TRA WAS
Rep By: Ross Atkins

Monroe, Louisiana, City of
Issues: AVI BUD ECN ROD SMB TRA WAS
Rep By: Ross Atkins

Ouachita Parish Police Jury
Issues: AVI BUD ECN ROD SMB TRA WAS
Rep By: Ross Atkins

The Atlantic Group, Public Affairs, Inc.

1317 I St. NW
Suite 300 W
Washington, DC 20005
Tel: (202)522-8606
Fax: (202)522-8669
Registered: LDA

E-mail: lfayres@attglobal.net

DC-Area Employees Representing Listed Clients
AYRES, Larry F., President

Clients

Carwell Products, Inc.
Issues: DEF
Rep By: Larry F. Ayres

Compuware Corp.
Issues: BUD CPI FIN LBR SCI TAX
Rep By: Larry F. Ayres

Dykema Gossett
Issues: BUD DEF
Rep By: Larry F. Ayres

Barbara A. Karmanos Cancer Institute
Issues: BUD HCR MED SCI
Rep By: Larry F. Ayres

Malden Mills Industries, Inc.
Issues: APP BUD DEF
Rep By: Larry F. Ayres

AWS Services

44965 Aviation Dr.
Suite 303
Dulles, VA 20166-7527
E-mail: uupna@ix.netcom.com
Tel: (703)260-3466
Fax: (703)260-3466
Registered: FARA

DC-Area Employees Representing Listed Clients
SMITH, Anne W., Bureau Coordinator

Clients

Ulster Unionist Party
Rep By: Anne W. Smith

Baach Robinson & Lewis, PLLC

One Thomas Circle NW
Suite 200
Washington, DC 20005-5802
Web: www.barole.com
E-mail: bachrob@barole.com
Tel: (202)833-8900
Fax: (202)466-5738
Registered: LDA

DC-Area Employees Representing Listed Clients
ROBINSON, Jeffrey D., Partner
ZELENKO, Benjamin L., Partner

Clients

American Soc. of Composers, Authors and Publishers
Rep By: Benjamin L. Zelenko

Equitas Reinsurance Ltd.
Issues: INS
Rep By: Benjamin L. Zelenko

Nat'l Football League Players Ass'n
Issues: GAM SPO TAX
Rep By: Benjamin L. Zelenko

Bachner Communications, Inc.

8811 Colesville Rd.
Suite G 106
Silver Spring, MD 20910
E-mail: john@bachner.com
Tel: (301)589-9121
Fax: (301)589-2017

DC-Area Employees Representing Listed Clients
BACHNER, John P., President

Clients

ASFE
Rep By: John P. Bachner

Bacino & Associates

112 Southwest St.
Alexandria, VA 22314
Tel: (703)549-8454
Fax: (703)836-5255
Registered: LDA

DC-Area Employees Representing Listed Clients
BACINO, Geoff, President

Clients

Liberty Check Printers
Issues: BAN
Rep By: Geoff Bacino

Sense Technologies, Inc.
Issues: AUT TRA
Rep By: Geoff Bacino

World Sports Exchange
Issues: GAM
Rep By: Geoff Bacino

Norman A. Bailey, Inc.

1311 Dolly Madison Blvd.
Suite 2A
McLean, VA 22101
Web: www.summitconnect.com
Tel: (703)506-0779
Fax: (703)506-8085
Provides fundamental economic and financial analysis.

DC-Area Employees Representing Listed Clients
BAILEY, Norman A., President

Clients

The AES Corp.
Rep By: Norman A. Bailey

Bank of Tokyo-Mitsubishi
Rep By: Norman A. Bailey

Inter-Nation Capital Management
Rep By: Norman A. Bailey

Madeira Development Co.
Rep By: Norman A. Bailey

Bain and Associates, Inc.

913 King St.
Alexandria, VA 22314
Web: www.bainpr.com/bain
E-mail: bain@bainpr.com
Tel: (703)549-9592
Fax: (703)549-9601

DC-Area Employees Representing Listed Clients
ACKLEY, Steve, Senior V. President
BAIN, C. Jackson, Chairman
BAIN, Sandra Kyle, President

Clients

American Industrial Hygiene Ass'n

American Public Transportation Ass'n

Biotechnology Industry Organization
Rep By: C. Jackson Bain

The Boeing Co.

Cephalon, Inc.

Gray and Company II

Physicians for Peace

Baise + Miller, P.C.

1020 19th St. NW
Suite 400
Washington, DC 20036
Web: www.dclaw.net
E-mail: basiemille@aol.com
Tel: (202)331-9100
Fax: (202)331-9060
Registered: LDA

DC-Area Employees Representing Listed Clients
BAISE, Gary H., Partner
BOCK, Eric P., Partner
FORMICA, Michael, Associate
MILLER, Marshall L., Partner

Clients

California Refuse Removal Council
Issues: ENV TRU WAS
Rep By: Eric P. Bock

Citizens for Health
Rep By: Marshall L. Miller

Food Distributors Internat'l (NAWGA-IFDA)
Rep By: Gary H. Baise

Ice Ban America, Inc.
Issues: TRA
Rep By: Eric P. Bock, Marshall L. Miller

Martinizing Environmental Group
Issues: ENV
Rep By: Eric P. Bock, Michael Formica, Marshall L. Miller

Nat'l Ass'n of Wheat Growers
Issues: CAW ENV
Rep By: Gary H. Baise

Nat'l Calcium Council
Rep By: Marshall L. Miller

Norcal Waste Systems, Inc.
Issues: ENV TRU WAS
Rep By: Eric P. Bock

Solid Waste Ass'n of North America
Issues: TAX
Rep By: Eric P. Bock

West Coast Refuse and Recycling Coalition
Issues: ENV TRU WAS
Rep By: Eric P. Bock

Baker & Daniels

805 15th St. NW
Suite 700
Washington, DC 20005
Tel: (202)312-7440
Fax: (202)312-7460
Registered: LDA

DC-Area Employees Representing Listed Clients
DAWSON, Albert R., Partner
MANNEN, Ted R., In-House Counsel
PRUITT, Jana Lee, Partner
RICHARDSON, Charles T., Partner
SWAIN, Frank S., Partner
WELLER, Mark W., Partner
ZOOK, David R., Managing Partner, Washington Office

Clients

American College of Sports Medicine
Rep By: Frank S. Swain

American Orthotic and Prosthetic Ass'n
Rep By: Mark W. Weller

Chase Manhattan Bank
Rep By: Frank S. Swain

Federal Home Loan Mortgage Corp. (Freddie Mac)

Guidant Corp.
Rep By: Mark W. Weller

Indiana Medical Device Manufacturers Council
Issues: MED
Rep By: Mark W. Weller

Roche Diagnostics
Rep By: Mark W. Weller

Baker & Hostetler LLP

1050 Connecticut Ave. NW
Suite 1100
Washington, DC 20036-5304
Web: www.bakerlaw.com
Tel: (202)861-1500
Fax: (202)861-1790
Registered: LDA, FARA
Washington office of a Cleveland-based general practice law firm.

Political Action Committee
Baker & Hostetler Political Action Committee
1050 Connecticut Ave. NW
Suite 1100
Washington, DC 20036-5304
Contact: William H. Schweitzer
Tel: (202)861-1500
Fax: (202)861-1790

DC-Area Employees Representing Listed Clients
BARTRAM, Darin
BECKWITH, Edward J.
BLASEY, III, Ralph G.
BRADEN, E. Mark, Partner
CASEY, Lee A.
CONROY, William F., Partner
CYMROT, Mark A.
DOLAN, Matthew J., Partner
FORD, Anne K., Partner
GRAEFE, Frederick H., Partner
HAUSER, Richard H., Partner
KENNELLY, Hon. Barbara Bailey
KERRIGAN, Kathleen M.
KIRSTEIN, David M., Partner
LOTTERER, Steven A., Legislative Assistant
LYSTAD, Robert, Associate
MARSHALL, David L., Partner
MURPHY, Betty Southard, Partner
RIVKIN, Jr., David B.
SANFORD, Bruce W., Partner
SCHWEITZER, William H., Partner
SNYDER, Kenneth F., Partner
STEPHEN, Christopher T.
VANDER JAGT, Hon. Guy, Of Counsel
WICK, Ronald F., Partner
YOUNG, Joanne, Partner
ZAPRUDER, Henry G., Partner

Clients

The Aluminum Ass'n
Rep By: William H. Schweitzer

American Concrete Pavement Ass'n (ACPA)
Issues: TRA
Rep By: Frederick H. Graefe

American Dental Ass'n
Issues: HCR
Rep By: William H. Schweitzer

American Electric Power Co.
Issues: TAX
Rep By: William F. Conroy, Matthew J. Dolan, Frederick H. Graefe, David L. Marshall, Hon. Guy Vander Jagt

American Fidelity Life Insurance Co.
Issues: INS
Rep By: Frederick H. Graefe, Christopher T. Stephen

American Football Coaches Ass'n
Rep By: Matthew J. Dolan, Hon. Guy Vander Jagt

American Resort Development Ass'n
Issues: TAX
Rep By: E. Mark Braden, William F. Conroy, Matthew J. Dolan, Frederick H. Graefe, David L. Marshall, Kenneth F. Snyder, Hon. Guy Vander Jagt

Amwest Surety Insurance Co.
Rep By: Steven A. Lotterer

Bangor Internat'l Airport
Issues: AVI
Rep By: Joanne Young

Blue Cross and Blue Shield of Ohio
Rep By: Matthew J. Dolan, Steven A. Lotterer, Hon. Guy Vander Jagt

Bristol-Myers Squibb Co.
Rep By: Matthew J. Dolan, Steven A. Lotterer, Hon. Guy Vander Jagt

Cafaro Co.
Issues: TAX
Rep By: William F. Conroy, Matthew J. Dolan, Steven A. Lotterer, David L. Marshall, Hon. Guy Vander Jagt

Capitol American Financial Corp.
Rep By: Frederick H. Graefe

Central Reserve Life
Rep By: Frederick H. Graefe

Children's Mercy Hospital
Issues: MMM
Rep By: Frederick H. Graefe

The Chubb Corp.
Issues: INS TAX
Rep By: William F. Conroy, Matthew J. Dolan, Frederick H. Graefe, Steven A. Lotterer, David L. Marshall, Hon. Guy Vander Jagt

Citigroup
Issues: BNK TAX
Rep By: William F. Conroy, Matthew J. Dolan, Kathleen M. Kerrigan, Steven A. Lotterer, David L. Marshall, Hon. Guy Vander Jagt

Coalition for Shareholder Fairness
Rep By: Steven A. Lotterer, Hon. Guy Vander Jagt

The Council of Insurance Agents & Brokers
Issues: HCR TAX
Rep By: William F. Conroy, Matthew J. Dolan, Frederick H. Graefe, Kathleen M. Kerrigan, Steven A. Lotterer, David L. Marshall, Hon. Guy Vander Jagt

Croatia, Republic of
Rep By: Darin Bartram, Lee A. Casey, David B. Rivkin, Jr.

D. H. Blair Investment Banking Corp.
Rep By: Matthew J. Dolan, Frederick H. Graefe, Steven A. Lotterer, Hon. Guy Vander Jagt

Eagle-Picher Personal Injury Settlement Trust
Issues: TAX
Rep By: Matthew J. Dolan, Frederick H. Graefe, Richard H. Hauser, Steven A. Lotterer, David L. Marshall, Hon. Guy Vander Jagt

Edison Electric Institute
Issues: TAX
Rep By: William F. Conroy, Matthew J. Dolan, Frederick H. Graefe, Steven A. Lotterer, Hon. Guy Vander Jagt

Emmis Broadcasting Corp.
Rep By: Steven A. Lotterer, William H. Schweitzer, Hon. Guy Vander Jagt

Federation of American Hospitals
Issues: MMM
Rep By: Matthew J. Dolan, Frederick H. Graefe, Kathleen M. Kerrigan

Fireman's Fund Insurance Cos.

Flexi-Van Leasing
Issues: TAX
Rep By: William F. Conroy, Matthew J. Dolan, Frederick H. Graefe, Steven A. Lotterer, Hon. Guy Vander Jagt

Florida Residential and Casualty Joint Underwriting Ass'n
Issues: TAX
Rep By: William F. Conroy, Matthew J. Dolan, Frederick H. Graefe, Steven A. Lotterer, David L. Marshall, Hon. Guy Vander Jagt

Florida Windstorm Underwriting Ass'n
Issues: TAX
Rep By: William F. Conroy, Matthew J. Dolan, Frederick H. Graefe, Steven A. Lotterer, David L. Marshall, Hon. Guy Vander Jagt

Forest City Ratner Companies
Rep By: William F. Conroy, Matthew J. Dolan, Steven A. Lotterer, David L. Marshall, Hon. Guy Vander Jagt

Harvard University
Issues: TAX
Rep By: Steven A. Lotterer, William H. Schweitzer

The Hearst Corp.

I.O.T.A. Partners
Rep By: Steven A. Lotterer, Hon. Guy Vander Jagt

Inman, Steinberg, Nye & Stone
Issues: IMM
Rep By: Steven A. Lotterer, Hon. Guy Vander Jagt

Invacare Corp.
Rep By: Frederick H. Graefe, Kathleen M. Kerrigan

Jordache Enterprises, Inc.
Rep By: Hon. Guy Vander Jagt

Kettering Medical Center
Rep By: Frederick H. Graefe

KeyCorp, Inc.
Issues: TAX
Rep By: William F. Conroy, Matthew J. Dolan, Steven A. Lotterer, Kenneth F. Snyder, Hon. Guy Vander Jagt

Loeb & Loeb
Rep By: Matthew J. Dolan, Steven A. Lotterer, Hon. Guy Vander Jagt

Major League Baseball
Issues: CPT LBR SPO TEC
Rep By: William H. Schweitzer

Marsh & McLennan Cos.
Issues: TAX
Rep By: William F. Conroy, Matthew J. Dolan, Steven A. Lotterer, David L. Marshall, Hon. Guy Vander Jagt

Medical Mutual of Ohio
Issues: HCR
Rep By: Matthew J. Dolan, Frederick H. Graefe, Richard H. Hauser, Hon. Guy Vander Jagt

Moose Internat'l Inc.
Issues: IMM
Rep By: E. Mark Braden, Matthew J. Dolan, Steven A. Lotterer, Hon. Guy Vander Jagt

Motion Picture Ass'n of America
Issues: CPT TAX
Rep By: Matthew J. Dolan, Steven A. Lotterer, Hon. Guy Vander Jagt

Nat'l Ass'n of Insurance and Financial Advisors

Nat'l Ass'n of Optometrics and Opticians
Issues: HCR
Rep By: Matthew J. Dolan, Frederick H. Graefe, Richard H. Hauser, Hon. Guy Vander Jagt

Nat'l Ass'n of Real Estate Investment Trusts
Issues: TAX
Rep By: William F. Conroy, Matthew J. Dolan, Frederick H. Graefe, Kathleen M. Kerrigan, Steven A. Lotterer, David L. Marshall, Hon. Guy Vander Jagt

News Corporation Ltd.

PPG Industries

PSH Master L.P.I.
Rep By: William F. Conroy, Matthew J. Dolan, Steven A. Lotterer, David L. Marshall, Hon. Guy Vander Jagt

Republic Services, Inc.
Issues: ENV

RMS Disease Management Inc.
Issues: MMM
Rep By: Frederick H. Graefe, Kathleen M. Kerrigan

Rollins Hudig Hall
Rep By: Matthew J. Dolan, Steven A. Lotterer, Hon. Guy Vander Jagt

The Royal Jordanian Airline
Rep By: Joanne Young

Schering Berlin Inc.
Issues: MMM
Rep By: Frederick H. Graefe, Kathleen M. Kerrigan

Sedgwick James, Inc.
Rep By: Matthew J. Dolan, Steven A. Lotterer, Hon. Guy Vander Jagt

Shieldalloy Metallurgical Corp.
Issues: ENV

Soc. of Professional Journalists
Rep By: Robert Lystad, Bruce W. Sanford

Sutton & Sutton Solicitors
Issues: BUD
Rep By: Mark A. Cymrot, Steven A. Lotterer, Hon. Guy Vander Jagt

Trans World Assurance Co.
Issues: INS
Rep By: Frederick H. Graefe, Christopher T. Stephen

Transportation Institute
Issues: TAX
Rep By: William F. Conroy, Matthew J. Dolan, Frederick H. Graefe, Steven A. Lotterer, David L. Marshall, Hon. Guy Vander Jagt

United Fidelity Life Insurance

United Jewish Communities, Inc.
Issues: TAX
Rep By: Edward J. Beckwith, Matthew J. Dolan

United States Conference of Mayors
Issues: URB

Verizon Communications
Issues: TEC
Rep By: Frederick H. Graefe, Richard H. Hauser

Washington Regional Transplant Consortium
Rep By: Frederick H. Graefe

The Wireless Communications Council
Rep By: Frederick H. Graefe, Hon. Guy Vander Jagt

Baker & McKenzie

815 Connecticut Ave. NW
Suite 900
Washington, DC 20006-4078
Tel: (202)452-7000
Fax: (202)452-7073
Registered: LDA, FARA
Web: www.bakerinfo.com
E-mail: washingtoninfo@bakernet.com
Washington office of an international law firm headquartered in Chicago, IL.

DC-Area Employees Representing Listed Clients
BRADEN, Susan G., Of Counsel
COWARD, Nicholas F., Managing Partner
GLEASON, Teresa A., Partner
O'BRIEN, Kevin M., Partner
OUTMAN, II, William D., Partner
PEELE, III, B. Thomas, Partner
REILLY, John R., Of Counsel

Clients

R. G. Barry
Rep By: Teresa A. Gleason

British Columbia Softwood Lumber Trade Council
Issues: TRD
Rep By: B. Thomas Peele, III, John R. Reilly

ChemFirst Inc.
Issues: TRD
Rep By: Teresa A. Gleason

Drives Inc.
Issues: TRD
Rep By: Susan G. Braden, Kevin M. O'Brien

Gulf State Steel Inc.
Issues: ENV GOV
Rep By: Susan G. Braden

Storck U.S.A.
Issues: TRD
Rep By: Susan G. Braden, Teresa A. Gleason, Kevin M. O'Brien

Wm. Wrigley Jr. Co.
Issues: TRD
Rep By: Teresa A. Gleason, Kevin M. O'Brien

Baker Botts, L.L.P.

1299 Pennsylvania Ave. NW
Suite 1300 West
Washington, DC 20004-2400
Tel: (202)639-7700
Fax: (202)639-7890
Registered: LDA, FARA
Web: www.bakerbotts.com
Washington office of a Houston law firm.

DC-Area Employees Representing Listed Clients
BAKER, IV, James A., Partner
BERRY, J. Patrick, Partner
BUMPERS, William M., Partner
KIELY, Bruce F., Partner
STONEROCK, Jeffrey, Partner

Clients

Aventis Pharmaceutical Products
Rep By: James A. Baker, IV

Entergy Corp.
Rep By: William M. Bumpers

Harris, Texas, Metropolitan Transit Authority of
Rep By: James A. Baker, IV

IT Group, Inc.
Rep By: J. Patrick Berry

Mickey Leland Nat'l Urban Air Toxics Research Center
Rep By: James A. Baker, IV

Partnership for Early Climate Action
Issues: ENG ENV UTI
Rep By: William M. Bumpers

Trajen, Inc.
Issues: AVI DEF FUE GOV SMB TRA TRU
Rep By: Jeffrey Stonerock

C. Baker Consulting Inc.

901 15th Street NW
Washington, DC 20005
Tel: (202)371-6329
Fax: (202)312-3011
Registered: LDA
Defense consulting and analytical firm.

DC-Area Employees Representing Listed Clients
BAKER, Caleb, President

Clients

Allison Transmission Division, General Motors Corp.
Issues: AVI DEF MAN
Rep By: Caleb Baker

General Dynamics Corp.
Issues: AVI DEF MAN
Rep By: Caleb Baker

Honeywell Internat'l, Inc.
Issues: AVI DEF MAN
Rep By: Caleb Baker

Raytheon Co.
Issues: AVI DEF MAN
Rep By: Caleb Baker

Stewart & Stevenson Services, Inc.
Issues: AVI DEF MAN
Rep By: Caleb Baker

The Laurin Baker Group

526 Bellvue Pl.
Alexandria, VA 22314-1408
Tel: (703)548-5545
Fax: (703)548-1339
Registered: LDA
A government relations and public affairs consulting firm.

DC-Area Employees Representing Listed Clients
BAKER, Laurin M., President

Clients

Illinois Tool Works
Issues: MAN TRD
Rep By: Laurin M. Baker

Industrial Fasteners Institute
Issues: MAN
Rep By: Laurin M. Baker

Kinghorn & Associates, L.L.C.
Issues: BUD
Rep By: Laurin M. Baker

South Carolina Public Railways
Issues: BUD RRR
Rep By: Laurin M. Baker

Baker, Donelson, Bearman & Caldwell, P.C.

801 Pennsylvania Ave. NW
Suite 800
Washington, DC 20004
Tel: (202)508-3400
Fax: (202)508-3402
Registered: LDA, FARA
Web: www.bakerdonelson.com
Washington office of a law firm headquartered in Memphis, TN.

DC-Area Employees Representing Listed Clients
BAKER, Jr., Hon. Howard H., Shareholder
DASCHLE, Linda Hall, Senior Public Policy Advisor
DUFF, James C.
EAGLEBURGER, Lawrence S., Senior Foreign Policy Advisor
EDELMAN, Doreen M., Of Counsel
HOWARD, Thomas L., Shareholder
JOHNSTON, Jr., Charles R., Shareholder
KENNEDY, J. Keith, Senior Public Policy Advisor
LAMORIELLO, Francine, Senior Director, Internat'l Business Strategy
MCBRIDE, James W., Shareholder
MCENTEE, Joan M., Shareholder
MONTGOMERY, George Cranwell, Shareholder
PARKINSON, Charles R., Senior Public Policy Advisor
POWELL, Janet L., Senior Public Policy Advisor
RANDALL, Albert B., Of Counsel
RANGE, James D., Senior Advisor for Legislative, Regulatory and Environmental Affairs
STOLEE, Anne M., Shareholder
TUCK, John C., Senior Public Policy Advisor

Clients

AAAE-ACI
Issues: BUD
Rep By: Linda Hall Daschle, Albert B. Randall

Alameda Corridor-East Construction Authority
Issues: BUD TRA
Rep By: Janet L. Powell

American Airlines
Issues: BUD
Rep By: Linda Hall Daschle, Albert B. Randall

American Concrete Pavement Ass'n (ACPA)
Rep By: Linda Hall Daschle

American Fly Fishing Trade Ass'n
Rep By: James D. Range

American Friends of Turkey
Rep By: Charles R. Johnston, Jr.

American Standard Cos. Inc.
Issues: TRD
Rep By: Francine Lamoriello, Joan M. McEntee, George Cranwell Montgomery

American Trucking Ass'ns
Issues: TRA
Rep By: J. Keith Kennedy, Charles R. Parkinson

American-Turkish Council
Rep By: Doreen M. Edelman, Charles R. Johnston, Jr.

Amgen
Issues: MMM
Rep By: J. Keith Kennedy, Charles R. Parkinson

Azerbaijan, Embassy of the Republic of
Rep By: Charles R. Johnston, Jr., George Cranwell Montgomery

BAE Systems Controls
Issues: TRA
Rep By: Janet L. Powell

The Boeing Co.
Issues: AVI
Rep By: Linda Hall Daschle, Albert B. Randall

Bombardier, Inc.
Issues: BUD
Rep By: Janet L. Powell

Briartek, Inc.
Issues: TRA
Rep By: Janet L. Powell

Bridgestone/Firestone, Inc.
Issues: BUD ENV LBR
Rep By: Janet L. Powell, James D. Range

Buckeye Technologies
Rep By: Francine Lamoriello

Burger King Corp.
Issues: BUD LBR TRD
Rep By: Doreen M. Edelman

Cleveland, City of/Cleveland Hopkins Internat'l Airport
Issues: AVI BUD
Rep By: Linda Hall Daschle, Albert B. Randall

Day & Zimmermann, Inc.
Issues: BUD ENG
Rep By: George Cranwell Montgomery, John C. Tuck

Deutsche Telekom, Inc.
Issues: TEC
Rep By: Hon. Howard H. Baker, Jr., J. Keith Kennedy, John C. Tuck

Dillingham Construction, Inc.
Rep By: Charles R. Johnston, Jr.

E-Tech
Rep By: Doreen M. Edelman, Charles R. Johnston, Jr.

Fishable Waters Coalition
Issues: ENV
Rep By: James D. Range

FLIR Systems, Inc.
Issues: BUD
Rep By: J. Keith Kennedy

Foothill Transit
Issues: BUD
Rep By: Janet L. Powell

Gibson Guitar Corp.
Rep By: Charles R. Johnston, Jr.

Howard Energy Internat'l
Rep By: Doreen M. Edelman, Charles R. Johnston, Jr.

IMAX Corp.
Rep By: Francine Lamoriello, Joan M. McEntee

Indianapolis Rail Project
Issues: TRA
Rep By: Janet L. Powell

Internat'l Ass'n of Fish and Wildlife Agencies
Issues: ENV
Rep By: James D. Range

L-3 Communications Corp.
Issues: BUD
Rep By: Linda Hall Daschle, Albert B. Randall

Leap Wireless Internat'l
Issues: COM TEC
Rep By: J. Keith Kennedy

Lincoln Nat'l Corp.
Issues: INS
Rep By: Francine Lamoriello, Joan M. McEntee

Lockheed Martin Air Traffic Management
Rep By: Linda Hall Daschle, Albert B. Randall

Loral Space and Communications, Ltd.
Issues: GOV
Rep By: Hon. Howard H. Baker, Jr., Linda Hall Daschle, George Cranwell Montgomery, John C. Tuck

Monsanto Co.
Issues: AGR
Rep By: James D. Range

Montana Land Reliance
Issues: TAX
Rep By: James D. Range

Motorola, Inc.
Rep By: Joan M. McEntee

Nat'l Ecological Foundation
Issues: ENV
Rep By: James D. Range

Newspaper Ass'n of America
Issues: POS
Rep By: J. Keith Kennedy, Charles R. Parkinson, John C. Tuck

Nextwave Telecom
Issues: COM TEC
Rep By: J. Keith Kennedy

Northwest Airlines, Inc.
Issues: AVI
Rep By: Linda Hall Daschle, Albert B. Randall

The Pacific Forest Trust
Rep By: James D. Range

PacifiCorp
Issues: ENG TRD
Rep By: J. Keith Kennedy, Francine Lamoriello

Pakistani-American Business Ass'n
Rep By: Charles R. Johnston, Jr.

Pennsylvania Turnpike Commission
Issues: BUD
Rep By: Janet L. Powell

Phillips Petroleum Co.
Rep By: Francine Lamoriello, Joan M. McEntee, George Cranwell Montgomery

Prince William County, Virginia
Issues: TRA
Rep By: Janet L. Powell

Sikorsky Aircraft Corp.
Rep By: George Cranwell Montgomery

U.S.-Azerbaijan Council, Inc.
Rep By: Charles R. Johnston, Jr.

United Technologies Corp.
Issues: AVI
Rep By: Linda Hall Daschle

Ventura Port District
Issues: BUD
Rep By: J. Keith Kennedy

VoiceStream Wireless Corp.
Issues: TEC
Rep By: Hon. Howard H. Baker, Jr., J. Keith Kennedy, John C. Tuck

The Washington Post Co.
Issues: LBR
Rep By: J. Keith Kennedy, Charles R. Parkinson, John C. Tuck

World Wildlife Fund
Issues: ENV
Rep By: James D. Range

Balch & Bingham LLP

1275 Pennsylvania Ave. NW
Tenth Floor
Washington, DC 20004
Tel: (202)347-6000
Fax: (202)347-6001
Registered: LDA
Washington office of a Birmingham, AL law firm.

Political Action Committee
Balch & Bingham LLP Federal Political Committee
1275 Pennsylvania Ave. NW
Tenth Floor
Washington, DC 20004
Contact: William F. Stiers
Tel: (202)347-6000
Fax: (202)347-6001

DC-Area Employees Representing Listed Clients
CUNNINGHAM, Sean, Attorney
EAMES, Fred, Partner
HECK, Wade, Director, Federal Affairs
MCCORMICK, III, Patrick J., Partner
OLSON, Barbara K., Partner
ROGERS, Jr., Edward M., Of Counsel
STIERS, William F., Director, Government Relations

Clients

Alabama Space Science Exhibits Commission
Issues: DEF ECN EDU
Rep By: Wade Heck, William F. Stiers

Bay Harbor Management, L.C.
Issues: TEC
Rep By: Barbara K. Olson

Coleman Research Corp.
Issues: DEF
Rep By: Wade Heck, William F. Stiers

Computer Systems Technologies, Inc.
Issues: AER DEF
Rep By: Wade Heck, William F. Stiers

Elmco, Inc.
Issues: DEF
Rep By: Wade Heck, William F. Stiers

Emerging Technology Partners, LLC
Issues: MED
Rep By: Wade Heck, William F. Stiers

FirstEnergy Co.
Issues: UTI
Rep By: Sean Cunningham, Fred Eames, Patrick J. McCormick, III

informal coalition
Issues: UTI
Rep By: Sean Cunningham, Fred Eames, Patrick J. McCormick, III, Barbara K. Olson

Interstate Wine Coalition
Issues: BEV TRD TRU
Rep By: Barbara K. Olson

Madison Research Corp.
Issues: DEF
Rep By: Wade Heck, William F. Stiers

Mas-Hamilton Group
Issues: BUD
Rep By: Wade Heck, William F. Stiers

Potomac Electric Power Co.
Issues: UTI
Rep By: Sean Cunningham, Fred Eames, Patrick J. McCormick, III

Primerica, Inc.

SCANA Corp.
Issues: TRA UTI
Rep By: Patrick J. McCormick, III, William F. Stiers

Southern Co.
Issues: UTI
Rep By: Patrick J. McCormick, III

TVA Watch
Issues: ENG ENV UTI
Rep By: Sean Cunningham, Fred Eames, Patrick J. McCormick, III

Donald Baldwin Associates

888 16th St. NW
Suite 700
Washington, DC 20006-4103
Tel: (202)835-8020
Fax: (202)331-4291
Registered: LDA
A Washington-based government relations consulting firm.

DC-Area Employees Representing Listed Clients
BALDWIN, Donald, President

Clients

Citizens for Law and Order
Rep By: Donald Baldwin

Federal Criminal Investigators Ass'n
Issues: LAW
Rep By: Donald Baldwin

Nat'l Law Enforcement Council
Issues: LAW
Rep By: Donald Baldwin

Security on Campus, Inc.
Issues: EDU LAW
Rep By: Donald Baldwin

Ball Janik, LLP

1455 F St. NW
Suite 225
Washington, DC 20005
Tel: (202)638-3307
Fax: (202)783-6947
Registered: LDA

Washington office of a law firm headquartered in Portland, OR

DC-Area Employees Representing Listed Clients

BEALL, James A., D.C. Office Managing Partner
CRAM, M. Victoria, Government Relations Consultant
GIGUERE, Michelle E., Government Relations Specialist
HAYES, Robert G., Partner
HIEMSTRA, Hal D., Government Relations Consultant
JAMES, Dan, Government Relations Consultant
JOHNSON, Jay S., Of Counsel
RINGWOOD, Irene, Partner

Clients

Alcoa Inc.
Issues: ENG
Rep By: Robert G. Hayes, Irene Ringwood

American Dehydrated Onion and Garlic Ass'n
Issues: AGR FOO TRD
Rep By: Robert G. Hayes, Irene Ringwood

American Sportfishing Ass'n
Rep By: Robert G. Hayes, Irene Ringwood

ATOFINA
Issues: ENG
Rep By: Robert G. Hayes, Irene Ringwood

Basic American, Inc.
Issues: AGR TRD
Rep By: Irene Ringwood

Bellevue, Washington, City of
Issues: BUD CAW ECN HOU LAW LBR ROD URB
Rep By: M. Victoria Cram

Billfish Foundation
Issues: MAR
Rep By: Robert G. Hayes

Cascade General, Inc.
Issues: BUD DEF MAR
Rep By: James A. Beall, Michelle E. Giguere

City University
Issues: EDU FOR
Rep By: James A. Beall

Clackamas, Oregon, County of
Issues: BUD ECN ROD
Rep By: James A. Beall, Michelle E. Giguere, Hal D. Hiemstra

Clatsop Community College
Issues: BUD
Rep By: James A. Beall, Michelle E. Giguere

Coastal Conservation Ass'n
Issues: MAR NAT
Rep By: Robert G. Hayes, Irene Ringwood

Columbia Falls Aluminum Co.
Issues: ENG
Rep By: Robert G. Hayes, Irene Ringwood

Goldendale Aluminum
Issues: ENG
Rep By: Robert G. Hayes, Irene Ringwood

Grants Pass Irrigation District
Issues: BUD
Rep By: Michelle E. Giguere, Dan James

Greenbrier Companies
Issues: ENV MAR RRR TAX
Rep By: James A. Beall, M. Victoria Cram, Hal D. Hiemstra

Guardian Marine Internat'l LLC
Issues: BUD FOR
Rep By: James A. Beall, Michelle E. Giguere

Hager Hinge Co.
Rep By: Robert G. Hayes, Irene Ringwood

Highline School District Educational Resources
Issues: AVI
Rep By: Michelle E. Giguere, Hal D. Hiemstra

Hood River, Oregon, Port of
Issues: BUD MAR ROD TRA
Rep By: James A. Beall, Michelle E. Giguere

Icicle Seafoods, Inc.
Issues: MAR
Rep By: Jay S. Johnson

Kaiser Aluminum & Chemical Corp.
Issues: ENG
Rep By: Robert G. Hayes, Irene Ringwood

Las Vegas, Nevada, City of
Issues: ENG HOU TAX TEC TRA
Rep By: M. Victoria Cram

Modesto, California, City of
Issues: BUD CAW ECN LBR ROD URB
Rep By: M. Victoria Cram

Northwest Aluminum Co.
Issues: ENG
Rep By: Robert G. Hayes, Irene Ringwood

Northwest Woodland Owners Council
Issues: TAX
Rep By: James A. Beall, M. Victoria Cram

Oregon Department of Transportation
Issues: BUD ROD TRA
Rep By: James A. Beall, Michelle E. Giguere, Hal D. Hiemstra

Portland, Oregon, City of
Issues: BUD CAW ECN GOV HOU LAW TAX URB
Rep By: M. Victoria Cram

Restore America's Estuaries
Issues: ENV
Rep By: Robert G. Hayes, Hal D. Hiemstra

Tukwila, Washington, City of
Issues: BUD
Rep By: James A. Beall, Michelle E. Giguere, Hal D. Hiemstra

Whittier, California, City of
Issues: UTI
Rep By: M. Victoria Cram

The Baller Herbst Law Group

1820 Jefferson Pl. NW
Washington, DC 20036
Tel: (202)833-0166
Fax: (202)833-1180
Registered: LDA

DC-Area Employees Representing Listed Clients

STOKES, Sean A., Attorney

Clients

Hiawatha Broadband Communications Inc.
Issues: COM TEC
Rep By: Sean A. Stokes

Balzano Associates

1730 N. Lynn St.
Suite 504
Arlington, VA 22209
Tel: (703)276-1412
Fax: (703)276-1415
Registered: LDA

DC-Area Employees Representing Listed Clients

BALZANO, Christopher
BALZANO, Jr., Michael P., President
GOODMAN, Ruthanne, Account Executive
LIMAURO, Nancy, Account Executive
VERMEULEN, Janel, Account Executive

Clients

Boeing Defense and Space Group
Issues: AER
Rep By: Michael P. Balzano, Jr., Ruthanne Goodman, Janel Vermeulen

The Business Roundtable
Issues: TRD
Rep By: Christopher Balzano, Michael P. Balzano, Jr., Ruthanne Goodman, Janel Vermeulen

Lockheed Martin Corp.
Issues: DEF
Rep By: Michael P. Balzano, Jr., Ruthanne Goodman, Janel Vermeulen

Nat'l Institute for Aerospace Studies and Services Inc.
Issues: DEF
Rep By: Michael P. Balzano, Jr., Ruthanne Goodman, Nancy Limauro, Janel Vermeulen

Bannerman and Associates, Inc.

888 16th St. NW
Washington, DC 20006
Tel: (202)835-8177
Fax: (202)835-8161
Registered: LDA, FARA

DC-Area Employees Representing Listed Clients

ABINGTON, Edward G.
BANNERMAN, M. Graeme, President
HABEEB, W. Mark
HINGELEY, Anne
MINER, William A.
SCHULTZ, Valerie A.
SILVERS, Curt
SITTNICK, Tammy, Staff Assistant

Clients

Assurance Technology Corp.
Issues: DEF
Rep By: M. Graeme Bannerman, Anne Hingeley, William A. Miner, Valerie A. Schultz

Egypt, Government of the Arab Republic of
Rep By: M. Graeme Bannerman, Anne Hingeley, William A. Miner, Valerie A. Schultz, Curt Silvers, Tammy Sittnick

El Salvador, Embassy of the Republic of
Rep By: M. Graeme Bannerman, Anne Hingeley, William A. Miner, Valerie A. Schultz, Curt Silvers, Tammy Sittnick

Internat'l College
Issues: BUD EDU FOR
Rep By: M. Graeme Bannerman, Anne Hingeley, William A. Miner, Valerie A. Schultz, Curt Silvers, Tammy Sittnick

Lebanese American University
Issues: EDU
Rep By: M. Graeme Bannerman, Anne Hingeley, William A. Miner, Valerie A. Schultz, Curt Silvers, Tammy Sittnick

Palestinian Authority
Issues: FOR
Rep By: Edward G. Abington, M. Graeme Bannerman, W. Mark Habeeb, Anne Hingeley, William A. Miner, Valerie A. Schultz, Curt Silvers

Peter S. Barash Associates, Inc.

1440 New York Ave. NW
Suite 400
Washington, DC 20005
Tel: (202)466-2221
Fax: (202)466-4455
Registered: LDA

DC-Area Employees Representing Listed Clients

BARASH, Peter S., President

Clients

American Soc. of Appraisers
Issues: BAN TAX
Rep By: Peter S. Barash

CLT Appraisal Services, Inc.
Rep By: Peter S. Barash

Council of Appraisal and Property Professional Societies
Rep By: Peter S. Barash

Guest and Associates
Rep By: Peter S. Barash

Joint Venture Partners
Rep By: Peter S. Barash

Morris Communications
Rep By: Peter S. Barash

Pharmaceutical Products, Inc.
Rep By: Peter S. Barash

TRW Inc.
Rep By: Peter S. Barash

Village Enterprises
Rep By: Peter S. Barash

Barbour Griffith & Rogers, Inc.

1275 Pennsylvania Ave. NW
Tenth Floor
Washington, DC 20004
Tel: (202)333-4936
Fax: (202)833-9392
Registered: LDA, FARA

Specializes in state and federal government relations as well as corporate business development.

Political Action Committee

Barbour Griffith & Rogers PAC
1275 Pennsylvania Ave. NW
Tenth Floor
Washington, DC 20004
Tel: (202)333-4936
Fax: (202)833-9392
Contact: G. O. Lanny Griffith, Jr.

DC-Area Employees Representing Listed Clients

BARBOUR, Haley, Chairman and Chief Exec. Officer
BARNHART, Scott, Of Counsel
BIERSACK, Carl, Director, Government Affairs
GRIFFITH, Jr., G. O. Lanny, Chief Operating Officer
HIMPLER, Bill, Director, Legislative Affairs
JOHNSON, James H., Of Counsel
MONROE, Loren, V. President and Director, Federal Affairs
ROGERS, Jr., Edward M., V. Chairman
STEVENS, R. Greg
THOMPSON, Brent, Director, Legislative Affairs

Clients

Air Transport Ass'n of America
Issues: BUD TRA
Rep By: Haley Barbour, Carl Biersack, G. O. Lanny Griffith, Jr., Loren Monroe

Alliance for Quality Nursing Home Care
Issues: MMM
Rep By: Haley Barbour, G. O. Lanny Griffith, Jr., Bill Himpler, Loren Monroe, Edward M. Rogers, Jr.

American Maritime Congress
Issues: DEF MAR TAX
Rep By: Haley Barbour, Carl Biersack, G. O. Lanny Griffith, Jr., Bill Himpler, Edward M. Rogers, Jr.

American Trucking Ass'ns
Issues: TAX
Rep By: Haley Barbour, G. O. Lanny Griffith, Jr., Edward M. Rogers, Jr., Brent Thompson

Amgen
Issues: HCR MMM PHA
Rep By: Haley Barbour, G. O. Lanny Griffith, Jr., Loren Monroe, Edward M. Rogers, Jr.

Artists Coalition
Issues: CPT
Rep By: Haley Barbour, G. O. Lanny Griffith, Jr., R. Greg Stevens, Brent Thompson

Ass'n of Oil Pipelines
Issues: ENV FUE TRA
Rep By: Carl Biersack

Avioimpex
Issues: FOR GOV TRD
Rep By: G. O. Lanny Griffith, Jr., R. Greg Stevens

Bay Harbor Management, L.C.
Issues: TEC
Rep By: Haley Barbour, Carl Biersack, G. O. Lanny Griffith, Jr., Loren Monroe, Edward M. Rogers, Jr.

BellSouth Telecommunications, Inc.
Issues: TEC
Rep By: Haley Barbour, G. O. Lanny Griffith, Jr., Loren Monroe, Edward M. Rogers, Jr., Brent Thompson

Better World Campaign
Issues: FOR
Rep By: Haley Barbour, G. O. Lanny Griffith, Jr., Loren Monroe, Edward M. Rogers, Jr.

Bristol-Myers Squibb Co.
Rep By: Haley Barbour, G. O. Lanny Griffith, Jr., Loren Monroe, Edward M. Rogers, Jr.

Broadcast Music Inc. (BMI)
Issues: CPT
Rep By: Haley Barbour, G. O. Lanny Griffith, Jr., Brent Thompson

Brown and Williamson Tobacco Corp.
Issues: TOB
Rep By: Haley Barbour, G. O. Lanny Griffith, Jr., Loren Monroe, Edward M. Rogers, Jr.

Camp Dresser and McKee, Inc.
Issues: ENV
Rep By: Haley Barbour

Canadian Nat'l Railway Co.
Issues: TRA
Rep By: Haley Barbour, Carl Biersack, G. O. Lanny Griffith, Jr., Loren Monroe

DaimlerChrysler Corp.
Issues: EDU ENV TRA TRD
Rep By: Haley Barbour, Scott Barnhart, G. O. Lanny Griffith, Jr.

Education Networks of America
Issues: EDU
Rep By: Haley Barbour, G. O. Lanny Griffith, Jr.

ezgov.com

FM Watch
Issues: HOU
Rep By: Haley Barbour, G. O. Lanny Griffith, Jr., Bill Himpler, Loren Monroe, Edward M. Rogers, Jr.

GCG Partners
Issues: TRD
Rep By: Haley Barbour, Bill Himpler, Brent Thompson

GlaxoSmithKline
Issues: HCR
Rep By: Haley Barbour, G. O. Lanny Griffith, Jr., Loren Monroe, Edward M. Rogers, Jr.

Illinois State Board of Education
Issues: EDU
Rep By: Haley Barbour, Scott Barnhart, G. O. Lanny Griffith, Jr., Bill Himpler

INTELSAT - Internat'l Telecommunications Satellite Organization
Issues: TEC
Rep By: Haley Barbour, Carl Biersack, G. O. Lanny Griffith, Jr., Bill Himpler, Loren Monroe

Lockheed Martin Corp.
Issues: AER DEF GOV
Rep By: Haley Barbour, Carl Biersack, James H. Johnson

LVMH Moet Hennessy Louis Vuitton S.A.
Issues: TRD
Rep By: Haley Barbour, Loren Monroe, Brent Thompson

Lyondell Chemical Co.
Issues: CAW FUE
Rep By: Haley Barbour, Carl Biersack, G. O. Lanny Griffith, Jr., Bill Himpler, Loren Monroe, Edward M. Rogers, Jr., Brent Thompson

Makedonski Telekomunikacii
Issues: FOR GOV TRD
Rep By: G. O. Lanny Griffith, Jr., R. Greg Stevens

MassMutual Financial Group
Issues: BAN BNK FIN HCR LBR RET TAX TOR
Rep By: Haley Barbour, Loren Monroe

Microsoft Corp.
Issues: CPI CSP
Rep By: Haley Barbour, G. O. Lanny Griffith, Jr., Loren Monroe, Edward M. Rogers, Jr., Brent Thompson

Oxygenated Fuels Ass'n
Issues: CAW FUE
Rep By: Haley Barbour, G. O. Lanny Griffith, Jr., Bill Himpler, Loren Monroe, Edward M. Rogers, Jr., Brent Thompson

Professional Benefit Trust
Issues: TAX
Rep By: Haley Barbour, G. O. Lanny Griffith, Jr., Bill Himpler, Loren Monroe, Edward M. Rogers, Jr.

Qwest Communications
Issues: TEC
Rep By: Haley Barbour, G. O. Lanny Griffith, Jr., Loren Monroe, Edward M. Rogers, Jr.

RJR Co.
Issues: TOB
Rep By: Haley Barbour, G. O. Lanny Griffith, Jr., Loren Monroe, Edward M. Rogers, Jr.

Southern Co.
Issues: ENV UTI
Rep By: Haley Barbour, Carl Biersack, G. O. Lanny Griffith, Jr., Bill Himpler, Loren Monroe, Edward M. Rogers, Jr., Brent Thompson

State Street Bank and Trust Co.
Issues: RET
Rep By: Haley Barbour, G. O. Lanny Griffith, Jr., Edward M. Rogers, Jr., Brent Thompson

Tulane University
Issues: EDU
Rep By: Haley Barbour, Scott Barnhart, G. O. Lanny Griffith, Jr., Loren Monroe

United Health Group
Issues: HCR MMM
Rep By: Haley Barbour, G. O. Lanny Griffith, Jr., Loren Monroe

University of Mississippi
Issues: EDU
Rep By: Haley Barbour, Scott Barnhart, G. O. Lanny Griffith, Jr., Loren Monroe

University of Mississippi Medical Center
Issues: EDU
Rep By: Haley Barbour, G. O. Lanny Griffith, Jr., Loren Monroe

University of Southern Mississippi
Issues: ENV MAR
Rep By: G. O. Lanny Griffith, Jr., James H. Johnson, Loren Monroe

The Winterthur Group
Issues: BAN
Rep By: G. O. Lanny Griffith, Jr., Loren Monroe

Yazoo County, Mississippi Port Commission
Issues: BUD
Rep By: Haley Barbour, G. O. Lanny Griffith, Jr., Edward M. Rogers, Jr.

Barents Group LLC

2001 M St. NW
Fourth Floor
Washington, DC 20036
Tel: (202)533-5660
Fax: (202)533-8580
Registered: LDA
Web: www.barents.com

A national firm of tax and economic consultants whose clients include law firms, trade associations, and federal and state government agencies. A wholly owned subsidiary of KPMG USA.

DC-Area Employees Representing Listed Clients

CAHILL, Kenneth, Healthcare
GALPER, Harvey, Managing Director
JOHNSON, Darwin G., Chairman
SHERMAN, Daniel, Healthcare
SKANDERSON, David M., Manager
SLAWTER, Shannon E.
SMITH, Linden C., Managing Director

Clients

American Petroleum Institute
Issues: FUE TAX
Rep By: Shannon E. Slawter, Linden C. Smith

Gardere & Wayne, LLP
Issues: FUE NAT
Rep By: Linden C. Smith

General Ore Internat'l Corp. Ltd.
Issues: TAX
Rep By: Linden C. Smith

John T. O'Rourke Law Offices
Issues: TAX
Rep By: David M. Skanderson, Linden C. Smith

Verner, Liipfert, Bernhard, McPherson and Hand, Chartered
Issues: TOB
Rep By: David M. Skanderson, Linden C. Smith

Barksdale Ballard & Co., Inc.

1951 Kidwell Dr.
Suite 205
Vienna, VA 22182
Tel: (703)827-8771
Fax: (703)827-0783
Web: www.bballard.com
E-mail: mballard@bballard.com

DC-Area Employees Representing Listed Clients

BALLARD, D. Michael, President and General Manager
RELLER, Nancy, Senior V. President

Clients

Partnership for Caring
Issues: FAM HCR
Rep By: Nancy Reller

Robert Wood Johnson Foundation
Issues: FAM HCR RET
Rep By: Nancy Reller

Wiland-Bell Productions
Issues: ART HCR
Rep By: D. Michael Ballard

Barnes & Thornburg

1401 I St. NW
Suite 500
Washington, DC 20005
Tel: (202)289-1313
Fax: (202)289-1330
Registered: LDA, FARA
Web: www.btlaw.com

A law firm with offices in Chicago, Indianapolis, Fort Wayne, South Bend, and Elkhart, IN.

DC-Area Employees Representing Listed Clients

EDGELL, John R., Partner
STAYIN, Randolph J., Partner
TAYLOR, Jeffrey L., Chairman, Federal Relations Group

Clients

Capital Goods Standards Coalition
Issues: TRD
Rep By: Randolph J. Stayin

Food Processing Machinery and Supplies Ass'n
Issues: FOO GOV TOR TRD
Rep By: Randolph J. Stayin

Indiana Glass Co.
Issues: TRD
Rep By: Randolph J. Stayin

Kyocera Corp.
Issues: TRD
Rep By: Randolph J. Stayin

Nat'l Candle Ass'n
Issues: TRD
Rep By: Randolph J. Stayin

NATSO, Inc.
Issues: TAX TRA
Rep By: Randolph J. Stayin

Process Equipment Manufacturers' Ass'n
Issues: GOV TOR TRD
Rep By: Randolph J. Stayin

Quebec Lumber Manufacturers Ass'n
Issues: TRD
Rep By: Randolph J. Stayin

Special Committee for Workplace Product Liability Reform
Issues: TOR TRD
Rep By: Randolph J. Stayin

Water and Wastewater Equipment Manufacturers Ass'n
Issues: ENV
Rep By: Randolph J. Stayin

Wheat Gluten Industry Council
Issues: TRD
Rep By: John R. Edgell, Randolph J. Stayin, Jeffrey L. Taylor

Barnes, Richardson and Colburn

1225 I St. NW
Suite 1150
Washington, DC 20005
Tel: (202)457-0300
Fax: (202)331-8746
Registered: FARA
Web: www.barnesrichdson.com
E-mail: mmcgrath@brc-dc.com

Washington office of a New York law firm.

DC-Area Employees Representing Listed Clients

HELMANIS, Ansis M., Special Counsel
MCGRATH, Matthew T., Partner
O'KELLY, James S., Partner
VON CONRAD, Gunter, Counsel

Clients

Agouron Pharmaceuticals, Inc.
Rep By: Matthew T. McGrath

Alcan Aluminum Corp.
Rep By: Matthew T. McGrath

American Ass'n of Exporters & Importers
Rep By: Matthew T. McGrath

American Ass'n of Fastener Importers
Rep By: Matthew T. McGrath

American Tourister, Inc.
Rep By: Matthew T. McGrath
Budd Co.
Rep By: Matthew T. McGrath
Consolidated Diesel Corp.
Rep By: Matthew T. McGrath, Gunter Von Conrad
Cummins Engine Co.
Durand Internat'l, J. G.
Rep By: Matthew T. McGrath
Florida Citrus Mutual
Rep By: Matthew T. McGrath
Florida Citrus Packers
Rep By: Matthew T. McGrath
Florida Citrus Processors Ass'n
Rep By: Matthew T. McGrath
Florida Farm Bureau Federation
Rep By: Matthew T. McGrath
Gulf Citrus Growers Ass'n
Rep By: Matthew T. McGrath
Indian River Citrus League
Rep By: Matthew T. McGrath
IPSCO Inc.
Italy-America Chamber of Commerce
Rep By: Matthew T. McGrath
Mercedes-Benz of North America, Inc.
Issues: AUT
Rep By: Gunter Von Conrad
Polaroid Corp.
Rep By: Matthew T. McGrath
Voest Alpine Steel
Rep By: Gunter Von Conrad
Wyeth-Ayerst Laboratories
Rep By: Ansis M. Helmanis

Law Offices of Mark Barnes

1350 I St. NW
Suite 1255
Washington, DC 20005
Tel: (202)626-0089
Fax: (202)626-0088
Registered: LDA
E-mail: MarkB17@aol.com

DC-Area Employees Representing Listed Clients
BARNES, Mark J., Attorney
BEGUN, Tammy, Attorney
BURGASSER, Jessica
COLPITTS, Cindy
GRESHAM, Julie, Attorney at Law
NORRIS, Uley, Attorney at Law

Clients
Briklee Trading Co.
Issues: FIR
Rep By: Mark J. Barnes, Tammy Begun
Cash America Internat'l
Issues: FIR
Rep By: Mark J. Barnes, Tammy Begun
Century Internat'l Arms
Issues: FIR
Rep By: Mark J. Barnes
Firearms Importers Roundtable Trade Group
Issues: FIR
Rep By: Mark J. Barnes, Tammy Begun
Intrac Arms Internat'l LLC
Issues: FIR
Rep By: Mark J. Barnes, Jessica Burgasser, Cindy Colpitts
Lew Horton Distributing Co.
Issues: FIR
Rep By: Mark J. Barnes, Tammy Begun
Mossberg Group, LLC
Issues: FIR
Rep By: Mark J. Barnes, Cindy Colpitts
Nat'l Ass'n of Arms Shows
Issues: FIR
Rep By: Mark J. Barnes, Tammy Begun
Nat'l Rifle Ass'n of America
Issues: FIR
Rep By: Mark J. Barnes, Tammy Begun

Richard L. Barnes

5335 Wisconsin Ave. NW
Suite 440
Washington, DC 20015
Tel: (202)895-1513
Fax: (301)320-7565
Registered: LDA
E-mail: dbarnes@erols.com

Clients
Simpson Investment Co.
Rep By: Richard L. Barnes

Barnett & Sivon, P.C.

2000 M St. NW
Suite 740
Washington, DC 20036-3313
Tel: (202)463-6040
Fax: (202)785-5209
Registered: LDA

DC-Area Employees Representing Listed Clients
BARNETT, Robert E., Partner
RIVAS, Jose S., Legislative Specialist
SIVON, James C., Partner

Clients
ABA Insurance Ass'n
Issues: BAN INS
Rep By: James C. Sivon
Citigroup
Issues: BAN
Rep By: Robert E. Barnett, James C. Sivon
Community Financial Services Ass'n
Issues: BAN CSP FIN
Rep By: Robert E. Barnett, Jose S. Rivas, James C. Sivon
The Financial Services Roundtable
Issues: BAN FIN HOU
Rep By: Robert E. Barnett, Jose S. Rivas, James C. Sivon

Barrack Ass'n Management

112-J Elden St.
Herndon, VA 20170-4809
Tel: (703)709-1035
Fax: (703)709-1036
E-mail: baminc@erols.com

DC-Area Employees Representing Listed Clients
BARRACK, David W., Owner/President
CAMPBELL, Nancy A., Account Manager
GOLD, Josh, Account Executive
TRINGALI, Diana, Account Executive

Clients
American Edged Products Manufacturers Ass'n
Rep By: David W. Barrack
Metal Finishing Suppliers Ass'n
Rep By: Diana Tringali
Nat'l Ass'n of Metal Finishers
Rep By: David W. Barrack
Nat'l Ass'n of Public Insurance Adjusters
Rep By: David W. Barrack

Michael F. Barrett, Jr.

601 13th St. NW
Suite 1120
Washington, DC 20005
Tel: (202)639-8142
Fax: (202)639-9493
Registered: LDA
E-mail: barrett120@aol.com

Clients
Alyeska Pipeline Service Co.
Issues: ENG
Rep By: Michael F. Barrett, Jr.
Citigroup
Issues: BAN
Rep By: Michael F. Barrett, Jr.
Lockheed Martin Corp.
Issues: ENG
Rep By: Michael F. Barrett, Jr.

Barron-Birrell, Inc.

1101 30th St. NW
Suite 500
Washington, DC 20007
Tel: (202)338-5393
Fax: (202)338-5391
Registered: FARA
A public relations, government affairs and economic development consulting firm.

DC-Area Employees Representing Listed Clients
BARRON, David H., Chairman
BIRRELL, Jeffrey C., President and Chief Exec. Officer

Clients
Congo, Office of the President of the Democratic Republic of the
Congolese Rally for Democracy
Gabonese Republic, Government of the
Liberia, Office of the President of the Republic of
Rep By: David H. Barron, Jeffrey C. Birrell
Mali, Embassy of the Republic of
Nigeria, Government of the Federal Republic of

Roger V. Barth

1801 K St. NW
Suite 1205L
Washington, DC 20006
Tel: (202)452-7373
Fax: (202)452-7333
E-mail: rbarth@erols.com

The Barton Co.

1620 I St. NW
Suite 600
Washington, DC 20006
Tel: (202)861-6778
Fax: (202)429-0422
Registered: LDA
E-mail: sbarton@usmayors.org
A government affairs and association management firm specializing in public sector and urban affairs issues.

DC-Area Employees Representing Listed Clients
PALMER-BARTON, Stacy, President

Clients
Dayton, Ohio, Washington Office of the City of
Issues: AVI BAN BUD CAW DIS ECN EDU ENV FIN FIR HOU LAW RET ROD TAX TRA URB WAS WEL
Rep By: Stacy Palmer-Barton
Gary Public Transportation Corp.
Issues: BUD TRA WEL
Rep By: Stacy Palmer-Barton
Gary Sanitary District
Issues: BUD CAW ENV WAS
Rep By: Stacy Palmer-Barton
Gary, Indiana, Housing Authority of the City of
Issues: BUD HOU URB WEL
Rep By: Stacy Palmer-Barton
Gary, Indiana, Washington Office of the City of
Issues: ALC AVI BAN BUD CAW DIS ECN EDU ENV FIN FIR GAM HOU LAW ROD RRR TRA URB WAS WEL
Rep By: Stacy Palmer-Barton
Lynn, Massachusetts, City of
Issues: BUD ECN EDU FIR RET TRA URB
Rep By: Stacy Palmer-Barton

Bass and Howes, Inc.

1818 N St. NW
Suite 450
Washington, DC 20036
Tel: (202)530-2900
Fax: (202)530-2901
Registered: LDA
Web: www.basshowes.com
E-mail: bh@basshowes.com
A public policy and public affairs firm.

DC-Area Employees Representing Listed Clients
BASS, Marie, Principal
HOWES, Joanne M., Principal
LASER, Rachel, Senior Program Associate
LIPNER, Robyn, Senior Program Manager
MOORE, Kirsten, Program Manager
ROSENBLUM, Elyse, Program Manager
ZESIGER, Heather

Clients
Family Violence Prevention Fund
Issues: BUD HCR LBR
Rep By: Joanne M. Howes
Genentech, Inc.
Issues: HCR
Rep By: Joanne M. Howes
Institute for Civil Soc.
Issues: HCR
Rep By: Rachel Laser, Robyn Lipner
Nat'l Breast Cancer Coalition
Issues: HCR MED MMM
Rep By: Joanne M. Howes, Robyn Lipner
Nat'l Employment Lawyers Ass'n
Issues: TAX
Nat'l Partnership for Women and Families
Issues: HCR MMM
Rep By: Joanne M. Howes, Robyn Lipner
Physicians for Reproductive Choice and Health
Issues: FAM HCR
Rep By: Kirsten Moore
Reproductive Health Technologies Project
Issues: BUD HCR MED
Rep By: Kirsten Moore
Ross Abbott Laboratories
Issues: MMM
Rep By: Rachel Laser, Robyn Lipner

Bassman, Mitchell & Alfano

707 L St. NW
Suite 560
Washington, DC 20036
Tel: (202)466-6502
Fax: (202)331-7510
E-mail: basmitalf@aol.com

Clients
BP Oil Marketers Ass'n
Chevron Petroleum Marketers Ass'n
Petroleum Marketers Ass'n of America

Bastianelli, Brown & Kelley

Two Lafayette Center
1133 21st St. NW, Suite 500
Washington, DC 20036
Tel: (202)293-8815
Fax: (202)293-7994
Registered: LDA
Web: www.govconlaw.com

E-mail: bbk@govconlaw.com

DC-Area Employees Representing Listed Clients
SISK, Marcus W., Consultant

Clients

Tosco Corp.
Issues: FUE
Rep By: Marcus W. Sisk

Beacon Consulting Group, Inc.

507 C St. NE
Washington, DC 20002-5809
Tel: (202)544-7944
Fax: (202)544-7975
Registered: LDA

Provides comprehensive government relations consulting services.

DC-Area Employees Representing Listed Clients
HALPIN, Katherine L., Senior Legislative Assistant
HENRY, Jeffrey W., Legislative Director
MACDOUGALL, Gordon P., President
MOELLER, Julie Debolt, Legislative Director
STEWART, Lisa A., V. President
TURVAVILLE, Kyndel, Legislative Assistant

Clients

Access Community Health Network
Issues: BUD
Rep By: Gordon P. MacDougall, Julie Debolt Moeller, Lisa A. Stewart

Advance Paradigm
Issues: BUD
Rep By: Gordon P. MacDougall, Lisa A. Stewart, Kyndel Turvaville

American Trauma Soc.
Issues: BUD
Rep By: Jeffrey W. Henry, Gordon P. MacDougall, Lisa A. Stewart

Big Brothers/Big Sisters of America
Issues: BUD
Rep By: Gordon P. MacDougall, Lisa A. Stewart, Kyndel Turvaville

Boston Symphony Orchestra
Issues: BUD
Rep By: Katherine L. Halpin, Gordon P. MacDougall, Lisa A. Stewart

Carnegie Hall Corp.
Issues: BUD
Rep By: Katherine L. Halpin, Gordon P. MacDougall, Lisa A. Stewart

Center Point Inc.
Issues: BUD
Rep By: Gordon P. MacDougall, Lisa A. Stewart, Kyndel Turvaville

Civic Ventures
Issues: BUD
Rep By: Gordon P. MacDougall, Julie Debolt Moeller, Lisa A. Stewart

Cummins-Allison Corp.
Rep By: Jeffrey W. Henry, Gordon P. MacDougall, Lisa A. Stewart

Haymarket Center
Rep By: Gordon P. MacDougall, Julie Debolt Moeller, Lisa A. Stewart

Metropolitan Family Services
Issues: BUD
Rep By: Gordon P. MacDougall, Julie Debolt Moeller, Lisa A. Stewart

Museum of Science and Industry
Issues: BUD
Rep By: Jeffrey W. Henry, Gordon P. MacDougall, Lisa A. Stewart

Mystic Seaport Museum
Issues: BUD
Rep By: Katherine L. Halpin, Gordon P. MacDougall, Lisa A. Stewart

Nat'l Crime Prevention Council
Issues: BUD
Rep By: Jeffrey W. Henry, Gordon P. MacDougall, Lisa A. Stewart

Ohio Wesleyan University
Issues: BUD
Rep By: Katherine L. Halpin, Gordon P. MacDougall, Lisa A. Stewart

Old Sturbridge Village
Issues: BUD
Rep By: Katherine L. Halpin, Gordon P. MacDougall, Lisa A. Stewart

Oregon Health Sciences University
Issues: BUD
Rep By: Jeffrey W. Henry, Gordon P. MacDougall, Lisa A. Stewart

Public/Private Ventures
Issues: BUD LAW
Rep By: Jeffrey W. Henry, Gordon P. MacDougall, Lisa A. Stewart

Safer Foundation
Issues: BUD
Rep By: Gordon P. MacDougall, Julie Debolt Moeller, Lisa A. Stewart

Westcare Foundation, Inc.
Issues: BUD
Rep By: Gordon P. MacDougall, Lisa A. Stewart, Kyndel Turvaville

Bechtel & Cole

1901 L St. NW
Suite 250
Washington, DC 20036
E-mail: coleslaw@erols.com
Tel: (202)833-4190
Fax: (202)833-3084

DC-Area Employees Representing Listed Clients
BECHTEL, Gene A., Board Chair and Principal
COLE, Harry F., Principal
FARHAT, Ann C., Managing Principal

Clients

Advanced Cordless Technologies, Inc.
Rep By: Gene A. Bechtel

Shurberg Broadcasting of Hartford Inc.
Rep By: Harry F. Cole

Lee Bechtel and Associates

8506 Sundale Dr.
Silver Spring, MD 20910
E-mail: balobby@aol.com
Tel: (301)588-2822
Fax: (301)588-2822
Registered: LDA

DC-Area Employees Representing Listed Clients
BECHTEL, Lee, Principal

Clients

American Ass'n of Naturopathic Physicians
Issues: HCR
Rep By: Lee Bechtel

American Soc. of Extra-Corporeal Technology
Rep By: Lee Bechtel

Paradigm Support Corp.
Issues: HCR
Rep By: Lee Bechtel

Belew Law Firm

1150 Connecticut Ave. NW
Suite 900
Washington, DC 20036-4104
Web: www.belewlaw.com
E-mail: mail@belewlaw.com
Tel: (202)862-4348
Fax: (202)862-4130
Registered: LDA

DC-Area Employees Representing Listed Clients
BELEW, Joy Carabasi, Director, Government Relations
BELEW, Jr., M. Wendell, President

Clients

BAE SYSTEMS North America
Issues: DEF
Rep By: Joy Carabasi Belew, M. Wendell Belew, Jr.

Government Employees Hospital Ass'n
Issues: BUD HCR
Rep By: Joy Carabasi Belew, M. Wendell Belew, Jr.

Seedco
Issues: ECN WEL
Rep By: Joy Carabasi Belew, M. Wendell Belew, Jr.

Vikki Bell

P.O. Box 3228
Arlington, VA 22203
E-mail: vikkis@clark.net
Tel: (703)525-5067
Registered: LDA

Clients

Canberra Packard BioScience
Issues: BUD DEF ENG MED SCI WAS
Rep By: Vikki Bell

Timothy Bell & Co.

11479 Waterview Cluster
Suite 200
Reston, VA 20190
Tel: (703)476-8060
Fax: (703)709-3003
Registered: LDA

DC-Area Employees Representing Listed Clients
MABEE, Ph.D., Marcia S., President

Clients

Coalition for American Trauma Care
Issues: BUD CSP HCR TEC
Rep By: Marcia S. Mabee, Ph.D.

Coalition for Health Funding
Issues: BUD
Rep By: Marcia S. Mabee, Ph.D.

Council of State and Territorial Epidemiologists
Issues: BUD HCR
Rep By: Marcia S. Mabee, Ph.D.

Bell, Boyd & Lloyd

1615 L St. NW
Suite 1200
Washington, DC 20036
Web: www.bellboyd.com
E-mail: info@bellboyd.com
Tel: (202)466-6300
Fax: (202)463-0678
Registered: LDA

DC-Area Employees Representing Listed Clients
BOND, Langhorne M., Of Counsel
BUTTERFIELD, William
CARROCCIO, A. Thomas, Partner
GILBERTSON, Ronald
HILL, Richard E., Of Counsel
KILCULLEN, Peter
MAGUIRE, II, Stephen J., Legislative Representative
SANTARELLI, Donald E., Partner
WILSON, Walter
ZIELINSKI, Charles A., Partner

Clients

Computer Associates Internat'l
Issues: CPI IMM
Rep By: Stephen J. Maguire, II

Investment Co. Institute

KJAZ-FM
Rep By: A. Thomas Carroccio

Performing Arts Network of New Jersey
Rep By: A. Thomas Carroccio

The Bellamy Law Firm, P.C.

1100 Connecticut Ave. NW
Suite 1000
Washington, DC 20036
E-mail: bellamylaw@aol.com
Tel: (202)785-5222
Fax: (202)785-5224
Registered: LDA

Provides legislative advocacy before Congress and federal agencies and engages in international trade development.

DC-Area Employees Representing Listed Clients
BELLAMY, Lorenzo, Owner

Clients

Chevron, U.S.A.
Issues: TRD
Rep By: Lorenzo Bellamy

Benchmarks, Inc.

3248 Prospect St. NW
Washington, DC 20007
Tel: (202)965-3983
Fax: (202)965-3987
Registered: LDA

A consulting firm.

DC-Area Employees Representing Listed Clients
SCANLON, Thomas J., President

Clients

Grupo Industrial Alfa, S.A.
Rep By: Thomas J. Scanlon

Internat'l Health, Racquet and Sportsclub Ass'n
Issues: CPT TAX
Rep By: Thomas J. Scanlon

Bennett Turner & Coleman, LLP

1900 K St. NW
Suite 750
Washington, DC 20006
Tel: (202)833-4500
Fax: (202)833-2859
Registered: LDA

DC-Area Employees Representing Listed Clients
BENNETT, Alan R., Partner
BULTENA, Jayne P., Partner
COLEMAN, Terry S., Partner
GOSS, Elizabeth, Partner
LESKOVSEK, Natasha, Associate
MANHEIM, Bruce
PETTY, Michael D., Partner
SCHRODE, Kristi E., Associate
TURNER, Samuel D., Partner

Clients

Abbott Laboratories

American Soc. of Clinical Oncology
Issues: BUD HCR MED MMM
Rep By: Terry S. Coleman, Elizabeth Goss, Samuel D. Turner

AstraZeneca Inc.

Bristol-Myers Squibb Co.
Issues: ADV CPT MED MMM
Rep By: Alan R. Bennett, Elizabeth Goss, Samuel D. Turner

Cancer Leadership Council
Issues: BUD HCR MED MMM
Rep By: Elizabeth Goss, Kristi E. Schrode, Samuel D. Turner

Celgene Corp.

The Children's Cause Inc.
Issues: BUD HCR MED MMM
Rep By: Elizabeth Goss, Kristi E. Schrode, Samuel D. Turner

Cure for Lymphoma Foundation
Issues: BUD HCR MED MMM
Rep By: Elizabeth Goss, Natasha Leskovsek, Kristi E. Schrode, Samuel D. Turner

Cystic Fibrosis Foundation
Issues: BUD HCR MED MMM PHA
Rep By: Elizabeth Goss, Natasha Leskovsek, Bruce Manheim, Samuel D. Turner

Johnson & Johnson, Inc.

Leukemia & Lymphoma Soc.
Issues: BUD HCR MED MMM
Rep By: Elizabeth Goss, Natasha Leskovsek, Kristi E. Schrode, Samuel D. Turner

Eli Lilly and Co.

Nat'l Coalition for Cancer Survivorship
Issues: BUD HCR MED MMM
Rep By: Elizabeth Goss, Kristi E. Schrode, Samuel D. Turner

Nat'l Patient Advocate Foundation
Issues: BUD HCR MED MMM
Rep By: Elizabeth Goss, Samuel D. Turner

North American Brain Tumor Coalition
Issues: BUD HCR MED MMM
Rep By: Elizabeth Goss, Natasha Leskovsek, Kristi E. Schrode, Samuel D. Turner

Novartis Corp.

Pfizer, Inc.

Serono Laboratories, Inc.
Issues: CPT MED MMM
Rep By: Alan R. Bennett, Bruce Manheim, Michael D. Petty

SmithKline Beecham Consumer Healthcare, LLP
Issues: ADV CPT MED
Rep By: Alan R. Bennett, Jayne P. Bultena, Michael D. Petty

Bentley, Adams, Hargett, Riley and Co., Inc.

120 S. Payne St.
Alexandria, VA 22314
Tel: (703)684-7300
Fax: (703)684-7302
Registered: LDA
Web: www.bahrinc.com

A dynamic, multi-focused consulting firm specializing in government relations and business improvement services. It is comprised of former Congressional and Executive Branch officials.

DC-Area Employees Representing Listed Clients
BIESTEK, Jr., Frederick A., Deputy Director, Government Relations
HARGETT, Michael, Treasurer
RILEY, H. McGuire, V. President
ROSAMOND, John, Director, Government Relations

Clients

InWork Technologies
Issues: DEF GOV
Rep By: Frederick A. Biestek, Jr., Michael Hargett, H. McGuire Riley, John Rosamond

Munitions Industrial Base Task Force
Issues: DEF FIR
Rep By: Frederick A. Biestek, Jr., Michael Hargett, H. McGuire Riley, John Rosamond

Sister Cities Internat'l
Issues: GOV URB
Rep By: Frederick A. Biestek, Jr., Michael Hargett, H. McGuire Riley, John Rosamond

William S. Bergman Associates

1726 M St. NW
Suite 1101
Washington, DC 20036
Tel: (202)452-1520
Fax: (202)833-1577
Web: www.wsb_wsba.com

An association management firm.

DC-Area Employees Representing Listed Clients
BECK, Deborah, V. President
BERGMAN, CAE, William S., President

Clients

Nat'l Ass'n of Lottery Purchasers
Rep By: Deborah Beck, William S. Bergman, CAE

Nurses Organization of Veterans Affairs
Rep By: Deborah Beck

Outdoor Power Equipment Aftermarket Ass'n
Rep By: William S. Bergman, CAE

Bergner Bockorny Castagnetti and Hawkins

1101 16th St. NW
Suite 500
Washington, DC 20036
Tel: (202)659-9111
Fax: (202)659-6387
Registered: LDA, FARA

A government relations consulting firm.

DC-Area Employees Representing Listed Clients
BERGNER, Jeffrey T., President
BOCKORNY, David A., Chairman
CASTAGNETTI, David, Principal
HAWKINS, James W., Principal
JACKSON, Alvin B.
REESE, Brenda Benjamin, Legislative Coordinator
SCHULMAN, Melissa, V. President

Clients

AdvaMed
Rep By: Jeffrey T. Bergner, David A. Bockorny, David Castagnetti, James W. Hawkins, Melissa Schulman

Agilent Technologies
Issues: HCR MMM TRD
Rep By: Jeffrey T. Bergner, David A. Bockorny, David Castagnetti, James W. Hawkins, Brenda Benjamin Reese, Melissa Schulman

American Bankers Ass'n
Issues: BAN
Rep By: Jeffrey T. Bergner, David A. Bockorny, David Castagnetti, Melissa Schulman

American Hospital Ass'n
Issues: BUD HCR MMM
Rep By: Jeffrey T. Bergner, David A. Bockorny, David Castagnetti, Melissa Schulman

Amgen
Issues: VET
Rep By: James W. Hawkins, Melissa Schulman

Auaya, Inc.
Issues: TAX TEC TRD

Biogen, Inc.
Issues: HCR
Rep By: Jeffrey T. Bergner, David A. Bockorny, David Castagnetti, James W. Hawkins, Brenda Benjamin Reese, Melissa Schulman

The Boeing Co.
Issues: TAX TRD
Rep By: Jeffrey T. Bergner, David A. Bockorny, David Castagnetti, Alvin B. Jackson, Melissa Schulman

Bristol-Myers Squibb Co.
Issues: HCR
Rep By: Jeffrey T. Bergner, David A. Bockorny, David Castagnetti, James W. Hawkins

Business Executives for Nat'l Security
Issues: FOR
Rep By: Jeffrey T. Bergner, David A. Bockorny, David Castagnetti, Melissa Schulman

The Business Roundtable

Chicago Board Options Exchange
Issues: BAN
Rep By: Jeffrey T. Bergner, David A. Bockorny, David Castagnetti, James W. Hawkins, Alvin B. Jackson, Brenda Benjamin Reese, Melissa Schulman

Coalition Against Database Piracy
Issues: CPT

Computer Coalition for Responsible Exports
Issues: CPI DEF TRD
Rep By: Jeffrey T. Bergner, David A. Bockorny, David Castagnetti, Melissa Schulman

Dell Computer Corp.
Issues: CPI TRD
Rep By: Jeffrey T. Bergner, David A. Bockorny, David Castagnetti, James W. Hawkins, Melissa Schulman

Direct Marketing Ass'n, Inc.
Issues: TAX

Elanco Animal Health
Issues: ANI
Rep By: Jeffrey T. Bergner, David A. Bockorny, David Castagnetti, Melissa Schulman

Everglades Defense Council
Issues: ENV
Rep By: Jeffrey T. Bergner, David A. Bockorny, David Castagnetti, James W. Hawkins

First Health Group Corp.
Issues: HCR
Rep By: Jeffrey T. Bergner, David A. Bockorny, David Castagnetti, James W. Hawkins, Melissa Schulman

Genzyme Corp.
Issues: HCR
Rep By: James W. Hawkins

GlaxoSmithKline
Issues: MED
Rep By: Jeffrey T. Bergner, David A. Bockorny, David Castagnetti, Melissa Schulman

Goodyear Tire and Rubber Co.
Issues: ROD TRA

Hewlett-Packard Co.
Issues: CPI ENV TEC TRD
Rep By: Jeffrey T. Bergner, David A. Bockorny, David Castagnetti

Lucent Technologies
Issues: CPT ENV HCR SCI TAX TEC TRD
Rep By: Jeffrey T. Bergner, David A. Bockorny, David Castagnetti, Melissa Schulman

Monsanto Co.
Issues: AGR FOO PHA TAX TRD
Rep By: Jeffrey T. Bergner, David A. Bockorny, David Castagnetti, Melissa Schulman

Nat'l Ass'n of Real Estate Investment Trusts
Issues: TAX
Rep By: Jeffrey T. Bergner, David A. Bockorny, David Castagnetti, James W. Hawkins, Melissa Schulman

Nat'l Rural Electric Cooperative Ass'n

Nat'l Soft Drink Ass'n
Issues: BEV
Rep By: Jeffrey T. Bergner, David A. Bockorny, David Castagnetti, Melissa Schulman

News Corporation Ltd.
Issues: ADV ART COM CPT TRD
Rep By: Jeffrey T. Bergner, David A. Bockorny, David Castagnetti, Melissa Schulman

Northwest Airlines, Inc.
Issues: AVI BUD LBR
Rep By: Jeffrey T. Bergner, David A. Bockorny, David Castagnetti, Melissa Schulman

Ovations/United Health Group
Issues: MMM
Rep By: Jeffrey T. Bergner, David A. Bockorny, David Castagnetti, James W. Hawkins, Brenda Benjamin Reese, Melissa Schulman

Petroleum Marketers Ass'n of America
Issues: BAN ENV FUE GOV ROD TAX TOB
Rep By: Jeffrey T. Bergner, David A. Bockorny, David Castagnetti, Melissa Schulman

Premium Standard Farms
Issues: AGR
Rep By: Jeffrey T. Bergner, David A. Bockorny, David Castagnetti, James W. Hawkins, Brenda Benjamin Reese, Melissa Schulman

Prudential Insurance Co. of America
Issues: INS TAX

Qwest Communications
Issues: TEC
Rep By: Jeffrey T. Bergner, David A. Bockorny, David Castagnetti, James W. Hawkins, Melissa Schulman

Taipei Economic and Cultural Representative Office in the United States
Rep By: Jeffrey T. Bergner, David A. Bockorny, David Castagnetti, Melissa Schulman

UDV North America, Inc.
Issues: BEV LBR TAX
Rep By: Jeffrey T. Bergner, David A. Bockorny, David Castagnetti, James W. Hawkins

Bergson & Co.

190 Falcon Ridge Rd.
Great Falls, VA 22066
Tel: (703)757-9270
Fax: (703)757-9275
Registered: LDA
E-mail: brgmstr@erols.com

A government relations consulting firm.

DC-Area Employees Representing Listed Clients
BERGSON, Paul C., Principal

Clients

General Dynamics Corp.
Issues: DEF
Rep By: Paul C. Bergson

PriceWaterhouseCoopers
Issues: DEF
Rep By: Paul C. Bergson

S & B Infrastructure, Inc.
Issues: DEF
Rep By: Paul C. Bergson

Swisher Internat'l Inc.
Issues: TOB
Rep By: Paul C. Bergson

Berkshire Inc.

7800 Foxhound Rd.
McLean, VA 22102
Tel: (703)821-3179
Fax: (703)448-3515
Registered: LDA

An international and domestic business consulting firm.

DC-Area Employees Representing Listed Clients
KELLEY, Michael T., President

Clients

Advanced Refractory Technologies, Inc.
Issues: DEF
Rep By: Michael T. Kelley

Hydrocarbon Technologies Inc.
Issues: ENG
Rep By: Michael T. Kelley

IIT Research Institute
Issues: DEF TAX
Rep By: Michael T. Kelley

Synzyme Technologies, Inc.
Issues: DEF ENG HCR MED
Rep By: Michael T. Kelley

Berliner Corcoran & Rowe

1101 17th St. NW
Suite 1100
Washington, DC 20036-4798
Web: www.bcr-dc.com
E-mail: bcr@bcr-dc.com
Tel: (202)293-5555
Fax: (202)293-9035
Registered: FARA

Clients

Polygon, Ltd.

Berliner, Candon & Jimison

1225 19th St. NW
Suite 800
Washington, DC 20036
Formerly Brady & Berliner.
Tel: (202)955-6067
Fax: (202)293-0307
Registered: LDA, FARA

DC-Area Employees Representing Listed Clients

BERLINER, Roger A., Partner
CANDON, Mary Eva, Partner
HIRST, Peter G., Associate
JIMISON, John W., Partner
KISH, Carla, Director, Federal Legislative Affairs
MARGOLIN, Burt, Director, Public Policy

Clients

California Primary Care Ass'n
Issues: HCR
Rep By: Carla Kish, Burt Margolin

Guam, Territory of
Issues: GOV TRU
Rep By: Roger A. Berliner, Mary Eva Candon

Los Angeles, California, County of
Issues: FAM HCR IMM MMM WEL
Rep By: Roger A. Berliner, Carla Kish, Burt Margolin

Tarzana Treatment Center
Issues: HCR
Rep By: Carla Kish, Burt Margolin

Wireless Location Industry Ass'n
Issues: TEC
Rep By: John W. Jimison, Carla Kish

Berman and Company

1775 Pennsylvania Ave. NW
Suite 1200
Washington, DC 20006
Tel: (202)463-7100
Fax: (202)463-7107
Registered: LDA

DC-Area Employees Representing Listed Clients

BERMAN, Richard B., President
DILWORTH, Tom, V. President, Operations

Clients

American Beverage Institute
Issues: BEV
Rep By: Richard B. Berman

Employment Policies Institute Foundation
Rep By: Richard B. Berman

Berman Enterprises

1800 K St. NW
Suite 1124
Washington, DC 20006
E-mail: bermanent@aol.com
Tel: (202)833-4923
Fax: (202)223-8036
Registered: LDA

DC-Area Employees Representing Listed Clients

BERMAN, Wayne, Managing Director

Clients

Flo-Sun Sugar
Issues: AGR
Rep By: Wayne Berman

Greater New York Hospital Ass'n
Issues: HCR
Rep By: Wayne Berman

Bernstein Law Firm, PLLC

1730 K St. NW
Washington, DC 20006
Tel: (202)452-8010
Fax: (202)296-2065
Registered: FARA

DC-Area Employees Representing Listed Clients

BERNSTEIN, Caryl S., Parnter
BERNSTEIN, George K., Partner
SHAPIRO, Robert B.

Clients

X.L. Insurance Co.
Rep By: George K. Bernstein, Robert B. Shapiro

Max N. Berry Law Offices

3213 O St. NW
Washington, DC 20007
Tel: (202)298-6134
Fax: (202)333-3348
Registered: LDA, FARA
E-mail: onostreet@aol.com

DC-Area Employees Representing Listed Clients

BERRY, Max N., Attorney-at-Law

Clients

American Importers and Exporters/Meat Products Group
Rep By: Max N. Berry

Ass'n of Chocolate, Biscuit and Confectionery Industries of the EEC
Rep By: Max N. Berry

Atalanta Corp.
Rep By: Max N. Berry

AVEBE America, Inc.
Rep By: Max N. Berry

Centraal Bureau van de Tuinbouwveilingen

Centre National Interprofessionel de L'Economie Laitiere (French Dairy Ass'n)
Issues: AGR
Rep By: Max N. Berry

Chocolate, Biscuit and Confectionery Industries of the European Community

Committee to Assure the Availability of Casein
Issues: AGR
Rep By: Max N. Berry

Danish Meat Canners Export Ass'n

Florida Department of Citrus
Issues: AGR
Rep By: Max N. Berry

Gallard-Schlesinger Chemical Manufacturing Corp.
Rep By: Max N. Berry

Gist Brocades
Rep By: Max N. Berry

Junex Enterprises
Rep By: Max N. Berry

Nylo-Flex Manufacturing Co., Inc.
Rep By: Max N. Berry

Tilda Rice

Valio Finnish Co-operative Dairies Ass'n
Rep By: Max N. Berry

Robert Betz Associates, Inc.

1444 I St. NW
Suite 410
Washington, DC 20005
Tel: (202)347-1990
Fax: (202)628-2310
Registered: LDA

DC-Area Employees Representing Listed Clients

BETZ, Cathy Clark, Exec. Health Counsel
BETZ, Robert B., President

Clients

American Ass'n of Eye and Ear Hospitals
Issues: MMM
Rep By: Robert B. Betz

Council of Surgical Specialty Facilities and Institutes
Issues: MMM
Rep By: Cathy Clark Betz, Robert B. Betz

Health Industry Group Purchasing Ass'n
Issues: GOV MMM
Rep By: Robert B. Betz

Terry Bevels Consulting

1317 F St. NW
Suite 400
Washington, DC 20004
E-mail: tbevels@aol.com
A government relations and public affairs firm.
Tel: (202)737-5110
Fax: (202)737-6721
Registered: LDA

DC-Area Employees Representing Listed Clients

BEVELS, Terry D.

Clients

Chatham Area Transit Authority
Issues: BUD TRA
Rep By: Terry D. Bevels

Columbia University
Issues: AGR BUD ENV
Rep By: Terry D. Bevels

Internat'l Center for Clubhouse Development
Issues: BUD EDU MED
Rep By: Terry D. Bevels

Joslin Diabetes Center
Issues: BUD EDU MED
Rep By: Terry D. Bevels

Beveridge & Diamond, P.C.

1350 I St. NW
Suite 700
Washington, DC 20005
Tel: (202)789-6000
Fax: (202)789-6190
Registered: LDA

DC-Area Employees Representing Listed Clients

BEVERIDGE, III, Albert J., Partner
CANNON, Dean H.
DAVIS, Richard S., Partner
DIAMOND, Henry L., Partner
FRIEDLAND, David M., Partner
GUTTMANN, Jr., John S., Partner
HAGAN, Paul E., Partner
HANSON, John N., Partner
HIMMELMAN, Harold, Partner
JAWETZ, Steven M.
RICHICHI, Thomas, Partner
SEGALL, Harold L., Partner
TIPTON, Caroline, Associate

Clients

American Historical Ass'n

Big Sky Consulting, Inc.

4020 Ellicott St.
Alexandria, VA 22304-1012
E-mail: cafulton@erols.com
Tel: (703)845-0487
Registered: LDA

DC-Area Employees Representing Listed Clients

FULTON, Ralph Thomas, President

Clients

Nat'l Fastener Distributors Ass'n
Issues: AUT AVI CSP MAN SCI SMB TRD
Rep By: Ralph Thomas Fulton

Leon G. Billings, Inc.

1625 K St. NW
Suite 790
Washington, DC 20006
A government affairs firm.
Tel: (202)293-7800
Fax: (202)293-7808
Registered: LDA

DC-Area Employees Representing Listed Clients

BILLINGS, Leon G., President
STURBITTS, Charlene A.

Clients

Downey McGrath Group, Inc.
Issues: ENG ENV WAS
Rep By: Leon G. Billings

Industry Urban-Development Agency
Issues: BUD NAT
Rep By: Leon G. Billings, Charlene A. Sturbitts

Lincoln Pulp and Paper Co.
Issues: CAW NAT
Rep By: Leon G. Billings

Ray Billups

306 N. Columbus St.
Alexandria, VA 22314
E-mail: raybillups@aol.com
A government affairs consultant.
Tel: (202)255-5787
Registered: LDA

Clients

Edison Electric Institute
Issues: ENG UTI
Rep By: Ray Billups

Nuclear Energy Institute
Issues: ENG
Rep By: Ray Billups

Potomac Electric Power Co.
Issues: ENG UTI
Rep By: Ray Billups

Bingham Dana LLP

1120 20th St. NW
Suite 800
Washington, DC 20036
Web: www.bingham.com
E-mail: info@bingham.com
Tel: (202)778-6150
Fax: (202)778-6155
Registered: LDA

DC-Area Employees Representing Listed Clients

BOGER, William H.
QUINN, Paul S.
SULLIVAN, Neal E., Attorney

Clients

Fleet Financial Group, Inc.
Issues: BAN BNK
Rep By: William H. Boger, Paul S. Quinn

FleetBoston Financial
Issues: FIN
Rep By: William H. Boger, Paul S. Quinn

Charles Schwab & Co., Inc.,
Issues: FIN
Rep By: Neal E. Sullivan

Thomas L. Birch

733 15th St. NW
Suite 938
Washington, DC 20005
A self-employed public affairs consultant.
Tel: (202)347-3666
Registered: LDA

Clients

Nat'l Assembly of State Arts Agencies
Issues: ART
Rep By: Thomas L. Birch

Nat'l Child Abuse Coalition
Issues: FAM
Rep By: Thomas L. Birch

Birch, Horton, Bittner & Cherot

1155 Connecticut Ave. NW
Suite 1200
Washington, DC 20036
Tel: (202)659-5800
Fax: (202)659-1027
Registered: LDA, FARA
Web: www.dc.bhb.com

Washington office of a firm headquartered in Anchorage, AK. Specializes in natural resources issues.

DC-Area Employees Representing Listed Clients

ALBERT, Thomas L., Member
BIRCH, Ronald G., President and Shareholder
BITTNER, William, Shareholder
BURDIN, Douglas S., Member
ELLIS, Allison, Associate
GUSTAFSON, Julia
HORN, William P., Shareholder
JONES, Jr., Roy S., Shareholder
QUEVLI, Elizabeth, Legislative Assistant
ROSS, Elisabeth H., Shareholder

Clients

Alaska Aerospace
Issues: AER
Rep By: William Bittner

Alaska Communications Systems, Inc.
Issues: TEC
Rep By: William Bittner

Alaska Legislature
Issues: ANI BUD NAT RES ROD
Rep By: William P. Horn

Alaska Professional Hunters Ass'n
Issues: AVI RES
Rep By: Thomas L. Albert, William P. Horn

Alaska State Snowmobile Ass'n
Issues: RES
Rep By: Douglas S. Burdin, William P. Horn

Aleut Corp.
Issues: BUD DEF RES
Rep By: Thomas L. Albert, Ronald G. Birch

America Outdoors
Issues: RES
Rep By: Julia Gustafson, William P. Horn

American Public Transportation Ass'n
Issues: TRA
Rep By: Ronald G. Birch

Anchorage, Alaska, Municipality of
Issues: BUD CAW ENV RES ROD
Rep By: Thomas L. Albert, William P. Horn

Ass'n of American Railroads
Issues: TAX TRA
Rep By: Ronald G. Birch

Bibb, Georgia, Board of Commissioners of the County of
Issues: ROD
Rep By: Julia Gustafson, William P. Horn

Blue Ribbon Coalition
Rep By: Douglas S. Burdin, William P. Horn

Clearwater Environmental, Inc.
Issues: ENV
Rep By: Thomas L. Albert, William P. Horn

Cordova, Alaska, City of
Issues: URB
Rep By: Roy S. Jones, Jr.

Council Tree Communications, L.L.C.
Issues: TEC
Rep By: Thomas L. Albert, William Bittner

CSX Corp.
Issues: BUD TOU
Rep By: Thomas L. Albert, Ronald G. Birch, William P. Horn

Digital Matrix Corp.
Issues: TRD
Rep By: Thomas L. Albert, Ronald G. Birch

DuPont
Issues: RES
Rep By: Thomas L. Albert, William P. Horn

Elim Native Corp.
Issues: RES
Rep By: Roy S. Jones, Jr.

Emmonak Corp.
Issues: NAT
Rep By: Roy S. Jones, Jr.

The Eyak Corp.
Issues: RES
Rep By: Roy S. Jones, Jr.

Fairbanks, Alaska, North Star Borough of
Issues: BUD CAW TRA
Rep By: Thomas L. Albert, Ronald G. Birch, William P. Horn

Feld Entertainment Inc.
Issues: ANI BUD
Rep By: Thomas L. Albert, William P. Horn, Roy S. Jones, Jr.

Florida Power and Light Co.
Rep By: William P. Horn

ICRC Energy, Inc.
Issues: BUD
Rep By: Thomas L. Albert, Ronald G. Birch, William P. Horn

Internat'l Snowmobile Manufacturers Ass'n
Issues: RES
Rep By: Douglas S. Burdin, Julia Gustafson, William P. Horn

ITRI, Ltd.
Issues: FIR
Rep By: William P. Horn

Kent Gamebore
Rep By: William P. Horn

Leisnoi
Issues: IND
Rep By: Roy S. Jones, Jr.

Missouri Public Service Co.
Rep By: Elisabeth H. Ross

Old Harbor Native Corp.
Rep By: Thomas L. Albert, Roy S. Jones, Jr.

Optical Disc Corp.
Issues: TRD
Rep By: Thomas L. Albert, Ronald G. Birch

Pacific Telecom, Inc.
Rep By: William Bittner, Elisabeth H. Ross

Port of Tillamook Bay
Issues: BUD
Rep By: Thomas L. Albert, William Bittner

Prince William Sound Regional Citizen's Advisory Council
Issues: BUD ENV
Rep By: Roy S. Jones, Jr.

Quinnat Landing Hotel
Issues: BUD RES
Rep By: Thomas L. Albert, William Bittner, William P. Horn

Salt River Pima Maricopa Indian Community
Issues: RES
Rep By: William P. Horn, Roy S. Jones, Jr.

Science Applications Internat'l Corp. (SAIC)
Issues: BUD
Rep By: Thomas L. Albert, Ronald G. Birch

Space Mark
Issues: BUD
Rep By: Thomas L. Albert, Ronald G. Birch

Spectrum Astro, Inc.
Issues: AER
Rep By: William Bittner

Sportsmen's Legal Defense Fund
Rep By: William P. Horn

St. George Tanaq
Issues: RES
Rep By: William Bittner

Tanadgusix Corp.
Issues: BUD
Rep By: Thomas L. Albert, William P. Horn

Trimble Navigation, Ltd.
Issues: BUD
Rep By: Thomas L. Albert, William Bittner

Turlock Irrigation District
Rep By: William P. Horn

University of Alaska
Issues: BUD RES
Rep By: Thomas L. Albert, Ronald G. Birch, William P. Horn

Wildlife Legislative Fund of America
Issues: ANI NAT
Rep By: Thomas L. Albert, Douglas S. Burdin, Julia Gustafson, William P. Horn

Yukon Pacific
Issues: NAT
Rep By: Thomas L. Albert, Ronald G. Birch, William P. Horn

BKSH & Associates

1801 K St. NW
Suite 901-L
Washington, DC 20006
Tel: (202)530-0500
Fax: (202)530-4800
Registered: LDA, FARA

Formerly known as Black, Kelly, Scruggs & Healey. A public affairs and government relations consulting firm created in 1996 from the merger of Gold & Liebengood and Black, Manafort, Stone & Kelly. A wholly-owned subsidiary of Burson-Marsteller.

DC-Area Employees Representing Listed Clients

BLACK, Jr., Charles R., President and Chief Exec. Officer
BODE, Holly A., Director
CHICCEHITTO, Karen, Director
COTTER, Lisa M., Director
DISLER, Mark, Director
FENIG, David, Director
FRIESS, Katherine, Director
HEALEY, James C., Managing Director
KLEPNER, Jerry, Managing Director
KYTE, John, Managing Director
LEVINSON, Riva, Managing Director
MERIN, Charles L., Managing Director
PASTRICK, R. Scott, Managing Director
PECKHAM, Gardner, Managing Director
POWELL, Paul L., Director
SCZUDLO, Rebecca, Director
SHEA, Dennis, Director
SLONE, Peter B., Managing Director
TEMPLETON, Patrick A., Senior Consultant
TOMPKINS, J. Warren, Senior Counselor
WEBB, Heather L., Associate
WEBER, Ronna Sable, Associate
WEISS, Jeffrey C., Director

Clients

Accenture
Issues: IMM
Rep By: Mark Disler

Advertising Company ART-ERIA
Issues: ECN FIN FOR GOV TRD
Rep By: Lisa M. Cotter, Riva Levinson

American Hotel and Lodging Ass'n
Issues: BUD LBR TAX TOB TOU TRA

American Medical Response
Issues: HCR

American Psychological Ass'n
Issues: HCR MMM

APS Healthcare, Inc.

Ass'n of American Medical Colleges
Issues: BUD MED MMM

AT&T
Issues: BUD CPT ENV TAX TEC

Bethlehem Steel Corp.
Issues: ENG TAX TRD

Bristol-Myers Squibb Co.
Issues: HCR MMM

California School Employees Ass'n

Citizens for Liberty in Cuba (Cuba Libertad)
Issues: FOR
Rep By: Gardner Peckham

The Coca-Cola Company
Issues: CPT FOO IMM TAX

Cook Children's Health Care System
Issues: BUD HCR MED

Cummins Engine Co.
Issues: CAW ENV TAX

Delaware North Companies
Issues: BUD NAT

Denton, Texas, County of
Issues: BUD TAX TRA

Federal Home Loan Mortgage Corp. (Freddie Mac)
Issues: BAN FIN TAX

Fuji TV Network

Genentech, Inc.
Issues: BUD CPT GOV HCR MAN MED MMM TAX

General Development Corp.
Issues: AVI FOR TRD
Rep By: Gardner Peckham

General Electric Capital Services, Inc.
Issues: BNK DEF FIN TAX TEC TRD

GlaxoSmithKline
Issues: BUD HCR MED PHA

GTECH Corp.
Issues: BUD GAM

Honeywell Internat'l, Inc.

Importers Service Corp.
Issues: TRD

Internat'l Council of Shopping Centers
Issues: BNK CAW ENV RES TAX

Jigawa, Nigerian State of
Rep By: Lisa M. Cotter, Riva Levinson

Lumenos
Rep By: Charles R. Black, Jr.

MacAndrews & Forbes Holdings, Inc.
Issues: BUD HCR TAX TOB

J. P. Morgan Chase & Co.
Issues: FIN
Rep By: Charles R. Black, Jr., Karen Chiccehitto, Dennis Shea

Mortgage Bankers Ass'n of America

Nat'l Broadcasting Co.
Issues: BUD

Nat'l Football League
Issues: TAX

Nat'l Power
Issues: FOR TRD
Rep By: John Kyte, Riva Levinson

Nat'l Propane Gas Ass'n
Issues: ENV

Nat'l Restaurant Ass'n
Issues: CPT FOO HCR TAX TOB TOU

Nat'l School Transportation Ass'n
Issues: BUD TAX TRA

NEC USA, Inc.
Issues: TRD

Occidental Internat'l Corporation
Issues: GOV TAX

Philip Morris Management Corp.
Issues: GOV MAN TAX TOB

Puerto Rico Industrial Development Co.

Roaring Fork Railroad Holding Authority
Issues: BUD TRA

Safety-Kleen Corp.
Issues: FUE WAS
Rep By: Karen Chiccehitto, Jerry Klepner, John Kyte, Rebecca Sczudlo

Santa Clara Valley Transportation Authority
Issues: BUD ROD TAX TRA

Santa Clara, California, County of
Issues: BUD ENV GOV HCR HOU IMM WEL

Thales
Issues: AER DEF

Travel Business Roundtable
Issues: TAX TOU

Tripoli Rocketry Ass'n
Issues: CHM CSP SCI
Rep By: John Kyte

United Network for Organ Sharing
Issues: BUD HCR

UST Public Affairs, Inc.
Issues: TOB
Rep By: Mark Disler, Katherine Friess, James C. Healey

Washington Metropolitan Area Transit Authority
Issues: BUD DOC TAX TRA

Waste Control Specialists, Inc.
Issues: ENG ENV GOV WAS

The Williams Companies
Issues: CAW ENV

Woodmont, LLC

Blank Rome Comisky & McCauley, LLP

900 17th St. NW
Suite 1000
Washington, DC 20006
Tel: (202)530-7400
Fax: (202)463-6915
Registered: LDA
Web: www.blankrome.com
A law firm headquartered in Philadelphia, PA.

DC-Area Employees Representing Listed Clients
BOGGS, III, J. Caleb, Of Counsel
FARRELL, Edward J., Partner
HOLMAN, Mark, Principal, Government Relations
MYERS, Jr., George C., Partner
NORCROSS, David A., Partner
SOUTH, Rebecca F.
WIGMAN, Victor M., Partner

Clients

Aetna/U.S. Healthcare, Inc.
Rep By: David A. Norcross

Canadian Cattlemen's Ass'n
Rep By: Edward J. Farrell

CC Distributors
Issues: GOV

Countrywide Home Loans, Inc.
Issues: BAN
Rep By: J. Caleb Boggs, III

Delaware River and Bay Authority
Issues: MAR TRA
Rep By: David A. Norcross

Delaware River Port Authority
Issues: MAR
Rep By: David A. Norcross

Federal Nat'l Payables, Inc.
Issues: GOV HOU URB
Rep By: J. Caleb Boggs, III

LDW, Inc.
Issues: TAX TEC
Rep By: David A. Norcross, Rebecca F. South

Maritime Exchange for the Delaware River and Bay
Issues: MAR TRU
Rep By: David A. Norcross

Meat New Zealand
Issues: AGR FOO TRD
Rep By: Edward J. Farrell

The Nat'l Foundation for Teaching Entrepreneurship
Issues: EDU
Rep By: J. Caleb Boggs, III

New Zealand Dairy Board
Rep By: Edward J. Farrell

On-Line Investment Services
Issues: BAN
Rep By: J. Caleb Boggs, III, David A. Norcross

Pilots' Ass'n of the Bay and River Delaware
Issues: AVI MAR
Rep By: David A. Norcross

Southwire, Inc.
Rep By: George C. Myers, Jr., Victor M. Wigman

U.S. Healthcare
Issues: HCR
Rep By: David A. Norcross

Valley Forge Flag Co.
Issues: GOV
Rep By: Rebecca F. South

Richard W. Bliss

1079 Papermill Ct. NW
Washington, DC 20007
Tel: (202)337-6008
Fax: (202)337-6193
Registered: LDA
E-mail: RWBliss@aol.com
An attorney specializing in legislative and administrative law.

DC-Area Employees Representing Listed Clients
BLISS, Richard W.
FARKAN, Pani, Director, Legislative Affairs

Clients

ADCS, Inc.
Issues: BUD CPI DEF

Fluor Corp.
Issues: ENG TRD WAS

Nat'l Paint and Coatings Ass'n
Issues: ENV TOR
Rep By: Pani Farkan

Nat'l Spa and Pool Institute
Issues: CSP MAN RES
Rep By: Pani Farkan

Niki Trading Co.
Issues: TRD
Rep By: Pani Farkan

John L. Bloom

225 N. Manchester St.
Arlington, VA 22203
Tel: (703)276-6710
Fax: (703)276-6711
Registered: LDA

Clients

American Cancer Soc.
Issues: TOB
Rep By: John L. Bloom

Bloomfield Associates, Inc.

13712 Wagon Way
Silver Spring, MD 20906
Tel: (301)460-3285
Fax: (301)460-4187
Registered: LDA, FARA
E-mail: dmb@his.com
A lobbying and consulting firm.

DC-Area Employees Representing Listed Clients
BLOOMFIELD, Douglas M., President

Clients

Kazakhstan 21st Century Foundation
Issues: FOR
Rep By: Douglas M. Bloomfield

T & N Industries
Issues: AUT HCR MAN
Rep By: Douglas M. Bloomfield

World Jewish Congress
Rep By: Douglas M. Bloomfield

Blue Ridge Internat'l Group, L.L.C.

500 N. Washington St.
Alexandria, VA 22314
Tel: (703)551-2108
Fax: (703)551-2109
An international advisory and governmental relations firm providing strategic planning, political consultation, financing assistance, international marketing, trade promotion and risk assessment services, all in support of international trade, investment and privatization.

DC-Area Employees Representing Listed Clients
BLOOM, Daniel John, Managing Principal
BULOW, Kay, Managing Principal
CASSELMAN, II, William E., Managing Principal
SCHROTE, John E., Agricultural and Natural Resources Advisor
WASH, B. Scott, Associate Counsel

Blumenfeld & Cohen

1625 Massachusetts Ave. NW
Suite 300
Washington, DC 20036
Tel: (202)955-6300
Fax: (202)955-6460
Registered: LDA
A law firm.

DC-Area Employees Representing Listed Clients
KIELY, Elise P. W., Associate
KUNIN, Christy C., Associate
MANISHIN, Glenn B., Partner

Clients

Rhythms NetConnections
Rep By: Christy C. Kunin

Bode & Grenier LLP

1150 Connecticut Ave. NW
Suite 900
Washington, DC 20036-4182
Tel: (202)828-4100
Fax: (202)828-4130
Web: www.bode.com
E-mail: bodebeckman@bode.com

DC-Area Employees Representing Listed Clients
BODE, William H., Partner

Clients

The Environmental Business Ass'n
Rep By: William H. Bode

Independent Terminal Operators Ass'n
Rep By: William H. Bode

Mount Airy Refining Co.
Rep By: William H. Bode

Peerless Petrochemicals, Inc.
Rep By: William H. Bode

Petrojam Ltd.
Rep By: William H. Bode

Shepherd Oil Co.
Rep By: William H. Bode

Superfund Action Coalition
Rep By: William H. Bode

Boesch & Co.

1001 Pennsylvania Ave. NW
Suite 850 North
Washington, DC 20004
Tel: (202)347-2222
Fax: (202)347-4242
Registered: LDA
E-mail: doycebesh@aol.com

DC-Area Employees Representing Listed Clients
BOESCH, Doyce A., President

Clients

AT&T
Issues: TEC
Rep By: Doyce A. Boesch

The Business Roundtable
Issues: TRD
Rep By: Doyce A. Boesch

Children's Health Fund
Issues: HCR
Rep By: Doyce A. Boesch

Huron Hospital
Rep By: Doyce A. Boesch

Integris Health Systems
Issues: HCR
Rep By: Doyce A. Boesch

NetCoalition.Com
Issues: CPI
Rep By: Doyce A. Boesch

O'Gara-Hess & Eisenhardt
Issues: DEF
Rep By: Doyce A. Boesch

Oracle Corp.
Issues: CPI LBR TAX TEC
Rep By: Doyce A. Boesch

Public Policy Partners
Issues: AVI
Rep By: Doyce A. Boesch

Sabre Inc.
Issues: TOU
Rep By: Doyce A. Boesch

Stockton East Water District
Issues: NAT
Rep By: Doyce A. Boesch

U.S. Filter
Issues: CAW
Rep By: Doyce A. Boesch

University of Oklahoma
Issues: EDU
Rep By: Doyce A. Boesch

Boffa & Associates, Inc.

733 15th St. NW
Suite 500
Washington, DC 20005
E-mail: jboffa@boffapr.com

Tel: (202)466-6977
Fax: (202)637-9825

DC-Area Employees Representing Listed Clients
BOFFA, John, President

Clients

Internet Internat'l Trade Council
Rep By: John Boffa

Bogart Associates Inc.

1200 Trinity Dr.
Alexandria, VA 22314
E-mail: jbogart@mindspring.com

Tel: (703)823-8674
Fax: (703)823-2628

DC-Area Employees Representing Listed Clients
BOGART, Jennifer, President

Clients

New American Century PAC
Ripon Educational Fund
Ripon Society
Rep By: Jennifer Bogart
View PAC
Young Republican Hispanic Ass'n

James E. Boland

1155 Connecticut Ave. NW
Suite 300
Washington, DC 20036

Tel: (202)467-8507
Fax: (202)429-0977
Registered: LDA

Clients

Compaq Computer Corp.
Issues: EDU TAX
Rep By: James E. Boland, Jr.
Federal Home Loan Mortgage Corp. (Freddie Mac)
Issues: BNK
Rep By: James E. Boland, Jr.
The Limited Inc.
Issues: TAX TRD
Rep By: James E. Boland, Jr.
Morgan Stanley Dean Witter & Co.
Issues: BAN BNK FIN TAX
Rep By: James E. Boland, Jr.
Waste Management, Inc.
Issues: ENV TAX WAS
Rep By: James E. Boland, Jr.

Bond & Company, Inc.

919 Prince St.
Alexandria, VA 22314

Tel: (703)684-6098
Fax: (703)684-7138
Registered: LDA, FARA

E-mail: bondandco@aol.com
A government affairs consulting firm.

DC-Area Employees Representing Listed Clients
BOND, Richard N., Chairman
KEAN, Eileen, Senior V. President
MADDEN, Andy, V. President
TAYLOR, Jeffrey K.

Clients

The Century Council
Rep By: Richard N. Bond
Hackensack University Medical Center Foundation
Issues: HCR
Rep By: Richard N. Bond, Eileen Kean
HCR-Manor Care, Inc.
Rep By: Richard N. Bond
Northeast Utilities
Issues: ENG
Rep By: Richard N. Bond
openNET Coalition
Issues: CPI TEC
Rep By: Richard N. Bond, Eileen Kean
Service Employees Internat'l Union
Rep By: Richard N. Bond, Eileen Kean, Andy Madden
United Brotherhood of Carpenters and Joiners of America
Issues: LBR
Rep By: Richard N. Bond, Eileen Kean

Bonner & Associates

1101 17th St. NW
Eighth Floor
Washington, DC 20036

Tel: (202)463-8880
Fax: (202)833-3584
Registered: LDA

Firm specializes in organizing public outreach efforts at the federal, state and local levels on legislative and regulatory issues.

DC-Area Employees Representing Listed Clients
BONNER, Jack, President
BONNER, Sandy Cohen, General Counsel
GASTON, Carole, V. President
HEGYI, Gwynn Geiger, Partner
RISSING, Ed, V. President
SCHNEIDER, Gail, V. President

Clients

American Insurance Ass'n
American Psychiatric Ass'n
The Boeing Co.
Chase Manhattan Bank
CIGNA Corp.
ComEd
Exelon Corp.
General Motors Corp.
Merck & Co.
Merrill Lynch & Co., Inc.
Nat'l Ass'n of Realtors
Northrop Grumman Corp.
Pacific Telesis
Verizon Communications

Bonner Group, Inc.

729 15th St. NW
Third Floor
Washington, DC 20005
E-mail: jhanson@bonnergrp.com

Tel: (202)737-5877
Fax: (202)737-6061

A political and non-profit fundraising firm.

DC-Area Employees Representing Listed Clients
BONNER, Mary Pat, President
HANSON, Jennifer, Political Director
THOMAS, Wylie, National Director

Booher & Associates

11 Canal Center Plaza
Suite 110
Alexandria, VA 22314

Tel: (703)548-0280
Fax: (703)683-7939
Registered: LDA

E-mail: booandco@aol.com

Political Action Committee
NAVAPD PAC
11 Canal Center Plaza
Suite 110
Alexandria, VA 22314
Contact: C. William Booher, Jr.

Tel: (703)548-0280

DC-Area Employees Representing Listed Clients
BOOHER, Jr., C. William, Principal

Clients

Foundation for Veterans' Health Care
Rep By: C. William Booher, Jr.
Nat'l Ass'n of VA Physicians and Dentists
Issues: DEF GOV HCR MED MMM PHA VET
Rep By: C. William Booher, Jr.

The Borden Group, Inc.

1414 Prince St.
Suite 302
Alexandria, VA 22314

Tel: (703)548-3692
Fax: (703)548-8024
Registered: LDA

E-mail: enid@tbg.dgsys.com
A public relations/government relations firm.

DC-Area Employees Representing Listed Clients
BORDEN, Enid A., President
DOYLE, Elizabeth Z., Account Executive
INGRAHAM, Margaret B., Exec. V. President

Clients

Meals on Wheels Ass'n of America
Issues: HCR
Rep By: Margaret B. Ingraham
Project Meal Foundation
Issues: HCR
Rep By: Enid A. Borden

Boros & Garofalo

1201 Connecticut Ave. NW
Suite 700
Washington, DC 20036

Tel: (202)822-9070
Fax: (202)822-9075
Registered: FARA

E-mail: bgairlaw@aol.com
An aviation law practice.

DC-Area Employees Representing Listed Clients
GAROFALO, Gary B., Partner
SMITH, Victor H.

Clients

Great Britain, Government of
Rep By: Gary B. Garofalo

Bostrom Corp.

1444 I St. NW
Suite 700
Washington, DC 20005-2210
Web: www.bostrom.com

Tel: (202)216-9623
Fax: (202)216-9646

Washington office of a Chicago association management firm.

DC-Area Employees Representing Listed Clients
HARRISON, Kim, Director, Administration
HECKER, CAE, Larry, V. President
LINDNER, CAE, Randy, Senior V. President and General Manager
MCGRATH, CAE, Charles, V. President
POWELL, Lee, Operations Manager
SANTINI, David L., Executive Director
SHANLEY, Claire, Account Executive

Clients

American Soc. of Access Professionals
Rep By: Claire Shanley
Automotive Maintenance and Repair Ass'n
Rep By: Larry Hecker, CAE
Council of American Kidney Societies
Greater Washington D.C. Chapter of CLU & ChFC
Rep By: Claire Shanley
Home Automation Ass'n
Rep By: Charles McGrath, CAE
Interlocking Concrete Pavement Institute
Rep By: Charles McGrath, CAE
Internat'l Biometric Ass'n (Eastern North American Region)
Rep By: David L. Santini
Internat'l Coach Federation
Rep By: David L. Santini
Nat'l Ass'n of Boards of Examiners of Long Term Care Administrators
Rep By: Randy Lindner, CAE

Beau Boulter

6932 N. Fairfax Dr.
Suite 204
Arlington, VA 22213
E-mail: Beauro@aol.com

Tel: (703)533-5859
Registered: LDA

Clients

United Seniors Ass'n
Rep By: Hon. Beau Boulter

Bracewell & Patterson, L.L.P.

2000 K St. NW
Suite 500
Washington, DC 20006-1872

Tel: (202)828-5800
Fax: (202)223-1225
Registered: LDA, FARA

Bracewell & Patterson has other offices in Houston, Dallas, San Antonio, Ft. Worth, Corpus Christi, and Austin, TX; Reston, VA; Almaty and Astana, Kazakhstan; and London, England.

Political Action Committee
Bracewell and Patterson, L.L.P. Political Action Committee
2000 K St. NW
Suite 500
Washington, DC 20006-1872
Contact: Gene E. Godley

Tel: (202)828-5870
Fax: (202)223-1225

DC-Area Employees Representing Listed Clients
BETHUNE, Hon. Edwin R., Partner
CHAPMAN, Hon. Jim, Partner
CLARKE, Robert L., Partner
EWING, Kevin
FOOTE, George M.
GODLEY, Gene E., Partner
HEBERT, Marc C., Associate
HOUSMAN, Robert F., Associate
INGEBRETSON, Charles L., Associate
PATE, Michael L., Partner
RACICOT, Marc, Partner
SEGAL, Scott H., Partner
STROUD, Jr., D. Michael, Associate
WATKISS, J. Dan, Partner

Clients

Air Conditioning Contractors of America
Issues: UTI
Rep By: Hon. Edwin R. Bethune, Gene E. Godley, Marc C. Hebert, Charles L. Ingebretson, Michael L. Pate, Scott H. Segal, D. Michael Stroud, Jr.
Alltel Corporation
Issues: TEC
Rep By: Hon. Edwin R. Bethune, Hon. Jim Chapman, Gene E. Godley, Marc C. Hebert, Charles L. Ingebretson, Michael L. Pate, Scott H. Segal, D. Michael Stroud, Jr.
American Bus Ass'n
Issues: TAX
Rep By: Michael L. Pate
American Chemistry Council
Issues: CHM ENV TAX TRD
Rep By: Hon. Edwin R. Bethune, Michael L. Pate

American Registry for Internet Numbers (ARIN)
Issues: CPI
Rep By: Gene E. Godley, Marc C. Hebert, Michael L. Pate, D. Michael Stroud, Jr.

BP Amoco Corp.

Cement Kiln Recycling Coalition
Issues: ENG ENV FUE
Rep By: Gene E. Godley, Marc C. Hebert, Michael L. Pate, Scott H. Segal

Centex Corp.
Issues: BAN TAX
Rep By: Michael L. Pate

Continental Cement Co., Inc.
Issues: CAW ENG ENV FUE
Rep By: Gene E. Godley, Marc C. Hebert, Michael L. Pate, Scott H. Segal

Council of Industrial Boiler Owners (CIBO)
Issues: CAW ENG ENV FUE GOV NAT UTI WAS
Rep By: Hon. Edwin R. Bethune, Hon. Jim Chapman, Kevin Ewing, Gene E. Godley, Marc C. Hebert, Charles L. Ingebretson, Michael L. Pate, Scott H. Segal, D. Michael Stroud, Jr.

Electronic Commerce Ass'n

Enron Corp.
Issues: ENG FOR FUE TAX TRD
Rep By: Gene E. Godley, Marc C. Hebert, Michael L. Pate, Scott H. Segal, J. Dan Watkiss

Enron Wind Corp./Zond
Issues: TAX

Envirocare of Utah, Inc.
Issues: BUD ENG ENV NAT WAS
Rep By: Hon. Edwin R. Bethune, Hon. Jim Chapman, Gene E. Godley, Marc C. Hebert, Charles L. Ingebretson, Michael L. Pate, Scott H. Segal, D. Michael Stroud, Jr.

FBI Agents Ass'n
Issues: BUD RET TAX
Rep By: Hon. Edwin R. Bethune, Hon. Jim Chapman, Gene E. Godley, Marc C. Hebert, Charles L. Ingebretson, Michael L. Pate, Scott H. Segal, D. Michael Stroud, Jr.

Gary-Williams Energy Corp.
Issues: ENV
Rep By: Hon. Edwin R. Bethune, Hon. Jim Chapman, Gene E. Godley, Marc C. Hebert, Charles L. Ingebretson, Michael L. Pate, Scott H. Segal, D. Michael Stroud, Jr.

Gas Processors Ass'n
Issues: ENG FUE
Rep By: Gene E. Godley, Michael L. Pate, Scott H. Segal

Houston, Texas, Port Authority of the City of
Issues: BUD
Rep By: Hon. Edwin R. Bethune, Hon. Jim Chapman, Gene E. Godley, Marc C. Hebert, Charles L. Ingebretson, Michael L. Pate, Scott H. Segal, D. Michael Stroud, Jr.

Huntsman Corp.
Issues: ENV
Rep By: Hon. Edwin R. Bethune, Hon. Jim Chapman, Gene E. Godley, Marc C. Hebert, Charles L. Ingebretson, Michael L. Pate, Scott H. Segal, D. Michael Stroud, Jr.

Independent Oil and Gas Ass'n of Pennsylvania
Rep By: Gene E. Godley, Michael L. Pate, Scott H. Segal

Integrated Waste Services Ass'n
Issues: CAW ENG ENV

Lyondell Chemical Co.
Issues: ENV TRD
Rep By: Gene E. Godley, Marc C. Hebert, Charles L. Ingebretson, Michael L. Pate, Scott H. Segal, D. Michael Stroud, Jr.

Nat'l Cable Television Ass'n
Issues: TAX TEC
Rep By: Gene E. Godley, Marc C. Hebert, Michael L. Pate, Scott H. Segal

Nat'l Organization of Social Security Claimants' Representatives

Oxygenated Fuels Ass'n
Issues: ENV
Rep By: Hon. Edwin R. Bethune, Hon. Jim Chapman, Gene E. Godley, Marc C. Hebert, Charles L. Ingebretson, Michael L. Pate, Scott H. Segal, D. Michael Stroud, Jr.

Physician Insurers Ass'n of America
Issues: HCR INS MED TAX
Rep By: Hon. Edwin R. Bethune, Gene E. Godley, Marc C. Hebert

Placid Refining Co.
Issues: ENV
Rep By: Hon. Edwin R. Bethune, Hon. Jim Chapman, Gene E. Godley, Marc C. Hebert, Charles L. Ingebretson, Michael L. Pate, Scott H. Segal, D. Michael Stroud, Jr.

Raytheon Co.

San Antonio Water System

Shell Oil Co.
Issues: ENV

Solex Environmental Systems, Inc.
Issues: ENG ENV
Rep By: Hon. Edwin R. Bethune, Hon. Jim Chapman, Gene E. Godley, Marc C. Hebert, Charles L. Ingebretson, Michael L. Pate, Scott H. Segal, D. Michael Stroud, Jr.

Southdown, Inc.
Issues: ENV
Rep By: Gene E. Godley, Marc C. Hebert, Michael L. Pate, Scott H. Segal

Sterling Chemical Co.
Issues: ENV TAX TRD WAS
Rep By: Gene E. Godley, Marc C. Hebert, Michael L. Pate, Scott H. Segal

Texas Petrochemicals Corp.
Issues: ENV
Rep By: Hon. Edwin R. Bethune, Hon. Jim Chapman, Gene E. Godley, Marc C. Hebert, Charles L. Ingebretson, Michael L. Pate, Scott H. Segal, D. Michael Stroud, Jr.

Texas Windstorm Insurance Ass'n
Issues: BUD TAX
Rep By: Hon. Edwin R. Bethune, Hon. Jim Chapman, Gene E. Godley, Marc C. Hebert, Charles L. Ingebretson, Michael L. Pate, Scott H. Segal, D. Michael Stroud, Jr.

UST Public Affairs, Inc.
Issues: AGR BUD CSP HCR TAX TOB
Rep By: Hon. Jim Chapman, Charles L. Ingebretson, Michael L. Pate

Valero Energy Corp.
Issues: ENV TAX TRD
Rep By: Gene E. Godley, Marc C. Hebert, Michael L. Pate, Scott H. Segal

Welcon, Inc.
Issues: ENV
Rep By: Hon. Edwin R. Bethune, Hon. Jim Chapman, Gene E. Godley, Marc C. Hebert, Charles L. Ingebretson, Michael L. Pate, Scott H. Segal, D. Michael Stroud, Jr.

Marshall A. Brachman

444 Carbery Place NE
Washington, DC 20002
Tel: (202)365-1018
Fax: (202)544-1760
Registered: LDA
Web: www.mabrachman.com
E-mail: marshall@mabrachman.com

Clients

Adams County, Colorado
Issues: BUD DEF
Rep By: Marshall A. Brachman

Allied Marketing
Issues: BUD GOV POS
Rep By: Marshall A. Brachman

Arizona Mail Order Co.
Issues: BUD CSP GOV POS TAX TEC
Rep By: Marshall A. Brachman

Camelbak Products, Inc.
Issues: BUD DEF
Rep By: Marshall A. Brachman

Diamond Ventures
Rep By: Marshall A. Brachman

Direct Marketing Ass'n, Inc.
Issues: BUD CSP GOV POS TAX TEC
Rep By: Marshall A. Brachman

Edmund Scientific Co.
Issues: BUD CSP GOV POS TAX TEC
Rep By: Marshall A. Brachman

Interface Inc.
Issues: GOV SMB
Rep By: Marshall A. Brachman

Lockheed Martin Aeronautical Systems Co.
Issues: BUD DEF SCI
Rep By: Marshall A. Brachman

Nat'l Wholesale Co., Inc.
Issues: BUD CSP GOV POS TAX TEC
Rep By: Marshall A. Brachman

Zions Bank Co.
Issues: BAN
Rep By: Marshall A. Brachman

Bracy Williams & Co.

601 13th St. NW
Suite 900 South
Washington, DC 20005
Tel: (202)783-5588
Fax: (202)783-5595
Registered: LDA
Web: www.bracywilliams.com
A government affairs consulting firm.

DC-Area Employees Representing Listed Clients

BENFIELD, James C.
BRACY, Michael M.
BRACY, Terrence L., Chief Exec. Officer
BROWN, James P., V. President
FLAHERTY, Linda Doorfee, Associate
MADDEN, Laura L., Associate
NASSAR, Josh, Associate
TUCKER, Tracy P., Associate
WILLIAMS, Susan J., President

Clients

Allied Pilots Ass'n
Issues: AVI TRA
Rep By: Terrence L. Bracy, Josh Nassar, Susan J. Williams

American Institute for Foreign Studies
Issues: EDU
Rep By: Linda Doorfee Flaherty, Susan J. Williams

Atlanta, Georgia, City of
Issues: GOV
Rep By: Michael M. Bracy, Terrence L. Bracy, James P. Brown, Laura L. Madden, Tracy P. Tucker, Susan J. Williams

Bi-State Development Agency
Rep By: Terrence L. Bracy, James P. Brown, Laura L. Madden

Business Alliance for Internat'l Economic Development
Rep By: James C. Benfield, Terrence L. Bracy

The Coin Coalition
Issues: MON
Rep By: James C. Benfield

College Parents of America
Issues: EDU
Rep By: Linda Doorfee Flaherty, Susan J. Williams

Council on Internat'l Educational Exchange
Issues: EDU FOR
Rep By: Linda Doorfee Flaherty, Susan J. Williams

Daishowa America Co., Ltd.
Issues: ENV RES
Rep By: Michael M. Bracy, Terrence L. Bracy

Energy Absorption Systems, Inc.
Issues: ROD TRA
Rep By: Susan J. Williams

FedEx Pilots Ass'n
Issues: AVI
Rep By: Josh Nassar, Susan J. Williams

Fort Worth Transportation Authority
Issues: TRA
Rep By: Terrence L. Bracy, James P. Brown, Laura L. Madden, Susan J. Williams

Fort Worth, Texas, City of
Issues: GOV
Rep By: Terrence L. Bracy, James P. Brown, Laura L. Madden, Tracy P. Tucker, Susan J. Williams

Foundation for Integrated Medicine
Issues: HCR
Rep By: Terrence L. Bracy, James P. Brown

Girl Scouts of the U.S.A. - Washington Office
Issues: SPO
Rep By: Linda Doorfee Flaherty, Susan J. Williams

Lambert-St. Louis Internat'l Airport
Issues: AVI TRA
Rep By: James P. Brown

MedStar Health
Issues: MED
Rep By: Linda Doorfee Flaherty, Susan J. Williams

Michigan Consolidated Gas Co.
Issues: GOV
Rep By: James C. Benfield, Michael M. Bracy, Terrence L. Bracy

Nassif & Associates
Issues: RES
Rep By: James P. Brown, Linda Doorfee Flaherty, Susan J. Williams

Nat'l Ass'n for Girls and Women in Sport
Issues: SPO
Rep By: Linda Doorfee Flaherty, Susan J. Williams

St. Louis Airport Authority
Issues: AVI
Rep By: Terrence L. Bracy, James P. Brown, Laura L. Madden

St. Louis Metropolitan Sewer District
Issues: UTI
Rep By: Terrence L. Bracy, James P. Brown, Laura L. Madden

St. Louis, Missouri, City of
Issues: GOV
Rep By: James P. Brown

Tucson, Arizona, City of
Issues: GOV
Rep By: Michael M. Bracy, Terrence L. Bracy, James P. Brown, Laura L. Madden, Tracy P. Tucker, Susan J. Williams

Women's Sports Foundation
Issues: SPO
Rep By: Linda Doorfee Flaherty, Susan J. Williams

YWCA of the USA
Issues: SPO
Rep By: Linda Doorfee Flaherty, Susan J. Williams

Bradley Arant Rose & White LLP

801 Pennsylvania Ave. NW
Suite 230
Washington, DC 20004
Tel: (202)393-7150
Fax: (202)347-1684
Registered: LDA
Web: www.bradleyarant.com
A law firm based in Birmingham, AL.

DC-Area Employees Representing Listed Clients
BOLES, Anita Lacy, Director, Government Affairs
ECKERT, Doug, Partner
ERDREICH, Hon. Ben L., Partner
HARRIS, George, Partner
PATRICK, Amy, Coordinator, Washington Office
PEEPLES, Lloyd, Associate
SELDEN, Jack W., Partner
STEWART, David, Associate
STRANGE, Luther J., Partner

Clients

Bank of Alabama

Birmingham Airport Authority
Issues: AVI TRA

Birmingham Building Trades Towers, Inc.

BL Harbert Internat'l

Blount Parrish & Co., Inc.

Central Alabama Community College

Energen Corp.

Federation of American Hospitals

Russell Corp.

TMS Consulting, LLC

United Parcel Service
Issues: TAX

Vulcan Materials Co.
Issues: NAT ROD

Robert Branand Internat'l

Four E St. SE
Washington, DC 20003
Tel: (202)546-4100
Registered: LDA

DC-Area Employees Representing Listed Clients
BRANAND, Robert, Principal

Brand & Frulla, P.C.

923 15th St. NW
Washington, DC 20005
Tel: (202)662-9700
Fax: (202)737-7565
Registered: LDA

DC-Area Employees Representing Listed Clients
BRAND, Stanley M., Partner
FRULLA, David E., Partner
HERMAN, Andrew D., Associate

Clients

United Airlines
Issues: AVI LBR TOU TRA
Rep By: David E. Frulla, Andrew D. Herman

Robert M. Brandon and Associates

1730 Rhode Island Ave. NW
Suite 712
Washington, DC 20036
Tel: (202)331-1550
Fax: (202)331-1663
Registered: LDA
Web: www.robertbrandon.com
E-mail: main@robertbrandon.com
A full-service strategic consulting and public affairs firm specializing in technology and telecommunications, consumer and healthcare issues, international public policy, and business development.

DC-Area Employees Representing Listed Clients
BRANDON, Robert M., President
MOLLOY, Michelle
ROHDE, Clifford

Clients

A Greater Washington
Rep By: Robert M. Brandon, Michelle Molloy

Best Health Care Inc.
Issues: HCR
Rep By: Robert M. Brandon

Electric Consumers Alliance
Issues: CSP ENG
Rep By: Robert M. Brandon, Michelle Molloy

Localisation Industry Standards Ass'n
Issues: TRD
Rep By: Robert M. Brandon, Clifford Rohde

Lottery.com
Issues: GAM
Rep By: Robert M. Brandon

Nat'l Ass'n for Public Interest Law (NAPIL)
Rep By: Robert M. Brandon, Clifford Rohde

T. Edward Braswell

1800 N. Kent St.
Suite 907
Arlington, VA 22209
Tel: (703)528-0840
Fax: (703)524-1005
Registered: LDA
Provides legislative consulting services.

Clients

Newport News Shipbuilding Inc.
Issues: DEF
Rep By: T. Edward Braswell, Jr.

Bredhoff & Kaiser

1000 Connecticut Ave. NW
Suite 1300
Washington, DC 20036
Tel: (202)842-2600
Fax: (202)842-1888

DC-Area Employees Representing Listed Clients
BREDHOFF, Elliot, Senior Counsel
CLARK, Julia Penny, Partner
COHEN, George H., Partner
FREUND, Jeffrey R., Partner
GIBBS, Jeffrey L., Partner
GOLD, Laurence, Of Counsel

Clients

Bakery, Confectionery and Tobacco Workers Internat'l Union
Rep By: Jeffrey R. Freund

Major League Baseball Players Ass'n
Rep By: George H. Cohen

Pickands Mather and Co.
Rep By: Elliot Bredhoff

Brewer Consulting Group, Inc.

1200 New Hampshire Ave. NW
Suite 445
Washington, DC 20036
Tel: (202)822-8882
Fax: (202)822-8822
Registered: LDA
E-mail: mfbrewer@worldnet.att.net

DC-Area Employees Representing Listed Clients
BREWER, Michael F., President

Clients

ACNielsen Corp.
Rep By: Michael F. Brewer

Suzie Brewster & Associates

451 New Jersey Ave. SE
Washington, DC 20003
Tel: (202)544-6363
Fax: (202)544-3219
Registered: LDA, FARA
E-mail: suzie_brewster@msn.com
A self-employed public affairs consultant.

DC-Area Employees Representing Listed Clients
BREWSTER, Suzie, President

Clients

Collier Shannon Scott, PLLC
Rep By: Suzie Brewster

University of Oklahoma
Rep By: Suzie Brewster

Brickfield, Burchette, Ritts & Stone

1025 Thomas Jefferson St. NW
Eighth Floor, West Tower
Washington, DC 20007
Tel: (202)342-0800
Fax: (202)342-0807
Registered: LDA
Web: www.bbrslaw.com

DC-Area Employees Representing Listed Clients
BREW, James, Partner
BRICKFIELD, Peter J. P., Partner
BURCHETTE, William H., Partner
MCCARTY, Michael N., Partner
NEWMAN, Colleen, Government Relations Advisor
RITTS, Frederick H., Partner
RYAN, Christine C., Partner

Clients

American Medical Technologists
Issues: BUD HCR MED MMM
Rep By: Michael N. McCarty, Colleen Newman

Arizona Power Authority
Issues: ENG GOV NAT TAX UTI
Rep By: Michael N. McCarty, Colleen Newman

Arvin-Edison Water Storage District
Rep By: Michael N. McCarty, Colleen Newman

Colorado River Water Conservation District
Rep By: Michael N. McCarty, Colleen Newman

East Texas Electric Cooperative
Issues: BUD ENG GOV TAX UTI
Rep By: William H. Burchette, Colleen Newman, Christine C. Ryan

Merced Irrigation District
Rep By: Michael N. McCarty, Colleen Newman

Northeast Texas Electric Cooperative
Issues: BUD ENG GOV TAX UTI
Rep By: William H. Burchette, Colleen Newman, Christine C. Ryan

Sam Rayburn G&T Electric Cooperative, Inc.
Issues: BUD ENG GOV TAX UTI
Rep By: William H. Burchette, Colleen Newman, Christine C. Ryan

Steel Manufacturers Ass'n
Issues: ENG
Rep By: James Brew

Tex-La Electric Cooperative of Texas
Issues: BUD ENG GOV TAX UTI
Rep By: William H. Burchette, Colleen Newman, Christine C. Ryan

William V. Brierre

1101 Connecticut Ave. NW
Suite 900
Washington, DC 20036
E-mail: wvbrierre@aol.com
Tel: (202)296-7787
Fax: (202)296-7780
Registered: LDA

Clients

Ad Hoc Maritime Coalition
Rep By: William V. Brierre, Jr.

General Electric Co.
Issues: ENV
Rep By: William V. Brierre, Jr.

Labor Management Maritime Committee, Inc.
Issues: MAR
Rep By: William V. Brierre, Jr.

Maersk Inc.
Rep By: William V. Brierre, Jr.

Maritime Institute for Research and Industrial Development
Issues: MAR TAX TRD
Rep By: William V. Brierre, Jr.

Sea Bridge Internat'l LLC
Issues: MAR
Rep By: William V. Brierre, Jr.

Transportation Institute
Issues: MAR
Rep By: William V. Brierre, Jr.

Bristol Group, Inc.

1900 L St. NW
Suite 407
Washington, DC 20036
Tel: (202)293-3454
Fax: (202)393-3455
Registered: LDA
A strategic policy and business consulting firm.

DC-Area Employees Representing Listed Clients
AFONSO, Paul G., General Counsel
PAPADOPOULOS, Daniel G., V. President, Government Affairs
PINTO, Tiago, Managing Director

Clients

Angola, Embassy of

Boston Edison Co.
Issues: ENG TEC
Rep By: Paul G. Afonso, Daniel G. Papadopoulos

TAP/Air Portugal
Issues: AVI
Rep By: Paul G. Afonso, Daniel G. Papadopoulos

Broad-Band Solutions

606 E. Capitol St. NE
Washington, DC 20003
Tel: (202)546-1493
Fax: (202)546-7807
A government affairs and public relations firm.

DC-Area Employees Representing Listed Clients
HICKOX, Amy, Principal
RHODES, Sage, Principal

Clients

Register.com
Issues: SCI
Rep By: Amy Hickox, Sage Rhodes

Brown & Associates

11 Canal Center Plaza
Suite 103
Alexandria, VA 20005
E-mail: brojes@erols.com
Tel: (703)683-6990
Fax: (703)683-0645
Registered: LDA

DC-Area Employees Representing Listed Clients
BROWN, Jesse
CAROZZA, Shirley
SCOTT, Edward P.

Clients

GAF Corp.
Issues: VET
Rep By: Edward P. Scott

Onehealthbank.com
Issues: HCR VET
Rep By: Jesse Brown, Shirley Carozza, Edward P. Scott

Pharmaceutical Research and Manufacturers of America
Issues: VET
Rep By: Jesse Brown, Edward P. Scott

Problem-Knowledge Coupler
Issues: VET
Rep By: Shirley Carozza, Edward P. Scott

Brown and Company, Inc.

600 Pennsylvania Ave. SE
Suite 304
Washington, DC 20003
Tel: (202)544-9614
Fax: (202)544-9618
Registered: LDA

Political Action Committee
Brown and Co. Inc. PAC
600 Pennsylvania Ave. SE
Suite 304
Washington, DC 20003
Contact: Cynthia L. Brown
Tel: (202)544-9614
Fax: (202)544-9618

DC-Area Employees Representing Listed Clients
BROWN, Cynthia L., President
JOHNSON, Hugh N. "Rusty"
LOSEY, Frank W., General Counsel

Clients

American Defense Internat'l, Inc.
Issues: DEF
Rep By: Cynthia L. Brown, Hugh N. "Rusty" Johnson

American Shipbuilding Ass'n
Issues: CAW DEF LBR TRA TRD
Rep By: Cynthia L. Brown, Hugh N. "Rusty" Johnson, Frank W. Losey

Bird-Johnson Co.
Issues: DEF
Rep By: Cynthia L. Brown, Hugh N. "Rusty" Johnson, Frank W. Losey

Merant PVCS
Issues: DEF ENG
Rep By: Cynthia L. Brown, Hugh N. "Rusty" Johnson

Sperry Marine Inc.
Issues: DEF
Rep By: Cynthia L. Brown, Hugh N. "Rusty" Johnson, Frank W. Losey

Arthur W. Brownell

1932 Relda Ct.
Falls Church, VA 22043
Tel: (703)536-9352
Fax: (703)536-8176
Registered: LDA
E-mail: awbrownell@aol.com

Clients

Council of Industrial Boiler Owners (CIBO)
Rep By: Arthur W. Brownell

Brownstein Hyatt & Farber, P.C.

1615 L St. NW
Suite 450
Washington, DC 20036
Tel: (202)296-7353
Fax: (202)296-7009
Registered: LDA

DC-Area Employees Representing Listed Clients
BRACK, William T.
FINEGAN, P. Cole
HUDSON, Thomas H.
LEVY, Michael B.
SPIELMAN, Andrew

Clients

American Salvage Pool Ass'n
Issues: AUT
Rep By: William T. Brack, Michael B. Levy

Apollo Advisors
Rep By: William T. Brack, Michael B. Levy

AT&T Broadband & Internet Service
Rep By: William T. Brack, Thomas H. Hudson, Michael B. Levy

Colorado Credit Union Systems
Issues: BAN
Rep By: William T. Brack, Michael B. Levy

Delta Petroleum Corp.
Issues: ENG
Rep By: Thomas H. Hudson, Michael B. Levy

Discount Refrigerants Inc.
Issues: ENV
Rep By: P. Cole Finegan, Andrew Spielman

Express One Internat'l Inc.
Issues: POS TRA
Rep By: William T. Brack, Thomas H. Hudson, Michael B. Levy

First Data Corp./Telecheck
Issues: FIN
Rep By: William T. Brack, Michael B. Levy

Global Crossing North America, Inc.
Issues: TEC
Rep By: William T. Brack, Thomas H. Hudson, Michael B. Levy

Liggett Group, Inc.
Issues: TOB
Rep By: William T. Brack, Michael B. Levy

Mariner Post Acute Network
Issues: HCR
Rep By: William T. Brack, Thomas H. Hudson, Michael B. Levy

Nat'l Cable Television Ass'n
Issues: TEC
Rep By: William T. Brack, Thomas H. Hudson, Michael B. Levy

NL Industries
Issues: CHM CSP
Rep By: William T. Brack, Michael B. Levy

Oracle Corp.
Issues: CPI
Rep By: William T. Brack, Thomas H. Hudson, Michael B. Levy

Pacific Capital Group, Inc.
Issues: TRD
Rep By: William T. Brack, Thomas H. Hudson, Michael B. Levy

Pfizer, Inc.
Issues: HCR
Rep By: William T. Brack, Michael B. Levy

Rent-a-Center, Inc.
Issues: CSP
Rep By: Michael B. Levy

Rhythms NetConnections
Issues: TEC
Rep By: William T. Brack, Michael B. Levy, Andrew Spielman

Shaw Group
Issues: MAN TRD
Rep By: Thomas H. Hudson

Teletech Teleservices, Inc.
Issues: TAX
Rep By: William T. Brack, Thomas H. Hudson, Michael B. Levy

Timet-Titantium Metals Corp.
Issues: TRD
Rep By: William T. Brack, Michael B. Levy

Vail Associates
Rep By: William T. Brack, Michael B. Levy

Broydrick & Associates

444 N. Capitol St. NW
Suite 837
Washington, DC 20001
Tel: (202)637-0637
Fax: (202)544-5321
Registered: LDA

A lobbying and public affairs firm, also deals with military and national security affairs, public health, community relations, municipal planning, grass roots organizing, and government procurement. Also maintains an office in Milwaukee and Madison, WI.

DC-Area Employees Representing Listed Clients
BROYDRICK, William, President
DEMSKE, Amy, Director, Washington Office and Partner
VINEY, Bill, Associate

Clients

Barr Laboratories
Issues: PHA
Rep By: William Broydrick, Bill Viney

Bell Ambulance
Rep By: William Broydrick, Amy Demske

Blood Center of Southeastern Wisconsin
Issues: EDU HCR MED MMM
Rep By: William Broydrick, Amy Demske

Children's Hospital of Wisconsin
Issues: BUD HCR MMM
Rep By: William Broydrick, Amy Demske

Direct Supply
Issues: HCR
Rep By: William Broydrick, Amy Demske

Extendicare Health Services Inc.
Issues: HCR
Rep By: Amy Demske

Innovative Resource Group
Issues: DEF HCR VET
Rep By: William Broydrick, Amy Demske

Johnsburg, Illinois, Village of
Issues: WAS
Rep By: Bill Viney

Loyola University Health System
Issues: EDU HCR MED
Rep By: Amy Demske

Loyola University of Chicago
Issues: BUD EDU HCR MED
Rep By: Bill Viney

Milwaukee Metropolitan Sewerage District
Issues: BUD CAW ENV
Rep By: Bill Viney

Milwaukee Public Museum
Issues: BUD
Rep By: Bill Viney

Mount Sinai Hospital
Issues: HCR MED MMM
Rep By: William Broydrick, Amy Demske

Nat'l Ass'n of Children's Hospitals Inc.
Issues: DEF HCR
Rep By: William Broydrick, Amy Demske

Northland Cranberries, Inc.
Rep By: William Broydrick

Wisconsin Energy Corp.
Issues: CAW ENG FUE UTI WAS
Rep By: William Broydrick, Bill Viney

Brustein & Manasevit

3105 South St. NW
Washington, DC 20007
Tel: (202)965-3652
Fax: (202)965-8913
Registered: LDA
Web: www.bruman.com
E-mail: bruman@bruman.com

An education and administrative law practice with an emphasis on federal education programs, including Title I, IDEA, charter schools, vocational education, and all relevant funding, appropriations and budget issues.

DC-Area Employees Representing Listed Clients
BRUSTEIN, Michael, Managing Partner
MILNER, Claire, Associate

Clients

California Department of Education
Rep By: Michael Brustein, Claire Milner

Bryan Cave LLP

700 13th St. NW
Suite 700
Washington, DC 20005-3960
Tel: (202)508-6000
Fax: (202)508-6200
Registered: LDA, FARA
Web: www.bryancave.com

Washington Office of an international law firm, which was founded in St. Louis, MO.

Political Action Committee
Bryan Cave LLP Political Action Committee
700 13th St. NW
Suite 700
Washington, DC 20005-3960
Tel: (202)508-6000
Fax: (202)508-6200

DC-Area Employees Representing Listed Clients
BADAMI, Scott M., Counsel
BAVINGER, III, William F., Partner
COLE, James M., Partner
COOPER, J. Michael, Partner
DANFORTH, Hon. John C., Partner
DIXON, Hon. Alan J., Partner
EDGAR, William C., Partner
KASTNER, Kenneth M., Partner
KAYE, Stephen S., Partner
LUDWIG, Mark N., Congressional Liaison
MARCUSS, Stanley J., Partner
MURPHY, James J., Partner
NAEGLE, LaDawn, Partner
O'CONNOR, III, John J., Partner
PEELE, Jo Anne, Partner
QUATRINI, Phillip A., Associate
SCHWARTZ, Daniel C., Partner
STOER, Eric F., Partner
TOPELIUS, Kathleen E., Partner
VAN VOORHEES, Robert F., Partner
WILNER, John R., Partner
WILSON, N. Whitney, Assciate
WINTER, Douglas E., Of Counsel
WOLF, Kevin J., Partner
ZUCKER, Jill M., Counsel

Clients

American Council of State Savings Supervisors
Rep By: Hon. Alan J. Dixon

Bank United of Texas FSB

The Boeing Co.

Business Computer Training Institute
Rep By: Hon. Alan J. Dixon

Chicago Mercantile Exchange
Rep By: Hon. Alan J. Dixon

Coin Acceptors, Inc.
Issues: BUD
Rep By: Mark N. Ludwig

Electronics Consultants Inc.
Issues: DEF
Rep By: Hon. Alan J. Dixon

The Equitable Cos.

Exxon Mobil Corp.
Rep By: Stanley J. Marcuss

Fleishman-Hillard, Inc
Rep By: Stanley J. Marcuss

Glenview, Illinois, Village of
Issues: DEF
Rep By: Hon. Alan J. Dixon

Great Lakes Chemical Corp.
Rep By: Stanley J. Marcuss

Highland Park, Illinois, City of Highwood Local Redevelopment Authority and the City of
Issues: GOV NAT VET
Rep By: Hon. Alan J. Dixon

Highwood, Illinois, City of
Rep By: Hon. Alan J. Dixon

Edward Jones Co.

Kellogg Brown and Root

Laclede Gas Co.
Rep By: Mark N. Ludwig, James J. Murphy

Nabisco, Inc.
Rep By: Stanley J. Marcuss

Popejoy Construction Co.

Town of Fort Sheridan Co., LLC
Rep By: Hon. Alan J. Dixon

Wells Fargo Bank, N.A.
Rep By: Stanley J. Marcuss

Westex Inc.
Rep By: Hon. Alan J. Dixon

BSMG Worldwide

1501 M St. NW
Suite 600
Washington, DC 20005-1710
Tel: (202)739-0200
Fax: (202)659-8287
Registered: FARA
Web: www.bsmg.com

Formerly known as Bozell Sawyer Miller Group. Headquartered in New York, NY.

DC-Area Employees Representing Listed Clients

BLUMA, Stephanie, Senior Associate
CARR, Lisa, Senior Associate
COOPER, Ranny, Partner
DUCHENSE, Steve, Managing Director
KEHOE, Stephen, Managing Director
LATTIMORE, Neel, Senior Managing Director
LYNAM, Clare, Senior Managing Director
MACHAMER, Molly, Director, Public Affairs
MARONI, William, Managing Director
MASSEY, Paul, Senior Associate, Public Affairs Practice
MAY, Clifford D., Senior Managing Director
MESZAROS, James A., Principal
MORGAN, Lance I., President and Partner
OILMAN, Betsy, Senior Associate
OPINSKY, Howard S., Managing Director
SWINT, Jennifer, Senior Managing Director
WILLIAMS, Scott, Senior Managing Director

Clients

AdvaMed

American Council on Education

American Red Cross

Bahamas, Government of the Commonwealth of the

British Columbia Lumber Trade Council

Bulgaria, Embassy of the Republic of

Chiquita Brands Internat'l, Inc.

Colombia, Government of the Republic of

Grocery Manufacturers of America
Rep By: Lance I. Morgan

Heinz Family Foundation

Ingersoll-Rand Co.
Issues: DEF FOR HCR MAN TRD

Life and Health Insurance Foundation for Education

Microsoft Corp.

Nat'l Cable Television Ass'n

Nat'l Center for Children in Poverty
Issues: WEL

Pharmaceutical Research and Manufacturers of America

Philippines Long Distance Telephone Co.

Puerto Rico, Commonwealth of

Sara Lee Corp.

Taxpayers Against Fraud, The False Claims Legal Center

Buc & Beardsley

919 18th St. NW
Suite 600
Washington, DC 20006
Tel: (202)736-3615
Fax: (202)736-3608
Registered: LDA

A law firm.

DC-Area Employees Representing Listed Clients

BEARDSLEY, Kate C., Partner

Clients

CryoLife, Inc.
Rep By: Kate C. Beardsley

Buchanan Ingersoll, P.C.

1776 K St.
Washington, DC 20006
Tel: (202)452-7941
Fax: (202)452-7989
Registered: LDA

DC-Area Employees Representing Listed Clients

JOHNSON, Laurindo
SHARARA, Norma N.
SHORE, Linda K.

Clients

nPower Advisors, LLC
Issues: CPI LBR RET SMB TAX
Rep By: Norma N. Sharara, Linda K. Shore

Burdeshaw Associates, Ltd.

4701 Sangamore Rd.
Suite N100
Bethesda, MD 20816-2508
Tel: (301)229-5800
Fax: (301)229-5045
Registered: LDA
Web: www.burdeshaw.com
E-mail: jstacy@burdeshaw.com

A diversified, privately-owned professional services company assisting industrial clients in matching their technology and capabilities to domestic and international government requirements.

DC-Area Employees Representing Listed Clients

CONNALLY, James, Associate
DENEZZA, Eugene, Associate
GOETZE, Richard, Associate
ISRAEL, Kenneth, Senior V. President, Air Force Programs
LATIMER, Helen, Associate
STACY, Michael, V. President, Business Development

Clients

Martin-Baker Aircraft Co., Ltd.
Issues: AER AVI BUD MAN SCI TRD URB
Rep By: James Connally, Kenneth Israel, Michael Stacy

Burgess Consulting

1350 I St. NW
Suite 870
Washington, DC 20005
Tel: (202)638-2945
Fax: (202)737-1947
Registered: LDA
Web: www.capalliance.com
E-mail: burgess@capalliance.com

A government relations firm. A member of The Capitol Alliance.

DC-Area Employees Representing Listed Clients

BURGESS, Cathy L., President

Burk & Associates

1313 Dolly Madison Blvd.
Suite 402
McLean, VA 22101
Tel: (703)790-1745
Fax: (703)790-2672
E-mail: Society@Burkinc.com

A multiple association management firm.

DC-Area Employees Representing Listed Clients

BURK, Jr., Richard J., President

Clients

American Board of Health Physics
Rep By: Richard J. Burk, Jr.

Health Physics Soc.
Rep By: Richard J. Burk, Jr.

Soc. for Risk Analysis
Rep By: Richard J. Burk, Jr.

John G. "Toby" Burke

400 N. Capitol St. NW
Suite 585
Washington, DC 20001
Tel: (202)347-6607
Fax: (202)393-7718
Registered: LDA

Clients

North Dakota, Governor's Office of the State of
Issues: AGR BUD ECN EDU GOV NAT TRA TRD UTI
Rep By: John G. "Toby" Burke

Burridge Associates

5102 Yuma St. NW
Washington, DC 20016
Tel: (202)686-0262
Fax: (202)956-5235

DC-Area Employees Representing Listed Clients

BURRIDGE, James L.

Clients

FMC Corp.
Rep By: James L. Burridge

Burson-Marsteller

1801 K St. NW
Suite 1000L
Washington, DC 20006
Tel: (202)530-0400
Fax: (202)530-4500
Registered: FARA
Web: www.bm.com

Washington Office of a New York public relations firm. A subsidiary of Young and Rubicam.

Political Action Committee

Burson-Marsteller Political Action Committee
1801 K St. NW
Suite 1000L
Washington, DC 20006
Tel: (202)530-0400
Fax: (202)530-4500

DC-Area Employees Representing Listed Clients

AUXIER, Gary, Managing Director, Public Affairs
CUNNINGHAM, Don, Managing Director, Media Practice
FORD, Pat, Managing Director, Public Affairs Practice
GARMAN, Susan, Managing Director, Public Affairs Practice
GUIDO, George, Director, Public Affairs Practice
HUDSON, Cynthia, Managing Director, Public Affairs Practice
LOTT, Brian H., Director, Public Affairs
MINTZ, Richard, Managing Director, Public Affairs Practice
MULLANEY, Kelley, Manager, Public Affairs Practice
RAVIV, Sheila, Managing Director, Constituency Relations Practice
SHAINMAN, Larry, Manager, Public Affairs Practice
VEITH, Craig G., Managing Director, Media
WALLER, Karen, Managing Director, Health Care Practice
WILSON, Marsha T., Director, Public Affairs Practice

Clients

American Airlines
Rep By: Brian H. Lott, Richard Mintz

British Nuclear Fuels plc

Citizens Flag Alliance

Comision Ejecutiva Hidroelectrica del Rio Lempa CEL
Rep By: Craig G. Veith

HCA Healthcare Corp.

King Faisal Foundation

Eli Lilly and Co.

Monsanto Co.
Rep By: Brian H. Lott

Motorola, Inc.

Royal Norwegian Consulate General - New York

Burwell, Peters and Houston

1762 Church St. NW
Washington, DC 20036
Tel: (202)939-8984
Fax: (202)939-8983
Registered: LDA

DC-Area Employees Representing Listed Clients

MATTS, Dorothy Sharon, Partner
PETERS, Eugene F., Partner

Clients

Barker Enterprises
Issues: GAM
Rep By: Dorothy Sharon Matts, Eugene F. Peters

Butera & Andrews

1301 Pennsylvania Ave. NW
Suite 500
Washington, DC 20004
Tel: (202)347-6875
Fax: (202)347-6876
Registered: LDA, FARA
Web: www.butera-andrews.com
E-mail: info@butera-andrews.com

A law firm specializing in legislative matters (e.g. banking, housing, and tax) and litigation.

DC-Area Employees Representing Listed Clients

ANDREWS, Cliff W., Legislative Director
ANDREWS, Jr., Wright H., Partner
BUTERA, James J., Partner
CORWIN, Philip S.
HART, Dennis M., Partner
LECKAR, Stephen C., Partner
MCINESPIE, John, Partner
TILLOTSON, Frank, Associate

Clients

Advanta Corp.
Issues: BAN BNK HOU
Rep By: Cliff W. Andrews, Wright H. Andrews, Jr., James J. Butera, Frank Tillotson

American Bankers Ass'n
Issues: BNK
Rep By: Philip S. Corwin

American Council of State Savings Supervisors
Issues: BAN
Rep By: Cliff W. Andrews, James J. Butera, Frank Tillotson

Bluebonnet Savings Bank
Issues: BAN
Rep By: Cliff W. Andrews, James J. Butera, Frank Tillotson

British Nuclear Fuels plc
Issues: ENG ENV TRD
Rep By: Wright H. Andrews, Jr., James J. Butera, Dennis M. Hart, Stephen C. Leckar, John McInespie, Frank Tillotson

Charter One
Issues: BAN HOU TRA
Rep By: Cliff W. Andrews, Wright H. Andrews, Jr., James J. Butera, Frank Tillotson

Citizens Bank
Issues: TAX
Rep By: Cliff W. Andrews, Wright H. Andrews, Jr., James J. Butera, Frank Tillotson

Coalition to Amend the Financial Information Privacy Act (CAFPA)
Issues: BAN BNK
Rep By: Cliff W. Andrews, Wright H. Andrews, Jr., James J. Butera, Frank Tillotson

Commercial Finance Ass'n
Issues: BNK CPT
Rep By: Philip S. Corwin

Committee to Preserve Aspen
Issues: TRA
Rep By: Cliff W. Andrews, Wright H. Andrews, Jr., James J. Butera, Frank Tillotson

Community Banks Ass'n of New York State
Issues: BAN
Rep By: Cliff W. Andrews, Wright H. Andrews, Jr., James J. Butera, Frank Tillotson

Community Preservation Corp.
Issues: BAN FIN HOU
Rep By: Cliff W. Andrews, James J. Butera, Frank Tillotson

Countrywide Mortgage Corp.
Issues: BAN HOU
Rep By: Cliff W. Andrews, James J. Butera, Frank Tillotson

Derivatives Net, Inc.
Issues: BAN
Rep By: Cliff W. Andrews, Wright H. Andrews, Jr., James J. Butera, Frank Tillotson

Dime Savings Bank of New York
Issues: BAN TAX
Rep By: Cliff W. Andrews, Wright H. Andrews, Jr., James J. Butera, Frank Tillotson

Federal Home Loan Bank of Boston
Issues: BAN HOU
Rep By: Cliff W. Andrews, Wright H. Andrews, Jr., James J. Butera, Frank Tillotson

Federal Home Loan Bank of Topeka
Issues: BAN HOU
Rep By: Cliff W. Andrews, Wright H. Andrews, Jr., James J. Butera, Frank Tillotson

Federation for American Immigration Reform (FAIR)
Issues: IMM
Rep By: Cliff W. Andrews, Wright H. Andrews, Jr., Frank Tillotson

FM Watch
Issues: BAN FIN HOU
Rep By: Cliff W. Andrews, Wright H. Andrews, Jr., James J. Butera, Frank Tillotson

FRANMAC/Taco Pac
Issues: FOO HCR LBR SMB TAX
Rep By: Cliff W. Andrews, Wright H. Andrews, Jr., James J. Butera, Frank Tillotson

Independence Bank
Issues: BAN
Rep By: Cliff W. Andrews, Wright H. Andrews, Jr., James J. Butera, Frank Tillotson

Internat'l Swaps and Derivatives Dealers Ass'n
Issues: BAN FIN
Rep By: Cliff W. Andrews, Wright H. Andrews, Jr., James J. Butera, Frank Tillotson

Luse Lehman Gorman Pomerenk & Schick, P.C.
Issues: BAN
Rep By: Cliff W. Andrews, Wright H. Andrews, Jr., James J. Butera, Frank Tillotson

Nat'l Home Equity Mortgage Ass'n
Issues: BAN BNK CSP HOU TAX
Rep By: Cliff W. Andrews, Wright H. Andrews, Jr., James J. Butera, Frank Tillotson

North American Securities Administrators Ass'n (NASAA)
Issues: BAN
Rep By: James J. Butera, Frank Tillotson

Option One Mortgage Corp.
Issues: BAN
Rep By: Cliff W. Andrews, Wright H. Andrews, Jr., James J. Butera, Philip S. Corwin, Frank Tillotson

Pedestal
Issues: BAN
Rep By: Cliff W. Andrews, Wright H. Andrews, Jr., James J. Butera, Frank Tillotson

Peoples Bank
Issues: BAN TAX
Rep By: Wright H. Andrews, Jr., James J. Butera

Rent-a-Center, Inc.
Issues: BAN
Rep By: Wright H. Andrews, Jr., James J. Butera

Savings Banks Life Insurance Fund
Issues: BAN TAX
Rep By: Cliff W. Andrews, Wright H. Andrews, Jr., James J. Butera, Frank Tillotson

Silver, Freedman & Taff
Issues: BAN
Rep By: Cliff W. Andrews, Wright H. Andrews, Jr., James J. Butera, Frank Tillotson

Soc. for Human Resource Management
Issues: BAN
Rep By: Cliff W. Andrews, Wright H. Andrews, Jr., James J. Butera, Frank Tillotson

Superior Bank, FSB
Issues: BAN HOU TAX
Rep By: Cliff W. Andrews, Wright H. Andrews, Jr., James J. Butera, Frank Tillotson

Texas Savings and Community Bankers
Issues: BAN HOU
Rep By: Cliff W. Andrews, Wright H. Andrews, Jr., James J. Butera, Frank Tillotson

USPA & IRA
Issues: BAN
Rep By: Cliff W. Andrews, Wright H. Andrews, Jr., James J. Butera, Frank Tillotson

Butsavage & Associates, P.C.

1920 L St. NW
Suite 510
Washington, DC 20036
Tel: (202)861-9700
Fax: (202)861-9711
A law firm specializing in labor and employment matters.

DC-Area Employees Representing Listed Clients
BUTSAVAGE, Carey R., President

Clients

Labor for America PAC
Rep By: Carey R. Butsavage

Butterfield Carter & Associates

1010 Pennsylvania Ave. SE
Washington, DC 20003
Tel: (202)544-7845
Fax: (202)544-7847
Registered: LDA, FARA
Web: www.bcanda.com
A lobbying and public relations firm.

DC-Area Employees Representing Listed Clients
BUTTERFIELD, R. Ian, Principal
CARTER, Gavin J., Principal

Clients

Institute of Cetacean Research
Rep By: R. Ian Butterfield, Gavin J. Carter

Japan, Embassy of
Issues: FOR GOV TRD
Rep By: R. Ian Butterfield, Gavin J. Carter

Thomas Pink, Inc.
Issues: TRD
Rep By: R. Ian Butterfield, Gavin J. Carter

C&M Internat'l, Ltd.

1001 Pennsylvania Ave. NW
Suite 1275
Washington, DC 20004
Tel: (202)624-2895
Fax: (202)628-5116
Registered: LDA, FARA
Web: www.cmintl.com
An international trade and business consulting firm associated with the law firm Crowell & Moring.

DC-Area Employees Representing Listed Clients
CLEMANS, Kathryn B., Director
COOPER, Doral S., President
COYLE, Melissa, Director
SWEENEY, Garnett J., Director
WILSON, Christopher, Director

Clients

Avon Products, Inc.
Issues: TRD
Rep By: Doral S. Cooper, Melissa Coyle

DNA Plant Technology Corp.
Issues: AGR FOO SCI TRD
Rep By: Doral S. Cooper, Melissa Coyle, Garnett J. Sweeney, Christopher Wilson

Indonesia, Ministry of Trade of the Republic of

Korea Internat'l Trade Ass'n

The Limited Inc.
Issues: TRD
Rep By: Doral S. Cooper, Christopher Wilson

Novartis Corp.
Issues: TRD
Rep By: Kathryn B. Clemans, Doral S. Cooper, Melissa Coyle

Oracle Corp.
Rep By: Kathryn B. Clemans, Doral S. Cooper

Pacific Dunlop, Ltd./Pacific Brands

Philippines, Department of Trade and Industry of the Republic of

The C.L.A. Group, LLC

2020 Pennsylvania Ave. NW
Suite 323
Washington, DC 20006-1846
Tel: (202)262-5843
Registered: LDA
Web: www.theclagroup.com
E-mail: info@theclagroup.com

DC-Area Employees Representing Listed Clients
SOCCI, Laurence L.

Clients

Colombian American Service Ass'n
Issues: BUD IMM
Rep By: Laurence L. Socci

Colombian American Trade Center
Issues: ECN TRD
Rep By: Laurence L. Socci

C/R Internat'l, L.L.C

1150 17th St. NW
Suite 406
Washington, DC 20036
Tel: (202)261-2840
Fax: (202)861-6490
Registered: LDA, FARA
E-mail: consult@crinternational.com

DC-Area Employees Representing Listed Clients
CABELLY, Robert J., Managing Member
JACKSON, Nancy Izzo, V. President
RILEY, Stephen F., Managing Member

Clients

Angola, Government of the Republic of

Chamber of Mines of South Africa

South Africa Foundation

Cadwalader, Wickersham & Taft

1201 F St. NW
Suite 1100
Washington, DC 20004
Tel: (202)862-2200
Fax: (202)862-2400
Registered: LDA
Web: www.cadwalader.com
E-mail: infosource@cwt.com
An international law firm headquartered in New York, NY.

DC-Area Employees Representing Listed Clients
LEVINSON, Ellen S., Government Relations Advisor

Clients

Coalition for Food Aid
Issues: AGR FOR

New York Board of Trade
Issues: AGR FIN
Rep By: Ellen S. Levinson

Cambridge Internat'l, Inc.

4306 Wynwood Dr.
Annandale, VA 22003
Tel: (703)354-3121
Fax: (703)354-3121
Registered: LDA
E-mail: cambintl@aol.com

DC-Area Employees Representing Listed Clients
WHITE, Justus P., President

Clients

Stewart & Stevenson Services, Inc.
Issues: DEF
Rep By: Justus P. White

Cambridge Systematics, Inc

5225 Wisconsin Ave. NW
Suite 409
Washington, DC 20015
Tel: (202)466-5542
Fax: (202)466-5548
Registered: LDA

DC-Area Employees Representing Listed Clients
HUERTA, Michael P., Principal

Clients

Salt Lake City Olympic Organizing Committee
Issues: BUD TRA
Rep By: Michael P. Huerta

Arthur E. Cameron

225 C St. NE
Suite A
Washington, DC 20002
Tel: (202)543-7275
Fax: (703)759-2248
Registered: LDA

Clients

Minnesota Mining and Manufacturing Co. (3M Co.)
Rep By: Arthur E. Cameron, Sr.

Minnesota Mining and Manufacturing Co. (Traffic Control Materials Division)
Rep By: Arthur E. Cameron, Sr.

Potters Industries, Inc.
Issues: TRA
Rep By: Arthur E. Cameron, Sr.

Rush Presbyterian-St. Luke's Medical Center
Rep By: Arthur E. Cameron, Sr.

Safetran Systems Corp.
Issues: TRA
Rep By: Arthur E. Cameron, Sr.

Bruce P. Cameron & Associates

1725 17th St. NW
Suite 109
Washington, DC 20009
E-mail: bcameron@igc.org
Tel: (202)667-9563
Fax: (202)332-6544
Registered: LDA, FARA

DC-Area Employees Representing Listed Clients
CAMERON, Bruce P., Lobbyist

Clients

Mozambique, Government of the Republic of
Rep By: Bruce P. Cameron

Cameron McKenna

2175 K St. NW
Fifth Floor
Washington, DC 20037
Tel: (202)789-1100
Fax: (202)289-3928
Registered: LDA, FARA

DC-Area Employees Representing Listed Clients
WILLIAMS, Jr., George H., Partner
ZIPP, Joel F., Partner

Clients

Hydro-Quebec
Rep By: George H. Williams, Jr., Joel F. Zipp

Cammer and Associates

P.O. Box 68
Fairfax, VA 22039
E-mail: cammer@iamdigex.net
Tel: (703)802-3416
Fax: (703)631-8340
Registered: FARA

DC-Area Employees Representing Listed Clients
CAMMER, Paul A., President
CAMMER, Sandra S., V. President and Secretary

Clients

Business Council on Indoor Air
Rep By: Paul A. Cammer

Japan Industrial Conference for Ozone Layer Protection
Rep By: Paul A. Cammer

Japan Industrial Conference on Cleaning

Office of James I. Campbell

8610 Hidden Hill Lane
Potomac, MD 20854
Web: www.jcampbell.com
E-mail: office@jcampbell.com
Tel: (301)983-2538
Registered: LDA

DC-Area Employees Representing Listed Clients
CAMPBELL, Jr., James I., Principal

Jan Campbell

411 Independence Ave. SE
Washington, DC 20003
Tel: (202)546-6733
Fax: (202)546-6732
Registered: LDA

Clients

Save America's Fossils for Everyone, Inc.
Issues: ENV NAT
Rep By: Jan Campbell

W. Douglas Campbell

1776 K St. NW
Suite 300
Washington, DC 20006
E-mail: dougcgr@aol.com
Tel: (202)530-5505
Fax: (202)719-7270
Registered: LDA

Clients

AOL Time Warner
Issues: CON CPI CPT CSP GAM LAW MIA TOR
Rep By: W. Douglas Campbell

Thomas D. Campbell & Assoc.

517 Queen St.
Alexandria, VA 22314
Tel: (703)683-0773
Registered: LDA

DC-Area Employees Representing Listed Clients
CAMPBELL, Thomas D., President

Clients

RAG North America
Issues: NAT TAX
Rep By: Thomas D. Campbell

Smokers Pneumonoconiosis Council
Issues: TAX
Rep By: Thomas D. Campbell

Thompson Creek Metals Co.
Issues: NAT TAX
Rep By: Thomas D. Campbell

Campbell Crane & Associates

1010 Pennsylvania Ave. SE
Washington, DC 20003
E-mail: campcran@aol.com
Tel: (202)546-4991
Fax: (202)544-7926
Registered: LDA

Formerly Campbell-Raupe, Inc.

DC-Area Employees Representing Listed Clients
CAMPBELL, Jeanne M., President and Chief Exec. Officer
CRANE, Daniel M.

Clients

American Ass'n of Advertising Agencies
Issues: ADV TAX
Rep By: Jeanne M. Campbell, Daniel M. Crane

The Ass'n For Manufacturing Technology (AMT)
Issues: CSP TOR
Rep By: Jeanne M. Campbell

Celanese Government Relations Office
Rep By: Jeanne M. Campbell, Daniel M. Crane

The Chubb Corp.
Issues: BAN DIS ENV TAX TOR
Rep By: Jeanne M. Campbell, Daniel M. Crane

Citigroup
Issues: TAX
Rep By: Jeanne M. Campbell, Daniel M. Crane

Invest to Compete Alliance

Massachusetts Water Resources Authority
Issues: BUD CAW ENV
Rep By: Jeanne M. Campbell, Daniel M. Crane

Merck & Co.
Issues: HCR MMM TAX
Rep By: Jeanne M. Campbell, Daniel M. Crane

Providence Gas
Rep By: Jeanne M. Campbell

Raytheon Co.
Issues: TAX
Rep By: Jeanne M. Campbell, Daniel M. Crane

Securities Industry Ass'n
Issues: BAN TAX
Rep By: Jeanne M. Campbell, Daniel M. Crane

Shriners Hospital for Children
Issues: CSP HCR
Rep By: Jeanne M. Campbell, Daniel M. Crane

Statute of Repose Coalition (SORC)

University of Massachusetts
Issues: DEF FOO
Rep By: Jeanne M. Campbell, Daniel M. Crane

USX Corp.
Issues: RET TAX
Rep By: Jeanne M. Campbell, Daniel M. Crane

Westinghouse
Rep By: Jeanne M. Campbell

John G. Campbell, Inc.

9300-D Old Keene Mill Rd.
Burke, VA 22015
Web: www.jcampbellinc.com
E-mail: John@JCampbellinc.com
Tel: (703)455-8885
Fax: (703)440-9208
Registered: LDA

DC-Area Employees Representing Listed Clients
CAMPBELL, John G., President

Clients

Advanced Power Technologies, Inc.
Issues: DEF

Computer Sciences Corp.
Rep By: John G. Campbell

DDL OMNI Engineering Corp.
Issues: DEF

EWA Land Information Group, Inc.
Issues: DEF

General Electric Co.
Issues: DEF

GEO Centers, Inc.

GSE Systems, Inc.

IT Group, Inc.
Rep By: John G. Campbell

ManTech Internat'l
Issues: DEF

Northrop Grumman Corp.
Issues: DEF
Rep By: John G. Campbell

Raytheon Co.
Issues: DEF

SAIC

Sierra Nevada Corp.
Issues: DEF

Sippican, Inc.
Issues: DEF

Vredenburg
Issues: DEF
Rep By: John G. Campbell

The Campo Group, Ltd.

Crystal Park
Suite 410 South
Arlington, VA 22202-4460
E-mail: thecampogroup@compuserve.com
Tel: (703)486-2187
Fax: (703)979-5806

A public affairs consulting firm.

DC-Area Employees Representing Listed Clients
CAMPO, Terry T., President

Clients

S. A. Campo
Rep By: Terry T. Campo

Chicago Global, Ltd.
Rep By: Terry T. Campo

Crystal Group
Rep By: Terry T. Campo

Farrell & Campo
Rep By: Terry T. Campo

Windsock Research
Rep By: Terry T. Campo

CANAMCO (The Canadian-American Company)

1220 19th St. NW
Suite 400
Washington, DC 20036
Tel: (202)822-0707
Fax: (202)822-0714
Registered: LDA, FARA

Represents American, Canadian and foreign firms and governments in Washington and U.S. firms with interests in Canada and abroad.

DC-Area Employees Representing Listed Clients
ABRAMS, Matthew J., President

Clients

Aerospace Industries Ass'n of Canada
Issues: AER
Rep By: Matthew J. Abrams

Canfield & Associates, Inc.

801 Pennsylvania Ave. NW
Suite 625
Washington, DC 20004
Tel: (202)661-2100
Fax: (202)661-2101
Registered: LDA

DC-Area Employees Representing Listed Clients
BLAUWET, Roger, Principal
BOSTON, April, Director, Government Affairs
CANFIELD, Anne C., President

Clients

Air Transport Ass'n of America
Issues: TAX
Rep By: Roger Blauwet, April Boston, Anne C. Canfield

American Home Products Corp.
Issues: TAX
Rep By: Roger Blauwet, April Boston, Anne C. Canfield

Ass'n of Financial Guaranty Insurers
Issues: BNK ECN FIN TAX TRA
Rep By: Roger Blauwet, April Boston, Anne C. Canfield

Consumer Mortgage Coalition
Issues: BNK HOU
Rep By: Roger Blauwet, April Boston, Anne C. Canfield

GE Commercial Real Estate & Financial Services
Issues: HOU TAX
Rep By: Roger Blauwet, April Boston, Anne C. Canfield

Merck & Co.
Issues: HCR TAX
Rep By: Roger Blauwet, April Boston, Anne C. Canfield

Mutual of Omaha Insurance Companies
Issues: HCR INS TAX
Rep By: Roger Blauwet, Anne C. Canfield

Pfizer, Inc.
Issues: MMM TAX
Rep By: Roger Blauwet, April Boston, Anne C. Canfield

Canfield, Smith and Martin

1815 H St. NW
Suite 1001
Washington, DC 20006
Tel: (202)822-5080
Fax: (202)822-5085

DC-Area Employees Representing Listed Clients
SMITH, Daniel C., Attorney

Clients

Nat'l Field Selling Ass'n
Issues: ADV CSP GOV LAW SMB TAX
Rep By: Daniel C. Smith

Mark R. Cannon

1335 Murray Downs Way
Reston, VA 20194
E-mail: mark.cannon@mciworld.com
Tel: (703)787-9277
Registered: LDA

Clients

Resources and Instruction for Staff Excellence, Inc.
Issues: BUD COM CPI EDU HCR SCI TAX TEC WEL
Rep By: Mark R. Cannon

Cannon Consultants, Inc.

1300 Pennsylvania Ave. NW
Suite 700
Washington, DC 20004
E-mail: chacannon@aol.com
Tel: (202)204-3040
Fax: (202)204-3041
Registered: LDA

DC-Area Employees Representing Listed Clients
CANNON, Charles A., President

Clients

Allboxesdirect
Rep By: Charles A. Cannon

ISL Inc.
Rep By: Charles A. Cannon

Land Mine Detection Systems, Inc.
Issues: DEF
Rep By: Charles A. Cannon

N-VIRO Internat'l Corp.
Rep By: Charles A. Cannon

Nat'l Audubon Soc.
Rep By: Charles A. Cannon

New Product Development Consortium
Rep By: Charles A. Cannon

Capital Consultants Corp.

750 First St. NE
9th Floor
Washington, DC 20002
Web: www.capitalconsultantscorp.com
Tel: (202)745-2900
Fax: (202)745-2901
Registered: FARA

A management consulting and strategic planning firm.

DC-Area Employees Representing Listed Clients
BARNHARD, Seth, V. President
HODGSON, Barry, Senior Consultant
KAISER, Michael David, President
SCHOLL, Wayne, V. President

Clients

American Indian Ass'n
Issues: ECN GAM IND TOB
Rep By: Michael David Kaiser

Brookhill Redevelopment
Issues: ENV RES
Rep By: Michael David Kaiser, Wayne Scholl

Chehalis Reservation, Confederated Tribes of the
Issues: ECN GAM IND TOB
Rep By: Barry Hodgson, Michael David Kaiser

Cherokee Investment Partners, LLC
Issues: ENV RES
Rep By: Seth Barnhard, Michael David Kaiser, Wayne Scholl

Development Corporation of Nevada
Issues: GAM IND
Rep By: Michael David Kaiser

Dolce Internat'l
Issues: RES URB
Rep By: Seth Barnhard, Michael David Kaiser

Emory University, Department of Internat'l Health-PAMM, USAID
Issues: EDU FOR HCR
Rep By: Michael David Kaiser

Energy Conservation Program, Inc.
Issues: ENG
Rep By: Michael David Kaiser

Guaynabo, Puerto Rico, City of
Issues: DEF RES
Rep By: Michael David Kaiser

Hercules Development Corp.
Issues: ECN GAM IND TOB
Rep By: Michael David Kaiser

Moscow State University
Issues: EDU FOR
Rep By: Michael David Kaiser

Omaha Tribe of Nebraska
Issues: IND TOB
Rep By: Barry Hodgson, Michael David Kaiser

Sister Cities Internat'l
Issues: FOR
Rep By: Michael David Kaiser

South African Government/World Bank
Issues: DEF FOR GOV RES
Rep By: Michael David Kaiser

Sports Corp., Ltd.
Issues: SPO URB
Rep By: Seth Barnhard, Michael David Kaiser

Trinity Partners, Inc.
Issues: ENV RES
Rep By: Seth Barnhard, Michael David Kaiser

Capital Insights Group

1700 K St. NW
Suite 1200
Washington, DC 20006
Web: www.cig1.com
E-mail: cig@cig1.com
Tel: (202)857-0001
Fax: (202)857-0209

Consultants to institutional money managers.

DC-Area Employees Representing Listed Clients
KAMINOW, Ira P., President and Chief Exec. Officer
ROSEN, Gerald R., Managing Director, International
SEDKY, Julie, V. President
SIMON, Susan C., V. President

Capital Partnerships (VA) Inc.

11350 Random Hills Rd.
Suite 800
Fairfax, VA 22030
E-mail: kbutler@cpiva.com
Tel: (703)620-4914
Fax: (703)620-4709
Registered: LDA

A transportation consulting and government relations firm.

DC-Area Employees Representing Listed Clients
ANGLE, Robin, Associate
BUTLER, Kenneth W., Senior Principal
GRAVELY, Clay, Associate

Clients

Anoka County Regional Railroad Authority
Issues: TRA
Rep By: Robin Angle, Kenneth W. Butler, Clay Gravely

Denver, Colorado, City and County of
Issues: TRA
Rep By: Robin Angle, Kenneth W. Butler, Clay Gravely

Douglas, Colorado, County of
Rep By: Robin Angle, Kenneth W. Butler, Clay Gravely

Friedlob, Sanderson, Raskin, Paulson, Toutillott
Issues: TRA
Rep By: Robin Angle, Kenneth W. Butler, Clay Gravely

North Metro Mayors Coalition
Issues: ROD TRA
Rep By: Robin Angle, Kenneth W. Butler, Clay Gravely

Policy Advantage
Rep By: Robin Angle, Kenneth W. Butler, Clay Gravely

Southeast Business Partnership
Issues: TRA
Rep By: Robin Angle, Kenneth W. Butler, Clay Gravely

Taxicab, Limousine and Paratransit Ass'n
Issues: TRA
Rep By: Robin Angle, Kenneth W. Butler, Clay Gravely

Capital Strategies Group, Inc.

444 N. Capitol St. NW
Suite 841
Washington, DC 20001
Web: www.capitalstrategies.com
E-mail: tammi.hayes@capitalstrategiesgroup.com
Tel: (202)393-6412
Fax: (202)638-4584
Registered: LDA, FARA

Capital Strategies Group, Inc. focuses on government relations, foreign and domestic business development, strategic partnering and raising capital for high-tech start-up companies.

DC-Area Employees Representing Listed Clients
HAYES, Tammi, President/Chief Exec. Officer

Clients

3gi, Inc.
Issues: SCI
Rep By: Tammi Hayes

allacrossamerica.com
Issues: SCI
Rep By: Tammi Hayes

Allthane Technologies Internat'l
Issues: DEF
Rep By: Tammi Hayes

The Capital Hill Group, Inc.
Issues: GOV
Rep By: Tammi Hayes

The Castano Group
Issues: TOB TOR
Rep By: Tammi Hayes

China.com
Issues: SCI
Rep By: Tammi Hayes

Corel Corp.
Issues: SCI
Rep By: Tammi Hayes

Internat'l Public Relations Co.
Issues: AUT TEC
Rep By: Tammi Hayes

Millenium 2100
Issues: UTI
Rep By: Tammi Hayes

Toyota Motor Corp.
Issues: AUT
Rep By: Tammi Hayes

Visitalk.com
Issues: SCI
Rep By: Tammi Hayes

Capitol Advisors, Inc.

1156 15th St. NW
Suite 304
Washington, DC 20005
Tel: (202)986-0050
Fax: (202)986-0052
Registered: FARA

Clients

Georgia, Government of the Republic of

The Capitol Alliance

1350 I St. NW
Suite 870
Washington, DC 20005
Web: www.capalliance.com
Tel: (202)638-6012
Fax: (202)737-1947

An alliance of the following consulting and government relations firms: McNamara & Associates, Health Policy Analysts, Hannett & Associates, Managed Care Compliance Solutions, Patrick M. Murphy and Associates, Burgess Consulting, Spivey/HPG (see separate listings) and HPEN (located in Los Angeles, CA).

DC-Area Employees Representing Listed Clients
HANNETT, Frederick J., Managing Principal

Capitol Associates, Inc.

426 C St. NE
Washington, DC 20002
Web: www.capitolassociates.com
E-mail: cai@capitolassociates.com
Tel: (202)544-1880
Fax: (202)543-2565
Registered: LDA

A government relations and consulting firm.

DC-Area Employees Representing Listed Clients
BROOKS, Tricia, Associate
FINERFROCK, William A., V. President, Health Policy
GEMSKI, Liz, Associate
HARDY HAVENS, Debra M., Chief Exec. Officer
JACKSON, Pamela Patrice, V. President, Public Affairs
LONG, Ph.D., Edward R., V. President, Congressional Relations
MILO, Sara, V. President
PAWELCZYK, Julie P., V. President
SHROYER, Julie, V. President
TEPP, Ronnie Kovner, Associate
WEXLER, Daniel, V. President
WILLIAMS, Matthew

Clients

Academic Health Center Coalition
Issues: BUD MED MMM
Rep By: Debra M. Hardy Havens, Edward R. Long, Ph.D., Julie P. Pawelczyk

Albert Einstein Medical Center
Issues: BUD MED
Rep By: Edward R. Long, Ph.D., Julie P. Pawelczyk

American Ass'n for Marriage and Family Therapy
Issues: HCR MMM
Rep By: William A. Finerfrock, Debra M. Hardy Havens, Julie Shroyer

American Medical Informatics Ass'n

American Psychological Ass'n
Issues: BUD
Rep By: Liz Gemski, Edward R. Long, Ph.D.

American Soc. of Radiologic Technologists
Issues: MMM
Rep By: William A. Finerfrock, Matthew Williams

American Soc. of Tropical Medicine and Hygiene
Issues: BUD MED TOB
Rep By: Sara Milo

Ass'n of Surgical Technologists
Issues: HCR MMM
Rep By: William A. Finerfrock

Aunt Martha's Youth Service Center
Issues: BUD
Rep By: Debra M. Hardy Havens

Bastyr University
Issues: HCR
Rep By: Liz Gemski, Edward R. Long, Ph.D.

Bermuda Biological Station for Research
Rep By: Ronnie Kovner Tepp

Boys and Girls Clubs of America
Issues: BUD TRA
Rep By: Edward R. Long, Ph.D., Daniel Wexler

California Ass'n of Marriage and Family Therapists
Issues: HCR MMM
Rep By: Debra M. Hardy Havens, Julie Shroyer

Cell Therapeutics Inc.
Issues: BUD HCR MED TAX
Rep By: Tricia Brooks

College on Problems of Drug Dependence
Issues: ALC BUD CPT HCR LAW MED TOB
Rep By: Julie Shroyer

DeBrunner and Associates, Inc.
Issues: MMM
Rep By: William A. Finerfrock, Debra M. Hardy Havens, Julie Shroyer, Matthew Williams

FDA-NIH Council
Issues: BUD HCR
Rep By: Tricia Brooks, Pamela Patrice Jackson

Fishers Island Ferry District
Issues: BUD
Rep By: Ronnie Kovner Tepp

Friends of CDC
Issues: BUD
Rep By: Pamela Patrice Jackson, Edward R. Long, Ph.D., Matthew Williams

GlaxoSmithKline

Health Physics Soc.
Issues: BUD ENG ENV FOO VET WAS
Rep By: Liz Gemski

Health Quest
Issues: MMM
Rep By: William A. Finerfrock, Debra M. Hardy Havens

Healthcare Billing and Management Ass'n
Issues: MMM
Rep By: William A. Finerfrock, Debra M. Hardy Havens, Julie Shroyer, Matthew Williams

Fred Hutchinson Cancer Research Center
Issues: BUD HCR IMM MED TAX TOB
Rep By: Debra M. Hardy Havens

Illinois Collaboration on Youth
Issues: BUD COM ENV HCR LAW MMM TOB TRU
Rep By: Debra M. Hardy Havens

Johns Hopkins University & Hospital
Issues: BUD CPT FOR MED MMM

Joint Council of Allergy, Asthma and Immunology
Issues: BUD ENV HCR MED TOB
Rep By: Tricia Brooks, Debra M. Hardy Havens, Matthew Williams

Lymphoma Research Foundation of America, Inc.
Issues: BUD HCR MED TOB
Rep By: Liz Gemski, Edward R. Long, Ph.D.

MedReview, Inc.
Issues: MMM
Rep By: William A. Finerfrock, Debra M. Hardy Havens

Nat'l Alliance for Eye and Vision Research
Issues: BUD MED TOB
Rep By: Sara Milo

Nat'l Ass'n of Children's Hospitals Inc.
Issues: BUD
Rep By: Debra M. Hardy Havens, Julie P. Pawelczyk

Nat'l Ass'n of Community Health Centers
Issues: BUD EDU HCR MMM
Rep By: Liz Gemski, Edward R. Long, Ph.D.

Nat'l Ass'n of Rural Health Clinics
Issues: HCR MMM
Rep By: William A. Finerfrock, Matthew Williams

Nat'l Coalition for Cancer Research
Issues: BUD HCR MED TAX TOB
Rep By: Liz Gemski, Pamela Patrice Jackson, Ronnie Kovner Tepp

Nat'l Federation of High Schools
Rep By: Daniel Wexler

Nat'l Federation of State High School Ass'ns
Issues: EDU
Rep By: Julie P. Pawelczyk, Daniel Wexler

Nat'l Nutritional Foods Ass'n
Issues: AGR BUD HCR TOB
Rep By: Liz Gemski, Edward R. Long, Ph.D.

Neurofibromatosis
Rep By: Edward R. Long, Ph.D., Ronnie Kovner Tepp

New York Botanical Garden
Issues: BUD
Rep By: Edward R. Long, Ph.D., Ronnie Kovner Tepp

New York University Medical Center
Issues: BUD HCR MED MMM TOB
Rep By: Debra M. Hardy Havens, Edward R. Long, Ph.D., Ronnie Kovner Tepp

NF Inc. - Mass Bay Area
Issues: BUD HCR TOB
Rep By: Edward R. Long, Ph.D., Ronnie Kovner Tepp

Northwest Regional Education Laboratory
Issues: BUD EDU
Rep By: Edward R. Long, Ph.D., Julie P. Pawelczyk

Northwestern Memorial Hospital
Issues: BUD HCR TOB
Rep By: Debra M. Hardy Havens, Edward R. Long, Ph.D., Ronnie Kovner Tepp

Parkinson's Action Network
Issues: BUD MED TOB
Rep By: Liz Gemski, Edward R. Long, Ph.D.

Pennsylvania Higher Education Assistance Agency
Issues: BUD EDU
Rep By: Edward R. Long, Ph.D., Julie P. Pawelczyk

Research Soc. on Alcoholism
Issues: ALC BUD MED TOB
Rep By: Sara Milo, Julie Shroyer

Rotary Foundation
Issues: BUD
Rep By: Liz Gemski, Edward R. Long, Ph.D.

Soc. of Toxicology
Issues: BUD CAW ENV MED TOB
Rep By: Sara Milo

Susquehanna Health System
Issues: BUD
Rep By: Edward R. Long, Ph.D., Julie P. Pawelczyk

Texas NF Foundation
Issues: BUD HCR TOB
Rep By: Edward R. Long, Ph.D., Ronnie Kovner Tepp

Thomas Jefferson University Hospital
Issues: BUD
Rep By: Edward R. Long, Ph.D., Julie P. Pawelczyk

University of Pennsylvania/School of Dental Medicine
Issues: BUD HCR TOB
Rep By: Edward R. Long, Ph.D., Ronnie Kovner Tepp

Urban Health Care Coalition of Pennsylvania
Issues: HCR MMM
Rep By: William A. Finerfrock, Debra M. Hardy Havens

Western Michigan University
Issues: BUD
Rep By: Edward R. Long, Ph.D., Julie P. Pawelczyk, Julie Shroyer

Capitol Campaign Consultants

4000 Cathedral Ave. NW
Suite 705 B
Washington, DC 20016-5261
Tel: (202)337-6954
Fax: (202)337-6959
Registered: LDA

DC-Area Employees Representing Listed Clients
FAHY, Thomas E., President

Clients

Broadcast Compliance Services
Rep By: Thomas E. Fahy

Maryland, DC, Delaware Broadcasters Ass'n
Rep By: Thomas E. Fahy

Mid-Atlantic Broadcast Partners
Rep By: Thomas E. Fahy

Capitol Capital Group

3328 S. Second St.
Arlington, VA 22204
Tel: (703)521-8844
Fax: (703)521-8866
Registered: LDA
E-mail: capitolcapitalgroup@earthlink.net

DC-Area Employees Representing Listed Clients
JONES, Michael J.
MAI, Peter

Clients

Washington Consulting Group
Issues: AVI TRA TRD
Rep By: Michael J. Jones, Peter Mai

Capitol City Group

601 Pennsylvania Ave. NW
Suite 900 South Bldg.
Washington, DC 20004
Tel: (202)434-8211
Fax: (202)638-7124
Registered: LDA
E-mail: thogan@harringtonhogan.com
A government relations firm.

DC-Area Employees Representing Listed Clients
HARRINGTON, Gerald T.
HOGAN, John J.
HOGAN, Thomas P., Managing Director
VITALE, Christopher P.

Clients

American Biophysics Corp.
Issues: SCI
Rep By: Gerald T. Harrington, John J. Hogan, Thomas P. Hogan, Christopher P. Vitale

Cranston, Rhode Island, City of
Issues: ECN GOV
Rep By: Gerald T. Harrington, John J. Hogan, Thomas P. Hogan, Christopher P. Vitale

CVS, Inc.
Issues: PHA
Rep By: Gerald T. Harrington, John J. Hogan, Thomas P. Hogan, Christopher P. Vitale

Greater Providence Chamber of Commerce
Issues: ECN
Rep By: Gerald T. Harrington, John J. Hogan, Thomas P. Hogan, Christopher P. Vitale

Landmark Medical Center
Rep By: Gerald T. Harrington, John J. Hogan, Thomas P. Hogan, Christopher P. Vitale

Rhode Island Resource Recovery Center
Issues: ENV WAS
Rep By: Gerald T. Harrington, John J. Hogan, Thomas P. Hogan, Christopher P. Vitale

Capitol Coalitions Inc.

509 C St. NE
Washington, DC 20002
Tel: (202)546-3800
Fax: (202)544-6771
Registered: LDA
A bipartisan lobbying firm specializing in telecommunications, trade, labor and appropriations issues.

DC-Area Employees Representing Listed Clients
AARON, Rebecca, Manager, Congressional Affairs
MEHLMAN, Amy R., Principal
SCOTT, Brett P., President
STEWART, Jarvis C., Principal

Clients

Astro Vision Internat'l, Inc.
Issues: SCI
Rep By: Amy R. Mehlman, Brett P. Scott, Jarvis C. Stewart

Big Sky Economic Development Authority
Issues: BUD
Rep By: Amy R. Mehlman, Brett P. Scott, Jarvis C. Stewart

Corning Inc.
Issues: TEC
Rep By: Amy R. Mehlman, Brett P. Scott

Deaconess Billings Clinic
Issues: HCR
Rep By: Brett P. Scott

EarthWatch, Inc.
Issues: TEC
Rep By: Brett P. Scott

Fanatasy Elections
Issues: CPI GOV TAX
Rep By: Brett P. Scott, Jarvis C. Stewart

Final Analysis, Inc.
Issues: TEC
Rep By: Brett P. Scott

Golden Rule Insurance Co.

Houston, Texas, Department of Aviation of the City of
Issues: AVI
Rep By: Amy R. Mehlman, Brett P. Scott, Jarvis C. Stewart

INTELSAT - Internat'l Telecommunications Satellite Organization
Issues: TEC
Rep By: Amy R. Mehlman, Brett P. Scott

Memphis Area Chamber of Commerce

Municorp Healthcare Systems Inc.

One Economy Corp.
Issues: BUD ECN HOU TEC
Rep By: Amy R. Mehlman, Brett P. Scott, Jarvis C. Stewart

Pocket Science, Inc.
Issues: COM
Rep By: Brett P. Scott

Trimble Navigation, Ltd.
Issues: TEC
Rep By: Brett P. Scott

VeriSign/Network Solutions, Inc.
Issues: TEC
Rep By: Brett P. Scott

Westinghouse Government Services Group
Issues: WAS
Rep By: Amy R. Mehlman, Brett P. Scott, Jarvis C. Stewart

Capitol Counsel Group, L.L.C.

1201 New York Ave. NW
Suite 1000
Washington, DC 20005
Tel: (202)216-8524
Fax: (202)962-8300
Registered: LDA
E-mail: capitol.counsel@att.net
A legislative and government affairs firm.

DC-Area Employees Representing Listed Clients
BELMAR, Warren, Managing Partner

Clients

Boys and Girls Clubs of Greater Washington
Rep By: Warren Belmar

Crown Central Petroleum Corp.
Issues: ENG ENV
Rep By: Warren Belmar

Federal Home Loan Bank of Dallas
Issues: BAN HOU
Rep By: Warren Belmar

Gauff, LTD.
Issues: ENV

HKC, Inc.
Issues: TRA

Houston Galveston Area Council
Issues: ENV TRA
Rep By: Warren Belmar

M.B. Consultants, Inc.
Issues: AGR
Rep By: Warren Belmar

The Nordam Group
Issues: AVI

Pray, Walker, Jackman, Williamson & Marlar
Rep By: Warren Belmar

The Texas Wind Power Co.
Issues: ENG

Capitol Health Group, LLC

1100 New York Ave. NW
Suite 200M
Washington, DC 20005
Tel: (202)367-0440
Fax: (202)367-0470
Registered: LDA
E-mail: info@caphg.com

The phone and fax numbers given were not definite at the time this edition went to press. Please contact the firm via e-mail at info@caphg.com if unable to reach them using the phone or fax numbers shown.

DC-Area Employees Representing Listed Clients
BROMBERG, Michael D., Chairman
COUGHLIN, Shawn, Principal
JENNING, Steven, Principal
MCCONKEY PELTIER, Layna, Principal

Clients

Abbott Laboratories
Issues: HCR MMM PHA
Rep By: Michael D. Bromberg, Shawn Coughlin, Steven Jenning, Layna McConkey Peltier

Beverly Enterprises
Issues: HCR MMM
Rep By: Michael D. Bromberg, Shawn Coughlin, Steven Jenning, Layna McConkey Peltier

Bristol-Myers Squibb Co.
Issues: HCR MMM PHA
Rep By: Michael D. Bromberg, Shawn Coughlin, Steven Jenning, Layna McConkey Peltier

Express Scripts Inc.
Issues: HCR MMM
Rep By: Michael D. Bromberg, Shawn Coughlin, Steven Jenning, Layna McConkey Peltier

Greater New York Hospital Ass'n
Issues: HCR MMM
Rep By: Michael D. Bromberg, Shawn Coughlin, Steven Jenning, Layna McConkey Peltier

Healthcare Leadership Council
Issues: HCR MMM PHA
Rep By: Michael D. Bromberg, Shawn Coughlin, Steven Jenning, Layna McConkey Peltier

Humana Inc.
Issues: HCR MMM
Rep By: Michael D. Bromberg, Shawn Coughlin, Steven Jenning, Layna McConkey Peltier

Johnson & Johnson, Inc.
Issues: HCR MMM PHA
Rep By: Michael D. Bromberg, Shawn Coughlin, Steven Jenning, Layna McConkey Peltier

Medassets.com
Issues: HCR MMM TEC
Rep By: Michael D. Bromberg, Shawn Coughlin, Steven Jenning, Layna McConkey Peltier

Nat'l Ass'n of Psychiatric Health Systems
Rep By: Michael D. Bromberg, Shawn Coughlin, Steven Jenning, Layna McConkey Peltier

Northwestern Memorial Hospital
Issues: HCR MMM
Rep By: Michael D. Bromberg, Shawn Coughlin, Steven Jenning, Layna McConkey Peltier

Pfizer, Inc.
Issues: HCR MMM PHA
Rep By: Michael D. Bromberg, Shawn Coughlin, Steven Jenning, Layna McConkey Peltier

Soc. of Thoracic Surgeons
Issues: HCR MMM
Rep By: Michael D. Bromberg, Shawn Coughlin, Steven Jenning, Layna McConkey Peltier

Capitol Hill Advocates

P.O. Box 6594
Arlington, VA 22206
Tel: (703)593-3456
Fax: (703)534-7760
Registered: LDA
Web: www.washingtonlobbyists.com
E-mail: info@washingtonlobbyists.com

Headquartered in Falls Church, VA. A boutique lobbying firm providing government relations, state and federal legislative and regulatory monitoring, and political, lobbying, and PAC services to a variety of clients.

DC-Area Employees Representing Listed Clients
PENCE, Randall G., President

Clients

American Soc. of Home Inspectors (ASHI)
Issues: CSP HOU SMB
Rep By: Randall G. Pence

American Wood Preservers Institute
Issues: BUD CAW CHM CSP DIS ECN EDU ENV GOV HOU INS LBR MAN RES ROD SCI SMB TAX TRA TRD TRU URB WAS
Rep By: Randall G. Pence

Big Sky, Inc.
Issues: ECN
Rep By: Randall G. Pence

Nat'l Concrete Masonry Ass'n
Issues: LBR MAN SMB TAX TRA
Rep By: Randall G. Pence

Capitol Link, Inc.

831 S. King St.
Suite E
Leesburg, VA 20175
Tel: (703)443-2311
Fax: (703)443-2315
Registered: LDA, FARA
Web: www.caplink.com
E-mail: mick@caplink.com

Governmental affairs consulting.

DC-Area Employees Representing Listed Clients
STATON, Hon. David M., President
STATON, Lynn S., Senior V. President

Clients

Catamount Energy Corp.
Issues: ENG UTI
Rep By: Hon. David M. Staton

Durham, North Carolina, City of
Issues: LAW TRA URB
Rep By: Hon. David M. Staton

Madison County Commission
Issues: AGR LAW LBR URB
Rep By: Hon. David M. Staton

Micronesia, Embassy of the Federated States of
Issues: EDU FOR
Rep By: Hon. David M. Staton

Mobile Area Water and Sewer System
Issues: CAW ENV
Rep By: Hon. David M. Staton

Mobile, Alabama, City of
Issues: HOU LAW TRA URB
Rep By: Hon. David M. Staton

Capitol Partners

601 Pennsylvania Ave. NW
Suite 900 South
Washington, DC 20004
Tel: (202)220-3181
Registered: LDA

DC-Area Employees Representing Listed Clients
CUNNINGHAM, William, Principal
ORLOFF, Jonathan M., Principal

Clients

American Chiropractic Ass'n
Issues: MED
Rep By: Jonathan M. Orloff

Biochemics
Issues: MED
Rep By: William Cunningham, Jonathan M. Orloff

Biogen, Inc.
Issues: BUD
Rep By: William Cunningham, Jonathan M. Orloff

Biomatrix
Issues: HCR
Rep By: William Cunningham, Jonathan M. Orloff

Cambridge Redevelopment Authority
Issues: URB
Rep By: William Cunningham, Jonathan M. Orloff

Concord Family and Adolescent Services
Issues: FAM
Rep By: William Cunningham, Jonathan M. Orloff

Emmanuel College
Rep By: William Cunningham, Jonathan M. Orloff

FLIR Systems, Inc.
Issues: DEF TRD
Rep By: William Cunningham, Jonathan M. Orloff

Kessler Medical Rehabilitation Research & Education Corp.
Issues: MED
Rep By: Jonathan M. Orloff

Marsh USA, Inc.
Issues: INS
Rep By: William Cunningham

Smith & Wesson
Issues: SCI
Rep By: William Cunningham, Jonathan M. Orloff

Capitol Perspectives

1915 17th St. NW
Washington, DC 20009
Tel: (202)265-5276
Fax: (202)234-2108
Registered: LDA
E-mail: MaryElise@aol.com

DC-Area Employees Representing Listed Clients
DEGONIA, Mary Elise, President

Clients

Alternative Schools Network
Rep By: Mary Elise DeGonia

Jobs for Youth
Rep By: Mary Elise DeGonia

Nat'l Council of La Raza
Rep By: Mary Elise DeGonia

Capitol Solutions

805 15th St. NW
Suite 810
Washington, DC 20005
Tel: (202)347-0940
Fax: (202)347-0941
Registered: LDA
Web: www.uscapitolsolutions.com
E-mail: dtaylor@uscapitolsolutions.com

Government relations consultants.

DC-Area Employees Representing Listed Clients
TAYLOR, David F.

Clients

Cellular Telecommunications and Internet Ass'n
Issues: BUD COM CPT LAW SCI
Rep By: David F. Taylor

Intellectual Property Owners Ass'n
Issues: BUD CPT
Rep By: David F. Taylor

Maricopa, Arizona, County of
Issues: BUD ENV

Capitol Strategies

4201 Wilson Blvd.
Suite 110C
Arlington, VA 22203
Tel: (703)358-9570
Registered: LDA

DC-Area Employees Representing Listed Clients
TRIPP, Mary M., Managing Partner

Clients

California Correctional Peace Officers Ass'n
Issues: BUD GOV IMM LAW
Rep By: Mary M. Tripp

NYSCOPBA - New York State Correctional Officers & Police Benevolent Ass'n
Issues: BUD IMM LAW
Rep By: Mary M. Tripp

Capitolink, LLC

1156 15th St. NW
Suite 400
Washington, DC 20005
Tel: (202)872-3865
Fax: (202)296-0833
Registered: LDA
Web: www.capitolink.com

A legislative, regulatory and public affairs consulting firm.

DC-Area Employees Representing Listed Clients
ATWOOD, Deborah M., Senior Associate
HEBERT, Thomas R., Senior Associate
THORNE, Ph.D., John H., Managing Director

Clients

American Crop Protection Ass'n
Issues: AGR CAW ENV
Rep By: Thomas R. Hebert, John H. Thorne, Ph.D.

Aventis CropScience
Issues: AGR CAW
Rep By: John H. Thorne, Ph.D.

ConAgra Foods, Inc.
Issues: AGR CAW ENV FOO
Rep By: John H. Thorne, Ph.D.

The Fertilizer Institute
Issues: CAW
Rep By: John H. Thorne, Ph.D.

Nat'l Ass'n of Conservation Districts
Issues: AGR BUD
Rep By: Deborah M. Atwood, Thomas R. Hebert

Nat'l Cattleman's Beef Ass'n
Issues: AGR CAW
Rep By: John H. Thorne, Ph.D.

Nat'l Chicken Council
Issues: AGR CAW
Rep By: John H. Thorne, Ph.D.

Nat'l Pork Producers Council
Issues: AGR CAW ENV
Rep By: Deborah M. Atwood, John H. Thorne, Ph.D.

Nat'l Turkey Federation
Issues: AGR CAW
Rep By: John H. Thorne, Ph.D.

Premium Standard Farms
Issues: AGR CAW
Rep By: Deborah M. Atwood, John H. Thorne, Ph.D.

SePRO Corp.
Issues: AGR BUD CAW ENV
Rep By: Thomas R. Hebert, John H. Thorne, Ph.D.

Smithfield Foods Inc.
Issues: AGR CAW
Rep By: Deborah M. Atwood, John H. Thorne, Ph.D.

SQM North America Corp.

United Egg Producers
Issues: AGR CAW
Rep By: John H. Thorne, Ph.D.

Vantage Point Network, LLC
Issues: AGR CAW CPI
Rep By: Thomas R. Hebert, John H. Thorne, Ph.D.

Caplin & Drysdale, Chartered

One Thomas Circle NW
Suite 1100
Washington, DC 20005
Tel: (202)862-5000
Fax: (202)429-3301
Registered: LDA
Web: www.caplindrysdale.com
A law firm specializing in federal tax matters.

DC-Area Employees Representing Listed Clients
BOISTURE, Robert A., Member
DORAN, Michael, Member
GREEN, Seth, Member
LIVINGSTON, Catherine E., Member
MASON, Kent A., Member
ROSENBAUM, Daniel B., Member
ROSENBLOOM, H. David, Member
TROYER, Thomas A., Member

Clients

American Benefits Council
Issues: RET TAX
Rep By: Kent A. Mason

The Chubb Corp.
Issues: INS TAX
Rep By: Seth Green, Daniel B. Rosenbaum

Council on Foundations
Issues: TAX
Rep By: Robert A. Boisture

The Hartford
Issues: INS TAX
Rep By: Seth Green, H. David Rosenbloom

Independent Sector
Issues: TAX
Rep By: Robert A. Boisture, Catherine E. Livingston

Edward Jones Investments
Issues: LBR TAX
Rep By: Kent A. Mason

MedStar Health
Issues: TAX
Rep By: Daniel B. Rosenbaum

Nat'l Rural Electric Cooperative Ass'n
Issues: LBR TAX
Rep By: Kent A. Mason

Paul, Hastings, Janofsky & Walker LLP
Issues: RET TAX
Rep By: Kent A. Mason

Variable Annuity Life Insurance Co.
Issues: LBR TAX
Rep By: Kent A. Mason

CAREY/NEALON & Associates, L.L.C.

119 N. Henry St.
Third Floor
Alexandria, VA 22314-2903
Tel: (703)921-9111
Fax: (703)836-8009
Registered: LDA
Web: www.athene.com/Carey.Neal
E-mail: CareyNelon@aol.com
A government relations firm specializing in military, defense, transportaion and international issues.

DC-Area Employees Representing Listed Clients
CAREY, Arlene P., Exec. Director
CAREY, USN (Ret.), Rr. Adm. James J., Chairman
GILBERTSON, Richard, Senior Associate
NEALON, Robert B., Co-Chairman
NELSON, David, Senior Associate

Clients

Amtech Internat'l
Rep By: Rr. Adm. James J. Carey, USN (Ret.)

Media Fusion L.L.C.
Rep By: Rr. Adm. James J. Carey, USN (Ret.)

Carlsmith Ball Wichman Case & Ichiki

700 14th St. NW
Washington, DC 20005
Tel: (202)628-2228
Fax: (202)628-2071
Registered: FARA

Clients

Guam Bankers Ass'n

Robert E. Carlstrom

7800 Stable Way
Potomac, MD 20854
Tel: (301)767-5949
Fax: (301)983-5681
Registered: LDA

Clients

The Doe Run Co.
Issues: ENV NAT TAX
Rep By: Robert E. Carlstrom, Jr.

Human Capital Resources
Issues: BNK EDU TAX
Rep By: Robert E. Carlstrom, Jr.

Internat'l Lead Zinc Research Organization, Inc. (ILZRO)
Issues: AUT ENG TRA
Rep By: Robert E. Carlstrom, Jr.

Carlyle Consulting

3000 S. Randolph St.
Suite 517
Arlington, VA 22206
E-mail: TCR666@worldnet.att.net
Tel: (703)837-8187
Registered: LDA

DC-Area Employees Representing Listed Clients
RODGERS, Thomas C., Owner/President

Clients

Alabama-Coushatta Tribe of Texas

Kickapoo Tribe of Texas

Levi Strauss and Co.
Issues: TAX
Rep By: Thomas C. Rodgers

Nat'l Indian Gaming Ass'n
Issues: GAM GOV IND TAX
Rep By: Thomas C. Rodgers

North of Ireland Free Trade Initiative
Issues: TRD
Rep By: Thomas C. Rodgers

Tule River Tribal Council
Issues: IND TAX
Rep By: Thomas C. Rodgers

Carmen & Muss, P.L.L.C.

1901 Pennsylvania Ave. NW
Suite 300
Washington, DC 20006
Tel: (202)728-1001
Fax: (202)728-4055
Registered: LDA
A law and government relations firm.

DC-Area Employees Representing Listed Clients
CARMEN, Melinda L., Member

Clients

DM Electronics Recycling Corporation
Issues: DEF ENV GOV WAS
Rep By: Melinda L. Carmen

Square 3942 Associates Limited Partnership
Issues: DOC GOV RES WAS
Rep By: Melinda L. Carmen

The Carmen Group

1299 Pennsylvania Ave. NW
Suite 800 West
Washington, DC 20004
Tel: (202)785-0500
Fax: (202)785-5277
Registered: LDA, FARA
Web: www.carmengroup.com

DC-Area Employees Representing Listed Clients
ADESNIK, Ryan, V. President
BOULTER, Hon. Beau, Senior Associate
BROWN, Max, Exec. V. President and Chief Operating Officer
BURKETT, Bob, Senior Consultant
CARMEN, David M., President and Chief Exec. Officer
CARMEN, Gerald P., V. Chairman
CORCORAN, Lisa, Program Director
COTTONE, Mel
DESHIELDS, Vangie
DIUGOS, Barbara
EITER, Steve, Creative Director
ESHMAN, Carrie
GARFINKEL, Andrew, Associate
GILSON, Susan E.
HANNAFORD, Peter D., Public Relations Counsel
HARPER, Dal, Operations Manager
HASSELL, John
HUNTER, Caroline, Associate
JEMMOTT, Diane, V. President
KALEN, Pam, V. President
KEENE, David A., Managing Associate
KEENE, Kerry, Project Manager
KUNZ, David, Associate
LAGOMARCINO, John
LINTON, Ron M.
MILLER, Alison, Events Coordinator
O'CONNELL, Mia
REILLY, Shelia, Events Director
RUSSELL, Michael E., Chief Financial Officer
SMITH, Clifton, Managing Associate
STEVENS, Jack, Senior Associate
TAYLOR, Sharon
TYUS, Aisha, Associate
WARNER, Ann D., Associate
YOUNG, James B., Associate

Clients

ADVO, Inc.
Rep By: Ryan Adesnik, David M. Carmen, Ron M. Linton, Michael E. Russell

Air Transport Ass'n of America
Issues: BUD TRA
Rep By: David M. Carmen, Gerald P. Carmen, David A. Keene, Ron M. Linton

American Concrete Pavement Ass'n (ACPA)
Issues: AUT ROD TAX TRA
Rep By: Ann D. Warner

American Gas Ass'n
Issues: ENG
Rep By: Gerald P. Carmen

Citizens for State Power
Issues: ENG

Colorado Ass'n of Transit Agencies
Issues: TRA

Colorado Springs-Pikes Peak, City of
Issues: ENV

Community Transit Ass'n of Idaho
Issues: TRA

Dillard University
Issues: BUD
Rep By: Ryan Adesnik, David M. Carmen, Clifton Smith, Sharon Taylor, Aisha Tyus

GELCO Information Network GSD, Inc.
Issues: CPI GOV
Rep By: Ryan Adesnik, David M. Carmen, Andrew Garfinkel

Hyundai Precision & Industrial Co., Ltd.

Hyundai Space & Aircraft Co., Ltd.
Issues: AER BAN
Rep By: Hon. Beau Boulter, Gerald P. Carmen, Barbara Diugos

Illinois Department of Transportation
Issues: TRA
Rep By: Ryan Adesnik, Hon. Beau Boulter, David M. Carmen, David A. Keene, Sharon Taylor

Interstate Council on Water Policy
Issues: ENV
Rep By: Susan E. Gilson

Kazakhstan, Government of the Republic of
Rep By: Jack Stevens

Major Medicaid Hospital Coalition
Issues: MMM
Rep By: Ryan Adesnik, Gerald P. Carmen, Diane Jemmott

Maryland Department of Transportation
Issues: TRA
Rep By: John Hassell, Mia O'Connell, James B. Young

MedStar Health
Issues: MMM
Rep By: David M. Carmen

Metropolitan Washington Airports Authority
Issues: AVI GOV TRA
Rep By: Diane Jemmott, Aisha Tyus

Metropolitan Water Reclamation District of Greater Chicago
Issues: BUD
Rep By: Mia O'Connell

Missouri Highway and Transportation Department
Issues: TRA
Rep By: John Hassell, Diane Jemmott, Ann D. Warner, James B. Young

Napa County, California, Flood and Water Conservation District
Issues: BUD URB
Rep By: Mia O'Connell

Nat'l Ass'n of Flood and Stormwater Management Agencies
Issues: DIS ENV NAT
Rep By: Susan E. Gilson

Nevada Department of Transportation
Issues: TRA
Rep By: James B. Young

New York Roadway Improvement Coalition
Issues: ROD
Rep By: John Lagomarcino

Northeast Illinois Regional Commuter Railroad Corp.
Issues: TRA
Rep By: Gerald P. Carmen, David A. Keene, John Lagomarcino, James B. Young

Northwest Airlines, Inc.
Issues: AVI
Rep By: Ryan Adesnik, Gerald P. Carmen

Northwest Municipal Conference
Issues: BUD ENV URB
Rep By: Mia O'Connell

Omnitech Robotics Inc.
Issues: DEF
Rep By: John Lagomarcino

Pembroke Real Estate, Inc.
Issues: RES
Rep By: Max Brown, Gerald P. Carmen, Diane Jemmott

Renova Inc.
Issues: TRD
Rep By: Gerald P. Carmen, Jack Stevens

Riverside County, California, Flood Control and Water Conservation District
Issues: BUD
Rep By: Mia O'Connell

Riverside South Planning Corp.
Issues: ROD
Rep By: John Lagomarcino

Santa Clara Valley Water District
Issues: BUD
Rep By: Mia O'Connell

Stafford, Virginia, County of
Issues: TRA
Rep By: John Hassell, Diane Jemmott, John Lagomarcino

Starwood Hotels & Resorts Worldwide, Inc.
Issues: TOU
Rep By: Ryan Adesnik, David M. Carmen

Sunrise Assisted Living
Issues: HCR
Rep By: Ryan Adesnik, Diane Jemmott

United Seniors Ass'n
Issues: GOV
Rep By: David A. Keene

US Bancorp
Issues: BAN CSP FIN GOV
Rep By: Hon. Beau Boulter, Gerald P. Carmen, David A. Keene

Utah Department of Transportation
Issues: TRA
Rep By: James B. Young

Washington Sports & Entertainment, L.P.
Issues: ECN TAX
Rep By: Ryan Adesnik, Gerald P. Carmen, Diane Jemmott

Western Development
Issues: RES
Rep By: Ryan Adesnik, Diane Jemmott

Wisconsin Public Service Corp.
Issues: ENG
Rep By: Mel Cottone, David A. Keene

World Wrestling Federation Entertainment Inc.
Rep By: Bob Burkett, David A. Keene

Bill Carney & Co.

523 Seventh St. SE
Washington, DC 20003
Tel: (202)543-5237
Fax: (202)543-5269
Registered: LDA
Web: www.billcarneyco.com
E-mail: bill@billcarneyco.com
A public affairs and government relations firm.

DC-Area Employees Representing Listed Clients
CARNEY, Jacqueline, V. President
CARNEY, Hon. William, President

Clients

Clean Energy Group
Issues: CAW ENG
Rep By: Jacqueline Carney, Hon. William Carney

COGEMA, Inc.
Issues: ENG SCI
Rep By: Jacqueline Carney, Hon. William Carney

Edison Electric Institute
Issues: CAW ENG ENV TAX UTI
Rep By: Jacqueline Carney, Hon. William Carney

Lockheed Martin Naval Electronics Surveillance Systems
Issues: ENG
Rep By: Hon. William Carney

Nuclear Energy Institute
Issues: BUD ENG WAS
Rep By: Hon. William Carney

Repeal PUHCA Now Coalition
Issues: BAN ENG
Rep By: Jacqueline Carney, Hon. William Carney

Carol/Trevelyan Strategy Group

733 15th St. NW
Suite 700
Washington, DC 20005
Tel: (202)347-5280
Fax: (202)347-5283
Web: www.ctsg.com/
E-mail: reach_us@ctsg.com
A public affairs and political consulting firm headquartered in Eugene, OR.

DC-Area Employees Representing Listed Clients
NELSON, Greg, Director, DC Office

Carpi & Clay

1130 Connecticut Ave. NW
Suite 650
Washington, DC 20036
Tel: (202)728-1050
Fax: (202)728-1060
Registered: LDA
Web: www.carpiclay.com
E-mail: kcarpi@carpiclay.com
A government relations consulting firm.

DC-Area Employees Representing Listed Clients
CARPI, Kenneth A., Partner

Clients

California Children's Hospital Ass'n
Issues: HCR MMM
Rep By: Kenneth A. Carpi

El Centro Regional Medical Center
Issues: BUD HCR
Rep By: Kenneth A. Carpi

Encinitas, California, City of
Issues: BUD GOV NAT
Rep By: Kenneth A. Carpi

Hertz Corp.
Issues: INS LAW
Rep By: Kenneth A. Carpi

Hollis-Eden Pharmaceuticals, Inc.
Issues: BUD
Rep By: Kenneth A. Carpi

Mount High Hosiery, Ltd.
Issues: TRD
Rep By: Kenneth A. Carpi

Port of San Diego
Issues: AVI MAR TOU TRA TRU
Rep By: Kenneth A. Carpi

San Diego County Water Authority
Issues: ENV NAT
Rep By: Kenneth A. Carpi

San Diego Natural History Museum
Issues: BUD SCI
Rep By: Kenneth A. Carpi

U.S./Mexico Border Counties Coalition
Issues: BUD
Rep By: Kenneth A. Carpi

Water Replenishment District of Southern California
Issues: ENV NAT
Rep By: Kenneth A. Carpi

The Carter Group

1301 K St. NW
Suite 900
East Tower
Washington, DC 20005
Tel: (202)408-8007
Fax: (202)408-8719
Registered: LDA
Web: www.thecartergroup-dc.com
E-mail: info@thecartergroup-dc.com
A lobbying and consulting firm.

DC-Area Employees Representing Listed Clients
CARTER, Michael R., Principal
CARTER, Thomas L.
EIRING, Gene P.
LINDBERG, Ernest T.
MCCLEAN, Scott D.
SULLIVAN, Paul N., Member

Clients

Advanced Technology Systems
Issues: GOV
Rep By: Michael R. Carter

Airborne Tactical Advantage Co.
Issues: DEF
Rep By: Michael R. Carter, Scott D. McClean

Military Order of the Purple Heart of the U.S.A.
Issues: VET
Rep By: Michael R. Carter, Scott D. McClean

Safety Harbor, Florida, City of
Issues: ROD TRA
Rep By: Michael R. Carter

Sensor Technologies and Systems Inc.
Issues: DEF LAW
Rep By: Michael R. Carter

Sierra Nevada Corp.
Issues: DEF TRD
Rep By: Michael R. Carter

Specialized Technical Services, Inc.
Rep By: Michael R. Carter, Scott D. McClean

Stilman Advanced Strategies
Issues: AVI DEF
Rep By: Michael R. Carter

Veridian Corp.
Issues: AER DEF LAW
Rep By: Michael R. Carter

Veritect
Issues: CSP
Rep By: Michael R. Carter

Vortex, Inc.
Issues: DEF
Rep By: Michael R. Carter, Scott D. McClean

Cartwright & Riley

1140 Connecticut Ave.
Suite 502
Washington, DC 20036
Tel: (202)293-9101
Fax: (202)293-9111
Registered: LDA

DC-Area Employees Representing Listed Clients
CARTWRIGHT, Russell S., Principal
CULLEN, Maura, Partner
SECHRIST, Amber, Partner

Clients

Anthem, Inc.
Issues: DEF HCR
Rep By: Russell S. Cartwright, Maura Cullen

GTECH Corp.
Issues: GAM
Rep By: Russell S. Cartwright

Kentucky, Commonwealth of
Issues: BUD EDU HCR TOB TRA WEL
Rep By: Russell S. Cartwright, Maura Cullen

Nova Southeastern University
Issues: BUD HCR HOU
Rep By: Russell S. Cartwright

Cascade Associates

499 S. Capitol St. SW
Suite 606
Washington, DC 20003
Tel: (202)554-5828
Fax: (202)554-2896
Registered: LDA

DC-Area Employees Representing Listed Clients
SCHAFER, Jennifer A., President

Clients

American Gas Cooling Center
Issues: BUD CAW ENG ENV TAX
Rep By: Jennifer A. Schafer

Business Council for Sustainable Energy
Issues: ENG
Rep By: Jennifer A. Schafer

Integrated Building and Construction Solutions
Issues: ENG ENV
Rep By: Jennifer A. Schafer

Nat'l Fenestration Rating Council
Issues: ENG
Rep By: Jennifer A. Schafer

Robur Corp.
Issues: ENG
Rep By: Jennifer A. Schafer

University of Oregon
Issues: BUD DEF SCI
Rep By: Jennifer A. Schafer

Cash, Smith & Wages

913 E. Taylor Run Pkwy.
Suite 303
Alexandria, VA 22302
Tel: (703)548-3676
Fax: (703)548-0926
Registered: LDA
E-mail: jbwages@compuserv.com

DC-Area Employees Representing Listed Clients
JOLLIE, Susan
WAGES, Joan B., Principal

Clients

Ass'n of Professional Flight Attendants
Issues: AVI HCR LBR
Rep By: Joan B. Wages

Nat'l Women's History Museum
Issues: BUD EDU RES
Rep By: Susan Jollie, Joan B. Wages

Cashdollar-Jones & Co.

1629 K St. NW
Suite 1100
Washington, DC 20006
Tel: (202)728-4058
Fax: (202)466-5283
Registered: LDA
E-mail: rcashdollar@earthlink.net

DC-Area Employees Representing Listed Clients
CASHDOLLAR, Robert, President

Clients

American Bankers Ass'n
Issues: AGR
Rep By: Robert Cashdollar

Nat'l Farmers Organization
Issues: AGR
Rep By: Robert Cashdollar

Pheasants Forever
Issues: AGR
Rep By: Robert Cashdollar

Caspian Group

1455 F St. NW
Suite 225
Washington, DC 20005
Tel: (202)624-0016
Fax: (202)783-6947
Registered: LDA
E-mail: lborland@erols.com

DC-Area Employees Representing Listed Clients

BORLAND, Lydia

Clients

U.S.-Turkish Business Council of DEIK
Issues: FOR TRD
Rep By: Lydia Borland

William E. Casselman, II

P.O. Box 156
Aldie, VA 20105-0156
Tel: (703)551-2108
Fax: (703)327-3116
Registered: LDA
E-mail: weclawfirm@aol.com
Attorney-at-Law.

Clients

Agency-Internat'l, Ltd.
Rep By: William E. Casselman, II

Federal Systems Group, Inc.
Rep By: William E. Casselman, II

Ova Noss Family Partnership
Rep By: William E. Casselman, II

Cassidy & Associates, Inc.

700 13th St. NW
Suite 400
Washington, DC 20005
Tel: (202)347-0773
Fax: (202)347-0785
Registered: LDA, FARA
Web: www.cassidy.com
E-mail: cassidy@cassidy.com
A public affairs consulting firm owned by the Interpublic Group of companies (IPG) headquartered in New York, NY. Also maintains offices in Boston.

DC-Area Employees Representing Listed Clients

ADLER, Laurie J., V. President
BARSH, Jr., Harry E., Senior Consultant
BENNEWITH, Alex, Account Executive
BOBBITT, Douglass E., Senior V. President
CARLEY, Dr. David, Senior Consultant
CASSIDY, Gerald S. J., Chairman and C.E.O., Cassidy Companies, Inc.
CLAY, Sonya C., Associate
CRAYBAS, Marisa, Account Executive
CRUMBLISS, John A., Account Executive
DOYLE, Jr., John S., Senior V. President
EDWARDS, Shawn, Account Exec.
EVANS, Christy Carson, V. President
FABIANI, James P., Chairman and Chief Exec. Officer
FEINMAN, Dori, Account Executive
FRANCHOT, Peter, Consultant
GALEY, Shannon, Account Executive
GILL, Gregory M., Senior V. President, General Counsel
GIOFFRE, Michele, Associates
GIUGNI, Henry K., V. Chairman
GODFREY, Jr., Carl Franklin, Exec. V. President
GONELLA, Geoff, Senior V. President, New Business Development
GORDON, Al, Director, New Business Development Consulting
GROSSMAN, Lawrence C., Senior V. President
HATCH, Paul D., Senior Consultant
HOCHSTEIN, Amos, Sr. V. President
JACOBSON, Judith M., Consultant
JAMES, Marie, Senior Associate
KAUFMAN, IV, W. Campbell, V. President
KEDZIOR, Dennis M., Senior V. President
KELLEY, USMC (Ret.), General Paul X., V. Chairman Emeritus
KELLY-JOHNSON, Mary Kate, V. President
LAMOND, Christopher, Associate
LAWRENCE, Jeffrey, Senior V. President and Director, Aerospace and Technology Group
LAWRENCE, Lindsay, Account Executive
LOONEY, Jr. USMC (Ret.), Maj. Gen. Edmund P., Senior Consultant
MACCONOMY, Scott D., Associate
MASON, Arthur D., Senior V. President
MCNAMARA, Daniel J., Senior V. President
MEROLA, Michael, Senior Associate
MORIARTY, Betty, V. President and Dir., New Business Development Research
NEAL, Laura A., V. President
O'CONNOR, Christine A., Associate
O'SHEA, Sean, Account Executive
ONOFF, Tim, Director, Consultant Network
OSBORNE, Valerie Rogers, V. President
PAUL, USMC (Ret.), Brig. Gen. Terry, Senior V. President and Director, Defense Group
PERRY, Louie, V. President
PINTO-RIDDICK, Blenda, Sr. Account Executive
PURCELL, F. Eugene, Senior Consultant
RAHEB, Walter, Sr. V. President and Director of Global Trade Strategies
RINALDO, Diane, Account Exec.
ROONEY, Hon. Fred B., Senior Consultant
ROWAN, James, Senior Consultant for Government Affairs
ROZSA, Gabor J., Senior V. President
RUSS, Marnie, Sr. Account Executive
RUSSO, Hon. Martin A., Vice Chairman, President and Chief Operating Officer
SHAKIR, Adib A., Consultant
SHIELDS, Mary E., Senior V. President
SOTSKY, Rachel, Associate
SUTTON, Barbara, Senior V. President
TATE, Sr., Dan C., Senior V. President
TRANT, Matthew J., Chief of Staff to Chairman and C.E.O.
VAUGHAN, (Ret.), Rear Admiral G. Dennis, Consultant
WALSH, Maureen, Associate
WARBURG, Gerald Felix, Senior V. President
WENTWORTH, Lyllett, Account Executive
WHITAKER, Stephen, Sr. V. President and Director of Global Trade Strategies

Clients

Abtech Industries
Issues: BUD ENV
Rep By: John S. Doyle, Jr., Shawn Edwards, Christy Carson Evans, W. Campbell Kaufman, IV, Brig. Gen. Terry Paul, USMC (Ret.), Gabor J. Rozsa

Adelphi University
Issues: BUD
Rep By: Christopher Lamond, Arthur D. Mason, Hon. Martin A. Russo, Barbara Sutton

ADI Ltd.
Issues: DEF
Rep By: Dennis M. Kedzior, Arthur D. Mason, Brig. Gen. Terry Paul, USMC (Ret.)

AdMeTech
Issues: BUD
Rep By: W. Campbell Kaufman, IV, Dennis M. Kedzior

Agassi Enterprises, Inc.
Issues: HCR
Rep By: Lawrence C. Grossman, Christopher Lamond

Air Products and Chemicals, Inc.
Issues: DEF ENG FUE
Rep By: Christy Carson Evans, Lawrence C. Grossman, Sean O'Shea

Alcon Laboratories
Issues: MED
Rep By: Jeffrey Lawrence, Blenda Pinto-Riddick

Alenia Aerospazig
Issues: AER TRD
Rep By: Laurie J. Adler, Dennis M. Kedzior, Jeffrey Lawrence, Michael Merola, Marnie Russ, Hon. Martin A. Russo

Alfred University
Issues: BUD
Rep By: Scott D. MacConomy, Daniel J. McNamara, Laura A. Neal, Diane Rinaldo

American Chamber of Commerce in Egypt
Issues: FOR
Rep By: Gregory M. Gill

American Film Institute
Issues: BUD
Rep By: Laura A. Neal, Valerie Rogers Osborne, Marnie Russ

American Lung Ass'n of Minnesota
Issues: ENV HCR
Rep By: Daniel J. McNamara, Michael Merola, Diane Rinaldo

American Superconductor Corp.
Issues: DEF
Rep By: Harry E. Barsh, Jr., Lawrence C. Grossman, Dennis M. Kedzior, Lindsay Lawrence, Brig. Gen. Terry Paul, USMC (Ret.), Blenda Pinto-Riddick

Arizona State University
Issues: AER
Rep By: Jeffrey Lawrence, Scott D. MacConomy, Diane Rinaldo

Arnold & Porter
Issues: BUD
Rep By: Dennis M. Kedzior, Arthur D. Mason, Brig. Gen. Terry Paul, USMC (Ret.)

Auspice, Inc.
Rep By: Jeffrey Lawrence

The Auxiliary Service Corporations
Issues: ECN EDU
Rep By: Carl Franklin Godfrey, Jr., Arthur D. Mason, Marnie Russ

Babyland Family Services, Inc.
Issues: BUD
Rep By: Laura A. Neal, Blenda Pinto-Riddick

Barry University
Issues: BUD
Rep By: Sonya C. Clay, Mary Kate Kelly-Johnson

Beacon Skanska U.S.A.

Bishop Museum
Issues: SCI
Rep By: Henry K. Giugni, Jeffrey Lawrence

The Boeing Co.
Issues: AER
Rep By: Shawn Edwards, Henry K. Giugni, Lawrence C. Grossman, Amos Hochstein, Jeffrey Lawrence, Arthur D. Mason, Brig. Gen. Terry Paul, USMC (Ret.), Marnie Russ, Dan C. Tate, Sr.

The BOSE Corp.
Issues: GOV TAX TRD
Rep By: Laurie J. Adler, Marie James, Walter Raheb, Stephen Whitaker

Boston College
Issues: BUD
Rep By: Gerald S. J. Cassidy, James P. Fabiani, Lawrence C. Grossman, Christopher Lamond, Christine A. O'Connor, Hon. Martin A. Russo, Barbara Sutton

Boston University
Issues: BUD
Rep By: Gerald S. J. Cassidy, Henry K. Giugni, Carl Franklin Godfrey, Jr., Lawrence C. Grossman, Dennis M. Kedzior, Jeffrey Lawrence

California Hospital Medical Center Foundation
Issues: BUD
Rep By: Laura A. Neal, Valerie Rogers Osborne, Blenda Pinto-Riddick

California Institute for the Arts
Issues: BUD
Rep By: Blenda Pinto-Riddick, Barbara Sutton, Gerald Felix Warburg

California Museum Foundation
Issues: BUD
Rep By: Jeffrey Lawrence, Valerie Rogers Osborne

Carondelet Health System
Issues: BUD
Rep By: Marie James, Mary E. Shields, Lyllett Wentworth

Central College
Issues: SCI
Rep By: Daniel J. McNamara, Michael Merola, Gabor J. Rozsa, Marnie Russ

Central Piedmont Community College
Issues: BUD
Rep By: Laura A. Neal, Marnie Russ

Chlorine Chemistry Council
Issues: AGR
Rep By: Jeffrey Lawrence, Arthur D. Mason, Dan C. Tate, Sr.

City College of San Francisco
Issues: BUD
Rep By: Maureen Walsh, Gerald Felix Warburg

City of Hope Nat'l Medical Center
Issues: BUD
Rep By: Barbara Sutton, Maureen Walsh

CMS Defense Systems, Inc.
Issues: BUD DEF
Rep By: Shawn Edwards, Lawrence C. Grossman, Brig. Gen. Terry Paul, USMC (Ret.)

CNF Transportation, Inc.
Issues: POS
Rep By: Christy Carson Evans, Christopher Lamond, Arthur D. Mason

Columbia University
Issues: BUD
Rep By: Carl Franklin Godfrey, Jr., Dennis M. Kedzior, Jeffrey Lawrence, Valerie Rogers Osborne, Hon. Martin A. Russo

Community Bank League of New England

Community General Hospital of Sullivan County
Issues: HCR MED
Rep By: Marie James, Maureen Walsh

Community Health Partners of Ohio
Issues: ECN HCR
Rep By: Marie James, Christopher Lamond, Daniel J. McNamara, Hon. Martin A. Russo, Lyllett Wentworth

Community Hospital Telehealth Consortium
Issues: BUD HCR
Rep By: W. Campbell Kaufman, IV, Diane Rinaldo, Marnie Russ, Maureen Walsh

Condell Medical Center
Issues: HCR
Rep By: Carl Franklin Godfrey, Jr., Valerie Rogers Osborne, Marnie Russ

The Core Center
Issues: BUD
Rep By: Valerie Rogers Osborne, Marnie Russ, Hon. Martin A. Russo

Council on Superconductivity for American Competitiveness
Issues: ENG
Rep By: Lawrence C. Grossman, Christopher Lamond

Crane & Co.
Issues: MON
Rep By: Douglass E. Bobbitt, Gregory M. Gill, Dennis M. Kedzior, Christopher Lamond, Hon. Martin A. Russo

CVS, Inc.

D'Youville College
Issues: BUD
Rep By: Douglass E. Bobbitt, Arthur D. Mason, Maureen Walsh

Dakota Wesleyan University
Rep By: Dennis M. Kedzior

Dimensions Healthcare System
Issues: BUD HCR
Rep By: Gregory M. Gill, W. Campbell Kaufman, IV

Dominican College of Blauvelt
Issues: BUD
Rep By: Christine A. O'Connor, Diane Rinaldo, Mary E. Shields

Draft Worldwide
Issues: POS
Rep By: Gregory M. Gill, Michele Gioffre, Jeffrey Lawrence, Valerie Rogers Osborne, Hon. Martin A. Russo

DRAKA USA Corp.
Issues: MAR
Rep By: Carl Franklin Godfrey, Jr., Daniel J. McNamara

E Lottery
Issues: GAM
Rep By: Gerald S. J. Cassidy, Arthur D. Mason, Hon. Martin A. Russo, Dan C. Tate, Sr.

eCharge Corp.
Issues: FIN TEC
Rep By: Christy Carson Evans, W. Campbell Kaufman, IV, Maureen Walsh

Edward Health Services
Issues: BUD
Rep By: Christy Carson Evans, Christopher Lamond, Barbara Sutton, Lyllett Wentworth

El Segundo, California, City of
Issues: TRA
Rep By: Sonya C. Clay, John S. Doyle, Jr., Valerie Rogers Osborne

Electro Energy, Inc.
Issues: DEF ENG
Rep By: Lawrence C. Grossman

Elmira College
Issues: BUD
Rep By: Lindsay Lawrence, Arthur D. Mason, Louie Perry

Fairfield University
Issues: BUD
Rep By: Carl Franklin Godfrey, Jr., Laura A. Neal, Hon. Martin A. Russo

Fairview Hospital and Healthcare Services
Issues: BUD
Rep By: Dennis M. Kedzior, Sean O'Shea, Barbara Sutton, Maureen Walsh

FedEx Corp.
Rep By: Marie James, Walter Raheb, Stephen Whitaker

Henry Ford Health System
Issues: BUD
Rep By: Henry K. Giugni, Hon. Martin A. Russo, Mary E. Shields

Forum Health
Issues: BUD
Rep By: Douglass E. Bobbitt, Daniel J. McNamara, Maureen Walsh

Gabon, Nat'l Assembly of
Rep By: Gregory M. Gill

Gabonese Republic, Office of the President of the
Rep By: Gregory M. Gill, Carl Franklin Godfrey, Jr.

General Dynamics Corp.
Issues: AER BUD DEF
Rep By: Shawn Edwards, Lawrence C. Grossman, Arthur D. Mason, Hon. Martin A. Russo, Dan C. Tate, Sr.

Hampshire College
Issues: ECN EDU
Rep By: Gerald Felix Warburg

Hampton University
Issues: DEF ECN EDU SCI
Rep By: Gregory M. Gill, Carl Franklin Godfrey, Jr., Judith M. Jacobson

Hawaii, State of
Issues: EDU LBR TAX
Rep By: Gregory M. Gill, Henry K. Giugni, Maureen Walsh

Hospital for Special Surgery
Issues: HCR MED SCI
Rep By: Gregory M. Gill, Marie James, Christopher Lamond, Mary E. Shields

Hunterdon Medical Center

HWT Inc.

Idaho State University
Issues: BUD
Rep By: Lawrence C. Grossman, W. Campbell Kaufman, IV, Laura A. Neal, Marnie Russ

Immaculata College
Rep By: Douglass E. Bobbitt, Laura A. Neal, Mary E. Shields, Maureen Walsh

Institute for Student Achievement
Issues: BUD
Rep By: Dennis M. Kedzior, Hon. Martin A. Russo, Mary E. Shields, Dan C. Tate, Sr.

Internat'l Snowmobile Manufacturers Ass'n
Issues: NAT
Rep By: Douglass E. Bobbitt, Christy Carson Evans, Carl Franklin Godfrey, Jr., W. Campbell Kaufman, IV, Daniel J. McNamara, Michael Merola, Diane Rinaldo

Jewish Family Service Ass'n of Cleveland
Issues: BUD
Rep By: Laurie J. Adler, Sonya C. Clay, Christopher Lamond, Arthur D. Mason, Diane Rinaldo

Kraft Foods, Inc.

Kuakini Hospital
Rep By: Henry K. Giugni

Lake Charles Memorial Hospital
Issues: BUD
Rep By: W. Campbell Kaufman, IV

Lewis and Clark College
Issues: BUD ECN
Rep By: Arthur D. Mason, Maureen Walsh, Gerald Felix Warburg

Liberty Science Center
Issues: BUD SCI
Rep By: Laurie J. Adler, W. Campbell Kaufman, IV, Jeffrey Lawrence, Daniel J. McNamara, Michael Merola

Lifebridge Health
Issues: BUD
Rep By: Gregory M. Gill, Dennis M. Kedzior, Michael Merola, Lyllett Wentworth

Lockheed Martin Corp.
Issues: DEF
Rep By: Shawn Edwards, Lawrence C. Grossman, Brig. Gen. Terry Paul, USMC (Ret.)

Lockheed Martin IMS
Rep By: Arthur D. Mason, Dan C. Tate, Sr.

Lorain County Community College
Issues: ECN
Rep By: John A. Crumbliss, Daniel J. McNamara, Laura A. Neal, Christine A. O'Connor

M2 Technologies Inc.
Issues: DEF
Rep By: Shawn Edwards, Brig. Gen. Terry Paul, USMC (Ret.)

Maersk Inc.
Issues: DEF TAX
Rep By: John S. Doyle, Jr., Carl Franklin Godfrey, Jr., Maj. Gen. Edmund P. Looney, Jr. USMC (Ret.), Michael Merola, Hon. Fred B. Rooney, Gabor J. Rozsa, Hon. Martin A. Russo

Major League Baseball
Issues: LBR TAX
Rep By: Michele Gioffre, Christopher Lamond, Arthur D. Mason, Hon. Martin A. Russo, Dan C. Tate, Sr.

Marietta College
Issues: BUD
Rep By: Laura A. Neal

Marymount University
Issues: BUD
Rep By: Valerie Rogers Osborne, Mary E. Shields, Maureen Walsh

Massachusetts Soc. of Certified Public Accountants

Matthews Media Group, Inc.
Issues: HCR
Rep By: Dennis M. Kedzior

MedWerks.com

Memorial Health System
Issues: HCR
Rep By: Arthur D. Mason, Laura A. Neal, Diane Rinaldo

Memorial Hermann Health Care System
Issues: BUD
Rep By: Christy Carson Evans, W. Campbell Kaufman, IV, Louie Perry, Blenda Pinto-Riddick

Miami-Dade Community College
Issues: EDU LAW
Rep By: Gregory M. Gill, Laura A. Neal

Montefiore Medical Center
Issues: HCR
Rep By: Gregory M. Gill, Lindsay Lawrence, Valerie Rogers Osborne

Museum of Discovery and Science
Issues: BUD NAT
Rep By: Arthur D. Mason, Laura A. Neal, Gabor J. Rozsa

Nat'l Jewish Medical and Research Center
Issues: BUD
Rep By: Laura A. Neal, Sean O'Shea, Valerie Rogers Osborne

Nat'l SAFE KIDS Campaign
Issues: BUD
Rep By: Valerie Rogers Osborne, Mary E. Shields, Maureen Walsh

The Nature Conservancy
Rep By: Henry K. Giugni

Neumann College
Issues: BUD
Rep By: Michael Merola, Mary E. Shields, Lyllett Wentworth

New Jersey Institute of Technology
Issues: AVI DEF ENV TRA
Rep By: John A. Crumbliss, Gregory M. Gill, Christopher Lamond, Michael Merola, Brig. Gen. Terry Paul, USMC (Ret.), Blenda Pinto-Riddick, Gabor J. Rozsa

North American Datacom
Issues: TEC
Rep By: W. Campbell Kaufman, IV, Christopher Lamond

North Shore Long Island Jewish Health System
Issues: BUD
Rep By: Arthur D. Mason, Christine A. O'Connor, Diane Rinaldo, Hon. Martin A. Russo

Northern Essex Community College Foundation
Issues: BUD
Rep By: Dennis M. Kedzior, Christopher Lamond, Jeffrey Lawrence

Northwestern University
Issues: BUD
Rep By: Michael Merola, Sean O'Shea, Hon. Martin A. Russo, Rachel Sotsky

Ocean Spray Cranberries
Issues: AGR CAW ENV NAT
Rep By: Gerald S. J. Cassidy, John S. Doyle, Jr., Christy Carson Evans, Carl Franklin Godfrey, Jr., Mary Kate Kelly-Johnson, Arthur D. Mason, Daniel J. McNamara, Sean O'Shea, Louie Perry, James Rowan, Gabor J. Rozsa

Ohio State University
Issues: BUD
Rep By: Christy Carson Evans, Dennis M. Kedzior, Arthur D. Mason, Diane Rinaldo, Mary E. Shields, Rachel Sotsky

Orange, California, County of
Rep By: Laurie J. Adler, Christy Carson Evans

Palmdale, California, City of
Issues: ROD TRA
Rep By: Daniel J. McNamara, Gabor J. Rozsa, Lyllett Wentworth

Partnership for Better Schools

Pfizer, Inc.

The PGA Tour, Inc.
Issues: TAX
Rep By: Dan C. Tate, Sr., Maureen Walsh

Philadelphia College of Osteopathic Medicine
Issues: BUD
Rep By: Douglass E. Bobbitt, Christopher Lamond

Philadelphia College of Textiles and Science
Issues: DEF SCI
Rep By: Douglass E. Bobbitt, Carl Franklin Godfrey, Jr., Hon. Fred B. Rooney

Philadelphia University
Issues: BUD
Rep By: Douglass E. Bobbitt, Christine A. O'Connor, Blenda Pinto-Riddick

Phoenix, Arizona, City of
Issues: CAW ECN NAT
Rep By: John A. Crumbliss, John S. Doyle, Jr., Christine A. O'Connor, Gabor J. Rozsa, Dan C. Tate, Sr.

Pierce College
Issues: BUD
Rep By: Douglass E. Bobbitt, Gregory M. Gill

Polytechnic University
Issues: BUD
Rep By: Amos Hochstein, Scott D. MacConomy, Lyllett Wentworth

Proctor Hospital
Issues: BUD
Rep By: Arthur D. Mason, Laura A. Neal, Diane Rinaldo

Proteus Co.
Issues: MAR WAS
Rep By: John S. Doyle, Jr.

Ramo Defense Systems, LLC
Issues: DEF
Rep By: Shawn Edwards, Christopher Lamond, Brig. Gen. Terry Paul, USMC (Ret.)

Research Foundation of the City University of New York
Issues: BUD
Rep By: W. Campbell Kaufman, IV, Christopher Lamond, Michael Merola, Barbara Sutton

Rhode Island School of Design
Issues: BUD
Rep By: John A. Crumbliss, Christopher Lamond, Jeffrey Lawrence, Barbara Sutton

Riverside Medical Center

Rochester Institute of Technology
Issues: BUD
Rep By: Shawn Edwards, Judith M. Jacobson, Dennis M. Kedzior, Jeffrey Lawrence, Scott D. MacConomy, Blenda Pinto-Riddick

Rush Presbyterian-St. Luke's Medical Center
Issues: BUD
Rep By: Sonya C. Clay, Michele Gioffre, Hon. Martin A. Russo, Barbara Sutton, Maureen Walsh

Sacramento Area Flood Control Agency
Issues: BUD DIS
Rep By: John A. Crumbliss, John S. Doyle, Jr., Christy Carson Evans, Gabor J. Rozsa, Hon. Martin A. Russo

Saint Coletta of Greater Washington, Inc.
Issues: BUD
Rep By: Dennis M. Kedzior, Mary E. Shields, Rachel Sotsky

Saint Joseph's Health Center Foundation, Inc.
Issues: BUD
Rep By: Arthur D. Mason, Laura A. Neal

San Diego, University of
Rep By: Carl Franklin Godfrey, Jr., Valerie Rogers Osborne, Maureen Walsh, Gerald Felix Warburg

Santa Rosa Memorial Hospital
Issues: BUD DIS ECN HCR TEC
Rep By: Marie James, Valerie Rogers Osborne, Maureen Walsh, Gerald Felix Warburg

Saudi Arabia, Royal Embassy of
Rep By: Gerald S. J. Cassidy, Lawrence C. Grossman, Arthur D. Mason, Dan C. Tate, Sr., Gerald Felix Warburg

Securities Industry Ass'n

Sepracor, Inc.

Sherwin Williams Co.
Issues: CSP HCR
Rep By: Mary Kate Kelly-Johnson, Arthur D. Mason, Blenda Pinto-Riddick, Hon. Martin A. Russo, Dan C. Tate, Sr., Gerald Felix Warburg

Smartforce
Issues: BUD
Rep By: John A. Crumbliss, Shawn Edwards, Amos Hochstein, W. Campbell Kaufman, IV, Maureen Walsh

Southeastern Pennsylvania Consortium for Higher Education
Issues: BUD
Rep By: Michael Merola, Hon. Fred B. Rooney, Mary E. Shields

Subaru of America
Issues: CAW TRD
Rep By: Douglass E. Bobbitt, Christy Carson Evans, Arthur D. Mason, Michael Merola, Dan C. Tate, Sr.

Summit Technology
Issues: MED
Rep By: Jeffrey Lawrence, Laura A. Neal, Barbara Sutton

SWATH Ocean Systems, Inc.
Issues: DEF
Rep By: Shawn Edwards, Brig. Gen. Terry Paul, USMC (Ret.), Rear Admiral G. Dennis Vaughan, (Ret.)

Taiwan Research Institute
Rep By: James Rowan, Hon. Martin A. Russo, Gerald Felix Warburg

Taiwan Studies Institute
Issues: DEF FOR TRD
Rep By: Gerald S. J. Cassidy, Amos Hochstein, Hon. Martin A. Russo, Maureen Walsh, Gerald Felix Warburg, Stephen Whitaker

Texas Tech University System
Issues: BUD
Rep By: Carl Franklin Godfrey, Jr., Dennis M. Kedzior, Jeffrey Lawrence, Daniel J. McNamara, Valerie Rogers Osborne, Blenda Pinto-Riddick

Tiffany & Co.
Issues: CSP TRD
Rep By: Douglass E. Bobbitt, Christy Carson Evans, Gregory M. Gill, Lindsay Lawrence, Stephen Whitaker

Tougaloo College
Rep By: Gregory M. Gill

Trinity Health
Issues: BUD
Rep By: W. Campbell Kaufman, IV, Blenda Pinto-Riddick

Tufts University School of Veterinary Medicine
Rep By: Carl Franklin Godfrey, Jr.

Ultracard, Inc.
Issues: DEF
Rep By: John A. Crumbliss, Brig. Gen. Terry Paul, USMC (Ret.)

United Service Organization
Issues: BUD DEF
Rep By: Shawn Edwards, Lawrence C. Grossman, Dennis M. Kedzior, Arthur D. Mason, Brig. Gen. Terry Paul, USMC (Ret.), Hon. Martin A. Russo, Dan C. Tate, Sr.

United Space Alliance
Issues: AER
Rep By: Laurie J. Adler, Jeffrey Lawrence, Arthur D. Mason, Brig. Gen. Terry Paul, USMC (Ret.), Marnie Russ, Hon. Martin A. Russo

University Medical Center of Southern Nevada
Issues: HCR
Rep By: Lawrence C. Grossman, Christopher Lamond

University of Dubuque
Issues: BUD
Rep By: Douglass E. Bobbitt, Carl Franklin Godfrey, Jr., Laura A. Neal

University of Hawaii
Issues: BUD
Rep By: Shawn Edwards, Jeffrey Lawrence

University of Massachusetts Memorial Health System
Issues: BUD
Rep By: Marie James, Mary Kate Kelly-Johnson, Sean O'Shea, Hon. Martin A. Russo, Barbara Sutton

University of Nevada - Las Vegas
Issues: BUD
Rep By: Lawrence C. Grossman, Christopher Lamond

University of Pittsburgh Medical Center (UPMC)
Issues: BUD
Rep By: Michael Merola, Valerie Rogers Osborne, Maureen Walsh

University of Puerto Rico
Issues: BUD
Rep By: Carl Franklin Godfrey, Jr., Dennis M. Kedzior, Blenda Pinto-Riddick

University of San Diego
Issues: BUD
Rep By: Valerie Rogers Osborne, Gerald Felix Warburg

University of San Francisco
Issues: BUD
Rep By: Blenda Pinto-Riddick, Mary E. Shields, Gerald Felix Warburg

Valley Hospital Foundation
Issues: BUD
Rep By: John A. Crumbliss, W. Campbell Kaufman, IV, Dennis M. Kedzior, Michael Merola

Variable Annuity Life Insurance Co.

Villanova University
Rep By: Gerald S. J. Cassidy, Shawn Edwards, Daniel J. McNamara, Blenda Pinto-Riddick

VoiceStream Wireless Corp.
Issues: TEC TRD
Rep By: John A. Crumbliss, Christy Carson Evans, Lawrence C. Grossman, W. Campbell Kaufman, IV, Mary Kate Kelly-Johnson, Arthur D. Mason, Michael Merola, Hon. Martin A. Russo, Dan C. Tate, Sr.

Vollmer Public Relations
Rep By: W. Campbell Kaufman, IV

Westminster College
Rep By: Carl Franklin Godfrey, Jr.

Wheelchairs for the World Foundation
Rep By: Douglass E. Bobbitt, Carl Franklin Godfrey, Jr., Amos Hochstein

Widener University
Issues: BUD
Rep By: Douglass E. Bobbitt, Christy Carson Evans, Maureen Walsh

Carol Cataldo & Associates

1725 Duke St.
Suite 600
Alexandria, VA 22314-3457
E-mail: cataldo2@ix.netcom.com
Tel: (703)549-0124
Fax: (703)299-9115

DC-Area Employees Representing Listed Clients
CATALDO, Carol, President

Clients

Commission of Accredited Truck Driving Schools (CATDS)
Issues: EDU GOV
Rep By: Carol Cataldo

Cavarocchi Ruscio Dennis Associates

317 Massachusetts Ave. NE
Suite 200
Washington, DC 20002
Tel: (202)546-4732
Fax: (202)546-1257
Registered: LDA

A government and public relations firm.

DC-Area Employees Representing Listed Clients
BARTHELD, Elizabeth
CAVAROCCHI, Nicholas G., Senior Partner
DENNIS, Lyle B., Partner
RUSCIO, Domenic R., Senior Partner

Clients

Alzheimer's Ass'n
Issues: BUD HCR SCI
Rep By: Domenic R. Ruscio

American Ass'n for Dental Research
Issues: BUD HCR MED SCI
Rep By: Nicholas G. Cavarocchi

American Ass'n for the Study of Liver Diseases
Issues: BUD HCR MED MMM SCI
Rep By: Lyle B. Dennis

American Ass'n of Public Health Dentistry
Issues: HCR
Rep By: Nicholas G. Cavarocchi

American Indian Higher Education Consortium
Issues: BUD EDU HCR IND MED
Rep By: Nicholas G. Cavarocchi, Domenic R. Ruscio

American Soc. of General Surgeons
Issues: HCR MMM
Rep By: Nicholas G. Cavarocchi, Domenic R. Ruscio

American Soc. of Pediatric Nephrology
Issues: BUD HCR MMM
Rep By: Nicholas G. Cavarocchi, Domenic R. Ruscio

Ass'n of University Programs in Health Administration
Issues: BUD
Rep By: Lyle B. Dennis

Boys Town Nat'l Research Hospital
Issues: BUD HCR SCI
Rep By: Nicholas G. Cavarocchi, Domenic R. Ruscio

Cooley's Anemia Foundation
Issues: BUD HCR MED MMM SCI
Rep By: Lyle B. Dennis

Council of Colleges of Acupuncture and Oriental Medicine
Issues: EDU HCR
Rep By: Lyle B. Dennis

Delta Dental Plans Ass'n
Issues: HCR INS TAX
Rep By: Nicholas G. Cavarocchi, Domenic R. Ruscio

The Genome Action Coalition
Issues: BUD HCR MED SCI
Rep By: Lyle B. Dennis

The Jeffrey Modell Foundation
Issues: BUD HCR MED SCI
Rep By: Lyle B. Dennis

Nat'l Coalition for Osteoporosis and Related Bone Diseases
Issues: BUD HCR SCI
Rep By: Nicholas G. Cavarocchi

Rutgers University
Issues: BUD EDU
Rep By: Lyle B. Dennis

Soc. for Women's Health Research
Issues: BUD HCR MED
Rep By: Elizabeth Bartheld, Lyle B. Dennis

Software Productivity Consortium
Issues: BUD CPI
Rep By: Nicholas G. Cavarocchi, Domenic R. Ruscio

Ann Cecchetti

10420 Green Acres Dr.
Silver Spring, MD 20903
E-mail: acecchetti@aol.com
Tel: (301)434-2002
Fax: (301)434-2002

Clients

Battelle
Issues: BUD
Rep By: Ann Cecchetti

Century Communications, Inc.

2816 S. Joyce St.
Arlington, VA 22202
Tel: (703)684-7228
Fax: (703)684-2981
Registered: LDA
E-mail: geod@erols.com

Provides management consulting and government representation services to business firms, non-profit, and government organizations. Emphasis is on food and agriculture, natural resources, international trade and logistics, environmental engineering, and public policy affecting these areas.

DC-Area Employees Representing Listed Clients
DUNLOP, George S., V. President

Clients

Citizens Network for Foreign Affairs (CNFA)
Issues: AGR FOR
Rep By: George S. Dunlop

CGR Associates, Inc.

733 15th St. NW
Suite 912
Washington, DC 20005
Tel: (202)393-0683
Fax: (202)393-0922
Registered: LDA

DC-Area Employees Representing Listed Clients
FRANKOVICH, Kevin, Principal

Clients

Ass'n of Air Medical Services
Issues: MMM TAX
Rep By: Kevin Frankovich

Fringe Benefit Group, Inc
Rep By: Kevin Frankovich

Chadbourne and Parke LLP

1200 New Hampshire Ave. NW
Washington, DC 20036
Tel: (202)974-5600
Fax: (202)974-5602
Registered: LDA, FARA
Web: www.chadbourne.com
Washington office of a New York law firm.

DC-Area Employees Representing Listed Clients
BELDEN, Roy S.
HANSEN, Kenneth, Partner
HARGIS, Lynn, Counsel
HOHENTHANER, Thomas, Associate
MARTIN, Keith, Partner

Clients

The AES Corp.
Rep By: Keith Martin

Cogentrix, Inc.
Rep By: Keith Martin

Electric Power Supply Ass'n
Rep By: Keith Martin

Independent Power Tax Group
Issues: TAX
Rep By: Keith Martin

Magellan Carbon Fuels
Rep By: Keith Martin

Panda Energy Internat'l
Issues: TRD
Rep By: Keith Martin

The Purdue Frederick Co.
Rep By: Keith Martin

Ruan Leasing Co.
Issues: TRU
Rep By: Keith Martin

Sithe Energies
Rep By: Keith Martin

Chambers Associates Inc.

805 15th St. NW
Suite 500
Washington, DC 20005
Tel: (202)371-9770
Fax: (202)371-6601
Registered: LDA
Public policy consultants specializing in tax, budget and authorizing committee issues before the government. In addition, the firm provides litigation support for claims estimation in mass torts.

DC-Area Employees Representing Listed Clients
CHAMBERS, Letitia, President
DENTON, Janet A., Senior V. President
FARRELL, Richard, Senior V. President
HECKLER, Hon. Margaret, Senior Advisor
LYMAN, Mary S., Project Manager, Tax Counsel
POWERS, Tara, Management Associate
SIGNER, William A., Senior V. President
TIBBALS, Troy, Legislative Assistant

Clients

Alarm Industry Communications Committee
Issues: TEC
Rep By: William A. Signer

American Arts Alliance
Issues: ART BUD CPT GOV TAX TEC
Rep By: Letitia Chambers, Janet A. Denton, Troy Tibbals

APG, Inc.
Rep By: William A. Signer

Castaic Lakewater Agency
Rep By: Letitia Chambers

Coalition of Publicly Traded Partnerships
Issues: TAX
Rep By: Letitia Chambers, Mary S. Lyman

Council of Infrastructure Financing Authorities
Issues: ENV FIN GOV TAX
Rep By: Tara Powers

Covanta Energy Corporation

Crown American Properties
Rep By: Letitia Chambers

Cummins Engine Co.

Defenders of Wildlife
Rep By: Letitia Chambers

Francotyp-Postalia
Rep By: Letitia Chambers

Greater New York Hospital Ass'n
Issues: MMM TAX
Rep By: William A. Signer

High River Limited Partnership
Rep By: Letitia Chambers

Inmarsat
Issues: TEC

Izopoli

Marriott Internat'l, Inc.
Issues: BUD LBR TAX
Rep By: William A. Signer

Micros, Inc.
Rep By: William A. Signer

Nat'l Ass'n of Convenience Stores
Issues: TOB
Rep By: William A. Signer

Nat'l Committee to Preserve Social Security and Medicare

Nat'l Congress of American Indians
Rep By: Letitia Chambers

Nat'l Employment Opportunities Network
Issues: BUD LBR TAX
Rep By: William A. Signer

Nat'l Healthy Start Ass'n
Issues: BUD
Rep By: Janet A. Denton, William A. Signer

New York Presbyterian Hospital - Cornell Medical Center
Rep By: William A. Signer

Norfolk, Virginia, City of
Issues: BUD ECN EDU ENV HOU LAW ROD RRR SMB TAX TRA WEL
Rep By: Janet A. Denton

NUI Environmental Group Inc.
Issues: BUD ENV
Rep By: Letitia Chambers

Nuvotec

Pennsylvania Pharmaceutical Ass'n

PriceWaterhouseCoopers
Rep By: Letitia Chambers

Provident Communications, Inc.
Rep By: Letitia Chambers

Shea & Gardner
Rep By: Letitia Chambers, Mary S. Lyman

Sullivan & Cromwell
Rep By: Letitia Chambers

TMC, Inc.
Rep By: William A. Signer

U.S.-Turkmenistan Business Council

Chambers, Conlon & Hartwell

122 C St. NW
Suite 850
Washington, DC 20001
Tel: (202)638-7790
Fax: (202)638-1045
Registered: LDA
Web: www.cchinc.com
A government relations consulting firm.

DC-Area Employees Representing Listed Clients
CHAMBERS, Ray B., Chairman
CONLON, Jerome, Senior Partner
HARTWELL, Keith O., President
NORDEN, Don, Partner and Counsel
NORDSTROM, Adam, Legislative Assistant
ROOTS, John, Partner

Clients

Advanced Power Technologies, Inc.
Issues: DEF
Rep By: John Roots

Alaska Railroad
Issues: RRR
Rep By: Don Norden

American Short Line and Regional Railroad Ass'n
Issues: RRR TRA
Rep By: Ray B. Chambers, Keith O. Hartwell, Don Norden, Adam Nordstrom

Canadian Nat'l Railway Co.
Issues: RRR
Rep By: Keith O. Hartwell

Delaware Otsego System
Issues: RRR TRA
Rep By: Ray B. Chambers

Florida East Coast Industries Inc.
Issues: TRA
Rep By: Ray B. Chambers, Jerome Conlon, Don Norden, John Roots

Investment Counsel Ass'n of America
Issues: FIN GOV
Rep By: Don Norden

Juneau, Alaska, City of
Issues: BUD GOV
Rep By: John Roots

Michigan State Department of Transportation
Issues: GOV
Rep By: Don Norden

Nat'l Railroad and Construction Maintenance Ass'n
Issues: RRR TRA
Rep By: Ray B. Chambers, Keith O. Hartwell, Don Norden

New York Metropolitan Transportation Authority
Issues: TRA
Rep By: Don Norden

Norfolk Southern Corp.
Issues: RRR
Rep By: Ray B. Chambers, Jerome Conlon, Keith O. Hartwell, Don Norden

Rail Supply and Service Coalition
Issues: RRR TRA
Rep By: Keith O. Hartwell, Don Norden

Carolyn C. Chaney & Associates

1401 K St. NW
Suite 700
Washington, DC 20005
Tel: (202)842-4930
Fax: (202)842-5051
Registered: LDA
Web: www.capitaledge.com
E-mail: chaney@capitaledge.com

DC-Area Employees Representing Listed Clients
CHANEY, Carolyn C., President
GIGLIO, Christopher F., V. President

Clients

Beaumont, Texas, City of
Issues: HOU LAW TRA URB
Rep By: Carolyn C. Chaney, Christopher F. Giglio

Farmers Branch, Texas, City of
Issues: TRA URB
Rep By: Carolyn C. Chaney, Christopher F. Giglio

Lincoln, Nebraska, City of
Issues: ENV HOU TAX TRA URB
Rep By: Carolyn C. Chaney, Christopher F. Giglio

Pasadena, California, City of
Issues: HOU LAW TAX TRA URB
Rep By: Carolyn C. Chaney, Christopher F. Giglio

Reno, Nevada, City of
Issues: URB
Rep By: Carolyn C. Chaney, Christopher F. Giglio

Santa Cruz County Regional Transportation Commission
Issues: TRA
Rep By: Carolyn C. Chaney, Christopher F. Giglio

Santa Cruz Metropolitan Transit District
Issues: TRA
Rep By: Carolyn C. Chaney, Christopher F. Giglio

Santa Cruz Redevelopment Agency
Issues: URB
Rep By: Carolyn C. Chaney, Christopher F. Giglio

Santa Cruz, California, County of
Issues: DIS
Rep By: Carolyn C. Chaney, Christopher F. Giglio

Scottsdale, Arizona, City of
Issues: COM LAW RES SCI TAX TRA URB
Rep By: Carolyn C. Chaney, Christopher F. Giglio

N. Chapman Associates

1723 U St. NW
Washington, DC 20009
Tel: (202)659-1858
Fax: (202)387-5553
Registered: LDA

DC-Area Employees Representing Listed Clients
CHAPMAN, Nancy, President

Clients

Apple Processors Ass'n
Rep By: Nancy Chapman

Mycogen Corp.
Rep By: Nancy Chapman

Michael Chase Associates, LTD

601 Madison St.
Suite 200
Alexandria, VA 22314
Tel: (703)765-4147
Fax: (703)765-4148
Registered: LDA

DC-Area Employees Representing Listed Clients
CHASE, Michael T., President

Clients

Allison Transmission Division, General Motors Corp.
Issues: DEF
Rep By: Michael T. Chase

American Systems Internat'l Corp.
Issues: DEF
Rep By: Michael T. Chase

Carwell Products, Inc.
Issues: DEF
Rep By: Michael T. Chase

Stewart & Stevenson Services, Inc.
Issues: DEF
Rep By: Michael T. Chase

J. Cherian Consultants, Inc.

1030 15th St. NW
Washington, DC 20005-1503
Tel: (202)842-1030
Fax: (202)842-1225
Web: www.jccinc.org
E-mail: jcci@erols.com

An international government relations firm specializing in international trade in services with a focus on corporate activities of insurance companies abroad. Represents major U.S. insurers and their trade associations.

DC-Area Employees Representing Listed Clients
CHERIAN, Ph.D., Joy, President

Chernikoff and Co.

1320 18th St. NW
Suite 100
Washington, DC 20036
Tel: (202)223-9280
Fax: (202)223-6608
Registered: LDA

A lobbying and consulting firm.

DC-Area Employees Representing Listed Clients
CHERNIKOFF, Larry B., President

Clients

American Architectural Foundation
Issues: ART
Rep By: Larry B. Chernikoff

Arena Stage
Issues: ART
Rep By: Larry B. Chernikoff

The Choral Arts Soc. of Washington
Issues: ART
Rep By: Larry B. Chernikoff

The Corcoran Gallery of Art
Issues: ART
Rep By: Larry B. Chernikoff

Federal City Council
Issues: DOC
Rep By: Larry B. Chernikoff

Folger Shakespeare Library
Issues: ART
Rep By: Larry B. Chernikoff

Ford's Theatre
Issues: ART
Rep By: Larry B. Chernikoff

Independent Television Service
Issues: COM
Rep By: Larry B. Chernikoff

Meridian Internat'l Center
Issues: ART
Rep By: Larry B. Chernikoff

Thelonius Monk Institute of Jazz
Issues: ART
Rep By: Larry B. Chernikoff

Nat'l Building Museum
Issues: ART
Rep By: Larry B. Chernikoff

Nat'l Museum of Women in the Arts
Issues: ART
Rep By: Larry B. Chernikoff

The Phillips Collection
Issues: ART
Rep By: Larry B. Chernikoff

The Shakespeare Theatre
Issues: ART
Rep By: Larry B. Chernikoff

The Textile Museum
Issues: ART
Rep By: Larry B. Chernikoff

The Washington Ballet
Issues: ART
Rep By: Larry B. Chernikoff

The Washington Opera
Issues: ART
Rep By: Larry B. Chernikoff

Washington Performing Arts Society
Issues: ART
Rep By: Larry B. Chernikoff

Chesapeake Enterprises, Inc.

1800 K St. NW
Suite 1122
Washington, DC 20006
Tel: (202)463-9677
Fax: (202)463-9680
Registered: LDA, FARA

DC-Area Employees Representing Listed Clients
FLUHARTY, J. John, V. President
REED, Scott W., President

Clients

Diamond Games
Rep By: J. John Fluharty

GTECH Corp.
Issues: GAM
Rep By: Scott W. Reed

Internat'l Raw Materials
Issues: TRD
Rep By: J. John Fluharty

Ketchum
Issues: GOV
Rep By: J. John Fluharty, Scott W. Reed

Nat'l Airline Passenger Coalition
Issues: AVI
Rep By: Scott W. Reed

Paucatuck Eastern Pequot Tribal Nation
Issues: IND
Rep By: J. John Fluharty, Scott W. Reed

Republican Leadership Coalition
Issues: INS
Rep By: Scott W. Reed

SBC Communications Inc.
Rep By: Scott W. Reed

Shakopee Business Council
Rep By: Scott W. Reed

Shakopee Mdewakanton Sioux Tribe
Issues: GOV IND TAX
Rep By: J. John Fluharty

Sun Healthcare Group, Inc.
Issues: HCR
Rep By: Scott W. Reed

Tiger Fund
Issues: CDT
Rep By: J. John Fluharty

Chlopak, Leonard, Schechter and Associates

1850 M St. NW
Suite 550
Washington, DC 20036
Tel: (202)289-5900
Fax: (202)289-4141
Registered: LDA, FARA
Web: www.clsdc.com
E-mail: info@clsdc.com

DC-Area Employees Representing Listed Clients
CHLOPAK, Robert A., President
FASS, Heather
GAGLIARDI, Tiffany
GONZALEZ-NOGUERA, Maria Christina, Senior Associate
HAEFELI, Jennifer A., Senior Associate
HALL, Stephanie, Managing Associate
LEONARD, Charles G., Partner
ROWE, James H., Partner and General Counsel
SCHECHTER, Peter, Partner
SULLIVAN, Kelly, Managing Director

Clients

Assicurazioni Generali, S.p.A.

Cruz Enverga & Raboca
Rep By: Peter Schechter

GE Capital Mortgage Insurance Co. (GEMICO)
Rep By: Charles G. Leonard

General Electric Appliances
Rep By: Charles G. Leonard

General Electric Capital Mortgage Corp.
Issues: HOU
Rep By: Charles G. Leonard

General Electric Co.
Rep By: Charles G. Leonard

Hoechst Marion Roussel Deutschland GmbH
Rep By: Peter Schechter, Kelly Sullivan

Hyundai Electronics Industries Co., LTD
Issues: TRD
Rep By: Tiffany Gagliardi, Maria Christina Gonzalez-Noguera, Charles G. Leonard, Peter Schechter

Intuit, Inc.
Rep By: Robert A. Chlopak

Mexico, Office of the President of
Rep By: Charles G. Leonard

PromPeru
Rep By: Peter Schechter

University Science Alliance
Rep By: Robert A. Chlopak

Wilkie Farr & Gallagher
Issues: TRD
Rep By: Tiffany Gagliardi, Maria Christina Gonzalez-Noguera, Charles G. Leonard, Peter Schechter

World Health Organization
Rep By: Peter Schechter, Kelly Sullivan

Ernest S. Christian

800 Connecticut Ave. NW
Suite 705
Washington, DC 20006-2717
Tel: (202)898-2090
Fax: (202)898-2086

A solo lobbyist.

DC-Area Employees Representing Listed Clients
CHRISTIAN, Ernest S.

Clients

Cost Recovery Action Group

Chwat and Company, Inc.

635 Slaters Lane
Suite 140
Alexandria, VA 22314
Tel: (703)684-7703
Fax: (703)684-7594
Registered: LDA, FARA
Web: www.chwatco.com
E-mail: John.Chwat@chwatco.com

A government relations firm providing federal and state government relations, as well as grassroots, grasstops, and coalition building. Clients include corporations, trade associations, professional organizations, small businesses, non-profit and cultural arts organizatons, and individuals.

DC-Area Employees Representing Listed Clients
BIZUB, Scott, Director, Government Relations
CHWAT, John, President
RIKER, Derek, V. President, Government Relations

Clients

AccuWeather
Issues: SCI
Rep By: Scott Bizub, John Chwat, Derek Riker

American Friends of the Czech Republic
Issues: ART
Rep By: John Chwat, Derek Riker

American Radio Relay League
Issues: COM TEC
Rep By: John Chwat, Derek Riker

BCI, Inc.
Issues: SCI
Rep By: John Chwat, Derek Riker

Center for Regulatory Effectiveness
Issues: ENV GOV SCI
Rep By: John Chwat, Derek Riker

Federal Physicians Ass'n
Issues: GOV
Rep By: John Chwat, Derek Riker

Nat'l Ass'n of Assistant United States Attorneys
Issues: LAW
Rep By: Scott Bizub, John Chwat, Derek Riker

Newington-Cropsey Foundation
Issues: ART
Rep By: Scott Bizub, John Chwat, Derek Riker

Security Industry Ass'n
Issues: LAW
Rep By: Scott Bizub, John Chwat, Derek Riker

Citizen Strategies

1100 New York Ave. NW
Suite 750
West Tower
Washington, DC 20005
Tel: (202)223-2555
Registered: LDA

DC-Area Employees Representing Listed Clients
KEATING, David L., President

Clients

Nat'l Taxpayers Union
Issues: BUD ENV GOV INS TAX
Rep By: David L. Keating

Civic Service, Inc.

1050 Connecticut Ave. NW
Suite 870
Washington, DC 20036
Tel: (202)783-9150
Fax: (202)783-9150
Registered: LDA

A public affairs consulting firm headquartered in St. Louis, MO.

DC-Area Employees Representing Listed Clients
PFAUTCH, Roy, President
SCHICK, Michael W., Senior Associate

Clients

American Ass'n of Clinical Endocrinologists
Issues: HCR
Rep By: Roy Pfautch, Michael W. Schick

IPR Shandwick
Issues: FOR TEC TRD
Rep By: Roy Pfautch, Michael W. Schick

Japan Federation of Construction Contractors, Inc.
Issues: TRD
Rep By: Roy Pfautch, Michael W. Schick

Nippon Telegraph and Telephone Corp.
Issues: TEC
Rep By: Roy Pfautch, Michael W. Schick

The Sanwa Bank , Ltd.
Issues: BAN
Rep By: Roy Pfautch, Michael W. Schick

CLARION Management Resources, Inc.

515 King St.
Suite 420
Alexandria, VA 22314-3103
Web: www.clarionmr.com
E-mail: crogin@clarionmr.com
Tel: (703)684-5570
Fax: (703)684-6048
An association management firm.

DC-Area Employees Representing Listed Clients
BAILEY, Christopher
CATTANEO, Joseph J., Director of Marketing and Public Relations
JOHNSON, Haley, Account Executive
OLIVE, Jr., John T., Account Executive
ROGIN, Carole M., President
TRAPP, Stephanie, Account Executive
WILLIAMSON, Darla
WOODBURY, David E., Director, Government Relations

Clients

Alliance of Work/Life Professionals
Rep By: Carole M. Rogin, David E. Woodbury

Ass'n of Women in the Metal Industries
Rep By: Haley Johnson, Carole M. Rogin

Better Hearing Institute
Rep By: John T. Olive, Jr.

Closure Manufacturers Ass'n
Rep By: Darla Williamson

Glass Packaging Institute
Rep By: Joseph J. Cattaneo

Hearing Industries Ass'n
Rep By: Carole M. Rogin, David E. Woodbury

Internat'l Soc. of Hospitality Consultants
Rep By: Haley Johnson, Carole M. Rogin

Wireless Location Industry Ass'n
Rep By: Christopher Bailey, Carole M. Rogin

Clark & Weinstock, Inc.

1775 I St. NW
Suite 700
Washington, DC 20006
Tel: (202)261-4000
Fax: (202)261-4001
Registered: LDA
Washington office of a strategic communications and public affairs consulting firm headquartered in New York, NY.

DC-Area Employees Representing Listed Clients
BIERON, Brian
CLARK, Harry W., Managing Partner
FAZIO, Jr., Hon. Vic H., Partner
KUTLER, Ed, Managing Director
MATHEWS, James H., Director
STACH, Deirdre, Director
STUART, Sandi, Managing Director
SWIRSKI, Sandra, Managing Director
URBAN, Anne, Managing Director
WEBER, Hon. John Vincent "Vin", Partner

Clients

American Ass'n of Health Plans (AAHP)
Issues: HCR
Rep By: Ed Kutler, Deirdre Stach, Sandi Stuart, Hon. John Vincent "Vin" Weber

American Ass'n of Homes and Services for the Aging
Issues: BUD GOV HCR HOU IMM INS LBR MED MMM TAX
Rep By: Hon. Vic H. Fazio, Jr., Ed Kutler, Sandi Stuart, Sandra Swirski, Anne Urban, Hon. John Vincent "Vin" Weber

AT&T
Issues: ENV TEC
Rep By: Hon. Vic H. Fazio, Jr., Ed Kutler, Deirdre Stach, Sandi Stuart, Hon. John Vincent "Vin" Weber

Calpine Corp.
Issues: CAW ENG ENV NAT
Rep By: Hon. Vic H. Fazio, Jr.

CapCURE
Issues: BUD HCR
Rep By: Ed Kutler, Deirdre Stach, Sandi Stuart, Hon. John Vincent "Vin" Weber

Cargill, Inc.
Issues: ENV
Rep By: Hon. Vic H. Fazio, Jr., Deirdre Stach, Sandi Stuart, Hon. John Vincent "Vin" Weber

Copeland, Lowery & Jacquez
Issues: CAW ENV RES ROD TRA URB
Rep By: Sandi Stuart

Delta Wetlands Project
Issues: AGR BUD CAW NAT RES
Rep By: Hon. Vic H. Fazio, Jr., Sandi Stuart, Hon. John Vincent "Vin" Weber

Edison Electric Institute
Issues: ENG
Rep By: Ed Kutler, Deirdre Stach, Sandi Stuart, Hon. John Vincent "Vin" Weber

Federal Home Loan Mortgage Corp. (Freddie Mac)
Issues: TAX
Rep By: Hon. John Vincent "Vin" Weber

Foundation Health Federal Services, Inc.
Issues: DEF HCR INS
Rep By: Hon. Vic H. Fazio, Jr., Sandi Stuart, Hon. John Vincent "Vin" Weber

Guidant Corp.
Issues: HCR MED MMM
Rep By: Ed Kutler, Hon. John Vincent "Vin" Weber

The Island ECN
Issues: CSP FIN GOV
Rep By: Ed Kutler

Lockheed Martin Corp.
Issues: AER DEF
Rep By: Hon. Vic H. Fazio, Jr., Ed Kutler, Deirdre Stach, Sandi Stuart, Hon. John Vincent "Vin" Weber

Microsoft Corp.
Issues: BUD CPI IMM TAX TRD
Rep By: Hon. Vic H. Fazio, Jr., Ed Kutler, Deirdre Stach, Sandi Stuart, Hon. John Vincent "Vin" Weber

Nat'l Center for Tobacco-Free Kids
Issues: BUD TOB
Rep By: Ed Kutler, Hon. John Vincent "Vin" Weber

Nat'l Prostate Cancer Coalition Co.
Issues: BUD HCR
Rep By: Hon. Vic H. Fazio, Jr., Sandi Stuart, Hon. John Vincent "Vin" Weber

Pharmaceutical Research and Manufacturers of America
Issues: HCR MED MMM
Rep By: Hon. Vic H. Fazio, Jr., Ed Kutler, Deirdre Stach, Sandi Stuart, Hon. John Vincent "Vin" Weber

Rubber Manufacturers Ass'n
Issues: TRA
Rep By: Hon. Vic H. Fazio, Jr., Sandi Stuart, Anne Urban, Hon. John Vincent "Vin" Weber

Sacramento, California, City of
Rep By: Hon. Vic H. Fazio, Jr.

Sallie Mae, Inc.
Issues: EDU
Rep By: Ed Kutler, Deirdre Stach, Hon. John Vincent "Vin" Weber

Schering-Plough Corp.
Issues: BUD CPT HCR MED MMM PHA TAX
Rep By: Hon. Vic H. Fazio, Jr., Ed Kutler, Deirdre Stach, Sandi Stuart, Hon. John Vincent "Vin" Weber

Sodexho Marriott Services, Inc.
Issues: DEF
Rep By: Hon. Vic H. Fazio, Jr., Sandi Stuart, Hon. John Vincent "Vin" Weber

Vivendi Universal
Issues: TOU
Rep By: Hon. Vic H. Fazio, Jr., Sandi Stuart, Hon. John Vincent "Vin" Weber

Clay and Associates

12116 Kerwood Rd.
Silver Spring, MD 20904
E-mail: mcclay217@aol.com
Tel: (301)622-5472
Fax: (301)622-5140
Registered: LDA

DC-Area Employees Representing Listed Clients
CLAY, Michelle C., President

Clients

Lambert-St. Louis Internat'l Airport
Issues: AVI TRA
Rep By: Michelle C. Clay

St. Louis, Missouri, City of
Issues: ECN ENV GOV HCR HOU TRA URB
Rep By: Michelle C. Clay

Clay Associates, Inc.

1701 Pennsylvania Ave. NW
Suite 1200
Washington, DC 20006
Web: www.clayassociates.com
E-mail: info@clayassociates.com
Tel: (202)861-0160
Fax: (202)861-3101
A public policy firm specializing in solid waste and hazardous waste disposal issues.

DC-Area Employees Representing Listed Clients
DENIT, Jeffery D., V. President and Technical Director
HORINKO, Marianne Lamont, President
STRAUS, Matthew A., V. President

Clients

Koch Industries, Inc.

RCRA Policy Forum

Cleary, Gottlieb, Steen and Hamilton

2000 Pennsylvania Ave. NW
Washington, DC 20006
Tel: (202)974-1500
Fax: (202)974-1999
Registered: LDA, FARA
Washington office of a multi-city, general practice law firm.

DC-Area Employees Representing Listed Clients
BACHMAN, Jr., Kenneth L., Partner
BENEDICT, Scott N., Special Counsel
BUSH, Derek, Associate
HINDS, Richard deC., Partner
LEBOURGEOIS, Ashton H., Legislative Analyst
LEDDY, Mark, Partner
MURPHY, Jr., John C., Partner

Clients

Asahi Glass Co.
Issues: TRD
Rep By: Kenneth L. Bachman, Jr., Mark Leddy

Champion Securities

Credit Suisse First Boston Corp.

CSFP Capital, Inc.

EBS Dealing Resources Inc.

Kuwait, Government of
Rep By: Kenneth L. Bachman, Jr.

Queensland Sugar, Ltd.

Securities Industry Ass'n
Issues: FIN TAX

The Clinton Group

1350 Connecticut Ave. NW
Suite 1102
Washington, DC 20036
Web: www.theclintongroup.com
Tel: (202)223-4747
Fax: (202)223-4245

DC-Area Employees Representing Listed Clients
CLINTON, Walter, President
KEEFFE, Mary Ann, V. President, Grassroots Services

William M. Cloherty

3211 Tennyson St. NW
Washington, DC 20015-2429
Tel: (202)966-0732
Fax: (202)363-1801
Registered: LDA

Clients

Alliance for the Prudent Use of Antibiotics (APUA)
Issues: EDU
Rep By: William M. Cloherty

Atom Sciences, Inc.
Issues: DEF EDU
Rep By: William M. Cloherty

Burstein Laboratories, Inc.
Issues: DEF
Rep By: William M. Cloherty

First Scientific Corp.
Issues: DEF EDU FOR HCR
Rep By: William M. Cloherty

Incyte Pharmaceuticals, Inc.
Issues: DEF
Rep By: William M. Cloherty

Lackawanna Junior College
Issues: EDU
Rep By: William M. Cloherty

Nat'l Bureau of Asian Research
Issues: TRA
Rep By: William M. Cloherty

Coan & Lyons

1100 Connecticut Ave. NW
Suite 1000
Washington, DC 20036
Web: www.coanlyons.com
Tel: (202)728-1070
Fax: (202)293-2448
Registered: LDA
A general practice law firm.

DC-Area Employees Representing Listed Clients
COAN, Jr., Carl A. S., Partner
COAN, III, Carl A. S., Partner
JAMES, Raymond K., Partner
LYONS, James A., Of Counsel
SALMON, Sheila C., Associate

Clients

Akron Tower Housing Partnership
Issues: HOU
Rep By: Carl A. S. Coan, Jr., Raymond K. James

Coalition for Affordable Housing Preservation
Issues: HOU
Rep By: Carl A. S. Coan, Jr., Raymond K. James

Council for Affordable and Rural Housing
Issues: HOU
Rep By: Raymond K. James

Hempstead, New York, Village of
Issues: HOU URB
Rep By: Carl A. S. Coan, Jr., Raymond K. James
Presidential Towers, Ltd.
Issues: HOU
Rep By: Carl A. S. Coan, Jr., Raymond K. James
Public Housing Authorities Directors Ass'n
Issues: HOU
Rep By: Carl A. S. Coan, Jr., Carl A. S. Coan, III, Raymond K. James
State Street Development Co. of Boston
Issues: HOU
Rep By: Carl A. S. Coan, Jr., Raymond K. James
Weinberg Investments, Inc.
Issues: HOU
Rep By: Carl A. S. Coan, Jr., Raymond K. James

Will Cofer Associates

4001 Pine Brook Rd.
Alexandria, VA 22310
Tel: (703)960-2331
Fax: (703)960-4611
Registered: LDA
E-mail: wilcofer@erols.com

DC-Area Employees Representing Listed Clients
COFER, Jr., Williston B., President

Clients
Gino Morena Enterprises
Rep By: Williston B. Cofer, Jr.

Alan F. Coffey

1800 M. St. NW
Washington, DC 20004
Tel: (202)467-7873

Clients
American Insurance Ass'n
Rep By: Alan F. Coffey, Jr.

Cohen and Woods Internat'l, Inc.

1621 N. Kent St.
Suite 1619
Arlington, VA 22209
Tel: (703)516-9510
Fax: (703)516-4547
Registered: LDA, FARA
Web: www.cohenandwoods.com
E-mail: cohenandwoods@cohenandwoods.com

DC-Area Employees Representing Listed Clients
COHEN, Herman J., President
WOODS, James L., Sr. V. President

Clients
Angola, Government of the Republic of
Rep By: Herman J. Cohen, James L. Woods
Burkina Faso, Government of
Rep By: Herman J. Cohen
Zimbabwe, Republic of
Rep By: Herman J. Cohen, James L. Woods

The Cohen Group

600 13th St. NW
Suite 640
Washington, DC 20005-3096
Tel: (202)756-8500
Fax: (202)756-8510
Web: www.cohengroup.net
An international strategic business and consulting firm headed by Former Defense Secretary William S. Cohen.

DC-Area Employees Representing Listed Clients
BODNER, James M., Senior V. President
COHEN, Hon. William S., Chairman and Chief Exec. Officer
PARK, H.K., Senior Associate
TYRER, Robert S., President, Chief Operating Officer

Cohen Mohr LLP

1055 Thomas Jefferson St. NW
Suite 504
Washington, DC 20007
Tel: (202)342-2550
Fax: (202)342-6147
Registered: LDA
Web: www.cohenmohr.com

DC-Area Employees Representing Listed Clients
COHEN, David S., Partner

Clients
Computer and Communications Industry Ass'n (CCIA)
Issues: COM CPI GOV SCI TEC
Rep By: David S. Cohen

Cohen, Gettings & Dunham, PC

2200 Wilson Blvd.
Suite 800
Arlington, VA 22201
Tel: (703)525-2260
Fax: (703)525-2489

DC-Area Employees Representing Listed Clients
DUBUC, Carroll E., Of Counsel

Clients
Air China Internat'l Corp., Ltd.
Issues: AVI TOR TOU TRD
Rep By: Carroll E. Dubuc
China Eastern Airlines
Issues: AVI TOR TOU TRD
Rep By: Carroll E. Dubuc

Scott Cohen

1801 N. Herndon St.
Arlington, VA 22201-5209
Tel: (703)527-0425
Government relations, public affairs and public relations consulting.

Clients
Federation of American Scientists
Issues: DEF FOR GOV SCI
Rep By: Scott Cohen
Rowe Signal Media
Issues: COM GOV MIA
Rep By: Scott Cohen

Cohn & Wolfe

1801 K St. NW
Suite 601 L
Washington, DC 20006
Tel: (202)756-7100
Fax: (202)756-7200
Web: www.cohnwolfe.com
A public relations firm affiliated with Burson-Marsteller.

DC-Area Employees Representing Listed Clients
HAWKINS, III, John R., Exec. V. President
KENNEDY, Brian, Senior Account Executive
NICHOLSON, Anne, V. President

Clients
Ladies Professional Golf Ass'n

Cohn and Marks

1920 N St. NW
Suite 300
Washington, DC 20036-1622
Tel: (202)293-3860
Fax: (202)293-4827
Registered: LDA
Web: www.cohnmarks.com
E-mail: rrr@cohnmarks.com
Law firm specializing in communications matters.

DC-Area Employees Representing Listed Clients
GOLDBERG, Kevin M., Associate
SCHMIDT, Jr., Richard M., Of Counsel

Clients
American Soc. of Newspaper Editors
Issues: CON GOV
Rep By: Kevin M. Goldberg, Richard M. Schmidt, Jr.
Internat'l Sign Ass'n
Rep By: Richard M. Schmidt, Jr.

Colex and Associates

1802 Fallbrook Rd.
Vienna, VA 22182
Tel: (202)295-9058
Fax: (202)295-9058
Registered: LDA

DC-Area Employees Representing Listed Clients
MACK, John P., Chief Exec. Officer

Clients
Bell, California, City of
Issues: POS
Rep By: John P. Mack
DynCorp Aerospace Technology
Issues: ENV
Rep By: John P. Mack
The NARAS Foundation
Issues: ART
Rep By: John P. Mack
Nat'l Rehabilitation Hospital
Issues: HCR
Rep By: John P. Mack
St. Bernard Port, Harbor and Terminal District
Issues: MAR
Rep By: John P. Mack
Triad Design Group
Issues: TRA
Rep By: John P. Mack

Collado Associates, Inc.

1405 Montague Dr.
Vienna, VA 22182
Tel: (703)759-3377
Registered: LDA

DC-Area Employees Representing Listed Clients
COLLADO, Emilio G., President

Clients
American Watch Ass'n
Rep By: Emilio G. Collado

Collier Shannon Scott, PLLC

3050 K St. NW
Washington, DC 20007
Tel: (202)342-8400
Fax: (202)342-8451
Registered: LDA, FARA
Web: www.colliershannon.com
E-mail: lawyers@colliershannon.com
A law firm specializing in antitrust, e-commerce, environment, energy, financial services, government relations, health care, intellectual property, international trade, occupational safety and health, privacy, tax, and telecommunications.

Political Action Committee
Collier Shannon Scott, LLC PAC
3050 K St. NW
Washington, DC 20007
Tel: (202)342-8555
Fax: (202)342-8451
Contact: R. Timothy Columbus

DC-Area Employees Representing Listed Clients
AUSTRIAN, Mark L., Member
BECKINGTON, Jeffrey S., Member
BLILEY, Jr., Hon. Thomas J., Senior Advisor, Gov't Relations and Public Pol.
BREW, John B., Member
COLUMBUS, R. Timothy, Member
CONWAY, Janice E., Government Relations Advisor
COURSEY, Michael J., Member
GILBERT, Robin H., Member
GUERRY, Jr., William M., Member
HARTQUIST, David A., Member
HOWARD, Lauren R., Member
KANTOR, Doug, Associate
KERSHOW, Michael R., Of Counsel
KIES, Kathleen Clark, Assistant Director, Government Relations
LASOFF, Laurence J., Member
LEITER, Jeffrey L., Member
MACLEOD, William C., Member
MATSUI, Doris O., Senior Advisor and Director, Government Relations and Public Policy
MCMAHON, Kathryn M. T., Member
OLDHAM, Judith L., Member
PAINTER, Dustin, Government Relations Advisor
PORTER, Robert W., Government Relations Advisor
ROSENTHAL, Paul C., Member
SCOTT, Gregory M., Associate
SCOTT, William W., Member
SHANNON, Thomas F., Of Counsel
SHERMAN, Michael D., Member
SINDER, Scott A., Member
SMITH, Jr., David C., Of Counsel
THOMPSON, Chet M., Associate
WITTENBORN, John L., Member
WOOD, Dana S., Director, Government Relations

Clients
AAAE-ACI
Rep By: Jeffrey L. Leiter
AdvaMed
Issues: TRD
Rep By: Doris O. Matsui, Paul C. Rosenthal
AKT Developments
Rep By: Robert W. Porter
Allegheny Technologies, Inc.
Rep By: David A. Hartquist, Robert W. Porter
Allied Products Corp.
Rep By: Paul C. Rosenthal
American Beekeeping Federation
Rep By: Michael J. Coursey
American Flange Producers Marking Coalition
Issues: TRD
Rep By: John B. Brew, Kathleen Clark Kies, Doris O. Matsui
American Honey Producers Ass'n
Rep By: Michael J. Coursey, Paul C. Rosenthal, David C. Smith, Jr.
American Iron and Steel Institute
Issues: DEF ENV
Rep By: Robert W. Porter, Dana S. Wood
American Land Title Ass'n
Issues: BAN INS
Rep By: Scott A. Sinder
American Sheep Industry Ass'n
Issues: AGR TRD
Rep By: Michael R. Kershow, Kathleen Clark Kies, Doris O. Matsui, Paul C. Rosenthal
American Textile Machinery Ass'n
Rep By: Lauren R. Howard, William W. Scott
Australian Dairy Corp.
Issues: AGR
Rep By: Robert W. Porter
Berry Amendment Glove Coalition
Rep By: Lauren R. Howard, Robert W. Porter
Bicycle Manufacturers Ass'n of America
Rep By: Janice E. Conway, David A. Hartquist, Michael R. Kershow, Kathleen Clark Kies
CARFAX, Inc.
Issues: LAW TRA
Rep By: R. Timothy Columbus, Gregory M. Scott

Cast Iron Soil Pipe Institute
Rep By: Paul C. Rosenthal

Chrome Coalition
Rep By: Kathryn M. T. McMahon, John L. Wittenborn

Coalition Against Australian Leather Subsidies
Issues: TRD
Rep By: Lauren R. Howard

Coalition for Fair Atlantic Salmon Trade
Issues: TRD
Rep By: Michael J. Coursey

Coalition for Safe Ceramicware
Rep By: David A. Hartquist, Michael R. Kershow, Robert W. Porter

Committee to Preserve American Color Television

COMPACT
Rep By: Jeffrey S. Beckington, Laurence J. Lasoff

Copper and Brass Fabricators Council
Issues: ENV GOV TRD
Rep By: Jeffrey S. Beckington, David A. Hartquist, Chet M. Thompson, John L. Wittenborn, Dana S. Wood

Copper Development Ass'n, Inc.
Issues: ENV
Rep By: Chet M. Thompson, John L. Wittenborn, Dana S. Wood

The Council of Insurance Agents & Brokers
Issues: BAN INS
Rep By: Scott A. Sinder

Damascus Tubular Products
Rep By: Jeffrey S. Beckington, David A. Hartquist

Fair Atlantic Salmon Trade
Rep By: Michael J. Coursey

Fannie Mae
Issues: BAN CDT FIN HOU TAX
Rep By: R. Timothy Columbus, Doug Kantor, Kathleen Clark Kies, Doris O. Matsui, Gregory M. Scott, Scott A. Sinder, Dana S. Wood

Federal Glove Contractors Coalition
Rep By: Lauren R. Howard

Flexel, Inc.
Rep By: Michael J. Coursey

Fresh Garlic Producer Ass'n
Rep By: Michael J. Coursey, Kathleen Clark Kies

Garden State Tanning, Inc.
Rep By: John L. Wittenborn

GATX Corp.
Issues: TAX
Rep By: Kathleen Clark Kies, Michael D. Sherman

Gerico
Rep By: Michael R. Kershow

Golden Gate Petroleum Internat'l, Ltd.
Rep By: Michael D. Sherman

Grocery Manufacturers of America
Rep By: William C. MacLeod

Idex Corp.
Rep By: Paul C. Rosenthal

Independent Insurance Agents of America, Inc.
Issues: BAN INS
Rep By: Scott A. Sinder

Independent Lubricant Manufacturers Ass'n
Issues: ENV
Rep By: Jeffrey L. Leiter

Inland Steel Industries, Inc.
Rep By: Dana S. Wood

Internat'l Ass'n of Emergency Managers

Internat'l Ass'n of Machinists and Aerospace Workers
Rep By: Laurence J. Lasoff

Internat'l Crystal Federation
Rep By: David A. Hartquist, Michael R. Kershow, Robert W. Porter

Internat'l Paper

Leather Industries of America
Issues: TRD
Rep By: Lauren R. Howard

Lion Oil Co.
Rep By: R. Timothy Columbus, Gregory M. Scott, Dana S. Wood

The Lykes Bros.
Rep By: Paul C. Rosenthal

Maui Pineapple Co.
Issues: DEF
Rep By: Lauren R. Howard, Robert W. Porter

Metals Industry Recycling Coalition
Rep By: William M. Guerry, Jr., Chet M. Thompson, John L. Wittenborn

Metro Internat'l Trade Services, Inc.
Rep By: Laurence J. Lasoff, Robert W. Porter

Military Footwear Coalition
Issues: APP BUD DEF
Rep By: Lauren R. Howard, Robert W. Porter

Military Glove Coalition
Issues: APP BUD DEF
Rep By: Lauren R. Howard, Robert W. Porter

Miller Co.
Rep By: Jeffrey S. Beckington, David A. Hartquist

Municipal Castings Fair Trade Council
Rep By: Robin H. Gilbert, Paul C. Rosenthal

NACCO Industries
Rep By: Paul C. Rosenthal

Nat'l Ass'n of Convenience Stores
Issues: ENV LBR TAX TOB
Rep By: R. Timothy Columbus, Kathleen Clark Kies, Jeffrey L. Leiter, Gregory M. Scott, Dana S. Wood

Nat'l Ass'n of Insurance and Financial Advisors
Issues: BAN INS
Rep By: Scott A. Sinder

Nat'l Ass'n of Professional Insurance Agents
Issues: BAN INS
Rep By: Scott A. Sinder

Nat'l Cosmetology Ass'n
Rep By: Lauren R. Howard, William W. Scott

Nat'l Juice Products Ass'n
Issues: TRD
Rep By: Kathleen Clark Kies, Robert W. Porter, Paul C. Rosenthal

Nat'l Pork Producers Council
Rep By: Paul C. Rosenthal

Oneida Ltd.
Rep By: Laurence J. Lasoff, Robert W. Porter

Outdoor Power Equipment Institute
Rep By: Mark L. Austrian, William M. Guerry, Jr., Laurence J. Lasoff, Judith L. Oldham

PC Strand Producers Coalition
Rep By: Paul C. Rosenthal

Pfaltzgraff
Rep By: David A. Hartquist, Michael R. Kershow

Planar Systems, Inc.
Issues: DEF
Rep By: Robert W. Porter, Paul C. Rosenthal

Propane Vehicle Council

Soc. of Independent Gasoline Marketers of America
Issues: BAN ENV LBR TAX TOB
Rep By: R. Timothy Columbus, Kathleen Clark Kies, Jeffrey L. Leiter, Gregory M. Scott, Dana S. Wood

Specialty Steel Industry of North America
Issues: DEF TRA
Rep By: David A. Hartquist, Lauren R. Howard, Laurence J. Lasoff, Robert W. Porter

Specialty Tubing Group
Rep By: Jeffrey S. Beckington, David A. Hartquist, Robert W. Porter

Steel Manufacturers Ass'n
Issues: ENV
Rep By: John L. Wittenborn, Dana S. Wood

Symbol Technologies, Inc.
Rep By: John B. Brew, Kathleen Clark Kies, Laurence J. Lasoff, Paul C. Rosenthal, Dana S. Wood

Tanners Countervailing Duty Coalition
Rep By: Lauren R. Howard

Toolex USA, Inc.
Issues: TRD
Rep By: John B. Brew, Kathleen Clark Kies, Robert W. Porter

United Parcel Service

Utica Cutlery Inc.

Valve Manufacturers Ass'n of America
Issues: CAW CPT ENG ENV FOR MAN TRD
Rep By: David A. Hartquist

Verizon Communications
Rep By: Doris O. Matsui

Vitol, S.A., Inc.
Rep By: Kathleen Clark Kies, Gregory M. Scott, Michael D. Sherman

Wickland Oil Co.
Issues: TAX
Rep By: Kathleen Clark Kies, Michael D. Sherman

The Williams Companies

Winner Internat'l
Rep By: Michael J. Coursey

World Floor Covering Ass'n
Issues: ENV SMB TAX
Rep By: R. Timothy Columbus, Scott A. Sinder

Colling Swift & Hynes

1331 F St. NW
Suite 800
Washington, DC 20004
Tel: (202)347-8000
Fax: (202)347-8920
Registered: LDA
Web: www.csandh.com
A public policy, government relations, and public affairs firm.

DC-Area Employees Representing Listed Clients
COLLING, Terese, Principal
COLLINS, Pablo, Senior Associate
HOAGLAND, Hon. Peter J., Principal
HYNES, Jr., Robert J., Principal
SWIFT, Hon. Allan B., Principal

Clients

Frank Beam and Co.
Issues: ENG URB
Rep By: Terese Colling, Robert J. Hynes, Jr., Hon. Allan B. Swift

Caraustar
Issues: CAW ENG ENV FUE GOV MAN TAX WAS
Rep By: Terese Colling, Pablo Collins, Robert J. Hynes, Jr., Hon. Allan B. Swift

Chuck & Rock Adventure Productions, Inc.
Issues: ART
Rep By: Terese Colling, Pablo Collins, Robert J. Hynes, Jr.

Garden State Paper Co., Inc.
Issues: ADV CAW ENG ENV FUE GOV MAN TAX WAS
Rep By: Terese Colling, Pablo Collins, Robert J. Hynes, Jr., Hon. Allan B. Swift

Greenman Technologies Inc.
Issues: ENV WAS
Rep By: Terese Colling, Pablo Collins, Robert J. Hynes, Jr.

Media General, Inc.
Issues: COM TAX TEC
Rep By: Terese Colling, Pablo Collins, Robert J. Hynes, Jr., Hon. Allan B. Swift

Molina Healthcare
Issues: GOV IMM MMM
Rep By: Hon. Peter J. Hoagland

The Newark Group
Issues: ADV CAW ENG ENV FUE GOV MAN TAX WAS
Rep By: Terese Colling, Pablo Collins, Robert J. Hynes, Jr., Hon. Allan B. Swift

NewsHunter.net, LLC
Issues: TEC
Rep By: Terese Colling, Robert J. Hynes, Jr., Hon. Allan B. Swift

Opportunity Internat'l
Issues: ECN
Rep By: Terese Colling, Robert J. Hynes, Jr.

Paper Recycling Coalition
Issues: ADV CAW ENG ENV FUE GOV MAN TAX WAS
Rep By: Terese Colling, Pablo Collins, Robert J. Hynes, Jr., Hon. Allan B. Swift

PrediWave
Issues: TEC
Rep By: Terese Colling, Pablo Collins, Robert J. Hynes, Jr., Hon. Allan B. Swift

Quest Diagnostics Inc.
Issues: MED MMM
Rep By: Terese Colling, Pablo Collins, Robert J. Hynes, Jr., Hon. Allan B. Swift

Rock-Tenn Co.
Issues: ADV CAW ENG ENV FUE GOV MAN TAX WAS
Rep By: Terese Colling, Pablo Collins, Robert J. Hynes, Jr., Hon. Allan B. Swift

Smurfit Stone Container Corp.
Issues: ADV CAW ENG ENV FUE GOV MAN TAX WAS
Rep By: Terese Colling, Pablo Collins, Robert J. Hynes, Jr., Hon. Allan B. Swift

Talgo
Issues: RRR
Rep By: Terese Colling, Pablo Collins, Robert J. Hynes, Jr., Hon. Allan B. Swift

White Pigeon Paper Co.
Issues: ADV CAW ENG ENV FUE GOV MAN TAX WAS
Rep By: Terese Colling, Pablo Collins, Robert J. Hynes, Jr., Hon. Allan B. Swift

Collins & Company, Inc.

2111 Wilson Blvd.
Suite 700
Arlington, VA 22201
Tel: (703)351-5057
Fax: (703)522-1738
Registered: LDA
Web: www.collinsandcompany.com
E-mail: info@collinsandcompany.com
Consultants on trade, defense, and foreign affairs issues.

DC-Area Employees Representing Listed Clients
BOND, James D., Exec. V. President
CASSEL, Scott
COLLINS, Richard L., President
HOOPER, Thomas A., Federal Privatization Programs
STAUTZ, Shay D., Programs and Legislation

Clients

The Boeing Co.
Issues: DEF
Rep By: James D. Bond, Richard L. Collins, Shay D. Stautz

Citizens Network for Foreign Affairs (CNFA)
Issues: FOR
Rep By: James D. Bond, Richard L. Collins, Thomas A. Hooper, Shay D. Stautz

EarthData Holdings
Issues: BUD
Rep By: James D. Bond, Richard L. Collins, Thomas A. Hooper, Shay D. Stautz

Hawaii Economic Development Alliance, State of
Issues: ECN
Rep By: James D. Bond, Richard L. Collins, Thomas A. Hooper, Shay D. Stautz

Internat'l Agriculture and Rural Development Group
Issues: FOR
Rep By: James D. Bond, Richard L. Collins, Thomas A. Hooper, Shay D. Stautz

Internat'l Fund for Agricultural Development
Rep By: James D. Bond, Richard L. Collins, Thomas A. Hooper, Shay D. Stautz

Loral Space and Communications, Ltd.
Issues: DEF
Rep By: James D. Bond, Richard L. Collins, Thomas A. Hooper, Shay D. Stautz

Mari-Flite Ferries, Inc.
Issues: DEF
Rep By: James D. Bond, Scott Cassel, Richard L. Collins, Shay D. Stautz

Marquette University
Issues: EDU
Rep By: James D. Bond, Richard L. Collins, Thomas A. Hooper, Shay D. Stautz

Nat'l Telephone Cooperative Ass'n
Issues: FOR
Rep By: James D. Bond, Richard L. Collins, Thomas A. Hooper, Shay D. Stautz

NewMarket Global Consulting Group
Issues: FOR
Rep By: James D. Bond, Richard L. Collins, Thomas A. Hooper, Shay D. Stautz

Northrop Grumman Corp.
Issues: DEF
Rep By: James D. Bond, Richard L. Collins, Thomas A. Hooper, Shay D. Stautz

Oracle Corp.
Issues: DEF
Rep By: James D. Bond, Scott Cassel, Richard L. Collins, Shay D. Stautz

Pacific Marine
Issues: DEF
Rep By: James D. Bond, Richard L. Collins, Thomas A. Hooper, Shay D. Stautz

PADCO, Inc.
Issues: FOR
Rep By: James D. Bond, Richard L. Collins, Thomas A. Hooper, Shay D. Stautz

Population Action Internat'l
Issues: FOR
Rep By: James D. Bond, Richard L. Collins, Thomas A. Hooper, Shay D. Stautz

Science Applications Internat'l Corp. (SAIC)
Issues: DEF
Rep By: James D. Bond, Scott Cassel, Richard L. Collins, Shay D. Stautz

Solipsys Corp.
Issues: DEF
Rep By: James D. Bond, Scott Cassel, Richard L. Collins, Shay D. Stautz

Textron Inc.
Issues: DEF
Rep By: Richard L. Collins

Textron Systems Division
Issues: DEF
Rep By: James D. Bond, Richard L. Collins, Thomas A. Hooper, Shay D. Stautz

Trex Enterprises
Rep By: James D. Bond, Richard L. Collins, Thomas A. Hooper, Shay D. Stautz

Columbus Public Affairs

2111 Wilson Blvd.
Suite 1200
Arlington, VA 22201
Tel: (703)522-1845
Fax: (703)351-6634
Registered: LDA
Web: www.columbuspublicaffairs.com

A domestic and international government affairs and consulting firm. A subsidiary of ColumbusNewport, LLC, a merchant banking and strategic business services firm.

DC-Area Employees Representing Listed Clients

ANTHES, Matthew D., Senior Associate
BRADSHAW, Richard, V. President
CONNOLLY, Gerald E., Exec. V. President
EFRUS, Robert G., Senior V. President
HATZIKONSTANTINOU, Maria E., Associate
JANGER, Lee J., Senior Associate
KEESE, III, James P., V. President
PLUNK, Daryl M., Senior V. President for Asia Operations
POLYAK, Jeffrey V., Associate
WERNER, Larry W., V. President
WIMER, David J., President

Clients

Advanced Telecom Group (ATG)

Alticor, Inc.

American Gaming Ass'n
Issues: GAM
Rep By: Larry W. Werner

Boost Technology

BuyMoreProduct

Cable & Wireless, Inc.

Changing World Technologies

CIGNA Corp.
Issues: FOR HCR SCI
Rep By: James P. Keese, III

Coalition of Independent Salvage Pools of America (CISPA)

Colorado River Commission of Nevada

Copyright Clearance Center, Inc.
Issues: CPT

Financial Accounting Standards Board

Gillette Co.

Greater Richmond Partnership

Guardsman Elevator Co.

Nat'l Cooperative Bank

Nat'l Football League Players Ass'n
Issues: TAX

Norsk Hydro

NTS Development Corporation

Ocwen Federal Savings Bank

Oracle Corp.

Rocky Research

Streampipe.com

TEVA Pharmaceuticals

Commerce Consultants Internat'l Ltd.

1025 Thomas Jefferson St. NW
Suite 410E
Washington, DC 20007
Tel: (202)342-3830
Fax: (202)318-0065
Registered: FARA
E-mail: cciltd@ix.netcom.com

A Washington and international consulting firm.

DC-Area Employees Representing Listed Clients

RICHARDS, Richard, Chairman
RICHARDS, Steve, V. President
WALKER, Laird, President

Clients

Integrated Microcomputer Systems, Inc.
Rep By: Steve Richards

Pratt & Whitney

Qwest Communications
Rep By: Laird Walker

Sunrider Internat'l
Rep By: Richard Richards

Thai Gypsum Products Co., Ltd.
Rep By: Steve Richards

Young Brothers Development (USA), Inc.
Rep By: Richard Richards

Commercial Associates Incorporated

P.O. Box 19001
Washington, DC 20036-9001
Tel: (202)331-1363

Serves domestic and foreign clientele as consultants on international commerce, sales development and marketing, patent licensing and exploitation and as representatives maintaining liaison with Congressional and Executive Branch offices as well as trade, financial and professional organizations in Washington, DC.

DC-Area Employees Representing Listed Clients

CHOSLOWSKY, V. S., Managing Director

Committee Management Associates

P.O. Box 7564
Arlington, VA 22207-7564
Tel: (703)241-1741
Fax: (703)241-1939
E-mail: MdB@Politechnic.com

A management consulting firm specializing in the management of political action committees. Also represents the political action committee of American General Corp. (see separate listing).

DC-Area Employees Representing Listed Clients

DE BLOIS, Michael, Director

Clients

Nat'l Ass'n of Independent Insurers
Rep By: Michael de Blois

United Pilots Political Action Committee
Rep By: Michael de Blois

Commonwealth Consulting Corp.

1800 N. Kent St.
Suite 907
Arlington, VA 22209
Tel: (703)524-0026
Fax: (703)524-1005
Registered: LDA
Web: www.commonwealthconsulting.com

DC-Area Employees Representing Listed Clients

LEHMAN, Christopher M., President

Clients

Alpha Technologies Group Inc.
Issues: TRD
Rep By: Christopher M. Lehman

Atlantic Marine Holding Co.
Issues: DEF
Rep By: Christopher M. Lehman

Delex Systems, Inc.
Issues: DEF DIS
Rep By: Christopher M. Lehman

IAI Internat'l
Issues: DEF
Rep By: Christopher M. Lehman

Lubbock, Texas, City of
Issues: DEF
Rep By: Christopher M. Lehman

Massa Products Corp.
Issues: DEF
Rep By: Christopher M. Lehman

Monroe, Florida, County of
Issues: DEF ENV
Rep By: Christopher M. Lehman

Newport News Shipbuilding Inc.
Issues: DEF
Rep By: Christopher M. Lehman

NoFire Technologies, Inc.
Issues: SCI
Rep By: Christopher M. Lehman

Sensor Research and Development Corp.
Issues: DEF ENV

Commonwealth Group, Ltd.

1001 Pennsylvania Ave. NW
Suite 450 North
Washington, DC 20004
Tel: (202)789-4040
Fax: (202)789-4242
Registered: LDA
Web: www.commonwealth-group.com

A merchant banking and corporate consulting firm specializing in political risk management, public policy advocacy, and international business consulting. Also maintains offices in Boston, MA and Providence, RI.

DC-Area Employees Representing Listed Clients

BELT, Bradley D., Managing Director
CUSHING, Christopher T., President
GREELEY, Christopher J.

Clients

American Management Services, Inc.
Issues: SMB
Rep By: Christopher T. Cushing

The Castano Group
Issues: TOB

Concord Family and Adolescent Services
Issues: WEL

Enron Corp.
Rep By: Bradley D. Belt

EXECUTONE Information Systems, Inc.
Issues: GAM
Rep By: Christopher T. Cushing

Maricopa, Arizona, County of
Issues: BUD CAW GOV
Rep By: Christopher T. Cushing

Nexia Biotechnologies, Inc.
Issues: SCI
Rep By: Christopher T. Cushing, Christopher J. Greeley

OraVax, Inc.
Issues: HCR
Rep By: Christopher T. Cushing, Christopher J. Greeley

D. E. Shaw & Co.
Issues: FIN
Rep By: Bradley D. Belt

Synkinetics, Inc.

Communications Consultants, Inc.

1730 Rhode Island Ave. NW
Suite 1000
Washington, DC 20036
Tel: (202)721-0999
Fax: (202)721-0995
Registered: LDA

DC-Area Employees Representing Listed Clients

SALEMME, R. Gerard

Clients

Eagle River, LLC
Issues: TEC
Rep By: R. Gerard Salemme

The Conaway Group LLC

P.O. Box 3008
Alexandria, VA 22302-0008
Tel: (703)931-4107
Fax: (703)931-3127
Registered: LDA

Consultants and advisors for the education and defense industries.

DC-Area Employees Representing Listed Clients

CONAWAY, USAF (Ret.), Lt. Gen. John B., President
FAIRCHILD, MacLellan, Consultant
HOBGOOD, James L., Consultant
MAYHEW, Howard, Consultant
RAMSEY, II, Forest, Consultant
WAITE, Michael S., Consultant

Clients

Accenture
Issues: DEF
Rep By: Lt. Gen. John B. Conaway, USAF (Ret.), James L. Hobgood, Michael S. Waite

AGS Defense, Inc.
Rep By: Lt. Gen. John B. Conaway, USAF (Ret.), James L. Hobgood

DFI Internat'l
Issues: GOV
Rep By: Lt. Gen. John B. Conaway, USAF (Ret.)

EDS Corp.
Issues: DEF
Rep By: Lt. Gen. John B. Conaway, USAF (Ret.), James L. Hobgood

Electronic Warfare Associates, Inc.

EMC Corp.

Essential Technologies, Inc.
Issues: DEF
Rep By: Lt. Gen. John B. Conaway, USAF (Ret.), James L. Hobgood

General Dynamics Corp.
Issues: DEF
Rep By: Lt. Gen. John B. Conaway, USAF (Ret.)

Gulfstream Aerospace Corp.
Issues: DEF
Rep By: Lt. Gen. John B. Conaway, USAF (Ret.)

Lockheed Martin Corp.
Issues: DEF
Rep By: Lt. Gen. John B. Conaway, USAF (Ret.), MacLellan Fairchild

Mountain Top Technologies, Inc.
Issues: DEF
Rep By: Lt. Gen. John B. Conaway, USAF (Ret.), James L. Hobgood

Science Applications Internat'l Corp. (SAIC)
Issues: DEF
Rep By: Lt. Gen. John B. Conaway, USAF (Ret.)

SRI Internat'l
Issues: DEF
Rep By: Lt. Gen. John B. Conaway, USAF (Ret.)

Condon and Forsyth

1016 16th St. NW
Suite 700
Washington, DC 20036
Tel: (202)289-0500
Fax: (202)289-4524
Web: www.condonlaw.com
E-mail: twhalen@condonlaw.com

Washington office of a New York-based law firm.

DC-Area Employees Representing Listed Clients

WHALEN, Thomas J., Managing Partner

Clients

Air Pacific Ltd.
Issues: AUT AVI INS TOR TOU TRA TRD
Rep By: Thomas J. Whalen

Iran Air
Issues: AUT AVI INS TOR TOU TRA TRD
Rep By: Thomas J. Whalen

Margaret Cone

1620 I St. NW
Suite 520
Washington, DC 20006
Tel: (202)265-3988
Fax: (202)833-4849
Registered: LDA
E-mail: margcone@aol.com

Clients

Artists Coalition
Issues: CPT
Rep By: Margaret Cone

Writers Guild of America
Issues: CPT
Rep By: Margaret Cone

Congressional Consultants

444 N. Capitol St. NW
Suite 532
Washington, DC 20001
Tel: (202)544-6264
Fax: (202)544-3610
Registered: LDA
E-mail: ccgampel@erols.com

A government relations firm specializing in federal health care issues.

DC-Area Employees Representing Listed Clients

GAMPEL, Gwen, President
LATE, Karen M., Senior Associate

Clients

Aksys, Ltd.
Issues: MED MMM
Rep By: Gwen Gampel, Karen M. Late

Alliance Medical Corp.
Issues: MED
Rep By: Gwen Gampel, Karen M. Late

Dialysis Clinic, Inc.
Issues: MMM
Rep By: Gwen Gampel

Nat'l Renal Administrators Ass'n
Issues: HCR MMM
Rep By: Gwen Gampel, Karen M. Late

Renal Leadership Council
Issues: HCR MMM
Rep By: Gwen Gampel

Schein Pharmaceutical, Inc.
Issues: MMM
Rep By: Gwen Gampel

SterilMed, Inc.
Issues: MED
Rep By: Gwen Gampel, Karen M. Late

Vanguard Medical Concepts, Inc.
Issues: MED
Rep By: Gwen Gampel, Karen M. Late

Conkling, Fiskum & McCormick

1275 K St. NW
Suite 810
Washington, DC 20005
Tel: (202)408-2100
Fax: (202)408-2115
Registered: LDA

DC-Area Employees Representing Listed Clients

CONKLING, Gary, President
EDER, Norm, Partner
FISKUM, David, Partner
JARMAN, Daniel, V. President, Federal Affairs

Clients

Electric Lightwave, Inc.
Issues: COM TAX
Rep By: Daniel Jarman

Electro Scientific Industries, Inc.
Issues: CPI CPT FIN IMM TAX TRD
Rep By: Gary Conkling, Norm Eder, Daniel Jarman

Industrial Customers of Northwest Utilities
Issues: BUD ENG TAX UTI
Rep By: Gary Conkling, Norm Eder, Daniel Jarman

Mentor Graphics Corp.
Issues: CPI CPT FIN IMM TAX TRD
Rep By: Gary Conkling, Daniel Jarman

New Edge Networks
Issues: COM TAX
Rep By: Gary Conkling, David Fiskum, Daniel Jarman

Oregon Graduate Institute of Science and Technology
Issues: BUD CPI EDU SCI
Rep By: Gary Conkling, Norm Eder, Daniel Jarman

Sisters of Providence Health Systems
Issues: BUD HCR IMM INS MMM TAX WEL
Rep By: Gary Conkling, Daniel Jarman

Conlon, Frantz, Phelan & Pires

1818 N St. NW
Suite 700
Washington, DC 20036
Tel: (202)331-7050
Fax: (202)331-9306
Registered: LDA
E-mail: firm@cfpllaw.com

A general practice law firm.

DC-Area Employees Representing Listed Clients

CONLON, Michael J., Partner
FRANTZ, David J., Partner
VARMA, Anurag

Clients

American Anthropological Ass'n
Rep By: David J. Frantz

American Ass'n of Physicians of Indian Origin
Issues: FOR HCR MED
Rep By: Anurag Varma

Automotive Engine Rebuilders Ass'n
Issues: AUT CAW TAX
Rep By: Michael J. Conlon

Automotive Parts Rebuilders Ass'n
Issues: AUT CAW TAX
Rep By: Michael J. Conlon

Automotive Refrigeration Products Institute
Issues: CAW
Rep By: Michael J. Conlon

Heavy Vehicle Maintenance Group
Issues: AUT CAW TRU
Rep By: Michael J. Conlon

Indian American Nat'l Foundation
Rep By: Anurag Varma

Internat'l Mobile Air Conditioning Ass'n
Rep By: Michael J. Conlon

Paper Machine Clothing Council
Rep By: David J. Frantz

Connerton & Ray

1401 New York Ave. NW
Tenth Floor
Washington, DC 20005-2102
Tel: (202)737-1900
Fax: (202)659-3458
Registered: LDA

A law firm specializing in labor and employment related matters.

DC-Area Employees Representing Listed Clients

CONNERTON, Robert J., Partner
CONNERTON, Terese M., Partner
KADROFSKE, Alan, Legislative Assistant
MALLINO, Sr., David L., Director, Government Affairs
MALLINO, Jr., David L., Legislative Representative
PAYNE, Phillis, Partner
RAY, James S., Partner

Clients

Brotherhood of Locomotive Engineers
Issues: LBR
Rep By: David L. Mallino, Sr., David L. Mallino, Jr.

Coalition for Workers' Health Care Funds
Issues: TOB
Rep By: David L. Mallino, Sr., David L. Mallino, Jr.

Internat'l Brotherhood of Teamsters
Issues: ENV WAS
Rep By: Alan Kadrofske, David L. Mallino, Jr., David L. Mallino, Sr.

Laborers Health & Safety Fund
Issues: HCR
Rep By: Alan Kadrofske, David L. Mallino, Sr., David L. Mallino, Jr.

Laborers Institute for Training and Education
Rep By: Alan Kadrofske, David L. Mallino, Sr.

Laborers-AGC Education and Training Fund
Issues: ENV LBR WAS
Rep By: Alan Kadrofske, David L. Mallino, Jr., David L. Mallino, Sr.

Laborers-Employers Cooperation & Education Trust
Issues: LBR
Rep By: David L. Mallino, Sr., David L. Mallino, Jr., Phillis Payne

Nat'l Energy Management Institute
Rep By: David L. Mallino, Sr.

Nat'l Environmental Education and Training Center
Rep By: Alan Kadrofske, David L. Mallino, Sr.

Conservation Strategies, LLC

1101 14th St. NW
Suite 420
Washington, DC 20005
Tel: (202)354-6457
Fax: (202)354-6441
Registered: LDA
E-mail: richinnes@aol.com

A government affairs consulting firm.

DC-Area Employees Representing Listed Clients

INNES, Richard, Principal

Clients

Ass'n of Nat'l Estuary Programs
Issues: CAW ENV GOV WAS

Environmental Defense Fund
Issues: CAW NAT

Nat'l Wildlife Federation - Office of Federal and Internat'l Affairs
Issues: CAW NAT
Rep By: Richard Innes

Northern Forest Alliance
Issues: NAT

Restore America's Estuaries
Issues: CAW ENV

World Wildlife Fund
Issues: CAW NAT

Consult

1714 N St. NW
Washington, DC 20036
Tel: (202)462-8990
Fax: (202)462-8995

A government and business relations consulting firm with offices in Washington and Jeruselem.

DC-Area Employees Representing Listed Clients

BEN-DAVID, Lenny, Managing Director

Contango LLC

3733 N. Tazewell St.
Arlington, VA 22207-4572
Tel: (703)241-4007
Registered: LDA

DC-Area Employees Representing Listed Clients
HOOPER, Candice Shy, Principal

Clients

Barrick Goldstrike Mines, Inc.
Issues: NAT TAX
Rep By: Candice Shy Hooper

Sherritt Internat'l
Issues: IMM TRD
Rep By: Candice Shy Hooper

Convergence Services, Inc.

110 S. Union St.
Suite 250
Alexandria, VA 22314
Tel: (703)548-0010
Fax: (703)548-0726
Registered: LDA
Web: www.convg.com
E-mail: info@convg.com

DC-Area Employees Representing Listed Clients
DUNN, Aura Kenny, Director, Federal Policy
LAWSON, John M., President
TICA-SANCHEZ, Debra, Project Manager, Education and Technology

Clients

Central Virginia Educational Telecommunications Corp.
Issues: COM EDU TEC
Rep By: John M. Lawson

CSRG Digital LLC
Issues: COM
Rep By: John M. Lawson

Detroit Public Television
Issues: BUD COM EDU TEC
Rep By: John M. Lawson

Family Communications, Inc.
Issues: BUD COM EDU TEC
Rep By: John M. Lawson

JASON Foundation for Education
Issues: EDU ENV SCI TEC
Rep By: John M. Lawson

KCTS
Issues: BUD COM EDU TEC
Rep By: John M. Lawson

Lancit Media/Junior Net
Issues: BUD COM EDU TEC
Rep By: John M. Lawson

Public Broadcasting Service
Issues: BUD COM EDU TEC
Rep By: John M. Lawson

Tequity
Issues: BUD COM EDU TEC
Rep By: John M. Lawson

WETA
Issues: EDU TEC
Rep By: John M. Lawson

WNVT/WNVC
Issues: BUD COM EDU TEC
Rep By: John M. Lawson

Cook and Associates

500 K St. NW
Suite 350
Washington, DC 20005-1209
Tel: (202)393-0159
Fax: (202)638-2780
Registered: LDA

DC-Area Employees Representing Listed Clients
HIXSON, Sheila E., President

Clients

Agr Foods
Rep By: Sheila E. Hixson

Duffy Internat'l
Rep By: Sheila E. Hixson

J. R. Gray & Co.
Rep By: Sheila E. Hixson

Learning Systems Internat'l

Metcor, Ltd.

Seamans-Rome
Rep By: Sheila E. Hixson

Cooney & Associates, Inc.

3910 Keller Ave.
Alexandria, VA 22302
Tel: (703)769-0020
Registered: LDA

A government relations consulting firm specializing in health policy and legislation.

DC-Area Employees Representing Listed Clients
COONEY, Patrick J., President

Clients

American College of Nurse-Midwives
Rep By: Patrick J. Cooney

American Physical Therapy Ass'n
Issues: HCR IMM LBR MMM SMB TAX VET
Rep By: Patrick J. Cooney

Nat'l Ass'n of Chain Drug Stores
Issues: HCR INS MMM PHA
Rep By: Patrick J. Cooney

J. T. Rutherford & Associates
Issues: HCR
Rep By: Patrick J. Cooney

Mitchell J. Cooper

1001 Connecticut Ave. NW
Washington, DC 20036
Tel: (202)331-1858
Fax: (202)331-1850
Registered: LDA

Clients

Rubber and Plastic Footwear Manufacturers Ass'n
Issues: TRD
Rep By: Mitchell J. Cooper

Cooper, Carvin & Rosenthal

1500 K St. NW
Suite 200
Washington, DC 20005
Tel: (202)220-9600
Fax: (202)220-9601
Registered: LDA

DC-Area Employees Representing Listed Clients
CARVIN, Michael A., Partner
COLATRIANO, Vincent, Partner
COOPER, Charles J., Partner
CYNKAR, Robert J., Partner
HUME, Hamish
KIRK, Michael W., Partner
ROSENTHAL, Steven S., Partner
THOMPSON, David H., Associate

Clients

Bank of America

Fleet Financial Group, Inc.

Real Access Alliance
Issues: COM RES
Rep By: Hamish Hume, Steven S. Rosenthal

Greg Copeland

2110 Yale Dr.
Alexandria, VA 22307
Tel: (703)768-3780
Fax: (703)765-8308
Registered: LDA

Clients

TVA Watch
Issues: UTI
Rep By: Greg Copeland

Copeland, Lowery & Jacquez

1341 G St. NW
Suite 200
Washington, DC 20005
Tel: (202)347-5990
Fax: (202)347-5941
Registered: LDA
Web: www.clj.com
E-mail: cljwash@clj.com

A government relations consulting firm.

DC-Area Employees Representing Listed Clients
ALCADE, Nancy, Legislative Associate
COPELAND, Jr., James M., Partner
DENTON, Jean Gingras, Partner
HANSEN, Linda, Assistant
JACQUEZ, Lynnette C., Partner
KIERIG, Chris, Legislative Associate
LARSON, Lance, Assistant
LOWERY, Hon. William D., Partner
SHOCKEY, Jeffrey S., Partner

Clients

Alameda, California, County of
Issues: HCR HOU IMM LBR RET TAX TOB TRA WEL
Rep By: James M. Copeland, Jr.

Bay Area Rapid Transit District
Issues: RET TRA
Rep By: James M. Copeland, Jr., Jean Gingras Denton

BeamHit America LLC
Issues: DEF FIR
Rep By: Jeffrey S. Shockey

Berkeley, California, City of
Issues: DIS ENV HOU LAW RET WEL
Rep By: James M. Copeland, Jr.

The Boeing Co.
Issues: BUD DEF
Rep By: Hon. William D. Lowery, Jeffrey S. Shockey

California State University, San Bernardino Foundation
Rep By: Jeffrey S. Shockey

CALSTART
Issues: BUD DEF ENG ENV SCI TRA
Rep By: Lynnette C. Jacquez

Cedars-Sinai Medical Center
Issues: BUD
Rep By: Jeffrey S. Shockey

Children's Hospital and Health Center of San Diego
Issues: BUD
Rep By: Hon. William D. Lowery, Jeffrey S. Shockey

Children's Hospital Los Angeles
Rep By: Hon. William D. Lowery, Jeffrey S. Shockey

Digital System Resources, Inc.
Rep By: Jean Gingras Denton, Hon. William D. Lowery

Disaster Insurance Coalition/City of Hope Nat'l Medical Center
Rep By: Jeffrey S. Shockey

El Toro Reuse Planning Authority
Issues: AVI DEF ECN
Rep By: Hon. William D. Lowery

Environmental Systems Research Institute, Inc.
Issues: DEF ENV
Rep By: Jeffrey S. Shockey

Hi-Desert Water District
Issues: BUD CAW ENV
Rep By: Hon. William D. Lowery, Jeffrey S. Shockey

Hollister Ranch Owners' Ass'n
Issues: NAT
Rep By: Lynnette C. Jacquez, Hon. William D. Lowery

Internation Securities Exchange
Issues: FIN
Rep By: James M. Copeland, Jr.

Jacobs & Co. Public Affairs/Loma Linda University
Issues: BUD HCR MMM
Rep By: Jeffrey S. Shockey

Large Public Power Council
Issues: TAX UTI
Rep By: Hon. William D. Lowery

Latham & Watkins
Issues: DIS
Rep By: Jeffrey S. Shockey

Loma Linda, California, City of
Issues: BUD ENV TRA
Rep By: Hon. William D. Lowery, Jeffrey S. Shockey

March Joint Powers Authority
Issues: AVI DEF ECN TRA
Rep By: Lynnette C. Jacquez

Merced, California, County of
Issues: CAW ECN EDU FAM HCR HOU IMM LBR TAX
Rep By: Lynnette C. Jacquez

Murrieta, California, City of
Rep By: Jeffrey S. Shockey

Orincon Corp.
Issues: AVI BUD DEF TRA
Rep By: Jean Gingras Denton, Hon. William D. Lowery

Pacific Life Insurance Co.
Issues: BUD FIN HCR TAX
Rep By: James M. Copeland, Jr.

Redlands, California, City of
Issues: BUD URB
Rep By: Hon. William D. Lowery, Jeffrey S. Shockey

Riverside Habitat Acquisition, County of
Rep By: Hon. William D. Lowery, Jeffrey S. Shockey

Riverside, California, City of
Issues: ANI BUD ECN FAM HCR HOU TRA
Rep By: Lynnette C. Jacquez

Salt Lake City Olympic Organizing Committee
Issues: BUD CAW CDT EDU ENG HCR HOU IMM TRA
Rep By: Jean Gingras Denton, Hon. William D. Lowery

San Bernardino Valley Municipal Water District
Issues: BUD CAW
Rep By: Jeffrey S. Shockey

San Diego Ass'n of Governments
Issues: TRA
Rep By: Jean Gingras Denton, Hon. William D. Lowery

San Diego State University Foundation
Issues: AGR BUD DEF EDU ENV
Rep By: Jean Gingras Denton, Hon. William D. Lowery

San Diego, California, City of
Issues: BUD CAW ECN EDU ENV HCR HOU IMM LBR NAT ROD TAX TRA URB
Rep By: Jean Gingras Denton, Hon. William D. Lowery

San Joaquin Council of Governments
Issues: RES TRA
Rep By: Jeffrey S. Shockey

San Joaquin Regional Rail Commission
Issues: TRA
Rep By: Jeffrey S. Shockey

Santa Barbara Electric Transit Institute
Issues: BUD TRA
Rep By: Lynnette C. Jacquez

Santa Barbara Metropolitan Transit District
Issues: BUD TRA
Rep By: Lynnette C. Jacquez

Science Applications Internat'l Corp. (SAIC)
Issues: BUD DEF ENG ENV
Rep By: Jean Gingras Denton, Hon. William D. Lowery

University of Redlands
Issues: BUD EDU SCI
Rep By: Jeffrey S. Shockey

Ventura County Community-Navy Action Partnership
Issues: BUD DEF
Rep By: Lynnette C. Jacquez

City of Victorville Redevelopment Agency
Issues: AVI BUD DEF TRA
Rep By: Jeffrey S. Shockey

Cordia Cos.

122 S. Royal St.
Alexandria, VA 22314-3328
Tel: (703)838-0373
Fax: (703)838-1698
Registered: LDA
E-mail: lou@cordia.com
A government relations and communications firm.

DC-Area Employees Representing Listed Clients
BILLINGSLEY, M. Scott, Counsel
CORDIA, Liz, V. President
CORDIA, Louis J., President and Chief Exec. Officer
FARAG, Kathleen N., Assistant
HILL, Karen K., Assistant
JOHNSON, Lori A., Exec. Assistant
WILSON, Marcia D., Associate

Clients

BI, Inc.

West Group
Rep By: Louis J. Cordia

Cormac Group, LLP

1620 L St. NW
Suite 1210
Washington, DC 20036
Tel: (202)721-9134
Fax: (202)955-6070
Registered: LDA

DC-Area Employees Representing Listed Clients
DERDERIAN, J.D.
TIMMONS, John W.
WILLIAMS, Patrick H.

Clients

America West Airlines
Amgen
Ass'n for Local Telecommunications Services
Ass'n of American Railroads
AT&T
AT&T Wireless Services, Inc.
Core Tec
FCN
ICO Global Communications
Nat'l Ass'n of Broadcasters
NCR Corp.
Orange County, California
PanAmSat Corp.
Issues: COM TEC
Rep By: Patrick H. Williams
SAIC
Telecommunications Industry Ass'n
Teligent, Inc.
Time Warner Telecom Inc.
XO Communications

Ernest J. Corrado

1801 K St. NW
Suite 1200
Washington, DC 20006
Tel: (202)736-2784
Fax: (202)223-8604
Registered: LDA
E-mail: ecorrado@erols.com

Clients

Bourgas Intermodal Feasability Study
Issues: ENV GOV TRA
Rep By: Ernest J. Corrado

Waesche, Sheinbaum, and O'Regan
Issues: ENV GOV TRA
Rep By: Ernest J. Corrado

Cortese PLLC

600 14th St. NW
Fifth Floor
Washington, DC 20005
Tel: (202)637-9696
Fax: (202)637-9797
Registered: LDA

DC-Area Employees Representing Listed Clients
CORTESE, Jr., Alfred W., Manager

Clients

American Competitiveness Institute
Issues: DEF
Rep By: Alfred W. Cortese, Jr.

Florida Department of Children & Families
Issues: WEL
Rep By: Alfred W. Cortese, Jr.

General Motors Corp.
Issues: AUT CSP GOV
Rep By: Alfred W. Cortese, Jr.

Cottone and Huggins Group

601 Pennsylvania Ave. NW
Suite 900
Washington, DC 20004
Tel: (202)547-3566
Fax: (202)639-8238
Registered: LDA
E-mail: jbhuggins@msn.com
An international government relations firm specializing in media production, public affairs, technology transfer, and project development.

DC-Area Employees Representing Listed Clients
BUGGS, Jesse, Senior V. President, Engineering and Environmental Systems
CARPENTIER, Patrick, V. President, International Security
COKER, Mary, V. President, Public Relations
COTTONE, Mel, Chairman
HUGGINS, James B., President and Chief Exec. Officer
MINGS, John, V. President, Proposal Development
NI, Ph.D., Chuanliu, Senior V. President, Economics and International Finance
RADER, Frederick A., V. President, Public Sector Relations and Training
SMITH, Nick, V. President, Media Production
SPEARS, Ph.D., John R., Senior V. President, Research and Technology

Clients

Alliant Energy
Issues: ENG
Rep By: Mel Cottone

Center for Sino-American Trade
Rep By: James B. Huggins

CESD/WVU
Issues: MIA
Rep By: James B. Huggins

Civil Air Patrol
Issues: GOV
Rep By: James B. Huggins

CTC Corp.
Issues: GOV
Rep By: James B. Huggins

Dulles Networking Associates
Issues: GOV
Rep By: James B. Huggins

EER Systems
Issues: AER GOV
Rep By: James B. Huggins

Galaxy Global Corp.
Rep By: James B. Huggins

Hardy County Industrial Ass'n
Issues: GOV
Rep By: James B. Huggins

HARSCO Corp.
Issues: DEF
Rep By: James B. Huggins

Marshall Research Corp.
Rep By: James B. Huggins

MICAH Software Systems
Issues: DEF GOV
Rep By: James B. Huggins

OAO Corp.
Issues: AER DEF
Rep By: James B. Huggins

Science Applications Internat'l Corp. (SAIC)
Issues: DEF GOV
Rep By: James B. Huggins

Spectrum Astro, Inc.
Issues: AER DEF GOV
Rep By: James B. Huggins

Strictly Business Software System
Issues: GOV
Rep By: James B. Huggins

TMC Technologies
Issues: GOV
Rep By: James B. Huggins

University of Tennessee
Rep By: James B. Huggins

Coudert Brothers

1627 I St. NW
Suite 1200
Washington, DC 20006
Tel: (202)775-5100
Fax: (202)775-1168
Registered: FARA
Web: www.coudert.com
Washington office of a New York law firm.

DC-Area Employees Representing Listed Clients
LIEBERMAN, Edward H., Partner

Clients

The Khazakstan 21st Century Foundation
Rep By: Edward H. Lieberman

Shawn Coulson

1850 M St. NW
Suite 280
Washington, DC 20036
Tel: (202)331-7900
Fax: (202)331-0726
Registered: LDA
Web: www.shawncoulson.com
E-mail: rcoleman@shawncoulson.com
International lawyers.

DC-Area Employees Representing Listed Clients
COLEMAN, Hon. Ronald D., Partner
WHEELER, William, Legislative Counsel

Clients

Domes Internat'l, Inc.
Issues: HOU
Rep By: Hon. Ronald D. Coleman, William Wheeler

People for the Ethical Treatment of Animals
Issues: ANI CHM ENV HCR SCI
Rep By: Hon. Ronald D. Coleman, William Wheeler

Counselors For Management, Inc.

1000 16th St. NW
Suite 400
Washington, DC 20036
Tel: (202)408-4998
Fax: (202)408-4997
Registered: LDA, FARA
E-mail: cfmincdc@aol.com

DC-Area Employees Representing Listed Clients
COOPERMAN, Richard M., Founder, Managing Director
LIPSEN, Janice C., President

Clients

Alternative Systems, Inc.
Rep By: Janice C. Lipsen

American Samoa, Government of
Rep By: Janice C. Lipsen

Campbell Estate
Rep By: Janice C. Lipsen

The Coursen Group

1133 Connecticut Ave. NW
Suite 900
Washington, DC 20036
Tel: (202)775-0880
Fax: (202)872-9372
Registered: LDA
E-mail: coursengroup@aol.com
A Washington government affairs and telecommunications consulting firm.

DC-Area Employees Representing Listed Clients
COURSEN, Hon. Christopher D., President

Clients

Cablevision Systems Corp.
Issues: TEC
Rep By: Hon. Christopher D. Coursen

Medium-Sized Cable Operators Group
Issues: TEC
Rep By: Hon. Christopher D. Coursen

Northcoast Communications, LLC
Issues: TEC
Rep By: Hon. Christopher D. Coursen

Northwest Energy Efficiency Alliance
Issues: ENG TEC
Rep By: Hon. Christopher D. Coursen

PSC Systems
Rep By: Hon. Christopher D. Coursen

The Washington Post Co.
Issues: TEC
Rep By: Hon. Christopher D. Coursen

Covington & Burling

1201 Pennsylvania Ave. NW
Washington, DC 20004-2401
Tel: (202)662-6000
Fax: (202)662-6291
Registered: LDA
Web: www.cov.com
Covington & Burling is a law firm dedicated to solving business and regulatory problems and to advising on sophisticated transactions. The firm has particular experience in mergers, acquisitions, securities, and financing transactions involving companies that provide or use Internet and information technology, communication services, and intellection.

DC-Area Employees Representing Listed Clients
APPLEBAUM, Harvey M., Partner
ATWOOD, James R., Partner
BAIRD, Bruce A., Partner
BARALD, Patricia A., Partner
BARNETT, Thomas O., Partner
BERMAN, Paul J., Partner
BLAKE, Jonathan D., Partner
BRADY, Richard A., Partner
BREUER, Lanny A., Partner

BROWN, David N., Partner
BRUCE, E. Edward, Partner
BUFFON, Charles E., Partner
CHESTER, Jr., George M., Partner
CLAGETT, Brice M., Partner
COHEN, Edwin S., Senior Counsel
COPAKEN, Richard D., Partner
CUTLER, Michael E., Partner
DEARMENT, Roderick A., Partner
DUGAN, John C., Partner
DUNKELBERGER, Jr., H. Edward, Partner
DYM, Herbert, Partner
EIZENSTADT, Stuart E.
ELLICOTT, John L., Senior Counsel
ELY, Jr., Clausen, Partner
FELS, Nicholas W., Partner
FLANNERY, Ellen J., Partner
GARRETT, Theodore L., Partner
GRACE, David R., Of Counsel
GRIBBON, Daniel M., Senior Counsel
HALL, John, Of Counsel
HORNE, Michael S., Partner
HUTT, Peter Barton, Partner
IVERSON, William D., Partner
JOHNSON, Jr., O. Thomas, Partner
KUHLIK, Bruce N., Partner
KUTCHER, Joan L., Legislative Counsel
LAMBERT, Eugene I., Partner
LEVERICH, Bingham B., Partner
LEVY, Gregg H., Partner
LEVY, Michael R., Partner
LIVINGSTON, Jr., S. William, Partner
MERRILL, Richard A., Special Counsel
MICHAELSON, Michael G., Special Counsel
MILLER, Charles A., Partner
MOORE, Amy N., Partner
NEWCOMER WILLIAMS, Mary, Associate
NICKLES, Peter J., Partner
OWEN, Roberts B., Of Counsel
PAUL, William M., Partner
PEARLMAN, Ronald A., Partner
PHILLIPS, Douglas E., Of Counsel
PLOTKIN, Mark, Partner
PORTNOY, James S., Associate
REMES, David H., Partner
ROSENBAUM, Steven J., Partner
RUPP, John P., Partner
SAILER, Henry P., Partner
SAYLER, Robert N., Partner
SCHENENDORF, Jack L.
SELF, Laurie C., Of Counsel
SMITH, II, John T., Partner
SNIPES, James C., Partner
STOCK, Stuart C., Partner
TAYLOR, Sarah E., Of Counsel
TEEL, Keith A., Partner
TEMKO, Stanley L., Partner
THOMPSON, Phyllis D., Partner
TOPOL, Allan J., Partner
TROOBOFF, Peter D., Partner
VINE, John M., Partner
WALDRON, Gerard J., Partner
WEINSTEIN, Harris, Partner
WEISS, Mark A., Partner
WEST, Jr., Togo D., Of Counsel
WESTBROOK, Reeves C., Partner
WILLIAMS, Jr., Wesley S., Partner
WILLIAMSON, Jr., Thomas S., Partner
WILSON, J. Randolph, Senior Counsel
WINNER, Sonya D., Partner

Clients

Ad Hoc Coalition on Intermarket Coordination
Issues: TAX
Rep By: William M. Paul

J. S. Alberici Construction Co.

American Ass'n of Oral and Maxillofacial Surgeons
Issues: HCR
Rep By: Roderick A. DeArment, Joan L. Kutcher

American Bankers Ass'n
Issues: FIN
Rep By: John C. Dugan

American Council on Education
Rep By: Roderick A. DeArment

American Tobacco Co.
Rep By: David H. Remes

American Watch Ass'n
Issues: TRD
Rep By: Roderick A. DeArment, David R. Grace

Anchorage Telephone Utility
Rep By: Paul J. Berman

The Ass'n For Manufacturing Technology (AMT)
Rep By: George M. Chester, Jr.

Ass'n for Maximum Service Television, Inc.
Rep By: Jonathan D. Blake

Ass'n of American Medical Colleges
Issues: HCR
Rep By: Roderick A. DeArment, Joan L. Kutcher

AT&T
Rep By: Harvey M. Applebaum, O. Thomas Johnson, Jr.

Attorneys' Liability Assurance Soc. Inc.
Issues: TAX
Rep By: Roderick A. DeArment

Bank of America
Issues: BAN
Rep By: Stuart C. Stock

Bazelon Center for Mental Health Law, Judge David L.
Rep By: Peter J. Nickles

British Columbia, Canada, Government of the Province of
Rep By: Harvey M. Applebaum

Brown Brothers Harriman & Co.
Issues: FIN
Rep By: John C. Dugan

Business Men's Assurance Co. of America

The Business Roundtable
Issues: TAX
Rep By: Roderick A. DeArment, Ronald A. Pearlman

C F Industries, Inc.

Canon USA, Inc.
Rep By: Harvey M. Applebaum, Thomas O. Barnett, David R. Grace, Sonya D. Winner

Canon, Inc.
Rep By: Thomas O. Barnett, David R. Grace, Sonya D. Winner

CBS Affiliates
Issues: COM
Rep By: Gerard J. Waldron

Chambre Syndicale des Producteurs d'Aciers Fins et Speciaux
Rep By: Harvey M. Applebaum

Coalition of Boston Teaching Hospitals
Issues: HCR
Rep By: Roderick A. DeArment, Joan L. Kutcher

Coalition on AFDC Quality Control Penalties
Rep By: Joan L. Kutcher

Coalition on EAF Funding
Rep By: Joan L. Kutcher, Phyllis D. Thompson

Coalition on Medicaid Reform
Rep By: Joan L. Kutcher, Charles A. Miller

Coalition to Preserve the Integrity of American Trademarks

Columbia Capital Corp.
Rep By: Michael E. Cutler

Consumer Healthcare Products Ass'n
Issues: HCR
Rep By: Peter Barton Hutt, Bruce N. Kuhlik

Copper and Brass Fabricators Council
Issues: ENV TRD
Rep By: J. Randolph Wilson

Cosmetic, Toiletry and Fragrance Ass'n
Rep By: Peter Barton Hutt

Council for Marketing and Opinion Research
Rep By: Laurie C. Self

Council for Responsible Nutrition
Rep By: Peter Barton Hutt

Cranston, Rhode Island, Department of Human Services

Direct Marketing Ass'n, Inc.

Dominion Resources, Inc.

Domtar, Inc.
Rep By: Harvey M. Applebaum

The ERISA Industry Committee (ERIC)
Issues: HCR RET
Rep By: John M. Vine

Exxon Co., U.S.A.
Rep By: Harvey M. Applebaum

Federal Home Loan Mortgage Corp. (Freddie Mac)
Issues: BUD FIN
Rep By: Roderick A. DeArment

The Financial Services Roundtable

General Electric Co.
Rep By: Roderick A. DeArment, Allan J. Topol

General Telephone Co. of California

Golden West Financial Corp.
Rep By: Stuart C. Stock, Harris Weinstein

Grocery Manufacturers of America
Issues: FOO
Rep By: Peter Barton Hutt

Honda Motor Co.

Internat'l Dairy Foods Ass'n
Issues: AGR FOO
Rep By: H. Edward Dunkelberger, Jr., Steven J. Rosenbaum

Internat'l Jelly and Preserve Ass'n
Rep By: David R. Grace

Internat'l Law Institute

Land Trust Alliance
Issues: TAX
Rep By: Roderick A. DeArment

Lansing, Michigan, Department of Social Services of the City of

Lederle Laboratories

Liggett Group, Inc.

Loews Corp.
Rep By: David H. Remes, Keith A. Teel

Louisiana Department of Social Services

Merck & Co.
Issues: MED
Rep By: Bruce N. Kuhlik

Microsoft Corp.
Issues: CPI CPT TRD
Rep By: Stuart C. Stock

Milk Industry Foundation
Rep By: H. Edward Dunkelberger, Jr.

Missouri Department of Social Services
Issues: WEL
Rep By: Joan L. Kutcher

Mountain West Savings Bank, F.S.B.
Rep By: John C. Dugan

Nat'l Ass'n for Biomedical Research

Nat'l Ass'n of Assistant United States Attorneys

Nat'l Food Processors Ass'n
Issues: FOO
Rep By: Clausen Ely, Jr.

Nat'l Football League
Issues: GAM TAX

Nat'l Hockey League

Nat'l Trust for Historic Preservation
Issues: TAX
Rep By: Roderick A. DeArment

Network Affiliated Stations Alliance
Issues: COM
Rep By: Gerard J. Waldron

New Jersey Department of Human Services

New Mexico Human Services Department

New York State Department of Social Services

Pharmaceutical Research and Manufacturers of America
Issues: HCR
Rep By: Peter Barton Hutt, Bruce N. Kuhlik

Philip Morris USA

Pizza Hut, Inc.
Rep By: Peter Barton Hutt

Public Broadcasting Service
Issues: COM CPT
Rep By: Joan L. Kutcher

Quebec, Canada, Government of the Province of
Rep By: Harvey M. Applebaum

Qwest Communications
Rep By: Roderick A. DeArment

Real Estate Roundtable
Rep By: John C. Dugan

Retirement Income Coalition
Issues: RET TAX
Rep By: Roderick A. DeArment, John M. Vine

Schering Corp.

Schering-Plough Corp.
Issues: CPT
Rep By: Ellen J. Flannery

Silver Group, Inc.

Sotheby's Holdings Inc.
Issues: ART TAX
Rep By: Roderick A. DeArment, David R. Grace

Synovus Financial Corp.
Rep By: John C. Dugan

Syntex (USA) Inc.
Rep By: Roderick A. DeArment

Union Pacific

Verizon Communications
Issues: TAX
Rep By: Roderick A. DeArment

The Washington Post Co.
Issues: LBR
Rep By: Roderick A. DeArment

WESTVACO
Issues: RET
Rep By: Roderick A. DeArment

Zeigler Coal Holding Co.
Rep By: Roderick A. DeArment, Ronald A. Pearlman

Law Office of C. Deming Cowles

316 South Carolina Ave. SE
Washington, DC 20003
Tel: (202)544-9660
Fax: (202)544-9661
Registered: LDA

E-mail: cowles@bellatlantic.com

DC-Area Employees Representing Listed Clients
COWLES, C. Deming, Owner

Clients

Alaska Fisheries Development Foundation

Alaska Longline Vessel Owners Ass'n

Bristol Bay Borough Fisheries Economic Development Corp

Elim, Alaska, City of
Issues: CAW ENV HCR IND MAR NAT WAS
Rep By: C. Deming Cowles

World Wildlife Fund
Issues: ENV MAR NAT
Rep By: C. Deming Cowles

Craig Associates

1001 Connecticut Ave. NW
Suite 507
Washington, DC 20036
Tel: (202)466-0001
Fax: (202)466-0002
Registered: LDA
E-mail: pcraig@bellatlantic.net
A firm specializing in legislative representation, grants consultation and federal agency liaison.

DC-Area Employees Representing Listed Clients
CRAIG, Patricia J., President
DYJAK, Kathryn, V. President
GROSS, Leslie Sacks, Legislative Analyst

Clients

County Welfare Directors Ass'n of California
Issues: FAM WEL
Rep By: Patricia J. Craig, Kathryn Dyjak, Leslie Sacks Gross

Dakota, Minnesota, County of
Issues: FAM GOV HCR HOU ROD
Rep By: Patricia J. Craig, Kathryn Dyjak, Leslie Sacks Gross

San Bernardino County Social Services Department
Issues: WEL
Rep By: Patricia J. Craig, Kathryn Dyjak, Leslie Sacks Gross

San Bernardino, California, County of
Issues: BUD FAM WEL
Rep By: Patricia J. Craig, Kathryn Dyjak

St. Louis, Minnesota, Social Services Department of the County of
Rep By: Patricia J. Craig

Cranwell & O'Connell

4113 Lee Hwy.
Arlington, VA 22207
Tel: (703)522-2255
Fax: (703)522-0765

DC-Area Employees Representing Listed Clients
CRANWELL, George E., Partner

Clients

American Soc. for Photogrammetry and Remote Sensing
Rep By: George E. Cranwell

Arlington Educational Ass'n Retirement Housing Corp.
Rep By: George E. Cranwell

Ass'n of Teacher Educators
Rep By: George E. Cranwell

Internat'l Council on Education for Teaching
Rep By: George E. Cranwell

Internat'l Geographic Information Foundation
Rep By: George E. Cranwell

Craver, Mathews, Smith and Co.

4121 Wilson Blvd.
11th Floor
Arlington, VA 22203
Tel: (703)258-0000
Fax: (703)258-0001
A direct-response and database marketing, fund-raising, and consulting firm for non-profit, progressive organizations.

DC-Area Employees Representing Listed Clients
AMTETTI, Rosemary I., President
CRAVER, Roger M., Chairman

Clients

Handgun Control, Inc.

Creative Associates Internat'l

5301 Wisconsin Ave. NW
Suite 700
Washington, DC 20015
Tel: (202)966-5804
Fax: (202)363-4771
Registered: LDA
Web: www.caii-dc.com
A professional services firm specializing in international development, education and civil society development.

DC-Area Employees Representing Listed Clients
HORBLITT, Steve, Director, External Relations

Creative Response Concepts

1150 S. Washington St.
Third Floor
Alexandria, VA 22314
Tel: (703)683-5004
Fax: (703)683-1703
A public relations and government affairs firm.

DC-Area Employees Representing Listed Clients
MUELLER, Gregory R., President

Clients

AT&T

Golden Rule Insurance Co.

Microsoft Corp.

Pharmaceutical Research and Manufacturers of America

Privacy Council

Stop MFN for China '96 Coalition

VISA U.S.A., Inc.

Women for Tax Reform

Law Offices of Thomas K. Crowe

2300 M St. NW
Suite 800
Washington, DC 20037
Tel: (202)973-2890
Fax: (202)973-2891
Registered: LDA
E-mail: tkcrowe@bellatlantic.net

DC-Area Employees Representing Listed Clients
CROWE, Thomas K.

Clients

Northern Mariana Islands, Commonwealth of the
Issues: COM SCI TEC
Rep By: Thomas K. Crowe

Crowell & Moring LLP

1001 Pennsylvania Ave. NW
Suite 1100
Washington, DC 20004-2595
Tel: (202)624-2500
Fax: (202)628-5116
Registered: LDA, FARA
Web: www.crowellmoring.com
A general practice law firm.

Political Action Committee
Crowell & Moring PAC
1001 Pennsylvania Ave. NW
Suite 1100
Washington, DC 20004-2595
Tel: (202)624-2500
Fax: (202)628-5116
Contact: Karen Hastie Williams

DC-Area Employees Representing Listed Clients
ALONGE, Shauna E., Partner
BEHRENS, Mark A., Partner
BIDDLE, Timothy M., Partner
BRYSON, Nancy S., Partner
CHARROW, Robert, Partner
COHEN, Barry E., Partner
CONTRATTO, Dana C., Partner
COOPER, Doral S., President, C & M International
COYLE, Melissa, Director, C & M International
ELMER, Brian C., Partner
GREEN, Edward M., Of Counsel
HALL, Jr., Ridgway M., Partner
HALLOWAY, Lorraine B., Partner
HELTZER, Harold J., Partner
JOHNSON, W. Stanfield, Partner
KATZ, Philip, Partner
KEINER, Jr., R. Bruce, Partner
LORBER, Leah
MCCRUM, R. Timothy, Partner
NEWBERGER, Stuart
QUARLES, Steven P., Partner
REGAN, James J., Partner
ROTH, Robert L., Partner
RYLAND, Barbara H., Of Counsel
SCHWARTZ, Victor E., Partner
SOUK, Fred S., Partner
STEEN, Ellen
SWEENEY, Garnett J.
WATERS, Jennifer, Partner
WEINERMAN, Lloyd, Of Counsel
WEINMAN, Howard M., Partner
WILLIAMS, Karen Hastie, Partner
WORK, Peter B., Partner

Clients

A.C.E. Insurance Co. (Bermuda) Ltd.
Rep By: Victor E. Schwartz, Howard M. Weinman

Aer Lingus
Rep By: R. Bruce Keiner, Jr.

Agricultural Air Group
Issues: ENV
Rep By: Steven P. Quarles

American Ass'n of Health Plans (AAHP)
Issues: CSP MED
Rep By: Mark A. Behrens, Leah Lorber, Victor E. Schwartz

American Forest & Paper Ass'n
Issues: NAT
Rep By: Steven P. Quarles

The American Land Conservancy
Rep By: Steven P. Quarles

American Tort Reform Ass'n
Issues: CSP
Rep By: Mark A. Behrens, Victor E. Schwartz

Associated Gas Distributors
Rep By: Dana C. Contratto

Avon Products, Inc.
Issues: TAX TRD
Rep By: Harold J. Heltzer

Bridgestone/Firestone, Inc.
Issues: CSP
Rep By: Mark A. Behrens, Victor E. Schwartz

Burlington Resources Oil & Gas Co.
Issues: NAT
Rep By: Steven P. Quarles

China, Board of Foreign Trade of the Republic of

CIGNA Corp.
Issues: CSP
Rep By: Victor E. Schwartz

Coalition for Fair Remedies
Issues: GOV
Rep By: Karen Hastie Williams

Committee on Federal Procurement of Architectural and Engineering Services
Issues: GOV
Rep By: Karen Hastie Williams

Cook Inlet Region Inc.
Rep By: Steven P. Quarles

Cosmetic, Toiletry and Fragrance Ass'n
Issues: ENV
Rep By: Nancy S. Bryson

Cyprus Amex Minerals Co.
Issues: NAT
Rep By: Edward M. Green, R. Timothy McCrum, Steven P. Quarles

Eagle-Picher Industries
Issues: TAX
Rep By: Harold J. Heltzer

Elastic Corp. of America

Endangered Species Coordinating Council
Issues: NAT
Rep By: Steven P. Quarles

The Feldspar Corp.
Rep By: Barry E. Cohen

Franco-Nevada Mining Corp., Inc.
Issues: NAT
Rep By: Edward M. Green, R. Timothy McCrum, Steven P. Quarles

Georgia-Pacific Corp.
Issues: NAT
Rep By: Steven P. Quarles

Guidant Corp.
Issues: CSP
Rep By: Mark A. Behrens, Victor E. Schwartz

Helicopter Ass'n Internat'l
Issues: GOV
Rep By: Timothy M. Biddle, Lorraine B. Halloway, Karen Hastie Williams

Holnam Inc.

Homestake Mining
Issues: NAT
Rep By: Edward M. Green, R. Timothy McCrum, Steven P. Quarles

ICF Consulting
Issues: TAX
Rep By: Harold J. Heltzer

Independence Mining Co., Inc.
Issues: NAT
Rep By: Edward M. Green, R. Timothy McCrum, Steven P. Quarles

Intermountain Forest Industry Ass'n
Issues: NAT
Rep By: Steven P. Quarles

KATY-FM
Issues: NAT
Rep By: Steven P. Quarles

Kenya Bombing Families
Issues: GOV
Rep By: Stuart Newberger, Karen Hastie Williams

KeySpan Energy
Rep By: Dana C. Contratto

Knoxville Utilities Board
Issues: ENG
Rep By: Dana C. Contratto, Jennifer Waters

Korea Internat'l Trade Ass'n

Lehn & Fink Products Group
Rep By: Dana C. Contratto

Eli Lilly and Co.
Issues: CSP
Rep By: Victor E. Schwartz

Lockheed Martin Corp.

Memphis Light, Gas and Water Division
Issues: ENG UTI
Rep By: Dana C. Contratto, Jennifer Waters

Meridian Oil Inc.

Multilec, S.A. de C.V.

Nashua Corp.
Rep By: Brian C. Elmer

Nat'l Ass'n of Psychiatric Health Systems

Nat'l Ass'n of Wholesaler-Distributors
Rep By: Mark A. Behrens

Nat'l Park Foundation
Issues: NAT
Rep By: Steven P. Quarles

Nat'l Pork Producers Council
Rep By: Steven P. Quarles, Victor E. Schwartz, Ellen Steen

Negev Phosphates

New York Life Insurance Co.

New York Life Internat'l Inc.
Issues: TRD
Rep By: Doral S. Cooper, Melissa Coyle, Garnett J. Sweeney

North Miami, Florida, City of
Rep By: Steven P. Quarles

Northwest Forestry Ass'n
Rep By: Steven P. Quarles

Pacific Dunlop, Ltd./Pacific Brands

Placer Dome U.S. Inc.
Issues: NAT
Rep By: Edward M. Green, R. Timothy McCrum, Steven P. Quarles

Product Liability Alliance, The
Rep By: Victor E. Schwartz

Product Liability Information Bureau
Rep By: Victor E. Schwartz

Reckitt & Colman Pharmaceuticals Inc.
Issues: ENV
Rep By: Nancy S. Bryson

Regional Airline Ass'n

Rocking K Development
Rep By: Steven P. Quarles

RTK Corp.
Rep By: Dana C. Contratto

Teledyne Controls, Inc.
Issues: GOV
Rep By: Karen Hastie Williams

Trust for Public Land

United Cities Gas Co.
Rep By: Harold J. Heltzer

United Technologies Corp.
Rep By: Brian C. Elmer, W. Stanfield Johnson, Karen Hastie Williams

USAA - United Services Automobile Ass'n
Issues: CSP INS
Rep By: Mark A. Behrens, Victor E. Schwartz

Del E. Webb Corp.
Issues: NAT
Rep By: Steven P. Quarles

Women Business Owners Corp. Inc.
Rep By: Karen Hastie Williams

The Wyatt Co.
Rep By: Harold J. Heltzer, Karen Hastie Williams

The Cullen Law Firm

1101 30th St. NW
Suite 300
Washington, DC 20007
Tel: (202)944-8600
Fax: (202)944-8611
Registered: LDA
Web: www.ecullenlaw.com

DC-Area Employees Representing Listed Clients
BLACK, Joseph A., Partner
CULLEN, Sr., Paul D., Partner

Clients

Committee to Preserve American Color Television
Issues: TRD

Owner-Operator Independent Drivers Ass'n, Inc.
Issues: CSP TEC TRA
Rep By: Paul D. Cullen, Sr.

The Cuneo Law Group, P.C.

317 Massachusetts Ave. NE
Suite 300
Washington, DC 20002
Tel: (202)789-3960
Fax: (202)789-1813
Registered: LDA, FARA
Web: www.cuneolaw.com
E-mail: contact@cuneolaw.com
A law firm.

DC-Area Employees Representing Listed Clients
COHEN, Daniel M., Attorney
CUNEO, Jonathan W.
JOSEPH, Joel, Of Counsel
LENETT, Michael G.
SCHWEITZER, James J.
STANLEY, David W., Attorney
TOSTRUD, Jon, Attorney

Clients

Committee to Support the Antitrust Laws
Issues: LBR
Rep By: Jonathan W. Cuneo

Nat'l Ass'n of Securities and Commercial Law Attorneys
Issues: BAN CSP FIN LAW
Rep By: Jonathan W. Cuneo, Michael G. Lenett, James J. Schweitzer

Songwriters Guild of America
Issues: ART CPT
Rep By: James J. Schweitzer

Taxpayers Against Fraud, The False Claims Legal Center
Issues: DEF GOV LAW MMM
Rep By: Jonathan W. Cuneo, Michael G. Lenett, James J. Schweitzer

Charles V. Cunningham & Assoc.

3797 Dade Dr.
Annandale, VA 22003
Tel: (703)204-2366
Fax: (703)204-2367
Registered: LDA
E-mail: ccunningham@cox.rr.com
An agricultural consultant.

DC-Area Employees Representing Listed Clients
CUNNINGHAM, Charles V., President

Clients

Dunavant Enterprises
Issues: AGR
Rep By: Charles V. Cunningham

Hohenberg Brothers, Co.
Issues: AGR
Rep By: Charles V. Cunningham

Curson Koopersmith Partners, Inc.

1300 Pennsylvania Ave. NW
Suite 700
Washington, DC 20004
Registered: LDA

DC-Area Employees Representing Listed Clients
GAUCLETTE, Eugene, Principal
KOOPERSMITH, Jeffrey M., Managing Partner
KOOPERSMITH, Theodore B., Principal

Clients

Internet Action PAC
Issues: ART BAN CIV CPI CPT CSP EDU GOV TEC TOR
Rep By: Eugene Gauclette, Jeffrey M. Koopersmith, Theodore B. Koopersmith

Underwriters Digital Research, Inc.
Issues: CON CPI CSP
Rep By: Jeffrey M. Koopersmith, Theodore B. Koopersmith

Law Offices of Kevin G. Curtin

700 13th St. NW
Suite 500
Washington, DC 20005
Tel: (202)508-6017
Fax: (202)508-6111
Registered: LDA

DC-Area Employees Representing Listed Clients
CURTIN, Kevin G.

Clients

Air Transport Ass'n of America
Issues: AVI
Rep By: Kevin G. Curtin

Anheuser-Busch Cos., Inc.
Issues: BEV
Rep By: Kevin G. Curtin

CSX Corp.
Issues: RRR TRA
Rep By: Kevin G. Curtin

Maersk Inc.
Issues: MAR
Rep By: Kevin G. Curtin

Nat'l Center for Tobacco-Free Kids
Issues: ADV TOB
Rep By: Kevin G. Curtin

Verizon Communications
Issues: TEC
Rep By: Kevin G. Curtin

Zenith Electronics Corp.
Issues: COM
Rep By: Kevin G. Curtin

Ralf Czepluch

P.O. Box 338
McLean, VA 22101
Tel: (703)827-8855
Registered: LDA

Clients

Edison Electric Institute
Issues: ENV TAX UTI
Rep By: Ralf W. K. Czepluch

The Da Vinci Group

20949 Lohengrin Court
Ashburn, VA 20147
Tel: (202)293-3144
Fax: (703)723-0916
Registered: LDA
Web: www.davincigroup.org
E-mail: dvg@aol.com
A political and legislative affairs consulting firm.

DC-Area Employees Representing Listed Clients
SMITH, Mark R., Director, Government Relations

Clients

Alliance for American Innovation, Inc.
Issues: CPT
Rep By: Mark R. Smith

Atlantic Shores Healthcare, Inc.
Issues: HCR
Rep By: Mark R. Smith

Einhorn, Yaffee, Prescott
Issues: RES

Lightguard Systems, Inc.
Issues: CSP TRA

N-Z Land Company
Rep By: Mark R. Smith

No-Wave, AB
Issues: CSP TEC

Oscoda Management
Issues: TOU

Soave Enterprises
Rep By: Mark R. Smith

Traffic.com
Issues: CPI TRA

Wackenhut Corrections Corp.
Issues: DOC LAW
Rep By: Mark R. Smith

Dalrymple and Associates, L.L.C.

1926 N St. NW
Third Floor
Washington, DC 20036
Tel: (202)833-1043
Fax: (202)833-0370
Registered: LDA
E-mail: dackdal@erols.com
A government and public relations consulting firm.

DC-Area Employees Representing Listed Clients
DALRYMPLE, Donald "Dack", Managing Director and Principal
WILBER, Scott, Associate

Clients

Aventis Pasteur
Issues: HCR MED MMM
Rep By: Donald "Dack" Dalrymple

BD
Rep By: Donald "Dack" Dalrymple

BioPort Corp.
Issues: DEF HCR PHA
Rep By: Donald "Dack" Dalrymple

Biotechnology Industry Organization
Issues: CPT HCR
Rep By: Donald "Dack" Dalrymple

Centocor, Inc.
Issues: MED
Rep By: Donald "Dack" Dalrymple

Edelman Public Relations Worldwide
Issues: FOO HCR MED PHA
Rep By: Donald "Dack" Dalrymple

Plasma Protein Therapeutics Ass'n
Rep By: Donald "Dack" Dalrymple

Daly Communications

4515 Willard Ave.
Suite 1903
Chevy Chase, MD 20815-3614
Tel: (301)656-2510
Fax: (301)656-8069
Web: www.johnjaydaly.com
E-mail: johndaly@erols.com

DC-Area Employees Representing Listed Clients
DALY, John Jay, President

Clients

Direct Marketing Ass'n of Washington

Darby Enterprises

5030 Gardner Dr.
Alexandria, VA 22304
Tel: (703)567-1000
Fax: (703)567-1022
Registered: LDA
E-mail: pbdarby@home.com

DC-Area Employees Representing Listed Clients
DARBY, Paul B., President

Clients

North American Bison Cooperative

Davidoff & Malito, LLP

444 N. Capitol St. NW
Washington, DC 20001
Tel: (202)347-1117
Fax: (202)638-4584
Registered: LDA

A government relations firm with offices also in New York, Long Island, and Albany, NY.

DC-Area Employees Representing Listed Clients
MALITO, Kenneth C., Assistant Director, Washington Office
MALITO, Robert J., Partner
SLADE, Stephen J., Director, Washington Office

Clients

American Museum of Natural History
Issues: BUD
Rep By: Kenneth C. Malito, Robert J. Malito, Stephen J. Slade

Forest City Ratner Companies
Rep By: Stephen J. Slade

Lou Levy & Sons Fashions, Inc.
Rep By: Kenneth C. Malito, Robert J. Malito, Stephen J. Slade

Magellan Health Services
Issues: MMM
Rep By: Kenneth C. Malito, Stephen J. Slade

New City Development
Rep By: Kenneth C. Malito, Robert J. Malito, Stephen J. Slade

New York Psychotherapy and Counseling Center
Issues: MMM
Rep By: Kenneth C. Malito, Robert J. Malito, Stephen J. Slade

Orangeburg, New York, Town of
Rep By: Stephen J. Slade

Project Return Foundation Inc.
Issues: HOU
Rep By: Kenneth C. Malito, Stephen J. Slade

Queens Borough Public Library
Issues: BUD CPT TEC
Rep By: Kenneth C. Malito, Stephen J. Slade

Soc. of Thoracic Surgeons
Issues: MMM
Rep By: Kenneth C. Malito, Robert J. Malito, Stephen J. Slade

SOS Interpreting Ltd.
Issues: LAW
Rep By: Kenneth C. Malito, Robert J. Malito, Stephen J. Slade

St. Vincent Catholic Medical Centers
Issues: HOU IMM MMM
Rep By: Kenneth C. Malito, Stephen J. Slade

Trans World Airlines, Inc.
Issues: AVI
Rep By: Robert J. Malito, Stephen J. Slade

Welch's Foods, Inc.
Issues: ENV TRD
Rep By: Kenneth C. Malito, Robert J. Malito, Stephen J. Slade

Davidson & Company, Inc.

1101 Pennsylvania Ave. NW
Suite 810
The Evening Star Building
Washington, DC 20004
Tel: (202)638-1101
Fax: (202)638-1102
Registered: LDA

A professional consulting firm specializing in government relations.

DC-Area Employees Representing Listed Clients
DAVIDSON, James H., Principal
HYNES, Jr., Robert J., Of Counsel
MAY, Richard E., Principal
SOKUL, Stanley, Principal

Clients

Advertising Tax Coalition
Issues: ADV TAX
Rep By: James H. Davidson, Richard E. May, Stanley Sokul

American Advertising Federation
Issues: ADV TAX
Rep By: James H. Davidson, Richard E. May, Stanley Sokul

American Ass'n for Homecare
Issues: HCR
Rep By: James H. Davidson, Richard E. May, Stanley Sokul

American Ass'n of Advertising Agencies
Issues: ADV TAX
Rep By: James H. Davidson, Richard E. May, Stanley Sokul

AOL Time Warner
Issues: LBR TAX
Rep By: James H. Davidson, Richard E. May, Stanley Sokul

Apria Healthcare Group
Issues: HCR
Rep By: James H. Davidson, Richard E. May, Stanley Sokul

Ass'n for Interactive Media

Ass'n of Nat'l Advertisers
Issues: ADV TAX
Rep By: James H. Davidson, Richard E. May, Stanley Sokul

The Business Roundtable
Issues: BUD TAX
Rep By: James H. Davidson, Richard E. May, Stanley Sokul

Corporation for Enterprise Development
Issues: BUD FIN TAX
Rep By: James H. Davidson, Richard E. May, Stanley Sokul

Direct Marketing Ass'n, Inc.
Issues: ADV TAX
Rep By: James H. Davidson, Richard E. May, Stanley Sokul

eBay Inc.
Issues: CPI TAX
Rep By: James H. Davidson, Richard E. May, Stanley Sokul

Ellicott Internat'l
Issues: BUD MAR TAX
Rep By: James H. Davidson, Richard E. May, Stanley Sokul

Federal Home Loan Mortgage Corp. (Freddie Mac)
Issues: BUD HOU TAX
Rep By: James H. Davidson, Richard E. May, Stanley Sokul

Grocery Manufacturers of America
Issues: ADV TAX
Rep By: James H. Davidson, Richard E. May, Stanley Sokul

The Hearst Corp.
Issues: LBR TAX
Rep By: James H. Davidson, Richard E. May, Stanley Sokul

Independent Contractor Coalition
Issues: LBR TAX
Rep By: James H. Davidson, Richard E. May, Stanley Sokul

Magazine Publishers of America
Issues: ADV LBR TAX
Rep By: James H. Davidson, Richard E. May, Stanley Sokul

Nat'l Ass'n of Broadcasters
Issues: ADV COM TAX
Rep By: James H. Davidson, Richard E. May, Stanley Sokul

Newspaper Ass'n of America
Issues: ADV TAX
Rep By: James H. Davidson, Richard E. May, Stanley Sokul

The Reader's Digest Ass'n
Issues: LBR TAX
Rep By: James H. Davidson, Richard E. May, Stanley Sokul

Paul Scherer & Co., LLP
Issues: LBR TAX
Rep By: James H. Davidson, Richard E. May, Stanley Sokul

The Washington Post Co.
Issues: LBR TAX
Rep By: James H. Davidson, Richard E. May, Stanley Sokul

Yellow Pages Publishers Ass'n
Issues: ADV TAX
Rep By: James H. Davidson, Richard E. May, Stanley Sokul

Mary E. Davis

5818 Bradley Blvd.
Bethesda, MD 20814
Tel: (301)229-5999
Registered: LDA

Clients

Interstate Natural Gas Ass'n of America
Issues: BUD CSP ENG TRA UTI
Rep By: Mary E. Davis

Bob Davis & Associates

2361 Jefferson Davis Hwy.
Suite 506
Arlington, VA 22202
Tel: (703)418-1410
Fax: (703)418-6882
Registered: LDA, FARA

DC-Area Employees Representing Listed Clients
DAVIS, Hon. Robert W., President

Clients

American Science and Engineering, Inc.
Issues: BUD DEF
Rep By: Hon. Robert W. Davis

Atlantic States Marine Fisheries Commission
Issues: MAR
Rep By: Hon. Robert W. Davis

British Aerospace
Issues: DEF
Rep By: Hon. Robert W. Davis

Casa Aircraft USA, Inc.
Issues: AVI
Rep By: Hon. Robert W. Davis

Environmental Research and Education Foundation
Issues: ENV
Rep By: Hon. Robert W. Davis

Fel Corp.
Rep By: Hon. Robert W. Davis

Florida Cruise and Ferry Service Inc.

Frequency Engineering Laboratories
Issues: DEF
Rep By: Hon. Robert W. Davis

Marquette General Hospital
Issues: MED
Rep By: Hon. Robert W. Davis

The Modernization Forum
Issues: MAN
Rep By: Hon. Robert W. Davis

Sippican, Inc.
Issues: DEF
Rep By: Hon. Robert W. Davis

Davis & Harman LLP

1455 Pennsylvania Ave. NW
Suite 1200
Washington, DC 20004
Tel: (202)347-2230
Fax: (202)393-3310
Registered: LDA

A law firm, focusing on federal income taxation and legislative matters.

DC-Area Employees Representing Listed Clients
ADNEY, John T., Partner
BELAS, Richard S., Partner
DAVIS, Thomas A., Partner
EWING, Hon. Thomas
GRIFFIN, Mark E., Partner
HARDOCK, Randolf H., Partner
HARMAN, Jr., William B., Partner
MATTOX, Barbara Groves, Partner
MCCLINTOCK, Janis K., Legislative Coordinator
MCKEEVER, III, Joseph F., Partner
SEYMON-HIRSCH, Barbara N., Partner
SPRINGFIELD, Craig R., Partner
VAN BRUNT, Kirk, Partner

Clients

Ad Hoc Life/Non-life Consolidation Group
Issues: TAX
Rep By: Richard S. Belas

Administaff
Issues: TAX
Rep By: Randolf H. Hardock

Aegon USA
Issues: TAX
Rep By: John T. Adney, Richard S. Belas, Barbara Groves Mattox

Allstate Insurance Co.
Issues: TAX
Rep By: Richard S. Belas, Thomas A. Davis, William B. Harman, Jr., Barbara Groves Mattox

American Benefits Council
Issues: RET TAX
Rep By: Randolf H. Hardock

American General Life Insurance Co.
Rep By: Richard S. Belas, Thomas A. Davis

American Horse Council, Inc.
Issues: TAX
Rep By: Thomas A. Davis

American Investors Life Insurance
Rep By: Richard S. Belas

Armco Inc.
Issues: TAX
Rep By: Thomas A. Davis

Bessemer Securities Corp.
Issues: TAX

Bethlehem Steel Corp.
Issues: TAX
Rep By: Richard S. Belas, Thomas A. Davis

Boston Capital
Issues: TAX
Rep By: Richard S. Belas

Chicago Board of Trade
Issues: TAX
Rep By: Thomas A. Davis

CIGNA Corp.
Issues: TAX
Rep By: Richard S. Belas

Citigroup
Rep By: Randolf H. Hardock, Craig R. Springfield

Committee of Annuity Insurers
Issues: TAX
Rep By: Richard S. Belas, Thomas A. Davis, Randolf H. Hardock, William B. Harman, Jr., Barbara Groves Mattox, Joseph F. McKeever, III, Kirk Van Brunt

Coors Brewing Company
Issues: TAX
Rep By: Randolf H. Hardock

Financial Executives International
Issues: RET
Rep By: Randolf H. Hardock

Florida Power and Light Co.
Issues: TAX
Rep By: Richard S. Belas, Thomas A. Davis

FMR Corp.
Issues: TAX
Rep By: Barbara Groves Mattox

General Aviation Manufacturers Ass'n
Issues: TAX
Rep By: Richard S. Belas

Greyhound Lines
Issues: TAX
Rep By: Randolf H. Hardock

Health Insurance Ass'n of America
Issues: TAX
Rep By: Randolf H. Hardock, Craig R. Springfield

Lincoln Nat'l Corp.
Issues: TAX
Rep By: Richard S. Belas, Randolf H. Hardock, Barbara Groves Mattox

Louisiana Workers' Compensation Corporation
Rep By: Richard S. Belas

Merrill Lynch & Co., Inc.
Issues: TAX
Rep By: Randolf H. Hardock

Mutual of Omaha Insurance Companies
Issues: TAX
Rep By: Randolf H. Hardock

Nat'l Ass'n of Professional Employer Organizations
Issues: RET TAX
Rep By: Randolf H. Hardock

Nat'l Business Aviation Ass'n
Rep By: Richard S. Belas

Nat'l Cattleman's Beef Ass'n
Rep By: Richard S. Belas, Thomas A. Davis

Nat'l Thoroughbred Racing Ass'n, Inc.
Issues: GAM TAX
Rep By: Thomas A. Davis

Paul, Hastings, Janofsky & Walker LLP
Issues: TAX
Rep By: Randolf H. Hardock

Pharmaceutical Research and Manufacturers of America
Issues: HCR
Rep By: Richard S. Belas, Thomas A. Davis, Barbara Groves Mattox

Stock Co. Information Group
Issues: TAX
Rep By: John T. Adney, Richard S. Belas, Thomas A. Davis, William B. Harman, Jr., Barbara Groves Mattox, Janis K. McClintock

United States Sugar Corp.
Issues: AGR
Rep By: Thomas A. Davis

Davis & Leiman, P.C.

5108 34th St. NW
Washington, DC 20008
Tel: (202)296-4790
Fax: (202)296-4791
E-mail: DLTrade@aol.com

A firm representing companies in international trade protection and customs litigation.

DC-Area Employees Representing Listed Clients

DAVIS, Mark D., Attorney
LEIMAN, Karmi, Consultant, International Trade

Clients

Corus Group Plc
Issues: TRD

Indalco Spa
Issues: TRD

Meter Spa
Issues: TRD

New Zealand Kiwifruit Marketing Board
Issues: TRD

Radix SA
Issues: TRD

W. Schulz GmbH
Issues: TRD

Sugiyama Chain Co., Ltd.
Issues: TRD

R. V. Davis and Associates

499 S. Capitol St. SW
Suite 504
Washington, DC 20003
Tel: (202)554-3626
Fax: (202)554-1961
Registered: LDA

An aerospace and hi-tech consulting firm.

DC-Area Employees Representing Listed Clients

DAVIS, Robert V., Principal
FOSTER, J. William, Principal

Clients

Ball Aerospace & Technology Corp.
Issues: AER
Rep By: Robert V. Davis, J. William Foster

Insyte Corp.
Issues: AER
Rep By: Robert V. Davis, J. William Foster

Motorola Space and Systems Technology Group
Issues: AER TEC
Rep By: Robert V. Davis

Spectrum Astro, Inc.
Issues: AER
Rep By: Robert V. Davis, J. William Foster

United Space Alliance
Issues: AER
Rep By: J. William Foster

Zenware Solutions, Inc.
Issues: AER
Rep By: Robert V. Davis, J. William Foster

Susan Davis Internat'l

1000 Vermont Ave. NW
Suite 700
Washington, DC 20005
Tel: (202)408-0808
Fax: (202)408-0876
Registered: LDA, FARA

DC-Area Employees Representing Listed Clients

CARY, Matthew J., Senior Associate
DAVIS, Susan A., Chairman
FOULKES, Tom, Senior Account Executive
RIXON, Gregory, Senior V. President
WHITTLESEY, Judy, Exec. V. President

Clients

Internet Council of Registrars
Issues: COM CPI SCI
Rep By: Susan A. Davis, Gregory Rixon

Register.com
Issues: CPI SCI TEC
Rep By: Susan A. Davis

Sabreliner Corp.
Issues: AVI
Rep By: Susan A. Davis

Westfield Corp.

Davis Manafort, Inc.

211 N. Union St.
Suite 250
Alexandria, VA 22314
Tel: (703)299-9100
Fax: (703)299-9110
Registered: LDA, FARA

DC-Area Employees Representing Listed Clients

BLOCKER, David, Director, Legislative Research
DAVIS, Richard H., Managing Partner
MANAFORT, Paul J., Chief Exec. Officer

Clients

GTECH Corp.
Issues: GAM
Rep By: Richard H. Davis

SBC Communications Inc.
Issues: COM TEC
Rep By: Richard H. Davis

Davis O'Connell, Inc.

444 N. Capitol St.
Suite 841
Washington, DC 20001
Tel: (202)638-5333
Fax: (202)638-5335
Registered: LDA
E-mail: docdc@davisoconnell.com

A bi-partisan government relations, lobbying and consulting firm providing strategic and technical advice and/or direct lobbying services to educational institutions, corporations, governments, and community and non-profit organizations on legislative and administrative issues.

DC-Area Employees Representing Listed Clients

DAVIS, Ph.D., Lynda C., President
GOLDEN, Jennifer, Counsel
O'CONNELL, Terrence M., Chief Operating Officer

Clients

CompTIA
Issues: CPT TAX
Rep By: Lynda C. Davis, Ph.D.

Constellation Technology Corp.
Issues: DEF
Rep By: Lynda C. Davis, Ph.D., Terrence M. O'Connell

Contra Costa Community College District
Issues: EDU ENV
Rep By: Lynda C. Davis, Ph.D., Jennifer Golden, Terrence M. O'Connell

Episcopal AIDS Ministry
Issues: HCR
Rep By: Lynda C. Davis, Ph.D.

Florida Community College of Jacksonville
Issues: EDU
Rep By: Lynda C. Davis, Ph.D.

Florida Department of Education
Issues: EDU
Rep By: Lynda C. Davis, Ph.D., Jennifer Golden

Illinois Community College Board
Issues: EDU WEL
Rep By: Lynda C. Davis, Ph.D., Terrence M. O'Connell

LifeLink Foundation
Issues: HCR
Rep By: Lynda C. Davis, Ph.D., Jennifer Golden

Lockheed Martin Corp.
Issues: DEF
Rep By: Terrence M. O'Connell

Los Angeles Community College District
Issues: EDU
Rep By: Lynda C. Davis, Ph.D.

Raydon Corp.
Issues: DEF SCI
Rep By: Lynda C. Davis, Ph.D., Terrence M. O'Connell

Science Applications Internat'l Corp. (SAIC)
Issues: DEF
Rep By: Lynda C. Davis, Ph.D., Terrence M. O'Connell

St. Petersburg Community College
Issues: DEF EDU
Rep By: Lynda C. Davis, Ph.D., Terrence M. O'Connell

Valencia Community College
Issues: EDU
Rep By: Lynda C. Davis, Ph.D.

Washington and Jefferson College
Issues: BUD ECN EDU SCI
Rep By: Lynda C. Davis, Ph.D., Terrence M. O'Connell

Davis Polk & Wardwell

1300 I St. NW
Suite 1000 East
Washington, DC 20005
Tel: (202)962-7000
Fax: (202)962-7111
Registered: LDA

Washington office of a New York general practice law firm.

DC-Area Employees Representing Listed Clients

DOREMUS, Jr., Theodore A., Of Counsel

Clients

Brown Brothers Harriman & Co.
Issues: BAN
Rep By: Theodore A. Doremus, Jr.

Wells Fargo Bank, N.A.
Issues: BAN
Rep By: Theodore A. Doremus, Jr.

Davis Wright Tremaine LLP

1500 K St. NW
Suite 450
Washington, DC 20005
Tel: (202)508-6600
Fax: (202)508-6699
Registered: LDA, FARA
Web: www.dwt.com

Washington, DC office of a Seattle, WA law firm.

Political Action Committee

Davis Wright Political Action Committee
1500 K St. NW
Suite 450
Washington, DC 20005
Tel: (202)508-6600
Fax: (202)508-6699
Contact: Richard L. Cys

DC-Area Employees Representing Listed Clients

CYS, Richard L., Partner
DEVORE, P. Cameron, Partner
GANNETT, Craig

Clients

American Tunaboat Owners' Coalition

Ass'n of Nat'l Advertisers
Rep By: P. Cameron DeVore

Ass'n of Oil Pipelines
Issues: ENV FUE TRA
Rep By: Craig Gannett

Brix Maritime, Inc.

Northwest Kidney Center/Northwest Organ Procurement Agency

Providence Health System

West Pac Vessel Owners Ass'n

Western Pioneer, Inc.

Davison, Cohen & Co.

1701 K St. NW
Suite 800
Washington, DC 20006
Tel: (202)835-8979
Fax: (202)833-9536
Registered: LDA
E-mail: US017486@mindspring.com

DC-Area Employees Representing Listed Clients
COHEN, Thomas W., President

Clients

Ass'n for Local Telecommunications Services
Issues: TEC
Rep By: Thomas W. Cohen

Corning Inc.
Rep By: Thomas W. Cohen

Donald S. Dawson & Associates

1133 Connecticut Ave. NW
Tenth Floor
Washington, DC 20036
Tel: (202)775-2370
Fax: (202)833-8491
Registered: LDA
A law firm specializing in general, legislative, and administrative representation before the federal government.

DC-Area Employees Representing Listed Clients
DAWSON, Donald S., Attorney

Clients

Leo A. Daly Co.
Issues: URB
Rep By: Donald S. Dawson

Opticians Ass'n of America
Issues: TRD
Rep By: Donald S. Dawson

St. Thomas/St. John Chamber of Commerce, Inc.
Issues: TRD
Rep By: Donald S. Dawson

Dawson & Associates, Inc.

1225 I St. NW
Suite 500
Washington, DC 20005
Tel: (202)312-2005
Fax: (202)289-8683
Registered: LDA
Web: www.dawsonassociates.com
E-mail: dawsonassociates@worldnet.att.net
A government relations firm.

DC-Area Employees Representing Listed Clients
BARROWS, David, Senior Advisor
BEVILL, Hon. Tom, Senior Advisor
CRABILL, Donald E., Senior Advisor
DAWSON, Robert K., President
DEASON, Ph.D., Jonathan P., Senior Advisor
DICKEY, Ph.D., Edward, Senior Advisor
DURKAY, James, Senior Advisor
DUSCHA, Lloyd, Senior Advisor
EDELMAN, Lester, Senior Counsel and Senior Advisor
GIANELLI, William R., Senior Advisor
GOODE, Bernard N., Senior Advisor
HEIBERG, Lt. Gen. Vald, Senior Advisor
LANSING, Olga, Senior Advisor
MYERS, Hon. John, Senior Advisor
PACKARD, Hon. Ron, Senior Advisor
POINTON, Henry, Senior Advisor
POLESE, Donald J., Senior Advisor
PORTER, Dr. Winston, Senior Advisor
ROMNEY, Clyde, Senior Advisor
WILLIAMS, USA (Ret.), Lt. Gen. Arthur E., Senior Advisor

Clients

AgriPartners
Issues: NAT RES
Rep By: David Barrows, Robert K. Dawson, Jonathan P. Deason, Ph.D., Hon. John Myers, Lt. Gen. Arthur E. Williams, USA (Ret.)

Chemical Land Holdings, Inc.
Issues: ENV NAT
Rep By: Donald E. Crabill, Robert K. Dawson, Jonathan P. Deason, Ph.D., Edward Dickey, Ph.D., James Durkay, Lt. Gen. Vald Heiberg, Hon. John Myers, Henry Pointon

Florida Citrus Mutual
Issues: ENV NAT RES
Rep By: Robert K. Dawson, Jonathan P. Deason, Ph.D., Edward Dickey, Ph.D., Lester Edelman, Lt. Gen. Vald Heiberg, Lt. Gen. Arthur E. Williams, USA (Ret.)

Florida Farm Bureau
Issues: ENV NAT RES
Rep By: Robert K. Dawson, Jonathan P. Deason, Ph.D., Edward Dickey, Ph.D., Lt. Gen. Vald Heiberg, Lt. Gen. Arthur E. Williams, USA (Ret.)

Florida Sugar Cane League, Inc.
Issues: ENV NAT RES
Rep By: Robert K. Dawson, Jonathan P. Deason, Ph.D., Edward Dickey, Ph.D., Lester Edelman, Lt. Gen. Vald Heiberg, Hon. John Myers, Lt. Gen. Arthur E. Williams, USA (Ret.)

Great Lakes Dredge & Dock
Issues: DIS ENV GOV MAR NAT SMB TRA
Rep By: Hon. Tom Bevill, Robert K. Dawson, James Durkay, Lester Edelman, Olga Lansing, Hon. John Myers

Sugar Cane Growers Cooperative of Florida
Issues: ENV NAT RES
Rep By: Robert K. Dawson, Jonathan P. Deason, Ph.D., Edward Dickey, Ph.D., Lester Edelman, Lt. Gen. Vald Heiberg, Hon. John Myers, Lt. Gen. Arthur E. Williams, USA (Ret.)

Osborne A. Day

2000 P St. NW
Suite 510
Washington, DC 20036
Tel: (202)466-6789
Fax: (202)296-3862
Registered: LDA

Clients

Recording for the Blind and Dyslexic, Inc.
Rep By: Osborne A. Day

DBH Consulting

P.O. Box 50037
Arlington, VA 22205
Tel: (703)536-2956
Fax: (703)241-0539
Registered: LDA
Web: www.dbhcon.com
E-mail: dHam@dbhcon.com
A transportation consultant.

DC-Area Employees Representing Listed Clients
HAM, Douglas B.

Clients

Alcalde & Fay
Issues: TRA
Rep By: Douglas B. Ham

The DCS Group

410 First St. SE
Third Floor
Washington, DC 20003
Tel: (202)484-2776
Fax: (202)484-7016
Registered: FARA
E-mail: dcs@dcsgroup.com
A public affairs and communications firm affiliated with The Dutko Group.

DC-Area Employees Representing Listed Clients
CUNNINGHAM, Sherri, Group Director
DUGGAN, Joseph P., Senior V. President
FILLIP, Christine, Senior V. President
GAY, Tim, Senior V. President
MADISON, Alan M., Partner
MALONI, Jason, Group Director
URBANSKI, Tina, Senior Acccount Executive
WAGNER, Joe, Director of Research/V. President

Clients

Ass'n for Competitive Technology

Birthright Israel

Council for Urban Economic Development

Longhorn Pipeline
Issues: ENG

Nutra-Park

Schering A.G.

United Jewish Communities, Inc.

Verizon Wireless

Worldwide E-Commerce Fraud Prevention Network

Dean Blakey & Moskowitz

1101 Vermont Ave. NW
Suite 400
Washington, DC 20005
Tel: (202)289-3900
Fax: (202)371-0197
Registered: LDA
E-mail: dbm@dbmlaw.com
A law firm specializing in governmental and educational matters.

DC-Area Employees Representing Listed Clients
AUSTIN, K. Sabrina, Senior Associate
BLAKEY, William A., Partner
DEAN, John E., Managing Partner
HARRIS-AIKENS, Donna, Associate Attorney
MOSKOWITZ, Saul L., Partner
NOLAN, Ellin J., Director, Government Relations
WHITE, Jacqueline M., Associate Attorney

Clients

American Psychological Ass'n
Issues: BUD EDU FAM
Rep By: Ellin J. Nolan

Ass'n of Technology Act Projects
Issues: BUD SCI
Rep By: Ellin J. Nolan

Bethune-Cookman College
Issues: EDU
Rep By: William A. Blakey

Bowie State University
Issues: EDU
Rep By: William A. Blakey

Chase Manhattan Bank
Rep By: John E. Dean

Chela Financial
Issues: EDU
Rep By: John E. Dean

Chicago State University
Issues: EDU
Rep By: William A. Blakey

Claflin College
Issues: EDU
Rep By: William A. Blakey

Clark Atlanta University
Issues: EDU
Rep By: William A. Blakey

Coalition of Higher Education Assistance Organizations
Issues: BUD EDU HCR
Rep By: Ellin J. Nolan

Consumer Bankers Ass'n
Issues: BUD EDU TAX
Rep By: John E. Dean, Saul L. Moskowitz

Council for Opportunity in Education
Rep By: William A. Blakey

DeVry, Inc.
Issues: BUD EDU
Rep By: William A. Blakey

Diversified Collection Services, Inc.
Issues: BAN BUD EDU
Rep By: K. Sabrina Austin, John E. Dean, Saul L. Moskowitz

Economics America
Issues: BUD EDU
Rep By: Ellin J. Nolan

Fair Share Coalition
Issues: TAX
Rep By: John E. Dean, Saul L. Moskowitz

Financial Collection Agencies
Issues: TAX
Rep By: Saul L. Moskowitz

HBCU/PAC
Rep By: William A. Blakey

Internat'l Technology Education Ass'n
Issues: BUD EDU
Rep By: Ellin J. Nolan

Knoxville College
Issues: BUD EDU
Rep By: William A. Blakey

Management Concepts, Inc.
Issues: AGR BUD
Rep By: John E. Dean, Ellin J. Nolan

Mendez University System, Ana G.
Issues: EDU
Rep By: William A. Blakey

Minority Males Consortium
Issues: LAW
Rep By: William A. Blakey

Nat'l Alliance of Sexual Assault Coalitions
Issues: BUD EDU LAW
Rep By: Ellin J. Nolan

Nat'l Collegiate Athletic Ass'n
Issues: EDU
Rep By: Ellin J. Nolan

Nat'l Council of Teachers of Mathematics
Issues: BUD EDU
Rep By: Ellin J. Nolan

Nat'l Science Teachers Ass'n
Issues: EDU
Rep By: Ellin J. Nolan

Nat'l Writing Project
Issues: BUD EDU
Rep By: Ellin J. Nolan

Paul Quinn College
Issues: EDU
Rep By: William A. Blakey

St. Augustine College
Issues: EDU
Rep By: William A. Blakey

Student Loan Funding Corp.
Issues: BUD EDU
Rep By: John E. Dean

Talladega College
Issues: BUD EDU
Rep By: William A. Blakey

Texas College
Issues: EDU
Rep By: William A. Blakey

UNIPAC Service Corp.
Issues: BUD EDU TAX
Rep By: John E. Dean

United Negro College Fund, Inc.
Issues: BUD EDU
Rep By: William A. Blakey

University of Louisville
Issues: BUD EDU
Rep By: William A. Blakey

University of Vermont
Issues: BUD EDU
Rep By: Ellin J. Nolan

Very Special Arts
Issues: BUD EDU
Rep By: Ellin J. Nolan

Voorhees College
Issues: BUD EDU WEL
Rep By: William A. Blakey

Wilberforce University
Issues: BUD EDU
Rep By: William A. Blakey

The Work Colleges
Issues: BUD EDU
Rep By: William A. Blakey

Debevoise and Plimpton

555 13th St. NW
1100 East
Washington, DC 20004-1179
Tel: (202)383-8000
Fax: (202)383-8118
Registered: FARA
Web: www.debevoise.com
Washington office of a general practice law firm headquartered in New York, NY.

DC-Area Employees Representing Listed Clients
CUNARD, Jeffrey P., Partner

Clients

Sony Corp.
Issues: CPT
Rep By: Jeffrey P. Cunard

DeBrunner and Associates, Inc.

Ten Pidgeon Hill Dr.
Suite 150
Sterling, VA 20165
Tel: (703)444-4091
Fax: (703)444-3029
Registered: LDA

DC-Area Employees Representing Listed Clients
DEBRUNNER, Charles L., President
HERR, Wendy W., Associate
KLUGH, Gloria J., Associate
KUGLER, Ellen J., Director, Government Affairs
ROONEY, Kathryn D., Associate

Clients

Albert Einstein Medical Center
Issues: BUD HCR MED MMM
Rep By: Charles L. DeBrunner, Ellen J. Kugler, Kathryn D. Rooney

Catholic Healthcare West
Issues: MMM
Rep By: Charles L. DeBrunner, Wendy W. Herr, Ellen J. Kugler, Kathryn D. Rooney

Health Quest
Issues: BUD MED
Rep By: Charles L. DeBrunner, Wendy W. Herr, Ellen J. Kugler, Kathryn D. Rooney

Nat'l Ass'n of Urban Hospitals
Issues: BUD MED MMM
Rep By: Charles L. DeBrunner, Wendy W. Herr, Gloria J. Klugh, Ellen J. Kugler, Kathryn D. Rooney

Private Essential Access Community Hospitals (PEACH) Inc.
Issues: BUD HCR MED MMM
Rep By: Charles L. DeBrunner, Ellen J. Kugler, Kathryn D. Rooney

Southcoast Health System
Issues: BUD HCR MED MMM
Rep By: Charles L. DeBrunner, Ellen J. Kugler, Kathryn D. Rooney

Susquehanna Health System
Issues: BUD HCR MED MMM
Rep By: Charles L. DeBrunner, Wendy W. Herr, Ellen J. Kugler, Kathryn D. Rooney

Thomas Jefferson University Hospital
Issues: BUD HCR MED MMM
Rep By: Charles L. DeBrunner, Ellen J. Kugler, Kathryn D. Rooney

Dechert

1775 I St. NW
Washington, DC 20006
Tel: (202)261-3300
Fax: (202)261-3333
Registered: LDA, FARA
Web: www.dechert.com
Washington office of an international general practice law firm.

DC-Area Employees Representing Listed Clients
BIEBER, Sander M., Partner
CURZON, Elliott R., Counsel
ERVIN, Susan C., Partner
FRIEDMAN, Paul H., Partner
HORWITZ, Reid B., Partner
JINDAL, Gorav, Associate
MOSTOFF, Allan S., Partner
MURPHY, Jack W., Partner
OMAN, Ralph, Counsel
SCHWARZ, Melvin, Partner
STEVENS, Paul Schott, Partner
TIMMENY, Wallace L., Partner

Clients

Broadcast Music Inc. (BMI)
Rep By: Ralph Oman

Dominion Resources, Inc.

Japan Bank for Internat'l Cooperation
Rep By: Allan S. Mostoff

Japan, Embassy of
Rep By: Allan S. Mostoff

Malta Development Corp.

Defense Health Advisors, Inc.

1717 Pennsylvania Ave. NW
Suite 1300
Washington, DC 20006
Tel: (202)452-6928
Registered: LDA
E-mail: cltval@aol.com
Health care consultant firm.

DC-Area Employees Representing Listed Clients
TSOUCALAS, Charlotte L.
WILLIS, Karin K.

Clients

Delta Dental Plan of California
Issues: DEF
Rep By: Charlotte L. Tsoucalas, Karin K. Willis

Johns Hopkins Medical Services
Issues: DEF
Rep By: Charlotte L. Tsoucalas

Tri West Healthcare Alliance
Rep By: Charlotte L. Tsoucalas

Vector Research, Inc.
Issues: DEF
Rep By: Charlotte L. Tsoucalas

Degnon Associates, Inc.

6728 Old McLean Village Dr.
McLean, VA 22101
Tel: (703)556-9222
Fax: (703)556-8729

DC-Area Employees Representing Listed Clients
DEGNON, CAE, George K., President
DEGNON, Laura, V. President
DEGNON, Marge, V. President

Clients

Academy for Eating Disorders
Rep By: George K. Degnon, CAE

Ambulatory Pediatric Ass'n
Rep By: Marge Degnon

American Academy on Physician and Patient

American Holistic Medical Ass'n

American Psychosomatic Soc.
Rep By: Laura Degnon

Ass'n of Christian Therapists

Ass'n of Pediatric Program Directors

Internat'l Soc. for Quality of Life Research

Multinat'l Working Team to Develop Criteria for Functional Gastrointestinal Disorders

Soc. for Occupational and Environmental Health

Soc. for Pediatric Pathology

DeHart and Darr Associates, Inc.

1360 Beverly Rd.
Suite 201
McLean, VA 22101
Tel: (703)448-1000
Fax: (703)790-3460

DC-Area Employees Representing Listed Clients
DARR, Anne
NEWBURG, Janice
SAVICH, Beverly
SMITH, Daniel

Clients

Direct Marketing Ass'n, Inc.

deKieffer & Horgan

729 15th St. NW
Suite 800
Washington, DC 20005
Tel: (202)783-6900
Fax: (202)783-6909
Registered: LDA
Web: www.dhlaw.com

DC-Area Employees Representing Listed Clients
DEKIEFFER, Donald E., Partner

Clients

Strategic Minerals Corp.
Issues: TRD
Rep By: Donald E. deKieffer

Glenn Roger Delaney

601 Pennsylvania Ave. NW
Suite 900
Washington, DC 20004
Tel: (202)434-8220
Fax: (202)639-8817
Registered: LDA

Clients

Blue Water Fishermen's Ass'n
Issues: MAR
Rep By: Glenn Roger Delaney

Internat'l Ass'n of Fish and Wildlife Agencies
Issues: NAT
Rep By: Glenn Roger Delaney

Louisiana Department of Wildlife and Fisheries - Fur and Refuse Division
Issues: NAT
Rep By: Glenn Roger Delaney

New England Aquarium
Issues: MAR
Rep By: Glenn Roger Delaney

Trident Seafood Corp.
Issues: FOO MAR
Rep By: Glenn Roger Delaney

Deloitte & Touche LLP Nat'l Office - Washington

555 12th St. NW
Suite 500
Washington, DC 20004-1207
Tel: (202)879-5600
Fax: (202)879-5309
Registered: LDA, FARA
Web: www.dttus.com

Political Action Committee
Deloitte & Touche LLP Federal PAC
555 12th St. NW
Suite 500
Washington, DC 20004-1207
Tel: (202)879-5600
Fax: (202)879-5309

DC-Area Employees Representing Listed Clients
EZZELL, William, Partner in Charge, Government Affairs
GARAY, Mark, Manager
SNOWLING, Randall, Partner
STEPHENSON, Gregory, Partner
STEVENS, Cindy M., Director, Federal Programs
STRETCH, C. Clinton, Partner, National Tax Services
WEISS, Randall D., Partner

Clients

Railroad Retirment Reform Working Group
Rep By: Randall D. Weiss

Liz Robbins Associates
Issues: TAX
Rep By: Mark Garay, C. Clinton Stretch

Torchmark Corp.
Issues: TAX
Rep By: Gregory Stephenson, Randall D. Weiss

George H. Denison

5910 Woodacres Dr.
Bethesda, MD 20816
Tel: (301)229-5791
Fax: (301)229-5792
Registered: LDA, FARA
A government relations consultant.

Clients

Bangor Internat'l Airport
Issues: AVI TRA
Rep By: George H. Denison

Congo, Democratic Republic of the
Issues: FOR
Rep By: George H. Denison

Federation of Electric Power Cos. of Japan
Issues: ENG
Rep By: George H. Denison

Mail 2000, Inc.
Issues: POS
Rep By: George H. Denison

Mauritania, Government of the Islamic Republic of
Rep By: George H. Denison

Med Images, Inc.
Issues: MMM
Rep By: George H. Denison

Pfluger Enterprises LLC
Issues: TEC TRD
Rep By: George H. Denison

Victims of Communism Memorial Foundation
Issues: FOR
Rep By: George H. Denison

Zimbabwe, Republic of
Issues: FOR
Rep By: George H. Denison

Denison, Scott and Cohen

2000 L St. NW
Suite 200
Washington, DC 20036

Tel: (202)416-1785
Fax: (202)546-6294
Registered: LDA, FARA

DC-Area Employees Representing Listed Clients

COHEN, Herman J., Partner
DENISON, George H., Partner
SCOTT, Ray, Partner

Clients

The Friends of Democratic Congo
Issues: FOR
Rep By: Herman J. Cohen, George H. Denison, Ray Scott

Denison, Scott Associates

Eight E St. SE
Washington, DC 20003

Tel: (202)543-4172
Fax: (202)546-6294
Registered: LDA, FARA

DC-Area Employees Representing Listed Clients

DENISON, George H., Partner
SCOTT, Ray, Partner

Clients

Bristol-Myers Squibb Co.
Issues: MMM
Rep By: George H. Denison, Ray Scott

Value Options Health Care Inc.
Issues: HCR

Denning & Wohlstetter

1700 K St. NW
Suite 301
Washington, DC 20006

Tel: (202)833-8884
Fax: (202)833-8886

A general practice law firm specializing in transportation, government contract, and trademark law.

DC-Area Employees Representing Listed Clients

GOLDMAN, Stanley I., Partner
WOHLSTETTER, Alan F., Managing Partner

Clients

American Red Bull Transit

Central Freight Forwarding
Rep By: Alan F. Wohlstetter

Express Forwarding and Storage, Inc.

Household Goods Forwarders Ass'n of America, Inc.
Rep By: Alan F. Wohlstetter

Household Goods Forwarders Tariff Bureau
Rep By: Stanley I. Goldman

Transconex, Inc.

Thomas J. Dennis

209 Tenth St. SE
Washington, DC 20003

Tel: (202)543-4541
Fax: (202)543-4457
Registered: LDA

E-mail: tomjdennis@aol.com
Provides government affairs consulting.

Clients

ARCO Products Co.
Issues: CAW ENG FUE GOV MAR
Rep By: Thomas J. Dennis

Edison Electric Institute
Issues: CAW TAX UTI
Rep By: Thomas J. Dennis

Energy East Management Corp.
Issues: UTI
Rep By: Thomas J. Dennis

PURPA Reform Group
Issues: UTI
Rep By: Thomas J. Dennis

Repeal PUHCA Now Coalition
Issues: UTI
Rep By: Thomas J. Dennis

John A. DeVierno

818 Connecticut Ave. NW
Suite 1100
Washington, DC 20006

Tel: (202)496-3459
Fax: (202)728-4044
Registered: LDA

Attorney at law, federal legal, regulatory and legislative practice.

Clients

CSX Corp.
Rep By: John A. DeVierno

Idaho, Department of Transportation of the State of
Rep By: John A. DeVierno

Montana, Department of Transportation of the State of
Rep By: John A. DeVierno

North Dakota, Department of Transportation of
Rep By: John A. DeVierno

Rural States Federal Transportation Policy Development Group
Rep By: John A. DeVierno

South Dakota, Department of Transportation of
Rep By: John A. DeVierno

Wyoming, Department of Transportation of
Rep By: John A. DeVierno

Devillier Communications

1899 L St. NW
Suite 200
Washington, DC 20036

Tel: (202)833-8121
Fax: (202)833-8155

A public relations/marketing firm.

DC-Area Employees Representing Listed Clients

DEVILLIER, Linda, President
HALLMAN, Kristina, V. President
LOHMAN, Barbara, V. President
OXLEY, Merri, V. President
SCHERGENS, Becky, V. President

Clients

All Kinds of Music
Issues: EDU
Rep By: Merri Oxley

Capital Concerts
Issues: COM
Rep By: Kristina Hallman

Lockheed Martin Corp.
Issues: EDU
Rep By: Linda Devillier, Merri Oxley, Becky Schergens

Nat'l Ass'n of Health Underwriters
Issues: HCR INS
Rep By: Merri Oxley

Perkins School for the Blind
Issues: EDU
Rep By: Barbara Lohman

Dewey Ballantine LLP

1775 Pennsylvania Ave. NW
Suite 200
Washington, DC 20006

Tel: (202)862-1000
Fax: (202)862-1093
Registered: LDA, FARA

Web: www.deweyballantine.com
Washington office of a New York-based general practice law firm.

Political Action Committee

Dewey Ballantine LLP Political Action Committee
1775 Pennsylvania Ave. NW
Suite 200
Washington, DC 20006

Tel: (202)862-1000
Fax: (202)862-1093

DC-Area Employees Representing Listed Clients

ANGELL, Margaret, Semiconductor Policy Specialist
BENTLEY, David, Associate
CLARK, Harry L., Counsel
CONRAD, Andrew, Associate
DEMPSEY, Kevin M., Partner
DOWLEY, Joseph K., Partner
HENDERSON, Basil W., Specialist
HOLMES, Diana, Associate
HOWELL, Thomas R., Partner
HUME, Greg, Economist
KENTZ, Andrew W., Partner
LEACH, David, Communications Industry Advisor
MAGNUS, John R., Partner
MCCALLION, Kerry, Legislative Assistant
MCFADDEN, II, W. Clark, Partner
MIANO, Andrea, Associate
O'CONNOR, Kevin M., Legislative Assistant
RAGOSTA, John A., Partner
RICCARDI, Jennifer, Associate
SALMON, John J., Partner
STEIN, Michael H., Partner
WICKETT, James M., Associate
WOLFF, Alan W., Managing Partner

Clients

AFLAC, Inc.
Issues: TRD
Rep By: Andrew Conrad, Joseph K. Dowley, Alan W. Wolff

American Forest & Paper Ass'n
Issues: TRD
Rep By: Kevin M. Dempsey, John A. Ragosta

American Natural Soda Ash Corp.
Issues: TRD
Rep By: Thomas R. Howell, Andrew W. Kentz, John R. Magnus

Automatic Data Processing, Inc
Issues: TAX
Rep By: Basil W. Henderson, Andrew W. Kentz, John J. Salmon, James M. Wickett

CAMECO Corp.
Rep By: W. Clark McFadden, II

Catholic Health Ass'n of the United States
Issues: TAX
Rep By: John J. Salmon

Citigroup
Rep By: John J. Salmon

Coalition for Fair Lumber Imports
Issues: TRD
Rep By: Kevin M. Dempsey, Andrew W. Kentz, John A. Ragosta

Development Resources, Inc.
Issues: TAX
Rep By: John J. Salmon

Dutch Produce Ass'n
Issues: TRD
Rep By: Jennifer Riccardi

GE Investment Corp.
Rep By: John J. Salmon

Labor-Industry Coalition for Internat'l Trade
Issues: TRD
Rep By: John R. Magnus, Kevin M. O'Connor, Alan W. Wolff

Nextwave Telecom
Issues: TEC
Rep By: David Leach

Norfolk Southern Corp.
Issues: RET TAX
Rep By: Joseph K. Dowley

Qwest Communications
Rep By: Joseph K. Dowley

Railroad Retirement Tax Working Group
Issues: RET
Rep By: Joseph K. Dowley, Basil W. Henderson, Andrew W. Kentz, John J. Salmon, James M. Wickett

SBC Communications Inc.
Rep By: David Leach

Scull Law Firm, David L.
Issues: TAX
Rep By: Andrew W. Kentz, James M. Wickett

SEMATECH, Inc.
Rep By: W. Clark McFadden, II

Semiconductor Equipment and Materials Internat'l
Rep By: Harry L. Clark

Semiconductor Industry Ass'n
Issues: BUD IMM TAX TOR TRD
Rep By: Margaret Angell, Kevin M. Dempsey, W. Clark McFadden, II, Alan W. Wolff

Solectron

Thompson Publishing, Inc.
Rep By: Andrew W. Kentz, John J. Salmon

Tribune Co.
Rep By: Joseph K. Dowley, Andrew W. Kentz

Union Pacific
Issues: BNK TAX TRA
Rep By: Andrew W. Kentz, John J. Salmon, James M. Wickett

United States Telecom Ass'n
Issues: TAX
Rep By: Joseph K. Dowley

Verizon Communications
Rep By: Joseph K. Dowley

Dewey Square Group

1001 G St. NW
Suite 300 East
Washington, DC 20001
Web: www.deweysquare

Tel: (202)638-5616
Fax: (202)638-5612
Registered: LDA

DC-Area Employees Representing Listed Clients

BAKER, III, Charles A., Partner
BASKETTE, Jon Patrick, Principal
CAMPION, Charles, Partner
MCLEAN, Catherine, Partner
REID, Morris, V. President
SHERIDAN, Anne, Principal
WHOULEY, Michael, Partner

Clients

AT&T
Issues: TEC
Rep By: Morris Reid

Northwest Airlines, Inc.
Issues: TRA TRD
Rep By: Charles A. Baker, III, Jon Patrick Baskette, Charles Campion, Michael Whouley

Dickstein Shapiro Morin & Oshinsky LLP

2101 L St. NW
Washington, DC 20037-1526

Tel: (202)785-9700
Fax: (202)887-0689
Registered: LDA, FARA

Web: www.legalinnovators.com
E-mail: ZausnerA@dsmo.com
A law firm providing comprehensive representation through its five core groups: Complex Dispute Resolution, Corporate and Finance, Litigation, Legislative and Regulatory Affairs, and Technology. Also maintains an office in New York, NY.

Political Action Committee
Dickstein Shapiro Morin & Oshinsky LLP Political Action Committee
2101 L St. NW Tel: (202)785-9700
Washington, DC 20037-1526 Fax: (202)887-0689
Contact: L. Andrew Zausner

DC-Area Employees Representing Listed Clients
ADAMS, Kenneth L., Partner
CASHEN, II, Henry C., Partner
DICKSTEIN, Sidney, Senior Counsel
EISENSTAT, Larry F., Partner
FEINSTEIN, Margaret
FORD, Hon. Wendell H., Senior Counsel
HAYWOOD, Elizabeth B., Associate
HUBBARD, Alan, Counsel
KADZIK, Peter J., Partner
KAYMAK, Alev, International Trade Consultant
KRAMER, Albert H., Partner
LOWTHER, Frederick M., Partner
MANGAS, Robert, Of Counsel
MATHEWS, Graham "Rusty", Senior Legislative Advisor
MCKAY, Laurie, Legislative Assistant
MILLER, Andrew P., Partner
NASH, Bernard, Partner
PARRIS, Hon. Stanford E., Of Counsel
POLATNICK, Eden, Associate
SAILER, Francis J., Partner
SHEPHERD, Rebecah Moore, Legislative Specialist
SIMON, Kenneth M., Partner
SZABO, Laura, Partner
TYDINGS, Hon. Joseph D., Senior Counsel
ZAUSNER, L. Andrew, Partner

Clients

American Greyhound Track Operators Ass'n
Issues: GAM IND SMB
Rep By: Henry C. Cashen, II, Margaret Feinstein, Elizabeth B. Haywood, Robert Mangas, Graham "Rusty" Mathews, Rebecah Moore Shepherd, L. Andrew Zausner

American Public Communications Council
Issues: TEC
Rep By: Elizabeth B. Haywood, Alan Hubbard, Albert H. Kramer, Robert Mangas, Rebecah Moore Shepherd

CaseNewHolland Inc.
Issues: AGR ECN FIN MAN TRD
Rep By: Peter J. Kadzik, Robert Mangas, Graham "Rusty" Mathews, L. Andrew Zausner

Cigar Ass'n of America
Issues: TOB
Rep By: Henry C. Cashen, II, Hon. Wendell H. Ford, Elizabeth B. Haywood, Robert Mangas, Graham "Rusty" Mathews, Laurie McKay, Hon. Stanford E. Parris, Rebecah Moore Shepherd, L. Andrew Zausner

Colakoglu Group
Issues: TRD
Rep By: Alev Kaymak, L. Andrew Zausner

Delta Air Lines
Issues: AVI
Rep By: Hon. Wendell H. Ford, Robert Mangas

DuPont
Rep By: Graham "Rusty" Mathews, Bernard Nash

Electric Power Supply Ass'n
Issues: UTI
Rep By: Hon. Wendell H. Ford, Elizabeth B. Haywood, Robert Mangas, Graham "Rusty" Mathews, Laurie McKay, Hon. Stanford E. Parris, Rebecah Moore Shepherd, Laura Szabo, L. Andrew Zausner

Exxon Valdez Oil Spill Litigation Plaintiffs
Issues: ENV FUE LAW MAR TAX
Rep By: Kenneth L. Adams, Bernard Nash

First USA Bank
Issues: BAN
Rep By: Henry C. Cashen, II, Graham "Rusty" Mathews, Bernard Nash, Hon. Joseph D. Tydings, L. Andrew Zausner

Habas Group
Issues: TRD
Rep By: Alev Kaymak, Francis J. Sailer, L. Andrew Zausner

Harbour Group Industries, Inc.
Issues: FIN
Rep By: Henry C. Cashen, II, Elizabeth B. Haywood, Peter J. Kadzik, Graham "Rusty" Mathews, L. Andrew Zausner

Home Box Office
Rep By: Bernard Nash, Rebecah Moore Shepherd, L. Andrew Zausner

Homestake Mining
Issues: FIN MON NAT
Rep By: Graham "Rusty" Mathews, Hon. Stanford E. Parris, L. Andrew Zausner

Hydro-Quebec
Issues: ENG UTI
Rep By: Hon. Wendell H. Ford, Elizabeth B. Haywood, Robert Mangas, Graham "Rusty" Mathews, Laurie McKay, Rebecah Moore Shepherd, L. Andrew Zausner

Incentive Federation Sweepstakes Trust Fund
Issues: POS
Rep By: Henry C. Cashen, II, Elizabeth B. Haywood, Graham "Rusty" Mathews, Rebecah Moore Shepherd, L. Andrew Zausner

Internat'l Brotherhood of Teamsters
Issues: LBR TRU
Rep By: Henry C. Cashen, II, Elizabeth B. Haywood, Peter J. Kadzik, Robert Mangas, Graham "Rusty" Mathews, Rebecah Moore Shepherd, L. Andrew Zausner

Kerr-McGee Corp.
Rep By: Hon. Wendell H. Ford, Robert Mangas, Graham "Rusty" Mathews, L. Andrew Zausner

Lorillard Tobacco Co.
Rep By: Henry C. Cashen, II, Hon. Wendell H. Ford, Elizabeth B. Haywood, Robert Mangas, Graham "Rusty" Mathews, Laurie McKay, Hon. Stanford E. Parris, Rebecah Moore Shepherd, L. Andrew Zausner

Luiginos
Rep By: Robert Mangas, Graham "Rusty" Mathews, L. Andrew Zausner

Malaysian Palm Oil Promotion Council
Rep By: Peter J. Kadzik

Nat'l Ass'n of Chain Drug Stores
Rep By: Henry C. Cashen, II, Peter J. Kadzik

Nat'l Ass'n of Water Companies
Issues: LAW TOR
Rep By: Robert Mangas, Graham "Rusty" Mathews, L. Andrew Zausner

PG&E Generating Co.
Issues: CAW ENG ENV UTI
Rep By: Sidney Dickstein, Larry F. Eisenstat, Hon. Wendell H. Ford, Elizabeth B. Haywood, Robert Mangas, Graham "Rusty" Mathews, Laurie McKay, Hon. Stanford E. Parris, Rebecah Moore Shepherd, Kenneth M. Simon, Laura Szabo, L. Andrew Zausner

Pipe Tobacco Council, Inc.
Issues: TOB
Rep By: Henry C. Cashen, II, Hon. Wendell H. Ford, Elizabeth B. Haywood, Robert Mangas, Graham "Rusty" Mathews, Laurie McKay, Hon. Stanford E. Parris, Rebecah Moore Shepherd, L. Andrew Zausner

Poseidon Resources Corp.
Rep By: Frederick M. Lowther, Bernard Nash, Hon. Stanford E. Parris, L. Andrew Zausner

Ratcliff Strategies
Rep By: Robert Mangas

The Reader's Digest Ass'n
Issues: POS
Rep By: Elizabeth B. Haywood, Robert Mangas, Graham "Rusty" Mathews, Andrew P. Miller, Hon. Stanford E. Parris, Rebecah Moore Shepherd, L. Andrew Zausner

Smokeless Tobacco Council
Issues: TOB
Rep By: Henry C. Cashen, II, Hon. Wendell H. Ford, Elizabeth B. Haywood, Robert Mangas, Graham "Rusty" Mathews, Laurie McKay, Hon. Stanford E. Parris, Rebecah Moore Shepherd, L. Andrew Zausner

William M. Diefenderfer

P.O. Box 1040 Tel: (703)759-0822
Great Falls, VA 22066 Fax: (703)438-3126
Registered: LDA

Clients

Nordstrom, Inc.
Issues: TAX
Rep By: William M. Diefenderfer, III

Weyerhaeuser Co.
Issues: TAX
Rep By: William M. Diefenderfer, III

Dierman, Wortley, and Zola

1776 K St. NW Tel: (202)296-7555
Suite 400 Fax: (202)785-0025
Washington, DC 20006 Registered: LDA
A consulting firm specializing in public policy and financial strategies.

DC-Area Employees Representing Listed Clients
WORTLEY, MC (Ret.), Hon. George C., Chairman
ZOLA, Hilliard A., President

Clients

Bangladesh Economic Program Zone Authority

Bangladesh Export Processing Zones Authority
Issues: FOR TRD
Rep By: Hon. George C. Wortley, MC (Ret.), Hilliard A. Zola

PriceWaterhouseCoopers
Issues: GOV

Space Media
Issues: EDU SCI

diGenova & Toensing

901 15th St. NW Tel: (202)289-7701
Suite 430 Fax: (202)289-7706
Washington, DC 20005 Registered: LDA
A law firm representing international and domestic clients before federal courts, federal departments and agencies, and Congress.

DC-Area Employees Representing Listed Clients
DIGENOVA, Joseph E., Partner
TOENSING, Brady, Associate
TOENSING, Victoria, Partner

Clients

American Hospital Ass'n
Issues: MMM
Rep By: Joseph E. diGenova, Brady Toensing, Victoria Toensing

Dillon, Hall & Lungershausen

1101 Pennsylvania Ave. NW Tel: (202)312-0600
Sixth Floor Fax: (202)312-0606
Washington, DC 20004
A law firm.

DC-Area Employees Representing Listed Clients
HALL, James E., Partner

Clients

DaimlerChrysler Corp.
Rep By: James E. Hall

Dilworth Paxson, LLP

1200 19th St. NW Tel: (202)452-0900
Suite 210 Fax: (202)452-0930
Washington, DC 20036 Registered: LDA
Web: www.dilworthlaw.com

DC-Area Employees Representing Listed Clients
DONNELLAN, Rebecca A., Partner

Clients

Alaska Federation of Natives
Rep By: Rebecca A. Donnellan

Bethel Native Corp.
Rep By: Rebecca A. Donnellan

Kuskokwim Corp.

The Direct Impact Co.

1029 N. Royal St. Tel: (703)684-1245
Suite 400 Fax: (703)684-1249
Alexandria, VA 22314
E-mail: JBrady@directimpact.com
A direct education, stakeholder mobilization, grassroots educations, online database management and fulfillment, and third-part ally recruitment firm.

DC-Area Employees Representing Listed Clients
AHEARN, Patrick, V. President, Field Operations
BENJAMIN, Thomas, V. President
BLOOMBERG, Mary Beth, Principal
BRADY, John, Chairman and Chief Exec. Officer
BRINTZENHOFE, Nicola, Chief Financial Officer
GIANINY, James, Senior V. President
GIBSON, Michael, V. President
HERRITY, Thomas M., President
MACFARLANE, Cathy, Exec. V. President
STRUBHAR, Keith, V. President
TUCKER, Michael, V. President, Client Relations

Clients

Air Quality Standards Coalition
American Apparel & Footwear Ass'n
American Ass'n of Health Plans (AAHP)
American Council of Life Insurers
American Forest & Paper Ass'n
American Petroleum Institute
American Plastics Council
Ass'n of American Railroads
Barona Indian Reservation
Bell Helicopter Textron, Inc.
Bristol-Myers Squibb Co.
Business Software Alliance
Cellular Telecommunications and Internet Ass'n
Citigroup
Coalition for Vehicle Choice
ComEd
Corporation for Public Broadcasting
D.A.R.E. America
Detroit Edison Co.
Eastman Chemical Co.
Greeting Card Ass'n

Health Insurance Ass'n of America
Independence Blue Cross
Ingalls Shipbuilding
Koch Industries, Inc.
Eli Lilly and Co.
Lockheed Martin Corp.
Merck & Co.
Nat'l Ass'n of Chain Drug Stores
Nat'l Ass'n of Convenience Stores
Nat'l Family Planning and Reproductive Health Ass'n
Issues: FAM
Rep By: Mary Beth Bloomberg
Newport News Shipbuilding Inc.
North American Venture Capital Ass'n
PacifiCare Health Systems
Pfizer, Inc.
Rhone-Polenc Inc.
Sempra Energy
Sierra Health Services
WellPoint Health Networks/Blue Cross of California/UNICARE
Wyeth-Ayerst Laboratories

Direct Impact, LLC

8503 Pelham Rd.
Bethesda, MD 20817
Tel: (301)564-9708
Fax: (301)564-9706
Registered: LDA

DC-Area Employees Representing Listed Clients
BAWDEN, Ben
CHARLES, Robert B., President
LITTLEFIELD, Sean

Clients

California, State of, Attorney General's Office
Issues: ALC LAW
Rep By: Ben Bawden, Robert B. Charles
D.A.R.E. America
Issues: ALC
Rep By: Robert B. Charles, Sean Littlefield

Dittus Communications

1150 17th St. NW
Suite 701
Washington, DC 20036
Tel: (202)775-1401
Fax: (202)775-1404
Registered: LDA
Web: www.dittus.com
Public affairs and communications.

DC-Area Employees Representing Listed Clients
BOYD, Trudi, V. President, Media Relations
CABRAL, Debra, Exec. V. President
CONWAY, Tom, Senior V. President
DITTUS, Gloria S., President and Chief Exec. Officer
ELSEN, Karine, Associate V. President
ESHELMAN, Jeffrey, Senior Director
FOX, Amy, Associate Director
GARFINKEL, Jennifer, Director
GIORGIO, Cynthia, Assistant V. President
JONES, Shelton, Senior Director
LITTERST, Kristin, Assistant V. President
MCNAMARA, Chris, V. President and Managing Director
MITCHELL, Erin, Associate Director
MOIRE, Jennifer, Director
MOORJANI, Neena, Associate Director
SCOTT, Leanne, Account Executive
SINGLETON, Roni, Director
SITES, Tim, V. President and Managing Director
SLATER, Alice, Associate Director
WIELAND, Paul, Manager & Editor, EIN
YOUNG, Kristin, Director

Clients

3Com Corp.
Rep By: Kristin Litterst
Alabama Power
Rep By: Gloria S. Dittus
American Ass'n of Preferred Provider Organizations
Rep By: Jennifer Garfinkel, Chris McNamara
American Business for Legal Immigration
Rep By: Trudi Boyd, Gloria S. Dittus
Americans for Computer Privacy
Rep By: Gloria S. Dittus, Kristin Litterst
Andrx Pharmaceutical Corp.
Rep By: Jennifer Garfinkel, Chris McNamara
Bizee.com
Rep By: Trudi Boyd
Business Software Alliance
Rep By: Tom Conway, Gloria S. Dittus, Cynthia Giorgio, Kristin Litterst, Jennifer Moire, Tim Sites
CapNet
Rep By: Gloria S. Dittus, Shelton Jones, Kristin Litterst
Citigroup
Rep By: Debra Cabral, Shelton Jones
Community Financial Services Ass'n
Rep By: Debra Cabral, Alice Slater, Kristin Young
Comptel
Rep By: Tom Conway, Gloria S. Dittus, Kristin Litterst, Jennifer Moire
COPA Commission
Rep By: Kristin Litterst, Jennifer Moire
Council for Affordable Reliable Energy (CARE)
Rep By: Shelton Jones
Dell Computer Corp.
Rep By: Gloria S. Dittus, Shelton Jones
Digital Focus
Rep By: Trudi Boyd, Tom Conway, Jeffrey Eshelman
DoubleClick
Rep By: Gloria S. Dittus
Editorial Information Network
Rep By: Trudi Boyd, Gloria S. Dittus, Paul Wieland
eLink
Rep By: Karine Elsen, Cynthia Giorgio, Leanne Scott
Exolve
Rep By: Jennifer Garfinkel, Chris McNamara
FM Watch
Rep By: Gloria S. Dittus, Shelton Jones
Hess
Rep By: Tom Conway, Jeffrey Eshelman
Intel Corp.
Rep By: Tom Conway, Shelton Jones, Kristin Litterst
Internat'l Limousine
Rep By: Tom Conway, Cynthia Giorgio
Kraft Foods, Inc.
Rep By: Gloria S. Dittus
Legend Airlines
Rep By: Gloria S. Dittus
Magazine Publishers of America
Rep By: Trudi Boyd, Debra Cabral, Amy Fox, Neena Moorjani
Microsoft Corp.
Rep By: Tom Conway, Cynthia Giorgio
Nat'l Alliance Against Blacklisting
Rep By: Debra Cabral, Kristin Litterst, Alice Slater
Nat'l Cooperative Business Ass'n
Rep By: Debra Cabral, Neena Moorjani
Pegasus Communications
Rep By: Kristin Litterst, Jennifer Moire
Pernod Ricard
Rep By: Gloria S. Dittus, Shelton Jones, Kristin Litterst, Jennifer Moire
Personal Watercraft Industry Ass'n
Rep By: Alice Slater, Kristin Young
R - Tech Veno
Rep By: Jennifer Garfinkel, Chris McNamara
Ronald Reagan Internat'l Center
Rep By: Roni Singleton, Tim Sites
Southern Co.
Rep By: Gloria S. Dittus
Statoil Energy
Rep By: Trudi Boyd, Gloria S. Dittus, Jeffrey Eshelman
SurfControl
Rep By: Gloria S. Dittus, Karine Elsen, Cynthia Giorgio, Erin Mitchell, Jennifer Moire, Tim Sites
SurfWatch
Rep By: Debra Cabral, Gloria S. Dittus
Surviving Selma
Rep By: Jeffrey Eshelman, Cynthia Giorgio, Chris McNamara, Tim Sites
TCS
Rep By: Tom Conway, Jeffrey Eshelman, Tim Sites
Uniformed Services Family Health Plan
Rep By: Debra Cabral, Jennifer Garfinkel, Chris McNamara
VeriSign/Network Solutions, Inc.
Rep By: Tom Conway, Gloria S. Dittus, Shelton Jones, Kristin Litterst
Yours.com
Rep By: Gloria S. Dittus

Doepken Keevican & Weiss

1620 L St. NW
Washington, DC 20036
Tel: (202)955-5080
Fax: (202)955-6070
Registered: LDA

DC-Area Employees Representing Listed Clients
SLEASE, III, Clyde H.

Clients

Allegheny County Airport Authority
Issues: GOV TOU TRA
Nat'l Liberty Museum
Issues: ECN EDU TOU URB
Rep By: Clyde H. Slease, III
Pittsburgh, University of
Issues: BUD
Please Touch Museum, The Children's Museum of Philadelphia
Issues: ECN EDU TOU URB
Rep By: Clyde H. Slease, III

Bob Dole Enterprises

901 15th St. NW
Suite 700
Washington, DC 20005-2301
Tel: (202)371-6000
Fax: (202)371-6279

DC-Area Employees Representing Listed Clients
HART, Vicki E.

Clients

Johnson & Johnson, Inc.
Issues: MMM
Rep By: Vicki E. Hart

Theodore A. Doremus, Jr.

1300 I St. NW
Suite 1000 East
Washington, DC 20005
Tel: (202)962-7160
Fax: (202)962-7111
Registered: LDA

Clients

The Financial Services Roundtable
Issues: FIN
Rep By: Theodore A. Doremus, Jr.
Wells Fargo Bank, N.A.
Rep By: Theodore A. Doremus, Jr.

Dorfman & O'Neal, Inc.

915 15th St. NW
Suite 600
Washington, DC 20005-2302
Tel: (202)393-8444
Fax: (202)393-8666
Registered: LDA
Web: www.dorfmanoneal.com
E-mail: mail@dorfmanoneal.com
A government relations, communications and marketing firm specializing in transportation, energy and environmental issues, and technology services.

DC-Area Employees Representing Listed Clients
DORFMAN, Ira H., President
MCCONAHY, Marc, V. President
NEVE, Maria F., Program Manager

Clients

American Honda Motor Co., Inc.
Issues: AUT ENV TRA
Rep By: Ira H. Dorfman, Marc McConahy, Maria F. Neve
FuelMaker Corp.
Issues: AUT ENV TRA
Rep By: Ira H. Dorfman, Marc McConahy, Maria F. Neve
Simula, Inc.
Issues: AUT AVI CSP RRR TRA
Rep By: Ira H. Dorfman

Dorsey & Whitney LLP

1001 Pennsylvania Ave. NW
Suite 300S
Washington, DC 20004
Tel: (202)824-8800
Fax: (202)824-8990
Registered: LDA, FARA
A law firm specializing in environmental, international trade, and legislative law.

DC-Area Employees Representing Listed Clients
BAKER-SHENK, Philip, Partner
BIEGING, David A., Partner
BOYLAN, Virginia W., Partner
DARCY, Cindy, Legislative Director
JARBOE, Mark
KARNS, Christopher, Partner
RIDLEY, Sarah, Legislative Assistant
SUGIYAMA, George, Partner
WADZINSKI, Kevin J., Associate

Clients

Bay Mills Indian Community
Issues: IND
Rep By: Virginia W. Boylan
Central Council of Tlingit and Haida Indian Tribes of Alaska
Issues: BUD IND
Rep By: Philip Baker-Shenk, David A. Bieging, Virginia W. Boylan, Cindy Darcy, Mark Jarboe, Christopher Karns, Kevin J. Wadzinski
Cow Creek Umpqua Tribe of Oregon
Issues: IND TAX
Rep By: Philip Baker-Shenk, David A. Bieging, Virginia W. Boylan, Cindy Darcy, Mark Jarboe, Christopher Karns, Kevin J. Wadzinski

Cuyapaipe Band of Mission Indians
Issues: IND
Rep By: Philip Baker-Shenk, David A. Bieging, Virginia W. Boylan, Cindy Darcy, Kevin J. Wadzinski

Delaware Tribe of Indians
Issues: IND
Rep By: Philip Baker-Shenk, David A. Bieging, Virginia W. Boylan, Cindy Darcy

Diamond Game Enterprises, Inc.
Issues: IND
Rep By: David A. Bieging, Virginia W. Boylan

Excelsior Gaming, Inc.
Rep By: David A. Bieging, Kevin J. Wadzinski

Grand Traverse Band of Chippewa and Ottawa Indians
Rep By: Philip Baker-Shenk, David A. Bieging, Virginia W. Boylan, Cindy Darcy, Christopher Karns, Kevin J. Wadzinski

Hoopa Valley Tribal Council
Issues: IND
Rep By: Philip Baker-Shenk, David A. Bieging, Cindy Darcy, Mark Jarboe, Christopher Karns, Sarah Ridley

Jamestown-S'Klallam Indian Tribe
Issues: IND
Rep By: Philip Baker-Shenk, David A. Bieging

Las Vegas Paiute Tribe
Rep By: David A. Bieging, Kevin J. Wadzinski

Little River Band of Ottawa Indians
Issues: IND
Rep By: Philip Baker-Shenk, David A. Bieging, Virginia W. Boylan, Cindy Darcy, Mark Jarboe, Sarah Ridley

Lower Elwaha S'Klallam Tribe
Issues: IND
Rep By: David A. Bieging, Virginia W. Boylan, Cindy Darcy, Sarah Ridley

Minneapolis-St. Paul Metropolitan Council
Issues: TRA
Rep By: David A. Bieging

Nez Perce Tribal Executive Committee
Rep By: Philip Baker-Shenk, David A. Bieging, Cindy Darcy, Sarah Ridley

Paucatuck Eastern Pequot Tribal Nation

Quinault Indian Nation
Issues: BUD IND
Rep By: Philip Baker-Shenk, David A. Bieging, Virginia W. Boylan, Cindy Darcy, Sarah Ridley

Red Lake Band of Chippewa Indians
Issues: GAM IND TAX
Rep By: Philip Baker-Shenk, David A. Bieging, Virginia W. Boylan, Cindy Darcy, Mark Jarboe, Christopher Karns, Kevin J. Wadzinski

Shakopee Mdewakanton Sioux Tribe
Issues: BUD GAM TAX
Rep By: Philip Baker-Shenk, David A. Bieging, Virginia W. Boylan, Cindy Darcy, Mark Jarboe, Sarah Ridley, Kevin J. Wadzinski

Southern Co.
Issues: ENV
Rep By: George Sugiyama

Spokane Tribe
Issues: TAX
Rep By: Philip Baker-Shenk, David A. Bieging, Virginia W. Boylan, Cindy Darcy, Sarah Ridley, Kevin J. Wadzinski

St. George Island Traditional Council
Issues: IND
Rep By: Philip Baker-Shenk, David A. Bieging, Christopher Karns, Kevin J. Wadzinski

Stockbridge-Munsee Community Band of Mohican Indians
Issues: BUD IND TAX
Rep By: Philip Baker-Shenk, David A. Bieging, Virginia W. Boylan, Cindy Darcy, Sarah Ridley, Kevin J. Wadzinski

Trading Cove Associates
Rep By: David A. Bieging, Virginia W. Boylan

Winnebago Tribe of Nebraska
Issues: BUD
Rep By: Philip Baker-Shenk, David A. Bieging, Virginia W. Boylan, Cindy Darcy, Sarah Ridley

Dow, Lohnes & Albertson, PLLC

1200 New Hampshire Ave. NW
Suite 800
Washington, DC 20036-6802
Tel: (202)776-2000
Fax: (202)776-2222
Registered: LDA, FARA
Web: www.dlalaw.com
E-mail: postmaster@dlalaw.com

DC-Area Employees Representing Listed Clients
ANTLEY, Corinne M., Member
BASILE, Michael D., Member
BAXT, Leonard J., Member
BENDER, Raymond G., Member
BRAUNSTEIN, Richard L., Member
BUREAU, Lisa C., Member
BURGER, James M., Member
BUTNER, Blain B., Member
BYRNES, John T., Member
CASSAT, Peter C., Member
DUDZINSKY, Jr., William S., Member
ESBIN, Barbara, Member
FEINBERG, Peter H., Member
FEORE, Jr., John R., Member
FRANCIS, Patricia A., Member
FRITTS, Linda A., Member
GLASS, Jonathan, Member
GOLDSTEIN, Michael B., Member
GRAY, Todd D., Member
GWADZ, Joyce T., Member
HARDY, Jr., Ralph W., Member
HART, Jonathan D., Member
HARTENBERGER, Werner K., Of Counsel
HAYS, Michael D., Member
HEPBURN, Michael A., Member
HILL, Jonathan B., Member
HINES, J. Michael, Member
JOST, John C., Member
KELLEY, Timothy J., Member
KOVAKA, Michael G., Member
KUZAS, Kevin J., Member
LANG, Paul R., Member
LOGAN, John S., Member
LONG, Bernard J., Member
LOUGHLIN, Stephanie M., Member
MATHER, Judith A., Member
MCGEARY, Elizabeth A., Member
MCHUGH, Richard P., Member
MILLER, Margaret L., Member
MILLS, David E., Member
O'CONNELL, Edward J., Member
O'ROURKE, Timothy J., Member
PHILLIPS, Laura H., Member
POMEROY, John H., Member
POST, Karen A., Senior Counsel
QUALIANA, Mary K., Member
REDDING, J. Christopher, Member
REED, Kevin F., Member
RITTER, Curtis A., Member
SALOMON, Kenneth D., Member
SAXENIAN, James R., Member
SHELDON, Stuart A., Member
STABBE, Michael H., Member
SWANSON, M. Anne, Member
TOOHEY, Daniel W., Senior Counsel
TREANOR, James A., Member
TRUONG, To-Quyen T., Member
TWEDT, Thomas D., Member
WADYKA, Christina S., Senior Counsel
WARD, John D., Member
WIESENFELDER, Leslie H., Member
WILD, David D., Member
WITTENSTEIN, David J., Member

Clients

American Ass'n of Cosmetology Schools

BET Holdings II, Inc.
Rep By: John R. Feore, Jr.

Cox Enterprises Inc.
Issues: GOV
Rep By: Kenneth D. Salomon

R. R. Donnelley & Sons
Rep By: J. Michael Hines, Paul R. Lang, Kenneth D. Salomon

Hawaiian Airlines
Issues: AVI BUD TAX
Rep By: Jonathan B. Hill

Iowa Telecommunications & Technology Commission
Issues: TEC
Rep By: Kenneth D. Salomon

Middlesex Community-Technical College
Issues: EDU
Rep By: Jonathan Glass

Nat'l ITFS Ass'n
Issues: COM EDU FOR TEC
Rep By: Todd D. Gray, Kenneth D. Salomon

Nat'l Technological University

Questcom
Rep By: Michael D. Hays

St. Louis Regional Education and Public Television Commission
Rep By: Todd D. Gray, Kenneth D. Salomon

St. Matthew's University School of Medicine
Issues: EDU
Rep By: Jonathan Glass, Michael B. Goldstein, Kenneth D. Salomon

Stelco Inc.
Rep By: Kenneth D. Salomon

Stoll Stoll Berne Lokting & Shlachter, P.C.
Issues: AVI FOR TOU TRA
Rep By: Michael D. Hays, Kenneth D. Salomon

University of Puerto Rico
Rep By: Todd D. Gray, Kenneth D. Salomon

Downey McGrath Group, Inc.

1225 I St. NW
Suite 350
Washington, DC 20005
Web: www.dmggroup.com
Tel: (202)789-1110
Fax: (202)789-1116
Registered: LDA, FARA

DC-Area Employees Representing Listed Clients
ACEVEDO, Elaine B., V. President
ALCRE, Jennifer
BERNIER, Delanne, V. President
DONALDSON, Nancy, V. President
DOWNEY, Jr., Hon. Thomas J., Chairman
MCCLOUD, Margaret M., Director
MCGRATH, Hon. Raymond J., President
MCLAUGHLIN, Kathleen Tynan, Chief Operating Officer
OLINGER, John Peter, V. President
PAINTER, Sally, Managing Director, International
WESSEL, Michael R., Senior V. President

Clients

American Foundation for AIDS Research
Issues: HCR
Rep By: Hon. Thomas J. Downey, Jr., John Peter Olinger

American Management Systems
Issues: CPI CPT DEF ENV FIN GOV SCI
Rep By: Nancy Donaldson, Hon. Thomas J. Downey, Jr.

American Soc. of Anesthesiologists
Issues: HCR MED MMM
Rep By: Delanne Bernier, Hon. Thomas J. Downey, Jr., Hon. Raymond J. McGrath, John Peter Olinger

AOL Time Warner
Issues: TEC
Rep By: Hon. Thomas J. Downey, Jr., John Peter Olinger

ASCAP

The Boeing Co.
Issues: BUD TRD
Rep By: Hon. Thomas J. Downey, Jr., Hon. Raymond J. McGrath

Breakthrough Technologies Institute
Issues: ENG
Rep By: Hon. Thomas J. Downey, Jr.

Chevron, U.S.A.
Issues: FUE
Rep By: Elaine B. Acevedo, Nancy Donaldson, Hon. Thomas J. Downey, Jr., Hon. Raymond J. McGrath

Dental Recycling North America
Issues: ENV HCR NAT
Rep By: Hon. Thomas J. Downey, Jr., Hon. Raymond J. McGrath, Michael R. Wessel

DuPont
Issues: AGR DEF ENV RRR
Rep By: Hon. Thomas J. Downey, Jr., John Peter Olinger

Energy Efficiency Systems, Inc.
Issues: ENV
Rep By: Hon. Thomas J. Downey, Jr., John Peter Olinger

Republic of Estonia

Fannie Mae
Issues: TAX
Rep By: Hon. Thomas J. Downey, Jr., John Peter Olinger

Fantasma Networks, Inc.
Issues: COM SCI TEC
Rep By: Elaine B. Acevedo, Hon. Thomas J. Downey, Jr., Hon. Raymond J. McGrath

Fuji Photo Film U.S.A., Inc.
Issues: TRD
Rep By: Hon. Thomas J. Downey, Jr., Margaret M. McCloud, John Peter Olinger

Hallmark Cards, Inc.
Issues: LAW
Rep By: Michael R. Wessel

Healthcare Ass'n of New York State
Issues: HCR MMM
Rep By: Hon. Thomas J. Downey, Jr., John Peter Olinger

Kalkines, Arky, Zall and Bernstein
Issues: BUD HCR HOU MMM
Rep By: Hon. Thomas J. Downey, Jr., John Peter Olinger

The Limited Inc.
Issues: LBR TRD
Rep By: Nancy Donaldson, Hon. Thomas J. Downey, Jr., John Peter Olinger

Merck & Co.
Issues: PHA
Rep By: Nancy Donaldson, Hon. Thomas J. Downey, Jr.

Metropolitan Life Insurance Co.
Issues: BAN FOR INS
Rep By: Hon. Thomas J. Downey, Jr., Hon. Raymond J. McGrath, John Peter Olinger

Microsoft Corp.
Issues: CPI CPT IMM TEC
Rep By: Hon. Thomas J. Downey, Jr., Hon. Raymond J. McGrath

Nat'l Cable Television Ass'n
Issues: COM
Rep By: Hon. Thomas J. Downey, Jr.

The New York Structural Biology Center
Issues: BUD
Rep By: Elaine B. Acevedo, Hon. Thomas J. Downey, Jr., Hon. Raymond J. McGrath, John Peter Olinger

Philipp Brothers Chemicals, Inc.
Issues: AGR CHM ENV PHA TRD
Rep By: Hon. Thomas J. Downey, Jr., John Peter Olinger

San Francisco, California, City and County of
Rep By: Hon. Thomas J. Downey, Jr.

SLM Holding Corp.
Issues: EDU
Rep By: Nancy Donaldson, Hon. Thomas J. Downey, Jr., Hon. Raymond J. McGrath, Michael R. Wessel

Teledesic Corp.
Issues: SCI TEC
Rep By: Hon. Thomas J. Downey, Jr.

The Timken Co.
Issues: TRD
Rep By: Delanne Bernier, Michael R. Wessel

U.S. Tour Operators Ass'n

United Brotherhood of Carpenters and Joiners of America
Issues: RET TAX
Rep By: Nancy Donaldson, Hon. Thomas J. Downey, Jr., Hon. Raymond J. McGrath

United Steelworkers of America
Issues: ECN LBR TRD
Rep By: Michael R. Wessel

World Federation of Free Latvians

W. B. Driggers & Associates, Inc.

9616 Burke View Ave.
Burke, VA 22015
Tel: (703)250-1852
Fax: (703)250-1857
Registered: LDA
E-mail: wbdassoc1@aol.com
Government relations consultant.

DC-Area Employees Representing Listed Clients
DRIGGERS, W. B., President

Clients

A. D. Butler and Associates, Inc.
Issues: DEF
Rep By: W. B. Driggers

Karta Technologies Inc.
Issues: DEF
Rep By: W. B. Driggers

Madison Government Affairs
Issues: DEF ENV URB
Rep By: W. B. Driggers

Photo Telesis
Issues: DEF
Rep By: W. B. Driggers

Raytheon Co.
Issues: DEF
Rep By: W. B. Driggers

SAVI Technology
Issues: DEF
Rep By: W. B. Driggers

Drinker Biddle & Reath LLP

1500 K St.
Suite 1100
Washington, DC 20005
Tel: (202)842-8800
Fax: (202)842-8465
Registered: LDA
Web: www.dbr.com
Washington office of a Philadelphia law firm.

DC-Area Employees Representing Listed Clients
BANKSON, Jr., John P., Of Counsel
BLUM, Jennifer L.
EDGE, Joe D., Partner
HUGHES, Timothy
MARQUEZ, Joaquin A., Partner
MELINSON, Gregg R.
MORSE, M. Howard, Partner
PETTIT, John W., Partner
REMINGTON, Michael J., Partner
SINGER, Richard M., Partner

Clients

Broadcast Music Inc. (BMI)
Issues: CPT
Rep By: Michael J. Remington

General Communications, Inc.
Rep By: Joe D. Edge

The Hearst Corp.
Issues: COM CPT MIA
Rep By: Jennifer L. Blum

KJVI
Rep By: John P. Bankson, Jr.

KKVI
Rep By: John P. Bankson, Jr.

KPVI

KTTY
Rep By: John P. Bankson, Jr.

Nat'l Community Capital Ass'n
Issues: TAX
Rep By: Timothy Hughes, Joaquin A. Marquez, Gregg R. Melinson

Printing Industries of America
Rep By: Michael J. Remington

Puerto Rico Bankers Ass'n
Rep By: Joaquin A. Marquez

Puerto Rico Chamber of Commerce
Rep By: Joaquin A. Marquez

Puerto Rico Manufacturers Ass'n
Rep By: Joaquin A. Marquez

Radio Shack Corp.
Issues: COM
Rep By: John W. Pettit

RioPort, Inc.
Rep By: M. Howard Morse, Michael J. Remington

WPXT
Rep By: John P. Bankson, Jr.

Drohan Management Group

11250 Roger Bacon Dr.
Suite Eight
Reston, VA 20190
Tel: (703)437-4377
Fax: (703)435-4390
Web: www.drohanmgmt.com/dmg/
E-mail: dmg@drohanmgmt.com
An association management and government relations firm.

DC-Area Employees Representing Listed Clients
DROHAN, CAE, William M., President
GUGGOLZ, Richard A., V. President
HOSKINS, Kathy, Account Executive
PRICE, CAE, Randall C., Account Executive

Clients

Ass'n of Nurses in AIDS Care
Rep By: Randall C. Price, CAE

Ass'n of Occupational Health Professionals in Healthcare
Rep By: Randall C. Price, CAE

Environmental Mutagen Soc.
Rep By: Randall C. Price, CAE

HIV/AIDS Nursing Certification Board
Rep By: Randall C. Price, CAE

Internat'l Biometric Ass'n (Eastern North American Region)
Rep By: Kathy Hoskins

Nat'l Ass'n of Corporate Treasurers

Nat'l Organization for Associate Degree Nursing
Rep By: Randall C. Price, CAE

Sports Lawyers Ass'n
Rep By: William M. Drohan, CAE, Richard A. Guggolz

DTB Associates, LLP

1001 Pennsylvania Ave. NW
Suite 600 North
Washington, DC 20004
Tel: (202)661-7092
Fax: (202)661-7093
Web: www.dtbassociates.com
E-mail: dtb@dtbassociates.com
Affiliated with the law firm of Powell, Goldstein, Frazer & Murphy (see separate listing). Focuses on international trade and agriculture policy issues.

DC-Area Employees Representing Listed Clients
BRENNER, Kyd D., Partner
BROSCH, Kevin, Partner
DRAZEK, Paul A., Partner
THORN, Craig A., Partner

Clients

American Farm Bureau Federation

Biotechnology Industry Organization

Duane, Morris & Heckscher LLP

1667 K St. NW
Suite 700
Washington, DC 20006
Tel: (202)776-7800
Fax: (202)776-7801
Registered: LDA
Web: www.duanemorris.com

DC-Area Employees Representing Listed Clients
AZIA, Stephen M.
BOHLKE, Gary, Partner
BRAD, Johnson, Partner
EASTWOOD, Valerie J.
MAPES, Jr., William R., Partner
QUILL, Terry, Partner

Clients

Mortgage Bankers Ass'n of America
Issues: HOU
Rep By: Johnson Brad

Power Mobility Coalition
Issues: BUD HCR
Rep By: Stephen M. Azia, Valerie J. Eastwood

The Duberstein Group, Inc.

2100 Pennsylvania Ave. NW
Suite 500
Washington, DC 20037
Tel: (202)728-1100
Fax: (202)728-1123
Registered: LDA
Government relations and corporate consulting.

DC-Area Employees Representing Listed Clients
ANGUS, III, John W., Senior V. President and General Counsel
BERMAN, Michael S., President
CHAMPLIN, Steven M., V. President
DUBERSTEIN, Kenneth M., Chairman and Chief Exec. Officer
GANDY, Henry M., V. President
HILL, John S., Director, Legislative Affairs
MEYER, Daniel P., V. President

Clients

Amerada Hess Corp.
Issues: FOR FUE
Rep By: John W. Angus, III, Michael S. Berman, Steven M. Champlin, Kenneth M. Duberstein, Henry M. Gandy, Daniel P. Meyer

American Apparel & Footwear Ass'n
Issues: APP TRD
Rep By: John W. Angus, III, Michael S. Berman, Steven M. Champlin, Kenneth M. Duberstein, Henry M. Gandy, Daniel P. Meyer

American Ass'n of Health Plans (AAHP)
Issues: HCR MED
Rep By: John W. Angus, III, Michael S. Berman, Steven M. Champlin, Kenneth M. Duberstein, Henry M. Gandy, Daniel P. Meyer

American Council of Life Insurers
Issues: BAN GOV HCR RET TAX
Rep By: John W. Angus, III, Michael S. Berman, Steven M. Champlin, Kenneth M. Duberstein, Henry M. Gandy, Daniel P. Meyer

American Gaming Ass'n
Issues: BNK GAM TAX
Rep By: John W. Angus, III, Michael S. Berman, Steven M. Champlin, Kenneth M. Duberstein, Henry M. Gandy, Daniel P. Meyer

The American Water Works Co.
Rep By: John W. Angus, III, Michael S. Berman, Steven M. Champlin, Kenneth M. Duberstein, Henry M. Gandy, Daniel P. Meyer

AOL Time Warner
Issues: CPT POS TAX TEC
Rep By: John W. Angus, III, Michael S. Berman, Steven M. Champlin, Kenneth M. Duberstein, Henry M. Gandy, Daniel P. Meyer

The Business Roundtable
Issues: BUD EDU ENV FIN GOV HCR LBR RET TAX TRD WEL
Rep By: John W. Angus, III, Michael S. Berman, Steven M. Champlin, Kenneth M. Duberstein, Henry M. Gandy, Daniel P. Meyer

Comcast Corp.
Issues: ART COM CPT MIA TEC
Rep By: John W. Angus, III, Michael S. Berman, Steven M. Champlin, Kenneth M. Duberstein, Henry M. Gandy, Daniel P. Meyer

Conoco Inc.
Issues: FOR FUE
Rep By: John W. Angus, III, Michael S. Berman, Steven M. Champlin, Kenneth M. Duberstein, Henry M. Gandy, Daniel P. Meyer

CSX Corp.
Issues: GOV MAR RRR
Rep By: John W. Angus, III, Michael S. Berman, Steven M. Champlin, Kenneth M. Duberstein, Henry M. Gandy, Daniel P. Meyer

Direct Marketing Ass'n, Inc.
Issues: ADV CPI POS TAX
Rep By: John W. Angus, III, Michael S. Berman, Steven M. Champlin, Kenneth M. Duberstein, Henry M. Gandy, Daniel P. Meyer

Dow Corning Corp.
Issues: GOV
Rep By: John W. Angus, III, Michael S. Berman, Steven M. Champlin, Kenneth M. Duberstein, Henry M. Gandy, Daniel P. Meyer

Fannie Mae
Issues: BNK HOU
Rep By: John W. Angus, III, Michael S. Berman, Steven M. Champlin, Kenneth M. Duberstein, Henry M. Gandy, Daniel P. Meyer

General Motors Corp.
Issues: AUT BNK ENV FOR GOV HCR TAX TRD
Rep By: John W. Angus, III, Michael S. Berman, Steven M. Champlin, Kenneth M. Duberstein, Henry M. Gandy, Daniel P. Meyer

Goldman, Sachs and Co.
Rep By: John W. Angus, III, Michael S. Berman, Steven M. Champlin, Kenneth M. Duberstein, Henry M. Gandy, Daniel P. Meyer

Marathon Oil Co.
Rep By: Michael S. Berman, Kenneth M. Duberstein, Henry M. Gandy, Daniel P. Meyer

Nat'l Cable Television Ass'n
Issues: COM
Rep By: John W. Angus, III, Michael S. Berman, Steven M. Champlin, Kenneth M. Duberstein, Henry M. Gandy, Daniel P. Meyer

Pharmacia Corp.
Issues: ANI CAW ENV HCR MED MMM TAX
Rep By: John W. Angus, III, Michael S. Berman, Steven M. Champlin, Kenneth M. Duberstein, Henry M. Gandy, Daniel P. Meyer

Project to Promote Competition and Innovation in the Digital Age
Issues: CPI CSP LBR SCI
Rep By: John W. Angus, III, Michael S. Berman, Steven M. Champlin, Kenneth M. Duberstein, Henry M. Gandy, Daniel P. Meyer

Sara Lee Corp.
Rep By: John W. Angus, III, Michael S. Berman, Steven M. Champlin, Kenneth M. Duberstein, Henry M. Gandy, Daniel P. Meyer

Transportation Institute
Issues: MAR
Rep By: John W. Angus, III, Michael S. Berman, Steven M. Champlin, Kenneth M. Duberstein, Henry M. Gandy, Daniel P. Meyer

United Airlines
Issues: AVI ENV TAX
Rep By: John W. Angus, III, Michael S. Berman, Steven M. Champlin, Kenneth M. Duberstein, Henry M. Gandy, Daniel P. Meyer

USX Corp.
Issues: FOR FUE
Rep By: John W. Angus, III, Michael S. Berman, Steven M. Champlin, Kenneth M. Duberstein, Henry M. Gandy, Daniel P. Meyer

Dublin Castle Group

1025 Connecticut Ave. NW
Suite 1012
Washington, DC 20036
E-mail: dcgmh@usa.net

DC-Area Employees Representing Listed Clients
HOGAN, Maureen Flatley, President

Clients

Adopt America
Issues: FAM
Rep By: Maureen Flatley Hogan

Bicopas, Ltd.
Issues: ECN FIN FOR
Rep By: Maureen Flatley Hogan

Catholic Alliance
Rep By: Maureen Flatley Hogan

Family Advocacy Services
Issues: FAM
Rep By: Maureen Flatley Hogan

Foster America, Inc.
Issues: FAM MMM WEL
Rep By: Maureen Flatley Hogan

Janus Solutions, Inc.
Issues: FAM MMM URB WEL
Rep By: Maureen Flatley Hogan

Link Romania, Inc.
Issues: ECN FOR TOU
Rep By: Maureen Flatley Hogan

Nat'l Adoption Foundation
Issues: FAM
Rep By: Maureen Flatley Hogan

Nat'l Ass'n of Foster Care Review Boards
Issues: FAM MMM
Rep By: Maureen Flatley Hogan

Romanian Orphans Connection, Inc.
Rep By: Maureen Flatley Hogan

Small Property Owners Ass'n of America
Rep By: Maureen Flatley Hogan

Ducheneaux, Taylor & Associates, Inc.

303 Massachusetts Ave. NE
Washington, DC 20002
Tel: (202)544-1353
Fax: (202)544-0620
Registered: LDA
E-mail: dtanet@aol.com

DC-Area Employees Representing Listed Clients
DUCHENEAUX, Franklin D., Partner
TAYLOR, Peter S., Partner

Clients

The Ashley Group
Issues: IND
Rep By: Franklin D. Ducheneaux, Peter S. Taylor

Gila River Farms
Issues: IND
Rep By: Peter S. Taylor

Grand Traverse Band of Chippewa and Ottawa Indians
Issues: IND
Rep By: Franklin D. Ducheneaux

Leech Lake Tribal Council
Issues: IND
Rep By: Franklin D. Ducheneaux

Minnesota Indian Gaming Ass'n
Issues: IND
Rep By: Franklin D. Ducheneaux

Mni-Sose Intertribal Water Rights Coalition
Issues: IND
Rep By: Peter S. Taylor

Pueblo of Laguna

Rosebud Sioux Tribal Council
Issues: IND
Rep By: Peter S. Taylor

Siletz Tribal Council
Issues: IND
Rep By: Franklin D. Ducheneaux

Timbisha Shoshone Tribe
Rep By: Peter S. Taylor

Tohono O'Odham Nation
Issues: IND
Rep By: Franklin D. Ducheneaux

Tulalip Tribes
Issues: IND
Rep By: Franklin D. Ducheneaux

Dr. John V. Dugan, Jr.

1730 M St. NW
Suite 911
Washington, DC 20036
Tel: (202)293-6116
Fax: (202)293-7444
Registered: LDA
E-mail: jackdugan@earthlink.net
A self-employed consultant.

Clients

American Institute of Chemical Engineers
Rep By: Dr. John V. Dugan, Jr.

Battelle
Issues: ENG ENV SCI
Rep By: Dr. John V. Dugan, Jr.

Dunaway & Cross

1700 K St. NW
Suite 800
Washington, DC 20006
Tel: (202)862-9700
Fax: (202)862-9710
Registered: LDA
E-mail: duncross@msn.com

DC-Area Employees Representing Listed Clients
DUNAWAY, Mac S., Managing Partner
SHAFER, Raymond P., General Counsel

Clients

Aerospace Industries Ass'n of America
Rep By: Mac S. Dunaway

Crown Controls Corp.
Rep By: Mac S. Dunaway

Goodman Manufacturing Co., L.P.
Rep By: Mac S. Dunaway

Industrial Truck Ass'n
Rep By: Mac S. Dunaway, Raymond P. Shafer

Portable Power Equipment Manufacturers Ass'n
Rep By: Mac S. Dunaway

The Toro Co.
Rep By: Mac S. Dunaway

Duncan and Associates

1213 29th St. NW
Washington, DC 20007
Tel: (202)333-5841
Fax: (202)333-5881

DC-Area Employees Representing Listed Clients
DUNCAN, Jack G., President

Clients

American Citizens for the Arts Political Action Committee
Rep By: Jack G. Duncan

American Network of Community Options and Resources (ANCOR)
Rep By: Jack G. Duncan

American Rehab Action
Rep By: Jack G. Duncan

Ass'n of Independent Colleges of Art and Design
Rep By: Jack G. Duncan

Conference of Educational Administrators of Schools and Programs for the Deaf
Rep By: Jack G. Duncan

Convention of American Instructors of the Deaf
Rep By: Jack G. Duncan

Council of State Administrators of Vocational Rehabilitation
Rep By: Jack G. Duncan

Nat'l Council of State Agencies for the Blind
Rep By: Jack G. Duncan

Nat'l Council on Rehabilitation Education
Rep By: Jack G. Duncan

Nat'l Rehabilitation Political Action Committee
Rep By: Jack G. Duncan

Duncan, Weinberg, Genzer & Pembroke, P.C.

1615 M St. NW
Suite 800
Washington, DC 20036-3203
Tel: (202)467-6370
Fax: (202)467-6379
Registered: LDA
E-mail: dwmp@dwgp.com
A law firm specializing in energy, natural resources, local government, communications, and environmental matters before federal and state courts and agencies.

DC-Area Employees Representing Listed Clients
ALLAN, Richmond F., Principal
DINERSTEIN, Paula N., Of Counsel
DUNCAN, Wallace L., President
EILBOTT, Eli D., Principal
FLUG, James F., Of Counsel
GAST, Lisa S., Associate
GENZER, Jeffrey C., Principal
HALL, Joseph C., Associate
LOWER, Janice L., Principal
MAZURE, Kathleen L., Of Counsel
PEMBROKE, James D., Secretary-Treasurer
POSTAR, Michael R., Principal
RUDEBUSCH, Thomas L., Principal
SHONKWILER, Tatjana M., Principal
SINGER, Ms. Terry E., Of Counsel
WEINBERG, Robert, Principal

Clients

Arab, Alabama, City of
Issues: GOV
Rep By: Janice L. Lower

Auburn, Avilla, Bluffton, Columbia City and Other Municipalities of Indiana
Issues: ENG GOV UTI
Rep By: Janice L. Lower, James D. Pembroke

Basin Electric Power Cooperative
Issues: ENG ENV UTI
Rep By: Richmond F. Allan

Bergen, New York, Village of
Issues: COM ENG ENV GOV UTI
Rep By: Richmond F. Allan, Jeffrey C. Genzer, Michael R. Postar, Thomas L. Rudebusch

Boonville, New York, Village of
Issues: GOV UTI
Rep By: Richmond F. Allan, Jeffrey C. Genzer

Braintree Electric Light Department
Issues: GOV UTI
Rep By: Janice L. Lower

Center for Clean Air Policy
Issues: ENV
Rep By: Jeffrey C. Genzer

Central Montana Electric Power Cooperative, Inc.
Issues: ENG UTI
Rep By: Janice L. Lower, James D. Pembroke

Central Virginia Electric Cooperative, Inc.
Issues: ENG UTI
Rep By: Robert Weinberg

Champlin Exploration, Inc.
Issues: FUE
Rep By: Kathleen L. Mazure

Churchville, New York, Village of
Issues: COM GOV
Rep By: Jeffrey C. Genzer, Michael R. Postar

Clayton, Dover, Lewes, Middletown, Milford, Newark, NewCastle, Seaford and Smyrna, Delaware, Municipalities of
Issues: COM ENG GOV UTI
Rep By: Janice L. Lower

College Station, Texas, City of
Issues: ENG GOV UTI
Rep By: Wallace L. Duncan, Michael R. Postar

Colorado Energy Assistance Foundation
Rep By: Jeffrey C. Genzer

Connecticut, Office of the Attorney General of the State of
Rep By: James F. Flug

Corn Belt Energy Corp.
Issues: ENG UTI
Rep By: Michael R. Postar

Craig-Botetourt Electric Cooperative, Inc.
Rep By: Robert Weinberg

Delaware Municipal Electric Corp. (DEMEC)
Issues: ENG GOV UTI
Rep By: Janice L. Lower

Eclipse Energy Systems, Inc./Insyte, Inc.
Issues: ENG
Rep By: Jeffrey C. Genzer

Energy House Capital Corp.
Rep By: Jeffrey C. Genzer

Energy Programs Consortium
Issues: ENG
Rep By: Jeffrey C. Genzer

EnerStar Power Corp.
Issues: ENG UTI
Rep By: Michael R. Postar

Export Council for Energy Efficiency
Issues: COM ENG TRD
Rep By: Jeffrey C. Genzer

Farmers' Electric Cooperative
Rep By: Robert Weinberg

Freeport, New York, Electric Department of the Village of
Issues: ENG ENV GOV UTI
Rep By: Richmond F. Allan, Jeffrey C. Genzer, Thomas L. Rudebusch

Front Royal, Virginia, Town of
Issues: GOV
Rep By: Janice L. Lower

Georgia, Office of the Attorney General of the State of
Rep By: James F. Flug

Geothermal Energy Ass'n
Rep By: Jeffrey C. Genzer

Greenport, New York, Village Electric Department of
Issues: ENG GOV UTI
Rep By: Richmond F. Allan, Thomas L. Rudebusch

Hagerstown, Maryland, Municipal Electric Light Plant of
Issues: ENG GOV UTI
Rep By: Janice L. Lower

Hawaii, Department of Business and Economic Development of the State of
Issues: ECN ENG GOV
Rep By: Jeffrey C. Genzer

Hoosier Energy Rural Electric Cooperative, Inc.
Issues: ENG UTI
Rep By: Robert Weinberg

Howard County, Maryland
Issues: COM GOV
Rep By: Janice L. Lower

Idaho, Office of the Attorney General of the State of
Rep By: James F. Flug

Indiana and Michigan Municipal Distributors Ass'n
Issues: ENG UTI
Rep By: Janice L. Lower, James D. Pembroke

Indiana, Office of the Attorney General of the State of
Rep By: James F. Flug

Internat'l Energy Consultants
Rep By: Jeffrey C. Genzer, Tatjana M. Shonkwiler

Jamestown, New York, Board of Public Utilities
Issues: ENG ENV GOV UTI
Rep By: Richmond F. Allan, Jeffrey C. Genzer, Thomas L. Rudebusch, Tatjana M. Shonkwiler

Knightstown, Indiana, Town of
Issues: COM GOV
Rep By: Michael R. Postar

Lea County Electric Cooperative, Inc.
Rep By: Robert Weinberg

M-S-R Public Power Agency
Issues: ENG GOV UTI
Rep By: Wallace L. Duncan, James D. Pembroke, Thomas L. Rudebusch

Maryland, Office of the Attorney General of the State of
Rep By: James F. Flug

Massena, New York, Town of
Issues: ENG GOV UTI
Rep By: Richmond F. Allan, Wallace L. Duncan, Jeffrey C. Genzer, Thomas L. Rudebusch

The Metropolitan Water District of Southern California
Issues: UTI
Rep By: Wallace L. Duncan, Michael R. Postar

Michigan, Office of the Attorney General of the State of
Rep By: James F. Flug

Mid-West Electric Consumers Ass'n
Issues: CSP ENG UTI
Rep By: Jeffrey C. Genzer

Mishawaka Utilities
Issues: ENG GOV UTI
Rep By: Janice L. Lower, James D. Pembroke

Modesto/Turlock Irrigation District
Issues: CSP ENG UTI
Rep By: Wallace L. Duncan, James D. Pembroke, Michael R. Postar

Municipal Electric Utilities Ass'n of New York State
Issues: COM ENG GOV UTI
Rep By: Wallace L. Duncan, Jeffrey C. Genzer, Kathleen L. Mazure, Thomas L. Rudebusch

Nat'l Ass'n of Energy Service Companies
Issues: ENG GOV UTI
Rep By: Jeffrey C. Genzer, Tatjana M. Shonkwiler

Nat'l Ass'n of State Energy Officials
Issues: ENG GOV
Rep By: Jeffrey C. Genzer

Nat'l Energy Assistance Directors' Ass'n
Issues: ENG GOV
Rep By: Jeffrey C. Genzer

Nevada, Office of the Attorney General
Rep By: James F. Flug

New York Municipal Power Agency
Issues: ENG GOV
Rep By: Jeffrey C. Genzer, Thomas L. Rudebusch

Ocala, Florida, City of
Issues: GOV
Rep By: Janice L. Lower

Ohio, Office of the Attorney General of the State of
Rep By: James F. Flug

ONEOK Bushton Processing, LLC
Issues: FUE
Rep By: Kathleen L. Mazure

ONEOK Energy Marketing & Trading Co.
Issues: FUE
Rep By: Kathleen L. Mazure

ONEOK Field Services, Inc.
Issues: FUE
Rep By: Kathleen L. Mazure

ONEOK Gas Transportation, LLC
Issues: FUE
Rep By: Kathleen L. Mazure

ONEOK Midcontinent Market Center, Inc.
Issues: FUE
Rep By: Kathleen L. Mazure

ONEOK Midstream Gas Supply, LLC
Issues: FUE
Rep By: Kathleen L. Mazure

ONEOK OkTex Pipeline Co.
Issues: FUE
Rep By: Kathleen L. Mazure

Orlando Utilities Commission
Issues: ENG GOV UTI
Rep By: Richmond F. Allan, Wallace L. Duncan, James D. Pembroke

Palo Alto, California, City of
Issues: ENG GOV UTI
Rep By: Wallace L. Duncan, James D. Pembroke

Penn Yan, New York, Village of
Issues: GOV
Rep By: Richmond F. Allan, Jeffrey C. Genzer, Michael R. Postar

Plattsburgh, New York, City of
Issues: ENG GOV UTI
Rep By: Jeffrey C. Genzer

Redding, California, Electric Department of the City of
Issues: ENG GOV UTI
Rep By: Wallace L. Duncan, James D. Pembroke, Michael R. Postar

Renewable Energy Policy Project
Rep By: Jeffrey C. Genzer

Rockville Centre, New York, Village of
Issues: ENG ENV GOV UTI
Rep By: Richmond F. Allan, Jeffrey C. Genzer, Thomas L. Rudebusch

Roosevelt County Rural Electric Cooperative
Rep By: Robert Weinberg

Salamanca, New York, City Board of Public Utilities of
Issues: ENG GOV
Rep By: Jeffrey C. Genzer, Tatjana M. Shonkwiler

Santa Clara, California, Electric Department of the City of
Issues: COM ENG GOV UTI
Rep By: Wallace L. Duncan, James D. Pembroke, Michael R. Postar

Sensor Oil and Gas Co.
Issues: ENG
Rep By: Richmond F. Allan

Sherburne, New York, Village of
Issues: UTI
Rep By: Jeffrey C. Genzer

City of Sherrill, New York
Rep By: Jeffrey C. Genzer

Solar Electric Light Co.
Issues: ENG
Rep By: Jeffrey C. Genzer

Solar Energy Industries Ass'n (SEIA)
Issues: ENG
Rep By: Jeffrey C. Genzer

Solar Energy Research and Education Foundation
Issues: EDU ENG
Rep By: Jeffrey C. Genzer, Tatjana M. Shonkwiler

Solvay, New York, Village of
Rep By: Jeffrey C. Genzer

South Dakota, Office of the Attorney General of the State of
Rep By: James F. Flug

South Mississippi Electric Power Ass'n
Issues: ENG UTI
Rep By: Robert Weinberg

Southern California Public Power Authority
Issues: ENG GOV UTI
Rep By: Richmond F. Allan, Wallace L. Duncan, James D. Pembroke, Michael R. Postar

Southern Maryland Electric Cooperative, Inc.
Issues: ENG UTI
Rep By: Robert Weinberg

Southwestern Electric Cooperative, Inc.
Issues: ENG UTI
Rep By: Michael R. Postar

Thurmont, Maryland, Town of
Issues: GOV
Rep By: Janice L. Lower

Transmission Agency of Northern California
Issues: ENG UTI
Rep By: Wallace L. Duncan, James D. Pembroke, Michael R. Postar

Trinity Public Utilities District
Issues: ENG GOV
Rep By: Jeffrey C. Genzer, James D. Pembroke

West Virginia, Office of the Attorney General of the State of
Rep By: James F. Flug

Williamsport, Maryland, Town of
Issues: GOV
Rep By: Janice L. Lower

Wisconsin, Office of the Attorney General of the State of
Rep By: James F. Flug

Wyoming, Office of the Attorney General of the State of
Rep By: James F. Flug

Yates County Cable TV Committee
Issues: COM GOV UTI
Rep By: Michael R. Postar

Dunlap & Browder, Inc.

418 Tenth St. SE
Washington, DC 20003
Tel: (202)546-3720
Fax: (202)546-5557
Registered: LDA
E-mail: dandb@intr.net

Consultants on public policy relationship to business opportunity and risk; emphasis on natural resources, energy and environment. Advisors to alternative fuels, energy efficiency, manufacturing, defense nuclear facilities management, chemical, utility, mining and energy companies; Native American and state governments; industry and public interest associations.

DC-Area Employees Representing Listed Clients

BROWDER, Joseph B., Partner
DUNLAP, Louise C., Partner

Clients

ARCADIS/California Energy Commission
Rep By: Louise C. Dunlap

BHP (USA) Inc.

Bones Brothers Ranch
Issues: NAT
Rep By: Joseph B. Browder, Louise C. Dunlap

Clean Air Campaign
Rep By: Joseph B. Browder, Louise C. Dunlap

Friends of the Everglades

Izaak Walton League of America (Mangrove and Florida Keys Chapters)
Rep By: Joseph B. Browder

Klamath Tribes
Rep By: Joseph B. Browder

Native American Rights Fund
Rep By: Joseph B. Browder

United Cement Corp.
Rep By: Joseph B. Browder, Louise C. Dunlap

Durante Associates

1925 N. Lynn St.
Suite 725
Arlington, VA 22209
E-mail: durantes@aol.com

Tel: (703)276-8444
Fax: (703)276-8447
Registered: LDA

DC-Area Employees Representing Listed Clients
DURANTE, Douglas A., V. President
DURANTE, Raymond W., President

Clients

ARK Energy, Inc.
Rep By: Douglas A. Durante

Clean Fuels Development Coalition
Issues: ENG
Rep By: Douglas A. Durante

Energy Pacific, Inc.
Rep By: Douglas A. Durante

Information Resources, Inc.
Rep By: Douglas A. Durante

Nebraska Ethanol Board
Rep By: Douglas A. Durante

Texas Corn Producers Board
Rep By: Douglas A. Durante

TRW Systems Integration Group
Rep By: Raymond W. Durante

World Wide Energy Group
Rep By: Douglas A. Durante

The Dutko Group, Inc.

412 First St. SE
Suite 100
Washington, DC 20003
Web: www.dutkogroup.com

Tel: (202)484-4884
Fax: (202)484-0109
Registered: LDA

A government affairs consulting firm.

DC-Area Employees Representing Listed Clients
ANDRES, Gary J., Senior Managing Partner
BAYLISS, Kim Koontz, Partner
BROWN, Peg
BROWN, Stephen H., V. President
CARD, Bradford, V. President
GLISSON, Laine
IRION, Mark S., President
KAUFMAN, Ronald C., Senior Managing Partner
LEHRMAN, Louis, V. President
PERLMUTTER, Deana, Senior V. President
PERRY, Steve, Chief Exec. Officer
RAFFENSPERGER, Juliette M., V. President
SAYLE, Stephen Craig, V. President
SILVERMAN, Arthur H., Senior Managing Partner and General Counsel
SIMMONS, William, Senior V. President
SPAULDING, Kimberly M., V. President
WATSON, Robert L., Partner

Clients

Accenture
Issues: BUD DEF
Rep By: Gary J. Andres, Juliette M. Raffensperger, Arthur H. Silverman, William Simmons

AES/CILCO

AIG Environmental

Alcatel USA
Issues: GOV LBR SCI TEC
Rep By: Gary J. Andres, Kim Koontz Bayliss, Mark S. Irion, Louis Lehrman, Steve Perry, Juliette M. Raffensperger, Stephen Craig Sayle

America's Community Bankers
Issues: BAN
Rep By: Gary J. Andres, Kimberly M. Spaulding

American Herbal Products Ass'n
Issues: FOO GOV
Rep By: Mark S. Irion, Kimberly M. Spaulding

ASCENT (Ass'n of Community Enterprises)
Issues: TEC
Rep By: Kim Koontz Bayliss, Louis Lehrman, Steve Perry, Juliette M. Raffensperger, Stephen Craig Sayle

Ass'n for Competitive Technology
Rep By: Kim Koontz Bayliss, Mark S. Irion, Louis Lehrman

AT&T
Issues: TEC
Rep By: Kim Koontz Bayliss, Louis Lehrman, Steve Perry, Juliette M. Raffensperger, Stephen Craig Sayle

AT&T Wireless Services, Inc.
Issues: TEC
Rep By: Kim Koontz Bayliss, Louis Lehrman, Steve Perry, Juliette M. Raffensperger, Stephen Craig Sayle

Biotech Research and Development Center
Issues: BUD
Rep By: Mark S. Irion, Arthur H. Silverman, William Simmons

Building America

Cable & Wireless, Inc.
Issues: TEC TRD
Rep By: Kim Koontz Bayliss, Louis Lehrman, Steve Perry, Juliette M. Raffensperger, Stephen Craig Sayle

Carolina PCS
Rep By: Louis Lehrman

Carpet and Rug Institute
Issues: CSP ENV
Rep By: Peg Brown, Mark S. Irion, Deana Perlmutter

CITGO Petroleum Corp.
Issues: CAW ENG ENV FUE MAR
Rep By: Mark S. Irion

Coalition for Auto Repair Equality (CARE)
Issues: AUT
Rep By: Stephen Craig Sayle

Coalition to Advance Sustainable Technology
Issues: ENV
Rep By: Peg Brown, Deana Perlmutter

Competitive Telecommunications Ass'n (COMPTEL)
Issues: TEC
Rep By: Kim Koontz Bayliss, Steve Perry, Juliette M. Raffensperger, Stephen Craig Sayle

CUBRC

Distilled Spirits Council of the United States, Inc.
Issues: TAX
Rep By: Gary J. Andres, Arthur H. Silverman, William Simmons, Kimberly M. Spaulding

Dominion Resources, Inc.
Issues: ENG UTI
Rep By: Robert L. Watson

Eastern Pequot Indians
Rep By: Ronald C. Kaufman, Kimberly M. Spaulding

European Telecommunications Standards Institute (ETSI)
Rep By: Kim Koontz Bayliss, Steve Perry, Juliette M. Raffensperger, Stephen Craig Sayle

EXCEL Communications Inc.
Issues: COM TEC TRD
Rep By: Kim Koontz Bayliss, Louis Lehrman, Steve Perry, Juliette M. Raffensperger, Stephen Craig Sayle

FedEx Corp.
Issues: AVI LBR POS ROD TRA TRU
Rep By: Gary J. Andres, Kimberly M. Spaulding

Food Distributors Internat'l (NAWGA-IFDA)
Issues: AGR BUD HCR TAX
Rep By: Gary J. Andres, Kimberly M. Spaulding

Household Internat'l, Inc.
Issues: BAN
Rep By: Gary J. Andres, Kimberly M. Spaulding

Hudson News

Internat'l Ass'n of Fire Fighters

JM Family Enterprises
Issues: AUT MAR TAX TRD
Rep By: Ronald C. Kaufman

L-3 Communications Corp.

The Lee Group, Inc.

Level 3 Communications LLC
Rep By: Peg Brown, Mark S. Irion, Deana Perlmutter

Longhorn Pipeline
Issues: ENV FUE NAT
Rep By: Mark S. Irion, Ronald C. Kaufman

Los Angeles Unified School District

Michigan Biotechnology Institute
Issues: AGR ENV
Rep By: Arthur H. Silverman, William Simmons

Mills Corporation
Issues: RES
Rep By: Ronald C. Kaufman

Nat'l Aviary in Pittsburgh
Rep By: Ronald C. Kaufman, Arthur H. Silverman, William Simmons

Nat'l Education Ass'n of the U.S.

Nat'l Ground Water Ass'n
Issues: ENV LBR SCI
Rep By: Gary J. Andres

Orange, Florida, County of
Rep By: Ronald C. Kaufman

Oregon Garden Foundation
Issues: BUD ECN EDU NAT
Rep By: Gary J. Andres, Mark S. Irion, Kimberly M. Spaulding

Organ Transplant Campaign

P2B Consulting

PacifiCare Health Systems
Issues: HCR MMM
Rep By: Gary J. Andres, Kimberly M. Spaulding

Partnership for Advanced Technology in Housing (PATH)

PlanetRx
Rep By: Gary J. Andres, Kimberly M. Spaulding

Prudential Securities, Inc.
Issues: GOV MIA TRD
Rep By: Gary J. Andres

QED Communications

Recording Industry Ass'n of America

Recovermat Technologies LLC
Issues: WAS
Rep By: Mark S. Irion

Sandy City, Utah, City of
Issues: BAN
Rep By: Arthur H. Silverman, William Simmons

Satellite Broadcasting and Communications Ass'n
Issues: CPT TEC
Rep By: Kim Koontz Bayliss, Steve Perry, Juliette M. Raffensperger, Stephen Craig Sayle

SEFBO Pipeline Bridge, Inc.
Issues: ENV FUE NAT
Rep By: Mark S. Irion

SkyBridge, LLC
Issues: COM TEC
Rep By: Kim Koontz Bayliss, Louis Lehrman, Steve Perry, Juliette M. Raffensperger, Stephen Craig Sayle

SpaceData Internat'l
Issues: COM SCI TEC
Rep By: Kim Koontz Bayliss, Louis Lehrman, Steve Perry, Juliette M. Raffensperger, Stephen Craig Sayle

Sprint Corp.
Issues: BUD LBR TAX TEC
Rep By: Gary J. Andres, Kimberly M. Spaulding

Todhunter Internat'l, Inc.
Issues: ENV TAX
Rep By: Arthur H. Silverman, William Simmons

Tufts University

TV Guide, Inc.
Issues: CDT CPT TEC
Rep By: Kim Koontz Bayliss, Steve Perry, Juliette M. Raffensperger, Stephen Craig Sayle

Union Pacific
Issues: TRA
Rep By: Gary J. Andres, Kimberly M. Spaulding

United Water Services

UPMC Health System
Issues: HCR
Rep By: Arthur H. Silverman, William Simmons

VeriSign/Network Solutions, Inc.
Issues: COM CPT TEC
Rep By: Kim Koontz Bayliss, Louis Lehrman, Steve Perry, Juliette M. Raffensperger, Stephen Craig Sayle

Virgin Islands, Government of the

The Washington Opera
Issues: ART
Rep By: Arthur H. Silverman, William Simmons

Western Governors Ass'n
Issues: HCR
Rep By: Arthur H. Silverman, William Simmons

Western Governors University
Issues: HCR
Rep By: Arthur H. Silverman, William Simmons

Winstar Communications, Inc.
Issues: COM GOV TEC
Rep By: Kim Koontz Bayliss, Louis Lehrman, Steve Perry, Juliette M. Raffensperger, Stephen Craig Sayle

XO Communications
Issues: TEC
Rep By: Kim Koontz Bayliss, Louis Lehrman, Steve Perry, Juliette M. Raffensperger, Stephen Craig Sayle

Dutton and Dutton, P.C.

5017 Tilden St. NW
Washington, DC 20016

Tel: (202)686-3500
Fax: (202)966-6621
Registered: FARA

DC-Area Employees Representing Listed Clients
DUTTON, Frederick G., Partner/President

Clients

Saudi Arabia, Royal Embassy of
Rep By: Frederick G. Dutton

Dyer Ellis & Joseph, P.C.

600 New Hampshire Ave. NW
11th Floor
Washington, DC 20037
Web: www.dyerellis.com
E-mail: info@dejlaw.com

Tel: (202)944-3000
Fax: (202)944-3068
Registered: LDA, FARA

A law firm specializing in domestic and international shipping, finance, corporate, securities, legislative, environmental, customs and trade matters.

Political Action Committee
Dyer Ellis & Joseph, P.C. PAC

600 New Hampshire Ave. NW
11th Floor
Washington, DC 20037
Contact: Duncan C. Smith, III
Tel: (202)944-3000
Fax: (202)944-3068

DC-Area Employees Representing Listed Clients
BANNON, Brian A., Partner
BONDAREFF, Joan, Counsel
CLICK, Joseph O., Partner
CRICK SAHATJIAN, Laurie, Partner
DANIEL, L. Maurice, Senior Government Affairs Advisor
DREWRY, James S. W., Partner
DYER, Thomas M., Partner
ELLIS, II, James B., Partner
ESBER, Brett M., Partner
GEREN, Natalia W., Associate
GRASSO, Jeanne Marie, Partner
GRAYKAUSKI, John
HENDERSON, John
JOSEPH, Michael, Partner
KEUP, Wayne A., Partner
MATHEWS, Lara Bernstein, Associate
NAFTZGER, J. Christopher, Associate
RIFKA, Margaret Dillenburg, Counsel
SALGADO, R. Anthony, Partner
SMITH, III, Duncan C., Partner and Treasurer
SOUTHWICK, Jennifer M., Government Affairs Analyst
WALDRON, Jonathan K., Partner
WALLACE, Sidney A., Counsel

Clients

Alaska Ship and Drydock, Inc.
Rep By: Brian A. Bannon, Duncan C. Smith, III

American Coke and Coal Chemicals Institute
Issues: ENV
Rep By: Laurie Crick Sahatjian, Jeanne Marie Grasso, Lara Bernstein Mathews, Duncan C. Smith, III, Jennifer M. Southwick, Sidney A. Wallace

Avondale Industries, Inc.
Issues: MAR
Rep By: Brian A. Bannon, Thomas M. Dyer, James B. Ellis, II, Michael Joseph, Duncan C. Smith, III

Bender Shipbuilding & Repair Co., Inc.
Issues: MAR
Rep By: James S. W. Drewry, James B. Ellis, II, Jeanne Marie Grasso, Margaret Dillenburg Rifka, Duncan C. Smith, III, Jennifer M. Southwick

BLNG, Inc.
Issues: MAR
Rep By: Laurie Crick Sahatjian, L. Maurice Daniel, James S. W. Drewry, Thomas M. Dyer, Duncan C. Smith, III, Jennifer M. Southwick

Browning Transport Management
Issues: ENV
Rep By: Laurie Crick Sahatjian, Duncan C. Smith, III, Jennifer M. Southwick, Sidney A. Wallace

China Shipping (Group) Co.
Rep By: Joseph O. Click, James S. W. Drewry, Thomas M. Dyer, Brett M. Esber, Duncan C. Smith, III, Jennifer M. Southwick

Clipper Cruise Line
Rep By: Thomas M. Dyer

John Crane-LIPS, Inc.
Issues: DEF
Rep By: Brian A. Bannon, James S. W. Drewry, Wayne A. Keup, Duncan C. Smith, III, Jennifer M. Southwick

Cross Sound Ferry Services, Inc.
Issues: MAR
Rep By: James S. W. Drewry, Lara Bernstein Mathews, Duncan C. Smith, III, Jennifer M. Southwick

DaimlerChrysler Corp.
Issues: DEF
Rep By: Brian A. Bannon, Brett M. Esber, Wayne A. Keup, Duncan C. Smith, III, Jennifer M. Southwick

Electronic Design Inc.
Issues: DEF
Rep By: Brian A. Bannon, Wayne A. Keup, Margaret Dillenburg Rifka, Duncan C. Smith, III, Jennifer M. Southwick

FastShip, Inc.
Issues: MAR
Rep By: Joan Bondareff, Laurie Crick Sahatjian, James S. W. Drewry, Thomas M. Dyer, James B. Ellis, II, John Graykauski, Lara Bernstein Mathews, J. Christopher Naftzger, Duncan C. Smith, III, Jennifer M. Southwick

Friede Goldman Halter
Issues: TAX
Rep By: James S. W. Drewry, John Graykauski, Duncan C. Smith, III, Jennifer M. Southwick

Fruit Shippers Ltd.
Issues: MAR
Rep By: James S. W. Drewry, Thomas M. Dyer, Brett M. Esber, Jeanne Marie Grasso, Duncan C. Smith, III, Jennifer M. Southwick

Glass Packaging Institute
Issues: ENV HCR
Rep By: Laurie Crick Sahatjian, Jeanne Marie Grasso, Duncan C. Smith, III, Jennifer M. Southwick, Jonathan K. Waldron

Heerema Marine Contractors Nederland B.V.
Issues: MAR
Rep By: James S. W. Drewry, Thomas M. Dyer, James B. Ellis, II, Natalia W. Geren, Jeanne Marie Grasso, Duncan C. Smith, III, Jennifer M. Southwick, Jonathan K. Waldron

Hornblower Marine Services, Inc.
Issues: MAR
Rep By: James S. W. Drewry, Jeanne Marie Grasso, Duncan C. Smith, III, Jennifer M. Southwick

Hvide Marine Inc.
Issues: MAR
Rep By: Laurie Crick Sahatjian, James S. W. Drewry, Thomas M. Dyer, James B. Ellis, II, Jeanne Marie Grasso, Lara Bernstein Mathews, Duncan C. Smith, III, Jennifer M. Southwick, Jonathan K. Waldron

Intermare Navigation SA
Issues: MAR
Rep By: James B. Ellis, II, R. Anthony Salgado, Duncan C. Smith, III

Kvaerner Shipholding, Inc.
Issues: MAR
Rep By: Thomas M. Dyer, James B. Ellis, II, John Henderson

Kvaerner Philadelphia Shipyard Inc.
Issues: MAR
Rep By: Thomas M. Dyer, James B. Ellis, II, Jeanne Marie Grasso, John Graykauski, Lara Bernstein Mathews, R. Anthony Salgado, Duncan C. Smith, III, Jennifer M. Southwick

Marine Spill Response Corporation
Issues: ENV
Rep By: Laurie Crick Sahatjian, Jeanne Marie Grasso, Lara Bernstein Mathews, Duncan C. Smith, III, Jennifer M. Southwick, Jonathan K. Waldron, Sidney A. Wallace

Nat'l Maritime Alliance
Rep By: Duncan C. Smith, III

Nat'l Oilseed Processors Ass'n
Issues: ENV
Rep By: Laurie Crick Sahatjian, Duncan C. Smith, III, Jennifer M. Southwick, Jonathan K. Waldron, Sidney A. Wallace

Nat'l Steel and Shipbuilding Co.
Rep By: James B. Ellis, II, Duncan C. Smith, III

Northrop Grumman Corp.
Issues: DEF
Rep By: Brian A. Bannon, James S. W. Drewry, Thomas M. Dyer, Duncan C. Smith, III, Jennifer M. Southwick

Offshore Rig Museum, Inc.
Issues: MAR
Rep By: Joan Bondareff, James S. W. Drewry, Duncan C. Smith, III, Jennifer M. Southwick

Put-in-Bay Boat Line Co.
Issues: TRA
Rep By: James S. W. Drewry, Lara Bernstein Mathews, Duncan C. Smith, III, Jennifer M. Southwick

Sea Ventures Inc.
Issues: MAR TAX
Rep By: James S. W. Drewry, Thomas M. Dyer, Duncan C. Smith, III, Jennifer M. Southwick

TI Group Inc.
Issues: DEF
Rep By: Brian A. Bannon, Joseph O. Click, Laurie Crick Sahatjian, Thomas M. Dyer, Wayne A. Keup, Margaret Dillenburg Rifka, Duncan C. Smith, III

TransAtlantic Lines - Iceland ehf
Issues: DEF
Rep By: Brian A. Bannon, James S. W. Drewry, Duncan C. Smith, III

The Trump Organization
Issues: MAR TAX
Rep By: Laurie Crick Sahatjian, Thomas M. Dyer, Jeanne Marie Grasso, Lara Bernstein Mathews, Duncan C. Smith, III, Jennifer M. Southwick, Jonathan K. Waldron

Wendella Sightseeing Boats Inc.
Issues: TRA
Rep By: James S. W. Drewry, Lara Bernstein Mathews, Duncan C. Smith, III, Jennifer M. Southwick

Dykema Gossett PLLC

1300 I St. NW
Suite 300 West
Washington, DC 20005
Tel: (202)522-8600
Fax: (202)522-8669
Registered: LDA, FARA

Washington office of a Michigan-based corporate law firm.

DC-Area Employees Representing Listed Clients
ARTHUR, David K., Legislative Associate
BARBOUR, Nancy R., Director, Federal Government Affairs
BERNARDINI, Charles R., Of Counsel
CARROLL, William H., Of Counsel
DIAZ, Steven A., Member
GROOBERT, Edward A., Member
JENKINS, Judy P., Associate
MACGUINEAS, D. Biard, Member
MARKWOOD, Tricia K., Legislative Associate
ZIMMERMAN, Stephen H., Member

Clients

Arvin Meritor Automotive
Issues: CSP ENV HCR LBR TRD
Rep By: David K. Arthur, Nancy R. Barbour

Calhoun County Community Development
Issues: TRA
Rep By: Nancy R. Barbour, Tricia K. Markwood

Citizen's Committee to Save the Federal Center
Issues: GOV TRA
Rep By: Nancy R. Barbour, Tricia K. Markwood

Comerica, Inc.
Issues: BAN
Rep By: David K. Arthur, Nancy R. Barbour

Detroit Public Schools
Issues: EDU
Rep By: David K. Arthur, Nancy R. Barbour

Detroit, Michigan, City of
Issues: AVI BUD DIS ENV FIR GOV HCR HOU IMM IND LAW TAX TRA TRD
Rep By: David K. Arthur, Nancy R. Barbour, Tricia K. Markwood

Equipment Leasing Ass'n of America

ERIM
Issues: DEF SCI
Rep By: Tricia K. Markwood

Ferris State University
Issues: EDU
Rep By: Nancy R. Barbour, Tricia K. Markwood

Great Lakes Corporate Resources
Issues: RRR TRA
Rep By: David K. Arthur, Nancy R. Barbour

Manulife USA
Rep By: Nancy R. Barbour, Stephen H. Zimmerman

Michigan Insurance Federation
Issues: TAX
Rep By: David K. Arthur, Stephen H. Zimmerman

Michigan Manufacturing Technology Center
Issues: MAN SCI
Rep By: Tricia K. Markwood

The Modernization Forum
Issues: BUD MAN SCI
Rep By: Tricia K. Markwood

Munson Healthcare

Southeastern Michigan Council of Government
Issues: ENV IMM RRR TAX TRA
Rep By: David K. Arthur, Nancy R. Barbour

Union Pacific
Issues: RRR
Rep By: Charles R. Bernardini

The Wellness Plan
Issues: HCR
Rep By: David K. Arthur, Nancy R. Barbour

E. E. & Company, L.L.C.

1101 30th St. NW
Suite 500
Washington, DC 20007
Tel: (202)625-8380
Fax: (202)274-1967
Registered: LDA

A government relations consulting firm.

DC-Area Employees Representing Listed Clients
MARTIN, Cynthia L., Managing Member

The Eagles Group

499 S. Capitol St. SW
Suite 518
Washington, DC 20003
E-mail: eag1@earthlink.net
Tel: (202)484-0082
Fax: (202)484-5696
Registered: LDA

Specializes in business development and government affairs.

DC-Area Employees Representing Listed Clients
COSTELLO, Terence, President

Clients

Diamond Head Financial Group
Issues: ECN TRD
Rep By: Terence Costello

Edmund Scientific Co.
Issues: DEF LBR TRD
Rep By: Terence Costello

Export Management Services, Inc.
Issues: DEF ECN GOV VET
Rep By: Terence Costello

Mainwave Technologies
Issues: GOV
Rep By: Terence Costello

Thomas Group Internat'l
Issues: DEF ECN GOV
Rep By: Terence Costello

University of South Carolina
Issues: SCI
Rep By: Terence Costello

Earle Palmer Brown Public Relations

6400 Goldsboro Rd.
Suite 500
Bethesda, MD 20817
Web: www.epb.com
E-mail: parmstro@epb.com
Tel: (301)263-2200
Fax: (301)263-2269

A national agency offering clients a complete suite of services, including corporate communications, public affairs, and integrated marketing. Provides clients with a comprehensive approach to get involved in the public policy process and shape decisions in their favor at every level of government. Campaigns involve research, message/creative development, media relations, grassroots organization, coalition building, issue advertising, and interactive advocacy.

DC-Area Employees Representing Listed Clients

ARMSTRONG, Philip C., Partner, Managing Director
BASS, Linda, Account Director, EPB PR
ENNIS, Kate, Account Director, EPB PR
GARTMAN, Heather, Director, Client Services/Group Director, EPB PR
RIOS, Jennifer, Account Service Manager, EPB PR
STEIMER, Mark, Account Director, EPB PR

Clients

American Forest & Paper Ass'n
Issues: ADV ENV
Blacksmith
Citibank, N.A.
Digital Access
Energy Cost Savings Council
Issues: EDU ENG
Fiberlink
Friedman Billings Ramsey
Potomac Electric Power Co.
Ruth's Chris Steak House
United Parcel Service
Issues: POS TRU

A. Blakeman Early

2212 Glasgow Rd.
Alexandria, VA 22307
Tel: (703)765-1031
Fax: (703)765-1031
Registered: LDA

Clients

American Lung Ass'n
Issues: ENV
Rep By: A. Blakeman Early

Bruce W. Eberle & Assoc., Inc.

1420 Spring Hill Rd.
Suite 490
McLean, VA 22102
Web: www.bruceeberle.com
E-mail: beberle@eberle1.com
Tel: (703)821-1550
Fax: (703)821-0920

Provides creative services for direct mail fundraising.

DC-Area Employees Representing Listed Clients

EBERLE, Bruce W., Chairman, Board of Directors
GRIFFITHS, William D., Chief Financial Officer

Joseph L. Ebersole

2101 Connecticut Ave. NW
Suite 63
Washington, DC 20008-1760
E-mail: jle2@aol.com
Tel: (202)265-9447
Fax: (202)265-7126
Registered: LDA

A lawyer and sole practitioner providing government relations services.

Clients

Coalition for Patent Information Dissemination
Issues: CPT
Rep By: Joseph L. Ebersole
Derwent, Inc.
Issues: CPT
Rep By: Joseph L. Ebersole
Dialoge Corp.
Issues: CPT
Rep By: Joseph L. Ebersole
IFI Claims Services
Issues: CPT
Rep By: Joseph L. Ebersole
Lexis-Nexis
Issues: CPT
Rep By: Joseph L. Ebersole
MicroPatent, LLC
Issues: CPT
Rep By: Joseph L. Ebersole
Questel-Orbit, Inc.
Issues: CPT
Rep By: Joseph L. Ebersole

Eckert Seamans Cherin & Mellott, LLC

1250 24th St. NW
Suite 700
Washington, DC 20037
Web: www.escm.com
Tel: (202)659-6600
Fax: (202)659-6699
Registered: LDA, FARA

A full service law firm headquartered in Pittsburgh, PA.

DC-Area Employees Representing Listed Clients

WALLACE, George J., Member
WEIGARD, Michael A., Member
WEINSTEIN, Jeffrey E., Member
ZIMMERMAN, LeRoy S., Senior Counsel

Clients

American Financial Services Ass'n
Rep By: George J. Wallace
CCI Construction
Issues: CON GOV RES TAX URB
Rep By: LeRoy S. Zimmerman
CSX Corp.
Issues: RRR TRA
Rep By: LeRoy S. Zimmerman
General Motors Corp.
Issues: AUT FIN FOR GOV
Rep By: LeRoy S. Zimmerman
GPA-1, LLC
Issues: DEF
Rep By: Jeffrey E. Weinstein
Kawasaki Motors Corp., USA
Issues: CSP ENV MAR
Rep By: Michael A. Weigard
PNH Associates
Issues: MED
Rep By: LeRoy S. Zimmerman

Edelman Public Relations Worldwide

1875 I St. NW
Suite 900
Washington, DC 20005
Web: www.edelman.com
Tel: (202)371-0200
Fax: (202)371-2858
Registered: LDA, FARA

Washington office of a firm headquartered in Chicago, IL.

DC-Area Employees Representing Listed Clients

CIMKO, Christine Kelly, V. President, Image and Events
DACH, Leslie, V. Chairman
DEAVER, Michael K., V. Chairman, International Relations
DIGGS, Carol, V. President
FLIEGER, Neal, General Manger
HAUPT, Chris, V. President
HOFFMAN, Eric, V. President
KEENUM, Rhonda, Senior V. President
KNOTT, Bob, V. President
MACHOWSKY, Martin, Senior V. President
PUZO, Daniel, Senior V. President
REHG, Robert, General Manager
SCHMIDT, John, Senior V. President
SEGALL, Peter, Exec. V. President and Deputy General Manager
SULLIVAN, Jere, Exec. V. President and Deputy General Manager
SURRELL, Jeffrey, Senior V. President
TAYLOR, Chuck, Senior V. President
TSAPATSARIS, Julianne, V. President
VANDYKE, Tish, V. President
ZINGMAN, Ben, Senior V. President, Public Affairs and Crisis Communications

Clients

American Health Care Ass'n
Rep By: Leslie Dach, John Schmidt, Peter Segall
American Plastics Council
Rep By: Carol Diggs
American Worldwide
Rep By: Robert Rehg
Americans for Sensible Estate Tax Solutions (ASSETS)
Issues: TAX
Rep By: Eric Hoffman
Ass'n for Advanced Life Underwriting
Rep By: Eric Hoffman
AT&T
Rep By: Michael K. Deaver
Bacardi Ltd.
Rep By: Leslie Dach, Michael K. Deaver, Jere Sullivan
California Health Care Foundation
Rep By: Peter Segall
Capital Confirmation
Rep By: Bob Knott
Church of Jesus Christ of Latter Day Saints
Rep By: Michael K. Deaver, Robert Rehg, Jeffrey Surrell
The Conference Board
Rep By: Christine Kelly Cimko
Disabled Veterens' LIFE Memorial Foundation Inc.
Rep By: Christine Kelly Cimko
Fleet Capital
Rep By: Robert Rehg
FleetBoston Financial
Rep By: Robert Rehg
Foodbrands America, Inc.
Rep By: Daniel Puzo
Fuji Photo Film U.S.A., Inc.
Rep By: Christine Kelly Cimko, Michael K. Deaver
Gyphon Networks
Rep By: Chuck Taylor
Korea Internat'l Trade Ass'n
Rep By: Jere Sullivan
Michel Richard's Citronell
Rep By: Daniel Puzo
Michelin North America
Rep By: Jere Sullivan
Microsoft Corp.
Rep By: Michael K. Deaver
Motorcycle Industry Council
Rep By: Carol Diggs
Nat'l Ass'n of Broadcasters
Rep By: Michael K. Deaver
Nat'l Hospice & Palliative Care Organization
Rep By: Peter Segall
Nat'l Hospice Foundation
Rep By: Peter Segall
Nat'l Nutritional Foods Ass'n
Rep By: Daniel Puzo
Nat'l Soc. of Professional Engineers
Rep By: Julianne Tsapatsaris
Nissan North America Inc.
Rep By: Leslie Dach, Michael K. Deaver, Jere Sullivan
Optinel Systems
Rep By: Chuck Taylor
Ortho-McNeil Pharmaceutical Corp.
Rep By: Peter Segall
Pfizer, Inc.
Lois Pope Life Foundation
Rep By: Christine Kelly Cimko
Portugal, Trade Commission of the Government of the Republic of
Rep By: Michael K. Deaver, Robert Rehg
Rheinmetall AG
Rep By: Christine Kelly Cimko
Rhythms NetConnections
Rep By: Eric Hoffman, Chuck Taylor
Schering-Plough Corp.
Rep By: Peter Segall
Speedway Motorsports
Rep By: Neal Flieger
Stewart & Stevenson Tactical Vehicle Systems, LP
Rep By: Christine Kelly Cimko
U.S. Senate Federal Credit Union
Rep By: Bob Knott
UKR Investments, Inc.
Rep By: Christine Kelly Cimko
Verizon Communications
Rep By: Neal Flieger
Windsor Group
Rep By: Bob Knott

Edington, Peel & Associates, Inc.

1317 F St. NW
Suite 200
Washington, DC 20004
Web: www.edingtonpeel.com
E-mail: contact@edingtonpeel.com
Tel: (202)737-1800
Fax: (202)737-2485
Registered: LDA

Public affairs consultants.

DC-Area Employees Representing Listed Clients

DAVIS, III, Delacroix "Del", Associate
EDINGTON, William H., Principal
MEYERS, Craig A., Associate
PEEL, Terry R., Principal

Clients

American Board of Trial Advocates
Rep By: William H. Edington
Firearms Training Systems, Inc.
Issues: BUD DEF
Rep By: William H. Edington
Florida State University
Issues: BUD FOR
Rep By: William H. Edington, Terry R. Peel
Helen Keller Worldwide
Issues: BUD HCR
Rep By: Terry R. Peel
Kettering Medical Center
Issues: BUD
Rep By: William H. Edington, Craig A. Meyers, Terry R. Peel

Kiwanis Internat'l
Issues: BUD HCR
Rep By: Terry R. Peel

Lockheed Martin Corp.
Issues: BUD DEF
Rep By: William H. Edington

Metropolitan Atlanta Rapid Transit Authority
Issues: BUD TRA
Rep By: William H. Edington

Nat'l Council for Eurasian and East European Research
Issues: BUD FOR
Rep By: Terry R. Peel

Pacific Union College
Issues: BUD
Rep By: William H. Edington, Craig A. Meyers, Terry R. Peel

Pan American Health Organization
Issues: BUD FOR
Rep By: Terry R. Peel

Paradise Valley Hospital
Issues: BUD ECN HCR MED
Rep By: William H. Edington, Craig A. Meyers

U.S. Fund for UNICEF
Issues: BUD FOR
Rep By: Terry R. Peel

United States Cane Sugar Refiners' Ass'n
Rep By: William H. Edington

Edwards Associates, Inc.

316 Pennsylvania Ave. SE
Suite 401
Washington, DC 20003
Tel: (202)546-1516
Fax: (202)546-1543
Registered: LDA

DC-Area Employees Representing Listed Clients
PHILLIPS, Mark, President

Clients

Confederated Tribes of the Grand Ronde
Rep By: Mark Phillips

Confederated Tribes of the Umatilla Reservation of Oregon
Rep By: Mark Phillips

Confederated Tribes of Warm Springs Reservation
Issues: BUD IND
Rep By: Mark Phillips

Coquille Indian Tribe
Rep By: Mark Phillips

Intertribal Timber Council
Rep By: Mark Phillips

The Macon Edwards Co.

600 Pennsylvania Ave. SE
Suite 320
Washington, DC 20003
Tel: (202)969-8110
Fax: (202)969-7036
Registered: LDA
A government affairs corporation specializing in agriculture, trade, and economic policy development.

DC-Area Employees Representing Listed Clients
EDWARDS, Macon T., President
PELTZ, Mara, V. President

Clients

American Soc. of Farm Managers and Rural Appraisers
Issues: AGR
Rep By: Macon T. Edwards, Mara Peltz

American Sugar Cane League of the U.S.A.
Issues: AGR
Rep By: Macon T. Edwards, Mara Peltz

Capital Equipment Legislative Coalition
Issues: BAN MAN TAX TRD
Rep By: Macon T. Edwards, Mara Peltz

Coalition for Crop Insurance Improvement
Rep By: Macon T. Edwards, Mara Peltz

First South Production Credit Ass'n
Issues: BAN
Rep By: Macon T. Edwards, Mara Peltz

Gildan Activewear
Issues: TRD
Rep By: Macon T. Edwards, Mara Peltz

Egan & Associates

1500 K St. NW
Suite 200
Washington, DC 20005
E-mail: cganpc@aol.com
Tel: (202)220-9610
Fax: (202)220-9608
Registered: LDA

DC-Area Employees Representing Listed Clients
EGAN, Joseph R., Chairman

Clients

ABB Combustion Engineering Nuclear Power
Rep By: Joseph R. Egan

Waste Control Specialists, Inc.
Issues: WAS

Egle Associates

1625 Beulah Rd.
Vienna, VA 22182
E-mail: egle@erols.com
Tel: (703)319-2276
Fax: (703)319-2283
Registered: LDA

DC-Area Employees Representing Listed Clients
EGLE, Richard, Principal Owner

Clients

NCR Corp.
Issues: BUD CPI
Rep By: Richard Egle

Planning Systems, Inc.
Issues: BUD CPI
Rep By: Richard Egle

Elias, Matz, Tiernan and Herrick

734 15th St. NW
12th Floor
Washington, DC 20005
Tel: (202)347-0300
Fax: (202)347-2172
A law firm specializing in banking and finance law.

DC-Area Employees Representing Listed Clients
EGE, Stephen M., Partner
MATZ, Timothy B., Managing Partner

Clients

Bayamon Federal Savings and Loan Ass'n
Beneficial Corp.
Coast Federal Savings and Loan Ass'n
Enterprise Bank
Entex, Inc.
Financial Corp. of America
First Federal Savings and Loan Ass'n of Raleigh
Haven Federal Savings and Loan Ass'n
Homestead Financial Corp.
Richardson Savings and Loan Ass'n

Rosalind K. Ellingsworth

1916 N. Daniel St.
Arlington, VA 22201
E-mail: rozhawk@aol.com
Tel: (703)524-0630
Registered: LDA

Clients

Coalition for a Global Standard on Aviation Noise
Issues: AVI
Rep By: Rosalind K. Ellingsworth

Ely & Co., Inc.

P.O. Box 21010
Alexandria, VA 22320
Tel: (703)836-4101
Fax: (703)836-1403
Registered: LDA
Web: www.ely-co.com
E-mail: bert@ely-co.com
Provides consulting services to financial institutions and trade associations on banking structure and monetary policy issues affecting banks, savings & loans and financial services firms. Also provides analyses of the Asian economic situation.

DC-Area Employees Representing Listed Clients
ELY, Bert, President

Clients

Ass'n of Bank Couriers
Issues: BAN
Rep By: Bert Ely

Adam Emanuel and Associates

2219 49th St. NW
Washington, DC 20007
E-mail: aceman8642@aol.com
Tel: (202)338-8642
Fax: (202)338-0196
Registered: LDA

DC-Area Employees Representing Listed Clients
EMANUEL, Adam, President

Clients

Ancore Corp.
Issues: DEF SCI TRA
Rep By: Adam Emanuel

EFW Corp.
Issues: DEF
Rep By: Adam Emanuel

Israel Aircraft Industries, Ltd.
Rep By: Adam Emanuel

Stanley J. Emerling

2713 Berryland Dr.
Oakton, VA 22124-1404
E-mail: SJEmerling@aol.com
Tel: (703)620-6036
Fax: (703)620-5989
Advisory services and project management for the meat and poultry services.

Clients

North American Meat Processors Ass'n
Issues: AGR FOO GOV
Rep By: Stanley J. Emerling

EMI Associates, Ltd.

P.O. Box 5748
Arlington, VA 22205-5748
E-mail: EMIwanciw@aol.com
Tel: (703)536-0725
Fax: (703)536-0738
Registered: LDA
A consulting firm specializing in government relations and international business development.

DC-Area Employees Representing Listed Clients
IWANCIW, Eugene M., President

Clients

Battelle Memorial Institute
Issues: BUD ENG FOR
Rep By: Eugene M. Iwanciw

Citizens Network for Foreign Affairs (CNFA)
Issues: AGR BUD FOR
Rep By: Eugene M. Iwanciw

ERIM
Issues: BUD FOR
Rep By: Eugene M. Iwanciw

Loyola College
Issues: BUD EDU FOR
Rep By: Eugene M. Iwanciw

Romyr Associates
Issues: GOV MIA
Rep By: Eugene M. Iwanciw

Scientech Corp.
Issues: BUD ENG FOR
Rep By: Eugene M. Iwanciw

Ukrainian Nat'l Ass'n, Inc.
Issues: BUD FOR
Rep By: Eugene M. Iwanciw

Emord & Associates, P.C.

1050 17th St. NW
Suite 600
Washington, DC 20036
Tel: (202)466-6937
Fax: (202)466-6938
Registered: LDA
Web: www.emord.com
E-mail: emordall@erols.com
A law firm.

DC-Area Employees Representing Listed Clients
EMORD, Jonathan W., President
KOLTON, Eleanor A., Senior Associate
LEWIS-ENG, Claudia A., Senior Associate

Clients

American Preventive Medical Ass'n
Issues: HCR
Rep By: Jonathan W. Emord, Eleanor A. Kolton, Claudia A. Lewis-Eng

The JAG Group, Inc.
Issues: HCR MMM PHA
Rep By: Jonathan W. Emord, Eleanor A. Kolton, Claudia A. Lewis-Eng

Meditrend, Inc.
Issues: HCR MMM PHA
Rep By: Jonathan W. Emord, Eleanor A. Kolton, Claudia A. Lewis-Eng

Pure Encapsulations, Inc.
Issues: HCR MMM PHA
Rep By: Jonathan W. Emord, Eleanor A. Kolton, Claudia A. Lewis-Eng

Rx Vitamins, Inc.
Issues: HCR MMM PHA
Rep By: Jonathan W. Emord, Eleanor A. Kolton, Claudia A. Lewis-Eng

Weider Nutritional Group
Issues: HCR MMM PHA
Rep By: Jonathan W. Emord, Eleanor A. Kolton, Claudia A. Lewis-Eng

XCEL Medical Pharmacy, Ltd.
Issues: HCR MMM PHA
Rep By: Jonathan W. Emord, Eleanor A. Kolton, Claudia A. Lewis-Eng

ENS Resources, Inc.

1747 Pennsylvania Ave. NW
Suite 420
Washington, DC 20006
Tel: (202)466-3755
Fax: (202)466-3787
Registered: LDA
An intergovernmental consulting and representation firm.

DC-Area Employees Representing Listed Clients
FRENCH, David
SAPIRSTEIN, Eric, President

Clients

California Ass'n of Sanitation Agencies
Issues: BUD CAW ENV
Rep By: Eric Sapirstein

East Bay Municipal Utility District
Issues: BUD CAW ENV NAT
Rep By: Eric Sapirstein

Las Virgenes Municipal Water District
Issues: BUD NAT
Rep By: Eric Sapirstein

Orange County Sanitation Districts
Issues: BUD NAT
Rep By: Eric Sapirstein

Poseidon Resources Corp.

Public Agencies for Audit Reform
Issues: BUD
Rep By: Eric Sapirstein

Sacramento, California, Department of Utilities of
Issues: BUD
Rep By: Eric Sapirstein

Sacramento, California, Public Works Agency of the County of
Issues: BUD NAT TRA
Rep By: Eric Sapirstein

South Tahoe Public Utility District
Issues: BUD
Rep By: Eric Sapirstein

Union Sanitary District
Issues: BUD NAT
Rep By: Eric Sapirstein

WateReuse Ass'n
Issues: BUD
Rep By: Eric Sapirstein

Western Research Institute
Issues: BUD TRA
Rep By: Eric Sapirstein

ENVIRON

4350 N. Fairfax Dr.
Suite 300
Arlington, VA 22203
Web: www.environcorp.com
Tel: (703)516-2300
Fax: (703)516-2345

Clients

Roussel-UCLAF

EOP Group, Inc.

819 Seventh St. NW
Washington, DC 20001
Tel: (202)833-8940
Fax: (202)833-8945
Registered: LDA

DC-Area Employees Representing Listed Clients
CAMPBELL, Chad
DELANEY, Shawn
GESSEMAN, Donald
GLEDHILL, Jonathan
HARTNESS, Norman
HEZIR, Joseph
HILLIER, Troy
IRBY, Richard
LAMSON, John
MARES, Jan
MCDANIEL, Corey
O'BANNON, Michael
OXENDINE, Tom
PULIZZI, Phil

Clients

American Petroleum Institute
Issues: BUD ENV WAS
Rep By: Donald Gesseman, Jonathan Gledhill, Joseph Hezir, Jan Mares, Corey McDaniel, Michael O'Bannon

Astaris

The Boeing Co.
Rep By: Donald Gesseman, Joseph Hezir

The Business Roundtable
Issues: BUD ENV
Rep By: Donald Gesseman, Norman Hartness, Joseph Hezir, John Lamson, Michael O'Bannon

Central Illinois Public Service Co.
Rep By: Joseph Hezir, Michael O'Bannon

Chlorine Chemistry Council
Rep By: Joseph Hezir, Michael O'Bannon

Continental Grain Co.
Issues: GOV
Rep By: Joseph Hezir, Michael O'Bannon, Phil Pulizzi

Dow AgroSciences
Rep By: Jonathan Gledhill, Michael O'Bannon

The Dow Chemical Co.
Rep By: Jonathan Gledhill, Michael O'Bannon

Edison Electric Institute
Issues: BUD ENG ENV
Rep By: Jonathan Gledhill, Joseph Hezir, Troy Hillier, Jan Mares, Corey McDaniel, Michael O'Bannon

FMC Corp.
Issues: CAW CHM ENV IND WAS
Rep By: Shawn Delaney, Jonathan Gledhill, Norman Hartness, Joseph Hezir, Troy Hillier, Jan Mares, Corey McDaniel, Michael O'Bannon, Tom Oxendine, Phil Pulizzi

Fort Howard Corp.
Rep By: Jonathan Gledhill, Michael O'Bannon, Tom Oxendine

Gas Research Institute
Issues: BUD ENG NAT
Rep By: Chad Campbell, Joseph Hezir, Richard Irby

Internat'l Food Additives Council
Issues: FOO
Rep By: Jonathan Gledhill, Joseph Hezir, Michael O'Bannon, Phil Pulizzi

Monsanto Co.
Rep By: Jonathan Gledhill, Joseph Hezir, Michael O'Bannon

Novartis Crop Protection
Issues: AGR CHM
Rep By: Jonathan Gledhill, Troy Hillier, Michael O'Bannon

Nuclear Energy Institute
Issues: BUD WAS
Rep By: Donald Gesseman, Joseph Hezir, Jan Mares, Corey McDaniel

Price Costco
Rep By: Jonathan Gledhill, Michael O'Bannon

Trident Seafood Corp.
Rep By: Michael O'Bannon

Uranium Producers of America
Issues: BUD
Rep By: Joseph Hezir, Richard Irby

Zirconia Sales America
Issues: WAS
Rep By: Joseph Hezir, Corey McDaniel, Michael O'Bannon

Ann Eppard Associates, Ltd.

211 N. Union St.
Suite 100
Alexandria, VA 22314
Tel: (703)739-2545
Fax: (703)739-2718
Registered: LDA

DC-Area Employees Representing Listed Clients
CHLOPECKI, Julie, Transportation Specialist
EPPARD, Ann, President
SCHECHTER, Karen, V. President

Clients

Air Transport Ass'n of America
Issues: TRA
Rep By: Julie Chlopecki, Ann Eppard

American Beverage Institute
Issues: TRA
Rep By: Julie Chlopecki, Ann Eppard

American Maritime Officers Service
Issues: MAR TRA
Rep By: Julie Chlopecki, Ann Eppard, Karen Schechter

Anthony Timberlands, Inc.
Issues: CAW
Rep By: Julie Chlopecki, Ann Eppard

Calspan University of Buffalo Research Center
Issues: AVI
Rep By: Julie Chlopecki, Ann Eppard, Karen Schechter

COMARCO Wireless Technology
Issues: SCI TRA
Rep By: Julie Chlopecki, Ann Eppard

Dade County Board of Commissioners
Issues: TRA
Rep By: Julie Chlopecki, Ann Eppard

Daniel, Mann, Johnson & Mendenhall
Issues: TRA
Rep By: Julie Chlopecki, Ann Eppard

Day & Zimmermann, Inc.
Rep By: Julie Chlopecki, Ann Eppard

Delta Development Group, Inc.
Issues: TRA URB
Rep By: Julie Chlopecki, Ann Eppard, Karen Schechter

FedEx Corp.
Issues: AVI POS
Rep By: Julie Chlopecki, Ann Eppard, Karen Schechter

George Zamias Developers
Rep By: Julie Chlopecki, Ann Eppard

Harlingen Area Chamber of Commerce
Issues: TRA
Rep By: Julie Chlopecki, Ann Eppard

Indiana County Development Corp.
Issues: TRA
Rep By: Julie Chlopecki, Ann Eppard

Jefferson Government Relations, L.L.C.
Issues: AVI
Rep By: Julie Chlopecki, Ann Eppard, Karen Schechter

Outdoor Advertising Ass'n of America
Issues: TRA
Rep By: Julie Chlopecki, Ann Eppard, Karen Schechter

Pennsylvania Pyrotechnics Ass'n
Issues: TRA
Rep By: Julie Chlopecki, Ann Eppard

Pennsylvania Turnpike Commission
Rep By: Julie Chlopecki, Ann Eppard

Pine Bluff Sand and Gravel Co.
Issues: TRA
Rep By: Julie Chlopecki, Ann Eppard

Thelen Reid & Priest LLP
Issues: AVI BUD TRA
Rep By: Julie Chlopecki, Ann Eppard

Traffic.com
Issues: COM SCI TRA
Rep By: Julie Chlopecki, Ann Eppard

Union Pacific
Issues: RRR
Rep By: Julie Chlopecki, Ann Eppard, Karen Schechter

United Airlines
Issues: AVI TRA
Rep By: Julie Chlopecki, Ann Eppard, Karen Schechter

Epstein Becker & Green, P.C.

1227 25th St. NW
Suite 700
Washington, DC 20037
Tel: (202)861-0900
Fax: (202)296-2882
Registered: LDA
Web: www.ebglaw.com
Washington office of a New York law firm.

DC-Area Employees Representing Listed Clients
ALEXANDER, Barry, Associate
BACHENHEIMER, Cara, Senior Counsel
BARNES, Clifford E., Member
COWAN, Joyce A., Associate
GRAY, Carolyn Doppelt, Partner
LEHRHOFF, Michael B.
LEWIS, Elizabeth A., Associate
NIX, Clayton J., Associate
SHATTUCK, Cathie A., Of Counsel
SNYDER, Lynn S., Member

Clients

AmSurg Corp.
Issues: BUD MMM
Rep By: Joyce A. Cowan

Coalition on Accessibility
Issues: ART CIV GOV SPO
Rep By: Carolyn Doppelt Gray, Michael B. Lehrhoff, Cathie A. Shattuck

Emergency Department Practice Management Ass'n (EDPMA)
Issues: BUD HCR MMM TAX
Rep By: Joyce A. Cowan

Fallon Community Health Plan
Issues: BUD HCR MMM
Rep By: Joyce A. Cowan

Federation of American Hospitals
Issues: BUD HCR MMM TAX
Rep By: Joyce A. Cowan

Health Insurance Ass'n of America

The Home Depot
Rep By: Cathie A. Shattuck

Nat'l Anti-Vivisection Soc.
Issues: ANI BUD HCR
Rep By: Joyce A. Cowan

Nat'l Funeral Directors Ass'n
Issues: DIS HCR MMM SMB VET WEL
Rep By: Joyce A. Cowan

Olsten Health Services
Issues: BUD HCR MMM VET
Rep By: Joyce A. Cowan, Elizabeth A. Lewis

Watts Health Foundation
Rep By: Joyce A. Cowan

Ernst & Young LLP

1225 Connecticut Ave. NW
Washington, DC 20036
Tel: (202)327-6000
Fax: (202)327-6200
Registered: LDA
Web: www.ey.com

Political Action Committee
Ernst & Young Political Action Committee
1225 Connecticut Ave. NW
Washington, DC 20036
Tel: (202)327-7584
Fax: (202)327-8863
Contact: Kathryn "K.C." Tominovich

DC-Area Employees Representing Listed Clients
BRORSEN, Les, National Director, Government Relations
DARLING, Lauren, Senior Manager
HECK, Patrick G., Senior Manager

MOSELEY, Phillip D., National Director, Legislative Services
NUEBIG, Tom S.
PEARSON, Mary Frances, Director, Federal Relations
PORTER, John D., Senior Manager
ROSENBLUM, Jay E., Director
RUEMPLER, Henry C., Partner
STEELE-FLYNN, Donna, Senior Manager
TOMINOVICH, Kathryn "K.C.", Political and Legislative Director

Clients

Bankruptcy Issues Council
Issues: BAN BNK
Rep By: Tom S. Nuebig

Cellular Depreciation Coalition
Issues: COM TEC
Rep By: Phillip D. Moseley, Tom S. Nuebig

E-Commerce Coalition
Issues: TAX
Rep By: Lauren Darling, Patrick G. Heck, Phillip D. Moseley, Henry C. Ruempler, Donna Steele-Flynn

Edison Electric Institute
Issues: TAX
Rep By: Lauren Darling, Patrick G. Heck, Phillip D. Moseley, Henry C. Ruempler, Donna Steele-Flynn

The Financial Services Roundtable

General Ore Internat'l Corp. Ltd.
Issues: TAX
Rep By: Lauren Darling, Patrick G. Heck, Phillip D. Moseley, John D. Porter, Henry C. Ruempler, Donna Steele-Flynn

Groom Law Group, Chartered
Issues: INS TAX
Rep By: Tom S. Nuebig

INCOL 2000
Issues: TAX
Rep By: Lauren Darling, Patrick G. Heck, Phillip D. Moseley, John D. Porter, Henry C. Ruempler, Donna Steele-Flynn

Interest Netting Coalition
Issues: TAX
Rep By: Lauren Darling, Patrick G. Heck, Phillip D. Moseley, Henry C. Ruempler, Donna Steele-Flynn

Koch Industries, Inc.
Issues: TAX
Rep By: Lauren Darling, Patrick G. Heck, Phillip D. Moseley, John D. Porter, Henry C. Ruempler, Donna Steele-Flynn

MassMutual Financial Group
Issues: BAN BNK FIN TAX
Rep By: Lauren Darling, Patrick G. Heck, Phillip D. Moseley, Henry C. Ruempler, Donna Steele-Flynn

Nordstrom, Inc.
Issues: TAX
Rep By: Lauren Darling, Patrick G. Heck, Phillip D. Moseley, Henry C. Ruempler, Donna Steele-Flynn

Repeal the Tax on Talking Coalition
Issues: TAX
Rep By: Lauren Darling, Patrick G. Heck, Phillip D. Moseley, John D. Porter, Henry C. Ruempler, Donna Steele-Flynn

Tax Policy Coalition
Issues: TAX
Rep By: Lauren Darling, Patrick G. Heck, Phillip D. Moseley, Henry C. Ruempler, Donna Steele-Flynn

Thelen Reid & Priest LLP
Issues: ENG TAX UTI
Rep By: Tom S. Nuebig

USAA - United Services Automobile Ass'n

Ervin Technical Associates, Inc. (ETA)

106 North Carolina Ave. SE
Washington, DC 20003
Tel: (202)863-0001
Fax: (202)863-0096
Registered: LDA, FARA

DC-Area Employees Representing Listed Clients

ANDAHAZY, William J.
EDWARDS, Hon. Jack
ERVIN, James L., President
MCDADE, Hon. Joseph M.
RICHBOURG, Donald E.

Clients

ACS Defense, Inc.
Issues: AER DEF SCI
Rep By: William J. Andahazy, James L. Ervin, Donald E. Richbourg

Chamberlain Manufacturing Corp.
Issues: BUD DEF MAN
Rep By: James L. Ervin, Hon. Joseph M. McDade

Computer Coalition for Responsible Exports
Issues: CPI DEF TRD
Rep By: William J. Andahazy, Hon. Jack Edwards, James L. Ervin, Donald E. Richbourg

General Dynamics Corp.
Issues: DEF TEC
Rep By: Hon. Jack Edwards, James L. Ervin, Hon. Joseph M. McDade

Ingalls Shipbuilding
Issues: DEF TRA
Rep By: William J. Andahazy, Hon. Jack Edwards, James L. Ervin, Hon. Joseph M. McDade, Donald E. Richbourg

Kaiser-Hill Co., L.L.C.
Issues: DEF ENG ENV
Rep By: Hon. Jack Edwards, James L. Ervin, Donald E. Richbourg

Kaman Diversified Technologies Corp.
Issues: AER DEF
Rep By: Hon. Jack Edwards, James L. Ervin, Donald E. Richbourg

Lister Bolt & Chain Co.
Issues: DEF MAR
Rep By: William J. Andahazy, Hon. Jack Edwards, James L. Ervin, Donald E. Richbourg

Lockheed Martin Corp.
Issues: AER DEF SCI
Rep By: William J. Andahazy, Hon. Jack Edwards, James L. Ervin, Hon. Joseph M. McDade, Donald E. Richbourg

Martins Point Health Care
Issues: DEF HCR
Rep By: Hon. Jack Edwards, James L. Ervin, Donald E. Richbourg

Northrop Grumman Corp.
Issues: AER DEF
Rep By: Hon. Jack Edwards, James L. Ervin, Hon. Joseph M. McDade, Donald E. Richbourg

Sarnoff Corp.
Issues: DEF
Rep By: William J. Andahazy, Hon. Jack Edwards, James L. Ervin

SKF USA, Inc.
Issues: AER DEF TRD
Rep By: James L. Ervin

United Defense, L.P.
Issues: DEF
Rep By: William J. Andahazy, Hon. Jack Edwards, James L. Ervin, Donald E. Richbourg

ViaTronix
Issues: HCR
Rep By: Hon. Joseph M. McDade

Video Network Communications
Issues: DEF
Rep By: William J. Andahazy, Hon. Jack Edwards, James L. Ervin

Winslow Press
Issues: EDU TAX
Rep By: Hon. Joseph M. McDade

Charles D. Estes & Associates

1600 Wilson Blvd.
Suite 900
Arlington, VA 22209-2505
Tel: (703)526-7850
Fax: (703)526-7805
Registered: LDA
E-mail: cestes@gri.org

Provides government affairs advice, principally on issues related to energy, environment and natural resources. Firm specializes in waste methane recovery from coal mines.

DC-Area Employees Representing Listed Clients

ESTES, Charles D., President

Clients

American Gas Ass'n
Issues: BUD
Rep By: Charles D. Estes

Appalachian-Pacific Coal Mine Methane Power Co., LLC
Rep By: Charles D. Estes

Gas Research Institute
Issues: BUD
Rep By: Charles D. Estes

Estes Associates

1300 Pennsylvania Ave. NW
Suite 600
Washington, DC 20004
Tel: (202)220-9798
Fax: (202)289-7675
Registered: LDA
E-mail: burntree@mindspring.com

Provides public affairs consulting services.

DC-Area Employees Representing Listed Clients

ESTES, John T., Exec. Director

Clients

Coalition for Competitive Rail Transportation
Rep By: John T. Estes

Main Street Coalition for Postal Fairness
Issues: POS
Rep By: John T. Estes

Etka Consulting

4502 Highland Green Ct.
Alexandria, VA 22312
Tel: (703)354-3303
Fax: (703)354-3336
Registered: LDA

DC-Area Employees Representing Listed Clients

ETKA, Steven D., Principal

Clients

Rural Advancement Foundation Internat'l - USA
Issues: AGR
Rep By: Steven D. Etka

Upper Midwest Dairy Coalition
Issues: AGR
Rep By: Steven D. Etka

Euroconsultants, Inc.

1150 18th St. NW
Suite 275
Washington, DC 20036
Tel: (202)466-6330
Fax: (202)466-6334
Registered: FARA
Web: www.tcfb.com/civ.international

DC-Area Employees Representing Listed Clients

ICHTER, Ralph, Partner/President

Clients

CNPA - Nat'l Center for the Promotion of Agricultural and Food Products

Evans & Black, Inc.

1615 L St. NW
Suite 1220
Washington, DC 20036-5610
Tel: (202)659-0946
Fax: (202)659-4972
Registered: LDA

DC-Area Employees Representing Listed Clients

BLACK, Judy A., Principal
DYER, Teresa J., Director, Government Affairs
EVANS, Rae Forker, President
MORRISSEY, Rafe, Director, Operations and Strategic Planning

Clients

American Business Media
Issues: CPT POS
Rep By: Rae Forker Evans, Rafe Morrissey

Brinker Internat'l
Issues: ALC CSP FOO LBR TAX
Rep By: Judy A. Black, Rae Forker Evans, Rafe Morrissey

Girl Scouts of the U.S.A. - Washington Office
Issues: BUD TAX
Rep By: Judy A. Black, Teresa J. Dyer, Rae Forker Evans

Hallmark Cards, Inc.
Issues: HCR LBR POS TAX
Rep By: Judy A. Black, Rae Forker Evans, Rafe Morrissey

Internat'l Council of Shopping Centers
Rep By: Judy A. Black, Teresa J. Dyer, Rafe Morrissey

Komen Breast Cancer Foundation, The Susan G.
Issues: BUD HCR MED MMM
Rep By: Teresa J. Dyer, Rae Forker Evans

Nat'l Osteoporosis Foundation
Issues: HCR
Rep By: Judy A. Black, Teresa J. Dyer, Rae Forker Evans

Newspaper Ass'n of America
Issues: POS
Rep By: Rae Forker Evans, Rafe Morrissey

Ticketmaster
Issues: ART TOU
Rep By: Judy A. Black, Teresa J. Dyer, Rafe Morrissey

Dave Evans Associates

406 Third St. SE
Washington, DC 20003
Tel: (202)546-9634
Registered: LDA

A government relations and political consulting firm.

DC-Area Employees Representing Listed Clients

EVANS, Hon. Dave, President

Clients

Dunn-Edwards Corp.
Issues: CAW
Rep By: Hon. Dave Evans

Harmon-Motive
Rep By: Hon. Dave Evans

Internat'l Game Technology
Issues: GAM
Rep By: Hon. Dave Evans

Manufactured Housing Ass'n for Regulatory Reform
Issues: HOU
Rep By: Hon. Dave Evans

United California Savings Bank
Rep By: Hon. Dave Evans

The Evans Group, Ltd.

700 13th St. NW
Suite 950
Washington, DC 20005
Tel: (202)333-8777
Fax: (202)333-8722
Registered: LDA, FARA
E-mail: tevans@theevansgroupltd.com

DC-Area Employees Representing Listed Clients
CARMINE, Ferrell D., Senior V. President
CHRISTIANSON, Geryld B., Senior Counselor
EVANS, JR., Hon. Thomas B., Chairman

Clients

Cyprus, Government of the Republic of
Issues: FOR
Rep By: Hon. Thomas B. Evans, Jr.

Kazakhstan 21st Century Foundation
Issues: FOR
Rep By: Geryld B. Christianson, Hon. Thomas B. Evans, Jr.

Naigai, Inc.
Issues: TRD
Rep By: Geryld B. Christianson, Hon. Thomas B. Evans, Jr.

PetrolRem, Inc.
Issues: CAW
Rep By: Ferrell D. Carmine, Hon. Thomas B. Evans, Jr.

Unideal Navitankers
Issues: MAR
Rep By: Geryld B. Christianson, Hon. Thomas B. Evans, Jr.

WorldWide Minerals Ltd.
Issues: TRD
Rep By: Geryld B. Christianson, Hon. Thomas B. Evans, Jr.

David V. Evans

3549 S. Utah St.
Arlington, VA 22206-1815
Tel: (703)998-0894
Registered: LDA
Governmental affairs consulting for elementary, secondary, vocational and higher education organizations.

Evergreen Associates, Ltd.

206 G St. NE
Washington, DC 20002
Tel: (202)543-3383
Fax: (202)544-7716
Registered: LDA
Web: www.evergreendc.com
E-mail: evergreen@intr.net

DC-Area Employees Representing Listed Clients
BROOKS, Robert M.
RICCELLI, Marcus M.

Clients

Central Kitsap School District
Issues: EDU
Rep By: Robert M. Brooks

Choctaw Nation of Oklahoma
Issues: IND
Rep By: Robert M. Brooks

Clover Park School District
Issues: EDU
Rep By: Robert M. Brooks, Marcus M. Riccelli

Medical Lake School District
Issues: EDU
Rep By: Robert M. Brooks, Marcus M. Riccelli

Military Impacted School Districts Ass'n
Issues: EDU
Rep By: Robert M. Brooks

Sun Innovations, Inc.
Issues: SMB TAX
Rep By: Robert M. Brooks

Washington State Impact Aid Ass'n
Issues: EDU
Rep By: Robert M. Brooks, Marcus M. Riccelli

Eversole Associates

3208 Park View Rd.
Chevy Chase, MD 20815
Tel: (301)951-3345
Fax: (301)951-1846
Registered: LDA
A government relations and public affairs firm.

DC-Area Employees Representing Listed Clients
BAKER, Benjamin, Associate
EVERSOLE, Kellye A., President

Clients

American Seed Trade Ass'n
Issues: AGR SCI
Rep By: Kellye A. Eversole

Nat'l Corn Growers Ass'n
Issues: AGR SCI
Rep By: Kellye A. Eversole

EZ's Solutions, Inc.

4141 N. Henderson Rd.
Suite 1101
Arlington, VA 22203
Tel: (703)522-1068
Fax: (703)527-1646
Registered: LDA

DC-Area Employees Representing Listed Clients
ZIEMBA, Elaine, President

Clients

NRG Energy, Inc.
Issues: BUD CAW ENG ENV FOR FUE NAT TAX UTI
Rep By: Elaine Ziemba

F&T Network, Inc.

15363 Worth Ct.
Centreville, VA 20120
Tel: (703)815-0954
Fax: (703)815-0970
Registered: LDA
E-mail: tshaw37@aol.com

DC-Area Employees Representing Listed Clients
SHAW, William A., President

Clients

KOSA
Issues: APP CAW CHM ENV FOO HCR MAN RRR TRA TRD WAS
Rep By: William A. Shaw

F.B.A.

1620 L St. NW
Suite 875
Washington, DC 20036
Tel: (202)833-5881
Fax: (202)833-5924
Registered: LDA
E-mail: fba@clark.net

DC-Area Employees Representing Listed Clients
KIRKLAND, J. R., President

Clients

Medco Containment Services, Inc.
Issues: PHA
Rep By: J. R. Kirkland

Ohio Supercomputing Center
Rep By: J. R. Kirkland

Old Dominion University
Rep By: J. R. Kirkland

RGK Foundation
Rep By: J. R. Kirkland

Science Applications Internat'l Corp. (SAIC)
Issues: CPI EDU
Rep By: J. R. Kirkland

Stetson University
Rep By: J. R. Kirkland

Sun Microsystems
Issues: CPI SCI
Rep By: J. R. Kirkland

University of Akron
Issues: EDU
Rep By: J. R. Kirkland

University of Alaska
Issues: EDU
Rep By: J. R. Kirkland

University of Nevada - Las Vegas
Issues: EDU
Rep By: J. R. Kirkland

University of Vermont
Issues: EDU
Rep By: J. R. Kirkland

Westinghouse Electric Co.
Rep By: J. R. Kirkland

F/P Research Associates

1700 K St. NW
Suite 1000
Washington, DC 20006
Tel: (202)296-5505
Fax: (202)296-6140
Registered: LDA

DC-Area Employees Representing Listed Clients
CRAWFORD, Ronald, President
CRAWFORD, Tim, V. President

Clients

American Bus Ass'n
Issues: TAX
Rep By: Ronald Crawford

Nat'l Cable Television Ass'n
Rep By: Ronald Crawford

Wiley, Rein & Fielding
Issues: TAX UTI
Rep By: Ronald Crawford

Falk Law Firm, plc

One Westin Center
2445 M St. NW
Suite 260
Washington, DC 20037
Tel: (202)833-8700
Fax: (202)872-1725
Registered: LDA
E-mail: falklaw@erols.com

DC-Area Employees Representing Listed Clients
FALK, Sr., James H., President

Marcus G. Faust, P.C.

332 Constitution Ave. NE
Washington, DC 20002
Tel: (202)547-5400
Fax: (202)543-5740
Registered: LDA

DC-Area Employees Representing Listed Clients
FAUST, Marcus G., President
FIRTH, Adrianne, Legislative Consultant

Clients

Central Utah Water Conservancy District
Issues: BUD
Rep By: Marcus G. Faust, Adrianne Firth

Clark County Department of Aviation
Rep By: Marcus G. Faust, Adrianne Firth

Clark County, Nevada, Office of the County Manager
Issues: RES TRA
Rep By: Marcus G. Faust, Adrianne Firth

Clark County-McCarran Internat'l Airport
Issues: AVI NAT RES TRA
Rep By: Marcus G. Faust

Colorado River Commission of Nevada
Issues: NAT RES
Rep By: Marcus G. Faust

Contra Costa Water District
Issues: CAW NAT
Rep By: Marcus G. Faust, Adrianne Firth

Las Vegas Valley Water District
Issues: NAT RES
Rep By: Marcus G. Faust

Public Service Co. of New Mexico
Issues: BUD UTI
Rep By: Marcus G. Faust, Adrianne Firth

Regional Transportation Commission
Issues: BUD TRA
Rep By: Marcus G. Faust, Adrianne Firth

Sierra Pacific Resources
Issues: BUD UTI
Rep By: Marcus G. Faust, Adrianne Firth

John J. Fausti & Associates, LLC

4301 Connecticut Ave. NW
Suite 453
Washington, DC 20008
Tel: (202)237-0505
Fax: (202)237-7566
Registered: LDA
E-mail: JFAusti@worldnet.att.net

DC-Area Employees Representing Listed Clients
FAUSTI, John J., Owner/Attorney
GRAY, Odyssey E., Law Clerk

Clients

Nat'l Ass'n of Aircraft and Communication Suppliers
Issues: AVI
Rep By: John J. Fausti, Odyssey E. Gray

G.W. Fauth & Associates Inc.

116 S. Royal St.
Alexandria, VA 22314
Tel: (703)549-6161
Fax: (703)549-6162
Registered: LDA
E-mail: gfauth@aol.com

DC-Area Employees Representing Listed Clients
FAUTH, III, Gerald W., President

Clients

U.S. Clay Producers Traffic Ass'n
Issues: TRA
Rep By: Gerald W. Fauth, III

Feder, Semo, Clarke & Bard

1350 Connecticut Ave. NW
Suite 600
Washington, DC 20036
Tel: (202)955-8305
Fax: (202)955-8311
Web: www.federlaw.com
A law firm specializing in employment, labor, and health care matters.

DC-Area Employees Representing Listed Clients
FEDER, Gerald, Senior Partner

Clients

Nat'l Employee Benefits Institute
Issues: FIN HCR LBR MMM RET TAX

Federal Access

4843 27th Rd. South
Arlington, VA 22206-1301
Tel: (703)998-8700
Fax: (703)998-1896
Registered: LDA

Transportation consultants.

DC-Area Employees Representing Listed Clients

CARR, Alice J., Secretary-Treasurer
COLE, Timothy R., President

Clients

Lousville Airport

Regional Airport Authority of Louisville & Jefferson Co.
Issues: AVI
Rep By: Timothy R. Cole

United Parcel Service
Issues: AVI POS
Rep By: Timothy R. Cole

Federal Health Strategies, Inc.

1001 Pennsylvania Ave. NW
Suite 850N
Washington, DC 20004
Tel: (202)661-3593
Fax: (202)737-4242
Registered: LDA

DC-Area Employees Representing Listed Clients

MEISTER, Norbert M., President

Clients

USFHP Conference Group
Issues: BUD DEF HCR TRA
Rep By: Norbert M. Meister

Federal Legislative Associates, Inc.

1710 Rhode Island Ave. NW
Fourth Floor
Washington, DC 20036
Tel: (202)467-0045
Fax: (202)467-0065
Registered: LDA
Web: www.fedgovlink.com
E-mail: fla@fedgovlink.com

A government relations and public affairs consulting firm.

DC-Area Employees Representing Listed Clients

AMITAY, Stephen D., Associate
MILLER, David H., Principal
REHANZEL, Lenka, Legislative Coordinator

Clients

FIRSTPLUS Financial Group Inc.
Issues: BAN BNK
Rep By: Stephen D. Amitay, David H. Miller

Religious Technology Center
Issues: CIV CPT FOR
Rep By: Stephen D. Amitay, David H. Miller

TV Radio Now Corp. (i Crave TV)
Issues: COM
Rep By: Stephen D. Amitay, David H. Miller

Federal Management Strategies, Inc.

1440 N St. NW
Suite 1016
Washington, DC 20005
Tel: (202)462-5911
Fax: (202)588-8094
Registered: LDA
E-mail: ckelcan@navpoint.com

Headquartered in Elkins Park, PA.

DC-Area Employees Representing Listed Clients

CANAVAN, Robert P., Consultant
FLANNERY, Kellen, President

Clients

CAL-FED
Issues: EDU TAX
Rep By: Robert P. Canavan

Federal Advocacy for California Education
Issues: EDU
Rep By: Robert P. Canavan, Kellen Flannery

Forest Counties Schools Coalition
Rep By: Robert P. Canavan

Nat'l Board for Professional Teaching Standards (NBPTS)
Issues: EDU

Nat'l Education Ass'n of the U.S.
Issues: EDU
Rep By: Robert P. Canavan

Nat'l Forest Counties School Coalition
Issues: EDU
Rep By: Robert P. Canavan

Rebuild America's Schools
Issues: EDU TAX
Rep By: Robert P. Canavan

San Dieguito School Transportation Cooperative
Issues: EDU
Rep By: Robert P. Canavan

Temple University
Issues: EDU
Rep By: Robert P. Canavan

Federal Strategies Group

717 D St. NW
Suite 310
Washington, DC 20004
Tel: (202)628-4901
Fax: (202)393-5728
Registered: LDA, FARA

The Group provides lobbying and consulting services on issues related to international trade.

DC-Area Employees Representing Listed Clients

EQUIHUA, Xavier, V. President
POTTER, Philip H., President

Clients

AFINOA
Issues: TRD
Rep By: Xavier Equihua

Argentine Citrus Ass'n
Issues: TRD
Rep By: Xavier Equihua

Bruce Fein

6515 Sunny Hill Court
McLean, VA 22101
Tel: (703)448-1279
Fax: (703)448-5765
Registered: FARA
E-mail: bruce.fein@erols.com

Clients

Togo, Embassy of the Republic of
Rep By: Bruce Fein

Feith & Zell, P.C.

1300 19th St. NW
Suite 400
Washington, DC 20036
Tel: (202)293-1600
Fax: (202)293-8965
Registered: LDA
Web: www.fundz.com
E-mail: washington@fundz.com

A law firm specializing in international trade matters and legislation and civil litigation.

DC-Area Employees Representing Listed Clients

FEITH, Douglas J., Partner
FELDMAN, Mark B., Partner
MIRON, George, Partner
POLINER, Michael C.

Clients

Corporacion de Exportaciones Mexicanas, S.A. de C.V. and Marvin Roy Feldman
Issues: ECN FOR LAW TOB TRD
Rep By: Mark B. Feldman

Loral Space and Communications, Ltd.
Issues: AER DEF TEC TRD
Rep By: Douglas J. Feith, Mark B. Feldman, Michael C. Poliner

Mas-Hamilton Group
Issues: DEF
Rep By: Douglas J. Feith

Feldesman, Tucker, Leifer, Fidell & Bank

2001 L St. NW
Second Floor
Washington, DC 20036
Tel: (202)466-8960
Fax: (202)293-8103

A general practice law firm.

DC-Area Employees Representing Listed Clients

FELDESMAN, James L., Partner

Clients

American College of Nurse-Midwives

Nat'l Ass'n of Community Health Centers
Rep By: James L. Feldesman

Nat'l Family Planning and Reproductive Health Ass'n
Rep By: James L. Feldesman

Bruce Fennie & Associates

305 E. Capitol St. SE
Washington, DC 20003
Tel: (202)543-2143

DC-Area Employees Representing Listed Clients

FENNIE, Bruce

Clients

BAE SYSTEMS North America
Issues: DEF
Rep By: Bruce Fennie

Fensterheim & Bean, P.C.

1250 Connecticut Ave. NW
Suite 700
Washington, DC 20005
Tel: (202)637-6667
Fax: (202)842-2869

A law firm specializing in real estate transactions, government contracts and corporate law.

DC-Area Employees Representing Listed Clients

BEAN, Jr., Donald, Partner
FENSTERHEIM, G. David, Partner

Clients

RECRA
Rep By: Donald Bean, Jr., G. David Fensterheim

Frank Fenton

801 Pennsylvania Ave. NW
Suite 1117
Washington, DC 20004
Tel: (202)628-1117
Fax: (202)783-6309
Registered: LDA

Counsels clients on international trade and economic affairs.

Clients

Bethlehem Steel Corp.
Issues: ENV TAX TRA TRD
Rep By: Frank Fenton

USX Corp.
Issues: ENV TAX TRA TRD
Rep By: Frank Fenton

Jack Ferguson Associates, Inc.

203 Maryland Ave. NE
Washington, DC 20002
Tel: (202)544-6655
Fax: (202)544-5763
Registered: LDA
E-mail: jackferguson@mindspring.com

DC-Area Employees Representing Listed Clients

ELIM, Raga
FERGUSON, Jack, President

Clients

The 13th Regional Corp.
Issues: IND
Rep By: Jack Ferguson

Alaska Airlines
Issues: AVI TRA
Rep By: Jack Ferguson

Arctic Power
Issues: NAT
Rep By: Jack Ferguson

AT&T
Issues: TEC TEL
Rep By: Jack Ferguson

Dillingham Construction, Inc.
Issues: ECN
Rep By: Jack Ferguson

Edison Electric Institute
Issues: UTI WAS
Rep By: Jack Ferguson

Fantasma Networks, Inc.
Issues: COM
Rep By: Jack Ferguson

Global Marine, Inc.
Issues: FUE
Rep By: Jack Ferguson

Icicle Seafoods, Inc.
Issues: MAR
Rep By: Jack Ferguson

Kennecott/Borax
Issues: MON
Rep By: Jack Ferguson

Maersk Inc.
Rep By: Jack Ferguson

Mortgage Insurance Companies of America
Issues: BAN FIN
Rep By: Jack Ferguson

Nat'l Ski Area Ass'n
Issues: NAT
Rep By: Jack Ferguson

Northern Air Cargo
Issues: TRA
Rep By: Jack Ferguson

Northland Holdings, Inc.
Issues: MAR
Rep By: Raga Elim, Jack Ferguson

PanAmSat Corp.
Issues: COM TEC
Rep By: Jack Ferguson

Sea Containers America, Inc.
Issues: MAR
Rep By: Raga Elim, Jack Ferguson

U.S. Borax, Inc.
Rep By: Jack Ferguson

United Airlines
Issues: AVI TRA
Rep By: Jack Ferguson

University of Oklahoma
Issues: EDU
Rep By: Jack Ferguson

The Ferguson Group, LLC

1130 Connecticut Ave. NW
Suite 300
Washington, DC 20036

Tel: (202)331-8500
Fax: (202)331-1598
Registered: LDA

DC-Area Employees Representing Listed Clients
FERGUSON, Jr., William, Chief Exec. Officer
GELNOVATCH, Valerie, Senior Associate
GWINN, W. Roger, President
HAMM, Ron, Senior Associate
HANKA, William W., Principal
LEHMAN, Trent, Senior Associate
MACON, Charmayne, Principal
MILLER, Mike, Principal
MOZINGO, Leslie Waters, Principal
RAEDER, Joseph L., Principal
REUBMAN, Elizabeth, Associate
WANG, Greg, Principal
WEBB, Ralph

Clients

Alabama A & M University
Issues: EDU ENV SCI
Rep By: William Ferguson, Jr., Ron Hamm

Alcalde & Fay
Issues: BUD ENV NAT
Rep By: W. Roger Gwinn, Ralph Webb

Arcadia, California, City of
Issues: BUD ENV UTI
Rep By: William Ferguson, Jr., W. Roger Gwinn, Ralph Webb

Brea, California, City of
Issues: BUD LAW TRA
Rep By: William Ferguson, Jr., Charmayne Macon

Broward, Florida, County of
Issues: AVI BUD CAW ECN ENV HOU NAT ROD TRA URB
Rep By: William Ferguson, Jr.

California State University Fullerton
Issues: EDU
Rep By: William Ferguson, Jr.

Camp Dresser and McKee, Inc.
Issues: BUD CAW ENV NAT
Rep By: W. Roger Gwinn

Central Valley Project Water Ass'n
Issues: BUD CAW NAT
Rep By: William Ferguson, Jr., W. Roger Gwinn, Joseph L. Raeder

Colusa Basin Drainage District
Issues: BUD NAT
Rep By: W. Roger Gwinn, Joseph L. Raeder

Fairfield, California, City of
Issues: BUD DEF ECN TRA
Rep By: William Ferguson, Jr., W. Roger Gwinn, Charmayne Macon, Mike Miller, Leslie Waters Mozingo

Family Farm Alliance (Project Transfer Council)
Issues: BUD NAT
Rep By: W. Roger Gwinn, Joseph L. Raeder

Folsom, California, City of
Issues: BUD ECN ENV NAT TRA
Rep By: W. Roger Gwinn, Mike Miller, Leslie Waters Mozingo, Joseph L. Raeder

Glenn-Colusa Irrigation District
Issues: BUD CAW ENV NAT
Rep By: W. Roger Gwinn, Joseph L. Raeder

Gridley, California, City of/Northern California Power Agency
Issues: BUD ENG
Rep By: W. Roger Gwinn

Huntington Beach, California, City of
Issues: BUD ENV NAT WAS
Rep By: W. Roger Gwinn, Ralph Webb

Imperial Irrigation District
Issues: BUD CAW ENG IND NAT
Rep By: William Ferguson, Jr., W. Roger Gwinn, Joseph L. Raeder

Inglewood, California, City of
Issues: BUD ECN HOU LAW LBR SMB TRA URB
Rep By: William Ferguson, Jr., Leslie Waters Mozingo

Interstate 5 Consortium
Issues: BUD TRA
Rep By: William Ferguson, Jr., Charmayne Macon, Leslie Waters Mozingo

The Irvine Co.
Issues: DEF ENV NAT TRA
Rep By: William Ferguson, Jr., W. Roger Gwinn, Leslie Waters Mozingo, Joseph L. Raeder

Kaweah Delta Water Conservation District
Issues: BUD ENV
Rep By: W. Roger Gwinn, Joseph L. Raeder

Kings River Interests
Issues: ENG ENV NAT
Rep By: Joseph L. Raeder

Lake, Illinois, County of
Issues: BUD CAW ENV LAW NAT ROD TRA URB
Rep By: Trent Lehman, Leslie Waters Mozingo

Lennar Partners
Issues: BUD
Rep By: William Ferguson, Jr.

Logan, Utah, City of (Transit District)
Issues: BUD TRA
Rep By: William Ferguson, Jr., Charmayne Macon, Leslie Waters Mozingo

Long Beach Transit
Issues: BUD TRA
Rep By: William Ferguson, Jr., Charmayne Macon, Leslie Waters Mozingo

Mecklenburg, North Carolina, County of
Issues: BUD ENV
Rep By: William Ferguson, Jr., W. Roger Gwinn, Leslie Waters Mozingo

Metropolitan King County Council
Issues: BUD CAW ECN ENV HCR HOU LAW LBR NAT RES TEC TRA URB WEL
Rep By: Leslie Waters Mozingo

Modesto/Turlock Irrigation District
Issues: CAW ENG NAT
Rep By: William Ferguson, Jr., W. Roger Gwinn, Joseph L. Raeder

Mooresville, North Carolina, Town of
Issues: ECN LAW
Rep By: Charmayne Macon

Municipal Transit Operation Coalition
Issues: BUD TRA
Rep By: Charmayne Macon, Leslie Waters Mozingo

Natomas
Issues: BUD ENV NAT
Rep By: W. Roger Gwinn

Northern California Power Agency
Issues: BUD
Rep By: W. Roger Gwinn

Norwalk, California, City of
Issues: BUD
Rep By: William Ferguson, Jr., W. Roger Gwinn, Charmayne Macon, Leslie Waters Mozingo, Ralph Webb

Novato, California, City of
Issues: DEF
Rep By: William Ferguson, Jr.

Oakland, California, City of
Issues: DEF
Rep By: William Ferguson, Jr.

Oceanside, California, City of
Issues: DEF DIS ECN MAR NAT ROD
Rep By: William Ferguson, Jr., W. Roger Gwinn, Leslie Waters Mozingo

Palo Alto, California, City of
Issues: BUD CAW ECN HOU LAW NAT ROD TRA URB
Rep By: Charmayne Macon

Pico Rivera, California, City of
Issues: BUD
Rep By: William Ferguson, Jr., Charmayne Macon

Roseville, California, City of
Issues: CAW ECN ENV IND LAW NAT RES ROD RRR TRA URB
Rep By: Mike Miller

Sacramento Area Council of Governments
Issues: BUD
Rep By: Mike Miller

Sacramento, California, Public Works Agency of the County of
Issues: BUD CAW
Rep By: W. Roger Gwinn

San Diego, California, City of
Issues: AVI
Rep By: William Ferguson, Jr.

San Luis Obispo, California, County of
Issues: BUD
Rep By: W. Roger Gwinn

Santa Ana, California, City of
Issues: BUD ECN IMM LAW LBR TRA
Rep By: William Ferguson, Jr., Leslie Waters Mozingo

Santa Monica, California, City of
Issues: BUD TRA
Rep By: W. Roger Gwinn, Ralph Webb

Sierra Madre, California, City of
Issues: BUD CAW ENV LAW NAT ROD TRA URB
Rep By: William Ferguson, Jr., Trent Lehman

Somach, Simmons & Dunn
Issues: BUD NAT
Rep By: W. Roger Gwinn, Greg Wang

Southeast Water Coalition
Issues: BUD CAW ENV
Rep By: W. Roger Gwinn, Ralph Webb

Stop It Now!
Issues: FAM HCR
Rep By: William Ferguson, Jr., Ron Hamm

Sutter, California, County of
Issues: BUD ENV
Rep By: W. Roger Gwinn

Transportation Corridor Agencies
Issues: ENV TRA
Rep By: William Ferguson, Jr., W. Roger Gwinn, Mike Miller

Wake, North Carolina, County of
Issues: BUD CAW ENV HCR HOU LAW MMM NAT TRA URB WEL
Rep By: W. Roger Gwinn

Washoe County
Issues: BUD ENV NAT
Rep By: W. Roger Gwinn

West Valley City, Utah
Issues: BUD TRA
Rep By: W. Roger Gwinn, Leslie Waters Mozingo

Yuma, Arizona, City of
Issues: BUD
Rep By: William Ferguson, Jr.

Fierce and Isakowitz

600 New Hampshire Ave. NW
Tenth Floor
Washington, DC 20037

Tel: (202)333-8667
Fax: (202)298-9109
Registered: LDA

DC-Area Employees Representing Listed Clients
BRADEN, Kathryn, Senior Associate
COOK, Samantha
FIERCE, Donald L., President
ISAKOWITZ, Mark W., Partner
MOERY, Diane

Clients

American Ass'n of Nurse Anesthetists
Issues: HCR
Rep By: Kathryn Braden, Samantha Cook, Donald L. Fierce, Mark W. Isakowitz, Diane Moery

American Ass'n of Preferred Provider Organizations
Rep By: Mark W. Isakowitz

American Gaming Ass'n
Issues: GAM
Rep By: Kathryn Braden, Donald L. Fierce, Mark W. Isakowitz

Competition in Contracting Act Coalition
Issues: LAW

Credit Union Nat'l Ass'n, Inc.
Issues: BAN
Rep By: Samantha Cook, Donald L. Fierce, Mark W. Isakowitz, Diane Moery

DuPont
Issues: AGR CSP ENV FOO HCR SCI TRD
Rep By: Kathryn Braden, Samantha Cook, Donald L. Fierce, Mark W. Isakowitz

E.I. du Pont de Nemours & Co.

Edison Electric Institute
Issues: ENG ENV UTI
Rep By: Mark W. Isakowitz, Diane Moery

Edison Internat'l
Issues: ENG UTI
Rep By: Samantha Cook, Diane Moery

Federation of American Hospitals
Issues: HCR
Rep By: Kathryn Braden, Samantha Cook, Donald L. Fierce, Mark W. Isakowitz, Diane Moery

Generic Pharmaceutical Ass'n
Issues: PHA
Rep By: Kathryn Braden, Samantha Cook, Donald L. Fierce, Mark W. Isakowitz, Diane Moery

Health Insurance Ass'n of America
Issues: HCR
Rep By: Kathryn Braden, Samantha Cook, Donald L. Fierce, Mark W. Isakowitz, Diane Moery

Liberty Maritime Co.
Issues: MAR
Rep By: Kathryn Braden, Donald L. Fierce, Mark W. Isakowitz

MCI WorldCom Corp.
Issues: TEC
Rep By: Kathryn Braden, Samantha Cook, Donald L. Fierce, Mark W. Isakowitz, Diane Moery

Pegasus Communications
Issues: TEC
Rep By: Kathryn Braden, Samantha Cook, Donald L. Fierce, Mark W. Isakowitz, Diane Moery

Rubber Manufacturers Ass'n
Rep By: Donald L. Fierce

Tricon Global Restaurants Inc.
Issues: FOO LBR TAX
Rep By: Kathryn Braden, Samantha Cook, Donald L. Fierce, Mark W. Isakowitz, Diane Moery

Filler & Weller, P.C.

117 N. Henry St.
Alexandria, VA 22314
Tel: (703)299-0784
Fax: (703)299-0254
Registered: LDA
E-mail: jfa@fillerweller.com
A highly specialized firm whose attorneys engage exclusively in the practice of aviation law.

DC-Area Employees Representing Listed Clients
FILLER, Marshall S., President
WELLER, John Craig, Partner

Clients

Pratt & Whitney
Issues: AVI

Financial Programs, Inc.

8621 Silver Oak Ct.
Springfield, VA 22153
Tel: (800)403-3374
Fax: (703)455-8282
Registered: LDA
Web: www.assn-mgt.com
E-mail: dennis@assn-mgt.com

DC-Area Employees Representing Listed Clients
BOYD, Dennis W., Exec. Director

Clients

Nat'l Ass'n of Assistant United States Attorneys
Issues: GOV LAW RET
Rep By: Dennis W. Boyd

Hyman Fine Associates

8605 Cameron St.
Suite M5
Silver Spring, MD 20910
Tel: (301)562-3141
Fax: (301)562-3141
E-mail: hynat@aol.com
A management consulting firm.

DC-Area Employees Representing Listed Clients
FINE, Hyman

Finkelstein, Thompson & Loughran

1055 Thomas Jefferson St. NW
Suite 601
Washington, DC 20007
Tel: (202)337-8000
Fax: (202)265-9363
Registered: FARA
A law firm specializing in securities, consumer fraud class actions, and civil, criminal and administrative matters before federal and state agencies.

DC-Area Employees Representing Listed Clients
COSENTINO, Victor J., Associate
SATTERFIELD, L. Kendall, Partner

Clients

Canadian Broadcasting Corp.
Rep By: Victor J. Cosentino, L. Kendall Satterfield

Fishbein Associates, Inc.

9901 Avenel Farm Dr.
Potomac, MD 20854
Tel: (301)767-1690
Fax: (301)767-1692
Registered: LDA

DC-Area Employees Representing Listed Clients
FISHBEIN, Julie W., Chairman
FISHBEIN, Rand H., Partner

Clients

Chamberlain Manufacturing Corp.
Issues: BUD DEF

Day & Zimmermann, Inc.
Issues: BUD DEF

Royal Ordnance North America, Inc.
Issues: BUD DEF

Valentec Systems, Inc.
Issues: BUD DEF

Fisher Consulting

P.O. Box 76228
Washington, DC 20013-6228
Tel: (202)625-2102
Fax: (202)625-2104
Registered: LDA
Government affairs consulting.

DC-Area Employees Representing Listed Clients
FISHER, Steven A., Washington Representative

Clients

American Great Lakes Ports
Issues: AGR BUD MAR TAX TRA
Rep By: Steven A. Fisher

Ball State University
Issues: BUD EDU ROD
Rep By: Steven A. Fisher

Build Indiana Council
Issues: ROD
Rep By: Steven A. Fisher

Chicago Southshore and South Bend Railroad
Issues: RRR
Rep By: Steven A. Fisher

Nat'l Soft Drink Ass'n

John Fitzgerald

13826 Castle Cliff Way
Silver Spring, MD 20904-5464
Tel: (301)384-6629
Registered: LDA
E-mail: fitzgerald@igc.opc.org

Flack Associates

1200 19th St. NW
Seventh Floor
Washington, DC 20006
Tel: (202)822-6288
Fax: (202)659-2609
Registered: LDA
E-mail: sgflack@aol.com

DC-Area Employees Representing Listed Clients
FLACK, Susan Garber, Principal

Clients

Spiegel Inc.
Issues: APP BAN TRD
Rep By: Susan Garber Flack

Target Corp.
Issues: APP HCR TRD
Rep By: Susan Garber Flack

Ruth Frances Fleischer

5459 Nebraska Ave. NW
Washington, DC 20015
Tel: (202)966-9179
Registered: LDA

Clients

Scenic Hudson
Issues: CAW ENV NAT WAS
Rep By: Ruth Frances Fleischer

Fleischman and Walsh, L.L.P.

1400 16th St. NW
Suite 600
Washington, DC 20036
Tel: (202)939-7900
Fax: (202)745-0916
Registered: LDA
Web: www.fw-law.com
E-mail: fw@fw-law.com
A law firm specializing in communications, utilities, and transportation law and legislative matters before federal and state administrative agencies and courts.

DC-Area Employees Representing Listed Clients
DAVIDSON, Seth A., Partner
DUPART, Louis H., Partner
EMMER, Matthew D., Partner
FLEISCHMAN, Aaron I., Partner
MCALLISTER, John P.
STARK, Krista
TOPEL, Howard, Partner
WALSH, Charles S., Partner
WYMA, John

Clients

ACTA Technology
Issues: CPI
Rep By: Louis H. Dupart, John P. McAllister

American Airlines
Rep By: Louis H. Dupart, John P. McAllister

AOL Time Warner
Rep By: Louis H. Dupart

Currenex
Issues: BAN FIN
Rep By: Louis H. Dupart, John P. McAllister

EWA Land Information Group, Inc.
Issues: DEF
Rep By: Louis H. Dupart

Farallon Capital Management
Rep By: Louis H. Dupart

Forest Cities
Rep By: Louis H. Dupart, John P. McAllister

Guardian Industries Corp.
Rep By: Louis H. Dupart

Indigo
Issues: AVI
Rep By: Louis H. Dupart, John P. McAllister

Katten Muchin & Zavis
Issues: BAN FIN
Rep By: Louis H. Dupart, John P. McAllister

Midway Airlines Corp.
Rep By: Louis H. Dupart, John P. McAllister

mp3.com
Issues: CPI CPT
Rep By: Seth A. Davidson, Louis H. Dupart

Nat'l Cable Television Ass'n
Issues: CPT TEC
Rep By: Seth A. Davidson, Charles S. Walsh

ORBITZ
Rep By: Louis H. Dupart, Krista Stark, John Wyma

SBC Communications Inc.
Rep By: Louis H. Dupart, Krista Stark, John Wyma

Verizon Communications

Fleishman-Hillard, Inc

1615 L St. NW
Suite 1000
Washington, DC 20036
Tel: (202)659-0330
Fax: (202)296-6119
Registered: LDA, FARA
Web: www.fleishman.com

Political Action Committee
Fleishman-Hillard Political Action Committee
1615 L St. NW
Suite 1000
Washington, DC 20036
Tel: (202)659-0330
Fax: (202)296-6119

DC-Area Employees Representing Listed Clients
BLACK, William, Senior V. President
BOUDREAU, Martha L., Senior V. President and Partner
BOYLE, Joy Bates, V. President
COLLENDER, Stanley, Senior V. President
FINZEL, Ben, V. President
FRAZIER, Harry, Senior V. President
GOODMAN, Alan, V. President
HABER, Jon, Senior V. President
HANNON, Sandra, V. President
HARDISON, Ann, V. President
HUBBARD, Henry W., Senior V. President and Partner
JOHNSON, Paul W., Exec. V. President, Senior Partner and General Manager
KAUFFMAN, Frank, Senior V. President
KRAMER, Elizabeth, V. President
MANDIGO, Michael, V. President
MCLEARN, Donald, Senior V. President
MOONEY, Robby A., Senior V. President and Partner
MULHERN, Jim, Senior V. President
SIEDLECKI, Kathleen, V. President
THOMPSON, Sela, Senior Legislative Assistant
WICKENDEN, David, Senior V. President and Senior Partner

Clients

American Ambulance Ass'n
Issues: HCR
Rep By: William Black

Enron Corp.
Issues: CPI ENG
Rep By: Michael Mandigo

Iceland, Government of the Republic of

Jacobs Engineering Group Inc.
Issues: AER BUD
Rep By: Joy Bates Boyle, Paul W. Johnson

Kahl Pownall Advocates
Issues: HCR MMM
Rep By: William Black, Kathleen Siedlecki

Knoll Pharmaceutical Co.
Issues: HCR
Rep By: Paul W. Johnson, Kathleen Siedlecki

Nat'l Ass'n of Rehabilitation Professionals in the Private Sector

Return to Work Coalition

Rubber Manufacturers Ass'n

SBC Communications Inc.
Issues: TEC
Rep By: Paul W. Johnson, Frank Kauffman, Michael Mandigo

Sigma-Tau Pharmaceuticals, Inc.

Soc. of Thoracic Surgeons
Rep By: William Black

Telefonos de Mexico
Issues: TEC
Rep By: Michael Mandigo

Wheat Foods Council
Rep By: Jim Mulhern

R. G. Flippo and Associates, Inc.

1101 30th St. NW
Suite 500
Washington, DC 20007
Tel: (202)289-5490
Fax: (202)289-5495
Registered: LDA
E-mail: rgflippo@erols.com
A management and legislative consultant firm.

DC-Area Employees Representing Listed Clients
FLIPPO, Hon. Ronnie G., President
WALLACE, Vicki P., Senior Associate

Clients

Alabama Nursing Homes Ass'n
Issues: BUD MMM
Rep By: Hon. Ronnie G. Flippo, Vicki P. Wallace

Huntsville, Alabama, City of
Issues: ECN ROD TRA URB
Rep By: Hon. Ronnie G. Flippo, Vicki P. Wallace

Huntsville-Madison County Airport
Issues: AVI TRA
Rep By: Hon. Ronnie G. Flippo, Vicki P. Wallace

Spectrum Astro, Inc.
Issues: AER DEF
Rep By: Hon. Ronnie G. Flippo

Tensor Technologies, Inc.
Issues: AVI TRA
Rep By: Hon. Ronnie G. Flippo, Vicki P. Wallace

Troy State University - Montgomery
Issues: BUD EDU
Rep By: Hon. Ronnie G. Flippo, Vicki P. Wallace

Floyd Associates

5906 Ashby Manor Place
Alexandria, VA 22310-2267
Tel: (703)960-2223
Fax: (703)960-2696
Registered: LDA
E-mail: floyd4@erols.com
A self-employed governmental and legislative consultant.

DC-Area Employees Representing Listed Clients
FLOYD, Veronica McCann

Clients

Brunswick Corp.
Issues: CAW MAR NAT TAX
Rep By: Veronica McCann Floyd

Foley & Lardner

3000 K St. NW
Suite 500
Washington, DC 20007-5109
Tel: (202)672-5300
Fax: (202)672-5399
Registered: LDA
Web: www.foleylardner.com
Washington office of a national law firm specializing in corporate law, litigation, health care law, legislative and regulatory law, international trade, international and domestic patent law, and trademark and copyright law. Merged with Hopkins and Sutter in 2001.

DC-Area Employees Representing Listed Clients
BIERMAN, James N., Partner-in-Charge
BORNSTEIN, Theodore H., Partner
BROWN, Sharie, Partner
CHAMEIDES, Steven B., Partner
CHRISTIE, R. Lee, Partner
DEVINE, Thomas R., Partner
EDMONDSON, Jr., Joseph, Partner
ELLIS, William T., Partner
GREBE, Michael W., Chairman and Chief Exec. Officer
HANSON, Jodi L., Lobbyist
ITZKOFF, Donald M., Partner
LAMBERT, Steven C., Partner
LEONARD, Jerris, Partner
LEONARD, Kathleen, Lobbyist
MCDERMOTT, Francis O., Of Counsel
RALSTON, Jr., David, Partner
RILEY, Jr., Richard F., Partner
SCHNEIDERMAN, Michael, Partner
VARON, Jay N., Partner
VOM EIGEN, Robert P., Partner
WAPENSKY, Russell, Lobbyist

Clients

AAAE-ACI
Issues: AVI
Rep By: Thomas R. Devine, Jodi L. Hanson, Jerris Leonard, Kathleen Leonard, David Ralston, Jr., Michael Schneiderman

Aurora Health Care, Inc.
Issues: HCR
Rep By: Theodore H. Bornstein

Canadian Nat'l Railway Co.
Issues: RRR
Rep By: Jodi L. Hanson, Jerris Leonard, Robert P. vom Eigen

CMC/Heartland Partnership
Issues: RES TRA
Rep By: Theodore H. Bornstein

ComEd
Issues: RRR
Rep By: Jodi L. Hanson, Jerris Leonard, Richard F. Riley, Jr.

Correctional Vendors Ass'n
Issues: LAW
Rep By: Kathleen Leonard

Bruce Givner, Attorney
Issues: TAX
Rep By: Jodi L. Hanson, Jerris Leonard, Richard F. Riley, Jr.

Grand Trunk Corp.
Issues: RRR
Rep By: Jodi L. Hanson, Jay N. Varon

Illinois Housing Development Authority
Issues: HOU LAW TAX
Rep By: Jodi L. Hanson

Illinois Institute of Technology
Issues: BUD
Rep By: Jodi L. Hanson

Information Handling Services
Issues: GOV
Rep By: Kathleen Leonard, David Ralston, Jr.

Kerr-McGee Corp.
Issues: WAS
Rep By: Jodi L. Hanson

Kruger Internat'l (KI)
Issues: LAW
Rep By: Jerris Leonard, David Ralston, Jr.

Liquid Metal Technologies
Issues: DEF
Rep By: Theodore H. Bornstein

Milwaukee, City of
Issues: ECN EDU ENV GOV HCR LAW TRA WEL
Rep By: Theodore H. Bornstein

Nat'l Realty Committee
Issues: TAX
Rep By: Jodi L. Hanson

Northland Cranberries, Inc.
Issues: AGR
Rep By: Theodore H. Bornstein

Northwestern Memorial Hospital
Issues: HCR
Rep By: Jodi L. Hanson

Oshkosh Truck Corp.
Issues: DEF
Rep By: Theodore H. Bornstein

PG&E Nat'l Energy Group
Issues: ENG
Rep By: Theodore H. Bornstein, Jodi L. Hanson

Real Estate Services Providers Council
Rep By: Jay N. Varon

San Diego Hospice Corp.
Issues: HCR
Rep By: Theodore H. Bornstein

Sand County Foundation
Issues: ENG
Rep By: Theodore H. Bornstein

Save the Greenback Coalition
Issues: MON
Rep By: Jerris Leonard, Russell Wapensky

Siemens Transportation Systems, Inc.
Issues: TRA
Rep By: Donald M. Itzkoff

Sub-Zero Freezer Co. Inc.
Issues: ENG ENV
Rep By: Theodore H. Bornstein

TDS Telecommunications
Issues: TEC
Rep By: Theodore H. Bornstein

USAA - United Services Automobile Ass'n
Issues: TAX
Rep By: R. Lee Christie, Jodi L. Hanson, Richard F. Riley, Jr.

Wisconsin Gas Co.
Issues: ENG ENV UTI
Rep By: Theodore H. Bornstein

YouBet.com
Issues: CPI GAM
Rep By: Jodi L. Hanson, Jerris Leonard

Foley Government and Public Affairs, Inc.

P.O. Box 61303
Potomac, MD 20859
Tel: (301)294-0937
Registered: LDA
Web: www.FoleyCoInc.com
E-mail: info@FoleyCoInc.com
A legislative advocacy, public affairs and market research firm. Specializes in high-tech/biotechnology, health care services, infrastructure funding, international trade, Congressional political issue generation, and Federal-sector contract opportunity creation and procurement since 1986. Also maintains Annapolis, MD and Los Angeles, CA offices.

DC-Area Employees Representing Listed Clients
FOLEY, Joseph P., President
GERVASIO, Jr., Ralph J., Legislative Assistant
LAVERY, Paul C., Research Assistant

Clients

Megaseal Corp.
Issues: BUD DEF FOR GOV SCI
Rep By: Joseph P. Foley

Nat'l Federation of Croatian Americans
Issues: BUD FOR TRD
Rep By: Joseph P. Foley

Pyrocap International Corp., Inc.
Issues: SCI
Rep By: Joseph P. Foley, Ralph J. Gervasio, Jr.

Thompson Lighting Protection Inc.
Issues: GOV SCI SMB
Rep By: Joseph P. Foley, Paul C. Lavery

Unified Industries, Inc.
Issues: BUD DEF GOV SCI SMB
Rep By: Joseph P. Foley

Upland, California, City of
Issues: GOV HOU RES ROD
Rep By: Joseph P. Foley

Zone Therapeutics, Inc.
Issues: BUD GOV MED PHA SCI
Rep By: Joseph P. Foley

Foley, Hoag & Eliot LLP

1747 Pennsylvania Ave. NW
Suite 1200
Washington, DC 20006
Tel: (202)223-1200
Fax: (202)785-6687
Registered: LDA, FARA
Web: www.fhe.com

DC-Area Employees Representing Listed Clients
BRENNAN, Janis H., Partner
GRAUSE, Marie Beatrice, Counsel
HUMES, Traci D., Of Counsel
REICHLER, Paul S., Partner
SMITH, Gare A., Counsel

Clients

Guatemala, Government of the Republic of
Rep By: Gare A. Smith

Guyana, Government of the Co-operative Republic of
Issues: FOR
Rep By: Paul S. Reichler, Gare A. Smith

Massachusetts Hospital Ass'n
Issues: HCR MMM
Rep By: Marie Beatrice Grause

Massachusetts Water Resources Authority
Issues: CAW
Rep By: Marie Beatrice Grause

PET Coalition
Issues: MMM
Rep By: Gare A. Smith

THA: An Ass'n of Hospitals and Health Systems
Issues: HCR MMM
Rep By: Marie Beatrice Grause

Uganda, Embassy of the Republic of
Issues: FOR
Rep By: Traci D. Humes, Paul S. Reichler

Uganda, Government of the Republic of
Issues: FOR
Rep By: Traci D. Humes, Paul S. Reichler

Fontheim Internat'l, LLC

601 13th St. NW
Suite 110 North
Washington, DC 20005
Tel: (202)296-8100
Fax: (202)296-8727
Registered: LDA

DC-Area Employees Representing Listed Clients
FONTHEIM, Claude G. B., Managing Director
LEVINSON, Kenneth I., Director, International Trade and Finance

Clients

Enron Corp.
Issues: GOV
Rep By: Kenneth I. Levinson

Microsoft Corp.
Issues: TRD
Rep By: Claude G. B. Fontheim, Kenneth I. Levinson

Vivendi Universal
Issues: FIN TRD
Rep By: Claude G. B. Fontheim, Kenneth I. Levinson

Fontheim Partners, PC

601 13th St. NW
Suite 1100
Washington, DC 20005
Tel: (202)429-2217
Fax: (202)296-8727
Registered: LDA

DC-Area Employees Representing Listed Clients
BIEL, Eric
FONTHEIM, Claude G. B., Partner
HUTMAN, Ken, Director, International Trade and Finance
LEVINSON, Kenneth I., Director, International Trade and Finance
NANCE, D. Scott, Principal

Clients

American Internat'l Group, Inc.
Issues: FIN TRD
Rep By: Claude G. B. Fontheim, Kenneth I. Levinson

Citizen's Educational Foundation
Rep By: Claude G. B. Fontheim, Ken Hutman

The Limited Inc.
Issues: APP LBR POS TRD
Rep By: Claude G. B. Fontheim, Kenneth I. Levinson, D. Scott Nance

Susquehanna Investment Group
Issues: FIN
Rep By: Eric Biel, Kenneth I. Levinson

Forscey & Stinson, PLLC

818 Connecticut Ave. NW
Suite 1004
Washington, DC 20006
E-mail: main@forstin.com

Tel: (202)530-7185
Fax: (202)530-7189
Registered: LDA

DC-Area Employees Representing Listed Clients
FORSCEY, Michael A., Managing Partner
STINSON, John M., Partner

Clients

Adventist Health System/Sunbelt, Inc.
Issues: HCR
Rep By: Michael A. Forscey

Law Offices of Peter Angelos
Issues: SPO TAX TOR
Rep By: Michael A. Forscey

Ass'n of Trial Lawyers of America
Issues: TOR
Rep By: Michael A. Forscey

Barr Laboratories
Issues: MMM PHA
Rep By: Michael A. Forscey

Bituminous Coal Operators Ass'n
Issues: ENV HCR
Rep By: Michael A. Forscey

Westhill Partners
Issues: UTI
Rep By: Michael A. Forscey

Forster & Associates

827 25th St. South
Arlington, VA 22202
E-mail: forsterjr@aol.com

Tel: (703)548-1360
Fax: (703)836-2608

DC-Area Employees Representing Listed Clients
FORSTER, Johann R., President

Clients

Bruker Meerestechnik GmbH
Issues: MAR SCI
Rep By: Johann R. Forster

Fentek Internat'l Pty. Ltd.
Issues: MAR
Rep By: Johann R. Forster

Friede, Goldman, & Halter, Inc.
Issues: DEF MAR
Rep By: Johann R. Forster

In-Pipe Technology
Issues: CAW SCI
Rep By: Johann R. Forster

PMSC-Irby Steel
Issues: MAN TRA
Rep By: Johann R. Forster

The Fortier Group, LLC

601 Pennsylvania Ave. NW
Suite 900
South Bldg.
Washington, DC 20004
E-mail: mpfortier@erols.com

Tel: (202)338-1829
Fax: (202)338-1879
Registered: LDA

The Fortier Group provides legislative and strategic counsel to clients.

DC-Area Employees Representing Listed Clients
FORTIER, Michael P., Principal

Clients

Caretenders Health Corp.
Issues: HCR
Rep By: Michael P. Fortier

ClaimTraq, Inc.
Issues: MMM PHA
Rep By: Michael P. Fortier

CNA Insurance Cos.
Issues: INS
Rep By: Michael P. Fortier

Bob Foster and Associates

1800 Diagonal Rd.
Suite 600
Alexandria, VA 22314
E-mail: BOBFOSTER1@compuserve.com

Tel: (703)684-4446
Fax: (703)836-2450
Registered: LDA

DC-Area Employees Representing Listed Clients
FOSTER, Robert B., President

Clients

American Indian Higher Education Consortium
Issues: BUD
Rep By: Robert B. Foster

American Sugar Alliance
Issues: BUD
Rep By: Robert B. Foster

David E. Fox and Associates

1325 18th St. NW
Suite 103
Washington, DC 20036

Tel: (202)887-0725
Fax: (202)872-0200

A law firm specializing in personal injury and medical malpractice suits, and family, business, and immigration law.

DC-Area Employees Representing Listed Clients
FOX, David E., Principal

Clients

Institutional and Municipal Parking Congress
Internat'l Parking Institute

FoxKiser

750 17th St. NW
Suite 1100
Washington, DC 20006

Tel: (202)778-2300
Fax: (202)778-2330
Registered: LDA

A law firm specializing in legislative practice at the federal, state, and international levels, with an emphasis on biomedical research, health care, and food and drug matters.

DC-Area Employees Representing Listed Clients
ENGEL, John M.
FISH, Andrew C.
FORRER, Graydon G.
FOX, Allan M.
HOLTZ, William E.
KISER, John Daniel
MEADE, David
PETERSON, Matthew D.
ROBERTSON, Diane E.
SWANZEY, Genine
WALTZKIN, Michael B.

Clients

Bristol-Myers Squibb Co.
Issues: ADV BUD CPT CSP HCR MED MMM PHA TRD
Rep By: Allan M. Fox, John Daniel Kiser

NitroMed, Inc.
Issues: BUD HCR MED MMM PHA
Rep By: Allan M. Fox, John Daniel Kiser, Diane E. Robertson

Fraioli/Siggins

80 F St. NW
Suite 804
Washington, DC 20001

Tel: (202)347-3042
Fax: (202)347-3046

A Democratic Campaign consulting firm.

DC-Area Employees Representing Listed Clients
BENNETT, Blair A.
DUNCAN, Josh
FRAIOLI, Michael J., President
HILTY, Christine
SIGGINS, Robert G., V. President

Franklin & Burling

1101 Connecticut Ave. NW
Suite 1200
Washington, DC 20036

Tel: (202)298-8107
Fax: (202)298-8108
Registered: LDA

DC-Area Employees Representing Listed Clients
BURLING, William, Partner
FRANKLIN, C. Anson, Partner

Clients

Nat'l Energy Resources Organization

Fratkin Associates

2322 20th St. NW
Washington, DC 20009

Tel: (202)265-5410
Fax: (202)332-8538
Registered: LDA

E-mail: sue@internet2.edu

Technology and telecommunications public policy consultants for the academic research community.

DC-Area Employees Representing Listed Clients
FRATKIN, Susan, Principal

Clients

Coalition of Academic Scientific Computation (CASC)
Issues: SCI
Rep By: Susan Fratkin

Freedman, Levy, Kroll & Simonds

1050 Connecticut Ave. NW
Washington, DC 20036-5366

Tel: (202)672-5300
Fax: (202)672-5399
Registered: LDA

Web: www.flks.com
E-mail: flks@flks.com

A general practice law firm.

DC-Area Employees Representing Listed Clients
CHETTLE, John H., Partner
HUGHES, Phyllis E., Legislative Specialist
MCBRIDE, Lawrence G., Partner

Clients

Enron Corp.
Issues: FUE NAT
Rep By: Lawrence G. McBride

Medical University of Southern Africa
Rep By: John H. Chettle

Freedom Technologies, Inc.

555 12th St. NW
Suite 950N
Washington, DC 20004

Tel: (202)371-2220
Fax: (202)371-1497
Registered: LDA

Advises governments and companies worldwide on telecommunications structural, regulatory, and business strategy issues.

DC-Area Employees Representing Listed Clients
ALDEN, John, V. President
CHASIA, James, Director, Strategic Analysis
OBUCHOWSKI, Janice, President

Douglas Ward Freitag

21150 New Hampshire Ave.
Brookeville, MD 20833

Tel: (301)570-3821
Registered: LDA

Clients

Inter-Associates, Inc.
Issues: AER CHM DEF ENG MAN SCI
Rep By: Douglas Ward Freitag

French & Company

601 13th St. NW
Suite 370 South
Washington, DC 20005

Tel: (202)783-7272
Fax: (202)783-4345
Registered: LDA

A governmental affairs consulting firm.

DC-Area Employees Representing Listed Clients
DORNBUSCH, Rebecca, V. President
ELLIOT, Warren, Of Counsel
FRENCH, Verrick O., President
SMITH, Keith H., Exec. V. President

Clients

Bendich, Stobaugh & Strong
Issues: TAX
Rep By: Verrick O. French

Encapco Technologies, LLC
Issues: BUD DEF ENV
Rep By: Rebecca Dornbusch, Verrick O. French

Information Spectrum Inc.
Issues: IMM
Rep By: Rebecca Dornbusch, Verrick O. French

Internat'l Biometric Industry Ass'n
Issues: BAN CPI CSP FIN GOV HCR IMM MAN TRA
Rep By: Rebecca Dornbusch, Verrick O. French

Internat'l Electronics Manufacturers and Consumers of America
Issues: IMM TAX TRD
Rep By: Verrick O. French, Keith H. Smith

Levine-Fricke Restoration Corp.
Issues: RES TRA
Rep By: Rebecca Dornbusch, Verrick O. French

Montgomery Ward & Co., Inc.
Issues: TRD
Rep By: Verrick O. French

Nossaman, Gunther, Knox & Elliott
Issues: ENV RES TRA
Rep By: Rebecca Dornbusch, Verrick O. French

John Freshman Associates, Inc.

1050 Thomas Jefferson St. NW
Sixth Floor
Washington, DC 20007

Tel: (202)298-1895
Fax: (202)298-1699
Registered: LDA

DC-Area Employees Representing Listed Clients
FRESHMAN, John D., President
KAST, Lawrence P., Director
KIEFER, Catherine B.

Clients

#10 Enterprises LLC
Issues: NAT RES
Rep By: John D. Freshman, Lawrence P. Kast, Catherine B. Kiefer

Anheuser-Busch Cos., Inc.
Issues: AGR ANI ENV MAR
Rep By: John D. Freshman, Lawrence P. Kast, Catherine B. Kiefer

Gulf Coast Waste Disposal Authority
Issues: CAW ENV
Rep By: John D. Freshman, Lawrence P. Kast, Catherine B. Kiefer

Lewis and Clark Rural Water System, Inc.
Issues: NAT
Rep By: John D. Freshman, Lawrence P. Kast, Catherine B. Kiefer

Los Angeles County Sanitation District
Issues: BUD ENV WAS
Rep By: John D. Freshman, Lawrence P. Kast, Catherine B. Kiefer

Metropolitan St. Louis Sewer District
Issues: BUD CAW DIS
Rep By: John D. Freshman, Lawrence P. Kast, Catherine B. Kiefer

Mid Dakota Rural Water System
Issues: BUD NAT
Rep By: John D. Freshman, Lawrence P. Kast, Catherine B. Kiefer

Monterey County Water Resources Agency
Issues: BUD ENV
Rep By: John D. Freshman, Lawrence P. Kast, Catherine B. Kiefer

Nat'l Audubon Soc.
Issues: ENV NAT
Rep By: John D. Freshman, Lawrence P. Kast, Catherine B. Kiefer

Oregon Water Trust
Issues: BUD
Rep By: John D. Freshman, Lawrence P. Kast, Catherine B. Kiefer

Pharmacia Corp.
Issues: ENV
Rep By: John D. Freshman, Lawrence P. Kast, Catherine B. Kiefer

Sacramento, California, Department of Utilities of
Issues: BUD ENV
Rep By: John D. Freshman, Lawrence P. Kast, Catherine B. Kiefer

Fried, Frank, Harris, Shriver & Jacobson

1001 Pennsylvania Ave. NW
Suite 800
Washington, DC 20004-2505
Tel: (202)639-7000
Fax: (202)639-7008
Registered: LDA, FARA
Web: www.ffhsj.com
Washington office of a New York law firm.

DC-Area Employees Representing Listed Clients
ANSELL, David L., Partner
KADEN, Alan S., Partner
KRAEMER, Jay R., Partner
LEDIG, Robert H., Partner
PITT, Harvey L., Managing Partner
POLEBAUM, Elliot E., Partner
ROWDEN, Marcus A., Of Counsel
RULE, Charles F., Partner
SAUBER, Richard, Partner
VARTANIAN, Thomas P., Partner

Clients

GE Nuclear Energy
Issues: ENG TRD
Rep By: Jay R. Kraemer

Friedman Law Offices, P.L.L.C.

888 16th St. NW
Suite 400
Washington, DC 20006
Tel: (202)835-7466
Fax: (202)296-8791
E-mail: philip.friedman2@gte.net
A law firm specializing in civil litigation, election law and regulatory affairs.

DC-Area Employees Representing Listed Clients
FRIEDMAN, Philip S., Partner

Clients

American Israel Public Affairs Committee
Rep By: Philip S. Friedman

Cuban American Nat'l Foundation/Cuban American Foundation

Jim Frigiola

3602 Tristan Ct.
Annandale, VA 22003
Tel: (703)641-9455
Fax: (703)641-8831
Registered: LDA

Clients

Fifty Caliber Shooters Policy Institute, Inc.
Issues: FIR
Rep By: Jim Frigiola

Fulbright & Jaworski L.L.P.

801 Pennsylvania Ave. NW
Washington, DC 20004-2604
Tel: (202)662-0200
Fax: (202)662-4643
Web: www.fulbright.com
E-mail: info@fulbright.com
Washington office of a Houston, TX-based general practice law firm.

Political Action Committee
Fulbright & Jaworski L.L.P. Federal Committee
801 Pennsylvania Ave. NW
Washington, DC 20004-2604
Tel: (202)662-4741
Fax: (202)662-4643
Contact: Peter V. B. Unger

DC-Area Employees Representing Listed Clients
BURGOYNE, Robert A., Partner
COHEN, Irwin, Partner
MANNING, Michael J., Partner
UNGER, Peter V. B., Partner
VOGT, Carl, Partner

Clients

The Philadelphia Stock Exchange, Inc.
Rep By: Peter V. B. Unger

The Furman Group

1401 K St. NW
Suite 450
Washington, DC 20005
Tel: (202)737-0700
Fax: (202)737-0455
Registered: LDA
A government relations and consulting firm specializing in water and infrastructure issues. Maintains offices in Washington, D.C., Las Vegas, NV, and San Diego, CA.

DC-Area Employees Representing Listed Clients
BROWDER, K. Link, Associate
FURMAN, II, Harold W., Chief Exec. Officer/President
JAMES, Thomas M., Senior V. President

Clients

California Water Service Co.
Issues: BUD DEF NAT
Rep By: K. Link Browder, Thomas M. James

Central Basin Municipal Water District
Issues: BUD TRA
Rep By: Thomas M. James

Fallon, Nevada, City of
Issues: BUD NAT
Rep By: K. Link Browder

Imperial Beach, California, City of
Issues: CAW
Rep By: Thomas M. James

Leucadia County Water District
Issues: BUD
Rep By: Thomas M. James

Mesquite Resort Ass'n
Issues: BUD NAT TRA
Rep By: K. Link Browder, Thomas M. James

Mesquite, Nevada, City of
Issues: BUD NAT TRA
Rep By: K. Link Browder, Thomas M. James

Moapa Valley Water District
Issues: BUD
Rep By: K. Link Browder

Olivenhain Municipal Water District
Issues: BUD NAT
Rep By: Thomas M. James

Paradise Canyon Resort
Issues: BUD NAT
Rep By: K. Link Browder, Thomas M. James

San Elijo Joint Powers Authority
Issues: BUD
Rep By: Thomas M. James

San Gabriel Basin Water Quality Authority
Issues: BUD
Rep By: Thomas M. James

Tooele, Utah, City of
Issues: BUD
Rep By: K. Link Browder, Thomas M. James

Upper San Gabriel Municipal Water District
Issues: BUD
Rep By: Thomas M. James

Virgin Valley Water District
Issues: BUD
Rep By: K. Link Browder, Thomas M. James

Watsonville, California, City of
Issues: BUD
Rep By: Thomas M. James

West Basin Municipal Water District
Issues: BUD
Rep By: Thomas M. James

West Hills Community College District
Issues: EDU
Rep By: Thomas M. James

G.R. Services

1100 New York Ave. NW
Suite 580
Washington, DC 20005
Tel: (202)898-1050
Fax: (202)789-4006
Registered: LDA
A transportation consulting firm.

DC-Area Employees Representing Listed Clients
EISENHART, Earl, President

Clients

American Bakers Ass'n
Rep By: Earl Eisenhart

Intermodal Ass'n of North America
Issues: FUE LBR MAR ROD RRR TAX TRA TRU
Rep By: Earl Eisenhart

Ryder System, Inc.
Issues: TRU
Rep By: Earl Eisenhart

Snack Food Ass'n
Issues: TRU
Rep By: Earl Eisenhart

Gainer & Rient

1920 N St. NW
Suite 250
Washington, DC 20036
Tel: (202)408-8000
Fax: (202)408-0888
E-mail: grh@us.net
A legal consulting firm specializing in criminal law.

DC-Area Employees Representing Listed Clients
GAINER, Ronald L., Partner
RIENT, Peter F., Partner

Linda Parke Gallagher & Assoc.

715 E. Capitol St. SE
Washington, DC 20003
Tel: (202)544-9489
Fax: (202)544-9490
E-mail: Eastcap@aol.com
A public relations and marketing communications firm, focusing on strategic communications consulting.

DC-Area Employees Representing Listed Clients
GALLAGHER, Linda Parke, President

Clients

Affordable Housing Preservation Center
Rep By: Linda Parke Gallagher

Multi-Family Housing Institute
Rep By: Linda Parke Gallagher

Nat'l Corp. for Housing Partnerships, Inc. (NCHP)
Rep By: Linda Parke Gallagher

The Gallagher Group, LLC

1800 N. Kent St.
Suite 907
Arlington, VA 22209
Tel: (703)527-1135
Fax: (703)524-1005
Registered: LDA

DC-Area Employees Representing Listed Clients
GALLAGHER, James P.

Clients

American Automar
Issues: DEF
Rep By: James P. Gallagher

Commonwealth Consulting Corp.
Issues: AER BUD DEF
Rep By: James P. Gallagher

General Dynamics Corp.
Issues: AER AVI DEF FOR
Rep By: James P. Gallagher

NoFire Technologies, Inc.
Issues: DEF
Rep By: James P. Gallagher

Gallagher, Boland and Meiburger

1023 15th St. NW
Suite 900
Washington, DC 20005-2602
Tel: (202)289-7200
Fax: (202)289-7698
E-mail: gbm@gbmdc.com
A law firm representing clients before federal regulatory agencies and departments and federal courts in energy-related matters.

DC-Area Employees Representing Listed Clients
BOLAND, Christopher T., Senior Counsel
BROADSTONE, James M., Partner
KELLY, Frank X., Partner
LESCH, Peter C., Partner
MEIBURGER, George J., Senior Counsel
STOJIC, Steve, Partner

Clients

Cinergy Corp.
Issues: ENG FUE NAT TRA UTI
Rep By: Peter C. Lesch, Steve Stojic

Enron Corp.
Issues: ENG FUE NAT TRA UTI
Rep By: Frank X. Kelly, Steve Stojic

Gas Research Institute
Issues: ENG FUE NAT TRA UTI
Rep By: James M. Broadstone

TECO Energy, Inc.
Issues: ENG FUE NAT TRA UTI
Rep By: Peter C. Lesch

Galland, Kharasch, Greenberg, Fellman & Swirsky, P.C.

1054 31st St. NW
Suite 200
Canal Square
Washington, DC 20007
Tel: (202)342-5200
Fax: (202)342-5219
Registered: LDA, FARA
Web: www.gkmg@gkmg.com
A law firm.

DC-Area Employees Representing Listed Clients
FELLMAN, Steven John, Managing Partner
STREET, David P., Partner

Clients

Air Canada

Air Jamaica Ltd.

Composites Fabricators Ass'n

Deutsche Lufthansa AG

Distribution Services, Ltd.
Rep By: David P. Street

Freight-Savers Shipping Co. Ltd.

Nat'l Ass'n of Theatre Owners
Rep By: Steven John Fellman

Orient Airlines Ass'n

Profit Freight Systems/LEP

Textile Rental Services Ass'n of America

Worldlink Logistics Inc.
Rep By: David P. Street

Gallant Co.

9506 Gauge Dr.
Fairfax Station, VA 22039
Tel: (703)690-4450
Fax: (703)690-4451

DC-Area Employees Representing Listed Clients
GALLANT, Karl, President

Clients

Alexander Strategy Group
Issues: ENG TAX
Rep By: Karl Gallant

Salem Communications Corp.
Rep By: Karl Gallant

Robert Garcia and Associates, Inc

1666 K St. NW
Suite 500
Washington, DC 20006
E-mail: garciaasoc@aol.com
Tel: (202)778-2149
Fax: (202)296-6907
Registered: LDA

DC-Area Employees Representing Listed Clients
GARCIA, Hon. Robert, Washington Representative

Clients

Verizon Communications
Rep By: Hon. Robert Garcia

Gardner, Carton and Douglas

1301 K St. NW
Suite 900
East Tower
Washington, DC 20005
Web: www.gcd.com
Tel: (202)408-7100
Fax: (202)289-1504
Registered: LDA

Gardner, Carton & Douglas is a law firm headquartered in Chicago, IL. Partners in the Washington office regularly represent clients before the federal government in tax, healthcare, environmental, telecommunications, the legislative process, actions by departments of the Executive Branch, general policy formation, and international trade and Indian law matters relating to administrative agency proceedings.

DC-Area Employees Representing Listed Clients
FLETCHER, Francis
MOW, Laura C., Partner
NILLES, Kathleen M., Partner
ROCK, Patrick, Partner
SULLIVAN, T. J., Partner

Clients

American Council on Education
Issues: TAX
Rep By: Kathleen M. Nilles

American Telecasting, Inc.
Issues: TEC

Andrew Corp.
Issues: TEC
Rep By: Francis Fletcher

Coalition for Nonprofit Health Care
Issues: HCR
Rep By: T. J. Sullivan

ComTech Communications, Inc.
Issues: TEC

The Council of Insurance Agents & Brokers
Issues: TAX
Rep By: Kathleen M. Nilles

DCT Communications, Inc.
Issues: TEC

Geotek Communications, Inc.
Issues: TEC

Nat'l Indian Gaming Ass'n
Issues: TAX
Rep By: Kathleen M. Nilles

Partnership Defense Fund Trust
Issues: TAX
Rep By: Kathleen M. Nilles

Pittencrieff Communications, Inc.

VHA Inc.
Issues: TAX
Rep By: Kathleen M. Nilles

Yukon Pacific
Issues: ENV
Rep By: Patrick Rock

Law Offices of Michael R. Gardner, P.C.

1150 Connecticut Ave. NW
Suite 710
Washington, DC 20036
E-mail: mrgpc@aol.com
Tel: (202)785-2828
Fax: (202)785-1504
Registered: LDA

A law firm.

DC-Area Employees Representing Listed Clients
GARDNER, Michael R.

Clients

Universal Wireless Communications Consortium
Issues: FOR SCI TEC TRD
Rep By: Michael R. Gardner

Sara Garland (and Associates)

418 C St. NE
Washington, DC 20002
Tel: (202)547-8530
Fax: (202)547-8532
Registered: LDA
Web: www.greystone-group.com
E-mail: sarag@mail.greystone-group.com

Also known as The Greystone Group, not affiliated with The Greystone Group (VA) also listed in this directory (see separate listing).

DC-Area Employees Representing Listed Clients
EMMONS, Rachel A., Exec. Associate
GARLAND, Sara G., Principal

Clients

Ad Hoc Public Television Group
Issues: AGR BUD
Rep By: Sara G. Garland

American Indian Higher Education Consortium
Issues: BUD COM EDU IND TEC
Rep By: Rachel A. Emmons, Sara G. Garland

Fort Abraham Lincoln Foundation
Issues: BUD
Rep By: Sara G. Garland

Minot State University
Issues: BUD EDU
Rep By: Rachel A. Emmons, Sara G. Garland

Oglala Lakota College
Issues: IND
Rep By: Sara G. Garland

Red River Trade Council
Issues: AGR BUD ECN ROD TEC TRA
Rep By: Sara G. Garland

Sesame Workshop
Issues: COM FOR
Rep By: Rachel A. Emmons, Sara G. Garland

Swope Parkway Health Center
Issues: BUD ECN HCR
Rep By: Rachel A. Emmons, Sara G. Garland

Turtle Mountain Community College
Issues: BUD
Rep By: Sara G. Garland

University of North Dakota
Issues: AER AGR AVI BUD EDU ENG ENV HCR
Rep By: Sara G. Garland

Anthony Garrett

1701 K St. NW
Suite 750
Washington, DC 20006
E-mail: agarrett@internews.org
Tel: (202)833-5740
Fax: (202)833-5745
Registered: LDA

Clients

Internews
Rep By: Anthony Garrett

Garrett Yu Hussein LLC

1825 Connecticut Ave. NW
Suite 650
Washington, DC 20009
Tel: (202)745-5100
Fax: (202)234-6159

DC-Area Employees Representing Listed Clients
GARRETT, Peter, Senior Partner
MCCABE, Patrick, Partner
REIS, Sharon, Partner
YU HUSSEIN, Pattie, Senior Partner

Clients

American Ass'n of University Women Legal Advocacy Fund

Bristol-Myers Squibb Co.

Campaign for Tobacco-Free Kids

Hoffmann-La Roche Inc.

Nat'l Academy of Social Insurance

Nat'l Asian Women's Health Organization

Nat'l Center for Tobacco-Free Kids

Robert Wood Johnson Foundation

The Garrison Group

1531 T St. NW
Washington, DC 20009
Tel: (202)234-6888
Fax: (202)234-6887
Registered: LDA

A public relations and lobbying firm specializing in agriculture and the food industry.

DC-Area Employees Representing Listed Clients
GARRISON, Charles, Consultant

Clients

Southeast Dairy Farmer Ass'n
Issues: AGR ENV FOO
Rep By: Charles Garrison

Garvey, Schubert & Barer

1000 Potomac St. NW
Suite 500
Washington, DC 20007
Web: www.gsblaw.com
Tel: (202)965-7880
Fax: (202)965-1729
Registered: LDA, FARA

Washington office of a Seattle law firm specializing in maritime, transportation, environmental regulation, and international trade matters before federal commissions, departments and agencies.

Political Action Committee
Garvey, Schubert & Barer Political Action Committee
1000 Potomac St. NW
Suite 500
Washington, DC 20007
Contact: Matthew R. Schneider
Tel: (202)965-7880
Fax: (202)965-1729

DC-Area Employees Representing Listed Clients
BAILEY, Jr., Harold G., Partner
CRIGLER, John, Partner
GLUCK, Richard D., Partner
GREENBERG, Eldon V. C., Partner
HOFF, Paul S., Partner
SCHNEIDER, Matthew R., Managing Director
WEGMAN, Richard A., Partner

Clients

American Internat'l Freight Ass'n
Issues: MAR
Rep By: Richard D. Gluck

Bermuda, Government of
Rep By: Richard A. Wegman

Canada, Embassy of
Rep By: Richard A. Wegman

Canada, Government of
Rep By: Richard A. Wegman

Canada, Trade Law Division of the Embassy of

Changing Paradigms
Rep By: Matthew R. Schneider

China Ocean Shipping Co.
Rep By: Richard D. Gluck

Coalition on the Implementation of the AFA
Issues: MAR
Rep By: Paul S. Hoff

Council of Appraisal and Property Professional Societies
Rep By: Matthew R. Schneider

East Coast Tuna Ass'n
Rep By: Eldon V. C. Greenberg

GoTo.com Inc.
Issues: MIA SCI
Rep By: Matthew R. Schneider

Interocean Management Co.

Japan Fisheries Ass'n
Rep By: Paul S. Hoff

Japan Wood-Products Information and Research Center
Rep By: Paul S. Hoff

Nat'l Academy of Sciences
Issues: GOV
Rep By: Richard A. Wegman

Nat'l Ass'n of Independent Fee Appraisers
Rep By: Matthew R. Schneider

Nat'l Fisheries Institute
Rep By: Eldon V. C. Greenberg

Natural Technologies
Rep By: Matthew R. Schneider

Primavera Laboratories, Inc.
Rep By: Matthew R. Schneider

USX Corp.
Issues: FOR HCR
Rep By: Richard A. Wegman

Harry Winston Research Foundation
Rep By: Matthew R. Schneider

GCS Inc.

5400 Albia Rd.
Bethesda, MD 20816
Tel: (301)320-4125
Fax: (301)320-0762
Registered: LDA

DC-Area Employees Representing Listed Clients
GINGRICH, Claud, President

Clients

Anheuser-Busch Cos., Inc.
Issues: TRD
Rep By: Claud Gingrich

Geddings Communications LLC

1655 N. Fort Myer Dr.
Suite 700
Arlington, VA 22209
Tel: (202)965-6680
Registered: LDA
Web: www.geddings.com
E-mail: kris@geddings.com
A full-service public affairs, advertising, and public relations agency headquartered in Columbia, SC.

DC-Area Employees Representing Listed Clients
GEDDINGS, Kristine Phillips, Co-Owner

Clients

Nat'l Coalition to Promote Physical Activity

Nat'l Committee to Preserve Social Security and Medicare
Rep By: Kristine Phillips Geddings

Genesis Consulting Group, LLC

P.O. Box 322
McLean, VA 22101
Tel: (703)444-2153
Fax: (703)444-6158
Registered: LDA

DC-Area Employees Representing Listed Clients
BENEDICT, Mark, President
DEBEAUMONT, Dana, Director, Communications

Clients

Elkem Materials Inc.
Issues: BUD ROD
Rep By: Mark Benedict, Dana DeBeaumont

FED Corp.
Issues: BUD DEF HCR
Rep By: Mark Benedict, Dana DeBeaumont

Integrated Skilled Care of Ohio
Issues: BUD HCR
Rep By: Mark Benedict, Dana DeBeaumont

Lennox Internat'l
Issues: BUD TRD
Rep By: Mark Benedict, Dana DeBeaumont

Lumber Fair Trade Group
Rep By: Mark Benedict

Norchem Concrete Products Inc.
Issues: BUD ROD
Rep By: Mark Benedict, Dana DeBeaumont

The Timken Co.
Issues: BAN BUD ENV HCR LBR TRD
Rep By: Mark Benedict, Dana DeBeaumont

Vandium Industry Coalition
Rep By: Mark Benedict, Dana DeBeaumont

GHL Inc.

1020 19th St. NW
Suite 520
Washington, DC 20036
Tel: (202)429-9714
Fax: (202)467-5469
Registered: LDA
Specialists in government relations, marketing and technical support. Provides services to high technology industries in the United States.

DC-Area Employees Representing Listed Clients
GOLDBERG, Thomas R., President

Clients

3Tex
Issues: DEF ROD SMB TRA
Rep By: Thomas R. Goldberg

Brewer Science Inc.
Issues: DEF SMB
Rep By: Thomas R. Goldberg

Foster-Miller, Inc.
Issues: DEF SMB
Rep By: Thomas R. Goldberg

Mississippi Polymer Technologies
Issues: DEF

Seemann Composites LLC
Issues: DEF
Rep By: Thomas R. Goldberg

Sensor Research and Development Corp.
Issues: CAW DEF DIS FOO MED
Rep By: Thomas R. Goldberg

Wilson Composites Group
Issues: DEF
Rep By: Thomas R. Goldberg

Gibbons & Company, Inc.

The Willard Office Bldg.
1455 Pennsylvania Ave. NW
Washington, DC 20004
Tel: (202)783-6000
Fax: (202)783-4171
Registered: LDA, FARA
Web: www.gibbonsco.com
E-mail: gibbons@gibbonsco.com
Provides counsel and assistance in government relations and public affairs to U.S. and international clients on a broad range of federal and international policy issues.

DC-Area Employees Representing Listed Clients
BAKER, Allison A.
CATTANEO, John M.
CHURCHILL, Christine M.
GIBBONS, Clifford S., President and Chief Exec. Officer
GIBBONS, Hon. Sam M., Chairman of the Board
PARZAKONIS, Joanna

Clients

Aso Corp.
Issues: TRD
Rep By: Clifford S. Gibbons, Hon. Sam M. Gibbons

Elettronica Veneta & IN.EL.
Issues: FOR TRD
Rep By: Clifford S. Gibbons

Kellogg Co.
Issues: FOR TAX TRD
Rep By: Clifford S. Gibbons, Joanna Parzakonis

Lloyd's of London
Rep By: Clifford S. Gibbons

Moffit Cancer Research Hospital
Issues: BUD HCR MMM
Rep By: Clifford S. Gibbons, Hon. Sam M. Gibbons

MONY Life Insurance Co.
Rep By: Clifford S. Gibbons, Hon. Sam M. Gibbons

Playtex Products, Inc.
Issues: CPA
Rep By: Clifford S. Gibbons, Hon. Sam M. Gibbons

Gibson, Dunn & Crutcher LLP

1050 Connecticut Ave. NW
Washington, DC 20036-5306
Tel: (202)955-8500
Fax: (202)467-0539
Registered: LDA, FARA
Web: www.gdclaw.com
An international law firm with offices in Century City, Los Angeles, Orange County, Palo Alto, San Diego and San Francisco, CA; Dallas, TX; Denver, CO; New York, NY; London, England; and Paris, France.

DC-Area Employees Representing Listed Clients
BAUMBUSCH, Peter L., Partner
BELLINI, Christopher J., Partner
COLLINS, Michael
COX, Douglas, Partner
EAGER, Robert C., Partner
FELLNER, Baruch A., Partner
GOODMAN, Amy, Of Counsel
HARRISON, Donald, Partner
KILBERG, William J., Partner
LEE, Judith A., Partner
LEVINE, Hon. Meldon E., Partner
LUDWISZEWSKI, Raymond B., Partner
MILLIAN, John C., Partner
MUCKENFUSS, III, Cantwell Faulkner, Partner
MUELLER, Ronald O., Partner
OLSON, John F., Partner
OLSON, Theodore B., Partner
PERRY, Mark A., Partner
PFUNDER, Malcolm R., Of Counsel
PLAINE, Daniel J., Partner
PLATT, Alan A., Principal
PRICE, Joseph H., Partner
ROSTOW, Victoria P., Of Counsel
RUDNICK, Amy G., Partner
SELEY, Peter E., Associate
SPARLIN, Jr., D. Dean, Associate
STURC, John H., Partner
TURZA, Peter H., Partner

Clients

The Boeing Co.
Rep By: Hon. Meldon E. Levine, Alan A. Platt

The Business Roundtable
Issues: FIN
Rep By: Amy Goodman, John F. Olson

California Federal Bank
Rep By: Robert C. Eager, Cantwell Faulkner Muckenfuss, III, Victoria P. Rostow

Civil Justice Reform Group
Rep By: Mark A. Perry

CNF Transportation, Inc.
Issues: TAX
Rep By: Michael Collins, Alan A. Platt, Peter H. Turza

Dollar Bank
Issues: BAN
Rep By: Robert C. Eager, Cantwell Faulkner Muckenfuss, III, Victoria P. Rostow

Hughes Electronics Corp.
Issues: AER
Rep By: Alan A. Platt

Investment Co. Institute
Issues: FIN
Rep By: Christopher J. Bellini

Lockheed Martin Corp.
Issues: ENV
Rep By: Raymond B. Ludwiszewski, Peter E. Seley

Loral Corp.
Rep By: Alan A. Platt

MacAndrews & Forbes Holdings, Inc.
Issues: BAN
Rep By: Cantwell Faulkner Muckenfuss, III, Victoria P. Rostow

Monterey Institute
Issues: DEF
Rep By: Alan A. Platt

New York Bankers Ass'n
Issues: BAN
Rep By: Robert C. Eager, Cantwell Faulkner Muckenfuss, III, Victoria P. Rostow

Northrop Grumman Corp.
Rep By: Hon. Meldon E. Levine, Alan A. Platt

Providian Financial Corp.
Rep By: Robert C. Eager

Prudential Insurance Co. of America
Issues: BAN
Rep By: Robert C. Eager, Cantwell Faulkner Muckenfuss, III

Southern California Organ Procurement Consortium
Issues: HCR
Rep By: Alan A. Platt

Tensiodyne Scientific Corp.
Issues: DEF
Rep By: Alan A. Platt

U.S. Business Alliance for Customs Modernization
Issues: TRD
Rep By: Judith A. Lee

Washington Mutual Bank
Issues: BAN
Rep By: Robert C. Eager, Cantwell Faulkner Muckenfuss, III

Thomas J. Gilligan

3513 McKinley St. NW
Washington, DC 20015-2513
Tel: (202)244-6450
Fax: (202)244-6570
Registered: LDA
Web: www.afec.com
E-mail: asehct@aol.com

Clients

Ass'n for Electronic Healthcare Transaction
Issues: HCR
Rep By: Thomas J. Gilligan

MBNA America Bank NA
Issues: HCR
Rep By: Thomas J. Gilligan

Gilman & Associates

600 Pennsylvania Ave. SE
Washington, DC 20003
Tel: (202)547-9080
Fax: (202)547-8944
E-mail: ndgilman@aol.com
A law firm emphasizing aviation and other transportation mode issues, injury and wrongful death, products liability, negligence law; and civil, criminal, and administrative matters.

DC-Area Employees Representing Listed Clients
GILMAN, Nicholas

GKRSE

1500 K St. NW
Suite 330
Washington, DC 20005
Tel: (202)408-5400
Fax: (202)408-5406
Registered: LDA
Web: www.gkrse-law.com
Formerly known as Grammer, Kissel, Robbins, Skancke & Edwards.

DC-Area Employees Representing Listed Clients
KISSEL, Peter C., Partner
SKANCKE, Nancy J., Partner

Clients

Kootenai Electric Cooperative, Inc.
Rep By: Peter C. Kissel, Nancy J. Skancke

Global Aviation Associates, Ltd.

1800 K St. NW
Suite 1104
Washington, DC 20006
Web: www.ga2online.com
Tel: (202)457-0212
Fax: (202)833-3183
Registered: FARA

DC-Area Employees Representing Listed Clients
ASH, Jon F., Managing Director
CHAMBERS, Charles R., Senior V. President

Clients

Ass'n of Asia Pacific Airlines
Issues: AVI
Rep By: Jon F. Ash, Charles R. Chambers

Austrian Airlines
Issues: AVI
Rep By: Jon F. Ash, Charles R. Chambers

Dallas/Fort Worth Internat'l Airport Board
Issues: AVI
Rep By: Jon F. Ash, Charles R. Chambers

Las Vegas/McCarran Internat'l Airport
Issues: AVI
Rep By: Jon F. Ash, Charles R. Chambers

Memphis-Shelby County Airport Authority
Issues: AVI
Rep By: Jon F. Ash, Charles R. Chambers

Norfolk, Virginia, City of
Issues: AVI
Rep By: Jon F. Ash, Charles R. Chambers

ORBITZ
Issues: AVI
Rep By: Jon F. Ash, Charles R. Chambers

Swissair
Issues: AVI
Rep By: Jon F. Ash, Charles R. Chambers

Global Communicators

901 15th St. NW
Suite 370
Washington, DC 20005
Tel: (202)371-9600
Fax: (202)371-0808
Registered: LDA, FARA

An international public affairs, economic development, and marketing communications consulting firm.

DC-Area Employees Representing Listed Clients
CHRISTIE, Katherine M., President
HARFF, James W., Chairman and Chief Exec. Officer
HEINE, Kristine E., Exec. V. President
HERRARA-DAVILA, Nina V.W.

Clients

Jordan Tourism Board
Rep By: James W. Harff, Nina V.W. Herrara-Davila

Switzerland, Economic Development, State of Vaud
Issues: ECN
Rep By: Katherine M. Christie, James W. Harff, Kristine E. Heine

Global Marketing and Development Solutions

2121 Eisenhower
Suite 600
Alexandria, VA 22314
Web: www.gmds.com
Tel: (703)299-6649
Fax: (703)299-9213
Registered: FARA

DC-Area Employees Representing Listed Clients
CARLBERG, Ronald L., Exec. V. President

Clients

Swiss Ordnance Enterprise
Rep By: Ronald L. Carlberg

Global Policy Group, Inc.

1101 16th St. NW
Washington, DC 20036
Web: www.globalpolicy.com
E-mail: gpg@globalpolicy.com
Tel: (202)496-1550
Fax: (202)496-1552
Registered: LDA, FARA

A research and consulting firm.

DC-Area Employees Representing Listed Clients
BERGNER, Douglas J., President
GRAIG, Ian C., Chief Exec.

Clients

Dana Corp.

Denso Internat'l America, Inc.

E.ON North America, Inc.
Issues: ECN ENG TRD
Rep By: Douglas J. Bergner

Fiat U.S.A., Inc.

JETRO New York

NEC USA, Inc.

Standard Chartered Bank
Issues: FIN
Rep By: Douglas J. Bergner

Global USA, Inc.

2121 K St. NW
Suite 650
Washington, DC 20037
Tel: (202)296-2400
Fax: (202)296-2409
Registered: LDA, FARA

A government relations and international consulting firm.

DC-Area Employees Representing Listed Clients
ANDERSON, Stanton D., Chairman
BROWN, Rosamond S., V. President
DENYSYK, Dr. Bohdan, President and Chief Exec. Officer
DUNCAN, Charles
EISELSBERG, David, Director, Research
JONES, Jerry H., Advisor
KOPP, George S., Senior V. President and General Counsel
ONES, Leyla, Senior Associate
SHACKELFORD, Lottie H., Exec. V. President
SMITH, Michael B., V. Chairman

Clients

All Nippon Airways Co.
Issues: AVI
Rep By: Dr. Bohdan Denysyk, George S. Kopp

Artel, Inc.
Issues: TEC
Rep By: George S. Kopp, Lottie H. Shackelford

Dade, Florida, County of
Issues: DIS ECN HOU
Rep By: Rosamond S. Brown, George S. Kopp, Lottie H. Shackelford

DRC, Inc.
Issues: DIS
Rep By: Charles Duncan, George S. Kopp

FM Watch
Issues: GOV HOU
Rep By: Lottie H. Shackelford

Hyundai Motor Co.
Issues: AUT TRD
Rep By: Rosamond S. Brown, George S. Kopp

Jacksonville Electric Authority
Issues: CAW UTI
Rep By: Rosamond S. Brown, Lottie H. Shackelford

Japan Federation of Construction Contractors, Inc.
Issues: TRD
Rep By: Dr. Bohdan Denysyk

K-Mortgage Corp.
Issues: HOU
Rep By: George S. Kopp, Lottie H. Shackelford

Komatsu Ltd.
Issues: TRD
Rep By: Dr. Bohdan Denysyk

Kyocera Corp.
Issues: DEF
Rep By: Dr. Bohdan Denysyk

Loral Space and Communications, Ltd.
Issues: SCI
Rep By: Dr. Bohdan Denysyk

Mazak Corp. & Mazak Sales and Service, Inc.
Issues: MAN TAX
Rep By: Dr. Bohdan Denysyk

Nippon Telegraph and Telephone Corp.

Psychemedics Corp.
Issues: ALC LBR SCI
Rep By: George S. Kopp, Lottie H. Shackelford

SBC Communications Inc.
Issues: TEC
Rep By: Rosamond S. Brown, Dr. Bohdan Denysyk, George S. Kopp, Lottie H. Shackelford

Taipei Economic and Cultural Representative Office in the United States
Issues: FOR
Rep By: Rosamond S. Brown, George S. Kopp

GLOBEMAC Associates

1011 Arlington Blvd.
Suite 304S
Arlington, VA 22209
Tel: (703)524-8293
Fax: (703)524-8398
Registered: LDA

DC-Area Employees Representing Listed Clients
MACKAY, Gordon D., Chairman

Clients

Massachusetts Software Council
Issues: CPI CPT TAX TEC
Rep By: Gordon D. MacKay

Metropolitan Life Insurance Co.
Issues: FIN INS TAX
Rep By: Gordon D. MacKay

New England Investment Co.
Issues: FIN TAX
Rep By: Gordon D. MacKay

New England Life Insurance Co.
Issues: FIN INS TAX
Rep By: Gordon D. MacKay

GMA Internat'l

1800 N. Beauregard St.
Suite 150
Alexandria, VA 22311
Tel: (703)250-0916
Fax: (703)239-0122
Registered: LDA

DC-Area Employees Representing Listed Clients
O'CONNOR, Edward C.

Clients

Singapore Technologies Automotive
Issues: BUD DEF TRD
Rep By: Edward C. O'Connor

Goddard Claussen

1150 Connecticut Ave. NW
Suite 201
Washington, DC 20036
Web: www.gcft.com
Tel: (202)955-6200
Fax: (202)955-6215

Washington office of a national public affairs and public relations firm.

DC-Area Employees Representing Listed Clients
ARMSTRONG, Edward, V. President
GLAUB, Richard, Senior V. President
PERKINS, Roy, Senior V. President and Deputy Director
SIEGEL, Elisa, Senior V. President
TIEGER, Carolyn C., Partner

Clients

American Council of Life Insurers

The Business Roundtable

Center for Claims Resolution

Chlorine Chemistry Council

Health Insurance Ass'n of America

David F. Godfrey

P.O. Box 6394
Alexandria, VA 22306
Tel: (703)780-2462
Fax: (703)780-6123
Registered: LDA

Clients

Dal Mac Investment Corp.
Issues: RES
Rep By: David F. Godfrey

Indian Pueblos Federal Development Corp.
Issues: RES
Rep By: David F. Godfrey

Keating Development Corp.
Issues: RES
Rep By: David F. Godfrey

W. G. Yates & Sons Construction Co.
Issues: RES
Rep By: David F. Godfrey

Goldberg & Associates, PLLC

888 16th St. NW
Suite 700
Washington, DC 20006-4103
Web: www.assnlaw.com
E-mail: jimcounsel@aol.com
Tel: (202)835-8282
Fax: (202)835-8293
Registered: LDA

A law firm.

DC-Area Employees Representing Listed Clients
GOLDBERG, James M., Partner

Clients

American Peanut Council
Rep By: James M. Goldberg

American School Counselor Ass'n
Rep By: James M. Goldberg

Michigan Retailers Ass'n
Rep By: James M. Goldberg

NAMM: Internat'l Music Products Ass'n

Nat'l Alcohol Beverage Control Ass'n
Issues: ALC TAX
Rep By: James M. Goldberg

Nat'l Ass'n of College Auxiliary Services

Nat'l Ass'n of School Music Dealers
Rep By: James M. Goldberg

North American Retail Dealers Ass'n
Issues: BNK CPT LBR
Rep By: James M. Goldberg

Goldberg, Godles, Wiener & Wright

1229 19th St. NW
Washington, DC 20036
E-mail: general@g2w2.com
Tel: (202)429-4900
Fax: (202)429-4912
Registered: LDA

A law firm.

DC-Area Employees Representing Listed Clients
GODLES, Joseph A., Partner
GOLDBERG, Henry, Partner

WIENER, Jonathan L., Partner
WRIGHT, Henrietta, Counsel

Clients

PanAmSat Corp.
Issues: COM TEC
Rep By: Henry Goldberg

Golin/Harris Internat'l

2300 Clarendon Blvd.
Suite 610
Arlington, VA 22201-3367
Tel: (703)351-5666
Fax: (703)351-5667
Registered: LDA, FARA
Web: www.golinharris.com
A strategic communications firm specializing in government, media and public relations. Recently merged with Weber McGinn, Inc.

DC-Area Employees Representing Listed Clients

BAILEY, R. Lane, Managing Director
BROWN, Marjorie Eilertsen, Senior V. President
FRAZER, Paul, Exec. V. President
FULTON, C. Michael, Exec. V. President
HYDE, Margaret, Account Exec.
KING-HOLMES, Alexis, Senior Account Exec.
MCLEOD, Bruce, V. President
MITCHELL, Carol C., V. President
SIX, Robert, Account Director
SKOLFIELD, Melissa T., V. President and Director, Health Care Practice Group
STENRUD, Chris, Account Group Supervisor
TAYLOR, Tracy L., Senior Account Exec.
VARNEY, Molly, Senior Account Exec.
VAVONESE, Jamie, Exec. Assistant
WALKER, Kevin L., Account Director

Clients

Alliance Community Hospital
Issues: HCR
Rep By: C. Michael Fulton

Brown General Hospital
Issues: HCR
Rep By: C. Michael Fulton

Center for the Arts and Sciences
Issues: EDU
Rep By: Carol C. Mitchell

Concord College
Issues: EDU
Rep By: Carol C. Mitchell

Flexsys America
Issues: ENV
Rep By: C. Michael Fulton

Go-Mart, Inc.
Issues: ENV TAX
Rep By: C. Michael Fulton

Grenada Lake Medical Center
Rep By: C. Michael Fulton

John Harland Co.
Issues: BAN EDU
Rep By: C. Michael Fulton, Carol C. Mitchell

Kent State University
Issues: EDU
Rep By: C. Michael Fulton

Michigan Technological University
Issues: EDU
Rep By: Carol C. Mitchell

Nat'l Ass'n of City and County Health Officials
Issues: HCR
Rep By: Carol C. Mitchell

Our Lady of the Lake Regional Medical Center
Issues: HCR
Rep By: C. Michael Fulton

Joel Pomerene Hospital
Issues: HCR
Rep By: C. Michael Fulton

Ruby Memorial Hospital
Issues: BUD
Rep By: Carol C. Mitchell

Sacred Heart University
Issues: EDU
Rep By: C. Michael Fulton

Southeast Missouri State University
Issues: EDU
Rep By: C. Michael Fulton

St. Mary's Hospital
Issues: HCR
Rep By: Carol C. Mitchell

University Health Associates, Inc.
Issues: EDU ENV
Rep By: C. Michael Fulton

West Virginia University Hospitals, Inc.
Rep By: Carol C. Mitchell

Good & Associates

1432 Fenwick Ln.
Suite 200
Silver Spring, MD 20910
Tel: (301)608-1141
E-mail: ligood@erols.com
A public affairs consulting firm.

DC-Area Employees Representing Listed Clients

GOOD, Larry, President

Mark W. Goodin

8617 Cross Chase Ct.
Fairfax Station, VA 22039
Tel: (703)690-3590
Registered: LDA
A political/government relations consultant.

Clients

American Ass'n of Health Plans (AAHP)
Issues: HCR
Rep By: Mark W. Goodin

Former Governors of Puerto Rico
Rep By: Mark W. Goodin

The PGA Tour, Inc.
Rep By: Mark W. Goodin

Puerto Rico, Commonwealth of
Issues: ECN GOV TAX
Rep By: Mark W. Goodin

Southern Auto Sales, Inc.
Rep By: Mark W. Goodin

Goodstein & Associates

1130 Connecticut Ave. NW
Suite 710
Washington, DC 20036
Tel: (202)659-1600
Fax: (202)659-1328
Registered: LDA
Web: www.rgoodstein.com
E-mail: goodstein8@aol.com
A lawyer, lobbyist, and consultant. Specializes in environmental and energy issues, both legislative and regulatory.

DC-Area Employees Representing Listed Clients

GOODSTEIN, Richard F., President

Clients

Air Products and Chemicals, Inc.
Issues: BUD CHM ENG ENV MAN TRD
Rep By: Richard F. Goodstein

American Ref-Fuel
Issues: CAW ENG ENV WAS

Bennett Environmental Inc.
Issues: ENV
Rep By: Richard F. Goodstein

Coeur d'Alene Mines Corp.
Issues: CAW ENV NAT

Lexmark Internat'l
Issues: ENV
Rep By: Richard F. Goodstein

Micell Technologies, Inc.
Issues: ENV TAX
Rep By: Richard F. Goodstein

U.S. Postal Service
Issues: ENV WAS
Rep By: Richard F. Goodstein

Goodwin, Procter & Hoar LLP

1717 Pennsylvania Ave. NW
Washington, DC 20006
Tel: (202)974-1000
Fax: (202)331-9330
Registered: LDA
Headquartered in Boston, MA. Acquired the firm Negroni & Kromer, PLLC, in 2000.

DC-Area Employees Representing Listed Clients

BUCKLEY, Jeremiah S.
KOLAR, Joseph M., Partner
KROMER, John P.
NAIMON, Jeffrey P., Associate
NEGRONI, Andrea Lee
RODERER, David W., Counsel
TANK, Margo, Associate

Clients

Consumer Mortgage Coalition
Issues: BAN HOU
Rep By: Joseph M. Kolar, Jeffrey P. Naimon

Electronic Financial Services Council
Issues: BAN FIN HOU INS SCI
Rep By: Jeremiah S. Buckley, Margo Tank

GE Capital Mortgage Services, Inc.

Massachusetts Bankers Ass'n
Issues: BAN HOU
Rep By: Jeremiah S. Buckley, Margo Tank

Mortgage Insurance Companies of America

Gordley Associates

600 Pennsylvania Ave. SE
Suite 320
Washington, DC 20003
Tel: (202)969-8900
Fax: (202)969-7036
Registered: LDA

DC-Area Employees Representing Listed Clients

GORDLEY, John, President
HARDEN, Krysta, Associate
KELLY, Maureen, Associate
MARQUET, Megan, Assistant Director
MCBETH, Daryn, Associate

Clients

American Soybean Ass'n
Issues: AGR ENV TRA
Rep By: John Gordley, Krysta Harden, Megan Marquet

Iowa Pork Producers Ass'n
Issues: AGR
Rep By: John Gordley, Krysta Harden, Megan Marquet

Nat'l Barley Growers Ass'n
Issues: AGR
Rep By: John Gordley, Krysta Harden, Maureen Kelly, Megan Marquet, Daryn McBeth

Nat'l BioDiesel Board

Nat'l Sunflower Ass'n
Issues: AGR
Rep By: John Gordley, Krysta Harden, Megan Marquet

Nebraska Wheat Board
Rep By: John Gordley, Daryn McBeth

U.S. Canola Ass'n
Issues: AGR
Rep By: John Gordley, Megan Marquet, Daryn McBeth

Wild Bird Feeding Institute
Issues: AGR NAT RES TAX
Rep By: John Gordley

Stuart J. Gordon

10005 Sorrel Ave.
Potomac, MD 20854
Tel: (301)299-8844
Fax: (301)983-8865
Registered: LDA

Clients

Major League Baseball
Issues: GOV LBR SPO TAX
Rep By: Stuart J. Gordon

The Gorlin Group

2300 M St. NW
Suite 800
Washington, DC 20037
Tel: (202)973-2870
Fax: (202)296-8407
Registered: LDA
E-mail: jgorlin@erols.com

DC-Area Employees Representing Listed Clients

GORLIN, Jacques, President

Clients

Bristol-Myers Squibb Co.
Issues: TRD
Rep By: Jacques Gorlin

Intellectual Property Committee
Issues: TRD
Rep By: Jacques Gorlin

Pfizer, Inc.
Issues: TRD
Rep By: Jacques Gorlin

Pharmaceutical Research and Manufacturers of America
Issues: TRD
Rep By: Jacques Gorlin

Gottehrer and Co.

115 S. Union St.
P310
Alexandria, VA 22314
Tel: (703)549-8280
Fax: (703)549-8271
Registered: LDA
E-mail: gottehrerandco@aol.com

DC-Area Employees Representing Listed Clients

GOTTEHRER, Barry, President

Clients

Bay State Health Systems
Issues: HCR
Rep By: Barry Gottehrer

Take The Field, Inc.
Issues: BUD SPO
Rep By: Barry Gottehrer

UST Public Affairs, Inc.
Issues: TAX TOB
Rep By: Barry Gottehrer

Wright, Lindsey & Jennings
Issues: BAN TAX
Rep By: Barry Gottehrer

Government Relations, Inc.

1050 17th St. NW
Suite 510
Washington, DC 20036
Tel: (202)775-0079
Fax: (202)785-0477
Registered: LDA
Web: www.govrelations.com
E-mail: TBulger825@aol.com

DC-Area Employees Representing Listed Clients
BULGER, Thomas J., President
HOWE, Allynn, Consultant
MILLER, Mark H., Associate
YOUNG, John N., Associate

Clients

Aldaron Inc.
Issues: AVI BUD ECN ROD TRA URB
Rep By: Thomas J. Bulger, Mark H. Miller, John N. Young

Ass'n for Commuter Transportation
Issues: BUD CAW ENV ROD TAX TRA
Rep By: Thomas J. Bulger, Mark H. Miller, John N. Young

Capital Area Transit Authority
Issues: BUD TRA
Rep By: Thomas J. Bulger, Mark H. Miller

Community Transit
Issues: TRA
Rep By: Thomas J. Bulger, Mark H. Miller, John N. Young

Fairfax, Virginia, County of
Issues: AVI BUD CAW ECN ENV HOU RES ROD TRA URB WAS
Rep By: Thomas J. Bulger, Mark H. Miller, John N. Young

Friends of ITS/ITS America
Issues: BUD TRA
Rep By: Thomas J. Bulger, Mark H. Miller, John N. Young

Gateway Cities
Issues: BUD TRA
Rep By: Thomas J. Bulger, Mark H. Miller, John N. Young

High Speed Ground Transportation Ass'n
Issues: BUD RRR TRA
Rep By: Thomas J. Bulger, Mark H. Miller

The Home Depot
Issues: BNK BUD CAW CSP ENV HOU IMM LBR NAT ROD TAX TRA TRD TRU
Rep By: Allynn Howe

Intelligent Transportation Soc. of America
Issues: SCI TRA
Rep By: Thomas J. Bulger

Mass Transit Authority
Issues: BUD RRR TRA
Rep By: Thomas J. Bulger, Mark H. Miller

Metropolitan Transportation Commission
Issues: AVI BUD CAW ECN ROD TRA URB
Rep By: Thomas J. Bulger, Mark H. Miller, John N. Young

Monroe, New York, County of
Issues: AVI BUD CAW ECN ENV RES ROD TRA URB
Rep By: Thomas J. Bulger, Mark H. Miller, John N. Young

Oakland County Board of Supervisors
Rep By: Thomas J. Bulger

Oakland, Michigan, County of
Issues: AVI BUD HOU ROD TRA
Rep By: Thomas J. Bulger, Mark H. Miller, John N. Young

Regional Public Tansportation Authority
Issues: BUD TRA
Rep By: Thomas J. Bulger, Mark H. Miller, John N. Young

Suburban Mobility Authority for Regional Transportation
Issues: BUD TRA
Rep By: Thomas J. Bulger, Mark H. Miller, John N. Young

Government Strategy Advisors

6701 Democracy Blvd.
Suite 300
Bethesda, MD 20817
Tel: (301)571-9404
Fax: (301)564-9619
Registered: LDA
E-mail: J_McNicholas@juno.com

A strategic marketing and government affairs firm specializing in information technology, telecommunications and health care industries.

DC-Area Employees Representing Listed Clients
MCNICHOLAS, John P., V. President

Governmental Strategies, Inc.

11803 Wayland St.
Oakton, VA 22124-2229
Tel: (703)716-4846
Fax: (703)716-0043
Registered: LDA
Web: www.govstrat.com
E-mail: gstrategies@compuserve.com

DC-Area Employees Representing Listed Clients
KENWORTHY, William D., V. President
SMITH, Timothy E., President

Clients

ComEd

Duke Energy

El Paso Electric Co.
Issues: UTI
Rep By: William D. Kenworthy, Timothy E. Smith

PSE&G

Gowran Internat'l Ltd.

1661 Crescent Place NW
Suite 608
Washington, DC 20009
Tel: (202)387-1971
Fax: (202)387-1396
Registered: FARA
E-mail: gowran@erols.com

DC-Area Employees Representing Listed Clients
LOIELLO, John P., President

Clients

Luso American Foundation
Issues: FOR SCI SMB

GPC Internat'l

1120 Connecticut Ave. NW
Suite 1100
Washington, DC 20036
Tel: (202)861-5899
Fax: (202)861-5795
Registered: LDA
Web: www.gpcusa.com

DC-Area Employees Representing Listed Clients
BERRY, Roger S.
CAHILL, John D., Senior V. President
CRANN, Daniel K., Director of Federal Relations
GEMMA, Suzanne
HALPIN, Peter G., V. President and Managing Director, Federal Relations
ITURREGUI, Carlos E., Senior Director
KING, Jennifer
MCLEAN, Sandy, V. President, Public Affairs
MCPHEE, Shelley
MORRISON, Bruce A.
NEE, Patrick, Account Executive/Office Manager
PAVEN, Andy, V. President

Clients

Alcan Aluminum Corp.
Issues: CAW ENG SCI
Rep By: John D. Cahill, Michael Day, Peter G. Halpin

Applied Terravision Systems
Issues: BUD
Rep By: Jennifer King, Bruce A. Morrison

Bechtel/Parsons Brinkeroff Joint Venture
Issues: TRA
Rep By: John D. Cahill, Andy Paven

Educational Video Conferencing, Inc.
Issues: EDU SCI
Rep By: Bruce A. Morrison

Fidelity Investments Co.
Issues: BAN
Rep By: John D. Cahill, Daniel K. Crann, Andy Paven

Harbor Philadelphia Center City Office, Ltd.
Issues: BAN RES
Rep By: Peter G. Halpin, Bruce A. Morrison

Massachusetts Port Authority
Issues: AVI
Rep By: John D. Cahill, Daniel K. Crann

Mineral Technologies, Inc.
Issues: ENV
Rep By: Shelley McPhee, Bruce A. Morrison

O'Grady Peyton Internat'l
Issues: IMM
Rep By: Bruce A. Morrison

PriceWaterhouseCoopers
Issues: AVI
Rep By: John D. Cahill, Daniel K. Crann

The Providence Plan
Issues: ECN ENC URB
Rep By: John D. Cahill, Daniel K. Crann, Suzanne Gemma

Providence Redevelopment Agency
Issues: BUD URB
Rep By: John D. Cahill, Daniel K. Crann, Suzanne Gemma

Puerto Rico, Commonwealth of
Issues: TRA
Rep By: John D. Cahill, Peter G. Halpin, Carlos E. Iturregui, Andy Paven

Roger Williams Medical Center
Issues: HCR
Rep By: John D. Cahill, Daniel K. Crann

Safety-Centered Solutions, Inc.
Issues: HCR
Rep By: John D. Cahill, Michael Day

Skadden, Arps, Slate, Meagher & Flom LLP
Issues: ENV
Rep By: Roger S. Berry, John D. Cahill, Michael Day

Sovereign Bank
Issues: FIN
Rep By: John D. Cahill

SWL Communications LLC
Issues: TEC

Tishman Construction Corp. of Washington D.C.
Issues: GOV
Rep By: Daniel K. Crann

Ultraprise.com
Issues: BAN SCI
Rep By: Bruce A. Morrison

YouBet.com
Issues: GAM
Rep By: John D. Cahill, Peter G. Halpin

Edmund C. Graber

2302 N. Jackson St.
Arlington, VA 22201
Tel: (703)469-3066
Fax: (703)469-3064
Registered: LDA
E-mail: egraber@erols.com

Provides government relations services primarily pertaining to transportation issues.

Clients

American Concrete Pavement Ass'n (ACPA)
Issues: TRA
Rep By: Edmund C. Graber

American Road and Transportation Builders Ass'n (ARTBA)
Issues: TRA
Rep By: Edmund C. Graber

Crown American Realty Trust
Issues: TRA
Rep By: Edmund C. Graber

Design-Build Institute of America
Issues: TRA
Rep By: Edmund C. Graber

Dredging Contractors of America
Issues: TRA
Rep By: Edmund C. Graber

Frederick Area Committee on Transportation (FACT)
Issues: TRA
Rep By: Edmund C. Graber

Illinois Public Transit Ass'n (IPTA)
Issues: TRA
Rep By: Edmund C. Graber

Nat'l Utility Contractors Ass'n (NUCA)
Issues: CAW TRA
Rep By: Edmund C. Graber

Safety Warning System, L.C.
Issues: TRA
Rep By: Edmund C. Graber

Jay Grant & Associates

801 Pennsylvania Ave. NW
Suite 245
Washington, DC 20005
Tel: (202)624-1512
Fax: (202)318-0338
Registered: LDA
Web: www.healthupdate.com
E-mail: jay@healthupdate.com

A legislative consulting firm headquartered in Seattle, WA.

DC-Area Employees Representing Listed Clients
GRANT, Jay B., Counsel
KEHL, David, Counsel
OLIVE, David M., Federal Counsel

Clients

AmeriPlan

Arkansas, Office of the Governor of the State of
Issues: CAW EDU ENV GOV HCR HOU LAW MMM NAT ROD TAX TRD
Rep By: Jay B. Grant, David Kehl, David M. Olive

Delta Dental Plans Ass'n

Fort Smith Regional Airport
Issues: AV AVI TRA
Rep By: Jay B. Grant, David M. Olive

Nat'l Ass'n of Dental Plans
Issues: HCR INS MMM TAX

Nat'l Ass'n of Insurance Commissioners
Issues: HCR MMM
Rep By: Jay B. Grant

The Nat'l Cathedral

Protective Life Insurance Co.
Issues: HCR INS
Rep By: Jay B. Grant

Travelocity.com
Issues: AVI
Rep By: Jay B. Grant, David M. Olive

Vision Technologies, Inc.
Issues: AVI COM CPI MAN SCI SMB TEC
Rep By: David M. Olive

Edwin C. Graves & Associates

1401 K St. NW
Suite 450
Washington, DC 20005
Tel: (202)737-0382
Fax: (202)737-0455
Registered: LDA, FARA

An independent consulting firm.

DC-Area Employees Representing Listed Clients
GRAVES, Edwin C., President

Clients

Azerbaijan, Embassy of the Republic of
Issues: FOR
Rep By: Edwin C. Graves

CBI Sugar Group
Issues: AGR TRD
Rep By: Edwin C. Graves

Charles H. Graves & Associates

1660 L St. NW
Suite 1050
Washington, DC 20036
E-mail: chg@foxislands.net
Tel: (202)659-2229
Fax: (202)659-5234
Registered: LDA

DC-Area Employees Representing Listed Clients
GRAVES, Charles H., President

Clients

Bridgeport, Connecticut, City of
Issues: TRA
Rep By: Charles H. Graves

Central Ohio Regional Transit Authority
Issues: TRA
Rep By: Charles H. Graves

Corpus Christi Regional Transportation Authority
Issues: TRA
Rep By: Charles H. Graves

Utah Transit Authority
Issues: TRA
Rep By: Charles H. Graves

Washoe County Regional Transportation Commission
Issues: TRA
Rep By: Charles H. Graves

The GrayWell Group, Inc.

205 S. Whiting St.
Suite 308
Alexandria, VA 22304
Tel: (703)751-8022
Fax: (703)751-5735
Registered: LDA

DC-Area Employees Representing Listed Clients
CALDWELL, Peter D., President
GRAY, Robert J.

Clients

Horizon Organic Dairy, Inc.
Issues: AGR
Rep By: Peter D. Caldwell, Robert J. Gray

Nat'l Cooperative Business Ass'n
Issues: AGR
Rep By: Peter D. Caldwell, Robert J. Gray

NCRI - Southeast/NCRI - Chesapeake
Issues: AGR
Rep By: Peter D. Caldwell

Visiting Nurse Service of New York
Issues: HCR

Donald R. Greeley

2801 Beechwood Circle
Arlington, VA 22207
Tel: (703)276-7184
A legislative consultant.

Clients

American Fiber Manufacturers Ass'n
Rep By: Donald R. Greeley

Law Offices of Carol Green

7315 Wisconsin Ave.
Suite 800W
Bethesda, MD 20814
Tel: (301)941-8038
Fax: (301)961-8648

DC-Area Employees Representing Listed Clients
GREEN, Carol Lynn, Attorney

Clients

Nat'l Funeral Directors Ass'n
Issues: CAW ENV
Rep By: Carol Lynn Green

Greenberg Traurig, LLP

800 Connecticut Ave. NW
Suite 500
Washington, DC 20006
Tel: (202)331-3100
Fax: (202)331-3101
Registered: LDA, FARA
Web: www.gtlaw.com
E-mail: Info@Gtlaw.com
Washington office of a full-service international law firm headquartered in Miami, FL.

DC-Area Employees Representing Listed Clients
ABRAMOFF, Jack, Senior Director, Government Affairs
BERGER, Amy F.
BLAGMAN, Diane J., Director, Legislative and Regulatory Affairs
BRECHER, Mitchell F., Shareholder
COHEN, Howard J., Shareholder
DRAPEAUX, Brian J., Assistant Director, Government Affairs
FINDER, Jodi
GARAGIOLA, Rob, Assistant Director, Government Affairs
GILLON, Peter M., Shareholder
ITURREGUI, Juan Carlos, Shareholder
KLEINMAN, Ronald W., Shareholder
MCDONALD, Gregory, Legislative Analyst
MCGOVERN, Elissa M., Of Counsel
MILLER, James F., Shareholder
MUELLER, Russell J., Director of Health and Retirement Policy
PLATT, Ronald L., Senior Director, Government Affairs
REEDER, Joseph
REIFF, Laura F., Shareholder
REYES, Victor, Shareholder
RING, Kevin, Associate
RUDY, Anthony C., Shareholder
SHIFFMAN, Gary M., Director, Governmental Affairs
SLOMOWITZ, Alan
TAYLOR, Nancy E., Shareholder
TESLER, Shana
TRYSLA, Timothy P., Assistant Director, Legislative Affairs
VAN HORNE, Jon W., Shareholder
VASELL, Shawn M.
VINE, Howard A., Managing Shareholder, Washington Office

Clients

Armando Alejandre, Estate of
Issues: FOR
Rep By: Ronald W. Kleinman

American Ass'n of Health Plans (AAHP)
Issues: HCR INS MMM
Rep By: Howard J. Cohen

American Health Care Ass'n
Issues: BUD HCR MMM
Rep By: Rob Garagiola, Russell J. Mueller, Nancy E. Taylor, Timothy P. Trysla

American Soc. of Anesthesiologists
Rep By: Howard J. Cohen

American Speech, Language, and Hearing Ass'n
Issues: BUD HCR MMM
Rep By: Rob Garagiola, Russell J. Mueller, Nancy E. Taylor, Timothy P. Trysla

Amgen
Issues: HCR MMM
Rep By: Howard J. Cohen, Russell J. Mueller

Applied Benefits Research Corp.
Issues: HCR
Rep By: Ronald L. Platt

ARAMARK Corp.
Issues: TAX
Rep By: Ronald L. Platt

Arbinet
Issues: TEC
Rep By: Mitchell F. Brecher

Associated Financial Corp.
Issues: HOU TAX
Rep By: Ronald L. Platt

ATOFINA Chemicals, Inc.
Rep By: Alan Slomowitz

Baxter Healthcare Corp.
Rep By: Howard J. Cohen

Bexar Metropolitan Water District
Issues: BUD
Rep By: Diane J. Blagman

Blue Cross and Blue Shield of California
Issues: TAX
Rep By: James F. Miller

Bowman Internat'l Corp.
Issues: GAM SPO
Rep By: Diane J. Blagman, James F. Miller, Ronald L. Platt

BUNAC USA, Inc.
Issues: IMM
Rep By: Elissa M. McGovern

The Business Roundtable
Issues: HCR
Rep By: Russell J. Mueller, Nancy E. Taylor, Timothy P. Trysla

Cable & Wireless U.S.A., Inc.
Issues: TEC

Cambridge Management Inc.
Issues: TRA
Rep By: Diane J. Blagman

Campbell Soup Co.
Issues: TAX
Rep By: Ronald L. Platt

Cellar Door Amphitheaters
Issues: TRA
Rep By: Diane J. Blagman

Channel One Network
Rep By: Jack Abramoff

Charter Schools Development Corp.
Issues: BUD DOC EDU FIN

Chicago Trust Co.
Issues: TAX
Rep By: James F. Miller

Chitimacha Tribe of Louisiana
Rep By: Jack Abramoff

Choctaw Indians, Mississippi Band of
Rep By: Jack Abramoff

Claire's Stores, Inc.
Issues: TRD
Rep By: Diane J. Blagman, Howard A. Vine

Clear Communications
Issues: TEC

Community Health Systems, Inc.
Issues: MMM
Rep By: Howard J. Cohen, Rob Garagiola, Russell J. Mueller, Nancy E. Taylor, Timothy P. Trysla

Coors Brewing Company
Issues: ALC FOO
Rep By: Nancy E. Taylor

Costa, Carlos Alberto, Estate of
Issues: FOR
Rep By: Ronald W. Kleinman

Coushatta Tribe of Louisiana
Rep By: Jack Abramoff

D&E Communications, Inc.
Issues: TEC

Mario M. de la Pena, Estate of
Issues: FOR
Rep By: Ronald W. Kleinman

Deloitte Consulting
Issues: HCR MMM
Rep By: Diane J. Blagman, Howard J. Cohen

Denver, Colorado, City of
Issues: TRD

E-Commerce Payment Coalition
Issues: GAM
Rep By: Ronald L. Platt, Shana Tesler

e.spire Communications, Inc.
Issues: TEC
Rep By: Mitchell F. Brecher

Englewood Hospital & Medical Center
Issues: HCR
Rep By: James F. Miller

Environmental Redevelopers Ass'n
Issues: ENV RES
Rep By: Peter M. Gillon

Epik Communications
Issues: TEC

Fannie Mae
Rep By: Anthony C. Rudy

Fashion Accessories Shippers Ass'n
Issues: TRD
Rep By: Ronald L. Platt

Florida Department of Agriculture and Consumer Services
Issues: TRD
Rep By: Diane J. Blagman, Howard A. Vine

Fresenius Medical Care North America
Issues: MMM
Rep By: Howard J. Cohen, Rob Garagiola, Russell J. Mueller, Nancy E. Taylor, Timothy P. Trysla

Genzyme Corp.
Issues: BUD PHA
Rep By: Russell J. Mueller, Nancy E. Taylor

GeoPhone, LLC
Issues: TEC
Rep By: Mitchell F. Brecher

Health Partners
Issues: HCR
Rep By: Peter M. Gillon, James F. Miller

Healtheon/Web MD
Issues: HCR
Rep By: Diane J. Blagman, Howard J. Cohen, Gregory McDonald, James F. Miller, Ronald L. Platt, Nancy E. Taylor, Shana Tesler, Timothy P. Trysla, Howard A. Vine

Humana Inc.
Issues: BUD DEF HCR MMM
Rep By: Howard J. Cohen, Russell J. Mueller, Nancy E. Taylor

Ingersoll-Rand Co.
Issues: IMM
Rep By: Laura F. Reiff

Internat'l Telecom Ltd.
Issues: TEC
Rep By: Mitchell F. Brecher

LDMI Telecommunications, Inc.
Issues: TEC
Rep By: Mitchell F. Brecher

LifePoint Hospitals, Inc.
Issues: MMM
Rep By: Howard J. Cohen, Rob Garagiola, Russell J. Mueller, Nancy E. Taylor, Timothy P. Trysla

Merck & Co.
Issues: HCR INS MMM PHA
Rep By: Howard J. Cohen

Miami, Florida, City of
Issues: EDU ENV IMM TAX TRA WEL
Rep By: Diane J. Blagman, Howard A. Vine

Miami-Dade, Florida, County of
Issues: EDU ENV IMM RET TAX TRA WEL
Rep By: Diane J. Blagman, Russell J. Mueller

Miller and Schroeder Financial, Inc.
Issues: HOU
Rep By: Ronald L. Platt

Mount Vernon, City of
Issues: EDU ENV IMM TAX TRA WEL
Rep By: Diane J. Blagman

Nat'l Ass'n for the Support of Long Term Care
Issues: BUD HCR MMM
Rep By: Rob Garagiola, Russell J. Mueller, Nancy E. Taylor, Timothy P. Trysla, Howard A. Vine

Nat'l Ass'n of Community Health Centers
Issues: BUD HCR MMM
Rep By: Diane J. Blagman, Howard J. Cohen, Rob Garagiola, Russell J. Mueller, Nancy E. Taylor, Timothy P. Trysla

Nat'l Ass'n of Computer Consultant Businesses
Issues: IMM TAX
Rep By: Diane J. Blagman, Ronald L. Platt, Nancy E. Taylor, Timothy P. Trysla, Howard A. Vine

Nat'l Ass'n of State & Provincial Lotteries
Issues: GAM
Rep By: Ronald L. Platt

Nat'l Center for Genome Research
Issues: AGR BUD FOO HCR
Rep By: Diane J. Blagman, Howard J. Cohen, Jodi Finder, Ronald L. Platt, Nancy E. Taylor, Timothy P. Trysla

Nat'l Housing Trust
Issues: HOU
Rep By: Ronald L. Platt

NeuLevel
Issues: CPI SCI
Rep By: Ronald L. Platt, Gary M. Shiffman

NICORE, Inc.
Issues: HCR
Rep By: Ronald L. Platt

Norlight Telecommunications, Inc.
Issues: TEC
Rep By: Mitchell F. Brecher

Oakland, California, City of
Issues: EDU ENV TRA WEL
Rep By: Diane J. Blagman

Operator Communications, Inc.
Issues: TEC
Rep By: Mitchell F. Brecher

Pharmaceutical Research and Manufacturers of America
Issues: HCR MMM PHA
Rep By: Howard J. Cohen

Playboy Enterprises, Inc.
Issues: GAM
Rep By: Diane J. Blagman, Ronald L. Platt

Prince George's, Maryland, County of
Issues: BUD HOU LAW LBR TRA URB
Rep By: Diane J. Blagman

Province Healthcare, Inc.
Issues: MMM
Rep By: Howard J. Cohen, Rob Garagiola, Russell J. Mueller, Nancy E. Taylor, Timothy P. Trysla

Questar InfoComm Inc.
Issues: TEC
Rep By: Mitchell F. Brecher

Rakisons, Ltd.
Issues: GAM
Rep By: Ronald L. Platt

Rural Hospital Coalition

Self-Insurance Institute of America, Inc.
Issues: HCR INS
Rep By: Russell J. Mueller

Severance Trust Executive Program
Issues: TAX
Rep By: Russell J. Mueller

Singapore Technologies, Inc.
Issues: MAN
Rep By: Joseph Reeder

Singer Asset Management Co., L.L.C.
Issues: TAX
Rep By: Ronald L. Platt

Smith Development, LLC
Issues: RES
Rep By: Diane J. Blagman, Gregory McDonald, Ronald L. Platt

Stanford Financial Group
Issues: TEC

Starnet Communications Internat'l
Issues: CPI GAM
Rep By: James F. Miller, Ronald L. Platt, Shana Tesler, Timothy P. Trysla

Starwood Hotels & Resorts Worldwide, Inc.
Issues: TAX
Rep By: James F. Miller

SunCruz Casino
Rep By: Jack Abramoff, Anthony C. Rudy

TECO Energy, Inc.
Issues: ENG TAX TRD

Time Warner Telecom Inc.
Issues: TEC
Rep By: Mitchell F. Brecher

TJTC Recovery Project Coalition
Issues: TAX
Rep By: Ronald L. Platt

Torrington Co.
Issues: DEF TRD
Rep By: Diane J. Blagman, Howard A. Vine

Unilever N.V.
Rep By: Howard A. Vine

Unilever United States, Inc.
Issues: BUD ENV FOO TRD
Rep By: Diane J. Blagman, Howard A. Vine

Uniroyal Technology Corp.
Rep By: Diane J. Blagman, Peter M. Gillon, Ronald W. Kleinman, Nancy E. Taylor, Howard A. Vine

United Healthcare
Issues: HCR
Rep By: James F. Miller

WellPoint Health Networks/Blue Cross of California/UNICARE
Rep By: James F. Miller

Western Pacific Economic Council
Rep By: Jack Abramoff

Wholesale Telecommunications Corp.
Issues: TEC
Rep By: Mitchell F. Brecher

Winstar Communications, Inc.
Issues: TEC

WOTC Project
Issues: TAX
Rep By: Ronald L. Platt

Yankton Sioux Tribe
Issues: IND
Rep By: Brian J. Drapeaux, Ronald L. Platt

Yipes Transmission, Inc.
Issues: TEC
Rep By: Mitchell F. Brecher

Greener and Hook, LLC

1875 I St. NW
Suite 540
Washington, DC 20006
Tel: (202)822-0655
Fax: (202)822-2022
Web: www.greenerandhook.com
E-mail: mailbox@greenerandhook.com

A communications consulting firm providing strategic counsel to corporations, trade associations, adhoc orgnizations, and political clients.

DC-Area Employees Representing Listed Clients
CZWARTACKI, John, Partner
GREENER, III, William I., Partner
HOOK, Michael J., Partner
HUGHES, Scott, Senior Associate
MARTINEZ, Jorge, Associate

Clients

Adshel, Inc.

Americans for Free Internat'l Trade (AFIT PAC)

BellSouth Corp.

Census Monitoring Board

Coors Brewing Company
Issues: ALC BEV CSP FOO GOV HCR MIA

Corporation for Public Broadcasting

Credit Union Nat'l Ass'n, Inc.

Data One Direct

The Justice Project, Inc.

Nat'l Beer Wholesalers Ass'n

Teligent, Inc.
Issues: COM GOV MIA TEC

Verizon Communications

Greer, Margolis, Mitchell, Burns & Associates

1010 Wisconsin Ave. NW
Suite 800
Washington, DC 20007
Tel: (202)338-8700
Fax: (202)338-2334

A media consulting firm.

DC-Area Employees Representing Listed Clients
BURNS, Annie, Partner
COLEMAN, Alison, Associate
GREER, Frank, Partner
GUENTHER, Kurt, Partner
MARGOLIS, Jim, Partner
MILANO, Madalene, Partner
MITCHELL, David E., Partner
OLSON, Raelynn, Partner
PINELO, Greg, Partner
RIEL, Elizabeth, Senior V. President
SMITH, David A., Partner
TALIAFERRO, Will, Partner
TOSCANO, J., Sr. V. President

Clients

Air Bag and Seat Belt Safety Campaign
Rep By: Madalene Milano, David E. Mitchell

American Ass'n of Family Physicians
Rep By: David E. Mitchell, J. Toscano

Campaign for the Northwest
Rep By: Frank Greer

Children's Action Network
Rep By: Jim Margolis, Elizabeth Riel

Communications Workers of America
Rep By: Jim Margolis, Greg Pinelo

Council for a Livable World

Democratic Nat'l Committee

NHTSA
Rep By: David E. Mitchell, Will Taliaferro

Nutrition Screening Initiative, The
Rep By: Alison Coleman, David A. Smith

Ross/Nutrition Screening Initiative
Rep By: David E. Mitchell, David A. Smith

The Gregory Co.

One Massachusetts Ave. NW
Suite 840
Washington, DC 20001
Tel: (202)371-0440
Fax: (202)371-0411
Registered: LDA

A public and government relations firm.

DC-Area Employees Representing Listed Clients
GREGORY, Neal, President

Clients

Benevolent and Protective Order of Elks (BPOE)
Rep By: Neal Gregory

Lake Preservation Coalition
Rep By: Neal Gregory

The Greystone Group (VA)

1000 Wilson Blvd.
Suite 2710
Arlington, VA 22209
Tel: (703)243-8242
Fax: (703)243-8377
Web: www.greystonegp.com
E-mail: gundersonsc@greystonegp.com

Local office of a consulting firm headquartered in Grand Rapids, MI. Provides strategic planning and research, communication, public relations, advertising, and leadership management and development services for non-profits and multinational corporations.

DC-Area Employees Representing Listed Clients
GUNDERSON, Hon. Steve, Managing Director

Clients

Republican Main Street Partnership
Rep By: Hon. Steve Gunderson

Griffin & Associates

1825 I St. NW
Suite 400
Washington, DC 20006
Tel: (202)857-5210
Fax: (202)429-6834
Registered: LDA

DC-Area Employees Representing Listed Clients
GRIFFIN, Janice B., President

Clients

Prudential Insurance Co. of America
Issues: FIN INS TAX
Rep By: Janice B. Griffin

Griffin, Johnson, Dover & Stewart

1300 Connecticut Ave. NW
Suite 600
Washington, DC 20036
Tel: (202)775-8116
Fax: (202)223-0358
Registered: LDA, FARA

A government relations firm.

DC-Area Employees Representing Listed Clients
DANVERS, William C., Lobbyist
DOVER, G. Jack, Lobbyist
GRIFFIN, Patrick J., President
HEARD, Keith, Lobbyist
JOHNSON, David E., V. President
KRASOW, Cristina L.
MADIGAN, Peter T., Principal
MANN, Susan O., Lobbyist
STEWART, Walter J. "Joe", Lobbyist
SWINEHART, Leonard, Lobbyist
ZESIGER, David W., Lobbyist

Clients

Air Transport Ass'n of America
Issues: AVI TRA
Rep By: David E. Johnson, Leonard Swinehart

Alaska Communications Systems, Inc.
Issues: TEC
Rep By: G. Jack Dover, Walter J. "Joe" Stewart

Alliance for Reasonable Regulation of Insecticides
Issues: AGR BUD CHM FOO
Rep By: Keith Heard

American Fish Spotters Ass'n
Issues: BUD MAR
Rep By: William C. Danvers, G. Jack Dover, Patrick J. Griffin, Keith Heard, David E. Johnson, Susan O. Mann, Walter J. "Joe" Stewart, Leonard Swinehart

American Petroleum Institute
Issues: ENV
Rep By: G. Jack Dover, Patrick J. Griffin, David E. Johnson, Susan O. Mann, Walter J. "Joe" Stewart

American Soc. of Anesthesiologists
Issues: BUD HCR MMM
Rep By: G. Jack Dover, Patrick J. Griffin, David E. Johnson, Walter J. "Joe" Stewart

Americans for Gun Safety

Arthur Andersen LLP
Rep By: Patrick J. Griffin, David E. Johnson, Walter J. "Joe" Stewart

Avue Technologies
Issues: GOV LBR
Rep By: William C. Danvers, G. Jack Dover, Patrick J. Griffin, Keith Heard, David E. Johnson, Susan O. Mann, Walter J. "Joe" Stewart, Leonard Swinehart

Coalition of Commercial and Investment Banks
Rep By: Keith Heard

Computer Coalition for Responsible Exports
Issues: CPI DEF TRD
Rep By: G. Jack Dover, David E. Johnson

Council of Smaller Enterprises
Issues: HCR SMB
Rep By: G. Jack Dover, David E. Johnson

Dell Computer Corp.
Issues: CPI DEF SCI TAX TRD
Rep By: William C. Danvers, G. Jack Dover, Patrick J. Griffin, Keith Heard, David E. Johnson, Susan O. Mann, Walter J. "Joe" Stewart, Leonard Swinehart

Deloitte Consulting
Issues: GOV HCR MMM
Rep By: William C. Danvers, G. Jack Dover, Patrick J. Griffin, Keith Heard, David E. Johnson, Susan O. Mann, Walter J. "Joe" Stewart, Leonard Swinehart

Delta Dental Plans Ass'n
Issues: CPI HCR
Rep By: G. Jack Dover, David E. Johnson

Deutsche Telekom, Inc.
Rep By: Patrick J. Griffin

Directors Guild of America
Issues: CPT MIA TAX
Rep By: William C. Danvers, G. Jack Dover, Patrick J. Griffin

Fannie Mae
Issues: BUD HOU TAX
Rep By: William C. Danvers, G. Jack Dover, Patrick J. Griffin, Keith Heard, David E. Johnson, Susan O. Mann, Walter J. "Joe" Stewart, Leonard Swinehart

Hong Kong Economic and Trade Office
Rep By: G. Jack Dover, David E. Johnson, Susan O. Mann, Walter J. "Joe" Stewart

Independent Telephone and Telecommunications Alliance
Issues: TEC
Rep By: G. Jack Dover, David W. Zesiger

The Justice Project, Inc.
Issues: LAW
Rep By: William C. Danvers, G. Jack Dover, Patrick J. Griffin, Keith Heard, David E. Johnson, Susan O. Mann, Walter J. "Joe" Stewart, Leonard Swinehart

Local Initiatives Support Corp.
Rep By: William C. Danvers, G. Jack Dover, Keith Heard

Lockheed Martin Corp.
Issues: DEF MAN
Rep By: Walter J. "Joe" Stewart

Lockheed Martin Global Telecommunications
Issues: TEC
Rep By: Walter J. "Joe" Stewart

Monsanto Co.
Rep By: G. Jack Dover, Patrick J. Griffin, Leonard Swinehart

Nat'l Music Publishers' Ass'n
Issues: CPT
Rep By: Patrick J. Griffin, David E. Johnson, Susan O. Mann

Philip Morris Management Corp.
Issues: BEV FOO TOB
Rep By: Walter J. "Joe" Stewart

PMX Corp.

Software Productivity Consortium
Issues: BUD CPI
Rep By: G. Jack Dover

United Technologies Corp.
Issues: DEF TRD
Rep By: William C. Danvers, G. Jack Dover, Patrick J. Griffin, Keith Heard, David E. Johnson, Susan O. Mann, Walter J. "Joe" Stewart, Leonard Swinehart

Wilmer, Cutler & Pickering
Issues: TEC
Rep By: William C. Danvers, G. Jack Dover, Patrick J. Griffin, Keith Heard, David E. Johnson, Susan O. Mann, Walter J. "Joe" Stewart, Leonard Swinehart

Wine and Spirits Wholesalers of America
Issues: ADV ALC BEV
Rep By: William C. Danvers, G. Jack Dover, Patrick J. Griffin, Keith Heard, David E. Johnson, Susan O. Mann, Walter J. "Joe" Stewart, Leonard Swinehart

J. Steven Griles & Associates

2600 Virginia Ave. NW
Suite 600
Washington, DC 20037
Tel: (202)333-2524
Fax: (202)338-5950
Registered: LDA

DC-Area Employees Representing Listed Clients
CANFIELD, IV, H. Spofford
GRILES, J. Steven, President
NORTHINGTON, John

Clients

Advanced Power Technologies, Inc.
Issues: RES
Rep By: J. Steven Griles

APTI
Issues: RES
Rep By: J. Steven Griles

Caithness Energy, LLC
Issues: ENG
Rep By: J. Steven Griles

Devon Energy Corp.
Issues: ENG
Rep By: J. Steven Griles

RAPOCA Energy Co.
Issues: TAX
Rep By: J. Steven Griles

Redstone
Issues: ENG
Rep By: H. Spofford Canfield, IV, J. Steven Griles, John Northington

Grisso Consulting

P.O. Box 230010
Centreville, VA 20120
Tel: (703)802-1682
Fax: (703)802-0289
Registered: LDA
Web: www.grissoconsulting.com
E-mail: mgrisso@grissoconsulting.com

DC-Area Employees Representing Listed Clients
GRISSO, Michael E., President

Clients

Commercial Service Co., Ltd.
Issues: FUE
Rep By: Michael E. Grisso

Health Policy Strategies
Issues: HCR
Rep By: Michael E. Grisso

Hees Interests, Ltd.
Issues: FUE NAT
Rep By: Michael E. Grisso

Medical Records Internat'l, Inc.
Issues: CPI CPT CSP HCR INS MED MMM PHA TAX TEC
Rep By: Michael E. Grisso

Nat'l Ass'n of Children's Hospitals Inc.
Rep By: Michael E. Grisso

TriWest Healthcare Alliance, Inc.
Rep By: Michael E. Grisso

The Grizzle Company

1400 16th St. NW
Suite 400
Washington, DC 20036
Tel: (202)234-2101
Fax: (202)234-1614
Registered: LDA
E-mail: grizzleco@aol.com

DC-Area Employees Representing Listed Clients
CANTOR, Richard A., President
GRIZZLE, Charles L., Chairman

Clients

al group Lonza
Rep By: Richard A. Cantor, Charles L. Grizzle

Ashland Inc.
Issues: BUD CAW ENV
Rep By: Richard A. Cantor, Charles L. Grizzle

California Steel Industries, Inc.

ENTEK Corp.
Rep By: Richard A. Cantor, Charles L. Grizzle

GSE Systems, Inc.
Issues: BUD
Rep By: Richard A. Cantor, Charles L. Grizzle

Internat'l Council of Shopping Centers
Issues: BUD CAW
Rep By: Richard A. Cantor, Charles L. Grizzle

ManTech Internat'l
Issues: BUD
Rep By: Richard A. Cantor, Charles L. Grizzle

Mas-Hamilton Group
Issues: BUD
Rep By: Richard A. Cantor, Charles L. Grizzle

NTS Mortgage Income Fund
Issues: BUD
Rep By: Richard A. Cantor, Charles L. Grizzle

Regional Airport Authority of Louisville & Jefferson Co.
Issues: BUD TRA
Rep By: Richard A. Cantor, Charles L. Grizzle

University of Louisville
Issues: BUD
Rep By: Richard A. Cantor, Charles L. Grizzle

WPC Brands, Inc.
Issues: CHM
Rep By: Richard A. Cantor, Charles L. Grizzle

Groom Law Group, Chartered

1701 Pennsylvania Ave. NW
Suite 1200
Washington, DC 20006
Tel: (202)857-0620
Fax: (202)659-4503
Registered: LDA
Web: www.groom.com
E-mail: info@groom.com
A law firm specializing in employee benefit and tax law.

DC-Area Employees Representing Listed Clients
BREYFOGLE, Jon W., Partner
FITZGERALD, Thomas F., Member
FORD, Gary M., Managing Principal
GROOM, Theodore R., Partner
LEONHARDT, Jill L., Consultant
MAZAWEY, Louis T.
THRASHER, Michael A.

Clients

American Benefits Council
Issues: HCR RET
Rep By: Jon W. Breyfogle

American Council of Life Insurers
Issues: LBR TAX
Rep By: Jon W. Breyfogle

Blue Cross Blue Shield Ass'n
Issues: HCR
Rep By: Jon W. Breyfogle, Thomas F. Fitzgerald

Buffalo Carpenters Pension Fund
Issues: LBR RET TAX
Rep By: Jon W. Breyfogle, Gary M. Ford

Mutual Tax Committee
Issues: TAX
Rep By: Theodore R. Groom

Production Service & Sales District Council Pension Fund
Issues: LBR RET TAX
Rep By: Jon W. Breyfogle, Gary M. Ford

Grove, Jaskiewicz, and Cobert

1730 M St. NW
Suite 400
Washington, DC 20036
Tel: (202)296-2900
Fax: (202)296-1370
Web: www.gjcobert.com
E-mail: rcobert@gjcobert.com
A general practice law firm.

DC-Area Employees Representing Listed Clients
COBERT, Ronald N., Partner
COPE, Robert L., Partner
DANAS, Andrew M., Partner
KILEY, Edward J., Partner

Clients

American Institute for Shippers' Ass'ns
Issues: MAR TRA TRU
Rep By: Ronald N. Cobert

GRQ, Inc.

5454 Wisconsin Ave.
Suite 1270
Chevy Chase, MD 20815
Tel: (301)718-0202
Fax: (301)718-2976
Registered: LDA

DC-Area Employees Representing Listed Clients
BOOTH, Patricia, Principal
PORTE, Phillip, Principal

Clients

American Ass'n of Cardiovascular and Pulmonary Rehabilitation
Issues: GOV HCR MMM
Rep By: Patricia Booth, Phillip Porte

American College of Chest Physicians
Issues: HCR MMM
Rep By: Patricia Booth, Phillip Porte

HCR-Manor Care, Inc.
Issues: GOV HCR MMM
Rep By: Patricia Booth, Phillip Porte

Mallinckrodt-Nellcor Puritan Bennett
Issues: HCR MMM
Rep By: Patricia Booth, Phillip Porte

Nat'l Ass'n for Medical Direction of Respiratory Care
Issues: GOV HCR MMM
Rep By: Patricia Booth, Phillip Porte

Transtracheal Systems
Issues: HCR MMM
Rep By: Patricia Booth, Phillip Porte

Tri Path Inc.
Issues: GOV HCR MMM
Rep By: Patricia Booth, Phillip Porte

Gryphon Internat'l

516 First St. SE
Washington, DC 20003
Tel: (202)546-5639
Fax: (202)544-0473
Registered: LDA
E-mail: whoffman@worldnet.att.net

DC-Area Employees Representing Listed Clients
HOFFMAN, William L.

Clients

American University of Beirut
Issues: BUD
Rep By: William L. Hoffman

Richardson Lawrie Associates
Rep By: William L. Hoffman

John C. Grzebien

1105 N. Pitt St.
Suite 3C
Alexandria, VA 22314
Tel: (703)836-7615
Registered: LDA

Clients

Dredging Contractors of America
Issues: ENV MAR NAT
Rep By: John C. Grzebien

Edison Community College
Issues: ECN
Rep By: John C. Grzebien

Heritage Harbor Museum
Issues: ART ECN EDU TOU
Rep By: John C. Grzebien

Professional Facilities Management
Issues: ECN
Rep By: John C. Grzebien

Providence City Arts for Youth, Inc.
Issues: ART ECN
Rep By: John C. Grzebien

Providence Performing Arts Center
Issues: ART ECN
Rep By: John C. Grzebien

SafeWorks, LLC
Issues: ECN
Rep By: John C. Grzebien

Save the Bay
Issues: ENV
Rep By: John C. Grzebien

Shea's Performing Arts Center
Issues: ART ECN
Rep By: John C. Grzebien

Tampa Bay Performing Arts Center
Issues: ECN
Rep By: John C. Grzebien

James E. Guirard

600 Water St. SW
Suite B 14
Washington, DC 20024
Tel: (202)488-2722
Fax: (202)488-2729
Registered: LDA
E-mail: justcauses@aol.com

Clients

Analytical Systems, Inc.
Issues: CHM DEF SCI
Rep By: James E. Guirard, Jr.

Newpark Resources/SOLOCO
Issues: DEF ENV FUE
Rep By: James E. Guirard, Jr.

SIGCOM, Inc.
Issues: ROD SCI TEC
Rep By: James E. Guirard, Jr.

Gustafson Associates

1175 Reston Ave.
Herndon, VA 20170
Tel: (703)450-9066
Registered: LDA

DC-Area Employees Representing Listed Clients
GUSTAFSON, Robert C., President

Clients

Center for Aging Policy
Issues: BUD
Rep By: Robert C. Gustafson

EarthVoice
Issues: FOR
Rep By: Robert C. Gustafson

Internat'l Campaign for Tibet
Issues: FOR
Rep By: Robert C. Gustafson

Internat'l Trust Fund for Demining and Mine Victims Assistance in Bosnia-Herzigovina
Issues: FOR
Rep By: Robert C. Gustafson

Interns for Peace Internat'l
Issues: FOR
Rep By: Robert C. Gustafson

Nat'l Spiritual Assembly of the Baha'is of the United States
Issues: FOR
Rep By: Robert C. Gustafson

Nature Islands, Inc.
Issues: FOR

Robert M. Guttman

219 Ninth St. SE
Washington, DC 20003
Tel: (202)547-1840
Fax: (202)547-7668

Clients

Nat'l Council for Adoption
Issues: FAM
Rep By: Robert M. Guttman

Daniel Guttman

1135 15th St. NW
Suite 410
Washington, DC 20006
Tel: (202)638-6050
Fax: (202)637-2977
Registered: LDA
An attorney.

Haake and Associates

1301 K St. NW
Suite 900, East Tower
Washington, DC 20005
Tel: (202)408-8700
Fax: (202)408-8704
Registered: LDA
A legislative consulting firm.

DC-Area Employees Representing Listed Clients
HAAKE, Timothy M., Counsel
OLSEN, Nathan M., Counsel

Clients

American Ass'n of Orthodontists
Issues: HCR POS
Rep By: Timothy M. Haake, Nathan M. Olsen

American Orthotic and Prosthetic Ass'n
Issues: HCR MMM
Rep By: Timothy M. Haake, Nathan M. Olsen

EMC Corp.
Rep By: Timothy M. Haake, Nathan M. Olsen

Free Trade Lumber Council
Rep By: Timothy M. Haake, Nathan M. Olsen

Jewelers of America
Issues: BNK TAX TRD
Rep By: Timothy M. Haake, Nathan M. Olsen

The Lansdale Company
Rep By: Timothy M. Haake, Nathan M. Olsen

North American Insulation Manufacturers Ass'n
Issues: ENG TAX
Rep By: Timothy M. Haake, Nathan M. Olsen

Ortho Concepts
Issues: MMM
Rep By: Timothy M. Haake, Nathan M. Olsen

The Pillsbury Co.
Issues: TAX TRD
Rep By: Timothy M. Haake

Saint-Gobain Corp.
Rep By: Timothy M. Haake, Nathan M. Olsen

Science Applications Internat'l Corp. (SAIC)
Issues: APP DEF
Rep By: Timothy M. Haake, Nathan M. Olsen

Seal Beach, California, City of
Issues: RES
Rep By: Timothy M. Haake, Nathan M. Olsen

Tanimura & Antle, Inc.
Issues: AGR TAX
Rep By: Timothy M. Haake, Nathan M. Olsen

Titan Corp.
Rep By: Timothy M. Haake, Nathan M. Olsen

C. McClain Haddow & Associates

2921 Mother Well Ct.
Herndon, VA 20171
Tel: (703)471-5210
Fax: (703)481-3682
Registered: LDA
E-mail: machaddow@erols.com

DC-Area Employees Representing Listed Clients
HADDOW, C. McClain, Director

Clients

Mylan Laboratories, Inc.
Issues: BUD CPT HCR

Somerset Pharmaceuticals
Rep By: C. McClain Haddow

Hadley & McKenna

1815 H St. NW
Suite 500
Washington, DC 20006-3604
Tel: (202)296-6300
Fax: (202)775-5929
A law firm.

DC-Area Employees Representing Listed Clients
HADLEY, Jr., Joseph E.

Clients

Aniline Ass'n, Inc.
Issues: CSP MAN WAS
Rep By: Joseph E. Hadley, Jr.

Ethylene Oxide Sterilization Ass'n, Inc.
Issues: CSP MAN MED WAS
Rep By: Joseph E. Hadley, Jr.

Nitrobenzene Ass'n
Issues: CSP MAN WAS
Rep By: Joseph E. Hadley, Jr.

Tetrahydrofuran Task Force
Issues: CSP MAN WAS
Rep By: Joseph E. Hadley, Jr.

Hager Sharp Inc.

1090 Vermont Ave. NW
Third Floor
Washington, DC 20005
Tel: (202)842-3600
Fax: (202)842-4032
Communications, public affairs and public relations.

DC-Area Employees Representing Listed Clients
CURTIS, Garry, Senior V. President
DEMENT, Polly, Senior Communications Counselor
HAGER, Susan, Chair and Chief Exec. Officer
HALL, Darcy, Account Assistant

Hale and Dorr LLP

1455 Pennsylvania Ave. NW
Suite 1000
Washington, DC 20004
Tel: (202)942-8400
Fax: (202)942-8484
Registered: LDA
Web: www.haledorr.com
A general practice law firm headquartered in Boston, MA.

DC-Area Employees Representing Listed Clients
BYERS, Bonnie B., Trade Economist
HELLER, Mark, Senior Partner
HOWE, Louise, Senior Partner
HUREWITZ, Barry J., Junior Partner
JAMESON, Paul W., Of Counsel
KAPLAN, Gilbert B., Senior Partner
LOWY, Karen, Associate
MAGRUDER, Meghan, Senior Partner
REVAZ, Cris R., Of Counsel
URWITZ, Jay P., Senior Partner

Clients

AdvaMed
Issues: GOV MED
Rep By: Mark Heller

Bethlehem Steel Corp.
Issues: TRD
Rep By: Gilbert B. Kaplan

Blyth Industries, Inc.
Issues: TRD
Rep By: Bonnie B. Byers, Jay P. Urwitz

Committee to Support U.S. Trade Laws
Issues: TRD
Rep By: Gilbert B. Kaplan

Cook Inc.
Issues: GOV MED
Rep By: Mark Heller, Louise Howe

Harcourt Inc.
Issues: EDU MIA
Rep By: Jay P. Urwitz

Hearing Industries Ass'n
Issues: GOV MED
Rep By: Mark Heller

Hillenbrand Industries, Inc.
Issues: GOV
Rep By: Mark Heller, Louise Howe

Lau Technologies
Issues: GOV
Rep By: Jay P. Urwitz

Micron Technology, Inc.
Issues: DEF TRD
Rep By: Bonnie B. Byers, Gilbert B. Kaplan, Jay P. Urwitz

Molecular BioSystems, Inc.
Issues: GOV MED
Rep By: Mark Heller

Neiman Marcus Group
Issues: APP
Rep By: Bonnie B. Byers, Gilbert B. Kaplan, Jay P. Urwitz

Northeastern University
Issues: EDU
Rep By: Jay P. Urwitz

Ostex Internat'l Inc.
Issues: MMM
Rep By: Barry J. Hurewitz, Jay P. Urwitz

Parametric Technology Corp.
Issues: CPI DEF
Rep By: Jay P. Urwitz

Pixtech, Inc.
Issues: DEF
Rep By: Bonnie B. Byers, Gilbert B. Kaplan

Psychological Corp.
Issues: EDU
Rep By: Jay P. Urwitz

SatCon Technology Corp.
Issues: AUT GOV
Rep By: Jay P. Urwitz

Thermedics Detection, Inc.
Issues: GOV
Rep By: Jay P. Urwitz

University College Dublin
Issues: EDU
Rep By: Jay P. Urwitz

Wang Laboratories Inc.
Issues: GOV
Rep By: Jay P. Urwitz

Wheelock College
Issues: EDU
Rep By: Jay P. Urwitz

Haley and Associates

412 First St. SE
Suite One
Washington, DC 20003
Tel: (202)484-7137
Fax: (202)484-0770
Registered: LDA

DC-Area Employees Representing Listed Clients
HALEY, Daniel D., President

Clients

CalCot
Issues: AGR TRD
Rep By: Daniel D. Haley

California Prune Board
Issues: AGR TRD
Rep By: Daniel D. Haley

California Strawberry Commission
Issues: AGR
Rep By: Daniel D. Haley

California Walnut Commission
Issues: AGR TRD
Rep By: Daniel D. Haley

Ingersoll-Rand Co.
Issues: DEF MAN TRD
Rep By: Daniel D. Haley

Sun Diamond Growers, Inc.
Issues: AGR
Rep By: Daniel D. Haley

SunSweet Growers, Inc.
Issues: AGR TRD
Rep By: Daniel D. Haley

Valley Fig Growers
Issues: AGR TRD
Rep By: Daniel D. Haley

Martin L. Hall

311 Maryland Ave. NE
Suite One
Washington, DC 20002
Tel: (202)544-4256
Fax: (202)544-4207
Registered: LDA

Clients

Gulfstream TLC, Inc.
Rep By: Martin L. Hall

Hall, Estill, Hardwick, Gable, Golden & Nelson

1120 20th St. NW
Suite 700 North
Washington, DC 20036-3406
Tel: (202)973-1200
Fax: (202)973-1212
Registered: LDA
Web: www.hallestill.com
A general and administrative practice law firm headquartered in Tulsa, OK.

DC-Area Employees Representing Listed Clients
CALLAHAN, John J., Associate
DINAN, Donald R., Partner
HEYWOOD, Christopher A., Associate
MEMBRINO, Joseph R., Partner
TAYLOR, Judith A., Associate
WILCOX, Jr., James B., Partner

Clients

Edison Internat'l

Hoopa Valley Tribal Council
Issues: IND
Rep By: Joseph R. Membrino

Penobscot Indian Nation
Rep By: Joseph R. Membrino

San Pasqual Band of Mission Indians
Issues: IND
Rep By: Joseph R. Membrino

Hall, Green, Rupli, LLC

1212 New York Ave. NW
Suite 350
Washington, DC 20005
Tel: (202)842-5077
Fax: (202)842-5010
Registered: LDA, FARA
A lobbying firm.

DC-Area Employees Representing Listed Clients
ALCALDE, Richard, Associate
GREEN, John M., Partner
HALL, G. Stewart, President and Partner
LEHMAN, David E., Associate
RUPLI, Timothy R., Partner

Clients

American Ass'n of Nurse Anesthetists
Issues: HCR
Rep By: John M. Green, G. Stewart Hall

Bay Area Rapid Transit District
Issues: TRA
Rep By: G. Stewart Hall

BellSouth Corp.
Issues: TEC
Rep By: John M. Green, G. Stewart Hall

BellSouth Telecommunications, Inc.
Issues: TEC
Rep By: John M. Green, G. Stewart Hall

Birmingham Airport Authority
Issues: AVI
Rep By: John M. Green, G. Stewart Hall

Colsa Corp.
Issues: CPI DEF
Rep By: John M. Green, G. Stewart Hall

Community Financial Services Ass'n
Issues: BAN
Rep By: John M. Green, G. Stewart Hall, Timothy R. Rupli

DaimlerChrysler Corp.
Rep By: John M. Green, G. Stewart Hall

FedEx Corp.
Issues: POS TRA
Rep By: John M. Green, G. Stewart Hall

Huntsville Madison Chamber of Commerce
Issues: AER DEF
Rep By: John M. Green, G. Stewart Hall

MemberWorks, Inc.
Issues: BAN
Rep By: John M. Green, G. Stewart Hall, Timothy R. Rupli

Nat'l Ass'n of Business Political Action Committees
Issues: CIV COM GOV
Rep By: John M. Green, G. Stewart Hall

Nat'l Rifle Ass'n of America
Issues: FIR
Rep By: John M. Green, G. Stewart Hall

Pernod Ricard
Issues: BEV
Rep By: John M. Green, G. Stewart Hall, Timothy R. Rupli

Philip Morris Management Corp.
Issues: FOO TOB
Rep By: John M. Green, G. Stewart Hall

Southern Research Institute
Issues: ENG MED
Rep By: John M. Green, G. Stewart Hall

U.S. Space & Rocket Center
Issues: EDU TOU
Rep By: John M. Green, G. Stewart Hall

United States Telecom Ass'n
Issues: TEC
Rep By: John M. Green, G. Stewart Hall

University of Alabama - Huntsville
Issues: EDU
Rep By: John M. Green, G. Stewart Hall

University of South Alabama
Issues: EDU
Rep By: John M. Green, G. Stewart Hall

UST Public Affairs, Inc.
Issues: TOB
Rep By: John M. Green

Halprin, Temple, Goodman & Maher

555 12th St. NW
Suite 950 North
Washington, DC 20004
Tel: (202)371-9100
Fax: (202)371-1497
Registered: LDA
Web: www.htgm.com
E-mail: law@htgm.com

DC-Area Employees Representing Listed Clients
BERNSTEIN, Joel H., Partner
GOODMAN, Stephen L., Partner
HALPRIN, Albert, Partner
MAHER, Jr., William F., Partner
TEMPLE, Riley K., Partner

Clients

Automated Credit Exchange
Issues: TEC
Rep By: Joel H. Bernstein

Telcordia Technologies, Inc.
Issues: TEC
Rep By: Joel H. Bernstein, Riley K. Temple

Verizon Communications
Issues: TEC
Rep By: Joel H. Bernstein, Riley K. Temple

Yellow Pages Publishers Ass'n
Issues: TEC
Rep By: Joel H. Bernstein, Albert Halprin

Halsey, Rains & Associates, LLC

2111 Wilson Blvd.
Suite 600
Arlington, VA 22201
Tel: (703)351-5077
Fax: (703)351-5827
Registered: LDA
E-mail: hra@halseyrains.com
A political consulting and issues management firm.

DC-Area Employees Representing Listed Clients
HALSEY, Steven C., Managing Member
HUBBARD, James, Member
RAINS, Laurie D., Member

Clients

American Board of Medical Specialties in Podiatry
Issues: GOV
Rep By: Steven C. Halsey, James Hubbard, Laurie D. Rains

American Medical Technologists
Issues: GOV
Rep By: Steven C. Halsey, James Hubbard, Laurie D. Rains

American Soc. of Military Comptrollers
Rep By: Steven C. Halsey, James Hubbard, Laurie D. Rains

Ass'n of Government Accountants
Issues: GOV
Rep By: Steven C. Halsey, James Hubbard, Laurie D. Rains

Board for Orthotists/Prosthetist Certification
Rep By: Steven C. Halsey, James Hubbard, Laurie D. Rains

Cardiovascular Credentialing Internat'l
Issues: GOV
Rep By: Steven C. Halsey, James Hubbard, Laurie D. Rains

The Chauncey Group Internat'l
Rep By: Steven C. Halsey, James Hubbard, Laurie D. Rains

Coalition for Professional Certification
Issues: GOV
Rep By: Steven C. Halsey, James Hubbard, Laurie D. Rains

Computer Adaptive Technologies
Issues: GOV
Rep By: Steven C. Halsey, James Hubbard, Laurie D. Rains

Internat'l Board of Lactation Consultant Examiners
Issues: GOV
Rep By: Steven C. Halsey, James Hubbard, Laurie D. Rains

Internat'l Electrical Testing Ass'n
Issues: GOV
Rep By: Steven C. Halsey, James Hubbard, Laurie D. Rains

Nat'l Ass'n of Portable X-Ray Providers
Issues: GOV HCR MMM SMB
Rep By: Steven C. Halsey, James Hubbard, Laurie D. Rains

Nat'l Commission for the Certification of Crane Operators
Issues: GOV
Rep By: Steven C. Halsey, James Hubbard, Laurie D. Rains

Nat'l Council on Family Relations
Rep By: Steven C. Halsey, James Hubbard, Laurie D. Rains

Nat'l Institute for Certification in Engineering Technologies
Issues: GOV
Rep By: Steven C. Halsey, James Hubbard, Laurie D. Rains

Martin G. Hamberger & Associates

227 Massachusetts Ave. NE
Suite One
Washington, DC 20002
Tel: (202)548-8470
Fax: (202)548-8472
Registered: LDA

A government affairs consulting firm.

DC-Area Employees Representing Listed Clients

HAMBERGER, Martin G., President
SEARS, William P., Consultant
TYNAN, Brian M.

Clients

American Public Transportation Ass'n
Issues: BUD TRA
Rep By: Martin G. Hamberger, Brian M. Tynan

Michael Baker Corp.
Issues: ENG ENV TRD
Rep By: Martin G. Hamberger, Brian M. Tynan

Eclipse Energy Systems, Inc./Insyte, Inc.
Issues: BUD ENG TRA
Rep By: Brian M. Tynan

Eschenbach USA, Inc.
Issues: TRD
Rep By: Martin G. Hamberger

Fortessa, Inc.
Issues: TRD
Rep By: Martin G. Hamberger

GATCO of VA, Inc.
Issues: TRD
Rep By: Martin G. Hamberger

Northrop Grumman Corp.
Issues: BUD DEF
Rep By: Martin G. Hamberger

Westinghouse Government Services Group
Issues: ENG ENV WAS
Rep By: Martin G. Hamberger, Brian M. Tynan

Charles A. Hamilton Associates LLC

5025 Overlook Rd. NW
Washington, DC 20016-1911
Tel: (202)237-8142
Fax: (202)237-8146
Registered: LDA, FARA
E-mail: cahallc@worldnet.att.net

An international trade consulting firm specializing in conflict avoidance and conflict resolution.

DC-Area Employees Representing Listed Clients

HAMILTON, Charles A., President

Clients

Airbus Industrie of North America, Inc.
Issues: AER AVI MAN TRA
Rep By: Charles A. Hamilton

Katherine Hamilton

3225 N. Pershing Dr.
Arlington, VA 22201
Tel: (703)516-4444
Fax: (703)516-4444
Registered: LDA
E-mail: hamiltongrp1@earthlink.net

DC-Area Employees Representing Listed Clients

HAMILTON, Katherine

Clients

American Bioenergy Ass'n
Issues: BUD ENG FUE SCI
Rep By: Katherine Hamilton

Bob Lawrence & Associates
Issues: BUD ENG FUE SCI
Rep By: Katherine Hamilton

Midwest Research Institute
Issues: BUD ENG FUE SCI
Rep By: Katherine Hamilton

Hammer & Co.

3231 Valley Lane
Falls Church, VA 22044
Tel: (703)532-9360
Fax: (703)532-9361
E-mail: hammerco@aol.com

A consulting firm.

DC-Area Employees Representing Listed Clients

HAMMER, Thomas A., President

Clients

Sweetener Users Ass'n
Rep By: Thomas A. Hammer

Hance, Scarborough & Wright

1150 17th St. NW
Suite 601
Washington, DC 20036
Tel: (202)296-2638
Fax: (202)296-9266
Registered: LDA

Washington office of a law firm headquartered in Austin, TX.

DC-Area Employees Representing Listed Clients

HANCE, Hon. Kent R., Partner
ROCK, James W.

Clients

American Soc. of Ass'n Executives
Issues: TAX
Rep By: Hon. Kent R. Hance

Hannett & Associates

1350 I St. NW
Suite 870
Washington, DC 20005
Tel: (202)638-6012
Fax: (202)737-1947
Registered: LDA
Web: www.capalliance.com
E-mail: hannett@capalliance.com

A government relations firm. Member of The Capitol Alliance.

DC-Area Employees Representing Listed Clients

HANNETT, Frederick J., President

Clients

Anthem Alliance
Issues: DEF MMM
Rep By: Frederick J. Hannett

Broadforum
Issues: EDU SCI

Healtheon/Web MD
Issues: CPI DEF HCR MMM TEC
Rep By: Frederick J. Hannett

Kaiser Permanente
Issues: HCR
Rep By: Frederick J. Hannett

The Harbour Group

3000 K St. NW
Suite 300
Washington, DC 20007
Tel: (202)295-8787
Fax: (202)295-8799
Web: www.harbourgrp.com

A lobbying, communications, and public relations subsidiary of Swidler Berlin Shereff Friedman (see separate listing).

DC-Area Employees Representing Listed Clients

CHANG, Audrey, Director
GORMAN, Teresa, Advisor
JOHNSON, Joel, Managing Director
MARCUS, Richard, Managing Director
RICHTER, Anna, Associate
SAKOL, Jodi, Senior Associate
SEXTON, Alan, Senior Associate
SLANEY, Joanna, Senior Associate

John D. Hardy

2000 Massachusetts Ave. NW
Washington, DC 20036
Tel: (202)785-1712
Fax: (202)785-1807
Registered: LDA

Clients

Marine Engineers Beneficial Ass'n (District No. 1 - PCD)
Issues: MAR TRA
Rep By: John D. Hardy

Hardy & Ellison, P.C.

9306 Old Keene Mill Rd.
Burke, VA 22015
Tel: (703)455-3600
Fax: (703)455-3603
Registered: LDA

DC-Area Employees Representing Listed Clients

ELLISON, Mark C., V. President

Clients

Consumer Satellite Systems, Inc.
Rep By: Mark C. Ellison

Hargett Consulting

1968 Crescent Park Dr.
Reston, VA 20190
Tel: (703)707-9793
Registered: LDA
E-mail: wjackhargett@msn.com

A consulting firm providing government relations, legislative strategy and business development services.

DC-Area Employees Representing Listed Clients

HARGETT, Jack, Principal

Clients

AAI Corp.
Issues: TRA
Rep By: Jack Hargett

Information Handling Services
Issues: SCI
Rep By: Jack Hargett

The Williamson Group
Rep By: Jack Hargett

Harles & Associates

P.O. Box 15318
Washington, DC 20003
Tel: (202)546-2847
Fax: (202)546-2854
Registered: LDA

DC-Area Employees Representing Listed Clients

HARLES, Charles, Director

Clients

Internat'l Ass'n of Business, Industry and Rehabilitation
Rep By: Charles Harles

Rehabilitation Engineering and Assistive Technology Soc. of North America
Rep By: Charles Harles

Harmon & Wilmot, L.L.P.

1010 Vermont Ave. NW
Suite 810
Washington, DC 20005
Tel: (202)783-9100
Fax: (202)783-9103
Registered: LDA

DC-Area Employees Representing Listed Clients

BROWN, II, Omer F., Partner
HARMON, Herbert, Partner
WILMOT, David W., Partner

Clients

Anheuser-Busch Cos., Inc.
Rep By: David W. Wilmot

Contractors Internat'l Group on Nuclear Liability
Issues: ENG FOR INS TRD
Rep By: Omer F. Brown, II

Energy Contractors Price-Anderson Group
Issues: ENG INS
Rep By: Omer F. Brown, II

Hotel Ass'n of Washington
Issues: DOC
Rep By: David W. Wilmot

MCI WorldCom Corp.
Rep By: David W. Wilmot

William D. Harris & Associates

818 Connecticut Ave. NW
Suite 818
Washington, DC 20006
Tel: (202)861-1922
Fax: (202)728-4040
Registered: LDA

Clients

Bolivia, Government of the Republic of

Leslie Harris & Associates

2120 L St. NW
Suite 400
Washington, DC 20037
Tel: (202)478-6301
Fax: (202)478-6171
Registered: LDA
Web: www.lharris.com
E-mail: lharris@lharris.com

A government relations and public policy firm. Provides a range of strategic services to nonprofit organizations, corporations, foundations and advocacy groups. Services include representation before Congress and the Executive Branch, planning and execution of strategic issue campaigns, strategic counseling, outreach and coalition development.

DC-Area Employees Representing Listed Clients

BOND, Jill, Managing Director and V. President, Strategic Initiatives
HARRIS, Leslie A., President
JOHNSON, Aleck, Senior Policy Analyst
KESSLER, Liza, Senior Policy Counsel
LEE, Jee Hang, Senior Legislative Associate
RAINES, Ghani, Legislative Associate
ZWERIN, Rachel, Associate

Clients

American Library Ass'n
Issues: CON
Rep By: Leslie A. Harris, Liza Kessler

AOL Time Warner
Issues: CPI TEC
Rep By: Jill Bond, Leslie A. Harris, Aleck Johnson, Rachel Zwerin

Consortium for School Networking
Issues: COM CPI EDU TEC
Rep By: Leslie A. Harris, Jee Hang Lee, Ghani Raines

EdLinc
Issues: TEC
Rep By: Jill Bond, Leslie A. Harris, Aleck Johnson, Jee Hang Lee, Ghani Raines

Internat'l Soc. for Technology in Education
Issues: COM CPI CPT EDU TAX TEC
Rep By: Leslie A. Harris, Jee Hang Lee, Ghani Raines

Leadership Conference on Civil Rights
Issues: CIV TEC
Rep By: Jill Bond, Leslie A. Harris, Aleck Johnson, Liza Kessler, Ghani Raines, Rachel Zwerin

Media Access Project
Issues: ART MIA TEC
Rep By: Leslie A. Harris

Nat'l School Boards Ass'n
Issues: CPT
Rep By: Leslie A. Harris

Verizon Communications
Issues: TEC
Rep By: Jill Bond, Leslie A. Harris

Harris Ellsworth & Levin

The Watergate
Suite 1113
2600 Virginia Ave. NW
Washington, DC 20037-1905
Web: www.internationaltrade-law.com
E-mail: hel@idt.net
Tel: (202)337-8338
Fax: (202)337-6685
Registered: LDA

A law firm.

DC-Area Employees Representing Listed Clients

ELLSWORTH, Cheryl N., Partner
HARRIS, II, Hon. Herbert E., Partner
LEVIN, Jeffrey S., Partner

Clients

American Railway Car Institute
Rep By: Hon. Herbert E. Harris, II

Ass'n of Food Industries, Inc.
Rep By: Cheryl N. Ellsworth, Hon. Herbert E. Harris, II, Jeffrey S. Levin

Cheese Importers Ass'n of America
Rep By: Hon. Herbert E. Harris, II

Coalition of Food Importers Ass'ns

Committee of Domestic Steel Wire Rope and Specialty Cable Manufacturers
Rep By: Cheryl N. Ellsworth, Hon. Herbert E. Harris, II, Jeffrey S. Levin

Shieldalloy Metallurgical Corp.
Rep By: Cheryl N. Ellsworth

Wood Corp.
Issues: TRD
Rep By: Hon. Herbert E. Harris, II, Jeffrey S. Levin

Harris, Wiltshire & Grannis LLP

1200 18th St. NW
Suite 1200
Washington, DC 20036
Web: www.harriswiltshire.com
Tel: (202)730-1300
Fax: (202)730-1301
Registered: LDA

A non-partisan firm specializing in telecommunications law and policy.

DC-Area Employees Representing Listed Clients

GRANNIS, Mark, Partner
GULICK, Karen, Partner
HARRIS, Scott Blake, Managing Partner
LADSON, Damon, Technology Policy Advisor
NAKAHATA, John T., Partner
WILTSHIRE, William, Partner
WRIGHT, Christopher

Clients

3Com Corp.
Issues: TEC
Rep By: Scott Blake Harris

Apple Computer, Inc.
Issues: TEC
Rep By: Scott Blake Harris

Cisco Systems Inc.
Issues: COM TEC
Rep By: Scott Blake Harris

Coalition for Affordable Local and Long Distance Services
Issues: TEC
Rep By: John T. Nakahata

North American GSM Alliance, LLC
Issues: COM TEC
Rep By: Scott Blake Harris

Time Domain Corp.
Issues: COM TEC
Rep By: Scott Blake Harris

VoiceStream Wireless Corp.
Issues: TEC
Rep By: Karen Gulick, Scott Blake Harris, John T. Nakahata

Winstar Communications, Inc.
Issues: COM TEC
Rep By: Scott Blake Harris

Hartke & Hartke

7637 Leesburg Pike
Falls Church, VA 22043
Tel: (703)734-2810
Registered: LDA

DC-Area Employees Representing Listed Clients

HARTKE, Vance
HARTKE, Wayne

Clients

Vortec Corp.
Issues: ENG
Rep By: Vance Hartke, Wayne Hartke

Hauck and Associates

1255 23rd St. NW
Suite 200
Washington, DC 20037-1174
Web: www.hauck.com
E-mail: info@hauck.com
Tel: (202)452-8100
Fax: (202)833-3636

A professional association management firm.

DC-Area Employees Representing Listed Clients

AILOR, David C., V. President, Regulatory Affairs
CUMMINGS, Kelly
FORBURGER, Melissa T., Account Exec.
HARACZNAK, Stephen R., Account Exec.
HAUCK, Graham S., Account Exec.
HAUCK, Jay, Account Exec.
HAUCK, Sheldon J., President
HOFFMAN, Carrie
HOVERMALE, David J., Director, Government Relations
JAMES, April, Senior Associate
JOHNSON, Allen F., Exec. V. President
LOUDY, Elizabeth A., V. President
MAHON, William J., Senior V. President
MURPHY, Christopher M., V. President and Chief Operating Officer
NORTH, Tristan M., Director, Government Affairs
ROBERTS, Brian
SAUNDERS, David A., V. President
VELANDER, Carol I., Director, Education and Training

Clients

American Academy of Wound Management
Rep By: Melissa T. Forburger

American Ambulance Ass'n
Rep By: Tristan M. North

American Ass'n of Residential Mortgage Regulators
Rep By: Christopher M. Murphy

American Coke and Coal Chemicals Institute
Rep By: David C. Ailor, David A. Saunders

DFK Internat'l/USA, Inc.
Rep By: Jay Hauck, William J. Mahon

Electromagnetic Energy Ass'n
Rep By: Melissa T. Forburger

Internat'l Ass'n of Seed Crushers
Rep By: Christopher M. Murphy

Internat'l Claim Ass'n
Rep By: Christopher M. Murphy

Internat'l Oxygen Manufacturers Ass'n
Rep By: David A. Saunders

Nat'l Ass'n of Healthcare Consultants
Rep By: Melissa T. Forburger, Carrie Hoffman

Nat'l Corrugated Steel Pipe Ass'n
Rep By: Brian Roberts

Nat'l Health Care Anti-Fraud Ass'n
Rep By: William J. Mahon, Carol I. Velander

Nat'l Oilseed Processors Ass'n
Rep By: David C. Ailor, Sheldon J. Hauck, Allen F. Johnson, David A. Saunders

Soy Protein Council
Rep By: Sheldon J. Hauck, David A. Saunders

State Government Affairs Council
Rep By: Kelly Cummings, Elizabeth A. Loudy

Hauser Group

1782 Columbia Rd. NW
Washington, DC 20009
Tel: (202)518-8047
Fax: (202)518-8048

DC-Area Employees Representing Listed Clients

HAUSER, Eric W., President
VALENTINE, Dawn, Associate
ZIMMERMAN, Tracy, Associate

Clients

20/20 Vision
Academy of Leadership
AFL-CIO - Transportation Trades Department
Americans Heritage Recreation
Annenberg Institute for School Reform, The
Bread for the World
Campaign for America
Campaign for Common Ground
Campaign Reform Project
The Century Foundation
Coalition of Private Safety-Net Hospitals
Coalition to Stop Gun Violence
The Commonwealth Fund
Congressional Exchange
Council on the Economic Impact of Health System Change
Education Commission of the States
Family Impact Seminar
Human Relations Foundation of Chicago
Indian Law Resource Center
Internat'l Fund for Agricultural Development
Kaiser Family Foundation
League of Women Voters of the United States
Missouri Democratic Party
Nat'l Coalition for Patient Rights
Nat'l Days of Dialogue on Race Relations
Nat'l Education Ass'n of the U.S.
Nat'l School Boards Ass'n
Newsday
Outdoor Recreation Coalition of America
Public Broadcasting Service
Street Law Inc.
Study Circles
Weidmann Associates
Working Today

Hawkins, Delafield & Wood

601 13th St. NW
Suite 800 North
Washington, DC 20005
Web: www.hdw.com
Tel: (202)682-1480
Fax: (202)682-1497
Registered: LDA

DC-Area Employees Representing Listed Clients

CONNORTON, John V., Partner
FREEDMAN, Anthony S., Partner
WOOD, Florence, Partner

Clients

Metropolitan Museum of Art

Mortgage Bankers Ass'n of America
Issues: HOU
Rep By: John V. Connorton

San Antonio, Texas, City of

The Hawthorn Group, L.C.

1199 N. Fairfax St.
Suite 1000
Alexandria, VA 22314
Web: www.hawthorngroup.com
E-mail: strategy@hawthorngroup.com
Tel: (703)299-4499
Fax: (703)299-4488
Registered: LDA

DC-Area Employees Representing Listed Clients

AERY, Shaila, President and Chief Operating Officer
ASHFORD, John, Chairman and Chief Exec. Officer
BONITATI, Robert, Senior V. President
COBB, Robert, Managing Principal, Hawthorn Southeast
FOER, Esther, Vice Chairman
GOODWIN, Thomas, Senior Counselor
HAMM, Peter, V. President
HAMMELMAN, Suzanne, V. President
KNIGHT, Delos, Senior Counselor
LAMBRIX, Thomas, Exec. V. President
MCPHEE, Jessica, Sr. Account Coordinator
MILLER, Mona, V. President, Communications
MOORE, W. John, Senior V. President, Communications Services
PORTER, Tola, Sr. Account Coordinator
STANLEY, Anne, Senior V. President
STICKLES, Peter, Senior Account Executive
ZAHN, Josh, Senior Account Executive

Clients

AT&T Wireless Services, Inc.
Rep By: Esther Foer

Commonwealth Atlantic Properties
Issues: RES

Electronic Industries Ass'n of Japan
Rep By: Esther Foer

Georgia-Pacific Corp.
Rep By: Suzanne Hammelman

Honda North America, Inc.
Rep By: Esther Foer

Nat'l Rural Telecom Ass'n

Salt River Project
Rep By: Robert Bonitati

Southern Co.
Rep By: John Ashford

Southern Generation
Rep By: John Ashford

Virgin Atlantic Airways

Hayward Internat'l

1350 Connecticut Ave. NW
Suite 605
Washington, DC 20036
Tel: (202)862-3952
Fax: (202)862-3956
Registered: FARA

DC-Area Employees Representing Listed Clients
HAYWARD, Barbara, President

Clients

Advanced Machinery Logistics, Inc.

Chad, Government of the Republic of
Rep By: Barbara Hayward

H.M.S. Rose Foundation

John Ashbrook Center for Public Policy

Market Access Ltd.

Nat'l Alliance of African-American Health Care Professions

Nat'l Islamic Front Afghanistan

Health and Medicine Counsel of Washington

507 Capitol Ct. NE
Suite 200
Washington, DC 20002
E-mail: ddirks@aol.com
Tel: (202)544-7499
Fax: (202)546-7105
Registered: LDA

DC-Area Employees Representing Listed Clients
DENNISON, Staci Sigman, Administrative Assistant
DIRKS, Dale P., President
DOBERT, Susie, Legislative Assistant
LINDBERG, Gavin, Legislative Director

Clients

American Academy of Family Physicians
Issues: BUD
Rep By: Staci Sigman Dennison, Dale P. Dirks

American Ass'n of Pharmaceutical Scientists
Issues: BUD HCR
Rep By: Staci Sigman Dennison, Dale P. Dirks

American Lung Ass'n
Issues: BUD HCR
Rep By: Staci Sigman Dennison, Dale P. Dirks

American Soc. of Clinical Pathologists
Issues: BUD HCR
Rep By: Staci Sigman Dennison, Dale P. Dirks

American Thoracic Soc.
Issues: BUD HCR
Rep By: Staci Sigman Dennison, Dale P. Dirks

Ass'n of Academic Health Sciences Library Directors
Rep By: Dale P. Dirks, Gavin Lindberg

Ass'n of Minority Health Profession Schools
Issues: BUD EDU HCR
Rep By: Staci Sigman Dennison, Dale P. Dirks, Susie Dobert, Gavin Lindberg

Coalition of Positive Outcomes in Pregnancy
Issues: HCR
Rep By: Dale P. Dirks

Crohn's and Colitis Foundation of America
Issues: BUD HCR
Rep By: Dale P. Dirks, Gavin Lindberg

Digestive Disease Nat'l Coalition
Issues: BUD HCR
Rep By: Staci Sigman Dennison, Dale P. Dirks, Susie Dobert, Gavin Lindberg

Dystonia Medical Research Foundation
Issues: BUD HCR
Rep By: Staci Sigman Dennison, Dale P. Dirks

ESA, Inc.
Issues: BUD HCR
Rep By: Dale P. Dirks, Gavin Lindberg

Immune Deficiency Foundation, Inc.
Issues: BUD
Rep By: Dale P. Dirks, Gavin Lindberg

Medical Library Ass'n/Ass'n of Academic Health Sciences Library Directors
Issues: BUD HCR MIA
Rep By: Dale P. Dirks, Gavin Lindberg

St. George's University School of Medicine
Issues: HCR
Rep By: Dale P. Dirks, Susie Dobert

Sudden Infant Death Syndrome Alliance
Issues: BUD
Rep By: Staci Sigman Dennison, Dale P. Dirks

Health Policy Alternatives, Inc.

444 N. Capitol St. NW
Suite 821
Washington, DC 20001
Tel: (202)737-3390
Fax: (202)628-3607
Registered: LDA

DC-Area Employees Representing Listed Clients
AULT, Thomas, Principal
FERMAN, John H., Principal
LAUDERBAUGH, Richard, Principal
MCCANN, Bart

Clients

AdvaMed
Issues: HCR
Rep By: Thomas Ault, Bart McCann

American College of Emergency Physicians
Issues: HCR
Rep By: Richard Lauderbaugh

American Hospital Ass'n
Issues: HCR
Rep By: Thomas Ault, Richard Lauderbaugh

American Nurses Ass'n
Issues: HCR
Rep By: Richard Lauderbaugh

Federation of American Hospitals
Rep By: Thomas Ault, Richard Lauderbaugh

Johnson & Johnson, Inc.
Rep By: Thomas Ault, Bart McCann

Medtronic, Inc.
Issues: HCR
Rep By: Thomas Ault, Bart McCann

Pharmaceutical Research and Manufacturers of America
Issues: HCR
Rep By: Thomas Ault

Health Policy Analysts

1350 I St. NW
Suite 870
Washington, DC 20005
Web: www.capalliance.com
E-mail: atkins@capalliance.com
Tel: (202)638-0551
Fax: (202)737-1947
Registered: LDA

A health policy consulting firm. Member of The Capitol Alliance.

DC-Area Employees Representing Listed Clients
ATKINS, G. Lawrence, President
NORTH, Nan F., Associate
SPOLARICH, Audrey, Principal
TILTON, Stephen G., Associate

Clients

Corporate Health Care Coalition
Issues: HCR
Rep By: G. Lawrence Atkins, Nan F. North

Employer Health Care Innovation Project
Issues: HCR
Rep By: G. Lawrence Atkins, Nan F. North

New Jersey Organ & Tissue Sharing Network
Issues: MMM
Rep By: G. Lawrence Atkins

Schering-Plough Legislative Resources L.L.C.
Issues: HCR MMM VET
Rep By: G. Lawrence Atkins, Audrey Spolarich, Stephen G. Tilton

Health Policy Group

1919 Pennsylvania Ave. NW
Suite 600
Washington, DC 20006
Tel: (202)326-1530
Fax: (202)547-1105
Registered: LDA

DC-Area Employees Representing Listed Clients
HUDSON, J. Michael, Senior Partner

Clients

Ass'n of Organ Procurement Organizations
Rep By: J. Michael Hudson

Ralin Medical
Rep By: J. Michael Hudson

Teletech Teleservices, Inc.
Rep By: J. Michael Hudson

University of Texas Health Systems
Rep By: J. Michael Hudson

Vector Research, Inc.
Issues: HCR
Rep By: J. Michael Hudson

Health Policy Strategies

888 17th St. NW
Suite 800
Washington, DC 20006
Tel: (202)452-8290
Fax: (202)822-9088
Registered: LDA

DC-Area Employees Representing Listed Clients
LANGLEY, Ann, President

Clients

Children's Hospital of Boston
Issues: BUD HCR MED
Rep By: Ann Langley

La Rabida Children's Hospital Research Center
Issues: HCR
Rep By: Ann Langley

Nat'l Ass'n of Children's Hospitals Inc.
Issues: BUD HCR MED
Rep By: Ann Langley

HearingRoom.com

1250 24th St. NW
Suite 300
Washington, DC 20037
Web: www.hearingroom.com
E-mail: info@hearingroom.com
Tel: (703)326-8219
Fax: (202)466-6249

An information company providing real-time text and audio of congressional hearings over the Internet.

DC-Area Employees Representing Listed Clients
ANGELL, Phillip S., Chairman
CHAPIN, Christopher K., Senior V. President
DEFIFE, Susan, President

Hecht, Spencer & Associates

499 S. Capitol St. SW
Suite 507
Washington, DC 20003
Tel: (202)554-2881
Registered: LDA, FARA

A government relations consulting firm. Allied to the Washington law firm of Patton Boggs and to the California-based political consulting firm of Spencer Roberts.

DC-Area Employees Representing Listed Clients
HECHT, Timothy P., V. President
HECHT, William H., President
HUDDLESTON, Hon. Walter D., Consultant
PHIFER, Franklin C., Senior V. President
SPENCER, Stuart K., Chairman

Clients

Boy Scouts of America
Issues: LAW
Rep By: Timothy P. Hecht, William H. Hecht, Franklin C. Phifer

Brown and Williamson Tobacco Corp.
Issues: TOB
Rep By: Timothy P. Hecht, William H. Hecht, Franklin C. Phifer, Stuart K. Spencer

Minnesota Mining and Manufacturing Co. (3M Co.)
Issues: HCR
Rep By: Timothy P. Hecht, William H. Hecht, Franklin C. Phifer

Norfolk Southern Corp.
Issues: RRR TAX TRA
Rep By: Timothy P. Hecht, William H. Hecht, Franklin C. Phifer

Patton Boggs, LLP
Issues: ADV BUD FOO TAX TRD
Rep By: William H. Hecht, Franklin C. Phifer

J. C. Penney Co., Inc.
Issues: APP LBR TAX TRA
Rep By: Timothy P. Hecht, William H. Hecht, Franklin C. Phifer

The Charles E. Smith Companies
Issues: BUD RES TAX
Rep By: Timothy P. Hecht, William H. Hecht, Franklin C. Phifer

TECO Energy, Inc.
Issues: TRA UTI
Rep By: Timothy P. Hecht, William H. Hecht, Franklin C. Phifer

Tulalip Tribes
Issues: ENV GAM IND
Rep By: Timothy P. Hecht, William H. Hecht, Franklin C. Phifer

Heenan, Althen & Roles

1110 Vermont Ave. NW
Suite 400
Washington, DC 20005
Web: www.harlaw.com
E-mail: info@harlaw.com
Tel: (202)887-0800
Fax: (202)775-8518
Registered: LDA

A law firm.

DC-Area Employees Representing Listed Clients
ALTHEN, William I., Partner
HEENAN, Michael T., Partner

Clients

American Institute of Biological Sciences

American League of Lobbyists
Rep By: William I. Althen

Eastern Pilots Ass'n

General Portland Inc.
Rep By: Michael T. Heenan

Hulcher Quarry, Inc.
Rep By: Michael T. Heenan

Lone Star Florida, Inc.
Rep By: Michael T. Heenan

Lone Star Industries
Rep By: Michael T. Heenan

Nemacolin Mines Corp.
Rep By: Michael T. Heenan

New York Trap Rock Co.

Olga Coal Co.

Peter White Coal Mining Co.
Rep By: Michael T. Heenan

The Pittston Co.

Youngstown Mines Corp.
Rep By: Michael T. Heenan

Law Office of Edward D. Heffernan

One Massachusetts Ave. NW
Suite 840
Washington, DC 20001
Tel: (202)842-4155
Fax: (202)842-3509
Registered: LDA

An attorney-at-law.

Clients

American Cast Iron Pipe Co.
Issues: BUD

Chicago Regional Transportation Authority
Issues: BUD TRA

DePaul University
Issues: BUD EDU IMM

Renewable Fuels Ass'n

Heidepriem & Mager, Inc.

888 17th St. NW
Suite 800
Washington, DC 20006
Tel: (202)822-8060
Fax: (202)822-9088
Registered: LDA
E-mail: nheidepriem@heimag.com

A public policy consulting firm.

DC-Area Employees Representing Listed Clients

BOLTE, Karin, Associate
FORD-ROEGNER, Pat, Senior Policy Analyst
FOSTER, Lisa, Associate
GOULD, Christopher, Associate
HEIDEPRIEM, Nikki, President
MAGER, Mimi, Chief Exec. Officer
ROEGNER, Pat Ford

Clients

American Home Products Corp.
Issues: PHA
Rep By: Karin Bolte, Nikki Heidepriem, Mimi Mager

CIGNA Corp.
Rep By: Lisa Foster, Nikki Heidepriem

Citigroup
Rep By: Nikki Heidepriem

Cytyc Corp.
Issues: HCR
Rep By: Karin Bolte, Mimi Mager

The Dow Chemical Co.
Issues: CSP
Rep By: Lisa Foster, Nikki Heidepriem

EXACT Laboratories
Issues: HCR
Rep By: Christopher Gould, Nikki Heidepriem

Nat'l Asian Women's Health Organization
Rep By: Pat Ford-Roegner, Mimi Mager

Nat'l Council of Juvenile and Family Court Judges
Rep By: Pat Ford-Roegner, Nikki Heidepriem

Pharmacia Corp.
Issues: HCR
Rep By: Karin Bolte, Pat Ford-Roegner, Christopher Gould, Nikki Heidepriem, Mimi Mager

R2 Technology, Inc.
Issues: MED
Rep By: Karin Bolte, Nikki Heidepriem, Mimi Mager, Pat Ford Roegner

Serono Laboratories, Inc.
Issues: EDU HCR MED
Rep By: Christopher Gould, Nikki Heidepriem

United Airlines
Issues: AVI
Rep By: Christopher Gould, Nikki Heidepriem, Mimi Mager

Wyeth-Ayerst Laboratories
Issues: PHA
Rep By: Karin Bolte, Mimi Mager

Heller & Rosenblatt

1101 15th St. NW
Suite 205
Washington, DC 20005-1714
Tel: (202)466-4700
Fax: (202)223-4826
Registered: FARA

A law firm specializing in international and federal government representation.

DC-Area Employees Representing Listed Clients

HELLER, Jack I., Partner
ROSENBLATT, Peter R., Partner

Clients

Taipei Economic and Cultural Representative Office in the United States

Helmsin & Yarwood Associates

2637 N. Marcey Rd.
Arlington, VA 22207
Tel: (202)898-2858
Fax: (202)842-3860
Registered: LDA
E-mail: byarwood@ahca.org

DC-Area Employees Representing Listed Clients

YARWOOD, Bruce, Partner

Clients

Alliance for Elder Care
Rep By: Bruce Yarwood

American Health Care Ass'n
Issues: HCR INS LBR MMM VET
Rep By: Bruce Yarwood

CaRess, Inc.
Issues: HCR MMM
Rep By: Bruce Yarwood

Crestwood Behavior Health, Inc.
Issues: HCR MMM
Rep By: Bruce Yarwood

DFG Group
Issues: HOU

Allen Herbert

2291 Wood Oak Dr.
Herndon, VA 20171
Tel: (703)709-4621
Registered: LDA
E-mail: allen.herbert@ca.com

Clients

Computer Associates Internat'l, Inc.
Issues: BUD CPI DEF LAW SCI TRD
Rep By: Allen Herbert

Law Offices of Robert T. Herbolsheimer

733 15th St. NW
Suite 1120
Washington, DC 20005
Tel: (202)628-9200
Fax: (202)628-9201
Registered: LDA
E-mail: rtherb@aol.com

DC-Area Employees Representing Listed Clients

HERBOLSHEIMER, Robert T., Partner

Clients

Bowling Proprietors' Ass'n of America
Issues: ART BEV LBR
Rep By: Robert T. Herbolsheimer

Dennis M. Hertel & Associates

1100 Connecticut Ave. NW
Suite 1000
Washington, DC 20036
Tel: (202)321-1800
Registered: LDA

A law firm.

DC-Area Employees Representing Listed Clients

HERTEL, Hon. Dennis M., President

Clients

Boysville
Issues: FAM LAW
Rep By: Hon. Dennis M. Hertel

Detroit Metropolitan Airport
Issues: TRA
Rep By: Hon. Dennis M. Hertel

Henry Ford Museum in Greenfield Village
Issues: TRA
Rep By: Hon. Dennis M. Hertel

Northwood Inc.
Issues: MMM
Rep By: Hon. Dennis M. Hertel

Hessel and Aluise, P.C.

1050 17th St. NW
Suite 900
Washington, DC 20036
Tel: (202)466-5300
Fax: (202)466-5508
Registered: LDA

A law firm specializing in housing, urban development, and real estate matters and legislative services.

DC-Area Employees Representing Listed Clients

ALUISE, Timothy J., Principal
HESSEL, Arthur R., Principal
LIBSON, Nancy, Director, Legislation and Public Policy

Clients

Massachusetts Housing Finance Agency
Issues: HOU
Rep By: Nancy Libson

Nat'l Cooperative Bank
Issues: HOU
Rep By: Timothy J. Aluise, Nancy Libson

Hewes, Gelband, Lambert & Dann, P.C.

1000 Potomac St. NW
Suite 300
Washington, DC 20007
Tel: (202)337-6200
Fax: (202)333-0871
Web: www.hewesgelband.com
E-mail: info@hewesgelband.com

A general and administrative law firm.

DC-Area Employees Representing Listed Clients

GELBAND, Stephen L., Partner
HEWES, Jr., C. Alexander, Managing Partner
PALMIERI, Andrew, President
SEAMON, Theodore I., Of Counsel
SORKIN, Stuart, Of Counsel
WILSON, Nancy B., Associate

Clients

American University

Arrow Air

Conquest Tours Ltd.
Rep By: Stephen L. Gelband

Orion Air
Rep By: Stephen L. Gelband

Pilgrim Airlines
Rep By: Theodore I. Seamon

Tower Air, Inc.
Rep By: Stephen L. Gelband

Wien Air Alaska
Rep By: Theodore I. Seamon

Hicks-Richardson Associates

P.O. Box 2115
Springfield, VA 22152
Tel: (703)866-4290
Fax: (703)866-4928
Registered: LDA

DC-Area Employees Representing Listed Clients

HICKS, Carol A., Managing Partner
HICKS, Fred B., Partner

Clients

California-American Water Co.

East Valley Water District
Issues: ENV
Rep By: Carol A. Hicks, Fred B. Hicks

San Gabriel Valley Water Ass'n
Issues: ENV
Rep By: Fred B. Hicks

Tarrant Regional Water District
Issues: AGR ENV
Rep By: Carol A. Hicks, Fred B. Hicks

Higgins, McGovern & Smith, LLC

1620 L St. NW
Suite 1210
Washington, DC 20036
Tel: (202)955-6062
Fax: (202)955-6070
Registered: LDA

DC-Area Employees Representing Listed Clients

BLISS, John S., Partner
HIGGINS, Lawrence, Partner
KOCH, Patrick C.
MCGOVERN, Jr., John J., Partner
ROSSO, Joseph L., Principal
SMITH, Carl M., Partner

Clients

APL Limited
Rep By: Carl M. Smith

AT&T
Issues: TEC
Rep By: Patrick C. Koch

Betac Corp.
Issues: DEF
Rep By: Carl M. Smith

Coalition Against Product Tampering
Issues: LAW
Rep By: John S. Bliss

Freightliner Corp.
Issues: BUD
Rep By: Joseph L. Rosso

Leprino Foods Co.
Issues: AGR

Metropolitan Life Insurance Co.
Issues: BAN INS TAX
Rep By: Lawrence Higgins

Mylan Laboratories, Inc.
Issues: PHA
Rep By: John J. McGovern, Jr.

New Skies Satellites N.V.
Issues: COM
Rep By: Patrick C. Koch

Northwestern Mutual Life Insurance Co.
Issues: FIN INS TAX TOR
Rep By: Lawrence Higgins

Preston Gates Ellis & Rouvelas Meeds LLP
Issues: TOU
Rep By: Carl M. Smith

Trident Systems Inc.
Issues: DEF
Rep By: Carl M. Smith

Highsaw, Mahoney & Clarke

1050 17th St. NW
Suite 590
Washington, DC 20036
Tel: (202)296-8500
Fax: (202)296-7143

DC-Area Employees Representing Listed Clients
CLARKE, Jr., John O., Partner
MAHONEY, William G., Partner

Clients

Railway Labor Executives' Ass'n
Rep By: William G. Mahoney

Hill and Knowlton, Inc.

600 New Hampshire Ave. NW
Suite 601
Washington, DC 20037
Tel: (202)333-7400
Fax: (202)333-1638
Registered: LDA, FARA
Web: www.hillandknowlton.com
Owned by WPP Group, a British communications conglomerate.

Political Action Committee
Hill and Knowlton, Inc. Political Action Committee (HILLPAC)
600 New Hampshire Ave. NW
Suite 601
Washington, DC 20037
Tel: (202)333-7400
Fax: (202)333-1638
Contact: Chad Tragakis

DC-Area Employees Representing Listed Clients
ANGAROLA, Christina
BAKER, Robin, Managing Director
BELKIN, Edward, Sr. Managing Director, Sr. Counselor Media Relations
BEYER, Alisa, Practice Leader
CLARK, Paul S., Senior Managing Director, Director of Media Relations
CLARKE, Victoria "Torrie", General Manager
COLFORD, Chris, Managing Director
COONS, Barbara, Senior Managing Director, U.S. Director Research Services
COSTIN, Sara, Managing Director
DHILLON, Neil, Managing Director
DUVAL, Fred, Sr. Counselor, Public Affairs and Government Relations
FOGELMAN-BEYER, Alisa, Sr. Managing Director, Director of Technology Practice
FRIEDMAN, Jim, Senior Managing Director, Director of Health Care
GILLIAM, Jr., Reginald E., Senior Managing Director, Public Affairs
GLICK, Nancy L., Sr. Managing Director, Sr. Counselor for Health, Nutrition and Consumer Issues
GRACE, Jennifer L., Sr. Managing Director, Technology Practice
GROOBERT, David, Senior Managing Director, Director of Marketing Communications
GULLEDGE, Lisa, Managing Director
HICKS, Nancy, Sr. Managing Director, Sr. Counselor Health
HILDEBRAND, Bruce, Senior Managing Director, Media Relations
HYMEL, Gary G., Chief Lobbyist and V. Chairman, Sr. Counselor Government Relations
JENNINGS, Jim, Exec. Managing Director, Co-Director, U.S. Healthcare Practice
KRAMER, Steve, Sr. Managing Director, Marketing Communications
MACKAY, David, Sr. Managing Director; Sr. Counselor, Marketing Communications; and Director, U.S. Client Services
MANKIEWICZ, Frank, V. Chairman
MARTIN, Krista, Sr. Account Supervisor
MEYER, Don, Senoir Account Supervisor
MINARD, Richard "Dick", Senior Managing Director and Deputy General Manager
MOEBIUS, Wanda, Senior Account Supervisor
MUNUZ, K.C., Managing Director
PARKER, Armetta, Managing Director
PASTER, Howard G., Chairman and Chief Exec. Officer
SHEEHAN, Maria, Managing Director
THORNELL, Paul, Senior Account Supervisor
TRAGAKIS, Chad, PAC Administrator
TRAMMELL, Jeffrey B., Sr. Managing Director, Sr. Counselor Public Affairs and Gov't Relations
VELASCO, Peter, Managing Director
VIORST, Marla, Senior Account Supervisor

Clients

The Aluminum Ass'n
Rep By: David MacKay

American Red Cross
Rep By: Nancy Hicks, Peter Velasco

Ariba
Issues: CPI
Rep By: Gary G. Hymel

Ass'n of American Publishers
Rep By: Bruce Hildebrand

Bell Atlantic Mobile
Issues: TEC

Blue Cross and Blue Shield of Florida
Issues: HCR
Rep By: Gary G. Hymel, Jeffrey B. Trammell

The Boeing Co.

Cadmus/Energy Star
Rep By: Bruce Hildebrand

Cleveland, Ohio, City of
Issues: GOV LAW
Rep By: Reginald E. Gilliam, Jr.

Debswana Diamond Co.

Eurapair International, Inc.
Issues: IMM
Rep By: Fred DuVal, Gary G. Hymel, Frank Mankiewicz

Ford Motor Co.
Rep By: Neil Dhillon, Jeffrey B. Trammell

Fresenius Medical Care North America
Issues: HCR
Rep By: Bruce Hildebrand

GlaxoSmithKline
Rep By: Jim Friedman, Lisa Gulledge

Great Lakes Science Center
Issues: GOV
Rep By: Reginald E. Gilliam, Jr.

Internat'l Olympic Committee
Issues: SPO
Rep By: Gary G. Hymel, Frank Mankiewicz, Jeffrey B. Trammell

Kohler Corp.
Issues: CAW
Rep By: Reginald E. Gilliam, Jr., Gary G. Hymel

Mazda Motor Corp.
Rep By: Gary G. Hymel

McAndrews and Forbes Holding, Inc.
Issues: ECN

Benjamin Moore & Co.

Motorola, Inc.
Rep By: Christina Angarola, Paul S. Clark, Richard "Dick" Minard

Orange, California, County of
Issues: URB
Rep By: Fred DuVal, Gary G. Hymel, Jeffrey B. Trammell

Petro-Canada
Issues: FUE
Rep By: Gary G. Hymel

Royal Netherlands, Embassy of the
Rep By: Gary G. Hymel

U.S. Mint
Rep By: Steve Kramer, David MacKay

Woods Hole Oceanographic Institution
Rep By: Neil Dhillon, Gary G. Hymel, Frank Mankiewicz

Hill, Betts & Nash L.L.P.

1615 New Hampshire Ave. NW
Suite 200
Washington, DC 20009
Tel: (202)319-0800
Fax: (202)319-0804
Washington office of a New York law firm.

DC-Area Employees Representing Listed Clients
KEHOE, Brien E., Counsel

Clients

Orient Overseas Container Line
Rep By: Brien E. Kehoe

Resources Trucking Inc.
Rep By: Brien E. Kehoe

Hills & Company, International Consultants

1200 19th St. NW
Suite 201
Washington, DC 20036-2065
Tel: (202)822-4700
Fax: (202)822-4710
Provides advice to U.S. businesses on investment, trade, and risk assessment issues abroad, particularly in emerging market economies.

DC-Area Employees Representing Listed Clients
CASEY, Edward A., Managing Director
ENDEAN, Erin M., Managing Director
FISHER, Robert, Managing Director
HILLS, Carla A., Chairman and Chief Exec. Officer

Clients

The Procter & Gamble Company
Issues: TRD
Rep By: Edward A. Casey, Robert Fisher, Carla A. Hills

Richard T. Hines Consulting, Inc.

809 Princess St.
Alexandria, VA 22314
Tel: (703)519-6165
Fax: (703)519-9669

DC-Area Employees Representing Listed Clients
HINES, Richard T.

Clients

Cambodian People's Party
Rep By: Richard T. Hines

Cornish F. Hitchcock

1100 17th St. NW
Tenth Floor
Washington, DC 20036-4601
Tel: (202)974-5111
Registered: LDA

Clients

Tax Analysis
Issues: MIA TAX
Rep By: Cornish F. Hitchcock

Hobbs, Straus, Dean and Walker, LLP

2120 L St. NW
Suite 700
Washington, DC 20037
Tel: (202)822-8282
Fax: (202)296-8834
Registered: LDA
E-mail: kbrooks@hsdwdc.com
A general and administrative law practice specializing in federal Indian and Alaskan native law.

DC-Area Employees Representing Listed Clients
BARBERO, Carol L., Partner
DEAN, S. Bobo, Partner
FUNK, Karen J., Legislative Affairs Specialist
JACOBSON, Craig A.
KANEGIS, Aura
OSCEOLA-BRANCH, Marie, Legislative Affairs Specialist
ROELS, Starla K.
ROY, Michael L., Partner
RYAN, Lisa F., Associate
SCHMIDT, Marsha K., Partner
SHAPIRO, Judith A., Partner
STRAUS, Jerry C., Partner
STROMMER, Geoffrey D., Partner
WALKER, Jr., Hans, Partner
WEBSTER, Joseph H., Associate
WILLIS, F. Michael, Associate

Clients

Alamo Navajo School Board
Issues: IND
Rep By: Carol L. Barbero, S. Bobo Dean, Karen J. Funk

Alaska Native Health Board
Issues: IND
Rep By: S. Bobo Dean, Karen J. Funk, Geoffrey D. Strommer

Black Mesa Community School Board
Rep By: Carol L. Barbero, Karen J. Funk, Aura Kanegis, Marie Osceola-Branch

Bristol Bay Area Health Corp.
Issues: IND
Rep By: Carol L. Barbero, S. Bobo Dean, Karen J. Funk, Aura Kanegis, Marie Osceola-Branch, Michael L. Roy, Marsha K. Schmidt, Jerry C. Straus, Geoffrey D. Strommer, Hans Walker, Jr., Joseph H. Webster, F. Michael Willis

Choctaw Indians, Mississippi Band of
Issues: IND
Rep By: Carol L. Barbero, S. Bobo Dean, Karen J. Funk, Marie Osceola-Branch, Michael L. Roy, Jerry C. Straus, Joseph H. Webster

Maniilaq Ass'n
Issues: IND
Rep By: Karen J. Funk, Geoffrey D. Strommer

Menominee Indian Tribe
Issues: IND
Rep By: S. Bobo Dean, Karen J. Funk, Marie Osceola-Branch, Judith A. Shapiro, Jerry C. Straus, Geoffrey D. Strommer, Hans Walker, Jr., Joseph H. Webster

Metlakatla Indian Community
Issues: IND
Rep By: Carol L. Barbero, S. Bobo Dean, Karen J. Funk, Marie Osceola-Branch, Marsha K. Schmidt, Jerry C. Straus, Geoffrey D. Strommer, Joseph H. Webster

Miccosukee Tribe of Indians of Florida
Issues: IND
Rep By: Carol L. Barbero, S. Bobo Dean, Karen J. Funk, Marie Osceola-Branch, Jerry C. Straus

Nat'l Indian Child Welfare Ass'n
Issues: IND
Rep By: Karen J. Funk

Norton Sound Health Corp.
Issues: IND
Rep By: Carol L. Barbero, S. Bobo Dean, Marie Osceola-Branch, Jerry C. Straus, Geoffrey D. Strommer, F. Michael Willis

Pinon Community School Board
Rep By: Carol L. Barbero, Karen J. Funk, Aura Kanegis

Pueblo de Conchiti
Issues: IND
Rep By: Aura Kanegis, Jerry C. Straus

Rock Point Community School
Rep By: Carol L. Barbero, Karen J. Funk, Aura Kanegis

Rough Rock Community School
Rep By: Carol L. Barbero, Karen J. Funk, Aura Kanegis

Seldovia Native Ass'n, Inc.
Rep By: Carol L. Barbero, S. Bobo Dean, Karen J. Funk, Marie Osceola-Branch, Geoffrey D. Strommer

Seminole Tribe of Indians of Florida
Issues: IND
Rep By: Carol L. Barbero, Karen J. Funk, Aura Kanegis, Marie Osceola-Branch, Michael L. Roy, Judith A. Shapiro, Jerry C. Straus, Joseph H. Webster

Shiprock Alternative Schools, Inc.
Issues: IND
Rep By: Carol L. Barbero, Karen J. Funk, Lisa F. Ryan

Shoalwater Bay Indian Tribe
Issues: IND
Rep By: Carol L. Barbero, S. Bobo Dean, Karen J. Funk, Craig A. Jacobson, Aura Kanegis, Marie Osceola-Branch, Starla K. Roels, Geoffrey D. Strommer, Joseph H. Webster

St. Regis Mohawk Tribe
Issues: IND
Rep By: Carol L. Barbero, S. Bobo Dean, Karen J. Funk

Susanville Indian Rancheria
Issues: IND
Rep By: S. Bobo Dean, Karen J. Funk, Marie Osceola-Branch, Michael L. Roy, Judith A. Shapiro, Geoffrey D. Strommer, Joseph H. Webster

Three Affiliated Tribes of Fort Berthold Reservation
Rep By: Karen J. Funk, Michael L. Roy, Hans Walker, Jr.

United Tribes Technical College
Rep By: Karen J. Funk

Lydia Hofer & Associates

151 D St. SE
Washington, DC 20003
Tel: (202)546-7255
Fax: (202)543-9289
Registered: LDA

DC-Area Employees Representing Listed Clients
HOFER, Lydia, Director, Washington Office

Clients

Piliero Mazza & Pargament
Issues: IND SMB
Rep By: Lydia Hofer

Sodak Gaming Inc.
Issues: GAM

Hoffman & Hoffman Public Relations

5683 Columbia Pike
Suite 200
Falls Church, VA 22041
Tel: (703)820-2244
Fax: (703)820-2271
Registered: FARA

DC-Area Employees Representing Listed Clients
HOFFMAN, Marshall, President
KIEL, Fred, V. President

Clients

Central Bank of Turkey
Rep By: Marshall Hoffman

Netherlands, Ministry of Foreign Affairs of the Government of

Turkey, Central Bank of

The Hoffman Group

1730 Rhode Island Ave. NW
Suite 717
Washington, DC 20036
Tel: (202)728-0800
Fax: (202)728-0802
Registered: LDA
Web: www.hoffmangroup.com
E-mail: webmaster@hoffmangroup.com
A full-service public affairs firm specializing in government relations and communications strategies.

DC-Area Employees Representing Listed Clients
FENTON, Anne, Senior Account Executive
HOFFMAN, Gail H., President

Clients

Saf T Hammer
Issues: FIR LAW
Rep By: Gail H. Hoffman

Hogan & Hartson L.L.P.

555 13th St. NW
Washington, DC 20004-1109
Tel: (202)637-5600
Fax: (202)637-5910
Registered: LDA, FARA
Web: www.hhlaw.com

Political Action Committee
Hogan & Hartson Political Action Committee
555 13th St. NW
Washington, DC 20004-1109
Tel: (202)637-5636
Fax: (202)637-5910
Contact: William Michael House

DC-Area Employees Representing Listed Clients
ABRAM, Jonathan
ARCHIBALD, Jeanne S., Managing Partner, Practice Administration
ASHFORD, Deborah
BANKS, James, Partner
BIANCHI, Melissa, Associate
BOSWELL, Donna A., Partner
BRADY, Robert P., Partner
BROWN, Stan
BULTENA, Lance D., Partner
CALAMARO, Raymond S., Partner
CARNEAL, George V., Director, Transportation Practice Group
CHANG, Irene, Associate
CHEN, James, Associate
COBB, Ty
CORN-REVERE, Robert
DOLAN, Edward, Partner
DOVER, Agnes, Partner
DUNST, Isabel P., Partner
ELLETT, E. Tazewell, Partner
FARQUHAR, Michele
FEAGLES, Prentiss, Partner
GILBERT, Gerald
GILLILAND, C. Michael, Partner
GORRELL, J. Warren, Chairman
GRANESE, Nancy, Government Affairs Advisor
GRINSTEAD, Darrel J., Partner
HAFT, William S.
HEFFERNAN, Elizabeth B., Partner
HENNING, Stephanie
HENSLER, David J.
HOLSTEIN, Howard
HOUSE, William Michael, Partner
HOWARD, Eve, Partner
JENKINS, John S.
KAPP, Robert H.
KUSHNER, Gary Jay, Partner
LARSON, Philip, Partner
LASKER, Helene C.
LEIBENLUFT, Robert, Partner
LEIBOWITZ, Lewis E., Partner
LEITCH, David G., Partner
LOEB, Laura E., Partner
MANG, Jeff, Legislative Services Manager
MARUYAMA, Warren H., Partner
MCBRIDE, Sharon, Legislative Specialist
MCCONNELL, Mark S., Partner
MCDAVID, Janet L.
MCINTOSH, Scott, Associate
MCMILLAN, James G., Partner
MEDINE, David, Partner
MICHAELSON, Martin
MICHEL, Hon. Robert H., Senior Advisor, Corporate and Governmental Affairs
MILLER, George W., Partner
MONTAGUE, R. Latane
MUNK, Jeffrey W., Counsel
NEVINS, Patrick, Associate
NEWMAN, Karol Lyn, Partner
ODLE, Bob Glen, Partner
OLIVER, Linda L., Partner
PAEMEN, Hugo, Senior Advisor
PENA, Humberto R., Partner
PONEMAN, Daniel B., Partner
PORTER, Hon. John Edward, Partner
RAHER, Patrick M., Partner
RITTS, Leslie Sue, Partner
ROBERTS, Beth L., Associate
ROGERS, Hon. Paul G., Partner
ROGGENSACK, Margaret E., Counsel
ROUSH, Corey, Associate
ROUTH, Steven S.
SCHNEIDER, Jeffrey G., Partner
SIEGLER, Ellen, Counsel
SILVERMAN, Richard S., Partner
SKAGGS, Hon. David E.
STANCEU, Timothy C., Partner
STANTON, John S., Partner
STROMBERG, Cliff
TODD, Kyra A., Associate
VAN HEUVEN, Catherine, Associate
VARNEY, Christine A., Partner
VICKERY, Ann Morgan, Partner
WARNKE, Christine M., Government Affairs Advisor
WEYMOUTH, T. Clark, Partner
WHEELER, Douglas
WINNIK, Joel S., Partner

Clients

AAA MidAtlantic
Issues: TEC TRA
Rep By: C. Michael Gilliland, William Michael House, Christine M. Warnke

Air Transport Ass'n of America
Rep By: E. Tazewell Ellett, William Michael House, Hon. Robert H. Michel, Jeffrey W. Munk

Algoma Steel, Inc.
Issues: ENV TRD
Rep By: Mark S. McConnell

American Academy of Pediatrics
Issues: HCR MED MMM

American Ambulance Ass'n
Issues: HCR MMM
Rep By: Darrel J. Grinstead

American Ass'n for Medical Transcription
Rep By: Beth L. Roberts, Cliff Stromberg

American Chemistry Council
Issues: CHM
Rep By: Christine M. Warnke

American College of Osteopathic Surgeons
Issues: BUD MED
Rep By: Laura E. Loeb

American Express Co.
Issues: BNK FIN
Rep By: William Michael House, Janet L. McDavid

American Frozen Food Institute
Issues: AGR ENV FOO LBR TRA TRD
Rep By: Gary Jay Kushner, Ellen Siegler, Timothy C. Stanceu

American Gaming Ass'n
Issues: TAX
Rep By: Robert H. Kapp, John S. Stanton

American Registry of Pathology
Issues: MED
Rep By: C. Michael Gilliland, Hon. Robert H. Michel, Hon. Paul G. Rogers

American Soc. of Orthopedic Physician Assistants
Rep By: Laura E. Loeb, Beth L. Roberts

Amgen
Issues: HCR MED PHA

Andalex Resources, Inc.
Issues: NAT
Rep By: C. Michael Gilliland, William Michael House, George W. Miller, Jeffrey W. Munk

Antitrust Coalition for Consumer Choice in Health Care
Issues: HCR LBR
Rep By: Robert Leibenluft

ASCENT (Ass'n of Community Enterprises)
Issues: TEC
Rep By: Linda L. Oliver

Ass'n of American Universities

Athens Casino and Hotel Consortium
Issues: GAM
Rep By: Christine M. Warnke

Biogen, Inc.
Issues: MED
Rep By: Humberto R. Pena

Biopure Corp.
Rep By: Raymond S. Calamaro

Blount Parrish & Co., Inc.
Issues: TAX
Rep By: Nancy Granese, William Michael House

Brandeis University
Issues: SCI
Rep By: C. Michael Gilliland, Martin Michaelson, Daniel B. Poneman

Bristol-Myers Squibb Co.
Issues: HCR
Rep By: Ann Morgan Vickery

BrokerTek Global, L.L.C.
Issues: AGR
Rep By: Lance D. Bultena, Humberto R. Pena

Brother Internat'l Co.
Issues: LBR MAN TRD
Rep By: William Michael House, Lewis E. Leibowitz, Jeff Mang, Jeffrey W. Munk

California State Teachers' Retirement System
Issues: BUD RET TAX
Rep By: John S. Stanton

Campaign for Medical Research
Issues: HCR
Rep By: Hon. Robert H. Michel, Hon. Paul G. Rogers

Cargill, Inc.

CELOTEX
Issues: MAN TAX
Rep By: Nancy Granese, William Michael House

Cendant Corp.
Issues: RES
Rep By: William Michael House, Jeffrey W. Munk

Chemical Manufacturers Ass'n

Chlorine Chemistry Council
Issues: CHM
Rep By: William Michael House, Christine M. Warnke

Coalition for the American Agricultural Producer (CAAP)
Issues: AGR
Rep By: Humberto R. Pena

Compaq Computer Corp.
Rep By: Christine A. Varney

CUNA Mutual Group
Issues: TAX
Rep By: C. Michael Gilliland, William Michael House

Dana Corp.
Issues: FOR
Rep By: Stan Brown, William Michael House, Warren H. Maruyama, Jeffrey W. Munk

Danaher Corp.
Issues: BUD CSP TRD
Rep By: Jeanne S. Archibald, C. Michael Gilliland

The Danny Foundation,
Issues: CSP
Rep By: C. Michael Gilliland, Christine M. Warnke

Defense Analyses Institute

DIAGEO
Rep By: Nancy Granese, William Michael House

Direct Selling Ass'n
Issues: TAX
Rep By: Deborah Ashford

Discovery Science Center
Issues: AER BUD EDU
Rep By: Hon. Robert H. Michel, Humberto R. Pena

Distilled Spirits Council of the United States, Inc.
Rep By: Leslie Sue Ritts

DNA Sciences, Inc.
Issues: CPI HCR
Rep By: Donna A. Boswell, Robert P. Brady, Lance D. Bultena, Raymond S. Calamaro

DoubleClick
Issues: CSP

eBay Inc.
Rep By: Lance D. Bultena, Nancy Granese, Hon. Robert H. Michel, Corey Roush, Christine A. Varney

Milton S. Eisenhower Foundation
Issues: LAW
Rep By: William Michael House, Christine M. Warnke

El Salvador, Embassy of the Republic of

El Toro Reuse Planning Authority
Rep By: George V. Carneal

Endocrine Soc.
Issues: HCR MMM
Rep By: Beth L. Roberts

Executive Jet
Issues: AVI
Rep By: E. Tazewell Ellett, William Michael House, Jeffrey W. Munk

Farm Credit Bank of Texas
Issues: BAN
Rep By: Humberto R. Pena

Farmland Industries, Inc.
Issues: AGR
Rep By: Humberto R. Pena

Federation of American Hospitals
Issues: MMM
Rep By: Darrel J. Grinstead

Financial Planning Ass'n
Issues: FIN TAX
Rep By: William Michael House, James G. McMillan

Fishable Waters Coalition
Issues: CAW
Rep By: James Banks, Catherine Van Heuven

FM Watch
Issues: HOU
Rep By: William Michael House, Sharon McBride, Jeffrey W. Munk, Christine M. Warnke

Foodmaker Internat'l Franchising Inc.
Issues: CPT
Rep By: J. Warren Gorrell, Mark S. McConnell

Fujisawa Health Care Inc.
Issues: MMM
Rep By: Hon. Robert H. Michel, Ann Morgan Vickery

GE Capital Aviation Services
Rep By: E. Tazewell Ellett, Hon. Robert H. Michel, Jeffrey W. Munk

Genentech, Inc.
Issues: HCR
Rep By: Donna A. Boswell, Ann Morgan Vickery

General Electric Co.
Issues: ENV
Rep By: Christine M. Warnke

General Motors Corp.
Rep By: Mark S. McConnell

Georal Internat'l Ltd.
Issues: BAN
Rep By: Christine M. Warnke

Golden Peanut Co.
Issues: AGR
Rep By: Humberto R. Pena

Grocery Manufacturers of America
Issues: FOO
Rep By: Jeanne S. Archibald, Lance D. Bultena, Raymond S. Calamaro, C. Michael Gilliland, Nancy Granese, William Michael House, Gary Jay Kushner, Jeffrey W. Munk, Richard S. Silverman

Guardian Industries Corp.
Issues: TRD
Rep By: Nancy Granese, Warren H. Maruyama

Health and Hospital Corp. of Marion County
Issues: HCR MMM
Rep By: C. Michael Gilliland, Jeffrey W. Munk, Ann Morgan Vickery

HMSHost Corp.
Issues: TAX
Rep By: Prentiss Feagles, C. Michael Gilliland, J. Warren Gorrell, Nancy Granese, William Michael House, Hon. Robert H. Michel, Jeffrey W. Munk

Infectious Diseases Soc. of America, Inc.
Issues: HCR MMM

Institute for Civil Soc.
Issues: HCR MED TAX
Rep By: Nancy Granese, Jeffrey W. Munk

Integra Life Sciences
Issues: TRD
Rep By: Raymond S. Calamaro

InterAmerica's Group LLC
Issues: NAT
Rep By: James Banks, Humberto R. Pena, Patrick M. Raher, Catherine Van Heuven

Internat'l Biometric Industry Ass'n

Irvine, California, City of
Issues: DEF
Rep By: C. Michael Gilliland, Christine M. Warnke

Kensey Nash Corp.
Issues: TRD
Rep By: Raymond S. Calamaro, Howard Holstein

Kinder-Care Learning Centers, Inc.
Issues: TAX
Rep By: Nancy Granese, William Michael House

Koch Industries, Inc.
Issues: FUE GOV TAX TRA
Rep By: Lance D. Bultena, Jeffrey W. Munk

Kongsberg Simrad
Issues: DEF MAR
Rep By: C. Michael Gilliland

Kraft Foods, Inc.
Issues: FOO TRD
Rep By: Timothy C. Stanceu

Laguna Woods, California, City of
Issues: ENV HCR
Rep By: C. Michael Gilliland, Christine M. Warnke

Lee County Port Authority
Issues: AVI
Rep By: E. Tazewell Ellett, C. Michael Gilliland, William Michael House

The McConnell Foundation
Issues: BUD
Rep By: C. Michael Gilliland, Douglas Wheeler

Meat New Zealand
Issues: AGR
Rep By: Humberto R. Pena

MedPro, Inc.
Issues: HCR LBR MED
Rep By: Nancy Granese

Medtronic, Inc.
Rep By: Ty Cobb, John S. Stanton

Mennonite Mutual Aid Ass'n
Issues: HCR
Rep By: Nancy Granese, Jeffrey W. Munk

Mercedes-Benz of North America, Inc.
Issues: ENV
Rep By: Patrick M. Raher

Michelin North America
Issues: ENV IMM MAN TAX
Rep By: Jeanne S. Archibald, C. Michael Gilliland, Nancy Granese, William Michael House, Lewis E. Leibowitz, Jeffrey W. Munk, Patrick M. Raher, Christine M. Warnke

Michigan Consolidated Gas Co.
Issues: ENG ENV TAX
Rep By: C. Michael Gilliland, David J. Hensler, Jeffrey W. Munk, Christine M. Warnke

Mortgage Insurance Companies of America
Issues: BAN HOU INS
Rep By: William Michael House, Christine M. Warnke

Nat'l Ass'n of Personal Financial Advisors
Issues: FIN
Rep By: James G. McMillan

Nat'l Board for Professional Teaching Standards (NBPTS)
Issues: EDU
Rep By: Nancy Granese, William Michael House, Hon. Robert H. Michel, Steven S. Routh

Nat'l Chicken Council
Issues: AGR ENV FOO LBR TRA
Rep By: C. Michael Gilliland, Gary Jay Kushner

Nat'l College Access Network
Issues: EDU
Rep By: Jonathan Abram, C. Michael Gilliland, Elizabeth B. Heffernan, Christine M. Warnke

Nat'l Environmental Development Ass'n, Inc.
Rep By: Leslie Sue Ritts, Ellen Siegler

Nat'l Foreign Trade Council, Inc.
Issues: FOR
Rep By: Warren H. Maruyama, Mark S. McConnell, Daniel B. Poneman

Nat'l Hospice & Palliative Care Organization
Issues: HCR
Rep By: Ann Morgan Vickery

Nat'l Pasta Ass'n
Rep By: Gary Jay Kushner

Nat'l Structured Settlements Trade Ass'n
Issues: HCR TAX
Rep By: Nancy Granese, Hon. Robert H. Michel, John S. Stanton

Nestle USA, Inc.
Issues: BEV FOO IMM LBR TRD
Rep By: Jeanne S. Archibald, C. Michael Gilliland, Nancy Granese, William Michael House, Richard S. Silverman

Network Advertising Initiative
Rep By: Christine A. Varney

New Zealand Dairy Board
Issues: AGR
Rep By: Humberto R. Pena

News Corporation Ltd.
Issues: CPT TRD
Rep By: Raymond S. Calamaro, Mark S. McConnell, Hon. Robert H. Michel, Daniel B. Poneman

Nippon Telegraph and Telephone Corp.

Nissan North America Inc.
Issues: MAN
Rep By: James Chen, William Michael House, R. Latane Montague, Jeffrey W. Munk, Patrick M. Raher

NTT America
Issues: COM TRD
Rep By: Lance D. Bultena, William Michael House, Jeffrey W. Munk, Joel S. Winnik

Olney Boys and Girls Club
Issues: BUD
Rep By: C. Michael Gilliland, Christine M. Warnke

Online Privacy Alliance
Rep By: Christine A. Varney

Ontario, Ministry of Economic Development and Trade

Parker Jewish Geriatric Institute
Rep By: Nancy Granese, Jeffrey G. Schneider

Payless Shoe Source
Issues: TRD
Rep By: Irene Chang, Stephanie Henning, Warren H. Maruyama, Mark S. McConnell, Daniel B. Poneman

Pharmaceutical Research and Manufacturers of America
Issues: TRD
Rep By: Jeanne S. Archibald, Donna A. Boswell, Irene Chang, Warren H. Maruyama, Beth L. Roberts, Ann Morgan Vickery

Plasma Protein Therapeutics Ass'n
Issues: HCR
Rep By: C. Michael Gilliland, Helene C. Lasker, Christine M. Warnke

Polaroid Corp.
Issues: TRD
Rep By: Jeanne S. Archibald

Polyisocyanurate Insulation Manufacturers Ass'n
Issues: ENV TAX
Rep By: Nancy Granese, William Michael House, Christine M. Warnke

Protein Technologies Internat'l
Issues: TRD
Rep By: Raymond S. Calamaro, Gary Jay Kushner

Public Service Co. of Colorado
Issues: ENG
Rep By: Lance D. Bultena, William Michael House, Hon. Robert H. Michel, Jeffrey W. Munk, Patrick Nevins, Karol Lyn Newman

Qwest Communications
Issues: COM TEC TRD
Rep By: William Michael House, Hon. Robert H. Michel, Jeffrey W. Munk

S1 Corp.
Issues: CPI
Rep By: Lance D. Bultena, C. Michael Gilliland, William S. Haft, William Michael House

Soap and Detergent Ass'n
Issues: ENV
Rep By: James Chen, Warren H. Maruyama, Humberto R. Pena

Southern Methodist University
Rep By: C. Michael Gilliland, William Michael House, Sharon McBride, Jeffrey W. Munk

The St. Joe Co.
Issues: APP AVI
Rep By: C. Michael Gilliland, William Michael House

Staff Builders, Inc.
Issues: BNK GOV HCR MMM
Rep By: Nancy Granese, Jeffrey G. Schneider

Taco Bell Corp.
Issues: FOO
Rep By: Humberto R. Pena

Taylor Packing Co., Inc.
Issues: AGR
Rep By: Gary Jay Kushner, Kyra A. Todd

Toyota Motor North America, U.S.A., Inc.
Issues: MAN TRD
Rep By: Jeanne S. Archibald, Raymond S. Calamaro, William Michael House

United Parcel Service
Issues: TRD
Rep By: Jeanne S. Archibald, Raymond S. Calamaro, Philip Larson

United States Sugar Corp.
Issues: AGR
Rep By: Humberto R. Pena

UPMC Presbyterian
Rep By: Isabel P. Dunst, Nancy Granese, Hon. Robert H. Michel

Vulcan Materials Co.
Issues: CHM NAT
Rep By: C. Michael Gilliland, William Michael House, Warren H. Maruyama, Jeffrey W. Munk, Christine M. Warnke

Warland Investment Co.
Issues: DEF RES
Rep By: David J. Hensler, John S. Jenkins, Jeffrey W. Munk

WebMD
Issues: CPI HCR
Rep By: Lance D. Bultena, C. Michael Gilliland, William S. Haft

Western Wireless Internat'l
Issues: TEC
Rep By: Michele Farquhar, Christine M. Warnke

Hohlt & Associates

1100 New York Ave. NW
Suite 700 East
Washington, DC 20005
Tel: (202)833-4146
Fax: (202)833-1587
Registered: LDA
Web: www.hohlt.com
E-mail: rick@hohlt.com

DC-Area Employees Representing Listed Clients
HOHLT, Richard F.

Clients

BMW Financial Services of North America, Inc.
Issues: AUT BAN BNK BUD CSP FIN TAX
Rep By: Richard F. Hohlt

Bristol-Myers Squibb Co.
Issues: BUD HCR MMM PHA TAX
Rep By: Richard F. Hohlt

Clark/Bardes, Inc.
Issues: BUD FIN INS TAX
Rep By: Richard F. Hohlt

Dime Savings Bank of New York
Issues: BAN BUD FIN HOU INS TAX
Rep By: Richard F. Hohlt

FISERV, Inc.
Issues: BAN CPI SCI SMB TAX
Rep By: Richard F. Hohlt

Guaranty Bank, SSB
Issues: BAN BNK BUD FIN HOU RES TAX
Rep By: Richard F. Hohlt

Kelly and Associates, Inc.
Issues: INS SMB TAX
Rep By: Richard F. Hohlt

J. P. Morgan Chase & Co.
Issues: BAN BUD FIN TAX
Rep By: Richard F. Hohlt

Northwest Airlines, Inc.
Issues: AVI ECN LBR TAX TOU TRA

Nuclear Energy Institute
Issues: BUD ENG TAX WAS
Rep By: Richard F. Hohlt

Sallie Mae, Inc.
Issues: BNK BUD EDU TAX
Rep By: Richard F. Hohlt

Washington Mutual Bank
Issues: BAN BUD FIN HOU INS TAX
Rep By: Richard F. Hohlt

Wilmington Savings Fund Society
Issues: BAN BNK BUD ECN FIN HOU TAX
Rep By: Richard F. Hohlt

Holland & Knight LLP

2099 Pennsylvania Ave. NW
Suite 100
Washington, DC 20006
Tel: (202)955-3000
Fax: (202)955-5564
Registered: LDA, FARA
Web: www.hklaw.com
E-mail: webmaster@hklaw.com

A commercial law firm with more than 1,150 lawyers in 22 offices in the U.S. Also maintains offices in Rio de Janeiro, Sao Paolo, Mexico City and Tokyo, and affiliates in Caracas and Tel Aviv.

DC-Area Employees Representing Listed Clients
ATCITTY, Shenan R.
BALL, Markham, Partner
BOOTHE, Jeffrey F., Partner
BRADLEY, Leigh A.
BRADNER, Robert Hunt, Senior Counsel
BUCHOLTZ, Harold R., Partner
BURKE, Brian E., Senior Counsel
BURKMAN, Jack M., Associate
CAVANAUGH, J. Michael, Partner
CLANCY, Michael W., Partner
CONNOLLY, Peter M., Partner
CUTLER, Lynn G., Senior Public Affairs Advisor
DYE, Stuart S., Partner
EWART, Andrea, Associate
FOWLER, Hon. Tillie K., Partner
GABA, Michael M., Partner
GALANO, Mike, Legislative Assistant
GILLILAND, David W., Senior Public Affairs Advisor
GILLIS, Michael, Legislative Assistant
GOLD, Richard M., Partner
GOODKIND, Arthur, Partner
HAN, Joanna S., Associate
HATCHER, Michael R., Partner
HILDEBRANT, Jeffrey P., Senior Counsel
HOGEN, Phillip N., Of Counsel
HUMMERS, Jr., Edward, Partner
HUMPHREY, Margot Smiley, Partner
JORDAN, Lloyd J., Senior Counsel
KILMER, Paul F., Partner
KITTO, Joseph L., Associate
KOTEEN, Bernard, Partner
LATHAM, Weldon H., Partner
LIND, Keith D., Senior Counsel
MARQUEZ, Jim J., Senior Counsel
MATTHEWS, Carol L. B., Partner
METZGER, David P., Partner
NAFTALIN, Alan, Partner
NAFTALIN, Charles, Partner
NEE, Amy B., Public Affairs Advisor
OLEYNIK, Ronald A., Partner
PALCHICK, Mark G., Partner
PATTON, Douglas J., Senior Counsel
RAILSBACK, Hon. Thomas F., Of Counsel
RHODES, Jr., Robert L., Partner
ROSENBERG, Marvin, Partner
SANTANA, Susan I., Associate
SIKORSKI, Hon. Gerald E., Partner
SLOVAK, Dorothy C., Associate
STUDLEY, Janet R., Partner
TOKER, P. J., Legislative Assistant
TRUEBLOOD, Travis W.
VIOLA, Beth, Senior Public Affairs Advisor
WHEELER, George Y., Partner
WHITESTONE, David C., Associate
WINSTEAD, David L., Partner
WOODSON, Roderic, Senior Counsel
WRIGHT, Steven H.

Clients

Air China Internat'l Corp., Ltd.

Air Malta Co. Ltd.

Allina Health Systems
Issues: HCR MMM TOB
Rep By: Hon. Gerald E. Sikorski, P. J. Toker

American Chemistry Council
Issues: ENV
Rep By: Robert Hunt Bradner, Jack M. Burkman, Mike Galano, Richard M. Gold, Hon. Thomas F. Railsback, Janet R. Studley, P. J. Toker, David C. Whitestone

Avianca Airlines

Benova, Inc.
Issues: MMM
Rep By: Jack M. Burkman, Richard M. Gold, Keith D. Lind

Bridgestone/Firestone, Inc.
Issues: CSP GOV TRA
Rep By: Robert Hunt Bradner, Jack M. Burkman, Hon. Gerald E. Sikorski, Janet R. Studley, Beth Viola, David C. Whitestone

Capitol Broadcasting Co.
Issues: TEC
Rep By: Michael Gillis, Hon. Thomas F. Railsback, Marvin Rosenberg, Hon. Gerald E. Sikorski, P. J. Toker

Cellular Telecommunications and Internet Ass'n
Issues: TEC
Rep By: Marvin Rosenberg

Central American Bank of Economic Integration
Issues: APP BUD ECN FOR LBR MAN TRD

Charter Schools Development Corp.
Issues: EDU
Rep By: Douglas J. Patton

Cheyenne and Arapahoe Tribes of Oklahoma
Issues: IND
Rep By: Hon. Gerald E. Sikorski

Clinical Laboratory Management Ass'n

Clyde's Restaurant Group
Issues: RES
Rep By: David C. Whitestone

Consortium for Plant Biotechnology Research
Issues: AGR BUD ENG FUE
Rep By: Jack M. Burkman, Richard M. Gold, David P. Metzger, Janet R. Studley

Consortium Plant Biotech Research
Rep By: Richard M. Gold, David P. Metzger, Janet R. Studley

DuPont
Issues: ENV
Rep By: Jack M. Burkman, Mike Galano, Richard M. Gold, David C. Whitestone

El Salvador, Embassy of the Republic of

El Salvador, Government of the Republic of

Envirotest Systems Corp.
Rep By: Janet R. Studley

ESPN, Inc.
Issues: COM
Rep By: Ronald A. Oleynik

FirstEnergy Co.
Issues: BUD ENG ENV UTI
Rep By: Richard M. Gold, Janet R. Studley, Beth Viola, David C. Whitestone

Florida Gas Utility
Issues: FUE TAX
Rep By: Harold R. Bucholtz, Richard M. Gold, Janet R. Studley, David C. Whitestone

FMC Corp.
Issues: BUD ENV
Rep By: Jack M. Burkman, Mike Galano, Richard M. Gold, P. J. Toker

General Mills
Issues: CSP FOO
Rep By: Hon. Gerald E. Sikorski

The Georgetown Partnership
Issues: TRA
Rep By: David C. Whitestone

Grand Rapids Area Transit Authority

Greater Jamaica Development Corp.
Rep By: Jim J. Marquez, David C. Whitestone

Hillsborough Area Regional Transit Authority
Issues: TRA

Hualapai Nation
Issues: BUD IND TRA
Rep By: Joseph L. Kitto, David C. Whitestone

Hubbard Broadcasting, Inc.
Issues: COM TEC
Rep By: Hon. Gerald E. Sikorski

Illinois Primary Health Care Ass'n
Issues: BUD HCR MMM
Rep By: Robert Hunt Bradner

Internat'l Intellectual Property Institute
Issues: BUD
Rep By: David C. Whitestone

Jamaica, Government of

S.C. Johnson and Son, Inc.
Issues: CAW CHM ENV TRD
Rep By: Jack M. Burkman, Mike Galano, Michael Gillis, Richard M. Gold, Janet R. Studley

Mille Lacs Band of Ojibwe Indians
Issues: IND
Rep By: Mike Galano, Richard M. Gold, Hon. Gerald E. Sikorski

Murphy Oil U.S.A.
Issues: CAW
Rep By: Jack M. Burkman, Mike Galano, Richard M. Gold, Janet R. Studley

Nassau County Health Care Corp.
Issues: BUD
Rep By: Jack M. Burkman, Mike Galano, Richard M. Gold, Keith D. Lind, Hon. Gerald E. Sikorski, P. J. Toker, David C. Whitestone

Nat'l Coalition of Minority Businesses
Issues: BUD CIV GOV SMB
Rep By: Joanna S. Han, Michael R. Hatcher, Jeffrey P. Hildebrant, Weldon H. Latham, Amy B. Nee

Nat'l Paint and Coatings Ass'n
Issues: CAW ENV HOU
Rep By: Jack M. Burkman, Mike Galano, Richard M. Gold, David C. Whitestone

PanAmSat Corp.
Issues: COM TEC
Rep By: Janet R. Studley

Placer, California, County of
Issues: BUD
Rep By: Jack M. Burkman, Mike Galano, Richard M. Gold, P. J. Toker, David C. Whitestone

Red Lake Band of Chippewa Indians
Issues: IND
Rep By: Hon. Gerald E. Sikorski

Rockdale, Georgia, County of, Board of Commissioners of
Issues: CAW
Rep By: Jack M. Burkman, Mike Galano, Richard M. Gold, David C. Whitestone

Sarasota, Florida, City of
Issues: CAW
Rep By: Jack M. Burkman, Richard M. Gold

Sarasota, Florida, County of
Issues: CAW
Rep By: Jack M. Burkman, Richard M. Gold, David C. Whitestone

Save America's Forests, Inc.
Issues: ENV
Rep By: Hon. Gerald E. Sikorski

Slim Fast Foods Co.
Issues: ADV FOO
Rep By: Hon. Gerald E. Sikorski

Somerville Housing Group
Issues: BUD
Rep By: Robert Hunt Bradner, Jack M. Burkman, Mike Galano, Michael Gillis, Richard M. Gold, Douglas J. Patton, P. J. Toker, Beth Viola

Southern Coalition for Advanced Transportation
Issues: BUD
Rep By: Richard M. Gold, David C. Whitestone

Spaceport Florida Authority
Issues: AER TAX
Rep By: Harold R. Bucholtz

Spirit Airlines
Rep By: Jack M. Burkman, Michael Gillis, Jim J. Marquez, Hon. Gerald E. Sikorski

Texaco Group Inc.
Issues: ENG ENV LBR
Rep By: Joanna S. Han, Michael R. Hatcher, Jeffrey P. Hildebrant, Weldon H. Latham

Thompson Publishing, Inc.
Issues: EDU
Rep By: Douglas J. Patton

Tichenor and Associates
Issues: DEF GOV
Rep By: Robert Hunt Bradner, Jack M. Burkman

Transportation District Commission of Hampton Roads
Issues: TRA

Tri-County Metropolitan Transportation District of Oregon

Unisys Corp.
Issues: GOV
Rep By: Hon. Gerald E. Sikorski

United Airlines
Issues: AVI BUD TRA
Rep By: Richard M. Gold, Hon. Gerald E. Sikorski, Janet R. Studley, David C. Whitestone

United Kingdom, Government of

UroMedica Corp.
Issues: MMM
Rep By: Keith D. Lind

Virologic, Inc.
Issues: HCR
Rep By: Jeffrey F. Boothe

Vitas Healthcare Corp.
Issues: HCR MMM
Rep By: Janet R. Studley

Water Systems Council
Issues: AGR BUD ENV MAN
Rep By: Mike Galano, Richard M. Gold

West Group
Issues: MIA
Rep By: Jack M. Burkman, Hon. Gerald E. Sikorski

West Palm Beach, Florida, City of
Issues: CAW
Rep By: Jack M. Burkman, Richard M. Gold, David C. Whitestone

West*Group Management LLC
Issues: RES
Rep By: David C. Whitestone

Wyeth-Ayerst Laboratories
Issues: BUD
Rep By: Steven H. Wright

Wyeth-Ayerst Pharmaceuticals
Issues: BUD HCR
Rep By: Robert Hunt Bradner, Michael Gillis, Richard M. Gold, Steven H. Wright

Peter Homer

4004 David Lane
Alexandria, VA 22311
Tel: (703)998-8177
Registered: LDA

Clients

Colorado River Indian Tribes
Issues: BUD ECN GOV IND MAN ROD SMB TEC UTI
Rep By: Peter Homer

Honberger and Walters, Inc.

440 First St. NW
Suite 430
Washington, DC 20001
Tel: (202)737-7523
Fax: (202)737-6788
Registered: LDA

DC-Area Employees Representing Listed Clients

CAMPBELL, Greg, Associate
GILCHREST, Donald, Associate
HONBERGER, Roger F., Partner
WALTERS, Thomas P., President

Clients

Calleguas Municipal Water District, California
Rep By: Donald Gilchrest, Thomas P. Walters

Monterey Salinas Transit
Issues: BUD TRA
Rep By: Greg Campbell, Donald Gilchrest, Thomas P. Walters

North San Diego County Transit Development Board
Issues: BUD DIS TRA
Rep By: Donald Gilchrest, Thomas P. Walters

Pechanga Band of Luiseno Mission Indians
Rep By: Donald Gilchrest, Roger F. Honberger, Thomas P. Walters

Port of San Diego
Rep By: Thomas P. Walters

Riverside, California, County of
Issues: GOV
Rep By: Greg Campbell, Donald Gilchrest, Thomas P. Walters

San Diego Metropolitan Transit Development Board
Issues: BUD RRR TRA
Rep By: Donald Gilchrest, Thomas P. Walters

San Diego, California, County of
Issues: GOV
Rep By: Greg Campbell, Donald Gilchrest, Thomas P. Walters

San Joaquin, California, County of
Issues: GOV
Rep By: Greg Campbell, Donald Gilchrest, Thomas P. Walters

Sweetwater Authority
Issues: BUD
Rep By: Donald Gilchrest, Thomas P. Walters

Ventura, California, County of
Issues: GOV
Rep By: Greg Campbell, Donald Gilchrest, Thomas P. Walters

Hooper Owen & Winburn

801 Pennsylvania Ave. NW
Suite 730
Washington, DC 20004
Tel: (202)638-7780
Fax: (202)638-7787
Registered: LDA, FARA

A legislative consulting firm.

DC-Area Employees Representing Listed Clients

DECAIN, Ann, Senior Legislative Specialist
GLAZE, Steve, Principal
GOMEZ, Esperanza, Senior Legislative Specialist
HOOPER, Lindsay D., Principal
OWEN, Daryl H., Principal
RUDD, David, Principal
WILSON, Hon. Charles, Principal
WINBURN, John P., Principal
WYMAN, Lucia A., Principal

Clients

AFL-CIO (American Federation of Labor and Congress of Industrial Organizations)
Issues: TAX
Rep By: Steve Glaze, Lindsay D. Hooper, John P. Winburn

American Soc. of Pension Actuaries
Issues: TAX
Rep By: Steve Glaze

Apple Computer, Inc.
Issues: TAX
Rep By: Steve Glaze, Lindsay D. Hooper, John P. Winburn

AT&T
Issues: COM TEC
Rep By: David Rudd

The Atlantic Co.
Issues: ENG
Rep By: Daryl H. Owen

Azerbaijan, Embassy of the Republic of
Issues: FOR
Rep By: Esperanza Gomez, Hon. Charles Wilson

Barrick Goldstrike Mines, Inc.
Issues: NAT RES TAX
Rep By: Lindsay D. Hooper

Bessemer Securities Corp.
Issues: TAX
Rep By: Steve Glaze

Borden Chemicals & Plastics, Inc.
Issues: CHM
Rep By: Lindsay D. Hooper, Daryl H. Owen

Comcast Corp.
Issues: COM
Rep By: David Rudd

Construction Management Ass'n of America
Issues: BUD GOV

Cox Enterprises Inc.
Issues: TAX
Rep By: Steve Glaze

Duke Energy
Issues: ENG
Rep By: Daryl H. Owen

El Paso Corporation

Entergy Corp.
Issues: ENG
Rep By: Daryl H. Owen

Entergy Services, Inc.
Rep By: Daryl H. Owen

Fantasma Networks, Inc.
Issues: COM TEC
Rep By: David Rudd

First Preston Management
Issues: TAX
Rep By: Lucia A. Wyman

Gary-Williams Energy Corp.
Issues: ENG
Rep By: Lindsay D. Hooper

GKN Westland Aerospace Inc.
Issues: AVI
Rep By: Hon. Charles Wilson

Hallmark Cards, Inc.
Issues: TAX
Rep By: Lindsay D. Hooper

The Hartford
Issues: INS TAX
Rep By: Steve Glaze, David Rudd, John P. Winburn

The Hillman Co.
Issues: TAX
Rep By: Lindsay D. Hooper

Houston Advanced Research Center
Issues: ENV
Rep By: Lucia A. Wyman

Hubbell, Inc.
Issues: TAX
Rep By: Lindsay D. Hooper

Hutchison Whampo, LTD
Issues: GOV
Rep By: David Rudd, John P. Winburn

IMI Services USA, Inc.
Issues: DEF
Rep By: Hon. Charles Wilson

Japan Nuclear Cycle Development Institute
Issues: ENG
Rep By: Daryl H. Owen

KPMG, LLP
Issues: TAX
Rep By: Steve Glaze, Lindsay D. Hooper, John P. Winburn

Latona Associates, Inc.
Issues: RES
Rep By: Hon. Charles Wilson

Lockheed Martin Corp.
Issues: AER DEF
Rep By: Hon. Charles Wilson

Metropolitan Life Insurance Co.
Issues: TAX
Rep By: Steve Glaze

Microsoft Corp.
Issues: CPI
Rep By: David Rudd

Morgan Stanley Dean Witter & Co.
Issues: TAX
Rep By: Lindsay D. Hooper

Nat'l Cable Television Ass'n
Issues: TEC
Rep By: David Rudd

Nat'l Coordinating Committee for Multiemployer Plans
Issues: TAX
Rep By: John P. Winburn

Norfolk Southern Railroad
Issues: RRR TAX TRD
Rep By: David Rudd, John P. Winburn

Pakistan, Government of the Islamic Republic of
Issues: FOR
Rep By: Esperanza Gomez, Hon. Charles Wilson

PanAmSat Corp.
Issues: TEC
Rep By: David Rudd, John P. Winburn

Parsons Corp.
Issues: TAX
Rep By: Steve Glaze, Lindsay D. Hooper, John P. Winburn

Pfizer, Inc.
Issues: PHA TAX TRA
Rep By: David Rudd, John P. Winburn

Philip Morris Management Corp.
Issues: TAX TOB TRA
Rep By: Lindsay D. Hooper, John P. Winburn

Shipston Group, LTD
Issues: TAX
Rep By: Hon. Charles Wilson

Stephens Group, Inc.
Issues: TAX
Rep By: Steve Glaze

Stilwell Financial Inc.
Issues: TAX TRA
Rep By: Lindsay D. Hooper

TECO Energy, Inc.
Issues: ENG TAX UTI
Rep By: Lindsay D. Hooper, Daryl H. Owen

TerraPoint
Issues: BUD
Rep By: Lindsay D. Hooper

Trizec Hahn Corp.
Issues: RES TAX
Rep By: Lindsay D. Hooper

United Airlines
Rep By: David Rudd

Waste Control Specialists, Inc.
Issues: TAX WAS
Rep By: Daryl H. Owen

Waste Management, Inc.
Issues: TAX WAS
Rep By: Steve Glaze

Wine and Spirits Wholesalers of America
Issues: TAX
Rep By: Steve Glaze, Lindsay D. Hooper, John P. Winburn

Hoover Partners

888 16th St. NW
Suite 300
Washington, DC 20006
Tel: (202)363-6426
Fax: (202)296-7302
Registered: LDA
Web: www.hooverpartners.com
E-mail: kim@hooverpartners.com

DC-Area Employees Representing Listed Clients
HOOVER, Kimberly, Founder

Clients

Ass'n of Bank Couriers
Issues: BAN TRA
Rep By: Kimberly Hoover

Financial Technology Industry Council
Issues: BAN SCI
Rep By: Kimberly Hoover

UMonitor.com
Issues: BAN SCI
Rep By: Kimberly Hoover

Hoppel, Mayer and Coleman

1000 Connecticut Ave. NW
Suite 400
Washington, DC 20036
Tel: (202)296-5460
Fax: (202)296-5463
E-mail: hmc@hmc-law.com

DC-Area Employees Representing Listed Clients
COLEMAN, Paul D., Partner
MAYER, Neal Michael, Senior Partner

Clients

Companhia Maritima Nacional

P & O Nedlloyd Ltd.

Philadelphia Regional Port Authority

Tropical Shipping and Construction Co.
Rep By: Paul D. Coleman, Neal Michael Mayer

Christopher C. Horner

1001 Connecticut Ave. NW
Suite 1250
Washington, DC 20036
Tel: (202)331-1010
Fax: (202)331-0640
E-mail: CHornerLaw@aol.com

Clients

Competitive Enterprise Institute
Rep By: Christopher C. Horner

Cooler Heads Coalition
Issues: ENG ENV FOR SCI
Rep By: Christopher C. Horner

Oliver James Horton

1132 Valley Dr.
Alexandria, VA 22302
Tel: (703)671-1408
Fax: (202)429-4342
Registered: LDA
E-mail: azhorton@aol.com

Clients

Agri Business Council of Arizona
Issues: AGR CAW ENV
Rep By: Oliver James Horton, Jr.

Arizona Power Authority
Issues: ENG NAT TAX UTI
Rep By: Oliver James Horton, Jr.

Giant Industries, Inc.
Issues: ENG ENV FUE SCI SMB
Rep By: Oliver James Horton, Jr.

Houlihan Consulting L.L.C.

11654 Plaza America Dr.
Suite 200
Reston, VA 20190
Tel: (703)713-9410
Fax: (703)713-0263
Registered: LDA
Web: www.houlihanconsulting.com
E-mail: pah@houlihanconsulting.com
An international business consulting firm providing Washington representation.

DC-Area Employees Representing Listed Clients
HOULIHAN, Peggy A., President and Chief Exec. Officer

Howe, Anderson & Steyer, P.C.

1747 Pennsylvania Ave. NW
Suite 1050
Washington, DC 20006
Tel: (202)296-5680
Fax: (202)331-8049
Web: www.haspc.com
E-mail: info@haspc.com
A law firm specializing in labor, antitrust, and trade regulation.

DC-Area Employees Representing Listed Clients
ANDERSON, James E., Partner
HOWE, William H., Partner
STEYER, Richard A., Partner

Clients

Ass'n of Bituminous Contractors
Rep By: William H. Howe

Greater Washington Soc. of Ass'n Executives
Rep By: James E. Anderson

IBFI - The Internat'l Ass'n for Document and Information Management Solutions

Nat'l Ass'n of Bankruptcy Trustees
Issues: BNK
Rep By: Richard A. Steyer

Wire Reinforcement Institute
Rep By: James E. Anderson

Law Offices of Irene E. Howie

7321 Masonville Dr.
Annadale, VA 22003
Tel: (703)573-0635
Fax: (703)573-0066
Registered: LDA
A law firm.

DC-Area Employees Representing Listed Clients
HOWIE, Irene E., Principal

Clients

Air Methods/Mercy Air
Rep By: Irene E. Howie

El Toro Reuse Planning Authority
Issues: AVI

The Nordam Group
Issues: AER MAN

Howrey Simon Arnold & White

1299 Pennsylvania Ave. NW
Washington, DC 20004-2402
Tel: (202)783-0800
Fax: (202)383-6610
Registered: LDA, FARA
A law firm specializing in commercial and antitrust litigation, international trade, intellectual property, government contracts, environmental insurance coverage, white collar criminal defense, securities litigation and products liability.

DC-Area Employees Representing Listed Clients
ABRAMS, Robert G., Partner
BRIGGS, III, John DeQ., Partner
BRUCE, John F., Partner
ENGEL, III, Charles J., Partner
FERGUSON, Edward L.
GRIMALDI, Alan M., Partner
HARRIS, Stuart H., Partner
HERTZBERG, Michael A., Partner
KERCHNER, George
LEVINE, Ezra C., Partner
MCMANUS, Katherine D., Partner
MOONEY, Saskia
NIELDS, Jr., John, Partner
OLSON, James W.
PIVIK, Robert, Chief Operating Officer
RILL, James, Partner
RUYAK, Robert, Chairman
SHEEHY, Terrence C., Partner
SHERZER, Harvey G., Partner
SMITH, Tracy Heinzman, Partner
WEINBERG, David B.
WOLFE, J. Thomas

Clients

Air & Water Technologies
Rep By: Alan M. Grimaldi

Allegheny Technologies, Inc.
Rep By: Harvey G. Sherzer

American Portland Cement Alliance
Rep By: John F. Bruce

Anheuser-Busch Cos., Inc.
Rep By: Terrence C. Sheehy

Bailey Corp.

Barker Brothers

Battery Council Internat'l
Issues: ENV WAS
Rep By: Edward L. Ferguson, David B. Weinberg, J. Thomas Wolfe

Environmental Treatment and Technologies Corp.

Exxon Co., U.S.A.
Rep By: Robert G. Abrams

Food Marketing Institute

General Signal Corp.
Rep By: Stuart H. Harris

H. J. Heinz Co.,

Huffy Corp.
Rep By: Alan M. Grimaldi

Kyocera Corp.
Rep By: Michael A. Hertzberg

LEP Scientific Ltd.
Rep By: Michael A. Hertzberg

Liberty Corp.
Rep By: John F. Bruce

Marine Preservation Ass'n
Rep By: Charles J. Engel, III

Nat'l Ass'n for Plastic Container Recovery
Rep By: Edward L. Ferguson, Saskia Mooney, David B. Weinberg

Non-Bank Funds Transmitters Group
Issues: FIN
Rep By: Ezra C. Levine

Portable Rechargeable Battery Ass'n
Rep By: George Kerchner, Saskia Mooney, Tracy Heinzman Smith, David B. Weinberg

Rockwell Collins
Rep By: John DeQ. Briggs, III

Sloan Valve Co.

Timex Corp.
Rep By: Stuart H. Harris

Uniroyal Chemical Co., Inc.
Rep By: John DeQ. Briggs, III

United States Beet Sugar Ass'n
Rep By: John F. Bruce

USA/Scientific Plastics Inc.
Rep By: Michael A. Hertzberg

Weight Watchers Internat'l, Inc.

Edwin E. Huddleson, III

1230 31st St. NW
Second Floor
Washington, DC 20007
Tel: (202)333-1360
Fax: (202)298-6699
Registered: LDA

E-mail: huddlesone@aol.com

Clients

Equipment Leasing Ass'n of America
Issues: ENV FIN
Rep By: Edwin E. Huddleson, III

R. J. Hudson Associates

P.O Box 20652
Alexandria, VA 22320-1652
Tel: (703)660-9246
Fax: (703)660-9240
Registered: LDA
E-mail: germroth@aol.com

DC-Area Employees Representing Listed Clients
GERMROTH, David S., Senior Lobbyist of Senior V. President
HUDSON, Rebecca J., President

Clients

American Council of Korean Travel Agents
Issues: CSP FOR GAM IMM TOU TRD
American Federation of Government Employees, Local 1689 Guam
Ass'n of American Shippers
Issues: DEF FOR GOV MAR TRA TRU
Coalition of Hawaii Movers
Issues: DEF MAR SMB TRA
Rep By: Rebecca J. Hudson
DeWitt Cos. of Guam and Saipan
Issues: DEF MAR
Rep By: Rebecca J. Hudson
Guam Internat'l Airport Authority
Government of Guam
Hawaii Food & Beverage Ass'n
Hawaiian Moving and Forwarding Ass'n
Honolulu Shipyard
Internat'l Facilities Management Ass'n
Nat'l Licensed Beverage Ass'n
Issues: ADV ALC ART BEV CPT CSP FOO GAM IND LBR MON SMB TAX TOB TOU TRA
Rep By: David S. Germroth
NAVATEK Ship Design Hawaii
Pacific Shipyards Internat'l, Hawaii
Philadelphia Hospitality & Business Alliance
T.W.Y. Co., Ltd.
Issues: DEF FOR IMM

Hughes Hubbard & Reed LLP

1775 I St. NW
Suite 600
Washington, DC 20006-2401
Tel: (202)721-4600
Fax: (202)721-4646
Registered: LDA, FARA
Washington office of a New York general practice law firm.

Political Action Committee
Hughes Hubbard & Reed LLP PAC Inc.
1775 I St. NW
Suite 600
Washington, DC 20006-2401
Tel: (202)721-4600
Fax: (202)721-4646

DC-Area Employees Representing Listed Clients
CURTISS, Catherine, Partner
FOOTE, George M., Partner
KASHDAN, Alan, Of Counsel
KLEIN, Dennis, Managing Partner
TOWNSEND, John M., Partner

Clients

Ajinomoto Co., Inc.
Rep By: John M. Townsend
Canada, Government of
Rep By: Catherine Curtiss
Ecuador, Government of the Republic of
Rep By: Catherine Curtiss
Federal Home Loan Bank of Seattle
Issues: FIN
NBD Bank, N.A.
Nikon Corp.
UNR Asbestos-Disease Trust

Hulshart & Associates

3009 Federal Hill Dr.
Falls Church, VA 22044
Tel: (703)241-5501
A government relations firm specializing in public policy strategies and lobbying for telecommunications, computer and interactive multimedia companies.

DC-Area Employees Representing Listed Clients
HULSHART, Mark, Principal

Robert R. Humphreys

4319 Reno Rd. NW
Washington, DC 20008
Tel: (202)363-2200
Fax: (202)363-7464
Registered: LDA
E-mail: humphreyslaw@worldnet.att.net
A sole practitioner providing legal and consulting services.

Clients

Helen Keller Nat'l Center for Deaf Blind Youths and Adults
Issues: EDU
Rep By: Robert R. Humphreys

Derrick Humphries

1025 Vermont Ave. NW
Suite 910
Washington, DC 20005
Tel: (202)347-7000
Fax: (202)347-2424
Web: www.humphreysandbrooks.com
E-mail: hblawyers@aol.com

Clients

Internat'l Ass'n of Black Professional Fire Fighters
Rep By: Derrick Humphries

Hunt Management Systems

Two Wisconsin Circle
Suite 670
Chevy Chase, MD 20815-7003
Tel: (301)718-7722
Fax: (301)718-9440
Acts as the office and staff for trade associations involved in employee benefit and related issues.

DC-Area Employees Representing Listed Clients
HUNT, Jr., Frederick D., President
LEIGHT, Elizabeth Ysla, Director, Government Relations
LENNAN, Anne C., V. President and Director of Federal Affairs

Clients

Soc. of Professional Benefit Administrators
Issues: GOV HCR INS LBR RET
Rep By: Frederick D. Hunt, Jr., Elizabeth Ysla Leight, Anne C. Lennan

Hunton & Williams

1900 K St. NW
Washington, DC 20006-1109
Tel: (202)955-1500
Fax: (202)778-2201
Registered: LDA, FARA
Web: www.hunton.com
E-mail: info@hunton.com

DC-Area Employees Representing Listed Clients
ADAMS, John J., Senior Counsel
ALBRECHT, Virginia S., Partner
BALILES, Gerald L., Partner
BROWNELL, F. William, Partner
DEJARNETTE, Jr., Edmund T., Counsel
FICHTHORN, Norman W., Partner
GENESON, David F., Partner
MALLORY, III, C. King, Partner
MAY, Richard E., Partner
NICKEL, Henry V., Partner
PRINCIPATO, Gregory, Trade and Transportation Specialist
SMITH, Jr., Turner T., Partner

Clients

Almont Shipping Terminals
Issues: MAR
Rep By: John J. Adams
American Electric Power Co.
Issues: TAX
Rep By: C. King Mallory, III, Richard E. May
American Road and Transportation Builders Ass'n (ARTBA)
Issues: CAW TRA
Rep By: F. William Brownell, Norman W. Fichthorn
California State University at Monterey Bay
CareFirst Blue Cross Blue Shield
Central Arizona Water Conservation District
Central West Virginia Regional Airport Authority
Clean Air Regulatory Information Group
Issues: CAW
Rep By: F. William Brownell, Norman W. Fichthorn, Henry V. Nickel
Coalition for a Global Standard on Aviation Noise
Issues: AVI
Rep By: Gerald L. Baliles, Gregory Principato
Edison Electric Institute
Rep By: John J. Adams, F. William Brownell, C. King Mallory, III, Henry V. Nickel, Turner T. Smith, Jr.
Envirotest Systems Corp.
Issues: CAW
The Foundation for Environmental and Economic Progress
Issues: BUD CAW ENV NAT RES
Rep By: Virginia S. Albrecht
The Irvine Co.
Issues: BUD CAW ENV NAT RES
Rep By: Virginia S. Albrecht
KeySpan Energy
Issues: UTI
Mills Corporation
Issues: RES
Rep By: Virginia S. Albrecht
Sempra Energy
Rep By: John J. Adams
United States Sugar Corp.
Issues: BUD CAW NAT RES
Rep By: Virginia S. Albrecht
Utility Air Regulatory Group
Rep By: Henry V. Nickel

Hurt, Norton & Associates

505 Capitol Ct. NE
Suite 200
Washington, DC 20002
Tel: (202)543-9398
Fax: (202)543-7844
Registered: LDA
E-mail: hna@hurtnorton.com

DC-Area Employees Representing Listed Clients
HURT, Robert H., Partner
NORTON, Frank, Partner
SIRACUSE, Helen C., Senior Associate
TAKAKOSHI, William K., Senior Associate
WOOD, Katharine Calhoun, Senior Associate

Clients

21st Century Partnership
Issues: DEF
Rep By: Robert H. Hurt, Frank Norton
Air Tran Airways
Issues: AVI TAX
Rep By: Robert H. Hurt, Frank Norton
Auburn University
Issues: AGR AVI LAW TRA
Rep By: Robert H. Hurt, Frank Norton, Katharine Calhoun Wood
Caswell Internat'l Corp.
Issues: DEF
Rep By: Robert H. Hurt, Frank Norton, William K. Takakoshi
The Coca-Cola Company
Issues: BEV
Rep By: Robert H. Hurt, Frank Norton, William K. Takakoshi, Katharine Calhoun Wood
Georgia Ports Authority
Issues: BUD TRA
Rep By: Robert H. Hurt, Frank Norton, Katharine Calhoun Wood
Intergraph Corp. Federal Systems Division
Issues: CPI DEF
Rep By: Robert H. Hurt, Frank Norton, William K. Takakoshi
Lockheed Martin Aeronautical Systems Co.
Issues: BUD DEF
Rep By: Robert H. Hurt, Frank Norton, Katharine Calhoun Wood
Mercer Engineering Research Center
Issues: BUD DEF
Rep By: Robert H. Hurt, Frank Norton, Katharine Calhoun Wood
Mercer University
Rep By: Robert H. Hurt, Frank Norton, Katharine Calhoun Wood
Pemco Aviation Group, Inc.
Issues: DEF
Rep By: Robert H. Hurt, Frank Norton, Helen C. Siracuse, William K. Takakoshi
Phoenix Air Group, Inc.
Issues: DEF
Rep By: Robert H. Hurt, Frank Norton
Quad City Development Group
Issues: BUD DEF ECN
Rep By: Robert H. Hurt, Frank Norton, William K. Takakoshi
Savannah Airport Commission
Issues: AVI DEF
Rep By: Robert H. Hurt, Frank Norton
Scientific Research Corp.
Issues: DEF
Rep By: Robert H. Hurt, Frank Norton
Sierra Military Health Services, Inc.
Issues: DEF
Rep By: Robert H. Hurt, Frank Norton, Helen C. Siracuse, William K. Takakoshi

Visiting Nurses Health System
Issues: HCR
Rep By: Robert H. Hurt, Frank Norton

Westinghouse Electric Co.
Issues: TRD
Rep By: Robert H. Hurt, Frank Norton, Katharine Calhoun Wood

Hyjek & Fix, Inc.

2100 Pennsylvania Ave. NW
Suite 560
Washington, DC 20037
Tel: (202)223-4800
Fax: (202)223-2011
Registered: LDA, FARA
E-mail: hyjekfix@hyjekfix.com
A federal marketing/government procurement lobbying firm.

DC-Area Employees Representing Listed Clients
FIX, Donald J., Partner
FIX, Michael W., Financial Director
HYJEK, Steven M., Partner
SCHECTER, Irene D., Senior Consultant
STEGENGA, Karl H., Director, Federal Marketing

Clients

BAE SYSTEMS North America
Issues: DEF
Rep By: Donald J. Fix, Steven M. Hyjek, Irene D. Schecter, Karl H. Stegenga

Bombardier Aerospace
Issues: DEF
Rep By: Donald J. Fix, Steven M. Hyjek

Gelco Government Services
Rep By: Donald J. Fix, Steven M. Hyjek

IT Group, Inc.
Rep By: Donald J. Fix, Steven M. Hyjek, Irene D. Schecter

Mobile Climate Control
Issues: DEF
Rep By: Donald J. Fix, Steven M. Hyjek

Niagara Area Chamber of Commerce
Issues: DEF
Rep By: Steven M. Hyjek, Irene D. Schecter, Karl H. Stegenga

Pilkington Thorn
Issues: DEF
Rep By: Steven M. Hyjek, Karl H. Stegenga

Shelby, Tennessee, County of
Issues: EDU GOV LAW
Rep By: Donald J. Fix, Steven M. Hyjek, Karl H. Stegenga

Shorts Missile Systems
Issues: DEF
Rep By: Steven M. Hyjek, Irene D. Schecter

U.S. Display Consortium
Issues: DEF
Rep By: Donald J. Fix, Steven M. Hyjek, Karl H. Stegenga

Hyman, Phelps & McNamara, P.C.

700 13th St. NW
Suite 1200
Washington, DC 20005
Tel: (202)737-5600
Fax: (202)737-9329
Registered: LDA
Web: www.hpm.com
A law firm specializing in food, drug and pharmaceutical matters before federal courts and government agencies and international regulatory authorities.

DC-Area Employees Representing Listed Clients
FARQUHAR, Douglas B., Partner
GIBBS, Jeffrey N., Partner
GILBERT, Jr., John A., Partner
PHELPS, James R., Partner
SIEGNER, Jr., A. Wes, Partner

Clients

Dietary Supplement Safety and Science Coalition
Issues: FOO
Rep By: A. Wes Siegner, Jr.

Hoffmann-La Roche Inc.
Issues: LAW
Rep By: John A. Gilbert, Jr.

Medeva Pharmaceuticals
Issues: MED
Rep By: Douglas B. Farquhar, John A. Gilbert, Jr., James R. Phelps

Ibex Internat'l, Inc.

1620 I St. NW
Suite 202
Washington, DC 20006
Tel: (202)452-8811
Fax: (202)659-5427
Registered: LDA, FARA

DC-Area Employees Representing Listed Clients
PAGONIS, George G., President

Clients

Chase Manhattan Bank
Rep By: George G. Pagonis

The Ickes & Enright Group

1300 Connecticut Ave. NW
Suite 600
Washington, DC 20036
Tel: (202)887-6726
Fax: (202)223-0358
Registered: LDA
E-mail: jenright@griffinjohnson.com
A government affairs consultanting firm.

DC-Area Employees Representing Listed Clients
ENRIGHT, Janice Ann, Partner
ICKES, Harold M., Partner

Clients

4C Foods Corp.
Issues: TRD
Rep By: Janice Ann Enright, Harold M. Ickes

American Federation of Teachers
Issues: BUD EDU
Rep By: Janice Ann Enright, Harold M. Ickes

Brooklyn Public Library
Issues: EDU
Rep By: Janice Ann Enright, Harold M. Ickes

Consortium for Worker Education
Issues: EDU LBR
Rep By: Janice Ann Enright, Harold M. Ickes

Deloitte Consulting
Issues: HCR
Rep By: Janice Ann Enright, Harold M. Ickes

Farallon Capital Management
Issues: FIN
Rep By: Janice Ann Enright, Harold M. Ickes

Greater New York Hospital Ass'n
Issues: BUD HCR MED
Rep By: Janice Ann Enright, Harold M. Ickes

HiSynergy Communications, Inc.
Issues: COM CPI MIA
Rep By: Janice Ann Enright, Harold M. Ickes

New York City, New York, Council of
Issues: EDU LBR TRA
Rep By: Janice Ann Enright, Harold M. Ickes

The New York Historical Soc.
Issues: EDU
Rep By: Janice Ann Enright, Harold M. Ickes

Service Employees Internat'l Union
Issues: BUD HCR IMM LBR MMM
Rep By: Janice Ann Enright, Harold M. Ickes

United Airlines
Issues: AVI
Rep By: Janice Ann Enright, Harold M. Ickes

Ietan Consulting

1300 Pennsylvania Ave. NW
Suite 600
Washington, DC 20005
Tel: (202)898-0875
A lobbying firm specializing in the representation of American Indian tribes.

DC-Area Employees Representing Listed Clients
PIPESTEM, Wilson
ROSENTHAL, Larry

Clients

Cabazon Band of Mission Indians
Rep By: Wilson Pipestem, Larry Rosenthal

Mashantucket Pequot Tribal Nation
Rep By: Wilson Pipestem, Larry Rosenthal

Oklahoma Indian Gaming Ass'n
Rep By: Wilson Pipestem, Larry Rosenthal

Frederick L. Ikenson, P.C.

1621 New Hampshire Ave. NW
Washington, DC 20009
Tel: (202)483-8900
Fax: (202)483-9368
Web: www.ikenson.com
E-mail: fikenson@ikenson.com

Clients

Cooper Tire and Rubber Co.
Rep By: Frederick L. Ikenson

GE Lighting Group
Rep By: Frederick L. Ikenson

General Electric Co.
Rep By: Frederick L. Ikenson

Hand Tools Institute
Rep By: Frederick L. Ikenson

Zenith Electronics Corp.
Rep By: Frederick L. Ikenson

Ikon Public Affairs

1101 30th St. NW
Suite 220
Washington, DC 20007
Tel: (202)337-6600
Fax: (202)337-6660
Registered: LDA

DC-Area Employees Representing Listed Clients
DEL PAPA, Dominic, Principal
STONE, Roger J., President
STUCKY, Edward J., Secretary/Treasurer

Clients

Argentina, The Secretary of Intelligence of

Committee for Good Common Sense
Issues: DEF TAX
Rep By: Edward J. Stucky

Cure Autism Now
Issues: HCR

Cytometrics, Inc.
Issues: HCR

Denver Children's Hospital
Issues: HCR
Rep By: Dominic Del Papa

Muhlenberg College
Issues: EDU

Piasecki Aircraft Corp.
Issues: DEF

RIM
Rep By: Dominic Del Papa

Tensiodyne Scientific Corp.
Issues: DEF

The Trump Organization
Issues: GAM
Rep By: Roger J. Stone

The ILEX Group

1173 Huntover Ct.
Suite 200
McLean, VA 22102
Tel: (703)356-8697
Fax: (703)356-4519
Registered: LDA
E-mail: bjilex@aol.com
A federal, state and local government relations and high tech business development consulting firm.

DC-Area Employees Representing Listed Clients
CANTUS, H. Hollister, President and Chief Exec. Officer

Clients

Applied Knowledge Group
Issues: CPI SCI
Rep By: H. Hollister Cantus

Digital Commerce Corp.
Issues: CPI GOV SMB TEC
Rep By: H. Hollister Cantus

European Aeronautics, Defence and Space, Inc.
Issues: AER AVI DEF
Rep By: H. Hollister Cantus

Net Results, Inc.
Issues: TEC UTI
Rep By: H. Hollister Cantus

Orbital Resources, LLC
Issues: AER COM TEC
Rep By: H. Hollister Cantus

Washington Infrastructure Services, Inc.
Issues: ROD RRR TRA
Rep By: H. Hollister Cantus

Impact Strategies

3927 Old Lee Hwy.
Suite 102
Fairfax, VA 22030
Tel: (703)503-4000
Registered: LDA
E-mail: impctstrat@aol.com
Provides corporate communications, government affairs, and political consulting services.

DC-Area Employees Representing Listed Clients
DOYLE, Shannon, Legislative Director
FEDORCHAK, Jeff, President

Clients

R. R. Donnelley & Sons
Issues: GOV HCR POS SCI
Rep By: Shannon Doyle, Jeff Fedorchak

Environmental Commonsense Coalition
Issues: BUD CAW ENV RES
Rep By: Shannon Doyle, Jeff Fedorchak

Placer County Water Agency
Issues: BUD ENV
Rep By: Jeff Fedorchak

South Tahoe Public Utility District
Issues: BUD CAW ENV

The Tekamah Corp.
Issues: DEF
Rep By: Jeff Fedorchak

The Timken Co.
Issues: HCR LBR TRD UTI
Rep By: Shannon Doyle, Jeff Fedorchak

IMPACT, LLC

1250 24th St. NW
Suite 350
Washington, DC 20037
Tel: (202)776-7740
Fax: (202)776-7741
Registered: FARA

E-mail: tarim@erols.com
A communications consulting and public relations firm.

DC-Area Employees Representing Listed Clients
TUNCATA-TARIMCILAR, Arzu, Managing Member

Clients

Turkey, Government of the Republic of

Turkish Industrialists and Businessmen's Ass'n (TUSIAD)
Issues: ECN FOR FUE TOU TRD
Rep By: Arzu Tuncata-Tarimcilar

Infotech Strategies, Inc.

1341 G St. NW
Suite 1100
Washington, DC 20005
Web: www.itstrategies.com
Tel: (202)393-2260
Fax: (202)393-0712
Registered: LDA

DC-Area Employees Representing Listed Clients
ANDREWS, Nicole, Account Supervisor
BARRON, Katie M., Senior Director, Communications
BERNHARDT, Pamela Fandel, V. President, Finance
CUMMINGS, Marc D., Director, E-Government and E-Business
GREESON, Jennifer, Director, Communications
KAY, Kenneth R., Chairman
KENNY, John, President
MAGGI, Philip, Coalition Policy Director
MORGAN, Moya G., Director, Coalition
QUILLAN, Mary
RAFFETTO, John K., Senior V. President, Public Relations
RODI, `Katherine G., Coalition Director

Clients

CEO Forum on Education and Technology
Issues: EDU
Rep By: Kenneth R. Kay

Computer Coalition for Responsible Exports
Issues: CPI TRD
Rep By: Jennifer Greeson, Kenneth R. Kay, Philip Maggi

Computer Systems Policy Project
Issues: GOV TRD
Rep By: Jennifer Greeson, Kenneth R. Kay, Philip Maggi, Moya G. Morgan

Infrastructure Management Group

4733 Bethesda Ave.
Suite 600
Bethesda, MD 20814
Tel: (301)907-2900
Fax: (301)907-2906
Advises on development, finance and operation of public-use infrastructure.

DC-Area Employees Representing Listed Clients
WHEELER, Porter K., Director, Transportation Policy and Economics

Clients

Canton Railroad Co.
Issues: RRR TRA
Rep By: Porter K. Wheeler

I-49 Roadbuilders Coalition
Issues: ROD
Rep By: Porter K. Wheeler

Institute for Certified Investment Management Consultants
Issues: FIN
Rep By: Porter K. Wheeler

Investment Program Ass'n
Issues: FIN
Rep By: Porter K. Wheeler

Money Management Institute
Issues: FIN
Rep By: Porter K. Wheeler

Edwin T. C. Ing

2121 K St. NW
Suite 800
Washington, DC 20037
Tel: (202)457-6630
Fax: (202)293-0027
Registered: LDA

Clients

Hawaiian Electric Co.
Rep By: Edwin T. C. Ing

Kamehameha Schools
Rep By: Edwin T. C. Ing

United States Windpower, Inc.
Rep By: Edwin T. C. Ing

Institutional Development Associates

1079 Old Cedar Rd.
McLean, VA 22102
Tel: (703)827-5932
Fax: (703)448-6983
Registered: FARA
E-mail: idajal@aol.com
A management consulting and support services firm specializing in international program management.

DC-Area Employees Representing Listed Clients
LUCAS, Jr., John A., President

Clients

Saudi Arabia, Royal Embassy of
Rep By: John A. Lucas, Jr.

Institutional Labor Advisors

1497 Chain Bridge Rd.
Suite 300
McLean, VA 22101
E-mail: mbarnes@ilalaw.com
Tel: (703)893-7071
Fax: (703)893-8020
Registered: LDA

DC-Area Employees Representing Listed Clients
COWEN, William B., Member of Firm
GREEN, Merritt J., Associate
OSSI, Gregory J., Associate
SMITH, David S., Member of Firm
STURNER, Jan W., Associate

Clients

Coal Act Fairness Alliance
Issues: TAX
Rep By: Merritt J. Green, Gregory J. Ossi, David S. Smith, Jan W. Sturner

Freeman United Coal Mining Co.
Issues: TAX
Rep By: Merritt J. Green, Gregory J. Ossi, David S. Smith, Jan W. Sturner

Retiree Benefits Alliance
Issues: TAX
Rep By: William B. Cowen, Merritt J. Green, Gregory J. Ossi, David S. Smith, Jan W. Sturner

Integrated Strategies/Strategic Communications

426 C St. NE
Washington, DC 20002
E-mail: BFFreed@att.net
Tel: (202)544-1880
Fax: (202)543-2565
A strategic public affairs and planning firm.

DC-Area Employees Representing Listed Clients
FREED, Bruce F., Principal
MERKOWITZ, David R., Principal

Inter-Associates, Inc.

1801 N. Hartford St.
Arlington, VA 22201-5206
Tel: (703)522-4995
Registered: LDA
E-mail: wwerst@interassociates.ioffice.com
An association management firm.

DC-Area Employees Representing Listed Clients
WERST, Jr., William H., President

Clients

Vacuum Insulation Ass'n
Issues: ENG FOO MED
Rep By: William H. Werst, Jr.

Interface Inc.

8403 Arlington Blvd.
Suite 100
Fairfax, VA 22031
Web: www.interfacinc.com
E-mail: dknapp@interfacinc.com
Tel: (703)876-6800
Fax: (703)876-0515
Provides sales and marketing support to clients represented in their dealings with federal government agencies.

DC-Area Employees Representing Listed Clients
KNAPP, David C., President
NESSEL, Rudy R., Chief Exec. Officer
ROSENBAUM, III, Albert B., Government Representative
WALSH, Brian, Secretary
WILLIAMS, Robert G., V. President

Clients

Airguard Industries
Rep By: Robert G. Williams

Bacharach
Rep By: David C. Knapp

Church and Dwight ArmaKleen
Rep By: David C. Knapp

Diebold, Inc.
Rep By: Albert B. Rosenbaum, III

Douglas Battery
Rep By: Albert B. Rosenbaum, III

Ecology and Environment
Rep By: Rudy R. Nessel

EO Tech
Rep By: Albert B. Rosenbaum, III

Everpure
Rep By: Robert G. Williams

Foamex
Rep By: David C. Knapp

General Cable Industries, Inc.
Rep By: Robert G. Williams

Heil Trucks
Rep By: Albert B. Rosenbaum, III

Hunter Ceiling Fans
Rep By: David C. Knapp

Lifeline
Rep By: Albert B. Rosenbaum, III

Maytag Corp.
Rep By: Robert G. Williams

Pressure Island
Rep By: David C. Knapp

QuikWater
Rep By: Albert B. Rosenbaum, III

Reckitt Benckiser Professional
Rep By: Rudy R. Nessel

Rheem Water Heaters
Rep By: Robert G. Williams

Safety-Kleen Corp.
Rep By: David C. Knapp, Brian Walsh

Scot Pump
Rep By: Robert G. Williams

USF Surface Preparation
Rep By: David C. Knapp, Robert G. Williams

Weld-It Trucks
Rep By: Albert B. Rosenbaum, III

Internat'l Advisory Services Group Ltd.

1707 L St. NW
Suite 725
Washington, DC 20036
Web: www.iasworldtrade.com
E-mail: iasg@erols.com
Tel: (202)296-6625
Fax: (202)659-3904
Registered: LDA
A trade, investment and political counseling firm.

DC-Area Employees Representing Listed Clients
BLUM, Charles H., President

Clients

European Confederation of Iron and Steel Industries (EUROFER)
Issues: TRD
Rep By: Charles H. Blum

Steel Service Center Institute
Issues: TRD
Rep By: Charles H. Blum

Internat'l Business and Economic Research Corp.

1317 F St. NW
Third Floor
Washington, DC 20004
Web: www.iberc.com
E-mail: staff@iberc.com
Tel: (202)955-6155
Fax: (202)955-5786
Registered: FARA

DC-Area Employees Representing Listed Clients
HANEY, Mark, President

Clients

Footwear Distributors and Retailers of America

Nat'l Retail Federation

Toy Manufacturers of America

Internat'l Business-Government Counsellors, Inc.

818 Connecticut Ave. NW
Suite 1200
Washington, DC 20006
Web: www.ibgc.com
Tel: (202)872-8181
Fax: (202)872-8696
Registered: LDA
An international government relations consulting firm established in 1972.

DC-Area Employees Representing Listed Clients
ELWELL, Robert G., V. President and Special Advisor
FROMYER, Mary O., V. President
MCDERMID, John F., President and Chief Operating Officer
REGAN, James, Senior V. President
SPIELMANN, Solveig Bjorke, Chairman/Chief Exec. Officer

Clients

ANSAC
Issues: TRD
Rep By: John F. McDermid

Campbell Soup Co.
Rep By: John F. McDermid

ConAgra Foods, Inc.
Issues: TRD
Rep By: John F. McDermid

Herbalife Internat'l, Inc.
Issues: TRD
Rep By: John F. McDermid

PepsiCo, Inc.
Rep By: John F. McDermid

Polaroid Corp.
Issues: TRD
Rep By: John F. McDermid

The Procter & Gamble Company
Issues: TRD
Rep By: John F. McDermid

Internat'l Capital Strategies

1450 G St. NW
Suite 210
Washington, DC 20005
Tel: (202)383-0090
Fax: (202)383-0093
Registered: LDA

A consulting firm.

DC-Area Employees Representing Listed Clients
SIMMONS, Audrea, Government Relations
WILLIAMS, Hon. Lyle, V. President

Clients

PPL

Internat'l Registries, Inc.

11495 Commerce Park Dr.
Reston, VA 20191-1507
Tel: (703)620-4880
Fax: (703)476-8522
Registered: LDA, FARA
Web: www.register-iri.com
E-mail: info@register-iri.com

DC-Area Employees Representing Listed Clients
CAMP, Larry E.

Clients

Marshall Islands, Republic of the
Rep By: Larry E. Camp

Mark S. Israel

1620 I St. NW
Suite 300
Washington, DC 20006
Tel: (202)429-0160
Fax: (202)293-3109
E-mail: misrael@elinkisp.com

DC-Area Employees Representing Listed Clients
GOODMAN, Joni, Legislative Analyst
ISRAEL, Mark S.

Clients

Hemet, California, City of
Riverside Community College
Riverside Unified School District
San Jacinto, California, City of

Issue Dynamics Inc.

919 18th St. NW
Tenth Floor
Washington, DC 20006
Tel: (202)263-2900
Fax: (202)263-2960
Registered: LDA
Web: www.idi.net
E-mail: info@idi.net

A consumer affairs consulting firm specializing in coalition building, grassroots organizing, public affairs and public relations on the Internet, and association management.

DC-Area Employees Representing Listed Clients
CRAWLEY, Penny, Senior Consultant, Grassroots Organizing Team
DEUTSCH, Kenneth, Senior V. President
GONZALES, Bridget, Senior Consultant
HARGRAVES, Dirck, Senior Consultant
HOWELL, Chandler, Assistant V. President
HULL, Bob, Assistant V. President
MANUAL, Cleo A., Senior Consultant
NORDHEIMER, Jennifer, Senior Consultant
ROSENTHAL, Sylvia, V. President
SIMON, Samuel A., President
SINOWAY, Linda, Senior Consultant

Clients

Alliance for Public Technology
American Telemedicine Ass'n
Bell Atlantic Internet Solutions
CapWeb
Consumers First
Democratic Senatorial Campaign Committee
Maryland Ass'n of the Deaf
Metricom, Inc.
New York State Democratic Committee
South Africa, Embassy of the Republic of
Verizon Communications
World Institute on Disability

Issues Management Ass'n

1390 Chain Bridge Rd.
Suite 47
McLean, VA 22102
Tel: (703)448-6989
Fax: (703)448-3323
Registered: LDA
E-mail: Sdries@erols.com

Specializes in multi-faced lobbying campaigns, building and mobilizing grassroots, forming and managing coalitions and developing public relations programs.

DC-Area Employees Representing Listed Clients
DRIESLER, Marty, V. President
DRIESLER, Stephen D., President

IssueSphere

1100 Connecticut Ave. NW
12th Floor
Washington, DC 20036
Tel: (202)452-6500
Fax: (202)452-6502

A public affairs firm focusing on the health sciences. Headquartered in New York, NY.

DC-Area Employees Representing Listed Clients
DELPONTE, Paul, Partner
SANDMAN, Jeffrey M., Managing Partner

Clients

Bristol-Myers Squibb Co.
The Commonwealth Fund
Internat'l Bottled Water Ass'n
Kaiser Family Foundation

Ivins, Phillips & Barker

1700 Pennsylvania Ave. NW
Suite 600
Washington, DC 20006
Tel: (202)393-7600
Fax: (202)393-7601
Registered: LDA
Web: www.ipbtax.com
E-mail: IPB@mindspring.com

A law firm specializing in tax law, employee benefits, estate planning and related litigation.

DC-Area Employees Representing Listed Clients
BARKER, Rosina B., Associate
DUNN, Jr., H. Stewart, Partner
FOX, Eric R., Partner
GRANWELL, Alan, Partner
KEENAN, Laurie E., Partner
O'BRIEN, Kevin P., Partner
SCHNEIDER, Mr. Leslie J., Partner
SMITH, Patrick J., Partner
SURINGA, Dirk J. J., Associate

Clients

Allegheny Ludlum Corp.
Rep By: Mr. Leslie J. Schneider, Patrick J. Smith

Bass Hotels and Resorts, Inc.
Issues: TAX
Rep By: Eric R. Fox, Alan Granwell, Dirk J. J. Suringa

Family Co. Group

Teledyne, Inc.

J/T Group

2555 M St. NW
Suite 327
Washington, DC 20037
Tel: (202)223-3352
Registered: LDA

DC-Area Employees Representing Listed Clients
JULIANO, Robert E., Co-Chairman
TINER, Michael L., Co-Chairman

Clients

AFL-CIO - Food and Allied Service Trades Department

Coalition for Group Legal Services
Rep By: Robert E. Juliano

Internat'l Speedway Corp.
Rep By: Robert E. Juliano

University Village Ass'n/Near West Side Conservation Community Council
Rep By: Robert E. Juliano

James & Hoffman, P.C.

1146 19th St. NW
Suite 600
Washington, DC 20036
Tel: (202)496-0500
Fax: (202)496-0555
Registered: LDA
Web: www.jamhoff.com

A law firm specializing in labor issues.

DC-Area Employees Representing Listed Clients
JAMES, Edgar N., Partner
KRIEGER, Kathy L., Partner
SCOTT, Judith, Partner
VOGT, Jeffrey S., Associate

Clients

Federal Law Enforcement Officers Ass'n
Issues: LAW

Jamison and Sullivan, Inc.

306 Constitution Ave. NE
Washington, DC 20002
Tel: (202)546-9060
Fax: (202)546-9160
Registered: LDA, FARA

DC-Area Employees Representing Listed Clients
JAMISON, Delos Cy, Chairman
SULLIVAN, Jay R., President

Clients

Ass'n of O & C Counties
Issues: RES
Rep By: Delos Cy Jamison, Jay R. Sullivan

Ass'n of Oregon Counties
Issues: NAT
Rep By: Delos Cy Jamison, Jay R. Sullivan

Counterpart Internat'l
Rep By: Delos Cy Jamison, Jay R. Sullivan

Douglas, Oregon, County of
Issues: NAT
Rep By: Delos Cy Jamison, Jay R. Sullivan

FANCOR
Rep By: Jay R. Sullivan

The Fanning Corp.
Issues: AGR
Rep By: Delos Cy Jamison, Jay R. Sullivan

Flight Landata, Inc.
Issues: AER AGR DEF ENV NAT WAS
Rep By: Delos Cy Jamison, Jay R. Sullivan

Greystar Resources, Ltd.
Issues: FOR NAT
Rep By: Delos Cy Jamison, Jay R. Sullivan

Internat'l Utility Efficiency Partnerships (IUEP)
Issues: ENV
Rep By: Delos Cy Jamison, Jay R. Sullivan

D. R. Johnson Lumber
Issues: NAT TAX
Rep By: Delos Cy Jamison, Jay R. Sullivan

Malheur Timber Operators
Rep By: Delos Cy Jamison, Jay R. Sullivan

Money Tree, Inc.
Issues: BAN

Polk County, Oregon
Issues: TRA

Prairie Wood Products
Rep By: Delos Cy Jamison, Jay R. Sullivan

Santa Clarita, California, City of
Issues: GOV NAT

Touch America
Issues: TEC

Umatilla Irrigation Districts Coordinating Committee

Umatilla Water Users
Rep By: Delos Cy Jamison, Jay R. Sullivan

Upper Klamath Water Users
Issues: IND NAT
Rep By: Delos Cy Jamison, Jay R. Sullivan

Janus-Merritt Strategies, L.L.C.

1133 21st St. NW
Suite 700
Washington, DC 20036
Tel: (202)887-6900
Fax: (202)887-6970
Registered: LDA
Web: www.janus-merritt.com

Specializes in strategic political counseling and positioning for international and domestic clients on a global basis.

DC-Area Employees Representing Listed Clients
ABIDOS, Christy, Office Manager, Assistant Managing Partner
BRIERTON, Thomas W., Principal
COURTNEY, Kurt, Assistant, Research Director
GUZIK, John
HOFFMAN, Scott P., Principal
NASHASHIBI, Omar, Director, Research
NOBLE, Bethany, Principal, Campaign Finance Director
ROBERTSON, Mark J., Managing Partner
ROESING, William P., Strategic Counsel
WALSH, J. Daniel, Principal

Clients

AFIN Securities
Issues: BAN
Rep By: Scott P. Hoffman, Bethany Noble, Mark J. Robertson, J. Daniel Walsh

American Business for Legal Immigration
Issues: IMM
Rep By: Scott P. Hoffman, Bethany Noble

Banorte Casa de Bolsa
Issues: BAN FOR
Rep By: Scott P. Hoffman, Mark J. Robertson, J. Daniel Walsh

C.A. Vencemos
Issues: ENV ROD TRD
Rep By: Mark J. Robertson

Camara Nacional de la Industria Pesquera
Issues: NAT TRD
Rep By: Scott P. Hoffman, Mark J. Robertson, J. Daniel Walsh

Camara Nacional de las Industrias Azucarera y Alcoholera
Issues: TRD
Rep By: Scott P. Hoffman, Mark J. Robertson, J. Daniel Walsh

CDM Fantasy Sports
Issues: CPI
Rep By: Scott P. Hoffman

Cemento Bayano
Issues: ENV ROD TRD
Rep By: Mark J. Robertson

Cementos Monterrey, S.A.
Issues: ENV ROD TRD
Rep By: Mark J. Robertson, J. Daniel Walsh

CEMEX Central, S.A. de C.V.
Issues: ENV FOR ROD TRD
Rep By: Scott P. Hoffman, Bethany Noble, Mark J. Robertson, J. Daniel Walsh

CEMEX USA
Issues: ENV FOR ROD TRD
Rep By: Mark J. Robertson

Corporacion Valenciana de Cementos Portland, S.A.
Issues: ENV ROD TRD
Rep By: Mark J. Robertson, J. Daniel Walsh

Corporacion Venezolana de Cementos, SACA
Issues: ENV ROD TRD
Rep By: Mark J. Robertson, J. Daniel Walsh

COVAD Communications Co.
Issues: TEC
Rep By: Scott P. Hoffman, Mark J. Robertson, J. Daniel Walsh

DSL Access Telecommunications Ass'n (DATA)
Issues: TEC
Rep By: Scott P. Hoffman, Mark J. Robertson, J. Daniel Walsh

EchoStar Communications Corp.
Issues: COM TEC
Rep By: Scott P. Hoffman, Bethany Noble, Mark J. Robertson, J. Daniel Walsh

Fannie Mae
Issues: FIN HOU
Rep By: John Guzik, Scott P. Hoffman, Mark J. Robertson

First Amendment Coalition for Expression
Issues: CIV COM CON GOV MIA REL TAX TEC
Rep By: Scott P. Hoffman, Bethany Noble

Fraternal Order of Police (U.S. Park Police Labor Committee)
Issues: BUD LAW
Rep By: Scott P. Hoffman, Mark J. Robertson, J. Daniel Walsh

Free ANWAR Campaign
Issues: FOR
Rep By: Scott P. Hoffman, Omar Nashashibi, Mark J. Robertson

Fundacion para la Preservacion de Flora y Fauna Marina
Issues: ENV NAT
Rep By: Mark J. Robertson, J. Daniel Walsh

Grupo Carrousel (Mexico)
Issues: FIN TRD
Rep By: Mark J. Robertson

Grupo Empresarial Maya
Issues: ENV ROD TRD
Rep By: Mark J. Robertson

Grupo Financiero Banorte
Issues: FOR
Rep By: Scott P. Hoffman, Mark J. Robertson, J. Daniel Walsh

Grupo Maseca
Issues: FOR TRD
Rep By: Mark J. Robertson, J. Daniel Walsh

Gulf Coast Portland Cement Co.
Issues: ENV ROD TRD
Rep By: Mark J. Robertson

HarvardNet, Inc.
Issues: TEC
Rep By: Scott P. Hoffman, Mark J. Robertson, J. Daniel Walsh

Houston Shell and Concrete
Issues: ENV ROD TRD
Rep By: Mark J. Robertson, J. Daniel Walsh

Interactive Gaming Council
Issues: COM CPI GAM TEC
Rep By: Scott P. Hoffman, Bethany Noble, Mark J. Robertson, J. Daniel Walsh

Interactive Services Ass'n
Rep By: Scott P. Hoffman, Bethany Noble

Islamic Institute
Issues: FOR

Mexam Trade, Inc.
Issues: ENV ROD TRD
Rep By: Mark J. Robertson

Mexican Crab Industry
Issues: FOR NAT TRD
Rep By: Mark J. Robertson

Mexican Nat'l Spiny Lobster Industry
Issues: FOR NAT TRD
Rep By: Mark J. Robertson

Napster, Inc.
Issues: LAW TEC
Rep By: Thomas W. Brierton, John Guzik, Scott P. Hoffman, Mark J. Robertson, J. Daniel Walsh

Nat'l Indian Gaming Ass'n
Issues: GAM TAX
Rep By: Scott P. Hoffman, Bethany Noble, Mark J. Robertson, J. Daniel Walsh

Pacific Coast Cement
Issues: ENV ROD TRD
Rep By: Mark J. Robertson, J. Daniel Walsh

PINSA, S.A de CD
Issues: ENV TRD
Rep By: Mark J. Robertson

Pretium S.C (Mexico)
Issues: ECN FOR TRD
Rep By: Mark J. Robertson

Rhythms NetConnections
Issues: TEC
Rep By: Scott P. Hoffman, Mark J. Robertson, J. Daniel Walsh

Scribe Communications, Inc.
Issues: BAN FOR TAX
Rep By: Scott P. Hoffman, Bethany Noble, Mark J. Robertson, J. Daniel Walsh

Secured Access Portals, Inc.
Issues: CSP
Rep By: Scott P. Hoffman, Bethany Noble, Mark J. Robertson

Sunbelt Cement
Issues: ENV ROD TRD
Rep By: Mark J. Robertson, J. Daniel Walsh

Szlavik, Hogan & Miller
Rep By: Bethany Noble

Tolmex
Issues: ENV ROD TRD
Rep By: Mark J. Robertson

Viejas Band of Kumeyaay Indians
Issues: GAM IND
Rep By: Thomas W. Brierton, Scott P. Hoffman, Omar Nashashibi, Bethany Noble, Mark J. Robertson, J. Daniel Walsh

Vivendi Universal
Issues: ADV ART BEV CPT TAX
Rep By: Scott P. Hoffman, Bethany Noble, Mark J. Robertson, J. Daniel Walsh

Jar-Mon Consultants, Inc.

208 N. Patrick St.
Alexandria, VA 22314
Tel: (703)548-4904
Fax: (703)548-1424
Registered: LDA
E-mail: jarmoninc@aol.com

DC-Area Employees Representing Listed Clients
JARMIN, Gary L., President
JARMIN, Gina, Senior V. President

Clients

American Federation of Senior Citizens
Issues: BUD HCR IMM INS MMM RET TAX
Rep By: Gina Jarmin

Christian Voice, Inc.
Issues: CIV CPI EDU FAM FOR HCR MMM REL RET WEL

Jarboe & Associates

711 Tenth St. SE
Washington, DC 20003
Tel: (202)547-7064
Registered: LDA

DC-Area Employees Representing Listed Clients
JARBOE, Kenan Patrick

Clients

Fontheim Internat'l
Issues: ECN LBR MAN SCI TRD URB
Rep By: Kenan Patrick Jarboe

JBC Internat'l

1620 I St. NW
Suite 615
Washington, DC 20006
Tel: (202)463-8493
Fax: (202)463-8497
Registered: LDA
Web: www.jbcinternational.com
E-mail: jbc@moinc.com

A trade consultancy providing strategic counsel, monitoring and advocacy services on trade issues to corporations, businesses and trade associations seeking opportunities in the global marketplace. Provides services to clients on a broad range of commercial issues.

Political Action Committee
JBC Internat'l Trade Development PAC
1620 I St. NW
Suite 615
Washington, DC 20006
Tel: (202)463-8493
Fax: (202)463-8497
Contact: Jason B. Clawson

DC-Area Employees Representing Listed Clients
ATKINSON, Alan R., Trade Analyst
BOONE, Jeannie M., Exec. Administrator
CARR, Courtenay, Trade Analyst
CLAWSON, James B., Chief Exec. Officer
CLAWSON, Jason B., President and Chief of Staff
EADS, Michael, V. President
LANIER, Robin W.
MATTINGLEY, Jr., George M. "Matt", V. President, Government Affairs

Clients

Allen-Bradley
Issues: TRD
Rep By: James B. Clawson, George M. "Matt" Mattingley, Jr.

The BOSE Corp.
Issues: TRD
Rep By: James B. Clawson, George M. "Matt" Mattingley, Jr.

California Ass'n of Winegrape Growers
Issues: TRD
Rep By: Jeannie M. Boone, James B. Clawson

Coalition for Intellectual Property Rights (CIPR)
Issues: TRD
Rep By: Courtenay Carr, James B. Clawson

DIAGEO
Issues: BEV FOO TRD
Rep By: Jeannie M. Boone, James B. Clawson

Internat'l Mass Retailers Ass'n
Issues: APP AUT BEV CPI FOO MAN TEC TRD
Rep By: Robin W. Lanier

Joint Industry Group (JIG)
Rep By: Alan R. Atkinson, James B. Clawson, Jason B. Clawson

Meridian Worldwide
Issues: TRD
Rep By: James B. Clawson, George M. "Matt" Mattingley, Jr.

UDV/Heublein, Inc.
Issues: TRD
Rep By: Jeannie M. Boone, James B. Clawson

Uniroyal Chemical Co., Inc.
Issues: TRD
Rep By: James B. Clawson, Michael Eads, George M. "Matt" Mattingley, Jr.

Wine Institute
Issues: TRD
Rep By: Jeannie M. Boone, James B. Clawson, George M. "Matt" Mattingley, Jr.

JCP Associates

444 N. Capitol St. NW
Suite 841
Washington, DC 20001
Tel: (202)638-2000
Fax: (202)638-4584
Registered: LDA
E-mail: jpirius@bellatlantic.net

DC-Area Employees Representing Listed Clients
PIRIUS, James C.

Clients

Florida State University System
Issues: DEF DIS ECN EDU HCR IMM MAR MED SCI TEC TRA
Rep By: James C. Pirius

University of South Florida Research Foundation
Issues: DIS EDU HCR MAR MED
Rep By: James C. Pirius

Youth Guidance of Chicago
Issues: EDU
Rep By: James C. Pirius

Jefferson Consulting Group

1401 K St. NW
Suite 900
Washington, DC 20005
Tel: (202)626-8550
Fax: (202)626-8578
Registered: LDA
Web: www.jeffersonconsulting.com

DC-Area Employees Representing Listed Clients
BEEBE, Cora, V. President
BURMAN, Allan V., President, Jefferson Solutions, LLC
CHESCAVAGE, Dorsey, Director
CONRAD, Kathy P., V. President
KELLY, Ross, V. President
MCNAMARA, Angela V., V. President
NAVALON, Jose, V. President
SUSMAN, Julia T., President and Chief Exec. Officer
THOMPSON, Robert J., Chairman
WRIGHT, Joseph, V. Chairman

Clients

Apple Computer, Inc.
Issues: CPI
Rep By: Kathy P. Conrad, Robert J. Thompson

First Consulting Group
Issues: HCR MMM
Rep By: Dorsey Chescavage, Kathy P. Conrad, Julia T. Susman

Franklin Covey
Rep By: Cora Beebe, Dorsey Chescavage, Kathy P. Conrad

Golden Rule Insurance Co.
Issues: HCR INS MMM
Rep By: Robert J. Thompson

Human Capital Resources
Issues: EDU
Rep By: Robert J. Thompson

M.D. - I.P.A.
Issues: HCR MMM
Rep By: Dorsey Chescavage, Angela V. McNamara, Robert J. Thompson

Managed Care Solutions
Issues: HCR VET
Rep By: Julia T. Susman

Mitsubishi Electric Automation
Rep By: Robert J. Thompson

Nuclear Energy Institute
Rep By: Robert J. Thompson

Servo Corp. of America
Issues: TRD
Rep By: Robert J. Thompson

Stone Investments, Inc.
Issues: CPI CPT GAM HCR IND LAW
Rep By: Robert J. Thompson

Jefferson Government Relations, L.L.C.

1615 L St. NW
Suite 650
Washington, DC 20036
Tel: (202)626-8500
Fax: (202)626-8593
Registered: LDA
Web: www.jeffersongr.com
E-mail: info@jeffersongr.com

A bipartisan, independent government relations firm providing strategic counsel and advocacy on state, federal and international legislative and regulatory affairs to corporate, association, university, government and not-for-profit clients. Practice areas include trade and international relations. Practice issue areas include agriculture, colleges and universities, corporate support, counties and municipalities, customs, e-commerce, energy/utility, environment, financial, food quality, health care, housing, Indian tribes, international trade, medical products, privacy issues, public health, tax, telecommunications, transportation, workplace safety and health.

DC-Area Employees Representing Listed Clients

CUPPERNULL, Carolyn M., Principal and Chief Administrative Officer
DESSER, John D., V. President
DONNELLY, Jr., Thomas R., Principal and V. Chairman
DOUGLASS, Hugh M., V. President and Chief Financial Officer
GILMARTIN, William J., V. President
GREENBERG, Mark S., V. President
KRAUSER, Katherine M., Director
MCARVER, Jr., Robert D., V. President
MILNE, John D., V. President
MORIN, Jeanne L., Principal
POWER, Patricia A., V. President
RASMUSSEN, Erik, Director
RATCHFORD, Hon. William R.
ROBERTS, William A., Principal
SCHUMACHER, Randal P., Chairman and Principal
SHEEHAN, Daniel J., Director

Clients

ABB Daimler-Benz Transportation, N.A. (ADTRANZ)
Issues: BUD TRA
Rep By: William A. Roberts

ADTranz (Daimler Chrysler Rail Systems)
Issues: TRA
Rep By: William A. Roberts

AFL-CIO Housing Investment Trust
Issues: HOU
Rep By: William J. Gilmartin

An Achievable Dream, Inc.
Issues: EDU
Rep By: Mark S. Greenberg, William A. Roberts

Aurora, Colorado, City of
Issues: DEF ENV
Rep By: Mark S. Greenberg, William A. Roberts

Bass Hotels and Resorts, Inc.
Issues: CPT HCR LBR TAX TOU TRA UTI
Rep By: John D. Desser, Thomas R. Donnelly, Jr., Katherine M. Krauser, Jeanne L. Morin, Daniel J. Sheehan

Bethune-Cookman College
Issues: EDU
Rep By: William J. Gilmartin, William A. Roberts

Bowling Transportation
Issues: TRA
Rep By: Randal P. Schumacher

Carlsberg Management Co.
Issues: BUD GOV HOU RES
Rep By: William J. Gilmartin, William A. Roberts, Daniel J. Sheehan

Children's Hospital Medical Center Foundation

Christopher Newport University
Issues: EDU
Rep By: Mark S. Greenberg, William A. Roberts

Computer Intelligence 2
Issues: AVI CPI GOV TEC
Rep By: William A. Roberts

Cummins-Allison Corp.
Issues: BAN CPT FIN MAN TRD
Rep By: John D. Desser, Thomas R. Donnelly, Jr., Erik Rasmussen

Dallas Area Rapid Transit Authority
Issues: BUD TRA
Rep By: William A. Roberts

Daytona Beach, City of
Issues: BUD GOV HOU RES
Rep By: William J. Gilmartin, William A. Roberts

Edison Welding Institute
Issues: DEF
Rep By: William J. Gilmartin, Katherine M. Krauser

eHealth Insurance Services, Inc.
Issues: CPI HCR TEC
Rep By: John D. Desser, Thomas R. Donnelly, Jr., Erik Rasmussen

Embry-Riddle Aeronautical University
Issues: AVI BUD EDU
Rep By: William A. Roberts

Engineered Arresting Systems Corp.
Issues: AER AVI MAN SCI TRA

Ergodyne
Issues: LBR
Rep By: Robert D. McArver, Jr., Randal P. Schumacher

EV Rental Cars, LLC
Issues: AUT BUD ENV TRA
Rep By: William A. Roberts

Greater Orlando Aviation Authority
Issues: AVI BUD TRA
Rep By: William A. Roberts, Daniel J. Sheehan

Iredell Memorial Hospital
Issues: MMM
Rep By: John D. Desser, Thomas R. Donnelly, Jr.

JDA Aviation Technology Systems
Issues: AVI MAN SCI TRA
Rep By: William A. Roberts, Daniel J. Sheehan

Lafarge Corp.
Issues: LBR
Rep By: Robert D. McArver, Jr., Randal P. Schumacher

Minnesota Mining and Manufacturing Co. (3M Co.)
Issues: ENV ROD
Rep By: Robert D. McArver, Jr., Randal P. Schumacher

NAHB Research Center
Issues: HOU
Rep By: William J. Gilmartin

Nat'l Ass'n of Home Builders Research Center, Inc.
Issues: GOV HOU
Rep By: William J. Gilmartin

Nat'l Industries for the Blind
Issues: BUD EDU GOV LBR
Rep By: Thomas R. Donnelly, Jr., Jeanne L. Morin

Nat'l Quality Health Council
Issues: HCR MMM
Rep By: John D. Desser, Thomas R. Donnelly, Jr.

Seminole Tribe of Indians of Florida
Issues: BUD ENV GAM IND TAX
Rep By: Jeanne L. Morin, Patricia A. Power, William A. Roberts

University of Miami
Issues: EDU
Rep By: William A. Roberts

Vinyl Institute
Issues: CHM CSP HCR
Rep By: Thomas R. Donnelly, Jr., Robert D. McArver, Jr., Patricia A. Power, Randal P. Schumacher

Visalia, California, City of
Issues: GOV ROD TRD
Rep By: William A. Roberts, Daniel J. Sheehan

Volusia, Florida, County of
Issues: AVI BUD NAT TRA
Rep By: Patricia A. Power, William A. Roberts, Daniel J. Sheehan

Westmoreland Coal Co.
Issues: ENV NAT UTI
Rep By: Thomas R. Donnelly, Jr., Katherine M. Krauser, Randal P. Schumacher, Daniel J. Sheehan

Jefferson-Waterman Internat'l, LLC

1401 K St. NW
Tenth Floor
Washington, DC 20005
Tel: (202)216-2200
Fax: (202)216-2999
Registered: LDA, FARA

An international business consulting and government relations firm.

DC-Area Employees Representing Listed Clients

CALLWOOD, Kevin, Exec. V. President
CARPINELLI, Stephen, Director
HOSKINSON, Samuel M., Exec. V. President
KLASS, USAF (Ret.), Col. Richard L., Senior V. President
MERKEL, Claire Sechler, European Consultant
O'NEILL, Daniel J., Senior V. President
WATERMAN, Charles E., Chief Exec. Officer
WROBLESKI, Ann B., Chief Operating Officer
WYMAN, Jr., Samuel H., Exec. V. President
YATES, Kenneth A., Senior V. President

Clients

Alenia Marconi Systems
Issues: AER DEF
Rep By: Col. Richard L. Klass, USAF (Ret.)

AmLib United Minerals
Rep By: Charles E. Waterman

Bulgaria, Ministry of Foreign Affairs of the Republic of
Rep By: Samuel M. Hoskinson

Chevron Chemical Co., LLC
Issues: TRD
Rep By: Samuel M. Hoskinson

ComInternational Management Inc.
Issues: FOR
Rep By: Samuel H. Wyman, Jr.

Edison Mission Energy
Issues: FOR TRD
Rep By: Ann B. Wrobleski

GPU, Inc.
Issues: TRD
Rep By: Ann B. Wrobleski

Jamaica, Government of
Rep By: Ann B. Wrobleski

Japan External Trade Organization (JETRO)
Rep By: Daniel J. O'Neill

Matsushita Electric Corp. of America

Matsushita Electric Industrial Co., Ltd.
Issues: TRD
Rep By: Daniel J. O'Neill

Sithe Energies
Rep By: Ann B. Wrobleski

Sumitomo Corp. of America
Issues: TRD
Rep By: Daniel J. O'Neill

Vietnam Veterans of America Foundation
Issues: FOR
Rep By: Col. Richard L. Klass, USAF (Ret.)

Western Wireless Internat'l
Issues: FOR TRD
Rep By: Ann B. Wrobleski

Jellinek, Schwartz & Connolly

1525 Wilson Blvd.
Suite 600
Arlington, VA 22209
Tel: (703)527-1670
Fax: (703)527-5477
Registered: LDA, FARA

A consulting firm specializing in environmental science policy and management.

DC-Area Employees Representing Listed Clients

BRILL, II, Richard Budd, Research Assistant
GRAY, Edward C.
JELLINEK, Steven D., Chairman
PFIFFERLING, Sueanne, V. President
SCHWARTZ, Jeffrey H., V. President

Clients

FQPA Implementation Working Group
Issues: AGR CHM ENV FOO SCI
Rep By: Edward C. Gray

Japan Automobile Manufacturers Ass'n

Linda Jenckes & Associates

510 11th St. SE
Washington, DC 20003
Tel: (202)547-3887
Fax: (202)547-3330
Registered: LDA
E-mail: ljenckes@kesslerassoc.com

DC-Area Employees Representing Listed Clients

JENCKES, Linda, President

Clients

Henry H. Kessler Foundation
Issues: MED MMM
Rep By: Linda Jenckes

Kessler Medical Rehabilitation Research & Education Corp.
Issues: MMM

Jenkens & Gilchrist

1919 Pennsylvania Ave. NW
Suite 600
Washington, DC 20006-3404
Tel: (202)326-1500
Fax: (202)326-1555
Registered: LDA
Web: www.jenkens.com
A law firm.

DC-Area Employees Representing Listed Clients
BARNES, Donald M., Managing Shareholder
MALASKY, Alan R., Shareholder
MITCHELL, John T., Partner
ONDECK, Christopher, Associate, Federal Practice
ROMANO, Salvatore, Shareholder
RUGGIO, Michael, Partner

Clients

American Amusement Machine Ass'n
Rep By: Donald M. Barnes

American Film Marketing Ass'n
Rep By: John T. Mitchell

Nat'l Ass'n of Recording Merchandisers
Issues: ART CON CSP LAW
Rep By: John T. Mitchell

Jenner & Block

601 13th St. NW
12th Floor
Washington, DC 20005
Tel: (202)639-6000
Fax: (202)639-6066
Registered: LDA
Washington office of a Chicago general practice law firm.

DC-Area Employees Representing Listed Clients
NADLER, Carl S., Partner
PORTMAN, Robert M., Partner

Clients

American Ass'n of Electrodiagnostic Medicine

American Board of Pain Medicine

American Booksellers Ass'n

American College of Emergency Physicians
Rep By: Robert M. Portman

American College of Healthcare Executives

American Film Marketing Ass'n

American Library Ass'n

American Psychological Ass'n

American Soc. of Cataract and Refractive Surgery
Issues: MMM
Rep By: Robert M. Portman

Building Owners and Managers Ass'n Internat'l

Coin Laundry Ass'n

CTAM

Dental Gold Institute

Edenspace Systems Corp.

Human Factors Soc.

Mailing & Fulfillment Services Ass'n

Million Dollar Roundtable

NACHA - The Electronic Payments Ass'n

Nat'l Ass'n of Insurance and Financial Advisors
Issues: BAN INS

Nat'l Ass'n of Recording Merchandisers

Nat'l Board of Examiners in Optometry

Nat'l Coalition of Petroleum Dry Cleaners
Rep By: Robert M. Portman

Nat'l Retail Federation

Nat'l Soc. to Prevent Blindness

Soc. of American Florists

JFS Group, Ltd.

1666 K St. NW
Fifth Floor
Washington, DC 20006
Tel: (202)887-1427
Fax: (202)466-3215
Registered: LDA
E-mail: jakeseher@aol.com

DC-Area Employees Representing Listed Clients
SEHER, Jake, Principal

Clients

Aircraft Services Group
Issues: AVI GOV

Factiva
Issues: GOV

R. J. Reynolds Tobacco Co.
Issues: TAX TOB
Rep By: Jake Seher

TD Waterhouse Group
Issues: FIN

JGW Internat'l Ltd.

10640 Main St.
Suite 200
Fairfax, VA 22030
Tel: (703)352-3400
Fax: (703)385-6470
Registered: LDA
Web: www.jgwintl.com

DC-Area Employees Representing Listed Clients
GABRIEL, USAF (Ret.), Gen. Charles A.
O'NEIL, John M., V. President
SCHANTZ, Jeffery A., Associate
WILSON, Andrew M., President
WILSON, John G., Chairman/Chief Exec. Officer

Clients

GEC-Marconi Defense Systems Ltd.
Rep By: Andrew M. Wilson, John G. Wilson

Graseby Plc
Rep By: John M. O'Neil, Andrew M. Wilson, John G. Wilson

Per Udsen
Rep By: Andrew M. Wilson, John G. Wilson

JKB Communications

738 Ninth St. SE
Washington, DC 20003
Tel: (202)546-3452
Registered: LDA
A government relations and publications management consulting firm.

DC-Area Employees Representing Listed Clients
BYNUM, Judith Kloss, Owner

Clients

Academy of General Dentistry
Issues: BUD HCR LBR
Rep By: Judith Kloss Bynum

JMD Associates, Inc.

4600 N. Park Ave.
Suite 101
Chevy Chase, MD 20815
Tel: (301)654-8316
Fax: (301)654-8336
Registered: LDA
E-mail: dbjmdassoc@aol.com
Government relations and public affairs counseling firm.

DC-Area Employees Representing Listed Clients
BUSHNELL, David, Managing Director

Clients

Engelhard Corp.
Issues: CAW MAR
Rep By: David Bushnell

Parents for Public Schools
Rep By: David Bushnell

Law Offices of Mark S. Joffe

1800 K St. NW
Suite 720
Washington, DC 20006
Tel: (202)457-6633
Fax: (202)457-6636
Registered: LDA

DC-Area Employees Representing Listed Clients
BACK, Kelli D., Attorney
JOFFE, Mark S.

Clients

Medicare Cost Contractors Alliance
Issues: GOV HCR MMM
Rep By: Kelli D. Back

Mary P. Johannes

1350 I St. NW
Suite 1060
Washington, DC 20005
Tel: (202)962-5384
Fax: (202)336-7223
Registered: LDA

Clients

Ford Motor Credit Co. (Legal Department)
Issues: BNK FIN SCI
Rep By: Mary P. Johannes

Sue E. Johnson Associates

1090 Vermont Ave NW
Eighth Floor
Washington, DC 20005
Tel: (202)408-7038
Fax: (202)408-0948
Registered: LDA
E-mail: sjassocs@erols.com

DC-Area Employees Representing Listed Clients
JOHNSON, Susan E., Exec. Director

Clients

Council of Urban and Economic Development
Rep By: Susan E. Johnson

First Nationwide Bank
Rep By: Susan E. Johnson

Real Estate Services Providers Council
Issues: BAN
Rep By: Susan E. Johnson

Johnson Co.

1275 Pennsylvania Ave. NW
Tenth Floor
Washington, DC 20004
Tel: (202)347-1434
Fax: (202)347-1534
Registered: LDA

DC-Area Employees Representing Listed Clients
ARMISTEAD, Rex
JOHNSON, James H., Principal

Clients

Baker & Hostetler LLP
Issues: COM CPI MMM TEC

Coffee Reserve
Issues: TAX TRD
Rep By: James H. Johnson

DATRON, Inc.
Issues: HCR MMM
Rep By: Rex Armistead, James H. Johnson

Flexi-Van Leasing
Issues: TAX

Hattiesburg, Mississippi, City of
Issues: ECN ROD RRR TOU TRA URB
Rep By: James H. Johnson

KFx, Inc.
Issues: FIN FUE

Kongsberg Defense & Aerospace
Issues: DEF
Rep By: James H. Johnson

Lockheed Martin Global Telecommunications
Issues: TEC

Potomac Electric Power Co.
Issues: COM ENG UTI

SCANA Corp.
Issues: COM ENG TAX

Johnson, Rogers & Clifton, L.L.P.

Watergate Office Bldg.
Suite 508
2600 Virginia Ave. NW
Washington, DC 20037
Tel: (202)337-8400
Fax: (202)337-3462
Registered: LDA, FARA

DC-Area Employees Representing Listed Clients
JOHNSON, II, Robert W.

Clients

American Nonwovens Corp.

Boundary Healthcare Products Corp.

Central Romana Corp.

Delta Comercio, S.A.

Dominican Ass'n of Industrial Free Zones (ADOZONA)

Dominican State Sugar Council (CEA)

Dominicana de Aviacion

Impex Overseas

Internat'l Sugar Policy Coordinating Commission of the Dominican Republic

MEI Corp.

Noble Transoceanic Corp.

Simark Trading Co., Inc.

Skytruck, Inc.

Tri Nat'l Aviation

Johnston & Associates, LLC

The Willard Office Bldg.
1455 Pennsylvania Ave. NW,
Suite 200
Washington, DC 20004
Tel: (202)737-0683
Fax: (202)737-0693
Registered: LDA
A consulting and lobbying practice.

DC-Area Employees Representing Listed Clients
FLINT, Alex, Partner
JOHNSTON, Hon. J. Bennett, Partner
JOHNSTON, N. Hunter, Partner
JONES, W. Proctor, Partner
SMITH, Gregory A., Partner
TOBER, Eric, Partner

Clients

Aiken and Edgenfield Counties, South Carolina, Economic Development Partnership of
Issues: BUD DEF ECN ENG ENV SCI
Rep By: Hon. J. Bennett Johnston, N. Hunter Johnston, W. Proctor Jones, Eric Tober

Alliance for Competitive Electricity
Issues: ENG TAX UTI
Rep By: Hon. J. Bennett Johnston, N. Hunter Johnston, Eric Tober

Avondale Industries, Inc.
Issues: BUD DEF
Rep By: Hon. J. Bennett Johnston, N. Hunter Johnston, Eric Tober

Battelle Memorial Institute
Issues: BUD ENG SCI
Rep By: Hon. J. Bennett Johnston, W. Proctor Jones

Burns and Roe Enterprises, Inc.
Issues: BUD DEF ENG GOV
Rep By: Hon. J. Bennett Johnston, W. Proctor Jones

California, State of
Rep By: Hon. J. Bennett Johnston

COGEMA, Inc.
Issues: BUD ENG SCI
Rep By: Hon. J. Bennett Johnston, N. Hunter Johnston, W. Proctor Jones, Eric Tober

Coushatta Tribe of Louisiana
Issues: BUD ECN GAM HOU IND TAX TOU
Rep By: Hon. J. Bennett Johnston, N. Hunter Johnston, W. Proctor Jones, Eric Tober

Edison Internat'l
Issues: BUD ENG ENV GOV SCI TAX UTI
Rep By: Hon. J. Bennett Johnston, N. Hunter Johnston, Eric Tober

EG&G
Issues: ENG
Rep By: Alex Flint, Hon. J. Bennett Johnston, W. Proctor Jones

Enron Corp.
Issues: ENG
Rep By: Hon. J. Bennett Johnston

The Ickes & Enright Group
Issues: BUD
Rep By: Hon. J. Bennett Johnston, N. Hunter Johnston, W. Proctor Jones

Jefferson Parish Council
Issues: BUD ECN ENG ENV TRA URB
Rep By: Hon. J. Bennett Johnston, N. Hunter Johnston, W. Proctor Jones, Eric Tober

Minnesota Valley Alfalfa Producers
Issues: BUD ENG
Rep By: W. Proctor Jones

Morgan, Lewis & Bockius LLP
Issues: ENG
Rep By: Alex Flint, Hon. J. Bennett Johnston, W. Proctor Jones

MTS Systems Inc.
Issues: BUD DEF
Rep By: Hon. J. Bennett Johnston, W. Proctor Jones, Eric Tober

New Orleans Internat'l Airport
Issues: AVI BUD TRA
Rep By: Hon. J. Bennett Johnston, N. Hunter Johnston, W. Proctor Jones, Eric Tober

New Orleans, Louisiana, Regional Transit Authority of
Issues: TRA
Rep By: Hon. J. Bennett Johnston, N. Hunter Johnston, Eric Tober

Northrop Grumman Corp.
Issues: BUD DEF
Rep By: Hon. J. Bennett Johnston, N. Hunter Johnston, W. Proctor Jones, Eric Tober

Nuclear Energy Institute
Issues: BUD ENG GOV
Rep By: Hon. J. Bennett Johnston, N. Hunter Johnston, W. Proctor Jones, Eric Tober

Oregon, State of
Rep By: Hon. J. Bennett Johnston

Regional Planning Commission
Issues: AGR AVI BUD ECN ROD TRA
Rep By: N. Hunter Johnston, W. Proctor Jones, Eric Tober

Regional Transit Authority
Issues: BUD TRA
Rep By: Hon. J. Bennett Johnston, N. Hunter Johnston, Eric Tober

Riverdeep Inc.
Issues: BUD EDU
Rep By: Alex Flint, Hon. J. Bennett Johnston, N. Hunter Johnston, W. Proctor Jones, Eric Tober

Sewerage and Water Board of New Orleans
Issues: BUD CAW HOU URB
Rep By: N. Hunter Johnston, W. Proctor Jones, Eric Tober

Tulane University
Issues: BUD ENG ENV HOU TRA URB
Rep By: Hon. J. Bennett Johnston, N. Hunter Johnston, W. Proctor Jones, Eric Tober

Tunica Biloxi Indians of Louisiana
Issues: BUD ECN ENV GAM HOU IND TAX TOU
Rep By: Hon. J. Bennett Johnston, N. Hunter Johnston, W. Proctor Jones, Eric Tober

United Gamefowl Breeders Ass'n, Inc.
Issues: AGR
Rep By: Hon. J. Bennett Johnston, Eric Tober

University of New Orleans
Issues: BUD ENV
Rep By: Hon. J. Bennett Johnston, N. Hunter Johnston, W. Proctor Jones, Eric Tober

University of Southwestern Louisiana
Issues: AGR APP BUD EDU ENG ENV GOV NAT SCI
Rep By: Hon. J. Bennett Johnston, N. Hunter Johnston, Eric Tober

USEC, Inc.
Issues: ENG
Rep By: Alex Flint, Hon. J. Bennett Johnston, W. Proctor Jones

Washington, State of
Rep By: Hon. J. Bennett Johnston

Westinghouse Government Services Group
Issues: BUD ENV
Rep By: Alex Flint, W. Proctor Jones

Xcel Energy, Inc.
Issues: BUD ENG
Rep By: Alex Flint, Hon. J. Bennett Johnston, W. Proctor Jones

Philip W. Johnston Associates

1330 New Hampshire Ave. NW
Suite 122
Washington, DC 20036
Tel: (202)659-8008
Fax: (202)659-8519
Registered: LDA

A health and human services consulting firm headquartered in Boston, MA.

DC-Area Employees Representing Listed Clients
JOHNSTON, Philip W., President
WARSCHOFF, Merrill E., Policy Director

Clients

Dimock Community Health Center
Issues: BUD
Rep By: Philip W. Johnston, Merrill E. Warschoff

Holyoke Hospital
Issues: HCR MMM
Rep By: Philip W. Johnston, Merrill E. Warschoff

Nat'l Ass'n of Community Health Centers
Rep By: Philip W. Johnston, Merrill E. Warschoff

Springfield, Massachusetts, City of
Issues: BUD HCR
Rep By: Philip W. Johnston, Merrill E. Warschoff

Jolly/Rissler, Inc.

818 Connecticut Ave. NW
Tenth Floor
Washington, DC 20006
E-mail: jris@jollyrissler.com
Tel: (202)293-3330
Fax: (202)293-3515
Registered: LDA

DC-Area Employees Representing Listed Clients
JOLLY, Thomas R., Chairman
RISSLER, Patricia F., President

Clients

AFLAC, Inc.
Issues: BAN BUD FIN HCR INS MMM TAX TRD
Rep By: Thomas R. Jolly, Patricia F. Rissler

CNA Insurance Cos.
Issues: AGR BAN BUD CPI CSP DIS ENV FIN GOV HCR HOU INS LBR MMM TAX TOB WAS
Rep By: Thomas R. Jolly, Patricia F. Rissler

Internat'l Union of Police Ass'ns
Issues: LBR
Rep By: Thomas R. Jolly, Patricia F. Rissler

Sallie Mae, Inc.
Issues: BUD EDU
Rep By: Thomas R. Jolly, Patricia F. Rissler

Jones, Day, Reavis & Pogue

51 Louisiana Ave. NW
Washington, DC 20001
Tel: (202)879-3939
Fax: (202)626-1700
Registered: LDA, FARA

Web: www.jonesday.com
E-mail: counsel@jonesday.com
Washington office of a Cleveland-based general practice law firm.

DC-Area Employees Representing Listed Clients
BRADFIELD, Michael, Partner
BROGEN, Stephen
BROOKS, Teresa A., Partner
BROWN, Robert M., Government Affairs Representative
HANSELL, Herbert J., Senior Counsel
MCDERMOTT, Robert F., Partner
O'HARA, James T., Partner
ROSE, Jonathan C., Partner
SIMS, Joe, Partner
WIACEK, Raymond J., Partner
WILDEROTTER, James A., Partner

Clients

AOL Time Warner
Rep By: Joe Sims

China, Embassy of the People's Republic of
Rep By: Herbert J. Hansell

The Coal Coalition
Issues: TAX
Rep By: Jonathan C. Rose

Pfizer, Inc.
Rep By: Raymond J. Wiacek

Sakura Bank Ltd.
Rep By: Michael Bradfield

Systematics

TCI

Trinity Health
Issues: HCR
Rep By: Teresa A. Brooks

Jones, Walker, Waechter, Poitevent, Carrere & Denegre, L.L.P.

499 S. Capitol St. SW
Suite 600
Washington, DC 20003
Tel: (202)828-8363
Fax: (202)828-6907
Registered: LDA, FARA

Web: www.joneswalker.com
A general practice law firm specializing in government representation.

DC-Area Employees Representing Listed Clients
CAMBON, Paul, Director of Government Affairs
JASKOT, John J., Of Counsel
JOHNSEN, R. Christian, Managing Partner
OGSBURY, James, Special Counsel

Clients

ACS Government Solutions Group
Issues: BUD CPI DEF
Rep By: Paul Cambon, John J. Jaskot, R. Christian Johnsen, James Ogsbury

American Ass'n of Nurse Anesthetists
Issues: BUD HCR
Rep By: Paul Cambon, John J. Jaskot, R. Christian Johnsen

The Audubon Institute
Issues: BUD
Rep By: Paul Cambon, John J. Jaskot, R. Christian Johnsen

Avondale Industries, Inc.
Issues: DEF MAR
Rep By: Paul Cambon, John J. Jaskot, R. Christian Johnsen

Bailey Link
Issues: BUD CPI DEF
Rep By: Paul Cambon, John J. Jaskot, R. Christian Johnsen

Baton Rouge, Louisiana, City of
Issues: AVI BUD URB
Rep By: Paul Cambon, John J. Jaskot, R. Christian Johnsen, James Ogsbury

Boys Town USA
Issues: BUD
Rep By: Paul Cambon, John J. Jaskot, R. Christian Johnsen, James Ogsbury

Broward, Florida, County of
Issues: BUD TRD
Rep By: Paul Cambon, John J. Jaskot, R. Christian Johnsen, James Ogsbury

Burk-Kleinpeter, Inc.
Issues: BUD CAW URB
Rep By: Paul Cambon, John J. Jaskot, R. Christian Johnsen

Canal Barge Co., Inc.
Issues: MAR
Rep By: John J. Jaskot, R. Christian Johnsen

Columbus General, L.L.C.
Issues: CPI DEF
Rep By: Paul Cambon, John J. Jaskot, R. Christian Johnsen

Committee of Unsecured Creditors
Issues: BNK BUD
Rep By: Paul Cambon, John J. Jaskot, R. Christian Johnsen, James Ogsbury

General Category Tuna Ass'n
Issues: MAR
Rep By: Paul Cambon, John J. Jaskot, R. Christian Johnsen, James Ogsbury

General Electric Co.
Issues: BUD CAW ENV NAT TAX WAS
Rep By: Paul Cambon, John J. Jaskot, R. Christian Johnsen, James Ogsbury

Ingram Barge Company
Issues: MAR
Rep By: Paul Cambon, John J. Jaskot, R. Christian Johnsen

Internat'l Shipholding Corp.
Issues: BUD MAR
Rep By: John J. Jaskot, R. Christian Johnsen

Internat'l Technology Resources, Inc.
Issues: BUD CPI DEF
Rep By: Paul Cambon, John J. Jaskot, R. Christian Johnsen

Jacobus Tenbroek Memorial Fund
Issues: BUD MMM TAX
Rep By: Paul Cambon, John J. Jaskot, R. Christian Johnsen, James Ogsbury

JRL Enterprises
Issues: CPI EDU
Rep By: Paul Cambon, John J. Jaskot, R. Christian Johnsen

LA Center for the Blind
Issues: BUD
Rep By: Paul Cambon, John J. Jaskot, R. Christian Johnsen

Lockheed Martin Global Telecommunications
Issues: DEF TEC
Rep By: Paul Cambon, John J. Jaskot, R. Christian Johnsen

Louisiana Superdome
Issues: TRA
Rep By: John J. Jaskot, R. Christian Johnsen

Martinez and Curtis
Issues: BUD ENG
Rep By: Paul Cambon, John J. Jaskot, R. Christian Johnsen, James Ogsbury

Mechanical Equipment Co., Inc.
Issues: DEF
Rep By: John J. Jaskot, R. Christian Johnsen

Mesa, Arizona, City of
Issues: BUD
Rep By: Paul Cambon, John J. Jaskot, R. Christian Johnsen, James Ogsbury

The MetroVision Chamber
Issues: DEF
Rep By: John J. Jaskot, R. Christian Johnsen

New Orleans, Louisiana, Port of
Issues: BUD DEF MAR TRA
Rep By: John J. Jaskot, R. Christian Johnsen

Oracle Corp.
Issues: CPI
Rep By: Paul Cambon, John J. Jaskot, R. Christian Johnsen

Petroleum Helicopters
Issues: AVI TAX
Rep By: John J. Jaskot, R. Christian Johnsen

Raytheon Co.
Issues: BUD DEF
Rep By: Paul Cambon, John J. Jaskot, R. Christian Johnsen, James Ogsbury

Science & Engineering Associates, Inc.
Issues: BUD DEF SCI
Rep By: Paul Cambon, John J. Jaskot, R. Christian Johnsen

Sewerage and Water Board of New Orleans
Issues: BUD CAW
Rep By: Paul Cambon, John J. Jaskot, R. Christian Johnsen

St. Gabriel, Louisiana, Town of
Issues: BUD
Rep By: John J. Jaskot, R. Christian Johnsen

Stewart Enterprises, Inc.
Issues: CSP
Rep By: Paul Cambon, John J. Jaskot, R. Christian Johnsen, James Ogsbury

TransOceanic Shipping
Issues: TRA
Rep By: John J. Jaskot, R. Christian Johnsen

Tulane University
Issues: BUD EDU
Rep By: Paul Cambon, John J. Jaskot, R. Christian Johnsen

Turkey, Government of the Republic of

United Special Transport Air Resources, LLC (USTAR)
Issues: AVI DEF TRA
Rep By: Paul Cambon, John J. Jaskot, R. Christian Johnsen

University of New Orleans Foundation
Issues: BUD EDU
Rep By: Paul Cambon, John J. Jaskot, R. Christian Johnsen

Jordan & Associates, Inc.

1401 K St. NW
Suite 700
Washington, DC 20005
E-mail: pjordan757@aol.com
Tel: (202)842-5030
Fax: (202)842-5048
Registered: LDA

A government affairs consulting firm.

DC-Area Employees Representing Listed Clients
JORDAN, Patricia, President

Clients

Livermore Amador Valley Transit Ass'n
Issues: TRA
Rep By: Patricia Jordan

Livermore, California, City of
Issues: AVI CAW TRA
Rep By: Patricia Jordan

Provo, Utah, City of
Issues: AVI ECN TRA URB UTI
Rep By: Patricia Jordan

South Salt Lake, Utah, City of
Issues: URB
Rep By: Patricia Jordan

Jorden Burt LLP

1025 Thomas Jefferson St. NW
Suite 400 East
Washington, DC 20007-0805
Web: www.jordenburtusa.com
Tel: (202)965-8100
Fax: (202)965-6403
Registered: LDA

DC-Area Employees Representing Listed Clients
BRANCH, Patricia, Legislative Coordinator
DILLON, Alanna, Legislative Coordinator
GETTLEMAN, Marna, Assistant Director, Grant Services
HAAKER, Ryan, Director of Administration and Special Projects
KUTNIK, Marc, Grant Services Specialist
THOMPSON, Marilyn Berry, Principal and Head, Government Relations Department
TIDMAN, Rebecca, Director, Federal Grants and Information Services
TURNER, Marion, Legislative Coordinator

Clients

American Museum of Natural History
Issues: AER ALC ANI ART AVI BUD CPT DEF EDU ENG FOR HCR IMM IND MAR MED MMM SCI TAX TEC URB VET
Rep By: Patricia Branch, Alanna Dillon, Marna Gettleman, Marilyn Berry Thompson, Rebecca Tidman

Assurant Group
Issues: BAN DIS ENV FIN HOU INS LAW TAX UTI
Rep By: Patricia Branch, Marna Gettleman, Marilyn Berry Thompson, Rebecca Tidman, Marion Turner

Atlantic Health Systems
Rep By: Patricia Branch, Alanna Dillon, Marna Gettleman, Marilyn Berry Thompson, Rebecca Tidman

The Colonial Williamsburg Foundation
Rep By: Patricia Branch, Alanna Dillon, Marna Gettleman, Marilyn Berry Thompson, Rebecca Tidman

Florida State University System
Issues: AER ALC ANI ART AVI BUD CPT DEF EDU ENG ENV FOR HCR IMM MAR MED MMM SCI TAX TEC URB VET
Rep By: Patricia Branch, Alanna Dillon, Marna Gettleman, Marilyn Berry Thompson, Rebecca Tidman

Gainesville Regional Utilities
Issues: UTI
Rep By: Patricia Branch, Alanna Dillon, Marna Gettleman, Marilyn Berry Thompson, Rebecca Tidman

Gainesville, Florida, City of
Issues: ALC ART AVI BUD CAW ECN EDU ENV GAM HCR HOU IMM LAW LBR MMM NAT POS ROD TAX TEC TRA URB WAS WEL
Rep By: Patricia Branch, Marna Gettleman, Marilyn Berry Thompson, Rebecca Tidman, Marion Turner

Lovelace Respiratory Research Institute
Issues: AER ALC ANI ART AVI BUD CPT DEF EDU ENG ENV FOR HCR IMM MAR MED MMM SCI TAX TEC URB VET
Rep By: Patricia Branch, Alanna Dillon, Marna Gettleman, Marilyn Berry Thompson, Rebecca Tidman

Miami Beach, Florida, City of
Issues: ALC ART AVI BUD CAW ECN EDU ENV GAM HCR HOU IMM LAW LBR MMM NAT POS ROD TAX TEC TRA URB WAS WEL
Rep By: Patricia Branch, Marna Gettleman, Marilyn Berry Thompson, Rebecca Tidman, Marion Turner

New York University
Issues: AER ALC ANI ART AVI BUD CPT DEF EDU ENG ENV FOR HCR IMM MAR MED MMM SCI TAX TEC URB VET
Rep By: Patricia Branch, Alanna Dillon, Marna Gettleman, Marilyn Berry Thompson, Rebecca Tidman

Newark, New Jersey, City of
Issues: ALC ART AVI BUD CAW ECN EDU ENV GAM HCR HOU IMM LAW LBR MMM NAT POS ROD TAX TEC TRA URB WAS WEL
Rep By: Patricia Branch, Marna Gettleman, Marilyn Berry Thompson, Rebecca Tidman

Southeastern Universities Research Ass'n

University Health System of New Jersey

University of Medicine and Dentistry of New Jersey
Issues: AER ALC ANI ART AVI BUD CPT DEF EDU ENG ENV FOR HCR IMM MAR MED MMM SCI TAX TEC URB VET
Rep By: Patricia Branch, Alanna Dillon, Marna Gettleman, Marilyn Berry Thompson, Rebecca Tidman

University of Miami
Issues: AER ALC ANI ART AVI BUD CPT DEF ECN EDU ENG ENV FOR HCR IMM MAR MED MMM SCI TAX TEC URB VET
Rep By: Alanna Dillon, Marna Gettleman, Marilyn Berry Thompson, Rebecca Tidman

University of Tulsa
Issues: AER ALC ANI ART AVI BUD CPT DEF EDU ENG ENV FOR HCR IMM MAR MED MMM SCI TAX TEC URB VET
Rep By: Patricia Branch, Alanna Dillon, Marna Gettleman, Marilyn Berry Thompson, Rebecca Tidman

University of Virginia
Issues: AER ALC ANI ART AVI BUD CPT DEF ECN EDU ENG ENV FOR HCR IMM MAR MED MMM SCI TAX TEC URB VET
Rep By: Patricia Branch, Alanna Dillon, Marna Gettleman, Marilyn Berry Thompson, Rebecca Tidman

UNUM/Provident Corp.

JSA-I, Inc.

1133 Connecticut Ave. NW
Suite 1010
Washington, DC 20036
Tel: (202)775-2360
Fax: (202)775-2364
Registered: LDA

DC-Area Employees Representing Listed Clients
AUTRY, John S., President and Chief Exec. Officer
BARKER, William B., Senior Associate

Clients

Newhall Land and Farming Co.
Issues: TRA
Rep By: John S. Autry, William B. Barker

Robert E. Juliano Associates

2555 M St. NW
Suite 327
Washington, DC 20037
Tel: (202)223-3352
Registered: LDA

DC-Area Employees Representing Listed Clients
JULIANO, Robert E., Chairman

Clients

AFL-CIO - Food and Allied Service Trades Department

Hotel Employees and Restaurant Employees Internat'l Union
Issues: ENV LBR TAX TOB TOU

Kalik Lewin

5247 Wisconsin Ave. NW
Suite Five
Washington, DC 20015
E-mail: rkalik@kaliklewin.com
Tel: (202)537-2290
Fax: (202)537-2291
Registered: LDA

DC-Area Employees Representing Listed Clients
KALIK, Robert G., Partner

Clients

American Vintners Ass'n
Rep By: Robert G. Kalik

American Wine Heritage Alliance
Issues: TAX TRD
Rep By: Robert G. Kalik

Citrosuco North America, Inc.
Issues: TRD
Rep By: Robert G. Kalik

The Kamber Group

1920 L St. NW
Washington, DC 20036
Web: www.kamber.com
E-mail: dc@kamber.com
Tel: (202)223-8700
Fax: (202)659-5559
Registered: LDA

Political Action Committee
Kamber Group PAC (TKG PAC)
1920 L St. NW
Washington, DC 20036
Contact: Victor S. Kamber
Tel: (202)223-8700
Fax: (202)659-5559

DC-Area Employees Representing Listed Clients
BENNETT, Kimberly, Senior Account Exec.
CUMMINS, James, V. President, Senior Producer
ERLING, Christina, Exec. Assistant to the President
GREENWALT, Pamela, Senior V. President and Director, Media Production
JOHNSON, Steven A., V. President
KAMBER, Victor S., President, Chief Exec. Officer and Chairman of the Board
LAFONTAINE, Paul, Chief Financial Officer
MACKELL, Jr., Thomas, Exec. V. President and Senior Counselor
MCCLURE, Donovan, Senior V. President
MCDONALD, Gavin, V. President
OWENS, Dedra, Senior Account Executive
REICH, Sheara, Assistant Account Executive
RICHARDSON, Jeff, Staff Assistant
SCHUKER, Jill A., Managing Director, International Operations and Global Strategy Division
SHAPIRO, Joe, Staff Assistant

Clients

Amalgamated Transit Union
Rep By: Pamela Greenwalt, Victor S. Kamber

Bristol-Myers Squibb Co.
Rep By: Jill A. Schuker

Communications Workers of America
Rep By: Donovan McClure

D.C. Lottery
Rep By: Kimberly Bennett

Internat'l Longshoremen's Ass'n
Rep By: Pamela Greenwalt

Internat'l Union of Painters and Allied Trades
Rep By: Victor S. Kamber, Gavin McDonald

Laborers' Internat'l Union of North America
Rep By: Pamela Greenwalt, Victor S. Kamber
Nat'l Energy Management Institute
Rep By: Christina Erling, Jeff Richardson
North American Communications Corp.
Issues: BAN BUD CSP LAW
Rep By: Victor S. Kamber, Gavin McDonald
Retail, Wholesale and Department Store Workers Union
Rep By: Gavin McDonald
Sheet Metal Workers' Internat'l Ass'n
Rep By: Steven A. Johnson, Victor S. Kamber

Kambrod Associates Ltd.

1800 N. Kent St.
Suite 907
Arlington, VA 22209
Tel: (703)416-1401
Fax: (703)418-3649
Registered: LDA

DC-Area Employees Representing Listed Clients
KAMBROD, Mathew R., President

Clients
Microvision, Inc.
Issues: DEF
Rep By: Mathew R. Kambrod

Law Offices of James L. Kane

1315 Vincent Place
McLean, VA 22101
Tel: (703)790-5287
Registered: LDA
Legislative and marketing representation for architecture/engineering firms before Federal agencies and the U.S. Congress.

DC-Area Employees Representing Listed Clients
KANE, Jr., James L., Attorney

Clients
The Smith, Korach, Hayet, Haynie Partnership
Issues: DEF VET
Rep By: James L. Kane, Jr.

Betty Ann Kane & Co.

118 Fifth St. NE
Washington, DC 20002
Tel: (202)546-9062
Fax: (202)547-9598
Registered: LDA
E-mail: bettyannkane@sprintmail.com
Provides government relations and resource development for associations, businesses and local governments.

DC-Area Employees Representing Listed Clients
KANE, Betty Ann, President

Clients
DC Land Title Ass'n
Issues: DOC TAX
Rep By: Betty Ann Kane
Laredo, Texas, City of
Issues: BUD COM ECN ENV HOU ROD TRA TRD
Rep By: Betty Ann Kane
NCRIC, Inc.
Issues: DOC INS
Rep By: Betty Ann Kane
Sprint Corp.
Issues: DOC TEC
Rep By: Betty Ann Kane
Tort Reform Institute
Issues: DOC TOR
Rep By: Betty Ann Kane

Kanner & Associates

122 C St. NW
Suite 500
Washington, DC 20001
Tel: (202)347-6625
Fax: (202)347-6605
Registered: LDA
Web: www.kannerandassoc.com
E-mail: office@kannerandassoc.com
A consulting firm specializing in energy and environmental issues.

DC-Area Employees Representing Listed Clients
KANNER, Martin B., President

Clients
Eugene Water and Electric Board
Issues: ENG
Rep By: Martin B. Kanner
Idaho Energy Authority, Inc.
Issues: ENG
Rep By: Martin B. Kanner
Missouri River Energy Services
Issues: ENG
Rep By: Martin B. Kanner
Northern California Power Agency
Issues: ENG
Rep By: Martin B. Kanner
Ohio Municipal Electric Ass'n
Issues: ENG
Rep By: Martin B. Kanner
Oregon Utility Resource Coordination Ass'n (OURCA)
Issues: ENG NAT UTI
Rep By: Martin B. Kanner
Public Power Council
Issues: ENG
Rep By: Martin B. Kanner

Karalekas & Noone

1211 Connecticut Ave. NW
Suite 302
Washington, DC 20036
Tel: (202)466-7330
Fax: (202)955-5879
Registered: LDA, FARA
Web: www.kn1211.com
A law firm specializing in legislative law and lobbying, government relations, and administrative law.

DC-Area Employees Representing Listed Clients
KARALEKAS, S. Steven, Partner
NOONE, James A., Partner

Clients
American Retirees Ass'n
Issues: VET
Rep By: S. Steven Karalekas, James A. Noone
Johns Hopkins University & Hospital
Rep By: James A. Noone
Johns Hopkins University-Applied Physics Lab
Issues: DEF
Rep By: S. Steven Karalekas, James A. Noone

Kasten & Co.

888 16th St. NW
Suite 700
Washington, DC 20006
Tel: (202)223-9151
Fax: (202)223-9814
Registered: LDA
Web: www.kastenco.com

DC-Area Employees Representing Listed Clients
KASTEN, Jr., Robert W., President
RUTH, Frederick A., V. President

Clients
Information Practices Coalition of Washington, D.C.
Issues: GOV
Rep By: Robert W. Kasten, Jr., Frederick A. Ruth
Newsbank, Inc.
Issues: GOV MIA
Rep By: Robert W. Kasten, Jr., Frederick A. Ruth

Katten Muchin & Zavis

1025 Thomas Jefferson St. NW
Suite 700 East
Washington, DC 20007
Tel: (202)625-3500
Fax: (202)298-7570
Registered: LDA, FARA
Web: www.kmz.com
A law firm.

DC-Area Employees Representing Listed Clients
VAN CLEEF, Carol R., Partner

Clients
Fidelity Investments Co.
Issues: BNK
Rep By: Carol R. Van Cleef
Fujisawa USA, Inc.
London Clearinghouse, Ltd.
Issues: FIN
Rep By: Carol R. Van Cleef
Official Artist Inc.
Rep By: Carol R. Van Cleef
SunTrust Banks, Inc.
Issues: BAN
Rep By: Carol R. Van Cleef

Kaye Scholer LLP

The McPherson Bldg.
901 15th St. NW, Suite 1100
Washington, DC 20005
Tel: (202)682-3500
Fax: (202)682-3580
Registered: LDA, FARA
Web: www.kayescholer.com
Washington office of a New York general and administrative practice law firm.

DC-Area Employees Representing Listed Clients
BREWSTER, Christopher R., Counsel
CAMERON, Donald B.
GRINER, G Christopher, Managing Partner
HENRY, Ronald K., Partner
HOUSE, Michael P., Partner
LEVINAS, Randi
MENDOZA, Julie C.
SCANLON, Kerry, Partner
SHRINSKY, Jason, Partner
TORREY, Sarah, Legal Assistant

Clients
Barnstable Broadcasting
Rep By: Jason Shrinsky
Beasley Broadcast Group
BNFL, Inc.
Issues: ENG
Rep By: Christopher R. Brewster, G Christopher Griner
Dick Broadcasting Co., Inc.
Holt Communications Corp.
Rep By: Jason Shrinsky
Katz Communications, Inc.
Rep By: Jason Shrinsky
Keymarket Communications, Inc.
Rep By: Jason Shrinsky
Korean Iron and Steel Ass'n
Issues: TRD
Rep By: Donald B. Cameron, Julie C. Mendoza
Korean Semiconductor Industry Ass'n
Rep By: Christopher R. Brewster, Michael P. House, Randi Levinas, Sarah Torrey
The Lincoln Group
Rep By: Jason Shrinsky
Malrite Communications Group, Inc.
Rep By: Christopher R. Brewster, Jason Shrinsky
Matra Aerospace, Inc.
J. P. Morgan Chase & Co.
Rep By: Christopher R. Brewster
NewCity Communications, Inc.
Rep By: Jason Shrinsky
Omega Oil Co.
Issues: FUE NAT
Rep By: Christopher R. Brewster
Sage Broadcasting Corp./SBC Technologies, Inc.
Spanish Broadcasting System, Inc.
Issues: COM TAX
Rep By: Christopher R. Brewster

Kearns & West, Inc.

1030 15th St. NW
Suite 820
Washington, DC 20005-1503
Tel: (202)535-7800
Fax: (202)535-7801
Web: www.kearnswest.com
A public affairs consulting firm.

DC-Area Employees Representing Listed Clients
GUNNING, Anne C., V. President
KEARNS, Ph.D., Kenneth D., Principal

Keelen Communications

P.O. Box 2776
Arlington, VA 22202
Tel: (703)548-0092
Fax: (703)548-9821
E-mail: keelencommunications@erols.com
A government relations and fundraising firm.

DC-Area Employees Representing Listed Clients
KEELEN, Matthew B., President

Clients
Nat'l Ass'n of Convenience Stores
Rep By: Matthew B. Keelen
Nat'l Ass'n of Realtors

Kehoe & Hambel

159 D St. SE
Washington, DC 20003
Tel: (202)547-7566
Fax: (202)546-8630
Registered: LDA
E-mail: kehoeandhambel@aol.com

DC-Area Employees Representing Listed Clients
HAMBEL, John
KEHOE, Danea M.

Clients
American Soc. of Pension Actuaries
Issues: RET
Rep By: Danea M. Kehoe
Nat'l Ass'n of Insurance and Financial Advisors
Issues: INS TAX
Rep By: Danea M. Kehoe
Niche Plan Sponsors, Inc.
Issues: RET TAX
Rep By: John Hambel, Danea M. Kehoe

The Kellen Company

1101 15th St. NW
Suite 202
Washington, DC 20005
Tel: (202)785-3232
Fax: (202)223-9741
Web: www.assnhq.com
Washington office of an association management firm with offices in Atlanta, GA and New York, NY. The firm merged with Sumner, Ryder and Snyder and Resources for Group Management in January of 2001 and intends to combine its three offices in August of 2001. In the interim, it will also maintain offices at 1030 15th St., N.W., Suite 870, Washington, DC 20005 and at 4041 Powder Mill Rd., Suite 104, Calverton, MD 20705.

DC-Area Employees Representing Listed Clients
COOPER, Valerie, Senior Account Executive
CRISTOL, Richard E., Exec. V. President
DECAPRIO, Robert, Account Executive
JONES, Belva W., Account Executive
KENNY, Lynn, Account Executive
MCDERMOTT, Marianne, V. President
SNYDER, Russell K., Exec. V. President

Clients

American College of Construction Lawyers
Rep By: Lynn Kenny

American College of Tax Counsel
Rep By: Lynn Kenny

American Tax Policy Institute
Rep By: Lynn Kenny

Asphalt Roofing Manufacturers Ass'n
Rep By: Russell K. Snyder

Ass'n for Dressings and Sauces
Rep By: Richard E. Cristol

Ass'n of Fund-Raising Distributors and Suppliers
Rep By: Richard E. Cristol

Builders Hardware Manufacturers Ass'n
Rep By: Russell K. Snyder

Calorie Control Council
Rep By: Richard E. Cristol

Comic Magazine Ass'n of America
Rep By: Russell K. Snyder

Exhibit Designers and Producers Ass'n
Rep By: Richard E. Cristol

Food Update Foundation
Rep By: Richard E. Cristol

Greeting Card Ass'n
Rep By: Marianne McDermott

Healthcare Convention and Exhibitors Ass'n
Rep By: Richard E. Cristol

Home Fashion Products Ass'n
Rep By: Russell K. Snyder

Home Infusion Therapy Franchise Owners Ass'n
Rep By: Marianne McDermott

Internat'l Food Additives Council
Rep By: Richard E. Cristol

Internat'l Formula Council
Rep By: Richard E. Cristol

Internat'l Jelly and Preserve Ass'n
Rep By: Richard E. Cristol

Lignin Institute
Rep By: Richard E. Cristol

Messenger Courier Ass'n of the Americas
Rep By: Robert DeCaprio

Nat'l Ass'n of Margarine Manufacturers
Rep By: Richard E. Cristol

Nat'l Candle Ass'n
Rep By: Marianne McDermott

Nat'l Institute of Oilseed Products
Rep By: Richard E. Cristol

Nat'l Pecan Shellers Ass'n
Rep By: Richard E. Cristol

Nat'l Viatical Ass'n
Rep By: Valerie Cooper

Processed Apples Institute
Rep By: Richard E. Cristol

Roof Coatings Manufacturers Ass'n
Rep By: Russell K. Snyder

The Vinegar Institute
Rep By: Richard E. Cristol

Weather Risk Management Ass'n
Rep By: Valerie Cooper

Window Covering Manufacturers Ass'n
Rep By: Russell K. Snyder

Window Covering Safety Council
Rep By: Russell K. Snyder

Worldwide Printing Thermographers Ass'n
Rep By: Valerie Cooper

Keller and Heckman LLP

1001 G St. NW
Suite 500 West
Washington, DC 20001
Tel: (202)434-4100
Fax: (202)434-4646
Registered: LDA, FARA
Web: www.khlaw.com
A law firm specializing in regulatory law, litigation and business transactions on behalf of foreign and domestic clients.

DC-Area Employees Representing Listed Clients
BLACK, Wayne V., Partner
BORGHESANI, Jr., William H., Partner
DE LA CRUZ, Peter L., Partner
DROZEN, Mel S., Partner
DUBECK, John B., Partner
ELDRED, John S., Partner
HALPRIN, Lawrence P., Partner
JONES, Terry
LEIGHTON, Richard J., Partner
MANN, Richard F., Partner
MARRAPESE, Martha E., Partner
MILLAR, Sheila A., Partner
NIELSEN, Catherine R., Partner
REGNERY, Alfred S., Counsel
RICHARDS, John B., Partner
SIMMONS, Ralph A., Partner

Clients

Food Distributors Internat'l (NAWGA-IFDA)
Issues: TRA TRU
Rep By: Terry Jones

Grocery Manufacturers of America

Leprino Foods Co.
Rep By: Richard J. Leighton, Richard F. Mann

Produce Marketing Ass'n
Rep By: Mel S. Drozen, Sheila A. Millar, Ralph A. Simmons

Tea Ass'n of the U.S.A., Inc.
Rep By: Wayne V. Black, Martha E. Marrapese

Robert K. Kelley Law Offices

321 D. St. NE
Washington, DC 20002
Tel: (301)654-3734
Registered: FARA

DC-Area Employees Representing Listed Clients
KELLEY, Robert K.

Clients

Japan Automobile Manufacturers Ass'n
Issues: AUT CAW TRD
Rep By: Robert K. Kelley

Kelley, Drye & Warren LLP

1200 19th St. NW
Suite 500
Washington, DC 20036
Tel: (202)955-9600
Fax: (202)955-9792
Registered: FARA
Web: www.kelleydrye.com
A law firm.

DC-Area Employees Representing Listed Clients
AAMOTH, Robert, Of Counsel
ADAMS, Danny E., Partner
CANIS, Jonathan, Partner
JACKSON, Thomas C., Partner
MORELLI, Genevieve, Of Counsel
PERMUT, Philip V., Partner
ST. LEDGER-ROTY, Judith, Partner
STEINWAY, Daniel M., Partner
VAUGHAN, David L., Partner

Clients

Environmental Business Action Coalition
Rep By: Daniel M. Steinway

Institute of Internat'l Bankers

Martini & Rossi Corp.

New York Presbyterian Hospital - Cornell Medical Center

Kelly and Associates, Inc.

925 15th St. NW
5th Floor
Washington, DC 20005
Tel: (202)342-9610
Fax: (202)342-0650
Registered: LDA
E-mail: jkelly@kellylobbyshop.com
A government/public affairs firm.

DC-Area Employees Representing Listed Clients
EDWARDS, Jill, Associate
KELLY, John A., Chief Exec. Officer

Clients

Academic Medicine Development Corp.
Rep By: John A. Kelly

AMDeC Policy Group, Inc.
Issues: BUD ECN HCR MED MMM SCI
Rep By: John A. Kelly

BMW (U.S.) Holding Corp.
Issues: AUT IMM SCI TAX
Rep By: John A. Kelly

BMW Financial Services of North America, Inc.
Rep By: John A. Kelly

BMW Manufacturing Corp.
Issues: AUT BUD CAW CPT CSP ECN IMM LBR MAN TAX TRD
Rep By: John A. Kelly

BMW of North America, Inc.
Rep By: John A. Kelly

Internat'l Narcotic Enforcement Officers Ass'n
Rep By: John A. Kelly

Morse Diesel Internat'l Inc.
Issues: TAX
Rep By: John A. Kelly

Peachtree Settlement Funding
Issues: TAX
Rep By: John A. Kelly

Perdue Farms Inc.
Issues: BUD LBR TAX
Rep By: John A. Kelly

Qwest Communications
Issues: LBR TAX
Rep By: John A. Kelly

Showell Farms Inc.
Rep By: John A. Kelly

Singer Assett Finance, Inc.
Issues: TAX
Rep By: John A. Kelly

The Kemper Co.

2600 Virginia Ave. NW
Suite 210
Washington, DC 20037
Tel: (202)337-5019
Fax: (202)337-5310
Registered: LDA
E-mail: TKemperCo@aol.com

DC-Area Employees Representing Listed Clients
KEMPER, Jr., Jackson, President and Chief Exec. Officer

Clients

Circuit Services, Inc.
Issues: MAN
Rep By: Jackson Kemper, Jr.

CRYPTEK Secure Communications, LLC
Issues: CPI DEF
Rep By: Jackson Kemper, Jr.

Flight Safety Technologies, Inc.
Issues: AER TRA
Rep By: Jackson Kemper, Jr.

Kildare Corp.
Issues: DEF SCI
Rep By: Jackson Kemper, Jr.

Progeny Systems
Issues: DEF
Rep By: Jackson Kemper, Jr.

Qualtec, Inc.
Issues: DEF
Rep By: Jackson Kemper, Jr.

Science Applications Internat'l Corp. (SAIC)
Issues: DEF
Rep By: Jackson Kemper, Jr.

Scientific Fishery Systems, Inc.
Issues: DEF MAR
Rep By: Jackson Kemper, Jr.

Sonetech Corp.
Issues: AER DEF
Rep By: Jackson Kemper, Jr.

Technology Systems, Inc.
Issues: DEF SCI
Rep By: Jackson Kemper, Jr.

Kendall and Associates

50 E St. SE
Washington, DC 20003
Tel: (202)546-2600
Fax: (202)484-1979
Registered: LDA

DC-Area Employees Representing Listed Clients
ANDRUKITIS, Barbara C., President
KENDALL, William T., Chairman

Clients

Toyota Motor North America, U.S.A., Inc.
Issues: CSP
Rep By: William T. Kendall

Patricia C. Kennedy

3220 Juniper Ln.
Falls Church, VA 22044
Tel: (703)533-2035
Registered: LDA
A government relations consultant.

Clients

DaimlerChrysler Corp.
Issues: AUT
Rep By: Patricia C. Kennedy

PEI Electronics
Issues: DEF
Rep By: Patricia C. Kennedy

Kennedy Government Relations

313 South Carolina Ave. SE
Washington, DC 20003-4213
Tel: (202)547-0971
Fax: (202)547-2672
Registered: LDA
E-mail: kennedyj@bellatlantic.net

DC-Area Employees Representing Listed Clients
KENNEDY, Jerry W., Attorney

Clients

El Dorado Irrigation District
Issues: ENV NAT
Rep By: Jerry W. Kennedy

General Atomics
Issues: DEF
Rep By: Jerry W. Kennedy

Kent & O'Connor, Inc.

1990 M St. NW
Suite 340
Washington, DC 20036
Tel: (202)223-6222
Fax: (202)785-0687
Registered: LDA
E-mail: mj1026@aol.com
A corporate government affairs consulting firm.

DC-Area Employees Representing Listed Clients

FITZGERALD, Eileen, Consultant
KENT, Jonathan H., Chairman
O'CONNOR, Patrick C., President
THOMAS, Cindy, Attorney

Clients

American College of Occupational and Environmental Medicine
Issues: HCR LBR
Rep By: Patrick C. O'Connor

American Soc. of Plastic and Reconstructive Surgeons
Issues: HCR
Rep By: Jonathan H. Kent

American Supply Ass'n
Issues: CAW ENV LBR SMB TAX UTI
Rep By: Eileen Fitzgerald, Jonathan H. Kent, Patrick C. O'Connor

Ball Research, Inc.
Issues: CPT
Rep By: Cindy Thomas

Condea Vista Chemical Co.
Issues: TAX
Rep By: Jonathan H. Kent, Cindy Thomas

FedEx Corp.
Issues: CAW TRA
Rep By: Patrick C. O'Connor

GlaxoSmithKline
Issues: CPT
Rep By: Cindy Thomas

Internat'l Academy of Compounding Pharmacists
Issues: PHA
Rep By: Eileen Fitzgerald, Jonathan H. Kent

Internat'l Ass'n of Airport Duty Free Stores
Issues: TRD
Rep By: Jonathan H. Kent

Internat'l Trademark Ass'n
Issues: CPT
Rep By: Jonathan H. Kent, Cindy Thomas

Internat'l Warehouse Logistics Ass'n
Issues: ECN LBR TRU
Rep By: Patrick C. O'Connor, Cindy Thomas

Liz Claiborne Internat'l
Issues: TRD
Rep By: Jonathan H. Kent, Cindy Thomas

Mont Blanc, Inc.
Issues: CPT
Rep By: Patrick C. O'Connor

Nat'l Ass'n of Fleet Administrators
Issues: ENG ENV FUE TAX TRA
Rep By: Patrick C. O'Connor

Nat'l Customs Brokers and Forwarders Ass'n of America
Issues: MAR TRA TRD
Rep By: Jonathan H. Kent, Cindy Thomas

Richemont Internat'l Ltd.
Issues: CSP
Rep By: Patrick C. O'Connor

Kerrigan & Associates, Inc.

1104 Dapple Grey Court
Great Falls, VA 22066
Tel: (703)757-2829
Fax: (703)757-2884
Registered: LDA
Web: www.egovtech.com
E-mail: kerrigan@egovtech.com

DC-Area Employees Representing Listed Clients

KERRIGAN, Michael J., President

Clients

L. P. Conwood Co.
Issues: TOB
Rep By: Michael J. Kerrigan

GCI-Wisconsin
Issues: MAR
Rep By: Michael J. Kerrigan

Maptech
Issues: SCI
Rep By: Michael J. Kerrigan

New York Institute for Special Education
Issues: EDU
Rep By: Michael J. Kerrigan

Science Applications Internat'l Corp. (SAIC)
Issues: SCI
Rep By: Michael J. Kerrigan

Kessler & Associates Business Services, Inc.

210 Seventh St. SE
Washington, DC 20003
Tel: (202)547-6808
Fax: (202)546-5425
Registered: LDA

DC-Area Employees Representing Listed Clients

BARTLETT, Michael L., Senior Legislative Associate/Director, Corporate Communications
BERMAN, Howard, Senior V. President, Environmental Counsel
EVANS, Billy Lee
GROS, Simon
JENCKES, Linda
KESSLER, Richard S., President
MUSSER, James C., Senior V. President, Tax Policy
SPORIDIS, Harry, Legislative Associate

Clients

Amgen
Issues: BUD MED TAX
Rep By: Michael L. Bartlett, Richard S. Kessler, James C. Musser

Burlington Northern Santa Fe Railway
Issues: RRR TAX TRA
Rep By: Michael L. Bartlett, Billy Lee Evans, Richard S. Kessler, James C. Musser

Dunn-Edwards Corp.
Issues: BUD CAW ENV GOV SMB TAX
Rep By: Michael L. Bartlett, Howard Berman, Billy Lee Evans, Richard S. Kessler, James C. Musser, Harry Sporidis

Exelon Corp.
Issues: TAX
Rep By: Michael L. Bartlett, Billy Lee Evans, Richard S. Kessler, James C. Musser, Harry Sporidis

Future of Puerto Rico Inc.

Grocery Manufacturers of America
Issues: FCC FOO TAX TRU
Rep By: Michael L. Bartlett, Simon Gros, Richard S. Kessler, James C. Musser, Harry Sporidis

Henry H. Kessler Foundation
Issues: MED MMM
Rep By: Simon Gros, Richard S. Kessler, Harry Sporidis

Mercy Health System of Northwest Arkasas
Issues: GOV URB
Rep By: Michael L. Bartlett, Linda Jenckes, Richard S. Kessler, James C. Musser

Nat'l Ass'n of Securities Dealers, Inc. (NASD)
Issues: BAN
Rep By: Michael L. Bartlett, Billy Lee Evans, Richard S. Kessler, James C. Musser

Norway, Government of the Kingdom of

Novartis Corp.
Issues: BUD ENV HCR MMM TAX TRD
Rep By: Richard S. Kessler, Harry Sporidis

Pfizer, Inc.
Issues: HCR MMM TAX TRD
Rep By: Richard S. Kessler, James C. Musser

Pharmacia Corp.
Issues: BUD ENV HCR TAX WAS
Rep By: Howard Berman, Billy Lee Evans, Simon Gros, Richard S. Kessler, James C. Musser, Harry Sporidis

Philip Morris Management Corp.
Issues: BEV FOO TOB
Rep By: Michael L. Bartlett, Billy Lee Evans, Richard S. Kessler, James C. Musser

Planet Electric
Issues: ENV
Rep By: Michael L. Bartlett, Howard Berman, Billy Lee Evans, Richard S. Kessler

Ripon Society
Rep By: Richard S. Kessler

Sallie Mae, Inc.
Issues: BNK EDU TAX TEC
Rep By: Michael L. Bartlett, Richard S. Kessler

Tosco Corp.
Issues: CAW ENV
Rep By: Howard Berman, Harry Sporidis

Ketchum

2000 L St. NW
Suite 300
Washington, DC 20036-0646
Tel: (202)835-8800
Fax: (202)835-8879
Registered: LDA, FARA
Web: www.ketchum.com
Headquartered in New York, NY. Ketchum is a part of Ketchum Communications.

DC-Area Employees Representing Listed Clients

BRADFIELD, Daniel, Vice President and Group Manager; Director, Grassroots Communications
BRUNS, Kevin T., V. President and Group Manager, Public Affairs
COFFEY, Nancy, Senior V. President, Media Relations
DOLAN, Jr., Charles H., Senior V. President
DOYNE, Karen, Director, Litigation Communications
ERICKSON, Steve, Sr. V. President, Healthcare
HURSON, John, Consultant
KIRK, Keith A., V. President for Grassroots
LASKY, Samantha, Account Executive
LEIBENSPERGER, Jr., Thomas, Account Supervisor
LIEB, Bonnie, Sr. V. President, Technology
LUKE, Anne Forristall, Senior V. President, Public Affairs and Issues Management
ROBINSON, Peter, Sr. V. President and Counselor for Policy, Govt. Relations
SCHANNON, Mark, Partner and Director
SUTHERLAND, Julia K., Senior V. President
THELIAN, Lorraine, Sr. Partner, North America
WHALEN, Katie, Senior Counselor

Clients

Capital One Financial Corp.
Rep By: Bonnie Lieb

The Dow Chemical Co.

Regeneration Technologies Inc.
Issues: HCR
Rep By: Samantha Lasky

Kilpatrick Stockton LLP

700 13th St. NW
Suite 800
Washington, DC 20005
Tel: (202)508-5800
Fax: (202)508-5858
Registered: LDA
Washington office of a law firm headquartered in Atlanta, GA.

DC-Area Employees Representing Listed Clients

BARNETT, Richard, Director, Government Relations
BRADY, J. Christopher, Director, Legislative Affairs
FORTENBERRY, Amy
HORDELL, Michael A.
HUGHES, J. Vance, Partner
LEVIN, David R., Partner
LEVITAS, Hon. Elliott H., Partner
LEVY, Neil I., Partner
RAIDER, Ron, Partner
SIMMONS, Charles, Partner
VON UNWERTH, Frederick H., Partner
WINCEK, Mark D., Partner

Clients

American Realty Advisors
Issues: RES
Rep By: Richard Barnett, J. Christopher Brady

American Speech, Language, and Hearing Ass'n
Rep By: Neil I. Levy

Atlanta, Georgia, City of
Issues: ENV
Rep By: J. Christopher Brady, J. Vance Hughes, Ron Raider

Blake Construction Co.
Rep By: Hon. Elliott H. Levitas, Neil I. Levy

Capitol Concerts, Inc.
Issues: ART
Rep By: Richard Barnett

Elcor Inc.
Rep By: Neil I. Levy

Employers Council on Flexible Compensation
Rep By: Mark D. Wincek

The Freedom Forum
Issues: RES
Rep By: J. Christopher Brady

Georgia Ports Authority
Issues: ENV
Rep By: J. Vance Hughes

Hoffman Management, Inc.
Issues: RES
Rep By: J. Christopher Brady, Hon. Elliott H. Levitas, Neil I. Levy

Interface
Rep By: Charles Simmons

Internat'l Furniture Rental Ass'n
Rep By: Frederick H. von Unwerth

PepsiCo, Inc.
Rep By: Mark D. Wincek

Public Properties Policy Ass'n
Rep By: Hon. Elliott H. Levitas

Republic Properties Corp.
Issues: RES
Rep By: J. Christopher Brady, Hon. Elliott H. Levitas

Julien J. Studley, Inc.
Issues: RES
Rep By: Richard Barnett, J. Christopher Brady, Neil I. Levy

Transrapid Internat'l
Issues: TRA
Rep By: J. Christopher Brady, Neil I. Levy

Zirconium Environmental Committee (ZEC)
Issues: ENV
Rep By: J. Christopher Brady, J. Vance Hughes, Charles Simmons

Jeffrey J. Kimbell & Associates

3504 Whitehaven Pkwy. NW
Washington, DC 20007
Tel: (202)338-6066
Fax: (202)338-6446
Registered: LDA
Web: www.kimbell-associates.com
E-mail: jjkimbell@aol.com
Provides strategic counsel and assistance to medical technology firms seeking guidance through the federal government labyrinth.

DC-Area Employees Representing Listed Clients
KIMBELL, Jeffrey J., Chief Exec. Officer

Clients

Boston Scientific Corp.
Issues: HCR MMM TAX TRD

Elanex Pharmaceuticals
Issues: HCR MMM TRD

Gambro Healthcare
Issues: HCR MMM

HemaSure, Inc.
Issues: CPT HCR MED SCI
Rep By: Jeffrey J. Kimbell

Intrinsiq Data Corp.
Issues: HCR MMM VET

Lifecore Biomedical
Issues: HCR MMM

Pan Pacific Pharmaceuticals
Issues: HCR IMM

Sepracor, Inc.
Issues: CPT HCR MED SCI
Rep By: Jeffrey J. Kimbell

Kimberly Consulting, LLC

901 15th St. NW
Suite 440
Washington, DC 20005
Tel: (202)312-3026
Fax: (202)312-3027
Registered: LDA
E-mail: kimberlyconsulting@att.net
A government affairs, business consulting, and lobbying firm.

DC-Area Employees Representing Listed Clients
KIMBERLY, Richard H., President

Clients

The Asheville School
Issues: BUD EDU
Rep By: Richard H. Kimberly

Chesapeake Bay Maritime Museum
Issues: BUD EDU ENV MAR TOU
Rep By: Richard H. Kimberly

Easton Airport
Issues: AVI BUD
Rep By: Richard H. Kimberly

Georgetown University-McDonough School of Business
Issues: EDU
Rep By: Richard H. Kimberly

Georgetown University-School of Nursing
Issues: EDU
Rep By: Richard H. Kimberly

Kimberly-Clark Corp.
Issues: CAW ENG ENV FOR TAX TRD
Rep By: Richard H. Kimberly

Pinkering Corp.
Issues: AVI
Rep By: Richard H. Kimberly

Tricap Management Corp.
Issues: HOU URB
Rep By: Richard H. Kimberly

Wayland Academy
Issues: BUD EDU
Rep By: Richard H. Kimberly

Zamorano
Issues: AGR BUD FOR
Rep By: Richard H. Kimberly

Joseph S. Kimmitt

6004 Copely Lane
McLean, VA 22101-2507
Tel: (703)538-2507
Fax: (703)538-6472
Registered: LDA
E-mail: skimmitt@aol.com

Clients

The Boeing Co.
Issues: AER AVI DEF
Rep By: Joseph S. Kimmitt

Kimmitt, Coates & McCarthy

1730 M St. NW
Suite 911
Washington, DC 20036
Tel: (202)293-4761
Fax: (202)659-5760
Registered: LDA

DC-Area Employees Representing Listed Clients
COATES, Jr., Vincent J., President
KIMMITT, Joseph S., Chairman
MCCARTHY, George D., Secretary/Treasurer

Clients

Absaroka Trust
Issues: NAT
Rep By: Vincent J. Coates, Jr.

Alliant Techsystems, Inc.
Issues: FIR
Rep By: Vincent J. Coates, Jr.

MSE, Inc.
Issues: AER DEF
Rep By: Vincent J. Coates, Jr., George D. McCarthy

Kinder & Associates, Inc.

1250 H St. NW
Suite 901
Washington, DC 20005
Tel: (202)463-8162
Fax: (202)463-8155
Registered: LDA
Web: www.kinderassociates.com
E-mail: webmaster@kinderassociates.com
A diversified professional services firm specializing in association management, lobbying, and public affairs.

DC-Area Employees Representing Listed Clients
PANTOS, George, Washington Counsel
WILLIAMS, Ashley K., Associate

Clients

Self-Insurance Institute of America, Inc.
Issues: HCR LBR
Rep By: George Pantos, Ashley K. Williams

King & Spalding

1730 Pennsylvania Ave. NW
Suite 1200
Washington, DC 20006-4706
Tel: (202)737-0500
Fax: (202)626-3737
Registered: LDA
Web: www.kslaw.com
Washington office of an Atlanta law firm.

DC-Area Employees Representing Listed Clients
BREWER, Carol, International Trade Specialist
CAMBELL, Glenn
CROCKETT, Elizabeth Schmidtlein, Associate
DORN, Joseph W., Partner
DURST, Michael, Partner
GRAHAM, Thomas, Partner
HESTER, Theodore M., Partner
HILL, Eleanor
JAFARI, Beth
JONES, Stephen A., Partner
KASSIR, Allison, Government Affairs Representative
MABILE, Michael P., Partner
NORTON, Lisa K., Associate
NUNN, Hon. Sam, Partner
PFEIFER, Eugene M., Partner
RICHMAN, Dvorah A., Partner
SCHOTT, Anne, Associate
STRIBLING, Jess H., Partner
TALMADGE, William C., Counsel
WHITESIDES, Ashley, Associate

Clients

Agrium Inc.
Issues: ENG FUE LBR TRO
Rep By: Lisa K. Norton

Blue Cross Blue Shield Ass'n
Issues: HCR
Rep By: Theodore M. Hester, Eleanor Hill

Bridgestone/Firestone, Inc.
Issues: AUT
Rep By: Theodore M. Hester, Eleanor Hill, Beth Jafari, Allison Kassir

The Egg Factory, LLC
Issues: COM SCI TEC
Rep By: Glenn Cambell, William C. Talmadge

ESR Children's Health Care System
Issues: HCR MMM
Rep By: Allison Kassir, William C. Talmadge

Farm Market iD
Issues: AGR
Rep By: William C. Talmadge, Ashley Whitesides

Healthcare Recoveries Inc.
Rep By: Allison Kassir, William C. Talmadge

Internet Security Systems, Inc.
Issues: CPI
Rep By: Lisa K. Norton, William C. Talmadge

Minnesota Mining and Manufacturing (3M Pharmaceuticals)
Issues: HCR
Rep By: Theodore M. Hester, William C. Talmadge

Salt Lake City Olympic Organizing Committee
Issues: BUD LAW MON SPO TRA TRD
Rep By: Theodore M. Hester, Allison Kassir, Lisa K. Norton, William C. Talmadge

Southern Tier Cement Committee
Issues: TRA
Rep By: Carol Brewer, Joseph W. Dorn, Theodore M. Hester, Michael P. Mabile

Teledyne-Commodore, LLC
Issues: DEF
Rep By: Theodore M. Hester

Kinghorn & Associates, L.L.C.

900 Second St. NE
Suite 201
Washington, DC 20002
Tel: (202)842-0219
Fax: (202)842-0439
Registered: LDA
E-mail: tkinghorn@kinghornassociates.com
A governmental affairs consulting firm.

DC-Area Employees Representing Listed Clients
HILBERT, II, John W., V. President, Legislative and Regulatory Affairs
KINGHORN, Jr., Edward J., President
SCOTT, Jeremy, Legislative Associates

Clients

Advanced Technology Institute
Issues: DEF
Rep By: Edward J. Kinghorn, Jr., Jeremy Scott

American Metalcasting Consortium
Issues: DEF
Rep By: Edward J. Kinghorn, Jr.

Ferroalloys Ass'n
Issues: ENV TRD
Rep By: John W. Hilbert, II, Edward J. Kinghorn, Jr., Jeremy Scott

Non-Ferrous Founders' Soc.
Issues: CAW ENV LBR
Rep By: John W. Hilbert, II, Jeremy Scott

Remediation Financial, Inc.
Issues: CAW ENV
Rep By: Edward J. Kinghorn, Jr.

South Carolina Research Authority
Issues: DEF TRA
Rep By: John W. Hilbert, II, Edward J. Kinghorn, Jr., Jeremy Scott

South Carolina Technology Alliance
Rep By: Edward J. Kinghorn, Jr., Jeremy Scott

Tri-County Alliance
Issues: ECN
Rep By: John W. Hilbert, II, Edward J. Kinghorn, Jr., Jeremy Scott

Steven Kingsley

845 Ninovan Rd. SE
Vienna, VA 22180-2017
Tel: (703)284-5818
Fax: (703)284-5819
E-mail: kingst@erols.com

Clients

Citizens' Scholarship Foundation of America
Issues: EDU
Rep By: Steven Kingsley

Nat'l Computer Systems
Rep By: Steven Kingsley

Peter Kinzler

7310 Stafford Rd.
Alexandria, VA 22307
Tel: (703)660-0799
Fax: (703)660-0799
Registered: LDA
E-mail: kinzler@tidalwave.net
A sole proprietor.

Clients

Coalition for Auto-Insurance Reform
Issues: INS
Rep By: Peter Kinzler

Massachusetts Mutual Life Insurance Co.
Issues: INS TOR
Rep By: Peter Kinzler

Prudential Insurance Co. of America
Issues: FIN INS TAX TOR TRD
Rep By: Peter Kinzler

Kirkland & Ellis

655 15th St. NW
Suite 1200
Washington, DC 20005
Tel: (202)879-5000
Fax: (202)879-5200
Registered: LDA, FARA
Web: www.kirkland.com
A general practice law firm specializing in matters before federal courts, administrative agencies and departments.

DC-Area Employees Representing Listed Clients
DRAKE, Stuart A. C., Partner
GASAWAY, Robert R., Associate
HOSTETLER, James S., Partner

IRVING, John, Partner
MARCHANT, Dawn D., Associate
SANDERS, David P., Partner
SINGER, William S., Partner
SKUBEL, Marimichael O., Partner
WEIGEL, Kenneth G., Partner
YOUNG, Mark D., Partner

Clients

ACME - Ass'n of Management Consulting Firms
American Ass'n for Laboratory Accreditation
American Staffing Ass'n
Rep By: John Irving
American Trucking Ass'ns
C F Industries, Inc.
Chamber of Commerce of the U.S.A.
Issues: CON ENV
Rep By: Robert R. Gasaway
Chicago Board of Trade
Issues: FIN
Rep By: Mark D. Young
FMC Corp.
General Motors Corp.
Issues: ENV
Rep By: Stuart A. C. Drake, Robert R. Gasaway
Professional Services Council
Rep By: James S. Hostetler
Sara Lee Corp.
Issues: TAX
Rep By: William S. Singer

Kirkpatrick & Lockhart LLP

1800 Massachusetts Ave. NW
Second Floor
Washington, DC 20036-1800
Tel: (202)778-9000
Fax: (202)778-9100
Registered: LDA
Web: www.kl.com
E-mail: info@kl.com
A general practice law firm. Also maintains offices in Boston, MA; Dallas, TX; Harrisburg and Pittsburgh, PA; Los Angeles and San Francisco, CA; Miami, FL; Newark, NJ; and New York, NY.

DC-Area Employees Representing Listed Clients
KOCH, George W., Legislative Consultant
TANNENBAUM, Ira L., Partner

Clients

American Financial Group
Issues: BAN FIN INS
Rep By: George W. Koch, Ira L. Tannenbaum
Grocery Manufacturers of America
Rep By: George W. Koch
Independent Grocers' Alliance
Rep By: George W. Koch
Nat'l Court Reporters Ass'n
Issues: CON LAW
Rep By: George W. Koch

Klein & Saks, Inc.

1112 16th St. NW
Suite 240
Washington, DC 20036
Tel: (202)835-0952
Fax: (202)835-0155
Registered: LDA

DC-Area Employees Representing Listed Clients
BATEMAN, Paul W., President
DIRIENZO, Michael
FULLER, Douglas
LUTLEY, John H., Chairman
VARY, George F.

Clients

The Gold and Silver Institute
Issues: ENV MON NAT TAX
Rep By: Paul W. Bateman, Michael DiRienzo, Douglas Fuller

Kleinfeld, Kaplan and Becker

1140 19th St. NW
Suite 900
Washington, DC 20036
Tel: (202)223-5120
Fax: (202)223-5619
Web: www.kkblaw.com
E-mail: kkb@kkblaw.com
A law firm specializing in regulatory and administrative matters in the areas of food, drugs, cosmetics, medical devices, pesticides, controlled substances and consumer products.

DC-Area Employees Representing Listed Clients
DAVIDSON, Jennifer A., Associate
DWYER, Daniel R., Partner
EHRLICH, Stacy L., Partner
HENTELEFF, Thomas O., Partner
KAPLAN, Alan H., Partner
LASSMAN, Prescott M., Partner
MATHERS, Peter R., Partner
MOREY, Richard S., Partner
REAGAN, Kinsey S., Partner
SAFIR, Peter O., Partner
VALERIO, Stacey L., Associate

Clients

Adria Laboratories, Inc.
Rep By: Alan H. Kaplan
Aventis CropScience
Rep By: Peter O. Safir
Carter-Wallace, Inc.
Rep By: Alan H. Kaplan, Peter O. Safir
Contact Lens Institute
Issues: GOV HCR
Rep By: Thomas O. Henteleff, Peter R. Mathers
Cord Laboratories
Rep By: Alan H. Kaplan, Richard S. Morey
Inwood Laboratories, Inc.
Rep By: Peter R. Mathers
Jones Medical Industries, Inc.
Rep By: Peter R. Mathers
Mead Johnson and Co.
Rep By: Alan H. Kaplan, Richard S. Morey
Par Pharmaceutical, Inc.
Rep By: Alan H. Kaplan
Quad Pharmaceutical Inc.
Rep By: Alan H. Kaplan
E. R. Squibb and Sons, Inc.
Rep By: Kinsey S. Reagan, Peter O. Safir
Vitarine Pharmaceuticals Inc.
Rep By: Alan H. Kaplan

Marvin G. Klemow

1700 N. Moore St.
Suite 1210
Arlington, VA 22209
Tel: (703)875-3723
Fax: (703)875-3740
Registered: FARA

Clients

Israel Aircraft Industries, Ltd.
Issues: DEF
Rep By: Marvin G. Klemow

Theodore C. Knappen, P.C.

1001 G St. NW
Suite 400 East
Washington, DC 20001
Tel: (202)638-3490
Fax: (202)638-3516
Registered: LDA
E-mail: tknappen@peyser.com

Clients

Greyhound Lines
Issues: TRA
Rep By: Theodore C. Knappen
Martz Group
Issues: TRA
Rep By: Theodore C. Knappen
Mid-Atlantic Medical Services, Inc.
Issues: HCR
Rep By: Theodore C. Knappen

Patrick C. Koch

1620 L St. NW
Suite 1210
Washington, DC 20036
Tel: (202)833-7755
Fax: (202)955-6070
Registered: LDA

Clients

Mercy Health Corp.
Issues: BUD
Rep By: Patrick C. Koch

Kogovsek & Associates

1001 Pennsylvania Ave. NW
Suite 760 North
Washington, DC 20004
Tel: (202)661-7060
Fax: (202)661-7066
Registered: LDA, FARA
The Washington office of a lobbying firm headquartered in Greenwood Village, CO.

DC-Area Employees Representing Listed Clients
ARBOGAST, Christine Ann, V. President
KOGOVSEK, Hon. Raymond P., President

Clients

Bohemian Cos.
Issues: BEV CAW ENV RES TAX TEC
Foundation Health Federal Services, Inc.
Issues: HCR INS MMM PHA
The Legislative Strategies Group, LLC
Rep By: Christine Ann Arbogast, Hon. Raymond P. Kogovsek
Rio Grande Water Conservation District
Issues: CAW NAT
Rep By: Christine Ann Arbogast, Hon. Raymond P. Kogovsek
Signal Behavioral Health Network
Issues: ALC BUD HCR MMM WEL
Rep By: Christine Ann Arbogast, Hon. Raymond P. Kogovsek
Southern Ute Indian Tribe
Issues: AGR BUD CAW ENG FUE GAM HOU IND NAT TAX
Rep By: Christine Ann Arbogast, Hon. Raymond P. Kogovsek
Southwestern Water Conservation District
Issues: AGR BUD NAT
Rep By: Christine Ann Arbogast, Hon. Raymond P. Kogovsek
Upper Yampa Water Conservancy District
Issues: AGR BUD NAT
Ute Mountain Ute Indian Tribe
Issues: AGR BUD CAW ENG FUE GAM HOU IND NAT TAX
Rep By: Christine Ann Arbogast, Hon. Raymond P. Kogovsek
Wolf Springs Ranches, Inc.
Issues: AVI DEF NAT
Rep By: Christine Ann Arbogast, Hon. Raymond P. Kogovsek

Koleda Childress & Co.

1110 N. Glebe Rd.
Suite 610
Arlington, VA 22201
Tel: (703)276-0600
Fax: (703)276-7662

DC-Area Employees Representing Listed Clients
CHILDRESS, James M., Principal
KOLEDA, Michael S., Principal

Clients

Eastman Chemical Co.
Rep By: James M. Childress
Gasification Technologies Council
Rep By: James M. Childress
Propane Consumers Coalition
Rep By: James M. Childress

Michael J. Kopetski

517 Colecroft Ct.
Alexandria, VA 22314

Clients

The Boeing Co.
Issues: TRD
Rep By: Michael J. Kopetski
The Business Roundtable
Issues: FOR TRD
Rep By: Michael J. Kopetski
Downey McGrath Group, Inc.
Issues: TRD
Rep By: Michael J. Kopetski

Harry Kopp LLC

1101 Connecticut Ave. NW
Suite 1200
Washington, DC 20036
Tel: (202)739-0129
Registered: LDA
E-mail: harrykopp@earthlink.net
A consulting firm.

DC-Area Employees Representing Listed Clients
KOPP, Harry, President

Clients

Philippine Sugar Alliance
Rep By: Harry Kopp

Michael E. Korens

2201 Wisconsin Ave. NW
Suite 105
Washington, DC 20007
Tel: (202)965-9810
Fax: (202)965-9812
Registered: LDA

Clients

NAV Canada
Issues: AVI
Rep By: Michael E. Korens
Northwest Airlines, Inc.
Issues: AVI
Rep By: Michael E. Korens
United Airlines
Issues: AVI
Rep By: Michael E. Korens

Korth & Korth

1700 K St. NW
Suite 501
Washington, DC 20006
Tel: (202)223-3630
Fax: (202)223-1878

DC-Area Employees Representing Listed Clients
KORTH, Fritz-Alan, Principal

Clients

Bernard Johnson, Inc.

Del Norte Technology
Rep By: Fritz-Alan Korth

KPMG, LLP

2001 M St. NW
Washington, DC 20036
Tel: (202)467-3000
Fax: (202)533-8500
Registered: LDA

Web: www.kpmg.com
An accounting firm headquartered in New York, NY.

Political Action Committee
KPMG PAC
2001 M St. NW
Washington, DC 20036
Tel: (202)467-3000
Fax: (202)533-8500
Contact: Stephen Allis

DC-Area Employees Representing Listed Clients
ALLIS, Stephen, Partner
BONAR, Jennifer
BREAKS, Katherine M., Associate
BROCKWAY, David
BROWN, Robert M.
CALLAS, George
GALVAN, Gail
GUTMAN, Harry L., Partner
ROSENTHAL, Steven M., Partner, Washington National Tax
ROSS, Frank K., Managing Partner
SCHWARZ, Melbert E.
SLAWTER, Shannon E.
SMITH, Linden C.
SPOONER, Gillian, Partner, Washington National Tax
STIRRUP, John T., Manager, Government Affairs
STOUT, Jr., Thomas A.
WAGNER, Elizabeth

Clients

Air Transport Ass'n of America
Issues: TAX
Rep By: Harry L. Gutman, Gillian Spooner

Apple Computer, Inc.
Issues: TAX
Rep By: Katherine M. Breaks, Harry L. Gutman, Melbert E. Schwarz

Bracewell & Patterson, L.L.P.
Issues: TAX TRD
Rep By: Shannon E. Slawter, Linden C. Smith

Independent Telephone and Telecommunications Alliance

The INDOPCO Coalition
Issues: TAX
Rep By: Robert M. Brown, Harry L. Gutman, Melbert E. Schwarz, Thomas A. Stout, Jr.

Investment Program Ass'n

The KPMG FSC Coalition
Issues: TAX
Rep By: Jennifer Bonar, Katherine M. Breaks, George Callas, Gail Galvan, Harry L. Gutman, Melbert E. Schwarz, Thomas A. Stout, Jr., Elizabeth Wagner

Money Management Institute

Nat'l Council of Farmer Cooperatives
Issues: TAX
Rep By: Jennifer Bonar, Harry L. Gutman, Gillian Spooner, Thomas A. Stout, Jr.

Nat'l Geographic Soc.
Issues: TAX

Nextwave Telecom
Issues: TEC
Rep By: Linden C. Smith

Sara Lee Corp.
Issues: TAX
Rep By: Gail Galvan, Harry L. Gutman, Thomas A. Stout, Jr.

Krivit & Krivit, P.C.

1120 G St. NW
Suite 200
Washington, DC 20005
Tel: (202)544-1112
Fax: (202)737-4933
Web: www.smart-city.com
E-mail: krivlaw@iamdigex.net
A law firm specializing in housing and urban development, economic development, education, employment, and communications law.

DC-Area Employees Representing Listed Clients
KRIVIT, Daniel H., President
PEREZ, Barbara Zientek
STEPHENSON KRIVIT, Sandra M.

Clients

Applied Development Associates

Aspira, Inc. of New Jersey

Bayonne Housing Authority
Rep By: Daniel H. Krivit

Bayonne, New Jersey, City of
Rep By: Daniel H. Krivit

East Chicago Public Housing Authority
Rep By: Daniel H. Krivit

Hoboken, New Jersey, City of

Jersey City Economic Development Corp.

South Jersey Regional Council of Carpenters

Union City, New Jersey, City of

George Kroloff & Associates

9158 Rothbury Dr.
Suite 168
Gaithersburg, MD 20886
Tel: (301)977-5008
Fax: (301)258-0016
Registered: FARA
An advertising, public relations and consulting firm.

DC-Area Employees Representing Listed Clients
KROLOFF, George, Senior Principal

Clients

America's Blood Centers

America's Charities
Rep By: George Kroloff

Commission on Presidential Debates
Rep By: George Kroloff

Nat'l Rural Electric Cooperative Ass'n

Publicis Dialog

Theodore George Kronmiller

601 Pennsylvania Ave. NW
Suite 900
South Bldg.
Washington, DC 20004
E-mail: kroncyber@msn.com
Tel: (202)434-8208
Fax: (202)639-8238
Registered: LDA, FARA

Clients

Iceland, Government of the Republic of
Rep By: Theodore George Kronmiller

Marshall Islands, Republic of the
Rep By: Theodore George Kronmiller

Krooth & Altman

1850 M St. NW
Suite 400
Washington, DC 20036
Tel: (202)293-8200
Fax: (202)872-0145
Registered: LDA
A general, administrative, and business practice law firm.

DC-Area Employees Representing Listed Clients
BARSKY, David A., Partner
CLANCY, Patrick J., Partner
KNOLL, E. Joseph, Partner
LIBRETTA, Donald F., Partner
MAZER, Michael E., Managing Partner
TENNANT, William S., Of Counsel
VIHSTADT, John E., Partner

Clients

District of Columbia Hospital Ass'n
Rep By: Patrick J. Clancy

Healthcare Financing Study Group
Issues: HCR
Rep By: David A. Barsky, Patrick J. Clancy, E. Joseph Knoll, Donald F. Libretta, Michael E. Mazer, William S. Tennant, John E. Vihstadt

David William Kuhnsman

7900 Westpark Dr.
SuiteT-305
McLean, VA 22102
Tel: (703)506-8770
Registered: LDA

Clients

Integrated Management Resources Group, Inc.
Issues: FIN GOV SMB
Rep By: David William Kuhnsman

Kurzweil & Associates

1212 New York Ave. NW
Suite 350
Washington, DC 20005
Tel: (202)842-7663
Fax: (202)842-5010
Registered: LDA
A government relations firm.

DC-Area Employees Representing Listed Clients
KURZWEIL, Jeffrey, Principal

Clients

Cabazon Band of Mission Indians
Issues: GAM IND
Rep By: Jeffrey Kurzweil

Hilton Hotels Corp.
Issues: TAX
Rep By: Jeffrey Kurzweil

HMSHost Corp.
Issues: AVI
Rep By: Jeffrey Kurzweil

Marriott Internat'l, Inc.
Issues: RES TAX
Rep By: Jeffrey Kurzweil

Nordstrom, Inc.
Issues: TAX
Rep By: Jeffrey Kurzweil

Sodexho Marriott Services, Inc.
Issues: FOO TAX
Rep By: Jeffrey Kurzweil

Kutak Rock LLP

1101 Connecticut Ave. NW
Suite 1000
Washington, DC 20036
Tel: (202)828-2400
Fax: (202)828-2488
Registered: LDA
Web: www.kutakrock.com
A multi-faceted firm specializing in corporate/government liaison; representative of clients with interests in the private sector, federal and state governments. Consists of the law firm of Kutak, Rock, and the Government Relations Group, its government relations arm.

DC-Area Employees Representing Listed Clients
BOND-COLLINS, Rhonda
HANDLOS, Brian
KARNES, Dave
KIRSHENBERG, Seth, Partner
SCHLOSSBERG, George R., Partner
STEINBERG, Barry P., Partner

Clients

Alameda, California, City of
Issues: ECN
Rep By: Rhonda Bond-Collins, Seth Kirshenberg, George R. Schlossberg, Barry P. Steinberg

American Humane Ass'n

American Public Info-Highway Coalition

Colorado Hispanic League

Energy Communities Alliance, Inc.
Issues: ENG
Rep By: Seth Kirshenberg, George R. Schlossberg

Farm Progress Cos.
Issues: ECN
Rep By: Seth Kirshenberg, George R. Schlossberg, Barry P. Steinberg

First Nat'l of Nebraska
Issues: BAN
Rep By: Brian Handlos, Dave Karnes

Highland Park, Illinois, City of Highwood Local Redevelopment Authority and the City of
Issues: ECN
Rep By: Rhonda Bond-Collins, Seth Kirshenberg, George R. Schlossberg, Barry P. Steinberg

Loews CNA Financial

Los Alamos, New Mexico, County of
Issues: ECN
Rep By: Seth Kirshenberg

Louisiana Public Facilities Authority

Massachusetts Higher Education Assistance Corp.

Municipal Bond Insurance Ass'n

New London Development Corp.
Issues: ECN
Rep By: Seth Kirshenberg, George R. Schlossberg, Barry P. Steinberg

Oak Ridge, Tennessee, City of
Issues: ECN
Rep By: Seth Kirshenberg

Orange, Florida, County of
Issues: ECN
Rep By: George R. Schlossberg

Orlando, Florida, City of
Issues: ECN
Rep By: Seth Kirshenberg, George R. Schlossberg, Barry P. Steinberg

Pickett, Virginia, Local Redevelopment Authority
Rep By: Barry P. Steinberg

San Francisco, City of
Issues: ECN
Rep By: Seth Kirshenberg, George R. Schlossberg, Barry P. Steinberg

Seaside, California, City of
Issues: ECN
Rep By: Rhonda Bond-Collins, Seth Kirshenberg, George R. Schlossberg, Barry P. Steinberg

Smith Barney Harris Upham & Co.

Team Stratford
Issues: ECN
Rep By: Seth Kirshenberg, George R. Schlossberg, Barry P. Steinberg

Tustin, California, City of
Issues: ECN
Rep By: Rhonda Bond-Collins, Seth Kirshenberg, George R. Schlossberg

Kyros & Cummins Associates

2445 M St. NW
Suite 260
Washington, DC 20037
Tel: (202)342-0204
Fax: (202)337-0034
Registered: LDA
E-mail: pkyros@aol.com
A public and legislative affairs consulting firm.

DC-Area Employees Representing Listed Clients
FALK, John M., V. President
KYROS, Hon. Peter N., President

Clients

Allsup Inc.
Issues: INS
Rep By: John M. Falk, Hon. Peter N. Kyros

American Soc. for Biochemistry and Molecular Biology
Rep By: Hon. Peter N. Kyros

American Soc. for Cell Biology
Issues: SCI
Rep By: Hon. Peter N. Kyros

Ass'n of Administrative Law Judges
Issues: GOV
Rep By: John M. Falk, Hon. Peter N. Kyros

Board of Veterans Appeals Professional Ass'n
Issues: GOV
Rep By: John M. Falk, Hon. Peter N. Kyros

Cooperative of American Physicians
Issues: INS
Rep By: John M. Falk, Hon. Peter N. Kyros

Defense Administrative Judges Professional Ass'n
Issues: GOV
Rep By: John M. Falk, Hon. Peter N. Kyros

Joint Steering Committee for Public Policy
Issues: SCI
Rep By: John M. Falk, Hon. Peter N. Kyros

Merit Systems Protection Board
Issues: GOV
Rep By: John M. Falk, Hon. Peter N. Kyros

Lackman & Associates, L.L.C.

1101 30th St. NW
Suite 220
Washington, DC 20007
Tel: (202)337-3137
Fax: (202)337-6660
Registered: LDA

DC-Area Employees Representing Listed Clients
LACKMAN, Carey A., Manager

Clients

Please Touch Museum, The Children's Museum of Philadelphia
Issues: EDU URB
Rep By: Carey A. Lackman

Lafayette Group, Inc.

8150 Leesburg Pike
Suite 900
Vienna, VA 22182
Tel: (703)760-8866
Fax: (703)760-8870
Registered: LDA
Web: www.lafayettegroup.com
A public affairs consulting firm.

DC-Area Employees Representing Listed Clients
DEWITT, Charles B., Partner
GREEN, Scott H., Partner

Clients

Boys and Girls Clubs of America
Issues: LAW
Rep By: Scott H. Green

D.A.R.E. America
Issues: ALC
Rep By: Scott H. Green

Shannon M. Lahey Associates

2701 32nd St. NW
Washington, DC 20008
Tel: (202)333-6924
Registered: LDA

DC-Area Employees Representing Listed Clients
LAHEY, Shannon M., Principal

Clients

Ass'n for Los Angeles Deputy Sheriffs
Issues: LAW RET
Rep By: Shannon M. Lahey

California Correctional Peace Officers Ass'n
Issues: GOV LAW LBR RET
Rep By: Shannon M. Lahey

NYSCOPBA - New York State Correctional Officers & Police Benevolent Ass'n
Issues: LAW LBR
Rep By: Shannon M. Lahey

Landry, Creedon & Associates, Inc.

499 S. Capitol St. SW
Suite 600
Washington, DC 20003
Tel: (202)488-8001
Fax: (202)488-8003
Registered: LDA
E-mail: bholmes@lmcinc.org
A consulting firm based in Phoenix, AZ.

DC-Area Employees Representing Listed Clients
HOLMES, Robert, V. President/Managing Director

Lee Lane

1828 L St. NW
Suite 1000
Washington, DC 20036
Tel: (202)463-8453
Fax: (202)293-4598
Registered: LDA
Web: www.aecs-inc.org

Clients

Americans for Equitable Climate Solutions
Issues: AGR AUT CAW ECN ENG FOR LBR MAN NAT ROD RRR TRA TRU UTI
Rep By: Lee Lane

Fern M. Lapidus

8801 Montgomery Ave.
Chevy Chase, MD 20815
Tel: (301)986-5491
Fax: (301)986-1506
Registered: LDA

Clients

Ass'n of Proprietary Colleges
Issues: EDU
Rep By: Fern M. Lapidus

Los Alamitos Unified School District
Issues: EDU
Rep By: Fern M. Lapidus

Nat'l Council for Impacted Schools
Rep By: Fern M. Lapidus

School of Visual Arts
Issues: EDU
Rep By: Fern M. Lapidus

LaRocco & Associates

Six E St. SE
Washington, DC 20003
Tel: (202)547-6400
Fax: (202)547-8800
Registered: LDA
E-mail: lcmlarocco@aol.com

DC-Area Employees Representing Listed Clients
LAROCCO, Christine B., President
LAROCCO, Hon. Lawrence P., Chairman
LAROCCO, Matthew, Senior V. President

Clients

American Bankers Ass'n
Issues: BAN BNK BUD CDT FIN INS SMB
Rep By: Hon. Lawrence P. LaRocco, Matthew LaRocco

Chase Electronic Investments
Rep By: Matthew LaRocco

Education Assistance Foundation
Rep By: Christine B. LaRocco, Hon. Lawrence P. LaRocco, Matthew LaRocco

Netivation.com
Issues: ADV BUD COM CPI SCI
Rep By: Hon. Lawrence P. LaRocco, Matthew LaRocco

Spokane Area Chamber of Commerce
Issues: BUD CSP DEF DIS ECN MED MMM RES
Rep By: Hon. Lawrence P. LaRocco, Matthew LaRocco

LaRock Associates, Inc.

6728 Baron Rd.
McLean, VA 22101
Tel: (703)556-3324
Fax: (703)734-7763
Registered: LDA
E-mail: joanlarock@erols.com
An environmental affairs government relations consulting firm.

DC-Area Employees Representing Listed Clients
LAROCK, Joan W., President

Clients

American Plastics Council
Issues: WAS
Rep By: Joan W. LaRock

LaRoe, Winn, Moerman & Donovan

3900 Highwood Court NW
Washington, DC 20007
Tel: (202)298-8100
Fax: (202)298-8200

DC-Area Employees Representing Listed Clients
DONOVAN, Paul M., Partner

Clients

Chlorine Institute
Rep By: Paul M. Donovan

Port Authority of New York and New Jersey
Rep By: Paul M. Donovan

Lasa, Monroig & Veve

2121 K St. NW
Suite 800
Washington, DC 20037
Tel: (202)261-3521
Fax: (202)261-3523
Registered: LDA
Web: www.lmvlaw.com
E-mail: izapien@lmvlaw.com
International law firm.

DC-Area Employees Representing Listed Clients
ALPERSTEIN, Brian, Partner
ZAPIEN, E. Ivan, Director, Government and International Business Solutions

Clients

Mendez University System, Ana G.
Issues: EDU
Rep By: Brian Alperstein, E. Ivan Zapien

Latham & Watkins

555 11th St. NW
Suite 1000
Washington, DC 20004
Tel: (202)637-2200
Fax: (202)637-2201
Registered: LDA, FARA
Web: www.lw.com
Washington office of a Los Angeles law firm.

DC-Area Employees Representing Listed Clients
ALLARD, Nicholas W., Partner
BABBITT, Bruce E., Of Counsel
BAER, Teresa D., Counsel
BEASLEY, Vicky
BERNTHAL, Eric L., Managing Partner
BOYLE, Kevin Charles, Partner
BRINKMAN, Karen
CAMERON, Richard
CORREIA, Edward
EPSTEIN, Gary M., Partner
GRIGSBY, McGee, Partner
HAYES, David J., Partner
HOLMSTEAD, Jeff, Partner
KELLY, Jr., William C., Partner
KURLANDER, Stuart, Partner
LEIVE, David M., Senior Communications Counsel
MAHONEY, Maureen E., Partner
MANTHEI, John R., Senior Associate
MORTON, Andrew
SUSSMAN, Robert M., Partner
VANDENBERGH, Michael P., Counsel
WELLFORD, W. Harrison, Partner
WINIK, Peter L., Partner

Clients

American Public Communications Council
Issues: TEC
Rep By: Nicholas W. Allard, Vicky Beasley

Boston Scientific Corp.
Issues: MED
Rep By: John R. Manthei

ElderCare Companies
Issues: HCR
Rep By: Edward Correia, William C. Kelly, Jr.

General Cigar Holdings, Inc.
Issues: TOB
Rep By: Nicholas W. Allard

Independent Telephone and Telecommunications Alliance
Issues: TEC
Rep By: Nicholas W. Allard, Karen Brinkman, Richard Cameron

Leap Wireless Internat'l
Issues: COM TEC
Rep By: Nicholas W. Allard

Nat'l Orthotics Manufacturers Ass'n
Issues: HCR
Rep By: Edward Correia, Stuart Kurlander, Andrew Morton

Serono Laboratories, Inc.
Issues: PHA
Rep By: Nicholas W. Allard, Edward Correia, John R. Manthei

Wireless Communications Ass'n
Issues: COM CPT TAX
Rep By: Nicholas W. Allard

Lathrop & Gage, L.C.

1200 G St. NW
Suite 800
Washington, DC 20005
Tel: (202)833-1420
Fax: (202)434-8992
Registered: LDA
Web: www.latropgage.com
The Washington office of a Kansas City law firm.

DC-Area Employees Representing Listed Clients
GEORGE, W. Peyton, Member

Clients

Wendy's Internat'l, Inc.
Issues: LBR TAX
Rep By: W. Peyton George

Lawler, Metzger & Milkman, LLC

1909 K St. NW
Suite 820
Washington, DC 20006
Tel: (202)777-7700
Fax: (202)777-7763
Registered: LDA

A law firm.

DC-Area Employees Representing Listed Clients

ESPOSITO, Sante J., Partner
KEENEY, Regina M., Partner
LAWLER, Gregory E., Managing Partner
LOGAN, Charles, Partner
MALLEN, Richard, Associate
METZGER, Jr., A. Richard, Partner
MILKMAN, Ruth M., Partner
STROBEL, Gil M., Associate
YATES, Valerie, Associate

Clients

Advocates for Highway and Auto Safety
Issues: AUT ROD TRA
Rep By: Sante J. Esposito

Allegiance Telecom, Inc.
Issues: TEC
Rep By: Regina M. Keeney, A. Richard Metzger, Jr., Ruth M. Milkman

Assumption College
Issues: EDU TRA
Rep By: Sante J. Esposito

Brotherhood of Maintenance of Way Employees
Issues: RRR
Rep By: Sante J. Esposito, Gregory E. Lawler

Canadian Nat'l Railroad/Illinois Central Railroad
Issues: TRA
Rep By: Sante J. Esposito, Gregory E. Lawler

Canadian Nat'l Railway Co.
Issues: RRR TRA
Rep By: Sante J. Esposito, Gregory E. Lawler

Currie Technologies, Inc.
Issues: CSP TRA
Rep By: Sante J. Esposito, Gregory E. Lawler

Electric Transportation Co.
Issues: CSP TRA
Rep By: Sante J. Esposito

EVA Corp.
Rep By: Sante J. Esposito

Fairfield University
Issues: ECN
Rep By: Sante J. Esposito, Gregory E. Lawler

Gemini Networks, Inc.
Issues: TEC
Rep By: A. Richard Metzger, Jr., Valerie Yates

Great Projects Film Co., Inc.
Issues: ART TRA
Rep By: Sante J. Esposito, Gregory E. Lawler

Highway 53 Longrange Improvement Citizens' Task Force
Issues: ROD TRA
Rep By: Sante J. Esposito

INTELSAT - Internat'l Telecommunications Satellite Organization
Issues: TEC
Rep By: Ruth M. Milkman

MCI WorldCom Corp.
Issues: TEC
Rep By: Regina M. Keeney, Charles Logan, A. Richard Metzger, Jr., Ruth M. Milkman, Valerie Yates

NorthPoint Communications, Inc.
Issues: COM TEC
Rep By: Ruth M. Milkman

ORBITZ
Issues: TRA
Rep By: Sante J. Esposito

Portals Development Associates L.P.
Issues: RES TRA
Rep By: Sante J. Esposito, Gregory E. Lawler

Provideo Productions
Issues: TRA
Rep By: Sante J. Esposito, Gregory E. Lawler

Rutgers University
Issues: NAT TRA
Rep By: Sante J. Esposito, Gregory E. Lawler

ZapWorld.com
Issues: CSP TRA
Rep By: Sante J. Esposito

Zuckert, Scoutt and Rasenberger, L.L.P.
Issues: AVI TRA
Rep By: Sante J. Esposito

Bob Lawrence & Associates

345 S. Patrick St.
Alexandria, VA 22314
Tel: (703)836-3654
Fax: (703)836-6086
Registered: LDA

Web: www.bl-a.com/welcome

DC-Area Employees Representing Listed Clients

COX, Craig, Senior Associate
GOLDWATER, James, V. President
LAWRENCE, Jr., Dr. L. Robert, President
TAYLOR, Anthony, V. President

Clients

Brandegee, Inc.
Rep By: James Goldwater

Columbia Research Corp.
Rep By: Anthony Taylor

Irrigation Ass'n
Issues: AGR
Rep By: James Goldwater, Dr. L. Robert Lawrence, Jr.

Minnesota Mining and Manufacturing Co. (3M Co.)
Rep By: Craig Cox, Dr. L. Robert Lawrence, Jr.

Nat'l Ass'n of Tower Erectors
Issues: TEC
Rep By: James Goldwater

The Laxalt Corp.

801 Pennsylvania Ave. NW
Suite 750
Washington, DC 20004
Tel: (202)393-0688
Fax: (202)393-7224
Registered: LDA

A congressional/governmental consulting firm.

DC-Area Employees Representing Listed Clients

LAXALT, Michelle D., President

Clients

Academy of Rail Labor Attorneys
Issues: RRR
Rep By: Michelle D. Laxalt

Alliance for American Innovation, Inc.
Issues: CPT DEF
Rep By: Michelle D. Laxalt

BP Capital, LLC
Rep By: Michelle D. Laxalt

Motion Picture Ass'n of America
Issues: ART
Rep By: Michelle D. Laxalt

Pickens Fuel Corp.
Issues: FUE
Rep By: Michelle D. Laxalt

Unisite, Inc.
Issues: TEC
Rep By: Michelle D. Laxalt

The Paul Laxalt Group

801 Pennsylvania Ave. NW
Suite 750
Washington, DC 20004
Tel: (202)624-0640
Fax: (202)624-0659
Registered: LDA

A government relations consulting firm.

DC-Area Employees Representing Listed Clients

LAXALT, Hon. Paul D., President
LORANGER, Tom, V. President

Clients

AIG Environmental
Rep By: Hon. Paul D. Laxalt, Tom Loranger

The American Land Conservancy
Issues: ENV
Rep By: Hon. Paul D. Laxalt, Tom Loranger

American Soc. of Anesthesiologists
Issues: HCR MMM
Rep By: Hon. Paul D. Laxalt, Tom Loranger

Apria Healthcare Group
Issues: HCR MMM
Rep By: Hon. Paul D. Laxalt, Tom Loranger

CSX Corp.
Issues: RRR
Rep By: Hon. Paul D. Laxalt, Tom Loranger

IDT Corp.
Issues: TEC
Rep By: Hon. Paul D. Laxalt, Tom Loranger

Philip Morris Management Corp.
Issues: BEV FOO TOB
Rep By: Hon. Paul D. Laxalt

PolyMedica Corp.
Issues: HCR MMM
Rep By: Hon. Paul D. Laxalt, Tom Loranger

Sierra Pacific Resources
Issues: UTI
Rep By: Hon. Paul D. Laxalt, Tom Loranger

Sirius Satellite Radio, Inc.
Issues: ART COM CPT
Rep By: Hon. Paul D. Laxalt, Tom Loranger

Yukon Pacific
Issues: FUE
Rep By: Hon. Paul D. Laxalt, Tom Loranger

Leadership Counsel, LLC

1625 Prince St.
Fifth Floor
Alexandria, VA 22314
E-mail: jlichtenstein@erols.com
Tel: (703)518-1484
Fax: (703)518-1519

DC-Area Employees Representing Listed Clients

LICHTENSTEIN, Jack D. P., Principal

Clients

Aegis Research Corp.
Rep By: Jack D. P. Lichtenstein

American Soc. for Industrial Security
Rep By: Jack D. P. Lichtenstein

GenuOne
Rep By: Jack D. P. Lichtenstein

MindSim, Inc.
Rep By: Jack D. P. Lichtenstein

MPRI, Inc.
Rep By: Jack D. P. Lichtenstein

Marvin Leath Associates

2019 Mayfair McLean Ct.
Falls Church, VA 22043-1764
Tel: (703)536-5573
Fax: (703)536-8163
Registered: LDA

DC-Area Employees Representing Listed Clients

LEATH, Hon. Marvin

Clients

Periodical Management Group, Inc.
Issues: DEF
Rep By: Hon. Marvin Leath

Textron Inc.
Issues: DEF
Rep By: Hon. Marvin Leath

J. LeBlanc Internat'l, LLC

601 Pennsylvania Ave. NW
Suite 900
South Bldg.
Washington, DC 20004
Tel: (202)638-6959
Fax: (703)799-2950

A business development and government relations firm.

DC-Area Employees Representing Listed Clients

LEBLANC, James L., Managing Partner

Clients

APG Solutions and Technologies
Rep By: James L. LeBlanc

Canada, Government of
Rep By: James L. LeBlanc

CATA (Canadian Advanced Technology Ass'n)
Rep By: James L. LeBlanc

Newbridge Networks
Rep By: James L. LeBlanc

Veritas Communications
Rep By: James L. LeBlanc

LeBoeuf, Lamb, Greene & MacRae L.L.P.

1875 Connecticut Ave. NW
Suite 1200
Washington, DC 20009-5728
Tel: (202)986-8000
Fax: (202)986-8102
Registered: LDA, FARA

Web: www.llgm.com

Washington office of a New York law firm.

DC-Area Employees Representing Listed Clients

BENN, D. Randall, Partner
BRITELL, Peter
HAVENS, III, Charles W., Of Counsel
HOYLE, Peggy A.
JAMES, A. Everette, Partner
KELLIHER, Joseph T., Senior Counsel
KREY, James M., Legislative Assistant
LANDGRAF, L. Charles, Partner
ROBINSON, Davis R., Partner
SERRANTI, Tess, Consultant
WILCHER, LaJuana S., Partner
WOODY, Robert W., Counsel

Clients

Ass'n of Metropolitan Sewerage Agencies
Issues: BUD ENV
Rep By: D. Randall Benn

Candle Corp.
Issues: CPI SCI
Rep By: Peggy A. Hoyle, A. Everette James, Joseph T. Kelliher

Houston, Texas, Department of Public Works & Engineering of the City of
Issues: BUD ENV
Rep By: D. Randall Benn

Hydro-Quebec
Issues: BNK ENG
Rep By: L. Charles Landgraf, Robert W. Woody
Internat'l Underwriting Ass'n of London
Issues: ENV INS
Rep By: James M. Krey, L. Charles Landgraf, Robert W. Woody
Jazz at Lincoln Center Inc.
Issues: ART BUD URB
Rep By: D. Randall Benn
Lloyd's of London
Issues: BAN ENV INS TEC
Rep By: D. Randall Benn, A. Everette James, James M. Krey, L. Charles Landgraf, LaJuana S. Wilcher, Robert W. Woody
Nationwide Global
Rep By: A. Everette James
New York State Reliability Council
Rep By: L. Charles Landgraf
The Project Leadership Committee, Lincoln Center for the Performing Arts
Issues: TAX
Rep By: D. Randall Benn, Peter Britell
Water Environment Research Foundation
Issues: BUD ENV
Rep By: D. Randall Benn, LaJuana S. Wilcher

Ledge Counsel

600 14th St. NW
Sixth Floor
Washington, DC 20005
E-mail: LedgeCnsl@aol.com
Tel: (202)783-1980
Fax: (202)783-1918
Registered: LDA

DC-Area Employees Representing Listed Clients
LOPATIN, Alan G., Principal

Clients
Dalton & Dalton P.C.
Issues: DOC EDU
Fort James Corp.
Kaplan Companies, Inc.
Issues: BUD EDU GOV
Nat'l and Community Service Coalition
Issues: BUD EDU GOV
Nat'l Ass'n of Retired Federal Employees
Issues: GOV HCR RET
Nat'l Ass'n of Senior Companion Project Directors
Issues: BUD GOV HCR
Nat'l Ass'n of Thrift Savings Plan Participants
Issues: FIN GOV RET
Nat'l Center for Family Literacy
Issues: BUD EDU
Nat'l Center for Learning Disabilities (NCLD)
Issues: BUD EDU
Nat'l Education Ass'n of the U.S.
Issues: EDU
Nat'l Head Start Ass'n
Issues: BUD EDU WEL
Nat'l Senior Service Corps Directors Ass'n
Issues: BUD GOV
Nat'l Treasury Employees Union
Issues: GOV LBR

Lee & Smith P.C.

1101 30th St. NW
Suite 200
Washington, DC 20007
Tel: (202)293-4584
Fax: (202)293-4588
Registered: LDA

DC-Area Employees Representing Listed Clients
LEE, David B., President
SMITH, C. William

Clients
Environmental Land Technology Ltd.
Issues: ENV NAT RES
Rep By: David B. Lee
North Dakota State University
Issues: AGR ANI DEF EDU NAT PHA SCI TRA
Rep By: David B. Lee
Space Dynamics Laboratory
Issues: DEF
Rep By: David B. Lee, C. William Smith
Utah State University
Issues: AGR ANI DEF EDU LAW NAT RES SCI TRA
Rep By: David B. Lee, C. William Smith

Jessica S. Lefevre

908 King St.
Suite 200
Alexandria, VA 22314
An attorney.
Tel: (703)836-3515
Fax: (703)548-3181
Registered: LDA

Clients
Alaska Eskimo Whaling Commission
Issues: MAR
Rep By: Jessica S. Lefevre

Leftwich & Douglas

1401 New York Ave.
Suite 600
Washington, DC 20005
Tel: (202)434-9100
Registered: LDA

DC-Area Employees Representing Listed Clients
BOYKIN, Curtis A.
BRIDENBAUGH, Thomas D.
DOUGLAS, Frederick A., Parnter
LUDOWAY, Natalie O.
PENN, Nicolas S.
TAYLOR, Rebecca L.

Clients
Verizon Washington, DC, Inc.
Rep By: Natalie O. Ludoway

The Legacy Group

1713 Birch Rd.
McLean, VA 22101
E-mail: mjgovan@aol.com
Tel: (703)917-0942
Fax: (703)917-0947
Registered: LDA

DC-Area Employees Representing Listed Clients
GOVAN, Michael J., President

Clients
Puerto Rico House of Representatives
Rep By: Michael J. Govan

LegiServe

611 Pennsylvania Ave. SE
Suite 287
Washington, DC 20003
Web: www.legiserve.com
E-mail: legiserve@aol.com
A public policy research firm.
Tel: (202)544-3273
Fax: (202)544-3273

DC-Area Employees Representing Listed Clients
PETERSEN, LeeAnn M., President

Legislative Solutions

1733 King St.
Alexandria, VA 22314
Web: www.legislativesolutions.com
Tel: (703)549-7464
Fax: (703)549-6980
Registered: LDA

DC-Area Employees Representing Listed Clients
DECHAINE, Dr. James, Partner
FLEMING, Daniel J., Partner

Clients
Allied Charities of Minnesota
Issues: TAX
Rep By: Dr. James DeChaine
American Trucking Ass'ns
Issues: INS TAX TRA TRU
Rep By: Dr. James DeChaine
Intermodal Ass'n of North America
Issues: FUE LBR MAR ROD RRR TAX TRA TRU
Rep By: Daniel J. Fleming
Truck Renting and Leasing Ass'n
Issues: CAW INS TAX TOR TRA TRU
Rep By: Daniel J. Fleming

The Legislative Strategies Group, LLC

1001 Pennsylvania Ave. NW
Suite 760 North
Washington, DC 20004
A bi-partisan lobbying firm.
Tel: (202)661-7060
Fax: (202)661-7066
Registered: LDA

DC-Area Employees Representing Listed Clients
FRIEBERG, Ronna
GAVORA, Carrie J., Health Policy Analyst
GOLD, Martin B., Chairman
HENRY, Denise M., Lobbyist
HILTON, Steven M., Lobbyist
KOGOVSEK, Hon. Raymond P.
LITTIG, Melvin J.
MASON, G. David
SMITH, Larry E., President
VOLJAVEC, Patricia Jarvis, Lobbyist
WINTERLING, Grayson

Clients
Allscripts Inc.
Issues: HCR MMM
Rep By: Martin B. Gold, Denise M. Henry, Steven M. Hilton, G. David Mason
American College of Cardiology
Issues: HCR
Rep By: Martin B. Gold, Denise M. Henry
American Hospital Ass'n
Issues: HCR
Rep By: Martin B. Gold, Denise M. Henry
American Systems Internat'l Corp.
Rep By: Melvin J. Littig, Grayson Winterling
Americans for Responsible Recreational Areas
Rep By: Larry E. Smith
Amgen
Issues: HCR
Rep By: Denise M. Henry
Biogen, Inc.
Boston Scientific Corp.
Cardinal Health Inc.
Rep By: Larry E. Smith
ECC Internat'l Corp.
Issues: DEF
Rep By: Melvin J. Littig, Grayson Winterling
Eye Bank Ass'n of America
Issues: HCR MED MMM
Rep By: Martin B. Gold, Denise M. Henry
Federal Home Loan Bank of San Francisco
Issues: BAN
Rep By: Martin B. Gold, Steven M. Hilton
Harcourt General
Rep By: Martin B. Gold, Larry E. Smith
Healthcare Leadership Council
Hoffmann-La Roche Inc.
Issues: HCR
Rep By: Denise M. Henry
Hong Kong Economic and Trade Office
Issues: FOR TRD
Hong Kong Trade Development Council
Issues: TRD
Rep By: Larry E. Smith
Hopi Indian Tribe
Issues: IND LAW
Rep By: Martin B. Gold, Steven M. Hilton, Larry E. Smith, Patricia Jarvis Voljavec
Independent Telephone and Telecommunications Alliance
Issues: TEC
Rep By: Larry E. Smith
Institute for Human-Machine Cognition
Issues: DEF
Rep By: Melvin J. Littig, Grayson Winterling
Joint Commission on the Accreditation of Health Care Organizations
Issues: HCR
Rep By: Martin B. Gold, Denise M. Henry
Eli Lilly and Co.
Issues: HCR
Rep By: Denise M. Henry
MedPartners, Inc.
Issues: HCR
Rep By: Martin B. Gold, Denise M. Henry
Nat'l Football League
Issues: COM GAM TAX
Rep By: Martin B. Gold, Steven M. Hilton
Nat'l Orthotics Manufacturers Ass'n
Issues: HCR
Rep By: Martin B. Gold, Denise M. Henry, Steven M. Hilton, Larry E. Smith
Noesis Inc.
Issues: DEF
Rep By: Melvin J. Littig, Grayson Winterling
Novartis Corp.
Wheat First Butcher Singer

LegisLaw

1155 Connecticut Ave. NW
Suite 500
Washington, DC 20036
E-mail: LegisLaw@aol.com
A full-service public affairs and government relations law firm.
Tel: (202)466-4840
Fax: (202)466-4841
Registered: LDA

DC-Area Employees Representing Listed Clients
WOOLLEY, Esq., Linda A., Principal

Clients
Comerica, Inc.
Issues: FIN
Rep By: Linda A. Woolley, Esq.
ITT Conoflow
Issues: AUT ENG
ITT Industries
Issues: RET TAX
Rep By: Linda A. Woolley, Esq.
Lehigh Portland Cement Co.
Issues: ROD TAX TRD
Rep By: Linda A. Woolley, Esq.
McDonnell & Miller
Issues: HOU
Rep By: Linda A. Woolley, Esq.

TRW Inc.
Issues: TAX
Rep By: Linda A. Woolley, Esq.

Arnold H. Leibowitz

1875 I St. NW
12th Floor
Washington, DC 20006
Tel: (202)824-8183
Fax: (202)296-9246
Registered: LDA
E-mail: arnold_leibowitz@hias.org

Clients

Hebrew Immigrant Aid Soc.
Issues: BUD IMM
Rep By: Arnold H. Leibowitz

Lent Scrivner & Roth LLC

915 15th St. NW
Suite 800
Washington, DC 20005
Tel: (202)347-3030
Fax: (202)347-3133
Registered: LDA
A government relations and strategic planning firm.

DC-Area Employees Representing Listed Clients
LENT, III, Norman F., Partner
LENT, Hon. Norman F., Senior Partner
ROTH, Alan J., Partner
SCRIVNER, Michael S., Partner

Clients

American Soc. of Anesthesiologists
Issues: MMM
Rep By: Norman F. Lent, III, Hon. Norman F. Lent, Alan J. Roth, Michael S. Scrivner

AOL Time Warner
Issues: TEC TRD
Rep By: Norman F. Lent, III, Hon. Norman F. Lent, Alan J. Roth, Michael S. Scrivner

Burlington Northern Santa Fe Railway
Issues: RRR
Rep By: Norman F. Lent, III, Hon. Norman F. Lent, Alan J. Roth, Michael S. Scrivner

Cellular Telecommunications and Internet Ass'n
Issues: TEC
Rep By: Norman F. Lent, III, Hon. Norman F. Lent, Alan J. Roth, Michael S. Scrivner

Chevron, U.S.A.
Issues: ENV
Rep By: Norman F. Lent, III, Hon. Norman F. Lent, Alan J. Roth, Michael S. Scrivner

Futurewave General Partners, L.P.
Issues: TEC
Rep By: Norman F. Lent, III, Hon. Norman F. Lent, Michael S. Scrivner

Great Western Cellular Partnership
Issues: TEC
Rep By: Norman F. Lent, III, Hon. Norman F. Lent, Alan J. Roth, Michael S. Scrivner

Iroquois Gas Transmission System
Issues: UTI
Rep By: Norman F. Lent, III, Hon. Norman F. Lent, Alan J. Roth, Michael S. Scrivner

KeySpan Energy
Issues: TAX UTI
Rep By: Norman F. Lent, III, Hon. Norman F. Lent, Alan J. Roth, Michael S. Scrivner

Bernard L. Madoff Investment Securities
Issues: FIN GOV
Rep By: Norman F. Lent, III, Hon. Norman F. Lent, Alan J. Roth, Michael S. Scrivner

Monroe Telephone Services, L.P.
Issues: TEC
Rep By: Norman F. Lent, III, Hon. Norman F. Lent, Alan J. Roth, Michael S. Scrivner

Nassau University Medical Center
Issues: HCR
Rep By: Norman F. Lent, III, Hon. Norman F. Lent, Alan J. Roth, Michael S. Scrivner

Nat'l Center for Tobacco-Free Kids
Issues: TOB
Rep By: Norman F. Lent, III, Hon. Norman F. Lent, Alan J. Roth, Michael S. Scrivner

New Skies Satellites N.V.
Issues: TEC
Rep By: Norman F. Lent, III, Hon. Norman F. Lent, Alan J. Roth, Michael S. Scrivner

Pfizer, Inc.
Issues: CSP PHA TRD
Rep By: Hon. Norman F. Lent, Norman F. Lent, III, Alan J. Roth, Michael S. Scrivner

Leonard and Co.

3433 N. Albemarle St.
Arlington, VA 22207
Tel: (703)536-9118
Registered: LDA

DC-Area Employees Representing Listed Clients
LEONARD, Burleigh C. W., President and Chief Exec. Officer

Clients

Kraft Foods, Inc.

Philip Morris Management Corp.
Issues: AGR
Rep By: Burleigh C. W. Leonard

Leonard Hurt Frost Lilly & Levin, PC

1701 K St. NW
Suite 300
Washington, DC 20006
Tel: (202)223-2500
Fax: (202)223-2501
Registered: LDA

DC-Area Employees Representing Listed Clients
LEVIN, Michael H.

Clients

SBREFA Coalition
Issues: SMB
Rep By: Michael H. Levin

Leonard Resource Group

1199 N. Fairfax St.
Suite 702
Alexandria, VA 22314
Tel: (703)548-8535
Fax: (703)548-8536
Registered: LDA

DC-Area Employees Representing Listed Clients
MACDONALD, Catriona, V. President, Policy

Clients

Nat'l Job Corps Ass'n
Issues: ECN

Lepon McCarthy White & Holzworth, PLLC

1225 19th St. NW
Suite 600
Washington, DC 20036
Tel: (202)857-0242
Fax: (202)857-0189
Registered: LDA, FARA

DC-Area Employees Representing Listed Clients
HOLZWORTH, David A., Partner
LEPON, Jeffrey M., Partner

Clients

Chilean Exporters Ass'n
Issues: AGR
Rep By: David A. Holzworth

Lerch & Co., Inc.

1629 K St. NW
Suite 1100
Washington, DC 20006
Tel: (202)785-6705
Fax: (202)331-4212
Registered: FARA

DC-Area Employees Representing Listed Clients
LERCH, Donald G., President

Clients

Japan Internat'l Agricultural Council
Rep By: Donald G. Lerch

Lesher & Russell, Inc.

1919 S. Eads St.
Suite 103
Arlington, VA 22202-3028
Tel: (703)979-6900
Fax: (703)979-6906
Registered: LDA
Represents agriculture and food-related clients.

DC-Area Employees Representing Listed Clients
LESHER, William G., President
RUSSELL, Randall M.

Clients

Chicago Mercantile Exchange
Issues: AGR FIN
Rep By: William G. Lesher, Randall M. Russell

Commerce Ventures
Issues: AGR
Rep By: William G. Lesher, Randall M. Russell

Federal Agricultural Mortgage Corp. (Farmer Mac)
Issues: AGR
Rep By: William G. Lesher, Randall M. Russell

Monsanto Co.
Issues: AGR
Rep By: William G. Lesher, Randall M. Russell

Philip Morris Management Corp.
Issues: AGR BEV FOO TOB
Rep By: William G. Lesher, Randall M. Russell

USA Rice Federation
Issues: AGR
Rep By: William G. Lesher, Randall M. Russell

Leventhal, Senter & Lerman, P.L.L.C.

2000 K St. NW
Suite 600
Washington, DC 20006-1809
Tel: (202)429-8970
Fax: (202)293-7783
Registered: FARA

DC-Area Employees Representing Listed Clients
LERMAN, Steven, Managing Partner

Clients

Grupo Televisa, S.A.

Leonard B. Levine & Associates

4009 Mansion Dr. NW
Washington, DC 20007
Tel: (202)965-2788
Fax: (202)965-2672
Registered: LDA

DC-Area Employees Representing Listed Clients
LEVINE, Leonard B.

Clients

Express Pipeline Partnership and Platte Pipeline Co.
Issues: CAW ENG ENV FUE TRD
Rep By: Leonard B. Levine

Levine & Co.

1225 I St. NW
Suite 350
Washington, DC 20005
Tel: (202)712-9134
Fax: (202)189-1110
Registered: LDA, FARA
E-mail: klevinejd@aol.com
A government affairs consulting, political consulting, and public affair consulting firm.

DC-Area Employees Representing Listed Clients
LEVINE, Ken, Chairman

Clients

American Internat'l Group, Inc.
Issues: TAX
Rep By: Ken Levine

Bermuda, Government of
Issues: TAX
Rep By: Ken Levine

GAF Corp.
Issues: CHM
Rep By: Ken Levine

Kohlberg Kravis Roberts & Co.
Issues: GOV
Rep By: Ken Levine

Radiant Aviation Services, Inc.
Issues: ENV
Rep By: Ken Levine

Schering-Plough Corp.
Issues: CPT TAX
Rep By: Ken Levine

Virgin Atlantic Airways
Issues: TRA
Rep By: Ken Levine

The Michael Lewan Co.

1001 Pennsylvania Ave. NW
Suite 850N
Washington, DC 20004
Tel: (202)347-2222
Fax: (202)347-4242
Registered: LDA, FARA
E-mail: michaellewanco@worldnet.att.net
A government relations firm.

DC-Area Employees Representing Listed Clients
LEWAN, Michael, President
SAUNDERS, Anne, Director, Legislative and Corporate Affairs

Clients

BSMG Worldwide
Issues: WEL
Rep By: Michael Lewan, Anne Saunders

Capital City Economic Development Authority
Issues: BUD ENV HOU TRA URB
Rep By: Michael Lewan, Anne Saunders

Connecticut Resource Recovery Authority
Issues: BUD ENV HOU TRA URB
Rep By: Michael Lewan, Anne Saunders

McGraw-Hill Cos., The
Issues: MIA
Rep By: Michael Lewan

Nat'l Center for Children in Poverty
Issues: WEL
Rep By: Michael Lewan, Anne Saunders

NetCoalition.Com
Issues: CPI CPT CSP
Rep By: Michael Lewan, Anne Saunders

Oracle Corp.
Issues: TAX
Rep By: Michael Lewan, Anne Saunders

Phoenix Home Life Mutual Insurance Co.
Issues: BAN TAX
Rep By: Michael Lewan, Anne Saunders

Public Policy Partners
Issues: AVI
Rep By: Michael Lewan

Lewis-Burke Associates

1233 20th St. NW
Suite 610
Washington, DC 20036
Tel: (202)466-4111
Fax: (202)466-4123
Registered: LDA
Web: www.lewis-burke.org
E-mail: LBA@lewis-burke.org

DC-Area Employees Representing Listed Clients
BROWN, Rachel, Government Relations Assistant
BURKE, April L., Principal
BURNHAM, Mark A., Government Relations Assistant
LEDFORD, Michael
MARIN, Mark, Government Relations Assistant

Clients

Ass'n of Independent Research Institutes
Issues: BUD CPT HCR IMM MED SCI TAX
Rep By: Rachel Brown, April L. Burke, Mark Marin

Associated Universities Inc.
Issues: BUD CPT EDU GOV IMM SCI TAX
Rep By: Rachel Brown, April L. Burke, Mark A. Burnham, Michael Ledford, Mark Marin

California Institute of Technology
Issues: BUD CPT EDU IMM SCI TAX
Rep By: April L. Burke, Mark A. Burnham, Mark Marin

Soc. for Industrial & Applied Mathematics
Issues: BUD EDU IMM SCI
Rep By: April L. Burke, Mark Marin

Syracuse University
Issues: BUD CPT EDU SCI TAX
Rep By: Rachel Brown, April L. Burke

Universities Research Ass'n
Issues: BUD CPT EDU ENG GOV SCI TAX
Rep By: Rachel Brown, April L. Burke, Mark A. Burnham, Mark Marin

University Corp. for Atmospheric Research
Issues: BUD CPT IMM SCI
Rep By: Rachel Brown, April L. Burke, Mark A. Burnham

University of Cincinnati
Issues: BUD CPT EDU HCR IMM MED SCI TAX
Rep By: Rachel Brown, April L. Burke, Mark A. Burnham

University of Southern California
Issues: BUD CPT EDU IMM MED SCI TAX
Rep By: Rachel Brown, April L. Burke, Mark A. Burnham

Virginia Commonwealth University
Issues: BUD EDU HCR IMM SCI TAX
Rep By: Rachel Brown, April L. Burke, Mark A. Burnham, Michael Ledford

Jack D.P. Lichtenstein

10659 Muirfield Dr.
Potomac, MD 20854-4080
Tel: (301)518-1484
Registered: LDA

Clients

American Soc. for Industrial Security
Issues: CON DEF DIS GOV LAW
Rep By: Jack D. P. Lichtenstein

Lichtman, Trister, Singer & Ross

1666 Connecticut Ave. NW
Suite 500
Washington, DC 20009
Tel: (202)328-1666
Fax: (202)328-9162

DC-Area Employees Representing Listed Clients
MUNSAT, Susan Chertkof, Attorney
TRISTER, Michael, Partner

Clients

Alliance for Justice
Rep By: Michael Trister

Liebman & Associates, Inc.

4413 Lowell St. NW
Washington, DC 20016
Tel: (202)966-5851
Registered: LDA

DC-Area Employees Representing Listed Clients
LIEBMAN, Murray, President

Clients

American Gas Ass'n
Issues: ENG ENV FUE GOV NAT SCI UTI
Rep By: Murray Liebman

KeySpan Energy
Issues: ENG ENV FUE GOV NAT SCI UTI
Rep By: Murray Liebman

Northern Indiana Public Service Co.
Issues: ENG ENV FUE GOV NAT SCI UTI
Rep By: Murray Liebman

Lighthouse Energy Group LLC

1200 18th St. NW
Suite 850
Washington, DC 20036
Tel: (202)822-2000
Fax: (202)822-2156
Registered: LDA

DC-Area Employees Representing Listed Clients
ANDERSON, Tobyn J., V. President
AYRES, Merribel S., President

Clients

Alliance Pipeline, L.P.
Issues: ENG
Rep By: Tobyn J. Anderson, Merribel S. Ayres

Ballard Power Systems
Issues: ENG
Rep By: Tobyn J. Anderson, Merribel S. Ayres

The Beacon Group Energy Funds
Issues: ENG ENV
Rep By: Tobyn J. Anderson, Merribel S. Ayres

Calpine Corp.
Issues: ENG
Rep By: Tobyn J. Anderson, Merribel S. Ayres

Coleman Powermate
Issues: ENG TRA
Rep By: Tobyn J. Anderson, Merribel S. Ayres

PowerGen
Issues: ENG
Rep By: Tobyn J. Anderson, Merribel S. Ayres

Powerspan Corp.
Issues: ENG
Rep By: Tobyn J. Anderson, Merribel S. Ayres

Lindsay Hart Neil & Weigler

1275 Pennsylvania Ave. NW
Ninth Floor
Washington, DC 20004
Tel: (202)467-8383
Fax: (202)467-8381
Registered: LDA

DC-Area Employees Representing Listed Clients
BEAUBIEN, Kathryn, Regulatory Manager
FRIEDMANN, Peter, Of Counsel

Clients

Agriculture Ocean Transportation Coalition
Rep By: Kathryn Beaubien, Peter Friedmann

Coalition of New England Companies for Trade
Issues: TRD
Rep By: Kathryn Beaubien, Peter Friedmann

Maritime Fire and Safety Ass'n
Issues: DIS
Rep By: Kathryn Beaubien, Peter Friedmann

Oregon Economic Development Department
Issues: TRA
Rep By: Kathryn Beaubien, Peter Friedmann

Pacific Coast Council of Customs Brokers and Freight Forwarders Ass'n
Issues: TRA
Rep By: Kathryn Beaubien, Peter Friedmann

Redwood City, California, Port of
Issues: TRA
Rep By: Kathryn Beaubien, Peter Friedmann

Reebok Internat'l
Issues: TRD
Rep By: Kathryn Beaubien, Peter Friedmann

Linowes and Blocher LLP

1150 17th St. NW
Suite 302
Washington, DC 20036
Tel: (202)293-8510
Fax: (202)293-8513
Registered: LDA
Web: www.linowes-law.com
E-mail: inbox@linowes-law.com

DC-Area Employees Representing Listed Clients
DELANEY, John J., Partner
DESIDERIO, Duane J., Associate
LIEBESMAN, Lawrence R., Partner

Clients

Fire Island Ass'n
Issues: NAT
Rep By: Lawrence R. Liebesman

Law Office of Zel E. Lipsen

One Massachusetts Ave. NW
Suite 330
Washington, DC 20001
Tel: (703)448-3060
Fax: (703)448-3060
Registered: LDA, FARA

DC-Area Employees Representing Listed Clients
EMANUEL, Adam
LIPSEN, Zel E., Principal

Clients

Ancore Corp.
Issues: LAW
Rep By: Adam Emanuel

British Ministry of Defence
Issues: AER DEF
Rep By: Adam Emanuel, Zel E. Lipsen

Dames & Moore
Issues: DEF ENG ENV
Rep By: Zel E. Lipsen

EFW Corp.
Issues: AER DEF
Rep By: Adam Emanuel

Media Fusion L.L.C.
Issues: SCI
Rep By: Zel E. Lipsen

Northrop Grumman Corp.
Issues: AER MAN
Rep By: Adam Emanuel, Zel E. Lipsen

PulseTech Products Corp.
Issues: DEF MAN
Rep By: Zel E. Lipsen

Robert E. Litan

Three Golden Crest Ct.
Rockville, MD 20854
Tel: (202)797-6120
Fax: (202)797-6181
Registered: LDA

DC-Area Employees Representing Listed Clients
LITAN, Robert E.

Clients

Arnold & Porter
Issues: DIS
Rep By: Robert E. Litan

Littler Mendelson, P.C.

1225 I St. NW
Suite 1000
Washington, DC 20005
Tel: (202)842-3400
Fax: (202)842-0011
Registered: LDA
Web: www.Littler.com

DC-Area Employees Representing Listed Clients
HOLLRAH, Russell A., Shareholder
SUSSER, Peter A., Shareholder

Clients

American Bakers Ass'n
Issues: LBR
Rep By: Peter A. Susser

Food Distributors Internat'l (NAWGA-IFDA)
Issues: LBR
Rep By: Peter A. Susser

Independent Contractor Ass'n of America, Inc.
Issues: TAX
Rep By: Russell A. Hollrah

Institute for a Drug-Free Workplace
Issues: ALC LBR
Rep By: Peter A. Susser

Private Care Ass'n, Inc.
Issues: HCR TAX
Rep By: Russell A. Hollrah

The Livingston Group, LLC

499 S. Capitol St. SW
Suite 600
Washington, DC 20003
Tel: (202)289-9881
Fax: (202)289-9877
Registered: LDA, FARA
Web: www.livingstongroup.com

DC-Area Employees Representing Listed Clients
GOODWEATHER, Melvin, Associate
LEGENDRE, Richard, Principal
LIVINGSTON, Jr., Hon. Robert L., Principal
MARTIN, J. Allen, Principal
RODGERS, Richard L., Associate

Clients

ACS Government Solutions Group
Issues: BUD CPI DEF
Rep By: Richard Legendre, Hon. Robert L. Livingston, Jr., J. Allen Martin, Richard L. Rodgers

American Ass'n of Nurse Anesthetists
Issues: BUD HCR
Rep By: Melvin Goodweather, Hon. Robert L. Livingston, Jr., J. Allen Martin, Richard L. Rodgers

Avondale Industries, Inc.

Baton Rouge, Louisiana, City of
Issues: AVI BUD URB
Rep By: Richard Legendre, Hon. Robert L. Livingston, Jr., J. Allen Martin, Richard L. Rodgers

Bollinger Shipyards

Boys Town USA
Issues: BUD
Rep By: Richard Legendre, Hon. Robert L. Livingston, Jr., J. Allen Martin, Richard L. Rodgers

Broward, Florida, County of
Issues: BUD TRD
Rep By: Melvin Goodweather, Hon. Robert L. Livingston, Jr., J. Allen Martin, Richard L. Rodgers

Committee of Unsecured Creditors
Issues: BNK BUD
Rep By: Melvin Goodweather, Hon. Robert L. Livingston, Jr., J. Allen Martin, Richard L. Rodgers

Commonwealth Atlantic Properties
Issues: RES
Rep By: Hon. Robert L. Livingston, Jr., J. Allen Martin

General Category Tuna Ass'n
Issues: MAR
Rep By: Melvin Goodweather, Hon. Robert L. Livingston, Jr., J. Allen Martin, Richard L. Rodgers

General Electric Co.
Issues: BUD CAW ENV NAT TAX WAS
Rep By: Hon. Robert L. Livingston, Jr., J. Allen Martin, Richard L. Rodgers

Gray Morrison
Issues: DEF
Rep By: Melvin Goodweather, Hon. Robert L. Livingston, Jr., J. Allen Martin, Richard L. Rodgers

Great Western Cellular Partnership
Issues: TEC
Rep By: Melvin Goodweather, Richard Legendre, Hon. Robert L. Livingston, Jr., J. Allen Martin

Illinois Department of Human Services
Issues: AGR ALC BUD FAM GOV HCR MED MMM SCI WEL
Rep By: Richard Legendre, Hon. Robert L. Livingston, Jr., J. Allen Martin, Richard L. Rodgers

Internat'l Systems, Inc.
Rep By: Hon. Robert L. Livingston, Jr., J. Allen Martin, Richard L. Rodgers

Jacobus Tenbroek Memorial Fund
Issues: BUD MMM TAX
Rep By: Hon. Robert L. Livingston, Jr., J. Allen Martin, Richard L. Rodgers

Link Plus Co.
Issues: SCI
Rep By: Melvin Goodweather, Hon. Robert L. Livingston, Jr., J. Allen Martin, Richard L. Rodgers

Lockheed Martin Global Telecommunications

Marine Desalination Systems LLC
Issues: BUD CAW
Rep By: Melvin Goodweather, Hon. Robert L. Livingston, Jr., J. Allen Martin, Richard L. Rodgers

Mesa, Arizona, City of
Issues: BUD
Rep By: Melvin Goodweather, Hon. Robert L. Livingston, Jr., J. Allen Martin, Richard L. Rodgers

MidAmerican Energy Holdings Co.
Issues: ENG
Rep By: Hon. Robert L. Livingston, Jr., J. Allen Martin, Richard L. Rodgers

Nat'l Capitol Concerts
Issues: ART
Rep By: Hon. Robert L. Livingston, Jr., J. Allen Martin

New Orleans, Louisiana, Port of
Issues: BUD MAR
Rep By: Melvin Goodweather, Richard Legendre, Hon. Robert L. Livingston, Jr., Richard L. Rodgers

Oracle Corp.

Raytheon Co.
Issues: BUD DEF
Rep By: Hon. Robert L. Livingston, Jr., J. Allen Martin, Richard L. Rodgers

Schering-Plough Corp.
Issues: BUD CPT HCR
Rep By: Melvin Goodweather, Hon. Robert L. Livingston, Jr., J. Allen Martin, Richard L. Rodgers

Stewart Enterprises, Inc.
Issues: CSP
Rep By: Melvin Goodweather, Richard Legendre, Hon. Robert L. Livingston, Jr., J. Allen Martin, Richard L. Rodgers

Turkey, Government of the Republic of

U.S. Oil and Gas Ass'n
Issues: BUD ENG FUE
Rep By: Hon. Robert L. Livingston, Jr., J. Allen Martin

LMRC, Inc.

1299 Pennsylvania Ave. NW
Suite 800 West
Washington, DC 20004
Tel: (202)682-3901
Fax: (202)842-0621
Registered: LDA
Web: www.carmengroup.com
A government and public affairs firm.

DC-Area Employees Representing Listed Clients
ADESNIK, Ryan, Chief of Staff
BOULTER, Hon. Beau, Senior Associate
CARMEN, David M., President and Chief Exec. Officer
CARMEN, Gerald P., V. Chairman
GILSON, Susan E., Senior Associate
HARPER, Dal, Operations Manager
HUGEL, Max, Vice Chairman
KALEN, Pam, Senior Associate
KEENE, David A., Managing Associate
LAGOMARCINO, John, Associate
LINTON, Ron M.
O'CONNELL, Mia, Senior Associate
SMITH, Clifton, Managing Associate
YOUNG, James B., Associate

Clients

Chicago, Illinois, Department of the Environment of the City of
Issues: URB
Rep By: Mia O'Connell

Chicago, Illinois, Washington Office of the City of
Issues: ROD URB
Rep By: Mia O'Connell

Citizens for State Power

Colorado Ass'n of Transit Agencies
Rep By: John Lagomarcino

Colorado, Department of Transportation of the State of
Issues: TRA
Rep By: John Lagomarcino

Managed Health Care Ass'n
Rep By: Pam Kalen

Metra/Northeast Illinois Rail Corp.
Rep By: John Lagomarcino

Montgomery, Maryland, County of

Lockridge Grindal & Nauen, P.L.L.P.

601 Pennsylvania Ave. NW
South Bldg., Suite 900
Washington, DC 20004
Tel: (202)434-8163
Fax: (202)639-8238
Registered: LDA
Web: www.locklaw.com
E-mail: dmmcgrann@locklaw.com
Washington office of a law firm headquartered in Minneapolis, MN.

DC-Area Employees Representing Listed Clients
BURTON, John D., Specialist, Federal Relations
CHANDLER, Kathleen K.
GINSBERG, Richard W.
GRINDAL, H. Theodore, Partner
HARTLE, Allyson J.
JOHNSON, Amy, Senior Federal Relations Specialist
KRINKIE, Mary Ramsey
MCGRANN, Dennis, Director, Public Affairs

Clients

Ass'n of Minnesota Counties
Issues: AGR DIS HCR TRA WAS WEL
Rep By: Dennis McGrann

Evangelical Lutheran Good Samaritan Soc.
Issues: HCR
Rep By: Dennis McGrann

Hennipin County Board of Commissioners
Issues: ENV HCR UNM WAS WEL
Rep By: Dennis McGrann

Jerome Foods
Issues: AGR ENV
Rep By: Dennis McGrann

Joint Powers Board
Issues: BUD RRR TRA URB
Rep By: John D. Burton, Amy Johnson, Dennis McGrann

Metropolitan Joint Powers Board
Issues: TRA
Rep By: Dennis McGrann

Minneapolis, Minnesota, City of
Issues: ECN
Rep By: Dennis McGrann

Minnesota Medical Group Management
Rep By: Dennis McGrann

Minnesota Transportation Alliance
Issues: TRA
Rep By: Dennis McGrann

Parent Centers FYI
Issues: EDU
Rep By: Dennis McGrann

Ramsey, Minnesota, Board of Commissioners of the County of
Issues: ENV HCR TOB WAS WEL
Rep By: Dennis McGrann

St. Louis, Minnesota, Board of Commissioners of the County
Issues: HCR TAX TRA
Rep By: Dennis McGrann

St. Louis/Lake Counties Regional Rail Authority
Issues: BUD FUE RRR TRA
Rep By: John D. Burton, Amy Johnson, Dennis McGrann

St. Paul, Minnesota, City of
Issues: ENV TRA
Rep By: Dennis McGrann

Valley Pride Pack
Issues: AGR FOO
Rep By: John D. Burton, Dennis McGrann

Wakota Bridge Coalition
Issues: ROD
Rep By: Dennis McGrann

Washington, Minnesota, County of
Rep By: Dennis McGrann

London and Satagaj, Attorneys-at-Law

1156 15th St. NW
Suite 510
Washington, DC 20005
Tel: (202)639-8888
Fax: (202)296-5333
Registered: LDA

DC-Area Employees Representing Listed Clients
LONDON, Sheldon I., Senior Partner
SATAGAJ, John S., Managing Partner

Clients

American Hardware Manufacturers Ass'n
Rep By: Sheldon I. London

American Supply and Machinery Manufacturers' Ass'n
Rep By: Sheldon I. London, John S. Satagaj

Hand Tools Institute
Rep By: John S. Satagaj

Manufacturing Jewelers and Suppliers of America
Rep By: Sheldon I. London

Nat'l Lumber and Building Material Dealers Ass'n
Rep By: John S. Satagaj

Photo Marketing Ass'n-Internat'l
Rep By: Sheldon I. London, John S. Satagaj

Wood Machinery Manufacturers of America
Rep By: Sheldon I. London, John S. Satagaj

Richard Long & Associates

P.O. Box 5320
Arlington, VA 22205
Tel: (703)536-2060
Fax: (703)536-8519
E-mail: 70720.2522@compuserve.com

DC-Area Employees Representing Listed Clients
LONG, Richard

Clients

Nat'l Council of Teachers of Mathematics
Rep By: Richard Long

G. T. Long & Associates

1101 17th St. NW
Suite 500
Washington, DC 20036
Tel: (202)452-1102
Fax: (202)452-1885
Registered: LDA

DC-Area Employees Representing Listed Clients
LONG, G. Thomas, President

Long Law Firm

801 Pennsylvania Ave. NW
Suite 750
Washington, DC 20004
Tel: (202)737-9212
Fax: (202)624-0659
Registered: LDA
E-mail: LongLawFrm@aol.com

DC-Area Employees Representing Listed Clients
KIRKPATRICK, C. Kris, Partner
LONG, Hon. Russell B., Partner

Clients

Bristol-Myers Squibb Co.
Rep By: C. Kris Kirkpatrick

Employee Stock Ownership Assn
Rep By: C. Kris Kirkpatrick

Louisiana Tobacco Group
Rep By: C. Kris Kirkpatrick

United Companies Financial Corp.
Rep By: C. Kris Kirkpatrick

Long, Aldridge & Norman, LLP

701 Pennsylvania Ave. NW
Suite 600
Washington, DC 20004
Tel: (202)624-1200
Fax: (202)624-1298
Registered: LDA
Web: www.lanlaw.com
E-mail: Landc@lanlaw.com

DC-Area Employees Representing Listed Clients
ANDERSON, Karen, Public Policy Advisor
BENITEZ, Juan Carlos, Of Counsel

DARDEN, Hon. George "Buddy", Partner
MARCUS, Lindsey, Government Affairs Consultant
MASON, Keith W., Partner
NUCKOLLS, C. Randall, Partner
SHAPIRO, Ira S., Partner
SIMS, Edgar H., Partner
TURNER, Patrick C., Government Affairs Consultant

Clients

AFLAC, Inc.
Issues: BEV FOO
Rep By: Karen Anderson, Hon. George "Buddy" Darden, Keith W. Mason

BellSouth Corp.
Issues: TEC
Rep By: Karen Anderson, Keith W. Mason, Edgar H. Sims

Biotechnology Industry Organization
Issues: AGR TRD
Rep By: Karen Anderson, Lindsey Marcus

Consortium on Government Relations for Student Affairs
Issues: EDU
Rep By: C. Randall Nuckolls, Patrick C. Turner

DeChiaro Properties
Rep By: C. Randall Nuckolls, Patrick C. Turner

Florida Internat'l University
Issues: BUD EDU
Rep By: C. Randall Nuckolls, Patrick C. Turner

Lockheed Martin Aeronautical Systems Co.
Issues: DEF
Rep By: Hon. George "Buddy" Darden

Monsanto Co.
Issues: AGR TRD
Rep By: Karen Anderson, Edgar H. Sims

Nat'l Ass'n of Professional Forestry Schools and Colleges
Issues: BUD NAT
Rep By: C. Randall Nuckolls, Patrick C. Turner

Nat'l Franchisee Ass'n
Issues: SMB
Rep By: C. Randall Nuckolls, Patrick C. Turner

Santa Fe Natural Tobacco Co.
Rep By: C. Randall Nuckolls

University of Georgia
Issues: BUD EDU
Rep By: C. Randall Nuckolls, Patrick C. Turner

Weather Channel
Issues: BUD COM SCI
Rep By: C. Randall Nuckolls, Patrick C. Turner

The Lonington Group

218 N. Lee St.
Alexandria, VA 22314
Tel: (703)329-1670
Fax: (703)329-1670
E-mail: aggray@world.att.net
A Washington representation and consultancy firm.

DC-Area Employees Representing Listed Clients
GRAY, Alan G., Managing Director

Clients

Harborlink, LLC
Rep By: Alan G. Gray

Metromarine Holdings, Inc.
Rep By: Alan G. Gray

Lotstein Buckman, Attorneys At Law

5185 MacArthur Blvd. NW
Washington, DC 20016-3341
Tel: (202)237-6000
Fax: (202)237-8900
Registered: LDA
Web: www.lotsteinbuckman.com
E-mail: info@lotsteinbuckman.com

DC-Area Employees Representing Listed Clients
LOTSTEIN, Robert, Attorney At Law
TURNER, Susan, Manager, Government Affairs

Clients

Nat'l Ass'n of Mortgage Brokers
Issues: BAN HOU
Rep By: Robert Lotstein, Susan Turner

Lowe & Associates, Ltd.

1211 Connecticut Ave. NW
Suite 805
Washington, DC 20036
Tel: (202)862-9835
Fax: (202)862-9838
Registered: LDA
E-mail: LOWEDC@aol.com
A full-service governmental relations and financial consulting firm.

DC-Area Employees Representing Listed Clients
LOWE, Jr., George H., President

Clients

Washington Parking Ass'n
Issues: TRA
Rep By: George H. Lowe, Jr.

LPI Consulting, Inc.

3000 K St. NW
Suite 300
Washington, DC 20007-5116
Tel: (202)424-7820
Fax: (202)424-7723
Registered: LDA
E-mail: lpiconsulting@mindspring.com

DC-Area Employees Representing Listed Clients
GORMAN, Teresa, Advisor

Clients

Albright & Wilson Americas
Rep By: Teresa Gorman

General Electric Co.
Rep By: Teresa Gorman

Koch Industries, Inc.
Issues: BUD CAW
Rep By: Teresa Gorman

Swidler Berlin Shereff Friedman, LLP
Issues: BUD CAW ENV GOV
Rep By: Teresa Gorman

Manuel Lujan Associates

151 D St. SE
Washington, DC 20003
Tel: (202)546-7255
Fax: (202)543-9289
Registered: LDA

DC-Area Employees Representing Listed Clients
HOFER, Lydia, Associate

Clients

Legix Co.
Issues: IND
Rep By: Lydia Hofer

Pojoaque Pueblo
Issues: BUD IND
Rep By: Lydia Hofer

J. C. Luman and Assoc.

1660 L St. NW
Suite 506
Washington, DC 20036
Tel: (202)682-9191
Fax: (202)463-6328
E-mail: jcluman@erols.com
A firm representing various clients with interests in employment, engineering, education, federal consulting and other federal activities.

DC-Area Employees Representing Listed Clients
LUMAN, Joseph C., President

Clients

Distance Education and Training Council
Rep By: Joseph C. Luman

Nat'l Ass'n of Personnel Services
Rep By: Joseph C. Luman

NISH - Creating Employment Opportunities for People with Severe Disabilities

United Homeowners Ass'n

Luman, Lange & Wheeler

1660 L St. St. NW
Suite 506
Washington, DC 20036
Tel: (202)463-1260
Fax: (202)463-6328
E-mail: llw1660@aol.com

DC-Area Employees Representing Listed Clients
LANGE, Gene C., Managing Partner
LUMAN, Joseph C., Of Counsel
THOMAS, John W., Partner

Clients

American Wholesale Marketers Ass'n
Issues: AGR BUD FOO LBR SMB TAX TOB TRU
Rep By: Gene C. Lange

Ass'n of Schools of Public Health
Rep By: Gene C. Lange

Ass'n of Veterinary Biologics Cos.
Rep By: John W. Thomas

LunaCorp, Inc.

4350 N. Fairfax Dr.
Suite 900
Arlington, VA 22203
Tel: (703)207-4500
Registered: LDA
Provides marketing, public relations and government affairs services for space companies and commercial space projects.

DC-Area Employees Representing Listed Clients
BECKNER, Victoria, Director of External Affairs
GUMP, David, President

Clients

Rotary Rocket Co.
Issues: AER
Rep By: Victoria Beckner, David Gump

Luntz Research Cos.

1000 Wilson Blvd.
Suite 950
Arlington, VA 22209
Tel: (703)358-0080
Fax: (703)358-0089
A political polling, communication, and strategic services firm.

DC-Area Employees Representing Listed Clients
INGRAM, Chris, Senior V. President
LUNTZ, Frank I., President

Lutzker & Lutzker LLP

1000 Vermont Ave. NW
Suite 450
Washington, DC 20005
Tel: (202)408-7600
Fax: (202)408-7677
Registered: LDA

DC-Area Employees Representing Listed Clients
LUTZKER, Arnold P., Partner

Clients

Directors Guild of America
Issues: CPT
Rep By: Arnold P. Lutzker

Shared Legal Capability for Intellectual Property
Issues: COM CPT
Rep By: Arnold P. Lutzker

Marshall L. Lynam

P.O. Box 76440
Washington, DC 20013-6440
Tel: (202)544-7996
Fax: (202)544-7996
Registered: LDA
E-mail: mlynam@cais.com

Clients

Dallas/Fort Worth Internat'l Airport Board
Issues: AVI
Rep By: Marshall L. Lynam

Radio Shack Corp.
Issues: BNK TAX TEC TRD
Rep By: Marshall L. Lynam

Lyons & Co.

1717 K St. NW
Suite 500
Washington, DC 20006
Tel: (202)466-5636
Fax: (202)466-2331
Registered: LDA
Web: www.lyonsandco.com
E-mail: lac@lyonsandco.com
A public affairs consulting firm.

DC-Area Employees Representing Listed Clients
LYONS, William, Owner

Clients

Clariant Corp.
Issues: TRD
Rep By: William Lyons

Holnam Inc.
Issues: BUD CIV ENV TRD
Rep By: William Lyons

M & R Strategic Services

2120 L St. NW
Suite 400
Washington, DC 20037
Tel: (202)223-9541
Fax: (202)223-9579
Registered: LDA
A full service government affairs and public relations firm.

DC-Area Employees Representing Listed Clients
BAUMGARTNER, Lisa, Senior V. President
HACAJ, Sylvia, Director, Government Relations
PORRO, Jeff, V. President
ROSS, Donald K., Principal
WASSERMAN, William B., Senior V. President
WEISS, Daniel J., Senior V. President

Clients

Greater New York Automobile Dealers Ass'n
Issues: AUT CAW CSP EDU FUE SMB TOR
Rep By: Sylvia Hacaj

Internat'l Dairy Foods Ass'n
Issues: AGR
Rep By: William B. Wasserman

Lesbian & Gay Community Center Hetrick-Martin Institute
Rep By: Sylvia Hacaj

Nat'l Center for Tobacco-Free Kids
Issues: TOB

Nat'l Prostate Cancer Coalition Co.
Rep By: William B. Wasserman

The M Companies

3942 N. Upland St.
Arlington, VA 22207
Tel: (703)533-9539
Fax: (703)533-1612
Registered: LDA
E-mail: themcos@aol.com
A government affairs and association management firm.

DC-Area Employees Representing Listed Clients
BUSH, J.D., CAE, Milton M., Principal

Clients

Entela, Inc.
Issues: CPI CSP LBR TEC TRD
Rep By: Milton M. Bush, J.D., CAE

Internat'l Federation of Inspection Agencies, North American Committee
Issues: TRU
Rep By: Milton M. Bush, J.D., CAE

Nat'l Technical Systems
Issues: CPI CSP LBR TEC TRD
Rep By: Milton M. Bush, J.D., CAE

Retlif Testing Laboratory, Inc.
Issues: COM CPI DEF LBR TEC TRD
Rep By: Milton M. Bush, J.D., CAE

MacKenzie McCheyne, Inc.

P.O. Box 523225
Springfield, VA 22152
Tel: (703)913-7726
Fax: (703)913-7742
Registered: FARA

DC-Area Employees Representing Listed Clients
MACKENZIE, I. R., Partner

Clients

Argentina-Brazil Venture Services Corp.

Argentine Economic & Investment Council

South Atlantic-TransAndes Economic Committee

Macro Internat'l

11785 Beltsville Dr.
Calverton, MD 20705
Web: www.macroint.com
Tel: (301)572-0200
Fax: (301)572-0999

DC-Area Employees Representing Listed Clients
QUIRK, Frank, President

Clients

ABLEDATA

Turner D. Madden

1919 Pennsylvania Ave. NW
Suite 800
Washington, DC 20006
E-mail: maddesq@bellatlantic.net
Tel: (202)434-8988
Fax: (202)861-1274
Registered: LDA

Clients

Internat'l Ass'n of Assembly Managers
Issues: CIV CPT LBR
Rep By: Turner D. Madden

Madison Government Affairs

444 N. Capitol St.
Suite 545
Washington, DC 20001
E-mail: pjhmga@aol.com
A government affairs firm.
Tel: (202)347-1223
Fax: (202)347-1225
Registered: LDA

DC-Area Employees Representing Listed Clients
HIRSCH, Paul J., President
JACOBSON, Myron M., Director, Legislative Affairs
KEMPER, III, Jackson, V. President, Business Development

Clients

Clean Air Now
Issues: CAW ENG
Rep By: Paul J. Hirsch

DCH Technology Inc.
Issues: ENG FUE GOV MAR SCI TRA WAS
Rep By: Paul J. Hirsch, Myron M. Jacobson

Fairfield, California, City of
Issues: DEF ECN
Rep By: Paul J. Hirsch

Food Bank of the Virginia Peninsula
Issues: ECN GOV HCR
Rep By: Paul J. Hirsch

NASA Aeronautics Support Team
Issues: AER AVI BUD ECN SCI
Rep By: Paul J. Hirsch

Nat'l Community Reinvestment Coalition
Issues: BUD ECN HOU
Rep By: Paul J. Hirsch, Myron M. Jacobson, Jackson Kemper, III

Newport News, Virginia, Industrial Development Authority of the City of
Issues: DEF TRA
Rep By: Paul J. Hirsch, Jackson Kemper, III

Nottoway, Virginia, County of
Issues: BUD ECN EDU
Rep By: Paul J. Hirsch, Myron M. Jacobson

Pensacola Chamber of Commerce
Issues: DEF
Rep By: Paul J. Hirsch, Jackson Kemper, III

REM Engineering
Issues: SMB VET
Rep By: Paul J. Hirsch, Myron M. Jacobson, Jackson Kemper, III

SM&A
Issues: DEF LAW
Rep By: Paul J. Hirsch, Myron M. Jacobson, Jackson Kemper, III

Systems Simulation Solutions Inc.
Issues: AER DEF
Rep By: Paul J. Hirsch, Jackson Kemper, III

Team Santa Rosa Economic Development Council
Issues: DEF ECN
Rep By: Paul J. Hirsch, Jackson Kemper, III

University of West Florida
Issues: EDU ENV
Rep By: Paul J. Hirsch, Myron M. Jacobson, Jackson Kemper, III

USS Wisconsin Foundation
Issues: ECN EDU
Rep By: Paul J. Hirsch, Myron M. Jacobson, Jackson Kemper, III

Virginia Living Museum
Issues: ANI BUD ECN EDU ENV NAT SCI
Rep By: Paul J. Hirsch, Myron M. Jacobson

Roy F. Weston, Inc.
Issues: BUD ENV
Rep By: Paul J. Hirsch, Myron M. Jacobson

Cliff Madison Government Relations, Inc.

254A Maryland Ave. NE
Washington, DC 20002
Tel: (202)543-9395
Fax: (202)543-4297
Registered: LDA

DC-Area Employees Representing Listed Clients
MADISON, Cliff, Partner

Clients

FedEx Corp.
Issues: TRA

Los Angeles County Metropolitan Transportation Authority
Issues: TRA

Riverside County Transportation Commission
Issues: TRA

The Eddie Mahe Company

900 Second St. NE
Suite 200
Washington, DC 20002
Web: www.temc.com
E-mail: info@temc.com
Provides strategic communications focusing on clients facing opposition or confrontation.
Tel: (202)842-4100
Fax: (202)842-4442

DC-Area Employees Representing Listed Clients
LEE, Ladonna Y., President
MAHE, Jr., Eddie, Chairman
THOMPSON, Doug, Associate

Clients

American Insurance Ass'n
Rep By: Ladonna Y. Lee, Eddie Mahe, Jr.

Japan, Ministry of Foreign Affairs of

United Soybean Board

Gerald A. Malia

1660 L St. NW
Suite 506
Washington, DC 20036
Tel: (202)639-8000
Fax: (202)463-6328
Registered: LDA

Clients

American Bureau of Shipping
Issues: MAR
Rep By: Gerald A. Malia

Mallino Government Relations

1615 L St. NW
Suite 650
Washington, DC 20036
Tel: (202)626-8517
Registered: LDA

DC-Area Employees Representing Listed Clients
MALLINO, Sr., David L.

Clients

Internat'l Brotherhood of Teamsters
Issues: ENV LBR
Rep By: David L. Mallino, Sr.

Laborers Health & Safety Fund
Issues: BUD HCR LBR
Rep By: David L. Mallino, Sr.

Laborers' Internat'l Union of North America
Issues: LBR
Rep By: David L. Mallino, Sr.

Laborers-AGC Education and Training Fund
Issues: BUD ENV LBR
Rep By: David L. Mallino, Sr.

Laborers-Employers Cooperation & Education Trust
Issues: LBR
Rep By: David L. Mallino, Sr.

Nat'l Energy Management Institute
Issues: BUD ENV LBR
Rep By: David L. Mallino, Sr.

Maloney & Knox, LLP

5225 Wisconsin Ave. NW
Suite 316
Washington, DC 20015-2014
Web: www.maloneyknox.com
E-mail: BMaloney@maloneyknox.com
Tel: (202)293-1414
Fax: (202)293-1702

DC-Area Employees Representing Listed Clients
MALONEY, Barry C., Managing Partner

Clients

Ass'n of Sales & Marketing Companies
Issues: FOO GOV LBR SMB TAX
Rep By: Barry C. Maloney

Managed Care Compliance Solutions, Inc.

1350 I St. NW
Suite 870
Washington, DC 20005
Web: www.capalliance.com
E-mail: mccs@capalliance.com
A health care consulting firm. Member of The Capitol Alliance.
Tel: (202)638-0550
Fax: (202)737-1947

DC-Area Employees Representing Listed Clients
ATKINS, G. Lawrence, Principal
BALCERZAK, Steven, Principal
GORMAN, John K., President
HANNETT, Frederick J., Principal

Management Options, Inc.

1620 I St. NW
Suite 615
Washington, DC 20006
Tel: (202)463-8493
Registered: LDA

DC-Area Employees Representing Listed Clients
ATKINSON, Alan R.
CLAWSON, James B.
CLAWSON, Jason B.
LANIER, Robin W.
MATTINGLEY, Jr., George M. "Matt"
TODD, Jason

Clients

American Teleservices Ass'n
Issues: ACC ADV AER APP ART AUT AVI BAN BEV COM CPI CSP EDU ENG FIN FOO FUE HCR INS MAN MED MIA PHA RRR SCI SMB TEC TOU TRA TRD
Rep By: Alan R. Atkinson, James B. Clawson, Jason B. Clawson, George M. "Matt" Mattingley, Jr., Jason Todd

Manatos & Manatos, Inc.

601 13th St. NW
Suite 1150 South
Washington, DC 20005
Tel: (202)393-7790
Fax: (202)628-0225
Registered: LDA

DC-Area Employees Representing Listed Clients
FRASER, Kimberley M., V. President
MANATOS, Andrew E., President
MANATOS, Mike A., V. President

Clients

American University
Rep By: Kimberley M. Fraser, Andrew E. Manatos

Committee for Citizen Awareness
Rep By: Kimberley M. Fraser

MMV

Pancyprian Ass'n of America
Issues: BUD DEF FOR
Rep By: Andrew E. Manatos, Mike A. Manatos

PSEKA, Internat'l Coordinating Committee, Justice for Cyprus
Rep By: Andrew E. Manatos, Mike A. Manatos

United Hellenic American Congress
Issues: BUD DEF FOR
Rep By: Andrew E. Manatos, Mike A. Manatos

World Council of Hellenes

Manatt, Phelps & Phillips, LLP

1501 M St. NW
Suite 700
Washington, DC 20005-1702
Tel: (202)463-4300
Fax: (202)463-4394
Registered: LDA, FARA

Web: www.manatt.com/mpp.htm
A law firm headquartered in Los Angeles, CA.

DC-Area Employees Representing Listed Clients
ALTSCHULER, Irwin P., Partner
AMERINE, David R., Partner
BROWN, Michael T., Associate
BUECHNER, Hon. Jack W., Partner
COOK, William P., Partner
DEHART, June L., Partner
FARNSWORTH, Eric, Senior Advisor
GEHLMANN, Gregory, Partner
GENTRY, Margaret, Legislative Advisor
GILLEECE, Mary Ann, Attorney
GONZALES, Walter, Legislative Assistant
HUEY, Erik V., Associate
JONES, James R., Senior Counsel
KABEL, Robert J., Partner
KUHNREICH, Jeff, Legislative Advisor
LOWELL, Abbe David, Partner
MULDER, Steven J., Legislative Advisor
RAY, John L., Partner
ROBERTS, James H., Partner
ROSE, Luke, Legislative Advisor
RYAN, Stephen M., Partner
SCHMIDT, Susan M., Of Counsel
SILVERMAN, Stephanie E., Senior Advisor
STEIN, Donald S., Partner
WASSERMAN, Jessica A., Partner
WATTERS, Robb

Clients

Agilent Technologies
Issues: BUD CPI GOV
Rep By: Stephen M. Ryan, Robb Watters

AIS, Inc.
Issues: IMM
Rep By: Michael T. Brown, Hon. Jack W. Buechner, William P. Cook, Robert J. Kabel

Alameda Corridor Transportation Authority
Issues: TRA
Rep By: June L. DeHart, Robert J. Kabel

Asociacion Columbiana de Exportadores de Flores (ASOCOLFLORES)
Issues: TRD
Rep By: Irwin P. Altschuler, Hon. Jack W. Buechner, June L. DeHart, Eric Farnsworth, Robert J. Kabel, Susan M. Schmidt, Stephanie E. Silverman, Jessica A. Wasserman

AUGURA
Issues: AGR TRD
Rep By: Susan M. Schmidt, Jessica A. Wasserman

The Bank Private Equity Coalition
Issues: BAN
Rep By: Robert J. Kabel, Steven J. Mulder

BellSouth Corp.
Issues: TEC TED
Rep By: June L. DeHart, Eric Farnsworth, Erik V. Huey, James R. Jones, Susan M. Schmidt, Stephanie E. Silverman

Bolivia, Embassy of
Rep By: Hon. Jack W. Buechner, Eric Farnsworth, James R. Jones, Robert J. Kabel, Jeff Kuhnreich, Steven J. Mulder, Susan M. Schmidt, Jessica A. Wasserman

Campbell Foundry Co.
Issues: GOV TRD
Rep By: Walter Gonzales, Luke Rose, Robb Watters

Catellus Development Corp.
Rep By: Hon. Jack W. Buechner, June L. DeHart, Jessica A. Wasserman

CEMEX Central, S.A. de C.V.
Issues: TRD
Rep By: Irwin P. Altschuler, Hon. Jack W. Buechner, June L. DeHart, James R. Jones, Robert J. Kabel, Jeff Kuhnreich, Stephanie E. Silverman, Jessica A. Wasserman

Coalition for Global Perspectives
Issues: TAX
Rep By: Hon. Jack W. Buechner, Robert J. Kabel, Steven J. Mulder, Robb Watters

Computer and Communications Industry Ass'n (CCIA)
Issues: BUD CPI CSP GOV POS TAX TEC
Rep By: Walter Gonzales, Luke Rose, Stephen M. Ryan, Robb Watters

Congo, Republic of
Rep By: Michael T. Brown, June L. DeHart, Eric Farnsworth, Margaret Gentry, Erik V. Huey, James R. Jones, John L. Ray, Jessica A. Wasserman

Corrections Corp. of America
Issues: LAW
Rep By: John L. Ray

DAG Petroleum
Issues: ENG FUE SMB
Rep By: Michael T. Brown, Margaret Gentry, James R. Jones, John L. Ray

R. R. Donnelley & Sons
Issues: DEF
Rep By: Mary Ann Gilleece

Downey Financial Corp.
Issues: BAN
Rep By: Robert J. Kabel, Steven J. Mulder

Eaton Corp., Cutler Hammer
Issues: DEF
Rep By: Mary Ann Gilleece, Jeff Kuhnreich

Employee-Owned S Corporations of America
Issues: TAX
Rep By: Hon. Jack W. Buechner, Steven J. Mulder, John L. Ray, Stephanie E. Silverman

Hewlett-Packard Co.
Issues: BUD CPI GOV
Rep By: Stephen M. Ryan, Robb Watters

Honeywell Internat'l, Inc.
Issues: DEF
Rep By: Mary Ann Gilleece, Jeff Kuhnreich

Intuit, Inc.
Issues: BUD CPI GOV POS
Rep By: Hon. Jack W. Buechner, Stephen M. Ryan, Robb Watters

Jacobs Engineering Group Inc.
Issues: BUD DEF
Rep By: Mary Ann Gilleece, James H. Roberts

Kean Tracers, Inc.
Issues: BAN CSP FIN
Rep By: Michael T. Brown, Hon. Jack W. Buechner, Erik V. Huey, Robert J. Kabel, Steven J. Mulder

Keller Equity Group, Inc.
Issues: BUD ROD TRA
Rep By: Michael T. Brown, Hon. Jack W. Buechner, June L. DeHart

Land Grant Development
Issues: RES TRA
Rep By: Eric Farnsworth, James R. Jones, Robert J. Kabel

Los Angeles Unified School District
Issues: EDU TEC
Rep By: Luke Rose, Robb Watters

Mexico, Embassy of
Rep By: Hon. Jack W. Buechner, Eric Farnsworth, Abbe David Lowell, Steven J. Mulder, Susan M. Schmidt

Miami Valley Economic Coalition
Issues: DEF
Rep By: Mary Ann Gilleece, Jeff Kuhnreich

Mitsubishi Motors America, Inc.
Issues: AUT LBR TRD
Rep By: Hon. Jack W. Buechner, Eric Farnsworth, Steven J. Mulder

Oracle Corp.
Issues: BUD CPI GOV TAX
Rep By: Luke Rose, Stephen M. Ryan, Robb Watters

Pelican Butte Corp.
Issues: RES
Rep By: Hon. Jack W. Buechner, June L. DeHart, James R. Jones, Jeff Kuhnreich, Jessica A. Wasserman

Playa Vista
Issues: TRA
Rep By: Michael T. Brown, Hon. Jack W. Buechner, June L. DeHart, Jeff Kuhnreich

Poseidon Resources Corp.
Issues: ENV WAS
Rep By: Hon. Jack W. Buechner, James R. Jones

Racal Communications Inc.
Issues: DEF
Rep By: Mary Ann Gilleece, Jeff Kuhnreich

Reno, Nevada, City of
Issues: BUD
Rep By: Michael T. Brown, June L. DeHart

Royal Wine Co.
Issues: TRD
Rep By: June L. DeHart, Donald S. Stein

S-Corporation Ass'n
Issues: SMB TAX
Rep By: Steven J. Mulder, Stephanie E. Silverman

Sabreliner Corp.
Issues: DEF
Rep By: Mary Ann Gilleece, Jeff Kuhnreich

Secretaria de Agricultura, Granaderia y Desarrolo Rural (SAGAR)
Rep By: Susan M. Schmidt

Servicios Corporativos Cintra SA de CV
Rep By: Irwin P. Altschuler, Abbe David Lowell

SESAC, Inc.
Issues: ART CPT
Rep By: Robert J. Kabel, Susan M. Schmidt

Single Stick
Issues: TOB
Rep By: Hon. Jack W. Buechner

Stewart & Stevenson Services, Inc.
Issues: DEF
Rep By: Mary Ann Gilleece, Jeff Kuhnreich

SWIPCO, U.S.
Issues: FOR GOV
Rep By: Hon. Jack W. Buechner, June L. DeHart, Eric Farnsworth, Robert J. Kabel, Jeff Kuhnreich, Susan M. Schmidt, Jessica A. Wasserman

Thermo EcoTek Corp.
Issues: EBG ENV TAX
Rep By: Hon. Jack W. Buechner

Unisys Corp.
Issues: BUD CPI DEF GOV
Rep By: Stephen M. Ryan, Robb Watters

US Airways
Issues: AVI
Rep By: Hon. Jack W. Buechner, Robert J. Kabel

Verizon Communications
Issues: COM TEC
Rep By: William P. Cook, Erik V. Huey, James R. Jones, John L. Ray

Yakima, Washington, City of
Issues: TRA
Rep By: Hon. Jack W. Buechner, June L. DeHart, Jeff Kuhnreich

Manelli Denison & Selter PLLC

2000 M St. NW
Suite 700
Washington, DC 20036
Web: www.farkaslaw.com
Tel: (202)261-1000
Fax: (202)887-0336
Registered: LDA

DC-Area Employees Representing Listed Clients
MANELLI, Daniel J.

Clients

Contact Lens Manufacturers Ass'n
Rep By: Daniel J. Manelli

MARC Associates, Inc.

1101 17th St. NW
Suite 803
Washington, DC 20036
Web: www.marcassoc.com
E-mail: Randy@marcassoc.com
Tel: (202)833-0007
Fax: (202)833-0086
Registered: LDA

A lobbying firm representing clients in the fields of health, education, defense, transportation, housing, infrastructure, economic development and the environment.

DC-Area Employees Representing Listed Clients
ALLEN, Edwin, Senior Counsel
COLEMAN, Devon
FENNINGER, Randolph B., Exec. V. President
MADISON, Cliff
MALDONADO, Daniel C., President
O'TOOLE, Eve, Legislative Associate
PATASHNIK, Bernard, Senior Consultant
PENBERTHY, Shannon, Legislative Associate
RIKER, Ellen, Senior V. President

Clients

AdvaMed
Issues: MMM
Rep By: Edwin Allen

American Academy of Dermatology
Issues: MMM
Rep By: Bernard Patashnik

American Academy of Otolaryngic Allergy
Issues: MMM
Rep By: Bernard Patashnik, Ellen Riker

American Ass'n of Clinical Urologists, Inc.
Rep By: Randolph B. Fenninger

American Clinical Neurophysiology Soc.
Issues: MMM
Rep By: Ellen Riker

American Sleep Disorders Ass'n
Issues: BUD MMM
Rep By: Ellen Riker

American Soc. for Gastrointestinal Endoscopy
Issues: MMM
Rep By: Randolph B. Fenninger, Shannon Penberthy

American Soc. of Anesthesiologists
Issues: BUD HCR MMM
Rep By: Daniel C. Maldonado, Bernard Patashnik, Ellen Riker

American Soc. of Hematology
Issues: HCR MMM
Rep By: Bernard Patashnik, Ellen Riker

American Soc. of Nuclear Cardiology
Issues: HCR MMM
Rep By: Edwin Allen, Randolph B. Fenninger, Bernard Patashnik

American Speech, Language, and Hearing Ass'n
Issues: MMM
Rep By: Bernard Patashnik

American Urological Ass'n
Issues: BUD MMM
Rep By: Randolph B. Fenninger

Boehringer Ingelheim Pharmaceuticals, Inc.
Issues: ENV HCR
Rep By: Edwin Allen

Cerebral Palsy Council
Issues: MMM
Rep By: Edwin Allen, Daniel C. Maldonado, Shannon Penberthy

Coalition for Health Services Research
Rep By: Daniel C. Maldonado, Shannon Penberthy, Ellen Riker

Corporation for Supportive Housing
Rep By: Daniel C. Maldonado, Eve O'Toole, Shannon Penberthy

Federation of State Medical Boards of the U.S.
Issues: HCR IMM MMM TEC
Rep By: Edwin Allen, Ellen Riker

Fine Arts Museums of San Francisco
Rep By: Daniel C. Maldonado, Eve O'Toole, Shannon Penberthy

L.A. Care Health Plan
Issues: MMM
Rep By: Edwin Allen, Daniel C. Maldonado

League of California Cities
Issues: DIS GOV LAW LBR RES TAX TEC TRA
Rep By: Eve O'Toole

Los Angeles County Mass Transportation Authority
Issues: TRA
Rep By: Cliff Madison, Daniel C. Maldonado

Los Angeles County Office of Education
Issues: EDU
Rep By: Daniel C. Maldonado

Los Angeles to Pasadena Metro Blue Line Construction Authority
Issues: TRA
Rep By: Eve O'Toole

Los Angeles, California, Community Development Commission of the County of
Issues: HOU
Rep By: Daniel C. Maldonado, Eve O'Toole

Los Angeles, California, County of
Issues: HOU URB
Rep By: Daniel C. Maldonado, Eve O'Toole

Massachusetts Medical Device Industry Council
Rep By: Edwin Allen

Nat'l Ass'n of Epilepsy Centers
Issues: BUD HCR MMM
Rep By: Ellen Riker

Nat'l Hemophilia Foundation
Issues: BUD HCR
Rep By: Daniel C. Maldonado, Shannon Penberthy, Ellen Riker

NI Industries
Issues: DEF
Rep By: Daniel C. Maldonado

PhotoMEDEX

San Francisco, California, City and County of
Issues: BAN BUD ECN HCR HOU LBR TAX TOB TRA WEL
Rep By: Edwin Allen, Cliff Madison, Daniel C. Maldonado, Eve O'Toole, Ellen Riker

Sunstone Behavioral Health
Issues: MMM
Rep By: Randolph B. Fenninger

TELACU
Rep By: Daniel C. Maldonado, Eve O'Toole, Shannon Penberthy

University of California at Irvine Advanced Power and Energy Program
Issues: APP
Rep By: Cliff Madison, Daniel C. Maldonado, Eve O'Toole

Urologix, Inc.
Rep By: Bernard Patashnik

Barton William Marcois

2600 Virginia Ave. NW
Suite 404
Washington, DC 20037
Tel: (202)338-0211
Fax: (202)965-3463
Registered: FARA

Clients

Kuwait Information Office
Rep By: Barton William Marcois

Markcorp Inc.

1201 Pennsylvania Ave. NW
Suite 300
Washington, DC 20004
Tel: (202)661-4642
Fax: (202)661-4699
Registered: LDA

Firm plans to move its office in 2001. No further information was available at the time this edition went to press.

DC-Area Employees Representing Listed Clients
CLARK, Michael, President

Clients

Edenspace Systems Corp.
Issues: ENV
Rep By: Michael Clark

TWK
Rep By: Michael Clark

Market Strategies Inc.

1199 N. Fairfax St.
Suite 400
Alexandria, VA 22314
Tel: (703)535-8505
Fax: (703)535-8517
Web: www.marketstrategies.com

A Republican polling, corporate image, and communications research firm based in Livonia, MI. Also maintains offices in Portland, OR and Alexandria, VA.

DC-Area Employees Representing Listed Clients
ALLEN, Mark, Washington Partner
GAGE, Alexander P., President
STEEPER, Frederick T., Principal

Markey and Associates

1155 15th St. NW
Suite 1101
Washington, DC 20005
Tel: (202)822-9288
Fax: (202)822-0920
Registered: LDA

DC-Area Employees Representing Listed Clients
MARKEY, Barbara R., Legislative Consultant
MARKEY, Patricia E., Legislative Consultant

Clients

United Distribution Cos.
Issues: BUD CSP
Rep By: Patricia E. Markey

Ron C. Marlenee

10192B Ashbrooke Ct.
Oakton, VA 22124
Tel: (703)938-3797
Registered: LDA

Clients

Archery Manufactures & Merchants Organization
Issues: RES
Rep By: Hon. Ron C. Marlenee

Everglades Coordinating Council
Issues: NAT RES
Rep By: Hon. Ron C. Marlenee

Flathead Joint Board of Control
Issues: RES UTI
Rep By: Hon. Ron C. Marlenee

Lower Yellowstone Irrigation Project
Issues: NAT
Rep By: Hon. Ron C. Marlenee

Safari Club Internat'l
Issues: ANI RES
Rep By: Hon. Ron C. Marlenee

Marlowe and Co.

1667 K St. NW
Suite 480
Washington, DC 20006
Tel: (202)775-1796
Fax: (202)775-0214
Registered: LDA
Web: www.netlobby.com/marlowe
E-mail: marlowe@mail.netlobby.com

A government relations consulting firm.

DC-Area Employees Representing Listed Clients
MARLOWE, Howard, President
MAZZELLA, Jeffrey, Legislative Representative

Clients

American Coastal Coalition
Issues: BUD NAT
Rep By: Howard Marlowe, Jeffrey Mazzella

Avalon, New Jersey, City of
Issues: BUD NAT
Rep By: Howard Marlowe, Jeffrey Mazzella

Broward, Florida, Department of Natural Resource Protection of the County of
Issues: BUD
Rep By: Howard Marlowe, Jeffrey Mazzella

Encinitas, California, City of
Issues: BUD NAT
Rep By: Howard Marlowe

Fire Island Ass'n
Issues: BUD NAT
Rep By: Howard Marlowe, Jeffrey Mazzella

Galveston County, Texas
Issues: BUD ENV
Rep By: Howard Marlowe, Jeffrey Mazzella

Jefferson Texas, County of
Issues: BUD NAT
Rep By: Howard Marlowe, Jeffrey Mazzella

Lee County, Florida
Issues: BUD NAT
Rep By: Howard Marlowe

Manatee, Florida, County of
Issues: BUD NAT
Rep By: Howard Marlowe

MOTE Marine Lab
Issues: BUD ENV MAR
Rep By: Howard Marlowe, Jeffrey Mazzella

North Topsail Beach, North Carolina, Town of
Issues: BUD NAT
Rep By: Howard Marlowe, Jeffrey Mazzella

Ocean Isle Beach, North Carolina, Town of
Issues: BUD NAT
Rep By: Howard Marlowe, Jeffrey Mazzella

Ocean Village Property Owners Ass'n, Inc.
Issues: BUD NAT
Rep By: Howard Marlowe, Jeffrey Mazzella

Sarasota, Florida, City of
Issues: BUD NAT
Rep By: Howard Marlowe, Jeffrey Mazzella

Solana Beach, California, City of
Issues: BUD NAT
Rep By: Howard Marlowe, Jeffrey Mazzella

St. Augustine Beach, Florida, City of
Issues: BUD NAT
Rep By: Howard Marlowe, Jeffrey Mazzella

St. Lucie, Florida, County of
Issues: BUD NAT
Rep By: Howard Marlowe, Jeffrey Mazzella

Venice, Florida, City of
Issues: BUD NAT
Rep By: Howard Marlowe, Jeffrey Mazzella

Martin & Glantz LLC

888 17th St. NW
Suite 800
Washington, DC 20006
Tel: (202)296-7010
Fax: (202)296-9374

A national consulting firm headquartered in Mill Valley, CA. Specializes in grassroots organizing and communications strategies to affect public, opinion leader and policymaker attitudes and actions.

DC-Area Employees Representing Listed Clients
COUSINO, Janelle, V. President

Clients

California Wellness Foundation

Casey Family Program
Issues: FAM

Edna McConnell Clark Foundation
Issues: FAM

Council for Excellence in Government
Issues: GOV

Ford Foundation

Martin, Fisher & Associates, Inc.

1700 K St. NW
Suite 800
Washington, DC 20006
Tel: (202)862-9705
Fax: (202)862-9710
Registered: LDA
E-mail: dobmartin@aol.com

A government affairs consulting and marketing firm.

DC-Area Employees Representing Listed Clients
FISHER, J. Paris, Senior V. President
MARTIN, David O'B., President

Clients

AAI Corp.
Issues: BUD DEF
Rep By: J. Paris Fisher, David O'B. Martin

Nat'l Soft Drink Ass'n
Issues: AGR BEV FOO LBR
Rep By: J. Paris Fisher, David O'B. Martin

United Defense, L.P.
Issues: BUD DEF
Rep By: J. Paris Fisher, David O'B. Martin

Masaoka & Associates, Inc.

1000 Connecticut Ave. NW
Suite 304
Washington, DC 20036
Tel: (202)296-4484
Fax: (202)293-3060
Registered: LDA, FARA
Web: www.masaokadc.com

A business-to-business general service provider in regulatory/policy research; legislative analysis; data collection/retrieval; government/public/media relations. Emphasis is on international economics, trade issues, and the auto and food industries.

DC-Area Employees Representing Listed Clients
CALABIA, Ted, Associate
SMITH, Jennifer L., Senior Associate
YAMADA, T. Albert, President

Clients

Fresh Produce Ass'n of the Americas
Issues: AGR FOO TRD
Rep By: Jennifer L. Smith, T. Albert Yamada

Japan External Trade Organization (JETRO)
Issues: ECN MAN TRD

Maseng Communications

1501 M St. NW
Suite 700
Washington, DC 20005
Tel: (202)879-4109
Fax: (202)638-1976
Registered: FARA
E-mail: mailbox@masengcomm.com

DC-Area Employees Representing Listed Clients
WILL, Mari Maseng, Principal

Clients

Japan Automobile Manufacturers Ass'n
Rep By: Mari Maseng Will

Dawson Mathis & Associates

421 New Jersey Ave. SE
Washington, DC 20003
Tel: (202)547-2090
Fax: (202)547-2011
Registered: LDA
E-mail: dawson417@aol.com

DC-Area Employees Representing Listed Clients
MATHIS, Hon. M. Dawson, President

Clients

San Joaquin Regional Rail Commission
Issues: TRA
Rep By: Hon. M. Dawson Mathis

United Parcel Service
Issues: POS TAX
Rep By: Hon. M. Dawson Mathis

Mattox Woolfolk, LLC

513 Capitol Court NE
Suite 100
Washington, DC 20002
Tel: (202)547-9505
Fax: (202)478-0279
Registered: LDA
Web: www.mattoxwoolfolk.com
E-mail: advocate@mattoxwoolfolk.com

DC-Area Employees Representing Listed Clients
MATTOX, Richard B., Partner
SMITH, Deya
WILLIS, Gregory
WOOLFOLK, Brian P., Partner

Clients

Constituency for Africa
Issues: FOR
Rep By: Richard B. Mattox, Brian P. Woolfolk

ICG Communications, Inc.
Issues: TEC
Rep By: Richard B. Mattox, Brian P. Woolfolk

MCI WorldCom Corp.
Issues: TEC
Rep By: Richard B. Mattox, Brian P. Woolfolk

Voices, Inc.
Issues: ADV
Rep By: Richard B. Mattox, Deya Smith, Gregory Willis, Brian P. Woolfolk

Matz, Blancato & Associates, Inc.

1101 Vermont Ave. NW
Suite 1001
Washington, DC 20005
Tel: (202)789-0470
Fax: (202)682-3984
Registered: LDA
E-mail: msbrb@erols.com
Consulting firm that provides government relations, public affairs and advocacy services. Also maintains an office in New York, NY.

DC-Area Employees Representing Listed Clients
BLANCATO, Robert B., President
ROSS, Emily K., Senior Associate

Clients

AFLAC, Inc.
Rep By: Robert B. Blancato

Americans for Long Term Care Security
Rep By: Robert B. Blancato

City Meals on Wheels USA
Rep By: Robert B. Blancato

Council of Senior Centers and Services of New York City, Inc.
Rep By: Robert B. Blancato

Metlife Mature Market Group

Nat'l Ass'n of Nutrition and Aging Services and Programs

Nat'l Committee for the Prevention of Elder Abuse/Institute on Aging

Nat'l Ethnic Coalition of Organizations
Rep By: Robert B. Blancato

Nat'l Italian American Foundation
Rep By: Robert B. Blancato

Nat'l Silver Haired Congress

UNIVEC
Rep By: Robert B. Blancato

West Virginia University Center on Aging
Rep By: Robert B. Blancato

Alan Mauk Associates, Ltd.

2121 Jamieson Ave.
Suite 1405
Alexandria, VA 22314
Tel: (703)567-2021
Registered: LDA
E-mail: alanmauk@aol.com
Public affairs and government relations consultants.

DC-Area Employees Representing Listed Clients
MAUK, Alan R., President

Clients

Ann Eppard Associates, Ltd.
Issues: MAR TRA
Rep By: Alan R. Mauk

Cambridge Management Inc.
Issues: AVI
Rep By: Alan R. Mauk

Oklahoma Department of Transportation
Issues: ROD TRA
Rep By: Alan R. Mauk

Yukon City, Oklahoma, City of
Rep By: Alan R. Mauk

Mayberry & Associates LLC

252 N. Washington St.
Suite A
Falls Church, VA 22046
Tel: (703)538-8804
Fax: (703)538-6305
Registered: LDA
E-mail: pgmayberry@aol.com

DC-Area Employees Representing Listed Clients
MAYBERRY, Peter G., President

Clients

Ass'n of the Nonwoven Fabrics Industry - INDA
Issues: CAW ENV TRD
Rep By: Peter G. Mayberry

Healthcare Compliance Packaging Council
Issues: PHA
Rep By: Peter G. Mayberry

Virginia M. Mayer

1660 L St. NW
Suite 1050
Washington, DC 20036
Tel: (202)496-9610
Fax: (202)659-5234
Registered: LDA

Clients

Boston, Massachusetts, City of
Issues: BUD ECN EDU ENV GOV HCR HOU LAW URB
Rep By: Virginia M. Mayer

Mayer, Brown & Platt

1909 K St. NW
Washington, DC 20006
Tel: (202)263-3000
Fax: (202)263-3300
Registered: LDA
Web: www.mayerbrown.com
E-mail: ksheehan@mayerbrown.com
Washington office of a law firm headquartered in Chicago, IL.

DC-Area Employees Representing Listed Clients
BILZI, Carol J., Counsel
BLOOM, David I., Partner
BORDERS, Brian T., Counsel
BOYLAN, Kim Marie, Partner
D'ESPOSITO, Julian
DAVIS, Robert P., Partner
DEARYBURY, Sheila, Associate
EASTMAN, Penny L., Legislative Director
FALK, Donald M., Partner
FINNEGAN, David B., Senior Counsel
GEHMAN, Julian, Counsel
GELLER, Kenneth
GITENSTEIN, Mark H., Partner
HILDEBRAND, Daniel
JONES, Erika Z., Partner
KANTOR, Mickey, Partner
KEEHAN, Timothy E., Partner
KILEY, Roger J., Partner
KRIESBERG, Simeon M., Partner
KUSSKE, Kathryn A., Partner
LEWIS, Jeffrey H., Associate
NEMETZ, Miriam R., Partner
ORSECK, Gary A., Partner
OSOLINIK, Carolyn P., Partner
PARVEN, Scott, Counsel
PUNKE, Michael W., Partner
RECHT, Philip R., Partner
ROTHFELD, Charles A., Counsel
SCHER, Amb. Peter L., Partner
SCHMITZ, John P., Partner
TAYLOR, Mark R., Partner
TRIPLETT, Charles S., Partner
WILLIAMSON, Richard S., Partner

Clients

Accenture
Issues: TRD
Rep By: Carol J. Bilzi, Brian T. Borders, Mark H. Gitenstein, Jeffrey H. Lewis

ACE INA
Rep By: Mark H. Gitenstein

Ace Ltd.
Issues: TAX
Rep By: Penny L. Eastman, Mark H. Gitenstein, Amb. Peter L. Scher, Charles S. Triplett, Richard S. Williamson

Alliance of Automobile Manufacturers, Inc.
Issues: AUT
Rep By: Erika Z. Jones

American Farm Bureau Federation
Issues: TAX

Ameritech
Issues: TEC
Rep By: Mark H. Gitenstein

AOL Time Warner
Issues: TRD
Rep By: Scott Parven

Ass'n of Publicly Traded Companies
Issues: ACC FIN SMB TAX
Rep By: Brian T. Borders, Mark H. Gitenstein

Bertelsmann AG
Issues: ART COM MIA TEC TRD
Rep By: Penny L. Eastman, Julian Gehman, John P. Schmitz

The Boeing Co.
Issues: TRD
Rep By: Scott Parven

Burlington Northern Santa Fe Railway
Issues: RRR
Rep By: Mark H. Gitenstein

Cable & Wireless, Inc.
Issues: TEC
Rep By: David B. Finnegan, Mark H. Gitenstein, Erika Z. Jones

Chamber of Commerce of the U.S.A.
Issues: GOV
Rep By: Kenneth Geller

Chicago Stock Exchange, Inc.
Issues: FIN
Rep By: Penny L. Eastman, Mark H. Gitenstein

Citigroup
Issues: TRD
Rep By: Scott Parven

CoBank, ACB
Issues: AGR TRD
Rep By: Amb. Peter L. Scher

COMDISCO, Inc.
Issues: TAX

Deutsche Lufthansa AG
Rep By: John P. Schmitz

ED&F Man Inc.
Issues: TRD
Rep By: Penny L. Eastman, Jeffrey H. Lewis, Carolyn P. Osolinik, Richard S. Williamson

Edison Electric Institute
Issues: ENV
Rep By: David B. Finnegan

Edison Mission Energy
Rep By: John P. Schmitz

Elanco Animal Health
Issues: TRD
Rep By: Amb. Peter L. Scher

Enron Corp.
Issues: ENG TRD
Rep By: John P. Schmitz

Ernst & Young LLP
Issues: CPI TRD
Rep By: Carol J. Bilzi, Mark H. Gitenstein, Jeffrey H. Lewis, Carolyn P. Osolinik, Charles A. Rothfeld

Federal Home Loan Bank of Chicago
Issues: BAN
Rep By: Penny L. Eastman, Richard S. Williamson

First Church of Christ, Scientist
Issues: HCR
Rep By: Carolyn P. Osolinik

Ford Motor Co.
Issues: CAW ENG
Rep By: David B. Finnegan

GATX Corp.
Issues: TAX

General Dynamics Corp.
Rep By: Sheila Dearybury, Mark H. Gitenstein, Carolyn P. Osolinik

General Electric Co.
Issues: DEF FOR
Rep By: Carol J. Bilzi, Carolyn P. Osolinik, John P. Schmitz

Illinois, State of
Issues: IND
Rep By: Julian D'Esposito, Daniel Hildebrand

Internat'l Game Technology
Issues: TAX

KPMG, LLP
Issues: TRD
Rep By: Carol J. Bilzi, Brian T. Borders, Mark H. Gitenstein, Jeffrey H. Lewis

The Limited Inc.
Issues: TAX

Lockheed Martin Corp.
Issues: DEF
Rep By: Mark H. Gitenstein, Miriam R. Nemetz, Carolyn P. Osolinik

London Metal Exchange, Ltd.

Marathon Oil Co.
Issues: FOR
Rep By: John P. Schmitz

Monsanto Co.
Issues: TRD
Rep By: Amb. Peter L. Scher

New Life Corp. of America
Issues: FIN
Rep By: Timothy E. Keehan

New York Life Insurance Co.
Issues: TRD
Rep By: Scott Parven

News America Inc.
Issues: CPT
Rep By: Amb. Peter L. Scher

Nicor, Inc.
Rep By: Penny L. Eastman

Oracle Corp.
Issues: CPI
Rep By: Penny L. Eastman, Donald M. Falk, Mark H. Gitenstein, Jeffrey H. Lewis, Richard S. Williamson

Pharmacia Corp.
Issues: HCR TRD
Rep By: Amb. Peter L. Scher

PriceWaterhouseCoopers
Issues: CPI TRD
Rep By: Carol J. Bilzi, Brian T. Borders, Mark H. Gitenstein, Jeffrey H. Lewis, Charles A. Rothfeld

St. Paul Cos.
Issues: HCR
Rep By: Jeffrey H. Lewis, Carolyn P. Osolinik

Technology Network
Issues: CPI
Rep By: Brian T. Borders, Kim Marie Boylan, Mark H. Gitenstein, Jeffrey H. Lewis, Charles A. Rothfeld

United Airlines
Issues: TRA TRD
Rep By: Amb. Peter L. Scher

United Defense, L.P.
Issues: DEF
Rep By: Mark H. Gitenstein, Miriam R. Nemetz, Carolyn P. Osolinik

United Parcel Service
Issues: TRA TRD
Rep By: Amb. Peter L. Scher

United Technologies Corp.
Issues: DEF
Rep By: Mark H. Gitenstein, Miriam R. Nemetz, Carolyn P. Osolinik

Wheat Export Trade Education Committee
Issues: TRD
Rep By: Michael W. Punke

MBV, Inc.

3101 South St. NW
Washington, DC 20007
Tel: (202)293-1166
Fax: (202)293-1181
Registered: LDA
E-mail: wthreadgill@atlantech.net

DC-Area Employees Representing Listed Clients
THREADGILL, Walter L., President

Clients

Multimedia Broadcast Investment Corp.
Issues: TRD
Rep By: Walter L. Threadgill

Charlie McBride Associates, Inc.

1101 17th St. NW
Suite 705
Washington, DC 20036
Tel: (202)466-4210
Fax: (202)466-4213
Registered: LDA

DC-Area Employees Representing Listed Clients
MCBRIDE, Charlie, President

Clients

Biomedical Research Foundation of Northwest Louisiana
Issues: ENG PHA TRA
Rep By: Charlie McBride

Edison Chouest Offshore, Inc.
Issues: DEF LBR MAR
Rep By: Charlie McBride

ExtrudeHone Corp.
Issues: BUD DEF MAN
Rep By: Charlie McBride

Idaho Titanium Technologies, LLC
Issues: DEF
Rep By: Charlie McBride

Louisiana Center for Manufacturing Sciences
Issues: BUD DEF MAN
Rep By: Charlie McBride

North American Shipbuilding
Issues: DEF LBR MAR
Rep By: Charlie McBride

Science and Engineering Associates, Inc.
Issues: BUD ENG MAN SCI
Rep By: Charlie McBride

Science Applications Internat'l Corp. (SAIC)
Issues: DEF ENG WAS
Rep By: Charlie McBride

SRT Group
Issues: BUD ENG SCI
Rep By: Charlie McBride

University Heights Science Park
Issues: ECN SCI URB
Rep By: Charlie McBride

Waterworks Internat'l, Inc.
Issues: ENV FUE SCI
Rep By: Charlie McBride

Yukon Pacific
Issues: ENG
Rep By: Charlie McBride

Barbara T. McCall Associates

1401 K St. NW
Suite 700
Washington, DC 20005
Tel: (202)842-5430
Fax: (202)842-5051
Registered: LDA
Web: www.capitaledge.com
E-mail: mccall@capitaledge.com

DC-Area Employees Representing Listed Clients
GARBOUSHIAN, Ralph, Legislative Assistant
MCCALL, Barbara T., President

Clients

Austin, Texas, City of
Issues: ENG HOU LAW TRA URB
Rep By: Ralph Garboushian, Barbara T. McCall

Columbia, South Carolina, City of
Issues: HOU LAW TRA URB
Rep By: Ralph Garboushian, Barbara T. McCall

Dallas, Texas, City of
Issues: ECN HOU LAW TEC TRA URB
Rep By: Ralph Garboushian, Barbara T. McCall

Denton, Texas, City of
Issues: LAW TRA URB UTI
Rep By: Ralph Garboushian, Barbara T. McCall

Henderson, Nevada, City of
Issues: HOU TRA URB
Rep By: Ralph Garboushian, Barbara T. McCall

Huntsville, Alabama, City of
Issues: HOU LAW TRA URB
Rep By: Ralph Garboushian, Barbara T. McCall

Lubbock, Texas, City of
Issues: ENG HOU LAW TRA URB
Rep By: Ralph Garboushian, Barbara T. McCall

Plano, Texas, City of
Issues: HOU LAW TRA URB
Rep By: Ralph Garboushian, Barbara T. McCall

Texas Cities Legislative Coalition (TCLC)
Rep By: Barbara T. McCall

Bettie McCarthy and Associates

4845 Rock Spring Rd.
Arlington, VA 22207
Tel: (703)241-7977
Fax: (703)241-1035
Registered: LDA
E-mail: bettiemccarthy@msn.com

DC-Area Employees Representing Listed Clients
MCCARTHY, Elizabeth S. "Bettie", President

Clients

Great Lakes Composites Consortium
Rep By: Elizabeth S. "Bettie" McCarthy

Navy Joining Center
Issues: MAN
Rep By: Elizabeth S. "Bettie" McCarthy

Proprietary Industries Ass'n
Rep By: Elizabeth S. "Bettie" McCarthy

McClure, Gerard & Neuenschwander, Inc.

201 Maryland Ave. NE
Washington, DC 20002
Tel: (202)543-7200
Fax: (202)543-0616
Registered: LDA
E-mail: mgn@mgninc.com
A government relations, consulting, and strategic planning firm.

DC-Area Employees Representing Listed Clients
BARRINGER, Steven G., Principal
FINDARO, Joseph T., Principal
IANDOLI, Matthew
JOHNSON, Nils W., Principal
MCCLURE, Hon. James A., Principal
NEUENSCHWANDER, Tod O., Principal

Clients

American Gaming Ass'n
Rep By: Steven G. Barringer, Joseph T. Findaro, Matthew Iandoli, Nils W. Johnson, Hon. James A. McClure, Tod O. Neuenschwander

Barrick Goldstrike Mines, Inc.
Rep By: Steven G. Barringer, Joseph T. Findaro, Matthew Iandoli, Nils W. Johnson, Hon. James A. McClure, Tod O. Neuenschwander

Boise State University
Issues: BUD
Rep By: Steven G. Barringer, Joseph T. Findaro, Matthew Iandoli, Nils W. Johnson, Hon. James A. McClure, Tod O. Neuenschwander

Brush Wellman, Inc.
Issues: BUD DEF ENV HCR NAT
Rep By: Steven G. Barringer, Joseph T. Findaro, Matthew Iandoli, Nils W. Johnson, Hon. James A. McClure, Tod O. Neuenschwander

Coachella Valley Water District
Issues: BUD ENV IND NAT
Rep By: Steven G. Barringer, Joseph T. Findaro, Matthew Iandoli, Nils W. Johnson, Hon. James A. McClure, Tod O. Neuenschwander

Echo Bay Mining
Rep By: Steven G. Barringer, Joseph T. Findaro, Matthew Iandoli, Nils W. Johnson, Hon. James A. McClure, Tod O. Neuenschwander

Family Farm Alliance (Project Transfer Council)
Rep By: Steven G. Barringer, Joseph T. Findaro, Matthew Iandoli, Nils W. Johnson, Hon. James A. McClure, Tod O. Neuenschwander

Harquehala Irrigation District
Issues: NAT
Rep By: Steven G. Barringer, Joseph T. Findaro, Matthew Iandoli, Nils W. Johnson, Hon. James A. McClure, Tod O. Neuenschwander

Hecla Mining Co.
Issues: BUD ENV
Rep By: Steven G. Barringer, Joseph T. Findaro, Matthew Iandoli, Nils W. Johnson, Hon. James A. McClure, Tod O. Neuenschwander

Helli USA Airways
Rep By: Steven G. Barringer, Joseph T. Findaro, Matthew Iandoli, Nils W. Johnson, Hon. James A. McClure, Tod O. Neuenschwander

Henderson, Nevada, City of
Rep By: Steven G. Barringer, Joseph T. Findaro, Matthew Iandoli, Nils W. Johnson, Hon. James A. McClure, Tod O. Neuenschwander

Howard Hughes Corp.
Rep By: Steven G. Barringer, Joseph T. Findaro, Matthew Iandoli, Nils W. Johnson, Hon. James A. McClure, Tod O. Neuenschwander

Idaho Power Co.
Issues: BUD CAW ENG ENV NAT UTI WAS
Rep By: Steven G. Barringer, Joseph T. Findaro, Matthew Iandoli, Nils W. Johnson, Hon. James A. McClure, Tod O. Neuenschwander

Independence Mining Co., Inc.
Rep By: Steven G. Barringer, Joseph T. Findaro, Matthew Iandoli, Nils W. Johnson, Hon. James A. McClure, Tod O. Neuenschwander

Internat'l Bottled Water Ass'n
Issues: BEV CSP
Rep By: Steven G. Barringer, Joseph T. Findaro, Matthew Iandoli, Nils W. Johnson, Hon. James A. McClure, Tod O. Neuenschwander

LC Technologies
Issues: BUD SCI TRA
Rep By: Tod O. Neuenschwander

Nat'l Endangered Species Act Reform Coalition
Issues: AGR ANI BUD ENV NAT RES TAX
Rep By: Steven G. Barringer, Joseph T. Findaro, Matthew Iandoli, Nils W. Johnson, Hon. James A. McClure, Tod O. Neuenschwander

Nat'l Mining Ass'n
Issues: BUD ENV NAT

Native American Mohegans Inc.
Issues: IND
Rep By: Steven G. Barringer, Joseph T. Findaro, Matthew Iandoli, Nils W. Johnson, Hon. James A. McClure, Tod O. Neuenschwander

Nevada Test Site Development Corp.
Issues: ECN ENG
Rep By: Steven G. Barringer, Joseph T. Findaro, Matthew Iandoli, Nils W. Johnson, Hon. James A. McClure, Tod O. Neuenschwander

Newmont Mining Corp.
Issues: BUD ENV NAT
Rep By: Steven G. Barringer, Joseph T. Findaro, Matthew Iandoli, Nils W. Johnson, Hon. James A. McClure, Tod O. Neuenschwander

Pershing Co. Water Conservation District of Nevada
Rep By: Steven G. Barringer, Joseph T. Findaro, Matthew Iandoli, Nils W. Johnson, Hon. James A. McClure, Tod O. Neuenschwander

Placer Dome U.S. Inc.
Issues: ENV MON NAT TAX
Rep By: Steven G. Barringer, Joseph T. Findaro, Matthew Iandoli, Nils W. Johnson, Hon. James A. McClure, Tod O. Neuenschwander

Private Fuels Storage, L.L.C.
Issues: BUD ENG
Rep By: Steven G. Barringer, Joseph T. Findaro, Matthew Iandoli, Nils W. Johnson, Hon. James A. McClure, Tod O. Neuenschwander

Quest Nevada, Inc.
Rep By: Steven G. Barringer, Joseph T. Findaro, Matthew Iandoli, Nils W. Johnson, Hon. James A. McClure, Tod O. Neuenschwander

Space Imaging, Inc.
Issues: AER BUD FOR SCI
Rep By: Steven G. Barringer, Joseph T. Findaro, Matthew Iandoli, Nils W. Johnson, Hon. James A. McClure, Tod O. Neuenschwander

Stirling Energy Systems
Rep By: Steven G. Barringer, Joseph T. Findaro, Matthew Iandoli, Nils W. Johnson, Hon. James A. McClure, Tod O. Neuenschwander

Verizon Wireless
Issues: BUD NAT TEC
Rep By: Steven G. Barringer, Joseph T. Findaro, Matthew Iandoli, Nils W. Johnson, Hon. James A. McClure, Tod O. Neuenschwander

Wellton-Mohawk Irrigation and Drainage District
Issues: BUD ENG NAT
Rep By: Steven G. Barringer, Joseph T. Findaro, Matthew Iandoli, Nils W. Johnson, Hon. James A. McClure, Tod O. Neuenschwander

Westlands Water District
Issues: BUD ENV NAT
Rep By: Steven G. Barringer, Joseph T. Findaro, Matthew Iandoli, Nils W. Johnson, Hon. James A. McClure, Tod O. Neuenschwander

The Williams Companies
Rep By: Steven G. Barringer, Joseph T. Findaro, Matthew Iandoli, Nils W. Johnson, Hon. James A. McClure, Tod O. Neuenschwander

James F. McConnell

1130 Connecticut Ave. NW
Suite 300
Washington, DC 20036
Tel: (202)223-2451
Fax: (202)331-1598
Registered: LDA
E-mail: jmcconnell@tfgnet.com

Clients

Orange County Transportation Authority
Issues: TRA
Rep By: James F. McConnell

Orange County Water District
Issues: BUD
Rep By: James F. McConnell

Orange, California, County of
Rep By: James F. McConnell

Santa Ana River Flood Protection Agency
Issues: BUD
Rep By: James F. McConnell

Law Office of Robert A. McConnell

1155 Connecticut Ave. NW
Suite 420
Washington, DC 20036
Tel: (202)467-8018
Fax: (202)467-2766
Registered: LDA
E-mail: robert.mcconnell@hyi-usa.com

DC-Area Employees Representing Listed Clients

MCCONNELL, Robert A.

Clients

Civil Justice Reform Group
Issues: GOV TOR
Rep By: Robert A. McConnell

McConnell/Ferguson Group

1130 Connecticut Ave. NW
Suite 300
Washington, DC 20036
Tel: (202)331-8500
Fax: (202)331-1598
Registered: LDA

A government relations consulting firm.

DC-Area Employees Representing Listed Clients

FERGUSON, Jr., William
HANKA, William W.
MCCONNELL, James F., Partner

Clients

Transportation Corridor Agencies
Rep By: William Ferguson, Jr., James F. McConnell

Ruth McCormick

723 Upland Place
Alexandria, VA 22314
Tel: (703)549-1466
Fax: (703)549-1574
Registered: LDA
E-mail: RMcCorm713@aol.com

McDermott, Will and Emery

600 13th St. NW
Washington, DC 20005-3096
Tel: (202)756-8000
Fax: (202)756-8087
Registered: LDA, FARA
Web: www.mwe.com

Washington office of a national law firm headquartered in Chicago, IL. Also maintains offices in Boston, MA; London, England; Los Angeles, Silicon Valley, and Orange County, CA; Miami, FL; New York, NY; and Vilnius, Lithuania.

Political Action Committee

McDermott, Will & Emery PAC
600 13th St. NW
Washington, DC 20005-3096
Tel: (202)756-8255
Fax: (202)756-8087
Contact: Stanton D. Anderson

DC-Area Employees Representing Listed Clients

ADAMS, Matthew T., Counsel
ANDERSON, Stanton D., Partner
ARON, David E., Associate
BACO, Luis E., Attorney at Law
BALDWIN, Jana V. T., Partner
BARRETT, William H., Partner
BLOCH, Ronald, Counsel
CAGE, Kenneth L., Partner
CHEN, Jennifer C., Associate
CODD, Bernard P., Associate
COOK, Janine, Partner
DEVINSKY, Paul, Partner
FELDGARDEN, Robert, Partner
FILES, Amory, Law Clerk
FULLER, David R., Partner
GEORGE, Keith E., Partner
GLEASON, Carolyn B., Partner
GOEL, Ankur J., Partner
GOLDMAN, William L., Partner
GOMBAR, Robert C., Partner
GREENHOUSE, Robin L., Partner
GREENSTEIN, Seth D., Partner
GROSBERG, Joel R., Associate
HAMBURGER, Paul, Partner
HANNES, Steven P., Partner
HARDING, Robert B., Partner
HEMPHILL, Holly K., Partner
HIBBERT, Robert G., Partner
HILL, Jerry C., Partner
HORAN, John G., Partner
HORNING, Robert S., Partner
JACOBSEN, Jr., Raymond A., Partner
JOHNSON, Calvin P., Legislative Director
KIM, Richard Y., Associate
KRASNER, Wendy L., Partner
LAHIFF, Christopher M., Partner
LASTOWKA, James A., Partner
LAWRENCE, Gregg, Partner
LEVER, Jack Q., Partner
LEVINE, David J., Partner
LONGACRE, James B., Associate
LOUTHIAN, III, Robert, Partner
LUPO, Raphael V., Partner
MATTHEWS, Marsha Dula, Partner
MCCARTY, Philip A., Partner
MEGREGIAN, Scott S., Partner
MITCHELL, Maggie A., Associate Legislative Director
NICHOLAS, Robert B., Partner
NOLLA, Teresita, Associate Legislative Director
NORDBERG, Jr., Carl A., Counsel
O'KEEFE, Patricia, Associate Legislative Director
PATANO, Paul, Partner
PEGG, William D., Associate
PUGH, Martha G., Partner
QUINTER, Neil, Partner
RIEDY, James A., Partner
ROGERS, David, Partner
ROMANSKY, Michael A., Partner
ROSEN, David L., Partner
RUCKERT, Edward M., Partner
SAPPER, Arthur G., Partner
SCHEINESON, Cathy Zeman, Partner
SCHWARTZ, Robert S., Partner
SCHWARZ, Carl W., Partner
SEALANDER, Karen S., Legislative Counsel
SNEED, James, Partner
STEINDLER, Thomas, Partner
STEINER, Arthur J., Partner
STEWART, David L., Partner
SWITZER, Michael D., Associate
TENENBAUM, Ellen S., Partner
TOMPA, Peter K., Partner
WALTHER, Pamela D., Partner
WATERS, Timothy J., Managing Partner
WELLS, Stephen E., Partner, Tax Law Department
WILLIAMS, T. Raymond, Partner
WILSON, Jane E., Partner, Tax Law Department
WISE, Edward J., Partner
WORK, Charles R., Partner; Department Head, Regulation and Government Affairs
ZIMMERMAN, Eric P., Associate

Clients

Alaska Seafood Marketing Institute
Issues: TRD
Rep By: Carolyn B. Gleason, Pamela D. Walther

Allergan, Inc.
Issues: MMM
Rep By: Michael A. Romansky, Eric P. Zimmerman

American College of Gastroenterology
Rep By: Calvin P. Johnson, Michael A. Romansky

American Dental Hygienists' Ass'n
Issues: HCR
Rep By: Wendy L. Krasner, Maggie A. Mitchell, Karen S. Sealander

American Electronics Ass'n

American Gastroenterological Ass'n
Issues: BUD GOV HCR MED
Rep By: Michael A. Romansky, Eric P. Zimmerman

American Import Shippers Ass'n
Rep By: Calvin P. Johnson

American Soc. of Ambulatory Surgery Centers
Issues: MMM
Rep By: Michael A. Romansky, Eric P. Zimmerman

American Soc. of Echocardiography
Issues: MMM
Rep By: Eric P. Zimmerman

American Spice and Trade Ass'n
Issues: AGR
Rep By: Jerry C. Hill, Edward M. Ruckert

Applied Benefits Research Corp.
Rep By: Paul Hamburger, Calvin P. Johnson, Eric P. Zimmerman

Appraisal Institute

ARAMARK Corp.

Arthroscopy Ass'n of North America
Issues: MMM
Rep By: Michael A. Romansky, Eric P. Zimmerman

Ass'n of Freestanding Radiation Oncology Centers
Issues: MMM
Rep By: Eric P. Zimmerman

Ass'n of periOperative Registered Nurses
Issues: MMM
Rep By: Michael A. Romansky, Karen S. Sealander

Associated Financial Corp.

Bayer Corp. / Agriculture Division
Issues: AGR
Rep By: Robert B. Nicholas

Blue Anchor, Inc.
Rep By: Carolyn B. Gleason

Borden Chemicals & Plastics, Inc.

California Ass'n of Children's Hospitals

California Avocado Commission
Issues: TRD
Rep By: Jerry C. Hill, Edward M. Ruckert

California Canning Peach Ass'n
Rep By: Carolyn B. Gleason

California Children's Hospital Ass'n

California Cling Peach Growers Advisory Board
Issues: TRD
Rep By: Carolyn B. Gleason, Jerry C. Hill, Maggie A. Mitchell, Pamela D. Walther

California Kiwi Fruit Commission
Issues: AGR
Rep By: Jerry C. Hill

California Table Grape Commission
Rep By: Edward M. Ruckert

Campbell Soup Co.
Rep By: Robert G. Hibbert

Carnival Corp.

Cedar Fair LP

Chase Nat'l Kiwi Farms
Rep By: Carolyn B. Gleason

The Chevron Companies
Issues: TAX
Rep By: Robert B. Harding

Chiquita Brands Internat'l, Inc.
Issues: TRD
Rep By: Carolyn B. Gleason, Jerry C. Hill

Circuit City Stores, Inc.
Rep By: Robert S. Schwartz

Coalition for Employment Opportunities
Rep By: Calvin P. Johnson

Coalition for Reasonable and Fair Taxation (CRAFT)
Issues: TAX
Rep By: Calvin P. Johnson, David L. Rosen

Comprehensive Health Services
Rep By: Wendy L. Krasner

Council of Women's and Infant's Specialty Hospitals
Issues: HCR MMM
Rep By: Wendy L. Krasner, Maggie A. Mitchell, Karen S. Sealander

Crop Protection Coalition
Issues: BUD CAW
Rep By: Jerry C. Hill, Edward M. Ruckert

Digital Media Ass'n
Issues: CPI CPT MIA SCI TEC
Rep By: Seth D. Greenstein, Neil Quinter

Electronic Industries Ass'n of Japan
Issues: TRD
Rep By: Stanton D. Anderson, Seth D. Greenstein, Neil Quinter, Robert S. Schwartz, Thomas Steindler

Fashion Accessories Shippers Ass'n
Rep By: Calvin P. Johnson

Florida Fruit and Vegetable Ass'n
Issues: AGR TRD
Rep By: Carolyn B. Gleason, Jerry C. Hill

foot.com
Issues: MMM
Rep By: Eric P. Zimmerman

W. A. Foote Memorial Hospital
Issues: MMM
Rep By: Eric P. Zimmerman

H. B. Fuller Co.
Issues: TAX
Rep By: Robert B. Harding

Georgia-Pacific Corp.
Rep By: Calvin P. Johnson, Stephen E. Wells, Jane E. Wilson

The Good Sam Club
Rep By: Jerry C. Hill

Guatemalan Development Foundation (FUNDESA)
Rep By: Jerry C. Hill

Hitachi Semiconductors of America
Rep By: Neil Quinter

Huntington's Disease Soc. of America
Issues: BUD HCR MED
Rep By: Neil Quinter

Hutzel Medical Center
Issues: HCR MMM
Rep By: Wendy L. Krasner, Maggie A. Mitchell, Karen S. Sealander

Inova Fairfax Hospital
Issues: HCR MMM
Rep By: Wendy L. Krasner, Maggie A. Mitchell, Karen S. Sealander

InterMountain Health Care Inc.
Issues: HCR MMM
Rep By: Michael A. Romansky, Karen S. Sealander, Eric P. Zimmerman

Internat'l Ass'n of Professional Numismatists
Issues: LAW MON TRD
Rep By: Amory Files, Peter K. Tompa

Internat'l Council of Cruise Lines

Internat'l Hearing Soc.
Issues: HCR
Rep By: Calvin P. Johnson, Karen S. Sealander, Timothy J. Waters

Internat'l Mass Retailers Ass'n
Rep By: Timothy J. Waters

Juvenile Diabetes Foundation Internat'l

Kvaerner US Inc.
Issues: FOR
Rep By: Scott S. Megregian

Eli Lilly and Co.
Issues: TAX
Rep By: Robert B. Harding

Lockheed Martin Corp.
Rep By: William H. Barrett, Raymond A. Jacobsen, Jr., Scott S. Megregian

Magee Women's Health Foundation
Issues: HCR MMM
Rep By: Wendy L. Krasner, Maggie A. Mitchell, Karen S. Sealander

Mariner Health Group, Inc.
Rep By: Calvin P. Johnson

The Marshfield Clinic
Issues: MMM
Rep By: Eric P. Zimmerman

Maxus Energy Corp.
Issues: TAX
Rep By: Robert B. Harding

McGlotten & Jarvis
Issues: HCR
Rep By: Calvin P. Johnson

MedCentral Health System
Issues: MMM
Rep By: Eric P. Zimmerman

Minor Crop Farmer Alliance
Issues: CHM
Rep By: Jerry C. Hill, Edward M. Ruckert

Morgan Stanley Dean Witter & Co.
Rep By: Neil Quinter

Murphy Oil U.S.A.
Issues: TAX
Rep By: Robert B. Harding

The MWW Group

Nat'l Ass'n of Independent Diagnostic Services

Nat'l Ass'n of Professional Employer Organizations
Issues: RET TAX
Rep By: David R. Fuller, David Rogers

Nat'l Employment Opportunities Network

Nat'l Paint and Coatings Ass'n
Issues: BUD HCR HOU
Rep By: Neil Quinter

Nat'l Perinatal Ass'n
Rep By: Wendy L. Krasner, Karen S. Sealander, Eric P. Zimmerman

Nat'l Potato Council
Issues: AGR CHM FOO TRD
Rep By: Jerry C. Hill

Nat'l Potato Promotion Board
Rep By: Jerry C. Hill

Northside Hospital
Issues: HCR MMM
Rep By: Wendy L. Krasner, Maggie A. Mitchell, Karen S. Sealander

Northside Savings Bank
Rep By: Wendy L. Krasner, Karen S. Sealander, Eric P. Zimmerman

Northwest Airlines, Inc.
Issues: AVI LBR
Rep By: Teresita Nolla

Outpatient Ophthalmic Surgery Soc.
Issues: MMM
Rep By: Michael A. Romansky, Eric P. Zimmerman

PHP Healthcare Corp.
Rep By: Wendy L. Krasner

Prudential Insurance Co. of America
Issues: TAX
Rep By: Robert B. Harding

Public Employee Retirement Systems of Colorado
Rep By: Maggie A. Mitchell

Puerto Rico Hospital Ass'n

Puerto Rico, Commonwealth of
Rep By: Neil Quinter

Respiratory Medication Providers Coalition
Issues: MMM PHA
Rep By: Robert B. Nicholas, Michael A. Romansky, Eric P. Zimmerman

RJR Nabisco Holdings Co.
Rep By: Calvin P. Johnson, Stephen E. Wells, Jane E. Wilson

Rotary Internat'l

Rural Health Network Coalition
Rep By: Wendy L. Krasner, Eric P. Zimmerman

Rural Referral Centers Coalition
Issues: MMM
Rep By: Calvin P. Johnson, Wendy L. Krasner, Karen S. Sealander, Eric P. Zimmerman

Section 2039(e) Group

Solo Cup Co.

St. Peter's Medical Center
Issues: HCR MMM
Rep By: Wendy L. Krasner, Maggie A. Mitchell, Karen S. Sealander

Stamford Hospital
Issues: MMM
Rep By: Eric P. Zimmerman

Stroh Brewing Co.
Rep By: Jerry C. Hill, Maggie A. Mitchell, T. Raymond Williams

Telecorp PCS Inc.
Issues: TEC
Rep By: Calvin P. Johnson, Neil Quinter

Terra Chemicals Internat'l

TJTC Recovery Project Coalition
Rep By: Calvin P. Johnson

U.S. Apple Ass'n
Issues: AGR
Rep By: Edward M. Ruckert

U.S. Mink Export Development Council
Issues: AGR BUD TRD
Rep By: Carolyn B. Gleason, Jerry C. Hill

UBS Warburg
Rep By: Neil Quinter

United Development Corp.

VIVRA
Rep By: Calvin P. Johnson, Michael A. Romansky, Eric P. Zimmerman

Welch's Foods, Inc.
Rep By: Carolyn B. Gleason

Wells Manufacturing Co.

Women and Infants' Hospital
Issues: HCR MMM
Rep By: Wendy L. Krasner, Maggie A. Mitchell, Karen S. Sealander

Women's Hospital
Issues: HCR MMM
Rep By: Wendy L. Krasner, Maggie A. Mitchell, Karen S. Sealander

Women's Hospital of Greensboro
Issues: HCR MMM
Rep By: Wendy L. Krasner, Maggie A. Mitchell, Karen S. Sealander

WOTC Project
Rep By: Calvin P. Johnson

Jack H. McDonald

901 15th St. NW
Washington, DC 20005-2301
Tel: (202)371-6253
Fax: (202)371-6279
Registered: LDA, FARA

Clients

India, Government of the Republic of
Rep By: Hon. Jack H. McDonald

Mexico, Government of
Rep By: Hon. Jack H. McDonald

Thera Matrix
Issues: HCR
Rep By: Hon. Jack H. McDonald

Verner, Liipfert, Bernhard, McPherson and Hand, Chartered
Issues: AER AVI CPT ECN FIN FUE HCR HOU PHA POS TAX TEC TOB TRD
Rep By: Hon. Jack H. McDonald

McGlotten & Jarvis

1901 L St. NW
Suite 300
Washington, DC 20036
Tel: (202)452-9515
Fax: (202)466-8016
Registered: LDA

DC-Area Employees Representing Listed Clients
JARVIS, John T.
MCGLOTTEN, Robert M.

Clients

Chlorine Chemistry Council
Issues: CAW
Rep By: John T. Jarvis

Computer Sciences Corp.
Rep By: John T. Jarvis, Robert M. McGlotten

CSX Corp.
Issues: RRR
Rep By: John T. Jarvis, Robert M. McGlotten

Edison Electric Institute
Issues: UTI
Rep By: John T. Jarvis, Robert M. McGlotten

Forest Products Industry Nat'l Labor-Management Committee
Issues: ENV NAT
Rep By: John T. Jarvis

Internat'l Dairy Foods Ass'n
Issues: FOO
Rep By: John T. Jarvis, Robert M. McGlotten

Internat'l Franchise Ass'n
Rep By: John T. Jarvis, Robert M. McGlotten

Investment Co. Institute
Issues: FIN
Rep By: John T. Jarvis, Robert M. McGlotten

Office and Professional Employees Internat'l Union
Issues: HCR
Rep By: Robert M. McGlotten

Philip Morris Management Corp.
Issues: BEV FOO TOB
Rep By: Robert M. McGlotten

Seafarers Internat'l Union of North America
Issues: MAR
Rep By: Robert M. McGlotten

United Mine Workers of America
Issues: ENV HCR
Rep By: John T. Jarvis

McGuiness & Holch

400 N. Capitol St. NW
Suite 585
Washington, DC 20001
Tel: (202)783-5300
Fax: (202)393-5218
Registered: LDA

DC-Area Employees Representing Listed Clients
ERICKSON, Markham C., Associate
HOLCH, Niels C., Partner
MCGUINESS, Kevin S., Partner

Clients

Arch Mineral Corp.
Issues: HCR LBR
Rep By: Markham C. Erickson, Kevin S. McGuiness

Barr Laboratories
Issues: HCR PHA
Rep By: Markham C. Erickson, Kevin S. McGuiness

Council for Responsible Nutrition
Issues: FOO HCR
Rep By: Markham C. Erickson, Kevin S. McGuiness

Major League Baseball Players Ass'n
Issues: LBR SPO
Rep By: Markham C. Erickson, Kevin S. McGuiness

Nat'l Horse Show Commission
Issues: ANI BUD
Rep By: Niels C. Holch

NetCoalition.Com
Issues: COM CPI
Rep By: Markham C. Erickson, Kevin S. McGuiness

Oneida Indian Nation of New York
Issues: CPI GAM IND TAX
Rep By: Markham C. Erickson, Niels C. Holch

Project to Promote Competition and Innovation in the Digital Age
Issues: CPI CSP LBR SCI
Rep By: Markham C. Erickson, Kevin S. McGuiness

R. J. Reynolds Tobacco Co.
Issues: TOB
Rep By: Kevin S. McGuiness

RJR Co.
Issues: TOB
Rep By: Kevin S. McGuiness

Wine and Spirits Wholesalers of America
Issues: BEV
Rep By: Markham C. Erickson, Kevin S. McGuiness

McGuiness Norris & Williams, LLP

1015 15th St. NW
Suite 1200
Washington, DC 20005
Tel: (202)789-8600
Fax: (202)789-1708
Registered: LDA
Web: www.mnwlaw.net
E-mail: info@mnwlaw.net

DC-Area Employees Representing Listed Clients
BARTL, Timothy J., Associate
BIRD, Ronald E., Chief Economist
COOPER, Christine M., Partner
EASTMAN, Michael J., Associate
HABIB, Amy, Associate
HOLT, James S., Consultant
KESSLER, Lorence L., Of Counsel
LAFORGE, William N., Of Counsel
LAKE, Monte B., Partner
MCGUINESS, Jeffrey C., Partner
NORRIS, Jeffrey A., Partner
POTTER, Edward E., Partner
REESMAN, Ann Elizabeth, Partner
TYSSE, G. John, Partner
WILLIAMS, Robert E., Partner
YAGER, Daniel V., Partner

Clients

American Kennel Club
Issues: ANI
Rep By: James S. Holt, William N. LaForge

American Nursery and Landscape Ass'n
Issues: IMM LBR
Rep By: James S. Holt, William N. LaForge, Monte B. Lake

Celanese Government Relations Office
Issues: MAN TRD
Rep By: William N. LaForge

Garden Centers of America
Issues: LBR
Rep By: Monte B. Lake

Labor Policy Ass'n (LPA)
Rep By: Timothy J. Bartl, Michael J. Eastman, Amy Habib, Jeffrey C. McGuiness, G. John Tysse, Daniel V. Yager

Nat'l Club Ass'n
Rep By: G. John Tysse

Nat'l Council of Agricultural Employers
Issues: AGR IMM LBR
Rep By: Timothy J. Bartl, James S. Holt, William N. LaForge, Monte B. Lake

Nat'l Turfgrass Evaluation Program
Issues: AGR
Rep By: William N. LaForge, Monte B. Lake

Nisei Farmers League
Issues: AGR CAW TRA
Rep By: Timothy J. Bartl, William N. LaForge, Monte B. Lake

PepsiCo, Inc.
Issues: BEV
Rep By: William N. LaForge

San Joaquin Valley Wide Air Pollution Study Agency
Issues: CAW
Rep By: William N. LaForge, Monte B. Lake

Turfgrass Producers Internat'l
Issues: AGR IMM
Rep By: William N. LaForge, Monte B. Lake

United States Council for Internat'l Business
Rep By: Edward E. Potter

Western Range Ass'n
Issues: AGR IMM NAT
Rep By: James S. Holt

Western States Petroleum Ass'n
Issues: ENV
Rep By: William N. LaForge, Monte B. Lake

Wholesale Nursery Growers of America
Issues: LBR
Rep By: Monte B. Lake

Wilke, Fleury, Hoffelt, Gould & Birney, LLP
Issues: ENV
Rep By: William N. LaForge

Mary Lee McGuire

444 N. Capitol St. NW
Suite 837
Washington, DC 20001
Tel: (202)637-9330
Fax: (202)544-5321
Registered: LDA

Clients

Cook Inlet Region Inc.
Rep By: Mary Lee McGuire

The Metropolitan Water District of Southern California
Issues: CAW
Rep By: Mary Lee McGuire

McGuireWoods L.L.P.

1050 Connecticut Ave. NW
Suite 1200
Washington, DC 20036
Tel: (202)857-1700
Fax: (202)857-1737
Registered: LDA, FARA
Web: www.mcguirewoods.com
A full service law firm headquartered in Richmond, VA.

Political Action Committee
McGuire Woods PAC
1050 Connecticut Ave. NW
Suite 1200
Washington, DC 20036
Tel: (202)857-2906
Fax: (202)857-1737
Contact: Jeffrey L. Schlagenhauf

DC-Area Employees Representing Listed Clients
ATKINSON, Frank B., Chairman, Executive Committee, McGuire Woods Consulting, LLC
BOGOSIAN, Joseph H., V. President, McGuire Woods Consulting, LLC
BRILLIANT, Hana
CALAMITA, F. Paul, Partner
KATSURINIS, Stephen A., V. President, McGuire Woods Consulting
PAYNE, Jr., Hon. Lewis F., President, McGuire Woods Consulting, LLC
SCHLAGENHAUF, Jeffrey L., Senior V. President, McGuire Woods Consulting, LLC
WHITTEMORE, Anne Marie, Partner

Clients

Alexandria, Virginia, Sanitation Authority of the City of
Issues: BUD
Rep By: Hana Brilliant, Stephen A. Katsurinis, Hon. Lewis F. Payne, Jr., Jeffrey L. Schlagenhauf

Allegiance Healthcare Corp.
Issues: MED
Rep By: Joseph H. Bogosian, Stephen A. Katsurinis, Hon. Lewis F. Payne, Jr.

Center for Governmental Studies of the University of Virginia
Issues: EDU
Rep By: Joseph H. Bogosian, Stephen A. Katsurinis, Hon. Lewis F. Payne, Jr.

CSO Partnership
Issues: CAW
Rep By: Hana Brilliant, F. Paul Calamita, Stephen A. Katsurinis

CSX Corp.
Issues: TRA
Rep By: Frank B. Atkinson, Joseph H. Bogosian, Stephen A. Katsurinis, Hon. Lewis F. Payne, Jr.

Eastman Chemical Co.
Issues: TOB
Rep By: Frank B. Atkinson, Stephen A. Katsurinis, Anne Marie Whittemore

Fibrowatt, Inc.
Issues: CAW ENG ENV TAX WAS
Rep By: Joseph H. Bogosian, Stephen A. Katsurinis, Hon. Lewis F. Payne, Jr.

Financial Services Council
Issues: BAN
Rep By: Joseph H. Bogosian, Stephen A. Katsurinis, Jeffrey L. Schlagenhauf

GE Financial Assurance
Issues: TAX
Rep By: Stephen A. Katsurinis, Hon. Lewis F. Payne, Jr., Jeffrey L. Schlagenhauf

Georgia-Pacific Corp.
Issues: CAW
Rep By: Stephen A. Katsurinis, Hon. Lewis F. Payne, Jr.

Huntington Sanitary Board
Issues: CAW
Rep By: Joseph H. Bogosian, Stephen A. Katsurinis, Jeffrey L. Schlagenhauf

Korea, Embassy of
Rep By: Joseph H. Bogosian

Lynchburg, Virginia, City of
Issues: CAW
Rep By: Hana Brilliant, F. Paul Calamita, Stephen A. Katsurinis, Hon. Lewis F. Payne, Jr., Jeffrey L. Schlagenhauf

Prince William County Service Authority
Issues: RES UTI
Rep By: Hana Brilliant, Stephen A. Katsurinis, Jeffrey L. Schlagenhauf

Richmond, Virginia, City of
Issues: CAW
Rep By: Hana Brilliant, F. Paul Calamita, Stephen A. Katsurinis, Hon. Lewis F. Payne, Jr., Jeffrey L. Schlagenhauf

Smithfield Foods Inc.
Issues: AGR
Rep By: Stephen A. Katsurinis, Hon. Lewis F. Payne, Jr., Jeffrey L. Schlagenhauf

Trigon Healthcare Inc.
Issues: LBR
Rep By: Stephen A. Katsurinis, Hon. Lewis F. Payne, Jr.

University of Miami
Issues: EDU
Rep By: Joseph H. Bogosian, Stephen A. Katsurinis, Jeffrey L. Schlagenhauf

Verizon Communications
Issues: TEC
Rep By: Stephen A. Katsurinis, Jeffrey L. Schlagenhauf

Wheeling, West Virginia, City of
Issues: CAW
Rep By: Joseph H. Bogosian, F. Paul Calamita, Stephen A. Katsurinis, Hon. Lewis F. Payne, Jr., Jeffrey L. Schlagenhauf

McIntyre Law Firm, PLLC

1155 15th St. NW
Suite 1101
Washington, DC 20005
Tel: (202)659-3900
Fax: (202)659-5763
Registered: LDA, FARA

DC-Area Employees Representing Listed Clients
LEMON, Chrys D., Attorney
MCINTYRE, James T., Managing Partner

Clients

Ass'n of Banks in Insurance
Issues: BAN CSP ENV FIN INS MAN TAX
Rep By: Chrys D. Lemon, James T. McIntyre

Community Financial Services Ass'n
Issues: BAN CSP FIN
Rep By: Chrys D. Lemon, James T. McIntyre

Internat'l Ass'n for Financial Planning
Issues: FIN TAX
Rep By: Chrys D. Lemon, James T. McIntyre

MemberWorks, Inc.
Issues: CSP FIN INS
Rep By: Chrys D. Lemon, James T. McIntyre

Risk and Insurance Management Soc., Inc. (RIMS)
Issues: ENV FIN HCR INS
Rep By: Chrys D. Lemon, James T. McIntyre

McKay Walker

5612 S. 4th St.
Arlington, VA 22204
Tel: (202)347-2612
Fax: (703)998-6191
Registered: LDA

A legislative consulting firm specializing in federal tax policy.

DC-Area Employees Representing Listed Clients
WALKER, Lynda K., Principal

Clients

Citigroup
Issues: TAX
Rep By: Lynda K. Walker

The Rouse Company
Issues: TAX
Rep By: Lynda K. Walker

Sunoco, Inc.
Issues: TAX
Rep By: Lynda K. Walker

Jana McKeag

315 Queen St.
Alexandria, VA 22314
Tel: (703)684-1203
Fax: (703)684-1481
Registered: LDA

Clients

Sodak Gaming Inc.
Issues: GAM IND
Rep By: Jana McKeag

Venture Catalysts
Rep By: Jana McKeag

McKenna & Cuneo, L.L.P.

1900 K St. NW
Washington, DC 20006
Tel: (202)496-7500
Fax: (202)496-7756
Registered: LDA, FARA
Web: www.mckennacuneo.com

Washington based firm with offices in Los Angeles, San Francisco, San Diego, Denver and Brussels, Belgium.

DC-Area Employees Representing Listed Clients
ALTMAN, Jeffrey P., Partner
DAMERON, Del S., Managing Partner
DENNIN, Joseph F., Partner
FELLER, Peter Buck, Partner
HOE, E. Sanderson, Partner
LEASON, Chris, Partner
LEVY, Frederic, Managing Partner
PILOT, Larry R., Partner
SMOOTS, Carol A., Partner
YESNER, Donna Lee, Of Counsel

Clients

American Pipe Fittings Ass'n
Rep By: Peter Buck Feller

American Soc. of Clinical Pathologists
Rep By: Jeffrey P. Altman

American Wood Preservers Institute

Ass'n for the Advancement of Medical Instrumentation

Cast Iron Pipefittings Committee
Rep By: Peter Buck Feller

Centocor, Inc.
Issues: MED MMM

Cominco, Ltd.

Consumer Specialties Products Ass'n

Cypress Bioscience Inc.
Issues: MMM

The Dow Chemical Co.

Enerco, Inc.

The Fertilizer Institute

Fontana Bleu, S.p.A.

Nat'l Propane Gas Ass'n
Rep By: Chris Leason

Oshkosh Truck Corp.
Rep By: Del S. Dameron

Pharmaceutical Research and Manufacturers of America

St. Jude Medical, Inc.
Issues: MAN MED MMM

Sumitomo Chemical Co., Ltd.
Rep By: Joseph F. Dennin

U.S. Fittings Group
Rep By: Peter Buck Feller

McKinney & McDowell Associates

1612 K St. NW
Suite 904
Washington, DC 20006
Tel: (202)833-9771
Fax: (202)833-9770
Registered: FARA
Web: www.mcandmc.com

DC-Area Employees Representing Listed Clients
MCDOWELL, Leila, V. President
MCKINNEY, Gwen, President

Clients

Haiti, Embassy of the Republic of

NAACP Legal Defense and Educational Fund, Inc.

McLeod, Watkinson & Miller

One Massachusetts Ave. NW
Suite 800
Washington, DC 20001-1431
Tel: (202)842-2345
Fax: (202)408-7763
Registered: LDA
Web: www.mwmlaw.com

A law firm specializing in agricultural and agribusiness, food and drug, environmental, international trade, and administrative law and litigation. Also maintains an active government relations practice.

DC-Area Employees Representing Listed Clients
FRERICHS, Stephen, Economist/Budget Analyst
GREEN, Randy, Senior Government Relations Consultant
GREEN, Robert R.
MCLEOD, Michael R., Partner
MILLER, Marc E., Partner
PASCO, Richard E., Senior Associate
PHELPS, Laura L., Government Relations Consultant
ROSSIER, Richard T., Partner
WATKINSON, Wayne R., Partner

Clients

American Ass'n of Crop Insurers
Issues: AGR BUD INS
Rep By: Stephen Frerichs, Michael R. McLeod, Laura L. Phelps

American Mushroom Institute
Rep By: Michael R. McLeod, Marc E. Miller, Laura L. Phelps

American Peanut Product Manufacturers, Inc.
Issues: AGR BUD
Rep By: Michael R. McLeod, Richard E. Pasco, Laura L. Phelps

California Avocado Commission
Issues: AGR
Rep By: Michael R. McLeod, Richard E. Pasco

Cattlemen's Beef Promotion and Research Board
Rep By: Wayne R. Watkinson

Certified Angus Beef
Rep By: Wayne R. Watkinson

Chicago Board of Trade
Issues: AGR TRD
Rep By: Michael R. McLeod

Coalition for Sugar Reform
Issues: AGR
Rep By: Randy Green, Michael R. McLeod

Dairy Management, Inc.
Rep By: Wayne R. Watkinson

Nat'l Frozen Food Ass'n
Rep By: Michael R. McLeod, Richard E. Pasco

Nat'l Honey Board
Rep By: Wayne R. Watkinson

Popcorn Board
Rep By: Wayne R. Watkinson

United Dairy Industry Ass'n
Rep By: Wayne R. Watkinson

United Egg Ass'n
Issues: AGR BUD CAW FOO MAN TRD WEL
Rep By: Robert R. Green, Michael R. McLeod, Laura L. Phelps

United Egg Producers
Issues: AGR BUD CAW FOO MAN TRD WEL
Rep By: Robert R. Green, Michael R. McLeod, Laura L. Phelps

United Soybean Board
Rep By: Wayne R. Watkinson

McMahon and Associates

1924 N St. NW
Washington, DC 20036
Tel: (202)293-6464
Fax: (202)293-6475
E-mail: mcmahon@aol.com

A public affairs consulting firm focusing on community relations, minority civil rights, economic development, and housing/health issues.

DC-Area Employees Representing Listed Clients
MCMAHON, Joseph E., President

Clients

Covenant House
Issues: BUD HCR HOU
Rep By: Joseph E. McMahon

Rodale Press
Issues: AGR ENV FOO
Rep By: Joseph E. McMahon

Viacom Inc.

McMillan, Hill & Associates

P.O. Box 1807
Alexandria, VA 22313
Tel: (703)876-0920
Registered: LDA

DC-Area Employees Representing Listed Clients
HILL, Frank H.
MCMILLAN, Hon. J. Alex

Clients

Coalition for a Comprehensive Tobacco Solution (C-FACTS)
Issues: TOB

Mutual of America
Issues: TAX

Virtual Medical Group
Issues: HCR

McNamara & Associates

100 Daingerfield Rd.
Alexandria, VA 22314
Tel: (703)519-8197
Fax: (703)548-3227
Registered: LDA

A government relations consultant. Member of The Capitol Alliance.

DC-Area Employees Representing Listed Clients
MCNAMARA, Thomas J., President

Clients

The Nat'l Sports Center for the Disabled
Rep By: Thomas J. McNamara

Printing Industries of America
Issues: ENV HCR SMB TAX
Rep By: Thomas J. McNamara

The Sharing Network
Issues: HCR
Rep By: Thomas J. McNamara

Diane McRee Associates

601 Pennsylvania Ave. NW
Suite 900
South Bldg.
Washington, DC 20004
Tel: (202)434-8205
Fax: (202)628-0565
Registered: LDA
E-mail: dmcree@erols.com

A government relations consulting firm.

DC-Area Employees Representing Listed Clients
MCREE, Diane B., President

Clients

3001, Inc.
Issues: ENV MAR SCI
Rep By: Diane B. McRee

GREX, Inc.
Issues: HCR IMM
Rep By: Diane B. McRee

HUTCO, Inc.
Issues: IMM LBR
Rep By: Diane B. McRee

Metamorphix, Inc.
Issues: SCI
Rep By: Diane B. McRee

Northrop Grumman Corp.
Issues: BUD DEF
Rep By: Diane B. McRee

Port of Lake Charles
Issues: MAR TRA
Rep By: Diane B. McRee

United States Tuna Foundation
Issues: MAR
Rep By: Diane B. McRee

McSlarrow Consulting L.L.C.

6551 Kristina Ursula Court
Falls Church, VA 22044
Tel: (703)658-0138
Fax: (703)658-5040
Registered: LDA

DC-Area Employees Representing Listed Clients
MCSLARROW, Alison, Principal

Clients

American Trucking Ass'ns
Issues: TRA
Rep By: Alison McSlarrow

Fannie Mae
Issues: HOU
Rep By: Alison McSlarrow

Microsoft Corp.
Issues: CPI IMM TEC
Rep By: Alison McSlarrow

Qwest Communications
Issues: TEC
Rep By: Alison McSlarrow

U.S. Oncology
Issues: HCR MMM
Rep By: Alison McSlarrow

Medicaid Policy, L.L.C.

1450 G St. NW
Suite 215
Washington, DC 20005

Tel: (202)393-6898
Fax: (202)393-6899
Registered: LDA

DC-Area Employees Representing Listed Clients
SCHNEIDER, Andrew G., Principal

Clients

California Rural Indian Health Board, Inc.
Issues: MMM
Rep By: Andrew G. Schneider

Taxpayers Against Fraud, The False Claims Legal Center
Issues: MMM
Rep By: Andrew G. Schneider

Medical Advocacy Services, Inc.

2011 Pennsylvania Ave. NW
Suite 800
Washington, DC 20006

Tel: (202)835-0437
Fax: (202)835-0442
Registered: LDA

DC-Area Employees Representing Listed Clients
BACCHUS, Julie, Government Affairs Representative
BLASER, Robert, Director
OWEN, Holly, Government Affairs Representative

Clients

American Ass'n of Clinical Endocrinologists
Rep By: Robert Blaser

American College of Rheumatology
Issues: HCR MMM
Rep By: Robert Blaser, Holly Owen

Renal Physicians Ass'n
Issues: HCR MMM
Rep By: Robert Blaser, Holly Owen

Soc. of General Internal Medicine
Issues: BUD HCR MED VET
Rep By: Robert Blaser

Wayne Edward Mehl

2725 Carter Farm Ct.
Alexandria, VA 22306

Tel: (703)780-1025
Fax: (703)799-9404
Registered: LDA

E-mail: wemehl@aol.com

Clients

Nevada Resort Ass'n
Issues: GAM
Rep By: Wayne Edward Mehl

Mehl, Griffin & Bartek Ltd.

2001 Jefferson Davis Hwy.
Suite 209
Arlington, VA 22202

Tel: (703)413-0090
Fax: (703)413-4467
Registered: LDA

Web: www.mehlgriffinbartek.com
E-mail: mgb@mehlgriffinbartek.com
A lobbying and business development consulting firm.

DC-Area Employees Representing Listed Clients
BARTEK, Ronald J., V. President
BLOCK, Richard A. "Chip", V. President, Business Development and Technology
GRIFFIN, Molly, President
MARSH, William A., Director, Government Affairs
MEHL, Theodore J., V. President
WOLOWICZ, Kelly A., Director, Administration and Finance

Clients

AMI Aircraft Seating Systems
Issues: AVI
Rep By: Molly Griffin, William A. Marsh, Theodore J. Mehl

Battelle Memorial Institute
Issues: DEF ENG ENV
Rep By: Ronald J. Bartek, Molly Griffin, Theodore J. Mehl

Chandler Evans Control Systems
Issues: AVI DEF
Rep By: Ronald J. Bartek, Molly Griffin, Theodore J. Mehl

D3 Internat'l Energy, LLC
Issues: AER AVI DEF ENG
Rep By: Ronald J. Bartek, Molly Griffin, William A. Marsh, Theodore J. Mehl

El Camino Resources, Ltd.
Issues: DEF
Rep By: Ronald J. Bartek, Molly Griffin, Theodore J. Mehl

Exide Corp.
Issues: TRD
Rep By: Ronald J. Bartek, Molly Griffin, William A. Marsh, Theodore J. Mehl

Friedrich's Ataxia Research Alliance
Issues: MED
Rep By: Ronald J. Bartek

Galaxy Aerospace Co., LP
Issues: DEF
Rep By: Molly Griffin, William A. Marsh

General Atomics
Issues: DEF
Rep By: Molly Griffin, Theodore J. Mehl

Irvine Sensors Corp.
Issues: DEF LAW
Rep By: Molly Griffin, William A. Marsh, Theodore J. Mehl

LSP Technologies
Issues: DEF
Rep By: Molly Griffin

Motorola Space and Systems Technology Group
Issues: DEF
Rep By: Ronald J. Bartek, Molly Griffin, Theodore J. Mehl

Nat'l Veterans Foundation
Issues: VET
Rep By: Molly Griffin, Theodore J. Mehl

Pacific Northwest Nat'l Laboratory
Issues: DEF ENV
Rep By: Ronald J. Bartek, Molly Griffin, Theodore J. Mehl

Q Systems, Inc.
Issues: ENV
Rep By: Ronald J. Bartek

Turbine Controls, Inc.
Issues: DEF
Rep By: Molly Griffin, Theodore J. Mehl

John Melcher

230-B Maryland Ave. NE
Washington, DC 20002

Tel: (202)546-4084
Fax: (202)544-7609
Registered: LDA

Clients

American Veterinary Medical Ass'n
Issues: ANI
Rep By: Hon. John Melcher

William M. Mercer, Inc.

1255 23rd St. NW
Suite 250
Washington, DC 20037

Tel: (202)263-3900
Fax: (202)296-0909
Registered: LDA

Web: www.mercer.com

DC-Area Employees Representing Listed Clients
HAMELBURG, Mark, Attorney
MERCER, William M.

Clients

The Business Roundtable
Issues: HCR
Rep By: William M. Mercer

Nat'l Ass'n of Manufacturers
Issues: HCR
Rep By: Mark Hamelburg, William M. Mercer

Mercury Group

201 N. Union St.
Suite 510
Alexandria, VA 22314

Tel: (703)299-9470
Fax: (703)299-9478
Registered: LDA

DC-Area Employees Representing Listed Clients
MAKRIS, Tony, President
SCHROPP, Tyler, V. President

Clients

Air Force Memorial Foundation
Issues: GOV NAT

Arena PAC

Lockheed Martin Corp.
Issues: AER DEF FOR

Premier Parks, Inc.
Issues: CSP TOU

PrivacyRight
Issues: CPI CSP MIA

Law Offices of Pamela L. Meredith

1101 30th St. NW
Suite 500
Washington, DC 20007

Tel: (202)625-4890
Fax: (202)625-4363
Registered: LDA

DC-Area Employees Representing Listed Clients
FLEMING, Sean, Associate
MEREDITH, Pamela L., Attorney

Clients

Spectrum Astro, Inc.
Issues: DEF SCI
Rep By: Pamela L. Meredith

Meredith Concept Group, Inc.

601 King St.
Alexandria, VA 22314

Tel: (202)364-8892
Fax: (202)364-8922
Registered: LDA, FARA

A marketing and legislative consulting firm.

DC-Area Employees Representing Listed Clients
MEREDITH, Sandra K., President

Clients

Messier-Dowty Internat'l
Issues: AER DEF GOV
Rep By: Sandra K. Meredith

Societe Nationale d'Etude et Construction de Moteurs d'Aviation (SNECMA)
Issues: DEF
Rep By: Sandra K. Meredith

G.L. Merritt & Associates, Inc.

8100 Crestridge Rd.
Fairfax Station, VA 22039
E-mail: glmerritt@erols.com

Tel: (703)250-5224
Registered: LDA

DC-Area Employees Representing Listed Clients
MERRITT, Gordon L., Principal

Clients

American Systems Internat'l Corp.
Issues: DEF MAN
Rep By: Gordon L. Merritt

APTI
Issues: DEF
Rep By: Gordon L. Merritt

ASIC
Issues: DEF
Rep By: Gordon L. Merritt

Raytheon Missile Systems
Issues: DEF
Rep By: Gordon L. Merritt

Metcalf Federal Relations

321 S. Washington St.
Second Floor
Alexandria, VA 22314
E-mail: metfed@ix.netcom.com

Tel: (703)519-3983
Fax: (703)299-0857
Registered: LDA

DC-Area Employees Representing Listed Clients
METCALF, Anne, Principal
SANDERS, Amy Ford

Clients

Brain Research Foundation
Issues: BUD
Rep By: Anne Metcalf, Amy Ford Sanders

Brookfield Zoo/Chicago Zoological Soc.
Issues: ANI BUD
Rep By: Anne Metcalf

Chicago Botanic Garden
Issues: BUD ENV NAT
Rep By: Anne Metcalf

Columbia College Chicago
Issues: BUD EDU
Rep By: Anne Metcalf

Green Door
Issues: BUD HCR
Rep By: Anne Metcalf

Museum Campus Chicago
Issues: ANI BUD EDU NAT TRA
Rep By: Anne Metcalf

Natural History Museum of Los Angeles County
Issues: EDU NAT
Rep By: Anne Metcalf

Philadelphia Zoo
Issues: ANI BUD ENV TRA
Rep By: Anne Metcalf, Amy Ford Sanders

Meyer & Glitzenstein

1601 Connecticut Ave. NW
Suite 700
Washington, DC 20009-1056

Tel: (202)588-5206
Fax: (202)588-5049

A law firm specializing in animal rights and environmental issues.

DC-Area Employees Representing Listed Clients
GLITZENSTEIN, Eric, Partner
MEYER, Kathy, Partner

Clients

The Fund for Animals
Humane Soc. of the United States
Wildlife Advocacy Project

Meyer & Klipper, PLLC

923 15th St. NW
Washington, DC 20005
Tel: (202)637-0850
Fax: (202)637-0851
Registered: LDA

DC-Area Employees Representing Listed Clients

KLIPPER, Michael R.
MOHR, Christopher A.

Clients

Coalition Against Database Piracy
Issues: CPT
Rep By: Michael R. Klipper, Christopher A. Mohr

Magazine Publishers of America
Issues: CIV CON CPT GAM
Rep By: Michael R. Klipper, Christopher A. Mohr

Property Owners Remedy Alliance
Issues: CPT
Rep By: Michael R. Klipper, Christopher A. Mohr

Meyer, Suozzi, English & Klein, P.C.

1300 Connecticut Ave. NW
Suite 600
Washington, DC 20036
Tel: (202)955-6390
Fax: (202)223-0358
Web: www.msek.com
E-mail: meyersuozzi@msek.com
A law firm.

DC-Area Employees Representing Listed Clients

ENRIGHT, Janice Ann, Senior Advisor, Government Affairs
ICKES, Harold M., Partner

Meyers & Alterman

1220 19th St. NW
Suite 400
Washington, DC 20036
Tel: (202)466-8270
Fax: (202)293-4377
E-mail: nmmeyers@aol.com

DC-Area Employees Representing Listed Clients

ALTERMAN, Stephen A., Partner
MEYERS, N. Marshall, Partner

Clients

Pet Industry Joint Advisory Council
Rep By: N. Marshall Meyers

Meyers & Associates

412 First St. SE
Suite One
Washington, DC 20003
Tel: (202)484-2773
Fax: (202)484-0770
Registered: LDA
Web: www.meyersandassociates.com
E-mail: larrymeyers@meyersandassociates.com
A general practice lobbying firm since 1981.

DC-Area Employees Representing Listed Clients

BOYD, Fran, V. President
DODD, Shelley Wilson, Senior Associate, Higher Education
HALEY, Daniel D., General Counsel
MEYERS, Larry D., President
MEYERS, Richard L., Partner
SHEPARD, Jennifer, Outside Associate
SHIRLEY, Graham E., Senior Associate

Clients

The Alliance for I-69 Texas
Issues: TRA
Rep By: Larry D. Meyers, Jennifer Shepard

AMCOR Capital Corp.
Issues: TAX
Rep By: Larry D. Meyers, Richard L. Meyers

American Beekeeping Federation
Issues: AGR BUD TRD
Rep By: Fran Boyd, Larry D. Meyers, Richard L. Meyers

American Sheep Industry Ass'n
Issues: AGR APP BUD FOO NAT TAX TRD
Rep By: Fran Boyd, Larry D. Meyers

Canadian River Municipal Water Authority
Issues: BUD CAW GOV NAT RES
Rep By: Fran Boyd, Larry D. Meyers

Coalition for Maritime Education
Issues: BUD EDU MAR
Rep By: Shelley Wilson Dodd, Larry D. Meyers

Corpus Christi, City of
Issues: CAW DEF ECN NAT ROD URB
Rep By: Larry D. Meyers, Richard L. Meyers

Council for Agricultural Science and Technology
Issues: AGR BUD
Rep By: Fran Boyd, Larry D. Meyers, Richard L. Meyers

Finnish American Corporate Team (F.A.C.T.)
Issues: FOR
Rep By: Larry D. Meyers, Richard L. Meyers

Geo-Seis Helicopters Inc.
Issues: AVI GOV LAW
Rep By: Richard L. Meyers

Irrigation Projects Reauthorization Council
Issues: BUD GOV NAT
Rep By: Fran Boyd, Larry D. Meyers

Las Cruces, New Mexico, City of
Issues: AVI BUD CAW DEF DIS ECN HOU IMM ROD TRA TRU URB UTI
Rep By: Larry D. Meyers, Richard L. Meyers

Minor Use, Minor Species Coalition
Issues: ANI
Rep By: Fran Boyd, Larry D. Meyers, Richard L. Meyers

Nat'l Ass'n for Agricultural Stewardship
Issues: AGR
Rep By: Fran Boyd, Larry D. Meyers, Richard L. Meyers

New Mexico State Office of Research & Development
Issues: BUD CPI ECN EDU IND MAN SCI TEC
Rep By: Richard L. Meyers

New Mexico State University
Issues: BUD EDU
Rep By: Larry D. Meyers, Richard L. Meyers

New Mexico State University, Department of Agriculture
Issues: AGR BUD EDU NAT
Rep By: Richard L. Meyers

New Mexico State University, Department of Engineering
Issues: BUD CAW COM DEF DIS EDU ENG ENV MAN SCI TEC WAS
Rep By: Richard L. Meyers

NOKIA
Issues: TEC
Rep By: Larry D. Meyers, Richard L. Meyers

North Carolina Peanut Growers Ass'n
Issues: AGR BUD TRD
Rep By: Fran Boyd, Larry D. Meyers, Richard L. Meyers

Rice Belt Warehouses
Issues: AGR TRD
Rep By: Fran Boyd, Larry D. Meyers, Richard L. Meyers

Rio Grande Valley Chamber of Commerce
Issues: ECN
Rep By: Larry D. Meyers, Richard L. Meyers

Rio Grande Valley Irrigation
Issues: BUD GOV
Rep By: Larry D. Meyers

Southwest Peanut Growers
Issues: AGR BUD TRD
Rep By: Fran Boyd, Larry D. Meyers, Richard L. Meyers

Southwest Peanut PAC
Rep By: Larry D. Meyers

Space Access
Issues: AER AVI BUD COM FIN GOV TRA
Rep By: Larry D. Meyers, Richard L. Meyers

Texas A&M Research Foundation
Issues: AGR BUD CAW DEF DIS EDU ENG ENV FUE HCR HOU LAW MAR ROD TAX TRA TRD
Rep By: Shelley Wilson Dodd, Larry D. Meyers

United Gamefowl Breeders Ass'n, Inc.

University of North Carolina at Greensboro
Issues: AGR BUD EDU FAM
Rep By: Shelley Wilson Dodd, Larry D. Meyers, Richard L. Meyers

Virginia Peanut Growers Ass'n
Issues: AGR BUD TRD
Rep By: Fran Boyd, Larry D. Meyers, Richard L. Meyers

Virginia-Carolina's Peanut Political Action Committee
Rep By: Larry D. Meyers

Wool Fiber, Yarn Fabric Coalition
Issues: APP TRD
Rep By: Fran Boyd, Larry D. Meyers, Richard L. Meyers

MFJ Internat'l

1300 Connecticut Ave. NW
Suite 600
Washington, DC 20036
Tel: (202)223-7017
Fax: (202)223-7013
Registered: LDA
E-mail: mfjorge@aol.com

DC-Area Employees Representing Listed Clients

JORGE, M. Fabiana, Principal

Clients

Asociacion Nacional de Fabricantes de Medicamentos

Centro Industrial de Laboratorios Farmaceuticas Argentinos (CILFA)

Miles & Stockbridge, P.C.

1140 Connecticut Ave. NW
Suite 1212
Washington, DC 20036
Tel: (202)737-9600
Fax: (202)737-0097
Registered: LDA
Web: www.milesstockbridge.com
E-mail: dcook@milesstockbridge.com
Washington office of a regional law firm headquartered in Baltimore, MD. The firm maintains a total of nine offices in Maryland, Northern Virginia, and the District of Columbia.

DC-Area Employees Representing Listed Clients

BLEICHER, Samuel A., Principal

Clients

Black & Decker Corp., The
Issues: ENV
Rep By: Samuel A. Bleicher

Elmer Larson, Inc.
Issues: DIS ENV HOU RES URB
Rep By: Samuel A. Bleicher

Millennium Intermarket Group, LLC

1825 I St. NW
Suite 400
Washington, DC 20006
Tel: (202)429-2090
Fax: (202)429-9574
Registered: LDA

DC-Area Employees Representing Listed Clients

RUSBY, P. Baman

Clients

Infilco Degremont, Inc.
Issues: BUD CAW ENV
Rep By: P. Baman Rusby

Miller & Chevalier, Chartered

655 15th St. NW
Suite 900
Washington, DC 20005-5701
Tel: (202)626-5800
Fax: (202)628-0858
Registered: LDA, FARA
Web: www.millerchevalier.com
E-mail: inquiries@milchev.com

Political Action Committee

Miller & Chevalier PAC
655 15th St. NW
Suite 900
Washington, DC 20005-5701
Tel: (202)626-5800
Fax: (202)628-0858
Contact: Leonard Bickwit, Jr.

DC-Area Employees Representing Listed Clients

BATES, John D., Member
BICKWIT, Jr., Leonard, Member
CAMPBELL, Michael D., Exec. Director
CREECH, Catherine L., Member
DE GRAMONT, Jacqueline, Associate
GIBBS, Lawrence B., Member
HUFFMAN, Robert K., Member
LE BEAU, Josephine Aiello, Associate
MADSEN, Marcia G., Member
MANN, Phillip L., Member
MCGLONE, William M.
MOYER, Jr., Homer E., Member
O'SULLIVAN, Lynda Troutman, Member
OLIPHANT, III, C. Frederick, Member
PAWLOW, Jean A., Member
SHAPIRO, Hal S., Partner
TRENGA, Anthony J.
VOGHT, Brook, Member
ZAKUPOWSKY, Jr., Alexander, Member

Clients

American Staffing Ass'n
Issues: LBR RET TAX
Rep By: C. Frederick Oliphant, III

APA Coalition
Issues: TAX

Ass'n of Financial Services Holding Companies
Issues: BAN
Rep By: Leonard Bickwit, Jr.

Bahrain, Government of the State of

Blue Cross and Blue Shield of California
Issues: HCR
Rep By: Leonard Bickwit, Jr.

Boston Edison Co.
Issues: TAX
Rep By: Leonard Bickwit, Jr., Brook Voght

H. E. Butt Grocery Co.
Issues: WEL
Rep By: Leonard Bickwit, Jr.

Canada, Government of
Rep By: Homer E. Moyer, Jr.

Chevy Chase Bank, F.S.B.
Issues: BAN
Rep By: Leonard Bickwit, Jr.

Envirocare of Utah, Inc.
Issues: ENG
Rep By: Leonard Bickwit, Jr.

Export Source Coalition
Issues: TAX

Exxon Mobil Corp.
Issues: ENG
Rep By: Leonard Bickwit, Jr., Homer E. Moyer, Jr.

Framatome, S.A.
Issues: ENG
Rep By: Leonard Bickwit, Jr., Homer E. Moyer, Jr.

Ernest & Julio Gallo Winery
Issues: CSP FOO TAX TRA TRD
Rep By: Leonard Bickwit, Jr., Lawrence B. Gibbs

Keidanren
Rep By: Lawrence B. Gibbs

Monsanto Co.
Issues: TAX

Mutual of America
Issues: TAX
Rep By: Leonard Bickwit, Jr., Phillip L. Mann

Nat'l Foreign Trade Council, Inc.
Issues: TAX TRD
Rep By: Homer E. Moyer, Jr., Hal S. Shapiro

NFTC-FSC Coalition

Organization for Internat'l Investment
Issues: TAX

Pulte Home Corp.
Issues: BAN TAX
Rep By: Leonard Bickwit, Jr.

SABIC Americas, Inc.
Issues: TRD
Rep By: Leonard Bickwit, Jr., Homer E. Moyer, Jr.

Safeway, Inc.
Issues: TAX
Rep By: Leonard Bickwit, Jr.

Service Corp. Internat'l
Issues: TAX

U.S. Chamber Task Force on Punitive Damages
Issues: TAX
Rep By: Leonard Bickwit, Jr., Lawrence B. Gibbs

Wal-Mart Stores, Inc.
Issues: TAX
Rep By: Leonard Bickwit, Jr.

Miller & Co.

809 Princess St.
Alexandria, VA 22314
Tel: (703)683-1325
Fax: (703)519-9669
Registered: LDA

DC-Area Employees Representing Listed Clients
MILLER, Richard W., President

Clients

American Chiropractic Ass'n
Issues: HCR
Rep By: Richard W. Miller

Nat'l College
Issues: EDU HCR MED
Rep By: Richard W. Miller

Tobacco Fairness Coalition
Issues: TAX TOB TRD
Rep By: Richard W. Miller

Miller & Van Eaton, P.L.L.C.

1155 Connecticut Ave. NW
Suite 1000
Washington, DC 20036-4306
Tel: (202)785-0600
Fax: (202)785-1234
Registered: LDA, FARA
Web: www.millervaneaton.com
E-mail: info2@millervaneaton.com
Law firm specializing in federal and local telecommunications and cable television matters before Congress, the administrative agencies, the executive branch and the courts.

DC-Area Employees Representing Listed Clients
AMES, Matthew C., Director
ELLROD, III, Frederick E., Director
KANE, Betty Ann, Federal Relations Advisor
MALONE, William, Partner
MILLER, Nicholas P., Managing Partner
VAN EATON, Joseph, Partner

Clients

Building Owners and Managers Ass'n Internat'l
Issues: TEC
Rep By: Matthew C. Ames, William Malone, Nicholas P. Miller

Coral Springs, Florida, City of
Issues: TEC
Rep By: Joseph Van Eaton

Dayton, Ohio, Washington Office of the City of
Issues: TEC
Rep By: William Malone

Dearborn, Michigan, Department of Communication of
Issues: TEC
Rep By: Nicholas P. Miller

Dubuque, Iowa, Cable Television Division of
Issues: TEC
Rep By: Nicholas P. Miller

Harvard Radio Broadcasting Co.
Issues: TEC
Rep By: William Malone

Henrico County, Virginia
Rep By: Frederick E. Ellrod, III

Kansas Electric Power Cooperative
Rep By: William Malone, Nicholas P. Miller

Laredo, Texas, City of
Issues: TEC
Rep By: Betty Ann Kane, Nicholas P. Miller

Montgomery, Maryland, Cable Television Office of the County of
Issues: TEC
Rep By: Nicholas P. Miller

Nat'l Apartment Ass'n
Issues: TEC
Rep By: Matthew C. Ames, William Malone, Nicholas P. Miller

Nat'l Multi-Housing Council
Issues: TEC
Rep By: Matthew C. Ames, William Malone, Nicholas P. Miller

Nebraska Public Power District
Issues: TEC
Rep By: William Malone

Northern Mariana Islands, Commonwealth of the
Issues: TEC
Rep By: Betty Ann Kane, William Malone

Phoenix, Arizona, City of
Issues: TEC
Rep By: Joseph Van Eaton

Portland, Oregon, City of
Issues: TEC
Rep By: Joseph Van Eaton

Prince George's, Maryland, County of
Issues: TEC
Rep By: Nicholas P. Miller

Real Estate Roundtable
Issues: TEC
Rep By: Matthew C. Ames, William Malone, Nicholas P. Miller

San Francisco, California, City and County of
Rep By: Nicholas P. Miller

St. Louis Office of Cable Television
Issues: TEC
Rep By: Nicholas P. Miller

Tacoma, Washington, City of
Issues: TEC
Rep By: Joseph Van Eaton

Tallahassee, Florida, City of
Issues: TEC
Rep By: Joseph Van Eaton

Tucson, Arizona, City of
Issues: TEC
Rep By: William Malone, Joseph Van Eaton

Tulsa, Oklahoma, City of
Issues: TEC
Rep By: Matthew C. Ames

Miller and Miller, P.C.

1990 M St. NW
Suite 760
Washington, DC 20036-3404
Tel: (202)785-2720
Fax: (202)775-8519
E-mail: MILLAW@netkonnect.net
A communications law firm representing radio and television stations before the Federal Communications Commission.

Clients

KAIL-TV
Issues: COM

Denny Miller McBee Associates

400 N. Capitol St. NW
Suite 363
Washington, DC 20001
Tel: (202)783-0280
Fax: (202)737-4518
Registered: LDA
Web: www.dennymillermcbee.com
A public affairs and management consulting firm.

DC-Area Employees Representing Listed Clients
BAKER, Mark, Of Counsel
EAST, Emelie, V. President
GREENE, USA (Ret.), Col. Fred W., Consultant
LOVAIN, Timothy B., V. President and General Counsel
MATHIESEN, Sandra Windsor, V. President
MCBEE, Steve, Exec. V. President and Chief Operating Officer
MILLER, Denny M., President
MILLER, Sandra B., Exec. V. President
SPINA, Sam, V. President and Special Counsel

Clients

24/7 Media, Inc.
Issues: CPI

Alaska Air Group
Issues: AVI TAX TRA

apex.com
Issues: CPI EDU

Asbestos Recycling Inc.
Issues: DEF WAS
Rep By: Col. Fred W. Greene, USA (Ret.), Steve McBee, Denny M. Miller

Beyond.com
Issues: CPI

The Boeing Co.
Issues: AER AVI DEF TRD

Cell Therapeutics Inc.
Issues: HCR

Central Puget Sound Regional Transit Authority (Sound Transit)
Issues: TRA

Click2Learn.com
Issues: DEF

Cray Inc.

Dimension 4
Issues: DEF NAT

DuPont
Issues: DEF LBR

eNIC Corp.
Issues: COM

Everett, Washington, Port of
Issues: DEF MAR TRA TRD

ExtrudeHone Corp.
Issues: AER BUD DEF SCI

First Church of Christ, Scientist
Issues: HCR MMM

General Dynamics Corp.
Issues: DEF

Institute for Systems Biology
Issues: MED

King, Washington, County of
Issues: ENV NAT

NetCoalition.Com
Issues: COM CPI CPT SCI TEC

NetSchools
Issues: COM EDU

Northrop Grumman Corp.
Issues: DEF

Olin Corp.-Winchester Division

Omega Oil Co.
Issues: ENG FUE SCI

Pacific Science Center
Issues: ECN EDU

Pierce, Washington, County of
Issues: ENV NAT

Precision Aerospace Corp.
Issues: AVI DEF

Ramgen Power Systems, Inc.
Issues: ENG

Science Applications Internat'l Corp. (SAIC)
Issues: DEF

Seattle, Washington, City of

Sonomish, Washington, County of
Issues: ENV NAT

Survival Inc.
Issues: DEF

Tacoma, Washington, Port of
Issues: MAR TRA TRD

Todd Shipyards Inc.
Issues: DEF TRA

Toy Manufacturers of America
Issues: CSP TRD

Washington, Department of Transportation of the State of
Issues: MAR ROD RRR TRA

Miller Thomson Wickens & Lebow LLP

1919 Pennsylvania Ave. NW
Suite 610
Washington, DC 20006
Tel: (202)775-2400
Fax: (202)331-7538
A law firm specializing in litigation, international trade and customs issues. The Washington, D.C. branch of a full-service Canadian law firm.

DC-Area Employees Representing Listed Clients
LEBOW, Edward M.
WICKENS, William E.

Miller, Balis and O'Neil, P.C.

1140 19th St. NW
Suite 700
Washington, DC 20036
Tel: (202)296-2960
Fax: (202)296-0166
Web: www.mbolaw.com
An energy law firm.

DC-Area Employees Representing Listed Clients
BALIS, Stanley W., Principal
GREGG, John P., Managing Partner
MILLER, William T., Principal

Clients

American Public Gas Ass'n
Rep By: Stanley W. Balis, John P. Gregg, William T. Miller

Miller, Canfield, Paddock & Stone, P.L.C.

1900 K St. NW
Suite 1150
Washington, DC 20006
Tel: (202)429-5575
Fax: (202)331-1118
Registered: LDA
Web: www.millercanfield.com
The Washington office of a law firm headquartered in Detroit, MI.

DC-Area Employees Representing Listed Clients
LAY, Tillman L., Senior Counsel

Clients

Nat'l League of Cities
Issues: COM TEC
Rep By: Tillman L. Lay

Millian Byers Associates, LLC

1090 Vermont Ave. NW
Third Floor
Washington, DC 20005
Tel: (202)842-5000
Fax: (202)789-4293
Web: www.milbya.com
E-mail: kym@milbya.com
Public policy issue management.

DC-Area Employees Representing Listed Clients
BYERS, H. James, President
FLYNN, Jack, Senior Labor Advisor
GREALY, Robert F., Senior International Advisor
MILLIAN, Kenneth Y., Chairman
NASH, James A., Advisor, Social and Ecological Ethics
RECFORD, Thomas J., Senior International Advisor

Clients

American Chemistry Council
Rep By: H. James Byers, Kenneth Y. Millian
C F Industries, Inc.
Rep By: H. James Byers
Chlorine Chemistry Council
Rep By: H. James Byers, Kenneth Y. Millian
Ciba Specialty Chemicals Corp.
Federal Strategies Group
Rep By: H. James Byers
Hager Sharp Inc.
Issues: ENV FOR LBR
Rep By: H. James Byers
Patton Boggs, LLP
Rep By: Kenneth Y. Millian
Vulcan Chemicals

Mintz, Levin, Cohn, Ferris, Glovsky and Popeo, P.C.

701 Pennsylvania Ave. NW
Suite 900
Washington, DC 20004-2608
Tel: (202)434-7300
Fax: (202)434-7400
Registered: LDA, FARA
Web: www.mintz.com
Washington office of a Boston law firm.

DC-Area Employees Representing Listed Clients
ANTONE, IV, Thomas M., Partner
BRASHARES, William C., Partner
CASSERLY, James L., Partner
CHIN, Yee Wah, Of Counsel
COTTON, Raymond D., Partner
DARLING, Erin Lewis, Associate
FERRIS, Charles D., Chairman
FOSTER, Hope S., Partner
FOX, Russell H., Partner
HARVIE, Christopher J., Partner
HOPE, Patrick, Associate
KAZON, Peter M., Partner
KELLY, Bradley L., Partner
KIRKLAND, James A., Partner
KISER, Cherie R., Partner
KRATTENMAKER, Thomas G., Partner
LAGUARDA, Fernando R., Associate
LAVALLEE, Adrienne C., Of Counsel
LEIBMAN, Sara F., Partner
LEWIN, Nathan, Partner
LLOYD, Frank W., Partner
LORMAN, Alvin J., Partner
MUNDT, Michelle, Associate
OBERBROECKLING, Laura J., Partner
PRYOR, Michael H., Partner
SAMUELS, Charles A., Partner
SOKLER, Bruce D., Partner
SYMONS, Howard J., Partner
VALENTINO, James, Partner

Clients

ABAHG, Inc.
American Ass'n of Homeopathic Pharmacists
American Clinical Laboratory Ass'n
Rep By: Peter M. Kazon
American College of Chest Physicians
Issues: BUD HCR MED MMM TOB
Rep By: Raymond D. Cotton
American College of Nuclear Physicians
AOL Time Warner
Rep By: James A. Kirkland, Bruce D. Sokler
Ass'n of American Blood Banks
Issues: HCR MMM
Rep By: Peter M. Kazon, Charles A. Samuels
Ass'n of Governing Boards of Universities and Colleges
Rep By: Raymond D. Cotton
Ass'n of Home Appliance Manufacturers
Issues: BNK CSP ENG ENV TRD
Rep By: Charles A. Samuels
AT&T Broadband & Internet Service
AT&T Wireless Services, Inc.
Issues: TEC
Rep By: Sara F. Leibman, Howard J. Symons
Biogen, Inc.
Issues: MMM
Rep By: Charles A. Samuels
Cablevision Systems Corp.
Issues: TEC
Rep By: Charles D. Ferris, Howard J. Symons
California Cable Television Ass'n
Rep By: Frank W. Lloyd
California State University Institute
Rep By: Raymond D. Cotton
Cellular Telecommunications and Internet Ass'n
Issues: TEC
Rep By: Michelle Mundt, Howard J. Symons
Comcast Corp.
Rep By: James L. Casserly
Council for Advanced Agricultural Formulations, Inc.
Issues: FOO
Rep By: Alvin J. Lorman
CVS, Inc.
Issues: HCR MMM
Rep By: Raymond D. Cotton, Erin Lewis Darling, Patrick Hope
George Washington University, Office of Government Relations
Rep By: Raymond D. Cotton
Internat'l Ass'n of Jewish Lawyers and Jurists
Rep By: Nathan Lewin
Internat'l Specialty Products
Rep By: Alvin J. Lorman
M/A-COM, Inc.
Mariner Post Acute Network
Rep By: Raymond D. Cotton
Massachusetts Technology Park Corp.
Medical College of Virginia, Dept. of Neurology, Office of the Chairman
Issues: BUD DEF HCR MED
Rep By: Raymond D. Cotton, Erin Lewis Darling
Michigan Technological University
Rep By: Raymond D. Cotton
Monmouth University
Rep By: Raymond D. Cotton
Morehouse School of Medicine
Rep By: Raymond D. Cotton
N-Methylpyrrolidone Producers Group, Inc.
Rep By: Alvin J. Lorman
Nat'l Ass'n of Higher Educational Finance Authorities
Issues: FIN
Rep By: Charles A. Samuels
Nat'l Cable Television Ass'n
Issues: TEC
Rep By: Howard J. Symons
Nat'l Council of Health Facilities Finance Authorities
Issues: FIN
Rep By: Charles A. Samuels
Nat'l Network to End Domestic Violence
Rep By: Fernando R. Laguarda
New England Cable Television Ass'n
Rep By: Frank W. Lloyd
Public Health Policy Advisory Board
Issues: BUD HCR MED
Rep By: Raymond D. Cotton
Soc. of Nuclear Medicine
Rep By: Alvin J. Lorman
Television Ass'n of Programmers Latin America (TAP Latin America)
Issues: COM TRD
Rep By: Frank W. Lloyd

Moir & Hardman

1828 L St. NW
Suite 901
Washington, DC 20036
Tel: (202)872-8680
Fax: (202)870-8698
Registered: LDA
A law firm specializing in telecommunication, communication, antitrust, and trade regulation law.

DC-Area Employees Representing Listed Clients
HARDMAN, Kenneth E., Principal
MOIR, Brian R., Principal

Susan Molinari, L.L.P.

4004 Sharp Place
Alexandria, VA 22304
Registered: LDA

DC-Area Employees Representing Listed Clients
MOLINARI, Hon. Susan

Clients

American Heart Ass'n
Issues: HCR
Rep By: Hon. Susan Molinari
Americans for Consumer Education and Competition, Inc.
Issues: BAN EDU FIN
Ass'n of American Railroads
Federal Home Loan Mortgage Corp. (Freddie Mac)
SBC Communications Inc.
Rep By: Hon. Susan Molinari

James T. Molloy

9226 Ispahanloop
Laurel, MD 20708
Tel: (301)776-6128
Fax: (301)776-5070
Registered: LDA
A federal affairs representative.

Clients

Advanced Refractory Technologies, Inc.
Issues: DEF
Rep By: James T. Molloy
Norfolk Southern Corp.
Issues: RRR
Rep By: James T. Molloy
Philip Morris Management Corp.
Issues: BEV FOO TOB
Rep By: James T. Molloy
Stanton & Associates
Rep By: James T. Molloy
Union Pacific Railroad Co.
Rep By: James T. Molloy

Gunter W. Moltzan

6701 Democracy Blvd.
Suite 300
Bethesda, MD 20817
Tel: (301)977-6104
Fax: (301)330-0790
Registered: FARA
E-mail: moltzan@ix.netcom.com

Clients

Baden-Wuerttemberg Agency for International Economic Cooperation
Rep By: Gunter W. Moltzan

Monfort & Wolfe

499 S. Capitol St. SW
Suite 420
Washington, DC 20003
Tel: (202)302-0465
Registered: LDA

DC-Area Employees Representing Listed Clients
FRISA, Hon. Dan, Senior Political Advisor
MONFORT, Charles A., Associate
MURPHY, Lynda M., Associate

Clients

Federal Sources, Inc.
Heard Communications
Incorporated Research Institutions for Seismology
Issues: SCI
Rep By: Charles A. Monfort
Minnesota Life Insurance Co.
Issues: INS TAX
Minnesota Townships
St. Elizabeth's Medical Center
Issues: HCR
Rep By: Charles A. Monfort

The Montgomery Group

11 Canal Center Plaza
Suite 104
Alexandria, VA 22314
Tel: (703)549-7408
Fax: (703)549-7409
Registered: LDA
E-mail: gvmont@aol.com

DC-Area Employees Representing Listed Clients
MONTGOMERY, Hon. G. V. "Sonny", President

Clients

Blue Cross Blue Shield of Mississippi
Rep By: Hon. G. V. "Sonny" Montgomery

Lockheed Martin Corp.
Issues: DEF
Rep By: Hon. G. V. "Sonny" Montgomery

Raytheon Co.
Rep By: Hon. G. V. "Sonny" Montgomery

Moore & Bruce, LLP

1072 Thomas Jefferson St. NW
Washington, DC 20007
Tel: (202)965-7748
Fax: (202)965-7749
Registered: LDA

A law firm specializing in taxation, international trade, and customs matters.

DC-Area Employees Representing Listed Clients
MORRIS, William

Clients

Mutual of America
Issues: TAX

Nat'l Automobile Dealers Ass'n
Issues: TAX
Rep By: William Morris

Timothy X. Moore and Co.

2900 M St. NW
Suite 300
Washington, DC 20007
Tel: (202)333-4318
Fax: (202)342-0418
Registered: LDA
E-mail: timxavier@aol.com

A government relations consulting firm with special interest in telecommunications, commerce, electric utility industry, environment, intellectual property issues, and appropriations.

DC-Area Employees Representing Listed Clients
MOORE, Timothy X., President

Clients

Berkeley County Water & Sanitation Authority
Issues: CAW UTI
Rep By: Timothy X. Moore

Galena, Illinois, City of
Issues: BUD CAW
Rep By: Timothy X. Moore

Inventure Place
Issues: ART CPT
Rep By: Timothy X. Moore

Santee Cooper (South Carolina Public Service Authority)
Rep By: Timothy X. Moore

South Carolina Public Service Authority
Issues: ENG UTI
Rep By: Timothy X. Moore

The Moore Law Firm, PLLC

1911 North Fort Myer Dr.
Suite 702
Arlington, VA 22209
Tel: (703)243-1667
Fax: (703)243-1672
Registered: LDA

A government relations firm providing advocacy services on legislative and regulatory issues in the pension area.

DC-Area Employees Representing Listed Clients
MOORE, Cynthia L., President

Clients

Nat'l Council on Teacher Retirement
Issues: RET
Rep By: Cynthia L. Moore

Alan J. Moore, Washington Representative - Governmental Affairs

9534 Clement Rd.
Silver Spring, MD 20910
Tel: (301)585-3838
Fax: (301)585-3838
Registered: LDA

DC-Area Employees Representing Listed Clients
MOORE, Alan J., President

Clients

Burlington Northern Santa Fe Railway
Issues: RRR
Rep By: Alan J. Moore

Morgan Casner Associates, Inc.

1332 Independence Ave. SE
Washington, DC 20003-2365
Tel: (202)543-4600
E-mail: mca@casner.com

A political and public affairs consulting firm that specializes in Washington representation and Federal Government liaison. Also sets up and operates political action committees for clients.

DC-Area Employees Representing Listed Clients
CASNER, Bruce M., President
COLKER, Ed.D., Laura J., Senior Associate
HEWITT, Mary E., V. President
MCEWEN, Hon. Robert D., Senior Associate
WILLIAMS, Lucinda L., Senior Associate

Morgan Meguire, LLC

1225 I St. NW
Suite 600
Washington, DC 20005
Tel: (202)661-6180
Fax: (202)661-6182
Registered: LDA
Web: www.morganmeguire.com
E-mail: morganmeguire@morganmeguire.com

Energy consultants.

DC-Area Employees Representing Listed Clients
HONG, Jocelyn, Principal
JACOBSON, Jack, Legislative Assistant
LINDSAY, Scott, V. President
MICHEL, Kyle G., Senior V. President and General Counsel
MUSANTE, Ramola, V. President
PARROTT, Katie, Associate
SCHREPEL, Dawn, Director, Project Development
SIMPSON, C. Kyle, President and Chief Exec. Officer
SLIZ, Deborah R., Principal
WEAVER, Kiel, V. President

Clients

Adroit Systems Inc.
Issues: ENG
Rep By: Scott Lindsay, Kyle G. Michel, Katie Parrott, C. Kyle Simpson, Deborah R. Sliz, Kiel Weaver

Air-Conditioning and Refrigeration Institute
Issues: ENG
Rep By: Kyle G. Michel, Ramola Musante, C. Kyle Simpson

Arctic Resources Co.
Issues: ENG
Rep By: Kyle G. Michel, C. Kyle Simpson, Kiel Weaver

Baker Electromotive, Inc.
Issues: AUT ENG
Rep By: Scott Lindsay, Kyle G. Michel, Katie Parrott, C. Kyle Simpson, Deborah R. Sliz, Kiel Weaver

BellSouth Corp.
Issues: ENG
Rep By: Scott Lindsay, Kyle G. Michel, Katie Parrott, C. Kyle Simpson, Deborah R. Sliz, Kiel Weaver

Burke Venture Capital
Issues: FIN
Rep By: Jocelyn Hong, Jack Jacobson, Kyle G. Michel, C. Kyle Simpson

Colorado River Energy Distributors Ass'n
Issues: ENG
Rep By: Scott Lindsay, Kyle G. Michel, Katie Parrott, C. Kyle Simpson, Deborah R. Sliz, Kiel Weaver

Energy Affairs Administration
Issues: ENG
Rep By: Kyle G. Michel, Ramola Musante, C. Kyle Simpson, Deborah R. Sliz

Energy Northwest
Issues: ENG
Rep By: Scott Lindsay, Kyle G. Michel, Katie Parrott, C. Kyle Simpson, Deborah R. Sliz, Kiel Weaver

Florida Municipal Power Agency
Issues: ENG
Rep By: Scott Lindsay, Kyle G. Michel, Katie Parrott, C. Kyle Simpson, Deborah R. Sliz, Kiel Weaver

Goodman Manufacturing Co., L.P.
Issues: ENG
Rep By: Scott Lindsay, Kyle G. Michel, Katie Parrott, C. Kyle Simpson, Deborah R. Sliz, Kiel Weaver

GovWorks.com
Issues: CPT
Rep By: Kyle G. Michel, C. Kyle Simpson, Kiel Weaver

Just Valuations
Issues: GOV
Rep By: Kyle G. Michel

Longhorn Pipeline
Issues: TRA
Rep By: Jocelyn Hong, Jack Jacobson, Scott Lindsay, Kyle G. Michel, Katie Parrott, C. Kyle Simpson, Deborah R. Sliz, Kiel Weaver

LVS Power Ltd.
Rep By: C. Kyle Simpson

Madison Gas & Electric Co.
Issues: ENG
Rep By: Scott Lindsay, Kyle G. Michel, Katie Parrott, C. Kyle Simpson, Deborah R. Sliz, Kiel Weaver

Manatee, Florida, County of
Issues: BUD
Rep By: Jocelyn Hong, Jack Jacobson, Scott Lindsay, Kyle G. Michel, Katie Parrott, C. Kyle Simpson, Deborah R. Sliz, Kiel Weaver

Monsanto Co.
Rep By: C. Kyle Simpson

Northern California Power Agency
Issues: ENG
Rep By: Scott Lindsay, Kyle G. Michel, Katie Parrott, C. Kyle Simpson, Deborah R. Sliz, Kiel Weaver

Northwest Public Power Ass'n
Issues: ENG
Rep By: Scott Lindsay, Kyle G. Michel, Katie Parrott, C. Kyle Simpson, Deborah R. Sliz, Kiel Weaver

Nuevo Energy
Issues: ENG
Rep By: Scott Lindsay, Kyle G. Michel, Katie Parrott, C. Kyle Simpson, Deborah R. Sliz, Kiel Weaver

Puerto Rico Electric Power Authority
Issues: ENG
Rep By: Kyle G. Michel, C. Kyle Simpson, Deborah R. Sliz

Puerto Rico, Attorney General of
Rep By: Kyle G. Michel

Redding, California, City of
Issues: URB
Rep By: Scott Lindsay, Kyle G. Michel, Katie Parrott, C. Kyle Simpson, Deborah R. Sliz, Kiel Weaver

Sacramento Municipal Utility District
Issues: ENG
Rep By: Katie Parrott, C. Kyle Simpson, Deborah R. Sliz

Seven Seas Petroleum USA Inc.
Issues: ENG
Rep By: Kyle G. Michel, C. Kyle Simpson, Deborah R. Sliz, Kiel Weaver

Shell Oil Co.
Rep By: Kyle G. Michel, C. Kyle Simpson

Southern California Public Power Authority
Issues: ENG
Rep By: Scott Lindsay, Kyle G. Michel, Katie Parrott, C. Kyle Simpson, Deborah R. Sliz, Kiel Weaver

Springfield, Missouri, City Utilities of
Issues: ENG
Rep By: Scott Lindsay, Kyle G. Michel, Katie Parrott, C. Kyle Simpson, Deborah R. Sliz, Kiel Weaver

Tennessee Valley Public Power Ass'n
Issues: ENG
Rep By: Scott Lindsay, Kyle G. Michel, Katie Parrott, C. Kyle Simpson, Deborah R. Sliz, Kiel Weaver

Texas A&M Engineering Experiment Station
Issues: ENG
Rep By: Ramola Musante, Dawn Schrepel, C. Kyle Simpson

Transmission Access Policy Study Group
Issues: ENG
Rep By: Scott Lindsay, Kyle G. Michel, Katie Parrott, C. Kyle Simpson, Deborah R. Sliz, Kiel Weaver

Truckee Donner Electric Power Utility District
Issues: ENG
Rep By: Kyle G. Michel, C. Kyle Simpson, Deborah R. Sliz, Kiel Weaver

Washington Public Utility Districts Ass'n
Issues: ENG
Rep By: Scott Lindsay, Kyle G. Michel, Katie Parrott, C. Kyle Simpson, Deborah R. Sliz, Kiel Weaver

Morgan, Lewis & Bockius LLP

1800 M St. NW
Washington, DC 20036
Tel: (202)467-7000
Fax: (202)467-7176
Registered: LDA, FARA
Web: www.morganlewis.com
E-mail: postmaster@morganlewis.com

Washington office of a general practice law firm headquartered in Philadelphia, PA.

DC-Area Employees Representing Listed Clients
BAER, William E.
BERMINGHAM, Maya, Associate
DANIEL, John E., Of Counsel
DENNIS, Sandra J. P., Partner
FRIEDMAN, Margery Sinder
GLASGOW, James A.
GLEASON, Kathryn L., Partner
GLICK, Helene L., Associate
HOBBS, III, Caswell O., Partner, Washington Office
KUHN, Nancy R.
MATTHEWS, John E.
O'CONNOR, Charles P., Managing Partner
PETERSON, Charles H.
RING, John F.
ROADY, Celia, Partner
SANZO, Kathleen M., Partner
SILVERMAN, Donald J., Partner
STADULIS, Lawrence P.
ZARB, Jr., Frank G., Partner

Clients

Bituminous Coal Operators Ass'n
Issues: HCR RET
Rep By: Margery Sinder Friedman

Cell Pathways, Inc.
Issues: TRD

The Church Alliance
Rep By: Helene L. Glick

CNA Financial Corp.
Issues: FIN HCR INS LAW

CNA Insurance Cos.
Issues: FIN HCR INS LAW

Coalition of Supporters of the Shipping Act
Rep By: Helene L. Glick

Cord Blood Registry, Inc.
Issues: HCR
Rep By: Maya Bermingham, Kathryn L. Gleason, Kathleen M. Sanzo

Credit Suisse First Boston Corp.
Issues: BUD DEF ENG FOR TRD
Rep By: William E. Baer, James A. Glasgow, Charles H. Peterson

Florida Equipment Contractors Ass'n
Issues: LBR

Internat'l Franchise Ass'n
Issues: SMB

Bob Lawrence & Associates
Issues: IMM

Northern Ireland, Government of

Schwab Fund for Charitable Giving

U.S. Chamber Institute for Legal Reform
Issues: TOR

U.S. Gypsum Co.
Issues: CSP

UGI Utilities, Inc.
Issues: ENV
Rep By: John E. Daniel

Unitech Services Group, Inc.
Issues: ENG ENV WAS
Rep By: John E. Daniel

United Kingdom, Government of

Vanguard Charitable Endowment Program
Issues: TAX
Rep By: Celia Roady

Wine Institute
Issues: ALC BEV CON LAW

Kay Allan Morrell, Attorney-at-Law

1101 30th St. NW
Suite 200
Washington, DC 20007
E-mail: kmorrell@erols.com
Tel: (202)342-2787
Fax: (202)342-2789
Registered: LDA

Clients

Environmental Land Technology Ltd.
Issues: ENV NAT RES
Rep By: Kay Allan Morrell

Scott J. Esparza & Co.
Issues: CIV LAW
Rep By: Kay Allan Morrell

Space Dynamics Laboratory
Issues: AER BUD DEF ENV SCI
Rep By: Kay Allan Morrell

Utah State University
Issues: AER AGR ANI BUD DEF EDU ENV NAT SCI TRA
Rep By: Kay Allan Morrell

Morriset, Schlosser, Ayer & Jozwiak

1730 Rhode Island Ave. NW
Suite 209
Washington, DC 20036-3120
Web: www.masaj.com
Tel: (202)331-8690
Fax: (202)331-8738
Registered: LDA

Washington office of a Seattle law firm.

DC-Area Employees Representing Listed Clients
AYER, Fran, Attorney
HUGHES, Jennifer P., Attorney

Clients

Alaska Eskimo Whaling Commission
Issues: IND
Rep By: Fran Ayer, Jennifer P. Hughes

Bay Mills Indian Community
Issues: IND
Rep By: Fran Ayer

Kake, Alaska, Organized Village of
Issues: IND
Rep By: Fran Ayer, Jennifer P. Hughes

Little River Band of Ottawa Indians

Little Traverse Bay Band of Odawa Indians

Michigan Inter-Tribal Council

Oglala Sioux Tribe
Issues: IND
Rep By: Fran Ayer

Paucatuck Eastern Pequot Tribal Nation
Issues: IND
Rep By: Fran Ayer, Jennifer P. Hughes

Prairie Band of Potawatomi Indians
Issues: IND
Rep By: Fran Ayer

Quechan Indian Tribe
Issues: IND
Rep By: Fran Ayer, Jennifer P. Hughes

Saginaw Chippewa Indian Tribe of Michigan
Issues: IND
Rep By: Fran Ayer, Jennifer P. Hughes

Morrison & Foerster LLP

2000 Pennsylvania Ave. NW
Suite 5500
Washington, DC 20006
Web: www.mofo.com
Tel: (202)887-1500
Fax: (202)887-0763
Registered: LDA, FARA

Washington office of a San Francisco law firm.

DC-Area Employees Representing Listed Clients
ARNSBARGER, Linda A., Of Counsel
BAND, Jonathan, Partner
BUSEY, G. Brian, Partner
FISCHER, L. Richard, Partner
KURUCZA, Robert M., Partner
LOEFFLER, Robert H., Partner
MCCORMICK, Thomas C., Associate
SCHWARTZ, Bryan Alan, Of Counsel
SPILIOTES, Nicholas J., Partner
TRITT, Cheryl A., Partner
WARRINGTON, Joan, Of Counsel

Clients

American Library Ass'n
Rep By: Jonathan Band

Denver, Colorado, City of
Issues: AVI
Rep By: G. Brian Busey

eBay Inc.
Issues: CPT
Rep By: Jonathan Band

Fujitsu Limited
Issues: CPT
Rep By: Jonathan Band

ICO Global Communications
Issues: COM TEC
Rep By: Cheryl A. Tritt

NetCoalition.Com
Issues: COM CPI CPT LAW SCI TEC
Rep By: Jonathan Band

Norfolk, Virginia, City of
Issues: AVI
Rep By: G. Brian Busey

San Francisco, California, City and County of
Issues: AVI
Rep By: G. Brian Busey

Seiko Epson Corp.
Issues: CPT TRD
Rep By: Jonathan Band, G. Brian Busey

Storage Technology Corp.
Issues: CPI GOV
Rep By: Jonathan Band

VISA U.S.A., Inc.
Issues: BAN BNK CPT CSP FIN SCI TAX
Rep By: L. Richard Fischer, Thomas C. McCormick

Yahoo!
Issues: CPI
Rep By: Jonathan Band

The Morrison Group, Inc.

1012 Steeples Ct.
Falls Church, VA 22046
E-mail: mrsngroup@aol.com
Tel: (703)536-1848
Fax: (703)536-1849
Registered: LDA

Provides government affairs and public relations services, including publications management.

DC-Area Employees Representing Listed Clients
MORRISON, Ph.D., James W., Chief Exec. Officer

Clients

Nat'l Ass'n for the Self-Employed
Issues: CPT ECN SMB TAX
Rep By: James W. Morrison, Ph.D.

Small Business Exporters Ass'n
Rep By: James W. Morrison, Ph.D.

Bob Moss Associates

1150 Connecticut Ave. NW
Suite 201
Washington, DC 20036
Registered: LDA

DC-Area Employees Representing Listed Clients
MOSS, Bob

Clients

Advanced Vehicle Systems
Issues: DEF
Rep By: Bob Moss

American Chemistry Council
Issues: TRA
Rep By: Bob Moss

The Centech Group
Issues: DEF GOV
Rep By: Bob Moss

Enron Corp.
Issues: DEF ENG
Rep By: Bob Moss

General Motors Corp.
Issues: ENG ENV TRA
Rep By: Bob Moss

Oxygenated Fuels Ass'n
Issues: ENG ENV
Rep By: Bob Moss

The Kate Moss Company

1401 I St. NW
Suite 1100
Washington, DC 20005
Tel: (202)326-8908
Fax: (202)408-4797
Registered: LDA

DC-Area Employees Representing Listed Clients
MOSS, Kate, Principal

Clients

Bank of America
Issues: BAN BNK FIN TAX
Rep By: Kate Moss

GE Capital Corp.
Issues: HOU
Rep By: Kate Moss

Morgan Stanley Dean Witter & Co.
Issues: BAN BNK FIN
Rep By: Kate Moss

SBC Communications Inc.
Issues: TEC
Rep By: Kate Moss

Trans Union Corp.
Issues: BAN FIN
Rep By: Kate Moss

Moss McGee Bradley & Foley

810 First St. NE
Suite 530
Washington, DC 20002
Tel: (202)842-4721
Fax: (202)842-0551
Registered: LDA

DC-Area Employees Representing Listed Clients
BRADLEY, David A., Partner
FOLEY, III, Leander J., Partner

Clients

Center for Employment Training
Issues: BUD EDU LBR WEL
Rep By: Leander J. Foley, III

Committee for Farmworker Programs
Issues: LBR
Rep By: Leander J. Foley, III

Community Development Financial Institutions (CDFI)
Issues: BAN ECN
Rep By: Leander J. Foley, III

Green Thumb, Inc.
Issues: LBR
Rep By: Leander J. Foley, III

Greenpoint Manufacturing and Design Center (GMDC)
Issues: ECN
Rep By: Leander J. Foley, III

Indian Hills Community College
Issues: EDU
Rep By: Leander J. Foley, III

Internat'l Ass'n of Personnel in Employment Security
Issues: BUD LBR
Rep By: Leander J. Foley, III

Kake Tribal Corp.
Issues: IND
Rep By: David A. Bradley

The Learning Disabilities Ass'n
Issues: EDU
Rep By: Leander J. Foley, III

Nat'l Center for Appropriate Technology
Issues: BUD HOU
Rep By: Leander J. Foley, III

Nat'l Community Action Foundation
Issues: BUD WEL
Rep By: David A. Bradley, Leander J. Foley, III

TELACU
Issues: ECN
Rep By: Leander J. Foley, III

Telacu Carpenter
Rep By: Leander J. Foley, III

Three Affiliated Tribes of Fort Berthold Reservation
Issues: IND
Rep By: Leander J. Foley, III

USA WORKS!
Issues: LBR
Rep By: David A. Bradley, Leander J. Foley, III

Western Alliance of Farmworker Advocates, Inc. (WAFA)
Issues: AGR
Rep By: Leander J. Foley, III

Gerald J. Mossinghoff

1530 Key Blvd.
Penthouse 28
Arlington, VA 22209
Tel: (703)276-8280
Fax: (703)276-1536
Registered: LDA
E-mail: peatins@compuserve.com

Clients

Pharmaceutical Research and Manufacturers of America
Rep By: Gerald J. Mossinghoff

L. A. Motley, L.L.C.

1101 Connecticut Ave.
Suite 1200
Washington, DC 20036
Tel: (202)466-5529
Fax: (202)466-4144
Registered: LDA, FARA
Web: www.cari.compuserve.com

DC-Area Employees Representing Listed Clients
MOTLEY, Langhorne A., President and Chief Exec. Officer

Clients

Anheuser-Busch Cos., Inc.
Rep By: Langhorne A. Motley

The Boeing Co.
Rep By: Langhorne A. Motley

The Moyer Group

6907 Westmoreland Ave.
Takoma Park, MD 20912-4408
Tel: (301)270-8115
Fax: (301)270-8255
Registered: LDA
E-mail: bmoyer@ix.netcom.com
Provides government relations services and marketing solutions.

DC-Area Employees Representing Listed Clients
MOYER, Bruce L., President

Clients

Federal Bar Ass'n
Issues: CON
Rep By: Bruce L. Moyer

Nat'l Ass'n of Postal Supervisors
Rep By: Bruce L. Moyer

MSP Strategic Communications, Inc.

1133 Connecticut Ave. NW
Suite 1000
Washington, DC 20036
Tel: (202)775-2376
Fax: (202)775-2394
Registered: LDA
E-mail: mspettit@mspstrategic.com
Provides legislative, communications and business consulting services. The firm plans to move its office in May of 2001, but further information was unavailable at the time this edition went to press.

DC-Area Employees Representing Listed Clients
PETTIT, Mitchell S., Chief Exec. Officer

Clients

MasterCard Internat'l
Issues: BAN CSP GAM
Rep By: Mitchell S. Pettit

Netscape Communications Corp.
Issues: COM CPI CPT CSP
Rep By: Mitchell S. Pettit

Project to Promote Competition and Innovation in the Digital Age
Issues: CPI CSP LBR SCI
Rep By: Mitchell S. Pettit

Securify
Rep By: Mitchell S. Pettit

Verizon Communications
Rep By: Mitchell S. Pettit

MSS Consultants, LLC

1117 Alden Rd.
Alexandria, VA 22308
Tel: (202)467-6540
Fax: (202)467-6541
Registered: LDA
A government relations consulting firm.

DC-Area Employees Representing Listed Clients
SMITH, Megan S., President

Clients

Arkenol, Inc.
Issues: BUD
Rep By: Megan S. Smith

B.C. Internat'l Corp.
Issues: BUD
Rep By: Megan S. Smith

Battelle Memorial Institute
Issues: BUD ENG
Rep By: Megan S. Smith

Cargill Dow
Issues: BUD ENG NAT SCI TAX
Rep By: Megan S. Smith

Muldoon, Murphy & Faucette, LLP

5101 Wisconsin Ave. NW
Washington, DC 20016
Tel: (202)362-0840
Fax: (202)966-9409
Registered: LDA, FARA
A law firm specializing in banking, securities, and corporate matters before federal and state regulatory agencies and legislative bodies.

DC-Area Employees Representing Listed Clients
DALY, Joseph P., Partner
FAUCETTE, Douglas P., Partner
MULDOON, Sr., Joseph A., Partner

Clients

GreenPoint Bank
Issues: BAN
Rep By: Joseph A. Muldoon, Sr.

Queens County Bancorp Inc.
Issues: BAN
Rep By: Joseph A. Muldoon, Sr.

Roslyn Bancorp Inc.
Issues: BAN
Rep By: Joseph A. Muldoon, Sr.

Mullenholz, Brimsek & Belair

1150 Connecticut Ave. NW
Suite 700
Washington, DC 20036
Tel: (202)296-8000
Fax: (202)296-8803
Registered: LDA, FARA
A general practice law firm.

DC-Area Employees Representing Listed Clients
BELAIR, Robert R., Partner
BRIMSEK, John R., Partner
CONAWAY, John B.
HALLER, Susan C.
MULLENHOLZ, John J., Of Counsel

Clients

Aviateca Airline
Rep By: John R. Brimsek

Canadian Pacific

Center for Civic Education
Issues: BUD
Rep By: Robert R. Belair, John B. Conaway, Susan C. Haller

ChoicePoint
Issues: BAN
Rep By: Robert R. Belair, Susan C. Haller

The Coalition on Motor Vehicle Privacy
Issues: BUD
Rep By: Robert R. Belair, John R. Brimsek, Susan C. Haller

Constitutional Rights Foundation
Issues: BUD
Rep By: Robert R. Belair, John B. Conaway, Susan C. Haller

Copa Airline
Rep By: John R. Brimsek

Delaware and Hudson Railroad
Issues: BUD ENV IMM RRR TAX TRU WAS
Rep By: John R. Brimsek

Equifax Inc.
Issues: BAN CPI CSP
Rep By: Robert R. Belair, Susan C. Haller

Fergus Falls, Minnesota, City of
Rep By: John R. Brimsek

First Data Corp./Telecheck
Issues: CPT
Rep By: Robert R. Belair, Susan C. Haller

Nat'l Institute for Citizen Education in the Law
Rep By: Robert R. Belair

NICA Airline
Rep By: John R. Brimsek

Northstar Corridor Development Authority
Issues: BUD
Rep By: John R. Brimsek

SEARCH Group, Inc.
Issues: BUD LAW
Rep By: Robert R. Belair, Susan C. Haller

Soo Line Railroad, Inc.
Issues: BUD ENV IMM RRR TAX TRU WAS
Rep By: John R. Brimsek

Street Law Inc.
Issues: BUD
Rep By: Robert R. Belair, Susan C. Haller

TACA de Honduras
Rep By: John R. Brimsek

TACA Internat'l Airlines
Rep By: John R. Brimsek

Multinat'l Government Services, Inc.

11 Dupont Circle NW
Suite 700
Washington, DC 20036
Tel: (202)293-5886
Fax: (202)939-6969
Registered: LDA
A consulting firm which represents clients before Federal regulatory agencies.

DC-Area Employees Representing Listed Clients
BOWEN, Brooks J.
FELDMAN, Warren
FROMM, Chuck
GLOZER, Ken
KELLY, William G.
LEVINSON, Bruce
STAS, Eric
TOZZI, Jim J., Director

Clients

Cellular Telecommunications and Internet Ass'n
Rep By: Brooks J. Bowen, Jim J. Tozzi

CIGNA Corp.
Issues: BUD HCR
Rep By: Warren Feldman, Eric Stas, Jim J. Tozzi

Edison Electric Institute
Issues: BUD ENG GOV
Rep By: Ken Glozer

General Tire, Inc.
Rep By: Brooks J. Bowen, Jim J. Tozzi

Goodyear Tire and Rubber Co.
Issues: AUT BUD CSP ENV GOV
Rep By: Brooks J. Bowen, Jim J. Tozzi

Rhone-Polenc Inc.
Issues: CHM
Rep By: Brooks J. Bowen, Chuck Fromm, William G. Kelly, Eric Stas, Jim J. Tozzi

TRW Inc.
Issues: AUT GOV
Rep By: Bruce Levinson, Jim J. Tozzi

MultiState Associates

515 King St.
Suite 300
Alexandria, VA 22314
Tel: (703)684-1110
Fax: (703)684-7912
Web: www.multistate.com
E-mail: info@multistate.com
Through company staff in five regional offices and a 50-state network of over 1,500 professional lobbyists, the firm provides customized state and local government relations services to corporations and associations in order to meet their information and lobbying needs on legislative, regulatory, and procurement matters. Also provides a 50-state customized legislative and regulatory issue identification and tracking.

DC-Area Employees Representing Listed Clients
HALLMAN, Paul W., Principal
MCNELIS, Marcie M., Principal

Clients

Air Transport Ass'n of America

Goodyear Tire and Rubber Co.

TRW Inc.

Paul Muroyama & Assoc.

499 S. Capitol St. SW
Suite 506
Washington, DC 20003
Tel: (202)484-0785
Fax: (202)484-0788
E-mail: paulmuroyama.washington@worldnet.att.net
Specializes in U.S.-Japan political and business consultation, publication of Political Report..

DC-Area Employees Representing Listed Clients
MUROYAMA, Paul, President and Chief Exec. Officer

Clients

Dai-Ichi Life Insurance Co.
Rep By: Paul Muroyama

NTT America
Rep By: Paul Muroyama

Patrick M. Murphy & Associates

503 Second St. NE
Washington, DC 20002
Tel: (202)544-8490
Fax: (202)543-7804
Registered: LDA
Web: www.patrickmurphy.com
E-mail: email@patrickmurphy.com
Member of the Capitol Alliance. Specializes in government relations at the federal, state, and local levels.

DC-Area Employees Representing Listed Clients
GOEAS, Carole, Associate
MURPHY, Patrick M., President
SELFRIDGE, Greg, V. President

Clients

American Federation of Government Employees (AFL-CIO)
Issues: LBR

Education Networks of America
Issues: CPI EDU
Rep By: Patrick M. Murphy

Ericsson Inc.
Issues: TEC

Healtheon/Web MD
Issues: TEC

Internet Clearinghouse

Santa Fe, New Mexico, County of
Issues: GOV
Rep By: Patrick M. Murphy

WebMD
Issues: CPI
Rep By: Patrick M. Murphy

R. B. Murphy & Associates

1010 Pennsylvania Ave. SE
Washington, DC 20003
Tel: (202)547-1005
Fax: (202)547-0150
Registered: LDA
Web: www.rbmurphy.com
E-mail: rbmurphy1@mindspring.com

DC-Area Employees Representing Listed Clients
MURPHY, Rick, President

Clients

Vern Clark & Associates
Issues: TRA
Rep By: Rick Murphy

Internat'l Ass'n of Fire Fighters
Issues: LBR
Rep By: Rick Murphy

Philip Morris Management Corp.
Issues: BEV FOO TOB
Rep By: Rick Murphy

Pierre E. Murphy Law Offices

2445 M St. NW
Suite 260
Washington, DC 20037
Tel: (202)872-1679
Fax: (202)872-1725
Web: www.lopmurphy.com
E-mail: pmurphy@lopmurphy.com
Specializes in aviation, regulatory and commercial law.

DC-Area Employees Representing Listed Clients
MURPHY, Pierre E., Principal
RUIZ, Andrea, Associate

Clients

Aero Continente, S.A.

Aerofloral, Inc.

Aeroinversiones, S.A.

Aeropostal

AeroUnion, S.A. de C.V.

Air 3000, Inc.

Air Atlantic Dominicana

Air D'Ayiti

Air Namibia

AMSA

Andes

APA Internat'l Air, S.A.
Rep By: Pierre E. Murphy

Apple Vacations, Inc.
Rep By: Pierre E. Murphy

Arrow Air

Caraven Airlines (Carga Aerea Venezolana, S.A.)
Rep By: Pierre E. Murphy

Caribbean Airline Co. Ltd.
Rep By: Pierre E. Murphy

Equinoccial, S.A.

Falcon Air Express

Far West Airlines, LLC

Faucett Airlines (Compania de Aviacion Faucett, S.A.)
Rep By: Pierre E. Murphy

Fine Air Services, Inc.

Grand Bahama Vacations, Inc.

Grand Canyon Railway

Guyana Airways 2000

ICC

Jamaica Air Freighters, Ltd.

Jamaica Vacations (JAMVAC)

Laker Airways (Bahamas) Ltd.
Rep By: Pierre E. Murphy

LAPA (Lineas Aereas Privadas, S.A.)
Rep By: Pierre E. Murphy

Lynden Air Cargo, LLC

Oakland Airport

Southern Air Transport
Rep By: Pierre E. Murphy

Sun Jet Internat'l, Inc.
Rep By: Pierre E. Murphy

TAESA (Transportes Aereos Ejecutivos, S.A. de C.V.)

TRIBASA

Turks Air Limited

TV Azteca

Worldwide Aviation Services, Ltd.
Rep By: Pierre E. Murphy

Murray & Murray

2001 Cool Spring Dr.
Alexandria, VA 22308
Registered: LDA
A business and government relations firm.

DC-Area Employees Representing Listed Clients
MURRAY, Daniel H., Partner
MURRAY, Ty, Partner

Clients

SWIPCO, U.S.
Issues: GOV

Murray, Scheer, Montgomery, Tapia & O'Donnell

1200 New Hampshire Ave NW
Suite 430
Washington, DC 20036
Tel: (202)955-3030
Fax: (202)955-1147
Registered: LDA, FARA
A government relations/public affairs consulting firm.

DC-Area Employees Representing Listed Clients
CRAWFORD, Thomas R., Legislative Director
HOULE, Alison
KEEGAN, Michael G., Policy Analyst
MONTGOMERY, John H., Partner
MURRAY, D. Michael, President
O'DONNELL, John R., Partner
TAPIA, Raul R., Partner
ZELDEN, Mark

Clients

Advantica Inc.

Albuquerque, New Mexico, City of
Issues: BUD CAW ECN EDU HOU LAW ROD TAX TRA
Rep By: John R. O'Donnell

Allmerica Financial
Issues: BAN FIN INS RET TAX
Rep By: Thomas R. Crawford, D. Michael Murray

Ass'n of Industrialists and Businessmen of Tatarstan
Rep By: D. Michael Murray

Ass'n of Metropolitan Sewerage Agencies
Rep By: John H. Montgomery

Bernalillo, New Mexico, County of
Issues: BUD CAW HOU LAW TRA
Rep By: John R. O'Donnell

Brownsville Public Utilities Board
Issues: BUD CAW ECN ENV
Rep By: John R. O'Donnell

Brownsville, Texas, City of
Issues: ECN TRA
Rep By: John H. Montgomery, John R. O'Donnell

California State Assembly - Committee on Rules
Rep By: Thomas R. Crawford, D. Michael Murray, Raul R. Tapia

Carolina Panthers

Cellular Telecommunications and Internet Ass'n

Chino, California, City of
Rep By: Raul R. Tapia

Cleveland Cliffs Iron Co.
Issues: TAX
Rep By: Thomas R. Crawford, D. Michael Murray

El Paso Water Utilities - Public Service Board
Issues: BUD CAW ENV
Rep By: John H. Montgomery, John R. O'Donnell

Equitable Assurance Soc. of the United States
Rep By: Thomas R. Crawford, D. Michael Murray

The Equitable Cos.
Issues: BAN FIN INS RET TAX
Rep By: Thomas R. Crawford, D. Michael Murray

Freeport, New York, Village of
Issues: ECN MAR
Rep By: John R. O'Donnell

Future View, Inc.

Ground Water Protection Council
Issues: BUD CAW ENV
Rep By: Michael G. Keegan, John H. Montgomery

Hempstead, New York, Village of
Issues: CAW
Rep By: John R. O'Donnell

Humboldt Harbor Recreation
Issues: BUD CAW TRA
Rep By: John R. O'Donnell

Iron Ore Ass'n
Rep By: Thomas R. Crawford, D. Michael Murray

Jasper, Alabama, City of
Issues: BUD ECN
Rep By: Alison Houle, John H. Montgomery, John R. O'Donnell, Mark Zelden

KQC Properties
Rep By: D. Michael Murray

Lafayette Consolidated Government
Issues: BUD TRA
Rep By: Thomas R. Crawford, D. Michael Murray, Mark Zelden

Lockheed Martin Corp.

Long Beach, California, City of
Issues: ECN
Rep By: John H. Montgomery, John R. O'Donnell, Raul R. Tapia

Marshall, Alabama, County of
Issues: BUD ECN
Rep By: Alison Houle, John H. Montgomery, John R. O'Donnell, Mark Zelden

Metropolitan Life Insurance Co.
Issues: FIN INS RET TAX TRD
Rep By: Thomas R. Crawford, D. Michael Murray

Mine Safety Appliances
Rep By: Thomas R. Crawford, D. Michael Murray

Monterey, California, County of
Issues: DEF ECN
Rep By: John R. O'Donnell, Raul R. Tapia

MONY Life Insurance Co.
Issues: BAN FIN INS RET TAX
Rep By: Thomas R. Crawford, D. Michael Murray

Nat'l Council of Coal Lessors
Issues: TAX
Rep By: Thomas R. Crawford, D. Michael Murray

Nat'l Rural Water Ass'n
Issues: AGR BUD CAW ENV
Rep By: Michael G. Keegan, John H. Montgomery

Native American Cultural & Educational Authority
Issues: IND
Rep By: John H. Montgomery

New England Financial
Issues: BAN FIN INS RET TAX
Rep By: Thomas R. Crawford, D. Michael Murray

New England Life Insurance Co.
Issues: BAN FIN INS RET TAX
Rep By: Thomas R. Crawford, D. Michael Murray

Oklahoma City, Oklahoma, City of
Issues: BUD CAW HOU LAW ROD TAX TRA
Rep By: John H. Montgomery

Oklahoma State Medical Ass'n
Issues: BUD CAW FAM HCR MMM TOB
Rep By: John H. Montgomery

Oxnard Harbor District
Issues: BUD DEF MAR TRA
Rep By: John R. O'Donnell

Oxnard, California, City of
Issues: BUD CAW ECN HOU TRA
Rep By: John R. O'Donnell

Pacific Life Insurance Co.
Issues: BAN FIN INS RET TAX
Rep By: Thomas R. Crawford, D. Michael Murray

Passaic Valley Sewerage Commissioners
Issues: BUD CAW
Rep By: Thomas R. Crawford, John H. Montgomery, D. Michael Murray, John R. O'Donnell

Penn Mutual Life Insurance Co.
Rep By: Thomas R. Crawford, D. Michael Murray

PepsiCo, Inc.
Issues: HCR LBR TAX TRD
Rep By: Thomas R. Crawford, D. Michael Murray

Phoenix, Arizona, City of
Issues: BUD CAW ECN EDU ENV HOU LAW ROD TAX TRA
Rep By: John R. O'Donnell

Piedmont Environmental Council
Issues: RES TAX TRA
Rep By: Thomas R. Crawford, D. Michael Murray

PIMCO Advisors, L.P.
Issues: TAX
Rep By: Thomas R. Crawford, D. Michael Murray

Porsche Cars North America, Inc.
Issues: AUT TAX
Rep By: Thomas R. Crawford, D. Michael Murray

Port Hueneme, California, City of

Qualimetrics, Inc.
Issues: BUD TRA
Rep By: Thomas R. Crawford, D. Michael Murray

Salazar Associates Internat'l, Inc.
Issues: ENG
Rep By: Raul R. Tapia

Salinas, California, City of
Issues: BUD HOU LAW ROD TAX TRA
Rep By: John R. O'Donnell

San Jose, California, City of
Issues: BUD ENV HOU LAW ROD TRA
Rep By: John H. Montgomery

Santa Clarita, California, City of
Issues: BUD ENV HOU ROD TAX TEC TRA
Rep By: John H. Montgomery, John R. O'Donnell

Science & Engineering Associates, Inc.
Issues: BUD DEF
Rep By: Thomas R. Crawford, D. Michael Murray, Mark Zelden

Sherwin Williams Co.
Issues: INS TAX
Rep By: Thomas R. Crawford, D. Michael Murray

Shubert Organization Inc.
Issues: ART TAX
Rep By: Thomas R. Crawford, D. Michael Murray

Southern California Ass'n of Governments
Issues: ROD TRA
Rep By: Thomas R. Crawford, John H. Montgomery, D. Michael Murray, John R. O'Donnell, Raul R. Tapia

Swaziland Sugar Ass'n
Issues: TAX TRD
Rep By: Thomas R. Crawford, D. Michael Murray

Tatarstan, Republic of
Rep By: D. Michael Murray

Tricon Global Restaurants Inc.
Issues: TAX
Rep By: Thomas R. Crawford, D. Michael Murray

United Biscuit
Issues: TRD
Rep By: Thomas R. Crawford, D. Michael Murray

Water Replenishment District of Southern California
Issues: BUD
Rep By: John R. O'Donnell, Raul R. Tapia

West Jordan, Utah, City of
Issues: CAW ECN
Rep By: John H. Montgomery, John R. O'Donnell

Wheeling & Lake Erie Railway Co.
Issues: RRR
Rep By: Thomas R. Crawford, D. Michael Murray

Wisconsin Central Transportation Corp.
Issues: RRR
Rep By: Thomas R. Crawford, D. Michael Murray

Muse & Associates

1775 I St. NW
Suite 520
Washington, DC 20006
Web: www.muse-associates.com
E-mail: dnmuse@muse-associates.com
Tel: (202)496-0200
Fax: (202)496-0201

A full-service health policy and strategic planning consulting firm. Provides policy analysis, cost estimates, special studies, and information services to clients interested in healthcare issues.

DC-Area Employees Representing Listed Clients
BURKE, Robert E., V. President
MUSE, Donald N., President
PORTNER, MPA, Gregory A., Senior Research Manager

Clients

Data Niche Associates Inc.

Novartis Corp.
Issues: HCR MMM
Rep By: Donald N. Muse

Pharmaceutical Research and Manufacturers of America
Issues: HCR MMM
Rep By: Donald N. Muse

The Tri-Alliance of Rehabilitation Professionals
Issues: MMM
Rep By: Donald N. Muse, Gregory A. Portner, MPA

MV3 & Associates

Hamilton Square
600 14th St. NW, Fifth Floor
Washington, DC 20005
E-mail: MV3Assoc@aol.com
Tel: (202)783-1980
Fax: (202)783-1918
Registered: LDA

A government affairs firm.

DC-Area Employees Representing Listed Clients
VALENTE, III, Mark, Principal

Clients

Center for Disease Detection

Cohn & Wolfe

Dalton & Dalton P.C.

Devon Management Group Inc.

Fund for American Opportunity PAC

Keating Development Corp.

Kelly Anderson & Associates

Nat'l Ass'n of Thrift Savings Plan Participants

Nat'l Italian American Foundation

Orkand Corp.

Pennsylvania Economic Development Financing Authorities

Pepper Hamilton LLP

PriceWaterhouseCoopers

United Payors and United Providers

The MWW Group

1747 Pennsylvania Ave. NW
Suite 1150
Washington, DC 20006
Web: www.mwwpr.com
E-mail: jslade@mww.com
Tel: (202)296-6222
Fax: (202)296-4507
Registered: LDA, FARA

A public relations/government affairs firm.

DC-Area Employees Representing Listed Clients
BECKER, Tracey, Federal Affairs Representative
BERKOFF, Todd S., Legislative Associate
BOSTIC, Dana P., Deputy Director, Federal Affairs
GRAY, Davon, Legislative Associate
IADAROLA, Elizabeth A., Deputy Director, Federal Affairs
KEMPNER, Michael W., President and Chief Exec. Officer
PELLERIN, Christine A., V. President, Federal Affairs
SLADE, Jonathan B., Senior V. President
SOMMER, Robert G., Exec. V. President
WALTER, Jeffery M., V. President

Clients

Amerijet Internat'l Inc.
Issues: TRD
Rep By: Jonathan B. Slade

Bacardi-Martini, USA, Inc.
Issues: TRD
Rep By: Tracey Becker, Dana P. Bostic, Elizabeth A. Iadarola, Christine A. Pellerin, Jonathan B. Slade, Jeffery M. Walter

Century Financial Group
Issues: BAN
Rep By: Christine A. Pellerin, Jonathan B. Slade

Cuban American Nat'l Foundation/Cuban American Foundation
Issues: FOR
Rep By: Dana P. Bostic, Elizabeth A. Iadarola, Jonathan B. Slade

Delaware River Stevedores
Issues: ENV
Rep By: Christine A. Pellerin, Jonathan B. Slade

Detroit Medical Center
Issues: BUD HCR
Rep By: Todd S. Berkoff, Dana P. Bostic, Christine A. Pellerin, Jonathan B. Slade

Domino's Pizza
Issues: LBR TOU TRA
Rep By: Tracey Becker, Dana P. Bostic, Jonathan B. Slade

GAF Corp.
Issues: CSP MAN
Rep By: Todd S. Berkoff, Elizabeth A. Iadarola, Michael W. Kempner, Christine A. Pellerin, Jonathan B. Slade, Robert G. Sommer, Jeffery M. Walter

Green County Health Care, Inc.
Issues: BUD HCR
Rep By: Todd S. Berkoff, Dana P. Bostic, Christine A. Pellerin, Jonathan B. Slade

Hadassah Medical Relief Fund
Issues: FOR
Rep By: Elizabeth A. Iadarola, Jonathan B. Slade

Hadassah, The Women's Zionist Organization of America
Issues: FOR
Rep By: Jonathan B. Slade

Internat'l Distance Learning
Issues: EDU
Rep By: Tracey Becker, Dana P. Bostic, Jonathan B. Slade

Charles Klatskin and Co.
Issues: RES
Rep By: Jonathan B. Slade

Kmart Corp.
Issues: ALC TRD TRU
Rep By: Elizabeth A. Iadarola, Christine A. Pellerin, Jonathan B. Slade, Jeffery M. Walter

Little Havana Activities and Nutrition Centers
Issues: BUD WEL
Rep By: Dana P. Bostic, Davon Gray, Jonathan B. Slade

Michigan Bulb
Issues: POS
Rep By: Davon Gray, Elizabeth A. Iadarola, Jonathan B. Slade

Nat'l Ass'n of Community Health Centers
Issues: HCR MMM
Rep By: Dana P. Bostic, Christine A. Pellerin, Jonathan B. Slade

Nat'l Ass'n of Jai-Alai Frontons, Inc.
Issues: GAM
Rep By: Elizabeth A. Iadarola, Jonathan B. Slade

New Sea Escape
Issues: TOU
Rep By: Jonathan B. Slade

Park Place
Issues: GAM

Perry Tritech Inc.
Issues: COM DEF TRD
Rep By: Jonathan B. Slade

Puerto Ricans for Civic Action
Issues: GOV
Rep By: Tracey Becker, Dana P. Bostic, Elizabeth A. Iadarola, Christine A. Pellerin, Jonathan B. Slade, Robert G. Sommer, Jeffery M. Walter

Puerto Rico Senate
Issues: ENV GOV
Rep By: Jonathan B. Slade, Robert G. Sommer

Ross University School of Medicine in Dominica
Issues: EDU MMM
Rep By: Tracey Becker, Dana P. Bostic, Davon Gray, Jonathan B. Slade

Synapse
Issues: BAN POS
Rep By: Tracey Becker, Jonathan B. Slade, Robert G. Sommer

United States Education Finance Corp.
Issues: EDU
Rep By: Tracey Becker, Dana P. Bostic, Davon Gray, Christine A. Pellerin, Jonathan B. Slade

James Pierce Myers

1617 Courtland Rd.
Alexandria, VA 22306
Tel: (703)660-1002
Fax: (703)660-1037
Registered: LDA

An attorney.

Clients

Preston Gates Ellis & Rouvelas Meeds LLP
Issues: POS
Rep By: James Pierce Myers

Timothy D. Naegele & Associates

1201 Pennsylvania Ave. NW
Suite 300
Washington, DC 20004
Web: www.naegele.com
E-mail: naegelewdc@aol.com
Tel: (202)466-7500
Fax: (202)661-4699

A law firm.

DC-Area Employees Representing Listed Clients
NAEGELE, Timothy D., Principal

Clients

Home Federal Savings and Loan Ass'n
Issues: BAN CPI FIN GOV
Rep By: Timothy D. Naegele

Nat'l Environmental Strategies

2600 Virginia Ave. NW
Suite 600
Washington, DC 20037
Tel: (202)333-2524
Fax: (202)338-5950
Registered: LDA

DC-Area Employees Representing Listed Clients
GRILES, J. Steven, Principal
HANSEN, Charles M.
HIMMELSTEIN, Marc I., President
NORTHINGTON, John, V. President
WILSON, Richard D., V. President

Clients

American Chemistry Council
Issues: CHM
Rep By: Marc I. Himmelstein

American Gas Ass'n
Issues: CAW ENV WAS
Rep By: Marc I. Himmelstein

American Petroleum Institute
Issues: CAW WAS
Rep By: Marc I. Himmelstein

Baker, Donelson, Bearman & Caldwell, P.C.
Issues: ENV

Bristol-Myers Squibb Co.
Issues: CAW
Rep By: Marc I. Himmelstein

Center for Energy and Economic Development

Coors Brewing Company
Issues: CAW
Rep By: Marc I. Himmelstein

The Dow Chemical Co.

Edison Electric Institute
Issues: CAW
Rep By: Marc I. Himmelstein

Ethyl Petroleum Additives, Inc.
Issues: CAW ENV FUE
Rep By: Marc I. Himmelstein, Richard D. Wilson

Nat'l Mining Ass'n
Issues: BUD CAW ENV NAT
Rep By: Marc I. Himmelstein

OXY USA Inc.
Issues: ENG
Rep By: Marc I. Himmelstein

Oxygenated Fuels Ass'n
Issues: CAW FUE
Rep By: Marc I. Himmelstein, Richard D. Wilson

Reilly Industries
Issues: ENV
Rep By: Marc I. Himmelstein

Sunoco, Inc.
Issues: ENV
Rep By: Marc I. Himmelstein

Texaco Group Inc.

Tracer Research Corporation

Nat'l Grass Roots & Communications

4115 Wisconsin Ave. NW
Suite 211
Washington, DC 20016
Web: www.ngrc.com
E-mail: larry@ngrc.com
Tel: (202)966-0440
Fax: (202)966-3336

A public relations/grass roots lobbying firm.

DC-Area Employees Representing Listed Clients
CAMERON, Brad, Chief Exec. Officer
RICHARDSON, Jr., Lawrence S., President

Clients

U.S. Trade Law Study Group

The National Group, LLP

818 Connecticut Ave. NW
Suite 1100
Washington, DC 20006
Tel: (202)728-1010
Fax: (202)728-4044
Registered: LDA

A government relations firm.

DC-Area Employees Representing Listed Clients
BIDEN, Hunter, Partner
BLOUNT, John, Partner
DEVIERNO, John A., Partner
FORSCEY, Michael A., Partner
OLDAKER, William C., Partner
STINSON, John M., Partner
VERSAGE, Vincent M., Partner

Clients

Adventist Health System/Sunbelt, Inc.
Rep By: John Blount

Biotechnology Industry Organization
Rep By: John Blount, William C. Oldaker

Bituminous Coal Operators Ass'n
Rep By: John Blount

Corning Inc.
Rep By: Vincent M. Versage

Delta Air Lines
Rep By: John Blount

Eastman Kodak Co.
Rep By: Vincent M. Versage

Xerox Corp.
Rep By: Vincent M. Versage

Nat'l Strategies Inc.

888 17th St. NW
12th Floor
Washington, DC 20006
Tel: (202)429-8744
Fax: (202)296-2962
Registered: LDA
Web: www.natstrat.com
E-mail: info@natstrat.com

A government relations consulting firm.

DC-Area Employees Representing Listed Clients
AYLWARD, David K., President
CATON, Cary K., V. President
MCLEAN, Chris, V. President
SCHERR, Marsha, V. President

Clients

American Trucking Ass'ns
Rep By: David K. Aylward

ATX Technologies
Rep By: David K. Aylward

Cellular Telecommunications and Internet Ass'n
Issues: TEC
Rep By: David K. Aylward

The Comcare Alliance
Rep By: David K. Aylward, Marsha Scherr

General Reinsurance Corp.
Issues: ENV
Rep By: David K. Aylward

Marconi
Rep By: David K. Aylward

Maricopa, Arizona, County of
Rep By: David K. Aylward

The McGuffey Project
Rep By: David K. Aylward

Shenandoah Valley
Rep By: David K. Aylward, Marsha Scherr

Superfund Reform '95
Rep By: David K. Aylward

TruePosition Inc.
Issues: TEC
Rep By: David K. Aylward

Navarro Legislative & Regulatory Affairs

1742 N St. NW
Washington, DC 20036
Tel: (202)955-6006
Fax: (202)785-2210
Registered: LDA

A law practice providing legislative and regulatory advice and representation, specializing in product safety and public health issues. Clients include manufacturers, retailers and organizations conducting research on public health issues.

DC-Area Employees Representing Listed Clients
NAVARRO, Bruce C., Principal

Clients

Ass'n for Healthcare Philanthropy
Issues: HCR
Rep By: Bruce C. Navarro

Health Risk Management Group, Inc.
Issues: CSP HCR
Rep By: Bruce C. Navarro

Ross Stores, Inc.
Issues: CSP LBR

Navista, Inc.

One Thomas Circle NW
Tenth Floor
Washington, DC 20005
Web: www.navista.net
Tel: (202)530-5910
Fax: (202)530-0659
Registered: LDA

DC-Area Employees Representing Listed Clients
FLATLEY, John, V. President
HELLEM, Steven B., President

Clients

American Ceramics Soc.
Issues: ENV SCI
Rep By: John Flatley

Corporate Environmental Enforcement Council (CEEC)
Issues: ENV
Rep By: John Flatley, Steven B. Hellem

Nealon & Moran, L.L.P.

119 N. Henry St.
Alexandria, VA 22314
Tel: (703)684-5755
Fax: (703)684-0472
Registered: LDA
E-mail: nealonpc@nealon.com

DC-Area Employees Representing Listed Clients
MORAN, Brian J.

Clients

Washington Flyer Taxi Drivers Ass'n, Inc.
Issues: CIV IMM LBR TRA
Rep By: Brian J. Moran

David Nelson & Associates

400 N. Capitol St. NW
Suite 585
Washington, DC 20001
Tel: (202)237-8848
Fax: (202)393-5218
Registered: LDA

DC-Area Employees Representing Listed Clients
NELSON, David W., President

Clients

Barr Laboratories
Issues: HCR
Rep By: David W. Nelson

Nat'l Alliance for the Mentally Ill

Pfizer, Inc.
Issues: HCR
Rep By: David W. Nelson

NES, Inc.

111 Gresham Place
Falls Church, VA 22046
Registered: LDA

DC-Area Employees Representing Listed Clients
GRILES, J. Steven
HIMMELSTEIN, Marc I.
WILSON, Richard

Clients

Devon Energy Corp.
Issues: ENG

The Dow Chemical Co.
Issues: ENV
Rep By: Marc I. Himmelstein

Fierce & Isakowitz
Issues: PHA

Podesta/Mattoon
Issues: CAW ENG
Rep By: Richard Wilson

Western Gas Resources
Issues: FUE

Neuman and Co.

1317 F St. NW
Suite 900
Washington, DC 20004
E-mail: neumanco@aol.com
Tel: (202)628-2075
Fax: (202)628-2077
Registered: LDA

DC-Area Employees Representing Listed Clients
NEUMAN, Robert A., President

Clients

Amgen
Issues: HCR MED
Rep By: Robert A. Neuman

Center for Deliberative Polling
Rep By: Robert A. Neuman

The Economist Newspaper Group
Rep By: Robert A. Neuman

Episcopal Diocese of Washington
Rep By: Robert A. Neuman

The Frontier Press
Rep By: Robert A. Neuman

Johns Hopkins Center for Gun Policy and Research
Rep By: Robert A. Neuman

Joyce Foundation
Rep By: Robert A. Neuman

Kaiser Family Foundation

Kids Voting USA
Rep By: Robert A. Neuman

Nat'l Center on Addiction and Substance Abuse
Rep By: Robert A. Neuman

Pew Center for Civic Journalism
Rep By: Robert A. Neuman

White Mountain Apache Tribe
Issues: ECN ENV GAM IND TOU
Rep By: Robert A. Neuman

New Frontiers Communications Consulting

626 S. 25th St.
Arlington, VA 22202
E-mail: rdw@nfrontiers.com
Tel: (703)548-6636
Fax: (703)548-6747
Registered: LDA

DC-Area Employees Representing Listed Clients
WILSON, R. David, Principal

Clients

BellSouth Corp.
Issues: TEC
Rep By: R. David Wilson

PanAmSat Corp.
Issues: COM TEC
Rep By: R. David Wilson

Qwest Communications
Issues: TEC
Rep By: R. David Wilson

United Pan-Europe Communications, NV
Issues: COM FOR TEC TRD
Rep By: R. David Wilson

Verizon Communications
Issues: TEC
Rep By: R. David Wilson

William B. Newman Jr.

1000 Connecticut Ave. NW
Suite 302
McLean, VA 20036
Tel: (202)835-0740
Registered: LDA

Clients

Americans for Equitable Climate Solutions
Rep By: William B. Newman, Jr.

Elisabeth G. Newton

8370 Greensboro Dr.
Suite 4-814
McLean, VA 22102
Tel: (703)827-9597
Fax: (703)893-9557
E-mail: e.g.newton@worldnet.att

Provides government relations consulting services with emphasis on science and engineering.

Clients

Morgan Stanley Dean Witter & Co.
Issues: BAN TAX
Rep By: Elisabeth G. Newton

Hugh C. Newton & Assoc.

214 Massachusetts Ave. NE
Suite 520
Washington, DC 20002
Tel: (202)608-6150
Fax: (202)544-6979

DC-Area Employees Representing Listed Clients

NEWTON, Hugh C., President

Clients

Heritage Foundation
Rep By: Hugh C. Newton

Nichols-Dezenhall Communication Management Group, Ltd.

1130 Connecticut Ave. NW
Suite 600
Washington, DC 20036
Tel: (202)296-0263
Fax: (202)452-9371
Registered: FARA

DC-Area Employees Representing Listed Clients

DEZENHALL, Eric, President
EGNER, David, V. President
HERSHOW, Sheila, V. President
NICHOLS, David A., Chairman
WEBER, John W., Exec. V. President

Clients

Meat Industry Council
Rep By: David A. Nichols, John W. Weber

Michael E. Nix Consulting

1545 18th St. NW
Suite 711
Washington, DC 20036
Tel: (202)234-1086
Fax: (202)234-1088
Registered: LDA
E-mail: menix@gateway.net

DC-Area Employees Representing Listed Clients

NIX, Michael E., President

Clients

Distributed Power Coalition of America
Issues: ENG ENV UTI
Rep By: Michael E. Nix

Nixon Peabody LLP

401 Ninth St. NW
Suite 900
Washington, DC 20004
Tel: (202)585-8000
Fax: (202)585-8080
Registered: LDA
Web: www.nixonpeabody.com

A general practice law firm; merged with Peabody & Brown in 2000.

DC-Area Employees Representing Listed Clients

CUNNINGHAM, Susan O., Partner
EDSON, Charles L., Partner
EGGERS, Susan, Associate
GOLDSTEIN, Richard S., Partner
GUSTINI, Raymond J., Partner
HANCE, Kenneth G., Partner
KELLY, Harry J., Partner
LYNCH, II, Allen A.
PRICE, Richard M., Partner
SILVERBERG, Kenneth H., Partner
STANTON, Richard P., Partner
STEVENS, Herbert F., Partner
SUSSMAN, Monica Hilton, Partner
WALLACE, Stephen J., Partner

Clients

Affordable Housing Tax Credit Coalition
Issues: TAX
Rep By: Charles L. Edson, Richard S. Goldstein

Continental Wingate Co., Inc.
Issues: HOU
Rep By: Richard M. Price, Monica Hilton Sussman

Cornerstone Florida Corp., Ltd.
Issues: HOU
Rep By: Richard S. Goldstein, Monica Hilton Sussman

Council for Affordable and Rural Housing
Rep By: Charles L. Edson

Denhill DC LCC
Issues: RES

Edward A. Fish Associates
Issues: HOU
Rep By: Charles L. Edson, Monica Hilton Sussman, Stephen J. Wallace

Genesee Brewing Co.
Issues: TRD

Highland Mortgage Co.
Issues: HOU
Rep By: Richard M. Price, Monica Hilton Sussman

iCall, Inc.
Rep By: Richard P. Stanton

Institute for Responsible Housing Preservation
Issues: HOU
Rep By: Charles L. Edson, Stephen J. Wallace

Light Associates
Rep By: Charles L. Edson, Stephen J. Wallace

Marine Spill Response Corporation

Media Tax Group
Issues: TAX

Mellon Mortgage Co.
Issues: HOU
Rep By: Richard M. Price, Monica Hilton Sussman

MetroPlains Development, Inc.
Rep By: Charles L. Edson, Richard M. Price, Herbert F. Stevens

Mobile Diagnostic Testing Services
Issues: HCR

Nat'l Leased Housing Ass'n
Issues: HOU
Rep By: Charles L. Edson, Stephen J. Wallace

New England Education Loan Marketing Corp. (Nellie Mae)
Rep By: Stephen J. Wallace

New York State Housing Finance Agency
Issues: HOU
Rep By: Stephen J. Wallace

Project Funding Corp. (PFC)
Issues: HOU
Rep By: Richard M. Price, Monica Hilton Sussman

Reilly Mortgage Group Inc.
Issues: HOU
Rep By: Richard M. Price, Monica Hilton Sussman

Saf T Lok, Inc.
Issues: BUD CSP FIR LAW
Rep By: Richard P. Stanton

Starrett City Associates
Rep By: Stephen J. Wallace

TRI Capital Corp.
Issues: HOU
Rep By: Richard M. Price, Monica Hilton Sussman

Welch's Foods, Inc.
Issues: CAW ENV
Rep By: Richard P. Stanton

WMF/Huntoon, Paige Associates Ltd.
Issues: HOU
Rep By: Richard M. Price, Monica Hilton Sussman

Walker F. Nolan

818 Connecticut Ave. NW
Suite 1100
Washington, DC 20006
Tel: (202)496-3470
Registered: LDA

Clients

Edison Electric Institute
Issues: ENG ENV UTI
Rep By: Walker F. Nolan

NSTAR
Issues: UTI
Rep By: Walker F. Nolan

Reliant Energy, Inc.
Issues: ENG UTI
Rep By: Walker F. Nolan

TXU Business Services
Issues: ENG UTI
Rep By: Walker F. Nolan

Non-Profit Management Associates, Inc.

1555 Connecticut Ave. NW
Suite 200
Washington, DC 20036
Tel: (202)462-9600
Fax: (202)462-9043

DC-Area Employees Representing Listed Clients

BRYANT, Sr., M.D.., Thomas E., Chairman
KRUEGER, Keith, President

Clients

Aspirin Foundation of America, Inc.
Rep By: Thomas E. Bryant, Sr., M.D.,

Consortium for School Networking
Rep By: Keith Krueger

Friends of the Nat'l Library of Medicine
Issues: CPI HCR MED TEC
Rep By: Keith Krueger

Nordhaus Haltom Taylor Taradash & Bladh LLP

816 Connecticut Ave. NW
Suite 300
Washington, DC 20006
Tel: (202)530-1270
Fax: (202)530-1920
Registered: LDA

DC-Area Employees Representing Listed Clients

GRANT, Jill E., Partner
GROVE, Donald H., Associate
JOSHI, Sangeeta, Paralegal

Clients

Hualapai Nation
Issues: IND

Jicarilla Apache Tribe
Issues: IND

Navajo Nation Oil and Gas Co., Inc.
Issues: IND
Rep By: Jill E. Grant

Pueblo of Laguna
Issues: IND

Santa Ana Pueblo
Issues: IND
Rep By: Jill E. Grant

Julia J. Norrell & Associates

601 Pennsylvania Ave. NW
Suite 900, S. Bldg.
Washington, DC 20004
Tel: (202)434-8192
Fax: (202)783-6304
Registered: LDA
E-mail: jnorrell@erols.com

DC-Area Employees Representing Listed Clients

NORRELL, Julia J., President

Clients

The Chubb Corp.
Issues: AUT BAN BNK BUD CPI CSP DIS ENV FAM FIN INS LBR RET TAX TOB TRD
Rep By: Julia J. Norrell

Metropolitan Life Insurance Co.
Issues: INS
Rep By: Julia J. Norrell

Minnesota Mining and Manufacturing Co. (3M Co.)
Issues: HCR
Rep By: Julia J. Norrell

UNUM/Provident Corp.
Issues: BUD CSP FAM FIN INS LBR RET TAX TRD
Rep By: Julia J. Norrell

Novecon

1020 16th St. NW
Washington, DC 20036
Tel: (202)659-3200
Fax: (202)659-3215
E-mail: novmgtco@aol.com

Investment and consulting firm focused on Eastern Europe, Russia and the Commonwealth of Independent States.

DC-Area Employees Representing Listed Clients

RAHN, Richard W., President

Nurnberger and Associates

1735 New York Ave. NW
Suite 500
Washington, DC 20006
Tel: (202)661-3884
Fax: (202)331-1024
E-mail: rnurnberge@aol.com

DC-Area Employees Representing Listed Clients

NURNBERGER, Ralph D.

Clients

McDonald's Corp.
Issues: SMB
Rep By: Ralph D. Nurnberger

Nusgart Consulting, LLC

5225 Pooks Hill Rd.
Suite 1626 North
Bethesda, MD 20814
Tel: (301)530-7846
Fax: (301)530-7946
Registered: LDA
E-mail: nusgart@bellatlantic.net

DC-Area Employees Representing Listed Clients

NUSGART, Marcia, President

Clients

Augustine Medical
Issues: HCR MMM
Rep By: Marcia Nusgart

BD
Issues: HCR MMM
Rep By: Marcia Nusgart

Cascade Designs
Issues: HCR MMM
Rep By: Marcia Nusgart

Coloplast Corp.
Issues: HCR MMM
Rep By: Marcia Nusgart

Contemporary Products Inc.
Issues: HCR MMM
Rep By: Marcia Nusgart

ConvaTec
Issues: HCR MMM
Rep By: Marcia Nusgart

Crown Therapeutics, Inc.
Issues: HCR MMM
Rep By: Marcia Nusgart

Dumex Medical
Issues: HCR MMM
Rep By: Marcia Nusgart

Essex Medical Systems Plus
Issues: HCR MMM
Rep By: Marcia Nusgart

Freedom Designs
Issues: HCR MMM
Rep By: Marcia Nusgart

Hill-Rom Co., Inc.
Issues: HCR MMM
Rep By: Marcia Nusgart

Hollister Inc.
Issues: HCR MMM
Rep By: Marcia Nusgart

Hyperion Medical
Issues: HCR MMM
Rep By: Marcia Nusgart

Hyperion Software

Kendall Healthcare Products Co.
Issues: HCR MMM
Rep By: Marcia Nusgart

Medline Industries Inc.
Issues: HCR MMM
Rep By: Marcia Nusgart

Pegasus Airwave
Issues: HCR MMM
Rep By: Marcia Nusgart

Precision Medical
Issues: HCR MMM
Rep By: Marcia Nusgart

ReGin Manufacturing Inc.
Issues: HCR MMM
Rep By: Marcia Nusgart

Respironics
Issues: HCR MMM
Rep By: Marcia Nusgart

ROHO, Inc.
Issues: HCR MMM
Rep By: Marcia Nusgart

Smith & Nephew, Inc.
Issues: HCR MMM
Rep By: Marcia Nusgart

Sunrise Medical
Issues: HCR MMM
Rep By: Marcia Nusgart

Tempur-Medical Inc.
Issues: HCR MMM
Rep By: Marcia Nusgart

Nutter & Harris, Inc.

1455 Pennsylvania Ave. NW
Suite 225
Washington, DC 20004
Tel: (202)289-7400
Fax: (202)289-7414
Registered: LDA, FARA
A government relations and public affairs consulting firm.

DC-Area Employees Representing Listed Clients
HARRIS, Robert L., Exec. V. President
NUTTER, Jack O., President

Clients

The Aluminum Ass'n
Issues: ENV
Rep By: Robert L. Harris

Fisher Scientific Worldwide
Rep By: Jack O. Nutter

Lead Industries Ass'n
Issues: ENV
Rep By: Robert L. Harris

Plum Creek Timber Co.
Issues: ENV RES
Rep By: Robert L. Harris

Reheis, Inc.
Rep By: Jack O. Nutter

The OB-C Group, LLC

1350 I St. NW
Suite 690
Washington, DC 20005
Tel: (202)898-4746
Fax: (202)898-4756
Registered: LDA, FARA
A government consulting and legislative lobbying firm.

DC-Area Employees Representing Listed Clients
KEATING, Thomas, Principal
MCKERNAN, Kim F., Principal
MELLODY, Charles J., Principal
NELSON, Patricia A., Principal
O'BRIEN, III, Lawrence F.
TARPLIN, Linda E., Principal

Clients

American Airlines
Issues: AVI TAX TRD
Rep By: Thomas Keating, Kim F. McKernan, Charles J. Mellody, Patricia A. Nelson, Lawrence F. O'Brien, III, Linda E. Tarplin

Anheuser-Busch Cos., Inc.
Issues: ADV ENV TAX TRD
Rep By: Thomas Keating, Kim F. McKernan, Charles J. Mellody, Patricia A. Nelson, Lawrence F. O'Brien, III, Linda E. Tarplin

AT&T
Issues: CPT DEF ENV GOV SCI TAX TEC TRD
Rep By: Thomas Keating, Kim F. McKernan, Charles J. Mellody, Patricia A. Nelson, Lawrence F. O'Brien, III, Linda E. Tarplin

Biotechnology Industry Organization
Issues: CSP HCR MED SCI
Rep By: Thomas Keating, Kim F. McKernan, Charles J. Mellody, Patricia A. Nelson, Lawrence F. O'Brien, III, Linda E. Tarplin

Blue Cross Blue Shield Ass'n
Issues: BUD HCR
Rep By: Thomas Keating, Kim F. McKernan, Charles J. Mellody, Patricia A. Nelson, Lawrence F. O'Brien, III, Linda E. Tarplin

Deutsche Telekom, Inc.

Fannie Mae
Rep By: Thomas Keating, Kim F. McKernan, Charles J. Mellody, Patricia A. Nelson, Lawrence F. O'Brien, III, Linda E. Tarplin

Goodyear Tire and Rubber Co.
Issues: MAN
Rep By: Thomas Keating, Kim F. McKernan, Charles J. Mellody, Patricia A. Nelson, Lawrence F. O'Brien, III, Linda E. Tarplin

Healthcare Distribution Management Ass'n
Issues: PHA
Rep By: Thomas Keating, Kim F. McKernan, Charles J. Mellody, Patricia A. Nelson, Lawrence F. O'Brien, III, Linda E. Tarplin

Investment Co. Institute
Issues: TAX
Rep By: Thomas Keating, Kim F. McKernan, Charles J. Mellody, Patricia A. Nelson, Lawrence F. O'Brien, III, Linda E. Tarplin

Merrill Lynch & Co., Inc.
Issues: FIN TAX
Rep By: Thomas Keating, Kim F. McKernan, Charles J. Mellody, Patricia A. Nelson, Lawrence F. O'Brien, III, Linda E. Tarplin

Motorola, Inc.
Issues: TRD
Rep By: Thomas Keating, Kim F. McKernan, Charles J. Mellody, Patricia A. Nelson, Lawrence F. O'Brien, III, Linda E. Tarplin

Nat'l Thoroughbred Racing Ass'n, Inc.
Issues: GAM SCI
Rep By: Thomas Keating, Kim F. McKernan, Charles J. Mellody, Patricia A. Nelson, Lawrence F. O'Brien, III, Linda E. Tarplin

Newport News Shipbuilding Inc.
Issues: DEF
Rep By: Thomas Keating, Kim F. McKernan, Charles J. Mellody, Patricia A. Nelson, Lawrence F. O'Brien, III, Linda E. Tarplin

The Rouse Company
Issues: FIN HOU TAX
Rep By: Thomas Keating, Kim F. McKernan, Charles J. Mellody, Patricia A. Nelson, Lawrence F. O'Brien, III, Linda E. Tarplin

Sears, Roebuck and Co.
Issues: BNK BUD DEF LBR MAR SCI TAX TRD
Rep By: Thomas Keating, Kim F. McKernan, Charles J. Mellody, Patricia A. Nelson, Lawrence F. O'Brien, III, Linda E. Tarplin

Securities Industry Ass'n
Issues: FIN TAX TRD
Rep By: Thomas Keating, Kim F. McKernan, Charles J. Mellody, Patricia A. Nelson, Lawrence F. O'Brien, III, Linda E. Tarplin

TIAA-CREF
Issues: TAX
Rep By: Thomas Keating, Kim F. McKernan, Charles J. Mellody, Patricia A. Nelson, Lawrence F. O'Brien, III, Linda E. Tarplin

United Parcel Service
Issues: LBR POS TRD
Rep By: Thomas Keating, Kim F. McKernan, Charles J. Mellody, Patricia A. Nelson, Lawrence F. O'Brien, III, Linda E. Tarplin

WellPoint Health Networks/Blue Cross of California/UNICARE
Issues: BUD HCR TAX
Rep By: Thomas Keating, Kim F. McKernan, Charles J. Mellody, Patricia A. Nelson, Lawrence F. O'Brien, III, Linda E. Tarplin

Wilmer, Cutler & Pickering
Issues: TEC
Rep By: Thomas Keating, Kim F. McKernan, Charles J. Mellody, Patricia A. Nelson, Lawrence F. O'Brien, III, Linda E. Tarplin

Obadal and MacLeod, p.c.

121 N. Henry St.
Alexandria, VA 22314
Tel: (703)739-9485
Fax: (703)739-9488
Registered: LDA

DC-Area Employees Representing Listed Clients
KLEIN, Christian A., Senior Associate
MACLEOD, Sarah, Managing Counsel
OBADAL, Anthony J., Partner

Clients

Aeronautical Repair Station Ass'n
Issues: AER AVI TRA
Rep By: Sarah MacLeod

Alsatian American Chamber of Commerce
Issues: BEV FOR TOU TRD
Rep By: Christian A. Klein

American Concrete Pipe Ass'n
Rep By: Anthony J. Obadal

Associated Equipment Distributors
Issues: AVI CAW CSP ENV GOV ROD TAX TRA TRD
Rep By: Christian A. Klein, Anthony J. Obadal

Ober, Kaler, Grimes & Shriver

1401 H St. NW
Suite 500
Washington, DC 20005-3324
Tel: (202)408-8400
Fax: (202)408-0640
Registered: LDA
Web: www.ober.com
E-mail: info@ober.com
A law firm.

DC-Area Employees Representing Listed Clients
HYATT, Thomas K., Shareholder

Clients

European Space Agency

Health Industry Initiative
Rep By: Thomas K. Hyatt

Upper Midwest Dairy Coalition

David O'Brien and Associates

2600 Virginia Ave. NW
Suite 600
Washington, DC 20037
E-mail: dobrien1@aol.com
Tel: (202)338-6650
Fax: (202)338-5950
Registered: LDA, FARA

DC-Area Employees Representing Listed Clients
ARNY, Wayne, Partner
O'BRIEN, David D., President
SCOTT, Shannon L., Senior Associate

Clients

John Crane-LIPS, Inc.
Issues: DEF
Rep By: Wayne Arny, David D. O'Brien

Cruising America Coalition
Issues: TOU
Rep By: David D. O'Brien, Shannon L. Scott

DRS
Issues: DEF
Rep By: Wayne Arny, David D. O'Brien

Jered Industries, Inc.
Issues: DEF

MacGregor
Issues: DEF
Rep By: David D. O'Brien

Robbins-Gioia, Inc.
Issues: DEF
Rep By: David D. O'Brien, Shannon L. Scott

Wi-LAN, Inc.
Issues: COM CPI TEC
Rep By: David D. O'Brien, Shannon L. Scott

O'Brien, Butler, McConihe & Schaefer

888 17th St. NW
Suite 1000
Washington, DC 20006
Tel: (202)298-6161
Fax: (202)293-1640
E-mail: MMcConihe@aol.com
A law firm specializing in association, litigation, insurance, health care, and estate law.

DC-Area Employees Representing Listed Clients
MCCONIHE, Michael H., Senior Partner

Clients

American Pharmaceutical Ass'n
Rep By: Michael H. McConihe

American Soc. of Appraisers
Rep By: Jerome C. Schaefer

O'Brien, Klink & Associates

2600 Virginia Ave. NW
Suite 600
Washington, DC 20037
Tel: (202)338-6550
Fax: (202)338-5950
Specializes in strategic planning, public affairs, and government relations.

DC-Area Employees Representing Listed Clients
BYRNES, David, Associate
KLINK, Hon. Ron, Partner
O'BRIEN, David D., President
SCOTT, Shannon L., Senior Associate

Clients

The Kinetics Group
Issues: DEF ENG PHA TAX
Rep By: David D. O'Brien, Shannon L. Scott

PetrolRem, Inc.
Issues: DEF ENV MAR
Rep By: David D. O'Brien, Shannon L. Scott

Zinc Corp. of America
Issues: DEF ENV
Rep By: David D. O'Brien, Shannon L. Scott

O'Bryon & Co.

4424 Montgomery Ave.
Suite 102
Bethesda, MD 20814
Tel: (301)652-5066
Fax: (301)913-9146
E-mail: obryonco@aol.com

DC-Area Employees Representing Listed Clients
O'BRYON, David S., President

Clients

American Ass'n of Limited Partners
Issues: FIN TAX
Rep By: David S. O'Bryon

Ass'n of Chiropractic Colleges
Issues: BUD DEF EDU HCR MED MMM VET
Rep By: David S. O'Bryon

Retirement Industry Trust Ass'n
Issues: FIN RET TAX
Rep By: David S. O'Bryon

The Observatory Group

3604 Davis St. NW
Washington, DC 20007
Tel: (202)342-8282
Fax: (202)342-6056
Registered: LDA
Web: www.ogroup.com
E-mail: wsemple@ogroup.com

DC-Area Employees Representing Listed Clients
SEMPLE, Nathaniel M., President

Clients

Partnership for Organ Donation
Rep By: Nathaniel M. Semple

O'Connor & Fierce Associates

600 New Hampshire Ave. NW
Suite 1000
Washington, DC 20037
Tel: (202)333-4141
Fax: (202)298-9109
Registered: LDA

DC-Area Employees Representing Listed Clients
O'CONNOR, Michael J., President

Clients

American of Martinsville

Internat'l Power Machines

Miller Desk

Pennsylvania House

PNC Bank, N.A.

Power Distribution, Inc. (PDI)

Powerware
Rep By: Michael J. O'Connor

SSI Services, Inc.

Thorn Microwave Devices
Rep By: Michael J. O'Connor

O'Connor & Hannan, L.L.P.

1666 K St. NW
Suite 500
Washington, DC 20006-2803
Tel: (202)887-1400
Fax: (202)466-2198
Registered: LDA, FARA
Web: www.oconnorhannan.com
E-mail: oh@oconnorhannan.com
A general practice law firm.

DC-Area Employees Representing Listed Clients
ADLER, Gary C., Partner
ADLER, Robert M., Partner
BARRIE, Robert W., Senior Government Relations Advisor
BECK, Edward
COFFEE, Roy C., Partner
CORCORAN, Hon. Thomas J., Partner
DOMBO, Frederick T., Associate
FAGRE, Danielle, Associate
FLEPS, Christina W., Partner
HARMALA, Robert
HIMMELBERG, John M., Partner
JENKINS, Timothy W., Partner
KOENIGS, Craig A., Associate
LEE, F. Gordon, Partner
MANNINA, Jr., George J., Partner
MANTON, Hon. Thomas J., Of Counsel
MELINCOFF, David R., Partner
NICKERSON, William
O'CONNOR, Patrick J., Senior Partner
O'DONNELL, Patrick E., Partner
POTTER, J. Craig, Partner
PRESSLER, Hon. Larry, Partner
QUINN, Thomas H., Partner
REED, III, Morgan W., Legislative Consultant
SCHNEIDER, Thomas J., Of Counsel
SPRINGER, David E., Partner
SYMINGTON, Hon. James W., Partner

Clients

Allergan, Inc.
Rep By: Robert W. Barrie, Hon. Thomas J. Corcoran, Patrick E. O'Donnell, Thomas H. Quinn

Alliance of Marine Mammal Parks and Aquariums
Issues: ANI MAR
Rep By: George J. Mannina, Jr.

American Forest & Paper Ass'n
Issues: ENV NAT
Rep By: Robert W. Barrie, Hon. Thomas J. Corcoran, George J. Mannina, Jr., Patrick E. O'Donnell

American Free Trade Ass'n
Issues: APP CPI CPT CSP MAN TRD
Rep By: Hon. Thomas J. Corcoran, Frederick T. Dombo, Danielle Fagre, Patrick E. O'Donnell

Amgen
Issues: HCR MMM TAX
Rep By: Roy C. Coffee, Timothy W. Jenkins

Ass'n of Chiropractic Colleges
Rep By: George J. Mannina, Jr.

Associated Credit Bureaus, Inc.
Issues: BAN CSP
Rep By: Roy C. Coffee, Timothy W. Jenkins, Thomas H. Quinn

ATOFINA Chemicals, Inc.
Issues: ENV NAT
Rep By: Robert W. Barrie, Hon. Thomas J. Corcoran, George J. Mannina, Jr., Patrick E. O'Donnell

Bank of America
Issues: TAX
Rep By: Edward Beck

Bear, Stearns and Co.
Issues: BNK FIN TAX
Rep By: Hon. Thomas J. Corcoran, Danielle Fagre, Timothy W. Jenkins, Patrick E. O'Donnell, Thomas H. Quinn

BellSouth Corp.
Issues: COM TEC
Rep By: Roy C. Coffee

Brooks Tropicals, Inc.
Issues: AGR TRD
Rep By: Hon. Thomas J. Corcoran, John M. Himmelberg

Calhoun County, Alabama Commission
Rep By: Morgan W. Reed, III, David E. Springer

California Debt Limit Allocation Committee
Issues: TAX
Rep By: Frederick T. Dombo, Christina W. Fleps, Robert Harmala, Patrick E. O'Donnell, Thomas H. Quinn

California Tax Credit Allocation Committee
Rep By: Roy C. Coffee, Danielle Fagre, Thomas H. Quinn

Capital One Financial Corp.
Issues: BAN FIN
Rep By: Timothy W. Jenkins, Thomas H. Quinn

Celera Genomics
Issues: CPT SCI
Rep By: Roy C. Coffee, Robert Harmala, Timothy W. Jenkins, Patrick E. O'Donnell, Hon. Larry Pressler, Thomas H. Quinn

Coalition for Tax Equity
Issues: GOV TAX
Rep By: Danielle Fagre, Timothy W. Jenkins

CommSource Internat'l, Inc.
Rep By: Robert W. Barrie

Communication Service for the Deaf
Issues: TEC
Rep By: Hon. Larry Pressler

CompTIA
Issues: TAX
Rep By: Frederick T. Dombo, Hon. Thomas J. Manton, David E. Springer

CustomerLinx
Rep By: Hon. Larry Pressler

Dakota Minnesota and Eastern Railroad
Issues: TRA
Rep By: Hon. Larry Pressler

Edison Electric Institute
Rep By: Thomas H. Quinn

Education Finance Council
Issues: EDU
Rep By: Patrick E. O'Donnell

Exxon Mobil Corp.
Issues: ENV NAT
Rep By: Robert W. Barrie, Hon. Thomas J. Corcoran, George J. Mannina, Jr., Patrick E. O'Donnell

Fishing Vessel Owners' Ass'n
Rep By: George J. Mannina, Jr.

Florida Citrus Alliance
Issues: AGR BUD
Rep By: John M. Himmelberg

Florida Department of Citrus
Rep By: John M. Himmelberg

Florida Tomato Exchange
Issues: AGR TRD
Rep By: John M. Himmelberg

FMC Corp.
Issues: ENV NAT
Rep By: Robert W. Barrie, Hon. Thomas J. Corcoran, George J. Mannina, Jr., Patrick E. O'Donnell

Futurewave General Partners, L.P.
Issues: TEC
Rep By: Hon. Larry Pressler, Thomas H. Quinn

General Electric Co.
Issues: ENV NAT
Rep By: Robert W. Barrie, Hon. Thomas J. Corcoran, George J. Mannina, Jr., Patrick E. O'Donnell

Georgia-Pacific Corp.
Issues: ENV NAT
Rep By: Robert W. Barrie, Hon. Thomas J. Corcoran, George J. Mannina, Jr., Patrick E. O'Donnell

P. H. Glatfelter
Issues: ENV NAT
Rep By: Robert W. Barrie, Hon. Thomas J. Corcoran, George J. Mannina, Jr., Patrick E. O'Donnell

Great Western Cellular Partnership
Issues: TEC
Rep By: Hon. Larry Pressler, Thomas H. Quinn

Healthcare Financing Study Group
Issues: BUD HCR HOU MMM TAX
Rep By: Hon. Thomas J. Corcoran, Christina W. Fleps, Thomas H. Quinn

JSG Trading Co.
Rep By: Hon. Thomas J. Corcoran

Kanowitz Fruit & Produce Co.
Rep By: John M. Himmelberg

KEECO
Rep By: Hon. Thomas J. Corcoran

Kendall-Jackson Winery
Issues: AGR ALC BEV IMM LAW TAX TEC TRD
Rep By: Robert M. Adler, Hon. Thomas J. Corcoran, Frederick T. Dombo, Christina W. Fleps, John M. Himmelberg, Patrick E. O'Donnell

Kurdistan Democratic Party USA
Issues: FOR
Rep By: Hon. Thomas J. Corcoran, Frederick T. Dombo, Hon. James W. Symington

Lafarge Corp.
Issues: MAN
Rep By: Hon. Larry Pressler

Lockheed Martin Corp.
Issues: AER AVI BUD DEF ENV GOV SCI TEC
Rep By: Hon. Thomas J. Corcoran, Timothy W. Jenkins, George J. Mannina, Jr., Patrick E. O'Donnell, Thomas H. Quinn, Hon. James W. Symington

Marine Mammal Coalition
Issues: ANI MAR
Rep By: George J. Mannina, Jr.

The Metris Companies, Inc.
Issues: BAN BNK CPI FIN
Rep By: Danielle Fagre, Timothy W. Jenkins

Mirage Resorts, Inc.
Issues: ANI MAR
Rep By: George J. Mannina, Jr.

Monroe Telephone Services, L.P.
Issues: TEC

Montrose Chemical Co.
Issues: ENV NAT
Rep By: Robert W. Barrie, Hon. Thomas J. Corcoran, George J. Mannina, Jr., Patrick E. O'Donnell

Morepen Laboratories, Ltd.
Rep By: Hon. Larry Pressler

M. A. Mortenson Co.
Rep By: Hon. Thomas J. Corcoran

Muldoon, Murphy & Faucette, LLP
Issues: BAN FIN TAX
Rep By: Thomas H. Quinn

Nat'l Ass'n of Ticket Brokers
Rep By: Gary C. Adler, Thomas H. Quinn

Nat'l Federation for the Blind
Issues: TEC
Rep By: Hon. Larry Pressler

Nat'l Paint and Coatings Ass'n
Issues: ENV NAT
Rep By: Robert W. Barrie, Hon. Thomas J. Corcoran, George J. Mannina, Jr., Patrick E. O'Donnell

Nat'l Peach Council
Issues: AGR TRD
Rep By: Hon. Thomas J. Corcoran, John M. Himmelberg

Netherlands Antilles, Government of
Rep By: Patrick E. O'Donnell

New England Mobile X-Ray
Rep By: Hon. Thomas J. Corcoran, Christina W. Fleps

Nuclear Energy Institute
Issues: ENG ENV GOV SCI UTI
Rep By: Roy C. Coffee

Pacific Seafood Processors Ass'n
Rep By: George J. Mannina, Jr.

Perry Institute for Marine Science
Issues: MAR TAX
Rep By: George J. Mannina, Jr.

Plano Molding Co.
Rep By: George J. Mannina, Jr.

Portland Cellular Partnership
Issues: COM
Rep By: Patrick E. O'Donnell, Thomas H. Quinn

Santa Fe, New Mexico, County of
Issues: BUD ENV
Rep By: Timothy W. Jenkins

Sempra Energy
Issues: ENG FUE UTI
Rep By: Roy C. Coffee

Smith Dawson & Andrews, Inc.
Issues: ACC ART
Rep By: Hon. Thomas J. Corcoran

Solid Waste Agency of Northern Cook County
Issues: CAW WAS
Rep By: Hon. Thomas J. Corcoran, George J. Mannina, Jr.

Southeast Alaska Seiners Ass'n
Issues: MAR
Rep By: Robert W. Barrie, George J. Mannina, Jr., Patrick J. O'Connor

St. Croix Chippewa Indians of Wisconsin
Issues: GAM IND
Rep By: Roy C. Coffee, Hon. Thomas J. Corcoran, Patrick J. O'Connor

State Government Affairs Council
Rep By: Timothy W. Jenkins

State Street Bank and Trust Co.
Issues: BAN FIN RET
Rep By: Edward Beck, Danielle Fagre, Timothy W. Jenkins, Thomas H. Quinn

Stephens Group, Inc.
Issues: FIN
Rep By: Hon. Larry Pressler

Student Loan Funding Corp.
Issues: EDU GOV
Rep By: Hon. Thomas J. Corcoran, Patrick E. O'Donnell, Thomas H. Quinn, Thomas J. Schneider, Hon. James W. Symington

Taipei Economic and Cultural Representative Office in the United States
Rep By: Patrick E. O'Donnell, Thomas H. Quinn

Telecorp PCS Inc.
Rep By: Morgan W. Reed, III, David E. Springer

Trident Seafood Corp.
Rep By: Gary C. Adler, George J. Mannina, Jr.

Tyson's Governmental Sales, LLC
Issues: AUT BUD DEF FUE MAN
Rep By: Hon. Thomas J. Corcoran, Frederick T. Dombo, Danielle Fagre, Patrick E. O'Donnell

U.S. Central Credit Union
Rep By: Roy C. Coffee, Thomas H. Quinn

UBS Warburg
Issues: BAN CPI FIN
Rep By: Roy C. Coffee, Frederick T. Dombo, Danielle Fagre, Timothy W. Jenkins, William Nickerson, Thomas H. Quinn

University of Akron
Rep By: F. Gordon Lee, Patrick E. O'Donnell

Upper Sioux Indian Community
Issues: GAM IND
Rep By: Hon. Thomas J. Corcoran, J. Craig Potter

UST Public Affairs, Inc.
Issues: BEV TAX TOB
Rep By: Thomas H. Quinn

Verizon Communications
Issues: TEC
Rep By: Hon. Larry Pressler

VISA U.S.A., Inc.
Issues: BAN BNK FIN TAX
Rep By: Roy C. Coffee, Hon. Thomas J. Corcoran, Danielle Fagre, Timothy W. Jenkins, Patrick E. O'Donnell, Thomas H. Quinn

Wards Cove Packing Co.
Rep By: George J. Mannina, Jr.

Nidal Z. Zayed and Associates
Issues: COM GOV
Rep By: Robert W. Barrie, Hon. Thomas J. Corcoran, Timothy W. Jenkins, Patrick J. O'Connor, Patrick E. O'Donnell

Odin, Feldman, & Pittleman, P.C.

9302 Lee Hwy.
Fairfax, VA 22031-1215
Tel: (703)218-2100
Fax: (703)218-2160
Registered: LDA

E-mail: ofp@ofplaw.com
A general practice law firm.

DC-Area Employees Representing Listed Clients
DALY, Thomas R., Attorney

Clients

American Chiropractic Ass'n
Issues: HCR INS MMM
Rep By: Thomas R. Daly

O'Donnell, Schwartz & Anderson, P.C.

1300 L St. NW
Suite 1200
Washington, DC 20005-4178
Tel: (202)898-1707
Fax: (202)682-9276
Registered: LDA

A law firm specializing in labor relations, aviation and railroad law, and employee benefits.

DC-Area Employees Representing Listed Clients
ANDERSON, Darryl J., President
GANZGLASS, Martin
HAJJAR, Anton G., Principal
LUBY, Arthur M., Principal

Clients

American Postal Workers Union
Rep By: Darryl J. Anderson, Anton G. Hajjar

Eritrea, Government of

Transport Workers Union of America, AFL-CIO
Issues: LBR TRA
Rep By: Arthur M. Luby

O'Donoghue & O'Donoghue

4748 Wisconsin Ave. NW
Washington, DC 20016
Tel: (202)362-0041
Registered: LDA

DC-Area Employees Representing Listed Clients
BOARDMAN, Ellen O.
CAPUANO, Donald J.
GILLIGAN, Charles W.
HOPP, R. Richard
POWERS, Brian A.
TEDROW, Sally M.

Clients

Nat'l Coordinating Committee for Multiemployer Plans
Issues: HCR LBR TAX

Ogilvy Public Relations Worldwide

1901 L St. NW
Suite 300
Washington, DC 20036
Tel: (202)466-7590
Fax: (202)466-7598
Registered: LDA, FARA

Web: www.ogilvypr.com
A full service strategic communications firm supporting business, government, and trade association clients.

DC-Area Employees Representing Listed Clients
BEALL, Thomas, Managing Director, Global Health and Medical Practice
BENTO, Michael, Senior V. President
BRUCE, Teresa, V. President
CARSON, Peter, Senior V. President
COHEN, Steven A., V. President
DAHLLOF, Steven J., Managing Director, Washington Office
DAVIS, Kamer, Senior V. President, Internet Marketing
JENKINS, Pam, Senior V. President, Group Head, Health and Medical
LAPORTE, Yolan, Senior V. President
MOELLER, Jamie W., Managing Director, Global Public Affairs Practice
NALL, Mickey, Senior V. President
ROSS, Lisa Osborne, Senior V. President, Public Affairs Practice
RUOFF, Beth, Senior V. President
SILVERMAN, Marcia, President of the Americas
WENTZEL, Jon, Senior V. President

Clients

American Chemistry Council
Rep By: Jon Wentzel

The American Floral Marketing Council
Rep By: Steven J. Dahllof

American Forest & Paper Ass'n
Rep By: Jamie W. Moeller

ATOFINA Chemicals, Inc.

Chemical Manufacturers Ass'n
Issues: CHM
Rep By: Jon Wentzel

Forest Products Industry Nat'l Labor-Management Committee
Issues: ENV NAT

INTELSAT - Internat'l Telecommunications Satellite Organization
Issues: SCI
Rep By: Steven A. Cohen, Jamie W. Moeller

Internat'l Sleep Products Ass'n
Rep By: Mickey Nall

MCI WorldCom Corp.

Ogletree Governmental Affairs, Inc.

2400 N St. NW
Fifth Floor
Washington, DC 20037
Tel: (202)728-1164
Fax: (202)728-2992
Registered: LDA

DC-Area Employees Representing Listed Clients
COXSON, Harold P., Principal
DEAN, Maggie, Principal
LUNNIE, Jr., Francis M., Principal
ROUSH, Michael, Principal

Clients

Alliance to Keep Americans Working
Issues: LBR
Rep By: Harold P. Coxson

American Academy of Adoption Attorneys
Issues: FAM
Rep By: Michael Roush

Americans for Better Borders
Issues: IMM TOU
Rep By: Harold P. Coxson

Coalition on Occupational Safety and Health
Issues: LBR
Rep By: Francis M. Lunnie, Jr.

Council on Labor Law Equality
Issues: LBR
Rep By: Harold P. Coxson

Eka Chemicals
Issues: CHM ENV
Rep By: Maggie Dean

Electronic Industries Alliance
Rep By: Francis M. Lunnie, Jr.

First Tuesday Group
Issues: HCR LBR
Rep By: Harold P. Coxson

Nat'l Alliance Against Blacklisting
Issues: GOV LBR
Rep By: Harold P. Coxson, Maggie Dean, Francis M. Lunnie, Jr., Michael Roush

Printing Industries of America
Issues: LBR

SAFE Foundation - NMD Project
Issues: DEF
Rep By: Harold P. Coxson

Bartley M. O'Hara

1825 I St. NW
Suite 400
Washington, DC 20006
Tel: (202)429-2019
Fax: (202)775-4187
Registered: LDA

A government relations consultant.

Clients

Arctic Power
Issues: ENG
Rep By: Bartley M. O'Hara

Internat'l Union of Bricklayers and Allied Craftsworkers
Rep By: Bartley M. O'Hara
Norfolk Southern Corp.
Issues: RRR TAX TRA
Rep By: Bartley M. O'Hara
San Bernardino Valley Municipal Water District
Issues: BUD REL
Rep By: Bartley M. O'Hara
United Parcel Service
Issues: POS RRR TAX TRA
Rep By: Bartley M. O'Hara

Takashi Oka

2555 Pennsylvania Ave. NW
Suite 503
Washington, DC 20037
Tel: (202)463-9279
Fax: (202)463-9283
Registered: FARA

Clients

Liberal Party of Japan
Issues: FOR
Rep By: Mr. Takashi Oka

William O'Keefe

1461 Carrington Ridge Ln.
Vienna, VA 22182
E-mail: okeefew@worldnet.att.net
Tel: (703)893-1814
Registered: LDA

Oldaker and Harris, LLP

818 Connecticut Ave. NW
Suite 1100
Washington, DC 20006
Tel: (202)728-1010
Fax: (202)728-4044
Registered: LDA, FARA

A law and government relations firm.

DC-Area Employees Representing Listed Clients

HARRIS, William D., Partner
NOLAN, Walker F., Special Counsel
OLDAKER, William C., Partner

Clients

Committee for a Democratic Majority
Rep By: William C. Oldaker
Edison Electric Institute
Issues: ENG
Rep By: Walker F. Nolan, William C. Oldaker
Fajardo, Puerto Rico, Municipality of
Issues: TRA URB
Rep By: William D. Harris, William C. Oldaker
Guaynabo, Puerto Rico, City of
Issues: TRA URB
Rep By: William D. Harris, William C. Oldaker
Mayaguez, Puerto Rico, Municipality of
Issues: TRA URB
Rep By: William D. Harris, William C. Oldaker
Puerto Rico Senate
Issues: GOV
Rep By: William C. Oldaker
Searchlight Victory Fund
Rep By: William C. Oldaker
Tohono O'Odham Nation
Rep By: William C. Oldaker

Olsson, Frank and Weeda, P.C.

1400 16th St. NW
Suite 400
Washington, DC 20036-2220
Tel: (202)789-1212
Fax: (202)234-3550
Registered: LDA, FARA
Web: www.ofwlaw.com
E-mail: info@ofwlaw.com

A law firm specializing in food and drug, medical device, and agricultural law.

Political Action Committee

Olsson, Frank and Weeda Freedom PAC
1400 16th St. NW
Suite 400
Washington, DC 20036-2220
Tel: (202)518-6323
Fax: (202)234-1560
Contact: John W. Bode

Olsson, Frank and Weeda, P.C. Fund for American Values PAC
1400 16th St. NW
Suite 400
Washington, DC 20036-2220
Tel: (202)789-1212
Fax: (202)234-3550
Contact: Marshall L. Matz

DC-Area Employees Representing Listed Clients

ACKERMAN, Kenneth, Of Counsel
BODE, John W., Principal
BROOKS, Sharon D., Associate
BRUNNER, Jan M., Associate
CROWN, Michele F., Of Counsel
DURKIN, David L., Principal
EAGLE, Jacqueline H., Of Counsel
FRANK, Richard L., Managing Partner
FURMAN, Pamela J., Principal
GRYMES, Susan P., Associate
HAHN, Robert A., Associate
HALPERN, Naomi J. L., Associate
HARNED, Karen Reis, Associate
ITZKOFF, Mark L., Of Counsel
JOHNSON, Dennis R., Principal
LACEY, Stephen L., Associate
MATZ, Marshall L., Principal
O'FLAHERTY, Michael J., Principal
O'FLAHERTY, Neil F., Principal
OLSSON, Philip C., Principal
PAHL, Tish E., Associate
REDPATH, Tyson, Legislative Assistant
SCHWEMER, Brett T., Associate
SIEGEL, Richard D., Senior Attorney
STROBOS, M.D., Jur T., Of Counsel
STROSCHEIN, Ryan W., Associate
TERMAN, Stephen D., Principal
TSIEN, Arthur Y., Principal
WEEDA, David F., Principal

Clients

Adheris, Inc.
Issues: MIA PHA
Rep By: John W. Bode, Richard L. Frank, Susan P. Grymes, Karen Reis Harned, Stephen L. Lacey, Marshall L. Matz, Tyson Redpath
American Academy of Audiology
Issues: HCR
Rep By: John W. Bode, Pamela J. Furman, Susan P. Grymes, Stephen L. Lacey, Marshall L. Matz, Tyson Redpath
American Commodity Distribution Ass'n
Issues: AGR BUD
Rep By: John W. Bode, Susan P. Grymes, Karen Reis Harned, Stephen L. Lacey, Marshall L. Matz, Tyson Redpath
American School Food Service Ass'n
Issues: AGR BUD IMM WEL
Rep By: John W. Bode, Susan P. Grymes, Karen Reis Harned, Stephen L. Lacey, Marshall L. Matz, Tyson Redpath
Ass'n of Medical Device Reprocessors
Issues: MED
Rep By: John W. Bode, Pamela J. Furman, Susan P. Grymes, Karen Reis Harned, Stephen L. Lacey, Marshall L. Matz, Tyson Redpath, Ryan W. Stroschein, Stephen D. Terman
Aventis Pasteur
Rep By: John W. Bode, Susan P. Grymes, Karen Reis Harned, Stephen L. Lacey, Marshall L. Matz, Tyson Redpath, Ryan W. Stroschein, Arthur Y. Tsien, David F. Weeda
Beef Products, Inc.
Rep By: John W. Bode, Richard L. Frank, Susan P. Grymes, Karen Reis Harned, Stephen L. Lacey, Marshall L. Matz, Tyson Redpath, Ryan W. Stroschein
Black Hills Forest Resource Ass'n
Issues: AGR
Rep By: Stephen L. Lacey, Marshall L. Matz, Richard D. Siegel, Ryan W. Stroschein
California Canning Peach Ass'n
Issues: AGR
Rep By: John W. Bode, Susan P. Grymes, Karen Reis Harned, Stephen L. Lacey, Marshall L. Matz, Tyson Redpath, Ryan W. Stroschein
Chocolate Manufacturers Ass'n of the U.S.A.
Issues: AGR FOO WEL
Rep By: John W. Bode, Richard L. Frank, Susan P. Grymes, Karen Reis Harned, Stephen L. Lacey, Marshall L. Matz, Tyson Redpath, Ryan W. Stroschein
Clement Pappas & Co., Inc.
Issues: AGR
Rep By: Stephen L. Lacey
Cliffstar Corp.
Issues: AGR
Rep By: Stephen L. Lacey
Duramed Pharmaceuticals, Inc.
Issues: PHA
Rep By: John W. Bode, Susan P. Grymes, Karen Reis Harned, Stephen L. Lacey, Marshall L. Matz, Ryan W. Stroschein, Arthur Y. Tsien, David F. Weeda
Food Distributors Internat'l (NAWGA-IFDA)
Issues: AGR ALC BUD FOO WEL
Rep By: John W. Bode, Richard L. Frank, Susan P. Grymes, Karen Reis Harned, Stephen L. Lacey, Marshall L. Matz, Tyson Redpath
General Mills
Issues: AGR BUD FOO WEL
Rep By: John W. Bode, Susan P. Grymes, Stephen L. Lacey, Marshall L. Matz, Ryan W. Stroschein
Gentrac Inc.
Rep By: John W. Bode, Susan P. Grymes, Karen Reis Harned, Stephen L. Lacey, Marshall L. Matz, Tyson Redpath, Ryan W. Stroschein, Arthur Y. Tsien, David F. Weeda
Health Resource Publishing Co.
Issues: MIA
Rep By: John W. Bode, Richard L. Frank, Susan P. Grymes, Karen Reis Harned, Stephen L. Lacey, Marshall L. Matz, Tyson Redpath, Ryan W. Stroschein
Institute of Food Technologists
Issues: AGR BUD FOO
Rep By: John W. Bode, Susan P. Grymes, Karen Reis Harned, Stephen L. Lacey, Marshall L. Matz, Tyson Redpath, Ryan W. Stroschein
Kraft Foods, Inc.
Issues: BUD FOO
Rep By: John W. Bode, Susan P. Grymes, Karen Reis Harned, Stephen L. Lacey, Marshall L. Matz, Tyson Redpath, Ryan W. Stroschein
Lower Brule Sioux Tribe
Issues: IND
Rep By: John W. Bode, Susan P. Grymes, Karen Reis Harned, Stephen L. Lacey, Marshall L. Matz, Tyson Redpath, Ryan W. Stroschein
McDonald's Corp.
Issues: BUD FOO
Rep By: Tyson Redpath, Ryan W. Stroschein
Mead Johnson Nutritional Group
Issues: AGR FOO WEL
Rep By: John W. Bode, Susan P. Grymes, Karen Reis Harned, Stephen L. Lacey, Marshall L. Matz, Michael J. O'Flaherty, Tyson Redpath, Ryan W. Stroschein
Nat'l Ass'n of Margarine Manufacturers
Issues: FOO
Rep By: John W. Bode, Susan P. Grymes, Karen Reis Harned, Stephen L. Lacey, Marshall L. Matz, Philip C. Olsson, Tyson Redpath, Ryan W. Stroschein
Nat'l Ass'n of Pharmaceutical Manufacturers
Issues: BUD PHA
Rep By: John W. Bode, Pamela J. Furman, Susan P. Grymes, Karen Reis Harned, Stephen L. Lacey, Marshall L. Matz, Tyson Redpath, Ryan W. Stroschein, Arthur Y. Tsien, David F. Weeda
Nat'l Coalition of Food Importers Ass'n
Issues: FOO TRD
Rep By: John W. Bode, Susan P. Grymes, Karen Reis Harned, Stephen L. Lacey, Marshall L. Matz, Tyson Redpath, Ryan W. Stroschein
Nat'l Confectioners Ass'n
Rep By: John W. Bode, Richard L. Frank, Susan P. Grymes, Karen Reis Harned, Stephen L. Lacey, Marshall L. Matz, Tyson Redpath, Ryan W. Stroschein
Nat'l Food Processors Ass'n
Issues: AGR BUD FOO
Rep By: John W. Bode, Susan P. Grymes, Karen Reis Harned, Stephen L. Lacey, Marshall L. Matz, Tyson Redpath, Ryan W. Stroschein
Nat'l Frozen Pizza Institute
Rep By: John W. Bode, Richard L. Frank, Marshall L. Matz, Tyson Redpath, Ryan W. Stroschein
Nat'l Meat Ass'n
Issues: BUD FOO
Rep By: John W. Bode, Susan P. Grymes, Karen Reis Harned, Stephen L. Lacey, Marshall L. Matz, Philip C. Olsson, Tyson Redpath, Ryan W. Stroschein
PennField Oil Co.
Issues: PHA
Rep By: John W. Bode, Susan P. Grymes, Karen Reis Harned, Stephen L. Lacey, Marshall L. Matz, Tyson Redpath, Ryan W. Stroschein, David F. Weeda
Philip Morris Management Corp.
Issues: BEV FOO TOB
Rep By: John W. Bode, Tyson Redpath, Ryan W. Stroschein
The Pillsbury Co.
Issues: AGR BUD FOO
Rep By: John W. Bode, Richard L. Frank, Susan P. Grymes, Karen Reis Harned, Stephen L. Lacey, Marshall L. Matz, Tyson Redpath, Ryan W. Stroschein
San Tomo Group
Rep By: John W. Bode, Richard L. Frank, Susan P. Grymes, Karen Reis Harned, Stephen L. Lacey, Marshall L. Matz, Tyson Redpath, Ryan W. Stroschein
Schwan's Sales Enterprises
Issues: AGR FUE TAX
Rep By: John W. Bode, Susan P. Grymes, Karen Reis Harned, Dennis R. Johnson, Stephen L. Lacey, Marshall L. Matz, Tyson Redpath, Ryan W. Stroschein
SteriGenics Internat'l
Rep By: John W. Bode, Susan P. Grymes, Karen Reis Harned, Stephen L. Lacey, Marshall L. Matz, Tyson Redpath, Ryan W. Stroschein
Titan Scan
Issues: AGR FOO
Rep By: John W. Bode, Susan P. Grymes, Karen Reis Harned, Stephen L. Lacey, Marshall L. Matz, Tyson Redpath, Ryan W. Stroschein
Transhumance Holding Co., Inc.
Issues: FOO TRD
Rep By: John W. Bode, David L. Durkin, Susan P. Grymes, Karen Reis Harned, Stephen L. Lacey, Marshall L.

Matz, Philip C. Olsson, Tyson Redpath, Ryan W. Stroschein

United Fresh Fruit and Vegetable Ass'n
Issues: AGR BUD FOO
Rep By: John W. Bode, David L. Durkin, Susan P. Grymes, Karen Reis Harned, Stephen L. Lacey, Marshall L. Matz, Michael J. O'Flaherty, Tyson Redpath, Ryan W. Stroschein

O'Malley, Miles, Nylen & Gilmore, P.A.

11785 Beltsville Dr.
Tenth Floor
Calverton, MD 20705
Tel: (301)572-7900
Fax: (301)572-6655
Registered: LDA

DC-Area Employees Representing Listed Clients
DAVEY, John P., Managing Partner
GINGLES, Andre J., Senior Partner
LEVIN, Mark G., Deputy Managing Partner
MCDONOUGH, John P., Senior Partner

Clients

Peterson Cos., Inc.
Issues: TRA
Rep By: John P. Davey, Andre J. Gingles, John P. McDonough

O'Melveny and Myers LLP

555 13th St. NW
Suite 500 West
Washington, DC 20004
Tel: (202)383-5300
Fax: (202)383-5414
Registered: LDA, FARA
Web: www.omm.com
Washington office of a Los Angeles general practice law firm.

Political Action Committee
O'Melveny and Myers LLP Political Action Committee
555 13th St. NW
Suite 500 West
Washington, DC 20004
Contact: Donald T. Bliss
Tel: (202)383-5300
Fax: (202)383-5414

DC-Area Employees Representing Listed Clients
ALMSTEDT, Kermit W., Partner
ANDERSON, Brian, Partner
BECKER, Evelyn, Special Counsel
BEDDOW, David T., Partner
BEISNER, John H., Partner
BLISS, Donald T., Partner
BROOKS, Brian, Associate
BURTON, Joel Stephen, Of Counsel
CLARKE, Peggy A., Special Counsel
COLEMAN, Jr., William T., Senior Partner
CULVAHOUSE, Jr., Arthur B., Partner
DELLINGER, III, Walter E., Partner
ECCLES, Robert N., Partner
HILER, Bruce A., Partner
HORLICK, Gary N., Partner
KIM, Hwan
KLAIN, Ronald A., Partner
LAYTON, Elisabeth, Associate
LITT, David, Partner
PARKER, Richard G., Partner
RAPHAELSON, Ira R., Partner
RIORDAN, Kelly J., Associate
WURGLITZ, Alfred M., Partner

Clients

Advanced Micro Devices
Issues: CPI LBR
Rep By: David T. Beddow, Arthur B. Culvahouse, Jr.

American Consumers for Affordable Homes
Rep By: Gary N. Horlick

Canada, Government of
Rep By: Gary N. Horlick

Cargill, Inc.
Rep By: Gary N. Horlick

Chile, Government of the Republic of
Rep By: Gary N. Horlick

CIGNA Corp.
Issues: FOR INS TRD
Rep By: Donald T. Bliss, William T. Coleman, Jr., Gary N. Horlick, Elisabeth Layton, David Litt

Civil Justice Reform Group
Rep By: John H. Beisner, Arthur B. Culvahouse, Jr.

Coalition for Asbestos Resolution
Issues: BNK CSP HCR TOR
Rep By: Walter E. Dellinger, III, Ronald A. Klain

Coalition for Truth in Environmental Marketing Information, Inc.
Issues: CSP ENV TRD
Rep By: Peggy A. Clarke, Gary N. Horlick

Fannie Mae
Issues: FIN HOU INS TAX

Samsung Heavy Industries Co., Ltd.
Issues: DEF
Rep By: Donald T. Bliss, William T. Coleman, Jr., Hwan Kim, Kelly J. Riordan

US Airways
Issues: AVI LBR TRA
Rep By: Donald T. Bliss, Joel Stephen Burton, William T. Coleman, Jr., Ronald A. Klain, Kelly J. Riordan

Verizon Communications
Issues: LBR TEC
Rep By: Arthur B. Culvahouse, Jr.

John F. O'Neal Law Offices

One Massachusetts Ave. NW
Suite 800
Washington, DC 20001
Tel: (202)628-0210
Fax: (202)628-2482
Registered: LDA

DC-Area Employees Representing Listed Clients
O'NEAL, John F., President

Clients

Nat'l Rural Telecom Ass'n
Issues: AGR
Rep By: John F. O'Neal

O'Neill, Athy & Casey, P.C.

1310 19th St. NW
Washington, DC 20036
Tel: (202)466-6555
Fax: (202)466-6596
Registered: LDA, FARA
A general, administrative, and legislative practice law firm.

DC-Area Employees Representing Listed Clients
ATHY, Jr., Andrew, Partner
CASEY, Martha L., Partner
KNAPP, John
O'NEILL, Christopher R., Partner

Clients

American Hospital Ass'n
Issues: HCR LAW
Rep By: Christopher R. O'Neill

AT&T
Issues: BUD TEC
Rep By: Andrew Athy, Jr., Christopher R. O'Neill

Beth Israel/Deaconess Medical Center
Rep By: Martha L. Casey, Christopher R. O'Neill

Boston Museum of Science
Rep By: Martha L. Casey, Christopher R. O'Neill

Coalition of Boston Teaching Hospitals
Issues: BUD HCR MED MMM
Rep By: Martha L. Casey, Christopher R. O'Neill

Des Moines University, Osteopathic Medical Center
Rep By: Christopher R. O'Neill

Glass Packaging Institute
Rep By: Andrew Athy, Jr., Christopher R. O'Neill

Harvard University Washington Office
Issues: BUD SCI
Rep By: Andrew Athy, Jr., Martha L. Casey

Industry Union Glass Container Promotion Program
Issues: BEV
Rep By: Andrew Athy, Jr.

JM Family Enterprises
Issues: CSP LBR TAX TRA
Rep By: Andrew Athy, Jr., Christopher R. O'Neill

Lehman Brothers
Issues: FIN
Rep By: Andrew Athy, Jr., Christopher R. O'Neill

Marathon Oil Co.
Rep By: Andrew Athy, Jr., Christopher R. O'Neill

Massachusetts General/Brigham and Women's Hospital
Rep By: Martha L. Casey, Christopher R. O'Neill

McLean Hospital
Issues: BUD MMM
Rep By: Martha L. Casey

Museum of Science-Boston

New England Deaconess Hospital
Rep By: Martha L. Casey

New England Medical Center
Rep By: Martha L. Casey, Christopher R. O'Neill

Northeastern University
Issues: BUD DEF EDU
Rep By: Martha L. Casey, Christopher R. O'Neill

Northwestern Memorial Hospital
Rep By: Andrew Athy, Jr., Martha L. Casey

Partners Healthcare System, Inc.
Issues: BUD HCR MED
Rep By: Christopher R. O'Neill

Schepens Eye Research Institute
Issues: BUD
Rep By: Martha L. Casey

Spaulding Rehabilitation Hospital
Issues: HCR MMM
Rep By: Martha L. Casey

Temple University Health System
Issues: BUD HCR MED MMM
Rep By: Martha L. Casey, John Knapp

TXU Business Services
Issues: ENG ENV FUE NAT TAX TEC UTI WAS
Rep By: Andrew Athy, Jr., Christopher R. O'Neill

USX Corp.
Issues: ENV HCR TAX TRD
Rep By: Andrew Athy, Jr., Christopher R. O'Neill

Viacom Inc.
Issues: TEC
Rep By: Andrew Athy, Jr., Christopher R. O'Neill

Oppenheimer Wolff & Donnelly LLP

1620 L St. NW
Suite 600
Washington, DC 20036
Tel: (202)312-8000
Fax: (202)312-8100
Registered: LDA, FARA
Web: www.oppenheimer.com
A law firm specializing in international trade, taxation, environmental law and regulatory law. Formed by the merger of Oppenheimer Wolff & Donnelly and Bayh, Connaughton & Stewart, P.C.

DC-Area Employees Representing Listed Clients
BAYH, Hon. Birch, Partner
CLADOUHOS, Harry W., Partner
FALEY, Kevin O., Partner
KORNS, John H., Partner
LAWRENCE, III, Thomas
STRAND, Margaret N., Partner

Clients

Association des Constructeurs Europeens de Motocycles
Issues: TRD
Rep By: Hon. Birch Bayh, Harry W. Cladouhos, John H. Korns

Bio-Vascular, Inc.
Issues: HCR
Rep By: Hon. Birch Bayh

CBI Industries
Rep By: Hon. Birch Bayh, Kevin O. Faley, Margaret N. Strand

ComEd
Issues: WAS
Rep By: Hon. Birch Bayh, Kevin O. Faley

Cook Group
Issues: HCR
Rep By: Hon. Birch Bayh, Kevin O. Faley

Crown Butte Mines, Inc.
Rep By: Hon. Birch Bayh, Kevin O. Faley, Margaret N. Strand

Empresas Fonalledas
Issues: ENV
Rep By: Margaret N. Strand

Full House Resorts, Inc.

Government Leasing Co.

Hutchinson, Kansas, Municipalities of

ICN Pharmaceuticals, Inc.
Issues: FOR GOV
Rep By: Hon. Birch Bayh, Kevin O. Faley

Illinois Tool Works
Issues: MAN
Rep By: Hon. Birch Bayh, Kevin O. Faley

MGF Industries Inc.
Issues: TRD
Rep By: Harry W. Cladouhos

Nat'l Basketball Ass'n
Rep By: Hon. Birch Bayh, Kevin O. Faley

Nat'l Disease Research Interchange
Issues: HCR MED

Nat'l Mitigation Bankers Ass'n
Issues: CAW ENV NAT
Rep By: Margaret N. Strand

New Starts Working Group
Issues: BUD TRA

NISH - Creating Employment Opportunities for People with Severe Disabilities
Issues: LBR
Rep By: Hon. Birch Bayh, Kevin O. Faley

NYK Bulkship, Inc.
Rep By: Harry W. Cladouhos, John H. Korns

Pennsylvania Savings Ass'n Insurance Corp.

Real Estate Capital Resources Ass'n
Rep By: Hon. Birch Bayh, Kevin O. Faley

John T. O'Rourke Law Offices

801 Pennsylvania Ave. NW
Fifth Floor
Washington, DC 20004
Tel: (202)662-4720
Fax: (202)662-4748
Registered: LDA
A general practice law firm.

DC-Area Employees Representing Listed Clients
LAZARUS, Maggi A., Associate
O'ROURKE, John T., Principal

Clients

Alliance Data Systems
Issues: BAN
Rep By: John T. O'Rourke

First American
Issues: ECN FIN RES TAX
Rep By: John T. O'Rourke

Goldman, Sachs and Co.
Issues: FIN TAX
Rep By: John T. O'Rourke

Herzog, Heine, Geduld, Inc.
Issues: FIN
Rep By: John T. O'Rourke

Internat'l Game Technology
Issues: CPT GAM TAX
Rep By: John T. O'Rourke

The Limited Inc.
Issues: CSP LBR TAX TRD
Rep By: John T. O'Rourke

Securities Industry Ass'n
Issues: FIN
Rep By: John T. O'Rourke

Orrick Herrington & Sutcliffe LLP

Washington Harbour
3050 K St. NW, Suite 200
Washington, DC 20007
Web: www.orrick.com
Tel: (202)339-8400
Fax: (202)339-8500
Registered: LDA

DC-Area Employees Representing Listed Clients
COWAN, Cameron, Managing Partner

Clients

BHP (USA) Inc.

O'Toole Consulting

700 13th St. NW
Tenth Floor
Washington, DC 20005
E-mail: totoole@shandwick.com
Tel: (202)434-8564
Fax: (202)347-8713
A public policy firm.

DC-Area Employees Representing Listed Clients
O'TOOLE, Thomas, President

Clients

Discovery Communications, Inc.
Rep By: Thomas O'Toole

Ottosen and Associates

6916 Wolf Run Shoals
Fairfax Station, VA 22039
Tel: (703)978-8037
Fax: (703)978-8039
Registered: LDA
A government relations, political consulting and fundraising firm.

DC-Area Employees Representing Listed Clients
OTTOSEN, Karl J., Partner

Clients

Contran Corp.
Issues: WAS
Rep By: Karl J. Ottosen

EWI-Re Ltd.
Rep By: Karl J. Ottosen

Kronos, Inc.
Rep By: Karl J. Ottosen

NL Industries
Rep By: Karl J. Ottosen

U.S. Federation of Small Businesses, Inc.
Rep By: Karl J. Ottosen

Valhi, Inc.
Rep By: Karl J. Ottosen

Outdoor Media, Inc.

6707 Old Stage Rd.
North Bethesda, MD 20852
Tel: (301)770-6496
Fax: (301)770-6497
Registered: LDA
E-mail: tlrs@erols.com
A government and media relations firm.

DC-Area Employees Representing Listed Clients
RICHARDSON, Tim, President

Clients

Kodiak Brown Bear Trust
Issues: ENV
Rep By: Tim Richardson

Theodore Roosevelt Conservation Alliance
Rep By: Tim Richardson

Wildlife Forever
Issues: ENV
Rep By: Tim Richardson

PACE-CAPSTONE

300 N. Lee St.
Suite 500
Alexandria, VA 22314
Tel: (703)518-8600
Fax: (703)518-8611
Registered: LDA
Web: www.pace-capstone.com
A political consulting firm.

DC-Area Employees Representing Listed Clients
DACEY, Scott C., Partner
GERMROTH, David S., Partner
LANDRUM, J. Michael, Partner
ROGERS, John C., Partner
WISE, James W., Partner

Clients

Agua Caliente Band of Cahuilla Indians
Issues: IND
Rep By: Scott C. Dacey, James W. Wise

Barona Band of Mission Indians
Issues: IND
Rep By: Scott C. Dacey, James W. Wise

Colorado River Indian Tribes
Issues: IND
Rep By: Scott C. Dacey, James W. Wise

Guam AFGE
Issues: DEF GOV
Rep By: David S. Germroth, James W. Wise

Guam Internat'l Airport Authority
Issues: TRA
Rep By: David S. Germroth, James W. Wise

Guam, Washington Office of the Governor
Issues: DEF GOV TRA
Rep By: David S. Germroth, James W. Wise

Honolulu Shipyard
Issues: DEF TRA
Rep By: David S. Germroth, James W. Wise

Household Goods Forwarders Ass'n of America, Inc.
Issues: DEF
Rep By: James W. Wise

Independent Bankers Ass'n of Texas
Issues: BAN
Rep By: James W. Wise

Internat'l Facilities Management Ass'n
Rep By: David S. Germroth, James W. Wise

Kern, California, County of
Issues: GOV
Rep By: Scott C. Dacey, J. Michael Landrum, James W. Wise

Morongo Band of Mission Indians
Issues: IND
Rep By: Scott C. Dacey, James W. Wise

Multimedia Games, Inc.
Issues: GAM
Rep By: Scott C. Dacey, James W. Wise

Nat'l Ass'n of Credit Management
Issues: BAN BNK
Rep By: J. Michael Landrum, James W. Wise

Oneida Tribe of Indians of Wisconsin
Issues: IND
Rep By: Scott C. Dacey

San Francisco Bar Pilots Ass'n
Issues: MAR
Rep By: James W. Wise

Pacific Islands Washington Office

P.O. Box 26142
Alexandria, VA 22313-6142
E-mail: paciswashofc@mail.com
Tel: (703)519-7757
Fax: (703)548-0633
Strategic planning and government liaison for Pacific Islands clients.

DC-Area Employees Representing Listed Clients
RADEWAGEN, Fred, President

Clients

Forum for America's Island Republicans
Rep By: Fred Radewagen

Guam Legislature
Issues: BUD NAT
Rep By: Fred Radewagen

Guam, Washington Office of the Governor
Issues: EDU
Rep By: Fred Radewagen

Marshall Islands Nuclear Claims Tribunal
Issues: ENG
Rep By: Fred Radewagen

The Micronesia Institute
Issues: ECN
Rep By: Fred Radewagen

Washington Pacific Publications, Inc.
Issues: MIA
Rep By: Fred Radewagen

Pacquing Consulting Inc.

P.O. Box 2484
Fairfax, VA 22031
E-mail: Julie.Pacquing@erols.com
Tel: (703)573-4380
Registered: LDA

DC-Area Employees Representing Listed Clients
PACQUING, Juliet, President

Clients

AAI Corp.
Issues: MAN
Rep By: Juliet Pacquing

Armstrong Laser Technology
Issues: MAN
Rep By: Juliet Pacquing

Law Office of Zel E. Lipsen
Issues: DEF ENG ENV TRA
Rep By: Juliet Pacquing

The Potomac Advocates
Issues: AGR DEF
Rep By: Juliet Pacquing

Production Technology, Inc.
Issues: DEF
Rep By: Juliet Pacquing

PAI Management Corp.

4350 East West Hwy.
Suite 401
Bethesda, MD 20814-4411
Web: www.paimgmt.com
E-mail: PAI@paimgmt.com
Tel: (301)656-4224
Fax: (301)656-0989
A full-service association management and development company

DC-Area Employees Representing Listed Clients
EPSTEIN, Mark, Senior Account Executive
WALLIS, Ph.D., Norman E., President

Clients

American Board of Adolescent Psychiatry
Issues: HCR MED
Rep By: Norman E. Wallis, Ph.D.

American Nat'l Metric Council
Issues: SCI

Internat'l Soc. for Pharmacoepidemiology
Rep By: Mark Epstein

Soc. for Mucosal Immunology
Issues: HCR MED
Rep By: Norman E. Wallis, Ph.D.

John M. Palatiello & Associates

1760 Reston Pkwy.
Suite 515
Reston, VA 20190
E-mail: johnmapps@aol.com
Tel: (703)787-6665
Fax: (703)787-7550
Registered: LDA

DC-Area Employees Representing Listed Clients
PALATIELLO, John M., Principal

Clients

Council on Federal Procurement of Architectural and Engineering Services (COFPAES)
Issues: GOV
Rep By: John M. Palatiello

EarthData Holdings
Issues: AVI DOC ENV GOV
Rep By: John M. Palatiello

Management Ass'n for Private Photogrammetric Surveyors
Issues: GOV
Rep By: John M. Palatiello

MAPPS PAC
Rep By: John M. Palatiello

Navigational Electronic Chart Systems Ass'n (NECSA)
Issues: GOV MAR
Rep By: John M. Palatiello

Paley Rothman Goldstein Rosenberg & Cooper

4800 Hampden Ln.
Seventh Floor
One Bethesda Center
Bethesda, MD 20814-2922
E-mail: calimafd@paleyrothman.com
Tel: (301)656-7603
Fax: (301)654-7354
Registered: LDA

DC-Area Employees Representing Listed Clients
CALIMAFDE, Paula A.

Clients

Small Business Council of America
Issues: LBR RET SMB TAX
Rep By: Paula A. Calimafde

The Palmer Group

216 Justice Ct. NE
Suite A
Washington, DC 20002
Tel: (202)547-7721
Fax: (202)547-7835
Registered: LDA
E-mail: palmgrp@ix.netcom.com

DC-Area Employees Representing Listed Clients

PALMER, Clifford A., Director

Clients

Ascension, Louisiana, Parish of
Issues: GOV TRA
Rep By: Clifford A. Palmer

BOH Environmental, L.L.C.
Issues: ENG ENV WAS
Rep By: Clifford A. Palmer

Erin Engineering and Research, Inc.
Issues: ENG
Rep By: Clifford A. Palmer

Grand Isle Independent Levee District
Rep By: Clifford A. Palmer

Monroe, Louisiana, Chamber of Commerce of the City of
Issues: AVI BUD ECN TRA
Rep By: Clifford A. Palmer

Monroe, Louisiana, City of
Rep By: Clifford A. Palmer

Orleans Levee District
Issues: DIS
Rep By: Clifford A. Palmer

Professional Engineering
Issues: BUD DIS ENV
Rep By: Clifford A. Palmer

West Jefferson Levee District
Issues: DIS
Rep By: Clifford A. Palmer

Palumbo & Cerrell, Inc.

1717 K St. NW
Suite 500
Washington, DC 20006
Tel: (202)466-9000
Fax: (202)466-9009
Registered: LDA
E-mail: pnc@clark.net
Public affairs counselors.

DC-Area Employees Representing Listed Clients

DEITZ, William T., V. President, Legislative and Regulatory Affairs
O'REGAN, Charles R., V. President, Government Affairs
PALUMBO, Benjamin L., President
SKRABUT, Jr., Paul A., Senior V. President

Clients

American Soc. of Composers, Authors and Publishers
Issues: ART COM CPT REL SMB TEC
Rep By: William T. Deitz, Charles R. O'Regan, Benjamin L. Palumbo, Paul A. Skrabut, Jr.

American Trans Air
Issues: CSP TOU TRA
Rep By: William T. Deitz, Charles R. O'Regan, Benjamin L. Palumbo, Paul A. Skrabut, Jr.

HT Medical
Issues: HCR
Rep By: William T. Deitz, Charles R. O'Regan, Benjamin L. Palumbo, Paul A. Skrabut, Jr.

Jackson Hewitt
Issues: TAX

K Capital Partners
Issues: BUD GOV TEC
Rep By: Charles R. O'Regan, Benjamin L. Palumbo, Paul A. Skrabut, Jr.

Los Angeles, California, Metropolitan Transit Authority of
Issues: ROD TRA URB
Rep By: William T. Deitz, Benjamin L. Palumbo, Paul A. Skrabut, Jr.

Multistate Tax Commission
Issues: IND TAX TEC TOB TRA UTI

Music Educators Nat'l Conference
Issues: ART EDU
Rep By: Charles R. O'Regan, Benjamin L. Palumbo, Paul A. Skrabut, Jr.

Paradigm Research Group

4938 Hampden Ln.
Suite 161
Bethesda, MD 20814
Tel: (301)564-1820
Fax: (301)564-4066
Registered: LDA
Web: www.paradigmclock.com
E-mail: paradigmrg@aol.com
Consults clients on issues of extraterrestrial and U.F.O. related phenomena.

DC-Area Employees Representing Listed Clients

BASSETT, Stephen G., Consultant

Clients

Center for the Study of Extraterrestrial Intelligence
Issues: GOV
Rep By: Stephen G. Bassett

The Enterprise Mission
Issues: GOV
Rep By: Stephen G. Bassett

Hickman Report
Issues: AER DEF GOV SCI
Rep By: Stephen G. Bassett

Operation Right to Know
Issues: GOV
Rep By: Stephen G. Bassett

SKYWATCH Internat'l
Issues: GOV

Howard F. Park

1249 South Carolina Ave. SE
Washington, DC 20003
Tel: (202)544-6262
Fax: (202)544-6062
E-mail: hpark4@aol.com
Provides services in grassroots mobilization and media relations.

Clients

American Watercraft Ass'n
Rep By: Howard F. Park

Parry, Romani, DeConcini & Symms

233 Constitution Ave. NE
Washington, DC 20002
Tel: (202)547-4000
Fax: (202)543-5044
Registered: LDA
Web: www.lobbycongress.com
E-mail: PRDandS@aol.com

Political Action Committee

Parry, Romani & DeConcini, Inc. PAC
233 Constitution Ave. NE
Washington, DC 20002
Tel: (202)547-4000
Fax: (202)543-5044
Contact: Romano Romani

DC-Area Employees Representing Listed Clients

BAXTER, Edward H., V. President, Government Relations
DECONCINI, Hon. Dennis, Partner
HADDOW, John M., V. President
HATCH, Scott D., Research Director
HENDERSON, Shannon Davis, Director, Congressional Affairs
MARTIN, Jack W., V. President, Government Relations
ROMANI, Romano, President
SKLADANY, Linda Arey, V. President for Congressional Relations
SYMMS, Hon. Steven D., Partner

Clients

AIDS Healthcare Foundation
Issues: MED MMM
Rep By: Edward H. Baxter, Hon. Dennis DeConcini, John M. Haddow, Scott D. Hatch, Shannon Davis Henderson, Jack W. Martin, Romano Romani, Linda Arey Skladany, Hon. Steven D. Symms

American Ecology

Andrx Pharmaceutical Corp.
Issues: LBR PHA
Rep By: Edward H. Baxter, Hon. Dennis DeConcini, John M. Haddow, Scott D. Hatch, Shannon Davis Henderson, Jack W. Martin, Romano Romani, Linda Arey Skladany, Hon. Steven D. Symms

Armstrong World Industries, Inc.
Rep By: Edward H. Baxter, Hon. Dennis DeConcini, John M. Haddow, Scott D. Hatch, Shannon Davis Henderson, Jack W. Martin, Romano Romani, Linda Arey Skladany, Hon. Steven D. Symms

Asphalt Systems, Inc.
Issues: ROD
Rep By: Edward H. Baxter, Hon. Dennis DeConcini, John M. Haddow, Scott D. Hatch, Shannon Davis Henderson, Jack W. Martin, Romano Romani, Linda Arey Skladany, Hon. Steven D. Symms

Aventis Pharmaceutical Products
Issues: CPT
Rep By: Edward H. Baxter, Hon. Dennis DeConcini, John M. Haddow, Scott D. Hatch, Shannon Davis Henderson, Jack W. Martin, Romano Romani, Linda Arey Skladany, Hon. Steven D. Symms

Avondale, Arizona, City of
Issues: EDU ENV LAW URB
Rep By: Edward H. Baxter, Hon. Dennis DeConcini, John M. Haddow, Scott D. Hatch, Shannon Davis Henderson, Jack W. Martin, Romano Romani, Linda Arey Skladany, Hon. Steven D. Symms

Bank of New York
Issues: BAN FIN
Rep By: Edward H. Baxter, Hon. Dennis DeConcini, John M. Haddow, Scott D. Hatch, Shannon Davis Henderson, Jack W. Martin, Romano Romani, Linda Arey Skladany, Hon. Steven D. Symms

Bristol-Myers Squibb Co.
Issues: CPT
Rep By: Edward H. Baxter, Hon. Dennis DeConcini, John M. Haddow, Scott D. Hatch, Shannon Davis Henderson, Jack W. Martin, Romano Romani, Linda Arey Skladany, Hon. Steven D. Symms

Coalition Against Database Piracy
Rep By: Edward H. Baxter, Hon. Dennis DeConcini, John M. Haddow, Scott D. Hatch, Shannon Davis Henderson, Jack W. Martin, Romano Romani, Linda Arey Skladany, Hon. Steven D. Symms

Composites Fabricators Ass'n
Issues: CAW
Rep By: Edward H. Baxter, Hon. Dennis DeConcini, John M. Haddow, Scott D. Hatch, Shannon Davis Henderson, Jack W. Martin, Romano Romani, Linda Arey Skladany, Hon. Steven D. Symms

Conservation Trust Fund for Puerto Rico

E Lottery

Ferraro, USA
Issues: FOO
Rep By: Edward H. Baxter, Hon. Dennis DeConcini, John M. Haddow, Scott D. Hatch, Shannon Davis Henderson, Jack W. Martin, Romano Romani, Linda Arey Skladany, Hon. Steven D. Symms

Formosan Ass'n for Public Affairs
Issues: FOR
Rep By: Edward H. Baxter, Hon. Dennis DeConcini, John M. Haddow, Scott D. Hatch, Shannon Davis Henderson, Jack W. Martin, Romano Romani, Linda Arey Skladany, Hon. Steven D. Symms

Forschler Ass'n

GlaxoSmithKline
Issues: CPT MED TAX
Rep By: Edward H. Baxter, Hon. Dennis DeConcini, John M. Haddow, Scott D. Hatch, Shannon Davis Henderson, Jack W. Martin, Romano Romani, Linda Arey Skladany, Hon. Steven D. Symms

Hemenway Associates

Herbalife Internat'l, Inc.
Issues: FOO
Rep By: Edward H. Baxter, Hon. Dennis DeConcini, John M. Haddow, Scott D. Hatch, Shannon Davis Henderson, Jack W. Martin, Romano Romani, Linda Arey Skladany, Hon. Steven D. Symms

Hoechst Marion Roussel Deutschland GmbH
Issues: CPT
Rep By: Edward H. Baxter, Hon. Dennis DeConcini, John M. Haddow, Scott D. Hatch, Shannon Davis Henderson, Jack W. Martin, Romano Romani, Linda Arey Skladany, Hon. Steven D. Symms

Inter-Cal Corp.
Issues: ADV FOO
Rep By: Edward H. Baxter, Hon. Dennis DeConcini, John M. Haddow, Scott D. Hatch, Shannon Davis Henderson, Jack W. Martin, Romano Romani, Linda Arey Skladany, Hon. Steven D. Symms

Internat'l Dairy Foods Ass'n

Jones, Day, Reavis & Pogue

Katten Muchin & Zavis
Issues: BAN
Rep By: Edward H. Baxter, Hon. Dennis DeConcini, John M. Haddow, Scott D. Hatch, Shannon Davis Henderson, Jack W. Martin, Romano Romani, Linda Arey Skladany, Hon. Steven D. Symms

Motion Picture Ass'n of America
Issues: ART COM CON CPT TAX TRD
Rep By: Edward H. Baxter, Hon. Dennis DeConcini, John M. Haddow, Scott D. Hatch, Shannon Davis Henderson, Jack W. Martin, Romano Romani, Linda Arey Skladany, Hon. Steven D. Symms

Nat'l Air Cargo, Inc.
Issues: DEF
Rep By: Edward H. Baxter, Hon. Dennis DeConcini, John M. Haddow, Scott D. Hatch, Shannon Davis Henderson, Jack W. Martin, Romano Romani, Linda Arey Skladany, Hon. Steven D. Symms

Nat'l Nutritional Foods Ass'n
Issues: FOO
Rep By: Edward H. Baxter, Hon. Dennis DeConcini, John M. Haddow, Scott D. Hatch, Shannon Davis Henderson, Jack W. Martin, Romano Romani, Linda Arey Skladany, Hon. Steven D. Symms

Nat'l Retail Federation
Issues: BNK
Rep By: Edward H. Baxter, Hon. Dennis DeConcini, John M. Haddow, Scott D. Hatch, Shannon Davis Henderson, Jack W. Martin, Romano Romani, Linda Arey Skladany, Hon. Steven D. Symms

Nogales, Arizona, City of
Issues: ECN ENV IMM LAW URB
Rep By: Edward H. Baxter, Hon. Dennis DeConcini, John M. Haddow, Scott D. Hatch, Shannon Davis Henderson, Jack W. Martin, Romano Romani, Linda Arey Skladany, Hon. Steven D. Symms

Nu Skin Internat'l Inc.
Issues: ADV FOO
Rep By: Edward H. Baxter, Hon. Dennis DeConcini, John M. Haddow, Scott D. Hatch, Shannon Davis Henderson, Jack W. Martin, Romano Romani, Linda Arey Skladany, Hon. Steven D. Symms

Owens Corning
Issues: TAX
Rep By: Edward H. Baxter, Hon. Dennis DeConcini, John M. Haddow, Scott D. Hatch, Shannon Davis Henderson, Jack W. Martin, Romano Romani, Linda Arey Skladany, Hon. Steven D. Symms

Peoria, Arizona, City of
Issues: EDU ENV LAW RES URB
Rep By: Edward H. Baxter, Hon. Dennis DeConcini, John M. Haddow, Scott D. Hatch, Shannon Davis Henderson, Jack W. Martin, Romano Romani, Linda Arey Skladany, Hon. Steven D. Symms

Pfizer, Inc.
Issues: CPT HCR MED MMM TAX
Rep By: Edward H. Baxter, Hon. Dennis DeConcini, John M. Haddow, Scott D. Hatch, Shannon Davis Henderson, Jack W. Martin, Romano Romani, Linda Arey Skladany, Hon. Steven D. Symms

Pharmacia Corp.
Issues: CPT HCR MED MMM
Rep By: Edward H. Baxter, Hon. Dennis DeConcini, John M. Haddow, Scott D. Hatch, Shannon Davis Henderson, Jack W. Martin, Romano Romani, Linda Arey Skladany, Hon. Steven D. Symms

Policy Development Group, Inc.
Issues: AGR RES
Rep By: Edward H. Baxter, Hon. Dennis DeConcini, John M. Haddow, Scott D. Hatch, Shannon Davis Henderson, Jack W. Martin, Romano Romani, Linda Arey Skladany, Hon. Steven D. Symms

Project to Promote Competition and Innovation in the Digital Age
Issues: CPT LBR TEC
Rep By: Edward H. Baxter, Hon. Dennis DeConcini, John M. Haddow, Scott D. Hatch, Shannon Davis Henderson, Jack W. Martin, Romano Romani, Linda Arey Skladany, Hon. Steven D. Symms

Research & Development Laboratories
Issues: DEF SCI
Rep By: Edward H. Baxter, Hon. Dennis DeConcini, John M. Haddow, Scott D. Hatch, Shannon Davis Henderson, Jack W. Martin, Romano Romani, Linda Arey Skladany, Hon. Steven D. Symms

Research Corp. Technology
Issues: CPT
Rep By: Edward H. Baxter, Hon. Dennis DeConcini, John M. Haddow, Scott D. Hatch, Shannon Davis Henderson, Jack W. Martin, Romano Romani, Linda Arey Skladany, Hon. Steven D. Symms

Rexall Sundown
Issues: ADV FOO
Rep By: Edward H. Baxter, Hon. Dennis DeConcini, John M. Haddow, Scott D. Hatch, Shannon Davis Henderson, Jack W. Martin, Romano Romani, Linda Arey Skladany, Hon. Steven D. Symms

Rock Creek Psychiatric Hospital

SBC Communications Inc.
Issues: LBR TEC
Rep By: Edward H. Baxter, Hon. Dennis DeConcini, John M. Haddow, Scott D. Hatch, Shannon Davis Henderson, Jack W. Martin, Romano Romani, Linda Arey Skladany, Hon. Steven D. Symms

Schering-Plough Corp.

SOL Source Technologies, Inc.
Issues: ADV FOO
Rep By: Edward H. Baxter, Hon. Dennis DeConcini, John M. Haddow, Scott D. Hatch, Shannon Davis Henderson, Jack W. Martin, Romano Romani, Linda Arey Skladany, Hon. Steven D. Symms

Styrene Information and Research Center
Issues: ENV MAN
Rep By: Edward H. Baxter, Hon. Dennis DeConcini, John M. Haddow, Scott D. Hatch, Shannon Davis Henderson, Jack W. Martin, Romano Romani, Linda Arey Skladany, Hon. Steven D. Symms

Sullivan & Cromwell
Issues: BAN FIN

Taxpayers Against Fraud, The False Claims Legal Center
Issues: GOV LAW
Rep By: Edward H. Baxter, Hon. Dennis DeConcini, John M. Haddow, Scott D. Hatch, Shannon Davis Henderson, Jack W. Martin, Romano Romani, Linda Arey Skladany, Hon. Steven D. Symms

TCOM, L.P.
Rep By: Edward H. Baxter, Hon. Dennis DeConcini, John M. Haddow, Scott D. Hatch, Shannon Davis Henderson, Jack W. Martin, Romano Romani, Linda Arey Skladany, Hon. Steven D. Symms

Twin Laboratories, Inc.

Unilever United States, Inc.
Issues: AGR CSP DEF ENV FOO TRD
Rep By: Edward H. Baxter, Hon. Dennis DeConcini, John M. Haddow, Scott D. Hatch, Shannon Davis Henderson, Jack W. Martin, Romano Romani, Linda Arey Skladany, Hon. Steven D. Symms

Utah Natural Products Alliance
Issues: FOO
Rep By: Edward H. Baxter, Hon. Dennis DeConcini, John M. Haddow, Scott D. Hatch, Shannon Davis Henderson, Jack W. Martin, Romano Romani, Linda Arey Skladany, Hon. Steven D. Symms

Watson Pharmaceuticals, Inc.

Jim Pasco & Associates

309 Massachusetts Ave. NE
Washington, DC 20002
Tel: (202)547-8189
Fax: (202)547-8190
Registered: LDA

DC-Area Employees Representing Listed Clients
PASCO, Jr., James O.

Clients

Computer Associates Internat'l
Rep By: James O. Pasco, Jr.

Miller Brewing Co.
Issues: BEV
Rep By: James O. Pasco, Jr.

Nat'l Air Cargo, Inc.
Issues: TRA
Rep By: James O. Pasco, Jr.

Philip Morris Management Corp.
Issues: BEV FOO TOB
Rep By: James O. Pasco, Jr.

Sony Music Entertainment Inc.
Issues: CPT
Rep By: James O. Pasco, Jr.

Patton Boggs, LLP

2550 M St. NW
Washington, DC 20037-1350
Tel: (202)457-6000
Fax: (202)457-6315
Registered: LDA, FARA

Web: www.pattonboggs.com
E-mail: info@pattonboggs.com
A general practice law firm.

DC-Area Employees Representing Listed Clients
ABERNATHY, John
ADDISON, Daniel R., Partner
ANDERSON, Todd, Associate
ANDREW, Anne Slaughter, Partner
ARBUCKLE, J. Gordon, Partner
AUSTIN, Jr., John, Of Counsel
BALTZAN, Elizabeth, Associate
BANGERT, Philip A., Partner
BERNARD, Michelle D., Partner
BESOZZI, Paul C., Partner
BLOOMQUIST, Michael D., Associate
BOGGS, Jr., Thomas Hale, Chair, Executive Committee
BOYCE, Katharine R., Partner
BRAMS, Robert S., Partner
BRAND, Joseph L., Partner
BRIGHT, Bill, Legislative Specialist
BROWN, Michael A., International Trade and Public Policy Specialist
BRUGGE, Parker, Partner
CAMP, John C., Senior Counsel
CHAJET, Henry, Partner
CHORBA, Timothy A., Partner
CHRISTIAN, Jr., James B., Partner
COLE, Elliott H., Partner
COWAN, Mark D., Partner
CURTO, Michael A., Partner
DAVINE, Amy C., Associate
DAVIS, Geoffrey G., Partner
DAVIS, Lanny J., Partner
DESCHAUER, Jr., John J., Partner
DILLEY, Dean M., Partner
DINO, Michael, Policy Analyst
DOWNS, Thomas C., Associate
DRIVER, Michael J., Partner
DUNN, III, David E., Partner
EICHBERG, Ross E., Partner
FARBER, David J., Partner
FARTHING, Penelope S., Partner
FITHIAN, John F., Partner
GARRETT, John C., Defense Systems Consultant
GAVIN, Stephen Diaz, Partner
GIBERGA, Elena, Legislative Specialist
GIBSON, Shannon M., Legislative Affairs Specialist
GINSBERG, Benjamin L., Partner
GOLDSTEIN, Jennifer, Associate
GRADISON, Hon. Willis "Bill" D., Senior Public Policy Counselor
GRIGG, Kenneth A., Partner
HENDRIX, R. Brian, Associate
HETTINGER, Michael, Public Policy Counselor
HOOG, Michael, Associate
HOUGH, Clayton L., Partner
JOHNSON, Hon. C. Donald "Don", Partner
JONAS, John F., Partner
JONES, Robert C., Partner
KAPLAN, Philip S., Partner
KENDRICK, Martha M., Partner
KIM, Harold, Associate
KLAUSNER, Joseph A., Of Counsel
KOEHLER, Robert H., Partner
KRACOV, Daniel A., Partner
KUWANA, Eric A., Partner
LABOSCHIN, Debra, Associate
LAUGHLIN, Hon. Greg H., Of Counsel
LEE, III, Lansing B., Of Counsel
LIEBMAN, Ronald S., Partner
LOPINA, Brian C., Of Counsel
MARANGI, Karen L., Legislative Specialist
MARTIN, John C., Partner
MASSA, III, Cliff, Partner
MATHIASCHECK, Susan, Partner
MAY, Timothy J., Partner
MCDOWELL, G. Kendrick, Partner
MCGAHN, II, Donald F., Associate
MEANS, Kathleen, Senior Health Policy Advisor
MEDEROS, Carolina L., Transportation Consultant
MIANO, Anne, Counsel
MILLS, Timothy B., Partner
MOOREHEAD, Donald V., Partner
MORRIS, Jon Paul, Associate
MURRAY, Nancy A., Of Counsel
NARDOTTI, Michael J., Partner
NEWBERRY, Edward J., Partner
NIRENBERG, Darryl D., Partner
NORMAN, III, W. Caffey, Partner
O'DONNELL, Thomas P., Of Counsel
O'HARA, Marie "Mimi", Legislative Affairs Specialist
OBERDORFER, John L., Partner
PAPE, Stuart M., Managing Partner
PEARLMAN, Donald H., Partner
PETERS, Stephanie J., Associate
PHILLIPS, Charles M., Associate
PRIOLEAU, Florence W., Partner
RABOY, David G., Chief Economic Consultant
RANDLE, Russell V., Partner
RASSMUSSEN, Garrett G., Partner
REEDER, James A., Partner
RING, Elizabeth E., Associate
ROBERTSON, Peter D., Partner
ROSENBERG, Andrew M., Associate
ROTHROCK, III, Aubrey A., Partner
RUBIN, Paul, Partner
SAMOLIS, Frank R., Partner
SAVIT, Mark N., Partner
SCHAENGOLD, Michael J., Partner
SCHETTEWI, Jennifer B., Associate
SCHMITZ, Joseph E., Partner
SCHNEEBAUM, Steven M., Partner
SCHUTZER, George J., Partner
SHAW, John S., Associate
SILER, Duane A., Partner
SLATER, Rodney, Partner
SMITH, Jeffrey T., Partner
SPOKES, Jennifer J., Associate
STUART, III, James R., Partner
TALISMAN, Charles E., Partner
TAYLOR, Robert K., Partner
THORNTON, Leslie T., Partner, Public Policy
TODD, David C., Partner
TRAPASSO, Joseph, Partner
TURNER, Jeffrey L., Partner
TUTTLE, Alan A., Partner
VANDERVER, Jr., Timothy A., Partner
VANISON, Denise, Partner
VELLA, Elizabeth C., Associate
VOGEL, John H., Partner
WADE, J. Kirk, Partner
WALDEN, Gregory S.
WALTZ, Daniel E., Partner
WILLIS, JoAnn V., Senior Health Policy Advisor
WILSON, Paul A. J., Partner
WISNER, Graham G.
WOOD, Benjamin
YAROWSKY, Jonathan R., Partner

Clients

500 C Street Associates, L.P.
Issues: BUD DOC RES
Rep By: Robert C. Jones

Aera Energy LLC
Issues: FUE
Rep By: Thomas Hale Boggs, Jr., Donald V. Moorehead, James A. Reeder

African Coalition for Trade, Inc.
Issues: APP TRD
Rep By: Thomas Hale Boggs, Jr., Elena Giberga, Lansing B. Lee, III, Frank R. Samolis

Air Force Memorial Foundation
Issues: RES
Rep By: John J. Deschauer, Jr., Benjamin L. Ginsberg

AKZO Aramid Products Inc.
Rep By: Henry Chajet, Mark N. Savit

Alcatel
Issues: FOR
Rep By: Thomas Hale Boggs, Jr., Jeffrey L. Turner, Graham G. Wisner

Alliance of Catholic Health Care Systems
Issues: MMM
Rep By: Hon. Willis "Bill" D. Gradison

America's Blood Centers
Issues: HCR MMM
Rep By: Martha M. Kendrick

American Advertising Federation
Issues: ADV BEV TOB
Rep By: Thomas Hale Boggs, Jr., Penelope S. Farthing, Elena Giberga, Thomas P. O'Donnell

American Ass'n of Advertising Agencies
Issues: ADV
Rep By: Thomas Hale Boggs, Jr., Penelope S. Farthing, John F. Fithian, Elena Giberga

American College of Gastroenterology
Issues: HCR MMM
Rep By: John F. Jonas, Martha M. Kendrick, Elizabeth E. Ring, JoAnn V. Willis

American Committee for Peace and Justice in South Asia
Issues: FOR
Rep By: Katharine R. Boyce, Lanny J. Davis

American Family Mutual Insurance Co.
Issues: TAX
Rep By: John F. Jonas, Elizabeth E. Ring, Elizabeth C. Vella

American Feed Industry Ass'n
Issues: AGR
Rep By: Clayton L. Hough

American Insurance Ass'n
Rep By: Benjamin L. Ginsberg

American Management
Issues: TEC
Rep By: Darryl D. Nirenberg

American Medical Rehabilitation Providers Ass'n
Issues: MMM
Rep By: John F. Jonas, Martha M. Kendrick, Elizabeth E. Ring, JoAnn V. Willis

American Medical Security
Rep By: Martha M. Kendrick

American Soc. of Safety Engineers
Issues: LBR
Rep By: Parker Brugge

American Trans Air
Issues: AVI
Rep By: Thomas Hale Boggs, Jr., Michael A. Brown, Joseph E. Schmitz

AOL Time Warner
Issues: TEC TRD
Rep By: Thomas Hale Boggs, Jr., Elena Giberga, Karen L. Marangi, Frank R. Samolis, Jeffrey L. Turner, Jonathan R. Yarowsky

APL Limited
Issues: MAR TRA
Rep By: Philip A. Bangert, Jeffrey L. Turner

Ass'n for Advanced Life Underwriting
Issues: TAX
Rep By: John F. Jonas

Ass'n of Nat'l Advertisers
Issues: ADV BEV TOB
Rep By: Thomas Hale Boggs, Jr., Penelope S. Farthing, John F. Fithian, Elena Giberga

Ass'n of Trial Lawyers of America
Issues: AVI BNK BUD CPI CSP GOV HCR INS TAX TEC TOB TOR TRA
Rep By: Thomas Hale Boggs, Jr., Brian C. Lopina, Karen L. Marangi, Darryl D. Nirenberg, Andrew M. Rosenberg, Jonathan R. Yarowsky

Augusta-Richmond, Georgia, County of
Issues: VET
Rep By: John J. Deschauer, Jr., Lansing B. Lee, III

Austin, Texas, City of
Issues: ENV
Rep By: Parker Brugge, Michael J. Driver

AutoNation, Inc.
Issues: AUT EPA TAX TRA
Rep By: Parker Brugge, Penelope S. Farthing, Donald V. Moorehead, Florence W. Prioleau

Azurix
Issues: WAS
Rep By: Michael A. Brown

Baltimore Symphony Orchestra
Issues: BUD
Rep By: Shannon M. Gibson, Robert C. Jones, Elizabeth C. Vella

Barat College
Issues: BUD
Rep By: Robert C. Jones

Barringer Technologies
Issues: AVI LAW
Rep By: James B. Christian, Jr., Darryl D. Nirenberg, Aubrey A. Rothrock, III

Beauty and Barber Supply Industries, Inc.
Issues: CPT
Rep By: Lanny J. Davis, Clayton L. Hough

Benin, Government of the Republic of

BET Holdings II, Inc.
Issues: TEC TEL
Rep By: Stephen Diaz Gavin

BNFL, Inc.
Issues: CAW GOV
Rep By: Thomas Hale Boggs, Jr., Thomas C. Downs, Michael J. Driver

Brink's Inc.
Issues: TRD
Rep By: David J. Farber

Bristol-Myers Squibb Co.
Issues: HCR
Rep By: Thomas Hale Boggs, Jr., Hon. Willis "Bill" D. Gradison, John F. Jonas, Stuart M. Pape

Broe Companies, Inc.
Issues: RRR
Rep By: Michael J. Driver

Business Insurance Coalition
Issues: TAX
Rep By: John F. Jonas

California Restaurant Ass'n

Cambridge Technologies
Issues: BUD DEF
Rep By: Robert C. Jones

Cellular Telecommunications and Internet Ass'n
Issues: BUD TEC
Rep By: Robert C. Jones

Central American Bank of Economic Integration

Chesapeake Bay Foundation
Issues: ENV NAT
Rep By: Parker Brugge, R. Brian Hendrix

Cincinnati, Ohio, City of
Issues: AVI BUD EDU HOU LBR POS RES TAX TOU TRA URB
Rep By: Shannon M. Gibson, Hon. Willis "Bill" D. Gradison, Florence W. Prioleau

The Climate Council,
Issues: BUD DEF ECN ENG ENV FOR NAT SCI UTI
Rep By: Donald H. Pearlman

The Clorox Co.
Issues: CAW ENV HOU
Rep By: Florence W. Prioleau

Coalition for Electronic Commerce
Issues: DEF
Rep By: John J. Deschauer, Jr., Edward J. Newberry

Coalition for Fair Competition in Rural Markets
Issues: ENG
Rep By: Brian C. Lopina, Edward J. Newberry

Coalition to Preserve Mine Safety Standards
Issues: LBR
Rep By: Henry Chajet, Brian C. Lopina

Ronald J. Cohen Investments
Issues: BUD DOC RES
Rep By: Brian C. Lopina

College Savings Bank
Rep By: James B. Christian, Jr., George J. Schutzer

Commco, L.L.C.
Rep By: Paul C. Besozzi, Thomas Hale Boggs, Jr., Penelope S. Farthing, John F. Fithian, Stephen Diaz Gavin, Benjamin L. Ginsberg

Condor-Pacific Industries
Issues: DEF TRD
Rep By: James B. Christian, Jr., Darryl D. Nirenberg, Daniel E. Waltz

L. P. Conwood Co.
Issues: TAX TOB
Rep By: Thomas Hale Boggs, Jr., James B. Christian, Jr., Darryl D. Nirenberg, Stuart M. Pape

Corning Inc.
Issues: TEC
Rep By: James B. Christian, Jr.

Crane Co.
Issues: DEF LBR
Rep By: Todd Anderson, Lanny J. Davis, John J. Deschauer, Jr., Penelope S. Farthing, Clayton L. Hough, Hon. Greg H. Laughlin, Michael J. Nardotti, Garrett G. Rassmussen, Jonathan R. Yarowsky

Denver Regional Transportation District
Issues: TRA
Rep By: Philip A. Bangert, Anne Miano, Edward J. Newberry

Detroit, Michigan, Public School System of the County of
Issues: EDU
Rep By: Michael A. Brown

DFS Group Ltd.
Issues: BUD TOB TOU TRD
Rep By: Elizabeth Baltzan, Thomas Hale Boggs, Jr., Elena Giberga, Edward J. Newberry, Stuart M. Pape, Frank R. Samolis, Denise Vanison, Jonathan R. Yarowsky

Dictaphone Corp.
Issues: CPI GOV HCR
Rep By: Amy C. Davine, Lanny J. Davis, Clayton L. Hough, Karen L. Marangi

Dimensions Internat'l
Issues: AVI
Rep By: John J. Deschauer, Jr., Edward J. Newberry

Direct Marketing Ass'n, Inc.
Issues: TAX
Rep By: Thomas Hale Boggs, Jr., Brian C. Lopina, Cliff Massa, III

Discovery Place, Inc. (Charlotte Science Museum)
Issues: BUD
Rep By: Lansing B. Lee, III, Darryl D. Nirenberg, Elizabeth C. Vella

Dole Food Co.
Issues: HCR TRD
Rep By: Thomas Hale Boggs, Jr., Hon. Greg H. Laughlin, David G. Raboy, Frank R. Samolis

Dredging Contractors of America
Issues: ENV TRA
Rep By: Philip A. Bangert

drugstore.com
Issues: CPI HCR PHA
Rep By: Daniel A. Kracov, Stuart M. Pape, Florence W. Prioleau

Eagle-Picher Industries
Issues: TRA
Rep By: Eric A. Kuwana

EchoStar Communications Corp.
Issues: COM TEC
Rep By: Bill Bright, Elena Giberga, Clayton L. Hough, John S. Shaw, Jonathan R. Yarowsky

Electro Design Manufacturing, Inc.
Issues: DEF
Rep By: Darryl D. Nirenberg

European Energy Company Coalition
Rep By: Thomas Hale Boggs, Jr., Jeffrey L. Turner

Farmland Industries, Inc.
Issues: TRD
Rep By: Brian C. Lopina, Daniel E. Waltz

Federal Communications Bar Ass'n
Issues: RES
Rep By: Edward J. Newberry

First Flight Centennial Foundation
Issues: AVI

FM Watch
Rep By: Thomas Hale Boggs, Jr., Donald V. Moorehead

FMC Wyoming Corp.
Issues: LBR
Rep By: Henry Chajet

Forethought Group/Forethought Life Insurance Co.
Issues: INS TAX
Rep By: John F. Jonas, Martha M. Kendrick, Elizabeth E. Ring

Frederick Douglass Gardens, Inc.
Issues: NAT
Rep By: Thomas C. Downs

General Aviation Manufacturers Ass'n
Issues: BUD
Rep By: Robert C. Jones

General Chemical Corp.
Issues: LBR
Rep By: Henry Chajet

General Mills
Issues: FOO
Rep By: Stuart M. Pape

Genome Dynamics, Inc.
Issues: BUD
Rep By: Robert C. Jones

George Mason University Foundation
Issues: BUD
Rep By: Edward J. Newberry

Gilbarco, Inc.
Issues: TRD
Rep By: Darryl D. Nirenberg, Frank R. Samolis

GovWorks.com
Issues: GOV TEC
Rep By: Michael A. Brown

W. R. Grace & Co.
Issues: ENV
Rep By: Parker Brugge, Peter D. Robertson

Grocery Manufacturers of America
Rep By: Stuart M. Pape

H.A.H. of Wisconsin L.P.
Issues: GAM
Rep By: Philip A. Bangert, Thomas Hale Boggs, Jr., Katharine R. Boyce, Brian C. Lopina, James A. Reeder

Halogenated Solvents Industry Alliance
Issues: CHM
Rep By: W. Caffey Norman, III

Hankin, Persson & Darnell
Issues: AVI
Rep By: Carolina L. Mederos

HCR-Manor Care, Inc.
Issues: BUD MMM
Rep By: John F. Jonas, Martha M. Kendrick, Elizabeth E. Ring, JoAnn V. Willis

Alan Hilburg & Associates
Issues: LBR
Rep By: James B. Christian, Jr., Donald V. Moorehead, John S. Shaw

Hitachi Home Electronics, Inc.
Issues: CPT
Rep By: Thomas Hale Boggs, Jr., Jeffrey L. Turner

Hoffmann-La Roche Inc.
Issues: HCR MED MMM PHA
Rep By: John F. Jonas, Martha M. Kendrick, Daniel A. Kracov, Stuart M. Pape, JoAnn V. Willis

Homestake Mining
Rep By: Henry Chajet, John C. Martin, Mark N. Savit

Houston, Texas, City of
Issues: BUD ENV HOU TRA URB
Rep By: Parker Brugge, Shannon M. Gibson, Carolina L. Mederos, Florence W. Prioleau

I-69 Mid-Continent Highway Coalition
Issues: TRA
Rep By: Carolina L. Mederos

IIT Research Institute
Issues: DEF
Rep By: John J. Deschauer, Jr.

Illinois Department of Human Services
Issues: AGR ALC BMD FAM GOV HCR MED MMM SCI WEL
Rep By: Shannon M. Gibson, Hon. Willis "Bill" D. Gradison, John F. Jonas, Martha M. Kendrick, Debra Laboschin, Edward J. Newberry, Andrew M. Rosenberg

Information Technology Ass'n of America (ITAA)
Issues: IMM LBR
Rep By: Darryl D. Nirenberg, Jonathan R. Yarowsky

Intercultural Cancer Council
Issues: HCR
Rep By: Katharine R. Boyce, Martha M. Kendrick

Internat'l Olympic Committee
Issues: LAW SPO TRA
Rep By: Joseph Trapasso

Internat'l Swaps and Derivatives Dealers Ass'n
Issues: FIN
Rep By: Thomas Hale Boggs, Jr., Donald V. Moorehead, Edward J. Newberry, Aubrey A. Rothrock, III

Internet Safety Ass'n
Issues: CPI CSP
Rep By: Mark D. Cowan, Michael Hettinger, Brian C. Lopina, Jeffrey L. Turner

IVIDCO, LLC
Issues: TEC
Rep By: Stephen Diaz Gavin, John S. Shaw

Jacksonville, Florida, City of
Issues: DIS ECN ENV HOU NAT TOU TRA
Rep By: Thomas C. Downs, Benjamin L. Ginsberg, Edward J. Newberry

James Hardie Building Products Inc.
Issues: HCR LBR
Rep By: James B. Christian, Jr., David J. Farber, Hon. Greg H. Laughlin, Joseph Trapasso

Kaiser Aluminum & Chemical Corp.
Issues: LBR
Rep By: Donald V. Moorehead

Kansas City Southern Industries
Issues: BUD RRR TRA
Rep By: Robert C. Jones

Kickapoo Tribe of Oklahoma
Issues: IND
Rep By: Katharine R. Boyce

LA 1 Coalition
Issues: TRA
Rep By: Philip A. Bangert, James A. Reeder

Lancaster, California, City of
Issues: ENV TRA
Rep By: Philip A. Bangert

Laquidara & Edwards, P.A.
Issues: TRA
Rep By: Edward J. Newberry

The Limited Inc.
Rep By: Penelope S. Farthing, Lansing B. Lee, III, Nancy A. Murray

LOOP, Inc.
Rep By: Philip A. Bangert, James B. Christian, Jr., Daniel E. Waltz

Magazine Publishers of America
Issues: ADV BEV CON TAX TOB
Rep By: Thomas Hale Boggs, Jr., Penelope S. Farthing

Magnificent Research Inc.
Rep By: Parker Brugge, Paul A. J. Wilson

Major League Baseball Players Ass'n
Issues: GAM SPO
Rep By: John F. Fithian, Elena Giberga, Aubrey A. Rothrock, III

Mannesmann VDO
Rep By: Carolina L. Mederos, Edward J. Newberry

Mars, Inc.
Rep By: Thomas Hale Boggs, Jr., Michael A. Curto, David E. Dunn, III, John F. Fithian, Kenneth A. Grigg, Clayton L. Hough, John F. Jonas, Martha M. Kendrick, Lansing B. Lee, III, Cliff Massa, III, Donald V. Moorehead, Darryl D. Nirenberg, Stuart M. Pape, David G. Raboy, Aubrey A. Rothrock, III, Frank R. Samolis, Steven M. Schneebaum

Martin Marietta Aggregates
Rep By: Henry Chajet, Mark N. Savit

Massachusetts Maritime Academy
Issues: APP BUD
Rep By: Robert C. Jones

MassMutual Financial Group
Issues: BNK FIN RET TAX
Rep By: John F. Jonas

Matsushita Electric Corp. of America
Issues: CPT
Rep By: Thomas Hale Boggs, Jr., Brian C. Lopina, Jeffrey L. Turner

MCI WorldCom Corp.
Issues: TEC
Rep By: Thomas Hale Boggs, Jr., James B. Christian, Jr., John J. Deschauer, Jr., Penelope S. Farthing, John F. Fithian, Elena Giberga, Robert C. Jones, Donald F. McGahn, II

McKinsey & Co., Inc.
Issues: IMM
Rep By: Hon. Greg H. Laughlin, Thomas P. O'Donnell, Jonathan R. Yarowsky

Medical Device Manufacturers Ass'n
Issues: MED
Rep By: Andrew M. Rosenberg, Jonathan R. Yarowsky

Methane Awareness Resource Group
Issues: LBR
Rep By: Henry Chajet

Midcoast Interstate Transmission, Inc.
Issues: ENV FUE
Rep By: Philip A. Bangert, Thomas Hale Boggs, Jr., Michael A. Brown, James A. Reeder

Minimed, Inc.
Issues: MED
Rep By: John F. Jonas, Eric A. Kuwana, Aubrey A. Rothrock, III, JoAnn V. Willis

Mitsubishi Electronics America (Consumer Electronics Group)
Issues: CPT
Rep By: Thomas Hale Boggs, Jr., Brian C. Lopina, Jeffrey L. Turner

Morton Internat'l
Issues: LBR
Rep By: Henry Chajet

G. Murphy Trading
Issues: TRD
Rep By: Hon. Greg H. Laughlin, Darryl D. Nirenberg, Joseph Trapasso

Mutual Legislative Committee
Issues: INS TAX
Rep By: John F. Jonas

Nassau Broadcasting Inc.
Issues: TEC
Rep By: Stephen Diaz Gavin, John S. Shaw

Nat'l Aquarium
Issues: BUD
Rep By: Robert C. Jones, Elizabeth C. Vella

Nat'l Ass'n of Consumer Bankruptcy Attorneys
Issues: BNK
Rep By: Darryl D. Nirenberg, Jonathan R. Yarowsky

Nat'l Ass'n of Theatre Owners
Issues: ART LBR TRD
Rep By: John F. Fithian, Elena Giberga, Frank R. Samolis

Nat'l Ass'n of Uniform Manufacturers and Distributors
Issues: GOV MAN POS
Rep By: Thomas C. Downs

Nat'l Automatic Merchandising Ass'n
Rep By: Thomas Hale Boggs, Jr.

Nat'l Cable Television Ass'n
Issues: COM
Rep By: Thomas Hale Boggs, Jr.

Nat'l Center for Manufacturing Sciences
Issues: BUD MAN
Rep By: Daniel R. Addison, J. Gordon Arbuckle, Thomas Hale Boggs, Jr., John J. Deschauer, Jr., Edward J. Newberry

Nat'l Community Pharmacists Ass'n
Issues: PHA
Rep By: Jonathan R. Yarowsky

Nat'l Family Caregivers Ass'n

Nat'l Marrow Donor Program
Issues: BUD HCR
Rep By: Martha M. Kendrick, JoAnn V. Willis

Nat'l Oilheat Research Alliance (NORA)
Issues: FUE
Rep By: Thomas C. Downs, Elena Giberga, Edward J. Newberry, Elizabeth C. Vella

Nat'l Retail Federation
Rep By: Frank R. Samolis

Nat'l Soft Drink Ass'n
Issues: TRD
Rep By: Darryl D. Nirenberg, Stuart M. Pape, Daniel E. Waltz

Nat'l Stroke Ass'n
Issues: HCR MED
Rep By: Penelope S. Farthing, Hon. Willis "Bill" D. Gradison, Florence W. Prioleau

Nat'l Yogurt Ass'n
Rep By: Stuart M. Pape

Navajo Refining Co.

New York Life Insurance Co.
Issues: BAN INS RET TAX TRD
Rep By: John F. Jonas

New York State Ass'n of Health Care Providers
Issues: INS MMM
Rep By: John F. Jonas, Martha M. Kendrick, JoAnn V. Willis

New York State Department of Transportation
Issues: TRA
Rep By: Anne Miano

New York State Metropolitan Transportation Authority
Issues: TRA
Rep By: Anne Miano

New York State Thruway Authority
Issues: TRA
Rep By: Anne Miano

Newport Group
Issues: TAX
Rep By: John F. Jonas

Newspaper Ass'n of America
Rep By: Thomas Hale Boggs, Jr., John F. Jonas

Northwestern Mutual Life Insurance Co.
Issues: BAN BNK FIN INS RET TAX
Rep By: John F. Jonas

Oakland, California, Port of
Issues: TRA
Rep By: Philip A. Bangert

OCI Wyoming
Issues: LBR
Rep By: Henry Chajet

Oman, Sultanate of

The Pacific Lumber Co.
Issues: NAT
Rep By: Thomas Hale Boggs, Jr., Aubrey A. Rothrock, III

Pakistan, Embassy of the Islamic Republic of
Rep By: Katharine R. Boyce, John J. Deschauer, Jr.

Pakistan, Government of the Islamic Republic of
Rep By: Lanny J. Davis

Paraguay, Secretariat for Planning of the Republic of

Patient Access to Transplantation (PAT) Coalition
Issues: BUD HCR MMM
Rep By: John F. Jonas, Martha M. Kendrick, Elizabeth E. Ring, JoAnn V. Willis

Pechanga Band of California Luiseno Indians
Issues: GAM IND
Rep By: Katharine R. Boyce, Lanny J. Davis, Clayton L. Hough, Carolina L. Mederos, Jonathan R. Yarowsky

Pentachlorophenol Task Force
Issues: CHM
Rep By: Daniel R. Addison

Peru, Government of the Republic of

Pharmanex
Issues: FOO
Rep By: Daniel A. Kracov, Stuart M. Pape

Philippines, Department of Trade and Industry of the Republic of
Rep By: Philip S. Kaplan

Philippines, Government of the Republic of

Pioneer of North America
Issues: CPT
Rep By: Thomas Hale Boggs, Jr., Brian C. Lopina, Jeffrey L. Turner

Point of Purchase Advertising Institute
Issues: ADV BEV TOB
Rep By: Thomas Hale Boggs, Jr., Penelope S. Farthing, John F. Fithian, Elena Giberga, Darryl D. Nirenberg, Thomas P. O'Donnell, James A. Reeder

Potomac Heritage Partnership
Issues: NAT TOU
Rep By: Parker Brugge, Thomas C. Downs

Preneed Insurers Government Programs Coalition
Issues: INS
Rep By: John F. Jonas, Martha M. Kendrick, Elizabeth E. Ring

Prince George's, Maryland, County of
Rep By: Michael A. Brown

Professional Beauty Federation PAC
Issues: EDU
Rep By: Brian C. Lopina

Qatar, Embassy of

Qatar, Government of the State of
Rep By: David E. Dunn, III

QSP Inc.
Issues: EDU
Rep By: Hon. Greg H. Laughlin, Darryl D. Nirenberg, Joseph Trapasso

Retractable Technologies, Inc.
Issues: CSP HCR MED
Rep By: Karen L. Marangi, Andrew M. Rosenberg, Jonathan R. Yarowsky

Rock of Ages Corp.
Rep By: Henry Chajet, David J. Farber

Roizman & Cos.
Issues: HOU
Rep By: Thomas P. O'Donnell, Joseph Trapasso

Salt Lake City Olympic Organizing Committee
Issues: BUD ENV HOU LAW MON SPO TEC TRA
Rep By: Joseph Trapasso

Salton, Inc.
Issues: CSP
Rep By: Jennifer Goldstein, Daniel A. Kracov, Brian C. Lopina, Paul Rubin

San Bernardino Valley Municipal Water District
Issues: ENV
Rep By: Daniel R. Addison, Thomas C. Downs, Russell V. Randle

San Bernardino, California, City of
Rep By: Daniel R. Addison, Thomas C. Downs, Russell V. Randle

Sanyo North American Corp.
Issues: CPT
Rep By: Thomas Hale Boggs, Jr., Brian C. Lopina, Jeffrey L. Turner

Save Barton Creek
Issues: ENV
Rep By: Parker Brugge, John J. Deschauer, Jr., Thomas C. Downs, Michael J. Driver, Benjamin L. Ginsberg, John C. Martin, Carolina L. Mederos, Anne Miano, James A. Reeder, Paul A. J. Wilson

Schering-Plough Corp.
Issues: HCR
Rep By: Hon. Willis "Bill" D. Gradison

Schoenke & Associates
Rep By: John F. Jonas

Security Capital Group
Issues: TAX
Rep By: Benjamin L. Ginsberg, Donald V. Moorehead, Darryl D. Nirenberg, Aubrey A. Rothrock, III

Sharp Electronics Corp.
Issues: CPT
Rep By: Thomas Hale Boggs, Jr., Brian C. Lopina, Jeffrey L. Turner

Shell Oil Co.
Issues: FUE
Rep By: Thomas Hale Boggs, Jr., Donald V. Moorehead

Sheriff Jefferson Parrish, Louisiana
Issues: BUD LAW
Rep By: Robert C. Jones, Elizabeth C. Vella

Shreveport, Louisiana, City of
Issues: BUD TRA URB
Rep By: Carolina L. Mederos, Edward J. Newberry

Sierra Military Health Services, Inc.
Issues: DEF
Rep By: Thomas Hale Boggs, Jr., John J. Deschauer, Jr., Shannon M. Gibson, Robert H. Koehler, Stuart M. Pape, Florence W. Prioleau

The Charles E. Smith Companies
Issues: RES
Rep By: Thomas Hale Boggs, Jr., John J. Deschauer, Jr., Brian C. Lopina, Edward J. Newberry

Solvay Minerals
Issues: LBR
Rep By: Henry Chajet

Sony Electronics, Inc.
Issues: CPT
Rep By: Thomas Hale Boggs, Jr., Brian C. Lopina, Jeffrey L. Turner

South Coast Air Quality Management District

Supra Telecom & Information Systems, Inc.
Issues: TEC
Rep By: Paul C. Besozzi, John F. Fithian

Swan Creek River Confederated Ojibbwa Tribes of Michigan
Issues: IND
Rep By: Thomas Hale Boggs, Jr., Katharine R. Boyce, Harold Kim

Syntroleum Corp.
Issues: FUE
Rep By: John C. Garrett, Jeffrey T. Smith

Teligent, Inc.
Issues: COM TEC
Rep By: Thomas Hale Boggs, Jr.

Tg Soda Ash
Issues: LBR
Rep By: Henry Chajet

Time Domain Corp.
Issues: ENG SCI TEC
Rep By: Paul C. Besozzi, Thomas Hale Boggs, Jr., Jonathan R. Yarowsky

Tip Tax Coalition
Issues: TAX
Rep By: Clayton L. Hough, Brian C. Lopina, George J. Schutzer

Toshiba Consumer Products, Inc.
Issues: CPT
Rep By: Thomas Hale Boggs, Jr., Brian C. Lopina, Jeffrey L. Turner

Travel Industry Ass'n of America
Issues: TOU
Rep By: Thomas Hale Boggs, Jr., Thomas C. Downs, Edward J. Newberry, Jeffrey L. Turner, Elizabeth C. Vella

Tribune Co.
Issues: ART CPT MIA
Rep By: Clayton L. Hough

Unifinancial Internat'l, Inc.
Rep By: Daniel R. Addison

Union Pacific Railroad Co.
Issues: TRA
Rep By: Thomas Hale Boggs, Jr., Lanny J. Davis, Robert C. Jones, Hon. Greg H. Laughlin

United Airlines
Issues: AVI LBR
Rep By: Thomas Hale Boggs, Jr., Hon. Greg H. Laughlin, Jonathan R. Yarowsky

United Defense, L.P.
Rep By: Katharine R. Boyce, John J. Deschauer, Jr.

United States Enrichment Corp.
Issues: TRD
Rep By: Thomas P. O'Donnell, James A. Reeder, Frank R. Samolis

United Technologies Corp.
Issues: ENV
Rep By: Thomas C. Downs, Russell V. Randle

University Medical Associates
Issues: BUD HCR
Rep By: John F. Jonas, Martha M. Kendrick, Elizabeth E. Ring, JoAnn V. Willis

US Airways
Rep By: Thomas Hale Boggs, Jr., Penelope S. Farthing, Donald V. Moorehead

Valley Children's Hospital
Issues: HCR
Rep By: Hon. Willis "Bill" D. Gradison, Martha M. Kendrick, Edward J. Newberry

Venetian Casino Resort, LLC
Issues: AVI COM ENG ENV GAM TAX TRA WAS
Rep By: Donald V. Moorehead

Ventura County Citizens Against Radar Emissions (VCCARE)
Issues: BUD
Rep By: Thomas Hale Boggs, Jr., Elena Giberga, Clayton L. Hough, Lansing B. Lee, III, Edward J. Newberry

Vulcan Materials Co.
Rep By: George J. Schutzer

Wal-Mart Stores, Inc.

Walton Enterprises
Issues: BAN EDU TAX
Rep By: Thomas Hale Boggs, Jr., Donald V. Moorehead, Aubrey A. Rothrock, III

Wam!Net
Issues: SCI
Rep By: Michael J. Driver

Wayne, Michigan, County of
Issues: TRA URB
Rep By: Michael A. Brown, Parker Brugge, John F. Fithian, Martha M. Kendrick, Carolina L. Mederos

Wegmans Food Markets, Inc.
Issues: TAX
Rep By: Donald V. Moorehead, Aubrey A. Rothrock, III

Weider Nutritional Group
Issues: FOO
Rep By: Brian C. Lopina

Westinghouse
Issues: WAS
Rep By: Michael J. Driver

Wheeling Pittsburgh Steel Corp.
Issues: MAN TRD
Rep By: John J. Deschauer, Jr., Elena Giberga, Frank R. Samolis

Wild Alabama
Issues: NAT RES
Rep By: Michael D. Bloomquist, Amy C. Davine, Lanny J. Davis, Susan Mathiascheck, Peter D. Robertson

Paul, Hastings, Janofsky & Walker LLP

1299 Pennsylvania Ave. NW
Tenth Floor
Washington, DC 20004-2400
Tel: (202)508-9500
Fax: (202)508-9700
Registered: LDA, FARA
Web: www.phjw.com
E-mail: info@phjw.com

Washington office of an international law firm headquartered in Los Angeles, CA.

Political Action Committee

Paul, Hastings, Janofsky and Walker Political Action Committee
1299 Pennsylvania Ave. NW
Tenth Floor
Washington, DC 20004-2400
Contact: Ralph B. Everett
Tel: (202)508-9500
Fax: (202)508-9700

DC-Area Employees Representing Listed Clients

BALL, Daniel R., Associate
BARCELLA, Jr., E. Lawrence, Partner
BEHRE, Kirby D., Partner
BURNS, David D., Associate
COLE, Christopher A., Associate
CROWE, Christine Marie, Associate
DAYANIM, Behnam, Associate
DICKSON, R. Bruce, Partner
ELLIOTT, E. Donald, Partner
EVERETT, Ralph B., Partner
FARIA, Wendell M., Of Counsel
FLICKER, Scott M., Partner
HOPE, Judith Richards, Senior Counsel
JOHNSON, Jr., John Griffith, Partner
LIVELY, P. Susan, Associate
LOEB, G. Hamilton, Partner
NORTHROP, Carl W., Partner
PATRIZIA, Charles A., Partner
PERITO, Paul L., Senior Counsel
PLOTKIN, Robert, Of Counsel
POERIO, J. Mark, Of Counsel
RYAN, Bruce D., Partner
TOGNI, Patrick J.
WATCHMAN, Gregory R., Of Counsel
YAMADA, Gerald H., Of Counsel

Clients

Amdahl Corp.
Rep By: Behnam Dayanim, G. Hamilton Loeb

American Trucking Ass'ns
Issues: BUD ROD TAX TRU
Rep By: Ralph B. Everett

Aspirin Foundation of America, Inc.
Rep By: R. Bruce Dickson

Big Dog Sportswear
Rep By: R. Bruce Dickson

Bristol-Myers Squibb Co.
Rep By: R. Bruce Dickson

Canada, Government of
Rep By: G. Hamilton Loeb

CFSBdirect Inc.
Issues: FIN
Rep By: Behnam Dayanim, Ralph B. Everett, Patrick J. Togni

Chamber of Shipping of America
Rep By: Ralph B. Everett

Chlorobenzene Producers Ass'n
Rep By: R. Bruce Dickson, P. Susan Lively

Coalition for Truth in Environmental Marketing Information, Inc.
Rep By: E. Donald Elliott

Cumulus Media, Inc.
Issues: COM
Rep By: Ralph B. Everett, Bruce D. Ryan

FirstEnergy Co.
Rep By: E. Donald Elliott

General Aviation Manufacturers Ass'n
Rep By: Judith Richards Hope

INTELSAT - Internat'l Telecommunications Satellite Organization
Issues: TEC
Rep By: Ralph B. Everett

Kawasaki Motors Corp., USA
Rep By: Scott M. Flicker

The Marine and Fire Insurance Ass'n of Japan, Inc.
Issues: INS TRD
Rep By: Behnam Dayanim, Scott M. Flicker, G. Hamilton Loeb

Mead Johnson Nutritional Group
Rep By: Ralph B. Everett

Meyer Pharmaceuticals
Rep By: R. Bruce Dickson

Norfolk Southern Corp.
Issues: BUD RRR TEC TRA
Rep By: Ralph B. Everett

Pappas Telecasting Cos.
Rep By: John Griffith Johnson, Jr.

Personal Communications Industry Ass'n (PCIA)
Issues: BUD COM TEC
Rep By: Ralph B. Everett

SBC Communications Inc.
Issues: TEC
Rep By: Ralph B. Everett

SCC Communications Corp.
Issues: TEC
Rep By: Ralph B. Everett

Star Tobacco & Pharmaceuticals Inc.
Issues: TOB
Rep By: Paul L. Perito

Tubos de Acero de Mexico, S.A.
Rep By: G. Hamilton Loeb

U.S. Figure Skating Ass'n
Issues: SPO
Rep By: Ralph B. Everett, G. Hamilton Loeb

Union Pacific
Issues: BUD RRR TAX
Rep By: Ralph B. Everett

Paul, Weiss, Rifkind, Wharton & Garrison

1615 L St. NW
Suite 1300
Washington, DC 20036
Tel: (202)223-7300
Fax: (202)223-7420
Registered: LDA, FARA

A law firm specializing in international trade policy and regulation.

DC-Area Employees Representing Listed Clients

FORTUNE, Terence J., Partner
HAMPE, Carl W., Of Counsel
MCAULIFFE SMITH, Kate, Associate
MONTGOMERY, Jr., Robert E., Partner
OLMER, Lionel H., Partner
OLSON, Jeffrey H., Associate
RATIGAN, John
RUDMAN, Hon. Warren B., Partner
SPECTOR, Phillip L., Partner

Clients

Alliance of Motion Picture & Television Producers
Issues: IMM
Rep By: Carl W. Hampe

American Agip MTBE Sales Division
Rep By: Terence J. Fortune

Bouchard Transportation Co.
Rep By: Carl W. Hampe

Commission on Graduates of Foreign Nursing Schools
Issues: IMM
Rep By: Carl W. Hampe, John Ratigan

The Devereux Foundation
Rep By: Carl W. Hampe

Federation of Korean Industries
Rep By: Carl W. Hampe, Lionel H. Olmer, John Ratigan

General Atlantic Service Corp.
Issues: LBR
Rep By: Carl W. Hampe

IBP, Inc.
Issues: IMM
Rep By: Carl W. Hampe

INTELSAT - Internat'l Telecommunications Satellite Organization
Rep By: Carl W. Hampe, Phillip L. Spector

Korea Telecom

Korea, Embassy of

Le Groupe de Soleil
Rep By: Terence J. Fortune

Nat'l Music Publishers' Ass'n
Issues: CPT
Rep By: Carl W. Hampe

SkyBridge, LLC
Issues: COM
Rep By: Jeffrey H. Olson, Phillip L. Spector

SpaceData Internat'l
Issues: TEC
Rep By: Carl W. Hampe

PBN Company

2000 L St. NW
Suite 835
Washington, DC 20006
Tel: (202)466-6210
Fax: (202)466-6205
Registered: FARA
Web: www.pbnco.com
E-mail: pbnwashdc@pbnco.com

DC-Area Employees Representing Listed Clients

NATHANSON, Paul, V. President and Managing Director
NECAR SULMER, Peter, Chairman and Chief Exec. Officer
THURMAN, Susan, President

Clients

Srpska, Government of the Republic of
Rep By: Paul Nathanson

Pearson & Pipkin, Inc.

104 North Carolina Ave. SE
Washington, DC 20003
Tel: (202)547-7177
Registered: LDA, FARA
E-mail: govtrel@aol.com

A government relations, political and issues management firm.

DC-Area Employees Representing Listed Clients

PEARSON, Ronald W., President

Clients

The 60/Plus Ass'n, Inc.
Issues: GOV HCR MMM RET TAX
Rep By: Ronald W. Pearson

Conservative Victory Fund
Rep By: Ronald W. Pearson

Nat'l Research Center for College and University Admissions

Young America's Foundation
Rep By: Ronald W. Pearson

The Kerry S. Pearson LLC

1225 19th St. NW
Suite 825
Washington, DC 20036
Tel: (202)331-7080
Fax: (202)331-7082
Registered: LDA

DC-Area Employees Representing Listed Clients

PEARSON, Mr. Kerry S., Chairman and Chief Exec. Officer
VAUGHAN, Ms. Lauren C., President and Chief Operating Officer

Clients

Doctors Community Healthcare Corp.
Issues: DOC ECN HCR
Rep By: Mr. Kerry S. Pearson

Lee Peckarsky

11408 Stonewood Ln.
Rockville, MD 20852
Tel: (301)468-6965
Registered: LDA

Clients

HomeStreet Bank
Rep By: Lee Peckarsky

Peduzzi Associates, Ltd.

219 N. Washington St.
Alexandria, VA 22314
Tel: (703)836-7990
Fax: (703)836-9739
Registered: LDA
E-mail: pal@pal-aerospace.com

DC-Area Employees Representing Listed Clients

BRACKETT, Rick, Associate
CONNOLLY, Peter C., Associate
DONNELLI, Maury, Associate
ELLIOTT, Paul E., Associate
FERREIRA, Joseph L., Associate
LANGSTON, Ed, Associate
MEADOWS, C. V., Associate
PEDUZZI, Lawrence P., President
PUTNAM, Ronald A., Associate
SMITH, Gordon, Associate
STOHLMAN, Robert, Associate

Clients

Integrated Medical Systems
Issues: AER
Rep By: Paul E. Elliott, Joseph L. Ferreira, C. V. Meadows, Lawrence P. Peduzzi, Ronald A. Putnam

Lord Corp.
Issues: DEF
Rep By: Paul E. Elliott, Joseph L. Ferreira, C. V. Meadows, Lawrence P. Peduzzi, Ronald A. Putnam

Marconi Flight Systems, Inc.
Issues: DEF
Rep By: Paul E. Elliott, Joseph L. Ferreira, C. V. Meadows, Lawrence P. Peduzzi, Ronald A. Putnam

Skyhook Technologies, Inc.
Issues: DEF MAN
Rep By: Paul E. Elliott, Joseph L. Ferreira, C. V. Meadows, Lawrence P. Peduzzi, Ronald A. Putnam

Bradford A. Penney

1201 North Pitt St.
Number 1B
Alexandria, VA 22314
Tel: (703)532-1427
Fax: (703)471-8688
Registered: LDA
E-mail: bpenney@hpwoods.org

Clients

Classroom Publishers Ass'n
Issues: EDU POS
Rep By: Bradford A. Penney

Pepper Hamilton LLP

600 14th St. NW
Suite 500
Washington, DC 20005
Tel: (202)220-1200
Fax: (202)220-1665
Registered: LDA, FARA

DC-Area Employees Representing Listed Clients

CORTESE, Jr., Alfred W., Partner
DORRIS, Gregory, Partner
EVANS, Jr., K. Stewart, Partner
RINKERMAN, Gary, Partner
SHEEHAN, Kenneth, Partner
TECKLER, Martin D., Counsel

Clients

Biotechnology Industry Organization

Florida Department of Health and Rehabilitative Services

Quebec, Canada, Government of the Province of

Perkins Coie LLP

607 14th St. NW
Suite 700
Washington, DC 20005-2011
Tel: (202)628-6600
Fax: (202)434-1690
Registered: LDA, FARA

Washington office of a Seattle law firm specializing in government ethics, election, campaign finance, and lobbying law, as well as international trade regulation, environment and natural resources, antitrust and securities issues, and aviation.

Political Action Committee

Perkins Coie Political Action Committee
607 14th St. NW
Suite 700
Washington, DC 20005-2011
Tel: (202)628-6600
Fax: (202)434-1690
Contact: Guy R. Martin

DC-Area Employees Representing Listed Clients

BAUER, Robert F., Managing Partner
BAUR, Donald C., Partner
FAWCETT, W. H. "Buzz", Partner
HUGHES, Mary Rose, Partner
HUME, John P., Partner
MARTIN, Guy R., Partner
SACILOTTO, Kara, Partner
VAKERICS, Thomas V.
WEINTRAUB, Ellen L., Of Counsel
WILDMAN, Sloane, Associate

Clients

Alaska Forest Ass'n
Rep By: Guy R. Martin

American Forest & Paper Ass'n
Rep By: Guy R. Martin

AuctionWatch.com
Issues: CPI TEC
Rep By: W. H. "Buzz" Fawcett

Avenue A, Inc.
Issues: CPI
Rep By: W. H. "Buzz" Fawcett

Bay Delta Urban Coalition
Issues: NAT
Rep By: Guy R. Martin

Beyond BAT Group
Rep By: Sloane Wildman

The Boeing Co.
Rep By: Guy R. Martin

Delta Wetlands Project
Issues: NAT
Rep By: Guy R. Martin

The Doe Run Co.
Issues: NAT
Rep By: Guy R. Martin

East Bay Municipal Utility District
Issues: NAT
Rep By: Guy R. Martin

Fort James Corp.
Issues: NAT
Rep By: Guy R. Martin

Intermountain Forest Industry Ass'n
Issues: ANI BUD CAW ENV MAR NAT RES
Rep By: W. H. "Buzz" Fawcett

Kootznoowoo, Inc.
Rep By: Guy R. Martin

Ledyard, Connecticut, Town of
Issues: NAT
Rep By: Guy R. Martin

The Metropolitan Water District of Southern California
Issues: NAT
Rep By: Guy R. Martin

Nat'l Cattleman's Beef Ass'n
Rep By: Guy R. Martin

Ocean Futures Soc., Inc.
Issues: ANI
Rep By: W. H. "Buzz" Fawcett

Spokane, Washington, City of
Issues: ROD
Rep By: W. H. "Buzz" Fawcett

Western Urban Water Coalition
Issues: NAT
Rep By: Guy R. Martin

Weyerhaeuser Co.
Issues: NAT
Rep By: Guy R. Martin

Deborah L. Perry

1050 N. Taylor St.
Suite 306
Arlington, VA 22201
E-mail: perrydl@gateway.net
Tel: (202)668-4447
Registered: LDA

A self-employed government relations consultant.

Clients

The Nat'l Foundation for Teaching Entrepreneurship
Issues: EDU
Rep By: Deborah L. Perry

Susan B. Perry

141 12th St. NE
Washington, DC 20002
E-mail: perrysb@aol.com
Tel: (202)547-4808
Fax: (202)547-1698
Registered: LDA

Clients

American Public Transportation Ass'n
Issues: TRA
Rep By: Susan B. Perry

Persimmon Group Inc.

1155 15th St. NW
Suite 811
Washington, DC 20005
E-mail: corp@persimmongroupinc.com
Tel: (202)775-8130
Fax: (202)223-2662

International business development consultants.

DC-Area Employees Representing Listed Clients

AHN, Jin, President

Clients

Kia Motors Corp.
Rep By: Jin Ahn

The Peterson Group

321 D St. SE
Washington, DC 20003
E-mail: wpsears@bellatlantic.net
Tel: (202)548-4701
Fax: (202)548-4702
Registered: LDA

DC-Area Employees Representing Listed Clients

SEARS, William P., President
SNYDER, Craig

Clients

Allegheny County, Pennsylvania, Port Authority of

American Public Transportation Ass'n

Erie Internat'l Airport
Issues: AVI BUD ECN TRA URB
Rep By: William P. Sears, Craig Snyder

Franklin Institute
Issues: AER BUD EDU HER SCI
Rep By: William P. Sears, Craig Snyder

Klett Rooney Lieber & Schorling
Issues: DEF TRA
Rep By: William P. Sears

Seton Hill College
Issues: BUD DEF EDU FOR
Rep By: William P. Sears

Petito & Associates

6008 34th Place NW
Washington, DC 20015
E-mail: petito@erols.com
Tel: (202)537-1327
Fax: (202)362-2414
Registered: LDA, FARA

Federal and public affairs, consulting services, and government relations.

DC-Area Employees Representing Listed Clients

PETITO, Margaret L., Director/Principal

Clients

Cultural Partnership of the Americas
Issues: ART FOR
Rep By: Margaret L. Petito

The Petrizzo Group, Inc.

444 North Capitol St. NW
Suite 535
Washington, DC 20001
Web: www.petrizzogroup.com
E-mail: tj@petrizzogroup.com
Tel: (202)478-6859
Registered: LDA

DC-Area Employees Representing Listed Clients

KENNEDY, Kara, V. President
PETRIZZO, Thomas "T.J.", President

Clients

Airborne Express
Issues: AVI LBR TAX
Rep By: Kara Kennedy, Thomas "T.J." Petrizzo

Central Puget Sound Regional Transit Authority (Sound Transit)
Issues: TAX TRA
Rep By: Kara Kennedy, Thomas "T.J." Petrizzo

Coalition for American Financial Security
Issues: RET TAX
Rep By: Kara Kennedy, Thomas "T.J." Petrizzo

Eddie Bauer Co.
Issues: TAX TRD
Rep By: Kara Kennedy, Thomas "T.J." Petrizzo

Electronic Industries Alliance
Issues: TAX
Rep By: Kara Kennedy, Thomas "T.J." Petrizzo

Group Health Cooperative
Issues: HCR MMM
Rep By: Kara Kennedy, Thomas "T.J." Petrizzo

Renton, Washington, City of
Issues: BUD ECN
Rep By: Kara Kennedy, Thomas "T.J." Petrizzo

Frank Russell Co.
Issues: FIN RET TAX TRD
Rep By: Kara Kennedy, Thomas "T.J." Petrizzo

Vulcan Northwest Inc.
Rep By: Kara Kennedy, Thomas "T.J." Petrizzo

Peyser Associates, Inc.

1001 G St. NW
Suite 400 East
Washington, DC 20001
Web: www.peyser.com
E-mail: peter@peyser.com
Tel: (202)638-3730
Fax: (202)638-3516
Registered: LDA

A government relations consulting firm.

DC-Area Employees Representing Listed Clients

BUCCIERO, Jr., Michael
HOWARTH, Thomas J., V. President, Client Relations
MOHIB, Mona
PEYSER, Jr., Peter A., President
WEBER, Becky B., Counsel
YOUNG, Thane

Clients

Federal Home Loan Bank of Seattle
Issues: BAN
Rep By: Michael Bucciero, Jr., Thomas J. Howarth, Peter A. Peyser, Jr.

Indiana Department of Transportation
Issues: TRA
Rep By: Becky B. Weber

The Irvine Co.
Issues: ENV
Rep By: Thane Young

S.C. Johnson and Son, Inc.
Issues: TRA
Rep By: Peter A. Peyser, Jr.

LACDA Alliance
Issues: ENV GOV
Rep By: Thane Young

Macon, City of
Issues: HCR HOU LAW TRA WEL
Rep By: Michael Bucciero, Jr., Peter A. Peyser, Jr.

Mission Springs Water District
Issues: ENV GOV UTI
Rep By: Thane Young

Monroe Center, LLC
Issues: RES
Rep By: Michael Bucciero, Jr., Peter A. Peyser, Jr.

Mothers Against Drunk Driving (MADD)
Issues: TRA
Rep By: Thomas J. Howarth

Muncie, Indiana, City of (Delaware County)
Issues: AVI CAW DIS ECN ENV HOU LAW LBR RRR URB
Rep By: Peter A. Peyser, Jr.

Orange County Fire Authority
Issues: GOV
Rep By: Thane Young

Orange County Transportation Authority
Issues: ROD TRA
Rep By: Peter A. Peyser, Jr.

Philadelphia, Pennsylvania, City of
Issues: CAW ENV HCR HOU LAW ROD TEC TRA WAS WEL
Rep By: Thomas J. Howarth, Peter A. Peyser, Jr.

Portland Tri-Met
Rep By: Peter A. Peyser, Jr.

Ryder System, Inc.
Issues: TRA
Rep By: Becky B. Weber

San Joaquin Area Flood Agency
Issues: ENV GOV
Rep By: Thane Young

San Joaquin Regional Transit District
Issues: TRA
Rep By: Thane Young

Seattle, Washington, City of
Issues: CAW ENV HCR HOU LAW ROD TEC TRA WAS WEL
Rep By: Thomas J. Howarth, Peter A. Peyser, Jr.

Sound Transit
Issues: TRA
Rep By: Thomas J. Howarth, Peter A. Peyser, Jr., Becky B. Weber

Southeastern Pennsylvania Transit Authority
Issues: TRA
Rep By: Thomas J. Howarth, Peter A. Peyser, Jr., Becky B. Weber

Stockton, City of
Issues: ECN ENV GOV WEL
Rep By: Thane Young

TRI-MET Tri-County Metropolitan Transportation
Issues: TRA
Rep By: Peter A. Peyser, Jr.

Twentynine Palms Water District
Issues: UTI
Rep By: Peter A. Peyser, Jr., Thane Young

Westminster, California, City of
Issues: ENV GOV
Rep By: Thane Young

Woodland, California, City of
Issues: ENV GOV
Rep By: Thane Young

Piliero Mazza & Pargament

888 17th St. NW
Suite 1100
Washington, DC 20006
Web: www.pmplawfirm.com
E-mail: pmazza@pmplawfirm.com
Tel: (202)857-1000
Fax: (202)857-0200
Registered: LDA

A law firm with practice areas including corporate counseling, employment law, government contracts, government relations, litigation, and Native American law.

DC-Area Employees Representing Listed Clients

MAZZA, Pamela J., Senior Partner

Clients

Ysleta Del Sur Pueblo
Issues: IND
Rep By: Pamela J. Mazza

Pillsbury Winthrop LLP

1100 New York Ave. NW
Ninth Floor
East Tower
Washington, DC 20005
Web: www.cushman.com
Tel: (202)861-3000
Fax: (202)822-0944
Registered: LDA, FARA

Washington office of a San Francisco law firm.

Clients

The Chevron Companies
Issues: CAW

Securities Litigation Reform Coalition

Piper Marbury Rudnick & Wolfe LLP

1200 19th St. NW
Washington, DC 20036-2430
Web: www.piperrudnick.com
E-mail: lawfirm@piperrudnick.com
Tel: (202)861-3900
Fax: (202)223-2085
Registered: LDA

Washington office of a national law firm with offices in Chicago, Baltimore, New York, Philadelphia, Dallas, Tampa, and Los Angeles.

DC-Area Employees Representing Listed Clients

BROCKMEYER, Michael F., Partner
CIVIDANES, Emilio W., Of Counsel
COLGATE, Stephen, Exec. Director
EPSTIEN, Jay A., Co-Managing Partner
GREEN, Douglas H., Partner
HALPERT, James J., Partner

HAMILTON, Heather
INGIS, Stuart P., Associate
JAMIESON, Paul W., Associate
JENNINGS, Deborah E., Partner
LISS, Jeffrey F., Partner, Chief Operating Officer
PALADINI, Vincent M., Associate
PAULEY, Katharine A., Legal Assistant
PLESSER, Ronald L., Partner
STARLING, Kenneth G., Partner
WEISSMAN, William R., Partner
ZEIDMAN, Philip F., Partner

Clients

Acxiom Corp.
Issues: CSP MIA
Rep By: Stuart P. Ingis, Ronald L. Plesser

Alliant Energy
Issues: CAW ENV WAS
Rep By: Deborah E. Jennings, William R. Weissman

American Business Conference
Rep By: Philip F. Zeidman

AOL Time Warner
Issues: CPI
Rep By: Alisa M. Bergman, Emilio W. Cividanes, James J. Halpert, Stuart P. Ingis, Katharine A. Pauley, Ronald L. Plesser

Commercial Internet Exchange Ass'n
Issues: COM CPI CPT CSP FAM GAM TEC
Rep By: Emilio W. Cividanes, James J. Halpert, Stuart P. Ingis, Vincent M. Paladini, Ronald L. Plesser

Contract Services Ass'n of America

Direct Marketing Ass'n, Inc.
Issues: CPI CSP
Rep By: Alisa M. Bergman, Emilio W. Cividanes, James J. Halpert, Stuart P. Ingis, Katharine A. Pauley, Ronald L. Plesser

Edison Electric Institute
Issues: ENV WAS
Rep By: William R. Weissman

Individual Reference Services Group
Issues: CSP
Rep By: Alisa M. Bergman, Emilio W. Cividanes, James J. Halpert, Stuart P. Ingis, Paul W. Jamieson, Ronald L. Plesser

Internat'l Telecommunications, Inc.
Issues: TEC
Rep By: James J. Halpert

Lexis-Nexis
Issues: CPT CSP MIA
Rep By: Michael F. Brockmeyer, Emilio W. Cividanes, James J. Halpert, Stuart P. Ingis, Katharine A. Pauley, Ronald L. Plesser

NetCoalition.Com
Issues: COM CPI CSP
Rep By: Emilio W. Cividanes, James J. Halpert, Heather Hamilton, Stuart P. Ingis, Katharine A. Pauley, Ronald L. Plesser

PSINet Inc.
Issues: CPI TEC
Rep By: Alisa M. Bergman, James J. Halpert, Stuart P. Ingis, Paul W. Jamieson, Katharine A. Pauley, Ronald L. Plesser

Utility Solid Waste Activities Group
Issues: WAS
Rep By: Jeffrey F. Liss, William R. Weissman

Piper Pacific Internat'l

6121 Lincolnia Rd.
Suite 106
Alexandria, VA 22312-2707
Tel: (703)914-2680
Fax: (703)914-2610
Registered: FARA
E-mail: PiperPacif@aol.com
Operates international cooperative programs focused on defense-related technologies and transpacific relationships.

DC-Area Employees Representing Listed Clients
PIPER, W. Stephen, Owner/President

Charles L. Pizer

1530 Wilson Blvd.
Suite 900
Arlington, VA 22209
Tel: (703)312-4326
Fax: (703)312-4343
Registered: LDA
A self-employed public affairs consultant.

Clients

Chicago School Reform Board of Trustees
Issues: ALC BUD EDU FOO TEC
Rep By: Charles L. Pizer

City Colleges of Chicago
Issues: COM EDU TAX TEC
Rep By: Charles L. Pizer

Susan S. Platt Consulting

10110 Walker Lake Dr.
Great Falls, VA 22066
Tel: (703)759-9622
Fax: (703)759-2144
E-mail: ssrplatt@msn.com

DC-Area Employees Representing Listed Clients
PLATT, Susan S.

Clients

Philip Morris Management Corp.
Issues: AGR ALC BEV BUD FOO TAX TOB
Rep By: Susan S. Platt

The Plexus Consulting Group

1620 I Street NW
Suite 900
Washington, DC 20006
Tel: (202)785-8940
Fax: (202)785-8949
Web: www.plexusconsulting.com
E-mail: steve_worth@plexusconsulting.com
A strategic management consulting and government affairs firm serving associations and nonprofit entities worldwide.

DC-Area Employees Representing Listed Clients
HUTCHISON, Fred H., Senior Partner
QUIWZOW, Yasmin
WORTH, Steven M., Managing Partner

Clients

American Soc. for Bone and Mineral Research
Issues: HCR MED
Rep By: Yasmin Quiwzow

Ass'n of Foreign Investors in U.S. Real Estate

Ass'n of Publicly Traded Companies

Check Payment Systems Ass'n
Issues: BAN CSP MON
Rep By: Yasmin Quiwzow

Iceland, Ministry of Fisheries, Government of
Rep By: Fred H. Hutchison

Institute of Internal Auditors
Rep By: Fred H. Hutchison

Internat'l Institute of Ammonia Refrigeration

Nat'l Asphalt Pavement Ass'n

Nat'l Cosmetology Ass'n
Issues: HCR PHA
Rep By: Yasmin Quiwzow

Nat'l Organization for Competency Assurance
Issues: LBR
Rep By: Yasmin Quiwzow

Soc. for Research Administration

Soc. of Thoracic Surgeons
Issues: HCR MED MMM
Rep By: Yasmin Quiwzow

Space Station Associates
Rep By: Fred H. Hutchison

Wallcovering Ass'n
Issues: CHM MAN
Rep By: Fred H. Hutchison

The PMA Group

1755 Jefferson Davis Hwy.
Suite 1107
Arlington, VA 22202
Tel: (703)415-0344
Fax: (703)415-0182
Registered: LDA
Formerly known as Paul Magliocchetti Associates. Provides government relations and legislative counsel.

Political Action Committee
Paul Magliocchetti Associates PAC
1755 Jefferson Davis Hwy.
Suite 1107
Arlington, VA 22202
Contact: Joseph Littleton
Tel: (703)415-0344
Fax: (703)415-0182

DC-Area Employees Representing Listed Clients
BERL, William E., Associate
CLARK, Fred J., Associate
CUNNINGHAM, Daniel, Associate
FLEMING, Daniel E., Associate
FOGARTY, Sean, Associate
GREEN, Kaylene, Director
GWALTNEY, W. David
HANSEN, Gregory L., Associate
HIU, Patrick, Associate
LITTLETON, Joseph, Associate
LYNCH, Dr. John, Associate
MADEY, Stephen, Associate
MAGLIOCCHETTI, Paul J., President
MIODUSKI, Mark
MORGAN, Brian
ROKALA, Mark, Associate
SANDERS, Timothy K., Associate
SHADE, Briggs, Associate
SHORT, Kelli, Associate
SMITH, Charles, Associate
STEWART, Dana, Legislative Assistant
THIEL, Brian, Director
VELTRI, Thomas, Associate
WACLAWSKI, Mark, Associate
WELCH, Sandra, Associate
WOODS, Glen

Clients

ADSIL
Issues: BUD
Rep By: Kaylene Green, Gregory L. Hansen, Dr. John Lynch, Paul J. Magliocchetti

Advanced Acoustic Concepts, Inc.
Issues: DEF
Rep By: Sean Fogarty, Kaylene Green, Gregory L. Hansen, Paul J. Magliocchetti

Advanced Programming Concepts
Issues: DEF
Rep By: Kaylene Green, Paul J. Magliocchetti, Thomas Veltri

AEPTEC
Issues: DEF
Rep By: Sean Fogarty, Kaylene Green, Gregory L. Hansen, Paul J. Magliocchetti

Ag/Bio Con
Issues: AGR
Rep By: Kaylene Green, Paul J. Magliocchetti, Mark Rokala, Kelli Short

Alliance
Rep By: Kaylene Green, Paul J. Magliocchetti, Kelli Short, Brian Thiel, Sandra Welch

American Academy of Audiology
Issues: BUD
Rep By: Kaylene Green, Paul J. Magliocchetti, Timothy K. Sanders

American Crop Protection Ass'n
Issues: BUD
Rep By: Mark Rokala, Timothy K. Sanders

Applied Marine Technologies, Inc.
Issues: DEF LAW
Rep By: Kaylene Green, Paul J. Magliocchetti, Kelli Short, Thomas Veltri

ARC Global Technologies
Rep By: Sean Fogarty, Kaylene Green, Gregory L. Hansen, Paul J. Magliocchetti, Charles Smith, Dana Stewart, Brian Thiel

AsclepiusNet
Issues: DEF
Rep By: Kaylene Green, Patrick Hiu, Paul J. Magliocchetti, Sandra Welch

Ass'n of Medical Device Reprocessors
Issues: BUD MED
Rep By: Kaylene Green, Paul J. Magliocchetti, Timothy K. Sanders

Autometric Inc.
Issues: DEF LAW
Rep By: Kaylene Green, Patrick Hiu, Dr. John Lynch, Paul J. Magliocchetti, Kelli Short, Charles Smith, Thomas Veltri

Battelle
Issues: DEF
Rep By: Daniel Cunningham, Kaylene Green, Paul J. Magliocchetti, Kelli Short, Brian Thiel, Thomas Veltri, Sandra Welch

Biocontrol Technology, Inc.
Issues: DEF
Rep By: Daniel Cunningham, Kaylene Green, Patrick Hiu, Paul J. Magliocchetti

Cartwright Electronics
Issues: DEF
Rep By: Daniel Cunningham, Daniel E. Fleming, Kaylene Green, Paul J. Magliocchetti, Mark Waclawski

Caterpillar Inc.
Issues: DEF
Rep By: William E. Berl, Kaylene Green, Gregory L. Hansen, Paul J. Magliocchetti, Charles Smith, Mark Waclawski

Chamberlain Manufacturing Corp.
Issues: DEF
Rep By: Kaylene Green, Paul J. Magliocchetti, Charles Smith, Mark Waclawski

Cheese of Choice Coalition
Issues: FOO
Rep By: Fred J. Clark, Kaylene Green, Paul J. Magliocchetti, Mark Rokala, Timothy K. Sanders

Chicago Mercantile Exchange
Issues: AGR FIN
Rep By: Fred J. Clark, Kaylene Green, Paul J. Magliocchetti, Timothy K. Sanders

CHIM
Issues: CPI HCR
Rep By: Kaylene Green, Paul J. Magliocchetti, Kelli Short, Brian Thiel

CoBank, ACB
Rep By: Fred J. Clark, Kaylene Green, Paul J. Magliocchetti, Timothy K. Sanders

ConAgra Foods, Inc.
Rep By: Paul J. Magliocchetti, Timothy K. Sanders

Concurrent Technologies Corp.
Issues: DEF
Rep By: Daniel Cunningham, Sean Fogarty, Kaylene Green, Patrick Hiu, Dr. John Lynch, Paul J. Magliocchetti, Timothy K. Sanders, Thomas Veltri

Condor Systems
Issues: DEF
Rep By: Kaylene Green, Joseph Littleton, Paul J. Magliocchetti

Coronado, California, City of
Issues: DEF TRA
Rep By: William E. Berl, Sean Fogarty, Kaylene Green, Gregory L. Hansen, Dr. John Lynch, Paul J. Magliocchetti

CPU Technology
Issues: DEF
Rep By: Kaylene Green, Gregory L. Hansen, Joseph Littleton, Stephen Madey, Paul J. Magliocchetti, Briggs Shade, Thomas Veltri

CRYPTEK Secure Communications, LLC
Issues: DEF
Rep By: Daniel Cunningham, Daniel E. Fleming, Sean Fogarty, Kaylene Green, Patrick Hiu, Paul J. Magliocchetti, Briggs Shade, Kelli Short, Brian Thiel

Diamond Antenna & Microwave Corp.
Issues: TRA
Rep By: Kaylene Green, Dr. John Lynch, Paul J. Magliocchetti, Mark Waclawski

Dynacom Industries
Rep By: Daniel Cunningham, Kaylene Green, Paul J. Magliocchetti

Dynamics Research Corp.
Issues: DEF
Rep By: Daniel E. Fleming, Sean Fogarty, Kaylene Green, Dr. John Lynch, Stephen Madey, Paul J. Magliocchetti, Briggs Shade, Kelli Short, Brian Thiel, Sandra Welch

Electro-Radiation Inc.
Issues: DEF
Rep By: Daniel Cunningham, Daniel E. Fleming, Kaylene Green, Paul J. Magliocchetti, Charles Smith, Mark Waclawski

Electronic Warfare Associates, Inc.
Issues: DEF
Rep By: Kaylene Green, Paul J. Magliocchetti, Thomas Veltri, Mark Waclawski

Environmental Technology Unlimited
Issues: ENV
Rep By: Kaylene Green, Paul J. Magliocchetti, Kelli Short, Brian Thiel

Fidelity Technologies Corp.
Issues: DEF
Rep By: Daniel E. Fleming, Kaylene Green, Paul J. Magliocchetti, Briggs Shade

FLIR Systems, Inc.
Issues: BUD DEF
Rep By: Kaylene Green, Gregory L. Hansen, Dr. John Lynch, Paul J. Magliocchetti

Florida Sugar Cane League, Inc.
Rep By: Fred J. Clark, Kaylene Green, Paul J. Magliocchetti, Timothy K. Sanders

Foundation Health Federal Services, Inc.
Rep By: Kaylene Green, Patrick Hiu, Paul J. Magliocchetti, Brian Thiel

General Atomics
Issues: DEF
Rep By: Kaylene Green, Paul J. Magliocchetti, Timothy K. Sanders

General Dynamics Corp.
Issues: DEF

General Mills
Issues: BUD TRD
Rep By: Fred J. Clark, Paul J. Magliocchetti, Timothy K. Sanders

Generic Pharmaceutical Ass'n
Issues: BUD
Rep By: Fred J. Clark, Kaylene Green, Paul J. Magliocchetti, Mark Rokala, Timothy K. Sanders

Gentex Corp.
Issues: DEF
Rep By: Daniel Cunningham, Kaylene Green, Patrick Hiu, Dr. John Lynch, Stephen Madey, Paul J. Magliocchetti

B. F. Goodrich Co.
Issues: DEF
Rep By: Sean Fogarty, Kaylene Green, Gregory L. Hansen, Paul J. Magliocchetti

Guild Associates
Issues: DEF
Rep By: Daniel Cunningham, Daniel E. Fleming, Kaylene Green, Paul J. Magliocchetti

IIT Research Institute
Issues: DEF
Rep By: Kaylene Green, Patrick Hiu, Paul J. Magliocchetti, Charles Smith, Brian Thiel

IMSSCO Inc.
Issues: DEF
Rep By: William E. Berl, Kaylene Green, Paul J. Magliocchetti

Innovative Productivity, Inc.
Issues: DEF
Rep By: Kaylene Green, Gregory L. Hansen, Paul J. Magliocchetti, Charles Smith

Joint Healthcare Information Technology Alliance
Rep By: Kaylene Green, Paul J. Magliocchetti, Kelli Short, Brian Thiel, Sandra Welch

Kollsman, Inc.
Issues: DEF
Rep By: Daniel E. Fleming, Kaylene Green, Dr. John Lynch, Paul J. Magliocchetti

L-3 Communications Corp.
Issues: DEF
Rep By: Daniel Cunningham, Daniel E. Fleming, Kaylene Green, Gregory L. Hansen, Patrick Hiu, Joseph Littleton, Paul J. Magliocchetti, Briggs Shade, Kelli Short, Charles Smith, Thomas Veltri, Mark Waclawski

Laguna Industries, Inc.
Issues: DEF
Rep By: Daniel E. Fleming, Kaylene Green, Paul J. Magliocchetti, Mark Waclawski

Laguna, New Mexico, City of
Rep By: Daniel E. Fleming, Kaylene Green, Paul J. Magliocchetti

Life Cell
Issues: DEF
Rep By: Kaylene Green, Patrick Hiu, Paul J. Magliocchetti, Charles Smith

Lockheed Martin Corp.
Issues: DEF
Rep By: Daniel E. Fleming, Kaylene Green, Dr. John Lynch, Paul J. Magliocchetti, Briggs Shade, Thomas Veltri, Mark Waclawski

Lockheed Martin Federal Systems
Issues: DEF
Rep By: Sean Fogarty, Kaylene Green, Gregory L. Hansen, Joseph Littleton, Paul J. Magliocchetti, Briggs Shade, Charles Smith, Thomas Veltri

Lockheed Martin MS/Gaithersburg
Issues: BUD
Rep By: Kaylene Green, Dr. John Lynch, Paul J. Magliocchetti, Kelli Short, Thomas Veltri

Lucent Technologies
Issues: DEF
Rep By: Kaylene Green, Paul J. Magliocchetti, Mark Waclawski

Marconi Communications Federal
Issues: DEF
Rep By: William E. Berl, Sean Fogarty, Kaylene Green, Joseph Littleton

McLean Hospital
Issues: DEF
Rep By: Kaylene Green, Patrick Hiu, Paul J. Magliocchetti, Brian Thiel

MIC Industries, Inc.
Issues: DEF DIS ECN
Rep By: Daniel Cunningham, Daniel E. Fleming, Kaylene Green, Paul J. Magliocchetti, Mark Waclawski

Microvision, Inc.
Rep By: Daniel Cunningham, Kaylene Green, Patrick Hiu, Joseph Littleton, Stephen Madey, Paul J. Magliocchetti, Brian Thiel

J. E. Morgan Knitting Mills
Rep By: Kaylene Green, Paul J. Magliocchetti, Charles Smith, Mark Waclawski

MTS Systems Inc.
Issues: DEF
Rep By: Daniel Cunningham, Kaylene Green, Gregory L. Hansen, Patrick Hiu, Joseph Littleton, Paul J. Magliocchetti, Mark Waclawski

Nat'l Ass'n of RC&D Councils
Rep By: Fred J. Clark, Kaylene Green, Paul J. Magliocchetti, Mark Rokala

Nat'l Ass'n of Resource Conservation
Rep By: Fred J. Clark, Kaylene Green, Paul J. Magliocchetti, Mark Rokala, Timothy K. Sanders, Dana Stewart

Nat'l Cattleman's Beef Ass'n
Rep By: Fred J. Clark, Kaylene Green, Paul J. Magliocchetti, Mark Rokala, Timothy K. Sanders

Nat'l Cooperative Bank
Issues: BUD
Rep By: Kaylene Green, Patrick Hiu, Paul J. Magliocchetti, Timothy K. Sanders

Nat'l Pork Producers Ass'n
Rep By: Fred J. Clark, Kaylene Green, Paul J. Magliocchetti, Mark Rokala, Timothy K. Sanders, Dana Stewart

New Mexico Tech
Issues: BUD DEF
Rep By: Kaylene Green, Stephen Madey, Paul J. Magliocchetti, Charles Smith, Thomas Veltri, Sandra Welch

Northrop Marine
Rep By: Kaylene Green, Gregory L. Hansen, Paul J. Magliocchetti

Omega Air
Issues: DEF
Rep By: William E. Berl, Kaylene Green, Stephen Madey, Paul J. Magliocchetti, Briggs Shade

Opportunity Medical, Inc.
Rep By: Kaylene Green, Patrick Hiu, Paul J. Magliocchetti, Sandra Welch

Orange Shipbuilding Co., Inc.
Issues: DEF
Rep By: Kaylene Green, Gregory L. Hansen, Paul J. Magliocchetti

Oxley
Rep By: Kaylene Green, Paul J. Magliocchetti, Charles Smith

Pathfinder Technology Inc.
Issues: DEF
Rep By: Kaylene Green, Paul J. Magliocchetti, Briggs Shade, Thomas Veltri

Planning Systems, Inc.
Issues: DEF
Rep By: Daniel Cunningham, Sean Fogarty, Kaylene Green, Patrick Hiu, Paul J. Magliocchetti, Briggs Shade, Brian Thiel

Prologic
Rep By: Kaylene Green, Paul J. Magliocchetti, Kelli Short, Thomas Veltri

Sabreliner Corp.
Issues: AVI DEF
Rep By: Kaylene Green, Joseph Littleton, Paul J. Magliocchetti

SACO Defense
Issues: DEF
Rep By: Kaylene Green, Paul J. Magliocchetti, Charles Smith, Mark Waclawski

SatoTravel
Issues: DEF
Rep By: Daniel Cunningham, Kaylene Green, Paul J. Magliocchetti, Mark Waclawski

Schweizer Aircraft Corp.
Issues: AVI DEF
Rep By: Kaylene Green, Dr. John Lynch, Paul J. Magliocchetti, Kelli Short

Science Applications Internat'l Corp. (SAIC)
Issues: CPI
Rep By: Kaylene Green, Paul J. Magliocchetti, Timothy K. Sanders

SIGCOM, Inc.
Issues: DEF
Rep By: Daniel Cunningham, Daniel E. Fleming, Paul J. Magliocchetti, Brian Thiel, Mark Waclawski, Sandra Welch

Spatial Integrated Systems
Issues: DEF
Rep By: William E. Berl, Kaylene Green, Patrick Hiu, Paul J. Magliocchetti

Stanly County Airport Authority
Issues: AVI DEF DIS
Rep By: Daniel Cunningham, Kaylene Green, Paul J. Magliocchetti, Brian Thiel, Mark Waclawski

SVS, Inc.
Rep By: Kaylene Green, Joseph Littleton, Stephen Madey, Paul J. Magliocchetti

Teledyne Controls, Inc.
Issues: AVI
Rep By: Kaylene Green, Dr. John Lynch, Paul J. Magliocchetti

TeleFlex Canada, Ltd.
Issues: DEF
Rep By: Daniel Cunningham, Kaylene Green, Paul J. Magliocchetti, Charles Smith, Mark Waclawski

Textron Inc.
Issues: DEF
Rep By: Daniel Cunningham, Daniel E. Fleming, Kaylene Green, Paul J. Magliocchetti, Briggs Shade, Thomas Veltri

Titan Corp.
Rep By: William E. Berl, Sean Fogarty, Kaylene Green, Gregory L. Hansen, Paul J. Magliocchetti, Timothy K. Sanders

Trex Enterprises
Rep By: Kaylene Green, Patrick Hiu, Paul J. Magliocchetti, Thomas Veltri

Triosyn Corp.
Issues: DEF
Rep By: Kaylene Green, Patrick Hiu, Paul J. Magliocchetti, Brian Thiel, Sandra Welch

U.S. Rice Producers Ass'n
Rep By: Fred J. Clark, Kaylene Green, Paul J. Magliocchetti, Mark Rokala

University Emergency Medicine Foundation
Issues: HCR
Rep By: Kaylene Green, Patrick Hiu, Paul J. Magliocchetti, Dana Stewart, Brian Thiel

Weidlinger Associates, Inc.
Issues: DEF
Rep By: Kaylene Green, Stephen Madey, Paul J. Magliocchetti

Podesta/Mattoon

1001 G St. NW
Suite 900 E
Washington, DC 20001-4545
Tel: (202)393-1010
Fax: (202)393-5510
Registered: LDA, FARA
Web: www.podesta.com/
E-mail: podesta@podesta.com

Formerly know as podesta.com. A consulting firm specializing in government relations, public affairs, and grassroots advocacy.

DC-Area Employees Representing Listed Clients

BROWN, Paul, Principal
DELORY, Ann, Associate
FRITTS, Kimberley, Principal
GELMAN, Matthew, Principal
JAMES, Claudia, President
LEARY, Kristen, Senior Associate
LITTMAN, Andrew C., Principal
MADDOX, Lauren, Principal
MATTOON, Dan, Partner
MORRA, Elizabeth, Principal
PIANALTO, Antonella
PODESTA, Anthony T., Chairman
POWERS, Timothy, Principal
ROTHSCHILD, Edwin S., Associate
TESSIER, Missi, Principal

Clients

Alliance to Save Energy
Issues: ENG
Rep By: Edwin S. Rothschild

American Council of Life Insurers
Issues: INS TAX
Rep By: Matthew Gelman

American Psychological Ass'n
Issues: HCR
Rep By: Ann Delory, Kimberley Fritts, Anthony T. Podesta

AOL Time Warner
Issues: COM CPT
Rep By: Ann Delory, Kimberley Fritts, Matthew Gelman, Claudia James, Andrew C. Littman, Anthony T. Podesta

Ass'n for Local Telecommunications Services
Rep By: Claudia James, Kristen Leary, Timothy Powers

Ass'n of Directory Publishers
Issues: CPT
Rep By: Claudia James, Anthony T. Podesta

Aventis CropScience
Issues: AGR FOO
Rep By: Ann Delory, Anthony T. Podesta

Blue Cross and Blue Shield of Maine
Issues: BUD INS TAX

Blue Cross Blue Shield Ass'n
Issues: BUD HCR INS TAX

California Poultry Industry Federation
Issues: AGR
Rep By: Timothy Powers

Celera Genomics
Issues: CPT SCI
Rep By: Ann Delory, Kimberley Fritts, Anthony T. Podesta

Chiquita Brands Internat'l, Inc.
Rep By: Ann Delory, Matthew Gelman, Kristen Leary

Dow AgroSciences
Issues: AGR BUD ENV PHA TAX
Rep By: Anthony T. Podesta

The Dow Chemical Co.

E-LOAN, Inc.
Issues: BAN
Rep By: Timothy Powers, Edwin S. Rothschild

eBay Inc.
Issues: CPI
Rep By: Claudia James

Envirocare of Utah, Inc.
Issues: WAS

Federation of American Hospitals
Issues: HCR
Rep By: Lauren Maddox

FM Watch

Friends of Cancer Research
Issues: MED
Rep By: Anthony T. Podesta, Missi Tessier

GE Power Systems
Issues: ENG
Rep By: Ann Delory, Anthony T. Podesta

Genentech, Inc.
Issues: CAW PHA TAX
Rep By: Matthew Gelman, Andrew C. Littman, Anthony T. Podesta

Grassroots Enterprise, Inc.

Horsehead Industries, Inc.
Rep By: Anthony T. Podesta, Timothy Powers

Interactive Gaming Council
Issues: CPI
Rep By: Matthew Gelman, Andrew C. Littman, Timothy Powers

Janus-Merritt Strategies, L.L.C.

MCI WorldCom Corp.
Issues: CPT TEC
Rep By: Matthew Gelman, Claudia James, Kristen Leary, Anthony T. Podesta

Motion Picture Ass'n of America
Issues: CPT
Rep By: Ann Delory, Kimberley Fritts, Matthew Gelman, Claudia James, Kristen Leary

Mount Sinai/NYU Health
Issues: BUD HCR
Rep By: Matthew Gelman, Andrew C. Littman, Lauren Maddox, Anthony T. Podesta, Timothy Powers, Missi Tessier

Nat'l Ass'n of Broadcasters
Issues: COM CPT GOV
Rep By: Ann Delory, Kimberley Fritts, Matthew Gelman, Claudia James, Kristen Leary

Nat'l Broadcasting Co.

Nat'l Conference of Bankruptcy Judges
Issues: BNK RET

Nat'l Environmental Strategies
Issues: ENG ENV
Rep By: Anthony T. Podesta, Timothy Powers

Nat'l Food Processors Ass'n
Issues: FOO
Rep By: Ann Delory, Anthony T. Podesta

NCI Coalition
Rep By: Ann Delory, Missi Tessier

News America Inc.
Issues: COM CPT
Rep By: Ann Delory, Kimberley Fritts, Anthony T. Podesta

Newspaper Ass'n of America
Issues: CPT GOV
Rep By: Claudia James

Nextel Communications, Inc.
Rep By: Andrew C. Littman, Anthony T. Podesta

North American GSM Alliance, LLC
Issues: COM
Rep By: Claudia James

Northpoint Technology, Ltd.
Issues: COM
Rep By: Ann Delory, Kimberley Fritts, Claudia James, Kristen Leary

Pillowtex Corp.
Issues: TRD
Rep By: Timothy Powers

Recording Industry Ass'n of America
Rep By: Ann Delory, Kimberley Fritts, Matthew Gelman, Claudia James, Andrew C. Littman, Anthony T. Podesta, Timothy Powers

The Science Coalition
Issues: EDU

SiTV
Rep By: Ann Delory, Kimberley Fritts, Matthew Gelman, Claudia James, Andrew C. Littman

Southdown, Inc.

Teligent, Inc.
Rep By: Kimberley Fritts, Claudia James, Anthony T. Podesta, Timothy Powers

Trans World Airlines, Inc.
Issues: TRA
Rep By: Ann Delory, Matthew Gelman, Kristen Leary, Antonella Pianalto, Anthony T. Podesta

Vivendi Universal
Rep By: Ann Delory, Kimberley Fritts, Matthew Gelman, Claudia James, Andrew C. Littman, Anthony T. Podesta

Policy Consulting Services

7500 Woodmont Ave.
Suite L08
Bethesda, MD 20814
Tel: (202)675-3380
Fax: (301)986-9346
Registered: LDA

DC-Area Employees Representing Listed Clients

SMITH, Paul C.

Clients

American Automotive Leasing Ass'n
Issues: CAW ENG ENV
Rep By: Paul C. Smith

IPALCO Enterprises, Inc./Indianapolis Power & Light Co.
Issues: CAW ENG
Rep By: Paul C. Smith

United Parcel Service
Issues: CAW ENG FIN POS
Rep By: Paul C. Smith

Policy Directions, Inc.

818 Connecticut Ave. NW
Suite 325
Washington, DC 20006
Tel: (202)776-0071
Fax: (202)776-0083
Registered: LDA, FARA

A government relations firm.

DC-Area Employees Representing Listed Clients

HOLCOMBE, Kathleen "Kay", Exec. V. President
KOPPERUD, Steve, Senior V. President
MICHAEL, Stephen, V. President
TRULL, Frankie L., President

Clients

American Feed Industry Ass'n
Issues: AGR ANI BUD CAW ENV FOO LBR TRD TRU
Rep By: Steve Kopperud, Frankie L. Trull

Amgen
Issues: HCR MED MMM PHA SCI
Rep By: Kathleen "Kay" Holcombe, Frankie L. Trull

Anthra
Issues: HCR MED
Rep By: Stephen Michael, Frankie L. Trull

Aventis Pharmaceuticals, Inc.
Issues: CSP HCR MMM
Rep By: Kathleen "Kay" Holcombe, Frankie L. Trull

Bausch & Lomb
Issues: MED
Rep By: Stephen Michael, Frankie L. Trull

Baxter Healthcare Corp.
Issues: HCR MED MMM PHA SCI
Rep By: Kathleen "Kay" Holcombe, Frankie L. Trull

Bayer Diagnostic
Issues: HCR MED
Rep By: Stephen Michael, Frankie L. Trull

Baylor College of Medicine
Issues: AGR BUD FOO HCR MED
Rep By: Kathleen "Kay" Holcombe, Stephen Michael, Frankie L. Trull

Burger King Corp.
Issues: ANI
Rep By: Stephen Michael, Frankie L. Trull

Cosmetic, Toiletry and Fragrance Ass'n
Issues: HCR MED
Rep By: Kathleen "Kay" Holcombe, Stephen Michael, Frankie L. Trull

Genelabs Technologies, Inc.
Issues: HCR MED
Rep By: Kathleen "Kay" Holcombe, Frankie L. Trull

Grocery Manufacturers of America
Issues: BUD FOO
Rep By: Kathleen "Kay" Holcombe, Steve Kopperud, Frankie L. Trull

Kraft Foods, Inc.
Issues: AGR FOO
Rep By: Kathleen "Kay" Holcombe, Steve Kopperud, Frankie L. Trull

Merck & Co.
Issues: HCR MED MMM
Rep By: Kathleen "Kay" Holcombe, Frankie L. Trull

Nat'l Ass'n for Biomedical Research
Issues: ANI BUD MED
Rep By: Kathleen "Kay" Holcombe, Frankie L. Trull

Nestle USA, Inc.
Issues: BUD FOO
Rep By: Steve Kopperud, Stephen Michael, Frankie L. Trull

Orphan Medical, Inc.
Issues: HCR LAW MED
Rep By: Kathleen "Kay" Holcombe, Stephen Michael, Frankie L. Trull

Pharmaceutical Research and Manufacturers of America
Issues: HCR MED MMM
Rep By: Kathleen "Kay" Holcombe, Frankie L. Trull

Philip Morris Management Corp.
Issues: BEV FOO TOB
Rep By: Kathleen "Kay" Holcombe

Reckitt & Colman Pharmaceuticals Inc.
Issues: ALC HCR MED
Rep By: Kathleen "Kay" Holcombe, Frankie L. Trull

Soc. for Neuroscience
Issues: BUD MED
Rep By: Stephen Michael, Frankie L. Trull

State University of New York at Albany
Issues: BUD EDU
Rep By: Stephen Michael, Frankie L. Trull

U.S. Oncology
Issues: HCR MED MMM
Rep By: Kathleen "Kay" Holcombe, Stephen Michael, Frankie L. Trull

Visible Genetics
Issues: HCR MED MMM
Rep By: Kathleen "Kay" Holcombe, Stephen Michael, Frankie L. Trull

The Policy Group

1120 Connecticut Ave. NW
Suite 490
Washington, DC 20036
Tel: (202)457-0670
Fax: (202)457-0638

DC-Area Employees Representing Listed Clients
HANNAPEL, Jeff, V. President
RICHTER, Christian, Principal

Clients

Metal Finishing Suppliers Ass'n
Issues: ENV MAN
Rep By: Christian Richter

Policy Impact Communications

1275 Pennsylvania Ave. NW
Tenth Floor
Washington, DC 20004
Tel: (202)737-5339
Fax: (202)467-0810
Registered: LDA

A public relations firm affiliated with the law and lobbying firm of Barbour, Griffth, and Rogers.

DC-Area Employees Representing Listed Clients
LAKE, James, President and Chief Exec. Officer
SCHULTE, Benena
TRON, Barrie, V. President and Creative Director

Clients

Lake Worth Drainage District
Issues: ENV
Rep By: Benena Schulte

Nat'l Review Magazine

University of Miami
Issues: EDU GOV

PolicyCounsel.com

P.O. Box 77476
Washington, DC 20013
Tel: (202)486-0824
Web: www.policycounsel.com
E-mail: info@policycounsel.com

Provides strategic advice on policy and regulatory matters.

DC-Area Employees Representing Listed Clients
HARPER, James W., Founder and Principal

Polity Consulting

12609 Pentenville Rd.
Silver Spring, MD 20904-3526
Tel: (301)622-0433
Fax: (301)625-8711
Registered: LDA
E-mail: rpkingsley@aol.com

Provides government relations, legislative advocacy, and political consulting services to help organizations become effective participants in the federal policy-making process.

DC-Area Employees Representing Listed Clients
KINGSLEY, Ph.D., Roger P., Principal

Clients

Brain Injury Ass'n
Issues: BUD DEF EDU HCR VET
Rep By: Roger P. Kingsley, Ph.D.

Internat'l Code Council
Issues: BUD ENV MMM
Rep By: Roger P. Kingsley, Ph.D.

Internat'l Dyslexia Ass'n, The
Issues: BUD CIV EDU HCR MED MMM
Rep By: Roger P. Kingsley, Ph.D.

Nat'l Ass'n of Developmental Disabilities Councils
Issues: BUD EDU HCR
Rep By: Roger P. Kingsley, Ph.D.

The Polling Company

1220 Connecticut Ave. NW
Second Floor
Washington, DC 20036
Tel: (202)667-6557
Fax: (202)467-6551
Registered: LDA
Web: www.pollingcompany.com
E-mail: info@pollingcompany.com

A full service survey, research, and political consulting firm.

DC-Area Employees Representing Listed Clients
FITZPATRICK, Kellyanne, President
SCITCHIK, Brian, Research Analyst

Clients

Export Control Coalition
Issues: CPI
Rep By: Kellyanne Fitzpatrick

Ralph Pomerance, Jr.

2026 Allen Pl. NW
Washington, DC 20009
Tel: (202)232-6885
Fax: (202)298-8514
Registered: LDA

Clients

Corporation for Enterprise Development
Issues: CAW
Rep By: Ralph Pomerance, Jr.

Wolfgang Pordzik

4710 Bethesda Ave.
Suite 919
Bethesda, MD 20814
Registered: FARA

Clients

Deutsche Post AG
Rep By: Wolfgang Pordzik

Porter, Wright, Morris & Arthur, LLP

1919 Pennsylvania Ave. NW
Suite 500
Washington, DC 20006-3434
Tel: (202)778-3000
Fax: (202)778-3063
Registered: LDA, FARA
Web: www.porterwright.com
E-mail: dca@porterwright.com

Washington office of an Ohio-based general practice law firm.

DC-Area Employees Representing Listed Clients
FINKEL, E. Jay, Partner
FISHER, Bart S., Of Counsel
GLICK, Leslie Alan, Partner
KESSLER, Judd L., Partner
STEARN, Mitchell A., Partner

Clients

ACS Industries, Inc.
Rep By: Leslie Alan Glick

Asociacion Nacional de la Industria Quimica (ANIQ), A.C
Rep By: Leslie Alan Glick

Ass'n of Brazilian Ceramic Tile Producers
Rep By: Leslie Alan Glick

Ass'n of Brazilian Tire Producers
Rep By: Leslie Alan Glick

Atanor, S.A.
Rep By: E. Jay Finkel

Grupo Cydsa

Harza Engineering Co.
Rep By: E. Jay Finkel, Judd L. Kessler

Huffy Bicycles
Rep By: Bart S. Fisher

Huffy Sports
Rep By: Bart S. Fisher

Huntington Bancshares
Rep By: E. Jay Finkel

Industrial Minera Mexicana
Rep By: Leslie Alan Glick

Kemet Electronics Co.
Rep By: Leslie Alan Glick

Nature's Farm Products
Rep By: Bart S. Fisher

Scottish Nat'l Party

TEKSID/Fiat U.S.A.
Rep By: Leslie Alan Glick

Vishay Intertechnologies, Inc.
Rep By: Leslie Alan Glick

Porter/Novelli

1909 K St. NW
Fourth Floor
Washington, DC 20006
Tel: (202)973-5800
Fax: (202)973-5858
Registered: LDA, FARA
Web: www.pninternational.com
E-mail: mpfeil@porternovelli.com

DC-Area Employees Representing Listed Clients
BLANKLEY, Tony, Of Counsel
CADY, Donald H., Partner
DALEY, Steve, Senior V. President
DEFRANCIS, Suzanne, Senior V. President, Public Affairs
FRISBY, Michael, Senior V. President, Public Affairs
GOULD, Rob, Partner, Washington Health Care Practice
GREENER, Charles V., Senior Partner and General Manager
LOWE, Roger, V. President, Public Affairs
MARCHAND, Lorraine H., Sr. V. President, Healthcare Marketing and Patients First
MARSHALL, Stephanie, V. President, Public Affairs
NEDELL, Jackie R., V. President, MessageMark Media Services
POWERS, Charles H., Senior V. President
SNYDER, Dan, Partner, Food, Beverage and Nutrition
VOLES, Lorraine, Senior Counsel
VOSE, Kathryn Kahler, Senior V. President

Clients

American Fidelity Life Insurance Co.
Rep By: Michael Frisby

Federation of Electric Power Cos. of Japan
Rep By: Charles H. Powers

Japan Automobile Manufacturers Ass'n
Issues: AUT ENV TRD
Rep By: Charles H. Powers

The Steel Alliance
Rep By: Donald H. Cady

The Potomac Advocates

321 D St. NE
Washington, DC 20002
Tel: (202)547-4192
Fax: (202)547-4674
Registered: LDA

DC-Area Employees Representing Listed Clients
RYAN, Patricia, Partner
SCALERA, Charles, Partner
SOJKA, Gary L., Partner

Clients

Adroit Systems Inc.
Rep By: Charles Scalera, Gary L. Sojka

Argon Engineering Associates
Rep By: Charles Scalera, Gary L. Sojka

Brashear Systems, L.L.P.
Issues: DEF
Rep By: Charles Scalera, Gary L. Sojka

CUBRC
Issues: DEF
Rep By: Charles Scalera, Gary L. Sojka

Eastman Kodak Co.
Issues: AER DEF
Rep By: Charles Scalera, Gary L. Sojka

Eclipse
Rep By: Charles Scalera, Gary L. Sojka

General Dynamics Corp.
Issues: DEF
Rep By: Charles Scalera, Gary L. Sojka

B. F. Goodrich Co.
Rep By: Charles Scalera, Gary L. Sojka

GTS
Rep By: Charles Scalera, Gary L. Sojka

Northrop Grumman Corp.
Issues: DEF
Rep By: Charles Scalera, Gary L. Sojka

Raytheon Co.
Issues: DEF
Rep By: Gary L. Sojka

SAFT America Inc.
Issues: AER DEF
Rep By: Charles Scalera, Gary L. Sojka

SAFT R&D Center
Rep By: Charles Scalera, Gary L. Sojka

Spot Image Corp.
Rep By: Charles Scalera, Gary L. Sojka

SRI Internat'l
Issues: DEF
Rep By: Charles Scalera, Gary L. Sojka

Veridian Corp.
Issues: DEF
Rep By: Charles Scalera, Gary L. Sojka

Potomac Communications Group

2025 M St. NW
Suite 350
Washington, DC 20036
Tel: (202)466-7391
Fax: (202)429-0365
Registered: LDA
Web: www.pcgpr.com
E-mail: fmaisano@pcgpr.com

Specializes in public relations, public affairs, and legislative support.

DC-Area Employees Representing Listed Clients
GREENBERGER, Leonard
LIMBACH, Mary "Mimi"
MAISANO, Frank, Director

Clients

American Water Works Ass'n

The Business Roundtable

Global Climate Coalition

Potomac Consulting Group

17413 Collier Way
Poolesville, MD 20837
Tel: (301)605-0501
Fax: (301)605-0503
Web: www.potomac.com

DC-Area Employees Representing Listed Clients
ANZOATEGUI, Carlos, Managing Partner

Clients

Committee on Human Rights for the People of Nicaragua
Rep By: Carlos Anzoategui

Potomac Group

816 Connecticut Ave. NW
Tenth Floor
Washington, DC 20006
Tel: (202)783-3460
Fax: (202)783-2432
Registered: LDA
Web: www.ptomac.com

DC-Area Employees Representing Listed Clients
HEGG, Richard Y, Legislative Consultant
KARSTING, Philip C., Director, Federal Affairs
SMITH, G. Wayne, President and Chief Exec. Officer

Clients

American Psychological Ass'n
Issues: EDU HCR MMM
Rep By: Richard Y Hegg, Philip C. Karsting, G. Wayne Smith

Ass'n of American Railroads
Issues: RRR TAX TRA TRU
Rep By: Richard Y Hegg, Philip C. Karsting, G. Wayne Smith

Maersk Inc.
Issues: MAR
Rep By: Richard Y Hegg, Philip C. Karsting, G. Wayne Smith

Rapid Mat LLC
Issues: BUD DEF DIS
Rep By: Richard Y Hegg, Philip C. Karsting, G. Wayne Smith

R. J. Reynolds Tobacco Co.
Issues: TAX TOB
Rep By: Richard Y Hegg, Philip C. Karsting, G. Wayne Smith

Seafarers Internat'l Union of North America
Issues: LBR MAR TRU
Rep By: Richard Y Hegg, Philip C. Karsting, G. Wayne Smith

Seafarers Mobilization Action Research Team
Issues: LBR MAR
Rep By: Richard Y Hegg, Philip C. Karsting, G. Wayne Smith

Transportation Institute
Issues: MAR
Rep By: Richard Y Hegg, Philip C. Karsting, G. Wayne Smith

Union Pacific
Issues: RRR TAX TRU
Rep By: Richard Y Hegg, Philip C. Karsting, G. Wayne Smith

Walgreen Co.
Issues: HCR
Rep By: Richard Y Hegg, Philip C. Karsting, G. Wayne Smith

Watson Energy
Issues: ENG
Rep By: Richard Y Hegg, Philip C. Karsting, G. Wayne Smith

Potomac Incorporated

8120 Woodmont Ave.
Suite 650
Bethesda, MD 20814
Tel: (301)656-7900
Fax: (301)656-7903
E-mail: gkhaller@aol.com
An opinion and market research firm serving the media, business, political organizations and candidates.

DC-Area Employees Representing Listed Clients
HALLER, G. Keith, President

Clients

Allegheny Power Service Corp.

Southwestern Bell Corp., Media Ventures

The Potomac Research Group LLC

1030 15th St. NW
Suite 1028
Washington, DC 20005
Tel: (202)216-9116
Fax: (202)216-0363
Registered: LDA
E-mail: prg@his.com
A government relations firm.

DC-Area Employees Representing Listed Clients
JORDAN, G. Harris, Managing Partner
KINGSLEY, Daniel T., Senior Partner
ORR, Paul Welles, Partner

Clients

Bayer Corp.
Issues: TRD
Rep By: G. Harris Jordan, Paul Welles Orr

Biotechnology Industry Organization
Issues: MED SCI
Rep By: G. Harris Jordan, Paul Welles Orr

Safety Reasearch Center, Inc.
Issues: TRD
Rep By: G. Harris Jordan, Paul Welles Orr

Spatial Technologies Industry Ass'n
Issues: SCI
Rep By: G. Harris Jordan, Paul Welles Orr

United States Cane Sugar Refiners' Ass'n
Issues: AGR TRD
Rep By: G. Harris Jordan, Paul Welles Orr

Potomac Resource Consultants

4807 Wellington Dr.
Chevy Chase, MD 20815
Tel: (301)654-5661
Fax: (301)652-8710
E-mail: rbsmytheprc@cs.com
Consulting and representation on environmental and natural resources policy.

DC-Area Employees Representing Listed Clients
SMYTHE, Ph.D., Robert B., Owner/Principal

Potomac Resources, Inc.

1001 Connecticut Ave. NW
Washington, DC 20036
Tel: (202)429-8873
Registered: LDA

DC-Area Employees Representing Listed Clients
OSANN, Edward R., President

Clients

American Council for an Energy-Efficient Economy
Rep By: Edward R. Osann

California Urban Water Conservation Council
Issues: ENG NAT
Rep By: Edward R. Osann

Toto USA, Inc.
Issues: ENG NAT
Rep By: Edward R. Osann

Potomac Strategies & Analysis, Inc.

P.O. Box 383
Galesville, MD 20765-0383
Tel: (301)261-9990
Registered: LDA

DC-Area Employees Representing Listed Clients
OLESON, Peter C., President

Clients

Autometric Inc.
Rep By: Peter C. Oleson

Sarnoff Corp.
Issues: DEF
Rep By: Peter C. Oleson

Potomac Strategies Internat'l LLC

1717 Pennsylvania Ave. NW
12th Floor
Washington, DC 20006
Tel: (202)416-0150
Registered: LDA
Web: www.potomacstrategies.com
E-mail: admin@potomacstrategies.com
Provides strategic planning, marketing and financial consulting services with special emphasis on federal procurement in the areas of command, control, communications, computers, intelligence, surveillance and reconnaissance (C4ISR) and health informatics and telemedicine systems.

DC-Area Employees Representing Listed Clients
ALLARD, C. Kenneth, V. President
CURRAN, Robert J., V. President
DUBOIS, Jr., Raymond F., President
TRUTANIC, Cynthia, V. President
WHOLEY, James K., General Counsel

Clients

Ass'n of the United States Army
Issues: DEF DOC
Rep By: Raymond F. DuBois, Jr., James K. Wholey

Command Systems Inc.
Issues: CPI DEF
Rep By: Robert J. Curran, Raymond F. DuBois, Jr., James K. Wholey

GEO Centers, Inc.
Issues: DEF HCR MED
Rep By: Raymond F. DuBois, Jr., Cynthia Trutanic

Member-Link Systems, Inc.
Issues: CPI DEF HCR MED
Rep By: Raymond F. DuBois, Jr., Cynthia Trutanic, James K. Wholey

memorize.com
Issues: CPI DEF MED
Rep By: Raymond F. DuBois, Jr., Cynthia Trutanic

Nat'l Electrical Manufacturers Ass'n
Issues: GOV MAN SMB
Rep By: James K. Wholey

Omniflight Helicopters, Inc.
Issues: AVI DEF MED
Rep By: James K. Wholey

Orbital Sciences Corp., Fairchild Defense Division
Issues: AER CPI DEF
Rep By: C. Kenneth Allard, Robert J. Curran, Raymond F. DuBois, Jr.

Spacelabs Medical Inc.
Issues: CPI DEF HCR MED SCI VET
Rep By: Raymond F. DuBois, Jr., Cynthia Trutanic, James K. Wholey

V-ONE Corp.
Issues: CPI DEF HCR MED
Rep By: Cynthia Trutanic

Powell Tate

700 13th St. NW
Suite 1000
Washington, DC 20005
Tel: (202)347-6633
Fax: (202)347-8713
Registered: LDA, FARA
Web: www.shandwickpublicaffairs.com
Strategic public affairs and communications firm.

DC-Area Employees Representing Listed Clients
ABERNETHY, Stacey Colleen, V. President and Deputy Director of Research
BARRETT, Laurence I., V. President
BURGER, George, Principal
CASEY, Daniel L., Senior V. President, Director of Research
CISNEROS, Adrienne Laura, Manager, Media Relations
COLLINS, Mike, Exec. V. President
FELDMAN, Steven, V. President
FOLEY, Donald J., Managing Director and Chief Operating Officer
FRAKER, Mary E., V. President
FRANCIS, Barbara L.
GELB, Michael, Senior V. President and Director, Editorial Services and Media Relations
GEST, Kathryn Waters, Senior V. President and Director, International Issues Group
HARRISON, Gail, Principal
HART, Bill, Senior V. President
HARTZ, Michelle, Consultant
HOOPES, Jr., Robert B., Group V. President
JENSEN, Paul H., Consultant
KEETON, Pamela, Director, Defense Group
KOLSTAD, Katherine C., Account Executive
KRAWITZ, David, President
MCCORMICK, Kelley, Group V. President
MILLER, Andrew Clark, V. President
MILLER, Mark, V. President, Writing
MOSHER, Liese, V. President
O'TOOLE, Thomas, Consultant
POSTON, Ramsey, V. President
POWELL, Jody, Chairman and Chief Exec. Officer
RIEGLE, Jr., Hon. Donald W., Chairman
SCHWARTZ, Haidee, V. President
SHIELDS, Carolyn, Director, Special Events
TATE, Sheila B., President
WHITMORE, David, Senior V. President and Chief Financial Officer

Clients

Adaptec

Americans Against Unfair Family Taxation

Brita GmbH
Rep By: Stacey Colleen Abernethy

CertainTeed Corp.

Delta Air Lines
Rep By: Jody Powell

Fortis Healthcare

Gabonese Republic, Government of the
Rep By: Kathryn Waters Gest

Gabonese Republic, Office of the President of the

Internat'l Dairy Foods Ass'n

Microsoft Corp.

Monsanto Co.

Nat'l Pest Control Ass'n

Northwest Airlines, Inc.

Prime Time 24
Issues: COM CPT

RedCreek Communications Inc.
Issues: CPI

Saudi Arabia, Royal Embassy of
Rep By: Daniel L. Casey, Michael Gelb, Kathryn Waters Gest, Katherine C. Kolstad, Andrew Clark Miller, Jody Powell, Sheila B. Tate

Solectron

Taiwan Studies Institute
Issues: DEF FOR TRD
Rep By: Laurence I. Barrett, Barbara L. Francis, Kathryn Waters Gest, Katherine C. Kolstad

UDV North America, Inc.

Powell, Goldstein, Frazer & Murphy LLP

1001 Pennsylvania Ave. NW
Suite 600
Washington, DC 20004
Tel: (202)347-0066
Fax: (202)624-7222
Registered: LDA, FARA

Web: www.pgfm.com
Provides corporations, trade associations and foreign governments with legal and political advice and representation on a range of public policy matters. The firm also has a government ethics practice providing advice and legal representation on campaign finance, lobbying disclosure, gift rule, and other compliance matters.

DC-Area Employees Representing Listed Clients
ABRAHAMS, Jessica, Partner
ALEXANDROV, Stanimir, Foreign Counsel
CAMERON, Kelly, Partner
CLARK, Alice Slayton, International Trade Analyst
COCO, Jr., Leo, Senior Policy Advisor
COLLINS, Charlotte, Of Counsel
DANIELS, Michael P., Partner
DERRICK, Jr., Hon. Butler E., Partner
DIGIULIAN, Maria, Associate
DRAZEK, Paul A., Senior Policy Advisor
EFFGEN, Gretchen, Analyst
ELLIS, Neil, Partner
EYMAN, Barbara D. A., Counsel
FINE, Michael E., Partner
FISCHBECK, Kyra, Associate
FRIEDBACHER, Todd, Associate
FULLERTON, Lawrence R., Partner
GAGE, Larry S., Partner
GINSBURG, David, Senior Counsel
HAMMOND, David C., Partner
HORTON, Katie, Senior Policy Advisor
HOWARD, Elizabeth Johns, Trade Policy Analyst
HUGE, Harry, Partner
JACOBS, Brenda A., Partner
KAPPEL, Brett G., Partner
KNAPP, John J., Partner
KOFF, Alexander, Associate
KUSHAN, Jeff, Partner
LAZARUS, III, Simon, Partner
LUBAND, Charles, Associate
MCSHERRY, Carolyn, Analyst
PARVER, Alan K., Managing Partner
PRICE, Daniel M., Partner
QUAM, David C., Associate
ROISTACHER, Charles H., Partner
RUBIN, Leonard J., Partner
SANDERS, Michael, Partner
SHAPIRO, Lisa, Analyst
SHOYER, Andrew, Partner
SKILLINGTON, G. Lee, Counsel
SLAFSKY, Ted, Coalition Manager
STRANNE, Steve K., Partner
STRENIO, Andrew, Partner
SUCHMAN, Peter O., Consultant
THORN, Craig A., Senior Policy Advisor
TORRESEN, Jr., Robert, Partner
TRAPHAGEN, Mark, Partner
VON OEHSEN, William H. E., Partner
WALDERS, Larry, Partner

Clients

American Committee for the Weizmann Institute of Science
Issues: FOR
Rep By: Michael E. Fine, Elizabeth Johns Howard

Ass'n of Community Cancer Centers
Issues: MMM
Rep By: Alan K. Parver, Steve K. Stranne

Austin, Nichols & Co., Inc.
Issues: TRD
Rep By: Daniel M. Price

Bayer Corp. / Agriculture Division
Issues: FOO
Rep By: Kyra Fischbeck, Brett G. Kappel, Lisa Shapiro, William H. E. von Oehsen

Cargill, Inc.
Rep By: Hon. Butler E. Derrick, Jr., Carolyn McSherry

Carpet Export Promotion Council
Issues: TRD
Rep By: Alice Slayton Clark, Brenda A. Jacobs

Caterpillar Inc.

Cegetel, S.A.
Issues: TEC
Rep By: Kelly Cameron

China, Embassy of the People's Republic of
Issues: TRD
Rep By: Alice Slayton Clark, Maria DiGiulian, Gretchen Effgen, Brenda A. Jacobs

Concurrent Technologies Corp.
Issues: ECN
Rep By: Hon. Butler E. Derrick, Jr., David C. Quam

DCS Group
Issues: TRD
Rep By: Brenda A. Jacobs, Alexander Koff

Dekalb, Illinois, City of
Issues: AVI ROD

DuPont
Issues: TRD
Rep By: Alice Slayton Clark, Simon Lazarus, III

The DuPont Pharmaceutical Co.
Issues: TRD
Rep By: Alice Slayton Clark, Simon Lazarus, III

EUTELSAT
Issues: TEC
Rep By: Kelly Cameron, Brett G. Kappel, David C. Quam

Fluor Corp.
Issues: ENG ENV LBR NAT RRR TRA WAS
Rep By: Hon. Butler E. Derrick, Jr.

Footwear Distributors and Retailers of America
Issues: TRD
Rep By: Alice Slayton Clark, Michael P. Daniels, Maria DiGiulian, Brenda A. Jacobs

Genentech, Inc.
Issues: CPT
Rep By: Jeff Kushan

Hong Kong Economic and Trade Office
Rep By: Brenda A. Jacobs

Hong Kong Trade Development Council
Issues: TRD
Rep By: Alice Slayton Clark, Michael P. Daniels, Maria DiGiulian, Gretchen Effgen, Michael E. Fine, Robert Torresen, Jr.

Inmarsat
Issues: TEC
Rep By: Kelly Cameron

Joint Stock Company Severstal
Issues: TRD
Rep By: Neil Ellis, Michael E. Fine, Daniel M. Price, Peter O. Suchman

Kinetic Biosystems Inc.
Issues: SCI
Rep By: Hon. Butler E. Derrick, Jr., Brett G. Kappel

Koyo Seiko Co., Ltd.
Issues: TRD
Rep By: Michael E. Fine, Peter O. Suchman

Monsanto Co.
Issues: AGR
Rep By: Paul A. Drazek, Craig A. Thorn

Nat'l Alliance for Infusion Therapy
Issues: MMM
Rep By: Alan K. Parver, Steve K. Stranne

Nat'l Ass'n of Public Hospitals and Health Systems
Issues: IMM INS MMM TOB
Rep By: Charlotte Collins, Barbara D. A. Eyman, Simon Lazarus, III, Charles Luband, Ted Slafsky, William H. E. von Oehsen

Nat'l Foreign Trade Council, Inc.
Issues: TRD
Rep By: Daniel M. Price

Organization for Internat'l Investment
Issues: GOV TRD
Rep By: Kelly Cameron, Michael E. Fine, Daniel M. Price

Pernod Ricard
Issues: TRD
Rep By: Daniel M. Price, Mark Traphagen

Pharmaceutical Research and Manufacturers of America
Issues: TRD
Rep By: Jeff Kushan

PROEXPORT
Rep By: Alice Slayton Clark, Maria DiGiulian, Gretchen Effgen, Brenda A. Jacobs

PSI Services Inc.

Public Hospital Pharmacy Coalition
Issues: PHA
Rep By: Ted Slafsky, William H. E. von Oehsen

Qualcomm Inc.
Issues: TEC
Rep By: Kelly Cameron, Brett G. Kappel, Jeff Kushan, Simon Lazarus, III, David C. Quam, Andrew Shoyer

Rollerblade, Inc.
Issues: TRD
Rep By: Michael E. Fine, Robert Torresen, Jr.

Shaklee Corp.
Issues: FOR TRD
Rep By: Daniel M. Price, Andrew Shoyer

Singapore Trade Development Board

Singapore, Embassy of the Republic of

Starrett City Associates
Issues: HOU
Rep By: John J. Knapp

Theragenics Corp.
Issues: ENG GOV
Rep By: Hon. Butler E. Derrick, Jr.

U.S. Ass'n of Importers of Textiles and Apparel
Issues: TRD
Rep By: Brenda A. Jacobs

Union Pacific
Rep By: Hon. Butler E. Derrick, Jr.

Walker Digital Corp.
Issues: GAM
Rep By: Hon. Butler E. Derrick, Jr., Brett G. Kappel, Simon Lazarus, III, David C. Quam

Power & Power

2300 Clarendon Blvd.
Suite 1107
Arlington, VA 22201
Tel: (703)841-1330
Fax: (703)841-1822

DC-Area Employees Representing Listed Clients
POWER, Thomas W., Partner
POWER, Tracy, Partner

Clients

Morrison Inc.

Thomas G. Powers

2008 Rockingham St.
McLean, VA 22101
Tel: (703)532-2163
Registered: LDA

Clients

Ass'n of Small Business Development Centers
Issues: SMB
Rep By: Thomas G. Powers

Nat'l Ass'n of Government Guaranteed Lenders
Issues: SMB
Rep By: Thomas G. Powers

Powers Pyles Sutter & Verville, PC

1875 I St. NW
12th Floor
Washington, DC 20006
Tel: (202)466-6550
Fax: (202)785-1756
Registered: LDA
Web: www.ppsv.com
E-mail: ppsv@ppsv.com
Focuses its practice on health law and public policy, education law, the law of tax-exempt organizations, and the law relating to public health and the environment.

Political Action Committee
Powers Pyles Sutter & Verville P.C. PAC
1875 I St. NW
12th Floor
Washington, DC 20006
Tel: (202)466-6550
Fax: (202)785-1756
Contact: Judith Buckalew

DC-Area Employees Representing Listed Clients
ALLEN, Jeremy W., Legislative Director
BUCKALEW, Judith, Director, Public Policy and Legislation
HALL, J. Michael, Director, Government Relations
HAYWOOD, Alyson M., Legislative Director
HUNTER, Justin, Legislative Director
POWERS, Galen D., President
PYLES, James C., Principal
SANER, II, Robert J., Principal
THOMAS, Peter W., Principal
VERVILLE, Richard E., Principal

Clients

American Academy of Neurology
Issues: HCR
Rep By: Judith Buckalew, Peter W. Thomas, Richard E. Verville

American Academy of Physical Medicine and Rehabilitation
Issues: HCR
Rep By: Richard E. Verville

American Ass'n for Homecare
Rep By: James C. Pyles

American Ass'n of Colleges of Nursing
Issues: BUD HCR
Rep By: J. Michael Hall

American Congress of Community Supports and Employment Services
Issues: HCR MMM
Rep By: Peter W. Thomas

American Foundation for the Blind - Governmental Relations Group
Issues: BUD EDU HCR
Rep By: J. Michael Hall, Alyson M. Haywood

American Liver Foundation
Issues: BUD HCR
Rep By: J. Michael Hall, Alyson M. Haywood

American Medical Rehabilitation Providers Ass'n
Issues: HCR
Rep By: Jeremy W. Allen, Peter W. Thomas

American Psychoanalytic Ass'n
Issues: HCR
Rep By: James C. Pyles

American Psychological Ass'n
Issues: BUD HCR
Rep By: J. Michael Hall

Ass'n of Metropolitan Water Agencies
Issues: UTI
Rep By: Robert J. Saner, II

Bon Secours Charity Health System
Issues: HCR MMM
Rep By: Judith Buckalew

California School of Professional Psychology
Issues: BUD EDU HCR
Rep By: J. Michael Hall, Alyson M. Haywood

Coalition for Patient Rights
Rep By: James C. Pyles

Fresenius Medical Care North America
Issues: HCR INS MED MMM
Rep By: Peter W. Thomas

Hooper, Lundy and Bookman
Issues: BUD MMM
Rep By: Judith Buckalew

InterTribal Bison Cooperative
Rep By: Judith Buckalew

J & J Independence Technology
Rep By: Peter W. Thomas

Joint Council of Allergy, Asthma and Immunology
Rep By: Richard E. Verville

Medical Group Management Ass'n
Issues: HCR
Rep By: Robert J. Saner, II

Nat'l Ass'n for the Advancement of Orthotics and Prosthetics
Issues: HCR
Rep By: Peter W. Thomas

Nat'l Ass'n of Rehabilitation Research and Training Centers
Rep By: Richard E. Verville

Nat'l Ass'n of Victims of Transfusion-associated HIV
Rep By: Judith Buckalew

Nat'l Mental Health Ass'n
Issues: BUD
Rep By: J. Michael Hall, Alyson M. Haywood

Nat'l Psoriasis Foundation
Issues: HCR MMM
Rep By: Judith Buckalew

Pain Care Coalition
Issues: HCR MED MMM
Rep By: Robert J. Saner, II

Southeastern Universities Research Ass'n
Rep By: J. Michael Hall

St. Louis University, School of Public Health
Issues: BUD DIS HCR
Rep By: Judith Buckalew

Tourette Syndrome Ass'n, Inc.
Issues: HCR MMM
Rep By: Judith Buckalew

University of Findlay
Issues: BUD DIS HCR
Rep By: Judith Buckalew

University of Florida Health Science Center
Issues: AGR BUD HCR
Rep By: J. Michael Hall, Alyson M. Haywood

Yosemite Nat'l Institute
Rep By: Judith Buckalew

Preston Gates Ellis & Rouvelas Meeds LLP

1735 New York Ave. NW
Suite 500
Washington, DC 20006-4759
Tel: (202)628-1700
Fax: (202)331-1024
Registered: LDA, FARA
Web: www.prestongates.com

A federal legislative, administrative and litigation law firm with offices in Washington, DC and major Pacific Coast centers including Seattle, Anchorage, Portland, Spokane, San Francisco, and Los Angeles. The firm has an international office in Hong Kong.

Political Action Committee

Preston Gates Ellis & Rouvelas Meeds LLP PAC
1735 New York Ave. NW
Suite 500
Washington, DC 20006-4759
Tel: (202)628-1700
Fax: (202)331-1024

DC-Area Employees Representing Listed Clients

BLANK, Jonathan, Managing Partner
BRANDT, Werner W., Government Affairs Counselor
CAMPBELL, Gary, Associate
CARLSON, Amy, Partner
CONNER, Darrell, Government Affairs Counselor
CRAIN, Julie, Associate
DAVIS, Hon. Bob, Counselor
DIMOPOULOS, Arthur, Of Counsel
DORAN, Kelley P., Associate
FLEMING, Elizabeth W., Of Counsel
FRIEDLANDER, Lisa L., Associate
FUNDERBURK, Hon. David, Government Affairs Counselor
GARVIE, Pamela J., Partner
GEIGER, Susan B., Partner
HEIMAN, Bruce J., Partner
HOUCK, Caryn, Associate
HUTHER, Christopher S., Partner
HUTSON, Harrison D., Of Counsel
IVEY, Glenn, Partner
JACKSON, Kristie, Associate
KAPLAN, Donald A., Partner
LONGSTRETH, John L., Partner
MAGEE, Marybeth, Associate
MARKS, Jeffrey, Associate
MARSHALL, Rolf, Partner
MCCALMON, Brian K., Associate
MEEDS, Hon. Lloyd, Of Counsel
MILLER, Eugene P., Partner
MOSHER, Sol, Senior Advisor, Federal Affairs and International Trade
MYHRE, William N., Partner
NURNBERGER, Ralph D., Government Affairs Counselor
O'MALLEY, Cindy, Government Affairs Analyst
O'NEIL, Michael J., Partner
PARK, Hong, Associate
PECKINPAUGH, Tim L., Partner
PHILLIPS, Rosanne, Treasurer, Political Action Committee
RITTER, Daniel, Associate
RIZZO, Sandra, Of Counsel
ROMERO, Jorge, Associate
ROUVELAS, Emanuel L., Chairman and Partner
RUGE, Mark H., Partner
SABO, Melanie, Partner
SEE, Chad
SHOOK, William A., Partner
STEPHENS, W. Dennis, Government Affairs Analyst
STERN, Martin L., Partner
THOMAS, W. David, Associate
TROY, Megan, Associate
TUCKER, Lisa M., Partner
VALENTINE, Steven R. "Rick", Of Counsel
WEISS, James R., Partner

Clients

Acme Software
Rep By: Tim L. Peckinpaugh, W. David Thomas

Adobe
Rep By: Tim L. Peckinpaugh

Air Nauru
Rep By: Susan B. Geiger

Akzo Nobel Chemicals, Inc.
Issues: CHM HCR
Rep By: Werner W. Brandt, Ralph D. Nurnberger, Daniel Ritter, Mark H. Ruge, Steven R. "Rick" Valentine

Alaska Ocean Seafoods L.P.
Issues: MAR
Rep By: William N. Myhre, Daniel Ritter

American Classic Voyages Co.
Issues: MAR
Rep By: Darrell Conner, Bruce J. Heiman, William N. Myhre, Emanuel L. Rouvelas

American Nuclear Insurers
Issues: ENG
Rep By: Tim L. Peckinpaugh

American Seafoods Inc.
Issues: MAR
Rep By: William N. Myhre, Daniel Ritter

American Soc. for Therapeutic Radiology and Oncology
Issues: BUD HCR MED MMM
Rep By: Susan B. Geiger, Sandra Rizzo, Mark H. Ruge, W. David Thomas

Americans for Computer Privacy
Rep By: Amy Carlson, Hon. David Funderburk, Bruce J. Heiman, Steven R. "Rick" Valentine

Amgen
Issues: HCR MMM
Rep By: Jonathan Blank, Pamela J. Garvie, Tim L. Peckinpaugh, Sandra Rizzo

Aventis Pharmaceutical Products
Rep By: Mark H. Ruge

Averitt Express, Inc.
Issues: AVI

Ballard, Spahr, Andrews & Ingersoll LLP
Issues: BUD

Battelle Memorial Institute
Issues: WAS
Rep By: Cindy O'Malley, Tim L. Peckinpaugh

Blaine, Washington, City of
Issues: CAW
Rep By: Tim L. Peckinpaugh

Brown-Forman Corp.
Issues: ADV CSP TAX TRD
Rep By: Pamela J. Garvie, John L. Longstreth, Michael J. O'Neil, Emanuel L. Rouvelas, W. Dennis Stephens

Burlington Northern Santa Fe Railway
Issues: ROD RRR TAX TEC
Rep By: Werner W. Brandt, Pamela J. Garvie, Hon. Lloyd Meeds, Michael J. O'Neil, Emanuel L. Rouvelas, W. Dennis Stephens, Martin L. Stern, Steven R. "Rick" Valentine

Business Software Alliance
Issues: CPI CPT CSP SCI TEC TRD
Rep By: Amy Carlson, Bruce J. Heiman

BWXT, Inc.
Rep By: Cindy O'Malley, Tim L. Peckinpaugh

Capitol Cargo Internat'l Airlines, Inc.
Rep By: Jonathan Blank

Chicago Title & Trust Co.
Issues: FIN INS
Rep By: Susan B. Geiger, Emanuel L. Rouvelas

Chicago Title Insurance
Issues: FIN INS
Rep By: Susan B. Geiger, Emanuel L. Rouvelas, Steven R. "Rick" Valentine

Chitimacha Tribe of Louisiana
Issues: IND
Rep By: Jonathan Blank, Werner W. Brandt, Hon. David Funderburk, Daniel Ritter, Emanuel L. Rouvelas, W. Dennis Stephens, Steven R. "Rick" Valentine

Coalition for Stability in Marine Financing
Rep By: William N. Myhre

Coastal Transportation Inc.
Issues: MAR
Rep By: William N. Myhre

Corning Inc.
Issues: TAX

Delta Air Lines
Rep By: James R. Weiss

Dredging Contractors of America
Issues: MAR
Rep By: Bruce J. Heiman, Rolf Marshall, William N. Myhre, Mark H. Ruge

East Tennessee Economic Council
Issues: BUD ECN
Rep By: Tim L. Peckinpaugh

eLottery, Inc.
Issues: GAM
Rep By: Werner W. Brandt, Hon. David Funderburk, Michael J. O'Neil, W. Dennis Stephens

Envirocare of Utah, Inc.
Issues: ENG ENV
Rep By: Cindy O'Malley, Tim L. Peckinpaugh, William A. Shook, W. Dennis Stephens, Steven R. "Rick" Valentine

Environmental Business Action Coalition
Issues: ENV
Rep By: Tim L. Peckinpaugh

For Homes

Foster Wheeler Environmental Corp.
Issues: ENG ENV
Rep By: Cindy O'Malley, Tim L. Peckinpaugh

Future of Puerto Rico Inc.
Issues: GOV
Rep By: Werner W. Brandt, Hon. David Funderburk, Hon. Lloyd Meeds, Sol Mosher, Tim L. Peckinpaugh, Daniel Ritter, W. Dennis Stephens, Steven R. "Rick" Valentine

Grant County P.U.D., Washington
Issues: UTI
Rep By: Werner W. Brandt, Tim L. Peckinpaugh, W. David Thomas

Great Lakes Dredge & Dock
Rep By: Bruce J. Heiman, Rolf Marshall, William N. Myhre

Greater Orlando Aviation Authority
Rep By: Jonathan Blank

Interlake Holding Corp.
Rep By: Susan B. Geiger, Emanuel L. Rouvelas

Internat'l Council of Containership Operators
Rep By: John L. Longstreth, Emanuel L. Rouvelas

Island Express Boat Lines Ltd.
Issues: BUD MAR
Rep By: Susan B. Geiger, Mark H. Ruge

KB Holdings
Rep By: Arthur Dimopoulos, William N. Myhre, Steven R. "Rick" Valentine

Lake Carriers Ass'n
Issues: TRA
Rep By: Susan B. Geiger, Mark H. Ruge

Magazine Publishers of America
Issues: POS
Rep By: Werner W. Brandt, Hon. David Funderburk, Bruce J. Heiman, Hon. Lloyd Meeds, Ralph D. Nurnberger, Cindy O'Malley, Emanuel L. Rouvelas, W. Dennis Stephens, Steven R. "Rick" Valentine

Marine Resources Company Internat'l
Rep By: William N. Myhre

Marine Transport Corp.
Rep By: Jonathan Blank, Susan B. Geiger

Maryland Department of Transportation
Rep By: Jonathan Blank, Pamela J. Garvie, James R. Weiss

Maryland, Aviation Administration of the State of
Rep By: Jonathan Blank

McDonald's Corp.

MG Financial Group
Issues: FIN
Rep By: Tim L. Peckinpaugh, Daniel Ritter

Microsoft Corp.
Issues: CPI CPT IMM TAX TEC TRD
Rep By: Werner W. Brandt, Bruce J. Heiman, Michael J. O'Neil, Emanuel L. Rouvelas, W. Dennis Stephens, Steven R. "Rick" Valentine

Money Garden Corp.
Rep By: Tim L. Peckinpaugh, Steven R. "Rick" Valentine

Mount Vernon Barge Service
Issues: TRA
Rep By: John L. Longstreth, Rolf Marshall, William N. Myhre, Mark H. Ruge, James R. Weiss

Nat'l Center for Economic Freedom, Inc.
Issues: GOV
Rep By: Werner W. Brandt, Hon. David Funderburk, Hon. Lloyd Meeds, Sol Mosher, Ralph D. Nurnberger, Tim L. Peckinpaugh, Daniel Ritter, W. Dennis Stephens, Steven R. "Rick" Valentine

Nat'l Council on Compensation Insurance
Issues: HCR INS
Rep By: Susan B. Geiger

Nat'l Marine Manufacturers Ass'n
Issues: MAR
Rep By: Mark H. Ruge

Nat'l Produce Production Inc.
Issues: AGR BAN
Rep By: Werner W. Brandt, Hon. David Funderburk, Bruce J. Heiman, Ralph D. Nurnberger, Daniel Ritter, Emanuel L. Rouvelas, Steven R. "Rick" Valentine

New York Institute of Technology
Issues: BUD EDU
Rep By: Amy Carlson

Northern Michigan University
Issues: EDU
Rep By: Cindy O'Malley, Tim L. Peckinpaugh, Mark H. Ruge

Northpoint Technology, Ltd.
Issues: TEC
Rep By: Lisa L. Friedlander, Hon. Lloyd Meeds, Martin L. Stern

Northwestern Michigan College
Issues: BUD
Rep By: Mark H. Ruge

Pac Med Clinics
Issues: BUD DEF HCR
Rep By: Werner W. Brandt, Tim L. Peckinpaugh

PepsiCo, Inc.
Rep By: Werner W. Brandt

Personal Watercraft Industry Ass'n
Issues: MAR NAT RES
Rep By: Mark H. Ruge

Pitney Bowes, Inc.
Issues: CPT POS
Rep By: Werner W. Brandt, Amy Carlson, Bruce J. Heiman, Hon. Lloyd Meeds, Cindy O'Malley, Emanuel L. Rouvelas, W. Dennis Stephens, Steven R. "Rick" Valentine

Port Angeles, Washington, City of
Rep By: Tim L. Peckinpaugh

PPL
Rep By: Pamela J. Garvie, Tim L. Peckinpaugh, Emanuel L. Rouvelas, Steven R. "Rick" Valentine

Pulse Medical Instruments
Issues: DEF TRA
Rep By: Pamela J. Garvie, Ralph D. Nurnberger

Regional Railroads of America

Rhodia, Inc.
Issues: CHM TRD
Rep By: Mark H. Ruge

RSA Security Inc.
Rep By: Amy Carlson, Bruce J. Heiman

Schlumberger Technology Corp.
Rep By: Tim L. Peckinpaugh

Seattle Housing Authority
Rep By: Tim L. Peckinpaugh

Seattle, Washington, Port of
Issues: AVI MAR
Rep By: Jonathan Blank, Werner W. Brandt, John L. Longstreth, William N. Myhre, Tim L. Peckinpaugh, Emanuel L. Rouvelas, W. David Thomas

Silverline Technologies, Inc.
Issues: BUD
Rep By: Ralph D. Nurnberger

Simpson Investment Co.
Issues: ENV

Southeast Alaska Regional Health Corp. (SEARHC)
Issues: HCR IND
Rep By: Werner W. Brandt, Darrell Conner, Susan B. Geiger, Hon. Lloyd Meeds

St. Lawrence Seaway Pilots Ass'n
Issues: MAR
Rep By: Mark H. Ruge

Stone and Webster Engineering Corp.
Issues: ENG ENV
Rep By: Cindy O'Malley, Tim L. Peckinpaugh, W. Dennis Stephens

Sun Outdoor Advertising
Rep By: John L. Longstreth, James R. Weiss

Sunmar Shipping, Inc.
Rep By: William N. Myhre

Tacoma, Washington, Port of
Issues: MAR TAX
Rep By: Jonathan Blank, Mark H. Ruge

Tan Holdings Corp.
Rep By: Ralph D. Nurnberger

Tate and Lyle North American Sugars Inc.
Issues: AGR FOO TRD
Rep By: Werner W. Brandt, Bruce J. Heiman, Sol Mosher, W. Dennis Stephens

The Title XI Coalition
Issues: BUD MAR
Rep By: Darrell Conner, Mark H. Ruge

Transpacific Stabilization Agreement
Issues: MAR
Rep By: Darrell Conner, John L. Longstreth, Mark H. Ruge

Transportation Institute
Issues: MAR TRD
Rep By: Darrell Conner, Susan B. Geiger, Bruce J. Heiman, John L. Longstreth, Rolf Marshall, William N. Myhre, Emanuel L. Rouvelas, Mark H. Ruge

Tri-City Industrial Development Council
Issues: BUD WAS
Rep By: Tim L. Peckinpaugh

United States Maritime Coalition
Issues: MAR
Rep By: Werner W. Brandt, Darrell Conner, Pamela J. Garvie, Susan B. Geiger, Bruce J. Heiman, John L. Longstreth, Rolf Marshall, Hon. Lloyd Meeds, Sol Mosher, William N. Myhre, Tim L. Peckinpaugh, Daniel Ritter, Emanuel L. Rouvelas, Mark H. Ruge, W. Dennis Stephens

USFHP Conference Group
Issues: BUD DEF HCR
Rep By: Cindy O'Malley, Tim L. Peckinpaugh

H. D. Vest Financial Service
Rep By: Tim L. Peckinpaugh

VoiceStream Wireless Corp.
Issues: TEC
Rep By: Werner W. Brandt, Hon. David Funderburk, Pamela J. Garvie, Hon. Lloyd Meeds, Sol Mosher, Ralph D. Nurnberger, Michael J. O'Neil, Tim L. Peckinpaugh, Emanuel L. Rouvelas, Mark H. Ruge, Chad See, W. Dennis Stephens, W. David Thomas, Steven R. "Rick" Valentine

WABCO
Rep By: Brian K. McCalmon, James R. Weiss

Washington State Hospital Ass'n
Rep By: Hon. Lloyd Meeds

Western Great Lakes Pilots Ass'n
Issues: MAR
Rep By: John L. Longstreth, Mark H. Ruge

PriceWaterhouseCoopers

1301 K St. NW Tel: (202)414-1000
Washington, DC 20005-3333 Fax: (202)414-1301
Registered: LDA

An accounting and consulting firm. Formed from the merger of Price Waterhouse LLP and Coopers and Lybrand.

Political Action Committee

PriceWaterhouseCoopers Partners' Political Action Committee
1301 K St. NW Tel: (202)414-1000
Washington, DC 20005-3333 Fax: (202)414-1301

DC-Area Employees Representing Listed Clients

ANGUS, Barbara, Partner
ANSON, Tim, Partner
BELL, Beverly E., Director, Federal Government Affairs
CAMPBELL, Larry, Manager, Tax Policy
CARLISLE, Jim, Director
CARLSON, Donald G., Director, National Tax Service
CHURCH, Elaine K., Partner, Employee Benefits Services
HARMAN, John R., Senior Manager, Tax Policy
JENNER, Gregory F., Partner
JOHNSON, Kirt C., Director
KIES, Kenneth J., Managing Partner, Washington National Tax Service
LONGANO, Don R., Partner
MCCONAGHY, Mark, Partner, Washington National Tax Service
MERRILL, Peter R., Partner
NEWLAND, Dee E. "Ned", Manager, Tax Policy Economics
RAFFANIELLO, Pat, Managing Director
REPASS, David M., Senior Manager
SCHOENFELD, Howard, Director
SHANAHAN, James R., Partner
SHAPIRO, Bernard M., Managing Partner
STARR, Sam, Partner
WELTMAN, Allen, Partner
WERTZ, Ken, Partner

Clients

Alliance Capital Management LP
Issues: TAX
Rep By: Jim Carlisle, Kirt C. Johnson, Kenneth J. Kies, Pat Raffaniello

American Ass'n of Nurse Anesthetists
Issues: HCR
Rep By: Kirt C. Johnson, Kenneth J. Kies, Pat Raffaniello

American Council of Life Insurers
Issues: TAX
Rep By: Barbara Angus, Jim Carlisle, Kenneth J. Kies

American Resort Development Ass'n

Archery Manufactures & Merchants Organization

Automobile Manufacturers R&D Coalition
Issues: TAX
Rep By: Jim Carlisle, Kenneth J. Kies, Mark McConaghy, James R. Shanahan

Bank of America
Issues: TAX
Rep By: Tim Anson, Jim Carlisle, Kenneth J. Kies

Blue Cross Blue Shield Ass'n
Issues: TAX
Rep By: Jim Carlisle, Kenneth J. Kies

Cigar Ass'n of America
Issues: TAX
Rep By: Kenneth J. Kies, Pat Raffaniello

Clark/Bardes, Inc.
Issues: TAX
Rep By: Jim Carlisle, Kenneth J. Kies, Pat Raffaniello

Coalition for Fair Tax Credits
Issues: TAX
Rep By: Jim Carlisle, Kenneth J. Kies, Pat Raffaniello, James R. Shanahan

Coalition of Corporate Taxpayers
Issues: TAX
Rep By: Jim Carlisle, Kenneth J. Kies, Don R. Longano

Conoco Inc.
Issues: TAX
Rep By: Kenneth J. Kies

Contract Manufacturing Coalition
Rep By: Barbara Angus, Tim Anson, Kenneth J. Kies, Peter R. Merrill

Council for Energy Independence
Issues: TAX
Rep By: Kenneth J. Kies, Pat Raffaniello

DaimlerChrysler Corp.

Edison Electric Institute
Issues: TAX
Rep By: Kenneth J. Kies, Pat Raffaniello

Electronic Commerce Tax Study Group
Issues: TAX
Rep By: Jim Carlisle, Peter R. Merrill, James R. Shanahan

General Electric Co.

General Motors Corp.
Issues: TAX
Rep By: Jim Carlisle, Kenneth J. Kies

Goldman, Sachs and Co.
Issues: TAX
Rep By: Barbara Angus, Kenneth J. Kies

Household Internat'l, Inc.
Issues: TAX
Rep By: Kenneth J. Kies

Interest Allocation Coalition
Issues: TAX
Rep By: Barbara Angus, Kenneth J. Kies

Internat'l Business Machines Corp.

Latona Associates, Inc.
Issues: TAX
Rep By: Kenneth J. Kies, Don R. Longano

Nat'l Foreign Trade Council, Inc.
Issues: TAX
Rep By: Peter R. Merrill

Owens Corning
Issues: TAX
Rep By: Jim Carlisle, Kenneth J. Kies, Pat Raffaniello

Placid Refining Co.
Issues: TAX
Rep By: Jim Carlisle, Kenneth J. Kies, Bernard M. Shapiro

Plum Creek Timber Co.
Issues: TAX
Rep By: Jim Carlisle, Kirt C. Johnson, Kenneth J. Kies, Pat Raffaniello

Prudential Insurance Co. of America

PwC Contract Manufacturing Coalition
Issues: TAX
Rep By: Barbara Angus, Tim Anson, Kenneth J. Kies

PwC Leasing Coalition
Issues: TAX
Rep By: Barbara Angus, Jim Carlisle, Kenneth J. Kies

Ralston Purina Co.
Issues: TAX
Rep By: Kenneth J. Kies, Don R. Longano

Schering-Plough Corp.

Steam Generator Coalition
Issues: TRD
Rep By: Kirt C. Johnson, Pat Raffaniello

Tupperware Corp.
Issues: TAX
Rep By: Barbara Angus, Kenneth J. Kies

United Parcel Service
Issues: TAX
Rep By: Barbara Angus, Jim Carlisle, Kenneth J. Kies, Pat Raffaniello

Vanguard Charitable Endowment Program
Issues: TAX
Rep By: Howard Schoenfeld

Pro Advance Inc.

5810 Kingstowne Center Dr.
Suite 120-740
Alexandria, VA 22315
Tel: (703)921-5070
Fax: (703)921-9217
Registered: FARA
Web: www.proadvance.com

DC-Area Employees Representing Listed Clients
GARLIKOV, Andrew J., President

Clients

Tai Ji Men Qigong Academy
Issues: FOR
Rep By: Andrew J. Garlikov

Sydney Probst

1832 Belmont Rd. NW
Washington, DC 20009
Tel: (202)986-6666
Fax: (202)986-6608
Registered: LDA
E-mail: sydneyp446@aol.com

Clients

Arkansas Blue Cross and Blue Shield
Issues: HCR
Rep By: Sydney Probst

Kansas City Southern Industries
Issues: FIN RRR
Rep By: Sydney Probst

Stilwell Financial Inc.
Issues: FIN
Rep By: Sydney Probst

Projects Internat'l

1800 K St. NW
Suite 1018
Washington, DC 20006
Tel: (202)333-1277
Fax: (202)333-3128
Assists clients in establishing overseas business ventures and investments.

DC-Area Employees Representing Listed Clients
PLATT, Alexander, Exec. V. President and General Manager

Clients

The Boeing Co.
Rep By: Alexander Platt

Proskauer Rose LLP

1233 20th St. NW
Suite 800
Washington, DC 20036-2396
Tel: (202)416-6800
Fax: (202)416-6899
Registered: LDA
Web: www.proskauer.com

DC-Area Employees Representing Listed Clients
BAUMGARTEN, Jon A., Partner
BIROS, Mark J., Partner
BROCK, Thomas H., Senior Counsel
CASSON, Joseph E., Partner
DENNIS, Warren L., Partner
HARKINS, Malcolm J., Partner
PASHKOFF, Lionel E., Senior Counsel
ROWE, Richard H., Partner
WOLF, Christopher, Partner

Clients

Bell Atlantic Network Services, Inc.

Bell Atlantic Personal Communications, Inc.

Films By Jove

Nat'l Film Preservation Foundation

Reed-Elsevier Inc.
Issues: CPT MIA
Rep By: Jon A. Baumgarten

Public Affairs Group, Inc.

1146 19th St. NW
Third Floor
Washington, DC 20036
Tel: (202)466-8209
Fax: (202)466-6572

DC-Area Employees Representing Listed Clients
FRASER, Edie, President and Chief Exec. Officer
STRZYZWESKI, Sandy, Chief Operating Officer/Chief Financial Officer/Chief Administrator

Clients

Cushman & Wakefield, Inc.

Duke Energy

Public Affairs Management, Inc.

1000 16th St. NW
Suite 500
Washington, DC 20036
Tel: (202)293-2231
Fax: (202)293-2118
Registered: LDA

DC-Area Employees Representing Listed Clients
AIKENS, Joan D., Managing Director

Clients

Regeneration Technologies Inc.

Public Affairs Resources, Inc.

3686 King St.
Suite 170
Alexandria, VA 22302
Tel: (703)379-6444
Fax: (703)379-9728
Registered: LDA
E-mail: petniunas@bellatlantic.net
A public affairs consulting firm.

DC-Area Employees Representing Listed Clients
PETNIUNAS, Susan E., Managing Principal

Clients

Abitibi Consolidated Sales Corp.
Issues: CAW ENG ENV TAX TRA
Rep By: Susan E. Petniunas

American Consumers for Affordable Homes
Rep By: Susan E. Petniunas

Election Systems & Software
Rep By: Susan E. Petniunas

Free Trade Lumber Council
Rep By: Susan E. Petniunas

Public Opinion Strategies

277 S. Washington St.
Suite 320
Alexandria, VA 22314
Tel: (703)836-7655
Fax: (703)836-8117
Web: www.pos.org
E-mail: info@pos.org
Political polling consultants.

DC-Area Employees Representing Listed Clients
BOLGER, Glen, Partner
MCINTURFF, William D., Managing Partner
NEWHOUSE, Neil S., Partner
ULM, Gene, Partner

Clients

American Hospital Ass'n
Rep By: William D. McInturff

Cellular Telecommunications and Internet Ass'n
Rep By: Glen Bolger, Neil S. Newhouse

Health Insurance Ass'n of America
Rep By: William D. McInturff

Public Policy Partners, LLC

1001 Pennsylvania Ave. NW
Suite 850 North
Washington, DC 20004-2505
Tel: (202)661-3580
Fax: (202)737-4242
Registered: LDA
A public policy strategic consulting and advocacy firm specializing in health care and medical technology issues.

DC-Area Employees Representing Listed Clients
DURENBERGER, Hon. David, President
WALDMANN, Daniel, V. President
WEEKLY, Jeffrey, Sr. Policy Associate

Clients

Express Scripts Inc.
Issues: DEF HCR
Rep By: Hon. David Durenberger, Daniel Waldmann, Jeffrey Weekly

Johnson & Johnson, Inc.
Issues: MMM
Rep By: Hon. David Durenberger, Daniel Waldmann, Jeffrey Weekly

St. Jude Medical, Inc.
Issues: HCR MMM SCI
Rep By: Hon. David Durenberger, Daniel Waldmann, Jeffrey Weekly

TriWest Healthcare Alliance, Inc.
Issues: DEF HCR MMM VET
Rep By: Hon. David Durenberger

Urologix, Inc.
Issues: MMM
Rep By: Hon. David Durenberger, Daniel Waldmann, Jeffrey Weekly

Vertis Neuroscience
Issues: MED MMM
Rep By: Hon. David Durenberger, Daniel Waldmann, Jeffrey Weekly

Public Policy Resources

6309 Beachway Dr.
Falls Church, VA 22044
Tel: (703)998-7121
Fax: (703)998-7123
Registered: LDA
E-mail: spreisti@erols.com

DC-Area Employees Representing Listed Clients
PRESTI, Susan, President

Clients

Air Courier Conference of America
Rep By: Susan Presti

Business Alliance for Customs Modernization

Public Private Partnership

1825 I Street NW
Suite 400
Washington, DC 20006
Tel: (202)429-2732
Fax: (202)429-6834
Registered: LDA

DC-Area Employees Representing Listed Clients
COLLINS, Arthur R.

Clients

Brown and Williamson Tobacco Corp.
Issues: AGR BUD TAX TOB TRD
Rep By: Arthur R. Collins

Lorillard Tobacco Co.
Issues: AGR BUD TAX TOB TRD
Rep By: Arthur R. Collins

Public Strategies Washington, Inc.

633 Pennsylvania Ave. NW
Fourth Floor
Washington, DC 20004
Tel: (202)783-2596
Fax: (202)628-5379
Registered: LDA, FARA
Web: www.psw-inc.com
E-mail: joneill@psw-inc.com
A government affairs consulting firm.

DC-Area Employees Representing Listed Clients
COLLETT, Anne
MCCURRY, Mike, President
O'NEALL, Nancy
O'NEILL, Joseph P., President
SNYDER, Paul M.
VARNEY, Kevin P.

Clients

Advanced Micro Devices
Issues: TAX
Rep By: Paul M. Snyder

Affiliated Computer Services
Issues: FIN
Rep By: Joseph P. O'Neill

American Methanol Institute
Issues: AUT CAW ENG ENV FUE SCI TAX TRA
Rep By: Joseph P. O'Neill, Paul M. Snyder

AngloGold North America
Issues: NAT
Rep By: Nancy O'Neall, Joseph P. O'Neill

Anheuser-Busch Cos., Inc.
Issues: BEV
Rep By: Joseph P. O'Neill, Paul M. Snyder

Bristol-Myers Squibb Co.
Issues: HCR
Rep By: Joseph P. O'Neill, Paul M. Snyder

Chamber of Commerce of the U.S.A.
Issues: ECN
Rep By: Joseph P. O'Neill

Edison Electric Institute
Issues: UTI
Rep By: Nancy O'Neall, Joseph P. O'Neill, Paul M. Snyder

Greater El Paso Chamber of Commerce
Issues: ECN
Rep By: Anne Collett, Joseph P. O'Neill

Honda North America, Inc.
Issues: AUT
Rep By: Joseph P. O'Neill

Hutchison Whampo, LTD
Rep By: Joseph P. O'Neill

Lockheed Martin IMS
Issues: GOV
Rep By: Joseph P. O'Neill

Mexico, Secretaria de Comercio y Fomento Industrial (SECOFI)
Rep By: Anne Collett, Joseph P. O'Neill, Paul M. Snyder

Reuters America Inc.
Issues: COM
Rep By: Joseph P. O'Neill

Southwest Airlines
Issues: AVI
Rep By: Joseph P. O'Neill, Paul M. Snyder

Public Strategies, Inc.

1401 I St. NW
Suite 220
Washington, DC 20005
Web: www.publicstrategiesinc.com
Tel: (202)216-8910
Fax: (202)216-8901
Registered: LDA

DC-Area Employees Representing Listed Clients
COWAN, Glenn, Managing Director
ELLER, Jeff
HENDERSON, Wallace J.

Clients

Bridgestone/Firestone, Inc.
Issues: CPI EDU SCI TAX TEC
Rep By: Jeff Eller, Wallace J. Henderson

Cellular Telecommunications and Internet Ass'n
Issues: COM CSP LAW LBR SCI TAX TEC
Rep By: Wallace J. Henderson

Fantasma Networks, Inc.
Issues: AUT CSP GOV
Rep By: Wallace J. Henderson

ITRON, Inc.
Issues: CSP ENG FUE MAN TEC UTI
Rep By: Wallace J. Henderson

United States Telecom Ass'n
Rep By: Wallace J. Henderson

Robert N. Pyle & Associates

1223 Potomac St. NW
Washington, DC 20007-0231
Tel: (202)333-8190
Fax: (202)337-3809
Registered: LDA

A multi-service public relations and political consulting firm. Clients include associations and companies in the food, metals and housing industries.

DC-Area Employees Representing Listed Clients
HERSH, Alexis, Senior V. President
O'NEILL, Alison, V. President
PYLE, Robert N., Chairman

Clients

Bulgarian-American Business Center
Issues: FOR
Rep By: Alexis Hersh, Alison O'Neill, Robert N. Pyle

Elkem Metals Co.
Issues: DEF
Rep By: Alexis Hersh, Alison O'Neill, Robert N. Pyle

Eramet Marietta Inc.

Independent Bakers Ass'n
Issues: FOO
Rep By: Alexis Hersh, Alison O'Neill, Robert N. Pyle

Internat'l Dairy-Deli-Bakery Ass'n
Issues: FOO
Rep By: Alexis Hersh, Alison O'Neill, Robert N. Pyle

Mary Jane Bakeries

McKee Foods Corp.
Issues: FOO
Rep By: Alexis Hersh, Alison O'Neill, Robert N. Pyle

Nat'l Grape Co-operative Ass'n, Inc.

Orbex Resources
Rep By: Alexis Hersh, Alison O'Neill, Robert N. Pyle

Ort's, Inc.
Rep By: Robert N. Pyle

Stratcor
Rep By: Robert N. Pyle

Strategic Minerals Corp.
Issues: DEF
Rep By: Alexis Hersh, Alison O'Neill, Robert N. Pyle

Welch's Foods, Inc.
Issues: FOO
Rep By: Alexis Hersh, Alison O'Neill, Robert N. Pyle

Qorvis Communications

1211 Connecticut Ave. NW
Suite 608
Washington, DC 20036
Web: www.qorvis.com
E-mail: INFO@qorvis.com
Tel: (202)496-1000
Fax: (202)496-1300

A grassroots communications firm.

DC-Area Employees Representing Listed Clients
ALUISI, Toni, Director
BRUGGEN, Hilary, Managing Director
BUCKLEY, William, Managing Director
COLLETON, Maura, Director
FERGUSON, Sydney, Managing Director
FUSILIER, VeTalle, Managing Director
HEALY, Thomas R., Director, Business Development
MARR, Brendan, Director
MERRITT, Bernie, Partner
PETRUZZELLO, Michael, Managing Partner
SCHMIDT, Jeffrey, Director
SHUR, Stephen, Principal
SMITH, Judy, Partner
THOMPSON, Jeffrey, Director
WEBER, Jim, Partner

Charles W. Quatt Associates, Inc.

2233 Wisconsin Ave.
Suite 501
Washington, DC 20007
Tel: (202)363-7782
Fax: (202)338-1000
Registered: LDA

A management consulting/policy analysis and advocacy firm.

DC-Area Employees Representing Listed Clients
QUATT, Charles W., Principal
VOGEL, Brian H., Principal

Clients

Coalition Against Bigger Trucks
Issues: TRU
Rep By: Brian H. Vogel

Andrew F. Quinlan

6023 Shaffer Dr.
Alexandria, VA 22310
Tel: (202)285-0244
Fax: (603)971-9137
Registered: LDA

Clients

Swiss Investors Protection Ass'n
Issues: BAN BUD FIN TAX
Rep By: Andrew F. Quinlan

Quinn Gillespie & Associates

1133 Connecticut Ave. NW
Fifth Floor
Washington, DC 20036
Web: www.quinngillespie.com
Tel: (202)457-1110
Fax: (202)457-1130

Strategic public affairs consulting, including legislative and executive branch lobbying, communications strategy, message development and advertisement production and placement.

DC-Area Employees Representing Listed Clients
ANDREWS, Bruce H., Associate
CONNAUGHTON, Jeffrey J., Principal
GARRETT, Debbie, Public Relations Associate
GILLESPIE, Edward W., Principal
HUME, Virginia, Public Relations Associate
HYNES, Scott, Associate
JAMES, Harriet, Associate
LAMPKIN, Marc, Associate
LAYMAN, Heather, Public Relations Associate
LUGAR, David, Associate
MADUROS, Nicholas, Associate
MCGUIRE, Anne, Associate
MEECE, Ashley, Associate
POWELL, Richard, Managing Director
QUINN, John M. "Jack", Principal
SIMMONS, Kyle, Associate
THOMAS, Marti
ZOMESKY, Marla, Associate

Clients

Allegiance Healthcare Corp.

American Hospital Ass'n
Issues: HCR
Rep By: Bruce H. Andrews, Edward W. Gillespie

American Insurance Ass'n
Rep By: Edward W. Gillespie, Marc Lampkin

Americans for Better Education

Americans for Computer Privacy

The Ass'n For Manufacturing Technology (AMT)

Bell Atlantic Digital Spectrum

British Columbia Lumber Trade Council
Issues: TRD
Rep By: Edward W. Gillespie, Harriet James, David Lugar, John M. "Jack" Quinn

The Chubb Corp.
Issues: INS TRD
Rep By: Jeffrey J. Connaughton, John M. "Jack" Quinn

Cisco Systems Inc.

Coalition to Repeal the Tax on Talking
Rep By: Debbie Garrett

The Coca-Cola Company

DaimlerChrysler Corp.

Direct TV

The Dow Chemical Co.

Enron Corp.

Forest County Potawatomi Community

Health Insurance Ass'n of America

Instinet
Issues: FIN
Rep By: Bruce H. Andrews, Jeffrey J. Connaughton, Edward W. Gillespie, David Lugar, Anne McGuire, John M. "Jack" Quinn

LVMH Moet Hennessy Louis Vuitton S.A.
Issues: TRD
Rep By: Bruce H. Andrews, Edward W. Gillespie, Harriet James, Nicholas Maduros, Anne McGuire, John M. "Jack" Quinn, Marla Zomesky

Metropolitan Life Insurance Co.
Rep By: Jeffrey J. Connaughton, Nicholas Maduros, John M. "Jack" Quinn

Microsoft Corp.

Network Advertising Initiative

Recording Industry Ass'n of America
Issues: ART COM CPT LBR
Rep By: Edward W. Gillespie

SBC Communications Inc.
Rep By: Edward W. Gillespie

Technology Network
Issues: IMM TAX TRD
Rep By: Bruce H. Andrews, Edward W. Gillespie, David Lugar, John M. "Jack" Quinn

USEC, Inc.
Issues: BUD ENG
Rep By: Bruce H. Andrews, Edward W. Gillespie, David Lugar

Verizon Communications

Viacom Inc.

Mark J. Raabe

3300 Circle Hill Rd.
Alexandria, VA 22305
Tel: (202)638-4170
Fax: (202)638-3670
Registered: LDA

A self-employed government relations consultant.

Clients

Downey McGrath Group, Inc.
Issues: HCR TAX
Rep By: Mark J. Raabe

Merck & Co.
Issues: TAX
Rep By: Mark J. Raabe

Barbara Raimondo

P.O. Box 466
Washington Grove, MD 20880

A self-employed public affairs consultant

Clients

American Soc. for Deaf Children
Issues: EDU
Rep By: Barbara Raimondo

Conference of Educational Administrators of Schools and Programs for the Deaf
Issues: EDU
Rep By: Barbara Raimondo

Robert A. Rapoza Associates

1250 I St. NW
Suite 902
Washington, DC 20005
Web: www.rapoza.org
E-mail: Rapoza@Rapoza.org
Tel: (202)393-5225
Fax: (202)393-3034
Registered: LDA

DC-Area Employees Representing Listed Clients
FEIGHAN, Alison, V. President
MOODY, Christopher, Policy Associate
RAPOZA, Robert A., President
SINICROPI, Pat, Policy Associate
SWESNIK, Deidre, Policy Associate

Clients

Alaska Village Initiatives
Rep By: Robert A. Rapoza

Arkansas Enterprise Group
Rep By: Robert A. Rapoza

Bedford Stuyvesant Restoration Corp.
Rep By: Robert A. Rapoza

Bethel New Life
Rep By: Robert A. Rapoza

Chicanos Por La Causa
Rep By: Robert A. Rapoza

Community Development Venture Capital Ass'n
Issues: AGR ECN
Rep By: Alison Feighan, Robert A. Rapoza

Community Transportation Ass'n of America
Issues: BUD TRA
Rep By: Alison Feighan, Robert A. Rapoza

Corporation for Supportive Housing
Issues: BUD
Rep By: Robert A. Rapoza

Delta Foundation
Rep By: Robert A. Rapoza
The Enterprise Foundation
Issues: BUD
Rep By: Robert A. Rapoza
Impact Services
Rep By: Robert A. Rapoza
Kentucky Highlands Investment Corp.
Rep By: Robert A. Rapoza
Local Initiatives Support Corp.
Issues: BUD ECN
Rep By: Robert A. Rapoza
Massachusetts Housing Partnership Fund
Rep By: Robert A. Rapoza
Mercy Housing
Issues: HOU
Rep By: Robert A. Rapoza
Nat'l Ass'n of Housing Partnerships
Issues: BUD
Rep By: Robert A. Rapoza
Nat'l Ass'n of SBA Microloan Intermediaries
Issues: SMB
Rep By: Alison Feighan, Robert A. Rapoza
Nat'l Council of La Raza
Rep By: Robert A. Rapoza
Nat'l Migrant Head Start Ass'n
Issues: EDU
Rep By: Robert A. Rapoza
Nat'l Neighborhood Housing Network
Issues: HOU
Rep By: Robert A. Rapoza
Nat'l Rural Development & Finance Corp.
Issues: BUD
Rep By: Alison Feighan, Robert A. Rapoza
Nat'l Rural Housing Coalition
Issues: BUD HOU
Rep By: Alison Feighan, Robert A. Rapoza
NCALL Research
Northeast Entrepreneur Fund
Rep By: Robert A. Rapoza
Northeast Ventures Corp.
Rep By: Robert A. Rapoza
Northern Economic Initiatives Corp.
Rep By: Robert A. Rapoza
Rural Community Assistance Corp.
Issues: ECN
Rep By: Robert A. Rapoza
Shorebank Corp.
Issues: ECN
Rep By: Robert A. Rapoza
Suomi College
Issues: EDU
Rep By: Robert A. Rapoza, Deidre Swesnik
TELACU
Rep By: Robert A. Rapoza
Youthbuild, USA
Issues: BUD
Rep By: Robert A. Rapoza

Marvin S. Rappaport

1200 New Hampshire Ave. NW
Suite 800
Washington, DC 20036
Tel: (202)776-2911
Fax: (202)776-2222
Registered: LDA
A self-employed consultant.

Robert Rarog

1810 Plymouth St. NW
Washington, DC 20012
Tel: (202)882-0321
Fax: (202)882-1096
Registered: LDA
E-mail: rrarog@aol.com
An independant consultant. Specializes in export control matters.

Clients

Sun Microsystems
Issues: CPI TRD
Rep By: Robert Rarog

The Rasky/Baerlein Group

818 Connecticut Ave. NW
Suite 1006
Washington, DC 20006
Tel: (202)530-7700
Fax: (202)530-7714

DC-Area Employees Representing Listed Clients
SCOTT-MARTIN, Read, V. President

Bruce Ray & Company

636 A St. NE
Washington, DC 20002
Tel: (202)543-4935
Registered: LDA

DC-Area Employees Representing Listed Clients
RAY, Ph.D., Bruce A., President

Clients

Bayley Seton Hospital
Rep By: Bruce A. Ray, Ph.D.
Cumberland Packing Corp.
Issues: FOO
Rep By: Bruce A. Ray, Ph.D.
Fairview Hospital and Healthcare Services
Issues: DEF
Rep By: Bruce A. Ray, Ph.D.
Lutheran Medical Center
Rep By: Bruce A. Ray, Ph.D.

Pamela Ray-Strunk and Associates

4805 N. 20th Place
Arlington, VA 22207
Tel: (703)522-8278
Fax: (703)526-0355
Registered: LDA
E-mail: psray@msn.com
A state and federal government relations firm.

DC-Area Employees Representing Listed Clients
RAY-STRUNK, Pamela

Clients

Carr Public Affairs
Issues: BUD EDU HCR
Rep By: Pamela Ray-Strunk
Dallas Area Rapid Transit Authority
Issues: BUD TRA
Rep By: Pamela Ray-Strunk
Suffolk, New York, County of
Issues: AGR ECN TRA WEL
Rep By: Pamela Ray-Strunk
Touro Law Center
Issues: BUD
Rep By: Pamela Ray-Strunk

RBG Associates

2200 Foxhall Rd. NW
Washington, DC 20007
Tel: (202)337-1870
Fax: (202)337-0165
Registered: LDA

DC-Area Employees Representing Listed Clients
GRIFFIN, Jr., Richard B., Managing Director

Clients

Ultratech Stepper Inc.
Issues: CPI SCI
Rep By: Richard B. Griffin, Jr.
Wabtec Corp.
Issues: RRR
Rep By: Richard B. Griffin, Jr.

Rea, Cross & Auchincloss

1707 L St. NW
Suite 570
Washington, DC 20006
Tel: (202)785-3700
Fax: (202)659-4934

DC-Area Employees Representing Listed Clients
REA, Jr., Bryce, Partner

Clients

Middle Atlantic Conference
Rep By: Bryce Rea, Jr.
New England Motor Rate Bureau
Rep By: Bryce Rea, Jr.

George Reagle

10046 Cotton Mill Lane
Columbia, MD 21046
Tel: (301)596-0533
Fax: (301)596-0352
Registered: LDA

Clients

Chamber of Commerce of the U.S.A.
Rep By: George Reagle
Coalition for Vehicle Choice
Issues: TRA
Rep By: George Reagle
Nat'l Safety Council
Rep By: George Reagle

Real Trends

9200 Centerway Rd.
Gaithersburg, MD 20879
Tel: (301)840-6642
Fax: (301)840-8502
Web: www.zgram.net
E-mail: zhi@zgram.net

DC-Area Employees Representing Listed Clients
HAMBY, Zhi Marie, President

Clients

CyberWynd Publications
Rep By: Zhi Marie Hamby
Nat'l Military Intelligence Ass'n
Rep By: Zhi Marie Hamby
Operations Security Professionals Soc.
Rep By: Zhi Marie Hamby

Robert L. Redding

313 Massachusetts Ave. NE
Washington, DC 20002
Tel: (202)543-7464
Fax: (202)543-4575
Registered: LDA
E-mail: b.redding@worldnet.att.net
A self-employed consultant.

Clients

Automotive Service Ass'n
Issues: AUT
Rep By: Robert L. Redding, Jr.
CRT, Inc.
Issues: EDU TEC
Rep By: Robert L. Redding, Jr.
Georgia Commodity Commission for Peanuts
Issues: AGR
Rep By: Robert L. Redding, Jr.
Georgia Cotton Commission
Issues: AGR
Rep By: Robert L. Redding, Jr.
Nat'l Peanut Buying Point Ass'n
Issues: AGR
Rep By: Robert L. Redding, Jr.
SICPA Industries of America, Inc.
Issues: BAN
Rep By: Robert L. Redding, Jr.
Tobacco Quota Warehouse Alliance
Issues: AGR
Rep By: Robert L. Redding, Jr.
University of Georgia - College of Agricultural and Environmental Sciences
Rep By: Robert L. Redding, Jr.
Vidalia Onion Business Council
Issues: AGR
Rep By: Robert L. Redding, Jr.

Reddy, Begley, & McCormick, LLP

2175 K St. NW
Suite 350
Washington, DC 20037-1845
Tel: (202)659-5700
Fax: (202)659-5711
Web: www.rbmfcclaw.com
E-mail: rbmfcclaw@aol.com
A communications law firm.

DC-Area Employees Representing Listed Clients
BEGLEY, Dennis F., Managing Partner
MCCORMICK, Matthew H., Partner

Clients

Asterisk Communications
Rep By: Dennis F. Begley
GHB Broadcasting Corp.
Rep By: Dennis F. Begley
KTTW-TV and KTTM-TV
Rep By: Dennis F. Begley
Memphis Public Library and Information Center
Rep By: Matthew H. McCormick
Midwest Broadcasting Corp.
Rep By: Matthew H. McCormick

Redfern Resources

P.O. Box 818
Great Falls, VA 22066-1824
Tel: (703)759-9388
Fax: (703)832-0516
Registered: LDA
E-mail: eredfern@erols.com
Public affairs consultant.

DC-Area Employees Representing Listed Clients
REDFERN, Ed, Government Relations Director

Clients

Cedar Rapids, Iowa, City of
Issues: CAW ENV GOV
Rep By: Ed Redfern
Iowa Public Transit Ass'n
Issues: TRA
Rep By: Ed Redfern
Kansas City Area Transportation Authority
Issues: HLT
Rep By: Ed Redfern
Kansas Public Transit Ass'n
Issues: TRA
Rep By: Ed Redfern
Lennox Internat'l
Issues: ENG ENV
Rep By: Ed Redfern

Missouri Public Transit Ass'n
Issues: TRA
Rep By: Ed Redfern

The Ruan Companies
Issues: TRA
Rep By: Ed Redfern

Schering-Plough Corp.
Issues: HLT
Rep By: Ed Redfern

Stine Seed Co.
Issues: AGR
Rep By: Ed Redfern

Woodbury County, Iowa
Issues: CAW ENV GOV
Rep By: Ed Redfern

World Food Prize
Issues: SCI
Rep By: Ed Redfern

Redland Energy Group

700 13th St. NW
Suite 950
Washington, DC 20005
Tel: (202)434-8918
Fax: (202)638-5129

DC-Area Employees Representing Listed Clients
HOWES, John A.

Clients

TVA Watch
Issues: ENG GOV UTI
Rep By: John A. Howes

T. Dean Reed Co.

1155 15th St. NW
Suite 1003
Washington, DC 20005
Web: www.tdeanreed.com
Tel: (202)223-3532
Fax: (202)223-5609
Registered: FARA

DC-Area Employees Representing Listed Clients
REED, T. Dean, President

Clients

Singapore, Embassy of the Republic of

Reed, Smith, Hazel & Thomas

P.O. Box 12001
Falls Church, VA 22042
Web: www.hazelthomas.com
E-mail: lawinfo@hazelthomas.com
Tel: (703)641-4200
Fax: (703)641-4340

Clients

American Security Council

Reed, Smith, LLP

1301 K St. NW
Suite 1100-East Tower
Washington, DC 20005
Web: www.rs.com
E-mail: rssm@rs.com
Tel: (202)414-9200
Fax: (202)414-9299
Registered: LDA

Political Action Committee
Reed Smith PAC

1301 K St. NW
Suite 1100-East Tower
Washington, DC 20005
Contact: David C. Evans
Tel: (202)414-9200
Fax: (202)414-9299

DC-Area Employees Representing Listed Clients
EVANS, David C., Partner
GEOGHEGAN, William A., Counsel
HARRIS, Judith L., Counsel
MCCURDY, Debra A., Health Policy Analyst
PETER, Phillips S., Counsel, Government Relations and Federal Group Head
RISSETTO, Christopher L., Partner
SCHEINESON, Marc, Partner
SEALE, C. Stevens, Partner
THOMAS, William G., Partner

Clients

Agilent Technologies
Issues: HCR
Rep By: Phillips S. Peter

AKAL Security
Issues: BUD GOV LAW LBR
Rep By: C. Stevens Seale

American Ass'n for Homecare
Issues: HCR
Rep By: Phillips S. Peter

American Soc. of Consultant Pharmacists
Issues: HCR
Rep By: Phillips S. Peter

Ass'n of Health Information Outsourcing Services
Issues: MMM
Rep By: Phillips S. Peter, Marc Scheineson

Baltimore, Maryland, City of
Issues: BUD
Rep By: Christopher L. Rissetto

Boys and Girls Club of Brownsville, Inc.
Issues: BUD
Rep By: Phillips S. Peter

Brick Industry Ass'n
Issues: MAN
Rep By: David C. Evans

Calaveras County, California, Water District
Issues: BUD ENV NAT RES TOU
Rep By: Christopher L. Rissetto

Center for Research on Institutions and Social Policy
Issues: BUD LAW
Rep By: Phillips S. Peter, C. Stevens Seale

Detroit, Michigan, City of
Rep By: Christopher L. Rissetto

Dominion Resources, Inc.
Issues: ENG UTI
Rep By: Phillips S. Peter, C. Stevens Seale, William G. Thomas

Eclipse Surgical Technologies
Issues: HCR
Rep By: Phillips S. Peter

Eureka, California, City of
Issues: BUD ENV NAT RES TOU
Rep By: Christopher L. Rissetto

Federated Investors, Inc.
Issues: SCI
Rep By: Phillips S. Peter

Flint, Michigan, City of
Issues: BUD
Rep By: Christopher L. Rissetto

Golf Course Superintendents Ass'n of America
Issues: CAW ENV LBR TOU
Rep By: David C. Evans, Phillips S. Peter, C. Stevens Seale

Humboldt Bay Municipal Water District
Issues: BUD ENV NAT RES TOU
Rep By: Christopher L. Rissetto

Innovative Science Solutions
Issues: MED
Rep By: Marc Scheineson

Internat'l Hearing Soc.
Issues: HCR
Rep By: Marc Scheineson

Knoll Pharmaceutical Co.
Issues: PHA
Rep By: Phillips S. Peter, C. Stevens Seale

Landis, NJ Sewerage Authority
Issues: BUD
Rep By: Christopher L. Rissetto

Lason, Inc.
Issues: GOV
Rep By: Phillips S. Peter, C. Stevens Seale

Mercy Medical
Issues: HCR MMM
Rep By: Phillips S. Peter

Nat'l Ass'n of Dental Laboratories
Issues: GOV
Rep By: David C. Evans

Oce-USA, Inc.
Issues: MAN
Rep By: Marc Scheineson

Ocean County, NJ Utilities Authority
Issues: BUD ENV NAT RES TOU
Rep By: Christopher L. Rissetto

Omnicare, Inc.
Issues: HCR MMM
Rep By: Phillips S. Peter

Orlando, Florida, City of
Issues: BUD
Rep By: Christopher L. Rissetto

Owens-Illinois, Inc.
Issues: MAN
Rep By: David C. Evans, Phillips S. Peter, C. Stevens Seale

PCS Health Systems, Inc.
Issues: HCR
Rep By: Phillips S. Peter, Marc Scheineson

Pharmacia Corp.
Issues: HCR
Rep By: Marc Scheineson

Phoenix, Arizona, City of
Issues: BUD
Rep By: Christopher L. Rissetto

Professional Bail Agents of the United States
Issues: GOV LAW LBR
Rep By: C. Stevens Seale

Pure Energy Corp.
Issues: ENG
Rep By: Phillips S. Peter

Respironics
Issues: HCR MMM
Rep By: Phillips S. Peter

Ryder System, Inc.
Issues: TOR TRA TRU
Rep By: C. Stevens Seale

Solus Research, Inc.
Issues: FOO MED
Rep By: Marc Scheineson

Springettsbury, Pennsylvania, Township of
Issues: BUD ENV NAT RES TOU
Rep By: Christopher L. Rissetto

Sunrise Medical
Issues: MMM
Rep By: Phillips S. Peter

Techneglas, Inc.
Issues: TRD
Rep By: Phillips S. Peter

USX Corp.
Issues: FUE
Rep By: Phillips S. Peter, C. Stevens Seale

Washington, Department of Information of the State of
Issues: COM
Rep By: Judith L. Harris, Phillips S. Peter

J. G. Wentworth
Issues: TAX
Rep By: Phillips S. Peter

Law Office of Paige E. Reffe

1801 K St. NW
Suite 1205L
Washington, DC 20006
Tel: (202)452-7330
Fax: (202)542-7333
Registered: LDA

DC-Area Employees Representing Listed Clients
REFFE, Paige E., Attorney

Clients

Ass'n of Bankruptcy Professionals, Inc.
Issues: BNK
Rep By: Paige E. Reffe

Lithuania, Republic of
Rep By: Paige E. Reffe

Slovakia, Government of
Rep By: Paige E. Reffe

University of Colorado, Office of the President
Issues: BUD ECN EDU IND
Rep By: Paige E. Reffe

Russ Reid Co.

1420 New York Ave. NW
Suite 550
Washington, DC 20005
Tel: (202)783-4805
Fax: (202)783-4804
Registered: LDA

Washington office of a Pasadena, CA communications consulting firm.

DC-Area Employees Representing Listed Clients
KELLER, Thomas C., Account Supervisor
MARCONE, Paul
MCINTYRE, Mark D., V. President and Director, Washington Office
WENNER, Jovita, Supervisor

Clients

Alfalit Internat'l
Issues: EDU
Rep By: Thomas C. Keller, Mark D. McIntyre, Jovita Wenner

City Rescue Mission Inc.

Corporation for Business, Work and Learning
Issues: EDU LBR
Rep By: Thomas C. Keller, Paul Marcone, Mark D. McIntyre, Jovita Wenner

Detroit Rescue Mission Ministries
Issues: ALC HOU
Rep By: Thomas C. Keller, Mark D. McIntyre

The Doe Fund
Issues: HOU
Rep By: Mark D. McIntyre

Dream Center/City Help
Issues: HOU
Rep By: Mark D. McIntyre, Jovita Wenner

Earth University, Inc.
Issues: EDU
Rep By: Thomas C. Keller, Mark D. McIntyre, Jovita Wenner

Eastern College

Eastern Mennonite University

Fresno Pacific University

Fuller Theological Seminary
Issues: EDU
Rep By: Thomas C. Keller, Mark D. McIntyre

Futures for Children

Gospel Rescue Ministries of Washington
Issues: HOU
Rep By: Thomas C. Keller, Mark D. McIntyre

Hebrew Academy for Special Children
Issues: EDU
Rep By: Mark D. McIntyre

Light of Life Ministries
Issues: ALC HOU WEL
Rep By: Thomas C. Keller, Mark D. McIntyre

New College
Issues: EDU
Rep By: Thomas C. Keller, Mark D. McIntyre

Touro College
Issues: EDU
Rep By: Thomas C. Keller, Mark D. McIntyre

Vanguard University
Issues: EDU
Rep By: Thomas C. Keller, Mark D. McIntyre

Village of Kiryas Joel
Issues: MED
Rep By: Thomas C. Keller, Mark D. McIntyre, Jovita Wenner

William Tyndale College
Issues: EDU
Rep By: Thomas C. Keller, Mark D. McIntyre, Jovita Wenner

Yeshiva of South Shore

The Rendon Group, Inc.

1875 Connecticut Ave. NW
Suite 414
Washington, DC 20009
Tel: (202)745-4900
Fax: (202)745-0215
Registered: FARA
Web: www.rendon.com
E-mail: slibby@rendon.com
A global strategic communications consultancy assisting clients in developing their communications and public relations policy and objectives.

DC-Area Employees Representing Listed Clients
HERMAN, Doug
LIBBY, Sandra, Chief Financial Officer
RENDON, Jr., John W., President

Clients

Aruba, Government of
Rep By: John W. Rendon, Jr.

The Renkes Group, Ltd.

1330 Connecticut Ave. NW
Suite 200
Washington, DC 20036
Tel: (202)872-9380
Fax: (202)872-1377
Registered: LDA, FARA
Web: www.renkes.com
E-mail: gregg@renkes.com
A research and consulting firm.

DC-Area Employees Representing Listed Clients
RENKES, Gregg D., President

Clients

AIG Environmental
Issues: ENV INS
Rep By: Patrick Pettey, Gregg D. Renkes

Coeur d'Alene Mines Corp.
Issues: NAT
Rep By: Gregg D. Renkes

Cominco Alaska Inc.
Issues: CAW
Rep By: Gregg D. Renkes

Edison Electric Institute
Issues: ENG
Rep By: Gregg D. Renkes

Envirosource Technologies
Issues: ENV
Rep By: Patrick Pettey

FirstEnergy Co.
Issues: ENG ENV
Rep By: Gregg D. Renkes

Florida Power and Light Co.
Issues: UTI
Rep By: Patrick Pettey, Gregg D. Renkes

Fort Sumter Tours
Issues: TOU
Rep By: Gregg D. Renkes

Land Trust Alliance
Issues: RES
Rep By: Gregg D. Renkes

Lockheed Martin Idaho Technologies Corp.
Rep By: Gregg D. Renkes

NAC Internat'l
Issues: ENG
Rep By: Gregg D. Renkes

Nuclear Energy Institute
Issues: ENG
Rep By: Patrick Pettey, Gregg D. Renkes

Pinnacle West Capital Corp.
Issues: ENG
Rep By: Gregg D. Renkes

Princess Cruise Lines
Issues: TOU
Rep By: Gregg D. Renkes

Sealaska Corp.
Issues: NAT
Rep By: Gregg D. Renkes

Southern Co.
Issues: ENG
Rep By: Gregg D. Renkes

SunCor Development Co.
Issues: ENV
Rep By: Patrick Pettey

USA Biomass Power Producers Alliance
Issues: ENV TAX
Rep By: Patrick Pettey, Gregg D. Renkes

Reno & Cavanaugh, PLLC

1250 I St. NW
Suite 900
Washington, DC 20005
Tel: (202)783-2800
Fax: (202)783-0550
Registered: LDA
Web: www.renocavanaugh.com
E-mail: lreno@renocavanaugh.com
A law firm specializing in housing and real estate issues.

DC-Area Employees Representing Listed Clients
CAVANAUGH, Gordon, Of Counsel
GENO, Sharon, Associate
GLASHEEN, Megan, Member
MCGOVERN, Julie S., Associate
RENO, Lee P., Member

Clients

Council of Large Public Housing Authorities
Issues: BUD HOU
Rep By: Gordon Cavanaugh, Sharon Geno

Housing Assistance Council
Rep By: Lee P. Reno

Houston, Texas, Housing Authority of the City of

Representative of German Industry and Trade

1627 I St. NW
Suite 550
Washington, DC 20006
Tel: (202)659-4777
Fax: (202)659-4779
Registered: LDA, FARA

DC-Area Employees Representing Listed Clients
BERGMANN, Robert
ESSER, Peter J. C., Government Affairs Counsel

Clients

Ass'n of German Chambers of Industry & Commerce (DIHT)
Issues: TRD
Rep By: Robert Bergmann, Peter J. C. Esser

Deutscher Industrie-und Handelstag

Federation of German Industries (BDI)
Issues: TRD
Rep By: Robert Bergmann, Peter J. C. Esser

Resource Management Consultants, Inc.

205 S. Whiting St.
Suite 308
Alexandria, VA 22304
Tel: (703)751-8022
Fax: (703)751-5735
Registered: LDA

DC-Area Employees Representing Listed Clients
GRAY, Robert J., President

Clients

Council of Northeast Farmer Cooperatives
Issues: AGR
Rep By: Robert J. Gray

Nat'l Center for Appropriate Technology
Issues: AGR
Rep By: Robert J. Gray

Organic Trade Ass'n
Issues: AGR
Rep By: Robert J. Gray

Southeast Dairy Farmer Ass'n
Issues: AGR
Rep By: Robert J. Gray

Waves States Ratification Committee
Issues: AGR
Rep By: Robert J. Gray

Resources Development, Inc.

110 D St. SE
Suite 114
Washington, DC 20003
Tel: (202)547-2555
Fax: (202)547-1641
Registered: LDA

DC-Area Employees Representing Listed Clients
ZION, Hon. Roger H., President

Clients

The 60/Plus Ass'n, Inc.
Issues: TAX
Rep By: Hon. Roger H. Zion

Independent Oil Producers Ass'n-Tri State
Rep By: Hon. Roger H. Zion

Results Cubed

5103 Moorland Ln.
Bethesda, MD 20814
Tel: (301)657-2412
Fax: (301)426-2909
Registered: LDA

DC-Area Employees Representing Listed Clients
MAHONEY, James E., President

Clients

Matlack Systems, Inc.
Issues: TRA TRU
Rep By: James E. Mahoney

RFB, Inc.

3315 Cummings Ln.
Chevy Chase, MD 20815
Tel: (301)913-9012
Fax: (301)913-9041
Registered: LDA
E-mail: RayBragg@worldnet.att.net
A government affairs consulting and lobbying firm.

DC-Area Employees Representing Listed Clients
BRAGG, Raymond F., President

Clients

Circle K Convenience Stores
Issues: TOB
Rep By: Raymond F. Bragg

Dale Service Corp.
Issues: BUD
Rep By: Raymond F. Bragg

Progress Energy
Issues: CAW ENG UTI
Rep By: Raymond F. Bragg

Roecker Engineering Co.
Issues: BUD
Rep By: Raymond F. Bragg

Transit Mixed Concrete Co.
Issues: RES
Rep By: Raymond F. Bragg

RGS Enterprises, Inc.

819 Seventh St. NW
Suite 215
Washington, DC 20001
Tel: (202)682-1881
Fax: (202)682-2471
Registered: LDA
Web: www.rgsenterprises.com
E-mail: rgsentinc@aol.com
A government relations consulting firm.

DC-Area Employees Representing Listed Clients
SYKES, Ronald G., President/CEO

Clients

AAE Technologies, Inc.
Issues: FUE
Rep By: Ronald G. Sykes

ADA Consulting Services
Issues: CAW ENG ENV TAX
Rep By: Ronald G. Sykes

Edison Electric Institute
Issues: CAW ENG ENV
Rep By: Ronald G. Sykes

General Motors Corp.
Issues: AUT CAW ENV TOR WAS
Rep By: Ronald G. Sykes

Information Resources, Inc.
Issues: CAW ENG FUE
Rep By: Ronald G. Sykes

Rhoads Group

700 13th St. NW
Suite 350
Washington, DC 20005
Tel: (202)637-0040
Fax: (202)637-0041
Registered: LDA, FARA
Formerly known as Boland & Madigan. A lobbying unit of Shandwick International, which is part of The Interpublic Group.

DC-Area Employees Representing Listed Clients
BARRETT, Jr., Michael F., Of Counsel
BEHRENDS, Paul D., V. President
IRELAND, Kathleen, V. President
JOHNSON, Kristin A., Exec. Assistant
MCKNIGHT, Steven G., Associate
MOTT, Jason N., Staff Assistant
NAGLE, B. Callan, V. President, Finance and Operations
NORTHUP, Clifford R., V. President
RHOADS, Barry D., Senior V. President
SHARPSTENE, Elizabeth R., Associate
WORRALL, Thomas, V. President, Business Development

Clients

AAAE-ACI
Issues: AVI
Rep By: Paul D. Behrends, Kathleen Ireland, Steven G. McKnight, Clifford R. Northup, Barry D. Rhoads, Elizabeth R. Sharpstene, Thomas Worrall

ADI Ltd.

Air Products and Chemicals, Inc.

American Eurocopter Corp.

American Management Systems
Issues: DEF
Rep By: Paul D. Behrends, Kathleen Ireland, Steven G. McKnight, B. Callan Nagle, Clifford R. Northup, Barry D. Rhoads, Thomas Worrall

AOL Time Warner

Associates First Capital Corp.

Boston Communications Group, Inc.

Burbank Aeronautical Corp. II

CES

CMS Defense Systems, Inc.

Dick Corp.
Issues: BUD
Rep By: Paul D. Behrends, Kathleen Ireland, Steven G. McKnight, Clifford R. Northup, Barry D. Rhoads, Thomas Worrall

Internat'l Franchise Ass'n

InterVelocity.com

The Justice Project, Inc.
Issues: LAW
Rep By: Paul D. Behrends, Kathleen Ireland, Steven G. McKnight, Clifford R. Northup, Barry D. Rhoads, Elizabeth R. Sharpstene, Thomas Worrall

KAMAN Corp.

KPMG, LLP

Medley Global Advisors

Mississippi, State of

New Jersey, State of

Orange, California, County of
Rep By: Steven G. McKnight, Barry D. Rhoads

Pershing Division of DLJ Securities Corp.

PNC Bank, N.A.
Issues: FIN
Rep By: Paul D. Behrends, Kathleen Ireland, Steven G. McKnight, B. Callan Nagle, Clifford R. Northup, Barry D. Rhoads, Thomas Worrall

The Queen's Health System

Saudi Arabia, Royal Embassy of

Charles Schwab & Co., Inc.,

Southern Maryland Navy Alliance, Inc.

SWATH Ocean Systems, Inc.
Issues: DEF
Rep By: Paul D. Behrends, Kathleen Ireland, Steven G. McKnight, Clifford R. Northup, Barry D. Rhoads, Elizabeth R. Sharpstene, Thomas Worrall

Taiwan Research Institute

Taiwan Studies Institute
Issues: DEF FOR TRD
Rep By: Paul D. Behrends, Kathleen Ireland, Steven G. McKnight, Clifford R. Northup, Barry D. Rhoads, Elizabeth R. Sharpstene

United Space Alliance

United States Enrichment Corp.
Issues: ENG
Rep By: Paul D. Behrends, Kathleen Ireland, Steven G. McKnight, Clifford R. Northup, Barry D. Rhoads, Elizabeth R. Sharpstene, Thomas Worrall

University of Pittsburgh Medical Center (UPMC)

Verizon Communications

John J. Rhodes

c/o Hunton & Williams
1900 K St. NW
Washington, DC 20006-1109
Tel: (202)955-1523
Fax: (202)778-2201
Registered: LDA

Clients

Central Arizona Water Conservation District
Issues: BUD NAT
Rep By: Hon. John J. Rhodes, III

Garrison Diversion Conservancy District
Issues: GOV NAT
Rep By: Hon. John J. Rhodes, III

George Washington University, Office of Government Relations
Issues: EDU
Rep By: Hon. John J. Rhodes, III

Imperial Irrigation District
Issues: GOV NAT
Rep By: Hon. John J. Rhodes, III

San Carlos Irrigation and Drainage District
Issues: GOV NAT
Rep By: Hon. John J. Rhodes, III

Ricchetti Inc.

1001 G St. NW
Suite 700 E
Washington, DC 20001-4545
Tel: (202)879-9321
Fax: (202)879-9340

A lobbying firm.

DC-Area Employees Representing Listed Clients

HEIMBACH, Jay, V. President
RICCHETTI, Jeff, Principal
RICCHETTI, Steve, Principal

Clients

American Ass'n of Nurse Anesthetists

American Gastroenterological Ass'n
Issues: BUD MMM
Rep By: Jeff Ricchetti, Steve Ricchetti

American Hospital Ass'n

AT&T

Fannie Mae
Rep By: Steve Ricchetti

Eli Lilly and Co.

Novartis Corp.

Siemens Corp.

Sam Richardson

203 S. West St.
Alexandria, VA 22314-2826
Tel: (703)548-3055
Fax: (703)684-5191
E-mail: carlyler@swbell.net

A full-service federal government affairs, corporate affairs, public relations, and international business consultancy.

Clients

Asset Management Consultants
Rep By: Sam Richardson

Berwind Corp.
Rep By: Sam Richardson

The Bortz Corp.
Rep By: Sam Richardson

ESCO Corp.
Rep By: Sam Richardson

Jones, Day, Reavis & Pogue
Rep By: Sam Richardson

LTV Steel Co.
Rep By: Sam Richardson

Moberly-Randolph County Economic Development
Rep By: Sam Richardson

Mueller Industries, Inc.
Rep By: Sam Richardson

NACCO Industries
Rep By: Sam Richardson

Nat'l Federation of Pachyderm Clubs, Inc.
Rep By: Sam Richardson

Ninth Congressional District Republican Committee
Rep By: Sam Richardson

Palmer Coking & Coal Co.
Rep By: Sam Richardson

Sheesley Construction Corp.
Rep By: Sam Richardson

Riggs Government Relations Consulting LLC

7203 Ludwood Ct.
Alexandria, VA 22306
Tel: (703)768-4484
Fax: (703)765-6739
Registered: LDA

DC-Area Employees Representing Listed Clients

DAVIS, Mark
RIGGS, Cathy A.
RIGGS, Hon. Frank D.

Clients

Charter Schools Development Corp.
Issues: BUD EDU
Rep By: Cathy A. Riggs, Hon. Frank D. Riggs

Edupoint.com
Issues: EDU
Rep By: Mark Davis, Cathy A. Riggs, Hon. Frank D. Riggs

Matthew J. Rinaldo

700 New Hampshire Ave. NW
Washington, DC 20037
Tel: (202)965-4282
Fax: (202)965-7628
Registered: LDA

Provides telecommunications/finance and general public affairs consulting services.

Ritter and Bourjaily, Inc.

218 S. Fairfax St.
Alexandria, VA 22314
Tel: (703)549-2322
Fax: (703)519-8275
Registered: LDA
E-mail: mbourjaily@aol.com

A business development consulting firm.

DC-Area Employees Representing Listed Clients

BOURJAILY, III, Monte F., President

Clients

Microcosm, Inc.
Issues: AER BUD DEF
Rep By: Monte F. Bourjaily, III

NanoDynamics, Inc.
Issues: BUD DEF SCI
Rep By: Monte F. Bourjaily, III

NAVSYS Corp.
Issues: AER BUD DEF
Rep By: Monte F. Bourjaily, III

Nu Thena Systems, Inc.
Issues: AER BUD DEF
Rep By: Monte F. Bourjaily, III

Onconova Inc.
Issues: BUD DEF MED
Rep By: Monte F. Bourjaily, III

Scram Technologies Inc.
Issues: BUD DEF SMB
Rep By: Monte F. Bourjaily, III

ViaSat, Inc.
Issues: AER BUD DEF SCI
Rep By: Monte F. Bourjaily, III

RMA Internat'l, Inc.

5313 Lee Hwy.
Arlington, VA 22207
Tel: (703)536-8099
Fax: (703)536-8092
Registered: LDA
E-mail: rmaint@erols.com

A Washington-based strategic planning firm which advises foreign and domestic clients from both the public and private sectors. The firm's capabilities are complemented through a network of affiliates in the U.S. and key capitals of Europe, Asia, and Latin America.

DC-Area Employees Representing Listed Clients

REICH, Otto J., President

Clients

Bacardi-Martini, USA, Inc.
Issues: CPT
Rep By: Otto J. Reich

BATMark

British American Tobacco China Ltd.
Issues: TRD

Kellogg Brown and Root

Lockheed Martin Corp.
Rep By: Otto J. Reich

Marriott Internat'l, Inc.
Rep By: Otto J. Reich

Mobil Latin America & Caribbean, Inc.
Rep By: Otto J. Reich

Telegate, Inc.
Issues: TEC
Rep By: Otto J. Reich

Liz Robbins Associates

441 New Jersey Ave. SE
Washington, DC 20003
Tel: (202)544-6093
Fax: (202)544-1465
Registered: LDA
E-mail: liz@lizrobbins.com

A government affairs consulting firm since 1977.

DC-Area Employees Representing Listed Clients

DERR, Sallie, Chief of Staff
ROBBINS, Liz, President

Clients

EMI Music
Issues: ART CPT
Rep By: Liz Robbins

H. J. Heinz Co.,
Issues: HCR TAX TRD
Rep By: Liz Robbins

Illinois Hospital and Health Systems Ass'n
Issues: MMM
Rep By: Liz Robbins

Lexis-Nexis
Issues: CPT GOV
Rep By: Liz Robbins

Parkinson's Disease Foundation
Issues: HCR
Rep By: Liz Robbins

Reed-Elsevier Inc.
Rep By: Liz Robbins

Scholastic, Inc.
Issues: ART EDU TAX TEC
Rep By: Liz Robbins

Take The Field, Inc.
Issues: ENV
Rep By: Liz Robbins

The Thomson Corp.
Issues: CPT
Rep By: Liz Robbins

Warburg, Pincus & Co., Inc., E. M.
Issues: BUD TAX
Rep By: Liz Robbins

Weight Watchers Internat'l, Inc.

The Roberts Group

1620 I St. NW
Suite 925
Washington, DC 20006
Tel: (202)293-5800
Fax: (202)463-8998

An ass'n management firm specializing in industries regulated by the Food and Drug Administration.

DC-Area Employees Representing Listed Clients
COX, John H., Director, Government Relations
HALLAGAN, John B.
ROBERTS, Glenn

Clients

American Spice and Trade Ass'n
Rep By: John B. Hallagan, Glenn Roberts

Flavor and Extract Manufacturers Ass'n
Rep By: John B. Hallagan, Glenn Roberts

Fragrance Materials Ass'n
Rep By: John B. Hallagan, Glenn Roberts

Internat'l Ass'n of Color Manufacturers
Rep By: John B. Hallagan, Glenn Roberts

Robertson, Monagle & Eastaugh

2300 Clarendon Blvd.
Suite 1010
Arlington, VA 22201
Tel: (703)527-4414
Fax: (703)527-0421
Registered: LDA

DC-Area Employees Representing Listed Clients
CLARK, James F.
GILMAN, Bradley D., Director
MARKS, Rick E.
SILVER, Steven W., Director

Clients

Alaska Fisheries Development Foundation

Alaska Forest Ass'n
Issues: ENV
Rep By: James F. Clark, Steven W. Silver

Alaska Groundfish Data Bank
Issues: BUD
Rep By: Bradley D. Gilman, Rick E. Marks

Alaska Pulp Corp.
Issues: RES
Rep By: James F. Clark, Steven W. Silver

Alaska Sea Life Center

Aleutians East Borough
Issues: NAT
Rep By: Bradley D. Gilman, Rick E. Marks, Steven W. Silver

American Airlines

American Steamship Co.
Rep By: Bradley D. Gilman

Coalition Against Unfair U.S. Postal Service Competition
Issues: POS
Rep By: Steven W. Silver

Continental Airlines Inc.
Issues: AVI
Rep By: Steven W. Silver

Craig, Alaska, City of
Issues: BUD
Rep By: Steven W. Silver

CSX Corp.
Issues: MAR RRR
Rep By: Bradley D. Gilman, Rick E. Marks

CSX Lines LLC
Issues: BUD DEF MAR TAX TRA TRD TRU
Rep By: Bradley D. Gilman, Rick E. Marks

Echo Bay Mining
Rep By: James F. Clark, Steven W. Silver

Federal Administrative Law Judges Conference
Issues: GOV
Rep By: Steven W. Silver

Fort James Corp.
Issues: ENV
Rep By: Steven W. Silver

Four Dam Pool
Issues: UTI
Rep By: Steven W. Silver

Friede, Goldman, & Halter, Inc.
Issues: DEF MAR
Rep By: Bradley D. Gilman, Rick E. Marks

Garden State Seafood Ass'n
Issues: MAR
Rep By: Rick E. Marks

Greens Creek Mining Co.
Rep By: Steven W. Silver

Inter-Island Ferry Authority
Rep By: Rick E. Marks

Kenai Penninsula Borough
Rep By: Rick E. Marks

Ketchikan Gateway Borough
Issues: BUD MAR
Rep By: Steven W. Silver

Ketchikan Public Utilities
Issues: BUD UTI
Rep By: Steven W. Silver

Kodiak Island, Alaska, Borough of
Issues: BUD
Rep By: Bradley D. Gilman, Rick E. Marks

Kodiak, Alaska, City of
Issues: BUD
Rep By: Bradley D. Gilman, Rick E. Marks

Kotzebue, Alaska, City of
Issues: ENV
Rep By: Steven W. Silver

Lunds Fisheries, Inc.
Issues: MAR
Rep By: Bradley D. Gilman, Rick E. Marks

Maersk Inc.
Rep By: Bradley D. Gilman

MailBoxes Etc.
Issues: POS
Rep By: Steven W. Silver

Monroe County Commercial Fishermen, Inc.
Issues: BUD
Rep By: Rick E. Marks

Northwest Airlines, Inc.
Rep By: Steven W. Silver

Ocean Shipholding, Inc.
Issues: TRA
Rep By: Bradley D. Gilman, Rick E. Marks

Ounalashka Corp.
Issues: BUD TAX
Rep By: Bradley D. Gilman, Rick E. Marks, Steven W. Silver

Pacific States Marine Fisheries Commission
Issues: BUD
Rep By: Bradley D. Gilman, Rick E. Marks

Petersburg, Alaska, City of
Issues: NAT URB
Rep By: Bradley D. Gilman, Rick E. Marks

Preston Gates Ellis & Rouvelas Meeds LLP
Issues: IND
Rep By: Steven W. Silver

Seafreeze
Issues: MAR
Rep By: Bradley D. Gilman, Rick E. Marks

Seward, Alaska, City of
Issues: BUD
Rep By: Bradley D. Gilman, Rick E. Marks, Steven W. Silver

Southeast Conference
Issues: UTI
Rep By: Steven W. Silver

Temsco Helicopter, Inc.
Issues: TRA
Rep By: Steven W. Silver

Transportation Institute
Issues: TRA
Rep By: Bradley D. Gilman, Rick E. Marks

Trident Seafood Corp.
Issues: MAR
Rep By: Bradley D. Gilman, Rick E. Marks

TVX Mineral Hill Mine

U.S. Marine Corp.
Issues: DEF
Rep By: Bradley D. Gilman, Rick E. Marks

Unalaska, Alaska, City of
Issues: ECN
Rep By: Bradley D. Gilman, Rick E. Marks

Verner, Liipfert, Bernhard, McPherson and Hand, Chartered
Issues: GOV
Rep By: Bradley D. Gilman, Rick E. Marks, Steven W. Silver

Wasilla, Alaska, City of
Issues: URB
Rep By: Steven W. Silver

Wrangell, Alaska, City of
Issues: URB
Rep By: Bradley D. Gilman, Rick E. Marks

Robins, Kaplan, Miller & Ciresi L.L.P.

1801 K St. NW
Washington, DC 20006
Tel: (202)775-0725
Fax: (202)223-8604
Registered: LDA, FARA

Web: www.rkmc.com
A law firm.

Political Action Committee
Robins Kaplan PAC
1801 K St. NW
Washington, DC 20006
Contact: Harold E. Mesirow
Tel: (202)775-0725
Fax: (202)223-8604

DC-Area Employees Representing Listed Clients
CONNOR, G. Brent, Associate
HUNNICUTT, Charles A., Partner
MESIROW, Harold E., Partner
THOMAS, Matthew J., Associate

Clients

The Boat Co.
Issues: MAR
Rep By: Harold E. Mesirow

Cal Dive Internat'l Inc.
Issues: MAR
Rep By: Harold E. Mesirow

Crystal Cruises
Issues: MAR
Rep By: Harold E. Mesirow

Internat'l Group of P&I Clubs
Issues: ENV MAR
Rep By: Harold E. Mesirow

North Dakota Wheat Commission
Issues: AGR TRD
Rep By: Charles A. Hunnicutt

Northwest Airlines, Inc.
Issues: AVI
Rep By: Charles A. Hunnicutt

Pacific Maritime Ass'n
Issues: LBR MAR
Rep By: Charles A. Hunnicutt, Harold E. Mesirow

R.M.S. Titanic, Inc.
Issues: MAR
Rep By: Charles A. Hunnicutt, Harold E. Mesirow

Kip Robinson

444 N. Capitol St. NW
Suite 545
Washington, DC 20001
Tel: (202)347-9710
Fax: (202)347-1225
Registered: LDA

A self-employed consultant.

Clients

Nat'l Weather Service Employees Organization
Issues: SCI
Rep By: Kip Robinson

Gilbert A. Robinson, Inc.

6617 Jill Ct.
Suite 100
McLean, VA 22101
Tel: (703)917-9500
Fax: (703)442-0749

DC-Area Employees Representing Listed Clients
HOECK, Kenneth J., Exec. V. President
ROBINSON, Gilbert A., Chairman

Clients

21st Century Space Foundation
Rep By: Gilbert A. Robinson

Chemcrete Technologies Russia (RIS/NIS), Inc.
Rep By: Kenneth J. Hoeck

Corporations to End World Hunger Foundation
Rep By: Gilbert A. Robinson

Global Movies Corp.
Rep By: Gilbert A. Robinson

Internat'l Marketing for Russia and NIS
Rep By: Kenneth J. Hoeck

Robert Schenk Internat'l Russia
Rep By: Gilbert A. Robinson

Robison Internat'l, Inc.

One Massachusetts Ave. NW
Suite 880
Washington, DC 20001
Tel: (202)371-1695
Fax: (202)371-1178
Registered: LDA, FARA

A public and legislative affairs firm.

DC-Area Employees Representing Listed Clients
EVERED, Stephen A., V. President
GILBERT, Sandra A., Director, Government Relations
LADD, Richard B., President
WILLSON, J. David, Director, Government Programs

Clients

Alliant Techsystems, Inc.
Issues: BUD DEF
Rep By: Sandra A. Gilbert

Armtec Defense Products
Issues: BUD DEF
Rep By: Richard B. Ladd, J. David Willson

The Boeing Co.
Issues: BUD DEF
Rep By: Sandra A. Gilbert, Richard B. Ladd

The BOSE Corp.
Issues: BUD CSP DEF
Rep By: Richard B. Ladd

General Electric Co.
Issues: BUD DEF
Rep By: Sandra A. Gilbert, Richard B. Ladd

Honeywell Internat'l, Inc.
Issues: BUD DEF ENG TRA
Rep By: Stephen A. Evered, Sandra A. Gilbert, Richard B. Ladd

L-3 Communications Corp.
Issues: BUD DEF
Rep By: Richard B. Ladd

Lockheed Martin Tactical Systems
Issues: BUD DEF
Rep By: Sandra A. Gilbert, Richard B. Ladd, J. David Willson

Oshkosh Truck Corp.
Issues: BUD DEF
Rep By: Richard B. Ladd, J. David Willson

Simula, Inc.
Issues: BUD DEF TRA
Rep By: Stephen A. Evered, J. David Willson

United Defense, L.P.
Issues: BUD DEF
Rep By: Sandra A. Gilbert, Richard B. Ladd

Rock & Associates

1150 17th St. NW
Suite 601
Washington, DC 20036
Tel: (202)296-6363
Fax: (202)296-9266
Registered: LDA
Web: www.jameswrock.com
E-mail: JamesWRock@aol.com

A consulting firm specializing in trade, tax, health and energy issues.

DC-Area Employees Representing Listed Clients
ROCK, James W., President

Clients

American Soc. of Ass'n Executives
Rep By: James W. Rock

Coalition for Fair Taxation of Real Estate
Rep By: James W. Rock

eLottery, Inc.
Issues: GAM
Rep By: James W. Rock

Nat'l Ass'n of Industrial and Office Properties
Issues: TAX
Rep By: James W. Rock

Rode & Qualey

1742 N St. NW
Washington, DC 20036
Tel: (202)223-0957
Fax: (202)429-9574
E-mail: tradelaw@aol.com

A law firm also with an office in New York, NY, specializing in customs and international trade law.

DC-Area Employees Representing Listed Clients
BURKE, R. Brian

Clients

Greyfab (Bangladesh) Ltd.
Rep By: R. Brian Burke

Rodriguez O'Donnell Fuerst Gonzalez & Williams

1710 Rhode Island Ave. NW
Tenth Floor
Washington, DC 20036
Tel: (202)293-3300
Fax: (202)293-3307
Registered: LDA
Web: www.rofgw.com
E-mail: rodriguez@rofgw.com

A law firm specializing in international trade, maritime, admiralty, customs tax, tax litigation, and government affairs. Also maintains offices in Chicago, New York, and Miami.

DC-Area Employees Representing Listed Clients
ANGEL, Usbaldo, Associate
CRAIG, Ashley W., Associate
GONZALEZ, Henry P., Partner
LENEHAN, III, Daniel W., Attorney-at-Law
RODRIGUEZ, Carlos, Senior Partner

Clients

Bicycle Shippers Ass'n
Rep By: Carlos Rodriguez

Boston Consolidated Services, Inc.
Rep By: Carlos Rodriguez

Coalition for Fair Play in Ocean Shipping
Issues: TRA TRD TRU
Rep By: Ashley W. Craig, Carlos Rodriguez

Espee Trading Corp.
Rep By: Carlos Rodriguez

New York/New Jersey Foreign Freight Forwarders and Brokers Ass'n, Inc.
Rep By: Ashley W. Craig, Carlos Rodriguez

Ocean World Lines, Inc.
Rep By: Ashley W. Craig

Summary Agency, Ltd.
Rep By: Carlos Rodriguez

Trailer Marine Transport Corp.
Rep By: Carlos Rodriguez

Votainer Consolidation Service
Rep By: Carlos Rodriguez

Rogers & Wells

607 14th St. NW
Washington, DC 20005
Tel: (202)434-0700
Fax: (202)912-6000
Registered: LDA, FARA

Washington office of a New York-based general practice law firm.

DC-Area Employees Representing Listed Clients
ARQUIT, Kevin J., Partner
EGAN, Jr., James C., Counsel
FERRIN, Richard P., Associate
HANKS, Sara, Partner, Latin American Division
MEIGHAN, Katherine W., Associate
NEWBORN, Steven A., Partner, Anti-Trust Division
SILVERMAN, William, Partner
SIMON, Carrie A., Counsel
SNIDER, Virginia L., Consultant, Anti-Trust Division
TRAINER, Ryan T., Partner
WILKINSON, Laura A., Of Counsel

Clients

American Hellenic Institute Public Affairs Committee

American Hellenic Institute, Inc.

Banque Paribas New York Branch
Issues: BAN
Rep By: Katherine W. Meighan

Canadian Pulp and Paper Ass'n, Newsprint Section of
Rep By: William Silverman

Dofasco, Inc.
Rep By: Richard P. Ferrin, William Silverman

Internat'l Sleep Products Ass'n
Issues: CSP
Rep By: Ryan T. Trainer

Major League Baseball Players Ass'n
Rep By: Kevin J. Arquit

Nat'l Automobile Dealers Ass'n

R. L. Polk & Co.

Republic Nat'l Bank of New York

Royal Dutch Shell Group

Barbara J. Rohde

1101 17th St. NW
Suite 500
Washington, DC 20036
Tel: (202)833-5575
Registered: LDA

A self-employed consultant.

Clients

Fargo-Moorhead Metropolitan Council of Governments
Rep By: Barbara J. Rohde

Moorehead, Minnesota, City of
Issues: TRA
Rep By: Barbara J. Rohde

Romano & Associates, LLC

444 N. Capitol St. NW
Suite 840
Washington, DC 20001-1512
Tel: (202)434-8016
Fax: (202)434-8018
Registered: LDA
Web: jpromanojr@aol.com

Specializes in community based economic development advocacy, including Native American interests.

DC-Area Employees Representing Listed Clients
ROMANO, John, Principal

Clients

Housing Assistance Council
Issues: BUD HOU
Rep By: John Romano

Nat'l Rural Development Ass'n
Issues: BUD ECN
Rep By: John Romano

Sisseton-Wahpoton Sioux Indian Tribe
Issues: BUD HCR IND
Rep By: John Romano

Rooney Group Internat'l, Inc.

2000 N. 14th St.
Suite 250
Arlington, VA 22201
Tel: (703)522-9500
Fax: (703)522-6847
Registered: LDA
E-mail: rgirooney@aol.com

DC-Area Employees Representing Listed Clients
KAFFKA, Jerry L., Associate
ROONEY, James W., Chief Exec. Officer

Clients

Akers Laboratories, Inc.
Issues: DEF HCR MED
Rep By: James W. Rooney

Autometric Inc.
Issues: AER CPI DEF EDU
Rep By: James W. Rooney

Celsius Tech Electronics
Issues: DEF
Rep By: James W. Rooney

CHEMRING, Ltd.
Rep By: James W. Rooney

Deere & Co.

Deere Co. Worldwide Commercial & Consumer Equipment Division
Issues: AUT DEF
Rep By: Jerry L. Kaffka, James W. Rooney

DuPont Agricultural Products
Issues: AUT AVI DEF DIS EDU LBR TRU
Rep By: Jerry L. Kaffka, James W. Rooney

ECC Internat'l Corp.
Issues: AER CPI DEF
Rep By: James W. Rooney

Federal Procurement Consultants
Issues: DEF FIR MAN
Rep By: James W. Rooney

GEC-Marconi Avionics Group

General Atomics
Issues: AER AVI DEF
Rep By: Jerry L. Kaffka, James W. Rooney

Institute of Human and Machine Cognition
Issues: AER CPI DEF EDU
Rep By: James W. Rooney

Intermarine USA
Issues: DEF
Rep By: James W. Rooney

Lockheed Martin Fairchild Systems
Issues: DEF
Rep By: James W. Rooney

Nammo Inc.
Issues: CHM DEF FIR
Rep By: James W. Rooney

Noesis Inc.
Issues: AER BUD DEF MAN SCI
Rep By: Jerry L. Kaffka, James W. Rooney

Raufoss A/S, Defense Products Division
Issues: DEF
Rep By: James W. Rooney

Samsung Heavy Industries Co., Ltd.
Issues: DEF

Scepter Manufacturing Co. LTD
Rep By: James W. Rooney

Shelters, Inc.
Issues: DIS
Rep By: James W. Rooney

University of Phoenix
Issues: EDU

Ropes & Gray

1301 K St. NW
Suite 800 East
Washington, DC 20005
Tel: (202)626-3900
Fax: (202)626-3961
Registered: LDA, FARA
Web: www.ropesgray.com
E-mail: postmaster@ropesgray.com

A law firm specializing in litigation, financial services, environmental law, health care and legislative representation.

DC-Area Employees Representing Listed Clients
BERRY, J. Daniel, Partner
CHERNEY, Colburn T., Partner
GLOVER, Gregory J., Partner
GREENWOOD, Mark A., Partner
HENNESSEY, Mary C., Associate
KNOWLTON, William A., Partner
MICHELS, Dina L., Partner
SUSMAN, Thomas M., Partner

Clients

Alliance for Understandable, Sensible and Accountable Government Regulations
Issues: GOV
Rep By: Thomas M. Susman

American Library Ass'n
Issues: GOV MIA
Rep By: Thomas M. Susman
The Business Roundtable
Issues: GOV
Rep By: Thomas M. Susman
Coalition for Effective Environmental Information
Issues: ENV
Rep By: Mark A. Greenwood
New England Organ Bank
Rep By: Thomas M. Susman

Peter J. Rose

499 S. Capitol St. SW
Suite 520
Washington, DC 20003
Tel: (202)484-3537
Fax: (202)479-4657
Registered: LDA
E-mail: peterosedc@prodigy.net

Clients

ARINC, Inc.
Issues: DEF
Rep By: Peter J. Rose
Day Care Ass'n of Tarrant County and Fort Worth Texas
Issues: EDU
Rep By: Peter J. Rose
HAECO, Inc.
Issues: DEF
Rep By: Peter J. Rose
La Sen, Inc.
Issues: TRA
Rep By: Peter J. Rose
Litton Life Support
Issues: DEF
Rep By: Peter J. Rose
Lockheed Martin Corp.
Issues: DEF
Rep By: Peter J. Rose
NAAS
Issues: HCR TAX
Rep By: Peter J. Rose
NOW Solutions, Inc.
Issues: DEF TRA
Rep By: Peter J. Rose
Osteopathic Health System of Texas
Issues: HCR
Rep By: Peter J. Rose
QTEAM
Issues: DEF
Rep By: Peter J. Rose
Rapid Reporting, Inc.
Issues: TAX
Rep By: Peter J. Rose
S-TEC Sentry
Issues: DEF
Rep By: Peter J. Rose

Rose Communications

1625 K St. NW
Suite 725
Washington, DC 20006
Tel: (202)785-8972
Fax: (202)785-4313
Registered: LDA

DC-Area Employees Representing Listed Clients
ROSE, Robert R., President

Clients

Fuel Cells for Transportation
Issues: BUD ENG
Rep By: Robert R. Rose

Ross & Hardies

888 16th St. NW
Suite 400
Washington, DC 20006-8791
Tel: (202)296-8600
Fax: (202)296-8791
Registered: LDA
A general practice law firm.

DC-Area Employees Representing Listed Clients
ROSS, Steve, Hiring Attorney

Clients

United Parcel Service
Issues: TRD

A. L. Ross Associates, Inc.

1220 19th St. NW
Suite 400
Washington, DC 20036
Tel: (202)872-7300
Fax: (202)872-9030
Registered: LDA

DC-Area Employees Representing Listed Clients
ROSS, Alan L., President

Clients

EXPRO Chemical Products
Issues: BUD CHM DEF FIR
Rep By: Alan L. Ross

Ross, Dixon & Bell

601 Pennsylvania Ave. NW
North Bldg.
Washington, DC 20004-2688
Tel: (202)662-2000
Fax: (202)662-2190
Web: www.rdblaw.com
A general trial and appellate practice law firm.

DC-Area Employees Representing Listed Clients
ROSS, Stuart, Partner

Clients

Motorcycle Industry Council
Rep By: Stuart Ross

Ross-Robinson & Associates

1825 I St. NW
Suite 400
Washington, DC 20006
Tel: (202)429-2715
Fax: (202)682-3084
Registered: LDA, FARA
Web: www.rosro.com
E-mail: hrr@rosro.com
A foreign policy consulting and lobbying firm.

DC-Area Employees Representing Listed Clients
DUNCAN, Monica, Legislative Assistant
ROSS-ROBINSON, Hazel, President

Clients

Caribbean Banana Exporters Ass'n
Issues: TRD
Rep By: Monica Duncan, Hazel Ross-Robinson
Haiti, Office of the President of the Republic of
Issues: FOR
Rep By: Monica Duncan, Hazel Ross-Robinson

Caleb S. Rossiter

5235 Sherier Place NW
Washington, DC 20016
Tel: (202)537-5104
Registered: LDA

Clients

Jacksonville University, Davis College of Business
Issues: EDU
Rep By: Caleb S. Rossiter

The Roth Group

2131 K St. NW
Suite 710
Washington, DC 20037-1810
Tel: (202)347-6787
Fax: (202)737-4727
Registered: LDA
E-mail: rothgroup@erols.com

DC-Area Employees Representing Listed Clients
FINLAYSON, Joseph, Exec. Director
HENRICKS, Jayd, Legislative Director
ROTH, Sr., Hon. Toby, President

Clients

Appleton Papers, Inc.
Issues: ENV
Rep By: Hon. Toby Roth, Sr.
Ass'n of Retail Travel Agents
Issues: TOU
Rep By: Jayd Henricks, Hon. Toby Roth, Sr.
Hughes Electronics Corp.
Issues: TRD
Rep By: Hon. Toby Roth, Sr.
Johnson Controls, Inc.
Issues: ENV
Rep By: Joseph Finlayson, Jayd Henricks, Hon. Toby Roth, Sr.
Nat'l Cash Register
Issues: ENV
Rep By: Joseph Finlayson, Hon. Toby Roth, Sr.
San Juan, Puerto Rico, City of
Issues: TRA
Rep By: Hon. Toby Roth, Sr.

Rothleder Associates, Inc.

1200 G St. NW
Suite 800
Washington, DC 20005
Tel: (202)434-8756
Fax: (202)737-2055
Registered: LDA
Government and congressional relations consultants.

DC-Area Employees Representing Listed Clients
ROTHLEDER, Linda S., President

Clients

Cendant Mobility Services
Issues: DEF
Military Mobility Coalition
Issues: DEF
PenRose Corp.
Issues: RES

Royer & Babyak

925 15th St. NW
Fifth Floor
Washington, DC 20006
Tel: (202)296-0784
Fax: (202)293-2768
Registered: LDA
E-mail: rsroyer@royerandbabyak.com
A law firm specializing in government and regulatory affairs.

DC-Area Employees Representing Listed Clients
BABYAK, Gregory R., Partner
KINSELLA, Michael T., Partner
NELSON, Paul, Legislative Consultant
ROYER, Robert Stewart, Partner

Clients

American Collectors Ass'n
Issues: BAN
Rep By: Robert Stewart Royer
American Names Ass'n
Issues: FIN
Rep By: Robert Stewart Royer
Associated Credit Bureaus, Inc.
Issues: FIN
Rep By: Paul Nelson
Bloomberg L.P.
Issues: CPT
Rep By: Gregory R. Babyak
Contact Lens Institute
Issues: BUD GOV HCR
Rep By: Gregory R. Babyak
Edison Properties L.L.C.
Issues: RES
Rep By: Robert Stewart Royer
Federal Home Loan Bank of New York
Issues: BAN
Rep By: Robert Stewart Royer
Federal Home Loan Mortgage Corp. (Freddie Mac)
Rep By: Robert Stewart Royer
Genentech, Inc.
Issues: BUD CPT HCR TAX
Rep By: Gregory R. Babyak
Internat'l Reciprocal Trade
Issues: FIN
Rep By: Robert Stewart Royer
Investment Co. Institute
Issues: FIN
MacAndrews & Forbes Holdings, Inc.
Issues: BAN
Rep By: Robert Stewart Royer
Michigan Trade Exchange
Rep By: Robert Stewart Royer
New York, State of
Rep By: Michael T. Kinsella
Rent-a-Center, Inc.
Issues: BAN
Rep By: Robert Stewart Royer
Trade Exchange of America
Rep By: Robert Stewart Royer
Tulane University
Rep By: Paul Nelson

RPB Co.

6001 Haverhill Ct.
Springfield, VA 22152
Tel: (703)644-7973

DC-Area Employees Representing Listed Clients
BEDELL, Robert P.

Clients

Dun & Bradstreet
Issues: CPI GOV
Rep By: Robert P. Bedell

RPH & Associates, L.L.C.

7268 Evans Mill Rd.
McLean, VA 22101-3423
Tel: (703)448-0931
Fax: (703)448-1141
Registered: LDA
Web: www.rphassociatesllc.com
E-mail: robert.casey.hanrahan@erols.com
Provides management consulting, lobbying, business development, marketing, public affairs, public relations, fund raising services and solutions, strategic planning, and capital sources for corporations and non-profits.

DC-Area Employees Representing Listed Clients
HANRAHAN, Hon. Robert P., President

Clients

Advantage Associates, Inc.
Issues: DEF
Rep By: Hon. Robert P. Hanrahan
entradia.com
Issues: TEC

Fon Digital Network Clearpoint Communications, Inc.
Issues: FIN TEC
Rep By: Hon. Robert P. Hanrahan

Hello Arabia Corp.
Issues: ECN
Rep By: Hon. Robert P. Hanrahan

Sonomedica, Inc.
Issues: HCR

RTC Direct

1055 Thomas Jefferson St. NW
Suite 500
Washington, DC 20007
Tel: (202)625-2111
Fax: (202)424-7900

Provides strategic communications consulting, grassroots organizing and volunteer recruitment designed to involve key target groups. Services offered to clients include constituency mobilization, corporate communications, product and service marketing and membership development. Works for clients on legislative, regulatory and administrative issues at federal, state and local levels. Provides direct mail and telephone contact services.

DC-Area Employees Representing Listed Clients

CHIDESTER, Becky, President
KEVILL, Paige, Management Supervisor
ROSS, Jeffrey, Senior V. President

Clients

American Psychological Ass'n

Philip Morris USA

US Airways

World Jewish Congress

RTS Consulting

Hamilton Square
600 14th St. NW, Fifth Floor
Washington, DC 20005
Tel: (202)783-1980
Fax: (202)783-1918
Registered: LDA
E-mail: RTSC@erols.com

A government affairs firm.

DC-Area Employees Representing Listed Clients

SCHULZE, Jr., Richard T., Principal

Clients

Aventis Behring

Cohn & Wolfe

Dalton & Dalton P.C.

Nat'l Ass'n of Thrift Savings Plan Participants

Orkand Corp.

OSHA Reform Coalition

Pepper Hamilton LLP

S-PAC

Rubin, Winston, Diercks, Harris & Cooke

1155 Connecticut Ave.
Sixth Floor
Washington, DC 20036
Tel: (202)861-0870
Fax: (202)429-0657

A law firm.

DC-Area Employees Representing Listed Clients

COOKE, Jr., Frederick D., Partner
DIERCKS, Walter E., Partner
HARRIS, Jeffrey, Partner
RUBIN, Eric M., Partner
WINSTON, James L., Partner

Clients

Fannie Mae

Nat'l Ass'n of Black-Owned Broadcasters
Issues: COM
Rep By: James L. Winston

Outdoor Advertising Ass'n of America
Rep By: Eric M. Rubin

Rainbow/Push Coalition (National Bureau)
Rep By: Frederick D. Cooke, Jr.

Ruddy & Associates

9106 Drumaldry Dr.
Bethesda, MD 20817
Tel: (301)530-1331
Fax: (301)530-9294
Registered: LDA
E-mail: bob_ruddy@yahoo.com

Legislative consultant.

DC-Area Employees Representing Listed Clients

RUDDY, Robert E., President

Clients

Mortgage Insurance Companies of America
Issues: BAN HOU INS
Rep By: Robert E. Ruddy

Nat'l Ass'n of Housing Cooperatives
Rep By: Robert E. Ruddy

Ruder Finn Washington

808 17th St. NW
Suite 600
Washington, DC 20006
Tel: (202)466-7800
Fax: (202)887-0905
Registered: FARA
Web: www.ruderfinn.com

The Washington office of a firm headquartered in New York, NY. An independent, full-service, worldwide public relations agency.

DC-Area Employees Representing Listed Clients

BURNETT, Helen, Senior V. President
GOSSENS, Myra Peabody, President, Public Relations, Washington
HAHN, Colleen, Senior V. President, Technology Practice
MARTIN, D. Craig, Managing Director
RABIN, Ken, Strategic Counselor

Clients

The Clorox Co.

Exportadora de Sal, S.A. de C.V.
Rep By: D. Craig Martin

Timothy R. Rupli and Associates, Inc.

1938 Great Falls
McLean, VA 20005
Tel: (703)534-9171
Registered: LDA
E-mail: tim@rupli.com

DC-Area Employees Representing Listed Clients

RUPLI, Timothy R.

Clients

R. Duffy Wall and Associates
Issues: EDU
Rep By: Timothy R. Rupli

University of Texas
Issues: EDU
Rep By: Timothy R. Rupli

J. T. Rutherford & Associates

46 S. Glebe Rd.
Suite 202
Arlington, VA 22204
Tel: (703)920-8001
Registered: LDA

DC-Area Employees Representing Listed Clients

LAVANTY, Deanna D., Senior Associate, Government Relations
LAVANTY, Donald F., President
RUTHERFORD, J. T., Founder

Clients

American College of Radiology
Issues: HCR MMM
Rep By: Deanna D. Lavanty, Donald F. Lavanty

American Optometric Ass'n
Issues: HCR MMM
Rep By: Deanna D. Lavanty, Donald F. Lavanty

American Soc. for Clinical Laboratory Science
Issues: HCR MMM
Rep By: Donald F. Lavanty

Glossco Free Zone, N.V.
Issues: TRD
Rep By: Donald F. Lavanty

Lawrence Ryan Internat'l, Inc.

P.O. Box 59558
Potomac, MD 20859
Tel: (301)299-1872
Fax: (301)299-1873
Registered: LDA

Clients

Amherst Systems Inc.
Issues: AER DEF

Assurance Technology Corp.
Issues: AER DEF

Sierra Technologies Inc.
Issues: AER DEF

Ryan, Phillips, Utrecht & MacKinnon

1133 Connecticut Ave. NW
Suite 300
Washington, DC 20036
Tel: (202)293-1177
Fax: (202)293-3411
Registered: LDA, FARA

A law firm specializing in legislative and administrative law, lobbying disclosure and ethics, and campaign finance.

DC-Area Employees Representing Listed Clients

HOPPE, Rodney, Legislative Associate
LAMB, James C., Associate
MACKINNON, Jeffrey M., Partner
PHILLIPS, William D., Partner
PLANNING, Mark D., Partner
RYAN, Thomas M., Partner
UTRECHT, Carolyn, Partner
VASAPOLI, Joseph V., Partner

Clients

Air Transport Ass'n of America
Issues: AER AVI LBR TRA
Rep By: Rodney Hoppe, Jeffrey M. MacKinnon, William D. Phillips, Mark D. Planning, Thomas M. Ryan

Ass'n of American Railroads
Issues: BUD ENV RRR TRA
Rep By: Rodney Hoppe, Jeffrey M. MacKinnon, William D. Phillips, Mark D. Planning, Thomas M. Ryan, Joseph V. Vasapoli

Coeur d'Alene Mines Corp.
Issues: CAW ENV NAT
Rep By: Rodney Hoppe, Jeffrey M. MacKinnon, William D. Phillips, Mark D. Planning, Thomas M. Ryan, Joseph V. Vasapoli

Cook Inlet Region Inc.
Issues: BUD COM FUE GAM IND MAR NAT RES SMB TEC TRA WEL
Rep By: Rodney Hoppe, Jeffrey M. MacKinnon, William D. Phillips, Mark D. Planning, Thomas M. Ryan, Joseph V. Vasapoli

R. R. Donnelley & Sons
Issues: DEF MAN POS
Rep By: Rodney Hoppe, Jeffrey M. MacKinnon, William D. Phillips, Mark D. Planning, Thomas M. Ryan, Joseph V. Vasapoli

Edison Electric Institute
Issues: ENG UTI
Rep By: Rodney Hoppe, Jeffrey M. MacKinnon, William D. Phillips, Mark D. Planning, Thomas M. Ryan, Joseph V. Vasapoli

Florida Power and Light Co.
Issues: ENG UTI
Rep By: Rodney Hoppe, Jeffrey M. MacKinnon, William D. Phillips, Mark D. Planning, Thomas M. Ryan, Joseph V. Vasapoli

General Communications, Inc.
Issues: BUD COM TAX TEC
Rep By: Rodney Hoppe, Jeffrey M. MacKinnon, William D. Phillips, Mark D. Planning, Thomas M. Ryan, Joseph V. Vasapoli

Investment Co. Institute
Issues: BAN FIN RET TAX
Rep By: Rodney Hoppe, Jeffrey M. MacKinnon, William D. Phillips, Mark D. Planning, Thomas M. Ryan, Joseph V. Vasapoli

Kerr-McGee Corp.
Rep By: Rodney Hoppe, Jeffrey M. MacKinnon, William D. Phillips, Mark D. Planning, Thomas M. Ryan, Joseph V. Vasapoli

Lockheed Martin Corp.
Rep By: Rodney Hoppe, Jeffrey M. MacKinnon, William D. Phillips, Mark D. Planning, Thomas M. Ryan, Joseph V. Vasapoli

MultiDimensional Imaging, Inc.
Issues: BUD HCR MED SCI
Rep By: Rodney Hoppe, Jeffrey M. MacKinnon, William D. Phillips, Mark D. Planning, Thomas M. Ryan, Joseph V. Vasapoli

Nat'l Cable Television Ass'n
Issues: BUD COM TEC
Rep By: Rodney Hoppe, Jeffrey M. MacKinnon, William D. Phillips, Mark D. Planning, Thomas M. Ryan, Joseph V. Vasapoli

New York Stock Exchange
Issues: FIN
Rep By: Rodney Hoppe, Jeffrey M. MacKinnon, Thomas M. Ryan, Joseph V. Vasapoli

Pfizer, Inc.
Issues: ENV HCR MMM PHA TAX TOU
Rep By: Rodney Hoppe, Jeffrey M. MacKinnon, William D. Phillips, Mark D. Planning, Thomas M. Ryan, Joseph V. Vasapoli

Philip Morris Management Corp.
Issues: BEV FOO TOB
Rep By: Rodney Hoppe, Jeffrey M. MacKinnon, Mark D. Planning, Thomas M. Ryan, Joseph V. Vasapoli

Pinnacle West Capital Corp.

Progress Energy
Issues: ENG UTI
Rep By: Rodney Hoppe, Jeffrey M. MacKinnon, William D. Phillips, Mark D. Planning, Thomas M. Ryan, Joseph V. Vasapoli

Sault Ste. Marie Tribe of Chippewa Indians
Issues: BUD GAM IND
Rep By: Rodney Hoppe, James C. Lamb, William D. Phillips, Mark D. Planning, Thomas M. Ryan, Joseph V. Vasapoli

Southern Co.
Issues: ENG WAS
Rep By: Rodney Hoppe, Jeffrey M. MacKinnon, William D. Phillips, Thomas M. Ryan, Joseph V. Vasapoli

TXU Business Services
Issues: UTI WAS
Rep By: Rodney Hoppe, Jeffrey M. MacKinnon, William D. Phillips, Mark D. Planning, Thomas M. Ryan, Joseph V. Vasapoli

U.S. Interactive
Issues: COM SCI TEC
Rep By: Rodney Hoppe, Jeffrey M. MacKinnon, William D. Phillips, Thomas M. Ryan, Joseph V. Vasapoli

United Pan-Europe Communications, NV
Issues: TEC
Rep By: Rodney Hoppe, Jeffrey M. MacKinnon, William D. Phillips, Mark D. Planning, Thomas M. Ryan, Joseph V. Vasapoli

VoiceStream Wireless Corp.
Issues: GOV TEC
Rep By: Rodney Hoppe, Jeffrey M. MacKinnon, William D. Phillips, Mark D. Planning, Thomas M. Ryan, Joseph V. Vasapoli

Ryberg and Smith LLP

1054 31st St. NW
Suite 300
Washington, DC 20007
Tel: (202)333-4000
Fax: (202)965-3445
Registered: LDA

DC-Area Employees Representing Listed Clients
RYBERG, Jr., Paul, Partner
SMITH, David, Partner

Clients

African Coalition for Trade, Inc.
Issues: TRD
Rep By: Paul Ryberg, Jr.

Mauritius Sugar Syndicate
Issues: AGR FOO TRD
Rep By: Paul Ryberg, Jr.

Mauritius, Chamber of Agriculture of
Issues: AGR FOO TRD
Rep By: Paul Ryberg, Jr.

Mauritius-U.S. Business Ass'n Inc.
Issues: TRD
Rep By: Paul Ryberg, Jr.

Sack & Harris, P.C.

8300 Greensboro Dr.
Suite 1080
McLean, VA 22102
Tel: (703)883-0102
Fax: (703)883-0108
Registered: FARA

DC-Area Employees Representing Listed Clients
HARRIS, IV, Robert A., V. President
SACK, James M., President
TRUITT, Michele E., Of Counsel

Clients

Thomas De La Rue, Inc.
Rep By: Michele E. Truitt

Sacramento-Potomac Consulting, Inc.

1341 G St. NW
Suite 200
Washington, DC 20005
Tel: (202)737-3655
Fax: (202)347-5941
Registered: LDA

DC-Area Employees Representing Listed Clients
GRIFFITH, Benjamin G., Senior Associate
LEHMAN, Hon. Richard H., President

Clients

Abide Internat'l, Inc.
Issues: URB
Rep By: Benjamin G. Griffith, Hon. Richard H. Lehman

California State University Fresno
Issues: ECN EDU
Rep By: Benjamin G. Griffith, Hon. Richard H. Lehman

Community Hospitals of Central California
Issues: BUD HCR WEL
Rep By: Benjamin G. Griffith, Hon. Richard H. Lehman

Federal Home Loan Mortgage Corp. (Freddie Mac)
Issues: FIN HOU INS
Rep By: Hon. Richard H. Lehman

Sagamore Associates, Inc.

805 15th St. NW
Suite 700
Washington, DC 20005
Tel: (202)312-7400
Fax: (202)312-7441
Registered: LDA
Web: www.bakerdaniels.com
A subsidiary of Baker & Daniels (see separate listing).

DC-Area Employees Representing Listed Clients
ATKINSON, Todd, V. President
BRISTOL, Theodore W., Senior V. President
CHURCH, Julia P., V. President
CODY, Ann E., V. President
DECKER, Carolyn Lee, V. President
GOGOL, David U., President
LEVINE, Lisa, Assistant V. President
LOWE, Serena, Assistant V. President
MINJACK, Greg, V. President
MORRIS, Dena S., Senior V. President
NICHOLS, David, V. President
SWAIN, Frank S., Senior V. President
TALLEY, Kevin D.
WASITIS, Doug, Senior V. President
WELLER, Mark W., Senior V. President
YOUNG, Audrey B., Senior V. President
ZOOK, David R., Managing Partner

Clients

2001 World Police and Fire Games
Issues: BUD
Rep By: Theodore W. Bristol, Julia P. Church, David U. Gogol

Allegheny County, Pennsylvania, Housing Authority
Issues: BUD HCR HOU TRA
Rep By: Todd Atkinson, David U. Gogol, Lisa Levine

Alltrista/Penny
Rep By: Mark W. Weller, Audrey B. Young

American Nuclear Soc.
Rep By: David Nichols, Doug Wasitis

Americans for Common Cents
Issues: MON
Rep By: Mark W. Weller

Arthritis Foundation
Issues: HCR MED
Rep By: Lisa Levine, Serena Lowe, Dena S. Morris, David Nichols, Kevin D. Talley

Asthma and Allergy Foundation of America

Autism Soc. of America, Inc.
Issues: BUD EDU HCR MED
Rep By: Dena S. Morris, David Nichols

Ball Aerospace & Technology Corp.
Issues: DEF
Rep By: Doug Wasitis, Mark W. Weller

Boehringer Mannheim Corp.
Issues: MED
Rep By: Doug Wasitis, Mark W. Weller

Chase Manhattan Bank
Issues: BAN BUD HOU SMB
Rep By: Frank S. Swain, Mark W. Weller

Cinergy PSI
Rep By: David U. Gogol

Fort Wayne, Indiana, City of
Issues: BUD HOU TRA
Rep By: Theodore W. Bristol, David U. Gogol

Geothermal Heat Pump Consortium
Issues: BUD ENG
Rep By: Todd Atkinson, Theodore W. Bristol, Doug Wasitis

Hill-Rom Co., Inc.
Issues: MED MMM
Rep By: David Nichols, Mark W. Weller

Hillenbrand Industries, Inc.

Historic Landmarks Foundation of Indiana
Issues: RES URB
Rep By: Todd Atkinson, David U. Gogol, Dena S. Morris

Huntingdon College
Issues: EDU SCI
Rep By: Julia P. Church, Doug Wasitis

Indiana Medical Device Manufacturers Council
Issues: MED
Rep By: Mark W. Weller

Indiana State University
Issues: BUD EDU LAW
Rep By: Dena S. Morris, David Nichols

Indiana University
Issues: BUD
Rep By: Doug Wasitis, Mark W. Weller

Indianapolis Neighborhood Housing Partnership
Issues: HOU
Rep By: Ann E. Cody, Dena S. Morris

Indianapolis Public Transportation Corp.
Issues: BUD TRA
Rep By: Dena S. Morris, David Nichols

Ispat Inland Steel Industries
Rep By: Mark W. Weller

Marion, Indiana, City of
Issues: BUD ECN URB
Rep By: David U. Gogol, Dena S. Morris

Medford, Oregon, City of
Issues: BUD HOU TRA
Rep By: Theodore W. Bristol, David U. Gogol

Nat'l Sleep Foundation
Issues: BUD HCR MED TRA
Rep By: Dena S. Morris, David Nichols

NextRX
Issues: HCR PHA
Rep By: Theodore W. Bristol, Frank S. Swain

Northern Indiana Commuter Transportation District
Rep By: Dena S. Morris, David Nichols

Nuclear Energy Institute
Issues: BUD ENG
Rep By: David Nichols, Doug Wasitis

Ohio River Valley Water Sanitation Commission
Issues: ENV
Rep By: Julia P. Church, Doug Wasitis

Polk, Iowa, County of
Issues: BUD
Rep By: Todd Atkinson, David U. Gogol

Purdue University
Issues: SCI
Rep By: Doug Wasitis, Mark W. Weller

Recreation Vehicle Industry Ass'n
Issues: TRA
Rep By: Ann E. Cody, David U. Gogol, Mark W. Weller

Shake-A-Leg
Issues: BUD SPO
Rep By: Ann E. Cody, David U. Gogol

South Bend, Indiana, City of
Issues: URB
Rep By: Dena S. Morris

Spring Hill Camps
Issues: TAX
Rep By: David U. Gogol, Frank S. Swain

TRANSPO
Rep By: Dena S. Morris, David Nichols

U.S. Disabled Athletes Fund
Issues: EDU HCR
Rep By: Dena S. Morris

U.S. Olympic Committee
Issues: SPO
Rep By: Ann E. Cody, David U. Gogol, Dena S. Morris

Union Hospital
Issues: AGR BUD HCR
Rep By: Julia P. Church, David Nichols, Mark W. Weller

Walsh Enterprises Internat'l
Issues: BUD FOR
Rep By: Theodore W. Bristol, David U. Gogol

Ways to Work
Issues: BUD WEL
Rep By: Todd Atkinson, David U. Gogol

West Lafayette, Indiana, City of
Issues: BUD HOU TRA
Rep By: Doug Wasitis

Wittenburg University
Issues: BUD EDU
Rep By: Todd Atkinson, Doug Wasitis

Saliba Action Strategies, LLC

5802 Grosvenor Lane
Bethesda, MD 20814
Tel: (301)581-1140
Fax: (301)571-5367
Registered: LDA
E-mail: khalil@salibastrategies.com

DC-Area Employees Representing Listed Clients
SALIBA, Khalil G. "Karl", Principal

Clients

Burger King Corp.
Issues: FOO HCR LBR SMB WEL
Rep By: Khalil G. "Karl" Saliba

GOPMarketplace.com
Rep By: Khalil G. "Karl" Saliba

New Media Strategies
Rep By: Khalil G. "Karl" Saliba

Welfare to Work Partnership
Issues: WEL

Samuels Internat'l Associates, Inc.

1133 21st St. NW
Suite 710
Washington, DC 20036
Tel: (202)223-7683
Fax: (202)223-7687
Registered: FARA
E-mail: mail@samuelsinternational.com

DC-Area Employees Representing Listed Clients
JULIHN, Lawrence, Senior V. President
SAMUELS, Michael, President

Clients

Angola, Government of the Republic of
Issues: GOV
Rep By: Lawrence Julihn, Michael Samuels

Sandifer and Co.

2419 Chain Bridge Rd. NW
Washington, DC 20016
Tel: (202)244-8736
Fax: (202)244-8736
Registered: LDA
E-mail: sandifer@erols.com
General legislative/regulatory consultants specializing in privacy, marketing, and electronic commerce issues, and grassroots lobbying at the federal and state level.

DC-Area Employees Representing Listed Clients
SANDIFER, Mike, President

Sandler & Travis Trade Advisory Services, Inc.

Ronald Reagan Bldg.
1300 Pennsylvania Ave. NW,
Suite 400
Washington, DC 20004

Tel: (202)638-2230
Fax: (202)638-2236
Registered: LDA, FARA

DC-Area Employees Representing Listed Clients
SCHAFFER, Robert P., President

Clients

Consejo Nacional de Zonas Frarcas de Exportacion
Rep By: Robert P. Schaffer

Haiti, Government of the Republic of
Rep By: Robert P. Schaffer

Sandler, Travis & Rosenberg, P.A.

1300 Pennsylvania Ave. NW
Suite 400
Ronald Reagan Bldg.
Washington, DC 20004
Web: www.strtrade.com

Tel: (202)638-2230
Fax: (202)638-2236
Registered: LDA, FARA

Washington office of a Miami, Florida law firm specializing in customs, international trade, transportation law, and copyright and trademark law.

DC-Area Employees Representing Listed Clients
COLLINSON, Nicole Bivens, Director, International Trade
FURA, Shannon, Trade Advisor
GALLAS, Philip, Member
GERDES, Ronald W., Senior Member
HOUSTON, III, William H., Trade Advisor
NAVARRO-BOWMAN, Chandri, Member
PAGE, Jeremy
PEREZ, Lauren, IPR Trade Advisor
RENTON, Susan, Associate
SAMET, Andrew
SANDLER, Gilbert Lee, Managing Director
SORINI, Ron, President, Trade Negotiations and Legislative Affairs
TRAVIS, Thomas G., Managing Director
WAKEMAN, Dennis, Director, Trade Data Division

Clients

American Apparel & Footwear Ass'n
Issues: APP TRD
Rep By: Nicole Bivens Collinson, Chandri Navarro-Bowman, Ron Sorini

American Free Trade Ass'n
Issues: TRD
Rep By: Lauren Perez, Gilbert Lee Sandler

American Textile Co.
Issues: APP TRD
Rep By: Nicole Bivens Collinson, Ron Sorini

Babcock & Wilcox
Issues: TRD
Rep By: Shannon Fura, Jeremy Page, Ron Sorini

Cambodia, Ministry of Commerce, Royal Kingdom of
Rep By: Nicole Bivens Collinson

Commercial Services Internat'l
Issues: TRD
Rep By: Shannon Fura, Jeremy Page

Confederation of Garment Exporters of the Philippines
Issues: TRD
Rep By: Nicole Bivens Collinson, William H. Houston, III, Ron Sorini

Consejo Nacional de Zonas Frarcas de Exportacion
Rep By: Chandri Navarro-Bowman

Elzay Ready Wear Manufacturing Co.
Issues: TRD
Rep By: Ron Sorini

Grupo "J" S.A.
Issues: APP TRD
Rep By: Ron Sorini

The Hosiery Ass'n
Issues: APP TRD
Rep By: Nicole Bivens Collinson, Ron Sorini

Intradeco
Issues: APP TRD
Rep By: Nicole Bivens Collinson, Chandri Navarro-Bowman, Ron Sorini

Skipps Cutting
Issues: APP TRD
Rep By: Nicole Bivens Collinson, Chandri Navarro-Bowman, Ron Sorini

Tailored Clothing Ass'n
Issues: APP TRD
Rep By: Nicole Bivens Collinson, Philip Gallas, Chandri Navarro-Bowman, Susan Renton

U.S. Apparel Industry Council
Rep By: Ronald W. Gerdes, Chandri Navarro-Bowman, Thomas G. Travis

Santini, Chartered

1101 King St.
Suite 350
Alexandria, VA 22314

Tel: (703)684-0755
Fax: (703)549-3682
Registered: LDA

DC-Area Employees Representing Listed Clients
SANTINI, Hon. James D.

Clients

Grand Canyon Air Tour Council
Issues: TOU
Rep By: Hon. James D. Santini

Nat'l Park Hospitality Ass'n
Issues: NAT TOU
Rep By: Hon. James D. Santini

Nat'l Tour Ass'n
Issues: TOU
Rep By: Hon. James D. Santini

United States Air Tour Ass'n
Issues: TOU
Rep By: Hon. James D. Santini

Michael L. Sauls

202 Jefferson St.
Alexandria, VA 22314

Tel: (202)543-2143
Registered: LDA

Clients

Itera Internat'l Energy Consultants
Issues: BAN ENG TRD
Rep By: Michael L. Sauls

Saunders and Company

1015 Duke St.
Alexandria, VA 22314-3551

Tel: (703)549-1555
Fax: (703)549-6526
Registered: FARA

Web: www.saunderscompany.com

DC-Area Employees Representing Listed Clients
SAUNDERS, Steven R., President

Clients

Air Freight Warehouse, Inc.
General Order Warehouse Coalition
Japan, Embassy of
Seiko Epson Corp.
U.S.-Mongolia Business Council, Inc.

Saunders Consulting

4806 Bentonbrook Dr.
Fairfax, VA 22030

Tel: (703)691-0898
Fax: (703)691-0898
Registered: LDA

E-mail: consulting@saunders.net

DC-Area Employees Representing Listed Clients
SAUNDERS, Albert C., Principal

Clients

Pharmaceutical Research and Manufacturers of America
Issues: HCR TAX
Rep By: Albert C. Saunders

Savarese & Associates

700 13th St. NW
Suite 1000
Washington, DC 20005

Tel: (202)347-6633
Fax: (202)347-2672
Registered: FARA

DC-Area Employees Representing Listed Clients
SAVARESE, James M.

R. Wayne Sayer & Associates

1400 I St. NW
Suite 540
Washington, DC 20005-2208
Web: www.sayer.com
E-mail: rws@sayer.com

Tel: (202)638-4434
Fax: (202)296-1074
Registered: LDA

DC-Area Employees Representing Listed Clients
KANIA, John, Director, Legislative Affairs
MORIN, William, V. President
SAYER, R. Wayne, President

Clients

Applied Materials
Issues: TAX TRD
Rep By: John Kania, William Morin, R. Wayne Sayer

Candescent Technologies
Rep By: John Kania, William Morin, R. Wayne Sayer

Coalition for Intelligent Manufacturing Systems (CIMS)
Rep By: William Morin, R. Wayne Sayer

IPC Washington Office
Issues: DEF SCI TAX TRD
Rep By: John Kania, William Morin, R. Wayne Sayer

MRS
Rep By: R. Wayne Sayer

Schott Corp.
Issues: DEF
Rep By: John Kania, William Morin, R. Wayne Sayer

Sheldahl, Inc.
Rep By: R. Wayne Sayer

Silicon Valley Group
Issues: BUD DEF SCI
Rep By: John Kania, William Morin, R. Wayne Sayer

Schagrin Associates

1100 15th St. NW
Suite 700
Washington, DC 20005
E-mail: schagrin@erols.com

Tel: (202)223-1700
Fax: (202)429-2522
Registered: LDA

A law and lobbying firm specializing in international trade issues.

DC-Area Employees Representing Listed Clients
BROWNE, Tamara L., Director, Governmental Affairs
SCHAGRIN, Roger B., Partner and President

Clients

Allied Tube & Conduit Corp.
Issues: TRA
Rep By: Roger B. Schagrin

Bitrek Corp.
Issues: TRA
Rep By: Tamara L. Browne, Roger B. Schagrin

Century Tube Corp.
Issues: TRA
Rep By: Roger B. Schagrin

Committee on Pipe and Tube Imports
Issues: TRA TRD
Rep By: Tamara L. Browne, Roger B. Schagrin

Geneva Steel Co.
Issues: TRA TRD
Rep By: Tamara L. Browne, Roger B. Schagrin

Hannibal Industries
Issues: TRA
Rep By: Tamara L. Browne, Roger B. Schagrin

IPSCO Tubulars, Inc.
Issues: TRA
Rep By: Tamara L. Browne, Roger B. Schagrin

LTV Copperweld
Issues: TRA
Rep By: Tamara L. Browne, Roger B. Schagrin

Maverick Tube Corp.
Issues: TRA
Rep By: Tamara L. Browne, Roger B. Schagrin

Sharon Tube Co.
Issues: TRA
Rep By: Roger B. Schagrin

Vest Inc.
Issues: TRA
Rep By: Tamara L. Browne, Roger B. Schagrin

Weirton Steel Corp.
Issues: TRA TRD
Rep By: Tamara L. Browne, Roger B. Schagrin

Western Tube & Conduit Co.
Issues: TRA
Rep By: Roger B. Schagrin

Wheatland Tube Co.
Issues: TRA
Rep By: Tamara L. Browne, Roger B. Schagrin

Schiff Hardin & Waite

1101 Connecticut Ave. NW
Suite 600
Washington, DC 20036

Tel: (202)778-6400
Fax: (202)778-6460
Registered: FARA

A general practice law firm.

DC-Area Employees Representing Listed Clients
JOURNEY, Drexel D., Partner
KLEIN, Andrew M., Partner
KNOWLES, Gearold L., Partner
ROCKEFELLER, Edwin S., Partner

Clients

China, Directorate General of Telecommunications, Ministry of Communications of the Republic of
Rep By: Gearold L. Knowles

Policy and Taxation Group

Wayne Schley

614 Massachusetts Ave. NE
Washington, DC 20002
Tel: (202)547-9476
Fax: (202)544-2454
Registered: LDA

Provides consulting services on the postal and legislative process.

Clients

United Parcel Service
Issues: POS
Rep By: Wayne Schley

Schmeltzer, Aptaker & Shepard, P.C.

2600 Virginia Ave. NW
Suite 1000
Washington, DC 20037-1905
Tel: (202)333-8800
Fax: (202)337-6065
Registered: LDA, FARA
Web: www.sasp.com
E-mail: sas@saslaw.com

A law firm specializing in labor and employment law, maritime law, and international and public sector policy..

DC-Area Employees Representing Listed Clients

CASE, III, Frank H., Partner
PAZ-SOLDAN, C. Mateo
SANFORD, Suzanne L., Associate
SCHMELTZER, Edward, Partner
SMITH, J. Anthony, Special Counsel

Clients

AfriSpace Corp.
Issues: FOR GOV TRD
Rep By: J. Anthony Smith

Ass'n of Maquiladores
Issues: APP GOV TRD
Rep By: C. Mateo Paz-Soldan, J. Anthony Smith

D.C. Historical Tourism Coalition
Issues: DOC TRD
Rep By: J. Anthony Smith

Honduras, Embassy of
Issues: FOR GOV TRD
Rep By: C. Mateo Paz-Soldan, J. Anthony Smith

Juneau, Alaska, City of
Issues: BUD MAR
Rep By: J. Anthony Smith

St. Paul, Alaska, City of
Issues: BUD ECN ENV FOR FUE IND MAR NAT URB
Rep By: C. Mateo Paz-Soldan, J. Anthony Smith

Schnader Harrison Segal & Lewis LLP

1300 I St. NW
11th Floor East
Washington, DC 20005-3314
Tel: (202)216-4200
Fax: (202)775-8741
Registered: LDA
E-mail: gmendenhall@schnader.com

DC-Area Employees Representing Listed Clients

GONZALEZ, Laura L.
MAGIELNICKI, Robert L.
MENDENHALL, Greggory B.

Clients

IATA U.S. Frequent Flyer Tax Interest Group
Issues: AVI SCI TEC TOU

Internat'l Air Transport Ass'n
Issues: AVI SCI TEC TOU
Rep By: Laura L. Gonzalez, Greggory B. Mendenhall

Marine Capital Management, LLC
Issues: MAR TRA
Rep By: Greggory B. Mendenhall

TECO Transport Corp.
Issues: AGR MAR TAX

Abraham Schneier and Associates

5765 F Burke Center Pkwy.
Suite 347
Burke, VA 22015
Tel: (202)822-0604
Fax: (703)323-7423
Registered: LDA

DC-Area Employees Representing Listed Clients

SCHNEIER, Abraham L., Principal

Clients

Bureau of Wholesale Sales Representatives
Issues: TAX
Rep By: Abraham L. Schneier

Kelly Services, Inc.
Issues: LBR TAX
Rep By: Abraham L. Schneier

Nat'l Federation of Independent Business
Issues: SMB TAX
Rep By: Abraham L. Schneier

Schramm, Williams & Associates, Inc.

517 C St. NE
Washington, DC 20002
Tel: (202)543-4455
Fax: (202)543-4586
Registered: LDA
E-mail: swaconsult@aol.com

A government relations consulting firm.

DC-Area Employees Representing Listed Clients

BROWN, Anita
LUDWIG, Gabriele
MUSSER, Duane L., Associate
SCHRAMM, Robert
WILLIAMS, Nancy

Clients

Alliance of Western Milk Producers
Issues: AGR BUD FOO
Rep By: Nancy Williams

The Ass'n Healthcare Coalition
Issues: HCR
Rep By: Duane L. Musser

California Asparagus Commission
Issues: AGR BUD TRD
Rep By: Anita Brown, Duane L. Musser, Robert Schramm

California Ass'n of Winegrape Growers
Issues: TRD
Rep By: Anita Brown, Nancy Williams

California Pistachio Commission
Issues: AGR BUD FOO TRD
Rep By: Anita Brown, Robert Schramm

California Tomato Commission
Issues: AGR IMM
Rep By: Duane L. Musser, Robert Schramm

Desert Grape Growers League
Issues: AGR TRD
Rep By: Robert Schramm

Dole Food Co.
Issues: AGR BUD
Rep By: Anita Brown, Robert Schramm

Kern County Water Agency
Issues: BUD ENV
Rep By: Nancy Williams

Kern River Watermaster
Issues: BUD ENV
Rep By: Nancy Williams

Lana'i Co.
Issues: BUD TRD
Rep By: Anita Brown, Robert Schramm

San Joaquin River Exchange Contractors Water Authority
Issues: BUD ENV
Rep By: Nancy Williams

U.S. Citrus Science Council
Issues: AGR BUD TRD
Rep By: Anita Brown, Gabriele Ludwig, Robert Schramm, Nancy Williams

Western Growers Ass'n
Issues: AGR BUD ENV FOO IMM TAX TRD
Rep By: Anita Brown, Gabriele Ludwig, Duane L. Musser, Robert Schramm, Nancy Williams

Western Growers Insurance Services
Issues: HCR
Rep By: Duane L. Musser, Robert Schramm

Western Pistachio Ass'n
Issues: AGR BUD ENV
Rep By: Duane L. Musser, Robert Schramm, Nancy Williams

Winegrape Growers of America
Issues: BUD TRD
Rep By: Anita Brown, Robert Schramm, Nancy Williams

Schrayer and Associates, Inc.

1920 L St. NW
Seventh Floor
Washington, DC 20036
Tel: (202)955-1381
Fax: (202)861-0811
Registered: LDA
E-mail: liz@schrayer.org

DC-Area Employees Representing Listed Clients

SCHRAYER, Elizabeth, President

Clients

Campaign to Preserve U.S. Global Leadership
Issues: BUD FOR
Rep By: Elizabeth Schrayer

Schroth & Associates

1101 30th St. NW
Washington, DC 20007
Tel: (202)333-9354
Fax: (202)333-9332
Registered: LDA

DC-Area Employees Representing Listed Clients

SNYDER, Craig, Contract Lobbyist

Clients

Thomas Jefferson University
Issues: BUD DEF HCR MED
Rep By: Craig Snyder

Elinor Schwartz

318 S. Abington St.
Arlington, VA 22204
Tel: (703)920-5389
Fax: (703)920-5402
Registered: LDA
E-mail: elinorschw@aol.com

A Washington representation consultant.

Clients

California State Lands Commission
Issues: ENG ENV FUE NAT RES
Rep By: Elinor Schwartz

New Mexico State Land Office
Rep By: Elinor Schwartz

Western States Land Commissioners Ass'n
Rep By: Elinor Schwartz

Schwartz & Ballen

1990 M St. NW
Suite 500
Washington, DC 20036
Tel: (202)776-0700
Fax: (202)776-0720
Registered: LDA

A law firm specializing in banking and financial services issues.

DC-Area Employees Representing Listed Clients

BALLEN, Robert G., Partner
FOX, Thomas A., Associate
SCHWARTZ, Gilbert T., Partner

Clients

American Council of Life Insurers
Issues: BAN INS
Rep By: Robert G. Ballen, Thomas A. Fox, Gilbert T. Schwartz

American Insurance Ass'n
Issues: BAN INS
Rep By: Robert G. Ballen, Thomas A. Fox, Gilbert T. Schwartz

Financial Services Coordinating Council
Issues: BAN INS
Rep By: Gilbert T. Schwartz

Schwensen and Associates

P.O. Box 17091
Alexandria, VA 22302
Tel: (703)683-3900
Fax: (703)549-8678

DC-Area Employees Representing Listed Clients

SCHWENSEN, Carl

The Scowcroft Group

900 17th St. NW
Suite 500
Washington, DC 20006
Tel: (202)296-9312
Fax: (202)296-9395
Web: www.scowcroft.com
E-mail: scowcroft@aol.com

DC-Area Employees Representing Listed Clients

GILLESPIE, Charles A., Senior Associate
KANSTEINER, Walter H., Principal
KANTER, Arnold, Principal
LAMPLEY, Virginia A., Principal and Managing Director
MELBY, Eric D.K., Principal
NEALER, Kevin G., Principal
SCOWCROFT, USAF (Ret.), Lt. Gen. Brent, President

Scribe Consulting & Communications

1341 Connecticut Ave. NW
Third Floor
Washington, DC 20036
Tel: (202)862-3900
Fax: (202)862-5500
E-mail: scribe2468@aol.com

Provides international and strategic consulting, communications, government affairs, and business and joint venture development.

DC-Area Employees Representing Listed Clients

BERNA, Rachel, Research and Project Manager
LARKINS, J. McKinney, Senior Associate
LEBLANC, Darian, Associate
SALA, Joseph L., Consultant
SINCERE, Richard E., Senior Consultant
SZLAVIK, Joseph J., President
WILKES, Alphie W., Director

Clients

The Boeing Co.
Rep By: Joseph J. Szlavik

Gabonese Republic, Government of the
Rep By: Joseph J. Szlavik

WorldSpace Corp.
Rep By: Joseph J. Szlavik

Scribner, Hall & Thompson, LLP

1875 I St. NW
Suite 1050
Washington, DC 20006-5409
Tel: (202)331-8585
Fax: (202)331-2032
Registered: LDA, FARA
Web: www.scribnerhall.com

A law firm specializing in federal and state tax practice.

DC-Area Employees Representing Listed Clients
BROWN, Lori J., Partner
DICKE, Stephen P., Partner
HOTINE, Susan J., Partner
KELLY, Biruta P., Partner
KOVEY, Mark H., Partner
MITCHELL, Samuel A., Associate
OYLER, Gregory K., Partner
SYKES, Thomas D., Partner
THOMPSON, Jr., Thomas C., Partner
WATSON, G. Norris, Of Counsel
WINSLOW, Peter H., Partner

Clients

CNA Financial Corp.
Rep By: Susan J. Hotine

Pacific Life Insurance Co.
Issues: TAX
Rep By: Susan J. Hotine, Thomas C. Thompson, Jr.

Transamerica Corp.
Rep By: Susan J. Hotine, Thomas C. Thompson, Jr.

The Secura Group

7799 Leesburg Pike
Suite 800 North
Falls Church, VA 22043
Tel: (703)749-0823
Fax: (703)749-1688

A consulting firm specializing in guidance to banks and other financial institutions in dealings with federal regulatory agencies.

DC-Area Employees Representing Listed Clients
ISAAC, William M., Chairman and Managing Director
MAGUIRE, Margaret, Managing Director
MANCUSI, Michael, Managing Director and Chief Exec. Officer

Clients

Bank of New England

SEDERHOLM Public Affairs, Inc.

1199 N. Fairfax St.
Suite 425
Alexandria, VA 22314
Tel: (703)548-8621
Fax: (703)236-1949
E-mail: sederholm@aol.com

Public affairs consulting and programming; issues management; legislative and political programming; association and coalition management; and event planning and management.

DC-Area Employees Representing Listed Clients
SEDERHOLM, Pamela, President

Clients

American Automotive Leasing Ass'n
Rep By: Pamela Sederholm

Internat'l Housewares Ass'n
Rep By: Pamela Sederholm

Leadership PAC 2002
Rep By: Pamela Sederholm

Wendy's Internat'l, Inc.
Rep By: Pamela Sederholm

The Segermark Associates, Inc.

904 Massachusetts Ave. NE
Washington, DC 20002-6228
Tel: (202)547-2222
Fax: (202)547-7417
Web: www.telecard.org

A government relations and association management firm.

DC-Area Employees Representing Listed Clients
SEGERMARK, Howard, President

Clients

Free Speech Coalition
Rep By: Howard Segermark

Internat'l Prepaid Communications Ass'n
Rep By: Howard Segermark

Sellery Associates, Inc.

1730 M St. NW
Suite 200
Washington, DC 20036-4530
Tel: (202)296-3522
Fax: (202)296-7713
Registered: LDA
E-mail: wsellery@selleryinc.com

Government relations consultants.

DC-Area Employees Representing Listed Clients
KIMBALL, Amy B., V. President
SABBATH, Lawrence E., V. President
SELLERY, Jr., William C., President

Clients

American Soc. for Quality
Issues: BUD EDU GOV HCR LBR SCI
Rep By: Amy B. Kimball, William C. Sellery, Jr.

Coalition for Uniform Product Liability Law
Issues: CSP TOR
Rep By: Amy B. Kimball, William C. Sellery, Jr.

Financial Service Centers of America
Issues: BAN
Rep By: Lawrence E. Sabbath, William C. Sellery, Jr.

Job Opportunities Business Symposium
Issues: TAX
Rep By: William C. Sellery, Jr.

The Mead Corp.
Issues: ENV MAN NAT TAX TRD
Rep By: Amy B. Kimball, William C. Sellery, Jr.

Nat'l Armored Car Ass'n
Issues: LBR TRA
Rep By: Lawrence E. Sabbath, William C. Sellery, Jr.

Nat'l Burglar and Fire Alarm Ass'n
Issues: COM LAW LBR
Rep By: Lawrence E. Sabbath, William C. Sellery, Jr.

Nat'l Council of Investigative and Security Services Inc.
Issues: LAW
Rep By: Lawrence E. Sabbath, William C. Sellery, Jr.

Pilkington North America
Issues: AUT ENG
Rep By: William C. Sellery, Jr.

Security Companies Organized for Legislative Action
Issues: LAW LBR
Rep By: Lawrence E. Sabbath, William C. Sellery, Jr.

SENSE, INC.

1111 14th St. NW
Suite 700
Washington, DC 20005
Tel: (202)628-1151
Fax: (202)638-4502
Registered: LDA
E-mail: sensetoo@aol.com

DC-Area Employees Representing Listed Clients
PITTMAN, C. Juliet, President

Clients

Choctaw Nation of Oklahoma
Rep By: C. Juliet Pittman

Hoopa Valley Tribal Council
Rep By: C. Juliet Pittman

Jamestown-S'Klallam Indian Tribe
Rep By: C. Juliet Pittman

Lummi Indian Nation
Rep By: C. Juliet Pittman

Noosack Indian Tribal council
Rep By: C. Juliet Pittman

Northwest Indian Fisheries Commission
Rep By: C. Juliet Pittman

Quinault Indian Nation
Rep By: C. Juliet Pittman

Sac & Fox Nation
Rep By: C. Juliet Pittman

Squaxin Island Indian Tribe
Rep By: C. Juliet Pittman

Swinomish Tribal Community
Rep By: C. Juliet Pittman

Sycuan Band of Mission Indians
Rep By: C. Juliet Pittman

Viejas Band of Kumeyaay Indians
Issues: GAM IND
Rep By: C. Juliet Pittman

David Senter & Associates

1730 M St. NW
Suite 911
Washington, DC 20036
Tel: (202)331-4348
Fax: (202)463-0862
Registered: LDA
E-mail: sntrada@aol.com

A government and public relations firm.

DC-Area Employees Representing Listed Clients
SENTER, Billy
SENTER, David L., Principal

Clients

American Corn Growers Ass'n
Issues: AGR TAX
Rep By: Billy Senter, David L. Senter

Edison Electric Institute
Issues: UTI
Rep By: David L. Senter

Nat'l Ass'n of Farmer Elected Committees (NAFEC)
Issues: AGR
Rep By: David L. Senter

Nat'l Ass'n of FSA County Office Employees

Severance Internat'l, Inc.

1120 C St. SE
Washington, DC 20003
Tel: (202)675-4585
Fax: (202)675-4586
Registered: FARA

Clients

Taiwan, Directorate General of Telecommunications

Seward & Kissel, LLP

1200 G St. NW
Suite 350
Washington, DC 20005
Tel: (202)737-8833
Fax: (202)737-5184
Registered: LDA

Washington office of a general practice law firm headquartered in New York City.

DC-Area Employees Representing Listed Clients
CLARK, Paul T., Partner

Clients

Merrill Lynch & Co., Inc.
Issues: BAN
Rep By: Paul T. Clark

Seyfarth, Shaw, Fairweather & Geraldson

815 Connecticut Ave. NW
Suite 500
Washington, DC 20006-4004
Tel: (202)463-2400
Fax: (202)828-5393
Registered: LDA, FARA
Web: www.seyfarth.com
E-mail: mailbox@seyfarth.com

Washington office of firm with eight addtional offices in the United States and one in Brussels, Belgium.

DC-Area Employees Representing Listed Clients
DYER, Joseph J., Partner
MCHALE, James M., Partner
ROSENTHAL, Donald L., Partner
SINGERMAN, Fredric S., Partner

Clients

Agricultural Producers
Rep By: Donald L. Rosenthal

Complete Business Solutions, Inc.
Rep By: Donald L. Rosenthal

Highmark Blue Cross/ Blue Shield

Hospitality Employers Ass'n
Rep By: Donald L. Rosenthal

Information Technology Ass'n of America (ITAA)
Issues: LBR
Rep By: Donald L. Rosenthal, Fredric S. Singerman

Sharretts, Paley, Carter and Blauvelt

1707 L St. NW
Suite 725
Washington, DC 20036
Tel: (202)223-4433
Fax: (202)659-3904
Registered: LDA

Washington office of a New York law firm.

DC-Area Employees Representing Listed Clients
BRICKELL, Beatrice A.
NIXON, Duncan A.

Clients

Toy Manufacturers of America
Issues: TRD
Rep By: Duncan A. Nixon

Daniel F. Shaw & Associates

c/o World Perspectives Inc.
1150 18th St. NW, Suite 275
Washington, DC 20036
Tel: (202)785-3345
Fax: (202)785-9227
Registered: LDA
E-mail: danshaw@agrilink.com

DC-Area Employees Representing Listed Clients
SHAW, Daniel F.

Clients

MacKenzie Agricultural Research
Rep By: Daniel F. Shaw

Nat'l Grain Sorgum Producers
Issues: AGR CAW GOV TRD
Rep By: Daniel F. Shaw

Shaw Pittman

2300 N St. NW
Washington, DC 20037-1128
Tel: (202)663-8000
Fax: (202)663-8007
Registered: LDA, FARA
Web: www.shawpittman.com
E-mail: info@shawpittman.com

A general practice law firm. Merged with Fisher Wayland Cooper Leader & Zaragoza, LLP in 2000.

Political Action Committee
Shaw Pittman Political Action Committee
2300 N St. NW
Washington, DC 20037-1128
Tel: (202)663-8000
Fax: (202)663-8007
Contact: Thomas J. Spulak

DC-Area Employees Representing Listed Clients
ANENBERG, Scott A., Partner
ARNOLD, Shannon, Associate
BAXTER, Thomas A., Partner
BECKER, Stephan E., Partner
BURKE, Ann Marie, Associate
CHARNOFF, Gerald, Partner
COHN, Robert E., Partner
CUSTER, Jr., B. Scott, Partner
DONALDSON, Richard C., Partner

EPSTEIN, Anita K., Government Relations Advisor
FRIED, Bruce, Partner
FUENTES, Rodolfo, Associate
HARRINGTON, Clifford M., Partner
HRVATIN, Claudia, Government Relations Advisor
ISRAEL, Sheryl R., Counsel
JENSEN, John E., Partner
JORDAN, Daryle, Associate
KLEIN, Allen J., Partner
KNAB, Karen, Exec. Director
LEADER, Martin R., Partner
MACK, III, Hon. Connie, Senior Policy Advisor
MENOTTI, David E., Partner
MICKEY, Jr., Paul, Managing Partner
MOETELL, Michael C.
MURDOCK, III, J. E., Partner
O'MALLEY, E. Michael, Government Relations Advisor
PEARL, Marc A., Partner
PEDERSEN, Jr., William F., Partner
POTTS, Ramsay D., Senior Counsel
RHINELANDER, John B., Senior Counsel
RUBIN, Harry, Partner
SAHR, David R., Partner
SCHMELTZER, Kathryn R., Partner
SCIARRINO, Dawn M., Counsel
SILBERG, Jay E., Partner
SMITH, Mark H., Sr. Corporate Relations Advisor
SPULAK, Thomas J., Partner
STERN, Elizabeth Espin, Partner
THOMPSON, Anthony J., Partner
WHELAN, Roger M., Senior Counsel
WHITFIELD, Milton B., Partner
WOODS, Andrew L., Partner
YABLON, Jeffery L., Partner
ZARAGOZA, Richard R., Partner

Clients

The Advocacy Group
Issues: EDU
Rep By: Thomas J. Spulak

Air Foyle, Ltd.
Rep By: Robert E. Cohn, B. Scott Custer, Jr., Sheryl R. Israel

American Ass'n for Homecare
Issues: HCR
Rep By: Bruce Fried

American Ass'n of Pharmaceutical Scientists

American Coke and Coal Chemicals Institute
Rep By: David E. Menotti

American College of Radiation Oncology
Issues: HCR
Rep By: Andrew L. Woods

American Consulting Engineers Council

American Dental Trade Ass'n

American Insurance Ass'n
Rep By: Marc A. Pearl

American Mobile Satellite Corp.

American Translators Ass'n

Ass'n of Banks of Israel
Issues: BAN TAX
Rep By: Scott A. Anenberg, Michael C. Moetell

Aviation Development Services
Rep By: J. E. Murdock, III

Bank Hapoalim B.M.
Issues: BAN TAX
Rep By: David R. Sahr

Bank Leumi le-Israel B.M.
Issues: BAN TAX
Rep By: Scott A. Anenberg

BET Holdings II, Inc.
Issues: ECN
Rep By: Thomas J. Spulak

Big Sky Airlines
Rep By: Robert E. Cohn, Sheryl R. Israel

The Boeing Co.
Rep By: Claudia Hrvatin

Buckley Broadcasting Corp.

Centerior Energy Corp.
Rep By: Jay E. Silberg

Chevy Chase Bank, F.S.B.
Issues: BAN
Rep By: Scott A. Anenberg, Thomas J. Spulak, Andrew L. Woods

Christian Broadcasting Network
Rep By: Clifford M. Harrington

Chromalloy Gas Turbine Corp.
Rep By: Sheryl R. Israel, J. E. Murdock, III

Colebrand, Ltd.

Cornerstone Television
Issues: TEC
Rep By: Kathryn R. Schmeltzer, Andrew L. Woods

Delta Air Lines
Issues: AVI
Rep By: Robert E. Cohn

Detroit Medical Center
Issues: BUD HCR MMM PHA TAX
Rep By: Bruce Fried, Thomas J. Spulak, Andrew L. Woods

DHL Airways, Inc.
Issues: AVI
Rep By: J. E. Murdock, III

Educational Media Foundation

Embraer Aircraft Corp.
Issues: AER AVI
Rep By: J. E. Murdock, III, Thomas J. Spulak

Empresa Estatal de Telecomunicaciones

Federation of Internat'l Trade Ass'ns (FITA)
Issues: TRD

Federation of Japanese Bankers Ass'ns
Rep By: David R. Sahr

Fisher Broadcasting, Inc.

General Motors Corp.
Issues: GOV

Glencairn, Ltd.
Issues: COM
Rep By: Martin R. Leader

Greenville-Spartanburg Airport District
Rep By: J. E. Murdock, III

Hawaii, State of
Issues: AVI
Rep By: Robert E. Cohn, J. E. Murdock, III, Thomas J. Spulak

Hunts Point Terminal Cooperative Ass'n

Tom Ingstead Broadcasting Group

Rob Ingstead Broadcasting, Inc.

The Ingstead Broadcasting, Inc.

Israel Aircraft Industries, Ltd.
Issues: AER AVI
Rep By: J. E. Murdock, III

Kansas City, Missouri, City of
Issues: AVI
Rep By: Robert E. Cohn

KATU

KDTV

KDUH-TV

KFAR-TV

KFTV

KHSD-TV

KLUZ-TV

KMEX-TV

KOMO-TV

KOMU-TV

KOTA-TV

KSGW-TV

KTUU

KTVW-TV

KUVN-TV

KWEX-TV

KXLN-TV

KXMA-TV

KXMB

KXMC-TV

KXMD-TV

KXTX-TV

Liberty Medical Supply
Issues: HCR
Rep By: Bruce Fried

Lucas Aerospace
Issues: AER AVI
Rep By: J. E. Murdock, III

MATEK
Rep By: Gerald Charnoff

Medicare Cost Contractors Alliance
Issues: HCR
Rep By: Shannon Arnold, Bruce Fried, Thomas J. Spulak, Andrew L. Woods

Mega Broadcasting Corp.

Memphis, Tennessee, City of
Issues: ECN URB
Rep By: Anita K. Epstein, Rodolfo Fuentes

Mexico, Secretaria de Comercio y Fomento Industrial (SECOFI)
Rep By: Anita K. Epstein, Claudia Hrvatin, E. Michael O'Malley, Thomas J. Spulak, Andrew L. Woods

Mexico, Secretariat of Commerce & Industrial Development of

Midway Airlines Corp.
Rep By: Robert E. Cohn, Sheryl R. Israel

The Money Store
Issues: FIN
Rep By: Andrew L. Woods

The MWW Group
Issues: GOV
Rep By: Thomas J. Spulak

Nat'l Air Transportation Ass'n
Rep By: Robert E. Cohn

Nat'l Ass'n of Broadcasters

Nat'l Automobile Dealers Ass'n

Nat'l Coalition for Minority Business
Rep By: Rodolfo Fuentes, John E. Jensen

Nat'l Glass Ass'n

Nat'l IPA Coalition
Issues: HCR
Rep By: Bruce Fried

Nat'l Marine Manufacturers Ass'n
Issues: CPT
Rep By: Thomas J. Spulak

Nat'l Oilseed Processors Ass'n
Issues: ENV
Rep By: David E. Menotti

The Nordam Group
Issues: AVI
Rep By: J. E. Murdock, III

Nortel Networks
Rep By: Stephan E. Becker, Thomas J. Spulak, Andrew L. Woods

North Carolina Global TransPark Authority
Issues: AVI
Rep By: J. E. Murdock, III

Pegasus Communications

Peninsula Airways, Inc.
Rep By: Robert E. Cohn

Pezold Management
Rep By: Dawn M. Sciarrino

Pilot Communications

Potomac Capital Investment Corp.

The Progress Freedom Foundation
Rep By: Jeffery L. Yablon

Raychem Corp.

Reiten Broadcasting, Inc.

R. J. Reynolds Tobacco Co.
Issues: TOB
Rep By: Thomas J. Spulak

San Jose, California, City of
Rep By: Robert E. Cohn, J. E. Murdock, III

SFX Broadcasting

Shell Oil Co.
Issues: LBR

Sibley Memorial Hospital
Issues: DOC
Rep By: Thomas J. Spulak

Sinclair Broadcast Group, Inc.
Issues: COM
Rep By: Martin R. Leader

Southern Ass'n of Forestry Economics
Issues: AGR
Rep By: Anita K. Epstein, Claudia Hrvatin, Thomas J. Spulak, Andrew L. Woods

Taiwan Power Co.

Texaco Group Inc.
Issues: CIV ENV LAW
Rep By: Rodolfo Fuentes

Toledo Edison Co.
Rep By: Jay E. Silberg

Triathlon Broadcasting

Universal Systems and Technology Inc.
Rep By: John E. Jensen

Univision Television Group Inc.

Univision Television Network

Vanguard Airlines, Inc.
Issues: AVI
Rep By: Robert E. Cohn, Sheryl R. Israel

VHA Inc.

Vulcan Chemicals
Rep By: Thomas J. Spulak

WBFF

WFMJ-TV

WGBO-TV

White Knight Broadcasting

WLTV

Wolf Creek Nuclear Operating Corp.
Rep By: Jay E. Silberg

WPTT-TV

WTTE

WXTV

Z Spanish Network

Shaw, Bransford, Veilleux & Roth

1100 Connecticut Ave. NW
Suite 900
Washington, DC 20036-4101
Tel: (202)463-8400
Fax: (202)833-8082
Registered: LDA
Web: www.shawbransford.com
E-mail: sbvr@shawbransford.com

A law firm specializing in labor and employment law.

DC-Area Employees Representing Listed Clients

BRANSFORD, William L., Partner
O'ROURKE, Thomas J., Of Counsel
ROTH, Debra L., Partner
SHAW, Jr., G. Jerry, Partner
SWIENCKI, Katherine E., Legislative Assistant
VEILLEUX, Diana J., Partner

Clients

Cendant Mobility Services
Issues: GOV
Rep By: G. Jerry Shaw, Jr.

Federal Employees Education and Assistance Fund
Rep By: G. Jerry Shaw, Jr.

Public Employees Roundtable
Rep By: G. Jerry Shaw, Jr.

Senior Executives Ass'n
Issues: GOV
Rep By: G. Jerry Shaw, Jr., Katherine E. Swiencki

Shea & Gardner

1800 Massachusetts Ave. NW
Washington, DC 20036
Tel: (202)828-2000
Fax: (202)828-2195
Registered: LDA, FARA

A general practice law firm.

DC-Area Employees Representing Listed Clients

ALDOCK, John D., Partner and Chair, Executive Committee
BASSECHES, Robert T., Partner
COOK, David B., Partner
GOODMAN, Collette C.
HANLON, Patrick M., Partner
HANLON, William R., Partner
RICH, John Townsend, Partner
WOOLSEY, R. James, Partner

Clients

APL Limited
Rep By: Robert T. Basseches

Center for Claims Resolution
Issues: CSP
Rep By: John D. Aldock, Patrick M. Hanlon, William R. Hanlon

Internat'l Federation of Inspection Agencies, North American Committee
Issues: TRD
Rep By: Patrick M. Hanlon

Iraqi Nat'l Congress
Rep By: Collette C. Goodman

North American Industrial Hemp Council, Inc.
Issues: AGR
Rep By: R. James Woolsey

SGS Government Programs, Inc.
Rep By: John D. Aldock, Patrick M. Hanlon

SGS North America, Inc.
Rep By: John D. Aldock, Patrick M. Hanlon

Societe Generale de Surveillance Holding S.A.
Issues: TRD
Rep By: John D. Aldock, Patrick M. Hanlon

Nijyar H. Shemdin

10903 Amherst Ave.
Suite 231
Silver Spring, MD 20902
Tel: (301)946-1383
Fax: (301)946-1383
Registered: FARA
Web: www.krg.org
E-mail: nshemdin@netscape.net

Clients

Kurdistan Regional Government
Rep By: Nijyar H. Shemdin

Sher & Blackwell

1850 M St. NW
Suite 900
Washington, DC 20036
Tel: (202)463-2500
Fax: (202)463-4950
Registered: LDA, FARA

A law and government relations firm specializing in transportation, natural resources, appropriations, telecommunications and maritime issues.

Political Action Committee

Sher & Blackwell PAC

1850 M St. NW
Suite 900
Washington, DC 20036
Contact: Marc J. Fink
Tel: (202)463-2500
Fax: (202)463-4950

DC-Area Employees Representing Listed Clients

ATWOOD, Mark, Partner
BLACKWELL, Sr., Robert J., Partner
BUTLER, John W., Partner
COMSTOCK, Earl W., Partner
FINK, Marc J., Partner
LAWRENCE, Jeffrey F., Partner
MICKEY, Anne E., Partner
NAH, Joseph, Associate
O'CONNOR, Kelly A., Associate
PIKE, Jeffrey R., Director, Government Relations
ROHDE, Wayne R., Associate
SHER, Stanley O., Partner
SMITH, David F., Partner
SPRING, Heather M., Associate
TROTTER, III, Antilla E., Associate
TSCHIRHART, Paul, Partner

Clients

AeroRepublica, S.A.
Issues: AVI
Rep By: Mark Atwood

Apex Marine Ship Management Co. LLC
Issues: MAR
Rep By: Marc J. Fink, Jeffrey R. Pike

ASCENT (Ass'n of Community Enterprises)
Issues: TEC
Rep By: Earl W. Comstock, Jeffrey R. Pike, Antilla E. Trotter, III

AUPS/Mo Hussain
Issues: MAR
Rep By: Earl W. Comstock, Jeffrey R. Pike

Carriers Against Harbor Tax
Issues: MAR
Rep By: Marc J. Fink, Jeffrey R. Pike, Stanley O. Sher

Casino Express Airlines
Issues: AVI
Rep By: Mark Atwood

Chapman Freeborn America
Issues: AVI
Rep By: Mark Atwood

Council of European and Japanese Nat'l Shipowners' Ass'ns
Issues: MAR
Rep By: Marc J. Fink, Stanley O. Sher

Custom Air Transport
Issues: AVI
Rep By: Mark Atwood

Dolphin Safe/Fair Trade Campaign
Issues: MAR
Rep By: Earl W. Comstock, Jeffrey R. Pike

Focal Communications
Issues: TEC
Rep By: Earl W. Comstock, Jeffrey R. Pike, Antilla E. Trotter, III

General Category Tuna Ass'n
Issues: MAR
Rep By: Jeffrey R. Pike

Humane Soc. of the United States
Rep By: Earl W. Comstock, Jeffrey R. Pike

Internat'l Brotherhood of Teamsters
Issues: GOV
Rep By: John W. Butler, Marc J. Fink

Internat'l Fund for Animal Welfare
Issues: ANI ENV
Rep By: Earl W. Comstock, Jeffrey R. Pike

Japan Internat'l Transport Institute
Issues: AVI
Rep By: Mark Atwood

Kalitta Air, L.L.C.
Issues: AVI
Rep By: Mark Atwood

Level 3 Communications LLC
Rep By: Earl W. Comstock, Jeffrey R. Pike

M K Airlines
Issues: AVI
Rep By: Mark Atwood

Martha's Vineyard Steamship Authority
Rep By: Jeffrey R. Pike

Nat'l Marine Life Center
Issues: ANI ENV
Rep By: Earl W. Comstock, Jeffrey R. Pike, Antilla E. Trotter, III

NCS Healthcare
Issues: HCR
Rep By: John W. Butler, Earl W. Comstock, Antilla E. Trotter, III

New York Waterways
Rep By: Robert J. Blackwell, Sr., Jeffrey F. Lawrence, Jeffrey R. Pike

Nippon Yusen Kaisha (NYK) Line
Issues: MAR
Rep By: Robert J. Blackwell, Sr., Jeffrey F. Lawrence, Jeffrey R. Pike, Stanley O. Sher

Noise Reduction Technology Coalition
Issues: AVI ENV TRD
Rep By: Mark Atwood

Nucentrix Broadband Networks
Rep By: Earl W. Comstock, Jeffrey R. Pike

Ocean Carriers Working Group
Issues: MAR
Rep By: John W. Butler, Marc J. Fink, Jeffrey R. Pike, Stanley O. Sher

Performing Animal Welfare Soc.
Issues: ANI
Rep By: Jeffrey R. Pike

Rowan Companies, Inc.
Issues: GOV
Rep By: Earl W. Comstock, Jeffrey F. Lawrence, Jeffrey R. Pike

Sanko Fisheries LLC

Sargeant Marine, Inc.
Issues: MAR
Rep By: Robert J. Blackwell, Sr., Earl W. Comstock, Jeffrey R. Pike, Antilla E. Trotter, III

Separation Technologies
Issues: ENG FIN
Rep By: Earl W. Comstock, Jeffrey R. Pike

Stuyvesant Dredging Co.
Issues: MAR
Rep By: Earl W. Comstock, Jeffrey F. Lawrence, Jeffrey R. Pike

Sun Pacific Internat'l
Issues: AVI
Rep By: Mark Atwood

Transpacific Stabilization Agreement
Issues: MAR
Rep By: Marc J. Fink, Stanley O. Sher

United Catcher Boats
Issues: MAR
Rep By: Earl W. Comstock, Jeffrey R. Pike

Winstar Communications, Inc.
Issues: GOV TEC
Rep By: Earl W. Comstock, Jeffrey R. Pike

Woods Hole Steamship Authority
Issues: MAR
Rep By: Earl W. Comstock, Jeffrey R. Pike

The Sheridan Group

1808 Swann St. NW
Washington, DC 20009
Tel: (202)462-7288
Fax: (202)483-1964
Registered: LDA
E-mail: SheridanGr@aol.com

DC-Area Employees Representing Listed Clients

BUCHHOLZ, Mary Beth, Senior Legislative Associate
SHERIDAN, Thomas F., President
VASILOFF, Jennifer, V. President
WETEKAM, James R., Senior Legislative Associate

Clients

American AIDS Political Action Committee
Rep By: Thomas F. Sheridan

American Cancer Soc.
Issues: BUD
Rep By: Thomas F. Sheridan, James R. Wetekam

Chronic Fatigue and Immune Dysfunction Syndrome Ass'n of America
Issues: BUD MED
Rep By: Mary Beth Buchholz, Thomas F. Sheridan

Cities Advocating Emergency AIDS Relief (CAEAR)
Issues: BUD
Rep By: Thomas F. Sheridan, Jennifer Vasiloff

Fenton Communications
Issues: MED
Rep By: Mary Beth Buchholz, Thomas F. Sheridan

Housing Works
Issues: BUD HOU TAX
Rep By: Thomas F. Sheridan

Nat'l Ryan White Title III (b) Coalition
Rep By: Thomas F. Sheridan

San Francisco AIDS Foundation
Issues: BUD HCR
Rep By: Thomas F. Sheridan

Sherman, Dunn, Cohen, Leifer & Yellig, P.C.

1125 15th St. NW
Suite 801
Washington, DC 20005
Tel: (202)785-9300
Fax: (202)775-1950

A law firm specializing in labor and employment law and occupational safety and health issues.

DC-Area Employees Representing Listed Clients

COHEN, Laurence J., Partner
CRANE, Martin J.
KURNICK, Robert D.
LEIFER, Elihu I., Partner
LEYLAND, Nora H.

RESNICK, Richard M.
RUBIN, James E.

Clients

AFL-CIO - Building and Construction Trades Department

Internat'l Brotherhood of Electrical Workers
Rep By: Laurence J. Cohen

Mary Katherine Shilton

3903 Gresham Place
Alexandria, VA 22305
Tel: (703)836-0279
Fax: (703)836-0831
Registered: LDA

Clients

Internat'l Community Corrections Ass'n
Issues: ALC GOV LAW
Rep By: Mary Katherine Shilton

Craig Shirley & Associates

122 S. Patrick St.
Alexandria, VA 22314
Tel: (703)739-5920
Fax: (703)739-5924
Registered: LDA

Web: www.craigshirley.com
E-mail: craigshirley@craigshirley.com
A public relations and government affairs firm.

DC-Area Employees Representing Listed Clients
BANISTER, Diana L., V. President
KEFAUVER, Jenny
SHIRLEY, Craig P., President

Clients

Citizens for State Power
Issues: UTI
Rep By: Craig P. Shirley

Nat'l Rifle Ass'n Institute for Legislative Action
Rep By: Diana L. Banister

Southeastern Legal Foundation
Rep By: Jenny Kefauver, Craig P. Shirley

Shook, Hardy & Bacon LLP

600 14th St. NW
Washington, DC 20005
Tel: (202)783-8400
Fax: (202)783-4211

DC-Area Employees Representing Listed Clients
DEMAREST, Jr., William F., Partner
WOODY, Robert J.

Clients

Molecular Separations Inc.
Issues: CAW ENG
Rep By: William F. Demarest, Jr., Robert J. Woody

Eric Shulman & Associates

5316 Edgewood Dr.
Alexandria, VA 22310
Tel: (703)971-7656
Registered: LDA
E-mail: eric8@erols.com

DC-Area Employees Representing Listed Clients
SHULMAN, Eric, President

Clients

Local 511 Professional Employees, AFGE
Issues: IMM
Rep By: Eric Shulman

Nat'l Border Patrol Council
Issues: IMM LAW LBR
Rep By: Eric Shulman

Nat'l Immigration and Naturalization Services Council
Issues: IMM
Rep By: Eric Shulman

Shutler and Low

14500 Avion Pkwy.
Suite 300
Chantilly, VA 20151
Tel: (703)818-1320
Fax: (703)818-8813
Registered: LDA

DC-Area Employees Representing Listed Clients
FAIRCHILD, Roger C.
JACKSON, Benjamin R., Partner
KALER, Robert G.
WEISSMAN, Robert A., Partner

Clients

Japan Automobile Standards Internat'l Center
Issues: AUT CAW ENG TRA
Rep By: Roger C. Fairchild, Robert G. Kaler

Nissan North America Inc.
Issues: AUT
Rep By: Roger C. Fairchild, Robert G. Kaler

Toyota Motor Manufacturing North America
Rep By: Roger C. Fairchild

Toyota Technical Center U.S.A. Inc.
Issues: AUT
Rep By: Roger C. Fairchild, Robert G. Kaler

Sidley & Austin

1722 I St. NW
Washington, DC 20006
Tel: (202)736-8000
Fax: (202)736-8711
Registered: LDA, FARA

Web: www.sidley.com
A general practice law firm headquartered in Chicago, IL.

DC-Area Employees Representing Listed Clients
BASS, I. Scott, Partner
BELL, Christopher, Partner
BUENTE, Jr., David T., Partner
CONLAN, Jr., Robert J., Partner
CONNAUGHTON, James, Partner
ECKLAND, William S., Partner
FLINT, Myles
GUTTER, Sam, Partner
HUIZINGA, James A., Partner
LEVY, David M., Partner
MACBETH, Angus, Partner
MILES, David M., Partner
NEMEROFF, Michael A., Partner
RAUL, Alan C., Partner
RISHE, Melvin, Partner
TEITELBAUM, David E., Partner
TOMPKINS, Jr., Joseph B., Partner
VAN WAZER, Thomas P., Partner
WARDEN, Michael P., Partner

Clients

Alliance of Nonprofit Mailers
Issues: POS
Rep By: David M. Levy

American Medical Informatics Ass'n
Rep By: Michael A. Nemeroff

American Petroleum Institute
Rep By: David T. Buente, Jr., Sam Gutter

Appleton Papers, Inc.
Issues: ENV
Rep By: Christopher Bell, David T. Buente, Jr., Myles Flint, Thomas M. McMahon, Andrew Schlickman

ARCO Coal Co.
Rep By: David T. Buente, Jr., James Connaughton

Arthur Andersen LLP

Cayman Islands, Government of
Rep By: Joseph B. Tompkins, Jr.

Chicago Board of Trade
Issues: TAX

Chicago Mercantile Exchange
Issues: TAX

Forensic Technology, Inc.

GE Lighting Group
Rep By: Angus Macbeth

General Electric Co.
Issues: ENV
Rep By: David T. Buente, Jr., James Connaughton

IBP, Inc.
Issues: ENV
Rep By: Alan C. Raul

Investment Co. Institute
Issues: FIN
Rep By: David M. Miles

Israel, Goverment of the State of
Rep By: Melvin Rishe

Israel, Ministry of Defense of the State of
Rep By: Melvin Rishe

MasterCard Internat'l

Medeva Pharmaceuticals
Issues: ENV
Rep By: Alan C. Raul

Nat'l Community Pharmacists Ass'n
Rep By: Michael A. Nemeroff

Nat'l Nutritional Foods Ass'n
Issues: FOO
Rep By: Alan C. Raul

Newell, Co.

Panama, Government of the Republic of

United States Cellular Corp.
Rep By: Michael A. Nemeroff

Wocom Commodities Limited

Mark A. Siegel & Associates

2103 O St. NW
Washington, DC 20037
Tel: (202)371-5600
Fax: (202)371-5608
Registered: LDA, FARA

DC-Area Employees Representing Listed Clients
SAILER, Brian, Exec. V. President
SIEGEL, Mark A., President

Clients

Maldives, Government of the Republic of
Rep By: Brian Sailer, Mark A. Siegel

Pakistan, Government of the Islamic Republic of

Jill Sigal Associates

P.O. Box 3037
Alexandria, VA 22302
Tel: (703)824-9013
Fax: (703)824-9014
Registered: LDA

A government relations consulting firm.

DC-Area Employees Representing Listed Clients
SIGAL, Jill, President

Franklin R. Silbey

9430 Sunnyfield Ct.
Potomac, MD 20854
Tel: (202)639-4494
Fax: (202)639-4495
Registered: LDA

Clients

Citigroup
Rep By: Franklin R. Silbey

Sills Associates

1700 K St. NW
Suite 1200
Washington, DC 20006
Tel: (202)857-0103
Fax: (202)857-0209
Registered: LDA

Web: www.cig1.com
E-mail: hsills@cig1.com
A public affairs consultant.

DC-Area Employees Representing Listed Clients
SILLS, Hilary, President

Clients

Jacksonville Electric Authority
Issues: CAW ENG ENV TAX UTI
Rep By: Hilary Sills

Municipal Electric Authority of Georgia
Issues: CAW ENG ENV TAX UTI
Rep By: Hilary Sills

Psychemedics Corp.
Issues: ALC LBR SCI
Rep By: Hilary Sills

Silverberg, Goldman & Bikoff, LLP

1101 30th St. NW
Suite 120
Washington, DC 20007
Tel: (202)944-3301
Fax: (202)944-3306
Registered: LDA
E-mail: mgoldman@sgbdc.com

DC-Area Employees Representing Listed Clients
BIKOFF, James, Partner
GOLDMAN, Michael, Partner

Clients

Societe Air France
Issues: TRA
Rep By: Michael Goldman

Silverstein and Mullens, P.L.L.C.

1776 K St. NW
Suite 700
Washington, DC 20006
Tel: (202)452-7900
Fax: (202)452-7989
Registered: LDA
E-mail: silvmul@capcon.net
A law firm specializing in taxation and legislative matters.

DC-Area Employees Representing Listed Clients
SHERMAN, Gerald H., Member
SILVERSTEIN, Leonard L., Member

Clients

Ass'n for Advanced Life Underwriting
Rep By: Gerald H. Sherman

Law Offices of David L. Simon

1000 Connecticut Ave. NW
Suite 412
Washington, DC 20006
Tel: (202)481-9000
Fax: (202)481-9010
Web: www.dlsimon.com
E-mail: DLSimon@dlsimon.com

DC-Area Employees Representing Listed Clients
SIMON, David L.

Clients

Chang Mien Industry Co., Ltd.
Issues: TRD
Rep By: David L. Simon

Eregli Demir ve Celik Fab.
Rep By: David L. Simon

Habas Group
Issues: TRD
Rep By: David L. Simon

Industrie Alimentare Molisane
Issues: TRD
Rep By: David L. Simon

Pastavilla Makarnacilik A.S.
Issues: TRD
Rep By: David L. Simon

Pastificio Antonio Pallante
Issues: TRD
Rep By: David L. Simon

Pastificio Pagani
Issues: TRD
Rep By: David L. Simon

Turkey, Government of the Republic of
Issues: TRD
Rep By: David L. Simon

The Yucel Group
Issues: TRD
Rep By: David L. Simon

Simon and Co., Inc.

1660 L St. NW
Suite 1050
Washington, DC 20036
E-mail: SimonCoDC@aol.com

Tel: (202)659-2229
Fax: (202)659-5234
Registered: LDA

DC-Area Employees Representing Listed Clients
BARBER, Heather, Director, Federal Affairs
DEGOOD, Alex, Director, Congressional Affairs
SIMON, Leonard S., President

Clients

AC Transit
Issues: BUD COM LBR TEC TRA
Rep By: Heather Barber, Alex DeGood, Leonard S. Simon

Alameda Corridor Transportation Authority
Issues: TRA
Rep By: Heather Barber, Alex DeGood, Leonard S. Simon

American Water Works Ass'n
Issues: BUD CAW ENV
Rep By: Heather Barber, Alex DeGood, Leonard S. Simon

Carmel, Indiana, City of
Issues: HOU TRA URB
Rep By: Heather Barber, Alex DeGood, Leonard S. Simon

Citrus Heights, California, City of
Issues: BUD
Rep By: Heather Barber, Alex DeGood, Leonard S. Simon

Easter Seals
Issues: TRA
Rep By: Heather Barber, Alex DeGood, Leonard S. Simon

Fresno, California, City of
Issues: TRA URB
Rep By: Heather Barber, Alex DeGood, Leonard S. Simon

Madison, Wisconsin, City of
Issues: BUD LBR TRA
Rep By: Heather Barber, Alex DeGood, Leonard S. Simon

Newark, California, City of
Rep By: Heather Barber, Alex DeGood, Leonard S. Simon

Oakley, California, City of
Issues: LAW
Rep By: Heather Barber, Alex DeGood, Leonard S. Simon

Pierce Transit
Issues: BUD TRA
Rep By: Heather Barber, Alex DeGood, Leonard S. Simon

Portland, Oregon, City of
Issues: BUD ENV NAT TRA
Rep By: Heather Barber, Alex DeGood, Leonard S. Simon

Sacramento Housing and Redeveloping Agency
Issues: BUD HOU URB
Rep By: Heather Barber, Alex DeGood, Leonard S. Simon

Salt Lake City, Utah, City of
Issues: BUD ECN ENV HOU TRA URB
Rep By: Heather Barber, Alex DeGood, Leonard S. Simon

San Leandro, California, City of
Issues: AVI BUD DIS POS
Rep By: Heather Barber, Alex DeGood, Leonard S. Simon

Tacoma, Washington, City of
Issues: BUD HOU TAX URB
Rep By: Heather Barber, Alex DeGood, Leonard S. Simon

Tacoma, Washington, Public Utilities Department of
Issues: UTI
Rep By: Heather Barber, Alex DeGood, Leonard S. Simon

Simon Strategies/Mindbeam

2100 Pennsylvania Ave. NW
Suite 535
Washington, DC 20037
Web: www.simoninc.com
E-mail: strategy@simoninc.com

Tel: (202)822-1700
Fax: (202)822-1919
Registered: LDA

DC-Area Employees Representing Listed Clients
BRODSKY, Art, Senior V. President
EISENLA, Kristofer, Communications Specialist
MORTON, Ann P., Senior V. President
SCHNEIDER, Kim, Policy Analyst
SIMON, Gregory C., Chief Exec. Officer
ULRICH, Christopher, V. President
VAN HOOK, Kristan, President

Clients

AirCell, Inc.
Rep By: Gregory C. Simon, Christopher Ulrich, Kristan Van Hook

Catholic Television Network
Issues: EDU TEC
Rep By: Ann P. Morton, Gregory C. Simon, Christopher Ulrich, Kristan Van Hook

Metricom, Inc.
Issues: CPI TEC
Rep By: Ann P. Morton, Gregory C. Simon, Kristan Van Hook

openNET Coalition
Issues: TEC
Rep By: Gregory C. Simon, Kristan Van Hook

Time Domain Corp.
Issues: TEC
Rep By: Gregory C. Simon, Kristan Van Hook

Traffic.com
Issues: CPI DIS ECN ROD TRA
Rep By: Ann P. Morton, Gregory C. Simon, Christopher Ulrich, Kristan Van Hook

Bill Simpson & Associates

1156 15th St. NW
Suite 315
Washington, DC 20005
E-mail: mcaden@erols.com

Tel: (202)452-1003
Fax: (202)452-1311
Registered: LDA

DC-Area Employees Representing Listed Clients
SIMPSON, William G., President

Clients

ChemFirst Inc.
Issues: CSP ENV
Rep By: William G. Simpson

FedEx Corp.
Issues: POS TRD
Rep By: William G. Simpson

Mississippi Chemical Corp.
Issues: AGR TRD
Rep By: William G. Simpson

Stephens Group, Inc.
Issues: BAN TAX
Rep By: William G. Simpson

Stephen F. Sims and Associates

400 N. Capitol St. NW
Suite 585
Washington, DC 20001
A lobbying and public affairs firm.

Tel: (202)783-5300
Fax: (202)393-5218
Registered: LDA

DC-Area Employees Representing Listed Clients
SIMS, Stephen F.

Clients

Barr Laboratories
Issues: CPT HCR
Rep By: Stephen F. Sims

Beerman, Swerdlove, Woloshin, Barezky, Becken, Genin & London
Issues: CPT HCR
Rep By: Stephen F. Sims

Polytec Group
Issues: TRD
Rep By: Stephen F. Sims

Victory Wholesale Grocers Inc.
Issues: CPT
Rep By: Stephen F. Sims

Robert H. Sindt

1850 M St. NW
Suite 400
Washington, DC 20036

Tel: (202)466-4500
Fax: (202)775-5872
Registered: LDA

Clients

Bethel Grain Co., LLC
Issues: SMB
Rep By: Robert H. Sindt

SISCORP

321 D St. NE
Washington, DC 20002

Tel: (202)548-8322
Fax: (202)548-8326
Registered: LDA

Provides representation before the legislative and executive branches of government.

DC-Area Employees Representing Listed Clients
JORDAN, Wendy
MASSEY, Donald F.
MEISSNER, Robert
SHOTTES, Fran

Clients

Biostar Group, The
Issues: COM DEF
Rep By: Robert Meissner, Fran Shottes

Dewey Electronics Corp.
Issues: DEF
Rep By: Robert Meissner

Global Environment Facility
Issues: ENV
Rep By: Donald F. Massey

Harbor Branch Institute
Issues: MAR
Rep By: Donald F. Massey

Infusion Dynamics
Issues: DEF
Rep By: Robert Meissner

Innovative Technical Solutions
Issues: DEF SCI
Rep By: Robert Meissner

Mercer Engineering Research Center
Issues: DEF
Rep By: Robert Meissner

Nintendo of America, Inc.
Issues: CPT TRD
Rep By: Donald F. Massey

Providence St. Vincent Medical Center
Issues: DEF
Rep By: Donald F. Massey

PSI
Issues: DEF
Rep By: Donald F. Massey

SAT
Issues: DEF
Rep By: Donald F. Massey

Science Applications Internat'l Corp. (SAIC)
Issues: DEF
Rep By: Wendy Jordan, Donald F. Massey, Fran Shottes

Textron Inc.
Issues: DEF
Rep By: Wendy Jordan, Fran Shottes

ThermoTrex Corp.
Rep By: Wendy Jordan, Robert Meissner, Fran Shottes

VLOC
Issues: DEF
Rep By: Robert Meissner

Skadden, Arps, Slate, Meagher & Flom LLP

1440 New York Ave. NW
Washington, DC 20005
Web: www.skadden.com
A general practice law firm.

Tel: (202)371-7000
Fax: (202)393-5760
Registered: LDA, FARA

Political Action Committee
Skadden Arps Political Action Committee
1440 New York Ave. NW
Washington, DC 20005
Contact: Lynn R. Coleman

Tel: (202)371-7000
Fax: (202)393-5760

DC-Area Employees Representing Listed Clients
BARNETTE, Curtis, Of Counsel
BENNETT, Robert S., Partner
BERLIN, Kenneth, Partner
BRUSCA, Richard L., Partner
COLEMAN, Lynn R., Partner
CUTRONE, Roseann M., Counsel
ESTES, III, John N., Partner
FLYNN, Brian, Legislative Consultant
GOLDBERG, Jr., Fred T., Partner
GOLDMAN, Leslie J., Partner
GROSS, Kenneth A., Partner
HAMILTON, Stephen W., Partner
HECHT, Jim, Partner
HOUGH, Jessica A.
LIGHTHIZER, Robert E., Partner
LOSEY, James A., Associate
MANGAN, John J., Partner
NAEVE, Clifford M., Partner
OOSTERHUIS, Paul W., Partner
QUALE, John C., Partner
SCHERMAN, William S., Partner
SCHLAGER, Ivan A.
STEPTOE, Mary Lou, Partner
SWEET, Jr., William J., Partner
WEIMER, Brian D., Associate

Clients

Akzo America, Inc.
Rep By: Robert E. Lighthizer

American Electronics Ass'n
Rep By: Roseann M. Cutrone

Amstel Hudson Management Corp.
Rep By: Robert E. Lighthizer

AOL Time Warner
Issues: TEC
Rep By: Ivan A. Schlager
Armco Inc.
Rep By: Robert E. Lighthizer
Bethlehem Steel Corp.
Issues: TRD
Rep By: Robert E. Lighthizer
Bull H.N. Information Services, Inc.
Cement Free Trade Ass'n
Century 21 Real Estate Corp.
Rep By: Kenneth A. Gross
Cinergy Corp.
Rep By: Clifford M. Naeve
Clark/Bardes, Inc.
Rep By: Roseann M. Cutrone, Fred T. Goldberg, Jr.
Colgate Palmolive
Issues: TRD
Rep By: Robert E. Lighthizer
Consolidated Freightways Corp.
Rep By: Lynn R. Coleman
Corning Inc.
Issues: TEC TRD
Rep By: Robert E. Lighthizer
Entergy Services, Inc.
Rep By: William S. Scherman
Fidelity Charitable Gift Fund
Issues: TAX
Rep By: Roseann M. Cutrone, Fred T. Goldberg, Jr., Jessica A. Hough
Fort Howard Corp.
Rep By: Roseann M. Cutrone, Fred T. Goldberg, Jr.
Fruit of the Loom, Inc.
Rep By: Robert E. Lighthizer
Georgia, Government of the Republic of
Rep By: Robert S. Bennett
Granite Broadcasting Co.
Issues: TEC
Hickey Freeman Co.
Inland Steel Industries, Inc.
Issues: TRD
Rep By: Robert E. Lighthizer
Ispat Inland Steel Industries
Rep By: Robert E. Lighthizer
LTV Steel Co.
Issues: TRD
Rep By: Robert E. Lighthizer
MCI WorldCom Corp.
Rep By: Roseann M. Cutrone, Fred T. Goldberg, Jr., Robert E. Lighthizer, Paul W. Oosterhuis
Meridian Oil Inc.
Milliken and Co.
Issues: TRD
Rep By: Robert E. Lighthizer, Ivan A. Schlager
Mitgo Corp.
Nat'l Ass'n of Broadcasters
Issues: COM
Nat'l Steel Corp.
Issues: TRD
Rep By: Robert E. Lighthizer, John J. Mangan
New World Communications Group, Inc.
News Corporation Ltd.
Issues: TEC
Rep By: Ivan A. Schlager
Pharmaceutical Research and Manufacturers of America
Rep By: Roseann M. Cutrone, Fred T. Goldberg, Jr., Robert E. Lighthizer, Paul W. Oosterhuis
Sara Lee Corp.
Rep By: Robert E. Lighthizer
SBC Communications Inc.
Rep By: Ivan A. Schlager
Sequent Computer Systems
Rep By: Roseann M. Cutrone
Silver King Communications
Rep By: John C. Quale
The Stanley Works
Issues: TRD
Rep By: Brian Flynn
State Universities Retirement System of Illinois Pension Fund
Rep By: Lynn R. Coleman
Tax Fairness Coalition
Issues: TAX
Rep By: Fred T. Goldberg, Jr.
TCI
Rep By: John C. Quale
Uniden Corp.
Union Pacific
Issues: TRA TRD
Rep By: Ivan A. Schlager
US Airways
Issues: AVI
Rep By: Curtis Barnette, Ivan A. Schlager
US Steel Group
Issues: TRD
Rep By: Robert E. Lighthizer
Verizon Washington, DC, Inc.
The Wing Group
Rep By: Lynn R. Coleman

Skol & Associates, Inc.

1133 Connecticut Ave. NW
Suite 650
Washington, DC 20036
Tel: (202)822-2077
Fax: (202)822-2078
Registered: LDA
An international consulting/strategy firm.

DC-Area Employees Representing Listed Clients
SKOL, Michael M., President

Clients
Colombian Banking and Financial Entities Ass'n (ASOBANCARIA)
Issues: BAN FIN FOR
Rep By: Michael M. Skol

Slagle & Associates

1200 N. Veitch St.
Suite 816
Arlington, VA 22201
Tel: (703)524-3495
Registered: LDA

DC-Area Employees Representing Listed Clients
SLAGLE, Jr., P. Roger, President

Clients
Dallas Area Rapid Transit Authority
Issues: TRA
Rep By: P. Roger Slagle, Jr.
Denver, Regional Transportation District of
Issues: TRA
Rep By: P. Roger Slagle, Jr.

Slover & Loftus

1224 17th St. NW
Washington, DC 20036
Tel: (202)347-7170
Fax: (202)347-3619
Registered: LDA
Web: www.sloverandloftus.com
A law firm.

DC-Area Employees Representing Listed Clients
LESEUR, John H., Partner
LOFTUS, C. Michael, Partner
MILLS, Christopher A.
PFOHL, Peter A., Associate

Clients
Western Coal Traffic League
Issues: RRR
Rep By: John H. LeSeur, Christopher A. Mills, Peter A. Pfohl

SLR Budget and Legislative Consulting

1420 New York Ave. NW
Suite 700
Washington, DC 20005
E-mail: sruhe@vsadc.com
Tel: (202)638-1950
Fax: (202)638-1928
Registered: LDA

DC-Area Employees Representing Listed Clients
RUHE, Shirley L., President

Clients
Powell, Goldstein, Frazer & Murphy LLP
Issues: BUD

David Smallen

141 12th St. NE
Suite 18
Washington, DC 20002
Tel: (202)547-9494
Fax: (202)366-7270
Registered: LDA
A self-employed public affairs consultant.

Anne V. Smith

1350 I St. NW
Suite 680
Washington, DC 20005
Tel: (202)371-0010
Fax: (202)393-5596
Registered: LDA, FARA

Clients
Baltic American Freedom League
Issues: DEF FOR
Rep By: Anne V. Smith
DeMil Internat'l
Issues: DEF FOR
Rep By: Anne V. Smith
Internat'l Research and Exchanges Board (IREX)
Rep By: Anne V. Smith
Japan, Embassy of
Rep By: Anne V. Smith
Partido Accion Nacional (PAN)
Rep By: Anne V. Smith

Leighton W. Smith

11 Canal Center Plaza
Suite 103
Alexandria, VA 22314
Tel: (703)683-4222
Fax: (703)683-0645
Registered: LDA
Web: www.spectrumgrp.com
E-mail: thespecgrp@aol.com

Clients
The Boeing Co.
Rep By: Adm. Leighton W. Smith, USN (Ret.)

Robert E. Smith

5903 Mount Eagle Dr.
Suite 1404
Alexandria, VA 22303
Tel: (703)329-9514
Fax: (703)329-1164
Registered: LDA

Clients
Arch Chemical Inc.
Issues: CHM
Rep By: Robert E. Smith
Olin Corp.
Issues: CHM FIR MON
Rep By: Robert E. Smith

Philip S. Smith & Associates, Inc.

611 Pennsylvania Ave. SE
Suite 340
Washington, DC 20003
Tel: (202)543-1444
Fax: (202)318-0652
Registered: LDA

DC-Area Employees Representing Listed Clients
KUE, Chia
KUE, Lisa
NADERI, Ms. Homa
SMITH, Jr., Philip J.
SMITH, Philip S., President

Clients
Afghanistan Foundation
Issues: DEF FOR IMM TRD
Rep By: Philip S. Smith
Lao Progressive Institute
Issues: FOR
Rep By: Chia Kue, Lisa Kue, Philip S. Smith
Lao Veterans of America, Inc.
Issues: FOR IMM TRD VET
Rep By: Chia Kue, Lisa Kue, Philip J. Smith, Jr., Philip S. Smith
United Lao Congress for Democracy
Issues: DEF FOR TRD VET
Rep By: Philip S. Smith

Smith & Harroff, Inc.

99 Canal Center Plaza
Suite 200
Alexandria, VA 22314
Tel: (703)683-8512
Fax: (703)683-4622
Registered: LDA
Web: www.smithharroff.com
E-mail: rmorris@smithharroff.com

DC-Area Employees Representing Listed Clients
BLAKELY, Ed, V. President
MCKERNAN, Robert T., Partner
MORRIS, Frederick E., Partner
POPOVICH, Luke, Senior V. President
SMITH, J. Brian, President and Chief Exec. Officer

Clients
Aluminum Co. of Canada
Sappi Fine Paper NA
Issues: CAW ENV LBR MAN NAT TAX TRA TRD WAS
Rep By: Luke Popovich

Smith & Metalitz, L.L.P.

1747 Pennsylvania Ave. NW
Suite 825
Washington, DC 20006-4604
Tel: (202)833-4198
Fax: (202)872-0546
Registered: LDA

DC-Area Employees Representing Listed Clients
METALITZ, Steven J., Partner
SCHLESINGER, Michael N., Associate
SCHWARTZ, Eric J., Partner
SMITH, Eric H., Managing Partner
STRONG, Maria S., Partner

Clients

eBay Inc.
Issues: CPI
Rep By: Steven J. Metalitz

Internat'l Intellectual Property Alliance
Issues: CPT TRD
Rep By: Steven J. Metalitz, Michael N. Schlesinger, Eric J. Schwartz, Eric H. Smith, Maria S. Strong

Smith Alling Lane, P.S.

1025 Connecticut Ave. NW
Suite 1012
Washington, DC 20036

Tel: (202)258-2301
Registered: LDA

DC-Area Employees Representing Listed Clients

HURST, Lisa
MACK, Robert
MCALEENAN, Michael
SCHELLBERG, Timothy

Clients

PE Biosystems
Issues: BUD CIV CPI LAW SCI
Rep By: Lisa Hurst, Robert Mack, Michael McAleenan, Timothy Schellberg

Sagem Morpho
Issues: BUD CIV CPI DEF ENG GOV IMM LAW SCI
Rep By: Lisa Hurst, Robert Mack, Michael McAleenan, Timothy Schellberg

Washington Ass'n of Sheriffs and Police Chiefs
Issues: BUD LAW
Rep By: Lisa Hurst, Robert Mack, Michael McAleenan, Timothy Schellberg

E. Del Smith and Co.

1130 Connecticut Ave. NW
Suite 650
Washington, DC 20036

Tel: (202)822-8300
Fax: (202)822-8315
Registered: LDA, FARA

Government relations consulting.

DC-Area Employees Representing Listed Clients

ALLEN, Margaret, Legislative Director
ALSOP, Ryan
CARPI, Kenneth A.
SMITH, E. Del, President

Clients

American Magline Group
Issues: RRR TRA
Rep By: E. Del Smith

Anaheim, California, City of
Issues: IMM TRA
Rep By: Margaret Allen, E. Del Smith

Anaheim, California, Public Utilities of the City of
Issues: TEC UTI
Rep By: Margaret Allen, E. Del Smith

Apple Valley, California, City of
Issues: TRA
Rep By: Margaret Allen, E. Del Smith

Aquarium of the Pacific
Issues: MAR SCI
Rep By: Ryan Alsop, E. Del Smith

Barstow, California, City of
Rep By: Margaret Allen, E. Del Smith

BEMS W/L Associates
Rep By: E. Del Smith

Bioelectromagnetics Soc.
Rep By: Margaret Allen, E. Del Smith

California Independent Petroleum Ass'n
Issues: ENG FUE
Rep By: Margaret Allen, E. Del Smith

California-American Water Co.
Issues: ENV
Rep By: Kenneth A. Carpi, E. Del Smith

Calleguas Creek Flood Prevention Committee
Rep By: E. Del Smith

Chep USA

Chino Hills, California, City of
Issues: TRA
Rep By: Margaret Allen, E. Del Smith

Contra Costa, California, Tenants of the County of
Issues: BUD MAR
Rep By: Margaret Allen, E. Del Smith

Corte Madera, California, Town of
Issues: BUD
Rep By: Margaret Allen, E. Del Smith

Downey, California, Economic Development of the City of
Issues: BUD
Rep By: Margaret Allen, E. Del Smith

Hesperia, California, City of
Issues: TRA
Rep By: Margaret Allen, E. Del Smith

Hollis-Eden Pharmaceuticals, Inc.
Issues: HCR MED
Rep By: Kenneth A. Carpi, E. Del Smith

InterMart Broadcasting
Rep By: E. Del Smith

Laguna Beach, California, City of
Issues: BUD CAW ENG
Rep By: Margaret Allen, E. Del Smith

Lake County Basin 2000
Issues: CAW
Rep By: E. Del Smith

Long Beach Naval Shipyard Employees Ass'n
Rep By: Margaret Allen, E. Del Smith

Long Beach Water Department
Issues: BUD
Rep By: Margaret Allen, E. Del Smith

Long Beach, California, City of
Issues: BUD DEF HOU
Rep By: Margaret Allen, E. Del Smith

Long Beach, California, Port of
Issues: BUD DEF TAX TRA
Rep By: Margaret Allen, E. Del Smith

Los Angeles, California, County of
Issues: BUD MAR TRA
Rep By: Margaret Allen, E. Del Smith

Lynwood, California, City of
Rep By: E. Del Smith

Morro Bay, California, City of
Issues: BUD
Rep By: Margaret Allen, E. Del Smith

Nat'l Independent Private Schools Ass'n
Issues: EDU
Rep By: Margaret Allen, E. Del Smith

Port Hueneme, California, City of
Issues: BUD
Rep By: Margaret Allen, E. Del Smith

Rancho Palos Verdes, California, City of
Issues: BUD
Rep By: E. Del Smith

Reusable Pallet and Container Coalition
Issues: DEF ENV TAX
Rep By: Margaret Allen, E. Del Smith

Santa Barbara, California, City of (Waterfront)
Issues: BUD
Rep By: Margaret Allen, E. Del Smith

Santa Barbara, California, Public Works Department
Issues: BUD
Rep By: Margaret Allen, E. Del Smith

Santa Cruz, California, Port of
Issues: BUD
Rep By: Margaret Allen, E. Del Smith

Seal Beach, California, City of
Issues: DEF
Rep By: E. Del Smith

Stockton, California, Port of
Issues: DEF
Rep By: E. Del Smith

Victorville, California, City of
Issues: BUD TRA
Rep By: Margaret Allen, E. Del Smith

Woods Hole Oceanographic Institution
Issues: SCI
Rep By: Margaret Allen, E. Del Smith

Xybernaut
Issues: COM
Rep By: E. Del Smith

Smith Dawson & Andrews, Inc.

1000 Connecticut Ave. NW
Suite 302
Washington, DC 20036

Tel: (202)835-0740
Fax: (202)775-8526
Registered: LDA, FARA

Web: www.sda-inc.com

A government relations and public affairs firm.

DC-Area Employees Representing Listed Clients

ANDREWS, Gregory B.
BAILEY, Kirk
DAWSON, Thomas C.
GAINES, Robert A.
LUGO, Ramon Luis
POWAR, Sherri
RILEY, Susan Mary
SMITH, James P.
WARNER, Ray

Clients

Alston & Bird, LLP
Issues: UTI
Rep By: Gregory B. Andrews, Thomas C. Dawson, James P. Smith

American Federation of Television and Radio Artists
Issues: ART COM CPT GOV LBR MIA
Rep By: James P. Smith

Avecia, Inc.
Issues: TRD
Rep By: Sherri Powar, James P. Smith

Bone Care Internat'l
Issues: MMM PHA
Rep By: James P. Smith

Caguas, Puerto Rico, City of
Issues: CAW HOU TRA
Rep By: Ramon Luis Lugo, James P. Smith

Carolina, Puerto Rico, City of
Issues: AGR BUD CAW ECN HOU TRA
Rep By: Ramon Luis Lugo, James P. Smith

Ceiba, Puerto Rico, City of
Issues: BUD DEF ECN
Rep By: Gregory B. Andrews, Ramon Luis Lugo, James P. Smith

Certified Automotive Parts Ass'n
Issues: AUT INS
Rep By: Gregory B. Andrews, Thomas C. Dawson, James P. Smith, Ray Warner

Children's Hospital and Medical Center
Issues: BUD HCR MMM
Rep By: Sherri Powar, James P. Smith

Council of Development Finance Agencies
Issues: FIN TAX
Rep By: Susan Mary Riley, James P. Smith

Eugene, Oregon, City of
Issues: BUD CAW LAW TRA URB
Rep By: Sherri Powar, James P. Smith

Fontana, California, City of
Issues: TRA
Rep By: Robert A. Gaines

George Washington University, Office of Government Relations
Issues: BUD TRA
Rep By: Gregory B. Andrews, James P. Smith, Ray Warner

Georgia Municipal Gas Ass'n
Rep By: Gregory B. Andrews, Thomas C. Dawson, James P. Smith

Georgia, State of
Issues: GOV
Rep By: Gregory B. Andrews, Thomas C. Dawson, Sherri Powar, James P. Smith

Haarmann & Reimer Corp.
Issues: BUD PHA TRA TRD
Rep By: Sherri Powar, James P. Smith

Hillwood Development Corp.
Issues: AVI TRA TRD
Rep By: Gregory B. Andrews, Thomas C. Dawson

Japan, Embassy of
Rep By: Gregory B. Andrews, James P. Smith

Kansas City Area Transportation Authority
Issues: BUD TRA
Rep By: Kirk Bailey, Thomas C. Dawson

Lane Transit District
Issues: BUD TRA
Rep By: Thomas C. Dawson, Sherri Powar, James P. Smith

Lane, Oregon, County of
Issues: BUD CAW DEF LAW
Rep By: Sherri Powar, James P. Smith

Litton Advanced Systems
Issues: AVI BUD
Rep By: Gregory B. Andrews, Thomas C. Dawson, Ray Warner

Litton Systems, Inc.
Issues: UTI
Rep By: Gregory B. Andrews, Thomas C. Dawson, Ray Warner

Mothers Against Drunk Driving (MADD)
Issues: ALC
Rep By: Gregory B. Andrews, Kirk Bailey, Thomas C. Dawson, James P. Smith

Nat'l Ass'n of Foreign Trade Zones
Issues: TRD
Rep By: Sherri Powar, James P. Smith

NeoPharm, Inc.
Issues: PHA
Rep By: Sherri Powar, James P. Smith

New York Metropolitan Transportation Authority
Issues: BUD TRA
Rep By: Thomas C. Dawson

Sacramento, California, City of
Issues: BUD TRA
Rep By: Thomas C. Dawson, James P. Smith

San Francisco Internat'l Airport
Issues: AVI BUD
Rep By: Gregory B. Andrews, Thomas C. Dawson

Springfield, Oregon, City of
Issues: BUD CAW
Rep By: Sherri Powar, James P. Smith

Springfield, Oregon, School District #19
Issues: EDU
Rep By: Gregory B. Andrews, Kirk Bailey, Thomas C. Dawson, Sherri Powar, James P. Smith

Upland, California, City of
Issues: DEF TRA
Rep By: Robert A. Gaines

Wound Ostomy Continence Nurses
Issues: HCR MMM
Rep By: Gregory B. Andrews, Sherri Powar

Smith Fairfield, Inc.

101 1/2 S. Union St.
Alexandria, VA 22314
Tel: (703)684-5100
Fax: (703)684-5424
Registered: LDA

Web: www.smithfairfield.com
A political and communications consulting firm that specializes in public, corporate, and political relations, event production and direct marketing.

DC-Area Employees Representing Listed Clients
DE POSADA, Robert
LARSON, Teresa J., Principal
SMITH, Jennifer K., President
WHITE, Kenneth, Principal

Smith Law Firm

1918 18th St. NW
Suite 24
Washington, DC 20009
Tel: (202)265-1551
Fax: (202)737-0693
Registered: LDA
E-mail: nativeamericans@compuserve.com

DC-Area Employees Representing Listed Clients
SMITH, Gregory A., Attorney at Law

Clients

Navajo Nation
Issues: IND
Rep By: Gregory A. Smith

Pueblo of Acoma
Issues: IND
Rep By: Gregory A. Smith

Smith Martin & Boyette

915 15th St. NW
Suite 800
Washington, DC 20005
Tel: (202)347-2980
Fax: (202)347-2992
Registered: LDA
E-mail: VanDesk@aol.com
Washington, DC office of a government relations/consulting firm headquartered in New Orleans, LA.

DC-Area Employees Representing Listed Clients
BOYETTE, Van R., Partner

Clients

Florida Crystals Corp.
Issues: AGR ENV TRD
Rep By: Van R. Boyette

Montana Land Reliance
Issues: RES TAX
Rep By: Van R. Boyette

Refined Sugars Inc.
Issues: AGR
Rep By: Van R. Boyette

Smith, Bucklin and Associates, Inc.

2025 M St. NW
Suite 800
Washington, DC 20036
Tel: (202)367-2100
Fax: (202)367-1200
Registered: LDA
Web: www.sba.com
A Chicago-headquartered association management firm.

Political Action Committee
Smith, Bucklin and Associates Political Action Committee
2025 M St. NW
Suite 800
Washington, DC 20036
Tel: (202)367-2100
Fax: (202)367-1200
Contact: Bonnie M. Aubin

DC-Area Employees Representing Listed Clients
AUBIN, Bonnie M.
CAMERA, CAE, Gaylen Millard, V. President, Health and Sciences
COLGAN, Corinne
DARIN, Anna
EKEDAHL, Duane H.
GAINE, John G.
GOLDBERG, Joan R.
HARMON, Linda
JANKO, Julie A.
KELLEY, William E.
KEMP, Steven C.
LYNCH, Scott
MALARKEY, Faye A.
MCELROY, Deborah C.
MCFARLAND, Jeff
MOORE, Frank M., Director, Public Policy Practice Group, Government Relations
MOYE, Stacey, Legislative Administrator, Government Relations
MURPHY, John C.
PAYNE, Michael L., Exec. V. President
RATHBUN, Jill, Director, Health Care Practice Group
REESE, Melissa
REISER, Tom, Account Executive
ROHN, David
VAZQUEZ, Frankie, Legislative Assistant, Government Relations
WILBUR, Robert H.

Clients

Academy of Osseointegration
Issues: BUD HCR
Rep By: Jill Rathbun

American Ass'n for the Study of Liver Diseases

American Ass'n of Health Care Administrative Management

American Bearing Manufacturers Ass'n
Rep By: Scott Lynch, David Rohn

American Federation for Medical Research

American Psychiatric Nurses Ass'n
Issues: BUD HCR MMM
Rep By: Jill Rathbun, Melissa Reese

American Soc. for Bone and Mineral Research
Rep By: Joan R. Goldberg

American Soc. of Nephrology
Issues: BUD MED MMM
Rep By: Jill Rathbun

American Urogynecologic Soc.
Issues: BUD HCR MED MMM
Rep By: Steven C. Kemp, Jill Rathbun

Ass'n for Governmental Leasing and Finance

Ass'n for Hospital Medical Education

Ass'n of Local Housing Finance Agencies
Issues: HOU
Rep By: Frank M. Moore, John C. Murphy

Ass'n of Telemessaging Services Internat'l

Check Payment Systems Ass'n

The Child Care Consortium
Issues: AGR EDU WEL
Rep By: Frank M. Moore, Stacey Moye

Community Financial Services Ass'n
Rep By: William E. Kelley

Council of Development Finance Agencies
Rep By: Anna Darin

Engine Manufacturers Ass'n

Foundation for Pavement Rehabilitation and Maintenance Research

Information Technology Resellers Ass'n

Internat'l Ass'n of Airport Duty Free Stores
Rep By: Michael L. Payne

Internat'l Bone and Mineral Soc.
Rep By: Tom Reiser

Internat'l District Energy Ass'n

Internat'l Furnishing & Design Ass'n (IFDA)

Internat'l Institute of Ammonia Refrigeration
Rep By: Frank M. Moore

Internat'l Slurry Surfacing Ass'n

Internat'l Soc. for Experimental Hematology
Rep By: Tom Reiser

Lamaze Internat'l
Rep By: Linda Harmon

Managed Funds Ass'n
Issues: FIN
Rep By: John G. Gaine

Mobile Communications Holdings, Inc.
Issues: SMB TEC
Rep By: Frank M. Moore

Museum Trustee Ass'n

Nat'l Ass'n of County Community and Economic Development
Issues: HOU
Rep By: John C. Murphy

Nat'l Ass'n of Food Equipment Manufacturers
Rep By: Robert H. Wilbur

Nat'l Ass'n of Healthcare Access Management
Rep By: Steven C. Kemp

Nat'l Child Care Ass'n
Rep By: Frank M. Moore, Stacey Moye

Nat'l Organization for Competency Assurance
Issues: SMB VET
Rep By: Bonnie M. Aubin, Frank M. Moore, Stacey Moye

Nat'l Vision Rehabilitation Cooperative
Rep By: Jill Rathbun

North American Ass'n of Food Equipment Manufacturers
Issues: LBR
Rep By: Robert H. Wilbur

Osteoarthritis Research Soc. Internat'l

Pet Food Institute
Rep By: Duane H. Ekedahl

Regional Airline Ass'n
Issues: AVI
Rep By: Faye A. Malarkey, Deborah C. McElroy

Soc. of Gynecologic Oncologists
Issues: BUD HCR MED MMM
Rep By: Jill Rathbun

Soc. of Maternal-Fetal Medicine
Rep By: Jill Rathbun

Soc. of Research Administrators
Rep By: Jeff McFarland

Soc. of Thoracic Surgeons
Issues: HCR MMM
Rep By: Corinne Colgan, Robert H. Wilbur

SonoSite
Issues: BUD EDU HCR
Rep By: Jill Rathbun

Viatical Ass'n of America
Rep By: William E. Kelley

Wireless Information Networks Forum (WinForum)
Rep By: Anna Darin

Smith, Hinaman & Associates

601 Madison St.
Suite 200
Alexandria, VA 22314
Tel: (703)684-9188
Registered: LDA

DC-Area Employees Representing Listed Clients
HINAMAN, Randy
SMITH, Don, Principal
SMITH, Todd

Clients

Burns and Roe Enterprises, Inc.
Issues: ENG
Rep By: Don Smith

Gadsden State Community College
Issues: EDU
Rep By: Don Smith

Ibex
Issues: AVI ENG
Rep By: Randy Hinaman, Don Smith, Todd Smith

US Acqua Sonics Corp.
Issues: CAW ENG
Rep By: Randy Hinaman, Don Smith

The Smith-Free Group

1401 K St. NW
12th Floor
Washington, DC 20005
Tel: (202)393-4760
Fax: (202)393-3516
Registered: LDA

DC-Area Employees Representing Listed Clients
BARTLETT, Doyle, Senior V. President
FREE, James C., President and Chief Exec. Officer
HICKMOTT, Robert, Senior V. President
LOCKE, W. Timothy, Senior V. President
SMITH, Alicia W., Senior V. President and Secretary
SMITH, James E., Chairman

Clients

Adriaen's Landing Management Co., LLC

American Franchisee Ass'n

American Petroleum Institute

AT&T
Issues: TEC TRD
Rep By: James C. Free, W. Timothy Locke, Alicia W. Smith

Broadcast Music Inc. (BMI)
Issues: CPT
Rep By: James C. Free, W. Timothy Locke, Alicia W. Smith

CSX Corp.
Issues: MAR RRR
Rep By: James C. Free, W. Timothy Locke, Alicia W. Smith

Federal Home Loan Mortgage Corp. (Freddie Mac)
Issues: BAN BUD TAX
Rep By: James E. Smith

HCA Healthcare Corp.
Issues: HCR
Rep By: James C. Free, W. Timothy Locke, Alicia W. Smith, James E. Smith

Kennecott/Borax
Issues: ENG ENV LBR WAS
Rep By: James C. Free, Alicia W. Smith

MasterCard Internat'l
Issues: BNK
Rep By: James C. Free, W. Timothy Locke, James E. Smith

MBNA America Bank NA
Issues: BAN BNK
Rep By: James C. Free, W. Timothy Locke, James E. Smith

Metropolitan Life Insurance Co.

Mortgage Bankers Ass'n of America

New Mexico Indian Gaming Ass'n

Northwestern Mutual Life Insurance Co.
Issues: FIN
Rep By: James E. Smith

Nuclear Energy Institute
Issues: ENG
Rep By: James C. Free, W. Timothy Locke, Alicia W. Smith

Paucatuck Eastern Pequot Tribal Nation
Issues: ECN HOU
Rep By: James C. Free, Robert Hickmott, W. Timothy Locke, Alicia W. Smith

J. P. Redd Inc.

Sandia Pueblo
Issues: BUD GAM IND NAT TAX TOU
Rep By: James C. Free, W. Timothy Locke, Alicia W. Smith

Sony Music Entertainment Inc.
Issues: BNK CPT TRD
Rep By: James C. Free, W. Timothy Locke, Alicia W. Smith

Sony Pictures Entertainment Inc.
Issues: CPT IMM TRD
Rep By: James C. Free, W. Timothy Locke, Alicia W. Smith

Southern Co.
Issues: BUD UTI
Rep By: James C. Free, W. Timothy Locke, Alicia W. Smith

Star Systems
Issues: BAN FIN
Rep By: Doyle Bartlett, James E. Smith

U.S. Wireless Data, Inc.
Issues: SMB
Rep By: Doyle Bartlett, James C. Free, Robert Hickmott, W. Timothy Locke, Alicia W. Smith

VISA U.S.A., Inc.
Issues: BNK
Rep By: James C. Free, W. Timothy Locke, James E. Smith

Washington Group Internat'l
Issues: ENG
Rep By: James C. Free, Robert Hickmott, W. Timothy Locke

Washington Mutual Bank
Issues: BAN FIN
Rep By: James C. Free, James E. Smith

Westinghouse Government Services Group
Issues: ENG
Rep By: James C. Free, Robert Hickmott, W. Timothy Locke

Xcel Energy, Inc.
Issues: ENG
Rep By: James C. Free, Robert Hickmott

Snavely, King, Majoros, O'Connor and Lee, Inc.

1220 L St. NW
Suite 410
Washington, DC 20005
Tel: (202)371-1111
Fax: (202)842-4966
Web: www.snavley-king.com
E-mail: skmoltom1@aol.com

A transportation and management consulting firm with further specializations in telecommunications, utility and economic issues.

DC-Area Employees Representing Listed Clients

KING, Charles W., President
LEE, Richard, V. President
MAJOROS, Michael, V. President
O'CONNOR, Tom, V. President

Clients

Canadian Pacific
Rep By: Tom O'Connor

Dow Jones & Co., Inc.
Rep By: Charles W. King

Kansas City Southern Industries
Rep By: Tom O'Connor

Montana, State of
Rep By: Tom O'Connor

Occidental Chemical Corporation
Rep By: Tom O'Connor

Puerto Rico Telephone Co.
Rep By: Michael Majoros

San Antonio City Public Service

Wall Street Journal
Rep By: Charles W. King

Washington Construction Co.
Rep By: Tom O'Connor

Robert D. Sneed

2404-D S. Walter Reed Dr.
Arlington, VA 22203
Tel: (703)820-6372
Fax: (703)820-6373
Registered: LDA

Clients

Advanced Power Technologies, Inc.
Issues: DEF
Rep By: Robert D. Sneed

General Electric Co.
Issues: DEF
Rep By: Robert D. Sneed

Hurt, Norton and Associates, Inc.
Issues: DEF
Rep By: Robert D. Sneed

Kaman Diversified Technologies Corp.
Issues: DEF
Rep By: Robert D. Sneed

Craig Snyder & Associates

1101 30th St. NW
Washington, DC 20006
Tel: (202)337-6600
Fax: (202)337-6660
Registered: LDA

DC-Area Employees Representing Listed Clients

SNYDER, Craig, President

Clients

Tensiodyne Scientific Corp.
Issues: AER BUD DEF TRA
Rep By: Craig Snyder

The Solomon Group, LLC

801 Pennsylvania Ave. NW
Suite 750
Washington, DC 20004
Tel: (202)628-3750
Fax: (202)624-0659
Registered: LDA, FARA
Web: www.solomongroup.com
E-mail: mail@solomongroup.com

An international public affairs consulting firm providing strategic counsel, lobbying, and media relations.

DC-Area Employees Representing Listed Clients

BAUER, Dana, Associate
CROSBY, Jr., William D., V. President and Chief Operating Officer
KINGSBURY, Cathryn J., Director, Research/Legislative Analyst
LONIE, David M., Principal Partner
ROHOLT WESTDORP, Lara, Associate
SOLOMON, Hon. Gerald B. H., President and Chief Exec. Officer
TEATOR, William R., Senior Director, Public and Media Affairs

Clients

AAI Corp.
Issues: DEF
Rep By: David M. Lonie, Hon. Gerald B. H. Solomon

Alliance for American Innovation, Inc.
Issues: CPT DEF
Rep By: William D. Crosby, Jr., David M. Lonie, Hon. Gerald B. H. Solomon

Apria Healthcare Group
Issues: HCR
Rep By: Hon. Gerald B. H. Solomon, William R. Teator

Ass'n of Small Business Development Centers
Issues: ECN FOR SMB
Rep By: David M. Lonie, Hon. Gerald B. H. Solomon, William R. Teator

Clough, Harbour & Associates LLP
Issues: DEF
Rep By: William D. Crosby, Jr., David M. Lonie, Hon. Gerald B. H. Solomon, William R. Teator

Espey Manufacturing and Electronics
Issues: DEF MAN TRD
Rep By: David M. Lonie, Hon. Gerald B. H. Solomon

Finch-Pruyn Paper Co.
Issues: ENV LBR NAT TRD TRU
Rep By: Hon. Gerald B. H. Solomon, William R. Teator

General Electric Co.
Issues: AVI BAN BNK DEF ENG FIN FOR HCR INS MAN TAX TRD UTI
Rep By: William D. Crosby, Jr., David M. Lonie, Hon. Gerald B. H. Solomon, William R. Teator

Institute for Entrepreneurship
Issues: BUD ECN EDU SMB
Rep By: Hon. Gerald B. H. Solomon, William R. Teator

Internat'l Medical Programs
Issues: BUD DEF FOR
Rep By: David M. Lonie, Lara Roholt Westdorp, Hon. Gerald B. H. Solomon

JBA Consulting, Inc.
Issues: ACC DEF GOV
Rep By: David M. Lonie, Hon. Gerald B. H. Solomon

"K" Line America, Inc.
Issues: MAR
Rep By: William D. Crosby, Jr., Hon. Gerald B. H. Solomon

Morocco, Foreign Ministry of the Kingdom of
Issues: FOR TRD
Rep By: David M. Lonie, Hon. Gerald B. H. Solomon

Nat'l Milk Producers Federation
Issues: AGR ANI TAX TRD
Rep By: Hon. Gerald B. H. Solomon, William R. Teator

Safe Environment of America
Issues: CHM DEF ENV WAS
Rep By: David M. Lonie, Lara Roholt Westdorp, Hon. Gerald B. H. Solomon

States Ratification Committee
Issues: AGR GOV TRD
Rep By: Hon. Gerald B. H. Solomon, William R. Teator

SUNY Empire State College
Issues: DEF EDU
Rep By: Hon. Gerald B. H. Solomon, William R. Teator

Taipei Economic and Cultural Representative Office in the United States
Issues: FOR TRD
Rep By: David M. Lonie, Hon. Gerald B. H. Solomon

Turkey, Embassy of the Republic of
Rep By: Hon. Gerald B. H. Solomon

Turkey, Government of the Republic of
Issues: FOR TRD
Rep By: Dana Bauer, David M. Lonie, Hon. Gerald B. H. Solomon

The Vandervort Group, LLC
Issues: BUD EDU HCR TEC
Rep By: Hon. Gerald B. H. Solomon, William R. Teator

Solutions Group

10335 Democracy Ln.
Fairfax, VA 22030
Tel: (703)352-0225
Fax: (703)352-8894
Registered: LDA

DC-Area Employees Representing Listed Clients

BURGESS, Robert, V. President
HERRITY, John F., President

Clients

Wheelabrator-Cleanwater Systems-BioGro Division
Rep By: Robert Burgess, John F. Herrity

Sonnenschein, Nath & Rosenthal

1301 K St. NW
Suite 600E
Washington, DC 20005
Tel: (202)408-6400
Fax: (202)408-6399

DC-Area Employees Representing Listed Clients

ROSENTHAL, Douglas E.

Clients

Quebec Lumber Manufacturers Ass'n
Issues: FOR GOV IND MAN TRD
Rep By: Douglas E. Rosenthal

Sonosky, Chambers, Sachse & Endreson

1250 I St. NW
Suite 1000
Washington, DC 20005
Tel: (202)682-0240
Fax: (202)682-0249
Registered: LDA

A law firm specializing in public land and natural resource law, energy, and Native American affairs.

DC-Area Employees Representing Listed Clients

CHAMBERS, Reid Peyton, Partner
ENDRESON, Douglas B. L., Partner
GLAZE, James E., Associate
MEGGESTO, James T., Associate
NOTO, Anne D., Partner
PAVEL, Mary J., Partner
PERRY, William R., Partner
SACHSE, Harry R., Partner
SIMON, Donald, Partner

Clients

Alaska Native Health Board

American Ass'n of Acupuncture and Oriental Medicine
Rep By: William R. Perry

Assiniboine and Sioux Tribes (Fort Peck Reservation)
Issues: BUD IND
Rep By: Mary J. Pavel, William R. Perry

Bad River Band of Lake Superior Chippewa
Rep By: William R. Perry

Colville Business Council
Rep By: William R. Perry

Common Cause
Rep By: Donald Simon

Cook Inlet Regional Citizen Advisory Council
Rep By: William R. Perry

Fond du Lac Reservation, Washington Office of the
Rep By: William R. Perry

Great Lakes Indian Fish and Wildlife Commission
Rep By: Reid Peyton Chambers

Ho-Chunk Nation
Issues: BUD IND
Rep By: Mary J. Pavel, William R. Perry

Hopi Indian Tribe
Issues: BUD IND
Rep By: Reid Peyton Chambers, Harry R. Sachse

Jemez, New Mexico, Pueblo of
Rep By: William R. Perry

Lac du Flambeau Chippewa Tribe

Mole Lake Band of the Sokaogon Chippewa Community
Rep By: William R. Perry

Multi-Housing Laundry Ass'n

Puyallup Tribe of Indians
Issues: IND
Rep By: Mary J. Pavel

Sault Ste. Marie, Michigan, City of
Rep By: William R. Perry

Shoshone-Bannock Tribes of the Fort Hall Indian Reservation
Rep By: William R. Perry

St. Croix Chippewa Indians of Wisconsin
Rep By: William R. Perry

Standing Rock Sioux Tribe
Issues: BUD IND
Rep By: Mary J. Pavel, William R. Perry

Yukon-Kuskokwim Health Corp.
Issues: BUD IND
Rep By: Mary J. Pavel, William R. Perry

Sparber and Associates

1319 F St. NW
Suite 301
Washington, DC 20004
Tel: (202)393-3240
Fax: (202)393-4385
Registered: LDA
E-mail: sparber@sparber.com
A public affairs firm.

DC-Area Employees Representing Listed Clients
O'ROURKE, Peter, V. President
SPARBER, Peter G., President
SUHR, Karen, Senior V. President

Clients

Great Lakes Chemical Corp.
Issues: CSP
Rep By: Peter O'Rourke, Peter G. Sparber

Marathon Ashland Petroleum, LLC
Issues: ENV
Rep By: Peter O'Rourke, Peter G. Sparber

Methyl Bromide Working Group
Issues: AGR
Rep By: Peter G. Sparber

Sleep Products Safety Council
Issues: CSP
Rep By: Peter G. Sparber, Karen Suhr

U.S. Steel
Issues: ENV
Rep By: Peter O'Rourke, Peter G. Sparber

Specialty Contractors Management, Inc.

P.O. Box 42558
Northwest Station
Washington, DC 20015-0558
Tel: (301)933-7430

DC-Area Employees Representing Listed Clients
KARDY, Walter M., President

Clients

Instrument Technicians Labor-Management Cooperation Fund
Rep By: Walter M. Kardy

Internat'l Council of Employers of Bricklayers and Allied Craftsmen
Rep By: Walter M. Kardy

Masonry Industry Ventures, Inc.
Rep By: Walter M. Kardy

The Spectrum Group

11 Canal Center Plaza
Suite 103
Alexandria, VA 22314
Tel: (703)683-4222
Fax: (703)683-0645
Registered: LDA
Web: www.spectrumgrp.com
E-mail: thespecgrp@aol.com
Marketing and legislative consultants for major U.S. manufacturers.

DC-Area Employees Representing Listed Clients
BACA, USA (Ret.), Lt. Gen Edward
BONDAREFF, Joan, Transportation Principal
CHAPMAN, P.E., Cheryl Kandaras
CIANCIOLO, USA (Ret.), Lt. Gen. Augustus
CONAWAY, USAF (Ret.), Lt. Gen. John B.
DADY, Gail
DAVIS, USAF (Ret.), Gen. J. B.
DELBRIDGE, USA (Ret.), Maj. Gen. Norman G.
FRATARANGELO, USMC (Ret.), Maj. Gen. Paul
GRANRUD, USA (Ret.), Lt. Gen. Jerome H.
HALL, Jr., USAF(Ret.), Lt. Gen. John B "Skip"
HICKMAN, USN (Ret.), RAdm. Donald "Smoke"
HINKLE, USN (Ret.), RAdm. James B.
HORD, Ben F.
LYNCH, Dr. John
MARQUEZ, USAF (Ret.), Lt. Gen. Leo
MCCOY, USA (Ret.), Maj. Gen. Ray
MCDONALD, USN (Ret.), Adm. Wesley
MCMANUS, Paul E., Chief Exec. Officer
MONTGOMERY, Hon. G. V. "Sonny"
ROONEY, James
SHARP, Gregory L., President
SHRIBER, Maurice N.
SMITH, USN (Ret.), Adm. Leighton W.
WHITE, D. Timothy

Clients

AAI Corp.
Issues: DEF
Rep By: Gen. J. B. Davis, USAF (Ret.), Ben F. Hord, Paul E. McManus, Gregory L. Sharp, Maurice N. Shriber

ADSI Inc.
Issues: TRA
Rep By: Joan Bondareff, Gen. J. B. Davis, USAF (Ret.), Maj. Gen. Paul Fratarangelo, USMC (Ret.), Lt. Gen. John B "Skip" Hall, Jr., USAF(Ret.), Lt. Gen. Leo Marquez, USAF (Ret.), Paul E. McManus, Gregory L. Sharp

Barksdale Foward
Issues: DEF GOV
Rep By: Gen. J. B. Davis, USAF (Ret.), Lt. Gen. Leo Marquez, USAF (Ret.), Paul E. McManus

Everett, Washington, Port of
Issues: TRA
Rep By: Joan Bondareff, Dr. John Lynch

KPMG, LLP
Issues: DEF
Rep By: Lt. Gen. Augustus Cianciolo, USA (Ret.), Gen. J. B. Davis, USAF (Ret.), RAdm. James B. Hinkle, USN (Ret.)

Nat'l Health Care Access Coalition
Issues: HCR IMM VET
Rep By: Joan Bondareff, Gregory L. Sharp

PESystems, Inc.
Issues: DEF
Rep By: Paul E. McManus, James Rooney

PKC
Issues: HCR
Rep By: Paul E. McManus, Gregory L. Sharp

Raydon Corp.
Issues: DEF
Rep By: Lt. Gen. Augustus Cianciolo, USA (Ret.), Maj. Gen. Paul Fratarangelo, USMC (Ret.), Gregory L. Sharp

The Refinishing Touch
Issues: DEF GOV
Rep By: Lt. Gen. Augustus Cianciolo, USA (Ret.), Maj. Gen. Ray McCoy, USA (Ret.), Paul E. McManus, Gregory L. Sharp

Robertson Aviation
Issues: DEF
Rep By: Lt. Gen. Augustus Cianciolo, USA (Ret.), Paul E. McManus, Gregory L. Sharp

Simula, Inc.
Issues: DEF
Rep By: Lt. Gen. Augustus Cianciolo, USA (Ret.), Lt. Gen. John B "Skip" Hall, Jr., USAF(Ret.), Paul E. McManus, James Rooney, Gregory L. Sharp

SRI Internat'l
Rep By: Gregory L. Sharp

Student Loan Finance Corp.
Issues: BAN EDU FIN
Rep By: Cheryl Kandaras Chapman, P.E., Gregory L. Sharp

System Planning Corp.
Issues: DEF

Tetra Tech
Issues: DEF
Rep By: Cheryl Kandaras Chapman, P.E., Lt. Gen. Augustus Cianciolo, USA (Ret.), Maj. Gen. Paul Fratarangelo, USMC (Ret.), RAdm. James B. Hinkle, USN (Ret.), Paul E. McManus

Titanium Metals Corp.
Issues: DEF
Rep By: Lt. Gen. Augustus Cianciolo, USA (Ret.), Adm. Wesley McDonald, USN (Ret.), Gregory L. Sharp

Tri-City Regional Port District
Issues: TRA
Rep By: Joan Bondareff, Lt. Gen. Augustus Cianciolo, USA (Ret.), Lt. Gen. Jerome H. Granrud, USA (Ret.), Dr. John Lynch, Gregory L. Sharp

TRW Inc.
Issues: DEF
Rep By: Gail Dady, RAdm. James B. Hinkle, USN (Ret.), James Rooney

SPECTRUM Science Public Relations, Inc.

1020 19th St. NW
Suite 800
Washington, DC 20036-6110
Tel: (202)955-6222
Fax: (202)955-0044
Web: www.spectrumscience.com
E-mail: jjs@spectrumscience.com
A public relations and public affairs counseling firm specializing in health care issues.

DC-Area Employees Representing Listed Clients
NORTON, Thomas C., Senior V. President
SENG, John J., President

Clients

Biotechnology Industry Organization
Issues: HCR MED MMM PHA SCI
Rep By: Thomas C. Norton

Soc. for Women's Health Research
Issues: HCR MED
Rep By: John J. Seng

Richard L. Spees, Inc.

801 Pennsylvania Ave. NW
Suite 750
Washington, DC 20004
Tel: (202)393-1132
Fax: (202)624-0659
Registered: LDA
E-mail: rspees@bellatlantic.net
A government relations firm.

DC-Area Employees Representing Listed Clients
MONRONEY, Beth
SPEES, Richard L.

Clients

American Psychological Ass'n
Issues: HCR
Rep By: Richard L. Spees

Chabot Space & Science Center
Issues: EDU SCI
Rep By: Richard L. Spees

Consortium for Regional Climate Centers
Issues: SCI
Rep By: Richard L. Spees

Council of American Overseas Research Centers
Issues: EDU
Rep By: Richard L. Spees

Desert Research Institute
Issues: ENG SCI
Rep By: Richard L. Spees

Internat'l Laboratory Technology Corp.
Issues: AGR
Rep By: Richard L. Spees

Miami Museum of Science & Space Transit Planetarium
Issues: EDU
Rep By: Richard L. Spees

Miami, Florida, City of
Issues: TRA
Rep By: Richard L. Spees

North American Interstate Weather Modification Council
Issues: SCI
Rep By: Richard L. Spees

Orange County Transportation Authority
Issues: TRA
Rep By: Richard L. Spees

Orange, Florida, County of
Issues: GOV
Rep By: Richard L. Spees

Pardee Construction Co.
Issues: TRA
Rep By: Richard L. Spees

Sensis Corp.
Issues: SCI TRA
Rep By: Richard L. Spees

Tallahassee, Florida, City of
Issues: GOV
Rep By: Richard L. Spees

University of Nevada - Reno
Issues: EDU
Rep By: Richard L. Spees

Spiegel & McDiarmid

1350 New York Ave. NW
Suite 1100
Washington, DC 20005-4798
Tel: (202)879-4000
Fax: (202)393-2866
Registered: LDA, FARA
Web: www.spiegelmcd.com
E-mail: spiegel@spiegelmcd.com
A law firm specializing in copyright and publishing; energy and public utility; international; and transportation issues.

DC-Area Employees Representing Listed Clients
BOGORAD, Cindy S., Partner
BROWN, Kenneth A., Public Affairs Director
CORBETT, Jr., John J., Partner
DOWDEN, Lisa, Partner
FINKELSTEIN, Ben, Partner
FRANCIS, Fran, Partner
JABLON, Robert A., Partner
MCDIARMID, Robert C., Partner
PETERS, Rise J., Partner
SETH, Andy, Legislative Coordinator
SMOLER, Barry, Of Counsel
TRAUGER, Thomas C., Partner
WARD, Matt, Associate
YARNELL, Christy, Head Librarian

Clients

CADDO Lake Institute
Rep By: John J. Corbett, Jr.

Centralia, Pennsylvania, Former Residents of
Rep By: Thomas C. Trauger

Des Moines Community School District
Rep By: John J. Corbett, Jr.

Des Moines, Iowa, City of

East Palo Alto, California, City of

Holyoke Department of Gas and Electricity
Issues: ENG
Rep By: Ben Finkelstein, Fran Francis

Lehigh-Northhampton Airport Authority
Issues: AVI
Rep By: John J. Corbett, Jr.

Michigan Municipal/Cooperative Group
Rep By: Robert A. Jablon

Minneapolis-St. Paul Metropolitan Airports Commission
Issues: AVI
Rep By: John J. Corbett, Jr.

Northern California Power Agency
Issues: ENG
Rep By: Lisa Dowden, Fran Francis, Robert C. McDiarmid

Ohio Municipal Electric Ass'n

Orange, California, County of
Rep By: John J. Corbett, Jr.

Piqua, Ohio, City of
Rep By: Kenneth A. Brown

St. Louis Airport Authority
Rep By: John J. Corbett, Jr.

Stamford, Connecticut, City of

Transmission Access Policy Study Group
Issues: ENG
Rep By: Cindy S. Bogorad, Robert C. McDiarmid

Spirer & Goldberg, P.C.

927 15th St. NW
Third Floor
Washington, DC 20005
Tel: (202)628-2900
Fax: (202)628-4608
A law firm.

DC-Area Employees Representing Listed Clients
SPIRER, Julian H., Managing Partner

Spivey/Health Policy Group

1350 I St. NW
Suite 870
Washington, DC 20005
Tel: (202)289-3522
A member of The Capitol Alliance focusing on health issues.

Spriggs & Hollingsworth

1350 I St. NW
Ninth Floor
Washington, DC 20005-3304
Tel: (202)898-5800
Fax: (202)682-1639
Web: www.spriggs.com
A general practice law firm.

DC-Area Employees Representing Listed Clients
COPLE, III, William J., Partner
HOLLINGSWORTH, Joe G., Senior Partner
SPRIGGS, William J., Senior Partner
STEWART, Rosemary, Partner

Clients

Glendale Federal Bank, FSB

Squire, Sanders & Dempsey L.L.P.

1201 Pennsylvania Ave. NW
P.O. Box 407
Washington, DC 20044-0407
Tel: (202)626-6600
Fax: (202)626-6780
Registered: LDA, FARA
Web: www.ssd.com
An international law firm.

DC-Area Employees Representing Listed Clients
BERGIN, Tim, Partner
BRIGGS, Alan L., Managing Partner
COSGROVE, Timothy
GELTMAN, Edward A., Partner
KRAGIE, Scott T., Partner
MARKS, Herbert E., Partner
NADLER, Jonathan J., Partner
NALL, David A., Partner
PAPKIN, Robert D., Partner
PUPKIN, Barry A., Partner
QUIGLEY, Thomas J., Counsel
SAUER, Edward W., Partner
SINICK, Marshall S., Partner
STOKES, Louis
THOMAS, Ritchie T., Partner
YOUNG, Glenn M., Partner

Clients

Aerolineas Argentinas
Rep By: Robert D. Papkin

Air India
Rep By: Marshall S. Sinick

Aloha Airlines

American Chamber of Commerce in Germany
Rep By: Ritchie T. Thomas

American Soc. of Anesthesiologists
Rep By: Scott T. Kragie

Ansett Transport Industries
Rep By: Robert D. Papkin, Edward W. Sauer

Ass'n of Research Libraries
Rep By: Ritchie T. Thomas

Avianca Airlines
Rep By: Robert D. Papkin

Belgium, Embassy of the Kingdom of
Rep By: Thomas J. Quigley, Ritchie T. Thomas

Case Western Reserve University School of Medicine
Issues: BUD MED
Rep By: Louis Stokes

Cleveland Clinic Foundation
Issues: BUD MMM
Rep By: Timothy Cosgrove

Compania Mexicana de Aviacion
Rep By: Robert D. Papkin

Cuyahoga Community College
Issues: BUD EDU
Rep By: Louis Stokes

Electronic Industries Alliance

Fast Air Carrier
Rep By: Marshall S. Sinick

Ferro Corp.

Independent Data Communications Manufacturers Ass'n
Rep By: Herbert E. Marks

Information Technology Ass'n of America (ITAA)
Issues: TEC
Rep By: Jonathan J. Nadler

Lineas Aereas Costarricicenes (Lasca Airlines)
Rep By: Robert D. Papkin, Edward W. Sauer

McGraw-Hill Cos., The
Issues: POS
Rep By: Tim Bergin

Nat'l City Corp.
Issues: BAN
Rep By: Louis Stokes

Nat'l Collegiate Athletic Ass'n
Issues: CPT
Rep By: Ritchie T. Thomas

Northeast Ohio Regional Sewer District

Polynesian Airlines
Rep By: Robert D. Papkin, Edward W. Sauer

Servicios Aereos de Honduras (SAHSA)
Rep By: Robert D. Papkin

Toyota Motor Corp.
Rep By: Ritchie T. Thomas

United Technologies Carrier
Rep By: Edward A. Geltman

VASP Airlines
Rep By: Robert D. Papkin, Edward W. Sauer

VIASA
Rep By: Robert D. Papkin, Edward W. Sauer

SRG & Associates

601 Pennsylvania Ave. NW
Suite 900 South
Washington, DC 20004
Tel: (202)434-8207
Fax: (202)639-8238
Registered: LDA

DC-Area Employees Representing Listed Clients
TANTILLO, Augustine D.

Clients

Celanese Government Relations Office
Rep By: Augustine D. Tantillo

Fieldcrest Cannon Inc.
Issues: APP
Rep By: Augustine D. Tantillo

Milliken and Co.
Issues: APP
Rep By: Augustine D. Tantillo

Northern Textile Ass'n
Issues: APP
Rep By: Augustine D. Tantillo

Textile/Clothing Technology Center
Issues: APP
Rep By: Augustine D. Tantillo

St. Maxens & Company

927 15th St. NW
12th Floor
Washington, DC 20015
Tel: (202)833-4466
Fax: (202)833-2833
E-mail: consultants@st.maxens.com
An international trade and government affairs consulting firm.

DC-Area Employees Representing Listed Clients
MIRANI, Viraj M.
SMITH, Julia
ST. MAXENS, II, Thomas F.

Clients

Binney & Smith Inc.
Rep By: Thomas F. St. Maxens, II

Hallmark Cards, Inc.
Rep By: Thomas F. St. Maxens, II

Mattel, Inc.
Issues: CSP HCR TRD
Rep By: Viraj M. Mirani, Julia Smith, Thomas F. St. Maxens, II

Thailand, Department of Foreign Trade of
Rep By: Thomas F. St. Maxens, II

US JVC Corp.
Issues: TRD
Rep By: Thomas F. St. Maxens, II

Staiger.com

P.O. Box 136
Scotland, MD 20687
Tel: (202)737-1004
Fax: (301)872-9843
Registered: LDA
E-mail: roger@staiger.com
Provides representation in the areas of fuel, natural resources, conservation and transportation.

DC-Area Employees Representing Listed Clients
STAIGER, Roger

Stanfield Tindal, Inc.

2346 Greenwich St.
Falls Church, VA 22046
Tel: (703)847-3664
Fax: (703)534-9461
Registered: LDA
Web: www.stanfieldtindal.com
E-mail: stantindal@aol.com
A government relations firm.

DC-Area Employees Representing Listed Clients
TINDAL, D'Anna, President

Clients

Recon/Optical, Inc.
Issues: BUD DEF FOR
Rep By: D'Anna Tindal

Stanton & Associates

1747 Pennsylvania Ave. NW
Suite 105
Washington, DC 20006
Tel: (202)467-4333
Fax: (202)467-4353
Registered: LDA

DC-Area Employees Representing Listed Clients
STANTON, Hon. James V., Principal

Clients

Nat'l Ass'n of Bankruptcy Trustees
Issues: BNK
Rep By: Hon. James V. Stanton

The State Affairs Co.

1600 Wilson Blvd.
Suite 205
Arlington, VA 22209
Tel: (703)358-8600
Fax: (703)358-8885
Registered: LDA
A consulting firm providing state legislative, regulatory and litigation expertise, as well as public relations and public affairs support.

DC-Area Employees Representing Listed Clients
CHAFE, Bonnie L.
MCCLOUD, David K., Managing Partner
MCCLOUD, Patrick, Associate
SMITH, Carol, General Counsel

Clients

Elk Valley Rancheria
Issues: GAM IND
Rep By: Bonnie L. Chafe

Hopland Band of Pomo Indians
Issues: IND
Rep By: Bonnie L. Chafe

Sheep Ranch Rancheria
Issues: GAM IND
Rep By: Bonnie L. Chafe, Carol Smith

Soboba Band of Mission Indians
Issues: IND
Rep By: Bonnie L. Chafe

Twentynine Palms Band of Mission Indians
Issues: IND
Rep By: Bonnie L. Chafe

Stein, Mitchell & Mezines

1100 Connecticut Ave. NW
Suite 1100
Washington, DC 20036
Tel: (202)737-7777
Fax: (202)296-8312
A law firm.

DC-Area Employees Representing Listed Clients
MEZINES, Basil J., Partner

Clients

American Collectors Ass'n

Automotive Warehouse Distributors Ass'n
Rep By: Basil J. Mezines

The Stella Group, Ltd.

706 N. Ivy St.
Arlington, VA 22201
Tel: (703)522-1195
Fax: (703)841-1634
Registered: LDA

E-mail: solarsklar@aol.com

DC-Area Employees Representing Listed Clients
SKLAR, Scott, President
SKLAR, Stella, V. President

Clients

Solar Energy Industries Ass'n (SEIA)
Issues: ENG ENV
Rep By: Stella Sklar

Stephens Law Firm

P.O. Box 1096
McLean, VA 22101-1096
Tel: (703)821-8700
Fax: (703)827-7761
Registered: LDA

E-mail: stelawfirm@aol.com

DC-Area Employees Representing Listed Clients
GRAHAM, Neil E., Senior Attorney
STEPHENS, William T., Managing Attorney
WILLIAMS, Michael A., Associate Attorney

Clients

American Rental Ass'n
Issues: BUD CSP GOV HCR LBR RES SMB TAX TOR TRA
Rep By: Neil E. Graham, William T. Stephens, Michael A. Williams

Stephens Law Offices

4700 N. 38th Pl.
Arlington, VA 22207-2915
Tel: (703)532-4900
Fax: (703)532-4986
Registered: LDA

E-mail: dooler@aol.com
A legal and government relations services firm.

DC-Area Employees Representing Listed Clients
STEPHENS, Jr., J. Gordon "Skip", Principal

Clients

Degussa Corp.
Rep By: J. Gordon "Skip" Stephens, Jr.

Harnischfeger Industries, Inc.
Issues: CAW NAT TAX
Rep By: J. Gordon "Skip" Stephens, Jr.

Joy Mining Machinery
Issues: CAW ENV NAT
Rep By: J. Gordon "Skip" Stephens, Jr.

OBWEO
Issues: AGR
Rep By: J. Gordon "Skip" Stephens, Jr.

P & H Mining Equipment
Issues: CAW ENV NAT

Roquette America
Issues: AGR RRR TRA TRU
Rep By: J. Gordon "Skip" Stephens, Jr.

Stephens, Cross, Ihlenfeld & Boring, Inc.

P.O. Box 57315
Washington, DC 20037
Tel: (202)679-6282
Fax: (202)872-1150
E-mail: ronstephens1@juno.com

DC-Area Employees Representing Listed Clients
STEPHENS, Ronald, Partner

Clients

Alliance for American Innovation, Inc.
Issues: CPT
Rep By: Ronald Stephens

Austin Professional Systems, Inc.
Issues: FIN GOV
Rep By: Ronald Stephens

J. Arthur Weber & Associates
Issues: GOV

Steptoe & Johnson LLP

1330 Connecticut Ave. NW
Washington, DC 20036-1795
Tel: (202)429-3000
Fax: (202)429-3902
Registered: LDA, FARA

Web: www.steptoe.com
E-mail: wrehm@Steptoe.com
A general practice law firm.

DC-Area Employees Representing Listed Clients
BAILEY, Arthur L., Partner
BAKER, Stewart A., Partner
BURKE, Edmund W., Partner
CHRISTIAN, Betty Jo, Partner
COBURN, David H., Partner
COLLIER, Jr., Thomas C., Partner
COLLINS, John T., Partner
CUNNINGHAM, Richard O., Partner
DIAMOND, Richard, Of Counsel
DUFFY, John J., Of Counsel
FLEISHMAN, Robert W., Partner
GOVER, Kevin, Partner
GRANDISON, W. George, Partner
HALVERSON, James, Partner
HOCHBERG, Sheldon E., Partner
HORNING, Mark F., Partner
HURST, Paul R., Associate
JORDAN, Robert, Partner
KAIL, Michael, Partner
KARAS, William, Partner
KRAULAND, Edward J., Partner
LAROCCA, Anthony J., Partner
LERNER, Matthew D., Partner
LICHTENBAUM, Peter, Partner
MACKIEWICZ, Edward R., Partner
MANUEL, Hilda, Special Counsel
MORAN, Anne E., Partner
MORAN, Mark A., Partner
NUSSDORF, Melanie Franco, Partner
POAG, Mary "Molly" Woodson, Of Counsel
ROBERTS, Richard L., Partner
SAAS, Richard, Partner
SILVERMAN, Mark J., Partner
SMILACK, Stanley, Of Counsel
TALENS, James M., Of Counsel
TAUB, Cynthia, Associate
VERMA, Richard R., Associate
WALLICK, Robert D., Partner
WETHINGTON, Olin L., Partner
WILKINSON, CPA, Catherine W., Partner
ZINN, Matthew J., Partner

Clients

Acoma Pueblo
Rep By: Thomas C. Collier, Jr.

Agua Caliente Band of Cahuilla Indians
Issues: IND
Rep By: John J. Duffy, Hilda Manuel

B.C. Softwood Lumber Trade Council
Issues: TRD
Rep By: W. George Grandison, Mark A. Moran

Bear, Stearns and Co.
Issues: BAN FIN TAX
Rep By: John T. Collins

British Columbia Softwood Lumber Trade Council
Rep By: W. George Grandison, Mark A. Moran

Burlington Northern Santa Fe Railway
Issues: TAX
Rep By: Catherine W. Wilkinson, CPA

Canada, Embassy of
Rep By: Mark A. Moran

Canadian Wheat Board
Issues: AGR TRD
Rep By: W. George Grandison, Edward J. Krauland

Canyon Forest Village Corp.

Central States Indemnity Co. of Omaha
Issues: FIN

Coach USA
Issues: TRA
Rep By: David H. Coburn

Coalition for Government Procurement
Issues: CPI DEF GOV PHA SMB
Rep By: Robert D. Wallick

EchoStar Communications Corp.

Federal Home Loan Bank of San Francisco
Issues: BAN FIN
Rep By: John T. Collins

FIAMM S.p.A.
Issues: TRD
Rep By: Edward J. Krauland

FIAMM Technologies, Inc.
Issues: TRD
Rep By: Edward J. Krauland

The Hillman Co.
Issues: TAX
Rep By: Edward R. Mackiewicz, Mark J. Silverman

Institute of Internat'l Bankers
Issues: BAN FIN
Rep By: John T. Collins

Internat'l R&D, Inc.

Isleta Pueblo
Rep By: Thomas C. Collier, Jr.

Jicarilla Apache Tribe
Rep By: Thomas C. Collier, Jr.

Mashpee Wampanoag Indian Tribal Council, Inc.
Issues: IND
Rep By: John J. Duffy, Hilda Manuel

Mazda North America Operations
Issues: AUT TRD

Mesalero Apache Tribe
Rep By: Thomas C. Collier, Jr.

Motorola, Inc.
Issues: TRD
Rep By: Stewart A. Baker, Paul R. Hurst, Peter Lichtenbaum

Mutual Tax Committee
Issues: TAX
Rep By: Matthew J. Zinn

Nambe Pueblo
Rep By: Thomas C. Collier, Jr.

Netscape Communications Corp.
Issues: TRD
Rep By: Stewart A. Baker, Paul R. Hurst, Peter Lichtenbaum

Pojoaque Pueblo
Rep By: Thomas C. Collier, Jr.

San Felipe Pueblo
Rep By: Thomas C. Collier, Jr.

San Juan Pueblo
Rep By: Thomas C. Collier, Jr.

Sandia Pueblo
Rep By: Thomas C. Collier, Jr.

Santa Ana Pueblo
Rep By: Thomas C. Collier, Jr.

Santa Clara Pueblo
Rep By: Thomas C. Collier, Jr.

Seaboard Corp.

Shakopee Mdewakanton Sioux Tribe
Rep By: Thomas C. Collier, Jr.

Sterling Internat'l Consultants, Inc.
Issues: APP BUD FOR
Rep By: Sheldon E. Hochberg, Edward J. Krauland, Richard R. Verma

Taos Pueblo
Rep By: Thomas C. Collier, Jr.

TAPS Renewal Task Force
Issues: ENV FUE NAT RES
Rep By: Thomas C. Collier, Jr., John J. Duffy, Robert Jordan, Cynthia Taub

Tesuque Pueblo
Rep By: Thomas C. Collier, Jr.

Trinidad and Tobago, Government of
Rep By: Mark A. Moran

United Asset Management Corp.
Issues: TAX
Rep By: Mark J. Silverman

USEC, Inc.
Rep By: Richard O. Cunningham

Western Financial/Westcorp Inc.
Issues: BAN FIN
Rep By: John T. Collins

Yavapai-Prescott Indian Tribe

Stevens Reed Curcio & Co.

305 Cameron St.
Alexandria, VA 22314
Tel: (703)683-8326
Fax: (703)683-8826
Web: www.srcmedia.com
A political/media consulting firm.

DC-Area Employees Representing Listed Clients
BURGER, Ben, Senior V. President
CURCIO, Paul, Partner
POTHOLM, Eric, Partner
REED, Rick, Partner
STEVENS, Greg, President

Clients

American Medical Ass'n

AXS Technologies

Citizens for Workers' Compensation Reform

Health Insurance Ass'n of America

Maine Pulp & Paper Ass'n

People For Montana

Republican Nat'l Committee

Straight Talk America

Wal-Mart Stores, Inc.

Stewart and Stewart

2100 M St. NW
Suite 200
Washington, DC 20037
Tel: (202)785-4185
Fax: (202)466-1286
Registered: LDA, FARA
Web: www.stewartlaw.com
E-mail: general@stewartlaw.com

DC-Area Employees Representing Listed Clients
DE PREST, Geert M., Partner
DUNN, Alan M., Partner
DWYER, Amy S., Of Counsel
HOLBEIN, James R., Of Counsel
HUREWITZ, Lane S., Of Counsel
JOHANSON, David S., Associate
MIRTCHEV, Alexander V., Division Director
MOYER, Carl, Trade Consultant
SALONEN, Eric, Of Counsel
STEWART, Terence P., Managing Partner

Clients

Bangladesh Economic Program Zone Authority

Dierman, Wortley, and Zola
Issues: TRD
Rep By: Alan M. Dunn

Floral Trade Council
Issues: TRD
Rep By: Geert M. De Prest, Amy S. Dwyer, David S. Johanson, Terence P. Stewart

The Gates Rubber Co.
Rep By: David S. Johanson, Carl Moyer, Terence P. Stewart

Libbey, Inc.
Issues: TRD
Rep By: Alan M. Dunn, David S. Johanson, Terence P. Stewart

PPG Industries
Issues: TRD
Rep By: Alan M. Dunn, David S. Johanson, Terence P. Stewart

Ranchers-Cattlemen Legal Action Fund
Issues: AGR TRD
Rep By: Alan M. Dunn, Amy S. Dwyer, David S. Johanson, Carl Moyer, Eric Salonen, Terence P. Stewart

The Timken Co.
Issues: TRD
Rep By: Alan M. Dunn, Amy S. Dwyer, David S. Johanson, Carl Moyer, Terence P. Stewart

Torrington Co.
Issues: TRD
Rep By: Geert M. De Prest, Alan M. Dunn, David S. Johanson, Carl Moyer

Kenneth F. Stinger

1730 M St. NW
Suite 911
Washington, DC 20036
Tel: (202)296-9158
Fax: (202)887-5378
Registered: LDA

Clients

PACCAR, Inc.
Issues: AUT CAW ENV HCR MAN ROD TAX TRA TRD TRU
Rep By: Kenneth F. Stinger

John M. Stinson

1667 K St. NW
Suite 460
Washington, DC 20006
Tel: (202)496-9688
Registered: LDA

Clients

American Iron and Steel Institute
Issues: ENG ENV
Rep By: John M. Stinson

Changing World Technologies
Issues: ENV TAX
Rep By: John M. Stinson

Nat'l Steel Corp.
Issues: ENG ENV HCR TAX TRD
Rep By: John M. Stinson

Northwest Pipe Co.
Issues: BUD
Rep By: John M. Stinson

RSR Corp.
Issues: ENV
Rep By: John M. Stinson

Stites & Harbison

1200 G St. NW
Suite 800
Washington, DC 20005
Tel: (202)434-8968
Fax: (202)737-5822
Registered: LDA

DC-Area Employees Representing Listed Clients
LEE, Kenneth G., Of Counsel

Clients

Family Place
Issues: BUD FAM
Rep By: Kenneth G. Lee

Montrose, Colorado, City of
Issues: BUD
Rep By: Kenneth G. Lee

Ogden, Utah, City of
Issues: BUD
Rep By: Kenneth G. Lee

Western Kentucky University
Issues: BUD
Rep By: Kenneth G. Lee

The Stone Group, Inc.

2760 Eisenhower Ave.
Suite 250
Alexandria, VA 22314
Tel: (703)329-1982
Fax: (703)329-2411
Registered: LDA, FARA
Web: www.tsgdirectresponse.com
E-mail: tsgrp@aol.com
A direct response marketing and advertising firm.

DC-Area Employees Representing Listed Clients
JONES, Lora Lynn, Senior V. President
STONE, Ann E. W., President

James T. Stovall

1725 N St. NW
Washington, DC 20036
Registered: FARA

Clients

Micronesia, Embassy of the Federated States of
Rep By: James T. Stovall, III

Strat@Comm (Strategic Communications Counselors)

818 Connecticut Ave. NW
Second Floor
Washington, DC 20006
Tel: (202)289-2001
Fax: (202)289-1327
Registered: LDA
Web: www.stratacomm.net

DC-Area Employees Representing Listed Clients
BOEKE, Elinore, Account Executive
CONLEY, Jeffrey B., Principal
DEFORE, Ron, Principal
FITZPATRICK, John F., Senior Counselor
LEWIS, James, Senior Counselor
PARKER, Mary Beth, Account Executive
SHIPLEY, Don, Senior Counselor
SLADE, David, Senior Account Executive
STEED, Diane K., Principal
UNDELAND, John R., Senior Counselor
WILLIAMS, Lynnette Johnson, V. President

Clients

American Ceramics Soc.
Issues: SCI

Americans for Responsible Alcohol Access
Rep By: Ron DeFore

Continental Teves
Issues: AUT CAW CSP ENG ENV ROD TRA
Rep By: Ron DeFore, Diane K. Steed

Corporate Environmental Enforcement Council (CEEC)
Issues: ENV

Nat'l Environmental Development Ass'n, Inc.

Sorptive Minerals Institute

Wine and Spirits Wholesalers of America
Issues: ALC BEV CSP GOV HCR TRD TRU
Rep By: Elinore Boeke

The Strategic Advocacy Group

2121 K St. NW
Suite 800
Washington, DC 20007
Tel: (202)261-6539
Fax: (202)261-6541
Registered: LDA

DC-Area Employees Representing Listed Clients
CHILDS, Blair G., President

Clients

Alliance for Affordable Services
Issues: SMB
Rep By: Blair G. Childs

American Small Businesses Ass'n
Issues: SMB
Rep By: Blair G. Childs

Americans for Financial Security
Issues: SMB
Rep By: Blair G. Childs

Strategic Choices, Inc.

2141 Wisconsin Ave. NW
Suite H
Washington, DC 20007
Tel: (202)337-9600
Fax: (202)337-9620
Registered: LDA

DC-Area Employees Representing Listed Clients
DEVINE, Thomas A.
MITROPOULOS, Nick
SHRUM, Robert M.

Clients

Colombian Coffee Federation
Issues: ADV MIA TRD
Rep By: Thomas A. Devine, Nick Mitropoulos, Robert M. Shrum

Strategic Energy Advisors

1350 New York Ave. NW
11th Floor
Washington, DC 20005
Tel: (202)628-3123
Fax: (202)628-3339
Registered: LDA
E-mail: bjhull@msn.com

DC-Area Employees Representing Listed Clients
HULL, Jeanine, Principal

Strategic Horizons Advisors, L.L.C.

1200 G St. NW
Suite 822
Washington, DC 20009
Tel: (202)434-8738
Registered: LDA

DC-Area Employees Representing Listed Clients
MCGRAW, Marvin A.

Clients

Guinea, Secretary General of the Presidency of the Republic of
Issues: AGR AVI BAN BUD CDT COM CPI DEF ECN EDU ENG ENV FIN FOO FOR FUE GOV HCR MAR NAT ROD RRR SCI TEC TOU TRA TRD TRU URB UTI
Rep By: Marvin A. McGraw

Strategic Impact, Inc.

444 N. Capitol St. NW
Suite 840
Washington, DC 20001
Tel: (202)434-8010
Fax: (202)434-8018
Registered: LDA
A full-service government affairs consulting firm focused on government relations, issues management and coalition building.

DC-Area Employees Representing Listed Clients
JIMENEZ, Michael C., Principal
MITCHELL, Patrick J., Principal

Clients

Cantelme and Kaasa
Rep By: Patrick J. Mitchell

Central Arizona Irrigation and Drainage District
Rep By: Michael C. Jimenez

ClaimTraq, Inc.
Rep By: Patrick J. Mitchell

Commercial Weather Services Ass'n (CWSA)
Issues: CPI NAT SCI
Rep By: Michael C. Jimenez, Patrick J. Mitchell

Hispanic Ass'n of Colleges and Universities
Issues: BUD EDU
Rep By: Michael C. Jimenez

Internat'l Arid Lands Consortium
Issues: EDU NAT
Rep By: Michael C. Jimenez, Patrick J. Mitchell

Investment Co. Institute
Issues: FIN RET TAX
Rep By: Patrick J. Mitchell

Maricopa-Stanfield Irrigation and Drainage District
Rep By: Michael C. Jimenez

Middle East Water and Energy Resource Institute
Rep By: Patrick J. Mitchell

Pascua Yaqui Tribe of Arizona
Rep By: Michael C. Jimenez, Patrick J. Mitchell

Santa Cruz Water and Power Districts Ass'n
Rep By: Michael C. Jimenez

Southwest Border Technology Project
Rep By: Michael C. Jimenez, Patrick J. Mitchell

Strategic Management Associates

112 S. West St.
Alexandria, VA 22314
Tel: (703)683-9600
Fax: (703)836-5255
Registered: LDA

DC-Area Employees Representing Listed Clients
KUNKO, Damian, Policy Assistant
O'SHAUGHNESSY, John J., President

Strategic Partners Inc.

499 S. Capitol St. SW
Suite 420
Washington, DC 20003
E-mail: ronkelley@aol.com
Tel: (202)256-5211
Fax: (703)827-7766
Registered: LDA

DC-Area Employees Representing Listed Clients
KELLEY, Ronald L., President

Clients

Materials Research Soc.
Issues: BUD
Rep By: Ronald L. Kelley

Strategy Group Internat'l

1710 N St. NW
Washington, DC 20036
Tel: (202)331-8460
Registered: LDA, FARA

DC-Area Employees Representing Listed Clients
GONZALEZ, Emilio, V. President

Clients

Partido de la Liberacion Dominica

Secure Wrap, Inc.
Issues: TOU TRD TRU
Rep By: Emilio Gonzalez

Richard Straus

3405 Rodman St. NW
Washington, DC 20008
E-mail: mcpgs@aol.com
Tel: (202)363-3495
Fax: (202)362-4513
Registered: LDA

Clients

American Soc. for Technion
Issues: BUD
Rep By: Richard Straus

Strother & Hosking, Inc.

6301 Stevenson Ave.
Suite One
Alexandria, VA 22304
Tel: (703)823-1732
Fax: (703)823-5064

DC-Area Employees Representing Listed Clients
HOSKING, James H., Assistant Exec. V. President
STROTHER, Michael E., Exec. V. President

Clients

Power and Communications Contractors Ass'n
Rep By: Michael E. Strother

Stuntz, Davis & Staffier, P.C.

1275 Pennsylvania Ave. NW
Ninth Floor
Washington, DC 20004
Tel: (202)662-6790
Fax: (202)624-0866
Registered: LDA, FARA

DC-Area Employees Representing Listed Clients
DAVIS, Randall E., President
RUNGE, Tom S., Of Counsel
SIFONTES, Marisa A., Associate
STAFFIER, John R., Principal
STUNTZ, Linda, Principal
YOUNG, Ellen S., Principal

Clients

Alliance for Competitive Electricity
Issues: UTI
Rep By: Randall E. Davis, Tom S. Runge

British Columbia Hydro and Power Authority
Issues: ENG UTI
Rep By: Linda Stuntz

Edison Electric Institute
Issues: ENG
Rep By: Ellen S. Young

Edison Internat'l
Issues: TAX UTI

GE Power Systems
Issues: ENG
Rep By: Linda Stuntz, Ellen S. Young

General Electric Appliances
Rep By: Linda Stuntz, Ellen S. Young

General Electric Industrial & Power Systems
Issues: BUD ENG SCI
Rep By: Linda Stuntz, Ellen S. Young

Los Angeles, California, County of
Issues: BUD DIS IMM LAW LBR RET URB
Rep By: Randall E. Davis

Nextel Communications, Inc.

North American Electric Reliability Council
Issues: ENG UTI
Rep By: Linda Stuntz

Pan-Alberta Gas Ltd.
Rep By: John R. Staffier

Pharmaceutical Research and Manufacturers of America
Issues: PHA
Rep By: Randall E. Davis

PURPA Reform Group
Issues: UTI
Rep By: Randall E. Davis, Linda Stuntz

R. J. Reynolds Tobacco Co.
Issues: TOB
Rep By: Randall E. Davis

Western Interconnection Coordination Forum
Issues: ENG UTI
Rep By: Linda Stuntz

Charlene A. Sturbitts

1625 K St. NW
Suite 790
Washington, DC 20006
Tel: (202)293-7800
Fax: (202)293-7808
Registered: LDA

A government relations firm.

Clients

Deere & Co.
Issues: CAW
Rep By: Charlene A. Sturbitts

Free Trade Lumber Council
Issues: AGR BUD CSP ENV HOU LBR NAT TRD
Rep By: Charlene A. Sturbitts

W. R. Grace & Co.
Issues: ENV
Rep By: Charlene A. Sturbitts

Sufka & Associates

1518 K St. NW
Suite 503
Washington, DC 20005
Web: www.sufka.com
E-mail: sufka1@aol.com
Tel: (202)737-0202
Fax: (202)638-4833

An association management company.

DC-Area Employees Representing Listed Clients
GREENE, Elizabeth
MCMAHON, Shaine, Account Executive
SUFKA, Kenneth M., President

Clients

American Soc. of Architectural Illustrators
Issues: ART

Associated Air Balance Council
Rep By: Kenneth M. Sufka

Internat'l Kitchen Exhaust Cleaning Ass'n
Rep By: Kenneth M. Sufka

Nat'l Air Duct Cleaners Ass'n
Rep By: Shaine McMahon, Kenneth M. Sufka

Nat'l Air Filtration Ass'n
Rep By: Kenneth M. Sufka

Patricia Sullivan

1155 15th St. NW
Suite 801
Washington, DC 20005
E-mail: psullivan@slsaservicers.org
Tel: (202)466-3639

Clients

Student Loan Servicing Alliance
Rep By: Patricia Sullivan

Sullivan & Cromwell

1701 Pennsylvania Ave. NW
Suite 800
Washington, DC 20006
Tel: (202)956-7500
Fax: (202)293-6330
Registered: LDA

A Washington office of a New York general practice law firm.

DC-Area Employees Representing Listed Clients
COHEN, H. Rodgin, Partner
CRAFT, Jr., Robert H., Managing Partner
HARITON, David P., Partner
LIBOW, Daryl, Partner
MCCALL, D. Mark, Of Counsel
PFEIFFER, Margaret K., Partner
RAISLER, Kenneth M., Partner
SIMMONS, Rebecca J., Partner
WILLIAMSON, Edwin D., Partner
WISEMAN, Michael, Partner
WOODALL, III, Samuel R., Government Affairs Specialist

Clients

British Airways Plc
Rep By: Daryl Libow, D. Mark McCall

First Fidelity Bancorporation
Rep By: Samuel R. Woodall, III

First Union Corp.
Issues: BAN
Rep By: H. Rodgin Cohen

The Foreign Exchange Committee
Issues: FIN
Rep By: Kenneth M. Raisler

Goldman, Sachs and Co.
Issues: BAN
Rep By: H. Rodgin Cohen, Michael Wiseman, Samuel R. Woodall, III

The Group of 20
Issues: FIN
Rep By: Kenneth M. Raisler, Rebecca J. Simmons, Michael Wiseman

Morgan Guaranty Trust Co.
Issues: BAN
Rep By: H. Rodgin Cohen, Michael Wiseman

N.V. Philips Gloeilampenfabrieken
Rep By: Margaret K. Pfeiffer

New York Clearing House Ass'n
Issues: FIN
Rep By: Samuel R. Woodall, III

Securities Industry Ass'n
Issues: FIN TAX
Rep By: David P. Hariton

Zions First Nat'l Bank
Issues: BAN
Rep By: Samuel R. Woodall, III

Sullivan & Mitchell, P.L.L.C.

1100 Connecticut Ave. NW
Suite 330
Washington, DC 20036
Tel: (202)861-5900
Fax: (202)861-6065
Registered: LDA

DC-Area Employees Representing Listed Clients
MITCHELL, Cleta, Attorney
SULLIVAN, Paul E.

Clients

Americans Back in Charge Foundation
Issues: CON GOV
Rep By: Cleta Mitchell, Paul E. Sullivan

Sullivan & Worcester LLP

1025 Connecticut Ave. NW
Suite 1000
Washington, DC 20036
Tel: (202)775-8190
Fax: (202)293-2275
Registered: LDA

A law firm.

DC-Area Employees Representing Listed Clients
KIRK, Jr., Paul G., Of Counsel

Francis J. Sullivan Associates

809 Cameron St.
Alexandria, VA 22314
Tel: (703)684-4707
Fax: (703)519-8084
Registered: LDA

DC-Area Employees Representing Listed Clients
SULLIVAN, Francis J.

Clients

Alexandria, Virginia, City of
Issues: ROD TRA
Rep By: Francis J. Sullivan

Flue-Cured Tobacco Cooperative Stabilization Corp.

Ingalls Shipbuilding
Issues: DEF
Rep By: Francis J. Sullivan

Textron Inc.
Issues: DEF
Rep By: Francis J. Sullivan

Sumlin Associates

112 West St.
Suite 400
Alexandria, VA 22204
Tel: (703)837-1384
Fax: (703)836-6550
Registered: LDA

DC-Area Employees Representing Listed Clients
NEDD, Council, Principal

Clients

The 60/Plus Ass'n, Inc.
Issues: TAX
Rep By: Council Nedd

The Anderson Group
Issues: GOV
Rep By: Council Nedd

Anglican Catholic Church
Issues: EDU FAM REL TAX
Rep By: Council Nedd

Council for Affordable Health Insurance
Issues: GOV HCR INS
Rep By: Council Nedd

Sunrise Research Corp.

2201 Wisconsin Ave. NW
Suite 105
Washington, DC 20007
Tel: (202)965-9810
Fax: (202)965-9812
Registered: LDA

DC-Area Employees Representing Listed Clients
PACKWOOD, Hon. Bob, President

Clients

American Business Is Local Enterprise
Issues: TAX
Rep By: Hon. Bob Packwood

American Public Power Ass'n
Issues: TAX
Rep By: Hon. Bob Packwood

The Coal Coalition
Rep By: Hon. Bob Packwood

GTE Service Corp.
Issues: TEC
Rep By: Hon. Bob Packwood

Jones, Day, Reavis & Pogue
Issues: RET
Rep By: Hon. Bob Packwood

Marriott Internat'l, Inc.
Issues: TAX
Rep By: Hon. Bob Packwood

Northwest Airlines, Inc.
Issues: AVI
Rep By: Hon. Bob Packwood

Paul Suplizio Associates

5920 Munson Ct.
Falls Church, VA 22041
Tel: (703)820-7707
Fax: (703)820-7726
E-mail: wotc@cox.rr.com
A government relations consulting firm.

DC-Area Employees Representing Listed Clients
SUPLIZIO, Paul E., President

Clients

Internat'l Barter and Countertrade Foundation
Issues: FIN TRD
Rep By: Paul E. Suplizio

Work Opportunity Tax Credit Coalition
Rep By: Paul E. Suplizio

Sutherland Asbill & Brennan LLP

1275 Pennsylvania Ave. NW
Washington, DC 20004-2415
Tel: (202)383-0100
Fax: (202)637-3593
Registered: LDA
Web: www.sablaw.com
E-mail: info@sablaw.com
A general practice law firm.

DC-Area Employees Representing Listed Clients
BERMAN, Daniel M., Partner
COHEN, N. Jerold, Partner
EGAN, Michael J., Of Counsel
GRENIER, Jr., Edward J., Partner
HOFFMAN, Joel E., Of Counsel
LIBIN, Jerome B., Partner
MOSSBERG, Christer L., Counsel
RODGERS, Peter H., Partner
THROWER, Randolph W., Partner
YARBROUGH, Katherine P., Partner

Clients

Armco Inc.
Rep By: Edward J. Grenier, Jr.

W. C. Bradley Co.
Issues: TAX
Rep By: Daniel M. Berman

Encyclopaedia Britannica, Inc.
Issues: TAX
Rep By: Daniel M. Berman

GAF Corp.

KN Energy Inc.

Nat'l Ass'n of Mutual Insurance Companies

New York Mercantile Exchange
Rep By: Katherine P. Yarbrough

Process Gas Consumers Group

Questar Corp.

WNHT

WSYT

Eugene F. Swanzey

11421 Cedar Ridge Dr.
Potomac, MD 20854
Tel: (301)983-3191
Fax: (301)983-3196
Registered: LDA

Clients

Mortgage Bankers Ass'n of America
Issues: BAN HOU
Rep By: Eugene F. Swanzey

Rick Swartz & Associates, Inc.

1869 Park Rd. NW
Washington, DC 20010
Tel: (202)328-1313
Fax: (202)797-9856
Registered: FARA
E-mail: rickswartz@aol.com

DC-Area Employees Representing Listed Clients
SWARTZ, Rick, President

David A. Sweeney

15209 Wycliffe Ct.
Rockville, MD 20853
Tel: (301)929-1665
Registered: LDA

Swidler Berlin Shereff Friedman, LLP

3000 K St. NW
Suite 300
Washington, DC 20007
Tel: (202)424-7500
Fax: (202)424-7643
Registered: LDA, FARA
Web: www.swidlaw.com
A law firm specializing in administrative, litigation, commercial and legislative practice.

Political Action Committee
Swidler & Berlin Political Action Committee
3000 K St. NW
Suite 300
Washington, DC 20007
Tel: (202)424-7500
Fax: (202)424-7643

DC-Area Employees Representing Listed Clients
BARNES, Peter, Member
BERLIN, Edward, Chairman
BLAU, Russell M., Partner
COLE, Keith N., Partner
COOPER, Kathy, Associate
DEBRY, Kristine, Associate
DELORENZO, James
DENIS, Paul T.
DIRENFELD, Barry B., Managing Partner
ERNST, Martin C.
FITZGERALD, Brian W., Partner
GALLAGHER, Lynn M., Counsel
GALLANT, Gary, Associate
GLEW, Jr., William B., Counsel
GOLDFIELD, Harold P., Senior Partner
HAMILTON, James, Partner
HYMAN, Lester S., Senior Counsel
JAFFE, Kenneth G., Partner
KIDDOO, Jean L., Partner
KNAUSS, Charles H., Partner
LEVY, Harold A., Of Counsel
LIPMAN, Andrew D., Partner
LORE, Kenneth G., Partner
MARSHALL, Jr., Thurgood, Partner
MILLER, Leonard A., Partner
POPKIN, Richard A., Partner
SCHANER, Kenneth I., Partner
SLAIMAN, Gary D., Partner
SPOONER, Nancy K., Partner
STEINWURTZEL, Robert N., Partner
TAYLOR, Katherine R., Associate
VALENTE, Thomas
WANG, Catherine, Member
WARD, Michael E., Counsel
WHITEHEAD, Priscilla A., Partner
WIGMORE, Michael B., Associate
WILHEIM, William B., Associate
ZENER, Robert V.

Clients

American Bakers Ass'n
Rep By: Barry B. Direnfeld, James Hamilton

Artichoke Enterprises, Inc.
Rep By: Barry B. Direnfeld, Harold P. Goldfield, James Hamilton, Lester S. Hyman, Michael E. Ward, Michael B. Wigmore

Ass'n of Community Cancer Centers

Associated Estates Co.
Rep By: Harold A. Levy, Kenneth G. Lore

Aventis Pharmaceuticals, Inc.
Issues: CPT
Rep By: Barry B. Direnfeld, Brian W. Fitzgerald, Harold P. Goldfield, Lester S. Hyman, Gary D. Slaiman

British Virgin Islands, Government of the
Rep By: Lester S. Hyman

BroadSpan Communications, Inc.
Issues: TEC
Rep By: James DeLorenzo, Harold P. Goldfield, Gary D. Slaiman

Cable & Wireless, Inc.
Rep By: Andrew D. Lipman

CAIS Internet
Rep By: Jean L. Kiddoo

California Independent System Operator
Issues: UTI
Rep By: Keith N. Cole, Barry B. Direnfeld, Kenneth G. Jaffe, Gary D. Slaiman

Coalition to Ensure Responsible Billing
Rep By: Kristine DeBry, Gary D. Slaiman, Katherine R. Taylor

Conoco Inc.
Issues: TAX TRD
Rep By: Harold P. Goldfield

Ry Cooder
Issues: TRD
Rep By: Gary Gallant, Harold P. Goldfield, Richard A. Popkin

Dairy.com
Issues: AGR COM
Rep By: James DeLorenzo, Paul T. Denis, Barry B. Direnfeld, Brian W. Fitzgerald, Thomas Valente

Electronic Industries Alliance

Entertainment Made Convenient
Rep By: Martin C. Ernst

Exxon Chemical Co.
Issues: CAW GOV
Rep By: Charles H. Knauss

Florida Power and Light Co.
Issues: CAW TAX UTI WAS
Rep By: Keith N. Cole, Barry B. Direnfeld, Brian W. Fitzgerald, Gary Gallant, Harold P. Goldfield, Lester S. Hyman, Gary D. Slaiman, Katherine R. Taylor

Frontier Communications Corp.
Issues: TEC
Rep By: Kristine DeBry, Gary D. Slaiman

General Electric Co.
Issues: BUD CAW ENV GOV TRA
Rep By: Barry B. Direnfeld, Charles H. Knauss

German Competitive Carriers Ass'n
Rep By: Andrew D. Lipman

H & R Executive Towers
Rep By: Harold A. Levy, Kenneth G. Lore

Hyundai Semiconductor America, Inc.
Rep By: Barry B. Direnfeld, Harold P. Goldfield, Lester S. Hyman

ICG Communications, Inc.
Issues: TEC
Rep By: Kristine DeBry, Gary D. Slaiman

Intersil Corp.
Issues: TEC
Rep By: Keith N. Cole, Nancy K. Spooner

Manhattan Plaza Associates
Rep By: Harold A. Levy, Kenneth G. Lore

Marconi plc
Issues: CPI MAN MMM TEC
Rep By: Keith N. Cole, Kristine DeBry

Matsushita Electric Corp. of America
Rep By: Barry B. Direnfeld, Harold P. Goldfield, Lester S. Hyman, Richard A. Popkin

MCI WorldCom Corp.
Rep By: Gary D. Slaiman

McLeod USA, Inc.
Issues: TEC
Rep By: Gary D. Slaiman

Merrill Lynch & Co., Inc.
Issues: FIN
Rep By: Barry B. Direnfeld, Brian W. Fitzgerald, Gary Gallant, Harold P. Goldfield, Lester S. Hyman, Gary D. Slaiman, Katherine R. Taylor

MFS Communications Co., Inc.

Microsoft Corp.
Issues: TAX
Rep By: Barry B. Direnfeld, Brian W. Fitzgerald, Harold P. Goldfield

Napster, Inc.
Issues: CPT TEC
Rep By: James DeLorenzo, Barry B. Direnfeld, Harold P. Goldfield, Gary D. Slaiman

Nat'l Ass'n of Chain Drug Stores
Issues: HCR PHA
Rep By: Barry B. Direnfeld, Harold P. Goldfield

Nat'l Grid USA
Issues: BUD ENV UTI

Nat'l Housing and Rehabilitation Ass'n
Rep By: Barry B. Direnfeld, James Hamilton, Harold A. Levy, Kenneth G. Lore

Nat'l Sediments Coalition
Issues: CAW ENV WAS
Rep By: Keith N. Cole, Barry B. Direnfeld, Harold P. Goldfield, Charles H. Knauss

Newman & Associates
Issues: TAX
Rep By: Keith N. Cole, Barry B. Direnfeld, Brian W. Fitzgerald, Gary Gallant, William B. Glew, Jr., Harold P. Goldfield, Lester S. Hyman, Harold A. Levy

Niagara Mohawk Power Corp.
Issues: BUD CAW TAX TRA UTI WAS
Rep By: Barry B. Direnfeld, Brian W. Fitzgerald, Gary Gallant, William B. Glew, Jr., Harold P. Goldfield, Gary D. Slaiman

Philip Morris Management Corp.
Issues: BEV FOO TOB
Rep By: Gary D. Slaiman, Katherine R. Taylor

Printing Industries of America
Issues: CAW
Rep By: Keith N. Cole

RCN Telecom Services Inc.
Issues: TEC
Rep By: Gary D. Slaiman

Recreational Equipment Inc.
Issues: RES
Rep By: Keith N. Cole

Renewable Fuels Ass'n
Issues: FUE TAX
Rep By: Keith N. Cole, Barry B. Direnfeld, Gary D. Slaiman, Michael E. Ward

Reusable Industrial Packaging Ass'n
Issues: BUD ENV
Rep By: Keith N. Cole, Brian W. Fitzgerald

Schering Corp.
Rep By: Brian W. Fitzgerald, Gary Gallant, Lester S. Hyman, Gary D. Slaiman

Shakopee Mdewakanton Sioux Tribe
Rep By: James Hamilton

Starrett Corp.
Issues: HOU
Rep By: Harold A. Levy

Suiza Foods Corp.
Issues: AGR FOO LBR
Rep By: Paul T. Denis, Barry B. Direnfeld, Brian W. Fitzgerald, Harold P. Goldfield, Gary D. Slaiman, Katherine R. Taylor

Transkaryotic Therapies Inc.
Issues: CPT
Rep By: Barry B. Direnfeld, Brian W. Fitzgerald, Gary Gallant, Harold P. Goldfield

US Airways
Issues: TRA
Rep By: Gary D. Slaiman, Katherine R. Taylor

Al Swift Consulting, Inc.

6301 Stevenson Ave.
Alexandria, VA 22304
Tel: (703)751-9181
Fax: (703)751-0299
Registered: LDA
Web: www.csandh.com
E-mail: swift@csandh.com
Also maintains a second e-mail address at alswift@home.com.

DC-Area Employees Representing Listed Clients
SWIFT, Hon. Allan B.

Clients

Institute of Scrap Recycling Industries, Inc.
Issues: ENV WAS
Rep By: Hon. Allan B. Swift

Symms, Lehn & Associates, Inc.

127 S. Fairfax St.
Suite 137
Alexandria, VA 22314
Tel: (703)495-0710
Fax: (703)495-9124
Registered: LDA, FARA

DC-Area Employees Representing Listed Clients
LEHN, Alfred M., Principal
SYMMS, Hon. Steven D., Principal

Clients

Amalgamated Sugar
Issues: AGR

Ass'n of American Railroads
Issues: RET TAX
Rep By: Alfred M. Lehn, Hon. Steven D. Symms

Berwind Corp.
Issues: LBR RET TAX

E-Prime Aerospace
Issues: AER

GAF Corp.

O'Connor & Hannan, L.L.P.
Issues: ENV

Snake River Sugar Co.
Issues: AGR TAX

Super Reachback Coalition
Issues: LBR TAX

Taipei Economic and Cultural Representative Office in the United States
Issues: FOR

System Planning Corp.

1000 Wilson Blvd.
Arlington, VA 22209
Tel: (703)351-8317
Fax: (703)351-8567
Registered: LDA

DC-Area Employees Representing Listed Clients
PURCELL, Theresa
ZAKHEIM, Dr. Dove, Corporate V. President

Clients

Hebrew University of Jerusalem
Issues: SCI
Rep By: Theresa Purcell

Mary-Rose Szoka de Valladares

P.O. Box 30452
Bethesda, MD 20824
Tel: (301)530-6591
Registered: LDA

Clients

Transconsortia
Issues: ENG FUE
Rep By: Mary-Rose Szoka de Valladares

George C. Tagg

1155 Connecticut Ave. NW
Suite 400
Washington, DC 20036
Tel: (301)656-1370
Fax: (301)657-3966
Registered: LDA

Clients

FedEx Corp.
Issues: POS
Rep By: George C. Tagg

Morgan Stanley Dean Witter & Co.
Issues: BAN FIN
Rep By: George C. Tagg

John T. O'Rourke Law Offices
Issues: TAX
Rep By: George C. Tagg

Waste Management, Inc.
Issues: TAX WAS
Rep By: George C. Tagg

Taggart and Associates, Inc.

2341 S. Ode St.
Arlington, VA 22202
Tel: (703)271-1940
Registered: LDA
E-mail: taggbill@erols.com
Represents firms interested in legislation and regulation in telecommunications, pharmaceuticals, healthcare, and agricultural production.

DC-Area Employees Representing Listed Clients
TAGGART, William A., President

Talley and Associates

2121 K St. NW
Suite 650
Washington, DC 20036
E-mail: tmg1@erols.com
Tel: (202)296-4114
Fax: (202)296-2409

DC-Area Employees Representing Listed Clients
TALLEY, Robert A. C., Principal

Clients

City Public Service
Issues: ENG TAX UTI
Rep By: Robert A. C. Talley

Colorado Springs Utilities
Issues: DEF ENG UTI
Rep By: Robert A. C. Talley

ElectriCities of North Carolina, Inc.
Issues: ENG TAX
Rep By: Robert A. C. Talley

Fair Trade Group
Rep By: Robert A. C. Talley

Tallon & Associates

305 C St. NE
Suite 305
Washington, DC 20002
Tel: (202)544-6873

DC-Area Employees Representing Listed Clients
TALLON, Hon. Robin

Clients

Philip Morris Management Corp.
Issues: BEV FOO TOB
Rep By: Hon. Robin Tallon

Tarne Powers & Associates

200 Daingerfield Rd.
Suite 100
Alexandria, VA 22314
Tel: (703)684-8352
Fax: (703)684-5812
E-mail: gtarne@tarnepowerspr.com
A public relations, communications and issue advocacy firm.

DC-Area Employees Representing Listed Clients
POWERS, Michelle R., V. President
TARNE, Gene, President

Clients

Americans for Integrity in Palliative Care
Issues: FAM MED
Rep By: Gene Tarne

Da Vinci's Notebook
Issues: ART
Rep By: Michelle R. Powers

Do No Harm: The Coalition of Americans for Research Ethics
Issues: MED
Rep By: Gene Tarne

Physicians Ad hoc Coalition for Truth (PHACT)
Issues: FAM MED
Rep By: Michelle R. Powers, Gene Tarne

Susan B. Anthony List
Issues: FAM
Rep By: Michelle R. Powers

TASC, Inc., Association Management

1420 16th St. NW
Suite 405
Washington, DC 20036
Tel: (202)328-7460
Fax: (202)332-2301

DC-Area Employees Representing Listed Clients
DYER, CAE, Randy, Exec. V. President

Clients

Early Learning Years Institute
Rep By: Randy Dyer, CAE

Internat'l Electronic Article Surveillance Manufacturers
Rep By: Randy Dyer, CAE

Nat'l Structured Settlements Trade Ass'n
Rep By: Randy Dyer, CAE

Unified Voice (Interior Designers)
Rep By: Randy Dyer, CAE

Tate-LeMunyon, LLC

233 Pennsylvania Ave. SE
Suite 300
Washington, DC 20003
Tel: (202)547-9050
Fax: (202)547-8991
Registered: LDA
Web: www.tatelemunyon.com

DC-Area Employees Representing Listed Clients
LEMUNYON, Glenn B., Principal
TATE, Jr., Dan C., Principal

Clients

Alliance Air Services
Issues: AVI TRA
Rep By: Glenn B. LeMunyon, Dan C. Tate, Jr.

Brownsville, Texas, Port of
Issues: MAR RRR TRA
Rep By: Glenn B. LeMunyon, Dan C. Tate, Jr.

Fannie Mae
Issues: HOU
Rep By: Glenn B. LeMunyon, Dan C. Tate, Jr.

Lockheed Martin Corp.
Issues: DEF TRA
Rep By: Glenn B. LeMunyon

North American Superhighway Coalition
Issues: ECN TRA
Rep By: Glenn B. LeMunyon, Dan C. Tate, Jr.

Orange, California, County of
Issues: DEF TRA
Rep By: Glenn B. LeMunyon

Patricia A. Taylor

7121 Sycamore Ave.
Takoma Park, MD 20912
Tel: (301)270-6105
Fax: (301)270-4207
Registered: LDA

A self-employed consultant.

Clients

Seedco
Issues: HOU
Rep By: Patricia A. Taylor

The Technical Group LLC

1300 I St. NW
Suite 1000 West
Washington, DC 20005
Tel: (202)962-8531
Fax: (202)962-8542
Registered: LDA

DC-Area Employees Representing Listed Clients
ANDERS, Michele, Senior Consultant
BRYANT, Chris, President

OVENDEN, Thomas D., Partner
SEARS, Fred, Senior Consultant

Clients

Kimberly-Clark Corp.
Issues: ENV
Rep By: Chris Bryant

Nat'l Environmental Development Ass'n, Inc.
Rep By: Thomas D. Ovenden

NEDA/Resource Conservation and Recovery Act Project

RSR Corp.
Issues: ENV TRA TRD WAS
Rep By: Michele Anders, Thomas D. Ovenden

Steel Shipping Container Institute

Technology Advocates, Inc.

P.O. Box 1408
Great Falls, VA 22066
Tel: (703)623-0698
Fax: (703)757-8274
Registered: LDA
Web: www.advocatesinc.com
E-mail: info@advocatesinc.com

DC-Area Employees Representing Listed Clients
ABBOUD, Jeffrey S., Principal

Clients

Fuel Cell Power Ass'n
Issues: ENG
Rep By: Jeffrey S. Abboud

Gas Turbine Ass'n, Inc.
Issues: ENG
Rep By: Jeffrey S. Abboud

Technology, Entertainment and Communications (TEC) Law Group

1140 Connecticut Ave. NW
Suite 1142
Washington, DC 20036
Tel: (202)862-4383
Fax: (202)331-5562
Registered: LDA
Web: www.teclawgroup.com
Provides counsel and representations to clients in the following industries: software, computer hardware, e-commerce, Internet, new media, telecommunications, music, TV, video, fashion, creative writing, professional sports, radio broadcasting, and Direct Broadcast Satellite. Also maintains offices in Greenville, SC and Atlanta, GA. Maintains an affiliated office in Detroit, MI.

DC-Area Employees Representing Listed Clients
KARIM, Talib I.
OFORI, Kofi Asiedu
PARKER, Rosalind
SESSION, Warner
WOODS, Jr., Fred W.

Clients

WorldSpace Corp.
Issues: TEC
Rep By: Talib I. Karim, Rosalind Parker

Teicher Consulting and Representation

4331 Reno Rd. NW
Washington, DC 20008
Tel: (202)244-8500
Fax: (202)244-8165
Registered: LDA
E-mail: teich@tmn.com
Business consulting and representation services for advanced technology companies.

DC-Area Employees Representing Listed Clients
TEICHER, Howard R., Principal

Clients

Coleman Research Corp.
Issues: AER DEF FOR
Rep By: Howard R. Teicher

Rafael U.S.A., Inc.
Issues: AER AVI GOV LAW MAR
Rep By: Howard R. Teicher

Sony Trans Com
Issues: AVI
Rep By: Howard R. Teicher

WESCAM
Issues: AER BUD MAR MIA
Rep By: Howard R. Teicher

Television Communicators

P.O. Box 5437
Friendship Station
Washington, DC 20016-5437
Tel: (202)966-6616
Fax: (202)966-6606
A total media and communications training, crisis and issues management consulting firm. Specializes in interview, spokesperson, presentation and government testimony communications training and candidate/political consulting.

DC-Area Employees Representing Listed Clients
WECHTER, Robert D., President

Clients

Random House
Rep By: Robert D. Wechter

Republic Nat'l Bank of New York
Rep By: Robert D. Wechter

Simon & Schuster Inc.
Rep By: Robert D. Wechter

Templeton & Co.

1801 K St. NW
Suite 901-L
Washington, DC 20006
Tel: (202)530-0500
Fax: (202)530-4800
Registered: LDA
E-mail: pat_templeton@bm.com

DC-Area Employees Representing Listed Clients
TEMPLETON, Patrick A., President

Terpstra Associates

1111 19th St. NW
12th Floor
Washington, DC 20036-4503
Tel: (202)828-9487
Fax: (202)828-8405
Registered: LDA
E-mail: gt@terpstraassociates.com

DC-Area Employees Representing Listed Clients
TERPSTRA, Grace, Principal

Clients

American Forest & Paper Ass'n
Issues: ENV WAS
Rep By: Grace Terpstra

Chesapeake Corp.
Issues: ENV
Rep By: Grace Terpstra

Fort James Corp.
Rep By: Grace Terpstra

Nat'l Hardwood Lumber Ass'n
Issues: ENV NAT TAX
Rep By: Grace Terpstra

TerraCom-Strategic Communications

1010 Wisconsin Ave. NW
Suite 210
Washington, DC 20007
Tel: (202)965-5151
Fax: (202)965-5252
Registered: LDA
A government and public relations consulting firm.

DC-Area Employees Representing Listed Clients
SANCHEZ, Felix R., Chief Exec. Officer

Clients

American Concrete Pavement Ass'n (ACPA)

Dallas/Fort Worth Internat'l Airport Board
Issues: AVI
Rep By: Felix R. Sanchez

Euro-Fulton, S.A.
Issues: TRD
Rep By: Felix R. Sanchez

Sidem International Ltd.
Issues: TRD
Rep By: Felix R. Sanchez

Thacher Proffitt & Wood

1700 Pennsylvania Ave. NW
Suite 800
Washington, DC 20006
Tel: (202)347-8400
Fax: (202)626-1930
Registered: LDA
Web: www.thacherproffitt.com
A law firm.

DC-Area Employees Representing Listed Clients
BURKE, Barbara D., Legislative/Regulatory Consultant

Clients

Water Quality Insurance Syndicate
Issues: ENV
Rep By: Barbara D. Burke

Susan R. Thau

6217 29th St. NW
Washington, DC 20015
Tel: (202)966-4361
Registered: LDA
A self-employed public interest consultant.

Clients

Community Anti-Drug Coalitions of America
Issues: ALC
Rep By: Susan R. Thau

Richard R. Thaxton

5112 Althea Dr.
Annandale, VA 22003
Tel: (703)425-5720
Fax: (703)425-2119
Registered: LDA
E-mail: dickthaxton@aol.com
A legislative consultant and lobbyist.

Clients

ANADAC
Issues: CPI
Rep By: Richard R. Thaxton

Chibank Service Inc.
Issues: BAN
Rep By: Richard R. Thaxton

Thelen Reid & Priest LLP

701 Pennsylvania Ave. NW
Suite 800
Washington, DC 20004
Tel: (202)508-4000
Fax: (202)508-4321
Registered: LDA, FARA
Web: www.thelenreid.com
A law firm. Also maintains offices in Los Angeles, San Francisco, and Silicon Valley, CA and in New York, NY.

Political Action Committee
Thelen Reid & Priest L.L.P. Political Action Committee
701 Pennsylvania Ave. NW
Suite 800
Washington, DC 20004
Tel: (202)508-4010
Fax: (202)508-4321
Contact: Stephan M. Minikes

DC-Area Employees Representing Listed Clients
BERKOFF, Barry I., Legislative Representative
COOPER, Howard A., Partner
DACEK, Raymond F., Of Counsel
ENGLISH, Jr., Charles M., Partner
ESTEVEZ, Mareza I.
EVENS, Mark F., Partner
GOODWIN, Lee M., Partner
HALL, III, Robert T., Partner
HONIGMAN, Steven S., Partner
JACOBSON, David E., Partner
KIRK, Jr., William A., Partner
LEIDL, Richard J., Partner
MINIKES, Stephan M., Partner
MITCHELL, James K., Partner
PITTMAN, Edward L., Of Counsel
PRAKASH, Ambari, Associate
REED, Alan J., Associate-Business & Finance
ROBERTS, Richard Y., Partner
SCHAEFGEN, John R., Partner
WEISENFELD, David J.
WEST, Nancy K., Senior Legislative Representative
YOVIENE, Wendy M., Associate

Clients

Abilene Industrial Foundation, Inc.
Issues: DEF
Rep By: Barry I. Berkoff, Richard J. Leidl, Stephan M. Minikes

Airport Minority Advisory Council
Issues: TRA
Rep By: Barry I. Berkoff, William A. Kirk, Jr., Richard J. Leidl, Stephan M. Minikes, Nancy K. West

Anderson Erickson Dairy Co.
Issues: AGR
Rep By: Charles M. English, Jr., Wendy M. Yoviene

Capital Dimensions Venture Fund Inc.
Rep By: William A. Kirk, Jr.

Capital Region Airport Commission
Issues: AVI BUD TRA
Rep By: Barry I. Berkoff, William A. Kirk, Jr., Richard J. Leidl, Stephan M. Minikes, Richard Y. Roberts, Nancy K. West

Charles Schwab & Co. Inc.
Issues: FIN
Rep By: Edward L. Pittman, Alan J. Reed, Richard Y. Roberts

Cincinnati Stock Exchange
Issues: FIN
Rep By: Edward L. Pittman, Ambari Prakash, Alan J. Reed, Richard Y. Roberts

Corpus Christi Port Authority
Issues: TRA
Rep By: Barry I. Berkoff, William A. Kirk, Jr., Richard J. Leidl, Stephan M. Minikes, Nancy K. West

Dayton Power and Light Co.
Rep By: John R. Schaefgen

Denver Internat'l Airport
Rep By: William A. Kirk, Jr., Richard J. Leidl, Stephan M. Minikes

Denver, Colorado, City of
Issues: AVI
Rep By: Barry I. Berkoff, William A. Kirk, Jr., Richard J. Leidl, Stephan M. Minikes, Richard Y. Roberts, Nancy K. West

Dominion Resources, Inc.
Issues: FIN UTI
Rep By: Richard Y. Roberts

DRS Precision Echo Inc.
Issues: DEF
Rep By: Barry I. Berkoff, Richard J. Leidl, Stephan M. Minikes

DRS Technologies, Inc.
Rep By: Barry I. Berkoff, Stephan M. Minikes, Nancy K. West

Duke Power Co.

E*TRADE Securities, Inc.
Issues: CPI FIN
Rep By: Richard Y. Roberts

Edison Electric Institute
Issues: TAX
Rep By: Howard A. Cooper, Raymond F. Dacek

Electronic Traders Ass'n
Issues: FIN UTI
Rep By: Richard Y. Roberts

L.B. Foster Co.
Issues: GOV
Rep By: Barry I. Berkoff, Richard J. Leidl, Stephan M. Minikes

Fulcrum Venture Capital Corp.
Issues: SMB
Rep By: William A. Kirk, Jr.

Green Mountain Power Corp.
Rep By: James K. Mitchell

Horizon Organic Holding Co.
Issues: AGR
Rep By: Charles M. English, Jr., Stephan M. Minikes, Nancy K. West, Wendy M. Yoviene

J. M. Huber Corp.

The Island ECN
Issues: FIN
Rep By: Edward L. Pittman, Richard Y. Roberts

J & B Management Co.
Rep By: Barry I. Berkoff, William A. Kirk, Jr.

The Jewelers' Security Alliance
Issues: BUD IMM LAW
Rep By: Barry I. Berkoff, William A. Kirk, Jr., Richard J. Leidl, Stephan M. Minikes, David J. Weisenfeld, Nancy K. West

LM Capital Corp.
Rep By: William A. Kirk, Jr.

MCA Inc.
Issues: TAX
Rep By: Barry I. Berkoff, William A. Kirk, Jr.

Medallion Funding Corp.
Issues: SMB
Rep By: William A. Kirk, Jr.

Metro Machine Corp. of Virginia
Issues: DEF
Rep By: Barry I. Berkoff, Steven S. Honigman, William A. Kirk, Jr., Richard J. Leidl, Stephan M. Minikes

Metro Machine of Pennsylvania, Inc.
Rep By: Barry I. Berkoff, William A. Kirk, Jr., Richard J. Leidl, Stephan M. Minikes

Metroplex Corp.
Rep By: Barry I. Berkoff, William A. Kirk, Jr., Richard J. Leidl, Stephan M. Minikes

MMG Ventures LP
Issues: SMB
Rep By: William A. Kirk, Jr.

Myriad Capital Inc.
Issues: SMB
Rep By: William A. Kirk, Jr.

Nat'l Ass'n of Investment Companies
Rep By: William A. Kirk, Jr.

Opportunity Capital Corp.
Issues: SMB
Rep By: Barry I. Berkoff, William A. Kirk, Jr., Richard Y. Roberts

Pacific 17
Issues: GOV
Rep By: William A. Kirk, Jr.

Parsons Brinckerhoff Inc.
Issues: BAN DEF DIS TRA
Rep By: Barry I. Berkoff, William A. Kirk, Jr., Stephan M. Minikes, Richard Y. Roberts

Philadelphia Industrial Development Corp.
Issues: DEF MAR TRA
Rep By: Barry I. Berkoff, Richard J. Leidl, Stephan M. Minikes

Philadelphia, Pennsylvania, City of
Rep By: Barry I. Berkoff, Richard J. Leidl, Stephan M. Minikes

Pinnacle West Capital Corp.
Issues: TAX
Rep By: Howard A. Cooper

Power Paragon Inc.
Rep By: Barry I. Berkoff, Richard J. Leidl, Stephan M. Minikes

Progress Energy
Issues: TAX
Rep By: David E. Jacobson

Recording Industry Ass'n of America
Issues: CPT
Rep By: William A. Kirk, Jr.

Charles Schwab & Co., Inc.,
Issues: FIN
Rep By: Edward L. Pittman, Alan J. Reed, Richard Y. Roberts

SEC Roundtable Group
Issues: UTI
Rep By: Richard Y. Roberts

SPD Technologies
Issues: DEF TRA
Rep By: Barry I. Berkoff, Richard J. Leidl, Stephan M. Minikes

Standard & Poor's Corp.
Rep By: Richard Y. Roberts

Suiza Foods Corp.
Issues: AGR
Rep By: Barry I. Berkoff, William A. Kirk, Jr., Stephan M. Minikes, Nancy K. West

Tillamook County Creamery Ass'n
Issues: AGR
Rep By: Charles M. English, Jr., Wendy M. Yoviene

TSG Ventures Inc.
Issues: SMB
Rep By: William A. Kirk, Jr.

Upper Midwest Coalition
Issues: AGR
Rep By: Charles M. English, Jr., Wendy M. Yoviene

Utility Decommissioning Tax Group
Issues: TAX

Washington Soccer Partners
Issues: IMM
Rep By: Barry I. Berkoff, Mareza I. Estevez, Richard J. Leidl, Nancy K. West

Thiemann Aitken Vohra & Rutledge, L.L.C.

908 King St.
Suite 300
Alexandria, VA 22314

Tel: (703)836-9400
Fax: (703)836-9410
Registered: LDA

DC-Area Employees Representing Listed Clients
AITKEN, Herve H., Member
THIEMANN, Alan J., Member

Clients

Ass'n of Test Publishers
Issues: CIV CPI CPT EDU LBR MIA
Rep By: Alan J. Thiemann

McGraw-Hill Cos., The
Issues: EDU
Rep By: Alan J. Thiemann

Midwest Motor Express, Inc.
Rep By: Herve H. Aitken

Nat'l Ass'n of Convenience Stores

Richard K. Thompson

1515 Jefferson Davis Hwy.
Suite 108
Arlington, VA 22202

Tel: (703)413-0710
Fax: (703)413-0712
Registered: LDA

A self-employed lobbyist.

Clients

Applied Graphics
Issues: CPI
Rep By: Richard K. Thompson

Thompson & Thompson

800 Connecticut Ave. NW
Suite 600
Washington, DC 20006

Tel: (202)783-1900
Fax: (202)783-5995
Registered: LDA

DC-Area Employees Representing Listed Clients
THOMPSON, David L., Partner
THOMPSON, Robert T., Partner

Clients

Small Business Survival Committee
Issues: GOV LBR
Rep By: David L. Thompson

Thompson and Naughton, Inc.

1155 15th St. NW
Suite 902
Washington, DC 20005

Tel: (202)775-5490
Fax: (202)822-9807
Registered: LDA

DC-Area Employees Representing Listed Clients
THOMPSON, Kenneth W., President

Clients

General Motors Corp.
Issues: ENG
Rep By: Kenneth W. Thompson

ITRON, Inc.
Issues: COM
Rep By: Kenneth W. Thompson

SEMCO
Issues: FIN TRA
Rep By: Kenneth W. Thompson

Thompson Coburn LLP

1909 K St. NW
Suite 600
Washington, DC 20006-1167

Tel: (202)585-6900
Fax: (202)585-6969
Registered: LDA

Web: www.thompsoncoburn.com
A law firm headquartered in St. Louis, MO.

DC-Area Employees Representing Listed Clients
ANDERSON, Anthony A., Partner
BELMAN, Murray J., Partner
COUGHLIN, Hon. R. Lawrence, Partner
DEAN, Warren L., Partner
GILL, Jr., Edward J., Partner
ROBERTS, Michael G., Partner
SEIDMAN, David, Associate
SNYDER, Patricia N., Partner
STRAUS, David, Partner
SUTTER-STARKE, Jane, Partner
WOODMAN, G. Kent, Partner
ZIEGLER, Sara, Legislative Specialist

Clients

Air Transport Ass'n of America
Issues: AVI ENV
Rep By: Warren L. Dean, Patricia N. Snyder

American Business Media
Issues: POS
Rep By: David Straus

American Trucking Ass'ns
Issues: TRA TRU
Rep By: Hon. R. Lawrence Coughlin

CEMEX USA
Issues: MAN RRR TRA TRD
Rep By: Hon. R. Lawrence Coughlin

Crowley Maritime Corp.
Issues: DEF FUE MAR TRA TRD

General Ore Internat'l Corp. Ltd.
Issues: MAR
Rep By: Warren L. Dean

Los Angeles County Metropolitan Transportation Authority
Issues: TRA
Rep By: Hon. R. Lawrence Coughlin, Jane Sutter-Starke, G. Kent Woodman

Massachusetts Bay Transportation Authority
Issues: TRA
Rep By: Hon. R. Lawrence Coughlin, Jane Sutter-Starke, G. Kent Woodman

Metropolitan Atlanta Rapid Transit Authority
Issues: TAX TRA
Rep By: Hon. R. Lawrence Coughlin, Jane Sutter-Starke

Regional Transportation Commission of South Nevada
Issues: TRA
Rep By: Hon. R. Lawrence Coughlin, Jane Sutter-Starke, G. Kent Woodman

Safegate Internat'l AB
Issues: AVI TRA
Rep By: Hon. R. Lawrence Coughlin

Special Vehicle Coalition
Issues: TRA
Rep By: Warren L. Dean

Taxicab, Limousine and Paratransit Ass'n
Issues: TRA
Rep By: Edward J. Gill, Jr.

UniGroup, Inc.
Issues: BNK TRA TRU
Rep By: Michael G. Roberts

Thompson, Hine and Flory LLP

1920 N St. NW
Washington, DC 20036

Tel: (202)331-8800
Fax: (202)331-8330

Web: www.thf.com
E-mail: attorneys@thf.com
Washington office of a Cleveland law firm.

DC-Area Employees Representing Listed Clients
BAKER, David H., Partner
COHEN, Irving P., Partner
FRIEDMAN, Barry A., Partner
LESSENCO, Gilbert B., Of Counsel
MARTINEZ, Michael L.
SANDSTROM, Mark Roy, Partner

Clients

Alliance for Responsible Cuba Policy
Rep By: David H. Baker

American Pyrotechnics Ass'n
Rep By: David H. Baker

Asphalt Emulsion Manufacturers Ass'n
Rep By: David H. Baker

Asphalt Recycling and Reclaiming Ass'n
Rep By: David H. Baker

Bridgeport and Port Jefferson Steamboat Co.
Rep By: David H. Baker

Home Baking Ass'n
Rep By: Gilbert B. Lessenco

Lighter Ass'n, Inc.
Rep By: David H. Baker

Lyme Disease Foundation
Rep By: Michael L. Martinez

Nat'l Council For Fireworks Safety
Rep By: David H. Baker

Plastic Container Institute
Rep By: David H. Baker

Plastic Shipping Container Institute
Rep By: David H. Baker

Tobacco Industry Labor Management Committee
Rep By: David H. Baker

Tobacco Industry Testing Laboratory, Inc.
Rep By: David H. Baker

The Toro Co.
Rep By: Gilbert B. Lessenco

Writing Instrument Manufacturers Ass'n
Rep By: David H. Baker

Yale Materials Handling Corp.
Rep By: Mark Roy Sandstrom

Tierney & Swift

1730 Rhode Island Ave. NW
Suite 200
Washington, DC 20036
Tel: (202)728-0401
Fax: (202)659-5711

DC-Area Employees Representing Listed Clients
SWIFT, Richard F., Partner

Clients

KCSM-TV
Rep By: Richard F. Swift

KVCR-TV
Rep By: Richard F. Swift

The Tierney Group

1200 G St. NW
Suite 800
Washington, DC 20005
Registered: LDA

DC-Area Employees Representing Listed Clients
WINSTON, Chriss H., V. President

Clients

Federal Home Loan Bank of Pittsburgh
Rep By: Chriss H. Winston

Valley Forge Flag Co.
Rep By: Chriss H. Winston

Tighe, Patton, Tabackman & Babbin

1747 Pennsylvania Ave. NW
Suite 300
Washington, DC 20006
Tel: (202)293-0398
Fax: (202)393-0363
Registered: LDA

DC-Area Employees Representing Listed Clients
BRUCE, Carol Elder, Partner
FRANZEL, Brent S.

Clients

The Boeing Co.
Issues: AER DEF
Rep By: Brent S. Franzel

Citigroup
Issues: TRD
Rep By: Brent S. Franzel

SPACEHAB, Inc.
Issues: SCI
Rep By: Brent S. Franzel

Timmons and Co., Inc.

1850 K St. NW
Suite 850
Washington, DC 20006
Tel: (202)331-1760
Fax: (202)822-9376
Registered: LDA
E-mail: mail@timmonsandco.com
Government relations consultants. Owned by the WPP Group, plc of London, England.

DC-Area Employees Representing Listed Clients
BATES, Michael J., V. President and General Counsel
BENNETT, Douglas F., Exec. V. President
FITZGIBBONS, Ellen B., V. President
HARLOW, Bryce L. "Larry", President and Managing Partner
KEATING, Timothy J., Chairman and Managing Partner
KOROLOGOS, Tom C., Chairman, Exec. Committee
TARPLIN, Richard J., V. President
TIMMONS, Sr., William E., Chairman Emeritus
TIMMONS, Jr., William E., Director, Research

Clients

American Council of Life Insurers
Issues: BAN FIN FOR INS RET TAX
Rep By: Michael J. Bates, Douglas F. Bennett, Ellen B. Fitzgibbons, Bryce L. "Larry" Harlow, Timothy J. Keating, Tom C. Korologos, Richard J. Tarplin, William E. Timmons, Jr., William E. Timmons, Sr.

American Petroleum Institute
Issues: CAW ENG TAX TRD
Rep By: Michael J. Bates, Douglas F. Bennett, Ellen B. Fitzgibbons, Bryce L. "Larry" Harlow, Timothy J. Keating, Tom C. Korologos, Richard J. Tarplin, William E. Timmons, Jr., William E. Timmons, Sr.

American Soc. of Anesthesiologists
Issues: HCR MMM
Rep By: Michael J. Bates, Douglas F. Bennett, Ellen B. Fitzgibbons, Bryce L. "Larry" Harlow, Timothy J. Keating, Tom C. Korologos, Richard J. Tarplin, William E. Timmons, Jr., William E. Timmons, Sr.

Anheuser-Busch Cos., Inc.
Issues: ADV BEV TAX TRD
Rep By: Michael J. Bates, Douglas F. Bennett, Ellen B. Fitzgibbons, Bryce L. "Larry" Harlow, Timothy J. Keating, Tom C. Korologos, Richard J. Tarplin, William E. Timmons, Jr., William E. Timmons, Sr.

Asbestos Working Group
Rep By: Michael J. Bates, Douglas F. Bennett, Ellen B. Fitzgibbons, Bryce L. "Larry" Harlow, Timothy J. Keating, Tom C. Korologos, Richard J. Tarplin, William E. Timmons, Sr., William E. Timmons, Jr.

AT&T
Issues: TEC
Rep By: Michael J. Bates, Douglas F. Bennett, Ellen B. Fitzgibbons, Bryce L. "Larry" Harlow, Timothy J. Keating, Tom C. Korologos, Richard J. Tarplin, William E. Timmons, Jr., William E. Timmons, Sr.

Bay Harbor Management, L.C.
Issues: TEC
Rep By: Michael J. Bates, Douglas F. Bennett, Ellen B. Fitzgibbons, Bryce L. "Larry" Harlow, Timothy J. Keating, Tom C. Korologos, Richard J. Tarplin, William E. Timmons, Jr., William E. Timmons, Sr.

Bristol-Myers Squibb Co.
Issues: HCR PHA
Rep By: Michael J. Bates, Douglas F. Bennett, Ellen B. Fitzgibbons, Bryce L. "Larry" Harlow, Timothy J. Keating, Tom C. Korologos, Richard J. Tarplin, William E. Timmons, Jr., William E. Timmons, Sr.

Cox Enterprises Inc.
Issues: COM CPT TAX
Rep By: Michael J. Bates, Douglas F. Bennett, Ellen B. Fitzgibbons, Bryce L. "Larry" Harlow, Timothy J. Keating, Tom C. Korologos, Richard J. Tarplin, William E. Timmons, Jr., William E. Timmons, Sr.

DaimlerChrysler Corp.
Issues: AUT BAN BUD CAW CSP ENG HCR IMM TAX TRD
Rep By: Michael J. Bates, Douglas F. Bennett, Ellen B. Fitzgibbons, Bryce L. "Larry" Harlow, Timothy J. Keating, Tom C. Korologos, Richard J. Tarplin, William E. Timmons, Jr., William E. Timmons, Sr.

Farallon Capital Management
Rep By: Michael J. Bates, Douglas F. Bennett, Ellen B. Fitzgibbons, Bryce L. "Larry" Harlow, Timothy J. Keating, Tom C. Korologos, Richard J. Tarplin, William E. Timmons, Sr., William E. Timmons, Jr.

Federal Home Loan Mortgage Corp. (Freddie Mac)
Issues: FIN HOU
Rep By: Michael J. Bates, Douglas F. Bennett, Ellen B. Fitzgibbons, Bryce L. "Larry" Harlow, Timothy J. Keating, Tom C. Korologos, Richard J. Tarplin, William E. Timmons, Jr., William E. Timmons, Sr.

Micron Technology, Inc.
Issues: CPI TAX TRD
Rep By: Michael J. Bates, Douglas F. Bennett, Ellen B. Fitzgibbons, Bryce L. "Larry" Harlow, Timothy J. Keating, Tom C. Korologos, Richard J. Tarplin, William E. Timmons, Jr., William E. Timmons, Sr.

Napster, Inc.
Rep By: Michael J. Bates, Douglas F. Bennett, Ellen B. Fitzgibbons, Bryce L. "Larry" Harlow, Timothy J. Keating, Tom C. Korologos, Richard J. Tarplin, William E. Timmons, Sr., William E. Timmons, Jr.

Nat'l Rifle Ass'n of America
Issues: CIV FIR LAW
Rep By: Michael J. Bates, Douglas F. Bennett, Ellen B. Fitzgibbons, Bryce L. "Larry" Harlow, Timothy J. Keating, Tom C. Korologos, Richard J. Tarplin, William E. Timmons, Jr., William E. Timmons, Sr.

New York Life Insurance Co.
Issues: FIN INS TAX TRD
Rep By: Michael J. Bates, Douglas F. Bennett, Ellen B. Fitzgibbons, Bryce L. "Larry" Harlow, Timothy J. Keating, Tom C. Korologos, Richard J. Tarplin, William E. Timmons, Jr., William E. Timmons, Sr.

Northrop Grumman Corp.
Issues: DEF TAX TRD
Rep By: Michael J. Bates, Douglas F. Bennett, Ellen B. Fitzgibbons, Bryce L. "Larry" Harlow, Timothy J. Keating, Tom C. Korologos, Richard J. Tarplin, William E. Timmons, Jr., William E. Timmons, Sr.

TruePosition Inc.
Issues: TEC
Rep By: Michael J. Bates, Douglas F. Bennett, Ellen B. Fitzgibbons, Bryce L. "Larry" Harlow, Timothy J. Keating, Tom C. Korologos, Richard J. Tarplin, William E. Timmons, Jr., William E. Timmons, Sr.

Union Pacific
Issues: NAT RRR TAX
Rep By: Michael J. Bates, Douglas F. Bennett, Ellen B. Fitzgibbons, Bryce L. "Larry" Harlow, Timothy J. Keating, Tom C. Korologos, Richard J. Tarplin, William E. Timmons, Jr., William E. Timmons, Sr.

University of Utah
Issues: BUD EDU
Rep By: Michael J. Bates, Douglas F. Bennett, Ellen B. Fitzgibbons, Bryce L. "Larry" Harlow, Timothy J. Keating, Tom C. Korologos, Richard J. Tarplin, William E. Timmons, Jr., William E. Timmons, Sr.

UNOCAL Corp.
Issues: ROF TAX TRD
Rep By: Michael J. Bates, Douglas F. Bennett, Ellen B. Fitzgibbons, Bryce L. "Larry" Harlow, Timothy J. Keating, Tom C. Korologos, Richard J. Tarplin, William E. Timmons, Jr., William E. Timmons, Sr.

VISA U.S.A., Inc.
Issues: BAN
Rep By: Michael J. Bates, Douglas F. Bennett, Ellen B. Fitzgibbons, Bryce L. "Larry" Harlow, Timothy J. Keating, Tom C. Korologos, Richard J. Tarplin, William E. Timmons, Sr., William E. Timmons, Jr.

Michael L. Tiner

1824 S St. NW
Suite 402
Washington, DC 20009
Tel: (202)546-8577
Fax: (202)387-0889
Registered: LDA
E-mail: tinerml@aol.com
A lobbying and labor consultant.

Clients

McDonald's Corp.
Issues: SMB
Rep By: Michael L. Tiner

Nuclear Energy Institute
Issues: WAS
Rep By: Michael L. Tiner

Philip Morris Management Corp.
Issues: BEV FOO TOB
Rep By: Michael L. Tiner

Bardyl R. Tirana

4401 Connecticut Ave. NW
Suite 700
Washington, DC 20008-2322
Tel: (202)244-0437
Fax: (202)363-8179
Registered: FARA
E-mail: btirana@aol.com

Clients

Kosovo, Government of the Republic of
Rep By: Bardyl R. Tirana

TKC Internat'l, Inc.

1775 Pennsylvania Ave. NW
Suite 1050
Washington, DC 20006
Tel: (202)638-7030
Fax: (202)318-0491
Web: www.tkci.com
E-mail: rkeefe@tkci.com
Manages the Global Strategies Group, an international organization of public affairs specialists.

DC-Area Employees Representing Listed Clients
KEEFE, Robert J., Chairman and Chief Exec. Officer

William J. Tobin and Associates

3612 Bent Branch Ct.
Falls Church, VA 22041-1006
Tel: (703)941-4329
Fax: (703)941-4329
Registered: LDA
Provides government, congressional and public relations services for clients in diversified industries.

DC-Area Employees Representing Listed Clients
TOBIN, Dr. William J.

Clients

Access Technology Ass'n
Issues: CIV CSP HCR LBR

American Ass'n of Early Childhood Educators
Issues: EDU FAM HCR

Americans for Choice in Education

Child Care Institute of America, Inc.

Early Childhood Development Center Legislative Coalition

Ecclesiastical Associates
Nat'l Accreditation Council for Early Childhood Professional Personnel and Programs
Nat'l Bible Ass'n
Nat'l Catholic Federation of Parents
Nat'l Childcare Parents Ass'n
Nat'l Released Time Project

Tongour Simpson Holsclaw Green

227 Massachusetts Ave. NE
Suite One
Washington, DC 20002
Tel: (202)544-7600
Fax: (202)544-6770
Registered: LDA

DC-Area Employees Representing Listed Clients
BURNS, Sascha M., V. President, Government Relations
GREEN, James F., Partner
HOLSCLAW, John Bradley "Brad", Partner
SIMPSON, Hon. Alan K., Partner
TONGOUR, Michael A., Managing Partner

Clients

American Ass'n of Nurse Anesthetists
Issues: HCR
Rep By: John Bradley "Brad" Holsclaw, Michael A. Tongour

Americans for Sensible Estate Tax Solutions (ASSETS)
Issues: TAX
Rep By: Hon. Alan K. Simpson

Ass'n for Advanced Life Underwriting
Issues: TAX
Rep By: Sascha M. Burns, Michael A. Tongour

Aventis Pharmaceuticals, Inc.
Issues: CPT
Rep By: John Bradley "Brad" Holsclaw, Michael A. Tongour

Communities in Schools, Inc.
Issues: BUD
Rep By: John Bradley "Brad" Holsclaw, Michael A. Tongour

Corning Inc.
Issues: TAX
Rep By: Sascha M. Burns, James F. Green, John Bradley "Brad" Holsclaw

CSX Corp.
Issues: TRA
Rep By: John Bradley "Brad" Holsclaw, Michael A. Tongour

Hydroelectric Licensing Reform Task Force
Issues: ENG
Rep By: Michael A. Tongour

Lancaster, California, City of
Issues: URB
Rep By: Michael A. Tongour

Pharmaceutical Research and Manufacturers of America
Issues: PHA
Rep By: John Bradley "Brad" Holsclaw, Michael A. Tongour

SBC Communications Inc.
Issues: TEC
Rep By: James F. Green, Michael A. Tongour

SCANA Corp.
Issues: ENG
Rep By: John Bradley "Brad" Holsclaw, Michael A. Tongour

TXU Business Services
Issues: UTI
Rep By: John Bradley "Brad" Holsclaw, Michael A. Tongour

TXU Inc.
Issues: UTI
Rep By: Michael A. Tongour

Union Switch and Signal, Inc.
Issues: TRA
Rep By: Michael A. Tongour

United States Telecom Ass'n
Issues: TEC
Rep By: Michael A. Tongour

Townsend Solheim

2817-D S. Woodrow St.
Arlington, VA 22206
Tel: (703)671-4228
Fax: (703)671-4424
Registered: LDA
E-mail: ltsolheim@earthlink.net
Provides clients legislative and regulatory lobbying and legal services in the areas of telecommunications and technology.

DC-Area Employees Representing Listed Clients
SOLHEIM, Linda T., Chief Exec.

Clients

Iridium, LLC
Issues: TEC
Rep By: Linda T. Solheim

Personal Communications Industry Ass'n (PCIA)
Rep By: Linda T. Solheim

VoiceStream Wireless Corp.
Issues: TEC
Rep By: Linda T. Solheim

Wireless Technology Research, L.L.C.
Issues: HCR MED
Rep By: Linda T. Solheim

The Trade Partnership

1775 Pennsylvania Ave. NW
Suite 1250
Washington, DC 20006
Tel: (202)347-1041
Fax: (202)628-0669
Registered: LDA
Web: www.tradepartnership.com

DC-Area Employees Representing Listed Clients
BAUGHMAN, Laura M., President
HOFFMANN, Justin, Trade Policy Analyst

Clients

The Business Roundtable
Issues: TRD
Rep By: Laura M. Baughman

Coalition for GSP
Issues: TRD
Rep By: Laura M. Baughman

Council of the Americas
Issues: TRD
Rep By: Laura M. Baughman

Nat'l Retail Federation
Issues: TRD
Rep By: Laura M. Baughman

TransNat'l Business Development Corp.

9608 Sotwood St.
Potomac, MD 20854
Tel: (301)983-1376
Registered: LDA
E-mail: transnational@compuserve.com

DC-Area Employees Representing Listed Clients
LEVINE, Peter J., President

Clients

Trans-Ona S.A.M.C.I.F.
Issues: MAR
Rep By: Peter J. Levine

Trippi, McMahon & Squier

1029 N. Royal St.
Suite 350
Alexandria, VA 22314
Tel: (703)519-8600
Fax: (703)519-8604
Web: www.thenewmedia.com
Political and media consulting.

DC-Area Employees Representing Listed Clients
MCMAHON, Steve, Partner
SQUIER, Mark R., Partner
TRIPPI, Joe, Partner

Troutman Sanders LLP

401 Ninth St. NW
Suite 1000
Washington, DC 20004
Tel: (202)274-2950
Fax: (202)274-2994
Registered: LDA, FARA
Web: www.troutmansanders.com
A law firm specializing in policy, legislation and regulation concerning energy, transportation and the environment; and power project development and finance. Firm headquartered in Atlanta, GA.

DC-Area Employees Representing Listed Clients
BROWN, Sandra L., Associate
COBB, Antoine P., Associate
CONNAUGHTON, Sean T., Of Counsel
DREHER, Robert, Of Counsel
FITZGERALD, Kevin C., Managing Partner
FITZGERALD, Mary Clare
GOMEZ, Diego A., Associate
ISRAEL, Benjamin L., Partner
JENSEN, Thomas C., Partner
MARSAN, William P., Associate
MOLM, John R., Partner
MOORHEAD, Eileen M., Associate
MULLINS, William A., Partner
REEVES, David C., Of Counsel
SIKORA, Clifford S., Partner
SUCHMAN, Bonnie, Of Counsel
SWEENEY, Jr., R. Michael, Associate
THOMPSON, Dionne E., Associate

Clients

American Institute of Certified Public Accountants
Issues: CPI TAX
Rep By: Mary Clare Fitzgerald

Canadian Electricity Ass'n
Issues: ENG
Rep By: William P. Marsan, Bonnie Suchman, Dionne E. Thompson

Cinergy Corp.
Issues: ENG ENV
Rep By: Thomas C. Jensen, Bonnie Suchman

Electronic Commerce Forum
Issues: CPI TAX
Rep By: Mary Clare Fitzgerald

ezgov.com
Rep By: Mary Clare Fitzgerald, William P. Marsan

Federal Home Loan Bank of Des Moines
Issues: FIN
Rep By: Mary Clare Fitzgerald

Kansas City Southern Industries
Rep By: Sandra L. Brown, William A. Mullins, David C. Reeves

Longhorn Pipeline
Issues: ENG ENV
Rep By: Thomas C. Jensen, Eileen M. Moorhead, Clifford S. Sikora

Minnesota Power
Issues: ENG
Rep By: Kevin C. Fitzgerald, William P. Marsan, Clifford S. Sikora

Otter Tail Power Co.
Rep By: Kevin C. Fitzgerald, William P. Marsan, Clifford S. Sikora

Paducah & Louisville Railroad
Issues: RRR
Rep By: Sandra L. Brown, William P. Marsan, William A. Mullins, David C. Reeves

PG&E Corp.
Issues: ENG
Rep By: Thomas C. Jensen, Bonnie Suchman, Dionne E. Thompson

Southern Co.
Issues: ENG
Rep By: Kevin C. Fitzgerald, William P. Marsan, Clifford S. Sikora, Bonnie Suchman

Trigen Energy Corp.
Issues: ENG
Rep By: Thomas C. Jensen, William P. Marsan, Bonnie Suchman, Dionne E. Thompson

Wisconsin Energy Corp.
Issues: ENG ENV GOV UTI
Rep By: Thomas C. Jensen, Clifford S. Sikora, Bonnie Suchman

Troutman Sanders Mays & Valentine L.L.P.

1660 Internat'l Dr.
Suite 600
McLean, VA 22102
Tel: (703)734-4334
Fax: (703)734-4340
Registered: LDA
Web: www.troutmansanders.com

DC-Area Employees Representing Listed Clients
DONAHUE, Kathleen, Of Counsel
KLEINE, Thomas C., Associate
TROY, Anthony F., Partner

Clients

ROCCO, Inc.
San Miguel Valley Corp.

Tucker & Flyer, P.C.

1615 L St. NW
Suite 400
Washington, DC 20036-5612
Tel: (202)452-8600
Fax: (202)429-3231
Registered: LDA
Web: www.tuckerflyer.com
E-mail: info@tuckerflyer.com

DC-Area Employees Representing Listed Clients
TUCKER, Stefan F., Partner

Christopher A.G. Tulou

2122 California St. NW
Suite 655
Washington, DC 20008-1803
Tel: (202)387-9440
Fax: (202)387-9445
Registered: LDA

Clients

Environmental Council of the States (ECOS)
Issues: CAW ENV NAT WAS
Rep By: Christopher A.G. Tulou

Sea Grant Ass'n
Issues: CAW EDU ENV MAR NAT SCI
Rep By: Christopher A.G. Tulou

David Turch & Associates

517 Second St. NE
Washington, DC 20002
Tel: (202)543-3744
Fax: (202)543-3509
Registered: LDA

A government relations consulting firm.

DC-Area Employees Representing Listed Clients

BOSCH, Kevin D., Associate
CAMPBELL, Marilyn E., Chief Operating Officer
GALLAGHER, Henry, Associate
MCLEAN, Joseph, Associate
TAMBONE, Victor, Associate
TURCH, David N. M., President

Clients

Digital Biometrics, Inc.
Issues: LAW
Rep By: Marilyn E. Campbell, Victor Tambone, David N. M. Turch

Dyno Nobel, Inc.
Rep By: Marilyn E. Campbell

Inland Valley Development Agency
Issues: ECN
Rep By: David N. M. Turch

Monrovia, California, City of

Rancho Cucamonga, California, City of

Recovery Engineering, Inc.
Issues: DEF
Rep By: Marilyn E. Campbell, David N. M. Turch

Rialto, California, City of
Issues: URB
Rep By: Kevin D. Bosch, Marilyn E. Campbell, Henry Gallagher, David N. M. Turch

Riverside County Transportation Commission
Rep By: Marilyn E. Campbell, David N. M. Turch

San Bernardino Airport Authority
Issues: AVI
Rep By: Marilyn E. Campbell, David N. M. Turch

San Bernardino Associated Governments
Issues: TRA
Rep By: Kevin D. Bosch, Marilyn E. Campbell, David N. M. Turch

San Bernardino, California, City of

San Bernardino, California, County of
Issues: GOV
Rep By: Kevin D. Bosch, Marilyn E. Campbell, Henry Gallagher, Victor Tambone, David N. M. Turch

Southern California Regional Rail Authority
Issues: TRA
Rep By: Marilyn E. Campbell, David N. M. Turch

St. Cloud, Minnesota, City of
Issues: URB
Rep By: Kevin D. Bosch, Marilyn E. Campbell, Victor Tambone, David N. M. Turch

Temecula, California, City of
Issues: URB
Rep By: Kevin D. Bosch, Marilyn E. Campbell, David N. M. Turch

Tuttle, Taylor & Heron

1025 Thomas Jefferson St. NW
Suite 407 West
Washington, DC 20007
Tel: (202)342-1300
Fax: (202)342-5880
Registered: LDA, FARA

A general practice law firm.

DC-Area Employees Representing Listed Clients

FRAAS, Phillip L., Of Counsel
HERON, Jr., Julian B., Senior Partner
TUTTLE, Julian B., Senior Partner
WESTWATER, Joseph J.

Clients

Bell Equipment Ltd.
Issues: TRD
Rep By: Phillip L. Fraas

Blue Diamond Growers
Issues: AGR
Rep By: Julian B. Heron, Jr.

California-Arizona Citrus League

Cheese Importers Ass'n of America
Rep By: Phillip L. Fraas

Crop Growers Insurance Co.
Issues: AGR
Rep By: Julian B. Heron, Jr.

Darigold, Inc.
Rep By: Phillip L. Fraas

DEIP (Dairy Export Incentive Program) Coalition
Issues: AGR
Rep By: Phillip L. Fraas

Nat'l Milk Producers Federation
Issues: AGR
Rep By: Julian B. Tuttle

Philip Morris Management Corp.
Issues: AGR
Rep By: Phillip L. Fraas

South African Sugar Ass'n
Issues: TRD
Rep By: Phillip L. Fraas

Sunkist Growers, Inc.
Issues: AGR
Rep By: Julian B. Heron, Jr.

Western United Dairymen
Rep By: Phillip L. Fraas

Tuvin Associates

2805 Washington Ave.
Chevy Chase, MD 20815
Tel: (301)588-8461
Fax: (301)495-6362
Registered: LDA

DC-Area Employees Representing Listed Clients

BENNETT, Raymond T., Associate
KUHN, James F., Associate
TUVIN, Carl R., President

Clients

Motion Picture and Television Fund
Issues: HCR HOU MED MMM
Rep By: Raymond T. Bennett, Carl R. Tuvin

Twenty-First Century Group

434 New Jersey Ave. SE
Washington, DC 20003
Tel: (202)488-2800
Fax: (202)488-3150
Registered: LDA
E-mail: twenty-firstcenturygroup@worldnet.att.net

DC-Area Employees Representing Listed Clients

FIELDS, Jr., Hon. Jack M., Chief Exec. Officer
WILKINSON, Cynthia M., President and General Counsel

Clients

Electronic Industries Alliance
Rep By: Hon. Jack M. Fields, Jr., Cynthia M. Wilkinson

Longhorn Pipeline
Issues: ENG
Rep By: Hon. Jack M. Fields, Jr., Cynthia M. Wilkinson

SBC Communications Inc.
Issues: TEC
Rep By: Hon. Jack M. Fields, Jr., Cynthia M. Wilkinson

Taxpayers Against Fraud, The False Claims Legal Center
Issues: GOV
Rep By: Hon. Jack M. Fields, Jr., Cynthia M. Wilkinson

Telecommunications Industry Ass'n
Issues: TEC
Rep By: Hon. Jack M. Fields, Jr., Cynthia M. Wilkinson

Verizon Communications
Issues: TEC
Rep By: Hon. Jack M. Fields, Jr., Cynthia M. Wilkinson

U.S. Strategies Corp.

1055 N. Fairfax St.
Suite 201
Alexandria, VA 22314-3563
Tel: (703)739-7999
Fax: (703)739-7995
Registered: LDA
Web: www.usstrategies.com

DC-Area Employees Representing Listed Clients

CAPISTRANT, Gary F., Senior V. President, Health
CAREY, Steven E., V. President, Legislative Affairs
GUENTHER-PETERSON, Nance, Senior V. President, Intergovernmental Relations
HANSON, Eric R., Chief Exec. Officer
HANSON, Heidi, Senior V. President, Public Affairs
RAMIREZ, Andres, Legislative Assistant
TRAVERSE, Brad, V. President, Federal Relations
WYRICK, Michael K., Consultant

Clients

Acute Long Term Hospital Ass'n
Issues: HCR MMM
Rep By: Gary F. Capistrant, Brad Traverse

AdvoServe
Issues: HCR
Rep By: Nance Guenther-Peterson, Heidi Hanson, Brad Traverse

American Institute for Public Safety
Issues: TRA
Rep By: Steven E. Carey, Michael K. Wyrick

American Nursery and Landscape Ass'n
Rep By: Steven E. Carey

Ash Britt
Issues: DIS ENV
Rep By: Steven E. Carey, Michael K. Wyrick

Caremark Rx, Inc.
Issues: HCR MMM PHA

Harrah's Entertainment, Inc.
Issues: GAM
Rep By: Steven E. Carey, Nance Guenther-Peterson, Heidi Hanson, Brad Traverse

Healthsouth Corp.
Issues: HCR
Rep By: Gary F. Capistrant, Steven E. Carey, Nance Guenther-Peterson, Heidi Hanson, Brad Traverse

Home Access Health
Issues: HCR
Rep By: Gary F. Capistrant, Nance Guenther-Peterson, Heidi Hanson, Brad Traverse

Integrated Health Services, Inc.
Issues: HCR
Rep By: Gary F. Capistrant, Steven E. Carey, Nance Guenther-Peterson, Heidi Hanson, Brad Traverse

IVAX Corp.
Issues: PHA
Rep By: Gary F. Capistrant

JRL Enterprises
Issues: EDU
Rep By: Steven E. Carey, Heidi Hanson

Kennedy Krieger Institute

Latino Strategies

Nat'l Ass'n of Community Health Centers
Issues: HCR MMM
Rep By: Gary F. Capistrant, Steven E. Carey, Heidi Hanson, Brad Traverse

Palm Beach, Florida, County of
Issues: CAW ECN HOU TRA
Rep By: Heidi Hanson

UBS Warburg
Issues: HCR
Rep By: Gary F. Capistrant, Steven E. Carey, Brad Traverse

The Udwin Group

2121 K St. NW
Suite 800
Washington, DC 20037
Tel: (202)261-6565
Fax: (202)466-7745
Registered: LDA
E-mail: gudwin@aol.com

Provides government and news media relations.

DC-Area Employees Representing Listed Clients

UDWIN, Gerald E., President

Clients

Verizon Communications
Issues: TEC
Rep By: Gerald E. Udwin

Ungaretti & Harris

1500 K St. NW
Suite 250
Washington, DC 20005-1714
Tel: (202)639-7500
Fax: (202)639-7505
Registered: LDA
Web: www.uhlaw.com
E-mail: infor@uhlaw.com

A full-service law firm headquartered in Chicago, IL.

DC-Area Employees Representing Listed Clients

BUCHER, Sheri, Legislative Director
CARI, Jr., Joseph A., Partner
FABERMAN, Edward P., Partner
FAULK, Page, Associate
FAUST, Michelle M., Associate
KONIGSBERG, Chuck, Partner
PERLMAN, Spencer, Legislative Affairs Manager
SCHULMAN, Joseph R., Legislative Counsel

Clients

Air Carrier Ass'n of America
Issues: AVI
Rep By: Edward P. Faberman, Page Faulk, Michelle M. Faust

Air Tran Airways
Issues: AVI
Rep By: Edward P. Faberman, Page Faulk, Michelle M. Faust

Akron-Canton Airport
Issues: AVI
Rep By: Edward P. Faberman

Allegiance Healthcare Corp.
Issues: MAN
Rep By: Sheri Bucher, Joseph A. Cari, Jr., Michelle M. Faust, Spencer Perlman

Cardinal Health Inc.
Issues: HCR
Rep By: Sheri Bucher, Page Faulk, Chuck Konigsberg, Spencer Perlman, Joseph R. Schulman

Colgan Air, Inc.
Issues: AVI
Rep By: Edward P. Faberman

Computer Communications Industry of America
Issues: SMB
Rep By: Sheri Bucher, Joseph A. Cari, Jr.

ComScore
Issues: SMB
Rep By: Joseph A. Cari, Jr.

Frontier Airlines
Rep By: Edward P. Faberman, Page Faulk, Michelle M. Faust

Frontier Communications Corp.
Issues: SMB

Lincoln Airport
Issues: RES
Rep By: Edward P. Faberman

Medical Research Laboratories
Issues: RES
Rep By: Sheri Bucher, Spencer Perlman

Premier Institute
Issues: ENV
Rep By: Joseph A. Cari, Jr.

Radius, The Global Travel Co.
Issues: AVI
Rep By: Edward P. Faberman, Michelle M. Faust

Stepan Co.
Rep By: Joseph A. Cari, Jr., Michelle M. Faust

United Defense, L.P.
Issues: GOV
Rep By: Sheri Bucher, Joseph A. Cari, Jr., Page Faulk, Chuck Konigsberg

USLaw.com

8555 16th St.
Suite 500
Silver Spring, MD 20910
Web: www.uslaw.com
Tel: (301)589-8100

DC-Area Employees Representing Listed Clients
KOTLOVE, Douglas, Director, Public Relations

Valanzano & Associates

601 13th St. NW
Suite 900 S.
Washington, DC 20005
Tel: (703)759-1966
Fax: (703)759-5101
Registered: LDA

DC-Area Employees Representing Listed Clients
VALANZANO, Anthony, President

Clients

American Council of Life Insurers
Issues: BAN INS TAX
Rep By: Anthony Valanzano

American Internat'l Group, Inc.
Issues: BAN ENV FIN INS RET TAX TRD
Rep By: Anthony Valanzano

American Land Title Ass'n
Issues: BAN
Rep By: Anthony Valanzano

Appraisal Institute
Issues: FIN HOU RES
Rep By: Anthony Valanzano

The Chubb Corp.
Issues: BAN CPI DIS ENV TAX TOB TRD
Rep By: Anthony Valanzano

The Council of Insurance Agents & Brokers
Issues: BAN DIS TAX
Rep By: Anthony Valanzano

Manufactured Housing Ass'n for Regulatory Reform
Issues: HOU
Rep By: Anthony Valanzano

Valente Lopatin & Schulze

Hamilton Square
600 14th St. NW, Fifth Floor
Washington, DC 20005
Tel: (202)783-1980
Fax: (202)783-1918
Registered: LDA
E-mail: VLandS@aol.com
A government affairs firm.

DC-Area Employees Representing Listed Clients
FEENEY, Susan
LOPATIN, Alan G., Principal
SCHULZE, Jr., Richard T., Principal
VALENTE, Claudia Barker
VALENTE, III, Mark, Principal

Clients

Alliance for Special Needs Children
Rep By: Alan G. Lopatin, Richard T. Schulze, Jr., Mark Valente, III

American Collectors Ass'n
Issues: BNK
Rep By: Alan G. Lopatin

Aventis Behring
Issues: HCR
Rep By: Richard T. Schulze, Jr.

Center for Disease Detection
Rep By: Mark Valente, III

Cohn & Wolfe
Rep By: Richard T. Schulze, Jr., Mark Valente, III

Columbus Educational Services
Rep By: Alan G. Lopatin, Richard T. Schulze, Jr., Mark Valente, III

Columbus Medical Services
Rep By: Alan G. Lopatin, Richard T. Schulze, Jr., Mark Valente, III

Dalton & Dalton P.C.
Issues: BUD
Rep By: Alan G. Lopatin, Richard T. Schulze, Jr., Mark Valente, III

Devon Management Group Inc.
Rep By: Mark Valente, III

FBV Group
Rep By: Richard T. Schulze, Jr., Claudia Barker Valente, Mark Valente, III

Fund for American Opportunity PAC
Rep By: Claudia Barker Valente, Mark Valente, III

Internat'l Tax and Investment Center
Rep By: Richard T. Schulze, Jr., Mark Valente, III

Kaplan Companies, Inc.
Rep By: Alan G. Lopatin

Keating Development Corp.
Rep By: Mark Valente, III

Keating Technologies Inc.
Rep By: Susan Feeney, Richard T. Schulze, Jr., Mark Valente, III

Kelly Anderson & Associates
Rep By: Mark Valente, III

The LTV Corp.
Issues: HCR
Rep By: Richard T. Schulze, Jr., Mark Valente, III

Mediware Information Systems, Inc.
Rep By: Richard T. Schulze, Jr., Mark Valente, III

Nat'l and Community Service Coalition
Rep By: Alan G. Lopatin

Nat'l Ass'n of Retired and Senior Volunteer Program Directors
Issues: BUD GOV
Rep By: Alan G. Lopatin

Nat'l Ass'n of Retired Federal Employees
Issues: BUD HCR RET
Rep By: Alan G. Lopatin

Nat'l Ass'n of Senior Companion Project Directors
Rep By: Alan G. Lopatin

Nat'l Ass'n of Thrift Savings Plan Participants
Rep By: Alan G. Lopatin, Richard T. Schulze, Jr., Mark Valente, III

Nat'l Center for Family Literacy
Issues: BUD EDU
Rep By: Alan G. Lopatin

Nat'l Center for Learning Disabilities (NCLD)
Rep By: Alan G. Lopatin

Nat'l Citizens Coalition for Nursing Home Reform

Nat'l Education Ass'n of the U.S.
Rep By: Alan G. Lopatin

Nat'l Head Start Ass'n
Issues: BUD EDU
Rep By: Alan G. Lopatin

Nat'l Italian American Foundation
Rep By: Mark Valente, III

North American Coal
Rep By: Mark Valente, III

O'Neill Properties Group
Rep By: Mark Valente, III

Orkand Corp.
Issues: BUD
Rep By: Alan G. Lopatin, Richard T. Schulze, Jr., Mark Valente, III

OSHA Reform Coalition
Rep By: Richard T. Schulze, Jr.

Pennsylvania Economic Development Financing Authorities
Rep By: Mark Valente, III

Pepper Hamilton LLP
Rep By: Richard T. Schulze, Jr., Mark Valente, III

PriceWaterhouseCoopers
Rep By: Mark Valente, III

S-PAC
Rep By: Richard T. Schulze, Jr.

System & Computer Technology Corp.
Rep By: Susan Feeney, Richard T. Schulze, Jr., Mark Valente, III

United Nations Development Programme
Rep By: Alan G. Lopatin, Richard T. Schulze, Jr., Mark Valente, III

United Payors and United Providers
Issues: HCR
Rep By: Alan G. Lopatin, Richard T. Schulze, Jr., Mark Valente, III

Valis Associates

1700 Pennsylvania Ave. NW
Suite 950
Washington, DC 20006
Tel: (202)393-5055
Fax: (202)393-0120
Registered: LDA
E-mail: valis@erols.com
A government relations and public affairs consulting firm.

DC-Area Employees Representing Listed Clients
CONTI, Jennifer, Senior Account Exec.
HUDSON, Dana W., Account Exec.
SCHAEFER, Hon. Dan, Senior Legislative Advisor
SCHULZE, Hon. Richard T., Senior Legislative Director
TOLSON, Todd, Account Executive
VALIS, Wayne H., President

Clients

American Bakers Ass'n
Issues: CAW ENV FOO LBR TRD
Rep By: Todd Tolson, Wayne H. Valis

American Consulting Engineers Council
Issues: ENV GOV LBR TOR
Rep By: Jennifer Conti, Hon. Richard T. Schulze, Todd Tolson, Wayne H. Valis

Ass'n for the Suppliers of Printing and Publishing Technology
Issues: ENV GOV TRD
Rep By: Hon. Richard T. Schulze, Todd Tolson, Wayne H. Valis

Ass'n of American Railroads
Issues: TRA
Rep By: Jennifer Conti, Hon. Dan Schaefer, Hon. Richard T. Schulze

CH2M Hill
Issues: TAX
Rep By: Jennifer Conti, Hon. Dan Schaefer, Hon. Richard T. Schulze, Wayne H. Valis

Citizens for Civil Justice Reform
Issues: GOV TOR
Rep By: Dana W. Hudson, Hon. Richard T. Schulze, Wayne H. Valis

Coalition for Open Markets and Expanded Trade
Issues: TRD
Rep By: Dana W. Hudson, Hon. Richard T. Schulze, Wayne H. Valis

Dairyland Power Cooperative
Issues: WAS
Rep By: Hon. Richard T. Schulze, Wayne H. Valis

The Doctors' Co.
Issues: GOV HCR
Rep By: Dana W. Hudson, Hon. Richard T. Schulze, Wayne H. Valis

Environmental Action Group
Issues: ENV GOV
Rep By: Hon. Richard T. Schulze, Todd Tolson, Wayne H. Valis

Exxon Mobil Corp.
Issues: CSP ENG GOV TAX TOR TRD
Rep By: Dana W. Hudson, Hon. Dan Schaefer, Hon. Richard T. Schulze, Wayne H. Valis

Grocery Manufacturers of America
Issues: BUD FOO TRD
Rep By: Hon. Dan Schaefer, Hon. Richard T. Schulze, Todd Tolson, Wayne H. Valis

Joint Southeast Public Improvement Council
Issues: TRA
Rep By: Jennifer Conti, Hon. Dan Schaefer, Wayne H. Valis

Kitchen Cabinet Manufacturers Ass'n
Issues: ENV TRD
Rep By: Todd Tolson, Wayne H. Valis

Nat'l Ass'n of Wholesaler-Distributors
Issues: TOR TRD
Rep By: Wayne H. Valis

New Majority Soc.
Issues: GOV
Rep By: Jennifer Conti, Dana W. Hudson, Hon. Richard T. Schulze

Norfolk Southern Corp.
Issues: RRR TRA
Rep By: Jennifer Conti, Hon. Richard T. Schulze, Wayne H. Valis

NPES, The Ass'n for Suppliers of Printing, Publishing, and Converting Technologies
Issues: CSP ENV TRD
Rep By: Hon. Richard T. Schulze, Todd Tolson, Wayne H. Valis

Regulatory Improvement Council
Issues: ENV GOV
Rep By: Todd Tolson, Wayne H. Valis

Renewable Fuels Ass'n
Issues: FUE
Rep By: Hon. Dan Schaefer, Hon. Richard T. Schulze, Todd Tolson, Wayne H. Valis

Soc. of the Plastics Industry
Issues: CAW ENV TOR
Rep By: Todd Tolson, Wayne H. Valis

Tax Action Group
Issues: TAX
Rep By: Hon. Richard T. Schulze, Todd Tolson, Wayne H. Valis

Telecommunications Industry Ass'n
Issues: TEC TRD
Rep By: Jennifer Conti, Hon. Richard T. Schulze, Wayne H. Valis

Trade Ass'n Liaison Council
Issues: GOV
Rep By: Dana W. Hudson, Wayne H. Valis

Transportation Reform Alliance
Issues: TRA
Rep By: Jennifer Conti, Hon. Richard T. Schulze, Wayne H. Valis

Van Fleet, Inc.

12809 Mill Meadow Ct.
Fairfax, VA 22033-3139
Tel: (703)802-2398
Fax: (703)802-9093
Registered: LDA, FARA
E-mail: frankc378@aol.com

DC-Area Employees Representing Listed Clients
VAN FLEET, Frank C., President

Clients

Calibre Corp.
Rep By: Frank C. Van Fleet

Crosby Internat'l
Rep By: Frank C. Van Fleet

The Van Fleet-Meredith Group

499 S. Capitol St. SW
Suite 520
Washington, DC 20003
Tel: (202)554-3714
Fax: (202)479-4657
Registered: LDA

DC-Area Employees Representing Listed Clients
MEREDITH, M. Bruce, Managing Partner
PAYETTE, Paul F., Partner
VAN FLEET, Townsend A., President

Clients

American Gas Ass'n
Issues: DEF
Rep By: M. Bruce Meredith, Paul F. Payette, Townsend A. Van Fleet

Donlee Technologies, Inc.
Issues: DEF
Rep By: M. Bruce Meredith, Paul F. Payette, Townsend A. Van Fleet

Lockheed Martin Corp.
Issues: DEF
Rep By: M. Bruce Meredith, Paul F. Payette, Townsend A. Van Fleet

Mantech Corp.
Issues: DEF
Rep By: M. Bruce Meredith, Paul F. Payette, Townsend A. Van Fleet

Miltope Corp.
Issues: DEF
Rep By: M. Bruce Meredith, Paul F. Payette, Townsend A. Van Fleet

PinPoint Systems Internat'l, LLC
Issues: DEF
Rep By: M. Bruce Meredith, Paul F. Payette, Townsend A. Van Fleet

United Defense, L.P.
Issues: DEF
Rep By: M. Bruce Meredith, Paul F. Payette, Townsend A. Van Fleet

Van Ness Feldman, P.C.

1050 Thomas Jefferson St. NW
Seventh Floor
Washington, DC 20007
Tel: (202)298-1800
Fax: (202)338-2416
Registered: LDA, FARA
Web: www.vnf.com
E-mail: vnf@vnf.com
A law firm providing legal and government policy counsel on energy, environmental, technology development, natural resources and tax issues.

Political Action Committee
Van Ness Feldman, P.C. Political Action Committee
1050 Thomas Jefferson St. NW
Seventh Floor
Washington, DC 20007
Tel: (202)298-1930
Fax: (202)338-2416
Contact: Thomas C. Roberts

DC-Area Employees Representing Listed Clients
ADDISON, Angela M., Associate
AGNEW, Richard A.
ANDERSON, Pamela Jo, Member
ARAUJO, Jaeleen K., Associate
ART, Andrew B., Associate
BACHMAN, Gary D., Member
BACON, Suzanne C., Associate Director, Gov't Issues
BENEKE, Patricia J., Member
BERNSTEIN, Mitch H., Member
BLEICHFELD, Howard S., Of Counsel
BOYD, Rebecca J., Associate
BUCHOVECKY, John J., Member
BURNES, Jr., John, Member
CHRISTOPH FRIEDMAN, Jessica, Associate
DANISH, Kyle W., Associate
DIETZ, Paula J., Associate Director, Governmental Issues
FELDMAN, Howard J., Member
FICHTNER, Shelley, Associate Director, Gov't Issues
FIDLER, Shelley N., Principal
FLEMING, Britt S., Associate
FLYNN, Kevin W., Associate
FOTIS, Stephen C., Member
GODLEY, Patricia Fry, Member
GOLDSTEIN, Nick, Associate
HICKEY, John A., Associate
HOWE, Shippen, Of Counsel
KALEN, Sam, Of Counsel
KORMAN, Paul I., Member
KOZLOWSKI, Richard G., Of Counsel
MCNALLY, Nancy Macan, Principal
MINTZ, Alan L., Member
MOFFATT, J. Curtis, Member
MOORE, Margaret A., Member
MOORE, Susan A., Associate
NELSON, Joseph B., Associate
NOGUEIRA, Ricardo, Associate
NORDHAUS, Robert, Member
PENNA, Richard A., Member
PRESS, Daniel S., Member
REESE, Evan, Associate
RICH, J. Curtis, Of Counsel
RICHARDSON, Julie R., Member
RICHARDSON, Steven, Member
ROBERTS, Thomas C., Member
RYAN, Cheryl Feik, Member
RYAN, Jay T., Associate
SENSIBA, Charles R., Associate
SHAPIRO, Howard Eliot, Member
SIMON, Jonathon D., Associate
SWIGER, Michael A., Member
SZABO, Robert G., Member
WOODKA, Janet L., Associate
YAFFE, David P., Member
YAMAGATA, Ben, Member
ZIMMETT, Brian, Associate
ZOLET, Theresa L., Member

Clients

Alaska North Slope LNG Project
Issues: FUE NAT
Rep By: Patricia Fry Godley, Alan L. Mintz, J. Curtis Moffatt, Thomas C. Roberts, Theresa L. Zolet

American Chemistry Council
Issues: TRA
Rep By: Margaret A. Moore, Thomas C. Roberts, Robert G. Szabo

American Electric Power Co.
Issues: ENG ENV
Rep By: Stephen C. Fotis

Arctic Slope Regional Corp.
Issues: BUD ENV FUE IND NAT RES TAX
Rep By: Howard J. Feldman, Alan L. Mintz

Barron Collier Co.
Issues: ENV NAT RES
Rep By: Alan L. Mintz

Bellingham, Washington, City of
Issues: ENG ENV
Rep By: Richard A. Agnew

Blackfeet Tribe of Montana
Issues: ENG ENV GOV IND NAT
Rep By: Daniel S. Press, J. Curtis Rich, Steven Richardson

Chelan County Public Utility District
Issues: ENV NAT UTI
Rep By: Robert Nordhaus

Cheyenne River Sioux Tribe
Issues: IND
Rep By: Daniel S. Press

Coal Utilization Research Council
Issues: BUD ENG ENV SCI
Rep By: Paula J. Dietz, Ben Yamagata

Consumers United for Rail Equity
Issues: BUD RRR TRA
Rep By: Nancy Macan McNally, Robert G. Szabo

Council for Conservation and Reinvestment of OCS Revenue
Issues: BUD ENG ENV FUE NAT
Rep By: Thomas C. Roberts, Robert G. Szabo

Delta Wetlands Project
Issues: IND NAT
Rep By: Joseph B. Nelson, Thomas C. Roberts, Robert G. Szabo

Doyon, Ltd.
Rep By: Alan L. Mintz

The Electric Vehicle Ass'n of the Americas (EVAA)
Issues: CAW ENG ENV SCI TAX TRA
Rep By: Britt S. Fleming, Ben Yamagata

Foothills Pipe Lines (Yukon), Ltd.
Issues: FUE
Rep By: J. Curtis Moffatt, Thomas C. Roberts

Geothermal Resources Ass'n
Issues: ENG TAX
Rep By: Howard J. Feldman

Hawaiian Electric Co.
Issues: ENG UTI
Rep By: Thomas C. Roberts

Intertribal Monitoring Ass'n on Indian Trust Funds
Issues: IND
Rep By: Daniel S. Press

Iowa, Dept. of Natural Resources of State of
Issues: AGR NAT
Rep By: Patricia J. Beneke

Koncor Forest Products Co.
Issues: NAT TRD
Rep By: Alan L. Mintz

Large Public Power Council
Issues: CAW ENV NAT TAX UTI WAS
Rep By: Howard J. Feldman, Stephen C. Fotis, Nancy Macan McNally, Robert Nordhaus

Mack Trucks, Inc.
Issues: CAW CSP ENG ENV SCI TAX
Rep By: Howard J. Feldman, Nancy Macan McNally, Richard A. Penna

McKesson Corp.
Issues: HCR MED MMM PHA TAX TRA
Rep By: Howard J. Feldman, Nancy Macan McNally

Methanex Inc.
Issues: CAW FUE
Rep By: Howard S. Bleichfeld, Thomas C. Roberts

Nat'l Endangered Species Act Reform Coalition
Issues: BUD ENV NAT RES
Rep By: Nancy Macan McNally, Joseph B. Nelson, J. Curtis Rich, Robert G. Szabo

Nat'l Rural Electric Cooperative Ass'n
Issues: ENG ENV NAT TAX
Rep By: J. Curtis Rich

The Nat'l Wetlands Coalition
Issues: CAW ENV NAT
Rep By: Howard S. Bleichfeld, Paula J. Dietz, Robert G. Szabo

Newport News, Virginia, City of
Issues: ENV IND
Rep By: Richard G. Kozlowski, Thomas C. Roberts

North Slope Borough, Alaska
Issues: BUD ECN EDU ENG ENV GOV HCR HOU IND MAR NAT POS RES TAX
Rep By: Alan L. Mintz

Petro Star, Inc.
Issues: DEF ENG ENV FUE RES SMB TAX
Rep By: Howard J. Feldman, Alan L. Mintz, Thomas C. Roberts, Jonathon D. Simon

Princess Tours
Issues: ENV RES
Rep By: Richard A. Agnew, Howard J. Feldman

Public Generating Pool
Issues: ENV NAT UTI
Rep By: Gary D. Bachman, Robert Nordhaus

Sacramento Municipal Utility District
Issues: ENG UTI
Rep By: Suzanne C. Bacon, Michael A. Swiger

Sealaska Corp.
Issues: BUD ENV IND NAT RES TAX
Rep By: Howard S. Bleichfeld, Rebecca J. Boyd, Howard J. Feldman, Alan L. Mintz, Thomas C. Roberts

Seattle City Light
Issues: ENG TAX UTI
Rep By: Richard A. Agnew

Sisters of Charity of Leavenworth Health Services
Issues: HCR MED MMM
Rep By: J. Curtis Rich

Sonoma County Water Agency
Issues: BUD
Rep By: Nancy Macan McNally, Robert G. Szabo

Tacoma, Washington, City of
Issues: ENG ENV NAT UTI
Rep By: Gary D. Bachman, Thomas C. Roberts, Michael A. Swiger

Tecumseh Products Co.
Issues: CAW ENV MAN
Rep By: Nancy Macan McNally, Richard A. Penna

Three Affiliated Tribes of Fort Berthold Reservation
Issues: BUD ENV IND NAT
Rep By: Patricia J. Beneke, Daniel S. Press, J. Curtis Rich, Steven Richardson

Toyota Motor Manufacturing North America
Issues: CAW ENV MAN
Rep By: Richard A. Penna, Robert G. Szabo

Toyota Motor North America, U.S.A., Inc.
Issues: CAW CSP ENG SCI
Rep By: Howard J. Feldman, Richard A. Penna, Robert G. Szabo

TransAlta Corp.
Issues: ENG ENV
Rep By: Richard A. Agnew

Van Scoyoc Associates, Inc.

1420 New York Ave. NW
Suite 1050
Washington, DC 20005
Tel: (202)638-1950
Fax: (202)638-7714
Registered: LDA, FARA

A legislative consulting firm.

DC-Area Employees Representing Listed Clients

ADCOCK, Michael W.
ANDERSON, Jason
BOBBITT, Jane
BOOTH, Carri, Legislative Assistant
CARTER, W. Minor, Of Counsel
COLE, Ray, Associate V. President
CRANE, Steve E., Legislative Associate
DOHONEY, James
ESTELL, Anita R., V. President
FULLER, Carolyn, V. President
GRIMM, Paul, V. President
HAWLEY, Buzz, Legislative Counsel
IARROBINO, Paul
JOHNSON, Kimberly, Legislative Counsel
KELLY, Kevin F., V. President
KLATT, III, Victor F.
KNISELY, Evan, Legislative Assistant
KNISELY, Robert L.
KOHLMOOS, James W., V. President
LANKFORD, Thomas L., V. President
MALOW, Jessica, Legislative Assistant
MORRISON, Keith, Special Assistant to the President, Legislative Assistant
PALMER, Steven O., V. President
PORTERFIELD, Lendell, Economist and Legislative Analyst
RUHE, Shirley L., Of Counsel
SCHOONMAKER, Jan, V. President
SCHULKEN, Chad, Legislative Assistant
SPEAR, Scott
STONE, John C. "Jay", V. President
THOMSON, Jasper, Legislative Assistant
TRINCA, Jeffrey S., V. President
VAN SCOYOC, H. Stewart, President
WELLS, Noreene, Program Assistant

Clients

Abrams & Co. Publishers Inc.
Issues: BUD EDU
Rep By: Victor F. Klatt, III, James W. Kohlmoos, H. Stewart Van Scoyoc

Alabama, Department of Transportation of the State of
Issues: BUD GOV ROD TRA
Rep By: Ray Cole, H. Stewart Van Scoyoc

Alabama Water and Wastewater Institute, Inc.
Issues: BUD
Rep By: Ray Cole, H. Stewart Van Scoyoc

Alameda-Contra Costa Transit District
Issues: BUD TRA
Rep By: Steven O. Palmer, Chad Schulken, H. Stewart Van Scoyoc

Alcoa Inc.
Issues: DEF
Rep By: Paul Grimm, Buzz Hawley, Thomas L. Lankford, H. Stewart Van Scoyoc

American Forest & Paper Ass'n
Issues: ENV NAT TAX
Rep By: John C. "Jay" Stone, Jeffrey S. Trinca, H. Stewart Van Scoyoc

American Library Ass'n
Issues: BUD EDU MIA
Rep By: Robert L. Knisely, James W. Kohlmoos, H. Stewart Van Scoyoc, Noreene Wells

American Psychological Ass'n
Issues: BUD HCR MED
Rep By: Evan Knisely, Robert L. Knisely, H. Stewart Van Scoyoc

Anheuser-Busch Cos., Inc.
Issues: ADV ALC ART MAN TAX
Rep By: Jeffrey S. Trinca, H. Stewart Van Scoyoc

APG Army Alliance
Issues: BUD DEF EDU TRA
Rep By: Steve E. Crane, Kevin F. Kelly, Thomas L. Lankford

Archimedes Technology Group
Issues: ENG SCI WAS
Rep By: Paul Grimm, Buzz Hawley, Paul Iarrobino, John C. "Jay" Stone, H. Stewart Van Scoyoc

Arista Knowledge Systems, Inc.
Issues: BUD EDU SCI
Rep By: Steve E. Crane, Kevin F. Kelly, H. Stewart Van Scoyoc

Ass'n of American Railroads
Issues: RRR
Rep By: Steven O. Palmer, H. Stewart Van Scoyoc

Ass'n of Schools of Public Health
Issues: BUD EDU HCR MED
Rep By: Steve E. Crane, Kevin F. Kelly, Evan Knisely, H. Stewart Van Scoyoc

Ass'n of Universities for Research in Astronomy, Inc.
Issues: BUD EDU TRD
Rep By: Steve E. Crane, Kevin F. Kelly, H. Stewart Van Scoyoc

The Audubon Institute
Issues: BUD GOV SCI
Rep By: Jan Schoonmaker, H. Stewart Van Scoyoc

Baltimore, Maryland, City of
Issues: ALC BUD EDU HOU TRA URB
Rep By: Steve E. Crane, Anita R. Estell, Kimberly Johnson, Kevin F. Kelly

Bethesda Academy for the Performing Arts
Issues: BUD
Rep By: Steve E. Crane, Kevin F. Kelly, H. Stewart Van Scoyoc

Board on Human Sciences
Issues: BUD EDU HCR SCI
Rep By: Steve E. Crane, Kevin F. Kelly, Jasper Thomson, H. Stewart Van Scoyoc

Brain Trauma Foundation
Issues: BUD HCR TRA
Rep By: Ray Cole, H. Stewart Van Scoyoc

Bristol-Myers Squibb Co.
Issues: BUD HCR
Rep By: Anita R. Estell, Kimberly Johnson, H. Stewart Van Scoyoc

British Trade and Commerce Bank
Issues: BAN
Rep By: Buzz Hawley, John C. "Jay" Stone, H. Stewart Van Scoyoc

Burns and Roe Enterprises, Inc.
Issues: DEF ENG
Rep By: Paul Grimm, Buzz Hawley, H. Stewart Van Scoyoc

Calspan University of Buffalo Research Center
Issues: AVI BUD ROD
Rep By: Steven O. Palmer, Chad Schulken, H. Stewart Van Scoyoc

Charter Schools Development Corp.
Issues: BUD EDU
Rep By: Victor F. Klatt, III, H. Stewart Van Scoyoc

Chesapeake Bay Foundation
Issues: BUD
Rep By: Kevin F. Kelly, Jasper Thomson, H. Stewart Van Scoyoc

Chicago State University
Issues: BUD EDU
Rep By: Anita R. Estell, Kimberly Johnson, H. Stewart Van Scoyoc

ChoicePoint
Issues: BNK

Clemson University
Issues: BUD EDU
Rep By: Paul Grimm, Steven O. Palmer, Chad Schulken, H. Stewart Van Scoyoc

Coalition of EPSCoR States
Issues: BUD
Rep By: Carolyn Fuller, Jan Schoonmaker, H. Stewart Van Scoyoc

The Colonial Williamsburg Foundation

Communications Training Analysis Corp. (C-TAC)
Issues: DEF ENG GOV
Rep By: Paul Grimm, Buzz Hawley, H. Stewart Van Scoyoc

Computer Data Systems, Inc.
Issues: CPI EDU
Rep By: Steve E. Crane, Kevin F. Kelly, H. Stewart Van Scoyoc

Computer Sciences Corp.
Issues: BUD CPI
Rep By: Steve E. Crane, Kevin F. Kelly, Jeffrey S. Trinca, H. Stewart Van Scoyoc

Davison Transport, Inc.
Issues: BUD EDU TRA
Rep By: John C. "Jay" Stone, H. Stewart Van Scoyoc

DGME Fairness Initiative
Issues: BUD HCR MMM
Rep By: Michael W. Adcock, Evan Knisely, Scott Spear, H. Stewart Van Scoyoc

Duke Solutions
Issues: ENG
Rep By: Paul Grimm

Education Leaders Council
Rep By: Victor F. Klatt, III

Fargo-Cass County Development Corp.
Issues: ECN
Rep By: Evan Knisely, H. Stewart Van Scoyoc

Federal Home Loan Bank of San Francisco
Issues: BAN BUD
Rep By: Kevin F. Kelly

Federation of State Humanities Councils
Issues: ART
Rep By: Carolyn Fuller, H. Stewart Van Scoyoc

FedEx Corp.
Issues: AVI BUD
Rep By: Ray Cole, Chad Schulken, H. Stewart Van Scoyoc

FMC Corp.
Issues: ENV
Rep By: H. Stewart Van Scoyoc

Glankler Brown, PLLC
Issues: AVI BUD TRA
Rep By: Jason Anderson, Ray Cole, Chad Schulken, H. Stewart Van Scoyoc

Great Cities' Universities
Issues: EDU URB
Rep By: Carolyn Fuller, H. Stewart Van Scoyoc

Greater New Orleans Expressway Commission
Issues: BUD DIS TRA
Rep By: Buzz Hawley, Paul Iarrobino, John C. "Jay" Stone, H. Stewart Van Scoyoc

Hughes Space & Communications Co.
Issues: AVI
Rep By: Steven O. Palmer, Chad Schulken, H. Stewart Van Scoyoc

Insight Technology, Inc.
Issues: BUD DEF SCI
Rep By: Thomas L. Lankford, H. Stewart Van Scoyoc

Intel Corp.
Issues: ENV
Rep By: H. Stewart Van Scoyoc

Internat'l Karate Federation
Rep By: Jeffrey S. Trinca

Internat'l Traditional Karate Federation
Issues: SPO
Rep By: Jeffrey S. Trinca, H. Stewart Van Scoyoc

Jackson State University
Issues: BUD EDU
Rep By: Anita R. Estell, Kimberly Johnson, H. Stewart Van Scoyoc

Jefferson County Commission
Issues: BUD
Rep By: Ray Cole, Chad Schulken, H. Stewart Van Scoyoc

Johns Hopkins School of Hygiene and Public Health
Issues: BUD MED
Rep By: Steve E. Crane, Kevin F. Kelly, H. Stewart Van Scoyoc

Johns Hopkins University-Applied Physics Lab
Issues: BUD
Rep By: Steve E. Crane, Kevin F. Kelly, Evan Knisely, H. Stewart Van Scoyoc

Johnson Controls, Inc.
Issues: BUD DEF ENG
Rep By: Paul Grimm, Buzz Hawley, H. Stewart Van Scoyoc

Krebs, LaSalle, LeMieux Consultants, Inc.
Issues: DIS
Rep By: Buzz Hawley, John C. "Jay" Stone, H. Stewart Van Scoyoc

Lehigh University
Issues: BUD DEF EDU TRA
Rep By: Steve E. Crane, Kevin F. Kelly, H. Stewart Van Scoyoc

Lockheed Martin Corp.
Issues: TEC
Rep By: H. Stewart Van Scoyoc

Lockheed Martin Government Electronics Systems
Issues: BUD DEF
Rep By: Thomas L. Lankford, H. Stewart Van Scoyoc

Lockheed Martin Hanford
Issues: ENG WAS
Rep By: Paul Grimm, Buzz Hawley, H. Stewart Van Scoyoc

Lockheed Martin Naval Electronics Surveillance Systems
Issues: BUD DEF
Rep By: Thomas L. Lankford, H. Stewart Van Scoyoc

Lockheed Martin Venture Star
Issues: AER BUD
Rep By: Kevin F. Kelly, Jessica Malow, Jasper Thomson, H. Stewart Van Scoyoc

Los Angeles County Metropolitan Transportation Authority
Issues: BUD TRA
Rep By: Ray Cole, H. Stewart Van Scoyoc

Memphis-Shelby County Airport Authority

Mentis Sciences Inc.
Issues: BUD DEF
Rep By: Thomas L. Lankford, H. Stewart Van Scoyoc

MilTec
Issues: BUD DEF
Rep By: Ray Cole, H. Stewart Van Scoyoc

Montana State University
Issues: BUD EDU
Rep By: Carri Booth, Carolyn Fuller, H. Stewart Van Scoyoc

Montgomery Airport Authority
Issues: AVI BUD ENV TRA
Rep By: Ray Cole, Chad Schulken, H. Stewart Van Scoyoc

Montgomery, Alabama, Chamber of Commerce of
Issues: BUD ECN ROD TRA URB
Rep By: Ray Cole, H. Stewart Van Scoyoc

Morgan State University
Issues: BUD EDU SCI TRA
Rep By: Steve E. Crane, Kevin F. Kelly, H. Stewart Van Scoyoc

Mount Sinai School of Medicine
Issues: BUD EDU HCR MED VET
Rep By: Steve E. Crane, Kevin F. Kelly, H. Stewart Van Scoyoc

NASA Aeronautics Support Team
Issues: AER AVI BUD SCI
Rep By: Steve E. Crane, Kevin F. Kelly, Steven O. Palmer, Chad Schulken, Jasper Thomson, H. Stewart Van Scoyoc

Nat'l Air Traffic Controllers Ass'n
Issues: AVI BUD
Rep By: Steven O. Palmer, Chad Schulken, H. Stewart Van Scoyoc

Nat'l Aircraft Resale Ass'n

Nat'l Asphalt Pavement Ass'n
Issues: BUD ROD
Rep By: Steven O. Palmer, Chad Schulken, H. Stewart Van Scoyoc

Nat'l Ass'n for Equal Opportunity in Higher Education
Issues: BUD EDU
Rep By: Steve E. Crane, Anita R. Estell, Kevin F. Kelly, H. Stewart Van Scoyoc

Nat'l Ass'n of Enrolled Agents
Issues: TAX
Rep By: Jeffrey S. Trinca, H. Stewart Van Scoyoc

Nat'l Ass'n of Foster Grandparent Program Directors
Issues: BUD LBR RET
Rep By: Evan Knisely, Robert L. Knisely, H. Stewart Van Scoyoc

Nat'l Ass'n of Independent Colleges and Universities
Issues: EDU
Rep By: H. Stewart Van Scoyoc

Nat'l Ass'n of Water Companies
Issues: CAW ENV TAX
Rep By: Jeffrey S. Trinca, H. Stewart Van Scoyoc

Nat'l Commission on Correctional Health Care
Issues: HCR
Rep By: Anita R. Estell, H. Stewart Van Scoyoc

Nat'l Environmental Development Ass'ns State & Federal Environmental Responsibility Project
Issues: ADV CAW ENV WAS
Rep By: H. Stewart Van Scoyoc

Nat'l Environmental Trust
Issues: CAW ENV
Rep By: H. Stewart Van Scoyoc

Nat'l Institute for Water Resources
Issues: BUD NAT
Rep By: Jan Schoonmaker, H. Stewart Van Scoyoc

The Nat'l Space Grant Alliance
Issues: AER BUD SCI
Rep By: Carri Booth, Carolyn Fuller, H. Stewart Van Scoyoc

New American School
Issues: BUD EDU
Rep By: Victor F. Klatt, III, Robert L. Knisely, H. Stewart Van Scoyoc

Ochsner Medical Institutions
Issues: BUD MED
Rep By: Jan Schoonmaker, H. Stewart Van Scoyoc

Oldcastle Materials Group
Issues: ROD
Rep By: Steven O. Palmer, H. Stewart Van Scoyoc

Orasure Technologies
Issues: BUD MED
Rep By: Steve E. Crane, Kevin F. Kelly, H. Stewart Van Scoyoc

Patient Access to Transplantation (PAT) Coalition
Issues: BUD HCR MMM
Rep By: Evan Knisely, H. Stewart Van Scoyoc

Quality Research

Recording for the Blind and Dyslexic, Inc.
Issues: EDU
Rep By: Robert L. Knisely, James W. Kohlmoos, H. Stewart Van Scoyoc, Noreene Wells

Regents College
Issues: BUD EDU
Rep By: Steve E. Crane, Robert L. Knisely, James W. Kohlmoos, H. Stewart Van Scoyoc

Regional Airport Authority of Louisville & Jefferson Co.
Issues: AVI BUD
Rep By: Steven O. Palmer, Chad Schulken, H. Stewart Van Scoyoc

Reno & Cavanaugh, PLLC
Issues: BUD HOU
Rep By: Steve E. Crane, Kevin F. Kelly, H. Stewart Van Scoyoc

Science Applications Internat'l Corp. (SAIC)
Issues: SCI
Rep By: Robert L. Knisely, H. Stewart Van Scoyoc

Sickle Cell Disease Ass'n of America
Issues: BUD HCR
Rep By: Anita R. Estell, Kimberly Johnson, H. Stewart Van Scoyoc

Space Explorers Inc.
Issues: EDU SCI
Rep By: Steve E. Crane, Kevin F. Kelly, H. Stewart Van Scoyoc

Space Grant Coalition
Issues: BUD
Rep By: Carolyn Fuller

Spelman College
Issues: BUD EDU
Rep By: Anita R. Estell, H. Stewart Van Scoyoc

Teach for America
Issues: BUD EDU
Rep By: Victor F. Klatt, III, Robert L. Knisely, James W. Kohlmoos, H. Stewart Van Scoyoc

Thompson Publishing, Inc.

Time Domain Corp.
Issues: SCI TRA
Rep By: Ray Cole, H. Stewart Van Scoyoc

TRAUX Engineering
Issues: SCI
Rep By: Thomas L. Lankford, H. Stewart Van Scoyoc

Tulane University
Issues: BUD DEF EDU MED MMM SCI
Rep By: Jan Schoonmaker, H. Stewart Van Scoyoc

Universal Systems, Inc.
Issues: AVI BUD DEF
Rep By: Thomas L. Lankford, Steven O. Palmer, H. Stewart Van Scoyoc

University of Alabama System
Issues: BUD EDU MED SCI
Rep By: Michael W. Adcock, Ray Cole, H. Stewart Van Scoyoc

University of Arizona
Issues: BUD
Rep By: Kevin F. Kelly

University of Connecticut
Issues: BUD EDU
Rep By: Steve E. Crane, Kevin F. Kelly

University of Idaho
Issues: BUD
Rep By: Carolyn Fuller, H. Stewart Van Scoyoc

University of Missouri
Issues: BUD SCI TRA
Rep By: Steve E. Crane, Kevin F. Kelly

University of Nebraska
Issues: BUD EDU MED SCI
Rep By: Carri Booth, Carolyn Fuller, Evan Knisely, H. Stewart Van Scoyoc

University of New Orleans Foundation
Issues: BUD
Rep By: Carolyn Fuller, Buzz Hawley, Kevin F. Kelly, John C. "Jay" Stone, H. Stewart Van Scoyoc

University of North Carolina at Chapel Hill
Issues: BUD EDU MED SCI
Rep By: Jane Bobbitt, Carri Booth, Carolyn Fuller, Keith Morrison, H. Stewart Van Scoyoc

University of Notre Dame
Issues: BUD EDU
Rep By: H. Stewart Van Scoyoc

University of Phoenix
Issues: BUD EDU
Rep By: Victor F. Klatt, III, Robert L. Knisely, H. Stewart Van Scoyoc

UNOCAL Corp.
Issues: CAW
Rep By: Kevin F. Kelly, H. Stewart Van Scoyoc

Veridian Engineering
Issues: BUD TRA
Rep By: Ray Cole, Steven O. Palmer, Chad Schulken, H. Stewart Van Scoyoc

Virginia Polytechnic Institute and State University
Issues: BUD EDU
Rep By: Paul Grimm, Buzz Hawley, Paul Iarrobino, H. Stewart Van Scoyoc

Virginia Tech Intellectual Properties, Inc.
Issues: BUD COM EDU SCI TRA
Rep By: Jan Schoonmaker, H. Stewart Van Scoyoc

Wackenhut Services, Inc.
Issues: ENG LAW
Rep By: Paul Grimm, Buzz Hawley, John C. "Jay" Stone, H. Stewart Van Scoyoc

Washington Consulting Group
Issues: AVI ENG TRA
Rep By: Buzz Hawley, Kevin F. Kelly, John C. "Jay" Stone, H. Stewart Van Scoyoc

Weyerhaeuser Co.
Issues: TAX
Rep By: H. Stewart Van Scoyoc

Xcellsis Corp.
Issues: BUD DEF TRA
Rep By: Ray Cole, Thomas L. Lankford, Steven O. Palmer

ZapMe! Corp.
Issues: EDU TEC
Rep By: James W. Kohlmoos, H. Stewart Van Scoyoc

Zuckert, Scoutt and Rasenberger, L.L.P.
Issues: TEC TOU
Rep By: Steven O. Palmer, Chad Schulken, H. Stewart Van Scoyoc

B. Wayne Vance

1203 Essex Manor
Alexandria, VA 22308
Tel: (703)765-2757
Fax: (703)765-2758
Registered: LDA

Joe Velasquez & Associates

1215 17th St. NW
Washington, DC 20036
Tel: (202)467-8068
Fax: (202)467-8067
Registered: LDA
E-mail: joevela@aol.com
A political consultant.

DC-Area Employees Representing Listed Clients
VELASQUEZ, Joe, President

Clients

1199 Nat'l Health & Human Services Employees Union
Issues: HCR LBR
Rep By: Joe Velasquez

ICF Consulting
Issues: ENG ENV LBR
Rep By: Joe Velasquez

South Gate, California, City of
Issues: GOV
Rep By: Joe Velasquez

The Velasquez Group

227 Massachusetts Ave. NE
Washington, DC 20006
Tel: (202)543-4780
Registered: LDA

DC-Area Employees Representing Listed Clients
VELASQUEZ, Jay

Clients

Arthur Andersen LLP

Deloitte & Touche LLP
Issues: ACC FIN
Rep By: Jay Velasquez

Deloitte Touche Tohmatsu Internat'l

Federal Home Loan Mortgage Corp. (Freddie Mac)
Issues: BUD HOU
Rep By: Jay Velasquez

Instinet
Issues: FIN
Rep By: Jay Velasquez

Interactive Brokers LLC
Issues: CDT FIN
Rep By: Jay Velasquez

Investment Co. Institute
Issues: FIN
Rep By: Jay Velasquez

KPMG, LLP

Mortgage Bankers Ass'n of America
Issues: BAN FIN
Rep By: Jay Velasquez

Mortgage Insurance Companies of America

Republicans for Clean Air
Issues: CAW UTI
Rep By: Jay Velasquez

VISA U.S.A., Inc.
Issues: BAN
Rep By: Jay Velasquez

Venable

1201 New York Ave. NW
Suite 1000
Washington, DC 20005
Tel: (202)962-4800
Fax: (202)962-8300
Registered: LDA, FARA
Web: www.venable.com
Washington office of a general practice law firm headquartered in Baltimore, MD.

DC-Area Employees Representing Listed Clients
ADAMS, David G., Partner
AMES, Robert G., Partner

BASKIN, Maurice, Partner
BASS, III, Kenneth C., Partner
CIVILETTI, Benjamin R., Partner
COSTON, William D., Partner
DUNN, Jeffrey A., Partner
FERRELL, Michael J.
HAILEY, Gary D., Of Counsel
HORTON, Hon. Frank J., Of Counsel
KNOWLES, Jeffrey D., Partner
LANDRY, Brock R., Partner
LEVITT, Geoffrey M., Partner
MADDEN, Thomas J., Partner
MCDOWELL, Heather L., Partner
MEYER, Lindsay B., Partner
SLAUGHTER, Kenneth S., Partner
TENENBAUM, Jeffrey S., Of Counsel
VOLNER, Ian D., Partner

Clients

Academy of Radiology Research
Issues: CPT GOV LBR TAX TOR
Rep By: Jeffrey S. Tenenbaum

Air Conditioning Contractors of America
Issues: CPT GOV LBR TAX TOR
Rep By: Jeffrey S. Tenenbaum

Amino and Phenolic Wood Adhesives Ass'n
Issues: CAW GOV
Rep By: Brock R. Landry

Ass'n for Postal Commerce
Rep By: Ian D. Volner

Ass'n of Clinical Research Professionals
Issues: CPT GOV LBR TAX TOR
Rep By: Jeffrey S. Tenenbaum

Associated Builders and Contractors
Rep By: Maurice Baskin

Bicycle Council
Issues: SPO
Rep By: Brock R. Landry

Bicycle Product Suppliers Ass'n
Issues: CSP GOV
Rep By: Brock R. Landry

Brazelton Foundation
Issues: CPT GOV LBR TAX TOR
Rep By: Jeffrey S. Tenenbaum

Carlson Wagonlit Travel, Inc.
Issues: TOU TRA

Cell Tech
Issues: ADV CSP FOO HCR SCI
Rep By: David G. Adams

Center for Energy and Economic Development
Issues: CPT GOV LBR TAX TOR
Rep By: Jeffrey S. Tenenbaum

Child Welfare League of America
Issues: CPT GOV LBR TAX TOR
Rep By: Jeffrey S. Tenenbaum

Chlorine Chemistry Council
Issues: CHM
Rep By: Brock R. Landry

Composite Panel Ass'n
Issues: CAW ENV
Rep By: Brock R. Landry

Connaught Laboratories Inc.
Rep By: Hon. Frank J. Horton

Cool Roof Rating Council
Issues: ENV
Rep By: Brock R. Landry

Direct Marketing Ass'n, Inc.
Rep By: Ian D. Volner

Eklof Marine Corp.
Issues: ENV LAW

Electronic Retailing Ass'n
Rep By: Jeffrey D. Knowles

Ergo Science Corp.
Issues: SCI
Rep By: David G. Adams

Hardwood Plywood and Veneer Ass'n
Issues: TOR
Rep By: Brock R. Landry

Information Technology Industry Council
Rep By: William D. Coston

Institute of Navigation
Issues: CPT GOV LBR TAX TOR
Rep By: Jeffrey S. Tenenbaum

Internat'l Bicycle Ass'n
Issues: TRD
Rep By: Brock R. Landry

Internat'l Council of Cruise Lines
Issues: CPT GOV LBR TAX TOR
Rep By: Jeffrey S. Tenenbaum

Internat'l Municipal Signal Ass'n
Issues: CPT GOV LBR TAX TOR
Rep By: Jeffrey S. Tenenbaum

Maryland Psychiatric Soc.
Issues: CPT GOV LBR TAX TOR
Rep By: Jeffrey S. Tenenbaum

Merck & Co.
Issues: ADV GOV HCR MED
Rep By: David G. Adams

Metal Building Manufacturers Ass'n
Issues: LBR MAN
Rep By: Brock R. Landry

Mid-Atlantic Toyota Distributors Inc.

Molecular BioSystems, Inc.
Issues: ADV CSP HCR MAN MED SCI
Rep By: David G. Adams

Nat'l Ass'n of Chain Drug Stores
Issues: CPT GOV LBR TAX TOR
Rep By: Jeffrey S. Tenenbaum

Nat'l Bicycle Dealers Ass'n
Issues: SMB TRD
Rep By: Brock R. Landry

Nat'l Coalition for Cancer Survivorship
Issues: CPT GOV LBR TAX TOR
Rep By: Jeffrey S. Tenenbaum

Nat'l Council of Juvenile and Family Court Judges
Issues: LAW
Rep By: Hon. Frank J. Horton, Thomas J. Madden

Nat'l Council of University Research Administrators
Issues: CPT GOV LBR TAX TOR
Rep By: Jeffrey S. Tenenbaum

Nat'l Criminal Justice Ass'n

Nat'l Electrical Safety Foundation
Issues: CPT GOV LBR TAX TOR
Rep By: Jeffrey S. Tenenbaum

North American Steel Framing Alliance
Issues: MAN
Rep By: Brock R. Landry

Recreation Vehicle Dealers Ass'n of North America
Issues: AUT CSP TOU
Rep By: Brock R. Landry

Roof Coatings Manufacturers Ass'n
Issues: CAW ENV GOV
Rep By: Brock R. Landry

SangStat Medical Corp.
Issues: HCR SCI
Rep By: David G. Adams

Special Libraries Ass'n
Issues: CPT GOV LBR TAX TOR
Rep By: Jeffrey S. Tenenbaum

USA Networks
Rep By: Ian D. Volner

Wood Products Indoor Air Consortium
Issues: ENV
Rep By: Brock R. Landry

Verner, Liipfert, Bernhard, McPherson and Hand, Chartered

901 15th St. NW
Suite 700
Washington, DC 20005-2301
Tel: (202)371-6000
Fax: (202)371-6279
Registered: LDA, FARA
Web: www.verner.com
E-mail: verner@verner.com
A general practice law firm.

Political Action Committee
Verner, Liipfert, Bernhard, McPherson and Hand PAC
901 15th St. NW
Suite 700
Washington, DC 20005-2301
Tel: (202)371-6000
Fax: (202)371-6279

DC-Area Employees Representing Listed Clients
BERG, Michael D., Member of Firm
BERNHARD, Berl, Co-Founder
BERNSTEIN, Matthew C., Member of Firm
BLANCHARD, Hon. James J., Member of Firm
BOGGS, Virginia R., Associate
BROOM, R. Stuart, Member of Firm
BROWN, Jamie E.
CARTWRIGHT, Suzanne D., Director, Legislative Affairs
COATS, Hon. Daniel R., Special Counsel
COE, Jo-Anne, Strategic Planner
DARNEILLE, III, Hopewell H., Member of Firm
DOLE, Hon. Robert J., Special Counsel
DUNCAN, III, Lawrence, Associate
DWYER, Denis J., Dir., Legislation and Federal Affairs
ESKIN, Andrew D., Member of Firm
EVANS, William C., Member of Firm
FITZGERALD, David A., Associate
FREEMAN, Rosemary B., Director, Public Affairs
FREILICH, Harold I., Member of Firm
GARON, Richard J., Senior Advisor, International Relations
GRANT, Andrea J., Member of Firm
GROSSMAN, Marla P., Member of Firm
HAND, Lloyd N., Member of Firm
HARRIS, Marshall F.
HART, Vicki E., Director, Legislation and Federal Affairs
HAWLEY, Noelle M., Associate
HICKIE, Jane, Member of Firm
HOCHBERG, Philip R., Of Counsel
JACOBSOHN, David B., Of Counsel
JOHNSON, Stephen R., Associate
KELLER, Thomas J., Member of Firm
KLEIN, Gary J., Member of Firm
KNEUER, John M. R.
KRAMER, William D., Member of Firm
LEGRO, Stanley W., Of Counsel
LEVINSON, Lawrence E., Member of Firm
LOUD, Ted, Public Relations Coordinator
LUTZ, Martin T., Member of Firm
MACKINNON, Douglas M., Director, Communications to the Office of Hon. Robert J. Dole
MANSON, III, Joseph L., Member of Firm
MARTIN, Jenifer, Associate
MCDONALD, Hon. Jack H., Consultant
MCGRATH, Edward J., Member of Firm
MCPHERSON, Harry C., Member of Firm
MEISTER, Brenda G., Member of Firm
MENDELSOHN, Martin, Member of Firm
MERRIGAN, John A., Member of Firm
MIETUS, John R., Member of Firm
MIGDAIL, Evan M., Member of Firm
MINOR, William H., Associate
MITCHELL, Hon. George J., Special Counsel
MIZOGUCHI, Brian A., Member of Firm
MORRIS, Sara W., Telecommunications Consultant
NATALIE, Ronald B., Member of Firm
NEILSON, Mikol S., Of Counsel
NORDSTROM, Paul E., Member of Firm
O'BRIEN, Michael E., Legislative Consultant
ORTMAN, Glen J., Member of Firm
PHILLIPS, Steven R., Member of Firm
PICARD, B. Donovan, Shareholder
PICKUP, James A., Associate
POMMER, Russell E., Member of Firm
PROTO, Neil T., Member of Firm
QUIRK, Sherry A., Member of Firm
RICHARDS, Ann W., Senior Advisor
ROBERTS, Michael J., Member of Firm
RUTTEN, Timothy M., Associate
SANCHEZ, Ignacio E.
SHAKOW, Susannah W., Associate
SHELIGA, Nancy A., Legislative Assistant
SIDDALL, David R., Member of Firm
SIDMAN, Lawrence R., Member of Firm
SPEED-BOST, Regina, Of Counsel
STERNE, Jr., John H., Of Counsel
SWANSTROM, Deborah A., Member of Firm
TEMKIN, Susan O., Member of Firm
VINCE, Clinton A., Member of Firm
WEINBERG, Linda M., Member of Firm
WEISS, David A., Director, Trade Policy
WERNER, Eric T., Member of Firm
YOUNGBLOOD, Theresa M., Associate
ZEITLER, William A., Member of Firm
ZENTAY, John H., Member of Firm

Clients

Accenture
Issues: FIN
Rep By: Berl Bernhard, William H. Minor, David A. Weiss, John H. Zentay

Aetna Inc.
Issues: HCR TAX

Alere Medical Inc.
Issues: HCR
Rep By: Andrew D. Eskin, Rosemary B. Freeman, Vicki E. Hart, Jenifer Martin, James A. Pickup

American Ass'n of Blood Banks
Issues: HCR MMM
Rep By: Vicki E. Hart

American Financial Group
Rep By: Berl Bernhard, Evan M. Migdail

American Share Insurance
Rep By: Andrew D. Eskin

American Soc. of Anesthesiologists
Issues: MMM
Rep By: Vicki E. Hart

Amgen
Issues: HCR
Rep By: Hon. Daniel R. Coats, Vicki E. Hart, Gary J. Klein, Harry C. McPherson, Martin Mendelsohn, John A. Merrigan

ArianeSpace, Inc.
Issues: AER
Rep By: Berl Bernhard

Atomic Energy of Canada
Rep By: Clinton A. Vince

Austin, Texas, City of
Issues: AVI FUE
Rep By: Vicki E. Hart, Jane Hickie, Ann W. Richards

Baca Land and Cattle Co.
Issues: NAT
Rep By: Jane Hickie

Bacardi-Martini, USA, Inc.
Issues: FOR
Rep By: Matthew C. Bernstein, Virginia R. Boggs, Gary J. Klein, John A. Merrigan

BellSouth Corp.
Issues: CPT
Rep By: Steven R. Phillips, David R. Siddall

BET Holdings II, Inc.
Rep By: Lawrence R. Sidman

Biovail Corp. Internat'l
Issues: PHA
Rep By: Matthew C. Bernstein, Hon. James J. Blanchard, Rosemary B. Freeman, Gary J. Klein, William H. Minor, Steven R. Phillips, James A. Pickup

Bombardier Transportation/Bombardier Transit Corporation
Issues: TRA
Rep By: Suzanne D. Cartwright, Denis J. Dwyer, Jenifer Martin, John R. Mietus, Neil T. Proto

CanWest
Issues: COM
Rep By: Hon. James J. Blanchard, Lawrence R. Sidman

Capital Metropolitan Transportation Authority
Issues: TRA
Rep By: Denis J. Dwyer, Jane Hickie, Ann W. Richards, Timothy M. Rutten

Caribe Waste Technologies
Rep By: Gary J. Klein

Chlorine Chemistry Council
Issues: ENV
Rep By: Rosemary B. Freeman, Stanley W. Legro, John H. Sterne, Jr.

Citigroup
Issues: ENV FIN HCR RET TAX
Rep By: Matthew C. Bernstein, Andrew D. Eskin, David B. Jacobsohn, Jenifer Martin, Martin Mendelsohn, John A. Merrigan

Coalition for America's Future

Commercial Information Systems, Inc.
Issues: CPI
Rep By: Timothy M. Rutten

Confederated Tribes of the Coos
Issues: IND
Rep By: Timothy M. Rutten

Continuum Healthcare Systems
Issues: MMM
Rep By: Vicki E. Hart

Cyprus, Government of the Republic of
Rep By: Berl Bernhard

The Walt Disney Co.
Issues: COM CPT TRD
Rep By: Berl Bernhard, Lawrence Duncan, III, Denis J. Dwyer, Harry C. McPherson

Equal Justice Coalition
Rep By: Jamie E. Brown, Lawrence E. Levinson, Harry C. McPherson, Neil T. Proto

EqualFooting.com
Issues: SMB
Rep By: Marla P. Grossman, Jenifer Martin

Federal Home Loan Bank of Indianapolis
Issues: BAN
Rep By: Hon. James J. Blanchard, Andrew D. Eskin, Rosemary B. Freeman, William H. Minor

Federal Home Loan Mortgage Corp. (Freddie Mac)
Issues: FIN HOU
Rep By: John A. Merrigan, William H. Minor

Firstdoor.com
Issues: SMB
Rep By: Marla P. Grossman

Flow Internat'l Corp.
Rep By: Gary J. Klein

Forest Soc. of Maine
Issues: NAT
Rep By: Jenifer Martin, James A. Pickup, Timothy M. Rutten

GenCorp
Issues: AER DEF HCR TRD
Rep By: Lloyd N. Hand

Genentech, Inc.
Issues: HCR
Rep By: Vicki E. Hart

General Cigar Holdings, Inc.

General Electric Co.
Issues: ENV
Rep By: Steven R. Phillips, Susannah W. Shakow, John H. Sterne, Jr., John H. Zentay

General Motors Corp.
Issues: CAW
Rep By: R. Stuart Broom, Rosemary B. Freeman, Clinton A. Vince

Genesee County Drain Commissioner
Issues: CAW
Rep By: Rosemary B. Freeman, Jenifer Martin

George Washington University, Office of Government Relations
Rep By: Denis J. Dwyer, Martin Mendelsohn, John H. Zentay

getpress.com
Issues: SMB
Rep By: Marla P. Grossman

Goldman, Sachs and Co.
Issues: TAX TRA
Rep By: Denis J. Dwyer, Noelle M. Hawley, Gary J. Klein, Jenifer Martin

The Hamilton Group
Issues: DEF
Rep By: Lawrence E. Levinson, Harry C. McPherson

Harris Corp.
Issues: COM
Rep By: Lawrence R. Sidman

G.E. Harris Harmon
Issues: ROD TRA
Rep By: Suzanne D. Cartwright, Denis J. Dwyer, Jenifer Martin

Healthcare Leadership Council
Rep By: Vicki E. Hart

Heritage Development
Issues: RES
Rep By: Suzanne D. Cartwright, Lawrence E. Levinson, Neil T. Proto

Home Warranty Coalition
Issues: HOU INS
Rep By: Matthew C. Bernstein, Harry C. McPherson, John A. Merrigan, Steven R. Phillips, James A. Pickup, Nancy A. Sheliga, John H. Zentay

"I Have a Dream" Foundation
Issues: EDU
Rep By: Rosemary B. Freeman

Independent Fuel Terminal Operators Ass'n
Issues: FUE
Rep By: Andrea J. Grant, Gary J. Klein, John R. Mietus, William H. Minor, Linda M. Weinberg, Theresa M. Youngblood, John H. Zentay

India, Government of the Republic of
Rep By: Berl Bernhard, Brenda G. Meister

Interactive Digital Software Ass'n
Rep By: Marla P. Grossman

Investment Co. Institute
Issues: FIN RET TAX
Rep By: John A. Merrigan

Kansas City, Missouri, City of
Issues: BUD HOU
Rep By: Timothy M. Rutten

Kasten Chase Applied Research Limited
Issues: CPI
Rep By: Hon. James J. Blanchard, Rosemary B. Freeman, David A. Weiss

Kellogg Co.
Issues: FOO TRA TRD
Rep By: Rosemary B. Freeman, Lawrence E. Levinson, Linda M. Weinberg, David A. Weiss, Theresa M. Youngblood

Kelly Services, Inc.
Issues: LBR
Rep By: Rosemary B. Freeman, Brenda G. Meister

Kmart Corp.
Issues: ALC
Rep By: Rosemary B. Freeman

Lehman Brothers
Issues: TAX
Rep By: Andrew D. Eskin, Vicki E. Hart, Gary J. Klein, John A. Merrigan, Mikol S. Neilson

The Limited Inc.
Issues: TRD
Rep By: Andrea J. Grant, Hon. George J. Mitchell

Lockheed Martin Corp.
Issues: TEC
Rep By: Denis J. Dwyer, Vicki E. Hart, Thomas J. Keller, Sara W. Morris, Steven R. Phillips, David R. Siddall, Lawrence R. Sidman, John H. Zentay

Lockheed Martin Tactical Systems
Issues: AVI
Rep By: Matthew C. Bernstein, Lloyd N. Hand, Jane Hickie, Harry C. McPherson, John A. Merrigan, Steven R. Phillips, Ann W. Richards, Theresa M. Youngblood, John H. Zentay

Lubrizol
Rep By: Andrea J. Grant

Magna Entertainment Corp.
Issues: GAM
Rep By: Jamie E. Brown, Marla P. Grossman, John H. Zentay

Management Insights, Inc.
Issues: TAX
Rep By: Evan M. Migdail

Mars, Inc.
Rep By: Andrew D. Eskin, Martin Mendelsohn, Nancy A. Sheliga

Merle Hay Mall Limited Partners
Issues: RES
Rep By: Suzanne D. Cartwright, Denis J. Dwyer, William H. Minor, Neil T. Proto

Merrill Lynch & Co., Inc.
Issues: BAN RET TAX
Rep By: Matthew C. Bernstein, Virginia R. Boggs, Andrew D. Eskin, Rosemary B. Freeman, Lloyd N. Hand, Vicki E. Hart, David B. Jacobsohn, Brenda G. Meister, Martin Mendelsohn, John A. Merrigan, William H. Minor, Steven R. Phillips, John H. Zentay

Mexico, Government of
Rep By: Vicki E. Hart

Microsoft Corp.
Issues: CPI
Rep By: Berl Bernhard

Midroc Ethiopia
Issues: TRD
Rep By: Lawrence E. Levinson, Harry C. McPherson

Mills Corporation
Issues: RES
Rep By: Jane Hickie, Ann W. Richards

Montenegro, Government of
Rep By: Lawrence E. Levinson

Muscular Dystrophy Ass'n
Rep By: Vicki E. Hart, Harry C. McPherson

Nat'l Ass'n of Government Guaranteed Lenders
Issues: SMB
Rep By: David B. Jacobsohn

Nat'l Basketball Ass'n
Issues: COM CPT SPO
Rep By: Philip R. Hochberg

Nat'l Broadcasting Co.
Issues: COM TEC
Rep By: Jane Hickie, Harry C. McPherson, John A. Merrigan, Sara W. Morris, Ann W. Richards, Lawrence R. Sidman, John H. Zentay

Nat'l Football League
Issues: COM CPT SPO
Rep By: Philip R. Hochberg

Nat'l Heritage Foundation
Issues: GOV
Rep By: Hon. Daniel R. Coats

Nat'l Hockey League
Issues: COM CPT SPO
Rep By: Philip R. Hochberg

New England Fuel Institute
Issues: FUE
Rep By: Andrea J. Grant, Nancy A. Sheliga, John H. Zentay

New Haven, Connecticut, City of
Issues: RES
Rep By: Suzanne D. Cartwright, Denis J. Dwyer, William H. Minor, Neil T. Proto

New Orleans, Louisiana, City of
Issues: ENG
Rep By: Paul E. Nordstrom, Glen J. Ortman, Sherry A. Quirk, Regina Speed-bost, Clinton A. Vince

New York Stock Exchange
Issues: CPT FIN TAX
Rep By: David B. Jacobsohn, John H. Zentay

Newport News Shipbuilding Inc.
Issues: BUD DEF
Rep By: Lloyd N. Hand

NOKIA
Issues: TEC
Rep By: John M. R. Kneuer, Lawrence R. Sidman

Northwest Airlines, Inc.
Issues: AVI
Rep By: Hon. James J. Blanchard, Denis J. Dwyer, Rosemary B. Freeman, Lloyd N. Hand, Harry C. McPherson, John A. Merrigan, Steven R. Phillips, Russell E. Pommer, David A. Weiss

NxtWave Communications
Issues: COM
Rep By: Sara W. Morris, David R. Siddall, Lawrence R. Sidman

Oerlikon Aerospace, Inc.
Issues: DEF TRD
Rep By: Lloyd N. Hand

Office of Hawaiian Affairs
Issues: EDU HCR HOU
Rep By: Denis J. Dwyer, Jenifer Martin

Oglethorpe Power Corp.
Issues: ENG
Rep By: David A. Fitzgerald, Sherry A. Quirk

Olympic Aid
Issues: FOR GOV
Rep By: Rosemary B. Freeman, Ted Loud, John H. Zentay

Parsons Brinckerhoff Inc.
Issues: TRA
Rep By: Denis J. Dwyer

Perry Tritech Inc.
Issues: TRD
Rep By: Steven R. Phillips, Theresa M. Youngblood

Peterson Cos., Inc.
Issues: TRA
Rep By: Denis J. Dwyer, Lloyd N. Hand

Petroleum Heat and Power Co., Inc.
Issues: TRA
Rep By: Gary J. Klein

Petroport, Inc.
Issues: NAT
Rep By: Andrea J. Grant, Vicki E. Hart, John H. Zentay

The PGA Tour, Inc.
Issues: TAX
Rep By: Evan M. Migdail

Pharmaceutical Research and Manufacturers of America
Issues: HCR
Rep By: Hon. Daniel R. Coats, Vicki E. Hart, Michael E. O'Brien

Philips Electronics North America Corp.
Issues: COM MAN
Rep By: Sara W. Morris, David R. Siddall, Lawrence R. Sidman, David A. Weiss

Platinum Guild Internat'l
Issues: MON
Rep By: Martin Mendelsohn

Polycistic Kidney Disease Foundation
Issues: HCR
Rep By: Hon. Daniel R. Coats, Vicki E. Hart

Port of Tillamook Bay
Issues: BUD
Rep By: Timothy M. Rutten, John H. Sterne, Jr.

Prowler Fisheries and Clipper Seafoods
Issues: NAT
Rep By: Steven R. Phillips, Timothy M. Rutten, John H. Sterne, Jr.

Public Broadcasting Entities
Issues: COM
Rep By: Vicki E. Hart, Lawrence R. Sidman

Raytheon Co.
Issues: DEF
Rep By: John H. Zentay

Rite Aid Corp.
Issues: HCR
Rep By: Matthew C. Bernstein, Andrew D. Eskin, Rosemary B. Freeman, Vicki E. Hart, Philip R. Hochberg, Jenifer Martin, John A. Merrigan, Sara W. Morris, Steven R. Phillips, Lawrence R. Sidman, John H. Zentay

Salt River Project
Issues: ENG
Rep By: Clinton A. Vince

Sarnoff Corp.
Issues: DEF
Rep By: Denis J. Dwyer, Lloyd N. Hand, Lawrence R. Sidman

SBC Communications Inc.
Rep By: Jane Hickie, Ann W. Richards

The Singer Group
Rep By: Lawrence E. Levinson

Site Inc.
Rep By: Linda M. Weinberg

Southeastern Federal Power Customers, Inc.
Issues: ENG
Rep By: David A. Fitzgerald, Sherry A. Quirk, John H. Sterne, Jr., Clinton A. Vince, John H. Zentay

Stanford Financial Group
Issues: FIN
Rep By: Lawrence E. Levinson, Harry C. McPherson

Staples, Inc.
Issues: TAX
Rep By: Denis J. Dwyer, Vicki E. Hart, Noelle M. Hawley, John H. Zentay

Starwood Lodging/Starwood Capital Group, L.P.
Issues: RES TAX
Rep By: Berl Bernhard, Virginia R. Boggs, Vicki E. Hart, Brenda G. Meister, Martin Mendelsohn, John A. Merrigan

Stewart & Stevenson Services, Inc.
Issues: DEF TAX TRD
Rep By: Virginia R. Boggs, Lloyd N. Hand, Brenda G. Meister, Steven R. Phillips

Taiwan, Government of

Texas Manufactured Housing Ass'n
Issues: HOU
Rep By: Jane Hickie, Ann W. Richards

Thomson Consumer Electronics, Inc.
Issues: COM MAN TRD
Rep By: Hon. James J. Blanchard, Vicki E. Hart, Philip R. Hochberg, John M. R. Kneuer, Sara W. Morris, David R. Siddall, Lawrence R. Sidman, David A. Weiss

Transportation Maritima Mexicana
Issues: ALC
Rep By: Lawrence E. Levinson, John A. Merrigan

United Arab Emirates, Government of

United Defense, L.P.
Issues: DEF
Rep By: Hon. Daniel R. Coats, Michael E. O'Brien, Steven R. Phillips

United Health Group
Issues: HCR MMM
Rep By: John A. Merrigan

United Pan-Europe Communications, NV
Issues: FOR TEC TRD
Rep By: Steven R. Phillips

University of Michigan Medical Center
Issues: MED
Rep By: Rosemary B. Freeman, Vicki E. Hart, Jenifer Martin

Vanderbilt University Medical Center
Issues: HCR
Rep By: Vicki E. Hart

Verizon Communications
Issues: TEC
Rep By: Lawrence R. Sidman

Vertical Net, Inc.
Rep By: John A. Merrigan

Virginia Commonwealth Trading Co.
Issues: CPT
Rep By: Lloyd N. Hand, Noelle M. Hawley, James A. Pickup, Linda M. Weinberg, David A. Weiss

VISA U.S.A., Inc.
Issues: CPT FIN HCR IMM TAX
Rep By: Andrew D. Eskin, Vicki E. Hart, Jenifer Martin, John A. Merrigan, Theresa M. Youngblood

Vitas Healthcare Corp.
Issues: HCR MMM
Rep By: Vicki E. Hart

Washington County, Oregon, Land Use and Transportation of
Issues: TRA
Rep By: Timothy M. Rutten

Washington Group Internat'l
Issues: ENG FOR
Rep By: Berl Bernhard, Marshall F. Harris, Douglas M. MacKinnon, Edward J. McGrath, Harry C. McPherson, Michael E. O'Brien, James A. Pickup

Simon Weisenthal Center/Museum of Tolerance
Rep By: Martin Mendelsohn

Winstar Petroleum
Issues: ENG
Rep By: Andrew D. Eskin, Steven R. Phillips

Woodfin Suite Hotels
Issues: TOU
Rep By: Lawrence E. Levinson

Yemen, Government of
Rep By: B. Donovan Picard

Michael E. Veve

2121 K St. NW
Suite 800
Washington, DC 20037
Tel: (202)261-3524
Fax: (202)261-3523
Registered: FARA

Clients

El Salvador, Government of the Republic of
Rep By: Michael E. Veve

Vickers and Vickers

1706 23rd St. South
Suite 100
Arlington, VA 22202-1552
Tel: (703)979-5542
Fax: (703)271-0072
Registered: LDA
E-mail: lorggvickers@mindspring.com

DC-Area Employees Representing Listed Clients
VICKERS, Linda, President

Clients

Rural Community Insurance Co.
Issues: AGR BUD
Rep By: Linda Vickers

Vickery Internat'l

1101 Pennsylvania Ave. NW
Suite 800
Washington, DC 20004
Tel: (202)639-1280
Registered: LDA

DC-Area Employees Representing Listed Clients
VICKERY, Jr., Raymond E.

Clients

Dow AgroSciences
Issues: TRD
Rep By: Raymond E. Vickery, Jr.

Brenda R. Viehe-Naess

1300 Pennsylvania Ave. NW
Suite 700
Washington, DC 20004-3024
Tel: (202)204-3023
Fax: (202)789-7349
Registered: LDA, FARA

Clients

Ass'n of British Insurers
Issues: FIN INS TAX
Rep By: Brenda R. Viehe-Naess

Fireman's Fund Insurance Cos.
Issues: INS TAX
Rep By: Brenda R. Viehe-Naess

Forces Vives
Issues: INS TAX
Rep By: Brenda R. Viehe-Naess

Zurich Financial Group
Issues: INS TAX
Rep By: Brenda R. Viehe-Naess

Vienna, Gregor & Associates

1020 N. Fairfax St.
Fourth Floor
Alexandria, VA 22314
Tel: (703)684-5236
Fax: (703)684-3417
Registered: LDA
E-mail: viennaassociates@pass1.com
Public affairs consultants.

DC-Area Employees Representing Listed Clients
GREGOR, Janet R., V. President
MARLAIS, Donald R., Senior Associate
MILLER, Nancy L., Senior Associate
VIENNA, Cheryl, V. President and Managing Partner
VIENNA, David P., President

Clients

California Board of Equalization
Rep By: Janet R. Gregor, Donald R. Marlais, Nancy L. Miller, David P. Vienna

California Franchise Tax Board
Rep By: Janet R. Gregor, Donald R. Marlais, Nancy L. Miller, David P. Vienna

California Public Employees' Retirement System
Rep By: Janet R. Gregor, Donald R. Marlais, Nancy L. Miller, David P. Vienna

California State Senate
Rep By: Janet R. Gregor, Donald R. Marlais, Nancy L. Miller, Cheryl Vienna, David P. Vienna

The Pacific Stock Exchange, Inc.
Rep By: Janet R. Gregor, Donald R. Marlais, Nancy L. Miller, Cheryl Vienna, David P. Vienna

Vierra Associates, Inc.

1825 I St. NW
Suite 400
Washington, DC 20006
Tel: (202)429-6830
Fax: (202)857-5233
Registered: LDA
A government and public relations consulting firm.

DC-Area Employees Representing Listed Clients
VIERRA, Dennis C., Chairman and Chief Exec. Officer

Clients

Dallas Area Rapid Transit Authority
Issues: TRA
Rep By: Dennis C. Vierra

Greater Orlando Aviation Authority
Issues: TRA
Rep By: Dennis C. Vierra

Memphis Area Transit Authority
Issues: TRA
Rep By: Dennis C. Vierra

New York Metropolitan Transportation Authority
Rep By: Dennis C. Vierra

Mary Vihstadt

P.O. Box 5685
1800 N. Patrick Henry Dr.
Arlington, VA 22205
Tel: (703)534-5211
Fax: (703)534-8152
Registered: LDA

Clients

The Dial Co.
Issues: CAW FOO
Rep By: Mary Vihstadt

Travelers Express Co., Inc.
Rep By: Mary Vihstadt

Vinson & Elkins L.L.P.

1455 Pennsylvania Ave. NW
Suite 700
Washington, DC 20004-1008
Tel: (202)639-6500
Fax: (202)639-6604
Registered: LDA
Web: www.vinson-elkins.com
Washington office of a Houston general practice law firm.

Political Action Committee
Nat'l Good Government Fund
1455 Pennsylvania Ave. NW
Suite 700
Washington, DC 20004-1008
Tel: (202)639-6500
Fax: (202)639-6604
Contact: Hon. Michael A. Andrews

DC-Area Employees Representing Listed Clients
ALMOND, Charles L., Partner
ANDREWS, Hon. Michael A., Partner

ANGLE, Stephen, Partner
BUXTON, C. Michael, Partner
CHAPOTON, John E., Partner
DAWE, Christopher M., Associate
LICHTENBAUM, Greta L. H., Of Counsel
MAZER, Robert A., Partner
ODAY, Larry A., Partner
TUOHEY, III, Mark H., Partner
VAUGHN, Christine L., Partner
WENNER, Adam, Partner

Clients

7-Eleven, Inc.
Issues: RET TOB
Rep By: Hon. Michael A. Andrews, Christine L. Vaughn

Aon Corp.
Issues: HCR MMM
Rep By: Larry A. Oday

Cheyne Walk Trust
Rep By: John E. Chapoton, Christine L. Vaughn

Enron Corp.
Issues: ENG
Rep By: Adam Wenner

Foundation for Hematopoietic Cell Therapy Accreditation
Rep By: Larry A. Oday

Goldman, Sachs and Co.
Rep By: Christine L. Vaughn

Greater Texas Student Loan Corp.
Issues: EDU
Rep By: Charles L. Almond

Kansas City Southern Industries
Issues: RRR TAX
Rep By: Hon. Michael A. Andrews, John E. Chapoton, Christine L. Vaughn

Lincoln Property Co.
Issues: RES
Rep By: Hon. Michael A. Andrews

Nat'l Ass'n of Settlement Purchasers
Issues: TAX
Rep By: Hon. Michael A. Andrews, John E. Chapoton, Christine L. Vaughn

Ohio Hospital Ass'n
Issues: MMM
Rep By: Larry A. Oday

Portland General Electric Co.
Issues: UTI
Rep By: Hon. Michael A. Andrews, Christopher M. Dawe

Scott & White Hospital
Issues: HCR
Rep By: Larry A. Oday

Southdown, Inc.
Issues: NAT RES
Rep By: Hon. Michael A. Andrews

Texas Veterans Land Board
Rep By: Charles L. Almond

University of Texas - Houston Health Science Center
Issues: BUD HCR TEC
Rep By: Hon. Michael A. Andrews

XL Capital Ltd
Issues: TAX
Rep By: John E. Chapoton, Christine L. Vaughn

Vinyard & Associates

555 13th St. NW
Third Floor
West Tower
Washington, DC 20004-1109
Tel: (202)637-6838
Fax: (202)637-5910
Registered: LDA

DC-Area Employees Representing Listed Clients
VINYARD, Jr., Walter D.

Clients

Lutheran Brotherhood
Issues: TAX
Rep By: Walter D. Vinyard, Jr.

Mennonite Mutual Aid Ass'n
Issues: HCR
Rep By: Walter D. Vinyard, Jr.

Viohl and Associates, Inc.

444 N. Capitol St. NW
Suite 428
Washington, DC 20001
Tel: (202)624-1478
Fax: (202)624-1475
Registered: LDA

A government relations consulting firm.

DC-Area Employees Representing Listed Clients
DEL ROSARIO, Gerald J.
VIOHL, Jeffrey C., President

Clients

Indiana, Office of the Governor of the State of
Issues: ALC AVI BUD CAW DIS ECN EDU ENV GAM GOV HCR HOU IMM IND LAW MMM NAT ROD TAX TEC TEL TOB TRA TRD UNM WAS WEL
Rep By: Gerald J. Del Rosario, Jeffrey C. Viohl

Ivy Tech State College
Issues: BUD EDU
Rep By: Gerald J. Del Rosario, Jeffrey C. Viohl

Vorys, Sater, Seymour and Pease, LLP

1828 L St. NW
Eleventh Floor
Washington, DC 20036-5109
Web: www.vssp.com
Tel: (202)467-8800
Fax: (202)467-8900
Registered: LDA

Washington office of an Ohio law firm. Maintains offices in Columbus, Cleveland, and Cincinnati.

DC-Area Employees Representing Listed Clients
ALFORD, James K., Counsel
GLICK, Warren W., Counsel
WILMER, Jr., John W., Partner

Clients

Advanced Material Resources, Inc.
Rep By: James K. Alford

Airborne Express

Alliance for Regional Transportation
Issues: BUD

American Ass'n of Enterprise Zones

Arab American Bank
Rep By: Warren W. Glick

Associated Insurance Cos., Inc.

Australia and New Zealand Banking Group
Rep By: Warren W. Glick

Banco Portugues do Atlantico, S.A.
Rep By: Warren W. Glick

Bob Evans Farms, Inc.

Brass and Bronze Ingot Manufacturers Ass'n
Issues: ENV

Camac Holdings, Inc.
Rep By: Warren W. Glick

Chadwick Internat'l, Inc.
Rep By: Warren W. Glick

Citizens Network for Foreign Affairs (CNFA)

Coalition for Employment through Exports

The Consulting Center
Rep By: James K. Alford

Fideicomiso de la Escuela de Agricultura de la Region Tropical Humeda, S.A.
Issues: BUD

Fund for American Studies

Honda North America, Inc.

Indotrade, Inc.
Rep By: James K. Alford

Internat'l Foundation for Election Systems (IFES)

M&W Pump Corp.
Rep By: Warren W. Glick

Motorists Insurance Cos.
Rep By: James K. Alford

Nat'l Ass'n for Nutritional Choice
Issues: CSP FOO HCR PHA

Ohio Cable Telecommunications Ass'n
Issues: COM

Ohio Insurance Institute

J. P. Redd Inc.
Rep By: Warren W. Glick

Salesian Missions of the Salesian Soc.

Texuna Internat'l USA Ltd.
Rep By: Warren W. Glick

Walmer Dollhouses, Inc.
Rep By: James K. Alford

VSAdc.com

1420 New York Ave. NW
Washington, DC 20005
Tel: (202)638-0326
Fax: (202)737-5154
Registered: LDA

Affiliated with the firm Van Scoyoc Associates (see separate listing).

DC-Area Employees Representing Listed Clients
MCDAID, Carol A.
RESKOVAC, J. R.
VAN SCOYOC, H. Stewart

Clients

59/Air Depot Road, Ltd.
Issues: GOV RES
Rep By: J. R. Reskovac

Caron Foundation
Issues: ALC BUD HCR INS TAX
Rep By: Carol A. McDaid

Betty Ford Center
Issues: ALC BUD HCR INS TAX
Rep By: Carol A. McDaid

Hazelden Foundation
Issues: ALC BUD HCR INS TAX
Rep By: Carol A. McDaid

Lawton/Fort Sill Chamber of Commerce & Industry
Issues: BUD DEF GOV VET
Rep By: J. R. Reskovac

Midwest City Municipal Authority
Issues: GOV URB
Rep By: J. R. Reskovac

Nat'l Council on Alcoholism and Drug Dependence
Issues: HCR
Rep By: Carol A. McDaid

Oklahoma, State of
Issues: BUD GOV
Rep By: J. R. Reskovac, H. Stewart Van Scoyoc

Partnership for Recovery Coalition
Issues: ALC BUD HCR INS TAX
Rep By: Carol A. McDaid

Texas Health Resources
Issues: CSP HCR INS MMM PHA TAX
Rep By: Carol A. McDaid, H. Stewart Van Scoyoc

Torchmark Corp.
Issues: HCR INS MMM PHA ROD TAX
Rep By: Carol A. McDaid, H. Stewart Van Scoyoc

Tulsa Airport Authority
Issues: AER AVI BUD GOV
Rep By: J. R. Reskovac

Valley Hope Ass'n
Issues: ALC BUD HCR INS TAX
Rep By: Carol A. McDaid

Vance Development Authority
Issues: AER BUD DEF
Rep By: J. R. Reskovac, H. Stewart Van Scoyoc

Visiting Nurse Service of New York
Issues: HCR MED
Rep By: Carol A. McDaid, H. Stewart Van Scoyoc

The Mike Waite Company

3457 S. Stafford St.
Arlington, VA 22206
Tel: (703)379-2859
Fax: (703)379-1014

DC-Area Employees Representing Listed Clients
WAITE, Michael S.

Clients

Arizona State University
Issues: ECN ECU
Rep By: Michael S. Waite

Oregon Military Department
Issues: DEF
Rep By: Michael S. Waite

R. Duffy Wall and Associates

601 13th St. NW
Suite 410 South
Washington, DC 20005
Tel: (202)737-0100
Fax: (202)628-3965
Registered: LDA, FARA

A wholly owned subsidiary of Fleishman-Hillard (see separate listing).

Political Action Committee
R. Duffy Wall and Associates Inc. Political Action Committee
601 13th St. NW
Suite 410 South
Washington, DC 20005
Contact: Julia E. Chaney
Tel: (202)737-0100
Fax: (202)628-3965

DC-Area Employees Representing Listed Clients
BREWSTER, Hon. Bill, Chairman
CHANDLER, Hon. Rodney D., President
CHANEY, Julia E., V. President
COOPER, Stephen, Senior V. President
EMERICK, Kelli, V. President
EMERY, Rodney, V. President
ENZI, Michael Bradley, V. President
GREGORY, Jack, V. President
GRISSO, Michael E., V. President
JACOB, Amy, V. President
JOHNSTON, Ann Thomas G., V. President
JORY, David C., Senior V. President
KRAUS, Angela, Assistant V. President
SCHUTE, Jr., William, Senior V. President
SWINDELLS, Grant, Senior Account Representative

Clients

American Ambulance Ass'n
Issues: HCR
Rep By: Stephen Cooper

American Gas Ass'n
Issues: ENV TAX
Rep By: Hon. Bill Brewster, Julia E. Chaney, Ann Thomas G. Johnston

American Internat'l Group, Inc.
Rep By: Hon. Rodney D. Chandler

Anderson Cancer Center, MD

AOL Time Warner
Issues: TEC
Barrett Resources
Beretta U.S.A. Corp.
Issues: DEF FIR MAN TAX
Rep By: Hon. Bill Brewster
BHP (USA) Inc.
Issues: TAX
Rep By: David C. Jory
California Central Coast Research Partnership
Issues: BUD EDU SCI
Children's Hospital Foundation
CIGNA Corp.
Issues: HCR
Rep By: Hon. Bill Brewster, Ann Thomas G. Johnston
Entergy Services, Inc.
Issues: CAW ENG ENV TAX UTI WAS
Rep By: Hon. Bill Brewster, Ann Thomas G. Johnston, David C. Jory
Fleishman-Hillard, Inc
Issues: AVI
Rep By: Hon. Bill Brewster, Hon. Rodney D. Chandler
Florence, South Carolina, City of
Issues: BUD
Rep By: Rodney Emery
Gardena, California, City of
Issues: BUD
Rep By: Rodney Emery
Home Care Ass'n of New York State
Issues: MMM
Rep By: Hon. Bill Brewster, Hon. Rodney D. Chandler, Stephen Cooper
M and K Oil Co., Inc.
Metropolitan Mortgage and Securities, Inc.
Issues: TAX
Rep By: Hon. Bill Brewster, Hon. Rodney D. Chandler, David C. Jory
Nat'l Ass'n of Counties
Issues: TAX
Rep By: Hon. Bill Brewster, Hon. Rodney D. Chandler, Julia E. Chaney
NCR Corp.
Issues: CPI ENV TRD
Rep By: Hon. Bill Brewster, Michael Bradley Enzi
Northwest Ecosystem Alliance
Issues: BUD
Rep By: Hon. Rodney D. Chandler
Novartis Corp.
Issues: HCR SCI
Rep By: Hon. Bill Brewster, Ann Thomas G. Johnston
Oracle Corp.
Issues: TAX TEC
Rep By: David C. Jory
Riddle Technology, Inc.
Software Finance and Tax Executives Council
Issues: TAX
Rep By: David C. Jory
St. Francis Hospital
St. Vincent Catholic Medical Centers
TriWest Healthcare Alliance, Inc.
United Airlines
Verizon Communications
Issues: COM HCR TAX TEC TRD
Rep By: Hon. Bill Brewster, David C. Jory
Waddell & Reed Financial, Inc.
Issues: FIN
Rep By: Hon. Bill Brewster, David C. Jory
World Wide Packets

Don Wallace Associates, Inc.

499 S. Capitol St. SW
Suite 600
Washington, DC 20003
Tel: (202)554-1222
Fax: (202)554-1230
Registered: LDA
E-mail: dwawashdc@aol.com
A government relations firm.

DC-Area Employees Representing Listed Clients
DAVIS, Rebecca
GILLILAND, John
WALLACE, Jr., Donald L., President

Clients
American Sugar Cane League of the U.S.A.
Issues: AGR
Rep By: John Gilliland, Donald L. Wallace, Jr.
Cotton Warehouse Ass'n of America
Issues: AGR
Rep By: Rebecca Davis, John Gilliland, Donald L. Wallace, Jr.
Service Corp. Internat'l
Issues: BUD LBR
Rep By: John Gilliland, Donald L. Wallace, Jr.

Wallman Strategic Consulting, LLC

555 12th St. NW
Washington, DC 20004
Tel: (202)347-4964
Fax: (202)347-4961
Registered: LDA

DC-Area Employees Representing Listed Clients
LOGAN, John E.
TARNUTZER, Brett
WALLMAN, Kathleen E.
ZAINA, Lisa M.

Clients
Intermedia Communications Inc.
Issues: TEC
Rep By: Kathleen E. Wallman, Lisa M. Zaina
Real Access Alliance
Issues: COM TEC
Rep By: Brett Tarnutzer, Kathleen E. Wallman

Warren and Company

3122 N St. NW
Washington, DC 20007
Tel: (202)333-9350
Fax: (202)333-9380
E-mail: werronen@aol.com
A strategic public affairs firm.

DC-Area Employees Representing Listed Clients
WERRONEN, Betsy Warren, President

Washington Alliance Group, Inc.

923 15th St. NW
Washington, DC 20005
Tel: (202)628-0752
Fax: (202)737-7565
Registered: LDA

DC-Area Employees Representing Listed Clients
SINGER, Bonnie, President

Clients
Central Michigan University
Issues: EDU HCR
Rep By: Bonnie Singer
Coachella Valley Economic Partnership
Issues: TRA
Rep By: Bonnie Singer
College of the Desert
Issues: EDU
Rep By: Bonnie Singer
Columbia University/Institute for Learning Technologies
Issues: EDU
Rep By: Bonnie Singer
Institute of Simulation and Training
Issues: EDU
Rep By: Bonnie Singer
Mort Community College
Issues: EDU MAN
Rep By: Bonnie Singer
New Orleans Environmental Systems Foundation
Issues: EDU ENV
Rep By: Bonnie Singer
Palm Desert, California, City of
Issues: EDU
Rep By: Bonnie Singer
The Readnet Foundation
Issues: EDU
Rep By: Bonnie Singer
Riverside County Schools
Issues: EDU
Rep By: Bonnie Singer
TI Group Inc.
Issues: EDU
Rep By: Bonnie Singer
University of California at Riverside
Issues: EDU
Rep By: Bonnie Singer

Washington Aviation Group

1707 H St. NW
Suite 703
Washington, DC 20006
Tel: (202)478-5425
Registered: LDA

DC-Area Employees Representing Listed Clients
BEAUJUIN, Arnolda
BIERMAN, Chad
DERKS, Paula
DICKSTEIN, Jason, President
SCHWEITZER, Michele

Clients
Aircraft Electronics Ass'n
Issues: AVI BUD GOV LBR MAN SMB TRA
Rep By: Arnolda Beaujuin, Chad Bierman, Paula Derks, Jason Dickstein
Airline Suppliers Ass'n
Issues: AVI GOV LBR SMB TRA
Rep By: Arnolda Beaujuin, Chad Bierman, Jason Dickstein, Michele Schweitzer
Professional Aviation Maintenance Ass'n
Issues: AVI GOV TRA
Rep By: Arnolda Beaujuin, Chad Bierman, Jason Dickstein

Washington Consulting Alliance, Inc.

421 New Jersey Ave. SE
Washington, DC 20003
Tel: (703)318-7169
Registered: LDA
E-mail: user3230@aol.com

DC-Area Employees Representing Listed Clients
BURGUM, Thomas L., V. President, Legislative Affairs
SAILER, Gill
WIGGINS, Shaun, President

Clients
Data Dynamics
Issues: GOV IND
Rep By: Thomas L. Burgum, Shaun Wiggins
EnerTech Industries Inc.
Issues: ENG ENV
Rep By: Thomas L. Burgum
Heartland Communications & Management Inc.
Issues: COM TEC
Rep By: Thomas L. Burgum, Shaun Wiggins
Metrocall Inc.
Issues: COM GOV
Rep By: Thomas L. Burgum, Gill Sailer
Norfolk Southern Corp.
Issues: LBR TRA
Rep By: Thomas L. Burgum
Pointe Coupee Police Jury
Issues: COM DIS
Rep By: Thomas L. Burgum
San Bernardino Valley Municipal Water District
Issues: CAW ENV
Rep By: Thomas L. Burgum
Synthetic Genetics
ThermoEnergy Corp.
Issues: CAW ENV
Rep By: Thomas L. Burgum

Washington Council Ernst & Young

1150 17th St. NW
Suite 601
Washington, DC 20036
Tel: (202)293-7474
Fax: (202)293-8811
Registered: LDA
A law and lobbying firm specializing in tax, budget and employee benefits, trade, telecommunications, environment and energy.

DC-Area Employees Representing Listed Clients
BADGER, Doug, Partner
DARLING, Lauren, Senior Manager
DONEY, John L., Senior Manager
FITZGERALD, Jayne T., Partner
GARRETT-NELSON, LaBrenda, Partner
GASPER, Gary J., Partner
GATES, Bruce A., Partner
GIORDANO, Nick, Partner
KOCH, Cathy, Senior Manager
LEONARD, Robert J., Partner
MASTRO, William
MCGUINESS, Martin, Senior Manager
MELTZER, Richard, Partner
MOSELEY, Phillip D., Partner
PORTER, John D., Senior Manager
ROZEN, Robert M., Partner
STEELE-FLYNN, Donna, Senior Manager
URBAN, Timothy J., Partner

Clients
Aetna Inc.
Issues: BUD HCR TAX
Rep By: Doug Badger, John L. Doney, Jayne T. Fitzgerald, LaBrenda Garrett-Nelson, Gary J. Gasper, Bruce A. Gates, Nick Giordano, Robert J. Leonard, Richard Meltzer, Robert M. Rozen, Timothy J. Urban
Aetna Life & Casualty Co.
Issues: BUD FIN HCR INS MMM TAX
Rep By: Doug Badger, Lauren Darling, John L. Doney, Jayne T. Fitzgerald, LaBrenda Garrett-Nelson, Gary J. Gasper, Bruce A. Gates, Nick Giordano, Cathy Koch, Robert J. Leonard, Richard Meltzer, Phillip D. Moseley, John D. Porter, Robert M. Rozen, Donna Steele-Flynn, Timothy J. Urban
Allegiance Healthcare Corp.
Rep By: John L. Doney, Jayne T. Fitzgerald, LaBrenda Garrett-Nelson, Gary J. Gasper, Bruce A. Gates, Robert J. Leonard, Richard Meltzer, Robert M. Rozen, Timothy J. Urban
American Insurance Ass'n
Issues: BUD ENV FIN INS TAX TRD
Rep By: Doug Badger, Lauren Darling, John L. Doney, Jayne T. Fitzgerald, LaBrenda Garrett-Nelson, Gary J. Gasper, Bruce A. Gates, Nick Giordano, Cathy Koch,

Robert J. Leonard, Richard Meltzer, Phillip D. Moseley, John D. Porter, Robert M. Rozen, Donna Steele-Flynn, Timothy J. Urban

American Staffing Ass'n
Issues: LBR RET TAX
Rep By: Doug Badger, Lauren Darling, John L. Doney, Jayne T. Fitzgerald, LaBrenda Garrett-Nelson, Gary J. Gasper, Bruce A. Gates, Nick Giordano, Cathy Koch, Robert J. Leonard, Richard Meltzer, Phillip D. Moseley, John D. Porter, Robert M. Rozen, Donna Steele-Flynn, Timothy J. Urban

Anheuser-Busch Cos., Inc.
Issues: BEV BUD TAX TRD
Rep By: Doug Badger, Lauren Darling, John L. Doney, Jayne T. Fitzgerald, LaBrenda Garrett-Nelson, Gary J. Gasper, Bruce A. Gates, Nick Giordano, Robert J. Leonard, Richard Meltzer, Phillip D. Moseley, John D. Porter, Robert M. Rozen, Donna Steele-Flynn, Timothy J. Urban

Antitrust Coalition for Consumer Choice in Health Care
Issues: HCR LBR
Rep By: Doug Badger, Lauren Darling, John L. Doney, Jayne T. Fitzgerald, LaBrenda Garrett-Nelson, Gary J. Gasper, Bruce A. Gates, Nick Giordano, Cathy Koch, Robert J. Leonard, Richard Meltzer, Phillip D. Moseley, John D. Porter, Robert M. Rozen, Donna Steele-Flynn, Timothy J. Urban

Apartment Investment and Management Co.
Issues: HOU TAX
Rep By: Doug Badger, Lauren Darling, John L. Doney, Jayne T. Fitzgerald, LaBrenda Garrett-Nelson, Gary J. Gasper, Bruce A. Gates, Nick Giordano, Cathy Koch, Robert J. Leonard, Richard Meltzer, Phillip D. Moseley, John D. Porter, Robert M. Rozen, Donna Steele-Flynn, Timothy J. Urban

Ass'n of American Railroads
Issues: BUD TAX
Rep By: Doug Badger, John L. Doney, Jayne T. Fitzgerald, LaBrenda Garrett-Nelson, Gary J. Gasper, Bruce A. Gates, Nick Giordano, Cathy Koch, Robert J. Leonard, Richard Meltzer, Phillip D. Moseley, John D. Porter, Robert M. Rozen, Donna Steele-Flynn, Timothy J. Urban

Ass'n of Home Appliance Manufacturers
Issues: ENG ENV TAX
Rep By: Doug Badger, Lauren Darling, John L. Doney, Jayne T. Fitzgerald, LaBrenda Garrett-Nelson, Gary J. Gasper, Bruce A. Gates, Nick Giordano, Robert J. Leonard, Richard Meltzer, Phillip D. Moseley, John D. Porter, Robert M. Rozen, Donna Steele-Flynn, Timothy J. Urban

AT&T
Issues: TAX
Rep By: Doug Badger, Lauren Darling, John L. Doney, Jayne T. Fitzgerald, LaBrenda Garrett-Nelson, Gary J. Gasper, Bruce A. Gates, Nick Giordano, Cathy Koch, Robert J. Leonard, Richard Meltzer, Phillip D. Moseley, John D. Porter, Robert M. Rozen, Donna Steele-Flynn, Timothy J. Urban

AT&T Capital Corp.
Rep By: Doug Badger, John L. Doney, Jayne T. Fitzgerald, LaBrenda Garrett-Nelson, Gary J. Gasper, Bruce A. Gates, Nick Giordano, Robert J. Leonard, Richard Meltzer, Robert M. Rozen, Timothy J. Urban

Avco Financial Services
Issues: TAX
Rep By: John L. Doney, Jayne T. Fitzgerald, LaBrenda Garrett-Nelson, Gary J. Gasper, Bruce A. Gates, Robert J. Leonard, Richard Meltzer, Robert M. Rozen, Timothy J. Urban

Aventis Pharmaceuticals, Inc.
Issues: HCR MMM
Rep By: Doug Badger, Lauren Darling, John L. Doney, Jayne T. Fitzgerald, LaBrenda Garrett-Nelson, Gary J. Gasper, Bruce A. Gates, Nick Giordano, Cathy Koch, Robert J. Leonard, Richard Meltzer, Phillip D. Moseley, John D. Porter, Robert M. Rozen, Donna Steele-Flynn, Timothy J. Urban

Baxter Healthcare Corp.
Issues: BUD HCR MMM TAX
Rep By: Doug Badger, Lauren Darling, John L. Doney, Jayne T. Fitzgerald, LaBrenda Garrett-Nelson, Gary J. Gasper, Bruce A. Gates, Nick Giordano, Cathy Koch, Robert J. Leonard, Richard Meltzer, Phillip D. Moseley, John D. Porter, Robert M. Rozen, Donna Steele-Flynn, Timothy J. Urban

BHC Communications, Inc.
Issues: TAX
Rep By: Doug Badger, Lauren Darling, John L. Doney, Jayne T. Fitzgerald, LaBrenda Garrett-Nelson, Gary J. Gasper, Bruce A. Gates, Nick Giordano, Cathy Koch, Robert J. Leonard, William Mastro, Richard Meltzer, Phillip D. Moseley, John D. Porter, Robert M. Rozen, Donna Steele-Flynn, Timothy J. Urban

Bulmer Holding PLC, H. P.
Issues: BEV BUD FOO TAX TRD
Rep By: Doug Badger, Lauren Darling, John L. Doney, Jayne T. Fitzgerald, LaBrenda Garrett-Nelson, Gary J. Gasper, Bruce A. Gates, Nick Giordano, Cathy Koch, Robert J. Leonard, Richard Meltzer, Phillip D. Moseley, John D. Porter, Robert M. Rozen, Donna Steele-Flynn, Timothy J. Urban

Cash Balance Coalition
Issues: RET TAX
Rep By: Doug Badger, Lauren Darling, John L. Doney, Jayne T. Fitzgerald, LaBrenda Garrett-Nelson, Gary J. Gasper, Bruce A. Gates, Nick Giordano, Robert J. Leonard, Richard Meltzer, Phillip D. Moseley, John D. Porter, Robert M. Rozen, Donna Steele-Flynn, Timothy J. Urban

Chamber of Shipping of America
Rep By: John L. Doney, Jayne T. Fitzgerald, LaBrenda Garrett-Nelson, Gary J. Gasper, Bruce A. Gates, Robert J. Leonard, Richard Meltzer, Robert M. Rozen, Timothy J. Urban

Citigroup
Issues: FIN TAX
Rep By: Doug Badger, Lauren Darling, John L. Doney, Jayne T. Fitzgerald, LaBrenda Garrett-Nelson, Gary J. Gasper, Bruce A. Gates, Nick Giordano, Cathy Koch, Robert J. Leonard, Richard Meltzer, Phillip D. Moseley, John D. Porter, Robert M. Rozen, Donna Steele-Flynn, Timothy J. Urban

Coalition for Fairness in Defense Exports
Issues: TAX
Rep By: Doug Badger, Lauren Darling, John L. Doney, Jayne T. Fitzgerald, LaBrenda Garrett-Nelson, Gary J. Gasper, Bruce A. Gates, Nick Giordano, Robert J. Leonard, Richard Meltzer, Phillip D. Moseley, John D. Porter, Robert M. Rozen, Donna Steele-Flynn, Timothy J. Urban

Coalition to Preserve Tracking Stock
Issues: TAX
Rep By: Doug Badger, Lauren Darling, John L. Doney, Jayne T. Fitzgerald, LaBrenda Garrett-Nelson, Gary J. Gasper, Bruce A. Gates, Nick Giordano, Robert J. Leonard, Richard Meltzer, Phillip D. Moseley, John D. Porter, Robert M. Rozen, Donna Steele-Flynn, Timothy J. Urban

ComEd
Issues: BUD TAX UTI
Rep By: Doug Badger, Lauren Darling, John L. Doney, Jayne T. Fitzgerald, LaBrenda Garrett-Nelson, Gary J. Gasper, Bruce A. Gates, Nick Giordano, Cathy Koch, Robert J. Leonard, Richard Meltzer, Phillip D. Moseley, John D. Porter, Robert M. Rozen, Donna Steele-Flynn, Timothy J. Urban

The Connell Co.
Issues: TAX
Rep By: Doug Badger, Lauren Darling, John L. Doney, Jayne T. Fitzgerald, LaBrenda Garrett-Nelson, Gary J. Gasper, Bruce A. Gates, Nick Giordano, Cathy Koch, Robert J. Leonard, Richard Meltzer, Phillip D. Moseley, John D. Porter, Robert M. Rozen, Donna Steele-Flynn, Timothy J. Urban

Deferral Group
Issues: TAX
Rep By: Doug Badger, Lauren Darling, John L. Doney, Jayne T. Fitzgerald, LaBrenda Garrett-Nelson, Gary J. Gasper, Bruce A. Gates, Nick Giordano, Robert J. Leonard, Richard Meltzer, Phillip D. Moseley, John D. Porter, Robert M. Rozen, Donna Steele-Flynn, Timothy J. Urban

Directors Guild of America
Issues: ART CIV TAX
Rep By: Doug Badger, Lauren Darling, John L. Doney, Jayne T. Fitzgerald, LaBrenda Garrett-Nelson, Gary J. Gasper, Bruce A. Gates, Nick Giordano, Cathy Koch, Robert J. Leonard, William Mastro, Richard Meltzer, Phillip D. Moseley, John D. Porter, Robert M. Rozen, Donna Steele-Flynn, Timothy J. Urban

Doris Duke Charitable Foundation
Issues: TAX
Rep By: Doug Badger, Lauren Darling, John L. Doney, Jayne T. Fitzgerald, LaBrenda Garrett-Nelson, Gary J. Gasper, Bruce A. Gates, Nick Giordano, Cathy Koch, Robert J. Leonard, Richard Meltzer, Phillip D. Moseley, John D. Porter, Robert M. Rozen, Donna Steele-Flynn, Timothy J. Urban

Eaton Vance Management Co.
Issues: BUD TAX
Rep By: Doug Badger, Lauren Darling, John L. Doney, Jayne T. Fitzgerald, LaBrenda Garrett-Nelson, Gary J. Gasper, Bruce A. Gates, Nick Giordano, Cathy Koch, Robert J. Leonard, Richard Meltzer, Phillip D. Moseley, John D. Porter, Robert M. Rozen, Donna Steele-Flynn, Timothy J. Urban

Eden Financial Corp.
Issues: TAX
Rep By: Doug Badger, Lauren Darling, John L. Doney, Jayne T. Fitzgerald, LaBrenda Garrett-Nelson, Gary J. Gasper, Bruce A. Gates, Nick Giordano, Robert J. Leonard, Richard Meltzer, Phillip D. Moseley, John D. Porter, Robert M. Rozen, Donna Steele-Flynn, Timothy J. Urban

The Enterprise Foundation
Issues: TAX
Rep By: Doug Badger, Lauren Darling, John L. Doney, Jayne T. Fitzgerald, LaBrenda Garrett-Nelson, Gary J. Gasper, Bruce A. Gates, Nick Giordano, Cathy Koch, Robert J. Leonard, Richard Meltzer, Phillip D. Moseley, John D. Porter, Robert M. Rozen, Donna Steele-Flynn, Timothy J. Urban

Fannie Mae
Issues: BAN BUD HOU TAX
Rep By: Doug Badger, Lauren Darling, John L. Doney, Jayne T. Fitzgerald, LaBrenda Garrett-Nelson, Gary J. Gasper, Bruce A. Gates, Nick Giordano, Cathy Koch, Robert J. Leonard, Richard Meltzer, Phillip D. Moseley, John D. Porter, Robert M. Rozen, Donna Steele-Flynn, Timothy J. Urban

FedEx Corp.
Issues: AVI BUD HCR LBR POS TAX TRD
Rep By: Doug Badger, Lauren Darling, John L. Doney, Jayne T. Fitzgerald, LaBrenda Garrett-Nelson, Gary J. Gasper, Bruce A. Gates, Nick Giordano, Cathy Koch, Robert J. Leonard, Richard Meltzer, Phillip D. Moseley, John D. Porter, Robert M. Rozen, Donna Steele-Flynn, Timothy J. Urban

Ford Motor Co.
Issues: BUD ENV HCR TAX TRD
Rep By: Doug Badger, Lauren Darling, John L. Doney, Jayne T. Fitzgerald, LaBrenda Garrett-Nelson, Gary J. Gasper, Bruce A. Gates, Nick Giordano, Robert J. Leonard, Richard Meltzer, Phillip D. Moseley, John D. Porter, Robert M. Rozen, Donna Steele-Flynn, Timothy J. Urban

General Electric Co.
Issues: BUD HCR TAX TRD
Rep By: Doug Badger, Lauren Darling, John L. Doney, Jayne T. Fitzgerald, LaBrenda Garrett-Nelson, Gary J. Gasper, Bruce A. Gates, Nick Giordano, Cathy Koch, Robert J. Leonard, Richard Meltzer, Phillip D. Moseley, John D. Porter, Robert M. Rozen, Donna Steele-Flynn, Timothy J. Urban

Global Competitiveness Coalition
Issues: TAX
Rep By: Doug Badger, Lauren Darling, John L. Doney, Jayne T. Fitzgerald, LaBrenda Garrett-Nelson, Gary J. Gasper, Bruce A. Gates, Nick Giordano, Cathy Koch, Robert J. Leonard, Richard Meltzer, Phillip D. Moseley, John D. Porter, Robert M. Rozen, Donna Steele-Flynn, Timothy J. Urban

Grasslands Water District
Issues: ENV NAT
Rep By: Doug Badger, Lauren Darling, John L. Doney, Jayne T. Fitzgerald, LaBrenda Garrett-Nelson, Gary J. Gasper, Bruce A. Gates, Nick Giordano, Cathy Koch, Robert J. Leonard, Richard Meltzer, Phillip D. Moseley, John D. Porter, Robert M. Rozen, Donna Steele-Flynn, Timothy J. Urban

Group Health, Inc.
Issues: BUD GOV HCR INS LBR MMM TAX
Rep By: Doug Badger, Lauren Darling, John L. Doney, Jayne T. Fitzgerald, LaBrenda Garrett-Nelson, Gary J. Gasper, Bruce A. Gates, Nick Giordano, Robert J. Leonard, Richard Meltzer, Phillip D. Moseley, John D. Porter, Robert M. Rozen, Donna Steele-Flynn, Timothy J. Urban

Health Benefits Coalition
Rep By: Bruce A. Gates

HEREIU
Issues: LBR
Rep By: Doug Badger, Lauren Darling, John L. Doney, Jayne T. Fitzgerald, LaBrenda Garrett-Nelson, Gary J. Gasper, Nick Giordano, Robert J. Leonard, Phillip D. Moseley, John D. Porter, Robert M. Rozen, Donna Steele-Flynn, Timothy J. Urban

Hewlett-Packard Co.
Issues: BUD TAX
Rep By: Nick Giordano

Gilbert P. Hyatt, Inventor
Issues: TAX
Rep By: Doug Badger, Lauren Darling, John L. Doney, Jayne T. Fitzgerald, LaBrenda Garrett-Nelson, Gary J. Gasper, Bruce A. Gates, Nick Giordano, Cathy Koch, Robert J. Leonard, Richard Meltzer, Phillip D. Moseley, John D. Porter, Robert M. Rozen, Donna Steele-Flynn, Timothy J. Urban

Investment Co. Institute
Issues: RET TAX
Rep By: Doug Badger, Lauren Darling, John L. Doney, Jayne T. Fitzgerald, LaBrenda Garrett-Nelson, Gary J. Gasper, Bruce A. Gates, Nick Giordano, Robert J. Leonard, Richard Meltzer, Phillip D. Moseley, John D. Porter, Robert M. Rozen, Donna Steele-Flynn, Timothy J. Urban

Large Public Power Council
Issues: ENG TAX
Rep By: Doug Badger, Lauren Darling, John L. Doney, Jayne T. Fitzgerald, LaBrenda Garrett-Nelson, Gary J. Gasper, Bruce A. Gates, Nick Giordano, Cathy Koch, Robert J. Leonard, Richard Meltzer, Phillip D. Moseley, John D. Porter, Robert M. Rozen, Donna Steele-Flynn, Timothy J. Urban

Local Initiatives Support Corp.
Issues: BAN TAX
Rep By: Doug Badger, Lauren Darling, John L. Doney, Jayne T. Fitzgerald, LaBrenda Garrett-Nelson, Gary J. Gasper, Bruce A. Gates, Nick Giordano, Cathy Koch, Robert J. Leonard, Richard Meltzer, Phillip D. Moseley, John D. Porter, Robert M. Rozen, Donna Steele-Flynn, Timothy J. Urban

MacAndrews & Forbes Holdings, Inc.
Issues: BAN BUD COM FIN MAN TAX TEC
Rep By: Doug Badger, Lauren Darling, John L. Doney, Jayne T. Fitzgerald, LaBrenda Garrett-Nelson, Gary J. Gasper, Bruce A. Gates, Nick Giordano, Cathy Koch, Robert J. Leonard, Phillip D. Moseley, John D. Porter, Robert M. Rozen, Donna Steele-Flynn, Timothy J. Urban

Marsh & McLennan Cos.
Issues: TAX
Rep By: Doug Badger, Lauren Darling, John L. Doney, Jayne T. Fitzgerald, LaBrenda Garrett-Nelson, Gary J. Gasper, Bruce A. Gates, Nick Giordano, Cathy Koch, Robert J. Leonard, Richard Meltzer, Phillip D. Moseley, John D. Porter, Robert M. Rozen, Donna Steele-Flynn, Timothy J. Urban

MCG Northwest, Inc.
Issues: TAX
Rep By: Doug Badger, Lauren Darling, John L. Doney, Jayne T. Fitzgerald, LaBrenda Garrett-Nelson, Gary J. Gasper, Bruce A. Gates, Nick Giordano, Cathy Koch, Robert J. Leonard, Richard Meltzer, Phillip D. Moseley, John D. Porter, Robert M. Rozen, Donna Steele-Flynn, Timothy J. Urban

McLane Co.
Issues: LBR TAX TOB
Rep By: Doug Badger, Lauren Darling, John L. Doney, Jayne T. Fitzgerald, LaBrenda Garrett-Nelson, Gary J. Gasper, Bruce A. Gates, Nick Giordano, Cathy Koch, Robert J. Leonard, Richard Meltzer, Phillip D. Moseley, John D. Porter, Robert M. Rozen, Donna Steele-Flynn, Timothy J. Urban

Merrill Lynch & Co., Inc.
Issues: BUD TAX
Rep By: Doug Badger, Lauren Darling, John L. Doney, Jayne T. Fitzgerald, LaBrenda Garrett-Nelson, Gary J. Gasper, Bruce A. Gates, Nick Giordano, Cathy Koch, Robert J. Leonard, Richard Meltzer, Phillip D. Moseley, John D. Porter, Robert M. Rozen, Donna Steele-Flynn, Timothy J. Urban

Metropolitan Banking Group
Issues: BAN FIN
Rep By: Doug Badger, Lauren Darling, John L. Doney, Jayne T. Fitzgerald, LaBrenda Garrett-Nelson, Gary J. Gasper, Bruce A. Gates, Nick Giordano, Robert J. Leonard, Richard Meltzer, Phillip D. Moseley, John D. Porter, Robert M. Rozen, Donna Steele-Flynn, Timothy J. Urban

Microsoft Corp.
Issues: TAX
Rep By: Doug Badger, John L. Doney, Jayne T. Fitzgerald, LaBrenda Garrett-Nelson, Gary J. Gasper, Bruce A. Gates, Nick Giordano, Robert J. Leonard, Richard Meltzer, Robert M. Rozen, Timothy J. Urban

Mutual of Omaha Insurance Companies
Issues: HCR TAX
Rep By: Doug Badger, Nick Giordano

Nat'l Ass'n for State Farm Agents
Issues: BUD GOV HCR INS LBR MMM TAX
Rep By: Doug Badger, Lauren Darling, John L. Doney, Jayne T. Fitzgerald, LaBrenda Garrett-Nelson, Gary J. Gasper, Bruce A. Gates, Nick Giordano, Cathy Koch, Robert J. Leonard, Richard Meltzer, Phillip D. Moseley, John D. Porter, Robert M. Rozen, Donna Steele-Flynn, Timothy J. Urban

Nat'l Ass'n of Professional Employer Organizations
Issues: HCR LBR RET TAX
Rep By: Doug Badger, Lauren Darling, John L. Doney, Jayne T. Fitzgerald, LaBrenda Garrett-Nelson, Gary J. Gasper, Bruce A. Gates, Nick Giordano, Cathy Koch, Robert J. Leonard, Richard Meltzer, Phillip D. Moseley, John D. Porter, Robert M. Rozen, Donna Steele-Flynn, Timothy J. Urban

Nat'l Ass'n of Real Estate Investment Trusts
Issues: TAX TEC
Rep By: Doug Badger, Lauren Darling, John L. Doney, Jayne T. Fitzgerald, LaBrenda Garrett-Nelson, Gary J. Gasper, Bruce A. Gates, Nick Giordano, Cathy Koch, Robert J. Leonard, Richard Meltzer, Phillip D. Moseley, John D. Porter, Robert M. Rozen, Donna Steele-Flynn, Timothy J. Urban

Nat'l Ass'n of State Farm Agents
Issues: TAX
Rep By: Doug Badger, Jayne T. Fitzgerald, LaBrenda Garrett-Nelson, Gary J. Gasper, Bruce A. Gates, Nick Giordano, Robert J. Leonard, Richard Meltzer

Nat'l Cable Television Ass'n
Issues: TEC
Rep By: Doug Badger, Jayne T. Fitzgerald, LaBrenda Garrett-Nelson, Gary J. Gasper, Bruce A. Gates, Nick Giordano, Robert J. Leonard, Richard Meltzer, Robert M. Rozen, Timothy J. Urban

Nat'l Defined Contribution Council
Issues: BUD FIN GOV LBR TAX
Rep By: Doug Badger, Lauren Darling, John L. Doney, Jayne T. Fitzgerald, LaBrenda Garrett-Nelson, Gary J. Gasper, Bruce A. Gates, Nick Giordano, Cathy Koch, Robert J. Leonard, Richard Meltzer, Phillip D. Moseley, John D. Porter, Robert M. Rozen, Donna Steele-Flynn, Timothy J. Urban

Nat'l Foreign Trade Council, Inc.
Issues: BUD TAX
Rep By: Doug Badger, Lauren Darling, John L. Doney, Jayne T. Fitzgerald, LaBrenda Garrett-Nelson, Gary J. Gasper, Bruce A. Gates, Nick Giordano, Cathy Koch, Robert J. Leonard, Richard Meltzer, Phillip D. Moseley, John D. Porter, Robert M. Rozen, Donna Steele-Flynn, Timothy J. Urban

Nat'l Multi-Housing Council
Issues: HOU TAX
Rep By: Doug Badger, Lauren Darling, John L. Doney, Jayne T. Fitzgerald, LaBrenda Garrett-Nelson, Gary J. Gasper, Bruce A. Gates, Nick Giordano, Cathy Koch, Robert J. Leonard, Richard Meltzer, Phillip D. Moseley, John D. Porter, Robert M. Rozen, Donna Steele-Flynn, Timothy J. Urban

NFTC-FSC Coalition

PaineWebber Group, Inc.
Rep By: Doug Badger, John L. Doney, Jayne T. Fitzgerald, LaBrenda Garrett-Nelson, Gary J. Gasper, Bruce A. Gates, Nick Giordano, Robert J. Leonard, Richard Meltzer, Robert M. Rozen, Timothy J. Urban

Pfizer, Inc.
Issues: HCR TAX TRD
Rep By: Doug Badger, Lauren Darling, John L. Doney, Jayne T. Fitzgerald, LaBrenda Garrett-Nelson, Gary J. Gasper, Bruce A. Gates, Nick Giordano, Cathy Koch, Robert J. Leonard, Richard Meltzer, Phillip D. Moseley, John D. Porter, Robert M. Rozen, Donna Steele-Flynn, Timothy J. Urban

R&D Tax Credit Coalition
Issues: TAX
Rep By: Doug Badger, Lauren Darling, John L. Doney, Jayne T. Fitzgerald, LaBrenda Garrett-Nelson, Gary J. Gasper, Bruce A. Gates, Nick Giordano, Cathy Koch, Robert J. Leonard, Richard Meltzer, Phillip D. Moseley, John D. Porter, Robert M. Rozen, Donna Steele-Flynn, Timothy J. Urban

R&D Tax Regulation Group
Issues: TAX
Rep By: Doug Badger, Lauren Darling, John L. Doney, Jayne T. Fitzgerald, LaBrenda Garrett-Nelson, Gary J. Gasper, Bruce A. Gates, Nick Giordano, Robert J. Leonard, Richard Meltzer, Phillip D. Moseley, John D. Porter, Robert M. Rozen, Donna Steele-Flynn, Timothy J. Urban

Recording Industry Ass'n of America
Issues: ART CIV CPT TAX
Rep By: Doug Badger, Lauren Darling, John L. Doney, Jayne T. Fitzgerald, LaBrenda Garrett-Nelson, Gary J. Gasper, Bruce A. Gates, Nick Giordano, Cathy Koch, Robert J. Leonard, Richard Meltzer, Phillip D. Moseley, John D. Porter, Robert M. Rozen, Donna Steele-Flynn, Timothy J. Urban

Reed-Elsevier Inc.
Issues: TAX
Rep By: Doug Badger, Lauren Darling, John L. Doney, Jayne T. Fitzgerald, LaBrenda Garrett-Nelson, Gary J. Gasper, Bruce A. Gates, Nick Giordano, Cathy Koch, Robert J. Leonard, Richard Meltzer, Phillip D. Moseley, John D. Porter, Robert M. Rozen, Donna Steele-Flynn, Timothy J. Urban

R. J. Reynolds Tobacco Co.
Issues: TAX TOB TRD
Rep By: Doug Badger, Lauren Darling, John L. Doney, Jayne T. Fitzgerald, LaBrenda Garrett-Nelson, Gary J. Gasper, Bruce A. Gates, Nick Giordano, Cathy Koch, Robert J. Leonard, Richard Meltzer, Phillip D. Moseley, John D. Porter, Robert M. Rozen, Donna Steele-Flynn, Timothy J. Urban

Charles Schwab & Co., Inc.,
Issues: TAX
Rep By: Doug Badger, Lauren Darling, John L. Doney, Jayne T. Fitzgerald, LaBrenda Garrett-Nelson, Gary J. Gasper, Bruce A. Gates, Nick Giordano, Cathy Koch, Robert J. Leonard, Richard Meltzer, Phillip D. Moseley, John D. Porter, Robert M. Rozen, Donna Steele-Flynn, Timothy J. Urban

Securities Industry Ass'n
Issues: RET TAX
Rep By: Doug Badger, Lauren Darling, John L. Doney, Jayne T. Fitzgerald, LaBrenda Garrett-Nelson, Gary J. Gasper, Bruce A. Gates, Nick Giordano, Cathy Koch, Robert J. Leonard, Richard Meltzer, Phillip D. Moseley, John D. Porter, Robert M. Rozen, Donna Steele-Flynn, Timothy J. Urban

Sierra Pacific Industries
Issues: BUD TAX
Rep By: Doug Badger, John L. Doney, Jayne T. Fitzgerald, LaBrenda Garrett-Nelson, Gary J. Gasper, Bruce A. Gates, Nick Giordano, Robert J. Leonard, Richard Meltzer, Robert M. Rozen, Timothy J. Urban

Skadden, Arps, Slate, Meagher & Flom LLP
Issues: TAX
Rep By: Doug Badger, Lauren Darling, John L. Doney, Jayne T. Fitzgerald, LaBrenda Garrett-Nelson, Gary J. Gasper, Bruce A. Gates, Nick Giordano, Robert J. Leonard, Richard Meltzer, Phillip D. Moseley, John D. Porter, Robert M. Rozen, Donna Steele-Flynn, Timothy J. Urban

Straddle Rules Tax Group
Issues: TAX
Rep By: Doug Badger, Lauren Darling, John L. Doney, Jayne T. Fitzgerald, LaBrenda Garrett-Nelson, Gary J. Gasper, Bruce A. Gates, Nick Giordano, Robert J. Leonard, Richard Meltzer, Phillip D. Moseley, John D. Porter, Robert M. Rozen, Donna Steele-Flynn, Timothy J. Urban

Tax Fairness Coalition
Issues: BUD TAX
Rep By: Doug Badger, Lauren Darling, John L. Doney, Jayne T. Fitzgerald, LaBrenda Garrett-Nelson, Gary J. Gasper, Bruce A. Gates, Nick Giordano, Cathy Koch, Robert J. Leonard, Richard Meltzer, Phillip D. Moseley, John D. Porter, Robert M. Rozen, Donna Steele-Flynn, Timothy J. Urban

Tax/Shelter Coalition
Rep By: Doug Badger, John L. Doney, Jayne T. Fitzgerald, LaBrenda Garrett-Nelson, Gary J. Gasper, Bruce A. Gates, Nick Giordano, Robert J. Leonard, Richard Meltzer, Robert M. Rozen, Timothy J. Urban

TransOceanic Shipping
Issues: TRD
Rep By: Doug Badger, John L. Doney, Jayne T. Fitzgerald, LaBrenda Garrett-Nelson, Gary J. Gasper, Bruce A. Gates, Nick Giordano, Robert J. Leonard, Richard Meltzer, Robert M. Rozen, Timothy J. Urban

TXU Business Services
Issues: TAX UTI
Rep By: Doug Badger, Lauren Darling, John L. Doney, Jayne T. Fitzgerald, LaBrenda Garrett-Nelson, Gary J. Gasper, Bruce A. Gates, Nick Giordano, Cathy Koch, Robert J. Leonard, Richard Meltzer, Phillip D. Moseley, John D. Porter, Robert M. Rozen, Donna Steele-Flynn, Timothy J. Urban

U.S. Oncology
Issues: HCR MED MMM
Rep By: Doug Badger, Lauren Darling, John L. Doney, Jayne T. Fitzgerald, LaBrenda Garrett-Nelson, Gary J. Gasper, Bruce A. Gates, Nick Giordano, Cathy Koch, Robert J. Leonard, Richard Meltzer, Phillip D. Moseley, John D. Porter, Robert M. Rozen, Donna Steele-Flynn, Timothy J. Urban

USA Biomass Power Producers Alliance
Issues: BUD TAX
Rep By: Doug Badger, Lauren Darling, John L. Doney, Jayne T. Fitzgerald, LaBrenda Garrett-Nelson, Gary J. Gasper, Bruce A. Gates, Nick Giordano, Cathy Koch, Robert J. Leonard, Richard Meltzer, Phillip D. Moseley, John D. Porter, Robert M. Rozen, Donna Steele-Flynn, Timothy J. Urban

Viaticus, Inc.
Issues: TAX
Rep By: Doug Badger, Lauren Darling, John L. Doney, Jayne T. Fitzgerald, LaBrenda Garrett-Nelson, Gary J. Gasper, Bruce A. Gates, Nick Giordano, Cathy Koch, Robert J. Leonard, Richard Meltzer, Phillip D. Moseley, John D. Porter, Robert M. Rozen, Donna Steele-Flynn, Timothy J. Urban

Wilkie Farr & Gallagher
Issues: TRD
Rep By: Doug Badger, Lauren Darling, John L. Doney, Jayne T. Fitzgerald, LaBrenda Garrett-Nelson, Gary J. Gasper, Bruce A. Gates, Nick Giordano, Cathy Koch, Robert J. Leonard, Richard Meltzer, Phillip D. Moseley, John D. Porter, Robert M. Rozen, Donna Steele-Flynn, Timothy J. Urban

Ziff Investors Partnership
Issues: BUD TAX
Rep By: Doug Badger, Lauren Darling, John L. Doney, Jayne T. Fitzgerald, LaBrenda Garrett-Nelson, Gary J. Gasper, Bruce A. Gates, Nick Giordano, Cathy Koch, Robert J. Leonard, Richard Meltzer, Phillip D. Moseley, John D. Porter, Robert M. Rozen, Donna Steele-Flynn, Timothy J. Urban

The Washington Group

1401 K St. NW
Suite 400
Washington, DC 20005
Tel: (202)789-2111
Fax: (202)789-4883
Registered: LDA, FARA

A government relations and strategic business development firm emphasizing corporate, banking, tax, trade, real estate, health, venture capital and international representation. Formerly the law firm of Raffaelli, Spees, Springer & Smith.

DC-Area Employees Representing Listed Clients

ALLEN, Kevin D., Senior V. President
BURKE, William J., Director, Legislative Affairs
EDWARDS, Missy, Senior V. President
FUNDERBURK, Tripp, Director, Policy
LEWIS, Rita M., Principal
O'HANLON, G. John, Principal

RAFFAELLI, John D., Principal
SAUNDERS, Tonya, V. President
SCHNABEL, Mark, Principal
SULLIVAN, Richard, V. President
WEST, Fowler, General Counsel

Clients

American Hospital Ass'n
Issues: BUD
Rep By: William J. Burke, Tripp Funderburk, Rita M. Lewis, G. John O'Hanlon, John D. Raffaelli, Tonya Saunders, Mark Schnabel

American Resort Development Ass'n
Issues: RES TAX
Rep By: Rita M. Lewis, G. John O'Hanlon, John D. Raffaelli, Tonya Saunders, Mark Schnabel, Fowler West

Ass'n of Progressive Rental Organizations
Issues: BAN BUD TAX
Rep By: John D. Raffaelli, Tonya Saunders, Mark Schnabel

AT&T
Issues: TEC
Rep By: Tripp Funderburk, Rita M. Lewis, G. John O'Hanlon, John D. Raffaelli, Tonya Saunders, Mark Schnabel

BD
Issues: HCR
Rep By: Tripp Funderburk, Rita M. Lewis, G. John O'Hanlon, John D. Raffaelli, Mark Schnabel

The Boeing Co.
Issues: AER HCR MMM TAX
Rep By: Rita M. Lewis, John D. Raffaelli, Tonya Saunders, Mark Schnabel

Bridgestone/Firestone, Inc.
Issues: AUT MAN TRA
Rep By: Rita M. Lewis, G. John O'Hanlon, John D. Raffaelli

California Ass'n of Winegrape Growers

Delta Air Lines
Issues: AVI TAX
Rep By: Rita M. Lewis, G. John O'Hanlon, John D. Raffaelli, Tonya Saunders, Mark Schnabel

Eastman Kodak Co.

Everglades Trust
Issues: ENV
Rep By: G. John O'Hanlon, Mark Schnabel, Fowler West

Global Waste Recycling, Inc.
Issues: ENV WAS
Rep By: Rita M. Lewis, G. John O'Hanlon, John D. Raffaelli, Tonya Saunders

Health Management Systems, Inc.

IVAX Corp.
Issues: HCR MED PHA VET
Rep By: William J. Burke, Tripp Funderburk, Rita M. Lewis, G. John O'Hanlon, John D. Raffaelli, Tonya Saunders, Mark Schnabel, Richard Sullivan, Fowler West

Korea Information & Communication, Ltd.
Issues: TEC
Rep By: Kevin D. Allen, William J. Burke, Tripp Funderburk, Rita M. Lewis, G. John O'Hanlon, John D. Raffaelli, Tonya Saunders, Mark Schnabel

LCOR, Inc.
Issues: RES
Rep By: Rita M. Lewis, G. John O'Hanlon, John D. Raffaelli

McGarr Capital Management Corp.

Media Fusion L.L.C.

Microsoft Corp.
Issues: CPI
Rep By: Kevin D. Allen, William J. Burke, Tripp Funderburk, Rita M. Lewis, G. John O'Hanlon, John D. Raffaelli, Tonya Saunders, Mark Schnabel, Richard Sullivan, Fowler West

Nat'l Ass'n of Real Estate Investment Trusts
Issues: RES TAX
Rep By: Rita M. Lewis, G. John O'Hanlon, John D. Raffaelli, Tonya Saunders, Mark Schnabel, Fowler West

News Corporation Ltd.
Rep By: Tripp Funderburk, Rita M. Lewis, G. John O'Hanlon, John D. Raffaelli, Tonya Saunders, Mark Schnabel, Richard Sullivan, Fowler West

Puerto Rico Hospital Ass'n

Real Estate Roundtable
Issues: RES TAX
Rep By: Rita M. Lewis, G. John O'Hanlon, John D. Raffaelli, Mark Schnabel

SAMPCO Companies
Issues: URB
Rep By: Tripp Funderburk, Rita M. Lewis, G. John O'Hanlon, John D. Raffaelli, Mark Schnabel, Richard Sullivan, Fowler West

SCAN Health Plan
Issues: HCR MMM
Rep By: John D. Raffaelli, Tonya Saunders, Mark Schnabel

Soft Telesis Inc.
Issues: TEC

Sun Healthcare Group, Inc.
Issues: HCR MMM

Texas Municipal Power Agency
Issues: ENG
Rep By: William J. Burke, Tripp Funderburk, Rita M. Lewis, G. John O'Hanlon, John D. Raffaelli, Tonya Saunders, Mark Schnabel

Westfield America, Inc.
Issues: RES TAX
Rep By: Richard Sullivan

WinStar Internat'l
Issues: TEC
Rep By: Kevin D. Allen, G. John O'Hanlon, John D. Raffaelli, Richard Sullivan

Yankton Sioux Tribe
Issues: IND
Rep By: Rita M. Lewis, G. John O'Hanlon, John D. Raffaelli, Tonya Saunders

Washington Health Advocates

227 Massachusetts Ave. NE
Suite 300
Washington, DC 20002
Tel: (202)543-7460
Fax: (202)543-5327
Registered: LDA
E-mail: healthadvocate@worldnet.att.net

DC-Area Employees Representing Listed Clients
MORRISON, Lynn, President
PEDDICORD, Ph.D., Douglas, V. President
SUMILAS, Michele

Clients

American Federation for Medical Research
Issues: BUD HCR MED MMM VET
Rep By: Lynn Morrison, Michele Sumilas

American Health Information Management Ass'n
Issues: HCR
Rep By: Douglas Peddicord, Ph.D.

American Medical Informatics Ass'n
Issues: BUD HCR MED TEC
Rep By: Douglas Peddicord, Ph.D., Michele Sumilas

American Soc. for Clinical Pharmacology and Therapeutics
Issues: BUD CSP MED
Rep By: Lynn Morrison, Douglas Peddicord, Ph.D., Michele Sumilas

Center for Healthcare Information Management
Issues: HCR
Rep By: Douglas Peddicord, Ph.D.

GCRC Program Directors Ass'n
Issues: BUD HCR MED
Rep By: Lynn Morrison, Douglas Peddicord, Ph.D., Michele Sumilas

Jewish Guild for the Blind
Issues: HCR MMM
Rep By: Douglas Peddicord, Ph.D., Michele Sumilas

Quintiles Transnational Corp.
Issues: MED
Rep By: Lynn Morrison, Douglas Peddicord, Ph.D., Michele Sumilas

Washington Healthcare Representatives

P.O. Box 25366
Washington, DC 20007-8366
Tel: (202)337-3185
Registered: LDA

DC-Area Employees Representing Listed Clients
BREMER, Heather H., President

Clients

Allergan, Inc.
Rep By: Heather H. Bremer

Cochlear Corp.
Rep By: Heather H. Bremer

Metra Biosystems, Inc.
Rep By: Heather H. Bremer

Washington Liaison Group, LLC

8000 Towers Crescent Dr.
Suite 1350
Tysons Corner, VA 22182
Tel: (703)760-7888
Fax: (703)760-4496
Registered: LDA
E-mail: washlg@aol.com
A public policy and political consulting firm.

DC-Area Employees Representing Listed Clients
DE BEARN, Gaston, President
JENKINS, II, David M., V. President and General Counsel
REED, Michael L., V. President and Secretary

Clients

Reckitt & Colman Pharmaceuticals Inc.
Issues: ALC HCR
Rep By: Gaston de Bearn, David M. Jenkins, II, Michael L. Reed

Serono Laboratories, Inc.
Issues: EDU HCR MED
Rep By: Gaston de Bearn, David M. Jenkins, II, Michael L. Reed

Washington Policy & Analysis, Inc.

1025 Thomas Jefferson St. NW
Suite 411 West
Washington, DC 20007
Tel: (202)965-1161
Fax: (202)965-1177
Registered: LDA, FARA
A government relations consulting firm.

DC-Area Employees Representing Listed Clients
CAMPBELL, Scott L., President
MARTIN, William F., Chairman

Clients

Federation of Electric Power Cos. of Japan

The Tokyo Electric Power Company, Inc.
Rep By: Scott L. Campbell, William F. Martin

Washington Policy Associates, Inc.

1600 Duke St.
Suite 220
Alexandria, VA 22314
Tel: (703)519-1715
Fax: (703)519-1716
Registered: LDA
Web: www.wpa.org
E-mail: wpa@wpa.org
A government relations and association management firm.

DC-Area Employees Representing Listed Clients
SMITH, Jeffrey C., President

Clients

Conference of Private Operators for Response Towing
Issues: MAR

The Maritime Consortium, Inc.
Rep By: Jeffrey C. Smith

Nat'l Ass'n of Charterboat Operators (NACO)
Issues: MAR
Rep By: Jeffrey C. Smith

Nat'l Ass'n of Collection Sites
Issues: ALC
Rep By: Jeffrey C. Smith

Washington Public Affairs Group

Eight E St. SE
Washington, DC 20003
Tel: (202)543-4172
Fax: (202)546-6294
Registered: LDA, FARA

DC-Area Employees Representing Listed Clients
DENISON, George H.
RATLIFF, J. O.
WRIGHT, Leo

Washington Resource Associates

8529 W. Oak Pl.
Vienna, VA 22182
Tel: (703)790-8093
Fax: (703)790-8257
Registered: LDA
Web: www.washingtonresource.com
E-mail: info@washingtonresource.com

DC-Area Employees Representing Listed Clients
LONG, Christopher T., President

Clients

Ass'n of Consulting Foresters of America
Issues: AGR ENV TAX

Sabre Inc.
Issues: CPI EDU GOV LBR TAX TOU TRA TRD
Rep By: Christopher T. Long

Sun Microsystems
Issues: CPI EDU GOV LBR TAX TRD
Rep By: Christopher T. Long

United States Marine Repair
Issues: BUD DEF
Rep By: Christopher T. Long

Washington Strategies, L.L.C.

2300 Clarendon Blvd.
Suite 401
Arlington, VA 22201
Tel: (703)516-4787
Fax: (703)522-2628
Registered: LDA
Web: www.washingtonstrategies.com
An association management and government affairs firm.

DC-Area Employees Representing Listed Clients
CALVERT, Jennifer Johnson
JARRELL, William P.
RICHARDSON, Craig
ZIEBART, Geoffrey C.

Clients

Ballard, Spahr, Andrews & Ingersoll LLP
Rep By: Jennifer Johnson Calvert, William P. Jarrell

Barrick Goldstrike Mines, Inc.
Issues: NAT
Rep By: Geoffrey C. Ziebart

Corning Inc.
Rep By: Jennifer Johnson Calvert, William P. Jarrell

Internat'l Longevity Center
Rep By: Jennifer Johnson Calvert, William P. Jarrell

Maersk Inc.
Rep By: Jennifer Johnson Calvert, William P. Jarrell

Nat'l Ass'n of Business Political Action Committees
Issues: CIV COM GOV
Rep By: Geoffrey C. Ziebart

New York Institute of Technology
Rep By: Jennifer Johnson Calvert, William P. Jarrell

Personal Watercraft Industry Ass'n
Rep By: Jennifer Johnson Calvert, William P. Jarrell

Recreational Fishing Alliance
Rep By: Jennifer Johnson Calvert, William P. Jarrell

University Technology Park
Rep By: Jennifer Johnson Calvert, William P. Jarrell

West Chester University
Rep By: Jennifer Johnson Calvert, William P. Jarrell

Widener University
Rep By: Jennifer Johnson Calvert, William P. Jarrell

Washington World Group, Ltd.

2120 L St. NW
Suite 208
Washington, DC 20037
E-mail: euk1@prodigy.net
Tel: (202)463-7820
Fax: (202)223-3794
Registered: FARA

DC-Area Employees Representing Listed Clients
VON KLOBERG, III, Edward J., Chairman and Founder

Clients

Argentina, Government of
Rep By: Edward J. von Kloberg, III

Asociacion Hondurena de Maquiladores
Rep By: Edward J. von Kloberg, III

Bahrain, Government of the State of
Rep By: Edward J. von Kloberg, III

Benin, Government of the Republic of
Issues: AVI

Biman Bangladesh Airlines
Rep By: Edward J. von Kloberg, III

Brunei Darussalam, Embassy of the State of
Rep By: Edward J. von Kloberg, III

Burkina Faso, Government of
Rep By: Edward J. von Kloberg, III

Burundi, Embassy of
Rep By: Edward J. von Kloberg, III

Cameroon, Government of the Republic of
Rep By: Edward J. von Kloberg, III

Cape Verde, Embassy of the Republic of
Rep By: Edward J. von Kloberg, III

Congo, Ministry of Foreign Affairs and Economic Cooperation of the Republic of
Rep By: Edward J. von Kloberg, III

Congo, Office of the Prime Minister of the Democratic Republic of the
Rep By: Edward J. von Kloberg, III

Costa Rica, Embassy of the Republic of
Rep By: Edward J. von Kloberg, III

Djibouti, Embassy of the Republic of
Rep By: Edward J. von Kloberg, III

Dominican Republic, Embassy of the
Rep By: Edward J. von Kloberg, III

Equitable Financial Co.
Rep By: Edward J. von Kloberg, III

Gabonese Republic, Office of the President of the
Rep By: Edward J. von Kloberg, III

Gambia Telecommunications
Rep By: Edward J. von Kloberg, III

Gambia, Government of the Republic of The
Rep By: Edward J. von Kloberg, III

Grenada, Government of the Republic of
Rep By: Edward J. von Kloberg, III

Guatemalan Development Foundation (FUNDESA)
Rep By: Edward J. von Kloberg, III

Guinea, Government of the Republic of
Rep By: Edward J. von Kloberg, III

Haiti, Provisional Government of the Republic of
Rep By: Edward J. von Kloberg, III

Kyrgyzstan, Government of the Republic of

Lesotho, Embassy of The Kingdom Of
Rep By: Edward J. von Kloberg, III

Lithuanian American Council
Rep By: Edward J. von Kloberg, III

Mali, Embassy of the Republic of
Rep By: Edward J. von Kloberg, III

Mauritania, Office of the Foreign Minister of
Rep By: Edward J. von Kloberg, III

Mongolian People's Republic, Embassy of
Rep By: Edward J. von Kloberg, III

Myanmar, Embassy of the Union of
Rep By: Edward J. von Kloberg, III

Nepal, Kingdom of
Rep By: Edward J. von Kloberg, III

Nepal, Royal Embassy of
Rep By: Edward J. von Kloberg, III

Nicaraguan Foundation for Democracy and Development
Rep By: Edward J. von Kloberg, III

Niger, Government of the Republic of
Rep By: Edward J. von Kloberg, III

Nigeria, Embassy of the Federal Republic of
Rep By: Edward J. von Kloberg, III

Pakistan, Embassy of the Islamic Republic of
Rep By: Edward J. von Kloberg, III

Panama, Government of the Republic of
Rep By: Edward J. von Kloberg, III

Papua New Guinea, Embassy of
Rep By: Edward J. von Kloberg, III

Picker Internat'l
Rep By: Edward J. von Kloberg, III

Rwanda, Government of the Republic of
Rep By: Edward J. von Kloberg, III

Senegal, Government of the Republic of
Rep By: Edward J. von Kloberg, III

Slovak Information Agency
Rep By: Edward J. von Kloberg, III

Slovenia, Republic of
Rep By: Edward J. von Kloberg, III

Suriname, Government of the Republic of
Rep By: Edward J. von Kloberg, III

Swaziland, Embassy of the Kingdom of
Rep By: Edward J. von Kloberg, III

Tanzania, Office of the Foreign Minister of the United Republic of
Rep By: Edward J. von Kloberg, III

Togo, Government of the Republic of
Rep By: Edward J. von Kloberg, III

Trinidad and Tobago, Embassy of the Republic of
Rep By: Edward J. von Kloberg, III

Zaire, Office of the President of the Republic of
Rep By: Edward J. von Kloberg, III

Wasserman and Associates

3626 Van Ness St. NW
Washington, DC 20008
E-mail: GWASSER115@aol.com
Tel: (202)966-9199
Fax: (202)362-7222
Registered: FARA

DC-Area Employees Representing Listed Clients
WASSERMAN, Gary

Clients

Taipei Economic and Cultural Representative Office in the United States
Rep By: Gary Wasserman

Waterman & Associates

900 Second St. NE
Suite 109
Washington, DC 20002
Tel: (202)898-1444
Fax: (202)898-0188
Registered: LDA

DC-Area Employees Representing Listed Clients
HOLLON, Michael
KRAHN, Joe, Associate
LUCAS, Amy, Senior Associate
SALMON, Stephanie, Senior Associate
WATERMAN, Diana L., V. President
WATERMAN, Ronald D., President

Clients

American Foundrymen's Soc.
Issues: CAW ENG ENV LBR MAN
Rep By: Amy Lucas, Diana L. Waterman

American Metalcasting Consortium
Issues: DEF
Rep By: Diana L. Waterman

California State Ass'n of Counties
Issues: DIS HCR HOU LAW TOB TRA WEL
Rep By: Michael Hollon, Joe Krahn, Ronald D. Waterman

Milwaukee, Wisconsin, County of
Issues: AVI HCR LAW LBR TOB TRA WEL
Rep By: Joe Krahn, Ronald D. Waterman

North American Die Casting Ass'n
Issues: CAW
Rep By: Amy Lucas, Diana L. Waterman

George Waters Consulting Service

1010 Massachusetts Ave. NW
Suite 210
Washington, DC 20001
E-mail: gwaters@knight.hub.com
Tel: (202)371-1153
Fax: (202)371-1032
Registered: LDA

DC-Area Employees Representing Listed Clients
DUGAN, Tom, Staff Attorney
WATERS, George, President

Clients

Chippewa Cree Tribe
Rep By: George Waters

Confederated Salish and Kootenai Tribes of the Flathead Nation

Eastern Band of Cherokee Indians
Rep By: George Waters

Passamaquoddy Tribe(s)(2)
Rep By: George Waters

Penobscot Indian Nation
Rep By: George Waters

Reno/Sparks Indian Colony
Rep By: George Waters

Walker River Paiute Tribe
Rep By: George Waters

Washoe Tribe of Nevada and California
Rep By: George Waters

Waterstone Strategies & Technologies

1200 New York Ave. NW
Suite 410
Washington, DC 20005
Tel: (202)682-9344
Fax: (202)689-9298
Registered: LDA

The Washington office of a firm headquartered in Niwot, CO.

DC-Area Employees Representing Listed Clients
STIRLING, Deborah J., Senior V. President

Wear & Associates

888 16th St. NW
Suite 400
Washington, DC 20006
Tel: (202)466-6015
Fax: (202)296-8791
Registered: LDA

DC-Area Employees Representing Listed Clients
WEAR, Terrance J., President

Clients

Dal-Tile Corp.
Rep By: Terrance J. Wear

InterMedia Partners
Rep By: Terrance J. Wear

Mobex Communications
Rep By: Terrance J. Wear

J. Arthur Weber & Associates

1140 23rd St. NW
Suite 806
Washington, DC 20037
Tel: (202)293-7187
Fax: (202)872-1150
Registered: LDA

DC-Area Employees Representing Listed Clients
WEBER, Joseph A., President

Clients

Citizens Against Research Bans
Issues: ENG NAT
Rep By: Joseph A. Weber

Coalition for Reliable Energy
Issues: ENG NAT
Rep By: Joseph A. Weber

Internat'l Technology Resources, Inc.
Rep By: Joseph A. Weber

Media Fusion L.L.C.
Issues: TEC UTI
Rep By: Joseph A. Weber

Stephens, Cross, Ihlenfeld and Boring, Inc.
Issues: GOV
Rep By: Joseph A. Weber

Webster, Chamberlain & Bean

1747 Pennsylvania Ave. NW
Suite 1000
Washington, DC 20006
Tel: (202)785-9500
Fax: (202)835-0243
Registered: LDA, FARA

A general practice law firm.

DC-Area Employees Representing Listed Clients
ABEGG, Heidi, Associate
DYE, Alan P., Partner
GOCH, David P., Partner
HAZARD, Jr., John W., Partner
HEROLD, Arthur, Partner
MACDONALD, Douglas, Associate
WATKINS, Charles M., Associate
WEBSTER, Hugh K., Partner

Clients

American Boiler Manufacturers Ass'n
Rep By: Hugh K. Webster

American Soc. of Nuclear Cardiology

American Soc. of Radiologic Technologists
Issues: HCR
Rep By: David P. Goch, Arthur Herold

American Staffing Ass'n
Rep By: Arthur Herold

Ass'n of Government Accountants

Ass'n of School Business Officials Internat'l
Rep By: Arthur Herold

Commercial Law League of America
Issues: BAN BNK
Rep By: David P. Goch

Internat'l Ass'n of Food Industry Suppliers
Rep By: Hugh K. Webster

Internat'l Safety Equipment Ass'n (ISEA)
Rep By: Arthur Herold

Nat'l Center for Homeopathy
Rep By: Alan P. Dye

Nat'l Tooling and Machining Ass'n
Rep By: Alan P. Dye

Packaging Machinery Manufacturers Institute
Rep By: Hugh K. Webster

Robotic Industries Ass'n
Rep By: Alan P. Dye

Screenprinting & Graphic Imaging Ass'n Internat'l
Rep By: Alan P. Dye

Skills USA-VICA

Taxicab, Limousine and Paratransit Ass'n
Issues: LBR
Rep By: Arthur Herold, Charles M. Watkins

Robert K. Weidner

1101 30th St. NW
Washington, DC 20007
Tel: (202)342-9240
Fax: (202)342-9241
Registered: LDA
E-mail: rkw57@msn.com

Provides natural resources, energy and environmental consulting and lobbying.

Clients

BP America, Inc.
Issues: ENV
Rep By: Robert K. Weidner

BP Exploration
Rep By: Robert K. Weidner

James W. Bunger & Associates
Issues: CHM FUE
Rep By: Robert K. Weidner

Questar Corp.
Issues: FUE
Rep By: Robert K. Weidner

Rural Public Lands County Council
Issues: NAT
Rep By: Robert K. Weidner

Donald Weightman

510 C St. NW
Washington, DC 20002
Tel: (202)544-1458
Fax: (202)544-1371
Registered: LDA
E-mail: dweightman@radix.net

Clients

Internet Ventures, Inc.
Issues: COM TEC
Rep By: Donald Weightman

Weil, Gotshal & Manges, LLP

1615 L St. NW
Suite 700
Washington, DC 20036-5610
Tel: (202)682-7000
Fax: (202)857-0939
Registered: LDA

Washington office of a New York general practice law firm.

DC-Area Employees Representing Listed Clients

AISTARS, Sandra M., Associate
ANDERSON, M. Jean, Partner
BEN-VENISTE, Richard, Partner
BETKE, Todd W., Associate
CONNOLLY, Annemargaret, Partner
HIRD, David B., Partner
JANOW, Joshua, Legislative Specialist
ODLE, Jr., Robert C., Partner
ROH, Jr., Charles E., Partner
TAYLOR, David, Legislative Specialist
TURNBULL, Bruce H., Partner
WILLIS, Larry I., Director, Legislative Services/Associate

Clients

Copyright Clearance Center, Inc.
Issues: CPT
Rep By: Sandra M. Aistars, Charles E. Roh, Jr., Bruce H. Turnbull

Empire Blue Cross and Blue Shield
Issues: HCR
Rep By: Sandra M. Aistars, Robert C. Odle, Jr.

GAF Corp.
Issues: CON
Rep By: Annemargaret Connolly, Robert C. Odle, Jr., Larry I. Willis

General Motors Corp.
Issues: TAX
Rep By: Robert C. Odle, Jr.

InterTrust, Inc.
Issues: CPT
Rep By: Sandra M. Aistars, Bruce H. Turnbull

Kimberly-Clark Corp.
Issues: TAX
Rep By: Larry I. Willis

Matsushita Electric Corp. of America
Issues: CPT
Rep By: Sandra M. Aistars, Bruce H. Turnbull

Nat'l Football League Players Ass'n
Issues: TAX
Rep By: Robert C. Odle, Jr.

Nomura Internat'l plc
Issues: TEC
Rep By: Joshua Janow, Robert C. Odle, Jr., Charles E. Roh, Jr., David Taylor, Larry I. Willis

Pinnacle West Capital Corp.

Real Estate Roundtable
Issues: ENV
Rep By: David B. Hird

Schering-Plough Corp.
Issues: CPT
Rep By: Richard Ben-Veniste

David M. Weiman

635 Maryland Ave. NE
Washington, DC 20002-5811
Tel: (202)546-5115
Registered: LDA

Clients

The Metropolitan Water District of Southern California
Issues: ENG UTI
Rep By: David M. Weiman

Bonnie H. Weinstein

1825 I St. NW
Suite 400
Washington, DC 20006
Tel: (202)293-4752
Fax: (202)530-0179
Registered: LDA

Clients

Air Tractor, Inc.
Issues: AVI
Rep By: Bonnie H. Weinstein

Edmund B. Welch

1600 Wilson Blvd.
Suite 1000A
Arlington, VA 22209
Tel: (703)807-0100
Fax: (703)807-0103
Registered: LDA

Clients

Dare County
Issues: RES
Rep By: Edmund B. Welch

Wells & Associates

1256 Pine Hill Rd.
McLean, VA 22101
Tel: (703)448-0935
Fax: (703)448-9322
Registered: LDA
E-mail: miltontwells@msn.com

DC-Area Employees Representing Listed Clients

WELLS, Milton T.

Clients

King & Spalding
Rep By: Milton T. Wells

Performance Food Group Inc.
Rep By: Milton T. Wells

Save the Greenback Coalition
Issues: MON
Rep By: Milton T. Wells

Carla L. West

666 Pennsylvania Ave. SE
Washington, DC 20003
Tel: (202)548-2311
Registered: LDA

Clients

Ag Biotech Planning Committee
Issues: AGR FOO
Rep By: Carla L. West

G. Frank West

406 First St. SE
Third Floor
Washington, DC 20003
Tel: (202)488-8562
Fax: (202)488-3803
Registered: LDA

A Washington representation consultant.

Clients

Kansas Gas Service
Rep By: G. Frank West

Oklahoma Natural Gas Co.
Rep By: G. Frank West

Jane West

4425 Walsh St.
Chevy Chase, MD 20815
Tel: (301)718-0979
Fax: (301)718-0980
Registered: LDA
E-mail: jewest@aol.com

Clients

Ass'n of TEH Act Projects
Issues: GOV
Rep By: Jane West, Ph.D.

Higher Education Consortium for Special Education
Issues: EDU
Rep By: Jane West, Ph.D.

Westerly Group

P.O. Box 2204
Washington, DC 20013
Tel: (202)628-9774
Fax: (202)628-9776
Registered: LDA
E-mail: westerly@slbrown.com

DC-Area Employees Representing Listed Clients

BROWN, Sarah, Senior Associate
CLINKENBEARD, Kirk L., President

Clients

Microcosm, Inc.
Issues: DEF
Rep By: Sarah Brown, Kirk L. Clinkenbeard

Sunset Properties, Inc.
Issues: AGR BUD GOV
Rep By: Sarah Brown, Kirk L. Clinkenbeard

Western Resources
Issues: ENG
Rep By: Sarah Brown, Kirk L. Clinkenbeard

The Wexler Group

1317 F St. NW
Suite 600
Washington, DC 20004
Tel: (202)638-2121
Fax: (202)638-7045
Registered: LDA, FARA
Web: www.wexlergroup.com

A government relations and public affairs consulting unit of Hill and Knowlton, Inc., which is in turn owned by the English firm WPP Group PLC.

Political Action Committee

The Wexler Group Political Action Committee
1317 F St. NW
Suite 600
Washington, DC 20004
Contact: Sena Fitzmaurice
Tel: (202)638-2121
Fax: (202)638-7045

DC-Area Employees Representing Listed Clients

BERRY, Cynthia E., Principal/General Counsel
EISGRAU, Adam, Principal/Director
FITZMAURICE, Sena, Principal
FLANAGAN, Hon. Michael Patrick, Principal/Senior Director
FOLSOM, R. D., Principal/Senior Director
HANNEGAN, Timothy, Principal/Senior Director
HEALY, Jr., Robert L., Principal/Senior Director
HOFFMAN, Jody A., Principal/Senior Director
HOLRAN, Peter T., Principal/Deputy General Manager
JONES, Anne, Principal/Director
LINK, Patric G., Principal/Senior Director
MALINA, Joel, Principal/Senior Director
MAROULIS, Christine, Senior Associate
MAY, Vicki, Principal
MCCANN, Patrick J., Principal/Senior Director
MELBERG, James K., Principal
MORITSUGU, Erika, Principal
PETERSON, Meg, Associate
SNAPE, Dale W., Principal/General Manager

WALKER, Hon. Robert S., Chairman and Chief Exec. Officer
WEXLER, Anne, Chairman of the Exec. Committee

Clients

AAAE-ACI
Issues: AVI
Rep By: Patrick J. McCann

Alaska, Washington Office of the State of
Rep By: Robert L. Healy, Jr., Joel Malina, Anne Wexler

Alliance for Understandable, Sensible and Accountable Government Regulations
Issues: GOV
Rep By: Joel Malina, Christine Maroulis

Alliance of Automobile Manufacturers, Inc.
Issues: AUT
Rep By: Hon. Michael Patrick Flanagan, Hon. Robert S. Walker

American Airlines
Issues: AVI
Rep By: Timothy Hannegan, Patrick J. McCann, Dale W. Snape, Anne Wexler

American Dental Ass'n
Issues: HCR
Rep By: Jody A. Hoffman

American Forest & Paper Ass'n
Issues: ENV
Rep By: Dale W. Snape, Anne Wexler

American Mobile Satellite Corp.
Issues: CPT TEC
Rep By: Adam Eisgrau

ARINC, Inc.
Issues: AVI
Rep By: Patrick J. McCann

Asea Brown Boveri, Inc.
Issues: ENV
Rep By: Robert L. Healy, Jr., Anne Wexler

AstroVision Inc.
Issues: AER SCI
Rep By: Peter T. Holran, Patric G. Link, Hon. Robert S. Walker

BP Amoco Corp.
Issues: ENG
Rep By: Robert L. Healy, Jr., Joel Malina

British Airways Plc
Issues: AVI
Rep By: Timothy Hannegan

British Columbia Hydro and Power Authority
Issues: FUE
Rep By: Joel Malina

Burger King Corp.
Issues: FOO HCR LBR TAX
Rep By: Hon. Michael Patrick Flanagan, Joel Malina, Anne Wexler

Burst Networks Inc.
Issues: COM
Rep By: Peter T. Holran, Anne Jones, Vicki May, Dale W. Snape

Caterpillar Inc.
Issues: ENV
Rep By: Joel Malina, Dale W. Snape, Anne Wexler

Chattanooga Metropolitan Airport Authority
Issues: AVI
Rep By: Timothy Hannegan

Chicago Transit Authority
Issues: TRA
Rep By: Patrick J. McCann

Comcast Corp.
Issues: TEC
Rep By: Sena Fitzmaurice, R. D. Folsom, Dale W. Snape, Hon. Robert S. Walker, Anne Wexler

CSX Corp.
Issues: RRR
Rep By: Patrick J. McCann, Anne Wexler

DCH Technology Inc.
Issues: ENG SCI
Rep By: Peter T. Holran, Anne Jones, Patric G. Link, Hon. Robert S. Walker

Digital Media Ass'n
Issues: SCI
Rep By: Adam Eisgrau

Dreamtime, Inc.
Issues: AER SCI TAX
Rep By: Peter T. Holran, Hon. Robert S. Walker

EarthWatch, Inc.
Issues: AER SCI
Rep By: Peter T. Holran, Anne Jones, Patric G. Link, Hon. Robert S. Walker

Electronic Industries Alliance
Issues: TRD
Rep By: R. D. Folsom, Hon. Robert S. Walker

Foothills Pipe Lines (Yukon), Ltd.
Issues: FUE
Rep By: Anne Wexler

General Motors Corp.
Issues: ENV GOV
Rep By: Hon. Michael Patrick Flanagan, Patrick J. McCann, Hon. Robert S. Walker, Anne Wexler

P. H. Glatfelter
Rep By: Hon. Robert S. Walker

Guardian Industries Corp.
Issues: TRD
Rep By: R. D. Folsom, Hon. Robert S. Walker, Anne Wexler

Hong Kong Economic and Trade Office
Issues: TRD
Rep By: R. D. Folsom, Joel Malina, Hon. Robert S. Walker

Hydroelectric Licensing Reform Task Force
Issues: ENG
Rep By: Joel Malina, Dale W. Snape, Hon. Robert S. Walker, Anne Wexler

Immunex Corp.
Issues: HCR
Rep By: Cynthia E. Berry, Jody A. Hoffman, Christine Maroulis, Erika Moritsugu, Anne Wexler

IMS Health Inc.
Issues: HCR IMM TAX
Rep By: Cynthia E. Berry, Jody A. Hoffman, Christine Maroulis, Anne Wexler

InVision Technologies
Issues: BUD
Rep By: Patrick J. McCann

Lockheed Martin Corp.
Issues: AER
Rep By: Peter T. Holran, Anne Jones, Dale W. Snape, Hon. Robert S. Walker

Mammoth Mountain
Issues: BUD TRA
Rep By: Timothy Hannegan, Patrick J. McCann

MENC: The Nat'l Ass'n for Music Education
Issues: EDU
Rep By: Cynthia E. Berry, Peter T. Holran, Joel Malina, Christine Maroulis, Hon. Robert S. Walker, Anne Wexler

Midwest Express Airlines
Issues: AVI
Rep By: Timothy Hannegan

Nat'l Ass'n of Music Merchants
Issues: EDU TAX
Rep By: Cynthia E. Berry, Peter T. Holran, Joel Malina, Christine Maroulis, Hon. Robert S. Walker, Anne Wexler

ORBITZ
Issues: AVI CPI SCI TRA
Rep By: Adam Eisgrau, Timothy Hannegan, Patric G. Link, Patrick J. McCann, Dale W. Snape, Hon. Robert S. Walker, Anne Wexler

PacifiCare Health Systems
Issues: HCR
Rep By: Cynthia E. Berry, Jody A. Hoffman, Christine Maroulis, Dale W. Snape, Anne Wexler

Rocket Development Co.
Issues: AER SCI
Rep By: Peter T. Holran, Hon. Robert S. Walker

Rosenbaum Trust
Issues: EDU
Rep By: Peter T. Holran, Christine Maroulis, Hon. Robert S. Walker

Sechan Electronics
Issues: DEF
Rep By: Peter T. Holran, Hon. Robert S. Walker

Shivwitz Band of the Paiute Indian Tribe of Utah
Issues: IND
Rep By: Dale W. Snape

Virginia Center for Innovative Technology
Issues: SCI
Rep By: Adam Eisgrau, Patric G. Link, Hon. Robert S. Walker

VISA U.S.A., Inc.
Issues: BAN CPT CSP HCR
Rep By: Cynthia E. Berry, Jody A. Hoffman

Wasatch Front Regional Council
Issues: BUD
Rep By: Patrick J. McCann

Wyeth-Ayerst Laboratories
Issues: MMM
Rep By: Cynthia E. Berry, Jody A. Hoffman, Christine Maroulis, Erika Moritsugu, Dale W. Snape

XM Satellite Radio, Inc.
Issues: COM
Rep By: Adam Eisgrau

Wheat & Associates, Inc.

1201 S. Eads St.
Suite Two
Arlington, VA 22202
Web: www.wheatgr.com

Tel: (703)271-8770
Fax: (703)271-9594
Registered: LDA

DC-Area Employees Representing Listed Clients

BEVVINO, Andrea, Director, Government Relations
KEEFE, Tom, Senior V. President
WHEAT, Hon. Alan D., President

Clients

Airgas, Inc.
Issues: ENV WAS
Rep By: Andrea Bevvino, Hon. Alan D. Wheat

AON Risk Services
Issues: FIN LBR WEL
Rep By: Hon. Alan D. Wheat

Apollo Group, Inc.
Issues: EDU
Rep By: Hon. Alan D. Wheat

Bay Mills Indian Community
Issues: GAM IND TAX
Rep By: Hon. Alan D. Wheat

The Century Council
Issues: ALC
Rep By: Andrea Bevvino, Hon. Alan D. Wheat

GE Capital Mortgage Insurance Co. (GEMICO)
Issues: HOU
Rep By: Andrea Bevvino, Hon. Alan D. Wheat

GlaxoSmithKline
Issues: HCR MED PHA
Rep By: Hon. Alan D. Wheat

Global Encasement, Inc.
Issues: TRA
Rep By: Tom Keefe, Hon. Alan D. Wheat

Nescrow.com Technologies
Issues: CSP
Rep By: Andrea Bevvino, Hon. Alan D. Wheat

Rainbow/Push Coalition (National Bureau)
Issues: ECN
Rep By: Hon. Alan D. Wheat

Susan J. White & Associates

1020 N. Fairfax
Suite 202
Alexandria, VA 22314

Tel: (703)683-2573
Fax: (703)683-0865
Registered: LDA

DC-Area Employees Representing Listed Clients

WHITE, Susan J., Principal

Clients

Cook, Illinois, County of
Issues: HCR LAW MMM RET TAX URB
Rep By: Susan J. White

Cuyahoga, Ohio, County of
Issues: HCR HOU LAW MMM RET TAX WEL
Rep By: Susan J. White

Los Angeles, California, County of
Issues: HCR MMM
Rep By: Susan J. White

Nat'l Ass'n of Government Deferred Compensation Administrators
Issues: RET TAX
Rep By: Susan J. White

Santa Barbara Regional Health Authority
Issues: HCR MMM
Rep By: Susan J. White

Shelby, Tennessee, County of
Issues: HCR MMM
Rep By: Susan J. White

White & Case LLP

601 13th St. NW
Suite 600 South
Washington, DC 20005
Web: www.whitecase.com
A general practice law firm.

Tel: (202)626-3600
Fax: (202)639-9355
Registered: LDA, FARA

Political Action Committee

White & Case PAC
601 13th St. NW
Suite 600 South
Washington, DC 20005
Contact: William P. McClure

Tel: (202)626-3600
Fax: (202)639-9355

DC-Area Employees Representing Listed Clients

BITTMAN, Robert
BOWEN, Vincent, Associate
BROWER, Charles N., Partner
BURKE, Richard J., Associate
CARLISLE, Linda E., Partner
CLINTON, William J., Partner
CORR, Christopher F., Partner
DESANTIS, Victor J., Partner
GILROY, Daniel T., Legislative Affairs Specialist
HILDEBRANDT, David A.
HOULIHAN, David P., Partner
HUNT, David W., Partner
LAMM, Carolyn B., Partner
LEGATO, Carmen D., Partner
MCCLURE, William P., Partner
MENTZ, J. Roger, Partner

NGUYEN, Mark D., Director, Multilateral Trade Service
PANOPOULOS, Frank
PAUL, Robert D., Partner
RITCEY-DONOHUE, Joanna M., Director, International Trade Service
SPAK, Gregory J., Partner
SPAK, Walter J., Partner
TERWILLIGER, III, George J.
ZISSIS, Kristina, Associate

Clients

Alticor, Inc.
Issues: TAX
Rep By: Linda E. Carlisle, J. Roger Mentz

American-Uzbekistan Chamber of Commerce
Rep By: Carolyn B. Lamm

Bank of Zaire

Bulgaria, Government of the Republic of

Bundesverband der Deutscher Banken

CalEnergy Co., Inc.
Rep By: David W. Hunt

The Coca-Cola Company
Issues: TAX
Rep By: William P. McClure

Costa Rica, Central Bank of

Dalmine
Rep By: David P. Houlihan

Employee-Owned S Corporations of America
Issues: TAX
Rep By: Linda E. Carlisle

Guinea, Government of the Republic of

Honduras, Government of the Republic of

Indonesia, Government of the Republic of
Rep By: Carolyn B. Lamm

Koniag, Inc.
Issues: TAX
Rep By: William P. McClure, J. Roger Mentz

Liberty Check Printers
Issues: TAX
Rep By: Linda E. Carlisle, J. Roger Mentz

Malaysia Ministry of Trade
Rep By: William J. Clinton, Walter J. Spak

Mercedes-Benz of North America, Inc.
Rep By: Linda E. Carlisle, J. Roger Mentz

Methanex Inc.
Issues: TAX
Rep By: Linda E. Carlisle, J. Roger Mentz

Minebea Thailand
Rep By: Walter J. Spak

Motion Picture Ass'n of America
Issues: TAX
Rep By: William P. McClure

Nigeria, Government of the Federal Republic of

Pakistan, Government of the Islamic Republic of

Parker Drilling Co.
Rep By: Charles N. Brower

Perpetual Corp.
Issues: TAX
Rep By: William P. McClure

Polyisocyanurate Insulation Manufacturers Ass'n
Rep By: Robert D. Paul

Profit Sharing/401 (k) Council of America
Rep By: David A. Hildebrandt

Scandinavian Airlines System (SAS)

Siderar S.A.I.C.
Rep By: David P. Houlihan

Siderca Corp.
Rep By: David P. Houlihan

Siderurgica del Orinoco (Sidor), C.A.
Rep By: David P. Houlihan

Singapore, Embassy of the Republic of
Rep By: William J. Clinton, Walter J. Spak

Singapore, Government of the Republic of
Rep By: William J. Clinton, Walter J. Spak

Suriname, Government of the Republic of

TAMSA
Rep By: David P. Houlihan

Techsnabexport, A.O.
Issues: ENG
Rep By: Carolyn B. Lamm, Frank Panopoulos

Thailand, Department of Foreign Trade of
Rep By: William J. Clinton, Walter J. Spak

Toshiba Corp.
Rep By: David P. Houlihan

Tunisia, Embassy of the Republic of

United States-China Chamber of Commerce

Uzbekistan, Government of the Republic of
Rep By: Carolyn B. Lamm

The Williams Companies
Rep By: Linda E. Carlisle, J. Roger Mentz

White House Writers Group

1030 15th St. NW
Suite 1100
Washington, DC 20005
Tel: (202)783-4600
Fax: (202)783-4601
Web: www.whwg.com

Provides writing services, strategic counsel, message management, and media relations for corporate and non-profit clients.

DC-Area Employees Representing Listed Clients

CASSE, Daniel, Senior Director
DAVIS, Mark W., Senior Director
DOHERTY, Eileen, Senior Director
GILDER, Josh, Senior Director
JUDGE, Clark S., Managing Director
MCGREGOR, Katy, Senior Director
MCGROARTY, Daniel, Senior Director
SANDERS BECKNER, Helen, Senior Director
STACH, Kevin, Senior Director
STINGER, Patti, Senior Director

R. H. White Public Affairs Consulting

13901 Piscataway Dr.
Fort Washington, MD 20744
Tel: (202)256-1293
Fax: (301)292-8598
Registered: LDA
E-mail: rhwhite@msn.com

Provides public affairs consulting for corporate and trade association clients.

DC-Area Employees Representing Listed Clients

WHITE, Richard H.

Clients

Brown and Williamson Tobacco Corp.
Issues: AGR HCR TAX TOB
Rep By: Richard H. White

R. C. Whitner and Associates, Inc.
Issues: DEF
Rep By: Richard H. White

John Thomas White

516 1/2 Oronoco St.
Alexandria, VA 22314
Tel: (703)684-2001
Fax: (703)739-7621
Registered: LDA

A self-employed legal and public affairs consultant.

Clients

The Boeing Co.
Rep By: John Thomas White, III

Nat'l Graduate University
Rep By: John Thomas White, III

Thomas R. "Randy" White

6305 26th St. North
Arlington, VA 22207
Tel: (703)532-4929
Fax: (703)532-1376
Registered: LDA
E-mail: trwhiteva@aol.com

Clients

Ass'n of Trial Lawyers of America
Issues: TOR
Rep By: Thomas R. "Randy" White

Whiteford, Taylor & Preston

1025 Connecticut Ave. NW
Suite 400
Washington, DC 20036
Tel: (202)659-6800
Fax: (202)331-0573
Registered: LDA
Web: www.wtplaw.com

A general practice law firm.

DC-Area Employees Representing Listed Clients

DUDLEY, Jane, Director, Governmental Affairs
SATTERFIELD, Lee A., Of Counsel

Clients

Accrediting Council for Continuing Education & Training

Suzanne Kay Whitehurst

3666 Gunston Rd.
Alexandria, VA 22302
Tel: (703)671-4795
Registered: LDA

R. C. Whitner and Associates, Inc.

1800 N. Kent St.
Suite 1104
Arlington, VA 22209
Tel: (703)243-1400
Fax: (703)525-0626
Registered: LDA
E-mail: whitner@erols.com

DC-Area Employees Representing Listed Clients

WHITNER, R. C., President

Clients

Condor Electronic Systems
Rep By: R. C. Whitner

Lockheed Martin Aeronautical Systems Co.
Issues: AER
Rep By: R. C. Whitner

Lockheed Martin Corp.
Rep By: R. C. Whitner

William F. Whitsitt Policy and Government Affairs

201 Maryland Ave. NE
Washington, DC 20002-5703
Tel: (202)544-3800
Fax: (202)543-0616
Registered: LDA
E-mail: wfwhitsitt@aol.com

Provides public policy advice and representation, with an emphasis on energy, environment, international travel matters, and government activities.

DC-Area Employees Representing Listed Clients

WHITSITT, William F., Principal

Clients

Burlington Resources Oil & Gas Co.
Issues: BUD ENG ENV FUE NAT TAX TRD
Rep By: William F. Whitsitt

Devon Energy Corp.
Issues: TRD
Rep By: William F. Whitsitt

Domestic Petroleum Council
Issues: BUD ENG ENV NAT TAX TRD UTI
Rep By: William F. Whitsitt

The Stanley Works
Issues: MAN TOR TRD
Rep By: William F. Whitsitt

Whitten & Diamond

1725 DeSales St. NW
Suite 800
Washington, DC 20036
Tel: (202)659-6540
Fax: (202)659-5730
Registered: LDA
E-mail: wd@cais.com

DC-Area Employees Representing Listed Clients

BLACKWELL, Hon. Lucien
DAWSON, Tom H., Consultant
DIAMOND, Robert M., Member
MELLON, Regina M., Government Affairs Representative
WHITTEN, Jamie L.
WILTRAUT, James

Clients

Aerolink, Inc.

Bombardier, Inc.
Issues: DEF
Rep By: Robert M. Diamond, Jamie L. Whitten

Can Manufacturers Institute
Issues: ENV
Rep By: Robert M. Diamond

Gas Technology Institute
Issues: ENG ENV
Rep By: Robert M. Diamond, Regina M. Mellon, Jamie L. Whitten

Lehigh Coal & Navigation Co.
Issues: DEF
Rep By: Robert M. Diamond, Jamie L. Whitten

Mountain Top Technologies, Inc.
Issues: DEF SCI
Rep By: Robert M. Diamond, Jamie L. Whitten

Norfolk Southern Corp.
Issues: TRA
Rep By: Robert M. Diamond

Philadelphia Internat'l Airport
Issues: TRA
Rep By: Robert M. Diamond, Regina M. Mellon

Philadelphia, Pennsylvania, City of
Issues: TRA
Rep By: Hon. Lucien Blackwell, Robert M. Diamond, Regina M. Mellon, Jamie L. Whitten

Pioneer Hi-Bred Internat'l, Inc.
Issues: AGR
Rep By: Robert M. Diamond, Regina M. Mellon, Jamie L. Whitten

St. Joseph University
Issues: EDU
Rep By: Robert M. Diamond, Jamie L. Whitten

Temple University
Issues: EDU HCR
Rep By: Robert M. Diamond, Regina M. Mellon, Jamie L. Whitten

Vernon, California, City of
Issues: IMM
Rep By: Robert M. Diamond, Jamie L. Whitten

Roy F. Weston, Inc.
Issues: DEF ENV
Rep By: Robert M. Diamond, Jamie L. Whitten

Burton V. Wides, P.C.

1225 I St. NW
Washington, DC 20005
Tel: (202)682-4763
Fax: (202)682-4707
Registered: LDA

DC-Area Employees Representing Listed Clients
WIDES, Burton V.

Clients
Guardian Life Insurance Co. of America
Issues: BAN BUD TAX TRD
Haiti, Embassy of the Republic of
Haiti, Government of the Republic of

Widmeyer Communications, Inc.

1825 Connecticut Ave. NW
Fifth Floor
Washington, DC 20009
Tel: (202)667-0901
Fax: (202)667-0902
Registered: LDA
Web: www.widmeyer.com
E-mail: info@widmeyer.com
A public relations and public affairs consulting firm. Also maintains an office in New York, NY.

DC-Area Employees Representing Listed Clients
ATKINSON, Jay, Chief Financial Officer
BLAUNSTEIN, Phyllis, Senior Counsel
BONDERUD, Kevin J., Senior V. President/Group Director
CHACON, Ruth W., Senior Counsel
CLAYTON, Joseph, President and Chief Operating Officer
COHEN, Gerry, Senior Counsel
DUNNING, Margaret Suzor, Senior V. President/Group Director
FAITH, Brian, V. President
FISKE, Edward, Senior Counsel
FRANK, David, Senior V. President and Group Director
INGLE, Cynthia, Assistant V. President
KELLY, James
SACKETT, Victoria A., V. President
SMITH, Jason, V. President
SULLIVAN, Tim, V. President
SUMMERS, David, V. President/Group Director
TIFFT, Susan, Senior Counsel
TINKER, Tim, V. President
WIDMEYER, Scott D., Chairman and Chief Exec. Officer

Clients
Aspen Institute
The Business Roundtable
Coalition to Protect Community Not-for-Profit Hospitals
The College Board
Education Communications, Inc.
Rep By: Kevin J. Bonderud
Inova Health Systems
Kellogg Foundation
Kennedy Center for the Performing Arts, John F.
Kids in the Know
Rep By: Kevin J. Bonderud
McGraw-Hill Cos., The
Nat'l Education Ass'n of the U.S.
Nat'l Institute for Literacy
Nat'l Research Center for College and University Admissions
Issues: EDU
Rep By: Kevin J. Bonderud
Pew Charitable Trust - Environmental Law & Policy Center of the Midwest
Primedia
Standard & Poor's Corp.
Teligent, Inc.
United Parcel Service
Washington Hospital Center
Wellesley College

The Wigglesworth Co.

9527 Liberty Tree Lane
Vienna, VA 22182
Tel: (703)319-7827
Fax: (703)319-8742
Registered: LDA

DC-Area Employees Representing Listed Clients
WIGGLESWORTH, Teresa N., President

Clients
SABIC Americas, Inc.
Issues: CHM FUE MAN TRD
Rep By: Teresa N. Wigglesworth

Bill Wight, LLC

P.O. Box 25204
Arlington, VA 22202
Tel: (703)920-4500
Fax: (703)920-8147
Registered: LDA
E-mail: wightllc@aol.com

DC-Area Employees Representing Listed Clients
WIGHT, Bill

Clients
General Motors Corp.
Issues: BUD DEF
Litton Electro Optical Systems
Issues: BUD DEF
Litton Electron Devices
Issues: BUD DEF
Litton Integrated Systems
Issues: BUD DEF
Litton Laser Systems
Issues: BUD DEF
Motorola Integrated Information Systems Group
Issues: BUD DEF

The Wilbur Group

4607 Connecticut Ave. NW
Suite 510
Washington, DC 20008
Tel: (202)364-1485
Registered: LDA
E-mail: vswilbur@earthlink.net

DC-Area Employees Representing Listed Clients
WILBUR, Valerie, President

Clients
Elderplan, Inc.
Issues: HCR
Rep By: Valerie Wilbur
Medicare Payment Coalition for Frail Beneficiaries
Issues: MED
Rep By: Valerie Wilbur
Nat'l Chronic Care Consortium
Issues: HCR
Rep By: Valerie Wilbur

Wilcox, Carroll & Froelich, PLLC

2011 Pennsylvania Ave. NW
Suite 301
Washington, DC 20006
Tel: (202)296-3005
Fax: (202)331-7479
Registered: LDA
E-mail: carroll@nmsa-usa.org

DC-Area Employees Representing Listed Clients
CARROLL, Jr., Charles T., Partner
FROELICH, M.D., F. Edwin, Partner

Clients
Nat'l Ass'n of Waterfront Employers
Rep By: Charles T. Carroll, Jr., F. Edwin Froelich, M.D.
Nat'l Maritime Safety Ass'n
Rep By: Charles T. Carroll, Jr., F. Edwin Froelich, M.D.

Wiley, Rein & Fielding

1776 K St. NW
Washington, DC 20006
Tel: (202)719-7000
Fax: (202)719-7049
Registered: LDA
Web: www.wrf.com
A law firm.

DC-Area Employees Representing Listed Clients
BARAN, Jan W., Partner
BAYES, James R., Partner
BODORFF, Richard
BOONE, Jr., Robert E., Of Counsel
BRADNER, Eileen P., Partner
BROWN, Tyrone, Of Counsel
BRUCE, III, James T., Partner
BRUNNER, Thomas W., Partner
BUCK, Susan C., Government Affairs Consultant
BURCHETT, Barbara G., Government Affairs Consultant
BUTLER, Robert J., Partner
DAWSON, Mimi W., Government Affairs Consultant
DESILVA, Eric W., Partner
FIELDING, Fred F., Partner
FINE, Sharon R.
GREGG, Donna C., Partner
HODGES, John A., Partner
JOHNSEN, Wayne D., Partner
JOSEPH, Bruce G., Partner
KAMP, John
KIRBY, Kathleen A., Counsel
KIRBY, Thomas W., Partner
KRUG, Peter
KRULWICH, Andrew S., Partner
LAHAM, Carol, Partner
LEWIS, Michael A., Consultant
MANNING, Mary Jo, Counsel
MCINTOSH, Lane
NAHRA, Kirk J., Partner
O'CONNELL, Pete, Of Counsel
PETTIT, Robert L., Partner
POTTER, Trevor, Partner
PRICE, Alan H., Partner
REIN, Bert W., Partner
REYNOLDS, III, John B., Partner
ROSS, Peter, Partner
SECREST, III, Lawrence W., Partner
SENKOWSKI, R. Michael, Partner
SHIELDS, Peter D., Partner
SLATTERY, Hon. Jim, Partner
TROY, Daniel E., Partner
VERRILL, Jr., Charles O., Partner
VICTORY, Nancy J., Partner
VOGT, Gregory J., Partner
WALLACE, Jr., James H., Partner
WILEY, Richard E., Partner

Clients
Advanced Integrated Technology, Inc.
Rep By: James T. Bruce, III
Aeronautical Radio, Inc.
AOL Time Warner
ARINC, Inc.
Issues: AVI COM TRA
Rep By: James T. Bruce, III, Barbara G. Burchett, Mimi W. Dawson, Hon. Jim Slattery
Ass'n of American Universities
Issues: CPT
Bell Atlantic Mobile
Issues: BUD COM CPT TAX TEC
Rep By: Mary Jo Manning
A. H. Belo Corp.
Issues: COM TEC
Rep By: James R. Bayes, Susan C. Buck, Mimi W. Dawson, Richard E. Wiley
Birmingham Steel Corp.
Issues: TRD
Rep By: Eileen P. Bradner, Sharon R. Fine, Hon. Jim Slattery
Blade Communications
Rep By: Donna C. Gregg
Chaparral Steel Co.
Rep By: Charles O. Verrill, Jr.
Club Car, Inc.
Rep By: Eileen P. Bradner, Charles O. Verrill, Jr.
Co-Steel Raritan
Issues: TRD
Rep By: Eileen P. Bradner, Sharon R. Fine, Hon. Jim Slattery
Columbia University
Issues: CPT MED
Rep By: James T. Bruce, III, Susan C. Buck, Hon. Jim Slattery
Connecticut Steel Corp.
Issues: TRD
Rep By: Eileen P. Bradner, Sharon R. Fine, Hon. Jim Slattery
Connecticut Student Loan Foundation
Issues: EDU
Rep By: Hon. Jim Slattery
Earth, Energy & Environment
Issues: ENG
Rep By: James T. Bruce, III, Hon. Jim Slattery
The Edison Project
Issues: EDU
Rep By: James T. Bruce, III
Electronic Industries Alliance
Engage Technologies
Issues: CPI CPT
Rep By: Mimi W. Dawson, Peter Ross
Gannett Co., Inc.
Issues: COM
Rep By: Susan C. Buck, Mimi W. Dawson, Pete O'Connell, Richard E. Wiley
Georgetown Industries
Rep By: Eileen P. Bradner, Charles O. Verrill, Jr.
Hearst-Argyle Television, Inc.
Issues: COM MIA
Rep By: Richard Bodorff, Susan C. Buck, Mimi W. Dawson, Robert L. Pettit
Industrial Telecommunications Ass'n, Inc.
Rep By: Robert L. Pettit
INTELSAT - Internat'l Telecommunications Satellite Organization
Issues: TEC
Rep By: Mimi W. Dawson, Bert W. Rein
Internat'l Paper
Rep By: Carol Laham
Internet Advertising Bureau
Issues: ADV CSP
Rep By: John Kamp
Kansas City Southern Industries
Rep By: Hon. Jim Slattery

Kansas City Southern Railway Co.
Issues: RRR TRA
Rep By: Hon. Jim Slattery

Keystone Consolidated Industries, Inc.
Issues: TRD
Rep By: Eileen P. Bradner, Sharon R. Fine, Hon. Jim Slattery

Marine Mammal Coalition
Rep By: John A. Hodges

MassMutual Financial Group
Issues: TAX
Rep By: Susan C. Buck

McGaw, Inc.

Merchant's Nat'l Bank

Mobile Telecommunications Technologies Corp.
Rep By: Mimi W. Dawson, Nancy J. Victory

Motorola, Inc.
Issues: TEC
Rep By: Mimi W. Dawson

Mutual of Omaha Insurance Companies
Issues: INS MED

Nat'l Religious Broadcasters
Issues: COM
Rep By: Richard E. Wiley

Nat'l Religious Broadcasters, Music License Committee
Rep By: Lawrence W. Secrest, III

NetCoalition.Com
Issues: CPI CPT
Rep By: Mimi W. Dawson

Newspaper Ass'n of America
Issues: COM POS
Rep By: James T. Bruce, III, Susan C. Buck, Mimi W. Dawson, Richard E. Wiley

Northwestern Steel and Wire Co.
Rep By: Eileen P. Bradner, Sharon R. Fine, Hon. Jim Slattery

Olan Mills Inc.

Open Group Electronic Messaging Ass'n (EMA) Forum
Issues: COM CPI CPT FIN GOV TEC
Rep By: James T. Bruce, III

Pacific Telesis

Personal Communications Industry Ass'n (PCIA)
Issues: TEC
Rep By: Susan C. Buck, Mimi W. Dawson, Hon. Jim Slattery, Nancy J. Victory

Prodigy
Rep By: Susan C. Buck, Robert J. Butler, Bruce G. Joseph, Nancy J. Victory

Professional Photographers of America

Qwest Communications
Issues: TEC
Rep By: Susan C. Buck, Barbara G. Burchett

Radio-Television News Directors Ass'n
Issues: COM MIA
Rep By: Kathleen A. Kirby

Raritan River Steel Co.
Rep By: Charles O. Verrill, Jr.

RENEW (Republican Network to Elect Women)
Rep By: Jan W. Baran

ROLITE, Inc.

Francis R. Ruddy Institute of Maritime Communications
Rep By: Mimi W. Dawson

Steel Manufacturers Ass'n

Syquest Technology, Inc.
Rep By: Charles O. Verrill, Jr.

Telephone Operators Caucus
Issues: ADV ART BUD COM CPT MIA
Rep By: Mary Jo Manning

Time Domain Corp.
Issues: TEC
Rep By: Susan C. Buck, Mimi W. Dawson, Mary Jo Manning

U.S. Banknote Corp.
Rep By: Fred F. Fielding

United Parcel Service
Rep By: Fred F. Fielding

United Student Aid Group

UTAM, Inc.
Rep By: Mimi W. Dawson

UtiliCorp United, Inc.
Issues: UTI
Rep By: James T. Bruce, III, Barbara G. Burchett, Mimi W. Dawson

Verizon Wireless
Issues: BUD COM CPT TAX TEC
Rep By: Mimi W. Dawson, Sharon R. Fine, Peter Krug, Mary Jo Manning, Lane McIntosh, Robert L. Pettit

Washington Citizens for World Trade
Issues: AGR
Rep By: Sharon R. Fine, Hon. Jim Slattery

Wheat Gluten Industry Council
Issues: TRD
Rep By: Hon. Jim Slattery

W. F. Young Inc.

Wilkinson, Barker and Knauer, LLP

2300 N St. NW
Suite 700
Washington, DC 20037-1128
Web: www.wbklaw.com
Tel: (202)783-4141
Fax: (202)783-5851
Registered: LDA, FARA

A law firm.

DC-Area Employees Representing Listed Clients
COHEN, Jonathan V., Partner
KELLER, L. Charles, Partner
KNAUER, Leon T., Partner
LINDSAY, J. Wade, Partner
PRIMOSCH, Robert, Partner
SINDERBRAND, Paul J., Partner

Clients

Colombia, Ministry of Communications of

Maine Cellular Telephone Co.
Issues: GOV

Panama, Public Service Regulatory Entity of the Government of the Republic of
Rep By: Leon T. Knauer

Wireless Communications Ass'n
Rep By: Jonathan V. Cohen, Robert Primosch, Paul J. Sinderbrand

Will and Carlson, Inc.

1015 18th St. NW
Suite 600
Washington, DC 20036
E-mail: willcarl@erols.com
Tel: (202)429-4344
Fax: (202)429-4342
Registered: LDA

DC-Area Employees Representing Listed Clients
CARLSON, Peter
JACKSON, Michael D., Senior Associate
MCLELLAN, Eileen
WILL, Robert P.

Clients

Animas-La Plata Water Conservancy District
Issues: BUD NAT
Rep By: Peter Carlson, Robert P. Will

Cambria Community Services District

Clark County Regional Flood Control District
Issues: BUD NAT
Rep By: Peter Carlson, Robert P. Will

Eastern Municipal Water District
Issues: BUD NAT
Rep By: Peter Carlson, Robert P. Will

Garrison Diversion Conservancy District
Issues: BUD NAT
Rep By: Peter Carlson, Robert P. Will

Kennedy/Jenks Consultants
Issues: BUD NAT
Rep By: Peter Carlson, Robert P. Will

The Metropolitan Water District of Southern California
Issues: BUD ENG
Rep By: Peter Carlson, Robert P. Will

Oregon Water Resources Congress
Issues: BUD NAT
Rep By: Peter Carlson

Salem, Oregon, City of
Issues: BUD
Rep By: Robert P. Will

Six Agency Committee
Issues: BUD IND NAT
Rep By: Peter Carlson, Robert P. Will

Southwest Water Conservation District of Colorado
Rep By: Peter Carlson, Robert P. Will

Tumalo Irrigation District
Issues: UTI

Western Coalition of Arid States
Issues: BUD ENV
Rep By: Peter Carlson, Robert P. Will

The Willard Group

1497 Chain Bridge Rd.
Suite 303
McLean, VA 22101
E-mail: dscherder@willardgroup.com
Tel: (703)893-8409
Fax: (703)893-8020
Registered: LDA

DC-Area Employees Representing Listed Clients
FALK, John M.
SCHERDER, Daniel, Managing Director

Clients

AEI Resources
Issues: ENG IND LBR NAT TAX
Rep By: Daniel Scherder

Bituminous Coal Operators Ass'n
Issues: ENV NAT TAX
Rep By: Daniel Scherder

Thomas D. Campbell & Assoc.
Issues: ENV NAT

Energy and Environment Coalition
Issues: ENV
Rep By: Daniel Scherder

EnviroPower
Issues: ENG ENV TAX
Rep By: Daniel Scherder

Kyros & Cummins Associates
Rep By: John M. Falk

The Peabody Group
Issues: ENG IND LBR NAT TAX
Rep By: Daniel Scherder

J. T. Rutherford & Associates
Issues: HCR TRD
Rep By: John M. Falk

Williams & Connolly

725 12th St. NW
Washington, DC 20005
Tel: (202)434-5000
Fax: (202)434-5029
Registered: LDA, FARA

A law firm.

DC-Area Employees Representing Listed Clients
BAINE, Kevin T., Partner
BARNETT, Robert B., Partner
COLLINS, Jeremiah C., Partner
COOPER, Richard M., Partner
CRAIG, Gregory B., Partner
DANIEL, III, Aubrey M., Partner
GALBRAITH, J. Alan, Partner
GENDERSON, Bruce R., Partner
GUTMAN, Howard W., Partner
KAHN, Peter J., Partner
KATZ, Daniel F., Partner
KENDALL, David E., Partner
KESTER, John G., Partner
MOGIN, Paul, Partner
SECHLER, Philip
SIMON, Barry S., Partner
SULLIVAN, Jr., Brendan V., Partner
URBANCZYK, Steve L., Partner
VARDAMAN, Jr., John W., Partner
WATKINS, Robert P., Partner

Clients

Archer Daniels Midland Co.
Rep By: Aubrey M. Daniel, III, Barry S. Simon

AutoNation, Inc.

Chamber of Independent Gas Stations of Argentina
Issues: CSP FUE
Rep By: Robert B. Barnett

General Motors Corp.
Rep By: Aubrey M. Daniel, III, Robert P. Watkins

Haiti, Chamber of Commerce of the Republic of
Rep By: Gregory B. Craig

Hatco Corp.
Rep By: Paul Mogin

Internat'l Truck and Engine Corp.
Rep By: Aubrey M. Daniel, III, J. Alan Galbraith

IVAX Corp.
Issues: PHA
Rep By: Richard M. Cooper

MCA Inc.
Rep By: David E. Kendall

McKechnie Brothers (South Africa) Ltd.
Rep By: Bruce R. Genderson

Motion Picture Ass'n of America

Omni Internat'l
Rep By: Brendan V. Sullivan, Jr.

R. J. Reynolds Tobacco Co.
Issues: TOB
Rep By: Richard M. Cooper, Philip Sechler

RJR Nabisco Holdings Co.
Rep By: Richard M. Cooper

Sentara Norfolk General Hospital

Special Olympics, Inc.
Rep By: Gregory B. Craig

United States Catholic Conference

Williams & Jensen, P.C.

1155 21st St. NW
Suite 300
Washington, DC 20036
Tel: (202)659-8201
Fax: (202)659-5249
Registered: LDA, FARA

A professional corporation engaged in general federal practice with activities in the areas of tax, antitrust, telecommunications, securities regulation, economic stabilization, education, transportation, energy and the environment, insurance, banking, health, food, drug, cosmetics, agriculture and related legislative matters.

Political Action Committee

Williams & Jensen Political Action Committee

1155 21st St. NW
Suite 300
Washington, DC 20036
Tel: (202)659-8201
Fax: (202)659-5249

DC-Area Employees Representing Listed Clients

ANDERSON, Rebecca L., Director, Government Affairs
BAKER, George D., Partner
BECHTEL, Philip E., Partner
BONFIGLIO, Barbara Wixon, Partner
CANFIELD, William B., Partner
CARP, Bertram W., Partner
FRANASIAK, David E., Partner
GLENNON, Jr., Robert E., Partner
HARRIS, II, A. J., Partner
HART, J. Steven, Chairman and Chief Exec. Officer
LANDERS, David M., Associate
LEWIS, Karen Judd, Partner
LYNCH, Karina, Associate
MARTINEZ, Robert J., Partner
MCMACKIN, Jr., John J., Partner
OLSEN, George G., Partner
RODA, Anthony J., Partner
ROSENKOETTER, Thomas J.
STARR, David A., Partner
TASSEY, Jeffrey A., Partner
TAYLOR, Tracy D., Associate
VLOSSAK, Frank C., Associate
WILLIAMS, J. D.

Clients

Abbott Laboratories
Rep By: George G. Olsen

ACE INA
Rep By: Robert E. Glennon, Jr.

Ad Hoc Coalition of Commercial and Investment Banks
Issues: CDT
Rep By: George D. Baker, William B. Canfield, J. Steven Hart

Aegon USA
Issues: BAN HCR INS TAX
Rep By: Rebecca L. Anderson, David E. Franasiak, Robert E. Glennon, Jr., J. Steven Hart, John J. McMackin, Jr., George G. Olsen, Anthony J. Roda

Alexander's Inc.
Rep By: David E. Franasiak, Robert E. Glennon, Jr., Anthony J. Roda

American Home Products Corp.
Issues: CAW CHM CPT CSP FOO HCR MMM PHA TAX
Rep By: David E. Franasiak, Robert E. Glennon, Jr., J. Steven Hart, Karen Judd Lewis, John J. McMackin, Jr., George G. Olsen, Anthony J. Roda, David A. Starr, Frank C. Vlossak

American Share Insurance
Issues: BNK
Rep By: Rebecca L. Anderson, J. Steven Hart, David M. Landers

The Anschutz Co.
Rep By: J. Steven Hart

AOL Time Warner
Issues: COM CPT TAX
Rep By: Bertram W. Carp, Robert E. Glennon, Jr., J. Steven Hart, Anthony J. Roda, Tracy D. Taylor

Applera Corp.
Issues: CPT
Rep By: J. Steven Hart, George G. Olsen, Anthony J. Roda

Arena PAC
Rep By: Barbara Wixon Bonfiglio, J. Steven Hart

Asahi Glass Co.
Issues: LBR TRD
Rep By: David E. Franasiak, J. Steven Hart, Anthony J. Roda

AstraZeneca Inc.
Issues: MMM
Rep By: George G. Olsen

Bass Enterprises Production Co.
Issues: AGR ENV MAR TAX
Rep By: George D. Baker, William B. Canfield, Robert E. Glennon, Jr., Anthony J. Roda

Bayer Corp.
Issues: CPT HCR MMM PHA TRD
Rep By: George G. Olsen

Chandis Securities Co.
Rep By: David E. Franasiak, Robert E. Glennon, Jr., Anthony J. Roda

Chicago Deferred Exchange Corp.
Issues: TAX
Rep By: David E. Franasiak

The Church Alliance
Issues: FIN HCR TAX
Rep By: William B. Canfield, David E. Franasiak, J. Steven Hart, George G. Olsen, David A. Starr

CIGNA Corp.
Issues: ENV HCR TAX
Rep By: George D. Baker, David E. Franasiak, Robert E. Glennon, Jr., J. Steven Hart, Karen Judd Lewis, George G. Olsen, Anthony J. Roda

The Coca-Cola Company
Issues: AGR BEV ENV FOO LBR TAX
Rep By: Bertram W. Carp, Robert E. Glennon, Jr., J. Steven Hart

Colonial Pipeline Co.
Issues: FUE TAX
Rep By: George D. Baker, David E. Franasiak, J. Steven Hart, Frank C. Vlossak

Continental Airlines Inc.
Issues: AVI BUD IMM TAX TRA
Rep By: J. Steven Hart, Karen Judd Lewis

Credit Suisse First Boston Corp.
Issues: BAN BNK FIN TAX
Rep By: Philip E. Bechtel, David E. Franasiak, Robert E. Glennon, Jr., J. Steven Hart, David M. Landers, George G. Olsen, Anthony J. Roda, Jeffrey A. Tassey

CT USA, Inc.
Issues: BAN
Rep By: David M. Landers

Dunn-Padre, Inc.
Issues: ENG ENV FUE NAT RES
Rep By: William B. Canfield, Robert J. Martinez

Estee Lauder, Inc.
Issues: TAX TRD
Rep By: George D. Baker, Robert E. Glennon, Jr.

Eurex Deutschland
Issues: CDT
Rep By: George D. Baker

Fannie Mae
Issues: BAN ECN HOU TAX
Rep By: Bertram W. Carp, David E. Franasiak, Robert E. Glennon, Jr., J. Steven Hart, John J. McMackin, Jr., J. D. Williams

Fidelity Investments Co.
Issues: FIN
Rep By: David M. Landers

First Union Corp.
Issues: BAN BNK EDU FIN TAX
Rep By: Philip E. Bechtel, David E. Franasiak, Robert E. Glennon, Jr., J. Steven Hart, David M. Landers, Anthony J. Roda, Jeffrey A. Tassey, J. D. Williams

Gateway, Inc.
Issues: CPT TAX TEC
Rep By: Bertram W. Carp, David E. Franasiak, J. Steven Hart, Anthony J. Roda, Tracy D. Taylor

Genentech, Inc.
Issues: PHA TAX
Rep By: David E. Franasiak, J. Steven Hart, Karina Lynch, George G. Olsen, Anthony J. Roda

Girling Health Care
Issues: MMM
Rep By: George G. Olsen

HP Global Workplaces, Inc.
Issues: POS
Rep By: William B. Canfield, J. Steven Hart, Anthony J. Roda

Human Rights Campaign
Issues: CIV
Rep By: Barbara Wixon Bonfiglio, Karen Judd Lewis, Anthony J. Roda

Internat'l Ass'n of Amusement Parks and Attractions
Rep By: Rebecca L. Anderson, Philip E. Bechtel, Bertram W. Carp, J. Steven Hart

Keystone, Inc.
Rep By: David E. Franasiak, Robert E. Glennon, Jr., J. Steven Hart, Karen Judd Lewis, George G. Olsen

Knight Trading Group
Issues: FIN
Rep By: David E. Franasiak, J. Steven Hart, Jeffrey A. Tassey

KSL Development Corp.
Rep By: George D. Baker, J. Steven Hart, Frank C. Vlossak

La Quinta Inns, Inc.
Issues: TAX
Rep By: Robert E. Glennon, Jr.

MeriStar Hospitality Corp.
Issues: TAX
Rep By: Robert E. Glennon, Jr.

J. P. Morgan Chase & Co.
Issues: TAX
Rep By: David E. Franasiak, Robert E. Glennon, Jr., George G. Olsen

J. P. Morgan Securities
Rep By: David E. Franasiak, Robert E. Glennon, Jr., George G. Olsen

Nat'l Ass'n of Rehabilitation Agencies
Issues: MMM
Rep By: George G. Olsen

Nat'l Audubon Soc.
Issues: ANI ENV NAT RES
Rep By: J. Steven Hart, John J. McMackin, Jr.

Nat'l Cable Television Ass'n
Issues: COM
Rep By: Bertram W. Carp, J. Steven Hart, Anthony J. Roda

Nat'l Underground Railroad Freedom Center
Issues: BUD EDU NAT
Rep By: William B. Canfield, J. Steven Hart, Robert J. Martinez, Anthony J. Roda

Norfolk Southern Corp.
Issues: RRR TAX
Rep By: Robert E. Glennon, Jr., Karen Judd Lewis, John J. McMackin, Jr., Frank C. Vlossak, J. D. Williams

Novartis Corp.
Issues: PHA
Rep By: George G. Olsen

Oklahoma Gas and Electric Co.
Issues: ENV UTI
Rep By: George D. Baker, David E. Franasiak, George G. Olsen

Owens-Illinois, Inc.
Issues: CSP TRD
Rep By: William B. Canfield, Robert E. Glennon, Jr., J. Steven Hart, Karen Judd Lewis, John J. McMackin, Jr., Anthony J. Roda, J. D. Williams

Perdue Farms Inc.
Rep By: David E. Franasiak, Robert E. Glennon, Jr., J. Steven Hart, Anthony J. Roda

Pharmaceutical Research and Manufacturers of America
Issues: CPT CSP HCR MMM PHA TRD
Rep By: William B. Canfield, J. Steven Hart, George G. Olsen, Anthony J. Roda

Pier 1 Imports
Issues: TRD
Rep By: Robert E. Glennon, Jr.

Pilgrim's Pride
Rep By: Robert E. Glennon, Jr.

The Pittston Co.
Issues: TAX
Rep By: J. Steven Hart, Karen Judd Lewis, Anthony J. Roda, David A. Starr

Private Practice Section of the American Physical Therapy Ass'n
Issues: HCR MMM
Rep By: George G. Olsen

Qwest Communications
Issues: TEC
Rep By: Bertram W. Carp, J. Steven Hart, Karen Judd Lewis, John J. McMackin, Jr.

Recording Industry Ass'n of America
Issues: ART BNK CPT
Rep By: Bertram W. Carp, J. Steven Hart, Anthony J. Roda

Reinsurance Ass'n of America
Issues: BAN BNK DIS FIN TAX
Rep By: William B. Canfield, David E. Franasiak, Robert E. Glennon, Jr., David M. Landers, Jeffrey A. Tassey

Reuters America Inc.
Issues: TEC
Rep By: Bertram W. Carp, J. Steven Hart, Anthony J. Roda, Tracy D. Taylor

Securities Traders Ass'n
Rep By: David E. Franasiak, J. Steven Hart, David A. Starr, Jeffrey A. Tassey

Smith Barney Harris Upham & Co.
Rep By: John J. McMackin, Jr.

Smithfield Foods Inc.
Rep By: William B. Canfield, Bertram W. Carp, J. Steven Hart, Anthony J. Roda

Superfund Reform '95
Rep By: George D. Baker

Tailored Clothing Ass'n
Issues: APP TRD
Rep By: J. Steven Hart, David A. Starr

Taxpayers Against Fraud, The False Claims Legal Center
Issues: DEF
Rep By: Karen Judd Lewis

Texaco Group Inc.
Issues: CAW ENV TAX
Rep By: George D. Baker, William B. Canfield, David E. Franasiak, Robert E. Glennon, Jr., J. Steven Hart

Texas Pacific Group
Issues: BUD TAX
Rep By: Robert E. Glennon, Jr., George G. Olsen

TTX Co.
Issues: RRR TRA
Rep By: Karen Judd Lewis, John J. McMackin, Jr., Anthony J. Roda

USAA - United Services Automobile Ass'n
Issues: FIN TAX
Rep By: George D. Baker, Philip E. Bechtel, Robert E. Glennon, Jr., David M. Landers, Karen Judd Lewis, Jeffrey A. Tassey, J. D. Williams

The Vantage Group, Inc.
Issues: POS
Rep By: William B. Canfield, Anthony J. Roda

Vornado Inc.
Issues: RES TAX
Rep By: Robert E. Glennon, Jr.

Western Coalition Political Action Committee
Rep By: Anthony J. Roda

James M. Williams, Jr.

10907 Forestgate Pl.
Glen Dale, MD 20769
Tel: (301)809-9052
Fax: (301)809-4368
Registered: LDA

Clients

Nat'l Ass'n of Minority Automobile Dealers
Issues: AUT CIV TRA TRD
Rep By: James M. Williams, Jr.

Willkie Farr & Gallagher

Three Lafayette Center
1155 21st St. NW
Washington, DC 20036-3384
Tel: (202)328-8000
Fax: (202)887-8979
Registered: LDA
Web: www.willkie.com
A general practice law firm headquartered in New York, NY.

DC-Area Employees Representing Listed Clients

BARRINGER, William H., Partner
BLOCK, Barbara, Senior Legislative Analyst
BLUMENFELD, Sue D., Partner
DUNN, Christopher A., Partner
DURLING, James P., Partner
MURRAY, David P., Partner
NICELY, Matthew, Associate Attorney
PIERCE, Kenneth J., Partner
PORTER, Daniel L., Partner
SMITH, Russell L., Special Counsel
VERVEER, Philip L., Partner
WHITEHOUSE, Theodore C., Partner

Clients

Ass'n of Directory Publishers
Issues: TEC
Rep By: Russell L. Smith

Bloomberg L.P.
Issues: CPT
Rep By: Russell L. Smith, Theodore C. Whitehouse

Branco Peres Citrus, S.A.
Rep By: Christopher A. Dunn

Cellular Telecommunications and Internet Ass'n
Rep By: Philip L. Verveer

Continuous Color Coat, Ltd.
Rep By: Christopher A. Dunn

Dun & Bradstreet
Issues: CPT MIA
Rep By: Theodore C. Whitehouse

Fuji Heavy Industries Ltd.
Rep By: William H. Barringer, Kenneth J. Pierce

Fuji Photo Film U.S.A., Inc.
Issues: TRD
Rep By: William H. Barringer, Daniel L. Porter, Russell L. Smith

Hyundai Electronics Industries Co., LTD
Issues: TRD
Rep By: James P. Durling, Daniel L. Porter, Russell L. Smith

ICF Industries, Inc.
Issues: TRD
Rep By: Russell L. Smith

Japan Automobile Manufacturers Ass'n
Issues: AUT TRD
Rep By: Russell L. Smith

Japan Iron and Steel Exporters Ass'n
Issues: TRD
Rep By: William H. Barringer, James P. Durling, Russell L. Smith

Matsushita Electric Industrial Co., Ltd.
Rep By: James P. Durling

Meat and Livestock Australia
Issues: AGR TRD
Rep By: William H. Barringer, Matthew Nicely, Russell L. Smith

J. P. Morgan Chase & Co.
Issues: FIN GOV
Rep By: Russell L. Smith

Sony Corp. of America
Rep By: Christopher A. Dunn

Sprint Corp.
Issues: GOV TEC
Rep By: Sue D. Blumenfeld, Russell L. Smith

Subaru-Isuzu Automotive, Inc.
Rep By: Kenneth J. Pierce

Telecommunications Industry Ass'n
Issues: TEC
Rep By: Philip L. Verveer

Yamaha Motor Corp. U.S.A.
Issues: CSP
Rep By: David P. Murray, Russell L. Smith

Wilmer, Cutler & Pickering

2445 M St. NW
Washington, DC 20037-1420
Tel: (202)663-6000
Fax: (202)663-6363
Registered: LDA, FARA
Web: www.wilmer.com
E-mail: law@wilmer.com
A general practice law firm.

DC-Area Employees Representing Listed Clients

BECKER, Brandon, Partner
BERMAN, Bruce M., Partner
CAMPBELL, James S., Partner
CASS, Richard W., Partner
CASSIDY, Jr., Robert C., Partner
CHARYTAN, Lynn, Partner
CHESTON, Sheila C.
CLAYTON, Carol, Associate
COLLINS, J. Barclay, Associate
COX, J. Edward, Commercial Analyst
CUTLER, Lloyd N., Partner
DUNNE, Steven M., Associate
GRAY, C. Boyden, Partner
GREENE, Ronald J., Partner
GREENWALD, John D., Partner
HARWOOD, Jr., John H., Partner
HOYT, Robert F., Associate
HUT, Stephen
HYDE, Terrill A., Partner
JETTON, Jr., C. Loring, Partner
KING, Neil J., Partner
KOLASKY, Jr., William J., Partner
LAKE, Jr., F. David, Partner
LAKE, William T., Partner
LANG, Jeffrey M., Partner
LEE, Yoon-Young, Partner
LEVY, Charles S., Partner
MANLEY, Jeffrey, Partner
MELTZER, Ronald I., Associate
MODE, Jr., Paul J., Partner
NURICK, Lester, Counsel
OLSON, Thomas P., Partner
PAYTON, John, Partner
PERLSTEIN, William J., Partner
PETERSON, Cathleen, Partner
PHYTHYON, Daniel
PICKER, Colin, Associate
PICKERING, John H., Senior Counsel
PRIBBLE, Robert, Legislative Specialist
RABINOVITZ, Bruce, Partner
RICHARDSON, Jr., William R., Partner
SHAMBON, Leonard M., Counsel
SHERBURNE, Jane C., Partner
SMYTHE, Marianne K., Partner
SQUIRE, Daniel H., Partner
STOEPPELWERTH, Ali M., Associate
TRENOR, John A., Associate
VOLLMER, Andrew N., Partner
WILKINS, William J., Partner
WILSON, Gary D., Partner
WITTEN, Roger M., Partner
WRATHALL, James R., Partner

Clients

ABC Inc.

AdvaMed
Issues: CSP
Rep By: Ronald J. Greene

American Civil Liberties Union
Issues: CIV FAM HCR
Rep By: Sheila C. Cheston

American Electric Power Co.
Issues: ENG FIN UTI
Rep By: Marianne K. Smythe

Amgen
Issues: HCR TAX
Rep By: C. Boyden Gray

AOL Time Warner
Issues: TRD
Rep By: Charles S. Levy

Atlantic Gulf Communities
Rep By: Daniel H. Squire

AutoNation, Inc.
Issues: TAX
Rep By: Terrill A. Hyde, William J. Wilkins

Best Foods
Rep By: William J. Wilkins

The Business Roundtable
Issues: TRD
Rep By: Charles S. Levy

The Center for Voting and Democracy

Citibank, N.A.
Rep By: Marianne K. Smythe

Clean Air Action Corp.
Rep By: C. Boyden Gray

Coalition of Service Industries
Issues: TRD
Rep By: Charles S. Levy

Common Cause
Rep By: Roger M. Witten

Computer Systems Policy Project
Issues: TRD
Rep By: Charles S. Levy

Cook Inlet Communications

Corporate Property Investors
Issues: TAX
Rep By: William J. Wilkins

Dallas Cowboys
Rep By: Richard W. Cass

Dell Computer Corp.
Issues: CPI
Rep By: Daniel Phythyon

Deutsche Telekom, Inc.
Issues: TEC
Rep By: Lloyd N. Cutler, C. Boyden Gray, John H. Harwood, Jr., William T. Lake, Charles S. Levy, Daniel Phythyon

DuPont
Rep By: John D. Greenwald

Educational Testing Service

Export Control Coalition
Issues: TRD
Rep By: Charles S. Levy

Fitch Investors Service, Inc.
Rep By: Marianne K. Smythe

Ernest & Julio Gallo Winery

Genzyme Corp.
Issues: HCR
Rep By: C. Boyden Gray

Hewlett-Packard Co.
Rep By: Charles S. Levy

Howard, Meedles, Tammen & Bergendoff
Rep By: Bruce M. Berman

IATA U.S. Frequent Flyer Tax Interest Group
Issues: TAX
Rep By: J. Barclay Collins, F. David Lake, Jr.

Intellectual Property Committee
Issues: TRD
Rep By: Charles S. Levy

Internat'l Metals Reclamation Co.
Rep By: Neil J. King

Intuit, Inc.

ITT World Directories, Inc.
Issues: TRD
Rep By: Robert C. Cassidy, Jr.

Lederle Laboratories
Rep By: Ronald J. Greene

Loral Space and Communications, Ltd.
Rep By: Lloyd N. Cutler, C. Boyden Gray

Managed Funds Ass'n
Issues: FIN
Rep By: Marianne K. Smythe

Marianas Political Status Commission

MCA Inc.

McDonald's Corp.
Issues: TAX
Rep By: William J. Wilkins

Milliken and Co.
Rep By: John D. Greenwald, Ronald I. Meltzer

Nat'l Press Foundation

PepsiCo, Inc.
Rep By: William J. Wilkins

Republic Industries, Inc.
Issues: TAX
Rep By: Terrill A. Hyde, William J. Wilkins

RKO General, Inc.

RMI Titanium Co.
Rep By: John D. Greenwald, Leonard M. Shambon

Scripps League Newspaper, Inc.

Sony Corp.

Superpharm Corp.

Swiss Bank Corp.
Issues: BAN
Rep By: Lloyd N. Cutler, Roger M. Witten

Swiss Bankers Ass'n
Issues: BAN
Rep By: Lloyd N. Cutler

Tax Information Group
Issues: TAX

Trans Ocean Leasing Corp.
Rep By: Ronald J. Greene

Union Bank of Switzerland
Issues: BAN
Rep By: Lloyd N. Cutler, Roger M. Witten

United Airlines

United Defense, L.P.
Issues: DEF FOR TRD
Rep By: Leonard M. Shambon

UNOCAL Corp.
Rep By: Paul J. Mode, Jr.

ValueVision Internat'l, Inc.
Rep By: William R. Richardson, Jr.

VeriSign/Network Solutions, Inc.
Issues: CPI CPT MIA SCI TEC
Rep By: Lloyd N. Cutler

Warburg, Pincus & Co., Inc., E. M.

Yamaha Motor Corp. U.S.A.
Rep By: Robert C. Cassidy, Jr.

Wilson & Wasserstein, Inc.

1401 K St. NW
Tenth Floor
Washington, DC 20005
Tel: (202)416-1720
Fax: (202)416-1719
Registered: LDA, FARA
E-mail: WilsonAsso@aol.com
A federal government relations and security consulting firm.

DC-Area Employees Representing Listed Clients
COOPER, Yurika S.
WASSERSTEIN, Glen D., V. President and General Counsel
WILSON, Russell J., President and Chief Exec. Officer

Clients

Bangladeshi-American Friendship Soc. of New York
Issues: IMM
Rep By: Yurika S. Cooper, Glen D. Wasserstein, Russell J. Wilson

Immigration Law Group, P.C.
Issues: IMM

Mortgage Investors Corp.
Issues: VET
Rep By: Glen D. Wasserstein, Russell J. Wilson

Scribe Communications, Inc.
Issues: FOR
Rep By: Russell J. Wilson

U.S. Fencing Ass'n
Issues: SPO
Rep By: Russell J. Wilson

West African Friends
Rep By: Glen D. Wasserstein, Russell J. Wilson

Wilson & Wilson

1155 15th St. NW
Suite 815
Washington, DC 20005
Tel: (202)835-1571
Fax: (202)296-2736
Registered: LDA
E-mail: editorwr@aol.com

DC-Area Employees Representing Listed Clients
WILSON, Robert Dale, Partner
WILSON, Sharon L., Partner

Clients

Boston University

Edison Industrial Systems Center
Issues: SCI
Rep By: Robert Dale Wilson

Environmental Industry Coalition

Falconbridge, Ltd.
Rep By: Robert Dale Wilson

Hecla Mining Co.
Rep By: Robert Dale Wilson

Nat'l Materials Advisory Board

Thermal Energy Systems, Inc.

Donald E. Wilson Consulting

7495 Covent Wood Ct.
Annandale, VA 22003
Tel: (703)866-9680
Fax: (703)451-8557
Registered: LDA
E-mail: donwilson@justicemail.com
The Washington Office of a defense consulting firm headquartered in Springfield, VA.

DC-Area Employees Representing Listed Clients
WILSON, Donald E.

Clients

Environmental Technologies Group
Issues: DEF

ITT Industries Defense
Issues: DEF

Northrop Grumman Corp.
Issues: DEF

The "Sandbagger" Corp.
Issues: DEF DIS
Rep By: Donald E. Wilson

Wilson Grand Communications

429 N. St. Asaph St.
Alexandria, VA 22314
Tel: (703)739-0330
Fax: (703)739-0332
A political media consulting firm.

DC-Area Employees Representing Listed Clients
WILSON, Paul O., Chairman/Chief Executive Officer

Clients

Ohio Senate Republican Caucus
Rep By: Paul O. Wilson

Wilson, Elser, Moskowitz, Edelman & Dicker LLP

1341 G St. NW
Fifth Floor
Washington, DC 20005
Tel: (202)626-7660
Fax: (202)628-3606
Registered: LDA

DC-Area Employees Representing Listed Clients
KRAUSE, Paul D., Managing Partner
STEEL, Laura N., Partner
WALLACE, Robert B., Partner

Clients

Albany Medical Center Hospital

Healthcare Ass'n of New York State
Issues: HCR

St. Benedictine Hospital

WinCapitol, Inc.

1022 29th St. NW
Washington, DC 20007
Tel: (202)333-3232
Fax: (202)333-5001
Registered: LDA
Web: www.wincapitol.com
E-mail: info@wincapitol.com

DC-Area Employees Representing Listed Clients
FLORY, David L., Chairman and Chief Exec. Officer
OLSEN, Christie, Principal
SIMS, James T., President

Clients

AFL-CIO (Union Label and Service Trades Department)
Issues: CSP
Rep By: David L. Flory, Christie Olsen, James T. Sims

American Green Network
Issues: ENV
Rep By: David L. Flory, Christie Olsen, James T. Sims

Danaher Corp.
Issues: TRD
Rep By: David L. Flory, Christie Olsen, James T. Sims

Kathleen Winn & Associates, Inc.

213 A St. NE
Washington, DC 20002
Tel: (202)547-3363
Fax: (202)544-6144
Registered: LDA

DC-Area Employees Representing Listed Clients
WINN, Kathleen

Clients

CSA America, Inc.
Issues: CSP ENG ENV FOO FUE GOV LBR MAN SCI
Rep By: Kathleen Winn

Methanex Inc.
Issues: CAW CHM ENV FUE TAX TRD

Pennzoil-Quaker State Co.
Issues: AUT CAW CSP ENV HCR LBR TAX TRA TRD

Winner & Associates

1341 G St. NW
Suite 200
Washington, DC 20005
Tel: (202)333-2533
Fax: (202)342-0763
Registered: LDA
E-mail: info@winnerdc.com
The Washington office of a firm headquartered in Encino, CA.

DC-Area Employees Representing Listed Clients
RAULSTON, Carol, Sr. V. President

Clients

Ass'n of Oil Pipelines

Educational Testing Service

Exxon Mobil Corp.

Global Mining Initiative

The Gold and Silver Institute

InterGen

Mashantucket Pequot Tribal Nation

Nat'l Soft Drink Ass'n

Phelps Dodge Corp.

RAND Corp.

Winning Strategies Washington, D.C., LLC

1200 G St. NW
Suite 800
Washington, DC 20005
Tel: (202)434-8768
Fax: (202)434-8707
Registered: LDA

DC-Area Employees Representing Listed Clients
BREWSTER, Brad
FLORIO, Dale
FOX, Jamie
GANNON, Richard
MCDONOUGH, Peter
MCQWEERY, James
MONES, Seth

Winstead, Sechrest & Minick, P.C.

1666 K St. NW
Suite 1200
Washington, DC 20005
Tel: (202)833-9200
Fax: (202)293-5939
Web: www.winstead.com
A law firm based in Dallas, TX.

DC-Area Employees Representing Listed Clients
CUSHING, Mark L., Of Counsel
MCCLURE, Frederick D., Shareholder

Deborah F. Winston

9210 Graceland Pl.
Fairfax, VA 22031
Tel: (202)879-9487
Fax: (202)393-7309
Registered: LDA

Clients

ING America Insurance Holdings, Inc.
Issues: FIN GOV INS RET TAX TOR
Rep By: Deborah F. Winston

Winston & Strawn

1400 L St. NW
Washington, DC 20005-3502
Tel: (202)371-5700
Fax: (202)371-5950
Registered: LDA, FARA
Web: www.winston.com
E-mail: postmaster@winston.com
Washington office of a Chicago law firm.

Political Action Committee
Winston & Strawn Political Action Committee
1400 L St. NW
Washington, DC 20005-3502
Tel: (202)371-5754
Fax: (202)371-5950
Contact: Hon. Beryl F. Anthony, Jr.

DC-Area Employees Representing Listed Clients
ANDERSON, II, William A., Partner, Environmental Practice
ANTHONY, Jr., Hon. Beryl F., Partner and Director, Legislative and Regulatory Practice
BERMAN, Jeffrey G., Partner, Corporate Practice
BLACK, III, H. Allen
BOR, Robert M., Of Counsel, Legislative and Regulatory Practice
BROAS, Timothy M., Partner
BROOME, David W., Political Advisor
BURNLEY, IV, Hon. James H., Partner, Transportation Practice
COOKE, Jr., Edmund D., Partner, Employment Relations Practice
CURTISS, James R., Partner, Energy Practice
FEHRENBACH, John, Partner, Environmental Practice
GERWIN, Jr., Edward F., Partner, Corporate Practice
HALL, William N., Partner, Environmental Practice
HIEBERT, Peter N., Partner, Legislative and Regulatory Practice
HIRSCHHORN, Eric L., Partner, Corporate Practice
KELLER, Jr., Roger A., Associate, Environmental
KIERN, Lawrence I., Of Counsel, Health Care Practice
KILLION, Frederick J.
KINNEY, Charles L., Partner, Legislative and Regulatory Practice
KIRTLAND, John C., Partner, Legislative and Regulatory Practice
LEMOV, Michael R., Partner, Legislative and Regulatory Practice
MARXUACH, Sergio
MCGARRY, III, J. Michael, Managing Partner, Washington Office (Energy)
MCLAUGHLIN, Michael J., Associate, Federal and Regulatory Affairs Practice

MCMICKLE, John D., Associate, Federal and Regulatory Affairs Practice
MILLS, Thomas L., Partner, Health Care Practice
NAPIER, Hon. John L., Of Counsel, Legislative and Regulatory Practice
O'LEARY, Joseph E., Consultant, Legislative and Regulatory Practice
PAPAVIZAS, Constantine G., Partner, Health Care Practice
PAVIA, Francisco J., Of Counsel, Legislative and Regulatory Practice
PITTS, James T., Partner, Federal Government Relations and Regulatory Affairs
REYNOLDS, Nicholas S., Partner, Energy Practice
RICHARDSON, Douglas C., Legislative Advisor, Legislative and Regulatory Practice
SMITH, Gregory K., Associate, Corporate Practice
WAITS, II, John A., Partner, Legislative and Regulatory Practice

Clients

Abilene, Texas, City of
Issues: TRA
Rep By: Hon. James H. Burnley, IV, John A. Waits, II

AirCell, Inc.
Issues: AVI
Rep By: Hon. Beryl F. Anthony, Jr., Jeffrey G. Berman

American Airlines
Issues: AVI
Rep By: Hon. James H. Burnley, IV, Roger A. Keller, Jr., Charles L. Kinney, Michael J. McLaughlin, John A. Waits, II

American General Financial Group
Issues: FIN INS
Rep By: Timothy M. Broas, Charles L. Kinney

American Healthways, Inc.
Rep By: Charles L. Kinney, Thomas L. Mills

American Honey Producers Ass'n
Issues: AGR
Rep By: Robert M. Bor, John A. Waits, II

American Lithotripsy Soc.
Rep By: Thomas L. Mills

Bank of America
Rep By: Hon. John L. Napier

Barr Laboratories
Issues: MMM PHA
Rep By: Hon. Beryl F. Anthony, Jr., Hon. James H. Burnley, IV, Eric L. Hirschhorn, Frederick J. Killion, Charles L. Kinney, Joseph E. O'Leary, Douglas C. Richardson, John A. Waits, II

Becker-Underwood, Inc.
Issues: ENV
Rep By: John Fehrenbach

Benrus Watch Co.
Issues: TRD
Rep By: Edward F. Gerwin, Jr., Peter N. Hiebert

CAMECO Corp.
Issues: ENG
Rep By: James R. Curtiss, Edward F. Gerwin, Jr.

Certified Airline Passenger Services, LLC
Issues: AVI
Rep By: Hon. James H. Burnley, IV, James T. Pitts, John A. Waits, II

Cheese Importers Ass'n of America
Issues: AGR
Rep By: Robert M. Bor, John A. Waits, II

Chicago, Regional Transportation Authority of
Rep By: Douglas C. Richardson

Columbia Ventures, LLC
Rep By: Hon. James H. Burnley, IV, Peter N. Hiebert, Roger A. Keller, Jr., Hon. John L. Napier

Cooper Tire and Rubber Co.
Issues: TRD
Rep By: Hon. Beryl F. Anthony, Jr., Hon. James H. Burnley, IV, John C. Kirtland, Hon. John L. Napier, James T. Pitts, John A. Waits, II

Corning Inc.
Issues: TRD
Rep By: Hon. Beryl F. Anthony, Jr., John C. Kirtland, Joseph E. O'Leary, John A. Waits, II

DHL Airways, Inc.
Rep By: Peter N. Hiebert, Eric L. Hirschhorn

DMJM + Harris
Rep By: Hon. James H. Burnley, IV, Charles L. Kinney, John D. McMickle, Joseph E. O'Leary

Eastern Band of Cherokee Indians
Issues: AGR IND
Rep By: Hon. Beryl F. Anthony, Jr., Hon. John L. Napier

The ESOP (Employee Stock Ownership Plan) Ass'n
Issues: GOV RET TAX
Rep By: Hon. Beryl F. Anthony, Jr., Charles L. Kinney

EyeTicket Corp.
Issues: SCI
Rep By: Hon. James H. Burnley, IV, Charles L. Kinney, Douglas C. Richardson

Federal Home Loan Bank of New York
Issues: BAN
Rep By: Hon. James H. Burnley, IV

Federal Judges Ass'n
Issues: GOV
Rep By: Hon. Beryl F. Anthony, Jr., Charles L. Kinney, Hon. John L. Napier, Douglas C. Richardson

Federal Magistrate Judges Ass'n
Issues: GOV
Rep By: Hon. Beryl F. Anthony, Jr., Charles L. Kinney, Hon. John L. Napier

First American Bulk Carriers Corp.
Issues: MAR
Rep By: Lawrence I. Kiern, Thomas L. Mills, Constantine G. Papavizas

Gildan Activewear
Issues: APP TRD
Rep By: Edward F. Gerwin, Jr., Charles L. Kinney, Douglas C. Richardson, John A. Waits, II

Heller Financial Inc.
Issues: SMB
Rep By: Charles L. Kinney, Douglas C. Richardson

Hill Internat'l, Inc.
Rep By: John A. Waits, II

Internat'l Council of Shopping Centers
Issues: BNK TAX
Rep By: Hon. Beryl F. Anthony, Jr., Charles L. Kinney, John D. McMickle

Jackson County, Mississippi Board of Supervisors
Issues: ENV TRA
Rep By: John C. Kirtland, John A. Waits, II

Jackson Municipal Airport Authority
Issues: TRA
Rep By: John C. Kirtland, John A. Waits, II

Jackson, Mississippi, City of
Issues: ENV HOU LAW TAX TRA
Rep By: John C. Kirtland, John A. Waits, II

Kirby Corp./Dixie Carriers
Issues: MAR
Rep By: Lawrence I. Kiern, Thomas L. Mills, Constantine G. Papavizas

Leukemia and Lymphoma Soc. of America
Rep By: Charles L. Kinney, Douglas C. Richardson

Liberty Maritime Co.
Issues: MAR
Rep By: Robert M. Bor, Hon. James H. Burnley, IV, Lawrence I. Kiern, Charles L. Kinney, John C. Kirtland, Thomas L. Mills, Hon. John L. Napier, Constantine G. Papavizas, James T. Pitts, Douglas C. Richardson, John A. Waits, II

Lockheed Martin Corp.
Issues: COM TEC
Rep By: Hon. Beryl F. Anthony, Jr., Charles L. Kinney

Marinette Marine Corp.
Issues: MAR
Rep By: Hon. James H. Burnley, IV, Lawrence I. Kiern, Charles L. Kinney, Thomas L. Mills, Constantine G. Papavizas

Maximum Information Technology Inc.
Issues: LAW
Rep By: Lawrence I. Kiern, John C. Kirtland, John A. Waits, II

Motor Coach Industries, Inc.
Issues: TRA
Rep By: Hon. Beryl F. Anthony, Jr., Hon. James H. Burnley, IV, Charles L. Kinney, Joseph E. O'Leary, James T. Pitts, Douglas C. Richardson, John A. Waits, II

Murphy Oil U.S.A.
Rep By: William A. Anderson, II, Hon. Beryl F. Anthony, Jr.

Nat'l Geographic Soc.
Issues: TAX
Rep By: Hon. Beryl F. Anthony, Jr., Charles L. Kinney

Nat'l Organization of Social Security Claimants' Representatives
Issues: GOV
Rep By: Hon. Beryl F. Anthony, Jr., Charles L. Kinney, Gregory K. Smith

Nat'l Paint and Coatings Ass'n
Issues: ENV
Rep By: William N. Hall, Roger A. Keller, Jr.

Norfolk Southern Corp.
Issues: RRR
Rep By: Hon. James H. Burnley, IV, Charles L. Kinney, Hon. John L. Napier, Joseph E. O'Leary, Douglas C. Richardson

Northland Holdings, Inc.
Issues: MAR
Rep By: H. Allen Black, III, Hon. James H. Burnley, IV, Lawrence I. Kiern, Thomas L. Mills, Joseph E. O'Leary, Constantine G. Papavizas, James T. Pitts, Douglas C. Richardson

ORBITZ
Rep By: Hon. James H. Burnley, IV

Panda Energy Internat'l
Issues: ENG FOR
Rep By: Hon. Beryl F. Anthony, Jr., David W. Broome, Charles L. Kinney, Hon. John L. Napier, Douglas C. Richardson, John A. Waits, II

Puerto Rico, Commonwealth of
Rep By: Hon. Beryl F. Anthony, Jr., Hon. James H. Burnley, IV, Peter N. Hiebert, Charles L. Kinney, John C. Kirtland, Michael J. McLaughlin, John D. McMickle, Francisco J. Pavia, Douglas C. Richardson, John A. Waits, II

Queensland Sugar, Ltd.
Issues: AGR
Rep By: Robert M. Bor, John A. Waits, II

Research Planning, Inc.
Issues: DIS
Rep By: Hon. James H. Burnley, IV, Charles L. Kinney, Hon. John L. Napier, Douglas C. Richardson

Rickenbacker Port Authority
Issues: TRA
Rep By: Hon. James H. Burnley, IV, Douglas C. Richardson, John A. Waits, II

Robinson Terminal
Issues: ROD
Rep By: Hon. James H. Burnley, IV, Joseph E. O'Leary

South Carolina Department of Transportation
Issues: TRA
Rep By: Roger A. Keller, Jr., Hon. John L. Napier

Southern Illinois University
Issues: AGR TRA
Rep By: Douglas C. Richardson

Spectrum Consulting, Inc.
Rep By: David W. Broome, John A. Waits, II

Traffic.com
Rep By: Hon. James H. Burnley, IV

University of California at Los Angeles
Issues: DIS
Rep By: Hon. Beryl F. Anthony, Jr., Peter N. Hiebert

USA Rice Federation
Issues: AGR ENV
Rep By: Robert M. Bor

Van Ommeren Shipping (USA), Inc.
Issues: MAR
Rep By: Thomas L. Mills, Constantine G. Papavizas

Virgin Islands Watch and Jewelry Manufacturers Ass'n
Rep By: Edward F. Gerwin, Jr., Peter N. Hiebert

Virgin Islands, Government of the
Issues: BUD DIS GOV TAX TRD
Rep By: Peter N. Hiebert, Charles L. Kinney, John C. Kirtland, John D. McMickle, John A. Waits, II

Waggoner Engineering, Inc.
Issues: ECN ENC ENV TRA
Rep By: John C. Kirtland, John A. Waits, II

Western Peanut Growers Ass'n
Issues: AGR
Rep By: Robert M. Bor, John A. Waits, II

Yellow Corp.
Issues: LBR MAR TAX TRU
Rep By: David W. Broome, Hon. James H. Burnley, IV, Charles L. Kinney, Michael J. McLaughlin, John D. McMickle, Joseph E. O'Leary, Douglas C. Richardson, Gregory K. Smith, John A. Waits, II

Winthrop, Stimson, Putnam & Roberts

1133 Connecticut Ave. NW
Suite 1200
Washington, DC 20036
Web: www.winstim.com
A general practice law firm.

Tel: (202)775-9800
Fax: (202)833-8491
Registered: LDA, FARA

DC-Area Employees Representing Listed Clients

BENKIN, Isaac D., Partner
CARR, Donald A., Managing Partner
CHRISTY, Jr., David S., Associate
DEBUTTS, Thomas M., Associate
ESPINOSA, William H., Associate
GALLAGHER, James L., Associate
GILLICK, John E., Partner
GRAY, Robert Reed, Of Counsel
GRIFF, Marvin T., Counsel
LEVITIN, Michael J., Associate
MATTHEWS, William L., Diretor, Non-Lawyer Trade Services
MEYER, Aileen "Chuca", Counsel
MORGAN, Jr., Gerald D., Partner
PARLIN, C. Christopher, Counsel
QUINN, Kenneth P., Partner
ROMANOW, Joshua I., Associate
TERRY, Paul W., Associate
THOMAS, William L., Associate
WALKER, Mary Ann, Partner
WALL, Christopher R., Partner
WATSON, Peter S., Counsel

Clients

Air Transat
Rep By: John E. Gillick

Caribbean Banana Exporters Ass'n
Rep By: C. Christopher Parlin

Chicago, Illinois, Department of Law, City of
Issues: AVI
Rep By: Kenneth P. Quinn

Corporate Health Care Coalition

El Al Israel Airlines, Ltd.
Rep By: John E. Gillick

Harris Chemical Group, Inc.

Korean Semiconductor Industry Ass'n
Issues: TRD
Rep By: David S. Christy, Jr., C. Christopher Parlin

LOT Polish Airlines
Rep By: John E. Gillick

Marshall Islands, Republic of the

Royal Caribbean Cruises, Ltd.
Rep By: Donald A. Carr

Sabre Inc.
Rep By: Kenneth P. Quinn

Sargeant Marine, Inc.
Rep By: William H. Espinosa

Share Our Strength

SKW Chemicals, Inc.
Issues: TRD
Rep By: William L. Matthews, C. Christopher Parlin, Christopher R. Wall

Transportes Aereos Mercantiles Panamericanos
Rep By: Robert Reed Gray

World Wildlife Fund
Rep By: Donald A. Carr

Wirthlin Worldwide

1363 Beverly Rd.
McLean, VA 22101
Tel: (703)556-0001
Fax: (703)893-3811
Web: www.wirthlin.com

A Republican political and corporate polling firm. Also engaged in strategic communications, consulting, and grass roots telephoning.

DC-Area Employees Representing Listed Clients

GRANGER, Jim, Chief Exec. Officer and President
HOSKINS, Jim, Senior V. President
STATLER, Jean, Senior V. President

Clients

American Plastics Council

General Motors Corp.

Republican Nat'l Committee

The Steel Alliance

Wise & Associates

400 N. Capitol St. NW
Suite 585
Washington, DC 20001
Tel: (202)737-1960
Fax: (202)737-5585
Registered: LDA

DC-Area Employees Representing Listed Clients

O'HARE, Patricia
RUBIN, Joshua
SATTLER, Dwayne
WISE, Nicholas P., President

Clients

American Soc. of Anesthesiologists
Issues: MMM
Rep By: Nicholas P. Wise

AT&T
Issues: TEC
Rep By: Nicholas P. Wise

Cleveland Growth Ass'n
Issues: LBR
Rep By: Joshua Rubin, Dwayne Sattler

Columbus State College
Issues: EDU
Rep By: Dwayne Sattler

Corrections Corp. of America
Issues: LAW
Rep By: Nicholas P. Wise

Greater Columbus Chamber
Issues: LBR
Rep By: Dwayne Sattler

Nat'l Hemophilia Foundation
Issues: HCR
Rep By: Nicholas P. Wise

Ohio Bureau of Employment Services
Issues: LBR
Rep By: Dwayne Sattler

Plaintiffs Committee for TWA 800 and Swissair Air III Crashes
Rep By: Dwayne Sattler, Nicholas P. Wise

Project to Promote Competition and Innovation in the Digital Age
Issues: LBR
Rep By: Nicholas P. Wise

RPM, Inc.
Issues: LAW
Rep By: Joshua Rubin, Nicholas P. Wise

Witeck * Combs Communications

2120 L St. NW
Suite 850
Washington, DC 20037
Tel: (202)887-0500
Fax: (202)887-5633
Web: www.witeckcombs.com
E-mail: bwiteck@witeckcombs.com

DC-Area Employees Representing Listed Clients

COMBS, Wesley I., President
WITECK, Robert V., Chairman

Clients

Cellular Telecommunications and Internet Ass'n

Coors Brewing Company

Christopher Reeve Paralysis Foundation

Witman Associates

2027 Massachusetts Ave. NW
Washington, DC 20036
Tel: (202)232-4962
Fax: (202)232-4963
Registered: LDA

Specializes in public policy, government relations and strategic planning.

DC-Area Employees Representing Listed Clients

WITMAN, Ellen G., President

Clients

Jewish Federation of Metropolitan Chicago
Issues: APP BUD HOU
Rep By: Ellen G. Witman

Partnership for Caring
Issues: HCR MMM
Rep By: Ellen G. Witman

United Jewish Communities, Inc.
Issues: IMM
Rep By: Ellen G. Witman

Womble Carlyle Sandridge & Rice, P.C.

1120 19th St. NW
Eighth Floor
Washington, DC 20036
Tel: (202)467-6900
Fax: (202)467-6910
Registered: LDA
Web: www.wcsr.com
E-mail: lawyers@wcsr.com

DC-Area Employees Representing Listed Clients

BRYANT, Debra, Director, Federal Government Relations
ERAT, Donna
JONES, Kevin Darrow
THRIFT, Ashley

Clients

Alameda Corridor-East Construction Authority
Issues: BUD TRA
Rep By: Kevin Darrow Jones

FedEx Corp.
Rep By: Ashley Thrift

North Carolina Electric Membership Corp.
Issues: BUD
Rep By: Debra Bryant, Donna Erat

North Carolina Global TransPark Authority
Issues: AVI BUD TRA
Rep By: Debra Bryant, Donna Erat, Kevin Darrow Jones

North Carolina State Ports Authority
Issues: BUD
Rep By: Debra Bryant

North Carolina, Hurricane Floyd Redevelopment Center of State of
Issues: BUD DIS
Rep By: Debra Bryant, Donna Erat

Working for the Future, LLC

7505 Inzer St.
Springfield, VA 22151
Tel: (703)256-0829
Registered: LDA
E-mail: workfuture@aol.com

DC-Area Employees Representing Listed Clients

GELAK, Deanna R.

Clients

Family and Medical Leave Act Technical Corrections Coalition
Rep By: Deanna R. Gelak

Soc. for Human Resource Management
Rep By: Deanna R. Gelak

Worldwide Associates, Inc

1155 15th St. NW
Suite 800
Washington, DC 20005
Tel: (202)429-9788
Fax: (202)833-5296
E-mail: wogoldberg@aol.com

DC-Area Employees Representing Listed Clients

GOLDBERG, Sherwood D., Managing Director
HAIG, Jr., Alexander M., Chairman and President

Wright & Talisman, P.C.

1200 G St. NW
Suite 600
Washington, DC 20005-3802
Tel: (202)393-1200
Fax: (202)393-1240
Registered: LDA
Web: www.wrightlaw.com
E-mail: Mail@Wrightlaw.com

A law firm.

DC-Area Employees Representing Listed Clients

BENNA, Robert H.
BUMGARNER, Carrie L.
DISCIULLO, Jeffrey G.
DUBOFF, Scott M.
FLYNN, Paul M.
GRADY, Gregory, V. President and Secretary
KAUFMAN, Kenneth S.
KOMAROW, Jeffrey D.
KOURY, Joseph S.
LAMB, Robert H.
MCMANUS, James T., President
PODGORSKY, Arnold B.
SMALL, Michael E., V. President and Assistant Secretary
SPECTOR, Barry S., V. President and Assistant Treasurer
STATMAN, Alan J., V. President and Treasurer
TALISMAN, Harold L., Counsel
THOMPSON, Michael J.
WAIKART, Douglas O.

Clients

Alabama Gas Corp.
Rep By: Jeffrey D. Komarow

Arizona Power Authority

Atlantic County Utilities Authority
Rep By: Scott M. DuBoff

Bangor Hydro-Electric Co.
Rep By: James T. McManus, Michael E. Small

Bristol Resource Recovery Facility Operating Committee
Rep By: Scott M. DuBoff, Robert H. Lamb

Columbia Gas Transmission Corp.
Rep By: Jeffrey G. DiSciullo

Columbia Gulf Transmission Corp.
Rep By: Jeffrey G. DiSciullo

Columbia Natural Resources
Issues: CAW ENG ENV WAS
Rep By: Robert H. Lamb

Delaware, Pennsylvania, Solid Waste Authority of the County of
Rep By: Scott M. DuBoff

Equitable Resources Energy Co.
Issues: CAW ENG ENV WAS
Rep By: Robert H. Lamb

GPM Gas Corp.
Rep By: Gregory Grady

Greater Detroit Resource Recovery Authority
Rep By: Scott M. DuBoff

Housatonic Resources Recovery Authority
Rep By: Scott M. DuBoff

Huntsville, Alabama, Solid Waste Disposal Authority of the City of
Rep By: Scott M. DuBoff

Indianapolis, Indiana, City of
Rep By: Scott M. DuBoff

Iroquois Gas Transmission System
Rep By: James T. McManus

Kern River Gas Transmission Co.
Rep By: Michael J. Thompson

Maine Public Service Co.
Rep By: James T. McManus, Michael E. Small

Marine Transport Lines, Inc.
Rep By: Arnold B. Podgorsky

Marion County Solid Waste Management
Rep By: Scott M. DuBoff

MidWest ISO Transmission Owners
Rep By: Michael E. Small

Montgomery County, Ohio/Montgomery County Solid Waste District
Rep By: Scott M. DuBoff, Robert H. Lamb

Northern Border Pipeline Co.
Rep By: Jeffrey G. DiSciullo

Northwest Pipeline Corp
Rep By: James T. McManus

Northwestern Public Service
Rep By: Michael E. Small

Ohio Prosecuting Attorneys Ass'n
Rep By: Scott M. DuBoff

PJM Interconnection, L.L.C.
Rep By: Robert H. Lamb, Barry S. Spector

Portland Metro Regional Government
Issues: WAS
Rep By: Scott M. DuBoff

Potlatch Corp.
Issues: CAW
Rep By: Robert H. Lamb

Solid Waste Authority of Central Ohio
Rep By: Scott M. DuBoff, Robert H. Lamb

Southwest Power Pool
Rep By: Michael E. Small

Southwestern Public Service Co.
Rep By: Alan J. Statman

Spokane Regional Solid Waste System
Rep By: Scott M. DuBoff

Sumner, Tennessee, Resource Authority of the County of
Rep By: Scott M. DuBoff

Sunoco, Inc.
Rep By: Robert H. Lamb

Tejon Ranch Co.
Rep By: Michael J. Thompson

Tesoro Petroleum Corp.
Rep By: Robert H. Benna

Texas Gas Transmission Corp.

Transcontinental Gas Pipeline Corp.
Rep By: Gregory Grady

Venice Gathering System, L.L.C.
Rep By: Jeffrey G. DiSciullo

Western Systems Coordinating Council
Rep By: Michael E. Small

Western Systems Power Pool
Rep By: Michael E. Small

Williams Field Services
Rep By: James T. McManus

Williams Pipelines Central, Inc.
Rep By: Gregory Grady

York County Solid Waste Authority
Rep By: Scott M. DuBoff

Leo Wright Associates

815 Connecticut Ave. NW
Suite 1200
Washington, DC 20006
Tel: (202)833-8128
Fax: (202)833-7924
Registered: LDA

A business, education, and government affairs consulting firm.

DC-Area Employees Representing Listed Clients
WRIGHT, F. Leo, President

Wuerthner Associates, Inc.

7207 Giles Pl.
Suite 100
Springfield, VA 22150-3708
Tel: (703)569-4840

A public affairs and concept development consulting firm.

DC-Area Employees Representing Listed Clients
WUERTHNER, Jr., J. J., President

Wunder & Lilley

1615 L St. NW
Suite 650
Washington, DC 20036
Tel: (202)659-3005
Fax: (202)659-1109
Registered: LDA

DC-Area Employees Representing Listed Clients
WUNDER, Jr., Bernard J., Partner

Clients

BellSouth Corp.
Issues: TEC
Rep By: Bernard J. Wunder, Jr.

Qwest Communications
Issues: TEC
Rep By: Bernard J. Wunder, Jr.

United States Telecom Ass'n
Issues: COM CPI GOV TAX TEC
Rep By: Bernard J. Wunder, Jr.

Young & Jatlow

2121 K St. NW
Suite 800
Washington, DC 20037
Tel: (202)261-3550
Fax: (202)261-3551
Registered: LDA

A law firm specializing in communications law.

DC-Area Employees Representing Listed Clients
YOUNG, Francis L., Partner

Clients

Alaska Network Systems
Rep By: Francis L. Young

Future of Puerto Rico Inc.
Rep By: Francis L. Young

Graphnet Inc.
Rep By: Francis L. Young

Zane & Associates

4616 Arlington Blvd.
Arlington, VA 22204
Tel: (703)521-7393
Fax: (703)521-1633
Registered: LDA

A lobbying and public affairs consulting firm. Also maintains an office in Anchorage, AK.

DC-Area Employees Representing Listed Clients
ZANE, Curtis J., Partner

Clients

Alaska Railroad
Issues: RRR
Rep By: Curtis J. Zane

Aleutian Pribilof Islands Community Development Ass'n
Issues: MAR
Rep By: Curtis J. Zane

Alyeska Pipeline Service Co.
Issues: NAT TAX
Rep By: Curtis J. Zane

Chugach Alaska Corp.
Issues: IND
Rep By: Curtis J. Zane

Holland America West-Tours
Issues: TOU
Rep By: Curtis J. Zane

Kake Tribal Corp.
Issues: IND
Rep By: Curtis J. Zane

Mashpee Wampanoag Indian Tribal Council, Inc.
Issues: IND

North American Sports Management, Inc.
Issues: GAM
Rep By: Curtis J. Zane

Ocean Services
Issues: MAR
Rep By: Curtis J. Zane

Parents Incorporated
Issues: HCR
Rep By: Curtis J. Zane

Seward, Alaska, City of
Issues: URB
Rep By: Curtis J. Zane

TDX Village Corp.
Issues: IND
Rep By: Curtis J. Zane

Union Pacific
Issues: RRR
Rep By: Curtis J. Zane

Wyandotte Tribe of Oklahoma
Issues: IND
Rep By: Curtis J. Zane

Bill Zavarela

2468 Ontario Rd. NW
Washington, DC 20009-2705
Tel: (202)328-1373
Registered: LDA

Clients

Ass'n for Enterprise Opportunity
Issues: ECN
Rep By: Bill Zavarela

Center for Community Change
Rep By: Bill Zavarela

Corporation for Enterprise Development
Rep By: Bill Zavarela

Death With Dignity Nat'l Center
Rep By: Bill Zavarela

Nat'l Employment Lawyers Ass'n
Issues: CIV
Rep By: Bill Zavarela

Nat'l Federation of Community Development of Credit Unions
Rep By: Bill Zavarela

Zeliff, Ireland, and Associates

499 S. Capitol St.
Suite 600
Washington, DC 20003
Tel: (202)554-0473
Fax: (202)554-0393
Registered: LDA

Government relations and marketing consultants.

DC-Area Employees Representing Listed Clients
IRELAND, Hon. Andy
ZELIFF, Jr., Hon. William H., Principal

Clients

Ass'n of Small Business Development Centers
Issues: SMB
Rep By: Hon. William H. Zeliff, Jr.

Boys Town USA
Issues: BUD
Rep By: Hon. Andy Ireland, Hon. William H. Zeliff, Jr.

Feld Entertainment Inc.
Issues: AGR BUD
Rep By: Hon. Andy Ireland

General Mills
Issues: SMB
Rep By: Hon. William H. Zeliff, Jr.

Schering-Plough Corp.
Issues: BUD CPT HCR
Rep By: Hon. Andy Ireland, Hon. William H. Zeliff, Jr.

SIG Arms
Issues: FIR
Rep By: Hon. William H. Zeliff, Jr.

The Zimmer Deshler Group

712 S. Adams St.
Arlington, VA 22204
Tel: (703)486-9555
Fax: (703)486-1666
Registered: LDA
E-mail: kzdeshler@aol.com

A consulting firm specializing in legislative, government relations and project management.

DC-Area Employees Representing Listed Clients
DESHLER, Kirsten Zimmer, President

Zuckerman Spaeder L.L.P.

1201 Connecticut Ave. NW
Suite 600
Washington, DC 20036
Tel: (202)778-1800
Fax: (202)822-8106
Registered: LDA, FARA
Web: www.zuckerman.com
E-mail: rweich@zuckerman.com

DC-Area Employees Representing Listed Clients
ANGULO, Charles
GULDI, Virginia
SCHULTZ, William B.
SMITH, Eleanor H., Partner
TAYLOR, III, William W., Partner
WEICH, Ronald H., Partner

Clients

American Civil Liberties Union
Issues: CIV CPI TEC
Rep By: Ronald H. Weich

American Psychological Soc.
Rep By: Ronald H. Weich

Amity, Inc.
Issues: ALC
Rep By: Charles Angulo, Ronald H. Weich

The Bureau of Nat'l Affairs, Inc.
Issues: GOV TAX
Rep By: Virginia Guldi, Eleanor H. Smith, Ronald H. Weich

Internat'l Brotherhood of Teamsters
Issues: LBR
Rep By: William W. Taylor, III, Ronald H. Weich

Mexico, Embassy of

Nat'l Board for Certification in Occupational Therapy, Inc.
Issues: IMM
Rep By: Ronald H. Weich

Nat'l Center for Tobacco-Free Kids
Issues: TOB
Rep By: Ronald H. Weich

Nat'l Pawnbrokers Ass'n
Issues: BNK FIR
Rep By: Ronald H. Weich

Nat'l Prison Project
Issues: CIV
Rep By: Ronald H. Weich

Oneida Indian Nation of New York
Issues: IND
Rep By: William W. Taylor, III, Ronald H. Weich

United States Pharmacopeia
Issues: MED
Rep By: Charles Angulo, Ronald H. Weich

Vietnam Veterans of America Foundation
Issues: LAW
Rep By: Charles Angulo, Ronald H. Weich

Zuckert, Scoutt and Rasenberger, L.L.P.

888 17th St. NW
Suite 600
Washington, DC 20006-3959
Tel: (202)298-8660
Fax: (202)342-0683
Registered: LDA, FARA

A law firm.

DC-Area Employees Representing Listed Clients
ALLEN, Richard A., Partner
BENGE, Malcolm L., Partner
CALDERWOOD, James A., Partner
CALLAWAY, Jr., William H., Partner
COSTELLO, Frank J., Partner
KISSICK, Ralph L., Partner
MATHIAS, Richard D., Partner
PERA, Lonnie E., Partner
PLUMP, Andrew R.
SCHOELLHAMER, Paul E., Partner and Director, Government Affairs
SCHWEITZER, Richard P., Partner
SIMPSON, Jr., Charles J., Partner
TRINDER, Rachel B., Partner
YINGLING, Monique E., Partner

Clients

Aerolineas Centrales de Colombia
Rep By: Richard D. Mathias

Air Afrique
Rep By: William H. Callaway, Jr.

Air Macau
Rep By: Rachel B. Trinder

Air Transport Ass'n of America
Issues: AVI
Rep By: Paul E. Schoellhamer

Airtours Internat'l
Rep By: Malcolm L. Benge, Richard D. Mathias

Alitalia
Rep By: Richard D. Mathias

All Nippon Airways Co.
Rep By: William H. Callaway, Jr., Andrew R. Plump, Charles J. Simpson, Jr., Rachel B. Trinder

American Bus Ass'n
Issues: ROD TAX TOU TRA
Rep By: Richard P. Schweitzer

Challenge Air Cargo
Rep By: William H. Callaway, Jr.

Columbia Helicopters, Inc.
Rep By: Rachel B. Trinder

Decatur Park District
Issues: AVI
Rep By: Paul E. Schoellhamer

Dunc LLC
Issues: AVI
Rep By: Paul E. Schoellhamer

Empresa Consolidada Cubana de Aviacion
Rep By: Lonnie E. Pera

Erickson Air-Crane Co.
Rep By: Rachel B. Trinder

Eva Airways Corp.
Rep By: Malcolm L. Benge, Rachel B. Trinder

Hong Kong Dragon Airlines Ltd.
Rep By: Rachel B. Trinder

Houston, Texas, Department of Aviation of the City of
Issues: AVI
Rep By: Paul E. Schoellhamer, Rachel B. Trinder

JMC Airlines, Ltd.
Rep By: Richard D. Mathias, Lonnie E. Pera

Kenya Airways
Rep By: Malcolm L. Benge, Richard D. Mathias

Korean Air Lines
Rep By: Malcolm L. Benge, William H. Callaway, Jr.

LADECO
Rep By: Charles J. Simpson, Jr.

Lan Chile
Rep By: Charles J. Simpson, Jr.

Macau, Civil Aviation Authority of
Rep By: Rachel B. Trinder

Malaysian Airline System
Rep By: Charles J. Simpson, Jr.

Martinair Holland
Rep By: Frank J. Costello, Rachel B. Trinder

Nat'l Business Aviation Ass'n
Rep By: Frank J. Costello

Nat'l Private Truck Council
Issues: TRA
Rep By: Richard P. Schweitzer

Nat'l Welding Supply Ass'n
Rep By: Richard P. Schweitzer

Nippon Cargo Airlines
Rep By: William H. Callaway, Jr., Charles J. Simpson, Jr., Rachel B. Trinder

Pakistan Internat'l Airlines
Rep By: Richard D. Mathias, Andrew R. Plump

Philippine Airlines
Rep By: Malcolm L. Benge

Rosemount, Inc.
Rep By: Rachel B. Trinder

Royal Brunei Airways
Rep By: Malcolm L. Benge, Charles J. Simpson, Jr.

Soc. of Glass and Ceramic Decorators
Rep By: James A. Calderwood

South African Airways
Rep By: Frank J. Costello

Truck Renting and Leasing Ass'n
Issues: TRU
Rep By: Richard P. Schweitzer

Turkish Airlines
Rep By: Charles J. Simpson, Jr.

UniGroup, Inc.
Issues: TRA
Rep By: James A. Calderwood

United Van Lines, Inc.
Rep By: James A. Calderwood

Zwerdling, Paul, Leibig, Kahn, Thompson & Wolly, P.C.

1025 Connecticut Ave. NW
Suite 712
Washington, DC 20036

Tel: (202)857-5000
Fax: (202)223-8417
Registered: LDA

DC-Area Employees Representing Listed Clients
LEIBIG, Michael, General Counsel

Clients

Internat'l Union of Police Ass'ns
Rep By: Michael Leibig

2001 Washington Representatives

The Clients

The following organizations may be headquartered anywhere in the United States (including Washington, DC) or abroad. They appear here because they either maintain a Washington office from which advocacy work is performed, or they retain someone in Washington to represent their interests before the federal government. Details on the firms who provide government relations or advocacy services on behalf of these organizations are set forth in the preceding section.

#10 Enterprises LLC

Houston, TX
Leg. Issues: NAT, RES

Outside Counsel/Consultants

John Freshman Associates, Inc.
Issues: NAT, RES
Rep By: John D. Freshman, Lawrence P. Kast, Catherine B. Kiefer

1199 Nat'l Health & Human Services Employees Union

New York, NY
Leg. Issues: HCR, LBR

Outside Counsel/Consultants

Joe Velasquez & Associates
Issues: HCR, LBR
Rep By: Joe Velasquez

1245 Foundation

1245 35th St. NW
Washington, DC 20007
A political action committee.

In-house, DC-area Employees

BARKER, Alec D.

The 13th Regional Corp.

Seattle, WA
Leg. Issues: IND

Outside Counsel/Consultants

Jack Ferguson Associates, Inc.
Issues: IND
Rep By: Jack Ferguson

20/20 Vision

1828 Jefferson Pl. NW
Washington, DC 20036
Tel: (202)833-2020
Fax: (202)833-5307
Registered: LDA
Web: www.2020vision.org
E-mail: vison@2020vision.org
Leg. Issues: CAW, CHM, DEF, ENV, FIR, FOO, HCR

In-house, DC-area Employees

WYERMAN, James: Exec. Director

Outside Counsel/Consultants

Hauser Group

2001 World Police and Fire Games

Indianapolis, IN
Leg. Issues: BUD

Outside Counsel/Consultants

Sagamore Associates, Inc.
Issues: BUD
Rep By: Theodore W. Bristol, Julia P. Church, David U. Gogol

21st Century Democrats

1311 L St. NW
Suite 300
Washington, DC 20005
Web: www.21stcenturydems.org
Tel: (202)626-5620
Fax: (202)347-0956

In-house, DC-area Employees

YOUNG, Kelly C.: Exec. Director

21st Century Partnership

Warner Robins, GA
Coordinates community support of military bases.

Leg. Issues: DEF

Outside Counsel/Consultants

Hurt, Norton & Associates
Issues: DEF
Rep By: Robert H. Hurt, Frank Norton

21st Century Space Foundation

Outside Counsel/Consultants

Gilbert A. Robinson, Inc.
Rep By: Gilbert A. Robinson

24/7 Media, Inc.

New York, NY
Leg. Issues: CPI

Outside Counsel/Consultants

Denny Miller McBee Associates
Issues: CPI

3001, Inc.

Sulphur, LA
A surveying and mapping firm. Formerly known as Vernon F. Meyer and Associates.

Leg. Issues: ENV, MAR, SCI

Outside Counsel/Consultants

Diane McRee Associates
Issues: ENV, MAR, SCI
Rep By: Diane B. McRee

3Com Corp.

1201 Pennsylvania Ave. NW
Suite 300
Washington, DC 20004
Web: www.3com.com
Tel: (202)661-4608
Fax: (202)661-4618

A high technology, networking company. Headquartered in Santa Clara, CA.

Leg. Issues: COM, CPI, CPT, CSP, ECN, EDU, FOR, GOV, IMM, LAW, LBR, MAN, SCI, SMB, TAX, TEC, TRD, URB, UTI

Political Action Committee/s

3Com Political Action Committee (3PAC)
1201 Pennsylvania Ave. NW
Suite 300
Washington, DC 20004
Contact: Dreama D. Towe
Tel: (202)661-4609
Fax: (202)661-4618

In-house, DC-area Employees

GARCIA, Greg: Director, Global Government Relations
TOWE, Dreama D.: Manager, Government Relations

Outside Counsel/Consultants

Dittus Communications
Rep By: Kristin Litterst

Harris, Wiltshire & Grannis LLP
Issues: TEC
Rep By: Scott Blake Harris

3D Metrics Inc.

Petaluma, CA
Leg. Issues: DEF

Outside Counsel/Consultants

American Defense Internat'l, Inc.
Issues: DEF
Rep By: Van D. Hipp, Jr., Dave Wilberding

3gi, Inc.

Washington, DC
Leg. Issues: SCI

Outside Counsel/Consultants

Capital Strategies Group, Inc.
Issues: SCI
Rep By: Tammi Hayes

3Tex

Cary, NC
Leg. Issues: DEF, ROD, SMB, TRA

Outside Counsel/Consultants

GHL Inc.
Issues: DEF, ROD, SMB, TRA
Rep By: Thomas R. Goldberg

4C Foods Corp.

New York, NY
Leg. Issues: TRD

Outside Counsel/Consultants

The Ickes & Enright Group
Issues: TRD
Rep By: Janice Ann Enright, Harold M. Ickes

500 C Street Associates, L.P.

Washington, DC
Leg. Issues: BUD, DOC, RES

Outside Counsel/Consultants

Patton Boggs, LLP
Issues: BUD, DOC, RES
Rep By: Robert C. Jones

59/Air Depot Road, Ltd.

Oklahoma City, OK
Leg. Issues: GOV, RES

Outside Counsel/Consultants

VSAdc.com
Issues: GOV, RES
Rep By: J. R. Reskovac

The 60/Plus Ass'n, Inc.

1655 N. Fort Myer Dr.
Suite 355
Arlington, VA 22209
Tel: (703)807-2070
Fax: (703)807-2073
Registered: LDA
Web: www.60plus.org

A grassroots organization that works for tax fairness for seniors.

Leg. Issues: BUD, FAM, FIN, GOV, HCR, HOU, INS, LAW, MMM, PHA, RET, TAX

Political Action Committee/s

Senior Power Campaign Committee
1655 N. Fort Myer Dr.
Suite 355
Arlington, VA 22209
Tel: (703)807-2070
Fax: (703)807-2073

In-house, DC-area Employees

HOUGH, Henry A.: Exec. V. President
MARTIN, James L.: President
NOONE, Amy E.: Assistant to the President
SENESE, Donald J.: V. President, Research
STEEL, Aimee N.: Communications Director
ZION, Hon. Roger H.: Honorary Chair

Outside Counsel/Consultants

Pearson & Pipkin, Inc.
Issues: GOV, HCR, MMM, RET, TAX
Rep By: Ronald W. Pearson

Resources Development, Inc.
Issues: TAX
Rep By: Hon. Roger H. Zion

Sumlin Associates
Issues: TAX
Rep By: Council Nedd

7-Eleven, Inc.

Dallas, TX
Leg. Issues: RET, TOB

Outside Counsel/Consultants

Vinson & Elkins L.L.P.
Issues: RET, TOB
Rep By: Hon. Michael A. Andrews, Christine L. Vaughn

A Greater Washington

Washington, DC

Outside Counsel/Consultants

Robert M. Brandon and Associates
Rep By: Robert M. Brandon, Michelle Molloy

AAA MidAtlantic

12600 Fair Lakes Circle
Fairfax, VA 22033-4904
Tel: (703)222-6000
Fax: (703)802-8621

Leg. Issues: TEC, TRA

In-house, DC-area Employees

ANDERSON, Mahlon G.: Director, Public and Government Relations
GRIMM, Jr., Norman E.: Director, Traffic Safety
KOSH, Ronald W.: V. President

Outside Counsel/Consultants

Anderson and Corrie
Rep By: Quentin R. Corrie

Hogan & Hartson L.L.P.
Issues: TEC, TRA
Rep By: C. Michael Gilliland, William Michael House, Christine M. Warnke

AAAE-ACI

601 Madison
Suite 400
Alexandria, VA 22314
Tel: (703)824-0500
Fax: (703)820-1395
Registered: LDA
Web: www.airportnet.org

The joint legislative affairs operation for the American Ass'n of Airport Executives and the Airports Council International - North America. Both groups continue to operate as two separate organizations, with the exception of their legislative affairs program.

Leg. Issues: AER, AVI, BUD, CAW, CPI, ENV, LAW, LBR, TRA

Political Action Committee/s

AAAE Good Government Committee
601 Madison
Suite 400
Alexandria, VA 22314
Contact: Todd J. Hauptli
Tel: (703)824-0500
Fax: (703)820-1395

In-house, DC-area Employees

BACON, Joel: Director, Legislative Affairs
HAUPTLI, Todd J.: Senior V. President, Federal Affairs
ORNST, Patty: Manager, Legislative Affairs
TRAVIS, Eryn: Director, Communications
VAN DAM, Brad: Director, Legislative Affairs

Outside Counsel/Consultants

AB Management Associates, Inc.
Issues: AVI
Rep By: Larry P. Barnett

Baker, Donelson, Bearman & Caldwell, P.C.
Issues: BUD
Rep By: Linda Hall Daschle, Albert B. Randall

Collier Shannon Scott, PLLC
Rep By: Jeffrey L. Leiter

Foley & Lardner
Issues: AVI
Rep By: Thomas R. Devine, Jodi L. Hanson, Jerris Leonard, Kathleen Leonard, David Ralston, Jr., Michael Schneiderman

Rhoads Group
Issues: AVI
Rep By: Paul D. Behrends, Kathleen Ireland, Steven G. McKnight, Clifford R. Northup, Barry D. Rhoads, Elizabeth R. Sharpstene, Thomas Worrall

The Wexler Group
Issues: AVI
Rep By: Patrick J. McCann

AAE Technologies, Inc.

Falls Church, VA
Leg. Issues: FUE

Outside Counsel/Consultants

RGS Enterprises, Inc.
Issues: FUE
Rep By: Ronald G. Sykes

AAI Corp.

1213 Jefferson Davis Hwy.
Suite 802
Arlington, VA 22202-4304
Tel: (703)412-4170
Fax: (703)416-4820
Registered: LDA, FARA
Web: www.aaicorp.com

A research, design, engineering and manufacturer of simulation trainers, automated hydraulic and electronic test systems, electric trolley buses and light rail trucks and shells headquartered in Hunt Valley, MD. The Washington office provides support for programs through the Congressional/Federal Budget Process.

Leg. Issues: BUD, DEF, MAN, TRA

Political Action Committee/s

AAI Corporation Political Action Committee (AAIPAC)
1213 Jefferson Davis Hwy.
Suite 802
Arlington, VA 22202-4304
Tel: (703)412-4170
Fax: (703)416-4820

In-house, DC-area Employees

BARRY, Albert P.: V. President, Washington Operations
EHUDIN, Marc L.: Director, Legislative Affairs

Outside Counsel/Consultants

Hargett Consulting
Issues: TRA
Rep By: Jack Hargett

Martin, Fisher & Associates, Inc.
Issues: BUD, DEF
Rep By: J. Paris Fisher, David O'B. Martin

Pacquing Consulting Inc.
Issues: MAN
Rep By: Juliet Pacquing

The Solomon Group, LLC
Issues: DEF
Rep By: David M. Lonie, Hon. Gerald B. H. Solomon

The Spectrum Group
Issues: DEF
Rep By: Gen. J. B. Davis, USAF (Ret.), Ben F. Hord, Paul E. McManus, Gregory L. Sharp, Maurice N. Shriber

AARP (American Ass'n of Retired Persons)

601 E St. NW
Washington, DC 20049
Tel: (202)434-2277
Fax: (202)434-6548
Registered: LDA
Web: www.aarp.org

A non-profit organization concerned with the needs and interests of persons 50 years and older.

Leg. Issues: BAN, BNK, BUD, CIV, CPI, CSP, ECN, ENG, FAM, FIN, FOO, GOV, HCR, HOU, INS, LAW, LBR, MMM, PHA, RET, TAX, TEC, TRA, VET

In-house, DC-area Employees

ALVAREZ, Debra: Legislative Specialist
BECKER, Mila: Legislative Representative
BLISS, Mary Ellen: Director, Federal Affairs, Economic Issues
CERTNER, David: Senior Coordinator, Federal Affairs
CLEMMER, Elizabeth: Associate Director, Public Policy Institute
CORRY, Martin C.: Director, Federal Affairs
DEETS, Horace B.: Exec. Director
DONNELLAN, Kevin J.: Director, Grassroots Advocacy
GIBSON, Mary Jo: Associate Director, Public Policy Institute
GIST, John: Associate Director, Public Policy Institute
GREEN, Roy: Legislative Representative
KEENAN, Theresa Anne: Senior Research Advisor
KRAMER, Jeff A.: Legislative Representative
LANE, Janet C.: Director, Communications Operations
MATHEIS, Cheryl: Director, State Legislation
MAYER, Marion R.: Legislative Representative
MORTON, Evelyn: Legislative Representative
NOVELLI, William D.: Associate Exec. Director
POLLAK, Michele: Legislative Representative
RAMSEY, Martha C.: Director, Publications
REED, Jo: Director, Federal Affairs, Consumer Issues
ROTHER, John C.: Director, Legislation and Public Policy Division
SLOAN, Kirsten A.: Deputy Director, Federal Affairs, Health Issues
SMITH, Patricia P.: Director, Federal Affairs, Health Issues
VARNER, Theresa: Director, Public Policy Institute
WHITE, Larry: Legislative Representative
ZALEZNICK, Steven: Chief Exec. Officer, AARP Services, Inc.

ABA Center on Children and the Law

740 15th St. NW
Washington, DC 20005
Tel: (202)662-1720
Fax: (202)662-1755
Web: www.abanet.org/child
E-mail: ctrchildlaw@attmail.com

In-house, DC-area Employees

DAVIDSON, Howard: Director

ABA Insurance Ass'n

Washington, DC
Leg. Issues: BAN, INS

Outside Counsel/Consultants

Barnett & Sivon, P.C.
Issues: BAN, INS
Rep By: James C. Sivon

ABAHG, Inc.

Brighton, MA

Outside Counsel/Consultants

Mintz, Levin, Cohn, Ferris, Glovsky and Popeo, P.C.

ABB Combustion Engineering Nuclear Power

Windsor, CT

Outside Counsel/Consultants

Egan & Associates
Rep By: Joseph R. Egan

ABB Daimler-Benz Transportation, N.A. (ADTRANZ)

Pittsburgh, PA
Leg. Issues: BUD, TRA

Outside Counsel/Consultants

Jefferson Government Relations, L.L.C.
Issues: BUD, TRA
Rep By: William A. Roberts

ABB, Inc.

555 12th St. NW
Suite 350
N. Tower
Washington, DC 20004
Tel: (202)638-1256
Fax: (202)737-1311
Registered: LDA
Leg. Issues: BUD, ENG, FOR, MMM, REL, TAX, TRD, UTI

Political Action Committee/s

ABB's Employees' Fund for Effective Government
555 12th St. NW
Suite 350
N. Tower
Washington, DC 20004
Contact: Bruce B. Talley
Tel: (202)639-4062
Fax: (202)737-1311

In-house, DC-area Employees

FENTON, Dawn D.H.: Manager, Government Affairs
HARSANYI, Dr. Fruzsina M.: V. President, Public Affairs and Corporate Communications
HOLZ, Hans: Director, Multilateral Project Finance
LOHMAN, Houda M.: Government Policy Analyst
TALLEY, Bruce B.: Director, Government Affairs and International Trade

Abbott Laboratories

1710 Rhode Island Ave. NW
Suite 300
Washington, DC 20036
Tel: (202)659-8524
Fax: (202)466-8386
Registered: LDA

Abbott Laboratories is a global, diversified health care company devoted to the discovery, development, manufacture, and marketing of pharmaceutical, diagnostic, nutritional, and hospital products.

Leg. Issues: AGR, BUD, CON, CPT, GOV, HCR, IMM, LBR, MAN, MED, MMM, PHA, TAX, TRD, WAS

Political Action Committee/s

Abbott Laboratories Better Government Fund
1710 Rhode Island Ave. NW
Suite 300
Washington, DC 20036
Contact: David W. Landsidle
Tel: (202)659-8524
Fax: (202)466-8386

In-house, DC-area Employees

HAAS, Rosemary T.: Regional Director, Government Affairs
LANDSIDLE, David W.: Divisional V. President, Federal Government Affairs
SENSIBAUGH, Cynthia B.: Director, Washington Affairs

Outside Counsel/Consultants

Bennett Turner & Coleman, LLP

Capitol Health Group, LLC
Issues: HCR, MMM, PHA
Rep By: Michael D. Bromberg, Shawn Coughlin, Steven Jenning, Layna McConkey Peltier

Williams & Jensen, P.C.
Rep By: George G. Olsen

ABC Inc.

New York, NY

Outside Counsel/Consultants

Wilmer, Cutler & Pickering

Abide Internat'l, Inc.

San Francisco, CA
Leg. Issues: URB

Outside Counsel/Consultants

Sacramento-Potomac Consulting, Inc.
Issues: URB
Rep By: Benjamin G. Griffith, Hon. Richard H. Lehman

Abilene Industrial Foundation, Inc.

Abilene, TX
Leg. Issues: DEF

Outside Counsel/Consultants

Thelen Reid & Priest LLP
Issues: DEF
Rep By: Barry I. Berkoff, Richard J. Leidl, Stephan M. Minikes

Abilene, Texas, City of

Leg. Issues: TRA

Outside Counsel/Consultants

Winston & Strawn
Issues: TRA
Rep By: Hon. James H. Burnley, IV, John A. Waits, II

Abitibi Consolidated Sales Corp.

Houston, TX

A paper manufacturer.

Leg. Issues: CAW, ENG, ENV, TAX, TRA

Outside Counsel/Consultants

Public Affairs Resources, Inc.
Issues: CAW, ENG, ENV, TAX, TRA
Rep By: Susan E. Petniunas

ABLEDATA

8630 Fenton St.
Suite 930
Silver Spring, MD 20910
Web: www.abledata.com
E-mail: abledata@macroint.com
Tel: (301)608-8998
Fax: (301)608-8958

Maintains an electronic database on assistive devices for people with disabilities.

In-house, DC-area Employees

BELKNAP, Katherine: Project Director

Outside Counsel/Consultants

Macro Internat'l

Abrams & Co. Publishers Inc.

Waterbury, CT
Leg. Issues: BUD, EDU

Outside Counsel/Consultants

Van Scoyoc Associates, Inc.
Issues: BUD, EDU
Rep By: Victor F. Klatt, III, James W. Kohlmoos, H. Stewart Van Scoyoc

Absaroka Trust

Portello Valley, CA
Leg. Issues: NAT

Outside Counsel/Consultants

Kimmitt, Coates & McCarthy
Issues: NAT
Rep By: Vincent J. Coates, Jr.

Abtech Industries

Scottsdale, AZ
Leg. Issues: BUD, ENV

Outside Counsel/Consultants

Cassidy & Associates, Inc.
Issues: BUD, ENV
Rep By: John S. Doyle, Jr., Shawn Edwards, Christy Carson Evans, W. Campbell Kaufman, IV, Brig. Gen. Terry Paul, USMC (Ret.), Gabor J. Rozsa

AC Transit

Oakland, CA
Leg. Issues: BUD, COM, LBR, TEC, TRA

Outside Counsel/Consultants

Simon and Co., Inc.
Issues: BUD, COM, LBR, TEC, TRA
Rep By: Heather Barber, Alex DeGood, Leonard S. Simon

Acacia Life Insurance Co.

7315 Wisconsin Ave.
Bethesda, MD 20814
Tel: (301)280-1000
Fax: (301)280-1031

Political Action Committee/s

Acacia Life Insurance Co. Political Action Committee
7315 Wisconsin Ave.
Bethesda, MD 20814
Contact: Ellen Jane Abromson
Tel: (301)280-1000
Fax: (301)280-1031

In-house, DC-area Employees

ABROMSON, Ellen Jane: Second V. President, Associate Counsel and Government Relations Representative

Academic Health Center Coalition

Baltimore, MD
Leg. Issues: BUD, MED, MMM

Outside Counsel/Consultants

Capitol Associates, Inc.
Issues: BUD, MED, MMM
Rep By: Debra M. Hardy Havens, Edward R. Long, Ph.D., Julie P. Pawelczyk

Academic Medicine Development Corp.

New York, NY

Outside Counsel/Consultants

Kelly and Associates, Inc.
Rep By: John A. Kelly

Academy for Eating Disorders

McLean, VA

Outside Counsel/Consultants

Degnon Associates, Inc.
Rep By: George K. Degnon, CAE

Academy for Educational Development - Nat'l Institute for Work and Learning

1825 Connecticut Ave. NW
Seventh Floor
Washington, DC 20009
Web: www.aed.org
Tel: (202)884-8186
Fax: (202)884-8422

A non-profit research and policy organization concerned primarily with the transition between education in the classroom and employment in the workplace. An Institute of the Academy for Educational Development.

In-house, DC-area Employees

CHARNER, Ivan: V. President and Director
FRASER, Bryna Shore: Deputy Director

Academy for Implants and Transplants

P.O. Box 223
Springfield, VA 22150
Tel: (703)451-0001
Fax: (703)451-0004

In-house, DC-area Employees

VISCIDO, Dr. Anthony J.: Exec. Director, Secretary/Treasurer

Academy for State and Local Government

444 N. Capitol St. NW
Suite 345
Washington, DC 20001
Tel: (202)434-4850
Fax: (202)434-4851

In-house, DC-area Employees

HATZER, Dawn: Coordinator
RUDA, Richard: Chief Counsel

Academy of General Dentistry

Chicago, IL
Leg. Issues: BUD, HCR, LBR

Outside Counsel/Consultants

JKB Communications
Issues: BUD, HCR, LBR
Rep By: Judith Kloss Bynum

Academy of Leadership

College Park, MD

Outside Counsel/Consultants

Hauser Group

Academy of Managed Care Pharmacy

100 N. Pitt
Suite 400
Alexandria, VA 22314
Web: www.amcp.org
Tel: (703)683-8416
Fax: (703)683-8417
Registered: LDA
Leg. Issues: CPT, HCR, MED, MMM, PHA

In-house, DC-area Employees

CAHILL, Judith: Exec. Director
FRY, Richard: Senior Director, Pharmacy Affairs
GEISSER, John E.: Director, Government Affairs

Academy of Osseointegration

Chicago, IL
Leg. Issues: BUD, HCR

Outside Counsel/Consultants

Smith, Bucklin and Associates, Inc.
Issues: BUD, HCR
Rep By: Jill Rathbun

Academy of Pharmaceutical Research and Science

2215 Constitution Ave. NW
Washington, DC 20037
Web: www.aphanet.org
E-mail: mka@mail.aphanet.org
Tel: (202)628-4410
Fax: (202)783-2351

An academy of the American Pharmaceutical Ass'n. Promotes scientific, technical and academic accomplishments in all disciplines, from basic biomedical and scientific research to applied, clinical, social and economic science, and integrates science into the profession of pharmacy.

Leg. Issues: HCR, INS, PHA

In-house, DC-area Employees

MAINE, Lucinda L.: Senior V. President

Academy of Radiology Research

1029 Vermont Ave. NW
Suite 505
Washington, DC 20005
Tel: (202)347-5872
Fax: (202)347-5876
Registered: LDA
Web: www.acadrad.org
E-mail: acadrad@aol.com

Works to advance research in radiology and related disciplines.

Leg. Issues: CPT, GOV, HCR, LBR, MED, TAX, TOR

In-house, DC-area Employees

NAGY, Edward C.: Exec. Director

Outside Counsel/Consultants

Arter & Hadden
Issues: HCR, MED
Rep By: Hon. Thomas G. Loeffler, Jon W. Plebani

Venable
Issues: CPT, GOV, LBR, TAX, TOR
Rep By: Jeffrey S. Tenenbaum

Academy of Rail Labor Attorneys

Leg. Issues: RRR

Outside Counsel/Consultants

The Laxalt Corp.
Issues: RRR
Rep By: Michelle D. Laxalt

ACB Government Employees

1155 15th St. NW
Suite 1004
Washington, DC 20005
Tel: (202)467-5081
Fax: (202)467-5085
Web: www.acb.org
E-mail: info@acb.org

In-house, DC-area Employees

POMERANTZ, Mitch

ACB Social Service Providers

1155 15th St. NW
Suite 1004
Washington, DC 20005
Tel: (202)467-5081
Fax: (202)467-5085
Web: www.acb.org
E-mail: info@acb.org

In-house, DC-area Employees

SHAW, Pam

Accenture

800 Connecticut Ave. NW
Washington, DC 20006
Tel: (202)533-1100
Fax: (202)533-1134
Registered: LDA
Web: www.andersenconsulting.com

Formerly Andersen Consulting LLP. Headquartered in Chicago, IL.

Leg. Issues: BUD, DEF, FIN, IMM, TRD

In-house, DC-area Employees

JOCHUM, Jim: Senior Manager, Government Affairs

Outside Counsel/Consultants

BKSH & Associates
Issues: IMM
Rep By: Mark Disler

The Conaway Group LLC
Issues: DEF
Rep By: Lt. Gen. John B. Conaway, USAF (Ret.), James L. Hobgood, Michael S. Waite

The Dutko Group, Inc.
Issues: BUD, DEF
Rep By: Gary J. Andres, Juliette M. Raffensperger, Arthur H. Silverman, William Simmons

Mayer, Brown & Platt
Issues: TRD
Rep By: Carol J. Bilzi, Brian T. Borders, Mark H. Gitenstein, Jeffrey H. Lewis

Verner, Liipfert, Bernhard, McPherson and Hand, Chartered
Issues: FIN
Rep By: Berl Bernhard, William H. Minor, David A. Weiss, John H. Zentay

Access Community Health Network

Chicago, IL
Leg. Issues: BUD

Outside Counsel/Consultants

Beacon Consulting Group, Inc.
Issues: BUD
Rep By: Gordon P. MacDougall, Julie Debolt Moeller, Lisa A. Stewart

Access Technology Ass'n

3612 Bent Branch Ct.
Falls Church, VA 22041
Tel: (703)941-4329
Fax: (703)941-4329
Registered: LDA

Members are producers of "access technology", i.e. products which help disabled employees to have greater access and effectiveness in the workplace.

Leg. Issues: CIV, CSP, HCR, LBR

In-house, DC-area Employees

TOBIN, Dr. William J.: Exec. Director

Outside Counsel/Consultants

William J. Tobin and Associates
Issues: CIV, CSP, HCR, LBR

The Accountability Project

1101 17th St. NW
Suite 203
Washington, DC 20036
Tel: (202)496-0280

A coalition of labor and other progressive groups that provides local communication tools for individuals and organizations to move public opinion and public policy in a more progressive direction. Participants include AFL-CIO; the American Federation of State County and Municipal Employees; the American Postal Workers Union; Clean Water Action; the Internat'l Ass'n of Machinists; the Internat'l Union of Electronic, Electrical, Salaried, Machine and Furniture Workers; Local 1199 Hospital Workers of New York; the Nat'l Ass'n of Social Workers; the Nat'l Council of Senior Citizens; the Service Employees Internat'l Union; the United Auto Workers; the United Mine Workers; and the United Steelworkers.

In-house, DC-area Employees

CAMPBELL, Bernie: Exec. Director

The Accountants Coalition

1200 G St. NW
Suite 800
Washington, DC 20005
Tel: (202)434-8759
Fax: (301)365-2864

A coalition seeking legislation to limit frivolous securities and other litigation in the current business environment. Members are: Arthur Andersen LLP, Coopers and Lybrand LLP, Deloitte and Touche LLP, Ernst and Young LLP, KPMG Peat Marwick LLP, and Price Waterhouse LLP.

In-house, DC-area Employees

BLAZEY, Leon: Exec. Director

Accrediting Commission on Education for Health Services Administration

730 11th St. NW
Fourth Floor
Washington, DC 20001
Tel: (202)638-5131
Fax: (202)638-3429
Web: www.acehsa.org
E-mail: acehsa@aupha.org

A not-for-profit corporation.

Leg. Issues: EDU, HCR

In-house, DC-area Employees

VOINEA-GRIFFIN, DDS, Andreea: Interim Exec. Director

Accrediting Council for Continuing Education & Training

1722 N St. NW
Washington, DC 20036
Tel: (202)955-1113
Fax: (202)955-1118
Web: www.accet.org
E-mail: rjwilliams@accet.org

Mission is to inspire and promote quality-oriented continuing education and training through the establishment of standards, policies and procedures for the objective and substantive evaluation of organizations seeking accredited status.

Leg. Issues: EDU

In-house, DC-area Employees

WILLIAMS, Roger J.: Exec. Director

Outside Counsel/Consultants

Whiteford, Taylor & Preston

Accuracy in Academia

4455 Connecticut Ave. NW
Suite 330
Washington, DC 20008
Tel: (202)364-3085
Fax: (202)364-4098
Web: www.academia.org
E-mail: cr@aim.org

Encourages students on college and university campuses to challenge professors who "misinform" or "propagandize" during the course of lectures and to report such incidents to its monthly newspaper, The Campus Report. A politically conservative organization which perceives a liberal and radical bias on college faculties, AIA asserts that it was founded "to promote accuracy, fairness, and balance in higher education." Founded in 1985.

In-house, DC-area Employees

FLYNN, Dan: Exec. Director

Accuracy in Media

4455 Connecticut Ave. NW
Suite 330
Washington, DC 20008
Tel: (202)364-4401
Fax: (202)364-4098
Web: www.aim.org
E-mail: ar1@aim.org

Conservative critics of news organizations. Organized in 1969.

In-house, DC-area Employees

IRVINE, Reed J.: Chairman of the Board

AccuWeather

State College, PA
Leg. Issues: SCI

Outside Counsel/Consultants

Chwat and Company, Inc.
Issues: SCI
Rep By: Scott Bizub, John Chwat, Derek Riker

ACE INA

1909 K Street NW
Suite 810
Washington, DC 20006
Tel: (202)530-2704
Fax: (202)872-0736
Registered: LDA
Web: www.ace-ina.com
E-mail: peter.o'connor@ace-ina.com
Leg. Issues: AGR, ENV, FIN, GOV, INS, TAX, TOR, TRD

In-house, DC-area Employees

FISHER, Tim: Assistant V. President, Global Government Affairs
MILLER, Knute Michael: V. President, Government and Industry Affairs
PRUITT, Penny: Federal Affairs Representative

Outside Counsel/Consultants

Mayer, Brown & Platt
Rep By: Mark H. Gitenstein

Williams & Jensen, P.C.
Rep By: Robert E. Glennon, Jr.

A.C.E. Insurance Co. (Bermuda) Ltd.

Hamilton, BERMUDA

Outside Counsel/Consultants

Crowell & Moring LLP
Rep By: Victor E. Schwartz, Howard M. Weinman

Ace Ltd.

Hamilton, BERMUDA

An insurance company.

Leg. Issues: TAX

Outside Counsel/Consultants

Mayer, Brown & Platt
Issues: TAX
Rep By: Penny L. Eastman, Mark H. Gitenstein, Amb. Peter L. Scher, Charles S. Triplett, Richard S. Williamson

ACME - Ass'n of Management Consulting Firms

New York, NY

Outside Counsel/Consultants

Kirkland & Ellis

Acme Software

Santa Clara, CA

Outside Counsel/Consultants

Preston Gates Ellis & Rouvelas Meeds LLP
Rep By: Tim L. Peckinpaugh, W. David Thomas

ACNielsen Corp.

Outside Counsel/Consultants

Brewer Consulting Group, Inc.
Rep By: Michael F. Brewer

Acoma Pueblo

Outside Counsel/Consultants

Steptoe & Johnson LLP
Rep By: Thomas C. Collier, Jr.

ACORN (Ass'n of Community Organizations for Reform Now)

739 Eighth St. SE
Washington, DC 20003
Tel: (202)547-2500
Fax: (202)546-2483
Web: www.acorn.org
E-mail: legnatacorn@acorn.org

A neighborhood-based organization of low and moderate income people in twenty-six states who are concerned with such issues as housing, banking, school reform and employment.

Leg. Issues: BAN, EDU, FIN, HOU, INS, LBR, WEL

In-house, DC-area Employees

KEST, Steven: Exec. Director
SAFFERT, Christopher: Legislative Director

ACS Defense, Inc.

Alexandria, VA
Leg. Issues: AER, DEF, SCI

Outside Counsel/Consultants

Ervin Technical Associates, Inc. (ETA)
Issues: AER, DEF, SCI
Rep By: William J. Andahazy, James L. Ervin, Donald E. Richbourg

ACS Government Solutions Group

Rockville, MD
Leg. Issues: BUD, CPI, DEF

Outside Counsel/Consultants

Jones, Walker, Waechter, Poitevent, Carrere & Denegre, L.L.P.
Issues: BUD, CPI, DEF
Rep By: Paul Cambon, John J. Jaskot, R. Christian Johnsen, James Ogsbury

The Livingston Group, LLC
Issues: BUD, CPI, DEF
Rep By: Richard Legendre, Hon. Robert L. Livingston, Jr., J. Allen Martin, Richard L. Rodgers

ACS Industries, Inc.

Woonsocket, RI

Outside Counsel/Consultants

Porter, Wright, Morris & Arthur, LLP
Rep By: Leslie Alan Glick

ACT, Inc.

One Dupont Circle NW
Suite 340
Washington, DC 20036-1170
Tel: (202)223-2318
Fax: (202)293-2223
Web: www.act.org
E-mail: critza@act.org

A non-profit organization dedicated to measurement and research primarily in support of individuals making decisions about education, training and careers starting in childhood and continuing throughout adulthood. ACT test instruments assist in college and university admission and placement and in school-to-work transitions. ACT maintains a large, historic database of educational performance records that is useful for research and evaluation of the American educational system. Headquartered in Iowa City, IA.

In-house, DC-area Employees

CRITZ, Anna: Director
JOHNSON, Adam: Government Relations Assistant

ACTA Technology

Mountain View, CA

A provider of database management for electronic commerce.

Leg. Issues: CPI

Outside Counsel/Consultants

Fleischman and Walsh, L.L.P.
Issues: CPI
Rep By: Louis H. Dupart, John P. McAllister

Action on Smoking and Health

2013 H St. NW
Washington, DC 20006
Tel: (202)659-4310
Fax: (202)833-3921
Web: www.ash.org

A national, non-profit contributor organization utilizing legal action and education to reduce the hazards of smoking and protect the rights of the non-smoking majority.

In-house, DC-area Employees

BANZHAF, III, John F.: Exec. Director and Chief Counsel

Acute Long Term Hospital Ass'n

1055 N. Fairfax St.
Suite 201
Alexandria, VA 22314-3563
Tel: (703)299-5571
Fax: (703)299-5574
Web: www.altha.org

Promotes the best interests of long term acute care hospitals and their patients.

Leg. Issues: HCR, MMM

In-house, DC-area Employees

TRAVERSE, Brad: Exec. Director

Outside Counsel/Consultants

U.S. Strategies Corp.
Issues: HCR, MMM
Rep By: Gary F. Capistrant, Brad Traverse

Acxiom Corp.

Little Rock, AR
Registered: LDA
Leg. Issues: CSP, MIA

Outside Counsel/Consultants

Arent Fox Kintner Plotkin & Kahn, PLLC
Issues: CSP
Rep By: Hon. Dale L. Bumpers, Michael T. McNamara

Piper Marbury Rudnick & Wolfe LLP
Issues: CSP, MIA
Rep By: Stuart P. Ingis, Ronald L. Plesser

Ad Hoc Coalition of Commercial and Investment Banks

Washington, DC
Leg. Issues: CDT

Outside Counsel/Consultants

Williams & Jensen, P.C.
Issues: CDT
Rep By: George D. Baker, William B. Canfield, J. Steven Hart

Ad Hoc Coalition on Intermarket Coordination

Chicago, IL
Leg. Issues: TAX

Outside Counsel/Consultants

Covington & Burling
Issues: TAX
Rep By: William M. Paul

Ad Hoc Life/Non-life Consolidation Group

Washington, DC
Leg. Issues: TAX

Outside Counsel/Consultants

Davis & Harman LLP
Issues: TAX
Rep By: Richard S. Belas

Ad Hoc Maritime Coalition

Outside Counsel/Consultants

William V. Brierre
Rep By: William V. Brierre, Jr.

Ad Hoc Nitrogen Committee

Washington, DC

Members include C F Industries, Mississippi Chemical Corp., Terra Industries Inc., J.R. Simplot Co., PCS Nitrogen Inc., and Coastal Chem Inc.

Leg. Issues: TRD

Outside Counsel/Consultants

Akin, Gump, Strauss, Hauer & Feld, L.L.P.
Issues: TRD
Rep By: Valerie A. Slater, S. Bruce Wilson

Ad Hoc Public Television Group

Leg. Issues: AGR, BUD

Outside Counsel/Consultants

Sara Garland (and Associates)
Issues: AGR, BUD
Rep By: Sara G. Garland

ADA Consulting Services

25461 Carberry Dr.
South Riding, VA 20152
Tel: (703)327-0598
Fax: (703)327-9477
Registered: LDA
E-mail: aduganstar@aol.com
Leg. Issues: CAW, ENG, ENV, TAX

In-house, DC-area Employees

DUGAN, Alicia A.: President

Outside Counsel/Consultants

RGS Enterprises, Inc.
Issues: CAW, ENG, ENV, TAX
Rep By: Ronald G. Sykes

Adams County, Colorado

Brighton, CO
Leg. Issues: BUD, DEF

Outside Counsel/Consultants

Marshall A. Brachman
Issues: BUD, DEF
Rep By: Marshall A. Brachman

Adaptec

Milipitas, CA

Outside Counsel/Consultants

Powell Tate

ADCS, Inc.

San Diego, CA
Leg. Issues: BUD, CPI, DEF

Outside Counsel/Consultants

Richard W. Bliss
Issues: BUD, CPI, DEF

Adelphi University

Garden City, NY
Leg. Issues: BUD

Outside Counsel/Consultants

Cassidy & Associates, Inc.
Issues: BUD
Rep By: Christopher Lamond, Arthur D. Mason, Hon. Martin A. Russo, Barbara Sutton

Adheris, Inc.

Woodburn, MA
Leg. Issues: MIA, PHA

Outside Counsel/Consultants

Olsson, Frank and Weeda, P.C.
Issues: MIA, PHA
Rep By: John W. Bode, Richard L. Frank, Susan P. Grymes, Karen Reis Harned, Stephen L. Lacey, Marshall L. Matz, Tyson Redpath

Adhesive and Sealant Council

7979 Old Georgetown Rd.
Suite 500
Bethesda, MD 20814
Tel: (301)986-9700
Fax: (301)986-9795
Web: www.ascouncil.org

A trade association representing manufacturers of adhesives and sealants and suppliers to the industry.

Leg. Issues: CHM

In-house, DC-area Employees

BARRY, Richard A.: President
ZANDO, Kate: Director, Administration and Finance

ADI Ltd.

Barton, AUSTRALIA
Leg. Issues: DEF

Outside Counsel/Consultants

Cassidy & Associates, Inc.
Issues: DEF
Rep By: Dennis M. Kedzior, Arthur D. Mason, Brig. Gen. Terry Paul, USMC (Ret.)

Rhoads Group

ADM Milling Co.

Shawnee Mission, KS

Outside Counsel/Consultants

Akin, Gump, Strauss, Hauer & Feld, L.L.P.

AdMeTech

Boston, MA
Leg. Issues: BUD

Outside Counsel/Consultants

Cassidy & Associates, Inc.
Issues: BUD
Rep By: W. Campbell Kaufman, IV, Dennis M. Kedzior

Administaff

Kingwood, TX

A professional employment organization.

Leg. Issues: TAX

Outside Counsel/Consultants

Davis & Harman LLP
Issues: TAX
Rep By: Randolf H. Hardock

Adobe

Outside Counsel/Consultants

Preston Gates Ellis & Rouvelas Meeds LLP
Rep By: Tim L. Peckinpaugh

Adopt America

1025 Connecticut Ave. NW
Suite 1012
Washington, DC 20036
Tel: (202)857-9709
Fax: (202)478-1838
Leg. Issues: FAM

In-house, DC-area Employees

HOGAN, Maureen Flatley: Exec. Director

Outside Counsel/Consultants

Dublin Castle Group
Issues: FAM
Rep By: Maureen Flatley Hogan

Adria Laboratories, Inc.

Columbus, OH

Outside Counsel/Consultants

Kleinfeld, Kaplan and Becker
Rep By: Alan H. Kaplan

Adriaen's Landing Management Co., LLC

Hartford, CT

Outside Counsel/Consultants

The Smith-Free Group

Adroit Systems Inc.

Bellevue, WA
Leg. Issues: ENG

Outside Counsel/Consultants

Morgan Meguire, LLC
Issues: ENG
Rep By: Scott Lindsay, Kyle G. Michel, Katie Parrott, C. Kyle Simpson, Deborah R. Sliz, Kiel Weaver

The Potomac Advocates
Rep By: Charles Scalera, Gary L. Sojka

Adshel, Inc.

Outside Counsel/Consultants

Greener and Hook, LLC

ADSI Inc.

Bethesda, MD
Leg. Issues: TRA

Outside Counsel/Consultants

The Spectrum Group
Issues: TRA
Rep By: Joan Bondareff, Gen. J. B. Davis, USAF (Ret.), Maj. Gen. Paul Fratarangelo, USMC (Ret.), Lt. Gen. John B "Skip" Hall, Jr., USAF(Ret.), Lt. Gen. Leo Marquez, USAF (Ret.), Paul E. McManus, Gregory L. Sharp

ADSIL

Palm Coast, FL
Leg. Issues: BUD

Outside Counsel/Consultants

The PMA Group
Issues: BUD
Rep By: Kaylene Green, Gregory L. Hansen, Dr. John Lynch, Paul J. Magliocchetti

ADTranz (Daimler Chrysler Rail Systems)

Pittsburgh, PA

A railcar manufacturer.

Leg. Issues: TRA

Outside Counsel/Consultants

Jefferson Government Relations, L.L.C.
Issues: TRA
Rep By: William A. Roberts

AdvaMed

1200 G St. NW
Suite 400
Washington, DC 20005
Web: www.advamed.org
Tel: (202)783-8700
Fax: (202)783-8750
Registered: LDA

Formerly known as the Health Industry Manufacturers Ass'n. Represents the medical device, diagnostics and healthcare information systems industry.

Leg. Issues: BUD, CSP, GOV, HCR, MED, MMM, TOB, TRD

Political Action Committee/s

Health Industry Manufacturers Ass'n PAC (HIMA-PAC)
1200 G St. NW
Suite 400
Washington, DC 20005
Contact: Stephen J. Ubl
Tel: (202)783-8700
Fax: (202)783-8750

In-house, DC-area Employees

ARNOLD, John: Director, e-Communications
BAILEY, Pamela G.: President
BARRY, Paul: Associate V. President, Global Strategy and Analysis
BENSON, James S.: Exec. V. President, Technology and Regulatory Affairs
CASTLE, Tess: Associate V. President, Technical and Regulatory Affairs
CERONE, Christopher: Director, Global Strategy and Analysis
FEDERICI, Tara: Associate V. President, Government Affairs
IVORY, Megan: Director, Federal Government Relations
JONES, Carolyn: Associate V. President, Technology and Regulatory Affairs
KELLY, Carol: Exec. V. President, Health Systems and Federal Legislative Policy
LIEBLER, Bernie: Director, Technology and Regulatory Affairs
PLOCK, Mary: V. President, Public Affairs
REILLY, Michael: Director, Government and Public Affairs
ROZYNSKI, Edward M.: Exec. V. President, Global Strategy and Analysis
SIMONS, Dee: Associate V. President, Payment and Policy
SMITH, Jim: V. President, Government Affairs
TREMBLE, Tom: Director, Government and Regional Affairs
TRUNZO, Janet: Associate V. President, Technology and Regulatory Affairs
UBL, Stephen J.: Exec. V. President, Federal Government Relations

Outside Counsel/Consultants

Bergner Bockorny Castagnetti and Hawkins
Rep By: Jeffrey T. Bergner, David A. Bockorny, David Castagnetti, James W. Hawkins, Melissa Schulman

BSMG Worldwide

Collier Shannon Scott, PLLC
Issues: TRD
Rep By: Doris O. Matsui, Paul C. Rosenthal

Hale and Dorr LLP
Issues: GOV, MED
Rep By: Mark Heller

Health Policy Alternatives, Inc.
Issues: HCR
Rep By: Thomas Ault, Bart McCann

MARC Associates, Inc.
Issues: MMM
Rep By: Edwin Allen

Wilmer, Cutler & Pickering
Issues: CSP
Rep By: Ronald J. Greene

Advance Paradigm

Hunt Valley, MD
Leg. Issues: BUD

Outside Counsel/Consultants

Beacon Consulting Group, Inc.
Issues: BUD
Rep By: Gordon P. MacDougall, Lisa A. Stewart, Kyndel Turvaville

Advanced Acoustic Concepts, Inc.

Ronkonkoma, NY
Leg. Issues: DEF

Outside Counsel/Consultants

The PMA Group
Issues: DEF
Rep By: Sean Fogarty, Kaylene Green, Gregory L. Hansen, Paul J. Magliocchetti

Advanced Cordless Technologies, Inc.

Montville, NJ

Outside Counsel/Consultants

Bechtel & Cole
Rep By: Gene A. Bechtel

Advanced Glassfiber Yarns

Aiken, SC
Leg. Issues: MAN

Outside Counsel/Consultants

Alston & Bird LLP
Issues: MAN
Rep By: Thomas M. Boyd

Advanced Integrated Technology, Inc.

Columbia, TN

Outside Counsel/Consultants

Wiley, Rein & Fielding
Rep By: James T. Bruce, III

Advanced Machinery Logistics, Inc.

Lima, PERU

Outside Counsel/Consultants

Hayward Internat'l

Advanced Material Resources, Inc.

Toronto, CANADA

Outside Counsel/Consultants

Vorys, Sater, Seymour and Pease, LLP
Rep By: James K. Alford

Advanced Micro Devices

Sunnyvale, CA
Leg. Issues: CPI, LBR, TAX

Outside Counsel/Consultants

O'Melveny and Myers LLP
Issues: CPI, LBR
Rep By: David T. Beddow, Arthur B. Culvahouse, Jr.

Public Strategies Washington, Inc.
Issues: TAX
Rep By: Paul M. Snyder

Advanced Power Technologies, Inc.

Washington, DC
Leg. Issues: DEF, RES

Outside Counsel/Consultants

John G. Campbell, Inc.
Issues: DEF

Chambers, Conlon & Hartwell
Issues: DEF
Rep By: John Roots

J. Steven Griles & Associates
Issues: RES
Rep By: J. Steven Griles

Robert D. Sneed
Issues: DEF
Rep By: Robert D. Sneed

Advanced Programming Concepts

Austin, TX

A developer of military command, control, communications, and intellegence systems.

Leg. Issues: DEF

Outside Counsel/Consultants

The PMA Group
Issues: DEF
Rep By: Kaylene Green, Paul J. Magliocchetti, Thomas Veltri

Advanced Refractory Technologies, Inc.

Buffalo, NY
Leg. Issues: DEF

Outside Counsel/Consultants

Berkshire Inc.
Issues: DEF
Rep By: Michael T. Kelley

James T. Molloy
Issues: DEF
Rep By: James T. Molloy

Advanced Technology Institute

Leg. Issues: DEF

Outside Counsel/Consultants

Kinghorn & Associates, L.L.C.
Issues: DEF
Rep By: Edward J. Kinghorn, Jr., Jeremy Scott

Advanced Technology Systems

McLean, VA
Leg. Issues: GOV

Outside Counsel/Consultants

The Carter Group
Issues: GOV
Rep By: Michael R. Carter

Advanced Telecom Group (ATG)

Outside Counsel/Consultants

Columbus Public Affairs

Advanced Transit Ass'n

9019 Hamilton Dr. Tel: (703)591-8328
Fairfax, VA 22031 Fax: (703)359-4244

Seeks encouragement and application of low cost, advanced transit technology and planning to meet the public transportation needs of metropolitan complexes. Headquartered in Palo Alto, CA.

Leg. Issues: TRA

In-house, DC-area Employees

KIEFFER, Dr. Jarold A.: Former Chairman

Advanced Vehicle Systems

Washington, DC
Leg. Issues: DEF

Outside Counsel/Consultants

Bob Moss Associates
Issues: DEF
Rep By: Bob Moss

Advanta Corp.

Horsham, PA Registered: LDA
Leg. Issues: BAN, BNK, HOU

Outside Counsel/Consultants

Butera & Andrews
Issues: BAN, BNK, HOU
Rep By: Cliff W. Andrews, Wright H. Andrews, Jr., James J. Butera, Frank Tillotson

Advantage Associates, Inc.

908 Pennsylvania Ave. SE Tel: (202)544-5666
Washington, DC 20003 Fax: (202)544-4647
Registered: LDA
Web: www.advantage-dc.com
E-mail: bsarpalius@advantage-dc.com
Leg. Issues: DEF

In-house, DC-area Employees

ALEXANDER, Jr., Hon. William V. "Bill": Associate
DICKINSON, Hon. Bill: Partner
GONZALEZ, USA (Ret.), Lt. Col. Roberto: Professional Staff
GRANT, Hon. James William "Bill": Partner
HANRAHAN, Hon. Robert P.: Partner
MCEWEN, Hon. Robert D.: Partner
ORTON, Hon. Bill: Partner
PATTERSON, Hon. Jerry M.: Partner
POLLOCK, Hon. Howard: Partner
SARPALIUS, Hon. Bill: President and Chief Exec. Officer
SCHULZE, Hon. Richard T.: Senior Legislative Director
TALLON, Hon. Robin: Partner
WORKS, George: Professional Staff

Outside Counsel/Consultants

RPH & Associates, L.L.C.
Issues: DEF
Rep By: Hon. Robert P. Hanrahan

Advantage Healthplan Inc.

P.O. Box 5939 Tel: (202)783-8191
Washington, DC 20016

A health maintenance organization

Leg. Issues: MMM

In-house, DC-area Employees

WOLFF, Elliot: President

Outside Counsel/Consultants

Morris J. Amitay, P.C.
Issues: MMM
Rep By: Morris J. Amitay, Stephen D. Amitay

Advantica Inc.

Spartanburg, SC

Outside Counsel/Consultants

Murray, Scheer, Montgomery, Tapia & O'Donnell

Adventist Development and Relief Agency Internat'l

12501 Old Columbia Pike Tel: (301)680-6380
Silver Spring, MD 20904 Fax: (301)680-6370
Web: www.adra.org

A non-governmental, independent organization established by the Seventh-day Adventist Church. Provides community development services and disaster relief in developing nations worldwide. ADRA provides services based on need, regardless of race or creed. Currently working in more than 130 nations around the world.

In-house, DC-area Employees

OCHOA, Mario: Exec. V. President
SCHEUNEMAN, Byron L.: Senior V. President
WATTS, Jr., Ralph S.: President

Adventist Health System/Sunbelt, Inc.

Orlando, FL
Leg. Issues: HCR

Outside Counsel/Consultants

Forscey & Stinson, PLLC
Issues: HCR
Rep By: Michael A. Forscey

The National Group, LLP
Rep By: John Blount

Advertising Company ART-ERIA

Kiev, UKRAINE
Leg. Issues: ECN, FIN, FOR, GOV, TRD

Outside Counsel/Consultants

BKSH & Associates
Issues: ECN, FIN, FOR, GOV, TRD
Rep By: Lisa M. Cotter, Riva Levinson

Advertising Tax Coalition

Washington, DC
Leg. Issues: ADV, TAX

Outside Counsel/Consultants

Davidson & Company, Inc.
Issues: ADV, TAX
Rep By: James H. Davidson, Richard E. May, Stanley Sokul

ADVO, Inc.

Windsor, CT

Outside Counsel/Consultants

The Carmen Group
Rep By: Ryan Adesnik, David M. Carmen, Ron M. Linton, Michael E. Russell

The Advocacy Group

1350 I St. NW Tel: (202)393-4841
Suite 680 Fax: (202)393-5596
Washington, DC 20005-3305 Registered: LDA
Web: www.advocacy.com
E-mail: info@advocacy.com
Leg. Issues: EDU

In-house, DC-area Employees

BOISCLAIR, Jon L.
DOTCHIN, Robert J.
MILLS, Robert E.
NUGENT, Jr., John M.
RAMONAS, George A.
SMITH, Anne V.

Outside Counsel/Consultants

Shaw Pittman
Issues: EDU
Rep By: Thomas J. Spulak

The Advocacy Institute

1629 K St. NW Tel: (202)777-7575
Suite 200 Fax: (202)777-7577
Washington, DC 20006-1629
Web: www.advocacy.org
E-mail: info@advocacy.org

Works to strengthen the capacity of social and economic justice advocates to influence and change public policy. This mission is realized through study, teaching, and counseling on effective advocacy tools and strategies.

In-house, DC-area Employees

ARNDORFER, Kay: Director, Tobacco Control Project
COHEN, David: Co-Director
PERTSCHUK, Michael: Co-Director
SHEEKEY, Kathleen D.: Co-Director

Advocates for Highway and Auto Safety

750 First St. NE Tel: (202)408-1711
Suite 901 Fax: (202)408-1699
Washington, DC 20002 Registered: LDA
Web: www.saferoads.org
E-mail: advocates@saferoads.org

A broad-based alliance of consumer, safety, health and law enforcement groups and insurance agents organizations. Supports highway safety legislation, standards, policies and programs at both the national and state levels in order to reduce deaths, injuries and economic costs associated with motor vehicle crashes. Financial support is from the property and casualty insurance industry, although leadership is shared equally between insurance and consumer/safety groups.

Leg. Issues: ALC, AUT, BUD, CSP, GOV, HCR, LAW, ROD, TRA, TRU

In-house, DC-area Employees

BABICS CHASE, Catherine C.: Director, State Affairs
DONALDSON, Ph.D., Gerald: Senior Research Director
GILLAN, Jacqueline S.: V. President
JASNY, Henry: Legal Counsel
MACKINTOSH, Stuart: Director, Communications
SHERWOOD, Lori: Manager, Legislative Affairs
STONE, Judith Lee: President

Outside Counsel/Consultants

Lawler, Metzger & Milkman, LLC
Issues: AUT, ROD, TRA
Rep By: Sante J. Esposito

Advocates for Youth

1025 Vermont Ave. NW Tel: (202)347-5700
Suite 200 Fax: (202)347-2263
Washington, DC 20005 Registered: LDA
Web: www.advocatesforyouth.org
E-mail: info@advocatesforyouth.org

Dedicated to creating and promoting policies which help young people make informed and responsible decisions about their reproductive and sexual health.

Leg. Issues: CIV, EDU, FAM, HCR, WEL

In-house, DC-area Employees

HAUSER, Debra: V. President
HOWELL, Marcela E.: Director, Public Affairs
WAGONER, James: President

AdvoServe

Leg. Issues: HCR

Outside Counsel/Consultants

U.S. Strategies Corp.
Issues: HCR
Rep By: Nance Guenther-Peterson, Heidi Hanson, Brad Traverse

AECL Technologies

481 N. Frederick Ave. Tel: (301)417-0047
Suite 405 Fax: (301)417-0746
Gaithersburg, MD 20877

Provides products and services to the nuclear industry, including complete reactor systems for power generation and research operations, plant control systems, and other specialized nuclear technology engineering services. The U.S. subsidiary of Atomic Energy of Canada Ltd.

In-house, DC-area Employees

GRISOLD, Ray: Treasurer and Acting President

Aegis Research Corp.

Outside Counsel/Consultants

Leadership Counsel, LLC
Rep By: Jack D. P. Lichtenstein

Aegon USA

Baltimore, MD
Leg. Issues: BAN, HCR, INS, TAX

Outside Counsel/Consultants

Davis & Harman LLP
Issues: TAX
Rep By: John T. Adney, Richard S. Belas, Barbara Groves Mattox

Williams & Jensen, P.C.
Issues: BAN, HCR, INS, TAX
Rep By: Rebecca L. Anderson, David E. Franasiak, Robert E. Glennon, Jr., J. Steven Hart, John J. McMackin, Jr., George G. Olsen, Anthony J. Roda

AEI Resources

Ashland, KY
Leg. Issues: ENG, IND, LBR, NAT, TAX

Outside Counsel/Consultants

The Willard Group
Issues: ENG, IND, LBR, NAT, TAX
Rep By: Daniel Scherder

AEPTEC

Rockville, MD
Leg. Issues: DEF

Outside Counsel/Consultants

The PMA Group
Issues: DEF
Rep By: Sean Fogarty, Kaylene Green, Gregory L. Hansen, Paul J. Magliocchetti

Aer Lingus
New York, NY
Outside Counsel/Consultants
Crowell & Moring LLP
Rep By: R. Bruce Keiner, Jr.

Aera Energy LLC
Bakersfield, CA
Leg. Issues: FUE
Outside Counsel/Consultants
Patton Boggs, LLP
Issues: FUE
Rep By: Thomas Hale Boggs, Jr., Donald V. Moorehead, James A. Reeder

Aero Continente, S.A.
Lima, PERU
Outside Counsel/Consultants
Pierre E. Murphy Law Offices

Aerofloral, Inc.
Miami, FL
Outside Counsel/Consultants
Pierre E. Murphy Law Offices

Aeroinversiones, S.A.
Lima, PERU
Outside Counsel/Consultants
Pierre E. Murphy Law Offices

Aerolineas Argentinas
New York, NY
Outside Counsel/Consultants
Squire, Sanders & Dempsey L.L.P.
Rep By: Robert D. Papkin

Aerolineas Centrales de Colombia
Bogota, COLOMBIA
Outside Counsel/Consultants
Zuckert, Scoutt and Rasenberger, L.L.P.
Rep By: Richard D. Mathias

Aerolink, Inc.
Washington, DC
Outside Counsel/Consultants
Whitten & Diamond

Aeromet, Inc.
Tulsa, OK
Leg. Issues: DEF
Outside Counsel/Consultants
Alford & Associates
Issues: DEF
Rep By: Marty Alford

Aeronautical Radio, Inc.
Annapolis, MD
Outside Counsel/Consultants
Wiley, Rein & Fielding

Aeronautical Repair Station Ass'n
Alexandria, VA
Web: www.arsa.org
E-mail: arsa@arsa.org
Leg. Issues: AER, AVI, TRA
Outside Counsel/Consultants
Obadal and MacLeod, p.c.
Issues: AER, AVI, TRA
Rep By: Sarah MacLeod

Aeropostal
Caracas, VENEZUELA
Outside Counsel/Consultants
Pierre E. Murphy Law Offices

AeroRepublica, S.A.
Bogota, COLOMBIA
Leg. Issues: AVI
Outside Counsel/Consultants
Sher & Blackwell
Issues: AVI
Rep By: Mark Atwood

The Aerospace Corp.
1000 Wilson Blvd.
Suite 2600
Arlington, VA 22209-3988
Tel: (703)812-0621
Fax: (703)812-9415
In-house, DC-area Employees
PULLIAM, Gary P.: General Manager, Corporate Business Division

Aerospace Education Foundation
1501 Lee Hwy.
Arlington, VA 22209-1198
Tel: (703)247-5839
Fax: (703)247-5853
Web: www.aef.org/aef/

An educational-outreach organization established by the Air Force Ass'n in 1956. Provides scholarships for Air Force enlisted personnel and officers, promotes elementary math and science education, and publishes reports concerning national defense issues. An affiliate of the Air Force Ass'n (see separate listing)..

In-house, DC-area Employees
MARRS, Danny D.: Temporary Managing Director

Aerospace Industries Ass'n of America
1250 I St. NW
Suite 1200
Washington, DC 20005-3924
Tel: (202)371-8400
Fax: (202)371-8470
Registered: LDA
Web: www.aia-aerospace.org
E-mail: aia@aia-aerospace.org

The trade association representing the nation's manufacturers of commercial, military and business aircraft, helicopters, aircraft engines, missiles, spacecraft materials, and related components and equipment.

Leg. Issues: AVI, DEF, FOR, MAN, TRD
In-house, DC-area Employees
ALLEN, Alexis B.: Director, Communications
BARSA, John D.: Manager, Legislative Affairs
CARNEY-TALLEY, Sandra: Assistant V. President, Policy and Planning
DOUGLASS, USAF (Ret.), Brig. Gen. John W.: President and Chief Exec. Officer
ETHERTON, Jonathan: Assistant V. President, Legislative Affairs
JOHNSON, Joel L.: V. President, International Affairs
LEWANDOWSKI, William: V. President, Supplier Management Council
NAPIER, David: Director, Research
PETERS, Robert A.: Director, Environmental Affairs and Occupational Safety and Health
ROBESON, Jr., Robert E.: V. President, Civil Aviation
SIEGEL, Stan: V. President, Technical Operations
TATE, Thomas N.: V. President, Legislative Affairs
Outside Counsel/Consultants
Dunaway & Cross
Rep By: Mac S. Dunaway

Aerospace Industries Ass'n of Canada
Ottawa, CANADA
Leg. Issues: AER
Outside Counsel/Consultants
CANAMCO (The Canadian-American Company)
Issues: AER
Rep By: Matthew J. Abrams

Aerospace Medical Ass'n
320 S. Henry St.
Alexandria, VA 22314
Tel: (703)739-2240
Fax: (703)739-9652
Web: www.asma.org

Founded in 1929. A professional organization of medical specialists, life scientists and engineers in the fields of aviation, space and environmental medicine. Seeks to stimulate study, exchange of information and cooperation among those involved in these disciplines.

In-house, DC-area Employees
RAYMAN, M.D., Russell B.: Exec. Director

AeroUnion, S.A. de C.V.
Mexico City, MEXICO
Outside Counsel/Consultants
Pierre E. Murphy Law Offices

The AES Corp.
Arlington, VA
Outside Counsel/Consultants
Norman A. Bailey, Inc.
Rep By: Norman A. Bailey
Chadbourne and Parke LLP
Rep By: Keith Martin

AES/CILCO
Outside Counsel/Consultants
The Dutko Group, Inc.

Aetna Inc.
1501 M St. NW
Suite 400
Washington, DC 20005
Tel: (202)223-2821
Fax: (202)331-4205
Registered: LDA

Headquartered in Hartford, CT.

Leg. Issues: BUD, HCR, MMM, RET, TAX
In-house, DC-area Employees
MCMURTRY, Vanda B.: Senior V. President, Federal Government Relations
TOPODAS, Jonathan M.: V. President and Counsel
Outside Counsel/Consultants
Verner, Liipfert, Bernhard, McPherson and Hand, Chartered
Issues: HCR, TAX
Washington Council Ernst & Young
Issues: BUD, HCR, TAX
Rep By: Doug Badger, John L. Doney, Jayne T. Fitzgerald, LaBrenda Garrett-Nelson, Gary J. Gasper, Bruce A. Gates, Nick Giordano, Robert J. Leonard, Richard Meltzer, Robert M. Rozen, Timothy J. Urban

Aetna Life & Casualty Co.
Hartford, CT
Leg. Issues: BUD, FIN, HCR, INS, MMM, TAX
Outside Counsel/Consultants
Washington Council Ernst & Young
Issues: BUD, FIN, HCR, INS, MMM, TAX
Rep By: Doug Badger, Lauren Darling, John L. Doney, Jayne T. Fitzgerald, LaBrenda Garrett-Nelson, Gary J. Gasper, Bruce A. Gates, Nick Giordano, Cathy Koch, Robert J. Leonard, Richard Meltzer, Phillip D. Moseley, John D. Porter, Robert M. Rozen, Donna Steele-Flynn, Timothy J. Urban

Aetna/U.S. Healthcare, Inc.
Blue Bell, PA
Web: www.aetnaushc.com
Outside Counsel/Consultants
Blank Rome Comisky & McCauley, LLP
Rep By: David A. Norcross

Affiliated Computer Services
Dallas, TX
Leg. Issues: FIN
Outside Counsel/Consultants
Public Strategies Washington, Inc.
Issues: FIN
Rep By: Joseph P. O'Neill

Affordable Housing Preservation Center
Outside Counsel/Consultants
Linda Parke Gallagher & Assoc.
Rep By: Linda Parke Gallagher

Affordable Housing Tax Credit Coalition
1255 23rd St. NW
Suite 800
Washington, DC 20037
Tel: (202)973-7739
Fax: (202)973-7750
Registered: LDA
E-mail: LIHTC@aol.com

Represents tax credit participants before Congress, the Treasury, and other regulatory bodies. The Coalition is involved in creating a positive image for the tax credit community and serving as the ethical voice of the tax credit industry. Membership includes syndicators, developers, institutional investors, lenders, and non-profits.

Leg. Issues: TAX
In-house, DC-area Employees
KERMAN, Candace: Director
Outside Counsel/Consultants
Nixon Peabody LLP
Issues: TAX
Rep By: Charles L. Edson, Richard S. Goldstein

Afghanistan Foundation
Washington, DC
Leg. Issues: DEF, FOR, IMM, TRD
Outside Counsel/Consultants
Philip S. Smith & Associates, Inc.
Issues: DEF, FOR, IMM, TRD
Rep By: Philip S. Smith

AFIN Securities

New York, NY
Leg. Issues: BAN

Outside Counsel/Consultants

Janus-Merritt Strategies, L.L.C.
Issues: BAN
Rep By: Scott P. Hoffman, Bethany Noble, Mark J. Robertson, J. Daniel Walsh

AFINOA

Buenos Aires, ARGENTINA
Leg. Issues: TRD

Outside Counsel/Consultants

Federal Strategies Group
Issues: TRD
Rep By: Xavier Equihua

AFL-CIO (American Federation of Labor and Congress of Industrial Organizations)

815 16th St. NW
Washington, DC 20006
Tel: (202)637-5000
Fax: (202)637-5058
Registered: LDA
Web: www.aflcio.org/

AFL-CIO was established in 1955 through a merger of the American Federation of Labor (1881) and the Congress of Industrial Organizations (1935). It consists of 51 state organizations and 614 local units broken into 87 separate unions with 13,100,000 members.

Leg. Issues: BAN, BNK, BUD, CIV, CON, CSP, DEF, ECN, EDU, ENG, ENV, FAM, FIN, FOR, GOV, HCR, IMM, LAW, LBR, MAR, MMM, POS, RET, TAX, TOR, TRA, TRD, UNM, UTI, WEL

Political Action Committee/s

AFL-CIO Committee on Political Education/Political Contribution Committee (COPE)
815 16th St. NW
Washington, DC 20006
Tel: (202)637-5000
Fax: (202)637-5058
Contact: Steve Rosenthal

In-house, DC-area Employees

ACKERMAN, Karen: Staff Director, Political Department
ANDERSON, Larry: Director, Support Services
BLACKWELL, Ron: Director, Corporate Affairs
CHAVEZ-THOMPSON, Linda: Exec. V. President
DION, Deborah: Outreach Specialist
DUNLOP, Susan: Assistant to the Exec. V. President
ELLENBERGER, James N.: Assistant Director, Occupational Safety & Health Department
FIORDELLISI, Maria: Legislative Representative
FLETCHER, Bill: Assistant to the President
GILLIAM, Arleen: Assistant to the President
HIATT, Jonathan: General Counsel
LEE, Thea: Assistant Director, Public Policy
MESTRICH, Keith: Press Secretary, Legislation Department
MITCHELL, Denise: Special Assistant to the President, Public Affairs
NUSSBAUM, Karen: Director, Working Women's Department
O'BRIEN, Shaun: Senior Policy Analyst
POWER, John "Jay": Legislative Representative
ROSENTHAL, Steve: Political Director
SAMUEL, William: Legislative Director
SEMINARIO, Margaret M.: Director, Occupational Safety & Health Department
SHAILOR, Barbara: Director, Internat'l Affairs Department
SHEA, Gerald M.: Exec. Assistant to the President, Political and Government Affairs
SWEENEY, John J.: President
TAYLOR, Peggy: Director, Legislation Department
TRUMKA, Richard L.: Secretary-Treasurer
WALSH, Richard: Deputy Director, Field Mobilization
WELSH, Robert: Exec. Assistant to the President
WOMACK, Richard: Civil Rights Director

Outside Counsel/Consultants

Hooper Owen & Winburn
Issues: TAX
Rep By: Steve Glaze, Lindsay D. Hooper, John P. Winburn

AFL-CIO (Union Label and Service Trades Department)

Washington, DC
Leg. Issues: CSP

Outside Counsel/Consultants

WinCapitol, Inc.
Issues: CSP
Rep By: David L. Flory, Christie Olsen, James T. Sims

AFL-CIO - Broadcast Division

815 16th St. NW
Suite 5090
Washington, DC 20006
Tel: (202)637-5334
Fax: (202)508-6962
E-mail: 71112.73@compuserve.com

The television production arm of the AFL-CIO.

In-house, DC-area Employees

MYERS-NELSON, Mary: Contact

AFL-CIO - Building and Construction Trades Department

815 16th St. NW
Suite 600
Washington, DC 20006
Tel: (202)347-1461
Fax: (202)628-0724
Registered: LDA
Leg. Issues: LBR

Political Action Committee/s

Political Education Fund of the Building and Construction Trade Department (AFL-CIO)
815 16th St. NW
Suite 600
Washington, DC 20006
Tel: (202)347-1461
Fax: (202)756-4607
Contact: Bob Powers

In-house, DC-area Employees

MALONEY, Joseph: Secretary-Treasurer
OZINGA, Bob: Chief of Staff
POWER, Ms. Bevin: Legislative Representative
POWERS, Bob: Legislative and Political Director
SULLIVAN, Edward C.: President

Outside Counsel/Consultants

Sherman, Dunn, Cohen, Leifer & Yellig, P.C.

AFL-CIO - Food and Allied Service Trades Department

815 16th St. NW
Washington, DC 20006
Tel: (202)737-7200
Fax: (202)737-7208
E-mail: fast3@fastaflcio.org

A trade union organization.

In-house, DC-area Employees

ANDERSON, Mark A.: President
BRUSKIN, Gene L.: Secretary-Treasurer

Outside Counsel/Consultants

J/T Group
Robert E. Juliano Associates

AFL-CIO Housing Investment Trust

Washington, DC
Leg. Issues: HOU

Outside Counsel/Consultants

Jefferson Government Relations, L.L.C.
Issues: HOU
Rep By: William J. Gilmartin

AFL-CIO Maritime Committee

1150 17th St. NW
Suite 700
Washington, DC 20036
Tel: (202)835-0404
Fax: (202)872-0912
Registered: LDA

Represents a group of seamen's unions in legislative matters.

Leg. Issues: BUD, DEF, MAR, VET

Political Action Committee/s

District No. 5 ITPE - NMU/MBA Political Action Committee
1150 17th St. NW
Suite 700
Washington, DC 20036
Tel: (202)835-0404
Fax: (202)872-0912

District No. 6 - PASS/NMEBA (AFL-CIO) Political Action Committee
1150 17th St. NW
Suite 700
Washington, DC 20036
Tel: (202)835-0404
Fax: (202)872-0912

National Maritime Union AFL-CIO Political & Legislative Organization On Watch
1150 17th St. NW
Suite 700
Washington, DC 20036
Tel: (202)835-0404
Fax: (202)872-0912

In-house, DC-area Employees

SIMPKINS, Talmage E.: Exec. Director

AFL-CIO - Maritime Trades Department

815 16th St. NW
Sixth Floor
Washington, DC 20006
Tel: (202)628-6300
Fax: (202)637-3989
Registered: LDA
Leg. Issues: BUD, CAW, DEF, ENG, GOV, HCR, LBR, MAN, MAR, TRA, TRD, VET

In-house, DC-area Employees

PECQUEX, Francis X.: Exec. Secretary-Treasurer

AFL-CIO - Professional Employees Department

815 16th St. NW
Washington, DC 20006
Tel: (202)638-0320
Fax: (202)628-4379
Registered: LDA
E-mail: dpeafl@aol.com

An association of labor unions.

Leg. Issues: ART, COM, CPI, CPT, IMM, LBR, TAX, TEC

In-house, DC-area Employees

ALMEIDA, Paul E.: President

AFL-CIO - Transportation Trades Department

888 16th Street NW
Suite 650
Washington, DC 20006
Tel: (202)628-9262
Fax: (202)628-0391
Registered: LDA
Web: www.ttd.org
Leg. Issues: AVI, BUD, CAW, GOV, LBR, MAR, ROD, RRR, TAX, TRA, TRD, WAS

Political Action Committee/s

AFL-CIO - Transportation Trades Department PAC
888 16th Street NW
Suite 650
Washington, DC 20006
Tel: (202)628-9262
Fax: (202)628-0391

In-house, DC-area Employees

INGRAO, Mike: Chief of Staff
PILE, Elizabeth: Manager, Legislative Affairs
WYTKIND, Edward: Exec. Director

Outside Counsel/Consultants

Hauser Group

AFLAC, Inc.

Columbus, GA

Insurance company.

Leg. Issues: BAN, BEV, BUD, FIN, FOO, HCR, INS, MMM, TAX, TRD

Outside Counsel/Consultants

Alston & Bird LLP
Issues: INS
Rep By: Thomas M. Boyd, Dwight C. Smith, III

Dewey Ballantine LLP
Issues: TRD
Rep By: Andrew Conrad, Joseph K. Dowley, Alan W. Wolff

Jolly/Rissler, Inc.
Issues: BAN, BUD, FIN, HCR, INS, MMM, TAX, TRD
Rep By: Thomas R. Jolly, Patricia F. Rissler

Long, Aldridge & Norman, LLP
Issues: BEV, FOO
Rep By: Karen Anderson, Hon. George "Buddy" Darden, Keith W. Mason

Matz, Blancato & Associates, Inc.
Rep By: Robert B. Blancato

The Africa-America Institute

1625 Massachusetts Ave. NW
Suite 400
Washington, DC 20036
Tel: (202)667-5636
Fax: (202)265-6332
Web: www.aaionline.org
E-mail: aainy@aaionline.org

Founded in 1953, AAI is a non-profit, multi-racial, multi-ethnic organization with the mission of promoting enlightened engagement between Africa and America, through education, training, and dialogue. Conducts a wide variety of Africa-oriented education, training, exchange, and public policy programs with funding from the U.S. Government, the private sector, and foundations. Headquartered in New York, NY.

In-house, DC-area Employees

HILL, Alyce: V. President
JACKSON, William D.: Director, Government Relations and Policy

Africa Policy Information Center

110 Maryland Ave. NE
Suite 509
Washington, DC 20002
Tel: (202)546-7961
Fax: (202)546-1545
Registered: LDA
Web: www.woaafrica.org

Founded in 1972 to help end minority rule in southern Africa. Advocates for a just American policy toward Africa.

In-house, DC-area Employees

MINTER, William: Acting Director

Africa Resources Trust USA

1400 16th St. NW
Suite 210
Washington, DC 20036
Tel: (202)939-3421
Fax: (202)939-3420
Registered: LDA
E-mail: artindc@aol.com

Headquartered in Harare, Zimbabwe.

Leg. Issues: BUD, ENV, TRD

In-house, DC-area Employees
CHRISTOFFERSEN, Nils: Director

African Coalition for Trade, Inc.

Washington, DC
Leg. Issues: APP, TRD

Outside Counsel/Consultants

Patton Boggs, LLP
Issues: APP, TRD
Rep By: Thomas Hale Boggs, Jr., Elena Giberga, Lansing B. Lee, III, Frank R. Samolis

Ryberg and Smith LLP
Issues: TRD
Rep By: Paul Ryberg, Jr.

African Wildlife Foundation

1400 16th St. NW
Suite 120
Washington, DC 20036
Web: www.awf.org
E-mail: africanwildlife@awf.org
Tel: (202)939-3333
Fax: (202)939-3332

Works with the people of Africa to conserve wildlife and habitat.

In-house, DC-area Employees
WRIGHT, R. Michael: President and Chief Exec. Officer

Africare

440 R St. NW
Washington, DC 20001
Web: www.africare.org
E-mail: africare@africare.org
Tel: (202)462-3614
Fax: (202)387-1034

Africare is a leader in aid to Africa, assisting families, villages, and nations in food, water, the environment, health, emergency humanitarian aid, private-sector development and governance, with a special emphasis on HIV/AIDS. Africare now supports more than 150 self-help development programs in 25 nations of Africa.

In-house, DC-area Employees
ALEMAIN, Alan C.: Director, Anglophone East and West Africa Region
BRYSON, Judy: Director, Food for Development
GOLDEN, Myron: Director, Francophone West Africa Region
HALL, Ph.D., Clarence: Director, HIV/AIDS Programs
LOWTHER, Kevin G.: Director, Southern Africa Region
LUCAS, C. Payne: President
RICHARDSON, Yolonda: Senior V. President

AfriSpace Corp.

Washington, DC
Leg. Issues: FOR, GOV, TRD

Outside Counsel/Consultants

Schmeltzer, Aptaker & Shepard, P.C.
Issues: FOR, GOV, TRD
Rep By: J. Anthony Smith

Ag Biotech Planning Committee

Washington, DC
Leg. Issues: AGR, FOO

Outside Counsel/Consultants

Carla L. West
Issues: AGR, FOO
Rep By: Carla L. West

Ag/Bio Con

Bozeman, MT
Leg. Issues: AGR

Outside Counsel/Consultants

The PMA Group
Issues: AGR
Rep By: Kaylene Green, Paul J. Magliocchetti, Mark Rokala, Kelli Short

Agassi Enterprises, Inc.

Las Vegas, NV
Leg. Issues: HCR

Outside Counsel/Consultants

Cassidy & Associates, Inc.
Issues: HCR
Rep By: Lawrence C. Grossman, Christopher Lamond

Agency-Internat'l, Ltd.

McLean, VA

Outside Counsel/Consultants

William E. Casselman, II
Rep By: William E. Casselman, II

Agilent Technologies

Palo Alto, CA
Leg. Issues: BUD, CPI, GOV, HCR, MMM, TRD

Outside Counsel/Consultants

Bergner Bockorny Castagnetti and Hawkins
Issues: HCR, MMM, TRD
Rep By: Jeffrey T. Bergner, David A. Bockorny, David Castagnetti, James W. Hawkins, Brenda Benjamin Reese, Melissa Schulman

Manatt, Phelps & Phillips, LLP
Issues: BUD, CPI, GOV
Rep By: Stephen M. Ryan, Robb Watters

Reed, Smith, LLP
Issues: HCR
Rep By: Phillips S. Peter

Agouron Pharmaceuticals, Inc.

La Jolla, CA

Outside Counsel/Consultants

Barnes, Richardson and Colburn
Rep By: Matthew T. McGrath

Agr Foods

New Orleans, LA

Outside Counsel/Consultants

Cook and Associates
Rep By: Sheila E. Hixson

Agri Business Council of Arizona

Phoenix, AZ
Leg. Issues: AGR, CAW, ENV

Outside Counsel/Consultants

Oliver James Horton
Issues: AGR, CAW, ENV
Rep By: Oliver James Horton, Jr.

Agribusiness Council

1312 18th St. NW
Suite 300
Washington, DC 20036
Web: www.agribusinesscouncil.org
E-mail: agenergy@aol.com
Tel: (202)296-4563
Fax: (202)887-9178

Founded in 1967, ABC is a non-profit, tax exempt organization dedicated to strengthening agricultural trade and development between the United States and lesser developed countries, with emphasis on production, processing and marketing of agro-food and allied industries. Coordinates with state/local agribusiness councils on international trade and investment promotion.

Leg. Issues: AGR, FOO, TRD

In-house, DC-area Employees
GRIFFITH, Patricia: Secretary-Treasurer
HOLLIS, Nicholas E.: President
JOHNSON, Frances Brigham: Director, Enterprise Policy and Development
STANTON, John: Director, Membership Services

Agricultural Air Group

Leg. Issues: ENV

Outside Counsel/Consultants

Crowell & Moring LLP
Issues: ENV
Rep By: Steven P. Quarles

Agricultural Biotechnology Forum

Washington, DC
Leg. Issues: AGR

Outside Counsel/Consultants

Agri/Washington
Issues: AGR
Rep By: Paul S. Weller, Jr.

Agricultural Producers

Valencia, CA

Outside Counsel/Consultants

Seyfarth, Shaw, Fairweather & Geraldson
Rep By: Donald L. Rosenthal

Agricultural Retailers Ass'n

1156 15th St. NW
Suite 302
Washington, DC 20005
Web: www.aradc.org
E-mail: ara@aradc.org
Tel: (202)457-0825
Fax: (202)457-0864
Registered: LDA

Leg. Issues: AGR, CAW, CHM, ENV, FOO, SMB, TRA

Political Action Committee/s

Agricultural Retailers Ass'n Political Action Committee (ARA-PAC)
1156 15th St. NW
Suite 302
Washington, DC 20005
Contact: Floyd D. Gaibler
Tel: (202)457-0825
Fax: (202)457-0864

In-house, DC-area Employees
GAIBLER, Floyd D.: V. President, Government Affairs
WEGMEYER, Tyler: Manager, Government Affairs

Agricultural Transporters Conference

2200 Mill Rd.
Alexandria, VA 22314
E-mail: fhall@trucking.org
Tel: (703)838-7990
Fax: (703)519-1866

Represents trucking companies who are transporters of agricultural commodities.

Leg. Issues: AGR, TRA

In-house, DC-area Employees
HALL, Fletcher R.: Exec. Director

Agriculture Ocean Transportation Coalition

Outside Counsel/Consultants

Lindsay Hart Neil & Weigler
Rep By: Kathryn Beaubien, Peter Friedmann

AgriPartners

Bonita Springs, FL
Leg. Issues: NAT, RES

Outside Counsel/Consultants

Dawson & Associates, Inc.
Issues: NAT, RES
Rep By: David Barrows, Robert K. Dawson, Jonathan P. Deason, Ph.D., Hon. John Myers, Lt. Gen. Arthur E. Williams, USA (Ret.)

Agrium Inc.

Calgary, CANADA
Leg. Issues: ENG, FUE, LBR, TRO

Outside Counsel/Consultants

King & Spalding
Issues: ENG, FUE, LBR, TRO
Rep By: Lisa K. Norton

AGS Defense, Inc.

Alexandria, VA

Outside Counsel/Consultants

The Conaway Group LLC
Rep By: Lt. Gen. John B. Conaway, USAF (Ret.), James L. Hobgood

Agua Caliente Band of Cahuilla Indians

Palm Springs, CA

An Indian tribal government.

Leg. Issues: IND

Outside Counsel/Consultants

PACE-CAPSTONE
Issues: IND
Rep By: Scott C. Dacey, James W. Wise

Steptoe & Johnson LLP
Issues: IND
Rep By: John J. Duffy, Hilda Manuel

Agudath Israel of America

1730 Rhode Island Ave. NW
Suite 504
Washington, DC 20036
E-mail: abbac5@cs.com
Tel: (202)835-0414
Fax: (202)835-0424

Sponsors a broad range of religious, educational, community, social service, and government advocacy projects in the Orthodox and general Jewish community. Headquarters are in New York, NY and the Washington office concentrates on government and legislative affairs.

Leg. Issues: CIV, CON, EDU, FAM, FOR

In-house, DC-area Employees
COHEN, Abba: Director and Counsel, Washington Office

AHL Shipping Co.

New Orleans, LA
Leg. Issues: FUE, TRA

Outside Counsel/Consultants

Adams and Reese LLP
Issues: FUE, TRA
Rep By: D. Lee Forsgren, Hon. James A. "Jimmy" Hayes

AIDS Action Council

1906 Sunderland Pl. NW
Washington, DC 20036
Tel: (202)530-8030
Fax: (202)530-8031
Registered: LDA

Web: www.aidsaction.com
E-mail: aidsaction@aidsaction.org

The Washington representative of over 1000 community-based AIDS service organizations. Works for enactment of fair and effective federal AIDS policies.

Leg. Issues: BUD, HCR, HOU, MED, MMM

In-house, DC-area Employees

FRENCH, Claudia: Exec. Director
SCHULER, Alexis: Director, Government Affairs
WATKINS, Venus: Director, Communications

AIDS Healthcare Foundation

Los Angeles, CA
Leg. Issues: MED, MMM

Outside Counsel/Consultants

Parry, Romani, DeConcini & Symms
Issues: MED, MMM
Rep By: Edward H. Baxter, Hon. Dennis DeConcini, John M. Haddow, Scott D. Hatch, Shannon Davis Henderson, Jack W. Martin, Romano Romani, Linda Arey Skladany, Hon. Steven D. Symms

AIG Environmental

New York, NY
Leg. Issues: ENV, INS

Outside Counsel/Consultants

The Dutko Group, Inc.

The Paul Laxalt Group
Rep By: Hon. Paul D. Laxalt, Tom Loranger

The Renkes Group, Ltd.
Issues: ENV, INS
Rep By: Patrick Pettey, Gregg D. Renkes

Aiken and Edgenfield Counties, South Carolina, Economic Development Partnership of

Aiken, SC
Leg. Issues: BUD, DEF, ECN, ENG, ENV, SCI

Outside Counsel/Consultants

Johnston & Associates, LLC
Issues: BUD, DEF, ECN, ENG, ENV, SCI
Rep By: Hon. J. Bennett Johnston, N. Hunter Johnston, W. Proctor Jones, Eric Tober

Air & Water Technologies

Somerville, NJ
Registered: LDA

Outside Counsel/Consultants

Howrey Simon Arnold & White
Rep By: Alan M. Grimaldi

Air 3000, Inc.

New Town Square, PA

Outside Counsel/Consultants

Pierre E. Murphy Law Offices

Air Afrique

Abidjan, COTE D'IVOIRE

Outside Counsel/Consultants

Zuckert, Scoutt and Rasenberger, L.L.P.
Rep By: William H. Callaway, Jr.

Air Atlantic Dominicana

Santo Domingo, DOMINICAN REPUBLIC

Outside Counsel/Consultants

Pierre E. Murphy Law Offices

Air Bag and Seat Belt Safety Campaign

Outside Counsel/Consultants

Greer, Margolis, Mitchell, Burns & Associates
Rep By: Madalene Milano, David E. Mitchell

Air Canada

Montreal, CANADA

Outside Counsel/Consultants

Galland, Kharasch, Greenberg, Fellman & Swirsky, P.C.

Air Carrier Ass'n of America

1500 K St. NW
Suite 250
Washington, DC 20005-1714
Tel: (202)639-7501
Fax: (202)639-7505
Registered: LDA
Leg. Issues: AVI

In-house, DC-area Employees

FABERMAN, Edward P.: Exec. Director

Outside Counsel/Consultants

Ungaretti & Harris
Issues: AVI
Rep By: Edward P. Faberman, Page Faulk, Michelle M. Faust

Air China Internat'l Corp., Ltd.

Beijing, CHINA (PEOPLE'S REPUBLIC)
Leg. Issues: AVI, TOR, TOU, TRD

Outside Counsel/Consultants

Cohen, Gettings & Dunham, PC
Issues: AVI, TOR, TOU, TRD
Rep By: Carroll E. Dubuc

Holland & Knight LLP

Air Conditioning Contractors of America

2800 Shirlington Rd.
Suite 300
Arlington, VA 22206
Tel: (703)575-4477
Fax: (703)575-4449
Registered: LDA
Web: www.acca.org
E-mail: govt@acca.org

ACCA is the trade association representing heating, ventilating, air conditioning and refrigeration contractors nationwide.

Leg. Issues: CAW, CPT, EDU, GOV, LBR, SMB, TAX, TOR, UTI

Political Action Committee/s

Air Conditioning Contractors of America Political Action Committee
2800 Shirlington Rd.
Suite 300
Arlington, VA 22206
Tel: (703)575-4477
Fax: (703)575-4449

In-house, DC-area Employees

HERZOG, John: Staff V. President, Public Policy
HONEYCUTT, Michael: Senior Staff V. President
SHUPING, CAE, Frances: Staff V. President, Communications and Technology

Outside Counsel/Consultants

Bracewell & Patterson, L.L.P.
Issues: UTI
Rep By: Hon. Edwin R. Bethune, Gene E. Godley, Marc C. Hebert, Charles L. Ingebretson, Michael L. Pate, Scott H. Segal, D. Michael Stroud, Jr.

Venable
Issues: CPT, GOV, LBR, TAX, TOR
Rep By: Jeffrey S. Tenenbaum

Air Courier Conference of America

Washington, DC
Web: www.aircour.org
E-mail: acca@aircour.org

Represents small package express carriers.

Outside Counsel/Consultants

Public Policy Resources
Rep By: Susan Presti

Air Cruisers, Inc.

Belmar, NJ
Leg. Issues: DEF

Outside Counsel/Consultants

Alford & Associates
Issues: DEF
Rep By: Marty Alford

Air D'Ayiti

Miami, FL

Outside Counsel/Consultants

Pierre E. Murphy Law Offices

Air Force Ass'n

1501 Lee Hwy.
Arlington, VA 22209-1198
Tel: (703)247-5800
Fax: (703)247-5853
Web: www.afa.org

An independent, non-profit, civilian organization. Primarily concerned with public understanding and acceptance of the pivotal role a well-equipped and well-trained Air Force plays in the security of the U.S. and its allies. Seeks to educate the public on the relevance of overall American military strength to global peace.

Leg. Issues: AER, AVI, DEF, SCI, VET

In-house, DC-area Employees

BRAXTON, Melissa: Manager, News and Information
BYARS, Napoleon: Director, Policy and Communications
GOSS, Kenneth A.: Director, Government Relations
LANGFELDT, Carl: Legislative Assistant
MARRS, Danny D.: Assistant Exec. Director
MCDONNELL, James A.: Chief, Military Relations
SHAUD, John A.: Exec. Director

Air Force Memorial Foundation

Arlington, VA
Leg. Issues: GOV, NAT, RES

Outside Counsel/Consultants

Mercury Group
Issues: GOV, NAT

Patton Boggs, LLP
Issues: RES
Rep By: John J. Deschauer, Jr., Benjamin L. Ginsberg

Air Force Sergeants Ass'n

5211 Auth Rd.
Suitland, MD 20746
Tel: (301)899-3500
Fax: (301)899-8136
Registered: LDA
Web: www.afsahq.org
E-mail: staff@afsahq.org

Represents some 165,000 active and retired Air Force enlisted members in more than 300 chapters worldwide before congressional and military decisionmakers, voicing their concerns over pay, benefits, advancement, retirement and living conditions.

Leg. Issues: BUD, DEF, EDU, HCR, MMM, PHA, TAX, VET

In-house, DC-area Employees

FAIRWEATHER, Allison: Manager, Legislative Affairs
LOKOVIC, James: Director, Military and Government Relations
SHOCKLEY, Ed: Director, Member and Field Services
STATON, James D.: Exec. Director
TASSONE, Lawrence: Director, Special Projects
TULL, Ron: Director, Marketing and Communications

Air Foyle, Ltd.

Luton, UNITED KINGDOM

Outside Counsel/Consultants

Shaw Pittman
Rep By: Robert E. Cohn, B. Scott Custer, Jr., Sheryl R. Israel

Air Freight Warehouse, Inc.

New York, NY

Outside Counsel/Consultants

Saunders and Company

Air India

Bombay, INDIA

Outside Counsel/Consultants

Squire, Sanders & Dempsey L.L.P.
Rep By: Marshall S. Sinick

Air Jamaica Ltd.

Kingston, JAMAICA

Outside Counsel/Consultants

Galland, Kharasch, Greenberg, Fellman & Swirsky, P.C.

Air Line Pilots Ass'n Internat'l

1625 Massachusetts Ave. NW
Washington, DC 20036
Tel: (202)797-4033
Fax: (202)797-4030
Registered: LDA
Web: www.alpa.org
Leg. Issues: AVI, LBR, TAX

Political Action Committee/s

Air Line Pilots Ass'n Political Action Committee
1625 Massachusetts Ave. NW
Washington, DC 20036
Tel: (202)797-4033
Fax: (202)797-4030
Contact: Paul L. Hallisay

In-house, DC-area Employees

BAKER, Gerald E.: Senior Legislative Representative
COHEN, Jonathan A.: Director, Legal Department
GASQUE, Henry: Manager, Communications
HALLISAY, Paul L.: Director, Government Affairs
KENNY, Brendan M.: Legislative Representative
MAZOR, John: Communications Specialist
SKIADOS, Don: Director, Communications
WOERTH, Capt. Duane E.: President

Air Macau

Andar, MACAU

Outside Counsel/Consultants

Zuckert, Scoutt and Rasenberger, L.L.P.
Rep By: Rachel B. Trinder

Air Malta Co. Ltd.

Luga, MALTA

Outside Counsel/Consultants

Holland & Knight LLP

Air Methods/Mercy Air

Englewood, CO

Outside Counsel/Consultants

Law Offices of Irene E. Howie
Rep By: Irene E. Howie

Air Namibia

Windhock, NAMIBIA

Outside Counsel/Consultants

Pierre E. Murphy Law Offices

Air Nauru

Yaren, NAURU

Outside Counsel/Consultants

Preston Gates Ellis & Rouvelas Meeds LLP
Rep By: Susan B. Geiger

Air Pacific Ltd.

Suva, FIJI
Leg. Issues: AUT, AVI, INS, TOR, TOU, TRA, TRD

Outside Counsel/Consultants

Condon and Forsyth
Issues: AUT, AVI, INS, TOR, TOU, TRA, TRD
Rep By: Thomas J. Whalen

Air Products and Chemicals, Inc.

1130 Connecticut Ave. NW
Suite 710
Washington, DC 20036
Tel: (202)659-1324
Fax: (202)659-1328
Registered: LDA
Web: www.airproducts.com
Leg. Issues: BUD, CHM, DEF, ENG, ENV, FUE, HCR, IMM, MAN, TAX, TRA, TRD

Political Action Committee/s

Air Products and Chemicals Inc. Political Alliance
1130 Connecticut Ave. NW
Suite 710
Washington, DC 20036
Contact: Pat Wilmer
Tel: (202)659-1324
Fax: (202)659-1328

In-house, DC-area Employees

GOODSTEIN, Richard F.: Washington Representative
WILMER, Pat: PAC Administrator

Outside Counsel/Consultants

Cassidy & Associates, Inc.
Issues: DEF, ENG, FUE
Rep By: Christy Carson Evans, Lawrence C. Grossman, Sean O'Shea

Goodstein & Associates
Issues: BUD, CHM, ENG, ENV, MAN, TRD
Rep By: Richard F. Goodstein

Rhoads Group

Air Quality Standards Coalition

Washington, DC

An alliance of electrical utility, manufacturing, transportation and oil companies.

Leg. Issues: CAW, ENV, SCI

Outside Counsel/Consultants

ADA Consulting Services
Issues: CAW, ENV, SCI
Rep By: Alicia A. Dugan

The Direct Impact Co.

Air Tractor, Inc.

Olney, TX
Leg. Issues: AVI

Outside Counsel/Consultants

Bonnie H. Weinstein
Issues: AVI
Rep By: Bonnie H. Weinstein

Air Traffic Control Ass'n

2300 Clarendon Blvd.
Suite 711
Arlington, VA 22201
Tel: (703)522-5717
Fax: (703)527-7251

Web: www.atca.org

E-mail: atca@worldnet.att.net

In-house, DC-area Employees

HARTL, Gabriel A.: President

MATTHEWS, Suzette: General Counsel

NEWMASTER, Carol: Senior V. President

Air Tran Airways

Orlando, FL

Leg. Issues: AVI, TAX

Outside Counsel/Consultants

Hurt, Norton & Associates

Issues: AVI, TAX

Rep By: Robert H. Hurt, Frank Norton

Ungaretti & Harris

Issues: AVI

Rep By: Edward P. Faberman, Page Faulk, Michelle M. Faust

Air Transat

Mirabel, CANADA

Outside Counsel/Consultants

Winthrop, Stimson, Putnam & Roberts

Rep By: John E. Gillick

Air Transport Ass'n of America

1301 Pennsylvania Ave. NW
Suite 1100
Washington, DC 20004-1707
Tel: (202)626-4000
Fax: (202)626-4208
Registered: LDA

Web: www.air-transport.org

Leg. Issues: AER, AVI, BUD, ENV, LBR, TAX, TRA

Political Action Committee/s

Air Transport Ass'n Employees Political Action Committee

1301 Pennsylvania Ave. NW
Suite 1100
Washington, DC 20004-1707
Tel: (202)626-4000
Fax: (202)626-4208

In-house, DC-area Employees

BROWNE, Thomas J.: Managing Director, Aviation Infrastructure

CASEY, James L.: V. President and Deputy General Counsel

COHEN, Roger: Managing Director, State Government Affairs

DOUBRAVA, Richard: Managing Director, Security

HALLETT, Carol B.: President and Chief Exec. Officer

HICKEY, Daniel: Director, Government Affairs

KOSTUK, Barbara M.: Director, Government Affairs

LA NAVE, Anna: Director, State Government Affairs

MEENAN, John M.: Senior V. President, Industry Policy

MERLIS, Edward A.: Senior V. President, Legislative and International Affairs

PREST, Albert H.: V. President, Operations

PYLPEC, Nestor N.: V. President, Industry Services

ROBERTS, Kim: Director, Communications

RYAN, John R.: V. President, Air Traffic Management

WARREN, Robert P.: Senior V. President, General Counsel, and Secretary

WASCOM, Michael D.: V. President, Communications

Outside Counsel/Consultants

Akin, Gump, Strauss, Hauer & Feld, L.L.P.
Rep By: Donald C. Alexander

Barbour Griffith & Rogers, Inc.
Issues: BUD, TRA
Rep By: Haley Barbour, Carl Biersack, G. O. Lanny Griffith, Jr., Loren Monroe

Canfield & Associates, Inc.
Issues: TAX
Rep By: Roger Blauwet, April Boston, Anne C. Canfield

The Carmen Group
Issues: BUD, TRA
Rep By: David M. Carmen, Gerald P. Carmen, David A. Keene, Ron M. Linton

Law Offices of Kevin G. Curtin
Issues: AVI
Rep By: Kevin G. Curtin

Ann Eppard Associates, Ltd.
Issues: TRA
Rep By: Julie Chlopecki, Ann Eppard

Griffin, Johnson, Dover & Stewart
Issues: AVI, TRA
Rep By: David E. Johnson, Leonard Swinehart

Hogan & Hartson L.L.P.
Rep By: E. Tazewell Ellett, William Michael House, Hon. Robert H. Michel, Jeffrey W. Munk

KPMG, LLP
Issues: TAX
Rep By: Harry L. Gutman, Gillian Spooner

MultiState Associates

Ryan, Phillips, Utrecht & MacKinnon
Issues: AER, AVI, LBR, TRA
Rep By: Rodney Hoppe, Jeffrey M. MacKinnon, William D. Phillips, Mark D. Planning, Thomas M. Ryan

Thompson Coburn LLP
Issues: AVI, ENV
Rep By: Warren L. Dean, Patricia N. Snyder

Zuckert, Scoutt and Rasenberger, L.L.P.
Issues: AVI
Rep By: Paul E. Schoellhamer

Air-Conditioning and Refrigeration Institute

4301 N. Fairfax Dr.
Suite 425
Arlington, VA 22203
Tel: (703)524-8800
Fax: (703)528-3816
Registered: LDA
Web: www.ari.org
E-mail: ari@ari.org

The Air-Conditioning and Refrigeration Institute (ARI) is a trade association that represents approximately 200 manufacturers of air-conditioning and refrigeration products. ARI members produce more than 90% of the central air-conditioning and commercial/industrial refrigeration equipment manufactured in the United States.

Leg. Issues: BUD, CAW, ENG, ENV, MAN, SCI, TAX, TRD, UTI

In-house, DC-area Employees

DOOLEY, Edward: V. President, Communication and Education
MCCOMBS, Julie: Director, International Trade
MILLER, Deborah E.: V. President, Government Affairs
REES, Jr., Clifford H. "Ted": President

Outside Counsel/Consultants

Morgan Meguire, LLC
Issues: ENG
Rep By: Kyle G. Michel, Ramola Musante, C. Kyle Simpson

Airborne Express

Seattle, WA
Leg. Issues: AVI, LBR, TAX

Outside Counsel/Consultants

The Petrizzo Group, Inc.
Issues: AVI, LBR, TAX
Rep By: Kara Kennedy, Thomas "T.J." Petrizzo

Vorys, Sater, Seymour and Pease, LLP

Airborne Tactical Advantage Co.

Virginia Beach, VA
Leg. Issues: DEF

Outside Counsel/Consultants

The Carter Group
Issues: DEF
Rep By: Michael R. Carter, Scott D. McClean

Airbus Industrie of North America, Inc.

198 Van Buren St.
Herndon, VA 20170
Tel: (703)834-3400
Fax: (703)834-3593
Leg. Issues: AER, AVI, MAN, TRA

In-house, DC-area Employees

COURPRON, Henri: President & Chief Operating Officer
GRECZYN, Mary Anne: Communications Manager

TOMASSETTI, Nick: Chief Exec. Officer
VENZ, David C.: V. President, Corporate Communications

Outside Counsel/Consultants

Charles A. Hamilton Associates LLC
Issues: AER, AVI, MAN, TRA
Rep By: Charles A. Hamilton

AirCell, Inc.

Louisville, CO
Leg. Issues: AVI

Outside Counsel/Consultants

Simon Strategies/Mindbeam
Rep By: Gregory C. Simon, Christopher Ulrich, Kristan Van Hook

Winston & Strawn
Issues: AVI
Rep By: Hon. Beryl F. Anthony, Jr., Jeffrey G. Berman

Aircraft Electronics Ass'n

Independence, MO
Leg. Issues: AVI, BUD, GOV, LBR, MAN, SMB, TRA

Outside Counsel/Consultants

Washington Aviation Group
Issues: AVI, BUD, GOV, LBR, MAN, SMB, TRA
Rep By: Arnolda Beaujuin, Chad Bierman, Paula Derks, Jason Dickstein

Aircraft Owners and Pilots Ass'n

421 Aviation Way
Frederick, MD 21701
Tel: (301)695-2000
Fax: (301)695-2375
Registered: LDA
Web: www.aopa.org
E-mail: aopahq@aopa.org

Represents the interests of over 365,000 pilots and aircraft owners who fly General Aviation aircrafts. Works with the Federal Aviation Administration, the Department of Transportation, the National Transportation Safety Board, the U.S. Congress and other local and national aviation organizations to ensure that the interests of its members and the entire General Aviation community are well represented.

Leg. Issues: AVI

Political Action Committee/s

Aircraft Owners and Pilots Ass'n Legislative Action PAC
421 Aviation Way
Frederick, MD 21701
Tel: (301)695-2000
Fax: (301)695-2375
Contact: John F. Williams

In-house, DC-area Employees

BOYER, Philip B.: President
CEBULA, Andrew V.: V. President, Government and Technical Affairs
CRIPPS, Corrie: Legislative Representative
DEERE, William R.: V. President and Exec. Director, AOPA Legislative Affairs
KRAUSS, Julia: Director, Legislative Affairs
MORDHOFF, Keith: Senior V. President, Communications
MORNINGSTAR, Warren: V. President, Communications
WILLIAMS, John F.: Manager, AOPA PAC

Aircraft Services Group

Leg. Issues: AVI, GOV

Outside Counsel/Consultants

JFS Group, Ltd.
Issues: AVI, GOV

Airgas, Inc.

Radner, PA
Leg. Issues: ENV, WAS

Outside Counsel/Consultants

Wheat & Associates, Inc.
Issues: ENV, WAS
Rep By: Andrea Bevvino, Hon. Alan D. Wheat

Airguard Industries

Louisville, KY

Outside Counsel/Consultants

Interface Inc.
Rep By: Robert G. Williams

Airline Suppliers Ass'n

Washington, DC
Web: www.airlinesuppliers.com
E-mail: info@airlinesuppliers.com
Leg. Issues: AVI, GOV, LBR, SMB, TRA

Outside Counsel/Consultants

Washington Aviation Group
Issues: AVI, GOV, LBR, SMB, TRA
Rep By: Arnolda Beaujuin, Chad Bierman, Jason Dickstein, Michele Schweitzer

Airport Consultants Council

908 King St.
Suite 100
Alexandria, VA 22314
Tel: (703)683-5900
Fax: (703)683-2564
Web: www.acconline.org
E-mail: info@acconline.org

In-house, DC-area Employees

HOCHSTETLER, Paula P.: Exec. Director

Airport Minority Advisory Council

Alexandria, VA
Leg. Issues: TRA

Outside Counsel/Consultants

Thelen Reid & Priest LLP
Issues: TRA
Rep By: Barry I. Berkoff, William A. Kirk, Jr., Richard J. Leidl, Stephan M. Minikes, Nancy K. West

Airports Council Internat'l - North America

1775 K St. NW
Suite 500
Washington, DC 20006
Tel: (202)293-8500
Fax: (202)887-5365
Registered: LDA
Web: www.aci-na.org
E-mail: postmaster@aci-na.org

Represents governmental entities that own and operate airports. The Council has combined its legislative affairs operations with the American Ass'n of Airport Executives (listed separately). See listing under AAAE-ACI for a list of the legislative affairs personnel and firms representing these two groups.

Political Action Committee/s

ACIPAC
1775 K St. NW
Suite 500
Washington, DC 20006
Tel: (202)293-8500
Fax: (202)887-5365

Airtours Internat'l

Manchester, UNITED KINGDOM

Outside Counsel/Consultants

Zuckert, Scoutt and Rasenberger, L.L.P.
Rep By: Malcolm L. Benge, Richard D. Mathias

AIS, Inc.

Greenbelt, MD
Leg. Issues: IMM

Outside Counsel/Consultants

Manatt, Phelps & Phillips, LLP
Issues: IMM
Rep By: Michael T. Brown, Hon. Jack W. Buechner, William P. Cook, Robert J. Kabel

Ajinomoto Co., Inc.

Tokyo, JAPAN

Outside Counsel/Consultants

Hughes Hubbard & Reed LLP
Rep By: John M. Townsend

Ajinomoto U.S.A., Inc.

Teaneck, NJ

Outside Counsel/Consultants

Akin, Gump, Strauss, Hauer & Feld, L.L.P.

AKAL Security

Santa Cruz, CA
Leg. Issues: BUD, GOV, LAW, LBR

Outside Counsel/Consultants

Reed, Smith, LLP
Issues: BUD, GOV, LAW, LBR
Rep By: C. Stevens Seale

Akers Laboratories, Inc.

Thorofare, NJ
Leg. Issues: DEF, HCR, MED

Outside Counsel/Consultants

Rooney Group Internat'l, Inc.
Issues: DEF, HCR, MED
Rep By: James W. Rooney

Akron-Canton Airport

Bloomington, IL
Registered: LDA
Leg. Issues: AVI

Outside Counsel/Consultants

Ungaretti & Harris
Issues: AVI
Rep By: Edward P. Faberman

Akron Tower Housing Partnership

Akron, OH
Leg. Issues: HOU

Outside Counsel/Consultants

Coan & Lyons
Issues: HOU
Rep By: Carl A. S. Coan, Jr., Raymond K. James

Aksys, Ltd.

Lincolnshire, IL
Leg. Issues: MED, MMM

Outside Counsel/Consultants

Congressional Consultants
Issues: MED, MMM
Rep By: Gwen Gampel, Karen M. Late

AKT Developments

Sacramento, CA

Outside Counsel/Consultants

Collier Shannon Scott, PLLC
Rep By: Robert W. Porter

Akzo America, Inc.

New York, NY

Outside Counsel/Consultants

Skadden, Arps, Slate, Meagher & Flom LLP
Rep By: Robert E. Lighthizer

AKZO Aramid Products Inc.

Clarks Summit, PA

Outside Counsel/Consultants

Patton Boggs, LLP
Rep By: Henry Chajet, Mark N. Savit

Akzo Nobel Chemicals, Inc.

Dobbs Ferry, NY
Leg. Issues: CHM, HCR

Outside Counsel/Consultants

Preston Gates Ellis & Rouvelas Meeds LLP
Issues: CHM, HCR
Rep By: Werner W. Brandt, Ralph D. Nurnberger, Daniel Ritter, Mark H. Ruge, Steven R. "Rick" Valentine

al group Lonza

Fairlawn, NJ

Outside Counsel/Consultants

The Grizzle Company
Rep By: Richard A. Cantor, Charles L. Grizzle

Alabama A & M University

Normal, AL
Leg. Issues: EDU, ENV, SCI

Outside Counsel/Consultants

The Ferguson Group, LLC
Issues: EDU, ENV, SCI
Rep By: William Ferguson, Jr., Ron Hamm

Alabama-Coushatta Tribe of Texas

Livingston, TX

Outside Counsel/Consultants

Carlyle Consulting

Alabama, Department of Transportation of the State of

Montgomery, AL
Leg. Issues: BUD, GOV, ROD, TRA

Outside Counsel/Consultants

Van Scoyoc Associates, Inc.
Issues: BUD, GOV, ROD, TRA
Rep By: Ray Cole, H. Stewart Van Scoyoc

Alabama Gas Corp.

Birmingham, AL

Outside Counsel/Consultants

Wright & Talisman, P.C.
Rep By: Jeffrey D. Komarow

Alabama Nursing Homes Ass'n

Montgomery, AL
Leg. Issues: BUD, MMM

Outside Counsel/Consultants

R. G. Flippo and Associates, Inc.
Issues: BUD, MMM
Rep By: Hon. Ronnie G. Flippo, Vicki P. Wallace

Alabama Power

Outside Counsel/Consultants

Dittus Communications
Rep By: Gloria S. Dittus

Alabama Space Science Exhibits Commission

Huntsville, AL
Leg. Issues: DEF, ECN, EDU

Outside Counsel/Consultants

Balch & Bingham LLP
Issues: DEF, ECN, EDU
Rep By: Wade Heck, William F. Stiers

Alabama Water and Wastewater Institute, Inc.

Montgomery, AL
Leg. Issues: BUD

Outside Counsel/Consultants

Van Scoyoc Associates, Inc.
Issues: BUD
Rep By: Ray Cole, H. Stewart Van Scoyoc

Alameda Corridor Transportation Authority

Glendale, CA
Leg. Issues: TRA

Outside Counsel/Consultants

Manatt, Phelps & Phillips, LLP
Issues: TRA
Rep By: June L. DeHart, Robert J. Kabel

Simon and Co., Inc.
Issues: TRA
Rep By: Heather Barber, Alex DeGood, Leonard S. Simon

Alameda Corridor-East Construction Authority

Irwindale, CA
Leg. Issues: BUD, TRA

Outside Counsel/Consultants

Baker, Donelson, Bearman & Caldwell, P.C.
Issues: BUD, TRA
Rep By: Janet L. Powell

Womble Carlyle Sandridge & Rice, P.C.
Issues: BUD, TRA
Rep By: Kevin Darrow Jones

Alameda, California, City of

Leg. Issues: ECN

Outside Counsel/Consultants

Kutak Rock LLP
Issues: ECN
Rep By: Rhonda Bond-Collins, Seth Kirshenberg, George R. Schlossberg, Barry P. Steinberg

Alameda, California, County of

Oakland, CA
Leg. Issues: HCR, HOU, IMM, LBR, RET, TAX, TOB, TRA, WEL

Outside Counsel/Consultants

Copeland, Lowery & Jacquez
Issues: HCR, HOU, IMM, LBR, RET, TAX, TOB, TRA, WEL
Rep By: James M. Copeland, Jr.

Alameda-Contra Costa Transit District

Oakland, CA
Leg. Issues: BUD, TRA

Outside Counsel/Consultants

Van Scoyoc Associates, Inc.
Issues: BUD, TRA
Rep By: Steven O. Palmer, Chad Schulken, H. Stewart Van Scoyoc

Alamo Navajo School Board

Magdalena, NM
Leg. Issues: IND

Outside Counsel/Consultants

Hobbs, Straus, Dean and Walker, LLP
Issues: IND
Rep By: Carol L. Barbero, S. Bobo Dean, Karen J. Funk

The Alan Guttmacher Institute

1120 Connecticut Ave. NW
Suite 460
Washington, DC 20036
Tel: (202)296-4012
Fax: (202)223-5756
Registered: LDA
Web: www.agi-usa.org
E-mail: policyinfo@agi-usa.org

A private, non-profit corporation for research, policy analysis and public education in the fields of fertility regulation, maternity care, population dynamics, and broadly-related areas of health and social policy. Founded in 1968 as the Center for Family Planning Program Development, AGI is an independent special affiliate of Planned Parenthood Federation of America. Maintains offices in New York City and Washington, DC.

Leg. Issues: BUD, FAM, HCR

In-house, DC-area Employees

COHEN, Susan A.: Senior Public Policy Associate
RICHARDS, Cory L.: V. President, Public Policy

Alarm Industry Communications Committee

440 Maple Ave. East
Suite 201
Vienna, VA 22180
Tel: (703)242-4670
Fax: (703)242-4675
Registered: LDA
Web: www.csaaul.org
E-mail: admin@csaaul.org
Leg. Issues: TEC

Political Action Committee/s

AICC PAC
440 Maple Ave. East
Suite 201
Vienna, VA 22180
Tel: (703)242-4670
Fax: (703)242-4675

In-house, DC-area Employees

DOYLE, Stephen P.: Exec. V. President

Outside Counsel/Consultants

Chambers Associates Inc.
Issues: TEC
Rep By: William A. Signer

Alaska Aerospace

Anchorage, AK
Leg. Issues: AER

Outside Counsel/Consultants

Birch, Horton, Bittner & Cherot
Issues: AER
Rep By: William Bittner

Alaska Air Group

Leg. Issues: AVI, TAX, TRA

Outside Counsel/Consultants

Denny Miller McBee Associates
Issues: AVI, TAX, TRA

Alaska Airlines

Seattle, WA
Leg. Issues: AVI, DIS, TRA

Outside Counsel/Consultants

APCO Worldwide
Issues: AVI, DIS
Rep By: Peter Goelz

Jack Ferguson Associates, Inc.
Issues: AVI, TRA
Rep By: Jack Ferguson

Alaska Communications Systems, Inc.

Anchorage, AK
Leg. Issues: TEC

Outside Counsel/Consultants

Birch, Horton, Bittner & Cherot
Issues: TEC
Rep By: William Bittner

Griffin, Johnson, Dover & Stewart
Issues: TEC
Rep By: G. Jack Dover, Walter J. "Joe" Stewart

Alaska Eskimo Whaling Commission

Barrow, AK
Registered: LDA
Leg. Issues: IND, MAR

Outside Counsel/Consultants

Jessica S. Lefevre
Issues: MAR
Rep By: Jessica S. Lefevre

Morriset, Schlosser, Ayer & Jozwiak
Issues: IND
Rep By: Fran Ayer, Jennifer P. Hughes

Alaska Federation of Natives

Outside Counsel/Consultants

Dilworth Paxson, LLP
Rep By: Rebecca A. Donnellan

Alaska Fisheries Development Foundation

Anchorage, AK

Outside Counsel/Consultants

Law Office of C. Deming Cowles

Robertson, Monagle & Eastaugh

Alaska Forest Ass'n

Ketchikan, AK
Leg. Issues: ENV

Outside Counsel/Consultants

Perkins Coie LLP
Rep By: Guy R. Martin

Robertson, Monagle & Eastaugh
Issues: ENV
Rep By: James F. Clark, Steven W. Silver

Alaska Groundfish Data Bank

Kodiak, AK
Leg. Issues: BUD

Outside Counsel/Consultants

Robertson, Monagle & Eastaugh
Issues: BUD
Rep By: Bradley D. Gilman, Rick E. Marks

Alaska Legislature

Juneau, AK
Leg. Issues: ANI, BUD, NAT, RES, ROD

Outside Counsel/Consultants

Birch, Horton, Bittner & Cherot
Issues: ANI, BUD, NAT, RES, ROD
Rep By: William P. Horn

Alaska Longline Vessel Owners Ass'n

Sitka, AK

Outside Counsel/Consultants

Law Office of C. Deming Cowles

Alaska Native Health Board

Anchorage, AK
Leg. Issues: IND

Outside Counsel/Consultants

Hobbs, Straus, Dean and Walker, LLP
Issues: IND
Rep By: S. Bobo Dean, Karen J. Funk, Geoffrey D. Strommer

Sonosky, Chambers, Sachse & Endreson

Alaska Network Systems

Anchorage, AK

Outside Counsel/Consultants

Young & Jatlow
Rep By: Francis L. Young

Alaska North Slope LNG Project

Anchorage, AK
Leg. Issues: FUE, NAT

Outside Counsel/Consultants

Van Ness Feldman, P.C.
Issues: FUE, NAT
Rep By: Patricia Fry Godley, Alan L. Mintz, J. Curtis Moffatt, Thomas C. Roberts, Theresa L. Zolet

Alaska Ocean Seafoods L.P.

Anacortes, WA
Leg. Issues: MAR

Outside Counsel/Consultants

Preston Gates Ellis & Rouvelas Meeds LLP
Issues: MAR
Rep By: William N. Myhre, Daniel Ritter

Alaska Professional Hunters Ass'n

Anchorage, AK
Leg. Issues: AVI, RES

Outside Counsel/Consultants

Birch, Horton, Bittner & Cherot
Issues: AVI, RES
Rep By: Thomas L. Albert, William P. Horn

Alaska Pulp Corp.

Sitka, AK
Leg. Issues: RES

Outside Counsel/Consultants

Robertson, Monagle & Eastaugh
Issues: RES
Rep By: James F. Clark, Steven W. Silver

Alaska Railroad

Anchorage, AK
Leg. Issues: RRR

Outside Counsel/Consultants

Chambers, Conlon & Hartwell
Issues: RRR
Rep By: Don Norden

Zane & Associates
Issues: RRR
Rep By: Curtis J. Zane

Alaska Rainforest Campaign

Washington, DC
Leg. Issues: ENG, ENV

Outside Counsel/Consultants

Arent Fox Kintner Plotkin & Kahn, PLLC
Issues: ENG, ENV
Rep By: Alison Kutler, Michael T. McNamara, Elliott I. Portnoy, Todd Weiss

Alaska Sea Life Center

Anchorage, AK

Outside Counsel/Consultants

Robertson, Monagle & Eastaugh

Alaska Seafood Marketing Institute

Seattle, WA
Leg. Issues: TRD

Outside Counsel/Consultants

McDermott, Will and Emery
Issues: TRD
Rep By: Carolyn B. Gleason, Pamela D. Walther

Alaska Ship and Drydock, Inc.

Ketchikan, AK

Outside Counsel/Consultants

Dyer Ellis & Joseph, P.C.
Rep By: Brian A. Bannon, Duncan C. Smith, III

Alaska State Snowmobile Ass'n

Anchorage, AK
Leg. Issues: RES

Outside Counsel/Consultants

Birch, Horton, Bittner & Cherot
Issues: RES
Rep By: Douglas S. Burdin, William P. Horn

Alaska Village Initiatives

Anchorage, AK

Outside Counsel/Consultants

Robert A. Rapoza Associates
Rep By: Robert A. Rapoza

Alaska Wilderness League

122 C Street NW
Suite 240
Washington, DC 20001
Tel: (202)544-5205
Fax: (202)544-5197
Registered: LDA
Web: www.alaskawild.org
E-mail: info@alaskawild.org
Leg. Issues: NAT

In-house, DC-area Employees

KOLTON, Adam
SHOGAN, Cindy: Exec. Director

Alaska, Washington Office of the State of

444 N. Capitol St. NW
Suite 336
Washington, DC 20001
Tel: (202)624-5858
Fax: (202)624-5857
Web: www.state.ak.us

In-house, DC-area Employees

KATZ, John W.: Director of State/Federal Relations
KERTTULA, Ph.D, Anna M.: Associate Director
SANDLER, Marideth J.: Associate Director
TABER, John: Associate Director

Outside Counsel/Consultants

The Wexler Group
Rep By: Robert L. Healy, Jr., Joel Malina, Anne Wexler

Albany Medical Center Hospital

Albany, NY

Outside Counsel/Consultants

Wilson, Elser, Moskowitz, Edelman & Dicker LLP

Albemarle Corp.

1155 15th St. NW
Suite 611
Washington, DC 20005
Tel: (202)223-1848
Fax: (202)223-1849
Registered: LDA
Web: www.albemarle.com
Leg. Issues: AUT, CAW, CHM, CSP, ENV, RRR, TRD

In-house, DC-area Employees

LITTLE, Barbara A.: V. President, Government Relations

J. S. Alberici Construction Co.

St. Louis, MO

Outside Counsel/Consultants

Covington & Burling

Albert Einstein Medical Center

Philadelphia, PA
Leg. Issues: BUD, HCR, MED, MMM

Outside Counsel/Consultants

Capitol Associates, Inc.
Issues: BUD, MED
Rep By: Edward R. Long, Ph.D., Julie P. Pawelczyk

DeBrunner and Associates, Inc.
Issues: BUD, HCR, MED, MMM
Rep By: Charles L. DeBrunner, Ellen J. Kugler, Kathryn D. Rooney

Albertson's Inc.

Boise, ID
Leg. Issues: LBR

Outside Counsel/Consultants

Akin, Gump, Strauss, Hauer & Feld, L.L.P.
Issues: LBR
Rep By: Barney J. Skladany, Jr.

Albright & Wilson Americas

Richmond, VA
A specialty chemical manufacturer.

Outside Counsel/Consultants

LPI Consulting, Inc.
Rep By: Teresa Gorman

Albuquerque, New Mexico, City of

Leg. Issues: BUD, CAW, ECN, EDU, HOU, LAW, ROD, TAX, TRA

Outside Counsel/Consultants

Murray, Scheer, Montgomery, Tapia & O'Donnell
Issues: BUD, CAW, ECN, EDU, HOU, LAW, ROD, TAX, TRA
Rep By: John R. O'Donnell

Alcalde & Fay

2111 Wilson Blvd.
Eighth Floor
Arlington, VA 22201-3058
Tel: (703)841-0626
Fax: (703)243-2874
Registered: LDA
Web: www.alcalde-fay.com
Leg. Issues: BUD, ENV, NAT, TRA

In-house, DC-area Employees

ALCALDE, Hector: Founder/Senior Partner
AUSTIN, Joe: Partner
BAFALIS, Hon. Louis A. "Skip": Partner
BILBRAY, Hon. James H.: Partner
BROWN, Shantrel
CANTUS, H. Hollister: Partner, Aerospace and Technology
COLEMAN, Rodney A.: Partner
COLENDA, Cynthia
CORTINA, Thomas A.: Partner
CRYE, J. Michael: Partner
DAVENPORT, Jim: Associate
FAY, Kevin J.: President
FOWLER, Mary Litton: Associate
HANCOCK, J. B.: Partner
HATHAWAY, Kris: Associate
HIRSHBERG, Jennefer A.: Partner
ISEMAN, Vicki L.: Partner
LEE, Jason: Associate
MCBETH, Danielle: Partner
MOORE, Lois: Partner
MUNOZ, Kathy Jurado: Partner
PATTERSON, Julie: Associate
PLOTT, Angela: Partner
PROWITT, Nancy Gibson: Partner
SCHLESINGER, Paul: Partner
STIRPE, David J.: Partner
STROUD, Tim: Associate
SULLIVAN, Bill: Partner
TURNER, Christopher L.: Associate
WALKER, Liz: Senior Associate
WEINSTEIN, Alana: Associate
ZORTHIAN, Barry: Partner

Outside Counsel/Consultants

DBH Consulting
Issues: TRA
Rep By: Douglas B. Ham

The Ferguson Group, LLC
Issues: BUD, ENV, NAT
Rep By: W. Roger Gwinn, Ralph Webb

Alcan Aluminum Corp.

99 Canal Center Plaza
Suite 200
Alexandria, VA 22314
Tel: (703)683-8512
Fax: (703)683-4622
Registered: LDA
Leg. Issues: CAW, ENG, SCI

In-house, DC-area Employees

MORRIS, Rick: Washington Representative

Outside Counsel/Consultants

Barnes, Richardson and Colburn
Rep By: Matthew T. McGrath

GPC Internat'l
Issues: CAW, ENG, SCI
Rep By: John D. Cahill, Michael Day, Peter G. Halpin

Alcatel

Paris, FRANCE
Leg. Issues: FOR

Outside Counsel/Consultants

Patton Boggs, LLP
Issues: FOR
Rep By: Thomas Hale Boggs, Jr., Jeffrey L. Turner, Graham G. Wisner

Alcatel USA

1909 K St. NW
Suite 800
Washington, DC 20006
Tel: (202)715-3707
Fax: (202)715-3715
Registered: LDA
Web: www.alcatel.com
E-mail: doug.wiley@usa.alcatel.com

Global telecommunications company with U.S. headquarters in Plano, TX.

Leg. Issues: COM, CPT, GOV, LBR, MAN, SCI, TEC, TRD

Political Action Committee/s

Alcatel USA Political Action Committee
1909 K St. NW
Suite 800
Washington, DC 20006
Tel: (202)715-3711
Fax: (202)715-3725
Contact: Douglas S. Wiley

In-house, DC-area Employees

GUNTHER, Jr., James J.: Senior Manager, Regulatory Affairs
WILEY, Douglas S.: Director, Government Relations, Alcatel Americas

Outside Counsel/Consultants

The Dutko Group, Inc.
Issues: GOV, LBR, SCI, TEC
Rep By: Gary J. Andres, Kim Koontz Bayliss, Mark S. Irion, Louis Lehrman, Steve Perry, Juliette M. Raffensperger, Stephen Craig Sayle

Alcoa Inc.

1909 K St. NW
Suite 500
Washington, DC 20006-1101
Tel: (202)956-5306
Fax: (202)956-5305
Registered: LDA

Headquartered in Pittsburgh, PA.

Leg. Issues: DEF, ENG, ENV, MAR, TAX, TRD, UTI

In-house, DC-area Employees

CALIFF, Lee H.: Manager, Government Affairs
WISOR, Russell C.: V. President, Government Affairs

Outside Counsel/Consultants

Ball Janik, LLP
Issues: ENG
Rep By: Robert G. Hayes, Irene Ringwood

Van Scoyoc Associates, Inc.
Issues: DEF
Rep By: Paul Grimm, Buzz Hawley, Thomas L. Lankford, H. Stewart Van Scoyoc

Alcon Laboratories

Leg. Issues: MED

Outside Counsel/Consultants

Cassidy & Associates, Inc.
Issues: MED
Rep By: Jeffrey Lawrence, Blenda Pinto-Riddick

Aldaron Inc.

Culver City, CA
Leg. Issues: AVI, BUD, ECN, ROD, TRA, URB

Outside Counsel/Consultants

Government Relations, Inc.
Issues: AVI, BUD, ECN, ROD, TRA, URB
Rep By: Thomas J. Bulger, Mark H. Miller, John N. Young

Armando Alejandre, Estate of

Leg. Issues: FOR

Outside Counsel/Consultants

Greenberg Traurig, LLP
Issues: FOR
Rep By: Ronald W. Kleinman

Alenia Aerospazig

Rome, ITALY
Leg. Issues: AER, TRD

Outside Counsel/Consultants

Cassidy & Associates, Inc.
Issues: AER, TRD
Rep By: Laurie J. Adler, Dennis M. Kedzior, Jeffrey Lawrence, Michael Merola, Marnie Russ, Hon. Martin A. Russo

Alenia Marconi Systems

Borehamwood, UNITED KINGDOM
Leg. Issues: AER, DEF

Outside Counsel/Consultants

Jefferson-Waterman Internat'l, LLC
Issues: AER, DEF
Rep By: Col. Richard L. Klass, USAF (Ret.)

Alere Medical Inc.

San Francisco, CA
Leg. Issues: HCR

Outside Counsel/Consultants

Verner, Liipfert, Bernhard, McPherson and Hand, Chartered
Issues: HCR
Rep By: Andrew D. Eskin, Rosemary B. Freeman, Vicki E. Hart, Jenifer Martin, James A. Pickup

Aleut Corp.

Anchorage, AK
Leg. Issues: BUD, DEF, RES

Outside Counsel/Consultants

Birch, Horton, Bittner & Cherot
Issues: BUD, DEF, RES
Rep By: Thomas L. Albert, Ronald G. Birch

Aleutian Pribilof Islands Community Development Ass'n

Juneau, AK
Leg. Issues: MAR

Outside Counsel/Consultants

Zane & Associates
Issues: MAR
Rep By: Curtis J. Zane

Aleutians East Borough

Anchorage, AK

A coalition of municipalities for this region.

Leg. Issues: NAT

Outside Counsel/Consultants

Robertson, Monagle & Eastaugh
Issues: NAT
Rep By: Bradley D. Gilman, Rick E. Marks, Steven W. Silver

Alexander Graham Bell Ass'n for the Deaf

3417 Volta Pl. NW
Washington, DC 20007
Tel: (202)337-5220
Fax: (202)337-8314
Web: www.agbell.org
E-mail: info@agbell.org

Founded by Alexander Graham Bell in 1890. A non-profit organization with membership in 57 countries which exists to promote the study, understanding and early detection of hearing loss in adults and children, as well as to work for better educational opportunities and teacher training for the hearing-impaired.

In-house, DC-area Employees

QUIGLEY, Elizabeth: Director, Marketing and Membership
TECKLENBURG, Michael: President

Alexander Strategy Group

Washington, DC
Leg. Issues: ENG, TAX

Outside Counsel/Consultants

Gallant Co.
Issues: ENG, TAX
Rep By: Karl Gallant

Alexander's Inc.

Saddle Brook, NJ

Outside Counsel/Consultants

Williams & Jensen, P.C.
Rep By: David E. Franasiak, Robert E. Glennon, Jr., Anthony J. Roda

Alexandria, Virginia, City of

Leg. Issues: ROD, TRA

Outside Counsel/Consultants

Francis J. Sullivan Associates
Issues: ROD, TRA
Rep By: Francis J. Sullivan

Alexandria, Virginia, Sanitation Authority of the City of

A public agency responsible for wastewater treatment in Alexandria and Fairfax County, VA.

Leg. Issues: BUD

Outside Counsel/Consultants

McGuireWoods L.L.P.
Issues: BUD
Rep By: Hana Brilliant, Stephen A. Katsurinis, Hon. Lewis F. Payne, Jr., Jeffrey L. Schlagenhauf

Alexis de Tocqueville Institution

1611 N. Kent St.
Suite 901
Arlington, VA 22209
Tel: (703)351-4969
Fax: (703)351-0090
Web: www.adti.net
E-mail: webmaster@adti.net

A non-partisan, non-profit educational research foundation established to conduct, publish and publicize research on the promotion and perfection of economic liberty, political freedom, opportunity and democracy in the United States and around the world.

In-house, DC-area Employees

BROWN, Ken: President
FOSSEDAL, Gregory: Chairman
MICHALOPOULOS, Dino: Visiting Fellow
PARKER, Larry: Senior Reporter
PRAWDZIK, Chris: V. President, Special Projects

Alfalit Internat'l

Miami, FL
Leg. Issues: EDU

Outside Counsel/Consultants

Russ Reid Co.
Issues: EDU
Rep By: Thomas C. Keller, Mark D. McIntyre, Jovita Wenner

Alfred University

Alfred, NY
Leg. Issues: BUD

Outside Counsel/Consultants

Cassidy & Associates, Inc.
Issues: BUD
Rep By: Scott D. MacConomy, Daniel J. McNamara, Laura A. Neal, Diane Rinaldo

Algoma Steel, Inc.

Sault Ste. Marie, CANADA
Leg. Issues: ENV, TRD

Outside Counsel/Consultants

Hogan & Hartson L.L.P.
Issues: ENV, TRD
Rep By: Mark S. McConnell

Alitalia

New York, NY

Outside Counsel/Consultants

Zuckert, Scoutt and Rasenberger, L.L.P.
Rep By: Richard D. Mathias

All Kinds of Music

Raleigh, NC
Leg. Issues: EDU

Outside Counsel/Consultants

Devillier Communications
Issues: EDU
Rep By: Merri Oxley

All Nippon Airways Co.

Tokyo, JAPAN
Leg. Issues: AVI

Outside Counsel/Consultants

Global USA, Inc.
Issues: AVI
Rep By: Dr. Bohdan Denysyk, George S. Kopp

Zuckert, Scoutt and Rasenberger, L.L.P.
Rep By: William H. Callaway, Jr., Andrew R. Plump, Charles J. Simpson, Jr., Rachel B. Trinder

allacrossamerica.com

Alexandria, VA
Leg. Issues: SCI

Outside Counsel/Consultants

Capital Strategies Group, Inc.
Issues: SCI
Rep By: Tammi Hayes

Allboxesdirect

Outside Counsel/Consultants

Cannon Consultants, Inc.
Rep By: Charles A. Cannon

Allegheny County Airport Authority

Pittsburgh, PA
Leg. Issues: GOV, TOU, TRA

Outside Counsel/Consultants

Doepken Keevican & Weiss
Issues: GOV, TOU, TRA

Allegheny County, Pennsylvania, Housing Authority

Pittsburgh, PA
Leg. Issues: BUD, HCR, HOU, TRA

Outside Counsel/Consultants

Sagamore Associates, Inc.
Issues: BUD, HCR, HOU, TRA
Rep By: Todd Atkinson, David U. Gogol, Lisa Levine

Allegheny County, Pennsylvania, Port Authority of

Outside Counsel/Consultants

The Peterson Group

Allegheny Energy, Inc.

1301 Pennsylvania Ave. NW
Suite 1030
Washington, DC 20004
Tel: (202)824-0404
Fax: (202)347-0132
Web: www.alleghenyenergy.com

In-house, DC-area Employees

LIMBACH, Dennis D.: Manager, Federal Legislative Affairs

Allegheny Ludlum Corp.

Pittsburgh, PA

Outside Counsel/Consultants

Ivins, Phillips & Barker
Rep By: Mr. Leslie J. Schneider, Patrick J. Smith

Allegheny Power Service Corp.

Greensburg, PA

Outside Counsel/Consultants

Potomac Incorporated

Allegheny River Mining Co.

Kittanning, PA

Outside Counsel/Consultants

Akin, Gump, Strauss, Hauer & Feld, L.L.P.

Allegheny Technologies, Inc.

Arlington, VA
Web: www.alleghenytechnologies.com

Headquartered in Pittsburgh, PA.

Outside Counsel/Consultants

Collier Shannon Scott, PLLC
Rep By: David A. Hartquist, Robert W. Porter

Howrey Simon Arnold & White
Rep By: Harvey G. Sherzer

Allegiance Healthcare Corp.

McGraw Park, IL
Leg. Issues: MAN, MED

Outside Counsel/Consultants

McGuireWoods L.L.P.
Issues: MED
Rep By: Joseph H. Bogosian, Stephen A. Katsurinis, Hon. Lewis F. Payne, Jr.

Quinn Gillespie & Associates

Ungaretti & Harris
Issues: MAN
Rep By: Sheri Bucher, Joseph A. Cari, Jr., Michelle M. Faust, Spencer Perlman

Washington Council Ernst & Young
Rep By: John L. Doney, Jayne T. Fitzgerald, LaBrenda Garrett-Nelson, Gary J. Gasper, Bruce A. Gates, Robert J. Leonard, Richard Meltzer, Robert M. Rozen, Timothy J. Urban

Allegiance Telecom, Inc.

1225 I St. NW
Washington, DC 20005
Tel: (202)289-0425
Leg. Issues: TEC

In-house, DC-area Employees

JOSEPH, Kevin: V. President, Government Affairs

Outside Counsel/Consultants

Lawler, Metzger & Milkman, LLC
Issues: TEC
Rep By: Regina M. Keeney, A. Richard Metzger, Jr., Ruth M. Milkman

Allen-Bradley

Milwaukee, WI
Leg. Issues: TRD

Outside Counsel/Consultants

JBC Internat'l
Issues: TRD
Rep By: James B. Clawson, George M. "Matt" Mattingley, Jr.

Allergan, Inc.

1030 15th St. NW
Suite 1028-A
Washington, DC 20005
Tel: (202)289-6772
Fax: (202)289-7129
Registered: LDA
Leg. Issues: MMM

In-house, DC-area Employees

GARY, W. Bradford: V. President, Government Affairs

Outside Counsel/Consultants

McDermott, Will and Emery
Issues: MMM
Rep By: Michael A. Romansky, Eric P. Zimmerman

O'Connor & Hannan, L.L.P.
Rep By: Robert W. Barrie, Hon. Thomas J. Corcoran, Patrick E. O'Donnell, Thomas H. Quinn

Washington Healthcare Representatives
Rep By: Heather H. Bremer

Allete

122 C St. NW
Suite 840
Washington, DC 20001
Web: www.allete.com
Tel: (202)638-7707
Fax: (202)638-7710

A multi-service company with operations in automotive, electric, water, and real estate.

In-house, DC-area Employees

LIBRO, William J.: Manager, Federal Affairs and Policy Development

Alliance

Outside Counsel/Consultants

The PMA Group
Rep By: Kaylene Green, Paul J. Magliocchetti, Kelli Short, Brian Thiel, Sandra Welch

Alliance Air Services

Fort Worth, TX
Leg. Issues: AVI, TRA

Outside Counsel/Consultants

Tate-LeMunyon, LLC
Issues: AVI, TRA
Rep By: Glenn B. LeMunyon, Dan C. Tate, Jr.

Alliance Capital Management LP

New York, NY
Leg. Issues: TAX

Outside Counsel/Consultants

PriceWaterhouseCoopers
Issues: TAX
Rep By: Jim Carlisle, Kirt C. Johnson, Kenneth J. Kies, Pat Raffaniello

Alliance Community Hospital

Alliance, OH
Leg. Issues: HCR

Outside Counsel/Consultants

Golin/Harris Internat'l
Issues: HCR
Rep By: C. Michael Fulton

Alliance Data Systems

Gahanna, OH
Leg. Issues: BAN

Outside Counsel/Consultants

John T. O'Rourke Law Offices
Issues: BAN
Rep By: John T. O'Rourke

Alliance for Affordable Services

1701 K St. NW
Suite 300
Washington, DC 20006
Tel: (202)347-4229
Fax: (202)463-7590
Registered: LDA
Web: www.membership.com/alliance
E-mail: alliance@membership.com
Leg. Issues: SMB

In-house, DC-area Employees

CHILDS, Blair G.: Washington Representative

Outside Counsel/Consultants

The Strategic Advocacy Group
Issues: SMB
Rep By: Blair G. Childs

Alliance for Aging Research

2021 K St. NW
Suite 305
Washington, DC 20006-1003
Web: www.agingresearch.org
E-mail: info@agingresearch.org
Tel: (202)293-2856
Fax: (202)785-8574

Founded in 1986, the Alliance for Aging Research is the nation's leading non-profit organization dedicated to improving the health and independence of Americans as they age, through public and private funding of medical research and geriatric education. At its core, the Washington, D.C. based Alliance promotes greater scientific and medical discovery to ensure a long and healthy life to every American.

Leg. Issues: HCR

In-house, DC-area Employees

KIMBALL, Mark: Director, Finance and Administration
PERRY, Daniel: Exec. Director
RHEINSTEIN, Valerie: Director of Communications
ZELDOW, Deborah: Senior Director, Strategies & Programs

Alliance for American Innovation, Inc.

236 Massachusetts Ave. NE
Suite 110
Washington, DC 20002
Tel: (202)546-8700
Fax: (202)546-7357
Registered: LDA
Leg. Issues: BUD, CPT, DEF, FAM, HCR, LAW, TAX, WEL

In-house, DC-area Employees

SELBY, Beverly M.: Exec. Director
SHORE, Steven M.: President

Outside Counsel/Consultants

The Da Vinci Group
Issues: CPT
Rep By: Mark R. Smith

The Laxalt Corp.
Issues: CPT, DEF
Rep By: Michelle D. Laxalt

The Solomon Group, LLC
Issues: CPT, DEF
Rep By: William D. Crosby, Jr., David M. Lonie, Hon. Gerald B. H. Solomon

Stephens, Cross, Ihlenfeld & Boring, Inc.
Issues: CPT
Rep By: Ronald Stephens

Alliance for Chemical Awareness

Washington, DC

Outside Counsel/Consultants

John Adams Associates Inc.
Rep By: Elizabeth McCarthy

Alliance for Children and Families

1701 K St. NW
Suite 200
Washington, DC 20006-1503
Tel: (202)223-3447
Fax: (202)331-7476

An 86-year old organization with 400 member not-for-profit family and child service agencies throughout North America. Headquartered in Milwaukee, WI. Formerly Family Service America, Inc.

Leg. Issues: ALC, BUD, CSP, EDU, FAM, HCR, HOU, IMM, LAW, TAX, WEL

In-house, DC-area Employees

BESSER, Marla: Policy Analyst
DELGADO VOTAW, Carmen: Senior V. President, Public Policy
MESSIH, Lillian: Policy Analyst
TOMLINSON, Ericka: Policy Analyst

Alliance for Community Media

666 11th St. NW
Suite 740
Washington, DC 20001-4542
Tel: (202)393-2650
Fax: (202)393-2653
Registered: LDA
Web: www.alliancecm.org
E-mail: acm@alliancecm.org

In-house, DC-area Employees

RIEDEL, Bunnie: Exec. Director

Alliance for Competitive Electricity

Members include Duke Power Co., New England Electric Systems, Pacific Gas and Electric Co. and Southern California Edison Co.

Leg. Issues: ENG, TAX, UTI

Outside Counsel/Consultants

Johnston & Associates, LLC
Issues: ENG, TAX, UTI
Rep By: Hon. J. Bennett Johnston, N. Hunter Johnston, Eric Tober

Stuntz, Davis & Staffier, P.C.
Issues: UTI
Rep By: Randall E. Davis, Tom S. Runge

Alliance for Elder Care

San Diego, CA

Outside Counsel/Consultants

Helmsin & Yarwood Associates
Rep By: Bruce Yarwood

Alliance for Health Reform

1900 L St. NW
Suite 512
Washington, DC 20036
Web: www.allhealth.org
Tel: (202)466-5626
Fax: (202)466-6525

A nonpartisan information clearinghouse on the health care issue. Chairman is Senator Jay Rockefeller (D-WV); V. Chairman is Sen. Bill Frist (R-TN).

In-house, DC-area Employees

HOWARD, Edward F.: Exec. V. President

The Alliance for I-69 Texas

Houston, TX
Leg. Issues: TRA

Outside Counsel/Consultants

Meyers & Associates
Issues: TRA
Rep By: Larry D. Meyers, Jennifer Shepard

Alliance for Internat'l Educational and Cultural Exchange, The

1776 Massachusetts Ave. NW
Suite 620
Washington, DC 20036
Tel: (202)293-6141
Fax: (202)293-6144
Registered: LDA
Web: www.alliance-exchange.org
E-mail: info@alliance-exchange.org
Leg. Issues: BUD, EDU, FOR

In-house, DC-area Employees

BARON, Kevin: Policy Specialist
MCCARRY, Michael: Exec. Director
TAIBER, Julie M.: Assistant Director/ Senior Policy Specialist

Alliance for Justice

11 Dupont Circle NW
Second Floor
Washington, DC 20036
Tel: (202)822-6070
Fax: (202)822-6068
Registered: LDA
Web: www.afj.org
E-mail: alliance@afj.org

An association of national, regional and local organizations working to provide equal access to government forums for all groups and individuals. Monitors and reports on federal judiciary, maintains an information clearinghouse, and creates training programs.

Leg. Issues: BUD, CIV, GOV

In-house, DC-area Employees

ARON, Nan: President
KLETTER, Joni: Law Fellow
POMERANZ, John: Non-Profit Advocacy Counsel

Outside Counsel/Consultants

Lichtman, Trister, Singer & Ross
Rep By: Michael Trister

Alliance for Nuclear Accountability

1801 18th St. NW
Suite 9-2
Washington, DC 20009
Web: www.ananuclear.org
Tel: (202)833-4668
Fax: (202)234-9536

A national alliance of over thirty organizations working to address issues of nuclear weapons production and waste clean-up. Many of the organizations are located in communities serving as home to one or more of the Department of Energy's nuclear weapon production/nuclear waste facilities.

Leg. Issues: BUD, CAW, DEF, ENV, HCR, SCI, WAS

In-house, DC-area Employees

BRIDGMAN, Jim: Program Director
CRANDALL, Kathy: Program Associate

Alliance for Public Technology

919 18th St. NW
Suite 900
Washington, DC 20006
Web: www.apt.org
Tel: (202)263-2970
Fax: (202)263-2960

A non-profit, tax exempt coalition of public interest groups and individuals whose goal is to foster broad access to affordable, usable information and communications services and technology.

In-house, DC-area Employees

SCHODER, Paul: President

Outside Counsel/Consultants

Issue Dynamics Inc.

Alliance for Quality Nursing Home Care

Atlanta, GA
Leg. Issues: MMM

Outside Counsel/Consultants

Akin, Gump, Strauss, Hauer & Feld, L.L.P.
Issues: MMM
Rep By: Karen E. Goldmeier Green, Joel Jankowsky, Dana E. Singiser, Jose H. Villarreal

Barbour Griffith & Rogers, Inc.
Issues: MMM
Rep By: Haley Barbour, G. O. Lanny Griffith, Jr., Bill Himpler, Loren Monroe, Edward M. Rogers, Jr.

Alliance for Rail Competition

1920 N St. NW
Suite 800
Washington, DC 20036
Web: www.railcompetition.org
E-mail: diane@railcompetition.org
Tel: (202)216-9270
Fax: (202)216-9662
Registered: LDA

Coalition of freight rail customers working to promote competition among freight railroads.

Leg. Issues: RRR

In-house, DC-area Employees

DUFF, Diane C.: Exec. Director
HEMPHILL, Melissa M.: Manager, Operations and Development

Alliance for Reasonable Regulation of Insecticides

Washington, DC
Leg. Issues: AGR, BUD, CHM, FOO

Outside Counsel/Consultants

Griffin, Johnson, Dover & Stewart
Issues: AGR, BUD, CHM, FOO
Rep By: Keith Heard

Alliance for Regional Transportation

Cincinnati, OH
Leg. Issues: BUD

Outside Counsel/Consultants

Vorys, Sater, Seymour and Pease, LLP
Issues: BUD

Alliance for Responsible Atmospheric Policy

2111 Wilson Blvd.
Eighth Floor
Arlington, VA 22201-3058
Web: www.arap.org
E-mail: alliance98@aol.com
Tel: (703)841-0626
Fax: (703)243-2874

The alliance is an industry coalition addressing issues of ozone protection and global climate change.

Leg. Issues: ENV

In-house, DC-area Employees

STIRPE, David J.: Exec. Director

Outside Counsel/Consultants

Alcalde & Fay
Issues: ENV
Rep By: Kevin J. Fay, David J. Stirpe

Alliance for Responsible Cuba Policy

Washington, DC

Outside Counsel/Consultants

Thompson, Hine and Flory LLP
Rep By: David H. Baker

Alliance for Retired Americans

8403 Colesville Rd.
Suite 1200
Silver Spring, MD 20910
Web: www.retiredamericans.org
Tel: (301)578-8422
Fax: (301)578-8847
Registered: LDA

Formed in 2001 by the AFL-CIO to replace the Nat'l Council for Senior Citizens. Advocates on behalf of union retirees.

Leg. Issues: MMM

In-house, DC-area Employees

SARMIENTO, Tony: Acting Exec. Director

Alliance for Special Needs Children

Outside Counsel/Consultants

Valente Lopatin & Schulze
Rep By: Alan G. Lopatin, Richard T. Schulze, Jr., Mark Valente, III

Alliance for Telecommunications Industry Solutions

1200 G St. NW
Suite 500
Washington, DC 20005
Web: www.atis.org
E-mail: atispr@atis.org
Tel: (202)628-6380
Fax: (202)393-5453

A member company organization whose work focus includes network interconnection standards, number portability, improved data transmission, wireless communication, Internet telephony, toll-free access, and order and billing issues. Members of ATIS and committee participants include, but are not limited to, telecommunications service providers, manufacturers, software developers, resellers, enhanced service providers, and providers of operations support.

In-house, DC-area Employees

BERNHARDS, John: Director, Public Relations
KLEIN, William: V. President, Finance and Operations
MILLER, Susan M.: President

Alliance for the Prudent Use of Antibiotics (APUA)

Boston, MA
Leg. Issues: EDU

Outside Counsel/Consultants

William M. Cloherty
Issues: EDU
Rep By: William M. Cloherty

Alliance for Understandable, Sensible and Accountable Government Regulations

Leg. Issues: GOV

Outside Counsel/Consultants

Ropes & Gray
Issues: GOV
Rep By: Thomas M. Susman

The Wexler Group
Issues: GOV
Rep By: Joel Malina, Christine Maroulis

Alliance Medical Corp.

Phoenix, AZ
Leg. Issues: MED

Outside Counsel/Consultants

Congressional Consultants
Issues: MED
Rep By: Gwen Gampel, Karen M. Late

Alliance of American Insurers

1211 Connecticut Ave. NW
Suite 400
Washington, DC 20036
Web: www.allianceai.org
Tel: (202)822-8811
Fax: (202)872-1885
Registered: LDA

A national property-casualty insurance trade ass'n representing more than 270 insurance companies in dealing with problems of common interest in the fields of legislation, regulation, litigation and public information. Headquartered in Downers Grove, IL.

Leg. Issues: AUT, ENV, FIN, HCR, HOU, INS, LBR, TOB, TOR, TRA

Political Action Committee/s

ALLPAC

1211 Connecticut Ave. NW
Suite 400
Washington, DC 20036
Tel: (202)822-8811
Fax: (202)872-1885

In-house, DC-area Employees

FARMER, David M.: Senior V. President, Federal Affairs
GARCIA, Nelson
SCHLOMAN, Kenneth D.: Counsel, Federal Affairs
WHITMAN, Lamar

Outside Counsel/Consultants

Akin, Gump, Strauss, Hauer & Feld, L.L.P.
Issues: ENV, HCR, INS
Rep By: Donald C. Alexander, Sean G. D'Arcy

Alliance of Arts Advocates

815 Connecticut Ave. NW
Suite 650
Washington, DC 20006
Tel: (202)822-6100
Fax: (202)822-6101

A political action committee.

In-house, DC-area Employees

WHITE, William R.

Alliance of Automobile Manufacturers, Inc.

1401 H St. NW
Suite 900
Washington, DC 20005
Web: www.autoalliance.org
Tel: (202)326-5500
Fax: (202)326-5595
Registered: LDA

Leg. Issues: AUT, BNK, BUD, CAW, CSP, ENV, FUE, MAN, TAX, TRA

In-house, DC-area Employees

ALIFERIS, Scott: Manager, Government Affairs
COOPER, Josephine: President and Chief Exec. Officer
HORNE, Katherine M.: Manager, Government Affairs
STANTON, Michael J.: V. President, Government Affairs

Outside Counsel/Consultants

Mayer, Brown & Platt
Issues: AUT
Rep By: Erika Z. Jones

The Wexler Group
Issues: AUT
Rep By: Hon. Michael Patrick Flanagan, Hon. Robert S. Walker

Alliance of Catholic Health Care Systems

Sacramento, CA
Leg. Issues: MMM

Outside Counsel/Consultants

Patton Boggs, LLP
Issues: MMM
Rep By: Hon. Willis "Bill" D. Gradison

Alliance of Marine Mammal Parks and Aquariums

418 N. Pitt St.
Alexandria, VA 22314
Web: www.ammpa.org
E-mail: ammpa@aol.com
Tel: (703)549-0137
Fax: (703)549-0488
Registered: LDA

An international association of 39 marine life parks, aquariums, zoos, research facilities, and professional organizations dedicated to the conservation of marine mammals and their habitats through public display, research, and education.

Leg. Issues: AGR, ANI, MAR

In-house, DC-area Employees

MENARD, Marilee: Exec. Director

Outside Counsel/Consultants

O'Connor & Hannan, L.L.P.
Issues: ANI, MAR
Rep By: George J. Mannina, Jr.

Alliance of Motion Picture & Television Producers

Encino, CA
Leg. Issues: IMM

Outside Counsel/Consultants

Paul, Weiss, Rifkind, Wharton & Garrison
Issues: IMM
Rep By: Carl W. Hampe

Alliance of Nonprofit Mailers

1211 Connecticut Ave. NW
Suite 620
Washington, DC 20036-2701
Tel: (202)462-5132
Fax: (202)462-0423
Registered: LDA
Web: www.nonprofitmailers.org
E-mail: alliance@nonprofitmailers.org

A national coalition of nonprofit organizations seeking to maintain reasonable and stable nonprofit mail rates and regulations.

Leg. Issues: POS

In-house, DC-area Employees

DENTON, Neal: Exec. Director

Outside Counsel/Consultants

Sidley & Austin
Issues: POS
Rep By: David M. Levy

Alliance of Western Milk Producers

Sacramento, CA
Registered: LDA
Leg. Issues: AGR, BUD, FOO

Outside Counsel/Consultants

Schramm, Williams & Associates, Inc.
Issues: AGR, BUD, FOO
Rep By: Nancy Williams

Alliance of Work/Life Professionals

Alexandria, VA

Outside Counsel/Consultants

CLARION Management Resources, Inc.
Rep By: Carole M. Rogin, David E. Woodbury

Alliance Pipeline, L.P.

Calgary, CANADA
Leg. Issues: ENG

Outside Counsel/Consultants

Lighthouse Energy Group LLC
Issues: ENG
Rep By: Tobyn J. Anderson, Merribel S. Ayres

Alliance to End Childhood Lead Poisoning

227 Massachusetts Ave. NE
Suite 200
Washington, DC 20002
Tel: (202)543-1147
Fax: (202)543-4466
Web: www.aeclp.org
E-mail: aeclp@aeclp.org

An educational, policy, and advocacy organization working to eliminate the problem of childhood lead poisoning.

Leg. Issues: ENV, HCR, HOU

In-house, DC-area Employees

GUTHRIE, Anne: Director, Health Policy
RYAN, Donald T.: Exec. Director

Alliance to Improve Medicare

900 17th St. NW
Suite 600
Washington, DC 20006
Tel: (202)452-1029
Fax: (202)296-9561
Registered: LDA
Web: www.reformmedicare.org
E-mail: tmoorehead@hlc.org

A coalition of organizations seeking comprehensive modernization of the traditional medicare system to offer more coverage choices, better benefits and access to the latest innovative medical practices.

Leg. Issues: MMM

In-house, DC-area Employees

MOORHEAD, Tracey: Director

Alliance to Keep Americans Working

Leg. Issues: LBR

Outside Counsel/Consultants

Ogletree Governmental Affairs, Inc.
Issues: LBR
Rep By: Harold P. Coxson

Alliance to Promote Software Innovations

1150 18th St. NW
Suite 700
Washington, DC 20036
Tel: (202)293-2700
Fax: (202)872-5501
Registered: LDA

In-house, DC-area Employees

GOULD, Rebecca M. J.: Manager, Public Policy

Alliance to Save Energy

1200 18th St. NW
Suite 900
Washington, DC 20036
Tel: (202)857-0666
Fax: (202)331-9588
Registered: LDA
Web: www.ase.org

Founded in 1977 by Senators Charles H. Percy and Hubert Humphrey, the Alliance is a non-profit coalition of government, business, consumer and labor leaders dedicated to increasing the efficiency of energy use. Conducts research and pilot projects to stimulate investment in energy efficiency, formulates policy initiatives and conducts educational programs.

Leg. Issues: BUD, ENG, ENV, FOR, SCI, UTI

In-house, DC-area Employees

HAMILTON, David: Director, State and Federal Policy
HOPKINS, Mark D.: V. President
NEMTZOW, David M.: President

Outside Counsel/Consultants

Podesta/Mattoon
Issues: ENG
Rep By: Edwin S. Rothschild

Alliant Energy

Madison, WI
Registered: LDA
Leg. Issues: CAW, ENG, ENV, WAS

Outside Counsel/Consultants

Cottone and Huggins Group
Issues: ENG
Rep By: Mel Cottone

Piper Marbury Rudnick & Wolfe LLP
Issues: CAW, ENV, WAS
Rep By: Deborah E. Jennings, William R. Weissman

Alliant Techsystems, Inc.

1911 Fort Myer Dr.
Suite 600
Arlington, VA 22209
Tel: (703)741-0546
Fax: (703)741-0529
Registered: LDA
Leg. Issues: AER, BUD, DEF, ENV, FIR, LBR, SCI, TAX, WAS

In-house, DC-area Employees

FEDOR, John D.: Director, Congressional Relations
MARTIN, William R.: V. President, Washington Operations
MASCH, Donald: Deputy Director, Government Relations

Outside Counsel/Consultants

Kimmitt, Coates & McCarthy
Issues: FIR
Rep By: Vincent J. Coates, Jr.

Robison Internat'l, Inc.
Issues: BUD, DEF
Rep By: Sandra A. Gilbert

Allied Charities of Minnesota

Minneapolis, MN
Leg. Issues: TAX

Outside Counsel/Consultants

Legislative Solutions
Issues: TAX
Rep By: Dr. James DeChaine

Allied Domecq

700 11th St. NW
Suite 680
Washington, DC 20001
Tel: (202)628-5877
Fax: (202)628-4847
Registered: LDA
Web: www.allieddomequ.plc.com

Involved in the manufacturing, importation and distribution of alcoholic beverages.

Leg. Issues: ADV, ALC, CAW, DEF, TAX, TRD

Political Action Committee/s

Allied Domecq PAC
700 11th St. NW
Suite 680
Washington, DC 20001
Tel: (202)628-5877
Fax: (202)628-4847
Contact: Chris R. Swonger

In-house, DC-area Employees

SWONGER, Chris R.: V. President and Director, Government Affairs
WALKER, Tracey: Manager, Government Affairs

Allied Marketing

Dallas, TX
Registered: LDA
Leg. Issues: BUD, GOV, POS

Outside Counsel/Consultants

Marshall A. Brachman
Issues: BUD, GOV, POS
Rep By: Marshall A. Brachman

Allied Pilots Ass'n

Arlington, TX

Represents American Airline pilots.

Leg. Issues: AVI, TRA

Outside Counsel/Consultants

Bracy Williams & Co.
Issues: AVI, TRA
Rep By: Terrence L. Bracy, Josh Nassar, Susan J. Williams

Allied Products Corp.

Chicago, IL

A machine tool manufacturing company.

Outside Counsel/Consultants

Collier Shannon Scott, PLLC
Rep By: Paul C. Rosenthal

Allied Tube & Conduit Corp.

Harvey, IL
Leg. Issues: TRA

Outside Counsel/Consultants

Schagrin Associates
Issues: TRA
Rep By: Roger B. Schagrin

Allina Health Systems

Minneapolis, MN
Leg. Issues: HCR, MMM, TOB

Outside Counsel/Consultants

Holland & Knight LLP
Issues: HCR, MMM, TOB
Rep By: Hon. Gerald E. Sikorski, P. J. Toker

Allison Transmission Division, General Motors Corp.

601 Madison St.
Suite 200
Alexandria, VA 22314
Tel: (703)549-9266
Fax: (703)549-9268
Leg. Issues: AVI, DEF, MAN

In-house, DC-area Employees

LOGAN, James A.: Director, Washington Operations

Outside Counsel/Consultants

C. Baker Consulting Inc.
Issues: AVI, DEF, MAN
Rep By: Caleb Baker

Michael Chase Associates, LTD
Issues: DEF
Rep By: Michael T. Chase

Allmerica Financial

Worcester, MA
Leg. Issues: BAN, FIN, INS, RET, TAX

Outside Counsel/Consultants

Murray, Scheer, Montgomery, Tapia & O'Donnell
Issues: BAN, FIN, INS, RET, TAX
Rep By: Thomas R. Crawford, D. Michael Murray

Allscripts Inc.

Libertyville, IL
Leg. Issues: HCR, MMM

Outside Counsel/Consultants

The Legislative Strategies Group, LLC
Issues: HCR, MMM
Rep By: Martin B. Gold, Denise M. Henry, Steven M. Hilton, G. David Mason

Allstate Insurance Co.

888 16th St. NW
Suite 700
Washington, DC 20006
Tel: (202)835-8126
Fax: (202)835-8227
Registered: LDA
Leg. Issues: BAN, BNK, CPT, CSP, DIS, ENV, INS, LAW, ROD, TAX, TOB

Political Action Committee/s

ALLPAC
888 16th St. NW
Suite 700
Washington, DC 20006
Tel: (202)835-8126
Fax: (202)835-8227
Contact: J. Charles Bruse

In-house, DC-area Employees

BRUSE, J. Charles: V. President and Assistant General Counsel

Outside Counsel/Consultants

Davis & Harman LLP
Issues: TAX
Rep By: Richard S. Belas, Thomas A. Davis, William B. Harman, Jr., Barbara Groves Mattox

Allsup Inc.

Belleville, IL
Leg. Issues: INS

Outside Counsel/Consultants

Kyros & Cummins Associates
Issues: INS
Rep By: John M. Falk, Hon. Peter N. Kyros

Alltel Corporation

601 Pennsylvania Ave. NW
Suite 720
Washington, DC 20004
Tel: (202)783-3970
Fax: (202)783-3982
Registered: LDA

Headquartered in Little Rock, AR

Leg. Issues: SCI, TAX, TEC

Political Action Committee/s

APAC

601 Pennsylvania Ave. NW
Suite 720
Washington, DC 20004
Contact: Sarah Versaggi
Tel: (202)783-3979
Fax: (202)783-3982

In-house, DC-area Employees

FRANKLIN, Bobby: V. President, Federal Legislative Affairs
HILL, Carolyn C.: V. President, Federal Government Affairs
RABIN, Glenn S.: Assistant V. President-Federal Regulatory Affairs
SMITH, Diane: Senior V. President-Federal Government Affairs
VERSAGGI, Sarah: Manager, Federal Legislation

Outside Counsel/Consultants

Bracewell & Patterson, L.L.P.
Issues: TEC
Rep By: Hon. Edwin R. Bethune, Hon. Jim Chapman, Gene E. Godley, Marc C. Hebert, Charles L. Ingebretson, Michael L. Pate, Scott H. Segal, D. Michael Stroud, Jr.

Allthane Technologies Internat'l

Oberholzer, SOUTH AFRICA
Leg. Issues: DEF

Outside Counsel/Consultants

Capital Strategies Group, Inc.
Issues: DEF
Rep By: Tammi Hayes

Alltrista/Penny

Greenville, TN

Outside Counsel/Consultants

Sagamore Associates, Inc.
Rep By: Mark W. Weller, Audrey B. Young

Almont Shipping Terminals

Wilmington, NC
Leg. Issues: MAR

Outside Counsel/Consultants

Hunton & Williams
Issues: MAR
Rep By: John J. Adams

Aloha Airlines

Honolulu, HI

Outside Counsel/Consultants

Squire, Sanders & Dempsey L.L.P.

Alpha Center for Health Planning

1350 Connecticut Ave. NW
Washington, DC 20036
Web: www.ac.org
E-mail: info@ac.org
Tel: (202)296-1818
Fax: (202)296-1825

In-house, DC-area Employees

HELMS, David: President

Alpha Technologies Group Inc.

Beverly Hills, CA
Leg. Issues: TRD

Outside Counsel/Consultants

Commonwealth Consulting Corp.
Issues: TRD
Rep By: Christopher M. Lehman

Alsatian American Chamber of Commerce

Alexandria, VA

Works to promote the culture, products, and industries of the Alsace region of France.

Leg. Issues: BEV, FOR, TOU, TRD

Outside Counsel/Consultants

Obadal and MacLeod, p.c.
Issues: BEV, FOR, TOU, TRD
Rep By: Christian A. Klein

Alston & Bird, LLP

Atlanta, GA
Leg. Issues: UTI

Outside Counsel/Consultants

Smith Dawson & Andrews, Inc.
Issues: UTI
Rep By: Gregory B. Andrews, Thomas C. Dawson, James P. Smith

Alternative Schools Network

Chicago, IL

Outside Counsel/Consultants

Capitol Perspectives
Rep By: Mary Elise DeGonia

Alternative Systems, Inc.

Half Moon Bay, CA

Outside Counsel/Consultants

Counselors For Management, Inc.
Rep By: Janice C. Lipsen

Alticor, Inc.

214 Massachusetts Ave. NE
Suite 210
Washington, DC 20002
Web: www.alticor.com
Tel: (202)547-5005
Fax: (202)547-3483
Registered: LDA

Formerly know as Amway Corporation. Headquartered in Ada, MI.

Leg. Issues: FAM, FOO, IMM, TAX, TEC, TRD

Political Action Committee/s

AMPAC

214 Massachusetts Ave. NE
Suite 210
Washington, DC 20002
Contact: John C. Gartland
Tel: (202)547-5005
Fax: (202)547-3483

In-house, DC-area Employees

GARTLAND, John C.: Director, Government Affairs
HOLWILL, Richard N.: Director, International Affairs

Outside Counsel/Consultants

Columbus Public Affairs

White & Case LLP
Issues: TAX
Rep By: Linda E. Carlisle, J. Roger Mentz

The Aluminum Ass'n

900 19th St. NW
Suite 300
Washington, DC 20006
Web: www.aluminum.org
Tel: (202)862-5100
Fax: (202)862-5164
Registered: LDA

Members represent virtually all domestic primary producers and about 85% of the semi-fabricated aluminum shipped in this country.

Leg. Issues: AUT, CAW, ENV, MAN, TRD

In-house, DC-area Employees

ADAMS, Nick: Director, Statistics and Economics
KING, Robin: V. President, Public Affairs
LARKIN, J. Stephen: President
STRIETER, Robert: V. President, Environmental Health and Safety

Outside Counsel/Consultants

Baker & Hostetler LLP
Rep By: William H. Schweitzer

Hill and Knowlton, Inc.
Rep By: David MacKay

Nutter & Harris, Inc.
Issues: ENV
Rep By: Robert L. Harris

Aluminum Co. of Canada

CANADA

Outside Counsel/Consultants

Smith & Harroff, Inc.

Alyeska Pipeline Service Co.

1667 K St. NW
Suite 1230
Washington, DC 20006
Web: www.alyeska-pipe.com
Tel: (202)466-3866
Fax: (202)466-3886
Registered: LDA

Operators of the Trans-Alaska Pipeline System. Headquartered in Anchorage, AK.

Leg. Issues: ENG, IND, NAT, TAX, TRA

In-house, DC-area Employees

HENSLEY, William L.: Manager, Federal Government Relations
SLAJER, Veronica A.: Assistant Manager, Federal Government Relations

Outside Counsel/Consultants

Michael F. Barrett, Jr.
Issues: ENG
Rep By: Michael F. Barrett, Jr.

Zane & Associates
Issues: NAT, TAX
Rep By: Curtis J. Zane

Alzheimer's Ass'n

1319 F St. NW
Suite 710
Washington, DC 20004
Web: www.alz.org
Tel: (202)393-7737
Fax: (202)393-2109
Registered: LDA

Leg. Issues: BUD, HCR, HOU, MED, MMM, PHA, SCI, TAX

In-house, DC-area Employees

HOGUE, Bonnie: Director, Federal and State Policy
MCCONNELL, Stephen R.: V. President, Public Policy

Outside Counsel/Consultants

Cavarocchi Ruscio Dennis Associates
Issues: BUD, HCR, SCI
Rep By: Domenic R. Ruscio

Amalgamated Sugar

Ogden, UT

A sugar beet producer.

Leg. Issues: AGR

Outside Counsel/Consultants

Symms, Lehn & Associates, Inc.
Issues: AGR

Amalgamated Transit Union

5025 Wisconsin Ave. NW
Washington, DC 20016
Web: www.atu.org
Tel: (202)537-1645
Fax: (202)244-7824
Registered: LDA

Leg. Issues: BUD, GOV, LBR, MAR, RRR, TRA

Political Action Committee/s

Amalgamated Transit Union Committee on Political Education

5025 Wisconsin Ave. NW
Washington, DC 20016
Tel: (202)537-1645
Fax: (202)244-7824

In-house, DC-area Employees

LA SALA, Jim: Internat'l President
MOLOFSKY, Robert A.: General Counsel
OWENS, Oscar: Internat'l Secretary-Treasurer
YORK, Amy: Legislative Representative

Outside Counsel/Consultants

The Kamber Group
Rep By: Pamela Greenwalt, Victor S. Kamber

Ambulatory Pediatric Ass'n

McLean, VA
Web: www.ambpeds.com
E-mail: ambpeds@aol.com

Outside Counsel/Consultants

Degnon Associates, Inc.
Rep By: Marge Degnon

AMCOR Capital Corp.

Coachello, CA

Provides financing for agriculture production efforts.

Leg. Issues: TAX

Outside Counsel/Consultants

Meyers & Associates
Issues: TAX
Rep By: Larry D. Meyers, Richard L. Meyers

Amdahl Corp.

Sunnyvale, CA
Web: www.amdahl.com

A California-based, international company that provides network services, designs, manufactures, sells and services large-scale mainframe computers, associated peripherals, and software.

Outside Counsel/Consultants

Paul, Hastings, Janofsky & Walker LLP
Rep By: Behnam Dayanim, G. Hamilton Loeb

AMDeC Policy Group, Inc.

New York, NY
Leg. Issues: BUD, ECN, HCR, MED, MMM, SCI

Outside Counsel/Consultants

Kelly and Associates, Inc.
Issues: BUD, ECN, HCR, MED, MMM, SCI
Rep By: John A. Kelly

Amerada Hess Corp.

New York, NY

A U.S.-based international oil and gas company with refining, marketing, exploration, and production interests.

Leg. Issues: FOR, FUE

Outside Counsel/Consultants

The Duberstein Group, Inc.
Issues: FOR, FUE
Rep By: John W. Angus, III, Michael S. Berman, Steven M. Champlin, Kenneth M. Duberstein, Henry M. Gandy, Daniel P. Meyer

Ameren Services

701 Pennsylvania Ave. NW
Suite 300
Washington, DC 20004
Tel: (202)508-5044
Registered: LDA
Headquartered in St. Louis, MO.

Leg. Issues: BUD, CAW, ENG, ENV, FUE, LBR, RRR, TAX, UTI, WAS

In-house, DC-area Employees

LABOMBARD, Susan: Federal Affairs Representative

America Outdoors

Knoxville, TN
Registered: LDA
Leg. Issues: RES, TAX

Outside Counsel/Consultants

The Argus Group, L.L.C.
Issues: TAX
Rep By: David R. Burton, Dan R. Mastromarco

Birch, Horton, Bittner & Cherot
Issues: RES
Rep By: Julia Gustafson, William P. Horn

America West Airlines

Phoenix, AZ

Outside Counsel/Consultants

Cormac Group, LLP

America's Blood Centers

725 15th St. NW
Suite 700
Washington, DC 20005
Tel: (202)393-5725
Fax: (202)393-1282
Registered: LDA
Web: www.americasblood.org
E-mail: abc@americasblood.org

Federation of independent blood centers that provide about half of the nation's volunteer donor blood supply.

Leg. Issues: HCR, MED, MMM

In-house, DC-area Employees

MACPHERSON, Jim: Chief Exec. Officer
SMITH, Kristen R.: Director, Government Affairs

Outside Counsel/Consultants

George Kroloff & Associates

Patton Boggs, LLP
Issues: HCR, MMM
Rep By: Martha M. Kendrick

America's Charities

Fairfax, VA

Outside Counsel/Consultants

George Kroloff & Associates
Rep By: George Kroloff

America's Community Bankers

900 19th St. NW
Suite 400
Washington, DC 20006
Tel: (202)857-3100
Fax: (202)296-8716
Registered: LDA
Web: www.acbankers.org
E-mail: info@acbankers.org

Represents savings and loan associations, savings banks, and thrift holding companies. Formed by the consolidation of the Nat'l Council of Community Bankers and the U.S. League of Savings Institutions.

Leg. Issues: BAN, BNK, BUD, DIS, EDU, FIN, HOU, SMB, TAX

Political Action Committee/s

ACB Compac
900 19th St. NW
Suite 400
Washington, DC 20006
Tel: (202)857-3100
Fax: (202)296-8716
Contact: Matthew D. Smyth

In-house, DC-area Employees

BAHIN, Charlotte M.: Regulatory Counsel
CASEY, Diane M.: President and Chief Exec. Officer
DAVIS, Robert R.: Director, Government Relations
ELDER, Albert: Government Relations
HONG, Peter: Government Relations
MAROULIS-CRONMILLER, Alexandra: Director, Membership
MONDRES, Eric M.: Government Relations
O'CONNOR, James E.: Government Relations
SCHMERMUND, Robert P.: Director, Public Affairs
SMYTH, Matthew D.: Government Relations
VERDIER, Stephen J.: Legislative Counsel

Outside Counsel/Consultants

The Dutko Group, Inc.
Issues: BAN
Rep By: Gary J. Andres, Kimberly M. Spaulding

America's Promise

909 N. Washington St.
Suite 400
Alexandria, VA 22314
Tel: (703)684-4500
Web: www.americaspromise.org

In-house, DC-area Employees

FORSHT, Ralph: V. President, Government Relations
RACICOT, Marc: Chairman

American Academy for Liberal Education

1700 K St. NW
Suite 901
Washington, DC 20006
Tel: (202)452-8611
Fax: (202)452-8620
Web: www.aale.org

Seeks improvement in academic standards at U.S. colleges and universities. Also accredits colleges and universities.

In-house, DC-area Employees

WALLIN, Jeffrey D.: President

American Academy of Actuaries

1100 17th St. NW
Seventh Floor
Washington, DC 20036
Tel: (202)223-8196
Fax: (202)872-1948
Registered: LDA
Web: www.actuaries.org
Leg. Issues: BAN, ENV, HCR, INS, MMM, RET, TAX

In-house, DC-area Employees

BLOOM, Lauren M.: General Counsel/Director, Professionalism
CARD, Noel R.: Director, Communications
ENGLISH, Stephen M.: Policy Analyst
GEBHARDTSBAUER, Ronald: Senior Pension Fellow
JOHANSEN, Lawrence A.: President
KWIATKOWSKI, Holly E.: Policy Analyst
LAWSON, Richard C.: Exec. Director
UCCELLO, Cori E.: Senior Health Fellow
VASS, Greg: Policy Analyst
WATTS, Meredith: Policy Analyst
WILDER, Thomas: Director, Public Policy

American Academy of Adoption Attorneys

Leg. Issues: FAM

Outside Counsel/Consultants

Ogletree Governmental Affairs, Inc.
Issues: FAM
Rep By: Michael Roush

American Academy of Audiology

8300 Greensboro Dr.
Suite 750
McLean, VA 22102
Tel: (703)790-8466
Fax: (703)790-8631
Registered: LDA
Web: www.audiology.org
E-mail: info@audiology.org

International association representing the legislative needs of professional audiologists.

Leg. Issues: BUD, HCR, INS, MMM

Political Action Committee/s

American Academy of Audiology PAC (AAA-PAC)
8300 Greensboro Dr.
Suite 750
McLean, VA 22102
Tel: (703)790-8466
Fax: (703)790-8631
Contact: Craig Johnson, Ph.D.

Audiology PAC
8300 Greensboro Dr.
Suite 750
McLean, VA 22102
Tel: (703)790-8466
Fax: (703)790-8631
Contact: Craig Johnson, Ph.D.

In-house, DC-area Employees

DAVIS, Sidney: Communications Director
FABRY, Ph.D., David: President
JOHNSON, Ph.D., Craig: Chair, Government Affairs Committee

Outside Counsel/Consultants

Olsson, Frank and Weeda, P.C.
Issues: HCR
Rep By: John W. Bode, Pamela J. Furman, Susan P. Grymes, Stephen L. Lacey, Marshall L. Matz, Tyson Redpath

The PMA Group
Issues: BUD
Rep By: Kaylene Green, Paul J. Magliocchetti, Timothy K. Sanders

American Academy of Child and Adolescent Psychiatry

3615 Wisconsin Ave. NW
Washington, DC 20016
Tel: (202)966-7300
Fax: (202)966-2891
Registered: LDA
Web: www.aacap.org
Leg. Issues: BUD, COM, EDU, ENV, FIN, HCR, HOU, IMM, LAW, LBR, MED, MMM, TOB

In-house, DC-area Employees

ANTHONY, Virginia Q.: Exec. Director
CROSBY, Mary: Director, Government Affairs/Deputy Exec. Director
MOORE, Nuala: Assistant Director, Government Affairs

American Academy of Dermatology

1350 I St. NW
Suite 880
Washington, DC 20005
Tel: (202)842-3555
Fax: (202)842-4355
Registered: LDA
Web: www.aad.org

Headquartered in Schaumburg, IL.

Leg. Issues: CPT, CSP, HCR, INS, LBR, MED, MMM

Political Action Committee/s

American Academy of Dermatology Ass'n PAC (Skin-PAC)
1350 I St. NW
Suite 880
Washington, DC 20005
Tel: (202)842-3555
Fax: (202)842-4355
Contact: John D. Barnes

In-house, DC-area Employees

BARNES, John D.: Associate Exec. Director, Government Affairs and Health Policy
EDWARDS, Laura Saul: Assistant Director, Federal Affairs
HAYDEN, Cheryl A.: Assistant Director, Federal Affairs

Outside Counsel/Consultants

MARC Associates, Inc.
Issues: MMM
Rep By: Bernard Patashnik

American Academy of Facial Plastic and Reconstructive Surgery

310 S. Henry St.
Alexandria, VA 22314
Tel: (703)299-9291
Fax: (703)299-8898
Web: www.aafprs.org
E-mail: mail@aafprs.org

In-house, DC-area Employees

DUFFY, Stephen C.: Exec. V. President

American Academy of Family Physicians

2021 Massachusetts Ave. NW
Washington, DC 20036
Tel: (202)232-9033
Fax: (202)232-9044
Registered: LDA
Web: www.aafp.org
Leg. Issues: BUD, EDU, HCR, INS, LAW, MED, MMM, SMB, TOB

In-house, DC-area Employees

BURKE, Kevin J.: Director, Washington Office
HILDEBRANDT, Susan: Assistant Director, Washington Office
JOHNSON, Michele I.: Government Relations Representative
LEE, Jennifer: Government Relations Analyst
SWEENEY, Rosemarie: V. President, Socioeconomics & Policy Analysis

Outside Counsel/Consultants

Health and Medicine Counsel of Washington
Issues: BUD
Rep By: Staci Sigman Dennison, Dale P. Dirks

American Academy of Neurology

Minneapolis, MN
Leg. Issues: HCR

Outside Counsel/Consultants

Powers Pyles Sutter & Verville, PC
Issues: HCR
Rep By: Judith Buckalew, Peter W. Thomas, Richard E. Verville

American Academy of Nurse Practitioners

P.O. Box 40130
Washington, DC 20016
Tel: (202)966-6414
Fax: (202)966-2856
Web: www.aanp.org
E-mail: dcoffice@aanp.org

Leg. Issues: HCR

Political Action Committee/s

American Academy of Nurse Practitioners PAC

P.O. Box 40473
Washington, DC 20024
Contact: Dee Swanson

In-house, DC-area Employees

JENNINGS, Ph.D., R.N, Carole P.: Washington Representative
SWANSON, Dee: PAC Treasurer
TOWERS, Ph.D., Jan: Director of Health Policy

American Academy of Ophthamology - Office of Federal Affairs

1101 Vermont Ave. NW
Suite 700
Washington, DC 20005
Tel: (202)737-6662
Fax: (202)737-7061
Registered: LDA
Web: www.eyenet.org

Headquartered in San Francisco, CA.

Leg. Issues: BUD, HCR, MED, MMM, VET

Political Action Committee/s

OPHTHPAC

1101 Vermont Ave. NW
Suite 700
Washington, DC 20005
Tel: (202)737-6662
Fax: (202)737-7061
Contact: Steve Miller

In-house, DC-area Employees

COHEN, Catherine Grealy: V. President, Governmental Affairs Division
COLMAN, Kim: Manager Reimbursement Policy
FOX, Leann: Political Affairs Coordinator
KOVAR, Carrie: Manager of Public Health Manpower Policy
MILLER, Steve: Director of OPHTPAC and Political Affairs
NELSON, Justin: Washington Representative
RICH, M.D., William L.: Secretary, Federal Affairs

American Academy of Optometry

6110 Executive Blvd.
Suite 506
Rockville, MD 20852
Tel: (301)984-1441
Fax: (301)984-4737
Web: www.aaopt.org/
E-mail: aaoptom@aol.com

In-house, DC-area Employees

SCHOENBRUN, Lois: Exec. Director

American Academy of Orthopaedic Surgeons

317 Massachusetts Ave. NE
Suite 100
Washington, DC 20002
Tel: (202)546-4430
Fax: (202)546-5051
Registered: LDA

Leg. Issues: BUD, HCR, INS, LBR, MED, MMM, SCI

In-house, DC-area Employees

LOVETT, David A.: Director

American Academy of Orthotists and Prosthetists

Leg. Issues: BUD, HCR

Outside Counsel/Consultants

Arent Fox Kintner Plotkin & Kahn, PLLC
Issues: BUD, HCR
Rep By: Katie Clarke, Douglas McCormack, Robert J. Waters

American Academy of Otolaryngic Allergy

1990 M St. NW
Suite 680
Washington, DC 20036
Tel: (202)955-5010
Fax: (202)955-5016
Web: www.allergy-ent.com
E-mail: aaoa@aol.com

Leg. Issues: MMM

In-house, DC-area Employees

LUCAS, Jami: Exec. Director

Outside Counsel/Consultants

MARC Associates, Inc.
Issues: MMM
Rep By: Bernard Patashnik, Ellen Riker

American Academy of Otolaryngology-Head and Neck Surgery

One Prince St.
Alexandria, VA 22314-3357
Tel: (703)836-4444
Fax: (703)683-5100
Registered: LDA
Web: www.entnet.org

Strives to advance the art and science of otolaryngology-head and neck surgery.

Leg. Issues: BUD, HCR, INS, MMM

Political Action Committee/s

American Academy of Otolaryngology-Head and Neck Surgery PAC

One Prince St.
Alexandria, VA 22314-3357
Tel: (703)836-4444
Fax: (703)683-5100
Contact: John R. Williams

In-house, DC-area Employees

HOLT, M.D., G. Richard: Exec. V. President
NISSENBAUM, Beverly: Director, Department of Health Policy and Government Affairs
WILLIAMS, John R.: Assistant Director, Congressional Affairs, Health Policy and Government Affairs

American Academy of Pediatrics

601 13th St. NW
Suite 400 North
Washington, DC 20005
Tel: (202)347-8600
Fax: (202)393-6137
Registered: LDA
Web: www.aap.org
E-mail: kids1st@aap.org

A professional membership organization whose 55,000 members advocate for the attainment of optimal physical and mental health for all infants, children, adolescents and young adults. Works to assure access to healthcare for all children and pregnant women.

Leg. Issues: HCR, MED, MMM

In-house, DC-area Employees

GUERNEY, Janis: Assistant Director
HENDRICKS, Karen: Assistant Director
HOLLAND, M. Elaine: Assistant Director, Government Liaison
NEWSON, Graham H.: Director, Government Liaison
NOYES, Elizabeth J.: Associate Exec.
THARP, Marjorie: Manager, Public Affairs

Outside Counsel/Consultants

Hogan & Hartson L.L.P.
Issues: HCR, MED, MMM

American Academy of Physical Medicine and Rehabilitation

Chicago, IL
Leg. Issues: HCR

Outside Counsel/Consultants

Powers Pyles Sutter & Verville, PC
Issues: HCR
Rep By: Richard E. Verville

American Academy of Physician Assistants

950 N. Washington St.
Alexandria, VA 22314-1552
Tel: (703)836-2272
Fax: (703)684-1924
Registered: LDA
Web: www.aapa.org
E-mail: aapa@aapa.org

Provides public education on the physician assistant profession and lobbies on federal legislation of importance to physician assistants and patients.

Leg. Issues: HCR

Political Action Committee/s

American Academy of Physician Assistants Political Action Committee

950 N. Washington St.
Alexandria, VA 22314-1552
Tel: (703)836-2272
Fax: (703)684-1924

In-house, DC-area Employees

CRANE, Stephen C.: Exec. V. President
GARA, Nicole: V. President, Government and Professional Affairs
HARDING, Sandra: Director, Federal Affairs
HUGHES, Nancy: V. President, Communication and Information Services
KASUNICH, Cheryl: V. President and Chief Operating Officer
MCGUIRE, Patricia: Administrator, Federal Affairs
O'CONNELL, Lynn: Foundation Director
THOMAS, Greg: V. President, Clinical Affairs and Education

American Academy of Wound Management

Washington, DC

Outside Counsel/Consultants

Hauck and Associates
Rep By: Melissa T. Forburger

American Academy on Physician and Patient

McLean, VA

Outside Counsel/Consultants

Degnon Associates, Inc.

American Accreditation Healthcare Commission/URAC

1275 K St. NW
Suite 1100
Washington, DC 20005
Tel: (202)216-9010
Web: www.urac.org

An independent, not-for-profit corporation engaged in the assessment of managed care organizations through a process of accreditation.

Leg. Issues: HCR

In-house, DC-area Employees

CARNEAL, Garry: President
GREEN, Kaylene: Chair

American Advertising Federation

1101 Vermont Ave. NW
Suite 500
Washington, DC 20005
Tel: (202)898-0089
Fax: (202)898-0159
Registered: LDA
Web: www.aaf.org
E-mail: aaf@aaf.org

Established in 1905. Represents all facets of the advertising industry: corporations, advertisers, advertising agencies, media, suppliers and related trade associations. Seeks to represent the industry's views, to prevent over regulation and promote a better understanding in government, education and the general public.

Leg. Issues: ADV, BEV, TAX, TOB

In-house, DC-area Employees

PENHILL, Laurel: Senior V. President, Operations
PERLMAN, Jeffry L.: Exec. V. President, Government Affairs and General Counsel
RECTOR, Clark E.: V. President, State Government Affairs
SNYDER, Wallace S.: President

Outside Counsel/Consultants

Davidson & Company, Inc.
Issues: ADV, TAX
Rep By: James H. Davidson, Richard E. May, Stanley Sokul

Patton Boggs, LLP
Issues: ADV, BEV, TOB
Rep By: Thomas Hale Boggs, Jr., Penelope S. Farthing, Elena Giberga, Thomas P. O'Donnell

American Agip MTBE Sales Division

New York, NY

Outside Counsel/Consultants

Paul, Weiss, Rifkind, Wharton & Garrison
Rep By: Terence J. Fortune

American AIDS Political Action Committee

1808 Swann St. NW
Washington, DC 20009
Tel: (202)462-7288
Fax: (202)483-1964

In-house, DC-area Employees

SHERIDAN, Thomas F.: President/Treasurer

Outside Counsel/Consultants

The Sheridan Group
Rep By: Thomas F. Sheridan

American Airlines

1101 17th St. NW
Suite 600
Washington, DC 20036
Tel: (202)496-5666
Fax: (202)496-5660
Registered: LDA

Leg. Issues: AVI, BUD, CPT, ENV, FIN, IMM, RET, TAX, TRD

Political Action Committee/s

American Airlines Political Action Committee

1101 17th St. NW
Suite 600
Washington, DC 20036
Tel: (202)496-5649
Fax: (202)496-5660
Contact: Julie L. Nichols

In-house, DC-area Employees

BLOCKER, Andy: Managing Director
NELSON, Carl A.: Associate General Counsel
NICHOLS, Julie L.: Managing Director, Government Affairs
RIS, Jr., William K.: Senior V. President, Government Affairs
STROTHER, Daniella: Managing Director, Government Affairs

Outside Counsel/Consultants

Akin, Gump, Strauss, Hauer & Feld, L.L.P.
Issues: AVI, FIN, RET, TAX
Rep By: Janet C. Boyd, Sean G. D'Arcy, Smith W. Davis, Sylvia A. de Leon, Barney J. Skladany, Jr.

Arent Fox Kintner Plotkin & Kahn, PLLC
Issues: AVI
Rep By: Hon. Dale L. Bumpers, Michael T. McNamara

Baker, Donelson, Bearman & Caldwell, P.C.
Issues: BUD
Rep By: Linda Hall Daschle, Albert B. Randall

Burson-Marsteller
Rep By: Brian H. Lott, Richard Mintz

Fleischman and Walsh, L.L.P.
Rep By: Louis H. Dupart, John P. McAllister

The OB-C Group, LLC
Issues: AVI, TAX, TRD
Rep By: Thomas Keating, Kim F. McKernan, Charles J. Mellody, Patricia A. Nelson, Lawrence F. O'Brien, III, Linda E. Tarplin

Robertson, Monagle & Eastaugh

The Wexler Group
Issues: AVI
Rep By: Timothy Hannegan, Patrick J. McCann, Dale W. Snape, Anne Wexler

Winston & Strawn
Issues: AVI
Rep By: Hon. James H. Burnley, IV, Roger A. Keller, Jr., Charles L. Kinney, Michael J. McLaughlin, John A. Waits, II

American Alliance for Health, Physical Education, Recreation and Dance

1900 Association Dr.
Reston, VA 20191-1598
Tel: (703)476-3400
Fax: (703)476-9527
Registered: LDA
Web: www.aahperd.org

In-house, DC-area Employees

DAVIS, Michael G.: Exec. V. President

American Amateur Karate Federation

Los Angeles, CA
Leg. Issues: SPO

Outside Counsel/Consultants

Akin, Gump, Strauss, Hauer & Feld, L.L.P.
Issues: SPO
Rep By: Marlene M. Colucci, Henry A. Terhune

American Ambulance Ass'n

1255 23rd St. NW
Suite 200
Washington, DC 20037
Tel: (202)452-8888
Fax: (202)452-0008
Registered: LDA
Web: www.the-aaa.org
E-mail: aaa911@the-aaa.org
Leg. Issues: HCR, MMM, TRA

Political Action Committee/s

American Ambulance Ass'n Federal PAC (AMBU-PAC)
1255 23rd St. NW
Suite 200
Washington, DC 20037
Tel: (202)452-8888
Fax: (202)452-0008
Contact: Tristan M. North

In-house, DC-area Employees

HARACZNAK, Stephen R.: Exec. V. President
HAUCK, Graham S.: Director of Meetings and Member Services
NORTH, Tristan M.: Director, Government Affairs

Outside Counsel/Consultants

Fleishman-Hillard, Inc
Issues: HCR
Rep By: William Black

Hauck and Associates
Rep By: Tristan M. North

Hogan & Hartson L.L.P.
Issues: HCR, MMM
Rep By: Darrel J. Grinstead

R. Duffy Wall and Associates
Issues: HCR
Rep By: Stephen Cooper

American Amusement Machine Ass'n

Elk Grove, IL
Leg. Issues: ART, CPT, MON

Outside Counsel/Consultants

Arent Fox Kintner Plotkin & Kahn, PLLC
Issues: ART, CPT, MON
Rep By: Alison Kutler, Michael T. McNamara, Elliott I. Portnoy, Todd Weiss

Jenkens & Gilchrist
Rep By: Donald M. Barnes

American Anthropological Ass'n

4350 N. Fairfax Dr.
Suite 640
Arlington, VA 22203-1620
Tel: (703)528-1902
Fax: (703)528-3546
Web: www.aaanet.org

In-house, DC-area Employees

DAVIS, Bill: Exec. Director
OVERBEY, Dr. Mary Margaret: Director, Government Relations

Outside Counsel/Consultants

Conlon, Frantz, Phelan & Pires
Rep By: David J. Frantz

American Apparel & Footwear Ass'n

1601 N. Kent St.
Suite 120
Arlington, VA 22209
Tel: (703)524-1864
Fax: (703)522-6741
Registered: LDA
Web: www.apparelandfootwear.org
E-mail: slamar@apperalandfootwear.org
Leg. Issues: APP, TRD

Political Action Committee/s

Clothes PAC
1601 N. Kent St.
Suite 120
Arlington, VA 22209
Tel: (703)524-1864
Fax: (703)522-6741
Contact: Stephen E. Lamar

In-house, DC-area Employees

LAMAR, Stephen E.: Director, Government Relations
MARTIN, Larry K.: President and Chief Operating Officer
MORGAN, Jack: Director, Communications
SUBLER, Rachel: Government Relations Representative

Outside Counsel/Consultants

The Direct Impact Co.

The Duberstein Group, Inc.
Issues: APP, TRD
Rep By: John W. Angus, III, Michael S. Berman, Steven M. Champlin, Kenneth M. Duberstein, Henry M. Gandy, Daniel P. Meyer

Sandler, Travis & Rosenberg, P.A.
Issues: APP, TRD
Rep By: Nicole Bivens Collinson, Chandri Navarro-Bowman, Ron Sorini

American Arbitration Ass'n

601 Pennsylvania Ave. NW
Suite 700
Washington, DC 20004-2676
Tel: (202)737-1460
Fax: (202)737-2418
Web: www.adr.org
E-mail: gallaghers@adr.org

Dedicated to the resolution of disputes through the use of arbitration, mediation, conciliation, negotiation, democratic elections, and other voluntary procedures. In 2000, 200,000 cases were filed with the Association in matters including commercial finance, construction, labor and employment, environmental, health care, insurance, real estate, and securities disputes. Maintains 40 offices nationwide and works in agreement with arbitral institutions in 38 other nations. Headquartered in New York, NY.

In-house, DC-area Employees

BAKER, P. Jean: V. President, Government Programs
GALLAGHER, Steven G.: Senior V. President
PARET, S. Pierre: Assistant V. President, Government Programs

American Architectural Foundation

Washington, DC
Leg. Issues: ART

Outside Counsel/Consultants

Chernikoff and Co.
Issues: ART
Rep By: Larry B. Chernikoff

American Arts Alliance

805 15th St. NW
Suite 500
Washington, DC 20005
Tel: (202)289-1776
Fax: (202)371-6601
Registered: LDA
Web: www.artswire/AAA
E-mail: aaa@artswire.org

A consortium of 2,600 professional non-profit arts institutions formed in 1977 and dedicated to advancing the arts.

Leg. Issues: ART, BUD, CPT, GOV, TAX, TEC

Political Action Committee/s

American Arts Alliance Political Action Committee (AAA PAC)
805 15th St. NW
Suite 500
Washington, DC 20005
Tel: (202)289-1776
Fax: (202)371-6601
Contact: Letitia Chambers

In-house, DC-area Employees

CHAMBERS, Letitia: Treasurer
DENTON, Janet A.: Director

Outside Counsel/Consultants

Chambers Associates Inc.
Issues: ART, BUD, CPT, GOV, TAX, TEC
Rep By: Letitia Chambers, Janet A. Denton, Troy Tibbals

American Ass'n for Active Lifestyles and Fitness

1900 Association Dr.
Reston, VA 20191
Tel: (703)476-3430
Fax: (703)476-9527
Web: www.aahperd.org/aaalf.html
E-mail: aaalf@aahperd.org

Affiliated with the American Alliance for Health, Physical Education, Recreation and Dance. Promotes active lifestyles for all ages, through professional members in school, community, corporate, and hospital settings.

Leg. Issues: BUD, EDU, HCR

In-house, DC-area Employees

SEAMAN, Dr. Janet: Exec. Director

American Ass'n for Adult and Continuing Education

1200 19th St. NW
Suite 300
Washington, DC 20036
Tel: (301)918-9193
Fax: (202)223-4579
Web: www.albany.edu/aaace

An international education association serving the field of adult and continuing education through advocacy, professional development and public information programs.

In-house, DC-area Employees

DARIN, Anna: Association Manager

American Ass'n for Clinical Chemistry, Inc.

2101 L St. NW
Suite 202
Washington, DC 20037
Tel: (202)857-0717
Fax: (202)887-5093
Registered: LDA
Web: www.aacc.org
E-mail: info@aacc.org
Leg. Issues: BUD, HCR, MED

In-house, DC-area Employees

FLAHERTY, Richard: Exec. V. President
GOLDSMITH, Jerry: V. President, Marketing Programs
NASH, Pamela A.: V. President, Policy and Programming
STINE, Vince: Government Affairs Program Director

American Ass'n for Dental Research

1619 Duke St.
Alexandria, VA 22314-3406
Tel: (703)548-0066
Fax: (703)548-1883
Web: www.dentalresearch.com
E-mail: research@iadr.com

A member organization of the Coalition for Health Funding in Washington.

Leg. Issues: BUD, HCR, MED, SCI

In-house, DC-area Employees

SCHWARZ, Eli: Exec. Director

Outside Counsel/Consultants

Cavarocchi Ruscio Dennis Associates
Issues: BUD, HCR, MED, SCI
Rep By: Nicholas G. Cavarocchi

American Ass'n for Geriatric Psychiatry

7910 Woodmont Ave.
Suite 1050
Bethesda, MD 20814-3004
Tel: (301)654-7850
Fax: (301)654-4137
Registered: LDA
Web: www.aagpgpa.org
E-mail: main@aagpgpa.org
Leg. Issues: ALC, BUD, HCR, MED, MMM, TAX

In-house, DC-area Employees

VANDERBILT, Marjorie W.: Director, Government Affairs

American Ass'n for Health Education

1900 Association Dr.
Reston, VA 20191
Tel: (703)476-3437
Fax: (703)476-6638
Web: www.aahperd.org/aahe
E-mail: aahe@aahperd.org

In-house, DC-area Employees

LANCE, J.: Coordinator, Government and Public Affairs
SMITH, Becky J.: Exec. Director and Coordinator, Government and Public Affairs

American Ass'n for Higher Education

One Dupont Circle NW
Suite 360
Washington, DC 20036-1110
Tel: (202)293-6440
Fax: (202)293-0073
Web: www.aahe.org

In-house, DC-area Employees

MOSES, Dr. Yalonda: President

American Ass'n for Homecare

625 Slaters Ln.
Suite 200
Alexandria, VA 22314-1171
Tel: (703)836-6263
Fax: (703)836-6730
Registered: LDA

Web: www.aahomecare.org
E-mail: info@aahomecare.org

The all-inclusive national association representing all elements of homecare under one roof.

Leg. Issues: HCR

Political Action Committee/s

American Ass'n for Homecare PAC

625 Slaters Ln.
Suite 200
Alexandria, VA 22314-1171
Contact: Heather Fraser
Tel: (703)836-6263
Fax: (703)836-6730

In-house, DC-area Employees

BENNER, Mara: V. President, Government Relations
CONNAUGHTON, Thomas A.: Chief Exec. Officer
CUERVO, Asela M.: V. President, Legal and Government Affairs
FRASER, Heather: PAC Contact
KELLY, Rusty: Director of Communications
VOYIAZIAKIS, Barbara: Membership Relations Assistant

Outside Counsel/Consultants

Davidson & Company, Inc.
Issues: HCR
Rep By: James H. Davidson, Richard E. May, Stanley Sokul

Powers Pyles Sutter & Verville, PC
Rep By: James C. Pyles

Reed, Smith, LLP
Issues: HCR
Rep By: Phillips S. Peter

Shaw Pittman
Issues: HCR
Rep By: Bruce Fried

American Ass'n for Laboratory Accreditation

5301 Buckeystown Pike
Suite 350
Frederick, MD 21704-8307
Web: www.a2la.org
Tel: (301)644-3248
Fax: (301)662-2974

Leg. Issues: AGR, AUT, CAW, COM, CSP, ENV, FOO, GOV, MAN, NAT, SCI, TEC, TRD, WAS

In-house, DC-area Employees

ROBINSON, Roxanne: V. President
UNGER, Peter S.: President

Outside Counsel/Consultants

Kirkland & Ellis

American Ass'n for Marriage and Family Therapy

1133 15th St. NW
Suite 300
Washington, DC 20005
Tel: (202)452-0109
Fax: (202)223-2329
Registered: LDA

Web: www.aamft.org
E-mail: central@aamft.org

Leg. Issues: ALC, FAM, GOV, HCR, INS, LBR, MED, MMM, PHA

Political Action Committee/s

American Ass'n for Marriage and Family Therapy PAC

1133 15th St. NW
Suite 300
Washington, DC 20005
Contact: John Ambrose
Tel: (202)452-0109
Fax: (202)223-2329

In-house, DC-area Employees

AMBROSE, John: Director, Legal and Government Affairs
BERGMAN, David: Manager, Government Affairs
BOWERS, Michael: Exec. Director

Outside Counsel/Consultants

Capitol Associates, Inc.
Issues: HCR, MMM
Rep By: William A. Finerfrock, Debra M. Hardy Havens, Julie Shroyer

American Ass'n for Medical Transcription

Modesto, CA

Outside Counsel/Consultants

Hogan & Hartson L.L.P.
Rep By: Beth L. Roberts, Cliff Stromberg

American Ass'n for Respiratory Care

1100 Duke Street
Alexandria, VA 22314
Tel: (703)548-8538
Fax: (703)548-8499
Registered: LDA

Web: www.aarc.org
E-mail: eicher@aarc.org

Headquartered in Dallas, TX.

Leg. Issues: BUD, HCR, MMM, TOB

In-house, DC-area Employees

EICHER, Jill A.: Director, Government Affairs

American Ass'n for the Advancement of Science

1200 New York Ave. NW
Washington, DC 20005
Tel: (202)326-6400
Fax: (202)371-9526

Web: www.aaas.org

In-house, DC-area Employees

BROADBENT, Nan: Director of Communications
NICHOLSON, Richard S.: Exec. Officer
TEICH, Albert H.: Director, Science and Policy Programs

American Ass'n for the Study of Liver Diseases

Washington, DC
Leg. Issues: BUD, HCR, MED, MMM, SCI

Outside Counsel/Consultants

Cavarocchi Ruscio Dennis Associates
Issues: BUD, HCR, MED, MMM, SCI
Rep By: Lyle B. Dennis

Smith, Bucklin and Associates, Inc.

American Ass'n of Acupuncture and Oriental Medicine

Raleigh, NC

Outside Counsel/Consultants

Sonosky, Chambers, Sachse & Endreson
Rep By: William R. Perry

American Ass'n of Advertising Agencies

1899 L St. NW
Suite 700
Washington, DC 20036
Tel: (202)331-7345
Fax: (202)857-3675
Registered: LDA

Web: www.aaaa.org
E-mail: wash@aaaadc.org

A trade association representing the advertising agency business. Headquartered in New York, NY.

Leg. Issues: ADV, COM, CPT, TAX

Political Action Committee/s

Professionals In Advertising PAC

1899 L St. NW
Suite 700
Washington, DC 20036
Tel: (202)331-7345
Fax: (202)857-3675

In-house, DC-area Employees

HOFFMAN, Adonis E.: Senior V. President and Counsel
O'BRIEN, Richard: Exec. V. President and Director, Government Relations

Outside Counsel/Consultants

Campbell Crane & Associates
Issues: ADV, TAX
Rep By: Jeanne M. Campbell, Daniel M. Crane

Davidson & Company, Inc.
Issues: ADV, TAX
Rep By: James H. Davidson, Richard E. May, Stanley Sokul

Patton Boggs, LLP
Issues: ADV
Rep By: Thomas Hale Boggs, Jr., Penelope S. Farthing, John F. Fithian, Elena Giberga

American Ass'n of Airport Executives

4212 King St.
Alexandria, VA 22312
Tel: (703)824-0500
Fax: (703)820-1395

Web: www.airportnet.org

The Association has combined its legislative affairs operations with the Airports Council International - North America (listed separately). See listing under AAAE-ACI for a list of the legislative affairs personnel and outside firms representing both groups.

In-house, DC-area Employees

BARCLAY, Charles: President

American Ass'n of Bank Directors

4701 Sangamore Rd.
Suite P15
Bethesda, MD 20816
Web: www.aabd.org
Tel: (301)263-9841
Fax: (301)229-2443

Provides information, education, advocacy and other services to directors of banks, and savings institutions nationwide.

Leg. Issues: BAN

In-house, DC-area Employees

BARIS, David H.: Exec. Director and General Counsel

American Ass'n of Bioanalysts

St. Louis, MO
Leg. Issues: MED, MMM

Outside Counsel/Consultants

Arent Fox Kintner Plotkin & Kahn, PLLC
Issues: MED, MMM
Rep By: Bill Applegate, Stacy Harbison, Robert J. Waters

American Ass'n of Black Women Entrepreneurs Corp.

P.O. Box 13858
Silver Spring, MD 20911-0858
Tel: (301)585-8051

The Association is concerned with the success of existing black women business owners. Provides information, professional training, networking and governmental development programs for members. Operates 20 chapters nationwide.

In-house, DC-area Employees

ALFORD, Brenda: Founding National President
WOODS, Anne B.: V. President for Membership Development

American Ass'n of Blacks in Energy

927 15th St. NW
Suite 200
Washington, DC 20005
Web: www.aabe.org
E-mail: bhill@aabe.org
Tel: (202)371-9530
Fax: (202)371-9218

A non-profit membership organization developed to encourage increased participation by blacks in developing national energy policy. Encourages research in energy use and development of energy technology.

Leg. Issues: ENG, ENV, FUE, UTI

In-house, DC-area Employees

HILL, Robert L.: Exec. Director
PARKER, Dionne: Director, Member Services

American Ass'n of Blood Banks

8101 Glenbrook Rd.
Bethesda, MD 20814-2749
Tel: (301)907-6977
Fax: (301)907-6895
Registered: LDA

Web: www.aabb.org
E-mail: aabb@aabb.org
Leg. Issues: BUD, HCR, MMM

In-house, DC-area Employees

GREGORY, Kay: Director, Regulatory Affairs
LIPTON, Karen Shoos: Chief Exec. Officer
OTTER, Jean: Division Director, Educational Programs
SCHIFF, Phil: Administration and Business Development
WIEGMANN, Theresa: General Counsel and Division Director, Government Affairs

Outside Counsel/Consultants

Verner, Liipfert, Bernhard, McPherson and Hand, Chartered
Issues: HCR, MMM
Rep By: Vicki E. Hart

American Ass'n of Cardiovascular and Pulmonary Rehabilitation

Middleton, WI
Leg. Issues: GOV, HCR, MMM

Outside Counsel/Consultants

GRQ, Inc.
Issues: GOV, HCR, MMM
Rep By: Patricia Booth, Phillip Porte

American Ass'n of Children's Residential Centers

122 C St. NW
Suite 820
Washington, DC 20001
E-mail: aacrc@dc.net
Tel: (202)628-1816
Fax: (202)638-0973

A national organization of agency and individual members concerned with residential treatment of children with emotional problems.

In-house, DC-area Employees

VICKERY, Allison: Exec. Director

American Ass'n of Clinical Endocrinologists

Jacksonville, FL
Leg. Issues: HCR

Outside Counsel/Consultants

Civic Service, Inc.
Issues: HCR
Rep By: Roy Pfautch, Michael W. Schick

Medical Advocacy Services, Inc.
Rep By: Robert Blaser

American Ass'n of Clinical Urologists, Inc.

Schaumburg, IL

Outside Counsel/Consultants

MARC Associates, Inc.
Rep By: Randolph B. Fenninger

American Ass'n of Colleges for Teacher Education

1307 New York Ave. NW
Suite 300
Washington, DC 20005-4701
Tel: (202)293-2450
Fax: (202)457-8095
Registered: LDA
Web: www.aacte.org
E-mail: aacte@aacte.org
Leg. Issues: BUD, EDU

In-house, DC-area Employees

EARLEY, Penelope: V. President, Government Relations
IMIG, David G.: President
TAAHAN, Chris: Program Associate, Governmental Affairs

American Ass'n of Colleges of Nursing

One Dupont Circle NW
Suite 530
Washington, DC 20036
Tel: (202)463-6930
Fax: (202)785-8320
Web: www.aacn.nche.edu

The only national organization devoted exclusively to furthering nursing education in America's universities and four-year colleges. Represents more than 470 member institutions nationwide. Works to advance the quality of baccalaureate and graduate nursing education, promote nursing research, and develop academic leaders.

Leg. Issues: BUD, HCR

In-house, DC-area Employees

BEDNASH, Geraldine: Exec. Director
CAMPBELL, Debbie: Director, Government Affairs
RHOME, Anne M.: Deputy Exec. Director

Outside Counsel/Consultants

Powers Pyles Sutter & Verville, PC
Issues: BUD, HCR
Rep By: J. Michael Hall

American Ass'n of Colleges of Osteopathic Medicine

5550 Friendship Blvd.
Suite 310
Chevy Chase, MD 20815-7231
Tel: (301)968-4100
Fax: (301)968-4101
Registered: LDA
Web: www.aacom.org

A non-profit medical education association.

Leg. Issues: BUD, EDU, HCR, MED, MMM, SCI

In-house, DC-area Employees

DYER, Michael J.: V. President, Government Relations
VUNK, Kari: Assistant Director, Government Relations
WOOD, D.O., Ph.D, Douglas L.: President

American Ass'n of Colleges of Pharmacy

1426 Prince St.
Alexandria, VA 22314
Tel: (703)739-2330
Fax: (703)836-8982
Registered: LDA
Web: www.aacp.org

A member organization of the Federation of Associations of Schools of the Health Professions in Washington.

Leg. Issues: EDU, HCR, IND, PHA, SCI

In-house, DC-area Employees

LANG, William G.: Director of Government Affairs
PENNA, Richard P.: Exec. V. President

American Ass'n of Colleges of Podiatric Medicine

1350 Piccard Dr.
Suite 322
Rockville, MD 20850
Tel: (301)990-7400
Fax: (301)990-2807
Web: www.aacpm.org
E-mail: aacpmas@aacpm.org

A non-profit educational association.

In-house, DC-area Employees

MCNEVIN, Anthony: President

American Ass'n of Collegiate Registrars and Admissions Officers

One Dupont Circle NW
Suite 520
Washington, DC 20036-1171
Tel: (202)263-0282
Fax: (202)872-8857
Web: www.aacrao.org
E-mail: gourleyj@aacrao.org

In-house, DC-area Employees

GOURLEY, Jacquelyn: Assistant Director, Government Relations and Communications
NASSIRIAN, Barmak: Associate Exec. Director
SULLIVAN, Jerome H.: Exec. Director

American Ass'n of Community Colleges

One Dupont Circle NW
Suite 410
Washington, DC 20036
Tel: (202)728-0200
Fax: (202)833-2467
Registered: LDA
Web: www.aacc.nche.edu
Leg. Issues: BUD, EDU, SCI, TAX, TEC, WEL

In-house, DC-area Employees

BAIME, David S.: Director, Government Relations
BOGGS, George R.: President
HERMES, James: Legislative Associate
KENT, Norma G.: Director, Communications
MANSO, Angela: Legislative Associate
MCKENNEY, James: Director, Workforce Development

American Ass'n of Cosmetology Schools

Phoenix, AZ
Web: www.beautyschools.org

An association of 615 cosmetology schools. Keeps members abreast of changes in laws and regulations, provides members with educational services, and promotes the welfare of cosmetology education in the United States.

Outside Counsel/Consultants

Dow, Lohnes & Albertson, PLLC

American Ass'n of Crop Insurers

One Massachusetts Ave. NW
Suite 800
Washington, DC 20001-1431
Tel: (202)789-4100
Fax: (202)408-7763
Registered: LDA
Web: www.aginsurance.org
E-mail: aaci@erols.com

A national, non-profit trade association which promotes agriculture through multiple peril crop insurance using the American agency system. The address given is that of the firm McLeod, Watkinson & Miller.

Leg. Issues: AGR, BUD, INS

Political Action Committee/s

American Ass'n of Crop Insurers Political Action Committee
One Massachusetts Ave. NW
Suite 800
Washington, DC 20001-1431
Tel: (202)789-4100
Fax: (202)408-7763
Contact: Laura L. Phelps

In-house, DC-area Employees

MCLEOD, Michael R.: Exec. Director
PHELPS, Laura L.

Outside Counsel/Consultants

McLeod, Watkinson & Miller
Issues: AGR, BUD, INS
Rep By: Stephen Frerichs, Michael R. McLeod, Laura L. Phelps

American Ass'n of Early Childhood Educators

3612 Bent Branch Ct.
Falls Church, VA 22041
Tel: (703)941-4329
Fax: (703)941-4329

Represents the interests of directors and teachers in early childhood centers.

Leg. Issues: EDU, FAM, HCR

In-house, DC-area Employees

TOBIN, Dr. William J.: Exec. Director

Outside Counsel/Consultants

Associated Child Care Consultants, Ltd.

William J. Tobin and Associates
Issues: EDU, FAM, HCR

American Ass'n of Electrodiagnostic Medicine

Rochester, NY

Outside Counsel/Consultants

Jenner & Block

American Ass'n of Engineering Societies

1111 19th St. NW
Suite 403
Washington, DC 20036
Tel: (202)296-2237
Fax: (202)296-1151
Registered: LDA
Web: www.aaes.org
E-mail: cblue@aaes.org

Federation of engineering societies representing more than 1,000,000 U.S. engineers in matters of public policy and public awareness. U.S. representative to the World Federation of Engineering Organizations.

Leg. Issues: BUD, DEF, ENV, GOV, SCI, TAX

In-house, DC-area Employees

BLUE, Chuck: Director, Communications and Public Awareness
JONES, Thomas: Director, Public Policy
MURRAY, Melissa R.: Public Policy Associate
PRICE, Thomas J.: Exec. Director

American Ass'n of Enterprise Zones

4717 Girton Ave.
Shady Side, MD 20764
Tel: (202)466-2687
Fax: (202)318-1103
E-mail: rhcowden@aol.com

In-house, DC-area Employees

COWDEN, Dick: Exec. Director

Outside Counsel/Consultants

Vorys, Sater, Seymour and Pease, LLP

American Ass'n of Entrepreneurs

1156 15th St. NW
Washington, DC 20005
Tel: (202)822-0180
Fax: (202)659-3029
Leg. Issues: SMB

Political Action Committee/s

American Ass'n of Entrepreneurs Federal PAC (ENTPAC)
1156 15th St. NW
Washington, DC 20005
Tel: (202)822-0180
Fax: (202)659-3029
Contact: James J. Albertine

In-house, DC-area Employees

ALBERTINE, James J.: Contact, Political Action Committee

Outside Counsel/Consultants

Albertine Enterprises, Inc.
Issues: SMB
Rep By: James J. Albertine, Dr. John M. Albertine, Aubrey C. King

American Ass'n of Exporters & Importers

New York, NY

Outside Counsel/Consultants

Barnes, Richardson and Colburn
Rep By: Matthew T. McGrath

American Ass'n of Eye and Ear Hospitals

Washington, DC
Web: www.aaeeh.com
E-mail: rbetz@aaeeh.org
Leg. Issues: MMM

Outside Counsel/Consultants

Robert Betz Associates, Inc.
Issues: MMM
Rep By: Robert B. Betz

American Ass'n of Family and Consumer Sciences

1555 King St.
Alexandria, VA 22314
Tel: (703)706-4600
Fax: (703)706-4663
Web: www.aafcs.org
E-mail: staff@aafcs.org

In-house, DC-area Employees

COLLINS CHADWICK, Ann: Director

American Ass'n of Family Physicians

Outside Counsel/Consultants

Greer, Margolis, Mitchell, Burns & Associates
Rep By: David E. Mitchell, J. Toscano

American Ass'n of Fastener Importers

Sayreville, NJ

Outside Counsel/Consultants

Barnes, Richardson and Colburn
Rep By: Matthew T. McGrath

American Ass'n of Grain Inspection and Weighing Agencies

Washington, DC
Web: www.agrwashington.com
E-mail: agriwash@aol.com
Leg. Issues: AGR

Outside Counsel/Consultants

Agri/Washington
Issues: AGR
Rep By: Andrea Ball, Jon Moore, Paul S. Weller, Jr.

American Ass'n of Health Care Administrative Management

Washington, DC
Web: www.aaham.org

Outside Counsel/Consultants

Smith, Bucklin and Associates, Inc.

American Ass'n of Health Plans (AAHP)

1129 20th St. NW
Suite 600
Washington, DC 20036-3421
Tel: (202)778-3200
Fax: (202)778-8508
Registered: LDA
Web: www.aahp.org

The merger of Group Health Ass'n of America and the American Managed Care and Review Ass'n formed AAHP. AAHP is a national trade association representing HMOs, PPOs, and similar network health plans.

Leg. Issues: CSP, HCR, INS, MED, MMM, PHA

Political Action Committee/s

HEALTH PLAN PAC (of AAHP)
1129 20th St. NW
Suite 600
Washington, DC 20036-3421
Tel: (202)778-3200
Fax: (202)778-8508

In-house, DC-area Employees

BIGGERT, Adrienne: Washington Representative
BOCCHINO, Carmella A.: Medical Director
DENNETT, Diana: Exec. V. President
GOON, Julie: V. President, Government Affairs
GORMAN, Tori: Director, Policy and Research
IGNAGNI, Karen M.: President and Chief Exec. Officer
LAMB, Tony: Director, Political Affairs
MERRITT, Mark: V. President and Chief, Strategic Planning and Public Affairs
PISANO, Susan: V. President, Communications
POMFRET, Jacqueline M.: Director, Legislative Affairs
REICHEL, Randi: Exec. Director, State Affairs
SCHALLER, Candy K.: V. President, Regulatory Affairs
SMITH, Rick: V. President, Public Policy and Research

Outside Counsel/Consultants

Clark & Weinstock, Inc.
Issues: HCR
Rep By: Ed Kutler, Deirdre Stach, Sandi Stuart, Hon. John Vincent "Vin" Weber

Crowell & Moring LLP
Issues: CSP, MED
Rep By: Mark A. Behrens, Leah Lorber, Victor E. Schwartz

The Direct Impact Co.

The Duberstein Group, Inc.
Issues: HCR, MED
Rep By: John W. Angus, III, Michael S. Berman, Steven M. Champlin, Kenneth M. Duberstein, Henry M. Gandy, Daniel P. Meyer

Mark W. Goodin
Issues: HCR
Rep By: Mark W. Goodin

Greenberg Traurig, LLP
Issues: HCR, INS, MMM
Rep By: Howard J. Cohen

American Ass'n of Healthcare Consultants

11208 Waples Mill Rd.
Suite 109
Fairfax, VA 22030
Tel: (703)691-2242
Fax: (703)691-2247
Web: www.aahc.net
E-mail: info@aahc.net

In-house, DC-area Employees

SMITH, Vaughan A.: President

American Ass'n of Homeopathic Pharmacists

Southeastern, PA

Outside Counsel/Consultants

Mintz, Levin, Cohn, Ferris, Glovsky and Popeo, P.C.

American Ass'n of Homes and Services for the Aging

2519 Connecticut Ave. NW
Washington, DC 20008-1520
Tel: (202)783-2242
Fax: (202)783-2255
Registered: LDA
Web: www.aahsa.org
E-mail: info@aahsa.org

The national ass'n of not-for-profit organizations dedicated to providing quality housing, health, community, and related services to the elderly.

Leg. Issues: BUD, GOV, HCR, HOU, IMM, INS, LBR, MED, MMM, TAX

In-house, DC-area Employees

BLOOM, Colleen C.: Housing Policy Analyst
BRUNO, William B.: Director, Congressional Affairs
CLOUD, Deborah: V. President, Communications
COUCH, Linda: Associate Director
GAY, Barbara L.: Director, Information
MCNICKLE, Larry: Director, Housing Policy
MINNIX, William L.: President and Chief Exec.
MUNLEY, Evelyn Fieman: Health Policy Analyst
PERES, Judith Rae: Director, Health Policy
POLNIASZEK, Susan E.: Reimbursement Policy Specialist
WEISS, Suzanne: Senior V. President, Advocacy

Outside Counsel/Consultants

Clark & Weinstock, Inc.
Issues: BUD, GOV, HCR, HOU, IMM, INS, LBR, MED, MMM, TAX
Rep By: Hon. Vic H. Fazio, Jr., Ed Kutler, Sandi Stuart, Sandra Swirski, Anne Urban, Hon. John Vincent "Vin" Weber

American Ass'n of Immunologists

9650 Rockville Pike
Bethesda, MD 20814-3994
Tel: (301)530-7178
Fax: (301)571-1816
Web: www.aai.org
E-mail: infoaai@aai.faseb.org

A professional association representing research scientists in immunology and related disciplines.

Leg. Issues: MED

In-house, DC-area Employees

GROSS, Lauren: Director, Public Policy and Government Affairs

American Ass'n of Law Libraries

E.B. Williams Law Library
Georgetown University Law Center
111 G St. NW
Washington, DC 20001-1417
Tel: (202)662-9200
Fax: (202)662-9202
Registered: LDA
Web: www.aallnet.org

An association headquartered in Chicago, IL providing education and professional support for law libraries.

Leg. Issues: BUD, CPT, GOV, TEC

In-house, DC-area Employees

BAISH, Mary Alice: Associate Washington Affairs Representative
OAKLEY, Robert L.: Washington Affairs Representative

American Ass'n of Limited Partners

Washington, DC
Leg. Issues: FIN, TAX

Outside Counsel/Consultants

O'Bryon & Co.
Issues: FIN, TAX
Rep By: David S. O'Bryon

American Ass'n of Motor Vehicle Administrators

4301 Wilson Blvd.
Suite 400
Arlington, VA 22203-1861
Tel: (703)522-4200
Fax: (703)522-1553
Web: www.aamva.org

An education association that promotes reasonable and uniform laws and regulations governing registration, certification of ownership, operation of motor vehicles, and the issuance of motor vehicle drivers' licenses. Promotes highway safety programs and efficient administration of state and provincial government programs. Membership consists of U.S., Canadian and Mexican state, provincial, and territorial motor vehicle and law enforcement agencies, and private companies engaged in providing services to motor vehicle and law enforcement agencies.

Leg. Issues: ALC, BUD, CAW, CON, CSP, ENV, IMM, IND, INS, LAW, ROD, RRR, SCI, TAX, TRA, TRU, WEL

In-house, DC-area Employees

LEWIS, Linda R.: President and Chief Exec. Officer
PETER, Brendan M.: Director, Government Affairs

American Ass'n of Museums

1575 I St. NW
Suite 400
Washington, DC 20005
Tel: (202)289-1818
Fax: (202)289-6578
Registered: LDA
Web: www.aam-us.org
Leg. Issues: ART, BAN, CPT, EDU, FOR, IND, SCI, TAX, TEC, TOU

In-house, DC-area Employees

ABLE, Jr., Edward H.: President and Chief Exec. Officer
FAULS, Brian J.: Senior Legislative Assistant
HALL, Jason Y.: Director, Government and Public Affairs
SCHULZE, Nichole A.: Government and Public Affairs Specialist
SZCZESNY, Barry G.: Assistant Director, Government Affairs Counsel

American Ass'n of Naturopathic Physicians

Seattle, WA
Web: www.naturopathic.org
Leg. Issues: HCR

Outside Counsel/Consultants

Lee Bechtel and Associates
Issues: HCR
Rep By: Lee Bechtel

American Ass'n of Neurological Surgeons/Congress of Neurological Surgeons

725 15th St. NW
Suite 800
Washington, DC 20005
Tel: (202)628-2072
Fax: (202)628-5264
Registered: LDA
Web: www.neurosurgery.org
E-mail: korrico@neurosurgery.org

Headquartered in Rolling Meadows, IL.

Leg. Issues: BUD, HCR, LBR, MED, MMM

Political Action Committee/s

American Neurological Surgery PAC
P.O. Box 136
Washington, DC 20044-0136
Tel: (202)628-1996

In-house, DC-area Employees

ORRICO, Kate O.: Director, Washington Office
SHOAF, Mary L.: Senior Washington Associate

American Ass'n of Nurse Anesthetists

412 First St. SE
Suite 12
Washington, DC 20003
Tel: (202)484-8400
Fax: (202)484-8408
Registered: LDA

Headquartered in Park Ridge, IL.

Leg. Issues: BUD, HCR

Political Action Committee/s

American Ass'n of Nurse Anesthetists PAC
412 First St. SE
Suite 12
Washington, DC 20003
Tel: (202)484-8400
Fax: (202)484-8408
Contact: Elisa Brewer

In-house, DC-area Employees

BREWER, Elisa: Political Action Coordinator
HEBERT, David E.: Director, Federal Government Affairs
PUGH, Kristen: Director, Federal Government Affairs
PURCELL, Frank J.: Director, Federal Government Affairs

Outside Counsel/Consultants

Fierce and Isakowitz
Issues: HCR
Rep By: Kathryn Braden, Samantha Cook, Donald L. Fierce, Mark W. Isakowitz, Diane Moery

Hall, Green, Rupli, LLC
Issues: HCR
Rep By: John M. Green, G. Stewart Hall

Jones, Walker, Waechter, Poitevent, Carrere & Denegre, L.L.P.
Issues: BUD, HCR
Rep By: Paul Cambon, John J. Jaskot, R. Christian Johnsen

The Livingston Group, LLC
Issues: BUD, HCR
Rep By: Melvin Goodweather, Hon. Robert L. Livingston, Jr., J. Allen Martin, Richard L. Rodgers

PriceWaterhouseCoopers
Issues: HCR
Rep By: Kirt C. Johnson, Kenneth J. Kies, Pat Raffaniello

Ricchetti Inc.

Tongour Simpson Holsclaw Green
Issues: HCR
Rep By: John Bradley "Brad" Holsclaw, Michael A. Tongour

American Ass'n of Occupational Health Nurses

Atlanta, GA
Leg. Issues: HCR, LBR

Outside Counsel/Consultants

Arent Fox Kintner Plotkin & Kahn, PLLC
Issues: HCR, LBR
Rep By: Bill Applegate, Douglas McCormack, Larri A. Short, Allison Shuren, Robert J. Waters

American Ass'n of Oral and Maxillofacial Surgeons

Rosemont, IL — Registered: LDA
Leg. Issues: HCR

Outside Counsel/Consultants

Covington & Burling
Issues: HCR
Rep By: Roderick A. DeArment, Joan L. Kutcher

American Ass'n of Orthodontists

St. Louis, MO
Leg. Issues: HCR, POS

Outside Counsel/Consultants

Haake and Associates
Issues: HCR, POS
Rep By: Timothy M. Haake, Nathan M. Olsen

American Ass'n of Pastoral Counselors

9504A Lee Hwy. — Tel: (703)385-6967
Fairfax, VA 22031-2303 — Fax: (703)352-7725
Web: www.aapc.org
E-mail: info@aapc.org

Organized in 1963 to ensure standards for the practice of pastoral counseling. An international, interfaith organization of professional pastoral counselors, parish clergy and other mental health professionals. Seeks to advance understanding of the mind-spirit connection.

Leg. Issues: HCR

In-house, DC-area Employees

WOODRUFF, Ph.D., C. Roy: Exec. Director

American Ass'n of Pharmaceutical Scientists

2107 Wilson Blvd. — Tel: (703)243-2800
Suite 700 — Fax: (703)243-9650
Arlington, VA 22201-3042
Web: www.aapspharmaceutica.com
E-mail: aaps@aaps.org
Leg. Issues: BUD, HCR

In-house, DC-area Employees

COX, CAE, John B.: Exec. Director

Outside Counsel/Consultants

Health and Medicine Counsel of Washington
Issues: BUD, HCR
Rep By: Staci Sigman Dennison, Dale P. Dirks

Shaw Pittman

American Ass'n of Physician Specialists

Leg. Issues: VET

Outside Counsel/Consultants

Arent Fox Kintner Plotkin & Kahn, PLLC
Issues: VET
Rep By: Edith Hambrick, Robert J. Waters, Todd Weiss

American Ass'n of Physicians of Indian Origin

Oakbrook Terrace, IL
Leg. Issues: FOR, HCR, MED

Outside Counsel/Consultants

Conlon, Frantz, Phelan & Pires
Issues: FOR, HCR, MED
Rep By: Anurag Varma

American Ass'n of Physics Teachers

One Physics Ellipse — Tel: (301)209-3300
College Park, MD 20740-3845 — Fax: (301)209-0845
Web: www.aapt.org
E-mail: aapt-exec@aapt.org

Founded in 1930 with the fundamental goal of ensuring the dissemination of the knowledge of physics; currently has over 11,000 members.

Leg. Issues: EDU, SCI

In-house, DC-area Employees

HEIN, Dr. Warren: Associate Exec. Officer
KHOURY, Dr. Bernard V.: Exec. Officer

American Ass'n of Political Consultants

600 Pennsylvania Ave. SE — Tel: (202)544-9815
Suite 330 — Fax: (202)544-9816
Washington, DC 20003
Web: www.theaapc.org
E-mail: info@theaapc.org

In-house, DC-area Employees

ALLMAN, Tracey: Exec. Director

American Ass'n of Port Authorities

1010 Duke St. — Tel: (703)684-5700
Alexandria, VA 22314-3589 — Fax: (703)684-6321
Registered: LDA
Web: www.aapa-ports.org
E-mail: info@aapa-ports.org
Leg. Issues: ENV, MAR, TAX, TRA, TRD

In-house, DC-area Employees

DENNE, Eileen E.: Director, Public Relations
GODWIN, Jean C.: Exec. V. President and General Counsel
NAGLE, Kurt: President and Chief Exec. Officer
O'CONNELL, Ed: Director, Membership Services
TURNER, Susan: Director, Government Relations
WILL, Mary Beth: Representative, Government Relations

American Ass'n of Preferred Provider Organizations

601 Pennsylvania Ave. NW — Tel: (202)220-3111
Suite 900 — Fax: (202)220-3112
South Bldg.
Washington, DC 20004
Web: www.aappo.org

Headquartered in Jeffersonville, IN.

Political Action Committee/s

American Ass'n of Preferred Provider Organizations PAC

601 Pennsylvania Ave. NW — Tel: (202)220-3111
Suite 900 — Fax: (202)220-3112
South Bldg.
Washington, DC 20004

Outside Counsel/Consultants

Dittus Communications
Rep By: Jennifer Garfinkel, Chris McNamara

Fierce and Isakowitz
Rep By: Mark W. Isakowitz

American Ass'n of Private Railroad Car Owners, Inc.

421 New Jersey Ave. SE — Tel: (202)547-5696
Washington, DC 20003 — Fax: (202)547-5623
Web: www.aaprco.com

In-house, DC-area Employees

ELLIOTT, M. Diane: Exec. Director

American Ass'n of Public Health Dentistry

Portland, OR
Leg. Issues: HCR

Outside Counsel/Consultants

Cavarocchi Ruscio Dennis Associates
Issues: HCR
Rep By: Nicholas G. Cavarocchi

American Ass'n of Residential Mortgage Regulators

1255 23rd St. NW — Tel: (202)452-8100
Suite 200 — Fax: (202)833-3636
Washington, DC 20037-1174

In-house, DC-area Employees

MURPHY, Christopher M.: Exec. Director

Outside Counsel/Consultants

Hauck and Associates
Rep By: Christopher M. Murphy

American Ass'n of School Administrators

1801 N. Moore St. — Tel: (703)528-0700
Arlington, VA 22209 — Fax: (703)528-2146
Registered: LDA
Web: www.aasa.org
E-mail: info@aasa.org
Leg. Issues: EDU

In-house, DC-area Employees

ADAMS-TAYLOR, Sharon: Director, Children's Initiatives
ARFSTROM, Kari: Project Director, Rural/Small Schools
CROSS, Jordan: Legislative Specialist
HOUSTON, Paul: Exec. Director
HUNTER, Bruce: Senior Associate Exec. Director
PENNING, Nicholas J.: Senior Legislative Analyst
SCHNEIDER, E. Joseph: Deputy Exec. Director
SELTZ, Judy: Director, Planning and Communications

American Ass'n of State Colleges and Universities

1307 New York Ave. — Tel: (202)293-7070
Fifth Floor — Fax: (202)296-5819
Washington, DC 20005-4701
Web: www.aascu.org
E-mail: info@aascu.org

Membership organization of public colleges and universities and university systems.

In-house, DC-area Employees

CHILCOTT, Susan: Director, Communications
CURRIS, Constantine: President
ELMENDORF, Edward M.: V. President, Government Relations

American Ass'n of State Highway and Transportation Officials

444 N. Capitol St. NW — Tel: (202)624-5800
Suite 249 — Fax: (202)624-5806
Washington, DC 20001
Web: www.aashto.org

In-house, DC-area Employees

HORSLEY, John: Exec. Director
OAKLEY, Janet: Director, Government Relations
SCHUST, Sunny Mays: Director, Communications and Publications

American Ass'n of Tissue Banks

1350 Beverly Rd. — Tel: (703)827-9582
Suite 220A — Fax: (703)356-2198
McLean, VA 22101
Web: www.aatb.org
E-mail: aatb@aatb.org

A scientific, non-profit peer group organization founded in 1976 to facilitate the provision of transplantable tissues of uniform high quality in quantities sufficient to meet national needs.

Leg. Issues: HCR

In-house, DC-area Employees

MOWE, Jeanne C.: Exec. Director
RIGNEY, P. Robert: Chief Exec. Officer

American Ass'n of University Affiliated Programs for Persons with Developmental Disabilities

8630 Fenton St. — Tel: (301)588-8252
Suite 410 — Fax: (301)588-2842
Silver Spring, MD 20910 — Registered: LDA
Web: www.aauap.org

A member organization of the Coalition for Health Funding in Washington.

Leg. Issues: BUD, EDU, HCR

In-house, DC-area Employees

JESIEN, George: Exec. Director
MELTZER, Donna Ledder: Director, Legislative Affairs

American Ass'n of University Professors

1012 14th St. NW — Tel: (202)737-5900
Suite 500 — Fax: (202)737-5526
Washington, DC 20005 — Registered: LDA
Web: www.aaup.org
Leg. Issues: CIV, CPT, EDU, SCI

In-house, DC-area Employees

FLOWER, Ruth L.: Director, Government Relations
MOLOTSKY, Iris F.: Director, Public Relations
SMITH, Mark F.: Associate Director, Government Relations

American Ass'n of University Women

1111 16th St. NW — Tel: (202)785-7793
Washington, DC 20036-4873 — Fax: (202)466-7618
Registered: LDA
Web: www.aauw.org
E-mail: info@aauw.org

An organization of 150,000 members working in over 1,500 communities. Works for the advancement of women and their transformations of American society. Current priorities include gender equity in education, reproductive choice, social security, and workplace and civil rights issues.

Leg. Issues: BUD, CIV, ECN, EDU, FAM, HCR, LBR, MMM, WEL

In-house, DC-area Employees

BERNARD, Sandy: President
BUCHMAN, Ellen: Field Director
PUESCHEL, Jamie: Manager, Government Relations
WOODS, Jacqueline E.: Exec. Director
ZIRKIN, Nancy M.: Director of Public Policy and Government Relations

American Ass'n of University Women Legal Advocacy Fund

Outside Counsel/Consultants

Garrett Yu Hussein LLC

American Ass'n on Mental Retardation

444 N. Capitol St. NW
Suite 846
Washington, DC 20001-1512
Web: www.aamr.org
Tel: (202)387-1968
Fax: (202)387-2193

In-house, DC-area Employees

CROSER, M. Doreen: Exec. Director

American Astronautical Soc.

6352 Rolling Mill Pl.
Suite 102
Springfield, VA 22152-2354
Web: www.astronautical.org
E-mail: aas@astronautical.org
Tel: (703)866-0020
Fax: (703)866-3526

A professional scientific and technical group dedicated to the advancement of space science and exploration.

Leg. Issues: AER, SCI

Political Action Committee/s

Public Policy Committee
6352 Rolling Mill Pl.
Suite 102
Springfield, VA 22152-2354
Contact: Marc Johansen
Tel: (703)866-0020
Fax: (703)866-3526

In-house, DC-area Employees

JOHANSEN, Marc: V. President, Public Policy
KIRKPATRICK, James R.: Exec. Director

American Astronomical Soc.

2000 Florida Ave. NW
Suite 400
Washington, DC 20009
Tel: (202)328-2010
Fax: (202)234-2560
Registered: LDA
Web: www.aas.org
E-mail: aas@aas.org
Leg. Issues: BUD, EDU, SCI

In-house, DC-area Employees

MARVEL, Ph.D., Kevin B.: Associate Officer, Public Policy
MILKEY, Dr. Robert: Exec. Officer

American Automar

Bethesda, MD
Leg. Issues: DEF

Outside Counsel/Consultants

The Gallagher Group, LLC
Issues: DEF
Rep By: James P. Gallagher

American Automobile Ass'n

1440 New York Ave. NW
Suite 200
Washington, DC 20005
Tel: (202)942-2050
Fax: (202)783-4798
Registered: LDA

Headquartered in Heathrow, FL.

Leg. Issues: AVI, CAW, COM, GOV, IMM, LBR, TEC, TOU, TRA

In-house, DC-area Employees

INGRASSIA, Jill: Manager, Congressional Relations
MARVASO, Kathleen: Managing Director
PIKRALLIDAS, Susan G.: V. President, Public and Government Relations
PLAUSHIN, Christopher: Manager, Regulatory Affairs
SRAMEK, Helen: Director, Federal Relations
WILLIAMS, Mantill: Director, Washington Public Relations

American Automotive Leasing Ass'n

Washington, DC
E-mail: amautolsg@aol.com

Represents the commercial automotive fleet leasing and management industry.

Leg. Issues: CAW, ENG, ENV

Outside Counsel/Consultants

Policy Consulting Services
Issues: CAW, ENG, ENV
Rep By: Paul C. Smith

SEDERHOLM Public Affairs, Inc.
Rep By: Pamela Sederholm

American Bakers Ass'n

1350 I St. NW
Suite 1290
Washington, DC 20005
Tel: (202)789-0300
Fax: (202)898-1164
Registered: LDA
Web: www.americanbakers.org
Leg. Issues: AGR, BUD, CAW, DEF, ENG, ENV, FOO, GOV, LBR, TAX, TRD, TRU

Political Action Committee/s

BREAD Political Action Committee
1350 I St. NW
Suite 1290
Washington, DC 20005
Contact: Paul Abenante
Tel: (202)789-0300
Fax: (202)898-1164

In-house, DC-area Employees

ABENANTE, Paul: President and Chief Exec. Officer
GIESECKE, Anne: V. President, Environmental Activities
MACKIE, II, Robb S.: V. President, Government Relations
SANDERS, Celetta Lee: V. President, Regulatory and Technical Services

Outside Counsel/Consultants

G.R. Services
Rep By: Earl Eisenhart

Littler Mendelson, P.C.
Issues: LBR
Rep By: Peter A. Susser

Swidler Berlin Shereff Friedman, LLP
Rep By: Barry B. Direnfeld, James Hamilton

Valis Associates
Issues: CAW, ENV, FOO, LBR, TRD
Rep By: Todd Tolson, Wayne H. Valis

American Bankers Ass'n

1120 Connecticut Ave. NW
Washington, DC 20036
Tel: (202)663-5000
Fax: (202)828-4548
Registered: LDA
Web: www.aba.com
Leg. Issues: AGR, BAN, BNK, BUD, CDT, EDU, FIN, GOV, HOU, INS, LAW, MON, POS, RET, SMB, TAX, TRD

Political Action Committee/s

American Bankers Ass'n BankPac
1120 Connecticut Ave. NW
Washington, DC 20036
Tel: (202)663-5000
Fax: (202)828-4548

In-house, DC-area Employees

BALLENTINE, James: Director, Center for Community Development
BARAN, Mark: Senior Tax Counsel
BLANCHFIELD, John: Director, Center for Agricultural and Rural Banking
BLEIER, Lisa: Senior Counsel
BLOCKLIN, Peter: Senior, Federal Legislative Representative-Senate Manager
BUTTERFIELD, Kristin: Associate Director, Grassroots
BYRNE, John J.: Senior Counsel and Compliance Manager
CAUSEY, Dawn: Director, Financial Institution Affairs, and Counsel
CHESSEN, James: Chief Economist and Group Director
CLAYTON, Kenneth J.: Chief Legislative Counsel
CLIMO, Beth L.: Exec. Director, ABA Securities Association and ABA Insurance Association
DAVIES, Dionne: Senior Federal Legislative Representative
DEAN, Virginia: Exec. Director, Communications
EARLY, Kerry P.: Associate Director, Washington Information
FEDDIS, Nessa E.: Senior Federal Counsel
FISHER, Donna J.: Director, Tax and Accounting
FOUBERG, Robert J.: Senior Counsel
GILL, John J.: General Counsel
GLAZA, Gordon: Regulatory Counsel
KOZLOW, Bess: Assistant Director, Grassroots
MCELLIGOTT, Tom: Program Manager, Washington Information
MCLAUGHLIN, James D.: Director, Regulatory and Trust Affairs
MILLER, Sarah: Director, Center for Securities, Trust and Investment
MULLINS, Geoff: Program Manager, Grassroots
NASER, Cristeena G.: Senior Counsel
OGILVIE, Donald G.: Exec. V. President
PEACE, Jr., J. Leon: Senior Counsel, Tax Legislation
PIGG, Joseph: Senior Counsel
RASMUS, John R.: Senior Federal Administrative Counsel
RAYMOND, Sharon: Director, Grassroots Programs and Washington Information
SHANNON, Deborah: Senior Federal Legislative Representative - House Manager
SMITH, Paul A.: Senior Federal Administrative Counsel
STONER, Floyd E.: Deputy Exec. Director, Government Relations
WATSON, Alison: Senior Federal Legislative Representative
YINGLING, Edward L.: Deputy Exec. V. President and Exec. Director, Government Relations

Outside Counsel/Consultants

Bergner Bockorny Castagnetti and Hawkins
Issues: BAN
Rep By: Jeffrey T. Bergner, David A. Bockorny, David Castagnetti, Melissa Schulman

Butera & Andrews
Issues: BNK
Rep By: Philip S. Corwin

Cashdollar-Jones & Co.
Issues: AGR
Rep By: Robert Cashdollar

Covington & Burling
Issues: FIN
Rep By: John C. Dugan

LaRocco & Associates
Issues: BAN, BNK, BUD, CDT, FIN, INS, SMB
Rep By: Hon. Lawrence P. LaRocco, Matthew LaRocco

American Bankruptcy Institute

44 Canal Center Plaza
Suite 404
Alexandria, VA 22314
Web: www.abiworld.org
E-mail: info@abrworld.org
Tel: (703)739-0800
Fax: (703)739-1060

A professional association of 7,800 attorneys, accountants, educators and others focusing on bankruptcy reorganization and insolvency matters.

Leg. Issues: BNK

In-house, DC-area Employees

GERDANO, Samuel J.: Exec. Director

American Bar Ass'n

740 15th St. NW
Ninth Floor
Washington, DC 20005
Tel: (202)662-1000
Fax: (202)662-1032
Registered: LDA
Web: www.abanet.org

Headquartered in Chicago, IL.

Leg. Issues: BNK, BUD, CIV, CON, CPI, CPT, EDU, ENV, FAM, FIR, FOR, GOV, HCR, HOU, IMM, INS, LAW, MMM, REL, RES, RET, TAX, TOR, TRA, TRD

In-house, DC-area Employees

CARDMAN, Denise A.: Senior Legislative Counsel
DRISCOLL, Kevin J.: Senior Legislative Counsel
EVANS, Robert D.: Associate Exec. Director
FRISBY, R. Larson: Legislative Counsel
GAINES, Kristi: Legislative Counsel
GASKIN, Lillian B.: Senior Legislative Counsel
GOLDSMITH, Kenneth: Staff Director, State Legislation
GREGORY, Hayden W.: Consultant
KAULBACK, Laura: Legislative Assistant
KUMBALA-FRASER, Mondi: Legislative Counsel
MCBARNETTE, Ellen: Legislative Counsel
NICHOLSON, E. Bruce: Legislative Counsel
STRANDLIE, Julie: Director, Grassroots Operations
WISE, Gail Alexander: Staff Director, Public Relations

American Bearing Manufacturers Ass'n

Washington, DC
Web: www.abma-dc.org
E-mail: abma@dc.sba.com

Outside Counsel/Consultants

Smith, Bucklin and Associates, Inc.
Rep By: Scott Lynch, David Rohn

American Beekeeping Federation

Jesup, GA
Leg. Issues: AGR, BUD, TRD

Outside Counsel/Consultants

Collier Shannon Scott, PLLC
Rep By: Michael J. Coursey

Meyers & Associates
Issues: AGR, BUD, TRD
Rep By: Fran Boyd, Larry D. Meyers, Richard L. Meyers

American Benefits Council

1212 New York Ave. NW
Suite 1250
Washington, DC 20005-3987
Tel: (202)289-6700
Fax: (202)289-4582
Registered: LDA
Web: www.americanbenefitscouncil.org
E-mail: info@abcstaff.org

Formerly known as the Ass'n of Private Pension and Welfare Plans.

Leg. Issues: HCR, RET, TAX

Political Action Committee/s

Americn Benefits Council PAC
1212 New York Ave. NW
Suite 1250
Washington, DC 20005-3987
Tel: (202)289-6700
Fax: (202)289-4582

In-house, DC-area Employees

DELAPLANE, James: V. President, Retirement Policy
DENNETT, Paul W.: V. President, Health Policy

GHAZAL, Maria M.: Director, Health Policy
KLEIN, James A.: President
SCOTT, John C.: Director, Retirement Policy

Outside Counsel/Consultants

Caplin & Drysdale, Chartered
Issues: RET, TAX
Rep By: Kent A. Mason

Davis & Harman LLP
Issues: RET, TAX
Rep By: Randolf H. Hardock

Groom Law Group, Chartered
Issues: HCR, RET
Rep By: Jon W. Breyfogle

American Beverage Institute

Washington, DC
Web: www.abionline.org
E-mail: abi@abionline.org
Leg. Issues: BEV, TRA

Outside Counsel/Consultants

Berman and Company
Issues: BEV
Rep By: Richard B. Berman

Ann Eppard Associates, Ltd.
Issues: TRA
Rep By: Julie Chlopecki, Ann Eppard

American Bioenergy Ass'n

Washington, DC
Leg. Issues: BUD, ENG, FUE, SCI

Outside Counsel/Consultants

Katherine Hamilton
Issues: BUD, ENG, FUE, SCI
Rep By: Katherine Hamilton

American Biophysics Corp.

East Greenwich, RI
Leg. Issues: SCI

Outside Counsel/Consultants

Capitol City Group
Issues: SCI
Rep By: Gerald T. Harrington, John J. Hogan, Thomas P. Hogan, Christopher P. Vitale

American Bird Conservancy

1250 24th St. NW
Suite 400
Washington, DC 20037
Tel: (202)778-9666
Fax: (202)778-9778
Registered: LDA
Web: www.abcbird.org
Leg. Issues: ANI

In-house, DC-area Employees

WINEGRAD, Gerald W.: V. President, Policy

American Board for Certification in Orthotics and Prosthetics, Inc. (ABC)

350 John Carlyle St.
Suite 200
Alexandria, VA 22314
Tel: (703)836-7114
Fax: (703)836-0838
Web: www.opoffice.org/abc
E-mail: opcertmail@opoffice.org

The ABC is the largest and most experienced credentialing organization for orthotic and prosthetic practitioners and facilities in the United States. Our organization has adopted rigorous education, clinical and testing requirements for providers of orthotic and prosthetic services and the highest organizational and safety standards for provider facilities available in the profession. Certification and accreditation by ABC assures provision of the highest quality of care of orthotic and prosthetic services.

In-house, DC-area Employees

DALY, Abbe: Director, Marketing
HOXIE, Lance: Exec. Director

American Board of Adolescent Psychiatry

Leg. Issues: HCR, MED

Outside Counsel/Consultants

PAI Management Corp.
Issues: HCR, MED
Rep By: Norman E. Wallis, Ph.D.

American Board of Health Physics

E-mail: abhpburkmgt@aol.com

Outside Counsel/Consultants

Burk & Associates
Rep By: Richard J. Burk, Jr.

American Board of Medical Specialties in Podiatry

Leg. Issues: GOV

Outside Counsel/Consultants

Halsey, Rains & Associates, LLC
Issues: GOV
Rep By: Steven C. Halsey, James Hubbard, Laurie D. Rains

American Board of Opticianry

6506 Lois Dale Rd.
Suite 209
Springfield, VA 22150
Tel: (703)719-5800
Fax: (703)719-9144
Web: www.abo-ncle.org

In-house, DC-area Employees

ROBEY, Michael: Exec. Director

American Board of Pain Medicine

Skokie, IL

Outside Counsel/Consultants

Jenner & Block

American Board of Trial Advocates

Encino, CA

Outside Counsel/Consultants

Edington, Peel & Associates, Inc.
Rep By: William H. Edington

American Boiler Manufacturers Ass'n

4001 North 9th St.
Suite 226
Arlington, VA 22203-1900
Tel: (703)522-7350
Fax: (703)522-2665
Registered: LDA
Web: www.abma.com
E-mail: abma@abma.com

An association of commercial, industrial, power-generating and heat-recovery boiler and fuel burning equipment manufacturers, as well as suppliers to the industry. Promotes common business interests of the industry and communicates with government in areas of mutual interest.

Leg. Issues: BUD, CAW, CSP, ECN, ENG, ENV, LBR, MAN, SCI, SMB, TAX, TRA, TRD, TRU, UTI

In-house, DC-area Employees

RAWSON, W. Randall: V. President

Outside Counsel/Consultants

Webster, Chamberlain & Bean
Rep By: Hugh K. Webster

American Booksellers Ass'n

Tarrytown, NY

Outside Counsel/Consultants

Jenner & Block

American Bureau of Shipping

1421 Prince St.
Suite 200
Alexandria, VA 22314
Tel: (703)519-0801
Fax: (703)519-1898
Registered: LDA
Leg. Issues: MAR

In-house, DC-area Employees

ASHE, Glenn M.: Director

Outside Counsel/Consultants

Gerald A. Malia
Issues: MAR
Rep By: Gerald A. Malia

American Bus Ass'n

1100 New York Ave. NW
Suite 1050
Washington, DC 20005
Tel: (202)842-1645
Fax: (202)842-0850
Registered: LDA
Web: www.buses.org
E-mail: abainfo@buses.org

Represents the intercity bus industry in its relations with the Congress, other elements of the transportation industry and the government. Formerly Nat'l Ass'n of Motor Bus Owners.

Leg. Issues: ROD, TAX, TOU, TRA

Political Action Committee/s

BUSPAC-Political Action Committee of the American Bus Ass'n
1100 New York Ave. NW
Suite 1050
Washington, DC 20005
Tel: (202)842-1645
Fax: (202)842-0850
Contact: Clyde J. Hart, Jr.

In-house, DC-area Employees

BRODERICK, Kelly: Legislative Assistant
DARR, Linda Bauer: V. President, Policy and External Affairs
HART, Jr., Clyde J.: V. President, Government Affairs
MAHORMEY, William: Director, Safety and Regulatory Programs
PANTUSO, Peter J.: President and Chief Exec. Officer

Outside Counsel/Consultants

Bracewell & Patterson, L.L.P.
Issues: TAX
Rep By: Michael L. Pate

F/P Research Associates
Issues: TAX
Rep By: Ronald Crawford

Zuckert, Scoutt and Rasenberger, L.L.P.
Issues: ROD, TAX, TOU, TRA
Rep By: Richard P. Schweitzer

American Business Conference

1730 K St. NW
Suite 1200
Washington, DC 20006
Tel: (202)822-9300
Fax: (202)467-4070
Registered: LDA
Web: www.americanbusinessconference.org

An organization limited to the Chief Executive Officers of midsize, high growth companies.

Leg. Issues: EDU, FIN, TAX, TRD

In-house, DC-area Employees

ENDEAN, Jr., Howard John: V. President, Policy
ROGSTAD, Barry K.: President

Outside Counsel/Consultants

Piper Marbury Rudnick & Wolfe LLP
Rep By: Philip F. Zeidman

American Business for Legal Immigration

Washington, DC
Leg. Issues: IMM

Outside Counsel/Consultants

Dittus Communications
Rep By: Trudi Boyd, Gloria S. Dittus

Janus-Merritt Strategies, L.L.C.
Issues: IMM
Rep By: Scott P. Hoffman, Bethany Noble

American Business Is Local Enterprise

Leg. Issues: TAX

Outside Counsel/Consultants

Sunrise Research Corp.
Issues: TAX
Rep By: Hon. Bob Packwood

American Business Media

New York, NY
Leg. Issues: CPT, POS

Outside Counsel/Consultants

Evans & Black, Inc.
Issues: CPT, POS
Rep By: Rae Forker Evans, Rafe Morrissey

Thompson Coburn LLP
Issues: POS
Rep By: David Straus

American Butter Institute

2101 Wilson Blvd.
Suite 400
Arlington, VA 22201
Tel: (703)243-5630
Fax: (703)841-9328
Web: www.butterinstitute.org
E-mail: aminer@nmpf.org

Represents manufacturers, packagers and distributors of butter and butter products.

Leg. Issues: CSP, ECN, FOO, TRD

In-house, DC-area Employees

KOZAK, Jerome J.: Exec. Director
MINER, Anuja: Program Administrator

American Cable Ass'n

Pittsburgh, PA
Registered: LDA
Leg. Issues: COM, CPT, GOV, SMB, TEC

Outside Counsel/Consultants

Alpine Group, Inc.
Issues: COM, CPT, GOV, SMB, TEC
Rep By: James Gregory Means, Rhod M. Shaw, Monica Skopec

American Camping Ass'n

Leg. Issues: AGR, CSP, EDU, IMM, IRA, NAT, TAX

Outside Counsel/Consultants

APCO Worldwide
Issues: AGR, CSP, EDU, IMM, IRA, NAT, TAX
Rep By: Danielle Ringwood

American Cancer Soc.

701 Pennsylvania Ave. NW
Suite 650
Washington, DC 20004
Tel: (202)661-5700
Fax: (202)661-5750
Registered: LDA
Web: www.cancer.org

Headquartered in Atlanta, GA, the ACS is the nationwide community-based health organization dedicated to eliminating cancer as a major health problem by preventing cancer, saving lives, and diminishing suffering from cancer, through research, education, advocacy, and service.

Leg. Issues: BUD, FOO, HCR, MED, MMM, TAX, TOB

In-house, DC-area Employees

CHAPMAN, Bob: Director, Operations
DOCANTO, Licy: Manager, Special Populations/Medically Underserved
GORDON, Megan: Manager, Federal Government Relations
LIEBERMAN, Unice B.: Director, Communications and Media Advocacy
ROUVELAS, Mary: Legislative Counsel
SELIG, Wendy: Managing Director, Federal Government Relations
SMITH, Daniel E.: National V. President, Federal and State Government Relations
WILLIAMS, Christine K.: Manager, Federal Government Affairs
WINICK, Seth: Managing Director, Advocacy Field Operations

Outside Counsel/Consultants

John L. Bloom
Issues: TOB
Rep By: John L. Bloom

The Sheridan Group
Issues: BUD
Rep By: Thomas F. Sheridan, James R. Wetekam

American Cast Iron Pipe Co.

Birmingham, AL
Leg. Issues: BUD

Outside Counsel/Consultants

Law Office of Edward D. Heffernan
Issues: BUD

American Center for Law and Justice

1650 Diagonal Rd.
Fifth Floor
Alexandria, VA 22314
Tel: (703)740-1450
Fax: (703)837-8510
Web: www.aclj.com

In-house, DC-area Employees

HENDERSON, Sr., James M.: Senior Counsel
SEKULOW, Jay Alan: Chief Counsel

American Ceramics Soc.

Washington, DC
Leg. Issues: ENV, SCI

Outside Counsel/Consultants

Navista, Inc.
Issues: ENV, SCI
Rep By: John Flatley

Strat@Comm (Strategic Communications Counselors)
Issues: SCI

American Chamber of Commerce Executives

4232 King St.
Alexandria, VA 22302
Tel: (703)998-0072
Fax: (703)931-5624
Web: www.acce.org
E-mail: info-request@acce.org

In-house, DC-area Employees

KLAHR, Pamela: V. President, Marketing
MULCKHUYSE, Marlies: V. President, Marketing and Association Development
PHILBIN, Tamara: V. President, Management Information Services
WHELAN, Edward: V. President, Benefits Services

American Chamber of Commerce in Egypt

Dokki, EGYPT
Leg. Issues: FOR

Outside Counsel/Consultants

Cassidy & Associates, Inc.
Issues: FOR
Rep By: Gregory M. Gill

American Chamber of Commerce in Germany

Frankfurt, GERMANY

Outside Counsel/Consultants

Squire, Sanders & Dempsey L.L.P.
Rep By: Ritchie T. Thomas

American Chemical Soc.

1155 16th St. NW
Washington, DC 20036
Tel: (202)872-4600
Fax: (202)872-4615
Registered: LDA
Web: www.acs.org
Leg. Issues: BUD, CHM, EDU, ENV, GOV, HCR, RET, SCI

In-house, DC-area Employees

CRUM, John: Exec. Director
DANIEL, David A.: Assistant Exec. Director and Chief Administrative Officer
DOUGHERTY, Brian J.
GERUM, Laura M.
GRAVELINE, Denise T.: Director, Communications
LEWIS, Flint H.: Director, Government Relations and Assistant Secretary
MERRELL, Halley A.: Assistant Exec. Director and Secretary
SCHUTT, David: Assistant Director, Government Relations
TRUPP GIL, Caroline M.

American Chemistry Council

1300 Wilson Blvd.
Arlington, VA 22209
Tel: (703)741-5000
Fax: (703)741-6000
Registered: LDA
Web: www.AmericanChemistry.com

Represents chemical manufacturers with operations in the U.S. and Canada. The Association brings together member company experts to help resolve public policy, technical and scientific problems. It communicates with government and the public and administers research studies and tests on chemical products and practices.

Leg. Issues: BUD, CAW, CHM, ENG, ENV, LAW, LBR, TAX, TRA, TRD, WAS

Political Action Committee/s

American Chemistry Council Political Action Committee (AmeriChem PAC)
1300 Wilson Blvd.
Arlington, VA 22209
Tel: (703)741-5936
Fax: (703)741-6097
Contact: Edward L. Murphy

In-house, DC-area Employees

BERNHARD, Mary E.: Director
BOUDRIAS, Claude P.: Director
CANAVAN, Colin: Coordinator, Federal Relations
FLAGG, Robert B.: Senior Director, Federal Relations
GOTTLIEB, Brian: Manager
GRIFFITH, Gary W.: Director
HOWLETT, Jr., C. T. "Kip": V. President, Chlorine Chemistry Council
KELLY, Kerry: Director
MCVANEY, Jim: Director
MURPHY, Edward L.: Senior Director, Grassroots and Political Activities
NELSON, Mark D.: V. President, Federal Relations
SANDERS, Rose Marie: Director
VAN VLACK, Charles W.: Exec. V. President and Chief Operating Officer
WEBBER, Frederick L.: President and Chief Exec. Officer
WILKINS, Timothy C.: Director, Grassroots
WINKELMAN, Eileen M.: Director

Outside Counsel/Consultants

Bracewell & Patterson, L.L.P.
Issues: CHM, ENV, TAX, TRD
Rep By: Hon. Edwin R. Bethune, Michael L. Pate

Hogan & Hartson L.L.P.
Issues: CHM
Rep By: Christine M. Warnke

Holland & Knight LLP
Issues: ENV
Rep By: Robert Hunt Bradner, Jack M. Burkman, Mike Galano, Richard M. Gold, Hon. Thomas F. Railsback, Janet R. Studley, P. J. Toker, David C. Whitestone

Millian Byers Associates, LLC
Rep By: H. James Byers, Kenneth Y. Millian

Bob Moss Associates
Issues: TRA
Rep By: Bob Moss

Nat'l Environmental Strategies
Issues: CHM
Rep By: Marc I. Himmelstein

Ogilvy Public Relations Worldwide
Rep By: Jon Wentzel

Van Ness Feldman, P.C.
Issues: TRA
Rep By: Margaret A. Moore, Thomas C. Roberts, Robert G. Szabo

American Chiropractic Ass'n

1701 Clarendon Blvd.
Arlington, VA 22209
Tel: (703)276-8800
Fax: (703)243-2593
Registered: LDA
Web: www.amerchiro.org
E-mail: MEMBERINFO@amerchiro.org

A national membership association representing the majority of licensed doctors of chiropractic in the United States.

Leg. Issues: HCR, INS, MED, MMM

Political Action Committee/s

American Chiropractic Ass'n Political Action Committee
1701 Clarendon Blvd.
Arlington, VA 22209
Tel: (703)276-8800
Fax: (703)243-2593

In-house, DC-area Employees

BURGESS-SMITH, Leslie: Director, Political Action Committee
CLANCY, Felicity Feather: V. President, Communications
CUNEO, Garrett: Exec. V. President
DE MARTINEZ, Julie Warner: V. President, Member Services
JACKSON, Patricia: V. President, Professional Development and Research
KAPLAN, Jim: Director, Political Action Committee
LUSIS, Ingrid: Director, Government Relations
WITTER, Jay: V. President, Government Relations

Outside Counsel/Consultants

Capitol Partners
Issues: MED
Rep By: Jonathan M. Orloff

Miller & Co.
Issues: HCR
Rep By: Richard W. Miller

Odin, Feldman, & Pittleman, P.C.
Issues: HCR, INS, MMM
Rep By: Thomas R. Daly

American Citizens Abroad

1051 N. George Mason Dr.
Arlington, VA 22205
Tel: (703)276-0949
Fax: (703)527-3269
E-mail: jacabr@aol.com

In-house, DC-area Employees

ABRAMS, Jacqueline M.: Director

American Citizens for the Arts Political Action Committee

Washington, DC

Outside Counsel/Consultants

Duncan and Associates
Rep By: Jack G. Duncan

American Civil Liberties Union

122 Maryland Ave. NE
Washington, DC 20002
Tel: (202)544-1681
Fax: (202)546-0738
Registered: LDA
Web: www.aclu.org

Headquartered in New York, NY.

Leg. Issues: CIV, CPI, FAM, HCR, TEC

In-house, DC-area Employees

ANDERS, Christopher: Legislative Counsel, Gay and Lesbian Issues
JOHNSON, Marvin: Legislative Counsel, Free Speech
KING, Rachel C.: Legislative Counsel, Criminal Justice
MURPHY, Laura W.: Director, Washington National Office
NOJEIM, Gregory T.: Associate Director and Chief Legislative Counsel
RUST-TIERNEY, Diann: Director, Death Penalty
SCHROEDER, Terri: Legislative Representative, Religious Freedom Issues

Outside Counsel/Consultants

Wilmer, Cutler & Pickering
Issues: CIV, FAM, HCR
Rep By: Sheila C. Cheston

Zuckerman Spaeder L.L.P.
Issues: CIV, CPI, TEC
Rep By: Ronald H. Weich

American Civil Liberties Union of the Nat'l Capital Area

1400 20th St. NW
Suite 119
Washington, DC 20036
Tel: (202)457-0800
Fax: (202)452-1868
Web: www.aclu-nca.org

Headquartered in New York, NY, the ACLU accepts civil liberties complaints by mail. Through a screening process will agree to represent qualified applicants at no charge. Recruits lawyers for specific cases on a voluntary basis. This office only deals with matters in Washington D.C., and Montgomery and Prince George's Counties in Maryland.

Leg. Issues: CIV

In-house, DC-area Employees
BARNES, Johnny: Exec. Director
SPITZER, Arthur: Legal Director

American Classic Voyages Co.

Chicago, IL
Leg. Issues: MAR

Outside Counsel/Consultants

Preston Gates Ellis & Rouvelas Meeds LLP
Issues: MAR
Rep By: Darrell Conner, Bruce J. Heiman, William N. Myhre, Emanuel L. Rouvelas

American Clinical Laboratory Ass'n

1250 H St. NW
Suite 880
Washington, DC 20005
Tel: (202)637-9466
Fax: (202)637-2050
Registered: LDA

ACLA represents the nation's largest state, local and regional independent laboratories.

Leg. Issues: HCR

Political Action Committee/s

American Clinical Laboratory Ass'n Political Action Committee
1250 H St. NW
Suite 880
Washington, DC 20005
Contact: JoAnne Glisson
Tel: (202)637-9466
Fax: (202)637-2050

In-house, DC-area Employees
GLISSON, JoAnne: V. President, Government Relations
SUNDWALL, M.D., David N.: President

Outside Counsel/Consultants

Mintz, Levin, Cohn, Ferris, Glovsky and Popeo, P.C.
Rep By: Peter M. Kazon

American Clinical Neurophysiology Soc.

Bloomfield, CT
Leg. Issues: MMM

Outside Counsel/Consultants

MARC Associates, Inc.
Issues: MMM
Rep By: Ellen Riker

American Coalition for Filipino Veterans

2500 Massachusetts Ave. NW
Washington, DC 20008
Tel: (202)246-1998
Fax: (301)963-1720
Registered: LDA
E-mail: ericlachica@msn.com

Leg. Issues: VET

In-house, DC-area Employees
LACHICA, Eric: Exec. Director

American Coastal Coalition

Washington, DC
Leg. Issues: BUD, NAT

Outside Counsel/Consultants

Marlowe and Co.
Issues: BUD, NAT
Rep By: Howard Marlowe, Jeffrey Mazzella

American Cocoa Research Institute

7900 Westpark Dr.
Suite A-320
McLean, VA 22102
Web: www.candyusa.org
Tel: (703)790-5011
Fax: (703)790-5752

The research institution of the Chocolate Manufacturers Ass'n of the U.S.A.

In-house, DC-area Employees
GLOWAKY, Ph.D., Raymond: Senior V. President, Scientific and Regulatory Affairs
GRAHAM, Lawrence T.: President

American Coke and Coal Chemicals Institute

1255 23rd St. NW
Suite 200
Washington, DC 20037-1174
Web: www.accci.org
Tel: (202)452-1140
Fax: (202)833-3636

Represents coke producers on regulatory and legislative issues and provides forum for international exchange.

Leg. Issues: ENV

In-house, DC-area Employees
SAUNDERS, David A.: President

Outside Counsel/Consultants

Dyer Ellis & Joseph, P.C.
Issues: ENV
Rep By: Laurie Crick Sahatjian, Jeanne Marie Grasso, Lara Bernstein Mathews, Duncan C. Smith, III, Jennifer M. Southwick, Sidney A. Wallace

Hauck and Associates
Rep By: David C. Ailor, David A. Saunders

Shaw Pittman
Rep By: David E. Menotti

American Collectors Ass'n

Minneapolis, MN
Leg. Issues: BAN, BNK

Outside Counsel/Consultants

Royer & Babyak
Issues: BAN
Rep By: Robert Stewart Royer

Stein, Mitchell & Mezines

Valente Lopatin & Schulze
Issues: BNK
Rep By: Alan G. Lopatin

American College of Cardiology

9111 Old Georgetown Rd.
Bethesda, MD 20814
Tel: (301)897-2692
Fax: (301)897-8757
Registered: LDA
Web: www.acc.org
E-mail: bgreen@acc.org

Leg. Issues: HCR, INS, MED, MMM, TOB

In-house, DC-area Employees
COLLISHAW, Karen: Associate Exec. V. President, Advocacy
GREENAN, Barbara: Director, Legislative Affairs
JACKSON, Ph.D., Marcia: Senior Associate Exec. V. President, Education
MCENTEE, Christine: Exec. V. President
MILLS, Penny: Senior Associate Exec. V. President, Strategy, Finance, and Operations
SOROSIAK, Camille: Associate Director, Legislative Affairs

Outside Counsel/Consultants

The Legislative Strategies Group, LLC
Issues: HCR
Rep By: Martin B. Gold, Denise M. Henry

American College of Chest Physicians

Northbrook, IL
Registered: LDA
Leg. Issues: BUD, HCR, MED, MMM, TOB

Outside Counsel/Consultants

GRQ, Inc.
Issues: HCR, MMM
Rep By: Patricia Booth, Phillip Porte

Mintz, Levin, Cohn, Ferris, Glovsky and Popeo, P.C.
Issues: BUD, HCR, MED, MMM, TOB
Rep By: Raymond D. Cotton

American College of Clinical Pharmacy

1101 Pennsylvania Ave. NW
Suite 700
Washington, DC 20004-2514
Tel: (202)756-2227
Fax: (202)756-7506
Registered: LDA
Web: www.accp.com
E-mail: ewebb@accp.com

Headquartered in Kansas City, MO.

Leg. Issues: HCR, MED, MMM, PHA, SCI

In-house, DC-area Employees
WEBB, C. Edwin: Director, Government and Professional Affairs

American College of Construction Lawyers

1030 15th St. NW
Suite 870
Washington, DC 20005
Tel: (202)638-3906
Fax: (202)393-0336

In-house, DC-area Employees
KENNY, Lynn: Exec. Director

Outside Counsel/Consultants

The Kellen Company
Rep By: Lynn Kenny

American College of Dentists

839 Quince Orchard Blvd.
Suite J
Gaithersburg, MD 20878
Web: www.acdentists.org
E-mail: saralls@facd.org
Tel: (301)977-3223
Fax: (301)977-3330

In-house, DC-area Employees
RALLS, Dr. Stephen A.: Exec. Director

American College of Emergency Physicians

2121 K Street NW
Suite 325
Washington, DC 20037
Tel: (202)728-0610
Fax: (202)728-0617
Registered: LDA
Web: www.acep.org

Headquartered in Dallas, Texas.

Leg. Issues: HCR, MED, MMM

Political Action Committee/s

Nat'l Emergency Medicine PAC
2121 K Street NW
Suite 325
Washington, DC 20037
Contact: Mark V. Cribben
Tel: (202)728-0610
Fax: (202)728-0617

In-house, DC-area Employees
CRIBBEN, Mark V.: Political Action Director
GORE, Laura: Director, Public Relations
HORN, Colleen: Manager, Public Relations
WHEELER, Gordon B.: Director, Public Affairs and Washington, DC Office

Outside Counsel/Consultants

Health Policy Alternatives, Inc.
Issues: HCR
Rep By: Richard Lauderbaugh

Jenner & Block
Rep By: Robert M. Portman

American College of Gastroenterology

4900-B South 31st. St.
Arlington, VA 22206
Tel: (703)820-7400
Fax: (703)931-4520
Registered: LDA
Web: www.acg.gi.org

The address given is that of the firm Ass'n and Government Relations Management, Inc.

Leg. Issues: HCR, MMM

Political Action Committee/s

Gastro Intestinal PAC (GIPAC)
4900-B South 31st. St.
Arlington, VA 22206
Contact: Deane A. Penn
Tel: (703)820-7400
Fax: (703)931-4520

In-house, DC-area Employees
FISE, Thomas F.: Exec. Director
PENN, Deane A.: PAC Contact

Outside Counsel/Consultants

Ass'n and Government Relations Management, Inc.
Rep By: Thomas F. Fise

McDermott, Will and Emery
Rep By: Calvin P. Johnson, Michael A. Romansky

Patton Boggs, LLP
Issues: HCR, MMM
Rep By: John F. Jonas, Martha M. Kendrick, Elizabeth E. Ring, JoAnn V. Willis

American College of Health Care Administrators

1800 Diagonal Rd.
Alexandria, VA 22314
Web: www.achca.org
E-mail: info@achca.org
Tel: (703)739-7900
Fax: (703)739-7901

The national professional society for long-term care administrators.

Leg. Issues: HCR

In-house, DC-area Employees
TUCKER, CAE, Karen S.: President and Chief Exec. Officer

American College of Healthcare Executives

Chicago, IL
Web: www.ache.org
E-mail: geninfo@ache.org

Outside Counsel/Consultants

Jenner & Block

American College of Nuclear Physicians

Outside Counsel/Consultants

Mintz, Levin, Cohn, Ferris, Glovsky and Popeo, P.C.

American College of Nurse Practitioners

503 Capitol Ct. NE
Suite 300
Washington, DC 20002
Web: www.nurse.org/acnp
E-mail: acnp@acnp.nurse.org
Tel: (202)546-4825
Fax: (202)546-4797

Mission is to unite and represent nurse practitioners across the United States.

Leg. Issues: HCR, MMM

In-house, DC-area Employees
SCHERS, Eric: Director

Outside Counsel/Consultants
Arent Fox Kintner Plotkin & Kahn, PLLC
Issues: HCR, MMM
Rep By: Bill Applegate, Stacy Harbison, Allison Shuren, Robert J. Waters

American College of Nurse-Midwives
818 Connecticut Ave. NW
Suite 900
Washington, DC 20006
Tel: (202)728-9860
Fax: (202)728-9897
Registered: LDA
Web: www.midwife.org
E-mail: info@acnm.org
Leg. Issues: HCR

Political Action Committee/s
Midwives PAC
P.O. Box 65111
Washington, DC 20037
Contact: Patricia Burkhardt

In-house, DC-area Employees
BURKHARDT, Patricia: PAC Administrator
FENNELL, Karen S.: Senior Policy Analyst
HARPS, Gina: Manager, Marketing/Public Relations
SILVER, Larry: Policy Analyst
WILLIAMS, Deanne R.: Exec. Director

Outside Counsel/Consultants
Cooney & Associates, Inc.
Rep By: Patrick J. Cooney
Feldesman, Tucker, Leifer, Fidell & Bank

American College of Obstetricians and Gynecologists
409 12th St. SW
P.O. Box 96920
Washington, DC 20090-6920
Tel: (202)863-2511
Fax: (202)488-3985
Registered: LDA
Web: www.acog.org

A non-profit membership organization of obstetricians and gynecologists.

Leg. Issues: FAM, GOV, HCR, IND, INS, MED, MMM, SCI, TOR

Political Action Committee/s
Physicians for Women's Health PAC
409 12th St. SW
P.O. Box 96920
Washington, DC 20090-6920
Tel: (202)863-2510
Fax: (202)488-3985
Contact: Lucia DiVenere

In-house, DC-area Employees
DARBOUZE, Farrah: Legislative Assistant
DIVENERE, Lucia: Manager, Federal Government Relations
HALE, M.D., Ralph: Exec. V. President
HESSBURG, Laura: Senior Federal Government Relations Representative
MARANO, Alyson: Grassroots Representative
MCKINNEY, Dawn: Senior Legislative Assistant
MURPHY, Penny: Director, Communications
SIMON, Marsha: Director, Government Relations and Outreach

American College of Occupational and Environmental Medicine
Arlington Heights, IL
Leg. Issues: HCR, LBR

Outside Counsel/Consultants
Kent & O'Connor, Inc.
Issues: HCR, LBR
Rep By: Patrick C. O'Connor

American College of Osteopathic Pediatricians
5550 Friendship Blvd.
Suite 300
Chevy Chase, MD 20815-7201
Tel: (301)968-4180
Fax: (301)968-4199
Web: www.aoha.org
E-mail: acop@osteohdq.org

In-house, DC-area Employees
KUSHNER, David L.: Exec. Director

American College of Osteopathic Surgeons
123 N. Henry St.
Alexandria, VA 22314-2903
Tel: (703)684-0416
Fax: (703)684-3280
Registered: LDA
Web: www.facos.org
E-mail: gbeaumont@theacos.org

Has over 1,800 members and represents osteopathic surgeons practicing in the specialities of general surgery, orthopedic surgery, urology, cardiothoracic and vascular surgery, neurosurgery, and plastic and reconstructive surgery.

Leg. Issues: BUD, HCR, MED, MMM

In-house, DC-area Employees
BEAUMONT, Guy D.: Exec. Director

Outside Counsel/Consultants
Hogan & Hartson L.L.P.
Issues: BUD, MED
Rep By: Laura E. Loeb

American College of Physicians-American Soc. of Internal Medicine (ACP-ASIM)
2011 Pennsylvania Ave. NW
Suite 800
Washington, DC 20006-1808
Tel: (202)261-4500
Fax: (202)835-0443
Registered: LDA
Web: acponline.org

Focuses on social, economic, and political developments that affect the practice of internal medicine. Formed by the merger of American College of Physicians and American Soc. of Internal Medicine. Headquartered in Philadelphia, PA.

Leg. Issues: BUD, HCR, MED, MMM

In-house, DC-area Employees
BAKER, Brett: Associate, Third Party Relations and Regulatory Affairs
BLASER, Robert: Senior Associate, Congressional Relations
CUNNINGHAM, Carl: Director, Competitiveness Advisory Services
DOHERTY, Robert B.: Senior V. President, Division of Governmental Affairs and Public Policy
DUMOULIN, John: Director, Managed Care and Regulatory Affairs
GINSBURG, Jack: Director, Health Policy Analysis and Research
GORDEN, Mark: Senior Associate, Managed Care and Regulatory Affairs
JENKINS, Jennifer: Associate, Grassroots Advocacy
OTT, Jim: Director, Operations
PREWITT, Elizabeth: Director, Governmental Affairs and Public Policy
SCHRIVER, Melinda L.: Associate, Public Policy
TRACHTMAN, Richard L.: Director, Congressional Affairs

American College of Preventive Medicine
1307 New York Ave. NW
Suite 200
Washington, DC 20005
Tel: (202)466-2044
Fax: (202)466-2662
Web: www.acpm.org
E-mail: info@acpm.org

A national professional society for physicians committed to disease prevention and health promotion. Seeks to advance the science and practice of preventive medicine by providing educational opportunities for its members, advocating public policies consistent with scientific principles of the discipline, and other activities.

Leg. Issues: HCR, MED, TOB

In-house, DC-area Employees
BARRY, Michael: Director, Public Affairs
RICHLAND, MPH, Jordan H.: Exec. Director

American College of Radiation Oncology
Oak Brook, IL
Leg. Issues: HCR

Outside Counsel/Consultants
Shaw Pittman
Issues: HCR
Rep By: Andrew L. Woods

American College of Radiology
1891 Preston White Dr.
Reston, VA 20191-9312
Tel: (703)648-8900
Fax: (703)262-9312
Web: www.acr.org
E-mail: info@acr.org
Leg. Issues: HCR, MMM

Political Action Committee/s
RADPAC
1891 Preston White Dr.
Reston, VA 20191-9312
Tel: (703)648-8900
Fax: (703)262-9312
Contact: Melanie Young

In-house, DC-area Employees
COOPER, Joshua: Director, Congressional Relations
CURRY, John J.: Exec. Director
ROSSER, Ann W.: Assistant Exec. Director
SHORT, Bradley W.: Director, Member Development and Chapter Relations
SHOWALTER, Charles: Senior Director, Government Relations
YOUNG, Melanie: Director, Radiology Advocacy Alliance

Outside Counsel/Consultants
J. T. Rutherford & Associates
Issues: HCR, MMM
Rep By: Deanna D. Lavanty, Donald F. Lavanty

American College of Rheumatology
Atlanta, GA
Leg. Issues: HCR, MMM

Outside Counsel/Consultants
Medical Advocacy Services, Inc.
Issues: HCR, MMM
Rep By: Robert Blaser, Holly Owen

American College of Sports Medicine
Indianapolis, IN

Outside Counsel/Consultants
Baker & Daniels
Rep By: Frank S. Swain

American College of Surgeons
1640 Wisconsin Ave. NW
Washington, DC 20007
Tel: (202)337-2701
Fax: (202)337-4271
Registered: LDA
Web: www.facs.org
E-mail: postmaster@facs.org

A voluntary educational and scientific organization headquartered in Chicago, IL. Established in 1913 to raise the standards of surgical practice and to improve the care of the surgical patient; has over 60,000 Fellows in this country and abroad.

Leg. Issues: HCR, INS, MED, MMM

In-house, DC-area Employees
BROWN, Cynthia A.: Interim Director, Health Policy and Advocacy Department
GALLAGHER, Christopher R.: Senior Government Affairs Associate
HARRIS, Jean A.: Regulatory and Coding Specialist
ROBERTS, Adrienne: Government Affairs Associate
SHALGIAN, Christian: Senior Government Affairs Associate

American College of Tax Counsel
1030 15th St. NW
Suite 870
Washington, DC 20005
Tel: (202)393-1780
Fax: (202)393-0336

In-house, DC-area Employees
KENNY, Lynn: Administrator

Outside Counsel/Consultants
The Kellen Company
Rep By: Lynn Kenny

American College Personnel Ass'n
One Dupont Circle NW
Suite 300
Washington, DC 20036-1110
Tel: (202)835-2272
Fax: (202)296-3286
Web: www.acpa.nche.edu
E-mail: info@acpa.nche.edu

The mission of ACPA is to serve student affairs professionals through the Association's programs, publications and services which are renowned for their focus on student learning, research, current issues and trends in higher education.

In-house, DC-area Employees
NEUBERGER, Ed.D., J.D, Carmen G.: Exec. Director

American Committee for Peace and Justice in South Asia
Laurel, MD
Leg. Issues: FOR

Outside Counsel/Consultants
Patton Boggs, LLP
Issues: FOR
Rep By: Katharine R. Boyce, Lanny J. Davis

American Committee for the Weizmann Institute of Science
1730 Rhode Island Ave. NW
Suite 409
Washington, DC 20036
Tel: (202)293-6883
Fax: (202)293-1753
Registered: LDA
Web: www.weizmann.ac.il
E-mail: dc@acwis.org
Leg. Issues: FOR

In-house, DC-area Employees
CHOTIN, Elizabeth E.: Director, Government Relations

Outside Counsel/Consultants
Powell, Goldstein, Frazer & Murphy LLP
Issues: FOR
Rep By: Michael E. Fine, Elizabeth Johns Howard

American Commodity Distribution Ass'n
New Smyrna Beach, FL
Leg. Issues: AGR, BUD

Outside Counsel/Consultants

Olsson, Frank and Weeda, P.C.
Issues: AGR, BUD
Rep By: John W. Bode, Susan P. Grymes, Karen Reis Harned, Stephen L. Lacey, Marshall L. Matz, Tyson Redpath

American Competitiveness Institute

Plymouth Meeting, PA
Leg. Issues: DEF

Outside Counsel/Consultants

Cortese PLLC
Issues: DEF
Rep By: Alfred W. Cortese, Jr.

American Concrete Pavement Ass'n (ACPA)

The above address is that of TerraCom-Strategic Communications.

Leg. Issues: AUT, ROD, TAX, TRA

Outside Counsel/Consultants

Baker & Hostetler LLP
Issues: TRA
Rep By: Frederick H. Graefe

Baker, Donelson, Bearman & Caldwell, P.C.
Rep By: Linda Hall Daschle

The Carmen Group
Issues: AUT, ROD, TAX, TRA
Rep By: Ann D. Warner

Edmund C. Graber
Issues: TRA
Rep By: Edmund C. Graber

TerraCom-Strategic Communications

American Concrete Pipe Ass'n

Irving, TX

Outside Counsel/Consultants

Obadal and MacLeod, p.c.
Rep By: Anthony J. Obadal

American Congress of Community Supports and Employment Services

Washington, DC Registered: LDA

A non-profit association created to support activities of the providers of vocational and community rehabilitation facilities.

Leg. Issues: HCR, MMM

Outside Counsel/Consultants

Powers Pyles Sutter & Verville, PC
Issues: HCR, MMM
Rep By: Peter W. Thomas

American Congress on Surveying and Mapping

Six Montgomery Village Ave.
Suite 403
Gaithersburg, MD 20879-3557
Tel: (240)632-9716
Fax: (240)632-1321
Registered: LDA
Leg. Issues: GOV

Political Action Committee/s

ACSM-NSPS Political Action Committee

Six Montgomery Village Ave.
Suite 403
Gaithersburg, MD 20879-3557
Tel: (240)632-9716
Fax: (240)632-1321
Contact: Susan Frank

In-house, DC-area Employees

FRANK, Susan: PAC Contact
SUMNER, Curtis: Exec. Director

American Conservative Union

1007 Cameron St.
Alexandria, VA 22314
Tel: (703)836-8602
Fax: (703)836-8606
Registered: LDA
Web: www.conservative.org
E-mail: acu@conservative.org

A lobbying organization with a membership of approximately 1,100,000; composed of people from all walks of life. Engages in political activity at the national level to advance conservative interests and views.

Political Action Committee/s

American Conservative Union Political Action Committee

1007 Cameron St.
Alexandria, VA 22314
Tel: (703)836-8602
Fax: (703)836-8606

In-house, DC-area Employees

JOSI, Christian: Exec. Director
KEENE, David A.

American Consulting Engineers Council

1015 15th St. NW
Suite 802
Washington, DC 20005
Tel: (202)347-7474
Fax: (202)898-0068
Registered: LDA
Web: www.acec.org
E-mail: acec@acec.org
Leg. Issues: AVI, BUD, CAW, CSP, ENV, GOV, HCR, LBR, ROD, SCI, SMB, TAX, TOR, TRA, TRD, URB, UTI, WAS

Political Action Committee/s

American Consulting Engineers Council Political Action Committee

1015 15th St. NW
Suite 802
Washington, DC 20005
Tel: (202)347-7474
Fax: (202)898-0068

In-house, DC-area Employees

BAJER, Ed: Director, Energy and Interprofessional Programs
BAKER, Emily A.: Deputy Director, Environmental Programs/EBAC
BANCROFT, David B.: Director, Environmental Programs/EBAC
BROWNE, Crystal M.: Administrative Assistant, Government Affairs
CARNEY, John: Director, Transportation and Infrastructure
FLEENOR, Camille: Director, Procurement Programs and Federal Markets
HERRING, Lee: Director, Public Affairs
KALAVRITINOS, Jack: Director, Government Affairs and General Counsel
KEENEY, Andrea: Webmaster
KERN, Thomas E.: Deputy Exec. V. President, Operations
KOURY, Kate: Director, Liability and Regulatory Affairs
MOORE, Michele: Assistant Director, International Affairs
PUVAK, Ken: Director, International Department
RAYMOND, David A.: Exec. V. President, and C.E.O.
SMITH, Glenore: Director, International Department
WALLEM, Kate: Director, Liability and Regulatory Affairs

Outside Counsel/Consultants

Akin, Gump, Strauss, Hauer & Feld, L.L.P.
Issues: GOV, SMB, TAX, TRA, WAS
Rep By: Marlene M. Colucci, Barney J. Skladany, Jr.

Shaw Pittman

Valis Associates
Issues: ENV, GOV, LBR, TOR
Rep By: Jennifer Conti, Hon. Richard T. Schulze, Todd Tolson, Wayne H. Valis

American Consumers for Affordable Homes

Outside Counsel/Consultants

O'Melveny and Myers LLP
Rep By: Gary N. Horlick

Public Affairs Resources, Inc.
Rep By: Susan E. Petniunas

American Corn Growers Ass'n

Washington, DC
Leg. Issues: AGR, TAX

Outside Counsel/Consultants

David Senter & Associates
Issues: AGR, TAX
Rep By: Billy Senter, David L. Senter

American Corporate Counsel Ass'n

1025 Connecticut Ave. NW
Suite 200
Washington, DC 20036
Tel: (202)293-4103
Fax: (202)293-4701
Web: www.acca.com

A bar association serving the diversified needs of in-house counsel.

Leg. Issues: CPT, ENV, FIN, INS, LAW, TOR

In-house, DC-area Employees

BRACKEN, Ann: V. President
HACKETT, Susan J.: Senior V. President and General Counsel
KREBS, Frederick J.: President and Chief Operating Officer
PHAH, Quan: Contact

American Correctional Ass'n

4380 Forbes Blvd.
Lanham, MD 20706-4322
Tel: (301)918-1800
Fax: (301)918-1900
Registered: LDA
Web: www.corrections.com/aca
E-mail: debbis@aca.org

A professional association representing all levels of corrections.

Leg. Issues: LAW

In-house, DC-area Employees

GONDLES, Jr., CAE, James A.: Exec. Director
TURPIN, Jim: Legislative Liaison

American Cotton Shippers Ass'n

1725 K St. NW
Suite 1404
Washington, DC 20006
Tel: (202)296-7116
Fax: (202)659-5322
Registered: LDA
Web: www.acsa-cotton.org
E-mail: acsa-mem-wmay@worldnet.att.net
Leg. Issues: AGR

Political Action Committee/s

Committee Organized for the Trading of Cotton (COTCO)

1725 K St. NW
Suite 1404
Washington, DC 20006
Tel: (202)296-7116
Fax: (202)659-5322
Contact: Neal P. Gillen

In-house, DC-area Employees

CRAWFORD, Rebecca B.
GILLEN, Neal P.: Exec. V. President and General Counsel
SMITH, Martha: Director, Congressional Relations

American Council for an Energy-Efficient Economy

1001 Connecticut Ave. NW
Suite 801
Washington, DC 20036
Tel: (202)429-8873
Fax: (202)429-2248
Registered: LDA
Web: www.aceee.org
E-mail: info@aceee.org

A non-profit research organization which gathers, evaluates, and disseminates information to stimulate use of energy-efficient technologies and policies.

Leg. Issues: ENG

In-house, DC-area Employees

GELLER, Howard S.: Exec. Director
LANGER, Therese: Senior Associate
NADEL, Steve: Exec. Director

Outside Counsel/Consultants

Potomac Resources, Inc.
Rep By: Edward R. Osann

American Council for Capital Formation

1750 K St. NW
Suite 400
Washington, DC 20006-2300
Tel: (202)293-5811
Fax: (202)785-8165
Registered: LDA
Web: www.accf.org
E-mail: info@accf.org

A non-profit, tax-exempt organization established in 1973. Seeks to eliminate the bias in the tax code against saving and investment. Maintains economic education programs to encourage public awareness of capital formation issues and advocates policy changes that would increase saving and investment.

Leg. Issues: ENV, TAX

In-house, DC-area Employees

BLOOMFIELD, Mark A.: President
DUNN, Mari Lee: Senior V. President
THORNING, Dr. Margo: Senior V. President and Chief Economist

American Council of Independent Laboratories

1629 K St. NW
Suite 400
Washington, DC 20006
Tel: (202)887-5872
Fax: (202)887-0021
Web: www.acil.org
E-mail: info@acil.org

ACIL is the national trade association of independent scientific and engineering laboratory, testing, R&D and consulting firms. Serves the interests of its members, their clients, and the public by promoting high standards of business practice and sound scientific and economic policy through education and advocacy.

Leg. Issues: AUT, CAW, CHM, COM, CSP, ENV, FOO, GOV, LBR, PHA, ROD, SCI, SMB, TEC, TRA

Political Action Committee/s

American Council of Independent Laboratories PAC

1629 K St. NW
Suite 400
Washington, DC 20006
Tel: (202)887-5872
Fax: (202)887-0021
Contact: Joan Walsh Cassedy

In-house, DC-area Employees

CASSEDY, Joan Walsh: Exec. Director

American Council of Korean Travel Agents

Torrance, CA
Leg. Issues: CSP, FOR, GAM, IMM, TOU, TRD

Outside Counsel/Consultants

R. J. Hudson Associates
Issues: CSP, FOR, GAM, IMM, TOU, TRD

American Council of Life Insurers

1001 Pennsylvania Ave. NW
Washington, DC 20004-2599
Tel: (202)624-2000
Fax: (202)624-2319
Registered: LDA
Web: www.acli.com

A national trade association that represents the interests of legal reserve life insurance companies in legislative, regulatory and judicial matters at the federal, state and municipal levels of government and at the NAIC. Its member companies hold the overwhelming majority of the life insurance in force in the United States.

Leg. Issues: BAN, BNK, CIV, DEF, EDU, ENV, FAM, FIN, FOR, GOV, HCR, INS, LAW, LBR, REL, RET, TAX, TOR, TRD

Political Action Committee/s

American Council of Life Insurers Political Action Committee (LifePAC)

1001 Pennsylvania Ave. NW
Washington, DC 20004-2599
Tel: (202)624-2000
Fax: (202)624-2319

In-house, DC-area Employees

ANDERSON, Philmore B.: V. President, Federal Relations
ARNETT, Angela: Senior Counsel
BATES, Douglas P.: Assistant V. President, Tax
BEY, Barbara: Senior V. President, Public Affairs and Publishing
BRADY, Cathleen: Senior Counsel
CAMPBELL, Jr., Hon. Carroll A.: President and Chief Exec. Officer
CANTER, Mark A.: Senior Counsel
CASKIE, Allen R.: Chief Counsel, Federal Relations
COMBS, Ann L.: V. President and Chief Counsel, Retirement and Pensions
DORGAN, Kimberly O.: Deputy V. President, Federal Relations
DURBIN, Margaret: Senior Counsel and Director, Federal Relations
EDWARDS, J. Brad: Director, Political Affairs and Federal Relations
ELAM, Mark R.: Exec. V. President, Government Relations and Chief Operating Officer
HAUSMAN, Shawn: Deputy Vice President, Public Affairs
HOENICKE, Jeanne E.: V. President and Deputy General Counsel
HUGHES, Gary E.: Senior V. President and General Counsel
LANAM, Linda L.: V. President and Chief Counsel, State Relations
LEWIS, Laurie D.: Senior Counsel
MCCONNAUGHEY, Robert S.: Senior Counsel
SMITH, L. Bradley: Managing Director, International Relations
WILKERSON, Carl B.: Chief Counsel, Securities

Outside Counsel/Consultants

The Direct Impact Co.

The Duberstein Group, Inc.
Issues: BAN, GOV, HCR, RET, TAX
Rep By: John W. Angus, III, Michael S. Berman, Steven M. Champlin, Kenneth M. Duberstein, Henry M. Gandy, Daniel P. Meyer

Goddard Claussen

Groom Law Group, Chartered
Issues: LBR, TAX
Rep By: Jon W. Breyfogle

Podesta/Mattoon
Issues: INS, TAX
Rep By: Matthew Gelman

PriceWaterhouseCoopers
Issues: TAX
Rep By: Barbara Angus, Jim Carlisle, Kenneth J. Kies

Schwartz & Ballen
Issues: BAN, INS
Rep By: Robert G. Ballen, Thomas A. Fox, Gilbert T. Schwartz

Timmons and Co., Inc.
Issues: BAN, FIN, FOR, INS, RET, TAX
Rep By: Michael J. Bates, Douglas F. Bennett, Ellen B. Fitzgibbons, Bryce L. "Larry" Harlow, Timothy J. Keating, Tom C. Korologos, Richard J. Tarplin, William E. Timmons, Jr., William E. Timmons, Sr.

Valanzano & Associates
Issues: BAN, INS, TAX
Rep By: Anthony Valanzano

American Council of State Savings Supervisors

Chicago, IL
Leg. Issues: BAN

Outside Counsel/Consultants

Bryan Cave LLP
Rep By: Hon. Alan J. Dixon

Butera & Andrews
Issues: BAN
Rep By: Cliff W. Andrews, James J. Butera, Frank Tillotson

American Council of the Blind

1155 15th St. NW
Suite 1004
Washington, DC 20005
Tel: (202)467-5081
Fax: (202)467-5085
Registered: LDA
Web: www.acb.org
E-mail: info@acb.org

In-house, DC-area Employees

CRAWFORD, Charles: Exec. Director
FESH, Anne C.: Administrative Coordinator

American Council of Young Political Leaders

1612 K St. NW
Suite 300
Washington, DC 20006
Tel: (202)857-0999
Fax: (202)857-0027
Web: www.acypl.org
E-mail: aglover@acypl.org

A bi-partisan council which selects emerging political leaders under the age of 41 to participate in bilateral educational study tours with other nations.

In-house, DC-area Employees

BLACK, Judy A.: President
MCDONALD, Danny Lee: Chairman
POOLE, Mark N.: Exec. Director

American Council on Education

One Dupont Circle NW
Suite 835
Washington, DC 20036-1193
Tel: (202)939-9300
Fax: (202)833-4760
Registered: LDA
Web: www.acenet.edu
Leg. Issues: EDU, TAX

In-house, DC-area Employees

HARTLE, Terry W.: Senior V. President, Government and Public Affairs
IKENBERRY, Stanley O.: President
MCDONOUGH, Timothy J.: Director, Public Affairs
STEINBACH, Sheldon Elliott: V. President and General Counsel
TIMMONS, Becky H.: Director, Government Relations

Outside Counsel/Consultants

BSMG Worldwide

Covington & Burling
Rep By: Roderick A. DeArment

Gardner, Carton and Douglas
Issues: TAX
Rep By: Kathleen M. Nilles

American Council on Internat'l Personnel, Inc.

1212 New York Ave. NW
Suite 425
Washington, DC 20005
Tel: (202)371-6789
Fax: (202)371-5524
Registered: LDA
Web: www.acip.com
E-mail: dcinfo@acip.com

An association devoted to employment-based immigration and national personnel mobility. Headquartered in New York, NY.

Leg. Issues: IMM

In-house, DC-area Employees

SHOTWELL, Lynn Frendt: Legal Counsel and Director, Government Relations
STEWART, Heather: Legislative Counsel

American Councils for Internat'l Education: ACTR/ACCELS

1776 Massachusetts Ave. NW
Suite 700
Washington, DC 20036
Tel: (202)833-7522
Fax: (202)833-7523
Registered: LDA
Web: www.actr.org
E-mail: general@actr.org

A private, not-for-profit educational association and exchange organization working to improve education, professional training, and research within and about the Russian-speaking world.

In-house, DC-area Employees

HERRIN, Carl A.: Director, Government Relations
HUBER, Robert T.: Consultant

American Counseling Ass'n

5999 Stevenson Ave.
Alexandria, VA 22304-3300
Tel: (703)823-9800
Fax: (703)823-0252
Registered: LDA
Web: www.counseling.org
E-mail: aca@counseling.org

Formerly known as the American Ass'n for Counseling and Development. Members work in educational settings, mental health agencies, community organizations, correctional institutions, employment agencies, rehabilitation programs, government, research facilities, and private practice. Includes 18 divisions, 56 branches, and four regions in the United States, Europe, Latin America, Puerto Rico, the Virgin Islands, and the Philippines. Works to promote public confidence and trust in the counseling profession. Currently has 51,000 members.

Leg. Issues: ALC, BUD, DEF, EDU, HCR, LAW, LBR, MMM

In-house, DC-area Employees

BARSTOW, Scott: Director, Public Policy and Legislation
LUM, Christie: Administrative Assistant, Public Policy and Legislation
WODISKA, Joan: Assistant Director, Public Policy and Legislation
YEP, Richard: Exec. Director

American Crop Protection Ass'n

1156 15th St. NW
Suite 400
Washington, DC 20005
Tel: (202)296-1585
Fax: (202)463-0474
Registered: LDA
Web: www.acpa.org

A non-profit trade organization representing the major manufacturers, formulators and distributors of crop protection and pest control products, including bioengineered products with crop production and protection characteristics. ACPA member companies produce, sell and distribute virtually all of the active compounds used in the crop protection chemicals registered for use in the U.S.

Leg. Issues: AGR, BUD, CAW, CHM, ENV, FOO, GOV, TRD

Political Action Committee/s

Crop Protection Political Action Committee (CPPAC)

1156 15th St. NW
Suite 400
Washington, DC 20005
Tel: (202)872-3844
Fax: (202)463-0474
Contact: Elin Peltz

In-house, DC-area Employees

FOSTER, Nancy E.: V. President, Legislative Affairs
GETTER, Pat: V. President, Communications
NOE, A. Allan: V. President, State Affairs, Biotechnology and Water Programs
PELTZ, Elin: Senior Director, Federal Legislative Affairs
ROLOFSON, George: Senior V. President, Government Affairs
VROOM, Jay J.: President

Outside Counsel/Consultants

Alpine Group, Inc.
Issues: AGR, ENV, FOO
Rep By: James D. Massie, Sam White

James Nicholas Ashmore & Associates
Issues: ENV, GOV, TRD
Rep By: James Nicholas Ashmore

Capitolink, LLC
Issues: AGR, CAW, ENV
Rep By: Thomas R. Hebert, John H. Thorne, Ph.D.

The PMA Group
Issues: BUD
Rep By: Mark Rokala, Timothy K. Sanders

American Defense Institute

1055 N. Fairfax St.
Suite 200
Alexandria, VA 22314
Tel: (703)519-7000
Fax: (703)519-8627
E-mail: ebm1@americandefins.org

Promotes awareness of and provides education on issues that affect US national defense and national security.

In-house, DC-area Employees

MCDANIEL, USN (Ret.), Capt. Eugene B.: President

American Defense Internat'l, Inc.

1800 K St. NW
Suite 1010
Washington, DC 20006
Tel: (202)296-5030
Fax: (202)296-4750
Registered: LDA, FARA
E-mail: amerdefint@aol.com
Leg. Issues: DEF

In-house, DC-area Employees

DAFFRON, Thomas
HERSON, Michael: President
HIPP, Jr., Van D.: Chairman
MARCINIK, Dr. Ed
PHILLIPS, George
SHINDELMAN, Bonnie
WILBERDING, Dave: V. President, Government Affairs

Outside Counsel/Consultants

Brown and Company, Inc.
Issues: DEF
Rep By: Cynthia L. Brown, Hugh N. "Rusty" Johnson

American Dehydrated Onion and Garlic Ass'n

San Francisco, CA
Leg. Issues: AGR, FOO, TRD

Outside Counsel/Consultants

Ball Janik, LLP
Issues: AGR, FOO, TRD
Rep By: Robert G. Hayes, Irene Ringwood

American Dental Ass'n

1111 14th St. NW
Suite 1200
Washington, DC 20005-5603
Web: www.ada.org
Tel: (202)898-2400
Fax: (202)898-2437
Registered: LDA

Headquartered in Chicago, IL.

Leg. Issues: HCR

Political Action Committee/s

American Dental Political Action Committee
1111 14th St. NW
Suite 1200
Washington, DC 20005-5603
Contact: Francis X. McLaughlin
Tel: (202)898-2424
Fax: (202)898-2437

In-house, DC-area Employees

GRAHAM, Michael A.: Senior Congressional Lobbyist
GREEN, Richard: Director, Washington Communications
MCLAUGHLIN, Francis X.: Director, Political Affairs
MCLEOD, Jonathan: Manager, Legislative and Regulatory Policy
MOSS, Dorothy J.: Director, Washington Office
PALMER, Craig A.: Washington Editor, ADA News
PRENTICE, William: Senior Congressional Lobbyist
RAIBLE, Robert: Coordinator, Washington Communications
RYAN, Frank E.: Manager, Political Education
SCOTT, Julie: Manager, Legislative and Regulatory Policy
SHERMAN, Judith C.: Senior Congressional Lobbyist
SPANGLER, Jr., Thomas J.: Director, Legislative and Regulatory Policy; CGA
TATE, Michael: Manager, Legislative and Regulatory Policy

Outside Counsel/Consultants

Baker & Hostetler LLP
Issues: HCR
Rep By: William H. Schweitzer

The Wexler Group
Issues: HCR
Rep By: Jody A. Hoffman

American Dental Education Ass'n

1625 Massachusetts Ave. NW
Washington, DC 20036
Web: www.adea.org
E-mail: adea@adea.org
Tel: (202)667-9433
Fax: (202)667-0642
Registered: LDA

Represents all dental schools in the U.S., as well as advanced education, hospital and allied dental institutions. Monitors relevant federal legislative and regulatory activities and maintains liaison with Congress, federal agencies, and other health and education ass'ns.

Leg. Issues: EDU, HCR, MED, MMM, TAX, TOB

In-house, DC-area Employees

LUKE, Gina G.: Director, State Government Relations
MOSS, Myla: Director, Federal Relations
VALACHOVIC, D.M.D., Richard W.: Exec. Director

American Dental Hygienists' Ass'n

Chicago, IL
Web: www.adha.org
Leg. Issues: HCR

Outside Counsel/Consultants

McDermott, Will and Emery
Issues: HCR
Rep By: Wendy L. Krasner, Maggie A. Mitchell, Karen S. Sealander

American Dental Trade Ass'n

4222 King St. West
Alexandria, VA 22302-1597
Web: www.adta.com
E-mail: bolan@adta.com
Tel: (703)379-7755
Fax: (703)931-9429

In-house, DC-area Employees

PRICE, Gary W.: President and Chief Exec. Officer

Outside Counsel/Consultants

Ass'n and Government Relations Management, Inc.
Rep By: Thomas F. Fise

Shaw Pittman

American Diabetes Ass'n

1701 N. Beauregard St.
Alexandria, VA 22311
Web: www.diabetes.org
Tel: (703)549-1500
Fax: (703)836-7439
Registered: LDA

Leg. Issues: BUD, CIV, HCR, MMM, TRA

In-house, DC-area Employees

BAUMAN, Carlea: Director, Grassroots Advocacy
FRANZ, Jerry: V. President, Communications
GRAHAM, IV, John H.: Chief Exec. Officer
MAWBY, Michael: V. President, Government Relations
TIBBITS, Paul: Manager, Government Relations

American Dietetic Ass'n

1120 Connecticut Ave. NW
Suite 480
Washington, DC 20036-3989
Web: www.eatright.org
E-mail: govaffairs@eatright.org
Tel: (202)775-8277
Fax: (202)775-8284
Registered: LDA

Headquartered in Chicago, IL.

Leg. Issues: AGR, FOO, HCR, MMM

Political Action Committee/s

American Dietetic Ass'n Political Action Committee
1120 Connecticut Ave. NW
Suite 480
Washington, DC 20036-3989
Contact: Alison S. Craighead
Tel: (202)775-8277
Fax: (202)775-8284

In-house, DC-area Employees

CRAIGHEAD, Alison S.: Manager, Government and Political Affairs
KETCH, Todd: Director, Government Affairs

American Ecology

Boise, ID

Outside Counsel/Consultants

Parry, Romani, DeConcini & Symms

American Edged Products Manufacturers Ass'n

112-J Elden St.
Herndon, VA 20170
Web: www.aepma.org
E-mail: aepma@erols.com
Tel: (703)709-8253
Fax: (703)709-1036

Formerly known as the American Cutlery Manufacturers Ass'n. Members are major U.S. manufacturers of cutlery products, edged hand tools, and scissors. The above address is that of the firm Barrack Ass'n Management.

In-house, DC-area Employees

BARRACK, David W.: Exec. Director
WILMOT, John: Deputy Director

Outside Counsel/Consultants

Barrack Ass'n Management
Rep By: David W. Barrack

American Educational Research Ass'n

1230 17th St. NW
Washington, DC 20036-3078
Web: www.aera.net
Tel: (202)223-9485
Fax: (202)775-1824

Leg. Issues: EDU

In-house, DC-area Employees

RUSSELL, William J.: Exec. Director
SROUFE, Gerald E.: Director, Government Relations

American Electric Power Co.

801 Pennsylvania Ave. NW
Suite 214
Washington, DC 20004
Tel: (202)628-1645
Fax: (202)628-4276
Registered: LDA

Headquartered in Columbus, OH.

Leg. Issues: ENG, ENV, FIN, TAX, UTI

Political Action Committee/s

American Electric Power Committee For Responsible Government
801 Pennsylvania Ave. NW
Suite 214
Washington, DC 20004
Tel: (202)628-1645
Fax: (202)628-4276

In-house, DC-area Employees

CAMPBELL, Sabrina V.: Director, Federal Agency Relations
KAVANAGH, Anthony P.: V. President, Governmental Affairs
MCBROOM, Marty: Director, Federal Environmental Affairs
MENEZES, Mark W.: V. President and Associate General Counsel

Outside Counsel/Consultants

Arter & Hadden
Issues: UTI

Baker & Hostetler LLP
Issues: TAX
Rep By: William F. Conroy, Matthew J. Dolan, Frederick H. Graefe, David L. Marshall, Hon. Guy Vander Jagt

Hunton & Williams
Issues: TAX
Rep By: C. King Mallory, III, Richard E. May

Van Ness Feldman, P.C.
Issues: ENG, ENV
Rep By: Stephen C. Fotis

Wilmer, Cutler & Pickering
Issues: ENG, FIN, UTI
Rep By: Marianne K. Smythe

American Electronics Ass'n

601 Pennsylvania Ave. NW
Suite 600
North Bldg.
Washington, DC 20004
Web: www.aeanet.org
E-mail: csc@aeanet.org
Tel: (202)682-9110
Fax: (202)682-9111
Registered: LDA

High tech trade association representing over 3,000 American companies in the U.S. and abroad.

Leg. Issues: BUD, COM, CPI, CPT, DEF, EDU, FIN, GOV, HCR, IMM, LBR, MAN, MED, MMM, SCI, TAX, TEC, TRD

In-house, DC-area Employees

ARCHEY, William T.: President and Chief Exec. Officer
BENNETT, B. Timothy: Senior V. President, International
BRAILOV, Marc: Director, Communications
GUHL, Jennifer: Manager, International Trade Policy
HURLEY GRAVES, Caroline: Tax Counsel and Director, Tax Policy
LAVET, Lorraine: Exec. V. President and Chief Operating Officer
MCINTYRE, Ann Marie: Director, Trade Regulation
PALAFOUTAS, John P.: V. President, Domestic Policy and Congressional Relations
PLATZER, Michaela: V. President, Research and Policy Analysis
STOHLER, Thomas: Director, Workforce and Education
STONE, Libby: Exec. Administrator

Outside Counsel/Consultants

McDermott, Will and Emery

Skadden, Arps, Slate, Meagher & Flom LLP
Rep By: Roseann M. Cutrone

American Enterprise Institute for Public Policy Research

1150 17th St. NW
Washington, DC 20036
Tel: (202)862-5800
Fax: (202)862-7177

A nonpartisan, nonprofit, research and educational organization founded in 1943. Conducts research, sponsors conferences and seminars, and publishes books and periodicals in economic policy, foreign policy, and social and political policy.

In-house, DC-area Employees

ARON, Leon: Resident Scholar
BARFIELD, Claude E.: Resident Scholar and Director, Science and Technology Policy Studies
BESHAROV, Douglas J.: Resident Scholar
BOLTON, John R.: Senior V. President
BORK, Robert H.: John M. Olin Scholar in Legal Studies
BOWMAN, Karlyn H.: Resident Fellow
CALFEE, John: Resident Scholar
CALOMIRIS, Charles: Visiting Scholar
CHENEY, Lynne V.: Senior Fellow
D'SOUZA, Dinesh: John Olin Research Fellow
EBERSTADT, Nicholas N.: Visiting Scholar
FALCOFF, Mark: Resident Scholar
FOSS, Murray F.: Visiting Scholar
FRADKIN, Hillel: Resident Scholar
FURCHTGOTT-ROTH, Diana: Resident Fellow
GARMENT, Suzanne: Resident Scholar
GEDMIN, Jeffrey: Research Fellow
GERSON, David: Exec. V. President
GINGRICH, Hon. Newt: Senior Fellow
GOLDWIN, Robert A.: Resident Scholar
HAHN, Robert W.: Resident Scholar
HASSETT, Kevin: Resident Scholar
HAZLETT, Thomas W.: Resident Scholar
HELMS, Robert: Resident Scholar and Director, Health Policy Studies
HICKS, Louis: Research Fellow
HUBBARD, R. Glenn: Visiting Scholar
JOHNSTON, James: Resident Fellow
KIRKPATRICK, Jeane J.: Senior Fellow and Director, Foreign Policy and Defense Studies
KOSTERS, Marvin H.: Resident Scholar and Director, Economic Policy
KRISTOL, Irving: John M. Olin Distinguished Fellow
LEDEEN, Michael A.: Resident Scholar
LILLEY, James: Resident Fellow and Director of Asian Studies
LINDSEY, Lawrence B.: Resident Scholar
LUTTER, Randall: Resident Scholar
MAKIN, John H.: Resident Scholar
MELTZER, Allan H.: Visiting Scholar
MURAVCHIK, Joshua: Resident Scholar
MURRAY, Charles: Bradley Fellow
NOVAK, Michael: Director, Social and Political Studies and G. F. Jewett Scholar
ORNSTEIN, Norman J.: Resident Scholar and Political Analyst
PERLE, Richard N.: Resident Fellow
RODMAN, Veronique: Director, Public Affairs
SCHNEIDER, William: Resident Fellow
SIDAK, J. Gregory: Director, Telecommunications Deregulation Project/F.K. Weyerhauser Fellow
SOMMERS, Christina Hoff: W. H. Brady Fellow
TROY, Daniel E.: Associate Scholar
WALDRON, Arthur: Visiting Scholar, Director of Asian Studies

WALKER, Graham: Visiting Scholar
WALLISON, Peter J.: Resident Fellow
WATTENBERG, Ben J.: Senior Fellow
WEAVER, Carolyn L.: Resident Scholar and Director, Social Security and Pension Studies
WURMSER, David: Resident Scholar

American Eurocopter Corp.

Grand Prairie, TX

Outside Counsel/Consultants

Rhoads Group

American Express Co.

801 Pennsylvania Ave.
Suite 650
Washington, DC 20004
Tel: (202)624-0761
Fax: (202)624-0775
Registered: LDA

Headquartered in New York, NY.

Leg. Issues: BAN, BNK, BUD, EDU, FIN, GOV, HCR, LBR, POS, RET, TAX, TEC, TOR, TOU, TRD

Political Action Committee/s

American Express Political Action Committee
801 Pennsylvania Ave.
Suite 650
Washington, DC 20004
Contact: Irene R. Bond
Tel: (202)624-0761
Fax: (202)624-0775

In-house, DC-area Employees

BOND, Irene R.: Manager, Government Affairs
DAVIS, Timothy S.: Senior V. President, Government Affairs
FERGUSON, Denise G.: V. President, Government Affairs
FLORES, Anna: Manager, Government Affairs
HANEY, Peggy: V. President, Public Responsibility
KAMEN, Laurel: V. President, Government Affairs
SHYCOFF, Barbara: V. President, Government Affairs
THOMSON, III, Robert B.: Director
WAILOO, A. Christopher: Director, Government Affairs

Outside Counsel/Consultants

Akin, Gump, Strauss, Hauer & Feld, L.L.P.
Issues: BAN, BUD, FIN, TOU
Rep By: Smith W. Davis, Sylvia A. de Leon, Joel Jankowsky, Barney J. Skladany, Jr.

Hogan & Hartson L.L.P.
Issues: BNK, FIN
Rep By: William Michael House, Janet L. McDavid

American Family Ass'n

227 Massachusetts Ave. NE
Suite 100-A
Washington, DC 20002
Web: www.afa.net
Tel: (202)544-0061
Fax: (202)544-0504

Based in Tupelo, Mississippi. Raises public awareness about explicit television programming and on such issues as child pornography.

In-house, DC-area Employees

TRUEMAN, Patrick: Director of Governmental Affairs

American Family Mutual Insurance Co.

Madison, WI
Leg. Issues: TAX

Outside Counsel/Consultants

Patton Boggs, LLP
Issues: TAX
Rep By: John F. Jonas, Elizabeth E. Ring, Elizabeth C. Vella

American Farm Bureau Federation

600 Maryland Ave. SW
Suite 800
Washington, DC 20024
Web: www.fb.org
Tel: (202)484-3600
Fax: (202)484-3604
Registered: LDA

An independent, voluntary organization comprised of farm and ranch families. Analyzes common problems and acts to improve education and encourage economic opportunities and social advancements in order to promote the national welfare.

Leg. Issues: AGR, BAN, BUD, CAW, CDT, EDU, ENV, FOO, FUE, GOV, HCR, IMM, LBR, MMM, NAT, POS, ROD, TAX, TOB, TRA, TRD, TRU, UTI, WAS, WEL

In-house, DC-area Employees

ANDERSON, Caroline: Director, Dairy Livestock, Poultry, and Aquaculture
CANSLER, Tim: Director, Commodities and Rural Development
DEMATTEO, Carl S.: Director, Political Education
DOGGETT, Jon: Senior Director, Natural Resources and Energy
ECKART, Brad: Deputy Director, Washington Office and Legislative Services
ERICKSON, Audrae: Director, International Trade, Policy, and Negotiations
GARZA, Chris: Assistant Director, Regulatory Affairs
JACKSON, Alex: Director, Trade Relations and Development
LITTLE, C. Bryan: Director, Agricultural Labor/Transportation/Regulatory Affairs
MASLYN, Mark A.: Deputy Exec. Director, Washington Office, Environment/Labor/Natural Resources
NEWPHER, Richard W.: Exec. Director, Washington Office
SALMONSEN, David: Director, Water Quality/Wetlands
SHARP, Adam: Director, Ag Chemicals/Biotechnology/Air Quality
THATCHER, Mary Kay: Deputy Director, Agriculture Policy/Budget/Taxes/Commodities/Trade
TOBIN, Merry M.: Director, Legislative Services
WATKINS, Rosemarie: Senior Dir., Conservation, Forestry, and Environmental Agriculture Issues
WOLFF, Patricia A.: Senior Director, Budget/Taxes/Appropriations

Outside Counsel/Consultants

DTB Associates, LLP

Mayer, Brown & Platt
Issues: TAX

American Farmland Trust

1200 18th St. NW
Suite 800
Washington, DC 20036
Web: www.farmland.org
Tel: (202)331-7300
Fax: (202)659-8339
Registered: LDA

Works to protect productive farmland through public education, policy development and private land conservancy transactions.

Leg. Issues: AGR, BUD, NAT

In-house, DC-area Employees

FLEEK, Susan: Director, Government Relations
GROSSI, Ralph E.: President
THOMPSON, Edward: Senior V. President, Public Policy
WARMAN, Timothy W.: V. President, Programs

American Federation for Medical Research

227 Massachusetts Ave. NE
Suite 303
Washington, DC 20002
Web: www.afmr.org
E-mail: admin@afmr.org
Tel: (202)543-7032
Fax: (202)543-7062

Leg. Issues: BUD, HCR, MED, MMM, VET

In-house, DC-area Employees

EISENBERG, Susan: Exec. Director

Outside Counsel/Consultants

Smith, Bucklin and Associates, Inc.

Washington Health Advocates
Issues: BUD, HCR, MED, MMM, VET
Rep By: Lynn Morrison, Michele Sumilas

American Federation of Government Employees (AFL-CIO)

80 F St. NW
Washington, DC 20001
Tel: (202)639-6419
Fax: (202)639-6441
Registered: LDA
Web: www.afge.org
E-mail: communications@afge.org

The largest union for federal workers and District of Columbia employees.

Leg. Issues: LBR

Political Action Committee/s

American Federation of Government Employees Political Action Committee
80 F St. NW
Washington, DC 20001
Contact: Bob Nicklas
Tel: (202)639-6457
Fax: (202)639-6490

In-house, DC-area Employees

BROOKS, Andrea: Director, Womens/Fair Practices Dept.
DAVIS, Jim: National Secretary-Treasurer
HARNAGE, Sr., Bobby L.: National President
MOTEN, Beth: Legislative Director
NICKLAS, Bob: PAC Director
ROTH, Mark D.: General Counsel
SEYMOUR, Magda Lynn: Director, Communications

Outside Counsel/Consultants

Patrick M. Murphy & Associates
Issues: LBR

American Federation of Government Employees, Local 1689 Guam

Outside Counsel/Consultants

R. J. Hudson Associates

American Federation of Home Care Providers

1320 Fenwick Ln.
Suite 100
Silver Spring, MD 20910
Tel: (301)588-1454
Fax: (301)588-4732
Registered: LDA

Leg. Issues: HCR

In-house, DC-area Employees

CUPPETT, Ted: President
HOWARD, Ann B.: Exec. Director

American Federation of Musicians of the United States and Canada

501 Third St. NW
Tenth Floor
Washington, DC 20001
Web: www.afm.org
E-mail: apollard@afm.org
Tel: (202)628-5460
Fax: (202)628-5461
Registered: LDA

An international labor union (U.S. and Canada) affiliated with the AFL-CIO representing more than 130,000 professional recording, radio, television, motion picture, symphonic, country, pop, alternative, rock and jazz musicians headquartered in New York, NY.

Leg. Issues: ART, BNK, CPT, GAM, HCR, LBR

Political Action Committee/s

TEMPO
501 Third St. NW
Tenth Floor
Washington, DC 20001
Contact: Alfonso M. Pollard
Tel: (202)628-5460
Fax: (202)628-5461

In-house, DC-area Employees

POLLARD, Alfonso M.: National Legislative Director

American Federation of Police & Concerned Citizens, Inc.

1090 Vermont Ave. Suite 800
Washington, DC 20005
Web: www.aphf.org
E-mail: policeinfo@aphf.org
Tel: (202)293-9088

In-house, DC-area Employees

SNYDER, John M.: V. President, Public Relations

American Federation of School Administrators

1729 21st St. NW
Washington, DC 20009-1101
Web: www.admin.org
E-mail: ddemond@admin.org
Tel: (202)986-4209
Fax: (202)986-4211

Political Action Committee/s

American Federation of School Administrators Political Action Committee
1729 21st St. NW
Washington, DC 20009-1101
Contact: Joseph Chagnon
Tel: (202)986-4209
Fax: (202)986-4211

In-house, DC-area Employees

CHAGNON, Joseph: Treasurer
GREENE, Joe L.: President

American Federation of Senior Citizens

Alexandria, VA
Leg. Issues: BUD, HCR, IMM, INS, MMM, RET, TAX

Outside Counsel/Consultants

Jar-Mon Consultants, Inc.
Issues: BUD, HCR, IMM, INS, MMM, RET, TAX
Rep By: Gina Jarmin

American Federation of State, County and Municipal Employees

1625 L St. NW
Washington, DC 20036-5687
Web: www.afscme.org
Tel: (202)429-1000
Fax: (202)429-1293
Registered: LDA

AFSCME's goal is to lobby all legislation affecting the welfare of state, county, municipal, and private workers.

Leg. Issues: BNK, BUD, CIV, DOC, EDU, ENV, FAM, GOV, HCR, HOU, IMM, LAW, LBR, MMM, RET, TAX, TRA, TRD, UNM, UTI, WEL

Political Action Committee/s

Public Employees Organized to Promote Legislative Equality (PEOPLE)
1625 L St. NW
Washington, DC 20036-5687
Contact: Charles M. Loveless
Tel: (202)429-1194
Fax: (202)223-3413

In-house, DC-area Employees

ALLEN, Marjorie D.: Legislative Affairs Specialist
BRADLEY, Cynthia P.: Legislative Affairs Specialist
BURKE, Diane B.: Assistant Director
CANAN, Linda: Assistant Director, Political Action
CLANCY, Jayne: Legislative Representative
COUFAL, Barbara: Legislative Affairs Specialist
COWAN, Frank: Assistant to the President
JAYNE, Jr., Edwin S.: Associate Director, Legislation
LOVELESS, Charles M.: Director, Department of Legislation
LUCY, William: Internat'l Secretary-Treasurer
MCENTEE, Gerald W.: Internat'l President

MEIKLEJOHN, Nanine: Legislative Affairs Specialist
NOLAN, Jean: Director, Public Affairs
SAUNDERS, Lee: Assistant to the President
SCANLON, Jr., Lawrence R.: Director, Political Action
YONTZ, Caryl: Legislative Affairs Specialist

American Federation of Teachers

555 New Jersey Ave. NW
Washington, DC 20001
Tel: (202)879-4400
Fax: (202)879-4402
Registered: LDA
Web: www.aft.org
Leg. Issues: AGR, BAN, BUD, CON, DEF, DIS, DOC, EDU, GOV, HCR, IMM, LAW, LBR, MMM, REL, RET, TAX, TEC, TOB, TRA, TRD, WEL

Political Action Committee/s

American Federation of Teachers Committee on Political Education
555 New Jersey Ave. NW
Washington, DC 20001
Tel: (202)393-6375
Fax: (202)879-4402
Contact: Elizabeth M. Smith

In-house, DC-area Employees

BIRDSALL, Cheryl C.: Associate Director, Legislation
CROSS, Mary: Associate Director, Legislative Affairs
CUNNINGHAM, William J.: Associate Director, Legislative Affairs
FELDMAN, Sandra: President
FREEMAN, Yvonne: Treasurer, Staff Union
HORWITZ, Jamie: Assistant Director, Public Affairs
KING, Gregory: Press Secretary
MCELROY, Edward: Secretary/Treasurer
MERONEY, Jane U.: Associate Director, Legislative Affairs
MORRIS, Gerald: Director, Legislative Research
SMITH, Elizabeth M.: Political Director
STROM, David: Counsel
TAMMELLEO, William F.: Associate Director, Legislation
WOHL, Alex: Director, Public Affairs

Outside Counsel/Consultants

The Ickes & Enright Group
Issues: BUD, EDU
Rep By: Janice Ann Enright, Harold M. Ickes

American Federation of Television and Radio Artists

New York, NY
Leg. Issues: ART, COM, CPT, GOV, LBR, MIA

Outside Counsel/Consultants

Smith Dawson & Andrews, Inc.
Issues: ART, COM, CPT, GOV, LBR, MIA
Rep By: James P. Smith

American Feed Industry Ass'n

1501 Wilson Blvd.
Suite 1100
Arlington, VA 22209-3199
Tel: (703)524-0810
Fax: (703)524-1921
Registered: LDA
Web: www.afia.org
E-mail: afia@afia.org

Provides leadership and service concerning the business, legislative, management, and global interests of the feed industry.

Leg. Issues: AGR, ANI, BUD, CAW, CSP, ENV, FOO, LBR, SCI, TRA, TRD, TRU, WAS

Political Action Committee/s

Feed Industry Political Action Committee
c/o Policy Directors Inc.
818 Connecticut Ave. NW
Washington, DC 20006
Tel: (202)776-0071
Fax: (202)776-0083
Contact: Steve Kopperud

In-house, DC-area Employees

BOSSMAN, David A.: President
KOPPERUD, Steve: PAC Contact
RUNYON, Rex A.: V. President, Public Relations
SELLERS, Richard: V. President, Feed Control and Nutrition

Outside Counsel/Consultants

Patton Boggs, LLP
Issues: AGR
Rep By: Clayton L. Hough

Policy Directions, Inc.
Issues: AGR, ANI, BUD, CAW, ENV, FOO, LBR, TRD, TRU
Rep By: Steve Kopperud, Frankie L. Trull

American Fiber Manufacturers Ass'n

1150 17th St. NW
Suite 310
Washington, DC 20036
Tel: (202)296-6508
Fax: (202)296-3052
Web: www.afma.org
E-mail: afma@afma.org

A trade organization representing domestic manufacturers of fibers, filaments and yarns. Manages programs on government relations, international trade policy, environmental concerns, technical issues and education.

In-house, DC-area Employees

BARKER, Robert H.: V. President
O'DAY, Paul T.: President

Outside Counsel/Consultants

Donald R. Greeley
Rep By: Donald R. Greeley

American Fidelity Life Insurance Co.

Pensacola, FL
Leg. Issues: INS

Outside Counsel/Consultants

Baker & Hostetler LLP
Issues: INS
Rep By: Frederick H. Graefe, Christopher T. Stephen

Porter/Novelli
Rep By: Michael Frisby

American Film Institute

Los Angeles, CA
Leg. Issues: BUD

Outside Counsel/Consultants

Cassidy & Associates, Inc.
Issues: BUD
Rep By: Laura A. Neal, Valerie Rogers Osborne, Marnie Russ

American Film Marketing Ass'n

Los Angeles, CA

Outside Counsel/Consultants

Jenkens & Gilchrist
Rep By: John T. Mitchell

Jenner & Block

American Financial Group

Cincinnati, OH
Leg. Issues: BAN, ENV, FIN, INS, TAX

Outside Counsel/Consultants

Akin, Gump, Strauss, Hauer & Feld, L.L.P.
Issues: ENV, INS, TAX
Rep By: Donald C. Alexander

Kirkpatrick & Lockhart LLP
Issues: BAN, FIN, INS
Rep By: George W. Koch, Ira L. Tannenbaum

Verner, Liipfert, Bernhard, McPherson and Hand, Chartered
Rep By: Berl Bernhard, Evan M. Migdail

American Financial Services Ass'n

919 18th St. NW
Suite 300
Washington, DC 20006
Tel: (202)296-5544
Fax: (202)223-0321
Registered: LDA
Web: www.afsaonline.org
E-mail: afsa@afsamail.org

AFSA is a national trade association for finance companies and other consumer and commercial lenders in the capital markets. Founded in 1916, AFSA's membership ranges from national financial services to independently owned consumer finance companies.

Leg. Issues: BAN, BNK, FIN

Political Action Committee/s

American Financial Services Ass'n Political Action Committee
919 18th St. NW
Suite 300
Washington, DC 20006
Tel: (202)296-5544
Fax: (202)223-0321
Contact: Danielle M. Koon

In-house, DC-area Employees

COVERT, Rick: V. President, State Government Affairs
KOON, Danielle M.: Director, Federal Government Affairs
LEHNER, Thomas J.: Exec. V. President, Government Affairs
LIVELY, Jr., H. R.: President and Chief Exec. Officer
MCELWEE, George S.: Manager, AFSAPAC & Gov't. Support
MCKEW, Robert E.: V. President and General Counsel
STRANGE, Lynne: Director, Communications

Outside Counsel/Consultants

Eckert Seamans Cherin & Mellott, LLC
Rep By: George J. Wallace

American Fish Spotters Ass'n

Chilmark, MA
Leg. Issues: BUD, MAR

Outside Counsel/Consultants

Griffin, Johnson, Dover & Stewart
Issues: BUD, MAR
Rep By: William C. Danvers, G. Jack Dover, Patrick J. Griffin, Keith Heard, David E. Johnson, Susan O. Mann, Walter J. "Joe" Stewart, Leonard Swinehart

American Fisheries Soc.

5410 Grosvenor Ln.
Suite 110
Bethesda, MD 20814-2199
Tel: (301)897-8616
Fax: (301)897-8096
Web: www.fisheries.org
E-mail: main@fisheries.org

An organization of more than 8,500 fisheries managers and aquatic scientists. Dedicated to strengthening the fisheries profession, advancing fisheries science, and conserving fisheries resources.

In-house, DC-area Employees

RASSAM, Dr. Gus: Exec. Director

American Flange Producers Marking Coalition

Washington, DC
Registered: LDA
Leg. Issues: TRD

Outside Counsel/Consultants

Collier Shannon Scott, PLLC
Issues: TRD
Rep By: John B. Brew, Kathleen Clark Kies, Doris O. Matsui

The American Floral Marketing Council

Alexandria, VA

Outside Counsel/Consultants

Ogilvy Public Relations Worldwide
Rep By: Steven J. Dahllof

American Fly Fishing Trade Ass'n

Kelso, WA

Outside Counsel/Consultants

Baker, Donelson, Bearman & Caldwell, P.C.
Rep By: James D. Range

American Football Coaches Ass'n

Waco, TX

Outside Counsel/Consultants

Baker & Hostetler LLP
Rep By: Matthew J. Dolan, Hon. Guy Vander Jagt

American Foreign Service Ass'n

2101 E St. NW
Washington, DC 20037
Tel: (202)338-4045
Fax: (202)338-6820
Registered: LDA
Web: www.afsa.org
E-mail: afsa@afsa.org

AFSA is the professional association of the U.S. Foreign Service, representing 23,000 active duty and retired Foreign Service employees.

Leg. Issues: BUD, FOR, GOV, LBR, TAX

In-house, DC-area Employees

ADAIR, Marshall P.: President
NAKAMURA, Kennon H.: Director, Congressional Relations
PAPP, Sharon: Legal Counsel
REARDON, Susan: Exec. Director

American Forest & Paper Ass'n

1111 19th St. NW
Suite 800
Washington, DC 20036
Tel: (202)463-2700
Fax: (202)463-2785
Registered: LDA
Web: www.afandpa.org
E-mail: info@afandpa.org

A national trade association of the forest, paper and wood products industry. Represents nearly 250 member companies and related trade associations which grow, harvest and process wood and wood fiber, manufacture pulp, paper and paperboard from both virgin and recycled fiber, and produce solid wood products.

Leg. Issues: ADV, BUD, CAW, ENV, NAT, RES, RRR, TAX, TRD, TRU, UTI, WAS

Political Action Committee/s

American Forest and Paper Ass'n Political Action Committee (AF&PA PAC)
1111 19th St. NW
Suite 800
Washington, DC 20036
Tel: (202)463-2779
Fax: (202)463-2424
Contact: Dylan Amo

In-house, DC-area Employees

AMO, Dylan: PAC Manager
BARNES, Gordon: Manager, Grassroots
COULOMBE, Mary: Director, Timber Access and Supply
DANIELSON, Jack: Director, Congressional Affairs
DUBENSKY, Mitch: Director, Forest and Wetlands
GUSLER, Dorothy: Director, International Trade
HANDLESMAN, Jacob: Director, International Research
HARCAR, Mary: Director, Tax Policy
HARRISON, Michael: Coordinator, Congressional Affairs

HEISSENBUTTEL, John: V. President, Forestry and Wood Products
HILDEBRAND, Sarah M.: V. President, Congressional Affairs
HUNT, Tim: Director, Air Quality Program
KIRSHNER, Robert: V. President and General Counsel
KNEISS, Sharon H.: V. President, Regulatory Affairs
LOVETT, Steve: V. President, Fiber Resources and Products
MADDEN, Suzanne: Director, State Government Affairs
MOFFETT-RIGOLI, Katy: Manager, Grassroots
MOORE, Hon. W. Henson: President and Chief Exec. Officer
MURRAY, Chip: Natural Resources Counsel
OLSON, Beth: Director, Regulatory Affairs
RITA, Pat: V. President, State Government Affairs
SCHAFFER, Amy E.: Senior Director, Environmental Program Coordinator and Industrial Waste
SCHWARTZ, Jerry: Director, Water Quality Program
SEEGER, Kristin: V. President, Communications
SERIE, Terry L.: V. President, Statistics
SMITH, Maureen H.: V. President, International Affairs
STISH, DeAnn: Director, Congressional Affairs

Outside Counsel/Consultants

The Accord Group
Issues: CAW, ENV, NAT
Rep By: Robert F. Hurley

Crowell & Moring LLP
Issues: NAT
Rep By: Steven P. Quarles

Dewey Ballantine LLP
Issues: TRD
Rep By: Kevin M. Dempsey, John A. Ragosta

The Direct Impact Co.

Earle Palmer Brown Public Relations
Issues: ADV, ENV

O'Connor & Hannan, L.L.P.
Issues: ENV, NAT
Rep By: Robert W. Barrie, Hon. Thomas J. Corcoran, George J. Mannina, Jr., Patrick E. O'Donnell

Ogilvy Public Relations Worldwide
Rep By: Jamie W. Moeller

Perkins Coie LLP
Rep By: Guy R. Martin

Terpstra Associates
Issues: ENV, WAS
Rep By: Grace Terpstra

Van Scoyoc Associates, Inc.
Issues: ENV, NAT, TAX
Rep By: John C. "Jay" Stone, Jeffrey S. Trinca, H. Stewart Van Scoyoc

The Wexler Group
Issues: ENV
Rep By: Dale W. Snape, Anne Wexler

American Forest Foundation

1111 19th St. NW
Suite 780
Washington, DC 20036
Web: www.affoundation.org
Tel: (202)463-2462
Fax: (202)463-2461

In-house, DC-area Employees

WISEMAN, Laurence: President

American Forests

910 17th St. NW
Suite 600
Washington, DC 20006
Web: www.amfor.org
Tel: (202)955-4500
Fax: (202)955-4588

American Forests, founded in 1875, is the oldest national nonprofit conservation group. It seeks to ensure the world the undiminished availability of all the benefits of trees and forests including clean air, clean water, and energy savings.

In-house, DC-area Employees

GANGLOFF, Deborah: Exec. Director
GRAY, Gerald: V. President, Resource Policy
MOLL, Gary: V. President, Urban Forestry

American Foundation for AIDS Research

1828 L St. NW
Suite 802
Washington, DC 20036
Tel: (202)331-8600
Fax: (202)331-8606
Registered: LDA

A national, not-for-profit public foundation for fighting AIDS through grant programs in basic and clinical research, education for AIDS prevention, and public policy.

Leg. Issues: HCR, MED

In-house, DC-area Employees

SILVER, Jane: Director, Public Policy

Outside Counsel/Consultants

Downey McGrath Group, Inc.
Issues: HCR
Rep By: Hon. Thomas J. Downey, Jr., John Peter Olinger

American Foundation for the Blind - Governmental Relations Group

820 First St. NE
Suite 400
Washington, DC 20002
Tel: (202)408-0200
Fax: (202)289-7880
Registered: LDA
Web: www.afb.org
E-mail: afbgov@afb.net

Mission is to help people who are blind or visually impaired achieve equality of access and opportunity that will ensure freedom of choice in their lives. Headquartered in New York, NY.

Leg. Issues: BUD, CIV, EDU, HCR, LBR, MMM, TEC

In-house, DC-area Employees

DINSMORE, Alan M.: Senior Governmental Relations Representative
LEMOINE, Barbara J.: Legislative Assistant
RICHERT, Mark D.: Governmental Relations Representative
SAJKA, Janina: Director, Technology Research and Development
SCHROEDER, Paul W.: V. President, Government Relations

Outside Counsel/Consultants

Powers Pyles Sutter & Verville, PC
Issues: BUD, EDU, HCR
Rep By: J. Michael Hall, Alyson M. Haywood

American Foundrymen's Soc.

Des Plaines, IL
Leg. Issues: CAW, ENG, ENV, LBR, MAN

Outside Counsel/Consultants

Waterman & Associates
Issues: CAW, ENG, ENV, LBR, MAN
Rep By: Amy Lucas, Diana L. Waterman

American Franchisee Ass'n

Chicago, IL

Outside Counsel/Consultants

The Smith-Free Group

American Free Trade Ass'n

Miami, FL
Leg. Issues: APP, CPI, CPT, CSP, MAN, TRD

Outside Counsel/Consultants

O'Connor & Hannan, L.L.P.
Issues: APP, CPI, CPT, CSP, MAN, TRD
Rep By: Hon. Thomas J. Corcoran, Frederick T. Dombo, Danielle Fagre, Patrick E. O'Donnell

Sandler, Travis & Rosenberg, P.A.
Issues: TRD
Rep By: Lauren Perez, Gilbert Lee Sandler

American Friends of Lubavitch

2110 Leroy Pl. NW
Washington, DC 20008
Tel: (202)332-5600
Fax: (202)332-5642

Represents the Washington interests of the Chabad-Lubavitch Movement and its centers in 44 states and over 60 foreign countries.

In-house, DC-area Employees

SHEMTOV, Rabbi Abraham: National Director
SHEMTOV, Rabbi Levi: Director, Washington Office

American Friends of the Czech Republic

Washington, DC
Leg. Issues: ART

Outside Counsel/Consultants

Chwat and Company, Inc.
Issues: ART
Rep By: John Chwat, Derek Riker

American Friends of Turkey

Washington, DC

Outside Counsel/Consultants

Baker, Donelson, Bearman & Caldwell, P.C.
Rep By: Charles R. Johnston, Jr.

American Friends Service Committee

1822 R St. NW
Washington, DC 20009
Tel: (202)483-3341
Fax: (202)232-3197

Seeks to maintain an effective presence in D.C. by bringing AFSC field experience, insights and advocacy to bear on policy-makers, opinion-shapers, the press and diplomats as well as by monitoring relevent developments in Washington. AFSC programs include humanitarian aid, development, economic and social justice and disarmament. AFSC is a Quaker-based agency with headquarters in Philadelphia, PA.

In-house, DC-area Employees

MATLACK, Jim: Director, Washington Office

American Frozen Food Institute

2000 Corporate Ridge
Suite 1000
McLean, VA 22102
Tel: (703)821-0770
Fax: (703)821-1350
Registered: LDA
Web: www.affi.com
E-mail: info@affi.com
Leg. Issues: AGR, ENV, FOO, LBR, MAN, TRA, TRD

Political Action Committee/s

American Frozen Food Institute Political Action Committee
2000 Corporate Ridge
Suite 1000
McLean, VA 22102
Contact: Leslie G. Sarasin, CAE
Tel: (703)821-0770
Fax: (703)821-1350

In-house, DC-area Employees

GARFIELD, Robert L.: Senior V. President, Regulatory and Technical Affairs
GILL, Michael: V. President, Legislative Affairs
PAGE, Jennie: Manager, Regulatory and Technical Affairs
SARASIN, CAE, Leslie G.: President and Chief Exec. Officer
TROWBRIDGE, Michelle: Senior Director, Communications

Outside Counsel/Consultants

Hogan & Hartson L.L.P.
Issues: AGR, ENV, FOO, LBR, TRA, TRD
Rep By: Gary Jay Kushner, Ellen Siegler, Timothy C. Stanceu

American Furniture Manufacturers Ass'n

1120 Connecticut Ave. NW
Suite 1080
Washington, DC 20036
Tel: (202)466-7362
Fax: (202)429-4915
Registered: LDA
Web: www.afmahp.org
E-mail: batsonr@afma4u.org

Headquartered in High Point, NC.

Leg. Issues: BNK, CSP, ENV, GOV, HCR, LBR, MAN, SMB, TAX, TOR, TRD

Political Action Committee/s

FurnPAC
1120 Connecticut Ave. NW
Suite 1080
Washington, DC 20036
Contact: Russell B. Batson
Tel: (202)466-7362
Fax: (202)429-4915

In-house, DC-area Employees

BATSON, Russell B.: V. President, Government Affairs
PEARCE, Christopher P.: Director, Congressional and Regulatory Affairs

American Gaming Ass'n

555 13th St. NW
Suite 1010 East
Washington, DC 20004
Tel: (202)637-6500
Fax: (202)637-6507
Registered: LDA
Web: www.americangaming.org
Leg. Issues: BNK, GAM, MAR, TAX, TOB

Political Action Committee/s

American Gaming Ass'n PAC
555 13th St. NW
Suite 1010 East
Washington, DC 20004
Contact: Judy L. Patterson
Tel: (202)637-6500
Fax: (202)637-6507

In-house, DC-area Employees

CHALMERS, Walton M.: V. President
FAHRENKOPF, Jr., Frank J.: President and Chief Exec. Officer
PATTERSON, Judy L.: V. President and Exec. Director
SHELK, John E.: V. President

Outside Counsel/Consultants

Arter & Hadden
Issues: GAM

Columbus Public Affairs
Issues: GAM
Rep By: Larry W. Werner

The Duberstein Group, Inc.
Issues: BNK, GAM, TAX
Rep By: John W. Angus, III, Michael S. Berman, Steven M. Champlin, Kenneth M. Duberstein, Henry M. Gandy, Daniel P. Meyer

Fierce and Isakowitz
Issues: GAM
Rep By: Kathryn Braden, Donald L. Fierce, Mark W. Isakowitz

Hogan & Hartson L.L.P.
Issues: TAX
Rep By: Robert H. Kapp, John S. Stanton

McClure, Gerard & Neuenschwander, Inc.
Rep By: Steven G. Barringer, Joseph T. Findaro, Matthew Iandoli, Nils W. Johnson, Hon. James A. McClure, Tod O. Neuenschwander

American Gas Ass'n

400 N. Capitol St. NW
Washington, DC 20001
Tel: (202)824-7000
Fax: (202)824-7115
Registered: LDA
Web: www.aga.org
E-mail: webmaster@aga.org

National trade association for natural gas utilities.

Leg. Issues: BUD, CAW, CSP, DEF, ENG, ENV, FIN, FUE, GOV, LBR, NAT, ROD, SCI, TAX, TEC, UTI, WAS

Political Action Committee/s

Gas Employees Political Action Committee
400 N. Capitol St. NW
Washington, DC 20001
Tel: (202)824-7220
Fax: (202)824-7090
Contact: Charles H. Fritts

In-house, DC-area Employees

BELFORD, Kevin B.: General Counsel
COOPER, Roger B.: Exec. V. President, Policy and Analysis
ESTES, Deborah M.: Managing Director, Government Relations
FREBERG, II, Douglas: Director, Government Relations
FRITTS, Charles H.: V. President, Government Relations
HENRY, Darrell: Director, Public Affairs
HILL, A. Karen: V. President, Regulatory Affairs
KABOUS, Julie: Manager, Government Relations
LACEY, Pamela A.: Senior Manging Counsel
LEWIS, Jane: Senior Managing Counsel and Director
PARKER, David N.: President and Chief Exec. Officer
ROGERS, Kyle: Director, Government Relations
SHELBY, Richard D.: Exec. V. President, Public Affairs
WILKINSON, Paul: V. President, Policy and Analysis
WISE, Eric: Senior Counsel and Director

Outside Counsel/Consultants

The Carmen Group
Issues: ENG
Rep By: Gerald P. Carmen

Charles D. Estes & Associates
Issues: BUD
Rep By: Charles D. Estes

Liebman & Associates, Inc.
Issues: ENG, ENV, FUE, GOV, NAT, SCI, UTI
Rep By: Murray Liebman

Nat'l Environmental Strategies
Issues: CAW, ENV, WAS
Rep By: Marc I. Himmelstein

The Van Fleet-Meredith Group
Issues: DEF
Rep By: M. Bruce Meredith, Paul F. Payette, Townsend A. Van Fleet

R. Duffy Wall and Associates
Issues: ENV, TAX
Rep By: Hon. Bill Brewster, Julia E. Chaney, Ann Thomas G. Johnston

American Gas Cooling Center

400 N. Capitol St. NW
Washington, DC 20001
Tel: (202)824-7140
Fax: (202)824-7093
Web: www.agcc.org
E-mail: tocchionero@agcc.org

A trade association promoting commercialization of natural gas cooling, dehumidification, and refrigeration equipment.

Leg. Issues: BUD, CAW, ENG, ENV, TAX

In-house, DC-area Employees

OCCHIONERO, Anthony: Exec. Director

Outside Counsel/Consultants

Cascade Associates
Issues: BUD, CAW, ENG, ENV, TAX
Rep By: Jennifer A. Schafer

American Gastroenterological Ass'n

7910 Woodmont Ave.
Suite 700
Bethesda, MD 20814
Tel: (301)654-2055
Fax: (301)654-5920
Registered: LDA
Web: www.gastro.org
Leg. Issues: BUD, GOV, HCR, MED, MMM

In-house, DC-area Employees

BACH, Dianne: V. President, Communications and Marketing
GREENBERG, Robert B.: Exec. V. President
ROBERTS, Mike: V. President, Public Policy and Government Relations
TEIXEIRA, Kathleen: Director, Government Affairs

Outside Counsel/Consultants

McDermott, Will and Emery
Issues: BUD, GOV, HCR, MED
Rep By: Michael A. Romansky, Eric P. Zimmerman

Ricchetti Inc.
Issues: BUD, MMM
Rep By: Jeff Ricchetti, Steve Ricchetti

American Gear Manufacturers Ass'n

1500 King St.
Suite 201
Alexandria, VA 22314
Tel: (703)684-0211
Fax: (703)684-0242
Web: www.agma.org
E-mail: webmaster@agma.org

An international trade association of 405 manufacturers and users of gears and gearing products.

Leg. Issues: CPT, ECN, MAN, SMB

Political Action Committee/s

American Gear Political Action Committee
1500 King St.
Suite 201
Alexandria, VA 22314
Tel: (703)838-0050
Fax: (703)684-0242
Contact: Joe T. Franklin, Jr.

In-house, DC-area Employees

FRANKLIN, Jr., Joe T.: President

American General Corp.

1101 Pennsylvania Ave. NW
Suite 515
Washington, DC 20004
Tel: (202)628-4600
Fax: (202)628-5410
Registered: LDA
Web: byron_anderson@agc.com
E-mail: banderson@clark.net

A financial services corporation. Headquartered in Houston, TX. The company's PAC is also represented by Committee Management Associates (see separate listing).

Leg. Issues: FIN, INS

Political Action Committee/s

American General Corp. PAC (AGCPAC)
1101 Pennsylvania Ave. NW
Suite 515
Washington, DC 20004
Tel: (202)628-4600
Fax: (202)628-5410
Contact: Jefferson D. Taylor

In-house, DC-area Employees

ANDERSON, Byron E.: Sr. V. President, Government Affairs
TAYLOR, Jefferson D.: V. President, Political Affairs; PAC Treasurer

American General Financial Group

Washington, DC
Leg. Issues: FIN, INS

Outside Counsel/Consultants

Winston & Strawn
Issues: FIN, INS
Rep By: Timothy M. Broas, Charles L. Kinney

American General Life Insurance Co.

Outside Counsel/Consultants

Davis & Harman LLP
Rep By: Richard S. Belas, Thomas A. Davis

American Geological Institute

4220 King St.
Alexandria, VA 22302-1502
Tel: (703)379-2480
Fax: (703)379-7563
Registered: LDA
Web: www.agiweb.org/
E-mail: agi@agiweb.org

A nonprofit 501(c)(3) federation of 37 geoscience societies.

Leg. Issues: ENV, FUE, NAT, SCI

In-house, DC-area Employees

APPLEGATE, David: Director, Government Affairs
DRAGONETTI, John J.: Senior Advisor, Government Affairs
MILLING, Marcus E.: Exec. Director

American Geophysical Union

2000 Florida Ave. NW
Washington, DC 20009
Tel: (202)462-6900
Fax: (202)328-0566
Registered: LDA
Web: www.agu.org
E-mail: service@agu.org

A scientific society with a worldwide membership of over 39,000 researchers, teachers, and administrators. AGU is dedicated to advancing the understanding of Earth and its environment in space.

Leg. Issues: AER, BUD, CPT, ENG, ENV, NAT, SCI

In-house, DC-area Employees

BIERLY, Ph.D., Eugene W.: Senior Scientist
DICKEY, Jr., Ph.D., John S.: Director, Outreach and Research Support
FOLGER, Ph.D., Peter: Manager, Public Affairs
HOLOVIAK, Judy: Director, Publications
LEIFERT, Harvey: Public Information Manager
SPILHAUS, Jr., Ph.D., A. F.: Exec. Director

WEAVER, Brenda: Director, Meetings
WHITE, Bill: Director, Information Technology

American Grain Inspection Institute

Leg. Issues: AGR

Outside Counsel/Consultants

Agri/Washington
Issues: AGR
Rep By: Jon Moore, Paul S. Weller, Jr.

American Great Lakes Ports

Washington, DC
Registered: LDA
Leg. Issues: AGR, BUD, MAR, TAX, TRA

Outside Counsel/Consultants

Fisher Consulting
Issues: AGR, BUD, MAR, TAX, TRA
Rep By: Steven A. Fisher

American Green Network

Washington, DC
Leg. Issues: ENV

Outside Counsel/Consultants

WinCapitol, Inc.
Issues: ENV
Rep By: David L. Flory, Christie Olsen, James T. Sims

American Greyhound Track Operators Ass'n

Birmingham, AL
Leg. Issues: GAM, IND, SMB

Outside Counsel/Consultants

Dickstein Shapiro Morin & Oshinsky LLP
Issues: GAM, IND, SMB
Rep By: Henry C. Cashen, II, Margaret Feinstein, Elizabeth B. Haywood, Robert Mangas, Graham "Rusty" Mathews, Rebecah Moore Shepherd, L. Andrew Zausner

American Hardware Manufacturers Ass'n

Schaumburg, IL
Web: www.ahma.org

Outside Counsel/Consultants

London and Satagaj, Attorneys-at-Law
Rep By: Sheldon I. London

American Health Assistance Foundation

15825 Shady Grove Rd.
Suite 140
Rockville, MD 20850
Tel: (301)948-3244
Fax: (301)258-9454
Web: www.ahaf.org

A national non-profit organization dedicated to funding research on and educating the public about age-related and degenerative diseases, and providing emergency financial assistance to Alzheimer's disease patients and their caregivers. Current programs include Alzheimer's Disease Research, National Glaucoma Research, National Heart Foundation, and Macular Degeneration Research.

In-house, DC-area Employees

HEROLD, Eve: Public Education Manager
MICHAELS, Janet: Exec. Director

American Health Care Ass'n

1201 L St. NW
Washington, DC 20005-4014
Tel: (202)842-4444
Fax: (202)842-3860
Registered: LDA
Web: www.ahca.org

Represents long term care facilities throughout the United States. Formerly (1974) American Nursing Home Ass'n.

Leg. Issues: BUD, HCR, INS, LBR, MMM, VET

Political Action Committee/s

American Health Care Ass'n Political Action Committee
1201 L St. NW
Washington, DC 20005-4014
Tel: (202)842-4444
Fax: (202)842-3860
Contact: Anna Lee

In-house, DC-area Employees

HOGAN, J. Michael: Senior Director, Legislative Affairs
LEE, Anna: PAC Administrator
MORTON, Cynthia: Director, Congressional Affairs
SCHAEFFLER, John: V. President, Legislative Affairs
SHOEMAKER, Priscilla: Senior Director, Legal Services, Clinical & Facility Operations
SMITH, Elise D.: Senior Director, Finance and Managed Care
SMITH, Todd: Director, Policy & Analysis
YARWOOD, Bruce: Legislative Counsel

Outside Counsel/Consultants

Edelman Public Relations Worldwide
Rep By: Leslie Dach, John Schmidt, Peter Segall

Greenberg Traurig, LLP
Issues: BUD, HCR, MMM
Rep By: Rob Garagiola, Russell J. Mueller, Nancy E. Taylor, Timothy P. Trysla

Helmsin & Yarwood Associates
Issues: HCR, INS, LBR, MMM, VET
Rep By: Bruce Yarwood

American Health Information Management Ass'n

1225 I St. NW
Suite 500
Washington, DC 20005
Tel: (202)218-3535
Fax: (202)682-0078
Registered: LDA
Web: www.ahima.org
E-mail: info@ahima.org

Headquartered in Chicago, IL.

Leg. Issues: HCR

In-house, DC-area Employees

ASMONGA, Donald D.: Manager, Government Relations
RODE, Daniel F.: V. President, Policy and Gov't Relations

Outside Counsel/Consultants

Washington Health Advocates
Issues: HCR
Rep By: Douglas Peddicord, Ph.D.

American Health Lawyers Ass'n

1025 Connecticut Ave. NW
Suite 600
Washington, DC 20036
Tel: (202)833-1100
Fax: (202)833-1105
Web: www.healthlawyers.org
E-mail: info@healthlawyers.org

In-house, DC-area Employees

LEIBOLD, Peter M.: Exec. V. President

American Health Quality Ass'n

1140 Connecticut Ave. NW
Suite 1050
Washington, DC 20036
Tel: (202)331-5790
Fax: (202)331-9334
Web: www.ahqa.org
E-mail: dschulke@ahqa.org

Promotes health care quality through community-based, independent quality evaluation and improvement programs.

In-house, DC-area Employees

DEUTSCH, Richard: Director, Communications
GAUDETTE, Sylvia: Director, Government Relations
MILGATE, Karen: Deputy Exec. V. President
PAGANELLI, Virginia: Director, Scientific and Technical Affairs
SCHULKE, David G.: Exec. V. President

American Healthways, Inc.

Nashville, TN

Outside Counsel/Consultants

Winston & Strawn
Rep By: Charles L. Kinney, Thomas L. Mills

American Heart Ass'n

1150 Connecticut Ave. NW
Suite 810
Washington, DC 20036
Tel: (202)785-7900
Fax: (202)785-7950
Registered: LDA
Web: www.americanheart.org
Leg. Issues: BUD, FOO, GOV, HCR, MED, SCI, TAX, TOB

In-house, DC-area Employees

CANOVA, Diane M.: V. President, Advocacy
HAMBURG, Richard S.: Director, Government Relations
KLEIN, Benjamin: Government Relations Representative
LOUIS, Claudia: Government Relations Manager
MOELLER, Karl: Manager, Government Relations
WILLIAMS, Brian: Government Relations Manager

Outside Counsel/Consultants

Susan Molinari, L.L.P.
Issues: HCR
Rep By: Hon. Susan Molinari

American Helicopter Soc. Internat'l

217 N. Washington St.
Alexandria, VA 22314
Tel: (703)684-6777
Fax: (703)739-9279
Web: www.vtol.org
E-mail: staff@vtol.org

An international professional technical society dedicated to the advancement and practical application of vertical flight worldwide.

In-house, DC-area Employees

FLATER, M. E. Rhett: Exec. Director

American Hellenic Educational Progressive Ass'n (AHEPA)

1909 Q St. NW
Suite 500
Washington, DC 20009-1007
Tel: (202)232-6300
Fax: (202)232-2140
Web: www.ahepa.org
E-mail: ahepa@ahepa.org

AHEPA is the largest Greek American association and a major community service organization in North America.

Political Action Committee/s

American Hellenic Educational Progressive Ass'n Political Action Committee (AHEPA-PAC)
1909 Q St. NW
Suite 500
Washington, DC 20009-1007
Tel: (202)232-6300
Fax: (202)232-2140

In-house, DC-area Employees

KOLARAS, Demo: Exec. Director

American Hellenic Institute Public Affairs Committee

1220 16th St. NW
Washington, DC 20036
Tel: (202)659-4608
Fax: (202)785-5178
Registered: LDA
Web: www.ahiworld.org

Provides an organization and program to strengthen relations between the U.S. and Greece and Cyprus, and within the American Hellenic Community.

Leg. Issues: FOR

In-house, DC-area Employees

CLARKE, Jonathan G.: Public Affairs Consultant
LARIGAKIS, Nicholas: Exec. Director

Outside Counsel/Consultants

Rogers & Wells

American Hellenic Institute, Inc.

1220 16th St. NW
Washington, DC 20036
Tel: (202)785-8430
Fax: (202)785-5178
Registered: LDA
Web: www.hri.org/ahipac
E-mail: info@ahiworld.org

Founded on August 1, 1974, as a 501 (C)(3) non-profit tax-exempt business league. An independent public policy trade association promoting commerce, investment and related matters between the U.S., Greece and Cyprus and within the American Hellenic Community.

In-house, DC-area Employees

LARIGAKIS, Nicholas: Exec. Director
MARKETOS, James: Chairman

Outside Counsel/Consultants

Rogers & Wells

American Herbal Products Ass'n

Los Angeles, CA
Web: www.ahpa.org
E-mail: ahpa@ahpa.org
Leg. Issues: FOO, GOV

Outside Counsel/Consultants

The Dutko Group, Inc.
Issues: FOO, GOV
Rep By: Mark S. Irion, Kimberly M. Spaulding

American Highway Users Alliance

1776 Massachusetts Ave. NW
Suite 500
Washington, DC 20036
Tel: (202)857-1200
Fax: (202)857-1220
Registered: LDA
Web: www.highways.org
E-mail: GOHighway@aol.com

Members generally include those connected with the automotive industry and other providers and users of highway transportation goods and services who stand to benefit from increased use of the nation's road system.

Leg. Issues: BUD, ENV, ROD, TAX, TRA

In-house, DC-area Employees

BOWLDEN, Taylor R.: V. President, Policy and Government Affairs
BUFF, Bill: Director, Communications and Government Affairs
FAY, William D.: President and Chief Exec. Officer
LAKIN, David N.: V. President, Public Liaison

American Hiking Soc.

1422 Fenwick Ln.
Silver Spring, MD 20910
Tel: (301)565-6704
Fax: (301)565-6714
Web: www.americanhiking.org

An advocacy and educational organization for hikers.

Leg. Issues: NAT, RES

In-house, DC-area Employees

MONTORFANO, Celina: Alliance Policy Coordinator
SLOAN, Mary Margaret: President

American Historical Ass'n

400 A St. SE
Washington, DC 20003
Tel: (202)544-2422
Fax: (202)544-8307
Web: www.theaha.org
E-mail: aha@theaha.org

The American Historical Association is a nonprofit membership organization founded in 1884 and incorporated by congress in 1889 for the promotion of historical studies, the collection and preservation of historical documents and artifacts, and the dissemination of historical research.

Leg. Issues: CPI, CPT, DOC, EDU, GOV, MIA

In-house, DC-area Employees

JONES, Arnita: Exec. Director

Outside Counsel/Consultants

Beveridge & Diamond, P.C.

American Holistic Medical Ass'n

McLean, VA

Outside Counsel/Consultants

Degnon Associates, Inc.

American Home Products Corp.

1667 K St. NW
Suite 1270
Washington, DC 20006
Tel: (202)659-8320
Fax: (202)496-2448
Registered: LDA
Leg. Issues: AGR, ANI, CAW, CHM, CPT, CSP, ENV, FOO, HCR, MMM, PHA, TAX, TRD

Political Action Committee/s

AHP Good Government Fund
1667 K St. NW
Suite 1270
Washington, DC 20006
Tel: (202)659-8320
Fax: (202)496-2448
Contact: Leo C. Jardot

In-house, DC-area Employees

JARDOT, Leo C.: V. President, Government Relations
KAYE, Bronwen A.: Director, Government Relations
MYRICK, Chris: Director, Government Relations
RABINOWITZ, Julie M.: Director, Government Relations and Counsel

Outside Counsel/Consultants

Akin, Gump, Strauss, Hauer & Feld, L.L.P.
Issues: CPT, HCR, PHA
Rep By: Elizabeth Hyman, Daniel L. Spiegel, S. Bruce Wilson

Canfield & Associates, Inc.
Issues: TAX
Rep By: Roger Blauwet, April Boston, Anne C. Canfield

Heidepriem & Mager, Inc.
Issues: PHA
Rep By: Karin Bolte, Nikki Heidepriem, Mimi Mager

Williams & Jensen, P.C.
Issues: CAW, CHM, CPT, CSP, FOO, HCR, MMM, PHA, TAX
Rep By: David E. Franasiak, Robert E. Glennon, Jr., J. Steven Hart, Karen Judd Lewis, John J. McMackin, Jr., George G. Olsen, Anthony J. Roda, David A. Starr, Frank C. Vlossak

American Homeowners Grassroots Alliance

6776 Little Falls Rd.
Arlington, VA 22213
Tel: (703)536-7776
Fax: (703)536-0003
Web: www.americanhomeowners.org
E-mail: Amerhome@aol.com

An advocacy organization representing the nation's 70 million homeowners. Focuses on issues impacting home ownership, buying, selling, building, remodeling, investing and financing.

Leg. Issues: BAN, BNK, CSP, HOU, INS, RES, TAX, TEC

In-house, DC-area Employees

HAHN, Beth D.: Exec. V. President

American Honda Motor Co., Inc.

Torrance, CA
Leg. Issues: AUT, ENV, TRA

Outside Counsel/Consultants

Dorfman & O'Neal, Inc.
Issues: AUT, ENV, TRA
Rep By: Ira H. Dorfman, Marc McConahy, Maria F. Neve

American Honey Producers Ass'n

Bruce, SD
Leg. Issues: AGR

Outside Counsel/Consultants

Collier Shannon Scott, PLLC
Rep By: Michael J. Coursey, Paul C. Rosenthal, David C. Smith, Jr.

Winston & Strawn
Issues: AGR
Rep By: Robert M. Bor, John A. Waits, II

American Horse Council, Inc.

1700 K St. NW
Suite 300
Washington, DC 20006
Tel: (202)296-4031
Fax: (202)296-1970
Registered: LDA
Web: www.horsecouncil.org
E-mail: ahc@horsecouncil.org

The trade association of the equine industry established in 1969 to monitor legislation and federal regulations affecting the horse industry and to keep its members informed.

Leg. Issues: AGR, ANI, BUD, CPT, GAM, IMM, TAX, TRA, TRD

Political Action Committee/s

American Horse Council Committee on Legislation and Taxation
1700 K St. NW
Suite 300
Washington, DC 20006
Tel: (202)296-4031
Fax: (202)296-1970
Contact: James J. Hickey, Jr.

In-house, DC-area Employees

HICKEY, Jr., James J.: President
ROBINSON, Brooke: Director, Legislative Affairs

Outside Counsel/Consultants

Davis & Harman LLP
Issues: TAX
Rep By: Thomas A. Davis

American Horse Protection Ass'n

1000 29th St. NW
Suite T-100
Washington, DC 20007
Tel: (202)965-0500
Fax: (202)965-9621

In-house, DC-area Employees

LOHNES, Robin C.: Exec. Director

American Hospital Ass'n

325 Seventh St. NW
Washington, DC 20004
Tel: (202)638-1100
Fax: (202)626-2254
Registered: LDA
Web: www.aha.org

The American Hospital Ass'n also serves as the contact point within the U.S. for the London-based Internat'l Hospital Federation.

Leg. Issues: BUD, HCR, LAW, MMM, TAX

Political Action Committee/s

American Hospital Ass'n Political Action Committee (AHA PAC)
325 Seventh St. NW
Washington, DC 20004
Tel: (202)638-1100
Fax: (202)626-2332
Contact: Mark Seklecki

In-house, DC-area Employees

AHNEN, Stephen: V. President, Special Assistant to the President
BENTLEY, James: Senior V. President, Strategic Policy Planning
COLLINS, Molly: Senior Associate Director, Public Policy Development
COYLE, Carmela: Senior V. President, Policy
DAVIDSON, Richard: President
GOLDMAN, Patricia R.: Senior Associate Director, Legislative Affairs
HATTON, Melinda Reid "Mindy": V. President and Chief Washington Counsel
LUGGIERO, Carla: Senior Associate Director, Legislative Affairs
MAGNO, Linda: Managing Director, Policy Development, Analysis, and Regulatory Affairs
MARONE, Barbara: Associate Director, Public Policy Development, Analysis, and Regulatory Affairs
MORRIS, Kristen: V. President, Legislative Affairs
MUDRON, Maureen: Senior Counsel
NICKLES, Thomas P.: Senior V. President, Federal Relations
POLLACK, Richard J.: Exec. V. President
PRYGA, Ellen A.: Director, Public Policy Development, Analysis, and Regulatory Affairs
REITER, Jim: Director, Advocacy and Member Communications
ROCK, Mike J.: Senior Associate Director, Legislative Affairs
ROONEY, Curtis: Senior Associate Director
SAVARY TAYLOR, Mary Beth: Director, Exec. Branch Relations
SEKLECKI, Mark: PAC Director
SIMPSON, Cal: Regional Exec.
WADE, Richard H.: Senior V. President, Strategic Communications
WEINER, Debbie: Director, AC and Grassroots Advocacy

Outside Counsel/Consultants

Arent Fox Kintner Plotkin & Kahn, PLLC
Issues: HCR
Rep By: Stacy Harbison, William A. Sarraille

Bergner Bockorny Castagnetti and Hawkins
Issues: BUD, HCR, MMM
Rep By: Jeffrey T. Bergner, David A. Bockorny, David Castagnetti, Melissa Schulman

diGenova & Toensing
Issues: MMM
Rep By: Joseph E. diGenova, Brady Toensing, Victoria Toensing

Health Policy Alternatives, Inc.
Issues: HCR
Rep By: Thomas Ault, Richard Lauderbaugh

The Legislative Strategies Group, LLC
Issues: HCR
Rep By: Martin B. Gold, Denise M. Henry

O'Neill, Athy & Casey, P.C.
Issues: HCR, LAW
Rep By: Christopher R. O'Neill

Public Opinion Strategies
Rep By: William D. McInturff

Quinn Gillespie & Associates
Issues: HCR
Rep By: Bruce H. Andrews, Edward W. Gillespie

Ricchetti Inc.

The Washington Group
Issues: BUD
Rep By: William J. Burke, Tripp Funderburk, Rita M. Lewis, G. John O'Hanlon, John D. Raffaelli, Tonya Saunders, Mark Schnabel

American Hotel and Lodging Ass'n

1201 New York Ave. NW
Suite 600
Washington, DC 20005-3931
Tel: (202)289-3100
Fax: (202)289-3199
Registered: LDA
Web: www.ahma.com
E-mail: infoctr@ahma.com

Formerly known as the American Hotel and Motel Ass'n.

Leg. Issues: BUD, CSP, FOO, GAM, IMM, LBR, RES, TAX, TEC, TOB, TOU, TRA

Political Action Committee/s

American Hotel and Motel Political Action Committee (AHMPAC)
1201 New York Ave. NW
Suite 600
Washington, DC 20005-3931
Tel: (202)289-3100
Fax: (202)289-3199
Contact: Lisa Costello

In-house, DC-area Employees

CONNORS, John P.: Exec. V. President, Governmental Affairs
COSTELLO, Lisa: PAC Director
ELLIOTT, Robert F.: Director, Regulatory Affairs
FISHER, William P.: President and Chief Exec. Officer
GAY, John F.: V. President, Government Affairs
HERMANN, Ronda: Manager, Legislative Communications
MAHER, Kevin L.: Director, Governmental Affairs
NELSON, Maura: V. President, Communications and marketing
POTTER, Kathryn: Director, Communications

Outside Counsel/Consultants

BKSH & Associates
Issues: BUD, LBR, TAX, TOB, TOU, TRA

American Humane Ass'n

236 Massachusetts Ave. NE
Suite 203
Washington, DC 20002-5702
Tel: (202)543-7780
Fax: (202)546-3266
Registered: LDA
Web: www.americanhumane.org

A non-profit organization working to protect both children and animals from abuse, neglect, and exploitation. Headquartered in Denver, CO.

Leg. Issues: ANI, ENV, FAM, WEL

In-house, DC-area Employees

BECK, Jennifer: Policy Analyst
DOUGLASS, Adele: Director, Washington Office
RIDINGS, Amy: Director, Legislative Affairs

Outside Counsel/Consultants

Kutak Rock LLP

American Immigration Lawyers Ass'n

918 F St. NW
Washington, DC 20004-1400
Tel: (202)216-2400
Fax: (202)371-9449
Registered: LDA
Web: www.aila.org

An association of 7,000 attorneys and law professors practicing and teaching in the field of immigration law. Advocates for fair and reasonable immigration law and policy.

Leg. Issues: IMM

In-house, DC-area Employees

AUERBACH, Randy: Director, Publications
BROWN, Theresa Cardinal: Associate Director, Advocacy
BUTTERFIELD, Jeanne A.: Exec. Director
GOLUB, Judith E.: Director, Advocacy and Public Affairs
KOLBE, Diane: Associate Director, Membership
NOVICK, Amy R.: Deputy Director for Programs
QUARLES, Susan D.: Deputy Director for Finance and Administration
TALLMER, Matt: Public Affairs Associate
WILLIAMS, Crystal: Director, Liaison and Information

American Import Shippers Ass'n

New Rochelle, NY

Outside Counsel/Consultants

Aitken, Irvin, Lewin, Berlin, Vrooman & Cohn
Rep By: Martin J. Lewin

McDermott, Will and Emery
Rep By: Calvin P. Johnson

American Importers and Exporters/Meat Products Group

Washington, DC

Outside Counsel/Consultants

Max N. Berry Law Offices
Rep By: Max N. Berry

American Indian Ass'n

Leg. Issues: ECN, GAM, IND, TOB

Outside Counsel/Consultants

Capital Consultants Corp.
Issues: ECN, GAM, IND, TOB
Rep By: Michael David Kaiser

American Indian Heritage Foundation

6051 Arlington Blvd.
Falls Church, VA 22044
Tel: (703)237-7500
Fax: (703)532-1921
Web: www.indians.org

Shares the cultural diversity of the American Indian with the non-Indian, and sponsors numerous special programs to benefit Indians. Has attracted more than 250,000 donors.

In-house, DC-area Employees

PALE MOON, Princess: President
ROSE, Dr. Wil: Chief Exec. Officer

American Indian Higher Education Consortium

121 Oronoco St.
Alexandria, VA 22314
Tel: (703)838-0400
Fax: (703)838-0388
Web: www.aihec.org
E-mail: aihec@aihec.org
Leg. Issues: BUD, COM, EDU, HCR, IND, MED, TEC

In-house, DC-area Employees

GIPP, Dr. Gerald: Exec. Director

Outside Counsel/Consultants

Cavarocchi Ruscio Dennis Associates
Issues: BUD, EDU, HCR, IND, MED
Rep By: Nicholas G. Cavarocchi, Domenic R. Ruscio

Bob Foster and Associates
Issues: BUD
Rep By: Robert B. Foster

Sara Garland (and Associates)
Issues: BUD, COM, EDU, IND, TEC
Rep By: Rachel A. Emmons, Sara G. Garland

American Industrial Hygiene Ass'n

2700 Prosperity Ave.
Suite 250
Fairfax, VA 22031
Tel: (703)849-8888
Fax: (703)207-3561
Registered: LDA
Web: www.aiha.org
E-mail: infonet@aiha.org
Leg. Issues: LBR, SMB

In-house, DC-area Employees

TRIPPLER, Aaron K.: Director, Government Affairs

Outside Counsel/Consultants

Bain and Associates, Inc.

American Institute for Conservation of Historic and Artistic Works

1717 K St. NW
Suite 200
Washington, DC 20006
Tel: (202)452-9545
Fax: (202)452-9328
Web: aic.stanford.edu
E-mail: info@aic-faic.org

Founded in 1959 as the American Group of the Internat'l Institute for Conservation of Historic and Artistic Works. A nonprofit professional membership organization whose purpose is to advance the knowledge and practice of conservation of cultural property.

Leg. Issues: ART

In-house, DC-area Employees
JONES, Elizabeth F.: Exec. Director

American Institute for Foreign Studies

Stamford, CT

Specializes in arranging and facilitating foreign exchange programs, including au pair programs.

Leg. Issues: EDU, FOR

Outside Counsel/Consultants

The Advocacy Group
Issues: FOR
Rep By: Robert J. Dotchin

Bracy Williams & Co.
Issues: EDU
Rep By: Linda Doorfee Flaherty, Susan J. Williams

American Institute for Public Safety

Leg. Issues: TRA

Outside Counsel/Consultants

U.S. Strategies Corp.
Issues: TRA
Rep By: Steven E. Carey, Michael K. Wyrick

American Institute for Shippers' Ass'ns

P.O. Box 33457
Washington, DC 20033
Tel: (202)628-0933
Fax: (202)296-7374
Web: www.shippers.org
E-mail: gcella@shippers.org

Represents the cooperative shipping industry.

Leg. Issues: MAR, TRA, TRU

In-house, DC-area Employees
CELLA, Glenn R.: Exec. Director
COBERT, Ronald N.: General Counsel

Outside Counsel/Consultants

Grove, Jaskiewicz, and Cobert
Issues: MAR, TRA, TRU
Rep By: Ronald N. Cobert

American Institute of Aeronautics and Astronautics

1801 Alexander Bell Dr.
Suite 500
Reston, VA 20191
Tel: (703)264-7500
Fax: (703)264-7551
Registered: LDA
Web: www.aiaa.org
E-mail: custserv@aiaa.org

A non-profit professional society for aerospace engineers and scientists. Membership: 40,000.

Leg. Issues: AER

In-house, DC-area Employees
CHATTMAN, Ray: Foundation Director
DE JONGH, Allison: Government Relations Representative
DUROCHER, Cort: Exec. Director
GREY, Jerry: Consultant
LEWIS, Michael J.: Business Development Group
LOONEY, Paul: Government Relations Representative

The American Institute of Architects

1735 New York Ave. NW
Washington, DC 20006
Tel: (202)626-7300
Fax: (202)626-7365
Registered: LDA
Web: www.aiaonline.com
E-mail: govaffs@aia.org

The AIA, founded in 1857, through education, government advocacy, community development, and public outreach activities works to achieve a more human built environment and a higher standard of professionalism for architects.

Leg. Issues: ART, BUD, CIV, DIS, EDU, ENV, GOV, HOU, RES, ROD, SMB, TAX, TOR, TRA, URB

Political Action Committee/s

ArchiPAC
1735 New York Ave. NW
Washington, DC 20006
Tel: (202)626-7300
Fax: (202)626-7365
Contact: Richard W. McDonnell

In-house, DC-area Employees
BLACKWELL, Lisa E.: Managing Director, Government Affairs
BUTLER, Tara A.: Legislative Analyst, Federal Affairs
DINEGAR, James C.: Chief Operating Officer
HAMLIN, Charles E.: Managing Director, Communications
KOONCE, Norman L.: Exec. V. President/C.E.O.
MCDONNELL, Richard W.: Program Manager, PAC/Grass Roots
WILSON, Daniel S.: Senior Director, Federal Affairs

American Institute of Biological Sciences

1444 I St. NW
Suite 200
Washington, DC 20005
Tel: (202)628-1500
Fax: (202)628-1509
Web: www.aibs.org

Fosters research and education in the biological sciences, including the medical, agricultural and environmental sciences and their applications to human welfare through meetings, publications and assistance to and cooperation with other science, health and environmental organizations.

In-house, DC-area Employees
O'GRADY, Richard: Exec. Director

Outside Counsel/Consultants

Heenan, Althen & Roles

American Institute of Certified Planners

1776 Massachusetts Ave. NW
Suite 400
Washington, DC 20036
Tel: (202)872-0611
Fax: (202)872-0643
Web: www.planning.org
E-mail: aicp@planning.org

The professional institute for city and regional planners within the American Planning Ass'n.

In-house, DC-area Employees
COYNE, Glenn: Director

American Institute of Certified Public Accountants

1455 Pennsylvania Ave. NW
Suite 400
Washington, DC 20004-1081
Tel: (202)737-6600
Fax: (202)638-4512
Registered: LDA
Web: www.aicpa.org

Leg. Issues: BAN, BNK, CPI, EDU, FIN, HCR, LBR, RET, TAX

Political Action Committee/s

AICPA Effective Legislation Committee
1455 Pennsylvania Ave. NW
Suite 400
Washington, DC 20004-1081
Tel: (202)737-6600
Fax: (202)638-4512

In-house, DC-area Employees
HIGGINBOTHAM, J. Thomas: V. President, Congressional and Political Affairs
HUNNICUTT, John E.: Senior V. President, Public Affairs
KARL, Edward: Director, Taxation
KRAVITZ, Peter: Director Congressional and Political Affairs
MACKAY, Ian: Director, Professional Standards and Services
PADWE, Gerry: V. President, Taxation
STROMSEM, William: Director, Taxation

Outside Counsel/Consultants

Troutman Sanders LLP
Issues: CPI, TAX
Rep By: Mary Clare Fitzgerald

American Institute of Chemical Engineers

1300 I St. NW
Suite 1090
East Tower
Washington, DC 20005-3314
Tel: (202)962-8690
Fax: (202)962-8699
Registered: LDA
Web: www.aiche.org
E-mail: dc@aiche.org

Headquartered in New York, NY.

Leg. Issues: BUD, EDU, ENV, HCR, MAN, RET, SCI, TAX

In-house, DC-area Employees
CLARK-SULLIVAN, Esq., Carla: Legislative Affairs
SCHUSTER, Ph.D., Darlene S.: Director, Government Relations

Outside Counsel/Consultants

Dr. John V. Dugan, Jr.
Rep By: Dr. John V. Dugan, Jr.

American Institute of Chemists

515 King St.
Suite 420
Alexandria, VA 22314
Tel: (703)836-2090
Fax: (703)684-6048
Web: www.theaic.org
E-mail: SDobson@Clarionmr.com

In-house, DC-area Employees
DOBSON, Sharon: Exec. Director
HENDRICKSON, Dr. Connie: President

American Institute of Chemists Foundation

515 King St.
Suite 420
Alexandria, VA 22314
Tel: (703)836-2090
Fax: (703)684-6048
Web: www.theaic.org
E-mail: aicoffice@theaic.org

The Foundation seeks to promote education in the chemical sciences.

In-house, DC-area Employees
DOBSON, Sharon: Contact

American Institute of Physics

One Physics Ellipse
College Park, MD 20740-3843
Tel: (301)209-3100
Fax: (301)209-0843
Registered: LDA
Web: www.aip.org
E-mail: aipinfo@aip.org

Leg. Issues: BUD, DEF, EDU, ENV, MED, SCI

In-house, DC-area Employees
BRODSKY, Marc H.: Exec. Director and Chief Exec. Officer
JONES, Richard M.: Senior Liaison, Government and Institutional Relations
LEATH, Audrey T.: Liaison, Government and Institutional Relations
TORRES, Alicia

American Institute of Ultrasound in Medicine

14750 Sweitzer Ln.
Suite 100
Laurel, MD 20707-5906
Tel: (301)498-4100
Fax: (301)498-4450
Web: www.aium.org
E-mail: cvalente@aium.org

AIUM is a non-profit organization dedicated to advancing the art and science of ultrasound in medicine and research. Its activities are professional, educational, literary, and scientific.

Leg. Issues: CSP, HCR, MED, MMM, SCI

In-house, DC-area Employees
BESSLING, Stacey: Public Relations Coordinator
VALENTE, Ph.D., CAE, Carmine M.: Exec. Director

American Institutes for Research

3333 K St. NW
Suite 300
Washington, DC 20007
Tel: (202)342-5000
Fax: (202)342-5033
Web: www.air-dc.org

A private, non-profit organization that conducts research in the behavioral and social sciences.

In-house, DC-area Employees
GOSLIN, Dr. David A.: President and Chief Exec. Officer
PELAVIN, Sol H.: Exec. V. President

American Insurance Ass'n

1130 Connecticut Ave. NW
Suite 1000
Washington, DC 20036
Tel: (202)828-7100
Fax: (202)293-1219
Registered: LDA
Web: www.aiadc.org

Leg. Issues: BAN, BUD, CSP, DIS, ENV, FIN, HCR, INS, LBR, TAX, TOB, TRA, TRD, URB

Political Action Committee/s

American Insurance Ass'n Political Action Committee
1130 Connecticut Ave. NW
Suite 1000
Washington, DC 20036
Tel: (202)828-7100
Fax: (202)293-1219

In-house, DC-area Employees
ARLINGTON, John G.: Assistant V. President, Federal Affairs
BALLEN, Debra T.: Senior V. President, Policy Development/Research
HERMAN, Angela D.: Director, Federal Affairs
MITCHELL, Gray: Director, Political Programs
NGUYEN, Natalie D.: Assistant V. President, Federal Affairs
PUSEY, Leigh Ann: Senior V. President, Federal Affairs
ROCHMAN, Julie: Senior V. President, Public Affairs
SAVERCOOL, John: V. President
SHELK, Melissa Wolford: V. President, Federal Affairs
VAGLEY, Robert E.: President

Outside Counsel/Consultants

Bonner & Associates

Alan F. Coffey
Rep By: Alan F. Coffey, Jr.

The Eddie Mahe Company
Rep By: Ladonna Y. Lee, Eddie Mahe, Jr.

Patton Boggs, LLP
Rep By: Benjamin L. Ginsberg

Quinn Gillespie & Associates
Rep By: Edward W. Gillespie, Marc Lampkin

Schwartz & Ballen
Issues: BAN, INS
Rep By: Robert G. Ballen, Thomas A. Fox, Gilbert T. Schwartz

Shaw Pittman
Rep By: Marc A. Pearl

Washington Council Ernst & Young
Issues: BUD, ENV, FIN, INS, TAX, TRD
Rep By: Doug Badger, Lauren Darling, John L. Doney, Jayne T. Fitzgerald, LaBrenda Garrett-Nelson, Gary J. Gasper, Bruce A. Gates, Nick Giordano, Cathy Koch, Robert J. Leonard, Richard Meltzer, Phillip D. Moseley,

John D. Porter, Robert M. Rozen, Donna Steele-Flynn, Timothy J. Urban

American Intellectual Property Law Ass'n

2001 Jefferson Davis Hwy.
Suite 203
Arlington, VA 22202
Tel: (703)415-0780
Fax: (703)415-0786
Registered: LDA
Web: www.aipla.org
E-mail: aipla@aipla.org
Leg. Issues: CPT

Political Action Committee/s

Intellectual Property Political Action Committee
2001 Jefferson Davis Hwy.
Suite 203
Arlington, VA 22202
Contact: Michael K. Kirk
Tel: (703)415-0780
Fax: (703)415-0786

In-house, DC-area Employees

KIRK, Michael K.: Exec. Director
SCHROEDER, Lee: Deputy Exec. Director

American Internat'l Automobile Dealers Ass'n

99 Canal Center Plaza
Suite 500
Alexandria, VA 22314-1538
Tel: (703)519-7800
Fax: (703)519-7810
Registered: LDA
Web: www.aiada.org
E-mail: goaiada@aiada.org

Founded in 1970, AIADA is the trade association representing the 10,000 American small businesses and their 300,000 employees who sell and service international nameplate vehicles. The association works to preserve a free market for international automobiles in the United States by advocating before the federal government. It also works to increase public awareness of the international automobile industry's value to the American economy.

Leg. Issues: AUT, ENV, TAX, TRD

In-house, DC-area Employees

BARNES, Lori Weaver: Manager, Public Relations
COLLIER, James A. "Jay": General Manager, AIADA Services
HUIZENGA, Walter E.: President
LANE, Scott H.: V. President, Government Relations
LUSK, Cody: Director, Legislative Affairs
OSTRONIC, Judith M.: Grassroots Program Manager

American Internat'l Freight Ass'n

Web: www.tianet.org
Leg. Issues: MAR

Outside Counsel/Consultants

Garvey, Schubert & Barer
Issues: MAR
Rep By: Richard D. Gluck

American Internat'l Group, Inc.

1399 New York Ave. NW
Suite 900
Washington, DC 20005
Tel: (202)585-5800
Fax: (202)585-5820
Registered: LDA

Headquartered in New York, NY.

Leg. Issues: BAN, BUD, CPI, DIS, ENV, FIN, INS, RET, TAX, TRD, WAS

In-house, DC-area Employees

BEATSON, Nora: Associate Director, Government Affairs
JOHNSON, L. Oakley: Senior V. President, Corporate and International Affairs
MERSKI, Richard P.: V. President, Governmental Affairs
MULVEY, Kevin C. W.: Director, International Government Affairs
NICKENS, Jacqueline: Receptionist, Government Affairs
WELLING, Brad G.: Director, Federal Government Affairs

Outside Counsel/Consultants

Fontheim Partners, PC
Issues: FIN, TRD
Rep By: Claude G. B. Fontheim, Kenneth I. Levinson

Levine & Co.
Issues: TAX
Rep By: Ken Levine

Valanzano & Associates
Issues: BAN, ENV, FIN, INS, RET, TAX, TRD
Rep By: Anthony Valanzano

R. Duffy Wall and Associates
Rep By: Hon. Rodney D. Chandler

American Investors Life Insurance

Topeka, KS

Outside Counsel/Consultants

Davis & Harman LLP
Rep By: Richard S. Belas

American Iron and Steel Institute

1101 17th St. NW
Suite 1300
Washington, DC 20036-4700
Tel: (202)452-7100
Fax: (202)463-6573
Registered: LDA
Web: www.steel.org

Affiliated with The Steel Recycling Institute (see separate listing).

Leg. Issues: AUT, CAW, DEF, ENG, ENV, GOV, HCR, LBR, ROD, TAX, TOR, TRD, TRU, UTI

Political Action Committee/s

SteelPAC
1101 17th St. NW
Suite 1300
Washington, DC 20036-4700
Contact: Jennifer G. Wright
Tel: (202)452-7133
Fax: (202)833-3661

In-house, DC-area Employees

MINARDI-MOSER, Tara: Manager, Government Relations
SCHULTZ, Jim: V. President, Environment and Energy
SHARKEY, III, Andrew G.: President and Chief Exec. Officer
SNEERINGER, Thomas M.: Senior V. President, Public Policy and General Counsel
SOLARZ, Barry D.: V. President, Tax and Trade
VISSCHER, Gary: V. President, Employee Relations
WRIGHT, Jennifer G.: PAC Contact

Outside Counsel/Consultants

Collier Shannon Scott, PLLC
Issues: DEF, ENV
Rep By: Robert W. Porter, Dana S. Wood

John M. Stinson
Issues: ENG, ENV
Rep By: John M. Stinson

American Israel Public Affairs Committee

440 First St. NW
Suite 600
Washington, DC 20001
Tel: (202)639-5200
Registered: LDA

A domestic, American organization of about 55,000 members which lobbies on legislation affecting U.S.-Israeli relations.

Leg. Issues: BUD, DEF, FOR

In-house, DC-area Employees

COLMAN, Jeffrey: Legislative Liaison/Lobbyist
FEUER, Marvin: Defense and Strategic Issues Director
GILLETTE, David: Senior Legislative Liaison
GORDON, Bradley: Legislative Director/Lobbyist
KAPLAN, Lionel: President
KOHR, Howard: Exec. Director
KURZ, Ester: Director, Legislative Strategy and Policy
ROSEN, Steve: Foreign Policy Issues Director

Outside Counsel/Consultants

Friedman Law Offices, P.L.L.C.
Rep By: Philip S. Friedman

American Jewish Committee

1156 15th St. NW
Suite 1201
Washington, DC 20005
Tel: (202)785-4200
Fax: (202)785-4115
Registered: LDA
Web: www.ajc.org
E-mail: ogia@ajc.org

Founded in 1906 by American Jews seeking to focus world attention on the pogroms in Russia, the Committee now claims about 50,000 members and maintains offices in 32 U.S. cities and Jerusalem. Generally supports pro-Israel policies, but takes independent positions on specific issues. International program includes efforts to assure well-being of Jewish communities around the world, and protection of minority rights generally. Domestic program covers broad range of human rights, civil liberties, social welfare, and education issues. Affiliated with Leadership Conference on Civil Rights and other coalitional groups in furtherance of a democratic, pluralistic society. Headquartered in New York, NY.

Leg. Issues: AGR, CIV, ENG, FAM, FOR, GOV, IMM, LAW, REL, WEL

In-house, DC-area Employees

BAKER, Rabbi Andrew: Director, European Affairs
BERNSTEIN, David: Director, Washington Chapter
FOLTIN, Richard T.: Director, Legislative Affairs and Counsel
ISAACSON, Jason F.: Director, Government and International Affairs
JACOBS, Barry: Director, Strategic Studies
KUPFERMAN, Alon: Assistant Director, Legislative Affairs

American Jewish Congress

2027 Massachusetts Ave. NW
Washington, DC 20036
Tel: (202)332-4001
Fax: (202)387-3434
Web: www.ajcongress.org
E-mail: washrep@ajcongress.org

National Jewish community relations and civil liberties membership organization dedicated to the preservation of all religious, racial and gender rights. It seeks to combat anti-Semitism and other forms of discrimination in the areas of employment, education, housing and voting. Areas of activity include: Church-State relations; government involvement in parochial schools; public school prayer; constitutional, minority and women's rights; Arab boycott of Israel; Middle East peace; and world Jewry. Headquartered in New York City.

Leg. Issues: BUD, CIV, DOC, EDU, FAM, FIR, FOR, GOV, HCR, IMM, LAW, MMM, UNM, WEL

In-house, DC-area Employees

ALEXANDER, Deborah: Special Assistant, Government and Public Affairs

American Kennel Club

New York, NY
Leg. Issues: ANI

Outside Counsel/Consultants

McGuiness Norris & Williams, LLP
Issues: ANI
Rep By: James S. Holt, William N. LaForge

American Koyo Corp.

Westlake, OH

Outside Counsel/Consultants

Arter & Hadden
Rep By: Daniel L. Cohen

American Kurdish Information Network (AKIN)

2600 Connecticut Ave. NW
Suite One
Washington, DC 20008-1558
Tel: (202)483-6444
Fax: (202)483-6476
Web: www.kurdistan.org
E-mail: akin@kurdistan.org

A non-profit organization serving the information needs of the United States relative to the Kurds.

Leg. Issues: EDU, FOR, IMM

In-house, DC-area Employees

XULAM, Kani: Director

American Labor Education Center

2000 P St. NW
Suite 300
Washington, DC 20036
Tel: (202)828-5170
Fax: (202)785-3862
E-mail: amlabor@mindspring.com

In-house, DC-area Employees

OHMANS, Karen: Director

The American Land Conservancy

San Francisco, CA
Leg. Issues: ENV

Outside Counsel/Consultants

Crowell & Moring LLP
Rep By: Steven P. Quarles

The Paul Laxalt Group
Issues: ENV
Rep By: Hon. Paul D. Laxalt, Tom Loranger

American Land Rights Ass'n

1217 E St. NE
Washington, DC 20002
Tel: (202)544-6156
Fax: (202)547-7513
E-mail: alra-dc@access.digex.net

Formed in 1978 as the National Park Inholders Association by individuals owning property in national parks. Expanded as the National Inholders Association in 1980 to include all persons owning property or some other equity interest within the boundary of any federally managed area or who is impacted by the management, regulation or access of that area. This includes all National Parks, Forests, Fish and Wildlife Areas, Bureau of Land Management and Corps of Engineers/Bureau of Reclamation areas. These people may own, lease or rent property or have a permit to graze, cut timber on, mine or otherwise use federal land.

In-house, DC-area Employees

GREFRATH, Bruce: Washington Representative

American Land Title Ass'n

1828 L St. NW
Suite 705
Washington, DC 20036
Tel: (202)296-3671
Fax: (202)223-5843
Registered: LDA
Web: www.alta.org
E-mail: service@alta.org
Leg. Issues: BAN, BNK, INS

Political Action Committee/s

Title Industry Political Action Committee
1828 L St. NW
Suite 705
Washington, DC 20036
Contact: Ann Hadley vom Eigen
Tel: (202)296-3671
Fax: (202)223-5843

In-house, DC-area Employees
FROHMAN, Charles: Director, Grassroots
MAHER, James R.: Exec. V. President
RAGAN, Lorri: V. President, Public Affairs
VOM EIGEN, Ann Hadley: Legislative Counsel

Outside Counsel/Consultants
Collier Shannon Scott, PLLC
Issues: BAN, INS
Rep By: Scott A. Sinder
Valanzano & Associates
Issues: BAN
Rep By: Anthony Valanzano

American League of Anglers and Boaters

c/o Amer. Recreation Coalition
1225 New York Ave. NW
Suite 450
Washington, DC 20005
Tel: (202)682-9530
Fax: (202)682-9529

In-house, DC-area Employees
CRANDALL, Derrick A.: Contact

American League of Financial Institutions

900 19th St. NW
Suite 400
Washington, DC 20006
Tel: (202)628-5624
Fax: (202)296-8716
Registered: LDA
Leg. Issues: BAN, BUD, FIN, HOU, RES, SMB, URB

In-house, DC-area Employees
CURTIS, Dina: President

American League of Lobbyists

P.O. Box 30005
Alexandria, VA 22310
Tel: (703)960-3011
Fax: (703)960-4070
Web: www.alldc.org
E-mail: alldc.org@erols.com

A non-profit membership organization whose purpose is to enhance the professionalism, competence, and ethical standards of lobbyists and to respond to challenges affecting First Amendment rights.

In-house, DC-area Employees
ALBERTINE, James J.: President
BABER, Patti Jo: Exec. Director

Outside Counsel/Consultants
Heenan, Althen & Roles
Rep By: William I. Althen

American Legion

1608 K St. NW
Washington, DC 20006
Tel: (202)861-2700
Fax: (202)861-2786
Registered: LDA

A major influential veterans organization established in 1919. Adopts resolutions, offers suggestions and presents testimony to Congress on foreign affairs and defense issues and veterans' benefits and programs. Co-headquartered in Indianapolis, IN and Washington, DC.

Leg. Issues: BUD, CON, CPT, DEF, DIS, ECN, EDU, ENV, FAM, FIR, FOR, GOV, HCR, IMM, IND, LAW, LBR, MED, MMM, POS, SCI, SMB, TAX, TOB, TRA, TRD, VET

In-house, DC-area Employees
BRUNE, Louis: Legislative Grassroots Coordinator
JEFFERSON, John: Assistant Legislative Director
ROBERTSON, Steve A.: Director, National Legislative Commission
SCHLEE, G. Michael: Director, National Security/Foreign Relations
SOMMER, Jr., John F.: Exec. Director, Washington Office
SPANOGLE, Robert W.: National Adjutant
WHEELER, Daniel: Exec. Director
WILLIAMS, Carroll L.: Director, National Veterans Affairs Commission

Outside Counsel/Consultants
Akin, Gump, Strauss, Hauer & Feld, L.L.P.
Issues: CON
Rep By: Marlene M. Colucci, Frank J. Donatelli, Joel Jankowsky, Charles W. Johnson, IV, Steven R. Ross

American Legislative Exchange Council

910 17th St. NW
Fifth Floor
Washington, DC 20006
Tel: (202)466-3800
Fax: (202)466-3801
Web: www.alec.org

Established in 1973; it is the largest individual membership organization of state legislators. Provides research and legislative analysis to state lawmakers and other state policy leaders. Serves as legislative liaison for its members.

In-house, DC-area Employees
BURNET, Lining: Director, Programs
FLYNN, Mike: Director, Legislation and Policy
LEE, Beverlee A.: Director, Finance and Administration
MOHUNLALL, Roop: Director, Project Development
PARDE, Duane A.: Exec. Director

American Leprosy Foundation

11600 Nebel St.
Suite 210
Rockville, MD 20852
Tel: (301)984-1336
Fax: (301)770-0580
E-mail: lwm-alf@erols.com

A Leprosy and TB research organization.

In-house, DC-area Employees
REED, Pris I.: Administrative Director
WALSH, Dr. Gerald P.: Scientific Director

American Library Ass'n

1301 Pennsylvania Ave. NW
Suite 403
Washington, DC 20004
Tel: (202)628-8410
Fax: (202)628-8419
Registered: LDA
Web: www.ala.org/alawashington.html
E-mail: alawash@alawash.org

A non-profit, educational organization with more than 58,000 members, including libraries, information specialists, library users, trustees and educators. Works toward the improvement of library and information services. Headquartered in Chicago, IL.

Leg. Issues: BUD, CON, CPT, EDU, GOV, MIA, POS, TEC

In-house, DC-area Employees
BRADLEY, Lynne E.: Director, Government Relations
COSTABILE, Mary R.: Associate Director
NISBET, Miriam M.: Legislative Counsel
SHEKETOFF, Emily: Exec. Director, Washington Office
TENNANT, Claudette: Assistant Director
WEINGARTEN, Frederick: Director, Office for Information Technology Policy

Outside Counsel/Consultants
Leslie Harris & Associates
Issues: CON
Rep By: Leslie A. Harris, Liza Kessler
Jenner & Block
Morrison & Foerster LLP
Rep By: Jonathan Band
Ropes & Gray
Issues: GOV, MIA
Rep By: Thomas M. Susman
Van Scoyoc Associates, Inc.
Issues: BUD, EDU, MIA
Rep By: Robert L. Knisely, James W. Kohlmoos, H. Stewart Van Scoyoc, Noreene Wells

American Lithotripsy Soc.

Manchester, MA

Outside Counsel/Consultants
Winston & Strawn
Rep By: Thomas L. Mills

American Liver Foundation

New York, NY
Leg. Issues: BUD, HCR

Outside Counsel/Consultants
Powers Pyles Sutter & Verville, PC
Issues: BUD, HCR
Rep By: J. Michael Hall, Alyson M. Haywood

American Logistics Ass'n

1133 15th St. NW
Suite 640
Washington, DC 20005
Tel: (202)466-2520
Fax: (202)296-4419
Registered: LDA
Web: www.ala-national.org

Lobbies for an improved military resale system.

Leg. Issues: BUD, DEF, VET

Political Action Committee/s
American Logistics Ass'n PAC
1133 15th St. NW
Suite 640
Washington, DC 20005
Tel: (202)466-2520
Fax: (202)296-4419
Contact: L. Maurice Branch

In-house, DC-area Employees
BRANCH, L. Maurice: V. President, Operations
BURTON, Alan J.: President
JEPSON, Frank: V. President, Exchange and MWR Affairs
NISSALKE, Alan: V. President, Government Relations and Commissary Affairs
WILLIAMS, Leonard B.: V. President, Legislative Affairs

American Logistics Infrastructure Improvement Consortium

Washington, DC
Registered: LDA
Leg. Issues: DEF

Outside Counsel/Consultants
Wayne Arny & Assoc.
Issues: DEF
Rep By: Wayne Arny

American Lung Ass'n

1726 M St. NW
Suite 902
Washington, DC 20036
Tel: (202)785-3355
Fax: (202)452-1805
Registered: LDA
Web: www.lungusa.org
Leg. Issues: BUD, ENV, HCR

In-house, DC-area Employees
BILLINGS, Paul: Assistant Director, Government Relations
DEMULLE, Fran: Director, Washington Office and Government Relations

Outside Counsel/Consultants
A. Blakeman Early
Issues: ENV
Rep By: A. Blakeman Early
Health and Medicine Counsel of Washington
Issues: BUD, HCR
Rep By: Staci Sigman Dennison, Dale P. Dirks

American Lung Ass'n of Minnesota

St. Paul, MN
Leg. Issues: ENV, HCR

Outside Counsel/Consultants
Cassidy & Associates, Inc.
Issues: ENV, HCR
Rep By: Daniel J. McNamara, Michael Merola, Diane Rinaldo

American Maglev Technology Inc.

Outside Counsel/Consultants
Alcalde & Fay
Rep By: Hector Alcalde, Vicki L. Iseman, Christopher L. Turner

American Magline Group

Los Angeles, CA
Leg. Issues: RRR, TRA

Outside Counsel/Consultants
Alcalde & Fay
Issues: TRA
Rep By: Hon. James H. Bilbray, Paul Schlesinger, Christopher L. Turner
E. Del Smith and Co.
Issues: RRR, TRA
Rep By: E. Del Smith

American Managed Behavioral Healthcare Ass'n

700 13th St. NW
Suite 950
Washington, DC 20005
Tel: (202)434-4565
Fax: (202)434-4564
Web: www.ambha.org

A trade association that represents managed behavioral health care organizations.

Leg. Issues: ALC, HCR, MED, MMM, PHA

In-house, DC-area Employees
GREENBERG, Pamela: Exec. Director

American Managed Care Pharmacy Ass'n

2300 Ninth St. South
Suite 210
Arlington, VA 22204
Tel: (703)920-8480
Fax: (703)920-8491

In-house, DC-area Employees
KONNOR, PharmMS, Delbert D.: President and Chief Exec. Officer

American Management

Torrance, CA
Leg. Issues: TEC

Outside Counsel/Consultants
Patton Boggs, LLP
Issues: TEC
Rep By: Darryl D. Nirenberg

American Management Services, Inc.

Waltham, MA
Leg. Issues: SMB

Outside Counsel/Consultants
Commonwealth Group, Ltd.
Issues: SMB
Rep By: Christopher T. Cushing

American Management Systems

4114 Legato Rd.
Fairfax, VA 22033
Tel: (703)267-8000
Fax: (703)227-5507
Web: www.amsinc.com
Leg. Issues: CPI, CPT, DEF, ENV, FIN, GOV, SCI

Political Action Committee/s

American Management Systems Inc. PAC (AMS PAC)

4114 Legato Rd. Fairfax, VA 22033 | Tel: (703)267-8000 | Fax: (703)227-5507

In-house, DC-area Employees

GILLCASH, Robert S.: Director, Government Affairs

Outside Counsel/Consultants

Downey McGrath Group, Inc.
Issues: CPI, CPT, DEF, ENV, FIN, GOV, SCI
Rep By: Nancy Donaldson, Hon. Thomas J. Downey, Jr.

Rhoads Group
Issues: DEF
Rep By: Paul D. Behrends, Kathleen Ireland, Steven G. McKnight, B. Callan Nagle, Clifford R. Northup, Barry D. Rhoads, Thomas Worrall

American Maritime Congress

1300 I St. NW
Suite 250 West
Washington, DC 20005
Tel: (202)842-4900
Fax: (202)842-3492
Registered: LDA

Leg. Issues: DEF, MAR, TAX

In-house, DC-area Employees

MASON, Michael D.: Director, Public Affairs
TOSI, Gloria Cataneo: President
VALLENDER, Prentiss W.: Director, Legislative Affairs

Outside Counsel/Consultants

Barbour Griffith & Rogers, Inc.
Issues: DEF, MAR, TAX
Rep By: Haley Barbour, Carl Biersack, G. O. Lanny Griffith, Jr., Bill Himpler, Edward M. Rogers, Jr.

American Maritime Officers Service

490 L'Enfant Plaza East SW
Suite 7204
Washington, DC 20024
Tel: (202)479-1133
Fax: (202)479-1136
Registered: LDA

A business league.

Leg. Issues: MAR, TAX, TRA

In-house, DC-area Employees

HOOVER, Karen: Assistant Legislative Director
MCKAY, Michael: President
SPENCER, Gordon: Legislative Director

Outside Counsel/Consultants

Ann Eppard Associates, Ltd.
Issues: MAR, TRA
Rep By: Julie Chlopecki, Ann Eppard, Karen Schechter

American Mathematical Soc.

1527 18th St. NW
Washington, DC 20036
Tel: (202)588-1100
Fax: (202)588-1853
Web: www.ams.org
E-mail: amsdc@ams.org

In-house, DC-area Employees

RANKIN, III, Samuel M.: Associate Exec. Director

American Meat Institute

1700 N. Moore St.
Suite 1600
Arlington, VA 22209
Tel: (703)841-2400
Fax: (703)527-0938
Registered: LDA
Web: www.meatami.com
E-mail: memberservices@meatami.com

Represents the interests of packers and processors of beef, pork, lamb, veal and turkey products and their suppliers.

Leg. Issues: BUD, ENV, FOO, IMM, TRD, TRU

Political Action Committee/s

American Meat Institute Political Action Committee

1700 N. Moore St.
Suite 1600
Arlington, VA 22209
Contact: Christina Scarmeas
Tel: (703)841-2400
Fax: (703)527-0938

In-house, DC-area Employees

BOYLE, J. Patrick: President and Chief Exec. Officer
BROWN, Michael J.: V. President, Legislative Affairs
CONDON, Leonard W.: V. President, International Trade
DAOUST, Josee: Manager, Public Affairs
HODGES, James H.: Senior V. President, Regulatory Affairs
LILYGREN, Sara J.: Senior V. President, Legislative and Public Affairs
RILEY, Janet M.: V. President, Public Affairs
SCARMEAS, Christina: Staff Assistant, Legislative and Public Affairs
WHEELER, Sandy: Director, Human Resources and Administration

American Medical Ass'n

1101 Vermont Ave. NW
12th Floor
Washington, DC 20005-3583
Tel: (202)789-7427
Fax: (202)789-7401
Registered: LDA
Web: www.ama-assn.org
E-mail: ron_szabat@ama_assn.org

Headquartered in Chicago, IL.

Leg. Issues: BUD, HCR, INS, LBR, MED, MMM, TOB

Political Action Committee/s

American Medical Political Action Committee

1101 Vermont Ave. NW
12th Floor
Washington, DC 20005-3583
Contact: Kevin L. Walker
Tel: (202)789-7467
Fax: (202)789-7469

In-house, DC-area Employees

ASKEW, Todd: Assistant Director, Congressional Affairs
CARVIN, Margaret L.: Assistant Director, Congressional Affairs
CIORLETTI, Julia: Assistant Director of Congressional Affairs
COX, III, George E.: Senior Washington Counsel, Division of Legislative Counsel
CRAINE, Brenda L.: Assistant Director, Division of Media and Information Services
DEEM, Richard A.: V. President, Government Affairs
ELLIOTT, Kinn: Director, Political and Grassroots Membership
EMERY, Jack M.: Assistant Director, Federal Affairs
GARIKES, Margaret: Director, Federal Affairs
HOBSON, Jr., Julius W.: Director, Congressional Affairs
KUFFNER, Mary: Washington Counsel
KURLAND, Pamela S.: Washington Counsel
LEETH, Timothy B.: Assistant Director, Congressional Affairs
MANTOOTH, Mark C.: Senior Washington Counsel
MCILRATH, Sharon: Assistant Director, Federal Affairs
MCMENAMIN, Peter: Director, Health Policy Development
MIROBALLI, Dana Lee: Washington Counsel, Division of Legislative Counsel
SHERMAN, Sandy L.: Assistant Director, Federal Affairs
SMITH, Conwell: Assistant Director of Congressional Affairs
SMOLEN, Maggie: Assistant Director, Congressional Affairs
STILLWELL, Lee J.: Senior V. President, Advocacy
SZABAT, Ronald P.: Director, Division of Legislative Counsel
TENOEVER, Katie: Washington Counsel
TIGHE, Margaret E. "Peggy": Assistant Director, Division of Congressional Affairs
TRIMMER, Joy: Assistant Director, Congressional Affairs Division
VARGO, Carol: Assistant Director, Federal Affairs
WALKER, Kevin L.: V. President, Political Affairs
WHITE, Annie: Assistant Director, Congressional Affairs

Outside Counsel/Consultants

Stevens Reed Curcio & Co.

American Medical Group Ass'n

1422 Duke St.
Alexandria, VA 22314
Tel: (703)838-0033
Fax: (703)548-1890
Registered: LDA
Web: www.amga.org

Leg. Issues: BUD, HCR, LBR, MMM, TAX

Political Action Committee/s

Group Practice Political Action Committee

1422 Duke St.
Alexandria, VA 22314
Contact: Dr. Donald W. Fisher, CAE
Tel: (703)838-0033
Fax: (703)548-1890

In-house, DC-area Employees

BARTLETT, J.D., Melissa: Legislative Counsel
FISHER, CAE, Dr. Donald W.: President and Chief Exec. Officer
FROELICH, Sara L.: V. President, Public Policy and Political Affairs
SANDERSON-AUSTIN, Julie: V. President, Quality Management, Research and Operations

American Medical Informatics Ass'n

4915 St. Elmo Ave.
Suite 401
Bethesda, MD 20814
Tel: (301)657-1291
Fax: (301)657-1296
Web: www.amia.org
E-mail: mail@mail.amia.org

Leg. Issues: BUD, HCR, MED, TEC

In-house, DC-area Employees

REYNOLDS, Dennis: Exec. Director

Outside Counsel/Consultants

Capitol Associates, Inc.

Sidley & Austin
Rep By: Michael A. Nemeroff

Washington Health Advocates
Issues: BUD, HCR, MED, TEC
Rep By: Douglas Peddicord, Ph.D., Michele Sumilas

American Medical Rehabilitation Providers Ass'n

1606 20th St. NW
Third Floor
Washington, DC 20009
Tel: (202)265-4404
Fax: (202)833-9168
Registered: LDA
Web: www.amrpa.org

Leg. Issues: HCR, MMM

In-house, DC-area Employees

ZOLLAR, Carolyn C.: V. President, Government Relations and Policy Development

Outside Counsel/Consultants

Patton Boggs, LLP
Issues: MMM
Rep By: John F. Jonas, Martha M. Kendrick, Elizabeth E. Ring, JoAnn V. Willis

Powers Pyles Sutter & Verville, PC
Issues: HCR
Rep By: Jeremy W. Allen, Peter W. Thomas

American Medical Response

Aurora, CO

Leg. Issues: HCR

Outside Counsel/Consultants

BKSH & Associates
Issues: HCR

American Medical Security

Green Bay, WI

Outside Counsel/Consultants

Patton Boggs, LLP
Rep By: Martha M. Kendrick

American Medical Student Ass'n

1902 Association Dr.
Reston, VA 20190
Tel: (703)620-6600
Fax: (703)620-5873
Registered: LDA
Web: www.amsa.org
E-mail: amsa@www.amsa.org

National organization representing physicians in training.

Leg. Issues: EDU, HCR, LBR, MED, MMM

In-house, DC-area Employees

CLARKE, Jr., Tim: Director of Public Relations
WRIGHT, Paul R.: Exec. Director

American Medical Technologists

Park Ridge, IL

Leg. Issues: BUD, GOV, HCR, MED, MMM

Outside Counsel/Consultants

Brickfield, Burchette, Ritts & Stone
Issues: BUD, HCR, MED, MMM
Rep By: Michael N. McCarty, Colleen Newman

Halsey, Rains & Associates, LLC
Issues: GOV
Rep By: Steven C. Halsey, James Hubbard, Laurie D. Rains

American Medical Women's Ass'n

801 N. Fairfax St.
Suite 400
Alexandria, VA 22314
Tel: (703)838-0500
Fax: (703)549-3864
Web: www.amwa-doc.org
E-mail: info@amwa-doc.org

In-house, DC-area Employees

LINCAMAOD, Melisa: Deputy Exec. Director, Governmental Affairs and Communications

American Metalcasting Consortium

Leg. Issues: DEF

Outside Counsel/Consultants

Kinghorn & Associates, L.L.C.
Issues: DEF
Rep By: Edward J. Kinghorn, Jr.

Waterman & Associates
Issues: DEF
Rep By: Diana L. Waterman

American Methanol Institute

800 Connecticut Ave. NW
Suite 620
Washington, DC 20006
Tel: (202)467-5050
Fax: (202)331-9055
Registered: LDA
Web: www.methanol.org
E-mail: ami@methanol.org

Supports the use of clean reformulated and oxygenated gasoline and encourages the development of emerging methanol-powered fuel cell technology.

Leg. Issues: AUT, CAW, CHM, ENG, ENV, FUE, SCI, TAX, TRA

In-house, DC-area Employees

CONDREY, Jr., Bailey L.: Director, Communications
LYNN, John E.: President and Chief Exec. Officer

Outside Counsel/Consultants

Public Strategies Washington, Inc.
Issues: AUT, CAW, ENG, ENV, FUE, SCI, TAX, TRA
Rep By: Joseph P. O'Neill, Paul M. Snyder

American Military Soc.

Springdale, MD
Leg. Issues: HCR, INS, RET, VET

Outside Counsel/Consultants

Ass'n Growth Enterprises
Issues: HCR, INS, RET, VET
Rep By: John Paul May, Thomas L. Pacino

American Mobile Satellite Corp.

Reston, VA
Leg. Issues: CPT, TEC

Outside Counsel/Consultants

Shaw Pittman

The Wexler Group
Issues: CPT, TEC
Rep By: Adam Eisgrau

American Mobile Telecommunications Ass'n

1150 18th St. NW
Suite 250
Washington, DC 20036
Tel: (202)331-7773
Fax: (202)331-9062
Web: www.amtaUSA.org
E-mail: arshark@atmausa.org

Represents the interests of business wireless telecommunications systems.

Leg. Issues: TEC

In-house, DC-area Employees

SHARK, Alan R.: President and Chief Exec. Officer

American Motorcyclist Ass'n

1225 I St. NW
Suite 500
Washington, DC 20005
Tel: (202)682-4759
Fax: (202)789-0406
Registered: LDA
Leg. Issues: AGR, BUD, EDU, GOV, INS, NAT, ROD, TRA, TRD

Political Action Committee/s

American Motorcyclist Political Action Committee
1225 I St. NW
Suite 500
Washington, DC 20005
Tel: (202)682-4750
Fax: (202)789-0406
Contact: Edward W. Moreland

In-house, DC-area Employees

HOLTZ, Patrick J.
MORELAND, Edward W.: Washington Representative

American Moving and Storage Ass'n

1611 Duke St.
Alexandria, VA 22314
Tel: (703)683-7410
Fax: (703)683-7527
Registered: LDA
Web: www.moving.org

An association for the moving and storage industry.

Leg. Issues: BUD, CSP, DEF, ENV, GOV, LBR, SMB, TAX, TRA

Political Action Committee/s

American Moving and Storage Political Action Committee
1611 Duke St.
Alexandria, VA 22314
Tel: (703)683-7410
Fax: (703)683-7527
Contact: Robert G. Drummer

In-house, DC-area Employees

DRUMMER, Robert G.: V. President, Government Affairs and General Counsel
HARRISON, Joseph M.: President
JENNINGS, Patricia: V. President, Programs and Services
MICHAEL, Scott: Assistant to the President
TREDWAY, Estelle: V. President, Industry Relations

American Museum of Natural History

New York, NY
Leg. Issues: AER, ALC, ANI, ART, AVI, BUD, CPT, DEF, EDU, ENG, FOR, HCR, IMM, IND, MAR, MED, MMM, SCI, TAX, TEC, URB, VET

Outside Counsel/Consultants

Davidoff & Malito, LLP
Issues: BUD
Rep By: Kenneth C. Malito, Robert J. Malito, Stephen J. Slade

Jorden Burt LLP
Issues: AER, ALC, ANI, ART, AVI, BUD, CPT, DEF, EDU, ENG, FOR, HCR, IMM, IND, MAR, MED, MMM, SCI, TAX, TEC, URB, VET
Rep By: Patricia Branch, Alanna Dillon, Marna Gettleman, Marilyn Berry Thompson, Rebecca Tidman

American Mushroom Institute

Washington, DC
Web: www.americanmushroom.org

Outside Counsel/Consultants

McLeod, Watkinson & Miller
Rep By: Michael R. McLeod, Marc E. Miller, Laura L. Phelps

American Music Therapy Ass'n

8455 Colesville Rd.
Suite 1000
Silver Spring, MD 20910-3392
Tel: (301)589-3300
Fax: (301)589-5175
Web: www.musictherapy.org
E-mail: info@musictherapy.org

Committed to the advancement of education, training, professional standards, and research in support of the music therapy profession.

In-house, DC-area Employees

BUMANIS, Al: Director, Conferences and Communications
FARBMAN, Andrea H.: Exec. Director

American Muslim Council

1212 New York Ave. NW
Suite 400
Washington, DC 20005
Tel: (202)789-2262
Fax: (202)789-2550
Registered: LDA
Web: www.amconline.org
E-mail: director@amconline.org
Leg. Issues: GOV

In-house, DC-area Employees

ABUZAAKOUK, Aly R.: Exec. Director

American Mutual Share Insurance Corp.

Dublin, OH

Outside Counsel/Consultants

Akin, Gump, Strauss, Hauer & Feld, L.L.P.

American Names Ass'n

Rancho Santa Fe, CA
Leg. Issues: FIN

Outside Counsel/Consultants

Royer & Babyak
Issues: FIN
Rep By: Robert Stewart Royer

American Nat'l Metric Council

4340 East West Hwy.
Suite 401
Bethesda, MD 20814-4411
Tel: (301)718-6539
Fax: (301)656-0989
E-mail: anmc@paimgmt.com
Leg. Issues: SCI

In-house, DC-area Employees

WALLIS, Ph.D., Norman E.: Exec. Director

Outside Counsel/Consultants

PAI Management Corp.
Issues: SCI

American Nat'l Standards Institute

1819 L St. NW
Sixth Floor
Washington, DC 20036
Tel: (202)293-8020
Fax: (202)293-9287
Web: www.ansi.org
E-mail: info@ansi.org

In-house, DC-area Employees

SCHWEIKER, Jane: Director, Public Policy and Government Relations

American Natural Soda Ash Corp.

Westport, CT
Leg. Issues: TRD

Outside Counsel/Consultants

Dewey Ballantine LLP
Issues: TRD
Rep By: Thomas R. Howell, Andrew W. Kentz, John R. Magnus

American Network of Community Options and Resources (ANCOR)

4200 Evergreen Ln.
Suite 315
Annandale, VA 22003
Tel: (703)642-6614
Fax: (703)642-0497
Registered: LDA
Web: www.ancor.org
E-mail: ancor@ancor.org

ANCOR members are agencies in 48 states and the District of Columbia that provide residential and other support services to people with mental retardation and other disabilities.

Leg. Issues: BUD, HCR, HOU, MMM, TAX, WEL

In-house, DC-area Employees

FREEBURG, Kara E.: Analyst, Public Policy
GALBRAITH, Suellen: Director, Public Policy
PIETRANGELO, Renee L.: Chief Executive Officer

Outside Counsel/Consultants

Thomas K. Arnold
Issues: TAX
Rep By: Thomas K. Arnold

Duncan and Associates
Rep By: Jack G. Duncan

American Nonwovens Corp.

Columbus, MS

Outside Counsel/Consultants

Johnson, Rogers & Clifton, L.L.P.

American Nuclear Insurers

Leg. Issues: ENG

Outside Counsel/Consultants

Preston Gates Ellis & Rouvelas Meeds LLP
Issues: ENG
Rep By: Tim L. Peckinpaugh

American Nuclear Soc.

LaGrange Park, IL

Outside Counsel/Consultants

Sagamore Associates, Inc.
Rep By: David Nichols, Doug Wasitis

American Nursery and Landscape Ass'n

1250 I St. NW
Suite 500
Washington, DC 20005
Tel: (202)789-2900
Fax: (202)789-1893
Registered: LDA
Web: www.anla.org
Leg. Issues: AGR, BUD, CAW, CHM, CPT, IMM, LBR, SMB, TAX

Political Action Committee/s

ANLA Nursery Industry Political Action Committee
1250 I St. NW
Suite 500
Washington, DC 20005
Tel: (202)789-2900
Fax: (202)789-1893
Contact: Heather Conti

In-house, DC-area Employees

ALBIZO, Joel: Senior Director, Membership and Marketing
BEDELL, Anthony: Director, Government Relations
CONTI, Heather: Govt. Relations Coordinator and PAC Contact
DOLIBOIS, Robert: Exec. V. President
EAGLE, Lindsay: Director of Communications
GALSTER, Geoff: Director, Regulatory Affairs
QUINN, Warren: Director, Operations
REGELBRUGGE, Craig J.: Senior Director, Government Relations
SCHECHTEL, Sharon: Director, Marketing and Retail Services

Outside Counsel/Consultants

McGuiness Norris & Williams, LLP
Issues: IMM, LBR
Rep By: James S. Holt, William N. LaForge, Monte B. Lake

U.S. Strategies Corp.
Rep By: Steven E. Carey

American Nurses Ass'n

600 Maryland Ave. SW
Suite 100 West
Washington, DC 20024-2571
Tel: (202)651-7000
Fax: (202)651-7001
Registered: LDA
Web: www.nursingworld.org

Works to improve health care, to foster high nursing standards and to improve nurses' economic and general welfare.

Leg. Issues: BUD, ECN, EDU, HCR, IMM, LBR, TRD

Political Action Committee/s

American Nurses Ass'n Political Action Committee (ANA-PAC)

600 Maryland Ave. SW
Suite 100 West
Washington, DC 20024-2571
Tel: (202)651-7000
Fax: (202)651-7001

In-house, DC-area Employees

ABOOD, Sheila: Associate Director, Federal Government Relations
GONZALEZ, Rose: Associate Director, Federal Government Relations
REED, Stephanie W.: Associate Director, Federal Government Relations
ROIT, Sheila: Political Action Specialist
STIERLE, MSN, RN, CNAA, Linda J.: Chief Exec. Officer

Outside Counsel/Consultants

Health Policy Alternatives, Inc.
Issues: HCR
Rep By: Richard Lauderbaugh

American Occupational Therapy Ass'n, Inc.

P.O. Box 31220
4720 Montgomery Ln.
Bethesda, MD 20824-1220
Web: www.aota.org
E-mail: praota@aota.org
Tel: (301)652-2682
Fax: (301)652-7711
Registered: LDA

Advances the quality, availability, use and support of occupational therapy through standard-setting, advocacy, education and research on behalf of its members and the public.

Leg. Issues: ALC, BUD, EDU, HCR, HOU, IMM, INS, LBR, MED, MMM, WEL

Political Action Committee/s

American Occupational Therapy Ass'n Political Action Committee

P.O. Box 31220
4720 Montgomery Ln.
Bethesda, MD 20824-1220
Contact: Darlene C. Dennis
Tel: (301)652-2682
Fax: (301)652-7711

In-house, DC-area Employees

BLUHM, Christopher: Assoc. Exec. Director for Business Operations Office
DENNIS, Darlene C.: Political Action Administrator
ISAACS, Joseph C.: Exec. Director
JACKSON, Leslie: Representative, Federal Affairs
METZLER, Christina A.: Director, Federal Affairs Department
SOMERS, Frederick P.: Associate Exec. Director for Professional Affairs
THOMAS, Judy: Director, Reimbursement Policy Program

American Oceans Campaign

600 Pennsylvania Ave. SE
Suite 210
Washington, DC 20003
Web: www.americanoceans.org
E-mail: info@americanoceans.org
Tel: (202)544-3526
Fax: (202)544-5625
Leg. Issues: ENV, MAR

In-house, DC-area Employees

MORTON, Ted: Director, Policy
POLO, Barbara Jeanne: Exec. Director

American of Martinsville

Martinsville, VA

Outside Counsel/Consultants

O'Connor & Fierce Associates

American Optometric Ass'n

1505 Prince St.
Suite 300
Alexandria, VA 22314
Web: www.aoanet.org
Tel: (703)739-9200
Fax: (703)739-9497
Registered: LDA

Headquartered in St. Louis, MO.

Leg. Issues: DEF, EDU, HCR, LBR, MMM, RET, VET

Political Action Committee/s

American Optometric Ass'n Political Action Committee

1505 Prince St.
Suite 300
Alexandria, VA 22314
Contact: Noel Brazil
Tel: (703)739-9200
Fax: (703)739-9497

In-house, DC-area Employees

BRAZIL, Noel: Manager, Political Action Committee
DANIELSON, David S.: Deputy Director, Government Relations
HIPP, Kelly: Assistant Director, Government Relations
MAYS, Jeffrey G.: Deputy Exec. Director
PETERSON, Alan D.: Assistant Director, Government Relations
WHITENER, John C.: Assistant Director, Government Relations

Outside Counsel/Consultants

J. T. Rutherford & Associates
Issues: HCR, MMM
Rep By: Deanna D. Lavanty, Donald F. Lavanty

American Organization of Nurse Executives

325 Seventh St. NW
Suite 700
Washington, DC 20004
Web: www.aone.org
Tel: (202)626-2240
Fax: (202)638-5499
Registered: LDA

A national organization for nurses who design, facilitate, and manage patient care. Headquartered in Chicago, IL.

Leg. Issues: BUD, EDU, HCR, LBR, MMM

In-house, DC-area Employees

WEBB, Jo Ann K.: Director, Federal Relations and Policy

American Orthotic and Prosthetic Ass'n

1650 King St.
Suite 500
Alexandria, VA 22314
Web: www.aopanet.org
Tel: (703)836-7116
Fax: (703)836-0838
Registered: LDA
Leg. Issues: HCR, MMM, VET

Political Action Committee/s

O & P PAC

1650 King St.
Suite 500
Alexandria, VA 22314
Contact: Kathy Dodson
Tel: (703)836-7116
Fax: (703)836-0838

In-house, DC-area Employees

DODSON, Kathy: Director, Government Relations
WILSON, Tyler J.: Exec. Director

Outside Counsel/Consultants

Baker & Daniels
Rep By: Mark W. Weller

Haake and Associates
Issues: HCR, MMM
Rep By: Timothy M. Haake, Nathan M. Olsen

American Osteopathic Academy of Addiction Medicine

5550 Friendship Blvd.
Suite 300
Chevy Chase, MD 20815-7201
Tel: (301)968-4160
Fax: (301)968-4199

In-house, DC-area Employees

KUSHNER, David L.: Exec. Director

American Osteopathic Ass'n

1090 Vermont Ave. NW
Suite 510
Washington, DC 20005
Web: www.aoa-net.org
Tel: (202)414-0140
Fax: (202)544-3525
Registered: LDA

A membership organization of osteopathic physicians headquartered in Chicago, IL.

Leg. Issues: HCR

Political Action Committee/s

Osteopathic Political Action Committee

1090 Vermont Ave. NW
Suite 510
Washington, DC 20005
Contact: Joanna Burton
Tel: (202)414-0140
Fax: (202)544-3525

In-house, DC-area Employees

BURTON, Joanna: PAC Director
FRIEDMAN, Susan: Deputy Director, Government Relations
JEANSONNE, Angela: Assistant Director, Federal Education Issues
MARTIN, R. Shawn: Assistant Director, Congressional Affairs
MAYERS, Michael: Assistant Director, Congressional Affairs
MONACO, Carol: Assistant Director, Regulatory Affairs
OLSON, Sydney: Director, Government Relations
STEWART, Erika: Office Manager, Government Relations

American Osteopathic Healthcare Ass'n

5550 Friendship Blvd.
Suite 300
Chevy Chase, MD 20815-7201
Web: www.aoha.org
E-mail: aoha@aoha.org
Tel: (301)968-2642
Fax: (301)968-4195
Registered: LDA

Trade association serving osteopathic hospitals and health systems.

Leg. Issues: MMM

Political Action Committee/s

Political Action Committee of the American Osteopathic Healthcare Ass'n

5550 Friendship Blvd.
Suite 300
Chevy Chase, MD 20815-7201
Tel: (301)968-2642
Fax: (301)968-4195

In-house, DC-area Employees

HARDY, Margaret: Director, Government Relations
KUSHNER, David L.: President and Chief Exec. Officer

American Paper Machinery Ass'n

111 Park Place
Falls Church, VA 22046-4513
Web: www.papermachinery.org
E-mail: apmahq@aol.com
Tel: (703)533-1787
Fax: (703)241-5603
Leg. Issues: MAN

In-house, DC-area Employees

ARMSTRONG, CAE, Elizabeth B.: Exec. Director

Outside Counsel/Consultants

Ass'n and Soc. Management Internat'l Inc.
Issues: MAN
Rep By: Elizabeth B. Armstrong, CAE

American Paperboard Packaging Environment Council

1111 19th St. NW
Suite 800
Washington, DC 20036
Tel: (202)463-2700
Fax: (202)463-2785

A special project of the American Forest & Paper Ass'n (see separate listing).

In-house, DC-area Employees

FOLEY, Cathy: Exec. Director, Bleached Paperboard

American Passenger Rail Coalition

900 Second St. NE
Suite 109
Washington, DC 20002
Tel: (202)408-1808
Fax: (202)408-9565
Registered: LDA

A national association of rail suppliers working for an improved, more efficient national Amtrak system and the development of a high speed rail in the Northeast Corridor and other federally designated high-speed rail corridors.

Leg. Issues: RRR

In-house, DC-area Employees

PARCELLS, Harriet: Exec. Director

American Payroll Ass'n

1225 I St. NW
Suite 500
Washington, DC 20005
Web: www.americanpayroll.org
E-mail: scottmapa@aol.com
Tel: (202)682-4775
Fax: (202)371-8892
Registered: LDA

Headquartered in New York, NY, the American Payroll Ass'n represents payroll professionals and businesses on tax and payroll issues. Coordinates with and lobbies the IRS, the Social Security Administration, State Legislatures and the U.S. Congress.

Leg. Issues: FAM, IMM, RET, TAX

In-house, DC-area Employees

MEZISTRANO, Scott: Manager, Government Relations
ZEIDNER, Rita L.: Manager, Government Relations

American Peanut Council

1500 King St.
Suite 301
Alexandria, VA 22314-2730
Web: www.peanutsusa.com
E-mail: generalinfo@peanutsusa.com
Tel: (703)838-9500
Fax: (703)838-9089

In-house, DC-area Employees

ANDERSON, Jeannette: President

Outside Counsel/Consultants

Goldberg & Associates, PLLC
Rep By: James M. Goldberg

American Peanut Product Manufacturers, Inc.

Washington, DC
Leg. Issues: AGR, BUD

Outside Counsel/Consultants

McLeod, Watkinson & Miller
Issues: AGR, BUD
Rep By: Michael R. McLeod, Richard E. Pasco, Laura L. Phelps

American Petroleum Institute

1220 L St. NW
Washington, DC 20005
Web: www.api.org
Tel: (202)682-8000
Fax: (202)682-8232
Registered: LDA

Established in 1919 as non-profit tax-exempt foundation, API has become the trade association and chief lobbying arm for over 300 corporations.

Leg. Issues: BUD, CAW, COM, ENG, ENV, FOR, FUE, GOV, LBR, MAR, NAT, TAX, TRA, TRD, WAS

In-house, DC-area Employees
ACQUINO, Edward: Senior Tax Accountant
BRAUN, Kathleen G.: Federal Relations Representative
BROWN, Rick: Senior Manager, Federal Agencies
BUSH, Barbara: Taxation Associate Director
CAVANEY, Byron "Red": President
CLOUD, Stephen J.: Legislative Research Manager
COLLELI, Ralph: Senior Attorney
COONEY, Philip: Senior Attorney
DEAL, David: Managing Attorney
DOLLINGER, Stephen: Senior Tax Attorney
ERIKSON, R. Brent: Washington Representative
FLAVIN, Lisa
FRICK, G. William: V. President, General Counsel and Secretary
ISAKOWER, Kyle
KIBBE, Mark: Legislative Analyst
LAFFLY-MURPHY, Genevieve: Washington Representative
MEADOWS, Stephanie: V. President, Head Assistant
PLATNER, Michael L.: Washington Representative
PRICE, Anne
ROSS, Michelle: Public Liaison Projects Manager
SALTZMAN, Joel: Washington Representative
SANDLER, Charles E.: V. President, Government Affairs
TRASK, Jeff: Senior Regulatory Analyst
WAGNER, John: Senior Attorney
YOOD, Andrew: Taxation Director

Outside Counsel/Consultants
Barents Group LLC
Issues: FUE, TAX
Rep By: Shannon E. Slawter, Linden C. Smith
The Direct Impact Co.
EOP Group, Inc.
Issues: BUD, ENV, WAS
Rep By: Donald Gesseman, Jonathan Gledhill, Joseph Hezir, Jan Mares, Corey McDaniel, Michael O'Bannon
Griffin, Johnson, Dover & Stewart
Issues: ENV
Rep By: G. Jack Dover, Patrick J. Griffin, David E. Johnson, Susan O. Mann, Walter J. "Joe" Stewart
Nat'l Environmental Strategies
Issues: CAW, WAS
Rep By: Marc I. Himmelstein
Sidley & Austin
Rep By: David T. Buente, Jr., Sam Gutter
The Smith-Free Group
Timmons and Co., Inc.
Issues: CAW, ENG, TAX, TRD
Rep By: Michael J. Bates, Douglas F. Bennett, Ellen B. Fitzgibbons, Bryce L. "Larry" Harlow, Timothy J. Keating, Tom C. Korologos, Richard J. Tarplin, William E. Timmons, Jr., William E. Timmons, Sr.

American Pharmaceutical Ass'n

2215 Constitution Ave. NW
Washington, DC 20037-2985
Tel: (202)628-4410
Fax: (202)783-2351
Registered: LDA
Web: www.aphanet.org

The national professional society of pharmacists.

Leg. Issues: HCR, MMM, PHA

Political Action Committee/s
American Pharmaceutical Ass'n Political Action Committee
2215 Constitution Ave. NW
Washington, DC 20037-2985
Tel: (202)628-4410
Fax: (202)783-2351
Contact: Susan Bishop

In-house, DC-area Employees
BISHOP, Susan: PAC Contact
GANS, John A.: Exec. V. President and Chief Exec. Officer
GEIGER, Lisa M.: Director, State and Federal Policy
MAINE, Lucinda L.: Senior V. President, Professional and Public Affairs
ROTHHOLZ, Mitchel C.: V. President, Professional Practice
WINCKLER, RPh, J.D., Susan: Group Director, Policy and Advocacy

Outside Counsel/Consultants
O'Brien, Butler, McConihe & Schaefer
Rep By: Michael H. McConihe

American Physical Soc.

529 14th St. NW
Suite 1050
Washington, DC 20045
Tel: (202)662-8700
Fax: (202)662-8711
Registered: LDA
Web: www.aps.org
E-mail: opa@aps.org

A non-profit scientific and educational society dedicated to the advancement and diffusion of the knowledge of physics.

Leg. Issues: BUD, DEF, EDU, ENG, FOR, SCI

In-house, DC-area Employees
LUBELL, Michael S.: Director, Public Affairs
PARK, Robert L.: Director, Public Information
SLAKEY, Francis: Associate Director, Public Affairs

American Physical Therapy Ass'n

1111 N. Fairfax St.
Alexandria, VA 22314
Tel: (703)684-2782
Fax: (703)684-7343
Registered: LDA
Web: www.apta.org
Leg. Issues: HCR, IMM, LBR, MMM, SMB, TAX, VET

Political Action Committee/s
American Physical Therapy Congressional Action Committee
1111 N. Fairfax St.
Alexandria, VA 22314
Tel: (703)706-3163
Fax: (703)838-8919
Contact: Michael Matlack

In-house, DC-area Employees
BEAUMONT, Nancy Perkin: Senior V. President, Communications Div.
BENNETT, John J.: General Counsel
BLACK, Joseph P. H.: Senior V. President, Education
DUNNE, Joanne E.: Exec. Director, Private Practice Section
GARLAND, Nancy: Director, Government Affairs
GUCCIONE, Andrew: Senior V. President, Practice and Research
LEE, Gayle: Assistant Director, Regulatory Affairs
MALLON, Francis J.: Chief Exec. Officer
MATLACK, Michael: PAC Contact
MEADOWS, Johnette L.: Director, Minority/International Affairs
O'BRIEN, Elizabeth: Assistant Director, Federal Regulatory Affairs
WATERS, Alexis B.: Director, Public Relations and Marketing Services

Outside Counsel/Consultants
Cooney & Associates, Inc.
Issues: HCR, IMM, LBR, MMM, SMB, TAX, VET
Rep By: Patrick J. Cooney

American Physiological Soc.

9650 Rockville Pike
Bethesda, MD 20814-3991
Tel: (301)530-7164
Fax: (301)571-8305
Web: www.faseb.org/aps/
E-mail: info@aps.faseb.org
Leg. Issues: MED

In-house, DC-area Employees
FRANK, Dr. Martin: Exec. Director

American Pilots Ass'n

499 S. Capitol St. SW
Suite 409
Washington, DC 20003
Tel: (202)484-0700
Fax: (202)484-9320
E-mail: apaxdir@aol.com

A trade association for state-licensed marine pilots.

Political Action Committee/s
American Pilots Ass'n Political Action Committee
499 S. Capitol St. SW
Suite 409
Washington, DC 20003
Tel: (202)484-0700
Fax: (202)484-9320
Contact: Capt. Michael R. Watson

In-house, DC-area Employees
WATSON, Capt. Michael R.: President

American Pipe Fittings Ass'n

111 Park Place
Falls Church, VA 22046
Tel: (703)538-1786
Fax: (703)241-5603
Web: www.apfa.com
E-mail: info@apfa.com
Leg. Issues: MAN

In-house, DC-area Employees
TYERYAR, CAE, Clay D.: Exec. Director

Outside Counsel/Consultants
Ass'n and Soc. Management Internat'l Inc.
Rep By: Clay D. Tyeryar, CAE
McKenna & Cuneo, L.L.P.
Rep By: Peter Buck Feller

American Planning Ass'n

1776 Massachusetts Ave. NW
Suite 400
Washington, DC 20036
Tel: (202)872-0611
Fax: (202)872-0643
Web: www.planning.org

An association seeking to advance the art and science of planning.

Leg. Issues: CAW, ECN, ENV, HOU, TEC, TOU, TRA, URB, WAS

In-house, DC-area Employees
JOHNSON, Denny: Information Coordinator
SOULE, AICP, Jeffrey: Director, Policy

American Plastics Council

1300 Wilson Blvd.
Suite 800
Arlington, VA 22209
Tel: (703)253-0700
Fax: (703)253-0701
Registered: LDA
Web: www.plastics.org
Leg. Issues: CAW, CHM, CSP, ENV, FOO, HCR, NAT, TRA, WAS

In-house, DC-area Employees
BERNSTEIN, Roger D.: V. President, Government Affairs
DURBIN, Martin J.: Director, Federal and International Affairs
ENNEKING, Patty: V. President, Non Durables
LIESEMER, Ph.D., Ronald N.: V. President, Technology
LOWMAN, Rodney W.: Exec. V. President and Chief Staff Officer
MCHUGH, Peter G.: Managing Counsel
MOORE, Susan P.: V. President, Communications
YOCUM, Ph.D., Ronald: President and Chief Exec. Officer

Outside Counsel/Consultants
The Direct Impact Co.
Edelman Public Relations Worldwide
Rep By: Carol Diggs
LaRock Associates, Inc.
Issues: WAS
Rep By: Joan W. LaRock
Wirthlin Worldwide

American Plywood Ass'n

Leg. Issues: HOU

Outside Counsel/Consultants
Arent Fox Kintner Plotkin & Kahn, PLLC
Issues: HOU
Rep By: Marc L. Fleischaker, Michael T. McNamara

American Podiatric Medical Ass'n

9312 Old Georgetown Rd.
Bethesda, MD 20814-1621
Tel: (301)571-9200
Fax: (301)530-2752
Registered: LDA
Web: www.apma.org
E-mail: askapma@apma.org
Leg. Issues: HCR

Political Action Committee/s
Podiatry Political Action Committee
9312 Old Georgetown Rd.
Bethesda, MD 20814-1621
Tel: (301)581-9232
Fax: (301)530-2752
Contact: Faye B. Frankfort

In-house, DC-area Employees
FRANKFORT, Faye B.: Director, Legislative Advocacy
GASTWIRTH, DPM, Glenn B.: Exec. Director
PARSLEY, Nancy L.: Director, Health Policy and Practice
RINKER, Martha L.: Director, Division of Policy, Practice and Advocacy

American Podiatric Medical Students Ass'n

9312 Old Georgetown Rd.
Bethesda, MD 20814
Tel: (301)493-9667
Fax: (301)530-2752
Web: www.apmsa.org
E-mail: betsyapmsa@aol.com

In-house, DC-area Employees
HERMAN, Betsy M.: Exec. Director

American Political Science Ass'n

1527 New Hampshire Ave. NW
Washington, DC 20036
Tel: (202)483-2512
Fax: (202)483-2657
Web: www.apsanet.org
E-mail: apsa@apsanet.org

In-house, DC-area Employees
RUDDER, Dr. Catherine E.: Exec. Director

American Portland Cement Alliance

1225 I St. NW
Suite 300
Washington, DC 20005
Tel: (202)408-9494
Fax: (202)408-0877
Registered: LDA
Leg. Issues: AVI, BUD, ENG, ENV, LBR, MAN, TAX, TRA, TRD

Political Action Committee/s
American Portland Cement Alliance Political Action Committee
1225 I St. NW
Suite 300
Washington, DC 20005
Tel: (202)408-9494
Fax: (202)408-0877
Contact: Richard C. Creighton

In-house, DC-area Employees
CREIGHTON, Richard C.: President
HUBBARD, David S.: Director, Legislative Affairs
HUDSON, Peggy Renken: V. President, Legislative Affairs
LOUDA, Dale: Director, Legislative Affairs
O'HARE, Andrew: V. President, Environmental Affairs
SULLIVAN, John J.: Director, Federal Affairs

Outside Counsel/Consultants

Howrey Simon Arnold & White
Rep By: John F. Bruce

American Postal Workers Union

1300 L St. NW
Washington, DC 20005
Tel: (202)842-4200
Fax: (202)842-4297
Registered: LDA
Web: www.apwu.org
E-mail: apwu.hq@worldnet.att.net

Political Action Committee/s

Commmittee on Political Action of the American Postal Workers Union, AFL-CIO
1300 L St. NW
Washington, DC 20005
Tel: (202)842-4200
Fax: (202)682-2528
Contact: Roy Braunstein

In-house, DC-area Employees

BILLER, Moe: President
BRAUNSTEIN, Roy: Legislative Director
BURRUS, William: Exec. V. President
REID, Myke: Assistant Legislative Director
TABBITA, Phil: Exec. Assistant to the President

Outside Counsel/Consultants

O'Donnell, Schwartz & Anderson, P.C.
Rep By: Darryl J. Anderson, Anton G. Hajjar

American Press Institute

11690 Sunrise Valley Dr.
Reston, VA 20191
Tel: (703)620-3611
Fax: (703)620-5814
E-mail: api@apireston.org

In-house, DC-area Employees

WINTER, William L.: President

American Preventive Medical Ass'n

9912 Georgetown Pike
Suite D-2
Great Falls, VA 22066
Tel: (703)759-0662
Fax: (703)759-6711
Registered: LDA
Web: www.apma.net
E-mail: apma@healthy.net
Leg. Issues: HCR

Political Action Committee/s

American Preventive Medical Ass'n PAC
9912 Georgetown Pike
Suite D-2
Great Falls, VA 22066
Tel: (703)759-0662
Fax: (703)759-6711
Contact: Candace Campbell

In-house, DC-area Employees

CAMPBELL, Candace: Exec. Director

Outside Counsel/Consultants

Emord & Associates, P.C.
Issues: HCR
Rep By: Jonathan W. Emord, Eleanor A. Kolton, Claudia A. Lewis-Eng

American Property Rights Alliance

1111 19th St. NW
Suite 800
Washington, DC 20036
Tel: (202)463-2748
Fax: (202)463-2424
Registered: LDA

In-house, DC-area Employees

LAIBLE, Myron: Contact
TURNER, Jane

American Psychiatric Ass'n

1400 K St. NW
Washington, DC 20005
Tel: (202)682-6000
Fax: (202)682-6850
Registered: LDA
Web: www.psych.org
E-mail: apa@psych.org
Leg. Issues: BUD, DEF, FAM, GOV, HCR, HOU, IND, INS, LAW, MED, MMM, SCI, VET

Political Action Committee/s

Corp. for the Advancement of Psychiatry Political Action Committee
1400 K St. NW
Washington, DC 20005
Tel: (202)682-6000
Fax: (202)682-6850

In-house, DC-area Employees

BOROUGHS, Lizbet: Associate Director, Government Relations
CUTLER, Jay B.: Director, Government Relations/Special Counsel
KUPER, Susan: Director, Membership
MEYERS, Nicholas: Deputy Director, Government Relations

Outside Counsel/Consultants

Bonner & Associates

American Psychiatric Nurses Ass'n

Washington, DC
Web: www.apna.org
E-mail: apna@dcsba.com
Leg. Issues: BUD, HCR, MMM

Outside Counsel/Consultants

Smith, Bucklin and Associates, Inc.
Issues: BUD, HCR, MMM
Rep By: Jill Rathbun, Melissa Reese

American Psychoanalytic Ass'n

New York, NY
Web: www.apsa.org
Leg. Issues: HCR

Outside Counsel/Consultants

Powers Pyles Sutter & Verville, PC
Issues: HCR
Rep By: James C. Pyles

American Psychological Ass'n

750 First St. NE
Washington, DC 20002-4242
Tel: (202)336-5500
Fax: (202)336-6069
Registered: LDA
Web: www.apa.org
E-mail: executiveoffice@apa.org
Leg. Issues: AER, ALC, AVI, BUD, CIV, COM, CPI, DEF, DOC, EDU, FAM, HCR, HOU, IMM, IND, LAW, LBR, MED, MIA, MMM, SCI, TAX, TOB, WEL

In-house, DC-area Employees

COTTER, Deborah: Legislative Assistant, Public Interest Policy
CULLEN, Elizabeth: Director, Congressional Affairs
DODGEN, Ph.D., Dan: Senior Legislative and Federal Affairs Officer
FARBERMAN, Rhea K.: Exec. Director, Public Communications
FRUMKIN, Lara
GARRISON, Ph.D., Ellen G.: Director, Public Interest Policy
GILFOYLE, Nathalie: Deputy General Counsel
GREEN, Lori Valencia: Senior Legislative/Federal Affairs Representative
HARTEL, Ph.D., Christine R.: Associate Exec. Director, Science
KELLY, Ph.D., Heather O'Beirne: Legislative and Federal Affairs Officer
KOBOR, Patricia C.: Senior, Science Policy
LEVITT, Ed.D., Nina Gail: Director, Education Policy
MCCARTY, Ph.D., Richard: Exec. Director, Science Directorate
MCINTYRE, Jeff: Senior Legislative Assistant, Public Policy
MUMFORD, Ph.D., Geoffrey: Legislative/Federal Affairs Officer
NELSON, David E.: Director, Federal Advocacy, Practice Directorate
NEWBOULD, Peter E.: Director, Congressional Affairs
PEDULLA, Diane
PRESTON, Camille: Policy Fellow
RICHMOND, Marilyn S.: Assistant Exec. Director, Government Relations
TOMES, Ph.D., Henry: Exec. Director, Public Interest Directorate
TRUBISKY, Paula: Legislative/Federal Affairs Officer
WALTER, Douglas: Legislative Counsel, Government Relations

Outside Counsel/Consultants

BKSH & Associates
Issues: HCR, MMM

Capitol Associates, Inc.
Issues: BUD
Rep By: Liz Gemski, Edward R. Long, Ph.D.

Dean Blakey & Moskowitz
Issues: BUD, EDU, FAM
Rep By: Ellin J. Nolan

Jenner & Block

Podesta/Mattoon
Issues: HCR
Rep By: Ann Delory, Kimberley Fritts, Anthony T. Podesta

Potomac Group
Issues: EDU, HCR, MMM
Rep By: Richard Y Hegg, Philip C. Karsting, G. Wayne Smith

Powers Pyles Sutter & Verville, PC
Issues: BUD, HCR
Rep By: J. Michael Hall

RTC Direct

Richard L. Spees, Inc.
Issues: HCR
Rep By: Richard L. Spees

Van Scoyoc Associates, Inc.
Issues: BUD, HCR, MED
Rep By: Evan Knisely, Robert L. Knisely, H. Stewart Van Scoyoc

American Psychological Soc.

1010 Vermont Ave. NW
Suite 1100
Washington, DC 20005-4907
Tel: (202)783-2077
Fax: (202)783-2083
Web: www.psychologicalscience.org
E-mail: APS@APS.Washington.dc.us

An organization dedicated to the promotion, protection and advancement of the interests of scientifically-oriented psychologists in research, appreciation and the improvement of human welfare.

Leg. Issues: ALC, BUD, EDU, HCR, MIA, SCI, TOB

In-house, DC-area Employees

BROOKHART, Sarah: Director, Policy and Communications

Outside Counsel/Consultants

Zuckerman Spaeder L.L.P.
Rep By: Ronald H. Weich

American Psychosomatic Soc.

McLean, VA
Web: www.psychosomatic.org
E-mail: info@psychosomatic.org

Outside Counsel/Consultants

Degnon Associates, Inc.
Rep By: Laura Degnon

American Public Communications Council

10302 Eaton Pl.
Suite 340
Fairfax, VA 22030
Tel: (703)385-5300
Fax: (703)385-5301
Web: www.apcc.net
E-mail: info@apcc.net
Leg. Issues: TEC

Political Action Committee/s

American Public Communications Council Political Action Committee
10302 Eaton Pl.
Suite 340
Fairfax, VA 22030
Tel: (703)385-5300
Fax: (703)385-5301
Contact: Vincent R. Sandusky

In-house, DC-area Employees

HALEDJIAN, Gregory: Government Relations Manager
RODDY-BURNS, Lisa M.: Exec. Director
SANDUSKY, Vincent R.: President

Outside Counsel/Consultants

Dickstein Shapiro Morin & Oshinsky LLP
Issues: TEC
Rep By: Elizabeth B. Haywood, Alan Hubbard, Albert H. Kramer, Robert Mangas, Rebecah Moore Shepherd

Latham & Watkins
Issues: TEC
Rep By: Nicholas W. Allard, Vicky Beasley

American Public Gas Ass'n

11094-D Lee Hwy.
Suite 102
Fairfax, VA 22030
Tel: (703)352-3890
Fax: (703)352-1271
Web: www.apga.org
E-mail: bcave@apga.org

A natural gas trade association.

Leg. Issues: DIS, NAT, UTI

In-house, DC-area Employees

CAVE, Bob: Exec. Director

Outside Counsel/Consultants

Miller, Balis and O'Neil, P.C.
Rep By: Stanley W. Balis, John P. Gregg, William T. Miller

American Public Health Ass'n

800 I St. NW
Washington, DC 20001
Tel: (202)777-2742
Fax: (202)777-2534
Registered: LDA
Web: www.apha.org/

A member organization of the Coalition for Health Funding in Washington. A member organization of the Nat'l Health Council.

Leg. Issues: BUD, ENV, FAM, FIR, FOO, HCR, MMM, ROD, TOB

In-house, DC-area Employees

AKHTER, M.D., Mohammed N.: Exec. Director
HOPPERT, Don: Federal Affairs Associate
LEVINSON, Dr. Richard: Associate Exec. Director, Programs and Policy
LISTER, V.D.M., Sarah: Director, Congressional Affairs
WALLACE, Mary L.: Director, Government Relations and Affiliate Affairs
ZIMMERMAN, Carole: Director, Communications

American Public Human Services Ass'n

810 First St. NE
Suite 500
Washington, DC 20002-4267
Tel: (202)682-0100
Fax: (202)289-6555
Web: www.aphsa.org

A non-profit association providing professional consultation to Congress and an active program of legislative monitoring and analysis on behalf of state and local human service departments.

In-house, DC-area Employees

RYAN, Elaine M.: Acting Exec. Director

American Public Info-Highway Coalition

A lobbying organization of municipal utility companies seeking legislation which would preserve a role for themselves in fiber-optic cable laying for the future "information superhighway".

Outside Counsel/Consultants

Kutak Rock LLP

American Public Power Ass'n

2301 M St. NW
Washington, DC 20037-1484
Tel: (202)467-2900
Fax: (202)467-2910
Registered: LDA

Web: www.APPAnet.org

Leg. Issues: BUD, CAW, ENG, RRR, SCI, TAX, TEC, UTI

Political Action Committee/s

Public Ownership of Electric Resources Political Action Committee

2301 M St. NW
Washington, DC 20037-1484
Tel: (202)467-2950
Fax: (202)467-2910
Contact: Anne-Marye Hastad

In-house, DC-area Employees

BLOOD, Rebecca: Senior Government Relations Representative
CAFRUNY, Madalyn B.: Director, Public Communications
CIRRINCIONE, Jane Dunn: Senior Government Relations Representative
DITTO, Joy: Government Relations
ECKL, Chris: Government Relations Representative
HASTAD, Anne-Marye: Legislative Research Assistant
NIPPER, James J.: Senior V. President, Government Relations
NOLAN, Michael J.: Government Relations Representative
PENN, David: Exec. V. President
PETTIT, Susan: Government Relations Representative
PREE, Curtis: Government Relations Representative
RICHARDSON, Alan H.: President/Chief Exec. Officer
TARBERT, Jeffrey: Senior V. President, Membership Services

Outside Counsel/Consultants

Arent Fox Kintner Plotkin & Kahn, PLLC
Issues: UTI
Rep By: Hon. Dale L. Bumpers, Mary Hope Davis, Michael T. McNamara

Sunrise Research Corp.
Issues: TAX
Rep By: Hon. Bob Packwood

American Public Transportation Ass'n

1666 K St. NW
Washington, DC 20006
Tel: (202)296-4700
Fax: (202)496-4324
Registered: LDA

Web: www.apta.com
E-mail: info@apta.com

APTA's mission is to serve and represent its members in making public transportation an effective path to economic opportunity, personal mobility, and improving the quality of life through partnerships, communications, technology, and advocacy.

Leg. Issues: BUD, TRA

In-house, DC-area Employees

ADKINS, Genesee: Government Relations Policy Specialist
DUFF, Daniel: Chief Counsel and V. President, Government Affairs
GUZZETTI, Arthur L.: Director, Policy Development and Member Mobilization
HEALY, Jr., Robert L.: Director, Government Relations
MILLAR, William W.: President
SHERIDAN, Rosemary: V. President, Communications and Marketing
YEDINAK, Tom: Senior Legislative Representative

Outside Counsel/Consultants

Bain and Associates, Inc.

Birch, Horton, Bittner & Cherot
Issues: TRA
Rep By: Ronald G. Birch

Martin G. Hamberger & Associates
Issues: BUD, TRA
Rep By: Martin G. Hamberger, Brian M. Tynan

Susan B. Perry
Issues: TRA
Rep By: Susan B. Perry

The Peterson Group

American Public Works Ass'n

1401 K St. NW
11th Floor
Washington, DC 20005
Tel: (202)408-9541
Fax: (202)408-9542
Web: www.apwa.net

Leg. Issues: CAW, DIS, ENV, NAT, ROD, TEC, TRA, URB, UTI, WAS

In-house, DC-area Employees

KING, Peter: Exec. Director

American Pyrotechnics Ass'n

4808 Moorlands Ln.
Bethesda, MD 20814
Tel: (301)907-8181
Fax: (301)907-9148
Registered: LDA

Web: www.americanpyro.com
E-mail: info@americanpyro.com

Fireworks importers, distributors, suppliers and manufacturers.

Leg. Issues: GOV

In-house, DC-area Employees

HECKMAN, Julie L.: Exec. Director

Outside Counsel/Consultants

Thompson, Hine and Flory LLP
Rep By: David H. Baker

American Radio Relay League

Newington, CT
Registered: LDA
Leg. Issues: COM, TEC

Outside Counsel/Consultants

Chwat and Company, Inc.
Issues: COM, TEC
Rep By: John Chwat, Derek Riker

American Railway Car Institute

Olympia Fields, IL

Outside Counsel/Consultants

Harris Ellsworth & Levin
Rep By: Hon. Herbert E. Harris, II

American Realty Advisors

Leg. Issues: RES

Outside Counsel/Consultants

Kilpatrick Stockton LLP
Issues: RES
Rep By: Richard Barnett, J. Christopher Brady

American Recreation Coalition

1225 New York Ave. NW
Suite 450
Washington, DC 20005
Tel: (202)682-9530
Fax: (202)682-9529
Web: www.funoutdoors.com
E-mail: arc@funoutdoors.com

A federation of recreation-related associations and companies that works to protect and enhance outdoor recreation opportunitites and resources.

Leg. Issues: NAT, TOU

In-house, DC-area Employees

AHERN, Catherine A.: V. President, Member Services
CRANDALL, Derrick A.: President

American Red Bull Transit

Indianapolis, IN

Outside Counsel/Consultants

Denning & Wohlstetter

American Red Cross

431 18th St. NW
Washington, DC 20006
Tel: (202)639-3125
Fax: (202)639-6116
Registered: LDA

Web: www.redcross.org

A humanitarian organization, led by volunteers, that provides relief to victims of disaster and helps people prevent, prepare for, and respond to emergencies.

Leg. Issues: AVI, BUD, DIS, GOV, HCR, LAW, LBR, MED, TAX

In-house, DC-area Employees

BABIARZ, Linda: Analyst
BLAIR, Alice K.: Manager, State Relations and Grass Roots Advocacy
BLAUL, William: V. President, Communications and Marketing
HOULE, Ronald G.: Director, Legislative Affairs
KROEMER, Kurt: Director, Regulatory Affairs
LANE, Jan: V. President, Government Relations

Outside Counsel/Consultants

BSMG Worldwide

Hill and Knowlton, Inc.
Rep By: Nancy Hicks, Peter Velasco

American Ref-Fuel

Houston, TX
Leg. Issues: CAW, ENG, ENV, WAS

Outside Counsel/Consultants

Goodstein & Associates
Issues: CAW, ENG, ENV, WAS

American Registry for Internet Numbers (ARIN)

Chantilly, VA
Leg. Issues: CPI

Outside Counsel/Consultants

Bracewell & Patterson, L.L.P.
Issues: CPI
Rep By: Gene E. Godley, Marc C. Hebert, Michael L. Pate, D. Michael Stroud, Jr.

American Registry of Pathology

Washington, DC
Leg. Issues: MED

Outside Counsel/Consultants

Hogan & Hartson L.L.P.
Issues: MED
Rep By: C. Michael Gilliland, Hon. Robert H. Michel, Hon. Paul G. Rogers

American Rehab Action

Washington, DC

Outside Counsel/Consultants

Duncan and Associates
Rep By: Jack G. Duncan

American Renewal

801 G St. NW
Washington, DC 20001
Tel: (202)393-2100
Fax: (202)393-2134
Web: www.american-renewal.org
E-mail: rlessner@american-renewal.org

A conservative advocacy organization. The legislative arm of the Family Research Council.

Leg. Issues: FAM

In-house, DC-area Employees

CONNOR, Kenneth L.: President
LESSNER, Richard: Exec. Director

American Rental Ass'n

Moline, IL
Web: www.ararental.org
Leg. Issues: BUD, CSP, GOV, HCR, LBR, RES, SMB, TAX, TOR, TRA

Outside Counsel/Consultants

Stephens Law Firm
Issues: BUD, CSP, GOV, HCR, LBR, RES, SMB, TAX, TOR, TRA
Rep By: Neil E. Graham, William T. Stephens, Michael A. Williams

American Resort Development Ass'n

1220 L St. NW
Suite 500
Washington, DC 20005
Tel: (202)371-6700
Fax: (202)289-8544
Registered: LDA
Web: www.arda.org

Represents the resort timeshare industry on issues such as purchase or right of use of units and time at resort condominiums/hotels.

Leg. Issues: ACC, BAN, CSP, DIS, LBR, RES, TAX, TEC, TOU

Political Action Committee/s

American Resort Development Ass'n Political Action Committee

1220 L St. NW
Suite 500
Washington, DC 20005
Tel: (202)371-6700
Fax: (202)289-8544
Contact: Sandra De Poy

American Resort Development Ass'n Resort Owners Coalition PAC (ARDA-ROC PAC)

1220 L St. NW
Suite 500
Washington, DC 20005
Contact: Sandra De Poy
Tel: (202)371-6700
Fax: (202)289-8544

In-house, DC-area Employees

DANIELS, Rhonda: Corporate Counsel
DE POY, Sandra: Director, Federal Relations and ARDA PAC
HUSSEY, Michael F.: Senior V. President, Public Affairs
NAUSBAUM, Howard: President

Outside Counsel/Consultants

Baker & Hostetler LLP
Issues: TAX
Rep By: E. Mark Braden, William F. Conroy, Matthew J. Dolan, Frederick H. Graefe, David L. Marshall, Kenneth F. Snyder, Hon. Guy Vander Jagt

PriceWaterhouseCoopers

The Washington Group
Issues: RES, TAX
Rep By: Rita M. Lewis, G. John O'Hanlon, John D. Raffaelli, Tonya Saunders, Mark Schnabel, Fowler West

American Restaurant China Council

P.O. Box 916
Alexandria, VA 22313
Tel: (703)893-4631

In-house, DC-area Employees

GRAYSON, Helen: Exec. Director

American Retirees Ass'n

2009 N. 14th St.
Suite 300
Arlington, VA 22201
Tel: (703)527-3065
Fax: (703)528-4229
Registered: LDA
Web: www.americanretireesassociation.org

Works for the amendment or repeal of the Uniformed Services Former Spouses Protection Act (USFSPA):10 USC 1408.

Leg. Issues: GOV, VET

In-house, DC-area Employees

AULT, USN (Ret.), Capt. Frank W.: Exec. Director

Outside Counsel/Consultants

Karalekas & Noone
Issues: VET
Rep By: S. Steven Karalekas, James A. Noone

American Rivers

1025 Vermont Ave.
Suite 720
Washington, DC 20005
Tel: (202)347-7550
Fax: (202)347-9240
Registered: LDA
Web: www.amrivers.org/amrivers/
E-mail: amrivers@amrivers.org

A public interest group working to preserve the nation's rivers, their landscapes, and their ecosystems.

In-house, DC-area Employees

BOWMAN, Margaret: Director, Hydropower Programs
SMITH, Chad: Associate Director
WODDER, Rebecca: President

American Road and Transportation Builders Ass'n (ARTBA)

1010 Massachusetts Ave. NW
Washington, DC 20001
Tel: (202)289-4434
Fax: (202)289-4435
Registered: LDA
Web: www.artba.org
E-mail: artba@aol.com
Leg. Issues: BUD, CAW, ENV, LBR, SMB, TRA

Political Action Committee/s

American Road and Transportation Builders Ass'n PAC
1010 Massachusetts Ave. NW
Washington, DC 20001
Contact: Martin Whitmer
Tel: (202)289-4434
Fax: (202)289-4435

In-house, DC-area Employees

BAUER, David: Director, Policy
BUECHNER, William: V. President, Economics and Research; Manager, Education and Research
DEASON, Ph.D., Jonathan P.: Environmental Consultant
JEANNERET, Matthew: V. President, Communications
MCCABE, Carrie: Editor, Transportation Builder
ROTHMAN, Eric: Marketing Consultant
RUANE, Dr. T. Peter: President and Chief Exec. Officer
WHITMER, Martin: V. President, Government Relations

Outside Counsel/Consultants

Edmund C. Graber
Issues: TRA
Rep By: Edmund C. Graber

Hunton & Williams
Issues: CAW, TRA
Rep By: F. William Brownell, Norman W. Fichthorn

American Running and Fitness Ass'n

4405 East-West Hwy.
Suite 405
Bethesda, MD 20814-9139
Tel: (301)913-9517
Fax: (301)913-9520
Web: www.americanrunning.org
E-mail: run@americanrunning.org

Founded in 1968 as the Nat'l Jogging Ass'n. Main goals include encouraging Americans to run and be fit, and to keep health professionals up-to-date on the latest in sports medicine.

In-house, DC-area Employees

BALDWIN, MPH, Barbara: Director, Information Services
KALISH, Susan: Exec. Director

American Salvage Pool Ass'n

Phoenix, AZ
Leg. Issues: AUT

Outside Counsel/Consultants

Brownstein Hyatt & Farber, P.C.
Issues: AUT
Rep By: William T. Brack, Michael B. Levy

American Samoa, Government of

Washington, DC

Outside Counsel/Consultants

Counselors For Management, Inc.
Rep By: Janice C. Lipsen

American School Counselor Ass'n

801 N. Fairfax St.
Suite 312
Alexandria, VA 22314
Tel: (703)683-2722
Fax: (703)683-1619
Web: www.schoolcounselor.org
E-mail: ASCA@erols.com
Leg. Issues: EDU

In-house, DC-area Employees

MELTON, Brenda: Chair, Public Relations
WONG, Richard: Exec. Director

Outside Counsel/Consultants

Goldberg & Associates, PLLC
Rep By: James M. Goldberg

American School Food Service Ass'n

700 S. Washington St.
Suite 300
Alexandria, VA 22314
Tel: (703)739-3900
Fax: (703)739-3915
Registered: LDA
Web: www.asfsa.org

A non-profit organization of state and local food-service directors and supervisors, cafeteria managers and food-service assistants and nutrition educators throughout the U.S. Dedicated to promoting the maintenance and improvement of children's health and nutrition by supporting implementation of nutritionally adequate, educationally sound, financially accountable school and nutrition programs.

Leg. Issues: AGR, BUD, IMM, WEL

Political Action Committee/s

American School Food Service Ass'n Political Action Committee (ASFSA PAC)
700 S. Washington St.
Suite 300
Alexandria, VA 22314
Contact: Barry Sackin
Tel: (703)739-3900
Fax: (703)739-3915

In-house, DC-area Employees

BELMONT, CAE, Barbara S.: Exec. Director
HAAS, Joseph: Government Affairs/Media Relations Specialist
SACKIN, Barry: Director, Government Affairs

Outside Counsel/Consultants

Olsson, Frank and Weeda, P.C.
Issues: AGR, BUD, IMM, WEL
Rep By: John W. Bode, Susan P. Grymes, Karen Reis Harned, Stephen L. Lacey, Marshall L. Matz, Tyson Redpath

American Science and Engineering, Inc.

Billerica, MA
Leg. Issues: BUD, DEF

Outside Counsel/Consultants

Bob Davis & Associates
Issues: BUD, DEF
Rep By: Hon. Robert W. Davis

American Seafoods Inc.

Seattle, WA
Leg. Issues: MAR

Outside Counsel/Consultants

Preston Gates Ellis & Rouvelas Meeds LLP
Issues: MAR
Rep By: William N. Myhre, Daniel Ritter

American Security Council

Boston, VA

A legislative advocacy group working to foster a bipartisan national security strategy for the U.S. Works on defense, foreign policy and international economic issues.

Outside Counsel/Consultants

Reed, Smith, Hazel & Thomas

American Security Resources, Inc.

Bethesda, MD

Outside Counsel/Consultants

Ashby and Associates
Rep By: William B. Montano

American Seed Research Foundation

601 13th St. NW
Suite 570 South
Washington, DC 20005
Tel: (202)638-3128
Fax: (202)638-3171
Web: www.amseed.org

In-house, DC-area Employees

NICOLAS, Suzanne: Secretary

American Seed Trade Ass'n

601 13th St. NW
Suite 570 South
Washington, DC 20005-3807
Tel: (202)638-3128
Fax: (202)638-3171
Web: www.amseed.org
Leg. Issues: AGR, SCI

In-house, DC-area Employees

CAHILL, Leslie C.: V. President, Government Affairs
CONDON, Mark: V. President of International Marketing
NICOLAS, Suzanne: Director, Programs and Services
URMSTON, Dean: Exec. V. President

Outside Counsel/Consultants

Eversole Associates
Issues: AGR, SCI
Rep By: Kellye A. Eversole

American Seniors Housing Ass'n

5100 Wisconsin Ave. NW
Suite 307
Washington, DC 20016
Tel: (202)237-0900
Registered: LDA
Web: www.seniorhousing.org
Leg. Issues: BUD, HCR, HOU, INS, LBR, MMM, RET, TAX

Political Action Committee/s

Senior Housing PAC
5100 Wisconsin Ave. NW
Suite 307
Washington, DC 20016
Contact: David S. Schless
Tel: (202)237-0900
Fax: (202)237-1616

In-house, DC-area Employees

PREEDE, Kenneth M.: Director, Research and Policy
SCHLESS, David S.: President

American Share Insurance

Leg. Issues: BNK

Outside Counsel/Consultants

Verner, Liipfert, Bernhard, McPherson and Hand, Chartered
Rep By: Andrew D. Eskin

Williams & Jensen, P.C.
Issues: BNK
Rep By: Rebecca L. Anderson, J. Steven Hart, David M. Landers

American Sheep Industry Ass'n

412 First St. SE
Suite One
Washington, DC 20003
Tel: (202)484-2773
Fax: (202)484-0770
Registered: LDA

Headquartered in Englewood, CO.

Leg. Issues: AGR, APP, BUD, FOO, NAT, TAX, TRD

Political Action Committee/s

American Sheep Industry Ass'n RAMSPAC
412 First St. SE
Suite One
Washington, DC 20003
Contact: Fran Boyd
Tel: (202)484-2773
Fax: (202)484-0770

In-house, DC-area Employees

BOYD, Fran: Contact, RAMSPAC

Outside Counsel/Consultants

Collier Shannon Scott, PLLC
Issues: AGR, TRD
Rep By: Michael R. Kershow, Kathleen Clark Kies, Doris O. Matsui, Paul C. Rosenthal

Meyers & Associates
Issues: AGR, APP, BUD, FOO, NAT, TAX, TRD
Rep By: Fran Boyd, Larry D. Meyers

American Shipbuilding Ass'n

600 Pennsylvania Ave. SE
Suite 305
Washington, DC 20003-4345
Tel: (202)544-8170
Fax: (202)544-8252
Registered: LDA
Web: www.americanshipbuilding.com
Leg. Issues: CAW, DEF, LBR, TRA, TRD

In-house, DC-area Employees
BROWN, Cynthia L.: President

Outside Counsel/Consultants
Brown and Company, Inc.
Issues: CAW, DEF, LBR, TRA, TRD
Rep By: Cynthia L. Brown, Hugh N. "Rusty" Johnson, Frank W. Losey

American Short Line and Regional Railroad Ass'n

1120 G St. NW
Suite 520
Washington, DC 20005-3889
Tel: (202)628-4500
Fax: (202)628-6430
Registered: LDA
Web: www.aslrra.org

Provides representation for small railroads before federal agencies, the Congress, and the courts.

Leg. Issues: RRR, TRA

Political Action Committee/s
PAC of the American Short Line and Regional Railroad Ass'n (ASLRRAA-PAC)
1120 G St. NW
Suite 520
Washington, DC 20005-3889
Tel: (202)628-4500
Fax: (202)628-6430
Contact: Alice C. Saylor

In-house, DC-area Employees
SAYLOR, Alice C.: V. President and General Counsel
TURNER, Frank: President and Treasurer

Outside Counsel/Consultants
Chambers, Conlon & Hartwell
Issues: RRR, TRA
Rep By: Ray B. Chambers, Keith O. Hartwell, Don Norden, Adam Nordstrom

American Sleep Disorders Ass'n

Rochester, MN
Registered: LDA
Leg. Issues: BUD, MMM

Outside Counsel/Consultants
MARC Associates, Inc.
Issues: BUD, MMM
Rep By: Ellen Riker

American Small Business Alliance

3417 1/2 M St. NW
Washington, DC 20007
Tel: (202)337-0037
Web: www.asbanet.org

An education and advocacy organization that offers a reasonable and responsible voice on small business issues.

In-house, DC-area Employees
MARKS, Joel: Exec. Director

American Small Businesses Ass'n

Grapevine, TX
Leg. Issues: SMB

Outside Counsel/Consultants
The Strategic Advocacy Group
Issues: SMB
Rep By: Blair G. Childs

American Soc. for Biochemistry and Molecular Biology

9650 Rockville Pike
Bethesda, MD 20814
Tel: (301)530-7145
Fax: (301)571-1824
Registered: LDA
Web: www.faseb.org/asbmb
E-mail: asbmb@asbmb.faseb.org
Leg. Issues: EDU, MED, SCI

In-house, DC-area Employees
FARNHAM, Peter: Public Affairs Officer
HANCOCK, Charles C.: Exec. Officer

Outside Counsel/Consultants
Kyros & Cummins Associates
Rep By: Hon. Peter N. Kyros

American Soc. for Bone and Mineral Research

Washington, DC
Web: www.asbmr.org
E-mail: asbmr@dc.sba.com
Leg. Issues: HCR, MED

Outside Counsel/Consultants
The Plexus Consulting Group
Issues: HCR, MED
Rep By: Yasmin Quiwzow
Smith, Bucklin and Associates, Inc.
Rep By: Joan R. Goldberg

American Soc. for Cell Biology

8120 Woodmont Ave.
Suite 750
Bethesda, MD 20814-2755
Tel: (301)347-9300
Fax: (301)347-9310
Web: www.ascb.org/ascb
E-mail: ascbinfo@ascb.org

Purpose is to promote and develop the field of cell biology.

Leg. Issues: EDU, HCR, MED, SCI

In-house, DC-area Employees
LESHAN, Timothy E.: Director, Public Policy
MARINCOLA, Elizabeth: Exec. Director

Outside Counsel/Consultants
Kyros & Cummins Associates
Issues: SCI
Rep By: Hon. Peter N. Kyros

American Soc. for Clinical Laboratory Science

7910 Woodmont Ave.
Suite 530
Bethesda, MD 20814
Tel: (301)657-2768
Fax: (301)657-2909
Web: www.ascls.org
E-mail: ascls@ascls.org

Represents clinical laboratory personnel.

Leg. Issues: HCR, MED, MMM

Political Action Committee/s
American Soc. for Clinical Laboratory Science Political Action Committee
7910 Woodmont Ave.
Suite 530
Bethesda, MD 20814
Tel: (301)657-2768
Fax: (301)657-2909
Contact: Constance Smith

In-house, DC-area Employees
PASSIMENT, Elissa: Exec. Director
SMITH, Constance: PAC Contact

Outside Counsel/Consultants
J. T. Rutherford & Associates
Issues: HCR, MMM
Rep By: Donald F. Lavanty

American Soc. for Clinical Nutrition

9650 Rockville Pike
Room 3300
Bethesda, MD 20814-3998
Tel: (301)530-7110
Fax: (301)571-1863
Web: www.faseb.org/ascn
E-mail: secretar@ascn.faseb.org.
Leg. Issues: HCR, MED

In-house, DC-area Employees
CLARK, Donald J.: Exec. Officer

American Soc. for Clinical Pharmacology and Therapeutics

Web: www.ascpt.org
E-mail: info@ascpt.org
Leg. Issues: BUD, CSP, MED

Outside Counsel/Consultants
Washington Health Advocates
Issues: BUD, CSP, MED
Rep By: Lynn Morrison, Douglas Peddicord, Ph.D., Michele Sumilas

American Soc. for Deaf Children

Leg. Issues: EDU

Outside Counsel/Consultants
Barbara Raimondo
Issues: EDU
Rep By: Barbara Raimondo

American Soc. for Engineering Education

1818 N St. NW
Suite 600
Washington, DC 20036
Tel: (202)331-3500
Fax: (202)265-8504
Web: www.asee.org
E-mail: aseeexec@asee.org

A professional society of institution administrators and faculty involved in engineering education. Activities include monitoring federal legislation affecting engineering education, providing faculty professional development, and managing federal government faculty and post-doctoral fellowship programs.

In-house, DC-area Employees
HUBAND, Dr. Frank L.: Exec. Director
TOLLERTON, Kathryn R.: Manager, Public Affairs

American Soc. for Gastrointestinal Endoscopy

Manchester, MA
Leg. Issues: MMM

Outside Counsel/Consultants
MARC Associates, Inc.
Issues: MMM
Rep By: Randolph B. Fenninger, Shannon Penberthy

American Soc. for Industrial Security

1625 Prince St.
Alexandria, VA 22314
Tel: (703)519-6200
Fax: (703)519-6299
Web: www.asisonline.org
Leg. Issues: CON, DEF, DIS, GOV, LAW

In-house, DC-area Employees
STACK, Michael J.: Exec. Director

Outside Counsel/Consultants
Leadership Counsel, LLC
Rep By: Jack D. P. Lichtenstein
Jack D.P. Lichtenstein
Issues: CON, DEF, DIS, GOV, LAW
Rep By: Jack D. P. Lichtenstein

American Soc. for Information Science

8720 Georgia Ave.
Suite 501
Silver Spring, MD 20910-3602
Tel: (301)495-0900
Fax: (301)495-0810
Web: www.asis.org
E-mail: asis@asis.org

In-house, DC-area Employees
HILL, Richard B.: Exec. Director

American Soc. for Investigative Pathology

9650 Rockville Pike
Bethesda, MD 20814-3993
Tel: (301)530-7130
Fax: (301)571-1879
Web: www.asip.uthscsa.edu
E-mail: asip@pathol.faseb.org

In-house, DC-area Employees
SOBEL, M.D., Ph.D, Mark E.: Exec. Officer

American Soc. for Microbiology

1752 N St. NW
Washington, DC 20036
Tel: (202)737-3600
Fax: (202)942-9333
Registered: LDA
Web: www.asmusa.org

A membership organization established in 1899 to promote scientific knowledge and research in the field of microbiology; its Public and Scientific Affairs Board monitors federal, state and local laws and informs the Society's members of the potential impact of proposed legislation and regulation.

Leg. Issues: CPT, MED, SCI

In-house, DC-area Employees
GOLDBERG, Michael I.: Exec. Director
SHOEMAKER, Janet: Director, Public Affairs

American Soc. for Nutritional Sciences

9650 Rockville Pike
Bethesda, MD 20814
Tel: (301)530-7050
Fax: (301)571-1892
Web: www.faseb.org/asns/
E-mail: allisonr@asns.faseb.org

The principal professional organization of nutrition research scientists in the U.S. Has approximately 3,000 members. Formerly known as American Institute of Nutrition.

In-house, DC-area Employees
ALLISON, Richard G.: Exec. Officer

American Soc. for Parenteral and Enteral Nutrition

8630 Fenton St.
Suite 412
Silver Spring, MD 20910
Tel: (301)587-6315
Fax: (301)587-2365
Web: www.clinnutr.org
E-mail: barneys@aspen.nutr.org

Seeks to gain Medicare/Medicaid coverage of nutrition services.

In-house, DC-area Employees
SELLERS, Barney: Exec. Director

American Soc. for Pharmacology and Experimental Therapeutics

9650 Rockville Pike
Bethesda, MD 20814-3995
Tel: (301)530-7060
Fax: (301)530-7061
Web: www.faseb.org/aspet
E-mail: info@aspet.org
Leg. Issues: MED

In-house, DC-area Employees
BERNSTEIN, James S.: Director, Public Affairs

American Soc. for Photogrammetry and Remote Sensing

Bethesda, MD
Web: www.asprs.org
E-mail: asprs@asprs.org

Outside Counsel/Consultants

Cranwell & O'Connell
Rep By: George E. Cranwell

American Soc. for Quality

Milwaukee, WI
Web: www.asq.org
E-mail: asq@asq.org
Leg. Issues: BUD, EDU, GOV, HCR, LBR, SCI

Outside Counsel/Consultants

Sellery Associates, Inc.
Issues: BUD, EDU, GOV, HCR, LBR, SCI
Rep By: Amy B. Kimball, William C. Sellery, Jr.

American Soc. for Reproductive Medicine

409 12th St. SW
Suite 203
Washington, DC 20024-2125
Tel: (202)863-4985
Fax: (202)484-4039
Web: www.asrm.com
E-mail: asrm-dc@asrm.org

A voluntary, non-profit organization of 11,500 physicians and scientists interested in reproductive healthcare. Headquartered in Birmingham, AL.

Leg. Issues: GOV, MIA

In-house, DC-area Employees

TIPTON, Sean B.: Public Affairs Director

American Soc. for Technion

New York, NY

A social welfare and fundraising organization.

Leg. Issues: BUD

Outside Counsel/Consultants

Richard Straus
Issues: BUD
Rep By: Richard Straus

American Soc. for the Prevention of Cruelty to Animals National Legislative Office

1755 Massachusetts Ave. NW
Suite 418
Washington, DC 20036
Tel: (202)232-5020
Fax: (202)797-8947
Registered: LDA
Web: www.aspca.org

Headquartered in New York, NY.

Leg. Issues: ANI

In-house, DC-area Employees

BLANEY, Nancy: Director, National Legislative Office
FALLETTA, Patricia: Coordinator, Fed. Govt. Affairs, Nat'l Legislative Office
RADZIEWICZ, Marianne: Associate Director, National Legislative Office

American Soc. for Therapeutic Radiology and Oncology

12500 Fair Lakes Circle
Suite 375
Fairfax, VA 22033
Tel: (703)502-1550
Fax: (703)502-7852
Registered: LDA
Web: www.astro.org
E-mail: meetings@astro.org

Promotes public health and the practice of radiation oncology.

Leg. Issues: BUD, HCR, MED, MMM

In-house, DC-area Employees

DALY, Nancy Riese: Director, Government Relations
FUSS, Wendy Smith: Director, Healthcare Policy
MALOUFF, Frank: Exec. Director
SIMONSON, Kristin: Coordinator, Government Relations

Outside Counsel/Consultants

Preston Gates Ellis & Rouvelas Meeds LLP
Issues: BUD, HCR, MED, MMM
Rep By: Susan B. Geiger, Sandra Rizzo, Mark H. Ruge, W. David Thomas

American Soc. for Training and Development

1640 King St.
P.O. Box 1443
Alexandria, VA 22313
Tel: (703)683-8100
Fax: (703)683-8103
Registered: LDA
Web: www.astd.org

A professional association that promotes workplace learning and performance.

Leg. Issues: EDU, IMM, LBR, TAX

In-house, DC-area Employees

BORKON, Lynn L.: Government Relations Associate
PANTAZIS, Cynthia: Director, Policy and Public Leadership

American Soc. of Access Professionals

Washington, DC
Web: www.accesspro.org
E-mail: asap@bostromdc.com

An independent professional organization working to enhance effective methods, techniques, and procedures for administering access statutes, i.e. Freedom of Information Act and The Privacy Act.

Outside Counsel/Consultants

Bostrom Corp.
Rep By: Claire Shanley

American Soc. of Ambulatory Surgery Centers

Chicago, IL

Formerly known as American Soc. of Outpatient Surgeons.

Leg. Issues: MMM

Outside Counsel/Consultants

McDermott, Will and Emery
Issues: MMM
Rep By: Michael A. Romansky, Eric P. Zimmerman

American Soc. of Anesthesiologists

1101 Vermont Ave. NW
Suite 606
Washington, DC 20005
Tel: (202)289-2222
Fax: (202)371-0384
Registered: LDA
Web: www.asahq.org
E-mail: mail@asawash.org

Washington office of a professional society headquartered in Park Ridge, IL.

Leg. Issues: BUD, HCR, MED, MMM

Political Action Committee/s

American Soc. of Anesthesiologists Political Action Committee (ASAPAC)
1101 Vermont Ave. NW
Suite 606
Washington, DC 20005
Tel: (202)289-2222
Fax: (202)371-0384
Contact: Manuel E. Bonilla

In-house, DC-area Employees

BONILLA, Manuel E.: Associate Director, Federal
SCOTT, Michael: Director, Governmental and Legal Affairs
TURPIN, S. Diane: Associate Director, State

Outside Counsel/Consultants

Downey McGrath Group, Inc.
Issues: HCR, MED, MMM
Rep By: Delanne Bernier, Hon. Thomas J. Downey, Jr., Hon. Raymond J. McGrath, John Peter Olinger

Greenberg Traurig, LLP
Rep By: Howard J. Cohen

Griffin, Johnson, Dover & Stewart
Issues: BUD, HCR, MMM
Rep By: G. Jack Dover, Patrick J. Griffin, David E. Johnson, Walter J. "Joe" Stewart

The Paul Laxalt Group
Issues: HCR, MMM
Rep By: Hon. Paul D. Laxalt, Tom Loranger

Lent Scrivner & Roth LLC
Issues: MMM
Rep By: Norman F. Lent, III, Hon. Norman F. Lent, Alan J. Roth, Michael S. Scrivner

MARC Associates, Inc.
Issues: BUD, HCR, MMM
Rep By: Daniel C. Maldonado, Bernard Patashnik, Ellen Riker

Squire, Sanders & Dempsey L.L.P.
Rep By: Scott T. Kragie

Timmons and Co., Inc.
Issues: HCR, MMM
Rep By: Michael J. Bates, Douglas F. Bennett, Ellen B. Fitzgibbons, Bryce L. "Larry" Harlow, Timothy J. Keating, Tom C. Korologos, Richard J. Tarplin, William E. Timmons, Jr., William E. Timmons, Sr.

Verner, Liipfert, Bernhard, McPherson and Hand, Chartered
Issues: MMM
Rep By: Vicki E. Hart

Wise & Associates
Issues: MMM
Rep By: Nicholas P. Wise

American Soc. of Appraisers

P.O. Box 17265
Washington, DC 20041
Tel: (703)478-2228
Fax: (703)742-8471
Web: www.appraisers.org
E-mail: asainfo@appraisers.org
Leg. Issues: BAN, TAX

Political Action Committee/s

American Soc. of Appraisers PAC
P.O. Box 17265
Washington, DC 20041
Tel: (703)478-2228
Fax: (703)742-8471
Contact: Leroy L. Ackermann

In-house, DC-area Employees

ACKERMANN, Leroy L.: PAC Administrator
BAKER, Edwin "Ted" W.: Exec. V. President

Outside Counsel/Consultants

Peter S. Barash Associates, Inc.
Issues: BAN, TAX
Rep By: Peter S. Barash

O'Brien, Butler, McConihe & Schaefer
Rep By: Jerome C. Schaefer

American Soc. of Architectural Illustrators

Washington, DC
Leg. Issues: ART

Outside Counsel/Consultants

Sufka & Associates
Issues: ART

American Soc. of Ass'n Executives

1575 I St. NW
Washington, DC 20005-1103
Tel: (202)626-2723
Fax: (202)371-1673
Registered: LDA
Web: www.asaenet.org
E-mail: pr@asaenet.org

An organization of 25,000 professionals who manage 12,000 leading trade, individual, and voluntary organizations in the U.S.

Leg. Issues: CIV, CON, CPT, GOV, HCR, INS, LBR, POS, RET, TAX, TOR, TOU

Political Action Committee/s

American Soc. of Ass'n Executives (A-PAC)
1575 I St. NW
Washington, DC 20005-1103
Tel: (202)626-2831
Fax: (202)371-1673
Contact: Andrea Cianfrani

In-house, DC-area Employees

CHANDLER, CAE, Linda C.: Exec. V. President
CIANFRANI, Andrea: PAC Manager
CLARKE, James L.: Senior V. President, Public Policy
CONSTANTINE, III, George E.: Staff Counsel
GARDNER, Courtney C.: Director, Public Relations
JACOBS, Jerald A.: General Counsel
JAMES, Diane: Director, Allied Partners
LANGFORD, Carrie: Associate Manager, Public Policy
LATHAM, Dawn: Associate Director, Public Policy
OLSON, CAE, Michael S.: President and Chief Exec. Officer
TOWLE, CAE, Raymond P.: Director, Public Policy
VEST, Chris: Manager, Media Relations

Outside Counsel/Consultants

Hance, Scarborough & Wright
Issues: TAX
Rep By: Hon. Kent R. Hance

Rock & Associates
Rep By: James W. Rock

American Soc. of Cataract and Refractive Surgery

4000 Legato Rd.
Suite 850
Fairfax, VA 22033
Tel: (703)591-2220
Fax: (703)591-0614
Registered: LDA
Web: www.ascrs.org
E-mail: ascrs@ascrs.org
Leg. Issues: BUD, HCR, MMM

Political Action Committee/s

American Soc. of Cataract and Refractive Surgery Political Action Committee (Eye PAC)
4000 Legato Rd.
Suite 850
Fairfax, VA 22033
Tel: (703)591-2220
Fax: (703)591-0614
Contact: Nancey K. McCann

In-house, DC-area Employees

KARCHER, David A.: Exec. Director
MCCANN, Nancey K.: Director, Government Relations

Outside Counsel/Consultants

Jenner & Block
Issues: MMM
Rep By: Robert M. Portman

American Soc. of Civil Engineers

1015 15th St. NW
Suite 600
Washington, DC 20005
Tel: (202)789-2200
Fax: (202)289-6797
Registered: LDA
Web: www.asce.org
E-mail: govwash@dc.asce.org
Leg. Issues: AVI, BUD, GOV, SCI, TRA

In-house, DC-area Employees

CHARLES, Michael: Senior Manager, Government Relations
DINGES, IV, Charles V.: Managing Director, Communications and Government Relations
HIGHT, Martin: Senior Manager, Government Relations
HOWELL, Jane: Director, Communications
PALLASCH, Brian T.: Director, Government Relations

American Soc. of Clinical Oncology

1900 Duke St.
Suite 200
Alexandria, VA 22314
Tel: (703)299-1050
Fax: (703)299-1044
Registered: LDA
Web: www.asco.org
E-mail: asco@asco.org
Leg. Issues: BUD, HCR, MED, MMM

In-house, DC-area Employees

BACON, Amy E.: Legislative Specialist
BALCH, M.D., Charles: Exec. V. President and Chief Exec. Officer
BRUINOOGE, Suanna: Senior Policy Analyst
KAMIN, Deborah: Senior Director, Public Policy
TAYLOR, Julia A.: Deputy Director, Public Policy

Outside Counsel/Consultants

Bennett Turner & Coleman, LLP
Issues: BUD, HCR, MED, MMM
Rep By: Terry S. Coleman, Elizabeth Goss, Samuel D. Turner

American Soc. of Clinical Pathologists

1225 New York Ave. NW
Suite 250
Washington, DC 20005-6156
Tel: (202)347-4450
Fax: (202)347-4453
Registered: LDA
Web: www.ascp.org

A non-profit medical society organized for educational and scientific purposes. Headquartered in Chicago, IL, its 75,000 members include board-certified pathologists, other physicians, clinical scientists, certified medical technologists and technicians.

Leg. Issues: BUD, HCR, LBR, MED, MMM

In-house, DC-area Employees

COX, Lisa: Manager, Congressional and Regulatory Affairs
STOMBLER, Robin E.: V. President, Government Affairs

Outside Counsel/Consultants

Health and Medicine Counsel of Washington
Issues: BUD, HCR
Rep By: Staci Sigman Dennison, Dale P. Dirks

McKenna & Cuneo, L.L.P.
Rep By: Jeffrey P. Altman

American Soc. of Composers, Authors and Publishers

New York, NY
Web: www.ascap.com
Leg. Issues: ART, COM, CPT, REL, SMB, TEC

Outside Counsel/Consultants

Baach Robinson & Lewis, PLLC
Rep By: Benjamin L. Zelenko

Palumbo & Cerrell, Inc.
Issues: ART, COM, CPT, REL, SMB, TEC
Rep By: William T. Deitz, Charles R. O'Regan, Benjamin L. Palumbo, Paul A. Skrabut, Jr.

American Soc. of Consultant Pharmacists

1321 Duke St.
Alexandria, VA 22314-3563
Tel: (703)739-1300
Fax: (703)739-1321
Registered: LDA
Web: www.ascp.com
E-mail: info@ascp.com

The national professional society representing more than 6,700 pharmacists who provide pharmacy and consulting services in a variety of health care settings, including nursing homes, home health care, prisons and jails, mental institutions, hospices and other long-term care institutions and organizations.

Leg. Issues: HCR, MMM, PHA

Political Action Committee/s

American Soc. of Consultant Pharmacists Political Action Committee
1321 Duke St.
Alexandria, VA 22314-3563
Tel: (703)739-1300
Fax: (703)739-1321
Contact: S. Leigh Davitian

In-house, DC-area Employees

DAVITIAN, S. Leigh: Director, Government Affairs
WEBSTER, R. Timothy: Exec. Director

Outside Counsel/Consultants

Reed, Smith, LLP
Issues: HCR
Rep By: Phillips S. Peter

American Soc. of Echocardiography

Raleigh, NC
E-mail: asc@mercury.interpath.net
Leg. Issues: MMM

Outside Counsel/Consultants

McDermott, Will and Emery
Issues: MMM
Rep By: Eric P. Zimmerman

American Soc. of Extra-Corporeal Technology

503 Carlisle Dr.
Suite 125
Herndon, VA 20170
Tel: (703)435-8556
Fax: (703)435-0056
Web: www.amsect.org
E-mail: webmaster@amsect.org

A non-profit medical association.

Leg. Issues: MED

In-house, DC-area Employees

CATE, George M.: Exec. Director

Outside Counsel/Consultants

Lee Bechtel and Associates
Rep By: Lee Bechtel

American Soc. of Farm Managers and Rural Appraisers

Denver, CO
Web: www.agri-associations.org/asfrma/
E-mail: asfmra@afri-associations.org
Leg. Issues: AGR

Outside Counsel/Consultants

The Macon Edwards Co.
Issues: AGR
Rep By: Macon T. Edwards, Mara Peltz

American Soc. of General Surgeons

Glenview, IL
Web: www.theasgs.org
E-mail: asgs-info@theasgs.org
Leg. Issues: HCR, MMM

Outside Counsel/Consultants

Cavarocchi Ruscio Dennis Associates
Issues: HCR, MMM
Rep By: Nicholas G. Cavarocchi, Domenic R. Ruscio

American Soc. of Health System Pharmacists

7272 Wisconsin Ave.
Bethesda, MD 20814
Tel: (301)657-3000
Fax: (301)657-1615
Registered: LDA
Web: www.ashp.org
Leg. Issues: HCR, MMM, PHA

Political Action Committee/s

American Soc. of Health System Pharmacists PAC
7272 Wisconsin Ave.
Bethesda, MD 20814
Tel: (301)657-3000
Fax: (301)657-1615
Contact: Brian M. Meyer

In-house, DC-area Employees

MANASSE, Ph.D., Sc., Henri R.: Exec. V. President and Chief Exec. Officer
MEYER, Brian M.: Director, Government Affairs Division
STEIN, Ph.D., Gary C.: Director, Federal Regulatory Affairs

American Soc. of Heating, Refrigerating and Air Conditioning Engineers

1828 L St. NW
Suite 906
Washington, DC 20036-5104
Tel: (202)833-1830
Fax: (202)833-0118
Web: www.ashrae.org

Headquartered in Atlanta, GA.

In-house, DC-area Employees

MIRO, Carlos R. "Chuck": Director, Government Affairs

American Soc. of Hematology

1900 M St. NW
Suite 200
Washington, DC 20036-2422
Tel: (202)776-0544
Fax: (202)776-0545
Registered: LDA
Web: www.hematology.org
E-mail: ash@dc.sba.com
Leg. Issues: BUD, HCR, MED, MMM, SCI

In-house, DC-area Employees

LIGGETT, Martha L.: Exec. Director
MAYRIDES, Maurice: Government Affairs Director

Outside Counsel/Consultants

MARC Associates, Inc.
Issues: HCR, MMM
Rep By: Bernard Patashnik, Ellen Riker

American Soc. of Home Inspectors (ASHI)

Des Plaines, IL
Leg. Issues: CSP, HOU, SMB

Outside Counsel/Consultants

Capitol Hill Advocates
Issues: CSP, HOU, SMB
Rep By: Randall G. Pence

American Soc. of Human Genetics

9650 Rockville Pike
Bethesda, MD 20814-3998
Tel: (301)571-1825
Fax: (301)530-7079
Web: www.faseb.org/genetics
E-mail: estrass@genetics.faseb.org

In-house, DC-area Employees

STRASS, Elaine: Exec. Director

American Soc. of Interior Designers

608 Massachusetts Ave. NE
Washington, DC 20002
Tel: (202)546-3480
Fax: (202)546-3240
Registered: LDA
Web: www.asid.org
E-mail: asid@asid.org

Represents 30,000 members, including interior design practitioners, students and manufacturers and distributors of materials specified by interior designers.

In-house, DC-area Employees

ALIN, Michael: Exec. Director

American Soc. of Internat'l Law

2223 Massachusetts Ave. NW
Washington, DC 20008-2864
Tel: (202)939-6000
Fax: (202)797-7133
Web: www.asil.org
E-mail: services@asil.org

In-house, DC-area Employees

KU, Charlotte: Exec. Director

American Soc. of Landscape Architects

636 I St. NW
Washington, DC 20001-3736
Tel: (202)898-2444
Fax: (202)898-1185
Web: www.asla.org

In-house, DC-area Employees

ARGUST, Marcia F.: Director, Public and Government Affairs
SOMERVILLE, Nancy: Exec. Director
TOLLIVER, Jim: Deputy Exec. Director
YOUNG, Beth: Manager, Public Relations

American Soc. of Mechanical Engineers

1828 L St. NW
Suite 906
Washington, DC 20036
Tel: (202)785-3756
Fax: (202)429-9417
Registered: LDA
Web: www.asme.org

Headquartered in New York, NY.

Leg. Issues: EDU, SCI

In-house, DC-area Employees

BURGIO, Patti
HAMILTON, Philip W.: Managing Director, Public Affairs
MEISINGER, Reese: Director, Public Affairs

American Soc. of Military Comptrollers

Alexandria, VA

Outside Counsel/Consultants

Halsey, Rains & Associates, LLC
Rep By: Steven C. Halsey, James Hubbard, Laurie D. Rains

American Soc. of Naval Engineers

1452 Duke St.
Alexandria, VA 22314-3458
Tel: (703)836-6727
Fax: (703)836-7491
Web: www.navalengineers.org
E-mail: asnehq@navalengineers.org

In-house, DC-area Employees

KRUSE, USN (Ret.), Capt. Dennis: Exec. Director

American Soc. of Nephrology

Washington, DC
Web: www.asn-online.com
E-mail: asn@dc.sba.com
Leg. Issues: BUD, MED, MMM

Outside Counsel/Consultants

Smith, Bucklin and Associates, Inc.
Issues: BUD, MED, MMM
Rep By: Jill Rathbun

American Soc. of Newspaper Editors

11690B Sunrise Valley Dr.
Reston, VA 20191
Tel: (703)453-1122
Fax: (703)453-1133
Web: www.asne.org
E-mail: asne@asne.org
Leg. Issues: CON, GOV

In-house, DC-area Employees

BOSLEY, Scott: Exec. Director
BOWMAN, Bobbi: Diversity Director

Outside Counsel/Consultants

Cohn and Marks
Issues: CON, GOV
Rep By: Kevin M. Goldberg, Richard M. Schmidt, Jr.

American Soc. of Nuclear Cardiology

9111 Old Georgetown Rd.
Bethesda, MD 20814-1699
Tel: (301)493-2360
Fax: (301)493-2376
Web: www.asnc.org
E-mail: admin@asnc.org

A professional medical sub-specialty society.

Leg. Issues: HCR, MMM

In-house, DC-area Employees

BOXALL, Jr., James A.: Director, Health Policy
NELLIGAN, William D.: Exec. Director

Outside Counsel/Consultants

MARC Associates, Inc.
Issues: HCR, MMM
Rep By: Edwin Allen, Randolph B. Fenninger, Bernard Patashnik

Webster, Chamberlain & Bean

American Soc. of Orthopedic Physician Assistants

Outside Counsel/Consultants

Hogan & Hartson L.L.P.
Rep By: Laura E. Loeb, Beth L. Roberts

American Soc. of Pediatric Nephrology

Cleveland, OH
Leg. Issues: BUD, HCR, MMM

Outside Counsel/Consultants

Cavarocchi Ruscio Dennis Associates
Issues: BUD, HCR, MMM
Rep By: Nicholas G. Cavarocchi, Domenic R. Ruscio

American Soc. of Pension Actuaries

4245 N. Fairfax Dr.
Suite 750
Arlington, VA 22203
Tel: (703)516-9300
Fax: (703)516-9308
Registered: LDA
Web: www.aspa.org
E-mail: aspa@aspa.org

Trade ass'n representing pension actuaries.

Leg. Issues: RET, TAX

Political Action Committee/s

American Soc. of Pension Actuaries PAC
4245 N. Fairfax Dr.
Suite 750
Arlington, VA 22203
Contact: Brian H. Graff
Tel: (703)516-9300
Fax: (703)516-9308

In-house, DC-area Employees

FLORES, Jolynne: Manager, Government Affairs
GRAFF, Brian H.: Exec. Director
TAYLOR, George: President

Outside Counsel/Consultants

Hooper Owen & Winburn
Issues: TAX
Rep By: Steve Glaze

Kehoe & Hambel
Issues: RET
Rep By: Danea M. Kehoe

American Soc. of Plant Physiologists

15501 Monona Dr.
Rockville, MD 20855
Tel: (301)251-0560
Fax: (301)279-2996
Registered: LDA
Web: www.aspp.org
E-mail: aspp@aspp.org
Leg. Issues: SCI

In-house, DC-area Employees

HYPS, Brian M.: Director, Public Affairs
LISACK, Jr., John: Exec. Director

American Soc. of Plastic and Reconstructive Surgeons

Arlington Heights, IL
Leg. Issues: HCR

Outside Counsel/Consultants

Kent & O'Connor, Inc.
Issues: HCR
Rep By: Jonathan H. Kent

American Soc. of Professional Estimators

11141 Georgia Ave.
Suite 412
Wheaton, MD 20902
Tel: (301)929-8848
Fax: (301)929-0231
Web: www.aspenational.com
E-mail: info@aspenational.com

In-house, DC-area Employees

PERRELL, Beverly S.: Director, Administration

American Soc. of Radiologic Technologists

Albuquerque, NM
Leg. Issues: HCR, MMM

Outside Counsel/Consultants

Capitol Associates, Inc.
Issues: MMM
Rep By: William A. Finerfrock, Matthew Williams

Webster, Chamberlain & Bean
Issues: HCR
Rep By: David P. Goch, Arthur Herold

American Soc. of Safety Engineers

Des Plaines, IL
Web: www.asae.org
Leg. Issues: LBR

Outside Counsel/Consultants

Patton Boggs, LLP
Issues: LBR
Rep By: Parker Brugge

American Soc. of Transplantation

1050 Connecticut Ave. NW
Washington, DC 20036-5339
Tel: (202)828-3460
Fax: (202)857-6395
Web: www.a-s-t.org

The above address is that of the firm Arent Fox Kintner Plotkin & Kahn. Headquartered in Mt. Laurel, NJ.

Leg. Issues: HCR

In-house, DC-area Employees

APPLEGATE, Bill: Director, Government Relations

Outside Counsel/Consultants

Arent Fox Kintner Plotkin & Kahn, PLLC
Issues: HCR
Rep By: Bill Applegate, Robert J. Waters

American Soc. of Travel Agents

1101 King St.
Alexandria, VA 22314
Tel: (703)739-2782
Fax: (703)684-8319
Registered: LDA
Web: www.astanet.com
Leg. Issues: AVI, CSP, MAR, SMB, TAX, TOU

Political Action Committee/s

American Soc. of Travel Agents Political Action Committee (ASTAPAC)
1101 King St.
Alexandria, VA 22314
Contact: Barbara E. O'Hara
Tel: (703)739-2782
Fax: (703)684-8319

In-house, DC-area Employees

LONG, Dina: V. President, Communications
MALONEY, William A.: Exec V. President and Chief Operating Officer
O'HARA, Barbara E.: V. President, Government Affairs
RUBIN, Burt: General Counsel
RUDEN, Paul M.: Senior V. President, Legal and Industry Affairs

Outside Counsel/Consultants

The Argus Group, L.L.C.
Issues: TAX, TOU
Rep By: David R. Burton, Dan R. Mastromarco

American Soc. of Tropical Medicine and Hygiene

Northbrook, IL
Leg. Issues: BUD, MED, TOB

Outside Counsel/Consultants

Capitol Associates, Inc.
Issues: BUD, MED, TOB
Rep By: Sara Milo

American Soc. of Women Accountants (ACC)

Outside Counsel/Consultants

Ass'n Management Bureau
Rep By: Laura Skoff

American Sociological Ass'n

1307 New York Ave. NW
Suite 700
Washington, DC 20005
Tel: (202)383-9005
Fax: (202)638-0882
Web: www.asanet.org
E-mail: executive.office@asanet

In-house, DC-area Employees

LEVINE, Dr. Felice J.: Exec. Officer

American Soybean Ass'n

St. Louis, MO

A national single-commodity association organized to assure a profitable soybean industry. Has approximately 30,000 dues-paying soybean-producer members; programs supported by over 450,000 soybean producers.

Leg. Issues: AGR, ENV, TRA

Outside Counsel/Consultants

Gordley Associates
Issues: AGR, ENV, TRA
Rep By: John Gordley, Krysta Harden, Megan Marquet

American Speech, Language, and Hearing Ass'n

10801 Rockville Pike
Rockville, MD 20852
Tel: (301)897-5700
Fax: (301)571-0469
Registered: LDA
Web: www.asha.org

A professional, scientific and accrediting organization representing 85,000 professionals in the field of speech, language, and hearing. A member organization of the Consortium for Citizens with Disabilities, the Nat'l Rehabilitation Coalition, and the Coalition for Health Care Choice and Accountability. The above address also serves as the office of the Council on Professional Standards in Speech-Language Pathology and Audiology, the Nat'l Student Speech Language Hearing Ass'n, Tri-Alliance of Rehabilitation Professionals, and the American Speech-Language-Hearing Foundation.

Leg. Issues: BUD, EDU, ENV, HCR, LAW, LBR, MED, MMM, SCI, TEC

Political Action Committee/s

American Speech-Language-Hearing Ass'n Political Action Committee
10801 Rockville Pike
Rockville, MD 20852
Tel: (301)897-5700
Fax: (301)571-0469

In-house, DC-area Employees

CHEROW, Evelyn: Director, Audiology Division
CLARKE, Catherine: Director, Federal Legislation Branch
DIGGS, Charles: Manager, Government Relations
FRANKLIN, Reed: Director, Congressional Constituent Relations
KANDER, Mark: Director, Medicare and Medicaid Branch
KARR, Susan: Director, School Services
PIETRANTON, Arlene: Associate Director for Speech Language Pathology
POTTER, James G.: Director, Government Relations and Public Policy
SPAHR, Frederick T.: Exec. Director
WHITE, Steven C.: Director, Healthcare Financing
WILLIAMS, Evelyn

Outside Counsel/Consultants

Greenberg Traurig, LLP
Issues: BUD, HCR, MMM
Rep By: Rob Garagiola, Russell J. Mueller, Nancy E. Taylor, Timothy P. Trysla

Kilpatrick Stockton LLP
Rep By: Neil I. Levy

MARC Associates, Inc.
Issues: MMM
Rep By: Bernard Patashnik

American Speech-Language-Hearing Foundation

10801 Rockville Pike
Rockville, MD 20852
Tel: (301)897-5700
Fax: (301)571-0457

The above address is that of the American Speech-Language-Hearing Ass'n (see separate listing).

In-house, DC-area Employees

MINGHETTI, Nancy: Exec. Director

American Spice and Trade Ass'n

Englewood Cliffs, NJ
Leg. Issues: AGR

Outside Counsel/Consultants

McDermott, Will and Emery
Issues: AGR
Rep By: Jerry C. Hill, Edward M. Ruckert

The Roberts Group
Rep By: John B. Hallagan, Glenn Roberts

American Sportfishing Ass'n

1033 N. Fairfax St.
Suite 200
Alexandria, VA 22314
Tel: (703)519-9691
Fax: (703)519-1872
Registered: LDA
Web: www.asafishing.org
E-mail: info@asafishing.org
Leg. Issues: MAR, NAT, SMB, TRD

Political Action Committee/s

American Sportfishing Association PAC
1033 N. Fairfax St.
Suite 200
Alexandria, VA 22314
Tel: (703)519-9691
Fax: (703)519-1872
Contact: J. Michael Nussman

In-house, DC-area Employees

HAYDEN, J. Michael: President
NUSSMAN, J. Michael: V. President for Government Affairs
PROSSER, Norville: V. President for Government Affairs

Outside Counsel/Consultants

Ball Janik, LLP
Rep By: Robert G. Hayes, Irene Ringwood

American Staffing Ass'n

277 S. Washington St.
Suite 200
Alexandria, VA 22314
Tel: (703)253-2020
Fax: (703)253-2053
Registered: LDA
Web: www.staffingtoday.net

ASA represents temporary help and staffing firms throughout the U.S. Formerly went by the name Nat'l Ass'n of Temporary and Staffing Services.

Leg. Issues: LBR, RET, TAX

Political Action Committee/s

StaffingPAC
277 S. Washington St.
Suite 200
Alexandria, VA 22314
Tel: (703)253-2035
Fax: (703)253-2053
Contact: Edward A. Lenz

In-house, DC-area Employees

GRECO, Dawn R.: Assistant Counsel
HARKINS, Elizabeth M.: Director, Government Affairs
LENZ, Edward A.: Senior V. President, Public Affairs and General Counsel

Outside Counsel/Consultants

Kirkland & Ellis
Rep By: John Irving

Miller & Chevalier, Chartered
Issues: LBR, RET, TAX
Rep By: C. Frederick Oliphant, III

Washington Council Ernst & Young
Issues: LBR, RET, TAX
Rep By: Doug Badger, Lauren Darling, John L. Doney, Jayne T. Fitzgerald, LaBrenda Garrett-Nelson, Gary J. Gasper, Bruce A. Gates, Nick Giordano, Cathy Koch, Robert J. Leonard, Richard Meltzer, Phillip D. Moseley, John D. Porter, Robert M. Rozen, Donna Steele-Flynn, Timothy J. Urban

Webster, Chamberlain & Bean
Rep By: Arthur Herold

American Standard Cos. Inc.

1500 Lee Hwy.
Suite 140
Arlington, VA 22209
Tel: (703)525-4015
Fax: (703)684-2037
Web: www.americanstandard.com
Leg. Issues: TRD

Political Action Committee/s

American Standard Cos Inc. PAC
1500 Lee Hwy.
Suite 140
Arlington, VA 22209
Tel: (703)525-4015
Fax: (703)684-2037

In-house, DC-area Employees

WOLF, James E.: V. President, Government Affairs

Outside Counsel/Consultants

American Continental Group, Inc.
Rep By: David A. Metzner, Shawn H. Smeallie

Baker, Donelson, Bearman & Caldwell, P.C.
Issues: TRD
Rep By: Francine Lamoriello, Joan M. McEntee, George Cranwell Montgomery

American Statistical Ass'n

1429 Duke St.
Alexandria, VA 22314-3402
Tel: (703)684-1221
Fax: (703)684-2037
Web: www.amstat.org
E-mail: asainfo@amstat.org

Advocates the development and application of statistics.

In-house, DC-area Employees

WALLER, Ph.D., Ray A.: Exec. Director

American Steamship Co.

Williamsville, NY

Outside Counsel/Consultants

Robertson, Monagle & Eastaugh
Rep By: Bradley D. Gilman

American Subcontractors Ass'n, Inc.

1004 Duke St.
Alexandria, VA 22314-3588
Tel: (703)684-3450
Fax: (703)836-3482
Registered: LDA
Web: www.asaonline.com
E-mail: asaoffice@asa-hq.com

A national trade association representing both union and non-union construction subcontractors. Founded in 1966, ASA serves more than 7,000 member companies through a nationwide network of local and state chapters.

Leg. Issues: GOV, LBR, ROD, SMB

Political Action Committee/s

American Subcontractors Ass'n PAC
1004 Duke St.
Alexandria, VA 22314-3588
Tel: (703)684-3450
Fax: (703)836-3482
Contact: Matt Wald

In-house, DC-area Employees

NELSON, E. Colette: Executive V. President
WALD, Matt: Director of Government and Industry Relations

American Sugar Alliance

2111 Wilson Blvd.
Suite 700
Arlington, VA 22201
Tel: (703)351-5055
Fax: (703)351-6698
Registered: LDA
Web: www.sugaralliance.org
E-mail: asainfo@aol.com

A national coalition backing America's cane, beet and corn farmers and processors.

Leg. Issues: AGR, APP, BUD, ENV, TRD

In-house, DC-area Employees

MARKWART, Luther A.: Chairman
MYERS, Vickie R.: Exec. Director
RONEY, John C. "Jack": Director, Economics
TERRELL, Joseph: Director, Public Affairs

Outside Counsel/Consultants

Bob Foster and Associates
Issues: BUD
Rep By: Robert B. Foster

American Sugar Cane League of the U.S.A.

Thibodaux, LA
Leg. Issues: AGR

Political Action Committee/s

American Sugar Cane League Political Action Committee
Thibodaux, LA

Outside Counsel/Consultants

The Macon Edwards Co.
Issues: AGR
Rep By: Macon T. Edwards, Mara Peltz

Don Wallace Associates, Inc.
Issues: AGR
Rep By: John Gilliland, Donald L. Wallace, Jr.

American Sugarbeet Growers Ass'n

1156 15th St. NW
Suite 1101
Washington, DC 20005
Tel: (202)833-2398
Fax: (202)833-2962
Registered: LDA
Web: www.hometown.aol.com/asga/sugar.htm
E-mail: asga@aol.com

A trade association representing U.S. sugarbeet producers in legislative, international, and public relations.

Leg. Issues: AGR

Political Action Committee/s

American Sugarbeet Growers Ass'n Political Action Committee
1156 15th St. NW
Suite 1101
Washington, DC 20005
Tel: (202)833-2398
Fax: (202)833-2962
Contact: Ruthann Geib

In-house, DC-area Employees

GEIB, Ruthann: V. President
MARKWART, Luther A.: Exec. V. President

American Superconductor Corp.

Westborough, MA
Leg. Issues: DEF

Outside Counsel/Consultants

Cassidy & Associates, Inc.
Issues: DEF
Rep By: Harry E. Barsh, Jr., Lawrence C. Grossman, Dennis M. Kedzior, Lindsay Lawrence, Brig. Gen. Terry Paul, USMC (Ret.), Blenda Pinto-Riddick

American Supply and Machinery Manufacturers' Ass'n

Cleveland, OH

Outside Counsel/Consultants

London and Satagaj, Attorneys-at-Law
Rep By: Sheldon I. London, John S. Satagaj

American Supply Ass'n

Chicago, IL
Web: www.asa.net
E-mail: asaemail@interserv.com
Leg. Issues: CAW, ENV, LBR, SMB, TAX, UTI

Outside Counsel/Consultants

Kent & O'Connor, Inc.
Issues: CAW, ENV, LBR, SMB, TAX, UTI
Rep By: Eileen Fitzgerald, Jonathan H. Kent, Patrick C. O'Connor

American Symphony Orchestra League

910 17th St. NW
Suite 800
Washington, DC 20006
Tel: (202)776-0212
Fax: (202)776-0224
Registered: LDA
Web: www.symphony.org
E-mail: league@symphony.org

The national service organization for the 1,800 symphony and chamber orchestras in America. Founded in 1942 and chartered by Congress in 1962, the League works to ensure the artistic and financial strength of American orchestras. The League provides professional training, management consulting, publications, artistic resources, and public policy information for orchestra management and volunteers and maintains an information center to respond to public inquiries. Headquartered in New York, NY.

Leg. Issues: ART, BUD, CPT, EDU, IMM, LBR, POS, TAX, TEC, TOU

In-house, DC-area Employees

SPARKS, John D.: V. President, Public and Government Affairs
WATTS, Heather C.: Associate Director, Government Affairs

American Systems Internat'l Corp.

2800 Shirlington Rd.
Suite 401
Arlington, VA 22206
Tel: (703)824-0300
Fax: (703)824-0320
Registered: LDA
Web: www.asic-dc.com
Leg. Issues: DEF, MAN

In-house, DC-area Employees

KHARE, Joe: Consultant
MCVEY, Robert D.: Chief Exec. Officer
SKIPPER, Jr., William H.: President
TESNOW, David: Consultant

Outside Counsel/Consultants

Michael Chase Associates, LTD
Issues: DEF
Rep By: Michael T. Chase

The Legislative Strategies Group, LLC
Rep By: Melvin J. Littig, Grayson Winterling

G.L. Merritt & Associates, Inc.
Issues: DEF, MAN
Rep By: Gordon L. Merritt

American Task Force for Lebanon

2213 M St. NW
Third Floor
Washington, DC 20037
Tel: (202)223-9333
Fax: (202)223-1399

A membership organization representing Americans of Lebanese ancestry.

In-house, DC-area Employees

CODY, Ph.D., George T.: Exec. Director
NASSIF, Thomas A.: Chairman

American Tax Policy Institute

1030 15th St. NW
Suite 870
Washington, DC 20005
Tel: (202)637-3243
Fax: (202)393-0336

In-house, DC-area Employees
KENNY, Lynn: Administrator

Outside Counsel/Consultants

The Kellen Company
Rep By: Lynn Kenny

American Telecasting, Inc.

Colorado Springs, CO
Leg. Issues: TEC

Outside Counsel/Consultants

Gardner, Carton and Douglas
Issues: TEC

American Telemedicine Ass'n

Washington, DC
Web: www.americantelemed.org
E-mail: info@americantelemed.org

Outside Counsel/Consultants

Issue Dynamics Inc.

American Teleservices Ass'n

Washington, DC
Leg. Issues: ACC, ADV, AER, APP, ART, AUT, AVI, BAN, BEV, COM, CPI, CSP, EDU, ENG, FIN, FOO, FUE, HCR, INS, MAN, MED, MIA, PHA, RRR, SCI, SMB, TEC, TOU, TRA, TRD

Outside Counsel/Consultants

Management Options, Inc.
Issues: ACC, ADV, AER, APP, ART, AUT, AVI, BAN, BEV, COM, CPI, CSP, EDU, ENG, FIN, FOO, FUE, HCR, INS, MAN, MED, MIA, PHA, RRR, SCI, SMB, TEC, TOU, TRA, TRD
Rep By: Alan R. Atkinson, James B. Clawson, Jason B. Clawson, George M. "Matt" Mattingley, Jr., Jason Todd

American Textile Co.

Pittsburgh, PA
Leg. Issues: APP, TRD

Outside Counsel/Consultants

Sandler, Travis & Rosenberg, P.A.
Issues: APP, TRD
Rep By: Nicole Bivens Collinson, Ron Sorini

American Textile Machinery Ass'n

111 Park Place
Falls Church, VA 22046
Tel: (703)538-1789
Fax: (703)241-5603
Web: www.webmasters.net/atma/
E-mail: armahq@aol.com

Political Action Committee/s

Textile Machinery Good Government Committee
111 Park Place
Falls Church, VA 22046
Tel: (703)538-1789
Fax: (703)241-5603
Contact: Clay D. Tyeryar, CAE

In-house, DC-area Employees
BUZZERD, Jr., CAE, Harry W.: Exec. V. President
TYERYAR, CAE, Clay D.: Secretary, Textile Machinery Good Government Committee

Outside Counsel/Consultants

Collier Shannon Scott, PLLC
Rep By: Lauren R. Howard, William W. Scott

American Textile Manufacturers Institute

1130 Connecticut Ave. NW
Suite 1200
Washington, DC 20036-3954
Tel: (202)862-0500
Fax: (202)862-0570
Registered: LDA
Web: www.atmi.org
E-mail: info@atmi.org
Leg. Issues: CAW, DEF, ENV, HCR, LBR, TRD

Political Action Committee/s

American Textile Industry Committee for Good Government
1130 Connecticut Ave. NW
Suite 1200
Washington, DC 20036-3954
Tel: (202)862-0500
Fax: (202)862-0537
Contact: Douglas W. Bulcao

In-house, DC-area Employees
BREMER, Charles V.: Director, International Trade
BULCAO, Douglas W.: Deputy Exec. V. President; Director, Government Relations Division
DUPREE, Jr., Robert F.: Associate Director, Government Relations
FLEMING, Julie: Assistant Director, Government Relations
JOHNSON, Cass: Assistant Director, International Trade Division
MOORE, Carlos: Exec. V. President
POOLE, Hardy: Director, Product Services Division

American Thoracic Soc.

1726 M St. NW
Suite 902
Washington, DC 20036
Tel: (202)785-3355
Fax: (202)452-1805
Registered: LDA

A member organization of the Coalition for Health Funding and the Nat'l Health Council.

Leg. Issues: BUD, CAW, HCR, TOB

In-house, DC-area Employees
DU MELLE, Fran: Exec. V. President
EWART, Gary: Legislative Representative
WENTWORTH, Marchant: Director, Health Care Policy, American Thoracic Soc.

Outside Counsel/Consultants

Health and Medicine Counsel of Washington
Issues: BUD, HCR
Rep By: Staci Sigman Dennison, Dale P. Dirks

American Tobacco Co.

Old Greenwich, CT

Outside Counsel/Consultants

Covington & Burling
Rep By: David H. Remes

American Tort Reform Ass'n

1850 M St. NW
Suite 1095
Washington, DC 20036
Tel: (202)682-1163
Fax: (202)682-1022
Registered: LDA
Web: www.atra.org
E-mail: SJoyce@ATRA.org
Leg. Issues: CSP, HCR

In-house, DC-area Employees
HOTRA, Michael: Director, Public Education
JOYCE, Sherman: President
LECLAIR, Larry: Director, Legislation

Outside Counsel/Consultants

Crowell & Moring LLP
Issues: CSP
Rep By: Mark A. Behrens, Victor E. Schwartz

American Tourister, Inc.

Warren, RI

Outside Counsel/Consultants

Barnes, Richardson and Colburn
Rep By: Matthew T. McGrath

American Trans Air

Indianapolis, IN
Leg. Issues: AVI, CSP, TOU, TRA

Outside Counsel/Consultants

Palumbo & Cerrell, Inc.
Issues: CSP, TOU, TRA
Rep By: William T. Deitz, Charles R. O'Regan, Benjamin L. Palumbo, Paul A. Skrabut, Jr.

Patton Boggs, LLP
Issues: AVI
Rep By: Thomas Hale Boggs, Jr., Michael A. Brown, Joseph E. Schmitz

American Transit Services Council

1090 Vermont Ave. NW
Suite 1225
Washington, DC 20005
Tel: (202)842-2818
Fax: (202)682-0168
Web: www.transitatsc.org

In-house, DC-area Employees
FOOTE, David: Managing Director

American Translators Ass'n

225 Reinekers Lane
Suite 590
Alexandria, VA 22314
Tel: (703)683-6100
Fax: (703)683-6122
Web: www.atanet.org
E-mail: ata@atanet.org

Fosters professional development and promotes translation and interpretation professions.

In-house, DC-area Employees
BACAK, Jr., Walter W.: Exec. Director

Outside Counsel/Consultants

Shaw Pittman

American Transportation Advisory Council (ATAC)

c/o ARTBA
1010 Massachusetts Ave. NW
Suite 600
Washington, DC 20001
Tel: (202)289-4434
Fax: (202)289-4435
Web: www.artba.org

A transportation lobbying group.

In-house, DC-area Employees
TOOHEY, William. D.

American Trauma Soc.

8903 Presidential Pkwy.
Suite 512
Upper Marlboro, MD 20772-2656
Tel: (301)420-4189
Fax: (301)420-0617
Web: www.amtruama.org
Leg. Issues: BUD

In-house, DC-area Employees
TETER, Harry: Exec. Director and General Counsel

Outside Counsel/Consultants

Beacon Consulting Group, Inc.
Issues: BUD
Rep By: Jeffrey W. Henry, Gordon P. MacDougall, Lisa A. Stewart

American Trucking Ass'ns

2200 Mill Rd.
Alexandria, VA 22314
Tel: (703)838-1880
Fax: (703)548-1841
Registered: LDA
Web: www.truckline.org
Leg. Issues: BUD, ENV, INS, LBR, ROD, SMB, TAX, TRA, TRU

Political Action Committee/s

Truck PAC
430 First St. SE
Washington, DC 20003
Tel: (202)544-6245
Fax: (202)675-6568
Contact: Royal R. Roth

In-house, DC-area Employees
BLAKELY, Regina: Senior V. President, Stategic and Litigation Communication
BROOKS, Steve: Counselor to the Senior V. President and Director, Political & External Affairs
DIGGES, Jr., Robert: V. President and Director, Litigation Center
DOVE, Stephen: Manager, Legislative Affairs
GILROY, Edwin J.: Director, Legislative Affairs
HART, Joe: V. President, Legislative and Government Affairs
KUNDU, Jai: V. President and Exec. Director, Safety Management Council
MCCORMICK, Jr., Walter B.: President and Chief Exec. Officer
PITCHER, Robert C.: Director, State Laws
ROTH, Royal R.: V. President, Political Affairs
SCOTT, Ted: Director, Highway Policy
STALKNECHT, Paul: Senior V. President, Federation Relations
STINGER, Kenneth F.: V. President, Federal and Federation Legislative Affairs
STRAWHORN, Larry: V. President, Engineering
WHITTINGHILL, James R. "Whit": Senior V. President, Legislative Affairs

Outside Counsel/Consultants

Baker, Donelson, Bearman & Caldwell, P.C.
Issues: TRA
Rep By: J. Keith Kennedy, Charles R. Parkinson

Barbour Griffith & Rogers, Inc.
Issues: TAX
Rep By: Haley Barbour, G. O. Lanny Griffith, Jr., Edward M. Rogers, Jr., Brent Thompson

Kirkland & Ellis

Legislative Solutions
Issues: INS, TAX, TRA, TRU
Rep By: Dr. James DeChaine

McSlarrow Consulting L.L.C.
Issues: TRA
Rep By: Alison McSlarrow

Nat'l Strategies Inc.
Rep By: David K. Aylward

Paul, Hastings, Janofsky & Walker LLP
Issues: BUD, ROD, TAX, TRU
Rep By: Ralph B. Everett

Thompson Coburn LLP
Issues: TRA, TRU
Rep By: Hon. R. Lawrence Coughlin

American Tunaboat Owners' Coalition

San Diego, CA

Outside Counsel/Consultants

Davis Wright Tremaine LLP

American University

4400 Massachusetts Ave. NW
Washington, DC 20016
Tel: (202)885-2166
Web: www.american.edu

In-house, DC-area Employees
KNIGHT, Yvonne: Director, Government Relations Office

Outside Counsel/Consultants

Hewes, Gelband, Lambert & Dann, P.C.

Manatos & Manatos, Inc.
Rep By: Kimberley M. Fraser, Andrew E. Manatos

American University of Beirut

Beirut, LEBANON

A New York educational corporation chartered by the New York Board of Regents, with a campus in Beirut, Lebanon.

Leg. Issues: BUD

Outside Counsel/Consultants

Gryphon Internat'l
Issues: BUD
Rep By: William L. Hoffman

American Urogynecologic Soc.

Chicago, IL
E-mail: AUGS@sba.com
Leg. Issues: BUD, HCR, MED, MMM

Outside Counsel/Consultants

Smith, Bucklin and Associates, Inc.
Issues: BUD, HCR, MED, MMM
Rep By: Steven C. Kemp, Jill Rathbun

American Urological Ass'n

Baltimore, MD
Leg. Issues: BUD, MMM

Outside Counsel/Consultants

MARC Associates, Inc.
Issues: BUD, MMM
Rep By: Randolph B. Fenninger

American Veterinary Medical Ass'n

1101 Vermont Ave. NW
Suite 710
Washington, DC 20005-3521
Tel: (202)789-0007
Fax: (202)842-4360
Registered: LDA
E-mail: 74232.57@compuserve.com
Leg. Issues: ANI

Political Action Committee/s

American Veterinary Medical Ass'n Political Action Committee
1101 Vermont Ave. NW
Suite 710
Washington, DC 20005-3521
Tel: (202)789-0007
Fax: (202)842-4360
Contact: Lavone Smith

In-house, DC-area Employees

ABNEY, D.V.M., Pamela: Assistant Director, Government Relations
DUNHAM, D.V.M., Bernadette M.: Assistant Director, Government Relations
FINNEGAN, Dr. Niall B.: Director, Governmental Relations Division
GOELDNER, Dean: Assistant Director, Government Relations
SMITH, Lavone: PAC Coordinator

Outside Counsel/Consultants

John Melcher
Issues: ANI
Rep By: Hon. John Melcher

American Vintners Ass'n

1200 G St. NW
Suite 360
Washington, DC 20005
Tel: (202)783-2756
Fax: (202)347-6341
Registered: LDA
Web: www.americanwineries.org
E-mail: info@americanwineries.org

Mission is to enhance the public perception and business environment of the American wine industry through marketing, public information and grassroots government representation initiatives.

Leg. Issues: AGR, ALC, BEV, BUD, TAX, TRD

In-house, DC-area Employees

NELSON, William: V. President
SIEGL, Simon: President

Outside Counsel/Consultants

Kalik Lewin
Rep By: Robert G. Kalik

American War Mothers

2615 Woodley Place NW
Washington, DC 20008
Tel: (202)462-2791

A non-political, non-sectarian, non-partisan, non-profit organization of mothers whose sons and daughters have served in the armed forces in World Wars I & II, the Korean War, Vietnam War, Persian Gulf War, and any future conflicts.

In-house, DC-area Employees

MCLAIN, Maydell E.: National President

American Watch Ass'n

P.O. Box 464
Washington, DC 20044-0464
Tel: (703)759-3377
Registered: LDA

A trade association of watch importers, assemblers and manufacturers.

Leg. Issues: TRD

Political Action Committee/s

American Watch Ass'n Political Action Committee
P.O. Box 464
Washington, DC 20044-0464
Contact: Emilio G. Collado

In-house, DC-area Employees

COLLADO, Emilio G.: Treasurer, Political Action Committee

Outside Counsel/Consultants

Collado Associates, Inc.
Rep By: Emilio G. Collado

Covington & Burling
Issues: TRD
Rep By: Roderick A. DeArment, David R. Grace

American Water Works Ass'n

1401 New York Ave. NW
Suite 640
Washington, DC 20005
Tel: (202)628-8303
Fax: (202)628-2846
Registered: LDA
Web: www.awwa.org
Leg. Issues: BUD, CAW, CSP, ENV, GOV, HCR, UTI

In-house, DC-area Employees

BAILEY, Jeanne: Regulatory Engineer
CURTIS, Tom: Deputy Exec. Director
HICKS, Fred B.: Washington Representative, American Water Works Foundation
HOLMES, Tommy: Legislative Programs Manager
ROBERSON, Alan: Director, Regulatory Affairs
VIA, Steve: Regulatory Engineer
WARBURTON, Albert E.: Director, Legislative Affairs

Outside Counsel/Consultants

Potomac Communications Group

Simon and Co., Inc.
Issues: BUD, CAW, ENV
Rep By: Heather Barber, Alex DeGood, Leonard S. Simon

The American Water Works Co.

Outside Counsel/Consultants

The Duberstein Group, Inc.
Rep By: John W. Angus, III, Michael S. Berman, Steven M. Champlin, Kenneth M. Duberstein, Henry M. Gandy, Daniel P. Meyer

American Watercraft Ass'n

Foothill Ranch, CA

Outside Counsel/Consultants

Howard F. Park
Rep By: Howard F. Park

American Waterways Operators

1600 Wilson Blvd.
Suite 1000
Arlington, VA 22209
Tel: (703)841-9300
Fax: (703)841-0389
Registered: LDA
Web: www.americanwaterways.com

The national trade ass'n representing the coastal and inland tugboat, towboat and barge industry.

Leg. Issues: BUD, CAW, CHM, ENV, LBR, MAR, NAT, TAX, TRA, TRD

Political Action Committee/s

American Waterways Operators Political Action Committee
1600 Wilson Blvd.
Suite 1000
Arlington, VA 22209
Tel: (703)841-9300
Fax: (703)841-0389
Contact: E. Boyd Hollingsworth, Jr.

In-house, DC-area Employees

ALLEGRETTI, Thomas A.: President
BURNS, Anne Davis: Director, Public Affairs
HOLLINGSWORTH, Jr., E. Boyd: V. President, Legislative Affairs
KELLY, Jennifer A.: Senior V. President, Government Affairs and Policy Analysis

American Wholesale Marketers Ass'n

1128 16th St. NW
Washington, DC 20036-4802
Tel: (202)463-2124
Fax: (202)467-0559
Registered: LDA
Web: www.awmanet.org

The major trade association for wholesale distributors of candy, groceries, tobacco products, health and beauty aids and other convenience store products.

Leg. Issues: AGR, BUD, FOO, LBR, SMB, TAX, TOB, TRU

Political Action Committee/s

American Wholesale Marketers Ass'n WHOLE PAC
1128 16th St. NW
Washington, DC 20036-4802
Tel: (202)463-2124
Fax: (202)467-0559
Contact: Jacqueline Cohen

In-house, DC-area Employees

COHEN, Jacqueline: V. President, Government and Industry Affairs

Outside Counsel/Consultants

Luman, Lange & Wheeler
Issues: AGR, BUD, FOO, LBR, SMB, TAX, TOB, TRU
Rep By: Gene C. Lange

American Wind Energy Ass'n

122 C St. NW
Suite 380
Washington, DC 20001
Tel: (202)383-2500
Fax: (202)383-2505
Registered: LDA
Web: www.awea.org
E-mail: windmail@awea.org
Leg. Issues: BUD, ENG, TAX

Political Action Committee/s

American Wind Energy Ass'n Political Action Committee (WindPAC)
122 C St. NW
Suite 380
Washington, DC 20001
Tel: (202)383-2500
Fax: (202)383-2505
Contact: Jaime Steve

In-house, DC-area Employees

STEVE, Jaime: Director, Government and Public Affairs
SWISHER, Randall S.: Exec. Director

American Wine Heritage Alliance

Canandaigua, NY
Leg. Issues: TAX, TRD

Outside Counsel/Consultants

Kalik Lewin
Issues: TAX, TRD
Rep By: Robert G. Kalik

American Women in Radio and Television

1595 Spring Hill Road
Suite 330, Tysons Corner
Vienna, VA 22182
Tel: (703)506-3290
Fax: (703)506-3266
Registered: LDA
Web: www.awrt.org
Leg. Issues: TEC

In-house, DC-area Employees

DUNCAN, Jacci: Exec. Director

Outside Counsel/Consultants

Ass'n Management Bureau

American Wood Preservers Institute

2750 Prosperity Ave.
Suite 550
Fairfax, VA 22031-4312
Tel: (703)204-0500
Fax: (703)204-4610
Registered: LDA
Web: www.awpi.org

A national trade association representing the United States wood preserving industry. Members include manufacturers of treated wood products, wood preservative pesticide registrants, and providers of allied services.

Leg. Issues: BUD, CAW, CHM, CSP, DIS, ECN, EDU, ENV, GOV, HOU, INS, LBR, MAN, RES, ROD, SCI, SMB, TAX, TRA, TRD, TRU, URB, WAS

Political Action Committee/s

American Wood Preservers Institute Political Action Committee
2750 Prosperity Ave.
Suite 550
Fairfax, VA 22031-4312
Tel: (703)204-0500
Fax: (703)204-4610

In-house, DC-area Employees

HOLLOWAY, Anne: Manager, Legislative Affairs
PARRIS, George E.: Director, Environmental and Regulatory Affairs
PINE, Mel: Manager, Communication
RAMMINGER, Scott: President

Outside Counsel/Consultants

Capitol Hill Advocates
Issues: BUD, CAW, CHM, CSP, DIS, ECN, EDU, ENV, GOV, HOU, INS, LBR, MAN, RES, ROD, SCI, SMB, TAX, TRA, TRD, TRU, URB, WAS
Rep By: Randall G. Pence

McKenna & Cuneo, L.L.P.

American Worldwide

Outside Counsel/Consultants

Edelman Public Relations Worldwide
Rep By: Robert Rehg

American Youth Policy Forum

1836 Jefferson Place NW
Washington, DC 20036
Web: www.aypf.org
Tel: (202)775-9731
Fax: (202)775-9733

In-house, DC-area Employees

BRAND, Betsy: Co-director
HALPERIN, Samuel: Senior Fellow
PARTEE, Glenda L.: Co-director

The American Youth Work Center

1200 17th St. NW
Fourth Floor
Washington, DC 20036
E-mail: info@youthtoday.org
Tel: (202)785-0764
Fax: (202)728-0657

Established in 1984 to promote youth service programs and to publish "Youth Today-The Newspaper on Youth Work."

In-house, DC-area Employees

TREANOR, William W.: Exec. Director

American Zinc Ass'n

1112 16th St. NW
Suite 240
Washington, DC 20036
Web: www.zinc.org
E-mail: gvary@zinc.org
Tel: (202)835-0164
Fax: (202)835-0155

In-house, DC-area Employees

DIRIENZO, Michael: Director, Public Affairs
VARY, George F.: Exec. Director

American Zoo and Aquarium Ass'n

8403 Colesville Rd.
Suite 710
Silver Spring, MD 20910
Web: www.aza.org
Tel: (301)562-0777
Fax: (301)562-0888
Registered: LDA

Leg. Issues: ANI

In-house, DC-area Employees

BUTLER, Sydney J.: Exec. Director
HUTCHINS, Dr. Michael: Dir., American Zoo and Aquarium Ass'n Conservation & Science
LATTIS, Richard: President/C.E.O. Zoo Atlanta
VEHRS, Kristin L.: Deputy Director

American-Arab Anti-Discrimination Committee (ADC)

4201 Connecticut Ave. NW
Suite 300
Washington, DC 20008
Web: www.adc.org
E-mail: adc@adc.org
Tel: (202)244-2990
Fax: (202)244-3196

The ADC is a non-sectarian, non-partisan civil rights organization committed to defending the rights of people of Arab descent and promoting their rich cultural heritage. Since its founding in 1980, the ADC has grown into the largest Arab-American grassroots organization in the United States, with more than 80 chapters nationwide. As the voice of Arab Americans, ADC regularly communicates issues of concern to the President of the United States and members of Congress.

Leg. Issues: CIV

In-house, DC-area Employees

MAKSOUD, Ph.D., Hala: President

American-Turkish Council

915 15th St. NW
7th Floor
Washington, DC 20005
E-mail: atcafot@aol.com
Tel: (202)783-0483
Fax: (202)783-0511

A business association dedicated to friendship and the promotion of U.S.-Turkish commercial, defense and cultural relations.

In-house, DC-area Employees

MCCURDY, G. Lincoln: President

Outside Counsel/Consultants

Baker, Donelson, Bearman & Caldwell, P.C.
Rep By: Doreen M. Edelman, Charles R. Johnston, Jr.

American-Uzbekistan Chamber of Commerce

Web: www.erols.com/aucc
E-mail: aucc@erols.com

Outside Counsel/Consultants

White & Case LLP
Rep By: Carolyn B. Lamm

Americans Against Unfair Family Taxation

Outside Counsel/Consultants

American Continental Group, Inc.

Powell Tate

Americans Against Union Control of Government

320-D Maple Ave. East
Vienna, VA 22180
E-mail: publicsrc@erols.com
Tel: (703)242-3575
Fax: (703)242-3579

Founded in 1973 by Carol Applegate, a Michigan public school teacher. Reports a current membership of 20,000. Operates as a division of the Public Service Research Council. Opposes collective bargaining for public employee unions.

Leg. Issues: LBR

In-house, DC-area Employees

DENHOLM, David Y.

Americans Back in Charge Foundation

Washington, DC

A non-profit, public foundation dedicated to overseeing research, education and legal efforts supporting term limits for public officials and campaign finance reform.

Leg. Issues: CON, GOV

Outside Counsel/Consultants

Sullivan & Mitchell, P.L.L.C.
Issues: CON, GOV
Rep By: Cleta Mitchell, Paul E. Sullivan

Americans for a Brighter Future

P.O. Box 2404
Washington, DC 20013
Tel: (202)543-7778
Fax: (202)543-7384

In-house, DC-area Employees

JACKSON, Raynard: Chairman

Americans for Affordable Electricity

c/o Internat'l Paper
1101 Pennsylvania Ave. NW, Suite 200
Washington, DC 20004
Web: www.a4ae.org
E-mail: HorneK@nrf.com
Tel: (202)347-6371
Registered: LDA

A broad-based coalition that advocates passage of legislation that creates an efficient, reliable and equitable interstate system for transmitting and distributing competitively priced electricity, including a date certain provision to assure that citizens in those states that fail to act reasonably soon will not lose out.

Leg. Issues: ENG, FUE, UTI

In-house, DC-area Employees

PAXON, Hon. William L.: Nat'l Chairman
SPRING, Andrea Leigh: Exec. Director

Outside Counsel/Consultants

Akin, Gump, Strauss, Hauer & Feld, L.L.P.
Issues: ENG, FUE, UTI
Rep By: Anthony Foti, Hon. William L. Paxon, James R. Tucker, Jr.

Americans for Better Borders

Leg. Issues: IMM, TOU

Outside Counsel/Consultants

Ogletree Governmental Affairs, Inc.
Issues: IMM, TOU
Rep By: Harold P. Coxson

Americans for Better Education

Outside Counsel/Consultants

Quinn Gillespie & Associates

Americans for Choice in Education

3612 Bent Branch Ct.
Arlington, VA 22041
Tel: (703)941-4329
Fax: (703)941-4329

In-house, DC-area Employees

TOBIN, Dr. William J.: V. President

Outside Counsel/Consultants

William J. Tobin and Associates

Americans for Common Cents

A coalition to preserve the one-cent coin.

Leg. Issues: MON

Outside Counsel/Consultants

Sagamore Associates, Inc.
Issues: MON
Rep By: Mark W. Weller

Americans for Computer Privacy

Washington, DC
Registered: LDA

Outside Counsel/Consultants

Dittus Communications
Rep By: Gloria S. Dittus, Kristin Litterst

Preston Gates Ellis & Rouvelas Meeds LLP
Rep By: Amy Carlson, Hon. David Funderburk, Bruce J. Heiman, Steven R. "Rick" Valentine

Quinn Gillespie & Associates

Americans for Consumer Education and Competition, Inc.

Washington, DC
Leg. Issues: BAN, EDU, FIN

Outside Counsel/Consultants

Susan Molinari, L.L.P.
Issues: BAN, EDU, FIN

Americans for Democratic Action

1625 K St. NW
Suite 210
Washington, DC 20006
Web: www.adaction.org
E-mail: adaction@ix.netcom.com
Tel: (202)785-5980
Fax: (202)785-5969
Registered: LDA

An independent political action group concerned with liberal domestic and foreign policies. Established in 1947.

Leg. Issues: GOV

Political Action Committee/s

Americans for Democratic Action Political Action Committee
1625 K St. NW
Suite 210
Washington, DC 20006
Contact: Valerie Dulk-Jacobs
Tel: (202)785-5980
Fax: (202)785-5969

In-house, DC-area Employees

DULK-JACOBS, Valerie: Special Assistant to the Director
FAGIN, Darryl H.: Legislative Director
ISAACS, Amy: National Director

Americans for Equitable Climate Solutions

Washington, DC
Leg. Issues: AGR, AUT, CAW, ECN, ENG, FOR, LBR, MAN, NAT, ROD, RRR, TRA, TRU, UTI

Outside Counsel/Consultants

Lee Lane
Issues: AGR, AUT, CAW, ECN, ENG, FOR, LBR, MAN, NAT, ROD, RRR, TRA, TRU, UTI
Rep By: Lee Lane

William B. Newman Jr.
Rep By: William B. Newman, Jr.

Americans for Fair Taxation

Houston, TX
Registered: LDA
Leg. Issues: TAX

Outside Counsel/Consultants

The Argus Group, L.L.C.
Issues: TAX
Rep By: David R. Burton, Dan R. Mastromarco

Arter & Hadden
Issues: TAX
Rep By: Daniel L. Cohen, Hon. Thomas G. Loeffler, Jon W. Plebani

Americans for Financial Security

A non-profit organization for individuals who seek a non-partisan source for financial resources.

Leg. Issues: SMB

Outside Counsel/Consultants

The Strategic Advocacy Group
Issues: SMB
Rep By: Blair G. Childs

Americans for Free Internat'l Trade (AFIT PAC)

112 S. West St.
Suite 310
Alexandria, VA 22314
E-mail: afitpac@aol.com
Tel: (703)684-8880
Fax: (703)836-5256

A political action committee representing auto import dealers.

Leg. Issues: AUT, TAX, TRD

In-house, DC-area Employees

HANAGAN, Mary Dreape: Exec. Director

Outside Counsel/Consultants

Greener and Hook, LLC

Americans for Gun Safety

Outside Counsel/Consultants

Griffin, Johnson, Dover & Stewart

Americans for Integrity in Palliative Care

Alexandria, VA

Leg. Issues: FAM, MED

Outside Counsel/Consultants

Tarne Powers & Associates

Issues: FAM, MED

Rep By: Gene Tarne

Americans for Long Term Care Security

Washington, DC

Outside Counsel/Consultants

Matz, Blancato & Associates, Inc.

Rep By: Robert B. Blancato

Americans for Medical Progress

908 King St.
Suite 201
Alexandria, VA 22314-3121
Tel: (703)836-9595
Fax: (703)836-9594

Web: www.AMProgress.org

E-mail: AMP@AMprogress.org

Educates the public, media and policymakers about the role of medical research in curing disease, easing pain and making quality medical care more affordable, and supports scientists use of animals in medical research.

Leg. Issues: ANI, HCR, MED, PHA, SCI

In-house, DC-area Employees

CALNAN, Jacqueline: President

Americans for Peace Now

1815 H St. NW
Suite 920
Washington, DC 20006
Tel: (202)728-1893
Fax: (202)728-1895
Registered: LDA

Web: www.peacenow.org

E-mail: APNDC@peacenow.org

A policy advocacy group which supports Israeli security through a peace agreement between Israel and her Arab neighbors.

Leg. Issues: FOR

In-house, DC-area Employees

DELEE, Debra: President and Chief Exec. Officer
FRIEDMAN, Laura: Legislative Director
ROSENBLUM, Mark: Founder, Political Director
ROTH, Lewis E.: Director, Public Affairs
SHELEF, Noam: Grassroots Coordinator

Americans for Political Participation

P.O. Box 19254
Alexandria, VA 22320

In-house, DC-area Employees

SULLIVAN, Frank: Contact, Political Action Committee

Americans for Responsible Alcohol Access

Outside Counsel/Consultants

Strat@Comm (Strategic Communications Counselors)

Rep By: Ron DeFore

Americans for Responsible Recreational Areas

A coalition of interests concerned about access to U.S. public lands and national parks.

Outside Counsel/Consultants

The Legislative Strategies Group, LLC

Rep By: Larry E. Smith

Americans for Sensible Estate Tax Solutions (ASSETS)

Washington, DC

A coliation of insurers, charitable institutions and other interests concerned with estate tax issues.

Leg. Issues: TAX

Outside Counsel/Consultants

Edelman Public Relations Worldwide

Issues: TAX

Rep By: Eric Hoffman

Tongour Simpson Holsclaw Green

Issues: TAX

Rep By: Hon. Alan K. Simpson

Americans for Tax Reform

1920 L St. NW
Suite 200
Washington, DC 20036
Tel: (202)785-0266
Fax: (202)785-0261
Registered: LDA

Web: www.atr.org

A taxpayer activist organization, ATR opposes all tax increases at the Federal, State and local level. Also serves as a clearinghouse for activist information nationwide.

Leg. Issues: AGR, BAN, BEV, BUD, CIV, COM, CON, CPI, CPT, DOC, EDU, ENG, ENV, FAM, FOR, GOV, HCR, INS, LAW, LBR, MAR, MMM, RET, ROD, SCI, TAX, TRA

In-house, DC-area Employees

ANSELL, Damon: V. President, Policy
FIKE, Robert: Manager, Federal Affairs
HORN, Ryan: Manager, Federal Affairs
KUHN, Jennifer: V. President, Finance
NEHRING, Ron: Senior Consultant
NORQUIST, Grover G.: President
SMITH, Loren: Operations Director
ZYSK, Jane: Director, Special Events

Americans for the Arts

1000 Vermont Ave. NW
12th Floor
Washington, DC 20005
Tel: (202)371-2830
Fax: (202)371-0424
Registered: LDA

Web: www.artsusa.org

Formed by the merger of the Nat'l Assembly of Local Arts Agencies and the American Council for the Arts. Represents and promotes local arts agencies through professional development, information, advocacy and formulation of national arts policy.

Leg. Issues: ART, EDU

Political Action Committee/s

Arts for America PAC

1000 Vermont Ave. NW
12th Floor
Washington, DC 20005
Contact: Robert L. Lynch
Tel: (202)371-2830
Fax: (202)371-0424

In-house, DC-area Employees

BLAKE, Linda: Director, Marketing and Public Relations
LYNCH, Robert L.: President/Chief Exec. Officer
OZLU, Nina: V. President, Government Affairs
VON RAGO, Lillian: Government Affairs Coordinator

Americans Heritage Recreation

Washington, DC

Outside Counsel/Consultants

Hauser Group

Americans Supporting the Pyrotechnics Industry

4808 Moorland Ln.
Suite 109
Bethesda, MD 20814

A political action committee.

In-house, DC-area Employees

HECKMAN, Julie L.

Americans United for Separation of Church and State

518 C St. NE
Washington, DC 20002
Tel: (202)466-3234
Fax: (202)466-2587
Registered: LDA

Web: www.au.org

A non-profit, non-sectarian, non-partisan organization founded in 1947 with the sole purpose of maintaining the Constitutional guarantee of religious freedom in the First Amendment. Opposes the support of church-related schools or other church-related activities with tax money.

Leg. Issues: ALC, BUD, CIV, CON, DOC, ECN, EDU, FOR, HCR, LAW, REL, URB, WEL

In-house, DC-area Employees

BOSTON, Robert: Assistant Director, Communications
CONN, Joseph L.: Managing Editor, Church and State Magazine
GREEN, Steven K.: Legal Director
JOSEPH, Rachel: Legislative Associate
KATZ, Daniel E.: Director, Legislative Affairs
KHAN, Ayesha: Litigator
LYNN, Barry W.: Exec. Director
MULLIGAN, Ann: State Legislative Coordinator

AmeriChoice Health Services, Inc.

8045 Leesburg Pike
Suite 650
Vienna, VA 22182
Tel: (703)506-3555
Fax: (703)506-3556

Web: www.americhoice.com

In-house, DC-area Employees

CHASKES, Deborah: V. President and Deputy General Counsel
WELTERS, Anthony: President

Amerijet Internat'l Inc.

Ft. Lauderdale, FL

Leg. Issues: TRD

Outside Counsel/Consultants

The MWW Group

Issues: TRD

Rep By: Jonathan B. Slade

AmeriPlan

Outside Counsel/Consultants

Jay Grant & Associates

Ameritech

Leg. Issues: TEC

Outside Counsel/Consultants

Mayer, Brown & Platt

Issues: TEC

Rep By: Mark H. Gitenstein

Ameron Internat'l Corp.

1090 Vermont Ave. NW
Suite 800
Washington, DC 20005
Tel: (202)408-7023
Fax: (202)289-2639

E-mail: hardisty@knight-hub.com

In-house, DC-area Employees

HARDISTY, John: Washington Representative

AMFM, Inc.

Austin, TX

Leg. Issues: COM, TEC

Outside Counsel/Consultants

Alcalde & Fay

Issues: COM, TEC

Rep By: Hector Alcalde, Jim Davenport, Vicki L. Iseman, Julie Patterson

Amgen

1300 I St. NW
Suite 470 East
Washington, DC 20005
Tel: (202)354-6100
Fax: (202)289-7448
Registered: LDA

Web: www.amgen.com

Headquartered in Thousand Oaks, CA.

Leg. Issues: BUD, CPT, GOV, HCR, MAN, MED, MMM, PHA, SCI, TAX, VET

Political Action Committee/s

Amgen Inc. PAC

1300 I St. NW
Suite 470 East
Washington, DC 20005
Contact: Peter B. Teeley
Tel: (202)354-6100
Fax: (202)289-7448

In-house, DC-area Employees

ANDERSON, Serena: Associate Director, Public Policy
CHEN, Kenneth: Director, Public Policy
NORTON, Rita E.: V. President, Government Relations
TEELEY, Peter B.: Government Affairs
TESKE, Judi A.: Senior Director, Reimbursement and Strategic Alliances

Outside Counsel/Consultants

Baker, Donelson, Bearman & Caldwell, P.C.
Issues: MMM
Rep By: J. Keith Kennedy, Charles R. Parkinson

Barbour Griffith & Rogers, Inc.
Issues: HCR, MMM, PHA
Rep By: Haley Barbour, G. O. Lanny Griffith, Jr., Loren Monroe, Edward M. Rogers, Jr.

Bergner Bockorny Castagnetti and Hawkins
Issues: VET
Rep By: James W. Hawkins, Melissa Schulman

Cormac Group, LLP

Greenberg Traurig, LLP
Issues: HCR, MMM
Rep By: Howard J. Cohen, Russell J. Mueller

Hogan & Hartson L.L.P.
Issues: HCR, MED, PHA

Kessler & Associates Business Services, Inc.
Issues: BUD, MED, TAX
Rep By: Michael L. Bartlett, Richard S. Kessler, James C. Musser

The Legislative Strategies Group, LLC
Issues: HCR
Rep By: Denise M. Henry

Neuman and Co.
Issues: HCR, MED
Rep By: Robert A. Neuman

O'Connor & Hannan, L.L.P.
Issues: HCR, MMM, TAX
Rep By: Roy C. Coffee, Timothy W. Jenkins

Policy Directions, Inc.
Issues: HCR, MED, MMM, PHA, SCI
Rep By: Kathleen "Kay" Holcombe, Frankie L. Trull

Preston Gates Ellis & Rouvelas Meeds LLP
Issues: HCR, MMM
Rep By: Jonathan Blank, Pamela J. Garvie, Tim L. Peckinpaugh, Sandra Rizzo

Verner, Liipfert, Bernhard, McPherson and Hand, Chartered
Issues: HCR
Rep By: Hon. Daniel R. Coats, Vicki E. Hart, Gary J. Klein, Harry C. McPherson, Martin Mendelsohn, John A. Merrigan

Wilmer, Cutler & Pickering
Issues: HCR, TAX
Rep By: C. Boyden Gray

Amherst Systems Inc.

Buffalo, NY
Leg. Issues: AER, DEF

Outside Counsel/Consultants

Lawrence Ryan Internat'l, Inc.
Issues: AER, DEF

AMI Aircraft Seating Systems

Colorado Springs, CO
Leg. Issues: AVI

Outside Counsel/Consultants

Mehl, Griffin & Bartek Ltd.
Issues: AVI
Rep By: Molly Griffin, William A. Marsh, Theodore J. Mehl

Amino and Phenolic Wood Adhesives Ass'n

Washington, DC
Leg. Issues: CAW, GOV

Outside Counsel/Consultants

Venable
Issues: CAW, GOV
Rep By: Brock R. Landry

Amity, Inc.

Tucson, AZ
Leg. Issues: ALC

Outside Counsel/Consultants

Zuckerman Spaeder L.L.P.
Issues: ALC
Rep By: Charles Angulo, Ronald H. Weich

AmLib United Minerals

Outside Counsel/Consultants

Jefferson-Waterman Internat'l, LLC
Rep By: Charles E. Waterman

Amnesty Internat'l U.S.A.

600 Pennsylvania Ave. SE
Fifth Floor
Washington, DC 20003
Tel: (202)544-0200
Fax: (202)546-7142
Registered: LDA

Works for the release of prisoners of conscience, fair trials for political prisoners, and an end to torture and execution.

Leg. Issues: FOR

In-house, DC-area Employees

AKWEI, Adotei: Advocacy Director for Africa
BURKE, Sharon: Advocacy Director for Middle East and North Africa
GREENWOOD, Maureen: Advocacy Director for Europe
KUMAR, T.: Advocacy Director for Asia
MCGRAW, Chris: Grassroots Advocacy Program Associate
MILLER, Andrew: Advocacy Director for Latin America
POWERS, Craig: Acting Grassroots Advocacy Director
SALINAS, Carlos: Acting Director, Washington Office

Amputee Coalition

Leg. Issues: BUD, HCR

Outside Counsel/Consultants

Arent Fox Kintner Plotkin & Kahn, PLLC
Issues: BUD, HCR
Rep By: Katie Clarke, Stacy Harbison, Douglas McCormack

AMSA

Miami, FL

Outside Counsel/Consultants

Pierre E. Murphy Law Offices

Amstel Hudson Management Corp.

New York, NY

Outside Counsel/Consultants

Skadden, Arps, Slate, Meagher & Flom LLP
Rep By: Robert E. Lighthizer

AmSurg Corp.

Nashville, TN

A healthcare company that operates ambulatory surgery centers.

Leg. Issues: BUD, MMM

Outside Counsel/Consultants

Epstein Becker & Green, P.C.
Issues: BUD, MMM
Rep By: Joyce A. Cowan

Amtech Internat'l

Outside Counsel/Consultants

CAREY/NEALON & Associates, L.L.C.
Rep By: Rr. Adm. James J. Carey, USN (Ret.)

AMTRAK (Nat'l Rail Passenger Corp.)

60 Massachusetts Ave. NE
Washington, DC 20002
Web: www.amtrak.com
Tel: (202)906-3000
Fax: (202)906-3175

In-house, DC-area Employees

BLACK, Clifford: Director, Special Projects
ELSBREE, Amy: Senior Director, Government Affairs
MCHUGH, Joe: Acting V. President, Government Affairs
SCHULZ, William: V. President, Corporate Communications
VAN VEEN, Karina: Manager, Media Relations

Amusement and Music Operators Ass'n

Chicago, IL
Leg. Issues: ART, COM, CON, CPT, GAM, MON

Outside Counsel/Consultants

Arent Fox Kintner Plotkin & Kahn, PLLC
Issues: ART, COM, CON, CPT, GAM, MON
Rep By: Alison Kutler, Michael T. McNamara, Elliott I. Portnoy, Todd Weiss

AMVETS (American Veterans of World War II, Korea and Vietnam)

4647 Forbes Blvd.
Lanham, MD 20706-4380
Tel: (301)459-9600
Fax: (301)459-7924
Registered: LDA
Web: www.amvets.org
E-mail: amvets@amvets.org

An organization, chartered by Congress, to represent all veterans and their dependents in matters concerning employment, hospitalization, rehabilitation, pension, disability compensation and housing. Also safeguards the welfare of American servicemen with respect to national security, immigration and naturalization, the combatting of subversive activities and national convention resolutions.

Leg. Issues: VET

In-house, DC-area Employees

FLANAGAN, Richard W.: National Public Relations Director
JONES, Richard: National Legislative Director
RAMSEY, Jr., Joe F.: Exec. Director, National Service Foundation
WOODBURY, David: National Exec. Director

Amwest Surety Insurance Co.

Woodland Hills, CA

Outside Counsel/Consultants

Baker & Hostetler LLP
Rep By: Steven A. Lotterer

An Achievable Dream, Inc.

Newport News, VA
Leg. Issues: EDU

Outside Counsel/Consultants

Jefferson Government Relations, L.L.C.
Issues: EDU
Rep By: Mark S. Greenberg, William A. Roberts

ANADAC

Arlington, VA
Leg. Issues: CPI

Outside Counsel/Consultants

Richard R. Thaxton
Issues: CPI
Rep By: Richard R. Thaxton

Anadarko Petroleum Corp.

800 Connecticut Ave. NW
Suite 700
Washington, DC 20006
Tel: (202)861-8064
Fax: (202)861-8065
Registered: LDA
Leg. Issues: ENG, NAT, TRD

In-house, DC-area Employees

PENSABENE, Gregory M.: V. President, Government Affairs and Corporate Communications

Anaheim, California, City of

Leg. Issues: IMM, TRA

Outside Counsel/Consultants

E. Del Smith and Co.
Issues: IMM, TRA
Rep By: Margaret Allen, E. Del Smith

Anaheim, California, Public Utilities of the City of

Leg. Issues: TEC, UTI

Outside Counsel/Consultants

E. Del Smith and Co.
Issues: TEC, UTI
Rep By: Margaret Allen, E. Del Smith

Analytical and Life Science Systems Ass'n

225 Reinekers Ln.
Suite 625
Alexandria, VA 22314
Tel: (703)836-1360
Fax: (703)836-6644
Registered: LDA
Web: www.alssa.org
E-mail: mduff@alssa.org

Members generally manufacture or market instruments and systems, including consumables, chemical reagents and software, used for analysis and measurement in chemical and life science applications.

Leg. Issues: ENV, TRD

In-house, DC-area Employees

DUFF, Michael J.: Exec. Director

Analytical Systems, Inc.

Baton Rouge, LA
Leg. Issues: CHM, DEF, SCI

Outside Counsel/Consultants

James E. Guirard
Issues: CHM, DEF, SCI
Rep By: James E. Guirard, Jr.

Anchorage Telephone Utility

Anchorage, AK

Outside Counsel/Consultants

Covington & Burling
Rep By: Paul J. Berman

Anchorage, Alaska, Municipality of

Leg. Issues: BUD, CAW, ENV, RES, ROD

Outside Counsel/Consultants

Birch, Horton, Bittner & Cherot
Issues: BUD, CAW, ENV, RES, ROD
Rep By: Thomas L. Albert, William P. Horn

Ancore Corp.

Santa Clara, CA
Leg. Issues: DEF, LAW, SCI, TRA

Outside Counsel/Consultants

Adam Emanuel and Associates
Issues: DEF, SCI, TRA
Rep By: Adam Emanuel

Law Office of Zel E. Lipsen
Issues: LAW
Rep By: Adam Emanuel

Andalex Resources, Inc.

Sandy, UT
Leg. Issues: NAT

Outside Counsel/Consultants

Hogan & Hartson L.L.P.
Issues: NAT
Rep By: C. Michael Gilliland, William Michael House, George W. Miller, Jeffrey W. Munk

Anderson Cancer Center, MD

Outside Counsel/Consultants

R. Duffy Wall and Associates

Anderson Erickson Dairy Co.

Des Moines, IA
Leg. Issues: AGR

Outside Counsel/Consultants

Thelen Reid & Priest LLP
Issues: AGR
Rep By: Charles M. English, Jr., Wendy M. Yoviene

The Anderson Group

Leg. Issues: GOV

Outside Counsel/Consultants

Sumlin Associates
Issues: GOV
Rep By: Council Nedd

Andes

Miami, FL

Outside Counsel/Consultants

Pierre E. Murphy Law Offices

Andrew Corp.

Orland Park, IL
Leg. Issues: TEC

Outside Counsel/Consultants

Gardner, Carton and Douglas
Issues: TEC
Rep By: Francis Fletcher

Andrx Pharmaceutical Corp.

Ft. Lauderdale, FL
Leg. Issues: LBR, PHA

Outside Counsel/Consultants

Dittus Communications
Rep By: Jennifer Garfinkel, Chris McNamara

Parry, Romani, DeConcini & Symms
Issues: LBR, PHA
Rep By: Edward H. Baxter, Hon. Dennis DeConcini, John M. Haddow, Scott D. Hatch, Shannon Davis Henderson, Jack W. Martin, Romano Romani, Linda Arey Skladany, Hon. Steven D. Symms

Law Offices of Peter Angelos

Baltimore, MD
Leg. Issues: SPO, TAX, TOR

Outside Counsel/Consultants

Forscey & Stinson, PLLC
Issues: SPO, TAX, TOR
Rep By: Michael A. Forscey

Anglican Catholic Church

Alexandria, VA
Leg. Issues: EDU, FAM, REL, TAX

Outside Counsel/Consultants

Sumlin Associates
Issues: EDU, FAM, REL, TAX
Rep By: Council Nedd

AngloGold North America

Englewood, CO
Leg. Issues: NAT

Outside Counsel/Consultants

Public Strategies Washington, Inc.
Issues: NAT
Rep By: Nancy O'Neall, Joseph P. O'Neill

Angola, Embassy of

Washington, DC

Outside Counsel/Consultants

Bristol Group, Inc.

Angola, Government of the Republic of

Luanda, ANGOLA
Leg. Issues: GOV

Outside Counsel/Consultants

C/R Internat'l, L.L.C

Cohen and Woods Internat'l, Inc.
Rep By: Herman J. Cohen, James L. Woods

Samuels Internat'l Associates, Inc.
Issues: GOV
Rep By: Lawrence Julihn, Michael Samuels

Anheuser-Busch Cos., Inc.

1776 I St. NW
Suite 200
Republic Place
Washington, DC 20006
Web: www.anheuser-busch.com
Tel: (202)293-9494
Fax: (202)223-9594
Registered: LDA

Leg. Issues: ADV, AGR, ALC, ANI, ART, BEV, BUD, ENV, MAN, MAR, TAX, TRD

In-house, DC-area Employees

HEFFERNAN, Barbara D.: Director, National Affairs
KEATING, Richard F.: V. President and Sr. Government Affairs Officer

Outside Counsel/Consultants

Law Offices of Kevin G. Curtin
Issues: BEV
Rep By: Kevin G. Curtin

John Freshman Associates, Inc.
Issues: AGR, ANI, ENV, MAR
Rep By: John D. Freshman, Lawrence P. Kast, Catherine B. Kiefer

GCS Inc.
Issues: TRD
Rep By: Claud Gingrich

Harmon & Wilmot, L.L.P.
Rep By: David W. Wilmot

Howrey Simon Arnold & White
Rep By: Terrence C. Sheehy

L. A. Motley, L.L.C.
Rep By: Langhorne A. Motley

The OB-C Group, LLC
Issues: ADV, ENV, TAX, TRD
Rep By: Thomas Keating, Kim F. McKernan, Charles J. Mellody, Patricia A. Nelson, Lawrence F. O'Brien, III, Linda E. Tarplin

Public Strategies Washington, Inc.
Issues: BEV
Rep By: Joseph P. O'Neill, Paul M. Snyder

Timmons and Co., Inc.
Issues: ADV, BEV, TAX, TRD
Rep By: Michael J. Bates, Douglas F. Bennett, Ellen B. Fitzgibbons, Bryce L. "Larry" Harlow, Timothy J. Keating, Tom C. Korologos, Richard J. Tarplin, William E. Timmons, Jr., William E. Timmons, Sr.

Van Scoyoc Associates, Inc.
Issues: ADV, ALC, ART, MAN, TAX
Rep By: Jeffrey S. Trinca, H. Stewart Van Scoyoc

Washington Council Ernst & Young
Issues: BEV, BUD, TAX, TRD
Rep By: Doug Badger, Lauren Darling, John L. Doney, Jayne T. Fitzgerald, LaBrenda Garrett-Nelson, Gary J. Gasper, Bruce A. Gates, Nick Giordano, Robert J. Leonard, Richard Meltzer, Phillip D. Moseley, John D. Porter, Robert M. Rozen, Donna Steele-Flynn, Timothy J. Urban

Aniline Ass'n, Inc.

Washington, DC
Leg. Issues: CSP, MAN, WAS

Outside Counsel/Consultants

Hadley & McKenna
Issues: CSP, MAN, WAS
Rep By: Joseph E. Hadley, Jr.

Animal Health Institute

1325 G St. NW
Suite 700
Washington, DC 20005
Web: www.ahi.org
Tel: (202)637-2440
Fax: (202)393-1667
Registered: LDA

AHI represents manufacturers of animal health products.

Leg. Issues: ANI, PHA

Political Action Committee/s

Animal Health Institute Political Action Committee
1325 G St. NW
Suite 700
Washington, DC 20005
Tel: (202)637-2440
Fax: (202)393-1667

In-house, DC-area Employees

AYERS, Carolyn S.: V. President, Administration and Finance
CARNEVALE, V.M.D., Richard A.: V. President, Regulatory, Scientific, and International Affairs
KEELING, John R.: V. President, Legislative Affairs
MATHEWS, Alexander S.: President and Chief Exec. Officer
MCCLURE, Kent D.: General Counsel

Animal Industry Foundation

1501 Wilson Blvd.
Suite 1100
Arlington, VA 22209
Web: www.aif.org
E-mail: aif@aif.org
Tel: (703)524-0810
Fax: (703)524-1921

A national education foundation that supports and promotes animal agriculture practices that provide for farm animal well-being through sound science and public education.

Leg. Issues: AGR, ANI

In-house, DC-area Employees

JOHNSON, Kay N.: V. President

Animas-La Plata Water Conservancy District

Durango, CO
Leg. Issues: BUD, NAT

Outside Counsel/Consultants

Will and Carlson, Inc.
Issues: BUD, NAT
Rep By: Peter Carlson, Robert P. Will

Ann Eppard Associates, Ltd.

211 N. Union St.
Suite 100
Alexandria, VA 22314
Tel: (703)739-2545
Fax: (703)739-2718
Registered: LDA

Leg. Issues: MAR, TRA

In-house, DC-area Employees

CHLOPECKI, Julie: Transportation Specialist
EPPARD, Ann: President
SCHECHTER, Karen: V. President

Outside Counsel/Consultants

Alan Mauk Associates, Ltd.
Issues: MAR, TRA
Rep By: Alan R. Mauk

Annenberg Institute for School Reform, The

Providence, RI

Outside Counsel/Consultants

Hauser Group

Anoka County Regional Railroad Authority

Anoka, MN
Leg. Issues: TRA

Outside Counsel/Consultants

Capital Partnerships (VA) Inc.
Issues: TRA
Rep By: Robin Angle, Kenneth W. Butler, Clay Gravely

ANSAC

Westport, CT
Leg. Issues: TRD

Outside Counsel/Consultants

Internat'l Business-Government Counsellors, Inc.
Issues: TRD
Rep By: John F. McDermid

ANSAR Inc.

Philadelphia, PA
Leg. Issues: DEF

Outside Counsel/Consultants

American Defense Internat'l, Inc.
Issues: DEF
Rep By: Van D. Hipp, Jr., Dave Wilberding

The Anschutz Co.

1747 Pennsylvania Ave. NW
Suite 850
Washington, DC 20006
Tel: (202)393-0100
Fax: (202)393-0102
Registered: LDA
E-mail: wiley.jones@qwestisp.net

Headquartered in Denver, CO.

In-house, DC-area Employees

JONES, Wiley N.: V. President and Washington Counsel

Outside Counsel/Consultants

Williams & Jensen, P.C.
Rep By: J. Steven Hart

Ansett Transport Industries

Melbourne, AUSTRALIA

Outside Counsel/Consultants

Squire, Sanders & Dempsey L.L.P.
Rep By: Robert D. Papkin, Edward W. Sauer

The Antarctica Project

1630 Connecticut Ave. NW
Third Floor
Washington, DC 20009
Tel: (202)234-2480
Fax: (202)387-4823
Web: www.asoc.org
E-mail: antarctica@igc.org

Seeks to preserve Antarctica through educating the public and governments on issues affecting the continent.

In-house, DC-area Employees

CLARK, Beth: Director

Anthem Alliance

Indianapolis, IN
Leg. Issues: DEF, MMM

Outside Counsel/Consultants

Hannett & Associates
Issues: DEF, MMM
Rep By: Frederick J. Hannett

Anthem, Inc.

Indianapolis, IN
Leg. Issues: DEF, HCR

Outside Counsel/Consultants

Cartwright & Riley
Issues: DEF, HCR
Rep By: Russell S. Cartwright, Maura Cullen

Anthony Timberlands, Inc.

Bearden, AR
Leg. Issues: CAW

Outside Counsel/Consultants

Ann Eppard Associates, Ltd.
Issues: CAW
Rep By: Julie Chlopecki, Ann Eppard

Anthra

Princeton, NJ
Leg. Issues: HCR, MED

Outside Counsel/Consultants

Policy Directions, Inc.
Issues: HCR, MED
Rep By: Stephen Michael, Frankie L. Trull

Anti-Defamation League

1100 Connecticut Ave. NW
Suite 1020
Washington, DC 20036
Tel: (202)452-8320
Fax: (202)296-2371
Registered: LDA
Web: www.adl.org

A Civil Rights Organization which fights anti-semetism and bigotry in the U.S. and abroad. A prime resource for information on Hate crimes, terrorism, religious liberty, and anti-bias education.

Leg. Issues: CIV, CON, DEF, FOR, IMM, LAW, REL

In-house, DC-area Employees

BURDETT, Stacy: Associate Director
FRIEDMAN, David: Director, Washington, DC, Maryland, Northern Virginia Region
HORDES, Jess N.: Director, Government and National Affairs Office
LIEBERMAN, Michael: Washington Counsel

Anti-Value Added Tax Coalition

1920 L St. NW
Suite 200
Washington, DC 20036
Tel: (202)785-0266
Fax: (202)785-0261
Registered: LDA

An affiliate of Americans for Tax Reform, drawing support from a variety of businesses, consumer organizations and trade associations. Works with the Congressional Anti VAT Caucus.

Leg. Issues: BUD, TAX

In-house, DC-area Employees

FIKE, Robert: Director

NORQUIST, Grover G.: Principal

Antitrust Coalition for Consumer Choice in Health Care

Washington, DC
Leg. Issues: HCR, LBR

Outside Counsel/Consultants

Hogan & Hartson L.L.P.
Issues: HCR, LBR
Rep By: Robert Leibenluft

Washington Council Ernst & Young
Issues: HCR, LBR
Rep By: Doug Badger, Lauren Darling, John L. Doney, Jayne T. Fitzgerald, LaBrenda Garrett-Nelson, Gary J. Gasper, Bruce A. Gates, Nick Giordano, Cathy Koch, Robert J. Leonard, Richard Meltzer, Phillip D. Moseley, John D. Porter, Robert M. Rozen, Donna Steele-Flynn, Timothy J. Urban

Anxiety Disorders Ass'n of America

11900 Parklawn Dr.
Suite 100
Rockville, MD 20852-2624
Tel: (301)231-9350
Fax: (301)231-7392
Web: www.adaa.org
E-mail: anxdis@aol.com

The only national non-profit organization dedicated to the interest of people who suffer from anxiety disorders. Members include people with anxiety disorders, clinicians, and researchers.

In-house, DC-area Employees

ROSS, Jerilyn: President, C.E.O.

AOC

1000 N. Payne St.
Alexandria, VA 22314
Tel: (703)549-1600
Fax: (703)549-2589
Web: www.crows.org

Formerly Ass'n of Old Crows; promotes electronic defense.

Leg. Issues: DEF

In-house, DC-area Employees

LUKE, Vern: Exec. Director

AOL Time Warner

1101 Connecticut Ave. NW
Suite 400
Washington, DC 20036-4303
Tel: (202)530-7878
Fax: (202)530-7879
Registered: LDA
Web: www.aol.com

Formed by the merger of America Online, Inc. and Time Warner, Inc. in 2001.

Leg. Issues: CIV, COM, CON, CPI, CPT, CSP, GAM, LAW, LBR, MIA, POS, TAX, TEC, TOR, TRD

Political Action Committee/s

Time Warner Inc. PAC

1101 Connecticut Ave. NW
Suite 400
Washington, DC 20036-4303
Tel: (202)530-7878
Fax: (202)530-7879

In-house, DC-area Employees

BARRY, Lisa B.: V. President, International Public Policy

EISNER, David: V. President, Corporate Communications

FISHBEIN, Ellen: Assistant General Counsel

FRAZEE, Elizabeth: Law and Public Affairs Group

JACOBSEN, Jennifer: Director, Domestic Public Policy

LESSER, Jill A.: V. President, Domestic Public Policy

NELSON, Lisa: Director, Domestic Public Policy

TEPLITZ, Steven N.: V. President, Telecommunications Policy

VRADENBURG, III, George: Senior V. President, Global and Strategic Policy

Outside Counsel/Consultants

Akin, Gump, Strauss, Hauer & Feld, L.L.P.
Issues: COM, TAX
Rep By: Janet C. Boyd, Joel Jankowsky, George R. Salem, Barney J. Skladany, Jr., Daniel L. Spiegel, Robin Weisman, S. Bruce Wilson

W. Douglas Campbell
Issues: CON, CPI, CPT, CSP, GAM, LAW, MIA, TOR
Rep By: W. Douglas Campbell

Davidson & Company, Inc.
Issues: LBR, TAX
Rep By: James H. Davidson, Richard E. May, Stanley Sokul

Downey McGrath Group, Inc.
Issues: TEC
Rep By: Hon. Thomas J. Downey, Jr., John Peter Olinger

The Duberstein Group, Inc.
Issues: CPT, POS, TAX, TEC
Rep By: John W. Angus, III, Michael S. Berman, Steven M. Champlin, Kenneth M. Duberstein, Henry M. Gandy, Daniel P. Meyer

Fleischman and Walsh, L.L.P.
Rep By: Louis H. Dupart

Leslie Harris & Associates
Issues: CPI, TEC
Rep By: Jill Bond, Leslie A. Harris, Aleck Johnson, Rachel Zwerin

Jones, Day, Reavis & Pogue
Rep By: Joe Sims

Lent Scrivner & Roth LLC
Issues: TEC, TRD
Rep By: Norman F. Lent, III, Hon. Norman F. Lent, Alan J. Roth, Michael S. Scrivner

Mayer, Brown & Platt
Issues: TRD
Rep By: Scott Parven

Mintz, Levin, Cohn, Ferris, Glovsky and Popeo, P.C.
Rep By: James A. Kirkland, Bruce D. Sokler

Patton Boggs, LLP
Issues: TEC, TRD
Rep By: Thomas Hale Boggs, Jr., Elena Giberga, Karen L. Marangi, Frank R. Samolis, Jeffrey L. Turner, Jonathan R. Yarowsky

Piper Marbury Rudnick & Wolfe LLP
Issues: CPI
Rep By: Alisa M. Bergman, Emilio W. Cividanes, James J. Halpert, Stuart P. Ingis, Katharine A. Pauley, Ronald L. Plesser

Podesta/Mattoon
Issues: COM, CPT
Rep By: Ann Delory, Kimberley Fritts, Matthew Gelman, Claudia James, Andrew C. Littman, Anthony T. Podesta

Rhoads Group

Skadden, Arps, Slate, Meagher & Flom LLP
Issues: TEC
Rep By: Ivan A. Schlager

R. Duffy Wall and Associates
Issues: TEC

Wiley, Rein & Fielding

Williams & Jensen, P.C.
Issues: COM, CPT, TAX
Rep By: Bertram W. Carp, Robert E. Glennon, Jr., J. Steven Hart, Anthony J. Roda, Tracy D. Taylor

Wilmer, Cutler & Pickering
Issues: TRD
Rep By: Charles S. Levy

Aon Corp.

Chicago, IL
Leg. Issues: HCR, MMM

Outside Counsel/Consultants

Vinson & Elkins L.L.P.
Issues: HCR, MMM
Rep By: Larry A. Oday

AON Risk Services

Kansas City, MO
Leg. Issues: FIN, LBR, WEL

Outside Counsel/Consultants

Wheat & Associates, Inc.
Issues: FIN, LBR, WEL
Rep By: Hon. Alan D. Wheat

APA Coalition

Washington, DC
Leg. Issues: TAX

Outside Counsel/Consultants

Miller & Chevalier, Chartered
Issues: TAX

APA Internat'l Air, S.A.

Miami, FL

Outside Counsel/Consultants

Pierre E. Murphy Law Offices
Rep By: Pierre E. Murphy

Apartment and Office Building Ass'n of Metropolitan Washington

1050 17th St. NW
Suite 300
Washington, DC 20036
Tel: (202)296-3390
Fax: (202)296-3399
Registered: LDA
Web: www.aoba-metro.org
Leg. Issues: RES

Political Action Committee/s

Apartment and Office Building Ass'n of Metropolitan Washington DC, Inc. Metro PAC - Federal
1050 17th St. NW
Suite 300
Washington, DC 20036
Tel: (202)296-3390
Fax: (202)296-3399
Contact: Thomas R. Hyland

In-house, DC-area Employees

CLARKE, Jeanne: Director, Finance and Membership
FRANCIS, Frann G.: General Counsel
HOOVER, Lesa N.: V. President, Governmental Affairs-MD
HYLAND, Thomas R.: V. President, Governmental Affairs-VA
JEFFERS, Margaret O.: Exec. V. President
PHARR, William Shaun: V. President, Governmental Affairs-DC

Apartment Investment and Management Co.

Washington, DC
Leg. Issues: HOU, TAX

Outside Counsel/Consultants

Washington Council Ernst & Young
Issues: HOU, TAX
Rep By: Doug Badger, Lauren Darling, John L. Doney, Jayne T. Fitzgerald, LaBrenda Garrett-Nelson, Gary J. Gasper, Bruce A. Gates, Nick Giordano, Cathy Koch, Robert J. Leonard, Richard Meltzer, Phillip D. Moseley, John D. Porter, Robert M. Rozen, Donna Steele-Flynn, Timothy J. Urban

Apex Marine Ship Management Co. LLC

Lake Success, NY
Leg. Issues: MAR

Outside Counsel/Consultants

Sher & Blackwell
Issues: MAR
Rep By: Marc J. Fink, Jeffrey R. Pike

apex.com

Bellevue, WA
Leg. Issues: CPI, EDU

Outside Counsel/Consultants

Denny Miller McBee Associates
Issues: CPI, EDU

APG Army Alliance

Leg. Issues: BUD, DEF, EDU, TRA

Outside Counsel/Consultants

Van Scoyoc Associates, Inc.
Issues: BUD, DEF, EDU, TRA
Rep By: Steve E. Crane, Kevin F. Kelly, Thomas L. Lankford

APG Solutions and Technologies

CANADA

Outside Counsel/Consultants

J. LeBlanc Internat'l, LLC
Rep By: James L. LeBlanc

APG, Inc.

Columbia, MD

Outside Counsel/Consultants

Chambers Associates Inc.
Rep By: William A. Signer

APICS - The Educational Soc. for Resource Management

5301 Shawnee Rd.
Alexandria, VA 22312
Tel: (703)354-8851
Fax: (703)354-8106
Web: www.apics.org
E-mail: service@apicsha.org

In-house, DC-area Employees

PRATS, Lisa: Director, Communications
RAYNES, CAE, Jeffry W.: Exec. Director and Chief Operating Officer

APKINDO

Jakarta, INDONESIA
Leg. Issues: FOR, TRD

Outside Counsel/Consultants

Akin, Gump, Strauss, Hauer & Feld, L.L.P.
Issues: FOR, TRD
Rep By: Sean G. D'Arcy, David Geanacopoulos, Barney J. Skladany, Jr.

APL Limited

1200 G St. NW
Suite 800
Washington, DC 20005
Tel: (202)434-8790
Fax: (202)775-8427
Registered: LDA
Web: www.apl.com
E-mail: lawrence_cosgriff@apl.com

A major intermodal container transportation and distribution services company headquartered in Oakland, CA.

Leg. Issues: MAR, TRA, TRD

Political Action Committee/s

APL Ltd. PAC
1200 G St. NW
Suite 800
Washington, DC 20005
Tel: (202)331-1424
Fax: (202)775-8427
Contact: Lawrence E. Cosgriff

In-house, DC-area Employees

COSGRIFF, Lawrence E.: V. President, Government Affairs
HONEYGOSKY, Paulette: Government Affairs Specialist

Outside Counsel/Consultants

Higgins, McGovern & Smith, LLC
Rep By: Carl M. Smith

Patton Boggs, LLP
Issues: MAR, TRA
Rep By: Philip A. Bangert, Jeffrey L. Turner

Shea & Gardner
Rep By: Robert T. Basseches

Apollo Advisors

Purchase, NY

Outside Counsel/Consultants

Brownstein Hyatt & Farber, P.C.
Rep By: William T. Brack, Michael B. Levy

Apollo Group, Inc.

666 Pennsylvania Ave. SE
Suite 202
Washington, DC 20003
Tel: (202)546-5488
Fax: (202)546-5281
Registered: LDA
Web: www.apollogroup.com
Leg. Issues: EDU

Political Action Committee/s

Apollo Group, Inc. Political Organization for Legislative Leadership
666 Pennsylvania Ave. SE
Suite 202
Washington, DC 20003
Tel: (202)546-5488
Fax: (202)546-5281
Contact: Scott Tominovich

In-house, DC-area Employees

SEIGEL, Charles: Senior V. President, National Affairs
TOMINOVICH, Scott: Associate Director, Government Affairs

Outside Counsel/Consultants

Wheat & Associates, Inc.
Issues: EDU
Rep By: Hon. Alan D. Wheat

Appalachian Regional Commission, Office of States' Washington Representative of

1666 Connecticut Ave. NW
Sixth Floor
Washington, DC 20235
Tel: (202)884-7746
Fax: (202)884-7695
E-mail: Bill_Walker@ARC.gov

In-house, DC-area Employees

WALKER, Bill: States' Washington Represntative

Appalachian-Pacific Coal Mine Methane Power Co., LLC

Arlington, VA

Outside Counsel/Consultants

Charles D. Estes & Associates
Rep By: Charles D. Estes

Apple Computer, Inc.

Cuppertino, CA
Leg. Issues: CPI, TAX, TEC

Outside Counsel/Consultants

Harris, Wiltshire & Grannis LLP
Issues: TEC
Rep By: Scott Blake Harris

Hooper Owen & Winburn
Issues: TAX
Rep By: Steve Glaze, Lindsay D. Hooper, John P. Winburn

Jefferson Consulting Group
Issues: CPI
Rep By: Kathy P. Conrad, Robert J. Thompson

KPMG, LLP
Issues: TAX
Rep By: Katherine M. Breaks, Harry L. Gutman, Melbert E. Schwarz

Apple Processors Ass'n

Washington, DC
Web: www.agriwashington.org
Leg. Issues: AGR

Outside Counsel/Consultants

Agri/Washington
Issues: AGR
Rep By: Andrea Ball, Jon Moore, Paul S. Weller, Jr.

N. Chapman Associates
Rep By: Nancy Chapman

Apple Vacations, Inc.

Elk Grove Village, IL

Outside Counsel/Consultants

Pierre E. Murphy Law Offices
Rep By: Pierre E. Murphy

Apple Valley, California, City of

Leg. Issues: TRA

Outside Counsel/Consultants

E. Del Smith and Co.
Issues: TRA
Rep By: Margaret Allen, E. Del Smith

Applera Corp.

Rockville, MD
Leg. Issues: CPT

Outside Counsel/Consultants

Williams & Jensen, P.C.
Issues: CPT
Rep By: J. Steven Hart, George G. Olsen, Anthony J. Roda

Appleton Papers, Inc.

Appleton, WI
Leg. Issues: ENV

Outside Counsel/Consultants

The Roth Group
Issues: ENV
Rep By: Hon. Toby Roth, Sr.

Sidley & Austin
Issues: ENV
Rep By: Christopher Bell, David T. Buente, Jr., Myles Flint, Thomas M. McMahon, Andrew Schlickman

Applied Benefits Research Corp.

Palm Harbor, FL
Leg. Issues: HCR

Outside Counsel/Consultants

Greenberg Traurig, LLP
Issues: HCR
Rep By: Ronald L. Platt

McDermott, Will and Emery
Rep By: Paul Hamburger, Calvin P. Johnson, Eric P. Zimmerman

Applied Development Associates

Hoboken, NJ

Outside Counsel/Consultants

Krivit & Krivit, P.C.

Applied Graphics

Washington, DC
Web: www.agt.com
Leg. Issues: CPI

Outside Counsel/Consultants

Richard K. Thompson
Issues: CPI
Rep By: Richard K. Thompson

Applied Knowledge Group

Reston, VA
Leg. Issues: CPI, SCI

Outside Counsel/Consultants

The ILEX Group
Issues: CPI, SCI
Rep By: H. Hollister Cantus

Applied Marine Technologies, Inc.

Virginia Beach, CA
Leg. Issues: DEF, LAW

Outside Counsel/Consultants

The PMA Group
Issues: DEF, LAW
Rep By: Kaylene Green, Paul J. Magliocchetti, Kelli Short, Thomas Veltri

Applied Materials

Santa Clara, CA
Leg. Issues: TAX, TRD

Outside Counsel/Consultants

R. Wayne Sayer & Associates
Issues: TAX, TRD
Rep By: John Kania, William Morin, R. Wayne Sayer

Applied Terravision Systems

Addison, TX
Leg. Issues: BUD

Outside Counsel/Consultants

GPC Internat'l
Issues: BUD
Rep By: Jennifer King, Bruce A. Morrison

Appraisal Institute

2600 Virginia Ave. NW
Suite 123
Washington, DC 20037
Tel: (202)298-6449
Fax: (202)298-5547
Registered: LDA
Web: www.appraisalinstitute.org

A participant in real estate appraisal and real property issues before the United States Congress, federal agencies, and within individual states headquartered in Chicago, IL.

Leg. Issues: BAN, FIN, HOU, RES

Political Action Committee/s

Appraisal Institute Political Action Committee (APPAC)
2600 Virginia Ave. NW
Suite 123
Washington, DC 20037
Tel: (202)298-5583
Fax: (202)298-5547
Contact: Donald E. Kelly

In-house, DC-area Employees

GARBER, Jr., William E.: Director, Government Affairs
KELLY, Donald E.: V. President, Public Affairs

Outside Counsel/Consultants

McDermott, Will and Emery

Valanzano & Associates
Issues: FIN, HOU, RES
Rep By: Anthony Valanzano

Apria Healthcare Group

Costa Mesa, CA

A home medical equipment supplier.

Leg. Issues: HCR, MMM

Outside Counsel/Consultants

Davidson & Company, Inc.
Issues: HCR
Rep By: James H. Davidson, Richard E. May, Stanley Sokul

The Paul Laxalt Group
Issues: HCR, MMM
Rep By: Hon. Paul D. Laxalt, Tom Loranger

The Solomon Group, LLC
Issues: HCR
Rep By: Hon. Gerald B. H. Solomon, William R. Teator

APS Healthcare, Inc.

Outside Counsel/Consultants

BKSH & Associates

APTI

Washington, DC
Leg. Issues: DEF, RES

Outside Counsel/Consultants

J. Steven Griles & Associates
Issues: RES
Rep By: J. Steven Griles

G.L. Merritt & Associates, Inc.
Issues: DEF
Rep By: Gordon L. Merritt

Aquarium of the Pacific

Long Beach, CA
Leg. Issues: MAR, SCI

Outside Counsel/Consultants

E. Del Smith and Co.
Issues: MAR, SCI
Rep By: Ryan Alsop, E. Del Smith

Arab American Bank

New York, NY

Outside Counsel/Consultants

Vorys, Sater, Seymour and Pease, LLP
Rep By: Warren W. Glick

Arab American Institute

1600 K St. NW
Suite 601
Washington, DC 20006
Tel: (202)429-9210
Fax: (202)429-9214
Web: www.aaiusa.org
E-mail: aai@aaiusa.org

The AAI was founded in 1985 to advance Arab American access to the political parties, participation in electoral politics, and to develop a political strategy with ethnic leaders nationwide to empower Arab Americans and their public policy concerns.

Political Action Committee/s

Arab American Leadership Political Action Committee
1600 K St. NW
Suite 601
Washington, DC 20006
Tel: (202)429-9210
Fax: (202)429-9214
Contact: James J. Zogby

In-house, DC-area Employees

BARWIG, Andrew: Communications Director
BERRY, Maya: Government Relations Director
SAMHAN, Helen Hatab: Exec. V. President
ZOGBY, James J.: President

Outside Counsel/Consultants

Akin, Gump, Strauss, Hauer & Feld, L.L.P.

Arab, Alabama, City of

Leg. Issues: GOV

Outside Counsel/Consultants

Duncan, Weinberg, Genzer & Pembroke, P.C.
Issues: GOV
Rep By: Janice L. Lower

ARAMARK Corp.

Philadelphia, PA
Leg. Issues: TAX

Outside Counsel/Consultants

Greenberg Traurig, LLP
Issues: TAX
Rep By: Ronald L. Platt

McDermott, Will and Emery

Aramco Services Co.

1667 K St. NW
Suite 1200
Washington, DC 20006
Tel: (202)223-7750
Fax: (202)223-7756

In-house, DC-area Employees

BOSCH, David D.: Director, Washington Office

Arbinet

New York, NY
Leg. Issues: TEC

Outside Counsel/Consultants

Greenberg Traurig, LLP
Issues: TEC
Rep By: Mitchell F. Brecher

ARC Global Technologies

Chicago, IL

Outside Counsel/Consultants

The PMA Group
Rep By: Sean Fogarty, Kaylene Green, Gregory L. Hansen, Paul J. Magliocchetti, Charles Smith, Dana Stewart, Brian Thiel

The Arc

1730 K St. NW
Washington, DC 20006
Tel: (202)785-3388
Fax: (202)467-4179
Registered: LDA
Web: www.thearc.org
E-mail: gaoinfo@thearc.org

The Arc of the United States works through education, research, and advocacy to improve the quality of life for children and adults with mental retardation and their family. The Arc also works to prevent both the causes and effects of mental retardation.

Leg. Issues: BUD, CIV, EDU, HCR, HOU, IMM, LAW, LBR, MMM, RET, TRA, UNM, WEL

In-house, DC-area Employees

FORD, Martha: Director of Legal Advocacy
MARCHAND, Paul: Assistant Exec. Director for Policy and Advocacy
MCGINLEY, Kathleen: Director, Health and Housing Policy
MUSHENO, Kim: Director of Governmental Affairs Communication

Arcadia, California, City of

Leg. Issues: BUD, ENV, UTI

Outside Counsel/Consultants

The Ferguson Group, LLC
Issues: BUD, ENV, UTI
Rep By: William Ferguson, Jr., W. Roger Gwinn, Ralph Webb

ARCADIS/California Energy Commission

Sacramento, CA

Outside Counsel/Consultants

Dunlap & Browder, Inc.
Rep By: Louise C. Dunlap

Arcata Associates, Inc.

North Las Vegas, NV
Leg. Issues: DEF

Outside Counsel/Consultants

Alcalde & Fay
Issues: DEF
Rep By: Hon. James H. Bilbray, Rodney A. Coleman

Arch Chemical Inc.

Norwalk, CA
Leg. Issues: CHM

Outside Counsel/Consultants

Robert E. Smith
Issues: CHM
Rep By: Robert E. Smith

Arch Mineral Corp.

St. Louis, MO
Leg. Issues: HCR, LBR

Outside Counsel/Consultants

McGuiness & Holch
Issues: HCR, LBR
Rep By: Markham C. Erickson, Kevin S. McGuiness

Archer Daniels Midland Co.

Decatur, IL

Outside Counsel/Consultants

Akin, Gump, Strauss, Hauer & Feld, L.L.P.

Williams & Connolly
Rep By: Aubrey M. Daniel, III, Barry S. Simon

Archery Manufactures & Merchants Organization

Gainesville, FL
Leg. Issues: RES

Outside Counsel/Consultants

Ron C. Marlenee
Issues: RES
Rep By: Hon. Ron C. Marlenee

PriceWaterhouseCoopers

Archimedes Technology Group

Leg. Issues: ENG, SCI, WAS

Outside Counsel/Consultants

Van Scoyoc Associates, Inc.
Issues: ENG, SCI, WAS
Rep By: Paul Grimm, Buzz Hawley, Paul Iarrobino, John C. "Jay" Stone, H. Stewart Van Scoyoc

ARCO Coal Co.

Denver, CO

Outside Counsel/Consultants

Sidley & Austin
Rep By: David T. Buente, Jr., James Connaughton

ARCO Products Co.

Long Beach, CA
Leg. Issues: CAW, ENG, FUE, GOV, MAR

Outside Counsel/Consultants

Thomas J. Dennis
Issues: CAW, ENG, FUE, GOV, MAR
Rep By: Thomas J. Dennis

Arctic Power

Anchorage, AK
Leg. Issues: ENG, NAT

Outside Counsel/Consultants

Jack Ferguson Associates, Inc.
Issues: NAT
Rep By: Jack Ferguson

Bartley M. O'Hara
Issues: ENG
Rep By: Bartley M. O'Hara

Arctic Resources Co.

Houston, TX
Leg. Issues: ENG

Outside Counsel/Consultants

Morgan Meguire, LLC
Issues: ENG
Rep By: Kyle G. Michel, C. Kyle Simpson, Kiel Weaver

Arctic Slope Regional Corp.

Barrow, AK

A largely Eskimo-owned Alaskan land company which has leased oil rights to its lands to some major petroleum producers.

Leg. Issues: BUD, ENV, FUE, IND, NAT, RES, TAX

Outside Counsel/Consultants

Van Ness Feldman, P.C.
Issues: BUD, ENV, FUE, IND, NAT, RES, TAX
Rep By: Howard J. Feldman, Alan L. Mintz

Arena PAC

1155 21st St. NW
Suite 300
Washington, DC 20036
Web: www.apac.org
Tel: (202)659-8201
Fax: (202)659-5249

The address given is that of the firm Williams & Jensen, P.C.

In-house, DC-area Employees

BONFIGLIO, Barbara Wixon: Treasurer
HART, J. Steven: Director

Outside Counsel/Consultants

Mercury Group

Williams & Jensen, P.C.
Rep By: Barbara Wixon Bonfiglio, J. Steven Hart

Arena Stage

Washington, DC
Web: www.arenastage.org
E-mail: arenastg@shirenet.com
Leg. Issues: ART

Outside Counsel/Consultants

Chernikoff and Co.
Issues: ART
Rep By: Larry B. Chernikoff

Argentina, Government of

Buenos Aires, ARGENTINA

Outside Counsel/Consultants

Arnold & Porter

Washington World Group, Ltd.
Rep By: Edward J. von Kloberg, III

Argentina, The Secretary of Intelligence of

Buenos Aires, ARGENTINA

Outside Counsel/Consultants

Ikon Public Affairs

Argentina-Brazil Venture Services Corp.

Buenos Aires, BRAZIL

Also based in Sao Paulo, Brazil.

Outside Counsel/Consultants

MacKenzie McCheyne, Inc.

Argentine Citrus Ass'n

Buenos Aires, ARGENTINA
Leg. Issues: TRD

Outside Counsel/Consultants

Federal Strategies Group
Issues: TRD
Rep By: Xavier Equihua

Argentine Economic & Investment Council

Buenos Aires, ARGENTINA

Outside Counsel/Consultants

MacKenzie McCheyne, Inc.

Argon Engineering Associates

Fairfax, VA

Outside Counsel/Consultants

The Potomac Advocates
Rep By: Charles Scalera, Gary L. Sojka

ArianeSpace, Inc.

601 13th St. NW
Suite 710 North
Washington, DC 20005
Web: www.arianespace.com
Tel: (202)628-3936
Fax: (202)628-3949
Registered: LDA

Headquartered in Evry, France, Arianespace Inc. promotes the marketing and sales of Ariane satellite launch services.

Leg. Issues: AER, TRD

In-house, DC-area Employees

BURCH, Jr., Charles F.: V. President, Sales
HEYDON, Douglas A.: Chairman

Outside Counsel/Consultants

Verner, Liipfert, Bernhard, McPherson and Hand, Chartered
Issues: AER
Rep By: Berl Bernhard

Ariba

Mountain Valley, CA
Leg. Issues: CPI

Outside Counsel/Consultants

Hill and Knowlton, Inc.
Issues: CPI
Rep By: Gary G. Hymel

ARINC, Inc.

Annapolis, MD
Leg. Issues: AVI, COM, DEF, TRA

Outside Counsel/Consultants

Peter J. Rose
Issues: DEF
Rep By: Peter J. Rose

The Wexler Group
Issues: AVI
Rep By: Patrick J. McCann

Wiley, Rein & Fielding
Issues: AVI, COM, TRA
Rep By: James T. Bruce, III, Barbara G. Burchett, Mimi W. Dawson, Hon. Jim Slattery

Arista Knowledge Systems, Inc.

Almeda, CA
Leg. Issues: BUD, EDU, SCI

Outside Counsel/Consultants

Van Scoyoc Associates, Inc.
Issues: BUD, EDU, SCI
Rep By: Steve E. Crane, Kevin F. Kelly, H. Stewart Van Scoyoc

Arizona Mail Order Co.

Tucson, AZ
Leg. Issues: BUD, CSP, GOV, POS, TAX, TEC

Outside Counsel/Consultants

Marshall A. Brachman
Issues: BUD, CSP, GOV, POS, TAX, TEC
Rep By: Marshall A. Brachman

Arizona Power Authority

Phoenix, AZ
Leg. Issues: ENG, GOV, NAT, TAX, UTI

Outside Counsel/Consultants

Brickfield, Burchette, Ritts & Stone
Issues: ENG, GOV, NAT, TAX, UTI
Rep By: Michael N. McCarty, Colleen Newman

Oliver James Horton
Issues: ENG, NAT, TAX, UTI
Rep By: Oliver James Horton, Jr.

Wright & Talisman, P.C.

Arizona Public Service Co.

800 Connecticut Ave. NW
Suite 610
Washington, DC 20006
Tel: (202)293-2655
Fax: (202)293-2666
Registered: LDA
E-mail: robbieaiken@pinnacledc.com

Headquartered in Phoenix, AZ.

Leg. Issues: BUD, CAW, TAX, TRA, UTI, WAS

In-house, DC-area Employees

AIKEN, Robert S.: V. President, Public Affairs

Arizona Science Center

Phoenix, AZ
Leg. Issues: EDU, SCI

Outside Counsel/Consultants

The Advocacy Group
Issues: EDU, SCI
Rep By: George A. Ramonas

Arizona State University

Tempe, AZ
Leg. Issues: AER, ECN, ECU

Outside Counsel/Consultants

Cassidy & Associates, Inc.
Issues: AER
Rep By: Jeffrey Lawrence, Scott D. MacConomy, Diane Rinaldo

The Mike Waite Company
Issues: ECN, ECU
Rep By: Michael S. Waite

ARK Energy, Inc.

Laguna Hills, CA

Outside Counsel/Consultants

Durante Associates
Rep By: Douglas A. Durante

Arkansas Blue Cross and Blue Shield

Little Rock, AR
Leg. Issues: HCR

Outside Counsel/Consultants

Sydney Probst
Issues: HCR
Rep By: Sydney Probst

Arkansas Enterprise Group

Arkadelphia, AR

Outside Counsel/Consultants

Robert A. Rapoza Associates
Rep By: Robert A. Rapoza

Arkansas, Office of the Governor of the State of

Little Rock, AR
Leg. Issues: CAW, EDU, ENV, GOV, HCR, HOU, LAW, MMM, NAT, ROD, TAX, TRD

Outside Counsel/Consultants

Jay Grant & Associates
Issues: CAW, EDU, ENV, GOV, HCR, HOU, LAW, MMM, NAT, ROD, TAX, TRD
Rep By: Jay B. Grant, David Kehl, David M. Olive

Arkenol, Inc.

Mission Viejo, CA
Leg. Issues: BUD

Outside Counsel/Consultants

MSS Consultants, LLC
Issues: BUD
Rep By: Megan S. Smith

Arlington Educational Ass'n Retirement Housing Corp.

Arlington, VA

Outside Counsel/Consultants

Cranwell & O'Connell
Rep By: George E. Cranwell

Armco Inc.

Pittsburgh, PA

A specialty steel producer.

Leg. Issues: TAX

Outside Counsel/Consultants

Davis & Harman LLP
Issues: TAX
Rep By: Thomas A. Davis

Skadden, Arps, Slate, Meagher & Flom LLP
Rep By: Robert E. Lighthizer

Sutherland Asbill & Brennan LLP
Rep By: Edward J. Grenier, Jr.

Armed Forces Benefit Ass'n

909 N. Washington St.
Alexandria, VA 22314
Web: www.afba.com
Tel: (703)549-4455
Fax: (703)706-5961

In-house, DC-area Employees

BLANTON, USAF (Ret), Lt. Gen. Charles C.: President
HASTY, Claudia: Exec. Officer

Armed Forces Communications and Electronics Ass'n Headquarters

4400 Fair Lakes Ct.
Fairfax, VA 22033
Web: www.afcea.org
E-mail: service@afcea.org
Tel: (703)631-6100
Fax: (703)631-4693

A professional membership association representing C4I, electronics, and IS/IT individuals in the military, government, and private industry.

In-house, DC-area Employees

WOOD, USAF, Ret., Lt. Gen. C. Norman: President and Chief Exec. Officer

Armenian Assembly of America

122 C St. NW
Suite 350
Washington, DC 20001
Web: www.aaainc.org
E-mail: info@aaainc.org
Tel: (202)393-3434
Fax: (202)638-4904
Registered: LDA

Acts as a conduit of information between the Armenian-American community and the federal government. Represents and promotes Armenian interests to governmental and nongovernmental policy makers through research, education, humanitarian, and advocacy programs.

Leg. Issues: FOR

In-house, DC-area Employees

ABAJIAN, Peter: Director, Western Region Office
ABLETT, Joan: Director, Public Affairs
ARDOUNY, Bryan: Director, Government Relations
VARTANIAN, Arpi: Acting Exec. Director

Armenian Nat'l Committee of America

888 17th St. NW
Suite 904
Washington, DC 20006
Web: www.anca.org
E-mail: anca@anca.org
Tel: (202)775-1918
Fax: (202)775-5648

A grassroots political organization with a network of regional affiliates across the U.S. and affiliated organizations throughout the world. Goals are threefold: to foster public awareness in support of a free, united and independent Armenia; to propose and guide public policy on matters of interest to Armenian Americans, including, but not limited to, overall human rights issues and Armenian political rights; to represent the collective Armenian American viewpoint on matters of public policy.

In-house, DC-area Employees

CHOULDJIAN, Elizabeth S.: Director, Communications
HAMPARIAN, Aram: Exec. Director
HEKIMIAN, Christopher M.: Director, Government Relations

Arms Control Ass'n

1726 M St. NW
Suite 201
Washington, DC 20036
Web: www.armscontrol.org
E-mail: aca@amrscontrol.org
Tel: (202)463-8270
Fax: (202)463-8273

A national membership organization promoting public education on arms control and disarmament. Not a lobbying organization.

Leg. Issues: DEF, ENG, FOR, GOV

In-house, DC-area Employees

KEENY, Jr., Spurgeon M.: President and Exec. Director
SCOBLIC, Peter: Editor, Arms Control Today Magazine

Armstrong Laser Technology

Freeport, PA
Leg. Issues: MAN

Outside Counsel/Consultants

Pacquing Consulting Inc.
Issues: MAN
Rep By: Juliet Pacquing

Armstrong World Industries, Inc.

1150 Connecticut Ave. NW
Suite 515
Washington, DC 20036
Tel: (202)296-2831
Fax: (202)294-4337
Registered: LDA

A manufacturing company headquartered in Lancaster, PA.

Leg. Issues: CSP, HCR, IMM, LBR, TRD

In-house, DC-area Employees

REID, Nancy S.: Government Relations Specialist
WEST, Gail Berry: Director, Government Relations

Outside Counsel/Consultants

Parry, Romani, DeConcini & Symms
Rep By: Edward H. Baxter, Hon. Dennis DeConcini, John M. Haddow, Scott D. Hatch, Shannon Davis Henderson, Jack W. Martin, Romano Romani, Linda Arey Skladany, Hon. Steven D. Symms

Armtec Defense Products

Coachella, CA
Leg. Issues: BUD, DEF

Outside Counsel/Consultants

Robison Internat'l, Inc.
Issues: BUD, DEF
Rep By: Richard B. Ladd, J. David Willson

Army & Air Force Mutual Aid Ass'n

102 Sheridan Ave.
Fort Myer, VA 22211-1110
Web: www.aafmaa.com
E-mail: info@aafmaa.com
Tel: (703)522-3060
Fax: (703)522-1336

Provides aid to families of deceased career officers by immediate payment of a fixed life insurance benefit, assistance with claims for federal compensation and similar matters.

In-house, DC-area Employees

LINCOLN, Walter: President

Arnold & Porter

555 12th St. NW
Washington, DC 20004-1206
Web: www.arnoldporter.com
Tel: (202)942-5000
Fax: (202)942-5999
Registered: LDA, FARA

Leg. Issues: BUD, DIS

Political Action Committee/s

Arnold & Porter Political Action Committee
555 12th St. NW
Washington, DC 20004-1206
Contact: Martha L. Cochran
Tel: (202)942-5228
Fax: (202)942-5999

In-house, DC-area Employees

ARONOW, Geoffrey: Partner
BAER, William J.: Partner
BAGLEY, Grant: Partner
BEERS, Donald O.: Partner
BENNETT, Alexander E.: Partner
BERGER, Paul S.: Partner
BERNSTEIN, Michael L.: Partner
BORN, Brooksley: Partner
BROMME, Jeffrey S.: Partner
CASSIDY, Susan Booth: Partner
COCHRAN, Martha L.: Partner
CULLEEN, Lawrence E.: Special Counsel
DANEKER, Michael: Partner
DEBEVOISE, II, Eli Whitney: Partner
DEWITT, Timothy: Partner
ENGLUND, Steven R.: Partner
EWING, Richard S.: Partner
FITZPATRICK, James F.: Partner
FLAX, Samuel A.: Partner
FOIS, Sonia P.: Partner
FRANK, Theodore: Partner
FREEMAN, Jr., David F.: Partner
FRESHOUR, Paul: Partner
GARRETT, Robert A.: Partner
GRANT, Patrick J.: Partner
GROSSI, Jr., Peter T.: Partner
HARKER, Drew A.: Partner
HUBBARD, Richard L.: Partner
HURLEY, Judith: Exec. Dir. and Chief Financial Officer
JOHNSON, Richard A.: Partner
JONES, Robert J.: Partner
KAHN, Sarah E.: Partner
KAPLAN, Steven L.: Partner
KENTOFF, David R.: Partner
KOTLER, Sarah B.: Associate
KRASH, Abe: Partner
LEDERMAN, Gordon N.: Associate
LEE, Susan G.: Partner
LETZLER, Kenneth A.: Partner
LEVINE, Arthur N.: Partner
LYONS, Dennis G.: Partner
NATHAN, Irvin B.: Partner
NICKEL, Leslie A.: Associate
OTT, Robert B.: Partner
PATTERSON, Donna E.: Partner
PERKINS, Nancy L.: Partner
READE, Claire E.: Partner
RICHMAN, Jeffrey W.: Associate
ROCKLER, Walter J.: Partner
ROGERS, William D.: Partner
ROSENBAUM, Robert D.: Partner
ROSS, Stanford G.: Partner
RUBEL, Eric A.: Partner
RUBIN, Blake D.: Partner
SACKS, Stephen M.: Partner
SANDMAN, James: Managing Partner
SCHMIDT, K. Peter
SCHNEIDER, Lawrence A.: Partner
SHOR, Michael T.: Partner
SINEL, Norman M.: Partner
SISSON, Edward: Partner
SMITH, Jeffrey H.: Partner
SOHN, Michael N.: Partner
VIETH, G. Duane: Partner
VODRA, William W.: Partner
WALDMAN, Daniel: Partner
ZENNER, Jr., Walter F.: Partner

Outside Counsel/Consultants

Cassidy & Associates, Inc.
Issues: BUD
Rep By: Dennis M. Kedzior, Arthur D. Mason, Brig. Gen. Terry Paul, USMC (Ret.)

Robert E. Litan
Issues: DIS
Rep By: Robert E. Litan

Arrow Air

Miami, FL

Outside Counsel/Consultants

Hewes, Gelband, Lambert & Dann, P.C.

Pierre E. Murphy Law Offices

Artel, Inc.

Reston, VA
Leg. Issues: TEC

Outside Counsel/Consultants

Global USA, Inc.
Issues: TEC
Rep By: George S. Kopp, Lottie H. Shackelford

Arthritis Foundation

Washington, DC
Leg. Issues: BUD, HCR, MED

Outside Counsel/Consultants

Arent Fox Kintner Plotkin & Kahn, PLLC
Issues: BUD
Rep By: Katie Clarke, Stacy Harbison, Alison Kutler, Douglas McCormack

Sagamore Associates, Inc.
Issues: HCR, MED
Rep By: Lisa Levine, Serena Lowe, Dena S. Morris, David Nichols, Kevin D. Talley

Arthroscopy Ass'n of North America

Rosemont, IL
Leg. Issues: MMM

Outside Counsel/Consultants

McDermott, Will and Emery
Issues: MMM
Rep By: Michael A. Romansky, Eric P. Zimmerman

Arthur Andersen LLP

1666 K St. NW
Suite 800
Washington, DC 20006
Web: www.arthurandersen.com
Tel: (202)481-7000
Fax: (202)862-7098
Registered: LDA

Leg. Issues: ACC

Political Action Committee/s

Arthur Andersen Political Action Committee
1666 K St. NW
Suite 800
Washington, DC 20006
Contact: Jeffrey J. Peck
Tel: (202)481-7000
Fax: (202)862-7098

In-house, DC-area Employees

BECCHI, Rosemary D.: Manager
BERNSTEIN, Rachelle: Tax Partner, Office of Federal Tax Services
CARLSON, George N.: Partner, Office of Federal Tax Services
CARRINGTON, Glenn: Partner
COHEN, Harrison J.: National Director
COLLINS, Bryan: Partner
COULAM, Weston J.: Manager
CRYAN, Thomas M.: Principal
DANCE, Glenn E.: Partner
FARB, Warren: Manager
FOGARASI, Andre P.: Managing Director, Office of Federal Tax Services
FULLER, Thomas D.: Principal
GORDON, Richard A.: Partner

GRAFMEYER, Richard: Partner
HEETER, Charles P.: Partner, Officer of Government Affairs
KLEIN, Carol Doran: Partner
KULISH, Carol: Principal
LAWSON, Peter H.: Director, Government Affairs
MACNEIL, C. Ellen: Partner
MULLET, Melinda R.: Congressional Specialist
PECK, Jeffrey J.: Managing Partner, Office of Government Affairs
PETERSON, Mark
PROUDFIT, Elizabeth M.: Congressional Specialist
TUERFF, T. Timothy: Partner

Outside Counsel/Consultants

Alpine Group, Inc.
Issues: ACC
Rep By: Dan Brouillette, James Gregory Means, Rhod M. Shaw

Griffin, Johnson, Dover & Stewart
Rep By: Patrick J. Griffin, David E. Johnson, Walter J. "Joe" Stewart

Sidley & Austin

The Velasquez Group

Artichoke Enterprises, Inc.

San Bruno, CA

Outside Counsel/Consultants

Swidler Berlin Shereff Friedman, LLP
Rep By: Barry B. Direnfeld, Harold P. Goldfield, James Hamilton, Lester S. Hyman, Michael E. Ward, Michael B. Wigmore

Artists Coalition

Burbank, CA
Leg. Issues: CPT

Outside Counsel/Consultants

Barbour Griffith & Rogers, Inc.
Issues: CPT
Rep By: Haley Barbour, G. O. Lanny Griffith, Jr., R. Greg Stevens, Brent Thompson

Margaret Cone
Issues: CPT
Rep By: Margaret Cone

Artists Rights Today (ART PAC)

408 Third St. SE
Washington, DC 20003
Tel: (202)546-1821
Fax: (202)543-2405

A political action committee organized to support the arts and the rights of artists before Congress and to aid the elected friends of the arts in Congress.

In-house, DC-area Employees
BEDARD, Robert: Treasurer

Aruba, Government of

Oranjestad, ARUBA

Outside Counsel/Consultants

The Rendon Group, Inc.
Rep By: John W. Rendon, Jr.

Arvin Meritor Automotive

Leg. Issues: CSP, ENV, HCR, LBR, TRD

Outside Counsel/Consultants

Dykema Gossett PLLC
Issues: CSP, ENV, HCR, LBR, TRD
Rep By: David K. Arthur, Nancy R. Barbour

Arvin-Edison Water Storage District

Arvin, CA

Outside Counsel/Consultants

Brickfield, Burchette, Ritts & Stone
Rep By: Michael N. McCarty, Colleen Newman

Asahi Glass Co.

Tokyo, JAPAN
Leg. Issues: LBR, TRD

Outside Counsel/Consultants

Cleary, Gottlieb, Steen and Hamilton
Issues: TRD
Rep By: Kenneth L. Bachman, Jr., Mark Leddy

Williams & Jensen, P.C.
Issues: LBR, TRD
Rep By: David E. Franasiak, J. Steven Hart, Anthony J. Roda

Asbestos Information Ass'n/North America

1235 Jefferson Davis Hwy.
Suite 406
Arlington, VA 22202
E-mail: aiabjpigg@aol.com
Tel: (703)412-1150
Fax: (703)412-1152

In-house, DC-area Employees
PIGG, B. J. "Bob": President

Asbestos Recycling Inc.

Kent, WA
Leg. Issues: DEF, WAS

Outside Counsel/Consultants

Denny Miller McBee Associates
Issues: DEF, WAS
Rep By: Col. Fred W. Greene, USA (Ret.), Steve McBee, Denny M. Miller

Asbestos Working Group

Chicago, IL

Outside Counsel/Consultants

Timmons and Co., Inc.
Rep By: Michael J. Bates, Douglas F. Bennett, Ellen B. Fitzgibbons, Bryce L. "Larry" Harlow, Timothy J. Keating, Tom C. Korologos, Richard J. Tarplin, William E. Timmons, Sr., William E. Timmons, Jr.

ASCAP

Outside Counsel/Consultants

Downey McGrath Group, Inc.

Ascension, Louisiana, Parish of

Gonzales, LA
Leg. Issues: GOV, TRA

Outside Counsel/Consultants

The Palmer Group
Issues: GOV, TRA
Rep By: Clifford A. Palmer

ASCENT (Ass'n of Community Enterprises)

1401 K St. NW
Suite 600
Washington, DC 20005
Tel: (202)835-9898
Fax: (202)853-9893
Registered: LDA

Formerly Telecommunications Resellers Ass'n.

Leg. Issues: TEC

In-house, DC-area Employees
DAVIS, Marianne: Manager, Conference Services
GUSKY, David: Exec. V. President
HILL, Julie S.: Director, Marketing
KELLY, III, Ernest B.: President
MCCARTHY, Amy: Director, Conference Services
MEDVED, Mary: Director of Administration
TROTMAN, Steve: V. President, Industry Relations
YANOFF, Leonard: V. President, Advanced Services

Outside Counsel/Consultants

The Dutko Group, Inc.
Issues: TEC
Rep By: Kim Koontz Bayliss, Louis Lehrman, Steve Perry, Juliette M. Raffensperger, Stephen Craig Sayle

Hogan & Hartson L.L.P.
Issues: TEC
Rep By: Linda L. Oliver

Sher & Blackwell
Issues: TEC
Rep By: Earl W. Comstock, Jeffrey R. Pike, Antilla E. Trotter, III

AsclepiusNet

McLean, VA
Leg. Issues: DEF

Outside Counsel/Consultants

The PMA Group
Issues: DEF
Rep By: Kaylene Green, Patrick Hiu, Paul J. Magliocchetti, Sandra Welch

Asea Brown Boveri, Inc.

Leg. Issues: ENV

Outside Counsel/Consultants

The Wexler Group
Issues: ENV
Rep By: Robert L. Healy, Jr., Anne Wexler

Aseptic Packaging Council

2120 L St. NW
Suite 400
Washington, DC 20037
Tel: (202)478-6158
Fax: (202)223-9579

In-house, DC-area Employees
PARKER, Erich: V. President, Communications

ASFE

Silver Spring, MD
Web: www.asfe.org
E-mail: info@asfe.org

Outside Counsel/Consultants

Bachner Communications, Inc.
Rep By: John P. Bachner

Ash Britt

Leg. Issues: DIS, ENV

Outside Counsel/Consultants

U.S. Strategies Corp.
Issues: DIS, ENV
Rep By: Steven E. Carey, Michael K. Wyrick

The Asheville School

Asheville, NC
Leg. Issues: BUD, EDU

Outside Counsel/Consultants

Kimberly Consulting, LLC
Issues: BUD, EDU
Rep By: Richard H. Kimberly

Ashland Inc.

601 Pennsylvania Ave. NW
Suite 540
North Bldg.
Washington, DC 20004
Tel: (202)223-8290
Fax: (202)293-2913
Registered: LDA

A diversified energy company headquartered in Covington, KY.

Leg. Issues: BUD, CAW, CHM, CPT, CSP, ENG, ENV, FOR, FUE, GOV, LBR, MAR, MMM, RET, ROD, TAX, TOR, TRA, TRD

Political Action Committee/s

Ashland Political Action Committee for Employees (PACE)
601 Pennsylvania Ave. NW
Suite 540
North Bldg.
Washington, DC 20004
Contact: Shannon M. Russell
Tel: (202)223-8290
Fax: (202)293-2913

In-house, DC-area Employees
ANDERSON, Brenda G.: Washington Representative
DUNTON, Holly S.: Public Affairs Coordinator
FONES, Linda L.: Administrative Coordinator
RUSSELL, Shannon M.: Senior Washington Representative
TOOHEY, Michael J.: Director, Federal Relations
YESH, Constance L.: Staff Assistant

Outside Counsel/Consultants

The Grizzle Company
Issues: BUD, CAW, ENV
Rep By: Richard A. Cantor, Charles L. Grizzle

The Ashley Group

Rochester, NY
A real estate developer.

Leg. Issues: IND

Outside Counsel/Consultants

Ducheneaux, Taylor & Associates, Inc.
Issues: IND
Rep By: Franklin D. Ducheneaux, Peter S. Taylor

The Asia Foundation

1779 Massachusetts Ave. NW
Suite 815
Washington, DC 20036
Web: www.asiafoundation.org
E-mail: tafwa@mcimail.com
Tel: (202)588-9420
Fax: (202)588-9409

In-house, DC-area Employees
YUAN, Nancy: Director of Washington Programs

Asia Pacific Policy Center

601 13th St. NW
Suite 1100 North
Washington, DC 20005
E-mail: appcusa@aol.com
Tel: (202)223-7258
Fax: (202)223-7280

Leg. Issues: ECN, FOR

In-house, DC-area Employees
PAAL, Douglas H.: President

Asia Society

1800 K St. NW
Suite 1102
Washington, DC 20006
Web: www.asiasociety.org
Tel: (202)833-2742
Fax: (202)833-0189

A private, non-profit educational organization which is dedicated to increasing American awareness of Asia and fostering communication between Asians and Americans.

In-house, DC-area Employees
SLOAN, Judith A.: Director, Washington Center
YAS, Penelope: Assistant Director, Development

Asian Development Bank - North American Representative Office

815 Connecticut Ave. NW
Suite 325
Washington, DC 20006
Web: www.adb.org
Tel: (202)728-1500
Fax: (202)728-0505

In-house, DC-area Employees
MOSER, Patricia: Senior Liaison Officer

Asian Pacific American Labor Alliance, AFL-CIO

815 16th St. NW
Washington, DC 20006
Web: www.apalanet.org
E-mail: apala@apalanet.org
Tel: (202)842-1263
Fax: (202)842-1462

First and only national organization representing Asian American and Pacific Islander trade unionists.

Leg. Issues: CIV, LBR

In-house, DC-area Employees
SOOK LEE, Jin: Exec. Director

ASIC

Arlington, VA
Leg. Issues: DEF

Outside Counsel/Consultants
G.L. Merritt & Associates, Inc.
Issues: DEF
Rep By: Gordon L. Merritt

Aso Corp.

Sarasota, FL
Manufactures first aid bandages.

Leg. Issues: TRD

Outside Counsel/Consultants
Gibbons & Company, Inc.
Issues: TRD
Rep By: Clifford S. Gibbons, Hon. Sam M. Gibbons

Asociacion Columbiana de Exportadores de Flores (ASOCOLFLORES)

Bogota, COLOMBIA
Leg. Issues: TRD

Outside Counsel/Consultants
Manatt, Phelps & Phillips, LLP
Issues: TRD
Rep By: Irwin P. Altschuler, Hon. Jack W. Buechner, June L. DeHart, Eric Farnsworth, Robert J. Kabel, Susan M. Schmidt, Stephanie E. Silverman, Jessica A. Wasserman

Asociacion de Productores de Salon y Truncha de Chile

Santiago, CHILE

Outside Counsel/Consultants
Arnold & Porter

Asociacion Hondurena de Maquiladores

San Pedro Sula, HONDURAS

Outside Counsel/Consultants
Washington World Group, Ltd.
Rep By: Edward J. von Kloberg, III

Asociacion Nacional de Fabricantes de Medicamentos

MEXICO

Outside Counsel/Consultants
MFJ Internat'l

Asociacion Nacional de la Industria Quimica (ANIQ), A.C

Mexico City, MEXICO

Outside Counsel/Consultants
Porter, Wright, Morris & Arthur, LLP
Rep By: Leslie Alan Glick

Asosiasi Panel Kayu Indonesia

Outside Counsel/Consultants
Akin, Gump, Strauss, Hauer & Feld, L.L.P.

Aspen Institute

One Dupont Circle NW Suite 700
Washington, DC 20036-1113
Web: www.aspeninstitute.org
Tel: (202)736-5800
Fax: (202)467-0790

A non-profit, nonpartisan global forum for leveraging the power of leaders to improve the human condition. Through its seminar and policy programs, the Institute fosters enlightened, morally repsonsible leadership and convenes leaders and policy makers to address new challenges.

In-house, DC-area Employees
CLARK, Peggy E.: Exec. V. President, Policy Programs
SPIEGELMAN, James M.: Director, Public Affairs

Outside Counsel/Consultants
Widmeyer Communications, Inc.

Asphalt Emulsion Manufacturers Ass'n

Annapolis, MD

Outside Counsel/Consultants
Thompson, Hine and Flory LLP
Rep By: David H. Baker

Asphalt Institute

6917 Arlington Rd.
Suite 210
Bethesda, MD 20814
Web: www.asphaltinstitute.org
E-mail: bmccarthy@asphaltinstitute.org
Tel: (301)656-5824
Fax: (301)656-5825

Headquartered in Lexington, KY.

In-house, DC-area Employees
MCCARTHY, Bernie: V. President

Asphalt Recycling and Reclaiming Ass'n

Annapolis, MD
Web: www.rampages.onramp.net/~prime/arra.htm

Outside Counsel/Consultants
Thompson, Hine and Flory LLP
Rep By: David H. Baker

Asphalt Roofing Manufacturers Ass'n

4041 Powder Mill Rd.
Suite 404
Calverton, MD 20705-3106
Web: www.asphaltroofing.org
Tel: (301)348-2002
Fax: (301)348-2020

In-house, DC-area Employees
HOBSON, Joseph W.: Director, Communications/Public Affairs
KELLY, Peter: General Manager
SNYDER, Russell K.: Exec. V. President

Outside Counsel/Consultants
The Kellen Company
Rep By: Russell K. Snyder

Asphalt Systems, Inc.

Salt Lake City, UT
Leg. Issues: ROD

Outside Counsel/Consultants
Parry, Romani, DeConcini & Symms
Issues: ROD
Rep By: Edward H. Baxter, Hon. Dennis DeConcini, John M. Haddow, Scott D. Hatch, Shannon Davis Henderson, Jack W. Martin, Romano Romani, Linda Arey Skladany, Hon. Steven D. Symms

ASPIRA Ass'n, Inc.

1444 I St. NW
Suite 800
Washington, DC 20005
Web: www.aspira.org
E-mail: info@aspira.org
Tel: (202)835-3600
Fax: (202)835-3613

A non-profit organization dedicated to encouraging education and leadership development among Hispanic youth.

In-house, DC-area Employees
BLACKBURN-MORENO, Ronald: President

Aspira, Inc. of New Jersey

Newark, NJ

Outside Counsel/Consultants
Krivit & Krivit, P.C.

Aspirin Foundation of America, Inc.

1555 Connecticut Ave. NW
Suite 200
Washington, DC 20036
Tel: (202)462-9600
Fax: (202)462-9043

A nonprofit organization made up of companies engaged in the manufacture, preparation, propagation, compounding or processing of aspirin and aspirin products. It informs members of scientific developments relating to aspirin and encourages an understanding of the potential health benefits of aspirin.

In-house, DC-area Employees
BRYANT, Sr., M.D.., Thomas E.: President

Outside Counsel/Consultants
Non-Profit Management Associates, Inc.
Rep By: Thomas E. Bryant, Sr., M.D.,
Paul, Hastings, Janofsky & Walker LLP
Rep By: R. Bruce Dickson

Ass'n for Advanced Life Underwriting

1922 F St. NW
Fourth Floor
Washington, DC 20006
Web: www.aalu.org
Tel: (202)331-6081
Fax: (202)331-2164

A trade association of highly qualified life insurance underwriters who wish to present to Congress and government agencies their position on estate and gift taxes, taxation of small business, retirement and employee benefit plans and other subjects related to formation of capital for security.

Leg. Issues: TAX

In-house, DC-area Employees
KORB, Thomas: Director, Government Affairs
STERTZER, David: Exec. V. President

Outside Counsel/Consultants
Edelman Public Relations Worldwide
Rep By: Eric Hoffman
Patton Boggs, LLP
Issues: TAX
Rep By: John F. Jonas
Silverstein and Mullens, P.L.L.C.
Rep By: Gerald H. Sherman
Tongour Simpson Holsclaw Green
Issues: TAX
Rep By: Sascha M. Burns, Michael A. Tongour

Ass'n for Ambulatory Behavioral Healthcare

2301 Mount Vernon Ave.
Suite 100
Alexandria, VA 22301
Web: www.aabh.org
E-mail: aabh@aabh.org
Tel: (703)836-2274
Fax: (703)836-0083

Trade association dealing with outpatient mental health services.

Leg. Issues: HCR, MED

In-house, DC-area Employees
KNIGHT, Mark A.: Exec. Director

Ass'n for Career and Technical Education

1410 King St.
Alexandria, VA 22314
Web: www.acteonline.org
E-mail: acte@acteonline.org
Tel: (703)683-3111
Fax: (703)683-7424
Registered: LDA

The Association for Career and Technical Education (ACTE) is the largest national education association dedicated to the advancement of education that prepares youth and adults for careers. Its mission is to provide leadership in developing a competitive workforce.

Leg. Issues: BUD, EDU, LBR, WEL

In-house, DC-area Employees
LOVEJOY, Bret D.: Exec. Director
O'BRIEN, Nancy: Assistant Exec. Director, Government Relations

Ass'n for Childhood Education Internat'l

17904 Georgia Ave.
Suite 215
Olney, MD 20832-2277
Web: www.acei.org
E-mail: aceihq@aol.com
Tel: (301)570-2111
Fax: (301)570-2212

A non-profit professional organization devoted to the education and well-being of children from infancy through early adolescence. Members include teachers, teacher educators, school administrators, students of education, parents and librarians. Through publications, conferences and other programs, it seeks to foster the professional growth of members and to inform members and the larger community on issues affecting children. Affiliate structure includes over 200 local, state, and national branches.

Leg. Issues: EDU, FAM

In-house, DC-area Employees
BAUER, Anne Watson: Editor/Director of Publications
GARDNER, Marilyn: Director, Membership and Marketing
ODLAND, Gerald C.: Exec. Director

Ass'n for Community Based Education

1805 Florida Ave. NW Tel: (202)462-6333
Washington, DC 20009

Formerly the Clearinghouse for Community Based Free Standing Educational Institutions. Dedicated to meeting the needs of non-traditional learners, the disadvantaged and minorities.

In-house, DC-area Employees

ZACHARIADIS, Christofer P.: Exec. Director

Ass'n for Commuter Transportation

Washington, DC
Leg. Issues: BUD, CAW, ENV, ROD, TAX, TRA

Outside Counsel/Consultants

Government Relations, Inc.
Issues: BUD, CAW, ENV, ROD, TAX, TRA
Rep By: Thomas J. Bulger, Mark H. Miller, John N. Young

Ass'n for Competitive Technology

1413 K St. NW 12th Floor Tel: (202)408-3370
Washington, DC 20005

Political Action Committee/s

Ass'n for Competitive Technology PAC

1413 K St. NW 12th Floor Tel: (202)408-3370
Washington, DC 20005
Contact: Jonathan V. Zuck

In-house, DC-area Employees

ZUCK, Jonathan V.

Outside Counsel/Consultants

The DCS Group

The Dutko Group, Inc.
Rep By: Kim Koontz Bayliss, Mark S. Irion, Louis Lehrman

Ass'n for Dressings and Sauces

1101 15th St. NW Tel: (202)785-3232
Suite 202 Fax: (202)223-9741
Washington, DC 20005
Web: www.dressings-sauces.org
E-mail: ads@@assnhq.com

In-house, DC-area Employees

CRISTOL, Richard E.: President

Outside Counsel/Consultants

The Kellen Company
Rep By: Richard E. Cristol

Ass'n for Education and Rehabilitation of the Blind & Visually Impaired

4600 Duke St. Tel: (703)823-9690
Suite 430 Fax: (703)823-9695
P.O. Box 22397
Alexandria, VA 22304
Web: www.aerbvi.org
E-mail: aer@laerbvi.org

An international organization formed in 1984 as a result of the consolidation of the American Ass'n of Workers for the Blind and the Ass'n for Education of the Visually Handicapped. Primary purpose is to promote quality services for blind children and adults.

Leg. Issues: CIV, EDU, HCR, TEC

In-house, DC-area Employees

FAIRBARNS, Jacqueline: Assistant Exec. Director
ROZELL, Denise M.: Exec. Director

Ass'n for Electronic Healthcare Transaction

Washington, DC
Web: www.afehct.org
E-mail: afehct@aol.com
Leg. Issues: HCR

Outside Counsel/Consultants

Thomas J. Gilligan
Issues: HCR
Rep By: Thomas J. Gilligan

Ass'n for Enterprise Opportunity

Chicago, IL
Web: www.microenterpriseworks.org
E-mail: aeo@assoceo.org
Leg. Issues: ECN

Outside Counsel/Consultants

Bill Zavarela
Issues: ECN
Rep By: Bill Zavarela

Ass'n for Financial Professionals, Inc.

7315 Wisconsin Ave. Tel: (301)907-2862
Suite 1250W Fax: (301)907-2864
Bethesda, MD 20814 Registered: LDA
Web: www.afponline.org
E-mail: afp@afponline.org

A professional association representing treasury professionals employed by corporations, non-profit organizations and government. Areas of interest include payment system and banking regulation, Federal Reserve, federal and state tax collection and filing requirements. Formerly the Treasury Management Ass'n, Inc.

Leg. Issues: BAN, FIN, TAX

In-house, DC-area Employees

CURRAN, Frank P.: V. President, Government Relations and Technical Services

Ass'n for Gerontology in Higher Education

1030 15th St. NW Tel: (202)289-9806
Suite 240 Fax: (202)289-9824
Washington, DC 20005
Web: www.aghe.org
E-mail: aghetemp@aghe.org

Formed to advance gerontology as a field of study in institutions of higher learning.

In-house, DC-area Employees

TOMPKINS, Dr. Catherine: Director

Ass'n for Governmental Leasing and Finance

Web: www.aglf.org
E-mail: aglf@aglf.org

Financiers and lessors of real and personal property to state and local government entities.

Outside Counsel/Consultants

Smith, Bucklin and Associates, Inc.

Ass'n for Healthcare Philanthropy

313 Park Ave. Tel: (703)532-6243
Suite 400 Fax: (703)532-7170
Falls Church, VA 22046
Web: www.go-ahp.org
E-mail: ahp@go-ahp.org

Membership includes 2,800 hospitals, nursing homes and health organizations.

Leg. Issues: HCR

In-house, DC-area Employees

MCGINLY, Ph.D, CAE, Dr. William C.: President and Chief Exec. Officer
SMITH, Ms. Bobbi: Director, Foundation and Government Relations

Outside Counsel/Consultants

Navarro Legislative & Regulatory Affairs
Issues: HCR
Rep By: Bruce C. Navarro

Ass'n for Hospital Medical Education

Washington, DC

Outside Counsel/Consultants

Smith, Bucklin and Associates, Inc.

Ass'n for Information and Image Management Internat'l

1100 Wayne Ave. Tel: (301)587-8202
Suite 1100 Fax: (301)587-2711
Silver Spring, MD 20910
Web: www.aiim.org
E-mail: aiim@aiim.org

The industry deals with the storage, retrieval, and manipulation of images of documents (business records, engineering drawings, etc.). The association monitors laws and regulations in these disciplines which could affect its members.

In-house, DC-area Employees

ARCURI, Jeff: V. President, Marketing and Meetings
MANCINI, John: President

Ass'n for Interactive Media

1301 Connecticut Ave. NW Tel: (202)408-0008
Fifth Floor Fax: (202)408-0111
Washington, DC 20036 Registered: LDA
Web: www.interactivehq.org
E-mail: info@interactivehq.org

Works with elected officials, senior lobbyists, critical congressional staff members and other power players to protect companies doing business on the Internet.

Leg. Issues: COM, CPI

In-house, DC-area Employees

ISAACSON, Ben: Exec. Director

Outside Counsel/Consultants

Davidson & Company, Inc.

Ass'n for Local Telecommunications Services

888 17th St. NW Tel: (202)969-2587
Suite 900 Fax: (202)969-2581
Washington, DC 20006 Registered: LDA
Web: www.alts.org
Leg. Issues: COM, CPI, TEC, UTI

Political Action Committee/s

Ass'n for Local Telecommunications Services PAC

888 17th St. NW Tel: (202)969-2587
Suite 900 Fax: (202)969-2581
Washington, DC 20006
Contact: John D. Windhausen, Jr.

In-house, DC-area Employees

ASKIN, Jonathan: General Counsel
GAUGLER, Tiki: Senior Attorney
STIFFLER, Alan: V. President, Association Affairs
WINDHAUSEN, Jr., John D.: President

Outside Counsel/Consultants

Cormac Group, LLP

Davison, Cohen & Co.
Issues: TEC
Rep By: Thomas W. Cohen

Podesta/Mattoon
Rep By: Claudia James, Kristen Leary, Timothy Powers

Ass'n for Los Angeles Deputy Sheriffs

Los Angeles, CA
Leg. Issues: LAW, RET

Outside Counsel/Consultants

Shannon M. Lahey Associates
Issues: LAW, RET
Rep By: Shannon M. Lahey

The Ass'n For Manufacturing Technology (AMT)

7901 Westpark Dr. Tel: (703)893-2900
McLean, VA 22102-4206 Fax: (703)893-1151
Registered: LDA
Web: www.mfgtech.org
E-mail: amt@mfgtech.org

Represents and promotes the interests of American builders of manufacturing machinery and allied technology.

Leg. Issues: BUD, CPT, CSP, DEF, ECN, FOR, MAN, SCI, SMB, TAX, TOR, TRD

Political Action Committee/s

MACHINE TOOLPAC

7901 Westpark Dr. Tel: (703)827-5225
McLean, VA 22102-4206 Fax: (703)749-2742
Contact: James H. Mack

In-house, DC-area Employees

CARLSON, Don F.: President
FREEDENBERG, Paul H.: Government Relations Director
GARDNER, Robert W.: V. President, Communications
KURRLE, Jonathan: Legislative Director
MACK, James H.: V. President, Government Relations
THOMAS, Amber L.: Legislative Analyst

Outside Counsel/Consultants

Campbell Crane & Associates
Issues: CSP, TOR
Rep By: Jeanne M. Campbell

Covington & Burling
Rep By: George M. Chester, Jr.

Quinn Gillespie & Associates

Ass'n for Maximum Service Television, Inc.

1776 Massachusetts Ave. NW Tel: (202)861-0344
Suite 310 Fax: (202)861-0342
Washington, DC 20036
Web: www.mstv.org

In-house, DC-area Employees

TAWIL, Victor: Senior V. President
WHITE, Margita E.: President

Outside Counsel/Consultants

Covington & Burling
Rep By: Jonathan D. Blake

Ass'n for Postal Commerce

1901 N. Fort Myer Dr. Tel: (703)524-0096
Suite 401 Fax: (703)524-1871
Arlington, VA 22209-1609 Registered: LDA
Web: www.postcom.org

Formerly known as the Third Class Mail Ass'n and then the Advertising Mail Marketing Ass'n. Represents those that

support the use of mail as a medium for business communication and commerce.

Leg. Issues: POS

In-house, DC-area Employees
DEL POLITO, Gene A.: President

Outside Counsel/Consultants

Venable
Rep By: Ian D. Volner

Ass'n for Professionals in Infection Control and Epidemiology

1275 K St. NW
Suite 1000
Washington, DC 20005
Tel: (202)789-1890
Fax: (202)789-1899
Registered: LDA
Web: www.apic.org
E-mail: apicinfo@apic.org

Promotes wellness and works to prevent illness and infection worldwide by advancing healthcare epidemiology through education, collaboration, research, practice and credentialing.

Leg. Issues: HCR, MED

In-house, DC-area Employees
LAXTON, Christopher E.: Exec. Director
THOMAS, Jennifer: Director, Government and Public Relations

Ass'n for Public Policy Analysis and Management

P.O. Box 18766
Washington, DC 20036-1876
Tel: (202)261-5788
Fax: (202)223-1149
Web: www.appam.org
E-mail: appam@ui.urban.org

The leading professional association for applied public policy and management research and education.

In-house, DC-area Employees
DEVEREUX, Erik: Exec. Director

Ass'n for Responsible Thermal Treatment

Wilmington, DE

Includes APTUS, Inc. of Pittsburgh, PA; ENSCO, Inc. of Lincolnshire, IL; Rollins Environmental Services of Wilmington, DE; Ross Environmental Services of Grafton, OH; ThermalKem of Rock Hill, SC; and USPCI of Houston, TX.

Outside Counsel/Consultants

Arter & Hadden
Rep By: Daniel L. Cohen, Jon W. Plebani

Ass'n for Supervision and Curriculum Development

1703 N. Beauregard St.
Alexandria, VA 22311-1714
Tel: (703)578-9600
Fax: (703)575-5400
Web: www.ascd.org
E-mail: info@ascd.org

Members are curriculum coordinators and consultants, superintendents, professors of education, educational administrators, school board members, principals, teachers, students and parents.

Leg. Issues: EDU

In-house, DC-area Employees
CARTER, Dr. Gene R.: Exec. Director
ERNST, Don: Government Relations Director
GLEASON, Barbara: Director, Public Information

Ass'n for the Advancement of Medical Instrumentation

3330 Washington Blvd.
Suite 400
Arlington, VA 22201-4598
Tel: (703)525-4890
Fax: (703)276-0793
Web: www.aami.org

In-house, DC-area Employees
MILLER, J.D., Michael J.: President

Outside Counsel/Consultants

McKenna & Cuneo, L.L.P.

Ass'n for the Study of Afro-American Life and History

7961 Eastern Ave.
Silver Spring, MD 20910
Tel: (301)587-5900
Fax: (301)587-5915
Web: www.asalh.org
E-mail: asalh@earthlink.net

Researches, collects, preserves and promotes the achievements and contributions of African Americans. Publishes the Journal of Negro History and the Negro History Bulletin and owns and maintains the Carter G. Woodson home in Washington, DC.

In-house, DC-area Employees
DICKINSON, Dr. Gloria: President
WEBSTER, Irena: Exec. Director

Ass'n for the Suppliers of Printing and Publishing Technology

Reston, VA
Leg. Issues: ENV, GOV, TRD

Outside Counsel/Consultants

Valis Associates
Issues: ENV, GOV, TRD
Rep By: Hon. Richard T. Schulze, Todd Tolson, Wayne H. Valis

Ass'n for Transportation, Law, Logistics and Policy

19564 Club House Rd.
Mont. Village, MD 20886
Tel: (301)670-6733
Fax: (301)670-6735
Web: www.transportlink.com/atllp
E-mail: atllp@aol.com

A global transportation and logistics organization.

Leg. Issues: TRA

In-house, DC-area Employees
JONES, E. Dale: Exec. Director

Ass'n for Unmanned Vehicle Systems International

3401 Columbia Pike
Suite 400
Arlington, VA 22204
Tel: (703)920-2720
Fax: (703)920-2889
Web: www.auvsi.org
E-mail: info@iaus.org

In-house, DC-area Employees
DAVIDSON, Daryl: Exec. Director
PULLEN, Rachel C.: Manager, Marketing

Ass'n for Women in Science

1200 New York Ave. NW
Suite 650
Washington, DC 20005
Tel: (202)326-8940
Fax: (202)326-8960
Web: www.awis.org
E-mail: awis@awis.org

A non-profit organization dedicated to achieving equity and full participation for women in the sciences, mathematics, engineering and technology. Publishes a variety of materials and sponsors conferences to inform girls and women about science programs, leadership skills and career advancement.

In-house, DC-area Employees
DIDION, Catherine J.: Exec. Director

The Ass'n Healthcare Coalition

Kansas City, MO
Leg. Issues: HCR

Outside Counsel/Consultants

Schramm, Williams & Associates, Inc.
Issues: HCR
Rep By: Duane L. Musser

Ass'n of Academic Health Centers

1400 16th St. NW
Suite 720
Washington, DC 20036
Tel: (202)265-9600
Fax: (202)265-7514
Web: www.ahcnet.org

A national nonprofit organization comprising health complexes with more than one hundred members at the nation's major universities; dedicated to improving health by education, biomedical and health services research, and healthcare delivery.

In-house, DC-area Employees
BULGER, M.D., Roger J.: President
OSTERWEIS, Ph.D., Marian: Exec. V. President
RAMSAY, M.D., David J.: Chair, Board of Directors

Ass'n of Academic Health Sciences Library Directors

Seattle, WA

Outside Counsel/Consultants

Health and Medicine Counsel of Washington
Rep By: Dale P. Dirks, Gavin Lindberg

Ass'n of Administrative Law Judges

Portland, OR
Leg. Issues: GOV

Outside Counsel/Consultants

Kyros & Cummins Associates
Issues: GOV
Rep By: John M. Falk, Hon. Peter N. Kyros

Ass'n of Air Medical Services

Pasadena, CA
Web: www.aams.org
E-mail: information@aams.org
Leg. Issues: MMM, TAX

Outside Counsel/Consultants

CGR Associates, Inc.
Issues: MMM, TAX
Rep By: Kevin Frankovich

Ass'n of America's Public Television Stations

1350 Connecticut Ave. NW
Suite 200
Washington, DC 20036
Tel: (202)887-1700
Fax: (202)293-2422
Registered: LDA
Web: www.apts.org
E-mail: info@apts.org

The association for America's public TV stations. Represents member stations' interests at federal agencies and before Congress. Provides lobbying, grassroots support, and research/planning support to member stations.

Leg. Issues: BUD, COM, EDU

In-house, DC-area Employees
DEWHIRST, Mary: V. President, Government Relations
ERSTLING, Mark D.: Senior V. President
KNUTSON, Marcia: Congressional Representative
MOHRMAN-GILLIS, Marilyn: V. President, Policy and Legal Affairs

Ass'n of American Blood Banks

Bethesda, MD
Leg. Issues: HCR, MMM

Outside Counsel/Consultants

Mintz, Levin, Cohn, Ferris, Glovsky and Popeo, P.C.
Issues: HCR, MMM
Rep By: Peter M. Kazon, Charles A. Samuels

Ass'n of American Chambers of Commerce in Latin America

1615 H St. NW
Washington, DC 20062
Tel: (202)463-5485
Fax: (202)463-3126
Web: www.aaccla.org
E-mail: inbox@aaccla.org

Represents 23 American Chambers of Commerce in 21 countries in the hemisphere and seeks to lower trade and investment barriers in the region.

Leg. Issues: ECN, FOR, GOV, TRD

In-house, DC-area Employees
MAGAN, Michael: Exec. V. President
MURPHY, John: Exec. Director

Ass'n of American Colleges and Universities

1818 R St. NW
Washington, DC 20009
Tel: (202)387-3760
Fax: (202)265-9532
Web: www.aacu-edu.org
E-mail: info@aacu.nw.dc.us

Founded in 1915, AAC&U is the national voice for liberal learning. It includes public and private colleges and universities. Through grants, national initiatives, publications and workshops, AAC&U strives to enhance undergraduate liberal education and to secure its integration with professional programs and courses of study.

In-house, DC-area Employees
GAFF, Jerry: V. President, Education and Institutional Renewal
HUMPHRYS, Deborah: V. President, Communications and Public Relations
MCTIGHE MUSIL, Caryn: V. President, Education and Diversity Initiatives
MERVES, Esther: Director, Membership and External Affairs
SCHNEIDER, Carol: President

Ass'n of American Geographers

1710 16th St. NW
Washington, DC 20009-3198
Tel: (202)234-1450
Fax: (202)234-2744
Web: www.aag.org
E-mail: gaia@aag.org
Leg. Issues: BAN, BUD, DEF, ECN, FIN, GOV, LBR, RET, SCI, TAX, TEC, TRD, UTI

In-house, DC-area Employees
ABLER, Ronald F.: Exec. Director

Ass'n of American Law Schools

1201 Connecticut Ave. NW
Suite 800
Washington, DC 20036
Tel: (202)296-8851
Fax: (202)296-8869
Web: www.aals.org
E-mail: aals@aals.org

In-house, DC-area Employees
MONK, Carl C.: Exec. Director and Exec. V. President
PRINCE, H. G.: Deputy Director

Ass'n of American Medical Colleges

2450 N St. NW
Washington, DC 20037-1126
Tel: (202)828-0400
Fax: (202)828-1125
Registered: LDA
Web: www.aamc.org

Composed of 125 medical schools, 400 teaching hospitals, 86 academic societies, the Organization of Student Representatives, and the Organization of Resident Representatives. Works with medical schools and teaching hospitals in developing national policies and goals in medical education, medical research and patient care.

Leg. Issues: ANI, BUD, EDU, HCR, MED, MMM, SCI, TAX, VET

In-house, DC-area Employees
COHEN, M.D., Jordan J.: President
DAVIS, Lynne: Director, Health Care Legislative Affairs
FISHBURNE, Jonathan: Senior Legislative Analyst
FROYD, Erica: Legislative Analyst
KEYES, Jr., J.D., Joseph A.: General Counsel, Senior V. President
KNAPP, Ph.D., Richard M.: Exec. V. President
MOORE, David B.: Associate V. President, Governmental Relations
NEELY, Susan: Sr. V. President, Communications

Outside Counsel/Consultants
BKSH & Associates
Issues: BUD, MED, MMM
Covington & Burling
Issues: HCR
Rep By: Roderick A. DeArment, Joan L. Kutcher

Ass'n of American Physicians and Surgeons

2111 Wisconsin Ave. NW
Suite 125
Washington, DC 20007
Tel: (202)333-3855
Web: www.aapsonline.com
E-mail: kdserkes@worldnet.att.net

An association representing doctors in private practice medicine headquartered in Tucson, AZ.

Leg. Issues: DIS, HCR, INS, MED, MMM, PHA

In-house, DC-area Employees
SERKES, Kathryn A.: Legislative Director

Ass'n of American Publishers

50 F St. NW
Fourth Floor
Washington, DC 20001-1564
Tel: (202)347-3375
Fax: (202)347-3690
Registered: LDA
Web: www.publishers.com

National trade association headquartered in New York, NY. Represents book and journal publishers.

Leg. Issues: CON, CPT, EDU, GOV, MIA, POS, TEC, TRD

In-house, DC-area Employees
ADLER, Allan R.: V. President, Legal and Government Affairs
SCHROEDER, Hon. Patricia: President and Chief Exec. Officer

Outside Counsel/Consultants
Hill and Knowlton, Inc.
Rep By: Bruce Hildebrand

Ass'n of American Railroads

50 F St. NW
12th Floor
Washington, DC 20001
Tel: (202)639-2525
Fax: (202)639-2526
Registered: LDA
Web: www.aar.com
Leg. Issues: BUD, CAW, ENV, RET, RRR, TAX, TRA, TRU

Political Action Committee/s
Ass'n of American Railroads PAC (Rail PAC)
50 F St. NW
Suite 12500
Washington, DC 20001
Tel: (202)639-2537
Fax: (202)639-2526
Contact: H. K. "Obie" O'Bannon

In-house, DC-area Employees
DETTMANN, Charles E.: Exec. V. President, Safety and Operations
HAMBERGER, Edward R.: President and Chief Exec. Officer
MACDONALD, Jennifer: Director, Government Affairs
O'BANNON, H. K. "Obie": V. President, Government Affairs
WARCHOT, Louis P.: Senior V. President, Law and General Counsel
WETZEL, John F.: Assistant V. President, Government Affairs
WHITE, Betsy: Acting V. President, Communications
WILSON, Nancy L.: Assistant V. President, Reguilatory Affairs

Outside Counsel/Consultants
The Accord Group
Issues: CAW, ENV, TAX, TRA
Rep By: Robert F. Hurley
American Continental Group, Inc.
Issues: TRA
Rep By: John A. Cline, Shawn H. Smeallie, Peter Terpeluk, Jr.
Birch, Horton, Bittner & Cherot
Issues: TAX, TRA
Rep By: Ronald G. Birch
Cormac Group, LLP
The Direct Impact Co.
Susan Molinari, L.L.P.
Potomac Group
Issues: RRR, TAX, TRA, TRU
Rep By: Richard Y Hegg, Philip C. Karsting, G. Wayne Smith
Ryan, Phillips, Utrecht & MacKinnon
Issues: BUD, ENV, RRR, TRA
Rep By: Rodney Hoppe, Jeffrey M. MacKinnon, William D. Phillips, Mark D. Planning, Thomas M. Ryan, Joseph V. Vasapoli
Symms, Lehn & Associates, Inc.
Issues: RET, TAX
Rep By: Alfred M. Lehn, Hon. Steven D. Symms
Valis Associates
Issues: TRA
Rep By: Jennifer Conti, Hon. Dan Schaefer, Hon. Richard T. Schulze
Van Scoyoc Associates, Inc.
Issues: RRR
Rep By: Steven O. Palmer, H. Stewart Van Scoyoc
Washington Council Ernst & Young
Issues: BUD, TAX
Rep By: Doug Badger, John L. Doney, Jayne T. Fitzgerald, LaBrenda Garrett-Nelson, Gary J. Gasper, Bruce A. Gates, Nick Giordano, Cathy Koch, Robert J. Leonard, Richard Meltzer, Phillip D. Moseley, John D. Porter, Robert M. Rozen, Donna Steele-Flynn, Timothy J. Urban

Ass'n of American Shippers

Alexandria, VA
Leg. Issues: DEF, FOR, GOV, MAR, TRA, TRU

Outside Counsel/Consultants
R. J. Hudson Associates
Issues: DEF, FOR, GOV, MAR, TRA, TRU

Ass'n of American Universities

1200 New York Ave. NW
Suite 550
Washington, DC 20005
Tel: (202)408-7500
Fax: (202)408-8184
Web: www.aau.org
Leg. Issues: CPT

In-house, DC-area Employees
HASSELMO, Nils: President
SMITH, Peter F.: Director, Public Affairs
TURMAN, Richard: Director, Federal Affairs
VAUGHN, John C.: Exec. V. President

Outside Counsel/Consultants
Hogan & Hartson L.L.P.
Wiley, Rein & Fielding
Issues: CPT

Ass'n of American Veterinary Medical Colleges

1101 Vermont Ave. NW
Suite 710
Washington, DC 20005
Tel: (202)371-9195
Fax: (202)842-0773
Web: www.aavmc.org
E-mail: aavmc@attmail.com

Central headquarters for the colleges of veterinary medicine, departments of veterinary science, and departments of comparative medicine of North America.

In-house, DC-area Employees
MANN, Curt: Exec. Director

Ass'n of Asia Pacific Airlines

Kuala Lumpur, MALAYSIA
Leg. Issues: AVI

Outside Counsel/Consultants
Global Aviation Associates, Ltd.
Issues: AVI
Rep By: Jon F. Ash, Charles R. Chambers

Ass'n of Bank Couriers

Washington, DC
Leg. Issues: BAN, TRA

Outside Counsel/Consultants
Ely & Co., Inc.
Issues: BAN
Rep By: Bert Ely
Hoover Partners
Issues: BAN, TRA
Rep By: Kimberly Hoover

Ass'n of Bankruptcy Professionals, Inc.

Lynchburg, VA
Leg. Issues: BNK

Outside Counsel/Consultants
Law Office of Paige E. Reffe
Issues: BNK
Rep By: Paige E. Reffe

Ass'n of Banks in Insurance

1155 15th St. NW
Suite 1101
Washington, DC 20005
Tel: (202)833-7756
Fax: (202)833-1429
Registered: LDA
Web: www.theabi.com
E-mail: abi@erols.com

A trade association dedicated to improving the ability of financial institutions to sell insurance.

Leg. Issues: BAN, CSP, ENV, FIN, INS, MAN, TAX

In-house, DC-area Employees
REYNOLDS, E. Kenneth: Exec. Director

Outside Counsel/Consultants
McIntyre Law Firm, PLLC
Issues: BAN, CSP, ENV, FIN, INS, MAN, TAX
Rep By: Chrys D. Lemon, James T. McIntyre

Ass'n of Banks of Israel

Tel Aviv, ISRAEL
A trade association serving the Israeli banking industry.

Leg. Issues: BAN, TAX

Outside Counsel/Consultants
Shaw Pittman
Issues: BAN, TAX
Rep By: Scott A. Anenberg, Michael C. Moetell

Ass'n of Bituminous Contractors

Washington, DC

Political Action Committee/s
Ass'n of Bituminous Contractors Political Action Committee
Washington, DC

Outside Counsel/Consultants
Howe, Anderson & Steyer, P.C.
Rep By: William H. Howe

Ass'n of Black Psychologists

P.O. Box 55999
Washington, DC 20040-5999
Tel: (202)722-0808
Fax: (202)722-5941
Web: www.abpsi.org
E-mail: admin@abpsi.org

Established in 1968, an organization of Black professionals and students in psychology working to improve the psychological health of black people.

Leg. Issues: EDU, HCR

In-house, DC-area Employees
ROBERTS, Michele: National Administrator

Ass'n of Brazilian Ceramic Tile Producers

Sao Paulo, BRAZIL

Outside Counsel/Consultants
Porter, Wright, Morris & Arthur, LLP
Rep By: Leslie Alan Glick

Ass'n of Brazilian Tire Producers

Sao Paulo, BRAZIL

Outside Counsel/Consultants
Porter, Wright, Morris & Arthur, LLP
Rep By: Leslie Alan Glick

Ass'n of British Insurers

London, UNITED KINGDOM
Leg. Issues: FIN, INS, TAX

Outside Counsel/Consultants
Brenda R. Viehe-Naess
Issues: FIN, INS, TAX
Rep By: Brenda R. Viehe-Naess

Ass'n of California Water Agencies

400 N. Capitol St. NW
Suite 357 South
Washington, DC 20001
Tel: (202)434-4760
Fax: (202)434-4763
Registered: LDA

Headquartered in Sacramento, CA.

Leg. Issues: BUD, CAW, NAT, TAX, UTI

In-house, DC-area Employees
MAUCIERI, Mat: Federal Relations Representative
REYNOLDS, David L.: Director, Federal Relations

Ass'n of Chiropractic Colleges

Bethesda, MD
Web: www.chirocolleges.org
E-mail: obyronco@aol.com
Leg. Issues: BUD, DEF, EDU, HCR, MED, MMM, VET

Outside Counsel/Consultants
The Advocacy Group
Issues: EDU
Rep By: Robert E. Mills
O'Bryon & Co.
Issues: BUD, DEF, EDU, HCR, MED, MMM, VET
Rep By: David S. O'Bryon
O'Connor & Hannan, L.L.P.
Rep By: George J. Mannina, Jr.

Ass'n of Chocolate, Biscuit and Confectionery Industries of the EEC

Brussels, BELGIUM

Outside Counsel/Consultants
Max N. Berry Law Offices
Rep By: Max N. Berry

Ass'n of Christian Therapists

McLean, VA

Outside Counsel/Consultants
Degnon Associates, Inc.

Ass'n of Clinical Research Professionals

Washington, DC
Web: www.acrpnet.org
Leg. Issues: CPT, GOV, HCR, LBR, TAX, TOR

Outside Counsel/Consultants
The Aker Partners Inc.
Issues: HCR
Rep By: G. Colburn Aker
Venable
Issues: CPT, GOV, LBR, TAX, TOR
Rep By: Jeffrey S. Tenenbaum

Ass'n of Collegiate Schools of Architecture

1735 New York Ave. NW
Third Floor
Washington, DC 20006
Web: www.acsa-arch.org
E-mail: acsanatl@aol.com
Tel: (202)785-2324
Fax: (202)628-0448

In-house, DC-area Employees
VIERRA, Stephanie: Exec. Director

Ass'n of Community Cancer Centers

11600 Nebel St.
Suite 201
Rockville, MD 20852
Web: www.assoc-cancer-ctrs.org
Tel: (301)984-9496
Fax: (301)770-1949
Leg. Issues: MMM

In-house, DC-area Employees
MORTENSON, Lee E.: Exec. Director

Outside Counsel/Consultants
Powell, Goldstein, Frazer & Murphy LLP
Issues: MMM
Rep By: Alan K. Parver, Steve K. Stranne
Swidler Berlin Shereff Friedman, LLP

Ass'n of Community College Trustees

1740 N St. NW
Washington, DC 20036
Tel: (202)775-4667
Fax: (202)223-1297
Registered: LDA
Web: www.acct.org
Leg. Issues: BUD, EDU, TAX

In-house, DC-area Employees
BROWN, J. Noah: Director, Public Policy
TAYLOR, Ray: President and Chief Exec. Officer
VAUGHAN, Katrina: Senior Associate, Public Policy

Ass'n of Consulting Foresters of America

732 N. Washington St.
Suite 4A
Alexandria, VA 22314
Web: www.acf-foresters.com
E-mail: director@acf-foresters.com
Tel: (703)548-0990
Fax: (703)548-6395

A 600+ organization working to advance the professionalism, ethics, and interests of professional foresters whose primary work is consulting to the public.

Leg. Issues: AGR, ENV, TAX

In-house, DC-area Employees
WILSON, Lynn: Executive Director

Outside Counsel/Consultants
Washington Resource Associates
Issues: AGR, ENV, TAX

Ass'n of Directory Publishers

Wrentham, MA
Leg. Issues: CPT, TEC

Outside Counsel/Consultants
Podesta/Mattoon
Issues: CPT
Rep By: Claudia James, Anthony T. Podesta
Willkie Farr & Gallagher
Issues: TEC
Rep By: Russell L. Smith

Ass'n of Disposable Device Manufacturers (ADDM)

1429 G St. NW
P.O. Box 344
Washington, DC 20005
Tel: (202)737-7554
Fax: (202)737-9329
Registered: LDA
Leg. Issues: HCR, MED

In-house, DC-area Employees
TORRENTE, Josephine M.: President

Ass'n of Farmworker Opportunity Programs

4350 N. Fairfax Dr.
Suite 410
Arlington, VA 22203
Web: www.afop.org
E-mail: afop@afop.org
Tel: (703)528-4141
Fax: (703)528-4145

A national federation of non-profit organizations and state agencies using federal dollars (under title IV, section 402 of the JTPA Act of 1982) to provide training leading to full-time employment for eligible migrant and seasonal farmworkers in 49 states and Puerto Rico. Founded in 1971.

In-house, DC-area Employees
DECARLO, Jacqueline: Senior Manager, AmeriCorps Program
MAKI, Reid: Manager, Department of Labor Project
STRAUSS, David: Exec. Director

Ass'n of Female Exhibit Contractors and Event Organizers

Outside Counsel/Consultants
Ass'n Management Bureau
Rep By: Maria E. Brennan

Ass'n of Financial Guaranty Insurers

New York, NY
Leg. Issues: BNK, ECN, FIN, TAX, TRA

Outside Counsel/Consultants
Canfield & Associates, Inc.
Issues: BNK, ECN, FIN, TAX, TRA
Rep By: Roger Blauwet, April Boston, Anne C. Canfield

Ass'n of Financial Services Holding Companies

888 17th St. NW
Suite 312
Washington, DC 20006
Web: www.afshc.org
E-mail: afshc@ibm.net
Tel: (202)223-6575
Fax: (202)331-3836
Registered: LDA

A non-profit trade organization made up of holding companies that own federally insured commercial banks, savings institutions and limited purpose institutions, as well as a variety of non-depository affiliates. Its members have combined assets in excess of $1.5 trillion.

Leg. Issues: BAN

Political Action Committee/s
Ass'n of Financial Services Holding Companies Political Action Committee
888 17th St. NW
Suite 312
Washington, DC 20006
Contact: Patrick A. Forte
Tel: (202)223-6575
Fax: (202)331-3836

In-house, DC-area Employees
FORTE, Patrick A.: President
GRAY, Geoffrey P.: Director, Government Relations
WILLIAMS, Harding deC.: Counsel

Outside Counsel/Consultants
Miller & Chevalier, Chartered
Issues: BAN
Rep By: Leonard Bickwit, Jr.

Ass'n of Flight Attendants

1275 K St. NW
Fifth Floor
Washington, DC 20005
Web: www.afanet.org
E-mail: afatalk@afanet.org
Tel: (202)712-9799
Fax: (202)712-9792
Registered: LDA
Leg. Issues: AVI, BUD, CAW, CIV, CSP, GOV, LAW, LBR, TOB

Political Action Committee/s
Ass'n of Flight Attendants Political Action Committee/Flight PAC
1275 K St. NW
Fifth Floor
Washington, DC 20005
Contact: Jo Ellen Deutsch
Tel: (202)712-9799
Fax: (202)712-9792

In-house, DC-area Employees
DEUTSCH, Jo Ellen: Director, Government Affairs
DONAHUE, George: V. President
FRIEND, Patricia: President
LARSON, Shane
MACKINNON, Paul: Secretary/Treasurer
WITKOWSKI, Christopher: Director, Air Safety

Ass'n of Floral Importers of Florida

Miami, FL

Outside Counsel/Consultants
Arnold & Porter

Ass'n of Food Industries, Inc.

Matawan, NJ

Outside Counsel/Consultants
Harris Ellsworth & Levin
Rep By: Cheryl N. Ellsworth, Hon. Herbert E. Harris, II, Jeffrey S. Levin

Ass'n of Foreign Investors in U.S. Real Estate

700 13th St. NW
Suite 950
Washington, DC 20005
Web: www.afire.org
E-mail: afire@afire.org
Tel: (202)434-4510
Fax: (202)434-4509

Established 1988 as the offical spokesman for the foreign real estate investment industry.

In-house, DC-area Employees
FETGATTER, James A.: Chief Executive

Outside Counsel/Consultants
The Plexus Consulting Group

Ass'n of Former Intelligence Officers

6723 Whittier Ave.
Suite 303A
McLean, VA 22101
Web: www.afio.com
E-mail: afio@his.com
Tel: (703)790-0320
Fax: (703)790-0264

Members are former personnel from all military and civilian intelligence and security agencies. Purpose is to promote public understanding and support for a strong and responsible national intelligence establishment. Conducts a number of essentially educational activities and projects.

In-house, DC-area Employees
JONKERS, Roy K.: Exec. Director

Ass'n of Freestanding Radiation Oncology Centers

Laguna Beach, CA
Leg. Issues: MMM

Outside Counsel/Consultants
McDermott, Will and Emery
Issues: MMM
Rep By: Eric P. Zimmerman

Ass'n of Fund Raising Professionals

1101 King St.
Suite 700
Alexandria, VA 22314
Web: www.afpnet.org
E-mail: afp@afpnet.org
Tel: (703)684-0410
Fax: (703)684-0540
Registered: LDA

Advances philanthropy through education, training and advocacy based on research, a code of ethical principles and standards of professional practice.

Leg. Issues: TAX

In-house, DC-area Employees
MAEHARA, Paulette V.: President and Chief Exec. Officer
NILSEN, Michael: Manager, Public Affairs
SCZUDLO, Walter: V. President, Public Affairs & General Counsel

Ass'n of Fund-Raising Distributors and Suppliers

1101 15th St. NW
Suite 202
Washington, DC 20005
Tel: (202)785-3232
Fax: (202)223-9741

In-house, DC-area Employees
CRISTOL, Richard E.: Washington Representative

Outside Counsel/Consultants
The Kellen Company
Rep By: Richard E. Cristol

Ass'n of German Chambers of Industry & Commerce (DIHT)

Berlin, GERMANY
Leg. Issues: TRD

Outside Counsel/Consultants
Representative of German Industry and Trade
Issues: TRD
Rep By: Robert Bergmann, Peter J. C. Esser

Ass'n of Governing Boards of Universities and Colleges

One Dupont Circle NW
Suite 400
Washington, DC 20036
Tel: (202)296-8400
Fax: (202)223-7053
Web: www.agb.org
Leg. Issues: EDU

In-house, DC-area Employees
INGRAM, Richard T.: President

Outside Counsel/Consultants
Mintz, Levin, Cohn, Ferris, Glovsky and Popeo, P.C.
Rep By: Raymond D. Cotton

Ass'n of Government Accountants

2208 Mount Vernon Ave.
Alexandria, VA 22301-1314
Tel: (703)684-6931
Fax: (703)548-9367
Web: www.agacgfm.org
Leg. Issues: ACC, GOV

In-house, DC-area Employees
CULKIN, Jr., Charles W.: Exec. Director

Outside Counsel/Consultants
Halsey, Rains & Associates, LLC
Issues: GOV
Rep By: Steven C. Halsey, James Hubbard, Laurie D. Rains
Webster, Chamberlain & Bean

Ass'n of Health Information Outsourcing Services

Malvern, PA
Leg. Issues: MMM

Outside Counsel/Consultants
Reed, Smith, LLP
Issues: MMM
Rep By: Phillips S. Peter, Marc Scheineson

Ass'n of Hispanic Advertising Agencies

E-mail: info@attaa.org

Outside Counsel/Consultants
Ass'n Management Group
Rep By: Horacio Gavilan

Ass'n of Home Appliance Manufacturers

1111 19th St. NW
Suite 402
Washington, DC 20036
Tel: (202)872-5955
Fax: (202)434-7400
Registered: LDA
Web: www.aham.org
E-mail: ahamdc@aham.org
Leg. Issues: BNK, BUD, CSP, ENG, ENV, MAN, TAX, TRD

Political Action Committee/s
Ass'n of Home Appliance Manufacturers Political Action Committee
1111 19th St. NW
Suite 402
Washington, DC 20036
Tel: (202)872-5955
Fax: (202)434-7400

In-house, DC-area Employees
KROMER, Kathi J.: Manager, Gov't Relations
SAMUELS, Charles A.: Government Relations Counsel

Outside Counsel/Consultants
Mintz, Levin, Cohn, Ferris, Glovsky and Popeo, P.C.
Issues: BNK, CSP, ENG, ENV, TRD
Rep By: Charles A. Samuels
Washington Council Ernst & Young
Issues: ENG, ENV, TAX
Rep By: Doug Badger, Lauren Darling, John L. Doney, Jayne T. Fitzgerald, LaBrenda Garrett-Nelson, Gary J. Gasper, Bruce A. Gates, Nick Giordano, Robert J. Leonard, Richard Meltzer, Phillip D. Moseley, John D. Porter, Robert M. Rozen, Donna Steele-Flynn, Timothy J. Urban

Ass'n of Independent Colleges of Art and Design

1213 29th St. NW
Washington, DC 20007
Tel: (202)333-5841
Fax: (202)333-5881
E-mail: bbaicad@best.com

In-house, DC-area Employees
DUNCAN, Jack G.: Legislative Counsel

Outside Counsel/Consultants
Duncan and Associates
Rep By: Jack G. Duncan

Ass'n of Independent Corrugated Converters

113 S. West St.
P.O. Box 25708
Alexandria, VA 22313
Tel: (703)836-2422
Fax: (703)836-2795
Web: www.aiccbox.org
E-mail: aicc@aiccbox.org
Leg. Issues: MAN, SMB

In-house, DC-area Employees
YOUNG, Steve: Exec. V. President

Ass'n of Independent Research Institutes

Westminster, MD
Web: www.airi.org
Leg. Issues: BUD, CPT, HCR, IMM, MED, SCI, TAX

Outside Counsel/Consultants
Lewis-Burke Associates
Issues: BUD, CPT, HCR, IMM, MED, SCI, TAX
Rep By: Rachel Brown, April L. Burke, Mark Marin

Ass'n of Industrialists and Businessmen of Tatarstan

Kazan, RUSSIA

Outside Counsel/Consultants
Murray, Scheer, Montgomery, Tapia & O'Donnell
Rep By: D. Michael Murray

Ass'n of Internat'l Automobile Manufacturers

1001 19th St. North
Suite 1200
Arlington, VA 22209
Tel: (703)525-7788
Fax: (703)525-3289
Registered: LDA
Web: www.aiam.org

A trade association representing the U.S. subsidiaries of internat'l automobile companies doing business in the United States. Member companies distribute passenger cars, multipurpose passenger vehicles and light trucks manufactured in the United States and overseas.

Leg. Issues: AUT, ENV, MAN, TRD

In-house, DC-area Employees
CABANISS, John: Director, Government and Energy
CAMMISA, Mike: Director, Safety
LOCKWOOD, II, Charles H.: V. President and General Counsel
MACCARTHY, Timothy C.: President and Chief Exec. Officer
RYAN, Paul D.: Director, Commercial Affairs

Ass'n of Jesuit Colleges and Universities

One Dupont Circle
Suite 405
Washington, DC 20036
Tel: (202)862-9893
Fax: (202)862-8523
Registered: LDA
Web: www.ajcunet.edu
E-mail: blkrobe@aol.com
Leg. Issues: BUD, EDU, TAX

In-house, DC-area Employees
LITTLEFIELD, Cynthia A.: Director, Federal Relations

Ass'n of Junior Leagues, Internat'l

1319 F St. NW
Suite 604
Washington, DC 20004
Tel: (202)393-3364
Fax: (202)393-4517
Web: www.ajli.org

An international organization of women committed to promoting voluntarism and the development of women and to improving the community through the effective action and leadership of trained volunteers.

In-house, DC-area Employees
DOUGLASS, Mary: Senior Associate/Meetings Manager

Ass'n of Legal Administrators, Capital Chapter

Web: www.alacapchap.org
E-mail: jenglish@alacapchap.org

Outside Counsel/Consultants
Ass'n Management Group

Ass'n of Local Air Pollution Control Officials

444 N. Capitol St. NW
Suite 307
Washington, DC 20001
Tel: (202)624-7864
Fax: (202)624-7863
Web: www.4cleanair.org
E-mail: 4clnair@sso.org

A national association of air pollution control officials with local jurisdiction.

Leg. Issues: ENV

In-house, DC-area Employees
BECKER, S. William: Exec. Director

Ass'n of Local Housing Finance Agencies

Washington, DC
Web: www.alhfa.com
E-mail: johnmurphy@dc.sba.com
Leg. Issues: HOU

Outside Counsel/Consultants
Smith, Bucklin and Associates, Inc.
Issues: HOU
Rep By: Frank M. Moore, John C. Murphy

Ass'n of Local Television Stations

1320 19th St. NW
Suite 300
Washington, DC 20036
Tel: (202)887-1970
Fax: (202)887-0950
Registered: LDA
Web: www.altv.com
Leg. Issues: COM, CPT

In-house, DC-area Employees
DONOVAN, David L.: V. President, Legal and Legislative Affairs
GIROUX, Angela: Director, Congressional Relations
HEDLUND, James B.: President
POPHAM, James: V. President, General Counsel

Ass'n of Maquiladores

San Pedro Sula, HONDURAS
Leg. Issues: APP, GOV, TRD

Outside Counsel/Consultants
Schmeltzer, Aptaker & Shepard, P.C.
Issues: APP, GOV, TRD
Rep By: C. Mateo Paz-Soldan, J. Anthony Smith

Ass'n of Maternal and Child Health Programs (AMCHP)

1220 19th St. NW
Washington, DC 20036
Tel: (202)775-0436
Fax: (202)775-0061
Registered: LDA
Web: www.amchp.org
E-mail: ddietrich@amchp.org
Leg. Issues: BUD, HCR, MED, MMM, WEL

In-house, DC-area Employees
DIETRICH, Deborah F.: Director, Legislative Affairs
GOLDSON, Christopher
HESS, Catherine

Ass'n of Medical Device Reprocessors

Washington, DC
Leg. Issues: BUD, MED

Outside Counsel/Consultants
Olsson, Frank and Weeda, P.C.
Issues: MED
Rep By: John W. Bode, Pamela J. Furman, Susan P. Grymes, Karen Reis Harned, Stephen L. Lacey, Marshall L. Matz, Tyson Redpath, Ryan W. Stroschein, Stephen D. Terman
The PMA Group
Issues: BUD, MED
Rep By: Kaylene Green, Paul J. Magliocchetti, Timothy K. Sanders

Ass'n of Meeting Professionals

1255 23rd St. NW
Suite 200
Washington, DC 20037
Tel: (202)452-8888
Fax: (202)452-0008

In-house, DC-area Employees
HAUCK, Graham S.: Exec. Director
MURPHY, Christopher M.: Senior Director

Ass'n of Metropolitan Sewerage Agencies

1816 Jefferson Place NW
Washington, DC 20036
Tel: (202)833-2672
Fax: (202)833-4657
Registered: LDA
Web: www.amsa-cleanwater.org
E-mail: kkirk@amsa-cleanwater.org

Members are publicly-owned wastewater treatment agencies. Assists its members in achieving efficient, cost-effective and sound public health and environmental goals for its users.

Leg. Issues: BUD, CAW, ENV, GOV, NAT, URB, UTI, WAS

In-house, DC-area Employees

DANNENFELDT, Paula: Deputy Exec. Director
GARRIGAN, Lee: Manager, Government Affairs
HORNBACK, Chris: Director, Government Affairs
KIRK, Ken: Exec. Director
SCHANER, Greg: Manager, Government Affairs

Outside Counsel/Consultants

LeBoeuf, Lamb, Greene & MacRae L.L.P.
Issues: BUD, ENV
Rep By: D. Randall Benn

Murray, Scheer, Montgomery, Tapia & O'Donnell
Rep By: John H. Montgomery

Ass'n of Metropolitan Water Agencies

1717 K St. NW
Suite 801
Washington, DC 20036
Tel: (202)331-2820
Fax: (202)785-1845
Registered: LDA
Web: www.amwa.net

Represents the nation's largest water suppliers before Congress and federal agencies and provides information on a national drinking water policy.

Leg. Issues: UTI

In-house, DC-area Employees

ARCENEAUX, Michael N.: Director, Legislative and Public Affairs
MOSHER, Jeffrey: Director, Technical Services
VANDE HEI, Diane: Exec. Director

Outside Counsel/Consultants

Powers Pyles Sutter & Verville, PC
Issues: UTI
Rep By: Robert J. Saner, II

Ass'n of Military Colleges and Schools of the U.S.

9429 Garden Ct.
Potomac, MD 20854-3964
Tel: (301)765-0695
Fax: (301)983-0583
Web: www.amcsus.org
E-mail: sorleydog@erols.com

Focuses on value-centered education for member military colleges and schools.

In-house, DC-area Employees

SORLEY, Dr. Lewis: Exec. Director

Ass'n of Military Surgeons of the U.S. (AMSUS)

9320 Old Georgetown Rd.
Bethesda, MD 20814
Tel: (301)897-8800
Fax: (301)530-5446
Web: www.amsus.org
E-mail: amsus@amsus.org

A membership organization comprised of healthcare professionals of all disciplines working in federal medicine. Works to increase the efficiency of its membership and advance the knowledge of federal medicine. Supports developments in technology, education, management and research involving federal medical services.

Leg. Issues: DEF, GOV, HCR, VET

In-house, DC-area Employees

MIRICK, USAF(Ret.), Col. Steven C.: Assistant Exec. Director
SANFORD, USN (Ret.), Rear Adm. Frederic G.: Exec. Director

Ass'n of Minnesota Counties

St. Paul, MN
Leg. Issues: AGR, DIS, HCR, TRA, WAS, WEL

Outside Counsel/Consultants

Lockridge Grindal & Nauen, P.L.L.P.
Issues: AGR, DIS, HCR, TRA, WAS, WEL
Rep By: Dennis McGrann

Ass'n of Minority Health Profession Schools

Washington, DC
Registered: LDA

Comprised of nine minority health professions schools in the U.S. whose mission is to help career development of health care professionals who come from disadvantaged backgrounds.

Leg. Issues: BUD, EDU, HCR

Outside Counsel/Consultants

Health and Medicine Counsel of Washington
Issues: BUD, EDU, HCR
Rep By: Staci Sigman Dennison, Dale P. Dirks, Susie Dobert, Gavin Lindberg

Ass'n of Nat'l Advertisers

1120 20th St. NW
Suite 520 South
Washington, DC 20036
Tel: (202)296-1883
Fax: (202)296-1430
Registered: LDA
Web: www.ana.net
Leg. Issues: ADV, BEV, COM, CPI, NAT, PHA, TAX, TOB

Political Action Committee/s

Pro-Ad PAC

1899 L Street NW
Suite 700
Washington, DC 20036
Contact: Carolyn W. Rae
Tel: (202)331-7345
Fax: (202)331-3675

In-house, DC-area Employees

BELLIS, James P.: Manager, Government Relations
JAFFE, Daniel L.: Exec. V. President, Director of Washington Office
RAE, Carolyn W.: PAC Contact
SCARBOROUGH, Keith A.: V. President, State Government Relations

Outside Counsel/Consultants

Davidson & Company, Inc.
Issues: ADV, TAX
Rep By: James H. Davidson, Richard E. May, Stanley Sokul

Davis Wright Tremaine LLP
Rep By: P. Cameron DeVore

Patton Boggs, LLP
Issues: ADV, BEV, TOB
Rep By: Thomas Hale Boggs, Jr., Penelope S. Farthing, John F. Fithian, Elena Giberga

Ass'n of Nat'l Estuary Programs

Palatka, FL
Leg. Issues: CAW, ENV, GOV, WAS

Outside Counsel/Consultants

Conservation Strategies, LLC
Issues: CAW, ENV, GOV, WAS

Ass'n of Nurses in AIDS Care

11250 Roger Bacon Dr.
Suite Eight
Reston, VA 20190
Tel: (703)437-4377
Fax: (703)435-4390
Web: www.anacnet.org/aids
E-mail: aidsnurses@aol.com

In-house, DC-area Employees

PRICE, CAE, Randall C.: Exec. Director

Outside Counsel/Consultants

Drohan Management Group
Rep By: Randall C. Price, CAE

Ass'n of O & C Counties

Roseburg, OR
Leg. Issues: RES

Outside Counsel/Consultants

Jamison and Sullivan, Inc.
Issues: RES
Rep By: Delos Cy Jamison, Jay R. Sullivan

Ass'n of Occupational and Environmental Clinics

1010 Vermont Ave. NW
Suite 513
Washington, DC 20005
Tel: (202)347-4976
Fax: (202)347-4950
Web: www.aoec.org
E-mail: aoec@aoec.org

Established in 1987, AOEC works to enhance the practice of occupational and environmental medicine through information sharing, education, and research.

In-house, DC-area Employees

KIRKLAND, Katherine H.: Exec. Director

Ass'n of Occupational Health Professionals in Healthcare

11250 Roger Bacon Dr.
Suite 8
Reston, VA 20190
Tel: (703)437-4377
Fax: (703)435-4390
Web: www.aohp.org/aohp/
E-mail: aohp@aohp.org

In-house, DC-area Employees

THOMPSON, Maureen: Exec. Director

Outside Counsel/Consultants

Drohan Management Group
Rep By: Randall C. Price, CAE

Ass'n of Oil Pipelines

1101 Vermont Ave. NW
Suite 604
Washington, DC 20005-3521
Tel: (202)408-7970
Fax: (202)408-7983
Registered: LDA
Web: www.aopl.org
E-mail: aopl@aopl.org

Represents common carrier, crude and product petroleum pipeline companies in Congress, before regulatory agencies, and in the federal courts. Provides information to the public on the oil pipeline industry.

Leg. Issues: ENV, FUE, TRA

In-house, DC-area Employees

COOPER, Benjamin S.: Exec. Director
JOY, Michele F.: General Counsel and Secretary
PAUL, Raymond: Director, Public Affairs

Outside Counsel/Consultants

Barbour Griffith & Rogers, Inc.
Issues: ENV, FUE, TRA
Rep By: Carl Biersack

Davis Wright Tremaine LLP
Issues: ENV, FUE, TRA
Rep By: Craig Gannett

Winner & Associates

Ass'n of Oregon Counties

Salem, OR
Leg. Issues: NAT

Outside Counsel/Consultants

Jamison and Sullivan, Inc.
Issues: NAT
Rep By: Delos Cy Jamison, Jay R. Sullivan

Ass'n of Organ Procurement Organizations

8110 Gatehouse Rd.
Suite 101 West
Falls Church, VA 22042
Tel: (703)573-2676
Fax: (703)573-0578
Web: www.aopo.org
E-mail: organdonation@aopo.org

In-house, DC-area Employees

SCHWAB, Paul: Exec. Director

Outside Counsel/Consultants

Health Policy Group
Rep By: J. Michael Hudson

Ass'n of Osteopathic Directors and Medical Educators

5550 Friendship Blvd.
Suite 300
Chevy Chase, MD 20815-7201
Tel: (301)968-2642
Fax: (301)968-4195
Web: www.aoha.org
E-mail: aodme@osteohdq.org

AODME provides leadership for the development, improvement, and evaluation of education and training of osteopathic physicians at all levels in order to further the quality of the osteopathic profession.

In-house, DC-area Employees

HARDY, Margaret: V. President, Federal Relations & Policy
KUSHNER, David L.: President and Chief Exec. Officer

Ass'n of Pain Management Anesthesiologist

Paducah, KY
Leg. Issues: MMM

Outside Counsel/Consultants

Arent Fox Kintner Plotkin & Kahn, PLLC
Issues: MMM
Rep By: Bill Applegate, Stacy Harbison, Alison Kutler, Jeff Peters, William A. Sarraille, Allison Shuren

Ass'n of Pediatric Program Directors

McLean, VA

Outside Counsel/Consultants

Degnon Associates, Inc.

Ass'n of periOperative Registered Nurses

Denver, CO
Leg. Issues: MMM

Outside Counsel/Consultants

McDermott, Will and Emery
Issues: MMM
Rep By: Michael A. Romansky, Karen S. Sealander

Ass'n of Professional Flight Attendants

Euless, TX
Leg. Issues: AVI, HCR, LBR

Outside Counsel/Consultants

Cash, Smith & Wages
Issues: AVI, HCR, LBR
Rep By: Joan B. Wages

Ass'n of Professors of Gynecology and Obstetrics

409 12th St. SW
Washington, DC 20024
Tel: (202)863-2507
Fax: (202)863-2514
Web: www.apgo.org
E-mail: webmaster@apgo.org

In-house, DC-area Employees

WACHTER, Donna D.: Exec. Director

Ass'n of Professors of Medicine

2501 M St. NW
Suite 550
Washington, DC 20037-1308
Tel: (202)861-7700
Fax: (202)861-9731
Registered: LDA
Web: www.im.org/apm
E-mail: APM@im.org

Represents the chairs of the departments of medicine at the U.S. medical schools and several of their affiliated teaching hospitals.

Leg. Issues: BUD, HCR, MED, MMM, SCI, TOB, VET

In-house, DC-area Employees

COUGHLIN, Jeffrey R.: Legislative Associate
IBRAHIM, Tod: Exec. Director

Ass'n of Progressive Rental Organizations

Austin, TX
Leg. Issues: BAN, BUD, TAX

Outside Counsel/Consultants

The Washington Group
Issues: BAN, BUD, TAX
Rep By: John D. Raffaelli, Tonya Saunders, Mark Schnabel

Ass'n of Proprietary Colleges

New York, NY
Leg. Issues: EDU

Outside Counsel/Consultants

Fern M. Lapidus
Issues: EDU
Rep By: Fern M. Lapidus

Ass'n of Publicly Traded Companies

Washington, DC
Web: www.aptc.org
E-mail: aptc@aptc.org

Members are smaller and mid-cap companies that trade their stock on U.S. stock markets. Acts as a voice for all publicly traded companies in regulatory and legislative matters which affect the fairness and efficiency of capital markets and the cost of capital. APTC focuses on the Securities and Exchange Commission and the congressional committees with jurisdiction over the securities laws. APTC also provides various services needed by publicly traded companies.

Leg. Issues: ACC, FIN, SMB, TAX

Outside Counsel/Consultants

Mayer, Brown & Platt
Issues: ACC, FIN, SMB, TAX
Rep By: Brian T. Borders, Mark H. Gitenstein

The Plexus Consulting Group

Ass'n of Reproductive Health Professionals

2401 Pennsylvania Ave. NW
Suite 350
Washington, DC 20037-1718
Tel: (202)466-3825
Fax: (202)466-3826
Web: www.arhp.org
E-mail: arhp@arhp.org

An interdisciplinary medical, professional association composed of obstetrician/gynecologists and other physicians, advanced practice clinicians, researchers, educators, and other professionals in reproductive health. Mission is to educate health care professionals and the public on family planning, contraception, and other reproductive health issues, including sexually transmitted diseases, HIV/AIDS, urogenital disorders, abortion, menopause, cancer prevention, sexual health, and infertility.

In-house, DC-area Employees

SHIELDS, Wayne C.: President and Chief Exec. Officer

Ass'n of Research Libraries

21 Dupont Circle NW
Suite 800
Washington, DC 20036
Tel: (202)296-2296
Fax: (202)872-0884
Registered: LDA
Web: www.arl.cni.org
E-mail: arlhq@arl.org
Leg. Issues: CPT, GOV

In-house, DC-area Employees

ADLER, Prudence: Assistant Exec. Director, Federal Relations and Information Policy
BARETT, Jaia: Deputy Exec. Director
WEBSTER, Duane: Exec. Director

Outside Counsel/Consultants

Squire, Sanders & Dempsey L.L.P.
Rep By: Ritchie T. Thomas

Ass'n of Retail Travel Agents

Lexington, KY
Leg. Issues: TOU

Outside Counsel/Consultants

The Roth Group
Issues: TOU
Rep By: Jayd Henricks, Hon. Toby Roth, Sr.

Ass'n of Sales & Marketing Companies

2100 Reston Pkwy.
Suite 400
Reston, VA 20191-1218
Tel: (703)758-7790
Fax: (703)758-7787
Web: www.asmc.org
E-mail: info@asmc.org

Association of Sales & Marketing Agencies.

Leg. Issues: FOO, GOV, LBR, SMB, TAX

In-house, DC-area Employees

ABRAHAM, Rick: President, ASMC Foodservice
BAUM, Mark W.: President
CONNELL, Karen: Exec. V. President

Outside Counsel/Consultants

Maloney & Knox, LLP
Issues: FOO, GOV, LBR, SMB, TAX
Rep By: Barry C. Maloney

Ass'n of School Business Officials Internat'l

11401 N. Shore Dr.
Reston, VA 20190-4200
Tel: (703)478-0405
Fax: (703)478-0205
Web: www.asbointl.org
E-mail: ditharpe@sprynet.com
Leg. Issues: ECN

In-house, DC-area Employees

THARPE, Ed.D., Don I.: Exec. Director

Outside Counsel/Consultants

Albertine Enterprises, Inc.
Issues: ECN
Rep By: James J. Albertine

Webster, Chamberlain & Bean
Rep By: Arthur Herold

Ass'n of Schools and Colleges of Optometry

6110 Executive Blvd.
Suite 510
Rockville, MD 20852
Tel: (301)231-5944
Fax: (301)770-1828
Web: www.opted.org
E-mail: mwall@opted.org

The national organization advancing and promoting optometric education. A member organization of the Federation of Associations of Schools of the Health Professions in Washington.

Leg. Issues: EDU

In-house, DC-area Employees

WALL, CAE, Martin A.: Exec. Director

Ass'n of Schools of Allied Health Professions

1730 M St. NW
Suite 500
Washington, DC 20036
Tel: (202)293-4848
Fax: (202)293-4852
Web: www.asahp.org
E-mail: asahp1@asahp.org

Membership consists primarily of institutions offering degrees in allied health fields, and faculty or academic staff employed by these institutions.

In-house, DC-area Employees

ELWOOD, Thomas W.: Exec. Director

Ass'n of Schools of Public Health

1101 15th St. NW
Suite 910
Washington, DC 20005
Tel: (202)296-1099
Fax: (202)296-1252
Web: www.asph.org
E-mail: info@asph.org

A member organization representing the 28 accredited graduate schools of Public Health in the U.S. and Puerto Rico. Its mission is to serve the collective needs of the Schools of Public Health as they pursue the education and training of public health professionals.

Leg. Issues: BUD, EDU, HCR, MED

In-house, DC-area Employees

GEMMELL, Michael K.: Exec. Director

Outside Counsel/Consultants

Luman, Lange & Wheeler
Rep By: Gene C. Lange

Van Scoyoc Associates, Inc.
Issues: BUD, EDU, HCR, MED
Rep By: Steve E. Crane, Kevin F. Kelly, Evan Knisely, H. Stewart Van Scoyoc

Ass'n of Science Technology Centers, Inc.

1025 Vermont Ave. NW
Suite 500
Washington, DC 20005
Tel: (202)783-7200
Fax: (202)783-7207
Web: www.astc.org
E-mail: info@astc.org

A non-profit association of science centers and museums dedicated to the public understanding of science to all people.

Leg. Issues: EDU, SCI

In-house, DC-area Employees

VANDORN, Bonnie: Exec. Director

Ass'n of Small Business Development Centers

8990 Burke Lake Rd.
Burke, VA 22015
Tel: (703)764-8950
Fax: (703)764-1234
Web: www.asbdc-us.org
E-mail: info@asbdc-us.org
Leg. Issues: ECN, FOR, SMB

In-house, DC-area Employees

MCCUTCHEN, Woodrow: President/Chief Exec. Officer

Outside Counsel/Consultants

Thomas G. Powers
Issues: SMB
Rep By: Thomas G. Powers

The Solomon Group, LLC
Issues: ECN, FOR, SMB
Rep By: David M. Lonie, Hon. Gerald B. H. Solomon, William R. Teator

Zeliff, Ireland, and Associates
Issues: SMB
Rep By: Hon. William H. Zeliff, Jr.

Ass'n of State and Interstate Water Pollution Control Administrators

750 First St. NE
Suite 1010
Washington, DC 20002
Tel: (202)898-0905
Fax: (202)898-0929
Web: www.asiwpca.org
E-mail: admin1@asiwpca.org

In-house, DC-area Employees

HALEY, Roberta: Exec. Director

Ass'n of State and Territorial Chronic Disease Program Directors

Outside Counsel/Consultants

Ass'n and Soc. Management Internat'l Inc.
Rep By: Michael Stewart

Ass'n of State and Territorial Health Officials

1275 K St. NW
Suite 800
Washington, DC 20005
Tel: (202)371-9090
Fax: (202)371-9797
Registered: LDA
Web: www.astho.org
E-mail: jhohl@astho.org

Represents the interests of senior health officials in the states and territories of the U.S.

Leg. Issues: HCR

In-house, DC-area Employees

BRYAN, Jacalyn L.: Deputy Director for Policy & Programs
HARDY, Jr., George: Exec. Director

Ass'n of State and Territorial Public Health Laboratory Directors

1211 Connecticut Ave. NW
Suite 608
Washington, DC 20036
Tel: (202)822-5227
Fax: (202)887-5098
Web: www.astphld.org

In-house, DC-area Employees

BECKER, Scott: Exec. Director
CLARK, Carol J.: Director, Administration

Ass'n of State and Territorial Solid Waste Management Officials

444 N. Capitol St. NW
Suite 315
Washington, DC 20001
Tel: (202)624-5828
Fax: (202)624-7875
Web: www.astswmo.org
Leg. Issues: ENV

In-house, DC-area Employees

KENNEDY, Thomas: Exec. Director

Ass'n of State Dam Safety Officials

1015 15th St. NW
Suite 600
Washington, DC 20005
Tel: (202)789-2200
Fax: (202)289-6797

Headquartered in Lexington, KY.

Leg. Issues: BUD

In-house, DC-area Employees

PALLASCH, Brian T.: Washington Representative

Ass'n of Surgical Technologists

Englewood, CO
Web: www.ast@ast.org
E-mail: ast@ast.org
Leg. Issues: HCR, MMM

Outside Counsel/Consultants

Capitol Associates, Inc.
Issues: HCR, MMM
Rep By: William A. Finerfrock

Ass'n of Teacher Educators

1900 Association Dr.
Suite ATE
Reston, VA 20191-1502
Tel: (703)620-3110
Fax: (703)620-9530
Web: www.siu.edu/departments/coe/ate
E-mail: ate1@aol.com

A national, individual membership association dedicated to the improvement of teacher education. Founded in 1920, ATE provides opportunities for professional growth and development through publications and conferences, workshops, and academies on current issues in the field. Monitors and reports federal legislation.

In-house, DC-area Employees

MONTGOMERY, Lynn: Exec. Director

Outside Counsel/Consultants

Cranwell & O'Connell
Rep By: George E. Cranwell

Ass'n of Teachers of Preventive Medicine

1660 L St. NW
Suite 208
Washington, DC 20036
Tel: (202)463-0550
Fax: (202)463-0555
Web: www.atpm.org
E-mail: info@atpm.org

In-house, DC-area Employees

CALKINS, Barbara J.: Exec. Director

Ass'n of Technology Act Projects

Springfield, IL
Leg. Issues: BUD, SCI

Outside Counsel/Consultants

Dean Blakey & Moskowitz
Issues: BUD, SCI
Rep By: Ellin J. Nolan

Ass'n of TEH Act Projects

Leg. Issues: GOV

Outside Counsel/Consultants

Jane West
Issues: GOV
Rep By: Jane West, Ph.D.

Ass'n of Telemessaging Services Internat'l

Washington, DC
Web: www.atsi.org

Outside Counsel/Consultants

Smith, Bucklin and Associates, Inc.

Ass'n of Test Publishers

1201 Pennsylvania Ave. NW
Suite 300
Washington, DC 20004
Tel: (202)857-8444
Web: www.testpublishers.org

A nonprofit trade association representing providers of assessments and assessment services.

Leg. Issues: CIV, CPI, CPT, EDU, LBR, MIA

In-house, DC-area Employees

HARRIS, Ph.D., William G.: Exec. Director
SCHEIB, Lauren: Administrator

Outside Counsel/Consultants

Thiemann Aitken Vohra & Rutledge, L.L.C.
Issues: CIV, CPI, CPT, EDU, LBR, MIA
Rep By: Alan J. Thiemann

Ass'n of the Nonwoven Fabrics Industry - INDA

Cary, NC
Leg. Issues: CAW, ENV, TRD

Outside Counsel/Consultants

Mayberry & Associates LLC
Issues: CAW, ENV, TRD
Rep By: Peter G. Mayberry

Ass'n of the United States Army

2425 Wilson Blvd.
Arlington, VA 22201-3385
Tel: (703)841-4300
Fax: (703)525-9039
Registered: LDA
Web: www.ausa.org
E-mail: ausa-info@ausa.org
Leg. Issues: DEF, DOC

In-house, DC-area Employees

GRADY, John: Director, Communications
MOLINO, John: Director, Government Affairs
SULLIVAN, USA(Ret), General Gordon R.: President

Outside Counsel/Consultants

Potomac Strategies Internat'l LLC
Issues: DEF, DOC
Rep By: Raymond F. DuBois, Jr., James K. Wholey

Ass'n of Trial Lawyers of America

1050 31st St. NW
Washington, DC 20007
Tel: (202)965-3500
Fax: (202)342-5484
Registered: LDA
Web: www.atlanet.org
Leg. Issues: AVI, BNK, BUD, CPI, CSP, GOV, HCR, INS, TAX, TEC, TOB, TOR, TRA

Political Action Committee/s

Ass'n of Trial Lawyers of America Political Action Committee

1050 31st St. NW
Washington, DC 20007
Tel: (202)965-3500
Fax: (202)342-5484

In-house, DC-area Employees

CARL, Carlton: Director, Media Relations
COHEN, Dan: Director, National Affairs
HENDERSON, Jr., Thomas H.: Chief Exec. Officer
LEHRMAN, Margie: Senior Director, Legal Knowledge & Professional Development
LIPSEN, Linda A.: Senior Director, Public and National Affairs
PECK, Robert: Director, Legal Affairs
STARR, Michael: General Counsel
STEINMAN, Susan: Public Affairs Counsel
WALKER, Donald: Senior Director, Finance and Administration

Outside Counsel/Consultants

Forscey & Stinson, PLLC
Issues: TOR
Rep By: Michael A. Forscey

Patton Boggs, LLP
Issues: AVI, BNK, BUD, CPI, CSP, GOV, HCR, INS, TAX, TEC, TOB, TOR, TRA
Rep By: Thomas Hale Boggs, Jr., Brian C. Lopina, Karen L. Marangi, Darryl D. Nirenberg, Andrew M. Rosenberg, Jonathan R. Yarowsky

Thomas R. "Randy" White
Issues: TOR
Rep By: Thomas R. "Randy" White

Ass'n of Universities for Research in Astronomy, Inc.

Washington, DC
Leg. Issues: BUD, EDU, TRD

Outside Counsel/Consultants

Van Scoyoc Associates, Inc.
Issues: BUD, EDU, TRD
Rep By: Steve E. Crane, Kevin F. Kelly, H. Stewart Van Scoyoc

Ass'n of University Programs in Health Administration

730 11th St. NW
Fourth Floor
Washington, DC 20001-4510
Tel: (202)638-1448
Fax: (202)638-3429
Web: www.aupha-lc.com
E-mail: aupha@aupha.com

Includes 105 university programs in North America and 60 affiliated training centers in 32 countries around the world.

Leg. Issues: BUD, EDU, HCR, MED, MIA, PHA

In-house, DC-area Employees

DALSTON, Ph.D., FAC, Jeptha W.: President and Chief Exec. Officer
MCCAIN, Mark: Director, Marketing and Communications
REED, Lydia: V. President and Chief Operating Officer

Outside Counsel/Consultants

Cavarocchi Ruscio Dennis Associates
Issues: BUD
Rep By: Lyle B. Dennis

Ass'n of Veterinary Biologics Cos.

Washington, DC

Outside Counsel/Consultants

Luman, Lange & Wheeler
Rep By: John W. Thomas

Ass'n of Water Technologies

8201 Greensboro Dr.
Suite 300
McLean, VA 22102
Tel: (703)610-9012
Fax: (703)610-9005
Web: www.awt.org
E-mail: awt@awt.org

A non-profit trade organization representing small to medium-sized independent water treatment companies and suppliers catering to the water treatment industry.

In-house, DC-area Employees

LINDSEY, Elise: Exec. Director

Outside Counsel/Consultants

Ass'n Management Group
Rep By: Elise Lindsey

Ass'n of Women in the Metal Industries

Alexandria, VA
Web: www.awmi.com
E-mail: awmihq@aol.com

Outside Counsel/Consultants

CLARION Management Resources, Inc.
Rep By: Haley Johnson, Carole M. Rogin

Ass'n of Women's Health, Obstetric and Neonatal Nurses

2000 L St. NW
Suite 740
Washington, DC 20036
Tel: (202)261-2400
Fax: (202)728-0575
Registered: LDA
Web: www.awhonn.org

Includes more than 22,000 women's health, obstetric and neonatal nurses and allied health-care professionals in the U.S. and Canada. Promotes optimal health care for women and infants and their families through education, research, consumer services and health policy development.

Leg. Issues: HCR

In-house, DC-area Employees

KINCAIDE, Gail G.: Exec. Director
RAY, Melinda Mercer: Director, Health Policy and Advocacy
THOMAS, Karen Kelly: Deputy Exec. Director

Ass'n on Third World Affairs

1629 K St. NW
Suite 802
Washington, DC 20006
Tel: (202)331-8455
Fax: (202)775-7465

In-house, DC-area Employees

HAHN, Dr. Lorna: Exec. Director

Ass'n to Unite the Democracies

502 H St. SW
Washington, DC 20024-2726
Tel: (202)544-5150
Fax: (202)544-3742
Web: www.iaud.org
E-mail: atunite@aol.com

Promotes a federation of industrial democracies to secure peace and world order, utilizing the institutions and resources of existing international organizations such as NATO, EU, and OSCE.

Leg. Issues: CON, DEF, ECN, EDU, FOR

In-house, DC-area Employees

HUDGENS, Capt. Tom: President and Chief Exec. Officer

ASSE Internat'l Student Exchange Program

Laguna Beach, CA

Outside Counsel/Consultants

Akin, Gump, Strauss, Hauer & Feld, L.L.P.

Asset Management Consultants

Leawood, KS

Outside Counsel/Consultants

Sam Richardson
Rep By: Sam Richardson

Assicurazioni Generali, S.p.A.

Trieste, ITALY

Outside Counsel/Consultants

Chlopak, Leonard, Schechter and Associates

Assiniboine and Sioux Tribes (Fort Peck Reservation)

Poplar, MT
Leg. Issues: BUD, IND

Outside Counsel/Consultants

Sonosky, Chambers, Sachse & Endreson
Issues: BUD, IND
Rep By: Mary J. Pavel, William R. Perry

Assisted Living Federation of America

11200 Waples Mill Rd.
Suite 150
Fairfax, VA 22030-7407
Tel: (703)691-8100
Fax: (703)691-8106
Web: www.alfa.org
E-mail: info@alfa.org

A national trade association dedicated to the assisted living and senior housing industry and the population it serves.

Leg. Issues: HCR, HOU, MED, MMM, RET

Political Action Committee/s

Assisted Living Federation of America PAC (ALFA PAC)

11200 Waples Mill Rd.
Suite 150
Fairfax, VA 22030-7407
Tel: (703)691-8100
Fax: (703)691-8106
Contact: Beth Singley

In-house, DC-area Employees

REDDING, Whitney: Director, Media and Public Relations
SHEEHY, Edward: V. President, State Legislative and Regulatory Affairs
SINGLEY, Beth: Director, Federal Relations
WAYNE, Karen A.: President and Chief Exec. Officer

Outside Counsel/Consultants

Arent Fox Kintner Plotkin & Kahn, PLLC
Issues: MMM
Rep By: Bill Applegate, Susan Kayser, Robert J. Waters

Associated Air Balance Council

1518 K St. NW
Suite 503
Washington, DC 20005
Tel: (202)737-0202
Fax: (202)638-4833
Web: www.aabchq.com
E-mail: aabchq@aol.com

In-house, DC-area Employees

SUFKA, Kenneth M.: Exec. Director

Outside Counsel/Consultants

Sufka & Associates
Rep By: Kenneth M. Sufka

Associated Builders and Contractors

1300 N. 17th St.
Eighth Floor
Rosslyn, VA 22209-3801
Tel: (703)812-2000
Fax: (703)812-8202
Registered: LDA
Web: www.abc.org/
E-mail: info@abc.org
Leg. Issues: BUD, ENV, LBR, TRA, UTI

Political Action Committee/s

Associated Builders and Contractors Political Action Committee (ABC-PAC)

1300 N. 17th St.
Eighth Floor
Rosslyn, VA 22209-3801
Tel: (703)812-2000
Fax: (703)812-8202
Contact: Steve Hinton

In-house, DC-area Employees

BARRETT, Michelle: Regional Field Representative
BOUCHER JAMESON, Jennifer: Director, Legislative Affairs
BRADBURY, Anne: Director, Work Place Policy
GLAZER, Melinda: Legislative Assistant
HAAS, Richard T.: V. President, Public Affairs
HINTON, Steve: PAC Coordinator
LESCOTT, Jaqueline: Regulatory Representative
LEVY, Robin: Government Affairs Assistant
MARESCA, Charles A.: Director, Legal and Regulatory Affairs
MONROE, Ned: Director, Political Development
RITTLER, Andy: Regional Field Representative
ROSENDAHL, Erik: Regional Field Representative
SHUMSKI, Scot: Regional Field Representative
SPENCER, William B.: V. President, Government Affairs
YOB, John: Regional Field Representative

Outside Counsel/Consultants

Venable
Rep By: Maurice Baskin

Associated Credit Bureaus, Inc.

1090 Vermont Ave. NW
Suite 200
Washington, DC 20005-4905
Tel: (202)371-0910
Fax: (202)371-0134
Registered: LDA
Web: www.acb_credit.com
Leg. Issues: BAN, BNK, CSP, FIN, LAW

Political Action Committee/s

Associated Credit Bureaus Inc. Political Action Committee

1090 Vermont Ave. NW
Suite 200
Washington, DC 20005-4905
Tel: (202)371-0910
Fax: (202)371-0134
Contact: D. Barry Connelly

In-house, DC-area Employees

CONNELLY, D. Barry: President
CRESCENZO, Raymond T.: V. President, Industry Relations
ELLMAN, Eric J.: Senior Manager, State Government Relations
MAGNUSON, Norman G.: V. President, Public Affairs
PRATT, Stuart K.: V. President, Government Relations

Outside Counsel/Consultants

O'Connor & Hannan, L.L.P.
Issues: BAN, CSP
Rep By: Roy C. Coffee, Timothy W. Jenkins, Thomas H. Quinn

Royer & Babyak
Issues: FIN
Rep By: Paul Nelson

Associated Equipment Distributors

c/o Obadal and MacLeod p.c.
121 N. Henry St.
Alexandria, VA 22314
Tel: (703)739-9485
Fax: (703)739-9488
Web: www.aednet.org
E-mail: aed@crosslink.net

Headquartered in Oak Brook, IL. Below address, phone, and fax is that of the firm Obadal and MacLeod, p.c.

Leg. Issues: AVI, CAW, CSP, ENV, GOV, ROD, TAX, TRA, TRD

Political Action Committee/s

Associated Equipment Distributors PAC

c/o Obadal and MacLeod p.c.
121 N. Henry St.
Alexandria, VA 22314
Tel: (703)739-9485
Fax: (703)739-9488
Contact: Christian A. Klein

In-house, DC-area Employees

KLEIN, Christian A.: PAC Contact

Outside Counsel/Consultants

Obadal and MacLeod, p.c.
Issues: AVI, CAW, CSP, ENV, GOV, ROD, TAX, TRA, TRD
Rep By: Christian A. Klein, Anthony J. Obadal

Associated Estates Co.

Cleveland, OH

Outside Counsel/Consultants

Swidler Berlin Shereff Friedman, LLP
Rep By: Harold A. Levy, Kenneth G. Lore

Associated Financial Corp.

Los Angeles, CA
Leg. Issues: HOU, TAX

Outside Counsel/Consultants

Greenberg Traurig, LLP
Issues: HOU, TAX
Rep By: Ronald L. Platt

McDermott, Will and Emery

Associated Gas Distributors

Washington, DC

Outside Counsel/Consultants

Crowell & Moring LLP
Rep By: Dana C. Contratto

Associated General Contractors of America

333 John Carlyle St.
Suite 200
Alexandria, VA 22314
Tel: (703)548-3118
Fax: (703)548-3119
Registered: LDA
Web: www.agc.org
E-mail: info@agc.org

A national trade association established in 1918 that represents qualified building, highway, municipal utilities, and heavy industrial construction contractors and industry related companies.

Leg. Issues: BUD, CAW, ENV, FAM, FOR, GOV, HCR, IMM, LBR, NAT, ROD, SMB, TAX, TRA, TRD, UTI, WAS

Political Action Committee/s

Associated General Contractors Political Action Committee

333 John Carlyle St.
Suite 200
Alexandria, VA 22314
Tel: (703)837-5362
Fax: (703)837-5407
Contact: Jeffrey D. Shoaf

In-house, DC-area Employees

ACORD, Heather: Assistant Director, Public Affairs
CASEY, Cecelia M.: Legislative Assistant, Congressional Relations
LOUGHLIN, Peter J.: Director, Congressional Relations
LUKENS, David R.: Chief Operating Officer
SANDHERR, Stephen E.: Exec. V. President and Chief Operating Officer
SHOAF, Jeffrey D.: Exec. Director, Congressional Relations
SWEATT, Loren E.: Director, Congressional Relations/Procurement and Environment
THODEN, Philip E.: Director, Congressional Relations/Tax and Fiscal Affairs

Associated Industries of Massachusetts

1730 M St. NW
Suite 911
Washington, DC 20036
Tel: (202)966-6321
Registered: LDA
Leg. Issues: MAN

In-house, DC-area Employees

BRUNO, Joseph A.: Senior V. President, Federal Relations

Associated Insurance Cos., Inc.

Indianapolis, IN
Registered: LDA

Outside Counsel/Consultants

Vorys, Sater, Seymour and Pease, LLP

Associated Landscape Contractors of America

150 Elden St.
Suite 270
Herndon, VA 20170
Tel: (703)736-9666
Fax: (703)736-9668
Web: www.alca.org
E-mail: information@alca.org

In-house, DC-area Employees

HOLDER, Debra: Exec. Director

Associated Specialty Contractors

Three Bethesda Metro Center
Suite 1100
Bethesda, MD 20814
Tel: (301)657-3110
Fax: (301)215-4500
Web: www.necanet.org

In-house, DC-area Employees

GRAU, John: President

Associated Universities Inc.

Washington, DC
Leg. Issues: BUD, CPT, EDU, GOV, IMM, SCI, TAX

Outside Counsel/Consultants

Lewis-Burke Associates
Issues: BUD, CPT, EDU, GOV, IMM, SCI, TAX
Rep By: Rachel Brown, April L. Burke, Mark A. Burnham, Michael Ledford, Mark Marin

Associates First Capital Corp.

Irving, TX

Outside Counsel/Consultants

Rhoads Group

Association des Constructeurs Europeens de Motocycles

Brussels, BELGIUM
Leg. Issues: TRD

Outside Counsel/Consultants

Oppenheimer Wolff & Donnelly LLP
Issues: TRD
Rep By: Hon. Birch Bayh, Harry W. Cladouhos, John H. Korns

Association Trends

7910 Woodmont Ave.
Suite 1150
Bethesda, MD 20814-3062
Tel: (301)652-8666
Fax: (301)656-8654
E-mail: associationtrends@associationtrends.com

A weekly newspaper carrying news and articles of value to U.S. trade and professional association executives.

In-house, DC-area Employees

CORNISH, Jill: Publisher

Assumption College

Worcester, MA
Leg. Issues: EDU, TRA

Outside Counsel/Consultants

Lawler, Metzger & Milkman, LLC
Issues: EDU, TRA
Rep By: Sante J. Esposito

Assurance Technology Corp.

Carlisle, MA
Leg. Issues: AER, DEF

Outside Counsel/Consultants

Bannerman and Associates, Inc.
Issues: DEF
Rep By: M. Graeme Bannerman, Anne Hingeley, William A. Miner, Valerie A. Schultz

Lawrence Ryan Internat'l, Inc.
Issues: AER, DEF

Assurant Group

Miami, FL Registered: LDA
Leg. Issues: BAN, DIS, ENV, FIN, HOU, INS, LAW, TAX, UTI

Outside Counsel/Consultants

Jorden Burt LLP
Issues: BAN, DIS, ENV, FIN, HOU, INS, LAW, TAX, UTI
Rep By: Patricia Branch, Marna Gettleman, Marilyn Berry Thompson, Rebecca Tidman, Marion Turner

The Assurant Group

Atlanta, GA
Leg. Issues: BAN, FIN

Outside Counsel/Consultants

Alston & Bird LLP
Issues: BAN, FIN
Rep By: Thomas M. Boyd, Dwight C. Smith, III

Astaris

St. Louis, MO

Outside Counsel/Consultants

EOP Group, Inc.

Asterisk Communications

Fort Lauderdale, FL

Outside Counsel/Consultants

Reddy, Begley, & McCormick, LLP
Rep By: Dennis F. Begley

Asthma and Allergy Foundation of America

1233 20th St. NW
Suite 402
Washington, DC 20036-2330
Web: www.aafa.org
E-mail: info@aafa.org
Tel: (800)727-8462
Fax: (202)466-8940

Supports research dedicated to finding a cure for asthma and allergy and provides asthma and allergy patients with information, referrals and practical advice.

Leg. Issues: HCR, MED, MMM

In-house, DC-area Employees

CARSON, Richard: Director, Public Policy
WORSTELL, MPH, Mary E.: Exec. Director

Outside Counsel/Consultants

Sagamore Associates, Inc.

AstraZeneca Inc.

1250 I St. NW
Suite 804
Washington, DC 20005
Tel: (202)289-2570
Fax: (202)289-2580
Registered: LDA

Formerly part of ICI Americas Inc.

Leg. Issues: BUD, CPT, ENV, GOV, HCR, MMM, TAX

In-house, DC-area Employees

CAMPBELL, Michael W.: Federal Government Affairs Assistant
MCGRATH, Dyan: Senior Manager, Federal Government Affairs
MCMILLAN, Stephen: Senior Manager, Pharmaceutical Federal Government Affairs
SCHLICHT, James P.: V. President, Government Affairs

Outside Counsel/Consultants

Bennett Turner & Coleman, LLP

Williams & Jensen, P.C.
Issues: MMM
Rep By: George G. Olsen

Astro Vision Internat'l, Inc.

Tiburon, CA
Leg. Issues: SCI

Outside Counsel/Consultants

Capitol Coalitions Inc.
Issues: SCI
Rep By: Amy R. Mehlman, Brett P. Scott, Jarvis C. Stewart

AstroVision Inc.

Gaithersburg, MD
Leg. Issues: AER, SCI

Outside Counsel/Consultants

The Wexler Group
Issues: AER, SCI
Rep By: Peter T. Holran, Patric G. Link, Hon. Robert S. Walker

AT&T

1120 20th St. NW
Suite 1000
Washington, DC 20036
Tel: (202)457-3810
Fax: (202)457-2571
Registered: LDA

Headquartered in Basking Ridge, NJ.

Leg. Issues: BUD, COM, CPT, DEF, ENV, FIN, GOV, SCI, TAX, TEC, TEL, TRD

Political Action Committee/s

AT&T PAC

1120 20th St. NW
Suite 1000
Washington, DC 20036
Tel: (202)457-3810
Fax: (202)457-2571

In-house, DC-area Employees

ARNOLD, Mary: V. President, Congressional Affairs
BORRELLI, Alice: Director, Federal Government Affairs
BRADY, Betsy: V. President, Federal Government Affairs
CADE, Marilyn: Director, Federal Government Affairs
CALI, Leonard J.: V. President and Director, Federal Regulatory Affairs
CARPENTER, Jr., Jot D.: V. President, Congressional Affairs
CASSIDY, Paige: V. President, Congressional Affairs
CICCONI, James W.: General Counsel and Exec. V. President, Law and Government Affairs
COFFIN, Jane: Director, International Affairs
CRANE, Rhonda: Director, International Public Affairs
DIMARTINO, Rita: Director, Federal Government Affairs
GASSTER, Elizabeth: Director, Federal Government Affairs
GRIFFIN, Charles: Director, Federal Government Affairs
JACOBY, Peter G.: V. President, Congressional Affairs
JOHNSON, Broderick D.: V. President of Congressional Relations
JOHNSON, Jr., James L.: V. President, Congressional Affairs
LUBIN, J. E.: Regulatory V. President
MACKLIN, Alice Y.: Staff Manager, Federal Government Affairs
MACOMBER, Debbie: Staff Manager, Federal Govt. Affairs
MARKIEWICZ, Stephanie J.: V. President, Congressional Affairs
MARSH, Joan: Director, Federal Government Affairs
MCGANN, James P.: Director, Media Relations
MCINTOSH, Joanna K.: V. President, International Affairs
O'HOLLAREN, Hilary: Director, Federal Government Affairs
QUINN, Robert W.: Director, Federal Government Affairs
SCARABELLO, Judy: Director, Federal Government Affairs
SHIPP, Charlie: V. President, Congressional Affairs
SIMONE, Frank: Director, Federal Government Affairs
SPURLOCK, James: Director, Federal Government Affairs
WILNER, Carol W.: V. President, Exec. Branch Advocacy

Outside Counsel/Consultants

Akin, Gump, Strauss, Hauer & Feld, L.L.P.
Issues: TEC
Rep By: Marlene M. Colucci, Joel Jankowsky, Barney J. Skladany, Jr., Daniel L. Spiegel, Jose H. Villarreal, Robin Weisman

Alpine Group, Inc.

BKSH & Associates
Issues: BUD, CPT, ENV, TAX, TEC

Boesch & Co.
Issues: TEC
Rep By: Doyce A. Boesch

Clark & Weinstock, Inc.
Issues: ENV, TEC
Rep By: Hon. Vic H. Fazio, Jr., Ed Kutler, Deirdre Stach, Sandi Stuart, Hon. John Vincent "Vin" Weber

Cormac Group, LLP

Covington & Burling
Rep By: Harvey M. Applebaum, O. Thomas Johnson, Jr.

Creative Response Concepts

Dewey Square Group
Issues: TEC
Rep By: Morris Reid

The Dutko Group, Inc.
Issues: TEC
Rep By: Kim Koontz Bayliss, Louis Lehrman, Steve Perry, Juliette M. Raffensperger, Stephen Craig Sayle

Edelman Public Relations Worldwide
Rep By: Michael K. Deaver

Jack Ferguson Associates, Inc.
Issues: TEC, TEL
Rep By: Jack Ferguson

Higgins, McGovern & Smith, LLC
Issues: TEC
Rep By: Patrick C. Koch

Hooper Owen & Winburn
Issues: COM, TEC
Rep By: David Rudd

The OB-C Group, LLC
Issues: CPT, DEF, ENV, GOV, SCI, TAX, TEC, TRD
Rep By: Thomas Keating, Kim F. McKernan, Charles J. Mellody, Patricia A. Nelson, Lawrence F. O'Brien, III, Linda E. Tarplin

O'Neill, Athy & Casey, P.C.
Issues: BUD, TEC
Rep By: Andrew Athy, Jr., Christopher R. O'Neill

Ricchetti Inc.

The Smith-Free Group
Issues: TEC, TRD
Rep By: James C. Free, W. Timothy Locke, Alicia W. Smith

Timmons and Co., Inc.
Issues: TEC
Rep By: Michael J. Bates, Douglas F. Bennett, Ellen B. Fitzgibbons, Bryce L. "Larry" Harlow, Timothy J. Keating, Tom C. Korologos, Richard J. Tarplin, William E. Timmons, Jr., William E. Timmons, Sr.

Washington Council Ernst & Young
Issues: TAX
Rep By: Doug Badger, Lauren Darling, John L. Doney, Jayne T. Fitzgerald, LaBrenda Garrett-Nelson, Gary J. Gasper, Bruce A. Gates, Nick Giordano, Cathy Koch, Robert J. Leonard, Richard Meltzer, Phillip D. Moseley, John D. Porter, Robert M. Rozen, Donna Steele-Flynn, Timothy J. Urban

The Washington Group
Issues: TEC
Rep By: Tripp Funderburk, Rita M. Lewis, G. John O'Hanlon, John D. Raffaelli, Tonya Saunders, Mark Schnabel

Wise & Associates
Issues: TEC
Rep By: Nicholas P. Wise

AT&T Broadband & Internet Service

Outside Counsel/Consultants

Brownstein Hyatt & Farber, P.C.
Rep By: William T. Brack, Thomas H. Hudson, Michael B. Levy

Mintz, Levin, Cohn, Ferris, Glovsky and Popeo, P.C.

AT&T Capital Corp.

Morristown, NJ

Outside Counsel/Consultants

Washington Council Ernst & Young
Rep By: Doug Badger, John L. Doney, Jayne T. Fitzgerald, LaBrenda Garrett-Nelson, Gary J. Gasper, Bruce A. Gates, Nick Giordano, Robert J. Leonard, Richard Meltzer, Robert M. Rozen, Timothy J. Urban

AT&T Wireless Services, Inc.

1150 Connecticut Ave. NW
Fourth Floor
Washington, DC 20036-4104
Web: www.attws.com
Tel: (202)223-9222
Fax: (202)223-9095
Registered: LDA
Leg. Issues: TEC

In-house, DC-area Employees

BRANDON, Douglas: V. President, External Affairs and Law
TIMMONS, Paula Pleas: Manager, Federal Affairs

Outside Counsel/Consultants

Cormac Group, LLP

The Dutko Group, Inc.
Issues: TEC
Rep By: Kim Koontz Bayliss, Louis Lehrman, Steve Perry, Juliette M. Raffensperger, Stephen Craig Sayle

The Hawthorn Group, L.C.
Rep By: Esther Foer

Mintz, Levin, Cohn, Ferris, Glovsky and Popeo, P.C.
Issues: TEC
Rep By: Sara F. Leibman, Howard J. Symons

Atalanta Corp.

Elizabeth, NJ

Outside Counsel/Consultants

Max N. Berry Law Offices
Rep By: Max N. Berry

Atanor, S.A.

Buenos Aires, ARGENTINA

Outside Counsel/Consultants

Porter, Wright, Morris & Arthur, LLP
Rep By: E. Jay Finkel

Athens Casino and Hotel Consortium

Old Westbury, NY
Leg. Issues: GAM

Outside Counsel/Consultants

Hogan & Hartson L.L.P.
Issues: GAM
Rep By: Christine M. Warnke

Athletic Footwear Ass'n

c/o Sporting Goods Manufacturers Ass'n
1150 17th St. NW, Suite 407
Washington, DC 20006-1604
Web: www.sportlink.com
E-mail: tomsgma@aol.com
Tel: (202)775-1762
Fax: (202)296-7462
Registered: LDA

In-house, DC-area Employees

COVE, Thomas J.: V. President, Government Relations

Atlanta, Georgia, City of

Leg. Issues: ENV, GOV

Outside Counsel/Consultants

Bracy Williams & Co.
Issues: GOV
Rep By: Michael M. Bracy, Terrence L. Bracy, James P. Brown, Laura L. Madden, Tracy P. Tucker, Susan J. Williams

Kilpatrick Stockton LLP
Issues: ENV
Rep By: J. Christopher Brady, J. Vance Hughes, Ron Raider

The Atlantic Co.

Washington, DC
Leg. Issues: ENG

Outside Counsel/Consultants

Hooper Owen & Winburn
Issues: ENG
Rep By: Daryl H. Owen

Atlantic Corridor USA

Buffalo, NY
Leg. Issues: FOR

Outside Counsel/Consultants

The Advocacy Group
Issues: FOR
Rep By: Robert E. Mills

Atlantic Council of the United States

910 17th St. NW
Tenth Floor
Washington, DC 20006
E-mail: info@acus.org
Tel: (202)463-7226
Fax: (202)463-7241

A non-profit, public policy center, promoting constructive U.S. leadership and engagement in international affairs, based on the central role of the Atlantic Community in the contemporary world.

In-house, DC-area Employees

BURWELL, Frances G.: Director, Transatlantic Relations Program
CATTO, Amb. Henry E.: Chairman
COE, Bonnie L.: Director, Atlantic-Pacific Interrelationships Program
GUERTIN, Dr. Donald L.: Director, Economics, Energy and Environment Program
JUBERT, Drew Ann: Director, Finance and Administration
MAKINS, Christopher J.: President
NELSON, C. Richard: Director, International Security

Atlantic County Utilities Authority

Pleasantville, NJ

Outside Counsel/Consultants

Wright & Talisman, P.C.
Rep By: Scott M. DuBoff

Atlantic Gulf Communities

Miami, FL

Outside Counsel/Consultants

Wilmer, Cutler & Pickering
Rep By: Daniel H. Squire

Atlantic Health Systems

Florham Park, NJ

Outside Counsel/Consultants

Jorden Burt LLP
Rep By: Patricia Branch, Alanna Dillon, Marna Gettleman, Marilyn Berry Thompson, Rebecca Tidman

Atlantic Marine Holding Co.

Jacksonville, FL
Leg. Issues: DEF

Outside Counsel/Consultants

Commonwealth Consulting Corp.
Issues: DEF
Rep By: Christopher M. Lehman

Atlantic Shores Healthcare, Inc.

Palm Beach Gardens, FL
Leg. Issues: HCR

Outside Counsel/Consultants

The Da Vinci Group
Issues: HCR
Rep By: Mark R. Smith

Atlantic States Marine Fisheries Commission

Washington, DC
Leg. Issues: MAR

Outside Counsel/Consultants

Bob Davis & Associates
Issues: MAR
Rep By: Hon. Robert W. Davis

Atlas Iron Processing, Inc.

Cleveland, OH

Outside Counsel/Consultants

Arter & Hadden

ATOFINA

Portland, OR
Leg. Issues: ENG

Outside Counsel/Consultants

Ball Janik, LLP
Issues: ENG
Rep By: Robert G. Hayes, Irene Ringwood

ATOFINA Chemicals, Inc.

1200 N. Nash St.
Suite 1150
Arlington, VA 22209
Web: www.atofinachemicals.com
E-mail: charles.kitchen@atofina.com
Tel: (703)527-2099
Fax: (703)527-2092
Registered: LDA

Headquartered in Philadelphia, PA.

Leg. Issues: AGR, CHM, ENV, LBR, NAT, TAX, TRA, TRD

Political Action Committee/s

ATOPAC
1200 N. Nash St.
Suite 1150
Arlington, VA 22209
Tel: (703)527-2099
Fax: (703)527-2092

In-house, DC-area Employees

KITCHEN, Charles A.: Director, Government Relations

Outside Counsel/Consultants

Greenberg Traurig, LLP
Rep By: Alan Slomowitz

O'Connor & Hannan, L.L.P.
Issues: ENV, NAT
Rep By: Robert W. Barrie, Hon. Thomas J. Corcoran, George J. Mannina, Jr., Patrick E. O'Donnell

Ogilvy Public Relations Worldwide

Atom Sciences, Inc.

Oak Ridge, TN
Leg. Issues: DEF, EDU

Outside Counsel/Consultants

William M. Cloherty
Issues: DEF, EDU
Rep By: William M. Cloherty

Atomic Energy of Canada

Outside Counsel/Consultants

Verner, Liipfert, Bernhard, McPherson and Hand, Chartered
Rep By: Clinton A. Vince

Attorneys' Liability Assurance Soc. Inc.

Chicago, IL
Leg. Issues: TAX

Outside Counsel/Consultants

Covington & Burling
Issues: TAX
Rep By: Roderick A. DeArment

ATX Technologies

Outside Counsel/Consultants

Nat'l Strategies Inc.
Rep By: David K. Aylward

Auaya, Inc.

Washington, DC
Leg. Issues: TAX, TEC, TRD

Outside Counsel/Consultants

Bergner Bockorny Castagnetti and Hawkins
Issues: TAX, TEC, TRD

Auburn University

Auburn, AL
Leg. Issues: AGR, AVI, LAW, TRA

Outside Counsel/Consultants

Hurt, Norton & Associates
Issues: AGR, AVI, LAW, TRA
Rep By: Robert H. Hurt, Frank Norton, Katharine Calhoun Wood

Auburn, Avilla, Bluffton, Columbia City and Other Municipalities of Indiana

Full list of municipalities includes: Auburn, Avilla, Bluffton, Columbia City, Garrett, Gas City, Mishawaka, New Carlisle, South Haven and Warren, Indiana.

Leg. Issues: ENG, GOV, UTI

Outside Counsel/Consultants

Duncan, Weinberg, Genzer & Pembroke, P.C.
Issues: ENG, GOV, UTI
Rep By: Janice L. Lower, James D. Pembroke

AuctionWatch.com

San Bruno, CA
Leg. Issues: CPI, TEC

Outside Counsel/Consultants

Perkins Coie LLP
Issues: CPI, TEC
Rep By: W. H. "Buzz" Fawcett

The Audubon Institute

New Orleans, LA
Leg. Issues: BUD, GOV, SCI

Outside Counsel/Consultants

Jones, Walker, Waechter, Poitevent, Carrere & Denegre, L.L.P.
Issues: BUD
Rep By: Paul Cambon, John J. Jaskot, R. Christian Johnsen

Van Scoyoc Associates, Inc.
Issues: BUD, GOV, SCI
Rep By: Jan Schoonmaker, H. Stewart Van Scoyoc

AUGURA

Bogota, COLOMBIA
Leg. Issues: AGR, TRD

Outside Counsel/Consultants

Manatt, Phelps & Phillips, LLP
Issues: AGR, TRD
Rep By: Susan M. Schmidt, Jessica A. Wasserman

Augusta-Richmond, Georgia, County of

Augusta, GA
Leg. Issues: VET

Outside Counsel/Consultants

Patton Boggs, LLP
Issues: VET
Rep By: John J. Deschauer, Jr., Lansing B. Lee, III

Augustine Medical

Eden Prairie, MN
Leg. Issues: HCR, MMM

Outside Counsel/Consultants

Nusgart Consulting, LLC
Issues: HCR, MMM
Rep By: Marcia Nusgart

Aunt Martha's Youth Service Center

Mattison, IL
Leg. Issues: BUD

Outside Counsel/Consultants

Capitol Associates, Inc.
Issues: BUD
Rep By: Debra M. Hardy Havens

AUPS/Mo Hussain

San Diego, CA
Leg. Issues: MAR

Outside Counsel/Consultants

Sher & Blackwell
Issues: MAR
Rep By: Earl W. Comstock, Jeffrey R. Pike

Aurora Health Care, Inc.

Milwaukee, WI
Leg. Issues: HCR

Outside Counsel/Consultants

Foley & Lardner
Issues: HCR
Rep By: Theodore H. Bornstein

Aurora, Colorado, City of

Leg. Issues: DEF, ENV

Outside Counsel/Consultants

Jefferson Government Relations, L.L.C.
Issues: DEF, ENV
Rep By: Mark S. Greenberg, William A. Roberts

Auspice, Inc.

Framingham, MA

Outside Counsel/Consultants

Cassidy & Associates, Inc.
Rep By: Jeffrey Lawrence

Austin Professional Systems, Inc.

Lewisburg, WV
Leg. Issues: FIN, GOV

Outside Counsel/Consultants

Stephens, Cross, Ihlenfeld & Boring, Inc.
Issues: FIN, GOV
Rep By: Ronald Stephens

Austin, Nichols & Co., Inc.

New York, NY

A manufacturer and distributor of alcoholic and non-alcoholic beverages.

Leg. Issues: TRD

Outside Counsel/Consultants

Powell, Goldstein, Frazer & Murphy LLP
Issues: TRD
Rep By: Daniel M. Price

Austin, Texas, City of

Leg. Issues: AVI, ENG, ENV, FUE, HOU, LAW, TRA, URB

Outside Counsel/Consultants

Barbara T. McCall Associates
Issues: ENG, HOU, LAW, TRA, URB
Rep By: Ralph Garboushian, Barbara T. McCall

Patton Boggs, LLP
Issues: ENV
Rep By: Parker Brugge, Michael J. Driver

Verner, Liipfert, Bernhard, McPherson and Hand, Chartered
Issues: AVI, FUE
Rep By: Vicki E. Hart, Jane Hickie, Ann W. Richards

Australia and New Zealand Banking Group

New York, NY

Outside Counsel/Consultants

Vorys, Sater, Seymour and Pease, LLP
Rep By: Warren W. Glick

Australian Dairy Corp.

Glen Iris, AUSTRALIA
Leg. Issues: AGR

Outside Counsel/Consultants

Collier Shannon Scott, PLLC
Issues: AGR
Rep By: Robert W. Porter

Austrian Airlines

Vienna, AUSTRIA
Leg. Issues: AVI

Outside Counsel/Consultants

Global Aviation Associates, Ltd.
Issues: AVI
Rep By: Jon F. Ash, Charles R. Chambers

Authentica Inc.

Waltham, MA
Leg. Issues: CPI

Outside Counsel/Consultants

The Advocacy Group
Issues: CPI
Rep By: George A. Ramonas

Autism Soc. of America, Inc.

7910 Woodmont Ave. — Tel: (301)657-0881
Suite 300 — Fax: (301)657-0869
Bethesda, MD 20814-3015
Web: www.autism.org

Works to increase public awareness about autism and the day-to-day issues faced by individuals with autism, their families, and the professionals with whom they interact. Provides information and education, supports research, and advocates for programs and services for the autism population.

Leg. Issues: BUD, EDU, HCR, MED

In-house, DC-area Employees
BECK, Rob: Exec. Director

Outside Counsel/Consultants

Sagamore Associates, Inc.
Issues: BUD, EDU, HCR, MED
Rep By: Dena S. Morris, David Nichols

Automated Credit Exchange

Pasadena, CA
Leg. Issues: TEC

Outside Counsel/Consultants

Halprin, Temple, Goodman & Maher
Issues: TEC
Rep By: Joel H. Bernstein

Automatic Data Processing, Inc

Roseland, NJ
Leg. Issues: TAX

Outside Counsel/Consultants

Dewey Ballantine LLP
Issues: TAX
Rep By: Basil W. Henderson, Andrew W. Kentz, John J. Salmon, James M. Wickett

Autometric Inc.

Springfield, VA
Leg. Issues: AER, CPI, DEF, EDU, LAW

Outside Counsel/Consultants

The PMA Group
Issues: DEF, LAW
Rep By: Kaylene Green, Patrick Hiu, Dr. John Lynch, Paul J. Magliocchetti, Kelli Short, Charles Smith, Thomas Veltri

Potomac Strategies & Analysis, Inc.
Rep By: Peter C. Oleson

Rooney Group Internat'l, Inc.
Issues: AER, CPI, DEF, EDU
Rep By: James W. Rooney

Automobile Manufacturers R&D Coalition

Washington, DC
Leg. Issues: TAX

Outside Counsel/Consultants

PriceWaterhouseCoopers
Issues: TAX
Rep By: Jim Carlisle, Kenneth J. Kies, Mark McConaghy, James R. Shanahan

Automotive Aftermarket Industry Ass'n

4600 East-West Hwy. — Tel: (301)654-6664
Suite 300 — Fax: (301)654-3299
Bethesda, MD 20814 — Registered: LDA
Web: www.aftermarket.org
E-mail: aaia@aftermarket.org
Leg. Issues: AUT, BNK, BUD, CAW, CHM, CPI, EDU, ENV, GOV, HCR, LBR, MAN, ROD, SMB, TAX, TOR, TRA, TRD, TRU, UNM, UTI, WAS

In-house, DC-area Employees
KADRICH, Lee
LOWE, Aaron
NOLEN, Leslie
SCOTT, Charlie

Automotive Consumer Action Program

8400 Westpark Dr. — Tel: (703)821-7144
McLean, VA 22102

Third-party mediation service that helps consumers resolve disputes with participating new car dealerships or car manufacturers.

Leg. Issues: AUT, GOV

In-house, DC-area Employees
FAQIRI, Seena

Automotive Engine Rebuilders Ass'n

Buffalo Grove, IL
Leg. Issues: AUT, CAW, TAX

Outside Counsel/Consultants

Conlon, Frantz, Phelan & Pires
Issues: AUT, CAW, TAX
Rep By: Michael J. Conlon

Automotive Maintenance and Repair Ass'n

1444 I St. NW — Tel: (202)712-9042
Washington, DC 20005 — Fax: (202)216-9646
Web: www.motorist.org
E-mail: AMRA@bostromdc.com

Works to strengthen the relationship between the motorist and the automotive service and repair industry through education and the creation of industry standards.

In-house, DC-area Employees
HARRISON, Kim: Director of Accreditation
HECKER, CAE, Larry: President

Outside Counsel/Consultants

Bostrom Corp.
Rep By: Larry Hecker, CAE

Automotive Parts and Service Alliance

4600 East-West Hwy. — Tel: (301)986-1500
Suite 300 — Fax: (301)986-9633
Bethesda, MD 20814-3415 — Registered: LDA
Web: www.aftermarket.org
E-mail: aaron.lowe@aftermarket.org

Provides government relations for manufacturers, distributors and retailers of automotive replacement parts, equipment, supplies and accessories as well as for automotive service establishments.

Leg. Issues: AUT, BNK, BUD, CAW, CPT, CSP, DEF, EDU, ENV, FOR, FUE, GOV, HCR, LBR, MAN, ROD, SCI, SMB, TAX, TOR, TRA, TRD, UTI, WAS

Political Action Committee/s

Automotive Aftermarket Political Action Committee
4600 East-West Hwy. — Tel: (301)986-1500
Suite 300 — Fax: (301)986-9633
Bethesda, MD 20814-3415
Contact: Aaron M. Lowe

In-house, DC-area Employees
KADRICH, Lee: V. President, Government Affairs and International Trade
LOWE, Aaron M.: V. President, Government Affairs

Automotive Parts Rebuilders Ass'n

4401 Fair Lakes Ct.
Suite 210
Fairfax, VA 22033-3848
Tel: (703)968-2772
Fax: (703)968-2878
Registered: LDA
Web: www.apra.org
E-mail: gager@BuyReman.com

Represents the remanufacturing industry of automotive and truck parts. Also represents the non-automotive remanufacturing industry.

Leg. Issues: AUT, CAW, ENV, MAN, TAX

In-house, DC-area Employees
GAGER, William C.: President

Outside Counsel/Consultants
Conlon, Frantz, Phelan & Pires
Issues: AUT, CAW, TAX
Rep By: Michael J. Conlon

Automotive Recyclers Ass'n

3975 Fair Ridge Dr.
Suite 20-North
Fairfax, VA 22033-2906
Tel: (703)385-1001
Fax: (703)385-1494
Registered: LDA
Web: www.autorecyc.org

Provides information, education, legislative and support services which facilitate the continued growth and evolution of the automotive recycling industry. Represents and services 2,200 companies through direct membership and about 3,500 other companies through international affiliated chapters.

Leg. Issues: AUT, ENV, SMB

In-house, DC-area Employees
STEINKULLER, William P.: Exec. V. President
WILSON, Michael E.: Manager, Governmental and Industry Relations

Automotive Refrigeration Products Institute

Fort Worth, TX
Leg. Issues: CAW

Outside Counsel/Consultants
Conlon, Frantz, Phelan & Pires
Issues: CAW
Rep By: Michael J. Conlon

Automotive Service Ass'n

313 Massachusetts Ave. NE
Washington, DC 20002
Tel: (202)543-1440
Fax: (202)543-4575
Registered: LDA
Web: www.asashop.org
Leg. Issues: AUT

Political Action Committee/s
Automotive Service Ass'n Political Action Committee
313 Massachusetts Ave. NE
Washington, DC 20002
Tel: (202)543-1440
Fax: (202)543-4575
Contact: Robert L. Redding, Jr.

In-house, DC-area Employees
REDDING, Jr., Robert L.

Outside Counsel/Consultants
Robert L. Redding
Issues: AUT
Rep By: Robert L. Redding, Jr.

Automotive Trade Ass'n Executives

8400 Westpark Dr.
McLean, VA 22102
Tel: (703)821-7072
Fax: (703)556-8581
E-mail: atae@nada.org

In-house, DC-area Employees
MARLETTE, C. Alan: Exec. Director

Automotive Warehouse Distributors Ass'n

Kansas City, MO

Outside Counsel/Consultants
Stein, Mitchell & Mezines
Rep By: Basil J. Mezines

AutoNation, Inc.

Fort Lauderdale, FL

A waste collection, disposal and recycling company. Is also the parent company of Alamo Rent-a-Car, an auto rental dealership.

Leg. Issues: AUT, EPA, TAX, TRA

Outside Counsel/Consultants
Arthur Andersen LLP
Issues: TAX
Rep By: Rachelle Bernstein, Glenn Carrington, Bryan Collins
Patton Boggs, LLP
Issues: AUT, EPA, TAX, TRA
Rep By: Parker Brugge, Penelope S. Farthing, Donald V. Moorehead, Florence W. Prioleau
Williams & Connolly
Wilmer, Cutler & Pickering
Issues: TAX
Rep By: Terrill A. Hyde, William J. Wilkins

The Auxiliary Service Corporations

Morrisville, NY
Leg. Issues: ECN, EDU

Outside Counsel/Consultants
Cassidy & Associates, Inc.
Issues: ECN, EDU
Rep By: Carl Franklin Godfrey, Jr., Arthur D. Mason, Marnie Russ

Auyua Inc.

1450 G St. NW
Suite 500
Washington, DC 20005
Registered: LDA

A communications systems provider.

Leg. Issues: BUD, CPT, ENV, HCR, IMM, LBR, SCI, TAX, TEC, TRD

In-house, DC-area Employees
CROWDERS, Charles E.
KEEFE, Kenneth
TOWNSEND, II, John B.

Avalon, New Jersey, City of

Avalon, NJ
Leg. Issues: BUD, NAT

Outside Counsel/Consultants
Marlowe and Co.
Issues: BUD, NAT
Rep By: Howard Marlowe, Jeffrey Mazzella

Avax Technologies, Inc.

Kansas City, MO
Leg. Issues: HCR, MED

Outside Counsel/Consultants
Akin, Gump, Strauss, Hauer & Feld, L.L.P.
Issues: HCR, MED
Rep By: Karen E. Goldmeier Green

Avco Financial Services

Costa Mesa, CA
Leg. Issues: TAX

Outside Counsel/Consultants
Washington Council Ernst & Young
Issues: TAX
Rep By: John L. Doney, Jayne T. Fitzgerald, LaBrenda Garrett-Nelson, Gary J. Gasper, Bruce A. Gates, Robert J. Leonard, Richard Meltzer, Robert M. Rozen, Timothy J. Urban

AVEBE America, Inc.

Princeton, NJ

Outside Counsel/Consultants
Max N. Berry Law Offices
Rep By: Max N. Berry

Avecia, Inc.

Wilmington, DE
Leg. Issues: TRD

Outside Counsel/Consultants
Smith Dawson & Andrews, Inc.
Issues: TRD
Rep By: Sherri Powar, James P. Smith

Aventis Behring

King of Prussia, PA
Leg. Issues: HCR

Outside Counsel/Consultants
RTS Consulting
Valente Lopatin & Schulze
Issues: HCR
Rep By: Richard T. Schulze, Jr.

Aventis CropScience

801 Pennsylvania Ave. NW
Suite 725
Washington, DC 20004
Tel: (202)628-0500
Fax: (202)628-6622
Registered: LDA
Web: www.aventis.com

The North American unit of Rhone-Poulenc Agro, an international crop protection business, which is a subsidiary of Rhone-Poulenc S.A., a global human, animal, and plant health business.

Leg. Issues: AGR, BNK, BUD, CAW, CPT, ENV, FOO, GOV

In-house, DC-area Employees
REIMERS, Jean D.: Director, Government Affairs

Outside Counsel/Consultants
Capitolink, LLC
Issues: AGR, CAW
Rep By: John H. Thorne, Ph.D.
Kleinfeld, Kaplan and Becker
Rep By: Peter O. Safir
Podesta/Mattoon
Issues: AGR, FOO
Rep By: Ann Delory, Anthony T. Podesta

Aventis Pasteur

801 Pennsylvania Ave. NW
Suite 725
Washington, DC 20004
Tel: (202)898-3192
Fax: (202)371-1107
Registered: LDA, FARA

A vaccine manufacturer headquartered in Swiftwater, PA.

Leg. Issues: HCR, MED, MMM

In-house, DC-area Employees
PETERSON, Geoffrey G.: Director, Federal Government Relations

Outside Counsel/Consultants
Dalrymple and Associates, L.L.C.
Issues: HCR, MED, MMM
Rep By: Donald "Dack" Dalrymple
Olsson, Frank and Weeda, P.C.
Rep By: John W. Bode, Susan P. Grymes, Karen Reis Harned, Stephen L. Lacey, Marshall L. Matz, Tyson Redpath, Ryan W. Stroschein, Arthur Y. Tsien, David F. Weeda

Aventis Pharmaceutical Products

801 Pennsylvania Ave. NW
Suite 725
Washington, DC 20004
Tel: (202)628-0500
Registered: LDA

Formerly known as Rhodia, Inc.

Leg. Issues: AUT, CAW, CHM, CPT, ENV, FOO, TRD, WAS

In-house, DC-area Employees
STANLEY, Kathleen H.

Outside Counsel/Consultants
Baker Botts, L.L.P.
Rep By: James A. Baker, IV
Parry, Romani, DeConcini & Symms
Issues: CPT
Rep By: Edward H. Baxter, Hon. Dennis DeConcini, John M. Haddow, Scott D. Hatch, Shannon Davis Henderson, Jack W. Martin, Romano Romani, Linda Arey Skladany, Hon. Steven D. Symms
Preston Gates Ellis & Rouvelas Meeds LLP
Rep By: Mark H. Ruge

Aventis Pharmaceuticals, Inc.

801 Pennsylvania Ave. NW
Suite 725
Washington, DC 20004
Tel: (202)628-0500
Fax: (202)682-0538
Registered: LDA
Web: www.aventis.com

A subsidiary of Rhone-Poulenc (see separate listing) headquartered in Parsippany, NJ.

Leg. Issues: CPT, CSP, HCR, MED, MMM, TAX, VET

In-house, DC-area Employees
COOK, Judith Wise: Director, Health Policy and Biotechnology Programs
EVANS, Eddie D.: V. President, Federal Government Relations
ZOWADER, Donald: Senior Manager, Federal Government Relations

Outside Counsel/Consultants

Policy Directions, Inc.
Issues: CSP, HCR, MMM
Rep By: Kathleen "Kay" Holcombe, Frankie L. Trull

Swidler Berlin Shereff Friedman, LLP
Issues: CPT
Rep By: Barry B. Direnfeld, Brian W. Fitzgerald, Harold P. Goldfield, Lester S. Hyman, Gary D. Slaiman

Tongour Simpson Holsclaw Green
Issues: CPT
Rep By: John Bradley "Brad" Holsclaw, Michael A. Tongour

Washington Council Ernst & Young
Issues: HCR, MMM
Rep By: Doug Badger, Lauren Darling, John L. Doney, Jayne T. Fitzgerald, LaBrenda Garrett-Nelson, Gary J. Gasper, Bruce A. Gates, Nick Giordano, Cathy Koch, Robert J. Leonard, Richard Meltzer, Phillip D. Moseley, John D. Porter, Robert M. Rozen, Donna Steele-Flynn, Timothy J. Urban

Avenue A, Inc.

Seattle, WA
Leg. Issues: CPI

Outside Counsel/Consultants

Perkins Coie LLP
Issues: CPI
Rep By: W. H. "Buzz" Fawcett

Averitt Express, Inc.

Cookeville, TN
Leg. Issues: AVI

Outside Counsel/Consultants

Preston Gates Ellis & Rouvelas Meeds LLP
Issues: AVI

Avianca Airlines

New York, NY

Outside Counsel/Consultants

Holland & Knight LLP

Squire, Sanders & Dempsey L.L.P.
Rep By: Robert D. Papkin

Aviateca Airline

Guatemala City, GUATEMALA

Outside Counsel/Consultants

Mullenholz, Brimsek & Belair
Rep By: John R. Brimsek

Aviation Development Services

New York, NY

Outside Counsel/Consultants

Shaw Pittman
Rep By: J. E. Murdock, III

Avioimpex

Skopje, MACEDONIA
Leg. Issues: FOR, GOV, TRD

Outside Counsel/Consultants

Barbour Griffith & Rogers, Inc.
Issues: FOR, GOV, TRD
Rep By: G. O. Lanny Griffith, Jr., R. Greg Stevens

Avis, Inc.

Garden City, NY — Registered: LDA

Outside Counsel/Consultants

Armstrong Associates, Inc.
Rep By: Jan M. Armstrong

Avon Products, Inc.

New York, NY — Registered: LDA
Leg. Issues: TAX, TRD

Outside Counsel/Consultants

C&M Internat'l, Ltd.
Issues: TRD
Rep By: Doral S. Cooper, Melissa Coyle

Crowell & Moring LLP
Issues: TAX, TRD
Rep By: Harold J. Heltzer

Avondale Industries, Inc.

New Orleans, LA
Leg. Issues: BUD, DEF, MAR

Outside Counsel/Consultants

Dyer Ellis & Joseph, P.C.
Issues: MAR
Rep By: Brian A. Bannon, Thomas M. Dyer, James B. Ellis, II, Michael Joseph, Duncan C. Smith, III

Johnston & Associates, LLC
Issues: BUD, DEF
Rep By: Hon. J. Bennett Johnston, N. Hunter Johnston, Eric Tober

Jones, Walker, Waechter, Poitevent, Carrere & Denegre, L.L.P.
Issues: DEF, MAR
Rep By: Paul Cambon, John J. Jaskot, R. Christian Johnsen

The Livingston Group, LLC

Avondale, Arizona, City of

Leg. Issues: EDU, ENV, LAW, URB

Outside Counsel/Consultants

Parry, Romani, DeConcini & Symms
Issues: EDU, ENV, LAW, URB
Rep By: Edward H. Baxter, Hon. Dennis DeConcini, John M. Haddow, Scott D. Hatch, Shannon Davis Henderson, Jack W. Martin, Romano Romani, Linda Arey Skladany, Hon. Steven D. Symms

Avue Technologies

Tacoma, WA
Leg. Issues: GOV, LBR

Outside Counsel/Consultants

Griffin, Johnson, Dover & Stewart
Issues: GOV, LBR
Rep By: William C. Danvers, G. Jack Dover, Patrick J. Griffin, Keith Heard, David E. Johnson, Susan O. Mann, Walter J. "Joe" Stewart, Leonard Swinehart

AXS Technologies

Outside Counsel/Consultants

Stevens Reed Curcio & Co.

Azerbaijan, Embassy of the Republic of

927 15th St. NW
Suite 700
Washington, DC 20005
Tel: (202)842-0001
Fax: (202)842-0004
Web: www.azembassy.com
Leg. Issues: FOR

Outside Counsel/Consultants

Baker, Donelson, Bearman & Caldwell, P.C.
Rep By: Charles R. Johnston, Jr., George Cranwell Montgomery

Edwin C. Graves & Associates
Issues: FOR
Rep By: Edwin C. Graves

Hooper Owen & Winburn
Issues: FOR
Rep By: Esperanza Gomez, Hon. Charles Wilson

Azurix

Houston, TX
Leg. Issues: WAS

Outside Counsel/Consultants

Patton Boggs, LLP
Issues: WAS
Rep By: Michael A. Brown

B'nai B'rith Internat'l

1640 Rhode Island Ave. NW
Washington, DC 20036-3278
Tel: (202)857-6545
Fax: (202)857-6689
Registered: LDA
Web: www.bnaibrith.org
Leg. Issues: BUD, FOR, HOU

In-house, DC-area Employees

EPSTEIN, Jason: Director, Legislative Affairs
HEIDEMAN, Richard D.: President
MARIASCHIN, Daniel S.: Exec. V. President
MERIDY, Mark: Deputy Director, B'nai B'rith Center for Public Policy
OLSHAN, Mark: Director, Senior Housing and Services
ROZENMAN, Eric: Exec. Director, International Jewish Monthly Magazine, Associate Director, Communications of BBI
SIEGEL-VANN, Dina: Director, Latin American Affairs

B.C. Internat'l Corp.

Hingham, MA
Leg. Issues: BUD

Outside Counsel/Consultants

MSS Consultants, LLC
Issues: BUD
Rep By: Megan S. Smith

B.C. Softwood Lumber Trade Council

Leg. Issues: TRD

Outside Counsel/Consultants

Steptoe & Johnson LLP
Issues: TRD
Rep By: W. George Grandison, Mark A. Moran

Babcock & Wilcox

Cambridge, CANADA
Leg. Issues: TRD

Outside Counsel/Consultants

Sandler, Travis & Rosenberg, P.A.
Issues: TRD
Rep By: Shannon Fura, Jeremy Page, Ron Sorini

Babyland Family Services, Inc.

Newark, NJ

A community-based child care and family development organization.

Leg. Issues: BUD

Outside Counsel/Consultants

Cassidy & Associates, Inc.
Issues: BUD
Rep By: Laura A. Neal, Blenda Pinto-Riddick

Baca Land and Cattle Co.

Leg. Issues: NAT

Outside Counsel/Consultants

Verner, Liipfert, Bernhard, McPherson and Hand, Chartered
Issues: NAT
Rep By: Jane Hickie

Bacardi Ltd.

Miami, FL

Outside Counsel/Consultants

Edelman Public Relations Worldwide
Rep By: Leslie Dach, Michael K. Deaver, Jere Sullivan

Bacardi-Martini, USA, Inc.

Miami, FL
Leg. Issues: CPT, FOR, TRD

Outside Counsel/Consultants

The MWW Group
Issues: TRD
Rep By: Tracey Becker, Dana P. Bostic, Elizabeth A. Iadarola, Christine A. Pellerin, Jonathan B. Slade, Jeffery M. Walter

RMA Internat'l, Inc.
Issues: CPT
Rep By: Otto J. Reich

Verner, Liipfert, Bernhard, McPherson and Hand, Chartered
Issues: FOR
Rep By: Matthew C. Bernstein, Virginia R. Boggs, Gary J. Klein, John A. Merrigan

Bacharach

Pittsburgh, PA

Outside Counsel/Consultants

Interface Inc.
Rep By: David C. Knapp

Bad River Band of Lake Superior Chippewa

Odanah, WI

Outside Counsel/Consultants

Sonosky, Chambers, Sachse & Endreson
Rep By: William R. Perry

Baden-Wuerttemberg Agency for International Economic Cooperation

Stuttgart, GERMANY

Outside Counsel/Consultants

Gunter W. Moltzan
Rep By: Gunter W. Moltzan

BAE Systems Controls

Johnson City, NY
Leg. Issues: TRA

Outside Counsel/Consultants

Baker, Donelson, Bearman & Caldwell, P.C.
Issues: TRA
Rep By: Janet L. Powell

BAE SYSTEMS North America

1215 Jefferson Davis Hwy.
Suite 1500
Arlington, VA 22202
Tel: (703)416-7800
Fax: (703)415-1459
Registered: LDA
Web: www.na.baesystems.com

An international defense and aerospace company. Headquartered in Rockville, MD.

Leg. Issues: DEF

Political Action Committee/s

BAE SYSTEMS North America Inc. Political Action Committee (BAE SYSTEMS USA PAC)

1215 Jefferson Davis Hwy.
Suite 1500
Arlington, VA 22202
Tel: (703)418-6208
Fax: (703)415-1459
Contact: Sydelle Lyon

In-house, DC-area Employees

FITCH, Robert J.: V. President, Government Relations
HARTNETT, Barbara A.: Public Affairs Specialist
KELLY, Claire: Director, Legislative Initiatives
LYON, Sydelle: Legislative Coordinator, Government Relations
RAWLS, Rodger: V. President, Government Relations-Information Systems Sector
SOUCY, Philip E.: Director, Public Relations
WALSH, Robert: V. President, Government Relations-Information and Electronic Warfare Systems

Outside Counsel/Consultants

Belew Law Firm
Issues: DEF
Rep By: Joy Carabasi Belew, M. Wendell Belew, Jr.

Bruce Fennie & Associates
Issues: DEF
Rep By: Bruce Fennie

Hyjek & Fix, Inc.
Issues: DEF
Rep By: Donald J. Fix, Steven M. Hyjek, Irene D. Schecter, Karl H. Stegenga

Bahamas, Government of the Commonwealth of the

Nassau, BAHAMAS

Outside Counsel/Consultants

BSMG Worldwide

Bahrain, Government of the State of

Manama, BAHRAIN

Outside Counsel/Consultants

Miller & Chevalier, Chartered

Washington World Group, Ltd.
Rep By: Edward J. von Kloberg, III

Bailey Corp.

Seabrook, NH

Outside Counsel/Consultants

Howrey Simon Arnold & White

Bailey Link

Matairie, LA
Leg. Issues: BUD, CPI, DEF

Outside Counsel/Consultants

Jones, Walker, Waechter, Poitevent, Carrere & Denegre, L.L.P.
Issues: BUD, CPI, DEF
Rep By: Paul Cambon, John J. Jaskot, R. Christian Johnsen

Baker & Hostetler LLP

1050 Connecticut Ave. NW
Suite 1100
Washington, DC 20036-5304
Tel: (202)861-1500
Fax: (202)861-1790
Registered: LDA, FARA
Web: www.bakerlaw.com
Leg. Issues: COM, CPI, MMM, TEC

Political Action Committee/s

Baker & Hostetler Political Action Committee

1050 Connecticut Ave. NW
Suite 1100
Washington, DC 20036-5304
Tel: (202)861-1500
Fax: (202)861-1790
Contact: William H. Schweitzer

In-house, DC-area Employees

BARTRAM, Darin
BECKWITH, Edward J.
BLASEY, III, Ralph G.
BRADEN, E. Mark: Partner
CASEY, Lee A.
CONROY, William F.: Partner
CYMROT, Mark A.
DOLAN, Matthew J.: Partner
FORD, Anne K.: Partner
GRAEFE, Frederick H.: Partner
HAUSER, Richard H.: Partner
KENNELLY, Hon. Barbara Bailey
KERRIGAN, Kathleen M.
KIRSTEIN, David M.: Partner
LOTTERER, Steven A.: Legislative Assistant
LYSTAD, Robert: Associate
MARSHALL, David L.: Partner
MURPHY, Betty Southard: Partner
RIVKIN, Jr., David B.
SANFORD, Bruce W.: Partner
SCHWEITZER, William H.: Partner
SNYDER, Kenneth F.: Partner
STEPHEN, Christopher T.
VANDER JAGT, Hon. Guy: Of Counsel
WICK, Ronald F.: Partner
YOUNG, Joanne: Partner
ZAPRUDER, Henry G.: Partner

Outside Counsel/Consultants

Johnson Co.
Issues: COM, CPI, MMM, TEC

Michael Baker Corp.

Leg. Issues: ENG, ENV, TRD

Outside Counsel/Consultants

Martin G. Hamberger & Associates
Issues: ENG, ENV, TRD
Rep By: Martin G. Hamberger, Brian M. Tynan

Baker Electromotive, Inc.

Richmond, VA
Leg. Issues: AUT, ENG

Outside Counsel/Consultants

Morgan Meguire, LLC
Issues: AUT, ENG
Rep By: Scott Lindsay, Kyle G. Michel, Katie Parrott, C. Kyle Simpson, Deborah R. Sliz, Kiel Weaver

Baker Hughes Incorporated

816 Connecticut Ave. NW
Second Floor
Washington, DC 20006-2705
Tel: (202)785-8093
Fax: (202)785-4509
Registered: LDA
Web: www.bakerhughes.com

Headquartered in Houston, TX.

Leg. Issues: TRD

In-house, DC-area Employees

DOWNEY, Arthur T.: V. President, Government Affairs

Baker, Donelson, Bearman & Caldwell, P.C.

801 Pennsylvania Ave. NW
Suite 800
Washington, DC 20004
Tel: (202)508-3400
Fax: (202)508-3402
Registered: LDA, FARA
Web: www.bakerdonelson.com
Leg. Issues: ENV

In-house, DC-area Employees

BAKER, Jr., Hon. Howard H.: Shareholder
DASCHLE, Linda Hall: Senior Public Policy Advisor
DUFF, James C.
EAGLEBURGER, Lawrence S.: Senior Foreign Policy Advisor
EDELMAN, Doreen M.: Of Counsel
HOWARD, Thomas L.: Shareholder
JOHNSTON, Jr., Charles R.: Shareholder
KENNEDY, J. Keith: Senior Public Policy Advisor
LAMORIELLO, Francine: Senior Director, Internat'l Business Strategy
MCBRIDE, James W.: Shareholder
MCENTEE, Joan M.: Shareholder
MONTGOMERY, George Cranwell: Shareholder
PARKINSON, Charles R.: Senior Public Policy Advisor
POWELL, Janet L.: Senior Public Policy Advisor
RANDALL, Albert B.: Of Counsel
RANGE, James D.: Senior Advisor for Legislative, Regulatory and Environmental Affairs
STOLEE, Anne M.: Shareholder
TUCK, John C.: Senior Public Policy Advisor

Outside Counsel/Consultants

Nat'l Environmental Strategies
Issues: ENV

Bakery, Confectionery and Tobacco Workers Internat'l Union

10401 Connecticut Ave.
Kensington, MD 20895
Tel: (301)933-8600
Fax: (301)946-8452

Has 120,000 members who work in the bakery, confectionery, tobacco and food processing industries.

Political Action Committee/s

Bakery, Confectionery and Tobacco Workers Internat'l Union Political Action Committee

10401 Connecticut Ave.
Kensington, MD 20895
Tel: (301)933-8600
Fax: (301)946-8452
Contact: Carolyn Jacobson

In-house, DC-area Employees

DURKEE, David: Secretary-Treasurer
HURT, Frank: President
JACOBSON, Carolyn: Director, Publications
SCANNELL, Raymond F.: Director of Research

Outside Counsel/Consultants

Bredhoff & Kaiser
Rep By: Jeffrey R. Freund

Ball Aerospace & Technologies Corp.

2200 Clarendon Blvd.
Suite 1202
Arlington, VA 22201
Tel: (703)284-5400
Fax: (703)284-5449
Web: www.ball.com

A manufacturer of packaging, industrial, and technical products.

In-house, DC-area Employees

CAMPBELL, John D.: Manager, Legislative Affairs
HESCHELES, Heather: Manager, Lesgislative Affairs
MOORE, Jesse W.: V. President, Washington Operations

Ball Aerospace & Technology Corp.

Boulder, CO
Leg. Issues: AER, DEF

Outside Counsel/Consultants

R. V. Davis and Associates
Issues: AER
Rep By: Robert V. Davis, J. William Foster

Sagamore Associates, Inc.
Issues: DEF
Rep By: Doug Wasitis, Mark W. Weller

Ball Research, Inc.

East Lansing, MI
Leg. Issues: CPT

Outside Counsel/Consultants

Kent & O'Connor, Inc.
Issues: CPT
Rep By: Cindy Thomas

Ball State University

Muncie, IN
Leg. Issues: BUD, EDU, ROD

Outside Counsel/Consultants

Fisher Consulting
Issues: BUD, EDU, ROD
Rep By: Steven A. Fisher

Ballard Power Systems

British Columbia, CANADA
Leg. Issues: ENG

Outside Counsel/Consultants

Lighthouse Energy Group LLC
Issues: ENG
Rep By: Tobyn J. Anderson, Merribel S. Ayres

Ballard, Spahr, Andrews & Ingersoll LLP

Philadelphia, PA
Leg. Issues: BUD

Outside Counsel/Consultants

Preston Gates Ellis & Rouvelas Meeds LLP
Issues: BUD

Washington Strategies, L.L.C.
Rep By: Jennifer Johnson Calvert, William P. Jarrell

Baltic American Freedom League

Los Angeles, CA
Leg. Issues: DEF, FOR

Outside Counsel/Consultants

Anne V. Smith
Issues: DEF, FOR
Rep By: Anne V. Smith

Baltimore Symphony Orchestra

Baltimore, MD
Leg. Issues: BUD

Outside Counsel/Consultants

Patton Boggs, LLP
Issues: BUD
Rep By: Shannon M. Gibson, Robert C. Jones, Elizabeth C. Vella

Baltimore, Maryland, City of

Leg. Issues: ALC, BUD, EDU, HOU, TRA, URB

Outside Counsel/Consultants

Reed, Smith, LLP
Issues: BUD
Rep By: Christopher L. Rissetto

Van Scoyoc Associates, Inc.
Issues: ALC, BUD, EDU, HOU, TRA, URB
Rep By: Steve E. Crane, Anita R. Estell, Kimberly Johnson, Kevin F. Kelly

Banco Portugues do Atlantico, S.A.

New York, NY

Outside Counsel/Consultants

Vorys, Sater, Seymour and Pease, LLP
Rep By: Warren W. Glick

Bangladesh Economic Program Zone Authority

Outside Counsel/Consultants

Dierman, Wortley, and Zola

Stewart and Stewart

Bangladesh Export Processing Zones Authority

Dhaka, BANGLADESH
Leg. Issues: FOR, TRD

Outside Counsel/Consultants

Dierman, Wortley, and Zola
Issues: FOR, TRD
Rep By: Hon. George C. Wortley, MC (Ret.), Hilliard A. Zola

Bangladeshi-American Friendship Soc. of New York

New York, NY
Leg. Issues: IMM

Outside Counsel/Consultants

Wilson & Wasserstein, Inc.
Issues: IMM
Rep By: Yurika S. Cooper, Glen D. Wasserstein, Russell J. Wilson

Bangor Hydro-Electric Co.

Bangor, ME

Outside Counsel/Consultants

Wright & Talisman, P.C.
Rep By: James T. McManus, Michael E. Small

Bangor Internat'l Airport

Bangor, ME
Leg. Issues: AVI, TRA

Outside Counsel/Consultants

Baker & Hostetler LLP
Issues: AVI
Rep By: Joanne Young

George H. Denison
Issues: AVI, TRA
Rep By: George H. Denison

Bank Hapoalim B.M.

Tel Aviv, ISRAEL

An Israeli financial institution.

Leg. Issues: BAN, TAX

Outside Counsel/Consultants

Shaw Pittman
Issues: BAN, TAX
Rep By: David R. Sahr

Bank Leumi le-Israel B.M.

Tel Aviv, ISRAEL

An Israeli banking institution.

Leg. Issues: BAN, TAX

Outside Counsel/Consultants

Shaw Pittman
Issues: BAN, TAX
Rep By: Scott A. Anenberg

Bank of Alabama

Birmingham, AL

Outside Counsel/Consultants

Bradley Arant Rose & White LLP

Bank of America

730 15th St. NW
Fifth Floor
Washington, DC 20005
Tel: (202)624-4099
Fax: (202)383-3475
Registered: LDA
Web: www.bankofamerica.com

Headquartered in Charlotte, NC.

Leg. Issues: BAN, BNK, FIN, TAX

In-house, DC-area Employees

COUPER, William: President
HILL, Edward J.: V. President, Government Relations
KUO, Ellen: V. President, Government Relations
MURPHY, Jeanne-Marie: Senior V. President, Government Relations

Outside Counsel/Consultants

Cooper, Carvin & Rosenthal

Covington & Burling
Issues: BAN
Rep By: Stuart C. Stock

The Kate Moss Company
Issues: BAN, BNK, FIN, TAX
Rep By: Kate Moss

O'Connor & Hannan, L.L.P.
Issues: TAX
Rep By: Edward Beck

PriceWaterhouseCoopers
Issues: TAX
Rep By: Tim Anson, Jim Carlisle, Kenneth J. Kies

Winston & Strawn
Rep By: Hon. John L. Napier

Bank of New England

Boston, MA

Outside Counsel/Consultants

The Secura Group

Bank of New England Holding Company Trustee

Boston, MA

Outside Counsel/Consultants

Andrews and Kurth, L.L.P.

Bank of New York

New York, NY
Leg. Issues: BAN, FIN

Outside Counsel/Consultants

Parry, Romani, DeConcini & Symms
Issues: BAN, FIN
Rep By: Edward H. Baxter, Hon. Dennis DeConcini, John M. Haddow, Scott D. Hatch, Shannon Davis Henderson, Jack W. Martin, Romano Romani, Linda Arey Skladany, Hon. Steven D. Symms

Bank of Tokyo-Mitsubishi

Tokyo, JAPAN

Outside Counsel/Consultants

Norman A. Bailey, Inc.
Rep By: Norman A. Bailey

Bank of Zaire

Kinshasa, ZAIRE

Outside Counsel/Consultants

White & Case LLP

The Bank Private Equity Coalition

c/o Manatt Phelps
1501 M St. NW, Suite 700
Washington, DC 20005-1702
Tel: (202)463-4300
Fax: (202)463-4394
Registered: LDA

An organization of venture capital subsidiaries of the following banks: Bank of Boston Corp., BankAmerica Corp., Bankers Trust New York Corp., Chase Manhattan Corp., Fleet Financial Group, J. P. Morgan & Co., Norwest Corp. and PNC Financial Corp.

Leg. Issues: BAN

In-house, DC-area Employees

KABEL, Robert J.: Legislative Counsel
MULDER, Steven J.: Legislative Advisor

Outside Counsel/Consultants

Manatt, Phelps & Phillips, LLP
Issues: BAN
Rep By: Robert J. Kabel, Steven J. Mulder

Bank United of Texas FSB

Houston, TX

Outside Counsel/Consultants

Bryan Cave LLP

Bankers Trust Co.

New York, NY

Outside Counsel/Consultants

Akin, Gump, Strauss, Hauer & Feld, L.L.P.
Rep By: Joel Jankowsky

Bankers' Ass'n for Finance and Trade

2121 K St. NW
Suite 701
Washington, DC 20037
Tel: (202)452-0952
Fax: (202)452-0959
Registered: LDA
Web: www.baft.org
E-mail: baft@baft.org

An association, established in 1921, of banking institutions dedicated to fostering and promoting international trade, finance and investment between the U.S. and its trading partners.

Leg. Issues: BAN, BUD, FOR, TRD

In-house, DC-area Employees

BIERMAN, John: Director, Communication and Issues Management
CONDEELIS, Mary: Exec. Director
FARMER, Thomas L.: General Counsel

Bankruptcy Issues Council

Leg. Issues: BAN, BNK

Outside Counsel/Consultants

Ernst & Young LLP
Issues: BAN, BNK
Rep By: Tom S. Nuebig

Banorte Casa de Bolsa

Mexico City, MEXICO
Leg. Issues: BAN, FOR

Outside Counsel/Consultants

Janus-Merritt Strategies, L.L.C.
Issues: BAN, FOR
Rep By: Scott P. Hoffman, Mark J. Robertson, J. Daniel Walsh

Banque Paribas New York Branch

New York, NY
Leg. Issues: BAN

Outside Counsel/Consultants

Rogers & Wells
Issues: BAN
Rep By: Katherine W. Meighan

Baptist Joint Committee on Public Affairs

200 Maryland Ave. NE
Suite 303
Washington, DC 20002
Tel: (202)544-4226
Fax: (202)544-2094
Web: www.bjcpa.org
E-mail: james_dunn@bjcpa.org

Staffed in Washington, DC in 1946. A joint effort of nine major Baptist denominations with 25 million members to promote religious liberty and separation of church and state.

In-house, DC-area Employees

HOLLMAN, Holly: General Counsel
WALKER, J. Brent: Exec. Director

Baptist World Alliance

6733 Curran St.
McLean, VA 22101-6005
Tel: (703)790-8980
Fax: (703)893-5160
Web: www.bwanet.org
E-mail: BWA@bwanet.org

Founded in 1905 in London. An international alliance of 196 national Baptist unions with almost 100,000 members worldwide.

In-house, DC-area Employees

LOTZ, Denton: General Secretary
RYAN, Wendy: Director, Division of Communications

Bar Ass'n of the District of Columbia

1819 H St. NW
Suite 1250
Washington, DC 20006-3690
Tel: (202)223-6600
Fax: (202)293-3388
Web: www.badc.org
E-mail: BAofDC@aol.com

In-house, DC-area Employees

GREEN, Peter M.: Exec. Director

Barat College

Lake Forest, IL
Leg. Issues: BUD

Outside Counsel/Consultants

Patton Boggs, LLP
Issues: BUD
Rep By: Robert C. Jones

Barber Colman Co.

Loves Park, IL
Leg. Issues: DEF

Outside Counsel/Consultants

American Defense Internat'l, Inc.
Issues: DEF
Rep By: Michael Herson, Van D. Hipp, Jr., Dave Wilberding

Barker Brothers

Los Angeles, CA

Outside Counsel/Consultants

Howrey Simon Arnold & White

Barker Enterprises

Greenbelt, MD
Leg. Issues: GAM

Outside Counsel/Consultants

Burwell, Peters and Houston
Issues: GAM
Rep By: Dorothy Sharon Matts, Eugene F. Peters

Barksdale Foward

Shreveport, LA — Registered: LDA
Leg. Issues: DEF, GOV

Outside Counsel/Consultants

The Spectrum Group
Issues: DEF, GOV
Rep By: Gen. J. B. Davis, USAF (Ret.), Lt. Gen. Leo Marquez, USAF (Ret.), Paul E. McManus

Barnstable Broadcasting

Waltham, MA

Outside Counsel/Consultants

Kaye Scholer LLP
Rep By: Jason Shrinsky

Barona Band of Mission Indians

Lakeside, CA
Leg. Issues: IND

Outside Counsel/Consultants

PACE-CAPSTONE
Issues: IND
Rep By: Scott C. Dacey, James W. Wise

Barona Indian Reservation

Lakeside, CA

Outside Counsel/Consultants

The Direct Impact Co.

Barr Laboratories

444 N. Capitol St. NW
Suite 722
Washington, DC 20001-0000
Tel: (202)393-6599
Fax: (202)638-3386
Registered: LDA

A generic pharmaceutical manufacturer headquartered in Pomona, NY.

Leg. Issues: BUD, CPT, GOV, HCR, INS, LBR, MAN, MMM, PHA

In-house, DC-area Employees

HANSEN, Jake: V. President, Government Affairs

Outside Counsel/Consultants

Broydrick & Associates
Issues: PHA
Rep By: William Broydrick, Bill Viney

Forscey & Stinson, PLLC
Issues: MMM, PHA
Rep By: Michael A. Forscey

McGuiness & Holch
Issues: HCR, PHA
Rep By: Markham C. Erickson, Kevin S. McGuiness

David Nelson & Associates
Issues: HCR
Rep By: David W. Nelson

Stephen F. Sims and Associates
Issues: CPT, HCR
Rep By: Stephen F. Sims

Winston & Strawn
Issues: MMM, PHA
Rep By: Hon. Beryl F. Anthony, Jr., Hon. James H. Burnley, IV, Eric L. Hirschhorn, Frederick J. Killion, Charles L. Kinney, Joseph E. O'Leary, Douglas C. Richardson, John A. Waits, II

Barrett Resources

Denver, CO

Outside Counsel/Consultants

R. Duffy Wall and Associates

Barrick Goldstrike Mines, Inc.

801 Pennsylvania Ave. NW
Suite 730
Washington, DC 20004
Tel: (202)638-0026
Fax: (202)638-7787
Registered: LDA

U.S. subsidiary of Barrick Gold Corporation, a Canadian gold mining company with operations in Nevada and Utah; U.S headquarters in Elko, NV.

Leg. Issues: BUD, ENG, FOR, GOV, MON, NAT, RES, TAX

Political Action Committee/s

Barrick Goldstrike Mines Inc. PAC
801 Pennsylvania Ave. NW
Suite 730
Washington, DC 20004
Tel: (202)638-0026
Fax: (202)638-7787

In-house, DC-area Employees

BROWN, Michael J.: V. President, U.S. Public Affairs

Outside Counsel/Consultants

Akin, Gump, Strauss, Hauer & Feld, L.L.P.
Issues: ENG, FOR, GOV, TAX
Rep By: Janet C. Boyd, William J. Farah, Henry A. Terhune, S. Bruce Wilson

Contango LLC
Issues: NAT, TAX
Rep By: Candice Shy Hooper

Hooper Owen & Winburn
Issues: NAT, RES, TAX
Rep By: Lindsay D. Hooper

McClure, Gerard & Neuenschwander, Inc.
Rep By: Steven G. Barringer, Joseph T. Findaro, Matthew Iandoli, Nils W. Johnson, Hon. James A. McClure, Tod O. Neuenschwander

Washington Strategies, L.L.C.
Issues: NAT
Rep By: Geoffrey C. Ziebart

Barringer Technologies

New Providence, NJ

A manufacturer of anti-terrorist and anti-narcotics detection equipment.

Leg. Issues: AVI, LAW

Outside Counsel/Consultants

Patton Boggs, LLP
Issues: AVI, LAW
Rep By: James B. Christian, Jr., Darryl D. Nirenberg, Aubrey A. Rothrock, III

Barron Collier Co.

Naples, FL

A private partnership engaged in diversified investment activities.

Leg. Issues: ENV, NAT, RES

Outside Counsel/Consultants

Van Ness Feldman, P.C.
Issues: ENV, NAT, RES
Rep By: Alan L. Mintz

Barry University

Miami Shores, FL
Leg. Issues: BUD

Outside Counsel/Consultants

Cassidy & Associates, Inc.
Issues: BUD
Rep By: Sonya C. Clay, Mary Kate Kelly-Johnson

R. G. Barry

Columbus, OH

Outside Counsel/Consultants

Baker & McKenzie
Rep By: Teresa A. Gleason

Barstow, California, City of

Outside Counsel/Consultants

E. Del Smith and Co.
Rep By: Margaret Allen, E. Del Smith

Base Ten Systems, Inc.

Trenton, NJ
Leg. Issues: PHA

Outside Counsel/Consultants

Akin, Gump, Strauss, Hauer & Feld, L.L.P.
Issues: PHA
Rep By: Karen E. Goldmeier Green, Barney J. Skladany, Jr.

BASF Corporation

601 13th St. NW
Suite 200 North
Washington, DC 20005
Tel: (202)682-9462
Registered: LDA
Leg. Issues: FOO, GOV, HCR, LBR, TAX, TRD

In-house, DC-area Employees

ADAMS, Jane A.: Manager, State Government Relations
COLEMAN, Hon. E. Thomas: V. President, Government Relations
DESETA, Anne: Manager, Grassroots Program
HYSELL, Donald R.: Director, Government Relations
THIES, Gregory A.: Manager, Government Relations
TOLAND, William P.: Environment and Energy Advocate

Basic American, Inc.

Leg. Issues: AGR, TRD

Outside Counsel/Consultants

Ball Janik, LLP
Issues: AGR, TRD
Rep By: Irene Ringwood

Basin Electric Power Cooperative

Bismarck, ND — Registered: LDA
Leg. Issues: ENG, ENV, UTI

Outside Counsel/Consultants

Duncan, Weinberg, Genzer & Pembroke, P.C.
Issues: ENG, ENV, UTI
Rep By: Richmond F. Allan

Bass Enterprises Production Co.

Fort Worth, TX
Leg. Issues: AGR, ENV, MAR, TAX

Outside Counsel/Consultants

Williams & Jensen, P.C.
Issues: AGR, ENV, MAR, TAX
Rep By: George D. Baker, William B. Canfield, Robert E. Glennon, Jr., Anthony J. Roda

Bass Hotels and Resorts, Inc.

Atlanta, GA

Formerly operating as Holiday Inn Worldwide.

Leg. Issues: CPT, HCR, LBR, TAX, TOU, TRA, UTI

Outside Counsel/Consultants

Ivins, Phillips & Barker
Issues: TAX
Rep By: Eric R. Fox, Alan Granwell, Dirk J. J. Suringa

Jefferson Government Relations, L.L.C.
Issues: CPT, HCR, LBR, TAX, TOU, TRA, UTI
Rep By: John D. Desser, Thomas R. Donnelly, Jr., Katherine M. Krauser, Jeanne L. Morin, Daniel J. Sheehan

Bassett Healthcare

Leg. Issues: BUD, HCR

Outside Counsel/Consultants

Arent Fox Kintner Plotkin & Kahn, PLLC
Issues: BUD, HCR
Rep By: Katie Clarke, Douglas McCormack

Bastyr University

Kenmore, WA
Leg. Issues: HCR

Outside Counsel/Consultants

Capitol Associates, Inc.
Issues: HCR
Rep By: Liz Gemski, Edward R. Long, Ph.D.

Bath Iron Works Corp.

2341 Jefferson Davis Hwy.
Suite 1100
Arlington, VA 22202
Tel: (703)418-0808
Fax: (703)418-0811

In-house, DC-area Employees

BOWLER, III, R. T. E.: Director, Washington Operations

BATMark

London, UNITED KINGDOM

Outside Counsel/Consultants

RMA Internat'l, Inc.

Baton Rouge, Louisiana, City of

Baton Rouge, LA
Leg. Issues: AVI, BUD, CAW, ECN, TRA, URB

Outside Counsel/Consultants

Adams and Reese LLP
Issues: CAW, ECN, TRA
Rep By: B. Jeffrey Brooks, Charlotte Collins, D. Lee Forsgren, Hon. James A. "Jimmy" Hayes, Andrea Wilkinson

Jones, Walker, Waechter, Poitevent, Carrere & Denegre, L.L.P.
Issues: AVI, BUD, URB
Rep By: Paul Cambon, John J. Jaskot, R. Christian Johnsen, James Ogsbury

The Livingston Group, LLC
Issues: AVI, BUD, URB
Rep By: Richard Legendre, Hon. Robert L. Livingston, Jr., J. Allen Martin, Richard L. Rodgers

Battelle

Columbus, OH
Leg. Issues: BUD, DEF, ENG, ENV, SCI

Outside Counsel/Consultants

James Nicholas Ashmore & Associates
Rep By: James Nicholas Ashmore

Ann Cecchetti
Issues: BUD
Rep By: Ann Cecchetti

Dr. John V. Dugan, Jr.
Issues: ENG, ENV, SCI
Rep By: Dr. John V. Dugan, Jr.

The PMA Group
Issues: DEF
Rep By: Daniel Cunningham, Kaylene Green, Paul J. Magliocchetti, Kelli Short, Brian Thiel, Thomas Veltri, Sandra Welch

Battelle Memorial Institute

901 D St. SW
Suite 900
Washington, DC 20024
Tel: (202)479-0500
Fax: (202)646-5233
Registered: LDA
Web: www.battelle.org

Headquartered in Columbus, OH.

Leg. Issues: AER, AGR, BUD, CAW, CHM, DEF, ENG, ENV, FOO, FOR, MAN, SCI, TRA, WAS

In-house, DC-area Employees

BAGLEY, John F.: V. President, External Relations
YACON-HOPPER, Jill: Manager, Government Relations

Outside Counsel/Consultants

American Systems Internat'l Corp.
Issues: DEF, MAN
Rep By: Robert D. McVey, William H. Skipper, Jr.

James Nicholas Ashmore & Associates
Issues: AER, AGR, BUD, CAW, CHM, ENV, FOO, MAN, SCI, TRA
Rep By: James Nicholas Ashmore

EMI Associates, Ltd.
Issues: BUD, ENG, FOR
Rep By: Eugene M. Iwanciw

Johnston & Associates, LLC
Issues: BUD, ENG, SCI
Rep By: Hon. J. Bennett Johnston, W. Proctor Jones

Mehl, Griffin & Bartek Ltd.
Issues: DEF, ENG, ENV
Rep By: Ronald J. Bartek, Molly Griffin, Theodore J. Mehl

MSS Consultants, LLC
Issues: BUD, ENG
Rep By: Megan S. Smith

Preston Gates Ellis & Rouvelas Meeds LLP
Issues: WAS
Rep By: Cindy O'Malley, Tim L. Peckinpaugh

Battelle Memorial Labs

Arlington, VA
Leg. Issues: DEF, MAN

Outside Counsel/Consultants

American Systems Internat'l Corp.
Issues: DEF, MAN
Rep By: Robert D. McVey, William H. Skipper, Jr.

Battery Council Internat'l

1299 Pennsylvania Ave. NW
Washington, DC 20004-2402
Tel: (202)783-0800
Fax: (202)383-6610
Leg. Issues: ENV, WAS

Political Action Committee/s

Battery Council Internat'l Political Action Committee
1299 Pennsylvania Ave. NW
Washington, DC 20004-2402
Tel: (202)783-0800
Fax: (202)383-6610
Contact: David B. Weinberg

In-house, DC-area Employees

WEINBERG, David B.: Treasurer

Outside Counsel/Consultants

Howrey Simon Arnold & White
Issues: ENV, WAS
Rep By: Edward L. Ferguson, David B. Weinberg, J. Thomas Wolfe

Bausch & Lomb

Rochester, NY
Leg. Issues: MED

Outside Counsel/Consultants

Policy Directions, Inc.
Issues: MED
Rep By: Stephen Michael, Frankie L. Trull

Baxter Healthcare Corp.

800 Connecticut Ave. NW
Suite 1100
Washington, DC 20006
Tel: (202)223-4016
Fax: (202)296-7177
Registered: LDA
Web: www.baxter.com

Manufacturer and supplier of healthcare products.

Leg. Issues: BUD, HCR, MAN, MED, MMM, PHA, SCI, TAX, TOR, TRD

Political Action Committee/s

Baxter Healthcare Corp. PAC
800 Connecticut Ave. NW
Suite 1100
Washington, DC 20006
Tel: (202)223-4016
Fax: (202)296-7177
Contact: Elizabeth A. Fuller

In-house, DC-area Employees

CALDEIRA, Victoria: Director, Federal Legislative Affairs
FULLER, Elizabeth A.: PAC and Grassroots Associate
GREGG, Sarah Massengale: V. President, Federal Legislative Affairs and Payment Planning
ROSSIN, Bradley: Legislative Manager
SPEAR, Jonathan B.: V. President, Government Affairs and Public Policy

Outside Counsel/Consultants

Greenberg Traurig, LLP
Rep By: Howard J. Cohen

Policy Directions, Inc.
Issues: HCR, MED, MMM, PHA, SCI
Rep By: Kathleen "Kay" Holcombe, Frankie L. Trull

Washington Council Ernst & Young
Issues: BUD, HCR, MMM, TAX
Rep By: Doug Badger, Lauren Darling, John L. Doney, Jayne T. Fitzgerald, LaBrenda Garrett-Nelson, Gary J. Gasper, Bruce A. Gates, Nick Giordano, Cathy Koch, Robert J. Leonard, Richard Meltzer, Phillip D. Moseley, John D. Porter, Robert M. Rozen, Donna Steele-Flynn, Timothy J. Urban

Bay Area Rapid Transit District

Oakland, CA
Leg. Issues: RET, TRA

Outside Counsel/Consultants

Copeland, Lowery & Jacquez
Issues: RET, TRA
Rep By: James M. Copeland, Jr., Jean Gingras Denton

Hall, Green, Rupli, LLC
Issues: TRA
Rep By: G. Stewart Hall

Bay County, Florida

Leg. Issues: ENV, GOV, TRA

Outside Counsel/Consultants

Alcalde & Fay
Issues: ENV, GOV, TRA
Rep By: Hector Alcalde, Hon. Louis A. "Skip" Bafalis, Jim Davenport

Bay Delta Urban Coalition

San Jose, CA
Leg. Issues: NAT

Outside Counsel/Consultants

Perkins Coie LLP
Issues: NAT
Rep By: Guy R. Martin

Bay Harbor Management, L.C.

New York, NY
Leg. Issues: TEC

Outside Counsel/Consultants

Balch & Bingham LLP
Issues: TEC
Rep By: Barbara K. Olson

Barbour Griffith & Rogers, Inc.
Issues: TEC
Rep By: Haley Barbour, Carl Biersack, G. O. Lanny Griffith, Jr., Loren Monroe, Edward M. Rogers, Jr.

Timmons and Co., Inc.
Issues: TEC
Rep By: Michael J. Bates, Douglas F. Bennett, Ellen B. Fitzgibbons, Bryce L. "Larry" Harlow, Timothy J. Keating, Tom C. Korologos, Richard J. Tarplin, William E. Timmons, Jr., William E. Timmons, Sr.

Bay Mills Indian Community

Brimley, MI
Leg. Issues: GAM, IND, TAX

Outside Counsel/Consultants

Dorsey & Whitney LLP
Issues: IND
Rep By: Virginia W. Boylan

Morriset, Schlosser, Ayer & Jozwiak
Issues: IND
Rep By: Fran Ayer

Wheat & Associates, Inc.
Issues: GAM, IND, TAX
Rep By: Hon. Alan D. Wheat

Bay State Health Systems

Springfield, MA
Leg. Issues: HCR

Outside Counsel/Consultants

Gottehrer and Co.
Issues: HCR
Rep By: Barry Gottehrer

Bayamon Federal Savings and Loan Ass'n

San Juan, PR

Outside Counsel/Consultants

Elias, Matz, Tiernan and Herrick

Bayer Corp.

1275 Pennsylvania Ave. NW
Suite 801
Washington, DC 20004
Tel: (202)737-8900
Fax: (202)737-8909
Registered: LDA
Leg. Issues: AGR, BUD, CAW, CHM, CPT, ENG, ENV, HCR, MMM, PHA, TRD

In-house, DC-area Employees

DOCKSAI, Ph.D., Ronald F.: V. President, Federal Government Relations
VAN EGMOND, Juliane H.: Director, Federal Government Relations

Outside Counsel/Consultants

The Potomac Research Group LLC
Issues: TRD
Rep By: G. Harris Jordan, Paul Welles Orr

Williams & Jensen, P.C.
Issues: CPT, HCR, MMM, PHA, TRD
Rep By: George G. Olsen

Bayer Corp. / Agriculture Division

West Haven, CT
Leg. Issues: AGR, FOO

Outside Counsel/Consultants

McDermott, Will and Emery
Issues: AGR
Rep By: Robert B. Nicholas

Powell, Goldstein, Frazer & Murphy LLP
Issues: FOO
Rep By: Kyra Fischbeck, Brett G. Kappel, Lisa Shapiro, William H. E. von Oehsen

Bayer Diagnostic

Tarytown, NY
Leg. Issues: HCR, MED

Outside Counsel/Consultants

Policy Directions, Inc.
Issues: HCR, MED
Rep By: Stephen Michael, Frankie L. Trull

Bayley Seton Hospital

Staten Island, NY

Outside Counsel/Consultants

Bruce Ray & Company
Rep By: Bruce A. Ray, Ph.D.

Baylor College of Medicine

Houston, TX
Leg. Issues: AGR, BUD, FOO, HCR, MED

Outside Counsel/Consultants

Policy Directions, Inc.
Issues: AGR, BUD, FOO, HCR, MED
Rep By: Kathleen "Kay" Holcombe, Stephen Michael, Frankie L. Trull

Bayonne Housing Authority

Bayonne, NJ

Outside Counsel/Consultants

Krivit & Krivit, P.C.
Rep By: Daniel H. Krivit

Bayonne, New Jersey, City of

Outside Counsel/Consultants

Krivit & Krivit, P.C.
Rep By: Daniel H. Krivit

Bazelon Center for Mental Health Law, Judge David L.

1101 15th St. NW
Suite 1212
Washington, DC 20005
Tel: (202)467-5730
Fax: (202)223-0409
Registered: LDA
Web: www.bazelon.org
E-mail: hn1660@handsnet.org

A public interest organization which helps to define, establish, and implement legal and constitutional rights of children and adults with mental disabilities.

Leg. Issues: BUD, CIV, EDU, HCR, HOU, LAW, MMM

In-house, DC-area Employees

ALLEN, Michael: Staff Attorney, Housing Issues
BERNSTEIN, Ph.D., Robert: Exec. Director
BURNIM, Ira A.: Legal Director
CARTY, Lee: Director, Publications and Communications
GILIBERTI, Mary: Staff Attorney, Children's Issues
HARRIS, Ellen: Staff Attorney, Committee on Mental Health Issues
KOYANAGI, Christine: Policy Director
MATHIS, Jennifer: Staff Attorney, ADA Issues
SELTZER, Tammy: Staff Attorney
STINE, Laurel: Director, Federal Relations

Outside Counsel/Consultants

Covington & Burling
Rep By: Peter J. Nickles

BCI, Inc.

Moorestown, NJ
Leg. Issues: SCI

Outside Counsel/Consultants

Chwat and Company, Inc.
Issues: SCI
Rep By: John Chwat, Derek Riker

BD

Franklin Lakes, NJ
Leg. Issues: HCR, MMM

Outside Counsel/Consultants

Dalrymple and Associates, L.L.C.
Rep By: Donald "Dack" Dalrymple

Nusgart Consulting, LLC
Issues: HCR, MMM
Rep By: Marcia Nusgart

The Washington Group
Issues: HCR
Rep By: Tripp Funderburk, Rita M. Lewis, G. John O'Hanlon, John D. Raffaelli, Mark Schnabel

The Beacon Group Energy Funds

New York, NY
Leg. Issues: ENG, ENV

Outside Counsel/Consultants

Lighthouse Energy Group LLC
Issues: ENG, ENV
Rep By: Tobyn J. Anderson, Merribel S. Ayres

Beacon Skanska U.S.A.

Boston, MA

Outside Counsel/Consultants

Cassidy & Associates, Inc.

Frank Beam and Co.

Leg. Issues: ENG, URB

Outside Counsel/Consultants

Colling Swift & Hynes
Issues: ENG, URB
Rep By: Terese Colling, Robert J. Hynes, Jr., Hon. Allan B. Swift

BeamHit America LLC

Columbia, MD
Leg. Issues: DEF, FIR

Outside Counsel/Consultants

Copeland, Lowery & Jacquez
Issues: DEF, FIR
Rep By: Jeffrey S. Shockey

Bear, Stearns and Co.

New York, NY
Registered: LDA
Leg. Issues: BAN, BNK, FIN, TAX

Outside Counsel/Consultants

Akin, Gump, Strauss, Hauer & Feld, L.L.P.
Rep By: Donald C. Alexander, Janet C. Boyd, Sean G. D'Arcy, Frank J. Donatelli, Joel Jankowsky

O'Connor & Hannan, L.L.P.
Issues: BNK, FIN, TAX
Rep By: Hon. Thomas J. Corcoran, Danielle Fagre, Timothy W. Jenkins, Patrick E. O'Donnell, Thomas H. Quinn

Steptoe & Johnson LLP
Issues: BAN, FIN, TAX
Rep By: John T. Collins

Beasley Broadcast Group

Outside Counsel/Consultants

Kaye Scholer LLP

Beaumont, Texas, City of

Leg. Issues: HOU, LAW, TRA, URB

Outside Counsel/Consultants

Carolyn C. Chaney & Associates
Issues: HOU, LAW, TRA, URB
Rep By: Carolyn C. Chaney, Christopher F. Giglio

Beauty and Barber Supply Industries, Inc.

Phoenix, AZ
Leg. Issues: CPT

Outside Counsel/Consultants

Patton Boggs, LLP
Issues: CPT
Rep By: Lanny J. Davis, Clayton L. Hough

Bechtel Group, Inc.

1015 15th St. NW
Suite 700
Washington, DC 20005-2605
Tel: (202)828-5200
Fax: (202)785-2645
Registered: LDA
Web: www.bechtel.com
E-mail: rragan@bechtel.com

The Washington office handles domestic and international marketing, government affairs and international financing.

Leg. Issues: BUD, DEF, ENG, ENV, GOV, TAX, TRA, TRD, WAS

In-house, DC-area Employees

CROOKS, Edwin W.: V. President and Development and Finance Manager (Bechtel Enterprises)
DRAGGON, Robert O.: Assistant Managing Director (Bechtel Enterprises)
HOWARD, Jane A.: Senior International Trade Representative (BCorp)
KENNEDY, Daniel E.: V. President and Manager, Government Affairs (BNI)
MONROE, Robert R.: V. President and Manager, Government Operations (BNI)
PAROBEK, Dennis A.: Manager, Government Affairs (BINFRA)
PILZER, Arthur: V. President and Development and Finance Manager (Bechtel Enterprises)
RAGAN, Robert H.: Principal V. President and Manager (Bechtel Group, Inc.)
ROBERTS, Anne B.: Senior Government Affairs Representative (BNI)
VICE, Jaime M.: Government Affairs Representative

Outside Counsel/Consultants

Akin, Gump, Strauss, Hauer & Feld, L.L.P.
Issues: TAX
Rep By: Donald C. Alexander, Sean G. D'Arcy

Bechtel/Parsons Brinkeroff Joint Venture

Boston, MA
Leg. Issues: TRA

Outside Counsel/Consultants

GPC Internat'l
Issues: TRA
Rep By: John D. Cahill, Andy Paven

Becker-Underwood, Inc.

Ames, IA
Leg. Issues: ENV

Outside Counsel/Consultants

Winston & Strawn
Issues: ENV
Rep By: John Fehrenbach

Bedford Stuyvesant Restoration Corp.

New York, NY

Outside Counsel/Consultants

Robert A. Rapoza Associates
Rep By: Robert A. Rapoza

Beef Products, Inc.

Dakota Dunes, SD

Outside Counsel/Consultants

Olsson, Frank and Weeda, P.C.
Rep By: John W. Bode, Richard L. Frank, Susan P. Grymes, Karen Reis Harned, Stephen L. Lacey, Marshall L. Matz, Tyson Redpath, Ryan W. Stroschein

Beer Institute

122 C St. NW
Suite 750
Washington, DC 20001-2109
Tel: (202)737-2337
Fax: (202)737-7004
Registered: LDA
Web: www.beerinst.org
E-mail: info@beerinstitute.org

Represents brewers and suppliers to the brewing industry before Congress, the Administration, and federal agencies.

Leg. Issues: ALC, BEV

In-house, DC-area Employees

BECKER, Jeffrey G.: President
DECELLE, Arthur J.: Exec. V. President and General Counsel
LEVY, Lori C.: Director, Communications
STANTON, Joseph M.: V. President, Federal Government Affairs

Beerman, Swerdlove, Woloshin, Barezky, Becken, Genin & London

Chicago, IL
Leg. Issues: CPT, HCR

Outside Counsel/Consultants

Stephen F. Sims and Associates
Issues: CPT, HCR
Rep By: Stephen F. Sims

Belgium, Embassy of the Kingdom of

3330 Garfield St. NW
Washington, DC 20008
Tel: (202)333-6900
Fax: (202)333-3079
Web: www.diplobel.org/usa/
E-mail: washington@diplobel.org

Outside Counsel/Consultants

Squire, Sanders & Dempsey L.L.P.
Rep By: Thomas J. Quigley, Ritchie T. Thomas

Bell Ambulance

Milwaukee, WI

Outside Counsel/Consultants

Broydrick & Associates
Rep By: William Broydrick, Amy Demske

Bell Atlantic Digital Spectrum

Outside Counsel/Consultants

Quinn Gillespie & Associates

Bell Atlantic Internet Solutions

Reston, VA

Outside Counsel/Consultants

Issue Dynamics Inc.

Bell Atlantic Mobile

Bedminster, NJ
Leg. Issues: BUD, COM, CPT, TAX, TEC

Outside Counsel/Consultants

Hill and Knowlton, Inc.
Issues: TEC

Wiley, Rein & Fielding
Issues: BUD, COM, CPT, TAX, TEC
Rep By: Mary Jo Manning

Bell Atlantic Network Services, Inc.

Arlington, VA

Outside Counsel/Consultants

Proskauer Rose LLP

Bell Atlantic Personal Communications, Inc.

Outside Counsel/Consultants

Proskauer Rose LLP

Bell Equipment Ltd.

Empangeni, SOUTH AFRICA
Leg. Issues: TRD

Outside Counsel/Consultants

Tuttle, Taylor & Heron
Issues: TRD
Rep By: Phillip L. Fraas

Bell Helicopter Textron, Inc.

Fort Worth, TX

Outside Counsel/Consultants

The Direct Impact Co.

Bell, California, City of

Leg. Issues: POS

Outside Counsel/Consultants

Colex and Associates
Issues: POS
Rep By: John P. Mack

Bellevue, Washington, City of

Leg. Issues: BUD, CAW, ECN, HOU, LAW, LBR, ROD, URB

Outside Counsel/Consultants

Ball Janik, LLP
Issues: BUD, CAW, ECN, HOU, LAW, LBR, ROD, URB
Rep By: M. Victoria Cram

Bellingham, Washington, City of

Leg. Issues: ENG, ENV

Outside Counsel/Consultants

Van Ness Feldman, P.C.
Issues: ENG, ENV
Rep By: Richard A. Agnew

BellSouth Corp.

1133 21st St. NW
Suite 900
Washington, DC 20036
Tel: (202)463-4100
Fax: (202)463-4141
Registered: LDA
Web: www.bellsouthcorp.com

Leg. Issues: BUD, COM, CPT, ENG, HCR, LBR, TAX, TEC, TED

In-house, DC-area Employees

BLAU, Robert T.: V. President, Exec. and Federal Regulatory Affairs
BOOZER, Lyndon K.: Exec. Director, Federal Relations
BRADY, Hugh S.: Exec. Director, Legislative Affairs
COX, Cynthia K.: Exec. Director, Federal and State Relations
ENGLISH, Pepper: V. President, Congressional Relations
JORDAN, Whit: V. President, Federal Regulatory
MARKEY, David J.: V. President, Governmental Affairs
MCCLOSKEY, William J.: Director, Media Relations
POSSNER, Karen B.: V. President, Strategic Policy
SCHNEIDAWIND, John: Director, Media Relations
URBANY, Francis S.: V. President, International
WHITE, Ward H.: V. President, Federal Relations

Outside Counsel/Consultants

Greener and Hook, LLC
Hall, Green, Rupli, LLC
Issues: TEC
Rep By: John M. Green, G. Stewart Hall
Long, Aldridge & Norman, LLP
Issues: TEC
Rep By: Karen Anderson, Keith W. Mason, Edgar H. Sims
Manatt, Phelps & Phillips, LLP
Issues: TEC, TED
Rep By: June L. DeHart, Eric Farnsworth, Erik V. Huey, James R. Jones, Susan M. Schmidt, Stephanie E. Silverman
Morgan Meguire, LLC
Issues: ENG
Rep By: Scott Lindsay, Kyle G. Michel, Katie Parrott, C. Kyle Simpson, Deborah R. Sliz, Kiel Weaver
New Frontiers Communications Consulting
Issues: TEC
Rep By: R. David Wilson
O'Connor & Hannan, L.L.P.
Issues: COM, TEC
Rep By: Roy C. Coffee
Verner, Liipfert, Bernhard, McPherson and Hand, Chartered
Issues: CPT
Rep By: Steven R. Phillips, David R. Siddall
Wunder & Lilley
Issues: TEC
Rep By: Bernard J. Wunder, Jr.

BellSouth Telecommunications, Inc.

Atlanta, GA
Leg. Issues: TEC

Outside Counsel/Consultants

Barbour Griffith & Rogers, Inc.
Issues: TEC
Rep By: Haley Barbour, G. O. Lanny Griffith, Jr., Loren Monroe, Edward M. Rogers, Jr., Brent Thompson
Hall, Green, Rupli, LLC
Issues: TEC
Rep By: John M. Green, G. Stewart Hall

A. H. Belo Corp.

Dallas, TX
Leg. Issues: COM, TEC

Outside Counsel/Consultants

Wiley, Rein & Fielding
Issues: COM, TEC
Rep By: James R. Bayes, Susan C. Buck, Mimi W. Dawson, Richard E. Wiley

Belridge Water Storage District

Bakersfield, CA

Outside Counsel/Consultants

Akin, Gump, Strauss, Hauer & Feld, L.L.P.

BEMS W/L Associates

Frederick, MD

Outside Counsel/Consultants

E. Del Smith and Co.
Rep By: E. Del Smith

Benchmark Communications Radio LP

Baltimore, MD

Outside Counsel/Consultants

Arthur Andersen LLP

Bender Shipbuilding & Repair Co., Inc.

Mobile, AL
Leg. Issues: MAR

Outside Counsel/Consultants

Dyer Ellis & Joseph, P.C.
Issues: MAR
Rep By: James S. W. Drewry, James B. Ellis, II, Jeanne Marie Grasso, Margaret Dillenburg Rifka, Duncan C. Smith, III, Jennifer M. Southwick

Bendich, Stobaugh & Strong

Seattle, WA
Leg. Issues: TAX

Outside Counsel/Consultants

French & Company
Issues: TAX
Rep By: Verrick O. French

Beneficial Corp.

Peapack, NJ

Outside Counsel/Consultants

Elias, Matz, Tiernan and Herrick

Benevolent and Protective Order of Elks (BPOE)

Chicago, IL

Outside Counsel/Consultants

The Gregory Co.
Rep By: Neal Gregory

Benin, Government of the Republic of

Porto-Novo, BENIN
Leg. Issues: AVI

Outside Counsel/Consultants

Patton Boggs, LLP
Washington World Group, Ltd.
Issues: AVI

Bennett Environmental Inc.

Toronto, CANADA
Leg. Issues: ENV

Outside Counsel/Consultants

Goodstein & Associates
Issues: ENV
Rep By: Richard F. Goodstein

Benova, Inc.

Portland, OR
Leg. Issues: MMM

Outside Counsel/Consultants

Holland & Knight LLP
Issues: MMM
Rep By: Jack M. Burkman, Richard M. Gold, Keith D. Lind

Benrus Watch Co.

Chicago, IL

A manufacturer of watches and jewelry.

Leg. Issues: TRD

Outside Counsel/Consultants

Winston & Strawn
Issues: TRD
Rep By: Edward F. Gerwin, Jr., Peter N. Hiebert

Benton Foundation/Communications Policy Project

950 18th St. NW
Washington, DC 20006
Tel: (202)638-5770
Fax: (202)638-5771
Web: www.benton.org

The Benton Foundation, the legacy of Senator William Benton, is working to involve non-profits in shaping the National Information Infrastructure. Benton has created the Communications Policy Project with support from the John D. and Catherine T. MacArthur Foundation.

In-house, DC-area Employees

KIRKMAN, Larry: President
MENICHELLI, Karen: V. President
WILHELM, Anthony: Director, Communications Policy Project

Beretta U.S.A. Corp.

Accokeek, MD
Leg. Issues: DEF, FIR, MAN, TAX

Outside Counsel/Consultants

American Defense Internat'l, Inc.
Issues: DEF
Rep By: Michael Herson, Van D. Hipp, Jr., Dave Wilberding
R. Duffy Wall and Associates
Issues: DEF, FIR, MAN, TAX
Rep By: Hon. Bill Brewster

Bergen Community College

Leg. Issues: BUD, HCR

Outside Counsel/Consultants

Arent Fox Kintner Plotkin & Kahn, PLLC
Issues: BUD, HCR
Rep By: Douglas McCormack, William A. Sarraille

Bergen, New York, Village of

Leg. Issues: COM, ENG, ENV, GOV, UTI

Outside Counsel/Consultants

Duncan, Weinberg, Genzer & Pembroke, P.C.
Issues: COM, ENG, ENV, GOV, UTI
Rep By: Richmond F. Allan, Jeffrey C. Genzer, Michael R. Postar, Thomas L. Rudebusch

Berkeley County Water & Sanitation Authority
Goose Creek, SC
Leg. Issues: CAW, UTI

Outside Counsel/Consultants

Timothy X. Moore and Co.
Issues: CAW, UTI
Rep By: Timothy X. Moore

Berkeley, California, City of
Leg. Issues: DIS, ENV, HOU, LAW, RET, WEL

Outside Counsel/Consultants

Copeland, Lowery & Jacquez
Issues: DIS, ENV, HOU, LAW, RET, WEL
Rep By: James M. Copeland, Jr.

Bermuda Biological Station for Research

Outside Counsel/Consultants

Capitol Associates, Inc.
Rep By: Ronnie Kovner Tepp

Bermuda, Government of
Hamilton, BERMUDA
Leg. Issues: TAX

Outside Counsel/Consultants

Garvey, Schubert & Barer
Rep By: Richard A. Wegman

Levine & Co.
Issues: TAX
Rep By: Ken Levine

Bernalillo, New Mexico, County of
Albuquerque, NM
Leg. Issues: BUD, CAW, HOU, LAW, TRA

Outside Counsel/Consultants

Murray, Scheer, Montgomery, Tapia & O'Donnell
Issues: BUD, CAW, HOU, LAW, TRA
Rep By: John R. O'Donnell

Bernard Johnson, Inc.
Houston, TX

Outside Counsel/Consultants

Korth & Korth

Berry Amendment Glove Coalition

Outside Counsel/Consultants

Collier Shannon Scott, PLLC
Rep By: Lauren R. Howard, Robert W. Porter

Bert Corona Leadership Institute
1500 Farragut St. NW
Washington, DC 20011
Tel: (202)723-7241
Fax: (202)723-7246
Registered: LDA
Web: www.nild.org
E-mail: hnild@aol.com
Leg. Issues: CIV, ECN, EDU, HCR, HOU, IMM, LBR

In-house, DC-area Employees

LOPEZ, Earl Francisco: President

Bertelsmann AG
Brussels, BELGIUM
Leg. Issues: ART, COM, MIA, TEC, TRD

Outside Counsel/Consultants

Mayer, Brown & Platt
Issues: ART, COM, MIA, TEC, TRD
Rep By: Penny L. Eastman, Julian Gehman, John P. Schmitz

Berwind Corp.
Philadelphia, PA
Leg. Issues: LBR, RET, TAX

Outside Counsel/Consultants

Sam Richardson
Rep By: Sam Richardson

Symms, Lehn & Associates, Inc.
Issues: LBR, RET, TAX

Bessemer Securities Corp.
New York, NY
An investment company.
Leg. Issues: TAX

Outside Counsel/Consultants

Davis & Harman LLP
Issues: TAX

Hooper Owen & Winburn
Issues: TAX
Rep By: Steve Glaze

Best Foods
Englewood Cliffs, NJ
Registered: LDA

Outside Counsel/Consultants

Wilmer, Cutler & Pickering
Rep By: William J. Wilkins

Best Health Care Inc.
Philadelphia, PA
Leg. Issues: HCR

Outside Counsel/Consultants

Robert M. Brandon and Associates
Issues: HCR
Rep By: Robert M. Brandon

BET Holdings II, Inc.
One BET Plaza
1900 W Pl. NE
Washington, DC 20018
Web: www.bet.com
Tel: (202)608-2000
Fax: (202)608-2595

Media entertainment company serving the African-American community. BET Holdings II, Inc. includes cable networks, an interactive website, entertainment themed restaurants, and movies production.

Leg. Issues: ART, COM, ECN, GAM, MIA, TEC, TEL

In-house, DC-area Employees

JOHNSON, Robert L.: Chief Exec. Officer/Chairman
KELLY, Kimberly A.: Counsel, Government Affairs and Affiliate Regulations
MARCHANT, Byron: Exec. V. President and C.A.O.

Outside Counsel/Consultants

Dow, Lohnes & Albertson, PLLC
Rep By: John R. Feore, Jr.

Patton Boggs, LLP
Issues: TEC, TEL
Rep By: Stephen Diaz Gavin

Shaw Pittman
Issues: ECN
Rep By: Thomas J. Spulak

Verner, Liipfert, Bernhard, McPherson and Hand, Chartered
Rep By: Lawrence R. Sidman

Betac Corp.
Alexandria, VA
A defense consulting firm.
Leg. Issues: DEF

Outside Counsel/Consultants

Higgins, McGovern & Smith, LLC
Issues: DEF
Rep By: Carl M. Smith

Beth Israel/Deaconess Medical Center
Boston, MA

Outside Counsel/Consultants

O'Neill, Athy & Casey, P.C.
Rep By: Martha L. Casey, Christopher R. O'Neill

Bethel Grain Co., LLC
Benton, IL
Leg. Issues: SMB

Outside Counsel/Consultants

Robert H. Sindt
Issues: SMB
Rep By: Robert H. Sindt

Bethel Native Corp.

Outside Counsel/Consultants

Dilworth Paxson, LLP
Rep By: Rebecca A. Donnellan

Bethel New Life
Chicago, IL

Outside Counsel/Consultants

Robert A. Rapoza Associates
Rep By: Robert A. Rapoza

Bethesda Academy for the Performing Arts
Bethesda, MD
Leg. Issues: BUD

Outside Counsel/Consultants

Van Scoyoc Associates, Inc.
Issues: BUD
Rep By: Steve E. Crane, Kevin F. Kelly, H. Stewart Van Scoyoc

Bethlehem Steel Corp.
1667 K St. NW
Suite 550
Washington, DC 20006
Tel: (202)775-6200
Fax: (202)775-6221
Registered: LDA

A steel and steel product production company headquartered in Bethlehem, PA.

Leg. Issues: AUT, BUD, CAW, DEF, ENG, ENV, HCR, MMM, ROD, RRR, TAX, TOR, TRA, TRD, TRU

In-house, DC-area Employees

CARINO, Jr., Maurice E.: V. President, Federal Government Affairs

Outside Counsel/Consultants

BKSH & Associates
Issues: ENG, TAX, TRD

Davis & Harman LLP
Issues: TAX
Rep By: Richard S. Belas, Thomas A. Davis

Frank Fenton
Issues: ENV, TAX, TRA, TRD
Rep By: Frank Fenton

Hale and Dorr LLP
Issues: TRD
Rep By: Gilbert B. Kaplan

Skadden, Arps, Slate, Meagher & Flom LLP
Issues: TRD
Rep By: Robert E. Lighthizer

Bethune-Cookman College
Daytona Beach, FL
Registered: LDA
Leg. Issues: EDU

Outside Counsel/Consultants

Dean Blakey & Moskowitz
Issues: EDU
Rep By: William A. Blakey

Jefferson Government Relations, L.L.C.
Issues: EDU
Rep By: William J. Gilmartin, William A. Roberts

The Bethune-DuBois Institute, Inc.
8401 Colesville Rd.
Suite 400
Silver Spring, MD 20910
Tel: (301)562-8300
Fax: (301)562-8303

Encourages participation by young Blacks in the political process and provides leadership training for the 21st Century. Offers training programs in the formulation and shaping of socio-economic and public policy issues.

In-house, DC-area Employees

TUCKER, Dr. C. DeLores: President

Better Hearing Institute
515 King St.
Suite 420
Alexandria, VA 22314
Web: www.betterhearing.org
E-mail: mail@betterhearing.org
Tel: (703)684-3391
Fax: (703)684-6084

A non-profit organization founded in 1973 in Washington whose principal purpose is to provide public information on hearing loss and available medical, surgical, hearing aid and rehabilitation assistance for those with uncorrected problems. Maintains a toll-free Hearing HelpLine at 1-800 EAR WELL, that provides information on hearing loss and hearing help anywhere in the United States and Canada.

In-house, DC-area Employees

OLIVE, Jr., John T.: Exec. Director

Outside Counsel/Consultants

CLARION Management Resources, Inc.
Rep By: John T. Olive, Jr.

Better World Campaign
1301 Connecticut Ave. NW
Suite 700
Washington, DC 20036
Tel: (202)462-4900
Registered: LDA
Leg. Issues: BUD, FOR

In-house, DC-area Employees

CUTTINO, Phyllis: V. President, Public Affairs
MYERS, Susan: Legislative Director
WIRTH, Hon. Timothy E.: President

Outside Counsel/Consultants

Barbour Griffith & Rogers, Inc.
Issues: FOR
Rep By: Haley Barbour, G. O. Lanny Griffith, Jr., Loren Monroe, Edward M. Rogers, Jr.

Beverly Enterprises

555 12th St. NW
Suite 1230
Washington, DC 20004
Tel: (202)783-1115
Fax: (202)783-5411
Registered: LDA

Leg. Issues: HCR, MMM

Political Action Committee/s

BevPAC

555 12th St. NW
Suite 1230
Washington, DC 20004
Contact: Kay Cox
Tel: (202)783-1115
Fax: (202)783-5411

In-house, DC-area Employees

COX, Kay: V. President, Federal Government Relations

Outside Counsel/Consultants

Capitol Health Group, LLC
Issues: HCR, MMM
Rep By: Michael D. Bromberg, Shawn Coughlin, Steven Jenning, Layna McConkey Peltier

Beverly Hills Federal Savings Bank

Beverly Hills, CA

Outside Counsel/Consultants

Arnold & Porter

Bexar Metropolitan Water District

San Antonio, TX
Leg. Issues: BUD

Outside Counsel/Consultants

Greenberg Traurig, LLP
Issues: BUD
Rep By: Diane J. Blagman

Beyond BAT Group

Washington, DC

A group of companies in the pulp and paper manufacturing business.

Outside Counsel/Consultants

Perkins Coie LLP
Rep By: Sloane Wildman

Beyond.com

Sunnyvale, CA
Leg. Issues: CPI

Outside Counsel/Consultants

Denny Miller McBee Associates
Issues: CPI

BHC Communications, Inc.

Leg. Issues: TAX

Outside Counsel/Consultants

Washington Council Ernst & Young
Issues: TAX
Rep By: Doug Badger, Lauren Darling, John L. Doney, Jayne T. Fitzgerald, LaBrenda Garrett-Nelson, Gary J. Gasper, Bruce A. Gates, Nick Giordano, Cathy Koch, Robert J. Leonard, William Mastro, Richard Meltzer, Phillip D. Moseley, John D. Porter, Robert M. Rozen, Donna Steele-Flynn, Timothy J. Urban

BHP (USA) Inc.

1155 Connecticut Ave. NW
Suite 323
Washington, DC 20036
E-mail: whittedpj@aol.com
Tel: (202)467-8577
Fax: (202)463-8576

Leg. Issues: BUD, ENG, ENV, FUE, LBR, NAT, TAX, TRD, UTI

In-house, DC-area Employees

WHITTED, Pamela J.: Director, Federal Government Affairs

Outside Counsel/Consultants

Dunlap & Browder, Inc.

Orrick Herrington & Sutcliffe LLP

R. Duffy Wall and Associates
Issues: TAX
Rep By: David C. Jory

BI, Inc.

Boulder, CO

Outside Counsel/Consultants

Cordia Cos.

Bi-State Development Agency

St. Louis, MO

Outside Counsel/Consultants

Bracy Williams & Co.
Rep By: Terrence L. Bracy, James P. Brown, Laura L. Madden

Bibb, Georgia, Board of Commissioners of the County of

Macon, GA
Leg. Issues: ROD

Outside Counsel/Consultants

Birch, Horton, Bittner & Cherot
Issues: ROD
Rep By: Julia Gustafson, William P. Horn

Bicopas, Ltd.

Bucharest, ROMANIA
Leg. Issues: ECN, FIN, FOR

Outside Counsel/Consultants

Dublin Castle Group
Issues: ECN, FIN, FOR
Rep By: Maureen Flatley Hogan

Bicycle Council

Lyndon Station, WI
Leg. Issues: SPO

Outside Counsel/Consultants

Venable
Issues: SPO
Rep By: Brock R. Landry

Bicycle Manufacturers Ass'n of America

Outside Counsel/Consultants

Collier Shannon Scott, PLLC
Rep By: Janice E. Conway, David A. Hartquist, Michael R. Kershow, Kathleen Clark Kies

Bicycle Product Suppliers Ass'n

Philadelphia, PA
Leg. Issues: CSP, GOV

Outside Counsel/Consultants

Venable
Issues: CSP, GOV
Rep By: Brock R. Landry

Bicycle Shippers Ass'n

San Jose, CA

Outside Counsel/Consultants

Rodriguez O'Donnell Fuerst Gonzalez & Williams
Rep By: Carlos Rodriguez

Big Brothers/Big Sisters of America

Philadelphia, PA

A non-profit youth mentoring program.

Leg. Issues: BUD

Outside Counsel/Consultants

Beacon Consulting Group, Inc.
Issues: BUD
Rep By: Gordon P. MacDougall, Lisa A. Stewart, Kyndel Turvaville

Big Dog Sportswear

Santa Barbara, CA

Outside Counsel/Consultants

Paul, Hastings, Janofsky & Walker LLP
Rep By: R. Bruce Dickson

Big Sky Airlines

Billings, MT

Outside Counsel/Consultants

Shaw Pittman
Rep By: Robert E. Cohn, Sheryl R. Israel

Big Sky Economic Development Authority

Billings, MT
Leg. Issues: BUD

Outside Counsel/Consultants

Capitol Coalitions Inc.
Issues: BUD
Rep By: Amy R. Mehlman, Brett P. Scott, Jarvis C. Stewart

Big Sky, Inc.

Leg. Issues: ECN

Outside Counsel/Consultants

Capitol Hill Advocates
Issues: ECN
Rep By: Randall G. Pence

Billfish Foundation

Leg. Issues: MAR

Outside Counsel/Consultants

Ball Janik, LLP
Issues: MAR
Rep By: Robert G. Hayes

Billiard and Bowling Institute of America

c/o Sporting Goods Manufacturers Ass'n
1625 K St. NW, Suite 900
Washington, DC 20006-1604
Web: www.sportlink.com
E-mail: tomsgma@aol.com
Tel: (202)775-1762
Fax: (202)296-7462
Registered: LDA

In-house, DC-area Employees

COVE, Thomas J.

Billing Concepts, Inc.

San Antonio, TX
Leg. Issues: TEC

Outside Counsel/Consultants

Arter & Hadden
Issues: TEC
Rep By: Daniel L. Cohen, Hon. Thomas G. Loeffler

Biman Bangladesh Airlines

New York, NY

Outside Counsel/Consultants

Washington World Group, Ltd.
Rep By: Edward J. von Kloberg, III

Binney & Smith Inc.

Easton, PA

Outside Counsel/Consultants

St. Maxens & Company
Rep By: Thomas F. St. Maxens, II

Bio-Vascular, Inc.

St. Paul, MN
Leg. Issues: HCR

Outside Counsel/Consultants

Oppenheimer Wolff & Donnelly LLP
Issues: HCR
Rep By: Hon. Birch Bayh

Biochemics

Danvers, MA
Leg. Issues: MED

Outside Counsel/Consultants

Capitol Partners
Issues: MED
Rep By: William Cunningham, Jonathan M. Orloff

Biocontrol Technology, Inc.

Pittsburgh, PA
Leg. Issues: DEF

Outside Counsel/Consultants

The PMA Group
Issues: DEF
Rep By: Daniel Cunningham, Kaylene Green, Patrick Hiu, Paul J. Magliocchetti

Bioelectromagnetics Soc.

Baltimore, MD

Outside Counsel/Consultants

E. Del Smith and Co.
Rep By: Margaret Allen, E. Del Smith

Biogen, Inc.

Washington, DC
Registered: LDA
Leg. Issues: BUD, HCR, MED, MMM

Outside Counsel/Consultants

Bergner Bockorny Castagnetti and Hawkins
Issues: HCR
Rep By: Jeffrey T. Bergner, David A. Bockorny, David Castagnetti, James W. Hawkins, Brenda Benjamin Reese, Melissa Schulman

Capitol Partners
Issues: BUD
Rep By: William Cunningham, Jonathan M. Orloff

Hogan & Hartson L.L.P.
Issues: MED
Rep By: Humberto R. Pena

The Legislative Strategies Group, LLC

Mintz, Levin, Cohn, Ferris, Glovsky and Popeo, P.C.
Issues: MMM
Rep By: Charles A. Samuels

Biomatrix

Ridgefield, NJ
Leg. Issues: HCR

Outside Counsel/Consultants

Capitol Partners
Issues: HCR
Rep By: William Cunningham, Jonathan M. Orloff

Biomedical Research Foundation of Northwest Louisiana

Shreveport, LA
Leg. Issues: ENG, PHA, TRA

Outside Counsel/Consultants

Charlie McBride Associates, Inc.
Issues: ENG, PHA, TRA
Rep By: Charlie McBride

Biomedical Research Institute

Rockville, MD
Leg. Issues: BUD, HCR

Outside Counsel/Consultants

Arent Fox Kintner Plotkin & Kahn, PLLC
Issues: BUD, HCR
Rep By: Hon. John C. Culver, Douglas McCormack, Todd Weiss

Biophysical Soc.

9650 Rockville Pike
Bethesda, MD 20814-3998
Tel: (301)530-7114
Fax: (301)530-7133
Web: www.biophysics.org/biophys
E-mail: society@biophysics.faseb.org

The Biophysical Society is an organization of over 5,400 scientists. The Society represents a wide range of research areas, in particular, scientists who work on the physical-chemical basis of biological structure, including: chemical kinetics, electrophysiology, microscopy, structural biology, spectroscopy, and x-ray crystallography.

Leg. Issues: SCI

In-house, DC-area Employees

KAMPMAN, Rosalba: Exec. Director

BioPort Corp.

Lansing, MI
Leg. Issues: DEF, HCR, PHA

Outside Counsel/Consultants

Dalrymple and Associates, L.L.C.
Issues: DEF, HCR, PHA
Rep By: Donald "Dack" Dalrymple

Biopure Corp.

Outside Counsel/Consultants

Hogan & Hartson L.L.P.
Rep By: Raymond S. Calamaro

Biostar Group, The

Germantown, MD
Leg. Issues: COM, DEF

Outside Counsel/Consultants

SISCORP
Issues: COM, DEF
Rep By: Robert Meissner, Fran Shottes

Biotech Research and Development Center

Peoria, IL
Leg. Issues: BUD

Outside Counsel/Consultants

The Dutko Group, Inc.
Issues: BUD
Rep By: Mark S. Irion, Arthur H. Silverman, William Simmons

Biotechnology Industry Organization

1625 K St. NW
Suite 1100
Washington, DC 20006-1604
Tel: (202)857-0244
Fax: (202)857-0237
Registered: LDA
Web: www.bio.org
E-mail: bio@bio.org
Leg. Issues: AGR, CPT, CSP, DEF, ENV, FIN, FOO, HCR, IMM, MED, MMM, PHA, SCI, TAX, TOR, TRD

Political Action Committee/s

Biotechnology Industry Organization PAC
1625 K St. NW
Suite 1100
Washington, DC 20006-1604
Tel: (202)857-0244
Fax: (202)857-0237
Contact: Lee Rawls

In-house, DC-area Employees

BRISCUSO, Raymond: Exec. Director
COHEN, Sharon L.: V. President for Health Policy
DRY, Lisa J.: Director, Communication
ERAMIAN, Dan: V. President, Communications
ERICKSON, R. Brent: Director, Industrial and Environmental Section
FELDBAUM, Carl B.: President
GIDDINGS, L. Val: V. President, Food and Agriculture
LAWTON, Stephen E.: V. President, Regulatory Affairs and General Counsel
LYONS, Matthew D.: Director, Government Relations, Food and Agriculture Section
PHILLIPS, Michael: Director, Food and Agriculture Section
RAWLS, Lee: V. President, Government Relations
RUFFIN, Edmund: V. President, Business Development
UFHOLZ, Philip: Director, Government Relations and Tax Counsel
WERNER, Michael: Director, Federal Government Relations

Outside Counsel/Consultants

Arent Fox Kintner Plotkin & Kahn, PLLC
Issues: FOO
Rep By: Stanley H. Abramson

Bain and Associates, Inc.
Rep By: C. Jackson Bain

Dalrymple and Associates, L.L.C.
Issues: CPT, HCR
Rep By: Donald "Dack" Dalrymple

DTB Associates, LLP

Long, Aldridge & Norman, LLP
Issues: AGR, TRD
Rep By: Karen Anderson, Lindsey Marcus

The National Group, LLP
Rep By: John Blount, William C. Oldaker

The OB-C Group, LLC
Issues: CSP, HCR, MED, SCI
Rep By: Thomas Keating, Kim F. McKernan, Charles J. Mellody, Patricia A. Nelson, Lawrence F. O'Brien, III, Linda E. Tarplin

Pepper Hamilton LLP

The Potomac Research Group LLC
Issues: MED, SCI
Rep By: G. Harris Jordan, Paul Welles Orr

SPECTRUM Science Public Relations, Inc.
Issues: HCR, MED, MMM, PHA, SCI
Rep By: Thomas C. Norton

Biovail Corp. Internat'l

Ontario, CANADA
Leg. Issues: PHA

Outside Counsel/Consultants

Verner, Liipfert, Bernhard, McPherson and Hand, Chartered
Issues: PHA
Rep By: Matthew C. Bernstein, Hon. James J. Blanchard, Rosemary B. Freeman, Gary J. Klein, William H. Minor, Steven R. Phillips, James A. Pickup

Bird-Johnson Co.

Arlington, VA
Leg. Issues: DEF

Outside Counsel/Consultants

Brown and Company, Inc.
Issues: DEF
Rep By: Cynthia L. Brown, Hugh N. "Rusty" Johnson, Frank W. Losey

Birmingham Airport Authority

Birmingham, AL
Leg. Issues: AVI, TRA

Outside Counsel/Consultants

Bradley Arant Rose & White LLP
Issues: AVI, TRA

Hall, Green, Rupli, LLC
Issues: AVI
Rep By: John M. Green, G. Stewart Hall

Birmingham Building Trades Towers, Inc.

Birmingham, AL

Outside Counsel/Consultants

Bradley Arant Rose & White LLP

Birmingham Steel Corp.

Birmingham, AL
Leg. Issues: TRD

Outside Counsel/Consultants

Wiley, Rein & Fielding
Issues: TRD
Rep By: Eileen P. Bradner, Sharon R. Fine, Hon. Jim Slattery

Birthright Israel

Outside Counsel/Consultants

The DCS Group

Biscuit and Cracker Manufacturers Ass'n

8484 Georgia Ave.
Suite 700
Silver Spring, MD 20910
Tel: (301)608-1552
Fax: (301)608-1557
Web: www.thebcma.org
Leg. Issues: FOO, GOV

In-house, DC-area Employees

BLUE, Christina: Director, Government Relations
ROONEY, Francis P.: President

Bishop Museum

Honolulu, HI
Leg. Issues: SCI

Outside Counsel/Consultants

Cassidy & Associates, Inc.
Issues: SCI
Rep By: Henry K. Giugni, Jeffrey Lawrence

Bitrek Corp.

Waynesboro, PA
Leg. Issues: TRA

Outside Counsel/Consultants

Schagrin Associates
Issues: TRA
Rep By: Tamara L. Browne, Roger B. Schagrin

Bituminous Coal Operators Ass'n

1500 K St. NW
Suite 875
Washington, DC 20005
Tel: (202)783-3195
Fax: (202)783-4862
Leg. Issues: ENV, HCR, NAT, RET, TAX

In-house, DC-area Employees

FEIBUSCH, Morris D.: V. President, Public Affairs
PERKINS, III, Charles S.: Secretary-Treasurer
YOUNG, David: President

Outside Counsel/Consultants

Forscey & Stinson, PLLC
Issues: ENV, HCR
Rep By: Michael A. Forscey

Morgan, Lewis & Bockius LLP
Issues: HCR, RET
Rep By: Margery Sinder Friedman

The National Group, LLP
Rep By: John Blount

The Willard Group
Issues: ENV, NAT, TAX
Rep By: Daniel Scherder

BitWise Designs Inc.

Schenectady, NY
Leg. Issues: CPI

Outside Counsel/Consultants

The Advocacy Group
Issues: CPI
Rep By: Robert E. Mills, George A. Ramonas

Bizee.com

Outside Counsel/Consultants

Dittus Communications
Rep By: Trudi Boyd

BKK Corp.

Torrance, CA

Outside Counsel/Consultants

Arter & Hadden
Rep By: Daniel L. Cohen, Hon. Thomas G. Loeffler

BL Harbert Internat'l
Birmingham, AL
Outside Counsel/Consultants
Bradley Arant Rose & White LLP

Black & Decker Corp., The
Towson, MD
Leg. Issues: ENV
Outside Counsel/Consultants
Miles & Stockbridge, P.C.
Issues: ENV
Rep By: Samuel A. Bleicher

Black America's Political Action Committee
2029 P St. NW
Suite 202
Washington, DC 20036
Tel: (202)785-9619
Fax: (202)785-9621
Web: www.bampac.org
E-mail: bampac@bampac.org

Support primarily black conservative political candidates for the federal, state, and local levels of government.

In-house, DC-area Employees
WHITE, Douglas: Treasurer
WILLIAMS, Alvin: Exec. Director

Black Hills Forest Resource Ass'n
Rapid City, SD
Leg. Issues: AGR
Outside Counsel/Consultants
Olsson, Frank and Weeda, P.C.
Issues: AGR
Rep By: Stephen L. Lacey, Marshall L. Matz, Richard D. Siegel, Ryan W. Stroschein

Black Mesa Community School Board
Chinle, AZ
Outside Counsel/Consultants
Hobbs, Straus, Dean and Walker, LLP
Rep By: Carol L. Barbero, Karen J. Funk, Aura Kanegis, Marie Osceola-Branch

Blackfeet Tribe of Montana
Browning, MT
Leg. Issues: ENG, ENV, GOV, IND, NAT
Outside Counsel/Consultants
Van Ness Feldman, P.C.
Issues: ENG, ENV, GOV, IND, NAT
Rep By: Daniel S. Press, J. Curtis Rich, Steven Richardson

Blacks in Government
1820 11th St. NW
Washington, DC 20001-5015
Tel: (202)667-3280
Fax: (202)667-3705
Web: www.bignet.org

Serves as a watchdog organization to ensure the fair treatment of blacks working in federal, state and local governments, particularly with regard to hiring, training and promotion policies.

In-house, DC-area Employees
REED, Gerald R.: National President
REEVES, Gregg: Exec. V. President

Blacksmith
McLean, VA
Outside Counsel/Consultants
Earle Palmer Brown Public Relations

Blade Communications
Toledo, OH
Outside Counsel/Consultants
Wiley, Rein & Fielding
Rep By: Donna C. Gregg

Blaine, Washington, City of
Blaine, WA
Leg. Issues: CAW
Outside Counsel/Consultants
Preston Gates Ellis & Rouvelas Meeds LLP
Issues: CAW
Rep By: Tim L. Peckinpaugh

Blake Construction Co.
Washington, DC
Outside Counsel/Consultants
Kilpatrick Stockton LLP
Rep By: Hon. Elliott H. Levitas, Neil I. Levy

Blinded Veterans Ass'n
477 H St. NW
Washington, DC 20001-2694
Tel: (202)371-8880
Fax: (202)371-8258
Web: www.bva.org
E-mail: bva@bva.org

The only veterans service organization chartered by the U.S. Congress to represent and provide services for America's blinded veterans.

In-house, DC-area Employees
MILLER, Thomas H.: Exec. Director

BLNG, Inc.
Greenwich, CT
Leg. Issues: MAR
Outside Counsel/Consultants
Dyer Ellis & Joseph, P.C.
Issues: MAR
Rep By: Laurie Crick Sahatjian, L. Maurice Daniel, James S. W. Drewry, Thomas M. Dyer, Duncan C. Smith, III, Jennifer M. Southwick

H & R Block, Inc.
700 13th St. NW
Suite 700
Washington, DC 20005-5922
Tel: (202)508-6363
Fax: (202)508-6330
Registered: LDA
Web: www.hrblock.com
E-mail: RWeinberger@hrblock.com

A tax, accounting, and financial services company headquartered in Kansas City, MO.

Leg. Issues: ACC, CPI, FIN, TAX

Political Action Committee/s
Block PAC
700 13th St. NW
Suite 700
Washington, DC 20005-5922
Tel: (202)508-6363
Fax: (202)508-6330
Contact: Robert A. Weinberger

In-house, DC-area Employees
DECKER, Larry: Legislative Assistant
WEINBERGER, Robert A.: V. President, Government Relations

Blood Center of Southeastern Wisconsin
Milwaukee, WI
Leg. Issues: EDU, HCR, MED, MMM
Outside Counsel/Consultants
Broydrick & Associates
Issues: EDU, HCR, MED, MMM
Rep By: William Broydrick, Amy Demske

Bloomberg L.P.
New York, NY
Leg. Issues: CPT
Outside Counsel/Consultants
Royer & Babyak
Issues: CPT
Rep By: Gregory R. Babyak
Willkie Farr & Gallagher
Issues: CPT
Rep By: Russell L. Smith, Theodore C. Whitehouse

Blount Parrish & Co., Inc.
Montgomery, AL
Leg. Issues: TAX
Outside Counsel/Consultants
Bradley Arant Rose & White LLP
Hogan & Hartson L.L.P.
Issues: TAX
Rep By: Nancy Granese, William Michael House

Blue Anchor, Inc.
Sacramento, CA
Outside Counsel/Consultants
McDermott, Will and Emery
Rep By: Carolyn B. Gleason

Blue Cross and Blue Shield of California
Woodland Hills, CA
Leg. Issues: HCR, TAX
Outside Counsel/Consultants
Greenberg Traurig, LLP
Issues: TAX
Rep By: James F. Miller
Miller & Chevalier, Chartered
Issues: HCR
Rep By: Leonard Bickwit, Jr.

Blue Cross and Blue Shield of Florida
Jacksonville, FL
Registered: LDA
Leg. Issues: HCR
Outside Counsel/Consultants
Hill and Knowlton, Inc.
Issues: HCR
Rep By: Gary G. Hymel, Jeffrey B. Trammell

Blue Cross and Blue Shield of Maine
Portland, ME
Leg. Issues: BUD, INS, TAX
Outside Counsel/Consultants
Podesta/Mattoon
Issues: BUD, INS, TAX

Blue Cross and Blue Shield of Ohio
Cleveland, OH
Outside Counsel/Consultants
Baker & Hostetler LLP
Rep By: Matthew J. Dolan, Steven A. Lotterer, Hon. Guy Vander Jagt

Blue Cross Blue Shield Ass'n
1310 G St. NW
12th Floor
Washington, DC 20005
Tel: (202)626-4780
Fax: (202)626-4833
Registered: LDA
Web: www.bluecares.com

Serves as an association for the independent locally-based Blue Cross and Blue Shield plans. Association headquartered in Chicago, IL.

Leg. Issues: BUD, HCR, INS, LBR, MMM, PHA, TAX

Political Action Committee/s
BluePAC
1310 G St. NW
12th Floor
Washington, DC 20005
Tel: (202)626-4780
Fax: (202)626-4833
Contact: Berry Trimble

In-house, DC-area Employees
ALDRICH, Stephanie: Senior Policy Consultant II
CALANDRO, Tony: Director, Grassroots Program
CERISANO, John C.: Director, Congressional Relations
DRELLOW, Pam: Managing Director, Public Affairs
ERICKSEN, Jack: Exec. Director, Congressional Relations
FOX, Alissa: Exec. Director, Policy
GALVIN, Jane: Senior Regulatory Consultant
HALTMEYER, Kris: Senior Policy Consultant
LAPIERRE, Steven: Exec. Washington Representative
LEHNHARD, Mary Nell: Senior V. President, Office of Policy and Representation
MUSKER, Joe: Senior Legislative Policy Analyst
NYQUIST, Christina: Director, Policy
PIERCE, Bill: Director, Public Affairs
SLACKMAN, Joel: Director, Policy
TRIMBLE, Berry: Manager, Congressional Communications
WEBB, Brian: Senior Policy Consultant

Outside Counsel/Consultants
Groom Law Group, Chartered
Issues: HCR
Rep By: Jon W. Breyfogle, Thomas F. Fitzgerald
King & Spalding
Issues: HCR
Rep By: Theodore M. Hester, Eleanor Hill
The OB-C Group, LLC
Issues: BUD, HCR
Rep By: Thomas Keating, Kim F. McKernan, Charles J. Mellody, Patricia A. Nelson, Lawrence F. O'Brien, III, Linda E. Tarplin
Podesta/Mattoon
Issues: BUD, HCR, INS, TAX
PriceWaterhouseCoopers
Issues: TAX
Rep By: Jim Carlisle, Kenneth J. Kies

Blue Cross Blue Shield of Mississippi
Jackson, MS
Outside Counsel/Consultants
The Montgomery Group
Rep By: Hon. G. V. "Sonny" Montgomery

Blue Diamond Growers
Sacramento, CA
Registered: LDA
Leg. Issues: AGR
Outside Counsel/Consultants
Tuttle, Taylor & Heron
Issues: AGR
Rep By: Julian B. Heron, Jr.

Blue Ribbon Coalition

Boise, ID

Outside Counsel/Consultants

Birch, Horton, Bittner & Cherot
Rep By: Douglas S. Burdin, William P. Horn

Blue Water Fishermen's Ass'n

Barnegat Light, NJ
Leg. Issues: MAR

Outside Counsel/Consultants

Glenn Roger Delaney
Issues: MAR
Rep By: Glenn Roger Delaney

Bluebonnet Savings Bank

Dallas, TX
Leg. Issues: BAN

Outside Counsel/Consultants

Butera & Andrews
Issues: BAN
Rep By: Cliff W. Andrews, James J. Butera, Frank Tillotson

Blyth Industries, Inc.

Greenwich, CT
Leg. Issues: TRD

Outside Counsel/Consultants

Hale and Dorr LLP
Issues: TRD
Rep By: Bonnie B. Byers, Jay P. Urwitz

BMC Software

8405 Greensboro Dr.
Suite 100
McLean, VA 22102
Tel: (703)744-3500
Fax: (703)744-3501
Web: www.bmc.com

In-house, DC-area Employees

CLARKE, Harry: General Manager, Federal Operations

BMW (U.S.) Holding Corp.

1101 Pennsylvania Ave. NW
Washington, DC 20004
Tel: (202)872-3822
Fax: (202)756-7444
Web: www.bmw.com
Leg. Issues: AUT, IMM, SCI, TAX

In-house, DC-area Employees

HELSING, Craig R.: V. President

Outside Counsel/Consultants

Kelly and Associates, Inc.
Issues: AUT, IMM, SCI, TAX
Rep By: John A. Kelly

BMW Financial Services of North America, Inc.

Washington, DC
Leg. Issues: AUT, BAN, BNK, BUD, CSP, FIN, TAX

Outside Counsel/Consultants

Hohlt & Associates
Issues: AUT, BAN, BNK, BUD, CSP, FIN, TAX
Rep By: Richard F. Hohlt

Kelly and Associates, Inc.
Rep By: John A. Kelly

BMW Manufacturing Corp.

Spartanburg, SC
Leg. Issues: AUT, BUD, CAW, CPT, CSP, ECN, IMM, LBR, MAN, TAX, TRD

Outside Counsel/Consultants

Kelly and Associates, Inc.
Issues: AUT, BUD, CAW, CPT, CSP, ECN, IMM, LBR, MAN, TAX, TRD
Rep By: John A. Kelly

BMW of North America, Inc.

Woodcliff, NJ

Outside Counsel/Consultants

Kelly and Associates, Inc.
Rep By: John A. Kelly

BNFL, Inc.

1900 M St. NW
Suite 500
Washington, DC 20036
Tel: (202)785-2635
Fax: (202)785-4037
Registered: LDA
Web: www.bnflinc.com

A U.S. subsidiary of BNFL (British Nuclear Fuels plc) headquartered in Fairfax, VA. BNFL Inc. is a full service nuclear waste management, decommissioning, engineering, spent fuel storage, and nuclear materials handling company.

Leg. Issues: CAW, ENG, GOV

In-house, DC-area Employees

CAMPBELL, David A.: Manager, Corporate External Affairs
GUAY, Richard F.: V. President, Government Relations
MEIGS, Marilyn F.: V. President, Fuel Cycle and Materials Processing
PIERCY, Clare: Government and Media Relations Representative

Outside Counsel/Consultants

Kaye Scholer LLP
Issues: ENG
Rep By: Christopher R. Brewster, G Christopher Griner

Patton Boggs, LLP
Issues: CAW, GOV
Rep By: Thomas Hale Boggs, Jr., Thomas C. Downs, Michael J. Driver

Board for Orthotists/Prosthetist Certification

Baltimore, MD

Outside Counsel/Consultants

Halsey, Rains & Associates, LLC
Rep By: Steven C. Halsey, James Hubbard, Laurie D. Rains

Board of Veterans Appeals Professional Ass'n

Washington, DC

A professional development association of federal administrative law judges.

Leg. Issues: GOV

Outside Counsel/Consultants

Kyros & Cummins Associates
Issues: GOV
Rep By: John M. Falk, Hon. Peter N. Kyros

Board on Human Sciences

Leg. Issues: BUD, EDU, HCR, SCI

Outside Counsel/Consultants

Van Scoyoc Associates, Inc.
Issues: BUD, EDU, HCR, SCI
Rep By: Steve E. Crane, Kevin F. Kelly, Jasper Thomson, H. Stewart Van Scoyoc

The Boat Co.

Washington, DC

A non-profit operator of small passenger vessels in Alaska.

Leg. Issues: MAR

Outside Counsel/Consultants

Robins, Kaplan, Miller & Ciresi L.L.P.
Issues: MAR
Rep By: Harold E. Mesirow

Boat Owners Ass'n of The United States (BOAT/U.S.)

880 S. Pickett St.
Alexandria, VA 22304
Tel: (703)461-2864
Fax: (703)461-2845
Registered: LDA
Web: www.boatus.com
E-mail: boatus@boatus.com

With 515,000 members, BOAT/U.S. is the largest organization of recreational boat owners in the world

Leg. Issues: MAR

Political Action Committee/s

Boat Owners Ass'n of The U.S. Political Action Committee
880 S. Pickett St.
Alexandria, VA 22304
Tel: (703)461-2864
Fax: (703)461-2845
Contact: Michael G. Sciulla

In-house, DC-area Employees

DICKINSON, Elaine: Assistant V. President
OAKERSON, Bill: President
SCIULLA, Michael G.: V. President and Lobbyist

Bob Evans Farms, Inc.

Columbus, OH

Outside Counsel/Consultants

Vorys, Sater, Seymour and Pease, LLP

Boca Raton, Florida, City of

Leg. Issues: NAT

Outside Counsel/Consultants

Alcalde & Fay
Issues: NAT
Rep By: Hon. Louis A. "Skip" Bafalis, Jim Davenport

Boehringer Ingelheim Pharmaceuticals, Inc.

Ridgefield, CT
Leg. Issues: ENV, HCR

Outside Counsel/Consultants

MARC Associates, Inc.
Issues: ENV, HCR
Rep By: Edwin Allen

Boehringer Mannheim Corp.

Indianapolis, IN
Leg. Issues: MED

Outside Counsel/Consultants

Sagamore Associates, Inc.
Issues: MED
Rep By: Doug Wasitis, Mark W. Weller

The Boeing Co.

1200 Wilson Blvd.
Arlington, VA 22209-1989
Tel: (703)465-3500
Fax: (703)465-3001
Registered: LDA
Web: www.boeing.com

Headquartered in Seattle, WA.

Leg. Issues: AER, AVI, BUD, COM, CPT, DEF, FOR, HCR, LBR, MAN, MMM, SCI, TAX, TRA, TRD

Political Action Committee/s

Boeing Co. Political Action Committee, The (BPAC)
1200 Wilson Blvd.
Arlington, VA 22209-1989
Tel: (703)465-3625
Fax: (703)465-3002
Contact: Michael N. Matton

In-house, DC-area Employees

ABBOUD, Meggan: Director, Constituent Relations
AUSTELL, Theodore "Ted": V. President, International Policy
BACHELLER, Burt P.: Director, International Programs
BARAGAR, Emory W.: V. President, Government Relations Operations
BERGENHOLTZ, Stephen: Legal Counsel
BRUCE, Virnell A.: V. President, Communications
DOLE, Gregory S.: Director, Commercial Trade Policy
DUNN, Loretta L.
ELLIS, Andrew K.: V. President, Government Relations (Aircraft and Missles Group)
FALLON, Willard G.: Legislative Affairs, Army Programs/V-22
FRANK, Matthew: Director, Federal Health, Safety, and Environment
FULLER, Rick: Director, Communications
GLEASON, Donna: Director, Corporate Legislation
GOFF, Donald G.: Director, Legislative Affairs
HANSEN, Christopher W.: Senior V. President, Government Relations
HAY, John C.: Director, Legislative Affairs
HEILIG, Paul T.: Legislative Affairs, Navy/USMC/Joint Programs
HOFGARD, Jefferson F.: Director, International Policy
JANS, Megan C.: Legislative Affairs, Army Programs
MATTON, Michael N.: V. President, Legislative Affairs
MILLER, Kristine B.: PAC Manager
MURPHY, Meredith: Director, Business Affairs and Acquisition Policy
ROBERTS, Roselee N.: Director, Legislative Affairs - Space Legislation
RUPINSKI, Walter F.: V. President, Export Management and Compliance
RUSSELL, Cheryl: Director, Federal Affairs
SCHWAB, Richard F.: Legislative Affairs, Navy/USMC/Joint Programs
SCHWARTZ, Elizabeth Nash: Director, Legislative Affairs - International Issues
SOMMER, Peter R.: Director, International Defense Trade
STONE, Mr. J. Robin: Director, State and Local Government Relations
TRAYNHAM, David: Director, Commercial Regulatory Affairs
VILHAUER, Robert J.: Director, Commercial Airplane Programs
WEAVER, Frank C.: Director, Telecommunications Policy
WILSON, John K.: Legislative Affairs, Air Force Programs
WUNDERLY, Susan M.: Legislative Affairs, International Programs

Outside Counsel/Consultants

Akin, Gump, Strauss, Hauer & Feld, L.L.P.
Issues: TRD
Rep By: Sean G. D'Arcy, Barney J. Skladany, Jr., S. Bruce Wilson

James Nicholas Ashmore & Associates
Issues: DEF, MAN, TRD
Rep By: James Nicholas Ashmore

Bain and Associates, Inc.

Baker, Donelson, Bearman & Caldwell, P.C.
Issues: AVI
Rep By: Linda Hall Daschle, Albert B. Randall

Bergner Bockorny Castagnetti and Hawkins
Issues: TAX, TRD
Rep By: Jeffrey T. Bergner, David A. Bockorny, David Castagnetti, Alvin B. Jackson, Melissa Schulman

Bonner & Associates

Bryan Cave LLP

Cassidy & Associates, Inc.
Issues: AER
Rep By: Shawn Edwards, Henry K. Giugni, Lawrence C. Grossman, Amos Hochstein, Jeffrey Lawrence, Arthur D. Mason, Brig. Gen. Terry Paul, USMC (Ret.), Marnie Russ, Dan C. Tate, Sr.

Collins & Company, Inc.
Issues: DEF
Rep By: James D. Bond, Richard L. Collins, Shay D. Stautz

Copeland, Lowery & Jacquez
Issues: BUD, DEF
Rep By: Hon. William D. Lowery, Jeffrey S. Shockey

Downey McGrath Group, Inc.
Issues: BUD, TRD
Rep By: Hon. Thomas J. Downey, Jr., Hon. Raymond J. McGrath

EOP Group, Inc.
Rep By: Donald Gesseman, Joseph Hezir

Gibson, Dunn & Crutcher LLP
Rep By: Hon. Meldon E. Levine, Alan A. Platt

Hill and Knowlton, Inc.

Joseph S. Kimmitt
Issues: AER, AVI, DEF
Rep By: Joseph S. Kimmitt

Michael J. Kopetski
Issues: TRD
Rep By: Michael J. Kopetski

Mayer, Brown & Platt
Issues: TRD
Rep By: Scott Parven

Denny Miller McBee Associates
Issues: AER, AVI, DEF, TRD

L. A. Motley, L.L.C.
Rep By: Langhorne A. Motley

Perkins Coie LLP
Rep By: Guy R. Martin

Projects Internat'l
Rep By: Alexander Platt

Robison Internat'l, Inc.
Issues: BUD, DEF
Rep By: Sandra A. Gilbert, Richard B. Ladd

Scribe Consulting & Communications
Rep By: Joseph J. Szlavik

Shaw Pittman
Rep By: Claudia Hrvatin

Leighton W. Smith
Rep By: Adm. Leighton W. Smith, USN (Ret.)

Tighe, Patton, Tabackman & Babbin
Issues: AER, DEF
Rep By: Brent S. Franzel

The Washington Group
Issues: AER, HCR, MMM, TAX
Rep By: Rita M. Lewis, John D. Raffaelli, Tonya Saunders, Mark Schnabel

John Thomas White
Rep By: John Thomas White, III

Boeing Defense and Space Group

Seattle, WA
Leg. Issues: AER

Outside Counsel/Consultants

Balzano Associates
Issues: AER
Rep By: Michael P. Balzano, Jr., Ruthanne Goodman, Janel Vermeulen

Boeing Information Services

7910 Science Application Court
Vienna, VA 22182
Tel: (703)676-1100
Fax: (703)903-1525

In-house, DC-area Employees

DELANEY, Bill: President
MCCARTHY, Andrea: Director, Public Relations

Bofors Defence AB

Karlskoga, SWEDEN
Leg. Issues: DEF

Outside Counsel/Consultants

American Defense Internat'l, Inc.
Issues: DEF
Rep By: Michael Herson, Van D. Hipp, Jr., George Phillips, Dave Wilberding

BOH Environmental, L.L.C.

New Orleans, LA
Leg. Issues: ENG, ENV, WAS

Outside Counsel/Consultants

The Palmer Group
Issues: ENG, ENV, WAS
Rep By: Clifford A. Palmer

Bohemian Cos.

Fort Collins, CO
Leg. Issues: BEV, CAW, ENV, RES, TAX, TEC

Outside Counsel/Consultants

Kogovsek & Associates
Issues: BEV, CAW, ENV, RES, TAX, TEC

Boise State University

Boise, ID
Leg. Issues: BUD

Outside Counsel/Consultants

McClure, Gerard & Neuenschwander, Inc.
Issues: BUD
Rep By: Steven G. Barringer, Joseph T. Findaro, Matthew Iandoli, Nils W. Johnson, Hon. James A. McClure, Tod O. Neuenschwander

Bolivia, Embassy of

3014 Massachusetts Ave. NW
Washington, DC 20008
Tel: (202)483-4410
Fax: (202)328-3712

Outside Counsel/Consultants

Manatt, Phelps & Phillips, LLP
Rep By: Hon. Jack W. Buechner, Eric Farnsworth, James R. Jones, Robert J. Kabel, Jeff Kuhnreich, Steven J. Mulder, Susan M. Schmidt, Jessica A. Wasserman

Bolivia, Government of the Republic of

La Paz, BOLIVIA

Outside Counsel/Consultants

Akin, Gump, Strauss, Hauer & Feld, L.L.P.
Rep By: David Geanacopoulos, Barney J. Skladany, Jr.

William D. Harris & Associates

Bollinger Shipyards

Outside Counsel/Consultants

The Livingston Group, LLC

Bolt, Beranek and Newman, Inc.

Cambridge, MA

Outside Counsel/Consultants

Akin, Gump, Strauss, Hauer & Feld, L.L.P.

Bombardier Aerospace

Washington, DC
Registered: LDA
Web: www.aerospace.bombardier.com

An airplane manufacturer which designs and builds both jets and turboprops for regional airlines, the Global Express, Learjet, Challenger business jets, and the high-velocity Shorts Starstreak air defense missile.

Leg. Issues: DEF, GOV, TRA

Outside Counsel/Consultants

Hyjek & Fix, Inc.
Issues: DEF
Rep By: Donald J. Fix, Steven M. Hyjek

Bombardier Transportation/Bombardier Transit Corporation

1023 15th St. NW
Suite 1000
Washington, DC 20005
Tel: (202)289-3933
Fax: (202)289-3962

Headquartered in New York, NY. Represents U.S. offices and plants of Bombardier Transportation and Bombardier Transit Corporation. Bombardier Inc., the parent company, a diversified manufacturing and service company, is a world leader in the manufacturing of business jets, regional aircraft, rail transportation equipment and motorized recreational products. It is also a provider of financial services and asset management. The Corporation employs 56,000 people in twelve countries in North America, Europe, and Asia.

Leg. Issues: TRA

In-house, DC-area Employees

IPSEN, Jeanine: Government Relations Manager

Outside Counsel/Consultants

Verner, Liipfert, Bernhard, McPherson and Hand, Chartered
Issues: TRA
Rep By: Suzanne D. Cartwright, Denis J. Dwyer, Jenifer Martin, John R. Mietus, Neil T. Proto

Bombardier, Inc.

Montreal, CANADA

An international consumer product manufacturing company.

Leg. Issues: AVI, BUD, DEF, TRA

Outside Counsel/Consultants

Akin, Gump, Strauss, Hauer & Feld, L.L.P.
Issues: AVI
Rep By: Marlene M. Colucci, David Geanacopoulos, Charles W. Johnson, IV, Jonathan R. Joyce, Barney J. Skladany, Jr.

Arent Fox Kintner Plotkin & Kahn, PLLC
Issues: TRA
Rep By: Paul Jackson Rice

Baker, Donelson, Bearman & Caldwell, P.C.
Issues: BUD
Rep By: Janet L. Powell

Whitten & Diamond
Issues: DEF
Rep By: Robert M. Diamond, Jamie L. Whitten

Bon Secours Charity Health System

Suffern, NY
Leg. Issues: HCR, MMM

Outside Counsel/Consultants

Powers Pyles Sutter & Verville, PC
Issues: HCR, MMM
Rep By: Judith Buckalew

The Bond Market Ass'n

1399 New York Ave. NW
Eighth Floor
Washington, DC 20005-4711
Web: www.bondmarkets.com
Tel: (202)434-8400
Fax: (202)434-8456
Registered: LDA

Headquartered in New York, NY.

Leg. Issues: BNK, BUD, CDT, FIN, HOU, TAX, TRA

Political Action Committee/s

Bond Market Ass'n Political Action Committee (BONDPAC)
1399 New York Ave. NW
Eighth Floor
Washington, DC 20005-4711
Contact: John R. Vogt
Tel: (202)434-8400
Fax: (202)434-8456

In-house, DC-area Employees

ALEXANDER, Donna K.: V. President
DECKER, Michael B.: V. President, Research and Policy Analysis
GREEN, Micah S.: President
HAMPTON, Frank R.: V. President, Legislative Affairs
NICHOLAS, Michael: Director, Issues Relations and Grassroots Programs
SALTZMAN, Paul: Senior V. President and General Counsel
VOGT, John R.: Exec. V. President
WILLIAMS, Michael W.: V. President, Legislative Affairs

Bone Care Internat'l

Madison, WI
Leg. Issues: MMM, PHA

Outside Counsel/Consultants

Smith Dawson & Andrews, Inc.
Issues: MMM, PHA
Rep By: James P. Smith

Bones Brothers Ranch

Birney, MT
Leg. Issues: NAT

Outside Counsel/Consultants

Dunlap & Browder, Inc.
Issues: NAT
Rep By: Joseph B. Browder, Louise C. Dunlap

Boonville, New York, Village of

Leg. Issues: GOV, UTI

Outside Counsel/Consultants

Duncan, Weinberg, Genzer & Pembroke, P.C.
Issues: GOV, UTI
Rep By: Richmond F. Allan, Jeffrey C. Genzer

Boost Technology

Outside Counsel/Consultants

Columbus Public Affairs

Borden Chemicals & Plastics, Inc.

Geismar, LA
Leg. Issues: CHM

Outside Counsel/Consultants

Hooper Owen & Winburn
Issues: CHM
Rep By: Lindsay D. Hooper, Daryl H. Owen

McDermott, Will and Emery

The Bortz Corp.

Uniontown, PA

Outside Counsel/Consultants

Sam Richardson
Rep By: Sam Richardson

The BOSE Corp.

Framingham, MA
Leg. Issues: BUD, CSP, DEF, GOV, TAX, TRD

Outside Counsel/Consultants

Cassidy & Associates, Inc.
Issues: GOV, TAX, TRD
Rep By: Laurie J. Adler, Marie James, Walter Raheb, Stephen Whitaker

JBC Internat'l
Issues: TRD
Rep By: James B. Clawson, George M. "Matt" Mattingley, Jr.

Robison Internat'l, Inc.
Issues: BUD, CSP, DEF
Rep By: Richard B. Ladd

Boston Capital

Boston, MA
Leg. Issues: TAX

Outside Counsel/Consultants

Davis & Harman LLP
Issues: TAX
Rep By: Richard S. Belas

Boston College

Chestnut Hill, MA
Leg. Issues: BUD

Outside Counsel/Consultants

Cassidy & Associates, Inc.
Issues: BUD
Rep By: Gerald S. J. Cassidy, James P. Fabiani, Lawrence C. Grossman, Christopher Lamond, Christine A. O'Connor, Hon. Martin A. Russo, Barbara Sutton

Boston Communications Group, Inc.

Boston, MA

Outside Counsel/Consultants

Rhoads Group

Boston Consolidated Services, Inc.

Boston, MA

Outside Counsel/Consultants

Rodriguez O'Donnell Fuerst Gonzalez & Williams
Rep By: Carlos Rodriguez

Boston Edison Co.

Boston, MA Registered: LDA
Leg. Issues: ENG, TAX, TEC

Outside Counsel/Consultants

Bristol Group, Inc.
Issues: ENG, TEC
Rep By: Paul G. Afonso, Daniel G. Papadopoulos

Miller & Chevalier, Chartered
Issues: TAX
Rep By: Leonard Bickwit, Jr., Brook Voght

Boston Museum of Science

Boston, MA

Outside Counsel/Consultants

O'Neill, Athy & Casey, P.C.
Rep By: Martha L. Casey, Christopher R. O'Neill

Boston Scientific Corp.

Natick, MA
Leg. Issues: HCR, MED, MMM, TAX, TRD

Outside Counsel/Consultants

Jeffrey J. Kimbell & Associates
Issues: HCR, MMM, TAX, TRD

Latham & Watkins
Issues: MED
Rep By: John R. Manthei

The Legislative Strategies Group, LLC

Boston Stock Exchange

Boston, MA

Outside Counsel/Consultants

Akin, Gump, Strauss, Hauer & Feld, L.L.P.

Boston Symphony Orchestra

Boston, MA
Leg. Issues: BUD

Outside Counsel/Consultants

Beacon Consulting Group, Inc.
Issues: BUD
Rep By: Katherine L. Halpin, Gordon P. MacDougall, Lisa A. Stewart

Boston University

3211 Tennyson St. NW Tel: (202)363-1620
Washington, DC 20015-2429
Leg. Issues: BUD, EDU

In-house, DC-area Employees

CLOHERTY, William M.

Outside Counsel/Consultants

Cassidy & Associates, Inc.
Issues: BUD
Rep By: Gerald S. J. Cassidy, Henry K. Giugni, Carl Franklin Godfrey, Jr., Lawrence C. Grossman, Dennis M. Kedzior, Jeffrey Lawrence

Wilson & Wilson

Boston, Massachusetts, City of

1660 L St. NW Tel: (202)496-9610
Suite 1050 Fax: (202)659-5234
Washington, DC 20036 Registered: LDA
E-mail: bostonwash@worldnet.att.net
Leg. Issues: BUD, ECN, EDU, ENV, GOV, HCR, HOU, LAW, URB

In-house, DC-area Employees

MAYER, Virginia M.: Director, Washington Office

Outside Counsel/Consultants

Virginia M. Mayer
Issues: BUD, ECN, EDU, ENV, GOV, HCR, HOU, LAW, URB
Rep By: Virginia M. Mayer

Bouchard Transportation Co.

Hicksville, NY

Outside Counsel/Consultants

Paul, Weiss, Rifkind, Wharton & Garrison
Rep By: Carl W. Hampe

Boundary Healthcare Products Corp.

Columbus, MS

Outside Counsel/Consultants

Johnson, Rogers & Clifton, L.L.P.

Bourgas Intermodal Feasability Study

Bourgas, BULGARIA
Leg. Issues: ENV, GOV, TRA

Outside Counsel/Consultants

Ernest J. Corrado
Issues: ENV, GOV, TRA
Rep By: Ernest J. Corrado

Bowie State University

Bowie, MD
Leg. Issues: EDU

Outside Counsel/Consultants

Dean Blakey & Moskowitz
Issues: EDU
Rep By: William A. Blakey

Bowling Proprietors' Ass'n of America

Arlington, TX
Leg. Issues: ART, BEV, LBR

Outside Counsel/Consultants

Law Offices of Robert T. Herbolsheimer
Issues: ART, BEV, LBR
Rep By: Robert T. Herbolsheimer

Bowling Transportation

Leg. Issues: TRA

Outside Counsel/Consultants

Jefferson Government Relations, L.L.C.
Issues: TRA
Rep By: Randal P. Schumacher

Bowman Internat'l Corp.

Manchester, UNITED KINGDOM
Leg. Issues: GAM, SPO

Outside Counsel/Consultants

Greenberg Traurig, LLP
Issues: GAM, SPO
Rep By: Diane J. Blagman, James F. Miller, Ronald L. Platt

Boy Scouts of America

Irving, TX
Leg. Issues: LAW

Outside Counsel/Consultants

Hecht, Spencer & Associates
Issues: LAW
Rep By: Timothy P. Hecht, William H. Hecht, Franklin C. Phifer

Boys and Girls Club of Brownsville, Inc.

Brownsville, TX
Leg. Issues: BUD

Outside Counsel/Consultants

Reed, Smith, LLP
Issues: BUD
Rep By: Phillips S. Peter

Boys and Girls Clubs of America

600 Jefferson Plaza Tel: (301)251-6676
Suite 401 Fax: (301)294-3052
Rockville, MD 20852
Web: www.bgca.org
Leg. Issues: BUD, LAW, TRA

In-house, DC-area Employees

CALLAWAY, Robbie: Senior V. President
SALEM, Steve: V. President, Government Relations

Outside Counsel/Consultants

Capitol Associates, Inc.
Issues: BUD, TRA
Rep By: Edward R. Long, Ph.D., Daniel Wexler

Lafayette Group, Inc.
Issues: LAW
Rep By: Scott H. Green

Boys and Girls Clubs of Greater Washington

Silver Spring, MD

Outside Counsel/Consultants

Capitol Counsel Group, L.L.C.
Rep By: Warren Belmar

Boys Town Nat'l Research Hospital

Omaha, NE
Leg. Issues: BUD, HCR, SCI

Outside Counsel/Consultants

Cavarocchi Ruscio Dennis Associates
Issues: BUD, HCR, SCI
Rep By: Nicholas G. Cavarocchi, Domenic R. Ruscio

Boys Town USA

Boys Town, NE
Leg. Issues: BUD

Outside Counsel/Consultants

Jones, Walker, Waechter, Poitevent, Carrere & Denegre, L.L.P.
Issues: BUD
Rep By: Paul Cambon, John J. Jaskot, R. Christian Johnsen, James Ogsbury

The Livingston Group, LLC
Issues: BUD
Rep By: Richard Legendre, Hon. Robert L. Livingston, Jr., J. Allen Martin, Richard L. Rodgers

Zeliff, Ireland, and Associates
Issues: BUD
Rep By: Hon. Andy Ireland, Hon. William H. Zeliff, Jr.

Boysville

Clinton, MD
Leg. Issues: FAM, LAW

Outside Counsel/Consultants

Dennis M. Hertel & Associates
Issues: FAM, LAW
Rep By: Hon. Dennis M. Hertel

BP America, Inc.

Washington, DC
Leg. Issues: ENV

Outside Counsel/Consultants

Robert K. Weidner
Issues: ENV
Rep By: Robert K. Weidner

BP Amoco Corp.

1776 I St. NW
Suite 1000
Washington, DC 20006
Tel: (202)785-4888
Fax: (202)457-6597
Registered: LDA

An oil, gas and solar energy company formed by the merger of British Petroleum, Amoco Corp. and Atlantic Richfield Co.

Leg. Issues: CAW, CHM, ENG, ENV, FOR, FUE, IMM, LBR, MAR, NAT, TAX, TRD, UTI, WAS

Political Action Committee/s

BP Amoco Corporate PAC
1776 I St. NW
Suite 1000
Washington, DC 20006
Contact: Michael Brien
Tel: (202)785-4888
Fax: (202)457-6597

In-house, DC-area Employees

ALLEN, Fletcher: Director, Government Affairs
BRIEN, Michael: PAC Administrator
BURTON, Larry D.: V. President, Federal Government Affairs
HILL, Jerry W.: Director, Federal Government Affairs
MCADAMS, Michael J.: Director, Federal Government Affairs, Eastern U.S.
MEDAGLIA, III, Thomas J.: Director, Government Affairs
REICHERTS, Liz: Associate Director, Government Affairs
ROGERS, Susan: Senior Tax Advisor

Outside Counsel/Consultants

Alpine Group, Inc.
Issues: ENG, TAX
Rep By: Dan Brouillette, James D. Massie, James Gregory Means

Bracewell & Patterson, L.L.P.

The Wexler Group
Issues: ENG
Rep By: Robert L. Healy, Jr., Joel Malina

BP Capital, LLC

Dallas, TX

Outside Counsel/Consultants

The Laxalt Corp.
Rep By: Michelle D. Laxalt

BP Exploration

Anchorage, AK

An oil and gas exploration, development and production company.

Outside Counsel/Consultants

Robert K. Weidner
Rep By: Robert K. Weidner

BP Oil Marketers Ass'n

Moorhead City, NC

Outside Counsel/Consultants

Bassman, Mitchell & Alfano

Bracco Diagnostics

Princeton, NJ
Leg. Issues: HCR, MMM

Outside Counsel/Consultants

Alpine Group, Inc.
Issues: HCR, MMM
Rep By: James D. Massie, Richard C. White

Bracewell & Patterson, L.L.P.

2000 K St. NW
Suite 500
Washington, DC 20006-1872
Tel: (202)828-5800
Fax: (202)223-1225
Registered: LDA, FARA

Leg. Issues: TAX, TRD

Political Action Committee/s

Bracewell and Patterson, L.L.P. Political Action Committee
2000 K St. NW
Suite 500
Washington, DC 20006-1872
Contact: Gene E. Godley
Tel: (202)828-5870
Fax: (202)223-1225

In-house, DC-area Employees

BETHUNE, Hon. Edwin R.: Partner
CHAPMAN, Hon. Jim: Partner
CLARKE, Robert L.: Partner
EWING, Kevin
FOOTE, George M.
GODLEY, Gene E.: Partner
HEBERT, Marc C.: Associate
HOUSMAN, Robert F.: Associate
INGEBRETSON, Charles L.: Associate
PATE, Michael L.: Partner
RACICOT, Marc: Partner
SEGAL, Scott H.: Partner
STROUD, Jr., D. Michael: Associate
WATKISS, J. Dan: Partner

Outside Counsel/Consultants

KPMG, LLP
Issues: TAX, TRD
Rep By: Shannon E. Slawter, Linden C. Smith

W. C. Bradley Co.

Columbus, GA
Leg. Issues: TAX

Outside Counsel/Consultants

Sutherland Asbill & Brennan LLP
Issues: TAX
Rep By: Daniel M. Berman

Braille Revival League

1155 15th St. NW
Suite 1004
Washington, DC 20005
Web: www.acb.org
Tel: (202)467-5081
Fax: (202)467-5085

An affiliate of the American Council of the Blind.

In-house, DC-area Employees

GRAY, Chris: President

Brain Injury Ass'n

105 N. Alfred St.
Alexandria, VA 22314
Tel: (703)236-6000
Fax: (703)236-6001
Registered: LDA
Web: www.biausa.org

Non-profit ass'n advocating brain injury prevention, education, and research.

Leg. Issues: BUD, DEF, EDU, HCR, VET

In-house, DC-area Employees

BERGMAN, Allan I.: President and Chief Exec. Officer
HOFFER, Larry: Director, Communications
WARD, Lisa: Director, Communications

Outside Counsel/Consultants

Polity Consulting
Issues: BUD, DEF, EDU, HCR, VET
Rep By: Roger P. Kingsley, Ph.D.

Brain Research Foundation

Chicago, IL
Leg. Issues: BUD

Outside Counsel/Consultants

Metcalf Federal Relations
Issues: BUD
Rep By: Anne Metcalf, Amy Ford Sanders

Brain Trauma Foundation

New York, NY
Leg. Issues: BUD, HCR, TRA

Outside Counsel/Consultants

Van Scoyoc Associates, Inc.
Issues: BUD, HCR, TRA
Rep By: Ray Cole, H. Stewart Van Scoyoc

Braintree Electric Light Department

Braintree, MA
Leg. Issues: GOV, UTI

Outside Counsel/Consultants

Duncan, Weinberg, Genzer & Pembroke, P.C.
Issues: GOV, UTI
Rep By: Janice L. Lower

Branch Banking and Trust Co.

Washington, DC

Outside Counsel/Consultants

Arthur Andersen LLP

Branco Peres Citrus, S.A.

Sao Paulo, BRAZIL

Outside Counsel/Consultants

Willkie Farr & Gallagher
Rep By: Christopher A. Dunn

Brandegee, Inc.

Pittsburgh, PA

Outside Counsel/Consultants

Bob Lawrence & Associates
Rep By: James Goldwater

Brandeis University

Waltham, MA
Leg. Issues: SCI

Outside Counsel/Consultants

Hogan & Hartson L.L.P.
Issues: SCI
Rep By: C. Michael Gilliland, Martin Michaelson, Daniel B. Poneman

Brashear Systems, L.L.P.

Pittsburgh, PA
Leg. Issues: DEF

Outside Counsel/Consultants

The Potomac Advocates
Issues: DEF
Rep By: Charles Scalera, Gary L. Sojka

Brass and Bronze Ingot Manufacturers Ass'n

Chicago, IL
Leg. Issues: ENV

Outside Counsel/Consultants

Vorys, Sater, Seymour and Pease, LLP
Issues: ENV

Brazelton Foundation

Fairfax, VA
Leg. Issues: CPT, GOV, LBR, TAX, TOR

Outside Counsel/Consultants

Venable
Issues: CPT, GOV, LBR, TAX, TOR
Rep By: Jeffrey S. Tenenbaum

Brea, California, City of

Leg. Issues: BUD, LAW, TRA

Outside Counsel/Consultants

The Ferguson Group, LLC
Issues: BUD, LAW, TRA
Rep By: William Ferguson, Jr., Charmayne Macon

Bread for the World

50 F St. NW
Suite 500
Washington, DC 20001
Web: www.bread.org
E-mail: bread@bread.org
Tel: (202)639-9400
Fax: (202)639-9401
Registered: LDA

A Christian citizen's movement that organizes people at the grassroots level to lobby their members of Congress on legislation that addresses the causes of hunger.

Leg. Issues: BUD, FOR, WEL

In-house, DC-area Employees

ALMEIDA, Raymond A.: International Analyst
BECKMANN, David: President
HOWELL, Barbara: Director, Government Relations
MCDONALD, Jim: International Analyst
QUINONEZ, Jose: Policy Analyst
SALTER, Howard: Director, Communications
STOTT, Lynette Engelhardt: Domestic Policy Analyst

Outside Counsel/Consultants

Hauser Group

Breakthrough Technologies Institute

Washington, DC

Supports public understanding of advanced environmental and energy technologies.

Leg. Issues: ENG

Outside Counsel/Consultants

Downey McGrath Group, Inc.
Issues: ENG
Rep By: Hon. Thomas J. Downey, Jr.

Brewer Science Inc.

Rolla, MO
Leg. Issues: DEF, SMB

Outside Counsel/Consultants

GHL Inc.
Issues: DEF, SMB
Rep By: Thomas R. Goldberg

Briartek, Inc.

Alexandria, VA
Leg. Issues: TRA

Outside Counsel/Consultants

Baker, Donelson, Bearman & Caldwell, P.C.
Issues: TRA
Rep By: Janet L. Powell

Brick Industry Ass'n

11490 Commerce Park Dr.
Reston, VA 20191-1525
Tel: (703)620-0010
Fax: (703)620-3928
Web: www.brickinfo.org
E-mail: brickinfo@bia.org

Formed by the merger of Brick Institute of America and the Nat'l Ass'n of Brick Distributors.

Leg. Issues: MAN

In-house, DC-area Employees

COONEY, Nelson J.: President

Outside Counsel/Consultants

Reed, Smith, LLP
Issues: MAN
Rep By: David C. Evans

Bridgeport and Port Jefferson Steamboat Co.

Port Jefferson, NY

Outside Counsel/Consultants

Thompson, Hine and Flory LLP
Rep By: David H. Baker

Bridgeport, Connecticut, City of

Bridgeport, CT
Leg. Issues: TRA

Outside Counsel/Consultants

Charles H. Graves & Associates
Issues: TRA
Rep By: Charles H. Graves

Bridgestone/Firestone, Inc.

Nashville, TN
Registered: LDA
Leg. Issues: AUT, BUD, CPI, CSP, EDU, ENV, GOV, LBR, MAN, SCI, TAX, TEC, TRA

Outside Counsel/Consultants

Akin, Gump, Strauss, Hauer & Feld, L.L.P.
Issues: AUT, CSP, TRA
Rep By: J. David Carlin, David Geanacopoulos, Charles W. Johnson, IV, Susan H. Lent, Hon. William L. Paxon, Barney J. Skladany, Jr., Daniel L. Spiegel, Robin Weisman

Baker, Donelson, Bearman & Caldwell, P.C.
Issues: BUD, ENV, LBR
Rep By: Janet L. Powell, James D. Range

Crowell & Moring LLP
Issues: CSP
Rep By: Mark A. Behrens, Victor E. Schwartz

Holland & Knight LLP
Issues: CSP, GOV, TRA
Rep By: Robert Hunt Bradner, Jack M. Burkman, Hon. Gerald E. Sikorski, Janet R. Studley, Beth Viola, David C. Whitestone

King & Spalding
Issues: AUT
Rep By: Theodore M. Hester, Eleanor Hill, Beth Jafari, Allison Kassir

Public Strategies, Inc.
Issues: CPI, EDU, SCI, TAX, TEC
Rep By: Jeff Eller, Wallace J. Henderson

The Washington Group
Issues: AUT, MAN, TRA
Rep By: Rita M. Lewis, G. John O'Hanlon, John D. Raffaelli

Bright Beginnings, Inc.

128 M St. NW
First Floor
Washington, DC 20001
Tel: (202)842-9090
Fax: (202)842-9095
Web: www.brightbeginningsinc.org
E-mail: bbikids@aol.com

Provides child care and social services for homeless families.

In-house, DC-area Employees

SHAVIN, Karen: Exec. Director

Briklee Trading Co.

Sherman Oaks, CA
Leg. Issues: FIR

Outside Counsel/Consultants

Law Offices of Mark Barnes
Issues: FIR
Rep By: Mark J. Barnes, Tammy Begun

Brink's Inc.

Darien, CT
Leg. Issues: TRD

Outside Counsel/Consultants

Patton Boggs, LLP
Issues: TRD
Rep By: David J. Farber

Brinker Internat'l

Dallas, TX
Leg. Issues: ALC, CSP, FOO, LBR, TAX

Outside Counsel/Consultants

Evans & Black, Inc.
Issues: ALC, CSP, FOO, LBR, TAX
Rep By: Judy A. Black, Rae Forker Evans, Rafe Morrissey

Bristol Bay Area Health Corp.

Dillingham, AK
Leg. Issues: IND

Outside Counsel/Consultants

Hobbs, Straus, Dean and Walker, LLP
Issues: IND
Rep By: Carol L. Barbero, S. Bobo Dean, Karen J. Funk, Aura Kanegis, Marie Osceola-Branch, Michael L. Roy, Marsha K. Schmidt, Jerry C. Straus, Geoffrey D. Strommer, Hans Walker, Jr., Joseph H. Webster, F. Michael Willis

Bristol Bay Borough Fisheries Economic Development Corp

Naknek, AK

Outside Counsel/Consultants

Law Office of C. Deming Cowles

Bristol Resource Recovery Facility Operating Committee

Bristol, CT

Outside Counsel/Consultants

Wright & Talisman, P.C.
Rep By: Scott M. DuBoff, Robert H. Lamb

Bristol-Myers Squibb Co.

655 15th St. NW
Suite 300
Washington, DC 20005
Tel: (202)783-0900
Fax: (202)783-2308
Registered: LDA
Web: www.bms.com

Headquartered in New York, NY.

Leg. Issues: ADV, BUD, CAW, CPT, CSP, ENG, ENV, FOR, GOV, HCR, LAW, MED, MMM, PHA, TAX, TRD

In-house, DC-area Employees

CAROZZA, Michael C.: Vice President, Federal Relations

KEANEY, David: Director, Federal Government Affairs

KENNEY, Joan M.: Director, Regulatory Relations and Policy

MURPHY, Patricia: Administrator, Government Affairs, MIS Operations

PACOTTI, Linda: Associate Director, Government Affairs

RYAN, John G.: Senior Counsel and Director, Government Affairs

THOMPSON, Richard L.: V. President, Government Affairs

WARR, David E.: Associate Director, Internat'l Govt. Affairs

Outside Counsel/Consultants

Arter & Hadden
Rep By: Hon. Thomas G. Loeffler, Jon W. Plebani

Baker & Hostetler LLP
Rep By: Matthew J. Dolan, Steven A. Lotterer, Hon. Guy Vander Jagt

Barbour Griffith & Rogers, Inc.
Rep By: Haley Barbour, G. O. Lanny Griffith, Jr., Loren Monroe, Edward M. Rogers, Jr.

Bennett Turner & Coleman, LLP
Issues: ADV, CPT, MED, MMM
Rep By: Alan R. Bennett, Elizabeth Goss, Samuel D. Turner

Bergner Bockorny Castagnetti and Hawkins
Issues: HCR
Rep By: Jeffrey T. Bergner, David A. Bockorny, David Castagnetti, James W. Hawkins

BKSH & Associates
Issues: HCR, MMM

Capitol Health Group, LLC
Issues: HCR, MMM, PHA
Rep By: Michael D. Bromberg, Shawn Coughlin, Steven Jenning, Layna McConkey Peltier

Denison, Scott Associates
Issues: MMM
Rep By: George H. Denison, Ray Scott

The Direct Impact Co.

FoxKiser
Issues: ADV, BUD, CPT, CSP, HCR, MED, MMM, PHA, TRD
Rep By: Allan M. Fox, John Daniel Kiser

Garrett Yu Hussein LLC

The Gorlin Group
Issues: TRD
Rep By: Jacques Gorlin

Hogan & Hartson L.L.P.
Issues: HCR
Rep By: Ann Morgan Vickery

Hohlt & Associates
Issues: BUD, HCR, MMM, PHA, TAX
Rep By: Richard F. Hohlt

IssueSphere

The Kamber Group
Rep By: Jill A. Schuker

Long Law Firm
Rep By: C. Kris Kirkpatrick

Nat'l Environmental Strategies
Issues: CAW
Rep By: Marc I. Himmelstein

Parry, Romani, DeConcini & Symms
Issues: CPT
Rep By: Edward H. Baxter, Hon. Dennis DeConcini, John M. Haddow, Scott D. Hatch, Shannon Davis Henderson, Jack W. Martin, Romano Romani, Linda Arey Skladany, Hon. Steven D. Symms

Patton Boggs, LLP
Issues: HCR
Rep By: Thomas Hale Boggs, Jr., Hon. Willis "Bill" D. Gradison, John F. Jonas, Stuart M. Pape

Paul, Hastings, Janofsky & Walker LLP
Rep By: R. Bruce Dickson

Public Strategies Washington, Inc.
Issues: HCR
Rep By: Joseph P. O'Neill, Paul M. Snyder

Timmons and Co., Inc.
Issues: HCR, PHA
Rep By: Michael J. Bates, Douglas F. Bennett, Ellen B. Fitzgibbons, Bryce L. "Larry" Harlow, Timothy J. Keating, Tom C. Korologos, Richard J. Tarplin, William E. Timmons, Jr., William E. Timmons, Sr.

Van Scoyoc Associates, Inc.
Issues: BUD, HCR
Rep By: Anita R. Estell, Kimberly Johnson, H. Stewart Van Scoyoc

Brita GmbH

Outside Counsel/Consultants

Powell Tate
Rep By: Stacey Colleen Abernethy

British Aerospace

Arlington, VA
Leg. Issues: DEF

Outside Counsel/Consultants

Bob Davis & Associates
Issues: DEF
Rep By: Hon. Robert W. Davis

British Airways Plc

1850 K St. NW
Suite 300
Washington, DC 20006
Tel: (202)331-9068
Fax: (202)466-3745
Registered: LDA, FARA
Web: www.britishairways.com
Leg. Issues: AVI

In-house, DC-area Employees

FORTNAM, Anthony: V. President, Government and Industry Affairs

Outside Counsel/Consultants

Sullivan & Cromwell
Rep By: Daryl Libow, D. Mark McCall

The Wexler Group
Issues: AVI
Rep By: Timothy Hannegan

British American Security Information Council

1012 14th St. NW
Suite 900
Washington, DC 20005
Tel: (202)397-8340
Fax: (202)347-4688
Web: www.basicint.org
E-mail: basicus@basicint.org

An independent research organization that analyzes international security policy in Europe and North America. Works to promote public awareness of defense, disarmament, military strategy, and nuclear policies in order to foster informed debate on the issues. Facilitates the exchange of information and analysis among researchers, journalists and parliamentarians. Encourages decision makers to take full advantage of opportunities for disarmament and cooperation.

Leg. Issues: FOR

In-house, DC-area Employees

PLESCH, Daniel T.: Director

British American Tobacco China Ltd.

Hong Kong, CHINA (PEOPLE'S REPUBLIC)
Leg. Issues: TRD

Outside Counsel/Consultants

RMA Internat'l, Inc.
Issues: TRD

British Columbia Hydro and Power Authority

Vancouver, CANADA
Leg. Issues: ENG, FUE, UTI

Outside Counsel/Consultants

Stuntz, Davis & Staffier, P.C.
Issues: ENG, UTI
Rep By: Linda Stuntz

The Wexler Group
Issues: FUE
Rep By: Joel Malina

British Columbia Lumber Trade Council

Vancouver, CANADA
Leg. Issues: TRD

Outside Counsel/Consultants

BSMG Worldwide

Quinn Gillespie & Associates
Issues: TRD
Rep By: Edward W. Gillespie, Harriet James, David Lugar, John M. "Jack" Quinn

British Columbia Softwood Lumber Trade Council

Vancouver, CANADA
Leg. Issues: TRD

Outside Counsel/Consultants

Baker & McKenzie
Issues: TRD
Rep By: B. Thomas Peele, III, John R. Reilly

Steptoe & Johnson LLP
Rep By: W. George Grandison, Mark A. Moran

British Columbia, Canada, Government of the Province of

Victoria, CANADA

Outside Counsel/Consultants

Akin, Gump, Strauss, Hauer & Feld, L.L.P.
Rep By: Frank J. Donatelli, David Geanacopoulos, Spencer S. Griffith

Covington & Burling
Rep By: Harvey M. Applebaum

British Ministry of Defence

London, UNITED KINGDOM
Leg. Issues: AER, DEF

Outside Counsel/Consultants

Law Office of Zel E. Lipsen
Issues: AER, DEF
Rep By: Adam Emanuel, Zel E. Lipsen

British Nuclear Fuels plc

Cheshire, UNITED KINGDOM
Leg. Issues: ENG, ENV, TRD

Outside Counsel/Consultants

Burson-Marsteller

Butera & Andrews
Issues: ENG, ENV, TRD
Rep By: Wright H. Andrews, Jr., James J. Butera, Dennis M. Hart, Stephen C. Leckar, John McInespie, Frank Tillotson

British Trade and Commerce Bank

Bayfront Ropseau, DOMINICA
Leg. Issues: BAN

Outside Counsel/Consultants

Van Scoyoc Associates, Inc.
Issues: BAN
Rep By: Buzz Hawley, John C. "Jay" Stone, H. Stewart Van Scoyoc

British Virgin Islands, Government of the

Road Town, BRITISH WEST INDIES

Outside Counsel/Consultants

Swidler Berlin Shereff Friedman, LLP
Rep By: Lester S. Hyman

Brix Maritime, Inc.

Portland, OR

Outside Counsel/Consultants

Davis Wright Tremaine LLP

Broadcast Compliance Services

Columbia, MD

Outside Counsel/Consultants

Capitol Campaign Consultants
Rep By: Thomas E. Fahy

Broadcast Education Ass'n

1771 N St. NW
Washington, DC 20036
Tel: (202)429-5354
Fax: (202)775-2981
Web: www.beaweb.org

An association of professors preparing college students for careers in the broadcasting industry.

In-house, DC-area Employees

NIELSEN, Louisa A.: Exec. Director

Broadcast Music Inc. (BMI)

New York, NY
Registered: LDA
Leg. Issues: CPT

Outside Counsel/Consultants

Barbour Griffith & Rogers, Inc.
Issues: CPT
Rep By: Haley Barbour, G. O. Lanny Griffith, Jr., Brent Thompson

Dechert
Rep By: Ralph Oman

Drinker Biddle & Reath LLP
Issues: CPT
Rep By: Michael J. Remington

The Smith-Free Group
Issues: CPT
Rep By: James C. Free, W. Timothy Locke, Alicia W. Smith

Broadforum

New York, NY
Leg. Issues: EDU, SCI

Outside Counsel/Consultants

Hannett & Associates
Issues: EDU, SCI

BroadSpan Communications, Inc.

St. Louis, MO
Leg. Issues: TEC

Outside Counsel/Consultants

Swidler Berlin Shereff Friedman, LLP
Issues: TEC
Rep By: James DeLorenzo, Harold P. Goldfield, Gary D. Slaiman

Broadwave USA Inc.

Leg. Issues: TEC

Outside Counsel/Consultants

Akin, Gump, Strauss, Hauer & Feld, L.L.P.
Issues: TEC
Rep By: Barney J. Skladany, Jr., James R. Tucker, Jr.

Broe Companies, Inc.

Denver, CO
Leg. Issues: RRR

Outside Counsel/Consultants

Patton Boggs, LLP
Issues: RRR
Rep By: Michael J. Driver

BrokerTek Global, L.L.C.

Leg. Issues: AGR

Outside Counsel/Consultants

Hogan & Hartson L.L.P.
Issues: AGR
Rep By: Lance D. Bultena, Humberto R. Pena

Brookfield Zoo/Chicago Zoological Soc.

Brookfield, IL
Leg. Issues: ANI, BUD

Outside Counsel/Consultants

Metcalf Federal Relations
Issues: ANI, BUD
Rep By: Anne Metcalf

Brookhill Redevelopment

Leg. Issues: ENV, RES

Outside Counsel/Consultants

Capital Consultants Corp.
Issues: ENV, RES
Rep By: Michael David Kaiser, Wayne Scholl

The Brookings Institution

1775 Massachusetts Ave. NW
Washington, DC 20036-2188
Tel: (202)797-6000
Fax: (202)797-6004
Web: www.brookings.edu
E-mail: communications@brook.edu

An independent, nonpartisan research organization, seeks to improve the performance of American institutions, the effectiveness of government programs, and the quality of U.S. public policies. It addresses current and emerging policy challenges and offers practical recommendations for dealing with them, expressed in language that is accessible to policymakers and the general public alike.

Leg. Issues: ECN, FOR, GOV

In-house, DC-area Employees

AARON, Henry J.: Senior Fellow, Economic Studies
ARMACOST, Michael H.: President
AXTELL, Robert: Fellow, Economic Studies
BINDER, Sarah: Senior Fellow, Government Studies
BLAIR, Margaret: Non-Resident Senior Fellow, Economic Studies
BOSWORTH, Barry P.: Senior Fellow, Economic Studies
BRYANT, Ralph C.: Senior Fellow, Economic Studies
BURTLESS, Gary: Senior Fellow, Economic Studies
COHEN, Roberta: Guest Scholar, Foreign Policy Studies
COHEN, Stephen P.: Senior Fellow, Foreign Policy Studies
COLLINS, Susan M.: Senior Fellow, Economic Studies
CRANDALL, Robert W.: Senior Fellow, Economic Studies
DAALDER, Ivo H.: Visiting Fellow, Foreign Policy Studies
DICKENS, William T.: Senior Fellow, Economic Studies
DIONNE, E.J.: Senior Fellow, Government Studies
DOWNS, Anthony: Senior Fellow, Economic Studies
EPSTEIN, Joshua M.: Senior Fellow, Economic Studies
FAHERTY, Robert L.: Director, Brookings Institution Press
FERGUSON, Charles H.: Senior Fellow, Economic Studies
FOREMAN, Christopher: Senior Fellow, Governmental Studies
GADDY, Clifford: Fellow, Foreign Policy Studies
GALE, William: Senior Fellow, Economic Studies
GILL, Bates: Senior Fellow, Foreign Policy Studies/Director, Northeast Asian Policy Studies
GOLDGEIER, James M.: Non-Resident Senior Fellow, Foreign Policy Studies
GORDON, Lincoln: Guest Scholar, Foreign Policy Studies
GORDON, Philip H.: Senior Fellow, Foreign Policy Studies/Director, Center on the U.S. and France
GRAHAM, Carol: Sr. Fellow, Foreign Policy Studies/Co-Dir., Center on Social & Economic Dynamics
HAASS, Richard N.: V. President and Director, Foreign Policy Studies
HASKINS, Ronald T.: Senior Fellow, Economic Studies Program

HELM, Suzanne: Director, Development - External Affairs
HESS, Stephen: Senior Fellow, Governmental Studies
HILL, Fiona: Fellow, Foreign Policy Studies
HORNER, Constance J.: Guest Scholar, Governmental Studies
KATZ, Bruce J.: Senior Fellow, Econ. Studies & Director, Center on Urban & Metropolitan Policy
LADNER, Joyce A.: Senior Fellow, Governmental Studies
LARDY, Nicholas R.: Senior Fellow and Interim Director of Foreign Policy Studies
LIGHT, Paul C.: V. President and Director, Governmental Studies/Dir., Center for Public Service
LINCOLN, Edward J.: Senior Fellow, Foreign Policy Studies
LINDSAY, James M.: Senior Fellow, Foreign Policy Studies
LITTELL, Barbara: Senior Staff, Center for Public Policy Education
LOVELESS, Tom: Senior Fellow, Governmental Studies/Dir. Brown Center on Education Policy
MANN, Thomas E.: Senior Fellow, Governmental Studies
MAYER, Martin: Guest Scholar, Economic Studies
MOCHIZUKI, Mike: Non-Resident Senior Fellow, Foreign Policy Studies
NESSEN, Ronald H.: V. President, Communications
NIVOLA, Pietro S.: Senior Fellow, Governmental Studies
O'HANLON, Michael E.: Senior Fellow, Foreign Policy Studies
PERRY, George L.: Senior Fellow, Economic Studies
RICE, Lois Dickson: Guest Scholar, Economic Studies
RIVLIN, Alice: Senior Fellow, Economic Studies
SAWHILL, Isabel V.: Senior Fellow, Economic Studies
SCHICK, Allen: Visiting Scholar, Governmental Studies
SCHOETTLE, Peter D.: Senior Staff, Center for Public Policy Education
SCHULTZE, Charles L.: Senior Fellow Emeritus, Economic Studies
SONNENFELDT, Helmut: Guest Scholar, Foreign Policy Studies
STEINBRUNER, John D.: Non-Resident Senior Fellow, Economic Policy Studies
TELHAMI, Shibley: Nonresident Senior Fellow, Foreign Policy Studies
TRIPLETT, Jack E.: Visiting Fellow, Economic Studies
WEAVER, R. Kent: Senior Fellow, Governmental Studies
WINSTON, Clifford: Senior Fellow, Economic Studies
YOUNG, H. Peyton: Visiting Fellow, Economic Studies/Co-Dir., Center on Social & Economic Dynamics

Brooklyn Public Library

Brooklyn, NY
Leg. Issues: EDU

Outside Counsel/Consultants

The Ickes & Enright Group
Issues: EDU
Rep By: Janice Ann Enright, Harold M. Ickes

Brooks Tropicals, Inc.

Homestead, FL
A tropical and sub-tropical fruit company.

Leg. Issues: AGR, TRD

Outside Counsel/Consultants

O'Connor & Hannan, L.L.P.
Issues: AGR, TRD
Rep By: Hon. Thomas J. Corcoran, John M. Himmelberg

Brother Internat'l Co.

Somerset, NJ
Leg. Issues: LBR, MAN, TRD

Outside Counsel/Consultants

Hogan & Hartson L.L.P.
Issues: LBR, MAN, TRD
Rep By: William Michael House, Lewis E. Leibowitz, Jeff Mang, Jeffrey W. Munk

Brotherhood of Locomotive Engineers

Ten G St. NE
Suite 480
Washington, DC 20002
Tel: (202)347-7936
Fax: (202)347-5237
Registered: LDA
Web: www.ble.org
Leg. Issues: LBR, RRR

Political Action Committee/s

Brotherhood of Locomotive Engineers PAC
Ten G St. NE
Suite 480
Washington, DC 20002
Tel: (202)347-7936
Fax: (202)347-5237
Contact: Brent Boggs

In-house, DC-area Employees

BOGGS, Brent: PAC Contact
JONES, Leroy D.: V. President and National Legislative Representative

Outside Counsel/Consultants

Connerton & Ray
Issues: LBR
Rep By: David L. Mallino, Sr., David L. Mallino, Jr.

Brotherhood of Maintenance of Way Employees

Ten G St. NE
Suite 460
Washington, DC 20002
Tel: (202)638-2135
Fax: (202)737-3085
Registered: LDA
E-mail: bmwewash@wash.bmwe.org
Railroad labor union.

Leg. Issues: BUD, GOV, RRR, TRA

In-house, DC-area Employees

KNIGHT, James: Director, Government Affairs

Outside Counsel/Consultants

Lawler, Metzger & Milkman, LLC
Issues: RRR
Rep By: Sante J. Esposito, Gregory E. Lawler

Brotherhood of Railroad Signalmen

Ten G St. NE
Suite 440
Washington, DC 20002
Tel: (202)628-5935
Fax: (202)347-3548
Registered: LDA
Web: www.brs.org
Leg. Issues: BUD, GOV, TRA

In-house, DC-area Employees

BOSTON, Dennis: V. President
PARKER, Leonard: Legislative Representative

Broward, Florida, County of

Fort Lauderdale, FL
Leg. Issues: AVI, BUD, CAW, ECN, ENV, HOU, NAT, ROD, TRA, TRD, URB

Outside Counsel/Consultants

The Ferguson Group, LLC
Issues: AVI, BUD, CAW, ECN, ENV, HOU, NAT, ROD, TRA, URB
Rep By: William Ferguson, Jr.

Jones, Walker, Waechter, Poitevent, Carrere & Denegre, L.L.P.
Issues: BUD, TRD
Rep By: Paul Cambon, John J. Jaskot, R. Christian Johnsen, James Ogsbury

The Livingston Group, LLC
Issues: BUD, TRD
Rep By: Melvin Goodweather, Hon. Robert L. Livingston, Jr., J. Allen Martin, Richard L. Rodgers

Broward, Florida, Department of Natural Resource Protection of the County of

Fort Lauderdale, FL
Leg. Issues: BUD

Outside Counsel/Consultants

Marlowe and Co.
Issues: BUD
Rep By: Howard Marlowe, Jeffrey Mazzella

Brown and Williamson Tobacco Corp.

1701 Pennsylvania Ave. NW
Suite 960
Washington, DC 20006
Tel: (202)463-6674
Fax: (202)463-7130
Registered: LDA
Web: www.bw.com
A subsidiary of BAT Industries PLS of Great Britain.

Leg. Issues: AGR, BUD, HCR, TAX, TOB, TRD

In-house, DC-area Employees

PRESSNELL, Sissy: Manager, Government Affairs

Outside Counsel/Consultants

Barbour Griffith & Rogers, Inc.
Issues: TOB
Rep By: Haley Barbour, G. O. Lanny Griffith, Jr., Loren Monroe, Edward M. Rogers, Jr.

Hecht, Spencer & Associates
Issues: TOB
Rep By: Timothy P. Hecht, William H. Hecht, Franklin C. Phifer, Stuart K. Spencer

Public Private Partnership
Issues: AGR, BUD, TAX, TOB, TRD
Rep By: Arthur R. Collins

R. H. White Public Affairs Consulting
Issues: AGR, HCR, TAX, TOB
Rep By: Richard H. White

Brown Brothers Harriman & Co.

New York, NY
Leg. Issues: BAN, FIN

Outside Counsel/Consultants

Covington & Burling
Issues: FIN
Rep By: John C. Dugan

Davis Polk & Wardwell
Issues: BAN
Rep By: Theodore A. Doremus, Jr.

Brown General Hospital

Georgetown, OH
Leg. Issues: HCR

Outside Counsel/Consultants

Golin/Harris Internat'l
Issues: HCR
Rep By: C. Michael Fulton

Brown-Forman Corp.

Louisville, KY
Registered: LDA
Leg. Issues: ADV, CSP, TAX, TRD

Outside Counsel/Consultants

Preston Gates Ellis & Rouvelas Meeds LLP
Issues: ADV, CSP, TAX, TRD
Rep By: Pamela J. Garvie, John L. Longstreth, Michael J. O'Neil, Emanuel L. Rouvelas, W. Dennis Stephens

Browning Transport Management

Norfolk, VA
Leg. Issues: ENV

Outside Counsel/Consultants

Dyer Ellis & Joseph, P.C.
Issues: ENV
Rep By: Laurie Crick Sahatjian, Duncan C. Smith, III, Jennifer M. Southwick, Sidney A. Wallace

Brownsville Public Utilities Board

Brownsville, TX
Leg. Issues: BUD, CAW, ECN, ENV

Outside Counsel/Consultants

Murray, Scheer, Montgomery, Tapia & O'Donnell
Issues: BUD, CAW, ECN, ENV
Rep By: John R. O'Donnell

Brownsville, Texas, City of

Leg. Issues: ECN, TRA

Outside Counsel/Consultants

Murray, Scheer, Montgomery, Tapia & O'Donnell
Issues: ECN, TRA
Rep By: John H. Montgomery, John R. O'Donnell

Brownsville, Texas, Port of

Brownsville, TX
Leg. Issues: MAR, RRR, TRA

Outside Counsel/Consultants

Tate-LeMunyon, LLC
Issues: MAR, RRR, TRA
Rep By: Glenn B. LeMunyon, Dan C. Tate, Jr.

Bruce Vladek

New York, NY
Leg. Issues: GOV

Outside Counsel/Consultants

Arnold & Porter
Issues: GOV
Rep By: Martha L. Cochran, James F. Fitzpatrick

Bruker Meerestechnik GmbH

Karlsruhe, GERMANY
Leg. Issues: MAR, SCI

Outside Counsel/Consultants

Forster & Associates
Issues: MAR, SCI
Rep By: Johann R. Forster

Brunei Darussalam, Embassy of the State of

3520 International Ct. NW
Washington, DC 20008
Tel: (202)237-1838
Fax: (202)342-0158

Outside Counsel/Consultants

Washington World Group, Ltd.
Rep By: Edward J. von Kloberg, III

Brunswick Corp.

Lake Forest, IL
Leg. Issues: CAW, MAR, NAT, TAX, TRD

Outside Counsel/Consultants

Akin, Gump, Strauss, Hauer & Feld, L.L.P.
Issues: TRD
Rep By: William J. Farah, Valerie A. Slater, Daniel L. Spiegel

Floyd Associates
Issues: CAW, MAR, NAT, TAX
Rep By: Veronica McCann Floyd

Brush Wellman, Inc.

Delta, UT
Leg. Issues: BUD, DEF, ENV, HCR, NAT

Outside Counsel/Consultants

McClure, Gerard & Neuenschwander, Inc.
Issues: BUD, DEF, ENV, HCR, NAT
Rep By: Steven G. Barringer, Joseph T. Findaro, Matthew Iandoli, Nils W. Johnson, Hon. James A. McClure, Tod O. Neuenschwander

BSMG Worldwide

1501 M St. NW
Suite 600
Washington, DC 20005-1710
Tel: (202)739-0200
Fax: (202)659-8287
Registered: FARA
Web: www.bsmg.com
Leg. Issues: WEL

In-house, DC-area Employees

BLUMA, Stephanie: Senior Associate
CARR, Lisa: Senior Associate
COOPER, Ranny: Partner
DUCHENSE, Steve: Managing Director
KEHOE, Stephen: Managing Director
LATTIMORE, Neel: Senior Managing Director
LYNAM, Clare: Senior Managing Director
MACHAMER, Molly: Director, Public Affairs
MARONI, William: Managing Director
MASSEY, Paul: Senior Associate, Public Affairs Practice
MAY, Clifford D.: Senior Managing Director
MESZAROS, James A.: Principal
MORGAN, Lance I.: President and Partner
OILMAN, Betsy: Senior Associate
OPINSKY, Howard S.: Managing Director
SWINT, Jennifer: Senior Managing Director
WILLIAMS, Scott: Senior Managing Director

Outside Counsel/Consultants

The Michael Lewan Co.
Issues: WEL
Rep By: Michael Lewan, Anne Saunders

BT North America Inc.

601 Pennsylvania Ave. NW
Suite 625
North Bldg.
Washington, DC 20004
Web: www.bt.com
Tel: (202)639-8222
Fax: (202)434-8867
Registered: LDA

The Washington office for the North American operations of British Telecommunications plc, headquartered in London, England.

Leg. Issues: COM, TEC

In-house, DC-area Employees

GRAF, II, James E.: President, BT North America, Inc.
VERDERAME, Kristen Neller: Director, U.S. Regulation and Government Relations

Buckeye Technologies

Memphis, TN

Outside Counsel/Consultants

Baker, Donelson, Bearman & Caldwell, P.C.
Rep By: Francine Lamoriello

Buckley Broadcasting Corp.

Greenwich, CT

Outside Counsel/Consultants

Shaw Pittman

Budd Co.

Troy, MI

Outside Counsel/Consultants

Barnes, Richardson and Colburn
Rep By: Matthew T. McGrath

Buffalo Carpenters Pension Fund

Cheektowga, NY
Leg. Issues: LBR, RET, TAX

Outside Counsel/Consultants

Groom Law Group, Chartered
Issues: LBR, RET, TAX
Rep By: Jon W. Breyfogle, Gary M. Ford

Buffalo Sewer Authority

Buffalo, NY
Leg. Issues: ENV

Outside Counsel/Consultants

The Advocacy Group
Issues: ENV
Rep By: Robert E. Mills

Buffalo, New York, City of

Leg. Issues: ECN

Outside Counsel/Consultants

The Advocacy Group
Issues: ECN
Rep By: Robert E. Mills

Build Indiana Council

Indianapolis, IN

A trade association of highway construction companies.

Leg. Issues: ROD

Outside Counsel/Consultants

Fisher Consulting
Issues: ROD
Rep By: Steven A. Fisher

Builders Hardware Manufacturers Ass'n

4041 Powder Mill Rd.
Suite 104
Calverton, MD 20705
Tel: (301)348-2005
Fax: (301)348-2020

In-house, DC-area Employees

SNYDER, Russell K.: Washington Representative

Outside Counsel/Consultants

The Kellen Company
Rep By: Russell K. Snyder

Building America

Outside Counsel/Consultants

The Dutko Group, Inc.

Building Owners and Managers Ass'n Internat'l

1201 New York Ave. NW
Suite 300
Washington, DC 20005
Tel: (202)408-2662
Fax: (202)371-0181
Registered: LDA
Web: www.boma.org
E-mail: postmaster@boma.org
Leg. Issues: ENV, RES, SCI, TAX, TEC, TOB, UTI

Political Action Committee/s

Building Owners and Managers Ass'n Political Action Committee
1201 New York Ave. NW
Suite 300
Washington, DC 20005
Contact: Robert Houton
Tel: (202)326-6365
Fax: (202)371-0181

In-house, DC-area Employees

GIANBERARDINO, Marco: Assistant Exec. Director, Government and Industry Affairs
HOUTON, Robert: Manager, State and Local Affairs
LEDERER, Gerry: Exec. Director, Government and Industry Affairs
PENAFIEL, Karen: Assistant Exec. Director, Government and Industry Affairs
SHERIDAN, Richard: Assistant Exec. Director, Government and Industry Affairs

Outside Counsel/Consultants

Jenner & Block
Miller & Van Eaton, P.L.L.C.
Issues: TEC
Rep By: Matthew C. Ames, William Malone, Nicholas P. Miller

Building Service Contractors Ass'n Internat'l

10201 Lee Hwy.
Suite 225
Fairfax, VA 22030
Tel: (703)359-7090
Fax: (703)352-0493
Registered: LDA
Web: www.bscai.org

Represents companies that provide facility maintenance and related services to building owners and managers.

Leg. Issues: CSP, ENV, INS, LBR, SMB, TAX

Political Action Committee/s

Building Service Contractors Ass'n Internat'l PAC (BSCAI PAC)
10201 Lee Hwy.
Suite 225
Fairfax, VA 22030
Contact: Carol A. Dean
Tel: (703)359-7090
Fax: (703)352-0493

In-house, DC-area Employees

DEAN, Carol A.: Exec. V. President

Outside Counsel/Consultants

Arent Fox Kintner Plotkin & Kahn, PLLC
Issues: CSP, ENV, INS, LBR, SMB, TAX
Rep By: Michael T. McNamara, Elliott I. Portnoy

Bulgaria, Embassy of the Republic of

1621 22nd St. NW
Washington, DC 20008
Tel: (202)387-0174
Fax: (202)234-7973

Outside Counsel/Consultants

BSMG Worldwide

Bulgaria, Government of the Republic of

Sofia, BULGARIA

Outside Counsel/Consultants

White & Case LLP

Bulgaria, Ministry of Foreign Affairs of the Republic of

Sofia, BULGARIA

Outside Counsel/Consultants

Jefferson-Waterman Internat'l, LLC
Rep By: Samuel M. Hoskinson

Bulgarian-American Business Center

McLean, VA
Leg. Issues: FOR

Outside Counsel/Consultants

Robert N. Pyle & Associates
Issues: FOR
Rep By: Alexis Hersh, Alison O'Neill, Robert N. Pyle

Bull H.N. Information Services, Inc.

Billerica, MA

Outside Counsel/Consultants

Skadden, Arps, Slate, Meagher & Flom LLP

Bulmer Holding PLC, H. P.

Hereford, UNITED KINGDOM
Leg. Issues: BEV, BUD, FOO, TAX, TRD

Outside Counsel/Consultants

Washington Council Ernst & Young
Issues: BEV, BUD, FOO, TAX, TRD
Rep By: Doug Badger, Lauren Darling, John L. Doney, Jayne T. Fitzgerald, LaBrenda Garrett-Nelson, Gary J. Gasper, Bruce A. Gates, Nick Giordano, Cathy Koch, Robert J. Leonard, Richard Meltzer, Phillip D. Moseley, John D. Porter, Robert M. Rozen, Donna Steele-Flynn, Timothy J. Urban

BUNAC USA, Inc.

Southbury, CT
Leg. Issues: IMM

Outside Counsel/Consultants

Greenberg Traurig, LLP
Issues: IMM
Rep By: Elissa M. McGovern

Bundesverband der Deutscher Banken

Cologne, GERMANY

Outside Counsel/Consultants

White & Case LLP

Bunge Corp.

1101 15th St. NW
Suite 503
Washington, DC 20005
Web: www.bungecorp.com
E-mail: cnelson@bunge.com
Tel: (202)785-3885
Fax: (202)785-3887

Headquartered in St. Louis, MO. Specializes in agriculture and business.

Leg. Issues: AGR, TRD

In-house, DC-area Employees

NELSON, Charles A.: V. President and Washington Representative

James W. Bunger & Associates

Leg. Issues: CHM, FUE

Outside Counsel/Consultants

Robert K. Weidner
Issues: CHM, FUE
Rep By: Robert K. Weidner

Burbank Aeronautical Corp. II

Burbank, CA

Outside Counsel/Consultants

Rhoads Group

The Bureau of Nat'l Affairs, Inc.

Washington, DC
Registered: LDA
Leg. Issues: GOV, TAX

Outside Counsel/Consultants

Zuckerman Spaeder L.L.P.
Issues: GOV, TAX
Rep By: Virginia Guldi, Eleanor H. Smith, Ronald H. Weich

Bureau of Wholesale Sales Representatives

Atlanta, GA
Leg. Issues: TAX

Outside Counsel/Consultants

Abraham Schneier and Associates
Issues: TAX
Rep By: Abraham L. Schneier

Burger King Corp.

Miami, FL Registered: LDA
Leg. Issues: ANI, BUD, FOO, HCR, LBR, SMB, TAX, TRD, WEL

Outside Counsel/Consultants

Baker, Donelson, Bearman & Caldwell, P.C.
Issues: BUD, LBR, TRD
Rep By: Doreen M. Edelman

Policy Directions, Inc.
Issues: ANI
Rep By: Stephen Michael, Frankie L. Trull

Saliba Action Strategies, LLC
Issues: FOO, HCR, LBR, SMB, WEL
Rep By: Khalil G. "Karl" Saliba

The Wexler Group
Issues: FOO, HCR, LBR, TAX
Rep By: Hon. Michael Patrick Flanagan, Joel Malina, Anne Wexler

Burk-Kleinpeter, Inc.

New Orleans, LA
Leg. Issues: BUD, CAW, URB

Outside Counsel/Consultants

Jones, Walker, Waechter, Poitevent, Carrere & Denegre, L.L.P.
Issues: BUD, CAW, URB
Rep By: Paul Cambon, John J. Jaskot, R. Christian Johnsen

Burke Venture Capital

Ridgefield, CT
Leg. Issues: FIN

Outside Counsel/Consultants

Morgan Meguire, LLC
Issues: FIN
Rep By: Jocelyn Hong, Jack Jacobson, Kyle G. Michel, C. Kyle Simpson

Burkina Faso, Government of

Ouagadougou, BURKINA FASO

Outside Counsel/Consultants

Cohen and Woods Internat'l, Inc.
Rep By: Herman J. Cohen

Washington World Group, Ltd.
Rep By: Edward J. von Kloberg, III

Burlington Northern Santa Fe Railway

1001 G St. NW
Suite 1210-W
Washington, DC 20001-4545
Tel: (202)347-8662
Fax: (202)347-8675
Registered: LDA
Web: www.bnsf.com
Leg. Issues: AGR, BNK, BUD, CAW, CDT, CHM, COM, CSP, DIS, ECN, ENG, ENV, FIN, FUE, GOV, HCR, IND, INS, LAW, LBR, MAN, MAR, MMM, NAT, RES, RET, ROD, RRR, SCI, SMB, TAX, TEC, TRA, TRD, TRU, UNM, URB, UTI, WAS

In-house, DC-area Employees

ENDRES, Jr., Arthur P. "Skip": V. President, Government Affairs
STRICKLAND, Jr., Sidney L.: Associate General Counsel

Outside Counsel/Consultants

Kessler & Associates Business Services, Inc.
Issues: RRR, TAX, TRA
Rep By: Michael L. Bartlett, Billy Lee Evans, Richard S. Kessler, James C. Musser

Lent Scrivner & Roth LLC
Issues: RRR
Rep By: Norman F. Lent, III, Hon. Norman F. Lent, Alan J. Roth, Michael S. Scrivner

Mayer, Brown & Platt
Issues: RRR
Rep By: Mark H. Gitenstein

Alan J. Moore, Washington Representative - Governmental Affairs
Issues: RRR
Rep By: Alan J. Moore

Preston Gates Ellis & Rouvelas Meeds LLP
Issues: ROD, RRR, TAX, TEC
Rep By: Werner W. Brandt, Pamela J. Garvie, Hon. Lloyd Meeds, Michael J. O'Neil, Emanuel L. Rouvelas, W. Dennis Stephens, Martin L. Stern, Steven R. "Rick" Valentine

Steptoe & Johnson LLP
Issues: TAX
Rep By: Catherine W. Wilkinson, CPA

Burlington Resources Oil & Gas Co.

Houston, TX
Leg. Issues: BUD, ENG, ENV, FUE, NAT, TAX, TRD

Outside Counsel/Consultants

Crowell & Moring LLP
Issues: NAT
Rep By: Steven P. Quarles

William F. Whitsitt Policy and Government Affairs
Issues: BUD, ENG, ENV, FUE, NAT, TAX, TRD
Rep By: William F. Whitsitt

Burns and Roe Enterprises, Inc.

1400 K St. NW
Suite 910
Washington, DC 20005
Tel: (202)898-1500
Fax: (202)898-1561
Registered: LDA
E-mail: rbr1@worldnet.att.net
Leg. Issues: AER, BUD, CAW, CHM, DEF, ENG, FUE, GOV, PHA, SCI, UTI, WAS

Political Action Committee/s

Burns and Roe PAC
1400 K St. NW
Suite 910
Washington, DC 20005
Tel: (202)898-1500
Fax: (202)898-1561
Contact: Randall B. Roe

In-house, DC-area Employees

ROE, Randall B.: V. Chairman

Outside Counsel/Consultants

Johnston & Associates, LLC
Issues: BUD, DEF, ENG, GOV
Rep By: Hon. J. Bennett Johnston, W. Proctor Jones

Smith, Hinaman & Associates
Issues: ENG
Rep By: Don Smith

Van Scoyoc Associates, Inc.
Issues: DEF, ENG
Rep By: Paul Grimm, Buzz Hawley, H. Stewart Van Scoyoc

Burst Networks Inc.

Seattle, WA
Leg. Issues: COM

Outside Counsel/Consultants

The Wexler Group
Issues: COM
Rep By: Peter T. Holran, Anne Jones, Vicki May, Dale W. Snape

Burstein Laboratories, Inc.

Irvine, CA
Leg. Issues: DEF

Outside Counsel/Consultants

William M. Cloherty
Issues: DEF
Rep By: William M. Cloherty

Burundi, Embassy of

2233 Wisconsin Ave. NW
Suite 212
Washington, DC 20007
Tel: (202)342-2574
Fax: (202)342-2578

Outside Counsel/Consultants

Washington World Group, Ltd.
Rep By: Edward J. von Kloberg, III

Business Alliance for Customs Modernization

Escondido, CA

Outside Counsel/Consultants

Public Policy Resources

Business Alliance for Internat'l Economic Development

Outside Counsel/Consultants

Bracy Williams & Co.
Rep By: James C. Benfield, Terrence L. Bracy

Business and Professional Women/USA

2012 Massachusetts Ave. NW
Washington, DC 20036
Tel: (202)293-1100
Fax: (202)861-0298
Web: www.bpwusa.org
Leg. Issues: CIV, ECN, FAM, HCR, LBR, RET, SMB

Political Action Committee/s

Business & Professional Women/USA Political Action Committee
2012 Massachusetts Ave. NW
Washington, DC 20036
Tel: (202)293-1100
Fax: (202)861-0298
Contact: Louise Sienko

In-house, DC-area Employees

CORNISH, Pat: National President
SIENKO, Louise: Chair and PAC Contact

Business Computer Training Institute

Gig Harbor, WA

Outside Counsel/Consultants

Bryan Cave LLP
Rep By: Hon. Alan J. Dixon

Business Council for Sustainable Energy

1200 18th St. NW
Ninth Floor
Washington, DC 20036
Tel: (202)785-0507
Fax: (202)785-0514
Registered: LDA
E-mail: bcse@bcse.org

A coalition of associations and businesses in the natural gas, energy efficiency, renewable energy and electric utility industries committed to expanded use of clean, domestic, sustainable energy.

Leg. Issues: ENG

In-house, DC-area Employees

MARVIN, Michael L.: President

Outside Counsel/Consultants

Cascade Associates
Issues: ENG
Rep By: Jennifer A. Schafer

Business Council on Indoor Air

P.O. Box 68
Fairfax, VA 22039
Tel: (703)802-3419
Fax: (703)631-8340
E-mail: cammer@iamdigex.net

A trade association formed to address issues and problems of indoor air quality.

In-house, DC-area Employees

CAMMER, Paul A.: President

Outside Counsel/Consultants

Cammer and Associates
Rep By: Paul A. Cammer

The Business Council

888 17th St. NW
Suite 506
Washington, DC 20006
Tel: (202)298-7650
Fax: (202)785-0296
Web: www.businesscouncil.com

A forum for the exchange of ideas between top corporate executives and government officials. Established originally as the Business Advisory Council to the Department of Commerce, it assumed its present name in 1961.

In-house, DC-area Employees

CASSIDY, Philip E.: Exec. Director

Business Executives for Nat'l Security

1717 Pennsylvania Ave. NW
Suite 350
Washington, DC 20006
Tel: (202)296-2125
Fax: (202)296-2490
Registered: LDA
Web: www.bens.org
E-mail: bens@bens.org

Concerned with the use of sound business practices in national security policy and preparing for new threats of the 21st Century.

Leg. Issues: DEF, FOR, GOV

In-house, DC-area Employees

BEEKS, Kenneth: V. President, Policy
HEARNEY, Richard D.: President and Chief Exec. Officer
TAIBL, Paul E.: Assistant V. President
WEISS, Stanley A.: Chairman

Outside Counsel/Consultants

Bergner Bockorny Castagnetti and Hawkins
Issues: FOR
Rep By: Jeffrey T. Bergner, David A. Bockorny, David Castagnetti, Melissa Schulman

Business Insurance Coalition

Washington, DC
Leg. Issues: TAX

Outside Counsel/Consultants

Patton Boggs, LLP
Issues: TAX
Rep By: John F. Jonas

Business Men's Assurance Co. of America

Kansas City, MO

Outside Counsel/Consultants

Covington & Burling

Business News Publishing Co.

Troy, MI

Outside Counsel/Consultants

Ashby and Associates
Rep By: R. Barry Ashby

The Business Roundtable

1615 L St. NW
Suite 1100
Washington, DC 20036-5610
Tel: (202)872-1260
Fax: (202)466-3509
Registered: LDA
Web: www.brt.org

An association of chief executive officers of leading corporations with a combined workforce of more than ten million employees in the U.S. The chief executives are committed to advocating public policies that foster vigorous economic growth, a dynamic global economy, and a well-trained and productive U.S. workforce essential for future competitiveness.

Leg. Issues: BUD, CSP, EDU, ENV, FIN, FOR, GOV, HCR, LBR, RET, TAX, TRD, WEL

In-house, DC-area Employees

BURT, Robert N.: Chairman
DICONTI, Michael A.: Director, Administration
ENGMAN, Patricia H.: Exec. Director
GRAVES, Donet D.: Exec. Director, BusinessLINC
GWYN, Brigitte S.: Legislative Director
HOPKINS, Marian E.: Director, Legislation
MAURY, Samuel L.: President
SCHACHTER, John: Deputy Director, Communications
SCHNEIDER, Johanna: Director, Communications
TRAIMAN, Susan N.: Director, Education Initiative
ZURAWSKI, Paul R.: Legislative Counsel

Outside Counsel/Consultants

American Strategies, Inc.

Balzano Associates
Issues: TRD
Rep By: Christopher Balzano, Michael P. Balzano, Jr., Ruthanne Goodman, Janel Vermeulen

Bergner Bockorny Castagnetti and Hawkins

Boesch & Co.
Issues: TRD
Rep By: Doyce A. Boesch

Covington & Burling
Issues: TAX
Rep By: Roderick A. DeArment, Ronald A. Pearlman

Davidson & Company, Inc.
Issues: BUD, TAX
Rep By: James H. Davidson, Richard E. May, Stanley Sokul

The Duberstein Group, Inc.
Issues: BUD, EDU, ENV, FIN, GOV, HCR, LBR, RET, TAX, TRD, WEL
Rep By: John W. Angus, III, Michael S. Berman, Steven M. Champlin, Kenneth M. Duberstein, Henry M. Gandy, Daniel P. Meyer

EOP Group, Inc.
Issues: BUD, ENV
Rep By: Donald Gesseman, Norman Hartness, Joseph Hezir, John Lamson, Michael O'Bannon

Gibson, Dunn & Crutcher LLP
Issues: FIN
Rep By: Amy Goodman, John F. Olson

Goddard Claussen

Greenberg Traurig, LLP
Issues: HCR
Rep By: Russell J. Mueller, Nancy E. Taylor, Timothy P. Trysla

Michael J. Kopetski
Issues: FOR, TRD
Rep By: Michael J. Kopetski

William M. Mercer, Inc.
Issues: HCR
Rep By: William M. Mercer

Potomac Communications Group

Ropes & Gray
Issues: GOV
Rep By: Thomas M. Susman

The Trade Partnership
Issues: TRD
Rep By: Laura M. Baughman

Widmeyer Communications, Inc.

Wilmer, Cutler & Pickering
Issues: TRD
Rep By: Charles S. Levy

Business Software Alliance

1150 18th St. NW
Suite 700
Washington, DC 20036
Tel: (202)872-5500
Fax: (202)872-5501
Registered: LDA
Web: www.bsa.org
E-mail: software@bsa.org
Leg. Issues: COM, CPI, CPT, CSP, GOV, SCI, TAX, TEC, TRD

In-house, DC-area Employees

HOLLEYMAN, II, Robert W.: President and C.E.O.
KRUGER, Robert M.: V. President, Enforcement
LANVANHOVE, Scott: V. President, Global Operations
SMIROLDO, Diane: V. President, Public Affairs

Outside Counsel/Consultants

Alpine Group, Inc.
Issues: COM, CPI, CPT
Rep By: Dan Brouillette, Rhod M. Shaw

The Direct Impact Co.

Dittus Communications
Rep By: Tom Conway, Gloria S. Dittus, Cynthia Giorgio, Kristin Litterst, Jennifer Moire, Tim Sites

Preston Gates Ellis & Rouvelas Meeds LLP
Issues: CPI, CPT, CSP, SCI, TEC, TRD
Rep By: Amy Carlson, Bruce J. Heiman

Business-Higher Education Forum

One Dupont Circle NW
Suite 250
Washington, DC 20036
Tel: (202)939-9345
Fax: (202)833-4723
Registered: LDA
Web: www.bhef.edu
E-mail: bhef@ace.nche.edu

In-house, DC-area Employees

MURPHY, Jeremiah L.: Exec. Director

Business-Industry Political Action Committee

888 16th St. NW
Suite 305
Washington, DC 20006
Tel: (202)833-1880
Fax: (202)833-2338
Web: www.bipac.org
E-mail: info@bipac.org

*Founded in 1963. Supported by over 1,000 associations and corporations. Publishes The BIPAC Action Report (q.) and Elections In*Sight (m.).*

In-house, DC-area Employees

ARCHULETA, Mark: Director, Finance and Administration
BUDDE, Bernadette A.: Senior V. President
CASEY, Gregory S.: President and Chief Exec. Officer
FLAVIN, Deborah C.: V. President, Development and Marketing
MARGO, R.D. "Dee": Chairman
PAYNE, Jeanne H.: Director, Member Services
SHULL, Darrell A.: V. President, Political Operations

A. D. Butler and Associates, Inc.

Fairfax, VA
Leg. Issues: DEF

Outside Counsel/Consultants

W. B. Driggers & Associates, Inc.
Issues: DEF
Rep By: W. B. Driggers

H. E. Butt Grocery Co.

San Antonio, TX
Leg. Issues: WEL

Outside Counsel/Consultants

Miller & Chevalier, Chartered
Issues: WEL
Rep By: Leonard Bickwit, Jr.

Buyers Up

1600 20th St. NW
Washington, DC 20009-1001
Tel: (202)588-7780
Fax: (202)588-7798
Web: www.buyersup.org
E-mail: buyersup@citizen.org

Affiliated with Public Citizen, a national non-profit consumer advocacy group. Administers a 5,000 member group purchasing program for home heating oils.

In-house, DC-area Employees

AUTON, Garland: Program Manager

BuyMoreProduct

Outside Counsel/Consultants

Columbus Public Affairs

BWXT, Inc.

Outside Counsel/Consultants

Preston Gates Ellis & Rouvelas Meeds LLP
Rep By: Cindy O'Malley, Tim L. Peckinpaugh

C F Industries, Inc.

1401 I St. NW
Suite 340
Washington, DC 20005
Tel: (202)371-9279
Fax: (202)371-9169
Registered: LDA
Web: www.cfindustries.com
E-mail: robrien@cfindustries.com

A fertilizer manufacturer headquartered in Long Grove, IL.

Leg. Issues: AGR, BUD, ENG, ENV, LBR, TAX, TRA, TRD, UTI

In-house, DC-area Employees

O'BRIEN, Rosemary L.: V. President, Public Affairs

Outside Counsel/Consultants

Covington & Burling

Kirkland & Ellis

Millian Byers Associates, LLC
Rep By: H. James Byers

C.A. Vencemos

Caracas, VENEZUELA
Leg. Issues: ENV, ROD, TRD

Outside Counsel/Consultants

Janus-Merritt Strategies, L.L.C.
Issues: ENV, ROD, TRD
Rep By: Mark J. Robertson

Cabazon Band of Mission Indians

Indio, CA
Leg. Issues: GAM, IND

Outside Counsel/Consultants

Ietan Consulting
Rep By: Wilson Pipestem, Larry Rosenthal

Kurzweil & Associates
Issues: GAM, IND
Rep By: Jeffrey Kurzweil

Cable & Wireless U.S.A., Inc.

Leg. Issues: TEC

Outside Counsel/Consultants

Greenberg Traurig, LLP
Issues: TEC

Cable & Wireless, Inc.

8219 Leesburg Pike
Vienna, VA 22182-2625
Tel: (703)790-5300
Fax: (703)442-8819
Registered: LDA, FARA
Web: www.cwusa.com

A subsidiary of Cable and Wireless plc of London, England.

Leg. Issues: TEC, TRD

In-house, DC-area Employees

JOYCE, Chris: V. President, Chief Financial Officer and Treasurer
ROTHSTEIN, Rachel: V. President, Regulatory and Government Affairs

Outside Counsel/Consultants

Columbus Public Affairs

The Dutko Group, Inc.
Issues: TEC, TRD
Rep By: Kim Koontz Bayliss, Louis Lehrman, Steve Perry, Juliette M. Raffensperger, Stephen Craig Sayle

Mayer, Brown & Platt
Issues: TEC
Rep By: David B. Finnegan, Mark H. Gitenstein, Erika Z. Jones

Swidler Berlin Shereff Friedman, LLP
Rep By: Andrew D. Lipman

Cablevision Systems Corp.

Woodbury, NY
Leg. Issues: TEC

Outside Counsel/Consultants

The Coursen Group
Issues: TEC
Rep By: Hon. Christopher D. Coursen

Mintz, Levin, Cohn, Ferris, Glovsky and Popeo, P.C.
Issues: TEC
Rep By: Charles D. Ferris, Howard J. Symons

CADDO Lake Institute

Aspen, CO

Outside Counsel/Consultants

Spiegel & McDiarmid
Rep By: John J. Corbett, Jr.

Cadmus/Energy Star

Outside Counsel/Consultants

Hill and Knowlton, Inc.
Rep By: Bruce Hildebrand

Cafaro Co.

Youngstown, OH
Leg. Issues: TAX

Outside Counsel/Consultants

Baker & Hostetler LLP
Issues: TAX
Rep By: William F. Conroy, Matthew J. Dolan, Steven A. Lotterer, David L. Marshall, Hon. Guy Vander Jagt

Caguas, Puerto Rico, City of

Leg. Issues: CAW, HOU, TRA

Outside Counsel/Consultants

Smith Dawson & Andrews, Inc.
Issues: CAW, HOU, TRA
Rep By: Ramon Luis Lugo, James P. Smith

CAI Wireless

Albany, NY

Outside Counsel/Consultants

Arter & Hadden

CAIS Internet

1255 22nd St. NW
Fourth Floor
Washington, DC 20037
Web: www.cais.com
Tel: (202)715-1300
Fax: (202)463-7190

An Internet service provider.

In-house, DC-area Employees

DICKERSON, Shawn: Administrative Assistant for Legal Counsel

Outside Counsel/Consultants

Swidler Berlin Shereff Friedman, LLP
Rep By: Jean L. Kiddoo

Caithness Energy, LLC

Englewood, CO
Leg. Issues: ENG

Outside Counsel/Consultants

J. Steven Griles & Associates
Issues: ENG
Rep By: J. Steven Griles

Cal Dive Internat'l Inc.

Houston, TX
Leg. Issues: MAR

Outside Counsel/Consultants

Robins, Kaplan, Miller & Ciresi L.L.P.
Issues: MAR
Rep By: Harold E. Mesirow

CAL-FED

Sacramento, CA
Leg. Issues: EDU, TAX

Outside Counsel/Consultants

Federal Management Strategies, Inc.
Issues: EDU, TAX
Rep By: Robert P. Canavan

Calaveras County, California, Water District

Leg. Issues: BUD, ENV, NAT, RES, TOU

Outside Counsel/Consultants

Reed, Smith, LLP
Issues: BUD, ENV, NAT, RES, TOU
Rep By: Christopher L. Rissetto

CalCot

Bakersfield, CA

An agricultural cooperative.

Leg. Issues: AGR, TRD

Outside Counsel/Consultants

Haley and Associates
Issues: AGR, TRD
Rep By: Daniel D. Haley

CalEnergy Co., Inc.

Omaha, NE

Outside Counsel/Consultants

White & Case LLP
Rep By: David W. Hunt

Calhoun County Community Development

Marshall, MI
Leg. Issues: TRA

Outside Counsel/Consultants

Dykema Gossett PLLC
Issues: TRA
Rep By: Nancy R. Barbour, Tricia K. Markwood

Calhoun County, Alabama Commission

Outside Counsel/Consultants

O'Connor & Hannan, L.L.P.
Rep By: Morgan W. Reed, III, David E. Springer

Calibre Corp.

Falls Church, VA

Outside Counsel/Consultants

Van Fleet, Inc.
Rep By: Frank C. Van Fleet

California Asparagus Commission

Stockton, CA
Leg. Issues: AGR, BUD, TRD

Outside Counsel/Consultants

Schramm, Williams & Associates, Inc.
Issues: AGR, BUD, TRD
Rep By: Anita Brown, Duane L. Musser, Robert Schramm

California Ass'n of Children's Hospitals

San Diego, CA

Outside Counsel/Consultants

McDermott, Will and Emery

California Ass'n of Marriage and Family Therapists

San Diego, CA
Leg. Issues: HCR, MMM

Outside Counsel/Consultants

Capitol Associates, Inc.
Issues: HCR, MMM
Rep By: Debra M. Hardy Havens, Julie Shroyer

California Ass'n of Sanitation Agencies

Sacramento, CA
Leg. Issues: BUD, CAW, ENV

Outside Counsel/Consultants

ENS Resources, Inc.
Issues: BUD, CAW, ENV
Rep By: Eric Sapirstein

California Ass'n of Winegrape Growers

Sacramento, CA
Leg. Issues: TRD

Outside Counsel/Consultants

JBC Internat'l
Issues: TRD
Rep By: Jeannie M. Boone, James B. Clawson

Schramm, Williams & Associates, Inc.
Issues: TRD
Rep By: Anita Brown, Nancy Williams

The Washington Group

California Avocado Commission

Santa Ana, CA
Leg. Issues: AGR, TRD

Outside Counsel/Consultants

McDermott, Will and Emery
Issues: TRD
Rep By: Jerry C. Hill, Edward M. Ruckert

McLeod, Watkinson & Miller
Issues: AGR
Rep By: Michael R. McLeod, Richard E. Pasco

California Board of Equalization

Sacramento, CA

Outside Counsel/Consultants

Vienna, Gregor & Associates
Rep By: Janet R. Gregor, Donald R. Marlais, Nancy L. Miller, David P. Vienna

California Cable Television Ass'n

Oakland, CA
Registered: LDA

Outside Counsel/Consultants

Mintz, Levin, Cohn, Ferris, Glovsky and Popeo, P.C.
Rep By: Frank W. Lloyd

California Canning Peach Ass'n

LaFayette, CA
Leg. Issues: AGR

Outside Counsel/Consultants

McDermott, Will and Emery
Rep By: Carolyn B. Gleason

Olsson, Frank and Weeda, P.C.
Issues: AGR
Rep By: John W. Bode, Susan P. Grymes, Karen Reis Harned, Stephen L. Lacey, Marshall L. Matz, Tyson Redpath, Ryan W. Stroschein

California Central Coast Research Partnership

San Luis Obispo, CA
Leg. Issues: BUD, EDU, SCI

Outside Counsel/Consultants

R. Duffy Wall and Associates
Issues: BUD, EDU, SCI

California Children's Hospital Ass'n

San Diego, CA
Leg. Issues: HCR, MMM

Outside Counsel/Consultants

Carpi & Clay
Issues: HCR, MMM
Rep By: Kenneth A. Carpi

McDermott, Will and Emery

California Cling Peach Growers Advisory Board

Dinuba, CA
Leg. Issues: TRD

Outside Counsel/Consultants

McDermott, Will and Emery
Issues: TRD
Rep By: Carolyn B. Gleason, Jerry C. Hill, Maggie A. Mitchell, Pamela D. Walther

California Correctional Peace Officers Ass'n

West Sacramento, CA
Leg. Issues: BUD, GOV, IMM, LAW, LBR, RET

Outside Counsel/Consultants

Capitol Strategies
Issues: BUD, GOV, IMM, LAW
Rep By: Mary M. Tripp

Shannon M. Lahey Associates
Issues: GOV, LAW, LBR, RET
Rep By: Shannon M. Lahey

California Debt Limit Allocation Committee

Sacramento, CA
Leg. Issues: TAX

Outside Counsel/Consultants

O'Connor & Hannan, L.L.P.
Issues: TAX
Rep By: Frederick T. Dombo, Christina W. Fleps, Robert Harmala, Patrick E. O'Donnell, Thomas H. Quinn

California Department of Education

Sacramento, CA

Outside Counsel/Consultants

Ablondi, Foster, Sobin & Davidow, P.C.

Brustein & Manasevit
Rep By: Michael Brustein, Claire Milner

California Federal Bank

Outside Counsel/Consultants

Gibson, Dunn & Crutcher LLP
Rep By: Robert C. Eager, Cantwell Faulkner Muckenfuss, III, Victoria P. Rostow

California Franchise Tax Board

Sacramento, CA

Outside Counsel/Consultants

Vienna, Gregor & Associates
Rep By: Janet R. Gregor, Donald R. Marlais, Nancy L. Miller, David P. Vienna

California Health Care Foundation

Outside Counsel/Consultants

Edelman Public Relations Worldwide
Rep By: Peter Segall

California Hospital Medical Center Foundation

Leg. Issues: BUD

Outside Counsel/Consultants

Cassidy & Associates, Inc.
Issues: BUD
Rep By: Laura A. Neal, Valerie Rogers Osborne, Blenda Pinto-Riddick

California Independent Petroleum Ass'n

Sacramento, CA
Leg. Issues: ENG, FUE

Outside Counsel/Consultants

E. Del Smith and Co.
Issues: ENG, FUE
Rep By: Margaret Allen, E. Del Smith

California Independent System Operator

Fulsom, CA
Leg. Issues: UTI

Outside Counsel/Consultants

Swidler Berlin Shereff Friedman, LLP
Issues: UTI
Rep By: Keith N. Cole, Barry B. Direnfeld, Kenneth G. Jaffe, Gary D. Slaiman

California Institute for the Arts

Valencia, CA
Leg. Issues: BUD

Outside Counsel/Consultants

Cassidy & Associates, Inc.
Issues: BUD
Rep By: Blenda Pinto-Riddick, Barbara Sutton, Gerald Felix Warburg

California Institute of Technology

Pasadena, CA
Leg. Issues: BUD, CPT, EDU, IMM, SCI, TAX

Outside Counsel/Consultants

Lewis-Burke Associates
Issues: BUD, CPT, EDU, IMM, SCI, TAX
Rep By: April L. Burke, Mark A. Burnham, Mark Marin

California Kiwi Fruit Commission

Sacramento, CA
Leg. Issues: AGR

Outside Counsel/Consultants

McDermott, Will and Emery
Issues: AGR
Rep By: Jerry C. Hill

California Museum Foundation

Los Angeles, CA
Leg. Issues: BUD

Outside Counsel/Consultants

Cassidy & Associates, Inc.
Issues: BUD
Rep By: Jeffrey Lawrence, Valerie Rogers Osborne

California Pistachio Commission

Fresno, CA
Leg. Issues: AGR, BUD, FOO, TRD

Outside Counsel/Consultants

Schramm, Williams & Associates, Inc.
Issues: AGR, BUD, FOO, TRD
Rep By: Anita Brown, Robert Schramm

California Poultry Industry Federation

Modesto, CA
Leg. Issues: AGR

Outside Counsel/Consultants

Podesta/Mattoon
Issues: AGR
Rep By: Timothy Powers

California Primary Care Ass'n

Sacramento, CA
Leg. Issues: HCR

Outside Counsel/Consultants

Berliner, Candon & Jimison
Issues: HCR
Rep By: Carla Kish, Burt Margolin

California Prune Board

San Francisco, CA
Leg. Issues: AGR, TRD

Outside Counsel/Consultants

Haley and Associates
Issues: AGR, TRD
Rep By: Daniel D. Haley

California Public Employees' Retirement System

Sacramento, CA

Outside Counsel/Consultants

Vienna, Gregor & Associates
Rep By: Janet R. Gregor, Donald R. Marlais, Nancy L. Miller, David P. Vienna

California Refuse Removal Council

Sacramento, CA
Leg. Issues: ENV, TRU, WAS

Outside Counsel/Consultants

Baise + Miller, P.C.
Issues: ENV, TRU, WAS
Rep By: Eric P. Bock

California Restaurant Ass'n

Sacramento, CA

Outside Counsel/Consultants

Patton Boggs, LLP

California Rural Indian Health Board, Inc.

Sacramento, CA
Leg. Issues: MMM

Outside Counsel/Consultants

Medicaid Policy, L.L.C.
Issues: MMM
Rep By: Andrew G. Schneider

California School Employees Ass'n

Outside Counsel/Consultants

BKSH & Associates

California School of Professional Psychology

San Francisco, CA
Leg. Issues: BUD, EDU, HCR

Outside Counsel/Consultants

Powers Pyles Sutter & Verville, PC
Issues: BUD, EDU, HCR
Rep By: J. Michael Hall, Alyson M. Haywood

California State Ass'n of Counties

Sacramento, CA
Web: www.csac.counties.org
Leg. Issues: DIS, HCR, HOU, LAW, TOB, TRA, WEL

Outside Counsel/Consultants

Waterman & Associates
Issues: DIS, HCR, HOU, LAW, TOB, TRA, WEL
Rep By: Michael Hollon, Joe Krahn, Ronald D. Waterman

California State Assembly - Committee on Rules

Sacramento, CA

Outside Counsel/Consultants

Murray, Scheer, Montgomery, Tapia & O'Donnell
Rep By: Thomas R. Crawford, D. Michael Murray, Raul R. Tapia

California State Lands Commission

Sacramento, CA
Leg. Issues: ENG, ENV, FUE, NAT, RES

Outside Counsel/Consultants

Elinor Schwartz
Issues: ENG, ENV, FUE, NAT, RES
Rep By: Elinor Schwartz

California State Senate

Sacramento, CA

Outside Counsel/Consultants

Vienna, Gregor & Associates
Rep By: Janet R. Gregor, Donald R. Marlais, Nancy L. Miller, Cheryl Vienna, David P. Vienna

California State Teachers' Retirement System

Sacramento, CA
Leg. Issues: BUD, RET, TAX

Outside Counsel/Consultants

Hogan & Hartson L.L.P.
Issues: BUD, RET, TAX
Rep By: John S. Stanton

California State University at Monterey Bay

Seaside, CA

Outside Counsel/Consultants

Hunton & Williams

California State University Fresno

Fresno, CA
Leg. Issues: ECN, EDU

Outside Counsel/Consultants

Sacramento-Potomac Consulting, Inc.
Issues: ECN, EDU
Rep By: Benjamin G. Griffith, Hon. Richard H. Lehman

California State University Fullerton

Fullerton, CA
Leg. Issues: EDU

Outside Counsel/Consultants

The Ferguson Group, LLC
Issues: EDU
Rep By: William Ferguson, Jr.

California State University Institute

Long Beach, CA

Outside Counsel/Consultants

Mintz, Levin, Cohn, Ferris, Glovsky and Popeo, P.C.
Rep By: Raymond D. Cotton

California State University, San Bernardino Foundation

San Bernardino, CA

Outside Counsel/Consultants

Copeland, Lowery & Jacquez
Rep By: Jeffrey S. Shockey

California Steel Industries, Inc.

Fontana, CA

Outside Counsel/Consultants

The Grizzle Company

California Strawberry Commission

Watsonville, CA
Leg. Issues: AGR

Outside Counsel/Consultants

Haley and Associates
Issues: AGR
Rep By: Daniel D. Haley

California Table Grape Commission

Fresno, CA
E-mail: info@tablegrape.com

Outside Counsel/Consultants

McDermott, Will and Emery
Rep By: Edward M. Ruckert

California Tax Credit Allocation Committee

Sacramento, CA

Outside Counsel/Consultants

O'Connor & Hannan, L.L.P.
Rep By: Roy C. Coffee, Danielle Fagre, Thomas H. Quinn

California Tomato Commission

Fresno, CA
Leg. Issues: AGR, IMM

Outside Counsel/Consultants

Schramm, Williams & Associates, Inc.
Issues: AGR, IMM
Rep By: Duane L. Musser, Robert Schramm

California Urban Water Conservation Council

Sacramento, CA
Leg. Issues: ENG, NAT

Outside Counsel/Consultants

Potomac Resources, Inc.
Issues: ENG, NAT
Rep By: Edward R. Osann

California Walnut Commission

Sacramento, CA
Leg. Issues: AGR, TRD

Outside Counsel/Consultants

Haley and Associates
Issues: AGR, TRD
Rep By: Daniel D. Haley

California Water Service Co.

San Jose, CA
Leg. Issues: BUD, DEF, NAT

Outside Counsel/Consultants

The Furman Group
Issues: BUD, DEF, NAT
Rep By: K. Link Browder, Thomas M. James

California Wellness Foundation

Woodland Hills, CA

Outside Counsel/Consultants

Martin & Glantz LLC

California, State of

Sacramento, CA

Outside Counsel/Consultants

Johnston & Associates, LLC
Rep By: Hon. J. Bennett Johnston

California, State of, Attorney General's Office

Sacramento, CA
Leg. Issues: ALC, LAW

Outside Counsel/Consultants

Direct Impact, LLC
Issues: ALC, LAW
Rep By: Ben Bawden, Robert B. Charles

California, Washington Office of the State of

444 N. Capitol St. NW
Suite 134
Washington, DC 20001
Tel: (202)624-5270
Fax: (202)624-5280

In-house, DC-area Employees

KIM, David S.: Deputy Director
MILLER, Kimberly: Deputy Director
O'BRIEN, Tom: Deputy Director
SLON, Deborah: Legislative Affairs Liaison

California-American Water Co.

Monterey, CA
Leg. Issues: ENV

Outside Counsel/Consultants

Hicks-Richardson Associates

E. Del Smith and Co.
Issues: ENV
Rep By: Kenneth A. Carpi, E. Del Smith

California-Arizona Citrus League

Valencia, CA

Outside Counsel/Consultants

Tuttle, Taylor & Heron

Calleguas Creek Flood Prevention Committee

Camarillo, CA

Outside Counsel/Consultants

E. Del Smith and Co.
Rep By: E. Del Smith

Calleguas Municipal Water District, California

Outside Counsel/Consultants

Honberger and Walters, Inc.
Rep By: Donald Gilchrest, Thomas P. Walters

Calorie Control Council

1101 15th St. NW
Suite 202
Washington, DC 20005
Web: www.caloriecontrol.org
E-mail: ccc@assnhq.com
Tel: (202)785-3232
Fax: (202)223-9741

In-house, DC-area Employees

CRISTOL, Richard E.: Washington Representative

Outside Counsel/Consultants

The Kellen Company
Rep By: Richard E. Cristol

Calpine Corp.

1200 18th St. NW
Suite 850
Washington, DC 20036
Tel: (202)822-9400
Fax: (202)822-2156

An independent energy producer, headquartered in San Jose, CA

Leg. Issues: CAW, ENG, ENV, NAT

In-house, DC-area Employees

CONNELLY, Jeanne K.: V. President, Federal Relations

Outside Counsel/Consultants

Clark & Weinstock, Inc.
Issues: CAW, ENG, ENV, NAT
Rep By: Hon. Vic H. Fazio, Jr.

Lighthouse Energy Group LLC
Issues: ENG
Rep By: Tobyn J. Anderson, Merribel S. Ayres

Calspan University of Buffalo Research Center

Buffalo, NY
Leg. Issues: AVI, BUD, ROD

Outside Counsel/Consultants

Ann Eppard Associates, Ltd.
Issues: AVI
Rep By: Julie Chlopecki, Ann Eppard, Karen Schechter

Van Scoyoc Associates, Inc.
Issues: AVI, BUD, ROD
Rep By: Steven O. Palmer, Chad Schulken, H. Stewart Van Scoyoc

CALSTART

Irwindale, CA
Leg. Issues: BUD, DEF, ENG, ENV, SCI, TRA

Outside Counsel/Consultants

Copeland, Lowery & Jacquez
Issues: BUD, DEF, ENG, ENV, SCI, TRA
Rep By: Lynnette C. Jacquez

Camac Holdings, Inc.

Houston, TX

Outside Counsel/Consultants

Vorys, Sater, Seymour and Pease, LLP
Rep By: Warren W. Glick

Camara Nacional de la Industria Pesquera

Mexico City, MEXICO
Leg. Issues: NAT, TRD

Outside Counsel/Consultants

Janus-Merritt Strategies, L.L.C.
Issues: NAT, TRD
Rep By: Scott P. Hoffman, Mark J. Robertson, J. Daniel Walsh

Camara Nacional de las Industrias Azucarera y Alcoholera

Mexico City, MEXICO
Leg. Issues: TRD

Outside Counsel/Consultants

Janus-Merritt Strategies, L.L.C.
Issues: TRD
Rep By: Scott P. Hoffman, Mark J. Robertson, J. Daniel Walsh

Cambodia, Ministry of Commerce, Royal Kingdom of

Phnom Penh, CAMBODIA

Outside Counsel/Consultants

Sandler, Travis & Rosenberg, P.A.
Rep By: Nicole Bivens Collinson

Cambodian People's Party

Phnom Penh, CAMBODIA

Outside Counsel/Consultants

Richard T. Hines Consulting, Inc.
Rep By: Richard T. Hines

Cambria Community Services District

Cambria, CA

Outside Counsel/Consultants

Will and Carlson, Inc.

Cambridge Management Inc.

New York, NY
Leg. Issues: AVI, TRA

Outside Counsel/Consultants

Greenberg Traurig, LLP
Issues: TRA
Rep By: Diane J. Blagman

Alan Mauk Associates, Ltd.
Issues: AVI
Rep By: Alan R. Mauk

Cambridge Redevelopment Authority

Cambridge, MA
Leg. Issues: URB

Outside Counsel/Consultants

Capitol Partners
Issues: URB
Rep By: William Cunningham, Jonathan M. Orloff

Cambridge Technologies

McLean, VA
Leg. Issues: BUD, DEF

Outside Counsel/Consultants

Patton Boggs, LLP
Issues: BUD, DEF
Rep By: Robert C. Jones

CAMECO Corp.

Saskatoon, CANADA
Registered: LDA
Leg. Issues: ENG

Outside Counsel/Consultants

Dewey Ballantine LLP
Rep By: W. Clark McFadden, II

Winston & Strawn
Issues: ENG
Rep By: James R. Curtiss, Edward F. Gerwin, Jr.

Camelbak Products, Inc.

Leg. Issues: BUD, DEF

Outside Counsel/Consultants

Marshall A. Brachman
Issues: BUD, DEF
Rep By: Marshall A. Brachman

Cameroon, Government of the Republic of

Yaounde, CAMEROON

Outside Counsel/Consultants

Washington World Group, Ltd.
Rep By: Edward J. von Kloberg, III

Camp Dresser and McKee, Inc.

Houston, TX
Web: www.cdm.com
Leg. Issues: BUD, CAW, ENV, NAT

Outside Counsel/Consultants

Barbour Griffith & Rogers, Inc.
Issues: ENV
Rep By: Haley Barbour

The Ferguson Group, LLC
Issues: BUD, CAW, ENV, NAT
Rep By: W. Roger Gwinn

Campaign Accountability Project

818 Connecticut Ave. NW
Suite 1007
Washington, DC 20006

In-house, DC-area Employees

KERMAN, Leslie: Contact, Political Action Committee

Campaign Finance Reform Coalition

c/o Meredith McGehee
Common Cause
1250 Connecticut Ave. NW
Washington, DC 20036
Web: www.commoncause.org
Tel: (202)833-1200
Fax: (202)659-3716
Registered: LDA

A coalition of organizations working for legislation to reform election campaign financing laws. Supporting groups include Common Cause, Public Citizen, the American Ass'n of Retired Persons, the Sierra Club, the American Heart Ass'n, the League of Women Voters, Episcopal Church and the Union of American Hebrew Congregations.

Leg. Issues: CIV, GOV, LAW, SCI, TOB

In-house, DC-area Employees

MCGEHEE, Meredith: Contact

Campaign for America

50 F St. NW
Suite 1198
Washington, DC 20001
Tel: (202)628-0610
Fax: (202)628-0598
Registered: LDA
Web: www.campaignforamerica.org
E-mail: cdperrin@aol.com
Leg. Issues: GOV

In-house, DC-area Employees

PERRIN, Cheryl D.: Exec. Director

Outside Counsel/Consultants

Hauser Group

Campaign for Common Ground

Boulder, CO

Outside Counsel/Consultants

Hauser Group

Campaign for Medical Research

201 Massachusetts Ave. NE
Suite C-4
Washington, DC 20008
Tel: (202)547-5860
Fax: (202)547-5728
Registered: LDA
Leg. Issues: BUD, HCR, TOB

In-house, DC-area Employees
MATHIS, Kevin S.: Legislative Director

Outside Counsel/Consultants
Hogan & Hartson L.L.P.
Issues: HCR
Rep By: Hon. Robert H. Michel, Hon. Paul G. Rogers

Campaign for the Northwest

Outside Counsel/Consultants
Greer, Margolis, Mitchell, Burns & Associates
Rep By: Frank Greer

Campaign for Tobacco-Free Kids

1707 L St. NW
Suite 800
Washington, DC 20036
Web: www.tobaccofreekids.org
Tel: (202)296-5469
Fax: (202)296-5427
Leg. Issues: TOB

In-house, DC-area Employees
CORR, William V.: Exec. V. President
HAMMOND, Ross: Latin American Specialist
WILKENFELD, Judy

Outside Counsel/Consultants
American Continental Group, Inc.
Issues: TOB
Rep By: Shawn H. Smeallie, Peter Terpeluk, Jr.
Garrett Yu Hussein LLC

Campaign for United Nations Reform

420 Seventh St. SE
Suite C
Washington, DC 20003-0270
Web: www.cunr.org
E-mail: cunr@cunr.org
Tel: (202)546-3956
Fax: (202)546-8703
Registered: LDA

A bi-partisan political organization working to create support for an upgraded U.N. through legislation, lobbying, electioneering, and publications. Also conducts a rating system for House and Senate and operates a PAC.

Leg. Issues: BUD

Political Action Committee/s
CUNRPAC
420 Seventh St. SE
Suite C
Washington, DC 20003-0270
Contact: Don Kraus
Tel: (202)546-3956
Fax: (202)546-8703

In-house, DC-area Employees
KRAUS, Don: Exec. Director
RAWSON, Edward: Exec. V. President

Campaign Reform Project

Mount Kisco, NY
Web: www.campaign-reform.org

Outside Counsel/Consultants
Hauser Group

Campaign to Preserve U.S. Global Leadership

Washington, DC
Leg. Issues: BUD, FOR

Outside Counsel/Consultants
Schrayer and Associates, Inc.
Issues: BUD, FOR
Rep By: Elizabeth Schrayer

Thomas D. Campbell & Assoc.

517 Queen St.
Alexandria, VA 22314
Tel: (703)683-0773
Registered: LDA
Leg. Issues: ENV, NAT

In-house, DC-area Employees
CAMPBELL, Thomas D.: President

Outside Counsel/Consultants
The Willard Group
Issues: ENV, NAT

Campbell Estate

Outside Counsel/Consultants
Counselors For Management, Inc.
Rep By: Janice C. Lipsen

Campbell Foundry Co.

Harrison, NJ
Leg. Issues: GOV, TRD

Outside Counsel/Consultants
Manatt, Phelps & Phillips, LLP
Issues: GOV, TRD
Rep By: Walter Gonzales, Luke Rose, Robb Watters

Campbell Soup Co.

Camden, NJ
Leg. Issues: TAX

Outside Counsel/Consultants
Greenberg Traurig, LLP
Issues: TAX
Rep By: Ronald L. Platt
Internat'l Business-Government Counsellors, Inc.
Rep By: John F. McDermid
McDermott, Will and Emery
Rep By: Robert G. Hibbert

S. A. Campo

Washington, DC

Outside Counsel/Consultants
The Campo Group, Ltd.
Rep By: Terry T. Campo

Can Manufacturers Institute

1625 Massachusetts Ave. NW
Suite 500
Washington, DC 20036
Web: www.cancentral.com
E-mail: webmaster@cancentral.com
Tel: (202)232-4677
Fax: (202)232-5756
Registered: LDA
Leg. Issues: ENV

In-house, DC-area Employees
BUDWAY, Robert R.: President and General Counsel
CULLEN, Geoffrey: Director, Government Relations

Outside Counsel/Consultants
Whitten & Diamond
Issues: ENV
Rep By: Robert M. Diamond

Canada, Embassy of

501 Pennsylvania Ave. NW
Washington, DC 20001
Web: www.canadianembassy.org
Tel: (202)682-1740
Fax: (202)682-7726

Outside Counsel/Consultants
Garvey, Schubert & Barer
Rep By: Richard A. Wegman
Steptoe & Johnson LLP
Rep By: Mark A. Moran

Canada, Government of

Ottawa, CANADA

Outside Counsel/Consultants
Garvey, Schubert & Barer
Rep By: Richard A. Wegman
Hughes Hubbard & Reed LLP
Rep By: Catherine Curtiss
J. LeBlanc Internat'l, LLC
Rep By: James L. LeBlanc
Miller & Chevalier, Chartered
Rep By: Homer E. Moyer, Jr.
O'Melveny and Myers LLP
Rep By: Gary N. Horlick
Paul, Hastings, Janofsky & Walker LLP
Rep By: G. Hamilton Loeb

Canada, Trade Law Division of the Embassy of

Ottawa, CANADA

Outside Counsel/Consultants
Garvey, Schubert & Barer

Canadian Broadcasting Corp.

Ottawa, CANADA

Outside Counsel/Consultants
Finkelstein, Thompson & Loughran
Rep By: Victor J. Cosentino, L. Kendall Satterfield

Canadian Broiler Hatching Egg Marketing Agency

Ottawa, CANADA

Outside Counsel/Consultants
Arter & Hadden
Rep By: William K. Dabaghi

Canadian Cattlemen's Ass'n

Calgary, CANADA

Outside Counsel/Consultants
Blank Rome Comisky & McCauley, LLP
Rep By: Edward J. Farrell

Canadian Chicken Marketing Agency

Ottawa, CANADA

Outside Counsel/Consultants
Arter & Hadden
Rep By: William K. Dabaghi

Canadian Egg Marketing Agency

Ottawa, CANADA

Outside Counsel/Consultants
Arter & Hadden
Rep By: William K. Dabaghi

Canadian Electricity Ass'n

Montreal, CANADA
Leg. Issues: ENG

Outside Counsel/Consultants
Troutman Sanders LLP
Issues: ENG
Rep By: William P. Marsan, Bonnie Suchman, Dionne E. Thompson

Canadian Nat'l Railroad/Illinois Central Railroad

Chicago, IL
Leg. Issues: TRA

Outside Counsel/Consultants
Lawler, Metzger & Milkman, LLC
Issues: TRA
Rep By: Sante J. Esposito, Gregory E. Lawler

Canadian Nat'l Railway Co.

601 Pennsylvania Ave. NW
Suite 500
Washington, DC 20004
Web: www.cn.ca
Tel: (202)347-7196
Fax: (202)347-8237
Registered: LDA

Freight railroad with headquarters in Montreal, Canada.

Leg. Issues: BUD, RET, RRR, TAX, TRA, TRD

In-house, DC-area Employees
PHILLIPS, Karen Borlaug: V. President, U.S. Government Affairs

Outside Counsel/Consultants
Barbour Griffith & Rogers, Inc.
Issues: TRA
Rep By: Haley Barbour, Carl Biersack, G. O. Lanny Griffith, Jr., Loren Monroe
Chambers, Conlon & Hartwell
Issues: RRR
Rep By: Keith O. Hartwell
Foley & Lardner
Issues: RRR
Rep By: Jodi L. Hanson, Jerris Leonard, Robert P. vom Eigen
Lawler, Metzger & Milkman, LLC
Issues: RRR, TRA
Rep By: Sante J. Esposito, Gregory E. Lawler

Canadian Pacific

Montreal, CANADA

Outside Counsel/Consultants
Mullenholz, Brimsek & Belair
Snavely, King, Majoros, O'Connor and Lee, Inc.
Rep By: Tom O'Connor

Canadian Pulp and Paper Ass'n, Newsprint Section of

Montreal, CANADA

Outside Counsel/Consultants
Rogers & Wells
Rep By: William Silverman

Canadian River Municipal Water Authority

Sanford, TX
Leg. Issues: BUD, CAW, GOV, NAT, RES

Outside Counsel/Consultants
Meyers & Associates
Issues: BUD, CAW, GOV, NAT, RES
Rep By: Fran Boyd, Larry D. Meyers

Canadian Turkey Marketing Agency

Ottawa, CANADA

Outside Counsel/Consultants

Arter & Hadden
Rep By: William K. Dabaghi

Canadian Wheat Board

Winnipeg, CANADA
Leg. Issues: AGR, TRD

Outside Counsel/Consultants

Steptoe & Johnson LLP
Issues: AGR, TRD
Rep By: W. George Grandison, Edward J. Krauland

Canadian-American Business Council

Washington, DC
Web: www.canambusco.com
E-mail: canambusco@aol.com

Outside Counsel/Consultants

Agri/Washington
Rep By: Andrea Ball, Paul S. Weller, Jr.

Canal Barge Co., Inc.

New Orleans, LA
Leg. Issues: MAR

Outside Counsel/Consultants

Jones, Walker, Waechter, Poitevent, Carrere & Denegre, L.L.P.
Issues: MAR
Rep By: John J. Jaskot, R. Christian Johnsen

Canberra Packard BioScience

Meriden, CT
Leg. Issues: BUD, DEF, ENG, MED, SCI, WAS

Outside Counsel/Consultants

Vikki Bell
Issues: BUD, DEF, ENG, MED, SCI, WAS
Rep By: Vikki Bell

Cancer Leadership Council

Washington, DC
Leg. Issues: BUD, HCR, MED, MMM

Outside Counsel/Consultants

Bennett Turner & Coleman, LLP
Issues: BUD, HCR, MED, MMM
Rep By: Elizabeth Goss, Kristi E. Schrode, Samuel D. Turner

Candescent Technologies

San Jose, CA

Outside Counsel/Consultants

R. Wayne Sayer & Associates
Rep By: John Kania, William Morin, R. Wayne Sayer

Candle Corp.

El Segundo, CA
An information technology company.

Leg. Issues: CPI, SCI

Outside Counsel/Consultants

LeBoeuf, Lamb, Greene & MacRae L.L.P.
Issues: CPI, SCI
Rep By: Peggy A. Hoyle, A. Everette James, Joseph T. Kelliher

Canon USA, Inc.

Lake Success, NY

Outside Counsel/Consultants

Covington & Burling
Rep By: Harvey M. Applebaum, Thomas O. Barnett, David R. Grace, Sonya D. Winner

Canon, Inc.

Tokyo, JAPAN

Outside Counsel/Consultants

Covington & Burling
Rep By: Thomas O. Barnett, David R. Grace, Sonya D. Winner

Cantelme and Kaasa

Phoenix, AZ

Outside Counsel/Consultants

Strategic Impact, Inc.
Rep By: Patrick J. Mitchell

Canton Railroad Co.

Baltimore, MD
Leg. Issues: RRR, TRA

Outside Counsel/Consultants

Infrastructure Management Group
Issues: RRR, TRA
Rep By: Porter K. Wheeler

CanWest

Leg. Issues: COM

Outside Counsel/Consultants

Verner, Liipfert, Bernhard, McPherson and Hand, Chartered
Issues: COM
Rep By: Hon. James J. Blanchard, Lawrence R. Sidman

Canyon Forest Village Corp.

Scottsdale, AZ

Outside Counsel/Consultants

Steptoe & Johnson LLP

CapCURE

Santa Monica, CA
Leg. Issues: BUD, HCR

Outside Counsel/Consultants

Clark & Weinstock, Inc.
Issues: BUD, HCR
Rep By: Ed Kutler, Deirdre Stach, Sandi Stuart, Hon. John Vincent "Vin" Weber

Cape Verde, Embassy of the Republic of

3415 Massachusetts Ave. NW — Tel: (202)965-6820
Washington, DC 20007 — Fax: (202)965-1207

Outside Counsel/Consultants

Washington World Group, Ltd.
Rep By: Edward J. von Kloberg, III

Capital Area Transit Authority

Lansing, MI
Leg. Issues: BUD, TRA

Outside Counsel/Consultants

Government Relations, Inc.
Issues: BUD, TRA
Rep By: Thomas J. Bulger, Mark H. Miller

Capital Children's Museum

800 Third St. NE — Tel: (202)675-4120
Washington, DC 20002 — Fax: (202)675-4140
Web: www.ccm.org
Leg. Issues: ART, DOC, EDU, TOU

In-house, DC-area Employees

TAYLOR KIDD, Ruth: Director, Finance and External Relations

Capital City Economic Development Authority

Hartford, CT
Working to revitalize the downtown residential and business district of Hartford, CT.

Leg. Issues: BUD, ENV, HOU, TRA, URB

Outside Counsel/Consultants

The Michael Lewan Co.
Issues: BUD, ENV, HOU, TRA, URB
Rep By: Michael Lewan, Anne Saunders

Capital Concerts

Washington, DC
Leg. Issues: COM

Outside Counsel/Consultants

Devillier Communications
Issues: COM
Rep By: Kristina Hallman

Capital Confirmation

Outside Counsel/Consultants

Edelman Public Relations Worldwide
Rep By: Bob Knott

Capital Dimensions Venture Fund Inc.

Minneapolis, MN

Outside Counsel/Consultants

Thelen Reid & Priest LLP
Rep By: William A. Kirk, Jr.

Capital Equipment Legislative Coalition

Falls Church, VA
Leg. Issues: BAN, MAN, TAX, TRD

Outside Counsel/Consultants

The Macon Edwards Co.
Issues: BAN, MAN, TAX, TRD
Rep By: Macon T. Edwards, Mara Peltz

Capital Gaming Internat'l, Inc.

West Atlantic City, NJ
Leg. Issues: GAM

Outside Counsel/Consultants

Akin, Gump, Strauss, Hauer & Feld, L.L.P.
Issues: GAM
Rep By: Charles W. Johnson, IV, Henry A. Terhune, Leslie M. Turner

Capital Goods Standards Coalition

Falls Church, VA
Leg. Issues: TRD

Outside Counsel/Consultants

Ass'n and Soc. Management Internat'l Inc.

Barnes & Thornburg
Issues: TRD
Rep By: Randolph J. Stayin

The Capital Hill Group, Inc.

Ottawa, CANADA
Leg. Issues: GOV

Outside Counsel/Consultants

Capital Strategies Group, Inc.
Issues: GOV
Rep By: Tammi Hayes

Capital Metropolitan Transportation Authority

Austin, TX
Leg. Issues: TRA

Outside Counsel/Consultants

Verner, Liipfert, Bernhard, McPherson and Hand, Chartered
Issues: TRA
Rep By: Denis J. Dwyer, Jane Hickie, Ann W. Richards, Timothy M. Rutten

Capital One Financial Corp.

2980 Fairview Park Dr. — Tel: (703)205-1722
Suite 1400 — Fax: (703)205-1785
Falls Church, VA 22042 — Registered: LDA
Leg. Issues: BAN, FIN

Political Action Committee/s

Capital One Associates Political Fund
2980 Fairview Park Dr. — Tel: (703)289-7800
Suite 1400 — Fax: (703)205-1785
Falls Church, VA 22042
Contact: Scott Silverthorne

In-house, DC-area Employees

CURTIS, Chris: Associate General Counsel
SILVERTHORNE, Scott: Director, Government Relations

Outside Counsel/Consultants

Ketchum
Rep By: Bonnie Lieb

O'Connor & Hannan, L.L.P.
Issues: BAN, FIN
Rep By: Timothy W. Jenkins, Thomas H. Quinn

Capital Region Airport Commission

Richmond, VA
Leg. Issues: AVI, BUD, TRA

Outside Counsel/Consultants

Thelen Reid & Priest LLP
Issues: AVI, BUD, TRA
Rep By: Barry I. Berkoff, William A. Kirk, Jr., Richard J. Leidl, Stephan M. Minikes, Richard Y. Roberts, Nancy K. West

Capital Research Center

1513 16th St. NW — Tel: (202)483-6900
Washington, DC 20036 — Fax: (202)483-6902
Web: www.capitalresearc.org
E-mail: crc@capitalresearch.org

A research organization focusing on philanthropy, specializing in public interest groups, what they believe, how they are financed and how they and their financial supporters are affecting the political process and society.

Leg. Issues: EDU, GOV, HCR, LBR, NAT, TAX, WEL

In-house, DC-area Employees

HUBERTY, Robert M.: V. President and Director, Research
IVANCIE, Thomas: Director, Development
SCANLON, Terrence: Chairman and President
WALKER, Andrew: Director, Communications

Capitol American Financial Corp.

Cleveland, OH

Outside Counsel/Consultants

Baker & Hostetler LLP
Rep By: Frederick H. Graefe

Capitol Broadcasting Co.

Raleigh, NC
Leg. Issues: TEC

Outside Counsel/Consultants

Holland & Knight LLP
Issues: TEC
Rep By: Michael Gillis, Hon. Thomas F. Railsback, Marvin Rosenberg, Hon. Gerald E. Sikorski, P. J. Toker

Capitol Cargo Internat'l Airlines, Inc.

Outside Counsel/Consultants

Preston Gates Ellis & Rouvelas Meeds LLP
Rep By: Jonathan Blank

Capitol Concerts, Inc.

Leg. Issues: ART

Outside Counsel/Consultants

Kilpatrick Stockton LLP
Issues: ART
Rep By: Richard Barnett

CapitolWatch

727 Second St. NE
Washington, DC 20002
Tel: (202)544-2600
Fax: (202)544-7760
Registered: LDA
Web: www.capitolwatch.org

A grassroots association working to eliminate the estate tax and keep e-commerce free from taxation.

Leg. Issues: BUD, ECN, GOV, TAX

In-house, DC-area Employees

THIELEN, Michael B.: Legislative Director
WATTERS, Robb: President

CapNet

Outside Counsel/Consultants

Dittus Communications
Rep By: Gloria S. Dittus, Shelton Jones, Kristin Litterst

CapWeb

Outside Counsel/Consultants

Issue Dynamics Inc.

Caraustar

Austell, GA
Leg. Issues: CAW, ENG, ENV, FUE, GOV, MAN, TAX, WAS

Outside Counsel/Consultants

Colling Swift & Hynes
Issues: CAW, ENG, ENV, FUE, GOV, MAN, TAX, WAS
Rep By: Terese Colling, Pablo Collins, Robert J. Hynes, Jr., Hon. Allan B. Swift

Caraven Airlines (Carga Aerea Venezolana, S.A.)

Miami, FL

Outside Counsel/Consultants

Pierre E. Murphy Law Offices
Rep By: Pierre E. Murphy

Cardinal Health Inc.

Dublin, OH

A manufacturer of healthcare products.

Leg. Issues: HCR

Outside Counsel/Consultants

The Legislative Strategies Group, LLC
Rep By: Larry E. Smith

Ungaretti & Harris
Issues: HCR
Rep By: Sheri Bucher, Page Faulk, Chuck Konigsberg, Spencer Perlman, Joseph R. Schulman

Cardiovascular Credentialing Internat'l

Virginia Beach, VA
Leg. Issues: GOV

Outside Counsel/Consultants

Halsey, Rains & Associates, LLC
Issues: GOV
Rep By: Steven C. Halsey, James Hubbard, Laurie D. Rains

CARE (Cooperative for Assistance and Relief Everywhere)

1625 K St. NW
Suite 500
Washington, DC 20006
Tel: (202)223-2277
Fax: (202)296-8695
Registered: LDA
Web: www.care.org

An international relief and development organization headquartered in Atlanta, GA. Supports programs in over 60 countries. Its humanitarian programs include emergency relief and rehabilitation, health and family planning, girls' education, environment, agriculture and natural resource management, and small enterprise activity development.

Leg. Issues: AGR, FOR, HCR

In-house, DC-area Employees

BUNTING, Kate: Director, Public Policy Initiatives
LEACH, Marianne: Exec. Director, Office of Public Policy and Govt. Relations

Career College Ass'n

Ten G St. NE
Suite 750
Washington, DC 20002-4213
Tel: (202)336-6700
Fax: (202)336-6828
Registered: LDA
Web: www.career.org
E-mail: cca@career.org

A trade association representing private career schools and colleges.

Leg. Issues: BUD, EDU, GOV

Political Action Committee/s

Career College Ass'n Political Action Committee
Ten G St. NE
Suite 750
Washington, DC 20002-4213
Contact: Tim Burga
Tel: (202)336-6700
Fax: (202)336-6828

In-house, DC-area Employees

BROFF, Nancy B.: General Counsel
BURGA, Tim: Political Director
GLAKAS, Nicholas: President
LEFTWICH, Bruce: V. President, Government Relations

CareFirst Blue Cross Blue Shield

Owings Mills, MD

Outside Counsel/Consultants

Hunton & Williams

Caremark Rx, Inc.

Northbrook, IL
Leg. Issues: HCR, MMM, PHA

Outside Counsel/Consultants

U.S. Strategies Corp.
Issues: HCR, MMM, PHA

CaRess, Inc.

Garden Grove, CA
Leg. Issues: HCR, MMM

Outside Counsel/Consultants

Helmsin & Yarwood Associates
Issues: HCR, MMM
Rep By: Bruce Yarwood

Caretenders Health Corp.

Louisville, KY
Leg. Issues: HCR

Outside Counsel/Consultants

The Fortier Group, LLC
Issues: HCR
Rep By: Michael P. Fortier

CARFAX, Inc.

Fairfax, VA
Leg. Issues: LAW, TRA

Outside Counsel/Consultants

Collier Shannon Scott, PLLC
Issues: LAW, TRA
Rep By: R. Timothy Columbus, Gregory M. Scott

Cargill Dow

Minnetonka, MN
Leg. Issues: BUD, ENG, NAT, SCI, TAX

Outside Counsel/Consultants

MSS Consultants, LLC
Issues: BUD, ENG, NAT, SCI, TAX
Rep By: Megan S. Smith

Cargill, Inc.

1101 15th St. NW
Suite 1000
Washington, DC 20005
Tel: (202)530-8160
Fax: (202)530-8180
Registered: LDA
Web: www.cargill.com

Specializes in international commodity merchandising, processing and distribution. Headquartered in Minneapolis, MN.

Leg. Issues: AGR, ANI, CAW, CDT, CHM, ECN, ENV, FIN, FOO, FOR, HCR, IMM, LBR, MAN, MAR, SCI, TAX, TRA, TRD, UTI, WAS

In-house, DC-area Employees

EDWARDSON, Bryan B.: Director, Public Policy
HARRINGTON, W. Brendan: Assistant V. President
MULLINS, Mike: Director, Public Policy
THRASHER, Linda K.: Director, Public Policy
YEUTTER, Van: Director, Washington Operations and Internat'l Business Development

Outside Counsel/Consultants

Akin, Gump, Strauss, Hauer & Feld, L.L.P.
Issues: TRD
Rep By: Valerie A. Slater, Karen Bland Toliver, S. Bruce Wilson

Alcalde & Fay
Issues: TRA
Rep By: Hector Alcalde, Lois Moore

Clark & Weinstock, Inc.
Issues: ENV
Rep By: Hon. Vic H. Fazio, Jr., Deirdre Stach, Sandi Stuart, Hon. John Vincent "Vin" Weber

Hogan & Hartson L.L.P.

O'Melveny and Myers LLP
Rep By: Gary N. Horlick

Powell, Goldstein, Frazer & Murphy LLP
Rep By: Hon. Butler E. Derrick, Jr., Carolyn McSherry

Caribbean Airline Co. Ltd.

Miami, FL

Outside Counsel/Consultants

Pierre E. Murphy Law Offices
Rep By: Pierre E. Murphy

Caribbean American Leadership Council

1400 East West Hwy.
Silver Spring, MD 20910

In-house, DC-area Employees

LAMAUTE, Daniel

Caribbean Banana Exporters Ass'n

Middlesex, UNITED KINGDOM
Leg. Issues: TRD

Outside Counsel/Consultants

Ross-Robinson & Associates
Issues: TRD
Rep By: Monica Duncan, Hazel Ross-Robinson

Winthrop, Stimson, Putnam & Roberts
Rep By: C. Christopher Parlin

Caribbean/Latin American Action

1818 N St. NW
Suite 500
Washington, DC 20036
Tel: (202)466-7464
Fax: (202)822-0075
Web: www.claa.org
E-mail: info@claa.org

Seeks to encourage the American private sector to play a more active role in helping Caribbean basin countries develop their economies. Supported financially by several major U.S. corporations.

In-house, DC-area Employees

PLANTY, Ambassador Donald J.: Exec. Director

Caribe Waste Technologies

Outside Counsel/Consultants

Verner, Liipfert, Bernhard, McPherson and Hand, Chartered
Rep By: Gary J. Klein

Caring Institute

228 Seventh St. SE
Washington, DC 20003
Tel: (202)547-4273
Fax: (202)547-4510
Web: www.caring-institute.org
E-mail: inquiry@caring-institute.org

The Caring Institute was founded in 1985 to promote and honor people involved in community and public service. Through the National Caring Awards the Institute honors ten adults and ten young adults who are working to make meaningful change in their communities.

In-house, DC-area Employees

HALAMANDARIS, Val: Exec. Director

Carlsberg Management Co.

Los Angeles, CA
Leg. Issues: BUD, GOV, HOU, RES

Outside Counsel/Consultants

Jefferson Government Relations, L.L.C.
Issues: BUD, GOV, HOU, RES
Rep By: William J. Gilmartin, William A. Roberts, Daniel J. Sheehan

Carlson Cos.

Minneapolis, MN
Leg. Issues: TAX

Outside Counsel/Consultants

Albertine Enterprises, Inc.
Issues: TAX
Rep By: Aubrey C. King

Carlson Wagonlit Travel, Inc.

Minneapolis, MN
Leg. Issues: TOU, TRA

Outside Counsel/Consultants

Venable
Issues: TOU, TRA

The Carlyle Group

1001 Pennsylvania Ave. NW
Suite 220 South
Washington, DC 20004
Tel: (202)347-2626
Fax: (202)347-1818
Web: www.thecarlylegroup.com
Leg. Issues: TAX

In-house, DC-area Employees

BAKER, III, James A.: Senior Counselor
CARLUCCI, Frank C.: Chairman
DARMAN, Richard G.: Senior Advisor
MATHIAS, Edward J.: Managing Director

Outside Counsel/Consultants

Akin, Gump, Strauss, Hauer & Feld, L.L.P.
Issues: TAX
Rep By: Janet C. Boyd

Carmel, Indiana, City of

Leg. Issues: HOU, TRA, URB

Outside Counsel/Consultants

Simon and Co., Inc.
Issues: HOU, TRA, URB
Rep By: Heather Barber, Alex DeGood, Leonard S. Simon

Carnegie Endowment for Internat'l Peace

1779 Massachusetts Ave. NW
Washington, DC 20036
Tel: (202)483-7600
Fax: (202)483-1840
Web: www.ceip.org

In-house, DC-area Employees

CIRINCIONE, Joseph: Senior Associate
GOTTEMOELLER, Rose E.: Senior Associate
MATHEWS, Jessica: President
MEISSNER, Doris: Senior Associate, Global Policy
TANZI, Vito: Senior Associate

Carnegie Hall Corp.

New York, NY
Leg. Issues: BUD

Outside Counsel/Consultants

Beacon Consulting Group, Inc.
Issues: BUD
Rep By: Katherine L. Halpin, Gordon P. MacDougall, Lisa A. Stewart

Carnival Corp.

Miami, FL

Outside Counsel/Consultants

McDermott, Will and Emery

Carnival Foundation

Miami, FL
Leg. Issues: TAX

Outside Counsel/Consultants

Alcalde & Fay
Issues: TAX
Rep By: Hector Alcalde, Vicki L. Iseman

Carolina Panthers

Charlotte, NC
A Nat'l Football League franchise.

Outside Counsel/Consultants

Murray, Scheer, Montgomery, Tapia & O'Donnell

Carolina PCS

Greenville, SC

Outside Counsel/Consultants

The Dutko Group, Inc.
Rep By: Louis Lehrman

Carolina, Puerto Rico, City of

Leg. Issues: AGR, BUD, CAW, ECN, HOU, TRA

Outside Counsel/Consultants

Smith Dawson & Andrews, Inc.
Issues: AGR, BUD, CAW, ECN, HOU, TRA
Rep By: Ramon Luis Lugo, James P. Smith

Caron Foundation

Wernerville, PA
Leg. Issues: ALC, BUD, HCR, INS, TAX

Outside Counsel/Consultants

VSAdc.com
Issues: ALC, BUD, HCR, INS, TAX
Rep By: Carol A. McDaid

Carondelet Health System

St. Louis, MO
Leg. Issues: BUD

Outside Counsel/Consultants

Cassidy & Associates, Inc.
Issues: BUD
Rep By: Marie James, Mary E. Shields, Lyllett Wentworth

Carpet and Rug Institute

Dalton, GA
Leg. Issues: CSP, ENV

Outside Counsel/Consultants

The Dutko Group, Inc.
Issues: CSP, ENV
Rep By: Peg Brown, Mark S. Irion, Deana Perlmutter

Carpet Export Promotion Council

New Delhi, INDIA
Leg. Issues: TRD

Outside Counsel/Consultants

Powell, Goldstein, Frazer & Murphy LLP
Issues: TRD
Rep By: Alice Slayton Clark, Brenda A. Jacobs

Carr Public Affairs

Albany, NY
Leg. Issues: BUD, EDU, HCR

Outside Counsel/Consultants

Pamela Ray-Strunk and Associates
Issues: BUD, EDU, HCR
Rep By: Pamela Ray-Strunk

Carriers Against Harbor Tax

Washington, DC
Leg. Issues: MAR

Outside Counsel/Consultants

Sher & Blackwell
Issues: MAR
Rep By: Marc J. Fink, Jeffrey R. Pike, Stanley O. Sher

Carrying Capacity Network, Inc.

2000 P St. NW
Suite 310
Washington, DC 20036
Tel: (202)296-4548
Fax: (202)296-4609
Registered: LDA
Web: www.carryingcapacity.org
E-mail: ccn@us.net

An environmental, population stabilization, and immigration reduction organization.

Leg. Issues: IMM

In-house, DC-area Employees

LAZARO, Robin: Network Coordinator
PRIESTAS, Lauren: Associate Director

CarsDirect.com

Culver City, CA
Leg. Issues: AUT, TEC

Outside Counsel/Consultants

Alston & Bird LLP
Issues: AUT, TEC
Rep By: Thomas M. Boyd, Jonathan Winer

Rachel Carson Council, Inc.

8940 Jones Mill Rd.
Chevy Chase, MD 20815
Tel: (301)652-1877
Web: www.members.aol.com/rccouncil/ourpage/
E-mail: rccouncil@aol.com

An international clearinghouse for information on environmental issues of concern to scientists and laymen, particularly pesticides.

In-house, DC-area Employees

POST, Dr. Diana: Exec. Director

Carter-Wallace, Inc.

New York, NY

Outside Counsel/Consultants

Kleinfeld, Kaplan and Becker
Rep By: Alan H. Kaplan, Peter O. Safir

Cartwright Electronics

Fullerton, CA
Leg. Issues: DEF

Outside Counsel/Consultants

The PMA Group
Issues: DEF
Rep By: Daniel Cunningham, Daniel E. Fleming, Kaylene Green, Paul J. Magliocchetti, Mark Waclawski

Carwell Products, Inc.

Cheektowaga, NY
Leg. Issues: DEF

Outside Counsel/Consultants

The Atlantic Group, Public Affairs, Inc.
Issues: DEF
Rep By: Larry F. Ayres

Michael Chase Associates, LTD
Issues: DEF
Rep By: Michael T. Chase

Casa Aircraft USA, Inc.

Chantilly, VA
An aircraft manufacturer.

Leg. Issues: AVI

Outside Counsel/Consultants

Bob Davis & Associates
Issues: AVI
Rep By: Hon. Robert W. Davis

Casa del Pueblo Community Program

1459 Columbia Rd. NW
Washington, DC 20009
Tel: (202)332-1094
Fax: (202)667-7783
E-mail: cdelpueblo@aol.com

A community-based organization serving the Hispanic community in the metropolitan Washington area with educational, cultural and social service components including adult education and after school programs.

In-house, DC-area Employees

RECINOS, Maria: Exec. Director

Cascade Designs

Seattle, WA
Leg. Issues: HCR, MMM

Outside Counsel/Consultants

Nusgart Consulting, LLC
Issues: HCR, MMM
Rep By: Marcia Nusgart

Cascade General, Inc.

Portland, OR
A shipbuilding and ship repair company.

Leg. Issues: BUD, DEF, MAR

Outside Counsel/Consultants

Ball Janik, LLP
Issues: BUD, DEF, MAR
Rep By: James A. Beall, Michelle E. Giguere

Case Western Reserve University School of Medicine

Cleveland, OH
Leg. Issues: BUD, MED

Outside Counsel/Consultants

Squire, Sanders & Dempsey L.L.P.
Issues: BUD, MED
Rep By: Louis Stokes

CaseNewHolland Inc.

1001 G St. NW
Suite 100 East
Washington, DC 20001
Tel: (202)737-7575
Fax: (202)737-9090
Registered: LDA

Designer, manufacturer, and distributor of agricultural and construction equipment. Also offers financial products and services. Headquartered in Racine, WI.

Leg. Issues: AGR, ECN, FIN, FOR, HCR, IMM, MAN, ROD, TAX, TRD

Political Action Committee/s

CaseNewHolland Excellence in Government Committee
1001 G St. NW
Suite 100 East
Washington, DC 20001
Tel: (202)737-7575
Fax: (202)737-9090

In-house, DC-area Employees

NADHERNY, Steven T.: Manager, Government Affairs
SALMON, Scott R.: Manager, Government Affairs
SAMORA, Jr., Joseph E.: V. President, Government Affairs

Outside Counsel/Consultants

Dickstein Shapiro Morin & Oshinsky LLP
Issues: AGR, ECN, FIN, MAN, TRD
Rep By: Peter J. Kadzik, Robert Mangas, Graham "Rusty" Mathews, L. Andrew Zausner

Casey Family Program

Seattle, WA
Leg. Issues: FAM

Outside Counsel/Consultants

Martin & Glantz LLC
Issues: FAM

Cash America Internat'l

Fort Worth, TX
A publicly-owned pawn shop chain.

Leg. Issues: FIR

Outside Counsel/Consultants

Law Offices of Mark Barnes
Issues: FIR
Rep By: Mark J. Barnes, Tammy Begun

Cash Balance Coalition

Washington, DC
Leg. Issues: RET, TAX

Outside Counsel/Consultants

Washington Council Ernst & Young
Issues: RET, TAX
Rep By: Doug Badger, Lauren Darling, John L. Doney, Jayne T. Fitzgerald, LaBrenda Garrett-Nelson, Gary J. Gasper, Bruce A. Gates, Nick Giordano, Robert J. Leonard, Richard Meltzer, Phillip D. Moseley, John D. Porter, Robert M. Rozen, Donna Steele-Flynn, Timothy J. Urban

Casino Express Airlines

Elko, NV
Leg. Issues: AVI

Outside Counsel/Consultants

Sher & Blackwell
Issues: AVI
Rep By: Mark Atwood

Cast Iron Pipefittings Committee

Outside Counsel/Consultants

McKenna & Cuneo, L.L.P.
Rep By: Peter Buck Feller

Cast Iron Soil Pipe Institute

Chattanooga, TN

Outside Counsel/Consultants

Collier Shannon Scott, PLLC
Rep By: Paul C. Rosenthal

Castaic Lakewater Agency

Santa Clarita, CA

Outside Counsel/Consultants

Chambers Associates Inc.
Rep By: Letitia Chambers

The Castano Group

New Orleans, LA
Leg. Issues: TOB, TOR

Outside Counsel/Consultants

Capital Strategies Group, Inc.
Issues: TOB, TOR
Rep By: Tammi Hayes

Commonwealth Group, Ltd.
Issues: TOB

Caswell Internat'l Corp.

Minneapolis, MN
Leg. Issues: DEF

Outside Counsel/Consultants

Hurt, Norton & Associates
Issues: DEF
Rep By: Robert H. Hurt, Frank Norton, William K. Takakoshi

CATA (Canadian Advanced Technology Ass'n)

Ottawa, CANADA

Outside Counsel/Consultants

J. LeBlanc Internat'l, LLC
Rep By: James L. LeBlanc

Catamount Energy Corp.

Rutland, VT
Leg. Issues: ENG, UTI

Outside Counsel/Consultants

Capitol Link, Inc.
Issues: ENG, UTI
Rep By: Hon. David M. Staton

Catellus Development Corp.

San Francisco, CA

Outside Counsel/Consultants

Manatt, Phelps & Phillips, LLP
Rep By: Hon. Jack W. Buechner, June L. DeHart, Jessica A. Wasserman

Caterpillar Inc.

818 Connecticut Ave. NW
Suite 600
Washington, DC 20006-2702
Tel: (202)466-0670
Fax: (202)466-0684
Registered: LDA

Leg. Issues: AUT, CPT, DEF, ENG, ENV, IMM, LAW, LBR, MAN, NAT, ROD, TAX, TRD

In-house, DC-area Employees

BALL, Will N.: Washington Manager, Government Affairs
BRENT, Richard: Washington Manager, Solar
HALLORAN, James: Washington Manager, Governmental Affairs
LANE, William C.: Washington Director, Governmental Affairs
OREM, Bayly: Washington Manager, Government Marketing

Outside Counsel/Consultants

The PMA Group
Issues: DEF
Rep By: William E. Berl, Kaylene Green, Gregory L. Hansen, Paul J. Magliocchetti, Charles Smith, Mark Waclawski

Powell, Goldstein, Frazer & Murphy LLP

The Wexler Group
Issues: ENV
Rep By: Joel Malina, Dale W. Snape, Anne Wexler

Catholic Alliance

448 New Jersey Ave. SE
Washington, DC 20003
Tel: (202)544-9600
Fax: (202)318-0789
Registered: LDA
Web: www.catholicvote.org
E-mail: deallaw@aol.com

An educational and public policy organization dedicated to infusing the public debate with a Catholic perspective.

Leg. Issues: FAM, FOR, REL

In-house, DC-area Employees

FLYNN, Ray: President

Outside Counsel/Consultants

Dublin Castle Group
Rep By: Maureen Flatley Hogan

Catholic Charities Archdiocesan Legal Network

924 G St. NW
Washington, DC 20001
Tel: (202)772-4398
Fax: (202)772-4402
Web: www.catholiccharitiesdc.org/center/spec_services/arch_legal.html
E-mail: bishopj@catholiccharitiesdc.org

In-house, DC-area Employees

BISHOP, James: Program Administrator

Catholic Charities Immigration Legal Services

1221 Massachusetts Ave. NW
Washington, DC 20005
Tel: (202)772-4348
Fax: (202)772-4409
Web: www.catholiccharitiesdc.org/center/spec_services/immigration.html

Offers professional immigration legal services to low-income clients from every country and national group needing assistance with matters before the INS and the Immigration Court.

Leg. Issues: IMM

In-house, DC-area Employees

ATKINSON, Jeannie M.: Program Administrator

Catholic Charities USA

1731 King St.
Suite 200
Alexandria, VA 22314
Tel: (703)549-1390
Fax: (703)549-1656
Registered: LDA
Web: www.catholiccharitiesusa.org

The nation's largest private, social-service network. Made up of 1,400 agencies and institutions working to reduce poverty, support families and empower communities. Promotes public policies and strategies that address human needs and social injustices. Responds to domestic disasters on behalf of the U.S. Catholic community. The national office provides advocacy and management support for agencies.

In-house, DC-area Employees

BERG, Brother Joseph: Director for Leadership/Mission
COLLINS, Gerald: Director of Disaster Response
DALESSANDRI, Ruth: V. President, Social Service
DALY, Sharon M.: V. President, Social Policy
KAMMER, SJ, Father Fred: President
KEIGHTLEY, John: Director of Development
PECK, Carol: Program Dir. for Family Support
PEELER, Alexandra: Director of Communications
RIVAS, Andrew: Legislative Liaison
STENSON, Jane: Program Director for Community Services

Catholic Health Ass'n of the United States

1875 I St. NW
Suite 1000
Washington, DC 20006
Tel: (202)296-3993
Fax: (202)296-3997
Registered: LDA
Web: www.chausa.org

Leg. Issues: BUD, FAM, HCR, INS, MMM, TAX, WEL

In-house, DC-area Employees

BEALE, Joanne Elden: Co-Director, Sponsor Services
BROWN, Felicien "Fish": Director, Public Policy
ECKELS, Timothy J.: Senior V. President
TROCCHIO, Julie: Director, Long Term Care

Outside Counsel/Consultants

Dewey Ballantine LLP
Issues: TAX
Rep By: John J. Salmon

Catholic Healthcare West

Pasadena, CA
Leg. Issues: MMM

Outside Counsel/Consultants

DeBrunner and Associates, Inc.
Issues: MMM
Rep By: Charles L. DeBrunner, Wendy W. Herr, Ellen J. Kugler, Kathryn D. Rooney

Catholic News Service

3211 Fourth St. NE
Washington, DC 20017-1100
Tel: (202)541-3250
Fax: (202)541-3255
E-mail: cns@nccbuscc.org

A news service specializing in Catholic activities.

In-house, DC-area Employees

LORSUNG, Thomas N.: Director and Editor-in-Chief

Catholic Television Network

Brooklyn, NY
Leg. Issues: EDU, TEC

Outside Counsel/Consultants

Simon Strategies/Mindbeam
Issues: EDU, TEC
Rep By: Ann P. Morton, Gregory C. Simon, Christopher Ulrich, Kristan Van Hook

Catholic University of America

620 Michigan Ave. NE
Washington, DC 20064
Tel: (202)319-5000
Fax: (202)319-5579
Web: www.cua.edu

In-house, DC-area Employees

PARKER, Craig W.: General Counsel
SMITH, Anne: Exec. Director, Public Affairs

Catholic War Veterans of the U.S.A.

441 N. Lee St.
Alexandria, VA 22314
Tel: (703)549-3622
Fax: (703)684-5196
Web: www.cwv.org
E-mail: cwv/mt@aol.com

In-house, DC-area Employees
KRICHTEN, Leo: Exec. Director
WAMESTER, Robert: National Commander

Catholics for a Free Choice

1436 U St. NW
Suite 301
Washington, DC 20009
Tel: (202)986-6093
Fax: (202)332-7995
Web: www.catholicsforchoice.org
E-mail: cffc@catholicsforchoice.org

Advances sexual and reproductive ethics that are based on justice, reflect a commitment to women's well-being, and respect and affirm the moral capacity of women and men to make sound decisions about their lives. Through discourse, education, and advocacy, CFFC works in the U.S. and internationally to infuse these values into public policy, community life, feminist analysis, and Catholic social thinking and teaching.

In-house, DC-area Employees
KISSLING, Frances: President

Cato Institute

1000 Massachusetts Ave. NW
Washington, DC 20001
Tel: (202)842-0200
Fax: (202)842-3490
Web: www.cato.org
E-mail: cato@cato.org

A public policy research institution which favors a "market liberal" approach to political and economic issues.

In-house, DC-area Employees
BANDOW, Doug: Senior Fellow
BOAZ, David D.: Exec. V. President
CARPENTER, Ted Galen: V. President, Defense and Foreign Policy Studies
CHAMBERLIN, Susan E.: Director, External Affairs
CLERIHUE, Randy J.: Director, Public Affairs
CRANE, Edward H.: President and Chief Exec. Officer
CREWS, Clyde Wayne: Director, Technology Studies
DORN, James A.: V. President, Academic Affairs
HUDGINS, Edward L.: Director, Regulatory Studies
LYNCH, Timothy: Assistant Director, Center for Constitutional Studies
MAX, Derrick: Director, Government Affairs
MILLER, Thomas P.: Director of Health Policy Studies
NISKANEN, William A.: Chairman
OLSEN, Darcy: Director, Education and Child Policy
PALMER, Tom G.: Fellow in Social Thought
PILON, Roger: Senior Fellow and Director, Center for Constitutional Studies
POLLOCK, Richard: V. President, Communications
SAMPLES, John: Director of the Center for Representative Government
TANNER, Michael D.: Director, Health and Welfare Studies
TAYLOR, Jerry: Director, Natural Resource Studies
THIERER, Adam D.: Director, Telecommunications Studies
VASQUEZ, Ian: Director, Global Economic Liberty Project

Cattlemen's Beef Promotion and Research Board

Englewood, CO

Outside Counsel/Consultants
McLeod, Watkinson & Miller
Rep By: Wayne R. Watkinson

Cayman Islands, Government of

Georgetown, CAYMAN ISLANDS

Outside Counsel/Consultants
Sidley & Austin
Rep By: Joseph B. Tompkins, Jr.

CBI Industries

Oak Brook, IL

Outside Counsel/Consultants
Oppenheimer Wolff & Donnelly LLP
Rep By: Hon. Birch Bayh, Kevin O. Faley, Margaret N. Strand

CBI Sugar Group

Guatemala, GUATEMALA
Leg. Issues: AGR, TRD

Outside Counsel/Consultants
Edwin C. Graves & Associates
Issues: AGR, TRD
Rep By: Edwin C. Graves

CBS Affiliates

Washington, DC
Leg. Issues: COM

Outside Counsel/Consultants
Covington & Burling
Issues: COM
Rep By: Gerard J. Waldron

CC Distributors

Corpus Christ, TX
Leg. Issues: GOV

Outside Counsel/Consultants
Blank Rome Comisky & McCauley, LLP
Issues: GOV

CCI Construction

Camp Hill, PA
Leg. Issues: CON, GOV, RES, TAX, URB

Outside Counsel/Consultants
Eckert Seamans Cherin & Mellott, LLC
Issues: CON, GOV, RES, TAX, URB
Rep By: LeRoy S. Zimmerman

CDM Fantasy Sports

St. Louis, MO
Leg. Issues: CPI

Outside Counsel/Consultants
Janus-Merritt Strategies, L.L.C.
Issues: CPI
Rep By: Scott P. Hoffman

Cedar Fair LP

Sandusky, OH

Outside Counsel/Consultants
McDermott, Will and Emery

Cedar Rapids, Iowa, City of

Cedar Rapids, IA
Leg. Issues: CAW, ENV, GOV

Outside Counsel/Consultants
Redfern Resources
Issues: CAW, ENV, GOV
Rep By: Ed Redfern

Cedars-Sinai Medical Center

Los Angeles, CA
Leg. Issues: BUD

Outside Counsel/Consultants
Copeland, Lowery & Jacquez
Issues: BUD
Rep By: Jeffrey S. Shockey

Cegetel, S.A.

Leg. Issues: TEC

Outside Counsel/Consultants
Powell, Goldstein, Frazer & Murphy LLP
Issues: TEC
Rep By: Kelly Cameron

Ceiba, Puerto Rico, City of

Leg. Issues: BUD, DEF, ECN

Outside Counsel/Consultants
Smith Dawson & Andrews, Inc.
Issues: BUD, DEF, ECN
Rep By: Gregory B. Andrews, Ramon Luis Lugo, James P. Smith

Celanese Government Relations Office

1530 Wilson Blvd.
Suite 210
Arlington, VA 22209
Tel: (703)358-2890
Fax: (703)358-9786
Registered: LDA

An industrial company with business lines in commodity chemicals, acetate fibers and technical polymers headquartered in Dallas, TX.

Leg. Issues: CPT, DEF, ENG, ENV, FOO, HCR, MAN, POS, RRR, TAX, TOB, TRD, UTI

In-house, DC-area Employees
CARPENTER, Robert R.: Director, State and Federal Affairs
STEADMAN, Jr., Dr. Eugene: Director, Government Affairs
WILLIAMS, H. Newton: V. President, Government Relations

Outside Counsel/Consultants
Akin, Gump, Strauss, Hauer & Feld, L.L.P.
Campbell Crane & Associates
Rep By: Jeanne M. Campbell, Daniel M. Crane
McGuiness Norris & Williams, LLP
Issues: MAN, TRD
Rep By: William N. LaForge
SRG & Associates
Rep By: Augustine D. Tantillo

Celera Genomics

Rockville, MD
Leg. Issues: CPT, SCI

Outside Counsel/Consultants
O'Connor & Hannan, L.L.P.
Issues: CPT, SCI
Rep By: Roy C. Coffee, Robert Harmala, Timothy W. Jenkins, Patrick E. O'Donnell, Hon. Larry Pressler, Thomas H. Quinn
Podesta/Mattoon
Issues: CPT, SCI
Rep By: Ann Delory, Kimberley Fritts, Anthony T. Podesta

Celgene Corp.

Warren, NJ

Outside Counsel/Consultants
Bennett Turner & Coleman, LLP

Cell Pathways, Inc.

Horsham, PA
Leg. Issues: TRD

Outside Counsel/Consultants
Morgan, Lewis & Bockius LLP
Issues: TRD

Cell Tech

Klamath Falls, OR
Leg. Issues: ADV, CSP, FOO, HCR, SCI

Outside Counsel/Consultants
Venable
Issues: ADV, CSP, FOO, HCR, SCI
Rep By: David G. Adams

Cell Therapeutics Inc.

Seattle, WA
Leg. Issues: BUD, HCR, MED, TAX

Outside Counsel/Consultants
Capitol Associates, Inc.
Issues: BUD, HCR, MED, TAX
Rep By: Tricia Brooks
Denny Miller McBee Associates
Issues: HCR

Cellar Door Amphitheaters

Leg. Issues: TRA

Outside Counsel/Consultants
Greenberg Traurig, LLP
Issues: TRA
Rep By: Diane J. Blagman

Cellular Depreciation Coalition

Leg. Issues: COM, TEC

Outside Counsel/Consultants
Ernst & Young LLP
Issues: COM, TEC
Rep By: Phillip D. Moseley, Tom S. Nuebig

Cellular Telecommunications and Internet Ass'n

1250 Connecticut Ave. NW
Suite 800
Washington, DC 20036
Tel: (202)785-0081
Fax: (202)785-0721
Registered: LDA
Web: www.wow-com.com
Leg. Issues: BUD, COM, CPT, CSP, LAW, LBR, SCI, TAX, TEC

Political Action Committee/s
Cellular Telecommunications Industry Ass'n Political Action Committee
1250 Connecticut Ave. NW
Suite 800
Washington, DC 20036
Tel: (202)785-0081
Fax: (202)785-0721
Contact: Michael Dean

In-house, DC-area Employees
ALTSCHUL, Michael E.: Sr. V. President
ARMSTRONG, Julie: Manager, Congressional Affairs
BASILE, Jo-Anne R.: V. President, External and Industry Relations
BERRY, Steven K.: Senior V. President, Congressional Affairs

DEAN, Michael: PAC Contact
PUTALA, Chris: V. President, Congressional Affairs
WHEELER, Thomas E.: President/Chief Exec. Officer
WILLIAMS, Andrea: Assistant General Counsel

Outside Counsel/Consultants

Arnold & Porter
Issues: TAX, TEC

Arter & Hadden
Issues: TEC
Rep By: Daniel L. Cohen

Capitol Solutions
Issues: BUD, COM, CPT, LAW, SCI
Rep By: David F. Taylor

The Direct Impact Co.

Holland & Knight LLP
Issues: TEC
Rep By: Marvin Rosenberg

Lent Scrivner & Roth LLC
Issues: TEC
Rep By: Norman F. Lent, III, Hon. Norman F. Lent, Alan J. Roth, Michael S. Scrivner

Mintz, Levin, Cohn, Ferris, Glovsky and Popeo, P.C.
Issues: TEC
Rep By: Michelle Mundt, Howard J. Symons

Multinat'l Government Services, Inc.
Rep By: Brooks J. Bowen, Jim J. Tozzi

Murray, Scheer, Montgomery, Tapia & O'Donnell

Nat'l Strategies Inc.
Issues: TEC
Rep By: David K. Aylward

Patton Boggs, LLP
Issues: BUD, TEC
Rep By: Robert C. Jones

Public Opinion Strategies
Rep By: Glen Bolger, Neil S. Newhouse

Public Strategies, Inc.
Issues: COM, CSP, LAW, LBR, SCI, TAX, TEC
Rep By: Wallace J. Henderson

Willkie Farr & Gallagher
Rep By: Philip L. Verveer

Witeck * Combs Communications

CELOTEX

Tampa, FL
Leg. Issues: MAN, TAX

Outside Counsel/Consultants

Hogan & Hartson L.L.P.
Issues: MAN, TAX
Rep By: Nancy Granese, William Michael House

Celsius Tech Electronics

Jarfalla, SWEDEN
Leg. Issues: DEF

Outside Counsel/Consultants

Rooney Group Internat'l, Inc.
Issues: DEF
Rep By: James W. Rooney

Cement Free Trade Ass'n

Los Angeles, CA

Outside Counsel/Consultants

Skadden, Arps, Slate, Meagher & Flom LLP

Cement Kiln Recycling Coalition

1225 I St. NW
Suite 300
Washington, DC 20005
Web: www.ckrc.org
Tel: (202)789-1945
Fax: (202)408-9392
Registered: LDA

A coalition of cement manufacturers who recover energy from waste-derived fuels.

Leg. Issues: ENG, ENV, FUE, GOV, WAS

Political Action Committee/s

Cement Kiln Recycling Coalition PAC
1225 I St. NW
Suite 300
Washington, DC 20005
Tel: (202)789-1945
Fax: (202)408-9392

In-house, DC-area Employees

BENOIT, Michael R.: Exec. Director
LUSK, Michelle: Director, Regulatory Affairs

Outside Counsel/Consultants

Bracewell & Patterson, L.L.P.
Issues: ENG, ENV, FUE
Rep By: Gene E. Godley, Marc C. Hebert, Michael L. Pate, Scott H. Segal

Cemento Bayano

Panama City, PANAMA
Leg. Issues: ENV, ROD, TRD

Outside Counsel/Consultants

Janus-Merritt Strategies, L.L.C.
Issues: ENV, ROD, TRD
Rep By: Mark J. Robertson

Cementos Monterrey, S.A.

Monterrey, MEXICO
Leg. Issues: ENV, ROD, TRD

Outside Counsel/Consultants

Janus-Merritt Strategies, L.L.C.
Issues: ENV, ROD, TRD
Rep By: Mark J. Robertson, J. Daniel Walsh

CEMEX Central, S.A. de C.V.

Monterrey, MEXICO
Leg. Issues: ENV, FOR, ROD, TRD

Outside Counsel/Consultants

Janus-Merritt Strategies, L.L.C.
Issues: ENV, FOR, ROD, TRD
Rep By: Scott P. Hoffman, Bethany Noble, Mark J. Robertson, J. Daniel Walsh

Manatt, Phelps & Phillips, LLP
Issues: TRD
Rep By: Irwin P. Altschuler, Hon. Jack W. Buechner, June L. DeHart, James R. Jones, Robert J. Kabel, Jeff Kuhnreich, Stephanie E. Silverman, Jessica A. Wasserman

CEMEX USA

Houston, TX
Leg. Issues: ENV, FOR, MAN, ROD, RRR, TRA, TRD

Outside Counsel/Consultants

Janus-Merritt Strategies, L.L.C.
Issues: ENV, FOR, ROD, TRD
Rep By: Mark J. Robertson

Thompson Coburn LLP
Issues: MAN, RRR, TRA, TRD
Rep By: Hon. R. Lawrence Coughlin

Cendant Corp.

1225 I St. NW
Suite 500
Washington, DC 20005
Tel: (202)312-2006
Fax: (202)408-0861
Registered: LDA
E-mail: samuel.wright@cendant.com

A provider of consumer and business services headquartered in New York, NY. Operates in three principal segments: Travel Services, Real Estate Services and Alliance Marketing.

Leg. Issues: AUT, BAN, BNK, DEF, FIN, INS, LBR, RES, SMB, TAX, TOU

Political Action Committee/s

Cendant Corp. Political Action Committee
1225 I St. NW
Suite 500
Washington, DC 20005
Tel: (202)312-2006
Fax: (202)408-0861
Contact: Samuel H. Wright

In-house, DC-area Employees

WRIGHT, Samuel H.: Senior V. President

Outside Counsel/Consultants

Hogan & Hartson L.L.P.
Issues: RES
Rep By: William Michael House, Jeffrey W. Munk

Cendant Mobility Services

Bethesda, MD
Leg. Issues: DEF, GOV

Outside Counsel/Consultants

Rothleder Associates, Inc.
Issues: DEF

Shaw, Bransford, Veilleux & Roth
Issues: GOV
Rep By: G. Jerry Shaw, Jr.

CENEX, Inc.

1745 Jefferson Davis Hwy.
Suite 404
Arlington, VA 22202
Tel: (703)413-9620
Fax: (703)413-9626
E-mail: rlooney@cenexharveststates.com

In-house, DC-area Employees

LOONEY, Robert J.: Director, Federal Affairs

Census Monitoring Board

Outside Counsel/Consultants

Greener and Hook, LLC

The Centech Group

Leg. Issues: DEF, GOV

Outside Counsel/Consultants

Bob Moss Associates
Issues: DEF, GOV
Rep By: Bob Moss

Center for Aging Policy

Washington, DC
Leg. Issues: BUD

Outside Counsel/Consultants

Gustafson Associates
Issues: BUD
Rep By: Robert C. Gustafson

Center for Auto Safety

1825 Connecticut Ave. NW
Suite 330
Washington, DC 20009
Web: www.autosafety.org
Tel: (202)328-7700
Fax: (202)387-0140

In-house, DC-area Employees

DITLOW, Clarence M.: Exec. Director

Center for Civic Education

Calabasas, CA
Registered: LDA
Leg. Issues: BUD

Outside Counsel/Consultants

Mullenholz, Brimsek & Belair
Issues: BUD
Rep By: Robert R. Belair, John B. Conaway, Susan C. Haller

Center for Claims Resolution

Princeton, NJ
Leg. Issues: CSP

Outside Counsel/Consultants

Goddard Claussen

Shea & Gardner
Issues: CSP
Rep By: John D. Aldock, Patrick M. Hanlon, William R. Hanlon

Center for Clean Air Policy

750 First St. NE
Suite 940
Washington, DC 20002
Web: www.ccap.org
E-mail: general@ccap.org
Tel: (202)408-9260
Fax: (202)408-8896

Formed by a group of state governors in 1985 to develop and promote innovative policy approaches to major state, federal and international energy and environmental problems. The Center's work is guided by the belief that sound policy solutions serve both economic and environmental interests.

Leg. Issues: ENV

In-house, DC-area Employees

EARL, Tony: Chairman
HELME, Edward A. "Ned": Exec. Director
MORRIS, Catherine: Deputy Director

Outside Counsel/Consultants

Duncan, Weinberg, Genzer & Pembroke, P.C.
Issues: ENV
Rep By: Jeffrey C. Genzer

Center for Community Change

1000 Wisconsin Ave. NW
Washington, DC 20007
Web: www.communitychange.org
Tel: (202)342-0519
Fax: (202)342-1132

Renders assistance and advice on community investment and related issues of particular concern to minority groups and low and moderate income community organizations.

In-house, DC-area Employees

BHARGAVA, Deepak: Director, Public Policy
GOLDBERG, Deborah: Co-Director, Neighborhood Revitalization Project
MOTT, Andrew: Exec. Director
POULARD, Othello: Director, Public Housing Initiative

Outside Counsel/Consultants

Bill Zavarela
Rep By: Bill Zavarela

Center for Defense Information

1779 Massachusetts Ave. NW
Suite 615
Washington, DC 20036
E-mail: cdi@igc.apc.org
Tel: (202)332-0600
Fax: (202)462-4559

Founded in 1972, CDI exists to make independent, informed analyses of U.S. defense policies available to journalists, scholars, government officials and the executive branch. It proposes options for obtaining equal or greater security at reduced expense; priority projects include restraining internat'l traffic in conventional arms, cleaning up pollution on U.S. military and nuclear sites, and reducing the U.S. role as world policeman. The Center's mail greatest priority in the New Millennium is the campaign to de-alert U.S. and Russian strategic nuclear weapons and reduce the risk of unintentional nuclear war. Publishes Defense Monitor (10/yr.); each edition is devoted to a single military issue.

Leg. Issues: DEF

In-house, DC-area Employees

BLAIR, Bruce G.: President
CARROLL, USN (Ret.), Rear Adm. Eugene: Deputy Director
HELLMAN, Chris: Senior Analyst
JOHNSON, David T.: Research Director
LA ROCQUE, USN (Ret), Rear Adm. Gene R.: Founder
SMITH, Col. Dan M.: Chief of Research
STOHL, Rachel: Research Analyst
VALASEK, Tomas: Research Analyst

Center for Deliberative Polling

Austin, TX

Outside Counsel/Consultants

Neuman and Co.
Rep By: Robert A. Neuman

Center for Democracy

1101 15th St. NW
Suite 505
Washington, DC 20005
Tel: (202)429-9141
Fax: (202)293-1768
Web: www.centerfordemocracy.org
E-mail: center@centerfordemocracy.org

A non-profit, non-partisan foundation that undertakes programs and studies on major issues that confront democratic societies. Founded in 1985, the Center maintains a close working relationship with the Council of Europe. The Center's Board of Directors includes key Democratic and Republican members of both the House and Senate as well as private sector leaders.

In-house, DC-area Employees

WEINSTEIN, Allen: President and Chief Exec. Officer

Center for Democracy and Technology

1634 I St. NW
Suite 1100
Washington, DC 20006-4003
Tel: (202)637-9800
Fax: (202)637-0968
Web: www.cdt.org
E-mail: info@cdt.org

A civil liberties advocacy organization dealing with internet issues.

Leg. Issues: CIV, TEC

In-house, DC-area Employees

BERMAN, Jerry: Exec. Director
BRUENING, Paula: Staff Counsel
COURTNEY, Rob: Policy Analyst
DAVIDSON, Alan: Staff Counsel
DEMPSEY, Jim: Senior Staff Counsel
GODWIN, Mike: Senior Fellow
SCHWARTZ, Ari: Policy Analyst

Center for Disease Detection

Outside Counsel/Consultants

MV3 & Associates

Valente Lopatin & Schulze
Rep By: Mark Valente, III

Center for Dispute Settlement

1666 Connecticut Ave. NW
Suite 500
Washington, DC 20009
Tel: (202)265-9572
Fax: (202)328-9162
Web: www.cdsusa.org

Designs, implements and evaluates alternative methods of resolving disputes.

In-house, DC-area Employees

SINGER, Linda R.: President

Center for Economic Organizing

1705 DeSales St. NW
Washington, DC 20036
Tel: (202)775-9072
Fax: (202)775-9074

Founded in 1972 as the People's Bicentennial Commission, CEO promotes economic democracy, a goal which entails greater labor union and public sector control of capital and the work place through, among other things, investment of $800 billion in pension fund assets.

In-house, DC-area Employees

BARBER, Randy: Director

Center for Education Reform

1001 Connecticut Ave. NW
Suite 204
Washington, DC 20036
Tel: (202)822-9000
Fax: (202)822-5077
Web: www.edreform.com

Nonprofit advocacy organization ensuring that quality public education is available to all children.

Leg. Issues: EDU

In-house, DC-area Employees

HEINZE, Mary Kayne: Director, Media Relations

Center for Employment Training

San Jose, CA
Leg. Issues: BUD, EDU, LBR, WEL

Outside Counsel/Consultants

Moss McGee Bradley & Foley
Issues: BUD, EDU, LBR, WEL
Rep By: Leander J. Foley, III

Center for Energy and Economic Development

333 John Carlyle St.
Suite 530
Alexandria, VA 22314
Tel: (703)684-6292
Fax: (703)684-6297
Web: www.ceednet.org

A non-profit organization dedicated to producing educational programs, research and materials that describe the new technologies, broad economic benefits, and environmental compatibility of coal.

Leg. Issues: CPT, GOV, LBR, TAX, TOR

In-house, DC-area Employees

KLINGELHOFER, Philip T.: V. President, Finance and Administration
MILLER, Stephen L.: President and Chief Exec. Officer

Outside Counsel/Consultants

Nat'l Environmental Strategies

Venable
Issues: CPT, GOV, LBR, TAX, TOR
Rep By: Jeffrey S. Tenenbaum

Center for Freedom and Prosperity

6023 Shaffer Dr.
Alexandria, VA 22310
Tel: (202)285-0244
Registered: LDA
Web: www.freedomandprosperity.org
E-mail: cfp@freedomandprosperity.org
Leg. Issues: BAN, BUD, ECN, FIN, RET, TAX, TEC

In-house, DC-area Employees

QUINLAN, Andrew F.: President and Chief Exec. Officer

Center for Governmental Studies of the University of Virginia

Charlottesville, VA
Leg. Issues: EDU

Outside Counsel/Consultants

McGuireWoods L.L.P.
Issues: EDU
Rep By: Joseph H. Bogosian, Stephen A. Katsurinis, Hon. Lewis F. Payne, Jr.

Center for Health Care Practice in the Public Interest

9525 Georgia Ave.
Suite 203
Silver Spring, MD 20910-1439
Tel: (301)588-5800
Fax: (301)588-5870
Web: www.resourcebuilder.com
E-mail: dr-feg@resourcebuilder.com

Advocates maintaining the availability of private health care through small or individual practices and opposes most managed care plans, most third-party management of insurance disbursements, and all micro-management of health and mental health practice.

In-house, DC-area Employees

GUNZBURG, Dr. Frank: Exec. Director

Center for Health, Environment and Justice

150 S. Washington St.
Suite 300
P.O. Box 6806
Falls Church, VA 22046-6806
Tel: (703)237-2249
Fax: (703)237-8389
Web: www.chej.org
E-mail: chej@chej.org

A 501(c)(3) environmental advocacy group serving more than 8,000 affiliated grassroots organizations. Works to combat toxic polluters and other threats to the environment. Maintains a second web site at www.noharm.org.

Leg. Issues: ENV

In-house, DC-area Employees

GIBBS, Lois Marie: Exec. Director

Center for Healthcare Information Management

Ann Arbor, MI
Leg. Issues: HCR

Outside Counsel/Consultants

Washington Health Advocates
Issues: HCR
Rep By: Douglas Peddicord, Ph.D.

Center for Immigration Studies

1522 K St. NW
Suite 820
Washington, DC 20005
Tel: (202)466-8185
Fax: (202)466-8076
Web: www.cis.org
E-mail: center@cis.org

Dedicated to research and analysis about immigration and its relation to the national interest.

Leg. Issues: IMM

In-house, DC-area Employees

KRIKORIAN, Mark: Exec. Director

Center for Individual Rights

1233 20th St. NW
Suite 300
Washington, DC 20036
Tel: (202)833-8400
Fax: (202)833-8410
Web: www.cir-usa.org
E-mail: cir@mail.wdn.com

In-house, DC-area Employees

MCDONALD, Michael P.: President
ROSMAN, Michael: General Counsel

Center for Innovation and the Environment, Progressive Foundation

600 Pennsylvania Ave. SE
Suite 400
Washington, DC 20003
Tel: (202)546-4482
Fax: (202)544-5014
E-mail: dknopman@pf.org

In-house, DC-area Employees

KNOPMAN, Debra: Director

Center for Internat'l Policy

1755 Massachusetts Ave. NW
Suite 550
Washington, DC 20036
Tel: (202)232-3317
Fax: (202)232-3440
Web: www.ciponline.org
E-mail: cip@ciponline.org

A private, non-profit research, and public education organization concerned with the impact of U.S. foreign policies, particularly economic and military assistance, on human rights, social, and economic needs in the Third World.

Leg. Issues: FOR

In-house, DC-area Employees

GOODFELLOW, William C.: Director
WHITE, Robert E.: President

Center for Internat'l Private Enterprise

1155 15th St. NW
Suite 700
Washington, DC 20005
Tel: (202)721-9200
Fax: (202)721-9250
Web: www.cipe.org
E-mail: cipe@cipe.org

An affiliate of the U.S. Chamber of Commerce, CIPE was established in 1983 to promote private enterprise and market-oriented economic reform worldwide. Supports strategies and techniques that address market-based democratic development. Receives support from PEW Charitable Trusts and other private foundations.

In-house, DC-area Employees

SULLIVAN, Dr. John D.: Exec. Director

Center for Law and Education

1875 Connecticut Ave. NW
Suite 510
Washington, DC 20009
Tel: (202)986-3000
Fax: (202)986-6648
Web: www.cleweb.org
E-mail: cle@cleweb.org

In-house, DC-area Employees

WECKSTEIN, Paul: Co-Director

Center for Law and Social Policy

1616 P St. NW
Suite 150
Washington, DC 20036
Tel: (202)328-5140
Fax: (202)328-5195
Web: www.clasp.org
E-mail: info@clasp.org

Seeks to improve the economic conditions of low-income families with children and to secure access for the poor to the civil justice system.

Leg. Issues: BUD, EDU, FAM, LAW, MMM, WEL

In-house, DC-area Employees
GREENBERG, Mark H.: Senior Staff Attorney
HOUSEMAN, Alan W.: Exec. Director
LEVIN-EPSTEIN, Jodie: Senior State Policy Advocate
PERLE, Linda: Senior Staff Attorney
ROBERTS, Paula: Senior Staff Attorney
SAVNER, Steve: Senior Staff Attorney
TURETSKY, Vicki: Senior Staff Attorney

Center for Marine Conservation

1725 DeSales St. NW
Suite 600
Washington, DC 20036
Tel: (202)429-5609
Fax: (202)872-0619
Web: www.cmc-ocean.org
E-mail: dccmc@ix.netcom.com

Seeks to protect marine ecosystems, prevent marine pollution, preserve endangered marine species, manage fisheries for conservation and conserve marine biological diversity.

Leg. Issues: ANI, CAW, ENV, MAR, NAT, WAS

In-house, DC-area Employees
DAVIS, Kimberly
DICKSON, David
DONNELLY, Mary Adele
HOSKINS, David: V. President of Govt. Affairs and General Counsel
RUFE, Roger: President
STEWART, Tara
YOUNG, Nina: Director, Marine Wildlife Conservation

Center for Media and Public Affairs

2100 L St. NW
Washington, DC 20037
Tel: (202)223-2942
Fax: (202)872-4014
Web: www.cmpa.com
E-mail: cmpamm@aol.com

A non-profit, non-partisan research institute devoted to scientific content analysis of news and entertainment media.

In-house, DC-area Employees
LICHTER, S. Robert: President
MESSINA-BOYER, Christine: Managing Director
TALBERT, Donna: Director, Development
WILLI, Mary Carroll: Director, Political Studies

Center for Media Education

2120 L St. NW
Suite 200
Washington, DC 20037
Tel: (202)331-7833
Fax: (202)331-7841
Web: www.cme.org/cme
E-mail: cme@cme.org

A non-profit, 501(c)(3) public interest policy and research organization dedicated to promoting quality media culture for children.

In-house, DC-area Employees
MONTGOMERY, Ph.D., Kathryn: President

Center for Nat'l Policy

One Massachusetts Ave. NW
Suite 333
Washington, DC 20001
Tel: (202)682-1800
Fax: (202)682-1818
Web: www.cnponline.org
E-mail: thcenter@cnponline.org

A public policy organization committed to advancing America's common goals. Promotes debate and discussion on how government can best serve American interests both at home and abroad.

In-house, DC-area Employees
COONEY, Emily: Events Coordinator
FOX, Steve: Deputy Director, External Relations
STEINBRUNER, Maureen S.: President

Center for Patient Advocacy

1350 Beverly Rd.
Suite 108
McLean, VA 22101
Tel: (703)748-0400
Fax: (703)748-0402
Registered: LDA
Web: www.patientadvocacy.org
E-mail: advocate@patientadvocacy.org

A private, non-profit, grassroots organization founded to represent the interests of patients nationwide and dedicated to ensuring that all Americans have timely access to the highest quality medical care.

Leg. Issues: HCR, MMM

In-house, DC-area Employees
DIGIACINTO, Jacqui: Program Coordinator
HALL, Terre McFillen: President
KAHANOVITZ, M.D., Neil: Founder
TREVINO, Laura D.: Manager, Public Affairs

Center for Policy Alternatives

1875 Connecticut Ave. NW
Suite 710
Washington, DC 20009
Tel: (202)387-6030
Fax: (202)986-2539
Web: www.stateaction.org

Provides a forum for analysis and dissemination of progressive policies and programs for application at the state and local level.

In-house, DC-area Employees
GRUENEBAUM, Jane: Chief Operating Officer
TARR-WHELAN, Linda: President and Chair

Center for Public Dialogue

10615 Brunswick Ave.
Kensington, MD 20895
Tel: (301)933-0277
E-mail: waltrybeck@aol.com

Provides consulting and research in land economics for federal state and local officials; national organizations; and foreign governments. Special emphasis is placed on affordable housing, property tax reform, infrastructure finance, growth management, anti-poverty strategies and conservation.

Leg. Issues: CAW, DOC, ECN, ENV, GOV, HOU, RES, TAX, TRA, UNM, URB

In-house, DC-area Employees
RYBECK, Walter: Director

Center for Regulatory Effectiveness

Washington, DC
Leg. Issues: ENV, GOV, SCI

Outside Counsel/Consultants
Chwat and Company, Inc.
Issues: ENV, GOV, SCI
Rep By: John Chwat, Derek Riker

The Center for Religious Freedom

1319 18th St. NW
Washington, DC 20036
Tel: (202)296-5101
Fax: (202)296-5078
Web: www.freedomhouse.org/religion
E-mail: religion@freedomhouse.org

Formerly known as The Puebla Institute. An international non-profit human rights organization focusing on religious persecution worldwide. The Center is a self-sustaining program within Freedom House, America's oldest human rights group.

In-house, DC-area Employees
MARSHALL, Paul: Senior Fellow
SHEA, Nina H.: Director

Center for Reproductive Law and Policy

1146 19th St. NW
Washington, DC 20036
Tel: (202)530-2975
Fax: (202)530-2976
Web: www.crlp.org

Headquartered in New York, NY.

Leg. Issues: FAM, HCR

In-house, DC-area Employees
ERNST, Julia: International Legislative Counsel
HOBBS, Monica: Federal Legislative Counsel
NOORIGIAN, Nicole: Fellowship Attorney, Federal Legislative Program

Center for Research on Institutions and Social Policy

Scarsdale, NY
Leg. Issues: BUD, LAW

Outside Counsel/Consultants
Reed, Smith, LLP
Issues: BUD, LAW
Rep By: Phillips S. Peter, C. Stevens Seale

Center for Resource Economics

1718 Connecticut Ave. NW
Suite 300
Washington, DC 20009
Tel: (202)232-7933
Fax: (202)234-1328
Web: www.islandpress.org

A non-profit organization which produces and disseminates information concerned with local and global environmental problems and future planning.

In-house, DC-area Employees
DORRANCE, Jr., Samuel R.: Director, Marketing
SAVITT, Charles: President

Center for Responsive Politics

1101 14th St. NW
Suite 1030
Washington, DC 20005-5635
Tel: (202)857-0044
Fax: (202)857-7809
Web: www.opensecrets.org
E-mail: info@crp.org

Founded in 1983, the Center for Responsive Politics is a non-partisan, non-profit research group that tracks money in politics and its effect on elections and public policy. Conducts computer-based research on campaign finance for the news media, academics, activists, and the public at large.

In-house, DC-area Employees
KRUMHOLZ, Sheila: Research Director
MAKINSON, Larry: Senior Fellow
NOBLE, Lawrence M.: Exec. Director and General Counsel
WEISS, Steven C.: Director of Communications

Center for Science in the Public Interest

1875 Connecticut Ave. NW
Suite 300
Washington, DC 20009
Tel: (202)332-9110
Fax: (202)265-4954
Registered: LDA
Web: www.cspinet.org
E-mail: cspi@cspinet.org

A tax-exempt public interest organization set up to clarify the relationship between scientific issues and the public's health and safety. Its major thrust is to increase public awareness of food and nutrition problems and it is critical of certain food industry and government policies and practices.

Leg. Issues: ALC, FOO

In-house, DC-area Employees
HACKER, George A.: Director of Alchohol Policies Project
JACOBSON, Dr. Michael F.: Exec. Director
LIEBMAN, Bonnie F.: Director, Nutrition
SILVERGLADE, Bruce A.: Director, Legal Affairs
SMITH-DEWAAL, Caroline: Director, Programs on Food Safety
WOOTAN, Margo: Senior Staff Scientist

Center for Security Policy

1920 L St. NW
Suite 210
Washington, DC 20036
Tel: (202)835-9077
Fax: (202)835-9066
Web: www.security-policy.org
E-mail: info@security-policy.org

Concerned with strategically significant developments relating to international, national, and economic security. Specializes in products tailored to supply policymakers with immediately useable information.

In-house, DC-area Employees
GAFFNEY, Jr., Frank J.: President and C.E.O.

Center for Sickle Cell Disease

2121 Georgia Ave. NW
Washington, DC 20059
Tel: (202)806-7930
Fax: (202)806-4517

In-house, DC-area Employees
CASTRO, Dr. Oswaldo: Director

Center for Sino-American Trade

Washington, DC

Outside Counsel/Consultants
Cottone and Huggins Group
Rep By: James B. Huggins

Center for Strategic and Budgetary Assessments

1730 Rhode Island Ave.
Suite 912
Washington, DC 20036
Tel: (202)331-7990
Fax: (202)331-8019
Web: www.csbaonline.org

A non-partisan defense research and analysis group.

In-house, DC-area Employees
KOSIAK, Steven: Senior Budget Analyst
KREPINEVICH, Andrew: Exec. Director
SHEPARD, Stacey: Director, Public Affairs

Center for Strategic and Internat'l Studies

1800 K St. NW
Washington, DC 20005
Tel: (202)887-0200
Fax: (202)775-3199
Web: www.csis.org
E-mail: info@csis.org

Founded in 1962, a public policy research institution dedicated to analysis and policy impact. Conducts research in the areas of Africa, the Americas, Asia, U.S. policy issues, energy, national security, Europe, international business and economics, international communications, Middle East, political military studies, preventive diplomacy, Russia, Eurasia, South Asia, global organized crime, new global economy, environment, etc. Research findings and policy recommendations are disseminated through conferences and a variety of publications to policymakers, opinion leaders, and academic experts.

In-house, DC-area Employees
FARRAR, Jay C.: V. President, External Relations
HAMRE, Dr. John J.: President and Chief Exec. Officer
NIBLETT, Robin: V. President, Strategic Planning and Senior Fellow, Europe Program
PALMER, Brenda W.: Senior V. President, Operations

PETERSON, Erik R.: Senior V. President and Director of Studies; William A. Schreyer Chair in Global Analysis
VONDRACEK, M. Jon: V. President

Center for Studies in Health Policy

3223 Quesada St. NW
Washington, DC 20015
Tel: (202)244-5383
Fax: (202)364-1926

Offers research and advisory service to those who formulate and implement health policy in both the public and private sectors of the economy.

In-house, DC-area Employees
GONYEA, Dr. Meredith A.: President

Center for the Arts and Sciences

Charleston, WV
Leg. Issues: EDU

Outside Counsel/Consultants

Golin/Harris Internat'l
Issues: EDU
Rep By: Carol C. Mitchell

Center for the Study of Extraterrestrial Intelligence

Asheville, NC
Leg. Issues: GOV

Outside Counsel/Consultants

Paradigm Research Group
Issues: GOV
Rep By: Stephen G. Bassett

Center for the Study of Responsive Law

P.O. Box 19367
Washington, DC 20036
Tel: (202)387-8030
Fax: (202)234-5176
E-mail: csrl@essential.org

The first Nader organization to be established, in 1968, as a tax-exempt study group to conduct research and produce reports for public education on consumer, environmental, tax, health and other problems.

In-house, DC-area Employees
NADER, Ralph: Managing Trustee
ORR, Beverly: Business Manager
RICHARD, John: Exec. Director

Center for the Study of Social Policy

1575 I St. NW
Suite 500
Washington, DC 20006
Tel: (202)371-1565
Fax: (202)371-1472
Web: www.cssp.org

In-house, DC-area Employees
FARROW, Frank: Director, Washington Office

The Center for Voting and Democracy

P.O. Box 60037
Washington, DC 20039
Tel: (301)270-4616
Fax: (301)270-4133
Web: www.fairvote.org
E-mail: fairvote@compuserve.com

A tax-exempt educational organization that serves as a national clearinghouse on proportional representation and other democratic alternatives to the plurality voting systems that are currently used in most U.S. elections.

Leg. Issues: CIV, CON

In-house, DC-area Employees
ANDERSON, Hon. John B.: President
RICHIE, Robert: Exec. Director

Outside Counsel/Consultants

Wilmer, Cutler & Pickering

Center for Women Policy Studies

1211 Connecticut Ave. NW
Suite 312
Washington, DC 20036
Tel: (202)872-1770
Fax: (202)296-8962
Web: www.centerwomenpolicy.org

A non-profit, policy and research-oriented organization that works on specific issues affecting women, particularly women and girls of color.

In-house, DC-area Employees
WOLFE, Dr. Leslie R.: President

Center of Concern

1225 Otis St. NE
Washington, DC 20017
Tel: (202)635-2757
Fax: (202)832-9494
Web: www.coc.org
E-mail: coc@coc.org

Works for global economic justice, guided by the vision and values of Catholic Social Thought. It is engaged in research, social analysis, theological reflection, networking, advocacy, and education.

Leg. Issues: ECN, MIA, TRD

In-house, DC-area Employees
HUG, Jim: President
WARNER, Candy: Director, Administration

Center on Budget and Policy Priorities

820 First St. NE
Suite 510
Washington, DC 20002
Tel: (202)408-1080
Fax: (202)408-1056
Registered: LDA
Web: www.cbpp.org

An independent, non-profit research organization which studies a range of government policies and programs, with an emphasis on those affecting low- and moderate-income Americans. The Center publishes reports, fact sheets and analyses for use by policymakers, legislators and others.

Leg. Issues: AGR, BUD, HOU, IMM, MMM, RET, TAX, WEL

In-house, DC-area Employees
GREENSTEIN, Robert: Exec. Director
JAFFE, Jim: Director, Communications
KOGAN, Richard: Senior Fellow for Budge Policy
LAV, Iris J.: Deputy Director
MCNICHOL, Elizabeth: Director, State Fiscal Project
NISSENBAUM, Ellen: Legislative Director
PRIMUS, Wendell E.: Director, Income Security
WALSH, Suzanne: Legislative Associate

Center on Conscience and War/NISBCO

1830 Connecticut Ave. NW
Washington, DC 20009
Tel: (202)483-2220
Fax: (202)483-1246
Registered: LDA
Web: www.nisbco.org
E-mail: nisbco@nisbco.org

A nonprofit service organization begun by an association of 35 religious bodies. Disseminates information on draft registration and seeks to defend and extend the rights of conscientious objectors to war. Opposes any form of registration, the draft, or compulsory national service. Provides counseling and legal referral services to military personnel and others.

Leg. Issues: DEF

In-house, DC-area Employees
GALVIN, E. William
MCNEIL, J.E.: Exec. Director

Center on Nat'l Labor Policy

5211 Port Royal Rd.
Suite 103
Springfield, VA 22151
Tel: (703)321-9180
Fax: (703)321-9325

Supports employees, employers and consumers in legal and regulatory action opposing abuses of labor union power.

In-house, DC-area Employees
AVAKIAN, Michael: General Counsel

Center Point Inc.

San Rafael, CA
Leg. Issues: BUD

Outside Counsel/Consultants

Beacon Consulting Group, Inc.
Issues: BUD
Rep By: Gordon P. MacDougall, Lisa A. Stewart, Kyndel Turvaville

The Center to Prevent Handgun Violence

1225 I St. NW
Suite 1100
Washington, DC 20005
Tel: (202)289-7319
Fax: (202)408-1851
Web: www.cphv.org

Founded in 1983 to reduce gun violence through education, legal advocacy, research, and outreach to the entertainment community. The information, education, and legal arm of Handgun Control, Inc. (see separate listing).

In-house, DC-area Employees
BARNES, Hon. Michael D.: President
BRADY, Sarah: Chair
DEALY, Brendan: Director, Communications
HWA, Nancy: Assistant Director, Communications

Centerior Energy Corp.

Cleveland, OH

Formed from a merger of Cleveland Electric Illuminating and Toledo Edison.

Outside Counsel/Consultants

Arter & Hadden
Rep By: Daniel L. Cohen, Hon. Thomas G. Loeffler

Shaw Pittman
Rep By: Jay E. Silberg

Centex Corp.

Dallas, TX
Leg. Issues: BAN, TAX

Outside Counsel/Consultants

Bracewell & Patterson, L.L.P.
Issues: BAN, TAX
Rep By: Michael L. Pate

Centocor, Inc.

Malvern, PA
Leg. Issues: MED, MMM

Outside Counsel/Consultants

Dalrymple and Associates, L.L.C.
Issues: MED
Rep By: Donald "Dack" Dalrymple

McKenna & Cuneo, L.L.P.
Issues: MED, MMM

Centraal Bureau van de Tuinbouwveilingen

Zoetermeer, NETHERLANDS

Outside Counsel/Consultants

Max N. Berry Law Offices

Central Alabama Community College

Alexander City, AL

Outside Counsel/Consultants

Bradley Arant Rose & White LLP

Central American Bank of Economic Integration

Tegucigalpa, HONDURAS
Leg. Issues: APP, BUD, ECN, FOR, LBR, MAN, TRD

Outside Counsel/Consultants

Holland & Knight LLP
Issues: APP, BUD, ECN, FOR, LBR, MAN, TRD

Patton Boggs, LLP

Central Arizona Irrigation and Drainage District

Outside Counsel/Consultants

Strategic Impact, Inc.
Rep By: Michael C. Jimenez

Central Arizona Water Conservation District

Phoenix, AZ
Leg. Issues: BUD, NAT

Outside Counsel/Consultants

Hunton & Williams

John J. Rhodes
Issues: BUD, NAT
Rep By: Hon. John J. Rhodes, III

Central Bank of Turkey

Ankara, TURKEY

Outside Counsel/Consultants

Hoffman & Hoffman Public Relations
Rep By: Marshall Hoffman

Central Basin Municipal Water District

Carson, CA
Leg. Issues: BUD, TRA

Outside Counsel/Consultants

The Furman Group
Issues: BUD, TRA
Rep By: Thomas M. James

Central College

Pella, IA
Leg. Issues: SCI

Outside Counsel/Consultants

Cassidy & Associates, Inc.
Issues: SCI
Rep By: Daniel J. McNamara, Michael Merola, Gabor J. Rozsa, Marnie Russ

Central Council of Tlingit and Haida Indian Tribes of Alaska

Juneau, AK
Leg. Issues: BUD, IND

Outside Counsel/Consultants

Dorsey & Whitney LLP
Issues: BUD, IND
Rep By: Philip Baker-Shenk, David A. Bieging, Virginia W. Boylan, Cindy Darcy, Mark Jarboe, Christopher Karns, Kevin J. Wadzinski

Central European Media Enterprises

Leg. Issues: FOR

Outside Counsel/Consultants

American Continental Group, Inc.
Issues: FOR
Rep By: Shawn H. Smeallie

Central Freight Forwarding

Miami, FL

Outside Counsel/Consultants

Denning & Wohlstetter
Rep By: Alan F. Wohlstetter

Central Illinois Public Service Co.

Springfield, IL

An electrical power company.

Outside Counsel/Consultants

EOP Group, Inc.
Rep By: Joseph Hezir, Michael O'Bannon

Central Kitsap School District

Oak Harbor, WA
Leg. Issues: EDU

Outside Counsel/Consultants

Evergreen Associates, Ltd.
Issues: EDU
Rep By: Robert M. Brooks

Central Michigan University

Mt. Pleasant, MI
Leg. Issues: EDU, HCR

Outside Counsel/Consultants

Washington Alliance Group, Inc.
Issues: EDU, HCR
Rep By: Bonnie Singer

Central Montana Electric Power Cooperative, Inc.

Billings, MT
Leg. Issues: ENG, UTI

Outside Counsel/Consultants

Duncan, Weinberg, Genzer & Pembroke, P.C.
Issues: ENG, UTI
Rep By: Janice L. Lower, James D. Pembroke

Central Ohio Regional Transit Authority

Columbus, OH
Leg. Issues: TRA

Outside Counsel/Consultants

Charles H. Graves & Associates
Issues: TRA
Rep By: Charles H. Graves

Central Piedmont Community College

Charlotte, NC
Leg. Issues: BUD

Outside Counsel/Consultants

Cassidy & Associates, Inc.
Issues: BUD
Rep By: Laura A. Neal, Marnie Russ

Central Puget Sound Regional Transit Authority (Sound Transit)

Seattle, WA
Leg. Issues: TAX, TRA

Outside Counsel/Consultants

Denny Miller McBee Associates
Issues: TRA

The Petrizzo Group, Inc.
Issues: TAX, TRA
Rep By: Kara Kennedy, Thomas "T.J." Petrizzo

Central Reserve Life

Strongsville, OH

Outside Counsel/Consultants

Baker & Hostetler LLP
Rep By: Frederick H. Graefe

Central Romana Corp.

La Romana, DOMINICAN REPUBLIC

Outside Counsel/Consultants

Johnson, Rogers & Clifton, L.L.P.

Central Soya Co.

1722 I St. NW
Fourth Floor
Washington, DC 20006
Tel: (202)736-8584
Fax: (202)833-3831
Registered: LDA, FARA
Web: www.centralsoya.com

An affiliate of the agricultural products firm Eridania Beghin Say, headquartered in Paris, France. Lobbies Congress and federal agencies on agricultural, food, environmental, and energy issues.

Leg. Issues: AGR, ENG, ENV, FOO, TRD

Political Action Committee/s

Central Soya PAC

1722 I St. NW
Fourth Floor
Washington, DC 20006
Contact: M. Ann Tutwiler
Tel: (202)736-8584
Fax: (202)833-3831

In-house, DC-area Employees

TUTWILER, M. Ann: Director, Government Relations

Central States Indemnity Co. of Omaha

Omaha, NE
Leg. Issues: FIN

Outside Counsel/Consultants

Steptoe & Johnson LLP
Issues: FIN

Central Station Alarm Ass'n

440 Maple Ave. East
Suite 201
Vienna, VA 22188
Tel: (703)242-4670
Fax: (703)242-4675
Registered: LDA
Web: www.csaaul.org
E-mail: admin@csaaul.org

An association of major burglar and fire alarm companies.

Leg. Issues: TEC

Political Action Committee/s

Alarm Industry Communication Committee

440 Maple Ave. East
Suite 201
Vienna, VA 22188
Contact: Stephen P. Doyle
Tel: (703)242-4670
Fax: (703)242-4675

In-house, DC-area Employees

DOYLE, Stephen P.: Exec. V. President

Central Utah Water Conservancy District

Orem, UT
Leg. Issues: BUD

Outside Counsel/Consultants

Marcus G. Faust, P.C.
Issues: BUD
Rep By: Marcus G. Faust, Adrianne Firth

Central Valley Project Water Ass'n

Sacramento, CA
Leg. Issues: BUD, CAW, NAT

Outside Counsel/Consultants

The Ferguson Group, LLC
Issues: BUD, CAW, NAT
Rep By: William Ferguson, Jr., W. Roger Gwinn, Joseph L. Raeder

Central Virginia Educational Telecommunications Corp.

Falls Church, VA
Leg. Issues: COM, EDU, TEC

Outside Counsel/Consultants

Convergence Services, Inc.
Issues: COM, EDU, TEC
Rep By: John M. Lawson

Central Virginia Electric Cooperative, Inc.

Lovingston, VA
Leg. Issues: ENG, UTI

Outside Counsel/Consultants

Duncan, Weinberg, Genzer & Pembroke, P.C.
Issues: ENG, UTI
Rep By: Robert Weinberg

Central West Virginia Regional Airport Authority

Charleston, WV

Outside Counsel/Consultants

Hunton & Williams

Centralia, Pennsylvania, Former Residents of

Outside Counsel/Consultants

Spiegel & McDiarmid
Rep By: Thomas C. Trauger

Centre for Development and Population Activities

1400 16th St. NW
Suite 100
Washington, DC 20036
Web: www.cedpa.org
E-mail: cmail@cedpa.org
Tel: (202)667-1142
Fax: (202)332-4496

A non-profit organization that seeks to expand the participation of women in international development.

In-house, DC-area Employees

CURLIN, Peggy: President
SEARS, Patricia M.: Senior Advisor, Special Projects

Centre National Interprofessionel de L'Economie Laitiere (French Dairy Ass'n)

Paris, FRANCE
Leg. Issues: AGR

Outside Counsel/Consultants

Max N. Berry Law Offices
Issues: AGR
Rep By: Max N. Berry

Centro Industrial de Laboratorios Farmaceuticas Argentinos (CILFA)

Buenos Aires, ARGENTINA

Outside Counsel/Consultants

MFJ Internat'l

Century 21 Real Estate Corp.

Parsippany, NJ

Political Action Committee/s

Century 21 Political Action Committee (CEN-PAC)

Parsippany, NJ

Outside Counsel/Consultants

Skadden, Arps, Slate, Meagher & Flom LLP
Rep By: Kenneth A. Gross

The Century Council

Los Angeles, CA
Registered: LDA
Leg. Issues: ALC

Outside Counsel/Consultants

Bond & Company, Inc.
Rep By: Richard N. Bond

Wheat & Associates, Inc.
Issues: ALC
Rep By: Andrea Bevvino, Hon. Alan D. Wheat

Century Financial Group

Leg. Issues: BAN

Outside Counsel/Consultants

The MWW Group
Issues: BAN
Rep By: Christine A. Pellerin, Jonathan B. Slade

The Century Foundation

1755 Massachusetts Ave. NW
Suite 400
Washington, DC 20036
Web: www.tcf.org
Tel: (202)387-0400
Fax: (202)483-9430

Formerly the Twentieth Century Fund.

In-house, DC-area Employees

ABRAMOWITZ, Mort: Senior Fellow
FINLAY-DICK, Brian: Program Officer
HARRISON, Selig: Writer, Foreign Policy Background and Korean Issues
KAHLENBERG, Richard: Senior Fellow
NOLAN, Janne: Director, International Programs
TEIXEIRA, Ruy: Senior Fellow
WASOW, Bernard: Senior Fellow and Acting Director, Washington Office
ZGORSKI, Lisa-Joy: Manager, Communications

Outside Counsel/Consultants

Hauser Group

Century Internat'l Arms

Boca Raton, FL
Leg. Issues: FIR

Outside Counsel/Consultants

Law Offices of Mark Barnes
Issues: FIR
Rep By: Mark J. Barnes

Century Tube Corp.

Pine Bluff, AR
Leg. Issues: TRA

Outside Counsel/Consultants

Schagrin Associates
Issues: TRA
Rep By: Roger B. Schagrin

CEO Forum on Education and Technology

Washington, DC
Leg. Issues: EDU

Outside Counsel/Consultants

Infotech Strategies, Inc.
Issues: EDU
Rep By: Kenneth R. Kay

Cephalon, Inc.

West Chester, PA Registered: LDA

Outside Counsel/Consultants

Jeffrey M. Anders
Rep By: Jeffrey M. Anders

Bain and Associates, Inc.

Cerebral Palsy Council

Van Nuys, CA
Leg. Issues: MMM

Outside Counsel/Consultants

MARC Associates, Inc.
Issues: MMM
Rep By: Edwin Allen, Daniel C. Maldonado, Shannon Penberthy

Ceridian Corp.

1300 I St. NW
Suite 420 East
Washington, DC 20005
Tel: (202)789-6525
Fax: (202)789-6593
Registered: LDA
Web: www.ceridian.com

Government relations office for Minnesota-based Ceridian Corporation, specializing in human resources policy, workforce development policy, and tax policy.

Leg. Issues: BAN, LBR, TAX

In-house, DC-area Employees

O'CONNELL, James J.: V. President, Government Relations
WARD, Stephanie L.: Manager, Government Relations

CertainTeed Corp.

Valley Forge, PA

Outside Counsel/Consultants

Powell Tate

Certified Airline Passenger Services, LLC

Washington, DC
Leg. Issues: AVI

Outside Counsel/Consultants

Winston & Strawn
Issues: AVI
Rep By: Hon. James H. Burnley, IV, James T. Pitts, John A. Waits, II

Certified Angus Beef

Wooster, OH

Outside Counsel/Consultants

McLeod, Watkinson & Miller
Rep By: Wayne R. Watkinson

Certified Automotive Parts Ass'n

Washington, DC
Leg. Issues: AUT, INS

Outside Counsel/Consultants

Smith Dawson & Andrews, Inc.
Issues: AUT, INS
Rep By: Gregory B. Andrews, Thomas C. Dawson, James P. Smith, Ray Warner

CES

San Diego, CA

Outside Counsel/Consultants

Rhoads Group

CESD/WVU

Morgantown, WV
Leg. Issues: MIA

Outside Counsel/Consultants

Cottone and Huggins Group
Issues: MIA
Rep By: James B. Huggins

CFSBdirect Inc.

Jersey City, NJ
Leg. Issues: FIN

Outside Counsel/Consultants

Paul, Hastings, Janofsky & Walker LLP
Issues: FIN
Rep By: Behnam Dayanim, Ralph B. Everett, Patrick J. Togni

CH2M Hill

1250 H St. NW
Suite 575
Washington, DC 20005
Tel: (202)393-2426
Fax: (202)783-8410
Web: www.ch2m.com
E-mail: rcorriga@ch2m.com

An employee-owned firm headquartered in Denver, CO. Specializes in project development, contruction, and engineering services. Assists public and private sector clients in applying technology, safeguarding the environment, and developing infrastucture throughout the world.

Leg. Issues: ENG, ENV, ROD, TAX, WAS

In-house, DC-area Employees

CORRIGAN, Richard L.: Senior V. President, Governmental Affairs

Outside Counsel/Consultants

Valis Associates
Issues: TAX
Rep By: Jennifer Conti, Hon. Dan Schaefer, Hon. Richard T. Schulze, Wayne H. Valis

Chabot Space & Science Center

Oakland, CA
Leg. Issues: EDU, SCI

Outside Counsel/Consultants

Richard L. Spees, Inc.
Issues: EDU, SCI
Rep By: Richard L. Spees

Chad, Government of the Republic of

N'Djamena, CHAD

Outside Counsel/Consultants

Hayward Internat'l
Rep By: Barbara Hayward

Chadwick Internat'l, Inc.

Fairfax, VA

Outside Counsel/Consultants

Vorys, Sater, Seymour and Pease, LLP
Rep By: Warren W. Glick

Challenge Air Cargo

Miami, FL

Outside Counsel/Consultants

Zuckert, Scoutt and Rasenberger, L.L.P.
Rep By: William H. Callaway, Jr.

Challenger Center for Space Science Education

1250 N. Pitt St.
Alexandria, VA 22314
Tel: (703)683-9740
Fax: (703)683-7546
Web: www.challenger.org

An international, not-for-profit educational organization that uses space themed programs to inspire young people and their teachers to explore science, math, and technology.

Leg. Issues: EDU, SCI

In-house, DC-area Employees

ABLOTT, Vance: President
WAHLBERG, Howard: V. President, Marketing and Network Development

Chamber of Commerce of the U.S.A.

1615 H St. NW
Washington, DC 20062-2000
Tel: (202)659-6000
Fax: (202)463-5836
Registered: LDA
Web: www.uschamber.com

Leg. Issues: AGR, ALC, AVI, BAN, BNK, BUD, CAW, CIV, COM, CON, CPI, CSP, DEF, ECN, EDU, ENG, ENV, FIN, FOR, GOV, HCR, IMM, INS, LAW, LBR, MAN, MED, POS, REL, RES, RET, SCI, SMB, TAX, TEC, TOB, TOR, TRA, TRD, WAS

Political Action Committee/s

Nat'l Chamber Alliance for Politics of the Chamber of Commerce for the U.S.A.
1615 H St. NW
Washington, DC 20062-2000
Tel: (202)659-6000
Fax: (202)463-5836
Contact: Bill Miller

In-house, DC-area Employees

ADAMS, Cecelia: Director, Congressional and Public Affairs
BOKAT, Stephen A.: V. President and General Counsel
BRILLIANT, Myron A.: Manager, Asia
CLARK, Jack: Director, Congressional and Public Affairs
CLARK, Michael: Exec. Director of the U.S.-India Business Council (USIBC)
CONRAD, Robin S.: V. President, National Chamber Litigation Center
DEELEY, George: Assistant Director, Europe, International Division
DONOHUE, Thomas J.: President and Chief Exec. Officer
EIDE, Peter J.: Manager, Labor Law
FINKE, Rupert: Associate Director, Eurasia, International Division
GOULD, Patrick: Associate Director, Congressional and Public Affairs
GRANT, Dr. Carl N.: Senior V. President, Communications
HIRSCHMANN, David: Exec. V. President, National Chamber Foundation
HOWARD, John E.: Director, Policy and Programs International
JEFFERSON, Sally: Director, Congressional and Public Affairs
JOHNSON, Randel K.: V. President, Labor Policy
JORDAN, Stephen: Director, Trade Policy Latin America
JOSTEN, R. Bruce: Exec. V. President
KNIGHTS, Josh: Director, Asia Trade Policy, International Division
KOVACS, William L.: V. President for Environment and Regulatory Affairs
LANE, Patrick J.: Director, Congressional and Public Affairs
LEBEDEV, Gregori: Exec. V. President and Chief Operating Officer
LITMAN, Gary V.: Director, Central Eastern Europe and Eurasia, International
MAGAN, Michael: Manager, Western Hemisphere
MANEY, Timothy J.: Director, Congressional and Public Affairs
MCMAHON, Diane: Assistant Director, U.S.-India Business Council (USIBC)
MILLER, Bill: Political Director
MORLEY, William J.: V. President, Congressional and Public Affairs
MURPHY, John
REGALIA, Martin A.: V. President, Economic Policy and Chief Economist
ROZETT, Linda S.: V. President, Media Relations
SHERK, Jon Arthur: Director, Technology Policy
SINCLAIRE, William T.: Director, Tax Policy
SMITH, Mark T.: Associate Director, Latin American Affairs
THIESSEN, Joe: Director, Congressional and Public Affairs
VAN FLEET, Mark: Manager, International Business Services
WEBB, Matthew: Staff Attorney, General Counsel's Office
WILD, Brian: Associate Director, Congressional and Public Affairs
WORKMAN, Willard A.: V. President, International Division

Outside Counsel/Consultants

Kirkland & Ellis
Issues: CON, ENV
Rep By: Robert R. Gasaway

Mayer, Brown & Platt
Issues: GOV
Rep By: Kenneth Geller

Public Strategies Washington, Inc.
Issues: ECN
Rep By: Joseph P. O'Neill

George Reagle
Rep By: George Reagle

Chamber of Independent Gas Stations of Argentina

Buenos Aires, ARGENTINA
Leg. Issues: CSP, FUE

Outside Counsel/Consultants

Williams & Connolly
Issues: CSP, FUE
Rep By: Robert B. Barnett

Chamber of Mines of South Africa

Johannesburg, SOUTH AFRICA

Outside Counsel/Consultants

C/R Internat'l, L.L.C

Chamber of Shipping of America

1730 M St. NW
Suite 407
Washington, DC 20036
E-mail: jcox@knowships.org

Tel: (202)775-4399
Fax: (202)659-3795
Registered: LDA

Represents 18 U.S. based companies which own, operate or charter oceangoing tankers, container ships, and other merchant vessels engaged in both the domestic and international trades. Also represents other entities which maintain a commercial interest in the operation of such vessels. Formerly (1998) known as the U.S. Chamber of Shipping.

Leg. Issues: MAR

In-house, DC-area Employees

COX, Joseph J.: President
METCALF, Kathy J.: Director, Maritime Affairs

Outside Counsel/Consultants

Paul, Hastings, Janofsky & Walker LLP
Rep By: Ralph B. Everett

Washington Council Ernst & Young
Rep By: John L. Doney, Jayne T. Fitzgerald, LaBrenda Garrett-Nelson, Gary J. Gasper, Bruce A. Gates, Robert J. Leonard, Richard Meltzer, Robert M. Rozen, Timothy J. Urban

Chamberlain Manufacturing Corp.

Elmhurst, IL
Leg. Issues: BUD, DEF, MAN

Outside Counsel/Consultants

Ervin Technical Associates, Inc. (ETA)
Issues: BUD, DEF, MAN
Rep By: James L. Ervin, Hon. Joseph M. McDade

Fishbein Associates, Inc.
Issues: BUD, DEF

The PMA Group
Issues: DEF
Rep By: Kaylene Green, Paul J. Magliocchetti, Charles Smith, Mark Waclawski

Chambre Syndicale des Producteurs d'Aciers Fins et Speciaux

Paris, FRANCE

Outside Counsel/Consultants

Covington & Burling
Rep By: Harvey M. Applebaum

Champion Securities

San Francisco, CA

Outside Counsel/Consultants

Cleary, Gottlieb, Steen and Hamilton

Champlin Exploration, Inc.

Enid, OK
Leg. Issues: FUE

Outside Counsel/Consultants

Duncan, Weinberg, Genzer & Pembroke, P.C.
Issues: FUE
Rep By: Kathleen L. Mazure

Chandis Securities Co.

Los Angeles, CA

Outside Counsel/Consultants

Williams & Jensen, P.C.
Rep By: David E. Franasiak, Robert E. Glennon, Jr., Anthony J. Roda

Chandler Evans Control Systems

West Hartford, CT
Leg. Issues: AVI, DEF

Outside Counsel/Consultants

Mehl, Griffin & Bartek Ltd.
Issues: AVI, DEF
Rep By: Ronald J. Bartek, Molly Griffin, Theodore J. Mehl

Chang Mien Industry Co., Ltd.

Kaohsiung, CHINA (TAIWAN)
Leg. Issues: TRD

Outside Counsel/Consultants

Law Offices of David L. Simon
Issues: TRD
Rep By: David L. Simon

Changing Paradigms

West Chester, OH

Outside Counsel/Consultants

Garvey, Schubert & Barer
Rep By: Matthew R. Schneider

Changing World Technologies

West Hempstead, NY
Leg. Issues: ENV, TAX

Outside Counsel/Consultants

Columbus Public Affairs

John M. Stinson
Issues: ENV, TAX
Rep By: John M. Stinson

Channel One Network

Washington, DC

Outside Counsel/Consultants

Greenberg Traurig, LLP
Rep By: Jack Abramoff

Chaparral Steel Co.

Midlothian, TX

Outside Counsel/Consultants

Wiley, Rein & Fielding
Rep By: Charles O. Verrill, Jr.

Chapman Freeborn America

Atlanta, GA
Leg. Issues: AVI

Outside Counsel/Consultants

Sher & Blackwell
Issues: AVI
Rep By: Mark Atwood

Charity Lobbying in the Public Interest

2040 S St. NW
Washington, DC 20009

Tel: (202)387-5072
Fax: (202)387-5149
Registered: LDA

In-house, DC-area Employees

ARONS, Dave: Co-Director
SMUCKER, Bob: Co-Director

Charles Schwab & Co. Inc.

San Francisco, CA
Leg. Issues: FIN

Outside Counsel/Consultants

Thelen Reid & Priest LLP
Issues: FIN
Rep By: Edward L. Pittman, Alan J. Reed, Richard Y. Roberts

Charter Communications, Inc.

1200 New Hampshire Ave. NW
Suite 800
Washington, DC 20036
E-mail: mrappaport@chartercom.com

Tel: (202)776-2911
Fax: (202)776-3911
Registered: LDA

Headquartered in St. Lous, MO.

Leg. Issues: TEC

Political Action Committee/s

CharterPAC

1200 New Hampshire Ave. NW
Suite 800
Washington, DC 20036
Contact: Marvin S. Rappaport

Tel: (202)776-2911
Fax: (202)776-3911

In-house, DC-area Employees

RAPPAPORT, Marvin S.: V. President, Public Policy

Charter One

Cleveland, OH
Leg. Issues: BAN, HOU, TRA

Outside Counsel/Consultants

Butera & Andrews
Issues: BAN, HOU, TRA
Rep By: Cliff W. Andrews, Wright H. Andrews, Jr., James J. Butera, Frank Tillotson

Charter Schools Development Corp.

Washington, DC
Leg. Issues: BUD, DOC, EDU, FIN

Outside Counsel/Consultants

Greenberg Traurig, LLP
Issues: BUD, DOC, EDU, FIN

Holland & Knight LLP
Issues: EDU
Rep By: Douglas J. Patton

Riggs Government Relations Consulting LLC
Issues: BUD, EDU
Rep By: Cathy A. Riggs, Hon. Frank D. Riggs

Van Scoyoc Associates, Inc.
Issues: BUD, EDU
Rep By: Victor F. Klatt, III, H. Stewart Van Scoyoc

Chase Electronic Investments

New York, NY

Outside Counsel/Consultants

LaRocco & Associates
Rep By: Matthew LaRocco

Chase Manhattan Bank

New York, NY
Leg. Issues: BAN, BUD, HOU, SMB

Registered: LDA

Outside Counsel/Consultants

Baker & Daniels
Rep By: Frank S. Swain

Bonner & Associates

Dean Blakey & Moskowitz
Rep By: John E. Dean

Ibex Internat'l, Inc.
Rep By: George G. Pagonis

Sagamore Associates, Inc.
Issues: BAN, BUD, HOU, SMB
Rep By: Frank S. Swain, Mark W. Weller

Chase Nat'l Kiwi Farms

Marysville, CA

Outside Counsel/Consultants

McDermott, Will and Emery
Rep By: Carolyn B. Gleason

Chatham Area Transit Authority

Savannah, GA
Leg. Issues: BUD, TRA

Outside Counsel/Consultants

Terry Bevels Consulting
Issues: BUD, TRA
Rep By: Terry D. Bevels

Chattanooga Metropolitian Airport Authority

Chattanooga, TN
Leg. Issues: AVI

Outside Counsel/Consultants

The Wexler Group
Issues: AVI
Rep By: Timothy Hannegan

The Chauncey Group Internat'l

Princeton, NJ

Outside Counsel/Consultants

Halsey, Rains & Associates, LLC
Rep By: Steven C. Halsey, James Hubbard, Laurie D. Rains

Check Payment Systems Ass'n

Washington, DC
Leg. Issues: BAN, CSP, MON

Outside Counsel/Consultants

The Plexus Consulting Group
Issues: BAN, CSP, MON
Rep By: Yasmin Quiwzow

Smith, Bucklin and Associates, Inc.

Cheese Importers Ass'n of America

New York, NY
Leg. Issues: AGR

Outside Counsel/Consultants

Harris Ellsworth & Levin
Rep By: Hon. Herbert E. Harris, II

Tuttle, Taylor & Heron
Rep By: Phillip L. Fraas

Winston & Strawn
Issues: AGR
Rep By: Robert M. Bor, John A. Waits, II

Cheese of Choice Coalition

New York, NY
Leg. Issues: FOO

Outside Counsel/Consultants

The PMA Group
Issues: FOO
Rep By: Fred J. Clark, Kaylene Green, Paul J. Magliocchetti, Mark Rokala, Timothy K. Sanders

Chehalis Reservation, Confederated Tribes of the

Leg. Issues: ECN, GAM, IND, TOB

Outside Counsel/Consultants

Capital Consultants Corp.
Issues: ECN, GAM, IND, TOB
Rep By: Barry Hodgson, Michael David Kaiser

Chela Financial

San Francisco, CA
Leg. Issues: EDU

Outside Counsel/Consultants

Dean Blakey & Moskowitz
Issues: EDU
Rep By: John E. Dean

Chelan County Public Utility District

Ephrata, WA
Leg. Issues: ENV, NAT, UTI

Outside Counsel/Consultants

Van Ness Feldman, P.C.
Issues: ENV, NAT, UTI
Rep By: Robert Nordhaus

Chemcrete Technologies Russia (RIS/NIS), Inc.

Moscow, RUSSIA

Outside Counsel/Consultants

Gilbert A. Robinson, Inc.
Rep By: Kenneth J. Hoeck

ChemFirst Inc.

Jackson, MS
Leg. Issues: CSP, ENV, TRD

Outside Counsel/Consultants

Baker & McKenzie
Issues: TRD
Rep By: Teresa A. Gleason

Bill Simpson & Associates
Issues: CSP, ENV
Rep By: William G. Simpson

Chemical and Biological Arms Control Institute

2111 Eisenhower Ave.
Suite 302
Alexandria, VA 22314
Web: www.cbaci.org
E-mail: cbaci@cbach.org
Tel: (703)739-1538
Fax: (703)739-1525

In-house, DC-area Employees

MOODIE, Michael: President

Chemical Land Holdings, Inc.

East Brunswick, NJ
Leg. Issues: ENV, NAT

Outside Counsel/Consultants

Dawson & Associates, Inc.
Issues: ENV, NAT
Rep By: Donald E. Crabill, Robert K. Dawson, Jonathan P. Deason, Ph.D., Edward Dickey, Ph.D., James Durkay, Lt. Gen. Vald Heiberg, Hon. John Myers, Henry Pointon

Chemical Manufacturers Ass'n

Washington, DC
Leg. Issues: CHM

Outside Counsel/Consultants

Hogan & Hartson L.L.P.

Ogilvy Public Relations Worldwide
Issues: CHM
Rep By: Jon Wentzel

Chemical Producers and Distributors Ass'n

1430 Duke St.
Alexandria, VA 22314
Web: www.cpda.com
E-mail: warren@cpda.com
Tel: (703)548-7700
Fax: (703)548-3149
Leg. Issues: AGR, CHM, FOO

Political Action Committee/s

Chemical Producers and Distributors Ass'n Political Action Committee

1430 Duke St.
Alexandria, VA 22314
Tel: (703)548-7700
Fax: (703)548-3149

In-house, DC-area Employees

SCHUTE, Diane J.: Director, Legislative Affairs
STICKLE, Ph.D., Warren E.: President

CHEMRING, Ltd.

Portsmouth, UNITED KINGDOM

Outside Counsel/Consultants

Rooney Group Internat'l, Inc.
Rep By: James W. Rooney

Chep USA

2121 K St. NW
Suite 800
Washington, DC 20037
E-mail: scameron@us.chep.com
Tel: (202)261-6518
Registered: LDA

Headquartered in Orlando, FL. Rental of reusable pallets and containers.

Leg. Issues: ENV, NAT, TAX, WAS

In-house, DC-area Employees

CAMERON, Scott J.: Director, Government and Regulatory Affairs

Outside Counsel/Consultants

E. Del Smith and Co.

Cherokee Investment Partners, LLC

Leg. Issues: ENV, RES

Outside Counsel/Consultants

Capital Consultants Corp.
Issues: ENV, RES
Rep By: Seth Barnhard, Michael David Kaiser, Wayne Scholl

Chesapeake Bay Foundation

Annapolis, MD
Leg. Issues: BUD, ENV, NAT

Outside Counsel/Consultants

Patton Boggs, LLP
Issues: ENV, NAT
Rep By: Parker Brugge, R. Brian Hendrix

Van Scoyoc Associates, Inc.
Issues: BUD
Rep By: Kevin F. Kelly, Jasper Thomson, H. Stewart Van Scoyoc

Chesapeake Bay Maritime Museum

St. Michaels, MD
Leg. Issues: BUD, EDU, ENV, MAR, TOU

Outside Counsel/Consultants

Kimberly Consulting, LLC
Issues: BUD, EDU, ENV, MAR, TOU
Rep By: Richard H. Kimberly

Chesapeake Corp.

Richmond, VA
Leg. Issues: ENV

Outside Counsel/Consultants

Terpstra Associates
Issues: ENV
Rep By: Grace Terpstra

Chevron Chemical Co., LLC

Houston, TX
Leg. Issues: TRD

Outside Counsel/Consultants

Jefferson-Waterman Internat'l, LLC
Issues: TRD
Rep By: Samuel M. Hoskinson

The Chevron Companies

1401 I St. NW
Suite 1200
Washington, DC 20005-2225
E-mail: info@chevron.com
Tel: (202)408-5800
Fax: (202)408-5845
Registered: LDA

Subsidiary of Chevron Corp. Headquartered in San Francisco, CA.

Leg. Issues: CAW, FUE, TAX

In-house, DC-area Employees

BEYE, Mamadou: International Relations Representative
BLANCHARD, Judith A.: Federal Relation Manager
CAVANAUGH, Philip T.: V. President, Government Relations
FAGER, Dan L.: Federal Relations Manager
HAYDEN, Jr., Ludwig: Federal Relations Manager
HOPKINS, Mark D.: Federal Relations Manager
IRWIN, William: International Relations Manager
OMOREGIE, Zuwa: Director, International Relations
SEDNEY, Diana: International Relations Manager

Outside Counsel/Consultants

McDermott, Will and Emery
Issues: TAX
Rep By: Robert B. Harding

Pillsbury Winthrop LLP
Issues: CAW

Chevron Petroleum Marketers Ass'n

Bel Air, MD

Outside Counsel/Consultants

Bassman, Mitchell & Alfano

Chevron, U.S.A.

1401 I St. NW
Suite 1200
Washington, DC 20005
Web: www.chevron.com
Tel: (202)408-5800
Fax: (202)408-5845
Registered: LDA
Leg. Issues: BAN, BUD, CAW, ENG, ENV, FUE, GOV, LBR, MAR, NAT, TAX, TRD, WAS

In-house, DC-area Employees

CAVANAUGH, Philip T.: General Manager
FAGER, Dan L.
HAYDEN, Jr., Ludwig
HOPKINS, Mark D.

Outside Counsel/Consultants

The Bellamy Law Firm, P.C.
Issues: TRD
Rep By: Lorenzo Bellamy

Downey McGrath Group, Inc.
Issues: FUE
Rep By: Elaine B. Acevedo, Nancy Donaldson, Hon. Thomas J. Downey, Jr., Hon. Raymond J. McGrath

Lent Scrivner & Roth LLC
Issues: ENV
Rep By: Norman F. Lent, III, Hon. Norman F. Lent, Alan J. Roth, Michael S. Scrivner

Chevy Chase Bank, F.S.B.

Chevy Chase, MD

Provides financial services to individuals and businesses, including deposit, lending and investment services.

Leg. Issues: BAN

Outside Counsel/Consultants

Miller & Chevalier, Chartered
Issues: BAN
Rep By: Leonard Bickwit, Jr.

Shaw Pittman
Issues: BAN
Rep By: Scott A. Anenberg, Thomas J. Spulak, Andrew L. Woods

Cheyenne and Arapahoe Tribes of Oklahoma

Concho, OK
Leg. Issues: IND

Outside Counsel/Consultants

Holland & Knight LLP
Issues: IND
Rep By: Hon. Gerald E. Sikorski

Cheyenne River Sioux Tribe

Eagle Butte, SD
Leg. Issues: IND

Outside Counsel/Consultants

Van Ness Feldman, P.C.
Issues: IND
Rep By: Daniel S. Press

Cheyne Walk Trust

Reno, NV

Outside Counsel/Consultants

Vinson & Elkins L.L.P.
Rep By: John E. Chapoton, Christine L. Vaughn

Chibank Service Inc.

Chicago, IL
Leg. Issues: BAN

Outside Counsel/Consultants

Richard R. Thaxton
Issues: BAN
Rep By: Richard R. Thaxton

Chicago Board of Trade

1455 Pennsylvania Ave. NW
Suite 1225
Washington, DC 20004
Tel: (202)783-1190
Fax: (202)347-5835
Registered: LDA
Leg. Issues: AGR, FIN, TAX, TRD

Political Action Committee/s

Auction Markets Political Action Committee of the Chicago Board of Trade (AMPAC/CBT)

1455 Pennsylvania Ave. NW
Suite 1225
Washington, DC 20004
Contact: Julie Bauer
Tel: (202)783-1190
Fax: (202)347-5835

In-house, DC-area Employees

BAUER, Julie: Director, Government Relations
JURKOVICH, Celesta S.: Senior V. President, Government Relations

Outside Counsel/Consultants

Davis & Harman LLP
Issues: TAX
Rep By: Thomas A. Davis

Kirkland & Ellis
Issues: FIN
Rep By: Mark D. Young

McLeod, Watkinson & Miller
Issues: AGR, TRD
Rep By: Michael R. McLeod

Sidley & Austin
Issues: TAX

Chicago Board Options Exchange

Chicago, IL
Leg. Issues: BAN

Outside Counsel/Consultants

Bergner Bockorny Castagnetti and Hawkins
Issues: BAN
Rep By: Jeffrey T. Bergner, David A. Bockorny, David Castagnetti, James W. Hawkins, Alvin B. Jackson, Brenda Benjamin Reese, Melissa Schulman

Chicago Botanic Garden

Glencoe, IL
Leg. Issues: BUD, ENV, NAT

Outside Counsel/Consultants

Metcalf Federal Relations
Issues: BUD, ENV, NAT
Rep By: Anne Metcalf

Chicago Deferred Exchange Corp.

Chicago, IL
Leg. Issues: TAX

Outside Counsel/Consultants

Williams & Jensen, P.C.
Issues: TAX
Rep By: David E. Franasiak

Chicago Global, Ltd.

Chicago, IL

Outside Counsel/Consultants

The Campo Group, Ltd.
Rep By: Terry T. Campo

Chicago Mercantile Exchange

1299 Pennsylvania Ave. NW
Suite 1175
Washington, DC 20004
Tel: (202)638-3838
Fax: (202)638-5799
Registered: LDA

A leading financial futures and options exchange with offices in Chicago, Washington, London, and Tokyo. Headquartered in Chicago, IL.

Leg. Issues: AGR, FIN, TAX

Political Action Committee/s

Chicago Mercantile Exchange PAC (CME/PAC)

1299 Pennsylvania Ave. NW
Suite 1175
Washington, DC 20004
Contact: Heather McFarland

In-house, DC-area Employees

FRAZIER, Lita: Director, Government Relations
MAYCUMBER, Jill: Manager, Regulatory and Legislative Affairs

Outside Counsel/Consultants

Bryan Cave LLP
Rep By: Hon. Alan J. Dixon

Lesher & Russell, Inc.
Issues: AGR, FIN
Rep By: William G. Lesher, Randall M. Russell

The PMA Group
Issues: AGR, FIN
Rep By: Fred J. Clark, Kaylene Green, Paul J. Magliocchetti, Timothy K. Sanders

Sidley & Austin
Issues: TAX

Chicago Regional Transportation Authority

Chicago, IL
Leg. Issues: BUD, TRA

Outside Counsel/Consultants

Law Office of Edward D. Heffernan
Issues: BUD, TRA

Chicago School Reform Board of Trustees

Chicago, IL
Leg. Issues: ALC, BUD, EDU, FOO, TEC

Outside Counsel/Consultants

Charles L. Pizer
Issues: ALC, BUD, EDU, FOO, TEC
Rep By: Charles L. Pizer

Chicago Southshore and South Bend Railroad

Michigan City, IN
Leg. Issues: RRR

Outside Counsel/Consultants

Fisher Consulting
Issues: RRR
Rep By: Steven A. Fisher

Chicago State University

Chicago, IL
Leg. Issues: BUD, EDU

Outside Counsel/Consultants

Dean Blakey & Moskowitz
Issues: EDU
Rep By: William A. Blakey

Van Scoyoc Associates, Inc.
Issues: BUD, EDU
Rep By: Anita R. Estell, Kimberly Johnson, H. Stewart Van Scoyoc

Chicago Stock Exchange, Inc.

Chicago, IL
Leg. Issues: FIN

Outside Counsel/Consultants

Mayer, Brown & Platt
Issues: FIN
Rep By: Penny L. Eastman, Mark H. Gitenstein

Chicago Title & Trust Co.

Chicago, IL
Leg. Issues: FIN, INS

Outside Counsel/Consultants

Preston Gates Ellis & Rouvelas Meeds LLP
Issues: FIN, INS
Rep By: Susan B. Geiger, Emanuel L. Rouvelas

Chicago Title Insurance

Leg. Issues: FIN, INS

Outside Counsel/Consultants

Preston Gates Ellis & Rouvelas Meeds LLP
Issues: FIN, INS
Rep By: Susan B. Geiger, Emanuel L. Rouvelas, Steven R. "Rick" Valentine

Chicago Transit Authority

Chicago, IL
Leg. Issues: TRA

Outside Counsel/Consultants

The Wexler Group
Issues: TRA
Rep By: Patrick J. McCann

Chicago Trust Co.

Chicago, IL
Leg. Issues: TAX

Outside Counsel/Consultants

Greenberg Traurig, LLP
Issues: TAX
Rep By: James F. Miller

Chicago, Illinois, Department of Law, City of

Chicago, IL
Leg. Issues: AVI

Outside Counsel/Consultants

Winthrop, Stimson, Putnam & Roberts
Issues: AVI
Rep By: Kenneth P. Quinn

Chicago, Illinois, Department of the Environment of the City of

Chicago, IL
Leg. Issues: URB

Outside Counsel/Consultants

LMRC, Inc.
Issues: URB
Rep By: Mia O'Connell

Chicago, Illinois, Washington Office of the City of

1301 Pennsylvania Ave. NW
Suite 404
Washington, DC 20004-1727
Web: www.ci.chi.il.us
Tel: (202)783-0911
Fax: (202)783-3524

Leg. Issues: ROD, URB

In-house, DC-area Employees

GLUNZ, Kathleen: Deputy Director
MICHAUD, Jay: Deputy Director
POWELL, Aquila: Associate Director
WHITTON, Laura Y.: Deputy Director
YUDIN, David E.: Director

Outside Counsel/Consultants

LMRC, Inc.
Issues: ROD, URB
Rep By: Mia O'Connell

Chicago, Regional Transportation Authority of

Chicago, IL

Outside Counsel/Consultants

Winston & Strawn
Rep By: Douglas C. Richardson

Chicanos Por La Causa

Phoenix, AZ

Outside Counsel/Consultants

Robert A. Rapoza Associates
Rep By: Robert A. Rapoza

The Child Care Consortium

Conyers, GA
Leg. Issues: AGR, EDU, WEL

Outside Counsel/Consultants

Smith, Bucklin and Associates, Inc.
Issues: AGR, EDU, WEL
Rep By: Frank M. Moore, Stacey Moye

Child Care Institute of America, Inc.

Kansas City, MO

Outside Counsel/Consultants

Associated Child Care Consultants, Ltd.

William J. Tobin and Associates

Child Nutrition Forum, c/o FRAC

1875 Connecticut Ave. NW
Suite 540
Washington, DC 20009
Web: www.frac.org
E-mail: eteller@frac.org
Tel: (202)986-2200
Fax: (202)986-2525

Leg. Issues: AGR, EDU, WEL

In-house, DC-area Employees

TELLER, Ellen S.: Director, Government Affairs

Child Welfare League of America

440 First St. NW
Third Floor
Washington, DC 20001-2085
Web: www.cwla.org
Tel: (202)638-2952
Fax: (202)638-4004
Registered: LDA

An association of over 1,100 public and not-for-profit agencies devoted to improving life for at-risk kids and their families.

Leg. Issues: ALC, BUD, CIV, CPT, FAM, GOV, HCR, HOU, IND, LAW, LBR, MMM, TAX, TOB, TOR, WEL

In-house, DC-area Employees

ALLEN, Barbara: Senior Policy Analyst
BILCHIK, Shay: Exec. Director
BRICELAND-BETTS, Timothy: Senior Policy Analyst
JOHNSON, Joyce L.: Press Secretary
MEITNER, Elizabeth M.: Public Policy Director
SCIAMANNA, John M.: Senior Policy Analyst

Outside Counsel/Consultants

Venable
Issues: CPT, GOV, LBR, TAX, TOR
Rep By: Jeffrey S. Tenenbaum

Children and Adults with Attention Deficit Disorders (CHADD)

Plantation, FL
Leg. Issues: BUD, DEF, EDU, HCR

Outside Counsel/Consultants

Arent Fox Kintner Plotkin & Kahn, PLLC
Issues: BUD, DEF, EDU, HCR
Rep By: Elliott I. Portnoy

Children's Action Network

Los Angeles, CA

A nationwide coalition of health- and youth-related organizations sponsoring the National Immunization Campaign, whose goal is to increase access to immunization services through public education and grassroots organization.

Outside Counsel/Consultants

Greer, Margolis, Mitchell, Burns & Associates
Rep By: Jim Margolis, Elizabeth Riel

The Children's Cause Inc.

Brooklyn, NY
Leg. Issues: BUD, HCR, MED, MMM

Outside Counsel/Consultants

Bennett Turner & Coleman, LLP
Issues: BUD, HCR, MED, MMM
Rep By: Elizabeth Goss, Kristi E. Schrode, Samuel D. Turner

Children's Defense Fund

25 E St. NW
Washington, DC 20001
Tel: (202)628-8787
Fax: (202)662-3580
Registered: LDA
Web: www.childrensdefense.org

An organization concerned with promoting preventive investment policies for children and youth. Major program areas are: education, child health and mental health, child welfare, child care and family support,juvenile crime prevention and adolescent pregnancy prevention. Through research, public education, litigation, monitoring federal administrative policies and assistance to state and community organizations and parents, CDF seeks to improve policies and practices resulting in the neglect or mistreatment of children of all races and classes.

Leg. Issues: BUD, CIV, ECN, EDU, FAM, FIR, GOV, HCR, HOU, LAW, LBR, MMM, TAX, TOB, WEL

In-house, DC-area Employees

ALLEN, MaryLee: Director, Child Welfare and Mental Health
BLANK, Helen: Director, Child Care
EDELMAN, Marian Wright: President
GLUCK, Adam: Senior House Associate
HAIFLEY, Gregg: Senior Health Associate
LEWIS, Peggy: Director, Communications
MARTINEZ, Susanne M.: Director, Programs and Policy Department
REEF, Grace: Director, Department of Intergovernmental Relations
WEINSTEIN, Deborah: Director, Family Income Division

Children's Foundation

725 15th St. NW
Suite 505
Washington, DC 20005
Tel: (202)347-3300
Fax: (202)347-3382
E-mail: cfwashdc@aol.com

A national, non-profit organization working on issues of child care, child nutrition and child support enforcement. Conducts research on regulations for home-based or family day care providers and child care centers, and publishes annual studies on each. Provides information to parents seeking child care and to child care providers on job-specific problems. Offers information to family day care providers about the federal Child Care Food Program. (All child care materials available in Spanish.) Offers information to custodial parents seeking to collect court-ordered child support. Publications list available upon request.

In-house, DC-area Employees

HOLLESTELLE, Kay: Exec. Director

Children's Health Fund

New York, NY
Leg. Issues: HCR

Outside Counsel/Consultants

Boesch & Co.
Issues: HCR
Rep By: Doyce A. Boesch

Children's Hospice Internat'l

2202 Mount Vernon Ave.
Suite 3C
Alexandria, VA 22301
Tel: (703)684-0330
Fax: (703)684-0226
Web: www.chionline.org

Shares expertise and information with health care professionals, families and organizations within communities that offer care to children with life-threatening conditions and their families.

In-house, DC-area Employees

ARMSTRONG-DAILEY, Ann: Founding Director

Outside Counsel/Consultants

Arnold & Porter

Children's Hospital and Health Center of San Diego

San Diego, CA
Leg. Issues: BUD

Outside Counsel/Consultants

Copeland, Lowery & Jacquez
Issues: BUD
Rep By: Hon. William D. Lowery, Jeffrey S. Shockey

Children's Hospital and Medical Center

Seattle, WA
Leg. Issues: BUD, HCR, MMM

Outside Counsel/Consultants

Smith Dawson & Andrews, Inc.
Issues: BUD, HCR, MMM
Rep By: Sherri Powar, James P. Smith

Children's Hospital Foundation

Outside Counsel/Consultants

R. Duffy Wall and Associates

Children's Hospital Los Angeles

Los Angeles, CA

Outside Counsel/Consultants

Copeland, Lowery & Jacquez
Rep By: Hon. William D. Lowery, Jeffrey S. Shockey

Children's Hospital Medical Center Foundation

Oakland, CA

Outside Counsel/Consultants

Jefferson Government Relations, L.L.C.

Children's Hospital of Boston

Boston, MA
Registered: LDA
Leg. Issues: BUD, HCR, MED

Outside Counsel/Consultants

Health Policy Strategies
Issues: BUD, HCR, MED
Rep By: Ann Langley

Children's Hospital of Wisconsin

Milwaukee, WI
Leg. Issues: BUD, HCR, MMM

Outside Counsel/Consultants

Broydrick & Associates
Issues: BUD, HCR, MMM
Rep By: William Broydrick, Amy Demske

Children's Mercy Hospital

Kansas City, MO
Leg. Issues: MMM

Outside Counsel/Consultants

Baker & Hostetler LLP
Issues: MMM
Rep By: Frederick H. Graefe

Children's Nat'l Medical Center

111 Michigan Ave. NW
Washington, DC 20010
Tel: (202)884-4933
Fax: (202)884-5988
Web: www.dcchildrens.com

In-house, DC-area Employees

BOWENS, Jacqueline D.: V. President, Government and Public Affairs

Children's Rights Council

300 I St. NE
Suite 401
Washington, DC 20002
Tel: (202)547-6227
Fax: (202)546-4272
Web: www.gocrc.com
E-mail: crcdc@erols.com

A national, non-profit organization of professional and lay members assisting children and families of divorce and separation. Particular attention is paid to issues surrounding a child's right to have access to both parents after divorce or separation. Alternate web address at www.info4parents.com

Leg. Issues: DOC, FAM, GOV

In-house, DC-area Employees

LEVY, David L.: President

Chile, Government of the Republic of

Santiago, CHILE

Outside Counsel/Consultants

O'Melveny and Myers LLP
Rep By: Gary N. Horlick

Chilean Exporters Ass'n

Santiago, CHILE
Leg. Issues: AGR

Outside Counsel/Consultants

Akin, Gump, Strauss, Hauer & Feld, L.L.P.
Lepon McCarthy White & Holzworth, PLLC
Issues: AGR
Rep By: David A. Holzworth

Chilean Salmon Farmers Ass'n

Santiago, CHILE

Outside Counsel/Consultants

Arnold & Porter

CHIM

Ann Arbor, MI
Leg. Issues: CPI, HCR

Outside Counsel/Consultants

The PMA Group
Issues: CPI, HCR
Rep By: Kaylene Green, Paul J. Magliocchetti, Kelli Short, Brian Thiel

China Eastern Airlines

Shanghai, CHINA (PEOPLE'S REPUBLIC)
Leg. Issues: AVI, TOR, TOU, TRD

Outside Counsel/Consultants

Cohen, Gettings & Dunham, PC
Issues: AVI, TOR, TOU, TRD
Rep By: Carroll E. Dubuc

China Ocean Shipping Co.

Shanghai, CHINA (PEOPLE'S REPUBLIC)

Outside Counsel/Consultants

Garvey, Schubert & Barer
Rep By: Richard D. Gluck

China Shipping (Group) Co.

Outside Counsel/Consultants

Dyer Ellis & Joseph, P.C.
Rep By: Joseph O. Click, James S. W. Drewry, Thomas M. Dyer, Brett M. Esber, Duncan C. Smith, III, Jennifer M. Southwick

China, Board of Foreign Trade of the Republic of

Taipei, CHINA (TAIWAN)

Outside Counsel/Consultants

Ablondi, Foster, Sobin & Davidow, P.C.
Crowell & Moring LLP

China, Directorate General of Telecommunications, Ministry of Communications of the Republic of

Taipei, CHINA (TAIWAN)

Outside Counsel/Consultants

Schiff Hardin & Waite
Rep By: Gearold L. Knowles

China, Embassy of the People's Republic of

2300 Connecticut Ave. NW
Washington, DC 20008
Tel: (202)328-2500
Fax: (202)588-0032
Web: www.china-embassy.org
E-mail: chinaembassy-us@fmprc.gov.cn
Leg. Issues: TRD

Outside Counsel/Consultants

Jones, Day, Reavis & Pogue
Rep By: Herbert J. Hansell

Powell, Goldstein, Frazer & Murphy LLP
Issues: TRD
Rep By: Alice Slayton Clark, Maria DiGiulian, Gretchen Effgen, Brenda A. Jacobs

China.com

Hong Kong, CHINA (PEOPLE'S REPUBLIC)
Leg. Issues: SCI

Outside Counsel/Consultants

Capital Strategies Group, Inc.
Issues: SCI
Rep By: Tammi Hayes

Chino Hills, California, City of

Leg. Issues: TRA

Outside Counsel/Consultants

E. Del Smith and Co.
Issues: TRA
Rep By: Margaret Allen, E. Del Smith

Chino, California, City of

Outside Counsel/Consultants

Murray, Scheer, Montgomery, Tapia & O'Donnell
Rep By: Raul R. Tapia

Chippewa Cree Tribe

Box Elder, MT

Outside Counsel/Consultants

George Waters Consulting Service
Rep By: George Waters

Chiquita Brands Internat'l, Inc.

Cincinnati, OH
Leg. Issues: TRD

Outside Counsel/Consultants

Akin, Gump, Strauss, Hauer & Feld, L.L.P.

BSMG Worldwide

McDermott, Will and Emery
Issues: TRD
Rep By: Carolyn B. Gleason, Jerry C. Hill

Podesta/Mattoon
Rep By: Ann Delory, Matthew Gelman, Kristen Leary

Chitimacha Tribe of Louisiana

Charenton, LA
Leg. Issues: IND

Outside Counsel/Consultants

Greenberg Traurig, LLP
Rep By: Jack Abramoff

Preston Gates Ellis & Rouvelas Meeds LLP
Issues: IND
Rep By: Jonathan Blank, Werner W. Brandt, Hon. David Funderburk, Daniel Ritter, Emanuel L. Rouvelas, W. Dennis Stephens, Steven R. "Rick" Valentine

Chlorine Chemistry Council

1300 Wilson Blvd.
Arlington, VA 22209
Tel: (703)741-5850
Fax: (703)741-6084
Registered: LDA
Web: www.c3.org
Leg. Issues: AGR, CAW, CHM, ENV

In-house, DC-area Employees

CHRISTMAN, Keith A.: Director, Disinfection and Government Relations
FLYNN, Janet F.: Director, Public Affairs
HOWLETT, Jr., C. T. "Kip": V. President and Exec. Director
HURD, Frank: Managing Director, Operations and Finance and Director, Government Relations
LAPKIN, Ted: Senior Public Policy Analyst
MASON, Ann M.: Director, Science and Regulatory Policy
MERRILL, Greg: Director, State Chlorine Issues
STEARNS, Joe: Director, International Affairs

Outside Counsel/Consultants

Cassidy & Associates, Inc.
Issues: AGR
Rep By: Jeffrey Lawrence, Arthur D. Mason, Dan C. Tate, Sr.

EOP Group, Inc.
Rep By: Joseph Hezir, Michael O'Bannon

Goddard Claussen

Hogan & Hartson L.L.P.
Issues: CHM
Rep By: William Michael House, Christine M. Warnke

McGlotten & Jarvis
Issues: CAW
Rep By: John T. Jarvis

Millian Byers Associates, LLC
Rep By: H. James Byers, Kenneth Y. Millian

Venable
Issues: CHM
Rep By: Brock R. Landry

Verner, Liipfert, Bernhard, McPherson and Hand, Chartered
Issues: ENV
Rep By: Rosemary B. Freeman, Stanley W. Legro, John H. Sterne, Jr.

Chlorine Institute

2001 L St. NW
Suite 506
Washington, DC 20036-4919
Tel: (202)775-2790
Fax: (202)223-7225
Web: www.cl2.com

In-house, DC-area Employees

BATES, Gardner: Director, Public & Member Communications
DUNGAN, Arthur E.: V. Pres., Safety, Health & Environment
LYDEN, Michael E.: V. Pres., Storage and Transportation
SMERKO, Robert G.: President
TROJAK, Gary F.: V. President, Packaging & Technical Services

Outside Counsel/Consultants

LaRoe, Winn, Moerman & Donovan
Rep By: Paul M. Donovan

Chlorobenzene Producers Ass'n

1850 M St. NW
Suite 700
Washington, DC 20036
Tel: (202)721-4145
Fax: (202)296-8120

A trade association for producers of chlorobenzenes.

In-house, DC-area Employees

KORDOSKI, Ph.D, Edward W.: Exec. Director

Outside Counsel/Consultants

Paul, Hastings, Janofsky & Walker LLP
Rep By: R. Bruce Dickson, P. Susan Lively

Chocolate Manufacturers Ass'n of the U.S.A.

8320 Old Courthouse Rd.
Suite 300
Vienna, VA 22182
Tel: (703)790-5011
Fax: (703)790-5752
Registered: LDA
Web: www.candyusa.org/who_cma.html
Leg. Issues: AGR, FOO, WEL

In-house, DC-area Employees

GRAHAM, Lawrence T.: President
LODGE, Stephen G.: V. President, Legislative Affairs
SMITH, Susan Snyder: V. President, Public Affairs

Outside Counsel/Consultants

Olsson, Frank and Weeda, P.C.
Issues: AGR, FOO, WEL
Rep By: John W. Bode, Richard L. Frank, Susan P. Grymes, Karen Reis Harned, Stephen L. Lacey, Marshall L. Matz, Tyson Redpath, Ryan W. Stroschein

Chocolate, Biscuit and Confectionery Industries of the European Community

Brussels, BELGIUM

Outside Counsel/Consultants

Max N. Berry Law Offices

Choctaw Indians, Mississippi Band of

Philadelphia, MS
Leg. Issues: IND

Outside Counsel/Consultants

Greenberg Traurig, LLP
Rep By: Jack Abramoff

Hobbs, Straus, Dean and Walker, LLP
Issues: IND
Rep By: Carol L. Barbero, S. Bobo Dean, Karen J. Funk, Marie Osceola-Branch, Michael L. Roy, Jerry C. Straus, Joseph H. Webster

Choctaw Nation of Oklahoma

Durant, OK
Leg. Issues: IND

Outside Counsel/Consultants

Evergreen Associates, Ltd.
Issues: IND
Rep By: Robert M. Brooks

SENSE, INC.
Rep By: C. Juliet Pittman

ChoicePoint

Alpharetta, GA
Leg. Issues: BAN, BNK

Outside Counsel/Consultants

Mullenholz, Brimsek & Belair
Issues: BAN
Rep By: Robert R. Belair, Susan C. Haller

Van Scoyoc Associates, Inc.
Issues: BNK

The Choral Arts Soc. of Washington

Washington, DC
Leg. Issues: ART

Outside Counsel/Consultants

Chernikoff and Co.
Issues: ART
Rep By: Larry B. Chernikoff

Chris-Craft Broadcasting, Inc.

1101 Connecticut Ave. NW
Suite 900
Washington, DC 20036
Tel: (202)828-2300
Fax: (202)828-2322

In-house, DC-area Employees

GIESE, Robert B.: V. President and Counsel

Christian Broadcasting Network

Lynchburg, VA

Outside Counsel/Consultants

Shaw Pittman
Rep By: Clifford M. Harrington

Christian Coalition of America

499 S. Capitol St. SW
Suite 615
Washington, DC 20003
Tel: (202)479-6900
Fax: (202)479-4260
Registered: LDA
Web: www.cc.org

The Washington office of a conservative political action group based in Chesapeake, Virginia. Founded by Pat Robertson. Represents its 1.7 million members on a variety of issues including taxation, crime, education, and abortion.

Leg. Issues: ART, COM, DEF, FAM, GAM, GOV, HCR, LAW, REL, TAX

In-house, DC-area Employees

COMBS, Roberta: Exec. V. President
MUSKETT, Susan T.: Government Relations Representative

Christian Legal Soc.

4208 Evergreen Ln.
Suite 222
Annandale, VA 22003
Tel: (703)642-1070
Fax: (703)642-1075
Registered: LDA
Web: www.christianlegalsociety.org
E-mail: clshq@clsnet.org

A national grassroots network of lawyers and law students committed to proclaiming, loving and serving Jesus Christ in the practice of law and advocating biblical conflict reconciliation, public justice, religious freedom and the sanctity of human life.

Leg. Issues: CIV, FAM

In-house, DC-area Employees

BAYLOR, Gregory S.: Associate Director, Center for Law and Religious Freedom
ESBECK, Carl H.: Director, Center for Law and Religious Freedom

Christian Network, Inc.

Clearwater, FL
Leg. Issues: COM, REL

Outside Counsel/Consultants

Alcalde & Fay
Issues: COM, REL
Rep By: Jim Davenport, Vicki L. Iseman, Julie Patterson

Christian Voice, Inc.

Alexandria, VA
Leg. Issues: CIV, CPI, EDU, FAM, FOR, HCR, MMM, REL, RET, WEL

Outside Counsel/Consultants

Jar-Mon Consultants, Inc.
Issues: CIV, CPI, EDU, FAM, FOR, HCR, MMM, REL, RET, WEL

Christians' Israel Public Action Campaign, Inc.

2013 Q St. NW
Washington, DC 20009-1009
Tel: (202)234-3600
Fax: (202)332-3221
Registered: LDA
E-mail: rahmercl@tidalwave.net

The only nationwide Christian organization registered with the Congress to address elected officials regarding a strong U.S.-Israel relationship and related issues. Educates the American Christian community about current events affecting Israel and the Middle East. Promotes sound, biblical, U.S. laws and policies toward that region of the world.

In-house, DC-area Employees

HELLMAN, Richard A.: President and Exec. Director

Christopher Newport University

Newport News, VA
Leg. Issues: EDU

Outside Counsel/Consultants

Jefferson Government Relations, L.L.C.
Issues: EDU
Rep By: Mark S. Greenberg, William A. Roberts

Christus Health

Houston, TX
Leg. Issues: HCR, TRA

Outside Counsel/Consultants

Advantage Associates, Inc.
Issues: HCR, TRA
Rep By: Hon. Bill Sarpalius

Christus Santa Rosa Hospital

San Antonio, TX

Outside Counsel/Consultants

Arter & Hadden

Chromalloy Gas Turbine Corp.

Austin, TX

Outside Counsel/Consultants

Shaw Pittman
Rep By: Sheryl R. Israel, J. E. Murdock, III

Chrome Coalition

Outside Counsel/Consultants

Collier Shannon Scott, PLLC
Rep By: Kathryn M. T. McMahon, John L. Wittenborn

Chronic Fatigue and Immune Dysfunction Syndrome Ass'n of America

Charlotte, NC
Leg. Issues: BUD, MED

Outside Counsel/Consultants

The Sheridan Group
Issues: BUD, MED
Rep By: Mary Beth Buchholz, Thomas F. Sheridan

The Chubb Corp.

One Massachusetts Ave. NW
Suite 350
Washington, DC 20001
Tel: (202)408-8123
Fax: (202)296-7683
Registered: LDA
Web: www.chubb.com

An insurance holding company.

Leg. Issues: AUT, BAN, BNK, BUD, CPI, CSP, DIS, ENV, FAM, FIN, INS, LBR, RET, TAX, TOB, TOR, TRD

In-house, DC-area Employees

CONWAY, Daniel: Senior V. President
FREE, Brant: Senior V. President and Director, Internat'l External Affairs
KORKUCH, Marylou: Assistant V. President
MULLIGAN, Robert: Assistant V. President

Outside Counsel/Consultants

Baker & Hostetler LLP
Issues: INS, TAX
Rep By: William F. Conroy, Matthew J. Dolan, Frederick H. Graefe, Steven A. Lotterer, David L. Marshall, Hon. Guy Vander Jagt

Campbell Crane & Associates
Issues: BAN, DIS, ENV, TAX, TOR
Rep By: Jeanne M. Campbell, Daniel M. Crane

Caplin & Drysdale, Chartered
Issues: INS, TAX
Rep By: Seth Green, Daniel B. Rosenbaum

Julia J. Norrell & Associates
Issues: AUT, BAN, BNK, BUD, CPI, CSP, DIS, ENV, FAM, FIN, INS, LBR, RET, TAX, TOB, TRD
Rep By: Julia J. Norrell

Quinn Gillespie & Associates
Issues: INS, TRD
Rep By: Jeffrey J. Connaughton, John M. "Jack" Quinn

Valanzano & Associates
Issues: BAN, CPI, DIS, ENV, TAX, TOB, TRD
Rep By: Anthony Valanzano

Chubu Electric Power Co.

900 17th St. NW
Suite 1220
Washington, DC 20006
Tel: (202)775-1960
Fax: (202)331-9256

An electric utility company headquartered in Nagoya, Japan.

Leg. Issues: UTI

In-house, DC-area Employees

KUZE, Kazunori: Chief Representative

Chuck & Rock Adventure Productions, Inc.

Leg. Issues: ART

Outside Counsel/Consultants

Colling Swift & Hynes
Issues: ART
Rep By: Terese Colling, Pablo Collins, Robert J. Hynes, Jr.

Chugach Alaska Corp.

Anchorage, AK
Leg. Issues: IND

Outside Counsel/Consultants

Zane & Associates
Issues: IND
Rep By: Curtis J. Zane

The Church Alliance

Minneapolis, MN

A coalition of chief executive officers and program administrators of 31 Protestant and Jewish mainline denominations and a Catholic religious order.

Leg. Issues: FIN, HCR, TAX

Outside Counsel/Consultants

Morgan, Lewis & Bockius LLP
Rep By: Helene L. Glick

Williams & Jensen, P.C.
Issues: FIN, HCR, TAX
Rep By: William B. Canfield, David E. Franasiak, J. Steven Hart, George G. Olsen, David A. Starr

Church and Dwight ArmaKleen

Princeton, NJ

Outside Counsel/Consultants

Interface Inc.
Rep By: David C. Knapp

Church of Jesus Christ of Latter Day Saints

Outside Counsel/Consultants

Edelman Public Relations Worldwide
Rep By: Michael K. Deaver, Robert Rehg, Jeffrey Surrell

Church of Scientology Internat'l

1701 20th St. NW
Washington, DC 20009
Tel: (202)667-6404
Fax: (202)667-6314
Web: www.scientology.org
E-mail: osadc@aol.com

Represents the interests of the Church of Scientology before the executive and legislative branches of the federal government. Also handles public relations issues for the Church.

Leg. Issues: ALC, CIV, CSP, EDU, FOR, HCR, MIA

In-house, DC-area Employees

STANARD, Sylvia: Director
TAYLOR, Susan: Director, Public Affairs

Church of the Brethren Washington Office

337 North Carolina Ave. SE
Washington, DC 20003
Tel: (202)546-3202
Fax: (202)544-5852
Web: www.brethren.org/genbd/washofc
E-mail: washofc@aol.com

Headquartered in Elgin, Illinois.

In-house, DC-area Employees

LASZAKOVITS, Greg: Coordinator
RITTLE, Marc: Legislative Associate

Church World Service/Lutheran World Relief

110 Maryland Ave. NE
Building Box 45
Washington, DC 20002
Tel: (202)543-6336
Fax: (202)546-6232
Web: www.nccusa.org
E-mail: lisaw@nccusa.org

In-house, DC-area Employees

WRIGHT, Lisa: Associate Director, International Director and Global Issues

Churchville, New York, Village of

Leg. Issues: COM, GOV

Outside Counsel/Consultants

Duncan, Weinberg, Genzer & Pembroke, P.C.
Issues: COM, GOV
Rep By: Jeffrey C. Genzer, Michael R. Postar

Ciba Specialty Chemicals Corp.

1825 I St. NW
Suite 400
Washington, DC 20006
Tel: (202)857-5200
Fax: (202)857-5219
Registered: LDA
Leg. Issues: CAW, CHM, CSP, ENV, LBR, RRR, TAX, TRD, WAS

Political Action Committee/s

Ciba Specialty Chemicals Corp. Employee Good Government Fund
1825 I St. NW
Suite 400
Washington, DC 20006
Tel: (202)857-5200
Fax: (202)857-5219
Contact: John L. Deming

In-house, DC-area Employees

DEMING, John L.: V. President, Government Affairs

Outside Counsel/Consultants

The Accord Group
Issues: CHM, ENV, TRD
Rep By: Robert F. Hurley

Millian Byers Associates, LLC

Cigar Ass'n of America

1707 H St. NW
Suite 800
Washington, DC 20006
Tel: (202)223-8204
Fax: (202)833-0379
Registered: LDA
Leg. Issues: TAX, TOB

Political Action Committee/s

Cigar Political Action Committee
1707 H St. NW
Suite 800
Washington, DC 20006
Tel: (202)223-8204
Fax: (202)833-0379
Contact: Norman F. Sharp

In-house, DC-area Employees

SHARP, Norman F.: President

Outside Counsel/Consultants

Dickstein Shapiro Morin & Oshinsky LLP
Issues: TOB
Rep By: Henry C. Cashen, II, Hon. Wendell H. Ford, Elizabeth B. Haywood, Robert Mangas, Graham "Rusty" Mathews, Laurie McKay, Hon. Stanford E. Parris, Rebecah Moore Shepherd, L. Andrew Zausner

PriceWaterhouseCoopers
Issues: TAX
Rep By: Kenneth J. Kies, Pat Raffaniello

CIGNA Corp.

2001 Pennsylvania Ave. NW
Suite 350
Washington, DC 20006-1825
Tel: (202)296-7174
Fax: (202)296-2521
Registered: LDA

A major healthcare and related financial services company formed by the merger of Connecticut General Life Insurance Co. and INA in 1982.

Leg. Issues: BUD, CSP, ENV, FIN, FOR, HCR, INS, MMM, RET, SCI, TAX, TRD

In-house, DC-area Employees

CALDWELL, Barry H.: V. President, Government Relations
JACOBS, Lynn S.: V. President, Government Affairs
LIFSON, Arthur: V. President, Federal Affairs

Outside Counsel/Consultants

Bonner & Associates

Columbus Public Affairs
Issues: FOR, HCR, SCI
Rep By: James P. Keese, III

Crowell & Moring LLP
Issues: CSP
Rep By: Victor E. Schwartz

Davis & Harman LLP
Issues: TAX
Rep By: Richard S. Belas

HeideprIem & Mager, Inc.
Rep By: Lisa Foster, Nikki Heidepriem

Multinat'l Government Services, Inc.
Issues: BUD, HCR
Rep By: Warren Feldman, Eric Stas, Jim J. Tozzi

O'Melveny and Myers LLP
Issues: FOR, INS, TRD
Rep By: Donald T. Bliss, William T. Coleman, Jr., Gary N. Horlick, Elisabeth Layton, David Litt

R. Duffy Wall and Associates
Issues: HCR
Rep By: Hon. Bill Brewster, Ann Thomas G. Johnston

Williams & Jensen, P.C.
Issues: ENV, HCR, TAX
Rep By: George D. Baker, David E. Franasiak, Robert E. Glennon, Jr., J. Steven Hart, Karen Judd Lewis, George G. Olsen, Anthony J. Roda

Cincinnati Stock Exchange

Cincinnati, OH
Leg. Issues: FIN

Outside Counsel/Consultants

Thelen Reid & Priest LLP
Issues: FIN
Rep By: Edward L. Pittman, Ambari Prakash, Alan J. Reed, Richard Y. Roberts

Cincinnati, Ohio, City of

Leg. Issues: AVI, BUD, EDU, HOU, LBR, POS, RES, TAX, TOU, TRA, URB

Outside Counsel/Consultants

Patton Boggs, LLP
Issues: AVI, BUD, EDU, HOU, LBR, POS, RES, TAX, TOU, TRA, URB
Rep By: Shannon M. Gibson, Hon. Willis "Bill" D. Gradison, Florence W. Prioleau

CINE

1001 Connecticut Ave. NW
Suite 625
Washington, DC 20036
Web: www.cine.org
Tel: (202)785-1136
Fax: (202)785-4114

Also known as the Council on International Non-Theatrical Events.

In-house, DC-area Employees

WEISS, David: Exec. Director

Cinergy Corp.

1301 Pennsylvania Ave. NW
Suite 1030
Washington, DC 20004
Tel: (202)824-0402
Fax: (202)824-0418
Registered: LDA

Formerly known as PSI Energy, Inc. and the Cincinnati Gas & Electric Co.

Leg. Issues: ENG, ENV, FUE, NAT, TRA, UTI

In-house, DC-area Employees

DAVIS, Sheila: Manager, Federal Government Affairs
DEBOISSIERE, Alex: Manager, Federal Regulatory Affairs

Outside Counsel/Consultants

Alpine Group, Inc.
Issues: ENV
Rep By: James D. Massie

Gallagher, Boland and Meiburger
Issues: ENG, FUE, NAT, TRA, UTI
Rep By: Peter C. Lesch, Steve Stojic

Skadden, Arps, Slate, Meagher & Flom LLP
Rep By: Clifford M. Naeve

Troutman Sanders LLP
Issues: ENG, ENV
Rep By: Thomas C. Jensen, Bonnie Suchman

Cinergy PSI

Plainfield, IN

Outside Counsel/Consultants

Sagamore Associates, Inc.
Rep By: David U. Gogol

Cingular Wireless

1818 N St. NW
Eighth Floor
Washington, DC 20036
Tel: (202)293-1707

In-house, DC-area Employees

ALMOND, Ben G.: Regulatory Affairs
BUGEL, James
FONTES, Brian F.
PALMER, Susan: Regulatory Affairs
PHILLIPS, Barbara L.: Congressional Affairs
WELLS, Kent M.: Congressional Affairs

Circle K Convenience Stores

Stamford, CT
Leg. Issues: TOB

Outside Counsel/Consultants

RFB, Inc.
Issues: TOB
Rep By: Raymond F. Bragg

Circuit City Stores, Inc.

600 13th St. NW
Suite 1200
Washington, DC 20005
Tel: (202)756-8299
Fax: (202)756-8087
Registered: LDA

A retailer of brand-name consumer electronics, major appliances, and used cars and trucks in the U.S. Headquartered in Richmond, Virginia.

Leg. Issues: BNK, HCR, TAX, TEC

In-house, DC-area Employees

SMITH, Kelly L.: Washington Representative

Outside Counsel/Consultants

McDermott, Will and Emery
Rep By: Robert S. Schwartz

Circuit Services, Inc.

Kenner, LA
Leg. Issues: MAN

Outside Counsel/Consultants

The Kemper Co.
Issues: MAN
Rep By: Jackson Kemper, Jr.

Circus Circus Enterprises, Inc.

Las Vegas, NV

Outside Counsel/Consultants

Arter & Hadden
Rep By: Daniel L. Cohen, Hon. Thomas G. Loeffler, Jon W. Plebani

CIS Global

Silver Spring, MD
Leg. Issues: CPI

Outside Counsel/Consultants

Arent Fox Kintner Plotkin & Kahn, PLLC
Issues: CPI
Rep By: Michael T. McNamara, Todd Weiss

Cisco Systems Inc.

601 Pennsylvania Ave. NW
Suite 520
North Bldg.
Washington, DC 20004
Web: www.cisco.com
E-mail: mtimmeny@cisco.com
Tel: (202)661-4000
Fax: (202)661-4041
Registered: LDA

Headquartered in San Jose, CA, Cisco provides end-to-end networking solutions that customers use to build a unified information infrastructure of their own or to connect to someone else's network.

Leg. Issues: BUD, COM, CPI, CPT, EDU, FIN, GOV, MAN, SCI, TAX, TEC, TRD

In-house, DC-area Employees

MEHLMAN, Bruce P.: Assistant Washington Representatives, Policy Counsel
TIMMENY, Michael: Manager, Government Relations

Outside Counsel/Consultants

Harris, Wiltshire & Grannis LLP
Issues: COM, TEC
Rep By: Scott Blake Harris

Quinn Gillespie & Associates

CITGO Petroleum Corp.

Tulsa, OK
Leg. Issues: CAW, ENG, ENV, FUE, MAR

Outside Counsel/Consultants

The Dutko Group, Inc.
Issues: CAW, ENG, ENV, FUE, MAR
Rep By: Mark S. Irion

Citibank, N.A.

New York, NY

Outside Counsel/Consultants

Earle Palmer Brown Public Relations

Wilmer, Cutler & Pickering
Rep By: Marianne K. Smythe

Cities Advocating Emergency AIDS Relief (CAEAR)

Washington, DC
Leg. Issues: BUD

Outside Counsel/Consultants

The Sheridan Group
Issues: BUD
Rep By: Thomas F. Sheridan, Jennifer Vasiloff

Citigroup

1101 Pennsylvania Ave. NW
Suite 1000
Washington, DC 20004
Web: www.citi.com
Tel: (202)879-6800
Fax: (202)783-4460
Registered: LDA

Leg. Issues: BAN, BNK, ENV, FIN, HCR, HOU, LAW, RET, TAX, TEC, TRD

Political Action Committee/s

Citicorp Voluntary Political Fund - Federal

1101 Pennsylvania Ave. NW
Suite 1000
Washington, DC 20004
Contact: Catherine Mahoney
Tel: (202)879-6800
Fax: (202)783-4460

In-house, DC-area Employees

DOWLING, S. Colin: Sr. V. President and Dir., State Government Affairs
FRANK, Abe L.: State Government Relations Deputy Director
JOHNSON, Leah: Director, Public Affairs
JOHNSON, Lionel C.: V. President, International Government Relations
LEVEY, Jeffrey R.: V. President, Director, Tax Legislation
LEVY, Roger N.: S. V. President and Director, Federal Government Relations
MAHONEY, Catherine: Assistant Director, PAC
ROBERTS, Carole T.: V. President, Federal Government Affairs
SHAPIRO, Dina S.: V. President, Deputy Director, Tax Legislation

Outside Counsel/Consultants

Arter & Hadden
Issues: BAN
Rep By: Daniel L. Cohen, Hon. Thomas G. Loeffler, Jon W. Plebani

Baker & Hostetler LLP
Issues: BNK, TAX
Rep By: William F. Conroy, Matthew J. Dolan, Kathleen M. Kerrigan, Steven A. Lotterer, David L. Marshall, Hon. Guy Vander Jagt

Barnett & Sivon, P.C.
Issues: BAN
Rep By: Robert E. Barnett, James C. Sivon

Michael F. Barrett, Jr.
Issues: BAN
Rep By: Michael F. Barrett, Jr.

Campbell Crane & Associates
Issues: TAX
Rep By: Jeanne M. Campbell, Daniel M. Crane

Davis & Harman LLP
Rep By: Randolf H. Hardock, Craig R. Springfield

Dewey Ballantine LLP
Rep By: John J. Salmon

The Direct Impact Co.

Dittus Communications
Rep By: Debra Cabral, Shelton Jones

Heidepriem & Mager, Inc.
Rep By: Nikki Heidepriem

Mayer, Brown & Platt
Issues: TRD
Rep By: Scott Parven

McKay Walker
Issues: TAX
Rep By: Lynda K. Walker

Franklin R. Silbey
Rep By: Franklin R. Silbey

Tighe, Patton, Tabackman & Babbin
Issues: TRD
Rep By: Brent S. Franzel

Verner, Liipfert, Bernhard, McPherson and Hand, Chartered
Issues: ENV, FIN, HCR, RET, TAX
Rep By: Matthew C. Bernstein, Andrew D. Eskin, David B. Jacobsohn, Jenifer Martin, Martin Mendelsohn, John A. Merrigan

Washington Council Ernst & Young
Issues: FIN, TAX
Rep By: Doug Badger, Lauren Darling, John L. Doney, Jayne T. Fitzgerald, LaBrenda Garrett-Nelson, Gary J. Gasper, Bruce A. Gates, Nick Giordano, Cathy Koch, Robert J. Leonard, Richard Meltzer, Phillip D. Moseley, John D. Porter, Robert M. Rozen, Donna Steele-Flynn, Timothy J. Urban

Citizen's Committee to Save the Federal Center

Battle Creek, MI
Leg. Issues: GOV, TRA

Outside Counsel/Consultants

Dykema Gossett PLLC
Issues: GOV, TRA
Rep By: Nancy R. Barbour, Tricia K. Markwood

Citizen's Educational Foundation

Old San Juan, PR

Outside Counsel/Consultants

Akin, Gump, Strauss, Hauer & Feld, L.L.P.
Rep By: Marlene M. Colucci, Sean G. D'Arcy, Gary A. Heimberg, Steven R. Ross, Barney J. Skladany, Jr., Jose H. Villarreal

Fontheim Partners, PC
Rep By: Claude G. B. Fontheim, Ken Hutman

Citizens Against a Nat'l Sales Tax/Value-Added Tax

1920 L St. NW
Suite 200
Washington, DC 20036
E-mail: info@atr.org
Tel: (202)785-0266
Fax: (202)785-0261

An affiliate of Americans for Tax Reform, drawing support from trade associations. Works with Congressional Anti-VAT Caucus.

In-house, DC-area Employees
NORQUIST, Grover G.: Principal

Citizens Against Government Waste

1301 Connecticut Ave. NW
Fourth Floor
Washington, DC 20036
Tel: (202)467-5300
Fax: (202)467-4253
Registered: LDA
Web: www.cagw.org

A non-partisan, non-profit organization which educates the American people about the findings of the Grace Commission and government waste. The Council for Citizens Against Government Waste (CCAGW), is a grassroots lobby whose members actively pursue enactment of waste-cutting recommendations to reduce the Federal deficit. Combined membership exceeds 600,000.

Leg. Issues: BUD, COM, CPI, EDU, ENG, ENV, FIN, FOO, FUE, GOV, HCR, INS, LBR, MMM, NAT, PHA, RES, RET, ROD, TAX, TEC, TOB, TRD, UTI, WAS

In-house, DC-area Employees
FRYDENLUND, John: Fellow, Food and Agriculture Policy
MCBURNEY, Shawn: Director, Government Relations
SCHATZ, Thomas A.: President
WILLIAMS, David: Director, Research
WRIGHT, Elizabeth: Director, Health and Sciences

Citizens Against Research Bans

Washington, DC
Leg. Issues: ENG, NAT

Outside Counsel/Consultants

J. Arthur Weber & Associates
Issues: ENG, NAT
Rep By: Joseph A. Weber

Citizens Bank

Providence, RI
Leg. Issues: TAX

Outside Counsel/Consultants

Butera & Andrews
Issues: TAX
Rep By: Cliff W. Andrews, Wright H. Andrews, Jr., James J. Butera, Frank Tillotson

Citizens Coal Council

110 Maryland Ave. NE
Suite 408
Washington, DC 20002
E-mail: citzcoal@starpower.net
Tel: (202)544-6210
Fax: (202)544-7164

Represents the interests of people who live near coal fields.

In-house, DC-area Employees
MCCORMICK, John L.: Communications Coordinator

Citizens Committee for the Right to Keep and Bear Arms

1090 Vermont Ave. NW
Suite 800
Washington, DC 20005
Tel: (202)326-5259
Fax: (202)898-1939
Registered: LDA
Web: www.ccrkba.com
E-mail: gundean@aol.com

A conservative group that supports the right of law-abiding citizens to own and use firearms. Headquartered in Bellevue, WA.

Leg. Issues: CIV, FIR, LAW

In-house, DC-area Employees
SNYDER, John M.: Director, Public Affairs

Citizens Communications Center

600 New Jersey Ave. NW
Suite 312
Washington, DC 20001
Tel: (202)662-9535
Fax: (202)662-9634
Web: www.law.georgetown.edu\clinics\ipr
E-mail: gulcipr@law.georgetown.edu
Leg. Issues: COM

In-house, DC-area Employees
CAMPBELL, Angela J.: Associate Director

Citizens Flag Alliance

Indianapolis, IN

Outside Counsel/Consultants

Burson-Marsteller

Citizens for a Conservative Majority

444 N. Capitol St. NW
Suite 840
Washington, DC 20001

In-house, DC-area Employees
FRANZEN, IV, Nicholas J.: PAC Administrator

Citizens for a Republican Majority

8116 Arlington Blvd. Suite 901
Falls Church, VA 22042
A political action committee.

In-house, DC-area Employees
BARGANIER, III, Brooks C.

Citizens for a Sound Economy

1250 H St. NW
Suite 700
Washington, DC 20005-3908
Tel: (202)783-3870
Fax: (202)783-4687
Registered: LDA
Web: www.cse.org
E-mail: cse@cse.org

A non-profit, non-partisan citizen action and education organization promoting free market solutions to economic problems. Supported by individuals, foundations and corporations. Present membership is 250,000.

Leg. Issues: AGR, BUD, ENV, FIN, GOV, HCR, INS, LBR, PHA, TAX, TEC, TOB, TOR, TRD, UTI

Political Action Committee/s

Citizens for a Sound Economy PAC (CSE PAC)
1250 H St. NW
Suite 700
Washington, DC 20005-3908
Contact: Michele Mitola
Tel: (202)783-3870
Fax: (202)783-4687

In-house, DC-area Employees
BECKNER, Paul N.: President
BROUGH, Wayne: Chief Economist
BURNS, Patrick A.: Director, Environmental Policy
DONALDSON, Anita: Director, Public Affairs
FLAHERTY, Stephen: Director, Grassroots
GUSTAFSON, Erick: Director, Technology and Communications Policy
KIBBE, Matt: Exec. V. President, Public Policy
MILLER, III, James C.: Counselor
MITOLA, Michele: V. President, Public Policy
REISER, Marty: V. President, Public Affairs

Citizens for an Alternative Tax System

10600 A Crestwood Dr.
Manassas, VA 20109
Fax: (703)368-5843
Registered: LDA
Web: www.cats.org
E-mail: info@aol.com

A grassroots lobbying organization which advocates replacing the federal income tax with a national retail sales tax.

Leg. Issues: TAX

In-house, DC-area Employees
WAHLQUIST, Glenn: Director Operations

Citizens for Civil Justice Reform

Washington, DC
Leg. Issues: GOV, TOR

Outside Counsel/Consultants

Valis Associates
Issues: GOV, TOR
Rep By: Dana W. Hudson, Hon. Richard T. Schulze, Wayne H. Valis

Citizens for Health

Boulder, CO

Outside Counsel/Consultants

Baise + Miller, P.C.
Rep By: Marshall L. Miller

Citizens for Law and Order

Washington, DC

Outside Counsel/Consultants

Donald Baldwin Associates
Rep By: Donald Baldwin

Citizens for Liberty in Cuba (Cuba Libertad)

Arlington, VA
Leg. Issues: FOR

Outside Counsel/Consultants

BKSH & Associates
Issues: FOR
Rep By: Gardner Peckham

Citizens for Public Action on Cholesterol, Inc.

P.O. Box 37304
Bethesda, MD 20824
Tel: (301)309-2357
Fax: (301)309-1856
Registered: LDA

A parallel organization to Citizens for the Treatment of High Blood Pressure. A member organization of the Coalition for Health Funding and other consumer health coalitions.

Leg. Issues: BUD, CSP, FOO, HCR, MED, MIA, MMM, SCI

In-house, DC-area Employees
WILSON, Gerald J.: Exec. Director

Citizens for State Power

Alexandria, VA
Leg. Issues: ENG, UTI

Outside Counsel/Consultants

The Carmen Group
Issues: ENG

LMRC, Inc.

Craig Shirley & Associates
Issues: UTI
Rep By: Craig P. Shirley

Citizens for Tax Justice

1311 L St. NW
Fourth Floor
Washington, DC 20005
Tel: (202)626-3780
Fax: (202)638-3486
Registered: LDA
Web: www.ctj.org
E-mail: ctj@ctj.org

A coalition of national public interest organizations, labor unions and state and local groups seeking tax reform, with particular concern for low and middle income families.

Leg. Issues: BUD, TAX

In-house, DC-area Employees
GARDNER, Matthew: Analyst
HSU, Fiona: Tax Analyst
MCINTYRE, Robert S.: Director
MEYERS, Edward R.: Program Director
RUBENSTEIN, Bonnie: Development Director

Citizens for the Treatment of High Blood Pressure, Inc.

P.O. Box 30374
Bethesda, MD 20824
Tel: (301)309-2357
Fax: (301)309-1856
Registered: LDA
E-mail: libbase@aol.com

An organization for Heart Disease and Brain Injury Research and Services . A member organization of the Coalition for Health Funding in Washington. CTHBP is a nonprofit public advocacy organization.

Leg. Issues: BUD, HCR, MIA

In-house, DC-area Employees
WILSON, Gerald J.

Citizens for Workers' Compensation Reform

Outside Counsel/Consultants
Stevens Reed Curcio & Co.

Citizens Network for Foreign Affairs (CNFA)

1111 19th St. NW
Suite 900
Washington, DC 20036
Tel: (202)296-3920
Fax: (202)296-3948
Web: www.cnfa.org
E-mail: info@cnfa.org

A bi-partisan, non-profit public policy, international development and education organization aimed at involving Americans in the foreign affairs process. CNFA's programs engage leaders from agriculture, industry, education and government in public-private partnerships to foster economic growth and sustainable development worldwide.

Leg. Issues: AGR, BUD, FOR

In-house, DC-area Employees
COSTELLO, John H.: President
HOMMES, Caryn D.: Director, Operations and Compliance
WITTING, William N.: Director, Small Enterprise Development

Outside Counsel/Consultants
Century Communications, Inc.
Issues: AGR, FOR
Rep By: George S. Dunlop
Collins & Company, Inc.
Issues: FOR
Rep By: James D. Bond, Richard L. Collins, Thomas A. Hooper, Shay D. Stautz
EMI Associates, Ltd.
Issues: AGR, BUD, FOR
Rep By: Eugene M. Iwanciw
Vorys, Sater, Seymour and Pease, LLP

Citizens Trade Campaign

P.O. Box 77077
Washington, DC 20013-7077
Tel: (202)624-8136
Fax: (202)624-6901

A non-profit coalition whose mission is making trade policy more democratic.

In-house, DC-area Employees
ROSS, Mr. Kelly: Exec. Director

Citizens United

4101 Chain Bridge Rd.
Suite 312
Fairfax, VA 22030
Tel: (703)352-4788
Fax: (703)591-2505
Web: www.citizensunited.org
E-mail: citizensunited.citizensunited@verizon.net

An organization dedicated to restoring citizen control of government through a combination of education, advocacy, and grass roots organization. Seeks to assert the values of limited government, freedom of enterprise, strong families and national sovereignty and security.

In-house, DC-area Employees
BOOS, Michael: V. President

Citizens' Commission on Civil Rights

2000 M St. NW
Suite 400
Washington, DC 20036
Tel: (202)659-5565
Fax: (202)223-5302
Web: www.cccr.org

In-house, DC-area Employees
PICHE, Diane: Exec. Director
TAYLOR, William L.: V. Chairman

Citizens' Scholarship Foundation of America

St. Peter, MN
Leg. Issues: EDU

Outside Counsel/Consultants
Steven Kingsley
Issues: EDU
Rep By: Steven Kingsley

Citrosuco North America, Inc.

Lake Wales, FL
Leg. Issues: TRD

Outside Counsel/Consultants
Kalik Lewin
Issues: TRD
Rep By: Robert G. Kalik

Citrus Heights, California, City of

Leg. Issues: BUD

Outside Counsel/Consultants
Simon and Co., Inc.
Issues: BUD
Rep By: Heather Barber, Alex DeGood, Leonard S. Simon

City College of San Francisco

San Francisco, CA
Leg. Issues: BUD

Outside Counsel/Consultants
Cassidy & Associates, Inc.
Issues: BUD
Rep By: Maureen Walsh, Gerald Felix Warburg

City Colleges of Chicago

Chicago, IL
Leg. Issues: COM, EDU, TAX, TEC

Outside Counsel/Consultants
Charles L. Pizer
Issues: COM, EDU, TAX, TEC
Rep By: Charles L. Pizer

City Meals on Wheels USA

New York, NY

Outside Counsel/Consultants
Matz, Blancato & Associates, Inc.
Rep By: Robert B. Blancato

City of Hope Nat'l Medical Center

Duarte, CA
Leg. Issues: BUD

Outside Counsel/Consultants
Cassidy & Associates, Inc.
Issues: BUD
Rep By: Barbara Sutton, Maureen Walsh

City Public Service

Austin, TX
Leg. Issues: ENG, TAX, UTI

Outside Counsel/Consultants
Talley and Associates
Issues: ENG, TAX, UTI
Rep By: Robert A. C. Talley

City Rescue Mission Inc.

Jacksonville, FL

Outside Counsel/Consultants
Russ Reid Co.

City University

Bellevue, WA
Leg. Issues: EDU, FOR

Outside Counsel/Consultants
Ball Janik, LLP
Issues: EDU, FOR
Rep By: James A. Beall

Civic Ventures

San Francisco, CA
Leg. Issues: BUD

Outside Counsel/Consultants
Beacon Consulting Group, Inc.
Issues: BUD
Rep By: Gordon P. MacDougall, Julie Debolt Moeller, Lisa A. Stewart

Civil Air Patrol

Maxwell, AL
Leg. Issues: GOV

Outside Counsel/Consultants
Cottone and Huggins Group
Issues: GOV
Rep By: James B. Huggins

Civil Justice Reform Group

Washington, DC

A coalition of broad-based, large corporations lobbying for civil justice reform issues.

Leg. Issues: GOV, TOR

Outside Counsel/Consultants
Gibson, Dunn & Crutcher LLP
Rep By: Mark A. Perry
Law Office of Robert A. McConnell
Issues: GOV, TOR
Rep By: Robert A. McConnell
O'Melveny and Myers LLP
Rep By: John H. Beisner, Arthur B. Culvahouse, Jr.

The Civil War Preservation Trust

1331 H St. NW
Suite 1001
Washington, DC 20005
Tel: (202)367-1861
Web: www.civilwar.org
E-mail: civilwartrust@civilwar.org

Works for the preservation of significant Civil War battlefields and supports preservation and education programs.

In-house, DC-area Employees
CAMPI, Jim: Director, Communications
LIGHTHIZER, James: President

Clackamas, Oregon, County of

Oregon City, OR
Leg. Issues: BUD, ECN, ROD

Outside Counsel/Consultants
Ball Janik, LLP
Issues: BUD, ECN, ROD
Rep By: James A. Beall, Michelle E. Giguere, Hal D. Hiemstra

Claflin College

Orangeburg, SC
Leg. Issues: EDU

Outside Counsel/Consultants
Dean Blakey & Moskowitz
Issues: EDU
Rep By: William A. Blakey

ClaimTraq, Inc.

Middletown, CT
Leg. Issues: MMM, PHA

Outside Counsel/Consultants
The Fortier Group, LLC
Issues: MMM, PHA
Rep By: Michael P. Fortier
Strategic Impact, Inc.
Rep By: Patrick J. Mitchell

Claire's Stores, Inc.

Pembroke Pines, FL
Leg. Issues: TRD

Outside Counsel/Consultants
Greenberg Traurig, LLP
Issues: TRD
Rep By: Diane J. Blagman, Howard A. Vine

Clariant Corp.

Charlotte, NC

A specialty chemicals manufacturing company.

Leg. Issues: TRD

Outside Counsel/Consultants
Lyons & Co.
Issues: TRD
Rep By: William Lyons

Vern Clark & Associates

State Line, NV
Leg. Issues: TRA

Outside Counsel/Consultants
R. B. Murphy & Associates
Issues: TRA
Rep By: Rick Murphy

Clark Atlanta University

Atlanta, GA
Leg. Issues: EDU

Outside Counsel/Consultants
Dean Blakey & Moskowitz
Issues: EDU
Rep By: William A. Blakey

Clark County Department of Aviation
Las Vegas, NV
Outside Counsel/Consultants
Marcus G. Faust, P.C.
Rep By: Marcus G. Faust, Adrianne Firth

Clark County Regional Flood Control District
Las Vegas, NV
Leg. Issues: BUD, NAT
Outside Counsel/Consultants
Will and Carlson, Inc.
Issues: BUD, NAT
Rep By: Peter Carlson, Robert P. Will

Clark County, Nevada, Office of the County Manager
Las Vegas, NV
Leg. Issues: RES, TRA
Outside Counsel/Consultants
Marcus G. Faust, P.C.
Issues: RES, TRA
Rep By: Marcus G. Faust, Adrianne Firth

Clark County-McCarran Internat'l Airport
Las Vegas, NV
Leg. Issues: AVI, NAT, RES, TRA
Outside Counsel/Consultants
Marcus G. Faust, P.C.
Issues: AVI, NAT, RES, TRA
Rep By: Marcus G. Faust

The Clark Estates, Inc.
New York, NY
Leg. Issues: RES, SPO
Outside Counsel/Consultants
The Accord Group
Issues: RES, SPO
Rep By: Jeffery T. More

Edna McConnell Clark Foundation
New York, NY
Leg. Issues: FAM
Outside Counsel/Consultants
Martin & Glantz LLC
Issues: FAM

Clark/Bardes, Inc.
North Barrington, IL
Leg. Issues: BUD, FIN, INS, TAX
Outside Counsel/Consultants
Hohlt & Associates
Issues: BUD, FIN, INS, TAX
Rep By: Richard F. Hohlt
PriceWaterhouseCoopers
Issues: TAX
Rep By: Jim Carlisle, Kenneth J. Kies, Pat Raffaniello
Skadden, Arps, Slate, Meagher & Flom LLP
Rep By: Roseann M. Cutrone, Fred T. Goldberg, Jr.

Classroom Publishers Ass'n
5335 Wisconsin Ave. NW
Suite 920
Washington, DC 20015
Tel: (202)965-2650
Fax: (202)244-5167

Represents publishers of classroom publications before the Postal Rate Commission, the U.S. Postal Service and Congress.

Leg. Issues: EDU, POS
In-house, DC-area Employees
OWEN, Jr., Stephen F.: General Counsel and Secretary
Outside Counsel/Consultants
Bradford A. Penney
Issues: EDU, POS
Rep By: Bradford A. Penney

Clatsop Community College
Astoria, OR
Leg. Issues: BUD
Outside Counsel/Consultants
Ball Janik, LLP
Issues: BUD
Rep By: James A. Beall, Michelle E. Giguere

Clayton, Dover, Lewes, Middletown, Milford, Newark, NewCastle, Seaford and Smyrna, Delaware, Municipalities of
Leg. Issues: COM, ENG, GOV, UTI
Outside Counsel/Consultants
Duncan, Weinberg, Genzer & Pembroke, P.C.
Issues: COM, ENG, GOV, UTI
Rep By: Janice L. Lower

Clean Air Action Corp.
Tulsa, OK
Outside Counsel/Consultants
Wilmer, Cutler & Pickering
Rep By: C. Boyden Gray

Clean Air Campaign
New York, NY
Outside Counsel/Consultants
Dunlap & Browder, Inc.
Rep By: Joseph B. Browder, Louise C. Dunlap

Clean Air Now
Santa Monica, CA
Leg. Issues: CAW, ENG
Outside Counsel/Consultants
Madison Government Affairs
Issues: CAW, ENG
Rep By: Paul J. Hirsch

Clean Air Regulatory Information Group
Washington, DC
Leg. Issues: CAW
Outside Counsel/Consultants
Hunton & Williams
Issues: CAW
Rep By: F. William Brownell, Norman W. Fichthorn, Henry V. Nickel

Clean Energy Group
Concord, MA
Leg. Issues: CAW, ENG
Outside Counsel/Consultants
Bill Carney & Co.
Issues: CAW, ENG
Rep By: Jacqueline Carney, Hon. William Carney

Clean Fuels Development Coalition
Arlington, VA
E-mail: durante@aol.com
Leg. Issues: ENG
Outside Counsel/Consultants
Durante Associates
Issues: ENG
Rep By: Douglas A. Durante

Clean Water Act Reauthorization Coalition
Washington, DC
Leg. Issues: CAW, ENV, NAT
Outside Counsel/Consultants
The Accord Group
Issues: CAW, ENV, NAT
Rep By: Philip T. Cummings

Clean Water Action
4455 Connecticut Ave. NW
Suite A300
Washington, DC 20008
Tel: (202)895-0420
Fax: (202)895-0438
Registered: LDA
Web: www.essential.org/cwa
E-mail: katernol@cleanwater.org

A national citizen organization working for clean and safe water at an affordable cost, control of toxic chemicals and preservation of natural resources.

Political Action Committee/s
Clean Water Action Vote Environment (Clean WAVE)
4455 Connecticut Ave. NW
Suite A300
Washington, DC 20008
Tel: (202)895-0420
Fax: (202)895-0438
Contact: Kathy Aterno
In-house, DC-area Employees
ATERNO, Kathy: Managing Director

Clean Water Council
4301 N. Fairfax Dr.
Suite 360
Arlington, VA 22203-1627
Tel: (703)358-9300
Fax: (703)358-9307
Web: www.nuca.com

A coalition concerned with clean water program funding.

In-house, DC-area Employees
HILLMAN, A. William

Clean Water Network
1200 New York Ave. NW
Suite 400
Washington, DC 20005
Tel: (202)289-2395
Fax: (202)289-1060
Web: www.cwn.org

A nationwide coalition of environmental and other interest groups favoring strict pollution control measures in any reauthorization of the Clean Water Act.

In-house, DC-area Employees
SCHER, Eddie: Director

Clear Communications
Leg. Issues: TEC
Outside Counsel/Consultants
Greenberg Traurig, LLP
Issues: TEC

Clearwater Environmental, Inc.
Glennallen, AK
Leg. Issues: ENV
Outside Counsel/Consultants
Birch, Horton, Bittner & Cherot
Issues: ENV
Rep By: Thomas L. Albert, William P. Horn

Clearwater, Florida, City of
Leg. Issues: BUD, ECN, GOV, HOU, ROD, TRA, URB, WEL
Outside Counsel/Consultants
Alcalde & Fay
Issues: BUD, ECN, GOV, HOU, ROD, TRA, URB, WEL
Rep By: Hector Alcalde, Danielle McBeth, Lois Moore

Clement Pappas & Co., Inc.
Seabrook, NJ
Leg. Issues: AGR
Outside Counsel/Consultants
Olsson, Frank and Weeda, P.C.
Issues: AGR
Rep By: Stephen L. Lacey

Clemson University
Clemson, SC
Leg. Issues: BUD, EDU
Outside Counsel/Consultants
Van Scoyoc Associates, Inc.
Issues: BUD, EDU
Rep By: Paul Grimm, Steven O. Palmer, Chad Schulken, H. Stewart Van Scoyoc

Cleveland Advanced Manufacturing Program
Cleveland, OH
Leg. Issues: DEF, MAN
Outside Counsel/Consultants
Ainslie Associates
Issues: DEF, MAN
Rep By: Virginia J. Ainslie

Cleveland Cliffs Iron Co.
Cleveland, OH
Registered: LDA
Leg. Issues: TAX
Outside Counsel/Consultants
Murray, Scheer, Montgomery, Tapia & O'Donnell
Issues: TAX
Rep By: Thomas R. Crawford, D. Michael Murray

Cleveland Clinic Foundation
2000 L St. NW
Suite 200
Washington, DC 20036
Tel: (202)861-0955
Fax: (202)872-0834
Registered: LDA
E-mail: nickeld@ccf.org

Specializes in health care delivery, research, and education. Headquartered in Cleveland, Ohio.

Leg. Issues: BUD, DEF, HCR, MED, MMM, SCI, TAX
In-house, DC-area Employees
NICKELSON, Daniel E.: Director, Government Affairs

Outside Counsel/Consultants

Ainslie Associates
Issues: BUD, DEF, MED, SCI
Rep By: Virginia J. Ainslie

Squire, Sanders & Dempsey L.L.P.
Issues: BUD, MMM
Rep By: Timothy Cosgrove

Cleveland Growth Ass'n

Cleveland, OH
Leg. Issues: LBR

Outside Counsel/Consultants

Wise & Associates
Issues: LBR
Rep By: Joshua Rubin, Dwayne Sattler

Cleveland State University - College of Urban Affairs

Cleveland, OH
Leg. Issues: BUD, ECN, EDU, URB

Outside Counsel/Consultants

Ainslie Associates
Issues: BUD, ECN, EDU, URB
Rep By: Virginia J. Ainslie

Cleveland, City of/Cleveland Hopkins Internat'l Airport

Cleveland, OH
Leg. Issues: AVI, BUD

Outside Counsel/Consultants

Baker, Donelson, Bearman & Caldwell, P.C.
Issues: AVI, BUD
Rep By: Linda Hall Daschle, Albert B. Randall

Cleveland, Ohio, City of

Leg. Issues: GOV, LAW

Outside Counsel/Consultants

Hill and Knowlton, Inc.
Issues: GOV, LAW
Rep By: Reginald E. Gilliam, Jr.

Click2Learn.com

Leg. Issues: DEF

Outside Counsel/Consultants

Denny Miller McBee Associates
Issues: DEF

Cliffstar Corp.

Dunkirk, NY
Leg. Issues: AGR

Outside Counsel/Consultants

Olsson, Frank and Weeda, P.C.
Issues: AGR
Rep By: Stephen L. Lacey

The Climate Council,

Leg. Issues: BUD, DEF, ECN, ENG, ENV, FOR, NAT, SCI, UTI

Outside Counsel/Consultants

Patton Boggs, LLP
Issues: BUD, DEF, ECN, ENG, ENV, FOR, NAT, SCI, UTI
Rep By: Donald H. Pearlman

Climate Institute

333-1/2 Pennsylvania Ave. SE
Washington, DC 20003
Tel: (202)547-0104
Fax: (202)547-0111
Web: www.climate.org
E-mail: info@climate.org

An organization that conducts research, disseminates information and advocates societal and public policy action to respond to climate change and ozone depletion.

Leg. Issues: ENG, ENV

In-house, DC-area Employees

TOPPING, Jr., John C.: President

Clinical Laboratory Management Ass'n

Wayne, PA

Outside Counsel/Consultants

Holland & Knight LLP

Clipper Cruise Line

St. Louis, MO

Outside Counsel/Consultants

Dyer Ellis & Joseph, P.C.
Rep By: Thomas M. Dyer

The Clorox Co.

Oakland, CA
Registered: LDA
Leg. Issues: CAW, ENV, HOU

Outside Counsel/Consultants

Patton Boggs, LLP
Issues: CAW, ENV, HOU
Rep By: Florence W. Prioleau

Ruder Finn Washington

Close Up Foundation

44 Canal Center Plaza
Alexandria, VA 22314
Tel: (703)706-3567
Fax: (703)706-0000
Registered: LDA
Web: www.closeup.org

A nonprofit, nonpartisan citizenship education organization best known for bringing students, teachers and older Americans to Washington, D.C., for a close up look at government.

Leg. Issues: BUD, EDU

In-house, DC-area Employees

JANGER, Stephen A.: President and Chief Exec. Officer
JENNINGS, III, Horace: Director, Government Relations

Closure Manufacturers Ass'n

515 King St.
Suite 420
Alexandria, VA 22314
Tel: (703)684-6213
Fax: (703)684-6048
Web: www.cmadc.org
E-mail: cmadc@erols.com

An affiliate of the Glass Packaging Institute.

In-house, DC-area Employees

WILLIAMSON, Darla: V. President

Outside Counsel/Consultants

CLARION Management Resources, Inc.
Rep By: Darla Williamson

Clough, Harbour & Associates LLP

Albany, NY
Leg. Issues: DEF

Outside Counsel/Consultants

The Solomon Group, LLC
Issues: DEF
Rep By: William D. Crosby, Jr., David M. Lonie, Hon. Gerald B. H. Solomon, William R. Teator

Clover Park School District

Tacoma, WA
Leg. Issues: EDU

Outside Counsel/Consultants

Evergreen Associates, Ltd.
Issues: EDU
Rep By: Robert M. Brooks, Marcus M. Riccelli

CLT Appraisal Services, Inc.

Devon, PA

Outside Counsel/Consultants

Peter S. Barash Associates, Inc.
Rep By: Peter S. Barash

Club Car, Inc.

Augusta, GA

Outside Counsel/Consultants

Wiley, Rein & Fielding
Rep By: Eileen P. Bradner, Charles O. Verrill, Jr.

Club for Growth

1776 K St. NW
Suite 300
Washington, DC 20006
Tel: (202)955-5500
Fax: (202)955-9466
Web: www.clubforgrowth.org

The mission of the Club for Growth is to help support political candidates who are advocates of the Reagan vision of limited government and lower taxes. The Club is primarily dedicated to helping elect pro-growth, pro-freedom candidates through political contributions and issue advocacy campaigns. Among the major economic growth issues the Club emphasizes are fundamental income tax reduction and simplification; school choice for all families; and personal investment of Social Security.

In-house, DC-area Employees

KEATING, David: Exec. Director
MOORE, Stephen: President
SEXTON, Nicole: Membership Director

Club Managers Ass'n of America

1733 King St.
Alexandria, VA 22314
Tel: (703)739-9500
Fax: (703)739-0124
Web: www.cmaa.org

A professional association founded in 1927 for managers of private membership clubs. It represents over 5,000 professional managers of country, city, yacht, faculty, military and golf clubs worldwide.

In-house, DC-area Employees

DRIGGS, Kathi: V. President
GORMAN, Bridget: Manager, Public Affairs
PALERMO, Lou: Director, Education and Professional Development
SINGERLING, CCM, CEC, James B.: Exec. V. President and Chief Exec. Officer
WOODWARD, Anne: Manager, Education

Clyde's Restaurant Group

Washington, DC
Leg. Issues: RES

Outside Counsel/Consultants

Holland & Knight LLP
Issues: RES
Rep By: David C. Whitestone

CMC/Heartland Partnership

Chicago, IL
Leg. Issues: RES, TRA

Outside Counsel/Consultants

Foley & Lardner
Issues: RES, TRA
Rep By: Theodore H. Bornstein

CMS Defense Systems, Inc.

Winter Park, FL
Leg. Issues: BUD, DEF

Outside Counsel/Consultants

Cassidy & Associates, Inc.
Issues: BUD, DEF
Rep By: Shawn Edwards, Lawrence C. Grossman, Brig. Gen. Terry Paul, USMC (Ret.)

Rhoads Group

CNA Financial Corp.

818 Connecticut Ave. NW
Tenth Floor
Washington, DC 20006
Tel: (202)296-4662
Fax: (202)296-5547
Registered: LDA
Web: www.cna.com

Headquartered in Chicago, IL.

Leg. Issues: AGR, BAN, BUD, CPI, CSP, DIS, ENV, FIN, GOV, HCR, HOU, INS, LAW, LBR, MMM, TAX, TOB, WAS

In-house, DC-area Employees

PERNICK, Carol V.: V. President, Congressional Relations

Outside Counsel/Consultants

Morgan, Lewis & Bockius LLP
Issues: FIN, HCR, INS, LAW

Scribner, Hall & Thompson, LLP
Rep By: Susan J. Hotine

CNA Insurance Cos.

Leg. Issues: AGR, BAN, BUD, CPI, CSP, DIS, ENV, FIN, GOV, HCR, HOU, INS, LAW, LBR, MMM, TAX, TOB, WAS

Outside Counsel/Consultants

The Fortier Group, LLC
Issues: INS
Rep By: Michael P. Fortier

Jolly/Rissler, Inc.
Issues: AGR, BAN, BUD, CPI, CSP, DIS, ENV, FIN, GOV, HCR, HOU, INS, LBR, MMM, TAX, TOB, WAS
Rep By: Thomas R. Jolly, Patricia F. Rissler

Morgan, Lewis & Bockius LLP
Issues: FIN, HCR, INS, LAW

CNF Transportation, Inc.

Palo Alto, CA
Leg. Issues: LBR, POS, ROD, TAX, TRA, TRU

Outside Counsel/Consultants

Alcalde & Fay
Issues: LBR, POS, ROD, TAX, TRA, TRU
Rep By: Hector Alcalde, Paul Schlesinger, Tim Stroud

Cassidy & Associates, Inc.
Issues: POS
Rep By: Christy Carson Evans, Christopher Lamond, Arthur D. Mason

Gibson, Dunn & Crutcher LLP
Issues: TAX
Rep By: Michael Collins, Alan A. Platt, Peter H. Turza

CNPA - Nat'l Center for the Promotion of Agricultural and Food Products

Paris, FRANCE

Outside Counsel/Consultants

Euroconsultants, Inc.

Co-Steel Raritan

Perth Amboy, NJ
Leg. Issues: TRD

Outside Counsel/Consultants

Wiley, Rein & Fielding
Issues: TRD
Rep By: Eileen P. Bradner, Sharon R. Fine, Hon. Jim Slattery

Coach USA

Houston, TX
Leg. Issues: TRA

Outside Counsel/Consultants

Steptoe & Johnson LLP
Issues: TRA
Rep By: David H. Coburn

Coachella Valley Economic Partnership

Coachella, CA
Leg. Issues: TRA

Outside Counsel/Consultants

Washington Alliance Group, Inc.
Issues: TRA
Rep By: Bonnie Singer

Coachella Valley Water District

Coachella, CA
Leg. Issues: BUD, ENV, IND, NAT

Outside Counsel/Consultants

McClure, Gerard & Neuenschwander, Inc.
Issues: BUD, ENV, IND, NAT
Rep By: Steven G. Barringer, Joseph T. Findaro, Matthew Iandoli, Nils W. Johnson, Hon. James A. McClure, Tod O. Neuenschwander

Coal Act Fairness Alliance

McLean, VA
Leg. Issues: TAX

Outside Counsel/Consultants

Institutional Labor Advisors
Issues: TAX
Rep By: Merritt J. Green, Gregory J. Ossi, David S. Smith, Jan W. Sturner

The Coal Coalition

Washington, DC

Includes Berwind Corp., Eastern Enterprises, LTV Corp., Mueller Industries, North American Coal Corp., Cleveland-Cliffs, Inc. and The Pittson Co.

Leg. Issues: TAX

Outside Counsel/Consultants

Jones, Day, Reavis & Pogue
Issues: TAX
Rep By: Jonathan C. Rose

Sunrise Research Corp.
Rep By: Hon. Bob Packwood

Coal Exporters Ass'n of the U.S.

1130 17th St. NW
Fifth Floor
Washington, DC 20036
E-mail: mphelleps@nma.org
Tel: (202)463-2639
Fax: (202)833-9636

Information about CMA can be found on the internet under the Nat'l Mining Ass'n's (see separate listing) website: www.nma.org.

In-house, DC-area Employees

PHELLEPS, Moya: Exec. Director

Coal Utilization Research Council

Washington, DC
Leg. Issues: BUD, ENG, ENV, SCI

Outside Counsel/Consultants

Van Ness Feldman, P.C.
Issues: BUD, ENG, ENV, SCI
Rep By: Paula J. Dietz, Ben Yamagata

Coalinga Corp.

1801 K St. NW
Suite 901L
Washington, DC 20006
Web: www.bm.com
E-mail: pat_templeton@bm.com
Tel: (202)530-0500
Fax: (202)530-4800

In-house, DC-area Employees

TEMPLETON, Patrick A.: Washington Representative

Coalition Against Australian Leather Subsidies

Leg. Issues: TRD

Outside Counsel/Consultants

Collier Shannon Scott, PLLC
Issues: TRD
Rep By: Lauren R. Howard

Coalition Against Bigger Trucks

901 N. Pitt St.
Suite 310
Alexandria, VA 22314
Web: www.cabt.org
E-mail: cabt@earthlink.net
Tel: (703)535-3131
Fax: (703)535-3322
Registered: LDA

A non-profit citizen's organization opposed to the increase of truck size and weight.

Leg. Issues: TRA, TRU

Outside Counsel/Consultants

Charles W. Quatt Associates, Inc.
Issues: TRU
Rep By: Brian H. Vogel

Coalition Against Database Piracy

Washington, DC
Leg. Issues: CPT

Outside Counsel/Consultants

Bergner Bockorny Castagnetti and Hawkins
Issues: CPT

Meyer & Klipper, PLLC
Issues: CPT
Rep By: Michael R. Klipper, Christopher A. Mohr

Parry, Romani, DeConcini & Symms
Rep By: Edward H. Baxter, Hon. Dennis DeConcini, John M. Haddow, Scott D. Hatch, Shannon Davis Henderson, Jack W. Martin, Romano Romani, Linda Arey Skladany, Hon. Steven D. Symms

Coalition Against Insurance Fraud

1012 14th St. NW
Suite 200
Washington, DC 20005
Web: www.insurancefraud.org
E-mail: djay@insurancefraud.org
Tel: (202)393-7330
Fax: (202)393-7329

A national coalition of consumer groups, government organizations and insurance companies dedicated to combatting all forms of fraud through advocacy and public information.

In-house, DC-area Employees

GOLDBLATT, Howard I.: Director, Government Affairs
JAY, Dennis: Exec. Director

Coalition Against Product Tampering

Washington, DC
Registered: LDA
Leg. Issues: LAW

Outside Counsel/Consultants

Higgins, McGovern & Smith, LLC
Issues: LAW
Rep By: John S. Bliss

Coalition Against Unfair U.S. Postal Service Competition

Leg. Issues: POS

Outside Counsel/Consultants

Robertson, Monagle & Eastaugh
Issues: POS
Rep By: Steven W. Silver

Coalition for a Comprehensive Tobacco Solution (C-FACTS)

Alexandria, VA
Leg. Issues: TOB

Outside Counsel/Consultants

McMillan, Hill & Associates
Issues: TOB

Coalition for a Global Standard on Aviation Noise

c/o Hunton and Williams
1900 K St. NW, P.O Box 19230
Washington, DC 20006
Tel: (202)778-2245
Leg. Issues: AVI

In-house, DC-area Employees

PRINCIPATO, Gregory: Contact

Outside Counsel/Consultants

Rosalind K. Ellingsworth
Issues: AVI
Rep By: Rosalind K. Ellingsworth

Hunton & Williams
Issues: AVI
Rep By: Gerald L. Baliles, Gregory Principato

Coalition for a Procompetitive Stark Law

Leg. Issues: HCR, MMM

Outside Counsel/Consultants

Arent Fox Kintner Plotkin & Kahn, PLLC
Issues: HCR, MMM
Rep By: William A. Sarraille, Allison Shuren

Coalition for Affordable Housing Preservation

Omaha, NE
Leg. Issues: HOU

Outside Counsel/Consultants

Coan & Lyons
Issues: HOU
Rep By: Carl A. S. Coan, Jr., Raymond K. James

Coalition for Affordable Local and Long Distance Services

Washington, DC
Leg. Issues: TEC

Outside Counsel/Consultants

Harris, Wiltshire & Grannis LLP
Issues: TEC
Rep By: John T. Nakahata

Coalition for America's Children

601 13th St. NW
Suite 400 North
Washington, DC 20005
Web: www.connectforkids.org
E-mail: cac@usakids.org
Tel: (202)347-8600
Fax: (202)393-6137

An alliance of non-profit organizations working together to call attention to serious obstacles that impede children's health, education, safety and security and to evelate children's concerns to the top of the public policy agenda.

In-house, DC-area Employees

THARP, Marjorie: Chair

Coalition for America's Future

Washington, DC

Outside Counsel/Consultants

Verner, Liipfert, Bernhard, McPherson and Hand, Chartered

Coalition for American Financial Security

Leg. Issues: RET, TAX

Outside Counsel/Consultants

The Petrizzo Group, Inc.
Issues: RET, TAX
Rep By: Kara Kennedy, Thomas "T.J." Petrizzo

Coalition for American Leadership Abroad/American Foreign Affairs Organizations, Inc.

AFSA Bldg.
2101 E St. NW
Washington, DC 20037
Web: www.colead.org
E-mail: COLEAD@afsa.org
Tel: (202)944-5519
Fax: (202)338-6820
Leg. Issues: FOR

In-house, DC-area Employees

BLANEY, III, Harry C.: President

Coalition for American Trauma Care

Leg. Issues: BUD, CSP, HCR, TEC

Outside Counsel/Consultants

Timothy Bell & Co.
Issues: BUD, CSP, HCR, TEC
Rep By: Marcia S. Mabee, Ph.D.

Coalition for Asbestos Resolution

Washington, DC

A group of companies working to secure federal legislation that would resolve the asbestos litigation problem. Primary aim is a national claims facility, at no cost to taxpayers, to expedite compensation to individuals suffering from asbestos-related disease.

Leg. Issues: BNK, CSP, HCR, TOR

Outside Counsel/Consultants

O'Melveny and Myers LLP
Issues: BNK, CSP, HCR, TOR
Rep By: Walter E. Dellinger, III, Ronald A. Klain

Coalition for Auto Repair Equality (CARE)

119 Oronoco St.
Suite 300
Alexandria, VA 22314-2015
Tel: (703)519-7555
Fax: (703)519-7747
Registered: LDA
Web: www.careauto.org
E-mail: care@careauto.org

A coalition of aftermarket auto parts, service and repair industry corporations opposed to legislation which would create a monopoly on auto parts, service and repair for domestic and foreign original equipment manufacturers. Opposes "Junker-Clunker," "Vehicle-Scrappage," and "Crash-Parts" legislation.

Leg. Issues: AUT, CAW, CPT, ENV, SMB, TRA

In-house, DC-area Employees

BASS-CORS, Sandy: Exec. Director
JOHNSON, Sheldon: Operations Director
PARDE, David L.: President

Outside Counsel/Consultants

The Dutko Group, Inc.
Issues: AUT
Rep By: Stephen Craig Sayle

Coalition for Auto-Insurance Reform

7310 Stafford Rd.
Alexandria, VA 22307
Tel: (703)660-0799
Fax: (703)660-0799
Registered: LDA
E-mail: kinzler@tidalwave.net

Represents academics, insurers, consumer activists and business groups in effort tp provide motorists the opportunity to purchase more affordable auto insurance that provides more adequate and timely compensation for accident victims.

Leg. Issues: INS

In-house, DC-area Employees

KINZLER, Peter

Outside Counsel/Consultants

Peter Kinzler
Issues: INS
Rep By: Peter Kinzler

Coalition for Brain Injury Research and Services, Inc.

P.O. Box 30374
Bethesda, MD 20824
Tel: (301)309-2357
Fax: (301)309-1856
Leg. Issues: BUD, HCR, MIA

In-house, DC-area Employees

WILSON, Gerald J.: Director

Coalition for Competitive Rail Transportation

Outside Counsel/Consultants

Estes Associates
Rep By: John T. Estes

Coalition for Crop Insurance Improvement

Washington, DC

Outside Counsel/Consultants

The Macon Edwards Co.
Rep By: Macon T. Edwards, Mara Peltz

Coalition for Effective Environmental Information

Washington, DC
Leg. Issues: ENV

Outside Counsel/Consultants

Ropes & Gray
Issues: ENV
Rep By: Mark A. Greenwood

Coalition for Electronic Commerce

Cleveland, OH
Leg. Issues: DEF

Outside Counsel/Consultants

Patton Boggs, LLP
Issues: DEF
Rep By: John J. Deschauer, Jr., Edward J. Newberry

Coalition for Employment Opportunities

Washington, DC

Outside Counsel/Consultants

McDermott, Will and Emery
Rep By: Calvin P. Johnson

Coalition for Employment through Exports

1100 Connecticut Ave. NW
Suite 810
Washington, DC 20036
Tel: (202)296-6107
Fax: (202)296-9709
Registered: LDA

An organization of U.S. businesses interested in foreign trade and the competitive position of U.S. exports, especially relating to programs of the U.S. Export-Import Bank, the Overseas Private Investment Corp., the Trade and Development Agency and the Department of Commerce. Represents 37 major exporters.

Leg. Issues: BUD, FIN, TRD

In-house, DC-area Employees

RICE, Edmund B.: President
ROSKE, Monique M.: Director, Government Relations

Outside Counsel/Consultants

Vorys, Sater, Seymour and Pease, LLP

Coalition for Fair Atlantic Salmon Trade

Brewer, ME
Leg. Issues: TRD

Outside Counsel/Consultants

Collier Shannon Scott, PLLC
Issues: TRD
Rep By: Michael J. Coursey

Coalition for Fair Competition in Rural Markets

Washington, DC
Leg. Issues: ENG

Outside Counsel/Consultants

Patton Boggs, LLP
Issues: ENG
Rep By: Brian C. Lopina, Edward J. Newberry

Coalition for Fair Lumber Imports

1775 Pennsylvania Ave. NW
Suite 600
Washington, DC 20006
Tel: (202)862-4505
Fax: (202)862-1093
Registered: LDA
E-mail: fairlumber@cs.com

Supports the enforcement of the U.S.-Canada Softwood Lumber Agreement.

Leg. Issues: TRD

In-house, DC-area Employees

REAGAN, Deborah: Manager, Legislative Affairs
SHOTWELL, Scott: Exec. Director

Outside Counsel/Consultants

Dewey Ballantine LLP
Issues: TRD
Rep By: Kevin M. Dempsey, Andrew W. Kentz, John A. Ragosta

Coalition for Fair Play in Ocean Shipping

Washington, DC
Leg. Issues: TRA, TRD, TRU

Outside Counsel/Consultants

Rodriguez O'Donnell Fuerst Gonzalez & Williams
Issues: TRA, TRD, TRU
Rep By: Ashley W. Craig, Carlos Rodriguez

Coalition for Fair Remedies

Leg. Issues: GOV

Outside Counsel/Consultants

Crowell & Moring LLP
Issues: GOV
Rep By: Karen Hastie Williams

Coalition for Fair Tax Credits

Washington, DC
Leg. Issues: TAX

Outside Counsel/Consultants

PriceWaterhouseCoopers
Issues: TAX
Rep By: Jim Carlisle, Kenneth J. Kies, Pat Raffaniello, James R. Shanahan

Coalition for Fair Taxation of Real Estate

Outside Counsel/Consultants

Rock & Associates
Rep By: James W. Rock

Coalition for Fairness in Defense Exports

Washington, DC
Leg. Issues: TAX

Outside Counsel/Consultants

Washington Council Ernst & Young
Issues: TAX
Rep By: Doug Badger, Lauren Darling, John L. Doney, Jayne T. Fitzgerald, LaBrenda Garrett-Nelson, Gary J. Gasper, Bruce A. Gates, Nick Giordano, Robert J. Leonard, Richard Meltzer, Phillip D. Moseley, John D. Porter, Robert M. Rozen, Donna Steele-Flynn, Timothy J. Urban

Coalition for Federal Sentencing Reform

3125 Mount Vernon Ave.
Alexandria, VA 22305
Tel: (703)684-0373
Fax: (703)684-6037
Web: www.sentencing.org
E-mail: bholman@ncianet.org

A project of the Nat'l Center on Institutions and Alternatives. Promotes reform of the federal sentencing guidelines and alternative sentencing of criminals to reduce prison overcrowding.

Leg. Issues: LAW

In-house, DC-area Employees

HOLMAN, Barry R.: Project Coordinator

Coalition for Food Aid

Washington, DC
Leg. Issues: AGR, FOR

Outside Counsel/Consultants

Cadwalader, Wickersham & Taft
Issues: AGR, FOR

Coalition for Global Perspectives

Washington, DC
Leg. Issues: TAX

Outside Counsel/Consultants

Manatt, Phelps & Phillips, LLP
Issues: TAX
Rep By: Hon. Jack W. Buechner, Robert J. Kabel, Steven J. Mulder, Robb Watters

Coalition for Government Procurement

1990 M St. NW
Suite 400
Washington, DC 20036
Tel: (202)331-0975
Fax: (202)822-9788
Web: www.washmg.aol.com
E-mail: coalgovpro@aol.com

A nonprofit membership organization composed of small and large businesses which sell commercial products to the Federal Government. Concerned about preserving the Multiple Award Schedule contracting system and other policies affecting federal commercial product procurement. Backed by several trade associations.

Leg. Issues: CPI, DEF, GOV, PHA, SMB

In-house, DC-area Employees

ALLEN, Edward L.: Exec. Director
CAGGIANO, Paul J.: President

Outside Counsel/Consultants

Steptoe & Johnson LLP
Issues: CPI, DEF, GOV, PHA, SMB
Rep By: Robert D. Wallick

Coalition for Group Legal Services

Des Moines, IA

Outside Counsel/Consultants

J/T Group
Rep By: Robert E. Juliano

Coalition for GSP

Washington, DC
Leg. Issues: TRD

Outside Counsel/Consultants

The Trade Partnership
Issues: TRD
Rep By: Laura M. Baughman

Coalition for Health Funding

Reston, VA
Leg. Issues: BUD

Outside Counsel/Consultants

Timothy Bell & Co.
Issues: BUD
Rep By: Marcia S. Mabee, Ph.D.

Coalition for Health Services Research

1801 K St. NW
Suite 700-L
Washington, DC 20006
Tel: (202)292-6700
Fax: (202)292-6800
Registered: LDA
Web: www.chsr.org
Leg. Issues: ALC, BUD, INS, MED, MMM, PHA, VET

In-house, DC-area Employees

LAWNICZAK, Jonathan: Director, Government Relations

Coalition for Health Services Research

1801 K St. NW
Suite 701-L
Washington, DC 20006
Tel: (202)292-6700
Fax: (202)292-6800
Web: www.ahsr.com
E-mail: info@ahsr.org

In-house, DC-area Employees

HELMS, David: Chief Exec. Officer/President

Outside Counsel/Consultants

MARC Associates, Inc.
Rep By: Daniel C. Maldonado, Shannon Penberthy, Ellen Riker

Coalition for Intellectual Property Rights (CIPR)

Washington, DC
Leg. Issues: TRD

Outside Counsel/Consultants

JBC Internat'l
Issues: TRD
Rep By: Courtenay Carr, James B. Clawson

Coalition for Intelligent Manufacturing Systems (CIMS)

Outside Counsel/Consultants

R. Wayne Sayer & Associates
Rep By: William Morin, R. Wayne Sayer

Coalition for Internat'l Justice

740 15th St. NW
Washington, DC 20005
Tel: (202)662-1595
Fax: (202)662-1597
Registered: LDA
Web: www.cij.org
E-mail: coalition@cij.org

A non-profit organization supporting the United Nations War Crimes Tribunals for the former Yugoslavia and Rwanda, as well as accountability in Sierra Leone, Cambodia, and East Timor.

Leg. Issues: LAW

In-house, DC-area Employees

BANG-JENSEN, Nina: Exec. Director

Coalition for Job Growth and Internat'l Competitiveness Through AMT Reform

Outside Counsel/Consultants

Arthur Andersen LLP
Rep By: Carol Kulish

Coalition for Job Opportunities

1200 17th St. NW
Washington, DC 20036
Tel: (202)331-5900
Fax: (202)331-2429
Web: www.restaurant.org

A group of some 30 companies and business trade associations opposed to proposals to raise the starting wage.

In-house, DC-area Employees

CULPEPPER, R. Lee: Contact

Coalition for Maritime Education

Leg. Issues: BUD, EDU, MAR

Outside Counsel/Consultants

Meyers & Associates
Issues: BUD, EDU, MAR
Rep By: Shelley Wilson Dodd, Larry D. Meyers

Coalition for Networked Information

21 Dupont Circle NW
Suite 800
Washington, DC 20036
Tel: (202)296-5098
Fax: (202)872-0884
Web: www.cni.org
E-mail: info@cni.org

In-house, DC-area Employees

LIPPINCOTT, Joan K.: Associate Exec. Director
LYNCH, Clifford A.: Exec. Director

Coalition for Nonprofit Health Care

Washington, DC
Leg. Issues: HCR

Outside Counsel/Consultants

Gardner, Carton and Douglas
Issues: HCR
Rep By: T. J. Sullivan

Coalition for Open Markets and Expanded Trade

Washington, DC

A grassroots coalition that advocates the elimination of barriers to exports and imports, and urges internat'l market opening agreements.

Leg. Issues: TRD

Outside Counsel/Consultants

Valis Associates
Issues: TRD
Rep By: Dana W. Hudson, Hon. Richard T. Schulze, Wayne H. Valis

Coalition for Patent Information Dissemination

Leg. Issues: CPT

Outside Counsel/Consultants

Joseph L. Ebersole
Issues: CPT
Rep By: Joseph L. Ebersole

Coalition for Patient Rights

Outside Counsel/Consultants

Powers Pyles Sutter & Verville, PC
Rep By: James C. Pyles

Coalition for Professional Certification

Arlington, VA
Leg. Issues: GOV

Outside Counsel/Consultants

Halsey, Rains & Associates, LLC
Issues: GOV
Rep By: Steven C. Halsey, James Hubbard, Laurie D. Rains

Coalition for Reasonable and Fair Taxation (CRAFT)

New York, NY
Leg. Issues: TAX

Outside Counsel/Consultants

McDermott, Will and Emery
Issues: TAX
Rep By: Calvin P. Johnson, David L. Rosen

Coalition for Reliable Energy

Washington, DC
Leg. Issues: ENG, NAT

Outside Counsel/Consultants

J. Arthur Weber & Associates
Issues: ENG, NAT
Rep By: Joseph A. Weber

Coalition for Responsible Waste Incineration

1133 Connecticut Ave. NW
Suite 1023
Washington, DC 20036
Tel: (202)775-9869
Fax: (202)833-8491
Registered: LDA
Web: www.crwi.org
E-mail: crwi@erols.com

Purpose is to enhance the development and responsible use of the thermal treatment of hazardous waste. Membership includes Fortune 500 companies, academics and hazardous waste incinerators.

Leg. Issues: WAS

In-house, DC-area Employees

KEENER, Melvin E.: Exec. Director

Coalition for Safe Ceramicware

York, PA

Outside Counsel/Consultants

Collier Shannon Scott, PLLC
Rep By: David A. Hartquist, Michael R. Kershow, Robert W. Porter

Coalition for Shareholder Fairness

Washington, DC
Registered: LDA

Outside Counsel/Consultants

Baker & Hostetler LLP
Rep By: Steven A. Lotterer, Hon. Guy Vander Jagt

Coalition for Stability in Marine Financing

Seattle, WA

Outside Counsel/Consultants

Preston Gates Ellis & Rouvelas Meeds LLP
Rep By: William N. Myhre

Coalition for Sugar Reform

McLean, VA

A coalition of trade associations opposed to government-guaranteed prices for sugar growers. Members include Chocolate Maufacturers Ass'n, Grocery Manufacturers of America Inc., Independent Bakers Ass'n, Nat'l Soft Drink Ass'n, Citizens for a Sound Economy and Consumer Federation of America.

Leg. Issues: AGR

Outside Counsel/Consultants

McLeod, Watkinson & Miller
Issues: AGR
Rep By: Randy Green, Michael R. McLeod

Coalition for Tax Equity

Leg. Issues: GOV, TAX

Outside Counsel/Consultants

O'Connor & Hannan, L.L.P.
Issues: GOV, TAX
Rep By: Danielle Fagre, Timothy W. Jenkins

Coalition for the American Agricultural Producer (CAAP)

Austin, TX
Leg. Issues: AGR

Outside Counsel/Consultants

Hogan & Hartson L.L.P.
Issues: AGR
Rep By: Humberto R. Pena

Coalition for the Fair Taxation of Business Transactions

Washington, DC
Leg. Issues: TAX

Outside Counsel/Consultants

Arthur Andersen LLP
Issues: TAX
Rep By: Rachelle Bernstein, Weston J. Coulam

Coalition for the Homeless

1234 Massachusetts Ave. NW
Washington, DC 20005
Tel: (202)347-8870
Fax: (202)347-7279
Web: www.dccfh.org
E-mail: mferrell@dccfh.org

Operates centers and transitional houses for the homeless and persons at risk of being homeless. Provides a program by which homeless individuals can realize independent living status and become economically contributing members of the community.

Leg. Issues: ALC, HCR, HOU, WEL

In-house, DC-area Employees

FERRELL, Michael L.: Exec. Director

Coalition for the Prevention of Alcohol Problems

c/o Ctr. for Science in Public Interest
1875 Connecticut Ave. NW, Suite 300
Washington, DC 20009-5728
Tel: (202)332-9110
Fax: (202)265-4954
E-mail: ghacker@cspinet.org

Promotes national policies to reduce alcohol problems, including restrictions on alcoholic beverage promotion.

In-house, DC-area Employees

HACKER, George A.: Chairman

Coalition for Travel Industry Parity

Rockville Centre, NY
Leg. Issues: TOU

Outside Counsel/Consultants

American Continental Group, Inc.
Issues: TOU
Rep By: John A. Cline, Steve Colovas, Shawn H. Smeallie

Coalition for Truth in Environmental Marketing Information, Inc.

c/o Grocery Manufacturers of America
1010 Wisconsin Ave. NW, Suite 900
Washington, DC 20007
Tel: (202)337-9400
Fax: (202)337-4508

A coalition of trade associations representing 3,600 businesses which support ecolabeling of consumer products consistent with the Federal Trade Commission Guides for the Use of Environmental Marketing Claims. Members of the coalition include the Aluminum Ass'n; the American Forest and Paper Ass'n; the American Plastics Council; the Can Manufacturers Institute; the Chemical Specialties Manufacturers Ass'n; the Cosmetic, Toiletry, and Fragrance Ass'n; the Electronic Industries Ass'n ; the Flexible Packaging Ass'n; the Grocery Manufacturers Ass'n; the Nat'l Food Processors Ass'n; the Soap and Detergent Ass'n; and the Soc. of the Plastics Industry.

Leg. Issues: CSP, ENV, TRD

In-house, DC-area Employees

KOCHENDERFER, Karil L.: Contact

Outside Counsel/Consultants

O'Melveny and Myers LLP
Issues: CSP, ENV, TRD
Rep By: Peggy A. Clarke, Gary N. Horlick

Paul, Hastings, Janofsky & Walker LLP
Rep By: E. Donald Elliott

Coalition for Uniform Product Liability Law

Leg. Issues: CSP, TOR

Outside Counsel/Consultants

Sellery Associates, Inc.
Issues: CSP, TOR
Rep By: Amy B. Kimball, William C. Sellery, Jr.

Coalition for Vehicle Choice

Washington, DC
Leg. Issues: TRA

Outside Counsel/Consultants

The Direct Impact Co.

George Reagle
Issues: TRA
Rep By: George Reagle

Coalition for Workers' Health Care Funds

Leg. Issues: TOB

Outside Counsel/Consultants

Connerton & Ray
Issues: TOB
Rep By: David L. Mallino, Sr., David L. Mallino, Jr.

Coalition of Academic Scientific Computation (CASC)

Columbus, OH
Leg. Issues: SCI

Outside Counsel/Consultants

Fratkin Associates
Issues: SCI
Rep By: Susan Fratkin

Coalition of Black Trade Unionists

P.O. Box 66268
Washington, DC 20035-6268
Web: www.cbtu.org
Tel: (202)429-1203
Fax: (202)429-1102

Founded in 1972 to bring more blacks into active trade union participation. President is William Lucy of the American Federation of State, County and Municipal Employees.

In-house, DC-area Employees

BAKER, Willie: Exec. V. President
DUNCAN, Will: Special Assistant

Coalition of Boston Teaching Hospitals

Boston, MA
Leg. Issues: BUD, HCR, MED, MMM

Outside Counsel/Consultants

Covington & Burling
Issues: HCR
Rep By: Roderick A. DeArment, Joan L. Kutcher

O'Neill, Athy & Casey, P.C.
Issues: BUD, HCR, MED, MMM
Rep By: Martha L. Casey, Christopher R. O'Neill

Coalition of Commercial and Investment Banks

Washington, DC

Outside Counsel/Consultants

Griffin, Johnson, Dover & Stewart
Rep By: Keith Heard

Coalition of Corporate Taxpayers

Leg. Issues: TAX

Outside Counsel/Consultants

PriceWaterhouseCoopers
Issues: TAX
Rep By: Jim Carlisle, Kenneth J. Kies, Don R. Longano

Coalition of EPSCoR States

Leg. Issues: BUD

Outside Counsel/Consultants

Van Scoyoc Associates, Inc.
Issues: BUD
Rep By: Carolyn Fuller, Jan Schoonmaker, H. Stewart Van Scoyoc

Coalition of Food Importers Ass'ns

New York, NY

Outside Counsel/Consultants

Harris Ellsworth & Levin

Coalition of Hawaii Movers

Honolulu, HI
Leg. Issues: DEF, MAR, SMB, TRA

Outside Counsel/Consultants

R. J. Hudson Associates
Issues: DEF, MAR, SMB, TRA
Rep By: Rebecca J. Hudson

Coalition of Higher Education Assistance Organizations

Washington, DC
Web: www.coheao.com
Leg. Issues: BUD, EDU, HCR

Outside Counsel/Consultants

Dean Blakey & Moskowitz
Issues: BUD, EDU, HCR
Rep By: Ellin J. Nolan

Coalition of Independent Salvage Pools of America (CISPA)

Outside Counsel/Consultants

Columbus Public Affairs

Coalition of New England Companies for Trade

Framingham, MA
Leg. Issues: TRD

Outside Counsel/Consultants

Lindsay Hart Neil & Weigler
Issues: TRD
Rep By: Kathryn Beaubien, Peter Friedmann

Coalition of Northeastern Governors

400 N. Capitol St. NW
Suite 382
Washington, DC 20001
Web: www.coneg.org
Tel: (202)624-8450
Fax: (202)624-8463

A non-profit organization conducting regional research and programs for the Northeastern Governors. It does limited monitoring of federal issues.

In-house, DC-area Employees

STUBBS, Anne D.: Exec. Director

Coalition of Positive Outcomes in Pregnancy

Marietta, GA
Leg. Issues: HCR

Outside Counsel/Consultants

Health and Medicine Counsel of Washington
Issues: HCR
Rep By: Dale P. Dirks

Coalition of Private Safety-Net Hospitals

Outside Counsel/Consultants

Hauser Group

Coalition of Publicly Traded Partnerships

805 15th St. NW
Suite 500
Washington, DC 20005
Tel: (202)371-9770
Fax: (202)371-6601

A trade ass'n representing publicly traded partnerships, corporations which are general partners of PTPs, and attorneys, accountants, and others who work with them.

Leg. Issues: TAX

Political Action Committee/s

Coalition of Publicly Traded Partnerships Political Action Committee
805 15th St. NW
Suite 500
Washington, DC 20005
Tel: (202)371-9770
Fax: (202)371-6601

In-house, DC-area Employees

CHAMBERS, Letitia: President
LYMAN, Mary S.: Tax Counsel

Outside Counsel/Consultants

Chambers Associates Inc.
Issues: TAX
Rep By: Letitia Chambers, Mary S. Lyman

Coalition of Service Industries

805 15th St. NW
Suite 1110
Washington, DC 20005
Web: www.uscsi.org
E-mail: csi@uscsi.org
Tel: (202)289-7460
Fax: (202)775-1726
Registered: LDA

Represents 40 major service corporations on foreign and economic policy matters.

Leg. Issues: BAN, FIN, FOR, INS, TAX, TEC, TRA, TRD

In-house, DC-area Employees

SCHMID, Linda: V. President and Director, Electronic Commerce
VASTINE, J. Robert: President

Outside Counsel/Consultants

Wilmer, Cutler & Pickering
Issues: TRD
Rep By: Charles S. Levy

Coalition of Supporters of the Shipping Act

Outside Counsel/Consultants

Morgan, Lewis & Bockius LLP
Rep By: Helene L. Glick

Coalition on Accessibility

Washington, DC
Leg. Issues: ART, CIV, GOV, SPO

Outside Counsel/Consultants

Epstein Becker & Green, P.C.
Issues: ART, CIV, GOV, SPO
Rep By: Carolyn Doppelt Gray, Michael B. Lehrhoff, Cathie A. Shattuck

Coalition on AFDC Quality Control Penalties

A group of state agencies that administer human service programs.

Outside Counsel/Consultants

Covington & Burling
Rep By: Joan L. Kutcher

Coalition on EAF Funding

A group of state agencies that administer human services programs.

Outside Counsel/Consultants

Covington & Burling
Rep By: Joan L. Kutcher, Phyllis D. Thompson

Coalition on Human Needs

1120 Connecticut Ave. NW
Suite 910
Washington, DC 20006
Web: www.chn.org
E-mail: chn@chn.org
Tel: (202)223-2532
Fax: (202)223-2538

An alliance of over 170 national human needs organizations concerned about the needs of the poor, minorities, children, women, the aged and people with disabilities. Major issues include federal budget priorities, welfare reform, worker supports, tax policy and block grants/federalism questions.

In-house, DC-area Employees

CAMPBELL, Stuart P.: Exec. Director
LESTER, Patrick W.: Senior Legislative Associate

Coalition on Medicaid Reform

Outside Counsel/Consultants

Covington & Burling
Rep By: Joan L. Kutcher, Charles A. Miller

The Coalition on Motor Vehicle Privacy

Washington, DC
Leg. Issues: BUD

Outside Counsel/Consultants

Mullenholz, Brimsek & Belair
Issues: BUD
Rep By: Robert R. Belair, John R. Brimsek, Susan C. Haller

Coalition on Occupational Safety and Health

c/o Nat'l Ass'n of Manufacturers
1331 Pennsylvania Ave. NW, Suite 600
Washington, DC 20004
Tel: (202)728-1164
Fax: (202)728-2992

A coalition of some 400 business and industry interests contesting organized labor's efforts to revise and strengthen workplace safeguards under the Occupational Safety and Health Act.

Leg. Issues: LBR

In-house, DC-area Employees

LUNNIE, Pete: Exec. Director

Outside Counsel/Consultants

Ogletree Governmental Affairs, Inc.
Issues: LBR
Rep By: Francis M. Lunnie, Jr.

Coalition on Royalties Taxation

Washington, DC

Outside Counsel/Consultants

Arthur Andersen LLP
Rep By: Rachelle Bernstein, Richard A. Gordon, T. Timothy Tuerff

Coalition on the Implementation of the AFA

Washington, DC
Leg. Issues: MAR

Outside Counsel/Consultants

Garvey, Schubert & Barer
Issues: MAR
Rep By: Paul S. Hoff

Coalition to Advance Sustainable Technology

Englewood, CO
Leg. Issues: ENV

Outside Counsel/Consultants

The Dutko Group, Inc.
Issues: ENV
Rep By: Peg Brown, Deana Perlmutter

Coalition to Amend the Financial Information Privacy Act (CAFPA)

Mamaroneck, NY
Leg. Issues: BAN, BNK

Outside Counsel/Consultants

Butera & Andrews
Issues: BAN, BNK
Rep By: Cliff W. Andrews, Wright H. Andrews, Jr., James J. Butera, Frank Tillotson

Coalition to Ensure Responsible Billing

Outside Counsel/Consultants

Swidler Berlin Shereff Friedman, LLP
Rep By: Kristine DeBry, Gary D. Slaiman, Katherine R. Taylor

Coalition to Preserve Employee Ownership of S Corporation

Washington, DC
Leg. Issues: TAX

Outside Counsel/Consultants

Arthur Andersen LLP
Issues: TAX
Rep By: Weston J. Coulam, Carol Kulish

Coalition to Preserve Mine Safety Standards

Washington, DC
Leg. Issues: LBR

Outside Counsel/Consultants

Patton Boggs, LLP
Issues: LBR
Rep By: Henry Chajet, Brian C. Lopina

Coalition to Preserve the Integrity of American Trademarks

1405 Montague Dr.
Vienna, VA 22182
Tel: (703)759-3377

A group of U.S. trademark owners opposed to the unauthorized importation into the United States of goods bearing their trademarks.

In-house, DC-area Employees

COLLADO, Emilio G.: Exec. Director

Outside Counsel/Consultants

Covington & Burling

Coalition to Preserve Tracking Stock

Leg. Issues: TAX

Outside Counsel/Consultants

Washington Council Ernst & Young
Issues: TAX
Rep By: Doug Badger, Lauren Darling, John L. Doney, Jayne T. Fitzgerald, LaBrenda Garrett-Nelson, Gary J. Gasper, Bruce A. Gates, Nick Giordano, Robert J. Leonard, Richard Meltzer, Phillip D. Moseley, John D. Porter, Robert M. Rozen, Donna Steele-Flynn, Timothy J. Urban

Coalition to Protect Community Not-for-Profit Hospitals

Outside Counsel/Consultants

Widmeyer Communications, Inc.

Coalition to Repeal the Davis-Bacon Act

1300 N. 17th St.
Eighth Floor
Arlington, VA 22209
Tel: (703)812-2000
Fax: (703)812-8202
Registered: LDA

In-house, DC-area Employees

ANGELIER, Amy: Washington Representative
BOUCHER JAMESON, Jennifer: Legislative Director
BURR, Geoff: Legal Assistant
CRAWFORD, Brian: Washington Representative

Coalition to Repeal the Tax on Talking

Washington, DC

Outside Counsel/Consultants

Quinn Gillespie & Associates
Rep By: Debbie Garrett

Coalition to Stop Gun Violence

1023 15th St. NW
Suite 600
Washington, DC 20005
Web: www.csgv.org
E-mail: csgv@csgv.org
Tel: (202)408-0061
Registered: LDA

Works to reduce the supply of and demand for handguns and assault weapons in America.

Leg. Issues: BUD, CSP, EDU, FIR, LAW, TRD

In-house, DC-area Employees

BEARD, Michael K.: President and Chief Exec. Officer
PERTSCHUK, Mark: Director, Legislative Affairs

Outside Counsel/Consultants

Hauser Group

Coalitions for America

717 Second St. NE
Washington, DC 20002
Tel: (202)546-3003
Fax: (202)547-0392
Registered: LDA

A conservative lobbying organization which brings together a wide range of organizations for the purpose of coordinating strategy and organizing grass roots participation in the political process.

Leg. Issues: ENV, LAW, TOB

In-house, DC-area Employees

LICHT, Eric: President
THOMPSON, Bob: V. President

Coast Alliance

600 Pennsylvania Ave. SE
Suite 340
Washington, DC 20003
Web: www.coastalliance.org
E-mail: coast@coastalliance.org
Tel: (202)546-9554
Fax: (202)546-9609

A public interest organization working to raise public concerns about conservation of the nation's coastal resources.

Leg. Issues: ENV, NAT

In-house, DC-area Employees

HAZLEWOOD, Catherine: Counsel, Pollution Program
SAVITZ, Jacqueline: Exec. Director

Coast Federal Savings and Loan Ass'n

Sarasota, FL

Outside Counsel/Consultants

Elias, Matz, Tiernan and Herrick

Coastal Conservation Ass'n

Houston, TX

A group of recreational fisheries.

Leg. Issues: MAR, NAT

Outside Counsel/Consultants

Ball Janik, LLP
Issues: MAR, NAT
Rep By: Robert G. Hayes, Irene Ringwood

Coastal Impact Assistance & Reinvestment

Baton Rouge, LA
Leg. Issues: BUD, FUE, NAT, ROD

Outside Counsel/Consultants

Adams and Reese LLP
Issues: BUD, FUE, NAT, ROD
Rep By: B. Jeffrey Brooks, Hon. James A. "Jimmy" Hayes

Coastal States Organization

444 N. Capitol St. NW
Suite 322
Washington, DC 20001
Web: www.sso.org/cso
E-mail: cso@sso.org
Tel: (202)508-3860
Fax: (202)508-3843

A representative ass'n of governors of 35 states, commonwealths and territories of the U.S. which have an ocean, gulf or Great Lakes boundary. Dedicated to providing an effective voice in the formation of national coastal and marine resource programs and policies.

In-house, DC-area Employees

KEHOE, Kerry: Legislative Counsel
LOPEZ, John: Policy Analyst
MACDONALD, Tony: Exec. Director

Coastal Transportation Inc.

Leg. Issues: MAR

Outside Counsel/Consultants

Preston Gates Ellis & Rouvelas Meeds LLP
Issues: MAR
Rep By: William N. Myhre

CoBank, ACB

Denver, CO
Registered: LDA
Leg. Issues: AGR, TRD

Outside Counsel/Consultants

Mayer, Brown & Platt
Issues: AGR, TRD
Rep By: Amb. Peter L. Scher

The PMA Group
Rep By: Fred J. Clark, Kaylene Green, Paul J. Magliocchetti, Timothy K. Sanders

The Coca-Cola Company

800 Connecticut Ave. NW
Suite 711
Washington, DC 20006
Web: www.cocacola.com
Tel: (202)973-2660
Registered: LDA

Headquartered in Atlanta, GA.

Leg. Issues: AGR, BEV, CPT, ENV, FOO, FOR, IMM, LBR, TAX, TRD

In-house, DC-area Employees

ANDERSON, Bryan D.: Director, Government Relations
BROWNLEE, John T.: Manager, Government Relations
GOLTZMAN, Michael: International Relations
HOWARD, Janet: V. President, International Relations
RESLER, Barclay T.: Assistant V. President, Governmental Relations

Outside Counsel/Consultants

BKSH & Associates
Issues: CPT, FOO, IMM, TAX

Hurt, Norton & Associates
Issues: BEV
Rep By: Robert H. Hurt, Frank Norton, William K. Takakoshi, Katharine Calhoun Wood

Quinn Gillespie & Associates

White & Case LLP
Issues: TAX
Rep By: William P. McClure

Williams & Jensen, P.C.
Issues: AGR, BEV, ENV, FOO, LBR, TAX
Rep By: Bertram W. Carp, Robert E. Glennon, Jr., J. Steven Hart

Cochlear Corp.

Englewood, CO

Outside Counsel/Consultants

Washington Healthcare Representatives
Rep By: Heather H. Bremer

Coeur d'Alene Mines Corp.

Coeur d'Alene, ID
Leg. Issues: CAW, ENV, NAT

Outside Counsel/Consultants

Goodstein & Associates
Issues: CAW, ENV, NAT

The Renkes Group, Ltd.
Issues: NAT
Rep By: Gregg D. Renkes

Ryan, Phillips, Utrecht & MacKinnon
Issues: CAW, ENV, NAT
Rep By: Rodney Hoppe, Jeffrey M. MacKinnon, William D. Phillips, Mark D. Planning, Thomas M. Ryan, Joseph V. Vasapoli

Coffee Reserve

Little Rock, AR
Leg. Issues: TAX, TRD

Outside Counsel/Consultants

Johnson Co.
Issues: TAX, TRD
Rep By: James H. Johnson

COGEMA, Inc.

7401 Wisconsin Ave.
Suite 500
Bethesda, MD 20814
Web: www.cogema-inc.com
Tel: (301)986-8585
Fax: (301)652-5690
Registered: LDA, FARA

Formerly known as French-American Metals Corp. Owns Pathfinder Mines, Inc. in the U.S. Cogema provides supplies and services for all stages of nuclear fuel cycle.

Leg. Issues: BUD, ENG, SCI

In-house, DC-area Employees

BYERLY, Christi: Communications Manager
GUAIS, Jean Claude: V. President, Strategic Development
MCMURPHY, Michael A.: President and Chief Exec. Officer
PENNINGTON, Thomas W.: V. President and General Counsel

Outside Counsel/Consultants

Bill Carney & Co.
Issues: ENG, SCI
Rep By: Jacqueline Carney, Hon. William Carney

Johnston & Associates, LLC
Issues: BUD, ENG, SCI
Rep By: Hon. J. Bennett Johnston, N. Hunter Johnston, W. Proctor Jones, Eric Tober

Cogentrix, Inc.

Charlotte, NC

Outside Counsel/Consultants

Chadbourne and Parke LLP
Rep By: Keith Martin

Ronald J. Cohen Investments

Bethesda, MD
Leg. Issues: BUD, DOC, RES

Outside Counsel/Consultants

Patton Boggs, LLP
Issues: BUD, DOC, RES
Rep By: Brian C. Lopina

Cohn & Wolfe

1801 K St. NW
Suite 601 L
Washington, DC 20006
Web: www.cohnwolfe.com
Tel: (202)756-7100
Fax: (202)756-7200

In-house, DC-area Employees

HAWKINS, III, John R.: Exec. V. President
KENNEDY, Brian: Senior Account Executive
NICHOLSON, Anne: V. President

Outside Counsel/Consultants

MV3 & Associates

RTS Consulting

Valente Lopatin & Schulze
Rep By: Richard T. Schulze, Jr., Mark Valente, III

Coin Acceptors, Inc.

St. Louis, MO
Leg. Issues: BUD

Outside Counsel/Consultants

Bryan Cave LLP
Issues: BUD
Rep By: Mark N. Ludwig

The Coin Coalition

Washington, DC
Web: www.coincoalition.org
E-mail: info@mail.coincoalition.org

A lobbying group calling for a newly-designed one dollar coin and phasing out of the dollar bill.

Leg. Issues: MON

Outside Counsel/Consultants

Bracy Williams & Co.
Issues: MON
Rep By: James C. Benfield

Coin Laundry Ass'n

Downers Grove, IL
Web: www.coinlaundry.org
E-mail: info@coinlaundry.org

Outside Counsel/Consultants

Jenner & Block

Colakoglu Group

Istanbul, TURKEY
Leg. Issues: TRD

Outside Counsel/Consultants

Dickstein Shapiro Morin & Oshinsky LLP
Issues: TRD
Rep By: Alev Kaymak, L. Andrew Zausner

Cold Finished Steel Bar Institute

P.O. Box 70194
Washington, DC 20024-0914
Web: www.cfsbi.com
E-mail: info@cfsbi.com
Tel: (202)508-1030
Fax: (703)241-5603

Leg. Issues: MAN

In-house, DC-area Employees

TYERYAR, CAE, Clay D.: Executive Staff

Colebrand, Ltd.

London, UNITED KINGDOM

Outside Counsel/Consultants

Shaw Pittman

Coleman Aerospace Co.

Orlando, FL
Leg. Issues: SCI

Outside Counsel/Consultants

Albertine Enterprises, Inc.
Issues: SCI
Rep By: James J. Albertine, Dr. John M. Albertine

Coleman Powermate

Aurora, IL
Leg. Issues: ENG, TRA

Outside Counsel/Consultants

Lighthouse Energy Group LLC
Issues: ENG, TRA
Rep By: Tobyn J. Anderson, Merribel S. Ayres

Coleman Research Corp.

Fairfax, VA
Leg. Issues: AER, DEF, FOR

Outside Counsel/Consultants

Balch & Bingham LLP
Issues: DEF
Rep By: Wade Heck, William F. Stiers

Teicher Consulting and Representation
Issues: AER, DEF, FOR
Rep By: Howard R. Teicher

Colgan Air, Inc.

Manassas, VA
Leg. Issues: AVI

Outside Counsel/Consultants

Ungaretti & Harris
Issues: AVI
Rep By: Edward P. Faberman

Colgate Palmolive

New York, NY
Leg. Issues: TRD

Outside Counsel/Consultants

Aitken, Irvin, Lewin, Berlin, Vrooman & Cohn
Issues: TRD
Rep By: Bruce Aitken, Adam S. Apatoff, Martin J. Lewin, Kieran Sharpe

Skadden, Arps, Slate, Meagher & Flom LLP
Issues: TRD
Rep By: Robert E. Lighthizer

Collagen Corp.

Palo Alto, CA
Leg. Issues: HCR

Outside Counsel/Consultants

Akin, Gump, Strauss, Hauer & Feld, L.L.P.
Issues: HCR
Rep By: Gary A. Heimberg, Steven R. Ross, Barney J. Skladany, Jr.

College and University Professional Ass'n for Human Resources

1233 20th St. NW
Suite 301
Washington, DC 20036-1250
Web: www.cupahr.org
Tel: (202)429-0311
Fax: (202)429-0149

An association of more than 6,000 human resource administrators representing over 1,800 colleges and universities.

In-house, DC-area Employees

AITKEN, Michael P.: Associate Exec. Director, Government and External Relations
OTZENBURGER, Stephen J.: Exec. Director
ROTHSTEIN, Audrey R.: Assistant Exec. Director, Planning and Operations

The College Board

1233 20th St. NW
Washington, DC 20036-2304
Web: www.collegeboard.org
Tel: (202)822-5900
Fax: (202)822-5920

Leg. Issues: AGR, BUD, EDU, TAX, TEC

In-house, DC-area Employees

RASCO, Carol H.: Exec. Director for Government Relations

Outside Counsel/Consultants

Widmeyer Communications, Inc.

College Football Bowl Ass'n

Jacksonville, FL

Outside Counsel/Consultants

Akin, Gump, Strauss, Hauer & Feld, L.L.P.

College of American Pathologists

1350 I St. NW
Suite 590
Washington, DC 20005
Web: www.cap.org
Tel: (202)354-7100
Fax: (202)354-7155
Registered: LDA

Headquartered in Northfield, IL.

Leg. Issues: BUD, GOV, HCR, LBR, MED, MMM, TAX

Political Action Committee/s

PathPAC

1350 I St. NW
Suite 590
Washington, DC 20005
Contact: Rebecca Woodcock
Tel: (202)354-7105
Fax: (202)354-7155

In-house, DC-area Employees

BELL, Denise: Director, Government Affairs
BERRY, Ann: Manager, Political Development
BONGIORNO, Phillip: Policy Analyst, Professional Affairs
CARLILE, Jane: Assistant Director, Professional Affairs
MILLER, Charles R.: Director, Political Programs and Grassroots Communication
MONGILLO, David: Director, Public Health and Scientific Affairs
PALMER, Michael C.: Director, Professional Affairs
WOODCOCK, Rebecca: PAC Contact
ZIMAN, Barry: Assistant Director, State Affairs

College of the Desert

Palm Desert, CA
Leg. Issues: EDU

Outside Counsel/Consultants

Washington Alliance Group, Inc.
Issues: EDU
Rep By: Bonnie Singer

College on Problems of Drug Dependence

Philadelpha, PA

A professional medical research organization.

Leg. Issues: ALC, BUD, CPT, HCR, LAW, MED, TOB

Outside Counsel/Consultants

Capitol Associates, Inc.
Issues: ALC, BUD, CPT, HCR, LAW, MED, TOB
Rep By: Julie Shroyer

College Parents of America

Arlington, VA
Leg. Issues: EDU

Outside Counsel/Consultants

Bracy Williams & Co.
Issues: EDU
Rep By: Linda Doorfee Flaherty, Susan J. Williams

College Republican Nat'l Committee

600 Pennsylvania Ave. SE
Suite 301
Washington, DC 20003
Tel: (202)608-1411
Fax: (202)608-1429
Web: www.crnc.org
E-mail: mail@crnc.org

Promotes the Republican Party on college campuses.

In-house, DC-area Employees

HAMILTON, Parker: Exec. Director
STEWART, Scott: Chairman

College Savings Bank

Princeton, NJ

Outside Counsel/Consultants

Patton Boggs, LLP
Rep By: James B. Christian, Jr., George J. Schutzer

College Station, Texas, City of

Leg. Issues: ENG, GOV, UTI

Outside Counsel/Consultants

Duncan, Weinberg, Genzer & Pembroke, P.C.
Issues: ENG, GOV, UTI
Rep By: Wallace L. Duncan, Michael R. Postar

Collier Shannon Scott, PLLC

3050 K St. NW
Washington, DC 20007
Tel: (202)342-8400
Fax: (202)342-8451
Registered: LDA, FARA
Web: www.colliershannon.com
E-mail: lawyers@colliershannon.com

Political Action Committee/s

Collier Shannon Scott, LLC PAC
3050 K St. NW
Washington, DC 20007
Tel: (202)342-8555
Fax: (202)342-8451
Contact: R. Timothy Columbus

In-house, DC-area Employees

AUSTRIAN, Mark L.: Member
BECKINGTON, Jeffrey S.: Member
BLILEY, Jr., Hon. Thomas J.: Senior Advisor, Gov't Relations and Public Pol.
BREW, John B.: Member
COLUMBUS, R. Timothy: Member
CONWAY, Janice E.: Government Relations Advisor
COURSEY, Michael J.: Member
GILBERT, Robin H.: Member
GUERRY, Jr., William M.: Member
HARTQUIST, David A.: Member
HOWARD, Lauren R.: Member
KANTOR, Doug: Associate
KERSHOW, Michael R.: Of Counsel
KIES, Kathleen Clark: Assistant Director, Government Relations
LASOFF, Laurence J.: Member
LEITER, Jeffrey L.: Member
MACLEOD, William C.: Member
MATSUI, Doris O.: Senior Advisor and Director, Government Relations and Public Policy
MCMAHON, Kathryn M. T.: Member
OLDHAM, Judith L.: Member
PAINTER, Dustin: Government Relations Advisor
PORTER, Robert W.: Government Relations Advisor
ROSENTHAL, Paul C.: Member
SCOTT, Gregory M.: Associate
SCOTT, William W.: Member
SHANNON, Thomas F.: Of Counsel
SHERMAN, Michael D.: Member
SINDER, Scott A.: Member
SMITH, Jr., David C.: Of Counsel
THOMPSON, Chet M.: Associate
WITTENBORN, John L.: Member
WOOD, Dana S.: Director, Government Relations

Outside Counsel/Consultants

Suzie Brewster & Associates
Rep By: Suzie Brewster

Colombia Flower Council

Miami, FL
Registered: LDA

Outside Counsel/Consultants

Akin, Gump, Strauss, Hauer & Feld, L.L.P.

Colombia, Government of the Republic of

Bogota, COLOMBIA

Outside Counsel/Consultants

Akin, Gump, Strauss, Hauer & Feld, L.L.P.
Rep By: David Geanacopoulos, Barney J. Skladany, Jr.

BSMG Worldwide

Colombia, Ministry of Communications of

Bogota, COLOMBIA

Outside Counsel/Consultants

Wilkinson, Barker and Knauer, LLP

Colombian American Service Ass'n

Miami, FL
Leg. Issues: BUD, IMM

Outside Counsel/Consultants

The C.L.A. Group, LLC
Issues: BUD, IMM
Rep By: Laurence L. Socci

Colombian American Trade Center

Miami, FL
Leg. Issues: ECN, TRD

Outside Counsel/Consultants

The C.L.A. Group, LLC
Issues: ECN, TRD
Rep By: Laurence L. Socci

Colombian Banking and Financial Entities Ass'n (ASOBANCARIA)

Bogota, COLOMBIA
Leg. Issues: BAN, FIN, FOR

Outside Counsel/Consultants

Skol & Associates, Inc.
Issues: BAN, FIN, FOR
Rep By: Michael M. Skol

Colombian Coffee Federation

New York, NY
Leg. Issues: ADV, MIA, TRD

Outside Counsel/Consultants

Strategic Choices, Inc.
Issues: ADV, MIA, TRD
Rep By: Thomas A. Devine, Nick Mitropoulos, Robert M. Shrum

Colombian Government Trade Bureau

1701 Pennsylvania Ave. NW
Suite 560
Washington, DC 20006
Tel: (202)887-9000
Fax: (202)223-0526
Web: www.coltrade.org

The Washington, DC office of Colombia's Ministry of Foreign Trade.

In-house, DC-area Employees

JARAMILLO, Felipe: Director

Colonial Pipeline Co.

Atlanta, GA
Leg. Issues: FUE, TAX

Outside Counsel/Consultants

Williams & Jensen, P.C.
Issues: FUE, TAX
Rep By: George D. Baker, David E. Franasiak, J. Steven Hart, Frank C. Vlossak

The Colonial Williamsburg Foundation

Williamsburg, VA

Outside Counsel/Consultants

Jorden Burt LLP
Rep By: Patricia Branch, Alanna Dillon, Marna Gettleman, Marilyn Berry Thompson, Rebecca Tidman

Van Scoyoc Associates, Inc.

Coloplast Corp.

Marietta, GA
Leg. Issues: HCR, MMM

Outside Counsel/Consultants

Nusgart Consulting, LLC
Issues: HCR, MMM
Rep By: Marcia Nusgart

Color Marketing Group

5904 Richmond Hwy.
Suite 408
Alexandria, VA 22303
Tel: (703)329-8500
Fax: (703)329-0155
Web: www.colormarketing.org
E-mail: cmg@colormarketing.org

In-house, DC-area Employees

BURNS, C.A.E., Nancy A.: Exec. Director

Color Pigments Manufacturers Ass'n, Inc.

300 N. Washington St.
Suite 102
Alexandria, VA 22314
Tel: (703)684-4044
Fax: (703)684-1795
E-mail: info@cpma.com

Trade association representing manufacturers of color pigments in Canada, Mexico, and the U.S.

Leg. Issues: CHM, SCI

In-house, DC-area Employees

ROBINSON, J. Lawrence: President

Colorado Ass'n of Transit Agencies

Denver, CO
Leg. Issues: TRA

Outside Counsel/Consultants

The Carmen Group
Issues: TRA

LMRC, Inc.
Rep By: John Lagomarcino

Colorado Credit Union Systems

Arvada, CO
Leg. Issues: BAN

Outside Counsel/Consultants

Brownstein Hyatt & Farber, P.C.
Issues: BAN
Rep By: William T. Brack, Michael B. Levy

Colorado Energy Assistance Foundation

Denver, CO

Outside Counsel/Consultants

Duncan, Weinberg, Genzer & Pembroke, P.C.
Rep By: Jeffrey C. Genzer

Colorado Hispanic League

Denver, CO

Outside Counsel/Consultants

Kutak Rock LLP

Colorado Intermountain Fixed Guideway Authority

Dumont, CO
Leg. Issues: TRA

Outside Counsel/Consultants

American Continental Group, Inc.
Issues: TRA
Rep By: John A. Cline, Shawn H. Smeallie

Colorado River Commission of Nevada

Las Vegas, NV
Leg. Issues: NAT, RES

Outside Counsel/Consultants

Columbus Public Affairs

Marcus G. Faust, P.C.
Issues: NAT, RES
Rep By: Marcus G. Faust

Colorado River Energy Distributors Ass'n

Salt Lake City, UT
Leg. Issues: ENG

Outside Counsel/Consultants

Morgan Meguire, LLC
Issues: ENG
Rep By: Scott Lindsay, Kyle G. Michel, Katie Parrott, C. Kyle Simpson, Deborah R. Sliz, Kiel Weaver

Colorado River Indian Tribes

Parker, AZ
Leg. Issues: BUD, ECN, GOV, IND, MAN, ROD, SMB, TEC, UTI

Outside Counsel/Consultants

Peter Homer
Issues: BUD, ECN, GOV, IND, MAN, ROD, SMB, TEC, UTI
Rep By: Peter Homer

PACE-CAPSTONE
Issues: IND
Rep By: Scott C. Dacey, James W. Wise

Colorado River Water Conservation District
Glenwood Springs, CO
Outside Counsel/Consultants
Brickfield, Burchette, Ritts & Stone
Rep By: Michael N. McCarty, Colleen Newman

Colorado Springs Utilities
Colorado Springs, CO
Leg. Issues: DEF, ENG, UTI
Outside Counsel/Consultants
Talley and Associates
Issues: DEF, ENG, UTI
Rep By: Robert A. C. Talley

Colorado Springs-Pikes Peak, City of
Colorado Springs, CO
Leg. Issues: ENV
Outside Counsel/Consultants
The Carmen Group
Issues: ENV

Colorado, Department of Transportation of the State of
Denver, CO
Leg. Issues: TRA
Outside Counsel/Consultants
LMRC, Inc.
Issues: TRA
Rep By: John Lagomarcino

Colsa Corp.
Huntsville, AL
A computing services company.
Leg. Issues: CPI, DEF
Outside Counsel/Consultants
Hall, Green, Rupli, LLC
Issues: CPI, DEF
Rep By: John M. Green, G. Stewart Hall

Columbia Capital Corp.
Alexandria, VA
Outside Counsel/Consultants
Covington & Burling
Rep By: Michael E. Cutler

Columbia College Chicago
Chicago, IL
Leg. Issues: BUD, EDU
Outside Counsel/Consultants
Metcalf Federal Relations
Issues: BUD, EDU
Rep By: Anne Metcalf

Columbia Falls Aluminum Co.
Columbia Falls, MT
Leg. Issues: ENG
Outside Counsel/Consultants
Ball Janik, LLP
Issues: ENG
Rep By: Robert G. Hayes, Irene Ringwood

Columbia Gas Transmission Corp.
Ten G St. NE
Suite 580
Washington, DC 20002
Tel: (202)216-9760
Fax: (202)216-9786
A subsidiary of NiSource Inc.
In-house, DC-area Employees
ROYKA, Sharon: Regulatory Representative
Outside Counsel/Consultants
Wright & Talisman, P.C.
Rep By: Jeffrey G. DiSciullo

Columbia Gulf Transmission Corp.
Outside Counsel/Consultants
Wright & Talisman, P.C.
Rep By: Jeffrey G. DiSciullo

Columbia Helicopters, Inc.
Portland, OR
Outside Counsel/Consultants
Zuckert, Scoutt and Rasenberger, L.L.P.
Rep By: Rachel B. Trinder

Columbia Lighthouse for the Blind
1120 20th St. NW
Suite 750 South
Washington, DC 20036
Web: www.clb.org
E-mail: info@clb.org
Tel: (202)454-6400
Fax: (202)454-6401

The Columbia Lighthouse sponsors programs for infants, children, adults and senior citizens who are blind or have vision impairments. All activities are designed to assist visually impaired individuals in leading fulfilling, independent lives. The Columbia Lighthouse serves the District of Columbia, Maryland, and Virginia.

In-house, DC-area Employees
LEONARD, Tracy: Director, Communications
OTTO, Dale: President and Chief Exec. Officer
ZIMMER, Kim: V. President, Communications

Columbia Natural Resources
Charleston, WV
Leg. Issues: CAW, ENG, ENV, WAS
Outside Counsel/Consultants
Wright & Talisman, P.C.
Issues: CAW, ENG, ENV, WAS
Rep By: Robert H. Lamb

Columbia Research Corp.
Indian Head, MD
Outside Counsel/Consultants
Bob Lawrence & Associates
Rep By: Anthony Taylor

Columbia University
New York, NY
Leg. Issues: AGR, BUD, CPT, ENV, MED
Outside Counsel/Consultants
Terry Bevels Consulting
Issues: AGR, BUD, ENV
Rep By: Terry D. Bevels
Cassidy & Associates, Inc.
Issues: BUD
Rep By: Carl Franklin Godfrey, Jr., Dennis M. Kedzior, Jeffrey Lawrence, Valerie Rogers Osborne, Hon. Martin A. Russo
Wiley, Rein & Fielding
Issues: CPT, MED
Rep By: James T. Bruce, III, Susan C. Buck, Hon. Jim Slattery

Columbia University/Institute for Learning Technologies
New York, NY
Leg. Issues: EDU
Outside Counsel/Consultants
Washington Alliance Group, Inc.
Issues: EDU
Rep By: Bonnie Singer

Columbia Ventures, LLC
Columbia, SC
Outside Counsel/Consultants
Winston & Strawn
Rep By: Hon. James H. Burnley, IV, Peter N. Hiebert, Roger A. Keller, Jr., Hon. John L. Napier

Columbia, South Carolina, City of
Leg. Issues: HOU, LAW, TRA, URB
Outside Counsel/Consultants
Barbara T. McCall Associates
Issues: HOU, LAW, TRA, URB
Rep By: Ralph Garboushian, Barbara T. McCall

Columbus Educational Services
Outside Counsel/Consultants
Valente Lopatin & Schulze
Rep By: Alan G. Lopatin, Richard T. Schulze, Jr., Mark Valente, III

Columbus General, L.L.C.
New Orleans, LA
Leg. Issues: CPI, DEF
Outside Counsel/Consultants
Jones, Walker, Waechter, Poitevent, Carrere & Denegre, L.L.P.
Issues: CPI, DEF
Rep By: Paul Cambon, John J. Jaskot, R. Christian Johnsen

Columbus Medical Services
Outside Counsel/Consultants
Valente Lopatin & Schulze
Rep By: Alan G. Lopatin, Richard T. Schulze, Jr., Mark Valente, III

Columbus State College
Columbus, OH
Leg. Issues: EDU
Outside Counsel/Consultants
Wise & Associates
Issues: EDU
Rep By: Dwayne Sattler

Colusa Basin Drainage District
Woodland, CA
Leg. Issues: BUD, NAT
Outside Counsel/Consultants
The Ferguson Group, LLC
Issues: BUD, NAT
Rep By: W. Roger Gwinn, Joseph L. Raeder

Colville Business Council
Nespelem, WA
Outside Counsel/Consultants
Sonosky, Chambers, Sachse & Endreson
Rep By: William R. Perry

COMARCO Wireless Technology
Irvine, CA
Leg. Issues: SCI, TRA
Outside Counsel/Consultants
Ann Eppard Associates, Ltd.
Issues: SCI, TRA
Rep By: Julie Chlopecki, Ann Eppard

The Comcare Alliance
Outside Counsel/Consultants
Nat'l Strategies Inc.
Rep By: David K. Aylward, Marsha Scherr

Comcast Corp.
2001 Pennsylvania Ave. NW
Suite 500
Washington, DC 20006
Tel: (202)638-5678
Fax: (202)466-7718
Registered: LDA
Web: www.comcast.com
Leg. Issues: ART, COM, CPT, MIA, TEC
In-house, DC-area Employees
COLTHARP, James R.: Senior Director, Public Policy
WAZ, Jr., Joseph W.: V. President, External Affairs and Public Policy Counsel
Outside Counsel/Consultants
The Duberstein Group, Inc.
Issues: ART, COM, CPT, MIA, TEC
Rep By: John W. Angus, III, Michael S. Berman, Steven M. Champlin, Kenneth M. Duberstein, Henry M. Gandy, Daniel P. Meyer
Hooper Owen & Winburn
Issues: COM
Rep By: David Rudd
Mintz, Levin, Cohn, Ferris, Glovsky and Popeo, P.C.
Rep By: James L. Casserly
The Wexler Group
Issues: TEC
Rep By: Sena Fitzmaurice, R. D. Folsom, Dale W. Snape, Hon. Robert S. Walker, Anne Wexler

COMDISCO, Inc.
Rosemont, IL
Leases computer equipment.
Leg. Issues: TAX
Outside Counsel/Consultants
Mayer, Brown & Platt
Issues: TAX

ComEd
400 Seventh St. NW
Fourth Floor
Washington, DC 20004
Tel: (202)347-7500
Fax: (202)347-7501
Commonwealth Edison, headquartered in Chicago, IL.
Leg. Issues: BUD, RRR, TAX, UTI, WAS
In-house, DC-area Employees
CAPUTO, Annie: Strategic Issues Communicator

Outside Counsel/Consultants

Bonner & Associates

The Direct Impact Co.

Foley & Lardner
Issues: RRR
Rep By: Jodi L. Hanson, Jerris Leonard, Richard F. Riley, Jr.

Governmental Strategies, Inc.

Oppenheimer Wolff & Donnelly LLP
Issues: WAS
Rep By: Hon. Birch Bayh, Kevin O. Faley

Washington Council Ernst & Young
Issues: BUD, TAX, UTI
Rep By: Doug Badger, Lauren Darling, John L. Doney, Jayne T. Fitzgerald, LaBrenda Garrett-Nelson, Gary J. Gasper, Bruce A. Gates, Nick Giordano, Cathy Koch, Robert J. Leonard, Richard Meltzer, Phillip D. Moseley, John D. Porter, Robert M. Rozen, Donna Steele-Flynn, Timothy J. Urban

Comerica, Inc.

Detroit, MI
Leg. Issues: BAN, FIN

Outside Counsel/Consultants

Dykema Gossett PLLC
Issues: BAN
Rep By: David K. Arthur, Nancy R. Barbour

LegisLaw
Issues: FIN
Rep By: Linda A. Woolley, Esq.

Comic Magazine Ass'n of America

4041 Powder Mill Rd.
Suite 104
Calverton, MD 20705
Tel: (301)348-2005
Fax: (301)348-2020

In-house, DC-area Employees

SNYDER, Russell K.: Washington Representative

Outside Counsel/Consultants

The Kellen Company
Rep By: Russell K. Snyder

Cominco Alaska Inc.

Kotzebue, AK
Leg. Issues: CAW

Outside Counsel/Consultants

The Renkes Group, Ltd.
Issues: CAW
Rep By: Gregg D. Renkes

Cominco, Ltd.

Vancouver, CANADA

Outside Counsel/Consultants

McKenna & Cuneo, L.L.P.

ComInternational Management Inc.

Hamilton, BERMUDA
Leg. Issues: FOR

Outside Counsel/Consultants

Jefferson-Waterman Internat'l, LLC
Issues: FOR
Rep By: Samuel H. Wyman, Jr.

Comision Ejecutiva Hidroelectrica del Rio Lempa CEL

San Salvador, EL SALVADOR

Outside Counsel/Consultants

Burson-Marsteller
Rep By: Craig G. Veith

Command Systems Inc.

Fort Wayne, IN
Leg. Issues: CPI, DEF

Outside Counsel/Consultants

Potomac Strategies Internat'l LLC
Issues: CPI, DEF
Rep By: Robert J. Curran, Raymond F. DuBois, Jr., James K. Wholey

Commco, L.L.C.

Sioux Falls, SD

Outside Counsel/Consultants

Patton Boggs, LLP
Rep By: Paul C. Besozzi, Thomas Hale Boggs, Jr., Penelope S. Farthing, John F. Fithian, Stephen Diaz Gavin, Benjamin L. Ginsberg

Commerce Clause Coalition

Washington, DC

Campaigns against legislation that inhibits the exportation of garbage across state lines. Members include the Nat'l Solid Wastes Management Ass'n and Waste Management.

Outside Counsel/Consultants

Akin, Gump, Strauss, Hauer & Feld, L.L.P.
Rep By: Barney J. Skladany, Jr.

Commerce Ventures

Chicago, IL
Leg. Issues: AGR

Outside Counsel/Consultants

Lesher & Russell, Inc.
Issues: AGR
Rep By: William G. Lesher, Randall M. Russell

Commercial Finance Ass'n

New York, NY
Registered: LDA
Leg. Issues: BNK, CPT

Outside Counsel/Consultants

Butera & Andrews
Issues: BNK, CPT
Rep By: Philip S. Corwin

Commercial Information Systems, Inc.

Portland, OR
Leg. Issues: CPI

Outside Counsel/Consultants

Verner, Liipfert, Bernhard, McPherson and Hand, Chartered
Issues: CPI
Rep By: Timothy M. Rutten

Commercial Internet Exchange Ass'n

1301 K Street NW
Suite 325
Washington, DC 20005
Web: www.cix.org
E-mail: info@cix.org
Tel: (703)709-8200
Fax: (703)709-5249

An advocacy and trade association for Internet service providers.

Leg. Issues: COM, CON, CPI, CPT, CSP, FAM, GAM, SCI, SMB, TEC

In-house, DC-area Employees

DOOLEY, Barbara A.: President
LEE, Eric: Director, Public Policy

Outside Counsel/Consultants

Piper Marbury Rudnick & Wolfe LLP
Issues: COM, CPI, CPT, CSP, FAM, GAM, TEC
Rep By: Emilio W. Cividanes, James J. Halpert, Stuart P. Ingis, Vincent M. Paladini, Ronald L. Plesser

Commercial Law League of America

Millburn, NJ
Leg. Issues: BAN, BNK

Outside Counsel/Consultants

Webster, Chamberlain & Bean
Issues: BAN, BNK
Rep By: David P. Goch

Commercial Service Co., Ltd.

Houston, TX
Leg. Issues: FUE

Outside Counsel/Consultants

Grisso Consulting
Issues: FUE
Rep By: Michael E. Grisso

Commercial Services Internat'l

Ft. Lauderdale, FL
Leg. Issues: TRD

Outside Counsel/Consultants

Sandler, Travis & Rosenberg, P.A.
Issues: TRD
Rep By: Shannon Fura, Jeremy Page

Commercial Vehicle Safety Alliance

5430 Grosvenor Lane
Suite 130
Bethesda, MD 20814-2142
Web: www.cvsa.org
Tel: (301)564-1623
Fax: (301)564-0588

A North American trucking safety group.

In-house, DC-area Employees

CAMPBELL, Stephen F.: Exec. Director

Commercial Weather Services Ass'n (CWSA)

Alexandria, VA
Web: www.weather-industry.org
E-mail: CWSA@wpa.org

A trade association promoting private weather-related companies and services.

Leg. Issues: CPI, NAT, SCI

Outside Counsel/Consultants

Strategic Impact, Inc.
Issues: CPI, NAT, SCI
Rep By: Michael C. Jimenez, Patrick J. Mitchell

Commission of Accredited Truck Driving Schools (CATDS)

Alexandria, VA
E-mail: cataldo2@ix.netcom.com
Leg. Issues: EDU, GOV

Outside Counsel/Consultants

Carol Cataldo & Associates
Issues: EDU, GOV
Rep By: Carol Cataldo

Commission on Graduates of Foreign Nursing Schools

Philadelphia, PA
Leg. Issues: IMM

Outside Counsel/Consultants

Paul, Weiss, Rifkind, Wharton & Garrison
Issues: IMM
Rep By: Carl W. Hampe, John Ratigan

Commission on Presidential Debates

Outside Counsel/Consultants

George Kroloff & Associates
Rep By: George Kroloff

Commissioned Officers Ass'n of the U.S. Public Health Service

8201 Corporate Dr.
Suite 560
Landover, MD 20785
Web: www.coausphs.org
E-mail: mikecoa@aol.com
Tel: (301)731-9080
Fax: (301)731-9084
Registered: LDA

A professional association of public health service commissioned officers and health care professionals.

Leg. Issues: GOV, HCR

In-house, DC-area Employees

LORD, USN (Ret.), Michael W.: Exec. Director

Committee for a Democratic Majority

227 Massachusetts Ave. NE
Suite 101
Washington, DC 20002
Tel: (202)544-4889
Fax: (202)546-2285

In-house, DC-area Employees

LOPACH, Tom: Director
OLDAKER, William C.: Treasurer

Outside Counsel/Consultants

Oldaker and Harris, LLP
Rep By: William C. Oldaker

Committee for a Responsible Federal Budget

220 1/2 E St. NE
Washington, DC 20002
E-mail: crfb@aol.com
Tel: (202)547-4484
Fax: (202)547-4476

A non-profit, educational organization committed to educating the public regarding the budget issues and process that have significant fiscal policy impact. Founded in 1981, the Committee is governed by a bi-partisan board composed of former directors of the Office of Management and Budget and the Congressional Budget Office, former Chairmen and ranking members of the House and Senate Budget Committees, other former leaders of Federal institutions and leaders of private industry. Major activities include non-partisan analysis and research, educational symposia and the preparation and distribution of educational materials.

Leg. Issues: BUD, ECN, GOV, HCR, MMM, RET, TAX

In-house, DC-area Employees

WAIT, Carol Cox: President

Committee for Citizen Awareness

Washington, DC

A non-profit, non-partisan organization seeking to enhance public awareness of the legislative process and increase voter participation.

Outside Counsel/Consultants

Manatos & Manatos, Inc.
Rep By: Kimberley M. Fraser

Committee for Economic Development

2000 L St. NW
Suite 700
Washington, DC 20036
Web: www.ced.org
Tel: (202)296-5860
Fax: (202)223-0776

An independent research and educational organization whose 250 Trustees formulate business and public policies that can help solve the nation's most critical economic and social problems. Unique policy making process centers on the active participation of these corporate and university leaders. Currently study topics include K thru 12 education; campaign finance reform; immigration reform; globalization and trade; and e-commerce and the digital economy.

In-house, DC-area Employees

KOLB, Charles: President
OOMS, Van Doorn: Senior V. President, Director of Research
PETRO, Michael J.: Chief of Staff, V. President and Director, Business and Government Policy
SCHWARTZ, Elliot: V. President and Director, Economic Studies

Committee for Education Funding

122 C St. NW
Suite 280
Washington, DC 20001
Web: www.cef.org
E-mail: ekealy@cef.org
Tel: (202)383-0083
Fax: (202)383-0097
Registered: LDA

A coalition of 100 educational institutions, associations, and state departments of education advocating adequate federal funding for education.

Leg. Issues: BUD, EDU

In-house, DC-area Employees

KEALY, Edward R.: Exec. Director

Committee for Fair Ammonium Nitrate Trade

Washington, DC
Leg. Issues: TRD

Outside Counsel/Consultants

Akin, Gump, Strauss, Hauer & Feld, L.L.P.
Issues: TRD
Rep By: Valerie A. Slater, S. Bruce Wilson

Committee for Farmworker Programs

Rochester, NY
Leg. Issues: LBR

Outside Counsel/Consultants

Moss McGee Bradley & Foley
Issues: LBR
Rep By: Leander J. Foley, III

Committee for Good Common Sense

Washington, DC
Leg. Issues: DEF, TAX

Outside Counsel/Consultants

Ikon Public Affairs
Issues: DEF, TAX
Rep By: Edward J. Stucky

Committee for Humane Legislation

2000 P St. NW
Suite 415
Washington, DC 20036
Web: www.envirolink.org/arrs/foa
E-mail: foa@igc.apc.org
Tel: (202)296-2172
Fax: (202)296-2190

The lobbying arm of Friends of Animals, an international animal protection organization.

In-house, DC-area Employees

DOLLINGER, Bill: Washington Representative

Committee for Purchase from People Who Are Blind or Severely Disabled

1421 Jefferson Davis Hwy.
Suite 10800
Arlington, VA 22202
Web: www.jwod.gov
E-mail: lwilson@jwod.gov
Tel: (703)603-7740
Fax: (703)603-0655

The Committee administers a mandatory federal procurement program that generates employment and training opportunities for persons who are blind or have other severe disabilities. Committee members are representatives from eleven Federal Government Agencies and four private citizens.

In-house, DC-area Employees

WILSON, Jr., Leon A.: Exec. Director

Committee for the Study of the American Electorate

421 New Jersey Ave. SE
Washington, DC 20003
Web: www.gspm.org/csae
E-mail: csnag@erols.com
Tel: (202)546-3221
Fax: (202)546-3571

In-house, DC-area Employees

GANS, Curtis B.: Director

Committee of Annuity Insurers

Washington, DC
Web: www.annuity-insurers.org

A 48-member coalition of life insurance companies that issue annuities. Committee was formed in 1981 to address Federal legislative and regulatory issues confronting the annuity industry and to participate in the development of Federal tax policy affecting annuities.

Leg. Issues: TAX

Outside Counsel/Consultants

Davis & Harman LLP
Issues: TAX
Rep By: Richard S. Belas, Thomas A. Davis, Randolf H. Hardock, William B. Harman, Jr., Barbara Groves Mattox, Joseph F. McKeever, III, Kirk Van Brunt

Committee of Domestic Steel Wire Rope and Specialty Cable Manufacturers

Outside Counsel/Consultants

Harris Ellsworth & Levin
Rep By: Cheryl N. Ellsworth, Hon. Herbert E. Harris, II, Jeffrey S. Levin

Committee of Unsecured Creditors

White Plains, NY
Leg. Issues: BNK, BUD

Outside Counsel/Consultants

Jones, Walker, Waechter, Poitevent, Carrere & Denegre, L.L.P.
Issues: BNK, BUD
Rep By: Paul Cambon, John J. Jaskot, R. Christian Johnsen, James Ogsbury

The Livingston Group, LLC
Issues: BNK, BUD
Rep By: Melvin Goodweather, Hon. Robert L. Livingston, Jr., J. Allen Martin, Richard L. Rodgers

Committee on Federal Procurement of Architectural and Engineering Services

Washington, DC
Leg. Issues: GOV

Outside Counsel/Consultants

Crowell & Moring LLP
Issues: GOV
Rep By: Karen Hastie Williams

Committee on Human Rights for the People of Nicaragua

17413 Collier Way
Poolesville, MD 20837
Tel: (301)605-0501
Fax: (301)605-0503

Established in 1977 to monitor and publicize violations of human rights committed against the people of Nicaragua. Monitors, documents and reports human rights violations against Indian tribes of the east coast of Nicaragua such as the Miskitos, Sumos, Ramas and Creoles.

In-house, DC-area Employees

ANZOATEGUI, Carlos: Chairman

Outside Counsel/Consultants

Potomac Consulting Group
Rep By: Carlos Anzoategui

Committee on Pipe and Tube Imports

Washington, DC
Leg. Issues: TRA, TRD

Outside Counsel/Consultants

Schagrin Associates
Issues: TRA, TRD
Rep By: Tamara L. Browne, Roger B. Schagrin

Committee On State Taxation

122 C St. NW
Suite 330
Washington, DC 20001
Web: www.statetax.org
E-mail: dlindholm@statetax.org
Tel: (202)484-5212
Fax: (202)484-5229
Registered: LDA

In-house, DC-area Employees

LINDHOLM, Douglas: President and Exec. Director

Committee on the Constitutional System

1400 16th St. NW
Suite 715
Washington, DC 20036
Tel: (202)387-8787
Fax: (202)939-3458

Studies possible structural changes in the Constitution and other measures to improve the working relationship between the President and Congress designed to make the government more responsive to current problems.

In-house, DC-area Employees

SCHAUFFLER, Peter: Coordinator

The Committee on the Parthenon

1220 16th St. NW
Suite 400
Washington, DC 20036
Tel: (202)955-1052
Fax: (202)955-5562

A research center for the study of the Parthenon and to promote the restoration of the Parthenon marbles.

In-house, DC-area Employees

POULOS, Anthi: President

Committee to Assure the Availability of Casein

Leg. Issues: AGR

Outside Counsel/Consultants

Max N. Berry Law Offices
Issues: AGR
Rep By: Max N. Berry

Committee to Preserve American Color Television

Leg. Issues: TRD

Outside Counsel/Consultants

Collier Shannon Scott, PLLC

The Cullen Law Firm
Issues: TRD

Committee to Preserve Aspen

Aspen, CO
Leg. Issues: TRA

Outside Counsel/Consultants

Butera & Andrews
Issues: TRA
Rep By: Cliff W. Andrews, Wright H. Andrews, Jr., James J. Butera, Frank Tillotson

Committee to Support the Antitrust Laws

Washington, DC
Registered: LDA
Leg. Issues: LBR

Outside Counsel/Consultants

The Cuneo Law Group, P.C.
Issues: LBR
Rep By: Jonathan W. Cuneo

Committee to Support U.S. Trade Laws

A coalition of over 100 businesses, trade associations and labor unions that believe GATT and other international trade agreements will undermine the protection afforded U.S. companies against foreign dumping and other unfair trade practices.

Leg. Issues: TRD

Outside Counsel/Consultants

Hale and Dorr LLP
Issues: TRD
Rep By: Gilbert B. Kaplan

Common Cause

1250 Connecticut Ave. NW
Washington, DC 20036
Web: www.commoncause.org
Tel: (202)833-1200
Fax: (202)659-3716
Registered: LDA

A non-profit, non-partisan citizens' lobby fighting for honest and accountable government, limits on special-interest in government, and restoration of ethics and integrity.

Leg. Issues: BUD, CIV, COM, GOV, TAX

In-house, DC-area Employees

BOK, Derek: Chairman
CRONIN, Jeff: Press Secretary
DAVIS, Edwin H.: Associate Director, Issues Development
HARSHBARGER, Scott: President
KELLER, Matthew: Legislative Director
MALLOY, Claudia: Secretary to the National Governing Board
MCGEHEE, Meredith: Senior V. President
SWANSON, Eric: Exec. V. President
WEXLER, Celia Viggo: Lobbyist/Policy Analyst

Outside Counsel/Consultants

Sonosky, Chambers, Sachse & Endreson
Rep By: Donald Simon

Wilmer, Cutler & Pickering
Rep By: Roger M. Witten

Common Sense Common Solutions PAC

1155 21st St. NW
Suite 300
Washington, DC 20036
Tel: (202)659-8201
Fax: (202)659-5249

In-house, DC-area Employees

BONFIGLIO, Barbara Wixon

Commonwealth Atlantic Properties

Alexandria, VA
Leg. Issues: RES

Outside Counsel/Consultants

The Hawthorn Group, L.C.
Issues: RES

The Livingston Group, LLC
Issues: RES
Rep By: Hon. Robert L. Livingston, Jr., J. Allen Martin

Commonwealth Consulting Corp.

Arlington, VA
Leg. Issues: AER, BUD, DEF

Outside Counsel/Consultants

The Gallagher Group, LLC
Issues: AER, BUD, DEF
Rep By: James P. Gallagher

The Commonwealth Fund

New York, NY

Outside Counsel/Consultants

Hauser Group

IssueSphere

CommSource Internat'l, Inc.

Chicago, IL

Outside Counsel/Consultants

O'Connor & Hannan, L.L.P.
Rep By: Robert W. Barrie

Communication Service for the Deaf

Sioux Falls, SD
Leg. Issues: TEC

Outside Counsel/Consultants

O'Connor & Hannan, L.L.P.
Issues: TEC
Rep By: Hon. Larry Pressler

Communications Consortium

1200 New York Ave. NW
Suite 300
Washington, DC 20005
E-mail: info@ccmc.org
Tel: (202)326-8700
Fax: (202)682-2154

A non-profit public interest media organization working on several issues, including: family policy, health reform, global population, immigration, environment, and welfare reform.

In-house, DC-area Employees

BONK, Kathy: President and Chief Exec. Officer
TYNES, Emily: V. President

Communications Training Analysis Corp. (C-TAC)

Arlington, VA
Leg. Issues: DEF, ENG, GOV

Outside Counsel/Consultants

Van Scoyoc Associates, Inc.
Issues: DEF, ENG, GOV
Rep By: Paul Grimm, Buzz Hawley, H. Stewart Van Scoyoc

Communications Workers of America

501 Third St. NW
Washington, DC 20001-2797
Tel: (202)434-1100
Fax: (202)434-1318
Registered: LDA

Web: www.cwa-union.org
Leg. Issues: BUD, HCR, LBR, TEC

Political Action Committee/s

Communications Workers of America-Committee on Political Education
501 Third St. NW
Washington, DC 20001-2797
Contact: Kathy Wagner
Tel: (202)434-1100
Fax: (202)434-1139

In-house, DC-area Employees

BAHR, Morton: President
BEAUMONT, Dina: Exec. Assistant to the President
EASTERLING, Barbara J.: Secretary-Treasurer
GERBER, Louis M.: Administrative Assistant to Secretary-Treasurer/Chief Lobbyist
JOHNSON, Candice: Associate Director, Communications
LEGRANDE, David E.: Director, Occupational Safety and Health
MILLER, Jeff: Director, Communications
NOVOTNY, Louise: Research Economist (Health Policy Analyst)
SCANLON, Patrick M.: General Counsel
WAGNER, Kathy: Director, Politics and COPE
WALSH, Hugh Leo: President and Director of Political and Legislative Affairs

Outside Counsel/Consultants

Greer, Margolis, Mitchell, Burns & Associates
Rep By: Jim Margolis, Greg Pinelo

The Kamber Group
Rep By: Donovan McClure

Communities in Schools, Inc.

Alexandria, VA
Leg. Issues: BUD

Outside Counsel/Consultants

Tongour Simpson Holsclaw Green
Issues: BUD
Rep By: John Bradley "Brad" Holsclaw, Michael A. Tongour

Community Anti-Drug Coalitions of America

Alexandria, VA
Leg. Issues: ALC

Outside Counsel/Consultants

Susan R. Thau
Issues: ALC
Rep By: Susan R. Thau

Community Ass'ns Institute (CAI)

225 Reinekers Lane
Suite 300
Alexandria, VA 22314
Web: www.caionline.org
Tel: (703)548-8600
Fax: (703)684-1581
Registered: LDA

Founded in 1973, CAI acts as a voice for the 42 million people who live in 205,000 community associations of all sizes and architectural types throughout the U.S. In addition to individual homeowners, membership also includes community association managers and management firms, attorneys, accountants, engineers, builders/developers, and other providers of products and services for community homeowners and their associations. Represents their constituency on a range of issues such as taxation, bankruptcy, and insurance. Over 16,500 members participate in the public process through 57 local Chapters and 26 state Legislative Action Committees.

Leg. Issues: BNK, COM, ENV, HOU, INS, RES, TAX, TEC, UTI

Political Action Committee/s

Community Ass'ns Institute PAC
225 Reinekers Lane
Suite 300
Alexandria, VA 22314
Contact: Steven J. Erd
Tel: (703)548-8600
Fax: (703)684-1581

In-house, DC-area Employees

BYRD KEENAN, CAE, Barbara: President
ERD, Steven J.: Director, Government and Public Affairs

Community Bank League of New England

Boston, MA

Outside Counsel/Consultants

Cassidy & Associates, Inc.

Community Banks Ass'n of New York State

New York, NY
Leg. Issues: BAN

Outside Counsel/Consultants

Butera & Andrews
Issues: BAN
Rep By: Cliff W. Andrews, Wright H. Andrews, Jr., James J. Butera, Frank Tillotson

The Community Builders, Inc.

1200 G St. NW
Suite 800
Washington, DC 20005
Web: www.tcbinc.org
E-mail: cherylf@tcbinc.org
Tel: (202)661-6101
Fax: (202)628-2040
Registered: LDA

A non-profit housing developer headquartered in Boston, MA.

Leg. Issues: BUD, HOU, URB, WEL

In-house, DC-area Employees

FOX, Cheryl: Director of Policy

Community Development Financial Institutions (CDFI)

Philadelphia, PA
Leg. Issues: BAN, ECN

Outside Counsel/Consultants

Moss McGee Bradley & Foley
Issues: BAN, ECN
Rep By: Leander J. Foley, III

Community Development Venture Capital Ass'n

Duluth, MN
Leg. Issues: AGR, ECN

Outside Counsel/Consultants

Robert A. Rapoza Associates
Issues: AGR, ECN
Rep By: Alison Feighan, Robert A. Rapoza

Community Financial Services Ass'n

Washington, DC
Web: www.cfsa.net
E-mail: cfsa@dc.sba.com
Leg. Issues: BAN, CSP, FIN

Outside Counsel/Consultants

Barnett & Sivon, P.C.
Issues: BAN, CSP, FIN
Rep By: Robert E. Barnett, Jose S. Rivas, James C. Sivon

Dittus Communications
Rep By: Debra Cabral, Alice Slater, Kristin Young

Hall, Green, Rupli, LLC
Issues: BAN
Rep By: John M. Green, G. Stewart Hall, Timothy R. Rupli

McIntyre Law Firm, PLLC
Issues: BAN, CSP, FIN
Rep By: Chrys D. Lemon, James T. McIntyre

Smith, Bucklin and Associates, Inc.
Rep By: William E. Kelley

Community for Creative Non-Violence

425 Second St. NW
Washington, DC 20001
Web: www.erols.com/ccnv
Tel: (202)393-4409
Fax: (202)783-3254

In-house, DC-area Employees

BISHOP, Terri: President and Co-Spokesperson
HENRY, Fred: V. President and Co-Spokesperson

The Community Foundation for the Nat'l Capital Region

1112 16th St. NW
Suite 340
Washington, DC 20036
Web: www.cfncr.org
Tel: (202)955-5890
Fax: (202)955-8084

A public non-profit organization which receives, administers and distributes charitable funds for the DC Metro area.

In-house, DC-area Employees

FREEMAN, Terri Lee: President

Community General Hospital of Sullivan County

Harris, NY
Leg. Issues: HCR, MED

Outside Counsel/Consultants

Cassidy & Associates, Inc.
Issues: HCR, MED
Rep By: Marie James, Maureen Walsh

Community Health Partners of Ohio

Lorain, OH
Leg. Issues: ECN, HCR

Outside Counsel/Consultants

Cassidy & Associates, Inc.
Issues: ECN, HCR
Rep By: Marie James, Christopher Lamond, Daniel J. McNamara, Hon. Martin A. Russo, Lyllett Wentworth

Community Health Systems, Inc.

Brentwood, TN
Leg. Issues: MMM

Outside Counsel/Consultants

Greenberg Traurig, LLP
Issues: MMM
Rep By: Howard J. Cohen, Rob Garagiola, Russell J. Mueller, Nancy E. Taylor, Timothy P. Trysla

Community Hospital Telehealth Consortium

Lake Charles, LA
Leg. Issues: BUD, HCR

Outside Counsel/Consultants

Cassidy & Associates, Inc.
Issues: BUD, HCR
Rep By: W. Campbell Kaufman, IV, Diane Rinaldo, Marnie Russ, Maureen Walsh

Community Hospitals of Central California

Fresno, CA
Leg. Issues: BUD, HCR, WEL

Outside Counsel/Consultants

Sacramento-Potomac Consulting, Inc.
Issues: BUD, HCR, WEL
Rep By: Benjamin G. Griffith, Hon. Richard H. Lehman

Community Learning and Information Network, Inc.

1750 K St. NW
12th Floor East
Washington, DC 20006
Tel: (202)857-2330
Fax: (202)835-0643
Registered: LDA
Web: www.clin.org

In-house, DC-area Employees
HENDERSON, James E.: V. President, Operations
PIERCE, William F.: V. President, Education

Community Preservation Corp.

New York, NY
Leg. Issues: BAN, FIN, HOU

Outside Counsel/Consultants

Butera & Andrews
Issues: BAN, FIN, HOU
Rep By: Cliff W. Andrews, James J. Butera, Frank Tillotson

Community Transit

Lynnwood, WA
Leg. Issues: TRA

Outside Counsel/Consultants

Government Relations, Inc.
Issues: TRA
Rep By: Thomas J. Bulger, Mark H. Miller, John N. Young

Community Transit Ass'n of Idaho

Boise, ID
Leg. Issues: TRA

Outside Counsel/Consultants

The Carmen Group
Issues: TRA

Community Transportation Ass'n of America

1341 G St. NW
Tenth Floor
Washington, DC 20005
Tel: (202)628-1480
Fax: (202)737-9197
Web: www.ctaa.org

A national membership organization to promote individual mobility and public transit in rural and urban communities. Formerly (1989) known as Rural America.

Leg. Issues: BUD, HCR, IND, INS, LBR, ROD, SMB, TRA, UNM, URB, WEL

In-house, DC-area Employees
BOGREN, Scott: Associate Director, Communications
MARSICO, Dale J.: Exec. Director

Outside Counsel/Consultants

Robert A. Rapoza Associates
Issues: BUD, TRA
Rep By: Alison Feighan, Robert A. Rapoza

COMPACT

Outside Counsel/Consultants

Collier Shannon Scott, PLLC
Rep By: Jeffrey S. Beckington, Laurence J. Lasoff

Companhia Maritima Nacional

Rio de Janeiro, BRAZIL

Outside Counsel/Consultants

Hoppel, Mayer and Coleman

Compania Mexicana de Aviacion

Mexico City, MEXICO

Outside Counsel/Consultants

Squire, Sanders & Dempsey L.L.P.
Rep By: Robert D. Papkin

Compaq Computer Corp.

1300 I St. NW
Suite 900 East
Washington, DC 20005
Tel: (202)962-3830
Fax: (202)962-3838
Registered: LDA
Web: www.compaq.com

A computer manufacturer headquartered in Houston, TX.

Leg. Issues: CPT, EDU, FIN, GOV, IMM, TAX, TEC, TRD

In-house, DC-area Employees
ALBERT, Stacey Stern: Sr. Counsel, Government Affairs
BLAIR, Michele: Manager, Government Affairs
CAMPBELL, Jeffrey: Director, Federal Government Affairs
EHRGOOD, Jr., Thomas A.: Director, International Government Counsel

Outside Counsel/Consultants

James E. Boland
Issues: EDU, TAX
Rep By: James E. Boland, Jr.

Hogan & Hartson L.L.P.
Rep By: Christine A. Varney

Compass Internat'l Inc.

1730 M St. NW
Suite 911
Washington, DC 20036-4505
Tel: (202)785-3066
Fax: (202)659-5760

A Washington-based public relations, advertising and Washington representation firm established in 1974.

Leg. Issues: AER, CDT, DEF, ENV, GOV, MAN, SMB, TRD, WAS

In-house, DC-area Employees
FRANKLAND, Jr., Walter L.: Secretary-Treasurer
MORGAN, Herbert N.: Chairman

Competition in Contracting Act Coalition

Leg. Issues: LAW

Outside Counsel/Consultants

Fierce and Isakowitz
Issues: LAW

Competition Policy Institute

1156 15th St. NW
Suite 520
Washington, DC 20005
Tel: (202)835-0202
Fax: (202)835-1132
Web: www.cpi.org

Advocates competition in the telecommunications industry which will benefit the consumer.

In-house, DC-area Employees
BERLYN, Debra R.: Exec. Director
BINZ, Ronald J.: President and Policy Director

Competitive Broadband Coalition

Washington, DC

A coalition of long-distance companies who oppose revisions to the 1996 Telecommunications Act that would allow the "Baby Bells" to provide high-speed data services in the long-distance market.

Outside Counsel/Consultants

Akin, Gump, Strauss, Hauer & Feld, L.L.P.
Rep By: Hon. William L. Paxon

Competitive Consumer Lending Coalition

Washington, DC
Leg. Issues: HOU

Outside Counsel/Consultants

Akin, Gump, Strauss, Hauer & Feld, L.L.P.
Issues: HOU
Rep By: J. David Carlin, Smith W. Davis, Joel Jankowsky

Competitive Enterprise Institute

1001 Connecticut Ave. NW
Suite 1250
Washington, DC 20036
Tel: (202)331-1010
Fax: (202)331-0640
Web: www.cei.org

In-house, DC-area Employees
COLLINS, Dyann: Assistant Editor
CONKO, Gregory: Director of Food Safety Policy
DE ALESSI, Michael: Director of Center for Private Conservation
DELONG, James V.: Senior Fellow
DUKE, Emily: Director of Development
EBELL, Myron: Director Global Warming and International Environmental Policy
FREEMAN, Ali: Environmental Policy Analyst
GATTUSO, James: V. President for Policy and Management
GEORGIA, Paul J.: Environmental Policy Analyst
GILLIAM, Loralei: Director of Marketing for Development
GOLAB, Thomas: V. President for Development
KAZMAN, Sam: General Counsel
KENT, Judy: Media Contact, Center for Private Conservation
LANGER, Andrew: Associate Director for Development
LIEBERMAN, Ben Charles: Policy Analyst
LOGOMASINI, Angela: Director, Risk and Environmental Policy
MELUGIN, Jessica: Policy Analyst
MORRISON, Richard: Director of Media Relations
OKONSKI, Kendra: Research Assistant
PAIGE, Sean: Warren Brookes Fellow in Environmental Journalism
RIGGS, David: Director, Land and Natural Resource Policy
SANERA, Ph.D., Michael: Director of Center for Environmental Education Research
SCHULTZ, Max: Editorial Director
SINGLETON, Solveig: Senior Policy Analyst
SMITH, Jr., Fred L.: President and Founder
SMITH, R.J.: Sr. Environmental Scholar
ZAMBONE, Jennifer: Environmental Policy Analyst

Outside Counsel/Consultants

Christopher C. Horner
Rep By: Christopher C. Horner

Competitive Telecommunications Ass'n (COMPTEL)

1900 M St. NW
Suite 800
Washington, DC 20036-3508
Tel: (202)296-6650
Fax: (202)296-7585
Registered: LDA
Web: www.comptel.org

A national industry association representing competitive telecommunications carriers and their suppliers.

Leg. Issues: TEC

Political Action Committee/s

Comptel PAC
1900 M St. NW
Suite 800
Washington, DC 20036-3508
Tel: (202)296-6650
Fax: (202)296-7585
Contact: Carol Ann Bischoff

In-house, DC-area Employees
BISCHOFF, Carol Ann: Exec. V. President and General Counsel
FRANKLIN, Kathleen: Director, Communications
FRISBY, Jr., H. Russell: President
LAMB, Kathy: Director, Member Services
LEE, Jonathan: V. President, Regulatory Affairs
MCDOWELL, Robert: V. President and Assistant General Counsel
MONROE, Mr. Terry: V. President, Industry & Government Relations
VAN FLEET, Bonnie: Senior Manager, Public Relations

Outside Counsel/Consultants

The Dutko Group, Inc.
Issues: TEC
Rep By: Kim Koontz Bayliss, Steve Perry, Juliette M. Raffensperger, Stephen Craig Sayle

Compex Corp.

233 Constitution Ave. NE
Washington, DC 20002
Tel: (202)547-4000
Fax: (202)543-5044

In-house, DC-area Employees
DECONCINI, Hon. Dennis

Complete Business Solutions, Inc.

Farmington Hills, MI

Outside Counsel/Consultants

Seyfarth, Shaw, Fairweather & Geraldson
Rep By: Donald L. Rosenthal

Composite Can and Tube Institute

50 S. Picket St.
Suite 110
Alexandria, VA 22304-7206
Tel: (703)823-7234
Fax: (703)823-7237
Web: www.cctiwdc.org
E-mail: cctiwdc@erols.com

In-house, DC-area Employees
DANNAHEY, Mary: Associate Manager, Meetings, Publications and Programs
GARLAND, Kristine: Exec. V. President
WIGFALL, Cynthia: Director, Administration

Composite Innovations, Inc.

Woodland Hills, CA

Outside Counsel/Consultants

Ashby and Associates
Rep By: R. Barry Ashby

Composite Panel Ass'n

18928 Premiere Ct.
Gaithersburg, MD 20879
Tel: (301)670-0604
Fax: (301)840-1252
Web: www.pbmdf.com/cpa/
E-mail: info@pbmdf.com
Leg. Issues: CAW, ENV

In-house, DC-area Employees
JULA, Tom: President

Outside Counsel/Consultants
Venable
Issues: CAW, ENV
Rep By: Brock R. Landry

Composites Fabricators Ass'n

1655 N. Fort Meyer Dr.
Suite 510
Arlington, VA 22209
Tel: (703)525-0511
Fax: (703)525-0743
Web: www.cfa-hq.org
E-mail: cfa-info@cfa-hq.org
Leg. Issues: CAW

In-house, DC-area Employees
HENRIKSEN, Melissa: Exec. Director
ODETTE, Ken: Director, Government Affairs

Outside Counsel/Consultants
Galland, Kharasch, Greenberg, Fellman & Swirsky, P.C.
Parry, Romani, DeConcini & Symms
Issues: CAW
Rep By: Edward H. Baxter, Hon. Dennis DeConcini, John M. Haddow, Scott D. Hatch, Shannon Davis Henderson, Jack W. Martin, Romano Romani, Linda Arey Skladany, Hon. Steven D. Symms

Comprehensive Health Services

Detroit, MI

Outside Counsel/Consultants
McDermott, Will and Emery
Rep By: Wendy L. Krasner

Compressed Gas Ass'n

1725 Jefferson Davis Hwy.
Suite 1004
Arlington, VA 22202-4102
Tel: (703)412-0900
Fax: (703)412-0128
Registered: LDA
Web: www.cganet.com
E-mail: cga@cganet.com
Leg. Issues: NAT

In-house, DC-area Employees
JOHNSON, Carl T.: President

Comptel

Outside Counsel/Consultants
Dittus Communications
Rep By: Tom Conway, Gloria S. Dittus, Kristin Litterst, Jennifer Moire

CompTIA

Lombard, IL
Leg. Issues: CPT, TAX

Outside Counsel/Consultants
Davis O'Connell, Inc.
Issues: CPT, TAX
Rep By: Lynda C. Davis, Ph.D.
O'Connor & Hannan, L.L.P.
Issues: TAX
Rep By: Frederick T. Dombo, Hon. Thomas J. Manton, David E. Springer

Computer Adaptive Technologies

Evanston, IL
Leg. Issues: GOV

Outside Counsel/Consultants
Halsey, Rains & Associates, LLC
Issues: GOV
Rep By: Steven C. Halsey, James Hubbard, Laurie D. Rains

Computer and Communications Industry Ass'n (CCIA)

666 11th St. NW
Suite 600
Washington, DC 20001
Tel: (202)783-0070
Fax: (202)783-0534
Registered: LDA
Web: www.ccianet.org
E-mail: ccia@ccianet.org

An international association of firms that represent all aspects of the computer and communications industry. Member companies include equipment manufacturers, software developers, telecommunications service providers, systems integrators, and third party vendors.

Leg. Issues: BUD, COM, CPI, CPT, CSP, GOV, LAW, MIA, POS, SCI, TAX, TEC, TRD

Political Action Committee/s
Computer and Communications Industry Ass'n Political Action Committee
666 11th St. NW
Suite 600
Washington, DC 20001
Tel: (202)783-0070
Fax: (202)783-0534
Contact: Edward J. Black

In-house, DC-area Employees
BLACK, Edward J.: President, Chief Exec. Officer, and Treasurer
CINNAMOND, Bill: Staff Counsel
COX, William M.: Director, Operations
JACOBS, Stephen I.: V. President and Chief Counsel
LYMAN, Blair L.: Director, Public Policy
MAHLER, Jason M.: V. President and General Counsel
MARIN, Monica M.: Exec. Assistant
MILES, Leslie K.: V. President, Communications and Industry Relations
MINCHAK, Gregory N.: Senior Research Assistant
OBIECUNAS, Robert J.: Controller
RUBIN, Gabriel N.: Senior Associate

Outside Counsel/Consultants
Cohen Mohr LLP
Issues: COM, CPI, GOV, SCI, TEC
Rep By: David S. Cohen
Manatt, Phelps & Phillips, LLP
Issues: BUD, CPI, CSP, GOV, POS, TAX, TEC
Rep By: Walter Gonzales, Luke Rose, Stephen M. Ryan, Robb Watters

Computer Associates Internat'l

Islandia, NY
Leg. Issues: CPI, IMM

Outside Counsel/Consultants
Bell, Boyd & Lloyd
Issues: CPI, IMM
Rep By: Stephen J. Maguire, II
Jim Pasco & Associates
Rep By: James O. Pasco, Jr.

Computer Associates Internat'l, Inc.

Herndon, VA
Leg. Issues: BUD, CPI, DEF, LAW, SCI, TRD

Outside Counsel/Consultants
Allen Herbert
Issues: BUD, CPI, DEF, LAW, SCI, TRD
Rep By: Allen Herbert

Computer Coalition for Responsible Exports

1341 G St. NW
Suite 1100
Washington, DC 20005
Tel: (202)393-2260
Fax: (202)393-0712
Web: www.ccre.net
Leg. Issues: CPI, DEF, TRD

In-house, DC-area Employees
GREESON, Jennifer: Manager, Communications Outreach
KAY, Kenneth R.: Exec. Director
MAGGI, Philip: Coalition Policy Director

Outside Counsel/Consultants
Bergner Bockorny Castagnetti and Hawkins
Issues: CPI, DEF, TRD
Rep By: Jeffrey T. Bergner, David A. Bockorny, David Castagnetti, Melissa Schulman
Ervin Technical Associates, Inc. (ETA)
Issues: CPI, DEF, TRD
Rep By: William J. Andahazy, Hon. Jack Edwards, James L. Ervin, Donald E. Richbourg
Griffin, Johnson, Dover & Stewart
Issues: CPI, DEF, TRD
Rep By: G. Jack Dover, David E. Johnson
Infotech Strategies, Inc.
Issues: CPI, TRD
Rep By: Jennifer Greeson, Kenneth R. Kay, Philip Maggi

Computer Communications Industry of America

Leg. Issues: SMB

Outside Counsel/Consultants
Ungaretti & Harris
Issues: SMB
Rep By: Sheri Bucher, Joseph A. Cari, Jr.

Computer Data Systems, Inc.

Rockville, MD
Leg. Issues: CPI, EDU

Outside Counsel/Consultants
Van Scoyoc Associates, Inc.
Issues: CPI, EDU
Rep By: Steve E. Crane, Kevin F. Kelly, H. Stewart Van Scoyoc

Computer Intelligence 2

Atlanta, GA
Leg. Issues: AVI, CPI, GOV, TEC

Outside Counsel/Consultants
Jefferson Government Relations, L.L.C.
Issues: AVI, CPI, GOV, TEC
Rep By: William A. Roberts

Computer Sciences Corp.

3170 Fairview Park Dr.
Falls Church, VA 22042
Tel: (703)876-1000
Fax: (703)849-1005
Registered: LDA
Web: www.csc.com

Heaquartered in El Segundo, CA.

Leg. Issues: BUD, CPI

In-house, DC-area Employees
SULLIVAN, James: Director, Federal Public Relations
SWANN, Lance B.: V. President, Government Relations

Outside Counsel/Consultants
Alcalde & Fay
Issues: CPI
Rep By: Hector Alcalde, Jim Davenport, Vicki L. Iseman, Lois Moore, Julie Patterson
John G. Campbell, Inc.
Rep By: John G. Campbell
McGlotten & Jarvis
Rep By: John T. Jarvis, Robert M. McGlotten
Van Scoyoc Associates, Inc.
Issues: BUD, CPI
Rep By: Steve E. Crane, Kevin F. Kelly, Jeffrey S. Trinca, H. Stewart Van Scoyoc

Computer Systems Policy Project

1341 G St. NW
Suite 1100
Washington, DC 20005
Tel: (202)393-2260
Fax: (202)393-0712
Web: www.cspp.org

An affiliation of 13 computer company CEOs created to develop and advocate trade and technology public policies affecting the U.S. computer industry.

Leg. Issues: GOV, TRD

In-house, DC-area Employees
GREESON, Jennifer: Manager, Communications Outreach
KAY, Kenneth R.: Exec. Director
MORGAN, Moya G.: Deputy Director

Outside Counsel/Consultants
Infotech Strategies, Inc.
Issues: GOV, TRD
Rep By: Jennifer Greeson, Kenneth R. Kay, Philip Maggi, Moya G. Morgan
Wilmer, Cutler & Pickering
Issues: TRD
Rep By: Charles S. Levy

Computer Systems Technologies, Inc.

Huntsville, AL
Leg. Issues: AER, DEF

Outside Counsel/Consultants
Balch & Bingham LLP
Issues: AER, DEF
Rep By: Wade Heck, William F. Stiers

Computing Research Ass'n

1100 17th St. NW
Suite 507
Washington, DC 20036
Tel: (202)234-2111
Fax: (202)667-1066
Web: www.cra.org
E-mail: info@cra.org

Members are U.S. and Canadian academic departments of computer science and computer engineering and industrial laboratories engaging in basic computing research.

Leg. Issues: CPI, SCI

In-house, DC-area Employees
ASPRAY, Dr. William: Exec. Director

Computing Technology Industry Ass'n

6776 Little Falls Rd.
Arlington, VA 22213
Tel: (703)536-0002
Fax: (703)536-0003
Registered: LDA
Web: www.compTIA.org
E-mail: CompTIApol@aol.com

A trade association representng 8,000 U.S. and international computer and semiconductor manufacturers, distributors, software publishers, resellers, retailers, integrators, and Internet and other service providers located in 50 countries. Headquartered in Lombard, IL.

Leg. Issues: CPI, MAN, SMB, TAX, TEC, TRD

In-house, DC-area Employees
HAHN, Bruce N.: Director, Public Policy
MYDLAND, Grant: Manager, Government Affairs
SANTONIELLO, Tom: Manager, Public Policy

Compuware Corp.

Farmington Hills, MI
Leg. Issues: BUD, CPI, FIN, LBR, SCI, TAX

Outside Counsel/Consultants

The Atlantic Group, Public Affairs, Inc.
Issues: BUD, CPI, FIN, LBR, SCI, TAX
Rep By: Larry F. Ayres

ComScore

Leg. Issues: SMB

Outside Counsel/Consultants

Ungaretti & Harris
Issues: SMB
Rep By: Joseph A. Cari, Jr.

ComTech Communications, Inc.

Citrus Heights, CA
Leg. Issues: TEC

Outside Counsel/Consultants

Gardner, Carton and Douglas
Issues: TEC

ConAgra Foods, Inc.

1627 I St. NW
Suite 950
Washington, DC 20006
Tel: (202)223-5115
Fax: (202)223-5118
Registered: LDA

A diversified food company headquartered in Omaha, NE.

Leg. Issues: AGR, BUD, CAW, ENV, FOO, FOR, HCR, LBR, TRD, TRU

Political Action Committee/s

ConAgra Good Government Ass'n

1627 I St. NW
Suite 950
Washington, DC 20006
Contact: Terri R. Marshall
Tel: (202)223-5115
Fax: (202)223-5118

In-house, DC-area Employees

BAGLIEN, Brent A.: V. President, Government Affairs
BRUETT, Cameron: Government Affairs Analyst
MARINELLI, Michelle: Staff Assistant, Government Affairs
MARSHALL, Terri R.: Senior Representative, Government Affairs
WATERS, Mary Kirtley: Senior Director, Legislative Counsel
YABLUNOSKY, Andrea: Administrator, Regulatory Affairs

Outside Counsel/Consultants

Capitolink, LLC
Issues: AGR, CAW, ENV, FOO
Rep By: John H. Thorne, Ph.D.

Internat'l Business-Government Counsellors, Inc.
Issues: TRD
Rep By: John F. McDermid

The PMA Group
Rep By: Paul J. Magliocchetti, Timothy K. Sanders

Concern, Inc.

1794 Columbia Rd. NW
Washington, DC 20009
Tel: (202)328-8160
Fax: (202)387-3378

A nonprofit tax exempt organization that provides environmental information to individuals, community groups, educational institutions, public officials, and others involved with the environment and policy development.

In-house, DC-area Employees

BOYD, Susan: Exec. Director

Concerned Educators Against Forced Unionism

8001 Braddock Rd.
Springfield, VA 22160
Tel: (703)321-8519
Fax: (703)321-7342
E-mail: clj@nrtw.org
Leg. Issues: EDU, LBR

In-house, DC-area Employees

JONES, Cathy L.: Coordinator

Concerned Women for America

1015 15th St. NW
Suite 1100
Washington, DC 20005
Tel: (202)488-7000
Fax: (202)488-0806
Registered: LDA
Web: www.cwfa.org
E-mail: gputnam@cwfa.org

Acts to preserve, protect and promote traditional and Judeo-Christian values through education, legal defense, legislative programs, humanitarian aid and other activities.

Leg. Issues: BUD, CON, EDU, FAM, GOV, IMM, TAX, WEL

In-house, DC-area Employees

BLOWE, Felita: Legislative Coordinator
LAHAYE, Beverly: Founder and Chairman
NEFF, Julie: Legislative Coordinator
SCHWARTZ, Michael: President, Government Relations

Concert USA

1120 20th St. NW
Suite 1000
Washington, DC 20036
Registered: LDA
Leg. Issues: COM, CPI, FOR, TAX, TEC, TRD

In-house, DC-area Employees

BILLET, Steven
EVANS, Barbara
HOBERMAN, Mary
LOEB, Eric

Concord Coalition

1819 H St. NW
Suite 800
Washington, DC 20006
Tel: (202)467-6222
Fax: (202)467-6333
Web: www.concordcoalition.org
E-mail: concord@concordcoalition.org

A non-profit, non-partisan grassroots group advocating balanced federal budgets and reforms to make long-term fiscal policy generationally equitable, particularly Social Security and Medicare. Founded by former Senators Paul Tsongas (D-MA) and Warren Rudman (R-NH). Co-chaired by Senator Rudman and former Senator Sam Nunn (D-GA).

Leg. Issues: BUD, MMM, RET

In-house, DC-area Employees

BIXBY, Robert: Exec. Director

Concord College

Athens, WV
Leg. Issues: EDU

Outside Counsel/Consultants

Golin/Harris Internat'l
Issues: EDU
Rep By: Carol C. Mitchell

Concord Family and Adolescent Services

Acton, MA
Leg. Issues: FAM, WEL

Outside Counsel/Consultants

Capitol Partners
Issues: FAM
Rep By: William Cunningham, Jonathan M. Orloff

Commonwealth Group, Ltd.
Issues: WEL

Concrete Plant Manufacturers Bureau

900 Spring St.
Silver Spring, MD 20910
Tel: (301)587-1400
Fax: (301)587-1605
Web: www.cpmb.org
E-mail: nmaher@nrmca.org

In-house, DC-area Employees

GARBINI, Robert A.: Exec. Secretary

Concurrent Technologies Corp.

Johnstown, PA
Leg. Issues: DEF, ECN

Outside Counsel/Consultants

The PMA Group
Issues: DEF
Rep By: Daniel Cunningham, Sean Fogarty, Kaylene Green, Patrick Hiu, Dr. John Lynch, Paul J. Magliocchetti, Timothy K. Sanders, Thomas Veltri

Powell, Goldstein, Frazer & Murphy LLP
Issues: ECN
Rep By: Hon. Butler E. Derrick, Jr., David C. Quam

Condea Vista Chemical Co.

Houston, TX
Leg. Issues: TAX

Outside Counsel/Consultants

Kent & O'Connor, Inc.
Issues: TAX
Rep By: Jonathan H. Kent, Cindy Thomas

Condell Medical Center

Libertyville, IL
Leg. Issues: HCR

Outside Counsel/Consultants

Cassidy & Associates, Inc.
Issues: HCR
Rep By: Carl Franklin Godfrey, Jr., Valerie Rogers Osborne, Marnie Russ

Condor Electronic Systems

1755 Jefferson Davis Hwy.
Suite 1107
Arlington, VA 22202
Tel: (703)415-0146
Fax: (703)415-0147
Registered: LDA
E-mail: BJackM@aol.com

A defense and electronics manufacturing company headquartered in Simi Valley, California.

Leg. Issues: BUD, DEF, TRD

In-house, DC-area Employees

MILLER, B. Jack: V. President, Washington Operations

Outside Counsel/Consultants

R. C. Whitner and Associates, Inc.
Rep By: R. C. Whitner

Condor Systems

San Jose, CA
Leg. Issues: DEF

Outside Counsel/Consultants

The PMA Group
Issues: DEF
Rep By: Kaylene Green, Joseph Littleton, Paul J. Magliocchetti

Condor-Pacific Industries

West Lake Village, CA
Leg. Issues: DEF, TRD

Outside Counsel/Consultants

Patton Boggs, LLP
Issues: DEF, TRD
Rep By: James B. Christian, Jr., Darryl D. Nirenberg, Daniel E. Waltz

Confederated Salish and Kootenai Tribes of the Flathead Nation

Pablo, MT

Outside Counsel/Consultants

George Waters Consulting Service

Confederated Tribes of the Coos

Leg. Issues: IND

Outside Counsel/Consultants

Verner, Liipfert, Bernhard, McPherson and Hand, Chartered
Issues: IND
Rep By: Timothy M. Rutten

Confederated Tribes of the Grand Ronde

Grand Ronde, OR

Outside Counsel/Consultants

Edwards Associates, Inc.
Rep By: Mark Phillips

Confederated Tribes of the Umatilla Reservation of Oregon

Pendleton, OR

Outside Counsel/Consultants

Edwards Associates, Inc.
Rep By: Mark Phillips

Confederated Tribes of Warm Springs Reservation

Leg. Issues: BUD, IND

Outside Counsel/Consultants

Edwards Associates, Inc.
Issues: BUD, IND
Rep By: Mark Phillips

Confederation of Garment Exporters of the Philippines

Metro Manila, PHILIPPINES
Leg. Issues: TRD

Outside Counsel/Consultants

Sandler, Travis & Rosenberg, P.A.
Issues: TRD
Rep By: Nicole Bivens Collinson, William H. Houston, III, Ron Sorini

Conference Board of the Mathematical Sciences

1529 18th St. NW
Washington, DC 20036
Tel: (202)293-1170
Fax: (202)265-2384
Web: www.maa.org
E-mail: lkolbe@maa.org

Fifteen mathematical societies united to provide a two-way channel of communication between the mathematical community and the Washington scene, and to serve as a focus for projects of broad concern to the mathematical sciences.

In-house, DC-area Employees
ROSIER, Dr. Ronald: Administrative Officer

The Conference Board

Outside Counsel/Consultants
Edelman Public Relations Worldwide
Rep By: Christine Kelly Cimko

Conference of Educational Administrators of Schools and Programs for the Deaf

St. Augustine, FL
Leg. Issues: EDU

Outside Counsel/Consultants
Duncan and Associates
Rep By: Jack G. Duncan
Barbara Raimondo
Issues: EDU
Rep By: Barbara Raimondo

Conference of Private Operators for Response Towing

16 Duke St.
Suite 220
Alexandria, VA 22314
Tel: (703)519-1713
Fax: (703)519-1716
Registered: LDA
Web: www.c-port.org
E-mail: c-port@c-port.org

A trade group representing the private towing, salvage and rescue industry.

Leg. Issues: MAR

In-house, DC-area Employees
LAGANA, Brian: Exec. Director

Outside Counsel/Consultants
Washington Policy Associates, Inc.
Issues: MAR

Conference of State Bank Supervisors

1015 18th St. NW
Suite 1100
Washington, DC 20036-5725
Tel: (202)296-2840
Fax: (202)296-1928
Registered: LDA
Web: www.csbs.org
E-mail: nmilner@csbsdc.org

Organization's goals are (1) to improve and maintain capabilities of state banking departments and (2) maintain for states the right to determine their financial structure as best suits their needs and to exercise proper control over their financial resource base.

Leg. Issues: BAN, GOV

In-house, DC-area Employees
BERGAN, Tim N.: Senior V. President, Internat'l
GODDARD, Montrice D.: Senior V. President, Regulation
GORMAN, John S.: General Counsel
MILNER, Neil: President and Chief Exec. Officer
RYAN, John L.: Senior V. President, Policy

Congo, Democratic Republic of the

Kinshasa, CONGO
Leg. Issues: FOR

Outside Counsel/Consultants
George H. Denison
Issues: FOR
Rep By: George H. Denison

Congo, Ministry of Foreign Affairs and Economic Cooperation of the Republic of

Kinshasa, CONGO

Outside Counsel/Consultants
Washington World Group, Ltd.
Rep By: Edward J. von Kloberg, III

Congo, Office of the President of the Democratic Republic of the

Kinshasa, CONGO

Outside Counsel/Consultants
Barron-Birrell, Inc.

Congo, Office of the Prime Minister of the Democratic Republic of the

Kinshasa, CONGO

Outside Counsel/Consultants
Washington World Group, Ltd.
Rep By: Edward J. von Kloberg, III

Congo, Republic of

Brazzaville, CONGO

Outside Counsel/Consultants
Manatt, Phelps & Phillips, LLP
Rep By: Michael T. Brown, June L. DeHart, Eric Farnsworth, Margaret Gentry, Erik V. Huey, James R. Jones, John L. Ray, Jessica A. Wasserman

Congolese Rally for Democracy

Outside Counsel/Consultants
Barron-Birrell, Inc.

Congress of Nat'l Black Churches

1225 I St. NW
Suite 750
Washington, DC 20005-0908
Tel: (202)371-1091
Fax: (202)371-0908
Web: www.cnbc.org

Comprised of eight traditionally black denominations, including: African Methodist Episcopal; Christian Methodist Episcopal; Church of God In Christ; Nat'l Baptist Convention of America; Nat'l Missionary Baptist Convention in America; Progressive Nat'l Baptist Convention. African Methodist Episcopal Zion; Nat'l Baptist Convention, U.S.A., Inc. CNBC seeks to promote unity, charity, and fellowship among member denominations, and provides opportunities for the identification and implementation of program efforts that may be achieved more effectively through collective action than by any single denomination.

In-house, DC-area Employees
ROBINSON, Ms. Sullivan: Exec. Director

Congressional Accountability Project

1611 Connecticut Ave. NW
Suite 3A
Washington, DC 20009
Tel: (202)296-2787
Fax: (202)833-2406

A watchdog spinoff from Public Citizen Inc. Founded in 1987, CAP monitors and pursues Congressional reform, particularly regarding ethics issues.

In-house, DC-area Employees
RUSKIN, Gary: Director

Congressional Agenda: 90's

3220 N St. NW
Suite 178
Washington, DC 20007
Tel: (202)342-9192

In-house, DC-area Employees
WAGLEY, John R.: Treasurer

Congressional Black Caucus Foundation

1004 Pennsylvania Ave. SE
Washington, DC 20003
Tel: (202)675-6730
Fax: (202)547-3806
Web: www.cbcfnet.org
E-mail: cbcfonline.org

Supports and conducts research, technical assistance, training, education and informational activities and programs to encourage and increase participation by blacks in the political process.

In-house, DC-area Employees
EDELIN, Ph.D., Ramona H.: Exec. Director

Congressional Economic Leadership Institute

201 Massachusetts Ave. NE
Suite C-8
Washington, DC 20002
Tel: (202)546-5007
Fax: (202)546-7037
Web: www.celi.org
E-mail: celi@celi.org

An educational, private, and non-profit foundation. Serves as a link between Congress and the corporate and labor communities on economic issues.

Leg. Issues: AER, AUT, AVI, BAN, COM, CPI, CPT, DEF, ECN, EDU, FIN, FOR, IMM, INS, LBR, MAN, MED, MMM, PHA, TAX, TEC, TOR, TRA, TRD

In-house, DC-area Employees
HOUTON, Dan: Program Manager
WEINFURTER, John J.: President
WORSLEY, Joleen L.: Director

Congressional Exchange

Outside Counsel/Consultants
Hauser Group

Congressional Hispanic Caucus Institute (CHCI)

504 C St. NE
Washington, DC 20002
Tel: (202)543-1771
Fax: (202)546-2143
Web: www.chci.org
E-mail: info@chci.org

A non-profit and non-partisan education organization whose mission is to develop the next generation of Latino leaders.

Leg. Issues: EDU

In-house, DC-area Employees
DURAN, Ingrid: Exec. Director
HERRERA, Juan J.: Communications Director
JOGE, Carmen: Programs Director
VASQUEZ, DeAnna: Operations Director

Congressional Hunger Center

229 1/2 Pennsylvania Ave. SE
Washington, DC 20003
Tel: (202)547-7022
Fax: (202)547-7575
E-mail: nohungr@aol.com

The Congressional Hunger Center fights hunger by developing and placing anti-hunger leaders across the U.S. The center also conducts projects on international humanitarian matters.

In-house, DC-area Employees
COONEY, Edward: Exec. Director

Congressional Institute for the Future

444 N. Capitol St. NW
Suite 601B
Washington, DC 20001
Tel: (202)347-9001
Fax: (202)347-9004
Web: www.futuretrends.org
E-mail: info@futuretrends.org

A nonprofit, bipartisan research and education group which works regularly with 100 Members of Congress. Drawing together private and public policy leaders, the Institute addresses the implications of emerging environmental, demographic, and economic trends and related technologies and forecasts.

In-house, DC-area Employees
HENNESSY, Tom: Exec. Director
MCCORD, Rob: Senior Fellow

Congressional Institute, Inc.

316 Pennsylvania Ave. SE
Suite 403
Washington, DC 20003
Tel: (202)547-4600
Fax: (202)547-3556
Web: www.conginst.org
E-mail: change_leader@conginst.org

Founded in 1987, the Congressional Institute is a non-profit research organization focused specifically on the U.S. Congress. The Institute is attempting to better inform the public about the Congress and assist the Congress in better serving the needs of the nation.

Leg. Issues: CAW, ENV, GOV, HCR, SCI, TRD

In-house, DC-area Employees
CLIMER, Jerome F.: President

Congressional Management Foundation

513 Capitol Ct. NE
Suite 300
Washington, DC 20002
Tel: (202)546-0100
Fax: (202)547-0936
Web: www.cmfweb.org
E-mail: cmf@cmfweb.org

A nonprofit, non-partisan organization which provides management training, consulting, and publications for Members of Congress and their staffs.

In-house, DC-area Employees
CALLAHAN, Michael: IT Analyst
FOLK, Nicole: IT Writer/Analyst
GOLDSCHMIDT, Kathy: Director, IT Services
SHAPIRO, Richard H.: Exec. Director
SHEETZ, Patty: Management Consultant

Congressional Sportsmen's Foundation

303 Pennsylvania Ave. SE
Washington, DC 20003
Tel: (202)543-6850
Fax: (202)543-6853
Web: www.sportsmenslink.org
E-mail: csf@sportsmenslink.org

Works to ensure that current and future generations of Americans have the right and opportunity to hunt and fish by serving as the sportsman's link to Congress.

In-house, DC-area Employees
GABLE, Melinda D.: Exec. Director
HOGAN, Matt: Director, Conservation Policy

Connaught Laboratories Inc.

Swiftwater, PA

Outside Counsel/Consultants
Venable
Rep By: Hon. Frank J. Horton

Connectcuba

216 Justice Ct. NE
Suite A
Washington, DC 20002
Tel: (202)547-7721
Fax: (202)686-5421

Lobbies to normalize U.S. relations with Cuba.

In-house, DC-area Employees
ATKINS, Ross: Managing Director

Outside Counsel/Consultants

Ross Atkins
Rep By: Ross Atkins

Connecticut Resource Recovery Authority

Hartford, CT

Working to revitalize the downtown residential and business district of Hartford, CT.

Leg. Issues: BUD, ENV, HOU, TRA, URB

Outside Counsel/Consultants

The Michael Lewan Co.
Issues: BUD, ENV, HOU, TRA, URB
Rep By: Michael Lewan, Anne Saunders

Connecticut Steel Corp.

Wallingford, CT
Leg. Issues: TRD

Outside Counsel/Consultants

Wiley, Rein & Fielding
Issues: TRD
Rep By: Eileen P. Bradner, Sharon R. Fine, Hon. Jim Slattery

Connecticut Student Loan Foundation

Hartford, CT
Leg. Issues: EDU

Outside Counsel/Consultants

Wiley, Rein & Fielding
Issues: EDU
Rep By: Hon. Jim Slattery

Connecticut, Office of the Attorney General of the State of

Hartford, CT

Outside Counsel/Consultants

Duncan, Weinberg, Genzer & Pembroke, P.C.
Rep By: James F. Flug

Connecticut, Washington Office of the Governor of the State of

444 N. Capitol St. NW
Suite 317
Washington, DC 20001
E-mail: akaufman@sso.org
Tel: (202)347-4535
Fax: (202)347-7151

In-house, DC-area Employees
KAUFMAN, Alison: Director, Washington Office

The Connell Co.

Westfield, NJ
Leg. Issues: TAX

Outside Counsel/Consultants

Washington Council Ernst & Young
Issues: TAX
Rep By: Doug Badger, Lauren Darling, John L. Doney, Jayne T. Fitzgerald, LaBrenda Garrett-Nelson, Gary J. Gasper, Bruce A. Gates, Nick Giordano, Cathy Koch, Robert J. Leonard, Richard Meltzer, Phillip D. Moseley, John D. Porter, Robert M. Rozen, Donna Steele-Flynn, Timothy J. Urban

Conoco Inc.

800 Connecticut Ave. NW
Suite 900
Washington, DC 20006
Tel: (202)467-1060
Fax: (202)467-1080
Registered: LDA
Web: www.conoco.com

An international energy company headquartered in Houston, TX.

Leg. Issues: FOR, FUE, TAX, TRD

Political Action Committee/s

Conoco PAC

800 Connecticut Ave. NW
Suite 900
Washington, DC 20006
Tel: (202)467-1060
Fax: (202)467-1080

In-house, DC-area Employees
LARCOM, M. Kay
MACALISTER, Rodney J.: Manager, Federal Affairs

Outside Counsel/Consultants

The Duberstein Group, Inc.
Issues: FOR, FUE
Rep By: John W. Angus, III, Michael S. Berman, Steven M. Champlin, Kenneth M. Duberstein, Henry M. Gandy, Daniel P. Meyer

PriceWaterhouseCoopers
Issues: TAX
Rep By: Kenneth J. Kies

Swidler Berlin Shereff Friedman, LLP
Issues: TAX, TRD
Rep By: Harold P. Goldfield

Conquest Tours Ltd.

Toronto, CANADA

Outside Counsel/Consultants

Hewes, Gelband, Lambert & Dann, P.C.
Rep By: Stephen L. Gelband

Conscience of a Conservative PAC

2400 Clarendon Blvd.
Suite 616
Arlington, VA 22201

In-house, DC-area Employees
FINLEY, Elise K.: Contact

Consejo Nacional de Zonas Frarcas de Exportacion

Santo Domingo, DOMINICAN REPUBLIC

Outside Counsel/Consultants

Sandler & Travis Trade Advisory Services, Inc.
Rep By: Robert P. Schaffer

Sandler, Travis & Rosenberg, P.A.
Rep By: Chandri Navarro-Bowman

The Conservation Fund

1800 N. Kent St.
Suite 1120
Arlington, VA 22209
Web: www.conservationfund.org
E-mail: postmaster@conservationfund.org
Tel: (703)525-6300
Fax: (703)525-4610

A national nonprofit organization dedicated to land and water conservation and integrating economic goals with environmental principles.

Leg. Issues: ENV, RES, TAX

In-house, DC-area Employees
ERDMANN, Richard L.: Sr. V. President and General Counsel
SUTHERLAND, Dave: Senior V. President and Real Estate Director
TURNER, John F.: President and Chief Exec. Officer
WILLIAMS, Tom: Federal Project Coordinator

Conservation Internat'l Foundation

1919 M St. NW
Suite 200
Washington, DC 20036
Web: www.conservation.org
Tel: (202)912-1000
Fax: (202)912-1030

A private, non-profit organization with 7,000 members dedicated to the protection and preservation of natural ecosystems and the species that rely on these habitats for their survival.

In-house, DC-area Employees
HOODYE, Tanya R.: Operations Coordinator
MITTERMEIER, Russell A.: President
MURPHY, Robin: V. President
SEIGMANN, Peter A.: Chief Exec. Officer/Charman

Conservation Trust Fund for Puerto Rico

San Juan, PR

Outside Counsel/Consultants

Parry, Romani, DeConcini & Symms

Conservative Caucus Research, Analysis and Education Foundation

450 Maple Ave. East
Suite 309
Vienna, VA 22180
E-mail: corndorf@cais.com
Tel: (703)281-6782
Fax: (703)281-4108

Provides research and analysis of public policy issues.

In-house, DC-area Employees
ORNDORFF, Charles: Administrative V. President
PHILLIPS, Howard J.: President

The Conservative Caucus

450 Maple Ave. East
Suite 309
Vienna, VA 22180
Web: www.conservativeusa.org
E-mail: corndorf@cais.com
Tel: (703)938-9626
Fax: (703)281-4108

A national activist group promoting conservative causes. Lobbying activities specialize in organizing grassroots support.

Leg. Issues: BUD, DEF, FOR, TAX

In-house, DC-area Employees
ORNDORFF, Charles: Administrative V. Chairman

Conservative Political Action Conference

1007 Cameron St.
Alexandria, VA 22314
Web: www.cpac.org
E-mail: cpac@cpac.org
Tel: (703)739-2550
Fax: (703)836-8606

A non-partisan, educational conference. Annual gathering of conservative activists.

In-house, DC-area Employees
KEENE, David A.: Chairman

Conservative Republican Network

763-A Delaware Ave. SW
Washington, DC 20024

A political action committee.

In-house, DC-area Employees
DAVIS, Charlie: PAC Administrator

Conservative Victory Fund

104 North Carolina Ave. SE
Washington, DC 20003
E-mail: conservativevf@aol.com
Tel: (202)546-5833
Fax: (202)546-3091

A political action committee.

In-house, DC-area Employees
WINTER, Thomas S.: Treasurer

Outside Counsel/Consultants

Pearson & Pipkin, Inc.
Rep By: Ronald W. Pearson

Consolidated Administration and Security Services, Inc.

San Diego, CA

Outside Counsel/Consultants

Arnold & Porter
Rep By: Martha L. Cochran

Consolidated Diesel Corp.

Whitakers, NC

Outside Counsel/Consultants

Barnes, Richardson and Colburn
Rep By: Matthew T. McGrath, Gunter Von Conrad

Consolidated Edison Co. of New York

633 Pennsylvania Ave. NW
Sixth Floor
Washington, DC 20004
Tel: (202)783-9020
Fax: (202)783-1489
Registered: LDA
Web: www.coned.com
Leg. Issues: BUD, ENG, ENV, TAX, UTI, WAS

In-house, DC-area Employees
CHAMPION, Thomas J.: Manager, Federal Government Relations

Consolidated Freightways Corp.

Palo Alto, CA
Registered: LDA

Outside Counsel/Consultants

Skadden, Arps, Slate, Meagher & Flom LLP
Rep By: Lynn R. Coleman

Consortium for Child Welfare

300 I St. NE
Suite 106
Washington, DC 20002-4389
Web: www.consortiumdc.org
E-mail: wellsthos@aol.com
Tel: (202)547-1589
Fax: (202)547-1857

In-house, DC-area Employees
WELLS, Thomas: Exec. Director

Consortium for Oceanographic Research and Education (CORE)

1755 Massachusetts Ave. NW
Suite 800
Washington, DC 20036
Tel: (202)332-0063
Fax: (202)232-8203
Registered: LDA
Leg. Issues: BUD, SCI

In-house, DC-area Employees
RAYDER, Scott: Director, Government Affairs
SCHAFF, Terry: Assistant to the President

Consortium for Plant Biotechnology Research

Leg. Issues: AGR, BUD, ENG, FUE

Outside Counsel/Consultants
Holland & Knight LLP
Issues: AGR, BUD, ENG, FUE
Rep By: Jack M. Burkman, Richard M. Gold, David P. Metzger, Janet R. Studley

Consortium for Regional Climate Centers

Reno, NV
Leg. Issues: SCI

Outside Counsel/Consultants
Richard L. Spees, Inc.
Issues: SCI
Rep By: Richard L. Spees

Consortium for School Networking

1555 Connecticut Ave. NW
Suite 200
Washington, DC 20036
Web: www.cosn.org
E-mail: info@cosn.org
Tel: (202)462-0992
Fax: (202)462-9043

A nonprofit education association promoting the use of telecommunications and the Internet to improve primary and secondary education.

Leg. Issues: COM, CPI, EDU, TEC

In-house, DC-area Employees
KRUEGER, Keith: Exec. Director
MORRIS, Helen: Deputy Director

Outside Counsel/Consultants
Leslie Harris & Associates
Issues: COM, CPI, EDU, TEC
Rep By: Leslie A. Harris, Jee Hang Lee, Ghani Raines
Non-Profit Management Associates, Inc.
Rep By: Keith Krueger

Consortium for Worker Education

New York, NY
Leg. Issues: EDU, LBR

Outside Counsel/Consultants
The Ickes & Enright Group
Issues: EDU, LBR
Rep By: Janice Ann Enright, Harold M. Ickes

Consortium of Citizens with Disabilities

c/o The Arc
1730 K St. NW
Washington, DC 20005
Web: www.c-c-d.org
Tel: (202)785-3388
Fax: (202)467-4179

In-house, DC-area Employees
YOUNG, Tony: Chairperson

Consortium of Social Science Ass'ns

1522 K St. NW
Suite 836
Washington, DC 20005
Tel: (202)842-3525
Fax: (202)842-2788
Registered: LDA
Web: www.cossa.org
E-mail: socscience@cossa.org

Advocates increased federal funding for the social and behavioral sciences.

Leg. Issues: AGR, BUD, EDU, GOV, HCR, LAW, SCI

In-house, DC-area Employees
RYAN, Chris: Associate Director, Public Affairs
SHARPE, Angela L.: Associate Director, Government Affairs
SILVER, Howard J.: Exec. Director

Consortium of Universities of the Washington Metropolitan Area

One Dupont Circle NW
Suite 200
Washington, DC 20036-1131
Web: www.consortium.org
Tel: (202)331-8080
Fax: (202)331-7925

Membership is comprised of American University, The Catholic University of America, The George Washington University, Georgetown University, Howard University, University of the District of Columbia, University of Maryland (College Park), Gallaudet University, Trinity College, Marymount University, George Mason University and Southeastern University.

Leg. Issues: DOC, EDU, GOV

In-house, DC-area Employees
CHILDERS, John B.: President and Chief Exec. Officer
KRAM, Sally W.: Director, Government and Community Relations

Consortium on Government Relations for Student Affairs

Washington, DC
Leg. Issues: EDU

Outside Counsel/Consultants
Long, Aldridge & Norman, LLP
Issues: EDU
Rep By: C. Randall Nuckolls, Patrick C. Turner

Consortium Plant Biotech Research

West Lafayette, IN

Outside Counsel/Consultants
Holland & Knight LLP
Rep By: Richard M. Gold, David P. Metzger, Janet R. Studley

Constellation Energy Group

1301 Pennsylvania Ave. NW
Suite 1050
Washington, DC 20004
Tel: (202)942-9840
Fax: (202)942-9847
Registered: LDA

Utility headquartered in Baltimore, MD.

Leg. Issues: BUD, CAW, CPI, FIN, HCR, TAX, UTI, WAS

In-house, DC-area Employees
CHERRY, Jan E.: Federal Relations Assistant
GILBERT, David: Federal Relations Representative
PENSABENE, Judith K.: Director, Federal Relations and Washington Counsel

Constellation Technology Corp.

Largo, FL
Leg. Issues: DEF

Outside Counsel/Consultants
Davis O'Connell, Inc.
Issues: DEF
Rep By: Lynda C. Davis, Ph.D., Terrence M. O'Connell

Constituency for Africa

2400 N St. NW
Suite 510
Washington, DC 20037
Web: www.cfanet.org
E-mail: cfanet@cfanet.org
Tel: (202)371-0588
Fax: (202)371-9017

An organization devoted to mobilizing and fostering increased cooperation and coordination among a broadly-based coalition of American, African and international organizations, institutions and individuals committed to the progress and empowerment of Africa and African peoples.

Leg. Issues: FOR

In-house, DC-area Employees
FOOTE, Melvin P.: President and Chief Exec. Officer

Outside Counsel/Consultants
Mattox Woolfolk, LLC
Issues: FOR
Rep By: Richard B. Mattox, Brian P. Woolfolk

Constitution PAC

508 First St. SE
Washington, DC 20003

A political action committee.

In-house, DC-area Employees
HARDIMAN, Michael

Constitution Project

50 F St. NW
Suite 110
Washington, DC 20001
Web: www.constitutionproject.org
E-mail: info@constitutionproject.org
Tel: (202)662-4240
Fax: (202)662-4241

Affiliated with the Century Foundation (see separate listing).

In-house, DC-area Employees
DAHL, Elizabeth: Deputy Director
SLOAN, Virginia: Exec. Director

Constitutional Rights Foundation

Los Angeles, CA
Leg. Issues: BUD

Outside Counsel/Consultants
Mullenholz, Brimsek & Belair
Issues: BUD
Rep By: Robert R. Belair, John B. Conaway, Susan C. Haller

Construction Industry Manufacturers Ass'n

525 School St. SW
Suite 303
Washington, DC 20024
Web: www.cimanet.com
E-mail: cimadc@sprynet.com
Tel: (202)479-2666
Fax: (202)554-0885

Headquatered in Milwaukee, WI.

Leg. Issues: MAN, TRA, TRD

In-house, DC-area Employees
YAKSICH, Nick: V. President, Government Affairs

Construction Industry Round Table, Inc.

1101 17th St. NW
Suite 608
Washington, DC 20036
Tel: (202)466-6777
Fax: (202)466-6767
Registered: LDA
Web: www.cirt.org
E-mail: cirt@cirt.org
Leg. Issues: BUD, CAW, DEF, ECN, ENV, GOV, LBR, TOR, TRA, WAS

In-house, DC-area Employees
CASSO, Mark A.: President

Outside Counsel/Consultants
Akin, Gump, Strauss, Hauer & Feld, L.L.P.
Issues: ENV, GOV, WAS
Rep By: Marlene M. Colucci

Construction Management Ass'n of America

7918 Jones Branch Dr.
Suite 540
McLean, VA 22102-3307
Web: www.cmaanet.org
E-mail: info@cmaanet.org
Tel: (703)356-2622
Fax: (703)356-6388
Leg. Issues: AVI, BUD, EDU, GOV, ROD, SMB, TRA

In-house, DC-area Employees
D'AGOSTINO, Bruce: Exec. Director

Outside Counsel/Consultants
Hooper Owen & Winburn
Issues: BUD, GOV

The Consulting Center

Riyadh, SAUDI ARABIA

Outside Counsel/Consultants
Vorys, Sater, Seymour and Pease, LLP
Rep By: James K. Alford

Consulting Engineers Council of Metropolitan Washington

8201 Greensboro Dr.
Suite 300
McLean, VA 22102
Web: www.cecmw.org
E-mail: ksilberman@amg-inc.com
Tel: (703)610-9000
Fax: (703)610-9005

A local organization of the American Consulting Engineers Council.

Outside Counsel/Consultants
Ass'n Management Group
Rep By: Karen Silberman

Consumer Aerosol Products Council

99 Canal Center Plaza
Suite 200
Alexandria, VA 22314
Web: www.nocfcs.org
Tel: (703)683-1044
Fax: (703)683-4622

The purpose of the council is to educate consumers about aerosol products.

Leg. Issues: CSP, HCR, WAS

In-house, DC-area Employees
MORRIS, Rick

Consumer Bankers Ass'n

1000 Wilson Blvd.
Suite 2500
Arlington, VA 22209-3908
Tel: (703)276-1750
Fax: (703)528-1290
Registered: LDA
Web: www.cbanet.org
E-mail: cba@cbanet.org
Leg. Issues: BAN, BUD, EDU, TAX

Political Action Committee/s
Consumer Bankers Ass'n Political Action Committee
1000 Wilson Blvd.
Suite 2500
Arlington, VA 22209-3908
Contact: Nancy Holcombe Camm
Tel: (703)276-1750
Fax: (703)528-1290

In-house, DC-area Employees
BELEW, Joe D.: President
CAMM, Nancy Holcombe: Manager, Congressional Affairs
ELMENDORF, Fritz M.: V. President, Communications and Public Relations

MOORE, Kathleen: Manager, Communications
SULLIVAN, Marcia Z.: V. President/Director, Government Relations
ZEISEL, Steven I.: Senior Counsel and V. President

Outside Counsel/Consultants

Dean Blakey & Moskowitz
Issues: BUD, EDU, TAX
Rep By: John E. Dean, Saul L. Moskowitz

Consumer Coalition for Quality Health Care

1101 Vermont Ave. NW
Suite 1001
Washington, DC 20005
Web: www.consumers.org
Tel: (202)789-3606
Fax: (202)898-2389

In-house, DC-area Employees
LINDBERG, Brian: Exec. Director

Consumer Electronics Ass'n

2500 Wilson Blvd.
Arlington, VA 22201-3834
Tel: (703)907-7500
Fax: (703)907-7601
Registered: LDA
Web: www.ce.org

Represents companies involved in the design, development, manufacturing, and distribution of audio, video, mobile electronics, communications, information technology, multimedia and accessory products, as well as related services, that are sold through consumer channels.

Leg. Issues: COM, CPI, CPT, LBR, MAN, SCI, TAX, TEC, TRD

In-house, DC-area Employees
JOHNSON, Douglas K.: Director, Technology Policy
JOSEPH, Jeff: V. President, CEA Communications and Strategic Relationships
KLEIN, Gary S.: V. President, Government and Legal Affairs
PETRICONE, Michael D.: V. President, Technology Policy
SHAPIRO, Gary: President and Chief Exec. Officer

Outside Counsel/Consultants

The Advocacy Group
Issues: COM, MAN, TAX, TEC
Rep By: Jon L. Boisclair, Robert J. Dotchin

Consumer Energy Council of America Research Foundation

2000 L St. NW
Suite 802
Washington, DC 20036
E-mail: cecarf@hotmail.com
Tel: (202)659-0404
Fax: (202)659-0407

The nation's senior public interest energy policy organization, founded in 1973. Provides a national resource for information, analysis and technical expertise on a variety of energy and environmental policies. A non-profit organization with a primary commitment to the provision of reliable and affordable energy for all sectors of the country, with special regard for environmental consequences. Acts to further public policy objectives by building partnerships among public and private organizations, including government at all levels, business and industry, utilities, consumers, and environmentalists.

Leg. Issues: CSP, ENG, FUE, GOV, SCI, TEC, TRA, UTI

In-house, DC-area Employees
BERMAN, Ellen: President

Consumer Federation of America

1424 16th St. NW
Suite 604
Washington, DC 20036
Tel: (202)387-6121
Fax: (202)265-7989
Registered: LDA
Web: www.consumerfed.org
E-mail: cfa@essential.org

A federation of national, state, regional and community consumer organizations dedicated to consumer action through legislation, information and education.

Leg. Issues: ADV, AGR, ALC, APP, ART, AUT, AVI, BAN, BEV, BNK, BUD, CAW, CHM, COM, CPI, CPT, CSP, DIS, ECN, EDU, ENG, ENV, FIN, FIR, FOO, FUE, GOV, HCR, HOU, INS, LAW, LBR, MAN, MAR, MED, MIA, MMM, NAT, PHA, POS, RES, RET, ROD, RRR, SCI, SPO, TAX, TEC, TOB, TOU, TRA, TRD, TRU, URB, UTI, WAS, WEL

Political Action Committee/s

Consumer Federation of America Political Action Fund
1424 16th St. NW
Suite 604
Washington, DC 20036
Tel: (202)387-6121
Fax: (202)265-7989

In-house, DC-area Employees
BROBECK, Stephen: Exec. Director
COOPER, Mark N.: Research Director
FISE, Mary Ellen: General Counsel
GILLIS, Jack: Public Affairs Director
HUNTER, J. Robert: Director, Insurance
JAEGER, Arthur R.: Assistant Director
METZENBAUM, Hon. Howard M.: Chairman
ROPER, Barbara L. N.: Editor

Consumer Federation of America's Insurance Group

1424 16th St. NW
Suite 604
Washington, DC 20036
Web: www.consumerfed.org
E-mail: loonlakeme@aol.com
Tel: (703)528-0062

Issues publications which assist consumers in evaluating their insurance needs and options; provides some guidance for a fee; and acts as an advocate for the consumer population before legislative and regulatory bodies.

Leg. Issues: INS

In-house, DC-area Employees
HUNTER, J. Robert: Director

Consumer Healthcare Products Ass'n

1150 Connecticut Ave. NW
12th Floor
Washington, DC 20036
Tel: (202)429-9260
Fax: (202)223-6835
Registered: LDA
Web: www.chpa-info.org

Manufacturers and distributors of over-the-counter medicines and dietary supplements.

Leg. Issues: ADV, BUD, CHM, CSP, EDU, GOV, HCR, MAN, MED, PHA

Political Action Committee/s

Consumer Healthcare Products Ass'n Political Action Committee
1150 Connecticut Ave. NW
12th Floor
Washington, DC 20036
Contact: Kevin J. Kraushaar
Tel: (202)429-9260
Fax: (202)223-6835

In-house, DC-area Employees
BACHRACH, Eve E.: Senior V. President, General Counsel and Secretary
KRAUSHAAR, Kevin J.: V. President and Director, Government Relations
MAVES, M.D., Michael D.: President
MISTER, Steven M.: V. President
SOLLER, R. William: Director, Science and Technology and Senior V. President
SPANGLER, David C.: V. President-International and Assistant General Counsel

Outside Counsel/Consultants

Covington & Burling
Issues: HCR
Rep By: Peter Barton Hutt, Bruce N. Kuhlik

Consumer Mortgage Coalition

801 Pennsylvania Ave. NW
Suite 625
Washington, DC 20004
Tel: (202)544-3550
Fax: (202)543-1438
Leg. Issues: BAN, BNK, HOU

In-house, DC-area Employees
CANFIELD, Anne C.: Exec. Director

Outside Counsel/Consultants

Canfield & Associates, Inc.
Issues: BNK, HOU
Rep By: Roger Blauwet, April Boston, Anne C. Canfield

Goodwin, Procter & Hoar LLP
Issues: BAN, HOU
Rep By: Joseph M. Kolar, Jeffrey P. Naimon

Consumer Project on Technology

P.O. Box 19367
Washington, DC 20036
Web: www.cptech.org
Tel: (202)387-8030
Fax: (202)234-5176

Founded by Ralph Nader.

In-house, DC-area Employees
LOVE, James P.: Director

Consumer Satellite Systems, Inc.

Indianapolis, IN

Outside Counsel/Consultants

Hardy & Ellison, P.C.
Rep By: Mark C. Ellison

Consumer Specialties Products Ass'n

1913 I St. NW
Washington, DC 20006
Tel: (202)872-8110
Fax: (202)872-8114
Registered: LDA
Web: www.cspa.org
E-mail: info@cspa.org

Effective July 15, 2001, CSPA will be moving to: 900 17th St., NW, Third Floor, Washington, DC 20006.

Leg. Issues: ENV

Political Action Committee/s

Chem PAC
1913 I St. NW
Washington, DC 20006
Contact: Stephen S. Kellner
Tel: (202)872-8110
Fax: (202)872-8114

In-house, DC-area Employees
CATHCART, Chris: President
KELLNER, Stephen S.: Senior Vice President, Legal Affairs
KLEIN, Philip: Senior V. President, Federal and State Legislative Affairs
LAFIELD, Bill: V. President, State Legislative Affairs
LAWS, Danielle: Federal Legislative Specialist
MAIRENA, Mario D.: Federal Legislative Representative
YOST, Joe: Senior Representative, State Legislative Affairs

Outside Counsel/Consultants

McKenna & Cuneo, L.L.P.

Consumers Energy Co.

1016 16th St. NW
Fifth Floor
Washington, DC 20036
Tel: (202)293-5794
Fax: (202)223-6178
Registered: LDA
Web: www.consumersenergy.com

An electric and gas utility based in Michigan. A subsidiary of CMS Energy Corp.

In-house, DC-area Employees
EDELSON, Howard J.: Director, Regional State Governmental Affairs
KRIPOWICZ, Mary Jo: Director, Federal Affairs
MENGEBIER, David G.: V. President, Government and International Affairs

Consumers First

Outside Counsel/Consultants

Issue Dynamics Inc.

Consumers for World Trade

1620 I St. NW
Suite 615
Washington, DC 20006
Tel: (202)861-0703
Fax: (202)463-8498
Registered: LDA
Web: www.cwt.org
E-mail: cwt@cwt.org

In the interests of consumers, favors an open trading system and opposes the imposition of tariffs, quotas and other trade barriers.

Leg. Issues: TRD

In-house, DC-area Employees
LANIER, Robin W.: President

Consumers Union of the United States

1666 Connecticut Ave. NW
Suite 310
Washington, DC 20009
Tel: (202)462-6262
Fax: (202)265-9548
Registered: LDA
Web: www.consumersunion.org

A nonprofit membership organization chartered in 1936 to provide consumers with information, education, and counsel about goods, services, health, and personal finance. Publishes "Consumer Reports" and other publications about consumer welfare. Headquartered in Yonkers, NY.

Leg. Issues: AGR, AUT, AVI, BAN, BNK, CHM, COM, CPI, CPT, CSP, DIS, ENG, ENV, FIN, FOO, FOR, GOV, HCR, INS, LBR, MMM, PHA, POS, RET, TEC, TRD, UTI

In-house, DC-area Employees
DUNCAN, Janell Mayo: Legislative Counsel
GOLDBERG, Adam: Policy Analyst
GREENBERG, Sally: Senior Product Safety Counsel
HAHN, Adrienne M.: Sr. Legislative Counsel
KIMMELMAN, Gene: Co-Director, Washington Office
SHEARER, Gail E.: Director, Health Policy Analysis
SILBERGELD, Mark: Co-Director, Washington Office
TORRES, III, Frank C.: Legislative Counsel

Consumers United for Rail Equity

1050 Thomas Jefferson St. NW
Seventh Floor
Washington, DC 20007
Tel: (202)298-1981
Fax: (202)338-2416
Leg. Issues: BUD, RRR, TRA

In-house, DC-area Employees
SZABO, Robert G.

Outside Counsel/Consultants

Van Ness Feldman, P.C.
Issues: BUD, RRR, TRA
Rep By: Nancy Macan McNally, Robert G. Szabo

Contact Lens Institute

8201 Corporate Dr.
Suite 850
Landover, MD 20785
Web: www.contactlenscouncil.org
E-mail: cli@us.net
Tel: (301)459-1800
Fax: (301)459-1802

A trade association representing the contact lens industry.

Leg. Issues: BUD, GOV, HCR

In-house, DC-area Employees
SCHILLING, III, Edward L.: Exec. Director

Outside Counsel/Consultants
Kleinfeld, Kaplan and Becker
Issues: GOV, HCR
Rep By: Thomas O. Henteleff, Peter R. Mathers
Royer & Babyak
Issues: BUD, GOV, HCR
Rep By: Gregory R. Babyak

Contact Lens Manufacturers Ass'n

2000 M St. NW
Suite 700
Washington, DC 20036
Tel: (202)261-1000
Fax: (202)887-0336
Web: www.clma.net
E-mail: clma@mds.com

Political Action Committee/s
Contact Lens Manufacturers Ass'n Political Action Committee (CONPAC)
2000 M St. NW
Suite 700
Washington, DC 20036
Tel: (202)261-1000
Fax: (202)887-0336
Contact: Daniel J. Manelli

In-house, DC-area Employees
MANELLI, Daniel J.: Treasurer

Outside Counsel/Consultants
Manelli Denison & Selter PLLC
Rep By: Daniel J. Manelli

Container Recycling Institute

1911 Fort Myer Dr.
Suite 702
Arlington, VA 22209-1603
Tel: (703)276-9800
Fax: (703)276-9587
Web: www.container-recycling.org
E-mail: cri@container-recycling.org

CRI is a non-profit research and public education organization dedicated to supporting options to reduce packaging waste. Publishes "Packaging and Container UPDATE" and other reports. Second web site at www.bottlebill.org.

Leg. Issues: ENV, WAS

In-house, DC-area Employees
FRANKLIN, Pat: Director

Contemporary Products Inc.

Portland, ME
Leg. Issues: HCR, MMM

Outside Counsel/Consultants
Nusgart Consulting, LLC
Issues: HCR, MMM
Rep By: Marcia Nusgart

Continental Airlines Inc.

1350 I St. NW
Suite 1250
Washington, DC 20005
Tel: (202)289-6060
Fax: (202)289-1546
Registered: LDA
Web: www.continental.com

Headquartered in Houston, TX.

Leg. Issues: AVI, BUD, IMM, TAX, TRA

In-house, DC-area Employees
COX, Rebecca G.: V. President, Government Affairs
KAMEN, Hershel
VAN DUYNE, Nancy H.: Staff V. President, Congressional Affairs

Outside Counsel/Consultants
Robertson, Monagle & Eastaugh
Issues: AVI
Rep By: Steven W. Silver
Williams & Jensen, P.C.
Issues: AVI, BUD, IMM, TAX, TRA
Rep By: J. Steven Hart, Karen Judd Lewis

Continental Cement Co., Inc.

Hannibal, MO
Leg. Issues: CAW, ENG, ENV, FUE

Outside Counsel/Consultants
Bracewell & Patterson, L.L.P.
Issues: CAW, ENG, ENV, FUE
Rep By: Gene E. Godley, Marc C. Hebert, Michael L. Pate, Scott H. Segal

The Continental Corp.

New York, NY

Outside Counsel/Consultants
Arnold & Porter

Continental Grain Co.

Washington, DC
Registered: LDA
Leg. Issues: GOV

Outside Counsel/Consultants
EOP Group, Inc.
Issues: GOV
Rep By: Joseph Hezir, Michael O'Bannon, Phil Pulizzi

Continental Teves

Auburn Hills, MI
Leg. Issues: AUT, CAW, CSP, ENG, ENV, ROD, TRA

Outside Counsel/Consultants
Strat@Comm (Strategic Communications Counselors)
Issues: AUT, CAW, CSP, ENG, ENV, ROD, TRA
Rep By: Ron DeFore, Diane K. Steed

Continental Wingate Co., Inc.

Boston, MA
Leg. Issues: HOU

Outside Counsel/Consultants
Nixon Peabody LLP
Issues: HOU
Rep By: Richard M. Price, Monica Hilton Sussman

Continuous Color Coat, Ltd.

Toronto, CANADA

Outside Counsel/Consultants
Willkie Farr & Gallagher
Rep By: Christopher A. Dunn

Continuum Healthcare Systems

Houston, TX
Leg. Issues: MMM

Outside Counsel/Consultants
Verner, Liipfert, Bernhard, McPherson and Hand, Chartered
Issues: MMM
Rep By: Vicki E. Hart

Contra Costa Community College District

Martinez, CA
Leg. Issues: EDU, ENV

Outside Counsel/Consultants
Davis O'Connell, Inc.
Issues: EDU, ENV
Rep By: Lynda C. Davis, Ph.D., Jennifer Golden, Terrence M. O'Connell

Contra Costa Water District

Concord, CA
Leg. Issues: CAW, NAT

Outside Counsel/Consultants
Marcus G. Faust, P.C.
Issues: CAW, NAT
Rep By: Marcus G. Faust, Adrianne Firth

Contra Costa, California, Tenants of the County of

Martinez, CA
Leg. Issues: BUD, MAR

Outside Counsel/Consultants
E. Del Smith and Co.
Issues: BUD, MAR
Rep By: Margaret Allen, E. Del Smith

Contract Manufacturing Coalition

Washington, DC

Outside Counsel/Consultants
PriceWaterhouseCoopers
Rep By: Barbara Angus, Tim Anson, Kenneth J. Kies, Peter R. Merrill

Contract Services Ass'n of America

1200 G St. NW
Suite 510
Washington, DC 20005
Tel: (202)347-0600
Fax: (202)347-0608
Registered: LDA
Web: www.csa-dc.org
E-mail: gary@csa-dc.org

Membership consists of companies that provide technical and support services with the government. The association's function is to serve member companies by protecting the current market, finding new markets, and lobbying issues that impact the government services industry.

Leg. Issues: BUD, DEF, ENV, GOV, LBR, SMB, TEC, TRA

Political Action Committee/s
Contract Services Ass'n Political Action Committee (CSA-PAC)
1200 G St. NW
Suite 510
Washington, DC 20005
Tel: (202)347-0600
Fax: (202)347-0608
Contact: Gary D. Engebretson

In-house, DC-area Employees
BAEBLER, Paul: Director, Membership Services
ENGEBRETSON, Gary D.: President
GARMAN, Cathleen: V. President, Public Policy
MCMILLAN, Kurt: Director, Business Management
SHU, Cindy: Legislative/Regulatory Manager
SIGALOF, George: Director, Public Relations

Outside Counsel/Consultants
Piper Marbury Rudnick & Wolfe LLP

Contractors Internat'l Group on Nuclear Liability

An ad hoc group of U.S. contractors.

Leg. Issues: ENG, FOR, INS, TRD

Outside Counsel/Consultants
Harmon & Wilmot, L.L.P.
Issues: ENG, FOR, INS, TRD
Rep By: Omer F. Brown, II

Contran Corp.

Dallas, TX
Leg. Issues: WAS

Outside Counsel/Consultants
Ottosen and Associates
Issues: WAS
Rep By: Karl J. Ottosen

ConvaTec

Skillman, NJ
Leg. Issues: HCR, MMM

Outside Counsel/Consultants
Nusgart Consulting, LLC
Issues: HCR, MMM
Rep By: Marcia Nusgart

Convention of American Instructors of the Deaf

Austin, TX

Outside Counsel/Consultants
Duncan and Associates
Rep By: Jack G. Duncan

L. P. Conwood Co.

Memphis, TN
Leg. Issues: TAX, TOB

Outside Counsel/Consultants
Kerrigan & Associates, Inc.
Issues: TOB
Rep By: Michael J. Kerrigan
Patton Boggs, LLP
Issues: TAX, TOB
Rep By: Thomas Hale Boggs, Jr., James B. Christian, Jr., Darryl D. Nirenberg, Stuart M. Pape

Ry Cooder

Santa Monica, CA
Leg. Issues: TRD

Outside Counsel/Consultants
Swidler Berlin Shereff Friedman, LLP
Issues: TRD
Rep By: Gary Gallant, Harold P. Goldfield, Richard A. Popkin

Cook Children's Health Care System

Fort Worth, TX
Leg. Issues: BUD, HCR, MED

Outside Counsel/Consultants
BKSH & Associates
Issues: BUD, HCR, MED

Cook Group

Bloomington, IN
Leg. Issues: HCR

Outside Counsel/Consultants
Oppenheimer Wolff & Donnelly LLP
Issues: HCR
Rep By: Hon. Birch Bayh, Kevin O. Faley

Cook Inc.

Indianapolis, IN
Leg. Issues: GOV, MED

Outside Counsel/Consultants

Hale and Dorr LLP
Issues: GOV, MED
Rep By: Mark Heller, Louise Howe

Cook Inlet Communications

Los Angeles, CA

Outside Counsel/Consultants

Wilmer, Cutler & Pickering

Cook Inlet Region Inc.

Anchorage, AK
Leg. Issues: BUD, COM, FUE, GAM, IND, MAR, NAT, RES, SMB, TEC, TRA, WEL

Outside Counsel/Consultants

Crowell & Moring LLP
Rep By: Steven P. Quarles

Mary Lee McGuire
Rep By: Mary Lee McGuire

Ryan, Phillips, Utrecht & MacKinnon
Issues: BUD, COM, FUE, GAM, IND, MAR, NAT, RES, SMB, TEC, TRA, WEL
Rep By: Rodney Hoppe, Jeffrey M. MacKinnon, William D. Phillips, Mark D. Planning, Thomas M. Ryan, Joseph V. Vasapoli

Cook Inlet Regional Citizen Advisory Council

Kenai, AK

Outside Counsel/Consultants

Sonosky, Chambers, Sachse & Endreson
Rep By: William R. Perry

Cook, Illinois, County of

Chicago, IL
Leg. Issues: HCR, LAW, MMM, RET, TAX, URB

Outside Counsel/Consultants

Susan J. White & Associates
Issues: HCR, LAW, MMM, RET, TAX, URB
Rep By: Susan J. White

Cool Roof Rating Council

Calverton, MD
Leg. Issues: ENV

Outside Counsel/Consultants

Venable
Issues: ENV
Rep By: Brock R. Landry

Cooler Heads Coalition

Washington, DC
Leg. Issues: ENG, ENV, FOR, SCI

Outside Counsel/Consultants

Christopher C. Horner
Issues: ENG, ENV, FOR, SCI
Rep By: Christopher C. Horner

Cooley's Anemia Foundation

Flushing, NY
Leg. Issues: BUD, HCR, MED, MMM, SCI

Outside Counsel/Consultants

Cavarocchi Ruscio Dennis Associates
Issues: BUD, HCR, MED, MMM, SCI
Rep By: Lyle B. Dennis

Cooper Green Hospital

Birmingham, AL
Leg. Issues: BUD, HCR

Outside Counsel/Consultants

Michael W. Adcock
Issues: BUD, HCR
Rep By: Michael W. Adcock

Cooper Tire and Rubber Co.

Findlay, OH
Leg. Issues: TRD

Outside Counsel/Consultants

Frederick L. Ikenson, P.C.
Rep By: Frederick L. Ikenson

Winston & Strawn
Issues: TRD
Rep By: Hon. Beryl F. Anthony, Jr., Hon. James H. Burnley, IV, John C. Kirtland, Hon. John L. Napier, James T. Pitts, John A. Waits, II

Cooperative of American Physicians

Los Angeles, CA
Leg. Issues: INS

Outside Counsel/Consultants

Kyros & Cummins Associates
Issues: INS
Rep By: John M. Falk, Hon. Peter N. Kyros

Coors Brewing Company

801 Pennsylvania Ave. NW
North Bldg., Suite 252
Washington, DC 20004-2604
Tel: (202)737-4444
Fax: (202)737-0951
Registered: LDA

A beer manufacturer headquartered in Golden, CO.

Leg. Issues: AGR, ALC, BEV, CAW, CSP, ENG, ENV, FOO, GOV, HCR, LBR, MIA, RRR, TAX, TEC, TRD

Political Action Committee/s

Politcal Action Coors Employees (PACE)
801 Pennsylvania Ave. NW
North Bldg., Suite 252
Washington, DC 20004-2604
Contact: Stacey Kane
Tel: (202)737-4444
Fax: (202)737-0951

In-house, DC-area Employees

CRAWFORD, Richard C.: Director, Federal Government Affairs
KANE, Stacey: Manager, Federal Government Affairs

Outside Counsel/Consultants

Davis & Harman LLP
Issues: TAX
Rep By: Randolf H. Hardock

Greenberg Traurig, LLP
Issues: ALC, FOO
Rep By: Nancy E. Taylor

Greener and Hook, LLC
Issues: ALC, BEV, CSP, FOO, GOV, HCR, MIA

Nat'l Environmental Strategies
Issues: CAW
Rep By: Marc I. Himmelstein

Witeck * Combs Communications

Copa Airline

Panama City, PANAMA

Outside Counsel/Consultants

Mullenholz, Brimsek & Belair
Rep By: John R. Brimsek

COPA Commission

Outside Counsel/Consultants

Dittus Communications
Rep By: Kristin Litterst, Jennifer Moire

Copeland, Lowery & Jacquez

1341 G St. NW
Suite 200
Washington, DC 20005
Tel: (202)347-5990
Fax: (202)347-5941
Registered: LDA
Web: www.clj.com
E-mail: cljwash@clj.com
Leg. Issues: CAW, ENV, RES, ROD, TRA, URB

In-house, DC-area Employees

ALCADE, Nancy: Legislative Associate
COPELAND, Jr., James M.: Partner
DENTON, Jean Gingras: Partner
HANSEN, Linda: Assistant
JACQUEZ, Lynnette C.: Partner
KIERIG, Chris: Legislative Associate
LARSON, Lance: Assistant
LOWERY, Hon. William D.: Partner
SHOCKEY, Jeffrey S.: Partner

Outside Counsel/Consultants

Clark & Weinstock, Inc.
Issues: CAW, ENV, RES, ROD, TRA, URB
Rep By: Sandi Stuart

Copper and Brass Fabricators Council

1050 17th St. NW
Suite 440
Washington, DC 20036
E-mail: copbrass@aol.com
Tel: (202)833-8575
Fax: (202)331-8267

A trade association working to promote the interests of copper and brass fabricators.

Leg. Issues: ENV, GOV, MAN, TRD

In-house, DC-area Employees

MAYER, Joseph L.: President

Outside Counsel/Consultants

Collier Shannon Scott, PLLC
Issues: ENV, GOV, TRD
Rep By: Jeffrey S. Beckington, David A. Hartquist, Chet M. Thompson, John L. Wittenborn, Dana S. Wood

Covington & Burling
Issues: ENV, TRD
Rep By: J. Randolph Wilson

Copper Development Ass'n, Inc.

New York, NY
Leg. Issues: ENV

Outside Counsel/Consultants

Collier Shannon Scott, PLLC
Issues: ENV
Rep By: Chet M. Thompson, John L. Wittenborn, Dana S. Wood

Copyright Clearance Center, Inc.

Rosewood, MA
Leg. Issues: CPT

Outside Counsel/Consultants

Columbus Public Affairs
Issues: CPT

Weil, Gotshal & Manges, LLP
Issues: CPT
Rep By: Sandra M. Aistars, Charles E. Roh, Jr., Bruce H. Turnbull

Coquille Indian Tribe

North Bend, OR

Outside Counsel/Consultants

Edwards Associates, Inc.
Rep By: Mark Phillips

Coral Springs, Florida, City of

Leg. Issues: TEC

Outside Counsel/Consultants

Miller & Van Eaton, P.L.L.C.
Issues: TEC
Rep By: Joseph Van Eaton

The Corcoran Gallery of Art

500 17th St. NW
Washington, DC 20006-4804
Tel: (202)639-1700
Fax: (202)639-1779
Web: www.corcoran.org
E-mail: pr@corcoran.org
Leg. Issues: ART

In-house, DC-area Employees

LEVY, David C.: President and Director
MULLENS, Denise: Assoc. Dean, Corcoran School of Art
ROTHSCHILD, Jan: Chief Communications Officer
WERTZ, Martha: V. President, Development

Outside Counsel/Consultants

Chernikoff and Co.
Issues: ART
Rep By: Larry B. Chernikoff

Cord Blood Registry, Inc.

San Mateo, CA

Umbilical cord blood collection and storage services.

Leg. Issues: HCR

Outside Counsel/Consultants

Morgan, Lewis & Bockius LLP
Issues: HCR
Rep By: Maya Bermingham, Kathryn L. Gleason, Kathleen M. Sanzo

Cord Laboratories

Broomfield, CO

Outside Counsel/Consultants

Kleinfeld, Kaplan and Becker
Rep By: Alan H. Kaplan, Richard S. Morey

Cordova, Alaska, City of

Leg. Issues: URB

Outside Counsel/Consultants

Birch, Horton, Bittner & Cherot
Issues: URB
Rep By: Roy S. Jones, Jr.

The Core Center

Chicago, IL
Leg. Issues: BUD

Outside Counsel/Consultants

Cassidy & Associates, Inc.
Issues: BUD
Rep By: Valerie Rogers Osborne, Marnie Russ, Hon. Martin A. Russo

Core Tec

Outside Counsel/Consultants

Cormac Group, LLP

Corel Corp.

Ottawa, CANADA

Leg. Issues: SCI

Outside Counsel/Consultants

Capital Strategies Group, Inc.
Issues: SCI
Rep By: Tammi Hayes

CORFAC, Internat'l

Outside Counsel/Consultants

Alcalde & Fay
Rep By: J. B. Hancock

Corn Belt Energy Corp.

Bloomington, IL

Leg. Issues: ENG, UTI

Outside Counsel/Consultants

Duncan, Weinberg, Genzer & Pembroke, P.C.
Issues: ENG, UTI
Rep By: Michael R. Postar

Corn Refiners Ass'n, Inc.

1701 Pennsylvania Ave. NW
Suite 950
Washington, DC 20006
Tel: (202)331-1634
Fax: (202)331-2054
Registered: LDA

Web: www.corn.org
E-mail: details@corn.org

Represents the U.S. corn wet milling industry.

Leg. Issues: AGR, ENV, FOO, TRA, TRD

In-house, DC-area Employees

CONNER, Charles F.: President
LEHMAN, Sherri: Director, Congressional Affairs

Cornerstone Florida Corp., Ltd.

Coral Gales, FL

Leg. Issues: HOU

Outside Counsel/Consultants

Nixon Peabody LLP
Issues: HOU
Rep By: Richard S. Goldstein, Monica Hilton Sussman

Cornerstone Television

Wall, PA

Leg. Issues: TEC

Outside Counsel/Consultants

Shaw Pittman
Issues: TEC
Rep By: Kathryn R. Schmeltzer, Andrew L. Woods

Corning Inc.

1350 I St. NW
Suite 500
Washington, DC 20005-3305
Tel: (202)682-3200
Fax: (202)682-3130
Registered: LDA

Web: www.corning.com

Leg. Issues: COM, TAX, TEC, TRD

Political Action Committee/s

COREPAC

1350 I St. NW
Suite 500
Washington, DC 20005-3305
Tel: (202)682-3200
Fax: (202)682-3130
Contact: Holly Pitt Young

In-house, DC-area Employees

FENDLEY, Stan G.: Director, Legislative and Regulatory Policy
REGAN, Timothy J.: V. President and Director, Government Affairs
WAGGONER, Deborah L.: Director, Public Policy
YOUNG, Holly Pitt: Manager,CORE PAC and Grassroots

Outside Counsel/Consultants

Capitol Coalitions Inc.
Issues: TEC
Rep By: Amy R. Mehlman, Brett P. Scott

Davison, Cohen & Co.
Rep By: Thomas W. Cohen

The National Group, LLP
Rep By: Vincent M. Versage

Patton Boggs, LLP
Issues: TEC
Rep By: James B. Christian, Jr.

Preston Gates Ellis & Rouvelas Meeds LLP
Issues: TAX

Skadden, Arps, Slate, Meagher & Flom LLP
Issues: TEC, TRD
Rep By: Robert E. Lighthizer

Tongour Simpson Holsclaw Green
Issues: TAX
Rep By: Sascha M. Burns, James F. Green, John Bradley "Brad" Holsclaw

Washington Strategies, L.L.C.
Rep By: Jennifer Johnson Calvert, William P. Jarrell

Winston & Strawn
Issues: TRD
Rep By: Hon. Beryl F. Anthony, Jr., John C. Kirtland, Joseph E. O'Leary, John A. Waits, II

Coronado, California, City of

Coronado, CA
Leg. Issues: DEF, TRA

Outside Counsel/Consultants

The PMA Group
Issues: DEF, TRA
Rep By: William E. Berl, Sean Fogarty, Kaylene Green, Gregory L. Hansen, Dr. John Lynch, Paul J. Magliocchetti

Corporacion de Exportaciones Mexicanas, S.A. de C.V. and Marvin Roy Feldman

Col. Polanco, MEXICO
Leg. Issues: ECN, FOR, LAW, TOB, TRD

Outside Counsel/Consultants

Feith & Zell, P.C.
Issues: ECN, FOR, LAW, TOB, TRD
Rep By: Mark B. Feldman

Corporacion Valenciana de Cementos Portland, S.A.

Madrid, SPAIN
Leg. Issues: ENV, ROD, TRD

Outside Counsel/Consultants

Janus-Merritt Strategies, L.L.C.
Issues: ENV, ROD, TRD
Rep By: Mark J. Robertson, J. Daniel Walsh

Corporacion Venezolana de Cementos, SACA

Caracas, VENEZUELA
Leg. Issues: ENV, ROD, TRD

Outside Counsel/Consultants

Janus-Merritt Strategies, L.L.C.
Issues: ENV, ROD, TRD
Rep By: Mark J. Robertson, J. Daniel Walsh

Corporate Council on Africa

1100 17th St.
Suite 1100
Washington, DC 20036
Tel: (202)835-1115
Fax: (202)835-1117
Web: www.africacncl.org

Works to strengthen the commercial relationship between Africa and the United States.

Leg. Issues: FOR

In-house, DC-area Employees

HAYES, Stephen: President
MCCOY, Tim: Director, Communications
SAUNDERS, Greg: Director, Policy

Corporate Environmental Enforcement Council (CEEC)

Washington, DC
Leg. Issues: ENV

Outside Counsel/Consultants

Navista, Inc.
Issues: ENV
Rep By: John Flatley, Steven B. Hellem

Strat@Comm (Strategic Communications Counselors)
Issues: ENV

Corporate Health Care Coalition

Washington, DC

*Includes AlliedSignal, Amoco, Atlantic Richfield, Boeing, DuPont, General Electric, IBM, Ameritech, Bell Atlantic, Pacific Telesis Group, Digital Equipment, McDonnell Douglas, Hershey Foods, United Parcel Service, Intel, Dow Chemical US*WEST, Cox Enterprises, Eastman Kodak, Georgia-Pacific Corp., GTE, ICI Americas Inc., MCI Communications, NYNEX and SBC Communications.*

Leg. Issues: HCR

Outside Counsel/Consultants

Health Policy Analysts
Issues: HCR
Rep By: G. Lawrence Atkins, Nan F. North

Winthrop, Stimson, Putnam & Roberts

Corporate Property Investors

New York, NY
Leg. Issues: TAX

Outside Counsel/Consultants

Wilmer, Cutler & Pickering
Issues: TAX
Rep By: William J. Wilkins

Corporation for Business, Work and Learning

Boston, MA

A work force development organization.

Leg. Issues: EDU, LBR

Outside Counsel/Consultants

Russ Reid Co.
Issues: EDU, LBR
Rep By: Thomas C. Keller, Paul Marcone, Mark D. McIntyre, Jovita Wenner

Corporation for Enterprise Development

777 N. Capitol St. NE
Suite 410
Washington, DC 20002
Tel: (202)408-9788
Fax: (202)408-9793
Registered: LDA
Web: www.cfed.org
Leg. Issues: BUD, CAW, ECN, FIN, TAX

In-house, DC-area Employees

BOSHARA, Ray: Policy Director
DABSON, Brian: President
FRIEDMAN, Robert: Chair and Founder

Outside Counsel/Consultants

Davidson & Company, Inc.
Issues: BUD, FIN, TAX
Rep By: James H. Davidson, Richard E. May, Stanley Sokul

Ralph Pomerance, Jr.
Issues: CAW
Rep By: Ralph Pomerance, Jr.

Bill Zavarela
Rep By: Bill Zavarela

Corporation for Public Broadcasting

401 Ninth St.
Second Floor
Washington, DC 20004-2037
Tel: (202)879-9600
Fax: (202)879-9700
Web: www.cpb.org

In-house, DC-area Employees

BUNTON, Jeannie: Director, Communications
KILMER, Debbie: V. President, Government Relations

Outside Counsel/Consultants

The Direct Impact Co.

Greener and Hook, LLC

Corporation for Supportive Housing

New York, NY
Leg. Issues: BUD

Outside Counsel/Consultants

MARC Associates, Inc.
Rep By: Daniel C. Maldonado, Eve O'Toole, Shannon Penberthy

Robert A. Rapoza Associates
Issues: BUD
Rep By: Robert A. Rapoza

Corporations to End World Hunger Foundation

Outside Counsel/Consultants

Gilbert A. Robinson, Inc.
Rep By: Gilbert A. Robinson

Corpus Christi Port Authority

Corpus Christi, TX
Leg. Issues: TRA

Outside Counsel/Consultants

Thelen Reid & Priest LLP
Issues: TRA
Rep By: Barry I. Berkoff, William A. Kirk, Jr., Richard J. Leidl, Stephan M. Minikes, Nancy K. West

Corpus Christi Regional Transportation Authority

Corpus Christi, TX
Leg. Issues: TRA

Outside Counsel/Consultants

Charles H. Graves & Associates
Issues: TRA
Rep By: Charles H. Graves

Corpus Christi, City of

Corpus Christi, TX
Leg. Issues: CAW, DEF, ECN, NAT, ROD, URB

Outside Counsel/Consultants

Meyers & Associates
Issues: CAW, DEF, ECN, NAT, ROD, URB
Rep By: Larry D. Meyers, Richard L. Meyers

Correctional Vendors Ass'n

Washington, DC
Leg. Issues: LAW

Outside Counsel/Consultants

Foley & Lardner
Issues: LAW
Rep By: Kathleen Leonard

Corrections Corp. of America

Nashville, TN

Designs, builds and manages corrections facilities.

Leg. Issues: GOV, LAW

Outside Counsel/Consultants

Akin, Gump, Strauss, Hauer & Feld, L.L.P.
Issues: GOV, LAW
Rep By: Michael J. Madigan, Steven R. Ross, Barney J. Skladany, Jr., James R. Tucker, Jr.

Manatt, Phelps & Phillips, LLP
Issues: LAW
Rep By: John L. Ray

Wise & Associates
Issues: LAW
Rep By: Nicholas P. Wise

Corte Madera, California, Town of

Leg. Issues: BUD

Outside Counsel/Consultants

E. Del Smith and Co.
Issues: BUD
Rep By: Margaret Allen, E. Del Smith

Corus Group Plc

Rotherham, UNITED KINGDOM
Leg. Issues: TRD

Outside Counsel/Consultants

Davis & Leiman, P.C.
Issues: TRD

COSCO Americas Inc.

Secaucus, NJ
Leg. Issues: MAR

Outside Counsel/Consultants

APCO Worldwide
Issues: MAR
Rep By: Hon. Don L. Bonker, Barry J. Schumacher

Cosmetic, Toiletry and Fragrance Ass'n

1101 17th St. NW
Suite 300
Washington, DC 20036
Tel: (202)331-1770
Fax: (202)331-1969
Registered: LDA
Web: www.ctfa.org
Leg. Issues: BUD, CAW, CSP, ENV, HCR, MED

Political Action Committee/s

Cosmetic, Toiletry and Fragrance Ass'n Political Action Committee
1101 17th St. NW
Suite 300
Washington, DC 20036
Tel: (202)331-1770
Fax: (202)331-1969
Contact: Michael F. Thompson

In-house, DC-area Employees

CAVINS, Mary Jane: V. President, Legislative Services
DEAVER, Carolyn J.: V. President, Foundation
DONEGAN, Jr., Thomas J.: V. President, Legal and General Counsel
HARVEY, Linda: Director, Publications and Communications
KAVANAUGH, E. Edward: President
MALBIN, Irene L.: V. President, Public Affairs
MCEWEN, Jr., Dr. Gerald N.: V. President, Science
SANTUCCI, Louis G.: V. President, International Affairs
SCHIAPPA, Cheryl: V. President, Administration
THOMPSON, Michael F.: V. President, Legislative Relations

Outside Counsel/Consultants

Covington & Burling
Rep By: Peter Barton Hutt

Crowell & Moring LLP
Issues: ENV
Rep By: Nancy S. Bryson

Policy Directions, Inc.
Issues: HCR, MED
Rep By: Kathleen "Kay" Holcombe, Stephen Michael, Frankie L. Trull

Cost Recovery Action Group

Washington, DC

A coalition working toward more-favorable depreciation rules for capital purchases. Members include USX Corp., Advanced Micro Devices, Intel Corp. and the Semiconductor Industry Ass'n.

Outside Counsel/Consultants

Ernest S. Christian

Costa Rica, Central Bank of

San Jose, COSTA RICA

Outside Counsel/Consultants

White & Case LLP

Costa Rica, Embassy of the Republic of

2114 S St. NW
Washington, DC 20008
Tel: (202)234-2946
Fax: (202)265-4795
Web: www.costarica-embassy.com
E-mail: embassy@com

A diplomatic organization.

Outside Counsel/Consultants

Washington World Group, Ltd.
Rep By: Edward J. von Kloberg, III

Costa, Carlos Alberto, Estate of

Leg. Issues: FOR

Outside Counsel/Consultants

Greenberg Traurig, LLP
Issues: FOR
Rep By: Ronald W. Kleinman

Cotton Council Internat'l

1521 New Hampshire Ave. NW
Washington, DC 20036
Tel: (202)745-7805
Fax: (202)483-4040
Web: www.cottonusa.org
E-mail: cottonusa@cotton.org

The overseas operating arm of the Nat'l Cotton Council of America.

In-house, DC-area Employees

TERHAAR, Allen A.: Exec. Director

Cotton Warehouse Ass'n of America

499 S. Capitol St. SW
Suite 600
Washington, DC 20003-4037
Tel: (202)554-1233
Fax: (202)554-1230
Registered: LDA
E-mail: cwaaoffice@aol.com
Leg. Issues: AGR

Political Action Committee/s

Cotton Warehouse Government Relations Committee
499 S. Capitol St. SW
Suite 600
Washington, DC 20003-4037
Tel: (202)554-1233
Fax: (202)554-1230

In-house, DC-area Employees

WALLACE, Jr., Donald L.: Exec. V. President

Outside Counsel/Consultants

Don Wallace Associates, Inc.
Issues: AGR
Rep By: Rebecca Davis, John Gilliland, Donald L. Wallace, Jr.

Council for a Livable World

110 Maryland Ave. NE
Suite 409
Washington, DC 20002
Tel: (202)543-4100
Fax: (202)543-6297
Registered: LDA
Web: www.clw.org
E-mail: clw@clw.org

Registered national political lobbying organization working to reduce the danger posed by weapons of mass destruction; strengthen and reform multilateral conflict resolution and peacekeeping; and revise the military budget to meet current circumstances. Raises funds and otherwise assists sympathetic candidates, lobbies chiefly in the Senate, and publishes reports advocating its objectives.

Leg. Issues: DEF

Political Action Committee/s

PEACE PAC
110 Maryland Ave. NE
Suite 409
Washington, DC 20002
Tel: (202)543-4100
Fax: (202)543-6297
Contact: Suzanne S. Kerr

In-house, DC-area Employees

GROSSMAN, Jerome: Chairman
ISAACS, John D.: President and Lobbyist
KERR, Suzanne S.: Legislative Director

Outside Counsel/Consultants

Greer, Margolis, Mitchell, Burns & Associates

Council for a Livable World Education Fund

110 Maryland Ave. NE
Suite 201
Washington, DC 20002
Tel: (202)546-0795
Fax: (202)546-5142
Registered: LDA
Web: www.clw.org/pub/clw/ef/clwef.html
E-mail: clwef@clw.org

Educates the public and policy makers about the dangers of the arms race and alternative arms control policies.

Leg. Issues: BUD, DEF, ENG, FOR

In-house, DC-area Employees

CARDAMONE, Thomas: Director, Conventional Arms Transfers Project and Editor, Arms Trade News
ISAACS, John D.: Senior Director
KERR, Suzanne S.
KIMBALL, Daryl: Director, Coalition to Reduce Nuclear Dangers

Council for Advanced Agricultural Formulations, Inc.

Washington, DC
Leg. Issues: FOO

Outside Counsel/Consultants

Mintz, Levin, Cohn, Ferris, Glovsky and Popeo, P.C.
Issues: FOO
Rep By: Alvin J. Lorman

Council for Advancement and Support of Education

1307 New York Ave. NW
Suite 1000
Washington, DC 20005
Tel: (202)328-5900
Fax: (202)387-4973
Web: www.case.org

An organization of independent elementary and secondary schools and college and university alumni relations, communications and philanthropy officers concerned with educational legislation related to their functions at their institutions.

In-house, DC-area Employees

LONG, Matthew: Government Relations Analyst
PETERSON, Vance: President

Council for Affordable and Rural Housing

121 N. Washington St.
Suite 301
Alexandria, VA 22314
Tel: (703)837-9001
Fax: (703)837-8467
Registered: LDA
Web: www.carh.org
E-mail: carh@carh.org

Works to ensure the continuance of affordable rental housing in rural areas across the country.

Leg. Issues: HOU

Political Action Committee/s

Council for Affordable and Rural Housing PAC Inc. (CARH PAC)
121 N. Washington St.
Suite 301
Alexandria, VA 22314
Tel: (703)837-9001
Fax: (703)837-8467
Contact: Colleen M. Fisher

In-house, DC-area Employees

FISHER, Colleen M.: Exec. Director

Outside Counsel/Consultants

Coan & Lyons
Issues: HOU
Rep By: Raymond K. James

Nixon Peabody LLP
Rep By: Charles L. Edson

Council for Affordable Health Insurance

112 S. West St.
Fourth Floor
Alexandria, VA 22314
Tel: (703)836-6200
Fax: (703)836-6550
Registered: LDA
Web: www.cahi.org
E-mail: mali@cahi.org

A research and advocacy ass'n representing insurance carriers in the individual, small group, MSA and senior markets. CAHI encourages healthcare reform through government representation, education, economic research newsletters and an on-line service.

Leg. Issues: GOV, HCR, INS, MMM, TAX

In-house, DC-area Employees

HUNTER, Angie: Director, Federal Affairs
LOUSSEDES, Kelly: Director, Public Affairs
O'DONNELL, Kelly: Director, Operations
WEGNER, Nona: President

Outside Counsel/Consultants

Sumlin Associates
Issues: GOV, HCR, INS
Rep By: Council Nedd

Council for Affordable Reliable Energy (CARE)

Outside Counsel/Consultants

Dittus Communications
Rep By: Shelton Jones

Council for Agricultural Science and Technology

Ames, IA
Leg. Issues: AGR, BUD

Outside Counsel/Consultants

Meyers & Associates
Issues: AGR, BUD
Rep By: Fran Boyd, Larry D. Meyers, Richard L. Meyers

Council for American Private Education

13017 Wisteria Dr.
PMB 457
Germantown, MD 20874
Tel: (301)916-8460
Fax: (301)916-8485
Web: www.capenet.org
E-mail: cape@capenet.org

Comprised of 17 national organizations of private secondary and elementary schools and school personnel.

Leg. Issues: EDU

In-house, DC-area Employees

MCTIGHE, Joe: Exec. Director

Council for Basic Education

1319 F St. NW
Suite 900
Washington, DC 20004-1152
Tel: (202)347-4171
Fax: (202)347-5047
Web: www.c-b-e.org
E-mail: info@c-b-e.org

A national, non-profit organization that advocates high academic standards for all students in the nation's public schools. Publishes analytical periodicals and provides technical support and training regarding standards-based reform to policymakers and practitioners at the national, state, and local levels.

Leg. Issues: EDU

In-house, DC-area Employees

CROSS, Christopher T.: President

Council for Chemical Research, Inc.

1620 L St. NW
Suite 620
Washington, DC 20036
Tel: (202)429-3971
Fax: (202)429-3976
Registered: LDA
Web: www.ccrhq.org
E-mail: info@ccrhq.org

A non-profit science and engineering educational association.

Leg. Issues: BUD

In-house, DC-area Employees

PRATT, Megan: Public Affairs Representative
REAM, Kathleen A.: Public Affairs Representative
TABOR, Janis L.: Exec. Director

Council for Christian College and Universities

321 Eighth St. NE
Washington, DC 20002
Tel: (202)546-8713
Fax: (202)546-8913
Web: www.cccu.org
E-mail: council@cccu.org

A national association of 100 colleges and universities of the liberal arts and sciences committed to making the Christian faith relevant to all academic disciplines and daily life on campus. The Council publishes "Choosing a Christian College," "Christian College News" and other public relations materials. Monitors legislation and litigation of special concern to Christian colleges and coordinates an internship/seminar American Studies Program for students in Washington, DC; a Latin American Studies Program in San Jose, Costa Rica; a film studies center in Burbank, California; a Middle East Studies Program in Cairo, Egypt; a Russian Studies Program in Russia; a China studies program in Xiamen, China, an Oxford Honours Programme, and a comtemporary music program in Martha's Vineyard.

In-house, DC-area Employees

ANDRINGA, Dr. Robert C.: President

Council for Conservation and Reinvestment of OCS Revenue

Baton Rouge, LA
Leg. Issues: BUD, ENG, ENV, FUE, NAT

Outside Counsel/Consultants

Van Ness Feldman, P.C.
Issues: BUD, ENG, ENV, FUE, NAT
Rep By: Thomas C. Roberts, Robert G. Szabo

Council for Court Excellence

1717 K St. NW
Suite 510
Washington, DC 20036
Tel: (202)785-5917
Fax: (202)785-5922
Web: www.courtexcellence.org
E-mail: office@courtexcellence.org

A civic group seeking reforms and improvement in the administration of justice at the federal, state and local levels.

Leg. Issues: DOC, GOV, LAW

In-house, DC-area Employees

HARAHAN, Samuel F.: Exec. Director

Council for Energy Independence

Leg. Issues: TAX

Outside Counsel/Consultants

PriceWaterhouseCoopers
Issues: TAX
Rep By: Kenneth J. Kies, Pat Raffaniello

Council for Excellence in Government

1301 K St. NW
Suite 450 West
Washington, DC 20005
Tel: (202)728-0418
Fax: (202)728-0422
Web: www.excelgov.org

Non-partisan, non-profit, and national in scope organization working to improve the performance of American government. Programs aim at strong public-sector leadership and management and at greater citizen confidence and participation in government, achieved through better understanding of government and its role.

Leg. Issues: GOV

In-house, DC-area Employees

FILLICHIO, Carl A.: Director, Public Affairs
MCGINNIS, Patricia G.: President and Chief Exec. Officer

Outside Counsel/Consultants

Martin & Glantz LLC
Issues: GOV

Council for Exceptional Children

1110 N. Glebe Rd.
Arlington, VA 22201-5704
Tel: (703)620-3660
Fax: (703)264-9494
Registered: LDA
Web: www.cec.sped.org
E-mail: service@cec.sped.org

An international professional organization dedicated to improving educational outcomes for students with disabilities and/or the gifted. TTY: (703)264-9446

Leg. Issues: BUD, EDU

In-house, DC-area Employees

FOLEY, Beth: Policy Specialist, Government Relations
SAFER, Nancy: Exec. Director
ZIEGLER, Deborah A.: Assistant Exec. Director, Public Policy

Council for Government Reform

3124 N. Tenth St.
Arlington, VA 22201
Tel: (703)243-7400
Fax: (703)243-7403
Registered: LDA
Web: www.govreform.org

Seeks to encourage greater responsiveness by, and an overall reduction in the size and scope of, government at all levels. Its purpose is to bring about a system of government that is supported by a lower tax burden, more efficient, less intrusive, and less costly.

Leg. Issues: BUD, CON, GOV, MMM, POS, RET, TAX

Political Action Committee/s

Council for Government Reform PAC
3124 N. Tenth St.
Arlington, VA 22201
Tel: (703)243-7400
Fax: (703)243-7403
Contact: Charles G. Hardin

In-house, DC-area Employees

ELLIS, Ryan: Director, Government Relations
HARDIN, Charles G.: President and Chief Exec. Officer

Council for Internat'l Exchange of Scholars

3007 Tilden St. NW
Suite 5L
Washington, DC 20008-3009
Tel: (202)686-4000
Fax: (202)362-3442
Web: www.cies.org/
E-mail: scholars@cies.iie.org

A private non-profit organization that facilitates international exchange in higher education and assists the U.S. State Department's Bureau of Educational and Cultural Affairs in the administration of the Fulbright Scholar Program.

Leg. Issues: EDU

In-house, DC-area Employees

PEHRSON, Judy: Director, External Relations
PETERSON, Patti McGill: Exec. Director

Council for LAB/LAS Environmental Research (CLER)

529 14th St. NW
Suite 655
Washington, DC 20045
Tel: (202)737-0171
Fax: (202)737-8406
Web: www.cler.com
E-mail: cler@johnadams.com

An organization of scientists and technical specialists representing member companies Huntsman Corp., Petresa, CONDEA Vista, DETEN, and Venoco. Mission is to evaluate data, conduct research and distribut scientific information on the environmental safety of the world's number one surfactant, linear alkylbenzene sulfonate (LAS) and the material from which it is produced, linear alkylbenzene (LAB).

In-house, DC-area Employees

DELUCA, Gina: Associate

Outside Counsel/Consultants

John Adams Associates Inc.
Rep By: A. John Adams

Council for Marketing and Opinion Research

Mount Sinai, NY

Outside Counsel/Consultants

Covington & Burling
Rep By: Laurie C. Self

Council for Opportunity in Education

1025 Vermont Ave. NW
Suite 900
Washington, DC 20005
Tel: (202)347-7430
Fax: (202)347-0786
Registered: LDA
Web: www.trioprograms.org
E-mail: mailbox@hqcoe.org
Leg. Issues: BUD, EDU

In-house, DC-area Employees

HENDERSON, Debra: Director, Public Policy
HOYLER, Maureen: Exec. V. President
MITCHEM, Dr. Arnold L.: President

Outside Counsel/Consultants

Dean Blakey & Moskowitz
Rep By: William A. Blakey

Council for Responsible Nutrition

1875 I St. NW
Suite 400
Washington, DC 20006
Tel: (202)872-1488
Fax: (202)872-9594
Registered: LDA
Web: www.crnusa.org
E-mail: info@crnusa.org

A trade association of suppliers, manufacturers, and distributors of nutritional supplements.

Leg. Issues: FOO, HCR

In-house, DC-area Employees

CORDARO, John B.: President and Chief Exec. Officer

Outside Counsel/Consultants

Covington & Burling
Rep By: Peter Barton Hutt

McGuiness & Holch
Issues: FOO, HCR
Rep By: Markham C. Erickson, Kevin S. McGuiness

Council for the Nat'l Interest

1250 Fourth St. SW
Suite WG-1
Washington, DC 20024
Web: www.cnionline.org
E-mail: count@igc.apc.org
Tel: (202)863-2951
Fax: (202)863-2952

A grassroots organization working for peace and justice in the Middle East. CNI believes that land for peace and security, self-determination for Palestinians, weapons reductions, regional economic cooperation, and water resources development are among the goals of a comprehensive peace settlement, and will serve our own national interests, as well as those of Arabs and Israelis. CNI also believes Israel must become independent of U.S. aid and achieve normal relations with its neighbors and the U.S.

Leg. Issues: FOR

In-house, DC-area Employees

AHMED, Sarah: Program Assistant
BIRD, Eugene: President
FINDLEY, Hon. Paul: Founding Chairman

Council for Urban Economic Development

1730 K St. NW
Suite 700
Washington, DC 20006
Web: www.cued.org
E-mail: mail@urbandevelopment.com
Tel: (202)223-4735
Fax: (202)223-4745

Founded in 1967, CUED is an economic development association with a membership of over 2500. Through on-site technical assistance, publications, conferences, training courses, seminars and clearinghouses, CUED offers an information network for its members to assist in the development and revitalization of local economies.

Leg. Issues: ECN

In-house, DC-area Employees

FINKLE, Jeffrey A.: President, Chief Exec. Officer
KALOMIRIS, Paul: Legislative Director

Outside Counsel/Consultants

The DCS Group

Council of American Kidney Societies

Washington, DC

Outside Counsel/Consultants

Bostrom Corp.

Council of American Overseas Research Centers

Washington, DC
Web: www.caorc.org
Leg. Issues: EDU

Outside Counsel/Consultants

Richard L. Spees, Inc.
Issues: EDU
Rep By: Richard L. Spees

Council of Appraisal and Property Professional Societies

Washington, DC

Outside Counsel/Consultants

Peter S. Barash Associates, Inc.
Rep By: Peter S. Barash

Garvey, Schubert & Barer
Rep By: Matthew R. Schneider

Council of Better Business Bureaus

4200 Wilson Blvd.
Suite 800
Arlington, VA 22203-1838
Web: www.bbb.org
E-mail: info@bbb.org
Tel: (703)276-0100
Fax: (703)525-8277

In-house, DC-area Employees

CHERICO, Holly: V.President, Public Relations and Communications
COLE, Steven J.: Senior V. President and General Counsel
HUNTER, Kenneth: President and Chief Exec. Officer
ROSE, Stephen L.: V. President, Chief Information Officer
UNDERHILL, Charles: Senior V. President, Dispute Resolution Division, Chief Operating Officer, BBB Online

Council of Chief State School Officers

One Massachusetts Ave. NW
Suite 700
Washington, DC 20001-1431
Web: www.ccsso.org
E-mail: info@ccsso.org
Tel: (202)408-5505
Fax: (202)408-8072
Registered: LDA

A nationwide non-profit organization representing the public officials who head departments of elementary and secondary education in the states and territories of the United States.

Leg. Issues: EDU

In-house, DC-area Employees

AMBACH, Gordon M.: Exec. Director
HAYES, Carnie: Director, Federal-State Relations
MARTIN, Wayne H.: Director, State Education Assessment Center
ROLLINS, Billie: Director, Strategic Planning and Communications
SHEEKEY, Arthur: Coordinator, Learning Technologies
SMINK, Jeffrey: Legislative Associate

Council of Citizens with Low Vision, Internat'l

1155 15th St. NW
Suite 1004
Washington, DC 20005
Web: www.acb.org
E-mail: info@acb.org
Tel: (202)467-5081
Fax: (202)467-5085

An affiliate of the American Council of the Blind.

In-house, DC-area Employees

STEWART, Ken: President

Council of Colleges of Acupuncture and Oriental Medicine

Portland, OR
Web: www.ccaom.org
Leg. Issues: EDU, HCR

Outside Counsel/Consultants

Cavarocchi Ruscio Dennis Associates
Issues: EDU, HCR
Rep By: Lyle B. Dennis

Council of Development Finance Agencies

1299 Pennsylvania Ave. NW
Suite 800 West
Washington, DC 20004
E-mail: aaron_mindel@dc.sba.com
Tel: (202)682-3901
Fax: (202)842-0621

Membership open to any state, city, county, public agency or special authority whose primary purpose is the provision of economic development financing. Address is that of the Carmen Group (see separate listing under "Firms").

Leg. Issues: FIN, TAX

In-house, DC-area Employees

GILSON, Susan E.: Director, Communications

Outside Counsel/Consultants

Smith Dawson & Andrews, Inc.
Issues: FIN, TAX
Rep By: Susan Mary Riley, James P. Smith

Smith, Bucklin and Associates, Inc.
Rep By: Anna Darin

Council of European and Japanese Nat'l Shipowners' Ass'ns

E-mail: lars.kjaer@worldnet.att.net

A worldwide trade association of national shipowners associations from several European countries and Japan and of individual liner ship operators in these countries.

Leg. Issues: MAR

Outside Counsel/Consultants

Sher & Blackwell
Issues: MAR
Rep By: Marc J. Fink, Stanley O. Sher

Council of Federal Home Loan Banks

1255 23rd St. NW
Washington, DC 20037
Web: www.cfhlb.org
Tel: (202)955-0002
Fax: (202)835-1144
Registered: LDA

Leg. Issues: BAN, GOV, HOU, SMB, TAX

In-house, DC-area Employees

BROOKS, Michelle: V. President, Government Relations
VON SEGGERN, John L.: President and Chief Exec. Officer

Council of Graduate Schools

One Dupont Circle NW
Suite 430
Washington, DC 20036
Web: www.cgsnet.org
E-mail: dstewart@cgs.nche.edu
Tel: (202)223-3791
Fax: (202)331-7157
Registered: LDA

Leg. Issues: BUD, EDU, GOV, MED, SCI, TAX

In-house, DC-area Employees

LINNEY, Jr., Dr. Thomas J.: V. President and Director, Government and Association Relations
SMITH, Robin: V. President
STEWART, Debra: President

Council of Independent Colleges

One Dupont Circle NW
Suite 320
Washington, DC 20036
Web: www.cic.edu
Tel: (202)466-7230
Fax: (202)466-7238

The non-profit, international service association for independent liberal arts colleges and universities. Develops programs and provides practical services that strengthen and advance independent colleges, with a focus on leadership development and educational development. CIC also assists independent colleges in their efforts to promote and market themselves.

Leg. Issues: EDU

In-house, DC-area Employees

ECKMAN, Richard: President
WILCOX, Laura A.: Director, Communications

Council of Industrial Boiler Owners (CIBO)

6035 Burke Centre Pkwy.
Suite 360
Burke, VA 22015
Web: www.cibo.org
E-mail: cibo@cibo.org
Tel: (703)250-9042
Fax: (703)239-9042
Registered: LDA

CIBO is a broad-based association of industrial boiler owners, architect-engineers, related equipment manufacturers and university affiliates with 100 members representing 20 major industrial sectors.

Leg. Issues: CAW, ENG, ENV, FUE, GOV, LAW, NAT, RES, SCI, URB, UTI, WAS

In-house, DC-area Employees

ANDERSON, Richard F.
BESSETTE, Robert D.: President

Outside Counsel/Consultants

Bracewell & Patterson, L.L.P.
Issues: CAW, ENG, ENV, FUE, GOV, NAT, UTI, WAS
Rep By: Hon. Edwin R. Bethune, Hon. Jim Chapman, Kevin Ewing, Gene E. Godley, Marc C. Hebert, Charles L. Ingebretson, Michael L. Pate, Scott H. Segal, D. Michael Stroud, Jr.

Arthur W. Brownell
Rep By: Arthur W. Brownell

Council of Infrastructure Financing Authorities

805 15th St. NW
Suite 500
Washington, DC 20005
Web: www.cifanet.org
Tel: (202)371-9694
Fax: (202)371-6601
Registered: LDA

National non-profit association representing state, regional and local public infrastructure financing agencies organized to advance a shared national policy agenda and promote an exchange of information on emerging public financing techniques.

Leg. Issues: ENV, FIN, GOV, TAX

In-house, DC-area Employees

FARRELL, Richard: Exec. Director

Outside Counsel/Consultants

Chambers Associates Inc.
Issues: ENV, FIN, GOV, TAX
Rep By: Tara Powers

Council of Institutional Investors

1730 Rhode Island Ave. NW
Suite 512
Washington, DC 20036
Web: www.cii.org
E-mail: info@cii.org
Tel: (202)822-0800
Fax: (202)822-0801
Registered: LDA

Founded in 1985, the Council represents approximately 115 pension funds and follows investment issues of interest to its members.

Leg. Issues: FIN

In-house, DC-area Employees

TESLIK, Sarah A. B.: Exec. Director

The Council of Insurance Agents & Brokers

701 Pennsylvania Ave. NW
Suite 750
Washington, DC 20004
Tel: (202)783-4400
Fax: (202)783-4410
Registered: LDA
Web: www.ciab.com
E-mail: ciab@ciab.com

Represents the nation's largest insurance agencies and brokerages. Council members specialize in a wide range of insurance products and risk management services for business, industry, government and the public; group benefits and workers' compensation are a large part of the association's professional services.

Leg. Issues: BAN, CPI, DIS, ENV, FIN, HCR, INS, TAX

Political Action Committee/s

CouncilPAC
701 Pennsylvania Ave. NW
Suite 750
Washington, DC 20004
Tel: (202)783-4400
Fax: (202)783-4410
Contact: Mary Starr Ross

In-house, DC-area Employees

ALLEN, Nicole: Director, State Affairs
CRERAR, Ken A.: President and Chief Exec. Officer
ROSS, Mary Starr: PAC Contact
WOOD, Joel: Senior V. President, Government Affairs

Outside Counsel/Consultants

Baker & Hostetler LLP
Issues: HCR, TAX
Rep By: William F. Conroy, Matthew J. Dolan, Frederick H. Graefe, Kathleen M. Kerrigan, Steven A. Lotterer, David L. Marshall, Hon. Guy Vander Jagt

Collier Shannon Scott, PLLC
Issues: BAN, INS
Rep By: Scott A. Sinder

Gardner, Carton and Douglas
Issues: TAX
Rep By: Kathleen M. Nilles

Valanzano & Associates
Issues: BAN, DIS, TAX
Rep By: Anthony Valanzano

Council of Large Public Housing Authorities

1250 I St. NW
Suite 901A
Washington, DC 20005
Tel: (202)638-1300
Fax: (202)638-2364
Web: www.clpha.org

A non-profit public housing interest organization whose main mission is the preservation and improvement of public housing to serve the nation's low-income population.

Leg. Issues: BUD, HOU

In-house, DC-area Employees

GROSS, Dr. Debbie: Research Director
ZATERMAN, Sunia: Exec. Director

Outside Counsel/Consultants

Reno & Cavanaugh, PLLC
Issues: BUD, HOU
Rep By: Gordon Cavanaugh, Sharon Geno

Council of Northeast Farmer Cooperatives

Leg. Issues: AGR

Outside Counsel/Consultants

Resource Management Consultants, Inc.
Issues: AGR
Rep By: Robert J. Gray

Council of Professional Ass'ns on Federal Statistics

1429 Duke St.
Suite 402
Alexandria, VA 22314-3402
Tel: (703)836-0404
Fax: (703)684-3410
Web: www.copafs.org
E-mail: copafs@aol.com

Established to monitor the priorities, scope and compatibility of the Federal statistical effort.

In-house, DC-area Employees

SPAR, Edward J.: Exec. Director

Council of Scientific Society Presidents

1155 16th St. NW
Suite 1017
Washington, DC 20036
Tel: (202)872-4452
Fax: (202)872-4079
Web: www.science-presidents.org
E-mail: cssp@acs.org

An organization of presidents, presidents-elect, and immediate past presidents of about 60 scientific societies and federations. Acts as a national voice in fostering wise science policy, in support of science and science education, and as a forum for open, substantive exchanges on current scientific issues with national leaders, and as a leadership development institute for national science leaders.

Leg. Issues: SCI

In-house, DC-area Employees

APPLE, Dr. Martin A.: President

Council of Senior Centers and Services of New York City, Inc.

New York, NY

Outside Counsel/Consultants

Matz, Blancato & Associates, Inc.
Rep By: Robert B. Blancato

Council of Smaller Enterprises

Cleveland, OH
Leg. Issues: HCR, SMB

Outside Counsel/Consultants

Griffin, Johnson, Dover & Stewart
Issues: HCR, SMB
Rep By: G. Jack Dover, David E. Johnson

Council of State Administrators of Vocational Rehabilitation

P.O. Box 3776
Washington, DC 20007
Tel: (202)638-4634

In-house, DC-area Employees

OWENS, Joseph H.: Exec. Director

Outside Counsel/Consultants

Duncan and Associates
Rep By: Jack G. Duncan

Council of State and Territorial Epidemiologists

Atlanta, GA
Leg. Issues: BUD, HCR

Outside Counsel/Consultants

Timothy Bell & Co.
Issues: BUD, HCR
Rep By: Marcia S. Mabee, Ph.D.

Council of State Community Development Agencies

444 N. Capitol St. NW
Suite 224
Washington, DC 20001
Tel: (202)624-3630
Fax: (202)624-3639
Web: www.sso.org/coscda

A national association of state community development agencies, which administer housing, community development, economic development and public works programs which are designed to aid low and moderate income persons.

In-house, DC-area Employees

TAYLOR, Dianne: Exec. Director

Council of State Governments

444 N. Capitol St. NW
Suite 401
Washington, DC 20001
Tel: (202)624-5460
Fax: (202)624-5452
Web: www.csg.org
E-mail: info@csg.org

An instrumentality of state governments created and supported by the states to promote inter-governmental cooperation. Conducts research, publishes reports and assists in state-federal liaison. Headquartered in Lexington, Kentucky.

Leg. Issues: AGR, BUD, DIS, FIN, GOV, HCR, LBR

In-house, DC-area Employees

BROWN, James A.: Director, Washington Office and General Counsel
CORMIER, Kristin: Policy and Legislation Director

Council of Surgical Specialty Facilities and Institutes

Washington, DC
Leg. Issues: MMM

Outside Counsel/Consultants

Robert Betz Associates, Inc.
Issues: MMM
Rep By: Cathy Clark Betz, Robert B. Betz

Council of the Americas

1310 G St. NW
Suite 690
Washington, DC 20005-3000
Tel: (202)639-0724
Fax: (202)639-0794
Registered: LDA
Web: www.counciloftheamericas.org

The premier business organization dedicated to promoting regional economic integration, free trade, open markets and investment, democracy, and the rule of law throughout the Western Hemisphere. Headquartered in New York, NY.

Leg. Issues: TRD

In-house, DC-area Employees

KILLORIDE, Patrick: Director, Governmental Affairs
MILLER, Scott A.: Director, Public Affairs
PRYCE, William T.: V. President, Washington Operations

Outside Counsel/Consultants

The Trade Partnership
Issues: TRD
Rep By: Laura M. Baughman

Council of the Great City Schools

1301 Pennsylvania Ave. NW
Suite 702
Washington, DC 20004
Tel: (202)393-2427
Fax: (202)393-2400
Registered: LDA
Web: www.cgcs.org
E-mail: mcasserly@cgcr.org
Leg. Issues: BUD, EDU

In-house, DC-area Employees

CASSERLY, Michael: Exec. Director
DUVALL, Henry: Director, Communications
SIMERLING, Jeffrey: Director, Legislation
WRIGHT, Julie: Legislative Consultant

Council of Urban and Economic Development

Washington, DC

Outside Counsel/Consultants

Sue E. Johnson Associates
Rep By: Susan E. Johnson

Council of Volunteer Americans

P.O. Box 1222
Sterling, VA 20167
Tel: (703)379-9188
Web: www.impeachclinton.org

A non-profit grassroots education and petition-gathering organization.

In-house, DC-area Employees

CLAYTON, Jack: V. President
NEAL, Michael: Director, Field Operations

Council of Women's and Infant's Specialty Hospitals

Providence, RI
Leg. Issues: HCR, MMM

Outside Counsel/Consultants

McDermott, Will and Emery
Issues: HCR, MMM
Rep By: Wendy L. Krasner, Maggie A. Mitchell, Karen S. Sealander

Council on Competitiveness

1500 K St. NW
Suite 850
Washington, DC 20005
Tel: (202)682-4292
Fax: (202)682-5150
Web: www.compete.org
E-mail: council@compete.org

A nonpartisan, nonprofit coalition of chief executive officers from business, academia and labor working together to set a national action agenda to strengthen U.S. competitiveness. The Council's work program focuses on technological innovation, human resource development, trade, fiscal policy and the benchmarking of U.S. competitiveness.

In-house, DC-area Employees

BERMAN, Marshall: Exec. Director-Internet Learning Network
HOLMES, Bucky: Director, Administration
KASLOW, Amy: Senior Fellow
KHAN, Mohamed: Director, Information Technology
ROONEY, Peter: Exec. Director-Forum on Technology and Innovation
VAN OPSTAL, Debra: Senior V. President
WEST, Kimberly: Deputy Director
WINCE-SMITH, Deborah: Senior Fellow
YOCHELSON, John N.: President

Council on Federal Procurement of Architectural and Engineering Services (COFPAES)

Washington, DC
Leg. Issues: GOV

Outside Counsel/Consultants

John M. Palatiello & Associates
Issues: GOV
Rep By: John M. Palatiello

Council on Foreign Relations

1779 Massachusetts Ave. NW
Suite 710
Washington, DC 20036
Tel: (202)518-3400
Fax: (202)986-2984
Web: www.foreignrelations.org

The Washington office of the New York-based Council on Foreign Relations.

In-house, DC-area Employees
DOBRIANSKY, Paula: V. President/Washington Director
SWEIG, Julia: Deputy Director, Latin American Programs

Council on Foundations

1828 L St. NW
Suite 300
Washington, DC 20036
Web: www.cof.org
Tel: (202)466-6512
Fax: (202)785-3926
Leg. Issues: TAX

In-house, DC-area Employees
CURTIS, Jody: Managing Editor, "Foundation News and Commentary"
DADISMAN, Ellen C.: V. President, Government and Media Relations
EDIE, John A.: Senior V. President and General Counsel
RIDINGS, Dorothy S.: President

Outside Counsel/Consultants
Caplin & Drysdale, Chartered
Issues: TAX
Rep By: Robert A. Boisture

Council on Hemispheric Affairs

1444 I St. NW
Suite 211
Washington, DC 20005
Web: www.coha.org
E-mail: coha@coha.org
Tel: (202)216-9261
Fax: (202)216-9193

Founded in 1975. A non-profit research and information organization dedicated to promoting a more balanced U.S. policy towards Latin America and Canada. Seeks to increase respect for strong human rights standards; raise the visibility of the inter-American relationship; encourage Fair Trade practices, as well as regional and economic development; and strengthen democratic institutions. Emphasizes research and publishing on US hemispheric policy, drugs, economics, diplomacy, and national security.

In-house, DC-area Employees
BIRNS, Laurence R.: Director

Council on Internat'l Educational Exchange

New York, NY
Leg. Issues: EDU, FOR

Outside Counsel/Consultants
Bracy Williams & Co.
Issues: EDU, FOR
Rep By: Linda Doorfee Flaherty, Susan J. Williams

Council on Labor Law Equality

Leg. Issues: LBR

Outside Counsel/Consultants
Ogletree Governmental Affairs, Inc.
Issues: LBR
Rep By: Harold P. Coxson

Council on Radionuclides and Radiopharmaceuticals (CORAR)

Leg. Issues: BUD, ENG, HCR, MMM, TRA

Outside Counsel/Consultants
Alpine Group, Inc.
Issues: BUD, ENG, HCR, MMM, TRA
Rep By: James D. Massie, Richard C. White

Council on Religious Freedom

4545 42nd St. NW
Suite 201
Washington, DC 20016
Tel: (202)363-8098
Fax: (202)363-0304

Headquartered in Rockville, MD. Upholds constitutionality and practices of the two religion clauses of the First Amendment in a broad manner.

In-house, DC-area Employees
WILSON, Neil: President

Council on Resident Education in Obstetrics and Gynecology

P.O. Box 96920
Washington, DC 20090-6920
Web: www.acog.org
E-mail: dnehra@acog.org
Tel: (202)638-5577
Fax: (202)863-4994

The Council is located at the American College of Obstetricians and Gynecologists.

In-house, DC-area Employees
NEHRA, DeAnne: Associate Director

Council on Social Work Education

1725 Duke St.
Suite 500
Alexandria, VA 22314
Web: www.cswe.org
E-mail: info@cswe.org
Tel: (703)683-8080
Fax: (703)683-8099

A nonprofit organization committed to promoting quality in social work education. Representing 3000 educators and 600 schools and academic departments, it is the sole accrediting authority for social work education in the U.S. and facilitates faculty development and scholarly exchange through publications, conferences and workshops.

In-house, DC-area Employees
BELESS, Dr. Donald W.: Exec. Director

Council on Superconductivity for American Competitiveness

Washington, DC
Leg. Issues: ENG

Outside Counsel/Consultants
Cassidy & Associates, Inc.
Issues: ENG
Rep By: Lawrence C. Grossman, Christopher Lamond

Council on the Economic Impact of Health System Change

Waltham, MA

Outside Counsel/Consultants
Hauser Group

Council on Undergraduate Research

734 15th St. NW
Suite 550
Washington, DC 20005
Web: www.cur.org
E-mail: cur@cur.org
Tel: (202)783-4810
Fax: (202)783-4811

Scientific association promoting research at undergraduate institutions.

Leg. Issues: EDU, SCI

In-house, DC-area Employees
HOAGLAND, Dr. K. Elaine: National Exec. Officer

Council Tree Communications, L.L.C.

Longmont, CO
Leg. Issues: TEC

Outside Counsel/Consultants
Birch, Horton, Bittner & Cherot
Issues: TEC
Rep By: Thomas L. Albert, William Bittner

Counterpart Internat'l

Washington, DC

Outside Counsel/Consultants
Jamison and Sullivan, Inc.
Rep By: Delos Cy Jamison, Jay R. Sullivan

Countrywide Home Loans, Inc.

1101 Pennsylvania Ave. NW
Suite 700
Washington, DC 20004
Web: www.countrywide.com
E-mail: jimmie_williams@countrywide.com
Tel: (202)756-7755
Fax: (202)756-7505
Registered: LDA

The nation's largest independent mortgage originator and servicer. Headquartered in Calabasas, CA.

Leg. Issues: BAN, FIN, HOU, INS, TAX

Political Action Committee/s
Countrywide Credit Industries Inc. PAC (Countrywide PAC)
1101 Pennsylvania Ave. NW
Suite 700
Washington, DC 20004
Contact: Jimmie L. Williams
Tel: (202)756-7755
Fax: (202)756-7505

In-house, DC-area Employees
WILLIAMS, Jimmie L.: V. President, Legislative Affairs

Outside Counsel/Consultants
Blank Rome Comisky & McCauley, LLP
Issues: BAN
Rep By: J. Caleb Boggs, III

Countrywide Mortgage Corp.

Pasadena, CA
Leg. Issues: BAN, HOU

Outside Counsel/Consultants
Butera & Andrews
Issues: BAN, HOU
Rep By: Cliff W. Andrews, James J. Butera, Frank Tillotson

County Welfare Directors Ass'n of California

Sacramento, CA
Leg. Issues: FAM, WEL

Outside Counsel/Consultants
Craig Associates
Issues: FAM, WEL
Rep By: Patricia J. Craig, Kathryn Dyjak, Leslie Sacks Gross

Coushatta Tribe of Louisiana

Elton, LA
Leg. Issues: BUD, ECN, GAM, HOU, IND, TAX, TOU

Outside Counsel/Consultants
Greenberg Traurig, LLP
Rep By: Jack Abramoff
Johnston & Associates, LLC
Issues: BUD, ECN, GAM, HOU, IND, TAX, TOU
Rep By: Hon. J. Bennett Johnston, N. Hunter Johnston, W. Proctor Jones, Eric Tober

COVAD Communications Co.

600 14th Street NW
Suite 750
Washington, DC 20005
Tel: (202)220-0400
Fax: (202)220-0401
Registered: LDA
Leg. Issues: TEC

In-house, DC-area Employees
ATWELL, Meredith: Director, Legislative Affairs

Outside Counsel/Consultants
Janus-Merritt Strategies, L.L.C.
Issues: TEC
Rep By: Scott P. Hoffman, Mark J. Robertson, J. Daniel Walsh

Covanta Energy Corporation

3211 Jermantown Rd.
Suite 300
Fairfax, VA 22030
Web: www.covantaenergy.com
Tel: (703)246-0600
Fax: (703)246-0808
Registered: LDA

Formerly Ogden Corp. An international developer, owner, and operator of power generation projects and a provider of related infrastructure services. Headquartered in Fairfield, NJ.

Leg. Issues: ART, AVI, ENG, WAS

Political Action Committee/s
Covanta Political Action Committee
3211 Jermantown Rd.
Suite 300
Fairfax, VA 22030
Contact: B. Kent Burton
Tel: (703)246-0833
Fax: (703)246-0808

In-house, DC-area Employees
BURTON, B. Kent: Senior V. President, Policy and International Business Relations
EGAN, Irene M.: Community and Government Affairs Representative

Outside Counsel/Consultants
Chambers Associates Inc.

Covenant House

New York, NY
Leg. Issues: BUD, HCR, HOU

Outside Counsel/Consultants
McMahon and Associates
Issues: BUD, HCR, HOU
Rep By: Joseph E. McMahon

Coventry Health Care, Inc.

6705 Rockledge Dr.
Suite 900
Bethesda, MD 20817
Web: www.cvty.com
Tel: (301)581-0600

In-house, DC-area Employees
WISE, Allan: President

Cow Creek Umpqua Tribe of Oregon

Roseburg, OR
Leg. Issues: IND, TAX

Outside Counsel/Consultants
Dorsey & Whitney LLP
Issues: IND, TAX
Rep By: Philip Baker-Shenk, David A. Bieging, Virginia W. Boylan, Cindy Darcy, Mark Jarboe, Christopher Karns, Kevin J. Wadzinski

Coweta County (Georgia) School Board

Newnan, GA
Leg. Issues: EDU

Outside Counsel/Consultants

Adams and Reese LLP
Issues: EDU
Rep By: B. Jeffrey Brooks

Cox Enterprises Inc.

1225 19th St. NW
Suite 450
Washington, DC 20036
Tel: (202)296-4933
Fax: (202)296-4951
Registered: LDA

A diversified communications company headquartered in Atlanta, GA.

Leg. Issues: COM, CPT, ENV, GOV, LBR, MMM, POS, TAX, TEC

In-house, DC-area Employees

HUBBARD, Sherry L.: Director of Operations
NETCHVOLODOFF, Alexander V.: V. President, Public Policy
WILSON, Alexandra M.: Chief, Public Policy Counsel

Outside Counsel/Consultants

Dow, Lohnes & Albertson, PLLC
Issues: GOV
Rep By: Kenneth D. Salomon

Hooper Owen & Winburn
Issues: TAX
Rep By: Steve Glaze

Timmons and Co., Inc.
Issues: COM, CPT, TAX
Rep By: Michael J. Bates, Douglas F. Bennett, Ellen B. Fitzgibbons, Bryce L. "Larry" Harlow, Timothy J. Keating, Tom C. Korologos, Richard J. Tarplin, William E. Timmons, Jr., William E. Timmons, Sr.

CPU Technology

Leg. Issues: DEF

Outside Counsel/Consultants

The PMA Group
Issues: DEF
Rep By: Kaylene Green, Gregory L. Hansen, Joseph Littleton, Stephen Madey, Paul J. Magliocchetti, Briggs Shade, Thomas Veltri

Craig, Alaska, City of

Leg. Issues: BUD

Outside Counsel/Consultants

Robertson, Monagle & Eastaugh
Issues: BUD
Rep By: Steven W. Silver

Craig-Botetourt Electric Cooperative, Inc.

New Castle, VA

Outside Counsel/Consultants

Duncan, Weinberg, Genzer & Pembroke, P.C.
Rep By: Robert Weinberg

Crane & Co.

Dalton, MA
Leg. Issues: MON

Outside Counsel/Consultants

Cassidy & Associates, Inc.
Issues: MON
Rep By: Douglass E. Bobbitt, Gregory M. Gill, Dennis M. Kedzior, Christopher Lamond, Hon. Martin A. Russo

Crane Co.

Stamford, CT
Leg. Issues: DEF, LBR

Outside Counsel/Consultants

Patton Boggs, LLP
Issues: DEF, LBR
Rep By: Todd Anderson, Lanny J. Davis, John J. Deschauer, Jr., Penelope S. Farthing, Clayton L. Hough, Hon. Greg H. Laughlin, Michael J. Nardotti, Garrett G. Rassmussen, Jonathan R. Yarowsky

John Crane-LIPS, Inc.

Chesapeake, VA
Leg. Issues: DEF, GOV, TRD

Outside Counsel/Consultants

Wayne Arny & Assoc.
Issues: DEF, GOV, TRD
Rep By: Wayne Arny, David D. O'Brien

Dyer Ellis & Joseph, P.C.
Issues: DEF
Rep By: Brian A. Bannon, James S. W. Drewry, Wayne A. Keup, Duncan C. Smith, III, Jennifer M. Southwick

David O'Brien and Associates
Issues: DEF
Rep By: Wayne Arny, David D. O'Brien

Cranston, Rhode Island, City of

Leg. Issues: ECN, GOV

Outside Counsel/Consultants

Capitol City Group
Issues: ECN, GOV
Rep By: Gerald T. Harrington, John J. Hogan, Thomas P. Hogan, Christopher P. Vitale

Cranston, Rhode Island, Department of Human Services

Cranston, RI

Outside Counsel/Consultants

Covington & Burling

Cray Inc.

Silver Spring, MD
Registered: LDA

Outside Counsel/Consultants

Denny Miller McBee Associates

Credit Suisse First Boston Corp.

1401 I St. NW
Suite 910
Washington, DC 20005
Tel: (202)354-2800
Fax: (202)354-2808
Leg. Issues: BAN, BNK, BUD, DEF, ENG, FIN, FOR, TAX, TRD

Political Action Committee/s

Credit Suisse First Boston Corp. Government Action Fund
1401 I St. NW
Suite 910
Washington, DC 20005
Contact: Mary Lynne Whalen
Tel: (202)354-2600
Fax: (202)354-2622

In-house, DC-area Employees

SEIDEL, Joseph L.
WHALEN, Mary Lynne: Treasurer

Outside Counsel/Consultants

Cleary, Gottlieb, Steen and Hamilton

Morgan, Lewis & Bockius LLP
Issues: BUD, DEF, ENG, FOR, TRD
Rep By: William E. Baer, James A. Glasgow, Charles H. Peterson

Williams & Jensen, P.C.
Issues: BAN, BNK, FIN, TAX
Rep By: Philip E. Bechtel, David E. Franasiak, Robert E. Glennon, Jr., J. Steven Hart, David M. Landers, George G. Olsen, Anthony J. Roda, Jeffrey A. Tassey

Credit Union Council of the Nat'l Ass'n of State Credit Union Supervisors

1655 N. Fort Meyer Dr.
Suite 300
Arlington, VA 22209
Web: www.nascus.org
E-mail: offices@nascus.org
Tel: (703)528-8351
Fax: (703)528-3248
Registered: LDA

In-house, DC-area Employees

DUERR, Douglas: President and Chief Exec. Officer

Credit Union Nat'l Ass'n, Inc.

805 15th St. NW
Suite 300
Washington, DC 20005-2207
Tel: (202)682-4200
Fax: (202)682-9054
Registered: LDA

A national trade association composed of 50 state leagues and over 10,000 members. Represents more than 90% of the nation's 11,000 state and federally chartered credit unions.

Leg. Issues: BAN, BNK

Political Action Committee/s

Credit Union Legislative Action Council
805 15th St. NW
Suite 300
Washington, DC 20005-2207
Contact: Richard Gose
Tel: (202)682-4200
Fax: (202)682-9054

In-house, DC-area Employees

BLOCK, Jeffrey
DIMOS, John: Manager, Senate Legislative Affairs
DUNN, Mary Mitchell: Senior V. President and Associate General Counsel, Regulatory Advocacy
GORE, Jennifer: Manager, Public and Congressional Affairs
GOSE, Richard: V. President, Political Action and Grassroots
GRAFF, Gretchen: Grassroots Manager
HAMPTON, Maura: Manager, House Legislative Affairs
HYLAND, Gigi: Regulatory Staff Attorney
KELLY, Colleen: V. President, State Governmental Affairs
KOHN, Gary J.: V. President and Senior Legislative Counsel
MCKECHNIE, III, John J.: V. President, Legislative Affairs
MICA, Hon. Daniel A.: President and Chief Exec. Officer
NEWTON, Susan: Senior V. President, League Services
PARKS, Carl M.: Senior V. President, Governmental Affairs
PROFIT, Michelle
RICHARD, Eric: General Counsel
THOMPSON, Kathleen O.: Sr. V. President/Associate General Counsel, Federal Compliance and Legislative
WOLFF, Mark: Senior V. President, Communications

Outside Counsel/Consultants

Fierce and Isakowitz
Issues: BAN
Rep By: Samantha Cook, Donald L. Fierce, Mark W. Isakowitz, Diane Moery

Greener and Hook, LLC

Creme de la Creme, Inc.

Dallas, TX
Leg. Issues: ANI, FOR, TRD

Outside Counsel/Consultants

APCO Worldwide
Issues: ANI, FOR, TRD
Rep By: Barry J. Schumacher, Hon. Stephen J. Solarz

Crestwood Behavior Health, Inc.

Stockton, CA
Leg. Issues: HCR, MMM

Outside Counsel/Consultants

Helmsin & Yarwood Associates
Issues: HCR, MMM
Rep By: Bruce Yarwood

The Criminal Justice Policy Foundation

1225 I St. NW
Suite 500
Washington, DC 20005
Web: www.ndsn.org
Tel: (202)312-2015
Fax: (202)842-2620

Non-profit, educational foundation for innovative solutions to problems of the criminal justice system. Key issues are crime prevention, drug policy, federal law enforcement, sentencing, policing, prisons and juvenile delinquency.

In-house, DC-area Employees

STERLING, Eric E.: President

Croatia, Republic of

Zagreb, CROATIA

Outside Counsel/Consultants

Baker & Hostetler LLP
Rep By: Darin Bartram, Lee A. Casey, David B. Rivkin, Jr.

Crohn's and Colitis Foundation of America

New York, NY
Leg. Issues: BUD, HCR

Outside Counsel/Consultants

Health and Medicine Counsel of Washington
Issues: BUD, HCR
Rep By: Dale P. Dirks, Gavin Lindberg

Crop Growers Insurance Co.

Overland, KS
Leg. Issues: AGR

Outside Counsel/Consultants

Tuttle, Taylor & Heron
Issues: AGR
Rep By: Julian B. Heron, Jr.

Crop Protection Coalition

Watsonville, CA
Leg. Issues: BUD, CAW

Outside Counsel/Consultants

McDermott, Will and Emery
Issues: BUD, CAW
Rep By: Jerry C. Hill, Edward M. Ruckert

Crosby Internat'l

Alexandria, VA

Outside Counsel/Consultants

Van Fleet, Inc.
Rep By: Frank C. Van Fleet

Cross Sound Ferry Services, Inc.

New London, CT
Leg. Issues: MAR

Outside Counsel/Consultants

Dyer Ellis & Joseph, P.C.
Issues: MAR
Rep By: James S. W. Drewry, Lara Bernstein Mathews, Duncan C. Smith, III, Jennifer M. Southwick

Crowley Maritime Corp.

1800 Diagonal Rd. Tel: (703)684-3132
Suite 606 Fax: (703)549-6245
Alexandria, VA 22314
Leg. Issues: DEF, FUE, MAR, TRA, TRD

In-house, DC-area Employees

FORTUNATO, Edward: Washington Representative

Outside Counsel/Consultants

Thompson Coburn LLP
Issues: DEF, FUE, MAR, TRA, TRD

Crown American Properties

Johnstown, PA

Outside Counsel/Consultants

Chambers Associates Inc.
Rep By: Letitia Chambers

Crown American Realty Trust

Johnstown, PA
Leg. Issues: TRA

Outside Counsel/Consultants

Edmund C. Graber
Issues: TRA
Rep By: Edmund C. Graber

Crown Butte Mines, Inc.

Billings, MT

Outside Counsel/Consultants

Oppenheimer Wolff & Donnelly LLP
Rep By: Hon. Birch Bayh, Kevin O. Faley, Margaret N. Strand

Crown Central Petroleum Corp.

Baltimore, MD
Leg. Issues: ENG, ENV

Outside Counsel/Consultants

Capitol Counsel Group, L.L.C.
Issues: ENG, ENV
Rep By: Warren Belmar

Crown Controls Corp.

New Bremen, OH

Outside Counsel/Consultants

Dunaway & Cross
Rep By: Mac S. Dunaway

Crown Therapeutics, Inc.

Belleville, IL
Leg. Issues: HCR, MMM

Outside Counsel/Consultants

Nusgart Consulting, LLC
Issues: HCR, MMM
Rep By: Marcia Nusgart

CRT, Inc.

Atlanta, GA
Leg. Issues: EDU, TEC

Outside Counsel/Consultants

Robert L. Redding
Issues: EDU, TEC
Rep By: Robert L. Redding, Jr.

Cruise Industry Charitable Foundation

Outside Counsel/Consultants

Alcalde & Fay
Rep By: Hector Alcalde, Cynthia Colenda, Danielle McBeth, Lois Moore, Christopher L. Turner

Cruising America Coalition

San Francisco, CA
Leg. Issues: TOU

Outside Counsel/Consultants

Wayne Arny & Assoc.
Issues: TOU
Rep By: Wayne Arny, David D. O'Brien

David O'Brien and Associates
Issues: TOU
Rep By: David D. O'Brien, Shannon L. Scott

Cruz Enverga & Raboca

Makati City, PHILIPPINES

Outside Counsel/Consultants

Chlopak, Leonard, Schechter and Associates
Rep By: Peter Schechter

CryoLife, Inc.

Marietta, GA

Outside Counsel/Consultants

Buc & Beardsley
Rep By: Kate C. Beardsley

CRYPTEK Secure Communications, LLC

Chantilly, VA
Leg. Issues: CPI, DEF

Outside Counsel/Consultants

The Kemper Co.
Issues: CPI, DEF
Rep By: Jackson Kemper, Jr.

The PMA Group
Issues: DEF
Rep By: Daniel Cunningham, Daniel E. Fleming, Sean Fogarty, Kaylene Green, Patrick Hiu, Paul J. Magliocchetti, Briggs Shade, Kelli Short, Brian Thiel

Crystal Cruises

Los Angeles, CA
Leg. Issues: MAR

Outside Counsel/Consultants

Robins, Kaplan, Miller & Ciresi L.L.P.
Issues: MAR
Rep By: Harold E. Mesirow

Crystal Group

Arlington, VA

Outside Counsel/Consultants

The Campo Group, Ltd.
Rep By: Terry T. Campo

CSA America, Inc.

Cleveland, OH
Leg. Issues: CSP, ENG, ENV, FOO, FUE, GOV, LBR, MAN, SCI

Outside Counsel/Consultants

Kathleen Winn & Associates, Inc.
Issues: CSP, ENG, ENV, FOO, FUE, GOV, LBR, MAN, SCI
Rep By: Kathleen Winn

CSFP Capital, Inc.

New York, NY

Outside Counsel/Consultants

Cleary, Gottlieb, Steen and Hamilton

CSO Partnership

Richmond, VA

An organization of combined sewer overflow communities.

Leg. Issues: CAW

Outside Counsel/Consultants

McGuireWoods L.L.P.
Issues: CAW
Rep By: Hana Brilliant, F. Paul Calamita, Stephen A. Katsurinis

CSRG Digital LLC

Los Angeles, CA
Leg. Issues: COM

Outside Counsel/Consultants

Convergence Services, Inc.
Issues: COM
Rep By: John M. Lawson

CSX Corp.

1331 Pennsylvania Ave. NW Tel: (202)783-8124
Suite 560 Fax: (202)783-5929
Washington, DC 20004 Registered: LDA

A multimodal transportation company headquartered in Richmond, VA.

Leg. Issues: BUD, COM, CSP, ENV, GOV, MAR, RRR, TAX, TOR, TOU, TRA, TRD, TRU, UTI, WAS

Political Action Committee/s

CSX Transportation Inc. Political Action Committee
1331 Pennsylvania Ave. NW Tel: (202)783-8124
Suite 560 Fax: (202)783-5929
Washington, DC 20004
Contact: Alem Woldehawariat

In-house, DC-area Employees

HAVENS, Arnie I.: Corporate V. President, Federal Affairs
LIEBMAN, Diane S.: V. President, Railroad Federal Affairs
SMYTHERS, Mike: Director, Federal Affairs
WOLDEHAWARIAT, Alem: Manager, Public Affairs

Outside Counsel/Consultants

Birch, Horton, Bittner & Cherot
Issues: BUD, TOU
Rep By: Thomas L. Albert, Ronald G. Birch, William P. Horn

Law Offices of Kevin G. Curtin
Issues: RRR, TRA
Rep By: Kevin G. Curtin

John A. DeVierno
Rep By: John A. DeVierno

The Duberstein Group, Inc.
Issues: GOV, MAR, RRR
Rep By: John W. Angus, III, Michael S. Berman, Steven M. Champlin, Kenneth M. Duberstein, Henry M. Gandy, Daniel P. Meyer

Eckert Seamans Cherin & Mellott, LLC
Issues: RRR, TRA
Rep By: LeRoy S. Zimmerman

The Paul Laxalt Group
Issues: RRR
Rep By: Hon. Paul D. Laxalt, Tom Loranger

McGlotten & Jarvis
Issues: RRR
Rep By: John T. Jarvis, Robert M. McGlotten

McGuireWoods L.L.P.
Issues: TRA
Rep By: Frank B. Atkinson, Joseph H. Bogosian, Stephen A. Katsurinis, Hon. Lewis F. Payne, Jr.

Robertson, Monagle & Eastaugh
Issues: MAR, RRR
Rep By: Bradley D. Gilman, Rick E. Marks

The Smith-Free Group
Issues: MAR, RRR
Rep By: James C. Free, W. Timothy Locke, Alicia W. Smith

Tongour Simpson Holsclaw Green
Issues: TRA
Rep By: John Bradley "Brad" Holsclaw, Michael A. Tongour

The Wexler Group
Issues: RRR
Rep By: Patrick J. McCann, Anne Wexler

CSX Lines LLC

An ocean container transportation organization. Headquartered in Charlotte, NC.

Leg. Issues: BUD, DEF, MAR, TAX, TRA, TRD, TRU

Outside Counsel/Consultants

Robertson, Monagle & Eastaugh
Issues: BUD, DEF, MAR, TAX, TRA, TRD, TRU
Rep By: Bradley D. Gilman, Rick E. Marks

CT USA, Inc.

Rochester, NY
Leg. Issues: BAN

Outside Counsel/Consultants

Williams & Jensen, P.C.
Issues: BAN
Rep By: David M. Landers

CTAM

Alexandria, VA
Web: www.ctam.com

Formerly the Cable Television Administration and Marketing Society.

Outside Counsel/Consultants

Jenner & Block

CTC Corp.

Richwood, WV
Leg. Issues: GOV

Outside Counsel/Consultants

Cottone and Huggins Group
Issues: GOV
Rep By: James B. Huggins

Cuban American Nat'l Foundation/Cuban American Foundation

1822 Jefferson Place NW Tel: (202)530-1894
Washington, DC 20036 Fax: (202)530-2444
Web: www.canfnet.org
E-mail: dc@canf.org

An independent, non-profit research and educational institution dedicated to the gathering and dissemination of economic, political, social, and cultural data related to Cuba and its people.

Leg. Issues: FOR

In-house, DC-area Employees

HAYES, Dennis: Exec. V. President

Outside Counsel/Consultants

Friedman Law Offices, P.L.L.C.

The MWW Group
Issues: FOR
Rep By: Dana P. Bostic, Elizabeth A. Iadarola, Jonathan B. Slade

Cubic Defense

Crystal Gateway One
Suite 1102
1235 Jefferson Davis Hwy.
Arlington, VA 22202
Web: www.cubic.com
Tel: (703)415-1600
Fax: (703)415-1608

In-house, DC-area Employees

LIDDLE, Jack W.: V. President, Legislative Liaison

CUBRC

Buffalo, NY
Leg. Issues: DEF

Outside Counsel/Consultants

The Dutko Group, Inc.

The Potomac Advocates
Issues: DEF
Rep By: Charles Scalera, Gary L. Sojka

Cultural Alliance of Greater Washington

1436 U St. NW
Suite 103
Washington, DC 20009-3997
Web: www.cultural-alliance.org
E-mail: staff@cultural-alliance.org
Tel: (202)638-2406
Fax: (202)638-3388

In-house, DC-area Employees

PAYNE, Jennifer Cover: Exec. Director

Cultural Partnership of the Americas

Leg. Issues: ART, FOR

Outside Counsel/Consultants

Petito & Associates
Issues: ART, FOR
Rep By: Margaret L. Petito

Cumberland Packing Corp.

Brooklyn, NY
Leg. Issues: FOO

Outside Counsel/Consultants

Bruce Ray & Company
Issues: FOO
Rep By: Bruce A. Ray, Ph.D.

Cummins Engine Co.

Columbus, OH

A manufacturer of diesel engines.

Leg. Issues: CAW, ENV, LBR, RET, TAX

Outside Counsel/Consultants

Akin, Gump, Strauss, Hauer & Feld, L.L.P.
Issues: LBR, RET, TAX
Rep By: Donald C. Alexander, Janet C. Boyd, Henry A. Terhune

Barnes, Richardson and Colburn

BKSH & Associates
Issues: CAW, ENV, TAX

Chambers Associates Inc.

Cummins-Allison Corp.

Mt. Prospect, IL
Leg. Issues: BAN, CPT, FIN, MAN, TRD

Outside Counsel/Consultants

Beacon Consulting Group, Inc.
Rep By: Jeffrey W. Henry, Gordon P. MacDougall, Lisa A. Stewart

Jefferson Government Relations, L.L.C.
Issues: BAN, CPT, FIN, MAN, TRD
Rep By: John D. Desser, Thomas R. Donnelly, Jr., Erik Rasmussen

Cumulus Media, Inc.

Milwaukee, WI
Leg. Issues: COM

Outside Counsel/Consultants

Paul, Hastings, Janofsky & Walker LLP
Issues: COM
Rep By: Ralph B. Everett, Bruce D. Ryan

CUNA Mutual Group

Madison, WI
Leg. Issues: TAX

Outside Counsel/Consultants

Hogan & Hartson L.L.P.
Issues: TAX
Rep By: C. Michael Gilliland, William Michael House

Cure Autism Now

Los Angeles, CA
Leg. Issues: HCR

Outside Counsel/Consultants

Ikon Public Affairs
Issues: HCR

Cure for Lymphoma Foundation

New York, NY
Leg. Issues: BUD, HCR, MED, MMM

Outside Counsel/Consultants

Bennett Turner & Coleman, LLP
Issues: BUD, HCR, MED, MMM
Rep By: Elizabeth Goss, Natasha Leskovsek, Kristi E. Schrode, Samuel D. Turner

Currenex

Redwood, CA
Leg. Issues: BAN, FIN

Outside Counsel/Consultants

Fleischman and Walsh, L.L.P.
Issues: BAN, FIN
Rep By: Louis H. Dupart, John P. McAllister

Currie Technologies, Inc.

Van Nuys, CA
Leg. Issues: CSP, TRA

Outside Counsel/Consultants

Lawler, Metzger & Milkman, LLC
Issues: CSP, TRA
Rep By: Sante J. Esposito, Gregory E. Lawler

Cushman & Wakefield, Inc.

New York, NY

Outside Counsel/Consultants

Public Affairs Group, Inc.

Custom Air Transport

Fort Lauderdale, FL
Leg. Issues: AVI

Outside Counsel/Consultants

Sher & Blackwell
Issues: AVI
Rep By: Mark Atwood

CustomerLinx

Outside Counsel/Consultants

O'Connor & Hannan, L.L.P.
Rep By: Hon. Larry Pressler

Cuyahoga Community College

Cleveland, OH
Leg. Issues: BUD, EDU

Outside Counsel/Consultants

Squire, Sanders & Dempsey L.L.P.
Issues: BUD, EDU
Rep By: Louis Stokes

Cuyahoga, Ohio, County of

Cleveland, OH
Leg. Issues: HCR, HOU, LAW, MMM, RET, TAX, WEL

Outside Counsel/Consultants

Susan J. White & Associates
Issues: HCR, HOU, LAW, MMM, RET, TAX, WEL
Rep By: Susan J. White

Cuyapaipe Band of Mission Indians

Alpine, CA
Leg. Issues: IND

Outside Counsel/Consultants

Dorsey & Whitney LLP
Issues: IND
Rep By: Philip Baker-Shenk, David A. Bieging, Virginia W. Boylan, Cindy Darcy, Kevin J. Wadzinski

CVS, Inc.

Woonsocket, RI
Leg. Issues: HCR, MMM, PHA

Outside Counsel/Consultants

Capitol City Group
Issues: PHA
Rep By: Gerald T. Harrington, John J. Hogan, Thomas P. Hogan, Christopher P. Vitale

Cassidy & Associates, Inc.

Mintz, Levin, Cohn, Ferris, Glovsky and Popeo, P.C.
Issues: HCR, MMM
Rep By: Raymond D. Cotton, Erin Lewis Darling, Patrick Hope

CyberWynd Publications

Gaithersburg, MD

Outside Counsel/Consultants

Real Trends
Rep By: Zhi Marie Hamby

Cypress Bioscience Inc.

San Diego, CA
Leg. Issues: MMM

Outside Counsel/Consultants

McKenna & Cuneo, L.L.P.
Issues: MMM

Cyprus Amex Minerals Co.

Englewood, CO
Leg. Issues: NAT

Outside Counsel/Consultants

Crowell & Moring LLP
Issues: NAT
Rep By: Edward M. Green, R. Timothy McCrum, Steven P. Quarles

Cyprus, Government of the Republic of

Nicosia, CYPRUS
Leg. Issues: FOR

Outside Counsel/Consultants

The Evans Group, Ltd.
Issues: FOR
Rep By: Hon. Thomas B. Evans, Jr.

Verner, Liipfert, Bernhard, McPherson and Hand, Chartered
Rep By: Berl Bernhard

Cystic Fibrosis Foundation

6931 Arlington Rd.
Suite 200
Bethesda, MD 20814
Web: www.cff.org
E-mail: info@cff.org
Tel: (301)951-4422
Fax: (301)951-6378
Registered: LDA

Strives to improve the quality of life for those with cystic fibrosis, and to assure a means by which to cure and control the disease.

Leg. Issues: BUD, HCR, INS, MED, MMM, PHA

In-house, DC-area Employees

BEALL, Ph.D., Robert J.: President/Chief Exec. Officer
MATTINGLY, C. Richard: Exec. V. President/Chief Operating Officer
PATTEE, Suzanne R.: V. President, Public Policy and Patient Affairs

Outside Counsel/Consultants

Bennett Turner & Coleman, LLP
Issues: BUD, HCR, MED, MMM, PHA
Rep By: Elizabeth Goss, Natasha Leskovsek, Bruce Manheim, Samuel D. Turner

Cytometrics, Inc.

Philadelphia, PA
Leg. Issues: HCR

Outside Counsel/Consultants

Ikon Public Affairs
Issues: HCR

Cytyc Corp.

Boxborough, MA

A biotechnology firm.

Leg. Issues: HCR

Outside Counsel/Consultants

Heidepriem & Mager, Inc.
Issues: HCR
Rep By: Karin Bolte, Mimi Mager

D&E Communications, Inc.

Leg. Issues: TEC

Outside Counsel/Consultants

Greenberg Traurig, LLP
Issues: TEC

D'Youville College

Buffalo, NY
Leg. Issues: BUD

Outside Counsel/Consultants

Cassidy & Associates, Inc.
Issues: BUD
Rep By: Douglass E. Bobbitt, Arthur D. Mason, Maureen Walsh

D.A.R.E. America

Los Angeles, CA
Leg. Issues: ALC

Outside Counsel/Consultants

The Direct Impact Co.

Direct Impact, LLC
Issues: ALC
Rep By: Robert B. Charles, Sean Littlefield

Lafayette Group, Inc.
Issues: ALC
Rep By: Scott H. Green

D.C. Building Industry Ass'n Political Action Committee

5100 Wisconsin Ave. NW
Suite 301
Washington, DC 20016
Web: www.dcbia.org
Tel: (202)966-8665
Fax: (202)966-3222

In-house, DC-area Employees

MOORE, Jerry: PAC Treasurer

D.C. Catholic Conference - Archdiocese of Washington

P.O. Box 29260
Washington, DC 20017
Tel: (301)853-5342
Fax: (301)853-7671
Registered: LDA
E-mail: jacksonr@adw.org

Serves as a forum that communicates and promotes positions that are shaped by Catholic moral and religious beliefs on public issues in the District of Columbia.

Leg. Issues: DOC

In-house, DC-area Employees

JACKSON, Ronald G.: Exec. Director

D.C. Historical Tourism Coalition

Leg. Issues: DOC, TRD

Outside Counsel/Consultants

Schmeltzer, Aptaker & Shepard, P.C.
Issues: DOC, TRD
Rep By: J. Anthony Smith

D.C. Lottery

Washington, DC

Outside Counsel/Consultants

The Kamber Group
Rep By: Kimberly Bennett

D.C. Rape Crisis Center

P.O. Box 34125
Washington, DC 20043
Web: www.dcrcc.org
E-mail: dcrcc@erols.com
Tel: (202)232-0789
Fax: (202)387-3812

Provides assistance to victims of sexual violence and educates the community.

In-house, DC-area Employees

SNYDER, Denise: Exec. Director

D. H. Blair Investment Banking Corp.

New York, NY

Outside Counsel/Consultants

Baker & Hostetler LLP
Rep By: Matthew J. Dolan, Frederick H. Graefe, Steven A. Lotterer, Hon. Guy Vander Jagt

D3 Internat'l Energy, LLC

Media, PA
Leg. Issues: AER, AVI, DEF, ENG

Outside Counsel/Consultants

Mehl, Griffin & Bartek Ltd.
Issues: AER, AVI, DEF, ENG
Rep By: Ronald J. Bartek, Molly Griffin, William A. Marsh, Theodore J. Mehl

Da Vinci's Notebook

Arlington, VA
Leg. Issues: ART

Outside Counsel/Consultants

Tarne Powers & Associates
Issues: ART
Rep By: Michelle R. Powers

Dade County Board of Commissioners

Miami, FL
Leg. Issues: TRA

Outside Counsel/Consultants

Ann Eppard Associates, Ltd.
Issues: TRA
Rep By: Julie Chlopecki, Ann Eppard

Dade, Florida, County of

Miami, FL
Leg. Issues: DIS, ECN, HOU

Outside Counsel/Consultants

Global USA, Inc.
Issues: DIS, ECN, HOU
Rep By: Rosamond S. Brown, George S. Kopp, Lottie H. Shackelford

Daemen College

Amherst, NY
Leg. Issues: EDU, HCR, SCI

Outside Counsel/Consultants

The Advocacy Group
Issues: EDU, HCR, SCI
Rep By: Robert E. Mills

DAG Petroleum

Falls Church, VA
Leg. Issues: ENG, FUE, SMB

Outside Counsel/Consultants

Manatt, Phelps & Phillips, LLP
Issues: ENG, FUE, SMB
Rep By: Michael T. Brown, Margaret Gentry, James R. Jones, John L. Ray

Dai-Ichi Life Insurance Co.

New York, NY

Outside Counsel/Consultants

Paul Muroyama & Assoc.
Rep By: Paul Muroyama

DaimlerChrysler Corp.

1401 H St. NW
Suite 700
Washington, DC 20005
Tel: (202)414-6747
Fax: (202)414-6716
Registered: LDA
Web: www.daimlerchrysler.com

A global transportation company with the U.S. headquarters in Auburn Hills, MI.

Leg. Issues: AUT, BAN, BNK, BUD, CAW, CSP, DEF, ECN, EDU, ENG, ENV, FUE, HCR, IMM, INS, MAN, MMM, TAX, TOR, TRA, TRD, UNM, URB

In-house, DC-area Employees

BECKER, Linda M.: Senior Manager, Public Policy and Communications
DAY, Brenda T.: Director, Congressional Affairs
ESTEREICHER, Christine: Representative, External Affairs
FELRICE, Barry: Senior Manager, Regulatory Affairs
FITZGIBBONS, Dennis B.: Director, Public Policy
JONES, Jake: Sr. Manager, Legislative Affairs
LIBERATORE, Robert G.: Senior V. President, External Affairs and Public Policy
MCBRIDE, Timothy J.: V. President, Washington Office
MOLNAR, Yancy: Analyst, International Trade
OTTEN, Norbert: Director, International Affairs

Outside Counsel/Consultants

Barbour Griffith & Rogers, Inc.
Issues: EDU, ENV, TRA, TRD
Rep By: Haley Barbour, Scott Barnhart, G. O. Lanny Griffith, Jr.

Dillon, Hall & Lungershausen
Rep By: James E. Hall

Dyer Ellis & Joseph, P.C.
Issues: DEF
Rep By: Brian A. Bannon, Brett M. Esber, Wayne A. Keup, Duncan C. Smith, III, Jennifer M. Southwick

Hall, Green, Rupli, LLC
Rep By: John M. Green, G. Stewart Hall

Patricia C. Kennedy
Issues: AUT
Rep By: Patricia C. Kennedy

PriceWaterhouseCoopers

Quinn Gillespie & Associates

Timmons and Co., Inc.
Issues: AUT, BAN, BUD, CAW, CSP, ENG, HCR, IMM, TAX, TRD
Rep By: Michael J. Bates, Douglas F. Bennett, Ellen B. Fitzgibbons, Bryce L. "Larry" Harlow, Timothy J. Keating, Tom C. Korologos, Richard J. Tarplin, William E. Timmons, Jr., William E. Timmons, Sr.

Dairy Management, Inc.

Rosemont, IL

Outside Counsel/Consultants

McLeod, Watkinson & Miller
Rep By: Wayne R. Watkinson

Dairy Trade Advisory Council

Leg. Issues: AGR

Outside Counsel/Consultants

The Aegis Group, Ltd.
Issues: AGR
Rep By: A. Mario Castillo

The Dairy Trade Coalition

Leg. Issues: AGR

Outside Counsel/Consultants

The Aegis Group, Ltd.
Issues: AGR
Rep By: A. Mario Castillo

Dairy.com

Dallas, TX
Leg. Issues: AGR, COM

Outside Counsel/Consultants

Swidler Berlin Shereff Friedman, LLP
Issues: AGR, COM
Rep By: James DeLorenzo, Paul T. Denis, Barry B. Direnfeld, Brian W. Fitzgerald, Thomas Valente

Dairyland Power Cooperative

La Crosse, WI
Registered: LDA
Leg. Issues: WAS

Outside Counsel/Consultants

Valis Associates
Issues: WAS
Rep By: Hon. Richard T. Schulze, Wayne H. Valis

Daishowa America Co., Ltd.

Port Angeles, WA
Leg. Issues: ENV, RES

Outside Counsel/Consultants

Bracy Williams & Co.
Issues: ENV, RES
Rep By: Michael M. Bracy, Terrence L. Bracy

Dakota Minnesota and Eastern Railroad

Brookings, SD
Leg. Issues: TRA

Outside Counsel/Consultants

O'Connor & Hannan, L.L.P.
Issues: TRA
Rep By: Hon. Larry Pressler

Dakota Wesleyan University

Mitchell, SD

Outside Counsel/Consultants

Cassidy & Associates, Inc.
Rep By: Dennis M. Kedzior

Dakota, Minnesota, County of

Hastings, MN
Leg. Issues: FAM, GOV, HCR, HOU, ROD

Outside Counsel/Consultants

Craig Associates
Issues: FAM, GOV, HCR, HOU, ROD
Rep By: Patricia J. Craig, Kathryn Dyjak, Leslie Sacks Gross

Dal Mac Investment Corp.

Fort Worth, TX
Leg. Issues: RES

Outside Counsel/Consultants

David F. Godfrey
Issues: RES
Rep By: David F. Godfrey

Dal-Tile Corp.

Dallas, TX

Outside Counsel/Consultants

Wear & Associates
Rep By: Terrance J. Wear

Dale Service Corp.

Dale City, VA
Leg. Issues: BUD

Outside Counsel/Consultants

RFB, Inc.
Issues: BUD
Rep By: Raymond F. Bragg

Dallas Area Rapid Transit Authority

Dallas, TX
Leg. Issues: BUD, TRA

Outside Counsel/Consultants

Jefferson Government Relations, L.L.C.
Issues: BUD, TRA
Rep By: William A. Roberts

Pamela Ray-Strunk and Associates
Issues: BUD, TRA
Rep By: Pamela Ray-Strunk

Slagle & Associates
Issues: TRA
Rep By: P. Roger Slagle, Jr.

Vierra Associates, Inc.
Issues: TRA
Rep By: Dennis C. Vierra

Dallas Cowboys

Irving, TX

Outside Counsel/Consultants

Wilmer, Cutler & Pickering
Rep By: Richard W. Cass

Dallas, Texas, City of

Leg. Issues: BUD, CAW, ECN, HOU, LAW, NAT, RES, ROD, TEC, TRA, URB

Outside Counsel/Consultants

Alcalde & Fay
Issues: BUD, CAW, NAT, RES, ROD, URB
Rep By: Hector Alcalde, Paul Schlesinger, Tim Stroud

Barbara T. McCall Associates
Issues: ECN, HOU, LAW, TEC, TRA, URB
Rep By: Ralph Garboushian, Barbara T. McCall

Dallas/Fort Worth Internat'l Airport Board

DFW Int'l Airport, TX
Leg. Issues: AVI

Outside Counsel/Consultants

Global Aviation Associates, Ltd.
Issues: AVI
Rep By: Jon F. Ash, Charles R. Chambers

Marshall L. Lynam
Issues: AVI
Rep By: Marshall L. Lynam

TerraCom-Strategic Communications
Issues: AVI
Rep By: Felix R. Sanchez

Dalmine

Dalmine, ITALY

Outside Counsel/Consultants

White & Case LLP
Rep By: David P. Houlihan

Dalton & Dalton P.C.

Alexandria, VA
Leg. Issues: BUD, DOC, EDU

Outside Counsel/Consultants

Ledge Counsel
Issues: DOC, EDU

MV3 & Associates

RTS Consulting

Valente Lopatin & Schulze
Issues: BUD
Rep By: Alan G. Lopatin, Richard T. Schulze, Jr., Mark Valente, III

Leo A. Daly Co.

1201 Connecticut Ave. NW
Tenth Floor
Washington, DC 20036
Web: www.leoadaly.com
Tel: (202)861-4600
Fax: (202)872-8530

Offers planning, architecture, engineering, and interior design services.

Leg. Issues: URB

In-house, DC-area Employees

DALLUGE, Charles D.: V. President and Managing Principal

Outside Counsel/Consultants

Donald S. Dawson & Associates
Issues: URB
Rep By: Donald S. Dawson

Damascus Tubular Products

Greenville, PA

Outside Counsel/Consultants

Collier Shannon Scott, PLLC
Rep By: Jeffrey S. Beckington, David A. Hartquist

Dames & Moore

Bethesda, MD
Leg. Issues: DEF, ENG, ENV

Outside Counsel/Consultants

Law Office of Zel E. Lipsen
Issues: DEF, ENG, ENV
Rep By: Zel E. Lipsen

Dana Corp.

Toledo, OH
Leg. Issues: FOR

Outside Counsel/Consultants

Global Policy Group, Inc.

Hogan & Hartson L.L.P.
Issues: FOR
Rep By: Stan Brown, William Michael House, Warren H. Maruyama, Jeffrey W. Munk

Danaher Corp.

Washington, DC

A manufacturer of automotive, instrumentation and precision component products.

Leg. Issues: BUD, CSP, TRD

Outside Counsel/Consultants

Hogan & Hartson L.L.P.
Issues: BUD, CSP, TRD
Rep By: Jeanne S. Archibald, C. Michael Gilliland

WinCapitol, Inc.
Issues: TRD
Rep By: David L. Flory, Christie Olsen, James T. Sims

Dance/USA

1156 15th St. NW
Suite 820
Washington, DC 20005
Web: www.danceusa.org
E-mail: danceusa@danceusa.org
Tel: (202)833-1717
Fax: (202)833-2686

Dance/USA is the national service organization for non-profit, professional dance. It seeks to advance the art of dance by addressing the needs, concerns and interests of professional dance.

Leg. Issues: ART, EDU, IMM, TAX

In-house, DC-area Employees

RORKE, Rebecca M.: Director, Government Affairs
SNYDER, Andrea: Exec. Director

Daniel, Mann, Johnson & Mendenhall

Los Angeles, CA

An engineering firm.

Leg. Issues: TRA

Outside Counsel/Consultants

Ann Eppard Associates, Ltd.
Issues: TRA
Rep By: Julie Chlopecki, Ann Eppard

Danish Meat Canners Export Ass'n

Copenhagen, DENMARK

Outside Counsel/Consultants

Max N. Berry Law Offices

The Danny Foundation,

San Ramon, CA
Leg. Issues: CSP

Outside Counsel/Consultants

Hogan & Hartson L.L.P.
Issues: CSP
Rep By: C. Michael Gilliland, Christine M. Warnke

Dare County

Manteo, NC
Leg. Issues: RES

Outside Counsel/Consultants

Edmund B. Welch
Issues: RES
Rep By: Edmund B. Welch

Darigold, Inc.

Seattle, WA

Outside Counsel/Consultants

Tuttle, Taylor & Heron
Rep By: Phillip L. Fraas

Dartmouth-Hitchcock Medical Center

Lebanon, NH
Leg. Issues: BUD

Outside Counsel/Consultants

Arent Fox Kintner Plotkin & Kahn, PLLC
Issues: BUD
Rep By: Douglas McCormack, William A. Sarraille

Data Dynamics

Grafton, ND
Leg. Issues: GOV, IND

Outside Counsel/Consultants

Washington Consulting Alliance, Inc.
Issues: GOV, IND
Rep By: Thomas L. Burgum, Shaun Wiggins

Data Niche Associates Inc.

Northfield, IL

Outside Counsel/Consultants

Muse & Associates

Data One Direct

Outside Counsel/Consultants

Greener and Hook, LLC

Datahr Rehabilitation Institute

Leg. Issues: HCR

Outside Counsel/Consultants

Arent Fox Kintner Plotkin & Kahn, PLLC
Issues: HCR
Rep By: Stacy Harbison, Douglas McCormack, Connie A. Raffa

DATRON, Inc.

Jackson, MS
Leg. Issues: HCR, MMM

Outside Counsel/Consultants

Johnson Co.
Issues: HCR, MMM
Rep By: Rex Armistead, James H. Johnson

Daughters of the American Revolution

1776 D St. NW
Washington, DC 20006-5303
Web: www.dar.org
Tel: (202)628-1776
Fax: (202)879-3252

A non-governmental, non-profit, historic, educational, and patriotic organization whose members are women whose lineage can be traced back to a Revolutionary patriot who aided in the cause of American Independence. At the time this edition went to press, DAR was undergoing the process of voting in a new president. No further information was available at that time.

In-house, DC-area Employees

FERGUSON LOVE, Georgane: Immediate Past President General

Davison Transport, Inc.
Ruston, LA
Leg. Issues: BUD, EDU, TRA

Outside Counsel/Consultants

Van Scoyoc Associates, Inc.
Issues: BUD, EDU, TRA
Rep By: John C. "Jay" Stone, H. Stewart Van Scoyoc

Day & Zimmermann, Inc.
Philadelphia, PA
Leg. Issues: BUD, DEF, ENG

Outside Counsel/Consultants

Baker, Donelson, Bearman & Caldwell, P.C.
Issues: BUD, ENG
Rep By: George Cranwell Montgomery, John C. Tuck

Ann Eppard Associates, Ltd.
Rep By: Julie Chlopecki, Ann Eppard

Fishbein Associates, Inc.
Issues: BUD, DEF

Day Care Ass'n of Tarrant County and Fort Worth Texas
Fort Worth, TX
Leg. Issues: EDU

Outside Counsel/Consultants

Peter J. Rose
Issues: EDU
Rep By: Peter J. Rose

Dayton Power and Light Co.
Dayton, OH

Outside Counsel/Consultants

Thelen Reid & Priest LLP
Rep By: John R. Schaefgen

Dayton, Ohio, Washington Office of the City of
1620 I St. NW
Suite 600
Washington, DC 20006
Tel: (202)861-6778
Fax: (202)429-0422
Leg. Issues: AVI, BAN, BUD, CAW, DIS, ECN, EDU, ENV, FIN, FIR, HOU, LAW, RET, ROD, TAX, TEC, TRA, URB, WAS, WEL

In-house, DC-area Employees

PALMER-BARTON, Stacy: Associate Director

Outside Counsel/Consultants

The Barton Co.
Issues: AVI, BAN, BUD, CAW, DIS, ECN, EDU, ENV, FIN, FIR, HOU, LAW, RET, ROD, TAX, TRA, URB, WAS, WEL
Rep By: Stacy Palmer-Barton

Miller & Van Eaton, P.L.L.C.
Issues: TEC
Rep By: William Malone

Daytona Beach, City of
Daytona Beach, FL
Leg. Issues: BUD, GOV, HOU, RES

Outside Counsel/Consultants

Jefferson Government Relations, L.L.C.
Issues: BUD, GOV, HOU, RES
Rep By: William J. Gilmartin, William A. Roberts

DC Land Title Ass'n
Leg. Issues: DOC, TAX

Outside Counsel/Consultants

Betty Ann Kane & Co.
Issues: DOC, TAX
Rep By: Betty Ann Kane

DCH Technology Inc.
Valencia, CA
Leg. Issues: ENG, FUE, GOV, MAR, SCI, TRA, WAS

Outside Counsel/Consultants

Madison Government Affairs
Issues: ENG, FUE, GOV, MAR, SCI, TRA, WAS
Rep By: Paul J. Hirsch, Myron M. Jacobson

The Wexler Group
Issues: ENG, SCI
Rep By: Peter T. Holran, Anne Jones, Patric G. Link, Hon. Robert S. Walker

DCS Group
Washington, DC
Leg. Issues: TRD

Outside Counsel/Consultants

Powell, Goldstein, Frazer & Murphy LLP
Issues: TRD
Rep By: Brenda A. Jacobs, Alexander Koff

DCT Communications, Inc.
Los Angeles, CA
Leg. Issues: TEC

Outside Counsel/Consultants

Gardner, Carton and Douglas
Issues: TEC

DDL OMNI Engineering Corp.
McLean, VA
Leg. Issues: DEF

Outside Counsel/Consultants

John G. Campbell, Inc.
Issues: DEF

Mario M. de la Pena, Estate of
Leg. Issues: FOR

Outside Counsel/Consultants

Greenberg Traurig, LLP
Issues: FOR
Rep By: Ronald W. Kleinman

Thomas De La Rue, Inc.
Chantilly, VA

Outside Counsel/Consultants

Sack & Harris, P.C.
Rep By: Michele E. Truitt

Deaconess Billings Clinic
Leg. Issues: HCR

Outside Counsel/Consultants

Capitol Coalitions Inc.
Issues: HCR
Rep By: Brett P. Scott

Dearborn, Michigan, Department of Communication of
Leg. Issues: TEC

Outside Counsel/Consultants

Miller & Van Eaton, P.L.L.C.
Issues: TEC
Rep By: Nicholas P. Miller

Death Penalty Information Center
1320 18th St. NW
Fifth Floor
Washington, DC 20036
Web: www.deathpenaltyinfo.org
E-mail: dpic@essential.org
Tel: (202)293-6970
Fax: (202)822-4787

A non-profit organization serving the media and the public with analysis and information on issues concerning capital punishment. The Center prepares in-depth reports, issues press releases, conducts briefings for journalists, and serves as a resource to those working on the death penalty issue.

Leg. Issues: CIV

In-house, DC-area Employees

DIETER, Richard: Exec. Director

Death With Dignity Nat'l Center

Outside Counsel/Consultants

Bill Zavarela
Rep By: Bill Zavarela

DeBrunner and Associates, Inc.
Ten Pidgeon Hill Dr.
Suite 150
Sterling, VA 20165
Tel: (703)444-4091
Fax: (703)444-3029
Registered: LDA
Leg. Issues: MMM

In-house, DC-area Employees

DEBRUNNER, Charles L.: President
HERR, Wendy W.: Associate
KLUGH, Gloria J.: Associate
KUGLER, Ellen J.: Director, Government Affairs
ROONEY, Kathryn D.: Associate

Outside Counsel/Consultants

Capitol Associates, Inc.
Issues: MMM
Rep By: William A. Finerfrock, Debra M. Hardy Havens, Julie Shroyer, Matthew Williams

Debswana Diamond Co.
Gabrone, BOTSWANA

Outside Counsel/Consultants

Hill and Knowlton, Inc.

Decatur Park District
Decatur, IL
Leg. Issues: AVI

Outside Counsel/Consultants

Zuckert, Scoutt and Rasenberger, L.L.P.
Issues: AVI
Rep By: Paul E. Schoellhamer

DeChiaro Properties
Baltimore, MD

Outside Counsel/Consultants

Long, Aldridge & Norman, LLP
Rep By: C. Randall Nuckolls, Patrick C. Turner

Deere & Co.
1808 I St. NW
Eighth Floor
Washington, DC 20006
Web: www.deere.com
Tel: (202)223-4817
Fax: (202)296-0011
Registered: LDA

Headquartered in Moline, IL.

Leg. Issues: AGR, BAN, BNK, BUD, CAW, CPI, CPT, HCR, TAX, TRD

In-house, DC-area Employees

BEHAN, William M.: Director, Federal Government Affairs
CRAMER, Wendy Rice: Manager, Federal Government Affairs
DORT, II, Dean R.: V. President, International
NAYLOR, Michael W.: V. President, Washington Affairs

Outside Counsel/Consultants

Rooney Group Internat'l, Inc.

Charlene A. Sturbitts
Issues: CAW
Rep By: Charlene A. Sturbitts

Deere Co. Worldwide Commercial & Consumer Equipment Division
Wagram, NC
Leg. Issues: AUT, DEF

Outside Counsel/Consultants

Rooney Group Internat'l, Inc.
Issues: AUT, DEF
Rep By: Jerry L. Kaffka, James W. Rooney

Deerfield Beach, Florida, City of
Leg. Issues: ENV, TRA, TRD

Outside Counsel/Consultants

Alcalde & Fay
Issues: ENV, TRA, TRD
Rep By: Hon. Louis A. "Skip" Bafalis, Shantrel Brown, Jim Davenport, Angela Plott

Defenders of Property Rights
1350 Connecticut Ave. NW
Suite 410
Washington, DC 20036
Web: www.yourpropertyrights.org
Tel: (202)822-6770
Fax: (202)822-6774

In-house, DC-area Employees

MARZULLA, Nancie G.: President

Defenders of Wildlife
1101 14th St. NW
Suite 1400
Washington, DC 20005
Web: www.defenders.org
E-mail: rmiguel@defenders.org
Tel: (202)682-9400
Fax: (202)682-1331
Registered: LDA

A non-profit national environmental organization with a membership of 380,000 working for the natural diversity of wildlife and for the protection of wildlife habitat through education, litigation, research and advocacy. Publishes the quarterly magazine "Defenders."

Leg. Issues: BUD, ENV, MAR, RES, TRA, TRD

In-house, DC-area Employees

ANDERSON, Rennie: International Associate
BEETHAM, Mary Beth: Director, Legislative Affairs
CHAMPINE, Christopher: Grassroots Coordinator
DAVIES, Catherine: Manager, Publications
DEANE, James G.: V. President, Publications
DEWEY, Robert: V. President, Government Relations and External Affairs
FASCIONE, Nina: Director, Carnivore Conservation
FERRIS, Robert M.: V. President, Species Conservation
KENNEDY, Caroline: Program Associate
LAHEY, Michael: Counsel, Public Lands
LYTWAK, Ed: Policy Coordinator
MATSON, Noah: Science Policy Analyst

MUFFETT, Carroll: International Counsel
ORASIN, Charles: V. President, Operations
SCHLICKEISEN, Dr. Rodger O.: President and Chief Exec. Officer
SENATORE, Michael P.: Director, Legal Department
SHAFFER, Mark: Senior V. President, Programs
SNAPE, III, William: V. President, Law and Litigation
STODUTO, Nicole: Legal Coordinator
TEJADA, Claudia: Program Associate
WATCHMAN, Laura H.: Manager, Conservation Planning Program

Outside Counsel/Consultants

Chambers Associates Inc.
Rep By: Letitia Chambers

Defense Administrative Judges Professional Ass'n

Fairfax Station, VA
Leg. Issues: GOV

Outside Counsel/Consultants

Kyros & Cummins Associates
Issues: GOV
Rep By: John M. Falk, Hon. Peter N. Kyros

Defense Analyses Institute

Outside Counsel/Consultants

Hogan & Hartson L.L.P.

Defense Credit Union Council

805 15th St. NW — Tel: (202)682-5993
Washington, DC 20005-2207 — Fax: (202)354-7000
Web: www.dcuc.org
E-mail: dcuc1@cuna.com

An association representing defense credit unions.

Leg. Issues: DEF, FIN

In-house, DC-area Employees

ARTEAGA, Roland: President and Chief Exec. Officer

Defense Orientation Conference Ass'n

9271 Old Keene Mill Rd. — Tel: (703)451-1200
Suite 200 — Fax: (703)451-1201
Burke, VA 22015-4202

Composed of individuals interested in national security issues. Offers tours of defense installations in the U.S. and overseas and provides speakers for members.

In-house, DC-area Employees

OHLSEN, John W.: Exec. Vice President

Deferral Group

Washington, DC
Leg. Issues: TAX

Outside Counsel/Consultants

Washington Council Ernst & Young
Issues: TAX
Rep By: Doug Badger, Lauren Darling, John L. Doney, Jayne T. Fitzgerald, LaBrenda Garrett-Nelson, Gary J. Gasper, Bruce A. Gates, Nick Giordano, Robert J. Leonard, Richard Meltzer, Phillip D. Moseley, John D. Porter, Robert M. Rozen, Donna Steele-Flynn, Timothy J. Urban

Degussa Corp.

Ridgefield Park, NJ

Outside Counsel/Consultants

Stephens Law Offices
Rep By: J. Gordon "Skip" Stephens, Jr.

DEIP (Dairy Export Incentive Program) Coalition

Leg. Issues: AGR

Outside Counsel/Consultants

Tuttle, Taylor & Heron
Issues: AGR
Rep By: Phillip L. Fraas

Dekalb, Illinois, City of

Leg. Issues: AVI, ROD

Outside Counsel/Consultants

Powell, Goldstein, Frazer & Murphy LLP
Issues: AVI, ROD

Del Norte Technology

Euless, TX

Outside Counsel/Consultants

Korth & Korth
Rep By: Fritz-Alan Korth

Delaware and Hudson Railroad

Kingston, NY
Leg. Issues: BUD, ENV, IMM, RRR, TAX, TRU, WAS

Outside Counsel/Consultants

Mullenholz, Brimsek & Belair
Issues: BUD, ENV, IMM, RRR, TAX, TRU, WAS
Rep By: John R. Brimsek

Delaware Municipal Electric Corp. (DEMEC)

Dover, DE

A municipal electric joint action agency.

Leg. Issues: ENG, GOV, UTI

Outside Counsel/Consultants

Duncan, Weinberg, Genzer & Pembroke, P.C.
Issues: ENG, GOV, UTI
Rep By: Janice L. Lower

Delaware North Companies

Buffalo, NY
Leg. Issues: BUD, NAT

Outside Counsel/Consultants

BKSH & Associates
Issues: BUD, NAT

Delaware Otsego System

Cooperstown, NY
Leg. Issues: RRR, TRA

Outside Counsel/Consultants

Chambers, Conlon & Hartwell
Issues: RRR, TRA
Rep By: Ray B. Chambers

Delaware River and Bay Authority

New Castle, DE
Leg. Issues: MAR, TRA

Outside Counsel/Consultants

Blank Rome Comisky & McCauley, LLP
Issues: MAR, TRA
Rep By: David A. Norcross

Delaware River Port Authority

Camden, NJ
Leg. Issues: MAR

Outside Counsel/Consultants

Blank Rome Comisky & McCauley, LLP
Issues: MAR
Rep By: David A. Norcross

Delaware River Stevedores

Philadelphia, PA

A terminal management company.

Leg. Issues: ENV

Outside Counsel/Consultants

The MWW Group
Issues: ENV
Rep By: Christine A. Pellerin, Jonathan B. Slade

Delaware Tribe of Indians

Bartlesville, OK
Leg. Issues: IND

Outside Counsel/Consultants

Dorsey & Whitney LLP
Issues: IND
Rep By: Philip Baker-Shenk, David A. Bieging, Virginia W. Boylan, Cindy Darcy

Delaware, Pennsylvania, Solid Waste Authority of the County of

Media, PA

Outside Counsel/Consultants

Wright & Talisman, P.C.
Rep By: Scott M. DuBoff

Delaware, Washington Office of the State of

444 N. Capitol St. NW — Tel: (202)624-7724
Suite 230 — Fax: (202)624-5495
Washington, DC 20001

In-house, DC-area Employees

HAMRICK, David: Director, Washington Office

Delex Systems, Inc.

Vienna, VA
Leg. Issues: DEF, DIS

Outside Counsel/Consultants

Commonwealth Consulting Corp.
Issues: DEF, DIS
Rep By: Christopher M. Lehman

Dell Computer Corp.

1225 I St. NW — Tel: (202)408-5538
Suite 920 — Fax: (202)408-7664
Washington, DC 20005 — Registered: LDA
Web: www.dell.com

Designs, manufactures, sells, and services personal computers, laptop computers, and servers. Headquartered in Round Rock, TX.

Leg. Issues: CPI, DEF, FIN, IMM, SCI, TAX, TRA, TRD

In-house, DC-area Employees

GOULD, Rebecca M. J.: Director, Public Policy
MULLINS, Karey E.: Policy Advisor

Outside Counsel/Consultants

Bergner Bockorny Castagnetti and Hawkins
Issues: CPI, TRD
Rep By: Jeffrey T. Bergner, David A. Bockorny, David Castagnetti, James W. Hawkins, Melissa Schulman

Dittus Communications
Rep By: Gloria S. Dittus, Shelton Jones

Griffin, Johnson, Dover & Stewart
Issues: CPI, DEF, SCI, TAX, TRD
Rep By: William C. Danvers, G. Jack Dover, Patrick J. Griffin, Keith Heard, David E. Johnson, Susan O. Mann, Walter J. "Joe" Stewart, Leonard Swinehart

Wilmer, Cutler & Pickering
Issues: CPI
Rep By: Daniel Phythyon

Deloitte & Touche LLP

555 12th St. NW — Tel: (202)879-5600
Suite 500 — Fax: (202)879-5309
Washington, DC 20004-1207 — Registered: LDA, FARA
Web: www.dttus.com
Leg. Issues: ACC, FIN

Political Action Committee/s

Deloitte & Touche LLP Federal PAC
555 12th St. NW — Tel: (202)879-5600
Suite 500 — Fax: (202)879-5309
Washington, DC 20004-1207

In-house, DC-area Employees

EZZELL, William: Partner in Charge, Government Affairs
GARAY, Mark: Manager
SNOWLING, Randall: Partner
STEPHENSON, Gregory: Partner
STEVENS, Cindy M.: Director, Federal Programs
STRETCH, C. Clinton: Partner, National Tax Services
WEISS, Randall D.: Partner

Outside Counsel/Consultants

The Velasquez Group
Issues: ACC, FIN
Rep By: Jay Velasquez

Deloitte Consulting

Deerfield, IL
Leg. Issues: GOV, HCR, MMM

Outside Counsel/Consultants

Greenberg Traurig, LLP
Issues: HCR, MMM
Rep By: Diane J. Blagman, Howard J. Cohen

Griffin, Johnson, Dover & Stewart
Issues: GOV, HCR, MMM
Rep By: William C. Danvers, G. Jack Dover, Patrick J. Griffin, Keith Heard, David E. Johnson, Susan O. Mann, Walter J. "Joe" Stewart, Leonard Swinehart

The Ickes & Enright Group
Issues: HCR
Rep By: Janice Ann Enright, Harold M. Ickes

Deloitte Touche Tohmatsu Internat'l

New York, NY

Outside Counsel/Consultants

The Velasquez Group

Delta Air Lines

1275 K St. NW — Tel: (202)216-0700
Suite 1200 — Fax: (202)216-0824
Washington, DC 20005 — Registered: LDA
Web: www.delta-air.com

Headquartered in Atlanta, GA.

Leg. Issues: AVI, BAN, BUD, CAW, HCR, IMM, LBR, POS, TAX, TOU, TRA, TRD

In-house, DC-area Employees
KENNEDY, Charlene Dziak: Manager, Government Affairs
MOLONEY, John M.: General Manager, Government Affairs
PICCIONE, Mary Elizabeth: General Manager, Government Affairs
YOHE, D. Scott: Senior V. President, Government Affairs

Outside Counsel/Consultants

Dickstein Shapiro Morin & Oshinsky LLP
Issues: AVI
Rep By: Hon. Wendell H. Ford, Robert Mangas

The National Group, LLP
Rep By: John Blount

Powell Tate
Rep By: Jody Powell

Preston Gates Ellis & Rouvelas Meeds LLP
Rep By: James R. Weiss

Shaw Pittman
Issues: AVI
Rep By: Robert E. Cohn

The Washington Group
Issues: AVI, TAX
Rep By: Rita M. Lewis, G. John O'Hanlon, John D. Raffaelli, Tonya Saunders, Mark Schnabel

Delta Comercio, S.A.

Santo Domingo, DOMINICAN REPUBLIC

Outside Counsel/Consultants

Johnson, Rogers & Clifton, L.L.P.

Delta Dental Plan of California

Sacramento, CA
Leg. Issues: DEF

Outside Counsel/Consultants

Defense Health Advisors, Inc.
Issues: DEF
Rep By: Charlotte L. Tsoucalas, Karin K. Willis

Delta Dental Plans Ass'n

Chicago, IL
Leg. Issues: CPI, HCR, INS, TAX

Outside Counsel/Consultants

Cavarocchi Ruscio Dennis Associates
Issues: HCR, INS, TAX
Rep By: Nicholas G. Cavarocchi, Domenic R. Ruscio

Jay Grant & Associates

Griffin, Johnson, Dover & Stewart
Issues: CPI, HCR
Rep By: G. Jack Dover, David E. Johnson

Delta Development Group, Inc.

Camp Hill, PA
Leg. Issues: TRA, URB

Outside Counsel/Consultants

Ann Eppard Associates, Ltd.
Issues: TRA, URB
Rep By: Julie Chlopecki, Ann Eppard, Karen Schechter

Delta Foundation

Greenville, MS

Outside Counsel/Consultants

Robert A. Rapoza Associates
Rep By: Robert A. Rapoza

Delta Petroleum Corp.

Leg. Issues: ENG

Outside Counsel/Consultants

Brownstein Hyatt & Farber, P.C.
Issues: ENG
Rep By: Thomas H. Hudson, Michael B. Levy

Delta Wetlands Project

Lafayette, CA
Leg. Issues: AGR, BUD, CAW, IND, NAT, RES

Outside Counsel/Consultants

Clark & Weinstock, Inc.
Issues: AGR, BUD, CAW, NAT, RES
Rep By: Hon. Vic H. Fazio, Jr., Sandi Stuart, Hon. John Vincent "Vin" Weber

Perkins Coie LLP
Issues: NAT
Rep By: Guy R. Martin

Van Ness Feldman, P.C.
Issues: IND, NAT
Rep By: Joseph B. Nelson, Thomas C. Roberts, Robert G. Szabo

DeMil Internat'l

Huntsville, AL

Provides environmentally friendly technology to destroy unexploded ordnance.

Leg. Issues: DEF, FOR

Outside Counsel/Consultants

Anne V. Smith
Issues: DEF, FOR
Rep By: Anne V. Smith

Democracy 21

1825 I St. NW
Suite 400
Washington, DC 20006
Tel: (202)429-2008
Fax: (202)293-2660
Registered: LDA
E-mail: info@democracy21.org

A non-profit, public policy organization.

Leg. Issues: GOV

In-house, DC-area Employees
WERTHEIMER, Fred: President

Democratic Candidate Fund

1310 19th St. NW
Washington, DC 20036
Tel: (202)466-6555
Fax: (202)466-6596

Address is that of O'Neill, Athy and Casey, P.C. (see separate listing under "Firms").

In-house, DC-area Employees
O'NEILL, Christopher R.: Treasurer

Democratic Congressional Campaign Committee

430 S. Capitol St. SE
Second Floor
Washington, DC 20003
Tel: (202)863-1500
Fax: (202)485-3512
Web: www.takebackthehouse.org

In-house, DC-area Employees
GRAEFE, Erin: Director, Washington Fundraising
MANTZ, Jonathan: National Finance Director
MCGRARRITY, Gerard: Director, Harriman Community Center
SMITH, Erik: Director, Communications
WOLFSON, Howard: Exec. Director

Democratic Governors Ass'n

430 S. Capitol St. SE
Suite 422
Washington, DC 20003
Tel: (202)479-5153
Fax: (202)479-5156
Web: www.democraticgovernors.org
E-mail: dga@dnc.democrats.org

In-house, DC-area Employees
THORNBERRY, B. J.: Exec. Director

Democratic Leadership Council

600 Pennsylvania Ave. SE
Suite 400
Washington, DC 20003
Tel: (202)546-0007
Fax: (202)544-5002
Registered: LDA
Web: www.dlcppi.org
E-mail: webmaster@dlcppi.org

Works to reshape American politics by moving it beyond the left-right debate. Seeks to define and galvanize popular support for a new public philosophy built on progressive ideals mainstream values, and innovative, nonbureaucratic solutions.

In-house, DC-area Employees
ALSTON, Charles C.: Exec. Director
CALLAHAN, Jenifer L.: Director, Office of the President
CHILDRESS, Martina: Office Manager and Intern Coordinator
CULBERTSON, Eliza: Director, Information Systems
FITZPATRICK, Joan: Controller
FRANKEL, Matthew: Press Secretary
FROM, Alvin: Founder and C.E.O.
KILGORE, Ed: Policy Director
KIZER BALL, Julie L.: Administrative Director
MILBY, Helen Muir: Development Director
MIRGA, Tomas F.: Editor, Blueprint Magazine
PAGE, Holly: V. President, Strategy and Innovation
RANGE, Peter Ross: Editor, Blueprint Magazine
RUNG, Anne: Congressional Director
VALENZUELA, Jeff: Coordinator, Political Programing
YEDINKSY, Theo: Director, DLC Trade Project

Democratic Nat'l Committee

430 S. Capitol St. SE
Washington, DC 20003
Tel: (202)863-8000
Fax: (202)863-8174
Web: www.democrats.org

Political Action Committee/s

Democratic Victory Fund

430 S. Capitol St. SE
Washington, DC 20003
Tel: (202)863-8000
Fax: (202)863-8174
Contact: Laurie Moskowitz

In-house, DC-area Employees
BACKUS, Jeremy: Press Secretary
FOLEY, Leigh: Director, Specialty Media
KELLY, Doug: Director, Research
KENNGOTT, Chris: Director, State Party Fundraising
MOSKOWITZ, Laurie: PAC Administrator

Outside Counsel/Consultants

Arnold & Porter

Greer, Margolis, Mitchell, Burns & Associates

Democratic Senatorial Campaign Committee

430 S. Capitol St. SE
Washington, DC 20003
Tel: (202)224-2447
Fax: (202)485-3120
Web: www.dscc.org
E-mail: info@dscc.org

Nat'l Political Party Committee supporting Democratic candidates for the U.S. Senate.

In-house, DC-area Employees
GRINER, Allison: Director, DSCC Roundtable

Outside Counsel/Consultants

Issue Dynamics Inc.

Denhill DC LCC

Charlotte, NC
Leg. Issues: RES

Outside Counsel/Consultants

Nixon Peabody LLP
Issues: RES

Denso Internat'l America, Inc.

Southfield, MI

Outside Counsel/Consultants

Global Policy Group, Inc.

Dental Gold Institute

Butler, NJ

Outside Counsel/Consultants

Jenner & Block

Dental Recycling North America

New York, NY
Leg. Issues: ENV, HCR, NAT

Outside Counsel/Consultants

Downey McGrath Group, Inc.
Issues: ENV, HCR, NAT
Rep By: Hon. Thomas J. Downey, Jr., Hon. Raymond J. McGrath, Michael R. Wessel

Denton, Texas, City of

Leg. Issues: LAW, TRA, URB, UTI

Outside Counsel/Consultants

Barbara T. McCall Associates
Issues: LAW, TRA, URB, UTI
Rep By: Ralph Garboushian, Barbara T. McCall

Denton, Texas, County of

Dallas, TX
Leg. Issues: BUD, TAX, TRA

Outside Counsel/Consultants

BKSH & Associates
Issues: BUD, TAX, TRA

Denver Children's Hospital

Denver, CO
Leg. Issues: HCR

Outside Counsel/Consultants

Ikon Public Affairs
Issues: HCR
Rep By: Dominic Del Papa

Denver Internat'l Airport

Denver, CO

Outside Counsel/Consultants

Thelen Reid & Priest LLP
Rep By: William A. Kirk, Jr., Richard J. Leidl, Stephan M. Minikes

Denver Regional Transportation District

Denver, CO
Leg. Issues: TRA

Outside Counsel/Consultants

Patton Boggs, LLP
Issues: TRA
Rep By: Philip A. Bangert, Anne Miano, Edward J. Newberry

Denver, Colorado, City and County of
Leg. Issues: TRA

Outside Counsel/Consultants

Capital Partnerships (VA) Inc.
Issues: TRA
Rep By: Robin Angle, Kenneth W. Butler, Clay Gravely

Denver, Colorado, City of
Leg. Issues: AVI, TRD

Outside Counsel/Consultants

Greenberg Traurig, LLP
Issues: TRD

Morrison & Foerster LLP
Issues: AVI
Rep By: G. Brian Busey

Thelen Reid & Priest LLP
Issues: AVI
Rep By: Barry I. Berkoff, William A. Kirk, Jr., Richard J. Leidl, Stephan M. Minikes, Richard Y. Roberts, Nancy K. West

Denver, Regional Transportation District of
Denver, CO
Leg. Issues: TRA

Outside Counsel/Consultants

Slagle & Associates
Issues: TRA
Rep By: P. Roger Slagle, Jr.

DePaul University
Chicago, IL
Leg. Issues: BUD, EDU, IMM

Outside Counsel/Consultants

Law Office of Edward D. Heffernan
Issues: BUD, EDU, IMM

Derivatives Net, Inc.
Charlotte, NC
Leg. Issues: BAN

Outside Counsel/Consultants

Butera & Andrews
Issues: BAN
Rep By: Cliff W. Andrews, Wright H. Andrews, Jr., James J. Butera, Frank Tillotson

Derwent, Inc.
Leg. Issues: CPT

Outside Counsel/Consultants

Joseph L. Ebersole
Issues: CPT
Rep By: Joseph L. Ebersole

Des Moines Community School District
Des Moines, IA

Outside Counsel/Consultants

Spiegel & McDiarmid
Rep By: John J. Corbett, Jr.

Des Moines University, Osteopathic Medical Center
Des Moines, IA

Outside Counsel/Consultants

O'Neill, Athy & Casey, P.C.
Rep By: Christopher R. O'Neill

Des Moines, Iowa, City of

Outside Counsel/Consultants

Spiegel & McDiarmid

Desert Grape Growers League
Mecca, CA
Leg. Issues: AGR, TRD

Outside Counsel/Consultants

Schramm, Williams & Associates, Inc.
Issues: AGR, TRD
Rep By: Robert Schramm

Desert Research Institute
Reno, NV
Leg. Issues: ENG, SCI

Outside Counsel/Consultants

Richard L. Spees, Inc.
Issues: ENG, SCI
Rep By: Richard L. Spees

Design Cuisine
2659 S. Shirlington Rd.
Arlington, VA 22206
Web: www.designcuisine.com
Tel: (703)979-9400
Fax: (703)979-8632

A catering company.

In-house, DC-area Employees

HOMAN, Bill: President

Design Professionals Coalition
1250 H St. NW
Suite 575
Washington, DC 20005
Tel: (202)393-2426
Fax: (202)783-8410

Above address is that of CH2M HILL.

In-house, DC-area Employees

CORRIGAN, Richard L.: V. Chairman

Design-Build Institute of America
1010 Massachusetts Ave. NW
Suite 350
Washington, DC 20001
Web: www.dbia.org
E-mail: dbia@dbia.org
Tel: (202)682-0110
Fax: (202)682-5877
Leg. Issues: TRA

Political Action Committee/s

Design-Build Institute of America PAC
1010 Massachusetts Ave. NW
Suite 350
Washington, DC 20001
Contact: David A. Johnston
Tel: (202)682-0110
Fax: (202)682-5877

In-house, DC-area Employees

JOHNSTON, David A.: Director, Technical Programs and PAC

Outside Counsel/Consultants

Edmund C. Graber
Issues: TRA
Rep By: Edmund C. Graber

Designers & Planners, Inc.
2120 Washington Blvd.
Suite 200
Arlington, VA 22204
Web: www.dandp.com
Tel: (703)920-7070
Fax: (703)920-7177

A member of the BMT Group of Companies. An engineering consulting firm that provides design, engineering computing and logistics services, specialized training programs and safety and environmental protection programs for the U.S. Navy, Coast Guard and other government clients.

In-house, DC-area Employees

GALLAGHER, John: President

Detroit Edison Co.
601 Pennsylvania Ave. NW
Suite 350
North Bldg.
Washington, DC 20004
Web: www.dteenergy.com
Tel: (202)347-8420
Fax: (202)347-8423
Registered: LDA

An investor-owned electric utility company. Headquartered in Detroit, MI.

In-house, DC-area Employees

BRITTO, Karen: Washington Representative
DEANNA, Jennifer S.: Legislative Assistant
HORN, Robert J.: Assistant V. President and Manager, Federal Affairs

Outside Counsel/Consultants

The Direct Impact Co.

Detroit Internat'l Bridge Co./The Ambassador Bridge
Detroit, MI
Leg. Issues: TRD

Outside Counsel/Consultants

The Advocacy Group
Issues: TRD
Rep By: Jon L. Boisclair, Robert E. Mills

Detroit Medical Center
Detroit, MI
Leg. Issues: BUD, HCR, MMM, PHA, TAX

Outside Counsel/Consultants

The MWW Group
Issues: BUD, HCR
Rep By: Todd S. Berkoff, Dana P. Bostic, Christine A. Pellerin, Jonathan B. Slade

Shaw Pittman
Issues: BUD, HCR, MMM, PHA, TAX
Rep By: Bruce Fried, Thomas J. Spulak, Andrew L. Woods

Detroit Metropolitan Airport
Detroit, MI
Leg. Issues: TRA

Outside Counsel/Consultants

Dennis M. Hertel & Associates
Issues: TRA
Rep By: Hon. Dennis M. Hertel

Detroit Public Schools
Detroit, MI
Leg. Issues: EDU

Outside Counsel/Consultants

Dykema Gossett PLLC
Issues: EDU
Rep By: David K. Arthur, Nancy R. Barbour

Detroit Public Television
Detriot, MI
Leg. Issues: BUD, COM, EDU, TEC

Outside Counsel/Consultants

Convergence Services, Inc.
Issues: BUD, COM, EDU, TEC
Rep By: John M. Lawson

Detroit Rescue Mission Ministries
Detroit, MI
Leg. Issues: ALC, HOU

Outside Counsel/Consultants

Russ Reid Co.
Issues: ALC, HOU
Rep By: Thomas C. Keller, Mark D. McIntyre

Detroit, Michigan, City of
Leg. Issues: AVI, BUD, DIS, ENV, FIR, GOV, HCR, HOU, IMM, IND, LAW, TAX, TRA, TRD

Outside Counsel/Consultants

Dykema Gossett PLLC
Issues: AVI, BUD, DIS, ENV, FIR, GOV, HCR, HOU, IMM, IND, LAW, TAX, TRA, TRD
Rep By: David K. Arthur, Nancy R. Barbour, Tricia K. Markwood

Reed, Smith, LLP
Rep By: Christopher L. Rissetto

Detroit, Michigan, Public School System of the County of
Leg. Issues: EDU

Outside Counsel/Consultants

Patton Boggs, LLP
Issues: EDU
Rep By: Michael A. Brown

Deutsche Lufthansa AG
Cologne, GERMANY

Outside Counsel/Consultants

Galland, Kharasch, Greenberg, Fellman & Swirsky, P.C.

Mayer, Brown & Platt
Rep By: John P. Schmitz

Deutsche Post AG
Bonn, GERMANY

Outside Counsel/Consultants

Wolfgang Pordzik
Rep By: Wolfgang Pordzik

Deutsche Telekom, Inc.
1020 19th St. NW
Suite 850
Washington, DC 20036
Tel: (202)452-9100
Fax: (202)452-9555
Registered: FARA

Headquartered in Bonn, Germany, with American headquarters in New York, NY.

Leg. Issues: TEC

In-house, DC-area Employees

BREITFELD, Julie S.: Senior Manager, Regulatory and Govt. Affairs
JAKUBEK, Wolfgang: Managing Director
SHINGLETON, A. Bradley: Legal Counsel
TEGGE, Dr. Andreas: Managing Director

Outside Counsel/Consultants

Baker, Donelson, Bearman & Caldwell, P.C.
Issues: TEC
Rep By: Hon. Howard H. Baker, Jr., J. Keith Kennedy, John C. Tuck

Griffin, Johnson, Dover & Stewart
Rep By: Patrick J. Griffin

The OB-C Group, LLC

Wilmer, Cutler & Pickering
Issues: TEC
Rep By: Lloyd N. Cutler, C. Boyden Gray, John H. Harwood, Jr., William T. Lake, Charles S. Levy, Daniel Phythyon

Deutscher Industrie-und Handelstag

Berlin, GERMANY

Outside Counsel/Consultants

Representative of German Industry and Trade

Development Bank of Japan

1101 17th St. NW
Suite 1001
Washington, DC 20036
Tel: (202)331-8696
Fax: (202)293-3932
Registered: FARA

Headquartered in Tokyo, Japan.

In-house, DC-area Employees

KAWASHITA, Haruhisa: Chief Representative
WADA, Yasuhiro: Representative

Development Corporation of Nevada

Las Vegas, NY
Leg. Issues: GAM, IND

Outside Counsel/Consultants

Capital Consultants Corp.
Issues: GAM, IND
Rep By: Michael David Kaiser

Development Group for Alternative Policies

927 15th St. NW
Fourth Floor
Washington, DC 20005
Web: www.developmentgap.org
E-mail: dgap@igc.org
Tel: (202)898-1566
Fax: (202)898-1612

A development policy resource organization which involves local people in addressing international economic policies that affect them.

In-house, DC-area Employees

HANSEN-KUHN, Karen: Latin American Coordinator
HELLINGER, Douglas: Exec. Director
HELLINGER, Stephen: President
SUGAR, Kathleen: Communications Coordinator

Development Resources, Inc.

Washington, DC
Leg. Issues: TAX

Outside Counsel/Consultants

Dewey Ballantine LLP
Issues: TAX
Rep By: John J. Salmon

The Devereux Foundation

Outside Counsel/Consultants

Paul, Weiss, Rifkind, Wharton & Garrison
Rep By: Carl W. Hampe

Devon Energy Corp.

Oklahoma City, OK
Leg. Issues: ENG, TRD

Outside Counsel/Consultants

J. Steven Griles & Associates
Issues: ENG
Rep By: J. Steven Griles

NES, Inc.
Issues: ENG

William F. Whitsitt Policy and Government Affairs
Issues: TRD
Rep By: William F. Whitsitt

Devon Management Group Inc.

Outside Counsel/Consultants

MV3 & Associates

Valente Lopatin & Schulze
Rep By: Mark Valente, III

DeVry, Inc.

Oakbrook Terrace, IL
Registered: LDA

An institute of higher learning.

Leg. Issues: BUD, EDU

Outside Counsel/Consultants

Dean Blakey & Moskowitz
Issues: BUD, EDU
Rep By: William A. Blakey

Dewey Electronics Corp.

Oakland, NJ
Leg. Issues: DEF

Outside Counsel/Consultants

SISCORP
Issues: DEF
Rep By: Robert Meissner

DeWitt Cos. of Guam and Saipan

Maite, GU
Leg. Issues: DEF, MAR

Outside Counsel/Consultants

R. J. Hudson Associates
Issues: DEF, MAR
Rep By: Rebecca J. Hudson

DFG Group

Bethesda, MD
Leg. Issues: HOU

Outside Counsel/Consultants

Helmsin & Yarwood Associates
Issues: HOU

DFI Internat'l

Washington, DC
Leg. Issues: GOV

Outside Counsel/Consultants

The Conaway Group LLC
Issues: GOV
Rep By: Lt. Gen. John B. Conaway, USAF (Ret.)

DFK Internat'l/USA, Inc.

Washington, DC

Outside Counsel/Consultants

Hauck and Associates
Rep By: Jay Hauck, William J. Mahon

DFS Group Ltd.

San Francisco, CA
Leg. Issues: BUD, TOB, TOU, TRD

Outside Counsel/Consultants

Patton Boggs, LLP
Issues: BUD, TOB, TOU, TRD
Rep By: Elizabeth Baltzan, Thomas Hale Boggs, Jr., Elena Giberga, Edward J. Newberry, Stuart M. Pape, Frank R. Samolis, Denise Vanison, Jonathan R. Yarowsky

DGME Fairness Initiative

Washington, DC
Leg. Issues: BUD, HCR, MMM

Outside Counsel/Consultants

Van Scoyoc Associates, Inc.
Issues: BUD, HCR, MMM
Rep By: Michael W. Adcock, Evan Knisely, Scott Spear, H. Stewart Van Scoyoc

DHL Airways, Inc.

Redwood City, CA
Leg. Issues: AVI

Outside Counsel/Consultants

Shaw Pittman
Issues: AVI
Rep By: J. E. Murdock, III

Winston & Strawn
Rep By: Peter N. Hiebert, Eric L. Hirschhorn

DIAGEO

London, UNITED KINGDOM
Leg. Issues: BEV, FOO, TRD

Outside Counsel/Consultants

Hogan & Hartson L.L.P.
Rep By: Nancy Granese, William Michael House

JBC Internat'l
Issues: BEV, FOO, TRD
Rep By: Jeannie M. Boone, James B. Clawson

The Dial Co.

Scottsdale, AZ
Leg. Issues: CAW, FOO

Outside Counsel/Consultants

Mary Vihstadt
Issues: CAW, FOO
Rep By: Mary Vihstadt

Dialoge Corp.

Leg. Issues: CPT

Outside Counsel/Consultants

Joseph L. Ebersole
Issues: CPT
Rep By: Joseph L. Ebersole

Dialogic Communications Corp.

Franklin, TN
Leg. Issues: DEF

Outside Counsel/Consultants

American Defense Internat'l, Inc.
Issues: DEF
Rep By: Michael Herson, Van D. Hipp, Jr.

Dialysis Clinic, Inc.

Nashville, TN
Leg. Issues: MMM

Outside Counsel/Consultants

Congressional Consultants
Issues: MMM
Rep By: Gwen Gampel

Diamond Antenna & Microwave Corp.

Lowell, MA
Leg. Issues: TRA

Outside Counsel/Consultants

The PMA Group
Issues: TRA
Rep By: Kaylene Green, Dr. John Lynch, Paul J. Magliocchetti, Mark Waclawski

Diamond Game Enterprises, Inc.

Albion, MI
Leg. Issues: IND

Outside Counsel/Consultants

Dorsey & Whitney LLP
Issues: IND
Rep By: David A. Bieging, Virginia W. Boylan

Diamond Games

New York, NY

Outside Counsel/Consultants

Chesapeake Enterprises, Inc.
Rep By: J. John Fluharty

Diamond Head Financial Group

Los Angeles, CA
Leg. Issues: ECN, TRD

Outside Counsel/Consultants

The Eagles Group
Issues: ECN, TRD
Rep By: Terence Costello

Diamond Manufacturing, Inc.

Wyoming, PA
Leg. Issues: BUD, DEF, TRD

Outside Counsel/Consultants

Arent Fox Kintner Plotkin & Kahn, PLLC
Issues: BUD, DEF, TRD
Rep By: Douglas McCormack

Diamond Ventures

Tucson, AZ

Outside Counsel/Consultants

Marshall A. Brachman
Rep By: Marshall A. Brachman

Dick Broadcasting Co., Inc.

Knoxville, TN

Outside Counsel/Consultants

Kaye Scholer LLP

Dick Corp.

Pittsburgh, PA
Leg. Issues: BUD

Outside Counsel/Consultants

Rhoads Group
Issues: BUD
Rep By: Paul D. Behrends, Kathleen Ireland, Steven G. McKnight, Clifford R. Northup, Barry D. Rhoads, Thomas Worrall

Dictaphone Corp.

Stratford, CT
Leg. Issues: CPI, GOV, HCR

Outside Counsel/Consultants

Patton Boggs, LLP
Issues: CPI, GOV, HCR
Rep By: Amy C. Davine, Lanny J. Davis, Clayton L. Hough, Karen L. Marangi

Diebold, Inc.

Canton, OH

Outside Counsel/Consultants

Interface Inc.
Rep By: Albert B. Rosenbaum, III

Dierman, Wortley, and Zola

1776 K St. NW
Suite 400
Washington, DC 20006
Tel: (202)296-7555
Fax: (202)785-0025
Registered: LDA
Leg. Issues: TRD

In-house, DC-area Employees

WORTLEY, MC (Ret.), Hon. George C.: Chairman
ZOLA, Hilliard A.: President

Outside Counsel/Consultants

Stewart and Stewart
Issues: TRD
Rep By: Alan M. Dunn

Dietary Supplement Safety and Science Coalition

Los Angeles, CA
Leg. Issues: FOO

Outside Counsel/Consultants

Hyman, Phelps & McNamara, P.C.
Issues: FOO
Rep By: A. Wes Siegner, Jr.

Digestive Disease Nat'l Coalition

Washington, DC
Registered: LDA
Leg. Issues: BUD, HCR

Outside Counsel/Consultants

Health and Medicine Counsel of Washington
Issues: BUD, HCR
Rep By: Staci Sigman Dennison, Dale P. Dirks, Susie Dobert, Gavin Lindberg

Digital Access

Outside Counsel/Consultants

Earle Palmer Brown Public Relations

Digital Biometrics, Inc.

Minnetonka, MN
A manufacturer of fingerprinting equipment.
Leg. Issues: LAW

Outside Counsel/Consultants

David Turch & Associates
Issues: LAW
Rep By: Marilyn E. Campbell, Victor Tambone, David N. M. Turch

Digital Commerce Corp.

Reston, VA
Leg. Issues: CPI, GOV, SMB, TEC

Outside Counsel/Consultants

The ILEX Group
Issues: CPI, GOV, SMB, TEC
Rep By: H. Hollister Cantus

Digital Descriptor Services, Inc.

Langhorne, PA
Leg. Issues: CPI, DEF, LAW

Outside Counsel/Consultants

The Advocacy Group
Issues: CPI, DEF, LAW
Rep By: Robert E. Mills

Digital Focus

Outside Counsel/Consultants

Dittus Communications
Rep By: Trudi Boyd, Tom Conway, Jeffrey Eshelman

Digital Future Coalition

P.O. Box 7679
Washington, DC 20004
Tel: (202)628-9210
Fax: (202)628-9227
Web: www.dfc.org
E-mail: dfc@dfc.org

A 42 member coalition devoted to balanced intellectual property law.

In-house, DC-area Employees

RODGERS, Ruth: Contact

Digital Matrix Corp.

Hampstead, NY
Leg. Issues: TRD

Outside Counsel/Consultants

Birch, Horton, Bittner & Cherot
Issues: TRD
Rep By: Thomas L. Albert, Ronald G. Birch

Digital Media Ass'n

Washington, DC
Leg. Issues: CPI, CPT, MIA, SCI, TEC

Outside Counsel/Consultants

McDermott, Will and Emery
Issues: CPI, CPT, MIA, SCI, TEC
Rep By: Seth D. Greenstein, Neil Quinter

The Wexler Group
Issues: SCI
Rep By: Adam Eisgrau

Digital Privacy and Security Working Group

1634 I St. NW
Suite 1100
Washington, DC 20006-4003
Tel: (202)637-9800
Fax: (202)637-0968

An ad hoc coalition of computer industry interests concerned with preserving the privacy of computerized data and communications.

In-house, DC-area Employees

DEMPSEY, Jim: Contact

Digital System Resources, Inc.

Fairfax, VA

Outside Counsel/Consultants

Copeland, Lowery & Jacquez
Rep By: Jean Gingras Denton, Hon. William D. Lowery

Dignity/USA

1500 Massachusetts Ave. NW
Suite 11
Washington, DC 20005
Tel: (202)861-0017
Fax: (202)429-9808
Web: www.dignityusa.org
E-mail: dignity@aol.com

A group of gay, lesbian, bisexual and transgender Catholics advocating for change in the Catholic Church's teaching on homosexuality and presenting positive testimony from a Catholic perspective on civil rights legislation

In-house, DC-area Employees

DUDDY, Marianne T.: Exec. Director

Dillard University

New Orleans, LA
Leg. Issues: BUD

Outside Counsel/Consultants

The Carmen Group
Issues: BUD
Rep By: Ryan Adesnik, David M. Carmen, Clifton Smith, Sharon Taylor, Aisha Tyus

Dillingham Construction, Inc.

Pleasanton, CA
Leg. Issues: ECN

Outside Counsel/Consultants

Baker, Donelson, Bearman & Caldwell, P.C.
Rep By: Charles R. Johnston, Jr.

Jack Ferguson Associates, Inc.
Issues: ECN
Rep By: Jack Ferguson

Dime Savings Bank of New York

New York, NY
Leg. Issues: BAN, BUD, FIN, HOU, INS, TAX

Outside Counsel/Consultants

Butera & Andrews
Issues: BAN, TAX
Rep By: Cliff W. Andrews, Wright H. Andrews, Jr., James J. Butera, Frank Tillotson

Hohlt & Associates
Issues: BAN, BUD, FIN, HOU, INS, TAX
Rep By: Richard F. Hohlt

Dimension 4

Seattle, WA
Leg. Issues: DEF, NAT

Outside Counsel/Consultants

Denny Miller McBee Associates
Issues: DEF, NAT

Dimensions Healthcare System

Largo, MD
Leg. Issues: BUD, HCR

Outside Counsel/Consultants

Cassidy & Associates, Inc.
Issues: BUD, HCR
Rep By: Gregory M. Gill, W. Campbell Kaufman, IV

Dimensions Internat'l

Alexandria, VA
Leg. Issues: AVI

Outside Counsel/Consultants

Patton Boggs, LLP
Issues: AVI
Rep By: John J. Deschauer, Jr., Edward J. Newberry

Dimock Community Health Center

Roxbury, MA
Leg. Issues: BUD

Outside Counsel/Consultants

Philip W. Johnston Associates
Issues: BUD
Rep By: Philip W. Johnston, Merrill E. Warschoff

Diplomatic and Consular Officers, Retired (Dacor)

1801 F St. NW
Washington, DC 20006
Tel: (202)682-0500
Fax: (202)842-3295
E-mail: dacor@ix.netcom.com

In-house, DC-area Employees

SERVICE, Robert: Exec. Director

Direct Marketing Ass'n Nonprofit Federation

1111 19th St. NW
11th Floor
Washington, DC 20036
Tel: (202)628-4380
Fax: (202)628-4383
Web: www.federationofnonprofits.org
E-mail: nonprofitfederation@the-dma.org

Formed from a merger of The Nat'l Federation of Nonprofits and the Direct Marketing Ass'n (New York).

Leg. Issues: POS

In-house, DC-area Employees

CASSIDY, Lee M.: Exec. Director
MILLER, George E.: Postal Counsel

Direct Marketing Ass'n of Washington

Vienna, VA
Tel: (703)821-3629

Outside Counsel/Consultants

Daly Communications

Direct Marketing Ass'n, Inc.

1111 19th St. NW
Suite 1100
Washington, DC 20036
Tel: (202)955-5030
Fax: (202)955-0085
Registered: LDA
Web: www.the-dma.org
Leg. Issues: ADV, BUD, COM, CPI, CSP, GOV, POS, TAX, TEC

Political Action Committee/s

Direct Marketing Ass'n Political Action Committee
1111 19th St. NW
Suite 1100
Washington, DC 20036
Tel: (202)861-2422
Fax: (202)955-0085
Contact: Mark A. Micali

In-house, DC-area Employees

CERASALE, Gerald E.: Sr. V. President, Governmental Affairs
MICALI, Mark A.: V. President, Government Affairs
SCANLON, Elizabeth K.: Government Affairs
STAREK, III, Roscoe Burton: Senior V. President, Catalog Issues

Outside Counsel/Consultants

Bergner Bockorny Castagnetti and Hawkins
Issues: TAX

Marshall A. Brachman
Issues: BUD, CSP, GOV, POS, TAX, TEC
Rep By: Marshall A. Brachman

Covington & Burling

Davidson & Company, Inc.
Issues: ADV, TAX
Rep By: James H. Davidson, Richard E. May, Stanley Sokul

DeHart and Darr Associates, Inc.

The Duberstein Group, Inc.
Issues: ADV, CPI, POS, TAX
Rep By: John W. Angus, III, Michael S. Berman, Steven M. Champlin, Kenneth M. Duberstein, Henry M. Gandy, Daniel P. Meyer

Patton Boggs, LLP
Issues: TAX
Rep By: Thomas Hale Boggs, Jr., Brian C. Lopina, Cliff Massa, III

Piper Marbury Rudnick & Wolfe LLP
Issues: CPI, CSP
Rep By: Alisa M. Bergman, Emilio W. Cividanes, James J. Halpert, Stuart P. Ingis, Katharine A. Pauley, Ronald L. Plesser

Venable
Rep By: Ian D. Volner

Direct Selling Ass'n

1275 Pennsylvania Ave. NW
Suite 800
Washington, DC 20004
Tel: (202)347-8866
Fax: (202)347-0055
Registered: LDA
Web: www.dsa.org
E-mail: info@dsa.org

Trade association for companies that market consumer goods and services away from fixed retail locations, primarily in homes by independent salespersons and distributors.

Leg. Issues: CSP, FOR, SMB, TAX, TRD

Political Action Committee/s

Direct Selling Ass'n Political Action Committee
1275 Pennsylvania Ave. NW
Suite 800
Washington, DC 20004
Contact: Joseph N. Mariano
Tel: (202)293-5760
Fax: (202)463-4569

In-house, DC-area Employees

HESSE, III, John: Senior Attorney and Director, Government Relations
MARIANO, Joseph N.: Senior V. President and Legal Counsel
OFFEN, Neil H.: President
ROBINSON, Amy M.: Manager, Communications

Outside Counsel/Consultants

Hogan & Hartson L.L.P.
Issues: TAX
Rep By: Deborah Ashford

Direct Selling Education Foundation

1275 Pennsylvania Ave. NW
Suite 800
Washington, DC 20004
Tel: (202)347-8866
Fax: (202)347-0055

The public service arm of the direct selling industry. Provides educational information and research activities on matters of interest to consumer advocates, marketing professors and the public on consumer and marketplace matters.

In-house, DC-area Employees

TAYLOR, Jeremy: Exec. Director

Direct Supply

Milwaukee, WI
Leg. Issues: HCR

Outside Counsel/Consultants

Broydrick & Associates
Issues: HCR
Rep By: William Broydrick, Amy Demske

Direct TV

Arlington, VA

Outside Counsel/Consultants

Quinn Gillespie & Associates

Directors Guild of America

Los Angeles, CA
Leg. Issues: ART, CIV, CPT, MIA, TAX

Outside Counsel/Consultants

Griffin, Johnson, Dover & Stewart
Issues: CPT, MIA, TAX
Rep By: William C. Danvers, G. Jack Dover, Patrick J. Griffin

Lutzker & Lutzker LLP
Issues: CPT
Rep By: Arnold P. Lutzker

Washington Council Ernst & Young
Issues: ART, CIV, TAX
Rep By: Doug Badger, Lauren Darling, John L. Doney, Jayne T. Fitzgerald, LaBrenda Garrett-Nelson, Gary J. Gasper, Bruce A. Gates, Nick Giordano, Cathy Koch, Robert J. Leonard, William Mastro, Richard Meltzer, Phillip D. Moseley, John D. Porter, Robert M. Rozen, Donna Steele-Flynn, Timothy J. Urban

Disability Rights Education and Defense Fund

1629 K St. NW
Suite 802
Washington, DC 20006
Tel: (202)986-0375
Fax: (202)462-5624
Registered: LDA

In-house, DC-area Employees

WRIGHT, Patrisha: Director, Governmental Affairs

Disabled American Veterans

807 Maine Ave. SW
Washington, DC 20024
Tel: (202)554-3501
Fax: (202)554-3581
Registered: LDA
Web: www.dav.org
Leg. Issues: VET

In-house, DC-area Employees

AUSTIN, Brian E.: Associate National Service Director
AUTRY, David E.: Deputy National Director, Communications
BASKERVILLE, Anthony: Deputy National Service Director, Employment
GORMAN, David W.: Exec. Director, Washington Headquarters
HARTMAN, Edward E.: Assistant National Director, Volunteer Services
ILEM, Joy J.: Assistant National Legislative Director
PLANTE, Robert P.: Assistant National Service Director
STEELMAN, Jerry: National Director, Voluntary Services
SURRATT, Rick: Deputy National Legislative Director
VIOLANTE, Joseph: National Legislative Director
WILBORN, Thomas L.: Assistant National Director, Communications
WILSON, Arthur H.: National Adjutant
WOLFE, Kenneth: National Service Director

Disabled Veterens' LIFE Memorial Foundation Inc.

Outside Counsel/Consultants

Edelman Public Relations Worldwide
Rep By: Christine Kelly Cimko

Disaster Insurance Coalition/City of Hope Nat'l Medical Center

Outside Counsel/Consultants

Copeland, Lowery & Jacquez
Rep By: Jeffrey S. Shockey

Discount Refrigerants Inc.

Leg. Issues: ENV

Outside Counsel/Consultants

Brownstein Hyatt & Farber, P.C.
Issues: ENV
Rep By: P. Cole Finegan, Andrew Spielman

Discovery Communications, Inc.

7700 Wisconsin Ave.
Bethesda, MD 20814
Tel: (301)986-1999
Fax: (301)986-5998
Registered: LDA
Web: www.discovery.com
Leg. Issues: TEC

In-house, DC-area Employees

BAER, Don: Exec. V. President, Strategies
LAMOUREUX, Anne: V. President, Government Relations

Outside Counsel/Consultants

O'Toole Consulting
Rep By: Thomas O'Toole

Discovery Place, Inc. (Charlotte Science Museum)

Charlotte, NC
Leg. Issues: BUD

Outside Counsel/Consultants

Patton Boggs, LLP
Issues: BUD
Rep By: Lansing B. Lee, III, Darryl D. Nirenberg, Elizabeth C. Vella

Discovery Science Center

Santa Ana, CA
Leg. Issues: AER, BUD, EDU

Outside Counsel/Consultants

Hogan & Hartson L.L.P.
Issues: AER, BUD, EDU
Rep By: Hon. Robert H. Michel, Humberto R. Pena

The Walt Disney Co.

1150 17th St. NW
Suite 400
Washington, DC 20036
Tel: (202)222-4700
Fax: (202)222-4799

An entertainment company headquartered in Burbank, CA.

Leg. Issues: COM, CPI, CPT, GAM, HCR, IMM, TRD

Political Action Committee/s

Walt Disney Co. Employee's PAC, The
1150 17th St. NW
Suite 400
Washington, DC 20036
Contact: Jill Rowlison
Tel: (202)222-4700
Fax: (202)222-4799

In-house, DC-area Employees

BATES, Richard M.: V. President, Government Relations
CAREY, Mary G.: Manager
FOX, Susan: V. President, Government Relations
KELLY, Brian: Director, Government Relations
KUSIN, Susan: Assistant
MORGENWECK, Gail: Manager
PADDEN, Preston: Exec. V. President, Government Relations
ROSE, Mitch F.: V. President, Government Relations
ROWLISON, Jill: PAC Administrator
YAMAMOTO, Andrea: Assistant

Outside Counsel/Consultants

Verner, Liipfert, Bernhard, McPherson and Hand, Chartered
Issues: COM, CPT, TRD
Rep By: Berl Bernhard, Lawrence Duncan, III, Denis J. Dwyer, Harry C. McPherson

Distance Education and Training Council

1601 18th St. NW
Suite Two
Washington, DC 20009
Web: www.detc.org
E-mail: detc@detc.org
Tel: (202)234-5100
Fax: (202)332-1386

Nonprofit accrediting agency for distance learning.

Leg. Issues: EDU

In-house, DC-area Employees

LAMBERT, Michael P.: Exec. Director

Outside Counsel/Consultants

J. C. Luman and Assoc.
Rep By: Joseph C. Luman

Distilled Spirits Council of the United States, Inc.

1250 I St. NW
Suite 400
Washington, DC 20005-3998
Tel: (202)628-3544
Fax: (202)682-8888
Registered: LDA
Web: www.discus.org
Leg. Issues: ADV, ALC, CAW, CSP, DEF, TAX, TRA, TRD

Political Action Committee/s

Distilled Spirits Political Action Committee
1250 I St. NW
Suite 400
Washington, DC 20005-3998
Contact: Shane Schriefer
Tel: (202)682-8819
Fax: (202)682-8849

In-house, DC-area Employees

BAKER, Mark: V. President, International Trade
COLEMAN, Franklin L.: Senior V. President, Public Affairs and Communications
CRESSY, Peter H.: President and Chief Exec. Officer
GORMAN, Mark S.: Senior V. President, Office of Government Relations
LAMB, Deborah A.: V. President, Internat'l Issues and Trade
SCHRIEFER, Shane: V. President, Office of Government Relations and Congressional Liaison
STANTON, Matt: V. President, Office of Government Relations

Outside Counsel/Consultants

The Dutko Group, Inc.
Issues: TAX
Rep By: Gary J. Andres, Arthur H. Silverman, William Simmons, Kimberly M. Spaulding

Hogan & Hartson L.L.P.
Rep By: Leslie Sue Ritts

Distributed Power Coalition of America

Washington, DC
Leg. Issues: ENG, ENV, UTI

Outside Counsel/Consultants

Michael E. Nix Consulting
Issues: ENG, ENV, UTI
Rep By: Michael E. Nix

Distribution and LTL Carriers Ass'n

2200 Mill Rd.
Suite 600
Alexandria, VA 22314
E-mail: dltlca@aol.com
Tel: (703)838-1806
Fax: (703)684-8143

An affiliate of the American Trucking Ass'ns, Inc. Represents the interests of general freight motor common carriers.

In-house, DC-area Employees

WILLIAMS, Kevin M.: President and Chief Exec. Officer

Distribution Services, Ltd.

South Gate, CA

Outside Counsel/Consultants

Galland, Kharasch, Greenberg, Fellman & Swirsky, P.C.
Rep By: David P. Street

District of Columbia Chamber of Commerce

1213 K St. NW
Washington, DC 20005
Web: www.dcchamber.org
Tel: (202)347-7201
Fax: (202)638-6764

In-house, DC-area Employees

MONTEILH, Richard: President
REYNOLDS, Elizabeth: Coordinator, Special Events/Administration

District of Columbia Financial Responsibility and Management Assistance Authority

441 Fourth St. NW
Room 570N
Washington, DC 20001
Web: www.dcfra.gov
Tel: (202)504-3400
Fax: (202)504-3431
Leg. Issues: GOV

In-house, DC-area Employees

RIVLIN, Alice: Chair of the Board
SMITH, Francis: Exec. Director

District of Columbia Hospital Ass'n

1250 I St. NW
Suite 700
Washington, DC 20005-3922
Web: www.dcha.org
E-mail: info@dcha.org
Tel: (202)682-1581
Fax: (202)371-8151

A trade association for hospitals in the District of Columbia. Represents its members in hearings and negotiations with the D.C. Government and federal government as appropriate and provides information on local hospital matters.

Leg. Issues: HCR

In-house, DC-area Employees

LEWIS, Joan H.: Senior V. President
MALSON, Robert A.: President

Outside Counsel/Consultants

Krooth & Altman
Rep By: Patrick J. Clancy

District of Columbia Office of Intergovernmental Relations

441 Fourth St. NW
Room 1010
Washington, DC 20001
E-mail: jwareck-em@dc.gov.org
Tel: (202)727-6265
Fax: (202)727-6895

In-house, DC-area Employees

CLARK, J. R.: Deputy Director

District of Columbia Special Olympics

300 I St. NE
Suite 102
Washington, DC 20002
Web: www.specialolympics.com
E-mail: wdcso@aol.com
Tel: (202)544-7770
Fax: (202)546-8249

In-house, DC-area Employees

HOCKER, Stephen A.: Exec. Director

Diversified Collection Services, Inc.

San Leandro, CA
Leg. Issues: BAN, BUD, EDU, GOV

Outside Counsel/Consultants

Argo Public Enterprise
Issues: GOV
Rep By: Mark Beasher

Dean Blakey & Moskowitz
Issues: BAN, BUD, EDU
Rep By: K. Sabrina Austin, John E. Dean, Saul L. Moskowitz

Diversified Internat'l Sciences Corp.

Lanham, MD
Leg. Issues: AVI

Outside Counsel/Consultants

AB Management Associates, Inc.
Issues: AVI
Rep By: Larry P. Barnett

Djibouti, Embassy of the Republic of

1156 15th St. NW
Suite 515
Washington, DC 20005
Tel: (202)331-0270
Fax: (202)331-0302

Outside Counsel/Consultants

Washington World Group, Ltd.
Rep By: Edward J. von Kloberg, III

DM Electronics Recycling Corporation

Newfields, NH
Leg. Issues: DEF, ENV, GOV, WAS

Outside Counsel/Consultants

Carmen & Muss, P.L.L.C.
Issues: DEF, ENV, GOV, WAS
Rep By: Melinda L. Carmen

DMJM+Harris

New York, NY

Outside Counsel/Consultants

Winston & Strawn
Rep By: Hon. James H. Burnley, IV, Charles L. Kinney, John D. McMickle, Joseph E. O'Leary

DNA Plant Technology Corp.

Oakland, CA
Leg. Issues: AGR, FOO, SCI, TRD

Outside Counsel/Consultants

C&M Internat'l, Ltd.
Issues: AGR, FOO, SCI, TRD
Rep By: Doral S. Cooper, Melissa Coyle, Garnett J. Sweeney, Christopher Wilson

DNA Sciences, Inc.

Mountain View, CA
Leg. Issues: CPI, HCR

Outside Counsel/Consultants

Hogan & Hartson L.L.P.
Issues: CPI, HCR
Rep By: Donna A. Boswell, Robert P. Brady, Lance D. Bultena, Raymond S. Calamaro

Do No Harm: The Coalition of Americans for Research Ethics

Alexandria, VA
Leg. Issues: MED

Outside Counsel/Consultants

Tarne Powers & Associates
Issues: MED
Rep By: Gene Tarne

Doctors Community Healthcare Corp.

Scottsdale, AZ
Leg. Issues: DOC, ECN, HCR

Outside Counsel/Consultants

The Kerry S. Pearson LLC
Issues: DOC, ECN, HCR
Rep By: Mr. Kerry S. Pearson

The Doctors' Co.

Napa, CA
Leg. Issues: GOV, HCR

Outside Counsel/Consultants

Valis Associates
Issues: GOV, HCR
Rep By: Dana W. Hudson, Hon. Richard T. Schulze, Wayne H. Valis

The Doe Fund

New York, NY
Leg. Issues: HOU

Outside Counsel/Consultants

Russ Reid Co.
Issues: HOU
Rep By: Mark D. McIntyre

The Doe Run Co.

St. Louis, MO
Leg. Issues: ENV, NAT, TAX

Outside Counsel/Consultants

Robert E. Carlstrom
Issues: ENV, NAT, TAX
Rep By: Robert E. Carlstrom, Jr.

Perkins Coie LLP
Issues: NAT
Rep By: Guy R. Martin

Dofasco, Inc.

Hamilton, CANADA

Outside Counsel/Consultants

Rogers & Wells
Rep By: Richard P. Ferrin, William Silverman

Dolce Internat'l

Montvale, NJ
Leg. Issues: RES, URB

Outside Counsel/Consultants

Capital Consultants Corp.
Issues: RES, URB
Rep By: Seth Barnhard, Michael David Kaiser

Dole Food Co.

Westlake Village, CA
Leg. Issues: AGR, BUD, HCR, TRD

Outside Counsel/Consultants

Patton Boggs, LLP
Issues: HCR, TRD
Rep By: Thomas Hale Boggs, Jr., Hon. Greg H. Laughlin, David G. Raboy, Frank R. Samolis

Schramm, Williams & Associates, Inc.
Issues: AGR, BUD
Rep By: Anita Brown, Robert Schramm

Dollar Bank

Pittsburgh, PA
Leg. Issues: BAN

Outside Counsel/Consultants

Gibson, Dunn & Crutcher LLP
Issues: BAN
Rep By: Robert C. Eager, Cantwell Faulkner Muckenfuss, III, Victoria P. Rostow

Dolphin Safe/Fair Trade Campaign

Washington, DC
Lobbies in support of dolphin protection legislation.

Leg. Issues: MAR

Outside Counsel/Consultants

Sher & Blackwell
Issues: MAR
Rep By: Earl W. Comstock, Jeffrey R. Pike

Domes Internat'l, Inc.

Golden, MS
Leg. Issues: HOU

Outside Counsel/Consultants

Shawn Coulson
Issues: HOU
Rep By: Hon. Ronald D. Coleman, William Wheeler

Domestic Petroleum Council

Washington, DC
Tel: (202)544-7100
Fax: (202)543-0616
Leg. Issues: BUD, ENG, ENV, NAT, TAX, TRD, UTI

Outside Counsel/Consultants

William F. Whitsitt Policy and Government Affairs
Issues: BUD, ENG, ENV, NAT, TAX, TRD, UTI
Rep By: William F. Whitsitt

Dominican Ass'n of Industrial Free Zones (ADOZONA)

Santo Domingo, DOMINICAN REPUBLIC

Outside Counsel/Consultants

Johnson, Rogers & Clifton, L.L.P.

Dominican College of Blauvelt

Orangeburg, NY
Leg. Issues: BUD

Outside Counsel/Consultants

Cassidy & Associates, Inc.
Issues: BUD
Rep By: Christine A. O'Connor, Diane Rinaldo, Mary E. Shields

Dominican Republic, Embassy of the

1715 22nd St. NW
Washington, DC 20008
Tel: (202)332-6280
Fax: (202)265-8507
Web: www.domrep.org
E-mail: embdomrepusa@msn.com

Outside Counsel/Consultants

Washington World Group, Ltd.
Rep By: Edward J. von Kloberg, III

Dominican State Sugar Council (CEA)

Santo Domingo, DOMINICAN REPUBLIC

Outside Counsel/Consultants

Johnson, Rogers & Clifton, L.L.P.

Dominicana de Aviacion

Santo Domingo, DOMINICAN REPUBLIC

Outside Counsel/Consultants

Johnson, Rogers & Clifton, L.L.P.

Dominion Resources, Inc.

444 N. Capitol St. NW
Suite 729
Washington, DC 20001
Tel: (202)585-4200
Fax: (202)737-3874
Registered: LDA
Web: www.domres.com

Utility industry headquartered in Richmond, VA.

Leg. Issues: BUD, CAW, ENG, ENV, FIN, FUE, NAT, TAX, TRD, UTI

In-house, DC-area Employees

CHAPMAN, Kelly G.: Manager, Federal Policy
MCKAY, Bruce C.: Manager, Federal Policy
VICTOR, Jayne L.: Director, Dominion Federal and Political Affairs

Outside Counsel/Consultants

Adams and Reese LLP
Issues: FUE, TAX
Rep By: Beverly E. Jones

Covington & Burling

Dechert

The Dutko Group, Inc.
Issues: ENG, UTI
Rep By: Robert L. Watson

Reed, Smith, LLP
Issues: ENG, UTI
Rep By: Phillips S. Peter, C. Stevens Seale, William G. Thomas

Thelen Reid & Priest LLP
Issues: FIN, UTI
Rep By: Richard Y. Roberts

Domino's Pizza

Ann Arbor, MI
Leg. Issues: LBR, TOU, TRA

Outside Counsel/Consultants

The MWW Group
Issues: LBR, TOU, TRA
Rep By: Tracey Becker, Dana P. Bostic, Jonathan B. Slade

Domtar, Inc.

Montreal, CANADA

Outside Counsel/Consultants

Covington & Burling
Rep By: Harvey M. Applebaum

Donlee Technologies, Inc.

York, PA
Leg. Issues: DEF

Outside Counsel/Consultants

The Van Fleet-Meredith Group
Issues: DEF
Rep By: M. Bruce Meredith, Paul F. Payette, Townsend A. Van Fleet

R. R. Donnelley & Sons

Chicago, IL
Registered: LDA
Leg. Issues: DEF, GOV, HCR, MAN, POS, SCI

Outside Counsel/Consultants

Dow, Lohnes & Albertson, PLLC
Rep By: J. Michael Hines, Paul R. Lang, Kenneth D. Salomon

Impact Strategies
Issues: GOV, HCR, POS, SCI
Rep By: Shannon Doyle, Jeff Fedorchak

Manatt, Phelps & Phillips, LLP
Issues: DEF
Rep By: Mary Ann Gilleece

Ryan, Phillips, Utrecht & MacKinnon
Issues: DEF, MAN, POS
Rep By: Rodney Hoppe, Jeffrey M. MacKinnon, William D. Phillips, Mark D. Planning, Thomas M. Ryan, Joseph V. Vasapoli

Donohue Industries Inc.

Montreal, CANADA
Leg. Issues: ENV

Outside Counsel/Consultants

Akin, Gump, Strauss, Hauer & Feld, L.L.P.
Issues: ENV

Doris Day Animal League

227 Massachusetts Ave. NE
Suite 100
Washington, DC 20002
Tel: (202)546-1761
Fax: (202)546-2193
Web: www.ddal.org
E-mail: info@ddal.org

In-house, DC-area Employees

AMUNDSON, Sara Jane: Deputy Director
HAZARD, Holly Elisabeth: Exec. Director

DoubleClick

Washington, DC
Tel: (202)783-0808
Leg. Issues: CSP

Outside Counsel/Consultants

Dittus Communications
Rep By: Gloria S. Dittus

Hogan & Hartson L.L.P.
Issues: CSP

Douglas Battery

Winston Salem, NC

Outside Counsel/Consultants

Interface Inc.
Rep By: Albert B. Rosenbaum, III

Douglas, Colorado, County of

Outside Counsel/Consultants

Capital Partnerships (VA) Inc.
Rep By: Robin Angle, Kenneth W. Butler, Clay Gravely

Douglas, Oregon, County of

Roseburg, OR
Leg. Issues: NAT

Outside Counsel/Consultants

Jamison and Sullivan, Inc.
Issues: NAT
Rep By: Delos Cy Jamison, Jay R. Sullivan

Dow AgroSciences

1776 I St. NW
Suite 1050
Washington, DC 20006
Tel: (202)429-3438
Fax: (202)429-3467
Registered: LDA

An agricultural chemical manufacturer. Headquartered in Indianapolis, IN.

Leg. Issues: AGR, BUD, CHM, ENV, FOO, GOV, NAT, PHA, TAX, TRD

In-house, DC-area Employees

BARROW, Craig S.: Leader, Science Policy and Regulatory Affairs
CAMPBELL, C. Thomas: Manager, Federal Government Relations
DONNELLY, Patrick J.: Global Leader, Government and Public Relations

Outside Counsel/Consultants

Alpine Group, Inc.
Issues: TRD
Rep By: James D. Massie, Richard C. White

EOP Group, Inc.
Rep By: Jonathan Gledhill, Michael O'Bannon

Podesta/Mattoon
Issues: AGR, BUD, ENV, PHA, TAX
Rep By: Anthony T. Podesta

Vickery Internat'l
Issues: TRD
Rep By: Raymond E. Vickery, Jr.

The Dow Chemical Co.

1776 I St. NW
Suite 1050
Washington, DC 20006
Tel: (202)429-3400
Fax: (202)429-3467
Registered: LDA

Headquartered in Midland, MI.

Leg. Issues: CAW, CHM, CSP, ENG, ENV, FOO, FUE, HCR, LBR, TAX, TOR, TRA, TRD

In-house, DC-area Employees

DELANEY, Wilma: V. President, Federal and State Government Affairs
FARFONE, Frank: V. President, International Affairs
MOLINARO, Peter A.: Director, Government Relations
MURRAY, James V.: Director, Government Affairs
ROGERS, Margaret: Manager, Government Relations, Environmental Policy
SAMS, Larry L.: Director, Federal Technical/Business Development
STONE, Paul D.: Director, Federal Technical/Business Development
SUAZO, Vicky M.: Manager, Government Relations and Health Issues
ULRICH, John R.: Manager, Government Relations, Environmental Policy

Outside Counsel/Consultants

EOP Group, Inc.
Rep By: Jonathan Gledhill, Michael O'Bannon

Heidepriem & Mager, Inc.
Issues: CSP
Rep By: Lisa Foster, Nikki Heidepriem

Ketchum

McKenna & Cuneo, L.L.P.

Nat'l Environmental Strategies

NES, Inc.
Issues: ENV
Rep By: Marc I. Himmelstein

Podesta/Mattoon

Quinn Gillespie & Associates

Dow Corning Corp.

1133 Connecticut Ave. NW
Suite 200
Washington, DC 20036-4305
Tel: (202)785-0585
Fax: (202)785-0421
Registered: LDA
Web: www.dowcorning.com

Manufactures silicones. Headquartered in Midland, MI.

Leg. Issues: CHM, GOV, TAX, TOR, TRD

In-house, DC-area Employees

GORMAN-GRAUL, Faye: Director, Government Relations/Washington Office

Outside Counsel/Consultants

The Duberstein Group, Inc.
Issues: GOV
Rep By: John W. Angus, III, Michael S. Berman, Steven M. Champlin, Kenneth M. Duberstein, Henry M. Gandy, Daniel P. Meyer

Dow Jones & Co., Inc.

New York, NY
Leg. Issues: CPT, TRD

Outside Counsel/Consultants

Akin, Gump, Strauss, Hauer & Feld, L.L.P.
Issues: CPT, TRD
Rep By: Katherine D. Brodie, Smith W. Davis, Donald R. Pongrace

Snavely, King, Majoros, O'Connor and Lee, Inc.
Rep By: Charles W. King

Dowling College

Oakdale, NY
Leg. Issues: EDU

Outside Counsel/Consultants

The Advocacy Group
Issues: EDU
Rep By: Robert E. Mills

Downey Financial Corp.

Newport Beach, CA
A thrift holding company.

Leg. Issues: BAN

Outside Counsel/Consultants

Manatt, Phelps & Phillips, LLP
Issues: BAN
Rep By: Robert J. Kabel, Steven J. Mulder

Downey McGrath Group, Inc.

1225 I St. NW
Suite 350
Washington, DC 20005
Tel: (202)789-1110
Fax: (202)789-1116
Registered: LDA, FARA
Web: www.dmggroup.com
Leg. Issues: ENG, ENV, HCR, TAX, TRD, WAS

In-house, DC-area Employees

ACEVEDO, Elaine B.: V. President
ALCRE, Jennifer
BERNIER, Delanne: V. President
DONALDSON, Nancy: V. President
DOWNEY, Jr., Hon. Thomas J.: Chairman
MCCLOUD, Margaret M.: Director
MCGRATH, Hon. Raymond J.: President
MCLAUGHLIN, Kathleen Tynan: Chief Operating Officer
OLINGER, John Peter: V. President
PAINTER, Sally: Managing Director, International
WESSEL, Michael R.: Senior V. President

Outside Counsel/Consultants

Leon G. Billings, Inc.
Issues: ENG, ENV, WAS
Rep By: Leon G. Billings

Michael J. Kopetski
Issues: TRD
Rep By: Michael J. Kopetski

Mark J. Raabe
Issues: HCR, TAX
Rep By: Mark J. Raabe

Downey, California, Economic Development of the City of

Leg. Issues: BUD

Outside Counsel/Consultants

E. Del Smith and Co.
Issues: BUD
Rep By: Margaret Allen, E. Del Smith

Doyon, Ltd.

Fairbanks, AK

Outside Counsel/Consultants

Van Ness Feldman, P.C.
Rep By: Alan L. Mintz

Draft Worldwide

Chicago, IL
Leg. Issues: POS

Outside Counsel/Consultants

Cassidy & Associates, Inc.
Issues: POS
Rep By: Gregory M. Gill, Michele Gioffre, Jeffrey Lawrence, Valerie Rogers Osborne, Hon. Martin A. Russo

DRAKA USA Corp.

Franklin, MA
Leg. Issues: MAR

Outside Counsel/Consultants

Cassidy & Associates, Inc.
Issues: MAR
Rep By: Carl Franklin Godfrey, Jr., Daniel J. McNamara

DRC, Inc.

Mobile, AL
Leg. Issues: DIS

Outside Counsel/Consultants

Global USA, Inc.
Issues: DIS
Rep By: Charles Duncan, George S. Kopp

Dream Center/City Help

Los Angeles, CA
Leg. Issues: HOU

Outside Counsel/Consultants

Russ Reid Co.
Issues: HOU
Rep By: Mark D. McIntyre, Jovita Wenner

Dreamtime, Inc.

Moffet Field, CA
Leg. Issues: AER, SCI, TAX

Outside Counsel/Consultants

The Wexler Group
Issues: AER, SCI, TAX
Rep By: Peter T. Holran, Hon. Robert S. Walker

Dredging Contractors of America

643 S. Washington St.
Alexandria, VA 22314
Tel: (703)518-8408
Fax: (703)518-8490
Registered: LDA
E-mail: mdsdca@kreative.net
Leg. Issues: ENV, MAR, NAT, TRA

In-house, DC-area Employees

SICKLES, Mark D.: Exec. Director

Outside Counsel/Consultants

Edmund C. Graber
Issues: TRA
Rep By: Edmund C. Graber

John C. Grzebien
Issues: ENV, MAR, NAT
Rep By: John C. Grzebien

Patton Boggs, LLP
Issues: ENV, TRA
Rep By: Philip A. Bangert

Preston Gates Ellis & Rouvelas Meeds LLP
Issues: MAR
Rep By: Bruce J. Heiman, Rolf Marshall, William N. Myhre, Mark H. Ruge

Drexel University

Philadelphia, PA
Leg. Issues: DEF

Outside Counsel/Consultants

American Defense Internat'l, Inc.
Issues: DEF
Rep By: Michael Herson, Van D. Hipp, Jr., Dave Wilberding

Drives Inc.

Fulton, MI
A manufacturer of chains, conveyor belts and power transmissions.

Leg. Issues: TRD

Outside Counsel/Consultants

Baker & McKenzie
Issues: TRD
Rep By: Susan G. Braden, Kevin M. O'Brien

DRS

Ontario, CANADA
Leg. Issues: DEF

Outside Counsel/Consultants

David O'Brien and Associates
Issues: DEF
Rep By: Wayne Arny, David D. O'Brien

DRS Precision Echo Inc.

Santa Clara, CA
Leg. Issues: DEF

Outside Counsel/Consultants

Thelen Reid & Priest LLP
Issues: DEF
Rep By: Barry I. Berkoff, Richard J. Leidl, Stephan M. Minikes

DRS Technologies, Inc.

1215 Jefferson Davis Hwy.
Suite 1004
Arlington, VA 22202
Tel: (703)416-8000
Fax: (703)416-8010
Registered: LDA
Web: www.drs.com
Headquartered in Parsippany, NJ.

Leg. Issues: AVI, DEF, TRA, TRD

In-house, DC-area Employees

ATWELL, Robert: V. President, Army Programs
BOWMAN, Michael: Sr. V. President, Washington Operations
CROCKER, Michael: V. President, Navy Programs
HANSEN, Kip L.: V. President, Government Relations

Outside Counsel/Consultants

Wayne Arny & Assoc.
Issues: DEF, TRD
Rep By: Wayne Arny, David D. O'Brien

Thelen Reid & Priest LLP
Rep By: Barry I. Berkoff, Stephan M. Minikes, Nancy K. West

Drug Strategies

1575 I St. NW
Suite 210
Washington, DC 20005
Tel: (202)289-9070
Fax: (202)414-6199
Web: www.drugstrategies.org

In-house, DC-area Employees

BRANNIGAN, Rosalind: Senior V. President, Strategic Planning
FALCO, Mathea: President

drugstore.com

Bellevue, WA
Leg. Issues: CPI, HCR, PHA

Outside Counsel/Consultants

Patton Boggs, LLP
Issues: CPI, HCR, PHA
Rep By: Daniel A. Kracov, Stuart M. Pape, Florence W. Prioleau

DSL Access Telecommunications Ass'n (DATA)

Washington, DC
Leg. Issues: TEC

Outside Counsel/Consultants

Janus-Merritt Strategies, L.L.C.
Issues: TEC
Rep By: Scott P. Hoffman, Mark J. Robertson, J. Daniel Walsh

Dubuque, Iowa, Cable Television Division of

Dubuque, IA
Leg. Issues: TEC

Outside Counsel/Consultants

Miller & Van Eaton, P.L.L.C.
Issues: TEC
Rep By: Nicholas P. Miller

Ducks Unlimited Inc.

1301 Pennsylvania Ave. NW
Suite 402
Washington, DC 20004
Tel: (202)347-1530
Fax: (202)347-1533
Registered: LDA
Web: www.ducks.org
Promotes migratory bird conservation through activities aimed at conserving and restoring natural habitat. Headquartered in Memphis, TN.

Leg. Issues: AGR, ANI, BUD, ENV, NAT, RES, TAX

In-house, DC-area Employees

ABRAHAM, Fred: Director, Conservation Policy
SUTHERLAND, Scott A.: Director, Wash. Offices and Govt. Affairs
WRINN, Dan: Government Affairs Representative

Outside Counsel/Consultants

The Accord Group
Issues: ENV
Rep By: Jeffery T. More

Duffy Internat'l

Outside Counsel/Consultants

Cook and Associates
Rep By: Sheila E. Hixson

Doris Duke Charitable Foundation

New York, NY
Leg. Issues: TAX

Outside Counsel/Consultants

Washington Council Ernst & Young
Issues: TAX
Rep By: Doug Badger, Lauren Darling, John L. Doney, Jayne T. Fitzgerald, LaBrenda Garrett-Nelson, Gary J. Gasper, Bruce A. Gates, Nick Giordano, Cathy Koch, Robert J. Leonard, Richard Meltzer, Phillip D. Moseley, John D. Porter, Robert M. Rozen, Donna Steele-Flynn, Timothy J. Urban

Duke Energy

401 Ninth St. NW
Suite 1100
Washington, DC 20004
Tel: (202)331-8090
Fax: (202)331-1181
Registered: LDA
Web: www.duke-energy.com
Headquartered in Charlotte, NC.

Leg. Issues: CAW, COM, ENG, ENV, FUE, GOV, LBR, NAT, TAX, TRA, UTI, WAS

In-house, DC-area Employees

HAYWOOD, Michael S.: Director, Federal Governmental Affairs
HENRY, Wayne O.: Director, Federal Government Affairs
MARSHALL, Beverly: V. President, Federal Government Affairs

MITCHELL, David F.: Director, EHS Federal Government Affairs
PRENDA, Brian J.: Director, Federal Government Affairs

Outside Counsel/Consultants

Governmental Strategies, Inc.

Hooper Owen & Winburn
Issues: ENG
Rep By: Daryl H. Owen

Public Affairs Group, Inc.

Duke Power Co.

Charlotte, NC
Registered: LDA

Outside Counsel/Consultants

Thelen Reid & Priest LLP

Duke Solutions

Charlotte, NC
Leg. Issues: ENG

Outside Counsel/Consultants

Van Scoyoc Associates, Inc.
Issues: ENG
Rep By: Paul Grimm

Dulles Area Transportation Ass'n

1450I Lee Jackson Memorial Hwy.
Suite A
Chantilly, VA 20151-1512
Web: www.data-trans.org
E-mail: info@data-trans.org
Tel: (703)817-1307
Fax: (703)817-1407

A non-profit transportation management organization which informs, educates and advises public and private decision-makers on actions needed to preserve mobility in the 150 square miles surrounding Washington Dulles International Airport.

Leg. Issues: ECN, ROD, TRA, URB

In-house, DC-area Employees

SMITH, Jr., Myron: Exec. Director

Dulles Networking Associates

Chantilly, VA
Leg. Issues: GOV

Outside Counsel/Consultants

Cottone and Huggins Group
Issues: GOV
Rep By: James B. Huggins

Dumex Medical

Toronto, CANADA
Leg. Issues: HCR, MMM

Outside Counsel/Consultants

Nusgart Consulting, LLC
Issues: HCR, MMM
Rep By: Marcia Nusgart

Dun & Bradstreet

1200 New Hampshire Ave. NW
Suite 440
Washington, DC 20036
Web: www.dnb.com
E-mail: cantrellj@dnb.com
Tel: (202)463-7200
Fax: (202)463-2163
Registered: LDA

A provider of business information. Headquartered in Murray Hill, NJ.

Leg. Issues: CPI, CPT, GOV, MIA

Political Action Committee/s

Political Action Committee of the Dun & Bradstreet Corporation
1200 New Hampshire Ave. NW
Suite 440
Washington, DC 20036
Contact: Jean Cantrell
Tel: (202)463-2154
Fax: (202)463-2163

In-house, DC-area Employees

CANTRELL, Jean: Exec. Director, Government Affairs

Outside Counsel/Consultants

RPB Co.
Issues: CPI, GOV
Rep By: Robert P. Bedell

Willkie Farr & Gallagher
Issues: CPT, MIA
Rep By: Theodore C. Whitehouse

Dunavant Enterprises

Memphis, TN
Leg. Issues: AGR

Outside Counsel/Consultants

Charles V. Cunningham & Assoc.
Issues: AGR
Rep By: Charles V. Cunningham

Dunc LLC

Chicago, IL
Leg. Issues: AVI

Outside Counsel/Consultants

Zuckert, Scoutt and Rasenberger, L.L.P.
Issues: AVI
Rep By: Paul E. Schoellhamer

Dunn-Edwards Corp.

Los Angeles, CA
A paint retailer.

Leg. Issues: BUD, CAW, ENV, GOV, SMB, TAX

Outside Counsel/Consultants

Dave Evans Associates
Issues: CAW
Rep By: Hon. Dave Evans

Kessler & Associates Business Services, Inc.
Issues: BUD, CAW, ENV, GOV, SMB, TAX
Rep By: Michael L. Bartlett, Howard Berman, Billy Lee Evans, Richard S. Kessler, James C. Musser, Harry Sporidis

Dunn-Padre, Inc.

Corpus Christi, TX
Leg. Issues: ENG, ENV, FUE, NAT, RES

Outside Counsel/Consultants

Williams & Jensen, P.C.
Issues: ENG, ENV, FUE, NAT, RES
Rep By: William B. Canfield, Robert J. Martinez

DuPont

601 Pennsylvania Ave. NW
Suite 325, North Bldg.
Washington, DC 20004
Web: www.dupont.com
Tel: (202)728-3600
Fax: (202)728-3649
Registered: LDA

Headquartered in Wilmington, DE.

Leg. Issues: AGR, AUT, CHM, CSP, DEF, ENG, ENV, FOO, HCR, LBR, MAN, RES, RRR, SCI, TAX, TRD

In-house, DC-area Employees

BOYKIN, C.D.: Manager, Government Affairs
HEINE, Robert M.: Director, International Trade and Investment
JACKSON, Tami S.: Manager, State Government and Public Affairs
JACOB, Thomas R.: Manager, International and Industry Affairs
JOHNSON, Nancie S.: V. President, Government Affairs
PARR, Michael: Manager, Government Affairs
WHARTON, Ellan K.: Senior Washington Counsel

Outside Counsel/Consultants

The Accord Group
Issues: AUT
Rep By: Robert F. Hurley

Birch, Horton, Bittner & Cherot
Issues: RES
Rep By: Thomas L. Albert, William P. Horn

Dickstein Shapiro Morin & Oshinsky LLP
Rep By: Graham "Rusty" Mathews, Bernard Nash

Downey McGrath Group, Inc.
Issues: AGR, DEF, ENV, RRR
Rep By: Hon. Thomas J. Downey, Jr., John Peter Olinger

Fierce and Isakowitz
Issues: AGR, CSP, ENV, FOO, HCR, SCI, TRD
Rep By: Kathryn Braden, Samantha Cook, Donald L. Fierce, Mark W. Isakowitz

Holland & Knight LLP
Issues: ENV
Rep By: Jack M. Burkman, Mike Galano, Richard M. Gold, David C. Whitestone

Denny Miller McBee Associates
Issues: DEF, LBR

Powell, Goldstein, Frazer & Murphy LLP
Issues: TRD
Rep By: Alice Slayton Clark, Simon Lazarus, III

Wilmer, Cutler & Pickering
Rep By: John D. Greenwald

DuPont Agricultural Products

Wilmington, DE
Leg. Issues: AUT, AVI, DEF, DIS, EDU, LBR, TRU

Outside Counsel/Consultants

Rooney Group Internat'l, Inc.
Issues: AUT, AVI, DEF, DIS, EDU, LBR, TRU
Rep By: Jerry L. Kaffka, James W. Rooney

The DuPont Pharmaceutical Co.

Washington, DC
Leg. Issues: HCR, TRD

Outside Counsel/Consultants

Alpine Group, Inc.
Issues: HCR, TRD
Rep By: Richard C. White

Powell, Goldstein, Frazer & Murphy LLP
Issues: TRD
Rep By: Alice Slayton Clark, Simon Lazarus, III

Duramed Pharmaceuticals, Inc.

Cincinnati, OH
Leg. Issues: PHA

Outside Counsel/Consultants

Olsson, Frank and Weeda, P.C.
Issues: PHA
Rep By: John W. Bode, Susan P. Grymes, Karen Reis Harned, Stephen L. Lacey, Marshall L. Matz, Ryan W. Stroschein, Arthur Y. Tsien, David F. Weeda

Durand Internat'l, J. G.

Milville, NJ

Outside Counsel/Consultants

Barnes, Richardson and Colburn
Rep By: Matthew T. McGrath

Durham, North Carolina, City of

Durham, NC
Leg. Issues: LAW, TRA, URB

Outside Counsel/Consultants

Capitol Link, Inc.
Issues: LAW, TRA, URB
Rep By: Hon. David M. Staton

Dutch Produce Ass'n

Breda, NETHERLANDS
Leg. Issues: TRD

Outside Counsel/Consultants

Dewey Ballantine LLP
Issues: TRD
Rep By: Jennifer Riccardi

Dykema Gossett

Washington, DC
Leg. Issues: BUD, DEF

Outside Counsel/Consultants

The Atlantic Group, Public Affairs, Inc.
Issues: BUD, DEF
Rep By: Larry F. Ayres

Dynacom Industries

Johnstown, PA

Outside Counsel/Consultants

The PMA Group
Rep By: Daniel Cunningham, Kaylene Green, Paul J. Magliocchetti

Dynamics Research Corp.

Wilmington, MA
Leg. Issues: DEF

Outside Counsel/Consultants

The PMA Group
Issues: DEF
Rep By: Daniel E. Fleming, Sean Fogarty, Kaylene Green, Dr. John Lynch, Stephen Madey, Paul J. Magliocchetti, Briggs Shade, Kelli Short, Brian Thiel, Sandra Welch

DynCorp

2000 Edmund Halley Dr.
Reston, VA 20191
Web: www.dyncorp.com
Tel: (703)264-0330
Fax: (703)715-4450
Registered: LDA

Political Action Committee/s

DynCorp Federal Political Action Committee (DYNPAC)
2000 Edmund Halley Dr.
Reston, VA 20191
Contact: Richard E. Stephenson
Tel: (703)264-9314
Fax: (703)715-4450

In-house, DC-area Employees

REICHARDT, David L.: Senior V. President and General Counsel
STEPHENSON, Richard E.: V. President, Technology and Government Relations
WHEELESS, Charlene: Director, Corporate Communications

DynCorp Aerospace Technology

Fort Worth, TX
Leg. Issues: ENV

Outside Counsel/Consultants

Colex and Associates
Issues: ENV
Rep By: John P. Mack

Dynegy, Inc.

Houston, TX
Leg. Issues: ENG, UTI

Outside Counsel/Consultants

Alpine Group, Inc.
Issues: ENG, UTI
Rep By: Rhod M. Shaw

Dyno Nobel, Inc.

Salt Lake City, UT

Outside Counsel/Consultants

David Turch & Associates
Rep By: Marilyn E. Campbell

Dystonia Medical Research Foundation

Chicago, IL
Leg. Issues: BUD, HCR

Outside Counsel/Consultants

Health and Medicine Counsel of Washington
Issues: BUD, HCR
Rep By: Staci Sigman Dennison, Dale P. Dirks

E Lottery

New York, NY
Leg. Issues: GAM

Outside Counsel/Consultants

Cassidy & Associates, Inc.
Issues: GAM
Rep By: Gerald S. J. Cassidy, Arthur D. Mason, Hon. Martin A. Russo, Dan C. Tate, Sr.

Parry, Romani, DeConcini & Symms

E*TRADE Group, Inc.

1101 Pennsylvania Ave. NW
Sixth Floor
Washington, DC 20004
Web: www.etrade.com
E-mail: bbarclay@etrade.com
Tel: (202)756-7750
Fax: (202)756-7545
Registered: LDA

An online broker headquartered in Menlo Park, CA.

Leg. Issues: BAN, CPI, ECN, FIN, SCI

Political Action Committee/s

E*Trade PAC
1101 Pennsylvania Ave. NW
Sixth Floor
Washington, DC 20004
Contact: Betsy Barclay
Tel: (202)756-7750
Fax: (202)756-7545

In-house, DC-area Employees

BARCLAY, Betsy: V. President of Government Affairs
WADE, Tara: Legislative Policy Analyst

E*TRADE Securities, Inc.

Palo Alto, CA
Leg. Issues: CPI, FIN

Outside Counsel/Consultants

Thelen Reid & Priest LLP
Issues: CPI, FIN
Rep By: Richard Y. Roberts

E-Commerce Coalition

Washington, DC
Leg. Issues: TAX

Outside Counsel/Consultants

Ernst & Young LLP
Issues: TAX
Rep By: Lauren Darling, Patrick G. Heck, Phillip D. Moseley, Henry C. Ruempler, Donna Steele-Flynn

E-Commerce Payment Coalition

Washington, DC
Leg. Issues: GAM

Outside Counsel/Consultants

Greenberg Traurig, LLP
Issues: GAM
Rep By: Ronald L. Platt, Shana Tesler

E-LOAN, Inc.

Dublin, CA
Leg. Issues: BAN

Outside Counsel/Consultants

Podesta/Mattoon
Issues: BAN
Rep By: Timothy Powers, Edwin S. Rothschild

E-Prime Aerospace

Titusville, FL

An aerospace company marketing rocket booster for satellite placement.

Leg. Issues: AER

Outside Counsel/Consultants

Symms, Lehn & Associates, Inc.
Issues: AER

E-Tech

Hamilton, BERMUDA

Outside Counsel/Consultants

Baker, Donelson, Bearman & Caldwell, P.C.
Rep By: Doreen M. Edelman, Charles R. Johnston, Jr.

E.I. du Pont de Nemours & Co.

Wilmington, DE

Outside Counsel/Consultants

Fierce and Isakowitz

E.ON North America, Inc.

New York, NY
Leg. Issues: ECN, ENG, TRD

Outside Counsel/Consultants

Global Policy Group, Inc.
Issues: ECN, ENG, TRD
Rep By: Douglas J. Bergner

e.spire Communications, Inc.

Annapolis, MD
Leg. Issues: TEC

Outside Counsel/Consultants

Greenberg Traurig, LLP
Issues: TEC
Rep By: Mitchell F. Brecher

E.ssociation

Outside Counsel/Consultants

Alcalde & Fay
Rep By: J. B. Hancock

Eagle River, LLC

Kirkland, WA
Leg. Issues: TEC

Outside Counsel/Consultants

Communications Consultants, Inc.
Issues: TEC
Rep By: R. Gerard Salemme

Eagle-Picher Industries

Cincinnati, OH
Leg. Issues: TAX, TRA

Outside Counsel/Consultants

Crowell & Moring LLP
Issues: TAX
Rep By: Harold J. Heltzer

Patton Boggs, LLP
Issues: TRA
Rep By: Eric A. Kuwana

Eagle-Picher Personal Injury Settlement Trust

Savannah, GA
Leg. Issues: TAX

Outside Counsel/Consultants

Arthur Andersen LLP
Issues: TAX
Rep By: Rosemary D. Becchi, Rachelle Bernstein, Glenn Carrington, Weston J. Coulam, Warren Farb

Baker & Hostetler LLP
Issues: TAX
Rep By: Matthew J. Dolan, Frederick H. Graefe, Richard H. Hauser, Steven A. Lotterer, David L. Marshall, Hon. Guy Vander Jagt

Early Childhood Development Center Legislative Coalition

3612 Bent Branch Ct.
Falls Church, VA 22041
Tel: (703)941-4329
Fax: (703)941-4329
Registered: LDA

In-house, DC-area Employees

TOBIN, Dr. William J.: Exec. Director

Outside Counsel/Consultants

William J. Tobin and Associates

Early Learning Years Institute

Concerned with the education and administration of children from Headstart through third grade.

Outside Counsel/Consultants

TASC, Inc., Association Management
Rep By: Randy Dyer, CAE

Earth Share

3400 International Dr. NW
Suite 2K
Washington, DC 20008
Web: www.earthshare.org
E-mail: info@earthshare.org
Tel: (202)537-7100
Fax: (202)537-7101

A coalition of 44 environmental charities who work nationally and internationally to protect human health and the environment.

In-house, DC-area Employees

STEIN, Kalman: President

Earth University, Inc.

San Jose, COSTA RICA
Leg. Issues: EDU

Outside Counsel/Consultants

Russ Reid Co.
Issues: EDU
Rep By: Thomas C. Keller, Mark D. McIntyre, Jovita Wenner

Earth, Energy & Environment

Shawnee, KS
Leg. Issues: ENG

Outside Counsel/Consultants

Wiley, Rein & Fielding
Issues: ENG
Rep By: James T. Bruce, III, Hon. Jim Slattery

EarthData Holdings

45 W. Watkins Mill Rd.
Gaithersburg, MD 20878
Web: www.earthdata.com
Tel: (301)948-8550
Fax: (301)963-2064

Formerly known as Photo Science, Inc. A mapping/GIS consulting firm.

Leg. Issues: AVI, BUD, DOC, ENV, GOV

In-house, DC-area Employees

LOGAN, Bryan J.: Chief Exec. Officer

Outside Counsel/Consultants

Collins & Company, Inc.
Issues: BUD
Rep By: James D. Bond, Richard L. Collins, Thomas A. Hooper, Shay D. Stautz

John M. Palatiello & Associates
Issues: AVI, DOC, ENV, GOV
Rep By: John M. Palatiello

Earthjustice Legal Defense Fund

1625 Massachusetts Ave. NW
Suite 702
Washington, DC 20036
Web: www.earthjustice.org
E-mail: eajusdc@earthjustice.org
Tel: (202)667-4500
Fax: (202)667-2356
Registered: LDA

Formerly known as the Sierra Club Legal Defense Fund.

Leg. Issues: ANI, CAW, NAT

In-house, DC-area Employees

FOX, Howard I.: Managing Attorney
HAYDEN, Martin: Legislative Director

Earthshell Container Corp.

Santa Barbara, CA
Leg. Issues: ENV

Outside Counsel/Consultants

Alcalde & Fay
Issues: ENV
Rep By: Thomas A. Cortina, Kevin J. Fay, Kris Hathaway, Kathy Jurado Munoz

EarthVoice

Washington, DC
Leg. Issues: FOR

Outside Counsel/Consultants

Gustafson Associates
Issues: FOR
Rep By: Robert C. Gustafson

EarthWatch, Inc.

Longmont, CO
Leg. Issues: AER, SCI, TEC

Outside Counsel/Consultants

Capitol Coalitions Inc.
Issues: TEC
Rep By: Brett P. Scott

The Wexler Group
Issues: AER, SCI
Rep By: Peter T. Holran, Anne Jones, Patric G. Link, Hon. Robert S. Walker

East Bay Municipal Utility District

Oakland, CA
Wastewater treatment and water supply utility district.

Leg. Issues: BUD, CAW, ENV, NAT

Outside Counsel/Consultants

ENS Resources, Inc.
Issues: BUD, CAW, ENV, NAT
Rep By: Eric Sapirstein

Perkins Coie LLP
Issues: NAT
Rep By: Guy R. Martin

East Chicago Public Housing Authority

East Chicago, IN

Outside Counsel/Consultants

Krivit & Krivit, P.C.
Rep By: Daniel H. Krivit

East Coast Tuna Ass'n

Salem, NH

Outside Counsel/Consultants

Garvey, Schubert & Barer
Rep By: Eldon V. C. Greenberg

East Palo Alto, California, City of

Outside Counsel/Consultants

Spiegel & McDiarmid

East Tennessee Economic Council

Leg. Issues: BUD, ECN

Outside Counsel/Consultants

Preston Gates Ellis & Rouvelas Meeds LLP
Issues: BUD, ECN
Rep By: Tim L. Peckinpaugh

East Texas Electric Cooperative

Nacogdoches, TX
Leg. Issues: BUD, ENG, GOV, TAX, UTI

Outside Counsel/Consultants

Brickfield, Burchette, Ritts & Stone
Issues: BUD, ENG, GOV, TAX, UTI
Rep By: William H. Burchette, Colleen Newman, Christine C. Ryan

East Valley Water District

San Bernardino, CA
Leg. Issues: ENV

Outside Counsel/Consultants

Hicks-Richardson Associates
Issues: ENV
Rep By: Carol A. Hicks, Fred B. Hicks

East/West Industries

Leg. Issues: DEF

Outside Counsel/Consultants

American Defense Internat'l, Inc.
Issues: DEF
Rep By: Michael Herson, Van D. Hipp, Jr., Bonnie Shindelman, Dave Wilberding

Easter Seals

700 13th St. NW
Suite 200
Washington, DC 20005
Tel: (202)347-3066
Fax: (202)737-7914
Registered: LDA
Web: www.easter-seals.org

A nonprofit health organization headquartered in Chicago, Illinois.

Leg. Issues: AGR, BUD, CIV, EDU, HCR, HOU, INS, LBR, MMM, POS, SCI, TAX, TEC, TRA, WEL

In-house, DC-area Employees

DEXTER, Jennifer: Senior Government Relations Specialist
KRAMER, Donald J.: Senior Information Specialist
NEAS, Katy Beh: Assistant V. President, Government Relations
ROMER, Joseph D.: Exec. V. President, Public Affairs
RUTTA, Randall L.: Senior V. President, Government Relations
TIERNAN, Christopher: Assistant V. President, Government Relations

Outside Counsel/Consultants

Simon and Co., Inc.
Issues: TRA
Rep By: Heather Barber, Alex DeGood, Leonard S. Simon

Eastern Band of Cherokee Indians

Cherokee, NC
Leg. Issues: AGR, IND

Outside Counsel/Consultants

George Waters Consulting Service
Rep By: George Waters

Winston & Strawn
Issues: AGR, IND
Rep By: Hon. Beryl F. Anthony, Jr., Hon. John L. Napier

Eastern College

St. David's, PA

Outside Counsel/Consultants

Russ Reid Co.

Eastern Mennonite University

Harrisonburg, VA

Outside Counsel/Consultants

Russ Reid Co.

Eastern Municipal Water District

Perris, CA
Leg. Issues: BUD, NAT

Outside Counsel/Consultants

Will and Carlson, Inc.
Issues: BUD, NAT
Rep By: Peter Carlson, Robert P. Will

Eastern Pequot Indians

North Stonington, CT

Outside Counsel/Consultants

The Dutko Group, Inc.
Rep By: Ronald C. Kaufman, Kimberly M. Spaulding

Eastern Pilots Ass'n

A labor bargaining organization whose members are primarily company loyalists and pilots newly hired in 1989 and 1990 to replace striking pilots.

Outside Counsel/Consultants

Heenan, Althen & Roles

Eastman Chemical Co.

1300 Wilson Blvd.
Suite 900
Arlington, VA 22209
Tel: (703)524-7700
Fax: (703)524-7707
Registered: LDA
Web: www.eastman.com
Leg. Issues: BUD, CHM, CPT, CSP, ENG, ENV, FOO, GOV, HCR, IMM, LBR, SCI, TOB, TOR, TRD

Political Action Committee/s

EASTPAC
1300 Wilson Blvd.
Suite 900
Arlington, VA 22209
Tel: (703)524-7700
Fax: (703)524-7707

In-house, DC-area Employees

JOHNSON, D. Lynn: V. President, Government Relations
RIDDLE, Gregory A.: Government Relations Associate
SCHLOESSER, Lynn L.: Director, Federal Affairs

Outside Counsel/Consultants

The Direct Impact Co.

Koleda Childress & Co.
Rep By: James M. Childress

McGuireWoods L.L.P.
Issues: TOB
Rep By: Frank B. Atkinson, Stephen A. Katsurinis, Anne Marie Whittemore

Eastman Kodak Co.

1250 H St. NW
Suite 800
Washington, DC 20005
Tel: (202)857-3400
Fax: (202)857-3401
Registered: LDA
Web: www.kodak.com

Headquartered in Rochester, NY.

Leg. Issues: AER, CPT, DEF, ENV, HCR, LBR, MMM, TEC, TRD

In-house, DC-area Employees

ALEXANDER, Stephen: Director, Technology and Environmental Affairs
JARMAN, Richard B.: Director, Advanced Manufacturing Affairs
JONES, Diane R.: Director, Health Imaging Affairs
NORD, Nancy A.: Director, Federal Government Affairs
PADILLA, Christopher A.: Director, International Trade Relations
PLASTER, Amy S.: Director, Workforce Policy
TAYLOR, Sandra E.: V. President and Director, Public Affairs

Outside Counsel/Consultants

Arent Fox Kintner Plotkin & Kahn, PLLC
Issues: HCR, MMM, TEC
Rep By: Bill Applegate, Robert J. Waters

The National Group, LLP
Rep By: Vincent M. Versage

The Potomac Advocates
Issues: AER, DEF
Rep By: Charles Scalera, Gary L. Sojka

The Washington Group

Easton Airport

Easton, MD
Leg. Issues: AVI, BUD

Outside Counsel/Consultants

Kimberly Consulting, LLC
Issues: AVI, BUD
Rep By: Richard H. Kimberly

Eaton Corp., Cutler Hammer

Pittsburgh, PA
Leg. Issues: DEF

Outside Counsel/Consultants

Manatt, Phelps & Phillips, LLP
Issues: DEF
Rep By: Mary Ann Gilleece, Jeff Kuhnreich

Eaton Vance Management Co.

Boston, MA
Leg. Issues: BUD, TAX

Outside Counsel/Consultants

Washington Council Ernst & Young
Issues: BUD, TAX
Rep By: Doug Badger, Lauren Darling, John L. Doney, Jayne T. Fitzgerald, LaBrenda Garrett-Nelson, Gary J. Gasper, Bruce A. Gates, Nick Giordano, Cathy Koch, Robert J. Leonard, Richard Meltzer, Phillip D. Moseley, John D. Porter, Robert M. Rozen, Donna Steele-Flynn, Timothy J. Urban

eBay Inc.

555 13th St. NW
Suite 300
Washington, DC 20004
Tel: (202)637-5981
Fax: (202)637-5940
Registered: LDA
Web: www.ebay.com

Headquartered in San Jose, CA.

Leg. Issues: ADV, AUT, BAN, CPI, CPT, CSP, IMM, LAW, LBR, SCI, TAX, TRD

Political Action Committee/s

eBay Inc. Committee for Responsible Internet Commerce
555 13th St. NW
Suite 300
Washington, DC 20004
Tel: (202)637-5981
Fax: (202)637-5940

In-house, DC-area Employees

COHEN, Tod: Director of Government Affairs
SIGNORINO, Marc-Anthony: Policy Analyst

Outside Counsel/Consultants

Davidson & Company, Inc.
Issues: CPI, TAX
Rep By: James H. Davidson, Richard E. May, Stanley Sokul

Hogan & Hartson L.L.P.
Rep By: Lance D. Bultena, Nancy Granese, Hon. Robert H. Michel, Corey Roush, Christine A. Varney

Morrison & Foerster LLP
Issues: CPT
Rep By: Jonathan Band

Podesta/Mattoon
Issues: CPI
Rep By: Claudia James

Smith & Metalitz, L.L.P.
Issues: CPI
Rep By: Steven J. Metalitz

EBS Dealing Resources Inc.

London, UNITED KINGDOM
A foreign currency trader.

Outside Counsel/Consultants

Cleary, Gottlieb, Steen and Hamilton

EC-MAC

Outside Counsel/Consultants

Alcalde & Fay
Rep By: Paul Schlesinger, Tim Stroud

ECC Internat'l Corp.

Orlando, FL
Leg. Issues: AER, CPI, DEF

Outside Counsel/Consultants

The Legislative Strategies Group, LLC
Issues: DEF
Rep By: Melvin J. Littig, Grayson Winterling

Rooney Group Internat'l, Inc.
Issues: AER, CPI, DEF
Rep By: James W. Rooney

Ecclesiastical Associates

Garden City, NY

Outside Counsel/Consultants

William J. Tobin and Associates

eCharge Corp.

Seattle, WA
Leg. Issues: FIN, TEC

Outside Counsel/Consultants

Cassidy & Associates, Inc.
Issues: FIN, TEC
Rep By: Christy Carson Evans, W. Campbell Kaufman, IV, Maureen Walsh

Echo Bay Mining

Juneau, AK

Outside Counsel/Consultants

McClure, Gerard & Neuenschwander, Inc.
Rep By: Steven G. Barringer, Joseph T. Findaro, Matthew Iandoli, Nils W. Johnson, Hon. James A. McClure, Tod O. Neuenschwander

Robertson, Monagle & Eastaugh
Rep By: James F. Clark, Steven W. Silver

EchoStar Communications Corp.

1233 20th St. NW
Suite 701
Washington, DC 20036
Tel: (202)293-0981
Fax: (202)293-0984
Registered: LDA

A satellite broadcasting company headquartered in Littleton, CO.

Leg. Issues: COM, CPT, TEC

Political Action Committee/s

EchoStar Communications Corp. PAC
1233 20th St. NW
Suite 701
Washington, DC 20036
Tel: (202)293-0981
Fax: (202)293-0984

In-house, DC-area Employees

WATSON, Karen: Director, Government and Public Affairs

Outside Counsel/Consultants

Janus-Merritt Strategies, L.L.C.
Issues: COM, TEC
Rep By: Scott P. Hoffman, Bethany Noble, Mark J. Robertson, J. Daniel Walsh

Patton Boggs, LLP
Issues: COM, TEC
Rep By: Bill Bright, Elena Giberga, Clayton L. Hough, John S. Shaw, Jonathan R. Yarowsky

Steptoe & Johnson LLP

ECI Telecom Ltd.

Petah Tikva, ISRAEL

Develops, manufactures, and distributes products for the telecommunications industry.

Outside Counsel/Consultants

Arnold & Porter

Eclipse

St. Petersburg, FL

Outside Counsel/Consultants

The Potomac Advocates
Rep By: Charles Scalera, Gary L. Sojka

Eclipse Energy Systems, Inc./Insyte, Inc.

Tampa, FL
Leg. Issues: BUD, ENG, TRA

Outside Counsel/Consultants

Duncan, Weinberg, Genzer & Pembroke, P.C.
Issues: ENG
Rep By: Jeffrey C. Genzer

Martin G. Hamberger & Associates
Issues: BUD, ENG, TRA
Rep By: Brian M. Tynan

Eclipse Surgical Technologies

Leg. Issues: HCR

Outside Counsel/Consultants

Reed, Smith, LLP
Issues: HCR
Rep By: Phillips S. Peter

Ecological and Toxicological Ass'n of Dyes and Organic Pigments Manufacturers

1850 M St. NW
Suite 700
Washington, DC 20036
Web: www.etad.com
E-mail: info@etad.com
Tel: (202)721-4154
Fax: (202)296-8120

Formed to address health and environmental issues associated with dyes and headquartered in Basel, Switzerland.

In-house, DC-area Employees

HELMES, Dr. C. Tucker: Exec. Director

Ecological Soc. of America

1707 H St. NW
Suite 400
Washington, DC 20006
Web: www.esa.sdsc.edu
E-mail: esahq@esa.org
Tel: (202)833-8773
Fax: (202)833-8775

Promotes the scientific study of organisms in relation to their environment, facilitates the exchange of ideas among those interested in ecology, and increases public knowledge and understanding of the environment.

In-house, DC-area Employees

LYMN, Nadine: Director, Public Affairs
MCCARTER, Katherine S.: Exec. Director

Ecology and Environment

Lancaster, NY

Outside Counsel/Consultants

Interface Inc.
Rep By: Rudy R. Nessel

Economic Development Alliance of Jefferson County, Arkansas

Leg. Issues: TRA

Outside Counsel/Consultants

Arent Fox Kintner Plotkin & Kahn, PLLC
Issues: TRA
Rep By: Todd Weiss

Economic Policy Institute

1660 L St. NW
Suite 1200
Washington, DC 20036
Web: www.epinet.org
E-mail: epi@epinet.org
Tel: (202)775-8810
Fax: (202)775-0819

A non-profit, non-partisan think tank that seeks to broaden the public debate about strategies to achieve a prosperous and fair economy.

In-house, DC-area Employees

APPELBAUM, Eileen: Associate Research Director
BARRETT, Jim: Economist
BERNSTEIN, Jared: Economist
FAUX, Jeff: President
GIBSON, Nan: Communications Director
MISHEL, Lawrence R.: Research Director
RASELL, M. Edith: Economist
SAWICKY, Max B.: Economist
SCOTT, Robert E.: Economist

Economic Strategy Institute

1401 H St. NW
Suite 560
Washington, DC 20005
Web: www.econstrat.org
Tel: (202)289-1288
Fax: (202)289-1319

Founded to increase national awareness of underlying American economic problems. Non-partisan research and outreach activities focus on the development of a comprehensive strategy to maintain American economic competitiveness.

In-house, DC-area Employees

PRESTOWITZ, Jr., Clyde V.: President

Economics America

New York, NY
Leg. Issues: BUD, EDU

Outside Counsel/Consultants

Dean Blakey & Moskowitz
Issues: BUD, EDU
Rep By: Ellin J. Nolan

The Economist Newspaper Group

New York, NY

Outside Counsel/Consultants

Neuman and Co.
Rep By: Robert A. Neuman

Ecuador, Government of the Republic of

San Salvador, ECUADOR

Outside Counsel/Consultants

Hughes Hubbard & Reed LLP
Rep By: Catherine Curtiss

Ed XL PAC

1530 33rd St. NW
Washington, DC 20007

In-house, DC-area Employees

HATCH, Paul D.: PAC Administrator

ED&F Man Inc.

New York, NY
Leg. Issues: TRD

Outside Counsel/Consultants

Mayer, Brown & Platt
Issues: TRD
Rep By: Penny L. Eastman, Jeffrey H. Lewis, Carolyn P. Osolinik, Richard S. Williamson

Eddie Bauer Co.

Redmond, WA
Leg. Issues: TAX, TRD

Outside Counsel/Consultants

The Petrizzo Group, Inc.
Issues: TAX, TRD
Rep By: Kara Kennedy, Thomas "T.J." Petrizzo

Edelman Public Relations Worldwide

1875 I St. NW
Suite 900
Washington, DC 20005
Web: www.edelman.com
Tel: (202)371-0200
Fax: (202)371-2858
Registered: LDA, FARA

Leg. Issues: FOO, HCR, MED, PHA

In-house, DC-area Employees

CIMKO, Christine Kelly: V. President, Image and Events
DACH, Leslie: V. Chairman
DEAVER, Michael K.: V. Chairman, International Relations
DIGGS, Carol: V. President
FLIEGER, Neal: General Manger
HAUPT, Chris: V. President
HOFFMAN, Eric: V. President
KEENUM, Rhonda: Senior V. President
KNOTT, Bob: V. President
MACHOWSKY, Martin: Senior V. President
PUZO, Daniel: Senior V. President
REHG, Robert: General Manager
SCHMIDT, John: Senior V. President
SEGALL, Peter: Exec. V. President and Deputy General Manager
SULLIVAN, Jere: Exec. V. President and Deputy General Manager
SURRELL, Jeffrey: Senior V. President
TAYLOR, Chuck: Senior V. President
TSAPATSARIS, Julianne: V. President
VANDYKE, Tish: V. President
ZINGMAN, Ben: Senior V. President, Public Affairs and Crisis Communications

Outside Counsel/Consultants

Dalrymple and Associates, L.L.C.
Issues: FOO, HCR, MED, PHA
Rep By: Donald "Dack" Dalrymple

Eden Financial Corp.

San Angelo, TX
Leg. Issues: TAX

Outside Counsel/Consultants

Washington Council Ernst & Young
Issues: TAX
Rep By: Doug Badger, Lauren Darling, John L. Doney, Jayne T. Fitzgerald, LaBrenda Garrett-Nelson, Gary J. Gasper, Bruce A. Gates, Nick Giordano, Robert J. Leonard, Richard Meltzer, Phillip D. Moseley, John D. Porter, Robert M. Rozen, Donna Steele-Flynn, Timothy J. Urban

Edenspace Systems Corp.

Reston, VA
Leg. Issues: ENV

Outside Counsel/Consultants

Jenner & Block

Markcorp Inc.
Issues: ENV
Rep By: Michael Clark

Edison Chouest Offshore, Inc.

Galliano, LA
Leg. Issues: DEF, LBR, MAR

Outside Counsel/Consultants

Charlie McBride Associates, Inc.
Issues: DEF, LBR, MAR
Rep By: Charlie McBride

Edison Community College

Fort Myers, FL
Leg. Issues: ECN

Outside Counsel/Consultants

John C. Grzebien
Issues: ECN
Rep By: John C. Grzebien

Edison Electric Institute

701 Pennsylvania Ave. NW
Washington, DC 20004-2696
Tel: (202)508-5000
Registered: LDA
Web: www.eei.org

A trade association for U.S. shareholder-owned electric utility companies, international affiliates, and industry associates worldwide.

Leg. Issues: BUD, CAW, CSP, DEF, DOC, ENG, ENV, GOV, LBR, NAT, TAX, TRA, UTI, WAS

Political Action Committee/s

Power PAC of the Edison Electric Institute

701 Pennsylvania Ave. NW
Washington, DC 20004-2696
Tel: (202)508-5777
Fax: (202)508-5403
Contact: Hannah Spillman-Simone

In-house, DC-area Employees

ANTHONY, Edwin: V. President, Member Relations and Corporate Secretary
BAILEY, Paul: V. President, Environmental
BEHNKE, Carl D.: V. President, Human Resources and Corporate Services
BODDIE, Judith Ann: Senior Governmental Affairs Representative
BOZEK, C. Richard: Manager, Environmental Programs
BRIER, M. William: V. President, Communication
CLEMENTS, Ronald: Director, Governmental Affairs
COMER, Edward H.: V. President, General Counsel
DAVIS, Fred G.: Director, Governmental Affairs
EASTON, Jr., John J.: V. President, International Programs
FANG, William: Associate General Counsel, Industry Affairs
HAGMANN, Patrice: Media Relations Representative
HUNT, Margaret: Director, Government Relations
KELLY, Charles J.: Manager, Human Resource, Regulatory and Legislative Issues
KENKEL, Mary: Director, Public Policy and Issue Management
KINSMAN, John: Manager, Atmospheric Science
KUHN, Thomas R.: President
LEMASTER, Lynn: Senior V. President, Policy, Issue Management and Internal Operations
LOUGHERY, Richard M.: Director, Environmental Programs
LUKEN, David D.: Director, Government Relations
MCGRATH, K. Michael: Group Director, Energy Supply
MCMAHON, Richard: Group Director, Energy Supply
NEUMANN, E. John: V. President, Government Affairs
NOVAK, John: Director, Environmental Programs
ODOM, Jr., James C. "Cal": Senior Legislative Representative
OWENS, David K.: Exec. V. President, Business Operations
ROSSLER, Michael: Manager, Environmental Programs
SPILLMAN-SIMONE, Hannah: Manager, Political Programs
STECKELBERG, Kathryn A.: Director, Government Relations
YAWN, Edward R.: Director, Government Relations

Outside Counsel/Consultants

ADA Consulting Services
Issues: CAW, ENG, ENV

Arter & Hadden
Issues: UTI
Rep By: Daniel L. Cohen

Baker & Hostetler LLP
Issues: TAX
Rep By: William F. Conroy, Matthew J. Dolan, Frederick H. Graefe, Steven A. Lotterer, Hon. Guy Vander Jagt

Ray Billups
Issues: ENG, UTI
Rep By: Ray Billups

Bill Carney & Co.
Issues: CAW, ENG, ENV, TAX, UTI
Rep By: Jacqueline Carney, Hon. William Carney

Clark & Weinstock, Inc.
Issues: ENG
Rep By: Ed Kutler, Deirdre Stach, Sandi Stuart, Hon. John Vincent "Vin" Weber

Ralf Czepluch
Issues: ENV, TAX, UTI
Rep By: Ralf W. K. Czepluch

Thomas J. Dennis
Issues: CAW, TAX, UTI
Rep By: Thomas J. Dennis

EOP Group, Inc.
Issues: BUD, ENG, ENV
Rep By: Jonathan Gledhill, Joseph Hezir, Troy Hillier, Jan Mares, Corey McDaniel, Michael O'Bannon

Ernst & Young LLP
Issues: TAX
Rep By: Lauren Darling, Patrick G. Heck, Phillip D. Moseley, Henry C. Ruempler, Donna Steele-Flynn

Jack Ferguson Associates, Inc.
Issues: UTI, WAS
Rep By: Jack Ferguson

Fierce and Isakowitz
Issues: ENG, ENV, UTI
Rep By: Mark W. Isakowitz, Diane Moery

Hunton & Williams
Rep By: John J. Adams, F. William Brownell, C. King Mallory, III, Henry V. Nickel, Turner T. Smith, Jr.

Mayer, Brown & Platt
Issues: ENV
Rep By: David B. Finnegan

McGlotten & Jarvis
Issues: UTI
Rep By: John T. Jarvis, Robert M. McGlotten

Multinat'l Government Services, Inc.
Issues: BUD, ENG, GOV
Rep By: Ken Glozer

Nat'l Environmental Strategies
Issues: CAW
Rep By: Marc I. Himmelstein

Walker F. Nolan
Issues: ENG, ENV, UTI
Rep By: Walker F. Nolan

O'Connor & Hannan, L.L.P.
Rep By: Thomas H. Quinn

Oldaker and Harris, LLP
Issues: ENG
Rep By: Walker F. Nolan, William C. Oldaker

Piper Marbury Rudnick & Wolfe LLP
Issues: ENV, WAS
Rep By: William R. Weissman

PriceWaterhouseCoopers
Issues: TAX
Rep By: Kenneth J. Kies, Pat Raffaniello

Public Strategies Washington, Inc.
Issues: UTI
Rep By: Nancy O'Neall, Joseph P. O'Neill, Paul M. Snyder

The Renkes Group, Ltd.
Issues: ENG
Rep By: Gregg D. Renkes

RGS Enterprises, Inc.
Issues: CAW, ENG, ENV
Rep By: Ronald G. Sykes

Ryan, Phillips, Utrecht & MacKinnon
Issues: ENG, UTI
Rep By: Rodney Hoppe, Jeffrey M. MacKinnon, William D. Phillips, Mark D. Planning, Thomas M. Ryan, Joseph V. Vasapoli

David Senter & Associates
Issues: UTI
Rep By: David L. Senter

Stuntz, Davis & Staffier, P.C.
Issues: ENG
Rep By: Ellen S. Young

Thelen Reid & Priest LLP
Issues: TAX
Rep By: Howard A. Cooper, Raymond F. Dacek

Edison Industrial Systems Center

Toledo, OH
Leg. Issues: SCI

Outside Counsel/Consultants

Wilson & Wilson
Issues: SCI
Rep By: Robert Dale Wilson

Edison Internat'l

555 Twelfth St. NW
Suite 640
Washington, DC 20004
Tel: (202)393-3075
Fax: (202)393-1497
Registered: LDA

Headquartered in Rosemead, CA.

Leg. Issues: BUD, CAW, ENG, ENV, FOR, GOV, NAT, SCI, TAX, TRA, UTI

In-house, DC-area Employees

GAULT, Polly L.: V. President, Washington Region
QUINN, Gloria
SANTOS, Barbara J.: Business Analyst
STARCK, Leslie E.: Manager, Federal Regulatory Affairs, Southern California Edison

Outside Counsel/Consultants

Akin, Gump, Strauss, Hauer & Feld, L.L.P.

Fierce and Isakowitz
Issues: ENG, UTI
Rep By: Samantha Cook, Diane Moery

Hall, Estill, Hardwick, Gable, Golden & Nelson

Johnston & Associates, LLC
Issues: BUD, ENG, ENV, GOV, SCI, TAX, UTI
Rep By: Hon. J. Bennett Johnston, N. Hunter Johnston, Eric Tober

Stuntz, Davis & Staffier, P.C.
Issues: TAX, UTI

Edison Mission Energy

Washington, DC
Registered: LDA
Leg. Issues: FOR, TRD, UTI

Outside Counsel/Consultants

Jefferson-Waterman Internat'l, LLC
Issues: FOR, TRD
Rep By: Ann B. Wrobleski

Mayer, Brown & Platt
Rep By: John P. Schmitz

The Edison Project

New York, NY
Leg. Issues: EDU

Outside Counsel/Consultants

Wiley, Rein & Fielding
Issues: EDU
Rep By: James T. Bruce, III

Edison Properties L.L.C.

Newark, NJ
Leg. Issues: RES

Outside Counsel/Consultants

Royer & Babyak
Issues: RES
Rep By: Robert Stewart Royer

Edison Welding Institute

Columbus, OH
Leg. Issues: DEF

Outside Counsel/Consultants

Jefferson Government Relations, L.L.C.
Issues: DEF
Rep By: William J. Gilmartin, Katherine M. Krauser

Editorial Information Network

Outside Counsel/Consultants

Dittus Communications
Rep By: Trudi Boyd, Gloria S. Dittus, Paul Wieland

EdLinc

Washington, DC
Leg. Issues: TEC

Outside Counsel/Consultants

Leslie Harris & Associates
Issues: TEC
Rep By: Jill Bond, Leslie A. Harris, Aleck Johnson, Jee Hang Lee, Ghani Raines

Edmund Scientific Co.

Burke, VA
Leg. Issues: BUD, CSP, DEF, GOV, LBR, POS, TAX, TEC, TRD

Outside Counsel/Consultants

Marshall A. Brachman
Issues: BUD, CSP, GOV, POS, TAX, TEC
Rep By: Marshall A. Brachman

The Eagles Group
Issues: DEF, LBR, TRD
Rep By: Terence Costello

EDS Corp.

1331 Pennsylvania Ave. NW
Suite 1300 North
Washington, DC 20004
Tel: (202)637-6700
Fax: (202)637-6759
Registered: LDA

An information/technology services company headquartered in Plano, TX.

Leg. Issues: AVI, BAN, BUD, COM, CPI, CPT, DEF, EDU, FIN, GOV, HCR, HOU, IMM, INS, LAW, MMM, SCI, TAX, TEC, TRD

Political Action Committee/s

EDS PAC
1331 Pennsylvania Ave. NW
Suite 1300 North
Washington, DC 20004
Tel: (202)637-6702
Fax: (202)637-6759
Contact: Virginia D. Bancroft

In-house, DC-area Employees

ANDERSON, Jeffrey: Director, International Relations
BANCROFT, Virginia D.: Director, Global Government Affairs
DOVE, Randolph V.: Exec. Director, Government Relations
FRANZ, Liesyl: Director, Financial Industry Policy
JAMESON, Booth S.: Director, Global Government Affairs
LYNN, John B.: Director, Telecommunications Policy
MCALISTER-BUNN, Lynn: Director; Healthcare Policy
MYERS, Karen M.: Director, Tax Policy
POULOS, Bill N.: Director, Electronic Commerce Policy
REESE, Rebecca: Director, International Economic Policy
SWEENEY, Jr., William R.: V. President, Global Affairs
WARD, Stephen D.: Government Affairs Director, Navy and Federal Programs

Outside Counsel/Consultants

The Conaway Group LLC
Issues: DEF
Rep By: Lt. Gen. John B. Conaway, USAF (Ret.), James L. Hobgood

Education and Research Institute

800 Maryland Ave. NE
Washington, DC 20002
Tel: (202)546-1710
Fax: (202)546-3489
Web: www.eri.org
E-mail: njc@dc.infi.net

ERI is a tax-exempt educational organization devoted to advancing a greater awareness and understanding of America's traditional values. Main program is the National Journalism Center, a journalism internship training program.

In-house, DC-area Employees

EVANS, M. Stanton: Chairman

Education and Training Resources

Bowling Green, KY
Leg. Issues: BUD, LBR

Outside Counsel/Consultants

Arent Fox Kintner Plotkin & Kahn, PLLC
Issues: BUD, LBR
Rep By: Katie Clarke, Douglas McCormack

Education Assistance Foundation

Seattle, WA

Outside Counsel/Consultants

LaRocco & Associates
Rep By: Christine B. LaRocco, Hon. Lawrence P. LaRocco, Matthew LaRocco

Education Commission of the States

Denver, CO
Web: www.ecs.org
E-mail: ecs@ecs.org

Outside Counsel/Consultants

Hauser Group

Education Communications, Inc.

Lake Forest, IL

Outside Counsel/Consultants

Widmeyer Communications, Inc.
Rep By: Kevin J. Bonderud

Education Finance Council

1155 15th St. NW
Suite 801
Washington, DC 20005
Tel: (202)466-8621
Fax: (202)466-8643
Registered: LDA
Web: www.efc.org

An organization of student loan secondary market organizations..

Leg. Issues: BUD, EDU, FIN, GOV, TAX

In-house, DC-area Employees

CASILLAS, Conwey: Director, Communications and Membership Services
HANSEN, William D.: Exec. Director
SMITH, Kathleen A.: Director, Government Affairs
WADSWORTH, Harrison Morton: Deputy Exec. Director

Outside Counsel/Consultants

O'Connor & Hannan, L.L.P.
Issues: EDU
Rep By: Patrick E. O'Donnell

Education First Alliance

Washington, DC

Advocates support for federal funding for education.

Outside Counsel/Consultants

American Strategies, Inc.

Education Leaders Council

An association of top state education officials.

Outside Counsel/Consultants

Van Scoyoc Associates, Inc.
Rep By: Victor F. Klatt, III

Education Networks of America

Nashville, TN
Leg. Issues: CPI, EDU

Outside Counsel/Consultants

Barbour Griffith & Rogers, Inc.
Issues: EDU
Rep By: Haley Barbour, G. O. Lanny Griffith, Jr.

Patrick M. Murphy & Associates
Issues: CPI, EDU
Rep By: Patrick M. Murphy

Educational Foundation for Citizenship and Statehood Project

San Juan, PR

Outside Counsel/Consultants

Akin, Gump, Strauss, Hauer & Feld, L.L.P.
Rep By: Marlene M. Colucci, Sean G. D'Arcy, Gary A. Heimberg, Steven R. Ross, Barney J. Skladany, Jr.

Educational Fund to Stop Gun Violence

1023 15th St. NW
Suite 600
Washington, DC 20005
Tel: (202)408-7560
Fax: (202)408-0062
Web: www.endhandgunviolence.org
E-mail: edfund@aol.com

The Educational Fund to End Handgun Violence is a non-profit educational charity dedicated to ending firearm violence, particularly as it affects children. Their mission is to stop gun violence through fostering effective community and national action and to make America a safer nation for current and future generations with initiatives combining youth development, education, and litigation.

In-house, DC-area Employees

HORWITZ, Joshua M.: Exec. Director

Educational Media Foundation

Sacramento, CA

Outside Counsel/Consultants

Shaw Pittman

Educational Testing Service

1800 K St. NW
Suite 900
Washington, DC 20006
Tel: (202)659-0616
Fax: (202)659-8075

Headquartered in Princeton, NJ.

Leg. Issues: EDU

In-house, DC-area Employees

CARNEVALE, Anthony P.: V. President for Public Leadership
FRANCIS, Les: V. President, Communications and Public Affairs
MCALLISTER, Patricia H.: Exec. Director, State and Federal Relations Office

Outside Counsel/Consultants

Wilmer, Cutler & Pickering
Winner & Associates

Educational Video Conferencing, Inc.

Yonkers, NY
Leg. Issues: EDU, SCI

Outside Counsel/Consultants

GPC Internat'l
Issues: EDU, SCI
Rep By: Bruce A. Morrison

Edupoint.com

Solana Beach, CA
Leg. Issues: EDU

Outside Counsel/Consultants

Riggs Government Relations Consulting LLC
Issues: EDU
Rep By: Mark Davis, Cathy A. Riggs, Hon. Frank D. Riggs

Edward Health Services

Naperville, IL
Leg. Issues: BUD

Outside Counsel/Consultants

Cassidy & Associates, Inc.
Issues: BUD
Rep By: Christy Carson Evans, Christopher Lamond, Barbara Sutton, Lyllett Wentworth

EEI

Washinton, DC

Outside Counsel/Consultants

American Continental Group, Inc.
Rep By: Steve Colovas, Shawn H. Smeallie, Peter Terpeluk, Jr.

EER Systems

Vienna, VA
Leg. Issues: AER, GOV

Outside Counsel/Consultants

Cottone and Huggins Group
Issues: AER, GOV
Rep By: James B. Huggins

Effective Government Committee

P.O. Box 15187
Washington, DC 20003
Tel: (202)485-3437
Fax: (202)485-3427

In-house, DC-area Employees

MAMET, Noah: Treasurer

EFW Corp.

Fort Worth, TX
Leg. Issues: AER, DEF

Outside Counsel/Consultants

Adam Emanuel and Associates
Issues: DEF
Rep By: Adam Emanuel

Law Office of Zel E. Lipsen
Issues: AER, DEF
Rep By: Adam Emanuel

EG&G

Gaithersburg, MD
Leg. Issues: ENG

Outside Counsel/Consultants

Johnston & Associates, LLC
Issues: ENG
Rep By: Alex Flint, Hon. J. Bennett Johnston, W. Proctor Jones

The Egg Factory, LLC

Roanoke, VA
Leg. Issues: COM, SCI, TEC

Outside Counsel/Consultants

King & Spalding
Issues: COM, SCI, TEC
Rep By: Glenn Cambell, William C. Talmadge

Egypt, Government of the Arab Republic of

Washington, DC

Outside Counsel/Consultants

Afridi & Angell LLP

Bannerman and Associates, Inc.
Rep By: M. Graeme Bannerman, Anne Hingeley, William A. Miner, Valerie A. Schultz, Curt Silvers, Tammy Sittnick

eHealth Insurance Services, Inc.
Leg. Issues: CPI, HCR, TEC

Outside Counsel/Consultants

Jefferson Government Relations, L.L.C.
Issues: CPI, HCR, TEC
Rep By: John D. Desser, Thomas R. Donnelly, Jr., Erik Rasmussen

Eickhorn-Solingen
Solingen, GERMANY
Leg. Issues: DEF

Outside Counsel/Consultants

American Defense Internat'l, Inc.
Issues: DEF
Rep By: Van D. Hipp, Jr., Dave Wilberding

Einhorn, Yaffee, Prescott
Leg. Issues: RES

Outside Counsel/Consultants

The Da Vinci Group
Issues: RES

Milton S. Eisenhower Foundation
1660 L St. NW
Suite 200
Washington, DC 20036
Web: www.eisenhowerfoundation.org
E-mail: mseisenhower@msn.com
Tel: (202)429-0440
Fax: (202)452-0169

Conducts research into the causes and prevention of violence and crime.

Leg. Issues: LAW

In-house, DC-area Employees
CURTIS, Lynn A.: President

Outside Counsel/Consultants

Hogan & Hartson L.L.P.
Issues: LAW
Rep By: William Michael House, Christine M. Warnke

Eka Chemicals
Leg. Issues: CHM, ENV

Outside Counsel/Consultants

Ogletree Governmental Affairs, Inc.
Issues: CHM, ENV
Rep By: Maggie Dean

Eklof Marine Corp.
Staten Island, NY
Leg. Issues: ENV, LAW

Outside Counsel/Consultants

Venable
Issues: ENV, LAW

El Al Israel Airlines, Ltd.
Tel Aviv, ISRAEL

Outside Counsel/Consultants

Winthrop, Stimson, Putnam & Roberts
Rep By: John E. Gillick

El Camino Resources, Ltd.
Woodland Hills, CA
Leg. Issues: DEF

Outside Counsel/Consultants

Mehl, Griffin & Bartek Ltd.
Issues: DEF
Rep By: Ronald J. Bartek, Molly Griffin, Theodore J. Mehl

El Centro Regional Medical Center
El Centro, CA
Leg. Issues: BUD, HCR

Outside Counsel/Consultants

Carpi & Clay
Issues: BUD, HCR
Rep By: Kenneth A. Carpi

El Dorado Irrigation District
Placerville, CA
Leg. Issues: ENV, NAT

Outside Counsel/Consultants

Kennedy Government Relations
Issues: ENV, NAT
Rep By: Jerry W. Kennedy

El Paso Corporation
555 11th St. NW
Suite 750
Washington, DC 20005
Web: www.elpaso.com
Tel: (202)637-3506
Fax: (202)637-3504
Registered: LDA

Headquartered in Houston, TX.

Leg. Issues: CAW, CPI, ENG, ENV, FUE, NAT, TAX, TRA, TRD

Political Action Committee/s

El Paso Corp. Political Action Committee
555 11th St. NW
Suite 750
Washington, DC 20005
Contact: Lori E. Laudien
Tel: (202)637-3506
Fax: (202)637-3504

In-house, DC-area Employees
CHASE, Mike: Manager, Federal Agency Affairs
COLLINS, Daniel: V. President and Associate General Counsel
COOK, G. Mark: Associate General Counsel, Pipelines
HENNEBERRY, Brian: Federal Government Affairs Representative
LAUDIEN, Lori E.: Director, Federal Government Affairs
MOORE, Michael D.: Director, Federal Agency Affairs
SWIFT, Heather: Federal Government Affairs Representative

Outside Counsel/Consultants

Alpine Group, Inc.
Issues: ENG, ENV, FUE, NAT, TAX
Rep By: James D. Massie, Rhod M. Shaw

Hooper Owen & Winburn

El Paso Electric Co.
El Paso, TX
Leg. Issues: UTI

Outside Counsel/Consultants

Governmental Strategies, Inc.
Issues: UTI
Rep By: William D. Kenworthy, Timothy E. Smith

El Paso Natural Gas Co.
El Paso, TX
Registered: LDA

Outside Counsel/Consultants

Andrews and Kurth, L.L.P.

El Paso Water Utilities - Public Service Board
El Paso, TX
Leg. Issues: BUD, CAW, ENV

Outside Counsel/Consultants

Murray, Scheer, Montgomery, Tapia & O'Donnell
Issues: BUD, CAW, ENV
Rep By: John H. Montgomery, John R. O'Donnell

El Salvador, Embassy of the Republic of
2308 California St. NW
Washington, DC 20008
Tel: (202)265-9671
Fax: (202)234-3834

Outside Counsel/Consultants

Bannerman and Associates, Inc.
Rep By: M. Graeme Bannerman, Anne Hingeley, William A. Miner, Valerie A. Schultz, Curt Silvers, Tammy Sittnick

Hogan & Hartson L.L.P.

Holland & Knight LLP

El Salvador, Government of the Republic of
San Salvador, EL SALVADOR

Outside Counsel/Consultants

Holland & Knight LLP

Michael E. Veve
Rep By: Michael E. Veve

El Segundo, California, City of
Leg. Issues: TRA

Outside Counsel/Consultants

Cassidy & Associates, Inc.
Issues: TRA
Rep By: Sonya C. Clay, John S. Doyle, Jr., Valerie Rogers Osborne

El Toro Reuse Planning Authority
Irvine, CA
Leg. Issues: AVI, DEF, ECN

Outside Counsel/Consultants

Copeland, Lowery & Jacquez
Issues: AVI, DEF, ECN
Rep By: Hon. William D. Lowery

Hogan & Hartson L.L.P.
Rep By: George V. Carneal

Law Offices of Irene E. Howie
Issues: AVI

Elan Pharmaceutical Research Corp.
1140 Connecticut Ave. NW
Suite 350
Washington, DC 20036
Tel: (202)872-7800
Fax: (202)872-7808
Registered: LDA

Leg. Issues: ACC, ADV, ALC, CHM, CPT, HCR, MAN, MED, MMM, PHA, SCI, VET

In-house, DC-area Employees
BUDASHEWITZ, Philip
MYERS, Dennis
PENDERGAST, Mary

Elanco Animal Health
Washington, DC
Web: www.lilly.com

Researches, develops and markets animal health products. Headquartered in Indianapolis, IN.

Leg. Issues: ANI, TRD

Outside Counsel/Consultants

Bergner Bockorny Castagnetti and Hawkins
Issues: ANI
Rep By: Jeffrey T. Bergner, David A. Bockorny, David Castagnetti, Melissa Schulman

Mayer, Brown & Platt
Issues: TRD
Rep By: Amb. Peter L. Scher

Elanex Pharmaceuticals
Bothell, WA
Leg. Issues: HCR, MMM, TRD

Outside Counsel/Consultants

Jeffrey J. Kimbell & Associates
Issues: HCR, MMM, TRD

Elastic Corp. of America

Outside Counsel/Consultants

Crowell & Moring LLP

Elbet Forth Worth
Fort Worth, TX
Leg. Issues: DEF, MAN

Outside Counsel/Consultants

American Systems Internat'l Corp.
Issues: DEF, MAN
Rep By: Joe Khare, Robert D. McVey, William H. Skipper, Jr.

Elcor Inc.
Bethesda, MD

Outside Counsel/Consultants

Kilpatrick Stockton LLP
Rep By: Neil I. Levy

ElderCare Companies
Point Pleasant, MI
Leg. Issues: HCR

Outside Counsel/Consultants

Latham & Watkins
Issues: HCR
Rep By: Edward Correia, William C. Kelly, Jr.

Elderplan, Inc.
Brooklyn, NY
Leg. Issues: HCR

Outside Counsel/Consultants

The Wilbur Group
Issues: HCR
Rep By: Valerie Wilbur

Election Systems & Software
Omaha, NE

A manufacturer of election equipment.

Outside Counsel/Consultants

Public Affairs Resources, Inc.
Rep By: Susan E. Petniunas

Electric Consumers Alliance

Indianapolis, IN
Leg. Issues: CSP, ENG

Outside Counsel/Consultants

Robert M. Brandon and Associates
Issues: CSP, ENG
Rep By: Robert M. Brandon, Michelle Molloy

Electric Lightwave, Inc.

Vancouver, WA
Leg. Issues: COM, TAX

Outside Counsel/Consultants

Conkling, Fiskum & McCormick
Issues: COM, TAX
Rep By: Daniel Jarman

Electric Power Research Institute

2000 L St. NW
Suite 805
Washington, DC 20036
Tel: (202)872-9222
Fax: (202)293-2697
Registered: LDA
Web: www.epri.com

Manages science and technology for the energy and energy services industry worldwide. Established in 1973. Headquartered in Palo Alto, CA.

In-house, DC-area Employees

BAUMAN, Barbara: Director, Washington Office
HARRIS, Collette: Washington Representative

Electric Power Supply Ass'n

1401 New York Ave. NW
11th Floor
Washington, DC 20005
Tel: (202)628-8200
Fax: (202)628-8260
Registered: LDA
Web: www.epsa.org
E-mail: espa@mindspring.com

Formed by the merger of Electric Generation Ass'n and Nat'l Independent Energy Producers. Represents competitive electric power suppliers, including generators and power marketers. Advocates full retail electric competition.

Leg. Issues: UTI

Political Action Committee/s

Electric Power Supply Ass'n Political Action Committee
1401 New York Ave. NW
11th Floor
Washington, DC 20005
Tel: (202)628-8200
Fax: (202)628-8260
Contact: Lynne H. Church

In-house, DC-area Employees

CHURCH, Lynne H.: President
PETERS, Eugene: V. President, Legislative Affairs
SALVOSA, Donn: Manager, Government Affairs
SIMON, Julie: V. President, Policy

Outside Counsel/Consultants

Chadbourne and Parke LLP
Rep By: Keith Martin

Dickstein Shapiro Morin & Oshinsky LLP
Issues: UTI
Rep By: Hon. Wendell H. Ford, Elizabeth B. Haywood, Robert Mangas, Graham "Rusty" Mathews, Laurie McKay, Hon. Stanford E. Parris, Rebecah Moore Shepherd, Laura Szabo, L. Andrew Zausner

Electric Transportation Co.

Santa Barbara, CA
Leg. Issues: CSP, TRA

Outside Counsel/Consultants

Lawler, Metzger & Milkman, LLC
Issues: CSP, TRA
Rep By: Sante J. Esposito

The Electric Vehicle Ass'n of the Americas (EVAA)

701 Pennsylvania Ave. NW
Third Floor
Washington, DC 20004
Tel: (202)508-5995
Fax: (202)508-5924
Registered: LDA
Web: www.evaa.org
E-mail: evaa@evaa.org

A coalition of electric utilities, auto manufacturers, local and state governments and others encouraging support for the commercialization of electric vehicle technologies.

Leg. Issues: BUD, CAW, ENG, ENV, SCI, TAX, TRA

In-house, DC-area Employees

CALLAHAN, Kateri A.: Exec. Director
CHIPPS, Katie B.: Public Policy Associate
HENDRICKSON, Gail: Associate Director

Outside Counsel/Consultants

Van Ness Feldman, P.C.
Issues: CAW, ENG, ENV, SCI, TAX, TRA
Rep By: Britt S. Fleming, Ben Yamagata

Electricite de France Internat'l North America, Inc.

1730 Rhode Island Ave. NW
Suite 509
Washington, DC 20036
Web: www.edf.fr
Tel: (202)429-2527
Fax: (202)429-2532

Heaquartered in Paris, France.

In-house, DC-area Employees

GAUJACQ, Catherine: President
ROVERSI, Louis: V. President

ElectriCities of North Carolina, Inc.

Raleigh, NC
Leg. Issues: ENG, TAX

Outside Counsel/Consultants

Talley and Associates
Issues: ENG, TAX
Rep By: Robert A. C. Talley

Electricity Consumers Resource Council (ELCON)

1333 H St. NW
West Tower
Eighth Floor
Washington, DC 20005
Web: www.elcon.org
E-mail: elcon@elcon.org
Tel: (202)682-1390
Fax: (202)289-6370
Registered: LDA

Established in January, 1976 by a number of industrial consumers of electricity who support regulatory practices that assure adequate supplies of electricity at prices based on cost of service.

Leg. Issues: ENG, UTI

In-house, DC-area Employees

ANDERSON, Dr. John A.: Exec. Director
HUGHES, John P.: Director, Technical Affairs
YACKER, Marc D.: Director, Government and Public Affairs

Electro Design Manufacturing, Inc.

Decatur, AL
Leg. Issues: DEF

Outside Counsel/Consultants

Patton Boggs, LLP
Issues: DEF
Rep By: Darryl D. Nirenberg

Electro Energy, Inc.

Danbury, CT
Leg. Issues: DEF, ENG

Outside Counsel/Consultants

Cassidy & Associates, Inc.
Issues: DEF, ENG
Rep By: Lawrence C. Grossman

Electro Scientific Industries, Inc.

Portland, OR
Leg. Issues: CPI, CPT, FIN, IMM, TAX, TRD

Outside Counsel/Consultants

Conkling, Fiskum & McCormick
Issues: CPI, CPT, FIN, IMM, TAX, TRD
Rep By: Gary Conkling, Norm Eder, Daniel Jarman

Electro-Radiation Inc.

Fairfield, CT

A manufacturer of Global Position Satellite anti-jamming equipment.

Leg. Issues: DEF

Outside Counsel/Consultants

The PMA Group
Issues: DEF
Rep By: Daniel Cunningham, Daniel E. Fleming, Kaylene Green, Paul J. Magliocchetti, Charles Smith, Mark Waclawski

Electromagnetic Energy Ass'n

1255 23rd St. NW
Suite 200
Washington, DC 20037-1174
Web: www.elecenergy.com
E-mail: eea@elecenergy.com
Tel: (202)452-1070
Fax: (202)833-3636

Founding members include AT&T Bell Labs, GTE Corp., Motorola, Raytheon and the Nat'l Ass'n of Broadcasters.

Leg. Issues: ENG

In-house, DC-area Employees

FORBURGER, Melissa T.: Exec. Director

Outside Counsel/Consultants

Hauck and Associates
Rep By: Melissa T. Forburger

Electronic Commerce Ass'n

1432 Fenwick Lane
Suite 200
Silver Spring, MD 20910
Web: www.theeca.org
E-mail: lgood@theeca.org
Tel: (301)608-9600

Advocates the positions of E-commerce service providers.

In-house, DC-area Employees

GOOD, Larry: Senior V. President
THEVENOT, E. Wayne: President

Outside Counsel/Consultants

Bracewell & Patterson, L.L.P.

Electronic Commerce Forum

Washington, DC
Leg. Issues: CPI, TAX

Outside Counsel/Consultants

Troutman Sanders LLP
Issues: CPI, TAX
Rep By: Mary Clare Fitzgerald

Electronic Commerce Tax Study Group

Washington, DC
Leg. Issues: TAX

Outside Counsel/Consultants

PriceWaterhouseCoopers
Issues: TAX
Rep By: Jim Carlisle, Peter R. Merrill, James R. Shanahan

Electronic Design Inc.

Metairie, LA
Leg. Issues: DEF

Outside Counsel/Consultants

Dyer Ellis & Joseph, P.C.
Issues: DEF
Rep By: Brian A. Bannon, Wayne A. Keup, Margaret Dillenburg Rifka, Duncan C. Smith, III, Jennifer M. Southwick

Electronic Financial Services Council

Washington, DC
Leg. Issues: BAN, FIN, HOU, INS, SCI

Outside Counsel/Consultants

Goodwin, Procter & Hoar LLP
Issues: BAN, FIN, HOU, INS, SCI
Rep By: Jeremiah S. Buckley, Margo Tank

Electronic Funds Transfer Ass'n

950 Herndon Pkwy.
Suite 390
Herndon, VA 20170
Web: www.efta.org
E-mail: eftassn@aol.com
Tel: (703)435-9800
Fax: (703)435-7157

Trade association advocating the advancement of electronic payment systems and commerce.

Leg. Issues: BAN

In-house, DC-area Employees

HELWIG, H. Kurt: Exec. Director
PATTERSON, Walt: Chairman

Electronic Industries Alliance

2500 Wilson Blvd.
Arlington, VA 22201-3834
Tel: (703)907-7500
Fax: (703)907-7501
Registered: LDA
Web: www.eia.org
Leg. Issues: CPI, ENV, TAX, TEC, TRD, WAS

In-house, DC-area Employees

BOWMAN, Heather: Manager, Environmental Issues
EVANS, Holly: Director, Environmental Affairs
KELLY, Brian: Sr. V. President, Government Relations and Communications
MCCURDY, Dave: President
SERAFIN, James J.: Director, Marketing and Legislative Affairs
WORTMANN, Barbara E.: Senior V. President, Policy, Planning and Industry Relations

Outside Counsel/Consultants

Ogletree Governmental Affairs, Inc.
Rep By: Francis M. Lunnie, Jr.

The Petrizzo Group, Inc.
Issues: TAX
Rep By: Kara Kennedy, Thomas "T.J." Petrizzo

Squire, Sanders & Dempsey L.L.P.

Swidler Berlin Shereff Friedman, LLP

Twenty-First Century Group
Rep By: Hon. Jack M. Fields, Jr., Cynthia M. Wilkinson

The Wexler Group
Issues: TRD
Rep By: R. D. Folsom, Hon. Robert S. Walker

Wiley, Rein & Fielding

Electronic Industries Ass'n of Japan

Tokyo, JAPAN
Leg. Issues: TRD

Outside Counsel/Consultants

The Hawthorn Group, L.C.
Rep By: Esther Foer

McDermott, Will and Emery
Issues: TRD
Rep By: Stanton D. Anderson, Seth D. Greenstein, Neil Quinter, Robert S. Schwartz, Thomas Steindler

Electronic Privacy Information Center

1718 Connecticut Ave. NW
Suite 200
Washington, DC 20009
Web: www.epic.org
E-mail: info@epic.org
Tel: (202)483-1140
Fax: (202)483-1248

In-house, DC-area Employees

ANDREWS, Sarah: Policy Analyst
ROTENBERG, Marc: Exec. Director
SHEN, Andrew: Policy Analyst
SOBEL, David: Legal Counsel

Electronic Retailing Ass'n

2101 Wilson Blvd.
Suite 1002
Arlington, VA 22201
Web: www.retailing.org
E-mail: emyers@retailing.org
Tel: (703)841-1751
Fax: (703)841-1860

Strives to stimulate total retail sales; to increase the percent of those sales that occur electronically; to improve the profitability of those sales; and to create a favorable climate in which electronic retailers can operate successfully and consumer confidence is continually reinforced.

Leg. Issues: ADV, ART, COM, FOR, GOV, MIA, TAX, TEC, TRD, TRU

In-house, DC-area Employees

CAVARRETTA, Joseph: V. President, Membership
MYERS, Elissa Matulis: President and Chief Exec. Officer

Outside Counsel/Consultants

Venable
Rep By: Jeffrey D. Knowles

Electronic Traders Ass'n

Washington, DC
Leg. Issues: FIN, UTI

Outside Counsel/Consultants

Thelen Reid & Priest LLP
Issues: FIN, UTI
Rep By: Richard Y. Roberts

Electronic Warfare Associates, Inc.

Herndon, VA
Leg. Issues: DEF

Outside Counsel/Consultants

The Conaway Group LLC

The PMA Group
Issues: DEF
Rep By: Kaylene Green, Paul J. Magliocchetti, Thomas Veltri, Mark Waclawski

Electronics Consultants Inc.

Lake Zurich, IL
Leg. Issues: DEF

Outside Counsel/Consultants

Bryan Cave LLP
Issues: DEF
Rep By: Hon. Alan J. Dixon

Elettronica Veneta & IN.EL.

Treviso, ITALY
Leg. Issues: FOR, TRD

Outside Counsel/Consultants

Gibbons & Company, Inc.
Issues: FOR, TRD
Rep By: Clifford S. Gibbons

ELGARD Corp.

Chardon, OH

Outside Counsel/Consultants

Arter & Hadden

Elim Native Corp.

Elim, AK
Leg. Issues: RES

Outside Counsel/Consultants

Birch, Horton, Bittner & Cherot
Issues: RES
Rep By: Roy S. Jones, Jr.

Elim, Alaska, City of

Leg. Issues: CAW, ENV, HCR, IND, MAR, NAT, WAS

Outside Counsel/Consultants

Law Office of C. Deming Cowles
Issues: CAW, ENV, HCR, IND, MAR, NAT, WAS
Rep By: C. Deming Cowles

eLink

Outside Counsel/Consultants

Dittus Communications
Rep By: Karine Elsen, Cynthia Giorgio, Leanne Scott

Elk Valley Rancheria

Crescent City, CA

A native American tribal government.

Leg. Issues: GAM, IND

Outside Counsel/Consultants

The State Affairs Co.
Issues: GAM, IND
Rep By: Bonnie L. Chafe

Elkem Materials Inc.

Pittsburgh, PA
Leg. Issues: BUD, ROD

Outside Counsel/Consultants

Genesis Consulting Group, LLC
Issues: BUD, ROD
Rep By: Mark Benedict, Dana DeBeaumont

Elkem Metals Co.

Pittsburgh, PA
Leg. Issues: DEF

Outside Counsel/Consultants

Robert N. Pyle & Associates
Issues: DEF
Rep By: Alexis Hersh, Alison O'Neill, Robert N. Pyle

Ellicott Internat'l

Baltimore, MD
Leg. Issues: BUD, MAR, TAX

Outside Counsel/Consultants

Davidson & Company, Inc.
Issues: BUD, MAR, TAX
Rep By: James H. Davidson, Richard E. May, Stanley Sokul

Elmco, Inc.

Huntsville, AL
Leg. Issues: DEF

Outside Counsel/Consultants

Balch & Bingham LLP
Issues: DEF
Rep By: Wade Heck, William F. Stiers

Elmer Larson, Inc.

Sycamore, IL
Leg. Issues: DIS, ENV, HOU, RES, URB

Outside Counsel/Consultants

Miles & Stockbridge, P.C.
Issues: DIS, ENV, HOU, RES, URB
Rep By: Samuel A. Bleicher

Elmira College

Elmira, NY
Leg. Issues: BUD

Outside Counsel/Consultants

Cassidy & Associates, Inc.
Issues: BUD
Rep By: Lindsay Lawrence, Arthur D. Mason, Louie Perry

eLottery, Inc.

Milford, CT
Leg. Issues: GAM

Outside Counsel/Consultants

Preston Gates Ellis & Rouvelas Meeds LLP
Issues: GAM
Rep By: Werner W. Brandt, Hon. David Funderburk, Michael J. O'Neil, W. Dennis Stephens

Rock & Associates
Issues: GAM
Rep By: James W. Rock

Elzay Ready Wear Manufacturing Co.

Amman, JORDAN
Leg. Issues: TRD

Outside Counsel/Consultants

Sandler, Travis & Rosenberg, P.A.
Issues: TRD
Rep By: Ron Sorini

Embraer Aircraft Corp.

Fort Lauderdale, FL
Leg. Issues: AER, AVI

Outside Counsel/Consultants

Shaw Pittman
Issues: AER, AVI
Rep By: J. E. Murdock, III, Thomas J. Spulak

Embry-Riddle Aeronautical University

Daytona Beach, FL
Leg. Issues: AVI, BUD, EDU

Outside Counsel/Consultants

Jefferson Government Relations, L.L.C.
Issues: AVI, BUD, EDU
Rep By: William A. Roberts

EMC Corp.

6903 Rockledge Dr.
Suite 730
Bethesda, MD 20817
Tel: (301)272-2320
Fax: (301)272-2369
Registered: LDA
Web: www.emc.com
E-mail: salisbury_keith@emc.com
Leg. Issues: BUD, CPI, FIN, SCI, TAX

Political Action Committee/s

EMC Political Action Committee
6903 Rockledge Dr.
Suite 730
Bethesda, MD 20817
Contact: Timur Eads
Tel: (301)272-2836
Fax: (301)272-2369

In-house, DC-area Employees

BOMAR, Nora: Manager, Government Affairs
EADS, Timur: Director of Government Affairs
SALISBURY, Keith: Manager, Government Affairs

Outside Counsel/Consultants

Akin, Gump, Strauss, Hauer & Feld, L.L.P.
Issues: FIN, TAX
Rep By: Donald C. Alexander, Sean G. D'Arcy, Smith W. Davis, Christine Hesse, Barney J. Skladany, Jr.

The Conaway Group LLC

Haake and Associates
Rep By: Timothy M. Haake, Nathan M. Olsen

Emergency Committee for American Trade

1211 Connecticut Ave. NW
Suite 801
Washington, DC 20036
Tel: (202)659-5147
Fax: (202)659-1347
Registered: LDA
Web: www.ecattrade.com

A group supporting expanded international trade and investment, composed of 54 chairmen of U.S. companies operating internationally.

Leg. Issues: TRD

In-house, DC-area Employees

COHEN, Calman J.: President
MENGHETTI, Linda: V. President and Counsel

Emergency Department Practice Management Ass'n (EDPMA)

Vienna, VA
Web: www.edpma.org
E-mail: info@edpma.org
Leg. Issues: BUD, HCR, MMM, TAX

Outside Counsel/Consultants

Ass'n Management Bureau
Rep By: Thomas C. Gibson

Epstein Becker & Green, P.C.
Issues: BUD, HCR, MMM, TAX
Rep By: Joyce A. Cowan

Emerging Technology Partners, LLC

Birmingham, AL
Leg. Issues: MED

Outside Counsel/Consultants

Balch & Bingham LLP
Issues: MED
Rep By: Wade Heck, William F. Stiers

Emerson

700 13th St. NW
Suite 700
Washington, DC 20005-3960
Tel: (202)508-6303
Fax: (202)508-6305
Registered: LDA

A manufacturer of telecommunications network power reliability equipment, process controls, and tools. Headquartered in St. Louis, MO.

In-house, DC-area Employees

MCDONALD, Robert: V. President, Governmental Affairs
SIMON, Heather: Legislative Assistant

EMI Music

New York, NY
Leg. Issues: ART, CPT

Outside Counsel/Consultants

Liz Robbins Associates
Issues: ART, CPT
Rep By: Liz Robbins

EMILY'S List

805 15th St. NW
Suite 400
Washington, DC 20005
Web: www.emilyslist.org
Tel: (202)326-1400
Fax: (202)326-1415

An acronym for Early Money Is Like Yeast, the group is a political network for Democratic women candidates.

Political Action Committee/s

Emily's List Political Action Committee
805 15th St. NW
Suite 400
Washington, DC 20005
Contact: Ellen R. Malcolm
Tel: (202)326-1400
Fax: (202)326-1415

In-house, DC-area Employees

MALCOLM, Ellen R.: President
O'CONNELL, Sheila: Political Director
SOLMONESE, Joe: Chief Operating Officer

Emmanuel College

Boston, MA

Outside Counsel/Consultants

Capitol Partners
Rep By: William Cunningham, Jonathan M. Orloff

Emmis Broadcasting Corp.

Indianapolis, IN

Outside Counsel/Consultants

Baker & Hostetler LLP
Rep By: Steven A. Lotterer, William H. Schweitzer, Hon. Guy Vander Jagt

Emmonak Corp.

Emmonak, AK
Leg. Issues: NAT

Outside Counsel/Consultants

Birch, Horton, Bittner & Cherot
Issues: NAT
Rep By: Roy S. Jones, Jr.

Emory University, Department of Internat'l Health-PAMM, USAID

Atlanta, GA
Leg. Issues: EDU, FOR, HCR

Outside Counsel/Consultants

Capital Consultants Corp.
Issues: EDU, FOR, HCR
Rep By: Michael David Kaiser

Empire Blue Cross and Blue Shield

New York, NY
Leg. Issues: HCR

Outside Counsel/Consultants

Weil, Gotshal & Manges, LLP
Issues: HCR
Rep By: Sandra M. Aistars, Robert C. Odle, Jr.

Employee Assistance Professionals Ass'n

2101 Wilson Blvd.
Suite 500
Arlington, VA 22201-3062
Tel: (703)387-1000
Fax: (703)522-4585
Registered: LDA
Web: www.eap-association.org
E-mail: info@eap-association.org

Created in 1971, the largest professional association for persons practicing in the employee assistance program field.

In-house, DC-area Employees

HALES, Stuart: Director, Communications
MACDONALD, Sheila B.: Director, Legislation and Public Policy
SAMUEL, Antoinette: C.E.O.

Employee Benefit Research Institute

2121 K St. NW
Suite 600
Washington, DC 20037-2121
Tel: (202)659-0670
Fax: (202)775-6312
Web: www.ebri.org
E-mail: info@ebri.org

A private, nonprofit and nonpartisan organization sponsored by corporations, associations and unions that conducts research and educational programs on employee benefit issues.

In-house, DC-area Employees

DEVINE, Danny: Director, Public Relations
SALISBURY, Dallas L.: President and Chief Exec. Officer

Outside Counsel/Consultants

Arnold & Porter

Employee Stock Ownership Assn

Washington, DC

Outside Counsel/Consultants

Long Law Firm
Rep By: C. Kris Kirkpatrick

Employee-Owned S Corporations of America

Chicago, IL
Leg. Issues: TAX

Outside Counsel/Consultants

Manatt, Phelps & Phillips, LLP
Issues: TAX
Rep By: Hon. Jack W. Buechner, Steven J. Mulder, John L. Ray, Stephanie E. Silverman

White & Case LLP
Issues: TAX
Rep By: Linda E. Carlisle

Employer Health Care Innovation Project

Washington, DC
Leg. Issues: HCR

Outside Counsel/Consultants

Health Policy Analysts
Issues: HCR
Rep By: G. Lawrence Atkins, Nan F. North

Employers Council on Flexible Compensation

927 15th St. NW
Suite 1000
Washington, DC 20005
Tel: (202)659-4300
Registered: LDA
Web: www.ecfc.org
E-mail: infoecfc@ecfc.org

Established in 1981. Represents interests of employers who favor retention of flexible compensation programs whereby employees are offered a variety of compensation and benefit arrangements from which they can select those most suitable to their needs.

Leg. Issues: HCR, TAX

In-house, DC-area Employees

FELTMAN, Kenneth E.: Exec. Director
MITCHELL, Fran W.: Exec. Assistant
WHYTE, Bonnie: Chief Operations Officer

Outside Counsel/Consultants

Albertine Enterprises, Inc.
Issues: TAX
Rep By: James J. Albertine

Alston & Bird LLP

Kilpatrick Stockton LLP
Rep By: Mark D. Wincek

Employment Policies Institute Foundation

Dedicated to expanding employment opportunities at all levels of the economy. EPI believes that entry-level positions offer the best job training that young Americans will ever have. EPI provides non-partisan research-based information related to policy debates affecting entry-level employment.

Outside Counsel/Consultants

Berman and Company
Rep By: Richard B. Berman

Employment Policy Foundation

1015 15th St. NW
Suite 1200
Washington, DC 20005
Tel: (202)789-8685
Fax: (202)789-8684

A non profit, non-partisan economic research and educational foundation which focuses on workplace trends and policies.

Leg. Issues: ECN, GOV, LBR, UNM

In-house, DC-area Employees

BIRD, Ronald E.: Chief Economist
POTTER, Edward E.: President

Empower America

1701 Pennsylvania Ave. NW
Suite 900
Washington, DC 20006-5805
Web: www.empoweramerica.org
Tel: (202)452-8200
Fax: (202)833-0388

A conservative political research and advocacy group formed by Vin Weber, former Member, U.S. House of Representatives (R-MN); Jack Kemp, former Member, U.S. House of Representatives (R-NY) and former Secretary of Housing and Urban Development; William J. Bennett, former Secretary of Education and former Director, Office of Drug Control Policy; Jeane Kirkpatrick, former Ambassador to the United Nations.

Leg. Issues: EDU, GOV, TAX

In-house, DC-area Employees

KWITOWSKI, Jeff: Spokesperson
TAYLOR, James R. "J.T.": President and Chief Exec. Officer

Empresa Consolidada Cubana de Aviacion

Havana, CUBA

Outside Counsel/Consultants

Zuckert, Scoutt and Rasenberger, L.L.P.
Rep By: Lonnie E. Pera

Empresa Estatal de Telecomunicaciones

Quito, ECUADOR

Outside Counsel/Consultants

Shaw Pittman

Empresas Fonalledas

San Juan, PR
Leg. Issues: ENV

Outside Counsel/Consultants

Oppenheimer Wolff & Donnelly LLP
Issues: ENV
Rep By: Margaret N. Strand

Encapco Technologies, LLC

Dublin, CA
Leg. Issues: BUD, DEF, ENV

Outside Counsel/Consultants

French & Company
Issues: BUD, DEF, ENV
Rep By: Rebecca Dornbusch, Verrick O. French

Encinitas, California, City of

Leg. Issues: BUD, GOV, NAT

Outside Counsel/Consultants

Carpi & Clay
Issues: BUD, GOV, NAT
Rep By: Kenneth A. Carpi

Marlowe and Co.
Issues: BUD, NAT
Rep By: Howard Marlowe

Encyclopaedia Britannica, Inc.

Chicago, IL
Leg. Issues: TAX

Outside Counsel/Consultants

Sutherland Asbill & Brennan LLP
Issues: TAX
Rep By: Daniel M. Berman

Endangered Species Coordinating Council

A lobbying coalition for reform of the Endangered Species Act made up largely of timber, paper, mining, and livestock organizations and organized labor.

Leg. Issues: NAT

Outside Counsel/Consultants

Crowell & Moring LLP
Issues: NAT
Rep By: Steven P. Quarles

Endocrine Soc.

4350 East-West Hwy.
Suite 500
Bethesda, MD 20814-4110
Tel: (301)941-0200
Fax: (301)941-0259
Registered: LDA
Web: www.endo-society.org
E-mail: endostaff@endo-society.org
Leg. Issues: HCR, MMM

In-house, DC-area Employees

HUNT, Scott: Exec. Director
KOPPI, Susan: Director, Public Affairs
ZARO, Ph.D., CAE, Joan A.: Senior Director, Governance and Policy

Outside Counsel/Consultants

Hogan & Hartson L.L.P.
Issues: HCR, MMM
Rep By: Beth L. Roberts

Enerco, Inc.

Carrollton, GA

Outside Counsel/Consultants

McKenna & Cuneo, L.L.P.

Energen Corp.

Outside Counsel/Consultants

Bradley Arant Rose & White LLP

Energy Absorption Systems, Inc.

Chicago, IL
Leg. Issues: ROD, TRA

Outside Counsel/Consultants

Albertine Enterprises, Inc.
Issues: TRA
Rep By: James J. Albertine, Dr. John M. Albertine, Aubrey C. King

Bracy Williams & Co.
Issues: ROD, TRA
Rep By: Susan J. Williams

Energy Affairs Administration

Puerto De Tierra, PR
Leg. Issues: ENG

Outside Counsel/Consultants

Morgan Meguire, LLC
Issues: ENG
Rep By: Kyle G. Michel, Ramola Musante, C. Kyle Simpson, Deborah R. Sliz

Energy and Environment Coalition

Washington, DC
Leg. Issues: DIS, ENG, ENV, UTI

Outside Counsel/Consultants

The Accord Group
Issues: DIS, ENG, ENV, UTI
Rep By: Patrick H. Quinn

The Willard Group
Issues: ENV
Rep By: Daniel Scherder

Energy Communities Alliance, Inc.

Washington, DC
Leg. Issues: ENG

Outside Counsel/Consultants

Kutak Rock LLP
Issues: ENG
Rep By: Seth Kirshenberg, George R. Schlossberg

Energy Conservation Program, Inc.

Duluth, MN
Leg. Issues: ENG

Outside Counsel/Consultants

Capital Consultants Corp.
Issues: ENG
Rep By: Michael David Kaiser

Energy Contractors Price-Anderson Group

Washington, DC

An ad hoc group of energy contractors lobbying on legislation to extend the Price-Anderson Act's liability limits on damages from nuclear power accidents.

Leg. Issues: ENG, INS

Outside Counsel/Consultants

Harmon & Wilmot, L.L.P.
Issues: ENG, INS
Rep By: Omer F. Brown, II

Energy Cost Savings Council

Leg. Issues: EDU, ENG

Outside Counsel/Consultants

Earle Palmer Brown Public Relations
Issues: EDU, ENG

Energy East Management Corp.

801 Pennsylvania Ave. NW
N. Bldg., Suite 250
Washington, DC 20004
Tel: (202)783-5521
Fax: (202)783-5569
Registered: LDA

Headquartered in Albany, NY.

Leg. Issues: UTI

In-house, DC-area Employees

SPARKS, Angela M.: V. President, Government Affairs

Outside Counsel/Consultants

Thomas J. Dennis
Issues: UTI
Rep By: Thomas J. Dennis

Energy Efficiency Systems, Inc.

Westbury, NY
Leg. Issues: ENV

Outside Counsel/Consultants

Downey McGrath Group, Inc.
Issues: ENV
Rep By: Hon. Thomas J. Downey, Jr., John Peter Olinger

Energy House Capital Corp.

Bloomfield, NJ

Outside Counsel/Consultants

Duncan, Weinberg, Genzer & Pembroke, P.C.
Rep By: Jeffrey C. Genzer

Energy Northwest

Richland, WA
Leg. Issues: ENG

Outside Counsel/Consultants

Morgan Meguire, LLC
Issues: ENG
Rep By: Scott Lindsay, Kyle G. Michel, Katie Parrott, C. Kyle Simpson, Deborah R. Sliz, Kiel Weaver

Energy Pacific, Inc.

Boise, ID

Outside Counsel/Consultants

Durante Associates
Rep By: Douglas A. Durante

Energy Programs Consortium

Washington, DC
Leg. Issues: ENG

Outside Counsel/Consultants

Duncan, Weinberg, Genzer & Pembroke, P.C.
Issues: ENG
Rep By: Jeffrey C. Genzer

EnerStar Power Corp.

Paris, IL
Leg. Issues: ENG, UTI

Outside Counsel/Consultants

Duncan, Weinberg, Genzer & Pembroke, P.C.
Issues: ENG, UTI
Rep By: Michael R. Postar

EnerTech Industries Inc.

Youngsville, LA
Leg. Issues: ENG, ENV

Outside Counsel/Consultants

Washington Consulting Alliance, Inc.
Issues: ENG, ENV
Rep By: Thomas L. Burgum

Engage Technologies

Andover, MA
Leg. Issues: CPI, CPT

Outside Counsel/Consultants

Wiley, Rein & Fielding
Issues: CPI, CPT
Rep By: Mimi W. Dawson, Peter Ross

Engelhard Corp.

Iselin, NJ
Leg. Issues: CAW, MAR

Outside Counsel/Consultants

JMD Associates, Inc.
Issues: CAW, MAR
Rep By: David Bushnell

Engine Manufacturers Ass'n

Chicago, IL

Outside Counsel/Consultants

Smith, Bucklin and Associates, Inc.

Engineered Arresting Systems Corp.

Leg. Issues: AER, AVI, MAN, SCI, TRA

Outside Counsel/Consultants

Jefferson Government Relations, L.L.C.
Issues: AER, AVI, MAN, SCI, TRA

Engineered Support System, Inc. (ESSI)

1235 Jefferson Davis Hwy.
Suite 305
Arlington, VA 22202
Tel: (703)416-7600
Fax: (703)416-7606
Registered: LDA

Headquartered in St. Louis, MO.

Leg. Issues: DEF, TEC

In-house, DC-area Employees

HAY, Matt: V. President, Washington Operations

Englewood Hospital & Medical Center

Englewood, NJ
Leg. Issues: HCR

Outside Counsel/Consultants

Greenberg Traurig, LLP
Issues: HCR
Rep By: James F. Miller

English First, Inc.

8001 Forbes Pl.
Suite 109
Springfield, VA 22151
Tel: (703)321-8818
Fax: (703)321-8408
Registered: LDA
Web: www.englishfirst.com

An organization that is for the adoption of English as the official language of the United States and against bilingual education and making Puerto Rico a state.

Leg. Issues: BUD, CON, EDU, GOV, IMM

In-house, DC-area Employees

BOULET, Jr., James: Exec. Director

eNIC Corp.

Seattle, WA
Leg. Issues: COM

Outside Counsel/Consultants

Denny Miller McBee Associates
Issues: COM

Enlisted Ass'n of the Nat'l Guard of the United States

1219 Prince St.
Alexandria, VA 22314
Tel: (800)234-3264
Fax: (703)519-3849
Registered: LDA
Web: www.eangus.org
E-mail: eangus@eangus.org
Leg. Issues: DEF

In-house, DC-area Employees

BIRCH, Bryan: Office Administrator
CLINE, Michael P.: Exec. Director/Chief Exec. Officer
HARTING, Erin: Legislative Analyst

Enron Corp.

1775 I St. NW
Suite 800
Washington, DC 20006
Tel: (202)828-3360
Fax: (202)828-3372
Registered: LDA

Formerly HNG/Internorth. Headquartered in Houston, TX.

Leg. Issues: BNK, BUD, CAW, CDT, CPI, DEF, ENG, ENV, FOR, FUE, GOV, HCR, IND, LBR, NAT, SCI, TAX, TEC, TRA, TRD, UTI

Political Action Committee/s

Enron PAC
1775 I St. NW
Suite 800
Washington, DC 20006
Tel: (202)466-9146
Fax: (202)828-3372
Contact: Carolyn Cooney

In-house, DC-area Employees

BRIGGS, Tom: V. President, Government Affairs
BURNS, Steve: Director, Federal Government Affairs

HARTSOE, Joseph R.: V. President and Federal Regulatory Counsel
HILLINGS, E. Joseph: V. President and General Manager, Federal Government Affairs
KEELER, Jeffrey: Director, Federal Government Affairs
LONG, Christopher: Senior Director, Federal Government Affairs
NAVIN, Allison: Manager, Federal Government Affairs
ROBERTSON, Linda L.: V. President, Federal Government Affairs
SULLIVAN, Lora: Federal Government Affairs Representative

Outside Counsel/Consultants

Alexander Strategy Group
Issues: ENG, UTI
Rep By: Edwin A. Buckham

Bracewell & Patterson, L.L.P.
Issues: ENG, FOR, FUE, TAX, TRD
Rep By: Gene E. Godley, Marc C. Hebert, Michael L. Pate, Scott H. Segal, J. Dan Watkiss

Commonwealth Group, Ltd.
Rep By: Bradley D. Belt

Fleishman-Hillard, Inc
Issues: CPI, ENG
Rep By: Michael Mandigo

Fontheim Internat'l, LLC
Issues: GOV
Rep By: Kenneth I. Levinson

Freedman, Levy, Kroll & Simonds
Issues: FUE, NAT
Rep By: Lawrence G. McBride

Gallagher, Boland and Meiburger
Issues: ENG, FUE, NAT, TRA, UTI
Rep By: Frank X. Kelly, Steve Stojic

Johnston & Associates, LLC
Issues: ENG
Rep By: Hon. J. Bennett Johnston

Mayer, Brown & Platt
Issues: ENG, TRD
Rep By: John P. Schmitz

Bob Moss Associates
Issues: DEF, ENG
Rep By: Bob Moss

Quinn Gillespie & Associates

Vinson & Elkins L.L.P.
Issues: ENG
Rep By: Adam Wenner

Enron Wind Corp./Zond

Tehachapi, CA Registered: LDA

Formerly known as Zond Systems, Inc.

Leg. Issues: TAX

Outside Counsel/Consultants

Bracewell & Patterson, L.L.P.
Issues: TAX

Ensign-Bickford Co.

Simsbury, CT
Leg. Issues: DEF

Outside Counsel/Consultants

American Defense Internat'l, Inc.
Issues: DEF
Rep By: Michael Herson, Van D. Hipp, Jr., Dave Wilberding

ENTEK Corp.

Brea, CA

Outside Counsel/Consultants

The Grizzle Company
Rep By: Richard A. Cantor, Charles L. Grizzle

Entela, Inc.

Grand Rapids, MI
Leg. Issues: CPI, CSP, LBR, TEC, TRD

Outside Counsel/Consultants

The M Companies
Issues: CPI, CSP, LBR, TEC, TRD
Rep By: Milton M. Bush, J.D., CAE

Entergy Corp.

Washington, DC
Leg. Issues: ENG

Outside Counsel/Consultants

Baker Botts, L.L.P.
Rep By: William M. Bumpers

Hooper Owen & Winburn
Issues: ENG
Rep By: Daryl H. Owen

Entergy Services, Inc.

1776 I St. NW
Suite 275
Washington, DC 20006
Tel: (202)530-7300
Fax: (202)530-7350
Registered: LDA

Represents Entergy Corp.'s operating companies, including Entergy Arkansas, Inc., Entergy Louisiana, Inc., Entergy Mississippi, Inc., Entergy New Orleans, Inc., Entergy Gulf States, Inc., Entergy Texas, Inc., Entergy Operations, Inc. (a nuclear power management company), Entergy Power (an independent power production subsidiary) and Entergy Enterprises (an independent/unregulated company involved in international investments). Headquartered in New Orleans, LA.

Leg. Issues: BUD, CAW, ENG, ENV, LBR, NAT, SCI, TAX, UTI, WAS

In-house, DC-area Employees

BILLUPS, Karen K.: Director, Federal Affairs and Washington Counsel
BROWN, Jr., S. M. Henry: V. President, Governmental Affairs
CARROLL, Kenneth: Director, Federal Tax and Environmental Legislative Policy and Strategy
PRIDE, Ann L.: Director, Public Affairs Policy and Strategy
SIMMS, Kristine D.: Director, Federal Government Affairs
WILLIAMS, II, James A: Senior Research Legislative Analyst

Outside Counsel/Consultants

Hooper Owen & Winburn
Rep By: Daryl H. Owen

Skadden, Arps, Slate, Meagher & Flom LLP
Rep By: William S. Scherman

R. Duffy Wall and Associates
Issues: CAW, ENG, ENV, TAX, UTI, WAS
Rep By: Hon. Bill Brewster, Ann Thomas G. Johnston, David C. Jory

Enterprise Bank

Fairfax, VA

Outside Counsel/Consultants

Elias, Matz, Tiernan and Herrick

The Enterprise Foundation

415 Second St. NE
Second Floor
Washington, DC 20002
Tel: (202)543-4599
Fax: (202)543-8130
Registered: LDA
Web: www.enterprisefoundation.org

Promotes affordable housing for low-income people.

Leg. Issues: BUD, HOU, TAX

In-house, DC-area Employees

SOLIS, Ali: Deputy Director, Public Policy
WILLIAMS, Stockton: Senior Legislative and Policy Advisor

Outside Counsel/Consultants

Robert A. Rapoza Associates
Issues: BUD
Rep By: Robert A. Rapoza

Washington Council Ernst & Young
Issues: TAX
Rep By: Doug Badger, Lauren Darling, John L. Doney, Jayne T. Fitzgerald, LaBrenda Garrett-Nelson, Gary J. Gasper, Bruce A. Gates, Nick Giordano, Cathy Koch, Robert J. Leonard, Richard Meltzer, Phillip D. Moseley, John D. Porter, Robert M. Rozen, Donna Steele-Flynn, Timothy J. Urban

The Enterprise Mission

Albuquerque, NM
Leg. Issues: GOV

Outside Counsel/Consultants

Paradigm Research Group
Issues: GOV
Rep By: Stephen G. Bassett

Entertainment Made Convenient

Los Angeles, CA

Outside Counsel/Consultants

Swidler Berlin Shereff Friedman, LLP
Rep By: Martin C. Ernst

Entex, Inc.

Houston, TX

Outside Counsel/Consultants

Elias, Matz, Tiernan and Herrick

entradia.com

Santa Barbara, CA
Leg. Issues: TEC

Outside Counsel/Consultants

RPH & Associates, L.L.C.
Issues: TEC

Envelope Manufacturers Ass'n of America

300 N. Washington St.
Suite 500
Alexandria, VA 22314-2530
Tel: (703)739-2200
Fax: (703)739-2209
Registered: LDA
Web: www.envelope.org
Leg. Issues: POS

Political Action Committee/s

Envelope Manufacturers Ass'n of America PAC
300 N. Washington St.
Suite 500
Alexandria, VA 22314-2530
Tel: (703)739-2200
Fax: (703)739-2209
Contact: Maynard H. Benjamin

In-house, DC-area Employees

BENJAMIN, Maynard H.: President
MUSE, Tonya W.: V. President

Envirocare of Utah, Inc.

Salt Lake City, UT

Radioactive waste disposal facility.

Leg. Issues: BUD, ENG, ENV, NAT, WAS

Outside Counsel/Consultants

Arter & Hadden
Issues: WAS
Rep By: Daniel L. Cohen

Bracewell & Patterson, L.L.P.
Issues: BUD, ENG, ENV, NAT, WAS
Rep By: Hon. Edwin R. Bethune, Hon. Jim Chapman, Gene E. Godley, Marc C. Hebert, Charles L. Ingebretson, Michael L. Pate, Scott H. Segal, D. Michael Stroud, Jr.

Miller & Chevalier, Chartered
Issues: ENG
Rep By: Leonard Bickwit, Jr.

Podesta/Mattoon
Issues: WAS

Preston Gates Ellis & Rouvelas Meeds LLP
Issues: ENG, ENV
Rep By: Cindy O'Malley, Tim L. Peckinpaugh, William A. Shook, W. Dennis Stephens, Steven R. "Rick" Valentine

Environmental Action Group

Washington, DC

Promotes reasonable, market-based environmental policies.

Leg. Issues: ENV, GOV

Outside Counsel/Consultants

Valis Associates
Issues: ENV, GOV
Rep By: Hon. Richard T. Schulze, Todd Tolson, Wayne H. Valis

Environmental and Energy Study Institute

122 C St. NW
Suite 700
Washington, DC 20001
Tel: (202)628-1400
Fax: (202)628-1825
Web: www.eesi.org
E-mail: cwerner@eesi.org

Carries out research, analysis, and education programs. Publishes the Environment and Energy Weekly Bulletin digest of pending environmental legislation.

In-house, DC-area Employees

GRAY, Don: Director, Water and Sustainable Communities Program
WERNER, Carol: Exec. Director

Environmental Business Action Coalition

1015 15th St. NW
Suite 802
Washington, DC 20005
Tel: (202)347-7474
Fax: (202)898-0076
Registered: LDA
Web: www.ebac.org
E-mail: ebac@us.net

Formerly known as the Hazardous Waste Action Coalition. A coalition of the American Consulting Engineers Council aimed at serving engineering and science firms practicing hazardous environmental management and remediation.

Leg. Issues: ENV

In-house, DC-area Employees

BAKER, Emily A.: Deputy Exec. Director

Outside Counsel/Consultants

Kelley, Drye & Warren LLP
Rep By: Daniel M. Steinway

Preston Gates Ellis & Rouvelas Meeds LLP
Issues: ENV
Rep By: Tim L. Peckinpaugh

The Environmental Business Ass'n

1150 Connecticut Ave. NW
Suite 900
Washington, DC 20036
Tel: (202)828-4100
Fax: (202)828-4130

In-house, DC-area Employees
BODE, William H.: President

Outside Counsel/Consultants

Bode & Grenier LLP
Rep By: William H. Bode

The Environmental Co., Inc.

Charlottesville, VA

Outside Counsel/Consultants

Wayne Arny & Assoc.
Rep By: Wayne Arny

Environmental Commonsense Coalition

Sacramento, CA
Leg. Issues: BUD, CAW, ENV, RES

Outside Counsel/Consultants

Impact Strategies
Issues: BUD, CAW, ENV, RES
Rep By: Shannon Doyle, Jeff Fedorchak

Environmental Council of the States (ECOS)

Washington, DC
Leg. Issues: CAW, ENV, NAT, WAS

Outside Counsel/Consultants

Christopher A.G. Tulou
Issues: CAW, ENV, NAT, WAS
Rep By: Christopher A.G. Tulou

Environmental Defense Fund

1875 Connecticut Ave. NW
Suite 1016
Washington, DC 20009
Web: www.edf.org
Tel: (202)387-3500
Fax: (202)319-8590
Registered: LDA

A national membership organization staffed by scientists, economists and attorneys whose purpose is to protect environmental quality and public health. EDF's efforts are concentrated in four main areas: energy, toxic chemicals, water resources, and wildlife. Offices are maintained in New York City; Oakland, CA; Boulder, CO; and Austin, TX. Methods include scientific research, litigation, public education, and community organization.

Leg. Issues: CAW, ENV, MAR, NAT, TRA, UTI

In-house, DC-area Employees
BEAN, Michael: Chairman, Wildlife Program
FLORINI, Karen: Senior Staff Attorney, Toxics Program
PETSONK, Annie: Attorney
RICH, Bruce: Chairman, Internat'l Programs

Outside Counsel/Consultants

Conservation Strategies, LLC
Issues: CAW, NAT

Environmental Industry Ass'ns

4301 Connecticut Ave. NW
Suite 300
Washington, DC 20008
Web: www.envasns.org
Tel: (202)244-4700
Fax: (202)966-4818
Registered: LDA

Formerly the Nat'l Solid Wastes Management Ass'n. Restructured in 1994 to include the Nat'l Solid Wastes Management Ass'n and the Waste Equipment Technology Ass'n

Leg. Issues: CAW, ENV, GOV, LBR, TAX, TOR, TRU, WAS

In-house, DC-area Employees
BIDERMAN, David: General Counsel
JACOBSOHN, Alice P.: Acting Director, Industry Research and Communications
PARKER, Bruce J.: President and Chief Exec. Officer
REPA, Ph.D., Edward A.: Director, Environment Programs
SATTERFIELD, Gary T.: Exec. V. President, Waste Equipement Technology Ass'n
SELLS, Bill: Director, Federal Relations

Outside Counsel/Consultants

Akin, Gump, Strauss, Hauer & Feld, L.L.P.

Environmental Industry Coalition

Troy, NY

Outside Counsel/Consultants

Wilson & Wilson

Environmental Industry Council

Washington, DC

Outside Counsel/Consultants

John Adams Associates Inc.
Rep By: A. John Adams

Environmental Information Ass'n

4915 Auburn Ave.
Suite 204
Bethesda, MD 20814
Web: www.eia-usa.org
E-mail: info@eia-usa.org
Tel: (301)961-4999
Fax: (301)961-3094
Leg. Issues: ENV

In-house, DC-area Employees
KYNOCH, Brent: Managing Director

Environmental Land Technology Ltd.

Ketchum, ID

A land development firm.

Leg. Issues: ENV, NAT, RES

Outside Counsel/Consultants

Lee & Smith P.C.
Issues: ENV, NAT, RES
Rep By: David B. Lee

Kay Allan Morrell, Attorney-at-Law
Issues: ENV, NAT, RES
Rep By: Kay Allan Morrell

Environmental Law Institute

1616 P St. NW
Suite 200
Washington, DC 20036
Web: www.eli.org
E-mail: eli@eli.org
Tel: (202)939-3800
Fax: (202)939-3868

Maintains a program of research into current developments in environmental law and policy, provides a legal document service, and publishes journals for the bar, scholars, managers, public officials and other environmental affairs professionals.

In-house, DC-area Employees
DUJACK, Steve: Director, Communications
FUTRELL, J. William: President

Environmental Media Services

1320 18th St. NW
Suite 500
Washington, DC 20036
E-mail: ems@ems.org
Tel: (202)463-6670
Fax: (202)463-6671

Coordinates media campaigns for environmental and public health advocacy organizations.

In-house, DC-area Employees
SCHARDT, Arlie: President

Environmental Mutagen Soc.

11250 Roger Bacon Dr.
Suite Eight
Reston, VA 20190
E-mail: emsdmg@aol.com
Tel: (703)437-4377
Fax: (703)435-4390

Address, phone and fax are that of Drohan Management Group (see seperate listing).

In-house, DC-area Employees
PRICE, CAE, Randall C.: Exec. Director

Outside Counsel/Consultants

Drohan Management Group
Rep By: Randall C. Price, CAE

Environmental Redevelopers Ass'n

Washington, DC
Leg. Issues: ENV, RES

Outside Counsel/Consultants

Greenberg Traurig, LLP
Issues: ENV, RES
Rep By: Peter M. Gillon

Environmental Research and Education Foundation

Washington, DC
Leg. Issues: ENV

Outside Counsel/Consultants

Bob Davis & Associates
Issues: ENV
Rep By: Hon. Robert W. Davis

Environmental Systems Research Institute, Inc.

Redlands, CA
Leg. Issues: DEF, ENV

Outside Counsel/Consultants

Copeland, Lowery & Jacquez
Issues: DEF, ENV
Rep By: Jeffrey S. Shockey

Environmental Technologies Group

Baltimore, MD
Leg. Issues: DEF

Outside Counsel/Consultants

Donald E. Wilson Consulting
Issues: DEF

Environmental Technology Council

734 15th St. NW
Suite 720
Washington, DC 20005
Web: www.etc.org
Tel: (202)783-0870
Fax: (202)737-2038
Registered: LDA

Represents the hazardous waste disposal and treatment industries.

Leg. Issues: ENV, WAS

In-house, DC-area Employees
CASE, David: Exec. Director
SLESINGER, Scott: V. President, Government Affairs

Environmental Technology Unlimited

Slingerlands, NY
Leg. Issues: ENV

Outside Counsel/Consultants

The PMA Group
Issues: ENV
Rep By: Kaylene Green, Paul J. Magliocchetti, Kelli Short, Brian Thiel

Environmental Treatment and Technologies Corp.

Findlay, OH

Outside Counsel/Consultants

Howrey Simon Arnold & White

Environmental Working Group

1718 Connecticut Ave. NW
Suite 600
Washington, DC 20009
Web: www.ewg.org
E-mail: info@ewg.org
Tel: (202)667-6982
Fax: (202)232-2592

In-house, DC-area Employees
COOK, Kenneth A.: President
WILES, Richard: V. President

EnviroPower

Lexington, KY
Leg. Issues: ENG, ENV, TAX

Outside Counsel/Consultants

The Willard Group
Issues: ENG, ENV, TAX
Rep By: Daniel Scherder

Envirosource Technologies

Oregon, OH
Leg. Issues: ENV

Outside Counsel/Consultants

The Renkes Group, Ltd.
Issues: ENV
Rep By: Patrick Pettey

Envirotest Systems Corp.

6903 Rockledge Dr.
Suite 214
Bethesda, MD
Leg. Issues: CAW

Outside Counsel/Consultants

Holland & Knight LLP
Rep By: Janet R. Studley

Hunton & Williams
Issues: CAW

EO Tech

Ann Arbor, MI

Outside Counsel/Consultants

Interface Inc.
Rep By: Albert B. Rosenbaum, III

Ephedra Education Council

Washington, DC
Leg. Issues: FOO

Outside Counsel/Consultants

The Aker Partners Inc.
Issues: FOO
Rep By: G. Colburn Aker

Epik Communications
Leg. Issues: TEC

Outside Counsel/Consultants

Greenberg Traurig, LLP
Issues: TEC

Epilepsy Foundation of America
4351 Garden City Dr.
Landover, MD 20785
Tel: (301)459-3700
Fax: (301)577-2684
Registered: LDA
Web: www.epilepsyfoundation.org
E-mail: postmaster@efa.org

The only national, non-profit, voluntary agency in the U.S. specifically dedicated to the welfare of people with epilepsy. EFA is committed to the prevention and eventual cure of epilepsy and to improving the lives of epilepsy patients.

Leg. Issues: BUD, HCR

In-house, DC-area Employees

FINUCANE, Alexandra K.: V. President, Legal and Government Affairs
VAN HAVERBEKE, Peter: Director, Public Relations
WARD, Julie: Director, Government Affairs

Outside Counsel/Consultants

Arent Fox Kintner Plotkin & Kahn, PLLC
Issues: BUD, HCR
Rep By: Stacy Harbison, Douglas McCormack

Episcopal AIDS Ministry
Miami, FL
Leg. Issues: HCR

Outside Counsel/Consultants

Davis O'Connell, Inc.
Issues: HCR
Rep By: Lynda C. Davis, Ph.D.

Episcopal Church, Office of Government Relations
110 Maryland Ave. NE
Suite 309
Washington, DC 20002
Tel: (202)547-7300
Fax: (202)547-4457
Web: www.ecusa.anglican.org/eppn

Represents the positions of the Episcopal Church to the United States government. Headquartered in New York, NY.

In-house, DC-area Employees

HART, Thomas H.: Director, Government Relations

Episcopal Diocese of Washington
Washington, DC

Outside Counsel/Consultants

Neuman and Co.
Rep By: Robert A. Neuman

Equal Justice Coalition

Outside Counsel/Consultants

Verner, Liipfert, Bernhard, McPherson and Hand, Chartered
Rep By: Jamie E. Brown, Lawrence E. Levinson, Harry C. McPherson, Neil T. Proto

EqualFooting.com
Sterling, VA
Leg. Issues: SMB

Outside Counsel/Consultants

Verner, Liipfert, Bernhard, McPherson and Hand, Chartered
Issues: SMB
Rep By: Marla P. Grossman, Jenifer Martin

Equatorial Guinea, Republic of
Leg. Issues: FOR

Outside Counsel/Consultants

Africa Global Partners
Issues: FOR
Rep By: Mimi Nedelcovych

Equifax Inc.
Atlanta, GA
Registered: LDA
Leg. Issues: BAN, CPI, CSP

Outside Counsel/Consultants

Mullenholz, Brimsek & Belair
Issues: BAN, CPI, CSP
Rep By: Robert R. Belair, Susan C. Haller

Equinoccial, S.A.
Quito, ECUADOR

Outside Counsel/Consultants

Pierre E. Murphy Law Offices

Equipment Leasing Ass'n of America
4301 N. Fairfax Dr.
Suite 550
Arlington, VA 22203-1627
Tel: (703)527-8655
Fax: (703)527-2649
Registered: LDA
Web: www.elaonline.com/
Leg. Issues: BNK, ENV, FIN, TAX, TOR

Political Action Committee/s

Lease-PAC
4301 N. Fairfax Dr.
Suite 550
Arlington, VA 22203-1627
Contact: Steven I. Fier
Tel: (703)527-8655
Fax: (703)527-2649

In-house, DC-area Employees

FIER, Steven I.: Director, Federal Government Relations
FLEMING, Michael J.: President
MILLER, Amy: V. President, Communications

Outside Counsel/Consultants

Dykema Gossett PLLC
Edwin E. Huddleson, III
Issues: ENV, FIN
Rep By: Edwin E. Huddleson, III

Equitable Assurance Soc. of the United States
New York, NY

Outside Counsel/Consultants

Murray, Scheer, Montgomery, Tapia & O'Donnell
Rep By: Thomas R. Crawford, D. Michael Murray

The Equitable Cos.
New York, NY
Leg. Issues: BAN, FIN, INS, RET, TAX

Outside Counsel/Consultants

Bryan Cave LLP
Murray, Scheer, Montgomery, Tapia & O'Donnell
Issues: BAN, FIN, INS, RET, TAX
Rep By: Thomas R. Crawford, D. Michael Murray

Equitable Financial Co.
New York, NY

Outside Counsel/Consultants

Washington World Group, Ltd.
Rep By: Edward J. von Kloberg, III

Equitable Resources Energy Co.
Kingsport, TN
Leg. Issues: CAW, ENG, ENV, WAS

Outside Counsel/Consultants

Wright & Talisman, P.C.
Issues: CAW, ENG, ENV, WAS
Rep By: Robert H. Lamb

Equitas Reinsurance Ltd.
London, UNITED KINGDOM
Leg. Issues: INS

Outside Counsel/Consultants

Baach Robinson & Lewis, PLLC
Issues: INS
Rep By: Benjamin L. Zelenko

Eramet Marietta Inc.
Marietta, OH
A manganese smelter.

Outside Counsel/Consultants

Robert N. Pyle & Associates

Eregli Demir ve Celik Fab.
Istanbul, TURKEY

Outside Counsel/Consultants

Law Offices of David L. Simon
Rep By: David L. Simon

Ergo Science Corp.
Charlestown, MA
Leg. Issues: SCI

Outside Counsel/Consultants

Venable
Issues: SCI
Rep By: David G. Adams

Ergodyne
St. Paul, MN
Leg. Issues: LBR

Outside Counsel/Consultants

Jefferson Government Relations, L.L.C.
Issues: LBR
Rep By: Robert D. McArver, Jr., Randal P. Schumacher

Erickson Air-Crane Co.
Central Point, OR

Outside Counsel/Consultants

Zuckert, Scoutt and Rasenberger, L.L.P.
Rep By: Rachel B. Trinder

Ericsson Inc.
1634 I St. NW
Suite 600
Washington, DC 20006-4083
Tel: (202)783-2200
Fax: (202)783-2206
Registered: LDA
Web: www.ericsson.com

A telecommunications equipment manufacturer headquartered in Richardson, TX.

Leg. Issues: TEC

In-house, DC-area Employees

BAFFER, Barbara: Director, Public Affairs and Regulation
GIERE, John: V. President, Marketing and Public Affairs
LINDSTROM, Tom: Director, Regulatory Policy
PEPER, Jennifer: Manager, Legislative Affairs

Outside Counsel/Consultants

Patrick M. Murphy & Associates
Issues: TEC

Erie Internat'l Airport
Erie, PA
Leg. Issues: AVI, BUD, ECN, TRA, URB

Outside Counsel/Consultants

The Peterson Group
Issues: AVI, BUD, ECN, TRA, URB
Rep By: William P. Sears, Craig Snyder

ERIM
Arlington, VA
Leg. Issues: BUD, DEF, FOR, SCI

Outside Counsel/Consultants

Dykema Gossett PLLC
Issues: DEF, SCI
Rep By: Tricia K. Markwood
EMI Associates, Ltd.
Issues: BUD, FOR
Rep By: Eugene M. Iwanciw

Erin Engineering and Research, Inc.
Walnut Creek, CA
Leg. Issues: ENG

Outside Counsel/Consultants

The Palmer Group
Issues: ENG
Rep By: Clifford A. Palmer

The ERISA Industry Committee (ERIC)
1400 L St. NW
Suite 350
Washington, DC 20005
Tel: (202)789-1400
Fax: (202)789-1120
Registered: LDA
Web: www.eric.org
E-mail: eric@eric.org

A non-profit association committed to the advancement of employee retirement, health, and welfare benefit plans of America's largest "Fortune 200" employers. Provides comprehensive retirement, health care coverage and other economic security benefits directly to some 25 million active and retired workers and their families.

Leg. Issues: BUD, HCR, LBR, RET, TAX

In-house, DC-area Employees

GREGORY, Janice M.: V. President
KNETTEL, Anthony J.: V. President, Health Policy
UGORETZ, Mark J.: President

Outside Counsel/Consultants

Covington & Burling
Issues: HCR, RET
Rep By: John M. Vine

Eritrea, Government of
Asmara, ERITREA

Outside Counsel/Consultants

O'Donnell, Schwartz & Anderson, P.C.

Ernst & Young LLP

1225 Connecticut Ave. NW
Washington, DC 20036
Tel: (202)327-6000
Fax: (202)327-6200
Registered: LDA
Web: www.ey.com
Leg. Issues: BAN, CPI, TRD

Political Action Committee/s

Ernst & Young Political Action Committee
1225 Connecticut Ave. NW
Washington, DC 20036
Tel: (202)327-7584
Fax: (202)327-8863
Contact: Kathryn "K.C." Tominovich

In-house, DC-area Employees

BRORSEN, Les: National Director, Government Relations
DARLING, Lauren: Senior Manager
HECK, Patrick G.: Senior Manager
MOSELEY, Phillip D.: National Director, Legislative Services
NUEBIG, Tom S.
PEARSON, Mary Frances: Director, Federal Relations
PORTER, John D.: Senior Manager
ROSENBLUM, Jay E.: Director
RUEMPLER, Henry C.: Partner
STEELE-FLYNN, Donna: Senior Manager
TOMINOVICH, Kathryn "K.C.": Political and Legislative Director

Outside Counsel/Consultants

American Continental Group, Inc.
Issues: BAN
Rep By: David A. Metzner, Shawn H. Smeallie, Thaddeus E. Strom, Peter Terpeluk, Jr.

Mayer, Brown & Platt
Issues: CPI, TRD
Rep By: Carol J. Bilzi, Mark H. Gitenstein, Jeffrey H. Lewis, Carolyn P. Osolinik, Charles A. Rothfeld

ESA, Inc.

Chelmsford, MA
Leg. Issues: BUD, HCR

Outside Counsel/Consultants

Health and Medicine Counsel of Washington
Issues: BUD, HCR
Rep By: Dale P. Dirks, Gavin Lindberg

Eschenbach USA, Inc.

Leg. Issues: TRD

Outside Counsel/Consultants

Martin G. Hamberger & Associates
Issues: TRD
Rep By: Martin G. Hamberger

ESCO Corp.

Portland, OR

Outside Counsel/Consultants

Sam Richardson
Rep By: Sam Richardson

The ESOP (Employee Stock Ownership Plan) Ass'n

1726 M St. NW
Suite 501
Washington, DC 20036
Tel: (202)293-2971
Fax: (202)293-7568
Registered: LDA
Web: www.esopassociation.org
E-mail: esop@esopassociation.org
Leg. Issues: GOV, RET, TAX

Political Action Committee/s

ESOP PAC
1726 M St. NW
Suite 501
Washington, DC 20036
Tel: (202)293-2971
Fax: (202)293-7568
Contact: J. Michael Keeling

In-house, DC-area Employees

KEELING, J. Michael: President

Outside Counsel/Consultants

Winston & Strawn
Issues: GOV, RET, TAX
Rep By: Hon. Beryl F. Anthony, Jr., Charles L. Kinney

Scott J. Esparza & Co.

Ventura, CA
Leg. Issues: CIV, LAW

Outside Counsel/Consultants

Kay Allan Morrell, Attorney-at-Law
Issues: CIV, LAW
Rep By: Kay Allan Morrell

Espee Trading Corp.

Richmond Hill, NY

Outside Counsel/Consultants

Rodriguez O'Donnell Fuerst Gonzalez & Williams
Rep By: Carlos Rodriguez

Espey Manufacturing and Electronics

Saratoga Springs, NY
Leg. Issues: DEF, MAN, TRD

Outside Counsel/Consultants

The Solomon Group, LLC
Issues: DEF, MAN, TRD
Rep By: David M. Lonie, Hon. Gerald B. H. Solomon

ESPN, Inc.

New York, NY
Leg. Issues: COM

Outside Counsel/Consultants

Holland & Knight LLP
Issues: COM
Rep By: Ronald A. Oleynik

ESR Children's Health Care System

Atlanta, GA
Leg. Issues: HCR, MMM

Outside Counsel/Consultants

King & Spalding
Issues: HCR, MMM
Rep By: Allison Kassir, William C. Talmadge

Essential Information Inc.

P.O. Box 19405
Washington, DC 20036
Tel: (202)387-8030
Fax: (202)234-5176
Web: www.essential.org

A corporate watchdog organization started by Ralph Nader.

In-house, DC-area Employees

RICHARD, John: Secretary

Essential Technologies, Inc.

Leg. Issues: DEF

Outside Counsel/Consultants

The Conaway Group LLC
Issues: DEF
Rep By: Lt. Gen. John B. Conaway, USAF (Ret.), James L. Hobgood

Essex Medical Systems Plus

St. Louis, MO
Leg. Issues: HCR, MMM

Outside Counsel/Consultants

Nusgart Consulting, LLC
Issues: HCR, MMM
Rep By: Marcia Nusgart

Estee Lauder, Inc.

New York, NY
Leg. Issues: TAX, TRD

Outside Counsel/Consultants

Williams & Jensen, P.C.
Issues: TAX, TRD
Rep By: George D. Baker, Robert E. Glennon, Jr.

Republic of Estonia

Tallinn, ESTONIA

Outside Counsel/Consultants

Downey McGrath Group, Inc.

Ethics and Public Policy Center

1015 15th St. NW
Suite 900
Washington, DC 20005
Tel: (202)682-1200
Fax: (202)408-0632
Web: www.eppc.org
E-mail: ethics@eppc.org

An independent research and education organization established in 1976 and affiliated with Georgetown University until 1980. Does research and publishes studies on major national and international issues while affirming political relevance of fundamental Western ethical standards and giving special attention to the role of religious organizations in public policy formulation.

In-house, DC-area Employees

ABRAMS, Elliott: President
CROMARTIE, Michael: V. President

Ethics and Religious Liberty Commission of the Southern Baptist Convention

505 Second St. NE
Washington, DC 20002-4916
Tel: (202)547-8105
Fax: (202)547-8165
Web: www.erlc.com

Religious liberty and ethics advocate for the Southern Baptist Convention. Headquartered in Nashville, TN.

In-house, DC-area Employees

ROYCE, Shannon: Director of Government Relations and Legislative Counsel
SANDERS, Dr. S. King: Director of Constituent Relations
STRODE, Tom: Bureau Chief for Baptist Press

Ethics Resource Center Inc.

1747 Pennsylvania Ave. NW
Suite 400
Washington, DC 20006
Tel: (202)737-2258
Fax: (202)737-2227
Registered: LDA
Web: www.ethics.org
E-mail: ethics@ethics.org

Founded in 1977, the Ethics Resource Center is a non-profit, nonpartisan educational organization promoting ethical practices in individuals and institutions. Works in four core leadership areas: institution and coalition development, research and knowledge building, consulting and technical assistance, and education and advocacy.

Leg. Issues: EDU, FOR, GOV, LBR

In-house, DC-area Employees

DAIGNEAULT, Michael G.: President
HARNED, Ph.D., Patricia J.: Director of Character Development

Ethiopia, Government of

Addis Ababa, ETHIOPIA

Outside Counsel/Consultants

Akin, Gump, Strauss, Hauer & Feld, L.L.P.

Ethyl Corp.

1155 15th St. NW
Suite 611
Washington, DC 20005
Tel: (202)223-4411
Fax: (202)223-1849
Registered: LDA
Web: www.ethyl.com

Headquartered in Richmond, VA.

Leg. Issues: AUT, CAW, CHM, CSP, ENV, RRR, TRD

In-house, DC-area Employees

LITTLE, Barbara A.: V. President, Government Relations

Ethyl Petroleum Additives, Inc.

Richmond, VA
Leg. Issues: CAW, ENV, FUE

Outside Counsel/Consultants

Nat'l Environmental Strategies
Issues: CAW, ENV, FUE
Rep By: Marc I. Himmelstein, Richard D. Wilson

Ethylene Oxide Sterilization Ass'n, Inc.

Washington, DC
Web: www.eosa.org
Leg. Issues: CSP, MAN, MED, WAS

Outside Counsel/Consultants

Hadley & McKenna
Issues: CSP, MAN, MED, WAS
Rep By: Joseph E. Hadley, Jr.

Eugene Water and Electric Board

Eugene, OR
Leg. Issues: ENG

Outside Counsel/Consultants

Kanner & Associates
Issues: ENG
Rep By: Martin B. Kanner

Eugene, Oregon, City of

Leg. Issues: BUD, CAW, LAW, TRA, URB

Outside Counsel/Consultants

Smith Dawson & Andrews, Inc.
Issues: BUD, CAW, LAW, TRA, URB
Rep By: Sherri Powar, James P. Smith

Eurapair International, Inc.

Laguna Beach, CA
Leg. Issues: IMM

Outside Counsel/Consultants

Hill and Knowlton, Inc.
Issues: IMM
Rep By: Fred DuVal, Gary G. Hymel, Frank Mankiewicz

Eureka, California, City of
Leg. Issues: BUD, ENV, NAT, RES, TOU
Outside Counsel/Consultants
Reed, Smith, LLP
Issues: BUD, ENV, NAT, RES, TOU
Rep By: Christopher L. Rissetto

Eurex Deutschland
Frankfurt, GERMANY
Leg. Issues: CDT
Outside Counsel/Consultants
Williams & Jensen, P.C.
Issues: CDT
Rep By: George D. Baker

Euro-Fulton, S.A.
Brussels, BELGIUM
Leg. Issues: TRD
Outside Counsel/Consultants
TerraCom-Strategic Communications
Issues: TRD
Rep By: Felix R. Sanchez

European Aeronautics, Defence and Space, Inc.
815 Connecticut Ave. NW
Suite 700
Washington, DC 20006
Tel: (202)776-0988
Fax: (202)776-9080
Registered: LDA, FARA
Leg. Issues: AER, AVI, DEF
In-house, DC-area Employees
VON NORDHEIM, Manfred: President and Chief Exec. Officer
Outside Counsel/Consultants
The ILEX Group
Issues: AER, AVI, DEF
Rep By: H. Hollister Cantus

European Commission Delegation
2300 M St. NW
Third Floor
Washington, DC 20037-1434
Web: www.erunion.org
Tel: (202)862-9500
Fax: (202)429-1766
In-house, DC-area Employees
HELIN, Willy: Director, Office of Press and Public Affairs

European Confederation of Iron and Steel Industries (EUROFER)
Brussels, BELGIUM
The confederation of European steelmakers.
Leg. Issues: TRD
Outside Counsel/Consultants
Internat'l Advisory Services Group Ltd.
Issues: TRD
Rep By: Charles H. Blum

European Energy Company Coalition
Outside Counsel/Consultants
Patton Boggs, LLP
Rep By: Thomas Hale Boggs, Jr., Jeffrey L. Turner

European Space Agency
Paris, FRANCE
Outside Counsel/Consultants
Ober, Kaler, Grimes & Shriver

European Telecommunications Standards Institute (ETSI)
Sophia Antipolis Cedex, FRANCE
Outside Counsel/Consultants
The Dutko Group, Inc.
Rep By: Kim Koontz Bayliss, Steve Perry, Juliette M. Raffensperger, Stephen Craig Sayle

European-American Business Council
1333 H St. NW
Suite 630
Washington, DC 20004
Web: www.eabc.org
E-mail: eabc@eabc.org
Tel: (202)347-9292
Fax: (202)628-5498
Registered: LDA
A joint endeavor of 85 multinational corporations with operations in both Europe and the U.S. to promote and sustain a healthy and open business climate worldwide.
Leg. Issues: TRD
In-house, DC-area Employees
BERRY, Willard M.: President
SHEIRE, James B.: Director, Government Affairs

European-American Phytomedicine Coalition
Paris, FRANCE
Outside Counsel/Consultants
Akin, Gump, Strauss, Hauer & Feld, L.L.P.

EUTELSAT
Paris, FRANCE
Leg. Issues: TEC
Outside Counsel/Consultants
Powell, Goldstein, Frazer & Murphy LLP
Issues: TEC
Rep By: Kelly Cameron, Brett G. Kappel, David C. Quam

EV Rental Cars, LLC
Calabasas, CA
Leg. Issues: AUT, BUD, ENV, TRA
Outside Counsel/Consultants
Jefferson Government Relations, L.L.C.
Issues: AUT, BUD, ENV, TRA
Rep By: William A. Roberts

Eva Airways Corp.
Taipei, CHINA (TAIWAN)
Outside Counsel/Consultants
Zuckert, Scoutt and Rasenberger, L.L.P.
Rep By: Malcolm L. Benge, Rachel B. Trinder

EVA Corp.
Roseville, MN
Outside Counsel/Consultants
Lawler, Metzger & Milkman, LLC
Rep By: Sante J. Esposito

Evangelical Lutheran Good Samaritan Soc.
Sioux Falls, SD
A nonprofit, long-term care and associated health care facility company.
Leg. Issues: HCR
Outside Counsel/Consultants
Lockridge Grindal & Nauen, P.L.L.P.
Issues: HCR
Rep By: Dennis McGrann

Everett, Washington, Port of
Everett, WA
Leg. Issues: DEF, MAR, TRA, TRD
Outside Counsel/Consultants
Denny Miller McBee Associates
Issues: DEF, MAR, TRA, TRD
The Spectrum Group
Issues: TRA
Rep By: Joan Bondareff, Dr. John Lynch

Everglades Coordinating Council
Pembroke Pines, FL
Leg. Issues: NAT, RES
Outside Counsel/Consultants
Ron C. Marlenee
Issues: NAT, RES
Rep By: Hon. Ron C. Marlenee

Everglades Defense Council
Coral Gables, FL
Leg. Issues: ENV
Outside Counsel/Consultants
Bergner Bockorny Castagnetti and Hawkins
Issues: ENV
Rep By: Jeffrey T. Bergner, David A. Bockorny, David Castagnetti, James W. Hawkins

Everglades Trust
Orlando, FL
Leg. Issues: ENV
Outside Counsel/Consultants
The Washington Group
Issues: ENV
Rep By: G. John O'Hanlon, Mark Schnabel, Fowler West

Evergreen Internat'l Aviation
1629 K St. NW
Suite 301
Washington, DC 20006
Tel: (202)466-2929
Fax: (202)659-2184
Registered: LDA
A total aviation capabilities company specializing in airplane and helicopter operations, including sales, leasing, ground services, maintenance and storage.
In-house, DC-area Employees
LYDON, Tom: Director, Governmental Affairs

Everpure
Westmont, IL
Outside Counsel/Consultants
Interface Inc.
Rep By: Robert G. Williams

EWA Land Information Group, Inc.
Herndon, VA
Leg. Issues: DEF
Outside Counsel/Consultants
American Defense Internat'l, Inc.
Issues: DEF
Rep By: Michael Herson, Van D. Hipp, Jr., Dave Wilberding
John G. Campbell, Inc.
Issues: DEF
Fleischman and Walsh, L.L.P.
Issues: DEF
Rep By: Louis H. Dupart

EWI-Re Ltd.
New York, NY
A reinsurance company.
Outside Counsel/Consultants
Ottosen and Associates
Rep By: Karl J. Ottosen

Ex-Partners of Servicemembers for Equality
P.O. Box 11191
Alexandria, VA 22312
Tel: (703)941-5844
Fax: (703)212-6951
Members are former spouses of military personnel and other persons supporting the cause. Seeks federal laws to restore to ex-spouses military benefits lost through divorce. Disseminates information on federal laws and Department of Defense regulations impacting on military personnel divorces.
Leg. Issues: DEF, FAM
In-house, DC-area Employees
ROGERS, Kathleen: Director

EXACT Laboratories
Maynard, MA
Leg. Issues: HCR
Outside Counsel/Consultants
Heidepriem & Mager, Inc.
Issues: HCR
Rep By: Christopher Gould, Nikki Heidepriem

EXCEL Communications Inc.
Dallas, TX
Leg. Issues: COM, TEC, TRD
Outside Counsel/Consultants
The Dutko Group, Inc.
Issues: COM, TEC, TRD
Rep By: Kim Koontz Bayliss, Louis Lehrman, Steve Perry, Juliette M. Raffensperger, Stephen Craig Sayle

Excelsior Gaming, Inc.
Outside Counsel/Consultants
Dorsey & Whitney LLP
Rep By: David A. Bieging, Kevin J. Wadzinski

Executive Jet
Montvale, NJ
Leg. Issues: AVI
Outside Counsel/Consultants
Hogan & Hartson L.L.P.
Issues: AVI
Rep By: E. Tazewell Ellett, William Michael House, Jeffrey W. Munk

Executive Leadership Council and Foundation
1010 Wisconsin Ave. NW
Suite 520
Washington, DC 20007
Web: www.elcinfo.com
Tel: (202)298-8226
Fax: (202)298-8074

In-house, DC-area Employees
JOLLY, Ernest: Interim Exec. Director

Executive Life Insurance Co.
Englewood, CA
Outside Counsel/Consultants
Akin, Gump, Strauss, Hauer & Feld, L.L.P.

EXECUTONE Information Systems, Inc.
Milford, CT
Leg. Issues: GAM
Outside Counsel/Consultants
Commonwealth Group, Ltd.
Issues: GAM
Rep By: Christopher T. Cushing

Exelon Corp.
400 Seventh St. NW
Fourth Floor
Washington, DC 20004
Web: www.exeloncorp.com
Tel: (202)347-7500
Fax: (202)347-7501
Registered: LDA

A diversified energy company created in 2000 by the merger of PECO Energy Company of Philadelphia and Unicom Corporation, the parent company of Commonwealth Edison of Chicago. Headquartered in Chicago, IL.

Leg. Issues: CAW, ENG, ENV, FUE, GOV, LBR, NAT, RRR, TAX, TEC, TRA, UTI, WAS

Political Action Committee/s
Exelon PAC
400 Seventh St. NW
Fourth Floor
Washington, DC 20004
Contact: David C. Brown
Tel: (202)347-7500
Fax: (202)347-7501

In-house, DC-area Employees
BROWN, David C.: V. President, Congressional Affairs
CAPUTO, Annie: Manager, Congressional Affairs
MOLER, Elizabeth A.: Senior V. President, Government Affairs & Policy

Outside Counsel/Consultants
Bonner & Associates

Kessler & Associates Business Services, Inc.
Issues: TAX
Rep By: Michael L. Bartlett, Billy Lee Evans, Richard S. Kessler, James C. Musser, Harry Sporidis

Exeter Architectural Products
Leg. Issues: DIS
Outside Counsel/Consultants
Arent Fox Kintner Plotkin & Kahn, PLLC
Issues: DIS
Rep By: Stacy Harbison, Alison Kutler, Douglas McCormack, Michael T. McNamara, Todd Weiss

Exhibit Designers and Producers Ass'n
1101 15th St. NW
Suite 202
Washington, DC 20005
Tel: (202)785-3232
Fax: (202)223-9741
In-house, DC-area Employees
CRISTOL, Richard E.: Washington Representative
Outside Counsel/Consultants
The Kellen Company
Rep By: Richard E. Cristol

Exide Corp.
Ann Arbor, MI
Leg. Issues: TRD
Outside Counsel/Consultants
Mehl, Griffin & Bartek Ltd.
Issues: TRD
Rep By: Ronald J. Bartek, Molly Griffin, William A. Marsh, Theodore J. Mehl

Exolve
Outside Counsel/Consultants
Dittus Communications
Rep By: Jennifer Garfinkel, Chris McNamara

Export Control Coalition
Washington, DC
Leg. Issues: CPI, TRD
Outside Counsel/Consultants
The Polling Company
Issues: CPI
Rep By: Kellyanne Fitzpatrick

Wilmer, Cutler & Pickering
Issues: TRD
Rep By: Charles S. Levy

Export Council for Energy Efficiency
Washington, DC
Leg. Issues: COM, ENG, TRD
Outside Counsel/Consultants
Duncan, Weinberg, Genzer & Pembroke, P.C.
Issues: COM, ENG, TRD
Rep By: Jeffrey C. Genzer

Export Management Services, Inc.
Alexandria, VA
Leg. Issues: DEF, ECN, GOV, VET
Outside Counsel/Consultants
The Eagles Group
Issues: DEF, ECN, GOV, VET
Rep By: Terence Costello

Export Source Coalition
Washington, DC
E-mail: jtd@cat.com

A coalition concerned with retention of current export source rule and the ability of U.S. exporters to compete in world markets.

Leg. Issues: TAX, TRD
Outside Counsel/Consultants
Miller & Chevalier, Chartered
Issues: TAX

Exportadora de Sal, S.A. de C.V.
Guerrero Negro, MEXICO
Outside Counsel/Consultants
Ruder Finn Washington
Rep By: D. Craig Martin

Express Forwarding and Storage, Inc.
New York, NY
Outside Counsel/Consultants
Denning & Wohlstetter

Express One Internat'l Inc.
Dallas, TX
Leg. Issues: POS, TRA
Outside Counsel/Consultants
Brownstein Hyatt & Farber, P.C.
Issues: POS, TRA
Rep By: William T. Brack, Thomas H. Hudson, Michael B. Levy

Express Pipeline Partnership and Platte Pipeline Co.
Calgary, CANADA
Leg. Issues: CAW, ENG, ENV, FUE, TRD
Outside Counsel/Consultants
Leonard B. Levine & Associates
Issues: CAW, ENG, ENV, FUE, TRD
Rep By: Leonard B. Levine

Express Scripts Inc.
Leg. Issues: DEF, HCR, MMM
Outside Counsel/Consultants
Capitol Health Group, LLC
Issues: HCR, MMM
Rep By: Michael D. Bromberg, Shawn Coughlin, Steven Jenning, Layna McConkey Peltier

Public Policy Partners, LLC
Issues: DEF, HCR
Rep By: Hon. David Durenberger, Daniel Waldmann, Jeffrey Weekly

EXPRO Chemical Products
Quebec, CANADA
Leg. Issues: BUD, CHM, DEF, FIR
Outside Counsel/Consultants
A. L. Ross Associates, Inc.
Issues: BUD, CHM, DEF, FIR
Rep By: Alan L. Ross

Extendicare Health Services Inc.
Milwaukee, WI
Leg. Issues: HCR
Outside Counsel/Consultants
Broydrick & Associates
Issues: HCR
Rep By: Amy Demske

ExtrudeHone Corp.
Irwin, PA
Leg. Issues: AER, BUD, DEF, MAN, SCI
Outside Counsel/Consultants
Charlie McBride Associates, Inc.
Issues: BUD, DEF, MAN
Rep By: Charlie McBride

Denny Miller McBee Associates
Issues: AER, BUD, DEF, SCI

Exxon Chemical Co.
Houston, TX
Leg. Issues: CAW, GOV
Outside Counsel/Consultants
Swidler Berlin Shereff Friedman, LLP
Issues: CAW, GOV
Rep By: Charles H. Knauss

Exxon Co., U.S.A.
Houston, TX
A division of Exxon Mobil Corp.
Outside Counsel/Consultants
Covington & Burling
Rep By: Harvey M. Applebaum

Howrey Simon Arnold & White
Rep By: Robert G. Abrams

Exxon Mobil Corp.
2001 Pennsylvania Ave. NW
Suite 300
Washington, DC 20006
Tel: (202)862-0200
Fax: (202)862-0267
Registered: LDA

Leg. Issues: ANI, BUD, CAW, CHM, CPT, CSP, ENG, ENV, FIN, FOR, FUE, GOV, HCR, IMM, LAW, LBR, MAR, MMM, NAT, TAX, TOR, TRA, TRD, UTI

In-house, DC-area Employees
HAINES, Robert W.: Manager, International Relations
HAMMER, Amy R.: Washington Representative, U.S. Senate
JACKSON, Lorie D.: Washington Representative, International Issues
RANDOL, III, A. G.: Senior Washington Representative, Environmental Issues
ROUSE, James J.: V. President, Washington Office
SCHELLER, Nora: Washington Representative, Government Agencies
SMITH, Randy T.: Washington Representative, House of Representatives

Outside Counsel/Consultants
Akin, Gump, Strauss, Hauer & Feld, L.L.P.
Issues: ENG, ENV, FOR, FUE, NAT, TAX
Rep By: David P. Callett, Smith W. Davis, David Geanacopoulos, Barney J. Skladany, Jr., Henry A. Terhune, Robin Weisman

Bryan Cave LLP
Rep By: Stanley J. Marcuss

Miller & Chevalier, Chartered
Issues: ENG
Rep By: Leonard Bickwit, Jr., Homer E. Moyer, Jr.

O'Connor & Hannan, L.L.P.
Issues: ENV, NAT
Rep By: Robert W. Barrie, Hon. Thomas J. Corcoran, George J. Mannina, Jr., Patrick E. O'Donnell

Valis Associates
Issues: CSP, ENG, GOV, TAX, TOR, TRD
Rep By: Dana W. Hudson, Hon. Dan Schaefer, Hon. Richard T. Schulze, Wayne H. Valis

Winner & Associates

Exxon Valdez Oil Spill Litigation Plaintiffs
Cordova, AK

A group of 40,000 commercial fisherman, native Alaskans, and others injured by the 1989 Exxon Valdez oil spill in Prince William Sound, Alaska.

Leg. Issues: ENV, FUE, LAW, MAR, TAX
Outside Counsel/Consultants
Dickstein Shapiro Morin & Oshinsky LLP
Issues: ENV, FUE, LAW, MAR, TAX
Rep By: Kenneth L. Adams, Bernard Nash

The Eyak Corp.
Crodova, AK
Leg. Issues: RES
Outside Counsel/Consultants
Birch, Horton, Bittner & Cherot
Issues: RES
Rep By: Roy S. Jones, Jr.

Eye Bank Ass'n of America

1015 18th St. NW
Suite 1010
Washington, DC 20036
Web: www.restoresight.org
E-mail: sightebaa@aol.com

Tel: (202)775-4999
Fax: (202)429-6036

Provides donor awareness literature on corneal transplantation, funds scientific research, legislates medical standards, accredits eye banks and trains technicians.

Leg. Issues: GOV, HCR, MED, MMM, SCI

In-house, DC-area Employees

AIKEN-O'NEILL, Patricia: President and Chief Exec. Officer

Outside Counsel/Consultants

The Legislative Strategies Group, LLC
Issues: HCR, MED, MMM
Rep By: Martin B. Gold, Denise M. Henry

EyeTicket Corp.

McLean, VA
Leg. Issues: SCI

Outside Counsel/Consultants

Winston & Strawn
Issues: SCI
Rep By: Hon. James H. Burnley, IV, Charles L. Kinney, Douglas C. Richardson

ezgov.com

Atlanta, GA

Outside Counsel/Consultants

Barbour Griffith & Rogers, Inc.

Troutman Sanders LLP
Rep By: Mary Clare Fitzgerald, William P. Marsan

Factiva

Princeton, NJ
Leg. Issues: GOV

Outside Counsel/Consultants

JFS Group, Ltd.
Issues: GOV

Fair Atlantic Salmon Trade

Outside Counsel/Consultants

Collier Shannon Scott, PLLC
Rep By: Michael J. Coursey

Fair Government Foundation

1100 Connecticut Ave. NW
Suite 330
Washington, DC 20036

Tel: (202)955-9001

A non-profit, non-partisan organization engaged in research and public education about governmental restraints upon First Amendment rights of free speech, association and political action, including regulation of campaign finance, ethics and lobbying.

In-house, DC-area Employees

DAHL, Bob: President

Fair Share Coalition

Leg. Issues: TAX

Outside Counsel/Consultants

Dean Blakey & Moskowitz
Issues: TAX
Rep By: John E. Dean, Saul L. Moskowitz

Fair Trade Group

Washington, DC

Outside Counsel/Consultants

Talley and Associates
Rep By: Robert A. C. Talley

Fairbanks, Alaska, North Star Borough of

Leg. Issues: BUD, CAW, TRA

Outside Counsel/Consultants

Birch, Horton, Bittner & Cherot
Issues: BUD, CAW, TRA
Rep By: Thomas L. Albert, Ronald G. Birch, William P. Horn

Fairchild Aircraft, Inc.

San Antonio, TX
Registered: LDA

Outside Counsel/Consultants

Arter & Hadden
Rep By: Hon. Thomas G. Loeffler, Jon W. Plebani

Fairfax County Water Authority

Fairfax, VA
Leg. Issues: CAW

Outside Counsel/Consultants

Alcalde & Fay
Issues: CAW
Rep By: Kevin J. Fay, Mary Litton Fowler, Nancy Gibson Prowitt

Fairfax, Virginia, County of

Fairfax, VA
Leg. Issues: AVI, BUD, CAW, ECN, ENV, HOU, RES, ROD, TRA, URB, WAS

Outside Counsel/Consultants

Government Relations, Inc.
Issues: AVI, BUD, CAW, ECN, ENV, HOU, RES, ROD, TRA, URB, WAS
Rep By: Thomas J. Bulger, Mark H. Miller, John N. Young

Fairfield University

Fairfield, CT
Leg. Issues: BUD, ECN

Outside Counsel/Consultants

Cassidy & Associates, Inc.
Issues: BUD
Rep By: Carl Franklin Godfrey, Jr., Laura A. Neal, Hon. Martin A. Russo

Lawler, Metzger & Milkman, LLC
Issues: ECN
Rep By: Sante J. Esposito, Gregory E. Lawler

Fairfield, California, City of

Leg. Issues: BUD, DEF, ECN, TRA

Outside Counsel/Consultants

The Ferguson Group, LLC
Issues: BUD, DEF, ECN, TRA
Rep By: William Ferguson, Jr., W. Roger Gwinn, Charmayne Macon, Mike Miller, Leslie Waters Mozingo

Madison Government Affairs
Issues: DEF, ECN
Rep By: Paul J. Hirsch

Fairview Hospital and Healthcare Services

Minneapolis, MN
Leg. Issues: BUD, DEF

Outside Counsel/Consultants

Cassidy & Associates, Inc.
Issues: BUD
Rep By: Dennis M. Kedzior, Sean O'Shea, Barbara Sutton, Maureen Walsh

Bruce Ray & Company
Issues: DEF
Rep By: Bruce A. Ray, Ph.D.

Faith & Politics Institute

110 Maryland Ave. NE
Suite 304
Washington, DC 20002
E-mail: faithpol1@aol.com

Tel: (202)546-1299
Fax: (202)546-4025

The Institute is an interfaith, bi-partisan, and non-profit organization that offers members of Congress and others in politics a variety of activities to fortify their commitments to both conscience and constituents.

In-house, DC-area Employees

LAMBERT, Dennis: Exec. Director
TANNER, Rev. W. Douglas: President

Fajardo, Puerto Rico, Municipality of

Fajardo, PR
Leg. Issues: TRA, URB

Outside Counsel/Consultants

Oldaker and Harris, LLP
Issues: TRA, URB
Rep By: William D. Harris, William C. Oldaker

Falcon Air Express

Miami, FL

Outside Counsel/Consultants

Pierre E. Murphy Law Offices

Falconbridge, Ltd.

Toronto, CANADA

Outside Counsel/Consultants

Wilson & Wilson
Rep By: Robert Dale Wilson

Fallon Community Health Plan

Worchester, MA
Leg. Issues: BUD, HCR, MMM

Outside Counsel/Consultants

Epstein Becker & Green, P.C.
Issues: BUD, HCR, MMM
Rep By: Joyce A. Cowan

Fallon, Nevada, City of

Leg. Issues: BUD, NAT

Outside Counsel/Consultants

The Furman Group
Issues: BUD, NAT
Rep By: K. Link Browder

Families Against Mandatory Minimums

1612 K St. NW
Suite 1400
Washington, DC 20006
Web: www.famm.org
E-mail: famm@famm.org

Tel: (202)822-6700
Fax: (202)822-6704

Seeks repeal of laws mandating minimum prison sentences and a return to greater judicial discretion.

In-house, DC-area Employees

PRICE, Mary: General Counsel
STEWART, Julie A.: President

Families U.S.A. Foundation

1334 G St. NW
Suite 300
Washington, DC 20005-3169
Web: www.familiesusa.org
E-mail: info@familiesusa.org

Tel: (202)628-3030
Fax: (202)347-2417
Registered: LDA

A non-profit advocacy organization for providing access to affordable health and long-term care for America's families.

Leg. Issues: HCR, MMM

In-house, DC-area Employees

ALKER, Joan Christina: Deputy Director, Government Affairs
FAIRBANKS, John: Media Director
KIRSCH, Jeff: Field Director
MCCLOSKEY, Amanda: Director, Health Policy Analysis
POLLACK, Ronald F.: Exec. Director
WAXMAN, Judith G.: Director, Government Affairs

Family Advocacy Services

Leg. Issues: FAM

Outside Counsel/Consultants

Dublin Castle Group
Issues: FAM
Rep By: Maureen Flatley Hogan

Family and Medical Leave Act Technical Corrections Coalition

7505 Inzer St.
Springfield, VA 22151

Tel: (703)256-0829

In-house, DC-area Employees

GELAK, Deanna R.: Exec. Director

Outside Counsel/Consultants

Working for the Future, LLC
Rep By: Deanna R. Gelak

Family Co. Group

Outside Counsel/Consultants

Ivins, Phillips & Barker

Family Communications, Inc.

Pittsburgh, PA
Leg. Issues: BUD, COM, EDU, TEC

Outside Counsel/Consultants

Convergence Services, Inc.
Issues: BUD, COM, EDU, TEC
Rep By: John M. Lawson

Family Farm Alliance (Project Transfer Council)

Elk Grove, CA
Leg. Issues: BUD, NAT

Outside Counsel/Consultants

The Ferguson Group, LLC
Issues: BUD, NAT
Rep By: W. Roger Gwinn, Joseph L. Raeder

McClure, Gerard & Neuenschwander, Inc.
Rep By: Steven G. Barringer, Joseph T. Findaro, Matthew Iandoli, Nils W. Johnson, Hon. James A. McClure, Tod O. Neuenschwander

Family Health Internat'l

2101 Wilson Blvd.
Suite 700
Arlington, VA 22201
Web: www.fhi.org
Tel: (703)516-9779
Fax: (703)516-9781

In-house, DC-area Employees

LAMPTEY, Peter: Project Director, Impact HIV/AIDS Prevention & Care Programs

Family Impact Seminar

Outside Counsel/Consultants

Hauser Group

Family Place

Leg. Issues: BUD, FAM

Outside Counsel/Consultants

Stites & Harbison
Issues: BUD, FAM
Rep By: Kenneth G. Lee

Family Research Council, Inc.

801 G St. NW
Washington, DC 20001
Tel: (202)393-2100
Fax: (202)393-2134
Registered: LDA

Web: www.frc.org
E-mail: corrdept@frc.org

An independent non-profit educational organization dedicated to ensuring that the interests of the family are considered and respected in the formation of public policy.

Leg. Issues: BUD, DEF, EDU, FAM, FOR, REL

In-house, DC-area Employees

BOWMAN, Michael: V. President, Government Relations
CONNOR, Kenneth L.: President
DANNENFELSER, Martin J.: V. President, Public Affairs
DONOVAN, Charles: Exec. V. President
MACKEY, Connie: Director, Government Relations
MCGEE, Laura
MOLLINS, Stephanie
PARSHALL, Janet: National Spokeswoman
WOTOCHEK, Jennifer: Legislative Assistant

Family Violence Prevention Fund

1522 K St. NW
Suite 550
Washington, DC 20005
Tel: (202)682-1212
Fax: (202)682-4662
Registered: LDA

Leg. Issues: BUD, HCR, LBR

In-house, DC-area Employees

STEWART, Kiersten: Director, Public Policy

Outside Counsel/Consultants

Bass and Howes, Inc.
Issues: BUD, HCR, LBR
Rep By: Joanne M. Howes

Family, Career and Community Leaders of America

1910 Association Dr.
Reston, VA 20191
Tel: (703)476-4900
Fax: (703)860-2713
Web: www.fcclainc.org
E-mail: natlhdqtrs@fcclainc.org

In-house, DC-area Employees

RAINS, Alan T.: Exec. Director

Fanatasy Elections

Glendale, CO

A political website.

Leg. Issues: CPI, GOV, TAX

Outside Counsel/Consultants

Capitol Coalitions Inc.
Issues: CPI, GOV, TAX
Rep By: Brett P. Scott, Jarvis C. Stewart

FANCOR

Chicago, IL

Outside Counsel/Consultants

Jamison and Sullivan, Inc.
Rep By: Jay R. Sullivan

Fannie Mae

3900 Wisconsin Ave. NW
Washington, DC 20016
Tel: (202)752-7000
Fax: (202)752-6099
Registered: LDA

Web: www.fanniemae.com

Formerly the Federal Nat'l Mortgage Ass'n, the company legally changed its name in 1997.

Leg. Issues: BAN, BNK, BUD, CDT, ECN, FIN, HOU, INS, TAX, TRA

In-house, DC-area Employees

BANKS, Pamela F.: V. President, Regulatory Compliance
CARR, James H.: Senior V. President, Policy, Research, Evaluation & Training, Fannie Mae Foundation
CHRISTENSON, Arne L.: Senior V. President, Regulatory Policy
DAUE, Janice: V. President, Public Affairs
DUNCAN, Duane S.: V. President, Government and Industry Relations
GORELICK, Jamie S.: V. Chair
HINES, John: Manager, Government Relations
KELVIE, William C.: Exec. V. President, Chief Information Officer
KRAMER, Charlene K.: V. President, Corporate Communications
MALONEY, Robert: V. President, Government Relations
MALONI, William Robert: Senior V. President, Government and Industrial Relations
VAN ETTEN, Laura: Director, Government Relations

Outside Counsel/Consultants

Collier Shannon Scott, PLLC
Issues: BAN, CDT, FIN, HOU, TAX
Rep By: R. Timothy Columbus, Doug Kantor, Kathleen Clark Kies, Doris O. Matsui, Gregory M. Scott, Scott A. Sinder, Dana S. Wood

Downey McGrath Group, Inc.
Issues: TAX
Rep By: Hon. Thomas J. Downey, Jr., John Peter Olinger

The Duberstein Group, Inc.
Issues: BNK, HOU
Rep By: John W. Angus, III, Michael S. Berman, Steven M. Champlin, Kenneth M. Duberstein, Henry M. Gandy, Daniel P. Meyer

Greenberg Traurig, LLP
Rep By: Anthony C. Rudy

Griffin, Johnson, Dover & Stewart
Issues: BUD, HOU, TAX
Rep By: William C. Danvers, G. Jack Dover, Patrick J. Griffin, Keith Heard, David E. Johnson, Susan O. Mann, Walter J. "Joe" Stewart, Leonard Swinehart

Janus-Merritt Strategies, L.L.C.
Issues: FIN, HOU
Rep By: John Guzik, Scott P. Hoffman, Mark J. Robertson

McSlarrow Consulting L.L.C.
Issues: HOU
Rep By: Alison McSlarrow

The OB-C Group, LLC
Rep By: Thomas Keating, Kim F. McKernan, Charles J. Mellody, Patricia A. Nelson, Lawrence F. O'Brien, III, Linda E. Tarplin

O'Melveny and Myers LLP
Issues: FIN, HOU, INS, TAX

Ricchetti Inc.
Rep By: Steve Ricchetti

Rubin, Winston, Diercks, Harris & Cooke

Tate-LeMunyon, LLC
Issues: HOU
Rep By: Glenn B. LeMunyon, Dan C. Tate, Jr.

Washington Council Ernst & Young
Issues: BAN, BUD, HOU, TAX
Rep By: Doug Badger, Lauren Darling, John L. Doney, Jayne T. Fitzgerald, LaBrenda Garrett-Nelson, Gary J. Gasper, Bruce A. Gates, Nick Giordano, Cathy Koch, Robert J. Leonard, Richard Meltzer, Phillip D. Moseley, John D. Porter, Robert M. Rozen, Donna Steele-Flynn, Timothy J. Urban

Williams & Jensen, P.C.
Issues: BAN, ECN, HOU, TAX
Rep By: Bertram W. Carp, David E. Franasiak, Robert E. Glennon, Jr., J. Steven Hart, John J. McMackin, Jr., J. D. Williams

The Fanning Corp.

Chicago, IL
Leg. Issues: AGR

Outside Counsel/Consultants

Jamison and Sullivan, Inc.
Issues: AGR
Rep By: Delos Cy Jamison, Jay R. Sullivan

Fantasma Networks, Inc.

Palo Alto, CA
Leg. Issues: AUT, COM, CSP, GOV, SCI, TEC

Outside Counsel/Consultants

Downey McGrath Group, Inc.
Issues: COM, SCI, TEC
Rep By: Elaine B. Acevedo, Hon. Thomas J. Downey, Jr., Hon. Raymond J. McGrath

Jack Ferguson Associates, Inc.
Issues: COM
Rep By: Jack Ferguson

Hooper Owen & Winburn
Issues: COM, TEC
Rep By: David Rudd

Public Strategies, Inc.
Issues: AUT, CSP, GOV
Rep By: Wallace J. Henderson

Far West Airlines, LLC

Outside Counsel/Consultants

Pierre E. Murphy Law Offices

Farallon Capital Management

Leg. Issues: FIN

Outside Counsel/Consultants

Fleischman and Walsh, L.L.P.
Rep By: Louis H. Dupart

The Ickes & Enright Group
Issues: FIN
Rep By: Janice Ann Enright, Harold M. Ickes

Timmons and Co., Inc.
Rep By: Michael J. Bates, Douglas F. Bennett, Ellen B. Fitzgibbons, Bryce L. "Larry" Harlow, Timothy J. Keating, Tom C. Korologos, Richard J. Tarplin, William E. Timmons, Sr., William E. Timmons, Jr.

Fargo-Cass County Development Corp.

Fargo, ND
Leg. Issues: ECN

Outside Counsel/Consultants

Van Scoyoc Associates, Inc.
Issues: ECN
Rep By: Evan Knisely, H. Stewart Van Scoyoc

Fargo-Moorhead Metropolitan Council of Governments

Fargo, ND

Outside Counsel/Consultants

Barbara J. Rohde
Rep By: Barbara J. Rohde

Farm Animal Reform Movement (FARM)

P.O. Box 30654
Bethesda, MD 20824
Tel: (301)530-1737
Fax: (301)530-5747
Web: www.farmusa.org
E-mail: farm@farmusa.org

A national public interest organization dedicated to promoting a plant-based diet and to exposing animal abuse and other adverse impacts of animal agriculture.

Leg. Issues: AGR, ANI, CAW, ENV, HCR, MED

In-house, DC-area Employees

HERSHAFT, Alex: President

Farm Credit Bank of Texas

Austin, TX
Registered: LDA
Leg. Issues: AGR, BAN

Outside Counsel/Consultants

Akin, Gump, Strauss, Hauer & Feld, L.L.P.
Issues: AGR
Rep By: J. David Carlin

Hogan & Hartson L.L.P.
Issues: BAN
Rep By: Humberto R. Pena

Farm Credit Council

50 F St. NW
Suite 900
Washington, DC ,20001
Tel: (202)626-8710
Fax: (202)626-8718
Registered: LDA
Web: www.fccouncil.com
E-mail: boscia@fccouncil.com

Protects and promotes the business and interests of the cooperative farm credit system.

Leg. Issues: AGR, BAN, BNK, BUD, FIN, FOO

Political Action Committee/s

Farm Credit Political Action Committee
50 F St. NW
Suite 900
Washington, DC 20001
Tel: (202)879-0851
Fax: (202)626-8718
Contact: William Jeffry Shipp

In-house, DC-area Employees
AUER, Kenneth E.: C.E.O.
DANA, Charles: General Counsel
HAYS, John J.: V. President
MORRILL, Jennifer: Director of Communications
SHIPP, William Jeffry: Exec. V. President
VANHOOSE, Todd: V. President, Government Affairs

Farm Market iD

Palos Verdes Estates, CA
A provider of farming information.
Leg. Issues: AGR
Outside Counsel/Consultants
King & Spalding
Issues: AGR
Rep By: William C. Talmadge, Ashley Whitesides

Farm Progress Cos.

Carol Stream, IL
Leg. Issues: ECN
Outside Counsel/Consultants
Kutak Rock LLP
Issues: ECN
Rep By: Seth Kirshenberg, George R. Schlossberg, Barry P. Steinberg

Farmers Branch, Texas, City of

Leg. Issues: TRA, URB
Outside Counsel/Consultants
Carolyn C. Chaney & Associates
Issues: TRA, URB
Rep By: Carolyn C. Chaney, Christopher F. Giglio

Farmers Insurance Group

325 Seventh St. NW
Suite 1225
Washington, DC 20004
Tel: (202)737-1445
Registered: LDA
Web: www.farmersinsurance.com
E-mail: Talyor_Caswell@farmersinsurance.com
A major personal lines insurance carrier headquartered in Los Angeles, CA.
Leg. Issues: BAN, BUD, DIS, ENV, FIN, INS, TAX
In-house, DC-area Employees
CASWELL, Taylor: Director, Federal Affairs

Farmers' Electric Cooperative

Clovis, NM
Outside Counsel/Consultants
Duncan, Weinberg, Genzer & Pembroke, P.C.
Rep By: Robert Weinberg

Farmland Industries, Inc.

1350 I St. NW
Suite 1240
Washington, DC 20005
Tel: (202)783-5330
Fax: (202)783-4381
Registered: LDA
Web: www.farmland.com
Leg. Issues: AGR, ANI, ENV, FIN, FOO, FOR, IMM, INS, LBR, TAX, TRA, TRD
In-house, DC-area Employees
SEVCIK, Jesse J.: Government Relations Specialist
SHEARER, Scott: Director, National Relations
Outside Counsel/Consultants
Hogan & Hartson L.L.P.
Issues: AGR
Rep By: Humberto R. Pena
Patton Boggs, LLP
Issues: TRD
Rep By: Brian C. Lopina, Daniel E. Waltz

Farrell & Campo

Washington, DC
Outside Counsel/Consultants
The Campo Group, Ltd.
Rep By: Terry T. Campo

Fashion Accessories Shippers Ass'n

New York, NY
Leg. Issues: TRD
Outside Counsel/Consultants
Greenberg Traurig, LLP
Issues: TRD
Rep By: Ronald L. Platt
McDermott, Will and Emery
Rep By: Calvin P. Johnson

Fast Air Carrier

Santiago, CHILE
Outside Counsel/Consultants
Squire, Sanders & Dempsey L.L.P.
Rep By: Marshall S. Sinick

FastShip, Inc.

Philadelphia, PA
Leg. Issues: MAR
Outside Counsel/Consultants
Dyer Ellis & Joseph, P.C.
Issues: MAR
Rep By: Joan Bondareff, Laurie Crick Sahatjian, James S. W. Drewry, Thomas M. Dyer, James B. Ellis, II, John Graykauski, Lara Bernstein Mathews, J. Christopher Naftzger, Duncan C. Smith, III, Jennifer M. Southwick

Faucett Airlines (Compania de Aviacion Faucett, S.A.)

Miami, FL
Outside Counsel/Consultants
Pierre E. Murphy Law Offices
Rep By: Pierre E. Murphy

FBI Agents Ass'n

New Rochelle, NY
Leg. Issues: BUD, RET, TAX
Outside Counsel/Consultants
Bracewell & Patterson, L.L.P.
Issues: BUD, RET, TAX
Rep By: Hon. Edwin R. Bethune, Hon. Jim Chapman, Gene E. Godley, Marc C. Hebert, Charles L. Ingebretson, Michael L. Pate, Scott H. Segal, D. Michael Stroud, Jr.

FBV Group

Springfield, VA
Outside Counsel/Consultants
Valente Lopatin & Schulze
Rep By: Richard T. Schulze, Jr., Claudia Barker Valente, Mark Valente, III

FCN

Outside Counsel/Consultants
Cormac Group, LLP

FDA-NIH Council

Washington, DC
A coalition of pharmaceutical biotech food companies, professional research societies, and non-profit groups seeking to increase visibility for the FDA and increase its budget.
Leg. Issues: BUD, HCR
Outside Counsel/Consultants
Capitol Associates, Inc.
Issues: BUD, HCR
Rep By: Tricia Brooks, Pamela Patrice Jackson

FED Corp.

Hopewell Junction, NY
Leg. Issues: BUD, DEF, HCR
Outside Counsel/Consultants
Genesis Consulting Group, LLC
Issues: BUD, DEF, HCR
Rep By: Mark Benedict, Dana DeBeaumont

Federal Administrative Law Judges Conference

Washington, DC
Web: www.faljc.org
Leg. Issues: GOV
Outside Counsel/Consultants
Robertson, Monagle & Eastaugh
Issues: GOV
Rep By: Steven W. Silver

Federal Advocacy for California Education

Sacramento, CA
Leg. Issues: EDU
Outside Counsel/Consultants
Federal Management Strategies, Inc.
Issues: EDU
Rep By: Robert P. Canavan, Kellen Flannery

Federal Agricultural Mortgage Corp. (Farmer Mac)

919 18th St. NW
Suite 200
Washington, DC 20006
Tel: (202)872-7700
Fax: (202)872-7713
Registered: LDA
Web: www.farmermac.com
Farmer Mac is a federally chartered corporation created by Congress to establish a secondary market for agricultural real estate and rural housing mortgage loans, and facilitate capital market funding for USDA-guaranteed farm program and rural development loans.
Leg. Issues: AGR, FIN
Political Action Committee/s
Federal Agricultural Mortgage Corp. Political Action Committee
919 18th St. NW
Suite 200
Washington, DC 20006
Tel: (202)872-7700
Fax: (202)872-7713
Contact: Thomas R. Clark
In-house, DC-area Employees
CLARK, Thomas R.: V. President, Corporate Relations
Outside Counsel/Consultants
Lesher & Russell, Inc.
Issues: AGR
Rep By: William G. Lesher, Randall M. Russell

Federal Bar Ass'n

2215 M St. NW
Washington, DC 20037
Tel: (202)785-1614
Fax: (202)785-1568
Registered: LDA
Web: www.fedbar.org
E-mail: fba@fedbar.org
Leg. Issues: CON
In-house, DC-area Employees
GOFF, Jackie: President
MOYER, Bruce L.: Government Relations Columnist
Outside Counsel/Consultants
The Moyer Group
Issues: CON
Rep By: Bruce L. Moyer

Federal City Council

Washington, DC
Leg. Issues: DOC
Outside Counsel/Consultants
Chernikoff and Co.
Issues: DOC
Rep By: Larry B. Chernikoff

Federal Communications Bar Ass'n

1020 19th St. NW
Suite 325
Washington, DC 20036-6101
Tel: (202)293-4000
Fax: (202)293-4317
Web: www.fcba.org
E-mail: fcba@fcba.org
An association of attorneys and other professionals involved in the development, interpretation, and practice of communications law and policy.
Leg. Issues: RES
In-house, DC-area Employees
ZENOR, Stanley: Exec. Director and Chief Exec. Officer
Outside Counsel/Consultants
Patton Boggs, LLP
Issues: RES
Rep By: Edward J. Newberry

Federal Criminal Investigators Ass'n

Arlington, VA
Leg. Issues: LAW
Outside Counsel/Consultants
Donald Baldwin Associates
Issues: LAW
Rep By: Donald Baldwin

Federal Education Ass'n

1201 16th St. NW
Washington, DC 20036
Tel: (202)822-7850
Fax: (202)822-7867
Web: www.feaonline.org
E-mail: fea@feaonline.org
A state affiliate of the Nat'l Education Ass'n. Represents federal employees of the Department of Defense on military bases in the United States and abroad.
In-house, DC-area Employees
NGUYEN, H. T.: Exec. Director and General Counsel

Federal Employees Education and Assistance Fund

Littleton, CO

Outside Counsel/Consultants

Shaw, Bransford, Veilleux & Roth
Rep By: G. Jerry Shaw, Jr.

Federal Facilities Council

2101 Constitution Ave. NW
Washington, DC 20418
Tel: (202)334-3378
Fax: (202)334-3370
Web: www4.nas.edu/cets/ffc.nsf

Encourages cooperation among several federal construction agencies.

In-house, DC-area Employees

BORGER, Henry A.: Exec. Secretary

Federal Funds Information for States

444 N. Capitol St. NW
Suite 642
Washington, DC 20001
Tel: (202)624-5382
Fax: (202)624-7745
Web: www.ffis.org

A tracking service providing data on federal grants-in-aid to states. Sponsored by the Nat'l Conference of State Legislatures and the Nat'l Governors' Ass'n.

In-house, DC-area Employees

HOWARD, Marcia: Director

Federal Glove Contractors Coalition

Washington, DC

Outside Counsel/Consultants

Collier Shannon Scott, PLLC
Rep By: Lauren R. Howard

Federal Home Loan Bank of Boston

Boston, MA
Leg. Issues: BAN, HOU

Outside Counsel/Consultants

Butera & Andrews
Issues: BAN, HOU
Rep By: Cliff W. Andrews, Wright H. Andrews, Jr., James J. Butera, Frank Tillotson

Federal Home Loan Bank of Chicago

Chicago, IL
Leg. Issues: BAN

Outside Counsel/Consultants

Mayer, Brown & Platt
Issues: BAN
Rep By: Penny L. Eastman, Richard S. Williamson

Federal Home Loan Bank of Dallas

Dallas, TX
Leg. Issues: BAN, HOU

Outside Counsel/Consultants

Capitol Counsel Group, L.L.C.
Issues: BAN, HOU
Rep By: Warren Belmar

Federal Home Loan Bank of Des Moines

Des Moines, IA
Leg. Issues: FIN

Outside Counsel/Consultants

Troutman Sanders LLP
Issues: FIN
Rep By: Mary Clare Fitzgerald

Federal Home Loan Bank of Indianapolis

Indianapolis, IN
Leg. Issues: BAN

Outside Counsel/Consultants

Verner, Liipfert, Bernhard, McPherson and Hand, Chartered
Issues: BAN
Rep By: Hon. James J. Blanchard, Andrew D. Eskin, Rosemary B. Freeman, William H. Minor

Federal Home Loan Bank of New York

New York, NY
Leg. Issues: BAN

Outside Counsel/Consultants

Royer & Babyak
Issues: BAN
Rep By: Robert Stewart Royer

Winston & Strawn
Issues: BAN
Rep By: Hon. James H. Burnley, IV

Federal Home Loan Bank of Pittsburgh

Pittsburgh, PA

Outside Counsel/Consultants

The Tierney Group
Rep By: Chriss H. Winston

Federal Home Loan Bank of San Francisco

San Francisco, CA
Leg. Issues: BAN, BUD, FIN

Outside Counsel/Consultants

The Legislative Strategies Group, LLC
Issues: BAN
Rep By: Martin B. Gold, Steven M. Hilton

Steptoe & Johnson LLP
Issues: BAN, FIN
Rep By: John T. Collins

Van Scoyoc Associates, Inc.
Issues: BAN, BUD
Rep By: Kevin F. Kelly

Federal Home Loan Bank of Seattle

Seattle, WA
Leg. Issues: BAN, FIN

Outside Counsel/Consultants

Hughes Hubbard & Reed LLP
Issues: FIN

Peyser Associates, Inc.
Issues: BAN
Rep By: Michael Bucciero, Jr., Thomas J. Howarth, Peter A. Peyser, Jr.

Federal Home Loan Bank of Topeka

Topeka, KS
Leg. Issues: BAN, HOU

Outside Counsel/Consultants

Butera & Andrews
Issues: BAN, HOU
Rep By: Cliff W. Andrews, Wright H. Andrews, Jr., James J. Butera, Frank Tillotson

Federal Home Loan Mortgage Corp. (Freddie Mac)

8200 Jones Branch Dr.
McLean, VA 22102
Tel: (703)903-2000
Fax: (703)903-2447
Registered: LDA
Web: www.freddiemac.com
Leg. Issues: BAN, BNK, BUD, CPI, FIN, HOU, INS, TAX

In-house, DC-area Employees

BAKER, Maxine B.: President and CEO of Foundation and V. President of Community Relations
DELK, Mitchell: V. President, Government Relations
FISCHER, Danna S.: Director, Government and Industry Relations
FITZPATRICK, Eileen B.: Media Relations Specialist
FOX, Barbara: Director, Government Relations (Senate)
GERMAN, Brad: Manager, Public Relations
HILL, Carlisa: Grants Manager, Freddie Mac Foundation
MCHALE, Sharon: Director, Public Relations
NOE, Jeff: Manager
PALOMBI, David R.: V. President, Corporate Communications
ROBINSON, Douglas: Director, Public Relations
SHOWELL, Jill: Legislative Director
STEPHENS, William L.: V. President, Shareholder Relations
TENNES, Lauren: Director, Government Relations

Outside Counsel/Consultants

Baker & Daniels

BKSH & Associates
Issues: BAN, FIN, TAX

James E. Boland
Issues: BNK
Rep By: James E. Boland, Jr.

Clark & Weinstock, Inc.
Issues: TAX
Rep By: Hon. John Vincent "Vin" Weber

Covington & Burling
Issues: BUD, FIN
Rep By: Roderick A. DeArment

Davidson & Company, Inc.
Issues: BUD, HOU, TAX
Rep By: James H. Davidson, Richard E. May, Stanley Sokul

Susan Molinari, L.L.P.

Royer & Babyak
Rep By: Robert Stewart Royer

Sacramento-Potomac Consulting, Inc.
Issues: FIN, HOU, INS
Rep By: Hon. Richard H. Lehman

The Smith-Free Group
Issues: BAN, BUD, TAX
Rep By: James E. Smith

Timmons and Co., Inc.
Issues: FIN, HOU
Rep By: Michael J. Bates, Douglas F. Bennett, Ellen B. Fitzgibbons, Bryce L. "Larry" Harlow, Timothy J. Keating, Tom C. Korologos, Richard J. Tarplin, William E. Timmons, Jr., William E. Timmons, Sr.

The Velasquez Group
Issues: BUD, HOU
Rep By: Jay Velasquez

Verner, Liipfert, Bernhard, McPherson and Hand, Chartered
Issues: FIN, HOU
Rep By: John A. Merrigan, William H. Minor

Federal Judges Ass'n

New York, NY
Leg. Issues: GOV

Outside Counsel/Consultants

Winston & Strawn
Issues: GOV
Rep By: Hon. Beryl F. Anthony, Jr., Charles L. Kinney, Hon. John L. Napier, Douglas C. Richardson

Federal Law Enforcement Officers Ass'n

East Northport, NY
Leg. Issues: LAW

Outside Counsel/Consultants

James & Hoffman, P.C.
Issues: LAW

Federal Magistrate Judges Ass'n

Sherman, TX
Leg. Issues: GOV

Outside Counsel/Consultants

Winston & Strawn
Issues: GOV
Rep By: Hon. Beryl F. Anthony, Jr., Charles L. Kinney, Hon. John L. Napier

Federal Managers Ass'n

1641 Prince St.
Alexandria, VA 22314
Tel: (703)683-8700
Fax: (703)683-8707
Registered: LDA
Web: www.fedmanagers.org
E-mail: info@fedmanagers.org
Leg. Issues: GOV

Political Action Committee/s

Federal Managers Ass'n Political Action Committee
1641 Prince St.
Alexandria, VA 22314
Tel: (703)683-8700
Fax: (703)683-8707
Contact: Didier Trinh

In-house, DC-area Employees

TRINH, Didier: Director, Governmental Affairs

Federal Nat'l Payables, Inc.

Bethesda, MD
Leg. Issues: GOV, HOU, URB

Outside Counsel/Consultants

Blank Rome Comisky & McCauley, LLP
Issues: GOV, HOU, URB
Rep By: J. Caleb Boggs, III

Federal Physicians Ass'n

P.O. Box 45150
Washington, DC 20026
Tel: (800)403-3374
Fax: (703)426-8400
Registered: LDA

Web: www.fedphy.org
E-mail: info@fedphy.org

Seeks to improve federal health care programs. Exec. Director is Dennis W. Boyd of Financial Programs, Inc. (see separate listing). Headquartered in Springfield, VA.

Leg. Issues: GOV, LBR, MED

Outside Counsel/Consultants

Ass'n Management Group

Chwat and Company, Inc.
Issues: GOV
Rep By: John Chwat, Derek Riker

Federal Procurement Consultants

Kansas City, MO
Leg. Issues: DEF, FIR, MAN

Outside Counsel/Consultants

Rooney Group Internat'l, Inc.
Issues: DEF, FIR, MAN
Rep By: James W. Rooney

Federal Sources, Inc.

McLean, VA

Outside Counsel/Consultants

Monfort & Wolfe

Federal Strategies Group

717 D St. NW
Suite 310
Washington, DC 20004
Tel: (202)628-4901
Fax: (202)393-5728
Registered: LDA, FARA

In-house, DC-area Employees

EQUIHUA, Xavier: V. President
POTTER, Philip H.: President

Outside Counsel/Consultants

Millian Byers Associates, LLC
Rep By: H. James Byers

Federal Systems Group, Inc.

McLean, VA

Outside Counsel/Consultants

William E. Casselman, II
Rep By: William E. Casselman, II

Federal Victory Fund

6429 Downing Ct.
Annandale, VA 22003

In-house, DC-area Employees

SARGENT, Mary Jane: Contact, Political Action Committee

Federated Ambulatory Surgery Ass'n

700 N. Fairfax St.
Suite 306
Alexandria, VA 22314
Tel: (703)836-8808
Fax: (703)549-0976
Registered: LDA

Web: www.fasa.org
E-mail: fasa@fasa.org
Leg. Issues: HCR, MMM

In-house, DC-area Employees

BRYANT, Kathy J.: Exec. Director

Outside Counsel/Consultants

Arent Fox Kintner Plotkin & Kahn, PLLC
Issues: HCR, MMM
Rep By: Robert J. Waters, Ronald L. Wisor, Jr.

Federated Investors, Inc.

Pittsburgh, PA
Leg. Issues: SCI

Outside Counsel/Consultants

Arter & Hadden
Rep By: Daniel L. Cohen

Reed, Smith, LLP
Issues: SCI
Rep By: Phillips S. Peter

Federation for American Immigration Reform (FAIR)

1666 Connecticut Ave. NW
Suite 400
Washington, DC 20009
Tel: (202)328-7004
Fax: (202)387-3447
Registered: LDA

Web: www.fairus.org
E-mail: fair@fairus.org

A national, nonprofit, membership organization working to stop illegal immigration and conform U.S. legal immigration policy to reasonable levels.

Leg. Issues: AGR, ENV, IMM

In-house, DC-area Employees

DENSON, Jennifer: Associate Director
MCALPIN, K. C.: Deputy Director
STEIN, Daniel A.: Exec. Director
WASHINGTON, Veronica: Government Relations Assistant

Outside Counsel/Consultants

Butera & Andrews
Issues: IMM
Rep By: Cliff W. Andrews, Wright H. Andrews, Jr., Frank Tillotson

Federation of American Hospitals

801 Pennsylvania Ave. NW
Suite 245
Washington, DC 20004-2604
Tel: (202)624-1500
Fax: (202)737-6462
Registered: LDA

Web: www.americashospitals.com

Represents nearly 1,700 investor-owned and managed hospitals and health systems that offer traditional care, ambulatory care, psychiatric care, and allied companies involved in health insurance and healthcare systems.

Leg. Issues: BUD, HCR, MMM, TAX

Political Action Committee/s

Federation of American Hospitals Political Action Committee
801 Pennsylvania Ave. NW
Suite 245
Washington, DC 20004-2604
Tel: (202)624-1500
Fax: (202)737-6462
Contact: Miya Fennar

In-house, DC-area Employees

BOSTON, Dan: Assistant V. President, Legislation and Public Affairs
COHEN, Jeffrey E.: Assistant V. President, Legislation
FENNAR, Miya: Office Manager and PAC Contact
GOGAL, Laura S.: V. President and Chief Counsel
HIPP, Duke: Director, Communications
PARKER, Wendy C.: Assistant V. President, Legislation
SCULLY, Thomas A.: President and Chief Exec. Officer
SPEIL, Steven: Senior V. President, Health Financing and Policy
THEVENOT, Laura Ison: Exec. V. President and Chief Operating Officer

Outside Counsel/Consultants

Baker & Hostetler LLP
Issues: MMM
Rep By: Matthew J. Dolan, Frederick H. Graefe, Kathleen M. Kerrigan

Bradley Arant Rose & White LLP

Epstein Becker & Green, P.C.
Issues: BUD, HCR, MMM, TAX
Rep By: Joyce A. Cowan

Fierce and Isakowitz
Issues: HCR
Rep By: Kathryn Braden, Samantha Cook, Donald L. Fierce, Mark W. Isakowitz, Diane Moery

Health Policy Alternatives, Inc.
Rep By: Thomas Ault, Richard Lauderbaugh

Hogan & Hartson L.L.P.
Issues: MMM
Rep By: Darrel J. Grinstead

Podesta/Mattoon
Issues: HCR
Rep By: Lauren Maddox

Federation of American Scientists

307 Massachusetts Ave. NE
Washington, DC 20002
Tel: (202)546-3300
Fax: (202)675-1010
Registered: LDA

Web: www.fas.org/
E-mail: fas@fas.org

Organized in 1945 for the purpose of lobbying to help ensure civilian control of atomic energy. Conducts research on arms control and other issues of science and society.

Leg. Issues: DEF, FOR, GOV, SCI

In-house, DC-area Employees

AFTERGOOD, Steven: Project Director, Government Secrecy Project
GABELNICK, Tamar: Editor, Arms Sales Monitor
KELLY, Henry C.: President/Editor, FAS Public Interest Report

Outside Counsel/Consultants

Scott Cohen
Issues: DEF, FOR, GOV, SCI
Rep By: Scott Cohen

Federation of American Societies for Experimental Biology

9650 Rockville Pike
Bethesda, MD 20814-3998
Tel: (301)530-7000
Fax: (301)530-7001
Registered: LDA

Web: www.faseb.org
E-mail: sgolub@faseb.org
Leg. Issues: BUD, MED, SCI

In-house, DC-area Employees

GARRISON, Dr. Howard: Director, Office of Public Affairs
GOLUB, PhD, Sidney: Exec. Director
WHITE, Patrick: Director, Legislative Affairs

Federation of Behavioral, Psychological and Cognitive Sciences

750 First St. NE
Suite 5007
Washington, DC 20002-4242
Tel: (202)336-5920
Fax: (202)336-5953
Web: www.thefederationonline.org
E-mail: federation@apa.org

Seeks to encourage policy and legislation that enhance training and research on behavioral, psychological and cognitive processes and works to educate the public and private agencies on the need for such research.

Leg. Issues: BUD, HCR, SCI

In-house, DC-area Employees

O'TOOLE, Patrice: Acting Director

Federation of Electric Power Cos. of Japan

1901 L St. NW
Suite 600
Washington, DC 20036
Tel: (202)466-6781
Fax: (202)466-6758
Registered: LDA, FARA
E-mail: fepco@denjiren.com

Headquartered in Tokyo, Japan

Leg. Issues: ENG

In-house, DC-area Employees

KAJIKAWA, Makoto: Chief Representative

Outside Counsel/Consultants

George H. Denison
Issues: ENG
Rep By: George H. Denison

Porter/Novelli
Rep By: Charles H. Powers

Washington Policy & Analysis, Inc.

Federation of German Industries (BDI)

Berlin, GERMANY
Leg. Issues: TRD

Outside Counsel/Consultants

Representative of German Industry and Trade
Issues: TRD
Rep By: Robert Bergmann, Peter J. C. Esser

Federation of Government Information Processing Councils

3601E Chain Bridge Rd.
Fairfax, VA 22030
Tel: (703)218-1955
Fax: (703)218-1960
Web: www.fgipc.org
E-mail: fgipc@fgipc.org

In-house, DC-area Employees

BUSH, Charlotte: Manager, Operations

Federation of Internat'l Trade Ass'ns (FITA)

11800 Sunrise Valley Drive
Suite 210
Reston, VA 20191
Tel: (703)620-1588
Fax: (703)620-4922
Web: www.fita.org
E-mail: info@fita.org

Represents 425 world trade clubs and international trade associations located across the United States, Canada and Mexico.

Leg. Issues: TRD

In-house, DC-area Employees

JOYNER, Nelson T.: Chairman

Outside Counsel/Consultants

Shaw Pittman
Issues: TRD

Federation of Japanese Bankers Ass'ns

Tokyo, JAPAN

Outside Counsel/Consultants

Shaw Pittman
Rep By: David R. Sahr

Federation of Korean Industries

Seoul, KOREA

Outside Counsel/Consultants

Paul, Weiss, Rifkind, Wharton & Garrison
Rep By: Carl W. Hampe, Lionel H. Olmer, John Ratigan

Federation of Nurses and Health Professionals/AFT

555 New Jersey Ave. NW
Tenth Floor
Washington, DC 20001
Tel: (202)879-4491
Fax: (202)879-4597
Registered: LDA
Web: www.aft.org/FNHP/
E-mail: fnhpaft@aft.org

FNHP is a union which primarily represents registered nurses, but also LPNs, technicians, technologists, doctors, therapists, aides, clerical personnel, service and maintenance workers, and pharmacists in both the public and private sector.

Leg. Issues: HCR, LBR, MED, MMM

Political Action Committee/s

COPE/Governmental Relations Department
555 New Jersey Ave. NW
Tenth Floor
Washington, DC 20001
Contact: Liz Smith
Tel: (202)879-4436
Fax: (202)393-6375

In-house, DC-area Employees

FRAAS, Charlotte: Director, Federal Legislation
KETTER, Joni: Senior Associate
MACDONALD, Mary Lehman: Director
SMITH, Liz: PAC Contact

Federation of State Humanities Councils

1600 Wilson Blvd.
Suite 902
Arlington, VA 22209
Tel: (703)908-9700
Fax: (703)908-9706
Leg. Issues: ART

In-house, DC-area Employees

LEFTWICH, Gail: President

Outside Counsel/Consultants

Van Scoyoc Associates, Inc.
Issues: ART
Rep By: Carolyn Fuller, H. Stewart Van Scoyoc

Federation of State Medical Boards of the U.S.

Fort Worth, TX
Leg. Issues: HCR, IMM, MMM, TEC

Outside Counsel/Consultants

MARC Associates, Inc.
Issues: HCR, IMM, MMM, TEC
Rep By: Edwin Allen, Ellen Riker

Federation of Tax Administrators

444 N. Capitol St. NW
Suite 348
Washington, DC 20001
Web: www.taxadmin.org
Tel: (202)624-5890
Fax: (202)624-7888

An association of the tax departments of the 50 states, the District of Columbia, and New York City, with other municipal tax departments represented through associate memberships. Works to "improve the techniques of tax administrators and the work of their profession, and to advance the standards of tax administration."

In-house, DC-area Employees

DUNCAN, Harley T.: Exec. Director

FedEx Corp.

300 Maryland Ave. NE
Washington, DC 20002
Tel: (202)546-1631
Fax: (202)546-3309
Registered: LDA

Headquartered in Memphis, TN.

Leg. Issues: AVI, BUD, CAW, FUE, HCR, LBR, POS, ROD, TAX, TRA, TRD, TRU

In-house, DC-area Employees

ADAMS, Gina: Staff V. President, Government Affairs
LEDOUX, Marque I.: Senior Federal Affairs Representative
MASTERSON, Ken: Executive V. President
O'KEEFE, Rush: V. President, Regulatory
PRYOR, Jr., David: Senior Federal Affairs Representative
RODGERS, Richard F.: Senior Federal Affairs Representative
YADON, Shawn: Senior State and Local Affairs Representative

Outside Counsel/Consultants

Cassidy & Associates, Inc.
Rep By: Marie James, Walter Raheb, Stephen Whitaker

The Dutko Group, Inc.
Issues: AVI, LBR, POS, ROD, TRA, TRU
Rep By: Gary J. Andres, Kimberly M. Spaulding

Ann Eppard Associates, Ltd.
Issues: AVI, POS
Rep By: Julie Chlopecki, Ann Eppard, Karen Schechter

Hall, Green, Rupli, LLC
Issues: POS, TRA
Rep By: John M. Green, G. Stewart Hall

Kent & O'Connor, Inc.
Issues: CAW, TRA
Rep By: Patrick C. O'Connor

Cliff Madison Government Relations, Inc.
Issues: TRA

Bill Simpson & Associates
Issues: POS, TRD
Rep By: William G. Simpson

George C. Tagg
Issues: POS
Rep By: George C. Tagg

Van Scoyoc Associates, Inc.
Issues: AVI, BUD
Rep By: Ray Cole, Chad Schulken, H. Stewart Van Scoyoc

Washington Council Ernst & Young
Issues: AVI, BUD, HCR, LBR, POS, TAX, TRD
Rep By: Doug Badger, Lauren Darling, John L. Doney, Jayne T. Fitzgerald, LaBrenda Garrett-Nelson, Gary J. Gasper, Bruce A. Gates, Nick Giordano, Cathy Koch, Robert J. Leonard, Richard Meltzer, Phillip D. Moseley, John D. Porter, Robert M. Rozen, Donna Steele-Flynn, Timothy J. Urban

Womble Carlyle Sandridge & Rice, P.C.
Rep By: Ashley Thrift

FedEx Pilots Ass'n

Memphis, TN
Leg. Issues: AVI

Outside Counsel/Consultants

Bracy Williams & Co.
Issues: AVI
Rep By: Josh Nassar, Susan J. Williams

Fel Corp.

Farmingdale, NJ

An electronics manufacturer.

Outside Counsel/Consultants

Bob Davis & Associates
Rep By: Hon. Robert W. Davis

Feld Entertainment Inc.

8607 Westwood Center Dr.
Vienna, VA 22182
Tel: (703)448-4000
Fax: (703)448-4100
Registered: LDA
Web: www.ringling.com

The owner of Ringling Brothers/Barnum & Bailey Circus and Disney on Ice.

Leg. Issues: AGR, ANI, BUD, TRD

In-house, DC-area Employees

WILLENS, Todd: V. President, Government Relations

Outside Counsel/Consultants

Akin, Gump, Strauss, Hauer & Feld, L.L.P.
Issues: TRD

Birch, Horton, Bittner & Cherot
Issues: ANI, BUD
Rep By: Thomas L. Albert, William P. Horn, Roy S. Jones, Jr.

Zeliff, Ireland, and Associates
Issues: AGR, BUD
Rep By: Hon. Andy Ireland

The Feldspar Corp.

Spruce Pine, NC

Outside Counsel/Consultants

Crowell & Moring LLP
Rep By: Barry E. Cohen

Fellowship Square Foundation, Inc.

560 Herndon Pkwy.
Suite 340
Herndon, VA 20170
E-mail: fsf@unidial.com
Tel: (703)471-5370
Fax: (703)471-9895

Provides affordable housing and services to low income elderly and handicapped individuals.

In-house, DC-area Employees

HARTMANN, David: President

Feminist Majority

1600 Wilson Blvd.
Suite 801
Arlington, VA 22209
Web: www.feminist.org
E-mail: femmaj@feminist.org
Tel: (703)522-2214
Fax: (703)522-2219

Encourages women to seek leadership positions in all sectors of society and promotes a national feminist agenda; affiliated with Feminist Majority Foundation.

In-house, DC-area Employees

JACKMAN, Jennifer: Director, Policy and Research
SMEAL, Eleanor: President

Fentek Internat'l Pty. Ltd.

Brisbane, AUSTRALIA
Leg. Issues: MAR

Outside Counsel/Consultants

Forster & Associates
Issues: MAR
Rep By: Johann R. Forster

Fenton Communications

Washington, DC
Web: www.fenton.com
Leg. Issues: MED

Outside Counsel/Consultants

The Sheridan Group
Issues: MED
Rep By: Mary Beth Buchholz, Thomas F. Sheridan

Fergus Falls, Minnesota, City of

Outside Counsel/Consultants

Mullenholz, Brimsek & Belair
Rep By: John R. Brimsek

Ferraro, USA

Somerset, NJ

A candy manufacturer.

Leg. Issues: FOO

Outside Counsel/Consultants

Parry, Romani, DeConcini & Symms
Issues: FOO
Rep By: Edward H. Baxter, Hon. Dennis DeConcini, John M. Haddow, Scott D. Hatch, Shannon Davis Henderson, Jack W. Martin, Romano Romani, Linda Arey Skladany, Hon. Steven D. Symms

Ferris State University

Big Rapids, MI
Leg. Issues: EDU

Outside Counsel/Consultants

Dykema Gossett PLLC
Issues: EDU
Rep By: Nancy R. Barbour, Tricia K. Markwood

Ferro Corp.

Cleveland, OH

Outside Counsel/Consultants

Squire, Sanders & Dempsey L.L.P.

Ferroalloys Ass'n

Washington, DC
Web: www.ferroalloysassociation.com
Leg. Issues: ENV, TRD

Outside Counsel/Consultants

Kinghorn & Associates, L.L.C.
Issues: ENV, TRD
Rep By: John W. Hilbert, II, Edward J. Kinghorn, Jr., Jeremy Scott

The Fertilizer Institute

501 Second St. NE
Washington, DC 20002
Tel: (202)675-8250
Fax: (202)544-8123
Registered: LDA
Web: www.tfi.org
E-mail: information@tfi.org

Represents more than 90 percent of the nation's fertilizer industry, including producers, manufacturers, retailers, trading firms and equipment manufacturers.

Leg. Issues: AGR, CAW, CHM, CSP, ENG, ENV, FOO, FOR, FUE, MAN, MAR, NAT, ROD, RRR, SCI, TRA, TRD, TRU, UTI, WAS

Political Action Committee/s

Fertilizer Institute Political Action Committee (FERT PAC)

501 Second St. NE
Washington, DC 20002
Contact: Ford B. West

Tel: (202)675-8250
Fax: (202)544-8123

In-house, DC-area Employees
GUFFAIN, Pamela D.: Director, Government Relations
MYERS, Gary D.: President
O'HARA-MATHERS, Kathleen: V. President, Public Affairs
VROOMEN, Dr. Harry: V. President, Economic Services
WEST, Ford B.: Sr. V. President
ZILLINGER, F. Everett: Director, Government Relations

Outside Counsel/Consultants
Capitolink, LLC
Issues: CAW
Rep By: John H. Thorne, Ph.D.
McKenna & Cuneo, L.L.P.

FIAMM S.p.A.
Leg. Issues: TRD

Outside Counsel/Consultants
Steptoe & Johnson LLP
Issues: TRD
Rep By: Edward J. Krauland

FIAMM Technologies, Inc.
Cadillac, MI
Leg. Issues: TRD

Outside Counsel/Consultants
Steptoe & Johnson LLP
Issues: TRD
Rep By: Edward J. Krauland

Fiat U.S.A., Inc.
New York, NY

Outside Counsel/Consultants
Global Policy Group, Inc.

Fiberlink
Blue Bell, PA

Outside Counsel/Consultants
Earle Palmer Brown Public Relations

Fibernet LLC
Annapolis, MD

Outside Counsel/Consultants
American Defense Internat'l, Inc.
Rep By: Michael Herson, Van D. Hipp, Jr., Dave Wilberding

Fibrowatt, Inc.
Philadelphia, PA
Leg. Issues: CAW, ENG, ENV, TAX, WAS

Outside Counsel/Consultants
McGuireWoods L.L.P.
Issues: CAW, ENG, ENV, TAX, WAS
Rep By: Joseph H. Bogosian, Stephen A. Katsurinis, Hon. Lewis F. Payne, Jr.

Fideicomiso de la Escuela de Agricultura de la Region Tropical Humeda, S.A.
San Jose, COSTA RICA
Leg. Issues: BUD

Outside Counsel/Consultants
Vorys, Sater, Seymour and Pease, LLP
Issues: BUD

Fidelity Charitable Gift Fund
Boston, MA
Leg. Issues: TAX

Outside Counsel/Consultants
Skadden, Arps, Slate, Meagher & Flom LLP
Issues: TAX
Rep By: Roseann M. Cutrone, Fred T. Goldberg, Jr., Jessica A. Hough

Fidelity Investments Co.
Boston, MA
Leg. Issues: BAN, BNK, FIN

Outside Counsel/Consultants
GPC Internat'l
Issues: BAN
Rep By: John D. Cahill, Daniel K. Crann, Andy Paven
Katten Muchin & Zavis
Issues: BNK
Rep By: Carol R. Van Cleef
Williams & Jensen, P.C.
Issues: FIN
Rep By: David M. Landers

Fidelity Technologies Corp.
Reading, PA
Leg. Issues: DEF

Outside Counsel/Consultants
The PMA Group
Issues: DEF
Rep By: Daniel E. Fleming, Kaylene Green, Paul J. Magliocchetti, Briggs Shade

Fieldcrest Cannon Inc.
Kannapolis, NC
A textile manufacturer.
Leg. Issues: APP

Outside Counsel/Consultants
SRG & Associates
Issues: APP
Rep By: Augustine D. Tantillo

Fierce & Isakowitz
Washington, DC
Leg. Issues: PHA

Outside Counsel/Consultants
NES, Inc.
Issues: PHA

Fifty Caliber Shooters Policy Institute, Inc.
Riverside, CA
Leg. Issues: FIR

Outside Counsel/Consultants
Jim Frigiola
Issues: FIR
Rep By: Jim Frigiola

Films By Jove
Studio City, CA

Outside Counsel/Consultants
Proskauer Rose LLP

Final Analysis, Inc.
Lanham, MD
Leg. Issues: TEC

Outside Counsel/Consultants
Capitol Coalitions Inc.
Issues: TEC
Rep By: Brett P. Scott

Financial Accounting Standards Board
Norwalk, CT
An educational organization which sets accounting standards.

Outside Counsel/Consultants
Columbus Public Affairs

Financial Collection Agencies
Wayne, PA
Leg. Issues: TAX

Outside Counsel/Consultants
Dean Blakey & Moskowitz
Issues: TAX
Rep By: Saul L. Moskowitz

Financial Corp. of America
Los Angeles, CA

Outside Counsel/Consultants
Elias, Matz, Tiernan and Herrick

Financial Executives International
1615 L St. NW
Suite 1320
Washington, DC 20036
Web: www.fei.org

Tel: (202)659-3700
Fax: (202)857-0230
Registered: LDA

A professional organization of individuals who are senior financial and administrative officers in business organizations throughout the U.S. Headquartered in Morristown, NJ, FEI has about 14,000 members, affiliated with 8,000 companies throughout the United States and Canada, including almost all of the Fortune 1,000.

Leg. Issues: FIN, RET

In-house, DC-area Employees
HINCHMAN, Grace L.: Senior V. President, Public Affairs
ROSEN, Mark: Director, Govenment Relations
SHEPLER, Bob: Manager, Government Relations
THOMAS, Sherri: Manager, Administration and Meetings

Outside Counsel/Consultants
Agri/Washington
Issues: FIN
Rep By: Jeffrey Sawyer
Davis & Harman LLP
Issues: RET
Rep By: Randolf H. Hardock

Financial Guaranty Insurance Corp.
New York, NY

Outside Counsel/Consultants
Arter & Hadden
Rep By: Jon W. Plebani

Financial Planning Ass'n
Washington, DC
Web: www.fpa.net
E-mail: fpa@fpa.net
Leg. Issues: FIN, INS, RET, SMB, TAX

Outside Counsel/Consultants
Hogan & Hartson L.L.P.
Issues: FIN, TAX
Rep By: William Michael House, James G. McMillan

Financial Service Centers of America
Hackensack, NJ
A trade association for providers of financial services.
Leg. Issues: BAN

Outside Counsel/Consultants
Sellery Associates, Inc.
Issues: BAN
Rep By: Lawrence E. Sabbath, William C. Sellery, Jr.

Financial Services Coordinating Council
Washington, DC
Leg. Issues: BAN, INS

Outside Counsel/Consultants
Schwartz & Ballen
Issues: BAN, INS
Rep By: Gilbert T. Schwartz

Financial Services Council
E-mail: FINSERCO@aol.com

A broad-based coalition of U.S. financial institutions, which supports comprehensive, structural reform of the financial services industry that would remove artificial barriers to competition.

Leg. Issues: BAN

Outside Counsel/Consultants
McGuireWoods L.L.P.
Issues: BAN
Rep By: Joseph H. Bogosian, Stephen A. Katsurinis, Jeffrey L. Schlagenhauf

The Financial Services Roundtable
805 15th St. NW
Suite 600
Washington, DC 20005
Web: www.fsround.org

Tel: (202)289-4322
Fax: (202)289-1903
Registered: LDA

Formely The Bankers Roundtable, the organization was formed from the merger between the Ass'n of Bank Holding Companies and the Ass'n of Reserve City Bankers.

Leg. Issues: BAN, BNK, FIN, HOU, INS, TAX, TRD

Political Action Committee/s
Financial Services Roundtable Political Action Committee
805 15th St. NW
Suite 600
Washington, DC 20005

Tel: (202)289-4322
Fax: (202)289-1903

In-house, DC-area Employees
BARTLETT, Steve: President
MCGREEVY, Lisa: Director, Government and Public Affairs
SOLOMON, Maura K.: Director of Banking and Financial Services
TALBOT, Scott: Director, Tax Policy, Counsel
WHITING, Richard M.: Exec. Director

Outside Counsel/Consultants
Barnett & Sivon, P.C.
Issues: BAN, FIN, HOU
Rep By: Robert E. Barnett, Jose S. Rivas, James C. Sivon
Covington & Burling
Theodore A. Doremus, Jr.
Issues: FIN
Rep By: Theodore A. Doremus, Jr.
Ernst & Young LLP

Financial Technology Industry Council

Washington, DC
Leg. Issues: BAN, SCI

Outside Counsel/Consultants

Hoover Partners
Issues: BAN, SCI
Rep By: Kimberly Hoover

Financial Women Internat'l

200 N. Glebe Rd.
Suite 820
Arlington, VA 22203-3728
Web: www.fwi.org
E-mail: info@fwi.org
Tel: (703)807-2007
Fax: (703)807-0111

Founded in 1921 as the Nat'l Ass'n of Bank Women. Membership includes nearly 3,500 women financial executives.

In-house, DC-area Employees

MARDEN, Judith C.: Director, Public Affairs and Exec. Director, FWI Foundation

FINCA Internat'l Inc., The Foundation for Internat'l Community Assistance

1101 14th St. NW
11th Floor
Washington, DC 20005-5601
Web: www.villagebanking.org
E-mail: info@villagebanking.org
Tel: (202)682-1510
Fax: (202)682-1535

FINCA provides financial services to the world's poorest families so they can create their own jobs, raise household incomes, and improve their standard of living; delivers services through a global network of locally managed, self-supporting institutions. Provides small loans to over 171,000 families in 20 countries.

Leg. Issues: ECN

In-house, DC-area Employees

GOMPF, Soledad: Director, Development
LENOIR, Monique: Communications Coordinator
SCOFIELD, Rupert: Exec. Director
YANOVITCH, Lawrence: Director, Policy and Research

Finch-Pruyn Paper Co.

Glens Falls, NY
Leg. Issues: ENV, LBR, NAT, TRD, TRU

Outside Counsel/Consultants

The Solomon Group, LLC
Issues: ENV, LBR, NAT, TRD, TRU
Rep By: Hon. Gerald B. H. Solomon, William R. Teator

Fine Air Services, Inc.

Miami, FL

Outside Counsel/Consultants

Pierre E. Murphy Law Offices

Fine Arts Museums of San Francisco

San Francisco, CA

Outside Counsel/Consultants

MARC Associates, Inc.
Rep By: Daniel C. Maldonado, Eve O'Toole, Shannon Penberthy

Finnish American Corporate Team (F.A.C.T.)

Washington, DC
Leg. Issues: FOR

Outside Counsel/Consultants

Meyers & Associates
Issues: FOR
Rep By: Larry D. Meyers, Richard L. Meyers

Fire Island Ass'n

New York, NY
Leg. Issues: BUD, NAT

Outside Counsel/Consultants

Linowes and Blocher LLP
Issues: NAT
Rep By: Lawrence R. Liebesman

Marlowe and Co.
Issues: BUD, NAT
Rep By: Howard Marlowe, Jeffrey Mazzella

Firearms Importers Roundtable Trade Group

Washington, DC
Leg. Issues: FIR

Outside Counsel/Consultants

Law Offices of Mark Barnes
Issues: FIR
Rep By: Mark J. Barnes, Tammy Begun

Firearms Training Systems, Inc.

Suwanee, GA
Registered: LDA
Leg. Issues: BUD, DEF

Outside Counsel/Consultants

Edington, Peel & Associates, Inc.
Issues: BUD, DEF
Rep By: William H. Edington

Fireman's Fund Insurance Cos.

1101 Connecticut Ave. NW
Suite 950
Washington, DC 20036
Tel: (202)785-3575
Fax: (202)785-3023
Registered: LDA
Web: www.ffic.com
Leg. Issues: INS, TAX

In-house, DC-area Employees

HOLLY, William F.: Assistant V. President, Government and Industry Affairs
LEFKIN, Peter A.: Senior V. President, Government and Industry Affairs
LORENZ, Lance E.: Director, Government Affairs
ROE, Christopher P.: Assistant V. President, Government and Industry Affairs

Outside Counsel/Consultants

Baker & Hostetler LLP

Brenda R. Viehe-Naess
Issues: INS, TAX
Rep By: Brenda R. Viehe-Naess

First Amendment Coalition for Expression

Washington, DC
Leg. Issues: CIV, COM, CON, GOV, MIA, REL, TAX, TEC

Outside Counsel/Consultants

Janus-Merritt Strategies, L.L.C.
Issues: CIV, COM, CON, GOV, MIA, REL, TAX, TEC
Rep By: Scott P. Hoffman, Bethany Noble

First American

Santa Ana, CA
Leg. Issues: ECN, FIN, RES, TAX

Outside Counsel/Consultants

John T. O'Rourke Law Offices
Issues: ECN, FIN, RES, TAX
Rep By: John T. O'Rourke

First American Aircraft Title

New Orleans, LA
Leg. Issues: MAR

Outside Counsel/Consultants

Adams and Reese LLP
Issues: MAR
Rep By: D. Lee Forsgren, Hon. James A. "Jimmy" Hayes

First American Bulk Carriers Corp.

Reno, NV
Leg. Issues: MAR

Outside Counsel/Consultants

Winston & Strawn
Issues: MAR
Rep By: Lawrence I. Kiern, Thomas L. Mills, Constantine G. Papavizas

First American Real Estate Solutions LLC

St. Petersburg, FL
Leg. Issues: BAN, RES

Outside Counsel/Consultants

The Advocacy Group
Issues: BAN, RES
Rep By: George A. Ramonas

First American Title Aircraft

New Orleans, LA
Leg. Issues: INS, MAR

Outside Counsel/Consultants

Adams and Reese LLP
Issues: INS, MAR
Rep By: D. Lee Forsgren, Hon. James A. "Jimmy" Hayes

First Church of Christ, Scientist

Boston, MA
Leg. Issues: HCR, MMM

Outside Counsel/Consultants

Mayer, Brown & Platt
Issues: HCR
Rep By: Carolyn P. Osolinik

Denny Miller McBee Associates
Issues: HCR, MMM

First Consulting Group

Long Beach, CA
Leg. Issues: HCR, MMM

Outside Counsel/Consultants

Jefferson Consulting Group
Issues: HCR, MMM
Rep By: Dorsey Chescavage, Kathy P. Conrad, Julia T. Susman

First Data Corp./Telecheck

Omaha, NE
Leg. Issues: CPT, FIN

Outside Counsel/Consultants

Brownstein Hyatt & Farber, P.C.
Issues: FIN
Rep By: William T. Brack, Michael B. Levy

Mullenholz, Brimsek & Belair
Issues: CPT
Rep By: Robert R. Belair, Susan C. Haller

First Federal Savings and Loan Ass'n of Raleigh

Raleigh, NC

Outside Counsel/Consultants

Elias, Matz, Tiernan and Herrick

First Fidelity Bancorporation

Newark, NJ

Outside Counsel/Consultants

Sullivan & Cromwell
Rep By: Samuel R. Woodall, III

First Flight Centennial Foundation

RDU Int'l Airport, NC
Leg. Issues: AVI

Outside Counsel/Consultants

Patton Boggs, LLP
Issues: AVI

First Health Group Corp.

1133 21st St. NW
Suite 450
Washington, DC 20036
Tel: (202)872-0556
Fax: (202)872-0908
Registered: LDA

A full-service national health benefits company headquartered in Downers Grove, IL.

Leg. Issues: HCR

In-house, DC-area Employees

QUEALY, Patricia A.: V. President, Government Affairs

Outside Counsel/Consultants

Bergner Bockorny Castagnetti and Hawkins
Issues: HCR
Rep By: Jeffrey T. Bergner, David A. Bockorny, David Castagnetti, James W. Hawkins, Melissa Schulman

First Nat'l of Nebraska

Omaha, NE
Leg. Issues: BAN

Outside Counsel/Consultants

Kutak Rock LLP
Issues: BAN
Rep By: Brian Handlos, Dave Karnes

First Nationwide Bank

San Francisco, CA

Outside Counsel/Consultants

Akin, Gump, Strauss, Hauer & Feld, L.L.P.
Rep By: Janet C. Boyd, Marlene M. Colucci, Michael S. Mandel

Sue E. Johnson Associates
Rep By: Susan E. Johnson

First Preston Management

Dallas, TX
Leg. Issues: TAX

Outside Counsel/Consultants

Hooper Owen & Winburn
Issues: TAX
Rep By: Lucia A. Wyman

First Savings Bank, F.S.B.

Manhattan, KS

Outside Counsel/Consultants

Arnold & Porter
Rep By: Martha L. Cochran

First Scientific Corp.

Ogden, UT
Leg. Issues: DEF, EDU, FOR, HCR

Outside Counsel/Consultants

William M. Cloherty
Issues: DEF, EDU, FOR, HCR
Rep By: William M. Cloherty

First South Production Credit Ass'n

Ridgeland, MS
Leg. Issues: BAN

Outside Counsel/Consultants

The Macon Edwards Co.
Issues: BAN
Rep By: Macon T. Edwards, Mara Peltz

First Tuesday Group

Washington, DC

Group of 21 trade associations formed to discuss and coordinate workplace issues before Congress, federal agencies and the court system.

Leg. Issues: HCR, LBR

Outside Counsel/Consultants

Ogletree Governmental Affairs, Inc.
Issues: HCR, LBR
Rep By: Harold P. Coxson

First Union Corp.

Charlotte, NC
Leg. Issues: BAN, BNK, EDU, FIN, TAX

Outside Counsel/Consultants

Sullivan & Cromwell
Issues: BAN
Rep By: H. Rodgin Cohen

Williams & Jensen, P.C.
Issues: BAN, BNK, EDU, FIN, TAX
Rep By: Philip E. Bechtel, David E. Franasiak, Robert E. Glennon, Jr., J. Steven Hart, David M. Landers, Anthony J. Roda, Jeffrey A. Tassey, J. D. Williams

First USA Bank

Wilmington, DE
Leg. Issues: BAN

Outside Counsel/Consultants

Dickstein Shapiro Morin & Oshinsky LLP
Issues: BAN
Rep By: Henry C. Cashen, II, Graham "Rusty" Mathews, Bernard Nash, Hon. Joseph D. Tydings, L. Andrew Zausner

Firstdoor.com

Kennesaw, GA
Leg. Issues: SMB

Outside Counsel/Consultants

Verner, Liipfert, Bernhard, McPherson and Hand, Chartered
Issues: SMB
Rep By: Marla P. Grossman

FirstEnergy Co.

Akron, OH Registered: LDA

Formed from the merger of Ohio Edison and Centerior Energy.

Leg. Issues: BUD, ENG, ENV, LBR, UTI

Outside Counsel/Consultants

Akin, Gump, Strauss, Hauer & Feld, L.L.P.
Issues: LBR
Rep By: Barney J. Skladany, Jr.

Balch & Bingham LLP
Issues: UTI
Rep By: Sean Cunningham, Fred Eames, Patrick J. McCormick, III

Holland & Knight LLP
Issues: BUD, ENG, ENV, UTI
Rep By: Richard M. Gold, Janet R. Studley, Beth Viola, David C. Whitestone

Paul, Hastings, Janofsky & Walker LLP
Rep By: E. Donald Elliott

The Renkes Group, Ltd.
Issues: ENG, ENV
Rep By: Gregg D. Renkes

FIRSTPLUS Financial Group Inc.

Dallas, TX
Leg. Issues: BAN, BNK

Outside Counsel/Consultants

Federal Legislative Associates, Inc.
Issues: BAN, BNK
Rep By: Stephen D. Amitay, David H. Miller

FISERV, Inc.

Brookfield, WI
Leg. Issues: BAN, CPI, SCI, SMB, TAX

Outside Counsel/Consultants

Hohlt & Associates
Issues: BAN, CPI, SCI, SMB, TAX
Rep By: Richard F. Hohlt

Edward A. Fish Associates

Boston, MA
Leg. Issues: HOU

Outside Counsel/Consultants

Nixon Peabody LLP
Issues: HOU
Rep By: Charles L. Edson, Monica Hilton Sussman, Stephen J. Wallace

Fishable Waters Coalition

Alexandria, VA
Leg. Issues: CAW, ENV

Outside Counsel/Consultants

Baker, Donelson, Bearman & Caldwell, P.C.
Issues: ENV
Rep By: James D. Range

Hogan & Hartson L.L.P.
Issues: CAW
Rep By: James Banks, Catherine Van Heuven

Fisher Broadcasting, Inc.

Seattle, WA

Outside Counsel/Consultants

Shaw Pittman

Fisher Imaging

Denver, CO
Leg. Issues: HCR

Outside Counsel/Consultants

American Continental Group, Inc.
Issues: HCR
Rep By: Steve Colovas, David A. Metzner

Fisher Scientific Worldwide

Hampton, NH

Outside Counsel/Consultants

Nutter & Harris, Inc.
Rep By: Jack O. Nutter

Fishers Island Ferry District

Fishers Island, NY
Leg. Issues: BUD

Outside Counsel/Consultants

Capitol Associates, Inc.
Issues: BUD
Rep By: Ronnie Kovner Tepp

Fishing Vessel Owners' Ass'n

Seattle, WA

Outside Counsel/Consultants

O'Connor & Hannan, L.L.P.
Rep By: George J. Mannina, Jr.

Fitch Investors Service, Inc.

New York, NY

Outside Counsel/Consultants

Wilmer, Cutler & Pickering
Rep By: Marianne K. Smythe

Flathead Joint Board of Control

St. Ignacious, MT
Leg. Issues: RES, UTI

Outside Counsel/Consultants

Ron C. Marlenee
Issues: RES, UTI
Rep By: Hon. Ron C. Marlenee

Flavor and Extract Manufacturers Ass'n

Washington, DC

Outside Counsel/Consultants

The Roberts Group
Rep By: John B. Hallagan, Glenn Roberts

Fleet Capital

Outside Counsel/Consultants

Edelman Public Relations Worldwide
Rep By: Robert Rehg

Fleet Financial Group, Inc.

Providence, RI
Leg. Issues: BAN, BNK

Outside Counsel/Consultants

Bingham Dana LLP
Issues: BAN, BNK
Rep By: William H. Boger, Paul S. Quinn

Cooper, Carvin & Rosenthal

Fleet Reserve Ass'n

125 N. West St.
Alexandria, VA 22314-2754
Tel: (703)683-1400
Fax: (703)549-6610
Registered: LDA

Web: www.fra.org
E-mail: legfra@fra.org

A voluntary, non-profit association comprised of active duty, reserve, and retired members of the U.S. Navy, Marine Corps, and Coast Guard. Represents members before the U.S. Congress and governmental agencies with regard to pay, health care, and other benefits.

Leg. Issues: BUD, CON, DEF, EDU, HCR, MMM, RET, TRA, VET

In-house, DC-area Employees

BARNES, Joseph L.: Director, Legislative Programs
CALKINS, Charles L.: National Exec. Secretary
MCKINNEY, C.A. "Mack": Legislative Counsel
WASHINGTON, Robert: Director, Member Services
YANETTE, Terry: National Veterans Service Officer

FleetBoston Financial

Boston, MA
Leg. Issues: FIN

Outside Counsel/Consultants

Bingham Dana LLP
Issues: FIN
Rep By: William H. Boger, Paul S. Quinn

Edelman Public Relations Worldwide
Rep By: Robert Rehg

Fleishman-Hillard, Inc

1615 L St. NW
Suite 1000
Washington, DC 20036
Tel: (202)659-0330
Fax: (202)296-6119
Registered: LDA, FARA

Web: www.fleishman.com
Leg. Issues: AVI

Political Action Committee/s

Fleishman-Hillard Political Action Committee
1615 L St. NW
Suite 1000
Washington, DC 20036
Tel: (202)659-0330
Fax: (202)296-6119

In-house, DC-area Employees

BLACK, William: Senior V. President
BOUDREAU, Martha L.: Senior V. President and Partner
BOYLE, Joy Bates: V. President
COLLENDER, Stanley: Senior V. President
FINZEL, Ben: V. President
FRAZIER, Harry: Senior V. President
GOODMAN, Alan: V. President
HABER, Jon: Senior V. President
HANNON, Sandra: V. President
HARDISON, Ann: V. President
HUBBARD, Henry W.: Senior V. President and Partner
JOHNSON, Paul W.: Exec. V. President, Senior Partner and General Manager
KAUFFMAN, Frank: Senior V. President
KRAMER, Elizabeth: V. President
MANDIGO, Michael: V. President
MCLEARN, Donald: Senior V. President
MOONEY, Robby A.: Senior V. President and Partner
MULHERN, Jim: Senior V. President
SIEDLECKI, Kathleen: V. President
THOMPSON, Sela: Senior Legislative Assistant
WICKENDEN, David: Senior V. President and Senior Partner

Outside Counsel/Consultants

Bryan Cave LLP
Rep By: Stanley J. Marcuss

R. Duffy Wall and Associates
Issues: AVI
Rep By: Hon. Bill Brewster, Hon. Rodney D. Chandler

Flexel, Inc.

Atlanta, GA

A producer of cellophane.

Outside Counsel/Consultants

Collier Shannon Scott, PLLC
Rep By: Michael J. Coursey

Flexi-Van Leasing

Kenilworth, NJ
Leg. Issues: TAX

Outside Counsel/Consultants

Baker & Hostetler LLP
Issues: TAX
Rep By: William F. Conroy, Matthew J. Dolan, Frederick H. Graefe, Steven A. Lotterer, Hon. Guy Vander Jagt

Johnson Co.
Issues: TAX

Flexsys America

Akron, OH
Leg. Issues: ENV

Outside Counsel/Consultants

Golin/Harris Internat'l
Issues: ENV
Rep By: C. Michael Fulton

Flight Landata, Inc.

Lawrence, MA
Leg. Issues: AER, AGR, DEF, ENV, NAT, WAS

Outside Counsel/Consultants

Jamison and Sullivan, Inc.
Issues: AER, AGR, DEF, ENV, NAT, WAS
Rep By: Delos Cy Jamison, Jay R. Sullivan

Flight Safety Foundation

601 Madison St.
Suite 300
Alexandria, VA 22314-1756
Web: www.flightsafety.org
Tel: (703)739-6700
Fax: (703)739-6708

An international organization of airlines, aerospace manufacturers, corporate flight departments and others interested in flight safety.

In-house, DC-area Employees

HILL, Ann: Director, Membership and Development
MATTHEWS, Stuart: President, and Chief Exec. Officer

Flight Safety Technologies, Inc.

New London, CT
Leg. Issues: AER, TRA

Outside Counsel/Consultants

The Kemper Co.
Issues: AER, TRA
Rep By: Jackson Kemper, Jr.

FlightSafety Internat'l

1201 Pennsylvania Ave. NW
Suite 300
Washington, DC 20004-2401
Web: www.flightsafety.com
Tel: (202)661-4700
Fax: (202)661-4799

Company provides classroom, simulator, and flight training for aircraft pilots and maintenance technicians. MarineSafety subsidiary provides classroom and simulator training for deck and engineering officers in ship handling operations and procedures. Instructional Systems Division designs courseware. Simulations Systems Division manufactures advanced flight simulators and training devices. Visual Simulation Systems Division manufactures visual equipment for simulators. Headquartered in Flushing, NY.

Leg. Issues: AER, AVI

In-house, DC-area Employees

GLESKE, Elmer G.: V. President, Governmental Affairs

Flint, Michigan, City of

Leg. Issues: BUD

Outside Counsel/Consultants

Reed, Smith, LLP
Issues: BUD
Rep By: Christopher L. Rissetto

FLIR Systems, Inc.

1755 Jefferson Davis Highway
Suite 1101
Arlington, VA 22202
Web: www.flir.com
Tel: (703)416-6666
Fax: (703)416-1517
Registered: LDA

Leg. Issues: AER, AVI, BUD, DEF, LAW, MAN, TRA, TRD

Political Action Committee/s

Flir Systems Inc. Employee PAC
1755 Jefferson Davis Highway
Suite 1101
Arlington, VA 22202
Tel: (703)416-6666
Fax: (703)416-1517

In-house, DC-area Employees

GARNER, Bob
HOPPER, Gary B.

Outside Counsel/Consultants

Baker, Donelson, Bearman & Caldwell, P.C.
Issues: BUD
Rep By: J. Keith Kennedy

Capitol Partners
Issues: DEF, TRD
Rep By: William Cunningham, Jonathan M. Orloff

The PMA Group
Issues: BUD, DEF
Rep By: Kaylene Green, Gregory L. Hansen, Dr. John Lynch, Paul J. Magliocchetti

Flo-Sun Sugar

Palm Beach, FL
Leg. Issues: AGR

Outside Counsel/Consultants

Berman Enterprises
Issues: AGR
Rep By: Wayne Berman

Floral Trade Council

Haslett, MI
Leg. Issues: TRD

Outside Counsel/Consultants

Stewart and Stewart
Issues: TRD
Rep By: Geert M. De Prest, Amy S. Dwyer, David S. Johanson, Terence P. Stewart

Florence, South Carolina, City of

Florence, SC
Leg. Issues: BUD

Outside Counsel/Consultants

R. Duffy Wall and Associates
Issues: BUD
Rep By: Rodney Emery

Florida Atlantic University

Boca Raton, FL
Leg. Issues: EDU

Outside Counsel/Consultants

The Advocacy Group
Issues: EDU
Rep By: Robert E. Mills, George A. Ramonas

Florida Citrus Alliance

Lakeland, FL
Leg. Issues: AGR, BUD

Outside Counsel/Consultants

O'Connor & Hannan, L.L.P.
Issues: AGR, BUD
Rep By: John M. Himmelberg

Florida Citrus Mutual

Lakeland, FL
Leg. Issues: ENV, NAT, RES

Outside Counsel/Consultants

Barnes, Richardson and Colburn
Rep By: Matthew T. McGrath

Dawson & Associates, Inc.
Issues: ENV, NAT, RES
Rep By: Robert K. Dawson, Jonathan P. Deason, Ph.D., Edward Dickey, Ph.D., Lester Edelman, Lt. Gen. Vald Heiberg, Lt. Gen. Arthur E. Williams, USA (Ret.)

Florida Citrus Packers

Lakeland, FL

Outside Counsel/Consultants

Barnes, Richardson and Colburn
Rep By: Matthew T. McGrath

Florida Citrus Processors Ass'n

Winter Haven, FL

Outside Counsel/Consultants

Barnes, Richardson and Colburn
Rep By: Matthew T. McGrath

Florida Community College of Jacksonville

Jacksonville, FL
Leg. Issues: EDU

Outside Counsel/Consultants

Davis O'Connell, Inc.
Issues: EDU
Rep By: Lynda C. Davis, Ph.D.

Florida Cruise and Ferry Service Inc.

Tampa, FL

Outside Counsel/Consultants

Bob Davis & Associates

Florida Crystals Corp.

Palm Beach, FL
Leg. Issues: AGR, ENV, TRD

Outside Counsel/Consultants

Smith Martin & Boyette
Issues: AGR, ENV, TRD
Rep By: Van R. Boyette

Florida Department of Agriculture and Consumer Services

Tallahassee, FL
Leg. Issues: TRD

Outside Counsel/Consultants

Greenberg Traurig, LLP
Issues: TRD
Rep By: Diane J. Blagman, Howard A. Vine

Florida Department of Children & Families

Tallahassee, FL
Leg. Issues: WEL

Outside Counsel/Consultants

Cortese PLLC
Issues: WEL
Rep By: Alfred W. Cortese, Jr.

Florida Department of Citrus

Tallahassee, FL
Leg. Issues: AGR

Outside Counsel/Consultants

Max N. Berry Law Offices
Issues: AGR
Rep By: Max N. Berry

O'Connor & Hannan, L.L.P.
Rep By: John M. Himmelberg

Florida Department of Education

Tallahassee, FL
Leg. Issues: EDU

Outside Counsel/Consultants

Davis O'Connell, Inc.
Issues: EDU
Rep By: Lynda C. Davis, Ph.D., Jennifer Golden

Florida Department of Health and Rehabilitative Services

Tallahassee, FL

A state agency responsible for handling welfare matters.

Outside Counsel/Consultants

Pepper Hamilton LLP

Florida East Coast Industries Inc.

St. Augustine, FL
Leg. Issues: TRA

Outside Counsel/Consultants

Chambers, Conlon & Hartwell
Issues: TRA
Rep By: Ray B. Chambers, Jerome Conlon, Don Norden, John Roots

Florida Equipment Contractors Ass'n

Hollywood, FL
Leg. Issues: LBR

Outside Counsel/Consultants

Morgan, Lewis & Bockius LLP
Issues: LBR

Florida Farm Bureau

Okeechobee, FL
Leg. Issues: ENV, NAT, RES

Outside Counsel/Consultants

Dawson & Associates, Inc.
Issues: ENV, NAT, RES
Rep By: Robert K. Dawson, Jonathan P. Deason, Ph.D., Edward Dickey, Ph.D., Lt. Gen. Vald Heiberg, Lt. Gen. Arthur E. Williams, USA (Ret.)

Florida Farm Bureau Federation

Gainesville, FL

Outside Counsel/Consultants
Barnes, Richardson and Colburn
Rep By: Matthew T. McGrath

Florida Fruit and Vegetable Ass'n

Orlando, FL
Leg. Issues: AGR, TRD

Outside Counsel/Consultants
McDermott, Will and Emery
Issues: AGR, TRD
Rep By: Carolyn B. Gleason, Jerry C. Hill

Florida Gas Utility

Gainesville, FL
Leg. Issues: FUE, TAX

Outside Counsel/Consultants
Holland & Knight LLP
Issues: FUE, TAX
Rep By: Harold R. Bucholtz, Richard M. Gold, Janet R. Studley, David C. Whitestone

Florida Internat'l University

701 Pennsylvania Ave. NW
Suite 600
Washington, DC 20004
Tel: (202)624-1263
Fax: (202)624-1298
Registered: LDA
Web: www.fiu.edu
E-mail: mviana@lanlaw.com
Leg. Issues: BUD, EDU

In-house, DC-area Employees
SAULS, Stephen: Vice Provost

Outside Counsel/Consultants
Long, Aldridge & Norman, LLP
Issues: BUD, EDU
Rep By: C. Randall Nuckolls, Patrick C. Turner

Florida Municipal Power Agency

Orlando, FL
Leg. Issues: ENG

Outside Counsel/Consultants
Morgan Meguire, LLC
Issues: ENG
Rep By: Scott Lindsay, Kyle G. Michel, Katie Parrott, C. Kyle Simpson, Deborah R. Sliz, Kiel Weaver

Florida Power and Light Co.

801 Pennsylvania Ave. NW
Suite 220
Washington, DC 20004-2604
Tel: (202)347-7082
Fax: (202)347-7076
Registered: LDA
Web: www.fpl.com
Headquartered in Juno Beach, FL.
Leg. Issues: CAW, ENG, TAX, UTI, WAS

In-house, DC-area Employees
CHAPEL, Christopher: Manager, Governmental Affairs, Washington Office
WILSON, Michael M.: V. President, Governmental Affairs

Outside Counsel/Consultants
Birch, Horton, Bittner & Cherot
Rep By: William P. Horn
Davis & Harman LLP
Issues: TAX
Rep By: Richard S. Belas, Thomas A. Davis
The Renkes Group, Ltd.
Issues: UTI
Rep By: Patrick Pettey, Gregg D. Renkes
Ryan, Phillips, Utrecht & MacKinnon
Issues: ENG, UTI
Rep By: Rodney Hoppe, Jeffrey M. MacKinnon, William D. Phillips, Mark D. Planning, Thomas M. Ryan, Joseph V. Vasapoli
Swidler Berlin Shereff Friedman, LLP
Issues: CAW, TAX, UTI, WAS
Rep By: Keith N. Cole, Barry B. Direnfeld, Brian W. Fitzgerald, Gary Gallant, Harold P. Goldfield, Lester S. Hyman, Gary D. Slaiman, Katherine R. Taylor

Florida Residential and Casualty Joint Underwriting Ass'n

Tallahassee, FL
Leg. Issues: TAX

Outside Counsel/Consultants
Baker & Hostetler LLP
Issues: TAX
Rep By: William F. Conroy, Matthew J. Dolan, Frederick H. Graefe, Steven A. Lotterer, David L. Marshall, Hon. Guy Vander Jagt

Florida State University

Tallahassee, FL
Leg. Issues: BUD, EDU, FOR

Outside Counsel/Consultants
The Advocacy Group
Issues: EDU
Rep By: Robert E. Mills, George A. Ramonas
Edington, Peel & Associates, Inc.
Issues: BUD, FOR
Rep By: William H. Edington, Terry R. Peel

Florida State University System

Tallahassee, FL
Leg. Issues: AER, ALC, ANI, ART, AVI, BUD, CPT, DEF, DIS, ECN, EDU, ENG, ENV, FOR, HCR, IMM, MAR, MED, MMM, SCI, TAX, TEC, TRA, URB, VET

Outside Counsel/Consultants
JCP Associates
Issues: DEF, DIS, ECN, EDU, HCR, IMM, MAR, MED, SCI, TEC, TRA
Rep By: James C. Pirius
Jorden Burt LLP
Issues: AER, ALC, ANI, ART, AVI, BUD, CPT, DEF, EDU, ENG, ENV, FOR, HCR, IMM, MAR, MED, MMM, SCI, TAX, TEC, URB, VET
Rep By: Patricia Branch, Alanna Dillon, Marna Gettleman, Marilyn Berry Thompson, Rebecca Tidman

Florida Sugar Cane League, Inc.

1301 Pennsylvania Ave. NW
Suite 401
Washington, DC 20004-1729
Tel: (202)785-4070
Fax: (202)659-8581
Registered: LDA
Works to educate members of Congress and staff about sugar farming and U.S. policies and regulations affecting sugar farmers.
Leg. Issues: AGR, ENV, NAT, RES

Political Action Committee/s
Florida Sugar Cane League Political Action Committee
1301 Pennsylvania Ave. NW
Suite 401
Washington, DC 20004-1729
Tel: (202)785-4070
Fax: (202)659-8581
Contact: Windsor Freemyer

In-house, DC-area Employees
FREEMYER, Windsor: Director, Government Relations
SELL, Alisa M.: Washington Representative
YANCEY, Dalton: Exec. V. President

Outside Counsel/Consultants
Dawson & Associates, Inc.
Issues: ENV, NAT, RES
Rep By: Robert K. Dawson, Jonathan P. Deason, Ph.D., Edward Dickey, Ph.D., Lester Edelman, Lt. Gen. Vald Heiberg, Hon. John Myers, Lt. Gen. Arthur E. Williams, USA (Ret.)
The PMA Group
Rep By: Fred J. Clark, Kaylene Green, Paul J. Magliocchetti, Timothy K. Sanders

Florida Tomato Exchange

Orlando, FL
Leg. Issues: AGR, TRD

Outside Counsel/Consultants
O'Connor & Hannan, L.L.P.
Issues: AGR, TRD
Rep By: John M. Himmelberg

Florida Windstorm Underwriting Ass'n

Jacksonville, FL
Leg. Issues: TAX

Outside Counsel/Consultants
Baker & Hostetler LLP
Issues: TAX
Rep By: William F. Conroy, Matthew J. Dolan, Frederick H. Graefe, Steven A. Lotterer, David L. Marshall, Hon. Guy Vander Jagt

Florida, Washington Office of the State of

444 N. Capitol St. NW
Suite 349
Washington, DC 20001
Tel: (202)624-5885
Fax: (202)624-5886

In-house, DC-area Employees
OVIEDO, Nina: Director, Washington Office

Flow Internat'l Corp.

Outside Counsel/Consultants
Verner, Liipfert, Bernhard, McPherson and Hand, Chartered
Rep By: Gary J. Klein

Flue-Cured Tobacco Cooperative Stabilization Corp.

Raleigh, NC

Outside Counsel/Consultants
Francis J. Sullivan Associates

Fluor Corp.

555 12th St. NW
Suite 620 North
Washington, DC 20004
Tel: (202)955-9300
Fax: (202)833-1630
Registered: LDA
Web: www.fluor.com
A global engineering and construction company with investments in low-sulphur coal headquartered in Aliso Viejo, California.
Leg. Issues: CPI, ENG, ENV, FUE, GOV, LBR, NAT, RRR, TRA, TRD, WAS

In-house, DC-area Employees
FRENCH, Michael P.: Senior Director, Government Relations
HOLMES, Diane: Senior Washington Representative
VAUGHN, Philip: Senior Director, Government Affairs

Outside Counsel/Consultants
The Advocacy Group
Issues: ENG
Rep By: George A. Ramonas
Richard W. Bliss
Issues: ENG, TRD, WAS
Powell, Goldstein, Frazer & Murphy LLP
Issues: ENG, ENV, LBR, NAT, RRR, TRA, WAS
Rep By: Hon. Butler E. Derrick, Jr.

FM Watch

555 13th St. NW
13th Floor
Washington, DC 20004-1109
Tel: (202)637-5636
Fax: (202)637-5910
A coalition of banks and mortgage insurers. Address listed is that of the firm Hogan & Hartson. (see seperate listing)
Leg. Issues: BAN, FIN, GOV, HOU

In-house, DC-area Employees
HOUSE, William Michael: Exec. Director

Outside Counsel/Consultants
Akin, Gump, Strauss, Hauer & Feld, L.L.P.
Barbour Griffith & Rogers, Inc.
Issues: HOU
Rep By: Haley Barbour, G. O. Lanny Griffith, Jr., Bill Himpler, Loren Monroe, Edward M. Rogers, Jr.
Butera & Andrews
Issues: BAN, FIN, HOU
Rep By: Cliff W. Andrews, Wright H. Andrews, Jr., James J. Butera, Frank Tillotson
Dittus Communications
Rep By: Gloria S. Dittus, Shelton Jones
Global USA, Inc.
Issues: GOV, HOU
Rep By: Lottie H. Shackelford
Hogan & Hartson L.L.P.
Issues: HOU
Rep By: William Michael House, Sharon McBride, Jeffrey W. Munk, Christine M. Warnke
Patton Boggs, LLP
Rep By: Thomas Hale Boggs, Jr., Donald V. Moorehead
Podesta/Mattoon

FMC Corp.

1667 K St. NW
Suite 460
Washington, DC 20006
Tel: (202)956-5200
Fax: (202)956-5235
Registered: LDA
Web: www.fmc.com
Headquartered in Chicago, IL.
Leg. Issues: AER, AGR, AUT, AVI, BUD, CAW, CHM, ENG, ENV, FOO, FUE, IND, MAN, NAT, ROD, RRR, TRD, WAS

Political Action Committee/s
FMC Corp. Good Government Program
1667 K St. NW
Suite 460
Washington, DC 20006
Tel: (202)956-5208
Fax: (202)956-5235
Contact: Alise M. Troester

In-house, DC-area Employees
CHERRY, Edward T.: Director, Regulatory Affairs
DAVIS, Lizanne H.: Director, Government Affairs
PROUT, Gerald R.: V. President, Government Affairs
RIPPERGER, Patricia: Government Affairs Analyst
TROESTER, Alise M.: Manager, Government Affairs

Outside Counsel/Consultants
Burridge Associates
Rep By: James L. Burridge
EOP Group, Inc.
Issues: CAW, CHM, ENV, IND, WAS
Rep By: Shawn Delaney, Jonathan Gledhill, Norman Hartness, Joseph Hezir, Troy Hillier, Jan Mares, Corey

McDaniel, Michael O'Bannon, Tom Oxendine, Phil Pulizzi

Holland & Knight LLP
Issues: BUD, ENV
Rep By: Jack M. Burkman, Mike Galano, Richard M. Gold, P. J. Toker

Kirkland & Ellis

O'Connor & Hannan, L.L.P.
Issues: ENV, NAT
Rep By: Robert W. Barrie, Hon. Thomas J. Corcoran, George J. Mannina, Jr., Patrick E. O'Donnell

Van Scoyoc Associates, Inc.
Issues: ENV
Rep By: H. Stewart Van Scoyoc

FMC Wyoming Corp.

Green River, WY
Leg. Issues: LBR

Outside Counsel/Consultants

Patton Boggs, LLP
Issues: LBR
Rep By: Henry Chajet

FMR Corp.

Boston, MA
Leg. Issues: TAX

Outside Counsel/Consultants

Davis & Harman LLP
Issues: TAX
Rep By: Barbara Groves Mattox

FN Herstal, USA

Vienna, VA
Leg. Issues: DEF, MAN

Outside Counsel/Consultants

American Systems Internat'l Corp.
Issues: DEF, MAN
Rep By: Robert D. McVey, William H. Skipper, Jr.

Foamex

Linwood, PA

Outside Counsel/Consultants

Interface Inc.
Rep By: David C. Knapp

Focal Communications

Falls Church, VA
Leg. Issues: TEC

Outside Counsel/Consultants

Sher & Blackwell
Issues: TEC
Rep By: Earl W. Comstock, Jeffrey R. Pike, Antilla E. Trotter, III

Folger Shakespeare Library

201 E. Capitol St. SE
Washington, DC 20003
Tel: (202)544-4600
Fax: (202)544-4623
Web: www.folger.edu

Home to the world's largest collection of Shakespeare's printed works. The library is a major center for scholarly research, and a lively venue for exhibitions, cultural programs and performing arts.

Leg. Issues: ART

Outside Counsel/Consultants

Chernikoff and Co.
Issues: ART
Rep By: Larry B. Chernikoff

Folsom, California, City of

Leg. Issues: BUD, ECN, ENV, NAT, TRA

Outside Counsel/Consultants

The Ferguson Group, LLC
Issues: BUD, ECN, ENV, NAT, TRA
Rep By: W. Roger Gwinn, Mike Miller, Leslie Waters Mozingo, Joseph L. Raeder

Fon Digital Network Clearpoint Communications, Inc.

Winter Park, FL
Leg. Issues: FIN, TEC

Outside Counsel/Consultants

RPH & Associates, L.L.C.
Issues: FIN, TEC
Rep By: Hon. Robert P. Hanrahan

Fond du Lac Reservation, Washington Office of the

Duluth, MN

Outside Counsel/Consultants

Sonosky, Chambers, Sachse & Endreson
Rep By: William R. Perry

Fontana Bleu, S.p.A.

Caserta, ITALY

Outside Counsel/Consultants

McKenna & Cuneo, L.L.P.

Fontana Union Water Co.

Fontana, CA
Leg. Issues: NAT

Outside Counsel/Consultants

Akin, Gump, Strauss, Hauer & Feld, L.L.P.
Issues: NAT
Rep By: J. David Carlin, Joel Jankowsky

Fontana, California, City of

Leg. Issues: TRA

Outside Counsel/Consultants

Smith Dawson & Andrews, Inc.
Issues: TRA
Rep By: Robert A. Gaines

Fontheim Internat'l

601 13th St. NW
Suite 110 North
Washington, DC 20005
Tel: (202)296-8100
Fax: (202)296-8727
Registered: LDA
Leg. Issues: ECN, LBR, MAN, SCI, TRD, URB

In-house, DC-area Employees

FONTHEIM, Claude G. B.: Managing Director
LEVINSON, Kenneth I.: Director, International Trade and Finance

Outside Counsel/Consultants

Jarboe & Associates
Issues: ECN, LBR, MAN, SCI, TRD, URB
Rep By: Kenan Patrick Jarboe

Food Bank of the Virginia Peninsula

Newport News, VA
Leg. Issues: ECN, GOV, HCR

Outside Counsel/Consultants

Madison Government Affairs
Issues: ECN, GOV, HCR
Rep By: Paul J. Hirsch

Food Distributors Internat'l (NAWGA-IFDA)

201 Park Washington Ct.
Falls Church, VA 22046-4621
Tel: (703)532-9400
Fax: (703)538-4673
Registered: LDA
Web: www.fdi.org
E-mail: moreinfo@fdi.org

Food Distributors International, the umbrella name for the National-American Wholesale Grocers' Ass'n (NAWGA) and its foodservice partner organization, the International Foodservice Distributors Ass'n (IFDA), is an international trade association comprised of food distribution companies that primarily supply and service independent grocers and food service operations throughout the United States, Canada and more than 20 other countries.

Leg. Issues: AGR, ALC, BUD, FOO, GOV, HCR, LAW, LBR, SMB, TAX, TOB, TRA, TRU, UTI, WEL

Political Action Committee/s

Food Distributors Voice in Politics Committee (FOODVIP Committee)

201 Park Washington Ct.
Falls Church, VA 22046-4621
Tel: (703)532-9400
Fax: (703)538-4673
Contact: Jonathan B. Eisen

In-house, DC-area Employees

BLOCK, John R.: President
BURKE, Kevin M.: V. President, Government Relations
EISEN, Jonathan B.: Director, Government Relations
FRENCH, David: Director, Government Relations
GRAY, John M.: President, IFDA and Exec. V. President, General Counsel, FDI

Outside Counsel/Consultants

Baise + Miller, P.C.
Rep By: Gary H. Baise

The Dutko Group, Inc.
Issues: AGR, BUD, HCR, TAX
Rep By: Gary J. Andres, Kimberly M. Spaulding

Keller and Heckman LLP
Issues: TRA, TRU
Rep By: Terry Jones

Littler Mendelson, P.C.
Issues: LBR
Rep By: Peter A. Susser

Olsson, Frank and Weeda, P.C.
Issues: AGR, ALC, BUD, FOO, WEL
Rep By: John W. Bode, Richard L. Frank, Susan P. Grymes, Karen Reis Harned, Stephen L. Lacey, Marshall L. Matz, Tyson Redpath

Food Lion, Inc.

Salisbury, NC

Outside Counsel/Consultants

Akin, Gump, Strauss, Hauer & Feld, L.L.P.
Rep By: Thomas McLish, Michael Mueller, Richard Wyatt, Jr.

Food Marketing Institute

655 15th St. NW
Washington, DC 20005-5701
Tel: (202)452-8444
Fax: (202)220-0872
Registered: LDA
Web: www.fmi.org
E-mail: fmi@fmi.org

A non-profit association conducting programs in research, education and public affairs. Members are food retailers and wholesalers and their customers.

Leg. Issues: AGR, BUD, CPT, CSP, DEF, ENV, FOO, FUE, GOV, HCR, IND, LBR, MMM, PHA, SMB, TAX, TOB, TOR, TRD, TRU, UTI

Political Action Committee/s

Food Marketing Institute Political Action Committee (FoodPAC)

655 15th St. NW
Washington, DC 20005-5701
Tel: (202)220-0627
Fax: (202)220-0872
Contact: Karry LaViolette

In-house, DC-area Employees

BOURNE, Laura L.: Director, Government Relations
COLER, Kate: Director, Government Relations
CURRY, Anne McGhee: V. President, Legislative and Political Affairs
FARR, Dagmar T.: Group V. President, Legislative and Consumer Affairs
GREEN, George R.: V. President and General Counsel
HAMMONDS, Timothy M.: President and Chief Exec. Officer
HATCHER, Jennifer L.: Director, Government Relations
KELLEY, J. Tyrone: Director, Government Relations
LAVIOLETTE, Karry: Manager, Political Affairs
MANTERIA, Bill: V. President, State Government Relations
MOTLEY, III, John J.: Senior V. President, Government and Public Affairs
NICOLL, Eric: Director, Government Relations
SMITH, Brian G.: Director, Grassroots Advocacy
WHITE, Deborah R.: Regulatory Counsel
WISE-VAUGHAN, Elizabeth: Director, Government Relations
YANISH, Nancy Foster: Director, Government Relations

Outside Counsel/Consultants

Howrey Simon Arnold & White

Food Processing Machinery and Supplies Ass'n

200 Daingerfield Rd.
Alexandria, VA 22314
Tel: (703)684-1080
Fax: (703)548-6563
Web: www.fpmsa.com
E-mail: fpmsa@clark.net

Consists of over 500 member companies providing machinery, supplies and services to the food, beverage, pharmaceutical, and chemical processing and packaging industries. Sponsors an annual international trade show and various industry councils.

Leg. Issues: FOO, GOV, TOR, TRD

In-house, DC-area Employees

MELNYKOVICH, George O.: President

Outside Counsel/Consultants

Barnes & Thornburg
Issues: FOO, GOV, TOR, TRD
Rep By: Randolph J. Stayin

The Food Processors Institute

1350 I St. NW
Suite 300
Washington, DC 20005
Web: www.fpi-food.org
E-mail: fpi@nfpa-food.org
Tel: (202)393-0890
Fax: (202)639-5932

The educational provider for the Nat'l Food Processors Ass'n.

In-house, DC-area Employees

WEDDIG, Lisa: Exec. Director

Food Research and Action Center

1875 Connecticut Ave. NW
Suite 540
Washington, DC 20009
Web: www.frac.org
E-mail: foodresearch@frac.org
Tel: (202)986-2200
Fax: (202)986-2525
Registered: LDA

A national advocacy and public interest law center working to reduce hunger among low-income people in the United States.

Leg. Issues: AGR, BUD, DEF, EDU, IMM, LBR, TRA

In-house, DC-area Employees

HENCHY, Geraldine: Senior Policy Analyst
HENDRICK, Scott: Legislative Associate
HESS, Doug: Policy Analyst/Researcher
PARKER, Lynn: Director, Child Nutrition Programs/Nutritution Policy
TELLER, Ellen S.: Director, Government Affairs
VOLLINGER, Ellen M.: Legal/Foodstamp Director
WEILL, James D.: President

Food Update Foundation

1101 15th St. NW
Suite 202
Washington, DC 20005
Tel: (202)785-3232
Fax: (202)223-9741

In-house, DC-area Employees

CRISTOL, Richard E.: Exec. Director

Outside Counsel/Consultants

The Kellen Company
Rep By: Richard E. Cristol

Foodbrands America, Inc.

Outside Counsel/Consultants

Edelman Public Relations Worldwide
Rep By: Daniel Puzo

Foodmaker Internat'l Franchising Inc.

San Diego, CA
Leg. Issues: CPT

Outside Counsel/Consultants

Hogan & Hartson L.L.P.
Issues: CPT
Rep By: J. Warren Gorrell, Mark S. McConnell

Foodservice & Packaging Institute, Inc.

1550 Wilson Blvd.
Suite 701
Arlington, VA 22209
Web: www.fpi.org
E-mail: fpi@fpi.org
Tel: (703)527-7505
Fax: (703)527-7512

Manufacturers of disposable products for food service and packaging.

In-house, DC-area Employees

BURKE, John R.: President
PHILLIPS, Beth: Director, Administrative and Member Services
VASQUEZ, Carmen: Manager, Marketing and Communications

foot.com

Hackensack, NJ
Leg. Issues: MMM

Outside Counsel/Consultants

McDermott, Will and Emery
Issues: MMM
Rep By: Eric P. Zimmerman

W. A. Foote Memorial Hospital

Jackson, MI
Leg. Issues: MMM

Outside Counsel/Consultants

McDermott, Will and Emery
Issues: MMM
Rep By: Eric P. Zimmerman

Foothill Transit

West Covina, CA
Leg. Issues: BUD

Outside Counsel/Consultants

Baker, Donelson, Bearman & Caldwell, P.C.
Issues: BUD
Rep By: Janet L. Powell

Foothills Pipe Lines (Yukon), Ltd.

Calgary, CANADA

A diversified company that is parent company of Novacor Chemicals Ltd., a petrochemical manufacturer.

Leg. Issues: FUE

Outside Counsel/Consultants

Van Ness Feldman, P.C.
Issues: FUE
Rep By: J. Curtis Moffatt, Thomas C. Roberts

The Wexler Group
Issues: FUE
Rep By: Anne Wexler

Footwear Distributors and Retailers of America

1319 F St. NW
Suite 700
Washington, DC 20004
Web: www.fdra.org
E-mail: fdra2@aol.com
Tel: (202)737-5660
Fax: (202)638-2615
Registered: LDA
Leg. Issues: TRD

Political Action Committee/s

Footwear Distributors and Retailers of America Political Action Committee
1319 F St. NW
Suite 700
Washington, DC 20004
Contact: Peter T. Mangione
Tel: (202)737-5660
Fax: (202)638-2615

In-house, DC-area Employees

MANGIONE, Peter T.: President

Outside Counsel/Consultants

Internat'l Business and Economic Research Corp.

Powell, Goldstein, Frazer & Murphy LLP
Issues: TRD
Rep By: Alice Slayton Clark, Michael P. Daniels, Maria DiGiulian, Brenda A. Jacobs

For Homes

Washington, DC

Outside Counsel/Consultants

Preston Gates Ellis & Rouvelas Meeds LLP

Forces Vives

Lausanne, SWITZERLAND

A life insurance and annuities company.

Leg. Issues: INS, TAX

Outside Counsel/Consultants

Brenda R. Viehe-Naess
Issues: INS, TAX
Rep By: Brenda R. Viehe-Naess

Betty Ford Center

Rancho Mirage, CA
Leg. Issues: ALC, BUD, HCR, INS, TAX

Outside Counsel/Consultants

VSAdc.com
Issues: ALC, BUD, HCR, INS, TAX
Rep By: Carol A. McDaid

Ford Foundation

New York, NY

Outside Counsel/Consultants

Martin & Glantz LLC

Henry Ford Health System

Detroit, MI
Leg. Issues: BUD

Outside Counsel/Consultants

Cassidy & Associates, Inc.
Issues: BUD
Rep By: Henry K. Giugni, Hon. Martin A. Russo, Mary E. Shields

Ford Motor Co.

1350 I St. NW
Suite 1000
Washington, DC 20005
Web: www.ford.com
Tel: (202)962-5400
Fax: (202)336-7224
Registered: LDA

Headquartered in Dearborn, MI.

Leg. Issues: AUT, BNK, BUD, CAW, CPT, CSP, DEF, ENG, ENV, FIN, FUE, HCR, IMM, MMM, ROD, TAX, TEC, TRA, TRD, TRU, UTI

Political Action Committee/s

Ford Motor Company Civic Action Fund
1350 I St. NW
Suite 1000
Washington, DC 20005
Contact: Julie Helm-Khani
Tel: (202)962-5365
Fax: (202)336-7228

In-house, DC-area Employees

DICKSON, Ellen: Manager, Washington Communications
HELM-KHANI, Julie: Legislative Manager, Healthcare and Labor
IOVINO, Peter: Legislative Manager, International Trade and Tax
JOHANNES, Mary P.: Legislative Manager Financial Services
KING, William K.: Regulatory Manager, Safety and Energy
MAGLEBY, Curt N.: Legislative Manager, Clean Air and E-Commerce
MORAN, Mike: Director, Washington Regional Communications
MORGAN, J. Railton: Legislative Manager, Environmental Quality
MULLINS-GRISSOM, Janet: V. President, Washington Affairs
ROUSSEL, Jerry: Regulatory Manager, Environment
SOLOMON, Nicole: Director, Corporate Policy Communications

Outside Counsel/Consultants

Hill and Knowlton, Inc.
Rep By: Neil Dhillon, Jeffrey B. Trammell

Mayer, Brown & Platt
Issues: CAW, ENG
Rep By: David B. Finnegan

Washington Council Ernst & Young
Issues: BUD, ENV, HCR, TAX, TRD
Rep By: Doug Badger, Lauren Darling, John L. Doney, Jayne T. Fitzgerald, LaBrenda Garrett-Nelson, Gary J. Gasper, Bruce A. Gates, Nick Giordano, Robert J. Leonard, Richard Meltzer, Phillip D. Moseley, John D. Porter, Robert M. Rozen, Donna Steele-Flynn, Timothy J. Urban

Ford Motor Credit Co. (Legal Department)

Dearborn, MI
Registered: LDA
Leg. Issues: BNK, FIN, SCI

Outside Counsel/Consultants

Mary P. Johannes
Issues: BNK, FIN, SCI
Rep By: Mary P. Johannes

Henry Ford Museum in Greenfield Village

Dearborn, MI
Leg. Issues: TRA

Outside Counsel/Consultants

Dennis M. Hertel & Associates
Issues: TRA
Rep By: Hon. Dennis M. Hertel

Ford's Theatre

Washington, DC
Leg. Issues: ART

Outside Counsel/Consultants

Chernikoff and Co.
Issues: ART
Rep By: Larry B. Chernikoff

The Foreign Exchange Committee

New York, NY
Leg. Issues: FIN

Outside Counsel/Consultants

Sullivan & Cromwell
Issues: FIN
Rep By: Kenneth M. Raisler

Forensic Technology, Inc.

1 Massachusetts Ave. NW
Suite 310
Washington, DC 20001
Web: www.fti-ibis.com
E-mail: ibis@his.com

Tel: (202)589-0440
Fax: (202)589-0861
Registered: LDA

Headquartered in Montreal, Canada.

Leg. Issues: BUD

In-house, DC-area Employees

LIGHTFOOT, Jim R.

Outside Counsel/Consultants

Sidley & Austin

Forest Cities

Cleveland, OH

Outside Counsel/Consultants

Fleischman and Walsh, L.L.P.
Rep By: Louis H. Dupart, John P. McAllister

Forest City Ratner Companies

Brooklyn, NY

Outside Counsel/Consultants

Baker & Hostetler LLP
Rep By: William F. Conroy, Matthew J. Dolan, Steven A. Lotterer, David L. Marshall, Hon. Guy Vander Jagt

Davidoff & Malito, LLP
Rep By: Stephen J. Slade

Forest Counties Schools Coalition

Red Bluff, CA

Outside Counsel/Consultants

Federal Management Strategies, Inc.
Rep By: Robert P. Canavan

Forest County Potawatomi Community

Milwaukee, WI

Outside Counsel/Consultants

Quinn Gillespie & Associates

Forest Industries Council on Taxation

1111 19th St. NW
Suite 800
Washington, DC 20036
E-mail: kathy_elsen@afandpa.org

Tel: (202)463-2757
Fax: (202)463-2057
Registered: LDA

Represents the views of private forest landowners on federal timber tax issues and advocates policies that encourage and protect private ownership of timberland and the profitable growing, harvesting, and regeneration of trees.

Leg. Issues: TAX

In-house, DC-area Employees

WISEMAN, Laurence: Contact

Forest Products Industry Nat'l Labor-Management Committee

1901 L St. NW
Suite 300
c/o McGlotten & Jarvis
Washington, DC 20036

Tel: (202)452-9517
Fax: (202)466-8016
Registered: LDA

A coalition representing the shared policy interests of labor unions and management in the forest products industry. The Committee works to ensure that legislative, administrative, and judicial actions affecting the domestic timber supply balance environmental concerns with economic realities.

Leg. Issues: ENV, NAT

In-house, DC-area Employees

JARVIS, John T.: Exec. Director

Outside Counsel/Consultants

McGlotten & Jarvis
Issues: ENV, NAT
Rep By: John T. Jarvis

Ogilvy Public Relations Worldwide
Issues: ENV, NAT

Forest Resources Ass'n

600 Jefferson Plaza
Suite 350
Rockville, MD 20852
Web: www.forestresources.org

Tel: (301)838-9385
Fax: (301)838-9481

Formerly the American Pulpwood Ass'n. Represents interests of foresters and loggers working in the pulp and paper industry.

In-house, DC-area Employees

JARVIS, Steve: Director, Forestry Programs
LEWIS, Richard: President
WARD, Neil: Director, Communications

Forest Soc. of Maine

Bangor, ME
Leg. Issues: NAT

Outside Counsel/Consultants

Verner, Liipfert, Bernhard, McPherson and Hand, Chartered
Issues: NAT
Rep By: Jenifer Martin, James A. Pickup, Timothy M. Rutten

Forethought Group/Forethought Life Insurance Co.

Batesville, IN
Leg. Issues: INS, TAX

Outside Counsel/Consultants

Patton Boggs, LLP
Issues: INS, TAX
Rep By: John F. Jonas, Martha M. Kendrick, Elizabeth E. Ring

Former Governors of Puerto Rico

San Juan, PR

Monitors legislative activities of Congress relating to Puerto Rico.

Outside Counsel/Consultants

Mark W. Goodin
Rep By: Mark W. Goodin

Formosan Ass'n for Public Affairs

552 Seventh St. SE
Washington, DC 20003

Tel: (202)547-3686
Fax: (202)543-7891

A grassroots organization.

Leg. Issues: FOR

In-house, DC-area Employees

BLAAUW, Coen: Exec. Director

Outside Counsel/Consultants

APCO Worldwide
Rep By: Hon. Stephen J. Solarz

Parry, Romani, DeConcini & Symms
Issues: FOR
Rep By: Edward H. Baxter, Hon. Dennis DeConcini, John M. Haddow, Scott D. Hatch, Shannon Davis Henderson, Jack W. Martin, Romano Romani, Linda Arey Skladany, Hon. Steven D. Symms

Forschler Ass'n

Alexandria, VA

Outside Counsel/Consultants

Parry, Romani, DeConcini & Symms

Fort Abraham Lincoln Foundation

Mandan, ND

A foundation for the preservation and maintenance of historic Native American and military sites in North Dakota.

Leg. Issues: BUD

Outside Counsel/Consultants

Sara Garland (and Associates)
Issues: BUD
Rep By: Sara G. Garland

Fort Howard Corp.

Green Bay, WI

Registered: LDA

Outside Counsel/Consultants

EOP Group, Inc.
Rep By: Jonathan Gledhill, Michael O'Bannon, Tom Oxendine

Skadden, Arps, Slate, Meagher & Flom LLP
Rep By: Roseann M. Cutrone, Fred T. Goldberg, Jr.

Fort James Corp.

Deerfield, IL
Leg. Issues: ENV, NAT

Registered: LDA

Outside Counsel/Consultants

Arter & Hadden
Issues: ENV

Ledge Counsel

Perkins Coie LLP
Issues: NAT
Rep By: Guy R. Martin

Robertson, Monagle & Eastaugh
Issues: ENV
Rep By: Steven W. Silver

Terpstra Associates
Rep By: Grace Terpstra

Fort Smith Regional Airport

Fort Smith, AR
Leg. Issues: AV, AVI, TRA

Outside Counsel/Consultants

Jay Grant & Associates
Issues: AV, AVI, TRA
Rep By: Jay B. Grant, David M. Olive

Fort Sumter Tours

Charleston, SC
Leg. Issues: TOU

Outside Counsel/Consultants

The Renkes Group, Ltd.
Issues: TOU
Rep By: Gregg D. Renkes

Fort Wayne, Indiana, City of

Fort Wayne, IN
Leg. Issues: BUD, HOU, TRA

Outside Counsel/Consultants

Sagamore Associates, Inc.
Issues: BUD, HOU, TRA
Rep By: Theodore W. Bristol, David U. Gogol

Fort Worth Transportation Authority

Fort Worth, TX
Leg. Issues: TRA

Outside Counsel/Consultants

Bracy Williams & Co.
Issues: TRA
Rep By: Terrence L. Bracy, James P. Brown, Laura L. Madden, Susan J. Williams

Fort Worth, Texas, City of

Leg. Issues: GOV

Outside Counsel/Consultants

Bracy Williams & Co.
Issues: GOV
Rep By: Terrence L. Bracy, James P. Brown, Laura L. Madden, Tracy P. Tucker, Susan J. Williams

Fortessa, Inc.

Leg. Issues: TRD

Outside Counsel/Consultants

Martin G. Hamberger & Associates
Issues: TRD
Rep By: Martin G. Hamberger

Fortis Healthcare

Milwaukee, WI

Outside Counsel/Consultants

Powell Tate

Forum for America's Island Republicans

Outside Counsel/Consultants

Pacific Islands Washington Office
Rep By: Fred Radewagen

Forum for Internat'l Policy

900 17th St. NW
Suite 502
Washington, DC 20006
Web: www.sfip.com
E-mail: theforum@erols.com

Tel: (202)296-9365
Fax: (202)296-9395

In-house, DC-area Employees

KANSTEINER, Walter H.: Senior Associate
KANTER, Arnold: Senior Associate
LAMPLEY, Virginia A.: V. President
MELBY, Eric D.K.: Senior Associate
SCOWCROFT, USAF (Ret.), Lt. Gen. Brent: President

Forum For Investor Advice

7200 Wisconsin Ave.
Suite 709
Bethesda, MD 20814
Web: www.investoradvice.org

Tel: (301)656-7998
Fax: (301)656-5019

In-house, DC-area Employees

LEVIN, Barbara: Exec. Director
SIDDON, Arthur: Director, Communications Services

Forum Health

Youngstown, OH
Leg. Issues: BUD

Outside Counsel/Consultants

Cassidy & Associates, Inc.
Issues: BUD
Rep By: Douglass E. Bobbitt, Daniel J. McNamara, Maureen Walsh

Foster America, Inc.

Chalfont, PA
Leg. Issues: FAM, MMM, WEL

Outside Counsel/Consultants

Dublin Castle Group
Issues: FAM, MMM, WEL
Rep By: Maureen Flatley Hogan

L.B. Foster Co.

Pittsburgh, PA
Leg. Issues: GOV

Outside Counsel/Consultants

Thelen Reid & Priest LLP
Issues: GOV
Rep By: Barry I. Berkoff, Richard J. Leidl, Stephan M. Minikes

Foster Wheeler Corp.

1667 K St. NW
Suite 650
Washington, DC 20006
Tel: (202)296-9703
Fax: (202)296-7461
Registered: LDA
Web: www.fwc.com
E-mail: sherry_peske@fwc.com

Foster Wheeler Corporation is an international organization that provides engineering services and products to a broad range of industries, including petroleum and gas, petrochemical, pharmaceutical, chemical processing, and power generation. Headquartered in Clinton, NJ.

Leg. Issues: BUD, ENG, ENV, GOV, TRD, WAS

Political Action Committee/s

Foster Wheeler Corp. PAC
1667 K St. NW
Suite 650
Washington, DC 20006
Contact: Sherry E. Peske
Tel: (202)296-9703
Fax: (202)296-7461

In-house, DC-area Employees

PESKE, Sherry E.: V. President, Government Affairs

Foster Wheeler Environmental Corp.

Livingston, NJ
Leg. Issues: ENG, ENV

Outside Counsel/Consultants

Preston Gates Ellis & Rouvelas Meeds LLP
Issues: ENG, ENV
Rep By: Cindy O'Malley, Tim L. Peckinpaugh

Foster-Miller, Inc.

Waltham, MA
Leg. Issues: DEF, SMB

Outside Counsel/Consultants

GHL Inc.
Issues: DEF, SMB
Rep By: Thomas R. Goldberg

Foundation Endowment

611 Cameron St.
Alexandria, VA 22314
Tel: (703)683-1077
Fax: (703)683-1272
E-mail: pfe@laser.net

In-house, DC-area Employees

HORN, Joseph: President

Foundation for Democracy in Africa

1900 L St. NW
Suite 414
Washington, DC 20036
Tel: (202)331-1333
Fax: (202)331-8547
E-mail: portmgmt@erols.com

In-house, DC-area Employees

OLADEINDE, Fred: President

The Foundation for Environmental and Economic Progress

1900 K St. NW
Washington, DC 20006-1109
Tel: (202)955-1500
Fax: (202)778-2201
Registered: LDA
Web: www.hunton.com
E-mail: valbrecht@hunton.com

A coalition of major planned community developers, land users and landowners working to reform federal endangered species and wetlands programs. Address, phone and fax listed is that of the firm Hunton & Williams.

Leg. Issues: BUD, CAW, ENV, NAT, RES

In-house, DC-area Employees

ALBRECHT, Virginia S.: Director, Government Affairs and General Counsel

Outside Counsel/Consultants

Hunton & Williams
Issues: BUD, CAW, ENV, NAT, RES
Rep By: Virginia S. Albrecht

Foundation for Hematopoietic Cell Therapy Accreditation

Omaha, NE

Outside Counsel/Consultants

Vinson & Elkins L.L.P.
Rep By: Larry A. Oday

Foundation for Integrated Medicine

Tucson, AZ
Leg. Issues: HCR

Outside Counsel/Consultants

Bracy Williams & Co.
Issues: HCR
Rep By: Terrence L. Bracy, James P. Brown

Foundation for Internat'l Meetings

1110 N. Glebe Rd.
Suite 580
Arlington, VA 22201-4795
Tel: (703)908-0707
Fax: (703)908-0709
Web: www.imminetwork.com

An organization composed of executives whose ass'ns and corporations meet outside the United States on an ongoing basis.

In-house, DC-area Employees

SAMMIS, Jack C.: President

Foundation for Middle East Peace

1761 N St. NW
Washington, DC 20036
Tel: (202)835-3650
Fax: (202)835-3651
Web: www.fmep.org
E-mail: pcwilcox@fmep.org

A privately funded organization seeking to promote a peaceful solution to the Israeli-Palestinian conflict that takes into account the security of both Israelis and Palestinians and is in accord with U.S. national interests.

In-house, DC-area Employees

WILCOX, Jr., Philip C.: President

Foundation for Pavement Rehabilitation and Maintenance Research

Washington, DC
Web: www.pavementpreservation.org

Outside Counsel/Consultants

Smith, Bucklin and Associates, Inc.

Foundation for Public Affairs

2033 K St. NW
Suite 700
Washington, DC 20006
Tel: (202)872-1750
Fax: (202)835-8343
Web: www.pac.org

The research affiliate of the Public Affairs Council. A national information and research center on corporate public affairs programs, practices, and trends as well as public interest groups.

In-house, DC-area Employees

SWIFT-ROSENZWEIG, Leslie: Exec. Director

Foundation for the Advancement of Chiropractic Tenets and Science

1110 N. Glebe Rd.
Suite 1000
Arlington, VA 22201
Tel: (703)528-5000
Fax: (703)528-5023
Web: www.chiropractic.org
E-mail: chiro@erols.com

In-house, DC-area Employees

HENDRICKSON, Ron: Exec. Director

Foundation for Veterans' Health Care

Alexandria, VA

Outside Counsel/Consultants

Booher & Associates
Rep By: C. William Booher, Jr.

Foundation Health Federal Services, Inc.

Rancho Cordova, CA
Leg. Issues: DEF, HCR, INS, MMM, PHA

Outside Counsel/Consultants

Clark & Weinstock, Inc.
Issues: DEF, HCR, INS
Rep By: Hon. Vic H. Fazio, Jr., Sandi Stuart, Hon. John Vincent "Vin" Weber

Kogovsek & Associates
Issues: HCR, INS, MMM, PHA

The PMA Group
Rep By: Kaylene Green, Patrick Hiu, Paul J. Magliocchetti, Brian Thiel

Foundation on Economic Trends

1660 L St. NW
Suite 216
Washington, DC 20036
Tel: (202)466-2823
Fax: (202)429-9602
Web: www.biotechcentury.org

Seeks to encourage the examination of emerging technologies in their full social and economic context, taking both benefits and potential adverse impacts into consideration.

In-house, DC-area Employees

RIFKIN, Jeremy R.: President

Four Dam Pool

Petersburg, AK
Leg. Issues: UTI

Outside Counsel/Consultants

Robertson, Monagle & Eastaugh
Issues: UTI
Rep By: Steven W. Silver

FQPA Implementation Working Group

Washington, DC
Leg. Issues: AGR, CHM, ENV, FOO, SCI

Outside Counsel/Consultants

Jellinek, Schwartz & Connolly
Issues: AGR, CHM, ENV, FOO, SCI
Rep By: Edward C. Gray

Fragomen, Del Rey, Bernsen & Loewy, PC

1212 New York Ave. NW
Eighth Floor
Washington, DC 20005
Tel: (202)223-5515
Registered: LDA
Web: www.fragomen.com
E-mail: gmerson@fragomen.com
Leg. Issues: IMM

In-house, DC-area Employees

MERSON, Gary N.: Government Affairs Counsel

Fragrance Materials Ass'n

Washington, DC

Outside Counsel/Consultants

The Roberts Group
Rep By: John B. Hallagan, Glenn Roberts

Framatome, S.A.

Paris, FRANCE
Leg. Issues: ENG

Outside Counsel/Consultants

Miller & Chevalier, Chartered
Issues: ENG
Rep By: Leonard Bickwit, Jr., Homer E. Moyer, Jr.

France Telecom America do Sul Ltda.

Sao Paulo, BRAZIL
Leg. Issues: TEC

Outside Counsel/Consultants

Arent Fox Kintner Plotkin & Kahn, PLLC
Issues: TEC
Rep By: Bill Applegate, Alan Fishel, David Vidal-Cordero, Todd Weiss

France Telecom North America

1717 K St. NW
Suite 507
Washington, DC 20036
Tel: (202)822-2100
Fax: (202)822-2099
Registered: LDA
Web: www.francetelecomna.com

An international telecommunications carrier headquartered in New York, NY. A subsidiary of France Telecom headquartered in Paris, France.

Leg. Issues: TEC

In-house, DC-area Employees

AGUTO, Danielle: V. President and General Counsel
CELLI, Bernard: Associate, Regulatory and Policy Affairs

Franco-Nevada Mining Corp., Inc.

Reno, NV
Leg. Issues: NAT

Outside Counsel/Consultants

Crowell & Moring LLP
Issues: NAT
Rep By: Edward M. Green, R. Timothy McCrum, Steven P. Quarles

Francotyp-Postalia

Lisle, IL

Outside Counsel/Consultants

Chambers Associates Inc.
Rep By: Letitia Chambers

Franklin Covey

Provo, UT

Outside Counsel/Consultants

Jefferson Consulting Group
Rep By: Cora Beebe, Dorsey Chescavage, Kathy P. Conrad

Franklin Institute

Philadelphia, PA
Leg. Issues: AER, BUD, EDU, HER, SCI

Outside Counsel/Consultants

The Peterson Group
Issues: AER, BUD, EDU, HER, SCI
Rep By: William P. Sears, Craig Snyder

FRANMAC/Taco Pac

Shawnee Mission, KS
Leg. Issues: FOO, HCR, LBR, SMB, TAX

Outside Counsel/Consultants

Butera & Andrews
Issues: FOO, HCR, LBR, SMB, TAX
Rep By: Cliff W. Andrews, Wright H. Andrews, Jr., James J. Butera, Frank Tillotson

Fraternal Order of Police

309 Massachusetts Ave. NE
Washington, DC 20002
Tel: (202)547-8189
Fax: (202)547-8190
Registered: LDA
Leg. Issues: CON, FIR, LAW, LBR, RET, TAX, TEC

In-house, DC-area Employees

GALLEGOS, Gilbert G.: National President
GRANBERG, Chris: Legislative Assistant
PASCO, Jr., James O.: Exec. Director
RICHARDSON, Timothy M.: Legislative Assistant
TEODORSKI, Bernard: Chairman, National Legislative Committee

Fraternal Order of Police (U.S. Park Police Labor Committee)

Washington, DC
Leg. Issues: BUD, LAW

Outside Counsel/Consultants

Janus-Merritt Strategies, L.L.C.
Issues: BUD, LAW
Rep By: Scott P. Hoffman, Mark J. Robertson, J. Daniel Walsh

Frederick Area Committee on Transportation (FACT)

Frederick, MD
Leg. Issues: TRA

Outside Counsel/Consultants

Edmund C. Graber
Issues: TRA
Rep By: Edmund C. Graber

Frederick Douglass Gardens, Inc.

Washington, DC
Leg. Issues: NAT

Outside Counsel/Consultants

Patton Boggs, LLP
Issues: NAT
Rep By: Thomas C. Downs

Free ANWAR Campaign

Leg. Issues: FOR

Outside Counsel/Consultants

Janus-Merritt Strategies, L.L.C.
Issues: FOR
Rep By: Scott P. Hoffman, Omar Nashashibi, Mark J. Robertson

Free Congress Research and Education Foundation

717 Second St. NE
Washington, DC 20002
Tel: (202)546-3000
Fax: (202)543-5605
Web: www.freecongress.org
E-mail: info@freecongress.org

Political Action Committee/s

Free Congress Political Action Committee
717 Second St. NE
Washington, DC 20002
Tel: (202)546-3000
Fax: (202)543-5605
Contact: Paul M. Weyrich

In-house, DC-area Employees

DEAN, Lisa: V. President, Technology Policy
JIPPING, Thomas L.: V. President, Policy
LIND, William S.: Director, Center for Cultural Conservatism
WEYRICH, Paul M.: President

Free Speech Coalition

Washington, DC

Outside Counsel/Consultants

The Segermark Associates, Inc.
Rep By: Howard Segermark

Free Trade Lumber Council

Montreal, CANADA
Leg. Issues: AGR, BUD, CSP, ENV, HOU, LBR, NAT, TRD

Outside Counsel/Consultants

Haake and Associates
Rep By: Timothy M. Haake, Nathan M. Olsen
Public Affairs Resources, Inc.
Rep By: Susan E. Petniunas
Charlene A. Sturbitts
Issues: AGR, BUD, CSP, ENV, HOU, LBR, NAT, TRD
Rep By: Charlene A. Sturbitts

The Freedom Alliance

22570 Market Court
Suite 240
Dulles, VA 20166
Tel: (703)444-7940
Fax: (703)444-9893
Web: www.freedomalliance.org

In-house, DC-area Employees

KILGANNON, Thomas P.: Exec. Director

Freedom Designs

Simi Valley, CA
Leg. Issues: HCR, MMM

Outside Counsel/Consultants

Nusgart Consulting, LLC
Issues: HCR, MMM
Rep By: Marcia Nusgart

The Freedom Forum

Arlington, VA
Leg. Issues: RES

Outside Counsel/Consultants

Kilpatrick Stockton LLP
Issues: RES
Rep By: J. Christopher Brady

Freedom of Information Clearinghouse

P.O. Box 19367
Washington, DC 20036
Tel: (202)588-1000
Fax: (202)588-7795
Web: www.citizen.org
E-mail: FOIA@citizen.org

A project of Ralph Nader's Center for the Study of Responsive Law which assists citizens in making Freedom of Information Act requests from the U.S. Government and, less often, in litigation of cases arising therefrom.

In-house, DC-area Employees

AYERS, Stephanie: Contact

The Freedom Project

111 C St. SE
Lower Unit
Washington, DC 20003
Tel: (202)546-6335
Fax: (202)546-6401
E-mail: geduldig@erols.com

In-house, DC-area Employees

MATHIS, Joshua: Consultant
SINGERLING, Chris: Manager

Freeman United Coal Mining Co.

Springfield, IL

A subsidiary of General Dynamics Corp. (see separate listing).

Leg. Issues: TAX

Outside Counsel/Consultants

Institutional Labor Advisors
Issues: TAX
Rep By: Merritt J. Green, Gregory J. Ossi, David S. Smith, Jan W. Sturner

Freeport, New York, Electric Department of the Village of

Freeport, NY
Leg. Issues: ENG, ENV, GOV, UTI

Outside Counsel/Consultants

Duncan, Weinberg, Genzer & Pembroke, P.C.
Issues: ENG, ENV, GOV, UTI
Rep By: Richmond F. Allan, Jeffrey C. Genzer, Thomas L. Rudebusch

Freeport, New York, Village of

Leg. Issues: ECN, MAR

Outside Counsel/Consultants

Murray, Scheer, Montgomery, Tapia & O'Donnell
Issues: ECN, MAR
Rep By: John R. O'Donnell

Freeport-McMoRan Copper & Gold Inc.

50 F St. NW
Suite 1050
Washington, DC 20001
Tel: (202)737-1400
Fax: (202)737-1568
Registered: LDA
Web: www.fcx.com

Headquartered in New Orleans, LA.

Leg. Issues: AVI, BUD, CAW, CHM, CIV, DEF, ENV, FOR, FUE, LBR, MON, NAT, RES, TAX, TRD, WAS

Political Action Committee/s

Freeport-McMoRan Copper and Gold Citizenship Committee
50 F St. NW
Suite 1050
Washington, DC 20001
Tel: (202)737-1400
Fax: (202)737-1568

McMoRan Exploration Company
50 F St. NW
Suite 1050
Washington, DC 20001
Tel: (202)737-1400
Fax: (202)737-1568

In-house, DC-area Employees

GUIDRY, Jerene B.: Legislative Assistant
KING, W. Russell: Senior V. President, International Relations and Federal Affairs

Freight-Savers Shipping Co. Ltd.

Rutherford, NJ

Outside Counsel/Consultants

Galland, Kharasch, Greenberg, Fellman & Swirsky, P.C.

Freightliner Corp.

Portland, OR
Leg. Issues: BUD

Outside Counsel/Consultants

Higgins, McGovern & Smith, LLC
Issues: BUD
Rep By: Joseph L. Rosso

Fremont Group, Inc.

San Francisco, CA
Leg. Issues: TAX

Outside Counsel/Consultants

Akin, Gump, Strauss, Hauer & Feld, L.L.P.
Issues: TAX
Rep By: Kenneth Alderfer, Sean G. D'Arcy

Frequency Engineering Laboratories

Farmingdale, NJ
Leg. Issues: DEF

Outside Counsel/Consultants

Bob Davis & Associates
Issues: DEF
Rep By: Hon. Robert W. Davis

Fresenius Medical Care North America

1875 I St. NW
Twelfth Floor
Washington, DC 20006
Tel: (202)296-8632
Fax: (202)296-8634
Registered: LDA
Leg. Issues: HCR, INS, MED, MMM, PHA

In-house, DC-area Employees

SMITH, Kathleen T.: V. President, Government Affairs

Outside Counsel/Consultants

Greenberg Traurig, LLP
Issues: MMM
Rep By: Howard J. Cohen, Rob Garagiola, Russell J. Mueller, Nancy E. Taylor, Timothy P. Trysla

Hill and Knowlton, Inc.
Issues: HCR
Rep By: Bruce Hildebrand

Powers Pyles Sutter & Verville, PC
Issues: HCR, INS, MED, MMM
Rep By: Peter W. Thomas

Fresh Garlic Producer Ass'n

Washington, DC

Outside Counsel/Consultants

Collier Shannon Scott, PLLC
Rep By: Michael J. Coursey, Kathleen Clark Kies

Fresh Produce Ass'n of the Americas

Nogales, AZ
Leg. Issues: AGR, FOO, TRD

Outside Counsel/Consultants

Masaoka & Associates, Inc.
Issues: AGR, FOO, TRD
Rep By: Jennifer L. Smith, T. Albert Yamada

Fresno Community Hospital and Medical Center

Fresno, CA
Leg. Issues: BUD, HCR

Outside Counsel/Consultants

Arent Fox Kintner Plotkin & Kahn, PLLC
Issues: BUD, HCR
Rep By: Douglas McCormack, William A. Sarraille

Fresno Metropolitan Museum

Leg. Issues: BUD

Outside Counsel/Consultants

Arent Fox Kintner Plotkin & Kahn, PLLC
Issues: BUD
Rep By: Douglas McCormack

Fresno Pacific University

Fresno, CA

Outside Counsel/Consultants

Russ Reid Co.

Fresno, California, City of

Leg. Issues: TRA, URB

Outside Counsel/Consultants

Simon and Co., Inc.
Issues: TRA, URB
Rep By: Heather Barber, Alex DeGood, Leonard S. Simon

Friction Free Technologies Inc.

New York, NY
Leg. Issues: DEF

Outside Counsel/Consultants

American Defense Internat'l, Inc.
Issues: DEF
Rep By: Michael Herson, Van D. Hipp, Jr., Bonnie Shindelman, Dave Wilberding

Friede Goldman Halter

Gulfport, MS
Leg. Issues: TAX

Outside Counsel/Consultants

Dyer Ellis & Joseph, P.C.
Issues: TAX
Rep By: James S. W. Drewry, John Graykauski, Duncan C. Smith, III, Jennifer M. Southwick

Friede, Goldman, & Halter, Inc.

Gulfport, MS
Leg. Issues: DEF, MAR

Outside Counsel/Consultants

Forster & Associates
Issues: DEF, MAR
Rep By: Johann R. Forster

Robertson, Monagle & Eastaugh
Issues: DEF, MAR
Rep By: Bradley D. Gilman, Rick E. Marks

Friedlob, Sanderson, Raskin, Paulson, Toutillott

Leg. Issues: TRA

Outside Counsel/Consultants

Capital Partnerships (VA) Inc.
Issues: TRA
Rep By: Robin Angle, Kenneth W. Butler, Clay Gravely

Friedman Billings Ramsey

Reston, VA

Outside Counsel/Consultants

Earle Palmer Brown Public Relations

Friedrich Ebert Foundation

1155 15th St. NW
Suite 1100
Washington, DC 20005
Web: www.fesdc.org
E-mail: fesdc@fesdc.org
Tel: (202)331-1819
Fax: (202)331-1837

The Washington office of the Ebert Foundation, which is headquartered in Bonn, Germany, is a non-profit private educational institution, committed to the concepts and basic values of social democracy and the labor movement. Political and civic education, international understanding, scholarly research, and the granting of scholarships are among the Foundation's activities.

In-house, DC-area Employees

DETTKE, Dr. Dieter: Exec. Director, Washington Office

Friedrich's Ataxia Research Alliance

Washington, DC
Leg. Issues: MED

Outside Counsel/Consultants

Mehl, Griffin & Bartek Ltd.
Issues: MED
Rep By: Ronald J. Bartek

Friends Committee on Nat'l Legislation

245 Second St. NE
Washington, DC 20002
Web: www.fcnl.org
E-mail: fcnl@fcnl.org
Tel: (202)547-6000
Fax: (202)547-6019
Registered: LDA

Quaker peace lobby, founded 1943, carrying to Congress the Friends' concerns for peace and justice at home and abroad.

Leg. Issues: BUD, CIV, DEF, ECN, FOR, GOV, HCR, IMM, IND, LAW, MMM, REL

In-house, DC-area Employees

GUTHRIE, Kathy: Field Program Coordinator
KIMBALL, Florence: Legislative Education Secretary
STOWE, Edward W.: Legislative Secretary
VOLK, E. Joe: Exec. Secretary

Friends of Cancer Research

Washington, DC
Leg. Issues: MED

Outside Counsel/Consultants

Podesta/Mattoon
Issues: MED
Rep By: Anthony T. Podesta, Missi Tessier

Friends of CDC

Atlanta, GA
Leg. Issues: BUD

Outside Counsel/Consultants

Capitol Associates, Inc.
Issues: BUD
Rep By: Pamela Patrice Jackson, Edward R. Long, Ph.D., Matthew Williams

The Friends of Democratic Congo

Gaithersburg, MD
Leg. Issues: FOR

Outside Counsel/Consultants

Denison, Scott and Cohen
Issues: FOR
Rep By: Herman J. Cohen, George H. Denison, Ray Scott

Friends of Free China

P.O. Box 4134
Merrifield, VA 22116
Web: www.fofc.org
E-mail: information@fofc.org
Tel: (703)573-8677

Advocates U.S. support of the Republic of China.

In-house, DC-area Employees

SEWELL, Richard A.: Exec. Director

Friends of Higher Education Inc.

P.O. Box 65125
Washington, DC 20035
Tel: (202)466-8621

A political action committee supporting candidates who support higher education and the Federal Family Education Loan Program.

Leg. Issues: EDU, FIN

In-house, DC-area Employees

WADSWORTH, Harrison Morton: Treasurer

Friends of ITS/ITS America

Washington, DC
Leg. Issues: BUD, TRA

Outside Counsel/Consultants

Government Relations, Inc.
Issues: BUD, TRA
Rep By: Thomas J. Bulger, Mark H. Miller, John N. Young

Friends of the Earth

1025 Vermont Ave. NW
Third Floor
Washington, DC 20005
Web: www.foe.org
E-mail: foe@foe.org
Tel: (202)783-7400
Fax: (202)783-0444
Registered: LDA

A public interest group committed to the preservation, restoration and rational use of the ecosphere. Established in 1969 with headquarters in Washington. Merged with the Environmental Policy Institute.

Leg. Issues: BAN, BUD, CAW, CHM, DOC, ENV, NAT, ROD, TAX, TRD

Political Action Committee/s

Friends of the Earth Political Action Committee
1025 Vermont Ave. NW
Third Floor
Washington, DC 20005
Contact: Brent Blackwelder
Tel: (202)783-7400
Fax: (202)783-0444

In-house, DC-area Employees

BLACKWELDER, Brent: President
BOHLEN, Larry: Director, Community Health and Environmental Programs
HIRSCH, David: Transportation Policy Coordinator
KRIPKE, Gawain: Director, Appropriations Project
PEREZ, Esten F.
PICA, Erich: Policy Associate
WEISS, Chris: Director, DC Environmental Network
WELCH, Carol: Deputy Director, International Projects/MDB Trade

Friends of the Everglades

Miami, FL

Outside Counsel/Consultants

Dunlap & Browder, Inc.

Friends of the Nat'l Institute of Dental and Craniofacial Research

1555 Connecticut Ave.
Suite 200
Washington, DC 20036
E-mail: josie@fnider.org
Tel: (202)483-1057
Fax: (202)462-9043

In-house, DC-area Employees

HOFFMAN, Beverly R.: Exec. Director
JORDAN, Josie: Deputy Exec. Director

Friends of the Nat'l Library of Medicine

1555 Connecticut Ave. NW
Suite 200
Washington, DC 20036-1126
Web: www.fnlm.org
E-mail: info@fnlm.org
Tel: (202)462-0992
Fax: (202)462-9043

A broad based coalition of individuals, institutions, and corporations that support the Nat'l Library of Medicine.

Leg. Issues: CPI, HCR, MED, TEC

In-house, DC-area Employees

HOFFMAN, Beverly R.: Exec. Director

Outside Counsel/Consultants

Non-Profit Management Associates, Inc.
Issues: CPI, HCR, MED, TEC
Rep By: Keith Krueger

Fringe Benefit Group, Inc

Austin, TX

Outside Counsel/Consultants

CGR Associates, Inc.
Rep By: Kevin Frankovich

Front Royal, Virginia, Town of

Leg. Issues: GOV

Outside Counsel/Consultants

Duncan, Weinberg, Genzer & Pembroke, P.C.
Issues: GOV
Rep By: Janice L. Lower

Frontier Airlines

Denver, CO

Outside Counsel/Consultants

Ungaretti & Harris
Rep By: Edward P. Faberman, Page Faulk, Michelle M. Faust

Frontier Communications Corp.

Rochester, NY Registered: LDA

A telecommunications company.

Leg. Issues: SMB, TEC

Outside Counsel/Consultants

Swidler Berlin Shereff Friedman, LLP
Issues: TEC
Rep By: Kristine DeBry, Gary D. Slaiman

Ungaretti & Harris
Issues: SMB

The Frontier Press

New York, NY

Outside Counsel/Consultants

Neuman and Co.
Rep By: Robert A. Neuman

Frontiers of Freedom Institute

1401 Wilson Blvd.
Suite 1007
Arlington, VA 22209
Web: www.ff.org
E-mail: freedom@ff.org
Tel: (703)527-8282
Fax: (703)527-8388

A 501(c)(3) non-profit research and education organization promoting individual and economic freedom. Favors protection of property rights and such issues as the flat tax, privatization of Social Security, energy deregulation, no taxing of the Internet, telecommunications competition, and global warming.

In-house, DC-area Employees

LANDRITH, III, George C.: Exec. Director
WALLOP, Hon. Malcolm: Chairman

Frozen Potato Products Institute

2000 Corporate Ridge
Suite 1000
McLean, VA 22102
Tel: (703)821-0770
Fax: (703)821-1350

Represents U.S. frozen potato processors.

In-house, DC-area Employees

GILL, Michael

Fruit of the Loom, Inc.

Chicago, IL Registered: LDA

Outside Counsel/Consultants

Skadden, Arps, Slate, Meagher & Flom LLP
Rep By: Robert E. Lighthizer

Fruit Shippers Ltd.

Nassau, BAHAMAS
Leg. Issues: MAR

Outside Counsel/Consultants

Dyer Ellis & Joseph, P.C.
Issues: MAR
Rep By: James S. W. Drewry, Thomas M. Dyer, Brett M. Esber, Jeanne Marie Grasso, Duncan C. Smith, III, Jennifer M. Southwick

Fuel Cell Energy, Inc.

1800 M St. NW
Suite 300
Washington, DC 20036
Web: www.fuelcellenergy.com
Tel: (202)296-8790
Fax: (202)296-8681

Headquartered in Danbury, CT.

Leg. Issues: BUD, CAW, ENG, ENV

Political Action Committee/s

Fuel Cell Energy, Inc. PAC
1800 M St. NW
Suite 300
Washington, DC 20036
Contact: Eric L. Simpkins
Tel: (202)296-8790
Fax: (202)296-8681

In-house, DC-area Employees

SIMPKINS, Eric L.: V. President, Business Development

Fuel Cell Power Ass'n

Washington, DC
Leg. Issues: ENG

Outside Counsel/Consultants

Technology Advocates, Inc.
Issues: ENG
Rep By: Jeffrey S. Abboud

Fuel Cells for Transportation

Washington, DC
Leg. Issues: BUD, ENG

Outside Counsel/Consultants

Rose Communications
Issues: BUD, ENG
Rep By: Robert R. Rose

FuelMaker Corp.

Toronto, CANADA
Leg. Issues: AUT, ENV, TRA

Outside Counsel/Consultants

Dorfman & O'Neal, Inc.
Issues: AUT, ENV, TRA
Rep By: Ira H. Dorfman, Marc McConahy, Maria F. Neve

Fuels Management Inc.

Miami, FL
Leg. Issues: ENG

Outside Counsel/Consultants

The Advocacy Group
Issues: ENG
Rep By: John M. Nugent, Jr.

Fuji Heavy Industries Ltd.

Tokyo, JAPAN

Outside Counsel/Consultants

Willkie Farr & Gallagher
Rep By: William H. Barringer, Kenneth J. Pierce

Fuji Photo Film U.S.A., Inc.

Elmsford, NY Registered: LDA
Leg. Issues: TRD

Outside Counsel/Consultants

Downey McGrath Group, Inc.
Issues: TRD
Rep By: Hon. Thomas J. Downey, Jr., Margaret M. McCloud, John Peter Olinger

Edelman Public Relations Worldwide
Rep By: Christine Kelly Cimko, Michael K. Deaver

Willkie Farr & Gallagher
Issues: TRD
Rep By: William H. Barringer, Daniel L. Porter, Russell L. Smith

Fuji TV Network

Outside Counsel/Consultants

BKSH & Associates

Fujisawa Health Care Inc.

Deerfield, IL Registered: LDA
Leg. Issues: MMM

Outside Counsel/Consultants

Hogan & Hartson L.L.P.
Issues: MMM
Rep By: Hon. Robert H. Michel, Ann Morgan Vickery

Fujisawa USA, Inc.

Rosemont, IL

Outside Counsel/Consultants

Katten Muchin & Zavis

Fujitsu Limited

1776 I St. NW
Suite 880
Washington, DC 20006
Web: www.fujitsu.com
Tel: (202)331-8750
Fax: (202)331-8797
Registered: FARA

Leg. Issues: CPT

In-house, DC-area Employees

KATOH, Masanobu: General Manager
KONO, Makato: Liaison Representative
OLIVE, David A.: Deputy General Manager
WALLS-RIVAS, Kristen: Policy and Legal Analyst

Outside Counsel/Consultants

Akin, Gump, Strauss, Hauer & Feld, L.L.P.
Rep By: Warren E. Connelly

Morrison & Foerster LLP
Issues: CPT
Rep By: Jonathan Band

Fulcrum Venture Capital Corp.

Culver City, CA
Leg. Issues: SMB

Outside Counsel/Consultants

Thelen Reid & Priest LLP
Issues: SMB
Rep By: William A. Kirk, Jr.

Full House Resorts, Inc.

Indian Wells, CA

Outside Counsel/Consultants

Oppenheimer Wolff & Donnelly LLP

H. B. Fuller Co.

Arden Hills, MN
Leg. Issues: TAX

Outside Counsel/Consultants

McDermott, Will and Emery
Issues: TAX
Rep By: Robert B. Harding

Fuller Theological Seminary

Pasadena, CA
Leg. Issues: EDU

Outside Counsel/Consultants

Russ Reid Co.
Issues: EDU
Rep By: Thomas C. Keller, Mark D. McIntyre

Fund for American Opportunity PAC

Outside Counsel/Consultants

MV3 & Associates

Valente Lopatin & Schulze
Rep By: Claudia Barker Valente, Mark Valente, III

Fund for American Studies

1706 New Hampshire Ave. NW
Washington, DC 20009
Web: www.tfas.org
E-mail: rream@tfas.org
Tel: (202)986-0384
Fax: (202)986-0390

Sponsors the Bryce Harlow Institute and other educational programs in partnership with Georgetown University to educate college students about the political, economic, and moral principles upon which the United States was founded.

In-house, DC-area Employees

KEYES, IV, William A.: Exec. Director, Institute on Political Journalism
KHACHIGIAN, Kristy: Director, Engalitcheff Institute and Bryce Harlow Institute
REAM, Roger R.: President

Outside Counsel/Consultants

Vorys, Sater, Seymour and Pease, LLP

The Fund for Animals

8121 Georgia Ave.
Suite 301
Silver Spring, MD 20910-4933
Web: www.fund.org
E-mail: fundinfo@fund.org
Tel: (301)585-2591
Fax: (301)585-2595
Registered: LDA

A non-profit animal protection organization headquartered in New York, NY.

Leg. Issues: ANI, NAT

In-house, DC-area Employees

MARKARIAN, Michael: Exec. V. President
PRESCOTT, Heidi: National Director
WOLF, Christine M.: Director, Government and International Affairs

Outside Counsel/Consultants

Meyer & Glitzenstein

Fund for Assuring an Independent Retirement

100 Indiana Ave. NW
Washington, DC 20001
Tel: (202)393-4695
Fax: (202)756-7400

An ad-hoc coalition organized by 28 active and retired federal and postal employee organizations.

In-house, DC-area Employees

SOMBROTTO, Vincent R.: Chairman

Fund for Constitutional Government

122 Maryland Ave. NE
Suite 300
Washington, DC 20002
E-mail: funcongov@aol.com
Tel: (202)546-3799
Fax: (202)543-3156

Dedicated to the exposure and correction of corruption in the federal government, a task undertaken through research, public education and, when necessary, litigation. Looks for instances of corruption that have a large public impact, that have precedent-setting value, and that, if rectified, will preserve an open and accountable government.

In-house, DC-area Employees
MARTIN, Conrad: Exec. Director
MISSOURI, Montre Aza: Secretary
ZILL, Anne B.: President

The Fund for Peace

1701 K St. NW
Suite 1100
Washington, DC 20006
Web: www.fundforpeace.org
Tel: (202)223-7940
Fax: (202)223-7947

Works to promote public education and research on global problems that threaten human survival and to search for practical solutions to those problems.

In-house, DC-area Employees
BADER, Anne C.: V. President, Development and Communications
BAKER, Pauline H.: President

Fundacion para la Preservacion de Flora y Fauna Marina

Mexico City, MEXICO
Leg. Issues: ENV, NAT

Outside Counsel/Consultants
Janus-Merritt Strategies, L.L.C.
Issues: ENV, NAT
Rep By: Mark J. Robertson, J. Daniel Walsh

Future Business Leaders of America - Phi Beta Lambda

1912 Association Dr.
Reston, VA 20191-1591
Web: www.fbla-pbl.org
E-mail: general@fbla.org
Tel: (703)860-3334
Fax: (703)758-0749

In-house, DC-area Employees
BUCKLEY, Jean: President and Chief Exec. Officer

Future Fund

818 Connecticut Ave. NW
Suite 1100
Washington, DC 20006
Tel: (202)728-1010
Fax: (202)728-4044
A political action committee.

In-house, DC-area Employees
OLDAKER, William C.: PAC Administrator

Future Leaders of America

Oxnard, CA
Leg. Issues: EDU

Outside Counsel/Consultants
Alcalde & Fay
Issues: EDU
Rep By: Lois Moore

Future of Puerto Rico Inc.

Hato Rey, PR
Leg. Issues: GOV

Outside Counsel/Consultants
Kessler & Associates Business Services, Inc.
Preston Gates Ellis & Rouvelas Meeds LLP
Issues: GOV
Rep By: Werner W. Brandt, Hon. David Funderburk, Hon. Lloyd Meeds, Sol Mosher, Tim L. Peckinpaugh, Daniel Ritter, W. Dennis Stephens, Steven R. "Rick" Valentine
Young & Jatlow
Rep By: Francis L. Young

Future View, Inc.

Washington, DC

Outside Counsel/Consultants
Murray, Scheer, Montgomery, Tapia & O'Donnell

Futures for Children

Albuquerque, NM
A developer of education programs for Native American youths.

Outside Counsel/Consultants
Russ Reid Co.

Futures Industry Ass'n

2001 Pennsylvania Ave. NW
Suite 600
Washington, DC 20006-1807
Web: www.fiafii.org
E-mail: info@fiafii.org
Tel: (202)466-5460
Fax: (202)296-3184
Registered: LDA
Leg. Issues: FIN

Political Action Committee/s
Futures Industry Political Action Committee
2001 Pennsylvania Ave. NW
Suite 600
Washington, DC 20006-1807
Contact: John M. Damgard
Tel: (202)466-5460
Fax: (202)296-3184

In-house, DC-area Employees
DAMGARD, John M.: President
WIERZYNSKI, Barbara: Exec. V. President and General Counsel

Futurewave General Partners, L.P.

Big Canoe, GA
Leg. Issues: TEC

Outside Counsel/Consultants
Lent Scrivner & Roth LLC
Issues: TEC
Rep By: Norman F. Lent, III, Hon. Norman F. Lent, Michael S. Scrivner
O'Connor & Hannan, L.L.P.
Issues: TEC
Rep By: Hon. Larry Pressler, Thomas H. Quinn

Gabon, Nat'l Assembly of

Libreville, GABON

Outside Counsel/Consultants
Cassidy & Associates, Inc.
Rep By: Gregory M. Gill

Gabonese Republic, Government of the

Libreville, GABON

Outside Counsel/Consultants
Barron-Birrell, Inc.
Powell Tate
Rep By: Kathryn Waters Gest
Scribe Consulting & Communications
Rep By: Joseph J. Szlavik

Gabonese Republic, Office of the President of the

Libreville, GABON

Outside Counsel/Consultants
Cassidy & Associates, Inc.
Rep By: Gregory M. Gill, Carl Franklin Godfrey, Jr.
Powell Tate
Washington World Group, Ltd.
Rep By: Edward J. von Kloberg, III

Gadsden State Community College

Gadsden, AL
Leg. Issues: EDU

Outside Counsel/Consultants
Smith, Hinaman & Associates
Issues: EDU
Rep By: Don Smith

GAF Corp.

Wayne, NJ
Registered: LDA
Leg. Issues: CHM, CON, CSP, MAN, VET

Outside Counsel/Consultants
Brown & Associates
Issues: VET
Rep By: Edward P. Scott
Levine & Co.
Issues: CHM
Rep By: Ken Levine
The MWW Group
Issues: CSP, MAN
Rep By: Todd S. Berkoff, Elizabeth A. Iadarola, Michael W. Kempner, Christine A. Pellerin, Jonathan B. Slade, Robert G. Sommer, Jeffery M. Walter
Sutherland Asbill & Brennan LLP
Symms, Lehn & Associates, Inc.
Weil, Gotshal & Manges, LLP
Issues: CON
Rep By: Annemargaret Connolly, Robert C. Odle, Jr., Larry I. Willis

Gainesville Regional Utilities

Gainesville, FL
Leg. Issues: UTI

Outside Counsel/Consultants
Jorden Burt LLP
Issues: UTI
Rep By: Patricia Branch, Alanna Dillon, Marna Gettleman, Marilyn Berry Thompson, Rebecca Tidman

Gainesville, Florida, City of

Leg. Issues: ALC, ART, AVI, BUD, CAW, ECN, EDU, ENV, GAM, HCR, HOU, IMM, LAW, LBR, MMM, NAT, POS, ROD, TAX, TEC, TRA, URB, WAS, WEL

Outside Counsel/Consultants
Jorden Burt LLP
Issues: ALC, ART, AVI, BUD, CAW, ECN, EDU, ENV, GAM, HCR, HOU, IMM, LAW, LBR, MMM, NAT, POS, ROD, TAX, TEC, TRA, URB, WAS, WEL
Rep By: Patricia Branch, Marna Gettleman, Marilyn Berry Thompson, Rebecca Tidman, Marion Turner

Galaxy Aerospace Co., LP

2121 Crystal Dr.
Suite 706
Arlington, VA 22202
Tel: (703)746-0670
Fax: (703)746-0671
Registered: LDA
Headquartered in Fort Worth, TX.
Leg. Issues: AVI, DEF

In-house, DC-area Employees
HARRIS, Barry Lambert
KOLAR, Alexander Peter

Outside Counsel/Consultants
Mehl, Griffin & Bartek Ltd.
Issues: DEF
Rep By: Molly Griffin, William A. Marsh

Galaxy Global Corp.

Fairmont, WV

Outside Counsel/Consultants
Cottone and Huggins Group
Rep By: James B. Huggins

Galena, Illinois, City of

Galena, IL
Leg. Issues: BUD, CAW

Outside Counsel/Consultants
Timothy X. Moore and Co.
Issues: BUD, CAW
Rep By: Timothy X. Moore

Gallard-Schlesinger Chemical Manufacturing Corp.

Carle Place, NY

Outside Counsel/Consultants
Max N. Berry Law Offices
Rep By: Max N. Berry

Gallery Watch

Washington, DC
Leg. Issues: ADV, MIA

Outside Counsel/Consultants
Sally L. Albright
Issues: ADV, MIA
Rep By: Sally L. Albright

Ernest & Julio Gallo Winery

Modesto, CA
Leg. Issues: CSP, FOO, TAX, TRA, TRD

Outside Counsel/Consultants
Miller & Chevalier, Chartered
Issues: CSP, FOO, TAX, TRA, TRD
Rep By: Leonard Bickwit, Jr., Lawrence B. Gibbs
Wilmer, Cutler & Pickering

Galveston County, Texas

Leg. Issues: BUD, ENV

Outside Counsel/Consultants
Marlowe and Co.
Issues: BUD, ENV
Rep By: Howard Marlowe, Jeffrey Mazzella

Gambia Telecommunications

Banjul, THE GAMBIA

Outside Counsel/Consultants
Washington World Group, Ltd.
Rep By: Edward J. von Kloberg, III

Gambia, Government of the Republic of The

Banjul, THE GAMBIA

Outside Counsel/Consultants

Washington World Group, Ltd.
Rep By: Edward J. von Kloberg, III

Gambro Healthcare

Lakewood, CO
Leg. Issues: HCR, MMM

Outside Counsel/Consultants

Jeffrey J. Kimbell & Associates
Issues: HCR, MMM

Ganaden Biotech Inc.

Alexandria, VA
Leg. Issues: DEF

Outside Counsel/Consultants

American Defense Internat'l, Inc.
Issues: DEF
Rep By: Michael Herson, Van D. Hipp, Jr., Dave Wilberding

Gannett Co., Inc.

1100 Wilson Blvd.
Arlington, VA 22234
Web: www.gannett.com
Tel: (703)284-6046
Registered: LDA

Gannett Co., Inc. is an international news and information company that publishes daily newspapers in the USA and operates a number of television stations.

Leg. Issues: COM, LBR, TAX

In-house, DC-area Employees

FELLER, Mimi A.: Senior V. President, Public Affairs and Gov't Relations

Outside Counsel/Consultants

Wiley, Rein & Fielding
Issues: COM
Rep By: Susan C. Buck, Mimi W. Dawson, Pete O'Connell, Richard E. Wiley

Garden Centers of America

1250 I St. NW
Suite 500
Washington, DC 20005
Web: www.anla.org
Tel: (202)789-2900
Fax: (202)789-1893
Registered: LDA
Leg. Issues: AGR, IMM, LBR, TRU

In-house, DC-area Employees

DOLIBOIS, Robert: Exec. V. President
SCHECHTEL, Sharon: Administrator

Outside Counsel/Consultants

McGuiness Norris & Williams, LLP
Issues: LBR
Rep By: Monte B. Lake

Garden State Paper Co., Inc.

Elmwood Park, NJ
Leg. Issues: ADV, CAW, ENG, ENV, FUE, GOV, MAN, TAX, WAS

Outside Counsel/Consultants

Colling Swift & Hynes
Issues: ADV, CAW, ENG, ENV, FUE, GOV, MAN, TAX, WAS
Rep By: Terese Colling, Pablo Collins, Robert J. Hynes, Jr., Hon. Allan B. Swift

Garden State Seafood Ass'n

Trenton, NJ
Leg. Issues: MAR

Outside Counsel/Consultants

Robertson, Monagle & Eastaugh
Issues: MAR
Rep By: Rick E. Marks

Garden State Tanning, Inc.

King of Prussia, PA

Outside Counsel/Consultants

Collier Shannon Scott, PLLC
Rep By: John L. Wittenborn

Gardena Alfalfa Growers Ass'n

Touchet, WA
Leg. Issues: AGR, BNK

Outside Counsel/Consultants

James Nicholas Ashmore & Associates
Issues: AGR, BNK
Rep By: James Nicholas Ashmore

Gardena, California, City of

Gardena, CA
Leg. Issues: BUD

Outside Counsel/Consultants

R. Duffy Wall and Associates
Issues: BUD
Rep By: Rodney Emery

Gardere & Wayne, LLP

Dallas, TX
Leg. Issues: FUE, NAT

Outside Counsel/Consultants

Barents Group LLC
Issues: FUE, NAT
Rep By: Linden C. Smith

Garrison Diversion Conservancy District

Carrington, ND
Leg. Issues: BUD, GOV, NAT

Outside Counsel/Consultants

John J. Rhodes
Issues: GOV, NAT
Rep By: Hon. John J. Rhodes, III

Will and Carlson, Inc.
Issues: BUD, NAT
Rep By: Peter Carlson, Robert P. Will

Gary Public Transportation Corp.

Gary, IN
Leg. Issues: BUD, TRA, WEL

Outside Counsel/Consultants

The Barton Co.
Issues: BUD, TRA, WEL
Rep By: Stacy Palmer-Barton

Gary Sanitary District

Gary, IN
Leg. Issues: BUD, CAW, ENV, WAS

Outside Counsel/Consultants

The Barton Co.
Issues: BUD, CAW, ENV, WAS
Rep By: Stacy Palmer-Barton

Gary, Indiana, Housing Authority of the City of

Gary, IN
Leg. Issues: BUD, HOU, URB, WEL

Outside Counsel/Consultants

The Barton Co.
Issues: BUD, HOU, URB, WEL
Rep By: Stacy Palmer-Barton

Gary, Indiana, Washington Office of the City of

1620 I St. NW
Suite 600
Washington, DC 20006
Tel: (202)861-6778
Fax: (202)429-0422
Leg. Issues: ALC, AVI, BAN, BUD, CAW, DIS, ECN, EDU, ENV, FIN, FIR, GAM, HOU, LAW, ROD, RRR, TRA, URB, WAS, WEL

In-house, DC-area Employees

PALMER-BARTON, Stacy: Associate Director

Outside Counsel/Consultants

The Barton Co.
Issues: ALC, AVI, BAN, BUD, CAW, DIS, ECN, EDU, ENV, FIN, FIR, GAM, HOU, LAW, ROD, RRR, TRA, URB, WAS, WEL
Rep By: Stacy Palmer-Barton

Gary-Williams Energy Corp.

Denver, CO
Leg. Issues: ENG, ENV

Outside Counsel/Consultants

Bracewell & Patterson, L.L.P.
Issues: ENV
Rep By: Hon. Edwin R. Bethune, Hon. Jim Chapman, Gene E. Godley, Marc C. Hebert, Charles L. Ingebretson, Michael L. Pate, Scott H. Segal, D. Michael Stroud, Jr.

Hooper Owen & Winburn
Issues: ENG
Rep By: Lindsay D. Hooper

Gas Appliance Manufacturers Ass'n

2107 Wilson Blvd.
Suite 600
Arlington, VA 22201
Web: www.gamanet.org
E-mail: information@gamanet.org
Tel: (703)525-7060
Fax: (703)525-6790
Registered: LDA
Leg. Issues: MAN

In-house, DC-area Employees

AUTERY, C. Reuben: President
MATTINGLY, Joseph M.: V. President

Gas Processors Ass'n

Tulsa, OK
Leg. Issues: ENG, FUE

Outside Counsel/Consultants

Bracewell & Patterson, L.L.P.
Issues: ENG, FUE
Rep By: Gene E. Godley, Michael L. Pate, Scott H. Segal

Gas Research Institute

1600 Wilson Blvd.
Suite 900
Arlington, VA 22209
Web: www.gri.org
Tel: (703)526-7800
Fax: (703)526-7805
Registered: LDA

A not-for-profit membership organization of natural gas distribution, pipeline, and production companies. GRI plans, manages, and develops financing for a cooperative R&D program in gaseous fuels and their use. Headquartered in Chicago, IL.

Leg. Issues: BUD, ENG, FUE, NAT, TAX, TRA, UTI

In-house, DC-area Employees

KENDARDINE, Melanie: V. President, Government Relations

Outside Counsel/Consultants

EOP Group, Inc.
Issues: BUD, ENG, NAT
Rep By: Chad Campbell, Joseph Hezir, Richard Irby

Charles D. Estes & Associates
Issues: BUD
Rep By: Charles D. Estes

Gallagher, Boland and Meiburger
Issues: ENG, FUE, NAT, TRA, UTI
Rep By: James M. Broadstone

Gas Technology Institute

1116 E St. SE
Washington, DC 20003
Web: www.igt.org
Tel: (202)547-7288
Fax: (202)547-1454
Registered: LDA

A non-profit research and development organization concerned with all forms of energy production and utilization other than nuclear. Founded in 1941; headquartered in Des Plaines, IL.

Leg. Issues: ENG, ENV

In-house, DC-area Employees

WILLER, Jay D.: Director, Washington Operations

Outside Counsel/Consultants

Whitten & Diamond
Issues: ENG, ENV
Rep By: Robert M. Diamond, Regina M. Mellon, Jamie L. Whitten

Gas Turbine Ass'n, Inc.

Washington, DC
Web: www.gasturbines.org
E-mail: info@gasturbines.org
Leg. Issues: ENG

Outside Counsel/Consultants

Technology Advocates, Inc.
Issues: ENG
Rep By: Jeffrey S. Abboud

Gasification Technologies Council

Arlington, VA
Web: www.gasification.org
E-mail: jmchil@aol.com

Outside Counsel/Consultants

Koleda Childress & Co.
Rep By: James M. Childress

GATCO of VA, Inc.

Leg. Issues: TRD

Outside Counsel/Consultants

Martin G. Hamberger & Associates
Issues: TRD
Rep By: Martin G. Hamberger

The Gates Rubber Co.

Denver, CO

Outside Counsel/Consultants

Stewart and Stewart
Rep By: David S. Johanson, Carl Moyer, Terence P. Stewart

Gateway Cities

Paramount, CA
Leg. Issues: BUD, TRA

Outside Counsel/Consultants

Government Relations, Inc.
Issues: BUD, TRA
Rep By: Thomas J. Bulger, Mark H. Miller, John N. Young

Gateway, Inc.

707 D St. NW
Washington, DC 20004
Tel: (202)737-2000
Fax: (202)737-2688
Registered: LDA
Web: www.gateway.com

A computer direct marketing company headquartered in San Diego, CA.

Leg. Issues: BAN, COM, CPI, CPT, EDU, IMM, MAN, MIA, SCI, TAX, TEC, TRD

Political Action Committee/s

Gateway Good Government PAC
707 D St. NW
Washington, DC 20004
Tel: (202)737-2000
Fax: (202)737-2688
Contact: Donald W. McClellan, Jr.

In-house, DC-area Employees

MCCLELLAN, Jr., Donald W.: V. President, Government Relations

Outside Counsel/Consultants

Williams & Jensen, P.C.
Issues: CPT, TAX, TEC
Rep By: Bertram W. Carp, David E. Franasiak, J. Steven Hart, Anthony J. Roda, Tracy D. Taylor

GATX Corp.

Chicago, IL
Leg. Issues: TAX

Outside Counsel/Consultants

Collier Shannon Scott, PLLC
Issues: TAX
Rep By: Kathleen Clark Kies, Michael D. Sherman

Mayer, Brown & Platt
Issues: TAX

Gauff, LTD.

San Juan, PR
Leg. Issues: ENV

Outside Counsel/Consultants

Capitol Counsel Group, L.L.C.
Issues: ENV

Gay & Robinson, Inc.

1301 Pennsylvania Ave. NW
Suite 401
Washington, DC 20004
Tel: (202)785-4070
Fax: (202)659-8581
Registered: LDA

Leg. Issues: AGR

In-house, DC-area Employees

FREEMYER, Windsor: Washington Representative
SELL, Alisa M.: Washington Representative
YANCEY, Dalton: Washington Representative

Gay and Lesbian Alliance Against Defamation (GLAAD)

1700 Kalorama Dr. NW
#101
Washington, DC 20009
Tel: (202)986-0425
Fax: (202)986-0470
Web: www.glaad.org
E-mail: renna@glaad.org

In-house, DC-area Employees

PATTERSON, Romaine: Regional Media Manager

Gay and Lesbian Victory Fund

1012 14th St. NW
Suite 1000
Washington, DC 20005
Tel: (202)842-8679
Fax: (202)289-3863
Web: www.victoryfund.org
E-mail: victoryf@victoryfund.org

In-house, DC-area Employees

BOND, Brian: Exec. Director

GCG Partners

Chicago, IL
Leg. Issues: TRD

Outside Counsel/Consultants

Barbour Griffith & Rogers, Inc.
Issues: TRD
Rep By: Haley Barbour, Bill Himpler, Brent Thompson

GCI-Wisconsin

Waukesha, WI
Leg. Issues: MAR

Outside Counsel/Consultants

Kerrigan & Associates, Inc.
Issues: MAR
Rep By: Michael J. Kerrigan

GCRC Program Directors Ass'n

Washington, DC

A health care association.

Leg. Issues: BUD, HCR, MED

Outside Counsel/Consultants

Washington Health Advocates
Issues: BUD, HCR, MED
Rep By: Lynn Morrison, Douglas Peddicord, Ph.D., Michele Sumilas

GE Capital Aviation Services

Stamford, CT

Outside Counsel/Consultants

Hogan & Hartson L.L.P.
Rep By: E. Tazewell Ellett, Hon. Robert H. Michel, Jeffrey W. Munk

GE Capital Corp.

1299 Pennsylvania Ave. NW
Suite 1100
Washington, DC 20004
Tel: (202)637-4012
Fax: (202)637-4066
Registered: LDA
Web: www.ge.com
E-mail: kathryn.fulton@corporate.GE.com

Headquartered in Stamford, CT.

Leg. Issues: FIN, HOU, TAX, TEC, WAS

In-house, DC-area Employees

FULTON, Kathryn: Manager, Government Relations (GE Capital)

Outside Counsel/Consultants

Adams and Reese LLP
Issues: WAS
Rep By: B. Jeffrey Brooks, D. Lee Forsgren

The Kate Moss Company
Issues: HOU
Rep By: Kate Moss

GE Capital Mortgage Insurance Co. (GEMICO)

Raleigh, NC
Registered: LDA
Leg. Issues: HOU

Outside Counsel/Consultants

Chlopak, Leonard, Schechter and Associates
Rep By: Charles G. Leonard

Wheat & Associates, Inc.
Issues: HOU
Rep By: Andrea Bevvino, Hon. Alan D. Wheat

GE Capital Mortgage Services, Inc.

Cherry Hill, NJ
Registered: LDA

Outside Counsel/Consultants

Goodwin, Procter & Hoar LLP

GE Commercial Real Estate & Financial Services

Stamford, CT
Registered: LDA
Leg. Issues: HOU, TAX

Outside Counsel/Consultants

Canfield & Associates, Inc.
Issues: HOU, TAX
Rep By: Roger Blauwet, April Boston, Anne C. Canfield

GE Financial Assurance

Washington, DC
Leg. Issues: TAX

Outside Counsel/Consultants

McGuireWoods L.L.P.
Issues: TAX
Rep By: Stephen A. Katsurinis, Hon. Lewis F. Payne, Jr., Jeffrey L. Schlagenhauf

GE Investment Corp.

Stamford, CT
Registered: LDA

Outside Counsel/Consultants

Dewey Ballantine LLP
Rep By: John J. Salmon

GE Lighting Group

Cleveland, OH
Registered: LDA

Outside Counsel/Consultants

Frederick L. Ikenson, P.C.
Rep By: Frederick L. Ikenson

Sidley & Austin
Rep By: Angus Macbeth

GE Nuclear Energy

San Jose, CA
Leg. Issues: ENG, TRD

Outside Counsel/Consultants

Fried, Frank, Harris, Shriver & Jacobson
Issues: ENG, TRD
Rep By: Jay R. Kraemer

GE Power Systems

1299 Pennsylvania Ave. NW
Suite 1100
Washington, DC 20004
Tel: (202)637-4147
Fax: (202)637-4400
Registered: LDA
E-mail: rob.walle@corporate.ge.com

Headquartered in Atlanta, GA.

Leg. Issues: ENG

In-house, DC-area Employees

WALLACE, Rob: Director, Government Relations

Outside Counsel/Consultants

Podesta/Mattoon
Issues: ENG
Rep By: Ann Delory, Anthony T. Podesta

Stuntz, Davis & Staffier, P.C.
Issues: ENG
Rep By: Linda Stuntz, Ellen S. Young

GEC-Marconi Avionics Group

Stanmore, UNITED KINGDOM

Outside Counsel/Consultants

Rooney Group Internat'l, Inc.

GEC-Marconi Defense Systems Ltd.

Stanmore, UNITED KINGDOM

Outside Counsel/Consultants

JGW Internat'l Ltd.
Rep By: Andrew M. Wilson, John G. Wilson

GEICO Corp.

One GEICO Plaza
Washington, DC 20076-0001
Tel: (301)986-3424
Fax: (301)718-5234
E-mail: rsober@geico.com

Political Action Committee/s

GEICO Political Action Committee
One GEICO Plaza
Washington, DC 20076-0001
Tel: (301)986-3000
Contact: Walter R. Smith

In-house, DC-area Employees

COVELL, Andrea M.: V. President and Legislative Counsel
GOLEC, Janice: Director, Business and Government Relations
GORDON, Bonny Kanter: Senior Counsel
GOULDEN, Jody: Director, Public Relations
SMITH, Walter R.: Assistant V. President, Communications
SOBER, Rynthia Manning: V. President, Public Affairs

Gelco Government Services

Reston, VA

Outside Counsel/Consultants

Hyjek & Fix, Inc.
Rep By: Donald J. Fix, Steven M. Hyjek

GELCO Information Network GSD, Inc.

Reston, VA
Leg. Issues: CPI, GOV

Outside Counsel/Consultants

The Carmen Group
Issues: CPI, GOV
Rep By: Ryan Adesnik, David M. Carmen, Andrew Garfinkel

Gemini Networks, Inc.

Hartford, CT
Leg. Issues: TEC

Outside Counsel/Consultants

Lawler, Metzger & Milkman, LLC
Issues: TEC
Rep By: A. Richard Metzger, Jr., Valerie Yates

Gemma & Associates

56 McPherson Circle
Potomac Falls, VA 20165
Tel: (703)444-4445
Fax: (703)444-7887
E-mail: peterjo@ix.netcom.com

In-house, DC-area Employees

GEMMA, Jr., Peter B.: President

GenCorp

1025 Connecticut Ave. NW
Suite 501
Washington, DC 20036
Tel: (202)828-6800
Fax: (202)828-6849
Registered: LDA
Web: www.gencorp.com

Headquartered in Sacramento, CA.

Leg. Issues: AER, DEF, HCR, TRD

In-house, DC-area Employees

ABERNETHY, Charles: Manager, Automotive, Export, Administration
ALLEN, Meghan: Manager, Congressional Relations
BREINDEL, Barry: Director, BMD and Technology (Aerojet)
BROWNLEE, D.H.: Director, Tactical Weapons and Systems (Aerojet)
FISCHMAN, Brent: Director, International Marketing and Sales
PEOPLES, Thomas E.: Senior V. President, International and Washington Operations

Outside Counsel/Consultants

Verner, Liipfert, Bernhard, McPherson and Hand, Chartered
Issues: AER, DEF, HCR, TRD
Rep By: Lloyd N. Hand

Genelabs Technologies, Inc.

Redwood City, CA
Leg. Issues: HCR, MED

Outside Counsel/Consultants

Policy Directions, Inc.
Issues: HCR, MED
Rep By: Kathleen "Kay" Holcombe, Frankie L. Trull

Genentech, Inc.

808 17th St. NW
Suite 250
Washington, DC 20006
Tel: (202)296-7272
Fax: (202)296-7290
Registered: LDA
Web: www.gene.com

Biotechnology company headquartered in South San Francisco, CA.

Leg. Issues: BUD, CAW, CPT, GOV, HCR, MAN, MED, MMM, PHA, SCI, TAX

In-house, DC-area Employees

FARBSTEIN, Marcus: Federal Government Liaison
MOORE, Walter K.: V. President, Government Affairs

Outside Counsel/Consultants

Bass and Howes, Inc.
Issues: HCR
Rep By: Joanne M. Howes

BKSH & Associates
Issues: BUD, CPT, GOV, HCR, MAN, MED, MMM, TAX

Hogan & Hartson L.L.P.
Issues: HCR
Rep By: Donna A. Boswell, Ann Morgan Vickery

Podesta/Mattoon
Issues: CAW, PHA, TAX
Rep By: Matthew Gelman, Andrew C. Littman, Anthony T. Podesta

Powell, Goldstein, Frazer & Murphy LLP
Issues: CPT
Rep By: Jeff Kushan

Royer & Babyak
Issues: BUD, CPT, HCR, TAX
Rep By: Gregory R. Babyak

Verner, Liipfert, Bernhard, McPherson and Hand, Chartered
Issues: HCR
Rep By: Vicki E. Hart

Williams & Jensen, P.C.
Issues: PHA, TAX
Rep By: David E. Franasiak, J. Steven Hart, Karina Lynch, George G. Olsen, Anthony J. Roda

General Atlantic Service Corp.

Greenwich, CT
Leg. Issues: LBR

Outside Counsel/Consultants

Paul, Weiss, Rifkind, Wharton & Garrison
Issues: LBR
Rep By: Carl W. Hampe

General Atomics

2001 Pennsylvania Ave. NW
Suite 650
Washington, DC 20006
Tel: (202)496-8200
Fax: (202)659-1110
Registered: LDA
Web: www.generalatomics.com

Manufacturer of unmanned aircraft vehicles headquartered in San Diego, CA.

Leg. Issues: AER, AVI, DEF, ENG

In-house, DC-area Employees

HAYNES, Mark: V. President, Washington Operations
WILLIS, Wayne D.: V. President, Washington Operations

Outside Counsel/Consultants

Kennedy Government Relations
Issues: DEF
Rep By: Jerry W. Kennedy

Mehl, Griffin & Bartek Ltd.
Issues: DEF
Rep By: Molly Griffin, Theodore J. Mehl

The PMA Group
Issues: DEF
Rep By: Kaylene Green, Paul J. Magliocchetti, Timothy K. Sanders

Rooney Group Internat'l, Inc.
Issues: AER, AVI, DEF
Rep By: Jerry L. Kaffka, James W. Rooney

General Aviation Manufacturers Ass'n

1400 K St. NW
Suite 801
Washington, DC 20005-2485
Tel: (202)393-1500
Fax: (202)842-4063
Registered: LDA
Web: www.generalaviation.org

GAMA is a trade association that represents U.S. manufacturers of general aviation airplanes, engines, avionics, and other components.

Leg. Issues: AVI, BUD, MAN, TAX

Political Action Committee/s

General Aviation Manufacturers Ass'n Political Action Committee (GAMAPAC)

1400 K St. NW
Suite 801
Washington, DC 20005-2485
Tel: (202)393-1500
Fax: (202)842-4063
Contact: Edward M. Bolen

In-house, DC-area Employees

BECKER, Darby M. R.: General Counsel
BOLEN, Edward M.: President
SIMI, Shelly Snyder: V. President, Communications
SWANDA, Ronald L.: V. President, Operations
VALENTINE, Barry: Senior V. President, Internat'l Affairs

Outside Counsel/Consultants

Davis & Harman LLP
Issues: TAX
Rep By: Richard S. Belas

Patton Boggs, LLP
Issues: BUD
Rep By: Robert C. Jones

Paul, Hastings, Janofsky & Walker LLP
Rep By: Judith Richards Hope

General Cable Industries, Inc.

Highland Heights, KY

Outside Counsel/Consultants

Interface Inc.
Rep By: Robert G. Williams

General Category Tuna Ass'n

Boston, MA
Leg. Issues: MAR

Outside Counsel/Consultants

Jones, Walker, Waechter, Poitevent, Carrere & Denegre, L.L.P.
Issues: MAR
Rep By: Paul Cambon, John J. Jaskot, R. Christian Johnsen, James Ogsbury

The Livingston Group, LLC
Issues: MAR
Rep By: Melvin Goodweather, Hon. Robert L. Livingston, Jr., J. Allen Martin, Richard L. Rodgers

Sher & Blackwell
Issues: MAR
Rep By: Jeffrey R. Pike

General Chemical Corp.

Green River, WY
Leg. Issues: LBR

Outside Counsel/Consultants

Patton Boggs, LLP
Issues: LBR
Rep By: Henry Chajet

General Cigar Holdings, Inc.

New York, NY
Leg. Issues: TOB

Outside Counsel/Consultants

Latham & Watkins
Issues: TOB
Rep By: Nicholas W. Allard

Verner, Liipfert, Bernhard, McPherson and Hand, Chartered

General Communications, Inc.

Washington, DC
Registered: LDA
Leg. Issues: BUD, COM, TAX, TEC

Outside Counsel/Consultants

Drinker Biddle & Reath LLP
Rep By: Joe D. Edge

Ryan, Phillips, Utrecht & MacKinnon
Issues: BUD, COM, TAX, TEC
Rep By: Rodney Hoppe, Jeffrey M. MacKinnon, William D. Phillips, Mark D. Planning, Thomas M. Ryan, Joseph V. Vasapoli

General Conference of Seventh-day Adventists

12501 Old Columbia Pike
Silver Spring, MD 20904
Tel: (301)680-6000
Fax: (301)680-6090
Web: www.adventist.org

The world headquarters of the Seventh-day Adventist church.

Leg. Issues: ALC, CIV, COM, CON, CPT, DIS, EDU, FAM, FIN, FOR, GAM, HCR, INS, LBR, MED, MIA, MMM, RET, TAX, TEC, TOB, WEL

In-house, DC-area Employees

DABROWSKI, Ray: Director, Communication
GRAZ, John: Director, Public Affairs and Religious Liberty
STANDISH, James: Assistant Director

General Development Corp.

Amman, JORDAN
Leg. Issues: AVI, FOR, TRD

Outside Counsel/Consultants

BKSH & Associates
Issues: AVI, FOR, TRD
Rep By: Gardner Peckham

General Dynamics Corp.

3190 Fairview Park Dr.
Falls Church, VA 22042
Tel: (703)876-3000
Fax: (703)876-3600
Registered: LDA
Web: www.generaldynamics.com
Leg. Issues: AER, AVI, BUD, DEF, FOR, LBR, MAN, TAX, TEC, TRA

Political Action Committee/s

General Dynamics Voluntary Political Contribution Plan

3190 Fairview Park Dr.
Falls Church, VA 22042
Tel: (703)876-3305
Fax: (703)876-3600
Contact: Diane L. Mossler

In-house, DC-area Employees

BANKUS, G. Kent: V. President, Government Relations
COLBURN, Cork: Staff V. President, Congressional Relations
EATON, Charles H. S.: Manager, Government Relations
GARDEPE, William M.: Director, Legislative Affairs
HACK, Ted: Director, Government Relations - Submarine Programs
HEATON, Erin R.: Director, Legislative Affairs
LAMB, Gerry F.: Director, Government Relations - Naval Surface Warfare Programs
MOSSLER, Diane L.: Director, Government and Community Relations
PEASE, Kendall: V. President, Communications
RILEY, Carey J.: Staff V. President, Government Relations
SAVNER, David: Senior V. President and General Counsel
SHAW, Win: Director, Aerospace Programs
TEMENAK, James M.: Staff V. President, Marine Systems

Outside Counsel/Consultants

C. Baker Consulting Inc.
Issues: AVI, DEF, MAN
Rep By: Caleb Baker

Bergson & Co.
Issues: DEF
Rep By: Paul C. Bergson

Cassidy & Associates, Inc.
Issues: AER, BUD, DEF
Rep By: Shawn Edwards, Lawrence C. Grossman, Arthur D. Mason, Hon. Martin A. Russo, Dan C. Tate, Sr.

The Conaway Group LLC
Issues: DEF
Rep By: Lt. Gen. John B. Conaway, USAF (Ret.)

Ervin Technical Associates, Inc. (ETA)
Issues: DEF, TEC
Rep By: Hon. Jack Edwards, James L. Ervin, Hon. Joseph M. McDade

The Gallagher Group, LLC
Issues: AER, AVI, DEF, FOR
Rep By: James P. Gallagher

Mayer, Brown & Platt
Rep By: Sheila Dearybury, Mark H. Gitenstein, Carolyn P. Osolinik

Denny Miller McBee Associates
Issues: DEF

The PMA Group
Issues: DEF

The Potomac Advocates
Issues: DEF
Rep By: Charles Scalera, Gary L. Sojka

General Electric Appliances

Louisville, KY

Outside Counsel/Consultants

Chlopak, Leonard, Schechter and Associates
Rep By: Charles G. Leonard

Stuntz, Davis & Staffier, P.C.
Rep By: Linda Stuntz, Ellen S. Young

General Electric Capital Mortgage Corp.

Raleigh, NC
Leg. Issues: HOU

Outside Counsel/Consultants

Chlopak, Leonard, Schechter and Associates
Issues: HOU
Rep By: Charles G. Leonard

General Electric Capital Services, Inc.

Washington, DC
Leg. Issues: BNK, DEF, FIN, TAX, TEC, TRD

Outside Counsel/Consultants

BKSH & Associates
Issues: BNK, DEF, FIN, TAX, TEC, TRD

General Electric Co.

1299 Pennsylvania Ave. NW
Suite 1100 West
Washington, DC 20004-2407
Tel: (202)637-4000
Fax: (202)637-4006
Registered: LDA

Leg. Issues: AVI, BAN, BNK, BUD, CAW, COM, CPT, CSP, DEF, ENG, ENV, FIN, FOR, GOV, HCR, IMM, INS, LBR, MAN, NAT, RRR, SCI, SMB, TAX, TEC, TRA, TRD, UTI, WAS

Political Action Committee/s

General Electric Co. Political Action Committee
1299 Pennsylvania Ave. NW
Suite 1100 West
Washington, DC 20004-2407
Contact: Blaine A. Barron
Tel: (202)637-4000
Fax: (202)637-4006

In-house, DC-area Employees

BARRON, Blaine A.: Manager, Financial Analysis and Regulatory Operations
BOGGS, Larry A.: Counsel, Environmental, Legislative and Regulatory Affairs
CLEMENTS, Bill: Senior Manager, International Trade Regulation
COOPER, Thomas E.: V. President, Aerospace Technology
FARRELL, Pamela: Technology, Research and Development
FRENKEL, Orit: Senior Manager, International Law and Policy
FULTON, Kathryn: Manager, Federal Government Relations, GE Capital
GADBAW, R. Michael: V. President and Senior Counsel, International Law and Policy
GOLDSTEIN, Ellen: Manager, Federal Government Relations (GE Medical Systems)
LAPLANTE, Clifford C.: Manager, Congressional and Exec. Office Relations
MERBER, Selig S.: Counsel, International Trade Regulation
MESSICK, Neil: Manager, Federal Government Relations
OKUN, B. Robert: V. President, NBC Washington
PINDER, Susan D.: Manager, Government Relations
PROWITT, Peter D.: Manager, Federal Government Relations
RICHARDS, Timothy J.: Senior Manager, International Trade and Investment
RINGO, D. W. "Skip": Manager, Aircraft Engine Programs
RIORDAN, Kevin J.: Team Leader, Government Relations
SINGER, Ronald M.: Manager, International Programs
STERN, Ronald A.: V. President and Senior Counsel, Antitrust
THOMSON, Lynn Harding: Manager, Federal Government Relations
VECCHIO, Joseph J.: Director, Federal Government Programs (GE Medical Systems)
WALLACE, Rob: Manager, Government and Industry Programs
WALTER, Susan M.: V. President, Corporate Government Relations

Outside Counsel/Consultants

The Accord Group
Issues: BUD, CAW, ENV, NAT, WAS
Rep By: Philip T. Cummings

Alston & Bird LLP
Issues: CSP, MAN
Rep By: Thomas M. Boyd, Thomas E. Crocker, Jonathan Winer

William V. Brierre
Issues: ENV
Rep By: William V. Brierre, Jr.

John G. Campbell, Inc.
Issues: DEF

Chlopak, Leonard, Schechter and Associates
Rep By: Charles G. Leonard

Covington & Burling
Rep By: Roderick A. DeArment, Allan J. Topol

Hogan & Hartson L.L.P.
Issues: ENV
Rep By: Christine M. Warnke

Frederick L. Ikenson, P.C.
Rep By: Frederick L. Ikenson

Jones, Walker, Waechter, Poitevent, Carrere & Denegre, L.L.P.
Issues: BUD, CAW, ENV, NAT, TAX, WAS
Rep By: Paul Cambon, John J. Jaskot, R. Christian Johnsen, James Ogsbury

The Livingston Group, LLC
Issues: BUD, CAW, ENV, NAT, TAX, WAS
Rep By: Hon. Robert L. Livingston, Jr., J. Allen Martin, Richard L. Rodgers

LPI Consulting, Inc.
Rep By: Teresa Gorman

Mayer, Brown & Platt
Issues: DEF, FOR
Rep By: Carol J. Bilzi, Carolyn P. Osolinik, John P. Schmitz

O'Connor & Hannan, L.L.P.
Issues: ENV, NAT
Rep By: Robert W. Barrie, Hon. Thomas J. Corcoran, George J. Mannina, Jr., Patrick E. O'Donnell

PriceWaterhouseCoopers

Robison Internat'l, Inc.
Issues: BUD, DEF
Rep By: Sandra A. Gilbert, Richard B. Ladd

Sidley & Austin
Issues: ENV
Rep By: David T. Buente, Jr., James Connaughton

Robert D. Sneed
Issues: DEF
Rep By: Robert D. Sneed

The Solomon Group, LLC
Issues: AVI, BAN, BNK, DEF, ENG, FIN, FOR, HCR, INS, MAN, TAX, TRD, UTI
Rep By: William D. Crosby, Jr., David M. Lonie, Hon. Gerald B. H. Solomon, William R. Teator

Swidler Berlin Shereff Friedman, LLP
Issues: BUD, CAW, ENV, GOV, TRA
Rep By: Barry B. Direnfeld, Charles H. Knauss

Verner, Liipfert, Bernhard, McPherson and Hand, Chartered
Issues: ENV
Rep By: Steven R. Phillips, Susannah W. Shakow, John H. Sterne, Jr., John H. Zentay

Washington Council Ernst & Young
Issues: BUD, HCR, TAX, TRD
Rep By: Doug Badger, Lauren Darling, John L. Doney, Jayne T. Fitzgerald, LaBrenda Garrett-Nelson, Gary J. Gasper, Bruce A. Gates, Nick Giordano, Cathy Koch, Robert J. Leonard, Richard Meltzer, Phillip D. Moseley, John D. Porter, Robert M. Rozen, Donna Steele-Flynn, Timothy J. Urban

General Electric Industrial & Power Systems

Schenectady, NY
Leg. Issues: BUD, ENG, SCI

Outside Counsel/Consultants

Stuntz, Davis & Staffier, P.C.
Issues: BUD, ENG, SCI
Rep By: Linda Stuntz, Ellen S. Young

General Federation of Women's Clubs

1734 N St. NW
Washington, DC 20036-2990
Tel: (202)347-3168
Fax: (202)835-0246

Web: www.gfwc.org
E-mail: gfwc@gfwc.org

In-house, DC-area Employees

ALBERT, Sarah: Public Policy Director
KRANZ, Sally: Director, Public Relations

General Mills

601 Pennsylvania Ave. NW
Suite 420
North Bldg.
Washington, DC 20004
Tel: (202)737-8200
Fax: (202)638-4914
Registered: LDA

Headquartered in Minneapolis, MN.

Leg. Issues: AGR, BUD, CSP, FOO, SMB, TRD, WEL

In-house, DC-area Employees

BIRD, Robert S.: Director, Washington Office
TOKER, Mary Catherine: Deputy Director, Washington Office

Outside Counsel/Consultants

Holland & Knight LLP
Issues: CSP, FOO
Rep By: Hon. Gerald E. Sikorski

Olsson, Frank and Weeda, P.C.
Issues: AGR, BUD, FOO, WEL
Rep By: John W. Bode, Susan P. Grymes, Stephen L. Lacey, Marshall L. Matz, Ryan W. Stroschein

Patton Boggs, LLP
Issues: FOO
Rep By: Stuart M. Pape

The PMA Group
Issues: BUD, TRD
Rep By: Fred J. Clark, Paul J. Magliocchetti, Timothy K. Sanders

Zeliff, Ireland, and Associates
Issues: SMB
Rep By: Hon. William H. Zeliff, Jr.

General Motors Corp.

1660 L St. NW
Fourth Floor
Washington, DC 20036
Tel: (202)775-5092
Fax: (202)775-5095
Registered: LDA

Web: www.gm.com

Leg. Issues: ADV, AER, AUT, AVI, BAN, BNK, BUD, CAW, CHM, CIV, COM, CPI, CPT, CSP, DEF, ECN, EDU, ENG, ENV, FIN, FOR, FUE, GOV, HCR, IMM, INS, LAW, LBR, MAN, MAR, MMM, MON, NAT, RES, RET, ROD, RRR, SCI, TAX, TEC, TOR, TRA, TRD, TRU, UNM, URB, UTI, WAS

In-house, DC-area Employees

COLE, Kenneth W.: V. President, Government Relations
FLYNN, James C.: Washington Representative - Locomotive Group
KAVJIAN, Edward M.: Senior Washington Representative
KEMMER, Mark L.: Senior Washington Representative
MARSH, Robert H.: Deputy Director, Federal Affairs
MARTIN, Gregory: Manager, Media Relations
MORRISSEY, Michael: Director, Communications
NOACK, William H.: Director, Regional Offices, Corporate Communications
O'TOOLE, Stephen E.: Senior Washington Representative
WASHBURN, Barbara J.: Senior Washington Representative
ZEBROSKI, Shirley: Senior Washington Representative

Outside Counsel/Consultants

ADA Consulting Services
Issues: CAW, ENV

Bonner & Associates

Cortese PLLC
Issues: AUT, CSP, GOV
Rep By: Alfred W. Cortese, Jr.

The Duberstein Group, Inc.
Issues: AUT, BNK, ENV, FOR, GOV, HCR, TAX, TRD
Rep By: John W. Angus, III, Michael S. Berman, Steven M. Champlin, Kenneth M. Duberstein, Henry M. Gandy, Daniel P. Meyer

Eckert Seamans Cherin & Mellott, LLC
Issues: AUT, FIN, FOR, GOV
Rep By: LeRoy S. Zimmerman

Hogan & Hartson L.L.P.
Rep By: Mark S. McConnell

Kirkland & Ellis
Issues: ENV
Rep By: Stuart A. C. Drake, Robert R. Gasaway

Bob Moss Associates
Issues: ENG, ENV, TRA
Rep By: Bob Moss

PriceWaterhouseCoopers
Issues: TAX
Rep By: Jim Carlisle, Kenneth J. Kies

RGS Enterprises, Inc.
Issues: AUT, CAW, ENV, TOR, WAS
Rep By: Ronald G. Sykes

Shaw Pittman
Issues: GOV

Thompson and Naughton, Inc.
Issues: ENG
Rep By: Kenneth W. Thompson

Verner, Liipfert, Bernhard, McPherson and Hand, Chartered
Issues: CAW
Rep By: R. Stuart Broom, Rosemary B. Freeman, Clinton A. Vince

Weil, Gotshal & Manges, LLP
Issues: TAX
Rep By: Robert C. Odle, Jr.

The Wexler Group
Issues: ENV, GOV
Rep By: Hon. Michael Patrick Flanagan, Patrick J. McCann, Hon. Robert S. Walker, Anne Wexler

Bill Wight, LLC
Issues: BUD, DEF

Williams & Connolly
Rep By: Aubrey M. Daniel, III, Robert P. Watkins

Wirthlin Worldwide

General Order Warehouse Coalition

New York, NY

Outside Counsel/Consultants

Saunders and Company

General Ore Internat'l Corp. Ltd.

Amsterdam, NETHERLANDS
Leg. Issues: MAR, TAX

Outside Counsel/Consultants

Barents Group LLC
Issues: TAX
Rep By: Linden C. Smith

Ernst & Young LLP
Issues: TAX
Rep By: Lauren Darling, Patrick G. Heck, Phillip D. Moseley, John D. Porter, Henry C. Ruempler, Donna Steele-Flynn

Thompson Coburn LLP
Issues: MAR
Rep By: Warren L. Dean

General Portland Inc.

Dallas, TX

Outside Counsel/Consultants

Heenan, Althen & Roles
Rep By: Michael T. Heenan

General Reinsurance Corp.

Stamford, CT
Leg. Issues: ENV

Outside Counsel/Consultants

Nat'l Strategies Inc.
Issues: ENV
Rep By: David K. Aylward

General Signal Corp.

Stamford, CT

Outside Counsel/Consultants

Howrey Simon Arnold & White
Rep By: Stuart H. Harris

General Telephone Co. of California

Santa Monica, CA

Outside Counsel/Consultants

Covington & Burling

General Tire, Inc.

Akron, OH

Outside Counsel/Consultants

Multinat'l Government Services, Inc.
Rep By: Brooks J. Bowen, Jim J. Tozzi

Generations United

1222 C St. NW
#820
Washington, DC 20001
Web: www.gu.org
E-mail: gu@cwla.org
Tel: (202)638-1263
Fax: (202)638-7555

A coalition of groups concerned about the welfare of children and the aging. Moving forces in the coalition are the Child Welfare League of America, the Nat'l Council on the Aging, the American Ass'n of Retired Persons and the Children's Defense Fund.

In-house, DC-area Employees

BUTTS, Donna M.: Exec. Director

Generic Pharmaceutical Ass'n

1620 I St. NW
Suite 800
Washington, DC 20006
Tel: (202)833-9070
Fax: (202)833-9612
Registered: LDA
Leg. Issues: BUD, CPT, CSP, HCR, MED, MMM, PHA, SCI, TRD

In-house, DC-area Employees

COURTNEY, Jim: Director, Communications
MENN, III, Henry W. ("Buddy"): V. President, Government Affairs
NIXON, William: President and C.E.O.

Outside Counsel/Consultants

Fierce and Isakowitz
Issues: PHA
Rep By: Kathryn Braden, Samantha Cook, Donald L. Fierce, Mark W. Isakowitz, Diane Moery

The PMA Group
Issues: BUD
Rep By: Fred J. Clark, Kaylene Green, Paul J. Magliocchetti, Mark Rokala, Timothy K. Sanders

Genesee Brewing Co.

Rochester, NY
Leg. Issues: TRD

Outside Counsel/Consultants

Nixon Peabody LLP
Issues: TRD

Genesee County Drain Commissioner

Flint, MI
Leg. Issues: CAW

Outside Counsel/Consultants

Verner, Liipfert, Bernhard, McPherson and Hand, Chartered
Issues: CAW
Rep By: Rosemary B. Freeman, Jenifer Martin

Genetics Soc. of America

9650 Rockville Pike
Bethesda, MD 20814
Web: www.faseb.org/genetics
E-mail: estrass@genetics.faseb.org
Tel: (301)571-1825
Fax: (301)530-7079

In-house, DC-area Employees

STRASS, Elaine: Exec. Director

Geneva Steel Co.

Vineyard, UT
Leg. Issues: TRA, TRD

Outside Counsel/Consultants

Schagrin Associates
Issues: TRA, TRD
Rep By: Tamara L. Browne, Roger B. Schagrin

The Genome Action Coalition

A voluntary health coalition.

Leg. Issues: BUD, HCR, MED, SCI

Outside Counsel/Consultants

Cavarocchi Ruscio Dennis Associates
Issues: BUD, HCR, MED, SCI
Rep By: Lyle B. Dennis

Genome Dynamics, Inc.

Gaithersburg, MD
Leg. Issues: BUD

Outside Counsel/Consultants

Patton Boggs, LLP
Issues: BUD
Rep By: Robert C. Jones

Gentex Corp.

Carbondale, PA
Leg. Issues: DEF

Outside Counsel/Consultants

American Defense Internat'l, Inc.
Issues: DEF
Rep By: Van D. Hipp, Jr., Dave Wilberding

The PMA Group
Issues: DEF
Rep By: Daniel Cunningham, Kaylene Green, Patrick Hiu, Dr. John Lynch, Stephen Madey, Paul J. Magliocchetti

Gentrac Inc.

Outside Counsel/Consultants

Olsson, Frank and Weeda, P.C.
Rep By: John W. Bode, Susan P. Grymes, Karen Reis Harned, Stephen L. Lacey, Marshall L. Matz, Tyson Redpath, Ryan W. Stroschein, Arthur Y. Tsien, David F. Weeda

GenuOne

Outside Counsel/Consultants

Leadership Counsel, LLC
Rep By: Jack D. P. Lichtenstein

Genzyme Corp.

1020 19th St. NW
Suite 550
Washington, DC 20036
Web: www.genzyme.com
Tel: (202)296-3280
Fax: (202)296-3411
Registered: LDA

A biotechnology company focused on developing therapeutic and diagnostic products and services to treat major unmet medical needs. Headquartered in Cambridge, MA.

Leg. Issues: BUD, HCR, INS, MED, MMM, PHA, TAX

In-house, DC-area Employees

MCGRANE, Mary: V. President, Government Relations
RAINES, Lisa J.: Senior V. President, Government Relations

Outside Counsel/Consultants

Bergner Bockorny Castagnetti and Hawkins
Issues: HCR
Rep By: James W. Hawkins

Greenberg Traurig, LLP
Issues: BUD, PHA
Rep By: Russell J. Mueller, Nancy E. Taylor

Wilmer, Cutler & Pickering
Issues: HCR
Rep By: C. Boyden Gray

GEO Centers, Inc.

Rockville, MD
Leg. Issues: DEF, HCR, MED

Outside Counsel/Consultants

John G. Campbell, Inc.

Potomac Strategies Internat'l LLC
Issues: DEF, HCR, MED
Rep By: Raymond F. DuBois, Jr., Cynthia Trutanic

Geo-Seis Helicopters Inc.

Ft. Collins, CO
Leg. Issues: AVI, GOV, LAW

Outside Counsel/Consultants

Meyers & Associates
Issues: AVI, GOV, LAW
Rep By: Richard L. Meyers

GeoPhone, LLC

Baltimore, MD
Leg. Issues: TEC

Outside Counsel/Consultants

Greenberg Traurig, LLP
Issues: TEC
Rep By: Mitchell F. Brecher

Georal Internat'l Ltd.

Whitestone, NY

A manufacturer of security doors for airports, banks, and other high-risk areas.

Leg. Issues: BAN

Outside Counsel/Consultants

Hogan & Hartson L.L.P.
Issues: BAN
Rep By: Christine M. Warnke

George Mason University Foundation

Fairfax, VA
Leg. Issues: BUD

Outside Counsel/Consultants

Patton Boggs, LLP
Issues: BUD
Rep By: Edward J. Newberry

George Washington University Medical Center

Outside Counsel/Consultants

Arent Fox Kintner Plotkin & Kahn, PLLC
Rep By: Douglas McCormack, William A. Sarraille

George Washington University, Office of Government Relations

714 21st St. NW
Third Floor
Washington, DC 20052
Tel: (202)994-9132
Fax: (202)994-1229
Registered: LDA
Leg. Issues: BUD, EDU, TRA

In-house, DC-area Employees

DEMCZUK, Bernard: Assistant V. President, Government Relations
SAWAYA, Richard: Assistant V. President, Government Relations

Outside Counsel/Consultants

Mintz, Levin, Cohn, Ferris, Glovsky and Popeo, P.C.
Rep By: Raymond D. Cotton

John J. Rhodes
Issues: EDU
Rep By: Hon. John J. Rhodes, III

Smith Dawson & Andrews, Inc.
Issues: BUD, TRA
Rep By: Gregory B. Andrews, James P. Smith, Ray Warner

Verner, Liipfert, Bernhard, McPherson and Hand, Chartered
Rep By: Denis J. Dwyer, Martin Mendelsohn, John H. Zentay

George Zamias Developers

Johnstown, PA

Outside Counsel/Consultants

Ann Eppard Associates, Ltd.
Rep By: Julie Chlopecki, Ann Eppard

Georgetown Industries

Outside Counsel/Consultants

Wiley, Rein & Fielding
Rep By: Eileen P. Bradner, Charles O. Verrill, Jr.

The Georgetown Partnership

Washington, DC
Leg. Issues: TRA

Outside Counsel/Consultants

Holland & Knight LLP
Issues: TRA
Rep By: David C. Whitestone

Georgetown University

Healy Hall
Third Floor
Box 571243
37th & O Sts. NW
Washington, DC 20057
Web: www.georgetown.edu/admin/publicaffairs/federalrelations.htm
Tel: (202)687-3455
Fax: (202)687-1656

In-house, DC-area Employees

COLLINS, T. Bryon: Senior Counselor, Federal Relations
FLEMING, Scott S.: Assistant to the President for Federal Relations

Georgetown University-McDonough School of Business

Washington, DC
Leg. Issues: EDU

Outside Counsel/Consultants

Kimberly Consulting, LLC
Issues: EDU
Rep By: Richard H. Kimberly

Georgetown University-School of Nursing

Washington, DC
Leg. Issues: EDU

Outside Counsel/Consultants

Kimberly Consulting, LLC
Issues: EDU
Rep By: Richard H. Kimberly

Georgia Commodity Commission for Peanuts

Tifton, GA
Leg. Issues: AGR

Outside Counsel/Consultants

Robert L. Redding
Issues: AGR
Rep By: Robert L. Redding, Jr.

Georgia Cotton Commission

Perry, GA
Leg. Issues: AGR

Outside Counsel/Consultants

Robert L. Redding
Issues: AGR
Rep By: Robert L. Redding, Jr.

Georgia Institute of Technology

601 13th St. NW
Suite 300
Washington, DC 20005
Tel: (202)756-3670
Fax: (202)347-1420

In-house, DC-area Employees

BARTLETT, Patricia L.: Director, Federal Relations
MEIEHOEFER, Melissa G.: Analyst, Federal Policy

Georgia Municipal Gas Ass'n

Atlanta, GA

Outside Counsel/Consultants

Smith Dawson & Andrews, Inc.
Rep By: Gregory B. Andrews, Thomas C. Dawson, James P. Smith

Georgia Ports Authority

Savannah, GA
Leg. Issues: BUD, ENV, TRA

Outside Counsel/Consultants

Hurt, Norton & Associates
Issues: BUD, TRA
Rep By: Robert H. Hurt, Frank Norton, Katharine Calhoun Wood

Kilpatrick Stockton LLP
Issues: ENV
Rep By: J. Vance Hughes

Georgia, Government of the Republic of

Tbilisi, GEORGIA

Outside Counsel/Consultants

Capitol Advisors, Inc.

Skadden, Arps, Slate, Meagher & Flom LLP
Rep By: Robert S. Bennett

Georgia, Office of the Attorney General of the State of

Atlanta, GA

Outside Counsel/Consultants

Duncan, Weinberg, Genzer & Pembroke, P.C.
Rep By: James F. Flug

Georgia, State of

Atlanta, GA
Leg. Issues: GOV

Outside Counsel/Consultants

Smith Dawson & Andrews, Inc.
Issues: GOV
Rep By: Gregory B. Andrews, Thomas C. Dawson, Sherri Powar, James P. Smith

Georgia-Pacific Corp.

1120 G St. NW
Suite 1050
Washington, DC 20005
Tel: (202)347-4446
Registered: LDA
Leg. Issues: BUD, CAW, CSP, ENG, ENV, HCR, NAT, TAX, TRA, TRD, UNM

In-house, DC-area Employees

BELL, Jackie D.: Director, Federal Government Affairs
HILL, Patricia K.: Manager, Federal Regulatory Affairs
MODI, David T.: V. President, Government Affairs
MOORE, Susan F.: V. President, Environmental Affairs

Outside Counsel/Consultants

Crowell & Moring LLP
Issues: NAT
Rep By: Steven P. Quarles

The Hawthorn Group, L.C.
Rep By: Suzanne Hammelman

McDermott, Will and Emery
Rep By: Calvin P. Johnson, Stephen E. Wells, Jane E. Wilson

McGuireWoods L.L.P.
Issues: CAW
Rep By: Stephen A. Katsurinis, Hon. Lewis F. Payne, Jr.

O'Connor & Hannan, L.L.P.
Issues: ENV, NAT
Rep By: Robert W. Barrie, Hon. Thomas J. Corcoran, George J. Mannina, Jr., Patrick E. O'Donnell

Geotek Communications, Inc.

Montvale, NJ
Leg. Issues: TEC

Outside Counsel/Consultants

Gardner, Carton and Douglas
Issues: TEC

Geothermal Energy Ass'n

209 Pennsylvania Ave. SE
Washington, DC 20003
Web: www.geotherm.org
E-mail: geo@geo-energy.org
Tel: (202)454-5261
Fax: (202)454-5265

A trade association for the geothermal power industry.

Leg. Issues: BUD, ENG, TAX

In-house, DC-area Employees

GAWELL, Karl: Exec. Director

Outside Counsel/Consultants

Duncan, Weinberg, Genzer & Pembroke, P.C.
Rep By: Jeffrey C. Genzer

Geothermal Heat Pump Consortium

701 Pennsylvania Ave. NW
Third Floor
Washington, DC 20004
Tel: (202)508-5500
Fax: (202)508-5222
Leg. Issues: BUD, ENG

In-house, DC-area Employees

ABNEE, Conn: Exec. Director
QUINN, Sara: Director, Marketing, Public and Governmental Affairs

Outside Counsel/Consultants

Sagamore Associates, Inc.
Issues: BUD, ENG
Rep By: Todd Atkinson, Theodore W. Bristol, Doug Wasitis

Geothermal Resources Ass'n

Davis, CA
Leg. Issues: ENG, TAX

Outside Counsel/Consultants

Van Ness Feldman, P.C.
Issues: ENG, TAX
Rep By: Howard J. Feldman

Gerico

Outside Counsel/Consultants

Collier Shannon Scott, PLLC
Rep By: Michael R. Kershow

German American Business Ass'n

700 Princess St.
Suite Three
Alexandria, VA 22314-3129
Web: www.gaba.org
E-mail: info@gaba.org
Tel: (703)836-6120
Fax: (703)836-6160

In-house, DC-area Employees

ZSCHOCK, Charles W.: President

German Competitive Carriers Ass'n

Cologne, GERMANY

Outside Counsel/Consultants

Swidler Berlin Shereff Friedman, LLP
Rep By: Andrew D. Lipman

German Marshall Fund of the United States

11 Dupont Circle NW
Suite 750
Washington, DC 20036
Web: www.gmfus.org
Tel: (202)745-3950
Fax: (202)265-1662

In-house, DC-area Employees
KENNEDY, Craig R.: President

Gerontological Soc. of America

1030 15th St. NW
Suite 250
Washington, DC 20005-1503
Web: www.geron.org
E-mail: geron@geron.org
Tel: (202)842-1275
Fax: (202)842-1150

The national professional organization of researchers, educators, and practitioners in the field of aging, the Society publishes The Journals of Gerontology and the Gerontologist. Its annual scientific meeting attracts some 3,500 participants.

In-house, DC-area Employees
HAROOTYAN, Linda K.: Deputy Director
REYAZUDDIN, Mohammed: Information Specialist
SCHUTZ, Carol A.: Exec. Director

getpress.com

Norwell, MA
Leg. Issues: SMB

Outside Counsel/Consultants
Verner, Liipfert, Bernhard, McPherson and Hand, Chartered
Issues: SMB
Rep By: Marla P. Grossman

GHB Broadcasting Corp.

Atlanta, GA

Outside Counsel/Consultants
Reddy, Begley, & McCormick, LLP
Rep By: Dennis F. Begley

Giant Food Inc.

P.O. Box 1804
Department 599
Washington, DC 20013
Tel: (301)341-4100
Fax: (301)618-4967

Supermarket chain headquartered in Landover, MD.

In-house, DC-area Employees
BUCHSBAUM, Michael: V. President, General Counsel
FINK, Paula: Communications Manager
MATTHEWS, Odonna: V. President, Consumer Affairs
SCHER, Barry F.: V. President, Public Affairs

Giant Industries, Inc.

Scottsdale, AZ
Leg. Issues: ENG, ENV, FUE, SCI, SMB

Outside Counsel/Consultants
Oliver James Horton
Issues: ENG, ENV, FUE, SCI, SMB
Rep By: Oliver James Horton, Jr.

GIAT Industries

Versailles, FRANCE
Leg. Issues: DEF

Outside Counsel/Consultants
American Defense Internat'l, Inc.
Issues: DEF
Rep By: Michael Herson, Van D. Hipp, Jr., Dave Wilberding

Gibraltar Information Bureau

1156 15th St. NW
Suite 1100
Washington, DC 20005
E-mail: gibinfobur@msn.com
Tel: (202)452-1108
Fax: (202)452-1109
Registered: FARA
Leg. Issues: FOR

In-house, DC-area Employees
STIEGLITZ, Perry J.: Director

Gibson Guitar Corp.

Nashville, TN

Outside Counsel/Consultants
Baker, Donelson, Bearman & Caldwell, P.C.
Rep By: Charles R. Johnston, Jr.

Gifts In Kind Internat'l

333 N. Fairfax St.
Suite 100
Alexandria, VA 22314
Web: www.GiftsInKind.org
E-mail: ProductDonations@GiftsInKind.org
Tel: (703)836-2121
Fax: (703)549-1481
Registered: LDA

Serves as liaison between donor corporations and not-for-profit organizations in distribution of corporate product donations to the needy.

In-house, DC-area Employees
CORRIGAN, Susan: President and Chief Exec. Officer

Gila River Farms

Sacaton, AZ

Gila River farms is a farming enterprise of the Gila River Indian Community.

Leg. Issues: IND

Outside Counsel/Consultants
Ducheneaux, Taylor & Associates, Inc.
Issues: IND
Rep By: Peter S. Taylor

Gila River Indian Community

Sacaton, AZ
Leg. Issues: BUD, GAM, IND, ROD, TAX

Outside Counsel/Consultants
Akin, Gump, Strauss, Hauer & Feld, L.L.P.
Issues: BUD, GAM, IND, ROD, TAX
Rep By: Katherine D. Brodie, Smith W. Davis, Susan H. Lent, Ado A. Machida, Donald R. Pongrace, Barney J. Skladany, Jr.

Gilbane Building Co.

4330 East-West Hwy.
Suite 314
Bethesda, MD 20814
Tel: (301)718-8860
Fax: (301)718-8862

In-house, DC-area Employees
CHOQUETTE, William: V. President and Washington Contact

Gilbarco, Inc.

Greensboro, NC
Leg. Issues: TRD

Outside Counsel/Consultants
Patton Boggs, LLP
Issues: TRD
Rep By: Darryl D. Nirenberg, Frank R. Samolis

Gildan Activewear

Montreal, CANADA
Leg. Issues: APP, TRD

Outside Counsel/Consultants
The Macon Edwards Co.
Issues: TRD
Rep By: Macon T. Edwards, Mara Peltz

Winston & Strawn
Issues: APP, TRD
Rep By: Edward F. Gerwin, Jr., Charles L. Kinney, Douglas C. Richardson, John A. Waits, II

Gillette Co.

Boston, MA

Outside Counsel/Consultants
Columbus Public Affairs

Gino Morena Enterprises

South San Francisco, CA

A hair care and beauty company.

Outside Counsel/Consultants
Will Cofer Associates
Rep By: Williston B. Cofer, Jr.

Girl Scouts of the U.S.A. - Washington Office

1025 Connecticut Ave. NW
Suite 309
Washington, DC 20036
Web: www.girlscouts.org
E-mail: lalexander@girlscouts.org
Tel: (202)659-3780
Fax: (202)331-8065
Registered: LDA

A national organization for all girls ages 5-17, emphasizing service to society, development of values, self-awareness, and leadership skills headquartered in New York, NY.

Leg. Issues: BUD, CIV, EDU, FAM, GOV, HCR, NAT, POS, SCI, SPO, TAX, WEL

In-house, DC-area Employees
ALEXANDER, LaVerne: Director, Government Relations

Outside Counsel/Consultants
Bracy Williams & Co.
Issues: SPO
Rep By: Linda Doorfee Flaherty, Susan J. Williams

Evans & Black, Inc.
Issues: BUD, TAX
Rep By: Judy A. Black, Teresa J. Dyer, Rae Forker Evans

Girling Health Care

Austin, TX
Leg. Issues: MMM

Outside Counsel/Consultants
Williams & Jensen, P.C.
Issues: MMM
Rep By: George G. Olsen

Girls Incorporated

1001 Connecticut Ave. NW
Suite 412
Washington, DC 20036
Web: www.girlsinc.org
E-mail: mwurf@girls-inc.org
Tel: (202)463-1881
Fax: (202)463-8994

Provides programs and advocacy for school aged girls. Headquartered in New York, NY.

Leg. Issues: ALC, EDU, FAM, LAW, SPO, TOB

In-house, DC-area Employees
WURF, Mildred Kiefer: Director, Public Policy

Gist Brocades

Charlotte, NC

Outside Counsel/Consultants
Max N. Berry Law Offices
Rep By: Max N. Berry

Bruce Givner, Attorney

Los Angeles, CA
Leg. Issues: TAX

Outside Counsel/Consultants
Foley & Lardner
Issues: TAX
Rep By: Jodi L. Hanson, Jerris Leonard, Richard F. Riley, Jr.

GKN Westland Aerospace Inc.

Wallingford, CT
Leg. Issues: AVI

Outside Counsel/Consultants
Hooper Owen & Winburn
Issues: AVI
Rep By: Hon. Charles Wilson

Glacier PAC

818 Connecticut Ave. NW
Suite 1100
Washington, DC 20006

In-house, DC-area Employees
OLDAKER, William C.

Glankler Brown, PLLC

Memphis, TN
Leg. Issues: AVI, BUD, TRA

Outside Counsel/Consultants
Van Scoyoc Associates, Inc.
Issues: AVI, BUD, TRA
Rep By: Jason Anderson, Ray Cole, Chad Schulken, H. Stewart Van Scoyoc

Glass Packaging Institute

515 King St.
Suite 420
Alexandria, VA 22314
Web: www.gpi.org
E-mail: gpidc@erols.com
Tel: (703)684-6359
Fax: (703)684-6048
Registered: LDA
Leg. Issues: ENV, HCR

In-house, DC-area Employees
CATTANEO, Joseph J.: President

Outside Counsel/Consultants
CLARION Management Resources, Inc.
Rep By: Joseph J. Cattaneo

Dyer Ellis & Joseph, P.C.
Issues: ENV, HCR
Rep By: Laurie Crick Sahatjian, Jeanne Marie Grasso, Duncan C. Smith, III, Jennifer M. Southwick, Jonathan K. Waldron

O'Neill, Athy & Casey, P.C.
Rep By: Andrew Athy, Jr., Christopher R. O'Neill

P. H. Glatfelter

Spring Grove, PA
Leg. Issues: ENV, NAT

Outside Counsel/Consultants

O'Connor & Hannan, L.L.P.
Issues: ENV, NAT
Rep By: Robert W. Barrie, Hon. Thomas J. Corcoran, George J. Mannina, Jr., Patrick E. O'Donnell

The Wexler Group
Rep By: Hon. Robert S. Walker

GlaxoSmithKline

1500 K St. NW
Suite 650
Washington, DC 20005
Tel: (202)715-1000
Fax: (202)715-1001
Registered: LDA
Web: www.gsk.com

Researches, develops, manufactures, and markets pharmaceuticals, vaccines, over-the-counter medicines, and health-related consumer goods. Formed through the merger of Glaxo Wellcome and SmithKline Beecham in 2000. Headquartered in Philadelphia, PA and Research Triangle Park, NC.

Leg. Issues: BUD, CPT, HCR, MED, MMM, PHA, TAX, TOB, TRD

In-house, DC-area Employees

KINNEY, Janie Ann: V. President, Federal Government Relations and Public Policy
MCLAIN, Patrick M.: Federal Government Relations
RYAN, Mary Frances: Federal Government Relations
SCHUYLER, William J.: Federal Government Relations
WALSH, Sarah J.: Federal Government Relations
WILLIAMS, Kimberly A.: Federal Government Relations
YORK, Elizabeth: Federal Government Relations

Outside Counsel/Consultants

Barbour Griffith & Rogers, Inc.
Issues: HCR
Rep By: Haley Barbour, G. O. Lanny Griffith, Jr., Loren Monroe, Edward M. Rogers, Jr.

Bergner Bockorny Castagnetti and Hawkins
Issues: MED
Rep By: Jeffrey T. Bergner, David A. Bockorny, David Castagnetti, Melissa Schulman

BKSH & Associates
Issues: BUD, HCR, MED, PHA

Capitol Associates, Inc.

Hill and Knowlton, Inc.
Rep By: Jim Friedman, Lisa Gulledge

Kent & O'Connor, Inc.
Issues: CPT
Rep By: Cindy Thomas

Parry, Romani, DeConcini & Symms
Issues: CPT, MED, TAX
Rep By: Edward H. Baxter, Hon. Dennis DeConcini, John M. Haddow, Scott D. Hatch, Shannon Davis Henderson, Jack W. Martin, Romano Romani, Linda Arey Skladany, Hon. Steven D. Symms

Wheat & Associates, Inc.
Issues: HCR, MED, PHA
Rep By: Hon. Alan D. Wheat

Glencairn, Ltd.

Pittsburgh, PA
Leg. Issues: COM

Outside Counsel/Consultants

Alcalde & Fay
Rep By: Hector Alcalde, Jim Davenport, Vicki L. Iseman, Julie Patterson

Shaw Pittman
Issues: COM
Rep By: Martin R. Leader

Glendale Federal Bank, FSB

Glendale, CA

Outside Counsel/Consultants

Spriggs & Hollingsworth

Glenn-Colusa Irrigation District

Willows, CA
Leg. Issues: BUD, CAW, ENV, NAT

Outside Counsel/Consultants

The Ferguson Group, LLC
Issues: BUD, CAW, ENV, NAT
Rep By: W. Roger Gwinn, Joseph L. Raeder

Glenview, Illinois, Village of

Leg. Issues: DEF

Outside Counsel/Consultants

Bryan Cave LLP
Issues: DEF
Rep By: Hon. Alan J. Dixon

Global Associates

Irvine, CA
Leg. Issues: LBR

Outside Counsel/Consultants

Arent Fox Kintner Plotkin & Kahn, PLLC
Issues: LBR
Rep By: Alison Kutler, Douglas McCormack

Global Climate Coalition

1275 K St. NW
Suite 890
Washington, DC 20005
Tel: (202)682-9161
Fax: (202)638-1043
Registered: LDA
Web: www.globalclimate.org
E-mail: gcc@globalclimate.org

A coalition of trade associations seeking to present the views of U.S. industry in the global climate debate.

Leg. Issues: ENG, ENV

In-house, DC-area Employees

HOLDSWORTH, Eric: Deputy Director
KELLY, Glenn: Exec. Director
MONTESANO, Craig F.: Manager, Government Relations and Public Affairs

Outside Counsel/Consultants

Potomac Communications Group

Global Competitiveness Coalition

Leg. Issues: TAX

Outside Counsel/Consultants

Washington Council Ernst & Young
Issues: TAX
Rep By: Doug Badger, Lauren Darling, John L. Doney, Jayne T. Fitzgerald, LaBrenda Garrett-Nelson, Gary J. Gasper, Bruce A. Gates, Nick Giordano, Cathy Koch, Robert J. Leonard, Richard Meltzer, Phillip D. Moseley, John D. Porter, Robert M. Rozen, Donna Steele-Flynn, Timothy J. Urban

Global Crossing North America, Inc.

1615 L St. NW
Suite 450
Washington, DC 20036
Tel: (202)872-0063
Registered: LDA
Web: www.globalcrossing.com
E-mail: john_morabito@globalcrossing.com

Headquartered in Rochester, NY.

Leg. Issues: TEC

Political Action Committee/s

Global Crossing North America, Inc., PAC
1615 L St. NW
Suite 450
Washington, DC 20036
Tel: (202)872-0063
Contact: Renee Bennett

In-house, DC-area Employees

BENNETT, Renee: Manager, Federal Legislative and Regulatory Affairs
MORABITO, John S.: V. President, Federal Legislative & Regulatory Affairs

Outside Counsel/Consultants

Brownstein Hyatt & Farber, P.C.
Issues: TEC
Rep By: William T. Brack, Thomas H. Hudson, Michael B. Levy

Global Encasement, Inc.

Union City, NJ
Leg. Issues: TRA

Outside Counsel/Consultants

Wheat & Associates, Inc.
Issues: TRA
Rep By: Tom Keefe, Hon. Alan D. Wheat

Global Environment Facility

Washington, DC
Leg. Issues: ENV

Outside Counsel/Consultants

SISCORP
Issues: ENV
Rep By: Donald F. Massey

Global Health Council

1701 K St. NW
Suite 600
Washington, DC 20006-1503
Tel: (202)833-5900
Fax: (202)833-0075
Registered: LDA
Web: www.globalhealth.org
E-mail: ghc@globalhealthcouncil.org

Provides education, training and advocacy for individuals and organizations in the international health care industry. Formerly named Nat'l Council for Internat'l Health.

Leg. Issues: FAM, FOR

In-house, DC-area Employees

KELLY, Kenneth: Grassroots Officer
MILLER, Carol A.: Director, Public Policy
SUMILAS, Michele: Senior Legislative Associate

Global Marine, Inc.

Houston, TX
Leg. Issues: FUE

Outside Counsel/Consultants

Jack Ferguson Associates, Inc.
Issues: FUE
Rep By: Jack Ferguson

Global Mining Initiative

Outside Counsel/Consultants

Winner & Associates

Global Movies Corp.

New York, NY

Outside Counsel/Consultants

Gilbert A. Robinson, Inc.
Rep By: Gilbert A. Robinson

Global One

12490 Sunrise Valley Dr.
Reston, VA 22096
Tel: (703)689-6000
Fax: (703)689-6715
Web: www.global-one.net

A telecommunications partnership formed by Sprint, Deutsche Telecom and France Telecom.

In-house, DC-area Employees

PARKER, Donald: Sr. V. President and General Counsel

Global Waste Recycling, Inc.

Hope, RI
Leg. Issues: ENV, WAS

Outside Counsel/Consultants

The Washington Group
Issues: ENV, WAS
Rep By: Rita M. Lewis, G. John O'Hanlon, John D. Raffaelli, Tonya Saunders

GlobalNet Holdings Corp.

McLean, VA

Outside Counsel/Consultants

John Adams Associates Inc.
Rep By: Esperanza Escobedo

Glossco Free Zone, N.V.

Leg. Issues: TRD

Outside Counsel/Consultants

J. T. Rutherford & Associates
Issues: TRD
Rep By: Donald F. Lavanty

Go! Systems, Inc.

Tampa, FL
Leg. Issues: DEF

Outside Counsel/Consultants

Alford & Associates
Issues: DEF
Rep By: Marty Alford

Go-Mart, Inc.

Gassaway, WV
Leg. Issues: ENV, TAX

Outside Counsel/Consultants

Golin/Harris Internat'l
Issues: ENV, TAX
Rep By: C. Michael Fulton

The Gold and Silver Institute

1112 16th St. NW
Suite 240
Washington, DC 20036
Tel: (202)835-0185
Fax: (202)835-0155
Web: www.goldinstitute.org
E-mail: goldinfo@goldinstitute.org

Represents gold miners, refiners, fabricators and wholesalers of gold and silver.

Leg. Issues: ENV, MON, NAT, TAX

In-house, DC-area Employees

BATEMAN, Paul W.: President

Outside Counsel/Consultants

Klein & Saks, Inc.
Issues: ENV, MON, NAT, TAX
Rep By: Paul W. Bateman, Michael DiRienzo, Douglas Fuller

Winner & Associates

Golden Gate Bridge Highway and Transportation District

San Francisco, CA
Leg. Issues: NAT, ROD, RRR

Outside Counsel/Consultants

Alcalde & Fay
Issues: NAT, ROD, RRR
Rep By: Jason Lee, Paul Schlesinger

Golden Gate Petroleum Internat'l, Ltd.

Concord, CA

Outside Counsel/Consultants

Collier Shannon Scott, PLLC
Rep By: Michael D. Sherman

Golden Peanut Co.

Alpharetta, GA
Leg. Issues: AGR

Outside Counsel/Consultants

Hogan & Hartson L.L.P.
Issues: AGR
Rep By: Humberto R. Pena

Golden Rule Insurance Co.

Indianapolis, IN
Leg. Issues: HCR, INS, MMM

Outside Counsel/Consultants

Capitol Coalitions Inc.

Creative Response Concepts

Jefferson Consulting Group
Issues: HCR, INS, MMM
Rep By: Robert J. Thompson

Golden West Financial Corp.

Oakland, CA

Outside Counsel/Consultants

Covington & Burling
Rep By: Stuart C. Stock, Harris Weinstein

Goldendale Aluminum

Vancouver, WA
Leg. Issues: ENG

Outside Counsel/Consultants

Ball Janik, LLP
Issues: ENG
Rep By: Robert G. Hayes, Irene Ringwood

Goldman, Sachs and Co.

1101 Pennsylvania Ave. NW
Suite 900
Washington, DC 20004
Tel: (202)637-3700
Fax: (202)637-3773
Leg. Issues: BAN, FIN, TAX, TRA

Political Action Committee/s

Goldman Sachs Group Inc. PAC
1101 Pennsylvania Ave. NW
Suite 900
Washington, DC 20004
Contact: Judah C. Sommer
Tel: (202)637-3700
Fax: (202)637-3773

In-house, DC-area Employees

COSTELLO, Ann S.: V. President
DOSWELL, W. Carter: V. President
SOMMER, Judah C.: Managing Director

Outside Counsel/Consultants

The Duberstein Group, Inc.
Rep By: John W. Angus, III, Michael S. Berman, Steven M. Champlin, Kenneth M. Duberstein, Henry M. Gandy, Daniel P. Meyer

John T. O'Rourke Law Offices
Issues: FIN, TAX
Rep By: John T. O'Rourke

PriceWaterhouseCoopers
Issues: TAX
Rep By: Barbara Angus, Kenneth J. Kies

Sullivan & Cromwell
Issues: BAN
Rep By: H. Rodgin Cohen, Michael Wiseman, Samuel R. Woodall, III

Verner, Liipfert, Bernhard, McPherson and Hand, Chartered
Issues: TAX, TRA
Rep By: Denis J. Dwyer, Noelle M. Hawley, Gary J. Klein, Jenifer Martin

Vinson & Elkins L.L.P.
Rep By: Christine L. Vaughn

Golf Course Superintendents Ass'n of America

Lawrence, KS
Leg. Issues: CAW, ENV, LBR, TOU

Outside Counsel/Consultants

Reed, Smith, LLP
Issues: CAW, ENV, LBR, TOU
Rep By: David C. Evans, Phillips S. Peter, C. Stevens Seale

The Good Sam Club

Agoura, CA

Outside Counsel/Consultants

McDermott, Will and Emery
Rep By: Jerry C. Hill

Goodman Manufacturing Co., L.P.

Houston, TX

A gas appliance manufacturer.

Leg. Issues: ENG

Outside Counsel/Consultants

Dunaway & Cross
Rep By: Mac S. Dunaway

Morgan Meguire, LLC
Issues: ENG
Rep By: Scott Lindsay, Kyle G. Michel, Katie Parrott, C. Kyle Simpson, Deborah R. Sliz, Kiel Weaver

B. F. Goodrich Co.

1825 I St. NW
Suite 400
Washington, DC 20006
Tel: (202)429-2060
Fax: (202)331-9501
Registered: LDA

Headquartered in Charlotte, NC.

Leg. Issues: BUD, DEF, ENV, GOV, HCR, IMM, MAN

In-house, DC-area Employees

BJORNSON, Ms. Gerrie: V. President, Government Relations

Outside Counsel/Consultants

The PMA Group
Issues: DEF
Rep By: Sean Fogarty, Kaylene Green, Gregory L. Hansen, Paul J. Magliocchetti

The Potomac Advocates
Rep By: Charles Scalera, Gary L. Sojka

Goodwill Industries Internat'l, Inc.

9200 Rockville Pike
Bethesda, MD 20814-3896
Tel: (301)530-6500
Fax: (301)530-1516
Registered: LDA
Web: www.goodwill.org
E-mail: mgraul@goodwill.org
Leg. Issues: LBR, TAX, WEL

In-house, DC-area Employees

COX, Samuel W.: Exec. V. President and Chief Operating Officer
GRAUL, Michael R.: Director, Governmental Affairs

Goodyear Tire and Rubber Co.

1420 New York Ave. NW
Suite 200
Washington, DC 20005
Tel: (202)682-9250
Fax: (202)682-1533
Registered: LDA

A manufacturer of tires, rubber and chemical products, with a subsidiary operation in oil pipelines headquartered in Akron, OH.

Leg. Issues: AUT, AVI, BUD, CAW, CSP, ENV, GOV, HCR, HOU, LBR, MAN, ROD, TAX, TRA, TRD, TRU, UTI, WAS

In-house, DC-area Employees

BURTSCHI, Mark: Director, Federal and State Affairs
JASINOWSKI, Isabel H.: V. President, Governmental Relations

Outside Counsel/Consultants

Bergner Bockorny Castagnetti and Hawkins
Issues: ROD, TRA

Multinat'l Government Services, Inc.
Issues: AUT, BUD, CSP, ENV, GOV
Rep By: Brooks J. Bowen, Jim J. Tozzi

MultiState Associates

The OB-C Group, LLC
Issues: MAN
Rep By: Thomas Keating, Kim F. McKernan, Charles J. Mellody, Patricia A. Nelson, Lawrence F. O'Brien, III, Linda E. Tarplin

GOPAC

122 C St. NW
Suite 505
Washington, DC 20001
Tel: (202)484-2282
Fax: (202)783-3306
Web: www.gopac.com
E-mail: gopac@websys.com

In-house, DC-area Employees

ADKINS, Amanda: Political Director
DEIER, David: Chairman
MOONIS, Anthony T.: Treasurer

GOPMarketplace.com

Links campaigns and committees with telephone vendors online

Outside Counsel/Consultants

Saliba Action Strategies, LLC
Rep By: Khalil G. "Karl" Saliba

Gordon Investment Corp.

Toronto, CANADA

Outside Counsel/Consultants

Akin, Gump, Strauss, Hauer & Feld, L.L.P.

W. L. Gore & Associates

Newark, DE

A fabric manufacturer.

Leg. Issues: DEF

Outside Counsel/Consultants

Alford & Associates
Issues: DEF
Rep By: Marty Alford

Gospel Rescue Ministries of Washington

Washington, DC
Leg. Issues: HOU

Outside Counsel/Consultants

Russ Reid Co.
Issues: HOU
Rep By: Thomas C. Keller, Mark D. McIntyre

GoTo.com Inc.

Pasadena, CA
Leg. Issues: MIA, SCI

Outside Counsel/Consultants

Garvey, Schubert & Barer
Issues: MIA, SCI
Rep By: Matthew R. Schneider

Government Accountability Project (GAP)

1612 K St. NW
Suite 400
Washington, DC 20006
Tel: (202)408-0034
Fax: (202)408-9855
Web: www.whistleblower.org
E-mail: gap1@erols.com

An activity to assist and advise "whistleblowers" in government.

In-house, DC-area Employees

CLARK, Louis: Exec. Director
DEVINE, Thomas M.: Legal Director

Government Employees Hospital Ass'n

Kansas City, MO
Leg. Issues: BUD, HCR

Outside Counsel/Consultants

Belew Law Firm
Issues: BUD, HCR
Rep By: Joy Carabasi Belew, M. Wendell Belew, Jr.

Government Finance Officers Ass'n, Federal Liaison Center

1750 K St. NW
Suite 350
Washington, DC 20006
Tel: (202)429-2750
Fax: (202)429-2755
Web: www.gfoa.org
E-mail: federalliaison@gfoa.org

Headquartered in Chicago, IL.

In-house, DC-area Employees

GAFFNEY-CAMPANELLA, Susan: Director, Federal Liaison Center

Government Leasing Co.

Colorado Springs, CO

Outside Counsel/Consultants

Oppenheimer Wolff & Donnelly LLP

Government Purchasing Project

P.O. Box 19367
Washington, DC 20036
Tel: (202)387-8030
Fax: (202)234-5176
Web: www.gpp.org
E-mail: gpp@essential.org

Helps government agencies to purchase environmentally-sound, energy-efficient, innovative technologies.

In-house, DC-area Employees

HUTA, Leda: Director

GovWorks.com

Burlingame, CA
Leg. Issues: CPT, GOV, TEC

Outside Counsel/Consultants

Morgan Meguire, LLC
Issues: CPT
Rep By: Kyle G. Michel, C. Kyle Simpson, Kiel Weaver

Patton Boggs, LLP
Issues: GOV, TEC
Rep By: Michael A. Brown

GPA-I, LLC

Memphis, TN
Leg. Issues: DEF

Outside Counsel/Consultants

Eckert Seamans Cherin & Mellott, LLC
Issues: DEF
Rep By: Jeffrey E. Weinstein

GPM Gas Corp.

Houston, TX

Outside Counsel/Consultants

Wright & Talisman, P.C.
Rep By: Gregory Grady

GPU, Inc.

801 Pennsylvania Ave. NW
Suite 310
Washington, DC 20004
Tel: (202)434-8150
Fax: (202)434-8156
Registered: LDA
Web: www.gpu.com
Leg. Issues: TRD

Political Action Committee/s

GPU Power PAC

801 Pennsylvania Ave. NW
Suite 310
Washington, DC 20004
Tel: (202)434-8150
Fax: (202)434-8156
Contact: Joel Brubaker

In-house, DC-area Employees

BRUBAKER, Joel: Federal Affairs Representative
COHEN, John L.: Manager, Government Affairs
LOVENG, Jeff: Manager, Federal Government Affairs
STINGER, Cynthia Mansfield: V. President, Government Affairs

Outside Counsel/Consultants

Jefferson-Waterman Internat'l, LLC
Issues: TRD
Rep By: Ann B. Wrobleski

W. R. Grace & Co.

Columbia, MD
Registered: LDA

A global specialty chemical company manufacturing catalysts and silicas, construction chemicals and materials and container sealants and coatings.

Leg. Issues: CAW, CHM, ENV

Outside Counsel/Consultants

Patton Boggs, LLP
Issues: ENV
Rep By: Parker Brugge, Peter D. Robertson

Charlene A. Sturbitts
Issues: ENV
Rep By: Charlene A. Sturbitts

Grand Bahama Vacations, Inc.

Fort Lauderdale, FL

Outside Counsel/Consultants

Pierre E. Murphy Law Offices

Grand Canyon Air Tour Council

Las Vegas, NV
Leg. Issues: TOU

Outside Counsel/Consultants

Santini, Chartered
Issues: TOU
Rep By: Hon. James D. Santini

Grand Canyon Railway

Outside Counsel/Consultants

Pierre E. Murphy Law Offices

Grand Isle Independent Levee District

Grand Isle, LA

Outside Counsel/Consultants

The Palmer Group
Rep By: Clifford A. Palmer

Grand Rapids Area Transit Authority

Grand Rapids, MI

Outside Counsel/Consultants

Holland & Knight LLP

Grand Traverse Band of Chippewa and Ottawa Indians

Suttons Bay, MI
Leg. Issues: IND

Outside Counsel/Consultants

Dorsey & Whitney LLP
Rep By: Philip Baker-Shenk, David A. Bieging, Virginia W. Boylan, Cindy Darcy, Christopher Karns, Kevin J. Wadzinski

Ducheneaux, Taylor & Associates, Inc.
Issues: IND
Rep By: Franklin D. Ducheneaux

Grand Trunk Corp.

Detroit, MI

Subsidiaries include Grand Trunk Western Railroad Co.; Central Vermont Railway, Inc. and Duluth Winnipeg and Pacific Railway Co.

Leg. Issues: RRR

Outside Counsel/Consultants

Foley & Lardner
Issues: RRR
Rep By: Jodi L. Hanson, Jay N. Varon

Grand Valley State University

Outside Counsel/Consultants

Alcalde & Fay
Rep By: Jennefer A. Hirshberg, Tim Stroud, Christopher L. Turner

Granite Broadcasting Co.

New York, NY
Leg. Issues: COM, TEC

Outside Counsel/Consultants

Akin, Gump, Strauss, Hauer & Feld, L.L.P.
Issues: COM
Rep By: Marlene M. Colucci, Smith W. Davis, Karen E. Goldmeier Green, Joel Jankowsky, Charles W. Johnson, IV

Skadden, Arps, Slate, Meagher & Flom LLP
Issues: TEC

Grant County P.U.D., Washington

Ephrata, WA
Leg. Issues: UTI

Outside Counsel/Consultants

Preston Gates Ellis & Rouvelas Meeds LLP
Issues: UTI
Rep By: Werner W. Brandt, Tim L. Peckinpaugh, W. David Thomas

Grants Pass Irrigation District

Grants Pass, OR
Leg. Issues: BUD

Outside Counsel/Consultants

Ball Janik, LLP
Issues: BUD
Rep By: Michelle E. Giguere, Dan James

Graphic Communications Internat'l Union

1900 L St. NW
Ninth Floor
Washington, DC 20036
Tel: (202)462-1400
Fax: (202)721-0600
Web: www.gciu.org
Leg. Issues: LBR

Political Action Committee/s

Graphic Communications Internat'l Union Political Contributions Committee

1900 L St. NW
Ninth Floor
Washington, DC 20036
Tel: (202)462-1400
Fax: (202)721-0600
Contact: Lawrence Martinez

In-house, DC-area Employees

MARTINEZ, Lawrence: V. President
TEDESCHI, George: President

Graphnet Inc.

Teaneck, NJ

Outside Counsel/Consultants

Young & Jatlow
Rep By: Francis L. Young

Graseby Plc

London, UNITED KINGDOM

Defense, security and electronics equipment manufacturers.

Outside Counsel/Consultants

JGW Internat'l Ltd.
Rep By: John M. O'Neil, Andrew M. Wilson, John G. Wilson

Grasslands Water District

Los Banos, CA
Leg. Issues: ENV, NAT

Outside Counsel/Consultants

Washington Council Ernst & Young
Issues: ENV, NAT
Rep By: Doug Badger, Lauren Darling, John L. Doney, Jayne T. Fitzgerald, LaBrenda Garrett-Nelson, Gary J. Gasper, Bruce A. Gates, Nick Giordano, Cathy Koch, Robert J. Leonard, Richard Meltzer, Phillip D. Moseley, John D. Porter, Robert M. Rozen, Donna Steele-Flynn, Timothy J. Urban

Grassroots Enterprise, Inc.

633 Pennsylvania Ave. NW
Fourth Floor
Washington, DC 20004
Tel: (202)783-5910
Fax: (202)783-5911
Web: www.grassroots.com

Headquartered in San Francisco, CA. A non-partisan technology and services company providing Internet-based communications and mobilization products to political organizations and their constituents.

In-house, DC-area Employees

CHIU, David S.: Co-Founder and V. President, Political Services and Business Development
MCCURRY, Mike: Chairman and Chief Exec. Officer

Outside Counsel/Consultants

Podesta/Mattoon

J. R. Gray & Co.

Thibodeaux, LA

Outside Counsel/Consultants

Cook and Associates
Rep By: Sheila E. Hixson

Gray and Company II

Annapolis, MD

Outside Counsel/Consultants

Bain and Associates, Inc.

Gray Morrison

Metairie, LA
Leg. Issues: DEF

Outside Counsel/Consultants

The Livingston Group, LLC
Issues: DEF
Rep By: Melvin Goodweather, Hon. Robert L. Livingston, Jr., J. Allen Martin, Richard L. Rodgers

Gray Panthers Nat'l Office in Washington

733 15th St. NW Tel: (202)737-6637
Suite 437 Fax: (202)737-1160
Washington, DC 20005
Web: www.graypanthers.org
E-mail: info@graypanthers.org

An education and advocacy organization seeking an affordable national health system protecting people of all ages; the elimination of discrimination on the basis of age, race, sex or disability; economic justice; and peaceful resolution of international conflicts.

In-house, DC-area Employees
FULLER, Tim M.: Exec. Director

Great Britain, Government of

London, UNITED KINGDOM

Outside Counsel/Consultants

Boros & Garofalo
Rep By: Gary B. Garofalo

Great Cities' Universities

New Orleans, LA
Leg. Issues: EDU, URB

Outside Counsel/Consultants

Van Scoyoc Associates, Inc.
Issues: EDU, URB
Rep By: Carolyn Fuller, H. Stewart Van Scoyoc

Great Lakes Chemical Corp.

West Lafayette, IN
Leg. Issues: CSP

Outside Counsel/Consultants

Alcalde & Fay
Rep By: Thomas A. Cortina

Bryan Cave LLP
Rep By: Stanley J. Marcuss

Sparber and Associates
Issues: CSP
Rep By: Peter O'Rourke, Peter G. Sparber

Great Lakes Composites Consortium

West Columbia, SC

Outside Counsel/Consultants

Bettie McCarthy and Associates
Rep By: Elizabeth S. "Bettie" McCarthy

Great Lakes Corporate Resources

Grand Rapids, MI
Leg. Issues: RRR, TRA

Outside Counsel/Consultants

Dykema Gossett PLLC
Issues: RRR, TRA
Rep By: David K. Arthur, Nancy R. Barbour

Great Lakes Dredge & Dock

Oak Brook, IL
Leg. Issues: DIS, ENV, GOV, MAR, NAT, SMB, TRA

Outside Counsel/Consultants

Dawson & Associates, Inc.
Issues: DIS, ENV, GOV, MAR, NAT, SMB, TRA
Rep By: Hon. Tom Bevill, Robert K. Dawson, James Durkay, Lester Edelman, Olga Lansing, Hon. John Myers

Preston Gates Ellis & Rouvelas Meeds LLP
Rep By: Bruce J. Heiman, Rolf Marshall, William N. Myhre

Great Lakes Indian Fish and Wildlife Commission

Odanah, WI

Outside Counsel/Consultants

Sonosky, Chambers, Sachse & Endreson
Rep By: Reid Peyton Chambers

Great Lakes Science Center

Cleveland, OH
Leg. Issues: GOV

Outside Counsel/Consultants

Hill and Knowlton, Inc.
Issues: GOV
Rep By: Reginald E. Gilliam, Jr.

Great Northwest Classic Committee

818 Connecticut Ave. NW Tel: (202)728-1010
Suite 1100 Fax: (202)728-4044
Washington, DC 20006

A political action committee. Below address, phone, and fax is that of the firm Oldaker and Harris, LLP.

In-house, DC-area Employees
HARRIS, William D.: PAC Treasurer

Great Plains Leadership Fund

420 C St. NE Tel: (202)546-1086
Washington, DC 20002

A political action committee.

In-house, DC-area Employees
NELSON, Scott

Great Projects Film Co., Inc.

New York, NY
Leg. Issues: ART, TRA

Outside Counsel/Consultants

Lawler, Metzger & Milkman, LLC
Issues: ART, TRA
Rep By: Sante J. Esposito, Gregory E. Lawler

Great Western Cellular Partnership

New York, NY
Leg. Issues: TEC

Outside Counsel/Consultants

Lent Scrivner & Roth LLC
Issues: TEC
Rep By: Norman F. Lent, III, Hon. Norman F. Lent, Alan J. Roth, Michael S. Scrivner

The Livingston Group, LLC
Issues: TEC
Rep By: Melvin Goodweather, Richard Legendre, Hon. Robert L. Livingston, Jr., J. Allen Martin

O'Connor & Hannan, L.L.P.
Issues: TEC
Rep By: Hon. Larry Pressler, Thomas H. Quinn

Greater Cleveland Regional Transit Authority

Cleveland, OH
Leg. Issues: TRA

Outside Counsel/Consultants

The Advocacy Group
Issues: TRA
Rep By: George A. Ramonas

Greater Columbus Chamber

Columbus, OH
Leg. Issues: LBR

Outside Counsel/Consultants

Wise & Associates
Issues: LBR
Rep By: Dwayne Sattler

Greater Detroit Resource Recovery Authority

Lansing, MI

Outside Counsel/Consultants

Wright & Talisman, P.C.
Rep By: Scott M. DuBoff

Greater El Paso Chamber of Commerce

El Paso, TX
Leg. Issues: ECN

Outside Counsel/Consultants

Public Strategies Washington, Inc.
Issues: ECN
Rep By: Anne Collett, Joseph P. O'Neill

Greater Jamaica Development Corp.

Outside Counsel/Consultants

Holland & Knight LLP
Rep By: Jim J. Marquez, David C. Whitestone

Greater New Orleans Expressway Commission

Metarie, LA
Leg. Issues: BUD, DIS, TRA

Outside Counsel/Consultants

Van Scoyoc Associates, Inc.
Issues: BUD, DIS, TRA
Rep By: Buzz Hawley, Paul Iarrobino, John C. "Jay" Stone, H. Stewart Van Scoyoc

Greater New York Automobile Dealers Ass'n

Whitestone, NY
Leg. Issues: AUT, CAW, CSP, EDU, FUE, SMB, TOR

Outside Counsel/Consultants

M & R Strategic Services
Issues: AUT, CAW, CSP, EDU, FUE, SMB, TOR
Rep By: Sylvia Hacaj

Greater New York Hospital Ass'n

New York, NY Registered: LDA
Leg. Issues: BUD, HCR, MED, MMM, TAX

Outside Counsel/Consultants

Berman Enterprises
Issues: HCR
Rep By: Wayne Berman

Capitol Health Group, LLC
Issues: HCR, MMM
Rep By: Michael D. Bromberg, Shawn Coughlin, Steven Jenning, Layna McConkey Peltier

Chambers Associates Inc.
Issues: MMM, TAX
Rep By: William A. Signer

The Ickes & Enright Group
Issues: BUD, HCR, MED
Rep By: Janice Ann Enright, Harold M. Ickes

Greater Orlando Aviation Authority

Orlando, FL
Leg. Issues: AVI, BUD, TRA

Outside Counsel/Consultants

Jefferson Government Relations, L.L.C.
Issues: AVI, BUD, TRA
Rep By: William A. Roberts, Daniel J. Sheehan

Preston Gates Ellis & Rouvelas Meeds LLP
Rep By: Jonathan Blank

Vierra Associates, Inc.
Issues: TRA
Rep By: Dennis C. Vierra

Greater Providence Chamber of Commerce

Providence, RI
Leg. Issues: ECN

Outside Counsel/Consultants

Capitol City Group
Issues: ECN
Rep By: Gerald T. Harrington, John J. Hogan, Thomas P. Hogan, Christopher P. Vitale

Greater Richmond Partnership

Richmond, VA

Outside Counsel/Consultants

Columbus Public Affairs

Greater Texas Student Loan Corp.

Bryan, TX
Leg. Issues: EDU

Outside Counsel/Consultants

Vinson & Elkins L.L.P.
Issues: EDU
Rep By: Charles L. Almond

Greater Washington Board of Trade

1129 20th St. NW Tel: (202)857-5900
Suite 200 Fax: (202)223-2648
Washington, DC 20036 Registered: LDA
Web: www.bot.org
E-mail: info@bot.org
Leg. Issues: BUD, CPI, DOC, ECN, EDU, LBR, ROD, SCI, TAX, TRA, UTI

Political Action Committee/s

CapNet (Capital Network Political Action Committee)
1129 20th St. NW Tel: (202)857-5936
Suite 200 Fax: (202)223-2648
Washington, DC 20036
Contact: Timothy D. Hugo

Greater Washington Board of Trade Federal Political Action Committee (FedPAC)
1129 20th St. NW Tel: (202)857-5936
Suite 200 Fax: (202)223-2648
Washington, DC 20036
Contact: Timothy D. Hugo

In-house, DC-area Employees
HUGO, Timothy D.: Director, CapNet and Federal Affairs
LECOS, William D.: Senior V. President, Advocacy Group
ROBERTS, Karen: Director, The Potomac Conference
TYDINGS, John R.: President

Greater Washington D.C. Chapter of CLU & ChFC

Outside Counsel/Consultants

Bostrom Corp.
Rep By: Claire Shanley

Greater Washington Educational Telecommunications Ass'n

2775 S. Quincy St.
Arlington, VA 22206
Tel: (703)998-2600
Fax: (703)998-3401
Web: www.weta.org
E-mail: info@weta.org

In-house, DC-area Employees

ROCKEFELLER, Sharon: President and Chief Exec. Officer

Greater Washington Soc. of Ass'n Executives

1426 21st St. NW
Suite 200
Washington, DC 20036
Tel: (202)429-9370
Fax: (202)833-1129
Web: www.gwsae.org
Leg. Issues: TAX

In-house, DC-area Employees

BARRETT, Gina: Director, Public Affairs
SARFATI, CAE, Susan: President and Chief Exec. Officer
SCHULTZ, Jane: V. President, Communications

Outside Counsel/Consultants

Albertine Enterprises, Inc.
Issues: TAX
Rep By: James J. Albertine

Howe, Anderson & Steyer, P.C.
Rep By: James E. Anderson

Green County Health Care, Inc.

Snow Hill, NC
Leg. Issues: BUD, HCR

Outside Counsel/Consultants

The MWW Group
Issues: BUD, HCR
Rep By: Todd S. Berkoff, Dana P. Bostic, Christine A. Pellerin, Jonathan B. Slade

Green Door

Washington, DC
Leg. Issues: BUD, HCR

Outside Counsel/Consultants

Metcalf Federal Relations
Issues: BUD, HCR
Rep By: Anne Metcalf

Green Mountain Power Corp.

Burlington, VT

Outside Counsel/Consultants

Thelen Reid & Priest LLP
Rep By: James K. Mitchell

Green Thumb, Inc.

Arlington, VA
Leg. Issues: LBR

Outside Counsel/Consultants

Moss McGee Bradley & Foley
Issues: LBR
Rep By: Leander J. Foley, III

Greenbrier Companies

Lake Oswego, OR
A manufacturer of railroad equipment.

Leg. Issues: ENV, MAR, RRR, TAX

Outside Counsel/Consultants

Ball Janik, LLP
Issues: ENV, MAR, RRR, TAX
Rep By: James A. Beall, M. Victoria Cram, Hal D. Hiemstra

Greenman Technologies Inc.

Lynnfield, MA
Leg. Issues: ENV, WAS

Outside Counsel/Consultants

Colling Swift & Hynes
Issues: ENV, WAS
Rep By: Terese Colling, Pablo Collins, Robert J. Hynes, Jr.

Greenpeace, U.S.A.

702 H. Street NW
Suite 300
Washington, DC 20001
Tel: (202)462-1177
Fax: (202)462-4507
Web: www.greenpeace.org

Environmental protection organization concerned with chemical and nuclear waste, endangered species of marine mammals, nuclear weapons testing, Antarctica, acid rain, ocean incineration of hazardous wastes, and outercontinental shelf oil exploration.

In-house, DC-area Employees

HIND, Richard: Legislative Director, Toxics Campaign
PASSACANTANDO, John: Exec. Director
RICHARDSON, Bill: Manager, Office Facilities

GreenPoint Bank

Flushing, NY
Leg. Issues: BAN

Outside Counsel/Consultants

Muldoon, Murphy & Faucette, LLP
Issues: BAN
Rep By: Joseph A. Muldoon, Sr.

Greenpoint Manufacturing and Design Center (GMDC)

Brooklyn, NY
Leg. Issues: ECN

Outside Counsel/Consultants

Moss McGee Bradley & Foley
Issues: ECN
Rep By: Leander J. Foley, III

Greenport, New York, Village Electric Department of

Leg. Issues: ENG, GOV, UTI

Outside Counsel/Consultants

Duncan, Weinberg, Genzer & Pembroke, P.C.
Issues: ENG, GOV, UTI
Rep By: Richmond F. Allan, Thomas L. Rudebusch

Greens Creek Mining Co.

Juneau, AK

Outside Counsel/Consultants

Robertson, Monagle & Eastaugh
Rep By: Steven W. Silver

Greenville-Spartanburg Airport District

Greer, SC

Outside Counsel/Consultants

Shaw Pittman
Rep By: J. E. Murdock, III

Greenwich Capital Markets, Inc.

1101 30th St. NW
Suite 500
Washington, DC 20007
Tel: (202)625-4880
Fax: (202)625-4881

A trading, finance, and investment banking firm specializing in fixed income markets. Headquartered in Greenwich, CT.

In-house, DC-area Employees

CARPENTER, Pilar Maria: Policy Analyst, Legal and External Affairs
SILVERMAN, Ed: Senior V. President

Outside Counsel/Consultants

Arnold & Porter
Rep By: Martha L. Cochran

Greeting Card Ass'n

1030 15th St. NW
Suite 870
Washington, DC 20005
Tel: (202)939-1778
Web: www.greetingcard.org
E-mail: gca@rgminc.com

In-house, DC-area Employees

MCDERMOTT, Marianne: Exec. V. President

Outside Counsel/Consultants

The Direct Impact Co.

The Kellen Company
Rep By: Marianne McDermott

Grenada Lake Medical Center

Grenada, MS

Outside Counsel/Consultants

Golin/Harris Internat'l
Rep By: C. Michael Fulton

Grenada, Government of the Republic of

St. George's, GRENADA

Outside Counsel/Consultants

Washington World Group, Ltd.
Rep By: Edward J. von Kloberg, III

GREX, Inc.

Lake Charles, LA
Leg. Issues: HCR, IMM

Outside Counsel/Consultants

Diane McRee Associates
Issues: HCR, IMM
Rep By: Diane B. McRee

Greyfab (Bangladesh) Ltd.

Dhaka, BANGLADESH

Outside Counsel/Consultants

Rode & Qualey
Rep By: R. Brian Burke

Greyhound Lines

Dallas, TX
Leg. Issues: TAX, TRA

Outside Counsel/Consultants

Davis & Harman LLP
Issues: TAX
Rep By: Randolf H. Hardock

Theodore C. Knappen, P.C.
Issues: TRA
Rep By: Theodore C. Knappen

Greystar Resources, Ltd.

Vancouver, CANADA
Leg. Issues: FOR, NAT

Outside Counsel/Consultants

Jamison and Sullivan, Inc.
Issues: FOR, NAT
Rep By: Delos Cy Jamison, Jay R. Sullivan

Gridley, California, City of/Northern California Power Agency

Leg. Issues: BUD, ENG

Outside Counsel/Consultants

The Ferguson Group, LLC
Issues: BUD, ENG
Rep By: W. Roger Gwinn

Grocery Manufacturers of America

1010 Wisconsin Ave. NW
Ninth Floor
Washington, DC 20007
Tel: (202)337-9400
Fax: (202)337-4508
Registered: LDA
Web: www.gmabrands.com
E-mail: fedaffairs@gmabrands.com

The Grocery Manufacturers of America speaks for food and consumer product manufacturers at the state, federal, and international levels on legislative and regulatory issues. The association also leads efforts to increase productivity, efficiency and growth in the food, beverage and consumer products industry.

Leg. Issues: ADV, BUD, CAW, DIS, ENV, FCC, FOO, TAX, TRD, TRU

Political Action Committee/s

Grocery Manufacturers of America PAC (GMA-PAC)
1010 Wisconsin Ave. NW
Ninth Floor
Washington, DC 20007
Tel: (202)337-9400
Fax: (202)337-4508
Contact: Susan M. Stout

In-house, DC-area Employees

ALLEN, Lisa: Director, Member Communications
CLEARY, Peter: Manager, Public Policy Communications
FERENC, Sue: V. President, Science and Regulatory Affairs
FLANAGAN, Troy: Manager, State Affairs
FOGARTY, Sarah: Director, International Trade
FRAZIER, Adrienne: Representative, Government Affairs
GRABOWSKI, Gene: V. President, Communications
JOHNSON, David: Representative, Government Affairs
KATIC, Lisa: Director, Scientific and Nutrition Policy
KOCHENDERFER, Karil L.: Director, International Trade and Environmental Affairs
KUNDE, Gerald "Chip": V. President, State Affairs
MASTEN, Mia: Manager, Federal Affairs
MOLPUS, C. Manly: President and Chief Exec. Officer
PYLAK, Artur: Assistant, State Affairs and Internat'l Trade
ROBERTSON, Doug: Representative, State Affairs
SOPHOS, Mary C.: Senior V. President and Chief Government Affairs Officer
STOUT, Susan M.: V. President, Federal Affairs

Outside Counsel/Consultants

BSMG Worldwide
Rep By: Lance I. Morgan

Collier Shannon Scott, PLLC
Rep By: William C. MacLeod

Covington & Burling
Issues: FOO
Rep By: Peter Barton Hutt

Davidson & Company, Inc.
Issues: ADV, TAX
Rep By: James H. Davidson, Richard E. May, Stanley Sokul

Hogan & Hartson L.L.P.
Issues: FOO
Rep By: Jeanne S. Archibald, Lance D. Bultena, Raymond S. Calamaro, C. Michael Gilliland, Nancy Granese, William Michael House, Gary Jay Kushner, Jeffrey W. Munk, Richard S. Silverman

Keller and Heckman LLP

Kessler & Associates Business Services, Inc.
Issues: FCC, FOO, TAX, TRU
Rep By: Michael L. Bartlett, Simon Gros, Richard S. Kessler, James C. Musser, Harry Sporidis

Kirkpatrick & Lockhart LLP
Rep By: George W. Koch

Patton Boggs, LLP
Rep By: Stuart M. Pape

Policy Directions, Inc.
Issues: BUD, FOO
Rep By: Kathleen "Kay" Holcombe, Steve Kopperud, Frankie L. Trull

Valis Associates
Issues: BUD, FOO, TRD
Rep By: Hon. Dan Schaefer, Hon. Richard T. Schulze, Todd Tolson, Wayne H. Valis

Groom Law Group, Chartered

1701 Pennsylvania Ave. NW
Suite 1200
Washington, DC 20006
Tel: (202)857-0620
Fax: (202)659-4503
Registered: LDA
Web: www.groom.com
E-mail: info@groom.com
Leg. Issues: INS, TAX

In-house, DC-area Employees

BREYFOGLE, Jon W.: Partner
FITZGERALD, Thomas F.: Member
FORD, Gary M.: Managing Principal
GROOM, Theodore R.: Partner
LEONHARDT, Jill L.: Consultant
MAZAWEY, Louis T.
THRASHER, Michael A.

Outside Counsel/Consultants

Ernst & Young LLP
Issues: INS, TAX
Rep By: Tom S. Nuebig

Ground Water Protection Council

Oklahoma City, OK
Leg. Issues: BUD, CAW, ENV

Outside Counsel/Consultants

Murray, Scheer, Montgomery, Tapia & O'Donnell
Issues: BUD, CAW, ENV
Rep By: Michael G. Keegan, John H. Montgomery

Group Health Cooperative

Seattle, WA
Leg. Issues: HCR, MMM

Outside Counsel/Consultants

The Petrizzo Group, Inc.
Issues: HCR, MMM
Rep By: Kara Kennedy, Thomas "T.J." Petrizzo

Group Health, Inc.

New York, NY
Registered: LDA
Leg. Issues: BUD, GOV, HCR, INS, LBR, MMM, TAX

Outside Counsel/Consultants

Washington Council Ernst & Young
Issues: BUD, GOV, HCR, INS, LBR, MMM, TAX
Rep By: Doug Badger, Lauren Darling, John L. Doney, Jayne T. Fitzgerald, LaBrenda Garrett-Nelson, Gary J. Gasper, Bruce A. Gates, Nick Giordano, Robert J. Leonard, Richard Meltzer, Phillip D. Moseley, John D. Porter, Robert M. Rozen, Donna Steele-Flynn, Timothy J. Urban

The Group of 20

London, UNITED KINGDOM
Leg. Issues: FIN

Outside Counsel/Consultants

Sullivan & Cromwell
Issues: FIN
Rep By: Kenneth M. Raisler, Rebecca J. Simmons, Michael Wiseman

Group of 30

1990 M St. NW
Suite 450
Washington, DC 20036
Tel: (202)331-2472
Fax: (202)785-9423
Web: www.group30.org
E-mail: info@group30.org

A think tank focusing on international financial issues.

In-house, DC-area Employees

WALSH, John G.: Exec. Director

Grumman Olson

Sturgis, MI
Leg. Issues: GOV, TRA

Outside Counsel/Consultants

Alvarado & Gerken
Issues: GOV, TRA
Rep By: Susan E. Alvarado

Grupo "J" S.A.

Bethesda, MD
Leg. Issues: APP, TRD

Outside Counsel/Consultants

Sandler, Travis & Rosenberg, P.A.
Issues: APP, TRD
Rep By: Ron Sorini

Grupo Carrousel (Mexico)

MEXICO
Leg. Issues: FIN, TRD

Outside Counsel/Consultants

Janus-Merritt Strategies, L.L.C.
Issues: FIN, TRD
Rep By: Mark J. Robertson

Grupo Cydsa

Monterrey, MEXICO

Outside Counsel/Consultants

Porter, Wright, Morris & Arthur, LLP

Grupo Empresarial Maya

Monterrey, MEXICO
Leg. Issues: ENV, ROD, TRD

Outside Counsel/Consultants

Janus-Merritt Strategies, L.L.C.
Issues: ENV, ROD, TRD
Rep By: Mark J. Robertson

Grupo Financiero Banorte

Monterrey, MEXICO
Leg. Issues: FOR

Outside Counsel/Consultants

Janus-Merritt Strategies, L.L.C.
Issues: FOR
Rep By: Scott P. Hoffman, Mark J. Robertson, J. Daniel Walsh

Grupo Industrial Alfa, S.A.

Monterrey, MEXICO

Outside Counsel/Consultants

Benchmarks, Inc.
Rep By: Thomas J. Scanlon

Grupo Maseca

Monterrey, MEXICO
Leg. Issues: FOR, TRD

Outside Counsel/Consultants

Janus-Merritt Strategies, L.L.C.
Issues: FOR, TRD
Rep By: Mark J. Robertson, J. Daniel Walsh

Grupo Televisa, S.A.

Outside Counsel/Consultants

Leventhal, Senter & Lerman, P.L.L.C.

GSE Systems, Inc.

Columbia, MD
Leg. Issues: BUD

Outside Counsel/Consultants

John G. Campbell, Inc.

The Grizzle Company
Issues: BUD
Rep By: Richard A. Cantor, Charles L. Grizzle

GTE Mobilnet

Atlanta, GA

Outside Counsel/Consultants

Alston & Bird LLP
Rep By: Peter Kontio

GTE Service Corp.

Washington, DC
Leg. Issues: TEC

Outside Counsel/Consultants

Sunrise Research Corp.
Issues: TEC
Rep By: Hon. Bob Packwood

GTECH Corp.

Washington, DC
Leg. Issues: BUD, GAM

Outside Counsel/Consultants

Akin, Gump, Strauss, Hauer & Feld, L.L.P.

BKSH & Associates
Issues: BUD, GAM

Cartwright & Riley
Issues: GAM
Rep By: Russell S. Cartwright

Chesapeake Enterprises, Inc.
Issues: GAM
Rep By: Scott W. Reed

Davis Manafort, Inc.
Issues: GAM
Rep By: Richard H. Davis

GTS

Virginia Beach, VA

Outside Counsel/Consultants

The Potomac Advocates
Rep By: Charles Scalera, Gary L. Sojka

Guam AFGE

Leg. Issues: DEF, GOV

Outside Counsel/Consultants

PACE-CAPSTONE
Issues: DEF, GOV
Rep By: David S. Germroth, James W. Wise

Guam Bankers Ass'n

Agana, GU

Outside Counsel/Consultants

Carlsmith Ball Wichman Case & Ichiki

Guam Internat'l Airport Authority

Tamuning, GU
Leg. Issues: AER, AVI, TRA

Outside Counsel/Consultants

Wayne Arny & Assoc.
Issues: AER, AVI, TRA
Rep By: Wayne Arny

R. J. Hudson Associates

PACE-CAPSTONE
Issues: TRA
Rep By: David S. Germroth, James W. Wise

Guam Legislature

Leg. Issues: BUD, NAT

Outside Counsel/Consultants

Pacific Islands Washington Office
Issues: BUD, NAT
Rep By: Fred Radewagen

Government of Guam

Outside Counsel/Consultants

R. J. Hudson Associates

Guam, Territory of

Agana, GU
Leg. Issues: GOV, TRU

Outside Counsel/Consultants

Berliner, Candon & Jimison
Issues: GOV, TRU
Rep By: Roger A. Berliner, Mary Eva Candon

Guam, Washington Office of the Governor

1225 19th St. NW
Suite 800
Washington, DC 20036
Tel: (202)785-4826
Fax: (202)822-0109
E-mail: govguam1@bcjlaw.com

Leg. Issues: AVI, COM, DEF, DOC, EDU, ENG, ENV, FUE, GOV, HCR, IMM, MAR, NAT, TEC, TOU, TRA, TRD, TRU

In-house, DC-area Employees

CANDON, Mary Eva: Counsel
WHITT, John: Federal Affairs Specialist

Outside Counsel/Consultants

PACE-CAPSTONE
Issues: DEF, GOV, TRA
Rep By: David S. Germroth, James W. Wise

Pacific Islands Washington Office
Issues: EDU
Rep By: Fred Radewagen

Guaranty Bank, SSB

Brown Deer, WI
Leg. Issues: BAN, BNK, BUD, FIN, HOU, RES, TAX

Outside Counsel/Consultants

Hohlt & Associates
Issues: BAN, BNK, BUD, FIN, HOU, RES, TAX
Rep By: Richard F. Hohlt

Guardian Angel Holdings, Inc.

San Francisco, CA
Leg. Issues: ALC, BUD

Outside Counsel/Consultants

Arent Fox Kintner Plotkin & Kahn, PLLC
Issues: ALC, BUD
Rep By: Alison Kutler, Michael T. McNamara, Todd Weiss

Guardian Industries Corp.

Auburn Hills, MI
Leg. Issues: TRD

Outside Counsel/Consultants

Fleischman and Walsh, L.L.P.
Rep By: Louis H. Dupart

Hogan & Hartson L.L.P.
Issues: TRD
Rep By: Nancy Granese, Warren H. Maruyama

The Wexler Group
Issues: TRD
Rep By: R. D. Folsom, Hon. Robert S. Walker, Anne Wexler

Guardian Life Insurance Co. of America

New York, NY
Leg. Issues: BAN, BUD, TAX, TRD

Outside Counsel/Consultants

Burton V. Wides, P.C.
Issues: BAN, BUD, TAX, TRD

Guardian Marine Internat'l LLC

Edmonds, WA
Leg. Issues: BUD, FOR

Outside Counsel/Consultants

Ball Janik, LLP
Issues: BUD, FOR
Rep By: James A. Beall, Michelle E. Giguere

Guardsman Elevator Co.

Outside Counsel/Consultants

Columbus Public Affairs

Guatemala, Government of the Republic of

Guatemala City, GUATEMALA

Outside Counsel/Consultants

Foley, Hoag & Eliot LLP
Rep By: Gare A. Smith

Guatemalan Development Foundation (FUNDESA)

Tegucigalpa, GUATEMALA

Outside Counsel/Consultants

McDermott, Will and Emery
Rep By: Jerry C. Hill

Washington World Group, Ltd.
Rep By: Edward J. von Kloberg, III

Guaynabo, Puerto Rico, City of

Guaynabo, PR
Leg. Issues: DEF, RES, TRA, URB

Outside Counsel/Consultants

Capital Consultants Corp.
Issues: DEF, RES
Rep By: Michael David Kaiser

Oldaker and Harris, LLP
Issues: TRA, URB
Rep By: William D. Harris, William C. Oldaker

Guest and Associates

Front Royal, VA
Registered: LDA

Outside Counsel/Consultants

Peter S. Barash Associates, Inc.
Rep By: Peter S. Barash

Guidant Corp.

1310 G St. NW
Suite 770
Washington, DC 20005
Tel: (202)508-0800
Fax: (202)508-0818
Registered: LDA

A developer, manufacturer and marketer of medical devices. Headquartered in Indianapolis, IN.

Leg. Issues: BUD, CSP, FIN, HCR, IMM, LBR, MED, MMM, SCI, TAX, TRD

In-house, DC-area Employees

CANTOR-WEINBERG, Julie: Manager, Government Affairs
GOSIER, Ann M.: V. President, Government Affairs

Outside Counsel/Consultants

Baker & Daniels
Rep By: Mark W. Weller

Clark & Weinstock, Inc.
Issues: HCR, MED, MMM
Rep By: Ed Kutler, Hon. John Vincent "Vin" Weber

Crowell & Moring LLP
Issues: CSP
Rep By: Mark A. Behrens, Victor E. Schwartz

Guide Dog Users, Inc.

1155 15th St. NW
Suite 1004
Washington, DC 20005
Tel: (202)467-5081
Fax: (202)467-5085

An affiliate of the American Council of the Blind.

In-house, DC-area Employees

GRUBB, Debbie: President

Guild Associates

Dublin, OH
Leg. Issues: DEF

Outside Counsel/Consultants

The PMA Group
Issues: DEF
Rep By: Daniel Cunningham, Daniel E. Fleming, Kaylene Green, Paul J. Magliocchetti

Guilford Mills, Inc.

1200 G St. NW
Suite 800
Washington, DC 20005
Tel: (202)434-8779
Fax: (202)638-5127
Registered: LDA
Web: www.guilfordmills.com

Leg. Issues: APP

In-house, DC-area Employees

MARTINDALE, III, Walter Reed: Washington Liaison, Governmental Affairs Director

Guinea, Government of the Republic of

Conakry, GUINEA

Outside Counsel/Consultants

Washington World Group, Ltd.
Rep By: Edward J. von Kloberg, III

White & Case LLP

Guinea, Secretary General of the Presidency of the Republic of

Conakry, GUINEA
Leg. Issues: AGR, AVI, BAN, BUD, CDT, COM, CPI, DEF, ECN, EDU, ENG, ENV, FIN, FOO, FOR, FUE, GOV, HCR, MAR, NAT, ROD, RRR, SCI, TEC, TOU, TRA, TRD, TRU, URB, UTI

Outside Counsel/Consultants

Strategic Horizons Advisors, L.L.C.
Issues: AGR, AVI, BAN, BUD, CDT, COM, CPI, DEF, ECN, EDU, ENG, ENV, FIN, FOO, FOR, FUE, GOV, HCR, MAR, NAT, ROD, RRR, SCI, TEC, TOU, TRA, TRD, TRU, URB, UTI
Rep By: Marvin A. McGraw

Gulf Citrus Growers Ass'n

LaBelle, FL

Outside Counsel/Consultants

Barnes, Richardson and Colburn
Rep By: Matthew T. McGrath

Gulf Coast Portland Cement Co.

Houston, TX
Leg. Issues: ENV, ROD, TRD

Outside Counsel/Consultants

Janus-Merritt Strategies, L.L.C.
Issues: ENV, ROD, TRD
Rep By: Mark J. Robertson

Gulf Coast Waste Disposal Authority

Houston, TX
Leg. Issues: CAW, ENV

Outside Counsel/Consultants

John Freshman Associates, Inc.
Issues: CAW, ENV
Rep By: John D. Freshman, Lawrence P. Kast, Catherine B. Kiefer

Gulf State Steel Inc.

Gadsden, AL
Leg. Issues: ENV, GOV

Outside Counsel/Consultants

Baker & McKenzie
Issues: ENV, GOV
Rep By: Susan G. Braden

Gulfstream Aerospace Corp.

1000 Wilson Blvd.
Suite 2701
Arlington, VA 22209
Tel: (703)276-9500
Fax: (703)276-9504
Web: www.gulfstreamaerospace.com

Washington office of an aircraft manufacturer. Includes representatives responsible for military marketing, government relations, and Washington liaison.

Leg. Issues: AVI, DEF, TRA

In-house, DC-area Employees

NEWMAN, Helen L.: Senior V. President, Government Operations
SHAW, Edward W.: Director, Washington Operations

Outside Counsel/Consultants

The Conaway Group LLC
Issues: DEF
Rep By: Lt. Gen. John B. Conaway, USAF (Ret.)

Gulfstream TLC, Inc.

Palm Beach, FL
Registered: LDA

Outside Counsel/Consultants

Martin L. Hall
Rep By: Martin L. Hall

Gun Owners of America

8001 Forbes Pl.
Suite 102
Springfield, VA 22151
Tel: (703)321-8585
Fax: (703)321-8408
Registered: LDA
Web: www.gunowners.org

A lobbying group opposing the registration of firearms and other forms of gun control. Founded in 1976, it has a dues-paying membership of about 100,000 and has a budget of about 1 million dollars.

Leg. Issues: BUD, FIR, GOV, LAW

In-house, DC-area Employees

FIELDS, Craig: Director, Electronic Communications
HAMMOND, Mike: Counsel
PRATT, Eric M.: Director, Communications
PRATT, Lawrence D.: Exec. Director
TRAMONTANO, Jerry: Legislative Assistant
VELLECO, John: Federal Affairs
ZOMETSKY, Joseph: Federal Affairs

Guyana Airways 2000

Georgetown, GUYANA

Outside Counsel/Consultants

Pierre E. Murphy Law Offices

Guyana, Government of the Co-operative Republic of

Georgetown, GUYANA
Leg. Issues: FOR

Outside Counsel/Consultants

Foley, Hoag & Eliot LLP
Issues: FOR
Rep By: Paul S. Reichler, Gare A. Smith

Gyphon Networks

Outside Counsel/Consultants

Edelman Public Relations Worldwide
Rep By: Chuck Taylor

Gypsum Ass'n

810 First St. NE
Suite 510
Washington, DC 20002
Web: www.gypsum.org
E-mail: info@gypsum.org
Tel: (202)289-5440
Fax: (202)289-3707

In-house, DC-area Employees

BEEMER, Jennifer: Director, Government Regulatory Affairs
WALKER, Jerry A.: Exec. Director

H & R Executive Towers

New York, NY

Outside Counsel/Consultants

Swidler Berlin Shereff Friedman, LLP
Rep By: Harold A. Levy, Kenneth G. Lore

H.A.H. of Wisconsin L.P.

Miami, FL

A race track operator.

Leg. Issues: GAM

Outside Counsel/Consultants

Patton Boggs, LLP
Issues: GAM
Rep By: Philip A. Bangert, Thomas Hale Boggs, Jr., Katharine R. Boyce, Brian C. Lopina, James A. Reeder

H.M.S. Rose Foundation

Bridgeport, CT

Outside Counsel/Consultants

Hayward Internat'l

Haarmann & Reimer Corp.

Springfield, NJ
Leg. Issues: BUD, PHA, TRA, TRD

Outside Counsel/Consultants

Smith Dawson & Andrews, Inc.
Issues: BUD, PHA, TRA, TRD
Rep By: Sherri Powar, James P. Smith

Habas Group

Istanbul, TURKEY
Leg. Issues: TRD

Outside Counsel/Consultants

Dickstein Shapiro Morin & Oshinsky LLP
Issues: TRD
Rep By: Alev Kaymak, Francis J. Sailer, L. Andrew Zausner

Law Offices of David L. Simon
Issues: TRD
Rep By: David L. Simon

Habitat for Humanity Internat'l

1010 Vermont Ave. NW
Suite 900
Washington, DC 20005
Tel: (202)628-9171
Fax: (202)628-9169

HFHI's Washington Office was opened in 1991 to represent HFHI with its public, private and non-profit partners in the nation's capital.

Leg. Issues: DIS, HOU

In-house, DC-area Employees

RANDEL, Amy: Director, Government Relations
STEENSLAND, Ann M.: Director, External Relations

Hackensack University Medical Center Foundation

Hackensack, NJ
Leg. Issues: HCR

Outside Counsel/Consultants

Bond & Company, Inc.
Issues: HCR
Rep By: Richard N. Bond, Eileen Kean

Hadassah Medical Relief Fund

New York, NY
Leg. Issues: FOR

Outside Counsel/Consultants

The MWW Group
Issues: FOR
Rep By: Elizabeth A. Iadarola, Jonathan B. Slade

Hadassah, The Women's Zionist Organization of America

5100 Wisconsin Ave. NW
Washington, DC 20016
Tel: (202)363-4600
Fax: (202)363-4651
Registered: LDA
Web: www.hadassah.org
E-mail: washingtonoffice@hadassah.org

Headquartered in New York, NY.

Leg. Issues: BUD, CIV, FAM, FOR, GOV, HCR, INS, LBR, MED, TOB

In-house, DC-area Employees

GILSON, Marla: Director

Outside Counsel/Consultants

The MWW Group
Issues: FOR
Rep By: Jonathan B. Slade

HAECO, Inc.

Hillsborough, OH
Leg. Issues: DEF

Outside Counsel/Consultants

Peter J. Rose
Issues: DEF
Rep By: Peter J. Rose

Hager Hinge Co.

St. Louis, MO

Outside Counsel/Consultants

Ball Janik, LLP
Rep By: Robert G. Hayes, Irene Ringwood

Hager Sharp Inc.

1090 Vermont Ave. NW
Third Floor
Washington, DC 20005
Tel: (202)842-3600
Fax: (202)842-4032
Leg. Issues: ENV, FOR, LBR

In-house, DC-area Employees

CURTIS, Garry: Senior V. President
DEMENT, Polly: Senior Communications Counselor
HAGER, Susan: Chair and Chief Exec. Officer
HALL, Darcy: Account Assistant

Outside Counsel/Consultants

Millian Byers Associates, LLC
Issues: ENV, FOR, LBR
Rep By: H. James Byers

Hagerstown, Maryland, Municipal Electric Light Plant of

Hagerstown, MD
Leg. Issues: ENG, GOV, UTI

Outside Counsel/Consultants

Duncan, Weinberg, Genzer & Pembroke, P.C.
Issues: ENG, GOV, UTI
Rep By: Janice L. Lower

Hagglunds Moelv AS

Moelv, NORWAY
Leg. Issues: DEF

Outside Counsel/Consultants

American Defense Internat'l, Inc.
Issues: DEF
Rep By: Michael Herson, Van D. Hipp, Jr., Dave Wilberding

Haiti, Chamber of Commerce of the Republic of

Port au Prince, HAITI

Outside Counsel/Consultants

Williams & Connolly
Rep By: Gregory B. Craig

Haiti, Embassy of the Republic of

2311 Massachusettes Ave. NW
Washington, DC 20008
Tel: (202)332-4090
Fax: (202)745-7215

Outside Counsel/Consultants

McKinney & McDowell Associates

Burton V. Wides, P.C.

Haiti, Government of the Republic of

Port au Prince, HAITI

Outside Counsel/Consultants

Sandler & Travis Trade Advisory Services, Inc.
Rep By: Robert P. Schaffer

Burton V. Wides, P.C.

Haiti, Office of the President of the Republic of

Port au Prince, HAITI
Leg. Issues: FOR

Outside Counsel/Consultants

Ross-Robinson & Associates
Issues: FOR
Rep By: Monica Duncan, Hazel Ross-Robinson

Haiti, Provisional Government of the Republic of

Port au Prince, HAITI

Outside Counsel/Consultants

Washington World Group, Ltd.
Rep By: Edward J. von Kloberg, III

Halliburton/Brown & Root

1150 18th St. NW
Suite 200
Washington, DC 20036
Tel: (202)223-0820
Fax: (202)223-2385
Registered: LDA

Specializes in energy services, construction, engineering, and government services. Headquartered in Dallas, TX.

Leg. Issues: BAN, BUD, COM, CSP, DEF, ENG, ENV, FIN, FOR, GOV, HCR, IMM, LBR, ROD, TRD

Political Action Committee/s

Brownbuilder's PAC (BPAC)
1150 18th St. NW
Suite 200
Washington, DC 20036
Contact: Donald A. Deline
Tel: (202)223-0820
Fax: (202)223-2385

Halliburton PAC (HALPAC)
1150 18th St. NW
Suite 200
Washington, DC 20036
Contact: Barbara Jones
Tel: (202)223-0820
Fax: (202)223-2385

In-house, DC-area Employees

DELINE, Donald A.: Director, Government Affairs
DOMINY, Charles E.: V. President, Government Affairs
JONES, Barbara: Director, Government Affairs

Hallmark Cards, Inc.

Kansas City, MO

A greeting card company.

Leg. Issues: HCR, LAW, LBR, POS, TAX

Outside Counsel/Consultants

Downey McGrath Group, Inc.
Issues: LAW
Rep By: Michael R. Wessel

Evans & Black, Inc.
Issues: HCR, LBR, POS, TAX
Rep By: Judy A. Black, Rae Forker Evans, Rafe Morrissey

Hooper Owen & Winburn
Issues: TAX
Rep By: Lindsay D. Hooper

St. Maxens & Company
Rep By: Thomas F. St. Maxens, II

Halogenated Solvents Industry Alliance

2001 L St. NW
Suite 506A
Washington, DC 20036-4919
Web: www.hsia.org
E-mail: info@hsia
Tel: (202)775-0232
Fax: (202)833-0381

Represents the interests of users and producers of chlorinated solvents to promote the continued safe use of these products and to promote the use of sound science in assessing the potential health effects of chlorinated solvents.

Leg. Issues: CHM

In-house, DC-area Employees

RISOTTO, Stephen P.: Exec. Director

Outside Counsel/Consultants

Patton Boggs, LLP
Issues: CHM
Rep By: W. Caffey Norman, III

Halon Alternatives Research Corp.

2111 Wilson Blvd.
8th Floor
Arlington, VA 22201
Web: www.harc.org
E-mail: harc96@aol.com
Tel: (703)524-6636
Fax: (703)243-2874

A trade association representing users, producers and distributors of halons interested in finding replacement agents.

In-house, DC-area Employees

CORTINA, Thomas A.

Outside Counsel/Consultants

Alcalde & Fay
Rep By: Thomas A. Cortina

HALT-An Organization of Americans for Legal Reform

1612 K St. NW
Suite 510
Washington, DC 20006
Web: www.halt.org
E-mail: halt@halt.org
Tel: (202)887-8255
Fax: (202)887-9699

HALT is dedicated to helping all Americans handle their legal affairs simply, affordably and equitably.

Leg. Issues: CIV, CSP, GOV

In-house, DC-area Employees

RUDY, Theresa Meeham: Director of Programs
TURNER, James C.: Exec. Director

The Hamilton Group

Baltimore, MD
Leg. Issues: DEF

Outside Counsel/Consultants

Verner, Liipfert, Bernhard, McPherson and Hand, Chartered
Issues: DEF
Rep By: Lawrence E. Levinson, Harry C. McPherson

Hamilton Sundstrand

1401 I St. NW
Suite 600
Washington, DC 20005
E-mail: bullarde@corpdc.utc.com
Tel: (202)336-7468
Fax: (202)336-7518
Registered: LDA

Formerly Sundstrand Corp. Designs, manufactures and markets proprietary-technology components and subsystems for industrial and aerospace markets. Headquartered in Windsor Locks, CT.

Leg. Issues: AER, AVI, BUD, DEF, ENV, TRD

In-house, DC-area Employees

BULLARD, Edward M.: Director, Washington Operations

Hampshire College

Amherst, MA
Leg. Issues: ECN, EDU

Outside Counsel/Consultants

Cassidy & Associates, Inc.
Issues: ECN, EDU
Rep By: Gerald Felix Warburg

Hampton University

Hampton, VA
Leg. Issues: DEF, ECN, EDU, SCI

Outside Counsel/Consultants

Cassidy & Associates, Inc.
Issues: DEF, ECN, EDU, SCI
Rep By: Gregory M. Gill, Carl Franklin Godfrey, Jr., Judith M. Jacobson

Hand Tools Institute

Tarrytown, NY

Outside Counsel/Consultants

Frederick L. Ikenson, P.C.
Rep By: Frederick L. Ikenson

London and Satagaj, Attorneys-at-Law
Rep By: John S. Satagaj

Handgun Control, Inc.

1225 I St. NW
Suite 1100
Washington, DC 20005
Web: www.handguncontrol.org
Tel: (202)898-0792
Fax: (202)371-9615
Registered: LDA

A national membership, non-profit citizen lobby working to enact sensible gun laws, reform the gun industry, and educate the public about the dangers of guns.

Leg. Issues: FIR

Political Action Committee/s

Handgun Control Voter Education Fund
1225 I St. NW
Suite 1100
Washington, DC 20005
Tel: (202)898-0792
Fax: (202)371-9615

Handgun Control, Inc. Political Action Committee
1225 I St. NW
Suite 1100
Washington, DC 20005
Tel: (202)898-0792
Fax: (202)371-9615

In-house, DC-area Employees

ADLER, Wendy: Director, Law Enforcement Relations
BARNES, Hon. Michael D.: President
BRADY, Sarah: Chair
DALY, Brendan: Director, Communications
HENIGAN, Dennis: General Counsel and Director, Legal Action Project
ORZA, Tony: Director, Government Relations and Legislative Counsel

Outside Counsel/Consultants

Craver, Mathews, Smith and Co.

Hankin, Persson & Darnell

Sarasota, FL
Leg. Issues: AVI

Outside Counsel/Consultants

Patton Boggs, LLP
Issues: AVI
Rep By: Carolina L. Mederos

Hannibal Industries

Los Angeles, CA
Leg. Issues: TRA

Outside Counsel/Consultants

Schagrin Associates
Issues: TRA
Rep By: Tamara L. Browne, Roger B. Schagrin

Harbor Branch Institute

Ft. Pierce, FL
Leg. Issues: EDU, MAR, MED, SCI

Outside Counsel/Consultants

The Advocacy Group
Issues: EDU, MED, SCI
Rep By: Robert E. Mills

SISCORP
Issues: MAR
Rep By: Donald F. Massey

Harbor Philadelphia Center City Office, Ltd.

New York, NY
Leg. Issues: BAN, RES

Outside Counsel/Consultants

GPC Internat'l
Issues: BAN, RES
Rep By: Peter G. Halpin, Bruce A. Morrison

Harborlink, LLC

Hampton, VA

Outside Counsel/Consultants

The Lonington Group
Rep By: Alan G. Gray

Harbour Group Industries, Inc.

St. Louis, MO
Leg. Issues: FIN

Outside Counsel/Consultants

Dickstein Shapiro Morin & Oshinsky LLP
Issues: FIN
Rep By: Henry C. Cashen, II, Elizabeth B. Haywood, Peter J. Kadzik, Graham "Rusty" Mathews, L. Andrew Zausner

Harcourt General

Outside Counsel/Consultants

The Legislative Strategies Group, LLC
Rep By: Martin B. Gold, Larry E. Smith

Harcourt Inc.

Chestnut Hill, MA
Leg. Issues: EDU, MIA

Outside Counsel/Consultants

Hale and Dorr LLP
Issues: EDU, MIA
Rep By: Jay P. Urwitz

Hardwood Plywood and Veneer Ass'n

P.O. Box 2789
Reston, VA 20195-0789
Web: www.hpva.org
E-mail: hpva@hpva.org
Tel: (703)435-2900
Fax: (703)435-2537
Leg. Issues: TOR

In-house, DC-area Employees

ALT, Kurt: Director, Environmental Policy and Veneer Member Services
ALTMAN, E. T.: President

Outside Counsel/Consultants

Venable
Issues: TOR
Rep By: Brock R. Landry

Hardy County Industrial Ass'n

Moorefield, WV
Leg. Issues: GOV

Outside Counsel/Consultants

Cottone and Huggins Group
Issues: GOV
Rep By: James B. Huggins

John Harland Co.

Atlanta, GA
Leg. Issues: BAN, EDU

Outside Counsel/Consultants

Golin/Harris Internat'l
Issues: BAN, EDU
Rep By: C. Michael Fulton, Carol C. Mitchell

Harlingen Area Chamber of Commerce

Harlingen, TX
Leg. Issues: TRA

Outside Counsel/Consultants

Ann Eppard Associates, Ltd.
Issues: TRA
Rep By: Julie Chlopecki, Ann Eppard

Harmon-Motive

Martinsville, IN

Outside Counsel/Consultants

Dave Evans Associates
Rep By: Hon. Dave Evans

Harnischfeger Industries, Inc.

Milwaukee, WI
Leg. Issues: CAW, NAT, TAX

Outside Counsel/Consultants

Stephens Law Offices
Issues: CAW, NAT, TAX
Rep By: J. Gordon "Skip" Stephens, Jr.

Harquehala Irrigation District

Phoenix, AZ
Leg. Issues: NAT

Outside Counsel/Consultants

McClure, Gerard & Neuenschwander, Inc.
Issues: NAT
Rep By: Steven G. Barringer, Joseph T. Findaro, Matthew Iandoli, Nils W. Johnson, Hon. James A. McClure, Tod O. Neuenschwander

Harrah's Entertainment, Inc.

Las Vegas, NV

A casino/hotel/resort management company.

Leg. Issues: GAM

Outside Counsel/Consultants

U.S. Strategies Corp.
Issues: GAM
Rep By: Steven E. Carey, Nance Guenther-Peterson, Heidi Hanson, Brad Traverse

Harris Chemical Group, Inc.

New York, NY

Outside Counsel/Consultants

Winthrop, Stimson, Putnam & Roberts

Harris Corp.

1201 E. Abingdon Dr.
Suite 300
Alexandria, VA 22314
Web: www.harris.com
Tel: (703)739-1946
Fax: (703)739-2775
Registered: LDA

Harris Corporation is an international communications equipment company focused on providing product, system, and service solutions. The company provides a range of products and services for commercial and government communications markets. Headquartered in Melbourne, FL.

Leg. Issues: AVI, COM, DEF, ENV, GOV, HCR, TEC, TRD

In-house, DC-area Employees

HALL, Joseph M.: Director, Congressional Relations
RIKSEN, Michael R.: Director, Government Relations
ROSAY, Debra L.: Manager, Congressional Relations
WHITE, Jr., Raymon M.: V. President, Washington Operations

Outside Counsel/Consultants

Verner, Liipfert, Bernhard, McPherson and Hand, Chartered
Issues: COM
Rep By: Lawrence R. Sidman

G.E. Harris Harmon

Blue Springs, MO
Leg. Issues: ROD, TRA

Outside Counsel/Consultants

Verner, Liipfert, Bernhard, McPherson and Hand, Chartered
Issues: ROD, TRA
Rep By: Suzanne D. Cartwright, Denis J. Dwyer, Jenifer Martin

Harris, Beach & Wilcox

Rochester, NY
Leg. Issues: BUD, TRA

Outside Counsel/Consultants

Akin, Gump, Strauss, Hauer & Feld, L.L.P.
Issues: BUD, TRA
Rep By: Susan H. Lent

Frederic R. Harris, Inc.

New York, NY
Leg. Issues: ROD, TRA

Outside Counsel/Consultants

Akin, Gump, Strauss, Hauer & Feld, L.L.P.
Issues: ROD, TRA
Rep By: Sylvia A. de Leon, Elizabeth Hyman, Susan H. Lent

Harris, Texas, Metropolitan Transit Authority of

Houston, TX
Leg. Issues: BUD, TRA

Outside Counsel/Consultants

Akin, Gump, Strauss, Hauer & Feld, L.L.P.
Issues: BUD, TRA
Rep By: Sylvia A. de Leon, Susan H. Lent, Barney J. Skladany, Jr.

Baker Botts, L.L.P.
Rep By: James A. Baker, IV

HARSCO Corp.

Camp Hill, PA
Leg. Issues: DEF

Outside Counsel/Consultants

Cottone and Huggins Group
Issues: DEF
Rep By: James B. Huggins

The Hartford

1101 Connecticut Ave. NW
Suite 401
Washington, DC 20036
Tel: (202)296-7513
Fax: (202)296-7514
Registered: LDA
Web: www.thehartford.com
Leg. Issues: CSP, ENV, FIN, HCR, INS, RET, TAX, TOR, TRA

In-house, DC-area Employees

DETMER, Kyra Lee: Director, Federal Affairs
THOMPSON, Eric: V. President, Federal Affairs

Outside Counsel/Consultants

Caplin & Drysdale, Chartered
Issues: INS, TAX
Rep By: Seth Green, H. David Rosenbloom

Hooper Owen & Winburn
Issues: INS, TAX
Rep By: Steve Glaze, David Rudd, John P. Winburn

Harvard Radio Broadcasting Co.

Cambridge, MA
Leg. Issues: TEC

Outside Counsel/Consultants

Miller & Van Eaton, P.L.L.C.
Issues: TEC
Rep By: William Malone

Harvard University

Cambridge, MA
Leg. Issues: TAX

Outside Counsel/Consultants

Baker & Hostetler LLP
Issues: TAX
Rep By: Steven A. Lotterer, William H. Schweitzer

Harvard University Washington Office

499 S. Capitol St. SW
Suite 405
Washington, DC 20003
Tel: (202)863-1292
Fax: (202)863-1104
Registered: LDA
Leg. Issues: BUD, SCI

In-house, DC-area Employees

CASEY, Kevin: Director, Federal/State Government Relations

Outside Counsel/Consultants

O'Neill, Athy & Casey, P.C.
Issues: BUD, SCI
Rep By: Andrew Athy, Jr., Martha L. Casey

HarvardNet, Inc.

Boston, MA
Leg. Issues: TEC

Outside Counsel/Consultants

Janus-Merritt Strategies, L.L.C.
Issues: TEC
Rep By: Scott P. Hoffman, Mark J. Robertson, J. Daniel Walsh

Harza Engineering Co.

1060 Leigh Mill Rd.
Great Falls, VA 22066
Tel: (703)759-6746
Fax: (703)438-0743

In-house, DC-area Employees

HESSE, Richard J.: Manager, Washington Office and Senior Consultant

Outside Counsel/Consultants

Porter, Wright, Morris & Arthur, LLP
Rep By: E. Jay Finkel, Judd L. Kessler

Hatco Corp.

Fords, NJ

Outside Counsel/Consultants

Williams & Connolly
Rep By: Paul Mogin

Hattiesburg, Mississippi, City of

Hattiesburg, MS
Leg. Issues: ECN, ROD, RRR, TOU, TRA, URB

Outside Counsel/Consultants

Johnson Co.
Issues: ECN, ROD, RRR, TOU, TRA, URB
Rep By: James H. Johnson

Haven Federal Savings and Loan Ass'n

Winter Haven, FL

Outside Counsel/Consultants

Elias, Matz, Tiernan and Herrick

Hawaii Economic Development Alliance, State of

Honolulu, HI
Leg. Issues: ECN

Outside Counsel/Consultants

Collins & Company, Inc.
Issues: ECN
Rep By: James D. Bond, Richard L. Collins, Thomas A. Hooper, Shay D. Stautz

Hawaii Food & Beverage Ass'n

Outside Counsel/Consultants

R. J. Hudson Associates

Hawaii, Department of Business and Economic Development of the State of

Honolulu, HI
Leg. Issues: ECN, ENG, GOV

Outside Counsel/Consultants

Duncan, Weinberg, Genzer & Pembroke, P.C.
Issues: ECN, ENG, GOV
Rep By: Jeffrey C. Genzer

Hawaii, State of

Honolulu, HI
Leg. Issues: AVI, EDU, LBR, TAX

Outside Counsel/Consultants

Cassidy & Associates, Inc.
Issues: EDU, LBR, TAX
Rep By: Gregory M. Gill, Henry K. Giugni, Maureen Walsh

Shaw Pittman
Issues: AVI
Rep By: Robert E. Cohn, J. E. Murdock, III, Thomas J. Spulak

Hawaiian Airlines

Honolulu, HI
Leg. Issues: AVI, BUD, TAX

Outside Counsel/Consultants

Dow, Lohnes & Albertson, PLLC
Issues: AVI, BUD, TAX
Rep By: Jonathan B. Hill

Hawaiian Commercial and Sugar Company

1301 Pennsylvania Ave. NW
Suite 401
Washington, DC 20004
Tel: (202)785-4020
Fax: (202)659-8581
Registered: LDA

Works to educate memebers of Congress and staff regarding sugar farming and U.S. policies and regulations affecting sugar farmers.

Leg. Issues: AGR, TRD

In-house, DC-area Employees

FREEMYER, Windsor: Washington Representative
SELL, Alisa M.: Washington Representative
YANCEY, Dalton: Washington Representative

Hawaiian Electric Co.

Honolulu, HI
Leg. Issues: ENG, UTI

Outside Counsel/Consultants

Edwin T. C. Ing
Rep By: Edwin T. C. Ing

Van Ness Feldman, P.C.
Issues: ENG, UTI
Rep By: Thomas C. Roberts

Hawaiian Moving and Forwarding Ass'n

Outside Counsel/Consultants

R. J. Hudson Associates

Haymarket Center

Chicago, IL

Outside Counsel/Consultants

Beacon Consulting Group, Inc.
Rep By: Gordon P. MacDougall, Julie Debolt Moeller, Lisa A. Stewart

Hazardous Materials Advisory Council

1101 Vermont Ave. NW
Suite 301
Washington, DC 20005-3521
Web: www.hmac.org
E-mail: hmacinfo@hmac.org
Tel: (202)289-4550
Fax: (202)289-4074

An international, non-profit, membership organization representing shippers of varying size, carriers of all modes, container manufacturers and reconditioners, as well as emergency response and clean-up companies. Promotes safety in domestic and international transportation and handling of hazardous materials, substances and waste.

In-house, DC-area Employees

ROBERTS, Alan: President

Hazelden Foundation

Center City, MN
Leg. Issues: ALC, BUD, HCR, INS, TAX

Outside Counsel/Consultants

VSAdc.com
Issues: ALC, BUD, HCR, INS, TAX
Rep By: Carol A. McDaid

HBCU/PAC

Washington, DC

Outside Counsel/Consultants

Dean Blakey & Moskowitz
Rep By: William A. Blakey

HCA Healthcare Corp.

Dallas, TX
Leg. Issues: HCR

Outside Counsel/Consultants

Arter & Hadden
Rep By: Daniel L. Cohen, Hon. Thomas G. Loeffler, Jon W. Plebani

Burson-Marsteller

The Smith-Free Group
Issues: HCR
Rep By: James C. Free, W. Timothy Locke, Alicia W. Smith, James E. Smith

HCR-Manor Care, Inc.

7361 Calhoun Place
Suite 300
Rockville, MD 20855
Tel: (240)453-8500
Registered: LDA

Headquartered in Toledo, OH.

Leg. Issues: BUD, GOV, HCR, MMM

Political Action Committee/s

Manor Healthcare Federal Political Action Committee

7361 Calhoun Place
Suite 300
Rockville, MD 20855
Tel: (240)453-8500

In-house, DC-area Employees

MCDERMOTT, Ann: V. President, Government Relations

Outside Counsel/Consultants

Bond & Company, Inc.
Rep By: Richard N. Bond

GRQ, Inc.
Issues: GOV, HCR, MMM
Rep By: Patricia Booth, Phillip Porte

Patton Boggs, LLP
Issues: BUD, MMM
Rep By: John F. Jonas, Martha M. Kendrick, Elizabeth E. Ring, JoAnn V. Willis

Health and Hospital Corp. of Marion County

Indianapolis, IN
Leg. Issues: HCR, MMM

Outside Counsel/Consultants

Hogan & Hartson L.L.P.
Issues: HCR, MMM
Rep By: C. Michael Gilliland, Jeffrey W. Munk, Ann Morgan Vickery

Health Benefits Coalition

1150 17th St. NW
Suite 601
Washington, DC 20036
Tel: (202)293-7474
Fax: (202)293-8811

Address and phone is that of the firm of Washington Council Ernst & Young.

In-house, DC-area Employees

GATES, Bruce A.: Exec. Director

Outside Counsel/Consultants

Washington Council Ernst & Young
Rep By: Bruce A. Gates

Health Data Exchange Corp.

Malvern, PA

Outside Counsel/Consultants

Albertine Enterprises, Inc.
Rep By: James J. Albertine

Health Industry Distributors Ass'n

66 Canal Center Plaza
Suite 520
Alexandria, VA 22314-1591
Tel: (703)549-4432
Fax: (703)549-6495
Registered: LDA
Web: www.hidanetwork.org

Represents distributors of medical and health products and home care providers to hospitals, nursing homes, physicians, other health care sites, and for patients in the home.

Leg. Issues: HCR, MMM

Political Action Committee/s

Health Industry Distributors Ass'n Political Action Committee

66 Canal Center Plaza
Suite 520
Alexandria, VA 22314-1591
Tel: (703)549-4432
Fax: (703)549-6495

In-house, DC-area Employees

HILLA, Elizabeth B.: Exec. Director, HIDA Educational Foundation
MANN, Wendy: V. President, Communications and Editor-in-Chief
ROWAN, Matt: President and C.E.O.

Health Industry Group Purchasing Ass'n

Washington, DC
Web: www.higpa.org
Leg. Issues: GOV, MMM

Outside Counsel/Consultants

Robert Betz Associates, Inc.
Issues: GOV, MMM
Rep By: Robert B. Betz

Health Industry Initiative

Members include SmithKline Beecham Laboratories, Baxter International, the American Hospital Association, Johnson & Johnson and the Federation of American Healthcare Systems.

Outside Counsel/Consultants

Ober, Kaler, Grimes & Shriver
Rep By: Thomas K. Hyatt

Health Insurance Ass'n of America

1201 F St. NW
Suite 500
Washington, DC 20004
Tel: (202)824-1600
Fax: (202)824-1651
Registered: LDA
Web: www.hiaa.org
Leg. Issues: ALC, BAN, BNK, BUD, CSP, HCR, INS, LBR, MED, MMM, PHA, RET, SMB, TAX, TOR

Political Action Committee/s

Health Insurance Political Action Committee

1201 F St. NW
Suite 500
Washington, DC 20004
Tel: (202)824-1600
Fax: (202)824-1651

In-house, DC-area Employees

CASHDOLLAR, Winthrop
COORSH, Richard: V. President, Communications
CORONEL, Susan
DODSON, Melissa: Federal Legislative Director
FYFFE, Kathleen: Federal Regulatory Director
HARRINGTON, Kathleen: Senior V. President, Federal Affairs
JOHNSTON, Matthew: Assistant Federal Legislative Director/Political Affairs Director
KAHN, III, Charles N. "Chip": President
LANZA, Susanne: Director, Managed Care Policy
MARTIN, Josephine C.: Senior V. President for Public Affairs
MILLER, Marianne: Director, Federal Regulatory Affairs Progra
RONAN, Patrick: Legislative Director, Federal Affairs
VAN GELDER, Susan I.: Corporate Secretary
WELLER, William C.: Senior Actuary, Policy Development and Research
WILDSMITH, IV, Thomas F.: Policy Research Actuary, Policy Development and Research
YOUNG, M.D., Donald A.: Chief Operating Officer and Medical Director

Outside Counsel/Consultants

Davis & Harman LLP
Issues: TAX
Rep By: Randolf H. Hardock, Craig R. Springfield

The Direct Impact Co.

Epstein Becker & Green, P.C.

Fierce and Isakowitz
Issues: HCR
Rep By: Kathryn Braden, Samantha Cook, Donald L. Fierce, Mark W. Isakowitz, Diane Moery

Goddard Claussen

Public Opinion Strategies
Rep By: William D. McInturff

Quinn Gillespie & Associates

Stevens Reed Curcio & Co.

Health Management Systems, Inc.

New York, NY

Outside Counsel/Consultants

The Washington Group

Health Partners

Leg. Issues: HCR

Outside Counsel/Consultants

Greenberg Traurig, LLP
Issues: HCR
Rep By: Peter M. Gillon, James F. Miller

Health Physics Soc.

McLean, VA
Web: www.hps.org
E-mail: hps@burkince.com

A professional society of health physics and radiation scientists.

Leg. Issues: BUD, ENG, ENV, FOO, VET, WAS

Outside Counsel/Consultants

Burk & Associates
Rep By: Richard J. Burk, Jr.

Capitol Associates, Inc.
Issues: BUD, ENG, ENV, FOO, VET, WAS
Rep By: Liz Gemski

Health Policy Strategies

Washington, DC
Leg. Issues: HCR

Outside Counsel/Consultants

Grisso Consulting
Issues: HCR
Rep By: Michael E. Grisso

Health Promotion Institute

409 Third St. SW
Suite 200
Washington, DC 20024-6682
Tel: (202)479-6687

A constituent unit of the Nat'l Council on the Aging.

In-house, DC-area Employees

MCCLENDON, Carol

Health Quest

Poughkeepsie, NY
Leg. Issues: BUD, MED, MMM

Outside Counsel/Consultants

Capitol Associates, Inc.
Issues: MMM
Rep By: William A. Finerfrock, Debra M. Hardy Havens

DeBrunner and Associates, Inc.
Issues: BUD, MED
Rep By: Charles L. DeBrunner, Wendy W. Herr, Ellen J. Kugler, Kathryn D. Rooney

Health Resource Publishing Co.

Leg. Issues: MIA

Outside Counsel/Consultants

Olsson, Frank and Weeda, P.C.
Issues: MIA
Rep By: John W. Bode, Richard L. Frank, Susan P. Grymes, Karen Reis Harned, Stephen L. Lacey, Marshall L. Matz, Tyson Redpath, Ryan W. Stroschein

Health Risk Management Group, Inc.

Washington, DC
Leg. Issues: CSP, HCR

Outside Counsel/Consultants

Navarro Legislative & Regulatory Affairs
Issues: CSP, HCR
Rep By: Bruce C. Navarro

Health Services of Kansas and Mid Missouri

New York, NY
Leg. Issues: FAM, HCR

Outside Counsel/Consultants

Arnold & Porter
Issues: FAM, HCR
Rep By: James F. Fitzpatrick, Jeffrey W. Richman

Healthcare Ass'n of New York State

Albany, NY
Registered: LDA
Leg. Issues: HCR, MMM

Outside Counsel/Consultants

Downey McGrath Group, Inc.
Issues: HCR, MMM
Rep By: Hon. Thomas J. Downey, Jr., John Peter Olinger

Wilson, Elser, Moskowitz, Edelman & Dicker LLP
Issues: HCR

Healthcare Billing and Management Ass'n

Laguna Beach, CA
Web: www.hbma.com
E-mail: info@hbma.com
Leg. Issues: MMM

Outside Counsel/Consultants

Capitol Associates, Inc.
Issues: MMM
Rep By: William A. Finerfrock, Debra M. Hardy Havens, Julie Shroyer, Matthew Williams

Healthcare Compliance Packaging Council

7799 Leesburg Pike
Suite 900N
Falls Church, VA 22043
Registered: LDA
Web: www.unitdose.org
Leg. Issues: PHA

Outside Counsel/Consultants

Mayberry & Associates LLC
Issues: PHA
Rep By: Peter G. Mayberry

Healthcare Convention and Exhibitors Ass'n

1101 15th St. NW
Suite 202
Washington, DC 20005
Tel: (202)785-3232
Fax: (202)223-9741

In-house, DC-area Employees

CRISTOL, Richard E.: Washington Representative

Outside Counsel/Consultants

The Kellen Company
Rep By: Richard E. Cristol

Healthcare Council of the Nat'l Capital Area

8201 Corporate Dr.
Suite 410
Landover, MD 20785-2229
Tel: (301)731-4701
Fax: (301)731-8286
Web: www.healthcare-council.org
E-mail: hcss@erols.com

A healthcare provider association.

In-house, DC-area Employees

BURNS, Joseph P.: President and Chief Exec. Officer

Healthcare Distribution Management Ass'n

1275 K St. NW
Suite 1212
Washington, DC 20005
Tel: (703)787-0000
Fax: (202)312-5005
Registered: LDA
Web: www.HealthcareDistribution.org

Formerly Nat'l Wholesale Druggists' Ass'n. Headquartered in Reston, VA.

Leg. Issues: PHA

Political Action Committee/s

Healthcare Distribution Management Ass'n PAC
1275 K St. NW
Suite 1212
Washington, DC 20005
Tel: (703)787-0000
Fax: (202)312-5005
Contact: Robert J. Falb

In-house, DC-area Employees

BICKEL, Lori A.: Associate Director, Regulatory Affairs
DEAN, Roberta: Associate Director, Congressional Affairs
FALB, Robert J.: Director, Congressional Affairs
GOYETTE, Diane P.: Director, Regulatory Affairs
HABER, Sherry J.: V. President, Government and Professional Affairs
HILL, Joseph M.: Associate Director, State Legislative Affairs
KOSAR, David A.: Director, State Legislative Affairs
MILLONIG, Marsha K.: V. President, Research and Information
STRECK, Ronald J.: President and Chief Exec. Officer

Outside Counsel/Consultants

The OB-C Group, LLC
Issues: PHA
Rep By: Thomas Keating, Kim F. McKernan, Charles J. Mellody, Patricia A. Nelson, Lawrence F. O'Brien, III, Linda E. Tarplin

Healthcare Financial Management Ass'n

1301 Connecticut Ave. NW
Suite 300
Washington, DC 20036
Tel: (202)296-2920
Fax: (202)223-9771
Registered: LDA
Web: www.hfma.org
E-mail: knownet@hfma.org

An association headquartered in Westchester, IL representing almost 35,000 members with a professional interest in healthcare financial management, including chief financial officers of healthcare institutions, accountants and patient accounts managers.

Leg. Issues: HCR

In-house, DC-area Employees

GUNDLING, Rick: Technical Director
PROPP, Elizabeth: V. President

Healthcare Financing Study Group

Washington, DC
Leg. Issues: BUD, HCR, HOU, MMM, TAX

Outside Counsel/Consultants

Krooth & Altman
Issues: HCR
Rep By: David A. Barsky, Patrick J. Clancy, E. Joseph Knoll, Donald F. Libretta, Michael E. Mazer, William S. Tennant, John E. Vihstadt

O'Connor & Hannan, L.L.P.
Issues: BUD, HCR, HOU, MMM, TAX
Rep By: Hon. Thomas J. Corcoran, Christina W. Fleps, Thomas H. Quinn

Healthcare Leadership Council

900 17th St. NW
Suite 600
Washington, DC 20006
Tel: (202)452-8700
Fax: (202)296-9561
Registered: LDA
Web: www.hlc.org

A coalition of health care providers -- physicians, health insurers, hospitals and pharmaceutical and medical technology companies -- established in 1990 to promote incremental, private-sector reforms of the healthcare system.

Leg. Issues: HCR, MMM, PHA

In-house, DC-area Employees

EDWARDS, James R.: Communications Manager
FREEMAN, Michael: V. President, Communications
GREALY, Mary R.: President
MERTZ, Alan B.: Exec. V. President
ROLFE, Katherine Elizabeth: Policy Director
SPITZNAGEL, DeDe: V. President, Policy
WOLGEMUTH, Kristin: Director, Government Affairs/Grassroots

Outside Counsel/Consultants

Capitol Health Group, LLC
Issues: HCR, MMM, PHA
Rep By: Michael D. Bromberg, Shawn Coughlin, Steven Jenning, Layna McConkey Peltier

The Legislative Strategies Group, LLC

Verner, Liipfert, Bernhard, McPherson and Hand, Chartered
Rep By: Vicki E. Hart

Healthcare Recoveries Inc.

Louisville, KY

Outside Counsel/Consultants

King & Spalding
Rep By: Allison Kassir, William C. Talmadge

Healtheon/Web MD

Atlanta, GA
Leg. Issues: CPI, DEF, HCR, MMM, TEC

Outside Counsel/Consultants

Greenberg Traurig, LLP
Issues: HCR
Rep By: Diane J. Blagman, Howard J. Cohen, Gregory McDonald, James F. Miller, Ronald L. Platt, Nancy E. Taylor, Shana Tesler, Timothy P. Trysla, Howard A. Vine

Hannett & Associates
Issues: CPI, DEF, HCR, MMM, TEC
Rep By: Frederick J. Hannett

Patrick M. Murphy & Associates
Issues: TEC

HealthFEST of Maryland, Inc.

Rockville, MD

Outside Counsel/Consultants

Armstrong Associates, Inc.
Rep By: Jan M. Armstrong

Healthnow

Buffalo, NY

Outside Counsel/Consultants

American Continental Group, Inc.
Rep By: David A. Metzner, Shawn H. Smeallie

Healthsouth Corp.

Leg. Issues: HCR

Outside Counsel/Consultants

U.S. Strategies Corp.
Issues: HCR
Rep By: Gary F. Capistrant, Steven E. Carey, Nance Guenther-Peterson, Heidi Hanson, Brad Traverse

Heard Communications

Somerset, NJ

Outside Counsel/Consultants

Monfort & Wolfe

Heard Goggan Blair & Williams

Austin, TX

A law firm.

Leg. Issues: BNK, GOV

Outside Counsel/Consultants

Akin, Gump, Strauss, Hauer & Feld, L.L.P.
Issues: BNK, GOV
Rep By: Sean G. D'Arcy, Karen E. Goldmeier Green

Hearing Industries Ass'n

Alexandria, VA
Web: www.hearing.org
E-mail: crogin@clarionmr.com

Represents the manufacturers of hearing aids and component parts.

Leg. Issues: GOV, MED

Outside Counsel/Consultants

CLARION Management Resources, Inc.
Rep By: Carole M. Rogin, David E. Woodbury

Hale and Dorr LLP
Issues: GOV, MED
Rep By: Mark Heller

The Hearst Corp.

New York, NY
Leg. Issues: COM, CPT, LBR, MIA, TAX

Outside Counsel/Consultants

Baker & Hostetler LLP

Davidson & Company, Inc.
Issues: LBR, TAX
Rep By: James H. Davidson, Richard E. May, Stanley Sokul

Drinker Biddle & Reath LLP
Issues: COM, CPT, MIA
Rep By: Jennifer L. Blum

Hearst-Argyle Television, Inc.

New York, NY
Leg. Issues: COM, MIA

Outside Counsel/Consultants

Wiley, Rein & Fielding
Issues: COM, MIA
Rep By: Richard Bodorff, Susan C. Buck, Mimi W. Dawson, Robert L. Pettit

Hearth Products Ass'n

1601 N. Kent St.
Suite 1001
Arlington, VA 22209
Tel: (703)522-0086
Fax: (703)522-0548
Web: www.hearthassociation.org
E-mail: hpamail@hearthassociation.org

North American trade association for the hearth industry.

In-house, DC-area Employees

KEITHLEY, Carter E.: President and Chief Exec. Officer

Heartland Communications & Management Inc.

Arlington, VA
Leg. Issues: COM, TEC

Outside Counsel/Consultants

Washington Consulting Alliance, Inc.
Issues: COM, TEC
Rep By: Thomas L. Burgum, Shaun Wiggins

Heavy Vehicle Maintenance Group

1818 N St. NW
Suite 700
Washington, DC 20036
Tel: (202)331-7050
Fax: (202)331-9306
Web: www.hvmg.com
E-mail: mjc@cfppllaw.com

A political education association formed by ten trade associations in the heavy duty motor vehicle aftermarket. Keeps the associations and their members advised on legislative and regulatory issues in the industry.

Leg. Issues: AUT, CAW, ROD, TAX, TRA, TRU

In-house, DC-area Employees

CONLON, Michael J.: President

Outside Counsel/Consultants

Conlon, Frantz, Phelan & Pires
Issues: AUT, CAW, TRU
Rep By: Michael J. Conlon

Hebrew Academy for Special Children

Brooklyn, NY

Provides programs and services to developmentally disabled children and adults.

Leg. Issues: EDU

Outside Counsel/Consultants

Russ Reid Co.
Issues: EDU
Rep By: Mark D. McIntyre

Hebrew Immigrant Aid Soc.

Leg. Issues: BUD, IMM

Outside Counsel/Consultants

Arnold H. Leibowitz
Issues: BUD, IMM
Rep By: Arnold H. Leibowitz

Hebrew University of Jerusalem

Jerusalem, ISRAEL
Leg. Issues: SCI

Outside Counsel/Consultants

System Planning Corp.
Issues: SCI
Rep By: Theresa Purcell

Hecla Mining Co.

Coeur d'Alene, ID
Leg. Issues: BUD, ENV

Outside Counsel/Consultants

McClure, Gerard & Neuenschwander, Inc.
Issues: BUD, ENV
Rep By: Steven G. Barringer, Joseph T. Findaro, Matthew Iandoli, Nils W. Johnson, Hon. James A. McClure, Tod O. Neuenschwander

Wilson & Wilson
Rep By: Robert Dale Wilson

Heerema Marine Contractors Nederland B.V.

Leiden, NETHERLANDS
Leg. Issues: MAR

Outside Counsel/Consultants

Dyer Ellis & Joseph, P.C.
Issues: MAR
Rep By: James S. W. Drewry, Thomas M. Dyer, James B. Ellis, II, Natalia W. Geren, Jeanne Marie Grasso, Duncan C. Smith, III, Jennifer M. Southwick, Jonathan K. Waldron

Hees Interests, Ltd.

Round Rock, TX
Leg. Issues: FUE, NAT

Outside Counsel/Consultants

Grisso Consulting
Issues: FUE, NAT
Rep By: Michael E. Grisso

Heil Trucks

Chattanooga, TN

Outside Counsel/Consultants

Interface Inc.
Rep By: Albert B. Rosenbaum, III

H. J. Heinz Co.,

Pittsburgh, PA
Leg. Issues: HCR, TAX, TRD

Outside Counsel/Consultants

Howrey Simon Arnold & White

Liz Robbins Associates
Issues: HCR, TAX, TRD
Rep By: Liz Robbins

Heinz Family Foundation

Outside Counsel/Consultants

BSMG Worldwide

Helen Keller Nat'l Center for Deaf Blind Youths and Adults

Port Washington, NY
Leg. Issues: EDU

Outside Counsel/Consultants

Robert R. Humphreys
Issues: EDU
Rep By: Robert R. Humphreys

Helen Keller Worldwide

New York, NY
Leg. Issues: BUD, HCR

Outside Counsel/Consultants

Edington, Peel & Associates, Inc.
Issues: BUD, HCR
Rep By: Terry R. Peel

Helicopter Ass'n Internat'l

1635 Prince St.
Alexandria, VA 22314-3406
Tel: (703)683-4646
Fax: (703)683-4745
Registered: LDA
Web: www.rotor.com

Represents the civil helicopter operator community, both domestically and internationally.

Leg. Issues: AVI, BUD, GOV, SCI

In-house, DC-area Employees

CORRAO, Joe: Director, Regulations
MEADE, Elizabeth: Exec. V. President, Administration
RASAVAGE, Roy: President
RIZNER, Glenn: V. President, Operations

Outside Counsel/Consultants

Crowell & Moring LLP
Issues: GOV
Rep By: Timothy M. Biddle, Lorraine B. Halloway, Karen Hastie Williams

Heller Financial Inc.

Chicago, IL
Leg. Issues: SMB

Outside Counsel/Consultants

Winston & Strawn
Issues: SMB
Rep By: Charles L. Kinney, Douglas C. Richardson

Helli USA Airways

Outside Counsel/Consultants

McClure, Gerard & Neuenschwander, Inc.
Rep By: Steven G. Barringer, Joseph T. Findaro, Matthew Iandoli, Nils W. Johnson, Hon. James A. McClure, Tod O. Neuenschwander

Hello Arabia Corp.

Washington, DC
Leg. Issues: ECN

Outside Counsel/Consultants

RPH & Associates, L.L.C.
Issues: ECN
Rep By: Hon. Robert P. Hanrahan

HemaSure, Inc.

Marlborough, MA
Leg. Issues: CPT, HCR, MED, SCI

Outside Counsel/Consultants

Jeffrey J. Kimbell & Associates
Issues: CPT, HCR, MED, SCI
Rep By: Jeffrey J. Kimbell

Hemenway Associates

Washington, DC

Outside Counsel/Consultants

Parry, Romani, DeConcini & Symms

Hemet, California, City of

Outside Counsel/Consultants

Mark S. Israel

Hempstead, New York, Village of

Leg. Issues: CAW, HOU, URB

Outside Counsel/Consultants

Coan & Lyons
Issues: HOU, URB
Rep By: Carl A. S. Coan, Jr., Raymond K. James

Murray, Scheer, Montgomery, Tapia & O'Donnell
Issues: CAW
Rep By: John R. O'Donnell

Henderson, Nevada, City of

Leg. Issues: HOU, TRA, URB

Outside Counsel/Consultants

Barbara T. McCall Associates
Issues: HOU, TRA, URB
Rep By: Ralph Garboushian, Barbara T. McCall

McClure, Gerard & Neuenschwander, Inc.
Rep By: Steven G. Barringer, Joseph T. Findaro, Matthew Iandoli, Nils W. Johnson, Hon. James A. McClure, Tod O. Neuenschwander

Hennipin County Board of Commissioners

Minneapolis, MN
Leg. Issues: ENV, HCR, UNM, WAS, WEL

Outside Counsel/Consultants

Lockridge Grindal & Nauen, P.L.L.P.
Issues: ENV, HCR, UNM, WAS, WEL
Rep By: Dennis McGrann

Henrico County, Virginia

Richmond, VA

Outside Counsel/Consultants

Miller & Van Eaton, P.L.L.C.
Rep By: Frederick E. Ellrod, III

Herbalife Internat'l, Inc.

Los Angeles, CA
Leg. Issues: FOO, TRD

Outside Counsel/Consultants

Internat'l Business-Government Counsellors, Inc.
Issues: TRD
Rep By: John F. McDermid

Parry, Romani, DeConcini & Symms
Issues: FOO
Rep By: Edward H. Baxter, Hon. Dennis DeConcini, John M. Haddow, Scott D. Hatch, Shannon Davis Henderson, Jack W. Martin, Romano Romani, Linda Arey Skladany, Hon. Steven D. Symms

Hercules Development Corp.

Leg. Issues: ECN, GAM, IND, TOB

Outside Counsel/Consultants

Capital Consultants Corp.
Issues: ECN, GAM, IND, TOB
Rep By: Michael David Kaiser

HEREIU

Washington, DC
Leg. Issues: LBR

Outside Counsel/Consultants

Washington Council Ernst & Young
Issues: LBR
Rep By: Doug Badger, Lauren Darling, John L. Doney, Jayne T. Fitzgerald, LaBrenda Garrett-Nelson, Gary J. Gasper, Nick Giordano, Robert J. Leonard, Phillip D. Moseley, John D. Porter, Robert M. Rozen, Donna Steele-Flynn, Timothy J. Urban

Heritage Development

Chagrin Falls, OH
Leg. Issues: RES

Outside Counsel/Consultants

Verner, Liipfert, Bernhard, McPherson and Hand, Chartered
Issues: RES
Rep By: Suzanne D. Cartwright, Lawrence E. Levinson, Neil T. Proto

Heritage Foundation

214 Massachusetts Ave. NE
Washington, DC 20002
Web: www.heritage.org
Tel: (202)546-4400
Fax: (202)546-8328

Founded in 1973, the Heritage Foundation analyzes research and publishes studies on major economic and foreign policy issues generally, but not invariably, aligned with conservative views. Also publishes Policy Review; The Journal of American Citizenship; conducts scholars program; and provides media with analysis of issues and trends. Claims to be the most broadly-based policy think tank in the U.S. with more than 200,000 individual, corporate and foundation supporters.

Leg. Issues: DEF, EDU, MMM, TAX

In-house, DC-area Employees

BEACH, William: Director, Center for Data Analysis
BENNETT, William J.: Distinguished Fellow, Cultural Policy Studies
BERKOWITZ, Herbert: V. President, Public Relations
BERSHERS, Kristine: Media Relations Manager
BOWARD, Gary: Chief of Staff and Assistant to the President
BUTLER, Stuart M.: V. President, Domestic and Economic Policy Studies
COHEN, Ariel: Senior Policy Analyst, Russian and Eurasion Affairs
COON, Charli: Senior Policy Analyst, Energy and Environment
DAWSON, Tom: Educational Affairs Fellow
DOUGHERTY, Joseph: Public Relations Associate
DUNLOP, Becky Norton: V. President, External Affairs
EIRAS, Anna: Policy Analyst, Trade and Latin America
FAGAN, Patrick F.: William H.G. FitzGerald Senior Fellow in Family and Cultural Issues
FEULNER, Jr., Edwin J.: President and Chief Exec. Officer
FRANC, Michael G.: V. President, Government Relations
FROGUE, James: Health Care Policy Analyst
FRONING, Denise: Policy Analyst, Trade and Internat'l Economics
GAYNER, Lewis: V. President, Administration and Chief Financial Officer
GAZIANO, Todd: Director, Center for Legal and Judicial Studies
HOLMES, Dr. Kim R.: V. President, Foreign Policy and Defense Studies
HULSMAN, John: Research Fellow, NATO and Europe
JOHN, David: Senior Policy Analyst, Social Security
JOHNSON, Stephen: Latin America Policy Analyst
KAFER, Krista: Education Policy Analyst
KLUCSARTIS, Ann: Director, Development Programs
LARKIN, Jennifer: Director, Congressional Relations, U.S. House of Representatives
LOCONTE, Joseph: William E. Simon Fellow in Religion and a Free Society
MEESE, III, Edwin: Ronald Reagan Fellow in Public Policy
MEYERSON, Adam: V. President, Educational Affairs
MITCHELL, Daniel J.: McKenna Senior Fellow in Political Economy
MOFFIT, Dr. Robert: Director, Domestic Policy Studies
MOORE, Thomas G.: Director, Kathryn & Shelby Collom Davis International Studies Center
O'DRISCOLL, Gerald: Director, Center for International Trade and Economics
PHILLIPS, James A.: Research Fellow, Middle East
RECTOR, Robert: Senior Research Fellow, Welfare and Family Issues
RUBIN, Cheryl: Director of Public Relations
SCHAEFER, Brett: Jay Kingham Fellow in International Regulatory Affairs

SPALDING, Dr. Matthew: Director, Lectures and Educational Programs
SPENCER, Jack: Policy Analyst, Defense and National Security
SPRING, Herbert Baker: Kirby Research Fellow in National Security Policy
THOMAS, Virginia: Director, Executive Branch Relations
TRULUCK, Phillip N.: Exec. V. President
UTT, Ronald: Grover M. Hermann Fellow in Federal Budget Affairs
VONKANNON, John: V. President and Treasurer
WEIDMAN, Jame: Director of Public Relations
WILLIAMS, Liz: Deputy Director, House Relations
WILSON, D. Mark: Labor Economist
WORTZEL, Larry: Director, Kathryn & Shelby Collom Davis Internat'l Studies

Outside Counsel/Consultants

Hugh C. Newton & Assoc.
Rep By: Hugh C. Newton

Heritage Harbor Museum

Providence, RI
Leg. Issues: ART, ECN, EDU, TOU

Outside Counsel/Consultants

John C. Grzebien
Issues: ART, ECN, EDU, TOU
Rep By: John C. Grzebien

Hershey Foods Corp.

1130 Connecticut Ave. NW
Suite 710
Washington, DC 20036
Tel: (202)833-5724
Fax: (202)833-5728
Registered: LDA
Web: www.hersheys.com

A manufacturer of chocolate, confectionery, and chocolate-related grocery products headquartered in Hershey, PA.

Leg. Issues: AGR, BUD, FOO, HCR, TAX, TRD

In-house, DC-area Employees
GRAF, Ronald P.: Federal Government Relations Manager

Hertz Corp.

Park Ridge, NJ
A car rental company.

Leg. Issues: INS, LAW

Outside Counsel/Consultants

Carpi & Clay
Issues: INS, LAW
Rep By: Kenneth A. Carpi

Herzog, Heine, Geduld, Inc.

Jersey City, NJ
Leg. Issues: FIN

Outside Counsel/Consultants

John T. O'Rourke Law Offices
Issues: FIN
Rep By: John T. O'Rourke

Hesperia, California, City of

Leg. Issues: TRA

Outside Counsel/Consultants

E. Del Smith and Co.
Issues: TRA
Rep By: Margaret Allen, E. Del Smith

Hess

Outside Counsel/Consultants

Dittus Communications
Rep By: Tom Conway, Jeffrey Eshelman

Hewlett-Packard Co.

900 17th St. NW
Suite 1100
Washington, DC 20006
Tel: (202)884-7010
Fax: (202)884-7070
Registered: LDA
Web: www.hp.com
Leg. Issues: BUD, CPI, CPT, ENV, GOV, HCR, IMM, LBR, MED, RET, SCI, TAX, TEC, TOR, TRD

In-house, DC-area Employees
BERISH, Jim: Manager, Federal Procurement Policy
BOND, Phil: Director, Federal Public Policy
COOPER, Scott: Manager, Technology Policy
HUGHES, Kristin: Manager, Federal Public Policy
ISAACS, David: Manager, Government Policy
MAXWELL, William A.: Manager, International Trade Policy
SULLIVAN, M. Dianne: Manager, International Trade Policy
WHITTAKER, James: Director, International Government Affairs

Outside Counsel/Consultants

Bergner Bockorny Castagnetti and Hawkins
Issues: CPI, ENV, TEC, TRD
Rep By: Jeffrey T. Bergner, David A. Bockorny, David Castagnetti

Manatt, Phelps & Phillips, LLP
Issues: BUD, CPI, GOV
Rep By: Stephen M. Ryan, Robb Watters

Washington Council Ernst & Young
Issues: BUD, TAX
Rep By: Nick Giordano

Wilmer, Cutler & Pickering
Rep By: Charles S. Levy

Hexcel Corp.

9001 Braddock Rd.
Suite 390
Springfield, VA 22151
Tel: (703)239-1882
Fax: (703)239-1039
Web: www.hexcel.com

A producer of technologically sophisticated, advanced composite materials and reinforcement fabrics.

Political Action Committee/s

Hexcel Corp. PAC
9001 Braddock Rd.
Suite 390
Springfield, VA 22151
Tel: (703)239-1882
Fax: (703)239-1039
Contact: Hugh McGillicuddy

In-house, DC-area Employees
MCGILLICUDDY, Hugh: Contact, Hexel Corp. PAC

Hi-Desert Water District

Yucca Valley, CA
Leg. Issues: BUD, CAW, ENV

Outside Counsel/Consultants

Copeland, Lowery & Jacquez
Issues: BUD, CAW, ENV
Rep By: Hon. William D. Lowery, Jeffrey S. Shockey

Hiawatha Broadband Communications Inc.

Winona, MN
Leg. Issues: COM, TEC

Outside Counsel/Consultants

The Baller Herbst Law Group
Issues: COM, TEC
Rep By: Sean A. Stokes

Hickey Freeman Co.

Chicago, IL

Outside Counsel/Consultants

Skadden, Arps, Slate, Meagher & Flom LLP

Hickman Report

A UFO research organization.

Leg. Issues: AER, DEF, GOV, SCI

Outside Counsel/Consultants

Paradigm Research Group
Issues: AER, DEF, GOV, SCI
Rep By: Stephen G. Bassett

Hicks, Muse, Tate & Furst

Dallas, TX
Leg. Issues: BAN, COM, ENV, TEC

Outside Counsel/Consultants

Arter & Hadden
Issues: BAN, COM, ENV, TEC
Rep By: Daniel L. Cohen, Hon. Thomas G. Loeffler, Jon W. Plebani

High River Limited Partnership

New York, NY

Outside Counsel/Consultants

Chambers Associates Inc.
Rep By: Letitia Chambers

High Speed Ground Transportation Ass'n

1010 Massachusetts Ave. NW
Washington, DC 20001
Tel: (202)789-8107
Fax: (202)789-8109
Registered: LDA
Web: www.hsgt.org/
E-mail: info@hsgt.org
Leg. Issues: BUD, RRR, TRA

In-house, DC-area Employees
CHETTLE, J. Anne: Director, Public Affairs
DYSART, Mark: President

Outside Counsel/Consultants

Government Relations, Inc.
Issues: BUD, RRR, TRA
Rep By: Thomas J. Bulger, Mark H. Miller

Higher Education Consortium for Special Education

Leg. Issues: EDU

Outside Counsel/Consultants

Jane West
Issues: EDU
Rep By: Jane West, Ph.D.

Highland Mortgage Co.

Birmingham, AL
Leg. Issues: HOU

Outside Counsel/Consultants

Nixon Peabody LLP
Issues: HOU
Rep By: Richard M. Price, Monica Hilton Sussman

Highland Park, Illinois, City of Highwood Local Redevelopment Authority and the City of

Highland Park, IL
Leg. Issues: ECN, GOV, NAT, VET

Outside Counsel/Consultants

Bryan Cave LLP
Issues: GOV, NAT, VET
Rep By: Hon. Alan J. Dixon

Kutak Rock LLP
Issues: ECN
Rep By: Rhonda Bond-Collins, Seth Kirshenberg, George R. Schlossberg, Barry P. Steinberg

Highline School District Educational Resources

Burien, WA
Leg. Issues: AVI

Outside Counsel/Consultants

Ball Janik, LLP
Issues: AVI
Rep By: Michelle E. Giguere, Hal D. Hiemstra

Highmark Blue Cross/ Blue Shield

600 Pennsylvania Ave. SE
Suite 220
Washington, DC 20003
Tel: (202)544-8814
Fax: (202)544-8853
E-mail: donna.hoffmeier@highmark.com

In-house, DC-area Employees
ENGLERT, Greg: Senior Government Affairs Representative

Outside Counsel/Consultants

Seyfarth, Shaw, Fairweather & Geraldson

Highway 53 Longrange Improvement Citizens' Task Force

International Falls, MN
Leg. Issues: ROD, TRA

Outside Counsel/Consultants

Lawler, Metzger & Milkman, LLC
Issues: ROD, TRA
Rep By: Sante J. Esposito

Highwood, Illinois, City of

Outside Counsel/Consultants

Bryan Cave LLP
Rep By: Hon. Alan J. Dixon

Alan Hilburg & Associates

McLean, VA
Leg. Issues: LBR

Outside Counsel/Consultants

Patton Boggs, LLP
Issues: LBR
Rep By: James B. Christian, Jr., Donald V. Moorehead, John S. Shaw

Hill Internat'l, Inc.

1225 I St. NW
Suite 601
Washington, DC 20005
Tel: (202)408-3000
Fax: (202)408-3058
Web: www.hillintl.com
E-mail: markanderson@hillintl.com

Headquartered in Willingboro, N.J.

In-house, DC-area Employees
ANDERSON, Mark I.: Senior V. President

Outside Counsel/Consultants
Winston & Strawn
Rep By: John A. Waits, II

Hill-Rom Co., Inc.

Charleston, SC
Leg. Issues: HCR, MED, MMM

Outside Counsel/Consultants
Nusgart Consulting, LLC
Issues: HCR, MMM
Rep By: Marcia Nusgart

Sagamore Associates, Inc.
Issues: MED, MMM
Rep By: David Nichols, Mark W. Weller

Hillenbrand Industries, Inc.

Batesville, IN
A manufacturer of medical devices and products.

Leg. Issues: GOV

Outside Counsel/Consultants
Hale and Dorr LLP
Issues: GOV
Rep By: Mark Heller, Louise Howe

Sagamore Associates, Inc.

The Hillman Co.

Pittsburgh, PA
Leg. Issues: TAX

Outside Counsel/Consultants
Hooper Owen & Winburn
Issues: TAX
Rep By: Lindsay D. Hooper

Steptoe & Johnson LLP
Issues: TAX
Rep By: Edward R. Mackiewicz, Mark J. Silverman

Hillsborough Area Regional Transit Authority

Tampa, FL
Leg. Issues: TRA

Outside Counsel/Consultants
Holland & Knight LLP
Issues: TRA

Hillsborough, Florida, County of

Tampa, FL
Leg. Issues: ECN, NAT, TAX, TRA, WAS, WEL

Outside Counsel/Consultants
Alcalde & Fay
Issues: ECN, NAT, TAX, TRA, WAS, WEL
Rep By: Hector Alcalde, Rodney A. Coleman, Lois Moore

Hillwood Development Corp.

Fort Worth, TX
Leg. Issues: AVI, TRA, TRD

Outside Counsel/Consultants
Smith Dawson & Andrews, Inc.
Issues: AVI, TRA, TRD
Rep By: Gregory B. Andrews, Thomas C. Dawson

Hilton Hotels Corp.

Beverly Hills, CA
Leg. Issues: TAX

Outside Counsel/Consultants
Kurzweil & Associates
Issues: TAX
Rep By: Jeffrey Kurzweil

HIP Health Plans

625 Indiana Ave. NW Suite 200
Washington, DC 20004
Tel: (202)393-0660
Fax: (202)393-0533
Registered: LDA

Web: www.hipusa.com

Headquartered in New York, NY.

Leg. Issues: HCR

In-house, DC-area Employees
ABERNETHY, David S.: Senior V. President, Public Policy and Regulatory Affairs
STRUMPF, George: Director, Federal Relations

Hispanic Ass'n of Colleges and Universities

San Antonio, TX
Leg. Issues: BUD, EDU

Outside Counsel/Consultants
Strategic Impact, Inc.
Issues: BUD, EDU
Rep By: Michael C. Jimenez

Hispanic Broadcasting Inc.

Dallas, TX
Leg. Issues: COM, CPT, TEC

Outside Counsel/Consultants
Alcalde & Fay
Issues: COM, CPT, TEC
Rep By: Hector Alcalde, Jim Davenport, Vicki L. Iseman, Tim Stroud

Historic Landmarks Foundation of Indiana

Indianapolis, IN
Leg. Issues: RES, URB

Outside Counsel/Consultants
Sagamore Associates, Inc.
Issues: RES, URB
Rep By: Todd Atkinson, David U. Gogol, Dena S. Morris

HiSynergy Communications, Inc.

New York, NY
Leg. Issues: COM, CPI, MIA

Outside Counsel/Consultants
The Ickes & Enright Group
Issues: COM, CPI, MIA
Rep By: Janice Ann Enright, Harold M. Ickes

The Hitachi Foundation

1509 22nd St. NW
Washington, DC 20037-1073
Tel: (202)457-0588
Fax: (202)296-1098
Web: www.hitachi.org

In-house, DC-area Employees
DYER, Barbara: President and Chief Exec. Officer

Hitachi Home Electronics, Inc.

Norcross, GA
Leg. Issues: CPT

Outside Counsel/Consultants
Patton Boggs, LLP
Issues: CPT
Rep By: Thomas Hale Boggs, Jr., Jeffrey L. Turner

Hitachi Semiconductors of America

Outside Counsel/Consultants
McDermott, Will and Emery
Rep By: Neil Quinter

Hitachi, Ltd.

1900 K St. NW
Suite 800
Washington, DC 20006
Tel: (202)828-9272
Fax: (202)828-9277
Registered: LDA
Web: www.hitachi.com
Leg. Issues: FOR, MAN, TRD

In-house, DC-area Employees
GREEN, Carl J.: Deputy Senior Representative
ISHII, Tsutomu: Senior Representative and Director

HIV/AIDS Nursing Certification Board

11250 Roger Bacon Dr.
Suite Eight
Reston, VA 20190
Tel: (703)437-4377
Fax: (703)435-4390

In-house, DC-area Employees
PRICE, CAE, Randall C.: Exec. Director

Outside Counsel/Consultants
Drohan Management Group
Rep By: Randall C. Price, CAE

HKC, Inc.

Warrenton, VA
Leg. Issues: TRA

Outside Counsel/Consultants
Capitol Counsel Group, L.L.C.
Issues: TRA

HMSHost Corp.

6600 Rockledge Dr.
Bethesda, MD 20817
Tel: (240)694-4100
Fax: (240)694-4623
Web: www.hms.com
Leg. Issues: AVI, TAX

Political Action Committee/s
Host Marriott Corp. PAC

6600 Rockledge Dr.
Bethesda, MD 20817
Tel: (240)694-4100
Fax: (240)694-4623
Contact: Clark D. Sharpe

In-house, DC-area Employees
SHARPE, Clark D.: V. President, Government Affairs

Outside Counsel/Consultants
Hogan & Hartson L.L.P.
Issues: TAX
Rep By: Prentiss Feagles, C. Michael Gilliland, J. Warren Gorrell, Nancy Granese, William Michael House, Hon. Robert H. Michel, Jeffrey W. Munk

Kurzweil & Associates
Issues: AVI
Rep By: Jeffrey Kurzweil

Ho-Chunk Nation

Black River Falls, WI
Leg. Issues: BUD, IND

Outside Counsel/Consultants
Sonosky, Chambers, Sachse & Endreson
Issues: BUD, IND
Rep By: Mary J. Pavel, William R. Perry

Hoboken, New Jersey, City of

Outside Counsel/Consultants
Krivit & Krivit, P.C.

Hoechst Marion Roussel Deutschland GmbH

Bad Soden, GERMANY
Leg. Issues: CPT

Outside Counsel/Consultants
Chlopak, Leonard, Schechter and Associates
Rep By: Peter Schechter, Kelly Sullivan

Parry, Romani, DeConcini & Symms
Issues: CPT
Rep By: Edward H. Baxter, Hon. Dennis DeConcini, John M. Haddow, Scott D. Hatch, Shannon Davis Henderson, Jack W. Martin, Romano Romani, Linda Arey Skladany, Hon. Steven D. Symms

Hoffman Management, Inc.

Alexandria, VA
Leg. Issues: RES

Outside Counsel/Consultants
Kilpatrick Stockton LLP
Issues: RES
Rep By: J. Christopher Brady, Hon. Elliott H. Levitas, Neil I. Levy

Hoffmann-La Roche Inc.

1300 I St. NW
Suite 520 West
Washington, DC 20005-3314
Tel: (202)408-0090
Fax: (202)408-1750
Registered: LDA
Leg. Issues: ALC, CPT, HCR, LAW, MED, MMM, PHA, TAX, TRD

In-house, DC-area Employees
BURNS, Brian R.: Director, Federal Government Affairs
FRANKO, Sara: Director, Federal Government Affairs

Outside Counsel/Consultants
Garrett Yu Hussein LLC

Hyman, Phelps & McNamara, P.C.
Issues: LAW
Rep By: John A. Gilbert, Jr.

The Legislative Strategies Group, LLC
Issues: HCR
Rep By: Denise M. Henry

Patton Boggs, LLP
Issues: HCR, MED, MMM, PHA
Rep By: John F. Jonas, Martha M. Kendrick, Daniel A. Kracov, Stuart M. Pape, JoAnn V. Willis

Hohenberg Brothers, Co.

Memphis, TN
Leg. Issues: AGR

Outside Counsel/Consultants
Charles V. Cunningham & Assoc.
Issues: AGR
Rep By: Charles V. Cunningham

Holland America West-Tours

Anchorage, AK
Leg. Issues: TOU

Outside Counsel/Consultants
Zane & Associates
Issues: TOU
Rep By: Curtis J. Zane

Hollis-Eden Pharmaceuticals, Inc.

San Diego, CA
Leg. Issues: BUD, HCR, MED

Outside Counsel/Consultants

Carpi & Clay
Issues: BUD
Rep By: Kenneth A. Carpi

E. Del Smith and Co.
Issues: HCR, MED
Rep By: Kenneth A. Carpi, E. Del Smith

Hollister Inc.

Libertyville, IL
Leg. Issues: HCR, MMM

Outside Counsel/Consultants

Nusgart Consulting, LLC
Issues: HCR, MMM
Rep By: Marcia Nusgart

Hollister Ranch Owners' Ass'n

Gaviota, CA
Leg. Issues: NAT

Outside Counsel/Consultants

Copeland, Lowery & Jacquez
Issues: NAT
Rep By: Lynnette C. Jacquez, Hon. William D. Lowery

Holnam Inc.

Dundee, MI Registered: LDA
Leg. Issues: BUD, CIV, ENV, TRD

Outside Counsel/Consultants

Crowell & Moring LLP

Lyons & Co.
Issues: BUD, CIV, ENV, TRD
Rep By: William Lyons

Holt Communications Corp.

Allentown, PA

Outside Counsel/Consultants

Kaye Scholer LLP
Rep By: Jason Shrinsky

Holy Childhood Ass'n

1720 Massachusetts Ave. NW
Washington, DC 20036
Tel: (202)775-8637
Fax: (202)429-2987

HCA is the Catholic Church's mission organization for young people. Funds collected by HCA help missionaries serve impoverished children in the developing world.

In-house, DC-area Employees

WRIGHT, Rev. Francis W.: National Director

Holy Land Trust

San Diego, CA
Leg. Issues: FOR, TOU

Outside Counsel/Consultants

APCO Worldwide
Issues: FOR, TOU
Rep By: Hon. Don L. Bonker, Barry J. Schumacher

Holyoke Department of Gas and Electricity

Holyoke, MA
Leg. Issues: ENG

Outside Counsel/Consultants

Spiegel & McDiarmid
Issues: ENG
Rep By: Ben Finkelstein, Fran Francis

Holyoke Hospital

Holyoke, MA
Leg. Issues: HCR, MMM

Outside Counsel/Consultants

Philip W. Johnston Associates
Issues: HCR, MMM
Rep By: Philip W. Johnston, Merrill E. Warschoff

Home Access Health

Hoffman Estates, IL
Leg. Issues: HCR

Outside Counsel/Consultants

U.S. Strategies Corp.
Issues: HCR
Rep By: Gary F. Capistrant, Nance Guenther-Peterson, Heidi Hanson, Brad Traverse

Home Automation Ass'n

Outside Counsel/Consultants

Bostrom Corp.
Rep By: Charles McGrath, CAE

Home Baking Ass'n

Topeka, KS

Outside Counsel/Consultants

Thompson, Hine and Flory LLP
Rep By: Gilbert B. Lessenco

Home Box Office

New York, NY

Outside Counsel/Consultants

Dickstein Shapiro Morin & Oshinsky LLP
Rep By: Bernard Nash, Rebecah Moore Shepherd, L. Andrew Zausner

Home Builders Institute

1090 Vermont Ave. NW
Suite 600
Washington, DC 20005
Web: www.hbi.org
Tel: (202)371-0600
Fax: (202)898-7777
Leg. Issues: BUD, LBR

In-house, DC-area Employees

HUMPHREYS, Fred: President and Chief Exec. Officer
MCINTYRE, Maria: Director, Job Development and Outreach

Home Care Aide Ass'n of America

228 Seventh St. SE
Washington, DC 20003-4306
Tel: (202)547-7424
Fax: (202)547-9559
Registered: LDA
Web: www.nahc.org

An affiliate of the Nat'l Ass'n for Home Care.

In-house, DC-area Employees

BARNETTE, Marcia L.: Contact

Home Care Ass'n of New York State

Albany, NY
Leg. Issues: MMM

Outside Counsel/Consultants

R. Duffy Wall and Associates
Issues: MMM
Rep By: Hon. Bill Brewster, Hon. Rodney D. Chandler, Stephen Cooper

The Home Depot

Atlanta, GA
Leg. Issues: BNK, BUD, CAW, CSP, ENV, HOU, IMM, LBR, NAT, ROD, TAX, TRA, TRD, TRU

Outside Counsel/Consultants

Epstein Becker & Green, P.C.
Rep By: Cathie A. Shattuck

Government Relations, Inc.
Issues: BNK, BUD, CAW, CSP, ENV, HOU, IMM, LBR, NAT, ROD, TAX, TRA, TRD, TRU
Rep By: Allynn Howe

Home Fashion Products Ass'n

4041 Powder Mill Rd.
Suite 104
Calverton, MD 20705
Tel: (301)348-2005
Fax: (301)348-2020

In-house, DC-area Employees

SNYDER, Russell K.: Exec. V. President

Outside Counsel/Consultants

The Kellen Company
Rep By: Russell K. Snyder

Home Federal Savings and Loan Ass'n

Worcester, MA
Leg. Issues: BAN, CPI, FIN, GOV

Outside Counsel/Consultants

Timothy D. Naegele & Associates
Issues: BAN, CPI, FIN, GOV
Rep By: Timothy D. Naegele

Home Infusion Therapy Franchise Owners Ass'n

1030 15th St. NW
Suite 870
Washington, DC 20005
Tel: (202)393-1780
Fax: (202)393-0336

In-house, DC-area Employees

MCDERMOTT, Marianne: Exec. Director

Outside Counsel/Consultants

The Kellen Company
Rep By: Marianne McDermott

Home Office Ass'n of America

New York, NY

Outside Counsel/Consultants

Akin, Gump, Strauss, Hauer & Feld, L.L.P.

Home Recording Rights Coalition (HRRC)

1341 G St. NW
P.O. Box 14267
Washington, DC 20005
Web: www.hrrc.org
E-mail: info@hrrc.org
Tel: (202)628-9212
Fax: (202)628-9227

HRRC is a national coalition of consumers, retailers, servicers, and manufacturers of audio and video electronics products, dedicated to preserving the consumer's access to and use of home electronics equipment.

In-house, DC-area Employees

RODGERS, Ruth: Exec. Director

Home School PAC

119 C St. SE
Washington, DC 20003

In-house, DC-area Employees

TEEPELL, Timothy: Contact

Home Warranty Coalition

Washington, DC
Leg. Issues: HOU, INS

Outside Counsel/Consultants

Verner, Liipfert, Bernhard, McPherson and Hand, Chartered
Issues: HOU, INS
Rep By: Matthew C. Bernstein, Harry C. McPherson, John A. Merrigan, Steven R. Phillips, James A. Pickup, Nancy A. Sheliga, John H. Zentay

Homestake Mining

San Francisco, CA
Leg. Issues: FIN, MON, NAT

Outside Counsel/Consultants

Crowell & Moring LLP
Issues: NAT
Rep By: Edward M. Green, R. Timothy McCrum, Steven P. Quarles

Dickstein Shapiro Morin & Oshinsky LLP
Issues: FIN, MON, NAT
Rep By: Graham "Rusty" Mathews, Hon. Stanford E. Parris, L. Andrew Zausner

Patton Boggs, LLP
Rep By: Henry Chajet, John C. Martin, Mark N. Savit

Homestead Financial Corp.

San Francisco, CA

Outside Counsel/Consultants

Elias, Matz, Tiernan and Herrick

HomeStreet Bank

Outside Counsel/Consultants

Lee Peckarsky
Rep By: Lee Peckarsky

Honda Motor Co.

Tokyo, JAPAN

Outside Counsel/Consultants

Covington & Burling

Honda North America, Inc.

955 L'Enfant Plaza SW
Suite 5300
Washington, DC 20024
Tel: (202)554-1650
Fax: (202)488-3542
Registered: LDA
Leg. Issues: AUT, CAW, CSP, FUE, IMM, MAN, TRD

In-house, DC-area Employees

CALPIN, Patrick: Analyst, Government Relations
COHEN, Edward: V. President, Govt. and Industry Relations
DELLINGER, Kent: Manager, Government Relations
GERKE, Scott A.: Specialist, Government Relations
HARRINGTON, Toni: Assistant V. President, Government and Industry Relations

Outside Counsel/Consultants

The Hawthorn Group, L.C.
Rep By: Esther Foer

Public Strategies Washington, Inc.
Issues: AUT
Rep By: Joseph P. O'Neill

Vorys, Sater, Seymour and Pease, LLP

Honduras, Embassy of

3007 Tilden St. NW
Suite 4M
Washington, DC 20008
Tel: (202)966-7702
Fax: (202)966-9751
Web: www.hondurasemb.org
E-mail: embhondu@aol.com
Leg. Issues: FOR, GOV, TRD

Outside Counsel/Consultants

Schmeltzer, Aptaker & Shepard, P.C.
Issues: FOR, GOV, TRD
Rep By: C. Mateo Paz-Soldan, J. Anthony Smith

Honduras, Government of the Republic of

Tegucigalpa, HONDURAS

Outside Counsel/Consultants

White & Case LLP

Honey Users Council of America

Outside Counsel/Consultants

Akin, Gump, Strauss, Hauer & Feld, L.L.P.

Honeywell Internat'l, Inc.

1001 Pennsylvania Ave. NW
Suite 700 South
Washington, DC 20004
Tel: (202)662-2650
Fax: (202)662-2674
Registered: LDA
Web: www.honeywell.com
E-mail: ken.cole@honeywell.com

A diversified high technology company involved in energy and safety controls, defense, and aerospace and specialized instrumentation industries. Merged with AlliedSignal in 1999 and that company adopted the Honeywell name.

Leg. Issues: AER, AVI, BUD, CAW, DEF, ENG, ENV, HCR, MAN, SCI, TAX, TRA, TRD, WAS

Political Action Committee/s

Honeywell Internat'l, Inc. PAC
1001 Pennsylvania Ave. NW
Suite 700 South
Washington, DC 20004
Tel: (202)662-2650
Fax: (202)662-2674
Contact: Ellis T. Nottingham

In-house, DC-area Employees

BANTON, Linda W.: V. President, Aerospace Government Relations
BOUDREAU, Paul
GUARISCO, Annette J.: Corporate Director, Public Policy and Government Relations
HEFTI, M. L. "Buzz": Staff V. President, Government Relations
HICKEY, Christopher: Director, Aerospace Government Relations
MAY, Stephen L.: Director, Legislative and Regulatory Affairs
NOTTINGHAM, Ellis T.: Director, Aerospace Government Affairs
ROCHFORD, Susan P.: Director, International Affairs
RUFFING, Sheryl McCluney: Director, Aerospace Government Relations and Aviation Policy
SIMONETTI, Arthur J.: Manager, Trade Legislation and Regulation

Outside Counsel/Consultants

C. Baker Consulting Inc.
Issues: AVI, DEF, MAN
Rep By: Caleb Baker

BKSH & Associates

Manatt, Phelps & Phillips, LLP
Issues: DEF
Rep By: Mary Ann Gilleece, Jeff Kuhnreich

Robison Internat'l, Inc.
Issues: BUD, DEF, ENG, TRA
Rep By: Stephen A. Evered, Sandra A. Gilbert, Richard B. Ladd

Hong Kong Dragon Airlines Ltd.

Lantau, HONG KONG

Outside Counsel/Consultants

Zuckert, Scoutt and Rasenberger, L.L.P.
Rep By: Rachel B. Trinder

Hong Kong Economic and Trade Office

1520 18th St. NW
Washington, DC 20036
Tel: (202)331-8947
Fax: (202)331-8958
Web: www.hongkong.org
Leg. Issues: FOR, TRD

In-house, DC-area Employees

CHEUNG, Joanna: Trade Officer
JACKSON, Chris: Director General
MCATEE, Daniel: Senior Information Officer

Outside Counsel/Consultants

Arter & Hadden

Griffin, Johnson, Dover & Stewart
Rep By: G. Jack Dover, David E. Johnson, Susan O. Mann, Walter J. "Joe" Stewart

The Legislative Strategies Group, LLC
Issues: FOR, TRD

Powell, Goldstein, Frazer & Murphy LLP
Rep By: Brenda A. Jacobs

The Wexler Group
Issues: TRD
Rep By: R. D. Folsom, Joel Malina, Hon. Robert S. Walker

Hong Kong Trade Development Council

Wanchai, CHINA (PEOPLE'S REPUBLIC)
Leg. Issues: TRD

Outside Counsel/Consultants

The Legislative Strategies Group, LLC
Issues: TRD
Rep By: Larry E. Smith

Powell, Goldstein, Frazer & Murphy LLP
Issues: TRD
Rep By: Alice Slayton Clark, Michael P. Daniels, Maria DiGiulian, Gretchen Effgen, Michael E. Fine, Robert Torresen, Jr.

Hong Kong, Government of

Hong Kong, CHINA (PEOPLE'S REPUBLIC)

Outside Counsel/Consultants

Arter & Hadden

Honolulu Shipyard

Leg. Issues: DEF, TRA

Outside Counsel/Consultants

R. J. Hudson Associates

PACE-CAPSTONE
Issues: DEF, TRA
Rep By: David S. Germroth, James W. Wise

Hood River, Oregon, Port of

Hood River, OR
Leg. Issues: BUD, MAR, ROD, TRA

Outside Counsel/Consultants

Ball Janik, LLP
Issues: BUD, MAR, ROD, TRA
Rep By: James A. Beall, Michelle E. Giguere

Hoopa Valley Tribal Council

Hoopa, CA
Leg. Issues: IND

Outside Counsel/Consultants

Dorsey & Whitney LLP
Issues: IND
Rep By: Philip Baker-Shenk, David A. Bieging, Cindy Darcy, Mark Jarboe, Christopher Karns, Sarah Ridley

Hall, Estill, Hardwick, Gable, Golden & Nelson
Issues: IND
Rep By: Joseph R. Membrino

SENSE, INC.
Rep By: C. Juliet Pittman

Hooper, Lundy and Bookman

Los Angeles, CA
Leg. Issues: BUD, MMM

Outside Counsel/Consultants

Powers Pyles Sutter & Verville, PC
Issues: BUD, MMM
Rep By: Judith Buckalew

Hoosier Energy Rural Electric Cooperative, Inc.

Bloomington, IN
Leg. Issues: ENG, UTI

Outside Counsel/Consultants

Duncan, Weinberg, Genzer & Pembroke, P.C.
Issues: ENG, UTI
Rep By: Robert Weinberg

Hopi Indian Tribe

Kykotsmovi, AZ
Leg. Issues: BUD, IND, LAW

Outside Counsel/Consultants

Arnold & Porter

The Legislative Strategies Group, LLC
Issues: IND, LAW
Rep By: Martin B. Gold, Steven M. Hilton, Larry E. Smith, Patricia Jarvis Voljavec

Sonosky, Chambers, Sachse & Endreson
Issues: BUD, IND
Rep By: Reid Peyton Chambers, Harry R. Sachse

Hopland Band of Pomo Indians

Hopland, CA
Leg. Issues: IND

Outside Counsel/Consultants

The State Affairs Co.
Issues: IND
Rep By: Bonnie L. Chafe

Horatio Alger Ass'n of Distinguished Americans

99 Canal Center Plaza
Suite 320
Alexandria, VA 22314
Tel: (703)684-9444
Fax: (703)684-9445
Web: www.horatioalger.com

In-house, DC-area Employees

GIROUX, Terrence J.: Exec. Director

Horizon Organic Dairy, Inc.

Longmont, CO
Leg. Issues: AGR

Outside Counsel/Consultants

The GrayWell Group, Inc.
Issues: AGR
Rep By: Peter D. Caldwell, Robert J. Gray

Horizon Organic Holding Co.

Longmont, CO
Leg. Issues: AGR

Outside Counsel/Consultants

Thelen Reid & Priest LLP
Issues: AGR
Rep By: Charles M. English, Jr., Stephan M. Minikes, Nancy K. West, Wendy M. Yoviene

Hornblower Marine Services, Inc.

Jeffersonville, IN
Leg. Issues: MAR

Outside Counsel/Consultants

Dyer Ellis & Joseph, P.C.
Issues: MAR
Rep By: James S. W. Drewry, Jeanne Marie Grasso, Duncan C. Smith, III, Jennifer M. Southwick

Horsehead Industries, Inc.

New York, NY

Outside Counsel/Consultants

Podesta/Mattoon
Rep By: Anthony T. Podesta, Timothy Powers

Horticultural Research Institute

1250 I St. NW
Suite 500
Washington, DC 20005
Tel: (202)789-2900
Fax: (202)789-1893
Web: www.anla.org/research
E-mail: apamplin@anla.org

Conducts research to benefit the nursery industry and the environment.

Leg. Issues: AGR, ENV, NAT, SCI, SMB

In-house, DC-area Employees

DOLIBOIS, Robert: Exec. V. President
PAMPLIN, Ashby: Administrator and Director

The Hosiery Ass'n

Charlotte, NC
Leg. Issues: APP, TRD

Outside Counsel/Consultants

Sandler, Travis & Rosenberg, P.A.
Issues: APP, TRD
Rep By: Nicole Bivens Collinson, Ron Sorini

Hospice Ass'n of America

228 Seventh St. SE
Washington, DC 20003-4306
Tel: (202)546-4759
Fax: (202)547-9559
Registered: LDA
Web: www.nahc.org/haa
E-mail: kpw@nahc.org
Leg. Issues: HCR

In-house, DC-area Employees
WOODS, Karen: Exec. Director

Hospital for Special Surgery

New York, NY
Leg. Issues: HCR, MED, SCI

Outside Counsel/Consultants

Cassidy & Associates, Inc.
Issues: HCR, MED, SCI
Rep By: Gregory M. Gill, Marie James, Christopher Lamond, Mary E. Shields

Hospitality Employers Ass'n

Myrtle Beach, SC

Outside Counsel/Consultants

Seyfarth, Shaw, Fairweather & Geraldson
Rep By: Donald L. Rosenthal

Hospitality Sales and Marketing Ass'n Internat'l

1300 L St. NW
Suite 1020
Washington, DC 20005
Tel: (202)789-0089
Fax: (202)789-1725
Web: www.hsmai.org
E-mail: bgilbert@hsmai.org

In-house, DC-area Employees
GILBERT, Robert A.: President and Chief Exec. Officer
NORDSTROM, Jane: Director, Education
WHITTEMORE, Ilsa: Associate Exec. Director

Hotel Ass'n of Washington

1201 New York Ave. NW
Suite 601
Washington, DC 20005
Tel: (202)289-0584
Fax: (202)289-8849
Registered: LDA
E-mail: edvetter@aol.com
Leg. Issues: DOC

Political Action Committee/s

Hotel Organization to Elect Leaders
1201 New York Ave. NW
Suite 601
Washington, DC 20005
Tel: (202)289-0584
Fax: (202)289-8849

In-house, DC-area Employees
WALKER, Reba P.: President

Outside Counsel/Consultants

Harmon & Wilmot, L.L.P.
Issues: DOC
Rep By: David W. Wilmot

Hotel Employees and Restaurant Employees Internat'l Union

1219 28th St. NW
Washington, DC 20007
Tel: (202)393-4373
Fax: (202)333-0468
Registered: LDA
Web: www.hereiu.org
E-mail: hereiu@pop.erols.com
Leg. Issues: ENV, LBR, TAX, TOB, TOU

Political Action Committee/s

Hotel Employees and Restaurant Employees Internat'l Union TIP-T Insure Progress
1219 28th St. NW
Washington, DC 20007
Tel: (202)393-4373
Fax: (202)965-0868
Contact: John W. Wilhelm

In-house, DC-area Employees
WILHELM, John W.: President

Outside Counsel/Consultants

Robert E. Juliano Associates
Issues: ENV, LBR, TAX, TOB, TOU

Housatonic Resources Recovery Authority

Brookfield, CT

Outside Counsel/Consultants

Wright & Talisman, P.C.
Rep By: Scott M. DuBoff

House Majority Fund

2407 15th St. NW
Suite 406
Washington, DC 20009
Tel: (202)248-0305

In-house, DC-area Employees
COLLINS, Michael

Household Financial Group, Ltd.

1730 K St. NW
Suite 1106
Washington, DC 20006
Tel: (202)466-3561
Fax: (202)466-3583
Registered: LDA
Leg. Issues: BNK, FIN

In-house, DC-area Employees
HANLON, Blake: Federal Director
O'TOOLE, J. Denis: V. President, Federal Governmental Relations
ST. AMAND, Janet G.: Director/Counsel, Federal Government Relations
STEWARD, William R.: Director, Governmental Relations

Household Goods Forwarders Ass'n of America, Inc.

2320 Mill Rd.
Suite 102
Alexandria, VA 22314
Tel: (703)684-3780
Fax: (703)684-3784
Web: www.hhgfaa.org
E-mail: hhgfaa@aol.com

Represents regulated moving and storage companies household goods forwarders and ocean carriers. Members move commercial and Department of Defense personal property domestically and internationally.

Leg. Issues: DEF

In-house, DC-area Employees
HEAD, Terry: President

Outside Counsel/Consultants

Denning & Wohlstetter
Rep By: Alan F. Wohlstetter

PACE-CAPSTONE
Issues: DEF
Rep By: James W. Wise

Household Goods Forwarders Tariff Bureau

Outside Counsel/Consultants

Denning & Wohlstetter
Rep By: Stanley I. Goldman

Household Internat'l, Inc.

1730 K St. NW
Suite 1106
Washington, DC 20006
Tel: (202)466-3561
Fax: (202)466-3583
Registered: LDA

Headquartered in Prospect Heights, IL.

Leg. Issues: BAN, BNK, FIN, HCR, RET, TAX, TOR

Political Action Committee/s

Household Internat'l Political Action Committee
1730 K St. NW
Suite 1106
Washington, DC 20006
Tel: (202)466-3561
Fax: (202)466-3583
Contact: Micaela Isler

In-house, DC-area Employees
ISLER, Micaela: PAC Director
ST. AMAND, Janet G.: Federal Director/Counsel
STEWARD, William R.: Director, Governmental Relations

Outside Counsel/Consultants

The Dutko Group, Inc.
Issues: BAN
Rep By: Gary J. Andres, Kimberly M. Spaulding

PriceWaterhouseCoopers
Issues: TAX
Rep By: Kenneth J. Kies

Housing and Development Law Institute

630 I St. NW
Washington, DC 20001
Tel: (202)289-3400
Fax: (202)289-3401
E-mail: hdli2000@aol.com
Leg. Issues: HOU

In-house, DC-area Employees
MAHER, William F.: Exec. Director and Counsel

Housing Assistance Council

1025 Vermont Ave. NW
Suite 606
Washington, DC 20005
Tel: (202)842-8600
Fax: (202)347-3441
Web: www.ruralhome.org
E-mail: hac@ruralhome.org

A national non-profit organization that helps provide decent and affordable housing for the rural poor by using its loan funds, technical assistance and training to supplement the efforts of housing organizations serving the people of rural America.

Leg. Issues: BUD, HOU

In-house, DC-area Employees
BELDEN, Joe: Deputy Exec. Director
LOZA, Moises: Exec. Director

Outside Counsel/Consultants

Reno & Cavanaugh, PLLC
Rep By: Lee P. Reno

Romano & Associates, LLC
Issues: BUD, HOU
Rep By: John Romano

Housing Works

Washington, DC
Leg. Issues: BUD, HOU, TAX

Outside Counsel/Consultants

The Sheridan Group
Issues: BUD, HOU, TAX
Rep By: Thomas F. Sheridan

Houston Advanced Research Center

The Woodlands, TX
Leg. Issues: ENV

Outside Counsel/Consultants

Hooper Owen & Winburn
Issues: ENV
Rep By: Lucia A. Wyman

Houston Clearing House Ass'n

Houston, TX

Outside Counsel/Consultants

Arter & Hadden
Rep By: William K. Dabaghi

Houston Galveston Area Council

Houston, TX
Leg. Issues: ENV, TRA

Outside Counsel/Consultants

Capitol Counsel Group, L.L.C.
Issues: ENV, TRA
Rep By: Warren Belmar

Houston Independent School District

Houston, TX
Leg. Issues: EDU

Outside Counsel/Consultants

Alcalde & Fay
Issues: EDU
Rep By: Danielle McBeth, Lois Moore, Kathy Jurado Munoz, Tim Stroud

Houston Shell and Concrete

Houston, TX
Leg. Issues: ENV, ROD, TRD

Outside Counsel/Consultants

Janus-Merritt Strategies, L.L.C.
Issues: ENV, ROD, TRD
Rep By: Mark J. Robertson, J. Daniel Walsh

Houston, Texas, City of

Leg. Issues: BUD, ENV, HOU, TRA, URB

Outside Counsel/Consultants

Patton Boggs, LLP
Issues: BUD, ENV, HOU, TRA, URB
Rep By: Parker Brugge, Shannon M. Gibson, Carolina L. Mederos, Florence W. Prioleau

Houston, Texas, Department of Aviation of the City of

Houston, TX
Leg. Issues: AVI

Outside Counsel/Consultants

Capitol Coalitions Inc.
Issues: AVI
Rep By: Amy R. Mehlman, Brett P. Scott, Jarvis C. Stewart

Zuckert, Scoutt and Rasenberger, L.L.P.
Issues: AVI
Rep By: Paul E. Schoellhamer, Rachel B. Trinder

Houston, Texas, Department of Public Works & Engineering of the City of

Leg. Issues: BUD, ENV

Outside Counsel/Consultants

LeBoeuf, Lamb, Greene & MacRae L.L.P.
Issues: BUD, ENV
Rep By: D. Randall Benn

Houston, Texas, Housing Authority of the City of

Outside Counsel/Consultants

Reno & Cavanaugh, PLLC

Houston, Texas, Port Authority of the City of

Leg. Issues: BUD, TRA

Outside Counsel/Consultants
Arter & Hadden
Issues: TRA
Rep By: Hon. Thomas G. Loeffler, Jon W. Plebani
Bracewell & Patterson, L.L.P.
Issues: BUD
Rep By: Hon. Edwin R. Bethune, Hon. Jim Chapman, Gene E. Godley, Marc C. Hebert, Charles L. Ingebretson, Michael L. Pate, Scott H. Segal, D. Michael Stroud, Jr.

Howard County, Maryland
Ellicott City, MD
Leg. Issues: COM, GOV
Outside Counsel/Consultants
Duncan, Weinberg, Genzer & Pembroke, P.C.
Issues: COM, GOV
Rep By: Janice L. Lower

Howard Energy Internat'l
Oceanside, CA
Outside Counsel/Consultants
Baker, Donelson, Bearman & Caldwell, P.C.
Rep By: Doreen M. Edelman, Charles R. Johnston, Jr.

Howard, Meedles, Tammen & Bergendoff
Kansas City, MO
Outside Counsel/Consultants
Wilmer, Cutler & Pickering
Rep By: Bruce M. Berman

Howland Hook Container Terminal Inc.
Staten Island, NY
Leg. Issues: BUD, MAR, TRA
Outside Counsel/Consultants
Akin, Gump, Strauss, Hauer & Feld, L.L.P.
Issues: BUD, MAR, TRA
Rep By: Anthony Foti, Susan H. Lent, Ado A. Machida, Hon. William L. Paxon, Henry A. Terhune

HP Global Workplaces, Inc.
Dallas, TX
Leg. Issues: POS
Outside Counsel/Consultants
Williams & Jensen, P.C.
Issues: POS
Rep By: William B. Canfield, J. Steven Hart, Anthony J. Roda

HT Medical
Gaithersburg, MD
Recently aquired by Immersion Medical, headquartered in San Jose, CA.
Leg. Issues: HCR
Outside Counsel/Consultants
Palumbo & Cerrell, Inc.
Issues: HCR
Rep By: William T. Deitz, Charles R. O'Regan, Benjamin L. Palumbo, Paul A. Skrabut, Jr.

Hualapai Nation
Peach Springs, AZ
Leg. Issues: BUD, IND, TRA
Outside Counsel/Consultants
Holland & Knight LLP
Issues: BUD, IND, TRA
Rep By: Joseph L. Kitto, David C. Whitestone
Nordhaus Haltom Taylor Taradash & Bladh LLP
Issues: IND

Hubbard Broadcasting, Inc.
St. Paul, MN
Leg. Issues: COM, TEC
Outside Counsel/Consultants
Holland & Knight LLP
Issues: COM, TEC
Rep By: Hon. Gerald E. Sikorski

Hubbell, Inc.
Orange, CT
Leg. Issues: TAX
Outside Counsel/Consultants
Hooper Owen & Winburn
Issues: TAX
Rep By: Lindsay D. Hooper

J. M. Huber Corp.
Edison, NJ
Outside Counsel/Consultants
Thelen Reid & Priest LLP

Hudson Institute
1015 18th St. NW
Suite 300
Washington, DC 20036
Web: www.hudson.org
Tel: (202)223-7770
Fax: (202)223-8537
An Indianapolis-based "think tank".
Leg. Issues: AGR, CHM, CIV, DEF, ECN, EDU, ENV, HOU, RET, SCI, TAX, TEC, TRD, URB, WEL
In-house, DC-area Employees
FUMENTO, Michael: Senior Fellow
HORNER, Charles: Senior Fellow
HOROWITZ, Michael J.: Senior Fellow
KAUFFMAN, Amy: Research Fellow
ODOM, USA (Ret), Lt. Gen. William E.: Director, National Security Studies
REYNOLDS, Alan: Senior Fellow and Director, Economic Studies
STELZER, Irwin: Senior Fellow and Director, Regulatory Studies
WEICHER, John C.: Senior Fellow
WEINSTEIN, Kenneth: Director, Washington Office
WITTMANN, Marshall: Senior Fellow, Governmental Studies

Hudson News
Outside Counsel/Consultants
The Dutko Group, Inc.

Huffy Bicycles
Miamisburg, OH
Outside Counsel/Consultants
Porter, Wright, Morris & Arthur, LLP
Rep By: Bart S. Fisher

Huffy Corp.
Dayton, OH
Outside Counsel/Consultants
Howrey Simon Arnold & White
Rep By: Alan M. Grimaldi

Huffy Sports
Sussex, WI
Outside Counsel/Consultants
Porter, Wright, Morris & Arthur, LLP
Rep By: Bart S. Fisher

Howard Hughes Corp.
Las Vegas, NV
A land development company.
Outside Counsel/Consultants
McClure, Gerard & Neuenschwander, Inc.
Rep By: Steven G. Barringer, Joseph T. Findaro, Matthew Iandoli, Nils W. Johnson, Hon. James A. McClure, Tod O. Neuenschwander

Hughes Electronics Corp.
Los Angeles, CA
Leg. Issues: AER, TRD
Outside Counsel/Consultants
Gibson, Dunn & Crutcher LLP
Issues: AER
Rep By: Alan A. Platt
The Roth Group
Issues: TRD
Rep By: Hon. Toby Roth, Sr.

Howard Hughes Medical Institute
4000 Jones Bridge Rd.
Chevy Chase, MD 20815-6789
Web: www.hhmi.org
E-mail: potterr@hhmi.org
Tel: (301)215-8855
Fax: (301)215-8863
A philanthropic organization that conducts biomedical research in collaboration with universities in the United States. Also awards grants for science education, including individual fellowships, and to support biomedical researchers in selected foreign countries.
In-house, DC-area Employees
CECH, Ph.D., Thomas R.: President
POTTER, Robert A.: Director, Communications

Hughes Space & Communications Co.
Los Angeles, CA
Leg. Issues: AVI
Outside Counsel/Consultants
Van Scoyoc Associates, Inc.
Issues: AVI
Rep By: Steven O. Palmer, Chad Schulken, H. Stewart Van Scoyoc

Hulcher Quarry, Inc.
Nokomis, IL
Outside Counsel/Consultants
Heenan, Althen & Roles
Rep By: Michael T. Heenan

Human Capital Resources
New York, NY
Leg. Issues: BNK, EDU, TAX
Outside Counsel/Consultants
Robert E. Carlstrom
Issues: BNK, EDU, TAX
Rep By: Robert E. Carlstrom, Jr.
Jefferson Consulting Group
Issues: EDU
Rep By: Robert J. Thompson

Human Factors Soc.
Santa Monica, CA
Outside Counsel/Consultants
Jenner & Block

Human Genome Sciences Inc.
Rockville, MD
Leg. Issues: CPT
Outside Counsel/Consultants
Akin, Gump, Strauss, Hauer & Feld, L.L.P.
Issues: CPT
Rep By: Thaddeus Burns, Barney J. Skladany, Jr., Daniel L. Spiegel, Robin Weisman

Human Relations Foundation of Chicago
Chicago, IL
Outside Counsel/Consultants
Hauser Group

Human Rights Campaign
Washington, DC
Leg. Issues: CIV
Outside Counsel/Consultants
Williams & Jensen, P.C.
Issues: CIV
Rep By: Barbara Wixon Bonfiglio, Karen Judd Lewis, Anthony J. Roda

Human Rights Campaign Fund
919 18th St. NW
Suite 800
Washington, DC 20006
Web: www.hrc.org
E-mail: hrc@hrc.org
Tel: (202)628-4160
Fax: (202)347-5323
Registered: LDA
A national lesbian and gay political organization. Lobbies Congress, provides campaign support, and educates the public.
Leg. Issues: CIV, HCR, LBR
Political Action Committee/s
Human Rights Campaign PAC
919 18th St. NW
Suite 800
Washington, DC 20006
Contact: Mike Mings
Tel: (202)628-4160
Fax: (202)347-5323
In-house, DC-area Employees
BIRCH, Elizabeth M.: Exec. Director
BUERMEYER, Nancy: Deputy Director, Legislation
CRAWFORD, Michael: Western Field Organizer
GINGRICH, Candace: NCOP Associate Manager
GREEN, Sally: Northern Field Organizer
HITCHCOCK, Donald: Southern Field Organizer
HUDDLESTON, Andrew: Political Assistant
KILBOURN, Seth: National Field Director
LABONTE, Christopher: Senior Policy Advocate
LAYTON, Kevin: Senior Counsel
MENARD, Barbara: Senior Policy Advocate
MINGS, Mike: Deputy Director, PAC
NELSON, Cathy: Development Director
NESBITT, Elizabeth: Western Field Organizer
PAYNE, Donna: Constituent Field Organizer
PERRIELLO, Mark: PAC Manager
SEATON, Liz: Field Deputy Director
SMITH, David M.: Director, Communications/Senior Strategist
SNOWDEN, Courtney: Policy Assistant
SPEY, Adam: PAC Coordinator
ST. PIERRE, Tracey: Senior Policy Associate

STACHELBERG, Winnie: Political Director
VARONA, Anthony E.: General Counsel

Human Rights Watch

1630 Connecticut Ave. NW
Suite 500
Washington, DC 20009
Web: www.hrw.org
Tel: (202)612-4321
Fax: (202)612-4333

The umbrella human rights organization whose components include the Africa, Americas, Asia, Helsinki and Middle East divisions, as well as other special projects. Based in New York City.

In-house, DC-area Employees
FLEISCHMAN, Janet: Washington Director, Human Rights Watch - Africa Division
GOLDSTEIN, Ricky: Acting Director, Human Rights Watch - Middle East Division
GOOSE, Stephen D.: Program Director, Arms Project
JENDRZEJCZYK, Mike: Washington Director, Human Rights Watch - Asia Division
RALPH, Regan: Director, Women's Rights Division

Humana Inc.

800 Connecticut Ave. NW
Suite 200
Washington, DC 20006
Web: www.humana.com
Tel: (202)467-5821
Fax: (202)467-5825
Registered: LDA

A health insurance company including, HMOs, PPOs, POSs, and Dental coverage. Headquartered in Louisville, KY.

Leg. Issues: BUD, DEF, HCR, INS, MMM

Political Action Committee/s
Humana PAC
800 Connecticut Ave. NW
Suite 200
Washington, DC 20006
Contact: Mary McKenzie
Tel: (202)467-5821
Fax: (202)467-5825

In-house, DC-area Employees
MCKENZIE, Mary: Director, Federal Relations and Treasurer
WILSON, Kimberly: Government Affairs Assistant

Outside Counsel/Consultants
Capitol Health Group, LLC
Issues: HCR, MMM
Rep By: Michael D. Bromberg, Shawn Coughlin, Steven Jenning, Layna McConkey Peltier
Greenberg Traurig, LLP
Issues: BUD, DEF, HCR, MMM
Rep By: Howard J. Cohen, Russell J. Mueller, Nancy E. Taylor

Humane Soc. of the United States

2100 L St. NW
Washington, DC 20037
Web: www.hsus.org
Tel: (202)452-1100
Fax: (202)778-6132
Registered: LDA

A non-profit organization concerned with the protection of animals, both domestic and wild. Provides consultation and guidance to local animal welfare agencies and conducts investigations into major incidents of animal abuse. Actively pursues implementation of state and federal legislation and engages in litigation on behalf of animal welfare.

Leg. Issues: ANI, LAW, MAR

In-house, DC-area Employees
BRODY, Mimi A.: Director, Federal Legislation
GRANDY, Ph.D., John W.: V. President, Wildlife and Habitat Protection
HADIDIAN, John: Director, Suburban Wildlife Protection
HAGOOD, Susan: Wildlife Issues Specialist
IRWIN, Paul G.: President
KLEIN, D.V.M., Patrice: Wildlife Veterinarian
PACELLE, Wayne P.: Senior V. President, Communications and Government Affairs
PATCH, Richard: Legislative Specialist
ROSE, Ph.D., Naomi: Marine Mammal Scientist
TELECKY, Ph.D., Teresa: Director, Wildlife Trade Program

Outside Counsel/Consultants
Meyer & Glitzenstein
Sher & Blackwell
Rep By: Earl W. Comstock, Jeffrey R. Pike

Humboldt Bay Municipal Water District

Eureka, CA
Leg. Issues: BUD, ENV, NAT, RES, TOU

Outside Counsel/Consultants
Reed, Smith, LLP
Issues: BUD, ENV, NAT, RES, TOU
Rep By: Christopher L. Rissetto

Humboldt Harbor Recreation

Eureka, CA
Leg. Issues: BUD, CAW, TRA

Outside Counsel/Consultants
Murray, Scheer, Montgomery, Tapia & O'Donnell
Issues: BUD, CAW, TRA
Rep By: John R. O'Donnell

Hunt Valve Co., Inc.

Salem, OH

Outside Counsel/Consultants
Arter & Hadden

Hunter Ceiling Fans

Memphis, TN

Outside Counsel/Consultants
Interface Inc.
Rep By: David C. Knapp

Hunterdon Medical Center

Flemington, NJ

Outside Counsel/Consultants
Cassidy & Associates, Inc.

Huntingdon College

Montgomery, AL
Leg. Issues: EDU, SCI

Outside Counsel/Consultants
Sagamore Associates, Inc.
Issues: EDU, SCI
Rep By: Julia P. Church, Doug Wasitis

Huntington Bancshares

Columbus, OH

Outside Counsel/Consultants
Porter, Wright, Morris & Arthur, LLP
Rep By: E. Jay Finkel

Huntington Beach, California, City of

Leg. Issues: BUD, ENV, NAT, WAS

Outside Counsel/Consultants
The Ferguson Group, LLC
Issues: BUD, ENV, NAT, WAS
Rep By: W. Roger Gwinn, Ralph Webb

Huntington Sanitary Board

Huntington, WV
Leg. Issues: CAW

Outside Counsel/Consultants
McGuireWoods L.L.P.
Issues: CAW
Rep By: Joseph H. Bogosian, Stephen A. Katsurinis, Jeffrey L. Schlagenhauf

Huntington's Disease Soc. of America

New York, NY
Leg. Issues: BUD, HCR, MED

Outside Counsel/Consultants
McDermott, Will and Emery
Issues: BUD, HCR, MED
Rep By: Neil Quinter

Hunts Point Terminal Cooperative Ass'n

Bronx, NY

Outside Counsel/Consultants
Shaw Pittman

Huntsman Corp.

8201 Greensboro Dr.
Suite 1000
McLean, VA 22102
Web: www.huntsman.com
E-mail: patrick_h_mcnamara@huntsman.com
Tel: (703)394-8018
Fax: (703)394-8048
Registered: LDA

A chemical manufacturer headquartered in Salt Lake City, UT.

Leg. Issues: CAW, CHM, CSP, ENG, ENV, FOO, FUE, HCR, TRD, WAS

In-house, DC-area Employees
MCNAMARA, Patrick H.: Director, Government and Industry Relations

Outside Counsel/Consultants
Bracewell & Patterson, L.L.P.
Issues: ENV
Rep By: Hon. Edwin R. Bethune, Hon. Jim Chapman, Gene E. Godley, Marc C. Hebert, Charles L. Ingebretson, Michael L. Pate, Scott H. Segal, D. Michael Stroud, Jr.

Huntsville Madison Chamber of Commerce

Huntsville, AL
Leg. Issues: AER, DEF

Outside Counsel/Consultants
Hall, Green, Rupli, LLC
Issues: AER, DEF
Rep By: John M. Green, G. Stewart Hall

Huntsville, Alabama, City of

Leg. Issues: ECN, HOU, LAW, ROD, TRA, URB

Outside Counsel/Consultants
R. G. Flippo and Associates, Inc.
Issues: ECN, ROD, TRA, URB
Rep By: Hon. Ronnie G. Flippo, Vicki P. Wallace
Barbara T. McCall Associates
Issues: HOU, LAW, TRA, URB
Rep By: Ralph Garboushian, Barbara T. McCall

Huntsville, Alabama, Solid Waste Disposal Authority of the City of

Outside Counsel/Consultants
Wright & Talisman, P.C.
Rep By: Scott M. DuBoff

Huntsville-Madison County Airport

Huntsville, AL
Leg. Issues: AVI, TRA

Outside Counsel/Consultants
R. G. Flippo and Associates, Inc.
Issues: AVI, TRA
Rep By: Hon. Ronnie G. Flippo, Vicki P. Wallace

Huron Hospital

Cleveland, OH

Outside Counsel/Consultants
Boesch & Co.
Rep By: Doyce A. Boesch

Hurt, Norton and Associates, Inc.

Washington, DC
Leg. Issues: DEF

Outside Counsel/Consultants
Robert D. Sneed
Issues: DEF
Rep By: Robert D. Sneed

Fred Hutchinson Cancer Research Center

Seattle, WA
Leg. Issues: BUD, HCR, IMM, MED, TAX, TOB

Outside Counsel/Consultants
Capitol Associates, Inc.
Issues: BUD, HCR, IMM, MED, TAX, TOB
Rep By: Debra M. Hardy Havens

Hutchinson, Kansas, Municipalities of

Outside Counsel/Consultants
Oppenheimer Wolff & Donnelly LLP

Hutchison Whampo, LTD

Hong Kong, CHINA (PEOPLE'S REPUBLIC)
Leg. Issues: GOV

Outside Counsel/Consultants
Hooper Owen & Winburn
Issues: GOV
Rep By: David Rudd, John P. Winburn
Public Strategies Washington, Inc.
Rep By: Joseph P. O'Neill

HUTCO, Inc.

Lafayette, LA
Leg. Issues: IMM, LBR

Outside Counsel/Consultants
Diane McRee Associates
Issues: IMM, LBR
Rep By: Diane B. McRee

Hutzel Medical Center

Detroit, MI
Leg. Issues: HCR, MMM

Outside Counsel/Consultants
McDermott, Will and Emery
Issues: HCR, MMM
Rep By: Wendy L. Krasner, Maggie A. Mitchell, Karen S. Sealander

Hvide Marine Inc.
Fort Lauderdale, FL
Leg. Issues: MAR

Outside Counsel/Consultants

Dyer Ellis & Joseph, P.C.
Issues: MAR
Rep By: Laurie Crick Sahatjian, James S. W. Drewry, Thomas M. Dyer, James B. Ellis, II, Jeanne Marie Grasso, Lara Bernstein Mathews, Duncan C. Smith, III, Jennifer M. Southwick, Jonathan K. Waldron

HWT Inc.
Portland, ME
A healthcare monitoring firm.

Outside Counsel/Consultants

Cassidy & Associates, Inc.

Gilbert P. Hyatt, Inventor
Leg. Issues: TAX

Outside Counsel/Consultants

Washington Council Ernst & Young
Issues: TAX
Rep By: Doug Badger, Lauren Darling, John L. Doney, Jayne T. Fitzgerald, LaBrenda Garrett-Nelson, Gary J. Gasper, Bruce A. Gates, Nick Giordano, Cathy Koch, Robert J. Leonard, Richard Meltzer, Phillip D. Moseley, John D. Porter, Robert M. Rozen, Donna Steele-Flynn, Timothy J. Urban

Hybrid Branch Coalition
Washington, DC
Leg. Issues: TAX

Outside Counsel/Consultants

Arthur Andersen LLP
Issues: TAX
Rep By: Rachelle Bernstein, Weston J. Coulam, Thomas D. Fuller, Richard A. Gordon, T. Timothy Tuerff

Hydro-Quebec
Montreal, CANADA
Leg. Issues: BNK, ENG, UTI

Outside Counsel/Consultants

Cameron McKenna
Rep By: George H. Williams, Jr., Joel F. Zipp

Dickstein Shapiro Morin & Oshinsky LLP
Issues: ENG, UTI
Rep By: Hon. Wendell H. Ford, Elizabeth B. Haywood, Robert Mangas, Graham "Rusty" Mathews, Laurie McKay, Rebecah Moore Shepherd, L. Andrew Zausner

LeBoeuf, Lamb, Greene & MacRae L.L.P.
Issues: BNK, ENG
Rep By: L. Charles Landgraf, Robert W. Woody

Hydrocarbon Technologies Inc.
Lawrenceville, NJ
A chemical and energy research and development company.
Leg. Issues: ENG

Outside Counsel/Consultants

Berkshire Inc.
Issues: ENG
Rep By: Michael T. Kelley

Hydroelectric Licensing Reform Task Force
Washington, DC
Leg. Issues: ENG

Outside Counsel/Consultants

Tongour Simpson Holsclaw Green
Issues: ENG
Rep By: Michael A. Tongour

The Wexler Group
Issues: ENG
Rep By: Joel Malina, Dale W. Snape, Hon. Robert S. Walker, Anne Wexler

Hyperion Medical
Celebration, FL
Leg. Issues: HCR, MMM

Outside Counsel/Consultants

Nusgart Consulting, LLC
Issues: HCR, MMM
Rep By: Marcia Nusgart

Hyperion Software
Stamford, CT
A computer software designer.

Outside Counsel/Consultants

Nusgart Consulting, LLC

Hyundai Electronics Industries Co., LTD
Seoul, KOREA
Leg. Issues: TRD

Outside Counsel/Consultants

Chlopak, Leonard, Schechter and Associates
Issues: TRD
Rep By: Tiffany Gagliardi, Maria Christina Gonzalez-Noguera, Charles G. Leonard, Peter Schechter

Willkie Farr & Gallagher
Issues: TRD
Rep By: James P. Durling, Daniel L. Porter, Russell L. Smith

Hyundai Motor Co.
1667 K St. NW
Suite 1210
Washington, DC 20006
Tel: (202)296-5550
Registered: LDA
Leg. Issues: AUT, TRD

In-house, DC-area Employees

EULE, Margo Grimm
SHIN, Hyun Kyu

Outside Counsel/Consultants

Aitken, Irvin, Lewin, Berlin, Vrooman & Cohn
Rep By: Bruce Aitken

Global USA, Inc.
Issues: AUT, TRD
Rep By: Rosamond S. Brown, George S. Kopp

Hyundai Pipe Co.
Seoul, KOREA

Outside Counsel/Consultants

Akin, Gump, Strauss, Hauer & Feld, L.L.P.

Hyundai Precision & Industrial Co., Ltd.
Seoul, KOREA

Outside Counsel/Consultants

The Carmen Group

Hyundai Semiconductor America, Inc.

Outside Counsel/Consultants

Swidler Berlin Shereff Friedman, LLP
Rep By: Barry B. Direnfeld, Harold P. Goldfield, Lester S. Hyman

Hyundai Space & Aircraft Co., Ltd.
Seoul, KOREA
Leg. Issues: AER, BAN

Outside Counsel/Consultants

The Carmen Group
Issues: AER, BAN
Rep By: Hon. Beau Boulter, Gerald P. Carmen, Barbara Diugos

"I Have a Dream" Foundation
New York, NY
Leg. Issues: EDU

Outside Counsel/Consultants

Verner, Liipfert, Bernhard, McPherson and Hand, Chartered
Issues: EDU
Rep By: Rosemary B. Freeman

I-49 Roadbuilders Coalition
Fort Smith, AR
Leg. Issues: ROD

Outside Counsel/Consultants

Infrastructure Management Group
Issues: ROD
Rep By: Porter K. Wheeler

I-69 Mid-Continent Highway Coalition
Shreveport, LA
Leg. Issues: TRA

Outside Counsel/Consultants

Patton Boggs, LLP
Issues: TRA
Rep By: Carolina L. Mederos

I.O.T.A. Partners
Bellevue, WA
A maritime exploration and salvage company.

Outside Counsel/Consultants

Baker & Hostetler LLP
Rep By: Steven A. Lotterer, Hon. Guy Vander Jagt

IAI Internat'l
Tel Aviv, ISRAEL
Leg. Issues: DEF

Outside Counsel/Consultants

Commonwealth Consulting Corp.
Issues: DEF
Rep By: Christopher M. Lehman

IATA U.S. Frequent Flyer Tax Interest Group
Geneva, SWITZERLAND
Leg. Issues: AVI, SCI, TAX, TEC, TOU

Outside Counsel/Consultants

Schnader Harrison Segal & Lewis LLP
Issues: AVI, SCI, TEC, TOU

Wilmer, Cutler & Pickering
Issues: TAX
Rep By: J. Barclay Collins, F. David Lake, Jr.

Iberville Parish
Plaquemine, LA
Leg. Issues: BUD, ENV, NAT, TRA

Outside Counsel/Consultants

Adams and Reese LLP
Issues: BUD, ENV, NAT, TRA
Rep By: B. Jeffrey Brooks, Andrea Wilkinson

Ibex
Arlington, VA
Leg. Issues: AVI, ENG

Outside Counsel/Consultants

Smith, Hinaman & Associates
Issues: AVI, ENG
Rep By: Randy Hinaman, Don Smith, Todd Smith

IBFI - The Internat'l Ass'n for Document and Information Management Solutions
100 Daingerfield Rd.
Alexandria, VA 22314-2888
Web: www.ibfi.org
E-mail: ecover@ibfi.org
Tel: (703)684-9606
Fax: (703)684-9675

Formerly known as Internat'l Business Forms Industries.

In-house, DC-area Employees

FREITAS, Joseph: President

Outside Counsel/Consultants

Howe, Anderson & Steyer, P.C.

IBP, Inc.
Dakota Dunes, SD
Leg. Issues: ENV, IMM

Outside Counsel/Consultants

Paul, Weiss, Rifkind, Wharton & Garrison
Issues: IMM
Rep By: Carl W. Hampe

Sidley & Austin
Issues: ENV
Rep By: Alan C. Raul

iCall, Inc.

Outside Counsel/Consultants

Nixon Peabody LLP
Rep By: Richard P. Stanton

ICC

Outside Counsel/Consultants

Pierre E. Murphy Law Offices

Ice Ban America, Inc.
North Palm Beach, FL
Leg. Issues: TRA

Outside Counsel/Consultants

Baise + Miller, P.C.
Issues: TRA
Rep By: Eric P. Bock, Marshall L. Miller

Iceland, Government of the Republic of
Reykjavik, ICELAND

Outside Counsel/Consultants

Fleishman-Hillard, Inc

Theodore George Kronmiller
Rep By: Theodore George Kronmiller

Iceland, Ministry of Fisheries, Government of
Reykjavik, ICELAND

Outside Counsel/Consultants

The Plexus Consulting Group
Rep By: Fred H. Hutchison

ICF Consulting

Fairfax, VA
Leg. Issues: ENG, ENV, LBR, TAX

Outside Counsel/Consultants

Crowell & Moring LLP
Issues: TAX
Rep By: Harold J. Heltzer

Joe Velasquez & Associates
Issues: ENG, ENV, LBR
Rep By: Joe Velasquez

ICF Industries, Inc.

New York, NY
Leg. Issues: TRD

Outside Counsel/Consultants

Willkie Farr & Gallagher
Issues: TRD
Rep By: Russell L. Smith

ICG Communications, Inc.

Englewood, CO
Leg. Issues: TEC

Outside Counsel/Consultants

Mattox Woolfolk, LLC
Issues: TEC
Rep By: Richard B. Mattox, Brian P. Woolfolk

Swidler Berlin Shereff Friedman, LLP
Issues: TEC
Rep By: Kristine DeBry, Gary D. Slaiman

Icicle Seafoods, Inc.

Seattle, WA
Leg. Issues: MAR

Outside Counsel/Consultants

Ball Janik, LLP
Issues: MAR
Rep By: Jay S. Johnson

Jack Ferguson Associates, Inc.
Issues: MAR
Rep By: Jack Ferguson

The Ickes & Enright Group

1300 Connecticut Ave. NW
Suite 600
Washington, DC 20036
Tel: (202)887-6726
Fax: (202)223-0358
Registered: LDA
E-mail: jenright@griffinjohnson.com
Leg. Issues: BUD

In-house, DC-area Employees

ENRIGHT, Janice Ann: Partner
ICKES, Harold M.: Partner

Outside Counsel/Consultants

Johnston & Associates, LLC
Issues: BUD
Rep By: Hon. J. Bennett Johnston, N. Hunter Johnston, W. Proctor Jones

ICN Pharmaceuticals, Inc.

Costa Mesa, CA
Leg. Issues: FOR, GOV

Outside Counsel/Consultants

Oppenheimer Wolff & Donnelly LLP
Issues: FOR, GOV
Rep By: Hon. Birch Bayh, Kevin O. Faley

ICO Global Communications

Washington, DC
Registered: LDA
Leg. Issues: COM, TEC

Outside Counsel/Consultants

Cormac Group, LLP

Morrison & Foerster LLP
Issues: COM, TEC
Rep By: Cheryl A. Tritt

ICRC Energy, Inc.

Alexandria, VA
Leg. Issues: BUD

Outside Counsel/Consultants

Birch, Horton, Bittner & Cherot
Issues: BUD
Rep By: Thomas L. Albert, Ronald G. Birch, William P. Horn

Idaho Energy Authority, Inc.

Idaho Falls, ID
Leg. Issues: ENG

Outside Counsel/Consultants

Kanner & Associates
Issues: ENG
Rep By: Martin B. Kanner

Idaho Power Co.

Boise, ID
Registered: LDA
Leg. Issues: BUD, CAW, ENG, ENV, NAT, UTI, WAS

Outside Counsel/Consultants

McClure, Gerard & Neuenschwander, Inc.
Issues: BUD, CAW, ENG, ENV, NAT, UTI, WAS
Rep By: Steven G. Barringer, Joseph T. Findaro, Matthew Iandoli, Nils W. Johnson, Hon. James A. McClure, Tod O. Neuenschwander

Idaho State University

Pocatella, ID
Leg. Issues: BUD

Outside Counsel/Consultants

Cassidy & Associates, Inc.
Issues: BUD
Rep By: Lawrence C. Grossman, W. Campbell Kaufman, IV, Laura A. Neal, Marnie Russ

Idaho Titanium Technologies, LLC

Idaho Falls, ID
Leg. Issues: DEF

Outside Counsel/Consultants

Charlie McBride Associates, Inc.
Issues: DEF
Rep By: Charlie McBride

Idaho, Department of Transportation of the State of

Boise, ID

Outside Counsel/Consultants

John A. DeVierno
Rep By: John A. DeVierno

Idaho, Office of the Attorney General of the State of

Boise, ID

Outside Counsel/Consultants

Duncan, Weinberg, Genzer & Pembroke, P.C.
Rep By: James F. Flug

Idex Corp.

Northbrook, IL

A manufacturer of industrial products.

Outside Counsel/Consultants

Collier Shannon Scott, PLLC
Rep By: Paul C. Rosenthal

IDT Corp.

Newark, NJ
Leg. Issues: TEC

Outside Counsel/Consultants

The Paul Laxalt Group
Issues: TEC
Rep By: Hon. Paul D. Laxalt, Tom Loranger

IEEE Computer Society

1730 Massachusetts Ave. NW
Washington, DC 20036-1903
Tel: (202)371-0101
Fax: (202)728-9614
Web: www.computer.org

Established in 1946, the IEEE Computer Society is the oldest and largest association of computer professionals in the world. Provides technical information and services. Also maintains offices in Los Alamito, Ca; Brussels, Belgium; and Tokyo, Japan. Recently opened service centers in Beijing, China; Budapest, Hungary; and Moscow, Russia.

In-house, DC-area Employees

KELLY, Anne Marie: Acting Exec. Director

IFI Claims Services

Leg. Issues: CPT

Outside Counsel/Consultants

Joseph L. Ebersole
Issues: CPT
Rep By: Joseph L. Ebersole

IIT Research Institute

Chicago, IL
Leg. Issues: DEF, TAX

Outside Counsel/Consultants

Berkshire Inc.
Issues: DEF, TAX
Rep By: Michael T. Kelley

Patton Boggs, LLP
Issues: DEF
Rep By: John J. Deschauer, Jr.

The PMA Group
Issues: DEF
Rep By: Kaylene Green, Patrick Hiu, Paul J. Magliocchetti, Charles Smith, Brian Thiel

Illinois Collaboration on Youth

Chicago, IL
Leg. Issues: BUD, COM, ENV, HCR, LAW, MMM, TOB, TRU

Outside Counsel/Consultants

Capitol Associates, Inc.
Issues: BUD, COM, ENV, HCR, LAW, MMM, TOB, TRU
Rep By: Debra M. Hardy Havens

Illinois Community College Board

Springfield, IL
Leg. Issues: EDU, WEL

Outside Counsel/Consultants

Davis O'Connell, Inc.
Issues: EDU, WEL
Rep By: Lynda C. Davis, Ph.D., Terrence M. O'Connell

Illinois Department of Human Services

Springfield, IL
Leg. Issues: AGR, ALC, BMD, BUD, FAM, GOV, HCR, MED, MMM, SCI, WEL

Outside Counsel/Consultants

The Livingston Group, LLC
Issues: AGR, ALC, BUD, FAM, GOV, HCR, MED, MMM, SCI, WEL
Rep By: Richard Legendre, Hon. Robert L. Livingston, Jr., J. Allen Martin, Richard L. Rodgers

Patton Boggs, LLP
Issues: AGR, ALC, BMD, FAM, GOV, HCR, MED, MMM, SCI, WEL
Rep By: Shannon M. Gibson, Hon. Willis "Bill" D. Gradison, John F. Jonas, Martha M. Kendrick, Debra Laboschin, Edward J. Newberry, Andrew M. Rosenberg

Illinois Department of Transportation

Springfield, IL
Leg. Issues: TRA

Outside Counsel/Consultants

The Carmen Group
Issues: TRA
Rep By: Ryan Adesnik, Hon. Beau Boulter, David M. Carmen, David A. Keene, Sharon Taylor

Illinois Hospital and Health Systems Ass'n

Napierville, IL
Leg. Issues: MMM

Outside Counsel/Consultants

Liz Robbins Associates
Issues: MMM
Rep By: Liz Robbins

Illinois Housing Development Authority

Chicago, IL
Leg. Issues: HOU, LAW, TAX

Outside Counsel/Consultants

Foley & Lardner
Issues: HOU, LAW, TAX
Rep By: Jodi L. Hanson

Illinois Institute of Technology

Leg. Issues: BUD

Outside Counsel/Consultants

Foley & Lardner
Issues: BUD
Rep By: Jodi L. Hanson

Illinois Primary Health Care Ass'n

Springfield, IL
Leg. Issues: BUD, HCR, MMM

Outside Counsel/Consultants

Holland & Knight LLP
Issues: BUD, HCR, MMM
Rep By: Robert Hunt Bradner

Illinois Public Transit Ass'n (IPTA)

Springfield, IL
Leg. Issues: TRA

Outside Counsel/Consultants

Edmund C. Graber
Issues: TRA
Rep By: Edmund C. Graber

Illinois State Board of Education

Springfield, IL
Leg. Issues: EDU

Outside Counsel/Consultants

Barbour Griffith & Rogers, Inc.
Issues: EDU
Rep By: Haley Barbour, Scott Barnhart, G. O. Lanny Griffith, Jr., Bill Himpler

Illinois Tool Works

Glenview, IL
Leg. Issues: MAN, TRD

Outside Counsel/Consultants

The Laurin Baker Group
Issues: MAN, TRD
Rep By: Laurin M. Baker

Oppenheimer Wolff & Donnelly LLP
Issues: MAN
Rep By: Hon. Birch Bayh, Kevin O. Faley

Illinois, State of

Springfield, IL
Leg. Issues: IND

Outside Counsel/Consultants

Mayer, Brown & Platt
Issues: IND
Rep By: Julian D'Esposito, Daniel Hildebrand

Illinois, Washington Office of the State of

444 N. Capitol St. NW
Suite 240
Washington, DC 20001
Tel: (202)624-7760
Fax: (202)724-0689

In-house, DC-area Employees

PIZZANO, Winifred A.: Senior Assistant to the Governor
ROBINSON, Bernie: Assistant to the Governor

Imaging Technologies Inc.

Washington, DC

Outside Counsel/Consultants

Ashby and Associates
Rep By: R. Barry Ashby

IMAX Corp.

Toronto, CANADA
Leg. Issues: ART

Outside Counsel/Consultants

American Continental Group, Inc.
Issues: ART
Rep By: Peter Terpeluk, Jr.

Baker, Donelson, Bearman & Caldwell, P.C.
Rep By: Francine Lamoriello, Joan M. McEntee

IMC Global Inc.

201 Maryland Ave. NE
Washington, DC 20002
Tel: (202)543-8700
Fax: (202)543-1562
Registered: LDA

Web: www.imcglobal.com
E-mail: bleberly@imcglobal.com

A worldwide producer and supplier of agriculture products and salt, headquartered in Lake Forest, IL.

Leg. Issues: AGR, ANI, BUD, CAW, ECN, ENV, FOR, HCR, LBR, NAT, RES, TAX, TOR, TRA, TRD, UTI, WAS

Political Action Committee/s

IMC Global Operations Inc. Political Action Committee
201 Maryland Ave. NE
Washington, DC 20002
Tel: (202)543-8700
Fax: (202)543-1562
Contact: Brenda L. Eberly

In-house, DC-area Employees

EBERLY, Brenda L.: Manager, Government Affairs

IMI Services USA, Inc.

7910 Woodmont Ave.
Suite 1410
Bethesda, MD 20814
Tel: (301)215-4800
Fax: (301)657-1446
Registered: LDA

A manufacturer of defense products.

Leg. Issues: DEF

In-house, DC-area Employees

SHARON, Yehiam: President

Outside Counsel/Consultants

Hooper Owen & Winburn
Issues: DEF
Rep By: Hon. Charles Wilson

Immaculata College

Immaculata, PA

Outside Counsel/Consultants

Cassidy & Associates, Inc.
Rep By: Douglass E. Bobbitt, Laura A. Neal, Mary E. Shields, Maureen Walsh

Immigration and Refugee Service of America

1717 Massachusetts Ave. NW
Suite 200
Washington, DC 20036
Tel: (202)797-2105
Fax: (202)797-2363
Registered: LDA
E-mail: irsa@irsa-uscr.org

Formerly the American Council for Nationalities Service. A nonsectarian network of non-profit organizations serving immigrants, refugees and their descendants. Advocates fair and humane public policy and assists foreign-born and non-English speakers through the coordination of refugee resettlement and direct assistance programs.

Leg. Issues: FOR, IMM

In-house, DC-area Employees

MASON, Jana: Congressional Liaison
NEZER, Melanie R.: Attorney
WINTER, Roger: Exec. Director

Immigration Law Group, P.C.

Washington, DC
Leg. Issues: IMM

Outside Counsel/Consultants

Wilson & Wasserstein, Inc.
Issues: IMM

Immune Deficiency Foundation, Inc.

Towson, MD
Leg. Issues: BUD

Outside Counsel/Consultants

Health and Medicine Counsel of Washington
Issues: BUD
Rep By: Dale P. Dirks, Gavin Lindberg

Immunex Corp.

Seattle, WA
Leg. Issues: HCR

Outside Counsel/Consultants

The Wexler Group
Issues: HCR
Rep By: Cynthia E. Berry, Jody A. Hoffman, Christine Maroulis, Erika Moritsugu, Anne Wexler

Impact America

228 S. Washington St.
Suite 200
Alexandria, VA 22314

A political action committee.

In-house, DC-area Employees

LISKER, Lisa R.: Contact

Impact Services

Philadelphia, PA

Outside Counsel/Consultants

Robert A. Rapoza Associates
Rep By: Robert A. Rapoza

Imperial Beach, California, City of

Leg. Issues: CAW

Outside Counsel/Consultants

The Furman Group
Issues: CAW
Rep By: Thomas M. James

Imperial Irrigation District

Imperial, CA
Leg. Issues: BUD, CAW, ENG, GOV, IND, NAT

Outside Counsel/Consultants

The Ferguson Group, LLC
Issues: BUD, CAW, ENG, IND, NAT
Rep By: William Ferguson, Jr., W. Roger Gwinn, Joseph L. Raeder

John J. Rhodes
Issues: GOV, NAT
Rep By: Hon. John J. Rhodes, III

Impex Overseas

Bucharest, ROMANIA

Outside Counsel/Consultants

Johnson, Rogers & Clifton, L.L.P.

Importers Service Corp.

Jersey City, NJ
Leg. Issues: TRD

Outside Counsel/Consultants

BKSH & Associates
Issues: TRD

IMS Health Inc.

Westport, CT
Leg. Issues: HCR, IMM, TAX

Outside Counsel/Consultants

The Wexler Group
Issues: HCR, IMM, TAX
Rep By: Cynthia E. Berry, Jody A. Hoffman, Christine Maroulis, Anne Wexler

IMSSCO Inc.

San Diego, CA

A manufacturer of fire fighting equipment.

Leg. Issues: DEF

Outside Counsel/Consultants

The PMA Group
Issues: DEF
Rep By: William E. Berl, Kaylene Green, Paul J. Magliocchetti

In-Pipe Technology

Chicago, IL
Leg. Issues: CAW, SCI

Outside Counsel/Consultants

Forster & Associates
Issues: CAW, SCI
Rep By: Johann R. Forster

Incentive Federation Sweepstakes Trust Fund

New York, NY
Leg. Issues: POS

Outside Counsel/Consultants

Dickstein Shapiro Morin & Oshinsky LLP
Issues: POS
Rep By: Henry C. Cashen, II, Elizabeth B. Haywood, Graham "Rusty" Mathews, Rebecah Moore Shepherd, L. Andrew Zausner

INCOL 2000

Washington, DC
Leg. Issues: TAX

Outside Counsel/Consultants

Ernst & Young LLP
Issues: TAX
Rep By: Lauren Darling, Patrick G. Heck, Phillip D. Moseley, John D. Porter, Henry C. Ruempler, Donna Steele-Flynn

Incorporated Research Institutions for Seismology

Washington, DC
Leg. Issues: SCI

Outside Counsel/Consultants

Monfort & Wolfe
Issues: SCI
Rep By: Charles A. Monfort

Incyte Pharmaceuticals, Inc.

Palo Alto, CA
Leg. Issues: DEF

Outside Counsel/Consultants

William M. Cloherty
Issues: DEF
Rep By: William M. Cloherty

Indalco Spa

Campobasso, ITALY
Leg. Issues: TRD

Outside Counsel/Consultants

Davis & Leiman, P.C.
Issues: TRD

Independence Bank

New York, NY
Leg. Issues: BAN

Outside Counsel/Consultants

Butera & Andrews
Issues: BAN
Rep By: Cliff W. Andrews, Wright H. Andrews, Jr., James J. Butera, Frank Tillotson

Independence Blue Cross

Philadelphia, PA

Outside Counsel/Consultants

The Direct Impact Co.

Independence Mining Co., Inc.

Englewood, CO Registered: LDA
Leg. Issues: NAT

Outside Counsel/Consultants

Crowell & Moring LLP
Issues: NAT
Rep By: Edward M. Green, R. Timothy McCrum, Steven P. Quarles

McClure, Gerard & Neuenschwander, Inc.
Rep By: Steven G. Barringer, Joseph T. Findaro, Matthew Iandoli, Nils W. Johnson, Hon. James A. McClure, Tod O. Neuenschwander

Independent Action

1317 F St. NW Tel: (202)783-2900
Suite 900 Fax: (202)783-3477
Washington, DC 20004-1105
E-mail: ralsan@aol.com

A political action committee that supports democratic challengers or state open seat candidates.

In-house, DC-area Employees

SANTORA, Ralph: Exec. Director

Independent Bakers Ass'n

1223 Potomac St. NW Tel: (202)333-8190
Washington, DC 20007-0231 Fax: (202)337-3809
Web: www.mindspring.com/~independentbaker
E-mail: independentbaker@mindspring.com

The contact information given is that of the firm Robert N. Pyle & Associates.

Leg. Issues: FOO

In-house, DC-area Employees

PYLE, Robert N.: President

Outside Counsel/Consultants

Robert N. Pyle & Associates
Issues: FOO
Rep By: Alexis Hersh, Alison O'Neill, Robert N. Pyle

Independent Bankers Ass'n of Texas

Austin, TX
Leg. Issues: BAN

Outside Counsel/Consultants

PACE-CAPSTONE
Issues: BAN
Rep By: James W. Wise

Independent Community Bankers of America

One Thomas Circle NW Tel: (202)659-8111
Suite 400 Fax: (202)659-9216
Washington, DC 20005 Registered: LDA
Web: www.icba.org
E-mail: info@icba.org

Represents locally owned and operated financial institutions in the United States.

Leg. Issues: AGR, BAN, BNK, FIN, SMB, TAX

Political Action Committee/s

Independent Bankers Political Action Committee
One Thomas Circle NW Tel: (202)659-8111
Suite 400 Fax: (202)659-9216
Washington, DC 20005

In-house, DC-area Employees

COOK, Timothy: Senior Editor
ENCE, Ronald K.: Director, Legislative Affairs
FOURNIER, Susan: Director, Information Center
GROCHALA, Ann M.: Director of Bank Operations
GUENTHER, Kenneth A.: Exec. V. President
HANLEY, John: Legislative Counsel
MERSKI, Paul: Tax Counsel
SCANLAN, Mark K.: Agriculture-Rural America Representative
THOMAS, Karen M.: Director of Regulatory Affairs/Senior Regulatory Counsel
WARE, Viveca Y.: Director of Payment Systems

Independent Contractor Ass'n of America, Inc.

1225 I St. NW Tel: (202)842-3400
Suite 1000 Fax: (202)842-0011
Washington, DC 20005 Registered: LDA
Web: www.littler.com

A national association dedicated to preserving independent contractor status.

Leg. Issues: TAX

In-house, DC-area Employees

HOLLRAH, Russell A.

Outside Counsel/Consultants

Littler Mendelson, P.C.
Issues: TAX
Rep By: Russell A. Hollrah

Independent Contractor Coalition

Washington, DC
Leg. Issues: LBR, TAX

Outside Counsel/Consultants

Davidson & Company, Inc.
Issues: LBR, TAX
Rep By: James H. Davidson, Richard E. May, Stanley Sokul

Independent Data Communications Manufacturers Ass'n

Washington, DC

Outside Counsel/Consultants

Squire, Sanders & Dempsey L.L.P.
Rep By: Herbert E. Marks

Independent Educational Consultants Ass'n

3251 Old Lee Hwy Tel: (703)591-4850
Suite 510 Fax: (703)591-4860
Fairfax, VA 22030-1504
Web: www.iecaonline.com
E-mail: requests@iecaonline.com

Professional association representing educational placement counselors working in private practice.

Leg. Issues: EDU, FAM

In-house, DC-area Employees

SKLAROW, Mark H.: Exec. Director

Independent Electrical Contractors, Inc.

2010-A Eisenhower Ave. Tel: (703)549-7351
Alexandria, VA 22314 Fax: (703)549-7448
Registered: LDA
Web: www.ieci.org
E-mail: ikec@ieci.org
Leg. Issues: BUD, ENG, LBR, TAX

Political Action Committee/s

Independent Electrical Contractors Inc. PAC
2010-A Eisenhower Ave. Tel: (703)549-7351
Alexandria, VA 22314 Fax: (703)549-7448

In-house, DC-area Employees

NORTHCOTT, Hao: V. President, Government Affairs

Independent Fuel Terminal Operators Ass'n

Leg. Issues: FUE

Outside Counsel/Consultants

Verner, Liipfert, Bernhard, McPherson and Hand, Chartered
Issues: FUE
Rep By: Andrea J. Grant, Gary J. Klein, John R. Mietus, William H. Minor, Linda M. Weinberg, Theresa M. Youngblood, John H. Zentay

Independent Grocers' Alliance

Chicago, IL

Outside Counsel/Consultants

Kirkpatrick & Lockhart LLP
Rep By: George W. Koch

Independent Insurance Agents of America, Inc.

412 First St. SE Tel: (202)863-7000
Suite 300 Fax: (202)863-7015
Washington, DC 20003 Registered: LDA
Web: www.iiaa.org
E-mail: info@iiaa.org
Leg. Issues: AGR, BAN, DIS, ENV, FIN, HCR, INS, MMM, SMB, TAX

Political Action Committee/s

Independent Insurance Agents of America, Inc. Political Action Committee
412 First St. SE Tel: (202)863-7000
Suite 300 Fax: (202)863-7015
Washington, DC 20003
Contact: Elizabeth E. Leger

In-house, DC-area Employees

BERTHOUD, Maria: V. President, Federal Government Affairs
EQUALE, Paul A.: Chief Exec. Officer, Capitol Hill Office
LEGER, Elizabeth E.: Assistant V. President, Political Affairs
MYERS, Jeffrey A.: V. President, Public Affairs
RIZZO, Eric: Manager, Grassroots Programs
RUSBULDT, Robert A.: Exec. V. President

Outside Counsel/Consultants

Collier Shannon Scott, PLLC
Issues: BAN, INS
Rep By: Scott A. Sinder

Independent Liquid Terminals Ass'n

1444 I Street NW Tel: (202)842-9200
Suite 400 Fax: (202)326-8660
Washington, DC 20005
Web: www.ilta.org
E-mail: ilta@ilta.org

An international trade association which represents operators of bulk liquid terminals above ground tank storage and pipeline facilities. Member companies operate for-hire and proprietary terminals.

In-house, DC-area Employees

CALVERT, E. Bruce: Director, Administration
DOANE, E. David: V. President
PROKOP, John A.: President

Independent Lubricant Manufacturers Ass'n

651 S. Washington St. Tel: (703)684-5574
Alexandria, VA 22314 Fax: (703)836-8503
Web: www.ilma.org
E-mail: ilma@ilma.org

A trade association representing over 150 companies that manufacture lubricants such as automotive and industrial oils, greases and metalworking fluids. Regular members, by definition, are neither owned nor controlled by companies that explore for or refine crude oil.

Leg. Issues: ENV

In-house, DC-area Employees

METALLO, Michael C.: Exec. Director

Outside Counsel/Consultants

Collier Shannon Scott, PLLC
Issues: ENV
Rep By: Jeffrey L. Leiter

Independent Office Products and Furniture Dealers Ass'n

301 North Fairfax St. Tel: (703)549-9040
Alexandria, VA 22314 Fax: (703)683-7552
Registered: LDA
Leg. Issues: BUD, GOV, HCR, LBR, MAN, POS, SMB, TAX

In-house, DC-area Employees

MILLER, Paul A.: Director of Government Affairs

Independent Oil and Gas Ass'n of Pennsylvania

Harrisburg, PA

Outside Counsel/Consultants

Bracewell & Patterson, L.L.P.
Rep By: Gene E. Godley, Michael L. Pate, Scott H. Segal

Independent Oil Producers Ass'n-Tri State

Evansville, IN

Outside Counsel/Consultants

Resources Development, Inc.
Rep By: Hon. Roger H. Zion

Independent Petroleum Ass'n of America

1201 15th St. NW Tel: (202)857-4722
Third Floor Fax: (202)857-4799
Washington, DC 20005 Registered: LDA
Web: www.ipaa.org
E-mail: govrel@ipaa.org

A national trade association representing oil and natural gas producers.

Leg. Issues: BAN, BUD, CAW, ENG, ENV, FUE, NAT, TAX, TRD, UTI, WAS

Political Action Committee/s

Wildcatter's Fund, Political Action Committee
1201 15th St. NW Tel: (202)857-4722
Third Floor Fax: (202)857-4799
Washington, DC 20005
Contact: Cynthia Powers Grisso

In-house, DC-area Employees
DILLON, Ben: V. President, Public Resources
FULLER, Lee O.: V. President, Government Relations
GRISSO, Cynthia Powers: V. President, Administration
MCCAUGHEY, Michelle: V. President, Communications
RUSSELL, Barry: President
SWEET, David M.: V. President, Natural Gas
WHITEHURST, Suzanne Kay: Director, Government Relations

Independent Power Tax Group

Leg. Issues: TAX

Outside Counsel/Consultants
Chadbourne and Parke LLP
Issues: TAX
Rep By: Keith Martin

Independent Sector

1200 18th St. NW
Second Floor
Washington, DC 20036
Tel: (202)467-6100
Fax: (202)467-6101
Registered: LDA
Web: www.independentsector.org
E-mail: info@independentsector.org

Independent Sector is a national forum working to encourage philanthropy, volunteering, not-for-profit initiative, and citizen action.

Leg. Issues: GOV, TAX

In-house, DC-area Employees
DARLING, Colleen: Writer/Researcher, Office of the President
MELENDEZ, Sara E.: President and Chief Executive Officer
SHIRAS, Peter: Senior V. President, Programs
THOMAS, John H.: V. President, Communications

Outside Counsel/Consultants
Caplin & Drysdale, Chartered
Issues: TAX
Rep By: Robert A. Boisture, Catherine E. Livingston

Independent Telephone and Telecommunications Alliance

Washington, DC
Leg. Issues: TEC

Outside Counsel/Consultants
Griffin, Johnson, Dover & Stewart
Issues: TEC
Rep By: G. Jack Dover, David W. Zesiger
KPMG, LLP
Latham & Watkins
Issues: TEC
Rep By: Nicholas W. Allard, Karen Brinkman, Richard Cameron
The Legislative Strategies Group, LLC
Issues: TEC
Rep By: Larry E. Smith

Independent Television Service

San Francisco, CA
Leg. Issues: COM

Outside Counsel/Consultants
Chernikoff and Co.
Issues: COM
Rep By: Larry B. Chernikoff

Independent Terminal Operators Ass'n

Washington, DC

Outside Counsel/Consultants
Bode & Grenier LLP
Rep By: William H. Bode

Independent Visually Impaired Enterprisers

1155 15th St. NW
Suite 1004
Washington, DC 20005
Tel: (202)467-5081
Fax: (202)467-5085

An affiliate of the American Council of the Blind. Represents visually impaired people who operate their own businesses.

In-house, DC-area Employees
HAYES, Carla: President

Independent Women's Forum

P.O. Box 3058
Arlington, VA 22203-0058
Tel: (703)558-4991
Fax: (703)558-4994
Web: www.iwf.org
E-mail: iwf@iwf.org

Provides a voice for American women who believe in individual freedom and personal responsibility.

In-house, DC-area Employees
PFOTENHAUER, Nancy M.: President
SCHULD, Kimberly: Director of Policy

Independents Committee for Future America

2023 Q St. NW
Washington, DC 20009-1009
Tel: (202)387-3624
Fax: (202)387-3629
E-mail: genih@aol.com

In-house, DC-area Employees
KITTRIE, Nicholas N.: Treasurer
SOBEL, Georgette J.: Secretary

India, Government of the Republic of

New Delhi, INDIA
Leg. Issues: FOR

Outside Counsel/Consultants
APCO Worldwide
Issues: FOR
Rep By: Hon. Don L. Bonker, Barry J. Schumacher
Jack H. McDonald
Rep By: Hon. Jack H. McDonald
Verner, Liipfert, Bernhard, McPherson and Hand, Chartered
Rep By: Berl Bernhard, Brenda G. Meister

Indian American Nat'l Foundation

Washington, DC

Outside Counsel/Consultants
Conlon, Frantz, Phelan & Pires
Rep By: Anurag Varma

Indian Hills Community College

Ottumwa, IA
Leg. Issues: EDU

Outside Counsel/Consultants
Moss McGee Bradley & Foley
Issues: EDU
Rep By: Leander J. Foley, III

Indian Law Resource Center

Outside Counsel/Consultants
Hauser Group

Indian Pueblos Federal Development Corp.

Albuquerque, NM
Leg. Issues: RES

Outside Counsel/Consultants
David F. Godfrey
Issues: RES
Rep By: David F. Godfrey

Indian River Citrus League

Indian River, FL

Outside Counsel/Consultants
Barnes, Richardson and Colburn
Rep By: Matthew T. McGrath

Indiana and Michigan Municipal Distributors Ass'n

Niles, MI
Leg. Issues: ENG, UTI

Outside Counsel/Consultants
Duncan, Weinberg, Genzer & Pembroke, P.C.
Issues: ENG, UTI
Rep By: Janice L. Lower, James D. Pembroke

Indiana County Development Corp.

Indiana, PA
Leg. Issues: TRA

Outside Counsel/Consultants
Ann Eppard Associates, Ltd.
Issues: TRA
Rep By: Julie Chlopecki, Ann Eppard

Indiana Department of Transportation

Indianapolis, IN
Leg. Issues: TRA

Outside Counsel/Consultants
Peyser Associates, Inc.
Issues: TRA
Rep By: Becky B. Weber

Indiana Glass Co.

Cincinnati, OH
Leg. Issues: TRD

Outside Counsel/Consultants
Barnes & Thornburg
Issues: TRD
Rep By: Randolph J. Stayin

Indiana Medical Device Manufacturers Council

Indianapolis, IN
Leg. Issues: MED

Outside Counsel/Consultants
Baker & Daniels
Issues: MED
Rep By: Mark W. Weller
Sagamore Associates, Inc.
Issues: MED
Rep By: Mark W. Weller

Indiana State University

Terre Haute, IN
Leg. Issues: BUD, EDU, LAW

Outside Counsel/Consultants
Sagamore Associates, Inc.
Issues: BUD, EDU, LAW
Rep By: Dena S. Morris, David Nichols

Indiana University

Bloomington, IN
Leg. Issues: BUD

Outside Counsel/Consultants
Sagamore Associates, Inc.
Issues: BUD
Rep By: Doug Wasitis, Mark W. Weller

Indiana, Office of the Attorney General of the State of

Indianapolis, IN

Outside Counsel/Consultants
Duncan, Weinberg, Genzer & Pembroke, P.C.
Rep By: James F. Flug

Indiana, Office of the Governor of the State of

Indianapolis, IN
Leg. Issues: ALC, AVI, BUD, CAW, DIS, ECN, EDU, ENV, GAM, GOV, HCR, HOU, IMM, IND, LAW, MMM, NAT, ROD, TAX, TEC, TEL, TOB, TRA, TRD, UNM, WAS, WEL

Outside Counsel/Consultants
Viohl and Associates, Inc.
Issues: ALC, AVI, BUD, CAW, DIS, ECN, EDU, ENV, GAM, GOV, HCR, HOU, IMM, IND, LAW, MMM, NAT, ROD, TAX, TEC, TEL, TOB, TRA, TRD, UNM, WAS, WEL
Rep By: Gerald J. Del Rosario, Jeffrey C. Viohl

Indianapolis Neighborhood Housing Partnership

Indianapolis, IN
Leg. Issues: HOU

Outside Counsel/Consultants
Sagamore Associates, Inc.
Issues: HOU
Rep By: Ann E. Cody, Dena S. Morris

Indianapolis Public Transportation Corp.

Indianapolis, IN
Leg. Issues: BUD, TRA

Outside Counsel/Consultants
Sagamore Associates, Inc.
Issues: BUD, TRA
Rep By: Dena S. Morris, David Nichols

Indianapolis Rail Project

Indianapolis, IN
Leg. Issues: TRA

Outside Counsel/Consultants
Baker, Donelson, Bearman & Caldwell, P.C.
Issues: TRA
Rep By: Janet L. Powell

Indianapolis, Indiana, City of

Outside Counsel/Consultants
Wright & Talisman, P.C.
Rep By: Scott M. DuBoff

Indigo

Chicago, IL
Leg. Issues: AVI

Outside Counsel/Consultants
Fleischman and Walsh, L.L.P.
Issues: AVI
Rep By: Louis H. Dupart, John P. McAllister

Individual Reference Services Group

Washington, DC
Leg. Issues: CSP

Outside Counsel/Consultants

Piper Marbury Rudnick & Wolfe LLP
Issues: CSP
Rep By: Alisa M. Bergman, Emilio W. Cividanes, James J. Halpert, Stuart P. Ingis, Paul W. Jamieson, Ronald L. Plesser

Indonesia, Government of the Republic of

Jakarta, INDONESIA

Outside Counsel/Consultants

White & Case LLP
Rep By: Carolyn B. Lamm

Indonesia, Ministry of Trade of the Republic of

Jakarta, INDONESIA

Outside Counsel/Consultants

C&M Internat'l, Ltd.

The INDOPCO Coalition

Washington, DC
Leg. Issues: TAX

Outside Counsel/Consultants

KPMG, LLP
Issues: TAX
Rep By: Robert M. Brown, Harry L. Gutman, Melbert E. Schwarz, Thomas A. Stout, Jr.

Indotrade, Inc.

Sterling, VA

Outside Counsel/Consultants

Vorys, Sater, Seymour and Pease, LLP
Rep By: James K. Alford

Industrial Customers of Northwest Utilities

Portland, OR
Leg. Issues: BUD, ENG, TAX, UTI

Outside Counsel/Consultants

Conkling, Fiskum & McCormick
Issues: BUD, ENG, TAX, UTI
Rep By: Gary Conkling, Norm Eder, Daniel Jarman

Industrial Designers Soc. of America

1142 Walker Rd.
Suite E
Great Falls, VA 22066
Web: www.idsa.org
E-mail: IDSA@erols.com
Tel: (703)759-0100
Fax: (703)759-7679

In-house, DC-area Employees

GOODRICH, Kristina: Exec. Director

Industrial Fabrics Ass'n Internat'l

2300 M St. NW
Suite 800
Washington, DC 20037
Web: www.ifai.com
E-mail: mtrifai@aol.com
Tel: (202)861-0981
Fax: (202)973-2881
Registered: LDA

A trade association for the industrial/technical fabrics industry. Headquartered in Roseville, MN.

Leg. Issues: APP, DEF, ENV, LBR, MAN, ROD, TRD, WAS

In-house, DC-area Employees

ROUNSAVILLE, Marcia Thomson: Washington Representative

Industrial Fasteners Institute

Cleveland, OH
Leg. Issues: MAN

Outside Counsel/Consultants

The Laurin Baker Group
Issues: MAN
Rep By: Laurin M. Baker

Industrial Minera Mexicana

Mexico City, MEXICO

Outside Counsel/Consultants

Porter, Wright, Morris & Arthur, LLP
Rep By: Leslie Alan Glick

Industrial Telecommunications Ass'n, Inc.

1110 N. Glebe Rd.
Suite 500
Arlington, VA 22201-5720
Web: www.ita-relay.com
E-mail: info@ita-relay.com
Tel: (703)528-5115
Fax: (703)524-1074
Registered: LDA

Founded in 1953, ITA is an FCC-certified frequency advisory committee and national trade association. In addition to regulatory and legislative representations before the FCC and Congress, ITA provides a variety of telecommunications services, including system engineering, licensing, FCC research, license data and refarming transition strategies. Supported by more than 3,000 members and 11 trade associations. Publishes Telecom Exchange.

Leg. Issues: BUD, COM, TEC

In-house, DC-area Employees

DENTON, Jeremy W.: Director, Government Affairs
SMITH, J. Sharpe: Director, Industry and Public Affairs
SMITH, Laura L.: President and C.E.O.

Outside Counsel/Consultants

Wiley, Rein & Fielding
Rep By: Robert L. Pettit

Industrial Truck Ass'n

1750 K St. NW
Suite 460
Washington, DC 20006
Web: www.indtrk.org
E-mail: indtrk@earthlink.net
Tel: (202)296-9880
Fax: (202)286-9884
Registered: LDA

ITA represents the manufacturers of forklift trucks and their suppliers.

In-house, DC-area Employees

MONTWIELER, William J.: Exec. Director

Outside Counsel/Consultants

Dunaway & Cross
Rep By: Mac S. Dunaway, Raymond P. Shafer

Industrie Alimentare Molisane

Campobasso, ITALY
Leg. Issues: TRD

Outside Counsel/Consultants

Law Offices of David L. Simon
Issues: TRD
Rep By: David L. Simon

Industry Union Glass Container Promotion Program

Leg. Issues: BEV

Outside Counsel/Consultants

O'Neill, Athy & Casey, P.C.
Issues: BEV
Rep By: Andrew Athy, Jr.

Industry Urban-Development Agency

Industry, CA
Leg. Issues: BUD, NAT

Outside Counsel/Consultants

Leon G. Billings, Inc.
Issues: BUD, NAT
Rep By: Leon G. Billings, Charlene A. Sturbitts

Infectious Diseases Soc. of America, Inc.

99 Canal Center Plaza
Suite 210
Alexandria, VA 22314
Web: www.idsociety.org
E-mail: info@idsociety.org
Tel: (703)299-0200
Fax: (703)299-0204
Registered: LDA

Leg. Issues: AGR, CSP, FOO, HCR, MED, MMM, SCI

In-house, DC-area Employees

GUIDOS, Robert J.: Director, Public Policy
LEASURE, Mark A.: Exec. Director

Outside Counsel/Consultants

Hogan & Hartson L.L.P.
Issues: HCR, MMM

Infilco Degremont, Inc.

Richmond, VA
Leg. Issues: BUD, CAW, ENV

Outside Counsel/Consultants

Millennium Intermarket Group, LLC
Issues: BUD, CAW, ENV
Rep By: P. Baman Rusby

Infiltrator Systems, Inc.

Old Saybrook, CT
Leg. Issues: CAW, ENV, UTI

Outside Counsel/Consultants

Albers & Co.
Issues: CAW, ENV, UTI
Rep By: William E. Albers, Daniel B. Beardsley, M. Guy Rohling

informal coalition

Leg. Issues: UTI

Outside Counsel/Consultants

Balch & Bingham LLP
Issues: UTI
Rep By: Sean Cunningham, Fred Eames, Patrick J. McCormick, III, Barbara K. Olson

InformaTech, Inc.

Fairfax, VA
Leg. Issues: DEF

Outside Counsel/Consultants

American Defense Internat'l, Inc.
Issues: DEF
Rep By: Michael Herson, Van D. Hipp, Jr., Dave Wilberding

Information Handling Services

Englewood, CO
Leg. Issues: GOV, SCI

Outside Counsel/Consultants

Foley & Lardner
Issues: GOV
Rep By: Kathleen Leonard, David Ralston, Jr.

Hargett Consulting
Issues: SCI
Rep By: Jack Hargett

Information Practices Coalition of Washington, D.C.

Washington, DC
Leg. Issues: GOV

Outside Counsel/Consultants

Kasten & Co.
Issues: GOV
Rep By: Robert W. Kasten, Jr., Frederick A. Ruth

Information Resources, Inc.

Leg. Issues: CAW, ENG, FUE

Outside Counsel/Consultants

Durante Associates
Rep By: Douglas A. Durante

RGS Enterprises, Inc.
Issues: CAW, ENG, FUE
Rep By: Ronald G. Sykes

Information Spectrum Inc.

Annandale, VA
Leg. Issues: IMM

Outside Counsel/Consultants

French & Company
Issues: IMM
Rep By: Rebecca Dornbusch, Verrick O. French

Information Technology Ass'n of America (ITAA)

1401 Wilson Blvd.
Suite 1100
Arlington, VA 22209
Web: www.itaa.org
E-mail: hmiller@itaa.org
Tel: (703)522-5055
Fax: (703)525-2279
Registered: LDA

Formerly the Ass'n of Data Processing Service Organizations (ADAPSO).

Leg. Issues: CPI, IMM, LBR, TEC

Political Action Committee/s

Information Technology Ass'n of America's "NET" PAC
1401 Wilson Blvd.
Suite 1100
Arlington, VA 22209
Contact: Harris N. Miller
Tel: (703)522-5055
Fax: (703)525-2279

In-house, DC-area Employees

BYNUM, Marjorie
CAYO, Carol: Director, Government Affairs-Taxation Policy
CLAMAN, Kimberly: V. President, Global Affairs
COHEN, Bob: Senior V. President, Communications
COLTON, David: V. President, Strategic Initiatives
FRAZIER, Lauren: Exec. Assistant, Government Affairs
GRKAVAC, Olga: Exec. V. President, Enterprise Systems Division
HOOPER, Heidi
KIM, Baker

LANDE, Jeffrey S.: V. President
MILLER, Harris N.: President
RIDNOUER, Nathan: Sr. Program Manager, ASP Program
SABO, Douglas: V. President, Information Security Programs
UNCAPHER, Mark: V. President and Counsel, Internet Commerce and Communications Division

Outside Counsel/Consultants

Patton Boggs, LLP
Issues: IMM, LBR
Rep By: Darryl D. Nirenberg, Jonathan R. Yarowsky

Seyfarth, Shaw, Fairweather & Geraldson
Issues: LBR
Rep By: Donald L. Rosenthal, Fredric S. Singerman

Squire, Sanders & Dempsey L.L.P.
Issues: TEC
Rep By: Jonathan J. Nadler

Information Technology Industry Council

1250 I St. NW
Suite 200
Washington, DC 20005
Tel: (202)737-8888
Fax: (202)638-4922
Registered: LDA
Web: www.itic.org

An association of information technology providers.

Leg. Issues: BUD, CPI, CPT, CSP, ENV, FIN, IMM, SCI, TAX, TEC, TRA, TRD

In-house, DC-area Employees

ADKINS, Richard Brian: Government Relations Counsel
DAWSON, Rhett B.: President
GODFREY, John: Director, Technology Policy
HAUSER, Katheryn: Director, Internat'l Trade
SALAETS, Kenneth J.: Director of Domestic Policy Issues
SMOOT, Oliver R.: Exec. V. President and Treasurer
TANIELIAN, Matthew J.: Director, Government Affairs

Outside Counsel/Consultants

Venable
Rep By: William D. Coston

Information Technology Resellers Ass'n

Reston, VA
Web: www.itra.net/welcome.cfm

Outside Counsel/Consultants

Smith, Bucklin and Associates, Inc.

Information Trust

2620 Quebec St. NW
Washington, DC 20008-1221
Tel: (202)364-1100
Fax: (202)364-2438
E-mail: sarmst@cni.org

Promotes free expression in the U.S. and abroad, and seeks to ensure government accountability by obtaining access to information, particularly in the areas of foreign policy, defense and military relations, and human rights. Combats inappropriate uses of government secrecy and advises investors on legislation and regulation in communications, media, trade, energy and Native American affairs.

Leg. Issues: AER, COM, CON, DEF, ENG, FIN, FOR, IND, MED, MIA, TEC, TRD

In-house, DC-area Employees

ARMSTRONG, R. Scott: Exec. Director

Infusion Dynamics

Plymouth Meeting, PA
Leg. Issues: DEF

Outside Counsel/Consultants

SISCORP
Issues: DEF
Rep By: Robert Meissner

ING America Insurance Holdings, Inc.

Wilmington, DE
Leg. Issues: FIN, GOV, INS, RET, TAX, TOR

Outside Counsel/Consultants

Deborah F. Winston
Issues: FIN, GOV, INS, RET, TAX, TOR
Rep By: Deborah F. Winston

Ingalls Shipbuilding

1725 Jefferson Davis Hwy.
Suite 601
Arlington, VA 22202
Tel: (703)418-0300
Fax: (703)413-0607
Registered: LDA

Headquartered in Pascagoula, MS.

Leg. Issues: DEF, TRA

In-house, DC-area Employees

LANGKNECHT, John M.: Director, Government Relations

Outside Counsel/Consultants

The Direct Impact Co.

Ervin Technical Associates, Inc. (ETA)
Issues: DEF, TRA
Rep By: William J. Andahazy, Hon. Jack Edwards, James L. Ervin, Hon. Joseph M. McDade, Donald E. Richbourg

Francis J. Sullivan Associates
Issues: DEF
Rep By: Francis J. Sullivan

Ingersoll-Rand Co.

1627 K St. NW
Suite 900
Washington, DC 20006
Tel: (202)955-1450
Fax: (202)955-1457
Web: www.ingersoll-rand.com

A diversified manufacturer of industrial and commercial equipment and components. Headquartered in Woodcliff Lake, NJ.

Leg. Issues: DEF, FOR, HCR, IMM, MAN, TRD

In-house, DC-area Employees

STABLES, Jr., Gordon W.: Director, Government Affairs and Sales

Outside Counsel/Consultants

BSMG Worldwide
Issues: DEF, FOR, HCR, MAN, TRD

Greenberg Traurig, LLP
Issues: IMM
Rep By: Laura F. Reiff

Haley and Associates
Issues: DEF, MAN, TRD
Rep By: Daniel D. Haley

Inglewood, California, City of

Leg. Issues: BUD, ECN, HOU, LAW, LBR, SMB, TRA, URB

Outside Counsel/Consultants

The Ferguson Group, LLC
Issues: BUD, ECN, HOU, LAW, LBR, SMB, TRA, URB
Rep By: William Ferguson, Jr., Leslie Waters Mozingo

Ingram Barge Company

Nashville, TN
Leg. Issues: MAR

Outside Counsel/Consultants

Jones, Walker, Waechter, Poitevent, Carrere & Denegre, L.L.P.
Issues: MAR
Rep By: Paul Cambon, John J. Jaskot, R. Christian Johnsen

Tom Ingstead Broadcasting Group

Minnetonka, MN

Outside Counsel/Consultants

Shaw Pittman

Rob Ingstead Broadcasting, Inc.

Valley City, ND

Outside Counsel/Consultants

Shaw Pittman

The Ingstead Broadcasting, Inc.

Fargo, ND

Outside Counsel/Consultants

Shaw Pittman

Inland Steel Industries, Inc.

Chicago, IL
Leg. Issues: TRD

Outside Counsel/Consultants

Collier Shannon Scott, PLLC
Rep By: Dana S. Wood

Skadden, Arps, Slate, Meagher & Flom LLP
Issues: TRD
Rep By: Robert E. Lighthizer

Inland Valley Development Agency

San Bernardino, CA
Leg. Issues: ECN

Outside Counsel/Consultants

David Turch & Associates
Issues: ECN
Rep By: David N. M. Turch

Inman, Steinberg, Nye & Stone

Beverly Hills, CA
Leg. Issues: IMM

Outside Counsel/Consultants

Baker & Hostetler LLP
Issues: IMM
Rep By: Steven A. Lotterer, Hon. Guy Vander Jagt

Inmarsat

London, UNITED KINGDOM
Leg. Issues: TEC

Outside Counsel/Consultants

Chambers Associates Inc.
Issues: TEC

Powell, Goldstein, Frazer & Murphy LLP
Issues: TEC
Rep By: Kelly Cameron

Innovation Reform Group

Leg. Issues: CHM, ENV

Outside Counsel/Consultants

The Accord Group
Issues: CHM, ENV
Rep By: Patrick H. Quinn

Innovative Productivity, Inc.

Louisville, KY
Leg. Issues: DEF

Outside Counsel/Consultants

The PMA Group
Issues: DEF
Rep By: Kaylene Green, Gregory L. Hansen, Paul J. Magliocchetti, Charles Smith

Innovative Resource Group

Madison, WI
Leg. Issues: DEF, HCR, VET

Outside Counsel/Consultants

Broydrick & Associates
Issues: DEF, HCR, VET
Rep By: William Broydrick, Amy Demske

Innovative Science Solutions

Morristown, NJ
Leg. Issues: MED

Outside Counsel/Consultants

Reed, Smith, LLP
Issues: MED
Rep By: Marc Scheineson

Innovative Technical Solutions

Honolulu, HI
Leg. Issues: DEF, SCI

Outside Counsel/Consultants

SISCORP
Issues: DEF, SCI
Rep By: Robert Meissner

Inova Fairfax Hospital

Falls Church, VA
Leg. Issues: HCR, MMM

Outside Counsel/Consultants

McDermott, Will and Emery
Issues: HCR, MMM
Rep By: Wendy L. Krasner, Maggie A. Mitchell, Karen S. Sealander

Inova Health Systems

Fairfax, VA

Outside Counsel/Consultants

Widmeyer Communications, Inc.

Inoveon Corp.

Oklahoma City, OK
Leg. Issues: BUD, HCR

Outside Counsel/Consultants

Arent Fox Kintner Plotkin & Kahn, PLLC
Issues: BUD, HCR
Rep By: Douglas McCormack, Robert J. Waters

Insight Technology, Inc.

Londonderry, NH
Leg. Issues: BUD, DEF, SCI

Outside Counsel/Consultants

Van Scoyoc Associates, Inc.
Issues: BUD, DEF, SCI
Rep By: Thomas L. Lankford, H. Stewart Van Scoyoc

Instinet

Washington, DC
Leg. Issues: FIN

Outside Counsel/Consultants

Quinn Gillespie & Associates
Issues: FIN
Rep By: Bruce H. Andrews, Jeffrey J. Connaughton, Edward W. Gillespie, David Lugar, Anne McGuire, John M. "Jack" Quinn

The Velasquez Group
Issues: FIN
Rep By: Jay Velasquez

Institute for a Drug-Free Workplace

1225 I St. NW
Suite 1000
Washington, DC 20005-3914
Tel: (202)842-7400
Fax: (202)842-0022
Web: www.drugfreeworkplace.org
E-mail: pizanias@drugfreeworkplace.org
Leg. Issues: ALC, LBR

In-house, DC-area Employees

DE BERNARDO, Mark A.: Exec. Director
DELOGU, Nancy N.: Counsel
DODGE, Garen E.: Assistant Director
GOETEL, Katie: Assistant Counsel
PIZANIAS, Helen: Fulfillment Manager

Outside Counsel/Consultants

Littler Mendelson, P.C.
Issues: ALC, LBR
Rep By: Peter A. Susser

Institute for Advanced Studies in Aging and Geriatric Medicine

1819 Pennsylvania Ave. NW
Suite 400
Washington, DC 20006-3603
Tel: (202)333-8845
Fax: (202)333-8898
Web: www.iasia.org

A non-profit, educational and scientific organization whose mission is to define the linkages between the body's immune system, the brain, and aging, so as to improve the quality of life during the aging process. Services include educational programs for high school and graduate students, public information town forums, work group meetings on vaccines, international conferences on immunology and aging, and scientific symposia.

In-house, DC-area Employees

ROLAND, Catherine S.: Program Director
SMITH, Ada-Saran E.: Program Director

Institute for Alternative Futures

100 N. Pitt St.
Suite 235
Alexandria, VA 22314-3134
Tel: (703)684-5880
Fax: (703)684-0640
Web: www.altfutures.com
E-mail: futurist@altfutures.com

Established as a research and education organization focused on the future and on new approaches to future problems, including greater citizen involvement in the workplace and government. Directs attention to public and governmental audiences.

In-house, DC-area Employees

BEZOLD, Ph.D., Clement: President
PECK, Jonathan: V. President

Institute for Balkan Affairs

P.O. Box 32099
Washington, DC 20007
Tel: (301)424-3220
Fax: (301)424-0192
Web: www.balkanaffairs.org
E-mail: comments@balkanaffairs.org

Provides information to the public through media, forums, publications, and other means on issues relating to the Balkans.

Leg. Issues: FOR

In-house, DC-area Employees

SREMAC, Danielle: Director

Institute for Certified Investment Management Consultants

1101 17th St. NW
Suite 703
Washington, DC 20036
Tel: (202)452-8670
Fax: (202)331-8446
Web: www.icimc.org
E-mail: info@icimc.org
Leg. Issues: FIN

In-house, DC-area Employees

DAVIS, Christopher L.: Exec. Director

Outside Counsel/Consultants

Infrastructure Management Group
Issues: FIN
Rep By: Porter K. Wheeler

Institute for Civil Soc.

Newton, MA
Leg. Issues: HCR, MED, TAX

Outside Counsel/Consultants

Bass and Howes, Inc.
Issues: HCR
Rep By: Rachel Laser, Robyn Lipner

Hogan & Hartson L.L.P.
Issues: HCR, MED, TAX
Rep By: Nancy Granese, Jeffrey W. Munk

Institute for Conservation Leadership

6930 Carroll Ave.
Suite 420
Takoma Park, MD 20912
Tel: (301)270-2900
Fax: (301)270-0610
Web: www.icl.org
E-mail: icl@icl.org

Provides training, consulting, and facilitation to help environmental and conservation leaders build stronger organizations to protect the Earth.

In-house, DC-area Employees

RUSSELL, Dianne J.: Exec. Director
STRAUGHAN, Baird: Associate Director

Institute for Educational Leadership

1001 Connecticut Ave. NW
Suite 310
Washington, DC 20036
Tel: (202)822-8405
Fax: (202)872-4050
Web: www.iel.org
E-mail: iel@iel.org

In-house, DC-area Employees

HALE, Elizabeth: V. President
HODGKINSON, Harold L.: Director, Center for Demographic Policy
USDAN, Michael D.: President
WILLS, Joan L.: Director, Center for Workforce Development

Institute for Entrepreneurship

Albany, NY
Leg. Issues: BUD, ECN, EDU, SMB

Outside Counsel/Consultants

The Solomon Group, LLC
Issues: BUD, ECN, EDU, SMB
Rep By: Hon. Gerald B. H. Solomon, William R. Teator

Institute for Health Care Research and Policy

2233 Wisconsin Ave. NW
Suite 525
Georgetown University
Washington, DC 20007
Tel: (202)687-0880
Fax: (202)687-3110

In-house, DC-area Employees

GOLDMAN, Janlori: Director, Health Privacy Project
KOMIFAR, Harriet: Co-Director
POLLITZ, Karen: Co-Director

The Institute for Higher Education Policy

1320 19th St. NW
Suite 400
Washington, DC 20036
Tel: (202)861-8223
Fax: (202)861-9307
Web: www.ihep.com
E-mail: institute@ihep.com
Leg. Issues: EDU

In-house, DC-area Employees

MERISOTIS, Jamie P.: President
O'BRIEN, Colleen T.: V. President
PHIPPS, Dr. Ronald: Senior Associate
WELLMAN, Jane V.: Senior Associate
WOLANIN, Thomas R.: Senior Associate

Institute for Human-Machine Cognition

Pensacola, FL
Leg. Issues: DEF

Outside Counsel/Consultants

The Legislative Strategies Group, LLC
Issues: DEF
Rep By: Melvin J. Littig, Grayson Winterling

Institute for Internat'l Economics

11 Dupont Circle NW
Suite 620
Washington, DC 20036
Tel: (202)328-9000
Fax: (202)328-5432
Web: www.iie.com

Established in 1981 as a nonprofit research institution devoted to the study of international economics and to present its ideas to government policy makers and the public.

In-house, DC-area Employees

BERGSTEN, C. Fred: Director
ELLIOT, Kimberly Ann: Research Fellow
FROST, Ellen L.: Visiting Fellow
GOLDSTEIN, Morris: Senior Fellow
HENNING, C. Randall: Visiting Fellow
NOLAND, Marcus: Senior Fellow
SCHOTT, Jeffrey J.: Senior Fellow

Institute for Justice

1717 Pennsylvania Ave. NW
Suite 200
Washington, DC 20006
Tel: (202)955-1300
Fax: (202)955-1329
Web: www.ij.org
E-mail: general@instituteforjustice.org

A non-profit, public interest law center founded to seek a rule of law under which individuals control their own destinies as free and responsible members of society. Through strategic litigation and training, the Institute works to secure greater protection for individual liberty, challenge the scope of ideology of the current welfare system, and illustrate and extend the benefits of freedom to all individuals. The Institute proposes solutions to society's pressing concerns based on the merits of individual initiative and opportunity rather through government-mandated solutions.

In-house, DC-area Employees

BLUM, Maureen: Director, Outreach Programs
BOLICK, Clint: V. President and Director, Litigation
KRAMER, John E.: V. President, Communications
MELLOR, William H.: President and General Counsel

Institute for Local Self-Reliance

2425 18th St. NW
Washington, DC 20009-2096
Tel: (202)232-4108
Fax: (202)332-0463
Web: www.ilsr.org
E-mail: ilsr@igc.apc.org

Provides research, technical, and policy assistance to citizen groups and governments on environmentally sustainable local economic development.

Leg. Issues: AGR, DOC, ECN, URB, WAS

In-house, DC-area Employees

BUCKLEY, Jane: Director
SELDMAN, Neil N.: President

Institute for Palestine Studies

3501 M St. NW
Washington, DC 20007-2624
Tel: (202)342-3990
Fax: (202)342-3927
Web: www.ipsjps.org
E-mail: ips@ipsjps.org

A private, non-profit institute headquartered in Beirut, Lebanon. Promotes research, analysis and documentation on the Arab-Israeli conflict and Palestinian concerns and publishes the Journal of Palestine Studies.

In-house, DC-area Employees

MATTAR, Philip: Exec. Director

Institute for Policy Studies

733 15th St. NW
Suite 1020
Washington, DC 20005
Tel: (202)234-9382
Fax: (202)387-7915
Web: www.ips-dc.org

Founded in 1963, IPS describes itself as "a transnational center for research, education and social invention." Sponsors critical examination of assumptions and policies on domestic and international issues.

In-house, DC-area Employees

BARNET, Richard J.: Distinguished Fellow
CAVANAGH, John: Co-Director
HONEY, Martha: Fellow
RASKIN, Marcus G.: Distinguished Fellow
SCHUMAN, Michael: Fellow

Institute for Polyacrylate Absorbents, Inc.

1850 M St. NW
Suite 700
Washington, DC 20036
Tel: (202)721-4190
Fax: (202)296-8120

A trade association for producers and users of polyacrylate absorbents.

In-house, DC-area Employees

KORDOSKI, Ph.D, Edward W.: Exec. Director

Institute for Public Representation

600 New Jersey Ave. NW
Suite 312
Washington, DC 20001
Tel: (202)662-9535
Fax: (202)662-9634

Operates out of Georgetown University Law Center; Engages in federal administrative practice, encouraging the federal government to consider the views of otherwise unrepresented, or under-represented, groups and individuals.

In-house, DC-area Employees

PARKER, Douglas L.: Director

Institute for Research on the Economics of Taxation (IRET)

1730 K St. NW
Suite 910
Washington, DC 20006
Web: www.iret.org
Tel: (202)463-1400
Fax: (202)463-6199

A non-profit, non-partisan research organization dedicated to promoting tax and fiscal policies that will strengthen the nation's free market economy.

In-house, DC-area Employees
ALLEN, Carla C.: V. President, Communications
ENTIN, Stephen J.: President and Exec. Director
SCHUYLER, Michael A.: Senior Economist

Institute for Responsible Housing Preservation

E-mail: irhp@aol.com

Represents owners and participants in the Low-Income Housing Preservation and Resident Homeownership Act of 1990 before Congress and other federal agencies.

Leg. Issues: HOU

Outside Counsel/Consultants
Nixon Peabody LLP
Issues: HOU
Rep By: Charles L. Edson, Stephen J. Wallace

Institute for Science and Internat'l Security

236 Massachusetts Ave. NE
Suite 500
Washington, DC 20002
Web: www.isis-online.org
E-mail: isis@isis-online.org
Tel: (202)547-3633
Fax: (202)547-3634
Leg. Issues: DEF, ENG, FOR

In-house, DC-area Employees
ALBRIGHT, David H.: President

Institute for Student Achievement

Lake Success, NY
Leg. Issues: BUD

Outside Counsel/Consultants
Cassidy & Associates, Inc.
Issues: BUD
Rep By: Dennis M. Kedzior, Hon. Martin A. Russo, Mary E. Shields, Dan C. Tate, Sr.

Institute for Systems Biology

Leg. Issues: MED

Outside Counsel/Consultants
Denny Miller McBee Associates
Issues: MED

Institute of Cetacean Research

Tokyo, JAPAN

An organization of whale researchers.

Outside Counsel/Consultants
Butterfield Carter & Associates
Rep By: R. Ian Butterfield, Gavin J. Carter

Institute of Electrical and Electronics Engineers, Inc.

1828 L St. NW
Suite 1202
Washington, DC 20036-5104
Web: www.ieeeusa.org
E-mail: ieeeusa@ieee.org
Tel: (202)785-0017
Fax: (202)785-0835
Registered: LDA

A worldwide, non-profit organization which serves more then 310,000 members in computer, electrical engineering, and electronics professions. IEEE-USA promotes the career and technology policy interests of IEEE's U.S. members.

Leg. Issues: BUD, COM, CPT, ENG, IMM, RET, SCI, TAX, TOR

In-house, DC-area Employees
BRANTLEY, Chris J.: Director, Government Relations and Operations
MCCARTER, Pender M.: Director, Communications and Public Relations
O'NEILL, J. Vincent: Senior Legislative Representative, Career Activities
RUDOLPH, Deborah K.: Manager, Technology Policy Activities
SUTTLE, W. Thomas: Managing Director, Professional Activities

Institute of Food Technologists

Chicago, IL
Leg. Issues: AGR, BUD, FOO

Outside Counsel/Consultants
Olsson, Frank and Weeda, P.C.
Issues: AGR, BUD, FOO
Rep By: John W. Bode, Susan P. Grymes, Karen Reis Harned, Stephen L. Lacey, Marshall L. Matz, Tyson Redpath, Ryan W. Stroschein

Institute of Human and Machine Cognition

Pensacola, FL
Leg. Issues: AER, CPI, DEF, EDU

Outside Counsel/Consultants
Rooney Group Internat'l, Inc.
Issues: AER, CPI, DEF, EDU
Rep By: James W. Rooney

Institute of Internal Auditors

Outside Counsel/Consultants
The Plexus Consulting Group
Rep By: Fred H. Hutchison

Institute of Internat'l Bankers

New York, NY
Leg. Issues: BAN, FIN

Outside Counsel/Consultants
Kelley, Drye & Warren LLP
Steptoe & Johnson LLP
Issues: BAN, FIN
Rep By: John T. Collins

Institute of Makers of Explosives

1120 19th St. NW
Suite 310
Washington, DC 20036-3605
Web: www.ime.org
Tel: (202)429-9280
Fax: (202)293-2420

Political Action Committee/s
Institute of Makers of Explosives Political Action Committee
1120 19th St. NW
Suite 310
Washington, DC 20036-3605
Contact: Cynthia Hilton
Tel: (202)429-9280
Fax: (202)293-2420

In-house, DC-area Employees
FLANAGAN, Susan J.P.: Counsel, Environmental Affairs
HILTON, Cynthia: Exec. V. President
RONAY, J. Christopher: President

Institute of Navigation

Alexandria, VA
Web: www.ion.org
Leg. Issues: CPT, GOV, LBR, TAX, TOR

Outside Counsel/Consultants
Venable
Issues: CPT, GOV, LBR, TAX, TOR
Rep By: Jeffrey S. Tenenbaum

Institute of Scrap Recycling Industries, Inc.

1325 G St. NW
Suite 1000
Washington, DC 20005-3104
Web: www.isri.org
E-mail: isri@isri.org
Tel: (202)737-1770
Fax: (202)626-0900
Registered: LDA

Formed as the result of the merger of the Nat'l Ass'n of Recycling Industries and the Institute of Scrap Iron and Steel.

Leg. Issues: CAW, ENV, TRD, WAS

Political Action Committee/s
Institute of Scrap Recycling Industries Political Action Committee
1325 G St. NW
Suite 1000
Washington, DC 20005-3104
Contact: Robin K. Wiener
Tel: (202)737-1770
Fax: (202)626-0900

In-house, DC-area Employees
HESSLER, Clare: Director, Federal and State Policy
HORNE, Scott J.: Manager, Government Relations and Counsel
REITER, Mark: Director, Congressional and International Affairs
WIENER, Robin K.: President

Outside Counsel/Consultants
Al Swift Consulting, Inc.
Issues: ENV, WAS
Rep By: Hon. Allan B. Swift

Institute of Simulation and Training

Orlando, FL
Leg. Issues: EDU

Outside Counsel/Consultants
Washington Alliance Group, Inc.
Issues: EDU
Rep By: Bonnie Singer

Institute of Transportation Engineers

1099 14th St. NW
Suite 300 West
Washington, DC 20005-3438
Web: www.ite.org
E-mail: ite_staff@ite.org
Tel: (202)289-0222
Fax: (202)289-7722

In-house, DC-area Employees
BRAHMS, Thomas W.: Exec. Director
HOUSTON, Russell: Government Relations Associate

Institute on Religion and Democracy

1110 Vermont Ave. NW
Suite 1180
Washington, DC 20005-3544
Web: www.ird-renew.org
E-mail: mail@ird-renew.org
Tel: (202)969-8430
Fax: (202)969-8429

An interdenominational, non-partisan organization founded in 1981 to promote balanced and constructive church involvement in foreign policy issues. Opposes compromising basic Christian beliefs by linking them with partisan political positions and affirms democracy as the political system most consistent with these Christian values.

Leg. Issues: CIV, FOR

In-house, DC-area Employees
KNIPPERS, Diane L.: President
WISDOM, Alan: Senior Research Associate and V. President

Institute on Religion and Public Policy

1101 15th St. NW
Suite 115
Washington, DC 20005
Web: www.religionandpolicy.org
E-mail: irpp@religion and policy.org
Tel: (202)835-8760
Fax: (202)318-4017

A non-profit, non-partisan, inter-religious organization that seeks to shape the public participation in policy of the American community of faith.

Leg. Issues: ART, CIV, CON, DEF, ECN, EDU, ENG, FAM, FOR, HCR, MMM, RET, URB

In-house, DC-area Employees
GRIEBOSKI, Joseph K.: President
KLISMET, Kurt J.: Director of Research
SHAW, Douglas B.: V. President, Programs and Policy

Institutional and Municipal Parking Congress

Fredericksburg, VA

Outside Counsel/Consultants
David E. Fox and Associates

Institutions and Governance Program

Ten G St. NE
Eighth Floor
Washington, DC 20002
Web: www.wri.org/governance
Tel: (202)729-7600
Fax: (202)729-7759

A center within the World Resources Institute which serves as a catalyst for action on environment and development issues.

In-house, DC-area Employees
LASH, Jonathan: President

Instrument Technicians Labor-Management Cooperation Fund

P.O. Box 42558
Northwest Station
Washington, DC 20015-0558
Tel: (301)933-7430

A joint labor-management promotional organization involved with the installation and servicing of instruments and measuring devices in industrial facilities.

In-house, DC-area Employees
KARDY, Walter M.: Fund Administrator

Outside Counsel/Consultants
Specialty Contractors Management, Inc.
Rep By: Walter M. Kardy

Insurance Information Institute

1730 Rhode Island Ave.
Suite 710
Washington, DC 20036
Web: www.iii.org
Tel: (202)833-1580
Fax: (202)223-5779

Headquartered in New York, NY.

In-house, DC-area Employees
GORMAN, Carolyn: V. President, Washington Office
MARKSTEIN, Daniel: Public Affairs Specialist
MOSELY, Elizabeth: Communications Specialist

Insurance Institute for Highway Safety

1005 N. Glebe Rd.
Suite 800
Arlington, VA 22201
Web: www.highwaysafety.org
E-mail: iihs@highwaysafety.org
Tel: (703)247-1500
Fax: (703)247-1678

A non-profit public service organization working to reduce injury, death and property loss on the highways.

In-house, DC-area Employees
O'NEILL, Brian: President

Insurance Services Office, Inc.

1825 K St. NW
Suite 703
Washington, DC 20006
Web: www.iso.com
Tel: (202)466-2800
Fax: (202)466-2090

A provider of information on property/casualty insurance (statistical, actuarial, policy language, and related services) headquartered in New York, NY.

Leg. Issues: INS

In-house, DC-area Employees
BINDEMAN, CPCU, ARP, Deborah: Senior Federal Affairs Representative
LAVIE, Ann Ferrill: Assistant V. President, Federal Affairs

Insyte Corp.

St. Petersburg, FL
Leg. Issues: AER

Outside Counsel/Consultants
R. V. Davis and Associates
Issues: AER
Rep By: Robert V. Davis, J. William Foster

Integra Life Sciences

Leg. Issues: TRD

Outside Counsel/Consultants
Hogan & Hartson L.L.P.
Issues: TRD
Rep By: Raymond S. Calamaro

Integrated Building and Construction Solutions

Pittsburgh, PA
Leg. Issues: ENG, ENV

Outside Counsel/Consultants
Cascade Associates
Issues: ENG, ENV
Rep By: Jennifer A. Schafer

Integrated Health Services, Inc.

Hunt Valley, MD
Leg. Issues: HCR

Outside Counsel/Consultants
U.S. Strategies Corp.
Issues: HCR
Rep By: Gary F. Capistrant, Steven E. Carey, Nance Guenther-Peterson, Heidi Hanson, Brad Traverse

Integrated Management Resources Group, Inc.

Ft. Washington, MD
Leg. Issues: FIN, GOV, SMB

Outside Counsel/Consultants
David William Kuhnsman
Issues: FIN, GOV, SMB
Rep By: David William Kuhnsman

Integrated Medical Systems

Signal Hill, CA
Leg. Issues: AER

Outside Counsel/Consultants
Peduzzi Associates, Ltd.
Issues: AER
Rep By: Paul E. Elliott, Joseph L. Ferreira, C. V. Meadows, Lawrence P. Peduzzi, Ronald A. Putnam

Integrated Microcomputer Systems, Inc.

Rockville, MD

Outside Counsel/Consultants
Commerce Consultants Internat'l Ltd.
Rep By: Steve Richards

Integrated Skilled Care of Ohio

Columbus, OH
Leg. Issues: BUD, HCR

Outside Counsel/Consultants
Genesis Consulting Group, LLC
Issues: BUD, HCR
Rep By: Mark Benedict, Dana DeBeaumont

Integrated Waste Services Ass'n

1401 H St. NW
Suite 220
Washington, DC 20005
Web: www.wte.org
E-mail: iwsa@wte.org
Tel: (202)467-6240
Fax: (202)467-6225
Registered: LDA

Leg. Issues: CAW, ENG, ENV

Political Action Committee/s
REPAC Integrated Waste Services Ass'n
1401 H St. NW
Suite 220
Washington, DC 20005
Contact: Katie Cullen
Tel: (202)467-6240
Fax: (202)467-6225

In-house, DC-area Employees
CULLEN, Katie: V. President, Media Relations and Legislative Affairs
ZANNES, Maria: President

Outside Counsel/Consultants
Bracewell & Patterson, L.L.P.
Issues: CAW, ENG, ENV

Integris Health Systems

Oklahoma City, OK
Leg. Issues: HCR

Outside Counsel/Consultants
Boesch & Co.
Issues: HCR
Rep By: Doyce A. Boesch

Intel Corp.

1634 I St. NW
Suite 300
Washington, DC 20006
Tel: (202)628-3838
Fax: (202)628-2525
Registered: LDA

Leg. Issues: CPI, CPT, CSP, EDU, ENV, FIN, HCR, IMM, SCI, TEC, TRD

Political Action Committee/s
Intel Political Action Committee
1634 I St. NW
Suite 300
Washington, DC 20006
Contact: Jeremy Bonfini
Tel: (202)626-4393
Fax: (202)628-2525

In-house, DC-area Employees
BONFINI, Jeremy: Government Relations Manager
COMER, Douglas B.: Director, Legal Affairs
HARPER, Stephen F.: Manager, Environmental Health and Safety
MAIBACH, Michael C.: V. President, Government Affairs
RICHARD, Sue: Press Relations Manager
ROSE, David: Director, Export/Import Administration
VERDERY, Jennifer: Manager, Human Resources Policy

Outside Counsel/Consultants
Alcalde & Fay
Rep By: Thomas A. Cortina, Kevin J. Fay
Dittus Communications
Rep By: Tom Conway, Shelton Jones, Kristin Litterst
Van Scoyoc Associates, Inc.
Issues: ENV
Rep By: H. Stewart Van Scoyoc

Intellectual Property Committee

A lobbying group of 13 multinational corporations, including IBM, Pfizer, Johnson & Johnson, Texas Instruments, Procter & Gamble and Time Warner.

Leg. Issues: TRD

Outside Counsel/Consultants
The Gorlin Group
Issues: TRD
Rep By: Jacques Gorlin
Wilmer, Cutler & Pickering
Issues: TRD
Rep By: Charles S. Levy

Intellectual Property Owners Ass'n

1255 23rd St. NW
Suite 200
Washington, DC 20037
Web: www.ipo.org
E-mail: info@ipo.org
Tel: (202)466-2396
Fax: (202)466-2893
Registered: LDA

A trade association representing patent, trademark, copyright and trade secret owners. Members include large midsized companies, small businesses universities and inventors.

Leg. Issues: BUD, CPT

Political Action Committee/s
IPO Political Action Fund
1255 23rd St. NW
Suite 200
Washington, DC 20037
Contact: Herbert C. Wamsley
Tel: (202)466-2396
Fax: (202)466-2893

In-house, DC-area Employees
MYRICK, Ronald: President
PAUGH, Wayne: Intellectual Property Counsel, Government Affairs
WAMSLEY, Herbert C.: Exec. Director

Outside Counsel/Consultants
Capitol Solutions
Issues: BUD, CPT
Rep By: David F. Taylor

Intelligent Optical Systems, Inc.

Torrance, CA

Outside Counsel/Consultants
Ashby and Associates
Rep By: R. Barry Ashby

Intelligent Transportation Soc. of America

400 Virginia Ave. SW
Suite 800
Washington, DC 20024-2370
Web: www.itsa.org
Tel: (202)484-4847
Fax: (202)484-3483
Registered: LDA

An educational, scientific and technical society dealing with transportation, telecommunications and technology issues.

Leg. Issues: SCI, TEC, TRA

In-house, DC-area Employees
BASTARACHE, Gerald: Director, Communications
CATANGUI, Raul G.: Legislative and Regulatory Counsel
HENSING, David J.: President

Outside Counsel/Consultants
Government Relations, Inc.
Issues: SCI, TRA
Rep By: Thomas J. Bulger

INTELSAT - Internat'l Telecommunications Satellite Organization

3400 International Dr. NW
Washington, DC 20008-3090
Web: www.intelsat.int
Tel: (202)944-6800
Fax: (202)944-7898
Registered: LDA

INTELSAT, with 143 member countries, provides worldwide voice, data, video and internet satellite services to over 200 countries and territories around the world.

Leg. Issues: SCI, TEC

In-house, DC-area Employees
MELTZER, David: V. President and General Counsel
TRUJILLO, Jr., Tony A.: Sr. Director, Corporate Communications and Government Affairs

Outside Counsel/Consultants
Barbour Griffith & Rogers, Inc.
Issues: TEC
Rep By: Haley Barbour, Carl Biersack, G. O. Lanny Griffith, Jr., Bill Himpler, Loren Monroe
Capitol Coalitions Inc.
Issues: TEC
Rep By: Amy R. Mehlman, Brett P. Scott
Lawler, Metzger & Milkman, LLC
Issues: TEC
Rep By: Ruth M. Milkman
Ogilvy Public Relations Worldwide
Issues: SCI
Rep By: Steven A. Cohen, Jamie W. Moeller
Paul, Hastings, Janofsky & Walker LLP
Issues: TEC
Rep By: Ralph B. Everett
Paul, Weiss, Rifkind, Wharton & Garrison
Rep By: Carl W. Hampe, Phillip L. Spector
Wiley, Rein & Fielding
Issues: TEC
Rep By: Mimi W. Dawson, Bert W. Rein

Inter-American Bar Ass'n

1211 Connecticut Ave. NW
Suite 202
Washington, DC 20036
Web: www.iaba.org
E-mail: iaba@iaba.org
Tel: (202)466-5944
Fax: (202)466-5946

In-house, DC-area Employees
FERRAND, Louis G.: Secretary General
POVOLO, Cayetano: President

Inter-American Dialogue

1211 Connecticut Ave. NW
Suite 510
Washington, DC 20036
Tel: (202)822-9002
Fax: (202)822-9553
Web: www.iadialog.org
E-mail: iad@iadialog.org

A think tank focusing on the Western Hemisphere.

In-house, DC-area Employees

HAKIM, Peter: President
SHIFTER, Michael: V. President, Policy

Inter-American Institute for Cooperation on Agriculture

1775 K St. NW
Suite 320
Washington, DC 20006
Tel: (202)458-3767
Fax: (202)458-6335
Web: www.iicawash.org
E-mail: jmiranda@iicawash.org

IICA is the specialized agency of the Inter-American System dealing in agricultural development. Membership consists of 34 Western Hemisphere nations. The U.S. Representative monitors policies relating to agricultural trade and development in the region, and is IICA's principal contact with the U.S. government. IICA is headquartered in San Jose, Costa Rica.

Leg. Issues: AGR, FOO, TRD

In-house, DC-area Employees

MIRANDA, John Anthony: Director and U.S. Representative

Inter-Associates, Inc.

1801 N. Hartford St.
Arlington, VA 22201-5206
Tel: (703)522-4995
Registered: LDA
E-mail: wwerst@interassociates.ioffice.com
Leg. Issues: AER, CHM, DEF, ENG, MAN, SCI

In-house, DC-area Employees

WERST, Jr., William H.: President

Outside Counsel/Consultants

Douglas Ward Freitag
Issues: AER, CHM, DEF, ENG, MAN, SCI
Rep By: Douglas Ward Freitag

Inter-Cal Corp.

Prescott, AZ
Leg. Issues: ADV, FOO

Outside Counsel/Consultants

Parry, Romani, DeConcini & Symms
Issues: ADV, FOO
Rep By: Edward H. Baxter, Hon. Dennis DeConcini, John M. Haddow, Scott D. Hatch, Shannon Davis Henderson, Jack W. Martin, Romano Romani, Linda Arey Skladany, Hon. Steven D. Symms

Inter-Island Ferry Authority

Outside Counsel/Consultants

Robertson, Monagle & Eastaugh
Rep By: Rick E. Marks

Inter-Nation Capital Management

New York, NY

Outside Counsel/Consultants

Norman A. Bailey, Inc.
Rep By: Norman A. Bailey

InterAction

1717 Massachusetts Ave. NW
Suite 701
Washington, DC 20036
Tel: (202)667-8227
Fax: (202)667-8236
Registered: LDA
Web: www.interaction.org
E-mail: ihouston@interaction.org

An umbrella organization for more than 160 U.S.-based non-profit organizations working in 165 countries throughout the world.

Leg. Issues: FOR

In-house, DC-area Employees

BARUAH, Smita: Legislative Assistant
HOUSTON, Ian: Director, Public Policy
MCCLYMONT, Mary: President and Chief Exec. Officer
ZARAFONETIS, John: Director, Development Policy and Practice

Interactive Amusement and Tournament Video Game Coalition

Washington, DC
Leg. Issues: ART, GAM

Outside Counsel/Consultants

Arent Fox Kintner Plotkin & Kahn, PLLC
Issues: ART, GAM
Rep By: Michael T. McNamara, Elliott I. Portnoy, Todd Weiss

Interactive Brokers LLC

Chicago, IL
Leg. Issues: CDT, FIN

Outside Counsel/Consultants

The Velasquez Group
Issues: CDT, FIN
Rep By: Jay Velasquez

Interactive Digital Software Ass'n

1211 Connecticut Ave. NW
Suite 600
Washington, DC 20036
Registered: LDA
Web: www.idsa.com
E-mail: info@idsa.com
Leg. Issues: COM, CON, CPT, CSP, GAM, LAW, TRA, TRD

In-house, DC-area Employees

KARG, Kathlene: Director, Intellectual Property and Public Policy
LOWENSTEIN, Douglas S.: President

Outside Counsel/Consultants

Verner, Liipfert, Bernhard, McPherson and Hand, Chartered
Rep By: Marla P. Grossman

Interactive Gaming Council

St. Charles, MO
Leg. Issues: COM, CPI, GAM, TEC

Outside Counsel/Consultants

Janus-Merritt Strategies, L.L.C.
Issues: COM, CPI, GAM, TEC
Rep By: Scott P. Hoffman, Bethany Noble, Mark J. Robertson, J. Daniel Walsh

Podesta/Mattoon
Issues: CPI
Rep By: Matthew Gelman, Andrew C. Littman, Timothy Powers

Interactive Services Ass'n

Washington, DC

Outside Counsel/Consultants

Janus-Merritt Strategies, L.L.C.
Rep By: Scott P. Hoffman, Bethany Noble

InterAmerica's Group LLC

McAllen, TX
Leg. Issues: NAT

Outside Counsel/Consultants

Hogan & Hartson L.L.P.
Issues: NAT
Rep By: James Banks, Humberto R. Pena, Patrick M. Raher, Catherine Van Heuven

InterAmerican College of Physicians and Surgeons

1712 I St. NW
Suite 200
Washington, DC 20006
Tel: (202)467-4756
Fax: (202)467-4758
Web: www.icps.org

A national Hispanic medical association representing Hispanic physicians in the U.S. and Puerto Rico. Works to increase the number of Hispanics in the medical profession and to advocate equitable health care policy legislation and health care services for Hispanic Americans.

In-house, DC-area Employees

RODRIGUEZ, M.D., Rene F.: President

Intercultural Cancer Council

Houston, TX
Leg. Issues: HCR

Outside Counsel/Consultants

Patton Boggs, LLP
Issues: HCR
Rep By: Katharine R. Boyce, Martha M. Kendrick

Interest Allocation Coalition

Washington, DC
Leg. Issues: TAX

Outside Counsel/Consultants

PriceWaterhouseCoopers
Issues: TAX
Rep By: Barbara Angus, Kenneth J. Kies

Interest Netting Coalition

Leg. Issues: TAX

Outside Counsel/Consultants

Ernst & Young LLP
Issues: TAX
Rep By: Lauren Darling, Patrick G. Heck, Phillip D. Moseley, Henry C. Ruempler, Donna Steele-Flynn

Interface

Atlanta, GA

Outside Counsel/Consultants

Kilpatrick Stockton LLP
Rep By: Charles Simmons

Interface Inc.

Fairfax, VA
Leg. Issues: GOV, SMB

Outside Counsel/Consultants

Marshall A. Brachman
Issues: GOV, SMB
Rep By: Marshall A. Brachman

InterGen

Outside Counsel/Consultants

Winner & Associates

Intergraph Corp. Federal Systems Division

2051 Mercator Dr.
Reston, VA 22091
Tel: (703)264-5644
Fax: (703)264-5715
Leg. Issues: CPI, DEF

Political Action Committee/s

Intergraph Corp. PAC
2051 Mercator Dr.
Reston, VA 22091
Tel: (703)264-5644
Fax: (703)264-5715
Contact: Edward A. Wilkinson, Jr.

In-house, DC-area Employees

WILKINSON, Jr., Edward A.: Treasurer, Intergraph Corp. PAC

Outside Counsel/Consultants

Michael W. Adcock
Issues: DEF
Rep By: Michael W. Adcock

Hurt, Norton & Associates
Issues: CPI, DEF
Rep By: Robert H. Hurt, Frank Norton, William K. Takakoshi

Interlake Holding Corp.

Stamford, CT

Outside Counsel/Consultants

Preston Gates Ellis & Rouvelas Meeds LLP
Rep By: Susan B. Geiger, Emanuel L. Rouvelas

Interlocking Concrete Pavement Institute

Washington, DC
Web: www.icpi.org
E-mail: icpi@bostromdc.com

Outside Counsel/Consultants

Bostrom Corp.
Rep By: Charles McGrath, CAE

Intermare Navigation SA

London, UNITED KINGDOM
Leg. Issues: MAR

Outside Counsel/Consultants

Dyer Ellis & Joseph, P.C.
Issues: MAR
Rep By: James B. Ellis, II, R. Anthony Salgado, Duncan C. Smith, III

Intermarine USA

Savannah, GA
Leg. Issues: DEF

Outside Counsel/Consultants

Rooney Group Internat'l, Inc.
Issues: DEF
Rep By: James W. Rooney

InterMart Broadcasting

Punta Gorda, FL

Outside Counsel/Consultants

E. Del Smith and Co.
Rep By: E. Del Smith

Intermedia Communications Inc.

Tampa, FL
Leg. Issues: TEC

Outside Counsel/Consultants

Wallman Strategic Consulting, LLC
Issues: TEC
Rep By: Kathleen E. Wallman, Lisa M. Zaina

InterMedia Partners

San Francisco, CA

Outside Counsel/Consultants

Wear & Associates
Rep By: Terrance J. Wear

Intermodal Ass'n of North America

7501 Greenway Center Dr. Tel: (301)982-3400
S-720 Fax: (301)982-4815
Greenbelt, MD 20770-6705
Web: www.intermodal.org/~iana
E-mail: iana@intermodal.org

Represents the combined interests of intermodal freight transportation companies and their suppliers.

Leg. Issues: FUE, LBR, MAR, ROD, RRR, TAX, TRA, TRU

In-house, DC-area Employees

CASEY, Joanne F.: President

Outside Counsel/Consultants

G.R. Services
Issues: FUE, LBR, MAR, ROD, RRR, TAX, TRA, TRU
Rep By: Earl Eisenhart

Legislative Solutions
Issues: FUE, LBR, MAR, ROD, RRR, TAX, TRA, TRU
Rep By: Daniel J. Fleming

Intermountain Forest Industry Ass'n

Couer d'Alene, ID Registered: LDA
Leg. Issues: ANI, BUD, CAW, ENV, MAR, NAT, RES

Outside Counsel/Consultants

Crowell & Moring LLP
Issues: NAT
Rep By: Steven P. Quarles

Perkins Coie LLP
Issues: ANI, BUD, CAW, ENV, MAR, NAT, RES
Rep By: W. H. "Buzz" Fawcett

InterMountain Health Care Inc.

Salt Lake City, UT
Leg. Issues: HCR, MMM

Outside Counsel/Consultants

McDermott, Will and Emery
Issues: HCR, MMM
Rep By: Michael A. Romansky, Karen S. Sealander, Eric P. Zimmerman

Internat'l Academy of Compounding Pharmacists

Houston, TX
Leg. Issues: PHA

Outside Counsel/Consultants

Kent & O'Connor, Inc.
Issues: PHA
Rep By: Eileen Fitzgerald, Jonathan H. Kent

Internat'l Agriculture and Rural Development Group

East Lansing, MI
Leg. Issues: FOR

Outside Counsel/Consultants

Collins & Company, Inc.
Issues: FOR
Rep By: James D. Bond, Richard L. Collins, Thomas A. Hooper, Shay D. Stautz

Internat'l Air Transport Ass'n

Geneva, SWITZERLAND

A nonprofit trade association serving the international airline industry.

Leg. Issues: AVI, SCI, TEC, TOU

Outside Counsel/Consultants

Schnader Harrison Segal & Lewis LLP
Issues: AVI, SCI, TEC, TOU
Rep By: Laura L. Gonzalez, Greggory B. Mendenhall

Internat'l Arid Lands Consortium

Tucson, AZ
Leg. Issues: EDU, NAT

Outside Counsel/Consultants

Strategic Impact, Inc.
Issues: EDU, NAT
Rep By: Michael C. Jimenez, Patrick J. Mitchell

Internat'l Ass'n for Dental Research

1619 Duke St. Tel: (703)548-0066
Alexandria, VA 22314 Fax: (703)548-1883
Web: www.dentalresearch.com
E-mail: research@iadr.com
Leg. Issues: HCR, MED, SCI

In-house, DC-area Employees

SCHWARZ, Eli: Exec. Director

Internat'l Ass'n for Financial Planning

Atlanta, GA Registered: LDA
Leg. Issues: FIN, TAX

Outside Counsel/Consultants

McIntyre Law Firm, PLLC
Issues: FIN, TAX
Rep By: Chrys D. Lemon, James T. McIntyre

Internat'l Ass'n of Airport Duty Free Stores

Washington, DC
Web: www.iaadfs.org
E-mail: iaadfs@dc.sba.com
Leg. Issues: TRD

Outside Counsel/Consultants

Kent & O'Connor, Inc.
Issues: TRD
Rep By: Jonathan H. Kent

Smith, Bucklin and Associates, Inc.
Rep By: Michael L. Payne

Internat'l Ass'n of Amusement Parks and Attractions

1448 Duke St. Tel: (703)836-4800
Alexandria, VA 22314 Fax: (703)836-4801
Registered: LDA
Web: www.iaapa.org
Leg. Issues: BAN, CPT, LBR

Political Action Committee/s

Internat'l Ass'n of Amusement Parks and Attractions Political Action Committee
1448 Duke St. Tel: (703)836-4800
Alexandria, VA 22314 Fax: (703)836-4801
Contact: Randall P. K. Davis

In-house, DC-area Employees

DAVIS, Randall P. K.: V. President, Government Relations
GRAFF, John R.: President, Chief Exec. Officer and Counsel
MOSEDALE, Susan: V. President, Membership and Marketing

Outside Counsel/Consultants

Williams & Jensen, P.C.
Rep By: Rebecca L. Anderson, Philip E. Bechtel, Bertram W. Carp, J. Steven Hart

Internat'l Ass'n of Assembly Managers

1200 G Street NW Tel: (202)434-8988
Suite 800 Fax: (202)861-1274
Washington, DC 20005 Registered: LDA
Leg. Issues: CIV, CPT, LBR

In-house, DC-area Employees

MADDEN, Turner D.: General Counsel & Chief Lobbyist

Outside Counsel/Consultants

Turner D. Madden
Issues: CIV, CPT, LBR
Rep By: Turner D. Madden

Internat'l Ass'n of Black Professional Fire Fighters

8700 Central Ave. Tel: (301)808-0804
Suite 306 Fax: (301)808-0807
Landover, MD 20785
Web: www.iabpff.org
E-mail: IABPFF@msn.com

Founded to address concerns specific to Black firefighters. Works to increase the number of minority firefighters and to enhance public awareness of fire safety and prevention. Also coordinates fund-raising efforts on behalf of civil rights groups.

In-house, DC-area Employees

QUEEN, Nathan R.: Nat'l Legislative Liaison
SPAULDING, Romeo O.: Acting Exec. Director

Outside Counsel/Consultants

Derrick Humphries
Rep By: Derrick Humphries

Internat'l Ass'n of Bridge, Structural, Ornamental and Reinforcing Iron Workers

1750 New York Ave. NW Tel: (202)383-4800
Suite 400 Fax: (202)638-4856
Washington, DC 20006 Registered: LDA
Leg. Issues: CAW, EDU, ENG, IND, LBR, TAX, TRA, TRD, WAS

Political Action Committee/s

Iron Workers Political Action League
1750 New York Ave. NW Tel: (202)383-4800
Suite 400 Fax: (202)347-3569
Washington, DC 20006
Contact: Frank J. Voyack

In-house, DC-area Employees

ROBERTSON, Raymond J.: General V. President
VOYACK, Frank J.: Legislative and Political Director

Internat'l Ass'n of Business, Industry and Rehabilitation

Washington, DC

An association of training and placement providers for persons with disabilities.

Outside Counsel/Consultants

Harles & Associates
Rep By: Charles Harles

Internat'l Ass'n of Chiefs of Police

515 N. Washington St. Tel: (703)836-6767
Alexandria, VA 22314 Fax: (703)836-4543
Registered: LDA
Web: www.theiacp.org
E-mail: information@theiacp.org
Leg. Issues: LAW

In-house, DC-area Employees

HORNE, Jennifer: Legislative Assistant
ROSENBLATT, Daniel: Exec. Director
VOEGTLIN, Gene: Legislative Counsel

Internat'l Ass'n of Color Manufacturers

Washington, DC

Outside Counsel/Consultants

The Roberts Group
Rep By: John B. Hallagan, Glenn Roberts

Internat'l Ass'n of Convention and Visitor Bureaus

2225 M St. NW Tel: (202)296-7888
Suite 500 Fax: (202)296-7889
Washington, DC 20036
Web: www.iacvb.org
E-mail: info@iacvb.org

In-house, DC-area Employees

GEHRISCH, Michael: President and Chief Exec. Officer

Internat'l Ass'n of Drilling Contractors

1901 L St. NW Tel: (202)293-0670
Suite 702 Registered: LDA
Washington, DC 20036
Web: www.iadc.org
Leg. Issues: ENG, ENV, FUE, MAR, TAX, TRD

Political Action Committee/s

Internat'l Ass'n of Drilling Contractors Political Action Committee (IADC-PAC)
1901 L St. NW Tel: (202)293-0670
Suite 702
Washington, DC 20036
Contact: Brian T. Petty

In-house, DC-area Employees

PETTY, Brian T.: Senior V. President, Government Affairs

Internat'l Ass'n of Emergency Managers

111 Park Place Tel: (703)538-1795
Falls Church, VA 22046-4513 Fax: (703)241-5603
Web: www.iaem.com
E-mail: iaem@aol.com

IAEM is a professional society of emergency managers from all levels of government, private industry, the military and others.

Leg. Issues: DIS

In-house, DC-area Employees

ARMSTRONG, CAE, Elizabeth B.: Exec. Director

Outside Counsel/Consultants

Ass'n and Soc. Management Internat'l Inc.
Issues: DIS
Rep By: Elizabeth B. Armstrong, CAE, Amy Starchville

Collier Shannon Scott, PLLC

Internat'l Ass'n of Fire Chiefs

4025 Fair Ridge Dr.
Fairfax, VA 22033-2868
Tel: (703)273-0911
Fax: (703)273-9363
Registered: LDA
Web: www.ichiefs.org

A professional association representing fire chiefs, chief fire officers and other members of the fire and emergency medical services community.

Leg. Issues: BUD, DIS, HCR, LBR, MED, RET, SCI, TEC, TRA, WAS

In-house, DC-area Employees

BRIESE, Garry L.: Exec. Director
CALDWELL, Alan: Director, Government Relations
WHITE, Andrew H.: Manager, Counterterrorism Programs

Internat'l Ass'n of Fire Fighters

1750 New York Ave. NW
Washington, DC 20006
Tel: (202)737-8484
Fax: (202)737-8418
Registered: LDA

Labor union affiliated with AFL-CIO.

Leg. Issues: AVI, DEF, HCR, LBR, TRU, WAS

Political Action Committee/s

Internat'l Ass'n of Fire Fighters Interested in Registration and Education (FIREPAC)
1750 New York Ave. NW
Washington, DC 20006
Tel: (202)737-8484
Fax: (202)737-8418
Contact: Kevin O'Connor

In-house, DC-area Employees

BILLY, David B.: Political Action Director
BOLLON, Vincent J.: General Secretary-Treasurer
BURKE, George A.: Assistant to the General President, Communications
CROUSE, Michael J.: Chief of Staff
DUFFY, Richard M.: Assistant to the General President, Occupational Safety & Health
KASINITZ, Barry: Legislative Director
KIM, Hank
MOORE, Lori: Assistant to the General President, Membership Services, Technical Assistance, Information Resources
O'CONNOR, Kevin: Assistant to the General President, Govenmental and Public Affairs
O'NEILL, Sean: Governmental Affairs Representative
SCHAITBERGER, Harold A.: General President

Outside Counsel/Consultants

The Dutko Group, Inc.

R. B. Murphy & Associates
Issues: LBR
Rep By: Rick Murphy

Internat'l Ass'n of Fish and Wildlife Agencies

444 N. Capitol St. NW
Suite 544
Washington, DC 20001
Tel: (202)624-7890
Fax: (202)624-7891
Registered: LDA
Web: www.sso.org/iafwa
E-mail: iafwa@sso.org

A quasi-governmental organization of public agencies charged with the protection and management of North America's fish and wildlife resources.

Leg. Issues: AGR, ANI, BUD, CAW, ENV, FIR, MAR, NAT

In-house, DC-area Employees

PETERSON, R. Max: Exec. V. President
TAYLOR, Gary J.: Legislative Director

Outside Counsel/Consultants

Baker, Donelson, Bearman & Caldwell, P.C.
Issues: ENV
Rep By: James D. Range

Glenn Roger Delaney
Issues: NAT
Rep By: Glenn Roger Delaney

Internat'l Ass'n of Food Industry Suppliers

1451 Dolley Madison Blvd.
McLean, VA 22101-3850
Tel: (703)761-2600
Fax: (703)761-4334
Web: www.iafis.org
E-mail: info@iafis.org

In-house, DC-area Employees

BRAY, Charles W.: President
KOROLISHLIN, Jennifer: Director, Communications
PERRY, Steve: Senior V. President

Outside Counsel/Consultants

Webster, Chamberlain & Bean
Rep By: Hugh K. Webster

Internat'l Ass'n of Heat and Frost Insulators and Asbestos Workers

1776 Massachusetts Ave. NW
Suite 301
Washington, DC 20036
Tel: (202)785-2388
Fax: (202)429-0568
Web: www.insulators.org

Political Action Committee/s

Internat'l Ass'n of Heat and Frost Insulators and Asbestos Workers Political Action Committee
1776 Massachusetts Ave. NW
Suite 301
Washington, DC 20036
Tel: (202)785-2388
Fax: (202)429-0568
Contact: James Grogan

In-house, DC-area Employees

GROGAN, James: General Secretary-Treasurer

Internat'l Ass'n of Jewish Lawyers and Jurists

Outside Counsel/Consultants

Mintz, Levin, Cohn, Ferris, Glovsky and Popeo, P.C.
Rep By: Nathan Lewin

Internat'l Ass'n of Machinists and Aerospace Workers

9000 Machinists Pl.
Upper Marlboro, MD 20772-2687
Tel: (301)967-4500
Fax: (301)967-4588
Registered: LDA
Web: www.iamaw.org
Leg. Issues: AVI, CSP, DEF, GOV, HCR, IMM, LBR, MAN, MAR, TRA, TRD

Political Action Committee/s

Machinists Non-Partisan Political League
9000 Machinists Place
Upper Marlboro, MD 20772
Tel: (301)967-4575
Fax: (301)967-4595
Contact: Richard P. Michalski

In-house, DC-area Employees

BUFFENBARGER, R. Thomas: President
CARELLI, Frank: Assistant Legislative Director
FILIPOVIC, Mark: Railroad Coordinator
GIRARDOT, Dean: Exec. Assistant
HERRNSTADT, Owen: Director, International Affairs
MICHALSKI, Richard P.: Director, Legislation and Political Action
ROACH, Jr., Robert: General V. President, Transportation
SPRANG, James: Airline Coordinator
TROTTER, Tom: Assistant Director, Legislative Affairs

Outside Counsel/Consultants

Collier Shannon Scott, PLLC
Rep By: Laurence J. Lasoff

Internat'l Ass'n of Personnel in Employment Security

Frankfort, KY
Leg. Issues: BUD, LBR

Outside Counsel/Consultants

Moss McGee Bradley & Foley
Issues: BUD, LBR
Rep By: Leander J. Foley, III

Internat'l Ass'n of Professional Numismatists

Brussels, BELGIUM
Leg. Issues: LAW, MON, TRD

Outside Counsel/Consultants

McDermott, Will and Emery
Issues: LAW, MON, TRD
Rep By: Amory Files, Peter K. Tompa

Internat'l Ass'n of Refrigerated Warehouses

7315 Wisconsin Ave.
Suite 1200N
Bethesda, MD 20814
Tel: (301)652-5674
Fax: (301)652-7269
Web: www.iarw.org
E-mail: email@iarw.org

In-house, DC-area Employees

HUDSON, J. William: President and C.E.O.
MILK, Benjamin: V. President and Secretary

Internat'l Ass'n of Seed Crushers

1255 23rd St. NW
Suite 200
Washington, DC 20037-1174
Tel: (202)452-8100
Fax: (202)833-3636
Headquartered in London, England.

In-house, DC-area Employees

MURPHY, Christopher M.: V. President and Chief Operating Officer

Outside Counsel/Consultants

Hauck and Associates
Rep By: Christopher M. Murphy

Internat'l Banana Ass'n

727 N. Washington St.
Alexandria, VA 22314
Tel: (703)836-5499
Fax: (703)836-2049
Web: www.eatmorebananas.com
E-mail: info@eatmorebananas.com

In-house, DC-area Employees

DEBUS, Tim: V. President
STENZEL, Thomas E.: President

Internat'l Barter and Countertrade Foundation

5920 Munson Ct.
Falls Church, VA 22041
Tel: (703)820-7707
Fax: (703)820-7726
E-mail: wotc@cox.rr.com

A non-profit organization founded to provide technical assistance and training to countries whose economies are not adequately served by local barter and countertrade financial institutions. Works to foster development of a global electronic barter marketplace on the internet, and to develop one-stop service to barter and countertrade projects through the foreign trade ministries and central banks of nations that are short of hard currency.

Leg. Issues: FIN, TRD

Outside Counsel/Consultants

Paul Suplizio Associates
Issues: FIN, TRD
Rep By: Paul E. Suplizio

Internat'l Bicycle Ass'n

Lyndon Station, WI
Leg. Issues: TRD

Outside Counsel/Consultants

Venable
Issues: TRD
Rep By: Brock R. Landry

Internat'l Biometric Ass'n (Eastern North American Region)

11250 Roger Bacon Dr.
Suite Eight
Washington, DC 20190
Tel: (703)437-4377
Fax: (703)435-4390

In-house, DC-area Employees

HOSKINS, Kathy: Exec. Director

Outside Counsel/Consultants

Bostrom Corp.
Rep By: David L. Santini

Drohan Management Group
Rep By: Kathy Hoskins

Internat'l Biometric Industry Ass'n

Washington, DC
Leg. Issues: BAN, CPI, CSP, FIN, GOV, HCR, IMM, MAN, TRA

Outside Counsel/Consultants

French & Company
Issues: BAN, CPI, CSP, FIN, GOV, HCR, IMM, MAN, TRA
Rep By: Rebecca Dornbusch, Verrick O. French

Hogan & Hartson L.L.P.

Internat'l Board of Lactation Consultant Examiners

Falls Church, VA
Leg. Issues: GOV

Outside Counsel/Consultants

Halsey, Rains & Associates, LLC
Issues: GOV
Rep By: Steven C. Halsey, James Hubbard, Laurie D. Rains

Internat'l Bone and Mineral Soc.

Outside Counsel/Consultants

Smith, Bucklin and Associates, Inc.
Rep By: Tom Reiser

Internat'l Bottled Water Ass'n

1700 Diagonal Rd.
Suite 650
Alexandria, VA 22314
Tel: (703)683-5213
Fax: (703)683-4074
Web: www.bottledwater.org
Leg. Issues: BEV, CSP, FOO

In-house, DC-area Employees

DOSS, Joseph: President

Outside Counsel/Consultants

IssueSphere

McClure, Gerard & Neuenschwander, Inc.
Issues: BEV, CSP
Rep By: Steven G. Barringer, Joseph T. Findaro, Matthew Iandoli, Nils W. Johnson, Hon. James A. McClure, Tod O. Neuenschwander

Internat'l Bridge, Tunnel and Turnpike Ass'n

2120 L St. NW
Suite 305
Washington, DC 20037
Tel: (202)659-4620
Fax: (202)659-0500
Registered: LDA
Web: www.ibtta.org
E-mail: ibtta@ibtta.org

An autonomous organization to serve the needs of toll-supported bridge, tunnel and turnpike facilities. Concerns itself with member organizations' interest in financing, constructing and managing their facilities.

Leg. Issues: TRA

In-house, DC-area Employees

CANNON, Bruce: Director, Public Affairs
GRAY, Neil A.: Director, Government Relations
SCHUSTER, Neil D.: Exec. Director

Internat'l Brotherhood of Boilermakers, Iron Shipbuilders, Blacksmiths, Forgers and Helpers

2722 Merrilee Dr.
Suite 360
Fairfax, VA 22031
Tel: (703)560-1493
Fax: (703)560-2584
Registered: LDA
Web: www.boilermakers.org
Leg. Issues: BUD, DEF, ENV, FIN, GOV, HCR, IMM, LBR, MAR, RET, RRR, TAX, TRA, TRD, UTI

Political Action Committee/s

Internat'l Brotherhood of Boilermakers, Iron Shipbuilders, Blacksmiths, Forgers and Helpers PAC

2722 Merrilee Dr.
Suite 360
Fairfax, VA 22031
Tel: (703)560-1493
Fax: (703)560-2584
Contact: Ande M. Abbott

In-house, DC-area Employees

ABBOTT, Ande M.: Assistant to the International President
MARTIN, Bridget Powell: Deputy Director, Legislation

Internat'l Brotherhood of Electrical Workers

1125 15th St. NW
Washington, DC 20005
Tel: (202)833-7000
Fax: (202)467-6316
Registered: LDA
Web: www.ibew.org
E-mail: journal@ibew.org

Represents 750,000 workers in the U.S. and Canada in all branches of the electrical industry, including construction, utilities, manufacturing, telecommunications, broadcasting, railroads and the public sector.

Leg. Issues: AER, ART, BUD, CAW, CIV, COM, CPI, CSP, DEF, DIS, DOC, ECN, EDU, ENG, ENV, FIN, GOV, HCR, HOU, IMM, LBR, MAN, MAR, MMM, NAT, RET, ROD, RRR, SCI, SMB, TAX, TEC, TRA, TRD, UNM, URB, UTI, WAS, WEL

Political Action Committee/s

Internat'l Brotherhood of Electrical Workers Committee on Political Education

1125 15th St. NW
Washington, DC 20005
Tel: (202)833-7000
Fax: (202)467-6316
Contact: Jerry J. O'Connor

In-house, DC-area Employees

DIEGEL, Rick: Political/Legislative Director
O'CONNOR, Jerry J.: International Secretary-Treasurer
SHULER, Liz: Political/Legislative Assistant Director

Outside Counsel/Consultants

Sherman, Dunn, Cohen, Leifer & Yellig, P.C.
Rep By: Laurence J. Cohen

Internat'l Brotherhood of Police Officers

317 S. Patrick St.
Alexandria, VA 22314
Tel: (703)519-0300
Fax: (703)519-0311

A division of the Nat'l Ass'n of Government Employees.

In-house, DC-area Employees

DONNELLAN, Christopher M.
POOLER-JOHNSON, Susanne J.
SMITH, Edward J.

Internat'l Brotherhood of Teamsters

25 Louisiana Ave. NW
Washington, DC 20001-2198
Tel: (202)624-6800
Fax: (202)624-8973
Registered: LDA
Web: www.teamster.org

Sponsors a political action committee known as DRIVE.

Leg. Issues: AVI, BEV, BUD, CSP, DEF, ENG, ENV, FOO, FUE, GOV, HCR, HOU, IMM, LBR, MAR, POS, RET, ROD, TAX, TRA, TRD, TRU, UTI, WAS

Political Action Committee/s

Democratic-Republican-Independent Voter Education (DRIVE)

25 Louisiana Ave. NW
Washington, DC 20001-2198
Tel: (202)624-8741
Fax: (202)624-8973
Contact: Mike Mathis

In-house, DC-area Employees

CALDWELL, Bret: Government Affairs Dept.
HARPLE, Charles E.: Legislative Representative
HOFFA, James P.: President
MATHIS, Mike: Director, Government Affairs
MCLUCKIE, Jr., Frederick P.: Legislative Representative
OLIVER, Janice: Legislative Representative
ZELENKO, Carin: Director, Corporate Affairs

Outside Counsel/Consultants

Connerton & Ray
Issues: ENV, WAS
Rep By: Alan Kadrofske, David L. Mallino, Jr., David L. Mallino, Sr.

Dickstein Shapiro Morin & Oshinsky LLP
Issues: LBR, TRU
Rep By: Henry C. Cashen, II, Elizabeth B. Haywood, Peter J. Kadzik, Robert Mangas, Graham "Rusty" Mathews, Rebecah Moore Shepherd, L. Andrew Zausner

Mallino Government Relations
Issues: ENV, LBR
Rep By: David L. Mallino, Sr.

Sher & Blackwell
Issues: GOV
Rep By: John W. Butler, Marc J. Fink

Zuckerman Spaeder L.L.P.
Issues: LBR
Rep By: William W. Taylor, III, Ronald H. Weich

Internat'l Business Machines Corp.

1301 K St. NW
Suite 1200-West Tower
Washington, DC 20005-3307
Tel: (202)515-5000
Registered: LDA
Leg. Issues: BAN, BUD, CAW, CPI, CPT, CSP, DEF, EDU, ENG, ENV, GOV, HCR, IMM, LBR, POS, RET, SCI, TAX, TEC, TRD, WEL

In-house, DC-area Employees

CAINE, Christopher G.: V. President, Governmental Programs
COLOMBARO, Geri J.: Program Director, Public Affairs, Human Resources
COMEDY, Yolanda: Corporate Community Relations Manager
CROSS, Aaron W.: Public Policy Program Director
EVANS, Linda C.: Program Director, Taxes and Finance
FORLENZA, Paul P.: Government Relations Director, Latin America
GILLESPIE, Edward A.: Senior Program Manager, Environmental Issues
HACKMAN, Timothy B.: Director, Public Affairs, Science and Technology
HUNNICUTT, Patrick A.: Regional Manager, Government Relations
KINGSCOTT, Kathleen N.: Director, Public Policy Programs
MCCULLOCH, Ned: Program Manager, Public Affairs
MUSTAIN, Christopher: Program Manager, Public Affairs
PEARSON, Harriet P.: Chief Privacy Officer
PERRY, Edmund F.: Director, Government Relations
RAYMOND, Brian J.: Program Manager, Grassroots and Political Programs
REDIFER, Paul: Regional Manager, Government Relations
RHONE, Adrienne G.: Manager, Government Relations
SHEEHY, Timothy J.: Public Policy Program Director, Finance and Taxation
SIEMIETKOWSKI, Susan M.: Regional Manager, Government Relations
STEWART, Steve W.: Director, Market Access, Trade and Telecommunications
TUTTLE, Susan C.: Program Manager, Public Affairs, Trade and Investment
WADDELL, Gregory W.: Program Director, E-Commerce Policy
WILLIAMS, Marcus P.: Counsel, Governmental Programs

Outside Counsel/Consultants

PriceWaterhouseCoopers

Internat'l Cadmium Ass'n

P.O. Box 924
Great Falls, VA 22066-0924
Tel: (703)759-7400
Fax: (703)759-7003
Web: www.cadmium.org
E-mail: icdamorrow@aol.com

A marketing, research and promotional arm of the cadmium industry headquartered in Brussels, Belgium.

Leg. Issues: AER, AUT, CAW, ENG, ENV, MAN, NAT, SCI, WAS

In-house, DC-area Employees

MORROW, Hugh: President

Internat'l Campaign for Tibet

1825 K St. NW
Suite 520
Washington, DC 20006
Tel: (202)785-1515
Fax: (202)785-4343
Registered: LDA
Web: www.savetibet.org

A human rights organization.

Leg. Issues: CIV, FOR

In-house, DC-area Employees

ACKERLY, John: President
MARKEY, Marybeth: Director, Government Relations
TSERING, Bhuchung: Director

Outside Counsel/Consultants

Gustafson Associates
Issues: FOR
Rep By: Robert C. Gustafson

Internat'l Cast Polymer Ass'n

8201 Greensboro Dr.
Suite 300
McLean, VA 22102
Tel: (703)610-9034
Fax: (703)610-9005
Web: www.icpa-hq.com
E-mail: trugh@icpa-hq.com

Outside Counsel/Consultants

Ass'n Management Group
Rep By: Timothy R. Rugh

Internat'l Cemetery and Funeral Ass'n

1895 Preston White Dr.
Reston, VA 22091-5434
Tel: (703)391-8400
Fax: (703)391-8416
Web: www.icfa.org
E-mail: rfells@icfa.org

Formerly the American Cemetery Association.

In-house, DC-area Employees

FELLS, Robert M.: Chief Operating Officer, External Affairs

Internat'l Center

731 Eighth St. SE
Washington, DC 20003
Tel: (202)547-3800
Fax: (202)546-4784
Web: www.internationalcenter.com
E-mail: icnfp@erols.ocm

A private, non-profit organization which encourages normalization of relations with former Soviet Republics, Vietnam, Mongolia and others. Also promotes tree-planting and solar power in developing countries.

In-house, DC-area Employees

MATTISON, Lindsay: Exec. Director

Internat'l Center for Clubhouse Development

New York, NY
Leg. Issues: BUD, EDU, MED

Outside Counsel/Consultants

Terry Bevels Consulting
Issues: BUD, EDU, MED
Rep By: Terry D. Bevels

Internat'l Center for Journalists

1616 H St. NW
Third Floor
Washington, DC 20006
Tel: (202)737-3700
Fax: (202)737-0530
Web: www.icfj.org
E-mail: editor@icfj.org

Organizes and conducts training programs in the U.S. and overseas for foreign journalists. Offers information resources and referral services for visiting foreign journalists.

In-house, DC-area Employees

ANABLE, David: President
DILLEHAY, J. Whayne: V. President
GLENNON, Margie Fleming: Director, Communications
LAVERY, Susan: Senior Director, Programs
TALALAY, Susan: Director, Knight International Press Fellowship Program

Internat'l Center for Research on Women

1717 Massachusetts Ave. NW
Suite 302
Washington, DC 20036
Web: www.icrw.org
E-mail: icrw@igc.apc.org
Tel: (202)797-0007
Fax: (202)797-0020

An independent, non-profit organization seeking to promote full and equal economic and social development of women, and improve their health and social status in developing countries.

In-house, DC-area Employees
GUPTA, Geeta Rao: President
MEHRA, Rekha: V. President

Internat'l Chiropractors Ass'n

1110 N. Glebe Rd.
Suite 1000
Arlington, VA 22201
Web: www.chiropractic.org
E-mail: chiro@erols.com
Tel: (703)528-5000
Fax: (703)528-5023

Political Action Committee/s
Internat'l Chiropractors Political Action Committee
1110 N. Glebe Rd.
Suite 1000
Arlington, VA 22201
Contact: Ron Hendrickson
Tel: (703)528-5000
Fax: (703)528-5023

In-house, DC-area Employees
HENDRICKSON, Ron: Exec. Director

Internat'l City/County Management Ass'n

777 N. Capitol St. NE
Suite 500
Washington, DC 20002-4201
Web: www.icma.org
Tel: (202)289-4262
Fax: (202)962-3500

Professional and educational association for local government administrators.

In-house, DC-area Employees
HANSELL, Jr., William H.: Exec. Director
KELLER, Elizabeth: Deputy Director

Internat'l Claim Ass'n

1255 23rd St. NW
Suite 200
Washington, DC 20037-1174
Web: www.claim.org
E-mail: cmurphy@claim.org
Tel: (202)452-8100
Fax: (202)833-3636

In-house, DC-area Employees
MURPHY, Christopher M.: Director of Administration

Outside Counsel/Consultants
Hauck and Associates
Rep By: Christopher M. Murphy

Internat'l Climate Change Partnership

2111 Wilson Blvd.
Eighth Floor
Arlington, VA 22201-3058
Tel: (703)841-0626
Fax: (703)243-2874

An industry coalition addressing global climate change.

Leg. Issues: ENV

In-house, DC-area Employees
FAY, Kevin J.: Exec. Director

Outside Counsel/Consultants
Alcalde & Fay
Issues: ENV
Rep By: Thomas A. Cortina, Kevin J. Fay, Kris Hathaway, David J. Stirpe

Internat'l Coach Federation

Washington, DC

Outside Counsel/Consultants
Bostrom Corp.
Rep By: David L. Santini

Internat'l Code Council

5203 Leesburg Pike
Suite 600
Falls Church, VA 22041
Web: www.intlcode.org
E-mail: staff@intlcode.org
Tel: (703)931-4533
Fax: (703)379-1546
Leg. Issues: BUD, ENV, MMM

In-house, DC-area Employees
KUCHNICKI, Richard P.: Exec. V. President

Outside Counsel/Consultants
Polity Consulting
Issues: BUD, ENV, MMM
Rep By: Roger P. Kingsley, Ph.D.

Internat'l College

New York, NY
Leg. Issues: BUD, EDU, FOR

Outside Counsel/Consultants
Bannerman and Associates, Inc.
Issues: BUD, EDU, FOR
Rep By: M. Graeme Bannerman, Anne Hingeley, William A. Miner, Valerie A. Schultz, Curt Silvers, Tammy Sittnick

Internat'l Commission for the Prevention of Alcoholism and Drug Dependency

12501 Old Columbia Pike
Silver Spring, MD 20904-1600
E-mail: 74617.2242@compuserve.com
Tel: (301)680-6719
Fax: (301)680-6090

In-house, DC-area Employees
NESLUND, Thomas R.: Exec. Director

Internat'l Committee on Organization & Policy

Morgantown, WV
Leg. Issues: AGR

Outside Counsel/Consultants
AESOP Enterprises, Ltd.
Issues: AGR
Rep By: Terry Nipp

Internat'l Communications Industries Ass'n (ICIA)

11242 Waples Mill Rd.
Suite 200
Fairfax, VA 22030
Web: www.icia.org
E-mail: icia@icia.org
Tel: (703)273-7200
Fax: (703)278-8082

ICIA is the international trade association for the professional communications products industry representing over 2,600 dealers, manufacturers, producers and other firms selling products and services in the video, computer and audio-visual industries.

Leg. Issues: COM, SMB, TRD

In-house, DC-area Employees
LEMKE, Randal: Exec. V. President

Internat'l Community Corrections Ass'n

LaCrosse, WI
Leg. Issues: ALC, GOV, LAW

Outside Counsel/Consultants
Mary Katherine Shilton
Issues: ALC, GOV, LAW
Rep By: Mary Katherine Shilton

Internat'l Council of Containership Operators

London, UNITED KINGDOM

Outside Counsel/Consultants
Preston Gates Ellis & Rouvelas Meeds LLP
Rep By: John L. Longstreth, Emanuel L. Rouvelas

Internat'l Council of Cruise Lines

2111 Wilson Blvd.
Eighth Floor
Arlington, VA 22201
Web: www.iccl.org
E-mail: icclinfo@iccl.org
Tel: (703)522-8463
Fax: (703)522-3811
Registered: LDA

An industry association representing the deep-sea, overnight, foreign-flag passenger cruise ship industry.

Leg. Issues: CPT, ENV, GOV, HCR, IMM, LBR, MAR, TAX, TOR, TRA

Political Action Committee/s
Internat'l Council of Cruise Lines PAC (ICCL-PAC)
2111 Wilson Blvd.
Eighth Floor
Arlington, VA 22201
Tel: (703)522-8463
Fax: (703)522-3811

In-house, DC-area Employees
CRYE, J. Michael: President
DENO, Stanford: Director, Technical Operations
MCPHERSON, Molly: Director, Communications
THOMPSON, Thomas E.: Exec. V. President

Outside Counsel/Consultants
Alcalde & Fay
Issues: MAR, TAX
Rep By: Hector Alcalde, Hon. Louis A. "Skip" Bafalis, J. Michael Crye, Lois Moore, Nancy Gibson Prowitt, Alana Weinstein, Barry Zorthian
McDermott, Will and Emery
Venable
Issues: CPT, GOV, LBR, TAX, TOR
Rep By: Jeffrey S. Tenenbaum

Internat'l Council of Employers of Bricklayers and Allied Craftsmen

821 15th St. NW
Washington, DC 20005
Tel: (202)383-3913
Fax: (202)383-3122

Represents contractors who employ members of the Internat'l Union of Bricklayers and Allied Craftsmen. Also furnishes the management trustees of the Internat'l Masonry Institute.

In-house, DC-area Employees
AQUILINE, Matthew S.: Exec. Director

Outside Counsel/Consultants
Specialty Contractors Management, Inc.
Rep By: Walter M. Kardy

Internat'l Council of Shopping Centers

1033 N. Fairfax St.
Suite 404
Alexandria, VA 22314
Web: www.icsc.org
E-mail: govrel@icsc.org
Tel: (703)549-7404
Fax: (703)549-8712
Registered: LDA

A trade association representing owners, developers, retailers, lenders and all others having a professional interest in the shopping center industry. Headquartered in New York, NY.

Leg. Issues: BNK, BUD, CAW, ENV, RES, TAX, TEC

Political Action Committee/s
Internat'l Council of Shopping Centers Political Action Committee (ICSC-PAC)
1033 N. Fairfax St.
Suite 404
Alexandria, VA 22314
Contact: Judy Laniak
Tel: (703)549-7404
Fax: (703)549-8712

In-house, DC-area Employees
HOFFMAN, III, William H.: Manager, Environmental Issues
LANIAK, Judy: Government Relations Administrator
MEHLMAN, Wayne A.: Director, Economic Issues
SALAS, Carlos: Manager, State Relations
STEWART, Cynthia E.: Director, Local Government Relations
SULLIVAN, Rebecca M.: V. President, Government Relations
TYSON, Herbert L.: Senior Director, State and Local Government Relations
WESELEY, Lizabeth: Project Coordinator, State Relations

Outside Counsel/Consultants
BKSH & Associates
Issues: BNK, CAW, ENV, RES, TAX
Evans & Black, Inc.
Rep By: Judy A. Black, Teresa J. Dyer, Rafe Morrissey
The Grizzle Company
Issues: BUD, CAW
Rep By: Richard A. Cantor, Charles L. Grizzle
Winston & Strawn
Issues: BNK, TAX
Rep By: Hon. Beryl F. Anthony, Jr., Charles L. Kinney, John D. McMickle

Internat'l Council on Education for Teaching

Wheeling, IL

ICET is an international, non-governmental association of educational organizations, institutions, and individuals dedicated to the improvement of teacher education and all forms of education and training related to national development.

Outside Counsel/Consultants
Cranwell & O'Connell
Rep By: George E. Cranwell

Internat'l Crystal Federation

Washington, DC
Web: www.colshan.com
E-mail: mkershow@colliershannon.com

Outside Counsel/Consultants
Collier Shannon Scott, PLLC
Rep By: David A. Hartquist, Michael R. Kershow, Robert W. Porter

Internat'l Dairy Foods Ass'n

1250 H St. NW
Suite 900
Washington, DC 20005
Web: www.idfa.org
Tel: (202)737-4332
Fax: (202)331-7820
Registered: LDA

Represents manufacturers, distributors and marketers of ice cream and related products in legislative, regulatory, marketing, production and training activities.

Leg. Issues: AGR, BUD, ENV, FOO, GOV, LBR, TRD

Political Action Committee/s
Ice Cream, Milk & Cheese PAC

1250 H St. NW
Suite 900
Washington, DC 20005
Contact: Constance E. Tipton
Tel: (202)737-4332
Fax: (202)331-7820

In-house, DC-area Employees

DETLEFSEN, Clay: Director, Environmental and Worker Safety Issues
FRYE, Cary: V. President, Regulatory and Scientific Affairs
NELSON, Kathleen: Director, Legislative Affairs
NUZUM, Janet: V. President and General Counsel
RULAND, Susan: V. President, Communications and Meetings
SAYLER, Allen: Director, Regulatory Affairs and International Standards
TIPTON, Constance E.: Senior Group V. President
TIPTON, E. Linwood: President and Chief Exec. Officer
TORREY, Michael K.: Senior Director, Legislative Affairs
YONKERS, Bob: Chief Economist

Outside Counsel/Consultants

Covington & Burling
Issues: AGR, FOO
Rep By: H. Edward Dunkelberger, Jr., Steven J. Rosenbaum

M & R Strategic Services
Issues: AGR
Rep By: William B. Wasserman

McGlotten & Jarvis
Issues: FOO
Rep By: John T. Jarvis, Robert M. McGlotten

Parry, Romani, DeConcini & Symms

Powell Tate

Internat'l Dairy-Deli-Bakery Ass'n

Madison, WI
Leg. Issues: FOO

Outside Counsel/Consultants

Robert N. Pyle & Associates
Issues: FOO
Rep By: Alexis Hersh, Alison O'Neill, Robert N. Pyle

Internat'l Distance Learning

Palm Beach, FL
Leg. Issues: EDU

Outside Counsel/Consultants

The MWW Group
Issues: EDU
Rep By: Tracey Becker, Dana P. Bostic, Jonathan B. Slade

Internat'l District Energy Ass'n

Washington, DC
Web: www.energy.rochester.edu/idea
E-mail: idea@dc.sba.com

An 85 year-old association representing utilities, institutions, consultants, engineers and suppliers of the district energy industry. Promotes environmentally acceptable concept of supplying heating or cooling centrally to areas via piping networks.

Outside Counsel/Consultants

Smith, Bucklin and Associates, Inc.

Internat'l Downtown Ass'n

910 17th St. NW
Suite 210
Washington, DC 20006-2603
Web: www.ida-downtown.org
E-mail: question@ida-downtown.org
Tel: (202)293-4505
Fax: (202)293-4509

Purpose is to further the improvement of downtowns and their adjacent neighborhoods. Objectives include: the enhancement of the professionalism of its members, the communication of the importance of downtowns to the public, and the development of public and private policy to further the downtown improvement process.

Leg. Issues: ART, ECN, HOU, RES, ROD, SMB, SPO, TOU, TRA, URB

In-house, DC-area Employees

JACKSON, Elizabeth: President

Internat'l Dyslexia Ass'n, The

Baltimore, MD
Leg. Issues: BUD, CIV, EDU, HCR, MED, MMM

Outside Counsel/Consultants

Polity Consulting
Issues: BUD, CIV, EDU, HCR, MED, MMM
Rep By: Roger P. Kingsley, Ph.D.

Internat'l Electrical Testing Ass'n

Morrison, CO
Leg. Issues: GOV

Outside Counsel/Consultants

Halsey, Rains & Associates, LLC
Issues: GOV
Rep By: Steven C. Halsey, James Hubbard, Laurie D. Rains

Internat'l Electronic Article Surveillance Manufacturers

Washington, DC
Web: www.ieasma.org
E-mail: info@ieasma.org

Manufactures security equipment for retailers.

Outside Counsel/Consultants

TASC, Inc., Association Management
Rep By: Randy Dyer, CAE

Internat'l Electronics Manufacturers and Consumers of America

Washington, DC

An American trade association composed of the U.S. manufacturing subsidiaries of 18 major overseas electronics companies.

Leg. Issues: IMM, TAX, TRD

Outside Counsel/Consultants

French & Company
Issues: IMM, TAX, TRD
Rep By: Verrick O. French, Keith H. Smith

Internat'l Energy Consultants

Las Vegas, NV

Outside Counsel/Consultants

Duncan, Weinberg, Genzer & Pembroke, P.C.
Rep By: Jeffrey C. Genzer, Tatjana M. Shonkwiler

Internat'l Eye Foundation/Soc. of Eye Surgeons

7801 Norfolk Ave.
Bethesda, MD 20814
Web: www.iefusa.org
E-mail: info@iefusa.org
Tel: (301)986-1830
Fax: (301)986-1876

In-house, DC-area Employees

BARROWS, John: Director of Programs
SHEFFIELD, Victoria: Exec. Director

Internat'l Fabricare Institute

12251 Tech Rd.
Silver Spring, MD 20904
Web: www.ifi.org
E-mail: communications@ifi.org
Leg. Issues: ENV
Tel: (301)622-1900
Fax: (301)236-9320
Registered: LDA

In-house, DC-area Employees

FISHER, William E.: Chief Exec. Officer
SCALCO, Mary: Senior V. President
WILLIAMS, Patricia Randolph: V. President, Government Affairs

Internat'l Facilities Management Ass'n

Outside Counsel/Consultants

R. J. Hudson Associates

PACE-CAPSTONE
Rep By: David S. Germroth, James W. Wise

Internat'l Federation of Inspection Agencies, North American Committee

3942 N. Upland St.
Arlington, VA 22207
E-mail: ifianac@aol.com
Leg. Issues: TRD, TRU
Tel: (703)533-9539
Fax: (703)533-1612
Registered: LDA

In-house, DC-area Employees

BUSH, J.D., CAE, Milton M.: Exec. Director

Outside Counsel/Consultants

The M Companies
Issues: TRU
Rep By: Milton M. Bush, J.D., CAE

Shea & Gardner
Issues: TRD
Rep By: Patrick M. Hanlon

Internat'l Federation of Professional and Technical Engineers

8630 Fenton St.
Suite 400
Silver Spring, MD 20910-3803
Web: www.ifpte.org
Tel: (301)565-9016
Fax: (301)565-0018
Registered: LDA

Leg. Issues: AER, AVI, BUD, CHM, CIV, COM, CPI, DEF, ECN, ENG, FUE, GOV, HCR, IMM, LBR, MAN, MAR, MMM, PHA, POS, ROD, RRR, SCI, TRA, TRD, UTI, WAS

Political Action Committee/s

Internat'l Federation of Professional and Technical Engineers LEAP-PAC

8630 Fenton St.
Suite 400
Silver Spring, MD 20910-3803
Contact: Dolores A. Gorezyca
Tel: (301)565-9016
Fax: (301)565-0018

In-house, DC-area Employees

CLARK, Julia A.: General Counsel
GOREZYCA, Dolores A.: Secretary-Treasurer
JUNEMANN, Gregory J.: International President
RHETT, Candace M.: Communications Director

Internat'l Food Additives Council

1101 15th St. NW
Suite 202
Washington, DC 20005
Leg. Issues: FOO
Tel: (202)785-3232
Fax: (202)223-9741

In-house, DC-area Employees

CRISTOL, Richard E.: Washington Representative

Outside Counsel/Consultants

EOP Group, Inc.
Issues: FOO
Rep By: Jonathan Gledhill, Joseph Hezir, Michael O'Bannon, Phil Pulizzi

The Kellen Company
Rep By: Richard E. Cristol

Internat'l Food Information Council

1100 Connecticut Ave. NW
Suite 430
Washington, DC 20036
Web: www.ific.org
E-mail: foodinfo@ific.org
Tel: (202)296-6540
Fax: (202)296-6547

In-house, DC-area Employees

ALEXANDER, Nick: Director, Media Relations
BORRA, RD, Susan: Senior V. President, Director of Nutrition
ROWE, Sylvia: President
SCHMIDT, David: Senior V. President, Food Safety

Internat'l Food Policy Research Institute

2033 K St. NW
Washington, DC 20006
Web: www.ifpri.org
E-mail: ifpri@cgiar.org
Tel: (202)862-5600
Fax: (202)467-4439

Analyzes world food problems, especially in developing countries, and conducts research on policies to increase the availability of food to needy populations.

In-house, DC-area Employees

PINSTRUP-ANDERSEN, Per: Director General
RUBENSTEIN, Michael: Director of Information

Internat'l Formula Council

1101 15th St. NW
Suite 202
Washington, DC 20005
Tel: (202)785-3232
Fax: (202)223-9741

In-house, DC-area Employees

CRISTOL, Richard E.: Exec. V. President

Outside Counsel/Consultants

The Kellen Company
Rep By: Richard E. Cristol

Internat'l Foundation for Election Systems (IFES)

1101 15th St. NW
Third Floor
Washington, DC 20005
Web: www.ifes.org
Tel: (202)828-8507
Fax: (202)452-0804

A private, non-profit foundation dedicated to promoting democracy worldwide. Focuses on election assistance, civil society, governance, and rule of law. Maintains 20 offices around the world.

In-house, DC-area Employees

SOUDRIETTE, Richard W.: President

Outside Counsel/Consultants

Vorys, Sater, Seymour and Pease, LLP

Internat'l Franchise Ass'n

1350 New York Ave. NW
Suite 900
Washington, DC 20005
Tel: (202)628-8000
Fax: (202)628-0812
Registered: LDA
Web: www.franchise.org
E-mail: info@franchise.org
Leg. Issues: BAN, CPT, CSP, ECN, HCR, LBR, SMB, TAX

Political Action Committee/s

Franchising Political Action Committee
1350 New York Ave. NW
Suite 900
Washington, DC 20005
Tel: (202)628-8000
Fax: (202)628-0812
Contact: Matthew R. Shay

In-house, DC-area Employees

DEBOLT, Don J.: President
HILL, Terry: V. President, Communications
REYNOLDS, John R.: President, IFA Educational Foundation and Exec. V. President
SHAY, Matthew R.: V. President and Chief Counsel

Outside Counsel/Consultants

McGlotten & Jarvis
Rep By: John T. Jarvis, Robert M. McGlotten

Morgan, Lewis & Bockius LLP
Issues: SMB

Rhoads Group

Internat'l Frozen Food Ass'n

2000 Corporate Ridge
Suite 1000
McLean, VA 22102
Tel: (703)821-0770
Fax: (703)821-1350
E-mail: info@affi.com
Leg. Issues: AGR, FOO, TRD

In-house, DC-area Employees

SARASIN, CAE, Leslie G.: Deputy Director General

Internat'l Fund for Agricultural Development

Rome, ITALY

Outside Counsel/Consultants

Collins & Company, Inc.
Rep By: James D. Bond, Richard L. Collins, Thomas A. Hooper, Shay D. Stautz

Hauser Group

Internat'l Fund for Animal Welfare

Yarmouth Port, MA
Leg. Issues: ANI, ENV

Outside Counsel/Consultants

Sher & Blackwell
Issues: ANI, ENV
Rep By: Earl W. Comstock, Jeffrey R. Pike

Internat'l Furnishing & Design Ass'n (IFDA)

Washington, DC

Outside Counsel/Consultants

Smith, Bucklin and Associates, Inc.

Internat'l Furniture Rental Ass'n

Westerville, OH

Outside Counsel/Consultants

Kilpatrick Stockton LLP
Rep By: Frederick H. von Unwerth

Internat'l Game Technology

Reno, NV
Leg. Issues: CPT, GAM, TAX

Outside Counsel/Consultants

Dave Evans Associates
Issues: GAM
Rep By: Hon. Dave Evans

Mayer, Brown & Platt
Issues: TAX

John T. O'Rourke Law Offices
Issues: CPT, GAM, TAX
Rep By: John T. O'Rourke

Internat'l Geographic Information Foundation

South Bend, IN

Outside Counsel/Consultants

Cranwell & O'Connell
Rep By: George E. Cranwell

Internat'l Group of P&I Clubs

London, UNITED KINGDOM
Leg. Issues: ENV, MAR

Outside Counsel/Consultants

Robins, Kaplan, Miller & Ciresi L.L.P.
Issues: ENV, MAR
Rep By: Harold E. Mesirow

Internat'l Health, Racquet and Sportsclub Ass'n

Boston, MA
Leg. Issues: CPT, TAX

Outside Counsel/Consultants

Benchmarks, Inc.
Issues: CPT, TAX
Rep By: Thomas J. Scanlon

Internat'l Healthcare Safety Professional Certification Board

8009 Carita Ct.
Bethesda, MD 20817
Tel: (301)770-2540
Fax: (301)770-2183
Web: www.chcm-chsp.org
E-mail: bchcm@juno.com

Certifies Healthcare Safety Professionals, working or consulting in medical or related fields, who are charged with responsibility for hazard control activities at hospitals and other health care facilities.

In-house, DC-area Employees

GORDON, Harold: Exec. Director

Internat'l Hearing Soc.

Livonia, MI
Leg. Issues: HCR

Outside Counsel/Consultants

McDermott, Will and Emery
Issues: HCR
Rep By: Calvin P. Johnson, Karen S. Sealander, Timothy J. Waters

Reed, Smith, LLP
Issues: HCR
Rep By: Marc Scheineson

Internat'l Housewares Ass'n

Chicago, IL

Outside Counsel/Consultants

SEDERHOLM Public Affairs, Inc.
Rep By: Pamela Sederholm

The Internat'l Human Rights Law Group

1200 18th St. NW
Suite 602
Washington, DC 20036
Tel: (202)822-4600
Fax: (202)822-4606
Web: www.hrlawgroup.org
E-mail: humanrights@hrlawgroup.org

A non-profit organization of human rights and legal professionals engaged in advocacy, litigation and training around the world. Seeks to empower local advocates to expand the scope of human rights protection for men and women and to promote broad participation in building human rights standards and procedures at the national, regional and international levels.

In-house, DC-area Employees

MCDOUGALL, Gay: Exec. Director

Internat'l Institute for Energy Conservation

1015 15th St. NW
Suite 600
Washington, DC 20005
Tel: (202)842-3388
Fax: (202)842-3388
Web: www.iiec.org

A non-profit organization that implements and fosters sustainable development in developing countries, including Central and Eastern Europe, through energy conservation.

In-house, DC-area Employees

THOMPSON, Griffin: President

Internat'l Institute of Ammonia Refrigeration

Washington, DC
Web: www.iiar.org
E-mail: iiar@iiar.org

Outside Counsel/Consultants

The Plexus Consulting Group

Smith, Bucklin and Associates, Inc.
Rep By: Frank M. Moore

Internat'l Insurance Council

900 19th St. NW
Suite 250
Washington, DC 20006
Tel: (202)682-2345
Fax: (202)218-7730
Web: www.iicdc.org

An international trade development organization of U.S. insurance and reinsurance companies and insurance service companies that do business in international markets.

In-house, DC-area Employees

CRONIN, Kevin: President

Internat'l Intellectual Property Alliance

1747 Pennsylvania Ave. NW
Suite 825
Washington, DC 20006-4604
Tel: (202)833-4198
Fax: (202)872-0546
Registered: LDA
Web: www.iipa.com
E-mail: info@iipa.com

A coalition of trade associations including the Ass'n of American Publishers, the AFMA, the Business Software Alliance, the Interactive Digital Software Association, the Motion Picture Ass'n of America, the Nat'l Music Publishers' Ass'n and the Recording Industry Ass'n of America.

Leg. Issues: CPT, TRD

In-house, DC-area Employees

METALITZ, Steven J.: V. President and General Counsel
SCHLESINGER, Michael N.: Counsel
SCHWARTZ, Eric J.: Counsel
SMITH, Eric H.: President
STRONG, Maria S.: V. President and Associate General Counsel

Outside Counsel/Consultants

Smith & Metalitz, L.L.P.
Issues: CPT, TRD
Rep By: Steven J. Metalitz, Michael N. Schlesinger, Eric J. Schwartz, Eric H. Smith, Maria S. Strong

Internat'l Intellectual Property Institute

Washington, DC
Leg. Issues: BUD

Outside Counsel/Consultants

Holland & Knight LLP
Issues: BUD
Rep By: David C. Whitestone

Internat'l Jelly and Preserve Ass'n

1101 15th St. NW
Suite 202
Washington, DC 20005
Tel: (202)785-3232
Fax: (202)223-9741

In-house, DC-area Employees

CRISTOL, Richard E.: Washington Representative

Outside Counsel/Consultants

Covington & Burling
Rep By: David R. Grace

The Kellen Company
Rep By: Richard E. Cristol

Internat'l Karate Federation

Outside Counsel/Consultants

Akin, Gump, Strauss, Hauer & Feld, L.L.P.
Rep By: Henry A. Terhune

Van Scoyoc Associates, Inc.
Rep By: Jeffrey S. Trinca

Internat'l Kitchen Exhaust Cleaning Ass'n

Washington, DC

Outside Counsel/Consultants

Sufka & Associates
Rep By: Kenneth M. Sufka

Internat'l Labor Office

1828 L St. NW
Suite 600
Washington, DC 20036
Tel: (202)653-7652
Fax: (202)653-7687
Web: www.ilo.org
E-mail: washilo@ilowbo.org

A United Nations Specialized Agency with 160 member countries. Seeks to improve working conditions, create employment and promote human rights throughout the world. A tripartite structure involves member country governments as well as worker and employer groups in its decision-making process. The Washington branch maintains relations with agencies and organizations dealing with social and labor issues in the U.S.

In-house, DC-area Employees

FREEMAN, Anthony G.: Director

Internat'l Labor Rights Fund

733 15th St. NW
Suite 920
Washington, DC 20005
Tel: (202)347-4100
Fax: (202)347-4885
Web: www.laborrights.org
E-mail: laborrights@igc.org

A non-profit organization representing human rights and labor rights.

Leg. Issues: FOR, LAW, LBR, TRD

In-house, DC-area Employees

HARVEY, Pharis J.: Exec. Director

Internat'l Laboratory Technology Corp.

Hollywood, FL
Leg. Issues: AGR

Outside Counsel/Consultants

Richard L. Spees, Inc.
Issues: AGR
Rep By: Richard L. Spees

Internat'l Law Institute

1615 New Hampshire Ave. NW
Washington, DC 20009
Tel: (202)483-3036
Fax: (202)483-3029
Web: www.ili.org
E-mail: training@ili.org

A non-profit organization which conducts training programs in DC and abroad for government officials in developing countries. Publishes books on international commercial law, finance and development.

In-house, DC-area Employees

KERR, Stuart: Exec. Director
WHITTEN, Peter: Director of Publishing

Outside Counsel/Consultants

Covington & Burling

Internat'l Lead Zinc Research Organization, Inc. (ILZRO)

Research Triangle, NC
Leg. Issues: AUT, ENG, TRA

Outside Counsel/Consultants

Robert E. Carlstrom
Issues: AUT, ENG, TRA
Rep By: Robert E. Carlstrom, Jr.

Internat'l Limousine

Outside Counsel/Consultants

Dittus Communications
Rep By: Tom Conway, Cynthia Giorgio

Internat'l Longevity Center

Outside Counsel/Consultants

Washington Strategies, L.L.C.
Rep By: Jennifer Johnson Calvert, William P. Jarrell

Internat'l Longshore and Warehouse Union

1775 K St. NW
Suite 200
Washington, DC 20006
Tel: (202)463-6265
Fax: (202)467-4875
Registered: LDA
Web: www.ilwu.org
Leg. Issues: AGR, BAN, HCR, IMM, LBR, MAR, TRA, TRD

In-house, DC-area Employees

MCLAUGHLIN, Lindsay: Washington Representative and Legislative Director

Internat'l Longshoremen's Ass'n

1101 17th St. NW
Suite 400
Washington, DC 20036
Tel: (202)955-6304
Fax: (202)955-6048

Political Action Committee/s

Internat'l Longshoremen's Ass'n PAC
1101 17th St. NW
Suite 400
Washington, DC 20036
Contact: John Bowers, Jr.
Tel: (202)955-6304
Fax: (202)955-6048

In-house, DC-area Employees

BOWERS, Jr., John: Legislative Director
ESDERS, Ingolf G.: Legislative Representative
GLEASON, Robert E.: Secretary/Treasurer

Outside Counsel/Consultants

The Kamber Group
Rep By: Pamela Greenwalt

Internat'l Magnesium Ass'n

6731 Whittier Ave.
Suite C-100
McLean, VA 22101
Tel: (703)442-8888
Fax: (703)821-1824
Web: www.intlmag.org
E-mail: ima@bellatlantic.net

An international organization made up of the producers, die casters, marketers, and users of magnesium.

In-house, DC-area Employees

CLOW, Byron B.: Exec. V. President

Internat'l Management and Development Institute

1615 L St. NW
Suite 900
Washington, DC 20036
Tel: (202)337-1022
Fax: (202)337-6678
E-mail: imdimail@aol.com

Provides educational programs and services to strengthen the ability of business and government to deal with international issues of mutual interest.

In-house, DC-area Employees

BONKER, Hon. Don L.: President and Chief Exec. Officer
CRANE, Brent: Director, Programs and Publications
SCHLEIDT, Sabine: Exec. V. President

Internat'l Marketing for Russia and NIS

Moscow, RUSSIA

Outside Counsel/Consultants

Gilbert A. Robinson, Inc.
Rep By: Kenneth J. Hoeck

Internat'l Mass Retailers Ass'n

1700 N. Moore St.
Suite 2250
Arlington, VA 22209
Tel: (703)841-2300
Fax: (703)841-1183
Registered: LDA
Web: www.imra.org
E-mail: mcain@imra.org

The trade association representing the mass retail industry, the largest segment of general merchandise retailing.

Leg. Issues: APP, AUT, BEV, BUD, CPI, CPT, CSP, ENV, FOO, HCR, LAW, LBR, MAN, PHA, SCI, TAX, TEC, TOR, TRA, TRD, TRU, UTI

Political Action Committee/s

Internation'l Mass Retail Ass'n Political Action Committee (IMRA/PAC)
1700 N. Moore St.
Suite 2250
Arlington, VA 22209
Tel: (703)841-2300
Fax: (703)841-1183

In-house, DC-area Employees

CAIN, Morrison G.: Senior V. President, Government Affairs
GILBERTSON, Lisa: Director of Tax and Financial Issues
GOLD, Jonathan E.: Legislative Representative
TAMPIO, Christopher M.: Contact
VERDISCO, Robert J.: President
WOLSKI, Lisa: Counsel, Tax and Finance

Outside Counsel/Consultants

JBC Internat'l
Issues: APP, AUT, BEV, CPI, FOO, MAN, TEC, TRD
Rep By: Robin W. Lanier

McDermott, Will and Emery
Rep By: Timothy J. Waters

Internat'l Medical Programs

Albany, NY
Leg. Issues: BUD, DEF, FOR

Outside Counsel/Consultants

The Solomon Group, LLC
Issues: BUD, DEF, FOR
Rep By: David M. Lonie, Lara Roholt Westdorp, Hon. Gerald B. H. Solomon

Internat'l Metals Reclamation Co.

Ellwood City, PA

Outside Counsel/Consultants

Wilmer, Cutler & Pickering
Rep By: Neil J. King

Internat'l Microelectronics and Packaging Soc. - IMAPS

611 Second St. NE
Washington, DC 20002
Tel: (202)548-4001
Fax: (202)548-6115
Web: www.imaps.org
E-mail: imaps@aol.com

A 6,000 member Society dedicated to the advancement of the field of microelectronics research and study. Also provides ten to twelve $6,000 tuition scholarships.

In-house, DC-area Employees

BELL, Ann: Manager, Corporate Relations
BRECK, Richard: Exec. Director
PAUL, Doug: Manager, Marketing and Membership

Internat'l Mobile Air Conditioning Ass'n

Fort Worth, TX

Outside Counsel/Consultants

Conlon, Frantz, Phelan & Pires
Rep By: Michael J. Conlon

Internat'l Municipal Lawyers Ass'n

1110 Vermont Ave. NW
Suite 200
Washington, DC 20005
Tel: (202)466-5424
Fax: (202)785-0152
Web: www.imla.org
E-mail: info@imla.org

A non-profit organization rendering service, information, and assistance to local government attorneys in North America.

In-house, DC-area Employees

UNDERHILL, Jr., Henry W.: Exec. Director and General Counsel

Internat'l Municipal Signal Ass'n

Newark, NJ
Leg. Issues: CPT, GOV, LBR, TAX, TOR

Outside Counsel/Consultants

Venable
Issues: CPT, GOV, LBR, TAX, TOR
Rep By: Jeffrey S. Tenenbaum

Internat'l Narcotic Enforcement Officers Ass'n

Albany, NY

Outside Counsel/Consultants

Kelly and Associates, Inc.
Rep By: John A. Kelly

Internat'l Olympic Committee

Lausanne, SWITZERLAND
Leg. Issues: LAW, SPO, TRA

Outside Counsel/Consultants

Hill and Knowlton, Inc.
Issues: SPO
Rep By: Gary G. Hymel, Frank Mankiewicz, Jeffrey B. Trammell

Patton Boggs, LLP
Issues: LAW, SPO, TRA
Rep By: Joseph Trapasso

Internat'l Oxygen Manufacturers Ass'n

1255 23rd St. NW
Suite 200
Washington, DC 20037-1174
Tel: (202)521-9300
Fax: (202)833-3636
Web: www.iomaweb.org
E-mail: ioma@iomaweb.org

In-house, DC-area Employees

SAUNDERS, David A.: Exec. Director

Outside Counsel/Consultants

Hauck and Associates
Rep By: David A. Saunders

Internat'l Paint Inc.

Union, NJ
Leg. Issues: CAW, ENV, MAR

Outside Counsel/Consultants

The Accord Group
Issues: CAW, ENV, MAR
Rep By: Patrick H. Quinn

Internat'l Paper

1101 Pennsylvania Ave. NW
Suite 200
Washington, DC 20004
Tel: (202)628-1223
Fax: (202)628-1368
Registered: LDA
Web: www.internationalpaper.com

Headquartered in Purchase, NY.

Leg. Issues: CAW, ENG, LBR, MAN, NAT, TAX, TRD

Political Action Committee/s

Internat'l Paper Political Action Committee (IPPAC)
1101 Pennsylvania Ave. NW
Suite 200
Washington, DC 20004
Contact: John C. Runyan
Tel: (202)628-1223
Fax: (202)628-1368

In-house, DC-area Employees

GEHLHAART, Donna: Washington Representative
MANN, Mary M.: Washington Representative
RUNYAN, John C.: Washington Representative
SHAFFER, Erin E.: Counsel, Federal Corporate Affairs
WITHEY, Ms. Lyn M.: V. President, Public Affairs

Outside Counsel/Consultants

Collier Shannon Scott, PLLC

Wiley, Rein & Fielding
Rep By: Carol Laham

Internat'l Parking Institute

Fredericksburg, VA
Web: www.parking.org
E-mail: ipi@parking.org

Represents the public parking profession.

Outside Counsel/Consultants

David E. Fox and Associates

Internat'l Personnel Management Ass'n

1617 Duke St. Tel: (703)549-7100
Alexandria, VA 22314 Fax: (703)684-0948
Web: www.ipma-hr.org
E-mail: ipma@ipma-hr.org

A non-profit membership organization for agencies and individuals in the public sector human resources field and others interested in the IPMA's objectives.

Leg. Issues: LBR

In-house, DC-area Employees

CHIAPPETTA, Christina Ott: Director, Government Affairs
REICHENBERG, Neil E.: Exec. Director

Internat'l Policy Council on Agriculture, Food and Trade

1616 P St. NW Tel: (202)328-5056
Suite 100 Fax: (202)328-5133
Washington, DC 20036
Web: www.ipcaft.org
E-mail: ipcaft@rff.org

In-house, DC-area Employees

LACY, Peter: Exec. Director

Internat'l Power Machines

Garland, TX

A manufacturer of uninterruptible power sources.

Outside Counsel/Consultants

O'Connor & Fierce Associates

Internat'l Prepaid Communications Ass'n

Washington, DC
Web: www.telecard.org

Outside Counsel/Consultants

The Segermark Associates, Inc.
Rep By: Howard Segermark

Internat'l Public Relations Co.

Tokyo, JAPAN
Leg. Issues: AUT, TEC

Outside Counsel/Consultants

Capital Strategies Group, Inc.
Issues: AUT, TEC
Rep By: Tammi Hayes

Internat'l R&D, Inc.

Los Angeles, CA

Outside Counsel/Consultants

Steptoe & Johnson LLP

Internat'l Raw Materials

Philadelphia, PA
Leg. Issues: TRD

Outside Counsel/Consultants

Chesapeake Enterprises, Inc.
Issues: TRD
Rep By: J. John Fluharty

Internat'l Reading Ass'n

444 N. Capitol St. NW Tel: (202)624-8800
Suite 630 Fax: (202)624-8826
Washington, DC 20001 Registered: LDA
Web: www.reading.org
E-mail: irawash@reading.org

An association headquartered in Newark, Delaware working for increased literacy for all by improving the quality of literary instruction.

Leg. Issues: EDU

In-house, DC-area Employees

LONG, Richard: Director, Government Relations

Internat'l Reciprocal Trade

St. Charles, MO
Leg. Issues: FIN

Outside Counsel/Consultants

Royer & Babyak
Issues: FIN
Rep By: Robert Stewart Royer

Internat'l Religious Liberty Ass'n

12501 Old Columbia Pike Tel: (301)680-6680
Silver Spring, MD 20904-6600 Fax: (301)680-6695
Web: www.irla.org
E-mail: 74532,240@compuserve.com

The General Conference of Seventh-day Adventists provides salaried personnel for the office. John Graz of the General Conference serves as Secretary-General.

Leg. Issues: CIV, CON

In-house, DC-area Employees

BEACH, Dr. Bert B.: V. President
GRAZ, John: Secretary-General

Internat'l Republican Institute

1212 New York Ave. NW Tel: (202)408-9450
Suite 900 Fax: (202)408-9462
Washington, DC 20005
Web: www.iri.org
E-mail: iri@iri.org

Provides training in countries throughout the world in political party building, communications strategy, policy research, and election processes to encourage and support the evolution of the democratic political process.

In-house, DC-area Employees

CRANER, Lorne W.: President

Outside Counsel/Consultants

Akin, Gump, Strauss, Hauer & Feld, L.L.P.

Internat'l Rescue Committee Inc.

1612 K St. NW Tel: (202)822-0043
Suite 700 Fax: (202)822-0089
Washington, DC 20006 Registered: LDA
Web: www.intrescom.org
Leg. Issues: BUD, FOR, IMM

In-house, DC-area Employees

ABRAMOWITZ, Sheppie: Special Advisor
BARTOLINI, Mark Ryan: V. President, Government Relations

Internat'l Research and Exchanges Board (IREX)

1616 H St. NW Tel: (202)628-8188
Washington, DC 20006 Fax: (202)628-8189
Web: www.irex.org
E-mail: irex@irex.org

Arranges exchanges and partnership projects in the former Soviet Union, Eastern and Central Europe, Mongolia, and China.

Leg. Issues: EDU, FOR

In-house, DC-area Employees

MELLNICK, Keith: Communications Officer

Outside Counsel/Consultants

The Advocacy Group
Issues: EDU, FOR
Rep By: George A. Ramonas, Anne V. Smith

Anne V. Smith
Rep By: Anne V. Smith

Internat'l Road Federation

1010 Massachusetts Ave. NW Tel: (202)371-5544
Suite 410 Fax: (202)371-5565
Washington, DC 20001
Web: www.irfnet.org
E-mail: info@irfnet.org

In-house, DC-area Employees

SANKEY, C. Patrick: Director General & Chief Exec. Officer

Internat'l Safety Equipment Ass'n (ISEA)

1901 N. Moore St. Tel: (703)525-1695
Suite 808 Fax: (703)528-2148
Arlington, VA 22209 Registered: LDA
Web: www.safetyequipment.org
E-mail: isea@safetyequipment.org

A trade association that represents manufacturers of safety and personal protective equipment. These manufacturers produce clothing and equipment to protect workers from hazards: respirators, head protection, eye and face protection, hearing protection, safety wearing apparel, instruments, first aid kits, warning devices, fall protection, emergency eyewash and showers, ergonomic equipment, high-visibility products.

Leg. Issues: CSP, DIS, LBR, MAN, TRD

In-house, DC-area Employees

GLUCKSMAN, Daniel I.: Director, Public Affairs
SHIPP, Daniel K.: President

Outside Counsel/Consultants

Webster, Chamberlain & Bean
Rep By: Arthur Herold

Internat'l Service Agencies

66 Canal Center Plaza Tel: (703)548-2200
Suite 310 Fax: (703)548-7684
Alexandria, VA 22314
Web: www.charity.org
E-mail: isa@charity.org

A federation of American charitable organizations that provide health and welfare services to needy people overseas.

In-house, DC-area Employees

ACOSTA, Renee: President

Internat'l Shipholding Corp.

New Orleans, LA
Leg. Issues: BUD, MAR

Outside Counsel/Consultants

Jones, Walker, Waechter, Poitevent, Carrere & Denegre, L.L.P.
Issues: BUD, MAR
Rep By: John J. Jaskot, R. Christian Johnsen

Internat'l Sign Ass'n

707 N. Saint Asaph St. Tel: (703)836-4012
Alexandria, VA 22314 Fax: (703)836-8353
Web: www.signs.org

Represents sign users, sign supply distributors, product manufacturers, and sign companies manufacturing on-premise signs.

Leg. Issues: ADV, CAW, COM, CPT, ENV, HCR, INS, LBR, MAN, RES, SMB, TRU, WAS

In-house, DC-area Employees

BEAMER BOHNERT, Suzanne C.: V. President, Government Relations and Public Affairs
LAPPEN, Mark: President and Chief Exec. Officer

Outside Counsel/Consultants

Cohn and Marks
Rep By: Richard M. Schmidt, Jr.

Internat'l Sleep Products Ass'n

501 Wythe St. Tel: (703)683-8371
Alexandria, VA 22314 Fax: (703)683-4503
Registered: LDA
Web: www.sleepproducts.org
E-mail: info@sleepproducts.org
Leg. Issues: CSP

In-house, DC-area Employees

ABOLT, Russ: Exec. V. President
CONRAD, Shawn D.: V. President, Government Relations and Issues Management

Outside Counsel/Consultants

Ogilvy Public Relations Worldwide
Rep By: Mickey Nall

Rogers & Wells
Issues: CSP
Rep By: Ryan T. Trainer

Internat'l Slurry Surfacing Ass'n

Washington, DC

Represents the pavement maintenance industry specializing in slurry seal and micro-surfacing techniques.

Outside Counsel/Consultants

Smith, Bucklin and Associates, Inc.

Internat'l Snowmobile Manufacturers Ass'n

Haslett, MI
Leg. Issues: NAT, RES, SPO, TOU

Outside Counsel/Consultants

Albertine Enterprises, Inc.
Issues: NAT, SPO, TOU
Rep By: James J. Albertine, Dr. John M. Albertine, Aubrey C. King

Birch, Horton, Bittner & Cherot
Issues: RES
Rep By: Douglas S. Burdin, Julia Gustafson, William P. Horn

Cassidy & Associates, Inc.
Issues: NAT
Rep By: Douglass E. Bobbitt, Christy Carson Evans, Carl Franklin Godfrey, Jr., W. Campbell Kaufman, IV, Daniel J. McNamara, Michael Merola, Diane Rinaldo

Internat'l Soc. for Experimental Hematology

Washington, DC
Web: www.iseh.org
E-mail: iseh@dc.sba.com

Outside Counsel/Consultants

Smith, Bucklin and Associates, Inc.
Rep By: Tom Reiser

Internat'l Soc. for Performance Improvement

1400 Spring St.
Suite 260
Silver Spring, MD 20910
Web: www.ispi.org
E-mail: info@ispi.org
Tel: (301)587-8570
Fax: (301)587-8573

ISPI is the leading association dedicated to improving workplace productivity.

In-house, DC-area Employees

HILL, Jim: President

Internat'l Soc. for Pharmacoepidemiology

Outside Counsel/Consultants

PAI Management Corp.
Rep By: Mark Epstein

Internat'l Soc. for Quality of Life Research

McLean, VA

Outside Counsel/Consultants

Degnon Associates, Inc.

Internat'l Soc. for Technology in Education

Eugene, OR
Leg. Issues: COM, CPI, CPT, EDU, TAX, TEC

Outside Counsel/Consultants

Leslie Harris & Associates
Issues: COM, CPI, CPT, EDU, TAX, TEC
Rep By: Leslie A. Harris, Jee Hang Lee, Ghani Raines

Internat'l Soc. of Air Safety Investigators

Park Center
107 E. Holly Ave., Suite 11
Sterling, VA 20164
Web: www.isasi.org
E-mail: isasi@erols.com
Tel: (703)430-9668
Fax: (703)430-4970

In-house, DC-area Employees

DELGANDIO, Frank: President
MAYES, Paul: V. President

Internat'l Soc. of Hospitality Consultants

515 King St.
Suite 420
Alexandria, VA 22314-3103
Web: www.ishc.com
E-mail: ishc@ishc.com
Tel: (703)684-6681
Fax: (703)684-6048

In-house, DC-area Employees

BARNES, Gary L.: President
JOHNSON, Haley: Administrative Director
LUSTIG, Ron: Chairman

Outside Counsel/Consultants

CLARION Management Resources, Inc.
Rep By: Haley Johnson, Carole M. Rogin

Internat'l Soc. of Refractive Surgery

Altamonte, FL
Leg. Issues: HCR

Outside Counsel/Consultants

Arent Fox Kintner Plotkin & Kahn, PLLC
Issues: HCR
Rep By: Jeff Peters, Alan E. Reider

Internat'l Space Business Council

P.O. Box 5752
Bethesda, MD 20824-5752
Web: www.spacebusiness.com
E-mail: ISBC@spacebusiness.com
Tel: (703)524-2766
Fax: (703)524-2767
Leg. Issues: AER, COM, DEF, SCI, TEC

In-house, DC-area Employees

SACKNOFF, Scott: President

Internat'l Specialty Products

Wayne, NJ

Outside Counsel/Consultants

Mintz, Levin, Cohn, Ferris, Glovsky and Popeo, P.C.
Rep By: Alvin J. Lorman

Internat'l Speedway Corp.

Daytona Beach, FL

Outside Counsel/Consultants

J/T Group
Rep By: Robert E. Juliano

Internat'l Sugar Policy Coordinating Commission of the Dominican Republic

Santo Domingo, DOMINICAN REPUBLIC

Outside Counsel/Consultants

Johnson, Rogers & Clifton, L.L.P.

Internat'l Swaps and Derivatives Dealers Ass'n

New York, NY
Registered: LDA
Leg. Issues: BAN, FIN

Outside Counsel/Consultants

Butera & Andrews
Issues: BAN, FIN
Rep By: Cliff W. Andrews, Wright H. Andrews, Jr., James J. Butera, Frank Tillotson

Patton Boggs, LLP
Issues: FIN
Rep By: Thomas Hale Boggs, Jr., Donald V. Moorehead, Edward J. Newberry, Aubrey A. Rothrock, III

Internat'l Systems, Inc.

San Diego, CA

Outside Counsel/Consultants

The Livingston Group, LLC
Rep By: Hon. Robert L. Livingston, Jr., J. Allen Martin, Richard L. Rodgers

Internat'l Tax and Investment Center

Washington, DC

Outside Counsel/Consultants

Valente Lopatin & Schulze
Rep By: Richard T. Schulze, Jr., Mark Valente, III

Internat'l Technology & Trade Associates, Inc. (ITTA, Inc.)

1330 Connecticut Ave. NW
Suite 210
Washington, DC 20036-1704
Web: www.itta.com
E-mail: itta@itta.com
Tel: (202)828-2614
Fax: (202)828-2617

In-house, DC-area Employees

CHAMBERLAIN, Paul F.: V. President
DYKE, Charles W.: Chairman, C.E.O.
FUJITO, Wayne T.: President and C.O.O.
HIND, Edwin A.: Exec. V. President
WEINROD, W. Bruce: Managing Director and General Counsel

Internat'l Technology Education Ass'n

1914 Association Dr.
Suite 201
Reston, VA 20191
Web: www.iteawww.org
E-mail: itea@iris.org
Tel: (703)860-2100
Fax: (703)860-0353
Leg. Issues: BUD, EDU

In-house, DC-area Employees

STARKWEATHER, Kendall N.: Exec. Director

Outside Counsel/Consultants

Dean Blakey & Moskowitz
Issues: BUD, EDU
Rep By: Ellin J. Nolan

Internat'l Technology Resources, Inc.

Alexandria, VA
Leg. Issues: BUD, CPI, DEF

Outside Counsel/Consultants

Jones, Walker, Waechter, Poitevent, Carrere & Denegre, L.L.P.
Issues: BUD, CPI, DEF
Rep By: Paul Cambon, John J. Jaskot, R. Christian Johnsen

J. Arthur Weber & Associates
Rep By: Joseph A. Weber

Internat'l Telecom Ltd.

Seattle, WA
Leg. Issues: TEC

Outside Counsel/Consultants

Greenberg Traurig, LLP
Issues: TEC
Rep By: Mitchell F. Brecher

Internat'l Telecommunications, Inc.

Davie, FL
Leg. Issues: TEC

Outside Counsel/Consultants

Piper Marbury Rudnick & Wolfe LLP
Issues: TEC
Rep By: James J. Halpert

Internat'l Televent Inc.

1430 Spring Hill Rd.
Suite 500
McLean, VA 22102
Web: www.intelevent.com
Tel: (703)556-7778
Fax: (703)448-6692

A non-profit telecommunications organization.

In-house, DC-area Employees

COLEMAN, Ronald D.: Chairman & Chief Exec. Officer

Internat'l Trade Commission Trial Lawyers Ass'n

2000 Pennsylvania Ave.
Suite 5500
Washington, DC 20006
Web: www.itctla.org
E-mail: admin@itctla.org
Tel: (202)887-1557

In-house, DC-area Employees

SCHWARTZ, Bryan Alan: President

Internat'l Trade Council

3114 Circle Hill Rd.
Alexandria, VA 22305-1606
Web: www.itctrade.com
E-mail: wisdom@itctrade.com
Tel: (703)548-1234
Fax: (703)548-6216

A coalition of some 850 companies engaged in international commerce. Maintains contact with Congress and U.S. federal agencies and with foreign embassies and international organizations to promote principles of free trade and corporate/individual economic rights. Engages in economic research and forecasting of trade and investment opportunities in 400 countries and territories around the world. Holds trade and investment conferences in the United States and overseas.

In-house, DC-area Employees

CARMI, Vicky I.: Director, Research
GANTER, Mark: Director, Economic Research
LALONDE, Gregory: V. President and General Counsel
LAWRENCE, De'Arcy: Director, Administration
NELSEN, Dr. Peter T.: President
PFISTER, Gail W.: V. President, Research
QUACKENBUSH, Linda: V. President, Administration
TIDWELL, Robert L.: V. President

Internat'l Trademark Ass'n

New York, NY
Leg. Issues: CPT

Outside Counsel/Consultants

Kent & O'Connor, Inc.
Issues: CPT
Rep By: Jonathan H. Kent, Cindy Thomas

Internat'l Traditional Karate Federation

Los Angeles, CA
Leg. Issues: SPO

Outside Counsel/Consultants

Van Scoyoc Associates, Inc.
Issues: SPO
Rep By: Jeffrey S. Trinca, H. Stewart Van Scoyoc

Internat'l Truck and Engine Corp.

Chicago, IL
Registered: LDA

Formerly Navistar Internat'l Transportation Corp.; before that, Internat'l Harvester.

Outside Counsel/Consultants

Williams & Connolly
Rep By: Aubrey M. Daniel, III, J. Alan Galbraith

Internat'l Trust Fund for Demining and Mine Victims Assistance in Bosnia-Herzigovina

Ljubljana, SLOVENIA
Leg. Issues: FOR

Outside Counsel/Consultants

Gustafson Associates
Issues: FOR
Rep By: Robert C. Gustafson

Internat'l Underwriting Ass'n of London

London, UNITED KINGDOM
Leg. Issues: ENV, INS

Outside Counsel/Consultants

LeBoeuf, Lamb, Greene & MacRae L.L.P.
Issues: ENV, INS
Rep By: James M. Krey, L. Charles Landgraf, Robert W. Woody

Internat'l Union of Bricklayers and Allied Craftsworkers

815 15th St. NW
Washington, DC 20005
Tel: (202)783-3788
Fax: (202)393-0219
Registered: LDA

Web: www.bacweb.org
E-mail: askbac@bacweb.org
Leg. Issues: HCR, LBR, RET

Political Action Committee/s

Internat'l Union of Bricklayers and Allied Craftsmen Political Action Committee
815 15th St. NW
Washington, DC 20005
Tel: (202)783-3788
Fax: (202)393-0219
Contact: Debbie Matthews

In-house, DC-area Employees

DRISCOLL, Timothy: Program Assistant, Government Relations
FLYNN, John: President
MATTHEWS, Debbie: Program Assistant, Government Relations
REAGAN, Joanna E.: Director, Government Relations

Outside Counsel/Consultants

Bartley M. O'Hara
Rep By: Bartley M. O'Hara

Internat'l Union of Electronic, Electrical, Salaried, Machine, and Furniture Workers-Communications Workers of America

1275 K St. NW
Suite 600
Washington, DC 20005
Tel: (202)513-6300
Registered: LDA

Political Action Committee/s

IUE-CWA Committee on Political Education
501 Third St. NW
Washington, DC 20001
Tel: (202)434-9509
Fax: (202)434-1139
Contact: Kathy Wagner

In-house, DC-area Employees

FIRE, Ed: President
MEYER, Douglas: Director, Research and Public Policy
MITCHELL, Peter: General Counsel
WAGNER, Kathy: Director, COPE and Legislation

Internat'l Union of Operating Engineers

1125 17th St. NW
Washington, DC 20036
Tel: (202)429-9100
Fax: (202)778-2691
Registered: LDA

Web: www.iuoe.org
Leg. Issues: LBR, TAX, TRA, TRD, WAS

Political Action Committee/s

Engineers' Political and Education Committee
1125 17th St. NW
Washington, DC 20036
Tel: (202)429-9100
Fax: (202)778-2691
Contact: Michael J. Murphy

In-house, DC-area Employees

JAMES, Timothy P.: Director, Department of Politics, Corporate and Government Affairs
MURPHY, Michael J.: Treasurer, EPEC

Internat'l Union of Painters and Allied Trades

1750 New York Ave. NW
Washington, DC 20006
Tel: (202)637-0700
Fax: (202)637-0771
Registered: LDA

Web: www.ibpat.org
E-mail: mail@ibpat.org

An organizing labor union. Formerly the Internat'l Brotherhood of Painters and Allied Trades.

Leg. Issues: ART, BUD, CAW, CHM, CIV, ECN, EDU, FIN, GOV, HCR, IMM, LBR, MAR, MIA, MMM, RET, ROD, SMB, TAX, TOR, TRA, UNM, URB, UTI

Political Action Committee/s

Internat'l Brotherhood of Painters and Allied Trades Political Action Committee
1750 New York Ave. NW
Washington, DC 20006
Tel: (202)637-0700
Fax: (202)637-0771
Contact: Michael E. Monroe

In-house, DC-area Employees

ANDERSON, Bill: Assistant to the General President
BOND, Dennis
COURTIEN, William A.: Exec. Assistant to the General President
HACKNEY, Richard
MEEHAN, Bill: Exec. General V. President
MONROE, Gary: Administrator, Labor Management Cooperation Fund
MONROE, Michael E.: General President
RIGMAIDEN, Kenneth: Assistant to the General President
WEATHERS, Hugh M.
WILLIAMS, James A.: General Secretary-Treasurer

Outside Counsel/Consultants

The Kamber Group
Rep By: Victor S. Kamber, Gavin McDonald

Internat'l Union of Police Ass'ns

1421 Prince St.
Suite 400
Alexandria, VA 22314
Tel: (703)549-7473
Fax: (703)683-9048
Web: www.sddi.com
E-mail: sam@iupa.org
Leg. Issues: ALC, FIR, LAW, LBR, RET

Political Action Committee/s

Internat'l Union of Police Ass'ns Law Enforcement PAC
1421 Prince St.
Suite 400
Alexandria, VA 22314
Tel: (703)549-7473
Fax: (703)683-9048
Contact: Dennis Slocumb

In-house, DC-area Employees

CABRAL, Sam A.: President
SLOCUMB, Dennis: Exec. V. President

Outside Counsel/Consultants

Jolly/Rissler, Inc.
Issues: LBR
Rep By: Thomas R. Jolly, Patricia F. Rissler

Zwerdling, Paul, Leibig, Kahn, Thompson & Wolly, P.C.
Rep By: Michael Leibig

Internat'l Utility Efficiency Partnerships (IUEP)

701 Pennsylvania Ave. NW
Suite 500
Washington, DC 20004
Tel: (202)508-5507
Fax: (202)508-5080
Web: www.ji.org
E-mail: ronalsee@eei.org

Identifies international energy project development opportunities and supports joint implementation project investment and development activities.

Leg. Issues: ENV

In-house, DC-area Employees

ITRRALDE, Rodrigo: Project Manager
RIVERA, Wanda: Exec. Assistant and Accounting Officer
SHIFLETT, Jr., Ronald C.: Exec. Director

Outside Counsel/Consultants

Jamison and Sullivan, Inc.
Issues: ENV
Rep By: Delos Cy Jamison, Jay R. Sullivan

Internat'l Warehouse Logistics Ass'n

Park Ridge, IL
Leg. Issues: ECN, LBR, TRU

Outside Counsel/Consultants

Kent & O'Connor, Inc.
Issues: ECN, LBR, TRU
Rep By: Patrick C. O'Connor, Cindy Thomas

Internat'l Window Cleaning Ass'n

7801 Suffolk Ct.
Alexandria, VA 22315-4029
Tel: (703)971-7771
Fax: (703)971-7772
Web: www.iwca.org
E-mail: iwca@aol.com

In-house, DC-area Employees

PITZER, Jack: Exec. Director

Internation Securities Exchange

New York, NY
Leg. Issues: FIN

Outside Counsel/Consultants

Copeland, Lowery & Jacquez
Issues: FIN
Rep By: James M. Copeland, Jr.

Internet Action PAC

New York, NY
Leg. Issues: ART, BAN, CIV, CPI, CPT, CSP, EDU, GOV, TEC, TOR

Outside Counsel/Consultants

Curson Koopersmith Partners, Inc.
Issues: ART, BAN, CIV, CPI, CPT, CSP, EDU, GOV, TEC, TOR
Rep By: Eugene Gauclette, Jeffrey M. Koopersmith, Theodore B. Koopersmith

Internet Advertising Bureau

New York, NY
Leg. Issues: ADV, CSP

Outside Counsel/Consultants

Wiley, Rein & Fielding
Issues: ADV, CSP
Rep By: John Kamp

Internet Alliance Inc.

1111 19th St. NW
Suite 1180
Washington, DC 20036
Tel: (202)955-8091
Fax: (202)955-8081
Registered: LDA
Web: www.internetalliance.org
E-mail: ia@internetalliance.org

Devoted to promoting consumer trust and confidence in the online industry worldwide through public policy, advocacy, consumer outreach, and strategic alliances.

Leg. Issues: COM, CPI, CSP, SCI

In-house, DC-area Employees

RICHARDS, Jeff B.: Exec. Director

Internet Clearinghouse

Outside Counsel/Consultants

Patrick M. Murphy & Associates

Internet Council of Registrars

Carlsbad, CA
Leg. Issues: COM, CPI, SCI

Outside Counsel/Consultants

Susan Davis Internat'l
Issues: COM, CPI, SCI
Rep By: Susan A. Davis, Gregory Rixon

Internet Internat'l Trade Council

Washington, DC

Concerned with issues affecting use of the Internet, including taxation and regulation of Internet content.

Outside Counsel/Consultants

Boffa & Associates, Inc.
Rep By: John Boffa

Internet Policy Institute

601 N. Pennsylvania Ave. NW
Suite 250
Washington, DC 20004
Tel: (202)628-3900
Fax: (202)628-3922
Web: www.internetpolicy.org

A think tank concerned with building a consensus of American opinion on Internet policy.

In-house, DC-area Employees

JENKINS, Kimberly: President

Internet Safety Ass'n

Washington, DC
Leg. Issues: CPI, CSP

Outside Counsel/Consultants

Patton Boggs, LLP
Issues: CPI, CSP
Rep By: Mark D. Cowan, Michael Hettinger, Brian C. Lopina, Jeffrey L. Turner

Internet Security Systems, Inc.

Atlanta, GA
Leg. Issues: CPI

Outside Counsel/Consultants

King & Spalding
Issues: CPI
Rep By: Lisa K. Norton, William C. Talmadge

Internet Security, Privacy & Self-Regulation PAC

P.O. Box 10096
Alexandria, VA 22310

In-house, DC-area Employees

CAREY, USN (Ret.), Rr. Adm. James J.: PAC Administrator

Internet Ventures, Inc.

Redondo Beach, CA
Leg. Issues: COM, TEC

Outside Counsel/Consultants

Donald Weightman
Issues: COM, TEC
Rep By: Donald Weightman

Internews

Arcata, CA

Outside Counsel/Consultants

Anthony Garrett
Rep By: Anthony Garrett

Interns for Peace Internat'l

New York, NY
Leg. Issues: FOR

Outside Counsel/Consultants

Gustafson Associates
Issues: FOR
Rep By: Robert C. Gustafson

Interocean Management Co.

Philadelphia, PA

Outside Counsel/Consultants

Garvey, Schubert & Barer

Interregional Associates

Metairie, LA
Leg. Issues: ECN, TRD

Outside Counsel/Consultants

Adams and Reese LLP
Issues: ECN, TRD
Rep By: B. Jeffrey Brooks

Intersil Corp.

Palm Bay, FL
Leg. Issues: TEC

Outside Counsel/Consultants

Swidler Berlin Shereff Friedman, LLP
Issues: TEC
Rep By: Keith N. Cole, Nancy K. Spooner

Interstate 5 Consortium

Huntington Beach, CA
Leg. Issues: BUD, TRA

Outside Counsel/Consultants

The Ferguson Group, LLC
Issues: BUD, TRA
Rep By: William Ferguson, Jr., Charmayne Macon, Leslie Waters Mozingo

Interstate Council on Water Policy

Washington, DC
Web: www.icwp.org
Leg. Issues: ENV

Outside Counsel/Consultants

The Carmen Group
Issues: ENV
Rep By: Susan E. Gilson

Interstate Natural Gas Ass'n of America

Ten G St. NE
Suite 700
Washington, DC 20002
Tel: (202)216-5900
Fax: (202)216-0875
Registered: LDA
Web: www.ingaa.org

Represents North American interstate and interprovincial natural gas pipelines, as well as European, Asian, and South American natural gas companies.

Leg. Issues: BUD, CSP, ENG, ENV, FUE, TAX, TRA, UTI

Political Action Committee/s

Interstate Natural Gas Assoc. of America Political Action Committee (INGAA-PAC)

Ten G St. NE
Suite 700
Washington, DC 20002
Contact: Mica Evans
Tel: (202)216-5900
Fax: (202)216-0875

In-house, DC-area Employees

BEAL, Lisa S.: Director, Environmental Affairs
BOSS, Terry D.: V. President, Environment, Safety and Operations
EDWARDS, III, Martin E.: Director, Legislative Affairs
EVANS, Mica: PAC Administrator
FRIEDMANN, Gay H.: Senior V. President, Legislative Affairs and Secretary
HALVORSEN, Jerald V.: President

Outside Counsel/Consultants

Mary E. Davis
Issues: BUD, CSP, ENG, TRA, UTI
Rep By: Mary E. Davis

Interstate Wine Coalition

Scarsdale, NY
Leg. Issues: BEV, TRD, TRU

Outside Counsel/Consultants

Balch & Bingham LLP
Issues: BEV, TRD, TRU
Rep By: Barbara K. Olson

Interstitial Cystitis Ass'n

51 Monroe St.
Suite 1402
Rockville, MD 20850
Tel: (301)610-5300
Fax: (301)610-5308
Registered: LDA
Web: www.ichelp.org
E-mail: icamail@ichelp.org
Leg. Issues: HCR

In-house, DC-area Employees

MEHALL, Nicole: Administrative Manager

InterTribal Bison Cooperative

Outside Counsel/Consultants

Powers Pyles Sutter & Verville, PC
Rep By: Judith Buckalew

Intertribal Monitoring Ass'n on Indian Trust Funds

Juneau, AK
Leg. Issues: IND

Outside Counsel/Consultants

Van Ness Feldman, P.C.
Issues: IND
Rep By: Daniel S. Press

Intertribal Timber Council

Portland, OR

Outside Counsel/Consultants

Edwards Associates, Inc.
Rep By: Mark Phillips

InterTrust, Inc.

Leg. Issues: CPT

Outside Counsel/Consultants

Weil, Gotshal & Manges, LLP
Issues: CPT
Rep By: Sandra M. Aistars, Bruce H. Turnbull

InterVelocity.com

Boston, MA

Outside Counsel/Consultants

Rhoads Group

Intrac Arms Internat'l LLC

Knoxville, TN

A firearms importer and distributor.

Leg. Issues: FIR

Outside Counsel/Consultants

Law Offices of Mark Barnes
Issues: FIR
Rep By: Mark J. Barnes, Jessica Burgasser, Cindy Colpitts

Intradeco

Miami, FL
Leg. Issues: APP, TRD

Outside Counsel/Consultants

Sandler, Travis & Rosenberg, P.A.
Issues: APP, TRD
Rep By: Nicole Bivens Collinson, Chandri Navarro-Bowman, Ron Sorini

Intrinsiq Data Corp.

Waltham, MA
Leg. Issues: HCR, MMM, VET

Outside Counsel/Consultants

Jeffrey J. Kimbell & Associates
Issues: HCR, MMM, VET

Intuit, Inc.

San Diego, CA
Leg. Issues: BUD, CPI, GOV, POS

Outside Counsel/Consultants

Chlopak, Leonard, Schechter and Associates
Rep By: Robert A. Chlopak

Manatt, Phelps & Phillips, LLP
Issues: BUD, CPI, GOV, POS
Rep By: Hon. Jack W. Buechner, Stephen M. Ryan, Robb Watters

Wilmer, Cutler & Pickering

Invacare Corp.

Elyria, OH

Outside Counsel/Consultants

Baker & Hostetler LLP
Rep By: Frederick H. Graefe, Kathleen M. Kerrigan

InvenCom LLC

Charlotte, NC

Outside Counsel/Consultants

American Defense Internat'l, Inc.
Rep By: Michael Herson, Van D. Hipp, Jr., Dave Wilberding

Inventure Place

Akron, OH
Leg. Issues: ART, CPT

Outside Counsel/Consultants

Timothy X. Moore and Co.
Issues: ART, CPT
Rep By: Timothy X. Moore

Invest to Compete Alliance

1010 Pennsylvania Ave. SE
Washington, DC 20003
Tel: (202)546-4995
Fax: (202)544-7926

A group of individuals, corporations, academic institutions, and trade associations concerned about trade and tax issues. The group's goal is to educate Congress and the public on the need for American business to compete at home and abroad. A 501(c)(6) organization.

In-house, DC-area Employees

MILLER, Garland: Exec. Director

Outside Counsel/Consultants

Campbell Crane & Associates

Investment Co. Institute

1401 H St. NW
12th Floor
Washington, DC 20005-2148
Tel: (202)326-5800
Fax: (202)326-5899
Registered: LDA
Web: www.ici.org

The trade association for the mutual fund industry.

Leg. Issues: BAN, BUD, FIN, RET, TAX, TRD

Political Action Committee/s

Investment Management Political Action Committee (IMPAC)

1401 H St. NW
12th Floor
Washington, DC 20005-2148
Contact: Shannon Billings
Tel: (202)326-5892
Fax: (202)326-5899

In-house, DC-area Employees

BATEMAN, Marguerite: Associate Counsel
BILLINGS, Shannon: Director, Political Affairs
DOMENICK, Julie: Exec. V. President
FINK, Matthew P.: President
KEMPS, David: Legislative Representative - Pension
LAWSON, Keith: Senior Counsel
MORRISSEY, Donald J.: V. President, Legislative Affairs
REED, Tamara C.: Associate Counsel
SACKETT, III, Dean R.: Legislative Representative, Banking and Securitys
STERN, Michael: Legislative Representative - Taxation
TYLE, Craig S.: General Counsel

Outside Counsel/Consultants

Arter & Hadden
Issues: TAX

Bell, Boyd & Lloyd

Gibson, Dunn & Crutcher LLP
Issues: FIN
Rep By: Christopher J. Bellini

McGlotten & Jarvis
Issues: FIN
Rep By: John T. Jarvis, Robert M. McGlotten

The OB-C Group, LLC
Issues: TAX
Rep By: Thomas Keating, Kim F. McKernan, Charles J. Mellody, Patricia A. Nelson, Lawrence F. O'Brien, III, Linda E. Tarplin

Royer & Babyak
Issues: FIN

Ryan, Phillips, Utrecht & MacKinnon
Issues: BAN, FIN, RET, TAX
Rep By: Rodney Hoppe, Jeffrey M. MacKinnon, William D. Phillips, Mark D. Planning, Thomas M. Ryan, Joseph V. Vasapoli

Sidley & Austin
Issues: FIN
Rep By: David M. Miles

Strategic Impact, Inc.
Issues: FIN, RET, TAX
Rep By: Patrick J. Mitchell

The Velasquez Group
Issues: FIN
Rep By: Jay Velasquez

Verner, Liipfert, Bernhard, McPherson and Hand, Chartered
Issues: FIN, RET, TAX
Rep By: John A. Merrigan

Washington Council Ernst & Young
Issues: RET, TAX
Rep By: Doug Badger, Lauren Darling, John L. Doney, Jayne T. Fitzgerald, LaBrenda Garrett-Nelson, Gary J. Gasper, Bruce A. Gates, Nick Giordano, Robert J. Leonard, Richard Meltzer, Phillip D. Moseley, John D. Porter, Robert M. Rozen, Donna Steele-Flynn, Timothy J. Urban

Investment Counsel Ass'n of America

1050 17th St. NW
Suite 725
Washington, DC 20036
Web: www.icaa.org
E-mail: icaa@icaa.org
Tel: (202)293-4222
Fax: (202)293-4223

A non-profit association that exclusively represents the interests of federally registered investment adviser firms.

Leg. Issues: FIN, GOV

In-house, DC-area Employees

TITTSWORTH, David G.: Exec. Director/Exec. V. President

Outside Counsel/Consultants

Chambers, Conlon & Hartwell
Issues: FIN, GOV
Rep By: Don Norden

Investment Program Ass'n

1101 17th St. NW
Suite 703
Washington, DC 20036
Web: www.ipa-dc.org
Tel: (202)775-9750
Fax: (202)331-8446

Established in 1985, IPA represents investors in non-traded securities such as limited partnerships, trusts, and program sponsors raising capital for real estate, oil and gas, equipment leasing and research and development/venture capital. Its members include the leading sponsors of limited partnerships, REITs, brokerage firms, attorneys, accountants, specialty debt offerings, and others interested in the investment industry.

Leg. Issues: FIN

Political Action Committee/s

InvestAmerica
1101 17th St. NW
Suite 703
Washington, DC 20036
Contact: Christopher L. Davis
Tel: (202)775-9750
Fax: (202)331-8446

In-house, DC-area Employees

DAVIS, Christopher L.: President

Outside Counsel/Consultants

Infrastructure Management Group
Issues: FIN
Rep By: Porter K. Wheeler

KPMG, LLP

InVision Technologies

Newark, CA
Leg. Issues: BUD

Outside Counsel/Consultants

The Wexler Group
Issues: BUD
Rep By: Patrick J. McCann

Inwood Laboratories, Inc.

Inwood, NY

Outside Counsel/Consultants

Kleinfeld, Kaplan and Becker
Rep By: Peter R. Mathers

InWork Technologies

Amarillo, TX
Leg. Issues: DEF, GOV

Outside Counsel/Consultants

Bentley, Adams, Hargett, Riley and Co., Inc.
Issues: DEF, GOV
Rep By: Frederick A. Biestek, Jr., Michael Hargett, H. McGuire Riley, John Rosamond

Iowa Department of Public Health

Des Moines, IA
Leg. Issues: HCR

Outside Counsel/Consultants

Arent Fox Kintner Plotkin & Kahn, PLLC
Issues: HCR
Rep By: Douglas McCormack, Robert J. Waters

Iowa Pork Producers Ass'n

Des Moines, IA
Leg. Issues: AGR

Outside Counsel/Consultants

Gordley Associates
Issues: AGR
Rep By: John Gordley, Krysta Harden, Megan Marquet

Iowa Public Transit Ass'n

Des Moines, IA
Leg. Issues: TRA

Outside Counsel/Consultants

Redfern Resources
Issues: TRA
Rep By: Ed Redfern

Iowa Telecommunications & Technology Commission

Camp Dodge, IA
Leg. Issues: TEC

Outside Counsel/Consultants

Dow, Lohnes & Albertson, PLLC
Issues: TEC
Rep By: Kenneth D. Salomon

Iowa, Dept. of Natural Resources of State of

Des Moines, IA
Leg. Issues: AGR, NAT

Outside Counsel/Consultants

Van Ness Feldman, P.C.
Issues: AGR, NAT
Rep By: Patricia J. Beneke

Iowa, Washington Office of the State of

444 N. Capitol St. NW
Suite 359
Washington, DC 20001
Tel: (202)624-5442
Fax: (202)624-8189

In-house, DC-area Employees

BUCHAN, Philip: Director, Washington Office

IPALCO Enterprises, Inc./Indianapolis Power & Light Co.

Indianapolis, IN
Registered: LDA

A holding company for a variety of energy enterprises including the Indianapolis Power & Light Co., Mid America Capital Resources, and SHAPE, Inc.

Leg. Issues: CAW, ECN, ENG, ENV, TAX, UTI

Outside Counsel/Consultants

Andrews and Kurth, L.L.P.

Policy Consulting Services
Issues: CAW, ENG
Rep By: Paul C. Smith

IPC Washington Office

1400 I St. NW
Suite 540
Washington, DC 20005-2208
Web: www.ipc.org
E-mail: fabrams@ipc.org
Tel: (202)638-6219
Fax: (202)638-0145

An ass'n connecting electronics industries. Headquartered in Northbrook, IL.

Leg. Issues: DEF, ENV, LBR, SCI, TAX, TRD, WAS

In-house, DC-area Employees

ABRAMS, Fern: Director, Environmental Policy
CUMMINGS, Cassandra: Government Coordinator

Outside Counsel/Consultants

R. Wayne Sayer & Associates
Issues: DEF, SCI, TAX, TRD
Rep By: John Kania, William Morin, R. Wayne Sayer

IPR Shandwick

Tokyo, JAPAN
Leg. Issues: FOR, TEC, TRD

Outside Counsel/Consultants

Civic Service, Inc.
Issues: FOR, TEC, TRD
Rep By: Roy Pfautch, Michael W. Schick

IPSCO Inc.

Regina, CANADA

Outside Counsel/Consultants

Barnes, Richardson and Colburn

IPSCO Tubulars, Inc.

Camanche, IA
Leg. Issues: TRA

Outside Counsel/Consultants

Schagrin Associates
Issues: TRA
Rep By: Tamara L. Browne, Roger B. Schagrin

Iran Air

Tehran, IRAN
Leg. Issues: AUT, AVI, INS, TOR, TOU, TRA, TRD

Outside Counsel/Consultants

Condon and Forsyth
Issues: AUT, AVI, INS, TOR, TOU, TRA, TRD
Rep By: Thomas J. Whalen

Iraqi Nat'l Congress

London, UNITED KINGDOM

A coalition of Iraqi groups both in and outside the country opposed to the rule of Saddam Hussein.

Outside Counsel/Consultants

Shea & Gardner
Rep By: Collette C. Goodman

Iredell Memorial Hospital

Statesville, NC
Leg. Issues: MMM

Outside Counsel/Consultants

Jefferson Government Relations, L.L.C.
Issues: MMM
Rep By: John D. Desser, Thomas R. Donnelly, Jr.

Iridium, LLC

Tempe, AZ
Web: www.iridium.com
E-mail: iridiumtoday@iridium.com
Leg. Issues: TEC

Outside Counsel/Consultants

Townsend Solheim
Issues: TEC
Rep By: Linda T. Solheim

Irish American Democrats

3744 Oliver St. NW
Washington, DC 20015
Web: www.irishamericandemocrats.com
E-mail: irldems@erols.com
Tel: (202)362-9064
Fax: (202)237-5141

A political action committee supporting democratic candidates who promote peace, justice, and prosperity in Ireland. Lobbies Congress and White House in continued support of U.S. involvement in the Irish peace process.

In-house, DC-area Employees

BETZLER, Mary Roddy: Political Director
O'LEARY, Stella: President/Treasurer

Irish Nat'l Caucus

413 E. Capitol St. SE
Washington, DC 20003
Tel: (202)544-0568
Fax: (202)543-2491
Web: www.knight-hub.com/inc/
E-mail: inc@knight-hub.com

Describes itself as a non-violent organization seeking to educate the public, Congress and the Federal Government about "injustice and oppression in Northern Ireland and to get America to stand up for Irish justice, freedom and peace". Also initiated the MacBride Principles, a "code of conduct for U.S. companies doing business in Ireland." Has no foreign principal.

Political Action Committee/s

Irish Nat'l Caucus Political Action Committee (IRISH PAC)
413 E. Capitol St. SE
Washington, DC 20003
Tel: (202)544-0568
Fax: (202)543-2491
Contact: Fr. Sean McManus

In-house, DC-area Employees

MCMANUS, Fr. Sean: President

Iron Ore Ass'n

St. Paul, MN

Outside Counsel/Consultants

Murray, Scheer, Montgomery, Tapia & O'Donnell
Rep By: Thomas R. Crawford, D. Michael Murray

Iroquois Gas Transmission System

Shelton, CT
Leg. Issues: UTI

Outside Counsel/Consultants

Lent Scrivner & Roth LLC
Issues: UTI
Rep By: Norman F. Lent, III, Hon. Norman F. Lent, Alan J. Roth, Michael S. Scrivner

Wright & Talisman, P.C.
Rep By: James T. McManus

Irrigation Ass'n

6540 Arlington Blvd.
Falls Church, VA 22042
Tel: (703)536-7080
Fax: (703)536-7019
Web: www.irrigation.org

An irrigation trade and conservation organization.

Leg. Issues: AGR, ENV, RES

In-house, DC-area Employees

DORSEY, Laura: Director, Communications
KIMMELL, Thomas H.: Exec. Director

Outside Counsel/Consultants

Bob Lawrence & Associates
Issues: AGR
Rep By: James Goldwater, Dr. L. Robert Lawrence, Jr.

Irrigation Projects Reauthorization Council

Courtland, TX
Leg. Issues: BUD, GOV, NAT

Outside Counsel/Consultants

Meyers & Associates
Issues: BUD, GOV, NAT
Rep By: Fran Boyd, Larry D. Meyers

The Irvine Co.

Newport Beach, CA
Leg. Issues: BUD, CAW, DEF, ENV, NAT, RES, TRA

Outside Counsel/Consultants

The Ferguson Group, LLC
Issues: DEF, ENV, NAT, TRA
Rep By: William Ferguson, Jr., W. Roger Gwinn, Leslie Waters Mozingo, Joseph L. Raeder

Hunton & Williams
Issues: BUD, CAW, ENV, NAT, RES
Rep By: Virginia S. Albrecht

Peyser Associates, Inc.
Issues: ENV
Rep By: Thane Young

Irvine Sensors Corp.

Costa Mesa, CA
Leg. Issues: DEF, LAW

Outside Counsel/Consultants

Mehl, Griffin & Bartek Ltd.
Issues: DEF, LAW
Rep By: Molly Griffin, William A. Marsh, Theodore J. Mehl

Irvine, California, City of

Irvine, CA
Leg. Issues: DEF

Outside Counsel/Consultants

Hogan & Hartson L.L.P.
Issues: DEF
Rep By: C. Michael Gilliland, Christine M. Warnke

ISAR, Initiative for Social Action and Renewal in Eurasia

1601 Connecticut Ave. NW
Suite 301
Washington, DC 20009
Tel: (202)387-3034
Fax: (202)667-3291
Web: www.isar.org/isar
E-mail: postmaster@isar.org

ISAR is dedicated to supporting democratic processes and efforts to improve conditions for the peoples of Eurasia. ISAR promotes cooperative activities, bilateral and multilateral, which serve as a basis for solutions to the myriad problems of the region. ISAR collects and distributes information about joint efforts which address areas of critical need and encourage personal initiative and democratic approaches. Other projects include several grant-making programs and the quarterly journal "Give and Take".

In-house, DC-area Employees

CROSBY, Harriett: President
KLOSE, Eliza K.: Exec. Director
WATTERS, Kate: Director, Programs

ISL Inc.

Outside Counsel/Consultants

Cannon Consultants, Inc.
Rep By: Charles A. Cannon

Islamic Institute

1920 L St. NW
Suite 200
Washington, DC 20036
Tel: (202)955-7174
Fax: (202)785-0261
Registered: LDA
E-mail: general@islamicinstitute.org
Leg. Issues: CIV, EDU, FAM, FOR, TAX

In-house, DC-area Employees

SAFFURI, Khalid: Exec. Director

Outside Counsel/Consultants

Janus-Merritt Strategies, L.L.C.
Issues: FOR

The Island ECN

New York, NY
Leg. Issues: CSP, FIN, GOV

Outside Counsel/Consultants

Clark & Weinstock, Inc.
Issues: CSP, FIN, GOV
Rep By: Ed Kutler

Thelen Reid & Priest LLP
Issues: FIN
Rep By: Edward L. Pittman, Richard Y. Roberts

Island Express Boat Lines Ltd.

Sandusky, OH
Leg. Issues: BUD, MAR

Outside Counsel/Consultants

Preston Gates Ellis & Rouvelas Meeds LLP
Issues: BUD, MAR
Rep By: Susan B. Geiger, Mark H. Ruge

Isleta Pueblo

Outside Counsel/Consultants

Steptoe & Johnson LLP
Rep By: Thomas C. Collier, Jr.

Ispat Inland Steel Industries

East Chicago, IN

Outside Counsel/Consultants

Sagamore Associates, Inc.
Rep By: Mark W. Weller

Skadden, Arps, Slate, Meagher & Flom LLP
Rep By: Robert E. Lighthizer

Israel Aircraft Industries, Ltd.

Arlington, VA
Leg. Issues: AER, AVI, DEF

Outside Counsel/Consultants

American Systems Internat'l Corp.
Rep By: Robert D. McVey, William H. Skipper, Jr.

Morris J. Amitay, P.C.
Issues: DEF
Rep By: Morris J. Amitay

Adam Emanuel and Associates
Rep By: Adam Emanuel

Marvin G. Klemow
Issues: DEF
Rep By: Marvin G. Klemow

Shaw Pittman
Issues: AER, AVI
Rep By: J. E. Murdock, III

Israel Policy Forum

1030 15th St. NW
Suite 850
Washington, DC 20005
Tel: (202)842-1700
Fax: (202)842-1722
E-mail: ipfdc@ipforumdc.org

Headquartered in New York, NY.

In-house, DC-area Employees

SMERLING, Thomas: V. President, IDF Director, Washington Policy Center

Israel, Economic Mission of the Government of the State of

New York, NY

Outside Counsel/Consultants

Arnold & Porter
Rep By: Paul S. Berger

Israel, Embassy of the State of

Washington, DC

Outside Counsel/Consultants

Arnold & Porter

Israel, Goverment of the State of

Jerusalem, ISRAEL

Outside Counsel/Consultants

Arnold & Porter

Sidley & Austin
Rep By: Melvin Rishe

Israel, Ministry of Defense of the State of

Tel Aviv, ISRAEL

Outside Counsel/Consultants

Sidley & Austin
Rep By: Melvin Rishe

Israel, Ministry of Finance of the State of

Jerusalem, ISRAEL

Outside Counsel/Consultants

Arnold & Porter

IT Group, Inc.

1401 K St. NW
Suite 801
Washington, DC 20005
Tel: (202)682-1147
Fax: (202)682-1171
Registered: LDA
Web: www.theitgroup.com
E-mail: ccrotteau@theitgroup.com

An environmental and infrastructure management and services company headquartered in Monroeville, PA. Serves government and commercial clients in domestic and international markets.

Leg. Issues: BUD, DEF, ENG, ENV

In-house, DC-area Employees

CROTTEAU, Craig A.: V. President, Government Affairs
MULVEY, William: V. President, Communications
TODD, Sean: Director, Federal Agency Relations

Outside Counsel/Consultants

Baker Botts, L.L.P.
Rep By: J. Patrick Berry

John G. Campbell, Inc.
Rep By: John G. Campbell

Hyjek & Fix, Inc.
Rep By: Donald J. Fix, Steven M. Hyjek, Irene D. Schecter

Italian-American Democratic Leadership Council

1101 Vermont Ave. NW
Suite 1001
Washington, DC 20005
Tel: (202)296-8016
Fax: (202)682-3984
Web: www.iadlc.org
E-mail: iadlc@erols.com

Federal PAC that works to elect Italian American Democrats into Congress and qualified Italian Americans to serve in the Administration.

In-house, DC-area Employees
GUELI, Charles A.: Treasurer
PANVINI, Vincent A.: Chairman
ZINZI, Laura: Director, PAC

Italy-America Chamber of Commerce

New York, NY

Outside Counsel/Consultants
Barnes, Richardson and Colburn
Rep By: Matthew T. McGrath

Itera Internat'l Energy Consultants

Jacksonville, FL
Leg. Issues: BAN, ENG, TRD

Outside Counsel/Consultants
Michael L. Sauls
Issues: BAN, ENG, TRD
Rep By: Michael L. Sauls

ITRI, Ltd.

Middlesex, UNITED KINGDOM
Leg. Issues: FIR

Outside Counsel/Consultants
Birch, Horton, Bittner & Cherot
Issues: FIR
Rep By: William P. Horn

ITRON, Inc.

Spokane, WA
Leg. Issues: COM, CSP, ENG, FUE, MAN, TEC, UTI

Outside Counsel/Consultants
Public Strategies, Inc.
Issues: CSP, ENG, FUE, MAN, TEC, UTI
Rep By: Wallace J. Henderson

Thompson and Naughton, Inc.
Issues: COM
Rep By: Kenneth W. Thompson

ITT Conoflow

Upper Saddle River, NJ
Leg. Issues: AUT, ENG

Outside Counsel/Consultants
LegisLaw
Issues: AUT, ENG

ITT Industries

1650 Tysons Blvd.
Suite 1700
McLean, VA 22201
Tel: (703)790-6300
Fax: (703)790-6365
Web: www.itt.com
Leg. Issues: AER, BUD, DEF, RET, TAX, TRD

In-house, DC-area Employees
CRUMLEY, James: V. President, Government Relations
JENKINS, Jr., Harry: Director, Congressional Liaison and Business Development
ROGERS, Millie D.: Director, Communications

Outside Counsel/Consultants
LegisLaw
Issues: RET, TAX
Rep By: Linda A. Woolley, Esq.

ITT Industries Defense

1650 Tysons Blvd.
Suite 1700
McLean, VA 22102
Tel: (703)790-6300
Fax: (703)790-6365
Registered: LDA
Web: www.ittind.com
Leg. Issues: AER, BUD, DEF, MMM

Political Action Committee/s
ITT Industries PAC
1650 Tysons Blvd.
Suite 1700
McLean, VA 22102
Tel: (703)790-6300
Fax: (703)790-6365
Contact: Greg Pallas

In-house, DC-area Employees
DAHLJELM, Harvey: Director, Air Force and Space Programs
DAUKSZ, Edward: Director, Army and Marine Corps Programs
LEON, Paul: Director, Business Development, Technology, and Logistics
PALLAS, Greg: Director, Congressional Liaison and Business Development

Outside Counsel/Consultants
Donald E. Wilson Consulting
Issues: DEF

ITT World Directories, Inc.

New York, NY
Leg. Issues: TRD

Outside Counsel/Consultants
Wilmer, Cutler & Pickering
Issues: TRD
Rep By: Robert C. Cassidy, Jr.

IUCN - The World Conservation Union (US)

1630 Connecticut Ave. NW
Third Floor
Washington, DC 20009
Tel: (202)387-4826
Fax: (202)387-4823
Web: www.iucn.org
E-mail: postmaster@iucnus.org

A global conservation organization headquartered in Gland, Switzerland.

Leg. Issues: ENV, FOR

In-house, DC-area Employees
HAJOST, Scott A.: Exec. Director

IVAX Corp.

Miami, FL
A pharmaceutical manufacturer.
Leg. Issues: HCR, MED, PHA, VET

Outside Counsel/Consultants
U.S. Strategies Corp.
Issues: PHA
Rep By: Gary F. Capistrant

The Washington Group
Issues: HCR, MED, PHA, VET
Rep By: William J. Burke, Tripp Funderburk, Rita M. Lewis, G. John O'Hanlon, John D. Raffaelli, Tonya Saunders, Mark Schnabel, Richard Sullivan, Fowler West

Williams & Connolly
Issues: PHA
Rep By: Richard M. Cooper

IVIDCO, LLC

Tucson, AZ
Leg. Issues: TEC

Outside Counsel/Consultants
Patton Boggs, LLP
Issues: TEC
Rep By: Stephen Diaz Gavin, John S. Shaw

Ivy Tech State College

Indianapolis, IN
Leg. Issues: BUD, EDU

Outside Counsel/Consultants
Viohl and Associates, Inc.
Issues: BUD, EDU
Rep By: Gerald J. Del Rosario, Jeffrey C. Viohl

IWPA - The Internat'l Wood Products Ass'n

4214 King St. West
Alexandria, VA 22302
Tel: (703)820-6696
Fax: (703)820-8550
Registered: LDA
Web: www.ihpa.org
E-mail: info@ihpa.org

Represents companies that import wood and wood products. Performs such legislative and regulatory activities as may be required and provides forums for the exchange and dissemination of information concerning standards of quality, greater utilization of wood products, and sustainable management of forests around the world, especially those in the tropics.

Political Action Committee/s
INPAC
4214 King St. West
Alexandria, VA 22302
Tel: (703)820-6696
Fax: (703)820-8550
Contact: Wendy J. Baer

In-house, DC-area Employees
BAER, Wendy J.: Exec. Vice President
SHEY, Brigid: Director, Government Affairs

Izaak Walton League of America

707 Conservation Ln.
Gaithersburg, MD 20878
Tel: (301)548-0150
Fax: (301)548-0146
Web: www.iwla.org
E-mail: general@iwla.org

A 50,000-member nationwide, non-profit conservation education organization. Dedicated to sustaining the nation's natural resources.

In-house, DC-area Employees
HANSEN, Paul W.: Exec. Director
MOSHER, Jim: Conservation Director

Izaak Walton League of America (Mangrove and Florida Keys Chapters)

Miami and Islamarada, FL

Outside Counsel/Consultants
Dunlap & Browder, Inc.
Rep By: Joseph B. Browder

Izopoli

Istanbul, TURKEY

Outside Counsel/Consultants
Chambers Associates Inc.

J & B Management Co.

Fort Lee, NJ

Outside Counsel/Consultants
Thelen Reid & Priest LLP
Rep By: Barry I. Berkoff, William A. Kirk, Jr.

J & J Independence Technology

Outside Counsel/Consultants
Powers Pyles Sutter & Verville, PC
Rep By: Peter W. Thomas

Jackson County, Mississippi Board of Supervisors

Pascagoula, MS
Leg. Issues: ENV, TRA

Outside Counsel/Consultants
Winston & Strawn
Issues: ENV, TRA
Rep By: John C. Kirtland, John A. Waits, II

Jackson Hewitt

Virginia Beach, VA
Leg. Issues: TAX

Outside Counsel/Consultants
Palumbo & Cerrell, Inc.
Issues: TAX

Jackson Municipal Airport Authority

Jackson, MS
Leg. Issues: TRA

Outside Counsel/Consultants
Winston & Strawn
Issues: TRA
Rep By: John C. Kirtland, John A. Waits, II

Jackson Nat'l Life Insurance

Lansing, MI
Registered: LDA
Leg. Issues: BAN, FIN, LAW, TAX, TEC

Outside Counsel/Consultants
Alpine Group, Inc.
Issues: BAN, FIN, LAW, TAX, TEC
Rep By: James D. Massie, Richard C. White

Jackson State University

Jackson, MS
Leg. Issues: BUD, EDU

Outside Counsel/Consultants
Van Scoyoc Associates, Inc.
Issues: BUD, EDU
Rep By: Anita R. Estell, Kimberly Johnson, H. Stewart Van Scoyoc

Jackson, Mississippi, City of

Leg. Issues: ENV, HOU, LAW, TAX, TRA

Outside Counsel/Consultants
Winston & Strawn
Issues: ENV, HOU, LAW, TAX, TRA
Rep By: John C. Kirtland, John A. Waits, II

Jacksonville Chamber of Commerce
Jacksonville, FL
Leg. Issues: EDU

Outside Counsel/Consultants

Alcalde & Fay
Issues: EDU
Rep By: Lois Moore

Jacksonville Electric Authority
Jacksonville, FL
Leg. Issues: CAW, ENG, ENV, TAX, UTI

Outside Counsel/Consultants

Global USA, Inc.
Issues: CAW, UTI
Rep By: Rosamond S. Brown, Lottie H. Shackelford

Sills Associates
Issues: CAW, ENG, ENV, TAX, UTI
Rep By: Hilary Sills

Jacksonville University, Davis College of Business
Jacksonville, FL Registered: LDA
Leg. Issues: EDU

Outside Counsel/Consultants

Caleb S. Rossiter
Issues: EDU
Rep By: Caleb S. Rossiter

Jacksonville, Florida, City of
Leg. Issues: DIS, ECN, ENV, HOU, NAT, TOU, TRA

Outside Counsel/Consultants

Patton Boggs, LLP
Issues: DIS, ECN, ENV, HOU, NAT, TOU, TRA
Rep By: Thomas C. Downs, Benjamin L. Ginsberg, Edward J. Newberry

Jacksonville, Florida, Port Authority of the City of
Jacksonville, FL
Leg. Issues: TRA

Outside Counsel/Consultants

Alcalde & Fay
Issues: TRA
Rep By: Hector Alcalde, Lois Moore

Jacobs & Co. Public Affairs/Loma Linda University
Los Angeles, CA
Leg. Issues: BUD, HCR, MMM

Outside Counsel/Consultants

Copeland, Lowery & Jacquez
Issues: BUD, HCR, MMM
Rep By: Jeffrey S. Shockey

Jacobs Engineering Group Inc.
413 New York Ave. SE
Washington, DC 20003
Tel: (202)543-3866
Fax: (202)543-1680
Registered: LDA
Web: www.jacobs.com

A professional services firm.

Leg. Issues: AER, AVI, BUD, CAW, DEF, ENG, ENV, GOV, LAW, RES, ROD, SCI, TAX, TRA, TRD, WAS

In-house, DC-area Employees

BIRKHOFER, William J.: V. President and Director, Government Affairs
ONAGHISE, Tryphene: Exec. Assistant

Outside Counsel/Consultants

Fleishman-Hillard, Inc
Issues: AER, BUD
Rep By: Joy Bates Boyle, Paul W. Johnson

Manatt, Phelps & Phillips, LLP
Issues: BUD, DEF
Rep By: Mary Ann Gilleece, James H. Roberts

Jacobus Tenbroek Memorial Fund
Baltimore, MD
Leg. Issues: BUD, MMM, TAX

Outside Counsel/Consultants

Jones, Walker, Waechter, Poitevent, Carrere & Denegre, L.L.P.
Issues: BUD, MMM, TAX
Rep By: Paul Cambon, John J. Jaskot, R. Christian Johnsen, James Ogsbury

The Livingston Group, LLC
Issues: BUD, MMM, TAX
Rep By: Hon. Robert L. Livingston, Jr., J. Allen Martin, Richard L. Rodgers

The JAG Group, Inc.
San Clemente, CA
Leg. Issues: HCR, MMM, PHA

Outside Counsel/Consultants

Emord & Associates, P.C.
Issues: HCR, MMM, PHA
Rep By: Jonathan W. Emord, Eleanor A. Kolton, Claudia A. Lewis-Eng

Jam Shoe Concepts, Inc.
Dayton, OH
Leg. Issues: TAX, TRD

Outside Counsel/Consultants

Albertine Enterprises, Inc.
Issues: TAX, TRD
Rep By: Dr. John M. Albertine

Jamaica Air Freighters, Ltd.
Miami, FL

Outside Counsel/Consultants

Pierre E. Murphy Law Offices

Jamaica Vacations (JAMVAC)
Miami, FL

Outside Counsel/Consultants

Pierre E. Murphy Law Offices

Jamaica, Government of
Kingston, JAMAICA

Outside Counsel/Consultants

Holland & Knight LLP

Jefferson-Waterman Internat'l, LLC
Rep By: Ann B. Wrobleski

James Hardie Building Products Inc.
Mission Viejo, CA
Leg. Issues: HCR, LBR

Outside Counsel/Consultants

Patton Boggs, LLP
Issues: HCR, LBR
Rep By: James B. Christian, Jr., David J. Farber, Hon. Greg H. Laughlin, Joseph Trapasso

Jamestown, New York, Board of Public Utilities
Leg. Issues: ENG, ENV, GOV, UTI

Outside Counsel/Consultants

Duncan, Weinberg, Genzer & Pembroke, P.C.
Issues: ENG, ENV, GOV, UTI
Rep By: Richmond F. Allan, Jeffrey C. Genzer, Thomas L. Rudebusch, Tatjana M. Shonkwiler

Jamestown-S'Klallam Indian Tribe
Sequim, WA
Leg. Issues: IND

Outside Counsel/Consultants

Dorsey & Whitney LLP
Issues: IND
Rep By: Philip Baker-Shenk, David A. Bieging

SENSE, INC.
Rep By: C. Juliet Pittman

Janus Solutions, Inc.
Hopewell, NJ
Leg. Issues: FAM, MMM, URB, WEL

Outside Counsel/Consultants

Dublin Castle Group
Issues: FAM, MMM, URB, WEL
Rep By: Maureen Flatley Hogan

Janus-Merritt Strategies, L.L.C.
1133 21st St. NW
Suite 700
Washington, DC 20036
Tel: (202)887-6900
Fax: (202)887-6970
Registered: LDA
Web: www.janus-merritt.com

In-house, DC-area Employees

ABIDOS, Christy: Office Manager, Assistant Managing Partner
BRIERTON, Thomas W.: Principal
COURTNEY, Kurt: Assistant, Research Director
GUZIK, John
HOFFMAN, Scott P.: Principal
NASHASHIBI, Omar: Director, Research
NOBLE, Bethany: Principal, Campaign Finance Director
ROBERTSON, Mark J.: Managing Partner
ROESING, William P.: Strategic Counsel
WALSH, J. Daniel: Principal

Outside Counsel/Consultants

Podesta/Mattoon

Japan Automobile Manufacturers Ass'n
1050 17th St. NW
Suite 410
Washington, DC 20036
Tel: (202)296-8537
Fax: (202)872-1212
Registered: LDA
Web: www.jama.com
Leg. Issues: AUT, CAW, ENV, TRD

In-house, DC-area Employees

BOOKBINDER, Ronald B.: Director, Government Affairs
DUNCAN, William C.: General Director, Washington Office

Outside Counsel/Consultants

Jellinek, Schwartz & Connolly

Robert K. Kelley Law Offices
Issues: AUT, CAW, TRD
Rep By: Robert K. Kelley

Maseng Communications
Rep By: Mari Maseng Will

Porter/Novelli
Issues: AUT, ENV, TRD
Rep By: Charles H. Powers

Willkie Farr & Gallagher
Issues: AUT, TRD
Rep By: Russell L. Smith

Japan Automobile Standards Internat'l Center
1015 18th St. NW
Suite 505
Washington, DC 20036
Tel: (202)887-4830
Fax: (202)887-4834
Registered: LDA
Leg. Issues: AUT, CAW, ENG, TRA

In-house, DC-area Employees

SOEBAGJO, Adryani: Research Assistant

Outside Counsel/Consultants

Shutler and Low
Issues: AUT, CAW, ENG, TRA
Rep By: Roger C. Fairchild, Robert G. Kaler

Japan Bank for Internat'l Cooperation
Tokyo, JAPAN

Outside Counsel/Consultants

Dechert
Rep By: Allan S. Mostoff

Japan External Trade Organization (JETRO)
New York, NY
Leg. Issues: ECN, MAN, TRD

Outside Counsel/Consultants

Afridi & Angell LLP

Jefferson-Waterman Internat'l, LLC
Rep By: Daniel J. O'Neill

Masaoka & Associates, Inc.
Issues: ECN, MAN, TRD

Japan Federation of Construction Contractors, Inc.
1825 K St. NW
Suite 1203
Washington, DC 20006
Tel: (202)466-3585
Fax: (202)466-3586
Registered: FARA
Web: www.nikkenren.com

JFCC represents the construction industry in Japan. It includes both Japanese and foreign corporations engaged in general construction contracting in Japan. The federation promotes the sound development and growth of the construction industry, and concentrates on contributing to improved living standards and social welfare.

Leg. Issues: TRD

In-house, DC-area Employees

IKETA, Yukio: Representative

Outside Counsel/Consultants

Civic Service, Inc.
Issues: TRD
Rep By: Roy Pfautch, Michael W. Schick

Global USA, Inc.
Issues: TRD
Rep By: Dr. Bohdan Denysyk

Japan Federation of Economic Organizations
1900 K St. NW
Suite 1075
Washington, DC 20006
Tel: (202)293-8436
Fax: (202)293-8438
Registered: LDA, FARA
E-mail: takahashi@kkc-usa.org
Leg. Issues: TRD

In-house, DC-area Employees

TAKAHASHI, Hiroyuki: U.S. Representative

Japan Fisheries Ass'n

Tokyo, JAPAN

Outside Counsel/Consultants

Garvey, Schubert & Barer
Rep By: Paul S. Hoff

Japan Industrial Conference for Ozone Layer Protection

Tokyo, JAPAN

Outside Counsel/Consultants

Cammer and Associates
Rep By: Paul A. Cammer

Japan Industrial Conference on Cleaning

Tokyo, JAPAN

Outside Counsel/Consultants

Cammer and Associates

Japan Internat'l Agricultural Council

Outside Counsel/Consultants

Lerch & Co., Inc.
Rep By: Donald G. Lerch

Japan Internat'l Transport Institute

Washington, DC
Leg. Issues: AVI

Outside Counsel/Consultants

Sher & Blackwell
Issues: AVI
Rep By: Mark Atwood

Japan Iron and Steel Exporters Ass'n

1155 21st St. NW
Suite 600
Washington, DC 20036
Tel: (202)429-4766
Fax: (202)463-9032
Registered: FARA
E-mail: dcjisea@man.com
Leg. Issues: TRD

In-house, DC-area Employees

SATO, Kazuo: General Manager

Outside Counsel/Consultants

Willkie Farr & Gallagher
Issues: TRD
Rep By: William H. Barringer, James P. Durling, Russell L. Smith

Japan Nuclear Cycle Development Institute

Washington, DC
Leg. Issues: ENG

Outside Counsel/Consultants

Hooper Owen & Winburn
Issues: ENG
Rep By: Daryl H. Owen

Japan Productivity Center for Socio-Economic Development

1001 Connecticut Ave. NW
Suite 425
Washington, DC 20036
Tel: (202)955-5663
Fax: (202)955-6125

A non-profit foundation headquartered in Tokyo, Japan. Supports improvement in industrial productivity through increased education and training of corporate employees. Conducts an international exchange program for corporate managers and employees. Also conducts research on social and economic issues.

In-house, DC-area Employees

HARADA, Daisaku: Senior Advisor
SHINODA, Hiroshi: Director, U.S. Office

Japan Wood-Products Information and Research Center

Tokyo, JAPAN

Outside Counsel/Consultants

Garvey, Schubert & Barer
Rep By: Paul S. Hoff

Japan, Embassy of

2520 Massachusetts Ave. NW
Washington, DC 20008
Tel: (202)238-6700
Fax: (202)328-2187
Web: www.embjapan.org
Leg. Issues: FOR, GOV, TRD

Outside Counsel/Consultants

Butterfield Carter & Associates
Issues: FOR, GOV, TRD
Rep By: R. Ian Butterfield, Gavin J. Carter

Dechert
Rep By: Allan S. Mostoff

Saunders and Company

Anne V. Smith
Rep By: Anne V. Smith

Smith Dawson & Andrews, Inc.
Rep By: Gregory B. Andrews, James P. Smith

Japan, Ministry of Foreign Affairs of

Tokyo, JAPAN

Outside Counsel/Consultants

The Eddie Mahe Company

Japan-America Soc. of Washington

1020 19th St. NW
Lower Lobby-40
Washington, DC 20036
Tel: (202)833-2210
Fax: (202)833-2456
Web: www.us-japan.org/dc/
E-mail: jaswdc@intr.net

In-house, DC-area Employees

PHILLIPS, JoAnna: Exec. Director

Japanese American Citizens League

1001 Connecticut Ave. NW
Suite 704
Washington, DC 20036
Tel: (202)223-1240
Fax: (202)296-8082

A national, non-profit, educational and civil rights organization. Monitors legislation and other activities which affect civil and constitutional rights. Headquartered in San Francisco, CA.

In-house, DC-area Employees

MINAMI, Kristine: Washington Representative

JASON Foundation for Education

Waltham, MA
Leg. Issues: EDU, ENV, SCI, TEC

Outside Counsel/Consultants

Convergence Services, Inc.
Issues: EDU, ENV, SCI, TEC
Rep By: John M. Lawson

Jasper, Alabama, City of

Leg. Issues: BUD, ECN

Outside Counsel/Consultants

Murray, Scheer, Montgomery, Tapia & O'Donnell
Issues: BUD, ECN
Rep By: Alison Houle, John H. Montgomery, John R. O'Donnell, Mark Zelden

Jazz at Lincoln Center Inc.

New York, NY
Leg. Issues: ART, BUD, URB

Outside Counsel/Consultants

LeBoeuf, Lamb, Greene & MacRae L.L.P.
Issues: ART, BUD, URB
Rep By: D. Randall Benn

JBA Consulting, Inc.

Greensboro, NC
Leg. Issues: ACC, DEF, GOV

Outside Counsel/Consultants

The Solomon Group, LLC
Issues: ACC, DEF, GOV
Rep By: David M. Lonie, Hon. Gerald B. H. Solomon

JBG Real Estate Associates

5301 Wisconsin Ave. NW
Washington, DC 20015
Tel: (202)293-4584
Fax: (202)293-4588
Registered: LDA

The address given is that of the firm Lee & Smith (see separate listing).

Leg. Issues: RES

In-house, DC-area Employees

SMITH, C. William

JDA Aviation Technology Systems

Washington, DC
Leg. Issues: AVI, MAN, SCI, TRA

Outside Counsel/Consultants

Jefferson Government Relations, L.L.C.
Issues: AVI, MAN, SCI, TRA
Rep By: William A. Roberts, Daniel J. Sheehan

Jefferson County Commission

Birmingham, AL
Leg. Issues: BUD

Outside Counsel/Consultants

Van Scoyoc Associates, Inc.
Issues: BUD
Rep By: Ray Cole, Chad Schulken, H. Stewart Van Scoyoc

Jefferson Government Relations, L.L.C.

1615 L St. NW
Suite 650
Washington, DC 20036
Tel: (202)626-8500
Fax: (202)626-8593
Registered: LDA
Web: www.jeffersongr.com
E-mail: info@jeffersongr.com
Leg. Issues: AVI

In-house, DC-area Employees

CUPPERNULL, Carolyn M.: Principal and Chief Administrative Officer
DESSER, John D.: V. President
DONNELLY, Jr., Thomas R.: Principal and V. Chairman
DOUGLASS, Hugh M.: V. President and Chief Financial Officer
GILMARTIN, William J.: V. President
GREENBERG, Mark S.: V. President
KRAUSER, Katherine M.: Director
MCARVER, Jr., Robert D.: V. President
MILNE, John D.: V. President
MORIN, Jeanne L.: Principal
POWER, Patricia A.: V. President
RASMUSSEN, Erik: Director
RATCHFORD, Hon. William R.
ROBERTS, William A.: Principal
SCHUMACHER, Randal P.: Chairman and Principal
SHEEHAN, Daniel J.: Director

Outside Counsel/Consultants

Ann Eppard Associates, Ltd.
Issues: AVI
Rep By: Julie Chlopecki, Ann Eppard, Karen Schechter

Jefferson Parish Council

Harahan, LA

A county government.

Leg. Issues: BUD, DEF, ECN, ENG, ENV, LBR, TRA, URB

Outside Counsel/Consultants

Adams and Reese LLP
Issues: BUD, DEF, ENG, ENV, LBR, TRA, URB
Rep By: B. Jeffrey Brooks

Johnston & Associates, LLC
Issues: BUD, ECN, ENG, ENV, TRA, URB
Rep By: Hon. J. Bennett Johnston, N. Hunter Johnston, W. Proctor Jones, Eric Tober

Jefferson State Community College

Birmingham, AL
Leg. Issues: BUD, EDU

Outside Counsel/Consultants

Michael W. Adcock
Issues: BUD, EDU
Rep By: Michael W. Adcock

Jefferson Texas, County of

Leg. Issues: BUD, NAT

Outside Counsel/Consultants

Marlowe and Co.
Issues: BUD, NAT
Rep By: Howard Marlowe, Jeffrey Mazzella

Jemez, New Mexico, Pueblo of

Outside Counsel/Consultants

Sonosky, Chambers, Sachse & Endreson
Rep By: William R. Perry

Jeppesen Sanderson, Inc.

515 Prince St.
Alexandria, VA 22314-3115
Tel: (703)519-5295
Fax: (703)519-5296
Registered: LDA
E-mail: dave.goehler@jeppesen.com

Specializes in aeronautical flight information and services. Headquartered in Englewood, CO.

Leg. Issues: AER, AVI, MAR, TEC

In-house, DC-area Employees

GOEHLER, David J.: Director, Washington Office

Jered Industries, Inc.

Brunswick, GA

Developer of military logistics support equipment.

Leg. Issues: DEF

Outside Counsel/Consultants

Wayne Arny & Assoc.
Rep By: Wayne Arny, David D. O'Brien

David O'Brien and Associates
Issues: DEF

Jerome Foods

Barron, WI
Leg. Issues: AGR, ENV

Outside Counsel/Consultants

Lockridge Grindal & Nauen, P.L.L.P.
Issues: AGR, ENV
Rep By: Dennis McGrann

Jersey City Economic Development Corp.

Jersey City, NJ

Outside Counsel/Consultants

Krivit & Krivit, P.C.

Jesuit Conference

1616 P St. NW
Suite 300
Washington, DC 20036
Web: www.jesuit.org/advocacy
E-mail: outreach@jesuit.org
Tel: (202)462-0400
Fax: (202)328-9212

Advocate on behalf of poor and marginalized constituencies.

Leg. Issues: HOU, IMM, WEL

In-house, DC-area Employees

ROBINSON, British: Nat'l Director

JETRO New York

New York, NY

Outside Counsel/Consultants

Global Policy Group, Inc.

Jewelers of America

New York, NY
Leg. Issues: BNK, TAX, TRD

Outside Counsel/Consultants

Haake and Associates
Issues: BNK, TAX, TRD
Rep By: Timothy M. Haake, Nathan M. Olsen

The Jewelers' Security Alliance

New York, NY
Leg. Issues: BUD, IMM, LAW

Outside Counsel/Consultants

Thelen Reid & Priest LLP
Issues: BUD, IMM, LAW
Rep By: Barry I. Berkoff, William A. Kirk, Jr., Richard J. Leidl, Stephan M. Minikes, David J. Weisenfeld, Nancy K. West

Jewish Family Service Ass'n of Cleveland

Cleveland Heights, OH
Leg. Issues: BUD

Outside Counsel/Consultants

Cassidy & Associates, Inc.
Issues: BUD
Rep By: Laurie J. Adler, Sonya C. Clay, Christopher Lamond, Arthur D. Mason, Diane Rinaldo

Jewish Federation of Greater Washington

6101 Montrose Rd.
Rockville, MD 20852
Web: www.jewishfedwash.org
Tel: (301)230-7200
Fax: (301)230-7265

In-house, DC-area Employees

FARBER, Ted B.: Exec. V. President

Jewish Federation of Metropolitan Chicago

Chicago, IL
Leg. Issues: APP, BUD, HOU

Outside Counsel/Consultants

Witman Associates
Issues: APP, BUD, HOU
Rep By: Ellen G. Witman

Jewish Guild for the Blind

New York, NY
Leg. Issues: HCR, MMM

Outside Counsel/Consultants

Washington Health Advocates
Issues: HCR, MMM
Rep By: Douglas Peddicord, Ph.D., Michele Sumilas

Jewish Institute for Nat'l Security Affairs

1717 K St. NW
Suite 800
Washington, DC 20006
Web: www.jinsa.org
E-mail: info@jinsa.org
Tel: (202)833-0020
Fax: (202)296-6452

Provides information concerning U.S. defense to the American Jewish community. Supports strong U.S. defense posture. Supports cooperation between U.S. and Israel on defense and security issues.

Leg. Issues: DEF, FOR, LAW, TRD

In-house, DC-area Employees

AMITAY, Morris J.: V. Chair
BRYEN, Shoshana: Special Projects Director
COLBERT, James: Communications Director
HALTEMAN, Marsha: Director, Corporate and Community Relations
NEUMANN, Thomas: Exec. Director

Jewish Peace Lobby

8604 Second Ave.
PMB 317
Silver Spring, MD 20910
Web: www.peacelobby@org
E-mail: peacelobby@msn.com
Tel: (301)589-8764
Fax: (301)589-2722

The second largest Jewish peace organization, works for peace in the Middle East by influencing U.S. foreign policy. Lobbies in congressional districts in over 40 states. Has over 4000 members, including over 250 Rabbis.

In-house, DC-area Employees

SEGAL, Ph.D., Jerome M.: President

Jewish War Veterans of the U.S.A.

1811 R St. NW
Washington, DC 20009-1659
Web: www.jwv.org
E-mail: jwv@erols.com
Tel: (202)265-6280
Fax: (202)234-5662
Registered: LDA

Represents veterans' interests and acts on issues of concern to the American Jewish community.

Leg. Issues: DEF, VET

In-house, DC-area Employees

GROSS, Tarneisha: National Director, Public Relations
ROSENBLEETH, USA (Ret.), Col. Herb: National Exec. Director

Jewish Women Internat'l

1828 L St. NW
Suite 250
Washington, DC 20036
Web: www.jwi.org
E-mail: jwi@jwi.org
Tel: (202)857-1300
Fax: (202)857-1380

Formerly B'Nai B'Rith Women. A volunteer-based Jewish women's organization. Interested in women's and family issues, and also in policies/issues concerning Israel and separation of church and state.

In-house, DC-area Employees

RUBINSON, Gail: Exec. Director

JHP, Inc. (Jobs Have Priority)

1526 Pennsylvania Ave. SE
Washington, DC 20003
Tel: (202)544-5300
Fax: (202)544-6600

Jobs for Homeless People's mission is to provide comprehensive, shelter-based employment services to homeless people in the Washington metropolitan area and to help homeless people move to permanent housing.

In-house, DC-area Employees

FARBER, Judith: Exec. Director
PERCY-JARRETT, Stephanie: Deputy Director

Jicarilla Apache Tribe

Dulce, NM
Leg. Issues: IND

Outside Counsel/Consultants

Nordhaus Haltom Taylor Taradash & Bladh LLP
Issues: IND

Steptoe & Johnson LLP
Rep By: Thomas C. Collier, Jr.

Jigawa, Nigerian State of

Outside Counsel/Consultants

BKSH & Associates
Rep By: Lisa M. Cotter, Riva Levinson

JM Family Enterprises

Deerfield Beach, FL
Registered: LDA
Leg. Issues: AUT, CSP, LBR, MAR, TAX, TRA, TRD

Outside Counsel/Consultants

The Dutko Group, Inc.
Issues: AUT, MAR, TAX, TRD
Rep By: Ronald C. Kaufman

O'Neill, Athy & Casey, P.C.
Issues: CSP, LBR, TAX, TRA
Rep By: Andrew Athy, Jr., Christopher R. O'Neill

JMC Airlines, Ltd.

Manchester, UNITED KINGDOM

Outside Counsel/Consultants

Zuckert, Scoutt and Rasenberger, L.L.P.
Rep By: Richard D. Mathias, Lonnie E. Pera

Job Opportunities Business Symposium

A coalition of employers supporting the Targeted Jobs Tax Credit.

Leg. Issues: TAX

Outside Counsel/Consultants

Sellery Associates, Inc.
Issues: TAX
Rep By: William C. Sellery, Jr.

Jobs for Youth

Chicago, IL

Outside Counsel/Consultants

Capitol Perspectives
Rep By: Mary Elise DeGonia

John Ashbrook Center for Public Policy

Ashland, OH

Outside Counsel/Consultants

Hayward Internat'l

Johns Hopkins Center for Civilian Biodefense Studies

Baltimore, MD
Leg. Issues: AGR, BUD, DEF, DIS, HCR, LAW, SCI

Outside Counsel/Consultants

Arnold & Porter
Issues: AGR, BUD, DEF, DIS, HCR, LAW, SCI
Rep By: Jeffrey W. Richman, Jeffrey H. Smith

Johns Hopkins Center for Gun Policy and Research

Baltimore, MD

Outside Counsel/Consultants

Neuman and Co.
Rep By: Robert A. Neuman

Johns Hopkins Medical Services

Baltimore, MD
Leg. Issues: DEF

Outside Counsel/Consultants

Defense Health Advisors, Inc.
Issues: DEF
Rep By: Charlotte L. Tsoucalas

Johns Hopkins School of Hygiene and Public Health

Baltimore, MD
Leg. Issues: BUD, MED

Outside Counsel/Consultants

Van Scoyoc Associates, Inc.
Issues: BUD, MED
Rep By: Steve E. Crane, Kevin F. Kelly, H. Stewart Van Scoyoc

Johns Hopkins University & Hospital

Baltimore, MD
Registered: LDA
Leg. Issues: BUD, CPT, FOR, MED, MMM

Outside Counsel/Consultants

Capitol Associates, Inc.
Issues: BUD, CPT, FOR, MED, MMM

Karalekas & Noone
Rep By: James A. Noone

Johns Hopkins University Hospital, School of Hygiene and Public Health

Baltimore, MD
Leg. Issues: BUD

Outside Counsel/Consultants

Arent Fox Kintner Plotkin & Kahn, PLLC
Issues: BUD
Rep By: Douglas McCormack

Johns Hopkins University-Applied Physics Lab

Laurel, MD
Leg. Issues: BUD, DEF

Outside Counsel/Consultants

Karalekas & Noone
Issues: DEF
Rep By: S. Steven Karalekas, James A. Noone

Van Scoyoc Associates, Inc.
Issues: BUD
Rep By: Steve E. Crane, Kevin F. Kelly, Evan Knisely, H. Stewart Van Scoyoc

Johnsburg, Illinois, Village of

Leg. Issues: WAS

Outside Counsel/Consultants

Broydrick & Associates
Issues: WAS
Rep By: Bill Viney

Johnson & Johnson, Inc.

1350 I St. NW
Suite 1210
Washington, DC 20005-3305
Tel: (202)589-1000
Fax: (202)589-1001
Registered: LDA
Web: www.jnj.com
Leg. Issues: BUD, CPT, DEF, HCR, IMM, MMM, PHA, TAX, TRD, VET

In-house, DC-area Employees

BOHN, Donald W.: Exec. Director, Federal Affairs and Reimbursement
CARROLL, Bruce: Manager, Federal Affairs
DOOLEY, Cathleen M.: Director, Federal Affairs
JODREY, Darrel Cox: Director, Federal Affairs
KRAMER, Craig: Director, Federal Affairs
NAISMITH, Martha: Director, Federal Affairs
SALMON, Shannon: V. President, Federal Affairs

Outside Counsel/Consultants

Akin, Gump, Strauss, Hauer & Feld, L.L.P.
Issues: HCR, TAX
Rep By: Donald C. Alexander, Gary A. Heimberg, Jorge J. Lopez, Jr., Barney J. Skladany, Jr.

Bennett Turner & Coleman, LLP

Capitol Health Group, LLC
Issues: HCR, MMM, PHA
Rep By: Michael D. Bromberg, Shawn Coughlin, Steven Jenning, Layna McConkey Peltier

Bob Dole Enterprises
Issues: MMM
Rep By: Vicki E. Hart

Health Policy Alternatives, Inc.
Rep By: Thomas Ault, Bart McCann

Public Policy Partners, LLC
Issues: MMM
Rep By: Hon. David Durenberger, Daniel Waldmann, Jeffrey Weekly

S.C. Johnson and Son, Inc.

900 17th St. NW
Suite 402
Washington, DC 20006-5504
Tel: (202)331-1186
Fax: (202)659-2338
Registered: LDA
Web: www.scj.com

A global producer and marketer of consumer insect control, house storage and cleaning products headquartered in Racine, Wisconsin.

Leg. Issues: AGR, CAW, CHM, CSP, ENV, FOO, FOR, TRA, TRD

In-house, DC-area Employees

LEVENSON, Nancy R.: Director, U.S. Federal Government Relations

Outside Counsel/Consultants

Arent Fox Kintner Plotkin & Kahn, PLLC
Issues: AGR, ENV, FOR, TRD
Rep By: Alison Kutler, Michael T. McNamara, Todd Weiss

Holland & Knight LLP
Issues: CAW, CHM, ENV, TRD
Rep By: Jack M. Burkman, Mike Galano, Michael Gillis, Richard M. Gold, Janet R. Studley

Peyser Associates, Inc.
Issues: TRA
Rep By: Peter A. Peyser, Jr.

Johnson Controls, Inc.

400 N. Capitol St. NW
Suite 590
Washington, DC 20001
Tel: (202)393-3224
Fax: (202)393-7718
Web: www.jci.com

Headquartered in Milwaukee, WI.

Leg. Issues: BUD, DEF, ENG, ENV

In-house, DC-area Employees

BEIGHTOL, David J.: Director, Government Affairs
WAGNER, Mark: Manager, Federal Government Relations

Outside Counsel/Consultants

The Roth Group
Issues: ENV
Rep By: Joseph Finlayson, Jayd Henricks, Hon. Toby Roth, Sr.

Van Scoyoc Associates, Inc.
Issues: BUD, DEF, ENG
Rep By: Paul Grimm, Buzz Hawley, H. Stewart Van Scoyoc

D. R. Johnson Lumber

Riddle, OR
Leg. Issues: NAT, TAX

Outside Counsel/Consultants

Jamison and Sullivan, Inc.
Issues: NAT, TAX
Rep By: Delos Cy Jamison, Jay R. Sullivan

Joint Baltic American Nat'l Committee, Inc.

400 Hurley Ave.
Rockville, MD 20850
Tel: (301)340-1954
Fax: (301)309-1406
Registered: LDA
Web: www.jbanc.org
E-mail: jbanc@jbanc.org

Represents the American Latvian Ass'n, the Lithuanian American Council and the Estonian American Nat'l Council.

Leg. Issues: BUD, FOR

In-house, DC-area Employees

ALTAU, Karl S.: Managing Director
RIMES, Algis: Chairman

Joint Center for Political and Economic Studies

1090 Vermont Ave. NW
Suite 1100
Washington, DC 20005-4961
Tel: (202)789-3500
Fax: (202)789-6390
Web: www.jointcenter.org

A national, non-profit, and tax exempt organization which conducts research on issues of special concern to black Americans and promotes the informed and effective involvement of blacks in the political process. Provides non-partisan analyses to the public through conferences, publications and other information services.

In-house, DC-area Employees

ALLEN, William A.: V. President for Development
BOSITIS, David A.: Senior Research Associate
DUGAS, Denise L.: V. President, Communications & Marketing
SIMMS, Margaret: V. President, Research
WILLIAMS, Eddie N.: President

Joint Commission on the Accreditation of Health Care Organizations

Leg. Issues: HCR

Outside Counsel/Consultants

The Legislative Strategies Group, LLC
Issues: HCR
Rep By: Martin B. Gold, Denise M. Henry

Joint Corporate Committee on Cuban Claims

Stamford, CT
Leg. Issues: FOR

Outside Counsel/Consultants

Akin, Gump, Strauss, Hauer & Feld, L.L.P.
Issues: FOR
Rep By: Barney J. Skladany, Jr.

Joint Council of Allergy, Asthma and Immunology

Mount Prospect, IL
Leg. Issues: BUD, ENV, HCR, MED, TOB

Outside Counsel/Consultants

Capitol Associates, Inc.
Issues: BUD, ENV, HCR, MED, TOB
Rep By: Tricia Brooks, Debra M. Hardy Havens, Matthew Williams

Powers Pyles Sutter & Verville, PC
Rep By: Richard E. Verville

Joint Healthcare Information Technology Alliance

Ann Arbor, MI

Outside Counsel/Consultants

The PMA Group
Rep By: Kaylene Green, Paul J. Magliocchetti, Kelli Short, Brian Thiel, Sandra Welch

Joint Industry Group (JIG)

1620 I St. NW
Suite 615
Washington, DC 20006
Tel: (202)463-8493
Fax: (202)463-8497
Web: www.moinc.com/jig
E-mail: jig@moinc.com

A member-driven coalition of over 130 companies, trade associations, and businesses actively involved in international trade. Examines the concerns of the business community relative to current and proposed Customs-related policies, actions, legislation and regulations, and strives to improve them through direct contact with the U.S. Customs Service, government agencies, and Congress.

In-house, DC-area Employees

CLAWSON, James B.: Secretariat

Outside Counsel/Consultants

JBC Internat'l
Rep By: Alan R. Atkinson, James B. Clawson, Jason B. Clawson

Joint Nat'l Committee for Languages

4646 40th St. NW
Suite 310
Washington, DC 20016
Tel: (202)966-8477
Fax: (202)966-8310
Web: www.languagepolicy.org

In-house, DC-area Employees

EDWARDS, Ph.D., J. David: Exec. Director

Joint Powers Board

Minneapolis, MN
Leg. Issues: BUD, RRR, TRA, URB

Outside Counsel/Consultants

Lockridge Grindal & Nauen, P.L.L.P.
Issues: BUD, RRR, TRA, URB
Rep By: John D. Burton, Amy Johnson, Dennis McGrann

Joint Southeast Public Improvement Council

Greenwood Village, CO
Leg. Issues: TRA

Outside Counsel/Consultants

Valis Associates
Issues: TRA
Rep By: Jennifer Conti, Hon. Dan Schaefer, Wayne H. Valis

Joint Steering Committee for Public Policy

8120 Woodmont Ave.
Suite 750
Bethesda, MD 20814-2755
Tel: (301)347-9309
Fax: (301)347-9310
Web: www.jscpp.org

An association for non-profit scientific and educational associations.

Leg. Issues: SCI

In-house, DC-area Employees

LESHAN, Timothy E.: Director of Public Policy
MARINCOLA, Elizabeth: Exec. Director
ZONARICH, Matt: District Coordinator

Outside Counsel/Consultants

Kyros & Cummins Associates
Issues: SCI
Rep By: John M. Falk, Hon. Peter N. Kyros

Joint Stock Company Severstal

Leg. Issues: TRD

Outside Counsel/Consultants

Powell, Goldstein, Frazer & Murphy LLP
Issues: TRD
Rep By: Neil Ellis, Michael E. Fine, Daniel M. Price, Peter O. Suchman

Joint Venture Partners

Overton Park, KS

Outside Counsel/Consultants

Peter S. Barash Associates, Inc.
Rep By: Peter S. Barash

Edward Jones Co.

St. Louis, MO

Outside Counsel/Consultants

Bryan Cave LLP

Edward Jones Investments

St. Louis, MO
Leg. Issues: LBR, TAX

Outside Counsel/Consultants

Caplin & Drysdale, Chartered
Issues: LBR, TAX
Rep By: Kent A. Mason

Jones Medical Industries, Inc.

St. Louis, MO

Outside Counsel/Consultants

Kleinfeld, Kaplan and Becker
Rep By: Peter R. Mathers

Jones, Day, Reavis & Pogue

51 Louisiana Ave. NW
Washington, DC 20001
Tel: (202)879-3939
Fax: (202)626-1700
Registered: LDA, FARA

Web: www.jonesday.com
E-mail: counsel@jonesday.com
Leg. Issues: RET

In-house, DC-area Employees

BRADFIELD, Michael: Partner
BROGEN, Stephen
BROOKS, Teresa A.: Partner
BROWN, Robert M.: Government Affairs Representative
HANSELL, Herbert J.: Senior Counsel
MCDERMOTT, Robert F.: Partner
O'HARA, James T.: Partner
ROSE, Jonathan C.: Partner
SIMS, Joe: Partner
WIACEK, Raymond J.: Partner
WILDEROTTER, James A.: Partner

Outside Counsel/Consultants

Parry, Romani, DeConcini & Symms

Sam Richardson
Rep By: Sam Richardson

Sunrise Research Corp.
Issues: RET
Rep By: Hon. Bob Packwood

Jordache Enterprises, Inc.

New York, NY

Outside Counsel/Consultants

Baker & Hostetler LLP
Rep By: Hon. Guy Vander Jagt

Jordan Tourism Board

, JORDAN

Outside Counsel/Consultants

Global Communicators
Rep By: James W. Harff, Nina V.W. Herrara-Davila

Joslin Diabetes Center

Boston, MA
Leg. Issues: BUD, EDU, MED

Outside Counsel/Consultants

Terry Bevels Consulting
Issues: BUD, EDU, MED
Rep By: Terry D. Bevels

Jovan Broadcasting

Leg. Issues: COM

Outside Counsel/Consultants

Alcalde & Fay
Issues: COM
Rep By: Hector Alcalde, Shantrel Brown, Jim Davenport, Vicki L. Iseman, Julie Patterson, Christopher L. Turner

Joy Mining Machinery

Pittsburgh, PA
Leg. Issues: CAW, ENV, NAT

Outside Counsel/Consultants

Stephens Law Offices
Issues: CAW, ENV, NAT
Rep By: J. Gordon "Skip" Stephens, Jr.

Joyce Foundation

Chicago, IL

Outside Counsel/Consultants

Neuman and Co.
Rep By: Robert A. Neuman

JRL Enterprises

New Orleans, LA
Registered: LDA
Leg. Issues: CPI, EDU

Outside Counsel/Consultants

Jones, Walker, Waechter, Poitevent, Carrere & Denegre, L.L.P.
Issues: CPI, EDU
Rep By: Paul Cambon, John J. Jaskot, R. Christian Johnsen

U.S. Strategies Corp.
Issues: EDU
Rep By: Steven E. Carey, Heidi Hanson

JSG Trading Co.

Tinton Falls, NJ

Outside Counsel/Consultants

O'Connor & Hannan, L.L.P.
Rep By: Hon. Thomas J. Corcoran

Judicial Watch, Inc.

501 School St. SW
Suite 725
Washington, DC 20024
Tel: (202)646-5172
Fax: (202)646-5199
Web: www.judicialwatch.org
E-mail: info@judicialwatch.or

In-house, DC-area Employees

KLAYMAN, Larry: Chief Exec. Officer and General Counsel

Juneau, Alaska, City of

Leg. Issues: BUD, GOV, MAR

Outside Counsel/Consultants

Chambers, Conlon & Hartwell
Issues: BUD, GOV
Rep By: John Roots

Schmeltzer, Aptaker & Shepard, P.C.
Issues: BUD, MAR
Rep By: J. Anthony Smith

Junex Enterprises

Hartsdale, NY

Outside Counsel/Consultants

Max N. Berry Law Offices
Rep By: Max N. Berry

Just Valuations

Altamonte Springs, FL
Leg. Issues: GOV

Outside Counsel/Consultants

Morgan Meguire, LLC
Issues: GOV
Rep By: Kyle G. Michel

Justice Fellowship

P.O. Box 16069
Washington, DC 20041-6069
Tel: (703)904-7312
Fax: (703)478-9679
Registered: LDA

Web: www.justicefellowship.org

The criminal justice affiliate of Prison Fellowship Ministries. Promotes reforms that hold offenders responsible for their acts, protect the public, and help restore victims' losses. Also seeks restitution and community service punishments for nonviolent offenders and viable work programs in prisons.

Leg. Issues: REL

In-house, DC-area Employees

BELL, Mariam: National Director, Federal Affairs
NANCE, Penny: Lobbyist
NOLAN, Pat: President

The Justice Project, Inc.

50 F St. NW
Suite 1070
Washington, DC 20001
Tel: (202)638-5855
Fax: (202)638-6056
Registered: LDA
Leg. Issues: LAW

In-house, DC-area Employees

LOGE, Peter
SMITH, Wayne: Executive Director

Outside Counsel/Consultants

Greener and Hook, LLC

Griffin, Johnson, Dover & Stewart
Issues: LAW
Rep By: William C. Danvers, G. Jack Dover, Patrick J. Griffin, Keith Heard, David E. Johnson, Susan O. Mann, Walter J. "Joe" Stewart, Leonard Swinehart

Rhoads Group
Issues: LAW
Rep By: Paul D. Behrends, Kathleen Ireland, Steven G. McKnight, Clifford R. Northup, Barry D. Rhoads, Elizabeth R. Sharpstene, Thomas Worrall

Justice Research and Statistics Ass'n

777 N. Capitol St. NE
Suite 801
Washington, DC 20002
Tel: (202)842-9330
Fax: (202)842-9329
Web: www.jrsa.org
E-mail: cjinfo@jrsa.org

National organization of state statistical analysis center directors as well as analysts, researchers and practioners throughout the justice system. Maintains a clearinghouse on data concerning crime and criminal justice at the state level. Also conducts state-based research and provides technical assistance and training.

In-house, DC-area Employees

WEISS, Joan C.: Exec. Director

Juvenile Diabetes Foundation Internat'l

1400 I St. NW
Suite 530
Washington, DC 20005
Tel: (202)371-9746
Fax: (202)371-2760
Registered: LDA
Web: www.jdf.org

Headquartered in New York, NY.

Leg. Issues: BUD, MED, POS

In-house, DC-area Employees

ADAMS, Jane M.: Associate Director, Public Affairs and Government Relations
SCHMIDT, William: V. President, Public Affairs
SOLER, Lawrence A.: Director, Government Relations

Outside Counsel/Consultants

McDermott, Will and Emery

K Capital Partners

Boston, MA
Leg. Issues: BUD, GOV, TEC

Outside Counsel/Consultants

Palumbo & Cerrell, Inc.
Issues: BUD, GOV, TEC
Rep By: Charles R. O'Regan, Benjamin L. Palumbo, Paul A. Skrabut, Jr.

"K" Line America, Inc.

Glen Allen, VA
Leg. Issues: MAR

Outside Counsel/Consultants

The Solomon Group, LLC
Issues: MAR
Rep By: William D. Crosby, Jr., Hon. Gerald B. H. Solomon

K-Mortgage Corp.

Wall Township, NJ
Leg. Issues: HOU

Outside Counsel/Consultants

Global USA, Inc.
Issues: HOU
Rep By: George S. Kopp, Lottie H. Shackelford

Kahl Pownall Advocates

Sacramento, CA
Leg. Issues: HCR, MMM

Outside Counsel/Consultants

Fleishman-Hillard, Inc
Issues: HCR, MMM
Rep By: William Black, Kathleen Siedlecki

KAIL-TV

Fresno, CA
Leg. Issues: COM

Outside Counsel/Consultants

Miller and Miller, P.C.
Issues: COM

Kaiser Aluminum & Chemical Corp.

655 15th St. NW
Suite 200
Washington, DC 20005
Tel: (202)638-2020
Fax: (202)638-1991
Registered: LDA

Headquartered in Houston, TX.

Leg. Issues: AER, AUT, AVI, BEV, BUD, CAW, CDT, CHM, CSP, DEF, ECN, ENG, ENV, FIN, FOR, FUE, GOV, HCR, LBR, MAN, MAR, MED, MMM, NAT, RES, RET, ROD, RRR, SCI, TAX, TOR, TRA, TRD, TRU, UTI, WAS

In-house, DC-area Employees

COLE, Robert E.: V. President, Government Affairs

Outside Counsel/Consultants

Ball Janik, LLP
Issues: ENG
Rep By: Robert G. Hayes, Irene Ringwood

Patton Boggs, LLP
Issues: LBR
Rep By: Donald V. Moorehead

Kaiser Family Foundation

Menlo Park, CA

Outside Counsel/Consultants

Hauser Group

IssueSphere

Neuman and Co.

Kaiser Permanente

1700 K St. NW
Suite 601
Washington, DC 20006
Tel: (202)296-1314
Fax: (202)296-4067
Registered: LDA

Leg. Issues: HCR

In-house, DC-area Employees

BURNETT, Laird: Senior Legislative Representative
COLE, Steven R.: Director of Public Policy
FROH, Richard B.: V. President, Government Relations
WOODS, Mary: Director, Public Affairs (Mid-Atlantic)

Outside Counsel/Consultants

Hannett & Associates
Issues: HCR
Rep By: Frederick J. Hannett

Kaiser-Hill Co., L.L.C.

Golden, CO
Leg. Issues: DEF, ENG, ENV

Outside Counsel/Consultants

Ervin Technical Associates, Inc. (ETA)
Issues: DEF, ENG, ENV
Rep By: Hon. Jack Edwards, James L. Ervin, Donald E. Richbourg

Kake Tribal Corp.

Kake, AK
Leg. Issues: IND

Outside Counsel/Consultants

Moss McGee Bradley & Foley
Issues: IND
Rep By: David A. Bradley

Zane & Associates
Issues: IND
Rep By: Curtis J. Zane

Kake, Alaska, Organized Village of

Leg. Issues: IND

Outside Counsel/Consultants

Morriset, Schlosser, Ayer & Jozwiak
Issues: IND
Rep By: Fran Ayer, Jennifer P. Hughes

Kalitta Air, L.L.C.

Ypsilanti, MI
Leg. Issues: AVI

Outside Counsel/Consultants

Sher & Blackwell
Issues: AVI
Rep By: Mark Atwood

Kalkines, Arky, Zall and Bernstein

New York, NY
Leg. Issues: BUD, HCR, HOU, MMM

Outside Counsel/Consultants

Downey McGrath Group, Inc.
Issues: BUD, HCR, HOU, MMM
Rep By: Hon. Thomas J. Downey, Jr., John Peter Olinger

KAMAN Corp.

Bloomfield, CT

Outside Counsel/Consultants

Rhoads Group

Kaman Diversified Technologies Corp.

1111 Jefferson Davis Hwy.
Suite 700
Arlington, VA 22202-3225
Tel: (703)416-2500
Fax: (703)416-2512
Registered: LDA

Web: www.kaman.com

Headquartered in Bloomfield, Connecticut.

Leg. Issues: AER, DEF

In-house, DC-area Employees

VIILO, Jr., Michael W.: Assistant V. President, Congressional and Industrial Relations

Outside Counsel/Consultants

Ervin Technical Associates, Inc. (ETA)
Issues: AER, DEF
Rep By: Hon. Jack Edwards, James L. Ervin, Donald E. Richbourg

Robert D. Sneed
Issues: DEF
Rep By: Robert D. Sneed

Kamehameha Schools

Honolulu, HI

Outside Counsel/Consultants

Edwin T. C. Ing
Rep By: Edwin T. C. Ing

Kanowitz Fruit & Produce Co.

Brooklyn, NY

Outside Counsel/Consultants

O'Connor & Hannan, L.L.P.
Rep By: John M. Himmelberg

Kansas City Area Transportation Authority

Kansas City, MO
Leg. Issues: BUD, HLT, TRA

Outside Counsel/Consultants

Redfern Resources
Issues: HLT
Rep By: Ed Redfern

Smith Dawson & Andrews, Inc.
Issues: BUD, TRA
Rep By: Kirk Bailey, Thomas C. Dawson

Kansas City Power & Light Co.

701 Pennsylvania Ave. NW
Suite 300
Washington, DC 20004
Tel: (202)508-5275
Fax: (202)508-5278
Registered: LDA

Web: www.kcpl.com

Headquartered in Kansas City, MO. The above address is also the Washington office of Empire District Electric Co.

In-house, DC-area Employees

POLING, Michael: Manager, Federal Government Affairs

Kansas City Southern Industries

Kansas City, MO
Registered: LDA
Leg. Issues: BUD, FIN, RRR, TAX, TRA

Outside Counsel/Consultants

Patton Boggs, LLP
Issues: BUD, RRR, TRA
Rep By: Robert C. Jones

Sydney Probst
Issues: FIN, RRR
Rep By: Sydney Probst

Snavely, King, Majoros, O'Connor and Lee, Inc.
Rep By: Tom O'Connor

Troutman Sanders LLP
Rep By: Sandra L. Brown, William A. Mullins, David C. Reeves

Vinson & Elkins L.L.P.
Issues: RRR, TAX
Rep By: Hon. Michael A. Andrews, John E. Chapoton, Christine L. Vaughn

Wiley, Rein & Fielding
Rep By: Hon. Jim Slattery

Kansas City Southern Railway Co.

Kansas City, MO
Leg. Issues: RRR, TRA

Outside Counsel/Consultants

Wiley, Rein & Fielding
Issues: RRR, TRA
Rep By: Hon. Jim Slattery

Kansas City, Missouri, City of

Leg. Issues: AVI, BUD, HOU

Outside Counsel/Consultants

Shaw Pittman
Issues: AVI
Rep By: Robert E. Cohn

Verner, Liipfert, Bernhard, McPherson and Hand, Chartered
Issues: BUD, HOU
Rep By: Timothy M. Rutten

Kansas Electric Power Cooperative

Topeka, KS

Outside Counsel/Consultants

Miller & Van Eaton, P.L.L.C.
Rep By: William Malone, Nicholas P. Miller

Kansas Gas Service

Overland Park, KS

Outside Counsel/Consultants

G. Frank West
Rep By: G. Frank West

Kansas Public Transit Ass'n

Overland Park, KS
Leg. Issues: TRA

Outside Counsel/Consultants

Redfern Resources
Issues: TRA
Rep By: Ed Redfern

Kaplan Companies, Inc.

Lewisville, NC
Leg. Issues: BUD, EDU, GOV

Outside Counsel/Consultants

Ledge Counsel
Issues: BUD, EDU, GOV

Valente Lopatin & Schulze
Rep By: Alan G. Lopatin

Barbara A. Karmanos Cancer Institute

Detroit, MI
Leg. Issues: BUD, HCR, MED, SCI

Outside Counsel/Consultants

The Atlantic Group, Public Affairs, Inc.
Issues: BUD, HCR, MED, SCI
Rep By: Larry F. Ayres

Karta Technologies Inc.

San Antonio, TX
Leg. Issues: DEF

Outside Counsel/Consultants

W. B. Driggers & Associates, Inc.
Issues: DEF
Rep By: W. B. Driggers

Kashmiri American Council

733 15th St. NW
Suite 1100
Washington, DC 20005
Web: www.kashmiri.com
E-mail: kac@kashmiri.com
Tel: (202)628-6789
Fax: (202)393-0062

Supports Kashmiri self-determination through a free, fair and impartial plebiscite as promised under international law and agreements by both India and Pakistan. Seeks to raise the level of consciousness in the United States about the people of the Kashmir region.

Leg. Issues: FOR, GOV, MIA

In-house, DC-area Employees

NABI FAI, Ghulam: Exec. Director

Kasten Chase Applied Research Limited

Reston, VA
Leg. Issues: CPI

Outside Counsel/Consultants

Verner, Liipfert, Bernhard, McPherson and Hand, Chartered
Issues: CPI
Rep By: Hon. James J. Blanchard, Rosemary B. Freeman, David A. Weiss

Katten Muchin & Zavis

1025 Thomas Jefferson St. NW
Suite 700 East
Washington, DC 20007
Tel: (202)625-3500
Fax: (202)298-7570
Registered: LDA, FARA

Web: www.kmz.com
Leg. Issues: BAN, FIN

In-house, DC-area Employees

VAN CLEEF, Carol R.: Partner

Outside Counsel/Consultants

Fleischman and Walsh, L.L.P.
Issues: BAN, FIN
Rep By: Louis H. Dupart, John P. McAllister

Parry, Romani, DeConcini & Symms
Issues: BAN
Rep By: Edward H. Baxter, Hon. Dennis DeConcini, John M. Haddow, Scott D. Hatch, Shannon Davis Henderson, Jack W. Martin, Romano Romani, Linda Arey Skladany, Hon. Steven D. Symms

KATU
Portland, OR
Outside Counsel/Consultants
Shaw Pittman

KATY-FM
Hemet, CA
Leg. Issues: NAT
Outside Counsel/Consultants
Crowell & Moring LLP
Issues: NAT
Rep By: Steven P. Quarles

Katz Communications, Inc.
New York, NY
Outside Counsel/Consultants
Kaye Scholer LLP
Rep By: Jason Shrinsky

Kawasaki Motors Corp., USA
Irvine, CA
Leg. Issues: CSP, ENV, MAR
Outside Counsel/Consultants
Eckert Seamans Cherin & Mellott, LLC
Issues: CSP, ENV, MAR
Rep By: Michael A. Weigard
Paul, Hastings, Janofsky & Walker LLP
Rep By: Scott M. Flicker

Kaweah Delta Water Conservation District
Visalia, CA
Leg. Issues: BUD, ENV
Outside Counsel/Consultants
The Ferguson Group, LLC
Issues: BUD, ENV
Rep By: W. Roger Gwinn, Joseph L. Raeder

Kazakhstan 21st Century Foundation
Zurich, SWITZERLAND
Leg. Issues: FOR
Outside Counsel/Consultants
Bloomfield Associates, Inc.
Issues: FOR
Rep By: Douglas M. Bloomfield
The Evans Group, Ltd.
Issues: FOR
Rep By: Geryld B. Christianson, Hon. Thomas B. Evans, Jr.

Kazakhstan, Government of the Republic of
Astana, KAZAKHSTAN
Outside Counsel/Consultants
Arnold & Porter
The Carmen Group
Rep By: Jack Stevens

KB Holdings
Dania, FL
Outside Counsel/Consultants
Preston Gates Ellis & Rouvelas Meeds LLP
Rep By: Arthur Dimopoulos, William N. Myhre, Steven R. "Rick" Valentine

KCSM-TV
San Mateo, CA
Outside Counsel/Consultants
Tierney & Swift
Rep By: Richard F. Swift

KCTS
Seattle, WA
Leg. Issues: BUD, COM, EDU, TEC
Outside Counsel/Consultants
Convergence Services, Inc.
Issues: BUD, COM, EDU, TEC
Rep By: John M. Lawson

KDTV
San Francisco, CA
Outside Counsel/Consultants
Shaw Pittman

KDUH-TV
Scottsbluff, NE
Outside Counsel/Consultants
Shaw Pittman

Kean Tracers, Inc.
West Conshohocken, PA
Leg. Issues: BAN, CSP, FIN
Outside Counsel/Consultants
Manatt, Phelps & Phillips, LLP
Issues: BAN, CSP, FIN
Rep By: Michael T. Brown, Hon. Jack W. Buechner, Erik V. Huey, Robert J. Kabel, Steven J. Mulder

Keating Development Corp.
Bala Cynwyd, PA
Leg. Issues: RES
Outside Counsel/Consultants
David F. Godfrey
Issues: RES
Rep By: David F. Godfrey
MV3 & Associates
Valente Lopatin & Schulze
Rep By: Mark Valente, III

Keating Technologies Inc.
Tucson, AZ
Outside Counsel/Consultants
Valente Lopatin & Schulze
Rep By: Susan Feeney, Richard T. Schulze, Jr., Mark Valente, III

KEECO
Lynnwood, VA
Outside Counsel/Consultants
O'Connor & Hannan, L.L.P.
Rep By: Hon. Thomas J. Corcoran

Keidanren
Tokyo, JAPAN
Outside Counsel/Consultants
Miller & Chevalier, Chartered
Rep By: Lawrence B. Gibbs

Keizai Koho Center
1900 K St. NW
Suite 1075
Washington, DC 20006
Tel: (202)293-8430
Fax: (202)293-8438
Registered: LDA, FARA
Web: www.kkc.or.jp
Leg. Issues: ECN, FOR, TRD
In-house, DC-area Employees
TAKAHASHI, Hiroyuki

Keller Equity Group, Inc.
Los Angeles, CA
Leg. Issues: BUD, ROD, TRA
Outside Counsel/Consultants
Manatt, Phelps & Phillips, LLP
Issues: BUD, ROD, TRA
Rep By: Michael T. Brown, Hon. Jack W. Buechner, June L. DeHart

Kellogg Brown and Root
1150 18th St. NW
Suite 200
Washington, DC 20036
Tel: (202)223-0820
Fax: (202)223-2385
Registered: LDA
Web: www.halliburton.com/kbr/
E-mail: Jim.Andrews@halliburton.com

An international technology-based engineering and construction unit of Halliburton Co. Headquartered in Houston, it provides a full spectrum of services to the hydrocarbon, chemical, energy, and forest products industries as well as government.

Leg. Issues: BAN, BUD, CSP, DEF, ENG, ENV, FIN, FOR, GOV, HCR, IMM, LBR, MED, TAX, TRA, TRD
In-house, DC-area Employees
ANDREWS, James H.: V. President
Outside Counsel/Consultants
Bryan Cave LLP
RMA Internat'l, Inc.

Kellogg Co.
Battle Creek, MI
Registered: LDA
Leg. Issues: AGR, FOO, FOR, MAN, TAX, TRA, TRD
Outside Counsel/Consultants
Arent Fox Kintner Plotkin & Kahn, PLLC
Issues: AGR, FOO, MAN
Rep By: Michael T. McNamara
Gibbons & Company, Inc.
Issues: FOR, TAX, TRD
Rep By: Clifford S. Gibbons, Joanna Parzakonis
Verner, Liipfert, Bernhard, McPherson and Hand, Chartered
Issues: FOO, TRA, TRD
Rep By: Rosemary B. Freeman, Lawrence E. Levinson, Linda M. Weinberg, David A. Weiss, Theresa M. Youngblood

Kellogg Foundation
Battle Creek, MI
Outside Counsel/Consultants
Widmeyer Communications, Inc.

Kelly and Associates, Inc.
925 15th St. NW
5th Floor
Washington, DC 20005
Tel: (202)342-9610
Fax: (202)342-0650
Registered: LDA
E-mail: jkelly@kellylobbyshop.com
Leg. Issues: INS, SMB, TAX
In-house, DC-area Employees
EDWARDS, Jill: Associate
KELLY, John A.: Chief Exec. Officer
Outside Counsel/Consultants
Hohlt & Associates
Issues: INS, SMB, TAX
Rep By: Richard F. Hohlt

Kelly Anderson & Associates
Alexandria, VA
Outside Counsel/Consultants
MV3 & Associates
Valente Lopatin & Schulze
Rep By: Mark Valente, III

Kelly Services, Inc.
Troy, MI
A temporary employment agency.
Leg. Issues: LBR, TAX
Outside Counsel/Consultants
Abraham Schneier and Associates
Issues: LBR, TAX
Rep By: Abraham L. Schneier
Verner, Liipfert, Bernhard, McPherson and Hand, Chartered
Issues: LBR
Rep By: Rosemary B. Freeman, Brenda G. Meister

Kemet Electronics Co.
Greenville, SC
Outside Counsel/Consultants
Porter, Wright, Morris & Arthur, LLP
Rep By: Leslie Alan Glick

Kemper Insurance Cos.
325 Seventh St. NW
Suite 1250
Washington, DC 20004
Tel: (202)347-8193
Fax: (202)347-9304
Registered: LDA
Headquartered in Longrove, IL.
Political Action Committee/s
Kemper Insurance Campaign Fund
325 Seventh St. NW
Suite 1250
Washington, DC 20004
Tel: (202)347-8193
Fax: (202)347-9304
Contact: Michael F. Dineen
In-house, DC-area Employees
BROWDER, Marliss: Senior Federal Relations Specialist
DINEEN, Michael F.: V. President, Legislative Affairs

Kenai Penninsula Borough
Soldotna, AK
Outside Counsel/Consultants
Robertson, Monagle & Eastaugh
Rep By: Rick E. Marks

Kendall Healthcare Products Co.
Mansfield, MA
Leg. Issues: HCR, MMM
Outside Counsel/Consultants
Nusgart Consulting, LLC
Issues: HCR, MMM
Rep By: Marcia Nusgart

Kendall-Jackson Winery
Santa Rosa, CA
Leg. Issues: AGR, ALC, BEV, IMM, LAW, TAX, TEC, TRD

Outside Counsel/Consultants

O'Connor & Hannan, L.L.P.
Issues: AGR, ALC, BEV, IMM, LAW, TAX, TEC, TRD
Rep By: Robert M. Adler, Hon. Thomas J. Corcoran, Frederick T. Dombo, Christina W. Fleps, John M. Himmelberg, Patrick E. O'Donnell

Kennecott/Borax
1325 Pennsylvania Ave. NW
Seventh Floor
Washington, DC 20004
Tel: (202)393-0266
Fax: (202)393-0232
Registered: LDA

Kennecott is a mining company headquartered in Salt Lake City, UT and US Borax is a mining company headquartered in Valencia, CA.

Leg. Issues: ENG, ENV, LBR, MON, NAT, TAX, UTI, WAS

In-house, DC-area Employees

FLANNIGAN, Michael: Director, Federal Government Affairs

Outside Counsel/Consultants

Jack Ferguson Associates, Inc.
Issues: MON
Rep By: Jack Ferguson

The Smith-Free Group
Issues: ENG, ENV, LBR, WAS
Rep By: James C. Free, Alicia W. Smith

Kennedy Center for the Performing Arts, John F.
New Hampshire Ave. & F St. NW
Washington, DC 20566
Web: www.kennedy-center.org
Tel: (202)416-8000
Fax: (202)416-8205

In-house, DC-area Employees

GOLDSPIEL, Eileen: Associate Managing Director, Government Liaison

Outside Counsel/Consultants

Widmeyer Communications, Inc.

Kennedy Institute of Ethics
37th and O Sts. NW
Fourth Floor, Healy Hall
Washington, DC 20027
Web: www.georgetown.edu/research.kie
Tel: (202)687-8099
Fax: (202)687-8089

Sponsors research on ethical issues in medicine, including the legal and medical definitions of death, allocation of health resources and issues concerning recombinant DNA.

In-house, DC-area Employees

WALTERS, Dr. LeRoy B.: Director

Kennedy Institute, Lt. Joseph P.
801 Buchanan St. NE
Washington, DC 20017
Tel: (202)529-7600
Fax: (202)529-2028

Serves children and adults with developmental disabilities in the Metro region through education, training and employment, therapeutic and residential services, technical assistance, progressive development, and research.

In-house, DC-area Employees

BIRKEL, Richard C.: President and Chief Exec. Officer

Kennedy Krieger Institute
Baltimore, MD

Outside Counsel/Consultants

U.S. Strategies Corp.

Kennedy/Jenks Consultants
San Francisco, CA

An engineering consulting firm.

Leg. Issues: BUD, NAT

Outside Counsel/Consultants

Will and Carlson, Inc.
Issues: BUD, NAT
Rep By: Peter Carlson, Robert P. Will

Kensey Nash Corp.
Exton, PA

A manufacturer of medical devices.

Leg. Issues: TRD

Outside Counsel/Consultants

Hogan & Hartson L.L.P.
Issues: TRD
Rep By: Raymond S. Calamaro, Howard Holstein

Kent Gamebore
Stouffville, CANADA

Outside Counsel/Consultants

Birch, Horton, Bittner & Cherot
Rep By: William P. Horn

Kent State University
Kent, OH
Leg. Issues: EDU

Outside Counsel/Consultants

Golin/Harris Internat'l
Issues: EDU
Rep By: C. Michael Fulton

Kentucky Highlands Investment Corp.
London, KY

Outside Counsel/Consultants

Robert A. Rapoza Associates
Rep By: Robert A. Rapoza

Kentucky, Commonwealth of
Frankfort, KY
Leg. Issues: BUD, EDU, HCR, TOB, TRA, WEL

Outside Counsel/Consultants

Cartwright & Riley
Issues: BUD, EDU, HCR, TOB, TRA, WEL
Rep By: Russell S. Cartwright, Maura Cullen

Kenya Airways
Nairobi, KENYA

Outside Counsel/Consultants

Zuckert, Scoutt and Rasenberger, L.L.P.
Rep By: Malcolm L. Benge, Richard D. Mathias

Kenya Bombing Families
Bowie, MD

Lobbying on behalf of families who lost relatives in the bombing of the U.S. Embassy in Nairobi, Kenya in August 1998.

Leg. Issues: GOV

Outside Counsel/Consultants

Crowell & Moring LLP
Issues: GOV
Rep By: Stuart Newberger, Karen Hastie Williams

Kern County Water Agency
Bakersfield, CA
Leg. Issues: BUD, ENV

Outside Counsel/Consultants

Schramm, Williams & Associates, Inc.
Issues: BUD, ENV
Rep By: Nancy Williams

Kern River Gas Transmission Co.
Salt Lake City, UT

Outside Counsel/Consultants

Wright & Talisman, P.C.
Rep By: Michael J. Thompson

Kern River Watermaster
Bakersfield, CA
Leg. Issues: BUD, ENV

Outside Counsel/Consultants

Schramm, Williams & Associates, Inc.
Issues: BUD, ENV
Rep By: Nancy Williams

Kern, California, County of
Bakersfield, CA
Leg. Issues: GOV

Outside Counsel/Consultants

PACE-CAPSTONE
Issues: GOV
Rep By: Scott C. Dacey, J. Michael Landrum, James W. Wise

Kerr-McGee Corp.
1667 K St. NW
Suite 250
Washington, DC 20006
Tel: (202)728-9600
Fax: (202)728-9587
Registered: LDA

Headquartered in Oklahoma City, OK.

Leg. Issues: ENG, WAS

In-house, DC-area Employees

FRANK, Peter M.: V. President, Public Affairs

Outside Counsel/Consultants

Dickstein Shapiro Morin & Oshinsky LLP
Rep By: Hon. Wendell H. Ford, Robert Mangas, Graham "Rusty" Mathews, L. Andrew Zausner

Foley & Lardner
Issues: WAS
Rep By: Jodi L. Hanson

Ryan, Phillips, Utrecht & MacKinnon
Rep By: Rodney Hoppe, Jeffrey M. MacKinnon, William D. Phillips, Mark D. Planning, Thomas M. Ryan, Joseph V. Vasapoli

Henry H. Kessler Foundation
West Orange, NJ
Leg. Issues: MED, MMM

Outside Counsel/Consultants

Linda Jenckes & Associates
Issues: MED, MMM
Rep By: Linda Jenckes

Kessler & Associates Business Services, Inc.
Issues: MED, MMM
Rep By: Simon Gros, Richard S. Kessler, Harry Sporidis

Kessler Medical Rehabilitation Research & Education Corp.
West Orange, NJ
Leg. Issues: MED, MMM

Outside Counsel/Consultants

Capitol Partners
Issues: MED
Rep By: Jonathan M. Orloff

Linda Jenckes & Associates
Issues: MMM

Ketchikan Gateway Borough
Ketchikan, AK
Leg. Issues: BUD, MAR

Outside Counsel/Consultants

Robertson, Monagle & Eastaugh
Issues: BUD, MAR
Rep By: Steven W. Silver

Ketchikan Public Utilities
Ketchikan, AK
Leg. Issues: BUD, UTI

Outside Counsel/Consultants

Robertson, Monagle & Eastaugh
Issues: BUD, UTI
Rep By: Steven W. Silver

Ketchum
2000 L St. NW
Suite 300
Washington, DC 20036-0646
Web: www.ketchum.com
Tel: (202)835-8800
Fax: (202)835-8879
Registered: LDA, FARA
Leg. Issues: GOV

In-house, DC-area Employees

BRADFIELD, Daniel: Vice President and Group Manager; Director, Grassroots Communications
BRUNS, Kevin T.: V. President and Group Manager, Public Affairs
COFFEY, Nancy: Senior V. President, Media Relations
DOLAN, Jr., Charles H.: Senior V. President
DOYNE, Karen: Director, Litigation Communications
ERICKSON, Steve: Sr. V. President, Healthcare
HURSON, John: Consultant
KIRK, Keith A.: V. President for Grassroots
LASKY, Samantha: Account Executive
LEIBENSPERGER, Jr., Thomas: Account Supervisor
LIEB, Bonnie: Sr. V. President, Technology
LUKE, Anne Forristall: Senior V. President, Public Affairs and Issues Management
ROBINSON, Peter: Sr. V. President and Counselor for Policy, Govt. Relations
SCHANNON, Mark: Partner and Director
SUTHERLAND, Julia K.: Senior V. President
THELIAN, Lorraine: Sr. Partner, North America
WHALEN, Katie: Senior Counselor

Outside Counsel/Consultants

Chesapeake Enterprises, Inc.
Issues: GOV
Rep By: J. John Fluharty, Scott W. Reed

Kettering Foundation
444 N. Capitol St. NW
Suite 434
Washington, DC 20001
Web: www.kettering.com
Tel: (202)393-4478
Fax: (202)393-7644

An operating (not grant-making) foundation with research programs on governmental, educational and international issues. Works to increase citizen participation in politics. Headquartered in Dayton, Ohio.

In-house, DC-area Employees
SAUNDERS, Harold H.: Director, Internat'l Affairs
WILDER, James: Director, External Affairs

Kettering Medical Center

Kettering, OH
Leg. Issues: BUD

Outside Counsel/Consultants

Baker & Hostetler LLP
Rep By: Frederick H. Graefe

Edington, Peel & Associates, Inc.
Issues: BUD
Rep By: William H. Edington, Craig A. Meyers, Terry R. Peel

KeyCorp, Inc.

Cleveland, OH Registered: LDA
Leg. Issues: TAX

Outside Counsel/Consultants

Baker & Hostetler LLP
Issues: TAX
Rep By: William F. Conroy, Matthew J. Dolan, Steven A. Lotterer, Kenneth F. Snyder, Hon. Guy Vander Jagt

Keymarket Communications, Inc.

North Augusta, SC

Outside Counsel/Consultants

Kaye Scholer LLP
Rep By: Jason Shrinsky

KeySpan Energy

Brooklyn, NY
Leg. Issues: ENG, ENV, FUE, GOV, NAT, SCI, TAX, UTI

Outside Counsel/Consultants

Crowell & Moring LLP
Rep By: Dana C. Contratto

Hunton & Williams
Issues: UTI

Lent Scrivner & Roth LLC
Issues: TAX, UTI
Rep By: Norman F. Lent, III, Hon. Norman F. Lent, Alan J. Roth, Michael S. Scrivner

Liebman & Associates, Inc.
Issues: ENG, ENV, FUE, GOV, NAT, SCI, UTI
Rep By: Murray Liebman

Keystone Consolidated Industries, Inc.

Dallas, TX
Leg. Issues: TRD

Outside Counsel/Consultants

Wiley, Rein & Fielding
Issues: TRD
Rep By: Eileen P. Bradner, Sharon R. Fine, Hon. Jim Slattery

Keystone, Inc.

Fort Worth, TX

Outside Counsel/Consultants

Williams & Jensen, P.C.
Rep By: David E. Franasiak, Robert E. Glennon, Jr., J. Steven Hart, Karen Judd Lewis, George G. Olsen

KFAR-TV

Fairbanks, AK

Outside Counsel/Consultants

Shaw Pittman

KFTV

Hanford, CA

Outside Counsel/Consultants

Shaw Pittman

KFx, Inc.

Arlington, VA
Leg. Issues: FIN, FUE

Outside Counsel/Consultants

Johnson Co.
Issues: FIN, FUE

Khalistan, Council of

1901 Pennsylvania Ave. NW
Suite 802
Washington, DC 20006
Tel: (202)833-3262
Fax: (202)452-9161
Registered: FARA
Web: www.khalistan.com
E-mail: cok@prolificom.net

Supports the independence of the Sikh nation in Punjab (Khalistan) from India.

Leg. Issues: FOR

In-house, DC-area Employees
AULAKH, Dr. Gurmit Singh: President

The Khazakstan 21st Century Foundation

Outside Counsel/Consultants

Coudert Brothers
Rep By: Edward H. Lieberman

KHSD-TV

Rapid City, SD

Outside Counsel/Consultants

Shaw Pittman

Kia Motors Corp.

Seoul, KOREA

Outside Counsel/Consultants

Persimmon Group Inc.
Rep By: Jin Ahn

Kickapoo Tribe of Oklahoma

McLoud, OK
Leg. Issues: IND

Outside Counsel/Consultants

Patton Boggs, LLP
Issues: IND
Rep By: Katharine R. Boyce

Kickapoo Tribe of Texas

Eagle Pass, TX

Outside Counsel/Consultants

Carlyle Consulting

Kids in the Know

Washington, DC

Outside Counsel/Consultants

Widmeyer Communications, Inc.
Rep By: Kevin J. Bonderud

Kids Voting USA

Scottsdale, AZ

Outside Counsel/Consultants

Neuman and Co.
Rep By: Robert A. Neuman

Kildare Corp.

New London, CT
Leg. Issues: DEF, SCI

Outside Counsel/Consultants

The Kemper Co.
Issues: DEF, SCI
Rep By: Jackson Kemper, Jr.

Kimberly-Clark Corp.

Irving, TX Registered: LDA

A global manufacturer of tissue, personal care, and healthcare products.

Leg. Issues: AVI, BUD, CAW, CHM, CPT, CSP, ENG, ENV, FIN, FOR, HCR, MAN, TAX, TOB, TRA, TRD, TRU, WAS

Outside Counsel/Consultants

Kimberly Consulting, LLC
Issues: CAW, ENG, ENV, FOR, TAX, TRD
Rep By: Richard H. Kimberly

The Technical Group LLC
Issues: ENV
Rep By: Chris Bryant

Weil, Gotshal & Manges, LLP
Issues: TAX
Rep By: Larry I. Willis

Kinder-Care Learning Centers, Inc.

Montgomery, AL

A part of Private Child Care Providers Coalition.

Leg. Issues: TAX

Outside Counsel/Consultants

Hogan & Hartson L.L.P.
Issues: TAX
Rep By: Nancy Granese, William Michael House

Kinetic Biosystems Inc.

Atlanta, GA
Leg. Issues: SCI

Outside Counsel/Consultants

Powell, Goldstein, Frazer & Murphy LLP
Issues: SCI
Rep By: Hon. Butler E. Derrick, Jr., Brett G. Kappel

The Kinetics Group

Santa Clara, CA
Leg. Issues: CHM, CPI, DEF, ENG, ENV, MAN, PHA, TAX

Outside Counsel/Consultants

Wayne Arny & Assoc.
Issues: CHM, CPI, ENV, MAN
Rep By: Wayne Arny, David D. O'Brien

O'Brien, Klink & Associates
Issues: DEF, ENG, PHA, TAX
Rep By: David D. O'Brien, Shannon L. Scott

King & Spalding

1730 Pennsylvania Ave. NW
Suite 1200
Washington, DC 20006-4706
Tel: (202)737-0500
Fax: (202)626-3737
Registered: LDA
Web: www.kslaw.com

In-house, DC-area Employees
BREWER, Carol: International Trade Specialist
CAMBELL, Glenn
CROCKETT, Elizabeth Schmidtlein: Associate
DORN, Joseph W.: Partner
DURST, Michael: Partner
GRAHAM, Thomas: Partner
HESTER, Theodore M.: Partner
HILL, Eleanor
JAFARI, Beth
JONES, Stephen A.: Partner
KASSIR, Allison: Government Affairs Representative
MABILE, Michael P.: Partner
NORTON, Lisa K.: Associate
NUNN, Hon. Sam: Partner
PFEIFER, Eugene M.: Partner
RICHMAN, Dvorah A.: Partner
SCHOTT, Anne: Associate
STRIBLING, Jess H.: Partner
TALMADGE, William C.: Counsel
WHITESIDES, Ashley: Associate

Outside Counsel/Consultants

Wells & Associates
Rep By: Milton T. Wells

King Communications Corp.

Washington, DC

Outside Counsel/Consultants

John Adams Associates Inc.
Rep By: A. John Adams

King Faisal Foundation

Outside Counsel/Consultants

Burson-Marsteller

King, Washington, County of

Seattle, WA
Leg. Issues: ENV, NAT

Outside Counsel/Consultants

Denny Miller McBee Associates
Issues: ENV, NAT

Kinghorn & Associates, L.L.C.

900 Second St. NE
Suite 201
Washington, DC 20002
Tel: (202)842-0219
Fax: (202)842-0439
Registered: LDA
E-mail: tkinghorn@kinghornassociates.com
Leg. Issues: BUD

In-house, DC-area Employees
HILBERT, II, John W.: V. President, Legislative and Regulatory Affairs
KINGHORN, Jr., Edward J.: President
SCOTT, Jeremy: Legislative Associates

Outside Counsel/Consultants

The Laurin Baker Group
Issues: BUD
Rep By: Laurin M. Baker

Kings River Interests

Leg. Issues: ENG, ENV, NAT

Outside Counsel/Consultants

The Ferguson Group, LLC
Issues: ENG, ENV, NAT
Rep By: Joseph L. Raeder

Kirby Corp./Dixie Carriers

Houston, TX
Leg. Issues: MAR

Outside Counsel/Consultants

Winston & Strawn
Issues: MAR
Rep By: Lawrence I. Kiern, Thomas L. Mills, Constantine G. Papavizas

Kitchen Cabinet Manufacturers Ass'n

Reston, VA
Leg. Issues: ENV, TRD

Outside Counsel/Consultants

Valis Associates
Issues: ENV, TRD
Rep By: Todd Tolson, Wayne H. Valis

Kiwanis Internat'l

Indianapolis, IN
Leg. Issues: BUD, HCR

Outside Counsel/Consultants

Edington, Peel & Associates, Inc.
Issues: BUD, HCR
Rep By: Terry R. Peel

KJAZ-FM

San Francisco, CA

Outside Counsel/Consultants

Bell, Boyd & Lloyd
Rep By: A. Thomas Carroccio

KJVI

Jackson, NV

Outside Counsel/Consultants

Drinker Biddle & Reath LLP
Rep By: John P. Bankson, Jr.

KKVI

Twin Falls, ID

Outside Counsel/Consultants

Drinker Biddle & Reath LLP
Rep By: John P. Bankson, Jr.

Klamath Tribes

Chiloquin, OR

Outside Counsel/Consultants

Dunlap & Browder, Inc.
Rep By: Joseph B. Browder

Charles Klatskin and Co.

Teterboro, NJ
A real estate developer and property management company.

Leg. Issues: RES

Outside Counsel/Consultants

The MWW Group
Issues: RES
Rep By: Jonathan B. Slade

Klett Rooney Lieber & Schorling

Pittsburgh, PA — Registered: LDA
Leg. Issues: DEF, TRA

Outside Counsel/Consultants

The Peterson Group
Issues: DEF, TRA
Rep By: William P. Sears

KLUZ-TV

Albuquerque, NM

Outside Counsel/Consultants

Shaw Pittman

Kmart Corp.

Troy, MI — Registered: LDA
Leg. Issues: ALC, TRD, TRU

Outside Counsel/Consultants

The MWW Group
Issues: ALC, TRD, TRU
Rep By: Elizabeth A. Iadarola, Christine A. Pellerin, Jonathan B. Slade, Jeffery M. Walter

Verner, Liipfert, Bernhard, McPherson and Hand, Chartered
Issues: ALC
Rep By: Rosemary B. Freeman

KMEX-TV

Los Angeles, CA

Outside Counsel/Consultants

Shaw Pittman

KN Energy Inc.

Lakewood, CO — Registered: LDA

Outside Counsel/Consultants

Sutherland Asbill & Brennan LLP

Knight Trading Group

Jersey City, NJ
Leg. Issues: FIN

Outside Counsel/Consultants

Williams & Jensen, P.C.
Issues: FIN
Rep By: David E. Franasiak, J. Steven Hart, Jeffrey A. Tassey

Knightstown, Indiana, Town of

Leg. Issues: COM, GOV

Outside Counsel/Consultants

Duncan, Weinberg, Genzer & Pembroke, P.C.
Issues: COM, GOV
Rep By: Michael R. Postar

Knoll Pharmaceutical Co.

Mount Olive, NJ
Leg. Issues: HCR, PHA

Outside Counsel/Consultants

Fleishman-Hillard, Inc
Issues: HCR
Rep By: Paul W. Johnson, Kathleen Siedlecki

Reed, Smith, LLP
Issues: PHA
Rep By: Phillips S. Peter, C. Stevens Seale

Knoxville College

Knoxville, TN
Leg. Issues: BUD, EDU

Outside Counsel/Consultants

Dean Blakey & Moskowitz
Issues: BUD, EDU
Rep By: William A. Blakey

Knoxville Utilities Board

Knoxville, TN
Leg. Issues: ENG

Outside Counsel/Consultants

Crowell & Moring LLP
Issues: ENG
Rep By: Dana C. Contratto, Jennifer Waters

Koable Co., Ltd.

Kang Won ~ Do, KOREA
Leg. Issues: DEF

Outside Counsel/Consultants

American Defense Internat'l, Inc.
Issues: DEF
Rep By: Michael Herson, Van D. Hipp, Jr., Dave Wilberding

Koch Industries, Inc.

655 15th St. NW
Suite 445
Washington, DC 20005
Tel: (202)737-1977
Fax: (202)737-8111
Registered: LDA

Headquartered in Wichita, KS.

Leg. Issues: BUD, CAW, ENV, FIN, FUE, GOV, ROD, SCI, TAX, TRA

In-house, DC-area Employees

CLAY, Don R.: Director, Environmental and Regulatory Affairs
FINK, Richard H.: Exec. V. President
GABLE, Wayne E.: Managing Director, Federal Affairs
GRIBBIN, D. J.: Director, Government Affairs
HALL, III, Robert P.: Director, Government Affairs
TAYLOR, Christine: PAC Director

Outside Counsel/Consultants

Clay Associates, Inc.

The Direct Impact Co.

Ernst & Young LLP
Issues: TAX
Rep By: Lauren Darling, Patrick G. Heck, Phillip D. Moseley, John D. Porter, Henry C. Ruempler, Donna Steele-Flynn

Hogan & Hartson L.L.P.
Issues: FUE, GOV, TAX, TRA
Rep By: Lance D. Bultena, Jeffrey W. Munk

LPI Consulting, Inc.
Issues: BUD, CAW
Rep By: Teresa Gorman

Kodiak Brown Bear Trust

Kodiak, AK
Leg. Issues: ENV

Outside Counsel/Consultants

Outdoor Media, Inc.
Issues: ENV
Rep By: Tim Richardson

Kodiak Island, Alaska, Borough of

Leg. Issues: BUD

Outside Counsel/Consultants

Robertson, Monagle & Eastaugh
Issues: BUD
Rep By: Bradley D. Gilman, Rick E. Marks

Kodiak, Alaska, City of

Leg. Issues: BUD

Outside Counsel/Consultants

Robertson, Monagle & Eastaugh
Issues: BUD
Rep By: Bradley D. Gilman, Rick E. Marks

Kohlberg Kravis Roberts & Co.

New York, NY
Leg. Issues: GOV

Outside Counsel/Consultants

Levine & Co.
Issues: GOV
Rep By: Ken Levine

Kohler Corp.

Kohler, WI
A manufacturer of plumbing supplies.

Leg. Issues: CAW

Outside Counsel/Consultants

Hill and Knowlton, Inc.
Issues: CAW
Rep By: Reginald E. Gilliam, Jr., Gary G. Hymel

Kollsman, Inc.

Merrimack, NH
A U.S. corporation engaged in the manufacturing of aircraft instrumentation, electro-optics equipment and systems, and medical instrumentation.

Leg. Issues: DEF

Outside Counsel/Consultants

The PMA Group
Issues: DEF
Rep By: Daniel E. Fleming, Kaylene Green, Dr. John Lynch, Paul J. Magliocchetti

Komatsu Ltd.

Tokyo, JAPAN
A heavy construction equipment manufacturer. U.S. office is in Chattanooga, TN.

Leg. Issues: TRD

Outside Counsel/Consultants

Global USA, Inc.
Issues: TRD
Rep By: Dr. Bohdan Denysyk

Susan G. Komen Breast Cancer Foundation

Dallas, TX
Leg. Issues: HCR, MED, MMM

Outside Counsel/Consultants

Akin, Gump, Strauss, Hauer & Feld, L.L.P.
Issues: HCR, MED, MMM
Rep By: Marlene M. Colucci, Karen E. Goldmeier Green

Komen Breast Cancer Foundation, The Susan G.

Dallas, TX
Leg. Issues: BUD, HCR, MED, MMM

Outside Counsel/Consultants

Evans & Black, Inc.
Issues: BUD, HCR, MED, MMM
Rep By: Teresa J. Dyer, Rae Forker Evans

KOMO-TV

Seattle, WA

Outside Counsel/Consultants

Shaw Pittman

KOMU-TV

Columbia, MO

Outside Counsel/Consultants

Shaw Pittman

Koncor Forest Products Co.

Anchorage, AK
Leg. Issues: NAT, TRD

Outside Counsel/Consultants

Van Ness Feldman, P.C.
Issues: NAT, TRD
Rep By: Alan L. Mintz

Kongsberg Defense & Aerospace

Konsberg, NORWAY
Leg. Issues: DEF

Outside Counsel/Consultants

Johnson Co.
Issues: DEF
Rep By: James H. Johnson

Kongsberg Simrad

Aberdeen, UNITED KINGDOM
Leg. Issues: DEF, MAR

Outside Counsel/Consultants

Hogan & Hartson L.L.P.
Issues: DEF, MAR
Rep By: C. Michael Gilliland

Koniag, Inc.

Anchorage, AK
Leg. Issues: TAX

Outside Counsel/Consultants

White & Case LLP
Issues: TAX
Rep By: William P. McClure, J. Roger Mentz

Kootenai Electric Cooperative, Inc.

Hayden, ID

Outside Counsel/Consultants

GKRSE
Rep By: Peter C. Kissel, Nancy J. Skancke

Kootznoowoo, Inc.

Juneau, AK

Outside Counsel/Consultants

Perkins Coie LLP
Rep By: Guy R. Martin

Korea Economic Institute of America

1101 Vermont Ave. NW
Suite 401
Washington, DC 20005
Tel: (202)371-0690
Fax: (202)371-0692
Registered: FARA
Web: www.keia.org
E-mail: jabw@keia.org

KEI promotes economic relations between the U.S. and South Korea through seminars, conferences, and publications.

Leg. Issues: ECN, FIN, FOR, TRD

In-house, DC-area Employees

BECK, Peter M.: Director, Research and Academic Affairs
COOPER, Caroline G.: Director, Congressional Affairs
LISTER, James M.: V. President
LOWE, Florence Myeong-Hwa: Director, Financial Affairs, Publications
WEBER, R. Ben: Director, Business & Public Affairs
WINDER, Joseph A. B.: President

Korea Information & Communication, Ltd.

Seoul, KOREA
Leg. Issues: TEC

Outside Counsel/Consultants

The Washington Group
Issues: TEC
Rep By: Kevin D. Allen, William J. Burke, Tripp Funderburk, Rita M. Lewis, G. John O'Hanlon, John D. Raffaelli, Tonya Saunders, Mark Schnabel

Korea Internat'l Trade Ass'n

1800 K St. NW
Suite 700
Washington, DC 20006
Tel: (202)828-4400
Fax: (202)828-4404
Registered: FARA
Web: www.kita.org
E-mail: mfqn36a@prodigy.com

Founded in 1984, KFTA Washington Office collects information on U.S. and world trade trends, conducts research and surveys on the U.S. economy, and provides facilities to support the overseas activities of member companies.

In-house, DC-area Employees

KIN, Moo Han: V. President

Outside Counsel/Consultants

Akin, Gump, Strauss, Hauer & Feld, L.L.P.
C&M Internat'l, Ltd.
Crowell & Moring LLP
Edelman Public Relations Worldwide
Rep By: Jere Sullivan

Korea Telecom

Seoul, KOREA

Outside Counsel/Consultants

Paul, Weiss, Rifkind, Wharton & Garrison

Korea Trade Center

1129 20th St. NW
Suite 410
Washington, DC 20036
Tel: (202)857-7919
Fax: (202)857-7923
Web: www.kotra.or.kr
E-mail: dcktc@bellatlantic.net

A Korean governmental agency based in Seoul with 115 offices worldwide, including 14 U.S. cities. The Washington office is involved primarily with reporting trade policy developments, encouraging U.S. companies to invest in Korea.

In-house, DC-area Employees

PARK, Won-Kyung: Director General

Korea, Embassy of

2450 Massachusetts Ave. NW
Washington, DC 20008
Tel: (202)939-5600
Fax: (202)797-0595

Outside Counsel/Consultants

McGuireWoods L.L.P.
Rep By: Joseph H. Bogosian
Paul, Weiss, Rifkind, Wharton & Garrison

Korean Air Lines

Seoul, KOREA

Outside Counsel/Consultants

Zuckert, Scoutt and Rasenberger, L.L.P.
Rep By: Malcolm L. Benge, William H. Callaway, Jr.

Korean Iron and Steel Ass'n

Seoul, KOREA
Leg. Issues: TRD

Outside Counsel/Consultants

Kaye Scholer LLP
Issues: TRD
Rep By: Donald B. Cameron, Julie C. Mendoza

Korean Semiconductor Industry Ass'n

Seoul, KOREA
Leg. Issues: TRD

Outside Counsel/Consultants

Kaye Scholer LLP
Rep By: Christopher R. Brewster, Michael P. House, Randi Levinas, Sarah Torrey
Winthrop, Stimson, Putnam & Roberts
Issues: TRD
Rep By: David S. Christy, Jr., C. Christopher Parlin

KOSA

Charlotte, NC
Leg. Issues: APP, CAW, CHM, ENV, FOO, HCR, MAN, RRR, TRA, TRD, WAS

Outside Counsel/Consultants

F&T Network, Inc.
Issues: APP, CAW, CHM, ENV, FOO, HCR, MAN, RRR, TRA, TRD, WAS
Rep By: William A. Shaw

Kosovo, Government of the Republic of

Pristina, YUGOSLAVIA

Outside Counsel/Consultants

Arnold & Porter
Bardyl R. Tirana
Rep By: Bardyl R. Tirana

KOTA-TV

Rapid City, SD

Outside Counsel/Consultants

Shaw Pittman

Kotzebue, Alaska, City of

Leg. Issues: ENV

Outside Counsel/Consultants

Robertson, Monagle & Eastaugh
Issues: ENV
Rep By: Steven W. Silver

Koyo Corp. of U.S.A.

Westlake, OH

Outside Counsel/Consultants

Arter & Hadden
Rep By: Jon W. Plebani

Koyo Seiko Co., Ltd.

Osaka, JAPAN
Leg. Issues: TRD

Outside Counsel/Consultants

Powell, Goldstein, Frazer & Murphy LLP
Issues: TRD
Rep By: Michael E. Fine, Peter O. Suchman

The KPMG FSC Coalition

c/o Harry L. Gutman
KPMG
LLP
2001 M St. NW
Washington, DC 20036
E-mail: hgutman@KPMG.com
Tel: (202)533-3044
Fax: (202)533-8570
Leg. Issues: TAX

Outside Counsel/Consultants

KPMG, LLP
Issues: TAX
Rep By: Jennifer Bonar, Katherine M. Breaks, George Callas, Gail Galvan, Harry L. Gutman, Melbert E. Schwarz, Thomas A. Stout, Jr., Elizabeth Wagner

KPMG, LLP

2001 M St. NW
Washington, DC 20036
Tel: (202)467-3000
Fax: (202)533-8500
Registered: LDA
Web: www.kpmg.com
Leg. Issues: DEF, TAX, TRD

Political Action Committee/s

KPMG PAC
2001 M St. NW
Washington, DC 20036
Tel: (202)467-3000
Fax: (202)533-8500
Contact: Stephen Allis

In-house, DC-area Employees

ALLIS, Stephen: Partner
BONAR, Jennifer
BREAKS, Katherine M.: Associate
BROCKWAY, David
BROWN, Robert M.
CALLAS, George
GALVAN, Gail
GUTMAN, Harry L.: Partner
ROSENTHAL, Steven M.: Partner, Washington National Tax
ROSS, Frank K.: Managing Partner
SCHWARZ, Melbert E.
SLAWTER, Shannon E.
SMITH, Linden C.
SPOONER, Gillian: Partner, Washington National Tax
STIRRUP, John T.: Manager, Government Affairs
STOUT, Jr., Thomas A.
WAGNER, Elizabeth

Outside Counsel/Consultants

Hooper Owen & Winburn
Issues: TAX
Rep By: Steve Glaze, Lindsay D. Hooper, John P. Winburn

Mayer, Brown & Platt
Issues: TRD
Rep By: Carol J. Bilzi, Brian T. Borders, Mark H. Gitenstein, Jeffrey H. Lewis

Rhoads Group

The Spectrum Group
Issues: DEF
Rep By: Lt. Gen. Augustus Cianciolo, USA (Ret.), Gen. J. B. Davis, USAF (Ret.), RAdm. James B. Hinkle, USN (Ret.)

The Velasquez Group

KPVI

Pocatello, ID

Outside Counsel/Consultants

Drinker Biddle & Reath LLP

KQC Properties

Lewisville, NC

Outside Counsel/Consultants

Murray, Scheer, Montgomery, Tapia & O'Donnell
Rep By: D. Michael Murray

Kraft Foods, Inc.

1341 G St. NW
Ninth Floor
Washington, DC 20005
Tel: (202)637-1500
Fax: (202)637-1505
Registered: LDA
Web: www.philipmorris.com

Part of the Phillip Morris Companies, Inc.

Leg. Issues: AGR, BUD, FOO, TRD

In-house, DC-area Employees

NORRIS, Frances M.: V. President, Federal Government Affairs/Food
WESTFALL, Linda "Tuckie": Director, Federal Government Affairs/Food

Outside Counsel/Consultants

Cassidy & Associates, Inc.

Dittus Communications
Rep By: Gloria S. Dittus

Hogan & Hartson L.L.P.
Issues: FOO, TRD
Rep By: Timothy C. Stanceu

Leonard and Co.

Olsson, Frank and Weeda, P.C.
Issues: BUD, FOO
Rep By: John W. Bode, Susan P. Grymes, Karen Reis Harned, Stephen L. Lacey, Marshall L. Matz, Tyson Redpath, Ryan W. Stroschein

Policy Directions, Inc.
Issues: AGR, FOO
Rep By: Kathleen "Kay" Holcombe, Steve Kopperud, Frankie L. Trull

Krebs, LaSalle, LeMieux Consultants, Inc.

Metalce, LA
Leg. Issues: DIS

Outside Counsel/Consultants

Van Scoyoc Associates, Inc.
Issues: DIS
Rep By: Buzz Hawley, John C. "Jay" Stone, H. Stewart Van Scoyoc

Kronos, Inc.

Houston, TX

Outside Counsel/Consultants

Ottosen and Associates
Rep By: Karl J. Ottosen

Kruger Internat'l (KI)

Green Bay, WI
Leg. Issues: LAW

Outside Counsel/Consultants

Foley & Lardner
Issues: LAW
Rep By: Jerris Leonard, David Ralston, Jr.

KSGW-TV

Sheridan-Gillett, WY

Outside Counsel/Consultants

Shaw Pittman

KSL Development Corp.

La Quinta, CA

Outside Counsel/Consultants

Williams & Jensen, P.C.
Rep By: George D. Baker, J. Steven Hart, Frank C. Vlossak

KTTW-TV and KTTM-TV

Sioux Falls, SD

Outside Counsel/Consultants

Reddy, Begley, & McCormick, LLP
Rep By: Dennis F. Begley

KTTY

Chula Vista, CA

Outside Counsel/Consultants

Drinker Biddle & Reath LLP
Rep By: John P. Bankson, Jr.

KTUU

Anchorage, AK

Outside Counsel/Consultants

Shaw Pittman

KTVW-TV

Phoenix, AZ

Outside Counsel/Consultants

Shaw Pittman

Kuakini Hospital

Honolulu, HI

Outside Counsel/Consultants

Cassidy & Associates, Inc.
Rep By: Henry K. Giugni

Kurdistan Democratic Party - Iraq

1015 18th St. NW
Suite 704
Washington, DC 20036
Tel: (202)331-9505
Fax: (202)331-9506
Registered: FARA

In-house, DC-area Employees

BARZANI, Farhad: Representative

Kurdistan Democratic Party USA

Washington, DC
Leg. Issues: FOR

Outside Counsel/Consultants

O'Connor & Hannan, L.L.P.
Issues: FOR
Rep By: Hon. Thomas J. Corcoran, Frederick T. Dombo, Hon. James W. Symington

Kurdistan Regional Government

Kurdistan, IRAQ

Outside Counsel/Consultants

Nijyar H. Shemdin
Rep By: Nijyar H. Shemdin

Kuskokwim Corp.

Outside Counsel/Consultants

Dilworth Paxson, LLP

KUVN-TV

Garland, TX

Outside Counsel/Consultants

Shaw Pittman

Kuwait Information Office

KUWAIT

Outside Counsel/Consultants

Barton William Marcois
Rep By: Barton William Marcois

Kuwait, Government of

Safat, KUWAIT

Outside Counsel/Consultants

Cleary, Gottlieb, Steen and Hamilton
Rep By: Kenneth L. Bachman, Jr.

Kvaerner Shipholding, Inc.

Bridgewater, NJ
Leg. Issues: MAR

Outside Counsel/Consultants

Dyer Ellis & Joseph, P.C.
Issues: MAR
Rep By: Thomas M. Dyer, James B. Ellis, II, John Henderson

Kvaerner Philadelphia Shipyard Inc.

Philadelphia, PA
Leg. Issues: MAR

Outside Counsel/Consultants

Dyer Ellis & Joseph, P.C.
Issues: MAR
Rep By: Thomas M. Dyer, James B. Ellis, II, Jeanne Marie Grasso, John Graykauski, Lara Bernstein Mathews, R. Anthony Salgado, Duncan C. Smith, III, Jennifer M. Southwick

Kvaerner US Inc.

Bridgewater, NJ
Leg. Issues: FOR

Outside Counsel/Consultants

McDermott, Will and Emery
Issues: FOR
Rep By: Scott S. Megregian

KVCR-TV

San Bernardino, CA

Outside Counsel/Consultants

Tierney & Swift
Rep By: Richard F. Swift

KWEX-TV

San Antonio, TX

Outside Counsel/Consultants

Shaw Pittman

KXLN-TV

Rosenberg, TX

Outside Counsel/Consultants

Shaw Pittman

KXMA-TV

Dickinson, ND

Outside Counsel/Consultants

Shaw Pittman

KXMB

Bismarck, ND

Outside Counsel/Consultants

Shaw Pittman

KXMC-TV

Minot, ND

Outside Counsel/Consultants

Shaw Pittman

KXMD-TV

Williston, ND

Outside Counsel/Consultants

Shaw Pittman

KXTX-TV

Dallas, TX

Outside Counsel/Consultants

Shaw Pittman

Kyocera Corp.

Kyoto, JAPAN

An industrial ceramics manufacturer. U.S. office in San Diego, CA.

Leg. Issues: DEF, TRD

Outside Counsel/Consultants

Barnes & Thornburg
Issues: TRD
Rep By: Randolph J. Stayin

Global USA, Inc.
Issues: DEF
Rep By: Dr. Bohdan Denysyk

Howrey Simon Arnold & White
Rep By: Michael A. Hertzberg

Kyrgyzstan, Government of the Republic of

Bishkek, KYRGYZSTAN

Outside Counsel/Consultants

Washington World Group, Ltd.

Kyros & Cummins Associates

2445 M St. NW
Suite 260
Washington, DC 20037
E-mail: pkyros@aol.com
Tel: (202)342-0204
Fax: (202)337-0034
Registered: LDA

In-house, DC-area Employees

FALK, John M.: V. President
KYROS, Hon. Peter N.: President

Outside Counsel/Consultants

The Willard Group
Rep By: John M. Falk

L-3 Communications Corp.

New York, NY
Leg. Issues: BUD, DEF

Outside Counsel/Consultants

Baker, Donelson, Bearman & Caldwell, P.C.
Issues: BUD
Rep By: Linda Hall Daschle, Albert B. Randall

The Dutko Group, Inc.

The PMA Group
Issues: DEF
Rep By: Daniel Cunningham, Daniel E. Fleming, Kaylene Green, Gregory L. Hansen, Patrick Hiu, Joseph Littleton, Paul J. Magliocchetti, Briggs Shade, Kelli Short, Charles Smith, Thomas Veltri, Mark Waclawski

Robison Internat'l, Inc.
Issues: BUD, DEF
Rep By: Richard B. Ladd

L.A. Care Health Plan

Los Angeles, CA
Leg. Issues: MMM

Outside Counsel/Consultants

MARC Associates, Inc.
Issues: MMM
Rep By: Edwin Allen, Daniel C. Maldonado

L.L. Capital Partners, Inc.

New York, NY
Leg. Issues: TOB

Outside Counsel/Consultants

Akin, Gump, Strauss, Hauer & Feld, L.L.P.
Issues: TOB
Rep By: Smith W. Davis, Frank J. Donatelli

LA I Coalition

Thibodaux, LA
Leg. Issues: TRA

Outside Counsel/Consultants

Patton Boggs, LLP
Issues: TRA
Rep By: Philip A. Bangert, James A. Reeder

LA Center for the Blind

Ruston, LA
Leg. Issues: BUD

Outside Counsel/Consultants

Jones, Walker, Waechter, Poitevent, Carrere & Denegre, L.L.P.
Issues: BUD
Rep By: Paul Cambon, John J. Jaskot, R. Christian Johnsen

La Quinta Inns, Inc.

San Antonio, TX
Leg. Issues: TAX

Outside Counsel/Consultants

Williams & Jensen, P.C.
Issues: TAX
Rep By: Robert E. Glennon, Jr.

La Rabida Children's Hospital Research Center

Chicago, IL
Leg. Issues: HCR

Outside Counsel/Consultants

Health Policy Strategies
Issues: HCR
Rep By: Ann Langley

La Sen, Inc.

Las Cruces, NM
Leg. Issues: TRA

Outside Counsel/Consultants

Peter J. Rose
Issues: TRA
Rep By: Peter J. Rose

Labor Council for Latin American Advancement (LCLAA)

815 16th St. NW
Suite 310
Washington, DC 20006
Web: www.lclaa.org
Tel: (202)347-4223
Fax: (202)347-5095

A Hispanic trade union association representing about 40 unions in 80 chapters throughout the country. Linked to the AFL-CIO in working for voter registration, education and participation by Hispanic workers.

Leg. Issues: CIV, ECN, EDU, FAM, FOR, GOV, HCR, HOU, IMM, LBR, MMM, RET, TRD, URB, WEL

In-house, DC-area Employees

POLANKO, Anna: Assistant Director
SANCHEZ, Oscar: Exec. Director

Labor for America PAC

P.O. Box 18206
Washington, DC 20036
Tel: (202)861-9700
Fax: (202)861-9711

Phone and fax number given are those of Butsavage & Associates, P.C.

In-house, DC-area Employees

BUTSAVAGE, Carey R.: Treasurer

Outside Counsel/Consultants

Butsavage & Associates, P.C.
Rep By: Carey R. Butsavage

Labor Management Maritime Committee, Inc.

1150 17th St. NW
Suite 700
Washington, DC 20036
Tel: (202)955-5662
Fax: (202)872-0912
Registered: LDA

Established in 1950. Seeks to promote a vigorous U.S. merchant marine. Composed of a labor group called the AFL-CIO Maritime Committee and of steamship lines in both the liner and bulk trades.

Leg. Issues: BUD, MAR

In-house, DC-area Employees

SIMPKINS, Talmage E.: Exec. V. President

Outside Counsel/Consultants

William V. Brierre
Issues: MAR
Rep By: William V. Brierre, Jr.

Labor Policy Ass'n (LPA)

1015 15th St. NW
Suite 1200
Washington, DC 20005
Tel: (202)789-8670
Fax: (202)789-0064
Registered: LDA

Organized in 1939; includes 235 major U.S. companies interested in the development and implementation of the nation's human resource and labor-management relations policies; conducts extensive research and analysis of pending federal legislative issues.

Leg. Issues: LBR

In-house, DC-area Employees

EASTMAN, Michael J.: Director of Government Relations
MCGUINESS, Jeffrey C.: President

Outside Counsel/Consultants

McGuiness Norris & Williams, LLP
Rep By: Timothy J. Bartl, Michael J. Eastman, Amy Habib, Jeffrey C. McGuiness, G. John Tysse, Daniel V. Yager

Labor-Industry Coalition for Internat'l Trade

Washington, DC
Registered: LDA

A coalition of major industrial companies and labor organizations. Seeks trade policy changes and other measures to help U.S. industry to compete more effectively against foreign industry.

Leg. Issues: TRD

Outside Counsel/Consultants

Dewey Ballantine LLP
Issues: TRD
Rep By: John R. Magnus, Kevin M. O'Connor, Alan W. Wolff

Laborers Health & Safety Fund

Washington, DC
Leg. Issues: BUD, HCR, LBR

Outside Counsel/Consultants

Connerton & Ray
Issues: HCR
Rep By: Alan Kadrofske, David L. Mallino, Sr., David L. Mallino, Jr.

Mallino Government Relations
Issues: BUD, HCR, LBR
Rep By: David L. Mallino, Sr.

Laborers Institute for Training and Education

Washington, DC

Outside Counsel/Consultants

Connerton & Ray
Rep By: Alan Kadrofske, David L. Mallino, Sr.

Laborers' Internat'l Union of North America

905 16th St. NW
Washington, DC 20006
Web: www.liuna.org
Tel: (202)737-8320
Fax: (202)737-2754
Registered: LDA

Leg. Issues: EDU, ENV, LBR, POS, TAX, TRA

Political Action Committee/s

Laborers' Political League
905 16th St. NW
Washington, DC 20006
Contact: Donald Kaniewski
Tel: (202)737-8320
Fax: (202)737-2754

In-house, DC-area Employees

BEARSE, Michael: General Counsel
BLACKLOW, Roger: National Political Coordinator
BOGGS, Michael D.: Director, International Affairs
COIA, Arthur A.: General President
FISHER, Linda L.: Director, Public Affairs
KANIEWSKI, Donald: Legislative and Political Director
LEVI, Gerron: Legislative Representative
O'SULLIVAN, Terence M.: Staff Assistant to the General President

Outside Counsel/Consultants

The Kamber Group
Rep By: Pamela Greenwalt, Victor S. Kamber

Mallino Government Relations
Issues: LBR
Rep By: David L. Mallino, Sr.

Laborers-AGC Education and Training Fund

Pomfret Center, CT
Leg. Issues: BUD, ENV, LBR, WAS

Outside Counsel/Consultants

Connerton & Ray
Issues: ENV, LBR, WAS
Rep By: Alan Kadrofske, David L. Mallino, Jr., David L. Mallino, Sr.

Mallino Government Relations
Issues: BUD, ENV, LBR
Rep By: David L. Mallino, Sr.

Laborers-Employers Cooperation & Education Trust

905 16th St. NW
Washington, DC 20006
Web: www.lecet.org
Tel: (202)783-3545
Fax: (202)347-1721
Registered: LDA

Leg. Issues: LBR, TRA, WAS

In-house, DC-area Employees

DAVIS, Steven M.: Marketing Representative
ENGQUIST, Christopher P.: Exec. Director
GANNON, Leo J.: Legislative Director

Outside Counsel/Consultants

Connerton & Ray
Issues: LBR
Rep By: David L. Mallino, Sr., David L. Mallino, Jr., Phillis Payne

Mallino Government Relations
Issues: LBR
Rep By: David L. Mallino, Sr.

Lac du Flambeau Chippewa Tribe

Lac du Flambeau, MI

Outside Counsel/Consultants

Sonosky, Chambers, Sachse & Endreson

LACDA Alliance

Los Angeles, CA
Leg. Issues: ENV, GOV

Outside Counsel/Consultants

Peyser Associates, Inc.
Issues: ENV, GOV
Rep By: Thane Young

Lackawanna Junior College

Scranton, PA
Leg. Issues: EDU

Outside Counsel/Consultants

William M. Cloherty
Issues: EDU
Rep By: William M. Cloherty

Laclede Gas Co.

St. Louis, MO

Outside Counsel/Consultants

Bryan Cave LLP
Rep By: Mark N. Ludwig, James J. Murphy

LADECO

Santiago, CHILE

Outside Counsel/Consultants

Zuckert, Scoutt and Rasenberger, L.L.P.
Rep By: Charles J. Simpson, Jr.

Ladies Professional Golf Ass'n

Outside Counsel/Consultants

Cohn & Wolfe

Lafarge Corp.

12950 Worldgate Dr.
Suite 500
Herndon, VA 20170
Web: www.lafarge.com
Tel: (703)480-3600
Fax: (703)796-2214
Registered: LDA

A producer of construction materials including cement, ready-mix concrete, and gypsum wall board.

Leg. Issues: BUD, CAW, ENV, LBR, MAN, TRA, TRD, WAS

Political Action Committee/s

Lafarge PAC
12950 Worldgate Dr.
Suite 500
Herndon, VA 20170
Contact: David W. Carroll
Tel: (703)480-3600
Fax: (703)796-2214

In-house, DC-area Employees

CARROLL, David W.: V. President, Environment, Health and Safety and Public Affairs

Outside Counsel/Consultants

Alpine Group, Inc.
Issues: BUD, CAW, ENV, TRA, TRD, WAS
Rep By: James Gregory Means

Jefferson Government Relations, L.L.C.
Issues: LBR
Rep By: Robert D. McArver, Jr., Randal P. Schumacher

O'Connor & Hannan, L.L.P.
Issues: MAN
Rep By: Hon. Larry Pressler

Lafayette Airport Commission

Lafayette, LA
Leg. Issues: AVI, BUD

Outside Counsel/Consultants

Adams and Reese LLP
Issues: AVI, BUD
Rep By: B. Jeffrey Brooks, Hon. James A. "Jimmy" Hayes

Lafayette Consolidated Government

Lafayette, LA
Leg. Issues: BUD, TRA

Outside Counsel/Consultants

Murray, Scheer, Montgomery, Tapia & O'Donnell
Issues: BUD, TRA
Rep By: Thomas R. Crawford, D. Michael Murray, Mark Zelden

Laguna Beach, California, City of

Leg. Issues: BUD, CAW, ENG

Outside Counsel/Consultants

E. Del Smith and Co.
Issues: BUD, CAW, ENG
Rep By: Margaret Allen, E. Del Smith

Laguna Industries, Inc.

Laguna, NM
Leg. Issues: DEF

Outside Counsel/Consultants

The PMA Group
Issues: DEF
Rep By: Daniel E. Fleming, Kaylene Green, Paul J. Magliocchetti, Mark Waclawski

Laguna Woods, California, City of

Laguna Woods, CA
Leg. Issues: ENV, HCR

Outside Counsel/Consultants

Hogan & Hartson L.L.P.
Issues: ENV, HCR
Rep By: C. Michael Gilliland, Christine M. Warnke

Laguna, New Mexico, City of

Laguna, NM

Outside Counsel/Consultants

The PMA Group
Rep By: Daniel E. Fleming, Kaylene Green, Paul J. Magliocchetti

Lake Carriers Ass'n

Cleveland, OH

A Great Lakes shipping company.

Leg. Issues: TRA

Outside Counsel/Consultants

Preston Gates Ellis & Rouvelas Meeds LLP
Issues: TRA
Rep By: Susan B. Geiger, Mark H. Ruge

Lake Charles Memorial Hospital

Lake Charles, LA
Leg. Issues: BUD

Outside Counsel/Consultants

Cassidy & Associates, Inc.
Issues: BUD
Rep By: W. Campbell Kaufman, IV

Lake County Basin 2000

Portland, OR
Leg. Issues: CAW

Outside Counsel/Consultants

E. Del Smith and Co.
Issues: CAW
Rep By: E. Del Smith

Lake Preservation Coalition

Devils Lake, ND

A non-profit citizen's conservation group.

Outside Counsel/Consultants

The Gregory Co.
Rep By: Neal Gregory

Lake Worth Drainage District

Delray Beach, FL
Leg. Issues: ENV

Outside Counsel/Consultants

Policy Impact Communications
Issues: ENV
Rep By: Benena Schulte

Lake, California, County of

Lakeport, CA
Leg. Issues: BUD, POS, RES, ROD, TRA, URB

Outside Counsel/Consultants

Alcalde & Fay
Issues: BUD, POS, RES, ROD, TRA, URB
Rep By: Paul Schlesinger, Tim Stroud

Lake, Illinois, County of

Waukegan, IL
Leg. Issues: BUD, CAW, ENV, LAW, NAT, ROD, TRA, URB

Outside Counsel/Consultants

The Ferguson Group, LLC
Issues: BUD, CAW, ENV, LAW, NAT, ROD, TRA, URB
Rep By: Trent Lehman, Leslie Waters Mozingo

Lakeland Regional Medical Center

Leg. Issues: BUD, HCR

Outside Counsel/Consultants

Arent Fox Kintner Plotkin & Kahn, PLLC
Issues: BUD, HCR
Rep By: Stacy Harbison, Douglas McCormack

Laker Airways (Bahamas) Ltd.

Miami, FL

Outside Counsel/Consultants

Pierre E. Murphy Law Offices
Rep By: Pierre E. Murphy

Lamaze Internat'l

Washington, DC
Web: www.lamaze.com
E-mail: lamaze@dc.sba.com

A non-profit organization consisting of professional, provider, and family coalition members whose purpose is to promote an optimal childbirth and early-parenting experience for families through education, advocacy, and reform.

Outside Counsel/Consultants

Smith, Bucklin and Associates, Inc.
Rep By: Linda Harmon

Lambert-St. Louis Internat'l Airport

St. Louis, MO
Leg. Issues: AVI, TRA

Outside Counsel/Consultants

Bracy Williams & Co.
Issues: AVI, TRA
Rep By: James P. Brown

Clay and Associates
Issues: AVI, TRA
Rep By: Michelle C. Clay

Lan Chile

Santiago, CHILE

Outside Counsel/Consultants

Zuckert, Scoutt and Rasenberger, L.L.P.
Rep By: Charles J. Simpson, Jr.

Lana'i Co.

Lana'i City, HI
Leg. Issues: BUD, TRD

Outside Counsel/Consultants

Schramm, Williams & Associates, Inc.
Issues: BUD, TRD
Rep By: Anita Brown, Robert Schramm

Lancaster, California, City of

Leg. Issues: ENV, TRA, URB

Outside Counsel/Consultants

Patton Boggs, LLP
Issues: ENV, TRA
Rep By: Philip A. Bangert

Tongour Simpson Holsclaw Green
Issues: URB
Rep By: Michael A. Tongour

Lancit Media/Junior Net

New York, NY
Leg. Issues: BUD, COM, EDU, TEC

Outside Counsel/Consultants

Convergence Services, Inc.
Issues: BUD, COM, EDU, TEC
Rep By: John M. Lawson

Land Grant Development

San Diego, CA
Leg. Issues: RES, TRA

Outside Counsel/Consultants

Manatt, Phelps & Phillips, LLP
Issues: RES, TRA
Rep By: Eric Farnsworth, James R. Jones, Robert J. Kabel

Land Mine Detection Systems, Inc.

Washington, DC
Leg. Issues: DEF

Outside Counsel/Consultants

Cannon Consultants, Inc.
Issues: DEF
Rep By: Charles A. Cannon

Land Trust Alliance

1331 H St. NW
Suite 400
Washington, DC 20005-4711
Web: www.lta.org
E-mail: lta@lta.org
Tel: (202)638-4725
Fax: (202)638-4730

Dedicated to advancing the voluntary conservation of land resources through local and regional non-profit land conservation groups, known as land trusts. Provides services to land trusts, supports land conservation policies, and works to educate a broad constituency on the consequences of diminishing land resources and the role of land trusts in saving land.

Leg. Issues: NAT, RES, TAX

In-house, DC-area Employees
HOCKER, Jean: President
SHAY, Russell: Director, Public Policy

Outside Counsel/Consultants
Covington & Burling
Issues: TAX
Rep By: Roderick A. DeArment
The Renkes Group, Ltd.
Issues: RES
Rep By: Gregg D. Renkes

Landis, NJ Sewerage Authority
Leg. Issues: BUD

Outside Counsel/Consultants
Reed, Smith, LLP
Issues: BUD
Rep By: Christopher L. Rissetto

Landmark Legal Foundation Center for Civil Rights
445-B Carlisle Dr.
Herndon, VA 20170
Tel: (703)689-2370
Fax: (703)689-2373
Web: www.landmarklegal.org

Public interest law firm promoting the fair market, education choice, resident management of public housing, fair taxation and property rights.

In-house, DC-area Employees
CHRISTENSEN, Eric: V. President, Development and Communications
LEVIN, Mark R.: President

Landmark Medical Center
Woonsocket, RI Registered: LDA

Outside Counsel/Consultants
Capitol City Group
Rep By: Gerald T. Harrington, John J. Hogan, Thomas P. Hogan, Christopher P. Vitale

Landmine Survivors
Leg. Issues: BUD

Outside Counsel/Consultants
Arent Fox Kintner Plotkin & Kahn, PLLC
Issues: BUD
Rep By: Stacy Harbison, Douglas McCormack

Landscape Architecture Foundation
636 I St. NW
Washington, DC 20001
Tel: (202)216-9034
Fax: (202)292-1185
Web: www.asla.org/asla/

In-house, DC-area Employees
EVERETT, Susan: Exec. Director

Lane Transit District
Eugene, OR
A public transit authority.
Leg. Issues: BUD, TRA

Outside Counsel/Consultants
Smith Dawson & Andrews, Inc.
Issues: BUD, TRA
Rep By: Thomas C. Dawson, Sherri Powar, James P. Smith

Lane, Oregon, County of
Eugene, OR
Leg. Issues: BUD, CAW, DEF, LAW

Outside Counsel/Consultants
Smith Dawson & Andrews, Inc.
Issues: BUD, CAW, DEF, LAW
Rep By: Sherri Powar, James P. Smith

The Lansdale Company
Seal Beach, CA

Outside Counsel/Consultants
Haake and Associates
Rep By: Timothy M. Haake, Nathan M. Olsen

Lansing, Michigan, Department of Social Services of the City of
Lansing, MI

Outside Counsel/Consultants
Covington & Burling

Lao Progressive Institute
Providence, RI
Leg. Issues: FOR

Outside Counsel/Consultants
Philip S. Smith & Associates, Inc.
Issues: FOR
Rep By: Chia Kue, Lisa Kue, Philip S. Smith

Lao Veterans of America, Inc.
Fresno, CA
Leg. Issues: FOR, IMM, TRD, VET

Outside Counsel/Consultants
Philip S. Smith & Associates, Inc.
Issues: FOR, IMM, TRD, VET
Rep By: Chia Kue, Lisa Kue, Philip J. Smith, Jr., Philip S. Smith

LAPA (Lineas Aereas Privadas, S.A.)
Buenos Aires, ARGENTINA

Outside Counsel/Consultants
Pierre E. Murphy Law Offices
Rep By: Pierre E. Murphy

Laquidara & Edwards, P.A.
Jacksonville, FL
A law firm.
Leg. Issues: TRA

Outside Counsel/Consultants
Patton Boggs, LLP
Issues: TRA
Rep By: Edward J. Newberry

The Lared Group
Los Angeles, CA

Outside Counsel/Consultants
Ashby and Associates
Rep By: R. Barry Ashby

Laredo, Texas, City of
Leg. Issues: BUD, COM, ECN, ENV, HOU, ROD, TEC, TRA, TRD

Outside Counsel/Consultants
Betty Ann Kane & Co.
Issues: BUD, COM, ECN, ENV, HOU, ROD, TRA, TRD
Rep By: Betty Ann Kane
Miller & Van Eaton, P.L.L.C.
Issues: TEC
Rep By: Betty Ann Kane, Nicholas P. Miller

Large Public Power Council
Austin, TX
A consortium of 21 state and local government-owned utilities in Arizona, California, Colorado, Florida, Georgia, Nebraska, South Carolina, Tennessee, Texas, Washington State, and Puerto Rico, including the municipal power departments of New York City and Los Angeles.
Leg. Issues: CAW, ENG, ENV, NAT, TAX, UTI, WAS

Outside Counsel/Consultants
Copeland, Lowery & Jacquez
Issues: TAX, UTI
Rep By: Hon. William D. Lowery
Van Ness Feldman, P.C.
Issues: CAW, ENV, NAT, TAX, UTI, WAS
Rep By: Howard J. Feldman, Stephen C. Fotis, Nancy Macan McNally, Robert Nordhaus
Washington Council Ernst & Young
Issues: ENG, TAX
Rep By: Doug Badger, Lauren Darling, John L. Doney, Jayne T. Fitzgerald, LaBrenda Garrett-Nelson, Gary J. Gasper, Bruce A. Gates, Nick Giordano, Cathy Koch, Robert J. Leonard, Richard Meltzer, Phillip D. Moseley, John D. Porter, Robert M. Rozen, Donna Steele-Flynn, Timothy J. Urban

Large Scale Biology
Vacaville, CA
Leg. Issues: DEF

Outside Counsel/Consultants
American Defense Internat'l, Inc.
Issues: DEF
Rep By: Michael Herson, Van D. Hipp, Jr., Dr. Ed Marcinik, Dave Wilberding

Las Cruces, New Mexico, City of
Leg. Issues: AVI, BUD, CAW, DEF, DIS, ECN, HOU, IMM, ROD, TRA, TRU, URB, UTI

Outside Counsel/Consultants
Meyers & Associates
Issues: AVI, BUD, CAW, DEF, DIS, ECN, HOU, IMM, ROD, TRA, TRU, URB, UTI
Rep By: Larry D. Meyers, Richard L. Meyers

Las Vegas Convention and Visitors Authority
Las Vegas, NV
Leg. Issues: TOU

Outside Counsel/Consultants
Alcalde & Fay
Issues: TOU
Rep By: Hon. James H. Bilbray, Julie Patterson, Christopher L. Turner

Las Vegas Paiute Tribe
Las Vegas, NV

Outside Counsel/Consultants
Dorsey & Whitney LLP
Rep By: David A. Bieging, Kevin J. Wadzinski

Las Vegas Valley Water District
Las Vegas, NV
Leg. Issues: NAT, RES

Outside Counsel/Consultants
Marcus G. Faust, P.C.
Issues: NAT, RES
Rep By: Marcus G. Faust

Las Vegas, Nevada, City of
Leg. Issues: ENG, HOU, TAX, TEC, TRA

Outside Counsel/Consultants
Ball Janik, LLP
Issues: ENG, HOU, TAX, TEC, TRA
Rep By: M. Victoria Cram

Las Vegas/McCarran Internat'l Airport
Las Vegas, NV
Leg. Issues: AVI

Outside Counsel/Consultants
Global Aviation Associates, Ltd.
Issues: AVI
Rep By: Jon F. Ash, Charles R. Chambers

Las Virgenes Municipal Water District
Calabasas, CA
Leg. Issues: BUD, NAT

Outside Counsel/Consultants
ENS Resources, Inc.
Issues: BUD, NAT
Rep By: Eric Sapirstein

Lason, Inc.
Troy, MI
Leg. Issues: GOV

Outside Counsel/Consultants
Reed, Smith, LLP
Issues: GOV
Rep By: Phillips S. Peter, C. Stevens Seale

Latham & Watkins
555 11th St. NW
Suite 1000
Washington, DC 20004
Tel: (202)637-2200
Fax: (202)637-2201
Registered: LDA, FARA
Web: www.lw.com
Leg. Issues: DIS

In-house, DC-area Employees
ALLARD, Nicholas W.: Partner
BABBITT, Bruce E.: Of Counsel
BAER, Teresa D.: Counsel
BEASLEY, Vicky
BERNTHAL, Eric L.: Managing Partner
BOYLE, Kevin Charles: Partner
BRINKMAN, Karen
CAMERON, Richard
CORREIA, Edward
EPSTEIN, Gary M.: Partner
GRIGSBY, McGee: Partner
HAYES, David J.: Partner
HOLMSTEAD, Jeff: Partner
KELLY, Jr., William C.: Partner
KURLANDER, Stuart: Partner
LEIVE, David M.: Senior Communications Counsel
MAHONEY, Maureen E.: Partner
MANTHEI, John R.: Senior Associate
MORTON, Andrew
SUSSMAN, Robert M.: Partner
VANDENBERGH, Michael P.: Counsel
WELLFORD, W. Harrison: Partner
WINIK, Peter L.: Partner

Outside Counsel/Consultants
Copeland, Lowery & Jacquez
Issues: DIS
Rep By: Jeffrey S. Shockey

Latino Strategies

Outside Counsel/Consultants

U.S. Strategies Corp.

Latona Associates, Inc.

Hampton, NH
Leg. Issues: RES, TAX

Outside Counsel/Consultants

Hooper Owen & Winburn
Issues: RES
Rep By: Hon. Charles Wilson

PriceWaterhouseCoopers
Issues: TAX
Rep By: Kenneth J. Kies, Don R. Longano

Lau Technologies

Littleton, MA
Leg. Issues: GOV, SCI

Outside Counsel/Consultants

Morris J. Amitay, P.C.
Issues: SCI
Rep By: Morris J. Amitay

Hale and Dorr LLP
Issues: GOV
Rep By: Jay P. Urwitz

Law Enforcement Alliance of America

7700 Leesburg Pike
Suite 421
Falls Church, VA 22043
Web: www.leaa.org
E-mail: leaa.steve@erols.com
Tel: (703)847-2677
Fax: (703)556-6485

A non-profit, non-partisan membership association comprised of law enforcement professionals, victims of crime and other private citizens. Seeks criminal justice reform which "puts victims' rights above criminals' rights" and opposes what it considers to be "restrictive" gun control legislation which infringes the Second Amendment rights of law-abiding citizens.

Leg. Issues: FIR, LAW

In-house, DC-area Employees

CHAPMAN, John: President
DEEDS, Ted: Director, Operations
FOTIS, James J.: Exec. Director
GRIFFITH, Laura: Director, Federal Legislative
WATSON, Kevin: Special Projects Coordinator

Law Enforcement Steering Committee

317 S. Patrick St.
Alexandria, VA 22314
Tel: (703)519-0300
Fax: (703)519-0311

A non-partisan coalition of national law enforcement associations, representing over 500,000 police practitioners. Advances legislation and policy that will ensure the safety of citizens and officers. The Chair of the committee is on a rotation.

In-house, DC-area Employees

DONNELLAN, Christopher M.

Law Office of Zel E. Lipsen

One Massachusetts Ave. NW
Suite 330
Washington, DC 20001
Tel: (703)448-3060
Fax: (703)448-3060
Registered: LDA, FARA
Leg. Issues: DEF, ENG, ENV, TRA

In-house, DC-area Employees

EMANUEL, Adam
LIPSEN, Zel E.: Principal

Outside Counsel/Consultants

Pacquing Consulting Inc.
Issues: DEF, ENG, ENV, TRA
Rep By: Juliet Pacquing

Bob Lawrence & Associates

Alexandria, VA
Leg. Issues: BUD, ENG, FUE, IMM, SCI

Outside Counsel/Consultants

Katherine Hamilton
Issues: BUD, ENG, FUE, SCI
Rep By: Katherine Hamilton

Morgan, Lewis & Bockius LLP
Issues: IMM

Lawton/Fort Sill Chamber of Commerce & Industry

Lawton, OK
Leg. Issues: BUD, DEF, GOV, VET

Outside Counsel/Consultants

VSAdc.com
Issues: BUD, DEF, GOV, VET
Rep By: J. R. Reskovac

Lawyers Alliance for World Security

1901 Pennsylvania Ave. NW
Suite 201
Washington, DC 20006
Web: www.lawscns.org
E-mail: info@lawscns.org
Tel: (202)745-2450
Fax: (202)667-0444

A national, non-partisan membership organization of legal professionals dedicated to stopping unrestrained weapons proliferation and bringing the rule of law to the newly independent nations of the former Soviet Union.

In-house, DC-area Employees

GRAHAM, Jr., Thomas: President and Ambassador
SCHLEFER, Mark: Chairman
SLESAR, Alex: Director of Administration

Lawyers Committee for Human Rights

100 Maryland Ave. NE
Suite 500
Washington, DC 20002
Web: www.lchr.org
E-mail: wdc@lchr.org
Tel: (202)547-5692
Fax: (202)543-5999

An independent non-profit, nongovernmental human rights organization. Headquartered in New York, NY.

Leg. Issues: CIV, FOR, IMM

In-house, DC-area Employees

MASSIMINO, Elisa: Director, Washington Office

Lawyers for Civil Justice

1140 Connecticut Ave.
Suite 503
Washington, DC 20036
Tel: (202)429-0045
Fax: (202)429-6982
Registered: LDA

A group of defense trial lawyers, manufacturers, insurers and trade associations seeking tort reform legislation to protect companies against unfair product liability claims. Members include AT&T, Exxon, General Motors, Ford, and Pfizer. Associations included are the Internat'l Ass'n of Defense Counsel, the Federation of Insurance and Corporate Counsel and the Defense Research Institute.

Leg. Issues: MAN, TOR

In-house, DC-area Employees

BAUMAN, Barry H.: Exec. Director

Lawyers for the Republic

1020 19th St. NW
Suite 400
Washington, DC 20036
Tel: (202)331-9100
Fax: (202)331-9060

A non-profit group providing information and advice on election issues, including redistricting.

In-house, DC-area Employees

FREER, Jr., Robert E.: Principal Activist

Lawyers' Committee for Civil Rights Under Law

1401 New York Ave. NW
Suite 400
Washington, DC 20005
Web: www.lawyerscommittee.com
Tel: (202)662-8600
Fax: (202)783-0857

A national non-profit organization that works for the elimination of discrimination in areas of education, employment and voting rights through litigation in the courts under constitutional and civil rights laws.

In-house, DC-area Employees

ARNWINE, Barbara R.: Exec. Director
HENDERSON, Thomas J.: Deputy Director for Litigation
SEYMOUR, Richard T.: Director, Employment Discrimination Project
STILL, Edward: Director, Voting Rights Project

LC Technologies

9455 Silver King Ct.
Fairfax, VA 22031
Web: www.igaze.com
E-mail: info@igaze.com
Tel: (703)385-7133
Fax: (703)385-7137
Leg. Issues: BUD, SCI, TRA

In-house, DC-area Employees

CLEVELAND, Nancy: Medical Coordinator

Outside Counsel/Consultants

McClure, Gerard & Neuenschwander, Inc.
Issues: BUD, SCI, TRA
Rep By: Tod O. Neuenschwander

LCOR, Inc.

Berwyn, PA
Leg. Issues: RES

Outside Counsel/Consultants

Arter & Hadden
Issues: RES
Rep By: Daniel L. Cohen

The Washington Group
Issues: RES
Rep By: Rita M. Lewis, G. John O'Hanlon, John D. Raffaelli

LDMI Telecommunications, Inc.

Hamtranck, MI
Leg. Issues: TEC

Outside Counsel/Consultants

Greenberg Traurig, LLP
Issues: TEC
Rep By: Mitchell F. Brecher

LDW, Inc.

Bensalem, PA
Leg. Issues: TAX, TEC

Outside Counsel/Consultants

Blank Rome Comisky & McCauley, LLP
Issues: TAX, TEC
Rep By: David A. Norcross, Rebecca F. South

Le Groupe de Soleil

Montreal, CANADA

Outside Counsel/Consultants

Paul, Weiss, Rifkind, Wharton & Garrison
Rep By: Terence J. Fortune

Le Meilleur Co., Ltd.

Seoul, KOREA
Leg. Issues: DEF

Outside Counsel/Consultants

American Defense Internat'l, Inc.
Issues: DEF
Rep By: Michael Herson, Van D. Hipp, Jr., Dave Wilberding

Lea County Electric Cooperative, Inc.

Lovington, NM

Outside Counsel/Consultants

Duncan, Weinberg, Genzer & Pembroke, P.C.
Rep By: Robert Weinberg

Lead Industries Ass'n

New York, NY
Registered: LDA
Leg. Issues: ENV

Outside Counsel/Consultants

Nutter & Harris, Inc.
Issues: ENV
Rep By: Robert L. Harris

Leadership 2000

1625 K St. NW
Suite 210
Washington, DC 20006
Web: www.adaction.org
E-mail: l2k@adaction.org
Tel: (202)785-5980
Fax: (202)785-5969

Formerly known as Youth for Democratic Action, Leadership 2000 is the youth-oriented political action arm of Americans for Democratic Action. Main undertakings include a Summer Seminar Series on Capitol Hill; organizing students and youth for political action (including campaigns and grassroots lobbying); and an international exchange program.

In-house, DC-area Employees

STAHL, Rusty: V. Chairperson
WATSON, Jamal: National Chairperson

Leadership Conference on Civil Rights

1629 K St. NW
Suite 1010
Washington, DC 20006
Web: www.civilrights.org
Tel: (202)466-3311
Fax: (202)466-3435
Registered: LDA

Founded in 1950, the Coalition consists of 185 national groups advocating equal opportunity for women, minorities, older Americans and persons with disabilities. Also includes religious, labor, gay and lesbian, civil liberties; and human rights organizations.

Leg. Issues: CIV, TEC

In-house, DC-area Employees

DANSKY, Becky: Research Assistant
HEIGHT, Dr. Dorothy I.: Chairperson
HENDERSON, Wade J.: Exec. Director
KOMAR, Brian: Legislative Analyst
LAWSON, Karen McGill: Policy Research Associate

Outside Counsel/Consultants

Leslie Harris & Associates
Issues: CIV, TEC
Rep By: Jill Bond, Leslie A. Harris, Aleck Johnson, Liza Kessler, Ghani Raines, Rachel Zwerin

Leadership for the Future

1722 I St. NW
Washington, DC 20006
Tel: (202)736-8000
Fax: (202)736-8711

In-house, DC-area Employees

NEMEROFF, Michael A.: Treasurer

Leadership PAC 2002

1199 N. Fairfax St.
Suite 425
Alexandria, VA 22314
Tel: (703)548-8621
Fax: (703)236-1949

Below address is that of the firm SEDERHOLM PUBLIC AFFAIRS, Inc.

In-house, DC-area Employees

CONNOR, Christopher
SEDERHOLM, Pamela

Outside Counsel/Consultants

SEDERHOLM Public Affairs, Inc.
Rep By: Pamela Sederholm

League of American Bicyclists

1612 K St. NW
Suite 401
Washington, DC 20006
Tel: (202)822-1333

In-house, DC-area Employees

WILLIAMS, Mele: Director, Government Relations

League of Arab States/Arab Information Center

1100 17th St. NW
Suite 602
Washington, DC 20036
E-mail: arableague@aol.com
Tel: (202)265-3210
Fax: (202)331-1525
Registered: FARA

In-house, DC-area Employees

AL-MTWALI, Mounthir: Information Officer
HASSOUNA, Dr. Hussein: Chief Representative

League of California Cities

Sacramento, CA
Leg. Issues: DIS, GOV, LAW, LBR, RES, TAX, TEC, TRA

Outside Counsel/Consultants

MARC Associates, Inc.
Issues: DIS, GOV, LAW, LBR, RES, TAX, TEC, TRA
Rep By: Eve O'Toole

League of Conservation Voters

1920 L St. NW
Suite 800
Washington, DC 20036
Web: www.lcv.org
E-mail: lcv@lcv.org
Tel: (202)785-8683
Fax: (202)835-0491
Registered: LDA

Established in 1970, LCV is the national, non-partisan arm of the environmental movement. LCV works to elect pro-environmental candidates to Congress. LCV publishes annual ratings of Congress based on key votes concerning energy, environment and natural resource issues. The votes are selected by leaders from major national environmental organizations.

Leg. Issues: ENV

Political Action Committee/s

League of Conservation Voters Political Action Committee
1920 L St. NW
Suite 800
Washington, DC 20036
Contact: Betsy Loyless
Tel: (202)785-8683
Fax: (202)835-0491

In-house, DC-area Employees

CALLAHAN, Debra J.: President
LOYLESS, Betsy: Political Director

League of Private Property Voters

1217 E St. NE
Washington, DC 20002
E-mail: alra-dc@access.digex.net
Tel: (202)544-6156
Fax: (202)547-7513

Publishes an annual report rating Congressmen on votes concerning private property issues.

In-house, DC-area Employees

GREFRATH, Bruce

League of Women Voters of the United States

1730 M St. NW
Suite 1000
Washington, DC 20036
Web: www.lwv.org
Tel: (202)429-1965
Fax: (202)429-0854
Registered: LDA

A voluntary, non-partisan, grassroots organization established in 1920 "to promote political responsibility through informed and active participation of citizens in government." The League now has over 130,000 members and supporters.

Leg. Issues: BUD, CAW, CIV, ENG, ENV, FOR, GOV, HCR, TRA

In-house, DC-area Employees

BROOKS, Mary E.: Senior Lobbyist
CEBALLOS, Kelly L.: Senior Director, Communications
LAWSON, Elizabeth: Senior Lobbyist
LEONARD, Lloyd J.: Legislative Director
TATE, Nancy E.: Exec. Director

Outside Counsel/Consultants

Hauser Group

Leap Wireless Internat'l

San Diego, CA
Leg. Issues: COM, TEC

Outside Counsel/Consultants

Baker, Donelson, Bearman & Caldwell, P.C.
Issues: COM, TEC
Rep By: J. Keith Kennedy

Latham & Watkins
Issues: COM, TEC
Rep By: Nicholas W. Allard

The Learning Disabilities Ass'n

Pittsburgh, PA
Leg. Issues: EDU

Outside Counsel/Consultants

Moss McGee Bradley & Foley
Issues: EDU
Rep By: Leander J. Foley, III

Learning Systems Internat'l

Outside Counsel/Consultants

Cook and Associates

Leather Industries of America

1000 Thomas Jefferson St. NW
Suite 515
Washington, DC 20007
Web: www.leatherusa.com
E-mail: info@leatherusa.com
Tel: (202)342-8086
Fax: (202)342-9063

Formerly the Tanners' Council of America.

Leg. Issues: TRD

In-house, DC-area Employees

BURT, Christine: Coordinator, Membership
FIRESTONE, Jean Ann: Communications Coordinator
MYERS, Charles: President

Outside Counsel/Consultants

Collier Shannon Scott, PLLC
Issues: TRD
Rep By: Lauren R. Howard

Lebanese American University

New York, NY
Leg. Issues: EDU

Outside Counsel/Consultants

Bannerman and Associates, Inc.
Issues: EDU
Rep By: M. Graeme Bannerman, Anne Hingeley, William A. Miner, Valerie A. Schultz, Curt Silvers, Tammy Sittnick

Lebanese Information and Research Center

P.O. 57263
Washington, DC 20037
E-mail: lirc@erols.com
Tel: (202)255-3106
Fax: (703)751-5327
Registered: FARA

Promotes the views of the "Lebanese Forces".

In-house, DC-area Employees

FARAH, Robert: Exec. Director

Lederle Laboratories

Madison, NJ

A subsidiary of American Home Products Corp.

Outside Counsel/Consultants

Covington & Burling

Wilmer, Cutler & Pickering
Rep By: Ronald J. Greene

Ledyard, Connecticut, Town of

Leg. Issues: NAT

Outside Counsel/Consultants

Perkins Coie LLP
Issues: NAT
Rep By: Guy R. Martin

Lee County Port Authority

Philadelphia, PA

A consulting firm.

Leg. Issues: AVI

Outside Counsel/Consultants

Hogan & Hartson L.L.P.
Issues: AVI
Rep By: E. Tazewell Ellett, C. Michael Gilliland, William Michael House

Lee County, Florida

Fort Myers, FL
Leg. Issues: BUD, NAT

Outside Counsel/Consultants

Marlowe and Co.
Issues: BUD, NAT
Rep By: Howard Marlowe

The Lee Group, Inc.

Outside Counsel/Consultants

The Dutko Group, Inc.

Leech Lake Tribal Council

Cass Lake, MN
Leg. Issues: IND

Outside Counsel/Consultants

Ducheneaux, Taylor & Associates, Inc.
Issues: IND
Rep By: Franklin D. Ducheneaux

Legal Action Center of the City of New York, Inc.

236 Massachusetts Ave. NE
Suite 505
Washington, DC 20002
E-mail: lacdc@lac-dc.org
Tel: (202)544-5478
Fax: (202)544-5712

A not-for-profit law and policy organization fighting discrimination against people with substance abuse problems, people with HIV/AIDS, people with criminal records, and expanding access to services.. Headquartered in New York, NY.

Leg. Issues: ALC, CIV, HCR, LAW

In-house, DC-area Employees

COLLIER, Jennifer: Director, National Policy

Legal Services Corp.

750 First St. NE
Suite 1000
Washington, DC 20002-4250
Web: www.lsc.gov
E-mail: hn35552@handsnet.org
Tel: (202)336-8800
Fax: (202)336-8959

A non-profit organization funded by the Congress to provide grants to legal service programs that provide attorneys for those who cannot afford private attorneys in civil cases.

In-house, DC-area Employees

FORTUNO, Victor M.: V. President and General Counsel
MCKAY, John: President
VIVERO, Mauricio: Director, Government Relations and Public Affairs

Legend Airlines

Dallas, TX

Outside Counsel/Consultants

Dittus Communications
Rep By: Gloria S. Dittus

The Legislative Strategies Group, LLC

1001 Pennsylvania Ave. NW
Suite 760 North
Washington, DC 20004
Tel: (202)661-7060
Fax: (202)661-7066
Registered: LDA

In-house, DC-area Employees

FRIEBERG, Ronna
GAVORA, Carrie J.: Health Policy Analyst
GOLD, Martin B.: Chairman
HENRY, Denise M.: Lobbyist

HILTON, Steven M.: Lobbyist
KOGOVSEK, Hon. Raymond P.
LITTIG, Melvin J.
MASON, G. David
SMITH, Larry E.: President
VOLJAVEC, Patricia Jarvis: Lobbyist
WINTERLING, Grayson

Outside Counsel/Consultants

Kogovsek & Associates
Rep By: Christine Ann Arbogast, Hon. Raymond P. Kogovsek

Legix Co.

Albuquerque, NM
A law and lobbying firm.

Leg. Issues: IND

Outside Counsel/Consultants

Manuel Lujan Associates
Issues: IND
Rep By: Lydia Hofer

Lehigh Coal & Navigation Co.

Pottsville, PA
Leg. Issues: DEF

Outside Counsel/Consultants

Whitten & Diamond
Issues: DEF
Rep By: Robert M. Diamond, Jamie L. Whitten

Lehigh Portland Cement Co.

Allentown, PA
Leg. Issues: ROD, TAX, TRD

Outside Counsel/Consultants

LegisLaw
Issues: ROD, TAX, TRD
Rep By: Linda A. Woolley, Esq.

Lehigh University

Bethlehem, PA
Leg. Issues: BUD, DEF, EDU, TRA

Outside Counsel/Consultants

Van Scoyoc Associates, Inc.
Issues: BUD, DEF, EDU, TRA
Rep By: Steve E. Crane, Kevin F. Kelly, H. Stewart Van Scoyoc

Lehigh-Northhampton Airport Authority

Allentown, PA
Leg. Issues: AVI

Outside Counsel/Consultants

Spiegel & McDiarmid
Issues: AVI
Rep By: John J. Corbett, Jr.

Lehman Brothers

800 Connecticut Ave. NW
Suite 1200
Washington, DC 20006
Tel: (202)452-4700
Fax: (202)452-4791
Registered: LDA

A leading securities and investment banking firm serving individual, institutional, corporate and governmental clients worldwide.

Leg. Issues: FIN, TAX

Political Action Committee/s

Action Fund of Lehman Brothers Holding Inc.
800 Connecticut Ave. NW
Suite 1200
Washington, DC 20006
Tel: (202)452-4720
Fax: (202)452-4791
Contact: Judith A. Winchester

In-house, DC-area Employees

WINCHESTER, Judith A.: Managing Director, Government Affairs

Outside Counsel/Consultants

O'Neill, Athy & Casey, P.C.
Issues: FIN
Rep By: Andrew Athy, Jr., Christopher R. O'Neill

Verner, Liipfert, Bernhard, McPherson and Hand, Chartered
Issues: TAX
Rep By: Andrew D. Eskin, Vicki E. Hart, Gary J. Klein, John A. Merrigan, Mikol S. Neilson

Lehn & Fink Products Group

Montvale, NJ

Outside Counsel/Consultants

Crowell & Moring LLP
Rep By: Dana C. Contratto

Lehtinen O'Donnell

Miami, FL
Leg. Issues: ENV, GOV, NAT

Outside Counsel/Consultants

Adams and Reese LLP
Issues: ENV, GOV, NAT
Rep By: D. Lee Forsgren, Hon. James A. "Jimmy" Hayes

Leisnoi

Anchorage, AK
Leg. Issues: IND

Outside Counsel/Consultants

Birch, Horton, Bittner & Cherot
Issues: IND
Rep By: Roy S. Jones, Jr.

Lennar Partners

Mission Viejo, CA
Leg. Issues: BUD

Outside Counsel/Consultants

The Ferguson Group, LLC
Issues: BUD
Rep By: William Ferguson, Jr.

Lennox Internat'l

Richardson, TX
Leg. Issues: BUD, ENG, ENV, TRD

Outside Counsel/Consultants

Genesis Consulting Group, LLC
Issues: BUD, TRD
Rep By: Mark Benedict, Dana DeBeaumont

Redfern Resources
Issues: ENG, ENV
Rep By: Ed Redfern

LEP Scientific Ltd.

London, UNITED KINGDOM

Outside Counsel/Consultants

Howrey Simon Arnold & White
Rep By: Michael A. Hertzberg

Leprino Foods Co.

Denver, CO
Registered: LDA
Leg. Issues: AGR

Outside Counsel/Consultants

Higgins, McGovern & Smith, LLC
Issues: AGR

Keller and Heckman LLP
Rep By: Richard J. Leighton, Richard F. Mann

Lesbian & Gay Community Center Hetrick-Martin Institute

Outside Counsel/Consultants

M & R Strategic Services
Rep By: Sylvia Hacaj

Lesotho, Embassy of The Kingdom Of

2511 Massachusetts Ave. NW
Washington, DC 20008
Tel: (202)797-5533
Fax: (202)234-6815

Outside Counsel/Consultants

Washington World Group, Ltd.
Rep By: Edward J. von Kloberg, III

Leucadia County Water District

Carlsbad, CA
Leg. Issues: BUD

Outside Counsel/Consultants

The Furman Group
Issues: BUD
Rep By: Thomas M. James

Leukemia & Lymphoma Soc.

5845 Richmond Hwy.
Suite 630
Alexandria, VA 22303-1870
Web: www.leukemia.org
Tel: (703)960-1100
Registered: LDA

Formerly the Luekemia Society of America.

Leg. Issues: BUD, HCR, MED, MMM

In-house, DC-area Employees

ARD, Jean: V. President, Government Affairs

Outside Counsel/Consultants

Bennett Turner & Coleman, LLP
Issues: BUD, HCR, MED, MMM
Rep By: Elizabeth Goss, Natasha Leskovsek, Kristi E. Schrode, Samuel D. Turner

Leukemia and Lymphoma Soc. of America

Outside Counsel/Consultants

Winston & Strawn
Rep By: Charles L. Kinney, Douglas C. Richardson

Level 3 Communications LLC

McLean, VA

Outside Counsel/Consultants

The Dutko Group, Inc.
Rep By: Peg Brown, Mark S. Irion, Deana Perlmutter

Sher & Blackwell
Rep By: Earl W. Comstock, Jeffrey R. Pike

Levi Strauss and Co.

San Francisco, CA
Leg. Issues: TAX

Outside Counsel/Consultants

Carlyle Consulting
Issues: TAX
Rep By: Thomas C. Rodgers

Levine-Fricke Restoration Corp.

Emeryville, CA
Leg. Issues: RES, TRA

Outside Counsel/Consultants

French & Company
Issues: RES, TRA
Rep By: Rebecca Dornbusch, Verrick O. French

Lou Levy & Sons Fashions, Inc.

New York, NY

Outside Counsel/Consultants

Davidoff & Malito, LLP
Rep By: Kenneth C. Malito, Robert J. Malito, Stephen J. Slade

Lew Horton Distributing Co.

Westboro, MA
Leg. Issues: FIR

Outside Counsel/Consultants

Law Offices of Mark Barnes
Issues: FIR
Rep By: Mark J. Barnes, Tammy Begun

Lewis and Clark College

Portland, OR
Leg. Issues: BUD, ECN

Outside Counsel/Consultants

Cassidy & Associates, Inc.
Issues: BUD, ECN
Rep By: Arthur D. Mason, Maureen Walsh, Gerald Felix Warburg

Lewis and Clark Rural Water System, Inc.

Sioux Falls, SD
A non-profit organization working to develop rural water supplies.

Leg. Issues: NAT

Outside Counsel/Consultants

John Freshman Associates, Inc.
Issues: NAT
Rep By: John D. Freshman, Lawrence P. Kast, Catherine B. Kiefer

Lexis-Nexis

Dayton, OH
Web: www.lexis-nexis.com
Leg. Issues: CPT, CSP, GOV, MIA

Outside Counsel/Consultants

Joseph L. Ebersole
Issues: CPT
Rep By: Joseph L. Ebersole

Piper Marbury Rudnick & Wolfe LLP
Issues: CPT, CSP, MIA
Rep By: Michael F. Brockmeyer, Emilio W. Cividanes, James J. Halpert, Stuart P. Ingis, Katharine A. Pauley, Ronald L. Plesser

Liz Robbins Associates
Issues: CPT, GOV
Rep By: Liz Robbins

Lexmark Internat'l

Lexington, KY
Leg. Issues: ENV

Outside Counsel/Consultants

Goodstein & Associates
Issues: ENV
Rep By: Richard F. Goodstein

Libbey, Inc.

Toledo, OH

A manufacturer of glass products.

Leg. Issues: TRD

Outside Counsel/Consultants

Stewart and Stewart
Issues: TRD
Rep By: Alan M. Dunn, David S. Johanson, Terence P. Stewart

Liberal Party of Japan

Tokyo, JAPAN
Leg. Issues: FOR

Outside Counsel/Consultants

Takashi Oka
Issues: FOR
Rep By: Mr. Takashi Oka

Liberia, Office of the President of the Republic of

Monrovia, LIBERIA

Outside Counsel/Consultants

Barron-Birrell, Inc.
Rep By: David H. Barron, Jeffrey C. Birrell

Liberty Check Printers

Mounds View, MN
Leg. Issues: BAN, TAX

Outside Counsel/Consultants

Bacino & Associates
Issues: BAN
Rep By: Geoff Bacino

White & Case LLP
Issues: TAX
Rep By: Linda E. Carlisle, J. Roger Mentz

Liberty Corp.

Greenville, SC

Outside Counsel/Consultants

Howrey Simon Arnold & White
Rep By: John F. Bruce

Liberty Lobby

300 Independence Ave. SE
Washington, DC 20003
Web: www.spotlight.org
Tel: (202)546-5611
Registered: LDA

Founded in 1955 by Willis A. Carto and a group of supporters in California. Describes itself as standing for "America-First constitutionalism," and a "populist" domestic policy and a "nationalist" foreign policy.

Leg. Issues: CON

In-house, DC-area Employees

ARNOLD, Andrew: Editor
PETHERICK, Chris: Editor

Liberty Maritime Co.

Lake Success, NY
Leg. Issues: MAR

Outside Counsel/Consultants

Fierce and Isakowitz
Issues: MAR
Rep By: Kathryn Braden, Donald L. Fierce, Mark W. Isakowitz

Winston & Strawn
Issues: MAR
Rep By: Robert M. Bor, Hon. James H. Burnley, IV, Lawrence I. Kiern, Charles L. Kinney, John C. Kirtland, Thomas L. Mills, Hon. John L. Napier, Constantine G. Papavizas, James T. Pitts, Douglas C. Richardson, John A. Waits, II

Liberty Medical Supply

Palm City, FL
Leg. Issues: HCR

Outside Counsel/Consultants

Shaw Pittman
Issues: HCR
Rep By: Bruce Fried

Liberty Mutual Insurance Group

Boston, MA
Registered: LDA
Leg. Issues: ENV, HCR

Outside Counsel/Consultants

Akin, Gump, Strauss, Hauer & Feld, L.L.P.
Issues: ENV, HCR
Rep By: Sean G. D'Arcy, Barney J. Skladany, Jr.

Liberty Science Center

Jersey City, NJ
Leg. Issues: BUD, SCI

Outside Counsel/Consultants

Cassidy & Associates, Inc.
Issues: BUD, SCI
Rep By: Laurie J. Adler, W. Campbell Kaufman, IV, Jeffrey Lawrence, Daniel J. McNamara, Michael Merola

Library Users of America

1155 15th St. NW
Suite 1004
Washington, DC 20005
Web: www.acb.org
E-mail: info@acb.org
Tel: (202)467-5081
Fax: (202)467-5805

An affiliate of the American Council of the Blind.

In-house, DC-area Employees

CRAWFORD, Charles
DOWNING, Winifred: President

Life and Health Insurance Foundation for Education

Outside Counsel/Consultants

BSMG Worldwide

Life Cell

Leg. Issues: DEF

Outside Counsel/Consultants

The PMA Group
Issues: DEF
Rep By: Kaylene Green, Patrick Hiu, Paul J. Magliocchetti, Charles Smith

Lifebridge Health

Baltimore, MD
Leg. Issues: BUD

Outside Counsel/Consultants

Cassidy & Associates, Inc.
Issues: BUD
Rep By: Gregory M. Gill, Dennis M. Kedzior, Michael Merola, Lyllett Wentworth

Lifecore Biomedical

Chaska, MN
Leg. Issues: HCR, MMM

Outside Counsel/Consultants

Jeffrey J. Kimbell & Associates
Issues: HCR, MMM

Lifeline

Groveport, OH

Outside Counsel/Consultants

Interface Inc.
Rep By: Albert B. Rosenbaum, III

LifeLink Foundation

Tampa, FL
Leg. Issues: HCR

Outside Counsel/Consultants

Davis O'Connell, Inc.
Issues: HCR
Rep By: Lynda C. Davis, Ph.D., Jennifer Golden

LifePoint Hospitals, Inc.

Brentwood, TN
Leg. Issues: MMM

Outside Counsel/Consultants

Greenberg Traurig, LLP
Issues: MMM
Rep By: Howard J. Cohen, Rob Garagiola, Russell J. Mueller, Nancy E. Taylor, Timothy P. Trysla

Liggett Group, Inc.

Durham, NC
Leg. Issues: TOB

Outside Counsel/Consultants

Brownstein Hyatt & Farber, P.C.
Issues: TOB
Rep By: William T. Brack, Michael B. Levy

Covington & Burling

Light Associates

Chicago, IL

Outside Counsel/Consultants

Nixon Peabody LLP
Rep By: Charles L. Edson, Stephen J. Wallace

Light of Life Ministries

Pittsburgh, PA
Leg. Issues: ALC, HOU, WEL

Outside Counsel/Consultants

Russ Reid Co.
Issues: ALC, HOU, WEL
Rep By: Thomas C. Keller, Mark D. McIntyre

Lighter Ass'n, Inc.

Washington, DC

Outside Counsel/Consultants

Thompson, Hine and Flory LLP
Rep By: David H. Baker

Lightguard Systems, Inc.

Leg. Issues: CSP, TRA

Outside Counsel/Consultants

The Da Vinci Group
Issues: CSP, TRA

Lignin Institute

1101 15th St. NW
Suite 202
Atlanta, GA 20005
Tel: (202)785-3232
Fax: (202)223-9741

In-house, DC-area Employees

CRISTOL, Richard E.: Washington Representative

Outside Counsel/Consultants

The Kellen Company
Rep By: Richard E. Cristol

Eli Lilly and Co.

555 12th St. NW
Suite 650
Washington, DC 20004-1205
Web: www.lilly.com
Tel: (202)393-7950
Fax: (202)393-7960
Registered: LDA

Leg. Issues: AGR, BUD, CPT, CSP, DEF, ENG, ENV, HCR, LBR, MAN, MMM, PHA, TAX, TOR, TRD, VET

In-house, DC-area Employees

BONITT, John E.: Director, Federal Affairs
BRANDT, Irene M.: Senior Government Affairs Associate
BUCKLEY, Richard: Manager, Federal Affairs
FILIPPONE, Desiree: Manager, International and Public Government Relations
HUNTINGTON, Erin B.: Manager, International and Public Government Relations
KAROL, Kathryn Dickey: Director, International and Public Government Relations
KELLEY, Joseph B.: Director, State Government Affairs
LINTHICUM, Kimberly: Sr. Associate, Federal Affairs
MIHALSKI, Edmund J.: Director, Federal Affairs
STEELMAN, Deborah: V. President, Corporate Affairs
STOWE, Ronald F.: V. President, Government Relations

Outside Counsel/Consultants

Albers & Co.
Issues: PHA
Rep By: William E. Albers, Daniel B. Beardsley, M. Guy Rohling

Bennett Turner & Coleman, LLP

Burson-Marsteller

Crowell & Moring LLP
Issues: CSP
Rep By: Victor E. Schwartz

The Direct Impact Co.

The Legislative Strategies Group, LLC
Issues: HCR
Rep By: Denise M. Henry

McDermott, Will and Emery
Issues: TAX
Rep By: Robert B. Harding

Ricchetti Inc.

The Limited Inc.

Columbus, OH
Leg. Issues: APP, CSP, LBR, POS, TAX, TRD

Outside Counsel/Consultants

James E. Boland
Issues: TAX, TRD
Rep By: James E. Boland, Jr.

C&M Internat'l, Ltd.
Issues: TRD
Rep By: Doral S. Cooper, Christopher Wilson

Downey McGrath Group, Inc.
Issues: LBR, TRD
Rep By: Nancy Donaldson, Hon. Thomas J. Downey, Jr., John Peter Olinger

Fontheim Partners, PC
Issues: APP, LBR, POS, TRD
Rep By: Claude G. B. Fontheim, Kenneth I. Levinson, D. Scott Nance

Mayer, Brown & Platt
Issues: TAX

John T. O'Rourke Law Offices
Issues: CSP, LBR, TAX, TRD
Rep By: John T. O'Rourke

Patton Boggs, LLP
Rep By: Penelope S. Farthing, Lansing B. Lee, III, Nancy A. Murray

Verner, Liipfert, Bernhard, McPherson and Hand, Chartered
Issues: TRD
Rep By: Andrea J. Grant, Hon. George J. Mitchell

Lincoln Airport

Lincoln, NE
Leg. Issues: RES

Outside Counsel/Consultants

Ungaretti & Harris
Issues: RES
Rep By: Edward P. Faberman

The Lincoln Group

Syracuse, NY

Outside Counsel/Consultants

Kaye Scholer LLP
Rep By: Jason Shrinsky

Lincoln Nat'l Corp.

1455 Pennsylvania Ave. NW
Suite 1260
Washington, DC 20004
E-mail: jmorrill2@lnc.com
Tel: (202)783-0350
Fax: (202)783-3332
Registered: LDA

Headquartered in Philadelphia, PA.

Leg. Issues: FIN, INS, TAX

Political Action Committee/s

LNC PAC
1455 Pennsylvania Ave. NW
Suite 1260
Washington, DC 20004
Tel: (202)783-0350
Fax: (202)783-3332

In-house, DC-area Employees

MORRILL, James A.: V. President and Director, Federal Relations

Outside Counsel/Consultants

Baker, Donelson, Bearman & Caldwell, P.C.
Issues: INS
Rep By: Francine Lamoriello, Joan M. McEntee

Davis & Harman LLP
Issues: TAX
Rep By: Richard S. Belas, Randolf H. Hardock, Barbara Groves Mattox

Lincoln Property Co.

Arlington, VA
Leg. Issues: RES

Outside Counsel/Consultants

Vinson & Elkins L.L.P.
Issues: RES
Rep By: Hon. Michael A. Andrews

Lincoln Pulp and Paper Co.

Lincoln, ME
Leg. Issues: CAW, NAT

Outside Counsel/Consultants

Leon G. Billings, Inc.
Issues: CAW, NAT
Rep By: Leon G. Billings

Lincoln, Nebraska, City of

Leg. Issues: ENV, HOU, TAX, TRA, URB

Outside Counsel/Consultants

Carolyn C. Chaney & Associates
Issues: ENV, HOU, TAX, TRA, URB
Rep By: Carolyn C. Chaney, Christopher F. Giglio

Lindesmith Center- Drug Policy Foundation

4455 Connecticut Ave. NW
Suite B500
Washington, DC 20008-2328
Web: www.drugpolicy.org
E-mail: drugpolicy@drugpolicy.org
Tel: (202)537-5005
Fax: (202)537-3007

A research and educational organization headquartered in New York, NY, that opposes the "war on drugs" and favors more pragmatic drug policies, such as the harm reduction policies employed in Europe and Australia.

Leg. Issues: ALC, EDU, HCR, LAW

In-house, DC-area Employees

LAMPI, Ruth: Director of Finance & Administration
MCCOLL, William D.: Director, Legislative Affairs

Lineas Aereas Costarricicenes (Lasca Airlines)

San Jose, COSTA RICA

Outside Counsel/Consultants

Squire, Sanders & Dempsey L.L.P.
Rep By: Robert D. Papkin, Edward W. Sauer

Link Plus Co.

Ellicott City, MD
Leg. Issues: SCI

Outside Counsel/Consultants

The Livingston Group, LLC
Issues: SCI
Rep By: Melvin Goodweather, Hon. Robert L. Livingston, Jr., J. Allen Martin, Richard L. Rodgers

Link Romania, Inc.

Washington, DC
Leg. Issues: ECN, FOR, TOU

Outside Counsel/Consultants

Dublin Castle Group
Issues: ECN, FOR, TOU
Rep By: Maureen Flatley Hogan

Lion Oil Co.

Jackson, MS

Outside Counsel/Consultants

Collier Shannon Scott, PLLC
Rep By: R. Timothy Columbus, Gregory M. Scott, Dana S. Wood

Liquid Metal Technologies

Tampa, FL
Leg. Issues: DEF

Outside Counsel/Consultants

Foley & Lardner
Issues: DEF
Rep By: Theodore H. Bornstein

Lister Bolt & Chain Co.

Richmond, CANADA
Leg. Issues: DEF, MAR

Outside Counsel/Consultants

Ervin Technical Associates, Inc. (ETA)
Issues: DEF, MAR
Rep By: William J. Andahazy, Hon. Jack Edwards, James L. Ervin, Donald E. Richbourg

Lithuania, Republic of

Vilnius, LITHUANIA

Outside Counsel/Consultants

Law Office of Paige E. Reffe
Rep By: Paige E. Reffe

Lithuanian American Council

Chicago, IL

Outside Counsel/Consultants

Washington World Group, Ltd.
Rep By: Edward J. von Kloberg, III

Little Havana Activities and Nutrition Centers

Miami, FL
Leg. Issues: BUD, WEL

Outside Counsel/Consultants

The MWW Group
Issues: BUD, WEL
Rep By: Dana P. Bostic, Davon Gray, Jonathan B. Slade

Little River Band of Ottawa Indians

Manistee, MI
Leg. Issues: IND

Outside Counsel/Consultants

Dorsey & Whitney LLP
Issues: IND
Rep By: Philip Baker-Shenk, David A. Bieging, Virginia W. Boylan, Cindy Darcy, Mark Jarboe, Sarah Ridley

Morriset, Schlosser, Ayer & Jozwiak

Little Traverse Bay Band of Odawa Indians

Petoskey, MI

Outside Counsel/Consultants

Morriset, Schlosser, Ayer & Jozwiak

Litton Advanced Systems

College Park, MD
Leg. Issues: AVI, BUD

Outside Counsel/Consultants

Smith Dawson & Andrews, Inc.
Issues: AVI, BUD
Rep By: Gregory B. Andrews, Thomas C. Dawson, Ray Warner

Litton Electro Optical Systems

Leg. Issues: BUD, DEF

Outside Counsel/Consultants

Bill Wight, LLC
Issues: BUD, DEF

Litton Electron Devices

San Carlos, CA

A manufacturer of defense and consumer electronics and electronics components.

Leg. Issues: BUD, DEF

Outside Counsel/Consultants

Bill Wight, LLC
Issues: BUD, DEF

Litton Integrated Systems

Agoura Hills, CA
Leg. Issues: BUD, DEF

Outside Counsel/Consultants

Bill Wight, LLC
Issues: BUD, DEF

Litton Laser Systems

Apopka, FL
Leg. Issues: BUD, DEF

Outside Counsel/Consultants

Bill Wight, LLC
Issues: BUD, DEF

Litton Life Support

Davenport, IA
Leg. Issues: DEF

Outside Counsel/Consultants

Peter J. Rose
Issues: DEF
Rep By: Peter J. Rose

Litton Systems, Inc.

College Park, MD
Leg. Issues: UTI

Outside Counsel/Consultants

Smith Dawson & Andrews, Inc.
Issues: UTI
Rep By: Gregory B. Andrews, Thomas C. Dawson, Ray Warner

Livermore Amador Valley Transit Ass'n

Livermore, CA
Leg. Issues: TRA

Outside Counsel/Consultants

Jordan & Associates, Inc.
Issues: TRA
Rep By: Patricia Jordan

Livermore, California, City of

Leg. Issues: AVI, CAW, TRA

Outside Counsel/Consultants

Jordan & Associates, Inc.
Issues: AVI, CAW, TRA
Rep By: Patricia Jordan

Liz Claiborne Internat'l

Secaucus, NJ
Registered: LDA
Leg. Issues: TRD

Outside Counsel/Consultants

Kent & O'Connor, Inc.

Issues: TRD

Rep By: Jonathan H. Kent, Cindy Thomas

Lloyd's of London

London, UNITED KINGDOM

Leg. Issues: BAN, ENV, INS, TEC

Outside Counsel/Consultants

Gibbons & Company, Inc.

Rep By: Clifford S. Gibbons

LeBoeuf, Lamb, Greene & MacRae L.L.P.

Issues: BAN, ENV, INS, TEC

Rep By: D. Randall Benn, A. Everette James, James M. Krey, L. Charles Landgraf, LaJuana S. Wilcher, Robert W. Woody

LM Capital Corp.

New York, NY

Outside Counsel/Consultants

Thelen Reid & Priest LLP

Rep By: William A. Kirk, Jr.

Local 511 Professional Employees, AFGE

Springfield, NJ

Leg. Issues: IMM

Outside Counsel/Consultants

Eric Shulman & Associates

Issues: IMM

Rep By: Eric Shulman

Local Initiatives Support Corp.

1825 K St. NW
Suite 1100
Washingon, DC 20006

Tel: (202)785-2908
Fax: (202)835-8931
Registered: LDA

Web: www.liscnet.org

A national non-profit organization based in New York City. Concerns include housing and community development policies and programs.

Leg. Issues: BAN, BUD, ECN, FAM, HOU, TAX, WEL

In-house, DC-area Employees

HUNTER, David

O'KEEFE, Stephanie

ROBERTS, Benson F.: V. President, Policy

SINCLAIR-SMITH, Susan

Outside Counsel/Consultants

Griffin, Johnson, Dover & Stewart

Rep By: William C. Danvers, G. Jack Dover, Keith Heard

Robert A. Rapoza Associates

Issues: BUD, ECN

Rep By: Robert A. Rapoza

Washington Council Ernst & Young

Issues: BAN, TAX

Rep By: Doug Badger, Lauren Darling, John L. Doney, Jayne T. Fitzgerald, LaBrenda Garrett-Nelson, Gary J. Gasper, Bruce A. Gates, Nick Giordano, Cathy Koch, Robert J. Leonard, Richard Meltzer, Phillip D. Moseley, John D. Porter, Robert M. Rozen, Donna Steele-Flynn, Timothy J. Urban

Localisation Industry Standards Ass'n

Geneva, SWITZERLAND

Leg. Issues: TRD

Outside Counsel/Consultants

Robert M. Brandon and Associates

Issues: TRD

Rep By: Robert M. Brandon, Clifford Rohde

Lockheed Martin Aeronautical Systems Co.

Marietta, GA

Leg. Issues: AER, BUD, DEF, SCI

Outside Counsel/Consultants

Alford & Associates

Issues: DEF

Rep By: Marty Alford

Marshall A. Brachman

Issues: BUD, DEF, SCI

Rep By: Marshall A. Brachman

Hurt, Norton & Associates

Issues: BUD, DEF

Rep By: Robert H. Hurt, Frank Norton, Katharine Calhoun Wood

Long, Aldridge & Norman, LLP

Issues: DEF

Rep By: Hon. George "Buddy" Darden

R. C. Whitner and Associates, Inc.

Issues: AER

Rep By: R. C. Whitner

Lockheed Martin Air Traffic Management

Rockville, MD

Outside Counsel/Consultants

Baker, Donelson, Bearman & Caldwell, P.C.

Rep By: Linda Hall Daschle, Albert B. Randall

Lockheed Martin Corp.

1725 Jefferson Davis Hwy.
Crystal Square 2, Suite 300
Arlington, VA 22202

Tel: (703)413-5600
Fax: (703)413-5613
Registered: LDA

Headquartered in Bethesda, Md., Lockheed Martin is a highly diversified global enterprise principally engaged in the research, design, development, manufacture and intergration of advanced-technology systems, products and services. The Corporation's core businesses span space and telecommunications, electronics, information and services, aeronautics, energy and systems intergration. Lockheed Martin employees approximately 180,000 people worldwide. Also represented by Adam Emanuel, of Adam Emanuel and Associates, on behalf of the Office of Zel E. Lipsen.

Leg. Issues: AER, AVI, BUD, COM, DEF, EDU, ENG, ENV, FOR, GOV, HCR, LBR, MAN, MAR, MMM, SCI, TAX, TEC, TRA, TRD, WAS, WEL

Political Action Committee/s

Lockheed Martin Employees PAC

1725 Jefferson Davis Hwy.
Crystal Square 2, Suite 300
Arlington, VA 22202

Tel: (703)413-5947
Fax: (703)413-5847

Contact: Kenneth D. Phelps, III

In-house, DC-area Employees

ANDREWS, Beverly: Director, International Relations and Trade

BOLDEN, Darwin K.: Government Relations Representative

BURNS, Hugh P.: Director, Marketing Communications

CHAUDET, Stephen E.: V. President, State and Local Government Affairs and PAC

COVAIS, Ron: V. President, The Americas

DAILEY, Brian: V. President, Washington Operations

DESMOND, James M.: V. President, Energy Sector Legislation

FORTIER, Alison: V. President, Space and Strategic Missile Legislative Affairs

GEORGE, Larry: V. President, Classified Programs

HERMANDORFER, Wayne: Director, Legislative Affairs

INGLEE, William: V. President, Legislative Affairs

KIRTMAN, Deanna M.: Director, Legislative Affairs, Navy Programs

MALONE, Harry: Director, Legislative Affairs, Army Programs

MCCLEAN, Scott D.: Director, Aeronautics Legislative Affairs

MOHRMANN, George F.: V. President, Legislative Affairs, Navy Programs

MONRO, Jr., Charles B.: Director, Airlift Programs, Aeronautics Sector, Washington Operations

MORNINGSTAR, Mary P.: Assistant General Counsel, Environmental Law

MORRISON, Mark E.: Director, Space and Strategic Programs

MUSSARA, Gerald: V. President, Trade and Regulatory Affairs

OVERSTREET, Jack C.: V. President, Legislative Affairs - Aircraft Programs

PHELPS, III, Kenneth D.: Treasurer, Lockheed Martin Employees Political Action Committee

ROBBINS, Michelle E.: Director, NASA Programs

SAUER, Ann E.: Director, General Legislation and Budgetary Affairs

SCHLEGEL, Nancy: Director, International Legislation

SULLIVAN, Eugene T.: Director, Aircraft Mod. & Maritime Surveillance, Aeronautics Sector, Washington Operations

TINGLE, G. Wayne: V. President, Systems Integration

VESSELLA, Candace C.: Director, Electronics Legislation

Outside Counsel/Consultants

American Systems Internat'l Corp.

Rep By: Robert D. McVey, William H. Skipper, Jr.

Balzano Associates

Issues: DEF

Rep By: Michael P. Balzano, Jr., Ruthanne Goodman, Janel Vermeulen

Barbour Griffith & Rogers, Inc.

Issues: AER, DEF, GOV

Rep By: Haley Barbour, Carl Biersack, James H. Johnson

Michael F. Barrett, Jr.

Issues: ENG

Rep By: Michael F. Barrett, Jr.

Cassidy & Associates, Inc.

Issues: DEF

Rep By: Shawn Edwards, Lawrence C. Grossman, Brig. Gen. Terry Paul, USMC (Ret.)

Clark & Weinstock, Inc.

Issues: AER, DEF

Rep By: Hon. Vic H. Fazio, Jr., Ed Kutler, Deirdre Stach, Sandi Stuart, Hon. John Vincent "Vin" Weber

The Conaway Group LLC

Issues: DEF

Rep By: Lt. Gen. John B. Conaway, USAF (Ret.), MacLellan Fairchild

Crowell & Moring LLP

Davis O'Connell, Inc.

Issues: DEF

Rep By: Terrence M. O'Connell

Devillier Communications

Issues: EDU

Rep By: Linda Devillier, Merri Oxley, Becky Schergens

The Direct Impact Co.

Edington, Peel & Associates, Inc.

Issues: BUD, DEF

Rep By: William H. Edington

Ervin Technical Associates, Inc. (ETA)

Issues: AER, DEF, SCI

Rep By: William J. Andahazy, Hon. Jack Edwards, James L. Ervin, Hon. Joseph M. McDade, Donald E. Richbourg

Gibson, Dunn & Crutcher LLP

Issues: ENV

Rep By: Raymond B. Ludwiszewski, Peter E. Seley

Griffin, Johnson, Dover & Stewart
Issues: DEF, MAN
Rep By: Walter J. "Joe" Stewart

Hooper Owen & Winburn
Issues: AER, DEF
Rep By: Hon. Charles Wilson

Mayer, Brown & Platt
Issues: DEF
Rep By: Mark H. Gitenstein, Miriam R. Nemetz, Carolyn P. Osolinik

McDermott, Will and Emery
Rep By: William H. Barrett, Raymond A. Jacobsen, Jr., Scott S. Megregian

Mercury Group
Issues: AER, DEF, FOR

The Montgomery Group
Issues: DEF
Rep By: Hon. G. V. "Sonny" Montgomery

Murray, Scheer, Montgomery, Tapia & O'Donnell

O'Connor & Hannan, L.L.P.
Issues: AER, AVI, BUD, DEF, ENV, GOV, SCI, TEC
Rep By: Hon. Thomas J. Corcoran, Timothy W. Jenkins, George J. Mannina, Jr., Patrick E. O'Donnell, Thomas H. Quinn, Hon. James W. Symington

The PMA Group
Issues: DEF
Rep By: Daniel E. Fleming, Kaylene Green, Dr. John Lynch, Paul J. Magliocchetti, Briggs Shade, Thomas Veltri, Mark Waclawski

RMA Internat'l, Inc.
Rep By: Otto J. Reich

Peter J. Rose
Issues: DEF
Rep By: Peter J. Rose

Ryan, Phillips, Utrecht & MacKinnon
Rep By: Rodney Hoppe, Jeffrey M. MacKinnon, William D. Phillips, Mark D. Planning, Thomas M. Ryan, Joseph V. Vasapoli

Tate-LeMunyon, LLC
Issues: DEF, TRA
Rep By: Glenn B. LeMunyon

The Van Fleet-Meredith Group
Issues: DEF
Rep By: M. Bruce Meredith, Paul F. Payette, Townsend A. Van Fleet

Van Scoyoc Associates, Inc.
Issues: TEC
Rep By: H. Stewart Van Scoyoc

Verner, Liipfert, Bernhard, McPherson and Hand, Chartered
Issues: TEC
Rep By: Denis J. Dwyer, Vicki E. Hart, Thomas J. Keller, Sara W. Morris, Steven R. Phillips, David R. Siddall, Lawrence R. Sidman, John H. Zentay

The Wexler Group
Issues: AER
Rep By: Peter T. Holran, Anne Jones, Dale W. Snape, Hon. Robert S. Walker

R. C. Whitner and Associates, Inc.
Rep By: R. C. Whitner

Winston & Strawn
Issues: COM, TEC
Rep By: Hon. Beryl F. Anthony, Jr., Charles L. Kinney

Lockheed Martin Fairchild Systems

Syosset, NY
Leg. Issues: DEF

Outside Counsel/Consultants

Rooney Group Internat'l, Inc.
Issues: DEF
Rep By: James W. Rooney

Lockheed Martin Federal Systems

Manassas, VA
Leg. Issues: DEF

Outside Counsel/Consultants

The PMA Group
Issues: DEF
Rep By: Sean Fogarty, Kaylene Green, Gregory L. Hansen, Joseph Littleton, Paul J. Magliocchetti, Briggs Shade, Charles Smith, Thomas Veltri

Lockheed Martin Global Telecommunications

Arlington, VA
Leg. Issues: DEF, TEC

Outside Counsel/Consultants

Alpine Group, Inc.
Issues: TEC
Rep By: Dan Brouillette

Griffin, Johnson, Dover & Stewart
Issues: TEC
Rep By: Walter J. "Joe" Stewart

Johnson Co.
Issues: TEC

Jones, Walker, Waechter, Poitevent, Carrere & Denegre, L.L.P.
Issues: DEF, TEC
Rep By: Paul Cambon, John J. Jaskot, R. Christian Johnsen

The Livingston Group, LLC

Lockheed Martin Government Electronics Systems

Moorestown, NJ
Leg. Issues: BUD, DEF

Outside Counsel/Consultants

Van Scoyoc Associates, Inc.
Issues: BUD, DEF
Rep By: Thomas L. Lankford, H. Stewart Van Scoyoc

Lockheed Martin Hanford

Richland, WA
Leg. Issues: ENG, WAS

Outside Counsel/Consultants

Van Scoyoc Associates, Inc.
Issues: ENG, WAS
Rep By: Paul Grimm, Buzz Hawley, H. Stewart Van Scoyoc

Lockheed Martin Idaho Technologies Corp.

Idaho Falls, ID

Outside Counsel/Consultants

The Renkes Group, Ltd.
Rep By: Gregg D. Renkes

Lockheed Martin IMS

1200 K St. NW
Suite 1200
Washington, DC 20005
Tel: (202)414-3500
Registered: LDA
Leg. Issues: GOV

In-house, DC-area Employees

GUSS, Phyllis A.: V. President, Legislative Affairs and Marketing
SCHOLLENBERGER, Bard D.: Director, Government Relations, Children and Family Services

Outside Counsel/Consultants

Cassidy & Associates, Inc.
Rep By: Arthur D. Mason, Dan C. Tate, Sr.

Public Strategies Washington, Inc.
Issues: GOV
Rep By: Joseph P. O'Neill

Lockheed Martin MS/Gaithersburg

Gaithersburg, MD
Leg. Issues: BUD

Outside Counsel/Consultants

The PMA Group
Issues: BUD
Rep By: Kaylene Green, Dr. John Lynch, Paul J. Magliocchetti, Kelli Short, Thomas Veltri

Lockheed Martin Naval Electronics Surveillance Systems

Moorestown, NJ
Leg. Issues: BUD, DEF, ENG

Outside Counsel/Consultants

Bill Carney & Co.
Issues: ENG
Rep By: Hon. William Carney

Van Scoyoc Associates, Inc.
Issues: BUD, DEF
Rep By: Thomas L. Lankford, H. Stewart Van Scoyoc

Lockheed Martin Tactical Systems

Arlington, VA
Leg. Issues: AVI, BUD, DEF

Outside Counsel/Consultants

Robison Internat'l, Inc.
Issues: BUD, DEF
Rep By: Sandra A. Gilbert, Richard B. Ladd, J. David Willson

Verner, Liipfert, Bernhard, McPherson and Hand, Chartered
Issues: AVI
Rep By: Matthew C. Bernstein, Lloyd N. Hand, Jane Hickie, Harry C. McPherson, John A. Merrigan, Steven R. Phillips, Ann W. Richards, Theresa M. Youngblood, John H. Zentay

Lockheed Martin Venture Star

Arlington, VA
Leg. Issues: AER, BUD

Outside Counsel/Consultants

Van Scoyoc Associates, Inc.
Issues: AER, BUD
Rep By: Kevin F. Kelly, Jessica Malow, Jasper Thomson, H. Stewart Van Scoyoc

Loeb & Loeb

Los Angeles, CA
A law firm.

Outside Counsel/Consultants

Baker & Hostetler LLP
Rep By: Matthew J. Dolan, Steven A. Lotterer, Hon. Guy Vander Jagt

Loews CNA Financial

New York, NY

Outside Counsel/Consultants

Kutak Rock LLP

Loews Corp.

New York, NY

Outside Counsel/Consultants

Covington & Burling
Rep By: David H. Remes, Keith A. Teel

Log Cabin Republicans PAC (LCR PAC)

1633 Q St. NW
Suite 210
Washington, DC 20009
Web: www.lcr.org
E-mail: meverts@lcr.org
Tel: (202)347-5306
Fax: (202)347-5224

In-house, DC-area Employees

TAFEL, Richard Leonard: Exec. Director

Logan College of Chiropractic

Chesterfield, MO
Leg. Issues: EDU, MED

Outside Counsel/Consultants

The Advocacy Group
Issues: EDU, MED
Rep By: Robert E. Mills

Logan, Utah, City of (Transit District)

Leg. Issues: BUD, TRA

Outside Counsel/Consultants

The Ferguson Group, LLC
Issues: BUD, TRA
Rep By: William Ferguson, Jr., Charmayne Macon, Leslie Waters Mozingo

Logis-Tech, Inc.

Alexandria, VA
Leg. Issues: DEF, MAN

Outside Counsel/Consultants

American Systems Internat'l Corp.
Issues: DEF, MAN
Rep By: Robert D. McVey, William H. Skipper, Jr.

Loma Linda, California, City of

Leg. Issues: BUD, ENV, TRA

Outside Counsel/Consultants

Copeland, Lowery & Jacquez
Issues: BUD, ENV, TRA
Rep By: Hon. William D. Lowery, Jeffrey S. Shockey

London Clearinghouse, Ltd.

London, UNITED KINGDOM
Leg. Issues: FIN

Outside Counsel/Consultants

Katten Muchin & Zavis
Issues: FIN
Rep By: Carol R. Van Cleef

London Futures and Options Exchange

London, UNITED KINGDOM

Outside Counsel/Consultants

Arnold & Porter

London Metal Exchange, Ltd.

London, UNITED KINGDOM

Outside Counsel/Consultants

Mayer, Brown & Platt

Lone Star Florida, Inc.

Fort Lauderdale, FL

A subsidiary of Lone Star Industries.

Outside Counsel/Consultants

Heenan, Althen & Roles
Rep By: Michael T. Heenan

Lone Star Industries

Stamford, CT

Outside Counsel/Consultants

Heenan, Althen & Roles
Rep By: Michael T. Heenan

Long Beach Naval Shipyard Employees Ass'n

Long Beach, CA

Outside Counsel/Consultants

E. Del Smith and Co.
Rep By: Margaret Allen, E. Del Smith

Long Beach Transit

Long Beach, CA
Leg. Issues: BUD, TRA

Outside Counsel/Consultants

The Ferguson Group, LLC
Issues: BUD, TRA
Rep By: William Ferguson, Jr., Charmayne Macon, Leslie Waters Mozingo

Long Beach Water Department

Long Beach, CA
Leg. Issues: BUD

Outside Counsel/Consultants

E. Del Smith and Co.
Issues: BUD
Rep By: Margaret Allen, E. Del Smith

Long Beach, California, City of

Leg. Issues: BUD, DEF, ECN, HOU

Outside Counsel/Consultants

Murray, Scheer, Montgomery, Tapia & O'Donnell
Issues: ECN
Rep By: John H. Montgomery, John R. O'Donnell, Raul R. Tapia

E. Del Smith and Co.
Issues: BUD, DEF, HOU
Rep By: Margaret Allen, E. Del Smith

Long Beach, California, Port of

Long Beach, CA
Leg. Issues: BUD, DEF, TAX, TRA

Outside Counsel/Consultants

E. Del Smith and Co.
Issues: BUD, DEF, TAX, TRA
Rep By: Margaret Allen, E. Del Smith

Long Island University

Brookville, NY
Leg. Issues: EDU

Outside Counsel/Consultants

The Advocacy Group
Issues: EDU
Rep By: Robert J. Dotchin, George A. Ramonas

Long Term Care Campaign

601 E St. NW
A6-560
Washington, DC 20049
Tel: (202)434-3744
Fax: (202)434-6403
Web: www.ltccampaign.org
E-mail: info@ltccampaign.org

A coalition of 150 national organizations dedicated to ensuring that all American families have access to affordable, quality long term care.

Leg. Issues: HCR

In-house, DC-area Employees

DAUPHINE, Jonathan D.: Exec. Director

Longhorn Pipeline

Dallas, TX
Leg. Issues: ENG, ENV, FUE, NAT, TRA

Outside Counsel/Consultants

The DCS Group
Issues: ENG

The Dutko Group, Inc.
Issues: ENV, FUE, NAT
Rep By: Mark S. Irion, Ronald C. Kaufman

Morgan Meguire, LLC
Issues: TRA
Rep By: Jocelyn Hong, Jack Jacobson, Scott Lindsay, Kyle G. Michel, Katie Parrott, C. Kyle Simpson, Deborah R. Sliz, Kiel Weaver

Troutman Sanders LLP
Issues: ENG, ENV
Rep By: Thomas C. Jensen, Eileen M. Moorhead, Clifford S. Sikora

Twenty-First Century Group
Issues: ENG
Rep By: Hon. Jack M. Fields, Jr., Cynthia M. Wilkinson

Longworth Industries Inc.

Candor, NC

A manufacturer of military clothing.

Leg. Issues: DEF

Outside Counsel/Consultants

American Defense Internat'l, Inc.
Issues: DEF
Rep By: Michael Herson, Van D. Hipp, Jr., Dave Wilberding

LOOP, Inc.

New Orleans, LA

A transporter of petroleum products.

Outside Counsel/Consultants

Patton Boggs, LLP
Rep By: Philip A. Bangert, James B. Christian, Jr., Daniel E. Waltz

Lorain County Community College

North Elyria, OH
Leg. Issues: ECN

Outside Counsel/Consultants

Cassidy & Associates, Inc.
Issues: ECN
Rep By: John A. Crumbliss, Daniel J. McNamara, Laura A. Neal, Christine A. O'Connor

Loral Corp.

Outside Counsel/Consultants

Gibson, Dunn & Crutcher LLP
Rep By: Alan A. Platt

Loral Space and Communications, Ltd.

1755 Jefferson Davis Hwy.
Suite 1007
Arlington, VA 22202-4159
Tel: (703)414-1040
Fax: (703)416-5582
Registered: LDA

Headquartered in New York, NY.

Leg. Issues: AER, DEF, GOV, SCI, TEC, TRD

Political Action Committee/s

Loral Spacecom Civic Responsibility Fund
1755 Jefferson Davis Hwy.
Suite 1007
Arlington, VA 22202-4159
Tel: (703)414-1040
Fax: (703)416-5582

In-house, DC-area Employees

FLAJSER, Steven H.: V. President, Legislative Relations
RHODES, Frederick W.: V. President, Corporate Legislative Relations

Outside Counsel/Consultants

Akin, Gump, Strauss, Hauer & Feld, L.L.P.

Baker, Donelson, Bearman & Caldwell, P.C.
Issues: GOV
Rep By: Hon. Howard H. Baker, Jr., Linda Hall Daschle, George Cranwell Montgomery, John C. Tuck

Collins & Company, Inc.
Issues: DEF
Rep By: James D. Bond, Richard L. Collins, Thomas A. Hooper, Shay D. Stautz

Feith & Zell, P.C.
Issues: AER, DEF, TEC, TRD
Rep By: Douglas J. Feith, Mark B. Feldman, Michael C. Poliner

Global USA, Inc.
Issues: SCI
Rep By: Dr. Bohdan Denysyk

Wilmer, Cutler & Pickering
Rep By: Lloyd N. Cutler, C. Boyden Gray

Lord Corp.

Cary, NC
Leg. Issues: DEF

Outside Counsel/Consultants

Peduzzi Associates, Ltd.
Issues: DEF
Rep By: Paul E. Elliott, Joseph L. Ferreira, C. V. Meadows, Lawrence P. Peduzzi, Ronald A. Putnam

Lorillard Tobacco Co.

Greensboro, NC
Leg. Issues: AGR, BUD, TAX, TOB, TRD

Outside Counsel/Consultants

Dickstein Shapiro Morin & Oshinsky LLP
Rep By: Henry C. Cashen, II, Hon. Wendell H. Ford, Elizabeth B. Haywood, Robert Mangas, Graham "Rusty" Mathews, Laurie McKay, Hon. Stanford E. Parris, Rebecah Moore Shepherd, L. Andrew Zausner

Public Private Partnership
Issues: AGR, BUD, TAX, TOB, TRD
Rep By: Arthur R. Collins

Los Alamitos Unified School District

Los Alamitos, CA
Leg. Issues: EDU

Outside Counsel/Consultants

Fern M. Lapidus
Issues: EDU
Rep By: Fern M. Lapidus

Los Alamos, New Mexico, County of

Leg. Issues: ECN

Outside Counsel/Consultants

Kutak Rock LLP
Issues: ECN
Rep By: Seth Kirshenberg

Los Angeles Community College District

Los Angeles, CA
Leg. Issues: EDU

Outside Counsel/Consultants

Davis O'Connell, Inc.
Issues: EDU
Rep By: Lynda C. Davis, Ph.D.

Los Angeles County Mass Transportation Authority

Los Angeles, CA
Leg. Issues: TRA

Outside Counsel/Consultants

MARC Associates, Inc.
Issues: TRA
Rep By: Cliff Madison, Daniel C. Maldonado

Los Angeles County Metropolitan Transportation Authority

Los Angeles, CA
Leg. Issues: BUD, TRA

Outside Counsel/Consultants

American Continental Group, Inc.
Issues: TRA
Rep By: John A. Cline, Shawn H. Smeallie

Cliff Madison Government Relations, Inc.
Issues: TRA

Thompson Coburn LLP
Issues: TRA
Rep By: Hon. R. Lawrence Coughlin, Jane Sutter-Starke, G. Kent Woodman

Van Scoyoc Associates, Inc.
Issues: BUD, TRA
Rep By: Ray Cole, H. Stewart Van Scoyoc

Los Angeles County Office of Education

Downey, CA
Leg. Issues: EDU

Outside Counsel/Consultants

MARC Associates, Inc.
Issues: EDU
Rep By: Daniel C. Maldonado

Los Angeles County Sanitation District

Whittier, CA
Leg. Issues: BUD, ENV, WAS

Outside Counsel/Consultants

John Freshman Associates, Inc.
Issues: BUD, ENV, WAS
Rep By: John D. Freshman, Lawrence P. Kast, Catherine B. Kiefer

Los Angeles to Pasadena Metro Blue Line Construction Authority

South Pasadena, CA
Leg. Issues: TRA

Outside Counsel/Consultants

MARC Associates, Inc.
Issues: TRA
Rep By: Eve O'Toole

Los Angeles Unified School District

Los Angeles, CA
Leg. Issues: EDU, TEC

Outside Counsel/Consultants

The Dutko Group, Inc.

Manatt, Phelps & Phillips, LLP
Issues: EDU, TEC
Rep By: Luke Rose, Robb Watters

Los Angeles, California, Community Development Commission of the County of

Monterey Park, CA
Leg. Issues: HOU

Outside Counsel/Consultants

MARC Associates, Inc.
Issues: HOU
Rep By: Daniel C. Maldonado, Eve O'Toole

Los Angeles, California, County of

440 First St. NW
Suite 440
Washington, DC 20001
Tel: (202)393-2404
Fax: (202)393-2666
Leg. Issues: BUD, DIS, FAM, HCR, HOU, IMM, LAW, LBR, MAR, MMM, RET, TRA, URB, WEL

In-house, DC-area Employees

JOSEPH, III, Thomas L.: Deputy Chief Legislative Representative
TODD, Reginald N.: Chief Legislative Representative

Outside Counsel/Consultants

Berliner, Candon & Jimison
Issues: FAM, HCR, IMM, MMM, WEL
Rep By: Roger A. Berliner, Carla Kish, Burt Margolin

MARC Associates, Inc.
Issues: HOU, URB
Rep By: Daniel C. Maldonado, Eve O'Toole

E. Del Smith and Co.
Issues: BUD, MAR, TRA
Rep By: Margaret Allen, E. Del Smith

Stuntz, Davis & Staffier, P.C.
Issues: BUD, DIS, IMM, LAW, LBR, RET, URB
Rep By: Randall E. Davis

Susan J. White & Associates
Issues: HCR, MMM
Rep By: Susan J. White

Los Angeles, California, Metropolitan Transit Authority of

Los Angeles, CA
Leg. Issues: ROD, TRA, URB

Outside Counsel/Consultants

Palumbo & Cerrell, Inc.
Issues: ROD, TRA, URB
Rep By: William T. Deitz, Benjamin L. Palumbo, Paul A. Skrabut, Jr.

Los Angeles, California, Washington Office of the City of

1301 Pennsylvania Ave. NW
Suite 400
Washington, DC 20004
Tel: (202)347-0915
Fax: (202)347-0919

In-house, DC-area Employees

ALVAREZ, Diego: Legislative Representative
DORSEY, Deborah Wood: Legislative Representative
RYAN, John C.: Legislative Representative
SEELEY, James F.: Chief Legislative Representative

LOT Polish Airlines

Warsaw, POLAND

Outside Counsel/Consultants

Winthrop, Stimson, Putnam & Roberts
Rep By: John E. Gillick

Lottery.com

Cincinnati, OH
Leg. Issues: GAM

Outside Counsel/Consultants

Robert M. Brandon and Associates
Issues: GAM
Rep By: Robert M. Brandon

Lotus Development Corp.

1301 K St. NW
Suite 1200 West
Washington, DC 20005
Tel: (202)515-4031
Fax: (202)515-5078
Registered: LDA
Leg. Issues: CPI, CPT, IMM, LBR, SCI, TAX, TEC, TRD

In-house, DC-area Employees

BRUNER, Cheryl: Senior Director, Public Policy and Government Affairs

Louis Dreyfus Corporation

1350 I St. NW
Suite 1260
Washington, DC 20005-3305
Tel: (202)842-5114
Fax: (202)842-5099
Registered: LDA
E-mail: lyonsd@ldcorp.com

A worldwide merchant of agricultural commodities. Headquartered in Wilton, CT.

Leg. Issues: AGR, MAR, TRD

In-house, DC-area Employees

LYONS, David Curtis: V. President, Government Relations

Louisiana Center for Manufacturing Sciences

Shreveport, LA
Leg. Issues: BUD, DEF, MAN

Outside Counsel/Consultants

Charlie McBride Associates, Inc.
Issues: BUD, DEF, MAN
Rep By: Charlie McBride

Louisiana Credit Union Ass'n

Harahan, LA
Leg. Issues: BAN

Outside Counsel/Consultants

Adams and Reese LLP
Issues: BAN
Rep By: B. Jeffrey Brooks, Hon. James A. "Jimmy" Hayes, Andrea Wilkinson

Louisiana Department of Social Services

Baton Rouge, LA

Outside Counsel/Consultants

Covington & Burling

Louisiana Department of Wildlife and Fisheries - Fur and Refuse Division

Baton Rouge, LA
Leg. Issues: NAT

Outside Counsel/Consultants

Glenn Roger Delaney
Issues: NAT
Rep By: Glenn Roger Delaney

Louisiana Energy Services

2600 Virginia Ave. NW
Suite 610
Washington, DC 20037
Tel: (202)337-6644
Fax: (202)337-2421

In-house, DC-area Employees

LENNY, Peter L.: President

Louisiana Internat'l Group

Kenner, LA
Leg. Issues: BUD, DIS

Outside Counsel/Consultants

Adams and Reese LLP
Issues: BUD, DIS
Rep By: B. Jeffrey Brooks

Louisiana Pacific Corp.

607 14th St. NW
Suite 800
Washington, DC 20005
Tel: (202)347-1501
Fax: (202)347-1521
Registered: LDA
Web: www.LPCorp.com
E-mail: Terry.Davies@LPCorp.com

A producer of building products headquartered in Portland, OR.

Leg. Issues: BUD, ENV, NAT

In-house, DC-area Employees

DAVIES, Terry: Corporate Manager, Government Relations

Louisiana Public Facilities Authority

Baton Rouge, LA

Outside Counsel/Consultants

Kutak Rock LLP

Louisiana State University

Baton Rouge, LA
Leg. Issues: BUD, EDU, ENG, FIN, NAT, TRA

Outside Counsel/Consultants

Adams and Reese LLP
Issues: BUD, EDU, ENG, FIN, NAT, TRA
Rep By: B. Jeffrey Brooks, Hon. James A. "Jimmy" Hayes, Andrea Wilkinson

Louisiana Superdome

New Orleans, LA
Leg. Issues: TRA

Outside Counsel/Consultants

Jones, Walker, Waechter, Poitevent, Carrere & Denegre, L.L.P.
Issues: TRA
Rep By: John J. Jaskot, R. Christian Johnsen

Louisiana Tobacco Group

Lake Charles, LA

Outside Counsel/Consultants

Long Law Firm
Rep By: C. Kris Kirkpatrick

Louisiana Workers' Compensation Corporation

Baton Rouge, LA

Outside Counsel/Consultants

Davis & Harman LLP
Rep By: Richard S. Belas

Lousville Airport

Lousville, KY

Outside Counsel/Consultants

Federal Access

Lovelace Respiratory Research Institute

Leg. Issues: AER, ALC, ANI, ART, AVI, BUD, CPT, DEF, EDU, ENG, ENV, FOR, HCR, IMM, MAR, MED, MMM, SCI, TAX, TEC, URB, VET

Outside Counsel/Consultants

Jorden Burt LLP
Issues: AER, ALC, ANI, ART, AVI, BUD, CPT, DEF, EDU, ENG, ENV, FOR, HCR, IMM, MAR, MED, MMM, SCI, TAX, TEC, URB, VET
Rep By: Patricia Branch, Alanna Dillon, Marna Gettleman, Marilyn Berry Thompson, Rebecca Tidman

Low Power Radio Coalition

601 13th St. NW
Suite 900 South
Washington, DC 20005
Tel: (202)783-5588
Web: www.lowpowerradio.org

In-house, DC-area Employees
BRACY, Michael M.: Exec. Director

Lower Brule Sioux Tribe
Leg. Issues: IND

Outside Counsel/Consultants

Olsson, Frank and Weeda, P.C.
Issues: IND
Rep By: John W. Bode, Susan P. Grymes, Karen Reis Harned, Stephen L. Lacey, Marshall L. Matz, Tyson Redpath, Ryan W. Stroschein

Lower Elwaha S'Klallam Tribe
Port Angeles, WA
Leg. Issues: IND

Outside Counsel/Consultants

Dorsey & Whitney LLP
Issues: IND
Rep By: David A. Bieging, Virginia W. Boylan, Cindy Darcy, Sarah Ridley

Lower Yellowstone Irrigation Project
Sidney, MT
Leg. Issues: NAT

Outside Counsel/Consultants

Ron C. Marlenee
Issues: NAT
Rep By: Hon. Ron C. Marlenee

Loyola College
Baltimore, MD
Leg. Issues: BUD, EDU, FOR

Outside Counsel/Consultants

EMI Associates, Ltd.
Issues: BUD, EDU, FOR
Rep By: Eugene M. Iwanciw

Loyola University
New Orleans, LA
Leg. Issues: BUD, DEF, EDU, ENG, ENV, LAW

Outside Counsel/Consultants

Adams and Reese LLP
Issues: BUD, DEF, EDU, ENG, ENV, LAW
Rep By: B. Jeffrey Brooks

Loyola University Health System
Maywood, IL
Leg. Issues: EDU, HCR, MED

Outside Counsel/Consultants

Broydrick & Associates
Issues: EDU, HCR, MED
Rep By: Amy Demske

Loyola University of Chicago
Chicago, IL Registered: LDA
Leg. Issues: BUD, EDU, HCR, MED

Outside Counsel/Consultants

Broydrick & Associates
Issues: BUD, EDU, HCR, MED
Rep By: Bill Viney

LSP Technologies
Dublin, OH
Leg. Issues: DEF

Outside Counsel/Consultants

Mehl, Griffin & Bartek Ltd.
Issues: DEF
Rep By: Molly Griffin

LTV Copperweld
Youngstown, OH
Leg. Issues: TRA

Outside Counsel/Consultants

Schagrin Associates
Issues: TRA
Rep By: Tamara L. Browne, Roger B. Schagrin

The LTV Corp.
1155 Connecticut Ave. NW
Suite 502
Washington, DC 20036
Web: www.ltvsteel.com
Tel: (202)872-5522
Fax: (202)872-5521
Registered: LDA

Steel manufacturer headquartered in Cleveland, OH.

Leg. Issues: AUT, CAW, ENG, ENV, HCR, TAX, TRA, TRD

Political Action Committee/s

LTV Corp. Active Citizenship Campaign
1155 Connecticut Ave. NW
Suite 502
Washington, DC 20036
Contact: Douglas A. Brook
Tel: (202)872-5522
Fax: (202)872-5521

In-house, DC-area Employees
BROOK, Douglas A.: V. President, Government Affairs

Outside Counsel/Consultants

Valente Lopatin & Schulze
Issues: HCR
Rep By: Richard T. Schulze, Jr., Mark Valente, III

LTV Steel Co.
Cleveland, OH
Leg. Issues: TRD

Outside Counsel/Consultants

Sam Richardson
Rep By: Sam Richardson

Skadden, Arps, Slate, Meagher & Flom LLP
Issues: TRD
Rep By: Robert E. Lighthizer

Lubbock, Texas, City of
Leg. Issues: DEF, ENG, HOU, LAW, TRA, URB

Outside Counsel/Consultants

Commonwealth Consulting Corp.
Issues: DEF
Rep By: Christopher M. Lehman

Barbara T. McCall Associates
Issues: ENG, HOU, LAW, TRA, URB
Rep By: Ralph Garboushian, Barbara T. McCall

Lubrizol

Outside Counsel/Consultants

Verner, Liipfert, Bernhard, McPherson and Hand, Chartered
Rep By: Andrea J. Grant

Lucas Aerospace
Englewood, CA
Leg. Issues: AER, AVI

Outside Counsel/Consultants

Shaw Pittman
Issues: AER, AVI
Rep By: J. E. Murdock, III

Lucent Technologies
900 19th St. NW
Suite 700
Washington, DC 20006
Web: www.lucent.com
Tel: (202)530-7000
Fax: (202)530-7042
Registered: LDA

Headquartered in Murry Hill, NJ.

Leg. Issues: CPT, CSP, DEF, EDU, ENV, HCR, RET, SCI, TAX, TEC, TRD

Political Action Committee/s

Lucent Technologies Inc. PAC
900 19th St. NW
Suite 700
Washington, DC 20006
Contact: Joseph Priester
Tel: (202)530-7015
Fax: (202)530-7007

In-house, DC-area Employees
BRADFORD, Martina L.: Corporate V. President, Public Affairs
CHILDS, Stephanie: Director, Global Public Affairs
KOCH, Gary: Director, Global Public Affairs
MATHIAS, Charles: Director, EMEA Region
MCMANUS, Mary P.: V. President, Global Public Affairs
MCNEIL, Sue: Director, Global Public Affairs
PRIESTER, Joseph: Exec. Assistant, Corporate V. President and PAC Treasurer
RABON, Tom: V. President, Global Public Affairs
WARRINGTON, Darlene: Manager, Coporate Media Relations
WILSON, Joanne: Director, Global Public Affairs

Outside Counsel/Consultants

Akin, Gump, Strauss, Hauer & Feld, L.L.P.
Issues: TRD
Rep By: Daniel L. Spiegel, S. Bruce Wilson

Bergner Bockorny Castagnetti and Hawkins
Issues: CPT, ENV, HCR, SCI, TAX, TEC, TRD
Rep By: Jeffrey T. Bergner, David A. Bockorny, David Castagnetti, Melissa Schulman

The PMA Group
Issues: DEF
Rep By: Kaylene Green, Paul J. Magliocchetti, Mark Waclawski

Luiginos
Duluth, MN

Outside Counsel/Consultants

Dickstein Shapiro Morin & Oshinsky LLP
Rep By: Robert Mangas, Graham "Rusty" Mathews, L. Andrew Zausner

Lumber Fair Trade Group

Outside Counsel/Consultants

Genesis Consulting Group, LLC
Rep By: Mark Benedict

Lumbermens Mutual Casualty Co.
325 Seventh St. NW
Suite 1250
Washington, DC 20004
Tel: (202)347-8193
Fax: (202)347-9304
Registered: LDA

Headquartered in Long Grove, IL.

Leg. Issues: BUD, CSP, ENV, FIN, HCR, INS, LAW, MMM, TAX, TOR

In-house, DC-area Employees
DINEEN, Michael F.

Lumenos
Arlington, VA

Outside Counsel/Consultants

BKSH & Associates
Rep By: Charles R. Black, Jr.

Lummi Indian Nation
Bellingham, WA

Outside Counsel/Consultants

SENSE, INC.
Rep By: C. Juliet Pittman

Lunds Fisheries, Inc.
Cape May, NJ
Leg. Issues: MAR

Outside Counsel/Consultants

Robertson, Monagle & Eastaugh
Issues: MAR
Rep By: Bradley D. Gilman, Rick E. Marks

Lupus Foundation of America
1300 Piccard Dr.
Suite 200
Rockville, MD 20850
Web: www.lupus.org
E-mail: info@lupus.org
Tel: (301)670-9292
Fax: (301)670-9486
Registered: LDA

Leg. Issues: HCR, MED, MMM, PHA

In-house, DC-area Employees
PETERS, Duane: V. President for Advocacy and Communications

Luse Lehman Gorman Pomerenk & Schick, P.C.
Washington, DC
Leg. Issues: BAN

Outside Counsel/Consultants

Butera & Andrews
Issues: BAN
Rep By: Cliff W. Andrews, Wright H. Andrews, Jr., James J. Butera, Frank Tillotson

Luso American Foundation
Lisbon, PORTUGAL
Leg. Issues: FOR, SCI, SMB

Outside Counsel/Consultants

Gowran Internat'l Ltd.
Issues: FOR, SCI, SMB

Lutheran Brotherhood
Minneapolis, MN
Leg. Issues: TAX

Outside Counsel/Consultants

Vinyard & Associates
Issues: TAX
Rep By: Walter D. Vinyard, Jr.

Lutheran Medical Center
Cleveland, OH

Outside Counsel/Consultants

Bruce Ray & Company
Rep By: Bruce A. Ray, Ph.D.

Lutheran Office for Governmental Affairs/Evangelical Lutheran Church in America

122 C St. NW
Suite 125
Washington, DC 20001
Web: www.loga.org
E-mail: loga@ecunet.org
Tel: (202)783-7507
Fax: (202)783-7502

Represents the Evangelical Lutheran Church in America in matters involving the poor and vulnerable, human and civil rights, and peacemaking. Headquartered in Chicago, IL.

Leg. Issues: BUD, CAW, CIV, CON, DEF, EDU, ENV, FAM, FOR, GOV, HCR, HOU, IMM, LAW, LBR, MMM, WAS, WEL

In-house, DC-area Employees
BENGSTON, Kay: Assistant Director
BROWN, Mark B.: Assistant Director
CODDING, Faye: Assistant Director
SILER, Russell O.: Director

Luxcore Public Affairs

1725 K St. NW
Suite 402
Washington, DC 20006
E-mail: cnalls@erols.com
Tel: (202)466-5258
Fax: (202)466-5298
Leg. Issues: CPI, FOR, GOV, RES

In-house, DC-area Employees
NALLS, Charles H.: Director, Government Affairs

LVMH Moet Hennessy Louis Vuitton S.A.

Paris, FRANCE
Leg. Issues: TRD

Outside Counsel/Consultants
Barbour Griffith & Rogers, Inc.
Issues: TRD
Rep By: Haley Barbour, Loren Monroe, Brent Thompson
Quinn Gillespie & Associates
Issues: TRD
Rep By: Bruce H. Andrews, Edward W. Gillespie, Harriet James, Nicholas Maduros, Anne McGuire, John M. "Jack" Quinn, Marla Zomesky

LVS Power Ltd.

Outside Counsel/Consultants
Morgan Meguire, LLC
Rep By: C. Kyle Simpson

The Lykes Bros.

Tampa, FL

Outside Counsel/Consultants
Collier Shannon Scott, PLLC
Rep By: Paul C. Rosenthal

Lyme Disease Foundation

Hartford, CT

Outside Counsel/Consultants
Thompson, Hine and Flory LLP
Rep By: Michael L. Martinez

Lymphoma Research Foundation of America, Inc.

Los Angeles, CA
Leg. Issues: BUD, HCR, MED, TOB

Outside Counsel/Consultants
Capitol Associates, Inc.
Issues: BUD, HCR, MED, TOB
Rep By: Liz Gemski, Edward R. Long, Ph.D.

Lynchburg, Virginia, City of

Leg. Issues: CAW

Outside Counsel/Consultants
McGuireWoods L.L.P.
Issues: CAW
Rep By: Hana Brilliant, F. Paul Calamita, Stephen A. Katsurinis, Hon. Lewis F. Payne, Jr., Jeffrey L. Schlagenhauf

Lynden Air Cargo, LLC

Anchorage, AK

Outside Counsel/Consultants
Pierre E. Murphy Law Offices

Lynn, Massachusetts, City of

Leg. Issues: BUD, ECN, EDU, FIR, RET, TRA, URB

Outside Counsel/Consultants
The Barton Co.
Issues: BUD, ECN, EDU, FIR, RET, TRA, URB
Rep By: Stacy Palmer-Barton

Lynwood, California, City of

Outside Counsel/Consultants
E. Del Smith and Co.
Rep By: E. Del Smith

Lyondell Chemical Co.

700 13th St. NW
Suite 950
Washington, DC 20005
Web: www.lyondell.com
E-mail: edlu.thom@lyondell.com
Tel: (202)434-8938
Fax: (202)434-4585
Registered: LDA

Headquartered in Houston, TX. Formerly known as ARCO Chemical Co.

Leg. Issues: CAW, ENV, FUE, MAN, RRR, SCI, TRD

Political Action Committee/s
Lyondell PAC
700 13th St. NW
Suite 950
Washington, DC 20005
Contact: Christina Wisdom
Tel: (202)434-8938
Fax: (202)434-4585

In-house, DC-area Employees
THOM, Edlu J.: Director, Government Affairs
WISDOM, Christina: PAC Manager/Gov't Affairs Coordinator

Outside Counsel/Consultants
Barbour Griffith & Rogers, Inc.
Issues: CAW, FUE
Rep By: Haley Barbour, Carl Biersack, G. O. Lanny Griffith, Jr., Bill Himpler, Loren Monroe, Edward M. Rogers, Jr., Brent Thompson
Bracewell & Patterson, L.L.P.
Issues: ENV, TRD
Rep By: Gene E. Godley, Marc C. Hebert, Charles L. Ingebretson, Michael L. Pate, Scott H. Segal, D. Michael Stroud, Jr.

M and K Oil Co., Inc.

Gillette, WY

Outside Counsel/Consultants
R. Duffy Wall and Associates

M K Airlines

Accra, GHANA
Leg. Issues: AVI

Outside Counsel/Consultants
Sher & Blackwell
Issues: AVI
Rep By: Mark Atwood

M&W Pump Corp.

Deerfield Beach, FL

Outside Counsel/Consultants
Vorys, Sater, Seymour and Pease, LLP
Rep By: Warren W. Glick

M-S-R Public Power Agency

Modesto, CA
Leg. Issues: ENG, GOV, UTI

Outside Counsel/Consultants
Duncan, Weinberg, Genzer & Pembroke, P.C.
Issues: ENG, GOV, UTI
Rep By: Wallace L. Duncan, James D. Pembroke, Thomas L. Rudebusch

M.B. Consultants, Inc.

South Fallsburg, NY
Leg. Issues: AGR

Outside Counsel/Consultants
Capitol Counsel Group, L.L.C.
Issues: AGR
Rep By: Warren Belmar

M.D. - I.P.A.

Rockville, MD
Leg. Issues: HCR, MMM

Outside Counsel/Consultants
Jefferson Consulting Group
Issues: HCR, MMM
Rep By: Dorsey Chescavage, Angela V. McNamara, Robert J. Thompson

M/A-COM, Inc.

Lowell, MA

Outside Counsel/Consultants
Mintz, Levin, Cohn, Ferris, Glovsky and Popeo, P.C.

M2 Technologies Inc.

West Hyannisport, MA
Leg. Issues: DEF

Outside Counsel/Consultants
Cassidy & Associates, Inc.
Issues: DEF
Rep By: Shawn Edwards, Brig. Gen. Terry Paul, USMC (Ret.)

MacAndrews & Forbes Holdings, Inc.

1455 Pennsylvania Ave. NW
Suite 300
Washington, DC 20004
E-mail: maf8c@aol.com
Tel: (202)628-2600
Fax: (202)638-2072
Registered: LDA

Headquartered in New York, NY.

Leg. Issues: BAN, BUD, COM, FIN, HCR, MAN, TAX, TEC, TOB

In-house, DC-area Employees
GREEN, William J.: V. President, Government Affairs

Outside Counsel/Consultants
BKSH & Associates
Issues: BUD, HCR, TAX, TOB
Gibson, Dunn & Crutcher LLP
Issues: BAN
Rep By: Cantwell Faulkner Muckenfuss, III, Victoria P. Rostow
Royer & Babyak
Issues: BAN
Rep By: Robert Stewart Royer
Washington Council Ernst & Young
Issues: BAN, BUD, COM, FIN, MAN, TAX, TEC
Rep By: Doug Badger, Lauren Darling, John L. Doney, Jayne T. Fitzgerald, LaBrenda Garrett-Nelson, Gary J. Gasper, Bruce A. Gates, Nick Giordano, Cathy Koch, Robert J. Leonard, Phillip D. Moseley, John D. Porter, Robert M. Rozen, Donna Steele-Flynn, Timothy J. Urban

Macau, Civil Aviation Authority of

Outside Counsel/Consultants
Zuckert, Scoutt and Rasenberger, L.L.P.
Rep By: Rachel B. Trinder

MacGregor

Pinebrook, NJ
Leg. Issues: DEF, TRD

Outside Counsel/Consultants
Wayne Arny & Assoc.
Issues: DEF, TRD
Rep By: Wayne Arny, David D. O'Brien
David O'Brien and Associates
Issues: DEF
Rep By: David D. O'Brien

Machinery Dealers Nat'l Ass'n

315 S. Patrick St.
Alexandria, VA 22314-3501
Web: www.mdna.org
E-mail: office@mdna.org
Tel: (703)836-9300
Fax: (703)836-9303

International trade association representing used metal working machinery dealers.

Leg. Issues: MAN, SMB, TAX, TOR, TRD

In-house, DC-area Employees
DEAL, Martha P.: Exec. V. President

Mack Trucks, Inc.

Allentown, PA
Leg. Issues: CAW, CSP, ENG, ENV, SCI, TAX

Outside Counsel/Consultants
Van Ness Feldman, P.C.
Issues: CAW, CSP, ENG, ENV, SCI, TAX
Rep By: Howard J. Feldman, Nancy Macan McNally, Richard A. Penna

MacKenzie Agricultural Research

Maple Park, IL

Outside Counsel/Consultants
Daniel F. Shaw & Associates
Rep By: Daniel F. Shaw

Macon, City of

Macon, GA Registered: LDA
Leg. Issues: HCR, HOU, LAW, TRA, WEL

Outside Counsel/Consultants

Peyser Associates, Inc.
Issues: HCR, HOU, LAW, TRA, WEL
Rep By: Michael Bucciero, Jr., Peter A. Peyser, Jr.

Madeira Development Co.

Madeira, PORTUGAL

Outside Counsel/Consultants

Norman A. Bailey, Inc.
Rep By: Norman A. Bailey

Madison County Commission

Huntsville, AL
Leg. Issues: AGR, LAW, LBR, URB

Outside Counsel/Consultants

Capitol Link, Inc.
Issues: AGR, LAW, LBR, URB
Rep By: Hon. David M. Staton

Madison Gas & Electric Co.

Madison, WI
Leg. Issues: ENG

Outside Counsel/Consultants

Morgan Meguire, LLC
Issues: ENG
Rep By: Scott Lindsay, Kyle G. Michel, Katie Parrott, C. Kyle Simpson, Deborah R. Sliz, Kiel Weaver

Madison Government Affairs

Washington, DC
Leg. Issues: DEF, ENV, URB

Outside Counsel/Consultants

W. B. Driggers & Associates, Inc.
Issues: DEF, ENV, URB
Rep By: W. B. Driggers

Madison Research Corp.

Huntsville, AL
Leg. Issues: DEF

Outside Counsel/Consultants

Balch & Bingham LLP
Issues: DEF
Rep By: Wade Heck, William F. Stiers

Madison, Wisconsin, City of

Leg. Issues: BUD, LBR, TRA

Outside Counsel/Consultants

Simon and Co., Inc.
Issues: BUD, LBR, TRA
Rep By: Heather Barber, Alex DeGood, Leonard S. Simon

Bernard L. Madoff Investment Securities

New York, NY
Leg. Issues: FIN, GOV

Outside Counsel/Consultants

Lent Scrivner & Roth LLC
Issues: FIN, GOV
Rep By: Norman F. Lent, III, Hon. Norman F. Lent, Alan J. Roth, Michael S. Scrivner

Maersk Inc.

1101 17th St. NW
Suite 610
Washington, DC 20036
Tel: (202)887-6770
Fax: (202)887-5014
Registered: LDA

Headquartered in Madison, NJ. Formed from the merger of Maersk Inc. and Sea-Land Services Inc.

Leg. Issues: DEF, MAR, TAX, TRA, TRD, TRU

In-house, DC-area Employees

JOHNSON, Mark R.: V. President, Government Affairs

Outside Counsel/Consultants

William V. Brierre
Rep By: William V. Brierre, Jr.

Cassidy & Associates, Inc.
Issues: DEF, TAX
Rep By: John S. Doyle, Jr., Carl Franklin Godfrey, Jr., Maj. Gen. Edmund P. Looney, Jr. USMC (Ret.), Michael Merola, Hon. Fred B. Rooney, Gabor J. Rozsa, Hon. Martin A. Russo

Law Offices of Kevin G. Curtin
Issues: MAR
Rep By: Kevin G. Curtin

Jack Ferguson Associates, Inc.
Rep By: Jack Ferguson

Potomac Group
Issues: MAR
Rep By: Richard Y Hegg, Philip C. Karsting, G. Wayne Smith

Robertson, Monagle & Eastaugh
Rep By: Bradley D. Gilman

Washington Strategies, L.L.C.
Rep By: Jennifer Johnson Calvert, William P. Jarrell

Magazine Publishers of America

1211 Connecticut Ave. NW
Suite 610
Washington, DC 20036
Tel: (202)296-7277
Fax: (202)296-0343
Registered: LDA

Headquartered in New York, NY.

Leg. Issues: ADV, BEV, CIV, CON, CPI, CPT, CSP, ENV, GAM, LBR, MIA, POS, TAX, TOB

Political Action Committee/s

Magazine Publishers of America Political Action Committee

1211 Connecticut Ave. NW
Suite 610
Washington, DC 20036
Contact: James R. Cregan
Tel: (202)296-7277
Fax: (202)296-0343

In-house, DC-area Employees

COHEN, Rita D.: Senior V. President, Legislative and Regulatory Policy
CREGAN, James R.: Exec. V. President, Government Affairs

Outside Counsel/Consultants

Davidson & Company, Inc.
Issues: ADV, LBR, TAX
Rep By: James H. Davidson, Richard E. May, Stanley Sokul

Dittus Communications
Rep By: Trudi Boyd, Debra Cabral, Amy Fox, Neena Moorjani

Meyer & Klipper, PLLC
Issues: CIV, CON, CPT, GAM
Rep By: Michael R. Klipper, Christopher A. Mohr

Patton Boggs, LLP
Issues: ADV, BEV, CON, TAX, TOB
Rep By: Thomas Hale Boggs, Jr., Penelope S. Farthing

Preston Gates Ellis & Rouvelas Meeds LLP
Issues: POS
Rep By: Werner W. Brandt, Hon. David Funderburk, Bruce J. Heiman, Hon. Lloyd Meeds, Ralph D. Nurnberger, Cindy O'Malley, Emanuel L. Rouvelas, W. Dennis Stephens, Steven R. "Rick" Valentine

Magee Women's Health Foundation

Pittsburgh, PA
Leg. Issues: HCR, MMM

Outside Counsel/Consultants

McDermott, Will and Emery
Issues: HCR, MMM
Rep By: Wendy L. Krasner, Maggie A. Mitchell, Karen S. Sealander

Magellan Carbon Fuels

Fairfax, VA

Outside Counsel/Consultants

Chadbourne and Parke LLP
Rep By: Keith Martin

Magellan Health Services

Atlanta, GA Registered: LDA
Leg. Issues: MMM

Outside Counsel/Consultants

Davidoff & Malito, LLP
Issues: MMM
Rep By: Kenneth C. Malito, Stephen J. Slade

Magna Entertainment Corp.

Los Angeles, CA
Leg. Issues: GAM

Outside Counsel/Consultants

Verner, Liipfert, Bernhard, McPherson and Hand, Chartered
Issues: GAM
Rep By: Jamie E. Brown, Marla P. Grossman, John H. Zentay

Magnificent Research Inc.

White Plains, NY

Outside Counsel/Consultants

Patton Boggs, LLP
Rep By: Parker Brugge, Paul A. J. Wilson

Magnitude Information Systems

Chester, NJ
Leg. Issues: CPI, GOV, HCR

Outside Counsel/Consultants

Arent Fox Kintner Plotkin & Kahn, PLLC
Issues: CPI, GOV, HCR
Rep By: Katie Clarke, Douglas McCormack

Mail 2000, Inc.

Bethesda, MD
Leg. Issues: POS

Outside Counsel/Consultants

George H. Denison
Issues: POS
Rep By: George H. Denison

MailBoxes Etc.

San Diego, CA
Leg. Issues: POS

Outside Counsel/Consultants

Robertson, Monagle & Eastaugh
Issues: POS
Rep By: Steven W. Silver

Mailing & Fulfillment Services Ass'n

1421 Prince St.
Alexandria, VA 22314-2814
Web: www.mfsanet.org
Tel: (703)836-9200
Fax: (703)548-8204

In-house, DC-area Employees

BRENNAN, Barry: Director, Postal Affairs
CASEY, Eric: Director, Marketing
WEAVER, David A.: President

Outside Counsel/Consultants

Jenner & Block

Main Street Coalition for Postal Fairness

A coalition of publishers of small periodicals who support postal reform. Members include American Business Press, Greeting Card Association, Hallmark Cards, Inc., Knight-Ridder Inc., the National Federation of Nonprofits, the Newspaper Association of America, the Coalition of Religious Press Associations, and Penwell Publishing Co.

Leg. Issues: POS

Outside Counsel/Consultants

Estes Associates
Issues: POS
Rep By: John T. Estes

Maine Cellular Telephone Co.

Auburn, ME
Leg. Issues: GOV

Outside Counsel/Consultants

Wilkinson, Barker and Knauer, LLP
Issues: GOV

Maine Public Service Co.

Presque Isle, ME

Outside Counsel/Consultants

Wright & Talisman, P.C.
Rep By: James T. McManus, Michael E. Small

Maine Pulp & Paper Ass'n

Outside Counsel/Consultants

Stevens Reed Curcio & Co.

Mainstream, Inc.

6930 Carroll Ave.
Suite 240
Takoma Park, MD 20912
Web: www.mainstreaminc.org
E-mail: info@mainstream.org
Tel: (301)891-8777
Fax: (301)891-8778

Provides job placement and employment opportunities for people with disabilities and assists employees, disability organizations, and social service providers with information and training on disability issues.

In-house, DC-area Employees

PICHETTE, David A.: Exec. Director

Mainwave Technologies
Tysons, VA
Leg. Issues: GOV

Outside Counsel/Consultants

The Eagles Group
Issues: GOV
Rep By: Terence Costello

Major League Baseball
New York, NY
Headquartered in New York, NY.

Leg. Issues: CPT, GOV, LBR, SPO, TAX, TEC

Outside Counsel/Consultants

Baker & Hostetler LLP
Issues: CPT, LBR, SPO, TEC
Rep By: William H. Schweitzer

Cassidy & Associates, Inc.
Issues: LBR, TAX
Rep By: Michele Gioffre, Christopher Lamond, Arthur D. Mason, Hon. Martin A. Russo, Dan C. Tate, Sr.

Stuart J. Gordon
Issues: GOV, LBR, SPO, TAX
Rep By: Stuart J. Gordon

Major League Baseball Players Ass'n
New York, NY
Leg. Issues: GAM, LBR, SPO

Outside Counsel/Consultants

Bredhoff & Kaiser
Rep By: George H. Cohen

McGuiness & Holch
Issues: LBR, SPO
Rep By: Markham C. Erickson, Kevin S. McGuiness

Patton Boggs, LLP
Issues: GAM, SPO
Rep By: John F. Fithian, Elena Giberga, Aubrey A. Rothrock, III

Rogers & Wells
Rep By: Kevin J. Arquit

Major League Baseball, Office of the Commissioner of
New York, NY

Outside Counsel/Consultants

Arnold & Porter

Major Medicaid Hospital Coalition
Washington, DC
Leg. Issues: MMM

Outside Counsel/Consultants

The Carmen Group
Issues: MMM
Rep By: Ryan Adesnik, Gerald P. Carmen, Diane Jemmott

Makedonski Telekomunikacii
Skopje, MACEDONIA
Leg. Issues: FOR, GOV, TRD

Outside Counsel/Consultants

Barbour Griffith & Rogers, Inc.
Issues: FOR, GOV, TRD
Rep By: G. O. Lanny Griffith, Jr., R. Greg Stevens

Malaysia Ministry of Trade
Kuala Lumpur, MALAYSIA

Outside Counsel/Consultants

White & Case LLP
Rep By: William J. Clinton, Walter J. Spak

Malaysian Airline System
Kuala Lumpur, MALAYSIA

Outside Counsel/Consultants

Zuckert, Scoutt and Rasenberger, L.L.P.
Rep By: Charles J. Simpson, Jr.

Malaysian Palm Oil Promotion Council
Chicago, IL

Outside Counsel/Consultants

Dickstein Shapiro Morin & Oshinsky LLP
Rep By: Peter J. Kadzik

Malden Mills Industries, Inc.
Lawrence, MA
Leg. Issues: APP, BUD, DEF

Outside Counsel/Consultants

The Atlantic Group, Public Affairs, Inc.
Issues: APP, BUD, DEF
Rep By: Larry F. Ayres

Maldives, Government of the Republic of
Male, MALDIVES

Outside Counsel/Consultants

Mark A. Siegel & Associates
Rep By: Brian Sailer, Mark A. Siegel

Malheur Timber Operators
John Day, OR

Outside Counsel/Consultants

Jamison and Sullivan, Inc.
Rep By: Delos Cy Jamison, Jay R. Sullivan

Mali, Embassy of the Republic of
2130 R St. NW
Washington, DC 20008
Tel: (202)332-2249
Fax: (202)332-6603

Outside Counsel/Consultants

Barron-Birrell, Inc.

Washington World Group, Ltd.
Rep By: Edward J. von Kloberg, III

Mallinckrodt-Nellcor Puritan Bennett
Pleasanton, CA
Leg. Issues: HCR, MMM

Outside Counsel/Consultants

GRQ, Inc.
Issues: HCR, MMM
Rep By: Patricia Booth, Phillip Porte

Malrite Communications Group, Inc.
Cleveland, OH

Outside Counsel/Consultants

Arter & Hadden

Kaye Scholer LLP
Rep By: Christopher R. Brewster, Jason Shrinsky

Malta Development Corp.
Valletta, MALTA

Outside Counsel/Consultants

Dechert

Mammoth Mountain
Mammoth Lakes, CA
Leg. Issues: BUD, TRA

Outside Counsel/Consultants

The Wexler Group
Issues: BUD, TRA
Rep By: Timothy Hannegan, Patrick J. McCann

Managed Care Solutions
Phoenix, AZ
Leg. Issues: HCR, VET

Outside Counsel/Consultants

Jefferson Consulting Group
Issues: HCR, VET
Rep By: Julia T. Susman

Managed Funds Ass'n
Washington, DC
Web: www.mfainfo.org
E-mail: janice@mfainfo.org
Leg. Issues: FIN

Outside Counsel/Consultants

Smith, Bucklin and Associates, Inc.
Issues: FIN
Rep By: John G. Gaine

Wilmer, Cutler & Pickering
Issues: FIN
Rep By: Marianne K. Smythe

Managed Health Care Ass'n
1299 Pennsylvania Ave. NW
Suite 800 West
Washington, DC 20004
Tel: (202)682-3901
Fax: (202)478-1734

An organization of private-sector employers working to foster a more productive, accountable and cost-effective health care delivery system through the expansion and improvement of managed health care. Currently has as members over 120 of the nation's largest companies which have implemented, or are considering implementing, managed health care programs.

In-house, DC-area Employees

KALEN, Pam: Exec. Director

Outside Counsel/Consultants

LMRC, Inc.
Rep By: Pam Kalen

Management Ass'n for Private Photogrammetric Surveyors
Reston, VA
Web: www.mapps.org
E-mail: info@mapps.org

A trade association of private surveying and mapping firms.

Leg. Issues: GOV

Outside Counsel/Consultants

John M. Palatiello & Associates
Issues: GOV
Rep By: John M. Palatiello

Management Concepts, Inc.
Vienna, VA
Leg. Issues: AGR, BUD

Outside Counsel/Consultants

Dean Blakey & Moskowitz
Issues: AGR, BUD
Rep By: John E. Dean, Ellin J. Nolan

Management Insights, Inc.
Dallas, TX
Leg. Issues: TAX

Outside Counsel/Consultants

Verner, Liipfert, Bernhard, McPherson and Hand, Chartered
Issues: TAX
Rep By: Evan M. Migdail

Manatee, Florida, County of
Bradenton, FL
Leg. Issues: BUD, NAT

Outside Counsel/Consultants

Marlowe and Co.
Issues: BUD, NAT
Rep By: Howard Marlowe

Morgan Meguire, LLC
Issues: BUD
Rep By: Jocelyn Hong, Jack Jacobson, Scott Lindsay, Kyle G. Michel, Katie Parrott, C. Kyle Simpson, Deborah R. Sliz, Kiel Weaver

Mandela Group
6039 Riddle Walk
Alexandria, VA 22302
A political action committee.

In-house, DC-area Employees

BARROW, Larry

Manhattan Plaza Associates
New York, NY

Outside Counsel/Consultants

Swidler Berlin Shereff Friedman, LLP
Rep By: Harold A. Levy, Kenneth G. Lore

Maniilaq Ass'n
Kotzebue, AK
Leg. Issues: IND

Outside Counsel/Consultants

Hobbs, Straus, Dean and Walker, LLP
Issues: IND
Rep By: Karen J. Funk, Geoffrey D. Strommer

Mannesmann VDO
Villigen-Schwennigen, GERMANY

Outside Counsel/Consultants

Patton Boggs, LLP
Rep By: Carolina L. Mederos, Edward J. Newberry

Mantech Corp.
Lexington Park, MD
Leg. Issues: DEF

Outside Counsel/Consultants

The Van Fleet-Meredith Group
Issues: DEF
Rep By: M. Bruce Meredith, Paul F. Payette, Townsend A. Van Fleet

ManTech Internat'l
Fairfax, VA
Leg. Issues: BUD, DEF

Outside Counsel/Consultants

John G. Campbell, Inc.
Issues: DEF

The Grizzle Company
Issues: BUD
Rep By: Richard A. Cantor, Charles L. Grizzle

Manufactured Housing Ass'n for Regulatory Reform

1331 Pennsylvania Ave. NW
Suite 508
Washington, DC 20004
E-mail: mharrdg@aol.com
Tel: (202)783-4087
Fax: (202)783-4075

A trade association of about 30 companies which produce manufactured housing. Dedicated to reform of the regulatory framework as it affects the housing and building industries.

Leg. Issues: HOU

In-house, DC-area Employees

GHORBANI, Daniel D.: President

Outside Counsel/Consultants

Dave Evans Associates
Issues: HOU
Rep By: Hon. Dave Evans

Valanzano & Associates
Issues: HOU
Rep By: Anthony Valanzano

Manufactured Housing Institute

2101 Wilson Blvd.
Suite 610
Arlington, VA 22201
Tel: (703)558-0400
Fax: (703)558-0401
Registered: LDA
Web: www.manufacturedhousing.org
E-mail: info@mfghome.org
Leg. Issues: BNK, BUD, CAW, CSP, DIS, HOU, RES, TAX, TEC

Political Action Committee/s

Manufactured Housing Institute Political Action Committee
2101 Wilson Blvd.
Suite 610
Arlington, VA 22201
Contact: Lauren Lewis
Tel: (703)558-0400
Fax: (703)558-0401

In-house, DC-area Employees

CABRERA, Sherri: Director, Government Affairs
COONEY, Brian: V. President, Government Affairs
LEWIS, Lauren: Director, Grassroots and PAC Activities
SAVAGE, CAE, Bruce A.: V. President, Public Affairs
STINEBERT, Chris: President

Outside Counsel/Consultants

Akin, Gump, Strauss, Hauer & Feld, L.L.P.
Rep By: Joel Jankowsky, Jose H. Villarreal

Manufactured Imports Promotion Organization (MIPRO)

2501 M St. NW
Suite 350
Washington, DC 20037
Tel: (202)659-3729
Fax: (202)887-5159
Registered: FARA

Headquartered in Tokyo, Japan.

Leg. Issues: TRD

In-house, DC-area Employees

KEMP, Tonya: Research Analyst
NATSUME, Takeo: Director

Manufacturers Alliance/MAPI Inc.

1525 Wilson Blvd.
Suite 900
Arlington, VA 22209
Web: www.mapi.net
Tel: (703)841-9000
Fax: (703)841-9514

A policy research organization. Members are producers and users of capital goods and allied products with the membership heavily represented in automotive, aerospace, computers, telecommunications, heavy equipment, and machinery. Conducts original research in economics, law and management and provides professional analysis of issues critical to the economic performance of the private sector. Operates 35 councils in various management disciplines, conducts the annual Conference on Business and Economic Policies, and acts as national spokesman for policies which stimulate technological advancement and economic growth.

Leg. Issues: ACC, BUD, CAW, CPT, CSP, DEF, ECN, EDU, ENG, ENV, FIN, GOV, HCR, IMM, INS, LBR, MAN, RET, SCI, TAX, TEC, TRD, UNM

In-house, DC-area Employees

DUESTERBERG, Thomas J.: President and Chief Exec. Officer
HOLMAN, Jr., Francis W.: V. President and Secretary
MORRISSETTE, Peggy: Director, Public and Government Affairs
STOCKER, Frederick T.: V. President, Counsel

Manufacturers Radio Frequency Advisory Committee, Inc.

Herndon, VA
Leg. Issues: COM

Outside Counsel/Consultants

Arter & Hadden
Issues: COM
Rep By: William K. Keane

Manufacturers Standardization Soc. of the Valve and Fitting Industry, Inc.

127 Park St. NE
Vienna, VA 22180-4602
Web: www.mss-hq.com
E-mail: info@mss-hq.com
Tel: (703)281-6613
Fax: (703)281-6671

Develops and publishes standards/specifications for industry products, including valves, valve acuators, flanges, pipe fittings, pipe hangers and associated seals.

Leg. Issues: MAN

In-house, DC-area Employees

O'NEILL, Robert: Exec. Director

Manufacturing Jewelers and Suppliers of America

Providence, RI

Outside Counsel/Consultants

London and Satagaj, Attorneys-at-Law
Rep By: Sheldon I. London

Manulife USA

Outside Counsel/Consultants

Dykema Gossett PLLC
Rep By: Nancy R. Barbour, Stephen H. Zimmerman

MAPPS PAC

Reston, VA

Outside Counsel/Consultants

John M. Palatiello & Associates
Rep By: John M. Palatiello

Maptech

Andover, MA
Leg. Issues: SCI

Outside Counsel/Consultants

Kerrigan & Associates, Inc.
Issues: SCI
Rep By: Michael J. Kerrigan

Marathon Ashland Petroleum, LLC

Findlay, OH
Leg. Issues: ENV

Outside Counsel/Consultants

Sparber and Associates
Issues: ENV
Rep By: Peter O'Rourke, Peter G. Sparber

Marathon Oil Co.

1101 Pennsylvania Ave. NW
Suite 510
Washington, DC 20004
Tel: (202)783-6333
Fax: (202)783-6309

A subsidiary of USX Corp.

Leg. Issues: FOR

In-house, DC-area Employees

STRAUB, Terrence D.: Washington Representative

Outside Counsel/Consultants

The Duberstein Group, Inc.
Rep By: Michael S. Berman, Kenneth M. Duberstein, Henry M. Gandy, Daniel P. Meyer

Mayer, Brown & Platt
Issues: FOR
Rep By: John P. Schmitz

O'Neill, Athy & Casey, P.C.
Rep By: Andrew Athy, Jr., Christopher R. O'Neill

March Joint Powers Authority

Moreno Valley, CA
Leg. Issues: AVI, DEF, ECN, TRA

Outside Counsel/Consultants

Copeland, Lowery & Jacquez
Issues: AVI, DEF, ECN, TRA
Rep By: Lynnette C. Jacquez

March of Dimes Birth Defects Foundation

1901 L St. NW
Suite 200
Washington, DC 20036
Tel: (202)659-1800
Fax: (202)296-2964
Registered: LDA

A non-profit organization dedicated to the prevention of birth defects and infant mortality through research, education, community services, and advocacy. Headquartered in White Plains, NY.

Leg. Issues: BUD, HCR, INS, MED, MMM, TAX, TOB

In-house, DC-area Employees

KELLEY, W. Curtis: Deputy Director, Federal Affairs
MERRILL, Jo: Director, Government Affairs
POTETZ, Lisa: Director, Public Policy Research
WEISS, Marina L.: Senior V. President, Public Policy and Government Affairs
WIGODE, Emil: Associate Director, Federal Affairs

Marconi

Outside Counsel/Consultants

Nat'l Strategies Inc.
Rep By: David K. Aylward

Marconi Communications Federal

Vienna, VA

A high performance communications systems and data transmission company.

Leg. Issues: DEF

Outside Counsel/Consultants

The PMA Group
Issues: DEF
Rep By: William E. Berl, Sean Fogarty, Kaylene Green, Joseph Littleton

Marconi Flight Systems, Inc.

Mojave, CA
Leg. Issues: DEF

Outside Counsel/Consultants

Peduzzi Associates, Ltd.
Issues: DEF
Rep By: Paul E Elliott, Joseph L. Ferreira, C. V. Meadows, Lawrence P. Peduzzi, Ronald A. Putnam

Marconi plc

London, UNITED KINGDOM
Leg. Issues: CPI, MAN, MMM, TEC

Outside Counsel/Consultants

Swidler Berlin Shereff Friedman, LLP
Issues: CPI, MAN, MMM, TEC
Rep By: Keith N. Cole, Kristine DeBry

Mari-Flite Ferries, Inc.

San Diego, CA
Leg. Issues: DEF

Outside Counsel/Consultants

Collins & Company, Inc.
Issues: DEF
Rep By: James D. Bond, Scott Cassel, Richard L. Collins, Shay D. Stautz

Marianas Political Status Commission

Saipan, NORTHERN MARIANA ISLANDS

Outside Counsel/Consultants

Wilmer, Cutler & Pickering

Maricopa, Arizona, County of

Phoenix, AZ
Leg. Issues: BUD, CAW, ENV, GOV

Outside Counsel/Consultants

Capitol Solutions
Issues: BUD, ENV

Commonwealth Group, Ltd.
Issues: BUD, CAW, GOV
Rep By: Christopher T. Cushing

Nat'l Strategies Inc.
Rep By: David K. Aylward

Maricopa-Stanfield Irrigation and Drainage District

Outside Counsel/Consultants

Strategic Impact, Inc.
Rep By: Michael C. Jimenez

Marietta College

Marietta, OH
Leg. Issues: BUD

Outside Counsel/Consultants
Cassidy & Associates, Inc.
Issues: BUD
Rep By: Laura A. Neal

Marin, California, County of

San Rafael, CA
Leg. Issues: DEF, HOU, LAW, NAT, TRA

Outside Counsel/Consultants
Alcalde & Fay
Issues: DEF, HOU, LAW, NAT, TRA
Rep By: Paul Schlesinger

The Marine and Fire Insurance Ass'n of Japan, Inc.

Tokyo, JAPAN
Leg. Issues: INS, TRD

Outside Counsel/Consultants
Paul, Hastings, Janofsky & Walker LLP
Issues: INS, TRD
Rep By: Behnam Dayanim, Scott M. Flicker, G. Hamilton Loeb

Marine Capital Management, LLC

Lake Forest, IL
Leg. Issues: MAR, TRA

Outside Counsel/Consultants
Schnader Harrison Segal & Lewis LLP
Issues: MAR, TRA
Rep By: Greggory B. Mendenhall

Marine Corps League

P.O. Box 3070 Tel: (703)207-9588
Merrifield, VA 22116 Fax: (703)207-0047
Web: www.mcleague.org
E-mail: mcl@mcleague.org

In-house, DC-area Employees
CORLEY, Jr., William Brooks: Exec. Director

Marine Corps Reserve Officers Ass'n

110 N. Royal St. Tel: (703)548-7607
Suite 406 Fax: (703)519-8779
Alexandria, VA 22314
Web: www.mcroa.com
Leg. Issues: AER, AVI, BUD, DEF, EDU, GOV, RET, VET

In-house, DC-area Employees
SNOW, Howard: Exec. Director

Marine Desalination Systems LLC

Washington, DC
Leg. Issues: BUD, CAW, DEF

Outside Counsel/Consultants
American Defense Internat'l, Inc.
Issues: DEF
Rep By: Thomas Daffron, Michael Herson, Van D. Hipp, Jr., Dave Wilberding
The Livingston Group, LLC
Issues: BUD, CAW
Rep By: Melvin Goodweather, Hon. Robert L. Livingston, Jr., J. Allen Martin, Richard L. Rodgers

Marine Engineers Beneficial Ass'n (District No. I - PCD)

444 N. Capitol St. NW Tel: (202)638-5355
Suite 800 Fax: (202)638-5369
Washington, DC 20001 Registered: LDA
Web: www.d1meba.org
Leg. Issues: AGR, DEF, ENV, LBR, MAR, NAT, TAX, TOU, TRA, TRU

Political Action Committee/s
Marine Engineers Beneficial Ass'n Political Action Fund
444 N. Capitol St. NW Tel: (202)638-5355
Suite 800 Fax: (202)638-5369
Washington, DC 20001

In-house, DC-area Employees
MORRIS, W. Patrick: Director of Legislative and Legal Affairs
ZIMMERMAN, Malissa: Director, Government Affairs

Outside Counsel/Consultants
John D. Hardy
Issues: MAR, TRA
Rep By: John D. Hardy

Marine Mammal Coalition

Noank, CT
An association of aquariums.

Leg. Issues: ANI, MAR

Outside Counsel/Consultants
O'Connor & Hannan, L.L.P.
Issues: ANI, MAR
Rep By: George J. Mannina, Jr.
Wiley, Rein & Fielding
Rep By: John A. Hodges

Marine Preservation Ass'n

Scottsdale, AZ

Outside Counsel/Consultants
Howrey Simon Arnold & White
Rep By: Charles J. Engel, III

Marine Resources Company Internat'l

Seattle, WA

Outside Counsel/Consultants
Preston Gates Ellis & Rouvelas Meeds LLP
Rep By: William N. Myhre

Marine Spill Response Corporation

455 Spring Park Pl. Tel: (703)326-5600
Suite 200 Fax: (703)326-5660
Herndon, VA 20170
Web: www.msrc.org
A national, private, non-profit corporation which responds to oil spills.

Leg. Issues: ENV

In-house, DC-area Employees
BENZ, Steven T.: President
ROOS, Judith A.: Manager, Marketing and Customer Service
SAMPLE, Michael J.: V. President, General Counsel

Outside Counsel/Consultants
Dyer Ellis & Joseph, P.C.
Issues: ENV
Rep By: Laurie Crick Sahatjian, Jeanne Marie Grasso, Lara Bernstein Mathews, Duncan C. Smith, III, Jennifer M. Southwick, Jonathan K. Waldron, Sidney A. Wallace
Nixon Peabody LLP

Marine Technology Soc.

1828 L St. NW Tel: (202)775-5966
Suite 906 Fax: (202)429-9417
Washington, DC 20036-5104
Web: www.mtsociety.org
E-mail: mtspubs@aol.com
A multi-disciplinary international professional society. Encourages the development of the technology, education, operational expertise, and public awareness needed to advance capabilities to work in all ocean areas and depths.

Leg. Issues: MAR

In-house, DC-area Employees
CLARK, Dr. Andrew M.: President
KRAUTHAMER, Judith: Exec. Director

Marine Transport Corp.

Weehawken, NJ

Outside Counsel/Consultants
Preston Gates Ellis & Rouvelas Meeds LLP
Rep By: Jonathan Blank, Susan B. Geiger

Marine Transport Lines, Inc.

Secaucus, NJ

Outside Counsel/Consultants
Wright & Talisman, P.C.
Rep By: Arnold B. Podgorsky

Mariner Health Group, Inc.

New London, CT

Outside Counsel/Consultants
McDermott, Will and Emery
Rep By: Calvin P. Johnson

Mariner Post Acute Network

Atlanta, GA
Leg. Issues: HCR

Outside Counsel/Consultants
Brownstein Hyatt & Farber, P.C.
Issues: HCR
Rep By: William T. Brack, Thomas H. Hudson, Michael B. Levy
Mintz, Levin, Cohn, Ferris, Glovsky and Popeo, P.C.
Rep By: Raymond D. Cotton

Marinette Marine Corp.

Marinette, WI
Leg. Issues: MAR

Outside Counsel/Consultants
Winston & Strawn
Issues: MAR
Rep By: Hon. James H. Burnley, IV, Lawrence I. Kiern, Charles L. Kinney, Thomas L. Mills, Constantine G. Papavizas

Marion County Solid Waste Management

Salem, OR

Outside Counsel/Consultants
Wright & Talisman, P.C.
Rep By: Scott M. DuBoff

Marion, Indiana, City of

Leg. Issues: BUD, ECN, URB

Outside Counsel/Consultants
Sagamore Associates, Inc.
Issues: BUD, ECN, URB
Rep By: David U. Gogol, Dena S. Morris

The Maritime Consortium, Inc.

Alexandria, VA
Provides drug testing services in compliance with Department of Transportation regulations for marine firms.

Outside Counsel/Consultants
Washington Policy Associates, Inc.
Rep By: Jeffrey C. Smith

Maritime Exchange for the Delaware River and Bay

Philadelphia, PA Registered: LDA
Leg. Issues: MAR, TRU

Outside Counsel/Consultants
Blank Rome Comisky & McCauley, LLP
Issues: MAR, TRU
Rep By: David A. Norcross

Maritime Fire and Safety Ass'n

Leg. Issues: DIS

Outside Counsel/Consultants
Lindsay Hart Neil & Weigler
Issues: DIS
Rep By: Kathryn Beaubien, Peter Friedmann

Maritime Institute for Research and Industrial Development

1775 K St. NW Tel: (202)463-6505
Suite 200 Fax: (202)223-9093
Washington, DC 20006 Registered: LDA
E-mail: miraid2@worldnet.att.net
A research organization of the Internat'l Organization of Masters, Mates and Pilots American-flag shipping companies.

Leg. Issues: MAR, TAX, TRD

In-house, DC-area Employees
KJELLBERG, Sandra D.: Government Relations
PATTI, C. James: President
PATTI, Meredith L.: Government Relations
WINES, Stephen H.: Special Counsel

Outside Counsel/Consultants
William V. Brierre
Issues: MAR, TAX, TRD
Rep By: William V. Brierre, Jr.

Maritime Investment Corp.

1250 24th St. NW Tel: (202)835-1617
Suite 300 Registered: LDA
Washington, DC 20037
Leg. Issues: FIN, MAR

In-house, DC-area Employees
CANTOR, L. Michael: Managing Director

Market Access Ltd.

London, UNITED KINGDOM

Outside Counsel/Consultants
Hayward Internat'l

Marquette General Hospital

Marquette, MI
Leg. Issues: MED

Outside Counsel/Consultants
Bob Davis & Associates
Issues: MED
Rep By: Hon. Robert W. Davis

Marquette University

Milwaukee, WI Registered: LDA
Leg. Issues: EDU

Outside Counsel/Consultants

Collins & Company, Inc.
Issues: EDU
Rep By: James D. Bond, Richard L. Collins, Thomas A. Hooper, Shay D. Stautz

Marriott Internat'l, Inc.

One Marriott Dr. Tel: (202)380-3000
Department 977.01 Registered: LDA
Washington, DC 20058
Leg. Issues: BUD, IND, LBR, RES, TAX, TEC

Political Action Committee/s

Marriott Internat'l Political Action Committee
One Marriott Dr. Tel: (202)380-3000
Department 977.01
Washington, DC 20058
Contact: Thomas E. Ladd

In-house, DC-area Employees

HILL, Nick: Director, Corporate Information
KITTLEMAN, Trent
LADD, Thomas E.: V. President, Government Affairs
LADD, William D.: V. President, Legislative Affairs
LUNDBERG, Rolf: V. President and Assistant General Counsel, Government and International Relations
RYAN, Joseph: Exec. V. President and General Counsel
STERLING, Charlotte: Senior V. President, Corporate Relations

Outside Counsel/Consultants

Chambers Associates Inc.
Issues: BUD, LBR, TAX
Rep By: William A. Signer

Kurzweil & Associates
Issues: RES, TAX
Rep By: Jeffrey Kurzweil

RMA Internat'l, Inc.
Rep By: Otto J. Reich

Sunrise Research Corp.
Issues: TAX
Rep By: Hon. Bob Packwood

Mars, Inc.

6885 Elm St. Tel: (703)821-4900
McLean, VA 22101 Fax: (703)448-9678

In-house, DC-area Employees

STEGEMANN, E. J.: V. President

Outside Counsel/Consultants

Andrews Associates, Inc.
Rep By: Hon. Mark Andrews, Dr. Jacqueline Balk-Tusa

Patton Boggs, LLP
Rep By: Thomas Hale Boggs, Jr., Michael A. Curto, David E. Dunn, III, John F. Fithian, Kenneth A. Grigg, Clayton L. Hough, John F. Jonas, Martha M. Kendrick, Lansing B. Lee, III, Cliff Massa, III, Donald V. Moorehead, Darryl D. Nirenberg, Stuart M. Pape, David G. Raboy, Aubrey A. Rothrock, III, Frank R. Samolis, Steven M. Schneebaum

Verner, Liipfert, Bernhard, McPherson and Hand, Chartered
Rep By: Andrew D. Eskin, Martin Mendelsohn, Nancy A. Sheliga

Marsh & McLennan Cos.

New York, NY
Insurance brokers.
Leg. Issues: TAX

Outside Counsel/Consultants

Baker & Hostetler LLP
Issues: TAX
Rep By: William F. Conroy, Matthew J. Dolan, Steven A. Lotterer, David L. Marshall, Hon. Guy Vander Jagt

Washington Council Ernst & Young
Issues: TAX
Rep By: Doug Badger, Lauren Darling, John L. Doney, Jayne T. Fitzgerald, LaBrenda Garrett-Nelson, Gary J. Gasper, Bruce A. Gates, Nick Giordano, Cathy Koch, Robert J. Leonard, Richard Meltzer, Phillip D. Moseley, John D. Porter, Robert M. Rozen, Donna Steele-Flynn, Timothy J. Urban

Marsh USA, Inc.

Boston, MA
Leg. Issues: INS

Outside Counsel/Consultants

Capitol Partners
Issues: INS
Rep By: William Cunningham

Marshall Institute, George C.

1730 K St. NW Tel: (202)296-9655
Suite 905 Fax: (202)296-9714
Washington, DC 20006
Web: www.marshall.org

A non profit organization specializing in scientific issues that impact public policy.

In-house, DC-area Employees

O'KEEFE, William: Managing Director

Marshall Islands Nuclear Claims Tribunal

Leg. Issues: ENG

Outside Counsel/Consultants

Pacific Islands Washington Office
Issues: ENG
Rep By: Fred Radewagen

Marshall Islands, Republic of the

Majuro, MARSHALL ISLANDS

Outside Counsel/Consultants

Internat'l Registries, Inc.
Rep By: Larry E. Camp

Theodore George Kronmiller
Rep By: Theodore George Kronmiller

Winthrop, Stimson, Putnam & Roberts

Marshall Research Corp.

Huntington, WV

Outside Counsel/Consultants

Cottone and Huggins Group
Rep By: James B. Huggins

Marshall, Alabama, County of

Guntersville, AL
Leg. Issues: BUD, ECN

Outside Counsel/Consultants

Murray, Scheer, Montgomery, Tapia & O'Donnell
Issues: BUD, ECN
Rep By: Alison Houle, John H. Montgomery, John R. O'Donnell, Mark Zelden

The Marshfield Clinic

Marshfield, WI
Leg. Issues: MMM

Outside Counsel/Consultants

McDermott, Will and Emery
Issues: MMM
Rep By: Eric P. Zimmerman

Martha's Vineyard Steamship Authority

Woodshole, MA

Outside Counsel/Consultants

Sher & Blackwell
Rep By: Jeffrey R. Pike

Martin Color-Fi

Edgefield, SC
Leg. Issues: TRD

Outside Counsel/Consultants

American Continental Group, Inc.
Issues: TRD
Rep By: John A. Cline, Thaddeus E. Strom

Martin Marietta Aggregates

Raleigh, NC

Outside Counsel/Consultants

Patton Boggs, LLP
Rep By: Henry Chajet, Mark N. Savit

Martin-Baker Aircraft Co., Ltd.

Middlesex, UNITED KINGDOM
Leg. Issues: AER, AVI, BUD, MAN, SCI, TRD, URB

Outside Counsel/Consultants

Burdeshaw Associates, Ltd.
Issues: AER, AVI, BUD, MAN, SCI, TRD, URB
Rep By: James Connally, Kenneth Israel, Michael Stacy

Martinair Holland

Amsterdam, NETHERLANDS

Outside Counsel/Consultants

Zuckert, Scoutt and Rasenberger, L.L.P.
Rep By: Frank J. Costello, Rachel B. Trinder

Martinez and Curtis

Phoenix, AZ
Leg. Issues: BUD, ENG

Outside Counsel/Consultants

Jones, Walker, Waechter, Poitevent, Carrere & Denegre, L.L.P.
Issues: BUD, ENG
Rep By: Paul Cambon, John J. Jaskot, R. Christian Johnsen, James Ogsbury

Martini & Rossi Corp.

White Plains, NY

Outside Counsel/Consultants

Kelley, Drye & Warren LLP

Martinizing Environmental Group

Leg. Issues: ENV

Outside Counsel/Consultants

Baise + Miller, P.C.
Issues: ENV
Rep By: Eric P. Bock, Michael Formica, Marshall L. Miller

Martins Point Health Care

Portland, ME
Leg. Issues: DEF, HCR

Outside Counsel/Consultants

Ervin Technical Associates, Inc. (ETA)
Issues: DEF, HCR
Rep By: Hon. Jack Edwards, James L. Ervin, Donald E. Richbourg

Martz Group

Wilkes-Barre, PA
Leg. Issues: TRA

Outside Counsel/Consultants

Theodore C. Knappen, P.C.
Issues: TRA
Rep By: Theodore C. Knappen

Marubeni America Corp.

1776 I St. NW Tel: (202)331-1167
Suite 725 Fax: (202)331-1319
Washington, DC 20006

International trading, financial, investment and organizing projects.

In-house, DC-area Employees

MIYAZAWA, Mike K.: V. Preisdent and General Manager
PHIPPS, John G.: Manager, Internat'l Business Development and Strategic Planning
UEHARA, So: Senior Researcher

Mary Jane Bakeries

Norfolk, VA

Outside Counsel/Consultants

Robert N. Pyle & Associates

Maryland Ass'n of the Deaf

Baltimore, MD

Outside Counsel/Consultants

Issue Dynamics Inc.

Maryland Dairy Industry Ass'n

Washington, DC
Leg. Issues: AGR

Outside Counsel/Consultants

Agri/Washington
Issues: AGR
Rep By: Jon Moore, Paul S. Weller, Jr.

Maryland Department of Transportation

Baltimore, MD
Leg. Issues: TRA

Outside Counsel/Consultants

The Carmen Group
Issues: TRA
Rep By: John Hassell, Mia O'Connell, James B. Young

Preston Gates Ellis & Rouvelas Meeds LLP
Rep By: Jonathan Blank, Pamela J. Garvie, James R. Weiss

Maryland Nat'l Capitol Building Ass'n

1738 Elton Rd. Tel: (301)445-5400
Suite 200 Fax: (301)445-5499
Silver Spring, MD 20903
E-mail: submdbia@mncba.org

In-house, DC-area Employees
CAMPBELL, F. Hamer: Director, Government Affairs and Senior Legislative Representative
MATLICK, CAE, Susan J.: Exec. Director

Maryland Psychiatric Soc.
Baltimore, MD
Leg. Issues: CPT, GOV, LBR, TAX, TOR

Outside Counsel/Consultants
Venable
Issues: CPT, GOV, LBR, TAX, TOR
Rep By: Jeffrey S. Tenenbaum

Maryland Taxpayers Ass'n, Inc.
7831 Woodmont Ave.
Suite 395
Bethesda, MD 20814
Tel: (301)946-2918
Fax: (301)942-5341
Registered: LDA
Web: www.mdtaxes.org
E-mail: president@mdtaxes.org
Leg. Issues: TAX

In-house, DC-area Employees
TIMMERMAN, Kenneth: President

Maryland, Aviation Administration of the State of
BWI Airport, MD

Outside Counsel/Consultants
Preston Gates Ellis & Rouvelas Meeds LLP
Rep By: Jonathan Blank

Maryland, DC, Delaware Broadcasters Ass'n
Baltimore, MD

Outside Counsel/Consultants
Capitol Campaign Consultants
Rep By: Thomas E. Fahy

Maryland, Office of the Attorney General of the State of
Annapolis, MD

Outside Counsel/Consultants
Duncan, Weinberg, Genzer & Pembroke, P.C.
Rep By: James F. Flug

Marymount University
Arlington, VA
Leg. Issues: BUD

Outside Counsel/Consultants
Cassidy & Associates, Inc.
Issues: BUD
Rep By: Valerie Rogers Osborne, Mary E. Shields, Maureen Walsh

Mas-Hamilton Group
Lexington, KY
Leg. Issues: BUD, DEF

Outside Counsel/Consultants
Alvarado & Gerken
Issues: DEF
Rep By: Susan E. Alvarado, David A. Gerken
Balch & Bingham LLP
Issues: BUD
Rep By: Wade Heck, William F. Stiers
Feith & Zell, P.C.
Issues: DEF
Rep By: Douglas J. Feith
The Grizzle Company
Issues: BUD
Rep By: Richard A. Cantor, Charles L. Grizzle

Mashantucket Pequot Tribal Nation

Outside Counsel/Consultants
Ietan Consulting
Rep By: Wilson Pipestem, Larry Rosenthal
Winner & Associates

Mashpee Wampanoag Indian Tribal Council, Inc.
Mashpee, MA
Leg. Issues: IND

Outside Counsel/Consultants
Steptoe & Johnson LLP
Issues: IND
Rep By: John J. Duffy, Hilda Manuel
Zane & Associates
Issues: IND

Masonry Industry Ventures, Inc.
821 15th St. NW
Washington, DC 20005
Tel: (202)383-3907
Fax: (202)383-0433
A U.S. corporation formed by elements of the masonry construction industry to pursue offshore construction opportunities, particularly in third-world countries.

In-house, DC-area Employees
KARDY, Walter M.: President

Outside Counsel/Consultants
Specialty Contractors Management, Inc.
Rep By: Walter M. Kardy

Mass Transit Authority
Flint, MI
Leg. Issues: BUD, RRR, TRA

Outside Counsel/Consultants
Government Relations, Inc.
Issues: BUD, RRR, TRA
Rep By: Thomas J. Bulger, Mark H. Miller

Massa Products Corp.
Hingham, MA
A manufacturer of acoustic equipment and marine products.
Leg. Issues: DEF

Outside Counsel/Consultants
Commonwealth Consulting Corp.
Issues: DEF
Rep By: Christopher M. Lehman

Massachusetts Bankers Ass'n
Boston, MA
Leg. Issues: BAN, HOU

Outside Counsel/Consultants
Goodwin, Procter & Hoar LLP
Issues: BAN, HOU
Rep By: Jeremiah S. Buckley, Margo Tank

Massachusetts Bay Transportation Authority
Boston, MA
Leg. Issues: TRA

Outside Counsel/Consultants
Thompson Coburn LLP
Issues: TRA
Rep By: Hon. R. Lawrence Coughlin, Jane Sutter-Starke, G. Kent Woodman

Massachusetts General/Brigham and Women's Hospital
Boston, MA

Outside Counsel/Consultants
O'Neill, Athy & Casey, P.C.
Rep By: Martha L. Casey, Christopher R. O'Neill

Massachusetts Higher Education Assistance Corp.
Boston, MA

Outside Counsel/Consultants
Kutak Rock LLP

Massachusetts Hospital Ass'n
Burlington, MA
Leg. Issues: HCR, MMM

Outside Counsel/Consultants
Foley, Hoag & Eliot LLP
Issues: HCR, MMM
Rep By: Marie Beatrice Grause

Massachusetts Housing Finance Agency
Boston, MA
Leg. Issues: HOU

Outside Counsel/Consultants
Hessel and Aluise, P.C.
Issues: HOU
Rep By: Nancy Libson

Massachusetts Housing Partnership Fund
Boston, MA

Outside Counsel/Consultants
Robert A. Rapoza Associates
Rep By: Robert A. Rapoza

Massachusetts Maritime Academy
Buzzards Bay, MA
Leg. Issues: APP, BUD

Outside Counsel/Consultants
Patton Boggs, LLP
Issues: APP, BUD
Rep By: Robert C. Jones

Massachusetts Medical Device Industry Council
Boston, MA

Outside Counsel/Consultants
MARC Associates, Inc.
Rep By: Edwin Allen

Massachusetts Mutual Life Insurance Co.
Springfield, MA
Leg. Issues: INS, TOR

Outside Counsel/Consultants
Peter Kinzler
Issues: INS, TOR
Rep By: Peter Kinzler

Massachusetts Port Authority
Boston, MA
Leg. Issues: AVI

Outside Counsel/Consultants
GPC Internat'l
Issues: AVI
Rep By: John D. Cahill, Daniel K. Crann

Massachusetts Soc. of Certified Public Accountants
Boston, MA

Outside Counsel/Consultants
Cassidy & Associates, Inc.

Massachusetts Software Council
Boston, MA
Leg. Issues: CPI, CPT, TAX, TEC

Outside Counsel/Consultants
GLOBEMAC Associates
Issues: CPI, CPT, TAX, TEC
Rep By: Gordon D. MacKay

Massachusetts Technology Park Corp.
Westborough, MA

Outside Counsel/Consultants
Mintz, Levin, Cohn, Ferris, Glovsky and Popeo, P.C.

Massachusetts Water Resources Authority
Boston, MA
Leg. Issues: BUD, CAW, ENV

Outside Counsel/Consultants
Campbell Crane & Associates
Issues: BUD, CAW, ENV
Rep By: Jeanne M. Campbell, Daniel M. Crane
Foley, Hoag & Eliot LLP
Issues: CAW
Rep By: Marie Beatrice Grause

Massachusetts, Commonwealth of
444 N. Capitol St. NW
Suite 400
Washington, DC 20001
Tel: (202)624-7713
Fax: (202)624-7714
Headquartered in Boston, MA.

In-house, DC-area Employees
GAVIN, Anne: Director, Office of Federal-State Relations

Massena, New York, Town of
Leg. Issues: ENG, GOV, UTI

Outside Counsel/Consultants
Duncan, Weinberg, Genzer & Pembroke, P.C.
Issues: ENG, GOV, UTI
Rep By: Richmond F. Allan, Wallace L. Duncan, Jeffrey C. Genzer, Thomas L. Rudebusch

MassMutual Financial Group
325 Seventh St.
Suite 1225
Washington, DC 20004
Tel: (202)737-0440
Fax: (202)628-2313
Registered: LDA
Web: www.massmutual.com
Leg. Issues: BAN, BNK, FIN, HCR, LBR, RET, TAX, TOR

Political Action Committee/s
MassMutual Political Action Committee
325 Seventh St.
Suite 1225
Washington, DC 20004
Tel: (202)737-0440
Fax: (202)628-2313
Contact: Ellen Wilkins Ellis

In-house, DC-area Employees
ELLIS, Ellen Wilkins: Second V. President, Government Relations
WEISS, Alison B.: Director

Outside Counsel/Consultants

Barbour Griffith & Rogers, Inc.
Issues: BAN, BNK, FIN, HCR, LBR, RET, TAX, TOR
Rep By: Haley Barbour, Loren Monroe

Ernst & Young LLP
Issues: BAN, BNK, FIN, TAX
Rep By: Lauren Darling, Patrick G. Heck, Phillip D. Moseley, Henry C. Ruempler, Donna Steele-Flynn

Patton Boggs, LLP
Issues: BNK, FIN, RET, TAX
Rep By: John F. Jonas

Wiley, Rein & Fielding
Issues: TAX
Rep By: Susan C. Buck

MasterCard Internat'l

1401 I St. NW
Suite 240
Washington, DC 20005
Tel: (202)414-8000
Fax: (202)414-8010
Registered: LDA
Web: www.mastercard.com

Headquarters are in Purchase, NY.

Leg. Issues: BAN, BNK, CSP, FIN, GAM, LAW, LBR, SCI, TAX

In-house, DC-area Employees
BINZEL, William P.: V. President, Public Affairs
CORRIGAN, Angela: Legislative Assistant

Outside Counsel/Consultants

MSP Strategic Communications, Inc.
Issues: BAN, CSP, GAM
Rep By: Mitchell S. Pettit

Sidley & Austin

The Smith-Free Group
Issues: BNK
Rep By: James C. Free, W. Timothy Locke, James E. Smith

MATEK

Moscow, RUSSIA

Outside Counsel/Consultants

Shaw Pittman
Rep By: Gerald Charnoff

Materials Research Soc.

Warrendale, PA
Leg. Issues: BUD

Outside Counsel/Consultants

Strategic Partners Inc.
Issues: BUD
Rep By: Ronald L. Kelley

Matlack Systems, Inc.

Wilmington, DE
Leg. Issues: TRA, TRU

Outside Counsel/Consultants

Results Cubed
Issues: TRA, TRU
Rep By: James E. Mahoney

Matra Aerospace, Inc.

Germantown, MD

A subsidiary of Matra, S.A. of Paris, France.

Outside Counsel/Consultants

Kaye Scholer LLP

Matson Navigation Co.

1735 New York Ave. NW
Suite 500
Washington, DC 20006
Tel: (202)662-8455
Fax: (202)331-1024
Registered: LDA
Web: www.matson.com

Specializes in ocean transportation between the U.S. Pacific Coast and Hawaii/Guam.

Leg. Issues: MAR

In-house, DC-area Employees
GRILL, Philip M.: V. President, Government Relations

Matsushita Electric Corp. of America

1620 L St. NW
Suite 1150
Washington, DC 20036
Tel: (202)223-2575
Fax: (202)223-2614
Registered: LDA

Leg. Issues: CPT, ENV, TAX, TEC, TRD

In-house, DC-area Employees
ALEXANDER, Mary K.: Assistant General Manager, Government and Public Affairs
FANNON, Peter F.: V. President, Technology Policy and Regulatory Affairs
SCHOMBURG, Paul: Manager, Government and Public Affairs
SHARP, Mark: General Manager, Corporate Environmental Department

Outside Counsel/Consultants

Alston & Bird LLP
Issues: TAX
Rep By: Henry J. Birnkrant, Robert T. Cole

Jefferson-Waterman Internat'l, LLC

Patton Boggs, LLP
Issues: CPT
Rep By: Thomas Hale Boggs, Jr., Brian C. Lopina, Jeffrey L. Turner

Swidler Berlin Shereff Friedman, LLP
Rep By: Barry B. Direnfeld, Harold P. Goldfield, Lester S. Hyman, Richard A. Popkin

Weil, Gotshal & Manges, LLP
Issues: CPT
Rep By: Sandra M. Aistars, Bruce H. Turnbull

Matsushita Electric Industrial Co., Ltd.

1620 L St. NW
Suite 1150
Washington, DC 20036
Tel: (202)223-2575
Fax: (202)223-2614
Registered: LDA, FARA

The Washington liaison office of the Japanese electronics company headquartered in Osaka, Japan.

Leg. Issues: TRD

In-house, DC-area Employees
KARIS, Katherine: International Research Coordinator
KIKUCHI, Hiroshi "Andy": Director

Outside Counsel/Consultants

Jefferson-Waterman Internat'l, LLC
Issues: TRD
Rep By: Daniel J. O'Neill

Willkie Farr & Gallagher
Rep By: James P. Durling

Mattel, Inc.

El Segundo, CA
Leg. Issues: CSP, HCR, TRD

Outside Counsel/Consultants

St. Maxens & Company
Issues: CSP, HCR, TRD
Rep By: Viraj M. Mirani, Julia Smith, Thomas F. St. Maxens, II

Matthews Media Group, Inc.

Rockville, MD
Leg. Issues: HCR

Outside Counsel/Consultants

Cassidy & Associates, Inc.
Issues: HCR
Rep By: Dennis M. Kedzior

Maui Pineapple Co.

Kahului, HI
Leg. Issues: DEF

Outside Counsel/Consultants

Collier Shannon Scott, PLLC
Issues: DEF
Rep By: Lauren R. Howard, Robert W. Porter

Mauritania, Government of the Islamic Republic of

Nouakchott, MAURITANIA

Outside Counsel/Consultants

George H. Denison
Rep By: George H. Denison

Mauritania, Office of the Foreign Minister of

Nouakchott, MAURITANIA

Outside Counsel/Consultants

Washington World Group, Ltd.
Rep By: Edward J. von Kloberg, III

Mauritius Sugar Syndicate

Port Louis, MAURITIUS
Leg. Issues: AGR, FOO, TRD

Outside Counsel/Consultants

Ryberg and Smith LLP
Issues: AGR, FOO, TRD
Rep By: Paul Ryberg, Jr.

Mauritius, Chamber of Agriculture of

Port Louis, MAURITIUS
Leg. Issues: AGR, FOO, TRD

Outside Counsel/Consultants

Ryberg and Smith LLP
Issues: AGR, FOO, TRD
Rep By: Paul Ryberg, Jr.

Mauritius-U.S. Business Ass'n Inc.

Washington, DC
Leg. Issues: TRD

Outside Counsel/Consultants

Ryberg and Smith LLP
Issues: TRD
Rep By: Paul Ryberg, Jr.

Maverick Tube Corp.

Chesterfield, MO
Leg. Issues: TRA

Outside Counsel/Consultants

Schagrin Associates
Issues: TRA
Rep By: Tamara L. Browne, Roger B. Schagrin

Maximum Information Technology Inc.

Jackson, MS
Leg. Issues: LAW

Outside Counsel/Consultants

Winston & Strawn
Issues: LAW
Rep By: Lawrence I. Kiern, John C. Kirtland, John A. Waits, II

Maxus Energy Corp.

Dallas, TX
Leg. Issues: TAX

Outside Counsel/Consultants

McDermott, Will and Emery
Issues: TAX
Rep By: Robert B. Harding

May Department Stores Co.

St. Louis, MO
Leg. Issues: BNK

Outside Counsel/Consultants

Albers & Co.
Issues: BNK
Rep By: William E. Albers, M. Guy Rohling

Mayaguez, Puerto Rico, Municipality of

Mayaguez, PR
Leg. Issues: TRA, URB

Outside Counsel/Consultants

Oldaker and Harris, LLP
Issues: TRA, URB
Rep By: William D. Harris, William C. Oldaker

Maytag Corp.

1310 G St. NW
Suite 720
Washington, DC 20005
Tel: (202)639-9420
Fax: (202)639-9421
Registered: LDA
E-mail: dhorst@maytag.com

Headquartered in Newton, IA, Maytag Corporation is a leading producer of home and commercial appliances. Its products are sold throughout North America and international markets and its brands include Maytag, Hoover, Jenn-Air, Dixie-Narco, and Blodgett.

Leg. Issues: BNK, BUD, CAW, CSP, ENV, FOO, LBR, MAN, SCI, TAX, TRA, TRD

Political Action Committee/s

Maytag Corporation Employees for Good Government Fund
1310 G St. NW
Suite 720
Washington, DC 20005
Tel: (202)639-9420
Fax: (202)639-9421

In-house, DC-area Employees
HORSTMAN, Douglass C.: V. President, Government Affairs
STEINER, David P.: Director, Government Affairs

Outside Counsel/Consultants

Interface Inc.
Rep By: Robert G. Williams

Mazak Corp. & Mazak Sales and Service, Inc.

Florence, KY
Leg. Issues: MAN, TAX

Outside Counsel/Consultants

Global USA, Inc.
Issues: MAN, TAX
Rep By: Dr. Bohdan Denysyk

Mazda Motor Corp.

Hiroshima, JAPAN

Outside Counsel/Consultants

Hill and Knowlton, Inc.
Rep By: Gary G. Hymel

Mazda North America Operations

1025 Connecticut Ave. NW
Suite 910
Washington, DC 20036
Tel: (202)467-5088
Registered: LDA

Responsible for research and development, sales and marketing, and customer parts and service support of Mazda vehicles in the U.S. Headquartered in Irvine, CA.

Leg. Issues: AUT, BNK, CSP, ENV, FUE, TRD

In-house, DC-area Employees

BROWN, Annemarie: Government Affairs Representative
NOCERA, Barbara: Director, Government and Industry Affairs
RYAN, Dan: Manager, Government and Safety Affairs

Outside Counsel/Consultants

Steptoe & Johnson LLP
Issues: AUT, TRD

MBNA America Bank NA

Newark, DE
Registered: LDA
Leg. Issues: BAN, BNK, HCR

Outside Counsel/Consultants

Thomas J. Gilligan
Issues: HCR
Rep By: Thomas J. Gilligan

The Smith-Free Group
Issues: BAN, BNK
Rep By: James C. Free, W. Timothy Locke, James E. Smith

MCA Inc.

Washington, DC
Registered: LDA

Also known as Music Corp. of America.

Leg. Issues: TAX

Outside Counsel/Consultants

Akin, Gump, Strauss, Hauer & Feld, L.L.P.

Thelen Reid & Priest LLP
Issues: TAX
Rep By: Barry I. Berkoff, William A. Kirk, Jr.

Williams & Connolly
Rep By: David E. Kendall

Wilmer, Cutler & Pickering

McAndrews and Forbes Holding, Inc.

Leg. Issues: ECN

Outside Counsel/Consultants

Hill and Knowlton, Inc.
Issues: ECN

The McConnell Foundation

Redding, CA
Leg. Issues: BUD

Outside Counsel/Consultants

Hogan & Hartson L.L.P.
Issues: BUD
Rep By: C. Michael Gilliland, Douglas Wheeler

McDermott Internat'l, Inc./Babcock & Wilcox

1820 N. Fort Myer Dr.
Suite 804
Arlington, VA 22209
Tel: (703)528-6237
Fax: (703)351-6418
Registered: LDA

McDermott International provides marine construction services for the oil and gas industry, and power generation systems and equipment for the electric utility industry and the U.S. Government. Major subsidiaries include J. Ray McDermott, S.A., Babcock & Wilcox, BWX Technologies, and McDermott Technologies, Inc. Headquartered in New Orleans, LA.

Leg. Issues: AGR, DEF, ENG, ENV, FOR, HCR, MAR, NAT, TAX, TRD

Political Action Committee/s

Better Government Fund of McDermott, Inc.

1820 N. Fort Myer Dr.
Suite 804
Arlington, VA 22209
Contact: Jack Hoggard
Tel: (703)351-6301
Fax: (703)351-6417

Good Government Fund of Babcock & Wilcox

1820 N. Fort Myer Dr.
Suite 804
Arlington, VA 22209
Contact: Jack Hoggard
Tel: (703)351-6301
Fax: (703)351-6417

In-house, DC-area Employees

HATTON, Bruce N.: V. President and General Manager, Washington Operations
HOGGARD, Jack: Manager, Legislative Affairs
PILAND, Julius L. "Bud": Manager, Government Programs
RADEMACHER, Richard: Manager, Government Programs (BWX Technologies)
TELLO, Beth: Office Manager

McDonald's Corp.

1725 DeSales St. NW
Suite 802
Washington, DC 20036
Tel: (202)887-8900
Fax: (202)887-8907
Registered: LDA

Web: www.mcdonalds.com

Headquartered in Oak Brook, IL.

Leg. Issues: ADV, AGR, BUD, CPT, CSP, EDU, FIN, FOO, IMM, LBR, ROD, SMB, TAX, TRD

Political Action Committee/s

McDonald's Federal PAC

1725 DeSales St. NW
Suite 802
Washington, DC 20036
Contact: Richard L. "Dick" Crawford
Tel: (202)887-8900
Fax: (202)887-8907

In-house, DC-area Employees

CRAWFORD, Richard L. "Dick": Senior Director, Government Relations
RELIC, Becky: Staff Director, Federal Relations

Outside Counsel/Consultants

Nurnberger and Associates
Issues: SMB
Rep By: Ralph D. Nurnberger

Olsson, Frank and Weeda, P.C.
Issues: BUD, FOO
Rep By: Tyson Redpath, Ryan W. Stroschein

Preston Gates Ellis & Rouvelas Meeds LLP

Michael L. Tiner
Issues: SMB
Rep By: Michael L. Tiner

Wilmer, Cutler & Pickering
Issues: TAX
Rep By: William J. Wilkins

McDonnell & Miller

Chicago, IL
Leg. Issues: HOU

Outside Counsel/Consultants

LegisLaw
Issues: HOU
Rep By: Linda A. Woolley, Esq.

MCG Northwest, Inc.

Portland, OR
Leg. Issues: TAX

Outside Counsel/Consultants

Washington Council Ernst & Young
Issues: TAX
Rep By: Doug Badger, Lauren Darling, John L. Doney, Jayne T. Fitzgerald, LaBrenda Garrett-Nelson, Gary J. Gasper, Bruce A. Gates, Nick Giordano, Cathy Koch, Robert J. Leonard, Richard Meltzer, Phillip D. Moseley, John D. Porter, Robert M. Rozen, Donna Steele-Flynn, Timothy J. Urban

McGarr Capital Management Corp.

Dallas, TX

Outside Counsel/Consultants

The Washington Group

McGaw, Inc.

Irvine, CA

Outside Counsel/Consultants

Wiley, Rein & Fielding

McGlotten & Jarvis

1901 L St. NW
Suite 300
Washington, DC 20036
Tel: (202)452-9515
Fax: (202)466-8016
Registered: LDA

Leg. Issues: HCR

In-house, DC-area Employees

JARVIS, John T.
MCGLOTTEN, Robert M.

Outside Counsel/Consultants

McDermott, Will and Emery
Issues: HCR
Rep By: Calvin P. Johnson

McGraw-Hill Cos., The

1200 G St. NW
Suite 900
Washington, DC 20005-3802
Tel: (202)383-3700
Fax: (202)383-3718
Registered: LDA

Web: www.mcgraw-hill.com

Headquartered in New York, NY, McGraw Hill is a global information services provider meeting worldwide needs in the financial services, eduation and business information markets.

Leg. Issues: ADV, COM, CPT, EDU, FIN, GOV, HCR, IMM, LBR, MIA, POS, TAX, TRD

In-house, DC-area Employees

BRADDON, Cynthia H.: V. President, Washington Affairs
DEGIUSTI, Paul: Director, Washington Affairs
JORDAN, William: Director, Government Affairs and Communications

Outside Counsel/Consultants

The Michael Lewan Co.
Issues: MIA
Rep By: Michael Lewan

Squire, Sanders & Dempsey L.L.P.
Issues: POS
Rep By: Tim Bergin

Thiemann Aitken Vohra & Rutledge, L.L.C.
Issues: EDU
Rep By: Alan J. Thiemann

Widmeyer Communications, Inc.

The McGuffey Project

Outside Counsel/Consultants

Nat'l Strategies Inc.
Rep By: David K. Aylward

MCI WorldCom Corp.

1133 19th St. NW
Washington, DC 20036
Tel: (202)887-3830
Fax: (202)736-6880
Registered: LDA

E-mail: richard.fruchterman@wcom.com

Leg. Issues: COM, CPI, CPT, GOV, HCR, TAX, TEC

Political Action Committee/s

MCI Telecommunications PAC (MCI PAC)

1133 19th St. NW
Washington, DC 20036
Tel: (202)887-3830
Fax: (202)736-6880

WorldCom Inc. Federal Political Action Committee

1133 19th St. NW
Washington, DC 20036
Tel: (202)887-3830
Fax: (202)736-6880

In-house, DC-area Employees

BROWN, Mary L.: V. President, Federation Regulations
CANTREL, Jr., Francis J.: Director, Government Relations
CASTEEL, Jr., Carroll K.: V. President, State Regulatory Affairs and Governmental Affairs
CLAFFEY, Terri G.: Senior Policy Advisor, Government Relations
FRUCHTERMAN, III, Richard L.: Director, Government Relations
GIBSON, Barbara: Senior Manager, Coporate Communications
HOGAN, Liz: Senior Policy Advisor, Government Relations
HOLMAN, Linda P.: Manager, Tax Legislative Affairs
KOPPEL, Robert: V. President, Regulatory
LUCCI, Mary Catherine: Manager, Coporate Communications
MAIMAN, Seth E.: Government Affairs
MARMON, William F.: V. President, Public Policy
NUGENT, Patrick J.: Director, Tax Legislation and Regulation
O'NEIL, III, Thomas F.: General Counsel, MCI Division
PORTER, David N.: V. President, Government Affairs and Regulatory Economics
ROBINSON, Clint: Legislative Policy Advisor
SALSBURY, Michael: General Counsel
SCHULTZ, Catherine: Director, Tax Legislation and Regulations
SORGI, Donna: V. President, Federal Advocacy
STILLMAN, Bradley: Director, Strategic Policy Initiatives
WHITT, Richard S.: Director, Internet Policy
WRIGHT, Lori E.: Manager, FCC Regulatory

Outside Counsel/Consultants

Alvarado & Gerken
Issues: COM, TEC
Rep By: Susan E. Alvarado, David A. Gerken

Fierce and Isakowitz
Issues: TEC
Rep By: Kathryn Braden, Samantha Cook, Donald L. Fierce, Mark W. Isakowitz, Diane Moery

Harmon & Wilmot, L.L.P.
Rep By: David W. Wilmot

Lawler, Metzger & Milkman, LLC
Issues: TEC
Rep By: Regina M. Keeney, Charles Logan, A. Richard Metzger, Jr., Ruth M. Milkman, Valerie Yates

Mattox Woolfolk, LLC
Issues: TEC
Rep By: Richard B. Mattox, Brian P. Woolfolk

Ogilvy Public Relations Worldwide

Patton Boggs, LLP
Issues: TEC
Rep By: Thomas Hale Boggs, Jr., James B. Christian, Jr., John J. Deschauer, Jr., Penelope S. Farthing, John F. Fithian, Elena Giberga, Robert C. Jones, Donald F. McGahn, II

Podesta/Mattoon
Issues: CPT, TEC
Rep By: Matthew Gelman, Claudia James, Kristen Leary, Anthony T. Podesta

Skadden, Arps, Slate, Meagher & Flom LLP
Rep By: Roseann M. Cutrone, Fred T. Goldberg, Jr., Robert E. Lighthizer, Paul W. Oosterhuis

Swidler Berlin Shereff Friedman, LLP
Rep By: Gary D. Slaiman

McKechnie Brothers (South Africa) Ltd.

Johannesburg, SOUTH AFRICA

Outside Counsel/Consultants

Williams & Connolly
Rep By: Bruce R. Genderson

McKee Foods Corp.

Collegedale, TN
Leg. Issues: FOO

Outside Counsel/Consultants

Robert N. Pyle & Associates
Issues: FOO
Rep By: Alexis Hersh, Alison O'Neill, Robert N. Pyle

McKesson Corp.

San Francisco, CA Registered: LDA
Leg. Issues: HCR, MED, MMM, PHA, TAX, TRA

Outside Counsel/Consultants

Van Ness Feldman, P.C.
Issues: HCR, MED, MMM, PHA, TAX, TRA
Rep By: Howard J. Feldman, Nancy Macan McNally

McKinsey & Co., Inc.

New York, NY
Leg. Issues: IMM

Outside Counsel/Consultants

Patton Boggs, LLP
Issues: IMM
Rep By: Hon. Greg H. Laughlin, Thomas P. O'Donnell, Jonathan R. Yarowsky

McLane Co.

Temple, TX
Leg. Issues: LBR, TAX, TOB

Outside Counsel/Consultants

Washington Council Ernst & Young
Issues: LBR, TAX, TOB
Rep By: Doug Badger, Lauren Darling, John L. Doney, Jayne T. Fitzgerald, LaBrenda Garrett-Nelson, Gary J. Gasper, Bruce A. Gates, Nick Giordano, Cathy Koch, Robert J. Leonard, Richard Meltzer, Phillip D. Moseley, John D. Porter, Robert M. Rozen, Donna Steele-Flynn, Timothy J. Urban

McLean Hospital

Belmont, MA
Leg. Issues: BUD, DEF, MMM

Outside Counsel/Consultants

O'Neill, Athy & Casey, P.C.
Issues: BUD, MMM
Rep By: Martha L. Casey

The PMA Group
Issues: DEF
Rep By: Kaylene Green, Patrick Hiu, Paul J. Magliocchetti, Brian Thiel

McLeod USA, Inc.

Cedar Rapids, IA
Leg. Issues: TEC

Outside Counsel/Consultants

Swidler Berlin Shereff Friedman, LLP
Issues: TEC
Rep By: Gary D. Slaiman

The Mead Corp.

Dayton, OH
Leg. Issues: ENV, MAN, NAT, TAX, TRD

Outside Counsel/Consultants

Sellery Associates, Inc.
Issues: ENV, MAN, NAT, TAX, TRD
Rep By: Amy B. Kimball, William C. Sellery, Jr.

Mead Johnson and Co.

Evansvile, IN

Outside Counsel/Consultants

Kleinfeld, Kaplan and Becker
Rep By: Alan H. Kaplan, Richard S. Morey

Mead Johnson Nutritional Group

Evansville, IN
Leg. Issues: AGR, FOO, WEL

Outside Counsel/Consultants

Olsson, Frank and Weeda, P.C.
Issues: AGR, FOO, WEL
Rep By: John W. Bode, Susan P. Grymes, Karen Reis Harned, Stephen L. Lacey, Marshall L. Matz, Michael J. O'Flaherty, Tyson Redpath, Ryan W. Stroschein

Paul, Hastings, Janofsky & Walker LLP
Rep By: Ralph B. Everett

Meals on Wheels Ass'n of America

Web: www.mealsonwheelsassn.org
E-mail: mowaa@tbg.dgsys.com
Leg. Issues: HCR

Outside Counsel/Consultants

The Borden Group, Inc.
Issues: HCR
Rep By: Margaret B. Ingraham

Meat and Livestock Australia

Washington, DC
Leg. Issues: AGR, TRD

Outside Counsel/Consultants

Willkie Farr & Gallagher
Issues: AGR, TRD
Rep By: William H. Barringer, Matthew Nicely, Russell L. Smith

Meat Importers Council of America

1901 N. Fort Myer Dr. Tel: (703)522-1910
Arlington, VA 22209

In-house, DC-area Employees

MORRISON, William C.: Exec. Director

Meat Industry Council

111 Park Place Tel: (703)538-1789
Falls Church, VA 22046 Fax: (703)241-5603

In-house, DC-area Employees

TYERYAR, CAE, Clay D.: Exec. Director

Outside Counsel/Consultants

Nichols-Dezenhall Communication Management Group, Ltd.
Rep By: David A. Nichols, John W. Weber

Meat Industry Suppliers Ass'n

111 Park Place Tel: (703)538-1789
Falls Church, VA 22046 Fax: (703)241-5603
Leg. Issues: MAN

In-house, DC-area Employees

TYERYAR, CAE, Clay D.: Exec. Director

Outside Counsel/Consultants

Ass'n and Soc. Management Internat'l Inc.
Rep By: Clay D. Tyeryar, CAE

Meat New Zealand

8000 Towers Crescent Dr. Tel: (703)821-5002
Suite 680 Fax: (703)821-3795
Vienna, VA 22182 Registered: FARA
Web: www.meatnz.co.nz
E-mail: help@meatnz.com

Also known as the New Zealand Meat Board. A statutory board of New Zealand with a representative in Washington, DC. The board represents the meat farmers of New Zealand. Its primary functions are to observe, monitor, and report on the meat market in North America, particulary the import of New Zealand meat into the USA, Canada, and Mexico. Headquartered in Wellington, New Zealand.

Leg. Issues: AGR, FOO, TRD

In-house, DC-area Employees

BURTT, Andrew: Regional Manager, North America

Outside Counsel/Consultants

Blank Rome Comisky & McCauley, LLP
Issues: AGR, FOO, TRD
Rep By: Edward J. Farrell

Hogan & Hartson L.L.P.
Issues: AGR
Rep By: Humberto R. Pena

Mechanical Contractors Ass'n of America

1385 Piccard Dr. Tel: (301)869-5800
Rockville, MD 20850-4340 Fax: (301)990-9690
Registered: LDA
Web: www.mcaa.org
E-mail: info@mcaa.org
Leg. Issues: GOV, LBR, TAX, UTI

In-house, DC-area Employees

BREEDLOVE, Adrienne M.: Associate Director, MSCA
BUFFINGTON, Cynthia: Exec. Director, Strategic Events Management
CHANEY, Pete: Director Safety and Health
DOLIM, Barbara: Exec. Director, MSCA
FEIDLER, Linda: Director, Executive & Administrative Services
FINK, Patricia M.: Director, Affiliate Support Services
FINK, Seth D.: Exec. Director, Finance and Business Operations
GENTILLE, John R.: Exec. V. President & Chief Exec. Officer
KOONTZ, John R.: National Director, Project Management and Supervisory Education
LETOW, Jan: Director, Membership
MCNERNEY, John: Director, Government/Labor Relations
NEWCOMBE, Anne: Director, Communications
NIKPOURFAND, Dariush "Nick": Exec. Director, NCPWB

Mechanical Equipment Co., Inc.

New Orleans, LA
Leg. Issues: DEF

Outside Counsel/Consultants

Jones, Walker, Waechter, Poitevent, Carrere & Denegre, L.L.P.
Issues: DEF
Rep By: John J. Jaskot, R. Christian Johnsen

Mecklenburg, North Carolina, County of

Charlotte, NC
Leg. Issues: BUD, ENV

Outside Counsel/Consultants

The Ferguson Group, LLC
Issues: BUD, ENV
Rep By: William Ferguson, Jr., W. Roger Gwinn, Leslie Waters Mozingo

Med Images, Inc.

Knoxville, TN
Leg. Issues: MMM

Outside Counsel/Consultants

George H. Denison
Issues: MMM
Rep By: George H. Denison

Medallion Funding Corp.

New York, NY
Leg. Issues: SMB

Outside Counsel/Consultants

Thelen Reid & Priest LLP
Issues: SMB
Rep By: William A. Kirk, Jr.

Medassets.com

Alpharetta, GA
Leg. Issues: HCR, MMM, TEC

Outside Counsel/Consultants

Capitol Health Group, LLC
Issues: HCR, MMM, TEC
Rep By: Michael D. Bromberg, Shawn Coughlin, Steven Jenning, Layna McConkey Peltier

MedCentral Health System

Mansfield, OH
Leg. Issues: MMM

Outside Counsel/Consultants

McDermott, Will and Emery
Issues: MMM
Rep By: Eric P. Zimmerman

Medco Containment Services, Inc.

Montvale, NJ
Leg. Issues: PHA

Outside Counsel/Consultants

F.B.A.
Issues: PHA
Rep By: J. R. Kirkland

Medeva Pharmaceuticals

Rochester, NY
Leg. Issues: ENV, MED

Outside Counsel/Consultants

Hyman, Phelps & McNamara, P.C.
Issues: MED
Rep By: Douglas B. Farquhar, John A. Gilbert, Jr., James R. Phelps

Sidley & Austin
Issues: ENV
Rep By: Alan C. Raul

Medford, Oregon, City of

Medford, OR
Leg. Issues: BUD, HOU, TRA

Outside Counsel/Consultants

Sagamore Associates, Inc.
Issues: BUD, HOU, TRA
Rep By: Theodore W. Bristol, David U. Gogol

Media Access Project

950 18th St. NW
Suite 220
Washington, DC 20006
Tel: (202)232-4300
Fax: (202)466-7656
Web: www.mediaaccess.org
E-mail: webmaster@mediaaccess.org

A public interest, non-profit communications law firm that represents citizen, civil rights, and grass root organizations across the country who are trying to get access to the media under the fairness doctrine and through application of other legal principles.

Leg. Issues: ART, MIA, TEC

In-house, DC-area Employees

LIANZA, Cheryl: Deputy Director
SCHWARTZMAN, Andrew J.: President and Chief Exec. Officer

Outside Counsel/Consultants

Leslie Harris & Associates
Issues: ART, MIA, TEC
Rep By: Leslie A. Harris

Media Fusion L.L.C.

P.O. Box 10096
Alexandria, VA 22314
Leg. Issues: SCI, TEC, UTI

Political Action Committee/s

Media Fusion PAC
P.O. Box 10096
Alexandria, VA 22314
Contact: Rr. Adm. James J. Carey, USN (Ret.)

In-house, DC-area Employees

CAREY, USN (Ret.), Rr. Adm. James J.

Outside Counsel/Consultants

American Systems Internat'l Corp.

CAREY/NEALON & Associates, L.L.C.
Rep By: Rr. Adm. James J. Carey, USN (Ret.)

Law Office of Zel E. Lipsen
Issues: SCI
Rep By: Zel E. Lipsen

The Washington Group

J. Arthur Weber & Associates
Issues: TEC, UTI
Rep By: Joseph A. Weber

Media General, Inc.

Richmond, VA
Leg. Issues: COM, TAX, TEC

Outside Counsel/Consultants

Colling Swift & Hynes
Issues: COM, TAX, TEC
Rep By: Terese Colling, Pablo Collins, Robert J. Hynes, Jr., Hon. Allan B. Swift

Media Institute

1000 Potomac St. NW
Suite 301
Washington, DC 20007
Tel: (202)298-7512
Fax: (202)337-7092
Web: www.mediainst.org
E-mail: tmi@clark.net

A Washington-based, non-profit, research organization which publishes studies, convenes seminars, files court briefs and agency comments, and conducts other programs on a variety of communications policy issues.

Leg. Issues: COM, MIA, TEC

In-house, DC-area Employees

KAPLAR, Richard T.: V. President
MAINES, Patrick D.: President

Media Research Center

325 S. Patrick St.
Alexandria, VA 22314
Tel: (703)683-9733
Fax: (703)683-9736
Web: www.mediaresearch.org
E-mail: mrc@mediaresearch.org

Seeks to "bring balance to the media by documenting and exposing liberal bias in news reporting and the entertainment industry."

Political Action Committee/s

Conservative Victory Committee
325 S. Patrick St.
Alexandria, VA 22314
Tel: (703)683-9733
Fax: (703)683-9736
Contact: L. Brent Bozell

In-house, DC-area Employees

BOZELL, L. Brent: President

Media Tax Group

A trade group consisting of tax directors of television and newspaper corporations.

Leg. Issues: TAX

Outside Counsel/Consultants

Nixon Peabody LLP
Issues: TAX

Medical College of Virginia, Dept. of Neurology, Office of the Chairman

Richmond, VA
Leg. Issues: BUD, DEF, HCR, MED

Outside Counsel/Consultants

Mintz, Levin, Cohn, Ferris, Glovsky and Popeo, P.C.
Issues: BUD, DEF, HCR, MED
Rep By: Raymond D. Cotton, Erin Lewis Darling

Medical Device Manufacturers Ass'n

1900 K St. NW
Suite 100
Washington, DC 20006
Tel: (202)496-7150
Fax: (202)496-7756
Registered: LDA
Web: www.medicaldevices.org
E-mail: mdmainfo@medicaldevices.org

A national trade association that represents manufacturers of medical devices, diagnostic products, and health care information systems. Seeks to improve the quality of patient care by encouraging the development of new medical technology and fostering the availability of innovative products. Represents its members' interest with regard to the laws and regulations administered by the Food and Drug Administration.

Leg. Issues: MED

In-house, DC-area Employees

NORTHRUP, Steve: Exec. Director
REUTHER, Mary Lacey: Deputy Exec. Director

Outside Counsel/Consultants

Patton Boggs, LLP
Issues: MED
Rep By: Andrew M. Rosenberg, Jonathan R. Yarowsky

Medical Group Management Ass'n

1717 Pennsylvania Ave. NW
Suite 600
Washington, DC 20006
Tel: (202)293-3450
Fax: (202)293-2787
Registered: LDA
Web: www.mgma.com

Executive office located in Englewood, CO. Membership consists of more than 7000 group practices which represent more than 150,000 physicians. The MGMA's mission is to enhance health care delivery and administration through group practice leadership and professional development, education, information, communication, advocacy, networking and research.

Leg. Issues: HCR

In-house, DC-area Employees

BUSHMAN, Jesse: Field Representative
GILBERG, Anders K.: Field Representative
KRUPP, Aaron: Government Affairs Representative
RICHARDSON, Rayna H.: Government Affairs Representative
SMITH, Jr., Patrick F.: V. President, Government Affairs

Outside Counsel/Consultants

Powers Pyles Sutter & Verville, PC
Issues: HCR
Rep By: Robert J. Saner, II

Medical Imaging Contrast Agent Ass'ns

Washington, DC
Leg. Issues: HCR, MMM

Outside Counsel/Consultants

Alpine Group, Inc.
Issues: HCR, MMM
Rep By: James D. Massie, Monica Skopec, Richard C. White

Medical Lake School District

Medical Lake, WA
Leg. Issues: EDU

Outside Counsel/Consultants

Evergreen Associates, Ltd.
Issues: EDU
Rep By: Robert M. Brooks, Marcus M. Riccelli

Medical Library Ass'n/Ass'n of Academic Health Sciences Library Directors

Washington, DC
Registered: LDA
Leg. Issues: BUD, HCR, MIA

Outside Counsel/Consultants

Health and Medicine Counsel of Washington
Issues: BUD, HCR, MIA
Rep By: Dale P. Dirks, Gavin Lindberg

Medical Mutual of Ohio

Cleveland, OH
Leg. Issues: HCR

Outside Counsel/Consultants

Baker & Hostetler LLP
Issues: HCR
Rep By: Matthew J. Dolan, Frederick H. Graefe, Richard H. Hauser, Hon. Guy Vander Jagt

The Medical Protective Co.

Fort Wayne, IN

Outside Counsel/Consultants

Akin, Gump, Strauss, Hauer & Feld, L.L.P.

Medical Records Internat'l, Inc.

Austin, TX
Leg. Issues: CPI, CPT, CSP, HCR, INS, MED, MMM, PHA, TAX, TEC

Outside Counsel/Consultants

Grisso Consulting
Issues: CPI, CPT, CSP, HCR, INS, MED, MMM, PHA, TAX, TEC
Rep By: Michael E. Grisso

Medical Research Laboratories

Leg. Issues: RES

Outside Counsel/Consultants

Ungaretti & Harris
Issues: RES
Rep By: Sheri Bucher, Spencer Perlman

Medical Soc. of the District of Columbia

2175 K St. NW Suite 200
Washington, DC 20037
Tel: (202)466-1800
Fax: (202)452-1542
Web: www.msdc.org
E-mail: shanbacker@msdc.org

Political Action Committee/s

District of Columbia PAC of the Medical Soc. of the District of Columbia
2175 K St. NW Suite 200
Washington, DC 20037
Tel: (202)466-1800
Fax: (202)452-1542

In-house, DC-area Employees

SHANBACKER, K. Edward: Exec. Director

Medical University of Southern Africa

Cape Town, SOUTH AFRICA

Outside Counsel/Consultants

Freedman, Levy, Kroll & Simonds
Rep By: John H. Chettle

Medicare Cost Contractors Alliance
Washington, DC
Leg. Issues: GOV, HCR, MMM

Outside Counsel/Consultants

Law Offices of Mark S. Joffe
Issues: GOV, HCR, MMM
Rep By: Kelli D. Back

Shaw Pittman
Issues: HCR
Rep By: Shannon Arnold, Bruce Fried, Thomas J. Spulak, Andrew L. Woods

Medicare Payment Coalition for Frail Beneficiaries
Bloomington, MN
Leg. Issues: MED

Outside Counsel/Consultants

The Wilbur Group
Issues: MED
Rep By: Valerie Wilbur

Meditrend, Inc.
Albuquerque, NM
Leg. Issues: HCR, MMM, PHA

Outside Counsel/Consultants

Emord & Associates, P.C.
Issues: HCR, MMM, PHA
Rep By: Jonathan W. Emord, Eleanor A. Kolton, Claudia A. Lewis-Eng

Medium-Sized Cable Operators Group
Washington, DC
Leg. Issues: TEC

Outside Counsel/Consultants

The Coursen Group
Issues: TEC
Rep By: Hon. Christopher D. Coursen

Mediware Information Systems, Inc.
New York, NY

Outside Counsel/Consultants

Valente Lopatin & Schulze
Rep By: Richard T. Schulze, Jr., Mark Valente, III

Medix Pharmaceuticals
Leg. Issues: HCR

Outside Counsel/Consultants

Arent Fox Kintner Plotkin & Kahn, PLLC
Issues: HCR
Rep By: Stacy Harbison, Douglas McCormack

Medley Global Advisors
New York, NY

Outside Counsel/Consultants

Rhoads Group

Medline Industries Inc.
Mundelein, IL
Leg. Issues: HCR, MMM

Outside Counsel/Consultants

Nusgart Consulting, LLC
Issues: HCR, MMM
Rep By: Marcia Nusgart

MedPartners, Inc.
Northbrook, IL
Leg. Issues: HCR

Outside Counsel/Consultants

The Legislative Strategies Group, LLC
Issues: HCR
Rep By: Martin B. Gold, Denise M. Henry

MedPro, Inc.
Lexington, KY
Leg. Issues: HCR, LBR, MED

Outside Counsel/Consultants

Hogan & Hartson L.L.P.
Issues: HCR, LBR, MED
Rep By: Nancy Granese

MedReview, Inc.
New York, NY
Leg. Issues: MMM

Outside Counsel/Consultants

Capitol Associates, Inc.
Issues: MMM
Rep By: William A. Finerfrock, Debra M. Hardy Havens

MedStar Health
Washington, DC
Leg. Issues: MED, MMM, TAX

Outside Counsel/Consultants

Bracy Williams & Co.
Issues: MED
Rep By: Linda Doorfee Flaherty, Susan J. Williams

Caplin & Drysdale, Chartered
Issues: TAX
Rep By: Daniel B. Rosenbaum

The Carmen Group
Issues: MMM
Rep By: David M. Carmen

Medtronic, Inc.
1300 Pennsylvania Ave. NW
Suite 380
Washington, DC 20004-3002
Tel: (202)289-9000
Fax: (202)298-9222
Registered: LDA
Web: www.medtronic.com
Leg. Issues: CSP, FOR, HCR, MMM, TAX

Political Action Committee/s

Medtronic, Inc. Medical Technology Fund
1300 Pennsylvania Ave. NW
Suite 380
Washington, DC 20004-3002
Tel: (202)289-9216
Fax: (202)298-9222
Contact: Vince Ventimilgia

In-house, DC-area Employees
VENTIMILGIA, Vince: Director, Government Affairs

Outside Counsel/Consultants

Health Policy Alternatives, Inc.
Issues: HCR
Rep By: Thomas Ault, Bart McCann

Hogan & Hartson L.L.P.
Rep By: Ty Cobb, John S. Stanton

MedWerks.com

Outside Counsel/Consultants

Cassidy & Associates, Inc.

Mega Broadcasting Corp.
Englewood Cliffs, NJ

Outside Counsel/Consultants

Shaw Pittman

Megapulse, Inc.
Bedford, MA
Leg. Issues: AVI

Outside Counsel/Consultants

AB Management Associates, Inc.
Issues: AVI
Rep By: Larry P. Barnett

Megaseal Corp.
Miami, FL
Leg. Issues: BUD, DEF, FOR, GOV, SCI

Outside Counsel/Consultants

Foley Government and Public Affairs, Inc.
Issues: BUD, DEF, FOR, GOV, SCI
Rep By: Joseph P. Foley

MEGAXESS, Inc.
Germantown, MD
Leg. Issues: GOV

Outside Counsel/Consultants

American Defense Internat'l, Inc.
Issues: GOV
Rep By: Michael Herson, Van D. Hipp, Jr., Dave Wilberding

MEI Corp.
Clearwater, FL

Outside Counsel/Consultants

Johnson, Rogers & Clifton, L.L.P.

Mellon Mortgage Co.
Cleveland, OH
Leg. Issues: HOU

Outside Counsel/Consultants

Nixon Peabody LLP
Issues: HOU
Rep By: Richard M. Price, Monica Hilton Sussman

Member-Link Systems, Inc.
Washington, DC
Leg. Issues: CPI, DEF, HCR, MED

Outside Counsel/Consultants

Potomac Strategies Internat'l LLC
Issues: CPI, DEF, HCR, MED
Rep By: Raymond F. DuBois, Jr., Cynthia Trutanic, James K. Wholey

MemberWorks, Inc.
Stamford, CT
Leg. Issues: BAN, CSP, FIN, INS

Outside Counsel/Consultants

Hall, Green, Rupli, LLC
Issues: BAN
Rep By: John M. Green, G. Stewart Hall, Timothy R. Rupli

McIntyre Law Firm, PLLC
Issues: CSP, FIN, INS
Rep By: Chrys D. Lemon, James T. McIntyre

Memorial Health System
Springfield, IL
Leg. Issues: HCR

Outside Counsel/Consultants

Cassidy & Associates, Inc.
Issues: HCR
Rep By: Arthur D. Mason, Laura A. Neal, Diane Rinaldo

Memorial Hermann Health Care System
Houston, TX
Leg. Issues: BUD

Outside Counsel/Consultants

Cassidy & Associates, Inc.
Issues: BUD
Rep By: Christy Carson Evans, W. Campbell Kaufman, IV, Louie Perry, Blenda Pinto-Riddick

Memorial Sloan-Kettering Cancer Center
New York, NY
Registered: LDA
Leg. Issues: HCR, MED, MMM

Outside Counsel/Consultants

Akin, Gump, Strauss, Hauer & Feld, L.L.P.
Issues: HCR, MED, MMM
Rep By: Jorge J. Lopez, Jr., Barney J. Skladany, Jr.

memorize.com
Fairfax, VA
Leg. Issues: CPI, DEF, MED

Outside Counsel/Consultants

Potomac Strategies Internat'l LLC
Issues: CPI, DEF, MED
Rep By: Raymond F. DuBois, Jr., Cynthia Trutanic

Memphis Area Chamber of Commerce
Memphis, TN

Outside Counsel/Consultants

Capitol Coalitions Inc.

Memphis Area Transit Authority
Memphis, TN
Leg. Issues: TRA

Outside Counsel/Consultants

Vierra Associates, Inc.
Issues: TRA
Rep By: Dennis C. Vierra

Memphis Light, Gas and Water Division
Memphis, TN
Leg. Issues: ENG, UTI

Outside Counsel/Consultants

Crowell & Moring LLP
Issues: ENG, UTI
Rep By: Dana C. Contratto, Jennifer Waters

Memphis Public Library and Information Center
Memphis, TN

Outside Counsel/Consultants

Reddy, Begley, & McCormick, LLP
Rep By: Matthew H. McCormick

Memphis, Tennessee, City of
Memphis, TN
Leg. Issues: ECN, URB

Outside Counsel/Consultants

Shaw Pittman
Issues: ECN, URB
Rep By: Anita K. Epstein, Rodolfo Fuentes

Memphis-Shelby County Airport Authority

Memphis, TN
Leg. Issues: AVI

Outside Counsel/Consultants

Global Aviation Associates, Ltd.
Issues: AVI
Rep By: Jon F. Ash, Charles R. Chambers

Van Scoyoc Associates, Inc.

MENC: The Nat'l Ass'n for Music Education

1806 Robert Fulton Dr.
Reston, VA 20191
Web: www.menc.org
E-mail: elizabeth@menc.org
Tel: (703)860-4000
Fax: (703)860-1531

An arts education organization.

Leg. Issues: EDU

In-house, DC-area Employees

LASKO, Elizabeth W.: Senior Manager, Public Relations, Marketing, and Media
MAHLMANN, John J.: Exec. Director

Outside Counsel/Consultants

The Wexler Group
Issues: EDU
Rep By: Cynthia E. Berry, Peter T. Holran, Joel Malina, Christine Maroulis, Hon. Robert S. Walker, Anne Wexler

Mendez University System, Ana G.

Rio Piedras, PR
Leg. Issues: EDU

Outside Counsel/Consultants

Dean Blakey & Moskowitz
Issues: EDU
Rep By: William A. Blakey

Lasa, Monroig & Veve
Issues: EDU
Rep By: Brian Alperstein, E. Ivan Zapien

Mennonite Central Committee Washington Office

110 Maryland Ave. NE
Suite 502
Washington, DC 20002
Web: www.mcc.org
E-mail: mccwash@mcc.org
Tel: (202)544-6564
Fax: (202)544-2820

A public advocacy organization of the Mennonite and Brethren in Christ churches of the United States.

In-house, DC-area Employees

BYLER, J. Daryl: Director
SHLABACH, Rachelle: Legislative Assistant
SHUPACK, Martin: Legislative Associate, International Affairs
TOEWS-HARDER, Elisabeth: Legislative Assistant
WHETTSTONE, David: Legislative Associate, Domestic Affairs

Mennonite Mutual Aid Ass'n

Goshen, IN
Leg. Issues: HCR

Outside Counsel/Consultants

Hogan & Hartson L.L.P.
Issues: HCR
Rep By: Nancy Granese, Jeffrey W. Munk

Vinyard & Associates
Issues: HCR
Rep By: Walter D. Vinyard, Jr.

Menominee Indian Tribe

Kenshena, WI
Leg. Issues: IND

Outside Counsel/Consultants

Hobbs, Straus, Dean and Walker, LLP
Issues: IND
Rep By: S. Bobo Dean, Karen J. Funk, Marie Osceola-Branch, Judith A. Shapiro, Jerry C. Straus, Geoffrey D. Strommer, Hans Walker, Jr., Joseph H. Webster

Mental and Addictive Disorders Appropriations Coalition

1400 K St. NW
c/o American Psychiatric Ass'n
Washington, DC 20005
Tel: (202)682-6046
Fax: (202)682-6287

Concerned with funding for research in mental and substance abuse disorders.

In-house, DC-area Employees

BRUNO, William B.: Associate Director

Mentis Sciences Inc.

Manchester, NH
Leg. Issues: BUD, DEF

Outside Counsel/Consultants

Van Scoyoc Associates, Inc.
Issues: BUD, DEF
Rep By: Thomas L. Lankford, H. Stewart Van Scoyoc

Mentor Corp.

Santa Barbara, CA
Leg. Issues: MMM

Outside Counsel/Consultants

Arnold & Porter
Issues: MMM
Rep By: Grant Bagley

Mentor Graphics Corp.

Wilsonville, OR
Leg. Issues: CPI, CPT, FIN, IMM, TAX, TRD

Outside Counsel/Consultants

Conkling, Fiskum & McCormick
Issues: CPI, CPT, FIN, IMM, TAX, TRD
Rep By: Gary Conkling, Daniel Jarman

Merant PVCS

Rockville, MD
Leg. Issues: DEF, ENG

Outside Counsel/Consultants

Brown and Company, Inc.
Issues: DEF, ENG
Rep By: Cynthia L. Brown, Hugh N. "Rusty" Johnson

Merced Irrigation District

Merced, CA

Outside Counsel/Consultants

Brickfield, Burchette, Ritts & Stone
Rep By: Michael N. McCarty, Colleen Newman

Merced, California, County of

Merced, CA
Leg. Issues: CAW, ECN, EDU, FAM, HCR, HOU, IMM, LBR, TAX

Outside Counsel/Consultants

Copeland, Lowery & Jacquez
Issues: CAW, ECN, EDU, FAM, HCR, HOU, IMM, LBR, TAX
Rep By: Lynnette C. Jacquez

Mercedes-Benz of North America, Inc.

Montvale, NJ
Leg. Issues: AUT, ENV

Outside Counsel/Consultants

Barnes, Richardson and Colburn
Issues: AUT
Rep By: Gunter Von Conrad

Hogan & Hartson L.L.P.
Issues: ENV
Rep By: Patrick M. Raher

White & Case LLP
Rep By: Linda E. Carlisle, J. Roger Mentz

Mercer Engineering Research Center

Warner Robins, GA
Leg. Issues: BUD, DEF

Outside Counsel/Consultants

Hurt, Norton & Associates
Issues: BUD, DEF
Rep By: Robert H. Hurt, Frank Norton, Katharine Calhoun Wood

SISCORP
Issues: DEF
Rep By: Robert Meissner

Mercer University

Macon, GA

Outside Counsel/Consultants

Hurt, Norton & Associates
Rep By: Robert H. Hurt, Frank Norton, Katharine Calhoun Wood

Merchant's Nat'l Bank

Indianapolis, IN

Outside Counsel/Consultants

Wiley, Rein & Fielding

Merck & Co.

601 Pennsylvania Ave. NW
Suite 1200
North Bldg.
Washington, DC 20036
Tel: (202)638-4170
Fax: (202)638-3670
Registered: LDA
Leg. Issues: ADV, BUD, CAW, CPT, CSP, ENV, GOV, HCR, IMM, INS, LBR, MAN, MED, MMM, PHA, SCI, TAX, TRD, VET, WAS

Political Action Committee/s

Merck & Co., Inc. PAC (MERCK PAC)
601 Pennsylvania Ave. NW
Suite 1200
North Bldg.
Washington, DC 20036
Contact: Lana Garvin
Tel: (202)638-4170
Fax: (202)638-3670

In-house, DC-area Employees

BLATTER, Victoria: Director, Federal Policy and Government Relations
CARLTON, Nancy M.: Exec. Director, Federal Policy and Government Relations
GARVIN, Lana: PAC Administrator
MICHAEL, Laurie L.: Senior Director, Counsel, Federal Policy and Government Relations
OLIVER, R. Teel: V. President, Federal Policy and Government Relations
SPATZ, Ian D.: Exec. Director, Federal Policy

Outside Counsel/Consultants

Bonner & Associates

Campbell Crane & Associates
Issues: HCR, MMM, TAX
Rep By: Jeanne M. Campbell, Daniel M. Crane

Canfield & Associates, Inc.
Issues: HCR, TAX
Rep By: Roger Blauwet, April Boston, Anne C. Canfield

Covington & Burling
Issues: MED
Rep By: Bruce N. Kuhlik

The Direct Impact Co.

Downey McGrath Group, Inc.
Issues: PHA
Rep By: Nancy Donaldson, Hon. Thomas J. Downey, Jr.

Greenberg Traurig, LLP
Issues: HCR, INS, MMM, PHA
Rep By: Howard J. Cohen

Policy Directions, Inc.
Issues: HCR, MED, MMM
Rep By: Kathleen "Kay" Holcombe, Frankie L. Trull

Mark J. Raabe
Issues: TAX
Rep By: Mark J. Raabe

Venable
Issues: ADV, GOV, HCR, MED
Rep By: David G. Adams

Mercy Health Corp.

Bala Cynwyd, PA
Leg. Issues: BUD

Outside Counsel/Consultants

Patrick C. Koch
Issues: BUD
Rep By: Patrick C. Koch

Mercy Health System of Northwest Arkasas

Rogers, AR
Leg. Issues: GOV, URB

Outside Counsel/Consultants

Kessler & Associates Business Services, Inc.
Issues: GOV, URB
Rep By: Michael L. Bartlett, Linda Jenckes, Richard S. Kessler, James C. Musser

Mercy Hospital of Des Moines, Iowa

Des Moines, IA
Leg. Issues: ALC, BUD, EDU, HCR, MMM

Outside Counsel/Consultants

Arent Fox Kintner Plotkin & Kahn, PLLC
Issues: ALC, BUD, EDU, HCR, MMM
Rep By: Bill Applegate, Lisa Estrada, Douglas McCormack, Elliott I. Portnoy, Allison Shuren, Robert J. Waters

Mercy Housing

Denver, CO
Leg. Issues: HOU

Outside Counsel/Consultants

Robert A. Rapoza Associates
Issues: HOU
Rep By: Robert A. Rapoza

Mercy Medical

Leg. Issues: HCR, MMM

Outside Counsel/Consultants

Reed, Smith, LLP
Issues: HCR, MMM
Rep By: Phillips S. Peter

Meridian Internat'l Center

1630 Crescent Pl. NW
Washington, DC 20009-4099
Tel: (202)667-6800
Fax: (202)667-1475
Web: www.meridian.org

Meridian Internat'l Center is a nonprofit educational and cultural institution that promotes international understanding through the exchange of people, ideas, and the arts.

Leg. Issues: ART

In-house, DC-area Employees

CUTLER, Walter L.: President
KEITH, Kenton W.: Senior V. President
MATTHEWS, Nancy: V. President, Arts and Communication

Outside Counsel/Consultants

Chernikoff and Co.
Issues: ART
Rep By: Larry B. Chernikoff

Meridian Oil Inc.

Houston, TX
Registered: LDA
A subsidiary of Burlington Resources Inc.

Outside Counsel/Consultants

Crowell & Moring LLP

Skadden, Arps, Slate, Meagher & Flom LLP

Meridian Worldwide

Washington, DC
Leg. Issues: TRD

Outside Counsel/Consultants

JBC Internat'l
Issues: TRD
Rep By: James B. Clawson, George M. "Matt" Mattingley, Jr.

MeriStar Hospitality Corp.

Washington, DC
Leg. Issues: TAX

Outside Counsel/Consultants

Williams & Jensen, P.C.
Issues: TAX
Rep By: Robert E. Glennon, Jr.

Merit Systems Protection Board

New York, NY
A professional development association of federal administrative judges.

Leg. Issues: GOV

Outside Counsel/Consultants

Kyros & Cummins Associates
Issues: GOV
Rep By: John M. Falk, Hon. Peter N. Kyros

Merle Hay Mall Limited Partners

Chicago, IL
Leg. Issues: RES

Outside Counsel/Consultants

Verner, Liipfert, Bernhard, McPherson and Hand, Chartered
Issues: RES
Rep By: Suzanne D. Cartwright, Denis J. Dwyer, William H. Minor, Neil T. Proto

Merrill Lynch & Co., Inc.

1455 Pennsylvania Ave. NW
Suite 950
Washington, DC 20004-1087
Tel: (202)661-7100
Fax: (202)661-7110
Registered: LDA
Web: www.ml.com

Headquartered in New York, NY.

Leg. Issues: BAN, BUD, FIN, FOR, RET, TAX

Political Action Committee/s

Merrill Lynch & Co., Inc. Political Action Committee
1455 Pennsylvania Ave. NW
Suite 950
Washington, DC 20004-1087
Tel: (202)661-7100
Fax: (202)661-7110
Contact: William R. DeReuter

In-house, DC-area Employees

DEREUTER, William R.: V. President, Government Relations
KELLY, John F.: V. President, Government Relations
THIBAU, Janelle C. M.: V. President, Government Relations
THOMPSON, Jr., Bruce E.: V. President and Director, Government Relations

Outside Counsel/Consultants

Bonner & Associates

Davis & Harman LLP
Issues: TAX
Rep By: Randolf H. Hardock

The OB-C Group, LLC
Issues: FIN, TAX
Rep By: Thomas Keating, Kim F. McKernan, Charles J. Mellody, Patricia A. Nelson, Lawrence F. O'Brien, III, Linda E. Tarplin

Seward & Kissel, LLP
Issues: BAN
Rep By: Paul T. Clark

Swidler Berlin Shereff Friedman, LLP
Issues: FIN
Rep By: Barry B. Direnfeld, Brian W. Fitzgerald, Gary Gallant, Harold P. Goldfield, Lester S. Hyman, Gary D. Slaiman, Katherine R. Taylor

Verner, Liipfert, Bernhard, McPherson and Hand, Chartered
Issues: BAN, RET, TAX
Rep By: Matthew C. Bernstein, Virginia R. Boggs, Andrew D. Eskin, Rosemary B. Freeman, Lloyd N. Hand, Vicki E. Hart, David B. Jacobsohn, Brenda G. Meister, Martin Mendelsohn, John A. Merrigan, William H. Minor, Steven R. Phillips, John H. Zentay

Washington Council Ernst & Young
Issues: BUD, TAX
Rep By: Doug Badger, Lauren Darling, John L. Doney, Jayne T. Fitzgerald, LaBrenda Garrett-Nelson, Gary J. Gasper, Bruce A. Gates, Nick Giordano, Cathy Koch, Robert J. Leonard, Richard Meltzer, Phillip D. Moseley, John D. Porter, Robert M. Rozen, Donna Steele-Flynn, Timothy J. Urban

Mesa Inc.

Irving, TX

Outside Counsel/Consultants

Akin, Gump, Strauss, Hauer & Feld, L.L.P.

Mesa, Arizona, City of

Mesa, AZ
Leg. Issues: BUD

Outside Counsel/Consultants

Jones, Walker, Waechter, Poitevent, Carrere & Denegre, L.L.P.
Issues: BUD
Rep By: Paul Cambon, John J. Jaskot, R. Christian Johnsen, James Ogsbury

The Livingston Group, LLC
Issues: BUD
Rep By: Melvin Goodweather, Hon. Robert L. Livingston, Jr., J. Allen Martin, Richard L. Rodgers

Mesalero Apache Tribe

Outside Counsel/Consultants

Steptoe & Johnson LLP
Rep By: Thomas C. Collier, Jr.

Mesquite Resort Ass'n

Mesquite, NV
Leg. Issues: BUD, NAT, TRA

Outside Counsel/Consultants

The Furman Group
Issues: BUD, NAT, TRA
Rep By: K. Link Browder, Thomas M. James

Mesquite, Nevada, City of

Leg. Issues: BUD, NAT, TRA

Outside Counsel/Consultants

The Furman Group
Issues: BUD, NAT, TRA
Rep By: K. Link Browder, Thomas M. James

Messenger Courier Ass'n of the Americas

1101 15th St. NW
Suite 202
Washington, DC 20005
Tel: (202)785-3298
Fax: (202)223-9741

In-house, DC-area Employees

DECAPRIO, Robert: Exec. Director

Outside Counsel/Consultants

The Kellen Company
Rep By: Robert DeCaprio

Messier-Dowty Internat'l

Gloucester, UNITED KINGDOM
Leg. Issues: AER, DEF, GOV

Outside Counsel/Consultants

Meredith Concept Group, Inc.
Issues: AER, DEF, GOV
Rep By: Sandra K. Meredith

Metabolife

Los Angeles, CA
Leg. Issues: HCR

Outside Counsel/Consultants

Arter & Hadden
Issues: HCR
Rep By: Daniel L. Cohen, Hon. Thomas G. Loeffler

Metal Building Manufacturers Ass'n

Cleveland, OH
Leg. Issues: LBR, MAN

Outside Counsel/Consultants

Venable
Issues: LBR, MAN
Rep By: Brock R. Landry

Metal Finishing Suppliers Ass'n

112-J Elden St.
Herndon, VA 20170
Tel: (703)709-5729
Fax: (703)709-1036
Web: www.mfsa.org
E-mail: mfsa@mfsa.org
Leg. Issues: CHM, ENV, MAN

Political Action Committee/s

Finishers PAC
112-J Elden St.
Herndon, VA 20170
Tel: (703)709-5729
Fax: (703)709-1036

In-house, DC-area Employees

TRINGALI, Diana: Exec. Director

Outside Counsel/Consultants

Barrack Ass'n Management
Rep By: Diana Tringali

The Policy Group
Issues: ENV, MAN
Rep By: Christian Richter

Metals Industry Recycling Coalition

Palmerton, PA

Outside Counsel/Consultants

Collier Shannon Scott, PLLC
Rep By: William M. Guerry, Jr., Chet M. Thompson, John L. Wittenborn

Metamorphix, Inc.

Baltimore, MD
Leg. Issues: SCI

Outside Counsel/Consultants

Diane McRee Associates
Issues: SCI
Rep By: Diane B. McRee

Metcor, Ltd.

1500 K St. NW
Suite 350
Washington, DC 20005
Tel: (202)638-2788
Fax: (202)638-2780

In-house, DC-area Employees

MULDOON, James: Chief Exec. Officer

Outside Counsel/Consultants

Cook and Associates

Meter Spa

Torino, ITALY
Leg. Issues: TRD

Outside Counsel/Consultants

Davis & Leiman, P.C.
Issues: TRD

Methane Awareness Resource Group

Green River, WY
Leg. Issues: LBR

Outside Counsel/Consultants

Patton Boggs, LLP
Issues: LBR
Rep By: Henry Chajet

Methanex Inc.

1000 Wilson Blvd.
Suite 2705
Arlington, VA 22209
Tel: (703)248-6101
Fax: (703)248-6120
Registered: LDA
Web: www.methanex.com
E-mail: wwright@methanex.com

Headquartered in Dallas, TX

Leg. Issues: CAW, CHM, ENV, FUE, TAX, TRD

In-house, DC-area Employees

WRIGHT, Wayne: V. President, Government Relations

Outside Counsel/Consultants

Van Ness Feldman, P.C.
Issues: CAW, FUE
Rep By: Howard S. Bleichfeld, Thomas C. Roberts

White & Case LLP
Issues: TAX
Rep By: Linda E. Carlisle, J. Roger Mentz

Kathleen Winn & Associates, Inc.
Issues: CAW, CHM, ENV, FUE, TAX, TRD

Methyl Bromide Working Group

Washington, DC
Registered: LDA
Leg. Issues: AGR

Outside Counsel/Consultants

Sparber and Associates
Issues: AGR
Rep By: Peter G. Sparber

Metlakatla Indian Community

Metlakatla, AK
Leg. Issues: IND

Outside Counsel/Consultants

Hobbs, Straus, Dean and Walker, LLP
Issues: IND
Rep By: Carol L. Barbero, S. Bobo Dean, Karen J. Funk, Marie Osceola-Branch, Marsha K. Schmidt, Jerry C. Straus, Geoffrey D. Strommer, Joseph H. Webster

Metlife Mature Market Group

Westport, CT

Outside Counsel/Consultants

Matz, Blancato & Associates, Inc.

Metra Biosystems, Inc.

Mountain View, CA

Outside Counsel/Consultants

Washington Healthcare Representatives
Rep By: Heather H. Bremer

Metra/Northeast Illinois Rail Corp.

Chicago, IL

Outside Counsel/Consultants

LMRC, Inc.
Rep By: John Lagomarcino

Metricom, Inc.

Los Gatos, CA
Leg. Issues: CPI, TEC

Outside Counsel/Consultants

Issue Dynamics Inc.

Simon Strategies/Mindbeam
Issues: CPI, TEC
Rep By: Ann P. Morton, Gregory C. Simon, Kristan Van Hook

The Metris Companies, Inc.

St. Louis Park, MN
Leg. Issues: BAN, BNK, CPI, FIN

Outside Counsel/Consultants

O'Connor & Hannan, L.L.P.
Issues: BAN, BNK, CPI, FIN
Rep By: Danielle Fagre, Timothy W. Jenkins

Metro Internat'l Trade Services, Inc.

Romulus, MI

Outside Counsel/Consultants

Collier Shannon Scott, PLLC
Rep By: Laurence J. Lasoff, Robert W. Porter

Metro Machine Corp. of Virginia

Norfolk, VA
Leg. Issues: DEF

Outside Counsel/Consultants

Thelen Reid & Priest LLP
Issues: DEF
Rep By: Barry I. Berkoff, Steven S. Honigman, William A. Kirk, Jr., Richard J. Leidl, Stephan M. Minikes

Metro Machine of Pennsylvania, Inc.

Outside Counsel/Consultants

Thelen Reid & Priest LLP
Rep By: Barry I. Berkoff, William A. Kirk, Jr., Richard J. Leidl, Stephan M. Minikes

Metrocall Inc.

Leg. Issues: COM, GOV

Outside Counsel/Consultants

Washington Consulting Alliance, Inc.
Issues: COM, GOV
Rep By: Thomas L. Burgum, Gill Sailer

Metromarine Holdings, Inc.

Alexandria, VA

Outside Counsel/Consultants

The Lonington Group
Rep By: Alan G. Gray

Metromedia Co.

Outside Counsel/Consultants

Alcalde & Fay
Rep By: Jennefer A. Hirshberg

MetroPlains Development, Inc.

St. Paul, MN

Outside Counsel/Consultants

Nixon Peabody LLP
Rep By: Charles L. Edson, Richard M. Price, Herbert F. Stevens

Metroplex Corp.

Washington, DC

A railroad construction company.

Outside Counsel/Consultants

Thelen Reid & Priest LLP
Rep By: Barry I. Berkoff, William A. Kirk, Jr., Richard J. Leidl, Stephan M. Minikes

Metropolitan Atlanta Rapid Transit Authority

Atlanta, GA
Leg. Issues: BUD, TAX, TRA

Outside Counsel/Consultants

Edington, Peel & Associates, Inc.
Issues: BUD, TRA
Rep By: William H. Edington

Thompson Coburn LLP
Issues: TAX, TRA
Rep By: Hon. R. Lawrence Coughlin, Jane Sutter-Starke

Metropolitan Banking Group

Washington, DC
Leg. Issues: BAN, FIN

Outside Counsel/Consultants

Washington Council Ernst & Young
Issues: BAN, FIN
Rep By: Doug Badger, Lauren Darling, John L. Doney, Jayne T. Fitzgerald, LaBrenda Garrett-Nelson, Gary J. Gasper, Bruce A. Gates, Nick Giordano, Robert J. Leonard, Richard Meltzer, Phillip D. Moseley, John D. Porter, Robert M. Rozen, Donna Steele-Flynn, Timothy J. Urban

Metropolitan Family Services

Chicago, IL
Leg. Issues: BUD

Outside Counsel/Consultants

Beacon Consulting Group, Inc.
Issues: BUD
Rep By: Gordon P. MacDougall, Julie Debolt Moeller, Lisa A. Stewart

Metropolitan Joint Powers Board

Minneapolis, MN
Leg. Issues: TRA

Outside Counsel/Consultants

Lockridge Grindal & Nauen, P.L.L.P.
Issues: TRA
Rep By: Dennis McGrann

Metropolitan King County Council

Seattle, WA
Leg. Issues: BUD, CAW, ECN, ENV, HCR, HOU, LAW, LBR, NAT, RES, TEC, TRA, URB, WEL

Outside Counsel/Consultants

The Ferguson Group, LLC
Issues: BUD, CAW, ECN, ENV, HCR, HOU, LAW, LBR, NAT, RES, TEC, TRA, URB, WEL
Rep By: Leslie Waters Mozingo

Metropolitan Life Insurance Co.

1620 L St. NW
Suite 800
Washington, DC 20036-5617
Tel: (202)659-3575
Fax: (202)659-1026
Registered: LDA
Web: www.metlife.com

Headquartered in New York, NY.

Leg. Issues: BAN, BNK, FIN, FOR, INS, RET, TAX, TRD

Political Action Committee/s

Metropolitan Employees' Political Participation Fund
1620 L St. NW
Suite 800
Washington, DC 20036-5617
Tel: (202)659-3575
Fax: (202)659-1026
Contact: Kate H. Carey

In-house, DC-area Employees

CAREY, Kate H.: V. President, Government Relations
IUCULANO, Russel: V. President, Government and Industry Relations
KAHN, Melissa Jan: V. President
NOLAN, Martha: Assistant V. President
REUSING, Vincent P.: Senior V. President, Government and Industry Relations

Outside Counsel/Consultants

Downey McGrath Group, Inc.
Issues: BAN, FOR, INS
Rep By: Hon. Thomas J. Downey, Jr., Hon. Raymond J. McGrath, John Peter Olinger

GLOBEMAC Associates
Issues: FIN, INS, TAX
Rep By: Gordon D. MacKay

Higgins, McGovern & Smith, LLC
Issues: BAN, INS, TAX
Rep By: Lawrence Higgins

Hooper Owen & Winburn
Issues: TAX
Rep By: Steve Glaze

Murray, Scheer, Montgomery, Tapia & O'Donnell
Issues: FIN, INS, RET, TAX, TRD
Rep By: Thomas R. Crawford, D. Michael Murray

Julia J. Norrell & Associates
Issues: INS
Rep By: Julia J. Norrell

Quinn Gillespie & Associates
Rep By: Jeffrey J. Connaughton, Nicholas Maduros, John M. "Jack" Quinn

The Smith-Free Group

Metropolitan Mortgage and Securities, Inc.

Spokane, WA
Leg. Issues: TAX

Outside Counsel/Consultants

Arnold & Porter
Rep By: Martha L. Cochran, David F. Freeman, Jr.

R. Duffy Wall and Associates
Issues: TAX
Rep By: Hon. Bill Brewster, Hon. Rodney D. Chandler, David C. Jory

Metropolitan Museum of Art

New York, NY

Outside Counsel/Consultants

Hawkins, Delafield & Wood

Metropolitan St. Louis Sewer District

St. Louis, MO
Leg. Issues: BUD, CAW, DIS

Outside Counsel/Consultants

John Freshman Associates, Inc.
Issues: BUD, CAW, DIS
Rep By: John D. Freshman, Lawrence P. Kast, Catherine B. Kiefer

Metropolitan Transportation Commission

Oakland, CA
Leg. Issues: AVI, BUD, CAW, ECN, ROD, TRA, URB

Outside Counsel/Consultants

Government Relations, Inc.
Issues: AVI, BUD, CAW, ECN, ROD, TRA, URB
Rep By: Thomas J. Bulger, Mark H. Miller, John N. Young

Metropolitan Washington Airports Authority

Alexandria, VA
Leg. Issues: AVI, GOV, TRA

Outside Counsel/Consultants

The Carmen Group
Issues: AVI, GOV, TRA
Rep By: Diane Jemmott, Aisha Tyus

Metropolitan Washington Council of Governments

777 N. Capitol St. NE
Suite 300
Washington, DC 20002-4201
Web: www.mwcog.org
Tel: (202)962-3200
Fax: (202)962-3201

A regional organization of the Washington area's major local governments and governing officials. Provides a forum for addressing regional problems through discussion, formal agreement, policy implications and trend assessment.

In-house, DC-area Employees

BOSLEY, John J.: General Counsel

The Metropolitan Water District of Southern California

1015 18th St. NW
Suite 600
Washington, DC 20036
E-mail: bradhiltscher@mwd.dst.ca.us
Tel: (202)296-3551
Fax: (202)296-6741
Registered: LDA
Leg. Issues: BUD, CAW, ENG, ENV, MAR, NAT, RES, TRA, UTI

In-house, DC-area Employees

HILTSCHER, Brad L.: Principal Legislative Representative

Outside Counsel/Consultants

Duncan, Weinberg, Genzer & Pembroke, P.C.
Issues: UTI
Rep By: Wallace L. Duncan, Michael R. Postar

Mary Lee McGuire
Issues: CAW
Rep By: Mary Lee McGuire

Perkins Coie LLP
Issues: NAT
Rep By: Guy R. Martin

David M. Weiman
Issues: ENG, UTI
Rep By: David M. Weiman

Will and Carlson, Inc.
Issues: BUD, ENG
Rep By: Peter Carlson, Robert P. Will

Metropolitan Water Reclamation District of Greater Chicago

Chicago, IL
Leg. Issues: BUD

Outside Counsel/Consultants

The Carmen Group
Issues: BUD
Rep By: Mia O'Connell

The MetroVision Chamber

New Orleans, LA
Leg. Issues: DEF

Outside Counsel/Consultants

Jones, Walker, Waechter, Poitevent, Carrere & Denegre, L.L.P.
Issues: DEF
Rep By: John J. Jaskot, R. Christian Johnsen

Mexam Trade, Inc.

Houston, TX
Leg. Issues: ENV, ROD, TRD

Outside Counsel/Consultants

Janus-Merritt Strategies, L.L.C.
Issues: ENV, ROD, TRD
Rep By: Mark J. Robertson

Mexican Crab Industry

Leg. Issues: FOR, NAT, TRD

Outside Counsel/Consultants

Janus-Merritt Strategies, L.L.C.
Issues: FOR, NAT, TRD
Rep By: Mark J. Robertson

Mexican Nat'l Spiny Lobster Industry

Leg. Issues: FOR, NAT, TRD

Outside Counsel/Consultants

Janus-Merritt Strategies, L.L.C.
Issues: FOR, NAT, TRD
Rep By: Mark J. Robertson

Mexican-American Legal Defense and Educational Fund

1717 K St. NW
Suite 311
Washington, DC 20036
Web: www.maldef.org
E-mail: maldefdc@aol.com
Tel: (202)293-2828
Fax: (202)293-2849
Registered: LDA

A national, non-profit organization that promotes and protects the civil rights of Latinos in the United States in the areas of education, employment, political access, and immigration; headquartered in Los Angeles, CA.

Leg. Issues: CIV, CON, EDU, HCR, IMM, LBR, WEL

In-house, DC-area Employees

AMADOR, Angelo: Policy Analyst
D'ORAZIO, Triana R.: Public Affairs Coordinator
DEMEO, Marisa J.: Regional Counsel

Mexico, Embassy of

Washington, DC

Outside Counsel/Consultants

Manatt, Phelps & Phillips, LLP
Rep By: Hon. Jack W. Buechner, Eric Farnsworth, Abbe David Lowell, Steven J. Mulder, Susan M. Schmidt

Zuckerman Spaeder L.L.P.

Mexico, Government of

Mexico City, MEXICO

Outside Counsel/Consultants

Jack H. McDonald
Rep By: Hon. Jack H. McDonald

Verner, Liipfert, Bernhard, McPherson and Hand, Chartered
Rep By: Vicki E. Hart

Mexico, Office of the President of

Mexico City, MEXICO

Outside Counsel/Consultants

Chlopak, Leonard, Schechter and Associates
Rep By: Charles G. Leonard

Mexico, Secretaria de Comercio y Fomento Industrial (SECOFI)

Mexico City, MEXICO

Outside Counsel/Consultants

Public Strategies Washington, Inc.
Rep By: Anne Collett, Joseph P. O'Neill, Paul M. Snyder

Shaw Pittman
Rep By: Anita K. Epstein, Claudia Hrvatin, E. Michael O'Malley, Thomas J. Spulak, Andrew L. Woods

Mexico, Secretariat of Commerce & Industrial Development of

Mexico City, MEXICO

Outside Counsel/Consultants

Shaw Pittman

Mexico-U.S. Business Committee, U.S. Council

1310 G St. NW
Suite 690
Washington, DC 20005-3000
Web: www.counciloftheamericas.org
E-mail: smiller@as-coa.org
Tel: (202)639-0724
Fax: (202)639-0794

A binational business organization dedicated to increasing trade and investment between Mexico and the United States. Represents U.S. corporations with interests in Mexico.

Leg. Issues: TRD

In-house, DC-area Employees

JONES, James: Chairman
MILLER, Scott A.: Exec. Director
PRYCE, William T.: Exec. V. President

Meyer Pharmaceuticals

Newport Beach, CA

Outside Counsel/Consultants

Paul, Hastings, Janofsky & Walker LLP
Rep By: R. Bruce Dickson

MFS Communications Co., Inc.

Outside Counsel/Consultants

Swidler Berlin Shereff Friedman, LLP

MG Financial Group

New York, NY
Leg. Issues: FIN

Outside Counsel/Consultants

Preston Gates Ellis & Rouvelas Meeds LLP
Issues: FIN
Rep By: Tim L. Peckinpaugh, Daniel Ritter

MGF Industries Inc.

Commerce, CA
Leg. Issues: TRD

Outside Counsel/Consultants

Oppenheimer Wolff & Donnelly LLP
Issues: TRD
Rep By: Harry W. Cladouhos

Miami Beach, Florida, City of

Leg. Issues: ALC, ART, AVI, BUD, CAW, ECN, EDU, ENV, GAM, HCR, HOU, IMM, LAW, LBR, MMM, NAT, POS, ROD, TAX, TEC, TRA, URB, WAS, WEL

Outside Counsel/Consultants

Jorden Burt LLP
Issues: ALC, ART, AVI, BUD, CAW, ECN, EDU, ENV, GAM, HCR, HOU, IMM, LAW, LBR, MMM, NAT, POS, ROD, TAX, TEC, TRA, URB, WAS, WEL
Rep By: Patricia Branch, Marna Gettleman, Marilyn Berry Thompson, Rebecca Tidman, Marion Turner

Miami Heat

Outside Counsel/Consultants

Alcalde & Fay
Rep By: Cynthia Colenda, Nancy Gibson Prowitt, Christopher L. Turner, Alana Weinstein

Miami Museum of Science & Space Transit Planetarium

Miami, FL
Leg. Issues: EDU

Outside Counsel/Consultants

Richard L. Spees, Inc.
Issues: EDU
Rep By: Richard L. Spees

Miami Valley Economic Coalition

Dayton, OH
Leg. Issues: DEF

Outside Counsel/Consultants

Manatt, Phelps & Phillips, LLP
Issues: DEF
Rep By: Mary Ann Gilleece, Jeff Kuhnreich

Miami, Florida, City of

Leg. Issues: EDU, ENV, IMM, TAX, TRA, WEL

Outside Counsel/Consultants

Greenberg Traurig, LLP
Issues: EDU, ENV, IMM, TAX, TRA, WEL
Rep By: Diane J. Blagman, Howard A. Vine

Richard L. Spees, Inc.
Issues: TRA
Rep By: Richard L. Spees

Miami-Dade Community College

Miami, FL
Leg. Issues: EDU, LAW

Outside Counsel/Consultants

Cassidy & Associates, Inc.
Issues: EDU, LAW
Rep By: Gregory M. Gill, Laura A. Neal

Miami-Dade County Public Schools

Miami, FL

Outside Counsel/Consultants

Alcalde & Fay
Rep By: Danielle McBeth, Lois Moore, Kathy Jurado Munoz, Tim Stroud

Miami-Dade, Florida, County of

Miami, FL
Leg. Issues: EDU, ENV, IMM, RET, TAX, TRA, WEL

Outside Counsel/Consultants

Alcalde & Fay
Rep By: Hector Alcalde, Danielle McBeth, Lois Moore, Christopher L. Turner

Greenberg Traurig, LLP
Issues: EDU, ENV, IMM, RET, TAX, TRA, WEL
Rep By: Diane J. Blagman, Russell J. Mueller

MIC Industries, Inc.

11911 Freedom Dr.
Suite 1000
Reston, VA 20190
Tel: (703)318-1900
Fax: (703)318-9321
Leg. Issues: DEF, DIS, ECN

Outside Counsel/Consultants

The PMA Group
Issues: DEF, DIS, ECN
Rep By: Daniel Cunningham, Daniel E. Fleming, Kaylene Green, Paul J. Magliocchetti, Mark Waclawski

MICAH Software Systems

Falls Church, VA
Leg. Issues: DEF, GOV

Outside Counsel/Consultants

Cottone and Huggins Group
Issues: DEF, GOV
Rep By: James B. Huggins

Miccosukee Indians

Miami, FL
Leg. Issues: ENV, IND

Outside Counsel/Consultants

Adams and Reese LLP
Issues: ENV, IND
Rep By: D. Lee Forsgren, Hon. James A. "Jimmy" Hayes

Miccosukee Tribe of Indians of Florida

499 S. Capitol St. SW
Suite 417
Washington, DC 20003
Tel: (202)554-9494
Fax: (202)554-9454
Registered: LDA

Headquartered in Miami, FL.

Leg. Issues: CAW, ENV, GAM, IND, NAT

In-house, DC-area Employees

COOPER, R. Clarke: Director, Government Affairs
LAWRENCE, Amanda: Legislative Assistant

Outside Counsel/Consultants

Hobbs, Straus, Dean and Walker, LLP
Issues: IND
Rep By: Carol L. Barbero, S. Bobo Dean, Karen J. Funk, Marie Osceola-Branch, Jerry C. Straus

Micell Technologies, Inc.

Raleigh, NC
Leg. Issues: ENV, TAX

Outside Counsel/Consultants

Albertine Enterprises, Inc.

Goodstein & Associates
Issues: ENV, TAX
Rep By: Richard F. Goodstein

Michel Richard's Citronell

Outside Counsel/Consultants

Edelman Public Relations Worldwide
Rep By: Daniel Puzo

Michelin North America

Greenville, SC
Registered: LDA

The U.S. subsidiary of Compagnie General des Etablissements Michelin de Clermont-Ferrand, France.

Leg. Issues: ENV, IMM, MAN, TAX

Outside Counsel/Consultants

Edelman Public Relations Worldwide
Rep By: Jere Sullivan

Hogan & Hartson L.L.P.
Issues: ENV, IMM, MAN, TAX
Rep By: Jeanne S. Archibald, C. Michael Gilliland, Nancy Granese, William Michael House, Lewis E. Leibowitz, Jeffrey W. Munk, Patrick M. Raher, Christine M. Warnke

Michigan Biotechnology Institute

Lansing, MI
Leg. Issues: AGR, ENV

Outside Counsel/Consultants

The Dutko Group, Inc.
Issues: AGR, ENV
Rep By: Arthur H. Silverman, William Simmons

Michigan Bulb

Leg. Issues: POS

Outside Counsel/Consultants

The MWW Group
Issues: POS
Rep By: Davon Gray, Elizabeth A. Iadarola, Jonathan B. Slade

Michigan Consolidated Gas Co.

Detroit, MI
Registered: LDA
Leg. Issues: ENG, ENV, GOV, TAX

Outside Counsel/Consultants

Bracy Williams & Co.
Issues: GOV
Rep By: James C. Benfield, Michael M. Bracy, Terrence L. Bracy

Hogan & Hartson L.L.P.
Issues: ENG, ENV, TAX
Rep By: C. Michael Gilliland, David J. Hensler, Jeffrey W. Munk, Christine M. Warnke

Michigan Insurance Federation

Lansing, MI
Leg. Issues: TAX

Outside Counsel/Consultants

Dykema Gossett PLLC
Issues: TAX
Rep By: David K. Arthur, Stephen H. Zimmerman

Michigan Inter-Tribal Council

Brimley, MI

Outside Counsel/Consultants

Morriset, Schlosser, Ayer & Jozwiak

Michigan Manufacturing Technology Center

Ann Arbor, MI
Leg. Issues: MAN, SCI

Outside Counsel/Consultants

Dykema Gossett PLLC
Issues: MAN, SCI
Rep By: Tricia K. Markwood

Michigan Municipal/Cooperative Group

Outside Counsel/Consultants

Spiegel & McDiarmid
Rep By: Robert A. Jablon

Michigan Nat'l Corp.

Farmington Hills, MI

Outside Counsel/Consultants

Arnold & Porter

Michigan Retailers Ass'n

Lansing, MI

Outside Counsel/Consultants

Goldberg & Associates, PLLC
Rep By: James M. Goldberg

Michigan State Department of Transportation

Lansing, MI
Leg. Issues: GOV

Outside Counsel/Consultants

Chambers, Conlon & Hartwell
Issues: GOV
Rep By: Don Norden

Michigan Technological University

Houghton, MI
Registered: LDA
Leg. Issues: EDU

Outside Counsel/Consultants

Golin/Harris Internat'l
Issues: EDU
Rep By: Carol C. Mitchell

Mintz, Levin, Cohn, Ferris, Glovsky and Popeo, P.C.
Rep By: Raymond D. Cotton

Michigan Trade Exchange

Southfield, MI

A barter exchange.

Outside Counsel/Consultants

Royer & Babyak
Rep By: Robert Stewart Royer

Michigan, Office of the Attorney General of the State of

Lansing, MI

Outside Counsel/Consultants

Duncan, Weinberg, Genzer & Pembroke, P.C.
Rep By: James F. Flug

Michigan, Washington Office of the State of

444 N. Capitol St. NW
Suite 411
Washington, DC 20001
Tel: (202)624-5840
Fax: (202)624-5841

In-house, DC-area Employees

WILSON, LeAnne R.: Director

Mickey Leland Nat'l Urban Air Toxics Research Center

Houston, TX

Outside Counsel/Consultants

Baker Botts, L.L.P.
Rep By: James A. Baker, IV

Microcosm, Inc.

Torrance, CA
Leg. Issues: AER, BUD, DEF

Outside Counsel/Consultants

Ritter and Bourjaily, Inc.
Issues: AER, BUD, DEF
Rep By: Monte F. Bourjaily, III

Westerly Group
Issues: DEF
Rep By: Sarah Brown, Kirk L. Clinkenbeard

Micron Technology, Inc.

Boise, ID
Registered: LDA
Leg. Issues: CPI, DEF, TAX, TRD

Outside Counsel/Consultants

Hale and Dorr LLP
Issues: DEF, TRD
Rep By: Bonnie B. Byers, Gilbert B. Kaplan, Jay P. Urwitz

Timmons and Co., Inc.
Issues: CPI, TAX, TRD
Rep By: Michael J. Bates, Douglas F. Bennett, Ellen B. Fitzgibbons, Bryce L. "Larry" Harlow, Timothy J. Keating, Tom C. Korologos, Richard J. Tarplin, William E. Timmons, Jr., William E. Timmons, Sr.

The Micronesia Institute

Leg. Issues: ECN

Outside Counsel/Consultants

Pacific Islands Washington Office
Issues: ECN
Rep By: Fred Radewagen

Micronesia, Embassy of the Federated States of

1725 N St. NW
Washington, DC 20036
Tel: (202)223-4383
Fax: (202)223-4391
Leg. Issues: EDU, FOR

Outside Counsel/Consultants

Capitol Link, Inc.
Issues: EDU, FOR
Rep By: Hon. David M. Staton

James T. Stovall
Rep By: James T. Stovall, III

MicroPatent, LLC

Leg. Issues: CPT

Outside Counsel/Consultants

Joseph L. Ebersole
Issues: CPT
Rep By: Joseph L. Ebersole

Micros, Inc.

Boston, MA

Outside Counsel/Consultants

Chambers Associates Inc.
Rep By: William A. Signer

Microsoft Corp.

21 Dupont Circle NW
Fifth Floor
Washington, DC 20036
Tel: (202)263-5900
Fax: (202)263-5902
Registered: LDA
Web: www.microsoft.com

Headquartered in Redmond, WA.

Leg. Issues: BUD, CPI, CPT, CSP, IMM, TAX, TEC, TRD

In-house, DC-area Employees

BEREJKA, Marc: Senior Attorney
HOUTON, Jamie: Manager, Federal Government Affairs
INMAN, Julie: Legislative Assistant
JURKOVICH, Tom: Manager, Federal Government Affairs
KNOTT, Kerry: Senior Manager, Federal Affairs
KNUTSON, Kent: Manager, Federal Government Affairs
KOENIG, Eric: Senior Manager, Federal Government Affairs

KRUMHOLTZ, Jack: Associate General Counsel/Federal Affairs
MALLORY, Michelle: Manager, Multi-State Government Affairs
SAMPSON, John: Manager, Federal Government Affairs

Outside Counsel/Consultants

Arthur Andersen LLP
Issues: TAX
Rep By: Rachelle Bernstein, Richard A. Gordon

Barbour Griffith & Rogers, Inc.
Issues: CPI, CSP
Rep By: Haley Barbour, G. O. Lanny Griffith, Jr., Loren Monroe, Edward M. Rogers, Jr., Brent Thompson

BSMG Worldwide

Clark & Weinstock, Inc.
Issues: BUD, CPI, IMM, TAX, TRD
Rep By: Hon. Vic H. Fazio, Jr., Ed Kutler, Deirdre Stach, Sandi Stuart, Hon. John Vincent "Vin" Weber

Covington & Burling
Issues: CPI, CPT, TRD
Rep By: Stuart C. Stock

Creative Response Concepts

Dittus Communications
Rep By: Tom Conway, Cynthia Giorgio

Downey McGrath Group, Inc.
Issues: CPI, CPT, IMM, TEC
Rep By: Hon. Thomas J. Downey, Jr., Hon. Raymond J. McGrath

Edelman Public Relations Worldwide
Rep By: Michael K. Deaver

Fontheim Internat'l, LLC
Issues: TRD
Rep By: Claude G. B. Fontheim, Kenneth I. Levinson

Hooper Owen & Winburn
Issues: CPI
Rep By: David Rudd

McSlarrow Consulting L.L.C.
Issues: CPI, IMM, TEC
Rep By: Alison McSlarrow

Powell Tate

Preston Gates Ellis & Rouvelas Meeds LLP
Issues: CPI, CPT, IMM, TAX, TEC, TRD
Rep By: Werner W. Brandt, Bruce J. Heiman, Michael J. O'Neil, Emanuel L. Rouvelas, W. Dennis Stephens, Steven R. "Rick" Valentine

Quinn Gillespie & Associates

Swidler Berlin Shereff Friedman, LLP
Issues: TAX
Rep By: Barry B. Direnfeld, Brian W. Fitzgerald, Harold P. Goldfield

Verner, Liipfert, Bernhard, McPherson and Hand, Chartered
Issues: CPI
Rep By: Berl Bernhard

Washington Council Ernst & Young
Issues: TAX
Rep By: Doug Badger, John L. Doney, Jayne T. Fitzgerald, LaBrenda Garrett-Nelson, Gary J. Gasper, Bruce A. Gates, Nick Giordano, Robert J. Leonard, Richard Meltzer, Robert M. Rozen, Timothy J. Urban

The Washington Group
Issues: CPI
Rep By: Kevin D. Allen, William J. Burke, Tripp Funderburk, Rita M. Lewis, G. John O'Hanlon, John D. Raffaelli, Tonya Saunders, Mark Schnabel, Richard Sullivan, Fowler West

Microvision, Inc.

Seattle, WA
Leg. Issues: DEF

Outside Counsel/Consultants

Kambrod Associates Ltd.
Issues: DEF
Rep By: Mathew R. Kambrod

The PMA Group
Rep By: Daniel Cunningham, Kaylene Green, Patrick Hiu, Joseph Littleton, Stephen Madey, Paul J. Magliocchetti, Brian Thiel

Mid Dakota Rural Water System

Miller, SD
Concerned with the water supply in rural South Dakota.
Leg. Issues: BUD, NAT

Outside Counsel/Consultants

John Freshman Associates, Inc.
Issues: BUD, NAT
Rep By: John D. Freshman, Lawrence P. Kast, Catherine B. Kiefer

Mid-Atlantic Broadcast Partners

Baltimore, MD

Outside Counsel/Consultants

Capitol Campaign Consultants
Rep By: Thomas E. Fahy

Mid-Atlantic Medical Services, Inc.

Four Taft Ct.
Rockville, MD 20850
Tel: (800)331-2102
Fax: (301)762-5728
Web: www.mamsi.com
Leg. Issues: HCR

In-house, DC-area Employees

GORENFLO, Richard W.: V. President, Regulatory Affairs
GUARRIELLO, Joseph L.: Exec. V. President, General Counsel and Secretary
SAMMIS, Elizabeth: Senior Director, Communications

Outside Counsel/Consultants

Theodore C. Knappen, P.C.
Issues: HCR
Rep By: Theodore C. Knappen

Mid-Atlantic Regional Joint Board UNITE PAC

903 Russell Ave.
Suite 400
Gaithersburg, MD 20879

In-house, DC-area Employees

FORTH, Patrick: PAC Administrator

Mid-Atlantic Toyota Distributors Inc.

Glen Burnie, MD

Outside Counsel/Consultants

Venable

Mid-West Electric Consumers Ass'n

Denver, CO
Registered: LDA
Leg. Issues: CSP, ENG, UTI

Outside Counsel/Consultants

Duncan, Weinberg, Genzer & Pembroke, P.C.
Issues: CSP, ENG, UTI
Rep By: Jeffrey C. Genzer

MidAmerican Energy Holdings Co.

1200 New Hampshire Ave. NW
Suite 300
Washington, DC 20036
Tel: (202)828-1378
Fax: (202)828-1380
Headquartered in Des Moines, Iowa.

Leg. Issues: ENG

In-house, DC-area Employees

WEISGALL, Jonathan: Washington Office Contact

Outside Counsel/Consultants

The Livingston Group, LLC
Issues: ENG
Rep By: Hon. Robert L. Livingston, Jr., J. Allen Martin, Richard L. Rodgers

Midcoast Interstate Transmission, Inc.

Muscle Shoals, AL
Leg. Issues: ENV, FUE

Outside Counsel/Consultants

Patton Boggs, LLP
Issues: ENV, FUE
Rep By: Philip A. Bangert, Thomas Hale Boggs, Jr., Michael A. Brown, James A. Reeder

Middle Atlantic Conference

Riverdale, MD

Outside Counsel/Consultants

Rea, Cross & Auchincloss
Rep By: Bryce Rea, Jr.

Middle East Institute

1761 N St. NW
Washington, DC 20036-2882
Tel: (202)785-1141
Fax: (202)331-8861
Web: www.themiddleeastinstitute.org
E-mail: mideasti@mideasti.org

Founded in 1946 to foster American understanding of the Middle East through conferences, lectures, education and publications. By charter may not become an instrument of policy nor attempt to influence legislation.

In-house, DC-area Employees

DUNN, Dr. Michael: Editor, Middle East Journal
MACK, David L.: V. President, General Programs
PARKER, Richard B.: Resident Scholar Emeritus
SUDDARTH, Roscoe S.: President

Middle East Policy Council

1730 M St. NW
Suite 512
Washington, DC 20036
Tel: (202)296-6767
Fax: (202)296-5791
Web: www.mepc.org
E-mail: info@mepc.org

A non-profit organization to expand public debate on U.S. Middle East policy through its publications and conferences. Publishes the quarterly journal "Middle East Policy".

In-house, DC-area Employees

FREEMAN, Jr., Chas W.: President
WILSON, Richard F.: Exec. Director

Middle East Water and Energy Resource Institute

Washington, DC

Outside Counsel/Consultants

Strategic Impact, Inc.
Rep By: Patrick J. Mitchell

Middlesex Community-Technical College

Middletown, CT
Leg. Issues: EDU

Outside Counsel/Consultants

Dow, Lohnes & Albertson, PLLC
Issues: EDU
Rep By: Jonathan Glass

Middlesex Hospital Home Care

Leg. Issues: HCR

Outside Counsel/Consultants

Arent Fox Kintner Plotkin & Kahn, PLLC
Issues: HCR
Rep By: Stacy Harbison, Douglas McCormack, Connie A. Raffa

Midroc Ethiopia

Addis Ababa, ETHIOPIA
Leg. Issues: TRD

Outside Counsel/Consultants

Verner, Liipfert, Bernhard, McPherson and Hand, Chartered
Issues: TRD
Rep By: Lawrence E. Levinson, Harry C. McPherson

Midway Airlines Corp.

Durham, NC

Outside Counsel/Consultants

Fleischman and Walsh, L.L.P.
Rep By: Louis H. Dupart, John P. McAllister

Shaw Pittman
Rep By: Robert E. Cohn, Sheryl R. Israel

Midwest Broadcasting Corp.

Detroit, MI

Outside Counsel/Consultants

Reddy, Begley, & McCormick, LLP
Rep By: Matthew H. McCormick

Midwest City Municipal Authority

Midwest City, OK
Leg. Issues: GOV, URB

Outside Counsel/Consultants

VSAdc.com
Issues: GOV, URB
Rep By: J. R. Reskovac

Midwest Express Airlines

Oak Creek, WI
Leg. Issues: AVI

Outside Counsel/Consultants

The Wexler Group
Issues: AVI
Rep By: Timothy Hannegan

MidWest ISO Transmission Owners

Outside Counsel/Consultants

Wright & Talisman, P.C.
Rep By: Michael E. Small

Midwest Motor Express, Inc.

Bismarck, ND

Outside Counsel/Consultants

Thiemann Aitken Vohra & Rutledge, L.L.C.
Rep By: Herve H. Aitken

Midwest Research Institute

Kansas City, MO
Leg. Issues: BUD, ENG, FUE, SCI

Outside Counsel/Consultants

Katherine Hamilton
Issues: BUD, ENG, FUE, SCI
Rep By: Katherine Hamilton

Migrant Legal Action Program

P.O. Box 53308 Tel: (202)462-7744
Washington, DC 20009

A national legal services, support, and advocacy center that assists migrant and seasonal farm workers with legal representation.

In-house, DC-area Employees

ROSENTHAL, Roger C.: Exec. Director

Military Ad Hoc Committee

c/o American Legion Tel: (202)861-2700
1608 K St. NW Fax: (202)861-2786
Washington, DC 20006

Seeks to preserve military benefits.

In-house, DC-area Employees

SCHLEE, G. Michael: Contact

Military Chaplains Ass'n of the U.S.

P.O. Box 42660 Tel: (202)574-2423
Washington, DC 20015-0660 Fax: (202)574-2423
Web: www.mca-usa.org
E-mail: chaplains@erols.com

In-house, DC-area Employees

WHITE, David: Exec. Director

The Military Coalition

125 N. West St. Tel: (703)683-1400
Alexandria, VA 22314 Fax: (703)549-6610
Web: www.themilitarycoalition.org
E-mail: steves@troa.org

Concerned with the preservation of benefits for active, reserve, retired, and veteran military personnel.

Leg. Issues: BUD, DEF, HCR, MMM, RET, TAX, VET

In-house, DC-area Employees

CLINE, Michael P.: Co-Chairman
MCKINNEY, C.A. "Mack": Coordinator
STROBRIDGE, USAF (Ret.), Col. Steven P.: Co-Chairman

Military Footwear Coalition

Washington, DC
Leg. Issues: APP, BUD, DEF

Outside Counsel/Consultants

Collier Shannon Scott, PLLC
Issues: APP, BUD, DEF
Rep By: Lauren R. Howard, Robert W. Porter

Military Glove Coalition

Washington, DC
Leg. Issues: APP, BUD, DEF

Outside Counsel/Consultants

Collier Shannon Scott, PLLC
Issues: APP, BUD, DEF
Rep By: Lauren R. Howard, Robert W. Porter

Military Impacted School Districts Ass'n

Leg. Issues: EDU

Outside Counsel/Consultants

Evergreen Associates, Ltd.
Issues: EDU
Rep By: Robert M. Brooks

Military Mobility Coalition

Washington, DC
Leg. Issues: DEF

Outside Counsel/Consultants

Rothleder Associates, Inc.
Issues: DEF

Military Order of the Purple Heart of the U.S.A.

5413-B Backlick Rd. Tel: (703)642-5360
Springfield, VA 22151 Fax: (703)642-2054
Web: www.purpleheart.org
E-mail: info@purpleheart.org

A veterans service organization.

Leg. Issues: VET

In-house, DC-area Employees

BRESSER, Gregory A.: Nat'l Service Director
KIRBY, John B.: Adjutant General

Outside Counsel/Consultants

The Carter Group
Issues: VET
Rep By: Michael R. Carter, Scott D. McClean

Military Order of the World Wars

435 N. Lee St. Tel: (703)683-4911
Alexandria, VA 22314 Fax: (703)683-4501
Web: www.militaryorder.org
E-mail: mowwhq@aol.com

A patriotic group of commissioned officers who have served in the U.S. armed forces. Founded in 1919 by General Pershing, it now has more than 11,000 members. Advocates a strong national defense posture and active support of patriotic education.

In-house, DC-area Employees

BULTMAN, Brig. Gen. Roger: Chief of Staff

Milk Industry Foundation

1250 H St. NW Tel: (202)737-4332
Suite 900 Fax: (202)331-7820
Washington, DC 20005
Web: www.idfa.org

Although a separate and autonomous trade association, the Milk Industry Foundation shares offices and staff with the Internat'l Ice Cream Ass'n and the Nat'l Cheese Institute under the umbrella of the Internat'l Dairy Foods Ass'n.

Outside Counsel/Consultants

Covington & Burling
Rep By: H. Edward Dunkelberger, Jr.

Mille Lacs Band of Ojibwe Indians

Onamia, MN
Leg. Issues: IND

Outside Counsel/Consultants

Holland & Knight LLP
Issues: IND
Rep By: Mike Galano, Richard M. Gold, Hon. Gerald E. Sikorski

Millenium 2100

Melbourne, FL
Leg. Issues: UTI

Outside Counsel/Consultants

Capital Strategies Group, Inc.
Issues: UTI
Rep By: Tammi Hayes

Miller and Schroeder Financial, Inc.

Leg. Issues: HOU

Outside Counsel/Consultants

Greenberg Traurig, LLP
Issues: HOU
Rep By: Ronald L. Platt

Miller Brewing Co.

1341 G St. NW Tel: (202)637-1551
Suite 900 Fax: (202)637-1549
Washington, DC 20005 Registered: LDA

Leg. Issues: BEV

In-house, DC-area Employees

SCULLY, Jr., Timothy H.: V. President, Government Affairs

Outside Counsel/Consultants

Akin, Gump, Strauss, Hauer & Feld, L.L.P.

Arnold & Porter

Jim Pasco & Associates
Issues: BEV
Rep By: James O. Pasco, Jr.

Miller Co.

Meriden, CT

Outside Counsel/Consultants

Collier Shannon Scott, PLLC
Rep By: Jeffrey S. Beckington, David A. Hartquist

Miller Desk

High Point, NC

Outside Counsel/Consultants

O'Connor & Fierce Associates

Milliken and Co.

910 16th St. NW Tel: (202)775-0084
Suite 402 Fax: (202)775-0784
Washington, DC 20006 Registered: LDA

Headquarterd in Spartansburg, SC.

Leg. Issues: APP, TRD

In-house, DC-area Employees

CORCORAN, Melissa: Legislative Assistant
DUTILH, Katherine M.: Legislative Assistant
NASH, Jr., John F.: Washington Counsel

Outside Counsel/Consultants

Skadden, Arps, Slate, Meagher & Flom LLP
Issues: TRD
Rep By: Robert E. Lighthizer, Ivan A. Schlager

SRG & Associates
Issues: APP
Rep By: Augustine D. Tantillo

Wilmer, Cutler & Pickering
Rep By: John D. Greenwald, Ronald I. Meltzer

Million Dollar Roundtable

Park Ridge, IL

Outside Counsel/Consultants

Jenner & Block

Mills Corporation

Washington, DC
Leg. Issues: RES

Outside Counsel/Consultants

The Dutko Group, Inc.
Issues: RES
Rep By: Ronald C. Kaufman

Hunton & Williams
Issues: RES
Rep By: Virginia S. Albrecht

Verner, Liipfert, Bernhard, McPherson and Hand, Chartered
Issues: RES
Rep By: Jane Hickie, Ann W. Richards

MilTec

Huntsville, AL
Leg. Issues: BUD, DEF

Outside Counsel/Consultants

Van Scoyoc Associates, Inc.
Issues: BUD, DEF
Rep By: Ray Cole, H. Stewart Van Scoyoc

Miltope Corp.

Hope Hull, AL

Involved in research, development and acquisition of defense equipment.

Leg. Issues: DEF

Outside Counsel/Consultants

The Van Fleet-Meredith Group
Issues: DEF
Rep By: M. Bruce Meredith, Paul F. Payette, Townsend A. Van Fleet

Milwaukee Metropolitan Sewerage District

Milwaukee, WI
Leg. Issues: BUD, CAW, ENV

Outside Counsel/Consultants

Broydrick & Associates
Issues: BUD, CAW, ENV
Rep By: Bill Viney

Milwaukee Public Museum

Milwaukee, WI
Leg. Issues: BUD

Outside Counsel/Consultants

Broydrick & Associates
Issues: BUD
Rep By: Bill Viney

Milwaukee, City of

Milwaukee, WI
Leg. Issues: ECN, EDU, ENV, GOV, HCR, LAW, TRA, WEL

Outside Counsel/Consultants

Foley & Lardner
Issues: ECN, EDU, ENV, GOV, HCR, LAW, TRA, WEL
Rep By: Theodore H. Bornstein

Milwaukee, Wisconsin, County of

Milwaukee, WI
Leg. Issues: AVI, HCR, LAW, LBR, TOB, TRA, WEL

Outside Counsel/Consultants

Waterman & Associates
Issues: AVI, HCR, LAW, LBR, TOB, TRA, WEL
Rep By: Joe Krahn, Ronald D. Waterman

MindSim, Inc.

Outside Counsel/Consultants

Leadership Counsel, LLC
Rep By: Jack D. P. Lichtenstein

Mine Safety Appliances

Pittsburgh, PA

Outside Counsel/Consultants

Murray, Scheer, Montgomery, Tapia & O'Donnell
Rep By: Thomas R. Crawford, D. Michael Murray

Minebea Thailand

Bangkok, THAILAND

Outside Counsel/Consultants

White & Case LLP
Rep By: Walter J. Spak

Mineral Policy Center

1612 K St. NW
Suite 808
Washington, DC 20006
Web: www.mineralpolicy.org
E-mail: mpc@mineralpolicy.org
Tel: (202)887-1872
Fax: (202)887-1875

A national non-profit organization dedicated to preventing adverse environmental impacts from hardrock mining, and to the cleanup of existing damage.

In-house, DC-area Employees

D'ESPOSITO, Stephen: President

Mineral Technologies, Inc.

New York, NY
Leg. Issues: ENV

Outside Counsel/Consultants

GPC Internat'l
Issues: ENV
Rep By: Shelley McPhee, Bruce A. Morrison

Mineralogical Soc. of America

1015 18th St. NW
Suite 601
Washington, DC 20036-5212
Web: www.minsocam.org
E-mail: business@minsocam.org
Tel: (202)775-4344
Fax: (202)775-0018

Founded for the advancement of mineralogy, crystallography, geochemistry, and petrology and the promotion of their uses in other sciences, industry, and the arts.

In-house, DC-area Employees

SPEER, Dr. J. Alexander: Exec. Director

Minimed, Inc.

Sylmar, CA
Leg. Issues: MED

Outside Counsel/Consultants

Patton Boggs, LLP
Issues: MED
Rep By: John F. Jonas, Eric A. Kuwana, Aubrey A. Rothrock, III, JoAnn V. Willis

Minneapolis, Minnesota, City of

Leg. Issues: ECN

Outside Counsel/Consultants

Lockridge Grindal & Nauen, P.L.L.P.
Issues: ECN
Rep By: Dennis McGrann

Minneapolis-St. Paul Metropolitan Airports Commission

Minneapolis, MN
Leg. Issues: AVI

Outside Counsel/Consultants

Spiegel & McDiarmid
Issues: AVI
Rep By: John J. Corbett, Jr.

Minneapolis-St. Paul Metropolitan Council

St. Paul, MN
Leg. Issues: TRA

Outside Counsel/Consultants

Dorsey & Whitney LLP
Issues: TRA
Rep By: David A. Bieging

Minnesota Indian Gaming Ass'n

Cass Lake, MN
Leg. Issues: IND

Outside Counsel/Consultants

Ducheneaux, Taylor & Associates, Inc.
Issues: IND
Rep By: Franklin D. Ducheneaux

Minnesota Life Insurance Co.

St. Paul, MN
Leg. Issues: BAN, INS, TAX

Outside Counsel/Consultants

The Advocacy Group
Issues: BAN, INS, TAX
Rep By: Jon L. Boisclair

Monfort & Wolfe
Issues: INS, TAX

Minnesota Medical Group Management

Winona, MN

Outside Counsel/Consultants

Lockridge Grindal & Nauen, P.L.L.P.
Rep By: Dennis McGrann

Minnesota Mining and Manufacturing (3M Pharmaceuticals)

St. Paul, MN
Leg. Issues: HCR

Outside Counsel/Consultants

King & Spalding
Issues: HCR
Rep By: Theodore M. Hester, William C. Talmadge

Minnesota Mining and Manufacturing Co. (3M Co.)

1101 15th St. NW
Suite 1100
Washington, DC 20005
Tel: (202)331-6900
Fax: (202)331-2805
Registered: LDA
Leg. Issues: BUD, CHM, CPT, ENG, ENV, GOV, HCR, PHA, ROD, TAX, TOR, TRA, TRD

In-house, DC-area Employees

BEDDOW, Tom F.: V. President, Public Affairs and Government Affairs
D'ZURILLA, June: Manager, Government Relations
HAYNES, Mildred: Manager, Government Relations
HOOPER, Theresa: Manager, Government Relations
PETERSON, Helena Hutton: Manager, Government Relations

Outside Counsel/Consultants

Arthur E. Cameron
Rep By: Arthur E. Cameron, Sr.

Hecht, Spencer & Associates
Issues: HCR
Rep By: Timothy P. Hecht, William H. Hecht, Franklin C. Phifer

Jefferson Government Relations, L.L.C.
Issues: ENV, ROD
Rep By: Robert D. McArver, Jr., Randal P. Schumacher

Bob Lawrence & Associates
Rep By: Craig Cox, Dr. L. Robert Lawrence, Jr.

Julia J. Norrell & Associates
Issues: HCR
Rep By: Julia J. Norrell

Minnesota Mining and Manufacturing Co. (Traffic Control Materials Division)

St. Paul, MN

Outside Counsel/Consultants

Arthur E. Cameron
Rep By: Arthur E. Cameron, Sr.

Minnesota Power

Duluth, MN
Registered: LDA
Leg. Issues: ENG

Outside Counsel/Consultants

Troutman Sanders LLP
Issues: ENG
Rep By: Kevin C. Fitzgerald, William P. Marsan, Clifford S. Sikora

Minnesota Townships

St. Michael, MN

Outside Counsel/Consultants

Monfort & Wolfe

Minnesota Transportation Alliance

Leg. Issues: TRA

Outside Counsel/Consultants

Lockridge Grindal & Nauen, P.L.L.P.
Issues: TRA
Rep By: Dennis McGrann

Minnesota Valley Alfalfa Producers

Shoreview, MN
Leg. Issues: BUD, ENG

Outside Counsel/Consultants

Johnston & Associates, LLC
Issues: BUD, ENG
Rep By: W. Proctor Jones

Minnesota, Washington Office of the State of

400 N. Capitol St.
Suite 365
Washington, DC 20001
Tel: (202)624-5308
Fax: (202)624-5425
Headquartered in St. Paul, MN.

In-house, DC-area Employees

RANGER, William E.: Director
WEIERKE, Corey H.: Deputy Director

Minor Crop Farmer Alliance

A coalition of vegetable and fruit growers seeking federal government help to encourage pesticide producers to continue to produce the safe chemicals used for so-called minor crops. Leading elements in the group include the American Farm Bureau Federation and the United Fresh Fruit and Vegetable Ass'n, Nat'l Council of Farmer Cooperatives and various regional and local commodity groups.

Leg. Issues: CHM

Outside Counsel/Consultants

McDermott, Will and Emery
Issues: CHM
Rep By: Jerry C. Hill, Edward M. Ruckert

Minor Use, Minor Species Coalition

Washington, DC

Members include the Nat'l Aquaculture Ass'n, the Animal Health Institute, the American Veterinary Medical Ass'n, and the American Pet Products Manufacturing Ass'n.

Leg. Issues: ANI

Outside Counsel/Consultants

Meyers & Associates
Issues: ANI
Rep By: Fran Boyd, Larry D. Meyers, Richard L. Meyers

Minority Business Enterprise Legal Defense and Education Fund

300 I St. NE
Suite 400
Washington, DC 20002
Web: www.mbeldef.org
E-mail: staff@mbeldef.org
Tel: (202)289-1700
Fax: (202)289-1701

In-house, DC-area Employees

LEE, Franklin M.: Chief Counsel
MITCHELL, Parren: Founder and Chairman
ROBINSON, Anthony W.: President

Minority Males Consortium

Lincoln, NE

An institute of higher learning aimed at producing programs to reduce violence among minority males.

Leg. Issues: LAW

Outside Counsel/Consultants

Dean Blakey & Moskowitz
Issues: LAW
Rep By: William A. Blakey

Minot State University

Minot, ND
Leg. Issues: BUD, EDU

Outside Counsel/Consultants

Sara Garland (and Associates)
Issues: BUD, EDU
Rep By: Rachel A. Emmons, Sara G. Garland

Mirage Resorts, Inc.

Las Vegas, NV
Leg. Issues: ANI, MAR

Outside Counsel/Consultants

O'Connor & Hannan, L.L.P.
Issues: ANI, MAR
Rep By: George J. Mannina, Jr.

Mirant

901 F St. NW
Suite 800
Washington, DC 20004
Web: www.mirant.com
Tel: (202)585-3800
Fax: (202)585-3806

An energy provider formerly known as Southern Energy. Headquartered in Atlanta, GA.

In-house, DC-area Employees

O'MALIA, Scott: Director, Federal Legislative Affairs

Mishawaka Utilities

Mishawaka, IN
Leg. Issues: ENG, GOV, UTI

Outside Counsel/Consultants

Duncan, Weinberg, Genzer & Pembroke, P.C.
Issues: ENG, GOV, UTI
Rep By: Janice L. Lower, James D. Pembroke

Mission Springs Water District

CA
Leg. Issues: ENV, GOV, UTI

Outside Counsel/Consultants

Peyser Associates, Inc.
Issues: ENV, GOV, UTI
Rep By: Thane Young

Mississippi Chemical Corp.

Yazoo City, MS
Leg. Issues: AGR, TRD

Outside Counsel/Consultants

Bill Simpson & Associates
Issues: AGR, TRD
Rep By: William G. Simpson

Mississippi Polymer Technologies

San Dimas, CA
Leg. Issues: DEF

Outside Counsel/Consultants

GHL Inc.
Issues: DEF

Mississippi, State of

Jackson, MS

Outside Counsel/Consultants

Rhoads Group

Missouri Democratic Party

Outside Counsel/Consultants

Hauser Group

Missouri Department of Social Services

Jefferson City, MO
Leg. Issues: WEL

Outside Counsel/Consultants

Covington & Burling
Issues: WEL
Rep By: Joan L. Kutcher

Missouri Highway and Transportation Department

Jefferson City, MO
Leg. Issues: TRA

Outside Counsel/Consultants

The Carmen Group
Issues: TRA
Rep By: John Hassell, Diane Jemmott, Ann D. Warner, James B. Young

Missouri Public Service Co.

Kansas City, MO

Outside Counsel/Consultants

Birch, Horton, Bittner & Cherot
Rep By: Elisabeth H. Ross

Missouri Public Transit Ass'n

Kansas City, MO
Leg. Issues: TRA

Outside Counsel/Consultants

Redfern Resources
Issues: TRA
Rep By: Ed Redfern

Missouri River Energy Services

Sioux Falls, SD
Leg. Issues: ENG

Outside Counsel/Consultants

Kanner & Associates
Issues: ENG
Rep By: Martin B. Kanner

Missouri, Washington Office of the State of

400 N. Capitol St. NW
Suite 376
Washington, DC 20001
Web: www.gov.state.mo.us/dc/frameset.html
E-mail: missouri@sso.org
Tel: (202)624-7720
Fax: (202)624-5855

In-house, DC-area Employees

GALLAGHER, Cristy: Director, Washington Office

Mitgo Corp.

Sacramento, CA

Outside Counsel/Consultants

Skadden, Arps, Slate, Meagher & Flom LLP

Mitretek Systems

McLean, VA
Web: www.mitretek.org
E-mail: corpcomm@mitretek.org
Leg. Issues: LAW

Outside Counsel/Consultants

Alcalde & Fay
Issues: LAW
Rep By: Hector Alcalde, Hon. Louis A. "Skip" Bafalis, Rodney A. Coleman, Jim Davenport

Mitsubishi Corp.

Tokyo, JAPAN
Leg. Issues: ENV, FOR, MAR

Outside Counsel/Consultants

Akin, Gump, Strauss, Hauer & Feld, L.L.P.
Issues: ENV, FOR, MAR
Rep By: Larisa Dobriansky, Elizabeth Hyman, Ado A. Machida, David Quigley, Daniel L. Spiegel, S. Bruce Wilson

Mitsubishi Electric & Electronics, USA

1560 Wilson Blvd.
Suite 1175
Arlington, VA 22209
Web: www.mitsubishielectric-usa.com
Tel: (703)276-3519
Fax: (703)276-8168

In-house, DC-area Employees

AYLWARD, Rayna: Exec. Director, Mitsubishi Electric America Foundation
SALAVANTIS, Peter J.: Director, Public Affairs

Mitsubishi Electric Automation

Vernon Hills, IL

Outside Counsel/Consultants

Jefferson Consulting Group
Rep By: Robert J. Thompson

Mitsubishi Electronics America (Consumer Electronics Group)

Norcross, GA
Leg. Issues: CPT

Outside Counsel/Consultants

Patton Boggs, LLP
Issues: CPT
Rep By: Thomas Hale Boggs, Jr., Brian C. Lopina, Jeffrey L. Turner

Mitsubishi Internat'l Corp.

2001 Pennsylvania Ave. NW
Suite 700
Washington, DC 20006
Web: www.mic.com
Tel: (202)331-7301
Fax: (202)331-7277
Leg. Issues: AGR, AUT, CHM, ENG, FOR, FUE, TEC, TRD

In-house, DC-area Employees

CALL, Michael: V. President, Deputy General Manager
EPSTEIN, Gordon: Manager
SUGIURA, Yasuyuki: V. President and General Manager
TAKAHASHI, George: Manager
WHITE, Kazuko: Manager

Mitsubishi Motors America, Inc.

1560 Wilson Blvd.
Suite 1200
Arlington, VA 22209
Tel: (703)525-4800
Fax: (703)525-6772
Registered: LDA
Web: www.mitsucars.com
E-mail: aschneider@mmsa.com

Headquartered in Southfield, MI.

Leg. Issues: AUT, CSP, FUE, LBR, TRD

In-house, DC-area Employees

MONTALBAN, Katrina: Assistant Manager, Government Relations
SCHNEIDER, Anna-Maria: Exec. Director, Government Relations, U.S. Operations

Outside Counsel/Consultants

Manatt, Phelps & Phillips, LLP
Issues: AUT, LBR, TRD
Rep By: Hon. Jack W. Buechner, Eric Farnsworth, Steven J. Mulder

Mitsubishi Motors R&D of America, Inc.

1560 Wilson Blvd.
Suite 1200
Arlington, VA 22209
Tel: (703)525-4800
Fax: (703)525-6772
Registered: LDA

Headquarterd in Ann Arbor, MI.

Leg. Issues: AUT

In-house, DC-area Employees

NAGATA, Kenichiro: V. President and General Manager
SINKEZ, Stephen G.: V. President, Regulatory Affairs

Mitsubishi Research Institute

2001 Pennsylvania Ave. NW
Suite 750
Washington, DC 20006
E-mail: ykondoh@mriusa.com
Tel: (202)785-2424
Fax: (202)785-2426

The Washington, DC office is the liaison of a research institute based in Tokyo, Japan.

Leg. Issues: AER, AUT, AVI, CHM, CPI, CSP, DEF, DIS, ECN, EDU, ENG, ENV, FIN, FOO, GOV, HCR, MAN, NAT, SCI, TEC, TRA, URB, WAS

In-house, DC-area Employees

KONDOH, Yasushi: Chief Representative

Mitsui and Co. (U.S.A.), Inc.

1701 Pennsylvania Ave. NW
Suite 500
Washington, DC 20006
Tel: (202)861-0660
Fax: (202)861-0437

Headquartered in New York, NY.

In-house, DC-area Employees

BELL, William C.: International Projects Manager
BRUSER, Lawrence: Deputy General Manager, and Director, Government Affairs
EPSTEIN, Christopher: Export Controls Manager
MURAMATSU, Kazutoshi: V. President and General Manager

MMG Ventures LP

Baltimore, MD

A investment company.

Leg. Issues: SMB

Outside Counsel/Consultants

Thelen Reid & Priest LLP
Issues: SMB
Rep By: William A. Kirk, Jr.

MMV

Washington, DC

Outside Counsel/Consultants

Manatos & Manatos, Inc.

Mni-Sose Intertribal Water Rights Coalition

Rapid City, SD
Leg. Issues: IND

Outside Counsel/Consultants

Ducheneaux, Taylor & Associates, Inc.
Issues: IND
Rep By: Peter S. Taylor

Moapa Valley Water District

Logandale, NV
Leg. Issues: BUD

Outside Counsel/Consultants

The Furman Group
Issues: BUD
Rep By: K. Link Browder

Moberly-Randolph County Economic Development

Moberly, MO

Outside Counsel/Consultants

Sam Richardson
Rep By: Sam Richardson

Mobex Communications

Boise, ID

Outside Counsel/Consultants

Wear & Associates
Rep By: Terrance J. Wear

Mobil Latin America & Caribbean, Inc.

Fairfax, VA

Outside Counsel/Consultants

RMA Internat'l, Inc.
Rep By: Otto J. Reich

Mobile Area Water and Sewer System

Leg. Issues: CAW, ENV

Outside Counsel/Consultants

Capitol Link, Inc.
Issues: CAW, ENV
Rep By: Hon. David M. Staton

Mobile Climate Control

Utica, NY

Manufacturers of environmental control units for commercial and military applications.

Leg. Issues: DEF

Outside Counsel/Consultants

Hyjek & Fix, Inc.
Issues: DEF
Rep By: Donald J. Fix, Steven M. Hyjek

Mobile Communications Holdings, Inc.

Washington, DC
Leg. Issues: SMB, TEC

Outside Counsel/Consultants

Smith, Bucklin and Associates, Inc.
Issues: SMB, TEC
Rep By: Frank M. Moore

Mobile Diagnostic Testing Services

Buffalo, NY
Leg. Issues: HCR

Outside Counsel/Consultants

Nixon Peabody LLP
Issues: HCR

Mobile Telecommunications Technologies Corp.

Jackson, MS

Outside Counsel/Consultants

Wiley, Rein & Fielding
Rep By: Mimi W. Dawson, Nancy J. Victory

Mobile, Alabama, City of

Leg. Issues: HOU, LAW, TRA, URB

Outside Counsel/Consultants

Capitol Link, Inc.
Issues: HOU, LAW, TRA, URB
Rep By: Hon. David M. Staton

The Jeffrey Modell Foundation

New York, NY

A voluntary health foundation.

Leg. Issues: BUD, HCR, MED, SCI

Outside Counsel/Consultants

Cavarocchi Ruscio Dennis Associates
Issues: BUD, HCR, MED, SCI
Rep By: Lyle B. Dennis

The Modernization Forum

Dearborn, MI — Registered: LDA
Leg. Issues: BUD, MAN, SCI

Outside Counsel/Consultants

Bob Davis & Associates
Issues: MAN
Rep By: Hon. Robert W. Davis

Dykema Gossett PLLC
Issues: BUD, MAN, SCI
Rep By: Tricia K. Markwood

Modesto, California, City of

Leg. Issues: BUD, CAW, ECN, LBR, ROD, URB

Outside Counsel/Consultants

Ball Janik, LLP
Issues: BUD, CAW, ECN, LBR, ROD, URB
Rep By: M. Victoria Cram

Modesto/Turlock Irrigation District

Modesto, CA
Leg. Issues: CAW, CSP, ENG, NAT, UTI

Outside Counsel/Consultants

Duncan, Weinberg, Genzer & Pembroke, P.C.
Issues: CSP, ENG, UTI
Rep By: Wallace L. Duncan, James D. Pembroke, Michael R. Postar

The Ferguson Group, LLC
Issues: CAW, ENG, NAT
Rep By: William Ferguson, Jr., W. Roger Gwinn, Joseph L. Raeder

Moffit Cancer Research Hospital

Tampa, FL
Leg. Issues: BUD, HCR, MMM

Outside Counsel/Consultants

Gibbons & Company, Inc.
Issues: BUD, HCR, MMM
Rep By: Clifford S. Gibbons, Hon. Sam M. Gibbons

Mole Lake Band of the Sokaogon Chippewa Community

Crandon, WI

Outside Counsel/Consultants

Sonosky, Chambers, Sachse & Endreson
Rep By: William R. Perry

Molecular BioSystems, Inc.

San Diego, CA

A manufacturer and marketer of medical devices.

Leg. Issues: ADV, CSP, GOV, HCR, MAN, MED, SCI

Outside Counsel/Consultants

Hale and Dorr LLP
Issues: GOV, MED
Rep By: Mark Heller

Venable
Issues: ADV, CSP, HCR, MAN, MED, SCI
Rep By: David G. Adams

Molecular Separations Inc.

Sarasota, FL

A hazardous waste treatment firm.

Leg. Issues: CAW, ENG

Outside Counsel/Consultants

Shook, Hardy & Bacon LLP
Issues: CAW, ENG
Rep By: William F. Demarest, Jr., Robert J. Woody

Molina Healthcare

Long Beach, CA
Leg. Issues: GOV, IMM, MMM

Outside Counsel/Consultants

Colling Swift & Hynes
Issues: GOV, IMM, MMM
Rep By: Hon. Peter J. Hoagland

Molina Medical Centers

Leg. Issues: GOV, IMM, MMM

Outside Counsel/Consultants

Arent Fox Kintner Plotkin & Kahn, PLLC
Issues: GOV, IMM, MMM
Rep By: Bill Applegate, Michael T. McNamara, William A. Sarraille

The Robert Mondavi Winery

Oakville, CA — Registered: LDA
Leg. Issues: BEV, TAX

Outside Counsel/Consultants

Akin, Gump, Strauss, Hauer & Feld, L.L.P.
Issues: BEV, TAX
Rep By: David Geanacopoulos, Henry A. Terhune

Money Garden Corp.

New York, NY

Outside Counsel/Consultants

Preston Gates Ellis & Rouvelas Meeds LLP
Rep By: Tim L. Peckinpaugh, Steven R. "Rick" Valentine

Money Management Institute

1101 17th St. NW
Suite 703
Washington, DC 20036
Tel: (202)347-3858
Fax: (202)331-8446
Web: www.moneyinstitute.com

Membership comprises firms that offer comprehensive financial consulting services to individual investors, foundations, retirement plans and trusts.

Leg. Issues: FIN, RET

In-house, DC-area Employees

DAVIS, Christopher L.: Exec. Director

Outside Counsel/Consultants

Infrastructure Management Group
Issues: FIN
Rep By: Porter K. Wheeler

KPMG, LLP

The Money Store

Sacramento, CA
Leg. Issues: FIN

Outside Counsel/Consultants

Shaw Pittman
Issues: FIN
Rep By: Andrew L. Woods

Money Tree, Inc.

Seattle, WA
Leg. Issues: BAN

Outside Counsel/Consultants

Jamison and Sullivan, Inc.
Issues: BAN

Mongolian People's Republic, Embassy of

2833 M St. NW
Washington, DC 20007
Tel: (202)333-7117
Fax: (202)298-9220
E-mail: monemb@aol.com

Outside Counsel/Consultants

Washington World Group, Ltd.
Rep By: Edward J. von Kloberg, III

Thelonius Monk Institute of Jazz

Washington, DC
Leg. Issues: ART

Outside Counsel/Consultants

Chernikoff and Co.
Issues: ART
Rep By: Larry B. Chernikoff

Monmouth University

West Long Branch, NJ

Outside Counsel/Consultants

Mintz, Levin, Cohn, Ferris, Glovsky and Popeo, P.C.
Rep By: Raymond D. Cotton

Monroe Center, LLC

Hoboken, NJ — Registered: LDA
Leg. Issues: RES

Outside Counsel/Consultants

Peyser Associates, Inc.
Issues: RES
Rep By: Michael Bucciero, Jr., Peter A. Peyser, Jr.

Monroe County Commercial Fishermen, Inc.

Marathon, FL
Leg. Issues: BUD

Outside Counsel/Consultants

Robertson, Monagle & Eastaugh
Issues: BUD
Rep By: Rick E. Marks

Monroe Telephone Services, L.P.

College Station, TX
Leg. Issues: TEC

Outside Counsel/Consultants

Lent Scrivner & Roth LLC
Issues: TEC
Rep By: Norman F. Lent, III, Hon. Norman F. Lent, Alan J. Roth, Michael S. Scrivner

O'Connor & Hannan, L.L.P.
Issues: TEC

Monroe, Florida, County of

Key West, FL
Leg. Issues: DEF, ENV

Outside Counsel/Consultants

Commonwealth Consulting Corp.
Issues: DEF, ENV
Rep By: Christopher M. Lehman

Monroe, Louisiana, Chamber of Commerce of the City of

Monroe, LA
Leg. Issues: AVI, BUD, ECN, ROD, SMB, TRA, WAS

Outside Counsel/Consultants

Ross Atkins
Issues: AVI, BUD, ECN, ROD, SMB, TRA, WAS
Rep By: Ross Atkins

The Palmer Group
Issues: AVI, BUD, ECN, TRA
Rep By: Clifford A. Palmer

Monroe, Louisiana, City of

Leg. Issues: AVI, BUD, ECN, ROD, SMB, TRA, WAS

Outside Counsel/Consultants

Ross Atkins
Issues: AVI, BUD, ECN, ROD, SMB, TRA, WAS
Rep By: Ross Atkins

The Palmer Group
Rep By: Clifford A. Palmer

Monroe, New York, County of

Rochester, NY
Leg. Issues: AVI, BUD, CAW, ECN, ENV, RES, ROD, TRA, URB

Outside Counsel/Consultants

Government Relations, Inc.
Issues: AVI, BUD, CAW, ECN, ENV, RES, ROD, TRA, URB
Rep By: Thomas J. Bulger, Mark H. Miller, John N. Young

Monrovia, California, City of

Outside Counsel/Consultants

David Turch & Associates

Monsanto Co.

600 13th St. NW
Suite 660
Washington, DC 20005
Tel: (202)783-2460
Fax: (202)783-2468
Registered: LDA

Web: www.monsanto.com

Headquartered in St. Louis, MO. The company merged with Pharmacia & Upjohn (see separate listing) in April of 2000.

Leg. Issues: AGR, BUD, CHM, CPT, ENV, FOO, PHA, TAX, TRD

Political Action Committee/s

Monsanto Citizenship Fund

600 13th St. NW
Suite 660
Washington, DC 20005
Tel: (202)783-2460
Fax: (202)783-2468
Contact: Linda Strachan

In-house, DC-area Employees

DYKES, Michael: V. President, Government Affairs
STRACHAN, Linda: PAC Contact

Outside Counsel/Consultants

Arnold & Porter

Arter & Hadden

Baker, Donelson, Bearman & Caldwell, P.C.
Issues: AGR
Rep By: James D. Range

Bergner Bockorny Castagnetti and Hawkins
Issues: AGR, FOO, PHA, TAX, TRD
Rep By: Jeffrey T. Bergner, David A. Bockorny, David Castagnetti, Melissa Schulman

Burson-Marsteller
Rep By: Brian H. Lott

EOP Group, Inc.
Rep By: Jonathan Gledhill, Joseph Hezir, Michael O'Bannon

Griffin, Johnson, Dover & Stewart
Rep By: G. Jack Dover, Patrick J. Griffin, Leonard Swinehart

Lesher & Russell, Inc.
Issues: AGR
Rep By: William G. Lesher, Randall M. Russell

Long, Aldridge & Norman, LLP
Issues: AGR, TRD
Rep By: Karen Anderson, Edgar H. Sims

Mayer, Brown & Platt
Issues: TRD
Rep By: Amb. Peter L. Scher

Miller & Chevalier, Chartered
Issues: TAX

Morgan Meguire, LLC
Rep By: C. Kyle Simpson

Powell Tate

Powell, Goldstein, Frazer & Murphy LLP
Issues: AGR
Rep By: Paul A. Drazek, Craig A. Thorn

Mont Blanc, Inc.

Chatham, NJ
Leg. Issues: CPT

Outside Counsel/Consultants

Kent & O'Connor, Inc.
Issues: CPT
Rep By: Patrick C. O'Connor

Montana Land Reliance

Billings, MT
Leg. Issues: RES, TAX

Outside Counsel/Consultants

Baker, Donelson, Bearman & Caldwell, P.C.
Issues: TAX
Rep By: James D. Range

Smith Martin & Boyette
Issues: RES, TAX
Rep By: Van R. Boyette

Montana State University

Bozeman, MT
Leg. Issues: BUD, EDU

Outside Counsel/Consultants

Van Scoyoc Associates, Inc.
Issues: BUD, EDU
Rep By: Carri Booth, Carolyn Fuller, H. Stewart Van Scoyoc

Montana, Department of Transportation of the State of

Helena, MT

Outside Counsel/Consultants

John A. DeVierno
Rep By: John A. DeVierno

Montana, State of

Helena, MT

Outside Counsel/Consultants

Snavely, King, Majoros, O'Connor and Lee, Inc.
Rep By: Tom O'Connor

Montefiore Medical Center

Bronx, NY
Leg. Issues: HCR

Outside Counsel/Consultants

Cassidy & Associates, Inc.
Issues: HCR
Rep By: Gregory M. Gill, Lindsay Lawrence, Valerie Rogers Osborne

Montenegro, Government of

Outside Counsel/Consultants

Verner, Liipfert, Bernhard, McPherson and Hand, Chartered
Rep By: Lawrence E. Levinson

Montenegro, Trade Mission to the U.S.A. of the Republic of

1610 New Hampshire Ave. NW
Washington, DC 20009
Tel: (202)234-6108
Fax: (202)234-6109
Registered: FARA

In-house, DC-area Employees

MARIC, Zorica: Acting Director

Monterey County Water Resources Agency

Salinas, CA
Leg. Issues: BUD, ENV

Outside Counsel/Consultants

John Freshman Associates, Inc.
Issues: BUD, ENV
Rep By: John D. Freshman, Lawrence P. Kast, Catherine B. Kiefer

Monterey Institute

Monterey, CA
Leg. Issues: DEF

Outside Counsel/Consultants

Gibson, Dunn & Crutcher LLP
Issues: DEF
Rep By: Alan A. Platt

Monterey Salinas Transit

Monterey, CA
Leg. Issues: BUD, TRA

Outside Counsel/Consultants

Honberger and Walters, Inc.
Issues: BUD, TRA
Rep By: Greg Campbell, Donald Gilchrest, Thomas P. Walters

Monterey, California, County of

Salinas, CA
Leg. Issues: DEF, ECN

Outside Counsel/Consultants

Murray, Scheer, Montgomery, Tapia & O'Donnell
Issues: DEF, ECN
Rep By: John R. O'Donnell, Raul R. Tapia

Montgomery Airport Authority

Montgomery, AL
Leg. Issues: AVI, BUD, ENV, TRA

Outside Counsel/Consultants

Van Scoyoc Associates, Inc.
Issues: AVI, BUD, ENV, TRA
Rep By: Ray Cole, Chad Schulken, H. Stewart Van Scoyoc

Montgomery County, Maryland, Division of Consumer Affairs

100 Maryland Ave.
Suite 330
Rockville, MD 20850
Tel: (240)777-3636
Fax: (240)777-3768
Web: www.co.mo.md.us/hca

In-house, DC-area Employees

ROSE, George B.: Division Chief

Montgomery County, Ohio/Montgomery County Solid Waste District

Dayton, OH

Outside Counsel/Consultants

Wright & Talisman, P.C.
Rep By: Scott M. DuBoff, Robert H. Lamb

Montgomery Ward & Co., Inc.

Chicago, IL
Registered: LDA
Leg. Issues: TRD

Outside Counsel/Consultants

French & Company
Issues: TRD
Rep By: Verrick O. French

Montgomery Watson

819 Seventh St. NW
Suite 200
Washington, DC 20001
Tel: (202)296-5354
Fax: (202)296-7248
Registered: LDA

Web: www.mw.com

Engineering firm headquartered in Chicago, IL.

Leg. Issues: ENV

Political Action Committee/s

MW PAC

819 7th St. NW
Suite 200
Washington, DC 20001
Tel: (202)296-5354
Fax: (202)296-7248

In-house, DC-area Employees

LAPAILLE, Gary J.: V. President, National and State Affairs

Montgomery, Alabama, Chamber of Commerce of

Leg. Issues: BUD, ECN, ROD, TRA, URB

Outside Counsel/Consultants

Van Scoyoc Associates, Inc.
Issues: BUD, ECN, ROD, TRA, URB
Rep By: Ray Cole, H. Stewart Van Scoyoc

Montgomery, Maryland, Cable Television Office of the County of

20 W. Gude Dr.
Rockville, MD 20850-1151
Tel: (301)424-4400
Fax: (301)294-7697

Administers the Cable TV Franchise Agreement for Montgomery County.

Leg. Issues: TEC

In-house, DC-area Employees

LAWTON, Jane: Cable Communications Administrator

Outside Counsel/Consultants

Miller & Van Eaton, P.L.L.C.
Issues: TEC
Rep By: Nicholas P. Miller

Montgomery, Maryland, County of

Exec. Office Building
101 Monroe St.
Fourth Floor
Rockville, MD 20850
Tel: (240)777-6553
Fax: (240)777-6551
Registered: LDA

In-house, DC-area Employees

MORNINGSTAR, Sara Eileen: Federal Relations Coordinator

Outside Counsel/Consultants

LMRC, Inc.

Montrose Chemical Co.

Trumbull, CT
Leg. Issues: ENV, NAT

Outside Counsel/Consultants

O'Connor & Hannan, L.L.P.
Issues: ENV, NAT
Rep By: Robert W. Barrie, Hon. Thomas J. Corcoran, George J. Mannina, Jr., Patrick E. O'Donnell

Montrose, Colorado, City of

Leg. Issues: BUD

Outside Counsel/Consultants

Stites & Harbison
Issues: BUD
Rep By: Kenneth G. Lee

MONY Life Insurance Co.

New York, NY
Registered: LDA
Leg. Issues: BAN, FIN, INS, RET, TAX

Outside Counsel/Consultants

Gibbons & Company, Inc.
Rep By: Clifford S. Gibbons, Hon. Sam M. Gibbons

Murray, Scheer, Montgomery, Tapia & O'Donnell
Issues: BAN, FIN, INS, RET, TAX
Rep By: Thomas R. Crawford, D. Michael Murray

Benjamin Moore & Co.

Montvale, NJ

A manufacturer and distributor of paint.

Outside Counsel/Consultants

Hill and Knowlton, Inc.

Moore Medical Corp.

New Britain, CT
Leg. Issues: HCR

Outside Counsel/Consultants

The Aker Partners Inc.
Issues: HCR
Rep By: G. Colburn Aker

Moorehead, Minnesota, City of

Leg. Issues: TRA

Outside Counsel/Consultants

Barbara J. Rohde
Issues: TRA
Rep By: Barbara J. Rohde

Mooresville, North Carolina, Town of

Mooresville, NC
Leg. Issues: ECN, LAW

Outside Counsel/Consultants

The Ferguson Group, LLC
Issues: ECN, LAW
Rep By: Charmayne Macon

Moose Internat'l Inc.

London, UNITED KINGDOM
Leg. Issues: IMM

Outside Counsel/Consultants

Baker & Hostetler LLP
Issues: IMM
Rep By: E. Mark Braden, Matthew J. Dolan, Steven A. Lotterer, Hon. Guy Vander Jagt

Morehouse School of Medicine

Atlanta, GA

Outside Counsel/Consultants

Mintz, Levin, Cohn, Ferris, Glovsky and Popeo, P.C.
Rep By: Raymond D. Cotton

Morepen Laboratories, Ltd.

Outside Counsel/Consultants

O'Connor & Hannan, L.L.P.
Rep By: Hon. Larry Pressler

J. P. Morgan Chase & Co.

800 Connecticut Ave. NW
9th Floor
Washington, DC 20006
Tel: (202)533-2100
Fax: (202)533-2124
Registered: LDA

Leg. Issues: BAN, BUD, EDU, FIN, FUE, GOV, HOU, POS, TAX

In-house, DC-area Employees

LAWSON, IV, W. David: Managing Director
WARD, L. Courtney: V. President

Outside Counsel/Consultants

BKSH & Associates
Issues: FIN
Rep By: Charles R. Black, Jr., Karen Chiccehitto, Dennis Shea

Hohlt & Associates
Issues: BAN, BUD, FIN, TAX
Rep By: Richard F. Hohlt

Kaye Scholer LLP
Rep By: Christopher R. Brewster

Williams & Jensen, P.C.
Issues: TAX
Rep By: David E. Franasiak, Robert E. Glennon, Jr., George G. Olsen

Willkie Farr & Gallagher
Issues: FIN, GOV
Rep By: Russell L. Smith

Morgan Guaranty Trust Co.

New York, NY
Leg. Issues: BAN

Outside Counsel/Consultants

Sullivan & Cromwell
Issues: BAN
Rep By: H. Rodgin Cohen, Michael Wiseman

J. E. Morgan Knitting Mills

Tamaqua, PA

Outside Counsel/Consultants

The PMA Group
Rep By: Kaylene Green, Paul J. Magliocchetti, Charles Smith, Mark Waclawski

J. P. Morgan Securities

New York, NY

Outside Counsel/Consultants

Williams & Jensen, P.C.
Rep By: David E. Franasiak, Robert E. Glennon, Jr., George G. Olsen

Morgan Stanley Dean Witter & Co.

1300 I St. NW
12th Floor
Washington, DC 20005
Tel: (202)326-3980
Fax: (202)326-3981
Registered: LDA

Headquartered in New York, NY.

Leg. Issues: BAN, BNK, FIN, FOR, IMM, TAX, TRD

Political Action Committee/s

Morgan Stanley Dean Witter PAC
1300 I St. NW
12th Floor
Washington, DC 20005
Contact: Douglas Davidson
Tel: (202)326-3980
Fax: (202)326-3981

In-house, DC-area Employees

ALTMAN, Emily: Principal, International Government Relations
BAPTISTA, Samuel J.: Managing Director, Government Affairs
DAVIDSON, Douglas: Chairman, Morgan Stanley Dean Witter PAC
MESSINA, Raymond A.: Principal, Federal Government Affairs

Outside Counsel/Consultants

Alston & Bird LLP
Issues: FIN
Rep By: Thomas M. Boyd

James E. Boland
Issues: BAN, BNK, FIN, TAX
Rep By: James E. Boland, Jr.

Hooper Owen & Winburn
Issues: TAX
Rep By: Lindsay D. Hooper

McDermott, Will and Emery
Rep By: Neil Quinter

The Kate Moss Company
Issues: BAN, BNK, FIN
Rep By: Kate Moss

Elisabeth G. Newton
Issues: BAN, TAX
Rep By: Elisabeth G. Newton

George C. Tagg
Issues: BAN, FIN
Rep By: George C. Tagg

Morgan State University

Baltimore, MD
Leg. Issues: BUD, EDU, SCI, TRA

Outside Counsel/Consultants

Van Scoyoc Associates, Inc.
Issues: BUD, EDU, SCI, TRA
Rep By: Steve E. Crane, Kevin F. Kelly, H. Stewart Van Scoyoc

Morgan, Lewis & Bockius LLP

1800 M St. NW
Washington, DC 20036
Tel: (202)467-7000
Fax: (202)467-7176
Registered: LDA, FARA

Web: www.morganlewis.com
E-mail: postmaster@morganlewis.com
Leg. Issues: ENG

In-house, DC-area Employees

BAER, William E.
BERMINGHAM, Maya: Associate
DANIEL, John E.: Of Counsel
DENNIS, Sandra J. P.: Partner
FRIEDMAN, Margery Sinder
GLASGOW, James A.
GLEASON, Kathryn L.: Partner
GLICK, Helene L.: Associate
HOBBS, III, Caswell O.: Partner, Washington Office
KUHN, Nancy R.
MATTHEWS, John E.
O'CONNOR, Charles P.: Managing Partner
PETERSON, Charles H.
RING, John F.
ROADY, Celia: Partner
SANZO, Kathleen M.: Partner
SILVERMAN, Donald J.: Partner
STADULIS, Lawrence P.
ZARB, Jr., Frank G.: Partner

Outside Counsel/Consultants

Johnston & Associates, LLC
Issues: ENG
Rep By: Alex Flint, Hon. J. Bennett Johnston, W. Proctor Jones

Morning Star Institute, The

611 Pennsylvania Ave. SE
Washington, DC 20003
Tel: (202)547-5531
Fax: (202)546-6724

Educates the public regarding the cultural and traditional rights and arts of Native Americans. Also works with Native People to recover and protect sacred lands and other cultural property.

Leg. Issues: ART, CIV, GOV, IND

In-house, DC-area Employees

HARJO, Suzan Shown: President and Exec. Director

Morocco, Foreign Ministry of the Kingdom of

1601 21st St. NW
Washington, DC 20009
Leg. Issues: FOR, TRD

Outside Counsel/Consultants

The Solomon Group, LLC
Issues: FOR, TRD
Rep By: David M. Lonie, Hon. Gerald B. H. Solomon

Morongo Band of Mission Indians

Banning, CA
Leg. Issues: IND

Outside Counsel/Consultants

PACE-CAPSTONE
Issues: IND
Rep By: Scott C. Dacey, James W. Wise

Morris Communications

Augusta, GA

Outside Counsel/Consultants

Peter S. Barash Associates, Inc.
Rep By: Peter S. Barash

Morrison Inc.

Mobile, AL

Outside Counsel/Consultants

Power & Power

Morro Bay, California, City of

Leg. Issues: BUD

Outside Counsel/Consultants

E. Del Smith and Co.
Issues: BUD
Rep By: Margaret Allen, E. Del Smith

Morse Diesel Internat'l Inc.

New York, NY
Leg. Issues: TAX

Outside Counsel/Consultants

Kelly and Associates, Inc.
Issues: TAX
Rep By: John A. Kelly

Mort Community College

Flint, MI
Leg. Issues: EDU, MAN

Outside Counsel/Consultants

Washington Alliance Group, Inc.
Issues: EDU, MAN
Rep By: Bonnie Singer

M. A. Mortenson Co.

Minneapolis, MN

Outside Counsel/Consultants

O'Connor & Hannan, L.L.P.
Rep By: Hon. Thomas J. Corcoran

Mortgage Bankers Ass'n of America

1919 Pennsylvania Ave. NW
Seventh Floor
Washington, DC 20006-3488
Web: www.mbaa.org
Tel: (202)557-2700
Registered: LDA

The only national trade association devoted exclusively to real estate finance. Represents more than 2,400 members, including mortgage bankers, savings and loan associations, commercial banks, life insurance companies and others in the mortgage lending field.

Leg. Issues: BAN, BNK, BUD, CSP, ENV, FIN, HOU, INS, LAW, RES, SCI, TAX, VET

Political Action Committee/s

Mortgage Bankers Ass'n of America Political Action Committee
1919 Pennsylvania Ave. NW
Seventh Floor
Washington, DC 20006-3488
Tel: (202)557-2700

In-house, DC-area Employees

GLASER, Howard B.: Senior Staff V. President and General Counsel
GRAMLEY, Lyle E.: Consulting Economist
HOWE, Todd
KAPEN, Karen: Associate Director/Counsel
KAPPELER, Joyce: Senior Staff V. Prsident, Education
KEMPNER, Jonathan L.: Chief Operating Officer
LEREAH, David A.: Senior Staff V. President and Chief Economist
MCGEE, Christi C.
O'TOOLE, Robert M.: Senior Staff V. President, Residential Finance/Government Agency Relations
SLESINGER, Phyllis: Staff V. President and General Counsel
WOOD, Burton C.: Senior Staff V. President, Legislation

Outside Counsel/Consultants

BKSH & Associates

Duane, Morris & Heckscher LLP
Issues: HOU
Rep By: Johnson Brad

Hawkins, Delafield & Wood
Issues: HOU
Rep By: John V. Connorton

The Smith-Free Group

Eugene F. Swanzey
Issues: BAN, HOU
Rep By: Eugene F. Swanzey

The Velasquez Group
Issues: BAN, FIN
Rep By: Jay Velasquez

Mortgage Insurance Companies of America

727 15th St. NW
12th Floor
Washington, DC 20005
Web: www.micanews.com
Tel: (202)393-5566
Fax: (202)393-5557

The trade association representing the private mortgage insurance industry.

Leg. Issues: BAN, FIN, HOU, INS

Political Action Committee/s

Mortgage Insurance Political Action Committee
727 15th St. NW
12th Floor
Washington, DC 20005
Contact: Suzanne C. Hutchinson
Tel: (202)393-5566
Fax: (202)393-5557

In-house, DC-area Employees

HUTCHINSON, Suzanne C.: Exec. V. President
IRONFIELD, Susan B.: Director, Legislative and Regulatory Relations

Outside Counsel/Consultants

Akin, Gump, Strauss, Hauer & Feld, L.L.P.
Issues: BAN, HOU, INS
Rep By: Smith W. Davis, Christine Hesse, Joel Jankowsky, Barney J. Skladany, Jr.

Jack Ferguson Associates, Inc.
Issues: BAN, FIN
Rep By: Jack Ferguson

Goodwin, Procter & Hoar LLP

Hogan & Hartson L.L.P.
Issues: BAN, HOU, INS
Rep By: William Michael House, Christine M. Warnke

Ruddy & Associates
Issues: BAN, HOU, INS
Rep By: Robert E. Ruddy

The Velasquez Group

Mortgage Investors Corp.

St. Petersburg, FL
Leg. Issues: VET

Outside Counsel/Consultants

Wilson & Wasserstein, Inc.
Issues: VET
Rep By: Glen D. Wasserstein, Russell J. Wilson

Morton Internat'l

Chicago, IL
Leg. Issues: LBR

Outside Counsel/Consultants

Patton Boggs, LLP
Issues: LBR
Rep By: Henry Chajet

Moscow Interbank Currency Exchange (MICEX)

Moscow, RUSSIA

Outside Counsel/Consultants

Arnold & Porter

Moscow Internat'l Petroleum Club

3000 K St. NW
Suite 105
Washington, DC 20007-5116
Web: www.mmnk.org
Tel: (202)424-7820
Fax: (202)424-7763

Provides Washington-based support for MIPC members and information for Congress, the Administration, and the public regarding energy cooperation and related policy developments in Russia.

In-house, DC-area Employees

PUGLIARESI, Lucian: Director, Washington Representative Office

Moscow State University

Moscow, RUSSIA
Leg. Issues: EDU, FOR

Outside Counsel/Consultants

Capital Consultants Corp.
Issues: EDU, FOR
Rep By: Michael David Kaiser

Mossberg Group, LLC

Daytona Beach, FL
Leg. Issues: FIR

Outside Counsel/Consultants

Law Offices of Mark Barnes
Issues: FIR
Rep By: Mark J. Barnes, Cindy Colpitts

Most Group Limited

Moscow, RUSSIA

A holding company for operations in the banking, construction and media sectors.

Leg. Issues: FOR, MIA

Outside Counsel/Consultants

APCO Worldwide
Issues: FOR, MIA
Rep By: Hon. Don L. Bonker

MOTE Marine Lab

Sarasota, FL
Leg. Issues: BUD, ENV, MAR

Outside Counsel/Consultants

Marlowe and Co.
Issues: BUD, ENV, MAR
Rep By: Howard Marlowe, Jeffrey Mazzella

Mothers Against Drunk Driving (MADD)

Hurst, TX
Leg. Issues: ALC, TRA

Outside Counsel/Consultants

Peyser Associates, Inc.
Issues: TRA
Rep By: Thomas J. Howarth

Smith Dawson & Andrews, Inc.
Issues: ALC
Rep By: Gregory B. Andrews, Kirk Bailey, Thomas C. Dawson, James P. Smith

Motion Picture and Television Fund

Woodland Hills, CA
Leg. Issues: HCR, HOU, MED, MMM

Outside Counsel/Consultants

Tuvin Associates
Issues: HCR, HOU, MED, MMM
Rep By: Raymond T. Bennett, Carl R. Tuvin

Motion Picture Ass'n of America

1600 I St. NW
Washington, DC 20006
Tel: (202)293-1966
Fax: (202)296-7410
Registered: LDA
Web: www.mpaa.org
Leg. Issues: ART, COM, CON, CPT, NAT, TAX, TEC, TRD

Political Action Committee/s

Motion Picture Ass'n Political Action Committee
1600 I St. NW
Washington, DC 20006
Contact: Kelly O'Connell
Tel: (202)293-1966
Fax: (202)296-7410

In-house, DC-area Employees

ATTAWAY, Fritz E.: Senior V. President, Government Relations and General Counsel
HUYNH, Phuong: Director, Public Relations
MERIFIELD-TRIPOLDI, Cynthia E.: V. President, Congressional Relations
O'CONNELL, Kelly: PAC Contact
RICHARDSON, Bonnie: V. President, Trade and Federal Affairs
SAUNDERS, Jane V.: V. President, Commercial Affairs
TAYLOR, Richard L.: V. President, Public Affairs
THOMPSON, Nancy: V. President, Administration
VALENTI, Jack J.: President and Chief Exec. Officer

Outside Counsel/Consultants

Akin, Gump, Strauss, Hauer & Feld, L.L.P.
Issues: CPT
Rep By: Smith W. Davis, William J. Farah, Joel Jankowsky, Barney J. Skladany, Jr., Robin Weisman

Baker & Hostetler LLP
Issues: CPT, TAX
Rep By: Matthew J. Dolan, Steven A. Lotterer, Hon. Guy Vander Jagt

The Laxalt Corp.
Issues: ART
Rep By: Michelle D. Laxalt

Parry, Romani, DeConcini & Symms
Issues: ART, COM, CON, CPT, TAX, TRD
Rep By: Edward H. Baxter, Hon. Dennis DeConcini, John M. Haddow, Scott D. Hatch, Shannon Davis Henderson, Jack W. Martin, Romano Romani, Linda Arey Skladany, Hon. Steven D. Symms

Podesta/Mattoon
Issues: CPT
Rep By: Ann Delory, Kimberley Fritts, Matthew Gelman, Claudia James, Kristen Leary

White & Case LLP
Issues: TAX
Rep By: William P. McClure

Williams & Connolly

Motor and Equipment Manufacturers Ass'n

1225 New York Ave. NW
Suite 300
Washington, DC 20005
Tel: (202)393-6362
Fax: (202)737-3742
Registered: LDA

Headquartered in North Carolina.

Leg. Issues: AUT, CAW, CHM, ENV, LBR, TRD

In-house, DC-area Employees

DUGGAN, Brian: Director, Internat'l Programs
HEFFERNAN, Claire M.: V. President, Government Relations
LOPES, Ana: Director, Public Relations

Outside Counsel/Consultants

Arent Fox Kintner Plotkin & Kahn, PLLC
Issues: ENV, TRD
Rep By: Marc L. Fleischaker, Lawrence F. Henneberger, Matthew J. McConkey, Michael T. McNamara, Deanne M. Ottaviano, Todd Weiss

Motor Coach Industries, Inc.

Des Plaines, IL
Leg. Issues: TRA

Outside Counsel/Consultants

Winston & Strawn
Issues: TRA
Rep By: Hon. Beryl F. Anthony, Jr., Hon. James H. Burnley, IV, Charles L. Kinney, Joseph E. O'Leary, James T. Pitts, Douglas C. Richardson, John A. Waits, II

Motor Freight Carriers Ass'n

499 S. Capitol St. SW
Suite 502A
Washington, DC 20003
Tel: (202)554-3060
Fax: (202)554-3160
Registered: LDA
Web: www.mfca.org
E-mail: mfca@mfca.org

Formerly Trucking Management, Inc. A national trade association of unionized general freight LTL carriers. Promotes the economic interests of unionized motor freight carriers in the public policy and collective bargaining arenas.

Leg. Issues: LBR, TRA, TRU

In-house, DC-area Employees

BARNA, Elisabeth A.: Director, Communications
EVANS, Catherine A.: V. President, Government Affairs
LYNCH, Timothy P.: President and Chief Exec. Officer
RODGERS, Mark W.: V. President, Industry Relations and Exec. Director TMI Division
ROGERS, William C.: V. President, Safety Training and Technology

Motorcycle Industry Council

1235 Jefferson Davis Hwy.
Suite 600
Arlington, VA 22202
Tel: (703)416-0444
Fax: (703)416-2269
Registered: LDA
Web: www.mic.org

Liaison with federal and state governments on behalf of manufacturers and distributors of motorcycles and motorcycle parts and accessories, and of some members of allied trades.

Leg. Issues: AUT, BUD, ENV, MAR, NAT, RES, TOU, TRA

In-house, DC-area Employees

VAN KLEECK, Kathy R.: V. President, Government Relations

Outside Counsel/Consultants

Edelman Public Relations Worldwide
Rep By: Carol Diggs

Ross, Dixon & Bell
Rep By: Stuart Ross

Motorcycle Riders Foundation

P.O. Box 1808
Washington, DC 20013-1808
Tel: (202)546-0983
Fax: (202)546-0986
Registered: LDA
Web: www.mrf.org
E-mail: wyld@mrf.org
Leg. Issues: TRA

Political Action Committee/s

Motorcycle Rights Fund - Political Active Cyclists
P.O. Box 1808
Washington, DC 20013-1808
Tel: (202)546-0983
Fax: (202)546-0986
Contact: Thomas Wyld

In-house, DC-area Employees

WYLD, Thomas: V. President, Government Relations

Motorists Insurance Cos.

Columbus, OH

Outside Counsel/Consultants

Vorys, Sater, Seymour and Pease, LLP
Rep By: James K. Alford

Motorola Integrated Information Systems Group

Scottsdale, AZ
Leg. Issues: BUD, DEF

Outside Counsel/Consultants

Bill Wight, LLC
Issues: BUD, DEF

Motorola Space and Systems Technology Group

Scottsdale, AZ

A manufacturer of defense and consumer electronics and communications equipment.

Leg. Issues: AER, DEF, TEC

Outside Counsel/Consultants

R. V. Davis and Associates
Issues: AER, TEC
Rep By: Robert V. Davis

Mehl, Griffin & Bartek Ltd.
Issues: DEF
Rep By: Ronald J. Bartek, Molly Griffin, Theodore J. Mehl

Motorola, Inc.

1350 I St. NW
Suite 400
Washington, DC 20005-3306
Tel: (202)371-6900
Fax: (202)842-3578
Registered: LDA

One of the world's leading suppliers of electronic equipment, systems, components and services headquartered in Schaumburg, IL.

Leg. Issues: CAW, DEF, ENV, FIN, FOR, LBR, TEC, TOR, TRD, UTI

Political Action Committee/s

Motorola Civic Action Campaign Fund
1350 I St. NW
Suite 400
Washington, DC 20005-3306
Tel: (202)371-6900
Fax: (202)842-3578
Contact: Bruce Morgan

In-house, DC-area Employees

ANAYA, Bill: Manager, Federal Legislative Relations
BARTH, Richard C.: V. President and Director, Telecommunications Strategy and Regulation
BOYD, Evelyn Y.: Director, International Trade Relations (Latin America)
BRECHER, Richard: Director, International Trade Relations (Asia)
BROONER, Mary E.: Director, Telecommunications Strategy and Regulation
BULAWKA, Bohdan: V. President and Director, ITU Global Strategy
CHORLINS, Marjorie: Director, International Trade & Corporate Relations
CRAFTON, Ph.D., Christine G.: V. President and Director, Broadband Regulatory Policy
DILAPI, Christine: Senior Engineer, Satellite Regulatory Affairs
DOWELL, Jill: Manager, Federal Legislative Relations
EGER, Charles L.: Director, Regulatory Affairs
GOLDSTEIN, James: Director, U.S. Government Relations, CGISS
GRAB, Glenn: Director, U.S. Government Relations
HAGGART, Veronica: Corporate V. President and Director, One Motorola Ventures, Eastern Region
JOHNSON, Randy: Director, U.S. Human Resource Legislative Affairs
KENNEDY, Michael D.: Corporate V. President and Director, Global Government Relations
KUBIK, Rob: Manager, Spectrum and Regulatory Policy
LAMBERGMAN, Barry: Director, Satellite Regulatory Affairs
LYONS, John F.: Director, Telecommunications Strategy & Regulation
MARSHALL, C. Travis: Deputy, Motorola Chief Executive Office for Telecommunications Relations
MORGAN, Bruce: Manager, U.S. Government Relations
NELSON, Marian Barell: V. President and Director, Global Trade Policy
O'CONNOR, Teresa: Director, Global Regulatory Relations
PICCOLO, Joann: Corporate V. President and Director, North America Region Government Relations
WELCH, John F.: V. President and Director, Global EME Strategy and Regulatory Affairs

Outside Counsel/Consultants

Arnold & Porter

Baker, Donelson, Bearman & Caldwell, P.C.
Rep By: Joan M. McEntee

Burson-Marsteller

Hill and Knowlton, Inc.
Rep By: Christina Angarola, Paul S. Clark, Richard "Dick" Minard

The OB-C Group, LLC
Issues: TRD
Rep By: Thomas Keating, Kim F. McKernan, Charles J. Mellody, Patricia A. Nelson, Lawrence F. O'Brien, III, Linda E. Tarplin

Steptoe & Johnson LLP
Issues: TRD
Rep By: Stewart A. Baker, Paul R. Hurst, Peter Lichtenbaum

Wiley, Rein & Fielding
Issues: TEC
Rep By: Mimi W. Dawson

Mount Airy Refining Co.

Houston, TX

Outside Counsel/Consultants

Bode & Grenier LLP
Rep By: William H. Bode

Mount Carmel Health

Columbus, OH

Outside Counsel/Consultants

Arter & Hadden

Mount High Hosiery, Ltd.

San Diego, CA
Leg. Issues: TRD

Outside Counsel/Consultants

Carpi & Clay
Issues: TRD
Rep By: Kenneth A. Carpi

Mount Sinai Hospital

New York, NY
Leg. Issues: HCR, MED, MMM

Outside Counsel/Consultants

Broydrick & Associates
Issues: HCR, MED, MMM
Rep By: William Broydrick, Amy Demske

Mount Sinai School of Medicine

New York, NY
Leg. Issues: BUD, EDU, HCR, MED, VET

Outside Counsel/Consultants

Van Scoyoc Associates, Inc.
Issues: BUD, EDU, HCR, MED, VET
Rep By: Steve E. Crane, Kevin F. Kelly, H. Stewart Van Scoyoc

Mount Sinai/NYU Health

New York, NY
Leg. Issues: BUD, HCR

Outside Counsel/Consultants

Podesta/Mattoon
Issues: BUD, HCR
Rep By: Matthew Gelman, Andrew C. Littman, Lauren Maddox, Anthony T. Podesta, Timothy Powers, Missi Tessier

Mount Vernon Barge Service

Mount Vernon, NY
Leg. Issues: TRA

Outside Counsel/Consultants

Preston Gates Ellis & Rouvelas Meeds LLP
Issues: TRA
Rep By: John L. Longstreth, Rolf Marshall, William N. Myhre, Mark H. Ruge, James R. Weiss

Mount Vernon, City of

Mt. Vernon, NY
Leg. Issues: EDU, ENV, IMM, TAX, TRA, WEL

Outside Counsel/Consultants

Greenberg Traurig, LLP
Issues: EDU, ENV, IMM, TAX, TRA, WEL
Rep By: Diane J. Blagman

Mountain Top Technologies, Inc.

Johnstown, PA
Leg. Issues: DEF, SCI

Outside Counsel/Consultants

The Conaway Group LLC
Issues: DEF
Rep By: Lt. Gen. John B. Conaway, USAF (Ret.), James L. Hobgood

Whitten & Diamond
Issues: DEF, SCI
Rep By: Robert M. Diamond, Jamie L. Whitten

Mountain West Savings Bank, F.S.B.

Coeur d'Alene, ID

Outside Counsel/Consultants

Covington & Burling
Rep By: John C. Dugan

Mozambique, Government of the Republic of

Maputo, MOZAMBIQUE

Outside Counsel/Consultants

Bruce P. Cameron & Associates
Rep By: Bruce P. Cameron

mp3.com

6515 Haystack Rd.
Alexandria, VA 22310
Tel: (703)822-0575
Fax: (703)822-0576
Registered: LDA
Web: www.mp3.com
E-mail: billyp@mp3.com

Internet music company headquartered in San Diego, CA.

Leg. Issues: CPI, CPT, SCI

In-house, DC-area Employees

PITTS, William R. "Billy"
ROBERTS, David: Director, Government Relations

Outside Counsel/Consultants

Fleischman and Walsh, L.L.P.
Issues: CPI, CPT
Rep By: Seth A. Davidson, Louis H. Dupart

MPRI, Inc.

Outside Counsel/Consultants

Leadership Counsel, LLC
Rep By: Jack D. P. Lichtenstein

MRJ Technology Solutions

10560 Arrowhead Dr.
Fairfax, VA 22030
Tel: (703)385-0700
Fax: (703)385-4637

In-house, DC-area Employees

DRIESSEN, J. Kenneth: Chief Exec. Officer

MRS

Chelmsford, MA

Outside Counsel/Consultants

R. Wayne Sayer & Associates
Rep By: R. Wayne Sayer

MSE, Inc.

Butte, MT
Leg. Issues: AER, DEF

Outside Counsel/Consultants

Kimmitt, Coates & McCarthy
Issues: AER, DEF
Rep By: Vincent J. Coates, Jr., George D. McCarthy

MTS Systems Inc.

Eden Prairie, MN
A manufacturing company.

Leg. Issues: BUD, DEF

Outside Counsel/Consultants

Johnston & Associates, LLC
Issues: BUD, DEF
Rep By: Hon. J. Bennett Johnston, W. Proctor Jones, Eric Tober

The PMA Group
Issues: DEF
Rep By: Daniel Cunningham, Kaylene Green, Gregory L. Hansen, Patrick Hiu, Joseph Littleton, Paul J. Magliocchetti, Mark Waclawski

Mueller Industries, Inc.

Germantown, TN

Outside Counsel/Consultants

Sam Richardson
Rep By: Sam Richardson

Muhlenberg College

Allentown, PA
Leg. Issues: EDU

Outside Counsel/Consultants

Ikon Public Affairs
Issues: EDU

Muldoon, Murphy & Faucette, LLP

5101 Wisconsin Ave. NW
Washington, DC 20016
Tel: (202)362-0840
Fax: (202)966-9409
Registered: LDA, FARA

Leg. Issues: BAN, FIN, TAX

In-house, DC-area Employees

DALY, Joseph P.: Partner
FAUCETTE, Douglas P.: Partner
MULDOON, Sr., Joseph A.: Partner

Outside Counsel/Consultants

O'Connor & Hannan, L.L.P.
Issues: BAN, FIN, TAX
Rep By: Thomas H. Quinn

Multi Media Telecommunications Ass'n (MMTA)

2500 Wilson Blvd.
Suite 300
Arlington, VA 22201-3834
Tel: (703)907-7472
Fax: (703)907-7478
Web: www.mmta.org
E-mail: info@mmta.org

Promotes an open, competitive marketplace for industry communications equipment and services.

In-house, DC-area Employees

BRADSHAW, Mary: President

Multi-Family Housing Institute

Washington, DC

Outside Counsel/Consultants

Linda Parke Gallagher & Assoc.
Rep By: Linda Parke Gallagher

Multi-Housing Laundry Ass'n

Raleigh, NC

Outside Counsel/Consultants

Sonosky, Chambers, Sachse & Endreson

MultiDimensional Imaging, Inc.

Newport Beach, CA
Leg. Issues: BUD, HCR, MED, SCI

Outside Counsel/Consultants

Ryan, Phillips, Utrecht & MacKinnon
Issues: BUD, HCR, MED, SCI
Rep By: Rodney Hoppe, Jeffrey M. MacKinnon, William D. Phillips, Mark D. Planning, Thomas M. Ryan, Joseph V. Vasapoli

Multilec, S.A. de C.V.

San Nicolas de los Garza, MEXICO

Outside Counsel/Consultants

Crowell & Moring LLP

Multimedia Broadcast Investment Corp.

Luxembourg-Ville, LUXEMBOURG
Leg. Issues: TRD

Outside Counsel/Consultants

MBV, Inc.
Issues: TRD
Rep By: Walter L. Threadgill

Multimedia Games, Inc.

Tulsa, OK
Provides satellite broadcasts of Indian gaming activities.

Leg. Issues: GAM

Outside Counsel/Consultants

PACE-CAPSTONE
Issues: GAM
Rep By: Scott C. Dacey, James W. Wise

Multinat'l Working Team to Develop Criteria for Functional Gastrointestinal Disorders

McLean, VA

Outside Counsel/Consultants

Degnon Associates, Inc.

Multistate Tax Commission

444 N. Capitol St. NW
Suite 425
Washington, DC 20001
Tel: (202)624-8699
Fax: (202)624-8819
Web: www.mtc.gov
E-mail: mtc@mtc.gov
Leg. Issues: IND, TAX, TEC, TOB, TRA, UTI

In-house, DC-area Employees

BLOCKER, Rene: Deputy Director
BUCKS, Dan R.: Exec. Director
MINES, Paul: General Counsel

Outside Counsel/Consultants

Palumbo & Cerrell, Inc.
Issues: IND, TAX, TEC, TOB, TRA, UTI

Muncie, Indiana, City of (Delaware County)

Muncie, IN
Leg. Issues: AVI, CAW, DIS, ECN, ENV, HOU, LAW, LBR, RRR, URB

Outside Counsel/Consultants

Peyser Associates, Inc.
Issues: AVI, CAW, DIS, ECN, ENV, HOU, LAW, LBR, RRR, URB
Rep By: Peter A. Peyser, Jr.

Municipal Bond Insurance Ass'n

White Plains, NY

Outside Counsel/Consultants

Kutak Rock LLP

Municipal Castings Fair Trade Council

Pittsburgh, PA

Outside Counsel/Consultants

Collier Shannon Scott, PLLC
Rep By: Robin H. Gilbert, Paul C. Rosenthal

Municipal Electric Authority of Georgia

Atlanta, GA
Leg. Issues: CAW, ENG, ENV, TAX, UTI

Outside Counsel/Consultants

Sills Associates
Issues: CAW, ENG, ENV, TAX, UTI
Rep By: Hilary Sills

Municipal Electric Utilities Ass'n of New York State

Albany, NY
Leg. Issues: COM, ENG, GOV, UTI

Outside Counsel/Consultants

Duncan, Weinberg, Genzer & Pembroke, P.C.
Issues: COM, ENG, GOV, UTI
Rep By: Wallace L. Duncan, Jeffrey C. Genzer, Kathleen L. Mazure, Thomas L. Rudebusch

Municipal Financial Consultants Inc.

Grosse Pointe Farms, MI
Leg. Issues: TAX

Outside Counsel/Consultants

Akin, Gump, Strauss, Hauer & Feld, L.L.P.
Issues: TAX
Rep By: Donald C. Alexander

Municipal Securities Rulemaking Board

1150 18th St. NW
Suite 400
Washington, DC 20036
Tel: (202)223-9347
Fax: (202)872-0347
Web: www.msrb.org

In-house, DC-area Employees

KEATING, Daniel L.: Chairman
KLINKE, Diane G.: General Counsel

STANBERRY, Thomas E.: V. Chairman
TAYLOR, Christopher A.: Exec. Director

Municipal Transit Operation Coalition

Gardena, CA
Leg. Issues: BUD, TRA

Outside Counsel/Consultants

The Ferguson Group, LLC
Issues: BUD, TRA
Rep By: Charmayne Macon, Leslie Waters Mozingo

Municipal Treasurers Ass'n of the United States and Canada

1029 Vermont Ave. NW
Suite 710
Washington, DC 20005
Web: www.mtausc.org
Tel: (202)737-0660
Fax: (202)737-0662

In-house, DC-area Employees

CRANE, Stacey L.: Exec. Director

Municorp Healthcare Systems Inc.

New Orleans, LA

Outside Counsel/Consultants

Capitol Coalitions Inc.

Munitions Industrial Base Task Force

1800 N. Kent St.
Suite 1050
Arlington, VA 22209
E-mail: mibtf@erols.com
Tel: (703)276-1702
Fax: (703)276-1704
Registered: LDA
Leg. Issues: DEF, FIR

In-house, DC-area Employees

PALASCHAK, Richard G.: Director, Operations

Outside Counsel/Consultants

Bentley, Adams, Hargett, Riley and Co., Inc.
Issues: DEF, FIR
Rep By: Frederick A. Biestek, Jr., Michael Hargett, H. McGuire Riley, John Rosamond

Munson Healthcare

Traverse City, MI

Outside Counsel/Consultants

Dykema Gossett PLLC

Murphy Oil U.S.A.

El Dorado, AR
Leg. Issues: CAW, TAX

Outside Counsel/Consultants

Holland & Knight LLP
Issues: CAW
Rep By: Jack M. Burkman, Mike Galano, Richard M. Gold, Janet R. Studley

McDermott, Will and Emery
Issues: TAX
Rep By: Robert B. Harding

Winston & Strawn
Rep By: William A. Anderson, II, Hon. Beryl F. Anthony, Jr.

G. Murphy Trading

Sedona, AZ
Leg. Issues: TRD

Outside Counsel/Consultants

Patton Boggs, LLP
Issues: TRD
Rep By: Hon. Greg H. Laughlin, Darryl D. Nirenberg, Joseph Trapasso

Murrieta, California, City of

Murrieta, CA

Outside Counsel/Consultants

Copeland, Lowery & Jacquez
Rep By: Jeffrey S. Shockey

Murry's, Inc.

8300 Pennsylvania Ave.
Upper Marlboro, MD 20772
Tel: (301)420-6400
Fax: (301)967-4806

In-house, DC-area Employees

MENDELSON, Ira: President and Chief Exec. Officer

Muscular Dystrophy Ass'n

Outside Counsel/Consultants

Verner, Liipfert, Bernhard, McPherson and Hand, Chartered
Rep By: Vicki E. Hart, Harry C. McPherson

Museum Campus Chicago

Chicago, IL
Leg. Issues: ANI, BUD, EDU, NAT, TRA

Outside Counsel/Consultants

Metcalf Federal Relations
Issues: ANI, BUD, EDU, NAT, TRA
Rep By: Anne Metcalf

Museum of Discovery and Science

Fort Lauderdale, FL
Leg. Issues: BUD, NAT

Outside Counsel/Consultants

Cassidy & Associates, Inc.
Issues: BUD, NAT
Rep By: Arthur D. Mason, Laura A. Neal, Gabor J. Rozsa

Museum of Science and Industry

Chicago, IL
Leg. Issues: BUD

Outside Counsel/Consultants

Beacon Consulting Group, Inc.
Issues: BUD
Rep By: Jeffrey W. Henry, Gordon P. MacDougall, Lisa A. Stewart

Museum of Science-Boston

Boston, MA

Outside Counsel/Consultants

O'Neill, Athy & Casey, P.C.

Museum Trustee Ass'n

Washington, DC
Web: www.mta-hq.org

Outside Counsel/Consultants

Smith, Bucklin and Associates, Inc.

Music Educators Nat'l Conference

Reston, VA
Leg. Issues: ART, EDU

Outside Counsel/Consultants

Palumbo & Cerrell, Inc.
Issues: ART, EDU
Rep By: Charles R. O'Regan, Benjamin L. Palumbo, Paul A. Skrabut, Jr.

Mutual Broadcasting System

1755 S. Jefferson Davis Hwy.
Suite 1200
Arlington, VA 22202
Tel: (703)413-8300
Fax: (703)413-8445

In-house, DC-area Employees

SOLOMON, Peggy: V. President, Operations

Mutual Legislative Committee

Leg. Issues: INS, TAX

Outside Counsel/Consultants

Patton Boggs, LLP
Issues: INS, TAX
Rep By: John F. Jonas

Mutual of America

Two Democracy Center
6903 Rockledge Dr., Suite 1250
Bethesda, MD 20817-1831
Web: www.mutualofamerica.com
Tel: (301)571-1940
Fax: (301)571-8244

Life insurance company headquartered in New York, NY.

Leg. Issues: TAX

In-house, DC-area Employees

MANNION, Sean: Senior V. President
PENDLETON, Linda: Service Manager

Outside Counsel/Consultants

McMillan, Hill & Associates
Issues: TAX

Miller & Chevalier, Chartered
Issues: TAX
Rep By: Leonard Bickwit, Jr., Phillip L. Mann

Moore & Bruce, LLP
Issues: TAX

Mutual of Omaha Insurance Companies

1700 Pennsylvania Ave. NW
Suite 500
Washington, DC 20006-4771
Tel: (202)393-6200
Fax: (202)639-8808
Registered: LDA

Headquartered in Omaha, NE.

Leg. Issues: FIN, GOV, HCR, INS, MED, MMM, TAX, TOR

Political Action Committee/s

COMPAC
1700 Pennsylvania Ave. NW
Suite 500
Washington, DC 20006-4771
Contact: Russell C. Ring
Tel: (202)393-6205
Fax: (202)639-8808

IMPAC
1700 Pennsylvania Ave. NW
Suite 500
Washington, DC 20006-4771
Contact: Russell C. Ring
Tel: (202)393-6205
Fax: (202)639-8808

In-house, DC-area Employees

ANDERSON, Kathryn L.: Manager, Federal Government Affairs
MATTOX, William C.: Exec. V. President, Federal Government Affairs
RING, Russell C.: V. President and Deputy Head, Federal Government Affairs

Outside Counsel/Consultants

Canfield & Associates, Inc.
Issues: HCR, INS, TAX
Rep By: Roger Blauwet, Anne C. Canfield

Davis & Harman LLP
Issues: TAX
Rep By: Randolf H. Hardock

Washington Council Ernst & Young
Issues: HCR, TAX
Rep By: Doug Badger, Nick Giordano

Wiley, Rein & Fielding
Issues: INS, MED

Mutual Tax Committee

New York, NY
Leg. Issues: TAX

Outside Counsel/Consultants

Groom Law Group, Chartered
Issues: TAX
Rep By: Theodore R. Groom

Steptoe & Johnson LLP
Issues: TAX
Rep By: Matthew J. Zinn

The MWW Group

1747 Pennsylvania Ave. NW
Suite 1150
Washington, DC 20006
Web: www.mwwpr.com
E-mail: jslade@mww.com
Tel: (202)296-6222
Fax: (202)296-4507
Registered: LDA, FARA
Leg. Issues: GOV

In-house, DC-area Employees

BECKER, Tracey: Federal Affairs Representative
BERKOFF, Todd S.: Legislative Associate
BOSTIC, Dana P.: Deputy Director, Federal Affairs
GRAY, Davon: Legislative Associate
IADAROLA, Elizabeth A.: Deputy Director, Federal Affairs
KEMPNER, Michael W.: President and Chief Exec. Officer
PELLERIN, Christine A.: V. President, Federal Affairs
SLADE, Jonathan B.: Senior V. President
SOMMER, Robert G.: Exec. V. President
WALTER, Jeffery M.: V. President

Outside Counsel/Consultants

McDermott, Will and Emery

Shaw Pittman
Issues: GOV
Rep By: Thomas J. Spulak

Myanmar, Embassy of the Union of

2300 S St. NW
Washington, DC 20008
Tel: (202)332-9044
Fax: (202)332-9046

Outside Counsel/Consultants

Washington World Group, Ltd.
Rep By: Edward J. von Kloberg, III

Mycogen Corp.

San Diego, CA

Outside Counsel/Consultants

N. Chapman Associates
Rep By: Nancy Chapman

Mylan Laboratories, Inc.

Pittsburgh, PA
Leg. Issues: BUD, CPT, HCR, PHA

Outside Counsel/Consultants

C. McClain Haddow & Associates
Issues: BUD, CPT, HCR

Higgins, McGovern & Smith, LLC
Issues: PHA
Rep By: John J. McGovern, Jr.

Myriad Capital Inc.

Monterey Park, CA

A small business investment firm.

Leg. Issues: SMB

Outside Counsel/Consultants

Thelen Reid & Priest LLP
Issues: SMB
Rep By: William A. Kirk, Jr.

Mystic Seaport Museum

Mystic, CT
Leg. Issues: BUD

Outside Counsel/Consultants

Beacon Consulting Group, Inc.
Issues: BUD
Rep By: Katherine L. Halpin, Gordon P. MacDougall, Lisa A. Stewart

N-Methylpyrrolidone Producers Group, Inc.

Washington, DC

Outside Counsel/Consultants

Mintz, Levin, Cohn, Ferris, Glovsky and Popeo, P.C.
Rep By: Alvin J. Lorman

N-VIRO Internat'l Corp.

Toledo, OH

Outside Counsel/Consultants

Cannon Consultants, Inc.
Rep By: Charles A. Cannon

N-Z Land Company

Outside Counsel/Consultants

The Da Vinci Group
Rep By: Mark R. Smith

N.V. Philips Gloeilampenfabrieken

Amsterdam, NETHERLANDS

Outside Counsel/Consultants

Sullivan & Cromwell
Rep By: Margaret K. Pfeiffer

NAACP Legal Defense and Educational Fund, Inc.

1444 I St. NW
Tenth Floor
Washington, DC 20005
E-mail: ldfdc@earthlink.net
Tel: (202)682-1300
Fax: (202)682-1312

Established in 1939 as the legal arm of the Nat'l Ass'n for the Advancement of Colored People. Separated from the NAACP in 1957 at the behest of the IRS. At present the LDF is a civil rights law firm with no connection to the NAACP. Headquartered in New York, NY.

In-house, DC-area Employees

BYRD, Janell M.: Director, Washington Office

Outside Counsel/Consultants

McKinney & McDowell Associates

NAADAC, The Ass'n for Addiction Professionals

901 N. Washington St.
Suite 600
Alexandria, VA 22314
Web: www.naadac.org
E-mail: naadac@naadac.org
Tel: (703)741-7686
Fax: (703)741-7698
Registered: LDA

Dedicated to the advancement of alcoholism and drug abuse counselors; seeks to improve the quality of care to addicted persons. Founded in 1972, NAADAC has over 15,000 members in 50 states.

Leg. Issues: ALC, HCR

Political Action Committee/s

NAAA PAC

901 N. Washington St.
Suite 600
Alexandria, VA 22314
Tel: (703)741-7686
Fax: (703)741-7698

In-house, DC-area Employees

BURNETT, Bill B.: President

NAAS

Austin, TX
Leg. Issues: HCR, TAX

Outside Counsel/Consultants

Peter J. Rose
Issues: HCR, TAX
Rep By: Peter J. Rose

Nabisco, Inc.

Parsippany, NJ

Outside Counsel/Consultants

Bryan Cave LLP
Rep By: Stanley J. Marcuss

NAC Internat'l

Norcross, GA
Leg. Issues: ENG

Outside Counsel/Consultants

The Renkes Group, Ltd.
Issues: ENG
Rep By: Gregg D. Renkes

NACCO Industries

Mayfield Heights, OH

A forklift truck manufacturer.

Outside Counsel/Consultants

Collier Shannon Scott, PLLC
Rep By: Paul C. Rosenthal

Sam Richardson
Rep By: Sam Richardson

NACHA - The Electronic Payments Ass'n

13665 Dulles Technology Dr.
Suite 300
Herndon, VA 20171
Web: www.nacha.org
Tel: (703)561-1100
Fax: (703)787-0996

Develops electronic solutions to improve the payments system. NACHA represents more than 12,000 financial institution, through direct memberships and a network of regional payments associations, and 600 organizations through its six industry councils.

In-house, DC-area Employees

MACOY, Ian W.: Senior Director, Communications and Affiliate Services
MCENTEE, Elliott C.: President and Chief Exec. Officer
NELSON, William B.: Exec. V. President

Outside Counsel/Consultants

Jenner & Block

NAFSA: Ass'n of Internat'l Educators

1307 New York Ave. NW
Eighth Floor
Washington, DC 20009-5728
Web: www.nafsa.org
E-mail: inbox@nafsa.org
Tel: (202)737-3699
Fax: (202)737-3657
Registered: LDA

A membership association which provides training, information and advocacy to professionals and volunteers in the field of international educational exchange.

Leg. Issues: EDU

In-house, DC-area Employees

JOHNSON, Marlene M.: Exec. Director and Chief Exec. Officer
JOHNSON, Victor: Director, Government Relations
PELLETIER, Steve: Director, Publications

NAHB Research Center

Upper Marlboro, MD
Leg. Issues: HOU

Outside Counsel/Consultants

Jefferson Government Relations, L.L.C.
Issues: HOU
Rep By: William J. Gilmartin

Naigai, Inc.

Tokyo, JAPAN

A manufacturer of glass pharmaceutical ampules.

Leg. Issues: TRD

Outside Counsel/Consultants

The Evans Group, Ltd.
Issues: TRD
Rep By: Geryld B. Christianson, Hon. Thomas B. Evans, Jr.

Nambe Pueblo

Outside Counsel/Consultants

Steptoe & Johnson LLP
Rep By: Thomas C. Collier, Jr.

NAMM: Internat'l Music Products Ass'n

Outside Counsel/Consultants

Goldberg & Associates, PLLC

Nammo Inc.

Arlington, VA
Leg. Issues: CHM, DEF, FIR

Outside Counsel/Consultants

Rooney Group Internat'l, Inc.
Issues: CHM, DEF, FIR
Rep By: James W. Rooney

NanoDynamics, Inc.

New York, NY
Leg. Issues: BUD, DEF, SCI

Outside Counsel/Consultants

Ritter and Bourjaily, Inc.
Issues: BUD, DEF, SCI
Rep By: Monte F. Bourjaily, III

Napa County, California, Flood and Water Conservation District

Napa, CA
Leg. Issues: BUD, URB

Outside Counsel/Consultants

The Carmen Group
Issues: BUD, URB
Rep By: Mia O'Connell

Naples Community Hospital

Naples, FL

Outside Counsel/Consultants

Akin, Gump, Strauss, Hauer & Feld, L.L.P.

Napster, Inc.

San Mateo, CA
Leg. Issues: CPT, LAW, TEC

Outside Counsel/Consultants

Janus-Merritt Strategies, L.L.C.
Issues: LAW, TEC
Rep By: Thomas W. Brierton, John Guzik, Scott P. Hoffman, Mark J. Robertson, J. Daniel Walsh

Swidler Berlin Shereff Friedman, LLP
Issues: CPT, TEC
Rep By: James DeLorenzo, Barry B. Direnfeld, Harold P. Goldfield, Gary D. Slaiman

Timmons and Co., Inc.
Rep By: Michael J. Bates, Douglas F. Bennett, Ellen B. Fitzgibbons, Bryce L. "Larry" Harlow, Timothy J. Keating, Tom C. Korologos, Richard J. Tarplin, William E. Timmons, Sr., William E. Timmons, Jr.

The NARAS Foundation

Santa Monica, CA
Leg. Issues: ART

Outside Counsel/Consultants

Colex and Associates
Issues: ART
Rep By: John P. Mack

NASA Aeronautics Support Team

Hampton, VA
Leg. Issues: AER, AVI, BUD, ECN, SCI

Outside Counsel/Consultants

Madison Government Affairs
Issues: AER, AVI, BUD, ECN, SCI
Rep By: Paul J. Hirsch

Van Scoyoc Associates, Inc.
Issues: AER, AVI, BUD, SCI
Rep By: Steve E. Crane, Kevin F. Kelly, Steven O. Palmer, Chad Schulken, Jasper Thomson, H. Stewart Van Scoyoc

NASD Regulation

1735 K St. NW
Washington, DC 20006
Web: www.nasdr.com
Tel: (202)728-8140
Fax: (202)728-8075

In-house, DC-area Employees

SCHAPIRO, Mary: President

NASDAQ Stock Market

1735 K St. NW
11th Floor
Washington, DC 20006
Web: www.nasd.com
Tel: (202)496-2500

In-house, DC-area Employees

BERKELEY, III, Alfred R.: President

Nashua Corp.

Nashua, NH

Outside Counsel/Consultants

Crowell & Moring LLP
Rep By: Brian C. Elmer

Nassau Broadcasting Inc.

Princeton, NJ
Leg. Issues: TEC

Outside Counsel/Consultants

Patton Boggs, LLP
Issues: TEC
Rep By: Stephen Diaz Gavin, John S. Shaw

Nassau County Health Care Corp.

East Meadow, NY
Leg. Issues: BUD

Outside Counsel/Consultants

Holland & Knight LLP
Issues: BUD
Rep By: Jack M. Burkman, Mike Galano, Richard M. Gold, Keith D. Lind, Hon. Gerald E. Sikorski, P. J. Toker, David C. Whitestone

Nassau University Medical Center

East Meadow, NY
Leg. Issues: HCR

Outside Counsel/Consultants

Lent Scrivner & Roth LLC
Issues: HCR
Rep By: Norman F. Lent, III, Hon. Norman F. Lent, Alan J. Roth, Michael S. Scrivner

Nassif & Associates

Leg. Issues: RES

Outside Counsel/Consultants

Bracy Williams & Co.
Issues: RES
Rep By: James P. Brown, Linda Doorfee Flaherty, Susan J. Williams

Nat'l 4-H Council

7100 Connecticut Ave.
Chevy Chase, MD 20815
Tel: (301)961-2800
Fax: (301)961-2894
Web: www.fourhcouncil.edu
E-mail: info@fourhcouncil.edu

The national private, non-profit partner of 4-H, the youth development education program of the Cooperative Extension System.

In-house, DC-area Employees

FLOYD, Jr., Donald T.: President and Chief Exec. Officer
PHILLIPS, Christie: Director of Marketing

Nat'l Abortion and Reproductive Rights Action League

1156 15th St. NW
Suite 700
Washington, DC 20005
Tel: (202)973-3000
Fax: (202)973-3096
Registered: LDA
Web: www.naral.org

Largest national membership organization whose purpose is to keep abortion safe, legal and available. Also works to promote a comprehensive approach to reproductive health, focusing on prevention, contraceptive care and prenatal, maternal and child health. Works through 27 state affiliates to mobilize pro-choice citizens to become politically active and uses its Political Action Committee to bring contributions and volunteers to the campaigns of pro-choice Congressional and state legislative candidates.

Leg. Issues: CIV, CON, EDU, FAM, HCR, INS, MED, SCI, WEL

Political Action Committee/s

NARAL PAC

1156 15th St. NW
Suite 700
Washington, DC 20005
Tel: (202)973-3000
Fax: (202)973-3096
Contact: Gloria Totten

In-house, DC-area Employees

CAVENDISH, Elizabeth: V. President, Legal Director and General Counsel
GERMOND, Alice Travis: Exec. V. President
HERWITT, Allison: Director, Government Relations
MICHELMAN, Kate: President
PISCITELLI, Julie: Director of Communications
TOTTEN, Gloria: Political Director

Nat'l Abortion Federation

1755 Massachusetts Ave. NW
Suite 600
Washington, DC 20036
Tel: (202)667-5881
Fax: (202)667-5890
Web: www.prochoice.org
E-mail: naf@prochoice.org

A non-profit professional association of abortion service providers in the United States, Puerto Rico and Canada. NAF's mission is to ensure that abortion remains safe, legal, and accessible.

Leg. Issues: FAM, HCR, LAW

In-house, DC-area Employees

IRVIN, Nicole: Director, Government Relations
SAPORTA, Vicki A.: Exec. Director

Nat'l Academy of Engineering

2101 Constitution Ave. NW
Washington, DC 20418
Tel: (202)334-2000
Fax: (202)334-2158
Web: www.nae.edu
E-mail: news@nas.edu

A private organization established in 1964 under the Congressional charter of the National Academy of Sciences. An organization of distinguished engineers, autonomous in its administration and selection of members, and sharing with the National Academy of Sciences responsibility for advising the Federal Government. Most activities carried out through the National Research Council.

In-house, DC-area Employees

LUDWIG, Bob: Media Associate

Nat'l Academy of Opticianry

8401 Corporate Dr.
Suite 605
Landover, MD 20785
Tel: (301)577-4828
Fax: (301)577-3880
Web: www.nao.org
E-mail: info@nao.org

Provides educational opportunities for all ophthalmic dispensers.

In-house, DC-area Employees

ICIEK, James E.: Exec. Director

Nat'l Academy of Public Administration

1120 G St. NW
Suite 850
Washington, DC 20005
Tel: (202)347-3190
Fax: (202)393-0993
Web: www.napawash.org
E-mail: academy@napawash.org

Non-profit, nonpartisan organization chartered by Congress to identify emerging issues of goverence and provide assistance to federal, state and local governments to improve performance.

Leg. Issues: DEF, ECN, ENV, GOV, HOU, TRA, URB

In-house, DC-area Employees

CIPOLLA, Frank: Director, Center for HRM
GADSBY, William: Director, Management Studies
GARRISON, David F.: V. President
KEINER, Suellen Terrill: Director, Center for the Economy and Environment
O'NEILL, Robert J.: President
SHOCKET, Phyllis G.: Director, Academy Affairs
WYE, Christopher: Director, Center for Improving Government Performance

Nat'l Academy of Sciences

2101 Constitution Ave. NW
Washington, DC 20418
Tel: (202)334-2000
Fax: (202)334-1684
Registered: LDA
Web: www.nas.edu

Private honorary organization of scholars in scientific and engineering research, chartered by act of Congress March 3, 1863 to serve as an advisor to the federal government on questions of science and technology. Conducts studies in all disciplines of natural and social sciences and engineering, with special emphasis on science advisory role in public policy issues. Affiliated with the Nat'l Academy of Engineering and the Institute of Medicine. The Nat'l Research Council is the operating arm of the NAS.

Leg. Issues: GOV

In-house, DC-area Employees

ALBERTS, Dr. Bruce: President
FULTON, Kenneth R.: Exec. Director
JENSEN, James E.: Director, Congressional and Government Affairs
WRIGHT, James R.: General Counsel

Outside Counsel/Consultants

Garvey, Schubert & Barer
Issues: GOV
Rep By: Richard A. Wegman

Nat'l Academy of Social Insurance

Outside Counsel/Consultants

Garrett Yu Hussein LLC

Nat'l Accreditation Council for Early Childhood Professional Personnel and Programs

Falls Church, VA

Outside Counsel/Consultants

Associated Child Care Consultants, Ltd.
William J. Tobin and Associates

Nat'l Accrediting Commission of Cosmetology Arts & Sciences, Inc.

901 N. Stuart St.
Suite 900
Arlington, VA 22203
Tel: (703)527-7600
Fax: (703)527-8811
Registered: LDA
Web: www.naccas.org
E-mail: naccas@naccas.org

Recognized national accrediting agency for post-secondary cosmetology, barbering, massage, and esthetics schools.

Leg. Issues: EDU

In-house, DC-area Employees

BIRD, Mary E.: Director, Government Relations and Legal Dept.
GROSS, Mark C.: Chief Executive Officer

Nat'l Adoption Foundation

Danbury, CT
Leg. Issues: FAM

Outside Counsel/Consultants

Dublin Castle Group
Issues: FAM
Rep By: Maureen Flatley Hogan

Nat'l Aeronautic Ass'n of the U.S.A.

1815 N. Fort Myer Dr.
Suite 500
Arlington, VA 22209-1805
Tel: (703)527-0226
Fax: (703)527-0229
Web: www.naa-usa.org
E-mail: naa@naa-usa.org

In-house, DC-area Employees

BREAM, Joseph R.: Treasurer
GREENFIELD, Jr., Arthur W.: Secretary, Contest and Records Board
KORANDA, Donald J.: President
MCDONALD, USN (Ret.), Adm. Wesley: Chairman

Nat'l Affordable Housing Management Ass'n

526 King St.
Suite 511
Alexandria, VA 22314
Tel: (703)683-8630
Fax: (703)683-8634
Web: www.nahma.org
E-mail: george.caruso@nahma.org

A national organization with grassroots origins in local AHMAs operating throughout the country. Members manage over 50% of all privately-owned, government-assisted housing and provide quality housing to over 2 million Americans with low and moderate incomes.

Leg. Issues: RES

In-house, DC-area Employees

CARROLL, Phil: President
CARUSO, George C.: Exec. Director
FOX, Wayne: President Elect

Nat'l Agricultural Aviation Ass'n

1005 E St. SE
Washington, DC 20003
Tel: (202)546-5722
Fax: (202)546-5726
Registered: LDA
Web: www.agaviation.org
E-mail: information@agaviation.org

A 1200-member organization dedicated to advancing the interests of agricultural aviation.

Leg. Issues: AGR, AVI, ENV, GOV, TRA

Political Action Committee/s

AgAv PAC

1005 E St. SE
Washington, DC 20003
Tel: (202)546-5722
Fax: (202)546-5726

In-house, DC-area Employees

CALLAN, James: Exec. Director
MOORE, Andrew D.: Director, Government Relations

Nat'l AIDS Fund

1400 I St. NW
Suite 1220
Washington, DC 20005
Tel: (202)408-4848
Fax: (202)408-1818
Web: www.aidsfund.org
E-mail: info@aidsfund.org

In-house, DC-area Employees

BILOWITH, Karen: Program Officer
DE MATTIES, Catalan: Director, Development
FERREE, Kandy: President

Nat'l Air Cargo, Inc.

Buffalo, NY
Leg. Issues: DEF, TRA

Outside Counsel/Consultants

Parry, Romani, DeConcini & Symms
Issues: DEF
Rep By: Edward H. Baxter, Hon. Dennis DeConcini, John M. Haddow, Scott D. Hatch, Shannon Davis Henderson, Jack W. Martin, Romano Romani, Linda Arey Skladany, Hon. Steven D. Symms

Jim Pasco & Associates
Issues: TRA
Rep By: James O. Pasco, Jr.

Nat'l Air Carrier Ass'n

910 17th St. NW
Washington, DC 20006
Tel: (202)833-8200
Fax: (202)659-9479
Registered: LDA
E-mail: naca@erols.com

Members are airlines that engage in charter and scheduled service.

In-house, DC-area Employees

PRIDDY, Ronald N.: President

Nat'l Air Duct Cleaners Ass'n

Washington, DC
Web: www.nadca.com
E-mail: nadca@aol.com

Outside Counsel/Consultants

Sufka & Associates
Rep By: Shaine McMahon, Kenneth M. Sufka

Nat'l Air Filtration Ass'n

Washington, DC
Web: www.nafahq.org
E-mail: nafahq@aol.com

Outside Counsel/Consultants

Sufka & Associates
Rep By: Kenneth M. Sufka

Nat'l Air Traffic Controllers Ass'n

1325 Massachusetts Ave. NW
Washington, DC 20005
Tel: (202)628-5451
Fax: (202)628-5767
Registered: LDA
Web: www.natca.org

The collective bargaining agent for the nation's more than 13,500 air traffic controllers. Interests include legislation affecting air safety, the Federal Aviation Administration and Department of Transportation, and federal workers.

Leg. Issues: AVI, BUD, LBR, TRA

Political Action Committee/s

Nat'l Air Traffic Controllers Ass'n PAC
1325 Massachusetts Ave. NW
Washington, DC 20005
Tel: (202)628-5451
Fax: (202)628-5767
Contact: Ken Montoya

In-house, DC-area Employees

CARR, John: President
MARLIN, Ruth: V. President
MONTOYA, Ken: Legislative Director

Outside Counsel/Consultants

Van Scoyoc Associates, Inc.
Issues: AVI, BUD
Rep By: Steven O. Palmer, Chad Schulken, H. Stewart Van Scoyoc

Nat'l Air Transportation Ass'n

4226 King St.
Alexandria, VA 22302-1507
Tel: (703)845-9000
Fax: (703)845-8176
Registered: LDA
Web: www.nata-online.org
Leg. Issues: AVI, BUD, ENV, LBR, SMB, TAX, TRA

Political Action Committee/s

NATAPAC
4226 King St.
Alexandria, VA 22302-1507
Tel: (703)845-9000
Fax: (703)845-8176
Contact: Eric Byer

In-house, DC-area Employees

BYER, Eric: Government Specialist
COYNE, III, Hon. James K.: President
DARROW, Alan: V. President

Outside Counsel/Consultants

Shaw Pittman
Rep By: Robert E. Cohn

Nat'l Aircraft Resale Ass'n

Alexandria, VA

Outside Counsel/Consultants

Van Scoyoc Associates, Inc.

Nat'l Airline Passenger Coalition

Washington, DC
Leg. Issues: AVI

Outside Counsel/Consultants

Chesapeake Enterprises, Inc.
Issues: AVI
Rep By: Scott W. Reed

Nat'l Alcohol Beverage Control Ass'n

4216 King St. West
Alexandria, VA 22302-1507
Tel: (703)578-4200
Fax: (703)820-3551
Registered: LDA
Web: www.nabca.org
Leg. Issues: ALC, TAX

In-house, DC-area Employees

SGUEO, James M.: Exec. Director

Outside Counsel/Consultants

Goldberg & Associates, PLLC
Issues: ALC, TAX
Rep By: James M. Goldberg

Nat'l Alliance Against Blacklisting

c/o Chamber of Commerce of the U.S.
1615 H St. NW
Washington, DC 20062-2000
Tel: (202)463-5507
Fax: (202)463-5901
E-mail: peide@uschamber.com

Above address is that of the Chamber of Commerce of the U.S.A.

Leg. Issues: GOV, LBR

In-house, DC-area Employees

EIDE, Peter J.: Contact

Outside Counsel/Consultants

Dittus Communications
Rep By: Debra Cabral, Kristin Litterst, Alice Slater

Ogletree Governmental Affairs, Inc.
Issues: GOV, LBR
Rep By: Harold P. Coxson, Maggie Dean, Francis M. Lunnie, Jr., Michael Roush

Nat'l Alliance for Eye and Vision Research

Washington, DC
Leg. Issues: BUD, MED, TOB

Outside Counsel/Consultants

Capitol Associates, Inc.
Issues: BUD, MED, TOB
Rep By: Sara Milo

Nat'l Alliance for Hispanic Health

1501 16th St. NW
Washington, DC 20036-1401
Tel: (202)387-5000
Fax: (202)797-4353
Web: www.hispanichealth.org

A private, non-profit membership organization dedicated to improving the health and well-being of the nation's Hispanic population.

Leg. Issues: HCR, LAW, MED, MMM, SCI

In-house, DC-area Employees

DELGADO, Ph.D., Jane L.: President and Chief Exec. Officer
FALCON, M.P.P., Adolph P.: V. President for Science and Policy

Nat'l Alliance for Infusion Therapy

Washington, DC
Leg. Issues: MMM

Outside Counsel/Consultants

Powell, Goldstein, Frazer & Murphy LLP
Issues: MMM
Rep By: Alan K. Parver, Steve K. Stranne

Nat'l Alliance for the Mentally Ill

Colonial Place Three
2107 Wilson Blvd., Suite 300
Arlington, VA 22201-3042
Tel: (703)524-7600
Fax: (703)524-9094
Registered: LDA
Web: www.nami.org

A national network of 1,200 local and state affiliates of a self-help movement for familes and friends of people with serious mental illnesses and those persons themselves.

Leg. Issues: BUD, EDU, HCR, HOU, LAW, MMM, PHA, VET, WEL

In-house, DC-area Employees

CAROLLA, Bob: Director, Communications
COWDRY, M.D., Rex: Deputy Exec. Director, Research
EDGAR, Elizabeth: Director, State Health Care
HONBERG, Ron: Deputy Exec. Director, Legal Affairs
NAGLE, Ann: Deputy Exec. Director, Operations
SCHANTZ, Connie: Manager, Meetings and Exhibits
SPERLING, Andrew: Deputy Exec. Director, Public Policy

Outside Counsel/Consultants

David Nelson & Associates

Nat'l Alliance of African-American Health Care Professions

Ellicott City, MD

Outside Counsel/Consultants

Hayward Internat'l

Nat'l Alliance of Black School Educators

310 Pennsylvania Ave. SE
Washington, DC 20003
Tel: (202)608-6310
Fax: (202)608-6319
Web: www.nabse.org
E-mail: nabse@nabse.org

Seeks to improve the educational opportunities and achievements of black youth, through the professional development of black educators.

In-house, DC-area Employees

LAWSON, Quentin R.: Exec. Director

Nat'l Alliance of Blind Students

1155 15th St. NW
Suite 1004
Washington, DC 20005
Tel: (202)467-5081
Fax: (202)467-5085
Web: www.acb.org
E-mail: info@acb.org

An affiliate of the American Council of the Blind.

In-house, DC-area Employees

SHINHOLSTER, April: President

Nat'l Alliance of Business

1201 New York Ave. NW
Suite 700
Washington, DC 20005
Tel: (202)289-2888
Fax: (202)289-1303
Web: www.nab.com
E-mail: info@nab.com

A non-profit, business-led organization dedicated to building a quality workforce by improving American education, forging a smooth transition from school to work, expanding life-long learning opportunities for incumbent workers, and fostering strategies that simultaneously address worker security and employer flexibility.

In-house, DC-area Employees

JONES, Roberts T.: President and Chief Exec. Officer
LINDSLEY, Thomas A.: V. President, Policy and Government Relations

Nat'l Alliance of Nurse Practitioners

325 Pennsylvania Ave. SE
Washington, DC 20003
Tel: (202)675-6350

In-house, DC-area Employees

ONIEAL, Marie Eileen: Chair

Nat'l Alliance of Postal and Federal Employees

1628 11th St. NW
Washington, DC 20001
Tel: (202)939-6325
Fax: (202)939-6389
Web: www.napfe.com
E-mail: napfe@patriot.net

Political Action Committee/s

Nat'l Alliance for Political Action
1628 11th St. NW
Washington, DC 20001
Tel: (202)939-6325
Fax: (202)939-6389
Contact: James McGee

In-house, DC-area Employees

MCGEE, James: President

Nat'l Alliance of Sexual Assault Coalitions

East Hartford, CT

A non-profit coalition of organizations aimed at reducing sexual assault and domestic violence.

Leg. Issues: BUD, EDU, LAW

Outside Counsel/Consultants

Dean Blakey & Moskowitz
Issues: BUD, EDU, LAW
Rep By: Ellin J. Nolan

Nat'l Alliance of State and Territorial AIDS Directors

444 N. Capitol St. NW
Suite 339
Washington, DC 20001
Tel: (202)434-8090
Fax: (202)434-8092
Registered: LDA
Web: www.nastad.org
E-mail: nastad@aol.com
Leg. Issues: HCR, MMM, PHA

In-house, DC-area Employees

HANEN, Laura: Director, Government Relations

Nat'l Alliance to End Homelessness

1518 K St. NW
Suite 206
Washington, DC 20005
Tel: (202)638-1526
Fax: (202)638-4664
E-mail: naeh@naeh.org

A coalition of service providers, public agenices and national organizations, including leaders from business, social services, the professions, labor, religious and public interest groups and government. Researches, educates and advocates on issues affecting the homeless and works to find solutions to this problem.

Leg. Issues: HOU, URB

In-house, DC-area Employees

GIBSON, Churchill J.: Exec. Director
ROMAN, Nan: President

Nat'l and Community Service Coalition

Leg. Issues: BUD, EDU, GOV

Outside Counsel/Consultants

Ledge Counsel
Issues: BUD, EDU, GOV

Valente Lopatin & Schulze
Rep By: Alan G. Lopatin

Nat'l Anti-Vivisection Soc.

Chicago, IL
Leg. Issues: ANI, BUD, HCR

Outside Counsel/Consultants

Epstein Becker & Green, P.C.
Issues: ANI, BUD, HCR
Rep By: Joyce A. Cowan

Nat'l Apartment Ass'n

201 N. Union St.
Suite 200
Alexandria, VA 22314
Tel: (703)518-6141
Fax: (703)518-6191
Web: www.naahq.org
Leg. Issues: TEC

Political Action Committee/s

Apartment Political Action Committee of the Nat'l Apartment Ass'n
201 N. Union St.
Suite 200
Alexandria, VA 22314
Tel: (703)518-6141
Fax: (703)518-6191
Contact: Barbara Vassallo

In-house, DC-area Employees

VASSALLO, Barbara: Director, State/Local Government Policy
WALD, Ann: Director, Membership

Outside Counsel/Consultants

Miller & Van Eaton, P.L.L.C.
Issues: TEC
Rep By: Matthew C. Ames, William Malone, Nicholas P. Miller

Nat'l Aquarium

Baltimore, MD
Leg. Issues: BUD

Outside Counsel/Consultants

Patton Boggs, LLP
Issues: BUD
Rep By: Robert C. Jones, Elizabeth C. Vella

Nat'l Armored Car Ass'n

Washington, DC
Leg. Issues: LBR, TRA

Outside Counsel/Consultants

Sellery Associates, Inc.
Issues: LBR, TRA
Rep By: Lawrence E. Sabbath, William C. Sellery, Jr.

Nat'l Art Education Ass'n

1916 Association Dr.
Reston, VA 20191-1590
Tel: (703)860-8000
Fax: (703)860-2960
Web: www.naea-reston.org
E-mail: naea@dgs.dgsys.com

In-house, DC-area Employees

HATFIELD, Dr. Thomas A.: Exec. Director

Nat'l Asian American Political Empowerment Fund

800 Seventh St. NW, Suite 305
Washington, DC 20001

In-house, DC-area Employees

WONG, Yeni

Nat'l Asian Pacific American Legal Consortium

1140 Connecticut Ave. NW
Suite 1200
Washington, DC 20036
Tel: (202)296-2300
Fax: (202)296-2318
Web: www.napalc.org

In-house, DC-area Employees

NARASAKI, Karen K.: Exec. Director

Nat'l Asian Women's Health Organization

San Francisco, CA

Outside Counsel/Consultants

Garrett Yu Hussein LLC

Heidepriem & Mager, Inc.
Rep By: Pat Ford-Roegner, Mimi Mager

Nat'l Asphalt Pavement Ass'n

5100 Forbes Blvd.
Suite 200
Lanham, MD 20706
Tel: (301)731-4748
Fax: (301)731-4621
Registered: LDA
Web: www.hotmix.org
E-mail: napa@hotmix.org
Leg. Issues: BUD, ENV, ROD, TRA

In-house, DC-area Employees

ACOTT, Mike: President
HANSEN, Jay: V. President, Government Affairs

Outside Counsel/Consultants

The Plexus Consulting Group

Van Scoyoc Associates, Inc.
Issues: BUD, ROD
Rep By: Steven O. Palmer, Chad Schulken, H. Stewart Van Scoyoc

Nat'l Ass'n for Agricultural Stewardship

New York, NY
Leg. Issues: AGR

Outside Counsel/Consultants

Meyers & Associates
Issues: AGR
Rep By: Fran Boyd, Larry D. Meyers, Richard L. Meyers

Nat'l Ass'n for Bilingual Education

1220 L St. NW
Suite 605
Washington, DC 20005-4018
Tel: (202)898-1829
Fax: (202)789-2866
Registered: LDA
Web: www.nabe.org
E-mail: nabe@nabe.org

Founded in 1976 as an association of educators, parents, businessmen and women and professionals to promote bilingual education for the sector of the population with limited proficiency in English.

Leg. Issues: CIV, EDU, IMM

In-house, DC-area Employees

LOERA, Patricia: Legislative Director

Nat'l Ass'n for Biomedical Research

818 Connecticut Ave. NW
Suite 200
Washington, DC 20006
Tel: (202)857-0540
Fax: (202)659-1902
Registered: LDA
Web: www.NABR.org
E-mail: info@nabr.org
Leg. Issues: ANI, BUD, MED

In-house, DC-area Employees

FORTSON, Tracy: V. President
RICH, Barbara A.: Exec. V. President

Outside Counsel/Consultants

Covington & Burling

Policy Directions, Inc.
Issues: ANI, BUD, MED
Rep By: Kathleen "Kay" Holcombe, Frankie L. Trull

Nat'l Ass'n for College Admission Counseling

1631 Prince St.
Alexandria, VA 22314-2818
Tel: (703)836-2222
Fax: (703)836-8015
Registered: LDA
Web: www.nacac.com

An association of secondary school counselors, college and university admission officers and counselors and related individuals who work with students as they make the transition from secondary to postsecondary education. Sponsors the National College Fair program.

Leg. Issues: BUD, EDU, TAX

In-house, DC-area Employees

HAWKINS, David A.: Director, Government Relations
SMITH, Joyce E.: Exec. Director
WILLIAMS, Valerie: Assistant Director, Government Relations

Nat'l Ass'n for Environmental Management

1612 K St. NW
Suite 1102
Washington, DC 20006
Tel: (202)986-6616
Fax: (202)530-4408
Web: www.naem.org

National professional association for environmental managers. Promotes environmental management principles with programs and initiatives which provide professional development, recognition and opportunities.

In-house, DC-area Employees

SINGER, Carol S.: Exec. Director

Nat'l Ass'n for Equal Opportunity in Higher Education

8701 Georgia Ave.
Suite 200
Silver Spring, MD 20910
Tel: (301)650-2440
Fax: (301)495-3306
Registered: LDA

An association of historically Black colleges and universities. Purpose is to achieve equality in higher education for all races and social classes.

Leg. Issues: BUD, EDU, GOV, HCR

In-house, DC-area Employees

PONDER, Dr. Henry: President and Chief Exec. Officer
ROSCOE, Dr. Wilma J.: V. President
SMITH, Bea Pace: Director, Federal Relations

Outside Counsel/Consultants

Van Scoyoc Associates, Inc.
Issues: BUD, EDU
Rep By: Steve E. Crane, Anita R. Estell, Kevin F. Kelly, H. Stewart Van Scoyoc

Nat'l Ass'n for Gifted Children

1707 L St. NW
Suite 550
Washington, DC 20036
Tel: (202)785-4268
Fax: (202)785-4248
Web: www.nagc.org

Works to promote an appropriate education for gifted and talented children.

Leg. Issues: EDU

In-house, DC-area Employees

ROSENSTEIN, Peter D.: Exec. Director

Nat'l Ass'n for Girls and Women in Sport

1900 Association Dr.
Reston, VA 20191-1599
Tel: (703)476-3450
Fax: (703)476-4566
Web: www.aahperd.org/nagws
E-mail: nagws@aahperd.org
Leg. Issues: SPO

In-house, DC-area Employees

BORYSOWICZ, Mary Ann: Exec. Director

Outside Counsel/Consultants

Bracy Williams & Co.
Issues: SPO
Rep By: Linda Doorfee Flaherty, Susan J. Williams

Nat'l Ass'n for Home Care

228 Seventh St. SE
Washington, DC 20003-4306
Tel: (202)547-7424
Fax: (202)547-3540
Registered: LDA
Web: www.nahc.org

Represents the nation's home care agencies, home care aide organizations, home health patients, and hospices.

Leg. Issues: MMM

Political Action Committee/s

Nat'l Ass'n for Home Care Political Action Committee

228 Seventh St. SE
Washington, DC 20003-4306
Tel: (202)547-7424
Fax: (202)547-9559
Contact: Eric W. Sokol

In-house, DC-area Employees

DOMBI, William: Director, Center for Health Care Law
FORSTER, Theresa M.: V. President, Policy
HALAMANDARIS, Val: President
KINCHELOE, James Jeffrey: Deputy Director, Government Affairs
SANTA ANNA, Yvonne: Deputy Director, Gov't Affairs
SOKOL, Eric W.: Deputy Director, Government Affairs
ST. PIERRE, Mary: V. President, Regulatory Affairs

Nat'l Ass'n for Human Development

1424 16th St. NW
Suite 102
Washington, DC 20036
Tel: (202)328-2191
Fax: (202)265-6682
E-mail: nahdcf@worldnet.att.net

A self-help, health/education/employment-training organization primarily for older adults; develops and publishes a variety of health/fitness print and audiovisual materials for older adults and professionals who serve them; and conducts training and other special projects for these target groups.

In-house, DC-area Employees

BAKER, Jules Evan: President

Nat'l Ass'n for Medical Direction of Respiratory Care

Chevy Chase, MD
Web: www.namdrc.org
E-mail: namdrc@erols.com

Membership association of pulmonary physicians with varied educational interests.

Leg. Issues: GOV, HCR, MMM

Outside Counsel/Consultants

GRQ, Inc.
Issues: GOV, HCR, MMM
Rep By: Patricia Booth, Phillip Porte

Nat'l Ass'n for Nutritional Choice

Gahanna, OH
Leg. Issues: CSP, FOO, HCR, PHA

Outside Counsel/Consultants

Vorys, Sater, Seymour and Pease, LLP
Issues: CSP, FOO, HCR, PHA

Nat'l Ass'n for Plastic Container Recovery

Charlotte, NC

Outside Counsel/Consultants

Howrey Simon Arnold & White
Rep By: Edward L. Ferguson, Saskia Mooney, David B. Weinberg

Nat'l Ass'n for Proton Therapy

7910 Woodmont Ave.
Suite 1303
Bethesda, MD 20814
Tel: (301)913-9360
Fax: (301)913-0372
Web: www.proton-therapy.org
E-mail: lenarzt@compuserve.com
Leg. Issues: HCR, SCI

In-house, DC-area Employees

ARZT, Leonard: Exec. Director

Nat'l Ass'n for Public Interest Law (NAPIL)

2120 L St. NW
Suite 450
Washington, DC 20037
Tel: (202)466-3686
Fax: (202)429-9766
Web: www.napil.org
E-mail: napil@napil.org

The Association was founded in 1986 by law students dedicated to surmounting barriers to equal justice that affect millions of low-income individuals and families. Today, NAPIL is the country's leading organization engaged in organizing, training, and supporting public service minded law students, and is the national leader in creating summer jobs and postgraduate public interest jobs.

In-house, DC-area Employees

STERN, David: Exec. Director

Outside Counsel/Consultants

Robert M. Brandon and Associates
Rep By: Robert M. Brandon, Clifford Rohde

Nat'l Ass'n for Sport and Physical Education

1900 Association Dr.
Reston, VA 20191
Tel: (703)476-3410
Fax: (703)476-8316
Web: www.aahperd.org
E-mail: naspe@aahperd.org

A non-profit, professional organization of individuals engaged in the study of human movement, sports, and physical activity.

Leg. Issues: EDU, HCR, SPO

In-house, DC-area Employees

YOUNG, Judith: Exec. Director

Nat'l Ass'n for State Farm Agents

Atlanta, GA
Leg. Issues: BUD, GOV, HCR, INS, LBR, MMM, TAX

Outside Counsel/Consultants

Washington Council Ernst & Young
Issues: BUD, GOV, HCR, INS, LBR, MMM, TAX
Rep By: Doug Badger, Lauren Darling, John L. Doney, Jayne T. Fitzgerald, LaBrenda Garrett-Nelson, Gary J. Gasper, Bruce A. Gates, Nick Giordano, Cathy Koch, Robert J. Leonard, Richard Meltzer, Phillip D. Moseley, John D. Porter, Robert M. Rozen, Donna Steele-Flynn, Timothy J. Urban

Nat'l Ass'n for the Advancement of Colored People, Washington Bureau

1025 Vermont Ave. NW
Suite 1120
Washington, DC 20005
Tel: (202)638-2269
Fax: (202)638-5936
Registered: LDA
Web: www.naacp.org

A civil rights organization which seeks to end racial segregation and discrimination in all aspects of American life. Headquartered in Baltimore, MD.

Leg. Issues: BAN, CIV, CON, DEF, EDU, FOR, HOU, IMM, LBR

In-house, DC-area Employees

SHELTON, Hilary: Director

Nat'l Ass'n for the Advancement of Orthotics and Prosthetics

Washington, DC

A provider/consumer organization focusing on healthcare reform, Medicare policy, and rehabilitation research for people using artificial limbs and orthopedic braces.

Leg. Issues: HCR

Outside Counsel/Consultants

Powers Pyles Sutter & Verville, PC
Issues: HCR
Rep By: Peter W. Thomas

Nat'l Ass'n for the Education of Young Children

1509 16th St. NW
Washington, DC 20036-1426
Tel: (202)232-8777
Fax: (202)328-1846
Registered: LDA
Web: www.naeyc.org
E-mail: naeyc@naeyc.org
Leg. Issues: EDU, TOB, WEL

In-house, DC-area Employees

GINSBERG, Dr. Mark: Exec. Director
KAGEN, Lynn: President

Nat'l Ass'n for the Self-Employed

1225 I St. NW
Suite 500
Washington, DC 20005
Tel: (202)466-2100
Fax: (202)466-2123
Registered: LDA
Web: www.nase.org

A 330,000 member organization representing the interests of the nation's self-employed and its smallest businesses.

Leg. Issues: CPT, ECN, SMB, TAX

In-house, DC-area Employees

HUGHES, Robert: President

Outside Counsel/Consultants

The Morrison Group, Inc.
Issues: CPT, ECN, SMB, TAX
Rep By: James W. Morrison, Ph.D.

Nat'l Ass'n for the Support of Long Term Care

King of Prussia, PA
Web: www.nasl.org
Leg. Issues: BUD, HCR, MMM

Outside Counsel/Consultants

Greenberg Traurig, LLP
Issues: BUD, HCR, MMM
Rep By: Rob Garagiola, Russell J. Mueller, Nancy E. Taylor, Timothy P. Trysla, Howard A. Vine

Nat'l Ass'n for Uniformed Services

5535 Hempstead Way
Springfield, VA 22151
Tel: (703)750-1342
Fax: (703)354-4380
Registered: LDA
Web: www.naus.org
E-mail: naus@ix.netcom.com
Leg. Issues: BUD, DEF, HCR, MMM, RET, VET

Political Action Committee/s

Nat'l Ass'n for Uniformed Services Political Action Committee

5535 Hempstead Way
Springfield, VA 22151
Tel: (703)750-1342
Fax: (703)354-4380
Contact: Benjamin H. Butler

In-house, DC-area Employees

BUTLER, Benjamin H.: Associate Legislative Counsel
MORRISON, John W.: Legislative Counsel
MURRAY, (USAF-Ret.), Maj. Gen. Richard D.: President
PARTRIDGE, (Ret.), Col. Charles C.: Legislative Director
WILLIS, Gene R.: Legislative Director

Outside Counsel/Consultants

Ass'n Growth Enterprises
Rep By: John Paul May, Thomas L. Pacino

Nat'l Ass'n of Affordable Housing Lenders

2121 K St. NW
Suite 700
Washington, DC 20037
Tel: (202)293-9850
Fax: (202)293-9852
Registered: LDA
E-mail: naahl@naahl.org
Leg. Issues: BAN, BUD, HOU, TAX

In-house, DC-area Employees

KENNEDY, Judith A.: President

Nat'l Ass'n of Agricultural Educators (NAAE)

1410 King St.
Suite 400
Alexandria, VA 22314
Tel: (703)838-5885
Fax: (703)838-5888
Web: www.teamaged.org
E-mail: jjackman@teamaged.org

Provides opportunities, services and advocacy for the agricultural education of society. Formerly known as Nat'l Vocational Agricultural Teachers Ass'n.

In-house, DC-area Employees

JACKMAN, Ph.D., William Jay: Exec. Director

Nat'l Ass'n of Air Traffic Specialists

11303 Amherst Ave.
Suite Four
Wheaton, MD 20902
Tel: (301)933-6228
Fax: (301)933-3902
Web: www.naats.org

Political Action Committee/s

NAATS Political Action Committee

11303 Amherst Ave.
Suite Four
Wheaton, MD 20902
Tel: (301)933-6228
Fax: (301)933-3902

In-house, DC-area Employees

PIKE, Walter: President

Nat'l Ass'n of Aircraft and Communication Suppliers

North Hollywood, CA

An organization of small businesses that purchase military surplus aircraft parts.

Leg. Issues: AVI

Outside Counsel/Consultants

John J. Fausti & Associates, LLC
Issues: AVI
Rep By: John J. Fausti, Odyssey E. Gray

Nat'l Ass'n of Area Agencies on Aging

927 15th St. NW
Sixth Floor
Washington, DC 20036
Tel: (202)296-8130
Fax: (202)296-8134
Web: www.n4a.org

The national representative of 655 area agencies on aging and 230 Title VI Native American aging programs.

Leg. Issues: GOV, IND, MMM

In-house, DC-area Employees

JACKSON, Janice: Exec. Director
MCKINNON, Monette: Director, Field Communications

Nat'l Ass'n of Arms Shows

Palm Springs, CA
Leg. Issues: FIR

Outside Counsel/Consultants

Law Offices of Mark Barnes
Issues: FIR
Rep By: Mark J. Barnes, Tammy Begun

Nat'l Ass'n of Assistant United States Attorneys

9001 Braddock Rd.
Suite 380
Springfield, VA 22151
Tel: (800)455-5661
Fax: (800)528-3492
Web: www.naausa.org
E-mail: info@naausa.org
Leg. Issues: GOV, LAW, RET

In-house, DC-area Employees
BOYD, Dennis W.: Exec. Director

Outside Counsel/Consultants
Chwat and Company, Inc.
Issues: LAW
Rep By: Scott Bizub, John Chwat, Derek Riker
Covington & Burling
Financial Programs, Inc.
Issues: GOV, LAW, RET
Rep By: Dennis W. Boyd

Nat'l Ass'n of Attorneys General

750 First St. NE
Suite 1100
Washington, DC 20002
Tel: (202)326-6000
Fax: (202)408-7014
Web: www.naag.org

Expresses views of state attorneys general through resolutions, communications, and testimony on selected subjects to the executive and legislative agencies of state and federal governments.

Leg. Issues: ROD, SCI, TAX

In-house, DC-area Employees
ROSS, Lynne M.: Exec. Director

Nat'l Ass'n of Bankruptcy Trustees

Columbia, SC
Leg. Issues: BNK

Outside Counsel/Consultants
Howe, Anderson & Steyer, P.C.
Issues: BNK
Rep By: Richard A. Steyer
Stanton & Associates
Issues: BNK
Rep By: Hon. James V. Stanton

Nat'l Ass'n of Beverage Retailers

5101 River Rd.
Suite 108
Bethesda, MD 20816
Tel: (301)656-1494
Fax: (301)656-7539
Registered: LDA
Web: www.nabronline.org
E-mail: nabr@nabronline.org
Leg. Issues: BEV, SMB, TAX, TRA

Political Action Committee/s
NABRPAC
5101 River Rd.
Suite 108
Bethesda, MD 20816
Tel: (301)656-1494
Fax: (301)656-7539
Contact: John B. Burcham, Jr.

In-house, DC-area Employees
BURCHAM, Jr., John B.: Exec. Director
LECKER, Barbara A.: Manager, Government Affairs

Nat'l Ass'n of Biology Teachers

12030 Sunrise Valley Dr.
Suite 110
Reston, VA 20191-3409
Tel: (703)264-9696
Fax: (703)264-7778
Web: www.nabt.org
E-mail: nabter@aol.com

Dedicated to leadership for biology education. Its programs focus on enhancing the professional growth and development of biology/life science teachers at all levels.

Leg. Issues: EDU, SCI

In-house, DC-area Employees
CARLEY, Wayne W.: Exec. Director

Nat'l Ass'n of Black Accountants

7249-A Hanover Pkwy.
Greenbelt, MD 20770
Tel: (301)474-6222
Fax: (301)474-3114
Web: www.nabainc.org
E-mail: cquinn@nabainc.org

Formed to unite students and professionals in the accounting field who are dedicated to professional and academic excellence. Offers a wide variety of benefits including continuing professional education, career placement services, leadership development and college scholarships.

In-house, DC-area Employees
MATTHEWS, Sr., Darryl R.: Exec. Director

Nat'l Ass'n of Black County Officials

440 First St. NW
Suite 410
Washington, DC 20001
Tel: (202)347-6953
Fax: (202)393-6596

Membership is comprised of both elected and appointed black county officials. Provides a forum for the exchange of views and information concerning issues that may affect their constituency.

In-house, DC-area Employees
COOPER, Donna: Exec. Director

Nat'l Ass'n of Black-Owned Broadcasters

1155 Connecticut Ave. NW
Sixth Floor
Washington, DC 20036
Tel: (202)463-8970
Fax: (202)429-0657
Web: www.nabob.org
E-mail: nabob@abs.net

Trade association representing interests of African American owners of broadcast stations and cable television systems.

Leg. Issues: COM

In-house, DC-area Employees
WINSTON, James L.: Exec. Director

Outside Counsel/Consultants
Rubin, Winston, Diercks, Harris & Cooke
Issues: COM
Rep By: James L. Winston

Nat'l Ass'n of Blind Teachers

1155 15th St. NW
Suite 1004
Washington, DC 20005
Tel: (202)467-5081
Fax: (202)467-5085
Web: www.asc.org
E-mail: info@acb.org

An affiliate of the American Council of the Blind (see separate listing).

In-house, DC-area Employees
CRAWFORD, Charles
SLABY, Patty: President

Nat'l Ass'n of Boards of Examiners of Long Term Care Administrators

Washington, DC
Web: www.nabweb.org
E-mail: nab@bostromdc.com

Outside Counsel/Consultants
Bostrom Corp.
Rep By: Randy Lindner, CAE

Nat'l Ass'n of Bond Lawyers

601 13th St. NW
Suite 800 South
Washington, DC 20005
Tel: (202)682-1498
Fax: (202)637-0217
Registered: LDA
Web: www.nabl.org

Works on legislation and regulation impacting municipal finance, including tax and securities laws. Headquartered in Wheaton, IL.

Leg. Issues: FIN, TAX

In-house, DC-area Employees
LARSEN, William L.: Director, Governmental Affairs

Nat'l Ass'n of Broadcast Employees and Technicians-Communications Workers of America, AFL-CIO (NABET-CWA)

501 Third St. NW
Washington, DC 20001-2797
Tel: (202)434-1254
Fax: (202)434-1426
Web: www.nabetcwa.org
E-mail: nabet-cwa@cwa-union.org

A labor union representing the broadcasting, cable television, and associated industries.

In-house, DC-area Employees
CLARK, John S.: Sector President
MAHONEY, Daniel: Secretary-Treasurer

Nat'l Ass'n of Broadcasters

1771 N St. NW
Washington, DC 20036-2891
Tel: (202)429-5300
Registered: LDA
Web: www.nab.org

Established in 1922 to foster, promote and advance the progress of radio and television broadcasting in an ever changing environment; to represent the interests of the broadcasting industry before the government, and to strengthen broadcasters' abilities to serve the public.

Leg. Issues: ADV, ART, BUD, COM, CPI, CPT, ENV, GOV, TAX

Political Action Committee/s
Television and Radio Political Action Committee (TARPAC)
1771 N St. NW
Washington, DC 20036-2891
Tel: (202)495-5427
Fax: (202)775-2157
Contact: Amanda Kornegay

In-house, DC-area Employees
ALMGREN, Kenneth D.: Exec. V. President and Chief Financial Officer
BAUMANN, Henry L.: Exec. V. President, Law and Regulatory Policy
CLAUDY, Lynn: Senior V. President, Science and Technology
DAVID, John: Exec. V. President, Radio
FRITTS, Edward O.: President and Chief Exec. Officer
FULLUM, Karen: V. President, Regulatory Affairs
GOODMAN, Jack N.: Senior V. President, Policy Counsel
HOLY, Lori: Legislative Counsel
IVINS, II, Benjamin F. P.: Senior Associate, General Counsel
KNEBEL, John A.: Exec. V. President, Operations and Business Development
KORNEGAY, Amanda: TARPAC Manager
MAY, James C.: Exec. V. President, Government Relations
ORLANDO, John S.: Senior V. President, External Relations
OWEN, Rob: Director, Senate Congressional Liaison
RAMSEY, Kathleen: Senior V. President, Congressional Relations
REINSDORF, Andrew: Director, House Congressional Liaison
SCHULTE, Valerie: Senior Associate General Counsel
STRINGHAM, Bart: Associate General Counsel
TIMMERMAN, Jerianne: Associate General Counsel
WHARTON, Dennis: Senior V. President, Corporate Communications
WILLIAMS, Kelly: Director, Engineering, Science, and Technology

Outside Counsel/Consultants
Cormac Group, LLP
Davidson & Company, Inc.
Issues: ADV, COM, TAX
Rep By: James H. Davidson, Richard E. May, Stanley Sokul
Edelman Public Relations Worldwide
Rep By: Michael K. Deaver
Podesta/Mattoon
Issues: COM, CPT, GOV
Rep By: Ann Delory, Kimberley Fritts, Matthew Gelman, Claudia James, Kristen Leary
Shaw Pittman
Skadden, Arps, Slate, Meagher & Flom LLP
Issues: COM

Nat'l Ass'n of Business Political Action Committees

2300 Clarendon Blvd.
Suite 401
Arlington, VA 22201
Tel: (703)516-4708
Fax: (703)516-9855
Registered: LDA
Web: www.nabpac.org
E-mail: nabpac@aol.com
Leg. Issues: CIV, COM, GOV

In-house, DC-area Employees
ZIEBART, Geoffrey C.: Exec. Director

Outside Counsel/Consultants
Hall, Green, Rupli, LLC
Issues: CIV, COM, GOV
Rep By: John M. Green, G. Stewart Hall
Washington Strategies, L.L.C.
Issues: CIV, COM, GOV
Rep By: Geoffrey C. Ziebart

Nat'l Ass'n of Chain Drug Stores

P.O. Box 1417-D49
Alexandria, VA 22313-1417
Tel: (703)549-3001
Fax: (703)836-4869
Registered: LDA
Web: www.nacds.org
Leg. Issues: CPT, GOV, HCR, INS, LBR, MMM, PHA, TAX, TOR

Political Action Committee/s
Nat'l Ass'n of Chain Drug Stores Political Action Committee
P.O. Box 1417-D49
Alexandria, VA 22313-1417
Tel: (703)549-3001
Fax: (703)549-0772
Contact: S. Lawrence Kocot

In-house, DC-area Employees
COSTER, John M.: V. President, Federal and State Programs
FULLER, Craig L.: President and C.E.O.
GUITERMAN, Susan L.: Senior V. President, Communications and External Affairs
KOCOT, S. Lawrence: Senior V. President, Government Affairs and General Counsel
LAMBERT, III, David F.: V. President, Government Affairs
LINK, James E.: V. President, Federal Legislative Affairs

Outside Counsel/Consultants

Akin, Gump, Strauss, Hauer & Feld, L.L.P.
Rep By: Barney J. Skladany, Jr.

Cooney & Associates, Inc.
Issues: HCR, INS, MMM, PHA
Rep By: Patrick J. Cooney

Dickstein Shapiro Morin & Oshinsky LLP
Rep By: Henry C. Cashen, II, Peter J. Kadzik

The Direct Impact Co.

Swidler Berlin Shereff Friedman, LLP
Issues: HCR, PHA
Rep By: Barry B. Direnfeld, Harold P. Goldfield

Venable
Issues: CPT, GOV, LBR, TAX, TOR
Rep By: Jeffrey S. Tenenbaum

Nat'l Ass'n of Charterboat Operators (NACO)

Alexandria, VA
Web: www.charterboat.org
E-mail: naco@charterboat.org

A trade group representing sportfishing, diving and excursion vessels.

Leg. Issues: MAR

Outside Counsel/Consultants

Washington Policy Associates, Inc.
Issues: MAR
Rep By: Jeffrey C. Smith

Nat'l Ass'n of Chemical Distributors

1560 Wilson Blvd. Tel: (703)527-6223
Suite 1250 Fax: (703)527-7747
Arlington, VA 22209
Web: www.nacd.com
E-mail: postmaster@nacd.com

Mission is to enhance and communicate the professionalism of the chemical distributors industry.

Leg. Issues: CAW, CHM, ENV, TRA, TRU

In-house, DC-area Employees

KOLSTAND, James L.: President and Chief Operating Officer

Nat'l Ass'n of Children's Hospitals Inc.

401 Wythe St. Tel: (703)684-1355
Alexandria, VA 22314 Fax: (703)684-1589
Registered: LDA
Web: www.childrenshospitals.net

Legislative interest includes children's access to health care, child abuse prevention, pediatric research, Medicaid.

Leg. Issues: BUD, DEF, FIR, HCR, IMM, MED, MMM, TOB, TRA

In-house, DC-area Employees

FELDMAN, Laura S.: Director, Grants Project and Policy
HANSEN, Suzanne: Director, Medicaid and State Policy
KELLY, Clare M.: Associate, Public Policy
MCANDREWS, Lawrence A.: President and Chief Exec. Officer
WILLSON, Peters D.: V. President, Public Policy

Outside Counsel/Consultants

Broydrick & Associates
Issues: DEF, HCR
Rep By: William Broydrick, Amy Demske

Capitol Associates, Inc.
Issues: BUD
Rep By: Debra M. Hardy Havens, Julie P. Pawelczyk

Grisso Consulting
Rep By: Michael E. Grisso

Health Policy Strategies
Issues: BUD, HCR, MED
Rep By: Ann Langley

Nat'l Ass'n of City and County Health Officials

Washington, DC
Leg. Issues: HCR

Outside Counsel/Consultants

Golin/Harris Internat'l
Issues: HCR
Rep By: Carol C. Mitchell

Nat'l Ass'n of Collection Sites

Alexandria, VA

A national trade association for the drug collection and alcohol testing industry.

Leg. Issues: ALC

Outside Counsel/Consultants

Washington Policy Associates, Inc.
Issues: ALC
Rep By: Jeffrey C. Smith

Nat'l Ass'n of College and University Attorneys

One Dupont Circle NW Tel: (202)833-8390
Suite 620 Fax: (202)296-8379
Washington, DC 20036
Web: www.nacua.org
E-mail: nacua@nacua.org

Enhances legal assistance to colleges and universities by educating attorneys and administrators on the nature of campus legal issues.

Leg. Issues: EDU

In-house, DC-area Employees

SANTORA, Kathleen C.: Chief Exec. Officer

Nat'l Ass'n of College and University Business Officers

2501 M St. NW Tel: (202)861-2500
Suite 400 Fax: (202)861-2583
Washington, DC 20037
Web: www.nacubo.org

Represents chief financial officers at more than 2,100 colleges and universities across the U.S.

In-house, DC-area Employees

BACHINGER, Mary: Senior Policy Analyst
GROSS, Anne: Director, Policy Research and Analysis
LARGER, Christine: V. President, Public Policy and Government Relations
MADIA, Michelle: Information Manager
MORLEY, Jr., James E.: President

Nat'l Ass'n of College Auxiliary Services

Charlottesville, VA

Outside Counsel/Consultants

Goldberg & Associates, PLLC

Nat'l Ass'n of College Stores

Oberlin, OH Registered: LDA
Leg. Issues: TAX

Outside Counsel/Consultants

Arent Fox Kintner Plotkin & Kahn, PLLC
Issues: TAX
Rep By: Marc L. Fleischaker, Michael T. McNamara

Nat'l Ass'n of Commissions for Women

8630 Fenton St. Tel: (301)585-8101
Suite 934 Fax: (301)585-3445
Silver Spring, MD 20910-3803
Web: www.nacw.org
E-mail: nacw2@nacw.org

Membership organization composed of regional, state and local commissions created by government to improve the the status of women. Organized in 1970.

In-house, DC-area Employees

HENDEL, Patricia J.: President

Nat'l Ass'n of Community Action Agencies

1100 17th St. NW Tel: (202)265-7546
Suite 500 Fax: (202)265-8850
Washington, DC 20036
Web: www.nacaa.org
E-mail: info@nacaa.org

Members represent organizations created to fight poverty at the local level.

In-house, DC-area Employees

BUCKSTEAD, John: Exec. Director
HOLLAND, Lisa: Coordinator, Marketing and Public Relations

Nat'l Ass'n of Community Health Centers

1330 New Hampshire Ave. NW Tel: (202)659-8008
Suite 122 Fax: (202)659-8519
Washington, DC 20036 Registered: LDA
Web: www.nachc.com

Leg. Issues: BUD, EDU, GOV, HCR, IMM, MED, MMM, PHA, TAX, TOB, VET, WEL

In-house, DC-area Employees

HAWKINS, Jr., Daniel R.: V. President, Federal and State Affairs
KENNEDY, Craig: Federal Affairs Representative
KOPPEN, Christopher: Associate Director, Federal Affairs
MCNALLY, Susan V.: Director Federal Affairs and Legislative Counsel
MIZEUR, Heather: Director, State Affairs
VAN COVERDEN, Thomas: President and Chief Exec. Officer

Outside Counsel/Consultants

Capitol Associates, Inc.
Issues: BUD, EDU, HCR, MMM
Rep By: Liz Gemski, Edward R. Long, Ph.D.

Feldesman, Tucker, Leifer, Fidell & Bank
Rep By: James L. Feldesman

Greenberg Traurig, LLP
Issues: BUD, HCR, MMM
Rep By: Diane J. Blagman, Howard J. Cohen, Rob Garagiola, Russell J. Mueller, Nancy E. Taylor, Timothy P. Trysla

Philip W. Johnston Associates
Rep By: Philip W. Johnston, Merrill E. Warschoff

The MWW Group
Issues: HCR, MMM
Rep By: Dana P. Bostic, Christine A. Pellerin, Jonathan B. Slade

U.S. Strategies Corp.
Issues: HCR, MMM
Rep By: Gary F. Capistrant, Steven E. Carey, Heidi Hanson, Brad Traverse

Nat'l Ass'n of Computer Consultant Businesses

1800 Diagonal Rd. Tel: (703)838-2050
Suite 520 Fax: (703)838-3610
Alexandria, VA 22314 Registered: LDA
Web: www.naccb.org
E-mail: staff@naccb.org
Leg. Issues: CPI, IMM, LBR, TAX

Political Action Committee/s

Nat'l Ass'n of Computer Consultant Businesses High-Tech PAC

1800 Diagonal Rd. Tel: (703)838-2050
Suite 520 Fax: (703)838-3610
Alexandria, VA 22314
Contact: Mark B. Roberts

In-house, DC-area Employees

ROBERTS, Mark B.: General Counsel

Outside Counsel/Consultants

Greenberg Traurig, LLP
Issues: IMM, TAX
Rep By: Diane J. Blagman, Ronald L. Platt, Nancy E. Taylor, Timothy P. Trysla, Howard A. Vine

Nat'l Ass'n of Conservation Districts

509 Capitol Ct. NE Tel: (202)547-6223
Washington, DC 20002 Fax: (202)547-6450
Web: www.nacdnet.org
E-mail: washington@nacdnet.org

A non-governmental, non-profit organization representing 3,000 local soil and water, natural resource and conservation districts and their state associations in 50 states, Puerto Rico, the Virgin Islands, the Pacific Basin, and the District of Columbia.

Leg. Issues: AGR, BUD, CAW, NAT

In-house, DC-area Employees

LAMB, Eugene: Director, Programs
SHEA, Ernest C.: Chief Exec. Officer

Outside Counsel/Consultants

Capitolink, LLC
Issues: AGR, BUD
Rep By: Deborah M. Atwood, Thomas R. Hebert

Nat'l Ass'n of Consumer Agency Administrators

1010 Vermont Ave. NW Tel: (202)347-7395
Suite 514 Fax: (202)347-2563
Washington, DC 20005
Web: www.nacaanet.org
E-mail: nacaa@erols.com

Supports and promotes the role of government agencies at all levels of government responsible for ensuring an honest, safe, informed marketplace. Also promotes consumer and business responsibility in a competitive economy.

In-house, DC-area Employees

WEINBERG, Wendy J.: Exec. Director

Nat'l Ass'n of Consumer Bankruptcy Attorneys

San Jose, CA
Leg. Issues: BNK

Outside Counsel/Consultants

Patton Boggs, LLP
Issues: BNK
Rep By: Darryl D. Nirenberg, Jonathan R. Yarowsky

Nat'l Ass'n of Convenience Stores

1605 King St.
Alexandria, VA 22314-2792
Tel: (703)684-3600
Fax: (703)836-4564
Registered: LDA
Web: www.cstorecentral.com
E-mail: kerley@cstorescentral.com
Leg. Issues: ENV, LBR, TAX, TOB

Political Action Committee/s

Nat'l Ass'n of Convenience Stores Political Action Committee
1605 King St.
Alexandria, VA 22314-2792
Tel: (703)684-3600
Fax: (703)836-4564
Contact: Lyle Beckwith

In-house, DC-area Employees

BECKWITH, Lyle: Director, Government Relations
HUTTER, Lindsay: V. President, Industry Relations and Communications
KATZ, Marc N.: V. President, Government Relations
LEBOEUF, Kerley: President
RICHMAN, Teri F.: Senior V. President, Research and Industry Affairs
SCHULMAN, Allison: Legislative Representative

Outside Counsel/Consultants

Chambers Associates Inc.
Issues: TOB
Rep By: William A. Signer

Collier Shannon Scott, PLLC
Issues: ENV, LBR, TAX, TOB
Rep By: R. Timothy Columbus, Kathleen Clark Kies, Jeffrey L. Leiter, Gregory M. Scott, Dana S. Wood

The Direct Impact Co.

Keelen Communications
Rep By: Matthew B. Keelen

Thiemann Aitken Vohra & Rutledge, L.L.C.

Nat'l Ass'n of Corporate Directors

1828 L St. NW
Suite 801
Washington, DC 20036
Tel: (202)775-0509
Fax: (202)775-4857
Web: www.nacdonline.org
E-mail: info@nacdonline.org

Seeks to enhance the governance and performance of business entities. Since 1977, NACD has been the only not-for-profit organization focused on the needs of individuals serving on corporate boards of directors.

In-house, DC-area Employees

RABER, Dr. Roger W.: President and Chief Exec. Officer
SAVAGE, Shannon A.: Director, Marketing

Nat'l Ass'n of Corporate Treasurers

Reston, VA
Web: www.nact.org
E-mail: nact@nact.org

Outside Counsel/Consultants

Drohan Management Group

Nat'l Ass'n of Counties

440 First St. NW
Eighth Floor
Washington, DC 20001
Tel: (202)393-6226
Fax: (202)393-2630
Web: www.naco.org
Leg. Issues: TAX

In-house, DC-area Employees

ARNOLD, Jeffrey D.: Deputy Legislative Director
BOMBERG, Neil: Associate Legislative Director, Employment and Training
BOSAK, KathyAnn: Director, Finance and Administration
BRAATEN, Kaye: Representative, County Services
BULLARD, Shawn: Associate Legislative Director, Large Urban County Caucus
BYARS, Dottie: State Association Liaison
BYERS, Jacqueline: Director, Research
COLE, Lisa: Director, NACO Services
FERGUSON, Edward E.: Director, County Services
FOGEL, Robert: Associate Legislative Director, Transportation
GILBERTI, Eric: Assistant Legislative Director, Rural Action Caucus
GOODMAN, G. Thomas: Director, Public Affairs
HARRIS, Martin: Co-Director, Joint Center for Sustainable Development
JARREAU, Bert: Chief Technology Officer
KAMPINSKY, Lois: Director, Telecommunications and Training
LIPSCOMB, Renata: Associate, Corporate Relations
MARKWOOD, Sandy: Deputy Director, County Services Department
MATTHEWS, Cassandra: Associate Legislative Director, Community and Economic Development
MCELROY, Sally: Associate Legislative Director, Health
MCRUNNEL, Karen: Executive Assistant and Board Liaison
MURRAY, Donald: Associate Legislative Director, Employment Justice and Public Safety
NAAKE, Larry E.: Exec. Director
OSBOURN, Stephanie: Associate Legislative Director, Environment/Energy/Land Use
POWELL, Anne: Database Manager
RICCI, Tiffany
ROSADO, Edwin S.: Director, Legislative Affairs
SANZ, Marilina: Associate Legislative Director, Human Services and Education
SWEET, Tom: Director, Corporate Relations
TABOR, Ralph: Associate Legislative Director
WITT, John: Senior Project Manager, NACO's Radon/Indoor Air Project

Outside Counsel/Consultants

R. Duffy Wall and Associates
Issues: TAX
Rep By: Hon. Bill Brewster, Hon. Rodney D. Chandler, Julia E. Chaney

Nat'l Ass'n of County Administrators

440 First St. NW
Washington, DC 20001
Tel: (202)393-6226
Fax: (202)393-2630
Web: www.naco.org

In-house, DC-area Employees

FERGUSON, Edward E.: Director, County Services

Nat'l Ass'n of County Aging Programs

440 First St. NW
Eighth Floor
Washington, DC 20001
Tel: (202)393-6226
Fax: (202)393-2630
Web: www.naco.org

Composed of county elected and appointed officials with an interest or direct responsibility for the delivery of aging services. Develops policy position on aging issues, highlights and disseminates information on aging and offers training to its members.

In-house, DC-area Employees

MARKWOOD, Sandy: Contact

Nat'l Ass'n of County and City Health Officials

1100 17th St. NW
Second Floor
Washington, DC 20036
Tel: (202)783-5550
Fax: (202)783-1583
Web: www.naccho.org
E-mail: sschenck@naccho.org

Represents all local health departments throughout the country.

Leg. Issues: HCR

In-house, DC-area Employees

GROSSMAN, MPH, Donna Brown: Director, Public Health Advocacy

Nat'l Ass'n of County Civil Attorneys

440 First St. NW
Eighth Floor
Washington, DC 20001
Tel: (202)942-4247
Fax: (202)737-0480
Web: www.naco.org

In-house, DC-area Employees

MURRAY, Donald: Contact
NAAKE, Larry E.: Contact

Nat'l Ass'n of County Community and Economic Development

2025 M St. NW
Suite 800
Washington, DC 20036
Tel: (202)367-1149
Fax: (202)367-2149
Registered: LDA
E-mail: john_murphy@dc.sba.com
Leg. Issues: HOU

In-house, DC-area Employees

MURPHY, John C.: Exec. Director

Outside Counsel/Consultants

Smith, Bucklin and Associates, Inc.
Issues: HOU
Rep By: John C. Murphy

Nat'l Ass'n of County Engineers

440 First St. NW
Washington, DC 20001
Tel: (202)393-5041
Fax: (202)393-2630
Web: www.naco.org/asfils/nace
E-mail: nace@naco.org

Professional organization for county engineering and public works officials. Works to advance county engineering and management by providing a forum for the exchange of ideas and information, acts to foster the growth of individual state associations of county engineers, and works to improve communications between county engineers and other agencies.

In-house, DC-area Employees

FOGEL, Robert: Contact
GIANCOLA, Anthony R.: Exec. Director

Nat'l Ass'n of County Health Facility Administrators

440 First St. NW
Washington, DC 20001
Tel: (202)393-6226
Fax: (202)393-2630
Web: www.nachfa.org

In-house, DC-area Employees

SANZ, Marilina: Associate Legislative Director, Human Services

Nat'l Ass'n of County Human Services Administrators

440 First St. NW
Washington, DC 20001
Tel: (202)393-6226
Fax: (202)393-2630
Web: www.naco.org

In-house, DC-area Employees

SANZ, Marilina: Associate Legislative Director, Human Services

Nat'l Ass'n of County Information Officers

440 First St. NW
Washington, DC 20001
Tel: (202)393-6226
Fax: (202)393-2630
Web: www.naco.org

In-house, DC-area Employees

GOODMAN, G. Thomas

Nat'l Ass'n of County Information Technology Administrators

440 First St. NW
Eighth Floor
Washington, DC 20001
Tel: (202)942-4245
Fax: (202)393-2630
Web: www.naco.org
Leg. Issues: CPI

In-house, DC-area Employees

POWELL, Anne

Nat'l Ass'n of County Park and Recreation Officials

440 First St. NW
Washington, DC 20001
Tel: (202)393-6226
Fax: (202)393-2630
Web: www.naco.org

In-house, DC-area Employees

WITT, Lou: Contact

Nat'l Ass'n of County Planners

440 First St. NW
Washington, DC 20001
Tel: (202)393-6226
Fax: (202)942-4281
Web: www.naco.org
E-mail: jdavenpo@naco.org

In-house, DC-area Employees

MARKWOOD, Sandy: Contact

Nat'l Ass'n of County Recorders, Election Officials and Clerks

440 First St. NW
Washington, DC 20001
Tel: (202)393-6226
Fax: (202)737-0480

In-house, DC-area Employees

FERGUSON, Edward E.: Contact
HARKRADER, Mary: President

Nat'l Ass'n of County Training and Employment Professionals

440 First St. NW
Washington, DC 20001
Tel: (202)393-6226
Fax: (202)942-4281
Web: www.naco.org

In-house, DC-area Employees

BOMBERG, Neil: Contact
GORTENBURG, Gary: Director, Employment and Training

Nat'l Ass'n of County Treasurers and Finance Officers

440 First St. NW
Washington, DC 20001
Tel: (202)942-4290
Fax: (202)393-2630

In-house, DC-area Employees

SWEET, Tom: Contact
TABOR, Ralph: Contact

Nat'l Ass'n of Credit Management

Columbia, MD
Leg. Issues: BAN, BNK

Outside Counsel/Consultants

PACE-CAPSTONE
Issues: BAN, BNK
Rep By: J. Michael Landrum, James W. Wise

Nat'l Ass'n of Criminal Defense Lawyers

1025 Connecticut Ave. NW
Suite 901
Washington, DC 20036
Tel: (202)872-8600
Fax: (202)872-8690
Registered: LDA
Web: www.criminaljustice.org
E-mail: assist@nacdl.com
Leg. Issues: LAW

In-house, DC-area Employees

STATLER, Stuart M.: Exec. Director

Nat'l Ass'n of Dealers in Ancient, Oriental and Primitive Art

New York, NY
Leg. Issues: FOR, GOV

Outside Counsel/Consultants

Arnold & Porter
Issues: FOR, GOV
Rep By: James F. Fitzpatrick

Nat'l Ass'n of Dental Assistants

900 S. Washington St.
Suite G-13
Falls Church, VA 22046
Tel: (703)237-8616
Fax: (703)533-1153
Leg. Issues: HCR

In-house, DC-area Employees

HENDERSON, K.: Membership Director

Nat'l Ass'n of Dental Laboratories

McLean, VA
Web: www.nadl.org
E-mail: cbeeton@nadl.org
Leg. Issues: GOV

Outside Counsel/Consultants

Reed, Smith, LLP
Issues: GOV
Rep By: David C. Evans

Nat'l Ass'n of Dental Plans

Dallas, TX
Leg. Issues: HCR, INS, MMM, TAX

Outside Counsel/Consultants

Jay Grant & Associates
Issues: HCR, INS, MMM, TAX

Nat'l Ass'n of Development Companies

6764 Old McLean Village Dr.
McLean, VA 22101
Tel: (703)748-2575
Web: www.nadco.org
E-mail: windarrow@aol.com

Members provide lending services to small businesses under several Small Business Administration guarantee programs. NADCO represents the membership before Congress and government agencies and provides education, research, industry communications and insurance services to members.

Political Action Committee/s

Nat'l Ass'n of Development Companies PAC
6764 Old McLean Village Dr.
McLean, VA 22101
Tel: (703)748-2575
Contact: Christopher L. Crawford

In-house, DC-area Employees

CRAWFORD, Christopher L.: Exec. Director

Nat'l Ass'n of Development Organizations

400 N. Capitol St. NW
Suite 390
Washington, DC 20001
Tel: (202)624-7806
Fax: (202)624-8813
Web: www.nado.org
E-mail: info@nado.org

Members, numbering over 350, are mainly regional planning and development organizations. Objectives are to promote community and economic development, primarily in rural areas and small metropolitan areas, and to provide for communication and education. Updates members on legislative developments through its weekly newsletter, NADO NEWS.

In-house, DC-area Employees

CHASE, Matthew: Deputy Director, Legislative Affairs
WOHLBRUCK, Aliceann: Exec. Director

Nat'l Ass'n of Developmental Disabilities Councils

1234 Massachusetts Ave. NW
Suite 103
Washington, DC 20005
Tel: (202)347-1234
Fax: (202)347-4023
Web: www.naddc.org
E-mail: naddc@naddc.org
Leg. Issues: AVI, BUD, CIV, ECN, EDU, FAM, GOV, HCR, IND, LAW, MMM, SMB, TEC, TRA, UNM, WEL

In-house, DC-area Employees

GENNARO, Mary M.: Director, Governmental Affairs
HEUNEMAN, Donna Z.: Exec. Director

Outside Counsel/Consultants

Polity Consulting
Issues: BUD, EDU, HCR
Rep By: Roger P. Kingsley, Ph.D.

Nat'l Ass'n of Elementary School Principals

1615 Duke St.
Alexandria, VA 22314-3483
Tel: (703)684-3345
Fax: (703)548-6021
Registered: LDA
Web: www.naesp.org
E-mail: naesp@naesp.org
Leg. Issues: EDU

In-house, DC-area Employees

FERRANDINO, Dr. Vincent: Exec. Director
MCCONNELL, Sally N.: Director, Government Relations

Nat'l Ass'n of Energy Service Companies

1615 M St. NW
Suite 800
Washington, DC 20036
Tel: (202)822-0950
Fax: (202)822-0955
Registered: LDA
Web: www.naesco.org

A group of energy service companies (including utilities, equipment manufacturers, financial institutions, and government entities) interested in energy efficiency project development.

Leg. Issues: ENG, GOV, UTI

In-house, DC-area Employees

GENZER, Jeffrey C.
SINGER, Ms. Terry E.: Exec. Director

Outside Counsel/Consultants

Duncan, Weinberg, Genzer & Pembroke, P.C.
Issues: ENG, GOV, UTI
Rep By: Jeffrey C. Genzer, Tatjana M. Shonkwiler

Nat'l Ass'n of Enrolled Agents

200 Orchard Ridge Dr.
Suite 302
Gaithersburg, MD 20878
Tel: (301)212-9608
Fax: (301)990-1611
Registered: LDA
Web: www.naea.org
E-mail: info@naea.org
Leg. Issues: BUD, SMB, TAX

In-house, DC-area Employees

BRAY, Janet: Exec. V. President
CRANFORD, Sharon H.: Director, Public Policy and External Relations
DADE, Michael: Legislative Assistant

Outside Counsel/Consultants

Van Scoyoc Associates, Inc.
Issues: TAX
Rep By: Jeffrey S. Trinca, H. Stewart Van Scoyoc

Nat'l Ass'n of Epilepsy Centers

Minneapolis, MN
Leg. Issues: BUD, HCR, MMM

Outside Counsel/Consultants

MARC Associates, Inc.
Issues: BUD, HCR, MMM
Rep By: Ellen Riker

Nat'l Ass'n of Evangelicals

1001 Connecticut Ave. NW
Suite 522
Washington, DC 20036
Tel: (202)789-1011
Fax: (202)842-0392
Web: www.nae.net
E-mail: OGA@nae.net

Areas of interest include: religious freedom, morality, faith and ethics, Christian religion, justice for the poor and oppressed, abortion, tax issues, mediation, and parental choice in education. Publishes the monthly newsletter, NAE Washington Insight. The association is headquartered in Azusa, CA.

Leg. Issues: CIV, FAM, FOR, TAX, WEL

In-house, DC-area Employees

CIZIK, Richard: V. President, Governmental Affairs
THOMPSON, Lisa L.: Policy Representative

Nat'l Ass'n of Executive Secretaries and Administrative Assistants

900 S. Washington St.
Suite G-13
Falls Church, VA 22046
Tel: (703)237-8616
Fax: (703)533-1153
Web: www.naesaa.com
E-mail: naesaa@erols.com

A trade association assisting members in their careers.

Leg. Issues: FAM, RET

In-house, DC-area Employees

LUDEMAN, Ruth L.: Exec. Director

Nat'l Ass'n of Farmer Elected Committees (NAFEC)

Kinsman, OH
Leg. Issues: AGR

Outside Counsel/Consultants

David Senter & Associates
Issues: AGR
Rep By: David L. Senter

Nat'l Ass'n of Federal Credit Unions

3138 N. Tenth St.
Arlington, VA 22201
Tel: (703)522-4770
Fax: (703)522-0594
Registered: LDA
Web: www.nafcunet.org

The only national trade association which exclusively serves federally chartered credit unions. Primary purpose is to provide members with strong representation before Congress and the federal regulatory agencies that have an impact on the operations of this type of credit union.

Leg. Issues: BAN, BNK, CSP, FIN, TAX

Political Action Committee/s

Nat'l Ass'n of Federal Credit Unions Political Action Committee
3138 N. Tenth St.
Arlington, VA 22201
Tel: (703)522-4770
Fax: (703)522-0594
Contact: Murray S. Chanow

In-house, DC-area Employees

BAKER, Gwen: Director, Regulatory Affairs and Federal Regulatory Counsel
BECKER, Fred R.: President
CHANOW, Murray S.: Senior, Legislative Representative
DENT, Linda: Director, Regulatory Compliance
DONOVAN, William J.: Senior V. President and General Counsel
GARWOOD, Suzanne: Director, Regulatory Affairs
GRONOND, Gail: Editor Manager, Member Services
KEEFE, Patrick: V. President, Communications and Technology
SWENSON, Diane: Exec. V. President
THALER, Brad: Associate Director, Legislative Affairs

Nat'l Ass'n of Federal Education Program Administrators

1801 N. Moore St.
Arlington, VA 22209
Tel: (703)875-0774
Fax: (703)807-1849
Web: www.nafepa.org

In-house, DC-area Employees

PFAFF, John: President

Nat'l Ass'n of Federal Veterinarians

1101 Vermont Ave. NW
Suite 710
Washington, DC 20005-6308
Tel: (202)289-6334
Fax: (202)842-4360
Web: www.erols.com/nafv
E-mail: nafv@erols.com

The NAFV is a non-profit corporation formed to promote the veterinary profession, to improve the professional efficiency and material interests of its members, to acquaint the public with the activities of veterinarians in the federal service, and to cooperate with the Amercian Veterinary Medical Association, the United States Animal health Association and other similar groups with common interests.

Leg. Issues: AGR, FOO, MED

Political Action Committee/s

Nat'l Ass'n of Federal Veterinarians Political Action Committee
1101 Vermont Ave. NW
Suite 710
Washington, DC 20005-6308
Tel: (202)289-6334
Fax: (202)842-4360
Contact: Dale D. Boyle, D.V.M.

In-house, DC-area Employees

BOYLE, D.V.M., Dale D.: Executive V. President
HUGHES, William G.: General Counsel

Nat'l Ass'n of Federally Impacted Schools

444 N. Capitol St. NW
Suite 419
Washington, DC 20001
Tel: (202)624-5455
Fax: (202)624-5468
Registered: LDA
Web: www.sso.org/nafis
E-mail: nafis@sso.org

An education information association which represents those school districts located throughout the U.S. which educate children whose parents live and/or work on some type of federal property e.g. Indian reservations, military bases, federally subsidized housing projects, as well as those districts affected by national dams, forests, etc. which have experienced a decrease in their tax base.

Leg. Issues: EDU

In-house, DC-area Employees
FORKENBROCK, John: Exec. Director
KING, D. Brady: Director, Government Relations
MCSPADDEN, Gail: Legislative Analyst

Nat'l Ass'n of Fleet Administrators

Iselin, NJ
Leg. Issues: ENG, ENV, FUE, TAX, TRA

Outside Counsel/Consultants

Kent & O'Connor, Inc.
Issues: ENG, ENV, FUE, TAX, TRA
Rep By: Patrick C. O'Connor

Nat'l Ass'n of Flood and Stormwater Management Agencies

1299 Pennsylvania Ave. NW
Suite 800 West
Washington, DC 20004
Web: www.nafsma.org
Tel: (202)682-3901
Fax: (202)785-5277

Formed to interact with Congress and federal agencies on water resource management issues, flood prevention and damage mitigation in urban environments.

Leg. Issues: DIS, ENV, NAT

In-house, DC-area Employees
GILSON, Susan E.: Director of Legislative and Regulatory Affairs

Outside Counsel/Consultants

The Carmen Group
Issues: DIS, ENV, NAT
Rep By: Susan E. Gilson

Nat'l Ass'n of Food Equipment Manufacturers

Washington, DC

Outside Counsel/Consultants

Smith, Bucklin and Associates, Inc.
Rep By: Robert H. Wilbur

Nat'l Ass'n of Foreign Trade Zones

1000 Connecticut Ave. NW
Suite 1001
Washington, DC 20036
Web: www.naftz.org
E-mail: info@naftz.org
Tel: (202)331-1950
Fax: (202)331-1994

Works to promote, stimulate and improve FTZ's as tools for the economic development of communities and for assisting companies to become comptitive in world markets. Also strives to improve communication between the U.S. government's regulatory and legislative bodies and FTZ grantees, operators and users.

Leg. Issues: TRD

In-house, DC-area Employees
CAMPBELL, Randy: Exec. Director

Outside Counsel/Consultants

Smith Dawson & Andrews, Inc.
Issues: TRD
Rep By: Sherri Powar, James P. Smith

Nat'l Ass'n of Foster Care Review Boards

Atlanta, GA
Leg. Issues: FAM, MMM

Outside Counsel/Consultants

Dublin Castle Group
Issues: FAM, MMM
Rep By: Maureen Flatley Hogan

Nat'l Ass'n of Foster Grandparent Program Directors

Memphis, TN
Leg. Issues: BUD, LBR, RET

Outside Counsel/Consultants

Van Scoyoc Associates, Inc.
Issues: BUD, LBR, RET
Rep By: Evan Knisely, Robert L. Knisely, H. Stewart Van Scoyoc

Nat'l Ass'n of FSA County Office Employees

Ripley, WV

Outside Counsel/Consultants

David Senter & Associates

Nat'l Ass'n of Gas Chlorinators

Trabuco Canyon, CA
Leg. Issues: TRA

Outside Counsel/Consultants

Alcalde & Fay
Issues: TRA
Rep By: Paul Schlesinger, Tim Stroud

Nat'l Ass'n of Government Communicators

526 King St.
Suite 423
Alexandria, VA 22314-3143
Web: www.nagc.com
E-mail: info@nagc.com
Tel: (703)518-4369
Fax: (703)706-9583

Formed by a merger of the Armed Forces Writers League, Federal Editors Ass'n and the Government Information Organization. Furthers professional interests of communicators (writers, editors, public information officers, and audiovisual specialists) working in federal, state, county, city, and other governments.

In-house, DC-area Employees
MITCHEL, M. Lynn: Exec. Director

Outside Counsel/Consultants

The Alexandria Group

Nat'l Ass'n of Government Deferred Compensation Administrators

Lexington, KY
Leg. Issues: RET, TAX

Outside Counsel/Consultants

Susan J. White & Associates
Issues: RET, TAX
Rep By: Susan J. White

Nat'l Ass'n of Government Employees

317 S. Patrick St.
Alexandria, VA 22314
Tel: (703)519-0300
Fax: (703)519-0311
Registered: LDA
E-mail: nage@erols.com

Headquartered in Boston, MA.

Leg. Issues: GOV, LBR

In-house, DC-area Employees
DONNELLAN, Christopher M.: Legislative Director
LYONS, Kenneth T.: President
POOLER-JOHNSON, Susanne J.: V. President
SMITH, Edward J.: Counsel

Nat'l Ass'n of Government Guaranteed Lenders

Stillwater, OK
Registered: LDA
Leg. Issues: SMB

Outside Counsel/Consultants

Thomas G. Powers
Issues: SMB
Rep By: Thomas G. Powers

Verner, Liipfert, Bernhard, McPherson and Hand, Chartered
Issues: SMB
Rep By: David B. Jacobsohn

Nat'l Ass'n of Governors' Highway Safety Representatives

750 First St. NE
Suite 720
Washington, DC 20002
Web: www.naghsr.org
E-mail: dmaddox@naghsr.org
Tel: (202)789-0942
Fax: (202)789-0946

In-house, DC-area Employees
HARSHA, Barbara: Exec. Director

Nat'l Ass'n of Health Underwriters

2000 N. 14th St.
Suite 450
Arlington, VA 22201
Tel: (703)276-0220
Fax: (703)841-7797
Registered: LDA
Web: www.nahu.org
E-mail: nahu@nahu.org

Represents more than 17,000 insurance professionals involved in the sale and service of health insurance and other related plans.

Leg. Issues: HCR, INS, MMM

Political Action Committee/s

Nat'l Ass'n of Health Underwriters PAC (HUPAC)

2000 N. 14th St.
Suite 450
Arlington, VA 22201
Contact: Thomas P. Bruderle
Tel: (703)276-3805
Fax: (703)841-7797

In-house, DC-area Employees
BRUDERLE, Thomas P.: Director, Congressional Affairs
CARR, Martin: Manager, Communications
CORCORAN, Kevin P.: Exec. V. President
GREENE, John C.: Manager, Federal Regulatory Affairs
TRAUTWEIN, Janet Stokes: Director, State and Federal Policy, Analysis and State Government Affairs

Outside Counsel/Consultants

Devillier Communications
Issues: HCR, INS
Rep By: Merri Oxley

Nat'l Ass'n of Healthcare Access Management

Washington, DC
Web: www.naham.org
E-mail: qiana_cunningham@dc.sba.com

Outside Counsel/Consultants

Smith, Bucklin and Associates, Inc.
Rep By: Steven C. Kemp

Nat'l Ass'n of Healthcare Consultants

1255 23rd St. NW
Suite 200
Washington, DC 20037-1174
Web: www.healthcon.org
E-mail: consultants@healthcon.org
Tel: (202)452-8282
Fax: (202)833-3636

Members provide management to physicians and dentists.

Leg. Issues: ACC, MED, MMM, TAX

In-house, DC-area Employees
FORBURGER, Melissa T.: Exec. Director
HOFFMAN, Carrie: Director of Meetings

Outside Counsel/Consultants

Hauck and Associates
Rep By: Melissa T. Forburger, Carrie Hoffman

Nat'l Ass'n of Higher Educational Finance Authorities

Washington, DC
Leg. Issues: FIN

Outside Counsel/Consultants

Mintz, Levin, Cohn, Ferris, Glovsky and Popeo, P.C.
Issues: FIN
Rep By: Charles A. Samuels

Nat'l Ass'n of Hispanic County Officials

440 First St. NW
Washington, DC 20001
Web: www.naco.org
E-mail: msanz@naco.org
Tel: (202)942-4260
Fax: (202)942-4281

In-house, DC-area Employees
SANZ, Marilina: Associate Legislative Director, Human Services

Nat'l Ass'n of Hispanic Journalists

1193 Nat'l Press Building
Washington, DC 20045
Web: www.nahj.org
E-mail: nahj@nahj.org
Tel: (202)662-7145
Fax: (202)662-7144

Dedicated to the recognition and professional advancement of Hispanics in the news industry. Membership consists of working journalists, journalism students, other media-related professionals, and academic scholars.

In-house, DC-area Employees
LOPEZ, Anna M.: Exec. Director

Nat'l Ass'n of Home Builders of the U.S.

1201 15th St. NW
Washington, DC 20005-2800
Tel: (202)822-0200
Fax: (202)822-0572
Registered: LDA
Web: www.nahb.com
E-mail: info@nahb.com
Leg. Issues: BAN, BUD, CIV, ENG, ENV, HOU, TAX, TRD, VET

Political Action Committee/s

BUILD-Political Action Committee

1201 15th St. NW
Washington, DC 20005-2800
Contact: Peter Rintye
Tel: (202)822-0470
Fax: (202)822-0572

In-house, DC-area Employees
ASNANI, Rick: Senior Political Field Director
BURGER, Susan: Director, Finance and Operations
CROWE, David A.: Staff V. President, Housing Policy
DODDRIDGE, Kathy: Staff V. President, Legislative Affairs
EDDY, Tammy: Staff V. President, Congressional Affairs
ENGEL, Jeanne K.: V. President, Policy-Multi-Family Services Division
FALLON, Paul: Director, Public Opinion Research
GRAY, Delna: Legislative Director, Tax Policy
GUTHRIE, Susan: Acting Senior Staff V. President, Staff V. President, Operations and Communications (Multi-Family Services)
HAYDEN, Lou: Legislative Director, Energy, Environment and Trade
HOWARD, Gerald M.: Exec. V. President and Chief Exec. Officer
JADCZAK, Jeremy: Congressional Representative and Grassroots Regional Director

KEULEMAN, Christopher: Director, Political Affairs/Democrat
KILLMER, William P.: Senior Staff V. President, Government Affairs Division
KRISHNAMOORTI, Mala: Legislative Director, Labor, Small Business, and Health Care
LAMORUREUX, Nicole D.: Director of Operations, Government Affairs Division
LYNCH, Jessica: Staff V. President, Communication Operations Division
MACAULEY, Alastair: Senior Political Field Director
MADSEN, Grant: Legislative Director, Environment
RINTYE, Peter: Staff V. President, Political Affairs
SCHWALB, Kevin: Director, Political Affairs/Republican
TOBIN, Jim: Legislative Director, Environment
TRAYLOR, Clayton: Senior V. President, Political Operations
WAGNER, Heidi L.: Congressional Representative, Grassroots Regional Director
ZANOWSKI, Paul J.: Congressional Representative and Grassroots Regional Director

Nat'l Ass'n of Home Builders Research Center, Inc.

Upper Marlboro, MD
Leg. Issues: GOV, HOU

Outside Counsel/Consultants

Jefferson Government Relations, L.L.C.
Issues: GOV, HOU
Rep By: William J. Gilmartin

Nat'l Ass'n of Housing and Redevelopment Officials

630 I St. NW
Washington, DC 20001-3736
Tel: (202)289-3500
Fax: (202)289-8181
Web: www.nahro.org
E-mail: nahro@nahro.org

A non-profit professional membership association of 9,000 local public agency administrators, commissioners, and nonprofits who carry out HUD low and moderate income programs in communities across the country, including public housing, Section rental assistance, Community Development Block Grants, HOME, McKinney Homeless and other HUD programs. NAHRO, through its newsletter, magazine, professional development training, certification courses and conferences informs its members of HUD rulemaking and Congressional legislation affecting their localities.

In-house, DC-area Employees

BARRETO, Jr., Julio: Director, Legislative and Program Development
NELSON, Jr., Richard Y.: Exec. Director
PRESTON, Tawana: Policy Analyst, Housing
SIGAL, Marcia: Policy Analyst, Community Development
SISKA, Christine: Policy Analyst, Housing
THORESON, Karen: President

Nat'l Ass'n of Housing Cooperatives

1401 New York Ave. NW
Suite 1100
Washington, DC 20005
Tel: (202)737-0797
Fax: (202)783-7869
Registered: LDA
Web: www.coophousing.org
E-mail: info@coophousing.org

Represents the interests of housing cooperative members.

Leg. Issues: BUD, HOU, TAX, UTI, VET

In-house, DC-area Employees

KLEINE, Douglas M.: Exec. Director

Outside Counsel/Consultants

Ruddy & Associates
Rep By: Robert E. Ruddy

Nat'l Ass'n of Housing Partnerships

Boston, MA
Leg. Issues: BUD

Outside Counsel/Consultants

Robert A. Rapoza Associates
Issues: BUD
Rep By: Robert A. Rapoza

Nat'l Ass'n of Independent Colleges and Universities

1025 Connecticut Ave. NW
Suite 700
Washington, DC 20036
Tel: (202)785-8866
Fax: (202)835-0003
Registered: LDA
Web: www.naicu.edu

An 900-member organization representing independent colleges and universities on public policy issues with all branches of the federal government.

Leg. Issues: BUD, EDU, TAX

In-house, DC-area Employees

BALZ, Frank: V. President, Research and Policy Analysis
BUDETTI, Maureen R.: Director, Legislative Affairs for Student Aid Policy
FLANAGAN, Sarah A.: V. President, Government Relations
FULLER, Jon: Senior Fellow
GIESECKE, Stephanie: Director, Budget and Appropriations
JOHNS, Karin L.: Director, Tax Policy
KING, Roland H.: V. President, Public Affairs
NEWSOME, Robert "Bo": Outreach Coordinator
WARREN, David L.: President

Outside Counsel/Consultants

Van Scoyoc Associates, Inc.
Issues: EDU
Rep By: H. Stewart Van Scoyoc

Nat'l Ass'n of Independent Diagnostic Services

Winter Park, FL

Outside Counsel/Consultants

McDermott, Will and Emery

Nat'l Ass'n of Independent Fee Appraisers

St. Louis, MO

Outside Counsel/Consultants

Garvey, Schubert & Barer
Rep By: Matthew R. Schneider

Nat'l Ass'n of Independent Insurers

444 N. Capitol St. NW
Suite 801
Washington, DC 20001
Tel: (202)639-0490
Fax: (202)639-0494
Registered: LDA
Web: www.naii.org

A property/casualty insurance trade association headquartered in Des Plaines, IL.

Leg. Issues: BAN, CPT, CSP, DIS, ENV, GOV, HCR, HOU, INS, LAW, LBR, ROD, TAX, TOB

Political Action Committee/s

Nat'l Ass'n of Independent Insurers Political Action Committee
444 N. Capitol St. NW
Suite 801
Washington, DC 20001
Tel: (202)639-0490
Fax: (202)639-0494

In-house, DC-area Employees

FRITZEL, Charles H.: Assistant V. President, Government Relations
GACKENBACH, Julie Leigh: Director, Government Relations
RAMIREZ, Jack: President and Chief Exec. Officer
TAYLOR, III, Charles A.: Assistant V. President, Government Relations

Outside Counsel/Consultants

Committee Management Associates
Rep By: Michael de Blois

Nat'l Ass'n of Independent Life Brokerage Agency

8201 Greensboro Dr.
Suite 300
McLean, VA 22102
Tel: (703)610-9000
Fax: (703)610-9005
Web: www.nailba.org
E-mail: jnormandy@nailba.org

Member agencies wholesale insurance products to agents. Member agencies are responsible for 70% of the first year life premium sold in the U.S.

Leg. Issues: BAN, CPI, INS

In-house, DC-area Employees

NORMANDY, Joseph: Exec. Director

Outside Counsel/Consultants

Ass'n Management Group
Rep By: Joseph Normandy

Nat'l Ass'n of Independent Schools

1620 L St. NW
Suite 1100
Washington, DC 20036-5605
Tel: (202)973-9700
Fax: (202)973-9790
Web: www.nais.org

In-house, DC-area Employees

BASSETT, Patrick F.: President
BURNETT, Jefferson: Director, Government Relations

Nat'l Ass'n of Industrial and Office Properties

2201 Cooperative Way
Third Floor
Herndon, VA 22071
Tel: (703)904-7100
Fax: (703)904-7942
Registered: LDA
Web: www.naiop.org

The trade association for developers, owners and investors in industrial, office and related commercial real estate.

Leg. Issues: ENV, LBR, RES, TAX, TEC, URB

Political Action Committee/s

Nat'l Ass'n of Industrial and Office Properties American Development PAC
2201 Cooperative Way
Third Floor
Herndon, VA 22071
Tel: (703)904-7100
Fax: (703)904-7942
Contact: Reba A. Raffaelli

In-house, DC-area Employees

BISACQUINO, Thomas J.: President
GALLAGHER, Steve: Assistant V. President, State and Local Affairs
RAFFAELLI, Reba A.: V. President, Government Affairs
ROOT, Laurie: V. President, Education
SPECTOR, Jay R.: Director of Federal Affairs
VERTINO, Sheila K.: V. President, International Research

Outside Counsel/Consultants

Rock & Associates
Issues: TAX
Rep By: James W. Rock

Nat'l Ass'n of Installation Developers

1730 K St. NW
Suite 700
Washington, DC 20006
Tel: (202)822-5256
Fax: (202)822-8819
Registered: FARA
Web: www.naid.org
E-mail: naid@urbandevelopment.com

Works to bring together public- and private-sector professionals involved with the redevelopment, and privitization of former military bases.

Leg. Issues: BUD, DEF, ECN, ENV, URB

In-house, DC-area Employees

FINKLE, Jeffrey A.: Exec. Director
FORD, Tim: Deputy Exec. Director

Nat'l Ass'n of Insurance and Financial Advisors

Web: www.agents-online.com
Leg. Issues: BAN, COM, INS, TAX

Outside Counsel/Consultants

Alpine Group, Inc.
Issues: COM, INS, TAX
Rep By: James D. Massie, Rhod M. Shaw, Richard C. White

Baker & Hostetler LLP

Collier Shannon Scott, PLLC
Issues: BAN, INS
Rep By: Scott A. Sinder

Jenner & Block
Issues: BAN, INS

Kehoe & Hambel
Issues: INS, TAX
Rep By: Danea M. Kehoe

Nat'l Ass'n of Insurance Commissioners

444 N. Capitol St. NW
Suite 701
Washington, DC 20001
Tel: (202)624-7790
Fax: (202)624-8579
Web: www.naic.org

Headquartered in Kansas City, MO.

Leg. Issues: HCR, MMM

In-house, DC-area Employees

CHESSON, Jack: Senior Legislative Counsel
COOK, Jennifer: Assistant Counsel, Health Policy
FIELDING, John: Senior Counsel, Financial Services
JACKSON, Aletia: Assistant Counsel, Health Policy
SENKEWICZ, Mary Beth: Senior Counsel, Health Policy
WETMORE, David: Director, Federal and International Affairs

Outside Counsel/Consultants

Jay Grant & Associates
Issues: HCR, MMM
Rep By: Jay B. Grant

Nat'l Ass'n of Investment Companies

1300 Pennsylvania Ave. NW
Suite 700
Washington, DC 20004
Tel: (202)289-4336
Fax: (202)289-4329
Registered: LDA
Web: www.naichq.org
E-mail: naichqtrs@aol.com
Leg. Issues: FIN

Political Action Committee/s

Nat'l Ass'n of Investment Companies
1300 Pennsylvania Ave. NW
Suite 700
Washington, DC 20004
Tel: (202)289-4336
Fax: (202)289-4329

In-house, DC-area Employees

JOHNSON, Angela: Chief Administrator

Outside Counsel/Consultants

Thelen Reid & Priest LLP
Rep By: William A. Kirk, Jr.

Nat'l Ass'n of Investors Corporation (NAIC)

Madison Heights, MI
Leg. Issues: TAX

Outside Counsel/Consultants

Arthur Andersen LLP
Issues: TAX
Rep By: Rachelle Bernstein, Weston J. Coulam, Glenn E. Dance, Carol Kulish

Nat'l Ass'n of Jai-Alai Frontons, Inc.

Leg. Issues: GAM

Outside Counsel/Consultants

The MWW Group
Issues: GAM
Rep By: Elizabeth A. Iadarola, Jonathan B. Slade

Nat'l Ass'n of Jewish Legislators

P.O. Box 42442
Washington, DC 20015
E-mail: najleg@aol.com
Tel: (202)494-7991

Membership organization for Jewish state legislators, focusing on state and federal legislative issues important to the Jewish community. Those issues include: the security of Israel and relations with other civil rights organizations.

Leg. Issues: CIV, GOV

In-house, DC-area Employees

WICE, Jeffrey M.: Counsel

Nat'l Ass'n of Letter Carriers of the United States of America

100 Indiana Ave. NW
Washington, DC 20001
Web: www.nalc.org
Tel: (202)393-4695
Fax: (202)737-1540
Registered: LDA

A collective bargaining representative of city delivery letter carriers employed by the U.S. Postal Service.

Leg. Issues: ADV, BUD, HCR, LBR, MMM, POS, RET, VET

Political Action Committee/s

Committee on Letter Carriers' Political Education
100 Indiana Ave. NW
Washington, DC 20001
Contact: Don Tomlinson
Tel: (202)393-4695
Fax: (202)756-7400

In-house, DC-area Employees

BROWN, Ronald G.: V. President
GOULD, George B.: Assistant to the President for Legislative and Political Affairs
LAPLACA, Joseph: Director, Retired Members
SEGAL, Allen: Special Assistant, Legislation
SOMBROTTO, Vincent R.: President
TOMLINSON, Don: Special Assistant, Political Education
VON BERGEN, Drew: Director, Public Relations
YOUNG, William H.: Exec. V. President

Nat'l Ass'n of Lottery Purchasers

Washington, DC

Outside Counsel/Consultants

William S. Bergman Associates
Rep By: Deborah Beck, William S. Bergman, CAE

Nat'l Ass'n of Manufacturers

1331 Pennsylvania Ave. NW
Sixth Floor
Washington, DC 20004-1790
Web: www.nam.org
E-mail: manufacturing@nam.org
Tel: (202)637-3000
Fax: (202)637-3182
Registered: LDA

NAM's mission is to enhance the future competitiveness of manufacturers and improve the standard of living for working Americans by shaping a legislative and regulatory climate conducive to U.S. economic growth and increasing the level of understanding between policy makers, the media, and the general public about the importance of manufacturing to America's economic strength.

Leg. Issues: ANI, BUD, CAW, CPT, CSP, ECN, ENV, FIN, FOR, GOV, HCR, IMM, LBR, MAN, MMM, NAT, RES, RET, SMB, TAX, TOR, TRA, TRD, WAS

In-house, DC-area Employees

AMUNDSON, Jan S.: V. President, Law Department and General Counsel
BAROODY, Michael E.: Exec. V. President
BIRO, Ladd K.: Senior V. President, Marketing, Member Communications and Services
BOYD, Sandra: Assistant V. President, Employment Policy
CLEARY, Patrick J.: V. President, Human Resources Policy
COLEMAN, Dorothy: V. President, Tax Policy
GARRITSON, Dean: V. President, Small and Medium Manufacturers
GOLD, Stephen: Exec. Director, Associations Council
JASINOWSKI, Jerry J.: President
KURKUL, Douglas R.: Assistant V. President, Member Communications
NARVAIZ, Laura: V. President, Communications
NICHOLS, Frederic A.: V. President, Public Affairs and Political Director
PRENDERGAST, Jim: National Director, Field Division
VARGO, Franklin J.: V. President, International Economic Affairs
WHITENTON, Mark: V. President, Resources, Environment and Regulation

Outside Counsel/Consultants

William M. Mercer, Inc.
Issues: HCR
Rep By: Mark Hamelburg, William M. Mercer

Nat'l Ass'n of Margarine Manufacturers

1101 15th St. NW
Suite 202
Washington, DC 20005
Web: www.margarine.org
E-mail: namm@assnhq.com
Tel: (202)785-3232
Fax: (202)223-9741
Leg. Issues: FOO

In-house, DC-area Employees

CRISTOL, Richard E.: President

Outside Counsel/Consultants

The Kellen Company
Rep By: Richard E. Cristol

Olsson, Frank and Weeda, P.C.
Issues: FOO
Rep By: John W. Bode, Susan P. Grymes, Karen Reis Harned, Stephen L. Lacey, Marshall L. Matz, Philip C. Olsson, Tyson Redpath, Ryan W. Stroschein

Nat'l Ass'n of Medicaid Directors

810 First St. NE
Suite 500
Washington, DC 20002
Web: www.aphsa.org
Tel: (202)682-0100
Fax: (202)289-6555

Formerly known as State Medicaid Directors Ass'n.

In-house, DC-area Employees

PARTRIDGE, Lee: Director, Health Policy

Nat'l Ass'n of Metal Finishers

112 Elden St.
Unit J
Herndon, VA 20170
Web: www.namf.org
E-mail: info@namf.org
Tel: (703)709-8299
Fax: (703)709-1036
Registered: LDA

Represents independent member surface finishing firms. Purpose is to advance, protect and perpetuate the surface finishing industry, and to develop the highest standards of service, quality and conduct. The above address is that of Barrack Ass'n Management. David W. Barrack, Josh Gold, Sarah-Jane Ziaya, and Nancy Campbell, all of Barrack Ass'n Management, serve as Exec. Director, Deputy Director, Membership Coordinator, and Exec. Assistant respectively.

Political Action Committee/s

Nat'l Ass'n of Metal Finishers Political Action Committee
112 Elden St.
Unit J
Herndon, VA 20170
Tel: (703)709-8299
Fax: (703)709-1036

In-house, DC-area Employees

BARRACK, David W.: Exec. Director
CAMPBELL, Nancy A.: Membership Coordinator
GOLD, Josh: Deputy Director

Outside Counsel/Consultants

Barrack Ass'n Management
Rep By: David W. Barrack

Nat'l Ass'n of Military Widows

4023 25th Rd. North
Arlington, VA 22207
Tel: (703)527-4565
Fax: (703)527-3881

In-house, DC-area Employees

ARTHURS, Jean: Legislative Liaison-President

Nat'l Ass'n of Minority Automobile Dealers

Lanham, MD
Web: www.namad.com
E-mail: namad-dc@email.msn.com
Leg. Issues: AUT, CIV, TRA, TRD

Outside Counsel/Consultants

James M. Williams, Jr.
Issues: AUT, CIV, TRA, TRD
Rep By: James M. Williams, Jr.

Nat'l Ass'n of Minority Contractors

666 11th St. NW
Suite 520
Washington, DC 20001
Web: www.n-a-m-c.com
E-mail: namc@verizonmail.com
Tel: (202)347-8259
Fax: (202)628-1876

Established in 1969. A non-profit minority trade association which addresses the needs and concerns of minority construction companies and contractors nationwide. Offers a variety of services to its membership, including information dissemination, educational training and advocacy.

In-house, DC-area Employees

TRUITT, William: Exec. Director

Nat'l Ass'n of Minority Political Families, USA, Inc.

6120 Oregon Ave. NW
Washington, DC 20015
Tel: (202)686-1216
Fax: (202)686-0598

Membership includes registered voters without regard to political party affiliation. Education, research, training, and scholarship are primary focuses. Issue-oriented, 501(C)3 non-partisan organization.

Leg. Issues: CIV, EDU, HCR, HOU, MMM

In-house, DC-area Employees

IVEY, Mary E.: President and Chief Exec. Officer

Nat'l Ass'n of Miscellaneous, Ornamental and Architectural Products Contractors

10382 Main St.
Suite 200
P.O. Box 280
Fairfax, VA 22030
Tel: (703)591-1870
Fax: (703)591-1895
Leg. Issues: INS, LBR, TRA

In-house, DC-area Employees

CODDING, Fred H.

Nat'l Ass'n of Mortgage Brokers

5185 MacArthur Blvd. NW
Washington, DC 20016
Web: www.namb.org
E-mail: turner@lotsteinbuckman.com
Tel: (202)237-6000
Fax: (202)237-8900
Registered: LDA

Headquartered in McLean, VA. Below address is that of the firm Lotstein Buckman.

Leg. Issues: BAN, BNK, FIN, HOU, RES

Political Action Committee/s

Nat'l Ass'n of Mortgage Brokers PAC
5185 MacArthur Blvd. NW
Washington, DC 20016
Contact: Susan Turner
Tel: (202)237-6000
Fax: (202)237-8900

In-house, DC-area Employees

LOTSTEIN, Robert: V. President, Government Affairs
TURNER, Susan: PAC Contact

Outside Counsel/Consultants

Ass'n Management Group
Issues: BAN, BNK, FIN, HOU, RES
Rep By: Mike Nizankiewicz

Lotstein Buckman, Attorneys At Law
Issues: BAN, HOU
Rep By: Robert Lotstein, Susan Turner

Nat'l Ass'n of Music Merchants

Carlsbad, CA
Leg. Issues: EDU, TAX

Outside Counsel/Consultants

The Wexler Group
Issues: EDU, TAX
Rep By: Cynthia E. Berry, Peter T. Holran, Joel Malina, Christine Maroulis, Hon. Robert S. Walker, Anne Wexler

Nat'l Ass'n of Mutual Insurance Companies

122 C St. NW
Suite 540
Washington, DC 20001
Web: www.namic.org
Tel: (202)628-1558
Fax: (202)628-1601
Registered: LDA

Headquartered in Indianapolis, IN.

Leg. Issues: INS

Political Action Committee/s

Nat'l Ass'n of Mutual Insurance Companies Political Action Committee (NAMIC-PAC)
122 C St. NW
Suite 540
Washington, DC 20001
Contact: Pamela J. Allen
Tel: (202)628-1558
Fax: (202)628-1601

In-house, DC-area Employees
ALLEN, Pamela J.: V. President, Federal Affairs
GIBSON, Jennifer: Director, Federal Affairs
WARD, Monte N.: Director, Federal Affairs

Outside Counsel/Consultants
Sutherland Asbill & Brennan LLP

Nat'l Ass'n of Naturopathic Physicians

McLean, VA

Outside Counsel/Consultants
Ass'n Management Group
Rep By: Maria Bianchi

Nat'l Ass'n of Negro Business & Professional Women's Clubs, Inc.

1806 New Hampshire Ave. NW
Washington, DC 20009
Tel: (202)483-4206
Fax: (202)462-7253
Web: www.nanbpwc.org

A 10,000 member association of black business and professional women with a mission of improving the quality of life in American communities. Through seminars, publications and leadership training programs, the Association educates its constituencies about contemporary social issues and relevant legislation on the local, state and national levels of government.

Leg. Issues: ACC, ADV, AGR, ALC, ART, BAN, BUD, CAW, CIV, COM, CSP, DOC, ECN, EDU, FAM, FIN, FOR, GOV, HCR, HOU, IND, INS, LAW, LBR, MAN, MED, MIA, RES, RET, SCI, SMB, TAX, TRD, UNM, URB, WEL

In-house, DC-area Employees
IVORY, Glo: Exec. Director

Nat'l Ass'n of Neighborhoods

1651 Fuller St. NW
Washington, DC 20009
Tel: (202)332-7766
Fax: (202)332-2314

Urban and rural organizations and coalitions working to strengthen neighborhood rights and responsibilities.

In-house, DC-area Employees
BYRD, Ricardo: Exec. Director

Nat'l Ass'n of Nurse Practitioners in Women's Health

503 Capitol Ct. NE
Suite 300
Washington, DC 20002
Tel: (202)543-9693
Fax: (202)543-9858
Web: www.npwh.org
E-mail: npwhdc@aol.com

A national membership organization whose mission is to ensure the provision of quality reproductive and women's health by nurse practitioners and other nurses. Publishes Practice Guidelines and is recognized by the U.S. Department of Education to accredit women's health nurse practitioners programs. Formerly known as Nat'l Ass'n of Nurse Practitioners in Reproductive Health.

Leg. Issues: ALC, EDU, FAM, HCR, MMM, PHA, SCI, WEL

In-house, DC-area Employees
WYSOCKI, Susan: President

Nat'l Ass'n of Nutrition and Aging Services and Programs

Grand Rapids, MI
Web: www.nanasp.org
E-mail: rossem@erols.com

Outside Counsel/Consultants
Matz, Blancato & Associates, Inc.

Nat'l Ass'n of Older Worker Employment Services

409 Third St. SW
Second Floor
Washington, DC 20024-6682
Tel: (202)479-6632
Fax: (202)479-6664
Web: www.ncoa.org

An organization of the Nat'l Council on the Aging. Promotes expansion of voluntary placement programs to increase job opportunities for older adults.

In-house, DC-area Employees
DAVIS, Don: V. President

Nat'l Ass'n of Optometrics and Opticians

Marblehead, OH
Leg. Issues: HCR

Outside Counsel/Consultants
Baker & Hostetler LLP
Issues: HCR
Rep By: Matthew J. Dolan, Frederick H. Graefe, Richard H. Hauser, Hon. Guy Vander Jagt

Nat'l Ass'n of Partners in Education

901 N. Pitt St.
Suite 320
Alexandria, VA 22314
Tel: (703)836-4880
Fax: (703)836-6941
Web: www.partnersineducation.org
E-mail: napehq@napehq.org

Encourages partnerships between schools or school districts and community organizations, business, and civic groups.

Leg. Issues: EDU

In-house, DC-area Employees
HERSHMAN, Esther: Symposium Coordinator
MERENDA, Daniel W.: President and Chief Exec. Officer

Nat'l Ass'n of Pediatric Nurse Associates and Practitioners

Cherry Hill, NJ
Leg. Issues: HCR

Outside Counsel/Consultants
Arent Fox Kintner Plotkin & Kahn, PLLC
Issues: HCR
Rep By: Stacy Harbison, Allison Shuren

Nat'l Ass'n of People with AIDS, Inc.

1413 K St. NW
Seventh Floor
Washington, DC 20005-3442
Tel: (202)898-0414
Fax: (202)898-0435
Registered: LDA
Web: www.napwa.org
E-mail: napwa@napwa.org

A national advocacy and consumer health education resource for all people living with HIV and AIDS and those who care for them.

Leg. Issues: BUD, CAW, CIV, HCR, INS, MED, MMM, TAX

In-house, DC-area Employees
ANDERSON, Terje: Exec. Director
FARMER, Anthony: Deputy Exec. Director

Nat'l Ass'n of Personal Financial Advisors

Wolfboro, NH
Leg. Issues: FIN

Outside Counsel/Consultants
Hogan & Hartson L.L.P.
Issues: FIN
Rep By: James G. McMillan

Nat'l Ass'n of Personnel Services

3133 Mount Vernon Ave.
Alexandria, VA 22305
Tel: (703)684-0180
Fax: (703)684-0071
Web: www.napsweb.org
E-mail: dcallis@napsweb.org

Members are personnel service firms.

In-house, DC-area Employees
CALLIS, Dianne B.: President

Outside Counsel/Consultants
J. C. Luman and Assoc.
Rep By: Joseph C. Luman

Nat'l Ass'n of Pharmaceutical Manufacturers

New York, NY
Leg. Issues: BUD, PHA

Outside Counsel/Consultants
Olsson, Frank and Weeda, P.C.
Issues: BUD, PHA
Rep By: John W. Bode, Pamela J. Furman, Susan P. Grymes, Karen Reis Harned, Stephen L. Lacey, Marshall L. Matz, Tyson Redpath, Ryan W. Stroschein, Arthur Y. Tsien, David F. Weeda

Nat'l Ass'n of Physician Nurses

900 S. Washington St.
Suite G-13
Falls Church, VA 22046
Tel: (703)237-8616
Fax: (703)533-1153
Leg. Issues: HCR

In-house, DC-area Employees
YOUNG, S.: Director

Nat'l Ass'n of Plant Patent Owners

1250 I St. NW
Suite 500
Washington, DC 20005
Tel: (202)789-2900
Fax: (202)789-1893
Web: www.anla.org

In-house, DC-area Employees
DOLIBOIS, Robert: Exec. V. President
REGELBRUGGE, Craig J.: Administrator

Nat'l Ass'n of Police Organizations

750 First St. NE
Suite 920
Washington, DC 20002-4241
Tel: (202)842-4420
Fax: (202)842-4396
Registered: LDA
Web: www.napo.org
E-mail: napo@erols.com

A coalition of over 4,000 police unions and associations across the U.S., representing over 220,000 law enforcement officers. Purpose is to advance the interests of America's law enforcement officers through legislative advocacy, political action and education.

Leg. Issues: BNK, BUD, COM, DEF, EDU, FIN, FIR, LAW, LBR, MED, TAX, TEC, TOB, TRA, TRU

Political Action Committee/s

Nat'l Ass'n of Police Organizations Political Action Committee Inc.

750 First St. NE
Suite 920
Washington, DC 20002-4241
Tel: (202)842-4420
Fax: (202)842-4396
Contact: Robert T. Scully

In-house, DC-area Employees
MCSPADDEN, Steven: General Counsel
SCULLY, Robert T.: Exec. Director
TROUBH, Mikael: Legislative Assistant

Nat'l Ass'n of Portable X-Ray Providers

St. Joseph, MO
Leg. Issues: GOV, HCR, MMM, SMB

Outside Counsel/Consultants
Halsey, Rains & Associates, LLC
Issues: GOV, HCR, MMM, SMB
Rep By: Steven C. Halsey, James Hubbard, Laurie D. Rains

Nat'l Ass'n of Postal Supervisors

1727 King St.
Suite 400
Alexandria, VA 22314-2753
Tel: (703)836-9660
Fax: (703)836-9665
Registered: LDA
Web: www.naps.org
E-mail: napshq@naps.org

Political Action Committee/s

Nat'l Ass'n of Postal Supervisors Political Action Committee

1727 King St.
Suite 400
Alexandria, VA 22314-2753
Tel: (703)836-9660
Fax: (703)836-9665
Contact: Ted Keating

In-house, DC-area Employees
KEATING, Ted: Exec. V. President
PALLADINO, Vincent: President

Outside Counsel/Consultants
The Moyer Group
Rep By: Bruce L. Moyer

Nat'l Ass'n of Postmasters of the U.S.

Eight Herbert St.
Alexandria, VA 22305-2600
Tel: (703)683-9027
Fax: (703)683-6820
Registered: LDA
Web: www.napus.org
E-mail: napus6@napus.org
Leg. Issues: POS

Political Action Committee/s

Nat'l Ass'n of Postmasters of the U.S. PAC for Postmasters

Eight Herbert St.
Alexandria, VA 22305-2600
Tel: (703)683-9027
Fax: (703)683-6820

In-house, DC-area Employees
GOOF, Dale: Secretary-Treasurer
LEVI, Robert: Director, Government Relations
MOSER, Charles E.: National President

Nat'l Ass'n of Private Industry Councils

1201 New York Ave. NW
Suite 350
Washington, DC 20005
Tel: (202)289-2950
Fax: (202)289-2846
Web: www.nawb.org
E-mail: nawb@nawb.org

Founded in 1979 as a service organization representing local private industry councils created by the Job Training Partnership Act. Focuses on employment and training policy and programming.

In-house, DC-area Employees
KNIGHT, Robert: President

Nat'l Ass'n of Professional Employer Organizations

901 N. Pitt St.
Suite 150
Alexandria, VA 22314
Web: www.napeo.org
E-mail: info@napeo.org
Tel: (703)836-0466
Fax: (703)836-0976

Represents professional employer organizations and provides programs and services on human resource, pension, pay roll and benefit services.

Leg. Issues: HCR, LBR, RET, TAX

In-house, DC-area Employees

YAGER, Milan P.: Executive V. President

Outside Counsel/Consultants

Davis & Harman LLP
Issues: RET, TAX
Rep By: Randolf H. Hardock

McDermott, Will and Emery
Issues: RET, TAX
Rep By: David R. Fuller, David Rogers

Washington Council Ernst & Young
Issues: HCR, LBR, RET, TAX
Rep By: Doug Badger, Lauren Darling, John L. Doney, Jayne T. Fitzgerald, LaBrenda Garrett-Nelson, Gary J. Gasper, Bruce A. Gates, Nick Giordano, Cathy Koch, Robert J. Leonard, Richard Meltzer, Phillip D. Moseley, John D. Porter, Robert M. Rozen, Donna Steele-Flynn, Timothy J. Urban

Nat'l Ass'n of Professional Forestry Schools and Colleges

Leg. Issues: BUD, NAT

Outside Counsel/Consultants

Long, Aldridge & Norman, LLP
Issues: BUD, NAT
Rep By: C. Randall Nuckolls, Patrick C. Turner

Nat'l Ass'n of Professional Insurance Agents

400 N. Washington St.
Alexandria, VA 22314-9980
Tel: (703)836-9340
Fax: (703)836-1279
Registered: LDA
Web: www.pianet.com
E-mail: piaweb@pianet.org
Leg. Issues: BAN, INS

Political Action Committee/s

Professional Insurance Agents' Political Action Committee
400 N. Washington St.
Alexandria, VA 22314-9980
Contact: Kellie Bray
Tel: (703)836-9340
Fax: (703)836-1279

In-house, DC-area Employees

BRAY, Kellie: Director, Political Affairs
EBERHART, Gary: Exec. V. President
GREENWOOD, Sheila M.: Assistant V. President, Government Affairs

Outside Counsel/Consultants

Collier Shannon Scott, PLLC
Issues: BAN, INS
Rep By: Scott A. Sinder

Nat'l Ass'n of Protection and Advocacy Systems (NAPAS)

900 Second St. NE
Suite 211
Washington, DC 20002
Tel: (202)408-9514
Fax: (202)408-9520
Registered: LDA
Web: www.protectionandadvocacy.com
E-mail: napas@earthlink.net

An association of protection and advocacy agencies and client assistance programs throughout the nation. Members provide legal administration, information and referrals to people with disabilities. The Association provides guidance on and responses to legislation that affects people with disabilities.

Leg. Issues: ALC, BUD, CIV, CON, EDU, HCR, HOU, MMM, SCI, TRA

In-house, DC-area Employees

DECKER, Curtis: Exec. Director
SPOOR, Barbara: Deputy Director, Training and Technical Assistance
WARD, Jim: Deputy Director, Public Policy

Nat'l Ass'n of Psychiatric Health Systems

325 Seventh St. NW
Suite 625
Washington, DC 20004-2802
Tel: (202)393-6700
Fax: (202)783-6041
Registered: LDA
Web: www.naphs.org
E-mail: naphs@naphs.org

Advocates for behavioral health and represents provider systems that are committed to the delivery of responsive, accountable, and clinically effective prevention, treatment and care for children, adolescents and adults with mental and substance abuse disorders.

Leg. Issues: BUD, HCR, MMM

Political Action Committee/s

Nat'l Ass'n of Psychiatric Health Systems Political Action Committee
325 Seventh St. NW
Suite 625
Washington, DC 20004-2802
Tel: (202)393-6700
Fax: (202)783-6041

In-house, DC-area Employees

COVALL, Mark: Exec. Director
PERRIN, Cidette S.: Director, Legislative and Regulatory Affairs
SZPAK, Carole: Director, Communications

Outside Counsel/Consultants

Capitol Health Group, LLC
Rep By: Michael D. Bromberg, Shawn Coughlin, Steven Jenning, Layna McConkey Peltier

Crowell & Moring LLP

Nat'l Ass'n of Psychiatric Treatment Centers for Children

1025 Connecticut Ave. NW
Suite 1012
Washington, DC 20036
E-mail: naptcc@aol.com
Tel: (202)857-9735
Fax: (202)362-5145

Works for the availability of comprehensive treatment services for persons under the age of 21with emotional problems and their families through active lobbying, public policy development, education and political action.

Political Action Committee/s

Nat'l Ass'n of Psychiatric Treatment Centers for Children Political Action Committee
1025 Connecticut Ave. NW
Suite 1012
Washington, DC 20036
Contact: Joy Midman
Tel: (202)857-9735
Fax: (202)362-5145

In-house, DC-area Employees

MIDMAN, Joy: Exec. Director

Nat'l Ass'n of Public Hospitals and Health Systems

1301 Pennsylvania Ave. NW
Suite 950
Washington, DC 20004
Tel: (202)585-0100
Fax: (202)585-0101
Registered: LDA
Web: www.naph.org
E-mail: cburch@naph.org

Represents urban safety net hospitals and patients they serve.

Leg. Issues: HCR, IMM, INS, MMM, PHA, TOB

In-house, DC-area Employees

BURCH, Christine C.: Exec. Director
CARRIER, Elizabeth: V. President, Managed Care
FAGNANI, Lynn P.: V. President, Finance and Reimbursement

Outside Counsel/Consultants

Powell, Goldstein, Frazer & Murphy LLP
Issues: IMM, INS, MMM, TOB
Rep By: Charlotte Collins, Barbara D. A. Eyman, Simon Lazarus, III, Charles Luband, Ted Slafsky, William H. E. von Oehsen

Nat'l Ass'n of Public Insurance Adjusters

112 Elden St.
Unit J
Herndon, VA 20170
Web: www.napia.com
E-mail: napia@erols.com
Tel: (703)709-8254
Fax: (703)709-1036

Established in 1951 to promote and protect the interests of public insurance adjusting professionals. The above address is that of Barrack Ass'n Management.

In-house, DC-area Employees

BARRACK, David W.: Exec. Director
WILMOT, John: Deputy Director

Outside Counsel/Consultants

Barrack Ass'n Management
Rep By: David W. Barrack

Nat'l Ass'n of Railroad Passengers

900 Second St. NE
Suite 308
Washington, DC 20002-3557
Tel: (202)408-8362
Fax: (202)408-8287
Registered: LDA
Web: www.narprail.org
E-mail: narp@narprail.org

In-house, DC-area Employees

CAPON, Ross: Exec. Director
LEONARD, Scott: Assistant Director
YORKER, Alan M.: President

Nat'l Ass'n of RC&D Councils

Outside Counsel/Consultants

The PMA Group
Rep By: Fred J. Clark, Kaylene Green, Paul J. Magliocchetti, Mark Rokala

Nat'l Ass'n of Real Estate Brokers

1629 K St. NW
Suite 602
Washington, DC 20006
Web: www.nareb.com
E-mail: abrown@nareb.com
Tel: (202)785-4477
Fax: (202)785-1244

In-house, DC-area Employees

CLARK, Ernest: President and Chief Exec. Officer

Nat'l Ass'n of Real Estate Investment Trusts

1875 I St. NW
Suite 600
Washington, DC 20006
Tel: (202)739-9400
Fax: (202)739-9401
Registered: LDA
Web: www.nareit.com
Leg. Issues: RES, TAX, TEC

Political Action Committee/s

Nat'l Ass'n of Real Estate Investment Trusts PAC (NAREIT PAC)
1875 I St. NW
Suite 600
Washington, DC 20006
Contact: Martin L. DePoy
Tel: (202)739-9400
Fax: (202)739-9401

In-house, DC-area Employees

CHASON, Anna: Public Affairs Counsel
DEPOY, Martin L.: V. President, Government Relations
EDWARDS, Tony M.: Senior V. President and General Counsel
FREEDMAN, Dara: Counsel
GRUPE, Michael: Senior V. President, Research
LISSAU, Jacqueline: Political Affairs Coordinator
QUIGLEY, Jr., Joseph J.: Director, Government Relations
WECHSLER, Steven A.: President and Chief Exec. Officer

Outside Counsel/Consultants

Baker & Hostetler LLP
Issues: TAX
Rep By: William F. Conroy, Matthew J. Dolan, Frederick H. Graefe, Kathleen M. Kerrigan, Steven A. Lotterer, David L. Marshall, Hon. Guy Vander Jagt

Bergner Bockorny Castagnetti and Hawkins
Issues: TAX
Rep By: Jeffrey T. Bergner, David A. Bockorny, David Castagnetti, James W. Hawkins, Melissa Schulman

Washington Council Ernst & Young
Issues: TAX, TEC
Rep By: Doug Badger, Lauren Darling, John L. Doney, Jayne T. Fitzgerald, LaBrenda Garrett-Nelson, Gary J. Gasper, Bruce A. Gates, Nick Giordano, Cathy Koch, Robert J. Leonard, Richard Meltzer, Phillip D. Moseley, John D. Porter, Robert M. Rozen, Donna Steele-Flynn, Timothy J. Urban

The Washington Group
Issues: RES, TAX
Rep By: Rita M. Lewis, G. John O'Hanlon, John D. Raffaelli, Tonya Saunders, Mark Schnabel, Fowler West

Nat'l Ass'n of Realtors

700 11th St. NW
Washington, DC 20001-4507
Tel: (202)383-1000
Fax: (202)383-7540
Registered: LDA
Web: www.realtors.com
Leg. Issues: BAN, BNK, CIV, CON, ENV, FIN, HOU, RES, TAX, TEC, TOR

Political Action Committee/s

Nat'l Ass'n of REALTORS Political Action Committee
700 11th St. NW
Washington, DC 20001-4507
Contact: Greg Knopp
Tel: (202)383-1207
Fax: (202)383-7540

In-house, DC-area Employees

BROWN, Brenda: Housing Policy Representative
CLARKE, James B.: Political Representative
COOK, Steve: V. President, Public Affairs
DELGADO, Jeanne: Business Issues Policy Representative
DENNIS, Patrick: Political Representative
FERRUGIARO, John E.: Political Representative
FLETCHER, Amy: Legislative Representative
FRIDAY SCOTT, Lisa: Political Programs Representative
GIOVANIELLO, Gerard: V. President, Government Affairs
GOOLD, Linda: Director, Federal Taxation
GREGORY, Jamie: Legislative Representative
GRIFFIN, III, L. George: Real Estate Finance Policy Representative
KNOPP, Greg: Senior RPAC Representative
MAHEADY, Joseph: Environment Policy Representative
MCPHERSON, Laura: Legislative Representative
MILLER, Doug: Representative, Commercial Finance Policy
MILLER, Edward C.: Business Issues Policy Representative

MORGAN, Peter Denis: Senior Federal Regulations Representative
RIGGS, Russell: Environmental Policy Representative
SADLIER, Lizanne: Political Representative
SAUNDERS, Jane L.: Political Representative
SEBREE, John M.: Legislative Representative
UNDERWOOD, Fred: Senior Fair Housing Policy Representative
VERSTANDIG, Lee L.: Senior V. President, Government Affairs
WEAVER, Gary: Housing Policy Representative
WITEK, Walt: V. President, Government Affairs

Outside Counsel/Consultants

Bonner & Associates

Keelen Communications

Nat'l Ass'n of Recording Merchandisers

Marlton, NJ
Leg. Issues: ART, CON, CSP, LAW

Outside Counsel/Consultants

Jenkens & Gilchrist
Issues: ART, CON, CSP, LAW
Rep By: John T. Mitchell

Jenner & Block

Nat'l Ass'n of Regional Councils

1700 K St. NW
13th Floor
Washington, DC 20006-0011
Tel: (202)457-0710
Fax: (202)296-9352
Web: www.narc.org
E-mail: nykwst@narc.org

Represents councils of local governments for metropolitan and rural regions concerned with federal, state and local programs affecting housing; transportation; community, economic and rural development; air, water, solid waste, coastal zone management; criminal justice; health and aging with emphasis on area-wide planning. Also fosters regional cooperation among public, private, civic and other regional organizations and interests.

In-house, DC-area Employees

BOSLEY, John J.: Legal Counsel
CHAPPELEAR-MARSHALL, Patsy: Director of Operations
DODGE, Bill: Exec. Director
NYKWEST, Beverly C.: Director of Policy

Nat'l Ass'n of Regulatory Utility Commissioners

1101 Vermont Ave. NW
Suite 200
Washington, DC 20005
Tel: (202)898-2200
Fax: (202)898-2213
Web: www.naruc.org
E-mail: cgray@naruc.org

In-house, DC-area Employees

BARKLIND, Sharla M.: Assistant General Counsel
GRAY, Charles D.: Exec. Director
MALLOY, Michelle: Director, Meetings
MELE, Chris: Legislative Director
RAMSAY, James Bradford: General Counsel
ZUFOLO, Jessica: Legislative Director

Nat'l Ass'n of Rehabilitation Agencies

11250 Roger Bacon Dr.
Suite Eight
Reston, VA 20190
Tel: (703)437-4377
Fax: (703)435-4390
Web: www.naranet.org
E-mail: rruggolz@drohanmgmt.com
Leg. Issues: MMM

Political Action Committee/s

Nat'l Ass'n of Rehabilitation Agencies, Inc. Political Action Committee

11250 Roger Bacon Dr.
Suite Eight
Reston, VA 20190
Tel: (703)437-4377
Fax: (703)435-4390

In-house, DC-area Employees

GUGGOLZ, Richard A.: Exec. Director

Outside Counsel/Consultants

Williams & Jensen, P.C.
Issues: MMM
Rep By: George G. Olsen

Nat'l Ass'n of Rehabilitation Professionals in the Private Sector

Framingham, MA

Outside Counsel/Consultants

Fleishman-Hillard, Inc

Nat'l Ass'n of Rehabilitation Research and Training Centers

Lawrence, KS

Outside Counsel/Consultants

Powers Pyles Sutter & Verville, PC
Rep By: Richard E. Verville

Nat'l Ass'n of Reinforcing Steel Contractors

10382 Main St.
Suite 200
P.O. Box 280
Fairfax, VA 22030
Tel: (703)591-1870
Fax: (703)591-1895
Leg. Issues: INS, LBR, TRA

In-house, DC-area Employees

CODDING, Fred H.: Exec. Director and General Counsel

Nat'l Ass'n of Resource Conservation

Washington, DC

Outside Counsel/Consultants

The PMA Group
Rep By: Fred J. Clark, Kaylene Green, Paul J. Magliocchetti, Mark Rokala, Timothy K. Sanders, Dana Stewart

Nat'l Ass'n of Retail Collection Attorneys

8201 Greensboro Dr.
Suite 300
McLean, VA 22102
Tel: (703)610-9000
Fax: (703)610-9005
Web: www.narca.org
E-mail: ddarrow@narca.org

The address given is that of the firm Ass'n Management Group (see separate listing).

Leg. Issues: BAN, BNK, CSP

In-house, DC-area Employees

DARROW, Diane L.: Exec. Director

Outside Counsel/Consultants

Arent Fox Kintner Plotkin & Kahn, PLLC
Issues: CSP
Rep By: Michael T. McNamara, Deanne M. Ottaviano, Kerry Reichs

Ass'n Management Group
Rep By: Kathy Allison, Diane L. Darrow

Nat'l Ass'n of Retired and Senior Volunteer Program Directors

Newport News, VA
Leg. Issues: BUD, GOV

Outside Counsel/Consultants

Valente Lopatin & Schulze
Issues: BUD, GOV
Rep By: Alan G. Lopatin

Nat'l Ass'n of Retired Federal Employees

606 N. Washington St.
Alexandria, VA 22314
Tel: (703)838-7760
Fax: (703)838-7782
Registered: LDA
Web: www.narfe.org
E-mail: natlhq@narfe.org
Leg. Issues: BUD, GOV, HCR, MMM, RET, TAX

Political Action Committee/s

Nat'l Ass'n of Retired Federal Employees Political Action Committee

606 N. Washington St.
Alexandria, VA 22314
Tel: (703)838-7760
Fax: (703)838-7782
Contact: Judith E. Park

In-house, DC-area Employees

ADCOCK, Daniel C.: Assistant Director, Legislation
ATWATER, Frank G.: President
FARRELL, Chris: Legislative Representative
PARK, Judith E.: Director, Legislation

Outside Counsel/Consultants

Ledge Counsel
Issues: GOV, HCR, RET

Valente Lopatin & Schulze
Issues: BUD, HCR, RET
Rep By: Alan G. Lopatin

Nat'l Ass'n of Rural Health Clinics

Leg. Issues: HCR, MMM

Outside Counsel/Consultants

Capitol Associates, Inc.
Issues: HCR, MMM
Rep By: William A. Finerfrock, Matthew Williams

Nat'l Ass'n of RV Parks and Campgrounds

113 Park Ave.
Falls Church, VA 22046
Tel: (703)241-8801
Fax: (703)241-1004
Web: www.gocampingamerica.com
E-mail: arvc@erols.com
Leg. Issues: CAW, CPT, ENG, FUE, GOV, HCR, MAR, NAT, RES, SMB, TAX, TOU

In-house, DC-area Employees

GORIN, David: President and Chief Exec. Officer

Outside Counsel/Consultants

Albertine Enterprises, Inc.
Issues: TOU
Rep By: Aubrey C. King

Nat'l Ass'n of SBA Microloan Intermediaries

Columbus, OH
Leg. Issues: SMB

Outside Counsel/Consultants

Robert A. Rapoza Associates
Issues: SMB
Rep By: Alison Feighan, Robert A. Rapoza

Nat'l Ass'n of School Music Dealers

Dallas, TX

Outside Counsel/Consultants

Goldberg & Associates, PLLC
Rep By: James M. Goldberg

Nat'l Ass'n of School Nurses

Scarborough, ME
Leg. Issues: EDU, HCR

Outside Counsel/Consultants

Arent Fox Kintner Plotkin & Kahn, PLLC
Issues: EDU, HCR
Rep By: Stacy Harbison, Michael T. McNamara, Elliott I. Portnoy, Allison Shuren, Robert J. Waters

Nat'l Ass'n of School Psychologists

4340 East-West Hwy.
Suite 402
Bethesda, MD 20814
Tel: (301)657-0270
Fax: (301)657-0275
Registered: LDA
Web: www.naspweb.org
E-mail: nasp@naspweb.org

School psychologist professional association which covers areas to promote educationally and psychologically healthy environments for all children and youth by implementing research-based, effective programs that prevent problems, enhance independence and promote optional learning.

Leg. Issues: EDU, HCR

In-house, DC-area Employees

BARZIER, Marilyn: Deputy Exec. Director
GORIN, Susan: Exec. Director
MORGAN, Linda: Director, Communications & Professional Projects

Nat'l Ass'n of Schools of Art and Design

11250 Roger Bacon Dr.
Suite 21
Reston, VA 20190-5202
Tel: (703)437-0700
Fax: (703)437-6312
Web: www.arts-accredit.org
E-mail: info@arts-accredit.org

In-house, DC-area Employees

HOPE, Samuel: Exec. Director

Nat'l Ass'n of Schools of Dance

11250 Roger Bacon Dr.
Suite 21
Reston, VA 20190-5202
Tel: (703)437-0700
Fax: (703)437-6312
Web: www.arts-accredit.org
E-mail: info@arts-accredit.org

Accreditation of post-secondary educational programs in dance.

Leg. Issues: EDU

In-house, DC-area Employees

HOPE, Samuel: Exec. Director

Nat'l Ass'n of Schools of Music

11250 Roger Bacon Dr.
Suite 21
Reston, VA 20190-5202
Tel: (703)437-0700
Fax: (703)437-6312
Web: www.arts-accredit.org
E-mail: info@arts-accredit.org

Accreditation of educational programs in music.

Leg. Issues: EDU

In-house, DC-area Employees

HOPE, Samuel: Exec. Director

Nat'l Ass'n of Schools of Public Affairs and Administration

1120 G St. NW
Suite 730
Washington, DC 20005
Tel: (202)628-8965
Fax: (202)626-4978
Web: www.naspaa.org
E-mail: naspaa@naspaa.org

An academic association for public service education and research in public policy and administration on the college and university level.

In-house, DC-area Employees

BRINTNALL, Michael A.: Exec. Director

Nat'l Ass'n of Schools of Theatre

11250 Roger Bacon Dr.
Suite 21
Reston, VA 20190-5202
Tel: (703)437-0700
Fax: (703)437-6312
Web: www.arts-accredit.org
E-mail: info@arts-accredit.org

Accreditation of post-secondary educational programs in theatre.

Leg. Issues: EDU

In-house, DC-area Employees

HOPE, Samuel: Exec. Director

Nat'l Ass'n of Secondary School Principals

1904 Association Dr.
Reston, VA 20191
Tel: (703)860-0200
Fax: (703)476-5432
Registered: LDA
Web: www.principal.org
E-mail: nassp@nassp.org
Leg. Issues: BUD, EDU

In-house, DC-area Employees

DEWITT, Stephen Wright: Director, Federal Relations
LAMPHER, Michelle: Director, Communications
TAYLOR, Kelley: General Counsel
TIROZZI, Dr. Gerald: Exec. Director

Nat'l Ass'n of Securities and Commercial Law Attorneys

Washington,
Leg. Issues: BAN, CSP, FIN, LAW

Outside Counsel/Consultants

The Cuneo Law Group, P.C.
Issues: BAN, CSP, FIN, LAW
Rep By: Jonathan W. Cuneo, Michael G. Lenett, James J. Schweitzer

Nat'l Ass'n of Securities Dealers, Inc. (NASD)

1735 K St. NW
Washington, DC 20006-1506
Tel: (202)728-8000
Fax: (202)728-6993
Registered: LDA
Web: www.nasd.com

Owns, operates and regulates the NASDAQ stock market and Amex, the American Stock Exchange.

Leg. Issues: BAN, CPT, FIN, TAX

In-house, DC-area Employees

CROWLEY, Daniel F. C.: V. President, Governmental Affairs
KOMOROSKE, John H.: Director, Governmental Relations
RIVERA, Cindy: Administrative Assistant Governmental Affairs
STORCH, Stephen E.: Director, Governmental Relations

Outside Counsel/Consultants

Akin, Gump, Strauss, Hauer & Feld, L.L.P.

Kessler & Associates Business Services, Inc.
Issues: BAN
Rep By: Michael L. Bartlett, Billy Lee Evans, Richard S. Kessler, James C. Musser

Nat'l Ass'n of Senior Companion Project Directors

Salt Lake City, UT
Leg. Issues: BUD, GOV, HCR

Outside Counsel/Consultants

Ledge Counsel
Issues: BUD, GOV, HCR

Valente Lopatin & Schulze
Rep By: Alan G. Lopatin

Nat'l Ass'n of Service and Conservation Corps

666 11th St. NW
Suite 1000
Washington, DC 20001-4542
Tel: (202)737-6272
Fax: (202)737-6277
Web: www.nascc.org
E-mail: nascc@nascc.org

A national clearinghouse, technical assistance, and advocacy organization for youth conservation and service corps.

Leg. Issues: BUD, CAW, DIS, EDU, ENV, HOU, LBR, NAT, TRA, UNM, URB, WAS, WEL

In-house, DC-area Employees

MOORE, Andrew E.: V. President, Government Relations and Public Affairs
SELZ, Kathleen: President

Nat'l Ass'n of Settlement Purchasers

Washington, DC
Web: www.thenasp.org
Leg. Issues: TAX

Outside Counsel/Consultants

Vinson & Elkins L.L.P.
Issues: TAX
Rep By: Hon. Michael A. Andrews, John E. Chapoton, Christine L. Vaughn

Nat'l Ass'n of Small Business Investment Companies

666 11th St. NW
Suite 750
Washington, DC 20001
Tel: (202)628-5055
Fax: (202)628-5080
Registered: LDA
Web: www.nasbic.org
E-mail: nasbic@nasbic.org
Leg. Issues: FIN, SMB

Political Action Committee/s

Nat'l Ass'n of Small Business Investment Companies Political Action Committee
666 11th St. NW
Suite 750
Washington, DC 20001
Tel: (202)628-5055
Fax: (202)628-5080
Contact: Jeanette Diana Paschal

In-house, DC-area Employees

FREEDENBERG, Sam: Director, Communications
MERCER, Lee W.: President
PASCHAL, Jeanette Diana: V. President

Outside Counsel/Consultants

The Advocacy Group
Issues: SMB
Rep By: Robert J. Dotchin

Nat'l Ass'n of Social Workers

750 First St. NE
Suite 700
Washington, DC 20002
Tel: (202)408-8600
Fax: (202)336-8311
Registered: LDA
Web: www.socialworkers.org

A 145,000 member organization that represents the social work and human services profession.

Leg. Issues: BUD, CIV, EDU, FAM, HCR, LAW, LBR, MMM, TAX, WEL

Political Action Committee/s

Nat'l Ass'n of Social Workers Political Action Committee for Candidate Action
750 First St. NE
Suite 700
Washington, DC 20002
Tel: (202)408-8600
Fax: (202)336-8311
Contact: Kathryn Levy

In-house, DC-area Employees

CLARK, Ph.D., Elizabeth: Exec. Director
LEVY, Kathryn: Political Affairs Associate
MOORE, III, Lawrence: Congressional Lobbyist
WEISMILLER, Toby: Divisional Director
WOODSIDE, Cynthia: Congressional Lobbyist

Nat'l Ass'n of State & Provincial Lotteries

Cleveland, OH
Leg. Issues: GAM

Outside Counsel/Consultants

Greenberg Traurig, LLP
Issues: GAM
Rep By: Ronald L. Platt

Nat'l Ass'n of State Alcohol and Drug Abuse Directors (NASADAD)

808 17th St. NW
Suite 410
Washington, DC 20006
Tel: (202)293-0090
Fax: (202)293-1250
Web: www.nasadad.org
E-mail: dcoffice@nasadad.org

Supports the development of effective alcohol and other drug abuse prevention and treatment throughout the U.S.

In-house, DC-area Employees

GALLANT, Louis E.: Exec. Director
SHEEHAN, Kathleen: Director, Public Policy

Nat'l Ass'n of State Auditors, Comptrollers and Treasurers

444 N. Capitol St. NW
Suite 234
Washington, DC 20001
Tel: (202)624-5451
Fax: (202)624-5473
Web: www.sso.org/nasact
E-mail: nasactdc@sso.org

Represents state finance officials before Congress and Executive agencies.

Leg. Issues: FIN, GOV

In-house, DC-area Employees

SCHNEIDER, Cornelia: Director, Washington Office

Nat'l Ass'n of State Aviation Officials

8401 Colesville Rd.
Suite 505
Silver Spring, MD 20910
Tel: (301)588-0587
Fax: (301)585-1803
Web: www.nasao.org
E-mail: henryo@nasao.org

Seeks to foster cooperation and mutual aid among the states and the federal government in developing national and state air transportation systems that serve the public interest. Washington office serves in dual role of representing the states' interests to federal agencies and vice versa.

In-house, DC-area Employees

LEHNERD, Lori: V. President
OGRODZINSKI, Henry M.: President and Chief Exec. Officer

Nat'l Ass'n of State Boards of Education

277 S. Washington St.
Alexandria, VA 22314
Tel: (703)684-4000
Fax: (703)836-2313
Web: www.nasbe.org
E-mail: boards@nasbe.org
Leg. Issues: EDU

In-house, DC-area Employees

GRIFFITH, David: Director, Governmental Affairs
ROACH, Dr. Virginia: Deputy Exec. Director
WELBURN, Brenda L.: Exec. Director

Nat'l Ass'n of State Budget Officers

444 N. Capitol St. NW
Suite 642
Washington, DC 20001
Tel: (202)624-5382
Fax: (202)624-7745
Web: www.nasbo.org
E-mail: snichols@sso.org

In-house, DC-area Employees

MAZER, Stacey: Senior Staff Associate

Nat'l Ass'n of State Credit Union Supervisors

1655 N. Fort Myer Dr.
Suite 300
Arlington, VA 22209
Tel: (703)528-8351
Fax: (703)528-3248
Registered: LDA
Web: www.nascus.org
E-mail: offices@nascus.org
Leg. Issues: FIN

In-house, DC-area Employees

DUERR, Douglas: President and Chief Exec. Officer
FORTNEY, Mary Martha: V. President, Public Affairs and Accreditation

Nat'l Ass'n of State Departments of Agriculture

1156 15th St. NW
Suite 1020
Washington, DC 20005
Tel: (202)296-9680
Fax: (202)296-9686
Web: www.nasda-hq.org
E-mail: nasda@patriot.net

A non-profit, non-partisan association of public officials composed of the executive heads of the fifty state Departments of Agriculture and those from the territories of Puerto Rico, Guam, American Samoa, and the Virgin Islands. NASDA's mission is to support and promote the American agriculture industry while protecting consumers and the environment, through the development, implementation, and communication of sound public policy and programs.

Leg. Issues: AGR, ANI, CAW, ENV, FOO, NAT, RES, TRD

In-house, DC-area Employees

ANDERSON, Curtis M.: Chief Financial Officer
ATAGI, Patrick S.: Manager, Legislative and Regulatory Affairs
INGRAM, Charles W.: Manager, Legislative and Regulatory Affairs
KIRCHHOFF, Richard W.: Exec. V. President and C.E.O.

Nat'l Ass'n of State Development Agencies

12884 Harbor Dr. Tel: (703)490-6777
Woodside, VA 20192 Fax: (703)492-4404
Web: www.nasda.com
E-mail: dbosmans@nasda.com

In-house, DC-area Employees
BOSMANS, Denise M.: Director, Membership Services
FRIEDMAN, Miles: President and CEO

Nat'l Ass'n of State Directors of Developmental Disabilities Services, Inc.

113 Oronoco St. Tel: (703)683-4202
Alexandria, VA 22314 Fax: (703)684-1395

In-house, DC-area Employees
GETTINGS, Robert M.: Exec. Director

Nat'l Ass'n of State Directors of Special Education

1800 Diagonal Rd. Tel: (703)519-3800
Suite 320 Fax: (703)519-3808
Alexandria, VA 22314
Web: www.nasdse.org
E-mail: nasdse@nasdse.org

Membership consists of special education departments in all states and federal jurisdictions. Assists state agencies in educating individuals with disabilities.

Leg. Issues: EDU

In-house, DC-area Employees
EAST, Dr. Bill: Exec. Director
REDER, Nancy: Deputy Exec. Director, Director of Government Relations

Nat'l Ass'n of State Directors of Vocational Technical Education Consortium

444 N. Capitol St. NW Tel: (202)737-0303
Suite 830 Fax: (202)737-1106
Washington, DC 20001 Registered: LDA
Web: www.nasdvtec.org
E-mail: nasdvtec@iris.org
Leg. Issues: EDU

In-house, DC-area Employees
GREEN, Kimberly A.: Exec. Director

Nat'l Ass'n of State EMS Directors

111 Park Place Tel: (703)538-1799
Falls Church, VA 22046-4513 Fax: (703)241-5603
Web: www.nasemsd.org
E-mail: nasemsd@aol.com

In-house, DC-area Employees
ARMSTRONG, CAE, Elizabeth B.: Exec. Director

Outside Counsel/Consultants
Ass'n and Soc. Management Internat'l Inc.
Rep By: Elizabeth B. Armstrong, CAE

Nat'l Ass'n of State Energy Officials

1414 Prince St. Tel: (703)299-8800
Suite 200 Fax: (703)299-6208
Alexandria, VA 22314
Web: www.naseo.org
E-mail: info@naseo.org

A non-profit corporation promoting a balanced national energy policy including traditional energy sources as well as energy conservation, alternative fuels, renewable energy, and energy security.

Leg. Issues: ENG, GOV

In-house, DC-area Employees
BISHOP, Frank: Exec. Director

Outside Counsel/Consultants
Duncan, Weinberg, Genzer & Pembroke, P.C.
Issues: ENG, GOV
Rep By: Jeffrey C. Genzer

Nat'l Ass'n of State Farm Agents

Atlanta, GA
Leg. Issues: TAX

Outside Counsel/Consultants
Washington Council Ernst & Young
Issues: TAX
Rep By: Doug Badger, Jayne T. Fitzgerald, LaBrenda Garrett-Nelson, Gary J. Gasper, Bruce A. Gates, Nick Giordano, Robert J. Leonard, Richard Meltzer

Nat'l Ass'n of State Foresters

444 N. Capitol St. NW Tel: (202)624-5415
Suite 540 Fax: (202)624-5407
Washington, DC 20001
Web: www.stateforesters.org
E-mail: nasf@sso.org

In-house, DC-area Employees
IMBERGAMO, Bill: Exec. Director

Nat'l Ass'n of State Mental Health Program Directors

66 Canal Center Plaza Tel: (703)739-9333
Suite 302 Fax: (703)548-9517
Alexandria, VA 22314
Web: www.nasmhpd.org
Leg. Issues: HCR, MED, MMM

In-house, DC-area Employees
GLOVER, Ph.D., Robert W.: Exec. Director
URFF, Jenifer E.: Director, Government Relations

Nat'l Ass'n of State Units on Aging

1225 I St. NW Tel: (202)898-2578
Suite 725 Fax: (202)898-2583
Washington, DC 20005
Web: www.nasua.org
E-mail: dquirk@nasua.org

National, non-profit, public interest organization dedicated to providing general and specialized information, technical assistance and professional development support to State Units on Aging. The membership of the Association is comprised of the 57 state and territorial government agencies charged with advancing the social and economic agendas of older persons in their respective states.

Leg. Issues: BUD, CSP, HCR, HOU, LBR, MMM, RET

In-house, DC-area Employees
QUIRK, Daniel: Exec. Director

Nat'l Ass'n of State Universities and Land-Grant Colleges

1307 New York Ave. NW Tel: (202)478-6040
Suite 400 Fax: (202)478-6046
Washington, DC 20005-4722
Web: www.nasulgc.org
Leg. Issues: AGR, EDU, GOV

In-house, DC-area Employees
FIELDS, Cheryl: Director, Public Affairs
HARPEL, Richard: Director, Federal Relations-Higher Education
MAGRATH, C. Peter: President
NEUFVILLE, Mortimer H.: Exec. V. President

Nat'l Ass'n of State Utility Consumer Advocates (NASUCA)

8300 Colesville Rd. Tel: (301)589-6313
Suite 101 Fax: (301)589-6380
Silver Spring, MD 20910
Web: www.nasuca.org
E-mail: nasuca@nasuca.org

Members are designated by state status to represent the residential ratepayers in their state before public utility commissions, the courts, and federal regulatory agencies on utility issues.

Leg. Issues: CSP, ENG, FUE, TEC, UTI

In-house, DC-area Employees
ACQUARD, Charles A.: Exec. Director

Nat'l Ass'n of State Workforce Agencies

444 N. Capitol St. NW Tel: (202)434-8020
Suite 142 Fax: (202)434-8033
Washington, DC 20001

Members are officials who administer state workforce services industry, but not limited to unemployment insurance programs, employment and training services, and labor market information programs.

In-house, DC-area Employees
BISHOP, Mason: Director, Legislation and Marketing
CASHEN, Kathleen: Employment and Training Director
DEROCCO, Emily S.: Exec. Director
GERASSIMEDES, Pam: Marketing and Outreach Coordinator
HOBBIE, Ph.D., Richard: Unemployment Insurance Director
READ, Marcia: Fiscal and Administrative Director
TERRY, Sybil: Equal Opportunity Director
VICKERS, Mary Susan: Labor Market Information and Research Director

Nat'l Ass'n of Student Financial Aid Administrators

1129 20th St. NW Tel: (202)785-0453
Suite 400 Fax: (202)785-1487
Washington, DC 20036-3489 Registered: LDA
Web: www.nasfaa.org

An institutional-based postsecondary education membership association with over 3,000 members. Coordinates efforts nationally to improve the delivery of student assistance and to increase resources available to students. A non-profit corporation of postsecondary institutions, individuals, agencies, and students interested in promoting the effective administration of student financial aid in the U.S.

Leg. Issues: BUD, EDU

In-house, DC-area Employees
MARTIN, Jr., Dr. A. Dallas: President
ZAGLANICZNY, Lawrence S.: Associate Director, Government Affairs

Nat'l Ass'n of Student Personnel Administrators

1875 Connecticut Ave. NW Tel: (202)265-7500
Suite 418 Fax: (202)797-1157
Washington, DC 20009-5728
Web: www.naspa.org/
E-mail: office@naspa.org

NASPA is the leading voice for student affairs administration, policy, and practice. It addresses critical issues in student affairs and seeks to enrich the educational experience for all college and university students.

Leg. Issues: EDU

In-house, DC-area Employees
DUNGY, Gwendolyn J.: Exec. Director

Nat'l Ass'n of Surety Bond Producers

5225 Wisconsin Ave. NW Tel: (202)686-3700
Suite 600 Fax: (202)686-3656
Washington, DC 20015-2014 Registered: LDA
Web: www.nasbp.org
E-mail: nasbp@nasbp.org

Members are insurance agencies and brokerage firms that provide corporate surety bonding and insurance for construction contractors.

Leg. Issues: ENV, INS, LBR, MMM, ROD, SMB, TRA, WAS

Political Action Committee/s
Surety PAC
5225 Wisconsin Ave. NW Tel: (202)686-3700
Suite 600 Fax: (202)686-3656
Washington, DC 20015-2014
Contact: Connie Lynch

In-house, DC-area Employees
FOSS, Richard A.: Exec. V. President
LYNCH, Connie: Director, Government Relations

Nat'l Ass'n of Tax Practitioners

1200 G St. NW Tel: (202)434-8778
Suite 800 Fax: (202)434-8707
Washington, DC 20005-8707

In-house, DC-area Employees
BORGHESE, Phyllis: Government Affairs Representative

Nat'l Ass'n of Telecommunications Officers and Advisors

Vienna, VA
Web: www.natoa.org
E-mail: info@natoa.org

Outside Counsel/Consultants
Ass'n Management Bureau
Rep By: Elizabeth Beaty

Nat'l Ass'n of the Deaf

814 Thayer Ave. Tel: (301)587-1788
Suite 250 Fax: (301)587-1791
Silver Spring, MD 20910
Web: www.nad.org
E-mail: nadinfo@nad.org

The nation's largest organization safeguarding the accessibility and civil rights of 28 million deaf and hard-of-hearing Americans in education, employment, health care, and telecommunications. TTY number is (301) 587-1789.

In-house, DC-area Employees
BLOCH, Nancy J.: Exec. Director
CHARMATZ, Marc: Counsel
FARB, Anita B.: Associate Exec. Director, Administration
RARUS, Nancy B.: Associate Exec. Director, Programs

Nat'l Ass'n of Theatre Owners

North Hollywood, CA
Leg. Issues: ART, LBR, TRD

Outside Counsel/Consultants
Galland, Kharasch, Greenberg, Fellman & Swirsky, P.C.
Rep By: Steven John Fellman

Patton Boggs, LLP
Issues: ART, LBR, TRD
Rep By: John F. Fithian, Elena Giberga, Frank R. Samolis

Nat'l Ass'n of Thrift Savings Plan Participants

Washington, DC
Leg. Issues: FIN, GOV, RET

Outside Counsel/Consultants

Ledge Counsel
Issues: FIN, GOV, RET

MV3 & Associates

RTS Consulting

Valente Lopatin & Schulze
Rep By: Alan G. Lopatin, Richard T. Schulze, Jr., Mark Valente, III

Nat'l Ass'n of Ticket Brokers

Washington, DC
Web: www.natb.org

Outside Counsel/Consultants

O'Connor & Hannan, L.L.P.
Rep By: Gary C. Adler, Thomas H. Quinn

Nat'l Ass'n of Tower Erectors

Watertown, SD
Leg. Issues: TEC

Outside Counsel/Consultants

Bob Lawrence & Associates
Issues: TEC
Rep By: James Goldwater

Nat'l Ass'n of Towns and Townships

444 N. Capital St. NW
Suite 208
Washington, DC 20001
Tel: (202)624-3550
Fax: (202)624-3554
Web: www.natat.org
E-mail: natat@sso.org

A federation of state associations and direct members representing over 11,000 units of local government. Units are mostly small and rural. The association provides supporting research and advocates for flexible, fair, equitable legislation and regulations applying to smaller local governments.

Leg. Issues: CAW, ECN, ENV, GOV, ROD, TEC, TRA, WAS

In-house, DC-area Employees

HALICKI, Tom: Exec. Director
VANASEK, Robert: Federal Affairs Associate

Nat'l Ass'n of Uniform Manufacturers and Distributors

New York, NY
Leg. Issues: GOV, MAN, POS

Outside Counsel/Consultants

Patton Boggs, LLP
Issues: GOV, MAN, POS
Rep By: Thomas C. Downs

Nat'l Ass'n of Urban Bankers, Inc.

1300 L St. NW
Suite 825
Washington, DC 20005
Tel: (202)289-8335
Fax: (202)842-4439
Web: www.naub.org
E-mail: ufsc@ecol.com

In-house, DC-area Employees

GABRIEL, Anthony: Acting Exec. Director

Nat'l Ass'n of Urban Hospitals

10 Pidgeon Hill Dr.
Suite 150
Sterling, VA 20165
Tel: (703)444-0989
Fax: (703)444-3029
Registered: LDA
Leg. Issues: BUD, MED, MMM

Outside Counsel/Consultants

DeBrunner and Associates, Inc.
Issues: BUD, MED, MMM
Rep By: Charles L. DeBrunner, Wendy W. Herr, Gloria J. Klugh, Ellen J. Kugler, Kathryn D. Rooney

Nat'l Ass'n of VA Physicians and Dentists

11 Canal Center Plaza
Suite 110
Alexandria, VA 22314
Tel: (703)548-0280
Fax: (703)683-7939
Web: www.navapd.org
E-mail: navaprd@dgsys.com
Leg. Issues: DEF, GOV, HCR, MED, MMM, PHA, VET

In-house, DC-area Employees

CONROY, M.D., Robert M.: President

Outside Counsel/Consultants

Booher & Associates
Issues: DEF, GOV, HCR, MED, MMM, PHA, VET
Rep By: C. William Booher, Jr.

Nat'l Ass'n of Veterans Research and Education Foundations

5018 Sangamore Rd.
Suite 300
Bethesda, MD 20816
Tel: (301)229-1048
Fax: (301)229-0442
Web: www.navref.org
E-mail: navref@navref.org

An association of non-profit foundations affiliated with the Department of Veterans' Affairs.

Leg. Issues: MED, VET

In-house, DC-area Employees

WEST, Barbara F.: Exec. Director

Nat'l Ass'n of Victims of Transfusion-associated HIV

Outside Counsel/Consultants

Powers Pyles Sutter & Verville, PC
Rep By: Judith Buckalew

Nat'l Ass'n of Water Companies

1725 K St. NW
Suite 1212
Washington, DC 20006
Tel: (202)833-8383
Fax: (202)331-7442
Registered: LDA
Web: www.nawc.org

Formerly (1971) Nat'l Water Co. Conference. Represents investor-owned water utilities. Monitors relevant environmental and tax issues.

Leg. Issues: CAW, ENV, LAW, TAX, TOR

Political Action Committee/s

Nat'l Ass'n of Water Companies Political Action Committee
1725 K St. NW
Suite 1212
Washington, DC 20006
Tel: (202)833-8383
Fax: (202)331-7442
Contact: Louis J. Jenny

In-house, DC-area Employees

COOK, Peter L.: Exec. Director
GASCON, Sharon: Deputy Exec. Director
HORNER, Michael J.: Director, Administration and Membership
JENNY, Louis J.: Director, Congressional Relations
LEWIS, Robert J.: Deputy Exec. Director, Federal Relations

Outside Counsel/Consultants

Dickstein Shapiro Morin & Oshinsky LLP
Issues: LAW, TOR
Rep By: Robert Mangas, Graham "Rusty" Mathews, L. Andrew Zausner

Van Scoyoc Associates, Inc.
Issues: CAW, ENV, TAX
Rep By: Jeffrey S. Trinca, H. Stewart Van Scoyoc

Nat'l Ass'n of Waterfront Employers

2011 Pennyslvania Ave. NW
Suite 301
Washington, DC 20006
Tel: (202)296-2810
Fax: (202)331-7479
Registered: LDA
E-mail: nawewdc@msn.com
Leg. Issues: LBR

In-house, DC-area Employees

CARROLL, Jr., Charles T.: General Counsel
FROELICH, M.D., F. Edwin: Assistant General Counsel

Outside Counsel/Consultants

Wilcox, Carroll & Froelich, PLLC
Rep By: Charles T. Carroll, Jr., F. Edwin Froelich, M.D.

Nat'l Ass'n of Wheat Growers

415 Second St. NE
Suite 300
Washington, DC 20002-4993
Tel: (202)547-7800
Fax: (202)546-2638
Registered: LDA
Web: www.wheatworld.org
E-mail: wheatworld@wheatworld.org
Leg. Issues: AGR, CAW, CHM, ENV, RES, RRR, TAX, TRA, TRD, TRU

Political Action Committee/s

Nat'l Ass'n of Wheat Growers Political Action Committee
415 Second St. NE
Suite 300
Washington, DC 20002-4993
Tel: (202)547-7800
Fax: (202)546-2638
Contact: Wayne L. Hammon

In-house, DC-area Employees

BOWLAND, Amy R.: Director, Communications
EBERSPACHER, Jack: Chief Exec. Officer
HAMMON, Wayne L.: Director, Government Relations

Outside Counsel/Consultants

Baise + Miller, P.C.
Issues: CAW, ENV
Rep By: Gary H. Baise

Nat'l Ass'n of Wholesaler-Distributors

1725 K St. NW
Suite 300
Washington, DC 20006
Tel: (202)872-0885
Fax: (202)785-0586
Registered: LDA
Web: www.naw.org

The Association serves as a representative of the Product Liability Alliance.

Leg. Issues: BUD, GOV, HCR, LBR, TAX, TOB, TOR, TRD, UTI

Political Action Committee/s

Wholesaler-Distributor Political Action Committee
1725 K St. NW
Suite 300
Washington, DC 20006
Tel: (202)872-0885
Fax: (202)296-5940
Contact: Alan M. Kranowitz

In-house, DC-area Employees

ANDERSON, Jr., James A.: V. President, Government Relations
KRANOWITZ, Alan M.: Senior V. President, Government Relations
PETER, John: V. President, Corporate Relations
VAN DONGEN, Dirk: President

Outside Counsel/Consultants

Crowell & Moring LLP
Rep By: Mark A. Behrens

Valis Associates
Issues: TOR, TRD
Rep By: Wayne H. Valis

Nat'l Ass'n of WIC Directors

2001 S St. NW
Suite 580
Washington, DC 20009
Tel: (202)232-5492
Fax: (202)387-5281
Web: www.wicdirectors.org

Serves as a national forum for state and local WIC Directors. Acts to promote the improved health, well-being and nutritional status of women, infants and children.

In-house, DC-area Employees

GREENAWAY, Douglas A.: Exec. Director
MCDOWELL, Ella: Legislative Assistant

Nat'l Ass'n to Protect Individual Rights

P.O. Box 7371
Fairfax Station, VA 22039-7371
Tel: (703)425-5347
Web: www.individualrights.net
E-mail: policywonk27@go.com

NAPIR is a 501(c)(4) nonpartisan public policy think tank specializing in the study of government budget and tax policies and information privacy issues.

Leg. Issues: BUD, CPI, EDU, GOV, HCR

In-house, DC-area Employees

MORISON, Karen A.: President

Nat'l Assembly of Health and Human Service Organizations

1319 F St. NW
Suite 601
Washington, DC 20004
Tel: (202)347-2080
Fax: (202)393-4517
Web: www.nassembly.org
E-mail: nassembly@nassembly.org

The Nat'l Assembly provides a forum for the exchange of information among member agencies in order to advance the work of the human service sector.

Leg. Issues: BUD, CIV, ECN, EDU, FAM, GOV, HCR, HOU, IMM, IND, LAW, MED, MMM, UNM, URB, WEL

In-house, DC-area Employees

KATZ, Irv: President and Chief Exec. Officer

Nat'l Assembly of State Arts Agencies

1029 Vermont Ave. NW
Second Floor
Washington, DC 20005
Tel: (202)347-6352
Fax: (202)737-0526
Web: www.nasaa.arts.org
E-mail: nasaa@nasaa-arts.org
Leg. Issues: ART

In-house, DC-area Employees

KATZ, Jonathan: Chief Exec. Officer

Outside Counsel/Consultants

Thomas L. Birch
Issues: ART
Rep By: Thomas L. Birch

Nat'l Audubon Soc.

1901 Pennsylvania Ave. NW
Suite 1100
Washington, DC 20006
Tel: (202)861-2242
Fax: (202)861-4290
Registered: LDA
Web: www.audubon.org

One of the nation's largest (575,000 members) membership organizations dedicated to the conservation of wildlife and other natural resources and to the sound protection of the natural environment. Priority campaigns-migratory birds, ancient forests, wetlands preservation, Endangered Species Act reauthorization and Everglades restoration.

Leg. Issues: ANI, BUD, ENV, FOR, NAT, RES

In-house, DC-area Employees

BEARD, Dan: Senior V. President, Public Policy
HIRSCHE, Evan: Director, Foundation
PLUMART, Perry: Director, Government Affairs

Outside Counsel/Consultants

Cannon Consultants, Inc.
Rep By: Charles A. Cannon

John Freshman Associates, Inc.
Issues: ENV, NAT
Rep By: John D. Freshman, Lawrence P. Kast, Catherine B. Kiefer

Williams & Jensen, P.C.
Issues: ANI, ENV, NAT, RES
Rep By: J. Steven Hart, John J. McMackin, Jr.

Nat'l Automatic Merchandising Ass'n

783 Station St.
Suite 1-D
Herndon, VA 20170
Tel: (703)435-1210
Fax: (703)435-6389
E-mail: tmcmahon@vending.org

Headquartered in Chicago, IL.

In-house, DC-area Employees

MCMAHON, Thomas E.: Senior V. President and Chief Counsel

Outside Counsel/Consultants

Patton Boggs, LLP
Rep By: Thomas Hale Boggs, Jr.

Nat'l Automobile Dealers Ass'n

8400 W. Park Dr.
McLean, VA 22102
Tel: (703)821-7000
Registered: LDA
Leg. Issues: AUT, BAN, BUD, CAW, CPT, CSP, ENV, GOV, HCR, LBR, TAX, WAS

Political Action Committee/s

Dealers Election Action Committee of the Nat'l Automobile Dealers Ass'n
8400 W. Park Dr.
McLean, VA 22102
Tel: (703)821-7000

In-house, DC-area Employees

BECK, Andy: Director of Government Communications
BRAZIEL, Rob: Legislative Counsel
EUSTICE, Mary Jo: Senior Legislative Representative
GREENE, H. Thomas: Chief Operating Officer, Legislative Affairs
HYATT, David: Group Exec. Director, Public Affairs
KOBLENZ, Andrew: Exec. Director, Industry Affairs
NEWMAN, William A.: Chief Legal Counsel
NUTT, Fred: Legislative Representative
REGAN, David: Exec. Director, Legislative Affairs
RIVERA, Ivette E.: Director, Legislative Affairs
SPURGEON, Scott: Legislative Representative

Outside Counsel/Consultants

Moore & Bruce, LLP
Issues: TAX
Rep By: William Morris

Rogers & Wells

Shaw Pittman

Nat'l Aviary in Pittsburgh

Pittsburgh, PA

Outside Counsel/Consultants

The Dutko Group, Inc.
Rep By: Ronald C. Kaufman, Arthur H. Silverman, William Simmons

Nat'l Bankers Ass'n

1513 P St. NW
Washington, DC 20005-1909
Tel: (202)588-5432
Fax: (202)588-5443
Web: www.natbankers.com

Serves as an advocate for minority and women-owned banks, provides a forum for interaction between bankers.

Political Action Committee/s

Nat'l Bankers Ass'n Political Action Committee
1513 P St. NW
Washington, DC 20005-1909
Tel: (202)588-5432
Fax: (202)588-5443
Contact: Norma Alexander Hart

In-house, DC-area Employees

HART, Norma Alexander: President

Nat'l Bar Ass'n

1225 11th St. NW
Washington, DC 20001
Tel: (202)842-3900
Fax: (202)289-6170
Web: www.nationalbar.org
E-mail: nationalba@aol.com

Founded in 1925, the National Bar Ass'n is the nation's oldest and largest national organization of African American attorneys representing a professional network of over 18,000 judges, lawyers, legal educators and law students. The purpose of the National Bar Ass'n is to advance the science of jurisprudence, uphold the honor of the legal profession, promote social intercourse among the members of the bar, and protect the civil and political rights of all citizens of the several states of the United States.

Political Action Committee/s

Nat'l Bar Ass'n Political Action Committee
1225 11th St. NW
Washington, DC 20001
Tel: (202)842-3900
Fax: (202)289-6170
Contact: John Crump, CMP, CAE

In-house, DC-area Employees

CRUMP, CMP, CAE, John: Exec. Director

Nat'l Barley Growers Ass'n

Red Lake Falls, MN
Leg. Issues: AGR

Outside Counsel/Consultants

Gordley Associates
Issues: AGR
Rep By: John Gordley, Krysta Harden, Maureen Kelly, Megan Marquet, Daryn McBeth

Nat'l Basketball Ass'n

New York, NY
Leg. Issues: COM, CPT, IMM, SPO

Outside Counsel/Consultants

Akin, Gump, Strauss, Hauer & Feld, L.L.P.
Issues: IMM, SPO
Rep By: Frank J. Donatelli

Oppenheimer Wolff & Donnelly LLP
Rep By: Hon. Birch Bayh, Kevin O. Faley

Verner, Liipfert, Bernhard, McPherson and Hand, Chartered
Issues: COM, CPT, SPO
Rep By: Philip R. Hochberg

Nat'l Beer Wholesalers Ass'n

1100 S. Washington St.
First Floor
Alexandria, VA 22314-4494
Tel: (703)683-4300
Fax: (703)683-8965
Registered: LDA
Web: www.nbwa.org
Leg. Issues: ADV, ALC, BEV, BUD, COM, GOV, LAW, LBR, SMB, TAX, TRA, TRU

Political Action Committee/s

Nat'l Beer Wholesalers Ass'n Political Action Committee
1100 S. Washington St.
First Floor
Alexandria, VA 22314-4494
Tel: (703)683-4300
Fax: (703)683-8965
Contact: David K. Rehr, Ph.D.

In-house, DC-area Employees

AUGLIS, Linda M.: Director, Political Affairs
CAMPAGNA, Shannon: Washington Representative
DODSON, Andrew C.: Washington Representative
KNIGHT, Laurie: Washington Representative
MLYNARCZYK, Tamara Tyrrell: Director, Public Affairs
PURSER, Craig: V. President
REHR, Ph.D., David K.: President

Outside Counsel/Consultants

Greener and Hook, LLC

Nat'l Bible Ass'n

New York, NY

Outside Counsel/Consultants

William J. Tobin and Associates

Nat'l Bicycle Dealers Ass'n

Costa Mesa, CA
Leg. Issues: SMB, TRD

Outside Counsel/Consultants

Venable
Issues: SMB, TRD
Rep By: Brock R. Landry

Nat'l BioDiesel Board

Jefferson City, MO

Outside Counsel/Consultants

Gordley Associates

Nat'l Black Caucus of Local Elected Officials

c/o Nat'l League of Cities
1301 Pennsylvania Ave. NW, Suite 550
Washington, DC 20004
Tel: (202)626-3000
Fax: (202)626-3043
Web: www.nbc-leo.org
E-mail: gordon@nlc.org

A non-profit, non-partisan organization formed to influence the National League of Cities on issues concerning or affecting African-Americans.

In-house, DC-area Employees

GORDON, Mary F.: Manager, Constituency Groups

Nat'l Black Caucus of State Legislators

444 N. Capitol St. NW
Suite 622
Washington, DC 20001
Tel: (202)624-5457
Fax: (202)508-3826
Web: www.nbcsl.com
E-mail: staff@nbcsl.com

Established in 1977 as an information resource and network for African-American state legislators.

In-house, DC-area Employees

ABDULLAH, Khalil: Exec. Director
THOMAS, James: President

Nat'l Black Child Development Institute

1101 15th St. NW
Suite 900
Washington, DC 20005
Tel: (202)833-2220
Fax: (202)833-8222
Web: www.nbcdi.org

Serves as a critical resource for improving the quality of life of African-American children, youth and families through direct services, public education programs, leadership training, and research.

In-house, DC-area Employees

MOORE, Evelyn K.: President and Chief Exec. Officer

Nat'l Black Media Coalition

1738 Elton Rd.
Suite 314
Silver Spring, MD 20903
Tel: (301)445-2600
Fax: (301)445-1693
Web: www.nbmc.org
E-mail: nbmc2000@aol.com

In-house, DC-area Employees

MARSHALL, Carmen: Exec. Director

Nat'l Black Police Ass'n

3251 Mount Pleasant St. NW
Washington, DC 20010
Tel: (202)986-2070
Fax: (202)986-0410
Web: www.blackpolice.org
E-mail: nbpatofc@worldnett.att.net

An organization of over 100 police associations representing some 35,000 individual members. Serves as advocate for minority police officers.

In-house, DC-area Employees

HAMPTON, Ronald E.: Exec. Director

Nat'l Black Women's Health Project

600 Pennsylvania Ave. SE
Suite 310
Washington, DC 20003
Tel: (202)543-9311
Fax: (202)543-9743
Registered: LDA
E-mail: nbwhp@nbwhp.org

A self-help, health advocacy membership organization.

Leg. Issues: ALC, CSP, FAM, HCR, MED, MMM, WEL

In-house, DC-area Employees

CLARK, Sheila: Policy Associate

Nat'l Board for Certification in Occupational Therapy, Inc.

Gaithersburg, MD
Leg. Issues: IMM

Outside Counsel/Consultants

Zuckerman Spaeder L.L.P.
Issues: IMM
Rep By: Ronald H. Weich

Nat'l Board for Professional Teaching Standards (NBPTS)

2200 Clarendon Blvd.
Suite 1401
Arlington, VA 22201
Tel: (703)465-2700
Registered: LDA
Web: www.nbpts.org

Advocates the creation of a National Board Certification system.

Leg. Issues: EDU

In-house, DC-area Employees
GALLUBO, Gary: V. President

Outside Counsel/Consultants

Federal Management Strategies, Inc.
Issues: EDU

Hogan & Hartson L.L.P.
Issues: EDU
Rep By: Nancy Granese, William Michael House, Hon. Robert H. Michel, Steven S. Routh

Nat'l Board of Examiners in Optometry

Bethesda, MD
Web: www.optometry.org
E-mail: nbeo@optometry.org

Outside Counsel/Consultants

Jenner & Block

Nat'l Border Patrol Council

Campo, CA
Leg. Issues: IMM, LAW, LBR

Outside Counsel/Consultants

Eric Shulman & Associates
Issues: IMM, LAW, LBR
Rep By: Eric Shulman

Nat'l Breast Cancer Coalition

1707 L St. NW
Suite 1060
Washington, DC 20036
Tel: (202)296-7477
Fax: (202)265-6854
Registered: LDA
Web: www.stopbreastcancer.org
Leg. Issues: HCR, MED, MMM

Political Action Committee/s

Nat'l Breast Cancer Coalition PAC

1707 L St. NW
Suite 1060
Washington, DC 20036
Contact: Jennifer Katz
Tel: (202)296-7477
Fax: (202)265-6854

In-house, DC-area Employees
KATZ, Jennifer: Deputy Director, Government Relations
VISCO, Frances M.: President

Outside Counsel/Consultants

Bass and Howes, Inc.
Issues: HCR, MED, MMM
Rep By: Joanne M. Howes, Robyn Lipner

Nat'l Broadcasting Co.

1299 Pennsylvania Ave. NW
11th Floor
Washington, DC 20004
Tel: (202)637-4545
Fax: (202)637-4548
Registered: LDA

A wholly owned subsidiary of the General Electric Co.

Leg. Issues: BUD, COM, TEC

In-house, DC-area Employees
OKUN, B. Robert: V. President, NBC Washington Office
ZIPURSKY, Diane: V. President, Washington Counsel

Outside Counsel/Consultants

BKSH & Associates
Issues: BUD

Podesta/Mattoon

Verner, Liipfert, Bernhard, McPherson and Hand, Chartered
Issues: COM, TEC
Rep By: Jane Hickie, Harry C. McPherson, John A. Merrigan, Sara W. Morris, Ann W. Richards, Lawrence R. Sidman, John H. Zentay

Nat'l Building Museum

401 F St. NW
Washington, DC 20001
Tel: (202)272-2448
Fax: (202)272-2564
Web: www.nbm.org

Provides social and educational programs on the built environment.

Leg. Issues: ART, MIA, RES, TOU

In-house, DC-area Employees
DIXON, Jill: Director, Public Affairs
JONES, Susan Henshaw: President

Outside Counsel/Consultants

Chernikoff and Co.
Issues: ART
Rep By: Larry B. Chernikoff

Nat'l Bureau of Asian Research

Seattle, WA
Leg. Issues: TRA

Outside Counsel/Consultants

William M. Cloherty
Issues: TRA
Rep By: William M. Cloherty

Nat'l Burglar and Fire Alarm Ass'n

8300 Colesville Rd.
Suite 750
Silver Spring, MD 20910
Tel: (301)585-1855
Fax: (301)585-1866
Registered: LDA
Web: www.alarm.org
E-mail: staff@alarm.org
Leg. Issues: COM, LAW, LBR

Political Action Committee/s

Alarm Industry Communications Political Action Committee

8300 Colesville Rd.
Suite 750
Silver Spring, MD 20910
Contact: Susan Wright
Tel: (301)585-1855
Fax: (301)585-1866

Nat'l Burglar & Fire Alarm Ass'n PAC (NBFAA PAC)

8300 Colesville Rd.
Suite 750
Silver Spring, MD 20910
Contact: Susan Wright
Tel: (301)585-1855
Fax: (301)585-1866

In-house, DC-area Employees
AUZUNNE, Adrienne: Director, Government Relations
WRIGHT, Susan: Director, Government Relations

Outside Counsel/Consultants

Sellery Associates, Inc.
Issues: COM, LAW, LBR
Rep By: Lawrence E. Sabbath, William C. Sellery, Jr.

Nat'l Business Aviation Ass'n

1200 18th St. NW
Suite 400
Washington, DC 20036-2506
Tel: (202)783-9000
Fax: (202)331-8364
Registered: LDA
Web: www.nbaa.com
E-mail: info@nbaa.org

Represents the aviation interests of over 5,200 companies which own and operate general aviation aircraft as an aid to the conduct of their business, or are involved with business aviation. Formerly the Nat'l Business Aircraft Ass'n.

Leg. Issues: AVI, BUD, TAX

Political Action Committee/s

Nat'l Business Aviation Ass'n Political Action Committee

1200 18th St. NW
Suite 400
Washington, DC 20036-2506
Contact: Alexander A. Rushton
Tel: (202)783-9454
Fax: (202)331-8364

In-house, DC-area Employees
ALMY, David W.: V. President, Strategic Program
BLOUIN, Robert: Senior V. President, Operations
BOSCO, Cassandra: Director, Public Relations
CARR, Douglas: Director, Government Affairs manager
OLCOTT, John W.: President
PONTE, Joe: V. President, Membership and Marketing
RUSHTON, Alexander A.: Administrative Assistant, Government and Public Affairs
STINE, II, William H.: Director, International Issues and Corporate Secretary
WEST, Jr., William Preston: Senior V. President, Government and Public Affairs

Outside Counsel/Consultants

Davis & Harman LLP
Rep By: Richard S. Belas

Zuckert, Scoutt and Rasenberger, L.L.P.
Rep By: Frank J. Costello

Nat'l Business Coalition on Health

1015 18th St. NW
Suite 730
Washington, DC 20036
Web: www.nbch.org
Tel: (202)775-9300
Fax: (202)775-1569

An association comprised of 100 business coalitions nationwide seeking cost-effective, better quality healcare for employees and their families.

Leg. Issues: HCR

In-house, DC-area Employees
LEHMAN, Ph.D., Gregg: President and Chief Exec. Officer

Nat'l Business Education Ass'n

1914 Association Dr.
Reston, VA 20191-1596
Tel: (703)860-8300
Fax: (703)620-4483
Web: www.nbea.org
E-mail: nbea@nbea.org

In-house, DC-area Employees
TREICHEL, Janet M.: Exec. Director

Nat'l Business Owners Ass'n

820 Gibbon St.
Suite 204
Alexandria, VA 22314
Tel: (703)838-2850
Fax: (703)838-0149
Registered: LDA
Web: www.nboa.org
E-mail: info@nboa.org
Leg. Issues: EDU, GOV, SMB

In-house, DC-area Employees
RUMFELT, Chad: Director, Government Affairs

Nat'l Cable Television Ass'n

1724 Massachusetts Ave. NW
Washington, DC 20036-1969
Tel: (202)775-3550
Fax: (202)775-3695
Registered: LDA
Web: www.ncta.com
Leg. Issues: BUD, COM, CPT, TAX, TEC

Political Action Committee/s

Nat'l Cable Television Ass'n Political Action Committee

1724 Massachusetts Ave. NW
Washington, DC 20036-1969
Contact: Eleanor Winter
Tel: (202)775-3550
Fax: (202)775-3671

In-house, DC-area Employees
BECKWITH, David: V. President, Communications
BINZEL, Peggy K.: Exec. V. President
BRENNER, Daniel L.: Senior V. President, Law and Regulatory Policy
BURSTEIN, Diane B.: Deputy General Counsel
CRAIG, Daniel: Director, Legislative Policy
EWALT, Jim: V. President, Public Affairs
GOLDBERG, Neal M.: General Counsel
LUCKETT, Jill: V. President, Program Network Policy
NICOLL, David L.: Associate General Counsel
ORLANDO, Ron: Director, Industry Grassroots Development
PIERCE, David C.: Senior Director, Public Affairs
PINSON, Valerie: Director, Government Relations
POLK, Loretta P.: Associate General Counsel
RICHERSON, Lois: Director, Government Relations
SACHS, Robert J.: President and Chief Exec. Officer
SCHOENTHALER, Lisa W.: Senior Director and Counsel, Office of Small System Operators
TOWNSEND, Wanda: Director, Government Relations
TURNER, Pamela J.: Senior V. President, Government Relations
WINTER, Eleanor: Senior V. President, Special Projects

Outside Counsel/Consultants

Bracewell & Patterson, L.L.P.
Issues: TAX, TEC
Rep By: Gene E. Godley, Marc C. Hebert, Michael L. Pate, Scott H. Segal

Brownstein Hyatt & Farber, P.C.
Issues: TEC
Rep By: William T. Brack, Thomas H. Hudson, Michael B. Levy

BSMG Worldwide

Downey McGrath Group, Inc.
Issues: COM
Rep By: Hon. Thomas J. Downey, Jr.

The Duberstein Group, Inc.
Issues: COM
Rep By: John W. Angus, III, Michael S. Berman, Steven M. Champlin, Kenneth M. Duberstein, Henry M. Gandy, Daniel P. Meyer

F/P Research Associates
Rep By: Ronald Crawford

Fleischman and Walsh, L.L.P.
Issues: CPT, TEC
Rep By: Seth A. Davidson, Charles S. Walsh

Hooper Owen & Winburn
Issues: TEC
Rep By: David Rudd

Mintz, Levin, Cohn, Ferris, Glovsky and Popeo, P.C.
Issues: TEC
Rep By: Howard J. Symons

Patton Boggs, LLP
Issues: COM
Rep By: Thomas Hale Boggs, Jr.

Ryan, Phillips, Utrecht & MacKinnon
Issues: BUD, COM, TEC
Rep By: Rodney Hoppe, Jeffrey M. MacKinnon, William D. Phillips, Mark D. Planning, Thomas M. Ryan, Joseph V. Vasapoli

Washington Council Ernst & Young
Issues: TEC
Rep By: Doug Badger, Jayne T. Fitzgerald, LaBrenda Garrett-Nelson, Gary J. Gasper, Bruce A. Gates, Nick Giordano, Robert J. Leonard, Richard Meltzer, Robert M. Rozen, Timothy J. Urban

Williams & Jensen, P.C.
Issues: COM
Rep By: Bertram W. Carp, J. Steven Hart, Anthony J. Roda

Nat'l Calcium Council

Washington, DC

Outside Counsel/Consultants

Baise + Miller, P.C.
Rep By: Marshall L. Miller

Nat'l Campaign for a Peace Tax Fund

2121 Decatur Pl. NW
Washington, DC 20008
Tel: (202)483-3751
Fax: (202)986-0667
Registered: LDA

Web: www.peacetax.com
E-mail: info@peacetax.com

A citizens' lobby advocating passage of a law permitting people conscientiously opposed to war to have the military portion of their taxes put into a separate fund which could not be used to support the military.

Leg. Issues: FIR, REL, TAX

In-house, DC-area Employees

FRANZ, Marian C.: Exec. Director

Nat'l Campaign for Hearing Health

1050 17th St. NW
Suite 701
Washington, DC 20036
Tel: (202)289-5850
Registered: LDA
Leg. Issues: EDU, FAM, HCR, LBR, MMM, VET

In-house, DC-area Employees

CLEARY, Carrie: Deputy Director
STONE, Alec: Director, Government Affairs

Nat'l Campaign for Jobs and Income Support

1000 Wisconsin Ave. NW
Washington, DC 20007
Tel: (202)342-0567
Fax: (202)333-5462
Web: www.nationalcampaign.org
E-mail: info@nationalcampaign.org

A consortium of 1000 grassroots community organizations in 40 states, including neighborhood, faith-based, low-income, immigrant, and women's organizations concerned with issues of poverty and economic inequality.

In-house, DC-area Employees

BHARGAVA, Deepak: Contact

Nat'l Candle Ass'n

1030 15th St. NW
Suite 870
Washington, DC 20005
Tel: (202)393-2210
Fax: (202)393-0336
Web: www.candles.org
E-mail: nca@rgminc.com
Leg. Issues: TRD

In-house, DC-area Employees

MCDERMOTT, Marianne: Exec. V. President

Outside Counsel/Consultants

Barnes & Thornburg
Issues: TRD
Rep By: Randolph J. Stayin

The Kellen Company
Rep By: Marianne McDermott

Nat'l Capitol Concerts

Washington, DC
Leg. Issues: ART

Outside Counsel/Consultants

The Livingston Group, LLC
Issues: ART
Rep By: Hon. Robert L. Livingston, Jr., J. Allen Martin

Nat'l Cargo Security Council

Alexandria, VA
Web: www.clark.net/pub/ncsc
E-mail: ncsc@clark.net

Outside Counsel/Consultants

The Alexandria Group

Nat'l Cash Register

Leg. Issues: ENV

Outside Counsel/Consultants

The Roth Group
Issues: ENV
Rep By: Joseph Finlayson, Hon. Toby Roth, Sr.

The Nat'l Cathedral

Washington, DC

Outside Counsel/Consultants

Jay Grant & Associates

Nat'l Catholic Conference for Interracial Justice

1200 Varnum St. NE
Washington, DC 20017
Tel: (202)529-6480
Fax: (202)526-1262

In-house, DC-area Employees

CONRAD, Jr., Deacon Joseph M.: Exec. Director

Nat'l Catholic Educational Ass'n

1077 30th St. NW
Suite 100
Washington, DC 20007
Tel: (202)337-6232
Fax: (202)333-6706
Web: www.ncea.org
E-mail: nceaadmin@ncea.org

In-house, DC-area Employees

KEEBLER, Barbara: Director, Public Relations
MCDONALD, Dale: Public Policy Research Associate

Nat'l Catholic Federation of Parents

Falls Church, VA

Outside Counsel/Consultants

William J. Tobin and Associates

Nat'l Cattleman's Beef Ass'n

1301 Pennsylvania Ave. NW
Suite 300
Washington, DC 20004
Tel: (202)347-0228
Fax: (202)638-0607
Registered: LDA
Web: www.hill.beef.org

Headquartered in Denver, CO. Non-profit trade association representing all segments of the nation's cattle industry, including cattle breeders, producers and feeders. Services include government affairs, public information and market information.

Leg. Issues: AGR, CAW, ENV, FOO, NAT, TAX, TRD

Political Action Committee/s

Nat'l Cattlemen's Ass'n Poltical Action Committee
1301 Pennsylvania Ave. NW
Suite 300
Washington, DC 20004
Tel: (202)347-0228
Fax: (202)638-0607
Contact: Tandy Harrison

In-house, DC-area Employees

CAMPBELL, Jason: Director, Public Lands
DIERLAM, Bryan: Associate Director, Agriculture Policy
HARRISON, Alisa: Director, Public Affairs
HARRISON, Tandy: Associate, PACS and PES
HYDE, Myra: Director, Private Lands
KEYS, III, G. Chandler: V. President, Public Policy
LAMBERT, Chuck: Chief Economist
TRUITT, Jay: Exec. Director, Legislative Affairs
VOLDSETH, Sonia: Associate Director, Food Policy
WEBER, Gary M.: Exec. Director, Regulatory Affairs

Outside Counsel/Consultants

Capitolink, LLC
Issues: AGR, CAW
Rep By: John H. Thorne, Ph.D.

Davis & Harman LLP
Rep By: Richard S. Belas, Thomas A. Davis

Perkins Coie LLP
Rep By: Guy R. Martin

The PMA Group
Rep By: Fred J. Clark, Kaylene Green, Paul J. Magliocchetti, Mark Rokala, Timothy K. Sanders

Nat'l Caucus and Center on Black Aged

1424 K St. NW
Suite 500
Washington, DC 20005-2407
Tel: (202)637-8400
Fax: (202)347-0895
Web: www.ncba-blackaged.org
E-mail: ncba@aol.com

In-house, DC-area Employees

SIMMONS, Samuel J.: President

Nat'l Center for Advanced Technologies

1250 I St. NW
Suite 801
Washington, DC 20005
Tel: (202)371-8458
Fax: (202)371-8573
Web: www.ncat.org
E-mail: ncat@ncat.com

A non-profit educational and research foundation established in December 1988 to provide a national focal point for coordination of advanced technologies between industry, academia, and government.

In-house, DC-area Employees

SIEGEL, Stan: President

Nat'l Center for Appropriate Technology

Butte, MT
Leg. Issues: AGR, BUD, HOU

Outside Counsel/Consultants

Moss McGee Bradley & Foley
Issues: BUD, HOU
Rep By: Leander J. Foley, III

Resource Management Consultants, Inc.
Issues: AGR
Rep By: Robert J. Gray

Nat'l Center for Children in Poverty

Yonkers, NY
Leg. Issues: WEL

Outside Counsel/Consultants

BSMG Worldwide
Issues: WEL

The Michael Lewan Co.
Issues: WEL
Rep By: Michael Lewan, Anne Saunders

Nat'l Center for Economic Freedom, Inc.

Washington, DC
Leg. Issues: GOV

Outside Counsel/Consultants

Preston Gates Ellis & Rouvelas Meeds LLP
Issues: GOV
Rep By: Werner W. Brandt, Hon. David Funderburk, Hon. Lloyd Meeds, Sol Mosher, Ralph D. Nurnberger, Tim L. Peckinpaugh, Daniel Ritter, W. Dennis Stephens, Steven R. "Rick" Valentine

Nat'l Center for Education Information

4401A Connecticut Ave. NW
PMB 212
Washington, DC 20008-2322
Tel: (202)362-3444
Fax: (202)362-3493
Web: www.ncei.com

In-house, DC-area Employees

FEISTRITZER, C. Emily: Director

Nat'l Center for Family Literacy

Louisville, KY
Leg. Issues: BUD, EDU

Outside Counsel/Consultants

Ledge Counsel
Issues: BUD, EDU

Valente Lopatin & Schulze
Issues: BUD, EDU
Rep By: Alan G. Lopatin

Nat'l Center for Genome Research

Santa Fe, NM
Leg. Issues: AGR, BUD, FOO, HCR

Outside Counsel/Consultants

Greenberg Traurig, LLP
Issues: AGR, BUD, FOO, HCR
Rep By: Diane J. Blagman, Howard J. Cohen, Jodi Finder, Ronald L. Platt, Nancy E. Taylor, Timothy P. Trysla

Nat'l Center for Homeopathy

801 N. Fairfax St.
Suite 306
Alexandria, VA 22314
Tel: (703)548-7790
Fax: (703)548-7792
Web: www.homeopathic.org
E-mail: info@homeopathic.org

In-house, DC-area Employees

STEVENSON, Sharon: Exec. Director

Outside Counsel/Consultants

Webster, Chamberlain & Bean
Rep By: Alan P. Dye

Nat'l Center for Housing Management

1010 N. Glebe Rd.
Suite 160
Arlington, VA 22201
Tel: (703)516-4070
Fax: (703)516-4069

In-house, DC-area Employees

STEVENS, Glenn: President

Nat'l Center for Learning Disabilities (NCLD)

418 C St. NE
Washington, DC 20002
Tel: (202)546-2663
Fax: (202)546-0057
Registered: LDA
Web: www.ncld.org
E-mail: publicpolicy@ncld.org

A not-for-profit organization committed to improving the lives of those affected by learning disabilities headquartered in New York, NY.

Leg. Issues: BUD, EDU, HCR

In-house, DC-area Employees

KALOI, Laura W.: Director, Public Policy

Outside Counsel/Consultants

Ledge Counsel
Issues: BUD, EDU

Valente Lopatin & Schulze
Rep By: Alan G. Lopatin

Nat'l Center for Manufacturing Sciences

201 Massachusetts Ave. NE
Suite C-6
Washington, DC 20002
Web: www.ncms.org
Tel: (202)544-9244
Fax: (202)544-9247

Headquartered in Ann Arbor, MI.

Leg. Issues: BUD, MAN

In-house, DC-area Employees

RACOSKY, Rebecca M.: V. President, Government Relations

Outside Counsel/Consultants

Patton Boggs, LLP
Issues: BUD, MAN
Rep By: Daniel R. Addison, J. Gordon Arbuckle, Thomas Hale Boggs, Jr., John J. Deschauer, Jr., Edward J. Newberry

Nat'l Center for Missing and Exploited Children

699 Prince St.
Alexandria, VA 22314-3175
Web: www.missingkids.com
Tel: (703)235-3900
Fax: (703)274-2222

Provides information on missing and exploited child issues and offers direct assistance to parents and law-enforcement agencies investigating such cases.

Leg. Issues: FAM

In-house, DC-area Employees

ALLEN, Ernest: President
CARTWRIGHT, Julia: Legislative Counsel
HAMMER, Nancy: General Counsel
RABUN, John: V. President and Chief Operating Officer
SCHWARTZ, Gina: Media Director

Nat'l Center for Neighborhood Enterprise

1424 16th St. NW
Suite 300
Washington, DC 20036-2211
Web: www.ncne.com
E-mail: info@ncne.com
Tel: (202)518-6500
Fax: (202)588-0314

A non-profit organization that assists low-income self-help groups in solving the problems of their communities.

Leg. Issues: ECN, EDU, FAM, HOU, LAW, SMB, URB, WEL

In-house, DC-area Employees

HUMPHRIES, Heather: Public Relations Director
WOODSON, Robert L.: President

Nat'l Center for Nonprofit Boards

1828 L St. NW
Suite 900
Washington, DC 20036-5104
Web: www.ncnb.org
Tel: (202)452-6262
Fax: (202)452-6299

Works to improve the effectiveness of nonprofit organizations by strengthening their boards of directors. Publishes material on nonprofit governance.

In-house, DC-area Employees

O'CONNOR, Judith: President and Chief Exec. Officer

Nat'l Center for Policy Analysis

655 15th St. NW Suite 375
Washington, DC 20005
Web: www.ncpa.org
E-mail: ncpa@his.com
Tel: (202)628-6671
Fax: (202)628-6474

A public policy research institute that developes and promotes private alternatives to government regulation and control, solving problems by relying on the strengths of the private sector. Headquartered in Dallas, TX.

Leg. Issues: BUD, ECN, EDU, ENV, FIR, HCR, INS, LBR, MMM, TAX, WEL

In-house, DC-area Employees

BARTLETT, Bruce: Senior Fellow
DU PONT, Hon. Pete: Policy Chairman
SCANDLEN, Greg M.: Senior Fellow
STRAYER, Jack: V. President, External Affairs

Nat'l Center for Public Policy Research

777 N. Capitol St. NE
Suite 803
Washington, DC 20002
Web: www.nationalcenter.org
E-mail: info@nationalcenter.org
Tel: (202)371-1400
Fax: (202)408-7773

A conservative research and action foundation focusing on environmental and regulatory issues, legal issues, health care and social security, civil rights, technology issues, foreign affairs, and tax and budget policy. Publishes Scoop, Relief Report, Budget Watch, Legal Briefs and Political Money Monitor newsletters, issue briefs and other publications.

Leg. Issues: CIV, DEF, ENV, FAM, GOV, HCR, MMM, TOB, TOR

In-house, DC-area Employees

RIDENOUR, Amy Moritz: President
RIDENOUR, David A.: V. President

Nat'l Center for Tobacco-Free Kids

1707 L St. NW
Suite 800
Washington, DC 20036
Web: www.tobaccofreekids.org
E-mail: info@tobaccofreekids.org
Tel: (202)296-5469
Fax: (202)296-5427
Registered: LDA

An advocacy group and clearinghouse for the anti-tobacco movement. The organization works to eliminate smoking among young Americans.

Leg. Issues: ADV, BUD, TOB

In-house, DC-area Employees

FORD, Anne J.: Manager, Federal Relations
MYERS, Matthew: President

Outside Counsel/Consultants

Clark & Weinstock, Inc.
Issues: BUD, TOB
Rep By: Ed Kutler, Hon. John Vincent "Vin" Weber

Law Offices of Kevin G. Curtin
Issues: ADV, TOB
Rep By: Kevin G. Curtin

Garrett Yu Hussein LLC

Lent Scrivner & Roth LLC
Issues: TOB
Rep By: Norman F. Lent, III, Hon. Norman F. Lent, Alan J. Roth, Michael S. Scrivner

M & R Strategic Services
Issues: TOB

Zuckerman Spaeder L.L.P.
Issues: TOB
Rep By: Ronald H. Weich

Nat'l Center for Urban Ethnic Affairs

P.O. Box 20
Cardinal Station
Washington, DC 20064
Tel: (202)232-3600
Fax: (202)319-6289

An independent, national, non-profit organization affiliated with the United States Catholic Conference. Concerned with older industrial cities and particularly with neighborhoods founded by immigrants, ethnic studies, representation and cultural tradition and multi-cultural cooperation.

In-house, DC-area Employees

KROMKOWSKI, John A.: President

Nat'l Center on Addiction and Substance Abuse

New York, NY

Outside Counsel/Consultants

Neuman and Co.
Rep By: Robert A. Neuman

Nat'l Center on Education and the Economy

700 11th St. NW
Suite 750
Washington, DC 20001
Tel: (202)783-3668
Fax: (202)783-3672

In-house, DC-area Employees

BARNICLE, Timothy M.: Director, Workforce Services

Nat'l Center on Institutions and Alternatives

3125 Mount Vernon Ave.
Alexandria, VA 22305
Web: www.ncianet.org/ncia
E-mail: ncia@igc.apc.org
Tel: (703)684-0373
Fax: (703)684-6037
Registered: LDA

The organization seeks alternative, community-based sentencing for non-violent offenders.

In-house, DC-area Employees

HOELTER, Herbert J.: Director
MILLER, Ph.D., Jerome G.: President

Nat'l Certification Board for Therapeutic Massage and Bodywork

8201 Greensboro Dr.
Suite 300
McLean, VA 22102
Web: www.ncbtmb.com
E-mail: mdownes@ncbtmb.com
Tel: (703)610-9015
Fax: (703)610-9005

Outside Counsel/Consultants

Ass'n Management Group
Rep By: Christine Niero

Nat'l Certified Pipe Welding Bureau

1385 Piccard Dr.
Rockville, MD 20850-4340
Web: www.mcaa.org
E-mail: nick@mcaa.org
Tel: (301)869-5800
Fax: (301)990-9690

Provide technical support on pipe welding.

In-house, DC-area Employees

NIKPOURFAND, Dariush "Nick": Exec. Director

Nat'l Chamber Foundation

1615 H St. NW
Washington, DC 20062
Web: www.uschamber.com
E-mail: ncf@uschamber.com
Tel: (202)463-5500
Fax: (202)463-3129

The non-profit public policy research institute affiliated with the Chamber of Commerce of the U.S.A.

In-house, DC-area Employees

EIDEN, Matt: Program Coordinator
HARE, Neil: Director, Programs
HARTER, Kiran: Program Coordinator
HIRSCHMANN, David: Exec. V. President
HOWELL, Andrew: V. President
MCHALE, Jeanette: Development Director
STRATTON, Jane: Program Assistant

Nat'l Chicken Council

1015 15th St. NW
Suite 930
Washington, DC 20005
Tel: (202)296-2622
Fax: (202)293-4005
Registered: LDA

The Nat'l Chicken Council, established in 1954, is the U.S. poultry industry's national trade association.

Leg. Issues: AGR, CAW, ENV, FOO, IMM, LBR, TRA, TRD

Political Action Committee/s

Nat'l Chicken Council Political Action Committee
1015 15th St. NW
Suite 930
Washington, DC 20005
Contact: George B. Watts
Tel: (202)296-2622
Fax: (202)293-4005

In-house, DC-area Employees

COLVILLE, Mary: Director, Government Relations
WATTS, George B.: President

Outside Counsel/Consultants

Capitolink, LLC
Issues: AGR, CAW
Rep By: John H. Thorne, Ph.D.

Hogan & Hartson L.L.P.
Issues: AGR, ENV, FOO, LBR, TRA
Rep By: C. Michael Gilliland, Gary Jay Kushner

Nat'l Child Abuse Coalition

Leg. Issues: FAM

Outside Counsel/Consultants

Thomas L. Birch
Issues: FAM
Rep By: Thomas L. Birch

Nat'l Child Care Ass'n

Outside Counsel/Consultants

Smith, Bucklin and Associates, Inc.
Rep By: Frank M. Moore, Stacey Moye

Nat'l Child Support Enforcement Ass'n

444 N. Capitol St. NW
Suite 414
Washington, DC 20001
Web: www.ncsea.org
E-mail: ncsea@sso.org
Tel: (202)624-8180
Fax: (202)624-8828

Works to ensure that children receive financial and emotional support from both parents through education, training, and advocacy.

Leg. Issues: BNK, BUD, GOV, LBR, MMM, WEL

In-house, DC-area Employees

BANKES, Joel: Exec. Director

Nat'l Childcare Parents Ass'n

3612 Bent Branch Ct.
Falls Church, VA 22041
Tel: (703)941-4329
Fax: (703)941-4329

In-house, DC-area Employees

TOBIN, Dr. William J.: Exec. Director

Outside Counsel/Consultants

Associated Child Care Consultants, Ltd.

William J. Tobin and Associates

Nat'l Chronic Care Consortium

Bloomington, MN
Leg. Issues: HCR

Outside Counsel/Consultants

The Wilbur Group
Issues: HCR
Rep By: Valerie Wilbur

Nat'l Citizens Coalition for Nursing Home Reform

1424 16th St. NW
Suite 202
Washington, DC 20036
Web: www.nccnhr.org
E-mail: nccnhr@nccnhr.org
Tel: (202)332-2275
Fax: (202)332-2949

A consumer-governed membership organization working to improve health care and living conditions for the nation's institutionalized aged through public education and legislation.

In-house, DC-area Employees

BURGER, Sarah Greene: Interim Exec. Director

Outside Counsel/Consultants

Valente Lopatin & Schulze

Nat'l City Corp.

Cleveland, OH
Leg. Issues: BAN

Outside Counsel/Consultants

Squire, Sanders & Dempsey L.L.P.
Issues: BAN
Rep By: Louis Stokes

Nat'l Clay Pipe Institute

206 Vassar Pl.
Alexandria, VA 22314
Tel: (703)370-5750

In-house, DC-area Employees

NEWBOULD, E. Jack: Corporate Counsel

Nat'l Club Ass'n

1120 20th St. NW
Suite 725
Washington, DC 20007
Web: www.natlclub.org
E-mail: natlclub@natlclub.org
Tel: (202)822-9822
Fax: (202)822-9808
Registered: LDA

The Nat'l Club Ass'n represents the business, legal and legislative interests of private social, recreational and athletic clubs. Over 1,000 private clubs nationwide, with an estimated 1 million members, belong to NCA.

Leg. Issues: ART, BEV, CIV, CPT, GOV, LBR, SMB, TAX

Political Action Committee/s

Nat'l Club Ass'n Political Action Committee
1120 20th St. NW
Suite 725
Washington, DC 20007
Contact: Kevin D. Anderson
Tel: (202)822-9822
Fax: (202)822-9808

In-house, DC-area Employees

ANDERSON, Kevin D.: V. President, Legal and Government Relations
WEGRZYN, Susanne R.: Exec. V. President
WEXLER, Timothy W.: Assistant Director, Government Relations

Outside Counsel/Consultants

McGuiness Norris & Williams, LLP
Rep By: G. John Tysse

Nat'l Coalition Against Domestic Violence

1532 16th St. NW
Washington, DC 20036
Web: www.webmerchants.com/ncadv
Tel: (202)745-1211
Fax: (202)745-0088
Registered: LDA

A national grassroots membership organization working to end violence in the lives of women and children. Provides a clearinghouse for information and technical assistance, a unified voice on public policy issues, regional training, public education, and a national conference.

In-house, DC-area Employees

FULCHER, Juley: Director, Public Policy

Nat'l Coalition Against the Misuse of Pesticides

701 E St. SE
Suite 200
Washington, DC 20003
Web: www.beyondpesticides.org
E-mail: info@beyondpesticides.org
Tel: (202)543-5450
Fax: (202)543-4791

An organization of grassroots groups and people established to identify hazards of pesticides and reduce or eliminate unnecessary use of pesticides through safer alternatives.

In-house, DC-area Employees

FELDMAN, Jay: Exec. Director

Nat'l Coalition for Advanced Manufacturing

1201 New York Ave. NW
Suite 725
Washington, DC 20005
Web: www.bmptoe.org/ncfam
E-mail: ncfam@clark.net
Tel: (202)216-2740
Fax: (202)289-7618

Non-profit, non-partisan 501(c)(3) organization designed to advance the goal of industrial modernization through research, education, and services.

In-house, DC-area Employees

GERST, Leesa: Director, Communications
REDDY, Leo J.: President

Nat'l Coalition for Cancer Research

Leg. Issues: BUD, HCR, MED, TAX, TOB

Outside Counsel/Consultants

Capitol Associates, Inc.
Issues: BUD, HCR, MED, TAX, TOB
Rep By: Liz Gemski, Pamela Patrice Jackson, Ronnie Kovner Tepp

Nat'l Coalition for Cancer Survivorship

1010 Wayne Ave.
Suite 770
Silver Spring, MD 20910
Tel: (301)650-9127
Fax: (301)565-9670
Registered: LDA
Leg. Issues: BUD, CPT, GOV, HCR, LBR, MED, MMM, TAX, TOR

In-house, DC-area Employees

DONESKI, Donna: Director, Marketing and Communications
STOVALL, Ellen: President and Chief Exec. Officer

Outside Counsel/Consultants

Bennett Turner & Coleman, LLP
Issues: BUD, HCR, MED, MMM
Rep By: Elizabeth Goss, Kristi E. Schrode, Samuel D. Turner

Venable
Issues: CPT, GOV, LBR, TAX, TOR
Rep By: Jeffrey S. Tenenbaum

Nat'l Coalition for Homeless Veterans

333 1/2 Pennsylvania Ave. SE
Washington, DC 20003-1148
Web: www.nchv.org
E-mail: nchv@nchv.org
Tel: (202)546-1969
Fax: (202)546-2063
Registered: LDA

In-house, DC-area Employees

BOONE, Linda: Exec. Director

Nat'l Coalition for Minority Business

Outside Counsel/Consultants

Shaw Pittman
Rep By: Rodolfo Fuentes, John E. Jensen

Nat'l Coalition for Osteoporosis and Related Bone Diseases

Washington, DC
Leg. Issues: BUD, HCR, SCI

Outside Counsel/Consultants

Cavarocchi Ruscio Dennis Associates
Issues: BUD, HCR, SCI
Rep By: Nicholas G. Cavarocchi

Nat'l Coalition for Patient Rights

Outside Counsel/Consultants

Hauser Group

Nat'l Coalition for the Homeless

1012 14th St. NW
Suite 600
Washington, DC 20005-3471
Web: www.nationalhomeless.org
E-mail: info@nationalhomeless.org
Tel: (202)737-6444
Fax: (202)737-6445

The National Coalition for the Homeless, founded in 1982, is a national network of people who are or have been homeless, activists, advocates, service providers, and others committed to a single mission: to end homelessness. We are committed to creating the systemic and attitudinal changes necessary to prevent and end homelessness. At the same time, we work to meet the immediate needs of people who either are, or at risk of becoming, homeless. We take as our first principle of practice, that homeless and formerly homeless people must be actively involved in all of our work.

In-house, DC-area Employees

DUFFIELD, Barbara: Director, Education
STOOPS, Michael: Director Field Organizing Project
WATLOV PHILLIPS, Sue: Acting Exec. Director

Nat'l Coalition of Abortion Providers

206 King St.
Second Floor
Alexandria, VA 22314
Web: www.ncap.com
E-mail: ronncap@aol.com
Tel: (703)684-0055
Fax: (703)684-5051
Registered: LDA

An organization of approximately 200 independently-owned abortion clinics.

Political Action Committee/s

Nat'l Coalition of Abortion Providers PAC
206 King St.
Second Floor
Alexandria, VA 22314
Contact: Ron Fitzsimmons
Tel: (703)684-0055
Fax: (703)684-5051

In-house, DC-area Employees

FITZSIMMONS, Ron: Exec. Director

Nat'l Coalition of Black Meeting Planners

8630 Fenton St.
Suite 126
Silver Spring, MD 20910
Web: www.ncbmp.org
E-mail: ncbmp@compuserve.com
Tel: (202)628-3952
Fax: (301)588-0011

In-house, DC-area Employees

APONTE, Ana: President
CRUMP, CMP, CAE, John: Chairman

Nat'l Coalition of Consumer Organizations on Aging

409 Third St. SW
Second Floor
Washington, DC 20024
Tel: (202)479-1200
Fax: (202)479-0735

In-house, DC-area Employees

BEDLIN, Howard: Contact

Nat'l Coalition of Food Importers Ass'n

Matawan, NJ
Leg. Issues: FOO, TRD

Outside Counsel/Consultants

Olsson, Frank and Weeda, P.C.
Issues: FOO, TRD
Rep By: John W. Bode, Susan P. Grymes, Karen Reis Harned, Stephen L. Lacey, Marshall L. Matz, Tyson Redpath, Ryan W. Stroschein

Nat'l Coalition of Minority Businesses

Leg. Issues: BUD, CIV, GOV, SMB

Outside Counsel/Consultants

Holland & Knight LLP
Issues: BUD, CIV, GOV, SMB
Rep By: Joanna S. Han, Michael R. Hatcher, Jeffrey P. Hildebrant, Weldon H. Latham, Amy B. Nee

Nat'l Coalition of Petroleum Dry Cleaners

Washington, DC

Outside Counsel/Consultants

Jenner & Block
Rep By: Robert M. Portman

Nat'l Coalition on Black Civic Participation, Inc.

1629 K St. NW
Suite 801
Washington, DC 20006
Web: www.bigvote.org
E-mail: ncobvp@igc.apc.org
Tel: (202)659-4929
Fax: (202)659-5025

An organization that works to increase black voter registration and turnout with a goal of increasing political empowerment of blacks and other minorities.

In-house, DC-area Employees

CAMPBELL, Melanie L.: Exec. Director

Nat'l Coalition on E-Commerce and Privacy

Washington, DC
Leg. Issues: CSP, TEC

Outside Counsel/Consultants

Alston & Bird LLP
Issues: CSP, TEC
Rep By: Thomas M. Boyd, A.E. Lovett, John A. Schall, Dwight C. Smith, III, Jonathan Winer

Nat'l Coalition on Health Care

1200 G St. NW
Suite 750
Washington, DC 20005
Web: www.americashealth.org
Tel: (202)638-7151
Fax: (202)638-7166

Former Presidents George Bush, Jimmy Carter and Gerald Ford are honorary Co-Chairmen.

In-house, DC-area Employees
SIMMONS, M.D., Henry E.: President

Nat'l Coalition on Rural Aging

409 Third St. SW
Second Floor
Washington, DC 20024-6682
Tel: (202)479-6981
Fax: (202)479-0735

A membership unit of the Nat'l Council on the Aging.

In-house, DC-area Employees
MCCLENDON, Carol

Nat'l Coalition to Abolish the Death Penalty

1436 U St. NW
Suite 104
Washington, DC 20009
Web: www.ncadp.org
E-mail: info@ncadp.org
Tel: (202)387-3890
Fax: (202)387-5590

A grassroots organization working to end the use of capital punishment in the United States.

Leg. Issues: LAW

In-house, DC-area Employees
HAWKINS, Steven: Exec. Director

Nat'l Coalition to Promote Physical Activity

Outside Counsel/Consultants
Geddings Communications LLC

Nat'l Collaboration for Youth

1319 F St. NW
Suite 601
Washington, DC 20004
Web: www.nydic.org
E-mail: nassembly@nassembly.org
Tel: (202)347-2080
Fax: (202)393-4517

Can be contacted through The Nat'l Assembly of Health and Human Service Organizations of which it is an affinity group.

In-house, DC-area Employees
KATZ, Irv: Contact

Nat'l College

Lombard, IL
Leg. Issues: EDU, HCR, MED

Outside Counsel/Consultants
Miller & Co.
Issues: EDU, HCR, MED
Rep By: Richard W. Miller

Nat'l College Access Network

Baltimore, MD
Leg. Issues: EDU

Outside Counsel/Consultants
Hogan & Hartson L.L.P.
Issues: EDU
Rep By: Jonathan Abram, C. Michael Gilliland, Elizabeth B. Heffernan, Christine M. Warnke

Nat'l Collegiate Athletic Ass'n

One Dupont Circle NW
Suite 310
Washington, DC 20036
Web: www.ncaa.org
E-mail: ddixon@ncaa.org
Tel: (202)293-3050
Fax: (202)293-3075
Registered: LDA

An association which sponsors programs that contribute to the overall development and well being of the student-athlete headquartered in Indianapolis, IN.

Leg. Issues: CPT, EDU, GAM, SPO, TAX

In-house, DC-area Employees
DIXON, Doris L.: Director, Federal Relations
NESTEL, Daniel: Sr. Assistant Director, Federal Relations

Outside Counsel/Consultants
Dean Blakey & Moskowitz
Issues: EDU
Rep By: Ellin J. Nolan

Squire, Sanders & Dempsey L.L.P.
Issues: CPT
Rep By: Ritchie T. Thomas

Nat'l Commission for the Certification of Crane Operators

Fairfax, VA
Leg. Issues: GOV

Outside Counsel/Consultants
Halsey, Rains & Associates, LLC
Issues: GOV
Rep By: Steven C. Halsey, James Hubbard, Laurie D. Rains

Nat'l Commission on Correctional Health Care

Chicago, IL
Leg. Issues: HCR

Outside Counsel/Consultants
Van Scoyoc Associates, Inc.
Issues: HCR
Rep By: Anita R. Estell, H. Stewart Van Scoyoc

Nat'l Committee Against Repressive Legislation

3321 12th St. NE
Third Floor
Washington, DC 20017
E-mail: ncarl@aol.com
Tel: (202)529-4225
Fax: (202)526-4611

Established in 1960 to support and coordinate opposition to all threats to the First Amendment rights of freedom of speech and association. Headquartered in Los Angeles, CA.

Leg. Issues: CIV, CON, IMM

In-house, DC-area Employees
GAGE, Kit: Washington Representative

Nat'l Committee for a Human Life Amendment

733 15th St. NW
Suite 956
Washington, DC 20005
Tel: (202)393-0703
Fax: (202)347-1383

In-house, DC-area Employees
TAYLOR, Michael: Exec. Director

Nat'l Committee for an Effective Congress

122 C St. NW
Suite 650
Washington, DC 20001
Web: www.ncec.org
E-mail: info@ncec.org
Tel: (202)639-8300
Fax: (202)639-5038

Established in 1948 to provide funds and technical campaign services to progressive candidates for Congress. Has helped elect both liberal Republicans and Democrats.

In-house, DC-area Employees
BYRON, James E.: Treasurer
GERSH, Mark H.: Washington Director
HEMENWAY, Russell D.: National Director

Nat'l Committee for Quality Assurance

2000 L St. NW
Suite 500
Washington, DC 20036
Web: www.ncqa.org
Tel: (202)955-3500
Fax: (202)955-3599

A non-profit organization committed to assessing and improving the quality of care provided by managed care organizations.

In-house, DC-area Employees
PAWLSON, Greg: Exec. V. President
TORDA, Phyllis: Assistant V. President

Nat'l Committee for Quality Health Care

1100 Connecticut Ave. NW
Suite 545
Washington, DC 20036
Web: www.ncqhc.org
E-mail: ncqhc@erols.com
Tel: (202)331-7535
Fax: (202)331-7532

A broad-based coalition of hospitals, and related firms which supply goods and services to the health care industry.

In-house, DC-area Employees
MCDERMOTT, Catherine: President

Nat'l Committee for Responsive Philanthropy

2001 S St. NW
Suite 620
Washington, DC 20009
Web: www.ncrp.org
E-mail: info@ncrp.org
Tel: (202)387-9177
Fax: (202)332-5084

A non-profit organization working to make United Ways, foundations, and corporate giving programs more accountable, accessible, and responsive to socially, economically and politically disenfranchised people, and to the changing needs of increasingly diverse communities nationwide.

In-house, DC-area Employees
COHEN, Rick: President

Nat'l Committee for the Prevention of Elder Abuse/Institute on Aging

Worcester, MA

Outside Counsel/Consultants
Matz, Blancato & Associates, Inc.

Nat'l Committee on Pay Equity

3420 Hamilton Street
Suite 200
Hyattsville, MD 20782
Web: www.feminist.com/fairpay.htm
E-mail: fairpay@aol.com
Tel: (301)277-1033
Fax: (301)277-4451

A coalition working to eliminate sex- and race-based wage discrimination and achieve pay equity.

In-house, DC-area Employees
REED, Alyson: Exec. Director

Nat'l Committee to Preserve Social Security and Medicare

Ten G St. NE
Suite 600
Washington, DC 20002-4215
Tel: (202)216-0420
Fax: (202)216-0446
Registered: LDA

Leg. Issues: BUD, HCR, MMM, RET

Political Action Committee/s
Nat'l Committee to Preserve Social Security and Medicare Political Action Committee
Ten G St. NE
Suite 600
Washington, DC 20002-4215
Contact: Max Richtman
Tel: (202)216-0420
Fax: (202)216-0446

In-house, DC-area Employees
BRIGNER, Sharon: Senior Policy Analyst
CHATMAN, Priscilla: Senior Policy Analyst
DAVIS, Lisa: Senior Policy Analyst
FREY, Scott: Senior Legislative Representative
GANNON, Cheryl: Director, Government Relations and Policy
MCSTEEN, Martha A.: President
RICHTMAN, Max: Exec. V. President

Outside Counsel/Consultants
Chambers Associates Inc.

Geddings Communications LLC
Rep By: Kristine Phillips Geddings

Nat'l Communication Ass'n

1765 N St. NW
Washington, DC 20036
Web: www.natcom.org
E-mail: jgaudino@scassn.org
Tel: (202)464-4622
Fax: (202)464-4600

In-house, DC-area Employees
GAUDINO, Dr. James L.: Exec. Director

Nat'l Community Action Foundation

810 1st St. NW
Washington, DC 20002
Tel: (202)842-2092
Fax: (202)842-2095

A non-profit lobbying organization representing the concerns of 900 community action agencies on human service legislation, including the Community Service Block Grant, Low Income Energy Assistance, Community Food Distribution, Weatherization, Headstart, and other programs for the poor.

Leg. Issues: BUD, WEL

Political Action Committee/s
Community Action Program Political Action Committee
810 1st St. NW
Washington, DC 20002
Tel: (202)842-2092
Fax: (202)842-2095

In-house, DC-area Employees
BRADLEY, David A.: Exec. Director

Outside Counsel/Consultants
Moss McGee Bradley & Foley
Issues: BUD, WEL
Rep By: David A. Bradley, Leander J. Foley, III

Nat'l Community Capital Ass'n

Philadelphia, PA
Leg. Issues: TAX

Outside Counsel/Consultants
Drinker Biddle & Reath LLP
Issues: TAX
Rep By: Timothy Hughes, Joaquin A. Marquez, Gregg R. Melinson

Nat'l Community Development Ass'n

522 21st St. NW
Suite 120
Washington, DC 20006
Web: www.ncdaonline.org
E-mail: ncda@ncpaonline.org
Tel: (202)293-7587
Fax: (202)887-5546

In-house, DC-area Employees
SASSO, John A.: Exec. Secretary

Nat'l Community Education Ass'n

3929 Old Lee Hwy. Tel: (703)359-8973
Suite 91-A Fax: (703)359-0972
Fairfax, VA 22030-2401
Web: www.ncea.com
E-mail: ncea@ncea.com

Provides membership services for community education professionals.

Leg. Issues: BUD, EDU, LAW

In-house, DC-area Employees

JEWELL-KELLY, Starla: Exec. Director

Nat'l Community Pharmacists Ass'n

205 Daingerfield Rd. Tel: (703)683-8200
Alexandria, VA 22314 Fax: (703)683-3619
Registered: LDA
Web: www.ncpanet.org
E-mail: info@ncpanet.org
Leg. Issues: PHA

Political Action Committee/s

Nat'l Community Pharmacists Ass'n Political Action Committee
205 Daingerfield Rd. Tel: (703)683-8200
Alexandria, VA 22314 Fax: (703)683-3619
Contact: John M. Rector

In-house, DC-area Employees

ANTHONY, Calvin J.: Exec. V. President
RECTOR, John M.: Senior V. President, Government Affairs and General Counsel

Outside Counsel/Consultants

Patton Boggs, LLP
Issues: PHA
Rep By: Jonathan R. Yarowsky
Sidley & Austin
Rep By: Michael A. Nemeroff

Nat'l Community Reinvestment Coalition

733 15th St. NW Tel: (202)628-8866
Suite 540 Fax: (202)628-9800
Washington, DC 20005
E-mail: jtaylor192@aol.com
Leg. Issues: BUD, ECN, HOU

In-house, DC-area Employees

EDDINGTON, Robin: Director, Legislative and Regulatory Affairs
TAYLOR, John E.: President and Chief Exec. Officer

Outside Counsel/Consultants

Madison Government Affairs
Issues: BUD, ECN, HOU
Rep By: Paul J. Hirsch, Myron M. Jacobson, Jackson Kemper, III

Nat'l Computer Systems

Arlington, VA

Outside Counsel/Consultants

Steven Kingsley
Rep By: Steven Kingsley

Nat'l Concrete Masonry Ass'n

2302 Horse Pen Rd. Tel: (703)713-1900
Herndon, VA 20171-3499 Fax: (703)713-1910
Registered: LDA
Web: www.ncma.org
E-mail: ncma@ncma.org

Represents the manufacturers of concrete masonry products.

Leg. Issues: BUD, CAW, DIS, ECN, ENV, GOV, LBR, MAN, SMB, TAX, TRA

Political Action Committee/s

Nat'l Concrete Masonry Ass'n Political Action Committee
2302 Horse Pen Rd. Tel: (703)713-1900
Herndon, VA 20171-3499 Fax: (703)713-1910
Contact: Mark B. Hogan

In-house, DC-area Employees

DEITZER, Harry J.: Director, Marketing
HOGAN, Mark B.: President

Outside Counsel/Consultants

Capitol Hill Advocates
Issues: LBR, MAN, SMB, TAX, TRA
Rep By: Randall G. Pence

Nat'l Confectioners Ass'n

8320 Old Courthouse Rd. Tel: (703)790-5750
Suite 300 Fax: (703)790-5752
Vienna, VA 22182 Registered: LDA
Web: www.candyusa.com
E-mail: nca@candyusa.com
Leg. Issues: FOO

Political Action Committee/s

Nat'l Confectioners Ass'n Political Action Committee
8320 Old Courthouse Rd. Tel: (703)790-5750
Suite 300 Fax: (703)790-5752
Vienna, VA 22182
Contact: Stephen G. Lodge

In-house, DC-area Employees

GRAHAM, Lawrence T.: President
LODGE, Stephen G.: V. President, Legislative Affairs
SMITH, Susan Snyder: Senior V. President

Outside Counsel/Consultants

Olsson, Frank and Weeda, P.C.
Rep By: John W. Bode, Richard L. Frank, Susan P. Grymes, Karen Reis Harned, Stephen L. Lacey, Marshall L. Matz, Tyson Redpath, Ryan W. Stroschein

Nat'l Conference of Bankruptcy Judges

Nashville, TN
Leg. Issues: BNK, RET

Outside Counsel/Consultants

Podesta/Mattoon
Issues: BNK, RET

Nat'l Conference of Catholic Bishops, Secretariat for Pro-Life Activities

3211 Fourth St. NE Tel: (202)541-3070
Washington, DC 20017 Fax: (202)541-3054
Web: www.nccbuscc.org/prolife

Works to oppose abortion and euthanasia.

In-house, DC-area Employees

CHOPKO, Mark E.
MONAHAN, Frank
QUINN, Gail: Exec. Director, Secretariat for Pro-Life Activities

Nat'l Conference of Christians and Jews

1815 H St. NW Tel: (202)822-6110
Suite 1050 Fax: (202)822-6114
Washington, DC 20006

In-house, DC-area Employees

KRAVITZ, Cheryl: Exec. Director

Nat'l Conference of State Historic Preservation Officers

444 N. Capitol St. NW Tel: (202)624-5465
Suite 342 Fax: (202)624-5419
Washington, DC 20001
Web: www.sso.org/ncshpo

In-house, DC-area Employees

SCHAMU, Nancy: Exec. Director

Nat'l Conference of State Legislatures

444 N. Capitol St. NW Tel: (202)624-5400
Suite 515 Fax: (202)737-1069
Washington, DC 20001

A non-partisan organization funded by the states which works to improve the quality and effectiveness of state legislatures, assure states a strong and cohesive voice in the federal decision-making process, and foster inter-governmental communication and cooperation.

In-house, DC-area Employees

BIRD, Michael: Federal Affairs Counsel
OSTEN, Neal: Director of Commerce and Communications
TUBBESING, Carl: Deputy Exec. Director
WILSON, Joy Johnson: Senior Program Director, Health and Human Services

Nat'l Conference of States on Building Codes and Standards

505 Huntmar Park Dr. Tel: (703)437-0100
Suite 210 Fax: (703)481-3596
Herndon, VA 20170
Web: www.ncsbcs.org

In-house, DC-area Employees

DIBBER, Barbara: Communications Specialist
UTHANK, Mike: President
WIBLE, Robert C.: Exec. Director

Nat'l Congress for Community Economic Development

1030 15th St. NW Tel: (202)289-9020
Suite 325 Fax: (202)289-7051
Washington, DC 20005
Web: www.ncced.org
E-mail: rpriest@ncced.org

A national organization which supports community-based, non-profit economic development corporations known as Community Development Corporations (CDCs).

In-house, DC-area Employees

KELLY, Kevin S.: Assistant V. President, Programs

Nat'l Congress of American Indians

1301 Connecticut Ave. NW Tel: (202)466-7767
Suite 200 Fax: (202)466-7797
Washington, DC 20036
Web: www.ncai.org

Founded in 1944, NCAI is the oldest and largest national Indian organization. It works to educate the U.S. Congress and public on tribal issues on behalf of tribal governments in an effort to safeguard tribal sovereignty.

In-house, DC-area Employees

CHASE, JoAnn: Exec. Director
JACKSON, Jr., Jack C.: Director, Government Affairs

Outside Counsel/Consultants

Chambers Associates Inc.
Rep By: Letitia Chambers

Nat'l Congress of Parents and Teachers

1090 Vermont Ave. NW Tel: (202)289-6790
Suite 1200 Fax: (202)289-6791
Washington, DC 20005 Registered: LDA
Web: www.pta.org

Headquartered in Chicago, IL. The governmental relations office of the National PTA organization.

In-house, DC-area Employees

HENRICH, Carolyn: Government Relations Specialist
IGO, Shirley: President-Elect
OAKES, Maribeth: Director, Legislation

Nat'l Consumer Law Center

1629 K St. NW Tel: (202)986-6060
Suite 600 Fax: (202)463-9462
Washington, DC 20006
Web: www.consumerlaw.org
E-mail: consumerlaw@nclc.org

Headquartered in Boston, MA. Aids legal services programs and other low-income advocates in matters involving consumer and energy issues.

In-house, DC-area Employees

SAUNDERS, Margot Freeman: Managing Attorney

Nat'l Consumers League

1701 K St. NW Tel: (202)835-3323
Suite 1200 Fax: (202)835-0747
Washington, DC 20006
Web: www.nclnet.org
E-mail: ncl@nclnet.org

Founded in 1899, the National Consumer League identifies, protects, represents, and advances the economic and social interests of consumers and workers. As America's pioneer consumer advocacy organization, NCL represents consumers and workers on such issues as healthcare, e-commerce, fair labor standards, privacy, food and drug safety, technology, telecommunications, and fraud.

Leg. Issues: ADV, AGR, APP, BAN, BNK, CAW, CIV, CPI, CSP, EDU, ENV, FIN, FOO, HCR, LAW, LBR, MAN, MED, PHA, POS, SCI, TEC, TOU, TRD, UTI, WAS

In-house, DC-area Employees

GOLODNER, Linda F.: President
GRANT, Susan: V. President, Public Policy
MCKAY, Carol: Assistant Director, Communications

Nat'l Contact Lens Examiners

6506 Lois Dale Rd. Tel: (703)719-5800
Suite 209 Fax: (703)719-9144
Springfield, VA 22150
Web: www.abo-ncle.org

In-house, DC-area Employees

ROBEY, Michael: Exec. Director

Nat'l Cooperative Bank

1725 I St. NW Tel: (202)336-7700
Suite 600 Fax: (202)336-7801
Washington, DC 20006 Registered: LDA
Web: www.ncb.com
E-mail: corprel@ncb.com

A congressionally-chartered organization reconstituted as a privately-owned cooperative financial services company providing mortgage banking, commercial lending, capital markets and depository services to cooperatively structured enterprises nationwide.

Leg. Issues: BUD, HOU

In-house, DC-area Employees

HACKMAN, Charles H.: Managing Director

Outside Counsel/Consultants

Columbus Public Affairs

Hessel and Aluise, P.C.
Issues: HOU
Rep By: Timothy J. Aluise, Nancy Libson

The PMA Group
Issues: BUD
Rep By: Kaylene Green, Patrick Hiu, Paul J. Magliocchetti, Timothy K. Sanders

Nat'l Cooperative Business Ass'n

1401 New York Ave. NW
Suite 1100
Washington, DC 20005
Tel: (202)638-6222
Fax: (202)628-6726
Registered: LDA
Web: www.cooperative.org
E-mail: ncba@ncba.org

A national, cross-industry membership and trade association representing cooperatives, including about 46,000 businesses ranging in size from small buying clubs to Fortune 500 companies.

Leg. Issues: AGR, BAN, BUD, FOR, HOU, TAX

Political Action Committee/s

Cooperative Action for Congressional Trust (CO ACT)
1401 New York Ave. NW
Suite 1100
Washington, DC 20005
Tel: (202)638-6222
Fax: (202)628-6726
Contact: Richard J. Dines

In-house, DC-area Employees

DINES, Richard J.: Director of Cooperative Business Development
HAZEN, Paul: President and Chief Exec. Officer
KELLY, Jennine: Director of Communications and Public Policy

Outside Counsel/Consultants

Dittus Communications
Rep By: Debra Cabral, Neena Moorjani

The GrayWell Group, Inc.
Issues: AGR
Rep By: Peter D. Caldwell, Robert J. Gray

Nat'l Coordinating Committee for Multiemployer Plans

815 16th St. NW
Washington, DC 20006
Tel: (202)737-5315
Fax: (202)737-1308
E-mail: rdefrehn@nccmp.org

Interested in legislation and regulations affecting multi-employer pension plans, health, welfare and training plans, and their participants and sponsors.

Leg. Issues: HCR, LBR, TAX

In-house, DC-area Employees

DEFREHN, Randy G.: Exec. Director

Outside Counsel/Consultants

Hooper Owen & Winburn
Issues: TAX
Rep By: John P. Winburn

O'Donoghue & O'Donoghue
Issues: HCR, LBR, TAX

Nat'l Coordinating Committee for the Promotion of History

400 A St. SE
Washington, DC 20003
Tel: (202)544-2422
Fax: (202)544-8307
Registered: LDA
Web: www2.h-net.msu.edu/~ncc

The lobbying arm of the historical and archival professions.

Leg. Issues: BUD, CPT, EDU, GOV, NAT

In-house, DC-area Employees

CRAIG, Bruce: Director

Nat'l Corn Growers Ass'n

122 C St. NW
Suite 510
Washington, DC 20001
Tel: (202)628-7001
Fax: (202)628-1933
Registered: LDA
Web: www.ncga.com
E-mail: corninfo@ncga.com

Headquartered in St. Louis, MO.

Leg. Issues: AGR, BUD, CAW, FUE, NAT, ROD, RRR, SCI, TAX, TRA, TRD

In-house, DC-area Employees

DOUGHERTY, Ellen A.: Director, Washington Communications
FRANZ, Keira E.: Director, Public Policy
KEITH, Susan: Senior Director, Public Policy
KNIGHT, Bruce I.: V. President, Public Policy
MARTINS, Jaqueline: Director, Public Policy
MCCLELLAND, John: Director, Energy and Analysis

Outside Counsel/Consultants

Alpine Group, Inc.
Issues: CAW
Rep By: James D. Massie

Eversole Associates
Issues: AGR, SCI
Rep By: Kellye A. Eversole

Nat'l Corp. for Housing Partnerships, Inc. (NCHP)

Vienna, VA
Registered: LDA
Web: www.nhpi.com
E-mail: wash.nhpi.com

Concerned with multifamily housing ownership and management.

Outside Counsel/Consultants

Linda Parke Gallagher & Assoc.
Rep By: Linda Parke Gallagher

Nat'l Corrugated Steel Pipe Ass'n

Washington, DC

Outside Counsel/Consultants

Hauck and Associates
Rep By: Brian Roberts

Nat'l Cosmetology Ass'n

Chicago, IL
Leg. Issues: HCR, PHA

Outside Counsel/Consultants

Collier Shannon Scott, PLLC
Rep By: Lauren R. Howard, William W. Scott

The Plexus Consulting Group
Issues: HCR, PHA
Rep By: Yasmin Quiwzow

Nat'l Cotton Council of America

1521 New Hampshire Ave. NW
Washington, DC 20036
Tel: (202)745-7805
Fax: (202)483-4040
Registered: LDA
Web: www.cotton.org

Headquartered in Memphis, TN.

Political Action Committee/s

Committee for the Advancement of Cotton
1521 New Hampshire Ave. NW
Washington, DC 20036
Tel: (202)745-7805
Fax: (202)483-4040
Contact: A. John Maguire

In-house, DC-area Employees

MAGUIRE, A. John: V. President, Washington Operations
MENCHEY, Keith: Government Relations Representative
WAKELYN, Phillip J.: Manager, Environmental Health and Safety`

Nat'l Council for Accreditation of Teacher Education

2010 Massachusetts Ave. NW
Suite 500
Washington, DC 20036-1023
Tel: (202)466-7496
Fax: (202)296-6620
Web: www.ncate.org
E-mail: ncate@ncate.org
Leg. Issues: EDU

In-house, DC-area Employees

FRANCIS, Shari L.: V. President, State Relations
GOLLNICK, Donna M.: Senior V. President
LEIBBRAND, Jane: V. President, Communications
WILLIAMS, Boyce C.: V. President, Institutional Relations
WISE, Arthur E.: President

Nat'l Council for Adoption

1930 17th St. NW
Washington, DC 20009-6207
Tel: (202)328-1200
Fax: (202)332-0935
Web: www.ncfa-usa.org
E-mail: ncfadc@attglobal.nef

A non-profit membership organization for agencies which provide services to pregnant adolescents, unmarried parents and infertile couples as well as for individuals who support the promotion of adoption of all kinds-healthy infants, children with "special needs" and international.

Leg. Issues: FAM

In-house, DC-area Employees

PURTILL, Patrick: President and Chief Exec. Officer

Outside Counsel/Consultants

Robert M. Guttman
Issues: FAM
Rep By: Robert M. Guttman

Nat'l Council for Community Behavioral Healthcare

12300 Twinbrook Pkwy.
Suite 320
Rockville, MD 20852
Tel: (301)984-6200
Registered: LDA
Web: www.nccbh.org
E-mail: membership@nccbh.org
Leg. Issues: ALC, BUD, CIV, HCR, HOU, LBR, MMM

In-house, DC-area Employees

LIEBFRIED, Tom: Assistant V. President, Government Relations
RAY, Charles G.: President and Chief Exec. Officer
SIMMONS, Pope M.: V. President, Government Relations

Nat'l Council for Eurasian and East European Research

Washington, DC
Leg. Issues: BUD, FOR

Outside Counsel/Consultants

Edington, Peel & Associates, Inc.
Issues: BUD, FOR
Rep By: Terry R. Peel

Nat'l Council For Fireworks Safety

Bethesda, MD

Outside Counsel/Consultants

Thompson, Hine and Flory LLP
Rep By: David H. Baker

Nat'l Council for Impacted Schools

Lawton, OK

Outside Counsel/Consultants

Fern M. Lapidus
Rep By: Fern M. Lapidus

Nat'l Council for Languages and Internat'l Studies

4646 40th St. NW
Washington, DC 20016
Tel: (202)966-8477
Fax: (202)966-8310
Registered: LDA
Web: www.languagepolicy.org
E-mail: info@languagepolicy.org

Supported by 64 language and international studies organizations.

Leg. Issues: EDU

In-house, DC-area Employees

EDWARDS, Ph.D., J. David: Exec. Director

Nat'l Council for Science and the Environment

1725 K St. NW
Suite 212
Washington, DC 20006
Tel: (202)530-5810
Fax: (202)628-4311
Web: www.cnie.org
E-mail: info@cnie.org

Mission is to improve the scientific basis for environmental decision-making.

Leg. Issues: ENV, NAT, SCI

In-house, DC-area Employees

AHMED, Ph.D., Karim: Secretary/Treasurer
BENEDICK, Richard E.: President
BLOCKSTEIN, Ph.D., David E.: Senior Scientist
SAUNDRY, Ph.D., Peter D.: Exec. Director

Nat'l Council for the Social Studies

3501 Newark St. NW
Washington, DC 20016
Tel: (202)966-7840
Fax: (202)966-2061
Web: www.ncss.org
E-mail: ncss@ncss.org

The largest association in the country devoted solely to social studies education. Engages and supports educators in strengthening and advocating the highest quality social studies curriculum and instruction at all levels and in all settings.

Leg. Issues: EDU

In-house, DC-area Employees

FRASCELLA, Albert: Director, Communications and Government Relations
GRIFFIN, Susan: Exec. Director

Nat'l Council of Agricultural Employers

1112 16th St. NW
Suite 920
Washington, DC 20036
Tel: (202)728-0300
Fax: (202)728-0303
Registered: LDA
Web: www.agemployers.org
E-mail: agemployers@aol.com

A non-profit trade association founded in 1964 to represent the interests of employers of agricultural labor and to ensure an adequate and capable work force for agriculture.

Leg. Issues: AGR, IMM, LBR

In-house, DC-area Employees

HUGHES, Sharon M.: Exec. V. President

Outside Counsel/Consultants

McGuiness Norris & Williams, LLP
Issues: AGR, IMM, LBR
Rep By: Timothy J. Bartl, James S. Holt, William N. LaForge, Monte B. Lake

Nat'l Council of Catholic Women

1275 K St. NW
Suite 975
Washington, DC 20005
Tel: (202)682-0334
Fax: (202)682-0338
Web: www.nccw.org
E-mail: nccw01@winstarmail.com
Leg. Issues: CAW, ENV, FAM, FOO, FOR, GOV, HCR, MMM, NAT, WEL

In-house, DC-area Employees

KANE, Annette P.: Exec. Director
REDDEN, K. La Verne: President

Nat'l Council of Chain Restaurants

325 Seventh St. NW
Suite 1100
Washington, DC 20004
Tel: (202)626-8183
Fax: (202)626-8185
Registered: LDA
Leg. Issues: GOV, LBR, TAX

Political Action Committee/s

Nat'l Council of Chain Restaurants PAC
325 Seventh St. NW
Suite 1100
Washington, DC 20004
Tel: (202)626-8183
Fax: (202)626-8185
Contact: Terrie M. Dort

In-house, DC-area Employees

DORT, Terrie M.: President

Nat'l Council of Coal Lessors

Charleston, WV
Leg. Issues: TAX

Outside Counsel/Consultants

Murray, Scheer, Montgomery, Tapia & O'Donnell
Issues: TAX
Rep By: Thomas R. Crawford, D. Michael Murray

Nat'l Council of Commercial Plant Breeders

601 13th St. NW
Suite 570 South
Washington, DC 20005
Tel: (202)638-3128
Fax: (202)638-3171
Web: www.amseed.org/nccpb

In-house, DC-area Employees

NICOLAS, Suzanne: Secretary
URMSTON, Dean: Exec. V. President

Nat'l Council of County Ass'n Executives

440 First St. NW
Eighth Floor
Washington, DC 20001
Tel: (202)395-6226
Fax: (202)393-2630
Web: www.naco.org

In-house, DC-area Employees

BYARS, Dottie: Contact

Nat'l Council of Farmer Cooperatives

50 F St. NW
Suite 900
Washington, DC 20001
Tel: (202)626-8700
Fax: (202)626-8722
Registered: LDA
Web: www.ncfc.org
E-mail: info@ncfc.org
Leg. Issues: AGR, BUD, CAW, ENV, TAX, TRA, TRD

Political Action Committee/s

Nat'l Council of Farmer Cooperatives Political Action Committee (Co-op PAC)
50 F St. NW
Suite 900
Washington, DC 20001
Tel: (202)626-8700
Fax: (202)626-8722
Contact: Randall T. Jones

In-house, DC-area Employees

BARR, Terry N.: Chief Economist and V. President, Agriculture and Trade Policy
GRAVES, David: President
HOWELL, James P.: V. President, Congressional and Regulatory Affairs
JONES, Randall T.: Senior V. President, Government and Public Affairs
KRZYMINSKI, James S.: Senior V. President, Corporate Services, General Counsel and Secretary
SCHAFER, Larry: V. President, Legal, Tax and Accounting Policy
VALENZUELA, Pam: Director, Communications and Member Relations
VAN ARSDALL, R. Thomas: V. President, Environmental Policy

Outside Counsel/Consultants

KPMG, LLP
Issues: TAX
Rep By: Jennifer Bonar, Harry L. Gutman, Gillian Spooner, Thomas A. Stout, Jr.

Nat'l Council of Health Facilities Finance Authorities

Helena, MT
Leg. Issues: FIN

Outside Counsel/Consultants

Mintz, Levin, Cohn, Ferris, Glovsky and Popeo, P.C.
Issues: FIN
Rep By: Charles A. Samuels

Nat'l Council of Higher Education Loan Programs

1100 Connecticut Ave. NW
12th Floor
Washington, DC 20036
Tel: (202)822-2106
Fax: (202)822-2142
Registered: LDA
Web: www.nchelp.org

Represents a nationwide network of guaranty agencies, secondary markets, lenders, loan servicers, collectors, schools, and other organizations involved in the administration of the Federal Family Education Loan Program. Also represents its members on public policy and regulatory issues with the legislative and executive branches of the federal government.

Leg. Issues: BAN, BUD, EDU, FIN, TAX

In-house, DC-area Employees

LANNING, Karen: Communications Coordinator
LIEF, Brett E.: President
ROSS, Lisa: V. President, Government Relations and Deputy General Counsel

Nat'l Council of Investigative and Security Services Inc.

Sacramento, CA
Leg. Issues: LAW

Outside Counsel/Consultants

Sellery Associates, Inc.
Issues: LAW
Rep By: Lawrence E. Sabbath, William C. Sellery, Jr.

Nat'l Council of Jewish Women

1707 L St. NW
Suite 950
Washington, DC 20036
Tel: (202)296-2588
Fax: (202)331-7792
Registered: LDA
Web: www.ncjw.org
E-mail: ncjwdc@aol.com

A Jewish women's volunteer organization headquartered in New York, NY.

Leg. Issues: BUD, CIV, EDU, FAM

In-house, DC-area Employees

FELT, Emily: Legislative Associate
MOSHENBERG, Sammie: Director, Washington Operations
RABHAN, Jody: Associate Director

Nat'l Council of Juvenile and Family Court Judges

Reno, NV
Leg. Issues: LAW

Outside Counsel/Consultants

Heidepriem & Mager, Inc.
Rep By: Pat Ford-Roegner, Nikki Heidepriem

Venable
Issues: LAW
Rep By: Hon. Frank J. Horton, Thomas J. Madden

Nat'l Council of La Raza

1111 19th St. NW
Suite 1000
Washington, DC 20036
Tel: (202)785-1670
Fax: (202)776-1792
Registered: LDA
Web: www.nclr.org

An advocacy organization for Americans of Hispanic descent. Provides research services and technical assistance for community development groups.

Leg. Issues: CIV, ECN, EDU, HCR, HOU, IMM, TRD, WEL

In-house, DC-area Employees

KAMASAKI, Charles K.: Senior V. President, Office of Research, Advocacy and Legislation
MUNOZ, Cecilia: V. President, Office of Research, Advocacy and Legislation
NAVARRETE, Lisa: Deputy V. President, Public Information
RODRIGUEZ, Eric: Poverty Policy Analyst
YZAGUIRRE, Raul: President

Outside Counsel/Consultants

Capitol Perspectives
Rep By: Mary Elise DeGonia

Robert A. Rapoza Associates
Rep By: Robert A. Rapoza

Nat'l Council of Negro Women

633 Pennsylvania Ave. NW
Washington, DC 20004
Tel: (202)737-0120
Fax: (202)383-9182
E-mail: ceo@ncnw.com

A council of national organizations and community based sections, formed to improve the qualtiy of life of African-American women and their families.

Leg. Issues: CIV, ECN, EDU, HCR, TRA

In-house, DC-area Employees

HEIGHT, Dr. Dorothy I.: Chair and Chief Exec. Officer

Nat'l Council of Nonprofit Ass'ns

1900 L St. NW
Suite 605
Washington, DC 20036
Tel: (202)467-6262
Fax: (202)467-6261
Web: www.ncna.org
E-mail: ncna@ncna.org

A coalition of state associations of non-profit organizations. Represents over 20,000 non-profits whose purpose is to enhance the quality of life in their respective communities.

In-house, DC-area Employees

ALVARADO, Audrey: Exec. Director

Nat'l Council of State Agencies for the Blind

Washington, DC

Outside Counsel/Consultants

Duncan and Associates
Rep By: Jack G. Duncan

Nat'l Council of State Boards of Nursing

Leg. Issues: HCR

Outside Counsel/Consultants

Arent Fox Kintner Plotkin & Kahn, PLLC
Issues: HCR
Rep By: Allison Shuren, Robert J. Waters

Nat'l Council of State Housing Agencies

444 N. Capitol St. NW
Suite 438
Washington, DC 20001
Tel: (202)624-7710
Fax: (202)624-5899
Web: www.ncsha.org
E-mail: info@ncsha.org

Organization of state agencies financing low and moderate income housing.

Leg. Issues: HOU, TAX

In-house, DC-area Employees

MCEVOY, John T.: Exec. Director
RIEMAN, Garth B.: Director, Program Development
THOMPSON, Barbara J.: Director, Policy and Government Affairs

Nat'l Council of Teachers of Mathematics

1906 Association Dr.
Reston, VA 20191-1988
Tel: (703)620-9840
Fax: (703)476-9027
Web: www.nctm.org
E-mail: nctm@nctm.org

Mission is to provide the vision and leadership necessary to ensure a mathematics education of the highest quaility for all students. Also serves as an advocate for mathematics education. Has over 100,000 members and more than 250 Affiliated Groups throughout the U.S. and Canada.

Leg. Issues: BUD, EDU

In-house, DC-area Employees

THORPE, Ph.D., John A.: Exec. Director

Outside Counsel/Consultants

Dean Blakey & Moskowitz
Issues: BUD, EDU
Rep By: Ellin J. Nolan

Richard Long & Associates
Rep By: Richard Long

Nat'l Council of the Churches of Christ in the USA

110 Maryland Ave. NE
Washington, DC 20002
Tel: (202)544-2350
Fax: (202)543-1297
E-mail: ncc_washington.parti@ecunet.org

A community of national religious organizations including 36 member communions with a combined membership of 51 million people. Convenes policy formulation panels, makes policy statements on public issues, lobbies before Congress and petitions federal agencies. Headquartered in New York, NY.

In-house, DC-area Employees

GIRTON-MITCHELL, Brenda: Director, Washington Office

Nat'l Council of University Research Administrators

Washington, DC
Leg. Issues: CPT, GOV, LBR, TAX, TOR

Outside Counsel/Consultants

Venable
Issues: CPT, GOV, LBR, TAX, TOR
Rep By: Jeffrey S. Tenenbaum

Nat'l Council of Women of the U.S.

4341 Forest Ln. NW
Washington, DC 20007
Tel: (202)363-2192

A council of women's organizations founded in 1888; affiliated with the International Council of Women. Headquartered in New York, NY.

In-house, DC-area Employees

MOFFAT, Pamela: Washington Representative

Nat'l Council on Alcoholism and Drug Dependence

Washington, DC
Registered: LDA
Web: www.ncadd.org

Concerned with the causes, effects, and social consequences of alcohol and/or drug dependency. Headquartered in New York, NY.

Leg. Issues: HCR

Outside Counsel/Consultants

VSAdc.com
Issues: HCR
Rep By: Carol A. McDaid

Nat'l Council on Compensation Insurance

Boca Raton, FL
Leg. Issues: HCR, INS

Outside Counsel/Consultants

Preston Gates Ellis & Rouvelas Meeds LLP
Issues: HCR, INS
Rep By: Susan B. Geiger

Nat'l Council on Family Relations

Minneapolis, MN

Outside Counsel/Consultants

Halsey, Rains & Associates, LLC
Rep By: Steven C. Halsey, James Hubbard, Laurie D. Rains

Nat'l Council on Measurement in Education

1230 17th St. NW
Washington, DC 20036
Tel: (202)223-9485
Fax: (202)775-1824

Concerned with ensuring that appropriate measurement takes place in educational settings.

In-house, DC-area Employees

RUSSELL, William J.: Exec. Officer

Nat'l Council on Radiation Protection and Measurement

7910 Woodmont Ave.
Suite 800
Bethesda, MD 20814
Tel: (301)657-2652
Fax: (301)907-8768
Web: www.ncrp.com
E-mail: ncrp@ncrp.com

In-house, DC-area Employees

BECKNER, William M.: Exec. Director
MEINHOLD, Charles: President

Nat'l Council on Rehabilitation Education

Washington, DC

Outside Counsel/Consultants

Duncan and Associates
Rep By: Jack G. Duncan

Nat'l Council on Teacher Retirement

Austin, TX
Leg. Issues: RET

Outside Counsel/Consultants

The Moore Law Firm, PLLC
Issues: RET
Rep By: Cynthia L. Moore

Nat'l Council on the Aging

409 Third St. SW
Second Floor
Washington, DC 20024
Tel: (202)479-1200
Fax: (202)479-0735
Registered: LDA
Web: www.ncoa.org
E-mail: info@ncoa.org

Established in 1950; the national organization for professionals and volunteers who work to improve the quality of life for older Americans. Serves as central, national resource for planning, training, information dissemination, technical assistance, advocacy, program and standards development, and publications that relate to all aspects of aging.

Leg. Issues: BUD, HCR, MMM

In-house, DC-area Employees

BEDLIN, Howard: V. President, Policy and Advocacy
FIRMAN, Ed.D., James P.: President and Chief Exec. Officer
LISEY, Diane: Public Policy Associate
MCCLENDON, Carol: Staff Liaison

Nat'l Council on U.S.-Arab Relations

1140 Connecticut Ave. NW
Suite 1210
Washington, DC 20036
Tel: (202)293-0801
Fax: (202)293-0903
Web: www.ncusar.org
E-mail: info@ncusar.org

In-house, DC-area Employees

SANDERS, Wallace: Director, Programs

Nat'l Court Reporters Ass'n

8224 Old Courthouse Rd.
Vienna, VA 22182-3808
Tel: (703)556-6272
Fax: (703)556-6291
Registered: LDA
Web: www.ncraonline.org
E-mail: msic@nerahq.org

The professional association serving the court reporting and captioning professions. NCRA is committed to servings its members and the public through programs that promote excellence in reporting.

Leg. Issues: CON, LAW, LBR

Political Action Committee/s

Nat'l Court Reporters Ass'n Political Action Committee
8224 Old Courthouse Rd.
Vienna, VA 22182-3808
Tel: (703)556-6272
Fax: (703)556-6291
Contact: Mark J. Golden, CAE

In-house, DC-area Employees

GOLDEN, CAE, Mark J.: Exec. Director
JORPELAND, Marshall S.: Director, Communications
RENDALL, Shari: Assistant Manager, Government Relations
WENHOLD, Dave: Director, Government Relations and Public Policy

Outside Counsel/Consultants

Kirkpatrick & Lockhart LLP
Issues: CON, LAW
Rep By: George W. Koch

Nat'l Crime Prevention Council

1000 Connecticut Ave. NW
13th Floor
Washington, DC 20036
Tel: (202)466-6272
Fax: (202)296-1356
Web: www.ncpc.org

A crime and violence prevention organization whose mission is to enable people to prevent crime and build safer, more caring communities.

Leg. Issues: BUD

In-house, DC-area Employees

CALHOUN, John A.: President and C.E.O.

Outside Counsel/Consultants

Beacon Consulting Group, Inc.
Issues: BUD
Rep By: Jeffrey W. Henry, Gordon P. MacDougall, Lisa A. Stewart

Nat'l Criminal Justice Ass'n

444 N. Capitol St. NW
Suite 618
Washington, DC 20001
Tel: (202)624-1440
Fax: (202)508-3859
Web: www.ncja.org
E-mail: info@ncja.org

NCJA represents states on crime control and public safety matters; focuses primarily on helping develop and implement national policy in the criminal justice field and on helping address criminal justice-related problems.

Leg. Issues: ALC, BUD, GOV, LAW

In-house, DC-area Employees

CROPPER, Cabell: Exec. Director
O'HARA, Mark A.: Government Affairs Counsel

Outside Counsel/Consultants

Venable

Nat'l Customs Brokers and Forwarders Ass'n of America

Washington, DC
Leg. Issues: MAR, TRA, TRD

Outside Counsel/Consultants

Kent & O'Connor, Inc.
Issues: MAR, TRA, TRD
Rep By: Jonathan H. Kent, Cindy Thomas

Nat'l Days of Dialogue on Race Relations

Washington, DC

Outside Counsel/Consultants

Hauser Group

Nat'l Defense Council Foundation

1220 King St.
Suite 230
Alexandria, VA 22314
Tel: (703)836-3443
Fax: (703)836-5402
Web: www.ndcf.org
E-mail: ndcf@erols.com

A foundation studying low-intensity conflicts, drug trafficing and energy problems. Sponsors fact-finding and relief missions to third-world and developing nations and conducts an intern study program.

Leg. Issues: DEF, FOR

In-house, DC-area Employees

MESSING, Jr. USA (Ret.), Major F. Andy: Exec. Director

Nat'l Defense Industrial Ass'n

2111 Wilson Blvd.
Suite 400
Arlington, VA 22201-3061
Tel: (703)522-1820
Fax: (703)522-1885
Registered: LDA
Web: www.ndia.org

Formerly the American Defense Preparedness Ass'n/Nat'l Securities Industrial Ass'n.

Leg. Issues: BUD, CPI, DEF, FOR, GOV, LAW, LBR, TAX, TRD

In-house, DC-area Employees

SCRIVNER, Peter C.: Senior V. President, Government Policy
SKIBBIE, USAF (Ret.), Lt. Gen. Lawrence: President

Nat'l Defense Transportation Ass'n

50 S. Pickett St.
Suite 220
Alexandria, VA 22304
Tel: (703)751-5011
Fax: (703)823-8761
Web: www.ndtahq.com
E-mail: ndta@ndtahq.com

Since its founding in 1944, the NDTA has functioned as a channel of cooperation and communication between transportation and government executives who must rely upon industry's services.

In-house, DC-area Employees

HONOR, USA (Ret.), Lt. Gen. Edward: President

Nat'l Defined Contribution Council

Denver, CO
Leg. Issues: BUD, FIN, GOV, LBR, TAX

Outside Counsel/Consultants

Washington Council Ernst & Young
Issues: BUD, FIN, GOV, LBR, TAX
Rep By: Doug Badger, Lauren Darling, John L. Doney, Jayne T. Fitzgerald, LaBrenda Garrett-Nelson, Gary J. Gasper, Bruce A. Gates, Nick Giordano, Cathy Koch, Robert J. Leonard, Richard Meltzer, Phillip D. Moseley, John D. Porter, Robert M. Rozen, Donna Steele-Flynn, Timothy J. Urban

Nat'l Democratic Club

30 Ivy St. SE
Washington, DC 20003
Tel: (202)543-2035
Fax: (202)479-4273
Web: www.democlub.net

In-house, DC-area Employees

HEMMENDINGER, Henry: General Manager

Nat'l Democratic County Officials Organization

440 First St. NW
Washington, DC 20001
Tel: (202)942-4217
Fax: (202)942-4281
Leg. Issues: ROD, RRR, TRA

In-house, DC-area Employees

FOGEL, Robert: Contact

Nat'l Democratic Institute for Internat'l Affairs

1717 Massachusetts Ave. NW
Suite 503
Washington, DC 20036
Tel: (202)328-3136
Fax: (202)939-3166
Web: www.ndi.org

In-house, DC-area Employees

DUNN, Jean B.: V. President
MELIA, Thomas O.: V. President, Programs
WOLLACK, Kenneth D.: President

Nat'l Dental Ass'n

3517 16th St. NW
Washington, DC 20010
Tel: (202)588-1697
Fax: (202)588-1244
Web: www.ndaonline.org
E-mail: nda@bellatlantic.org

Founded in Virginia in 1913, the largest organization of minority dentists is dedicated to providing quality dental care to the unserved and underserved population. Representing the nation's 5,000 Black dentists, with 50 chapters, the NDA along with its four auxiliaries advocate the inclusion of dental care services in local, state and federal health care programs, foster the integration of minority dental health care providers into the profession and promote dentistry as a viable career for minorities through scholarship and support programs.

In-house, DC-area Employees

JOHNS, Robert S.: Exec. Director

Nat'l Deposit Insurance Corp.

Dublin, OH

Outside Counsel/Consultants

Akin, Gump, Strauss, Hauer & Feld, L.L.P.

Nat'l Diabetes Information Clearinghouse

One Information Way
Bethesda, MD 20892-3560
Tel: (301)654-3327
Fax: (301)907-8906
Web: www.niddk.nih.gov
E-mail: ndic@info.niddk.nih.gov

An information referral service of the National Institute of Diabetes and Digestive and Kidney Diseases (NIDDK). Responds to inquiries, develops and distributes publications, and provides referrals to diabetes organizations. Maintains a database of patient and professional education materials.

In-house, DC-area Employees

KRANZFELDER, Kathy: Project Director

Nat'l Digestive Diseases Information Clearinghouse

Two Information Way
Bethesda, MD 20892-3570
Tel: (301)654-3810
Fax: (301)907-8906
Web: www.niddk.nih.gov
E-mail: nddic@info.niddk.nih.gov

An information and referral service of the Nat'l Institute of Diabetes and Digestive and Kidney Diseases, one of the Nat'l Institutes of Health. A central information resource on the prevention and management of digestive diseases, the clearinghouse responds to written inquiries, develops and distributes publications about digestive diseases, and provides referrals to digestive disease organizations. The NDDIC maintains a database of patient and professional education materials, from which literature searches are generated.

In-house, DC-area Employees

KRANZFELDER, Kathy: Director

Nat'l Disease Research Interchange

Philadelphia, PA
Leg. Issues: HCR, MED

Outside Counsel/Consultants

Oppenheimer Wolff & Donnelly LLP
Issues: HCR, MED

Nat'l District Attorneys Ass'n

99 Canal Center Plaza
Suite 510
Alexandria, VA 22314
Tel: (703)549-9222
Fax: (703)836-3195
Web: www.ndaa-apri.org
E-mail: newman.flanagan@ndaa-apri.org

A membership association for local prosecutors.

Leg. Issues: ALC, CON, ENV, FAM, FIR, GOV, HCR, LAW, SCI, TEC, TRA

In-house, DC-area Employees

FLANAGAN, Newman: Exec. Director
POLLEY, James: Director, Government Affairs

Nat'l Ecological Foundation

Nashville, TN
Leg. Issues: ENV

Outside Counsel/Consultants

Baker, Donelson, Bearman & Caldwell, P.C.
Issues: ENV
Rep By: James D. Range

Nat'l Education Ass'n of the U.S.

1201 16th St. NW
Washington, DC 20036
Tel: (202)833-4000
Registered: LDA
Web: www.nea.org
Leg. Issues: AGR, BUD, CIV, EDU, HCR, LAW, LBR, RET, TAX, TEC, WEL

Political Action Committee/s

Nat'l Education Ass'n Political Action Committee
1201 16th St. NW
Washington, DC 20036
Tel: (202)833-4000
Contact: Mary Elizabeth Teasley

In-house, DC-area Employees

BREEDLOVE, Carolyn: Senior Professional Associate, Government Relations
BRYANT, David: Senior Professional Associate
CHASE, Bob: President
FIGUEROA, Darryl Lynette: Senior Professional Associate, Media Relations Staff
GARCIA, Isabelle: Senior Professional Associate, Government Relations
MATTOS, Kate: Director, Communications
MOODY, Randall: Senior Professional Associate
MURDOCK, Patricia C.: Manager, Information Resources and Advocacy
PACHECO, Jack: Manager, Political Affairs
PACKER, Joel: Senior Professional Associate, Government Relations
POLIDORI, Jack: Senior Professional Associate, Government Relations
SHUST, Diane M.: Senior Professional Associate, Government Relations
TEASLEY, Mary Elizabeth: Director, Government Relations
WALKER, Douglas: Senior Professional Associate
WEAVER, Reg: V. President
WILSON, John I.: Exec. Director

Outside Counsel/Consultants

The Dutko Group, Inc.

Federal Management Strategies, Inc.
Issues: EDU
Rep By: Robert P. Canavan

Hauser Group

Ledge Counsel
Issues: EDU

Valente Lopatin & Schulze
Rep By: Alan G. Lopatin

Widmeyer Communications, Inc.

Nat'l Education Knowledge Industry Ass'n (NEKIA)

1718 Connecticut Ave. NW
Suite 700
Washington, DC 20009
Tel: (202)518-0847
Fax: (202)785-3849
Web: www.nekia.org
E-mail: info@nekia.org

A national trade association committed to making cost-effective education innovation and expertise available to all communities.

In-house, DC-area Employees

JONES, C. Todd: President

Nat'l Electrical Contractors Ass'n

Three Bethesda Metro Center
Suite 1100
Bethesda, MD 20814
Tel: (301)657-3110
Fax: (301)215-4500
Registered: LDA
Web: www.necanet.org
E-mail: webmaster@necanet.org

Founded in 1901, NECA represents the electrical contracting industry with more than 4,000 member companies which install communications and electric power systems for business and industry. Includes 118 chapters in the U.S. and others around the world. Dedicated to enhancing the industry through continuing education, labor relations, current information and promotional activities.

Leg. Issues: CSP, ENG, ENV, GOV, LBR, SMB, TAX, UTI

Political Action Committee/s

Electrical Construction PAC-Nat'l Electrical Contractors Ass'n (ECPAC)
Three Bethesda Metro Center
Suite 1100
Bethesda, MD 20814
Tel: (301)657-3110
Fax: (301)215-4500
Contact: Robert L. White, Jr.

In-house, DC-area Employees

BELSCHNER, Shanna
DUNCAN, Bonnie: Director, Communications
GRAU, John: Exec. V. President and Chief Exec. Officer
WHITE, Jr., Robert L.: Director, Government Affairs

Nat'l Electrical Manufacturers Ass'n

1300 N. 17th St.
Suite 1847
Rosslyn, VA 22209
Tel: (703)841-3200
Fax: (703)841-3300
Registered: LDA
Web: www.nema.org
E-mail: webmaster@nema.org

The principal national association representing over 600 American electroindustry companies. A leading developer of US and international standards for electrical products and systems. Issue interests include international trade, energy, environment, safety, and liability.

Leg. Issues: BUD, CAW, CSP, ENG, ENV, FOR, GOV, HCR, LBR, MAN, MED, MMM, SMB, TEC, TRD, WAS

Political Action Committee/s

Nat'l Electrical Manufacturers Ass'n PAC (NEMA PAC)
1300 N. 17th St.
Suite 1847
Rosslyn, VA 22209
Tel: (703)841-3251
Fax: (703)841-3351
Contact: Timothy Feldman

In-house, DC-area Employees

BRITAIN, Robert G.: V. President, Medical Products
ERDHEIM, Eric: Senior Manager, Environmental Health and Safety
FELDMAN, Timothy: V. President, Government Affairs
HAMILTON, Rae M.: V. President, Communications and Publications
LALUMONDIER, Richard: Scientist, Environment, Health and Safety
MEAKEM, John: Manager, International Trade
O'HAGAN, Malcolm: President
SILCOX, Clark: Legal Counsel

Outside Counsel/Consultants

Potomac Strategies Internat'l LLC
Issues: GOV, MAN, SMB
Rep By: James K. Wholey

Nat'l Electrical Safety Foundation

1300 N. 17th St.
Suite 1847
Rosslyn, VA 22209
Tel: (703)841-3211
Fax: (703)841-3311
Leg. Issues: CPT, GOV, LBR, TAX, TOR

In-house, DC-area Employees

BIDDLE, CAE, Walter: Exec. Director

Outside Counsel/Consultants

Venable
Issues: CPT, GOV, LBR, TAX, TOR
Rep By: Jeffrey S. Tenenbaum

Nat'l Employee Benefits Institute

1350 Connecticut Ave. NW
Suite 600
Washington, DC 20036
Tel: (202)822-6432
Fax: (202)466-5109
Registered: LDA
Web: www.federlaw.com

Member companies include the Archer Daniels Midland, Atlantic Richfield, BellSouth Corp., Browning-Ferris Industries, Chevron, the Dial Corp., Dow Chemical, Fluor Corp., Georgia Pacific, Houston Industries, Hunt-Wesson, IBM Corp., Marathon Oil, Mobil Oil, Morton Internat'l, Potlatch Corp., TRW, Upjohn Co., and US West.

Leg. Issues: FIN, HCR, LBR, MMM, RET, TAX

In-house, DC-area Employees

MARK, Molly: Director, Government Affairs
SEMO, Joseph: Exec. Director

Outside Counsel/Consultants

Feder, Semo, Clarke & Bard
Issues: FIN, HCR, LBR, MMM, RET, TAX

Nat'l Employment Lawyers Ass'n

San Francisco, CA
Leg. Issues: CIV, TAX

Outside Counsel/Consultants

Bass and Howes, Inc.
Issues: TAX

Bill Zavarela
Issues: CIV
Rep By: Bill Zavarela

Nat'l Employment Opportunities Network

Gaithersburg, MD
Leg. Issues: BUD, LBR, TAX

Outside Counsel/Consultants

Chambers Associates Inc.
Issues: BUD, LBR, TAX
Rep By: William A. Signer

McDermott, Will and Emery

Nat'l Endangered Species Act Reform Coalition

1050 Thomas Jefferson St. NW
Sixth Floor
Washington, DC 20007
Tel: (202)333-7481
Fax: (202)338-2416
Registered: LDA
Web: www.nesarc.org

A coalition of industry, local governments, trade associations and agriculture groups seeking to reform the Endangered Species Act.

Leg. Issues: AGR, ANI, BUD, ENV, NAT, RES, TAX

In-house, DC-area Employees

MCCLURE, Hon. James A.: Chairman

Outside Counsel/Consultants

McClure, Gerard & Neuenschwander, Inc.
Issues: AGR, ANI, BUD, ENV, NAT, RES, TAX
Rep By: Steven G. Barringer, Joseph T. Findaro, Matthew Iandoli, Nils W. Johnson, Hon. James A. McClure, Tod O. Neuenschwander

Van Ness Feldman, P.C.
Issues: BUD, ENV, NAT, RES
Rep By: Nancy Macan McNally, Joseph B. Nelson, J. Curtis Rich, Robert G. Szabo

Nat'l Endowment for Democracy

1101 15th St. NW
Suite 700
Washington, DC 20005
Tel: (202)293-9072
Fax: (202)223-6042
Web: www.ned.org
E-mail: info@ned.org

A private, nonprofit grantmaking organization with substantial federal financial support which seeks to promote the growth of democracy abroad.

In-house, DC-area Employees

GERSHMAN, Carl S.: President

Nat'l Energy Assistance Directors' Ass'n

Washington, DC
Web: www.neada.org
Leg. Issues: ENG, GOV

Outside Counsel/Consultants

Duncan, Weinberg, Genzer & Pembroke, P.C.
Issues: ENG, GOV
Rep By: Jeffrey C. Genzer

Nat'l Energy Management Institute

Alexandria, VA
Leg. Issues: BUD, ENV, LBR

Outside Counsel/Consultants

Connerton & Ray
Rep By: David L. Mallino, Sr.

The Kamber Group
Rep By: Christina Erling, Jeff Richardson

Mallino Government Relations
Issues: BUD, ENV, LBR
Rep By: David L. Mallino, Sr.

Nat'l Energy Resources Organization

Outside Counsel/Consultants

Franklin & Burling

Nat'l Environmental Development Ass'n, Inc.

Washington, DC

Members are companies and others concerned with balancing environmental and economic interests to obtain both a clean environment and a strong economy.

Outside Counsel/Consultants

Hogan & Hartson L.L.P.
Rep By: Leslie Sue Ritts, Ellen Siegler

Strat@Comm (Strategic Communications Counselors)

The Technical Group LLC
Rep By: Thomas D. Ovenden

Nat'l Environmental Development Ass'ns State & Federal Environmental Responsibility Project

Washington, DC
Leg. Issues: ADV, CAW, ENV, WAS

Outside Counsel/Consultants

Van Scoyoc Associates, Inc.
Issues: ADV, CAW, ENV, WAS
Rep By: H. Stewart Van Scoyoc

Nat'l Environmental Education and Training Center

Indiana, PA

Outside Counsel/Consultants

Connerton & Ray
Rep By: Alan Kadrofske, David L. Mallino, Sr.

Nat'l Environmental Policy Institute

1401 K Street NW
M 103
Washington, DC 20005
Tel: (202)857-4784
Fax: (202)833-5977
E-mail: dritter@nep.org

A non-profit, 501(c)(3) organization of environmental leaders founded to promote efficient, effective environmental protection and build consensus for change. Through a bi-partisan approach, NEPI seeks to advance new ideas for developing environmental policies based upon sound science, consideration of risk, costs and benefits, and the involvement of new constituencies.

In-house, DC-area Employees

RITTER, Hon. Don: Chairman

Nat'l Environmental Strategies

2600 Virginia Ave. NW
Suite 600
Washington, DC 20037
Tel: (202)333-2524
Fax: (202)338-5950
Registered: LDA

Leg. Issues: ENG, ENV

In-house, DC-area Employees

GRILES, J. Steven: Principal
HANSEN, Charles M.
HIMMELSTEIN, Marc I.: President
NORTHINGTON, John: V. President
WILSON, Richard D.: V. President

Outside Counsel/Consultants

Podesta/Mattoon
Issues: ENG, ENV
Rep By: Anthony T. Podesta, Timothy Powers

Nat'l Environmental Trust

1200 18th St. NW
Washington, DC 20036
Tel: (202)887-8800
Fax: (202)887-8877
Registered: LDA
Web: www.environet.org

Formerly the Environmental Information Center.

Leg. Issues: CAW, ENG, ENV, UTI

In-house, DC-area Employees

CLAPP, Philip E.: President
CURTIS, Kevin: V. President, Government Affairs
LIDDLE, James: Government Relations Associate
READ, Debbie: Legislative Director
STANTON, John Maloney: V. President

Outside Counsel/Consultants

Van Scoyoc Associates, Inc.
Issues: CAW, ENV
Rep By: H. Stewart Van Scoyoc

Nat'l Ethnic Coalition of Organizations

New York, NY

Outside Counsel/Consultants

Matz, Blancato & Associates, Inc.
Rep By: Robert B. Blancato

Nat'l Fair Housing Alliance

1212 New York Ave. NW
Suite 525
Washington, DC 20005
Tel: (202)898-1661
Fax: (202)371-9744
Registered: LDA
E-mail: nfha@erols.com
Leg. Issues: BAN, CON, HOU, INS, URB

In-house, DC-area Employees

HUDSON, James H.: Director of Public Policy
SMITH, Shanna L.: Exec. Director

Nat'l Family Caregivers Ass'n

10400 Connecticut Ave.
Suite 500
Kensington, MD 20895-3944
Tel: (301)942-6430
Fax: (301)942-2302
Web: www.nfcacares.org
E-mail: info@nfcacares.org

A not-for-profit membership organization representing American family caregivers through education and information.

In-house, DC-area Employees

MINTZ, Suzanne G.: President

Outside Counsel/Consultants

Patton Boggs, LLP

Nat'l Family Farm Coalition

110 Maryland Ave NE
Suite 307
Washington, DC 20002
Tel: (202)543-5675
Fax: (202)543-0978
Web: www.nffc.net
E-mail: nffc@nffc.net

Seeks to strengthen the family farm system of agriculture by promoting federal policies that benefit family farms, protect the environment, and create economic stability in rural communities.

In-house, DC-area Employees

OZER, Kathy: Exec. Director

Nat'l Family Planning and Reproductive Health Ass'n

1627 K St. NW 12th Floor
Washington, DC 20006
Tel: (202)293-3114
Fax: (202)293-1990
Registered: LDA
Web: www.nfprha.org
E-mail: info@nfprha

A non-profit membership organization established to improve and expand the delivery of voluntary and comprehensive family planning and reproductive health care services. Members comprise almost all grantees funded by Title X of the Public Health Service Act, which serves more than four million low income women and adolescents yearly.

Leg. Issues: BUD, FAM, INS

In-house, DC-area Employees

DESARNO, Judith M.: President
FIGUA, Emily: Senior Public Policy Analyst
KEEFE, Marilyn J.: Director of Public Policy and Service Delivery

Outside Counsel/Consultants

The Direct Impact Co.
Issues: FAM
Rep By: Mary Beth Bloomberg

Feldesman, Tucker, Leifer, Fidell & Bank
Rep By: James L. Feldesman

Nat'l Farmers Organization

Ames, IA
Leg. Issues: AGR

Outside Counsel/Consultants

Cashdollar-Jones & Co.
Issues: AGR
Rep By: Robert Cashdollar

Nat'l Farmers Union (Farmers Educational & Co-operative Union of America)

400 N. Capitol St. NW
Suite 790
Washington, DC 20001
Tel: (202)554-1600
Fax: (202)554-1654
Registered: LDA
Web: www.nfu.org
E-mail: nfu@nfu.org

Washington office of an Aurora, CO-based organization. Dedicated to promoting and strengthening family farmers and a family farm system of agriculture through policies and programs.

Leg. Issues: AGR, BAN, BUD, CHM, CIV, CPT, DIS, ECN, EDU, ENV, FOO, HCR, HOU, IMM, IND, LBR, NAT, RES, SCI, SMB, TAX, TRA, TRD, UTI

Political Action Committee/s

NATFARMPAC
400 N. Capitol St. NW
Suite 790
Washington, DC 20001
Tel: (202)554-1600
Fax: (202)554-1654

In-house, DC-area Employees

BUIS, Tom: V. President, Government Relations
DANIELSON, Nancy: Senior Policy Analyst
MILLER, Jim: Chief Economist
NIEHOFF, Jodi: Government Relations Representative
SCHEPIS, Chris: Government Relations Representative
SWENSON, Leland: President
WHITE, Clarence: Communications Coordinator

Nat'l Fastener Distributors Ass'n

Cleveland, OH
Leg. Issues: AUT, AVI, CSP, MAN, SCI, SMB, TRD

Outside Counsel/Consultants

Big Sky Consulting, Inc.
Issues: AUT, AVI, CSP, MAN, SCI, SMB, TRD
Rep By: Ralph Thomas Fulton

Nat'l Federation for the Blind

Baltimore, MD
Leg. Issues: TEC

Outside Counsel/Consultants

O'Connor & Hannan, L.L.P.
Issues: TEC
Rep By: Hon. Larry Pressler

Nat'l Federation of Community Development of Credit Unions

Outside Counsel/Consultants

Bill Zavarela
Rep By: Bill Zavarela

Nat'l Federation of Croatian Americans

1329 Connecticut Ave. NW
Washington, DC 20036-1825
Tel: (202)331-2830
Fax: (202)331-0050
Registered: LDA
E-mail: ncfahdq@aol.com

Maintains a network linking Cro-American organizations. Promotes programs that strengthen and support cultural, educational, humanitarian, social, economical, and political activities important to the Cro-American community and Croatia.

Leg. Issues: BUD, FOR, TRD

In-house, DC-area Employees

LEPETIC, Alenna M.: National Coordinator
RUKAVINA, Steven: Exec. V. President

Outside Counsel/Consultants

Foley Government and Public Affairs, Inc.
Issues: BUD, FOR, TRD
Rep By: Joseph P. Foley

Nat'l Federation of Democratic Women

Political Action Committee/s

Nat'l Federation of Democratic Women PAC

P.O. Box 65153
Washington, DC 20035
Contact: Laura Comini

In-house, DC-area Employees

ANDERSON, Corinne: President
COMINI, Laura: Treasurer, PAC

Nat'l Federation of Federal Employees

1016 16th St. NW
Suite 300
Washington, DC 20036
Tel: (202)862-4400
Fax: (202)862-4432
Registered: LDA
Web: www.nffe.org

A labor union representing 100,000 federal workers in federal agencies throughout the country.

Political Action Committee/s

Nat'l Federation of Federal Employees Political Action Committee

1016 16th St. NW
Suite 300
Washington, DC 20036
Tel: (202)862-4400
Fax: (202)862-4432
Contact: Richard N. Brown

Nat'l Federation of Federal Employees Public Affairs Council

1016 16th St. NW
Suite 300
Washington, DC 20036
Tel: (202)862-4400
Fax: (202)862-4432

In-house, DC-area Employees

BJORKLUND, Laura: Business Representative
BROWN, Richard N.: National President
CARELLI, Frank: Legislative Liaison
COFFEY, Tiffany: Dir. of Publications & Public Relations
EXLEY, Robbie: Specialist, Labor Relations
RAY, Thomas: Secretary-Treasurer

Nat'l Federation of High Schools

Outside Counsel/Consultants

Capitol Associates, Inc.
Rep By: Daniel Wexler

Nat'l Federation of Independent Business

1201 F St. NW
Suite 200
Washington, DC 20004
Tel: (202)554-9000
Fax: (202)554-0496
Registered: LDA
Web: www.nfib.com
Leg. Issues: SMB, TAX

Political Action Committee/s

Nat'l Federation of Independent Business SAFE Trust

1201 F St. NW
Suite 200
Washington, DC 20004
Tel: (202)554-9000
Fax: (202)554-0496

In-house, DC-area Employees

BAHRET, Mary Ellen: Manager, Legislative Affairs/Senate
BLANKENBURG, Daniel W.: Manager, Government Relations
BLASINSKY, Mary: Chief of Staff
BOIAGIAN, Mindi: Director, Media Communications
BOSGRAAF, Kimberly: Counsel, Regulatory Policy
DANNER, Donald "Dan": Senior V. President, Federal Public Policy
DOUCET, Shane: Manager, Legislative Affairs
ECKERLY, Susan: Director, Federal Public Policy/Senate
EMLING, John: Manager, Legislative Affairs/House
FARIS, Jack: President and Chief Exec. Officer
JENSEN, Amy: Director, Public Policy/House
LEON, Mary Reed: Manager, Legislative Affairs/House
LYONS, Lisbeth: Manager, Legislative and Grassroots Services
SULLIVAN, Thomas M.: Exec. Director, NFIB Legal Foundation
WHITFIELD, Dennis: V. President, Grassroots and Media Communications
WOLFF, Sharon: Manager, Campaign Services
WOODS, Stephen P.: V. President, State Public Policy

Outside Counsel/Consultants

Abraham Schneier and Associates
Issues: SMB, TAX
Rep By: Abraham L. Schneier

Nat'l Federation of Pachyderm Clubs, Inc.

Moberly, MO

Outside Counsel/Consultants

Sam Richardson
Rep By: Sam Richardson

Nat'l Federation of Republican Women

124 N. Alfred St.
Alexandria, VA 22314
Tel: (703)548-9688
Fax: (703)548-9836
Web: www.nfrw.org
E-mail: mail@nfrw.org

Founded in 1938, the Federation has over 95,000 members in 1800 unit clubs throughout the 50 states, the District of Columbia, Puerto Rico, Guam and the Virgin Islands. Dedicated to the political education and training of women leaders.

Leg. Issues: EDU, MMM, RET

In-house, DC-area Employees

MILLER, Marian: President
TAYLOR, Kathleen: Political Director

Nat'l Federation of State High School Ass'ns

Kansas City, MO
Leg. Issues: EDU

Outside Counsel/Consultants

Capitol Associates, Inc.
Issues: EDU
Rep By: Julie P. Pawelczyk, Daniel Wexler

Nat'l Fenestration Rating Council

1300 Spring St.
Suite 500
Silver Spring, MD 20910
Tel: (301)589-6372
Fax: (301)588-0854
Web: www.nfrc.org
E-mail: NFRCUSA@aol.com

A nonprofit organization of manufacturers, state and federal energy regulators, utilities and others committed to developing and operating a program to rate and label window products for energy efficiency.

Leg. Issues: ENG

In-house, DC-area Employees

DOUGLAS, Susan: Administrator

Outside Counsel/Consultants

Cascade Associates
Issues: ENG
Rep By: Jennifer A. Schafer

Nat'l FFA Organization

1410 King St.
Suite 400
Alexandria, VA 22314
Tel: (703)838-5889
Fax: (703)838-5888
Web: www.ffa.org

Formerly known as Future Farmers of America. Primary purpose is the development of leadership, personal growth and career success among students preparing for careers in agriculture-related fields.

Leg. Issues: AGR, EDU, NAT

In-house, DC-area Employees

CASE, Dr. Larry D.: National Advisor and Chief Exec. Officer
HARRIS, C. Coleman: National Exec. Secretary

Nat'l Field Selling Ass'n

Philadelphia, PA
Leg. Issues: ADV, CSP, GOV, LAW, SMB, TAX

Outside Counsel/Consultants

Canfield, Smith and Martin
Issues: ADV, CSP, GOV, LAW, SMB, TAX
Rep By: Daniel C. Smith

Nat'l Film Preservation Foundation

Washington, DC
Web: www.cweb.loc.gov/film/
E-mail: sleg@loc.gov

Outside Counsel/Consultants

Proskauer Rose LLP

Nat'l Fire Protection Ass'n

1110 N. Glebe Rd.
Suite 210
Arlington, VA 22201
Tel: (703)516-4346
Fax: (703)516-4350
Registered: LDA

Educates the public with fire safety information through educational programs, and the distribution of the National Fire Codes. Headquartered in Quincy, Massachusetts.

Leg. Issues: CSP, DIS, HOU, SCI

In-house, DC-area Employees

BIECHMAN, John C.: V. President, Government Affairs

Nat'l Fisheries Institute

1901 N. Fort Myer Dr.
Suite 700
Arlington, VA 22209
Tel: (703)524-8884
Fax: (703)524-4619
Registered: LDA
Web: www.nfi.org
E-mail: office@nfi.org
Leg. Issues: BUD, FOO, LBR, MAR, NAT, TRD

Political Action Committee/s

Nat'l Fisheries Institute Political Action Committee

1901 N. Fort Myer Dr.
Suite 700
Arlington, VA 22209
Tel: (703)524-8884
Fax: (703)524-4619
Contact: Richard Gutting, Jr.

In-house, DC-area Employees

CANDLER, Linda: V. President, Communications
GUTTING, Jr., Richard: Exec. V. President
LEBLANC, Justin: V. President, Government Relations

Outside Counsel/Consultants

Garvey, Schubert & Barer
Rep By: Eldon V. C. Greenberg

Nat'l Food Processors Ass'n

1350 I St. NW
Suite 300
Washington, DC 20005
Tel: (202)639-5900
Fax: (202)639-5932
Registered: LDA
Web: www.nfpa-food.org
Leg. Issues: AGR, BUD, FOO, TAX, TRD

Political Action Committee/s

Nat'l Food Processors Ass'n Political Action Committee

1350 I St. NW
Suite 300
Washington, DC 20005
Tel: (202)639-5900
Fax: (202)639-5932

In-house, DC-area Employees

APPLEBAUM, Rhona: Exec. V. President, Scientific and Regulatory Affairs
CADY, John R.: President
ENGLISH, Marlene: Director, Political Affairs
HILDWINE, Regina: Director, Technical Regulatory Affairs-FDA
HONTZ, Lloyd: Director, Technical Regulatory Affairs-USDA
JARMAN, Rick: Senior Director, Technical Regulatory Affairs-EPA
JOHNSTON, Kelly D.: Exec. V. President, Government Affairs and Communications
MATTHYS, Allen: V. President, Regulatory Affairs
RIEHL, Scott: Senior Director, State Government Affairs

ROCHETTE, Peggy
SCOTT, Jenny: Senior Director, Food Safety Programs
WILLARD, Timothy: V. President, Communications

Outside Counsel/Consultants

Covington & Burling
Issues: FOO
Rep By: Clausen Ely, Jr.

Olsson, Frank and Weeda, P.C.
Issues: AGR, BUD, FOO
Rep By: John W. Bode, Susan P. Grymes, Karen Reis Harned, Stephen L. Lacey, Marshall L. Matz, Tyson Redpath, Ryan W. Stroschein

Podesta/Mattoon
Issues: FOO
Rep By: Ann Delory, Anthony T. Podesta

Nat'l Football League

New York, NY
Leg. Issues: COM, CPT, GAM, SPO, TAX

Outside Counsel/Consultants

BKSH & Associates
Issues: TAX

Covington & Burling
Issues: GAM, TAX

The Legislative Strategies Group, LLC
Issues: COM, GAM, TAX
Rep By: Martin B. Gold, Steven M. Hilton

Verner, Liipfert, Bernhard, McPherson and Hand, Chartered
Issues: COM, CPT, SPO
Rep By: Philip R. Hochberg

Nat'l Football League Players Ass'n

2021 L St. NW
Suite 600
Washington, DC 20036
Tel: (202)463-2200
Fax: (202)857-0673
Web: www.nflpa.org
Leg. Issues: GAM, SPO, TAX

In-house, DC-area Employees

UPSHAW, Gene: Exec. Director

Outside Counsel/Consultants

Baach Robinson & Lewis, PLLC
Issues: GAM, SPO, TAX
Rep By: Benjamin L. Zelenko

Columbus Public Affairs
Issues: TAX

Weil, Gotshal & Manges, LLP
Issues: TAX
Rep By: Robert C. Odle, Jr.

Nat'l Foreign Trade Council, Inc.

1625 K St. NW
Suite 1090
Washington, DC 20006-1604
Tel: (202)887-0278
Fax: (202)452-8160
Registered: LDA

Established 1914. Represents the foreign trade and investment interests of the 550-plus U.S. corporations who make up its membership. Favors open international economic system and expansion of international trade and investment. Formed the U.S.-South Africa Business Council in 1993.

Leg. Issues: BUD, FOR, TAX, TRD

In-house, DC-area Employees

IRACE, Mary: V. President, Trade and Export Finance
MURRAY, Fred F.: V. President, Tax Policy
O'FLAHERTY, J. Daniel: V. President and Exec. Director, U.S.-South Africa Business Council
REINSCH, William A.: President
SOLOMON, Emily B.: Managing Director, U.S.-South Africa Business Council
SWIFT, Richard J.: Chairman

Outside Counsel/Consultants

Alston & Bird LLP
Issues: TRD
Rep By: Robert T. Cole, Charles Wheeler

Hogan & Hartson L.L.P.
Issues: FOR
Rep By: Warren H. Maruyama, Mark S. McConnell, Daniel B. Poneman

Miller & Chevalier, Chartered
Issues: TAX, TRD
Rep By: Homer E. Moyer, Jr., Hal S. Shapiro

Powell, Goldstein, Frazer & Murphy LLP
Issues: TRD
Rep By: Daniel M. Price

PriceWaterhouseCoopers
Issues: TAX
Rep By: Peter R. Merrill

Washington Council Ernst & Young
Issues: BUD, TAX
Rep By: Doug Badger, Lauren Darling, John L. Doney, Jayne T. Fitzgerald, LaBrenda Garrett-Nelson, Gary J. Gasper, Bruce A. Gates, Nick Giordano, Cathy Koch, Robert J. Leonard, Richard Meltzer, Phillip D. Moseley, John D. Porter, Robert M. Rozen, Donna Steele-Flynn, Timothy J. Urban

Nat'l Forest Counties School Coalition

Red Bluff, CA
Leg. Issues: EDU

Outside Counsel/Consultants

Federal Management Strategies, Inc.
Issues: EDU
Rep By: Robert P. Canavan

Nat'l Forest Recreation Ass'n

325 Pennsylvannia Ave. SE
Washington, DC 20003
Tel: (202)546-8527
Fax: (202)546-8528
Registered: LDA
Web: www.nfra.org
E-mail: info@nfra.org

In-house, DC-area Employees

O'BRIEN, Patrick J.: Exec. Director

Nat'l Forum for Black Public Administrators

777 N. Capitol St. NE
Suite 807
Washington, DC 20002
Tel: (202)408-9300
Fax: (202)408-8558
Web: www.nfbpa.org
E-mail: nfbpa@erols.com

In-house, DC-area Employees

SAUNDERS, III, John E.: Exec. Director

Nat'l Foundation for Cancer Research

4600 East West Hwy.
Suite 525
Bethesda, MD 20814
Tel: (301)654-1250
Fax: (301)654-5824

In-house, DC-area Employees

SALISBURY, Franklin C.: President

Nat'l Foundation for Infectious Diseases

4733 Bethesda Ave.
Suite 750
Bethesda, MD 20814
Tel: (301)656-0003
Fax: (301)907-0878
Web: www.nfid.org
E-mail: info@nfid.org

In-house, DC-area Employees

HANRAHAN, Kathleen: Director, Special Projects
MARTONE, M.D., William J.: Senior Exec. Director
NOVICK, Len: Exec. Director

The Nat'l Foundation for Teaching Entrepreneurship

New York, NY
Leg. Issues: EDU

Outside Counsel/Consultants

Blank Rome Comisky & McCauley, LLP
Issues: EDU
Rep By: J. Caleb Boggs, III

Deborah L. Perry
Issues: EDU
Rep By: Deborah L. Perry

Nat'l Foundation for the Improvement of Education

1201 16th St. NW
Washington, DC 20036
Tel: (202)822-7840
Fax: (202)822-7779

A nonprofit organization whose mission is to improve teaching and learning in America's public schools by supporting innovations designed and carried out by teachers and increasing public awareness of the need for school changes. Created in 1969 by the Nat'l Education Ass'n.

In-house, DC-area Employees

DARLAND, Dallas L.: Director, Institutional Advancement
RENYI, Judith: Exec. Director

Nat'l Foundation for Women Business Owners

1411 K St. NW
Suite 1350
Washington, DC 20005-3407
Tel: (202)638-3060
Fax: (202)638-3064
Web: www.nfwbo.org
E-mail: pr@nfwbo.org

Provides research, consulting and public relations services on women business owners and their enterprises.

In-house, DC-area Employees

ROSENTHAL, Bruce G.: Manager, Public Relations

Nat'l Franchise Council

1341 G St. NW
Suite 1000
Washington, DC 20005
Tel: (202)626-8562
Fax: (202)626-8593
Registered: LDA
Leg. Issues: CSP, FIN, LBR, SMB

In-house, DC-area Employees

SIMON, Neil A.: Exec. Director

Nat'l Franchisee Ass'n

Atlanta, GA
Leg. Issues: SMB

Outside Counsel/Consultants

Long, Aldridge & Norman, LLP
Issues: SMB
Rep By: C. Randall Nuckolls, Patrick C. Turner

Nat'l Frozen Food Ass'n

Harrisburg, PA

Outside Counsel/Consultants

McLeod, Watkinson & Miller
Rep By: Michael R. McLeod, Richard E. Pasco

Nat'l Frozen Pizza Institute

2000 Corporate Ridge
Suite 1000
McLean, VA 22102
Tel: (703)821-0770
Fax: (703)821-1350
Registered: LDA

Represents manufacturers of frozen pizza and suppliers to the industry.

Leg. Issues: AGR, FOO

In-house, DC-area Employees

GARFIELD, Robert L.: Exec. Director

Outside Counsel/Consultants

Olsson, Frank and Weeda, P.C.
Rep By: John W. Bode, Richard L. Frank, Marshall L. Matz, Tyson Redpath, Ryan W. Stroschein

Nat'l Funeral Directors Ass'n

400 C St. NE
Washington, DC 20002
Tel: (202)547-0441
Fax: (202)547-0726
Registered: LDA
Web: www.afda.org
E-mail: jfitch@nfda.org

Headquartered in Brookfield, WI.

Leg. Issues: BNK, BUD, CAW, CSP, DIS, ENV, HCR, INS, LBR, MMM, SMB, TAX, VET, WAS, WEL

Political Action Committee/s

NFDA-PAC
400 C St. NE
Washington, DC 20002
Tel: (202)547-0441
Fax: (202)547-0726
Contact: John H. Fitch, Jr.

In-house, DC-area Employees

FITCH, Jr., John H.: Director, Government Relations
SALYER, Allison: Legislative Assistant

Outside Counsel/Consultants

Epstein Becker & Green, P.C.
Issues: DIS, HCR, MMM, SMB, VET, WEL
Rep By: Joyce A. Cowan

Law Offices of Carol Green
Issues: CAW, ENV
Rep By: Carol Lynn Green

Nat'l Gaucher Foundation

11140 Rockville Pike
Suite 101
Rockville, MD 20852
Tel: (301)816-1515
Fax: (301)816-1516
Web: www.gaucherdisease.org
E-mail: ngf@gaucherdisease.org

A non-profit organization that funds research for Gaucher Disease. Also provides listings of treatment centers and support groups for patients. Publishes a quarterly newsletter.

Leg. Issues: HCR, INS, MED

In-house, DC-area Employees

BERMAN, Dr. Robin Ely: Medical Director/President and Chief Exec. Officer
BUYERS, Rhonda: Exec. Director

Nat'l Gay and Lesbian Task Force

1700 Kalorama Rd.
Suite 101
Washington, DC 20009-2702
Tel: (202)332-6483
Fax: (202)332-0207

Dedicated to achieving full equality and civil rights for lesbians and gay men. Supports a related, non-lobbying group called NGLTF Policy Institute.

In-house, DC-area Employees

ELLIOT, David: Director, Public Information
TOLEDO, Elizabeth: Exec. Director

Nat'l Geographic Soc.

1145 17th St. NW
Washington, DC 20036
Tel: (202)857-7000
Fax: (202)775-6141

Founded in 1888 to facilitate the increase and diffusion of geographic and scientific knowledge. Reaches an international audience through its magazines, books, maps, television programming, and educational films and software.

Leg. Issues: TAX

In-house, DC-area Employees

ADAMSON, Terrence: Senior V. President, Law, Business and Government
FAHEY, John: President and Chief Exec. Officer
GROSVENOR, Gilbert M.: Chairman of the Board
HUDSON, Betty: Senior V. President, Communications
JACOBSEN, Mary Jeanne: V. President, Communications
MOFFET, Barbara S.: Director, Plans and Programs
SIMS, Robert B.: Exec. V. President and President, Magazine Group

Outside Counsel/Consultants

KPMG, LLP
Issues: TAX

Winston & Strawn
Issues: TAX
Rep By: Hon. Beryl F. Anthony, Jr., Charles L. Kinney

Nat'l Glass Ass'n

8200 Greensboro Dr.
Suite 302
McLean, VA 22102-3881
Tel: (703)442-4890
Fax: (703)442-0630
Registered: LDA
Web: www.glass.org
E-mail: nga@glass.org

Represents the flat glass industry including architectural, automotive, and specialty glass.

Political Action Committee/s

Nat'l Glass Ass'n Political Action Committee
8200 Greensboro Dr.
Suite 302
McLean, VA 22102-3881
Tel: (703)442-4890
Fax: (703)442-0630
Contact: Brenda Stempson

In-house, DC-area Employees

JAMES, Philip J.: President and Chief Exec. Officer
STEMPSON, Brenda: Exec. V. President

Outside Counsel/Consultants

Shaw Pittman

Nat'l Governors' Ass'n

444 N. Capitol St. NW
Suite 267
Washington, DC 20001-1512
Tel: (202)624-5300
Fax: (202)624-5313
Web: www.nga.org

Represents state governors and serves as liaison between state and federal governments. Formerly known as the Nat'l Governors Conference.

In-house, DC-area Employees

GANZGLASS, Evelyn: Policy Studies Director of Employment and Social Services
HENNEBERRY, Joan: Policy Studies Director for Health
JONES, Nolan: Director, Human Resources Group
LINN, Dane: Policy Studies Director, Education
PRINCIPI, Frank: Legislative Associate
SCHEPPACH, Raymond C.: Exec. Director
SEYBOLD, Catherine: Manager, Media Relations
THOMASIAN, John: Director, Center for Best Practices
WILEY, Peter: Director of State Services

Nat'l Graduate University

Arlington, VA

Outside Counsel/Consultants

John Thomas White
Rep By: John Thomas White, III

Nat'l Grain and Feed Ass'n

1250 I St. NW
Suite 1003
Washington, DC 20005-3917
Tel: (202)289-0873
Fax: (202)289-5388
Registered: LDA
Web: www.ngfa.org
E-mail: ngfa@ngfa.org

Ass'n of grain, feed and processing firms that store, handle, merchandise, mill, process, and export over 70% of U.S. grains and oilseeds.

Leg. Issues: AGR, CAW, FOO, GOV, HCR, LBR, MIA, ROD, RRR, TOU, TRA, TRD, TRU

Political Action Committee/s

GrainPAC
1250 I St. NW
Suite 1003
Washington, DC 20005-3917
Tel: (202)289-0873
Fax: (202)289-5388
Contact: David C. Lindsay

In-house, DC-area Employees

GORDON, Randall C.: V. President, Communications and Government Relations
KEITH, Kendell W.: President
LINDSAY, David C.: Director, Legislative Affairs

Outside Counsel/Consultants

Arent Fox Kintner Plotkin & Kahn, PLLC
Issues: AGR
Rep By: Marc L. Fleischaker

Nat'l Grain Sorgum Producers

Abernathy, TX
Leg. Issues: AGR, CAW, GOV, TRD

Outside Counsel/Consultants

Daniel F. Shaw & Associates
Issues: AGR, CAW, GOV, TRD
Rep By: Daniel F. Shaw

Nat'l Grain Trade Council

1300 L St. NW
Suite 925
Washington, DC 20005
Tel: (202)842-0400
Fax: (202)789-7223
Registered: LDA
Web: www.ngtc.org
E-mail: manager@ngtc.org
Leg. Issues: AGR, CDT, FIN, TRD

In-house, DC-area Employees

KINNAIRD, Jula J.: President
PETERSEN, Robert R.: President
WEILAND, Jennifer J.: Assistant to the President, Legal Counsel

Nat'l Grange

1616 H St. NW
Washington, DC 20006
Tel: (202)628-3507
Fax: (202)347-1091
Registered: LDA
Web: www.nationalgrange.org
E-mail: rfrederick@nationalgrange.org

A family-based community service organization with special interest in farm policies and programs. Concerned with legislation relating to agriculture and rural America.

Leg. Issues: AGR, ALC, ANI, BAN, BUD, CAW, COM, EDU, ENG, ENV, FIR, FOO, HCR, IND, MMM, NAT, POS, ROD, RRR, TAX, TEC, TOB, TRA, TRD, UTI, WEL

In-house, DC-area Employees

FREDERICK, Robert M.: Director, Administrative Services
RICHARDSON, Kermit: President
WATSON, LeRoy: Director, Legislative Activities

Nat'l Grape Co-operative Ass'n, Inc.

Westfield, NY

Outside Counsel/Consultants

Robert N. Pyle & Associates

Nat'l Grid USA

633 Pennsylvania Ave. NW
Sixth Floor
Washington, DC 20004
Tel: (202)783-7959
Fax: (202)783-1489
Registered: LDA
Web: www.us.ngrid.com

Formed by merger of New England Electric System and New England Power Service Co. in 2000. Headquartered in Westboro, MA.

Leg. Issues: BUD, ENG, ENV, TAX, UTI, WAS

In-house, DC-area Employees

ALFELDA, Margaret A.: Office Manager
LOOMIS, Ralph E.: V. President, Federal Affairs

Outside Counsel/Consultants

Swidler Berlin Shereff Friedman, LLP
Issues: BUD, ENV, UTI

Nat'l Grocers Ass'n

1825 Samuel Morse Dr.
Reston, VA 20190
Tel: (703)437-5300
Fax: (703)437-7768
Registered: LDA
Web: www.nationalgrocers.org
E-mail: info@nationalgrocers.org

Formed as result of a merger of the Cooperative Food Distributors of America and the Nat'l Ass'n of Retail Grocers of the United States. Represents independently operated grocery retailers and the retailer-owned cooperatives and voluntary wholesalers who service them.

Leg. Issues: AGR, ENG, FOO, HCR, LBR, TAX, TOB

Political Action Committee/s

Nat'l Grocers Ass'n Political Action Committee
1825 Samuel Morse Dr.
Reston, VA 20190
Tel: (703)437-5300
Fax: (703)437-7768
Contact: Thomas F. Wenning

In-house, DC-area Employees

DIPASQUALE, Frank: Senior V. President
WENNING, Thomas F.: Senior V. President and General Counsel
ZAUCHA, Thomas K.: President and Chief Exec. Officer
ZLOTNIKOFF, Stuart: Senior V. President

Nat'l Ground Water Ass'n

Westerville, OH
Registered: LDA
Leg. Issues: ENV, LBR, SCI

Outside Counsel/Consultants

The Dutko Group, Inc.
Issues: ENV, LBR, SCI
Rep By: Gary J. Andres

Nat'l Guard Ass'n of the U.S.

One Massachusetts Ave. NW
Washington, DC 20001
Tel: (202)789-0031
Fax: (202)682-9358
Registered: LDA
Leg. Issues: DEF

In-house, DC-area Employees

ALEXANDER, Maj. Gen. Richard C.: Exec. Director
GOHEEN, John: Director, Communications
GOSS, (Ret.), Col. Bill: Director, Legislative Affairs
ISBERG, Joan: Deputy Director, Army Activities
TIERNY, Jim: Deputy Director, Joint Activities

Nat'l Hardwood Lumber Ass'n

c/o Terpstra Associates
1111 19th St. NW, 12th Floor
Washington, DC 20036-4503
Tel: (202)828-9487
Fax: (202)828-8405

Headquartered in Memphis TN.

Leg. Issues: ENV, NAT, TAX

Political Action Committee/s

Nat'l Hardwood Lumber Ass'n PAC
c/o Terpstra Associates
1111 19th St. NW, 12th Floor
Washington, DC 20036-4503
Tel: (202)828-9487
Fax: (202)828-8405
Contact: Grace Terpstra

In-house, DC-area Employees

TERPSTRA, Grace: PAC Contact

Outside Counsel/Consultants

Terpstra Associates
Issues: ENV, NAT, TAX
Rep By: Grace Terpstra

Nat'l Head Start Ass'n

1651 Prince St.
Alexandria, VA 22314
Tel: (703)739-0875
Fax: (703)739-0878
Web: www.nhsa.org

Membership is comprised of staff, parents and friends involved in over 2,000 Head Start programs across the country.

Leg. Issues: BUD, EDU, GOV, HCR, INS, WEL

In-house, DC-area Employees

GREENE, Sarah: Chief Exec. Officer
MAILLAR, Townley: Director, Government Affairs
MCGRADY, Michael: Deputy Director

Outside Counsel/Consultants

Ledge Counsel
Issues: BUD, EDU, WEL

Valente Lopatin & Schulze
Issues: BUD, EDU
Rep By: Alan G. Lopatin

Nat'l Health Care Access Coalition

Washington, DC
Leg. Issues: HCR, IMM, VET

Outside Counsel/Consultants

The Spectrum Group
Issues: HCR, IMM, VET
Rep By: Joan Bondareff, Gregory L. Sharp

Nat'l Health Care Anti-Fraud Ass'n

1255 23rd St. NW
Suite 200
Washington, DC 20037-1174
Tel: (202)452-8100
Fax: (202)785-6764
Web: www.nhcaa.org
E-mail: fraud@nhcaa.org

Organized to improve the prevention, detection and prosecution of health care fraud offenders.

In-house, DC-area Employees

MAHON, William J.: Exec. Director

Outside Counsel/Consultants

Hauck and Associates
Rep By: William J. Mahon, Carol I. Velander

Nat'l Health Council

1730 M St. NW
Suite 500
Washington, DC 20036
Web: www.nhcouncil.org
E-mail: info@nhcouncil.org

Tel: (202)785-3910
Fax: (202)785-5923
Registered: LDA

A membership association of the nation's major health organizations, dedicated to promoting and enhancing the health of all Americans.

Leg. Issues: BUD, CSP, GOV, HCR, MED, MMM, PHA, SCI, TAX, TOB

In-house, DC-area Employees
SMEDBURG, Paul C.: Director, Governmental Affairs
WEINBERG, CAE, Myrl: President

Nat'l Health Law Program

1101 14th St. NW
Suite 405
Washington, DC 20005
Web: www.healthlaw.org
E-mail: nhelpdc@healthlaw.org

Tel: (202)289-7661
Fax: (202)289-7724

A non-profit law firm specializing in health law for low-income clients.

Leg. Issues: CIV, HCR, IMM, MMM

In-house, DC-area Employees
HITOV, Steve: Staff Attorney
LAVIN, Laurence: Director
MCTAGGART, Brendan: Director, Communications
NIOUS, Lionel: Administrative Assistant

Nat'l Health Lawyers Ass'n

1025 Connecticut Ave. NW
Suite 600
Washington, DC 20036
Web: www.healthlawyers.org

Tel: (202)833-1100
Fax: (202)833-1105

In-house, DC-area Employees
LEIBOLD, Peter M.: Exec. V. President and Chief Exec. Officer
MILLER, Wayne: Director, Finance and Administration

Nat'l Health Museum

133 H. St. NW
Suite 600
Washington, DC 20005
Web: www.nationalhealthmuseum.org

Tel: (202)737-2670
Fax: (202)347-4285

Concerned with the establishment of the new National Health Museum.

In-house, DC-area Employees
DUNHAM, J. Mark: Acting Director
HASELTINE, Ph.D., William: Chairman
KOOP, M.D., Sc.D, C. Everett: Chairman Emeritus

Nat'l Health Policy Forum

2131 K St. NW
Suite 500
Washington, DC 20006
Web: www.nhpf.org

Tel: (202)872-1390
Fax: (202)862-9837

In-house, DC-area Employees
MATHERLEE, Karen R.: Co-Director

Nat'l Healthy Start Ass'n

Baltimore, MD
Leg. Issues: BUD

Outside Counsel/Consultants
Chambers Associates Inc.
Issues: BUD
Rep By: Janet A. Denton, William A. Signer

Nat'l Hemophilia Foundation

New York, NY
Leg. Issues: BUD, HCR

Outside Counsel/Consultants
MARC Associates, Inc.
Issues: BUD, HCR
Rep By: Daniel C. Maldonado, Shannon Penberthy, Ellen Riker

Wise & Associates
Issues: HCR
Rep By: Nicholas P. Wise

Nat'l Heritage Foundation

Falls Church, VA
Leg. Issues: GOV

Outside Counsel/Consultants
Verner, Liipfert, Bernhard, McPherson and Hand, Chartered
Issues: GOV
Rep By: Hon. Daniel R. Coats

Nat'l Hispanic Council on Aging

2713 Ontario Rd. NW
Suite 200
Washington, DC 20009

Tel: (202)265-1288
Fax: (202)745-2522

Founded in 1980 as a national voluntary organization to serve the needs of the Hispanic elderly.

Leg. Issues: ALC, CAW, CIV, HCR, HOU, IMM, WEL

In-house, DC-area Employees
SOTOMAYOR, Dr. Marta: President

Nat'l Hockey League

New York, NY
Leg. Issues: COM, CPT, IMM, SPO

Outside Counsel/Consultants
Akin, Gump, Strauss, Hauer & Feld, L.L.P.
Issues: IMM, SPO
Rep By: Frank J. Donatelli

Covington & Burling

Verner, Liipfert, Bernhard, McPherson and Hand, Chartered
Issues: COM, CPT, SPO
Rep By: Philip R. Hochberg

Nat'l Home Equity Mortgage Ass'n

Chino, CA
Leg. Issues: BAN, BNK, CSP, HOU, TAX

Outside Counsel/Consultants
Butera & Andrews
Issues: BAN, BNK, CSP, HOU, TAX
Rep By: Cliff W. Andrews, Wright H. Andrews, Jr., James J. Butera, Frank Tillotson

Nat'l Honey Board

Longmont, CO

Outside Counsel/Consultants
McLeod, Watkinson & Miller
Rep By: Wayne R. Watkinson

Nat'l Horse Show Commission

Leg. Issues: ANI, BUD

Outside Counsel/Consultants
McGuiness & Holch
Issues: ANI, BUD
Rep By: Niels C. Holch

Nat'l Hospice & Palliative Care Organization

1700 Diagonal Rd.
Suite 300
Alexandria, VA 22314
Web: www.uhpco.org

Tel: (703)837-1500
Fax: (703)525-5762
Registered: LDA

A public benefit organization advocating on behalf of the nation's hospices, palliative care organizations and the terminally ill population.

Leg. Issues: HCR

In-house, DC-area Employees
DUNCAN, Andy: Manager, Government Relations
KEYSERLING, Jonathan: V. President, Legislative and Regulatory Affairs

Outside Counsel/Consultants
Edelman Public Relations Worldwide
Rep By: Peter Segall

Hogan & Hartson L.L.P.
Issues: HCR
Rep By: Ann Morgan Vickery

Nat'l Hospice Foundation

Outside Counsel/Consultants
Edelman Public Relations Worldwide
Rep By: Peter Segall

Nat'l Housing and Rehabilitation Ass'n

1625 Massachusetts Ave. NW
Suite 601
Washington, DC 20036-2244
Web: www.housingonline.com

Tel: (202)939-1750
Fax: (202)265-4435

In-house, DC-area Employees
BELL, Peter H.: Exec. Director

Outside Counsel/Consultants
Swidler Berlin Shereff Friedman, LLP
Rep By: Barry B. Direnfeld, James Hamilton, Harold A. Levy, Kenneth G. Lore

Nat'l Housing Conference

815 15th St. NW
Suite 538
Washington, DC 20005
Web: www.nhc.org
E-mail: nhc@nhc.org

Tel: (202)393-5772
Fax: (202)393-5656

Established in 1931, a nonpartisan organization that seeks to mobilize support for affordable housing and community development programs.

Leg. Issues: BAN, BNK, FIN, HOU, INS, RES, URB

In-house, DC-area Employees
FIORE, Maria: Policy Manager
REID, Robert J.: Exec. Director

Nat'l Housing Endowment

1201 15th St. NW
Washington, DC 20005-2800

Tel: (202)822-0274
Fax: (202)861-2177

In-house, DC-area Employees
SILVER, Bruce S.: President and Chief Exec. Officer

Nat'l Housing Trust

1101 30th St. NW
Suite 400
Washington, DC 20007
Web: www.nhtinc.org
E-mail: kmoloney@nhtinc.org

Tel: (202)333-8931
Fax: (202)833-1031
Registered: LDA

A national organization devoted to the preservation of affordable housing.

Leg. Issues: HOU

In-house, DC-area Employees
BODAKEN, Michael: President

Outside Counsel/Consultants
Greenberg Traurig, LLP
Issues: HOU
Rep By: Ronald L. Platt

Nat'l Humanities Alliance

21 Dupont Circle NW
Suite 604
Washington, DC 20036
Web: www.nhalliance.org
E-mail: jhammer@cni.org

Tel: (202)296-4994
Fax: (202)872-0884
Registered: LDA

Works to advance the humanities by promoting the common interests of its members with regard to national policy, programs, and legislation that affect the National Endowment for the Humanities and other related federal agencies.

Leg. Issues: ART, BUD, CPT, EDU

In-house, DC-area Employees
HAMMER, John H.: Director

Nat'l Hydropower Ass'n

One Massachusetts Ave. NW
Suite 850
Washington, DC 20001
Web: www.hydro.org
E-mail: info@hydro.org

Tel: (202)682-1700
Fax: (202)682-9478
Registered: LDA

NHA is a renewal energy trade association representing hydroelectric power.

Leg. Issues: BUD, CAW, ENG, MAR, NAT, SCI, UTI

In-house, DC-area Employees
CIOCCI, Linda Church: Exec. Director
STOVER, Mark R.: Director, Government Affairs
TUFT, David: Director, Communications

Nat'l Immigration Forum

220 I St. NE
Suite 220
Washington, DC 20002

Tel: (202)544-0004
Fax: (202)544-1905
Registered: LDA

Defends legal immigration; fights anti-immigrant prejudice; and preserves the American tradition of diversity.

Leg. Issues: IMM, WEL

In-house, DC-area Employees
KELLEY, Angela: Deputy Exec. Director
SHARRY, Frank P.: Exec. Director
YOUNG, Tara: Policy Assistant

Nat'l Immigration and Naturalization Services Council

Washington, DC
Leg. Issues: IMM

Outside Counsel/Consultants
Eric Shulman & Associates
Issues: IMM
Rep By: Eric Shulman

Nat'l Independent Private Schools Ass'n

Bradenton, FL
Leg. Issues: EDU

Outside Counsel/Consultants

E. Del Smith and Co.
Issues: EDU
Rep By: Margaret Allen, E. Del Smith

Nat'l Indian Child Welfare Ass'n

Portland, OR
Leg. Issues: IND

Outside Counsel/Consultants

Hobbs, Straus, Dean and Walker, LLP
Issues: IND
Rep By: Karen J. Funk

Nat'l Indian Education Ass'n

700 N. Fairfax St.
Suite 210
Alexandria, VA 22314
Tel: (703)838-2870
Fax: (703)838-1620
Registered: LDA
Web: www.niea.org
E-mail: niea@mindspring.com
Leg. Issues: EDU

In-house, DC-area Employees

CHEEK, John: Exec. Director

Nat'l Indian Gaming Ass'n

224 Second St. SE
Washington, DC 20003
Tel: (202)546-7711
Fax: (202)546-1755
Web: www.indiangaming.org
E-mail: niga@indiangaming.org

A trade association dedicated to improving the lives of Native Americans through economic development.

Leg. Issues: GAM, GOV, IND, TAX

In-house, DC-area Employees

HILL, Richard G.: Chairman
MORAGO, Sheila: Director, Public Relations
VAN NORMAN, Mark: Exec. Director

Outside Counsel/Consultants

Carlyle Consulting
Issues: GAM, GOV, IND, TAX
Rep By: Thomas C. Rodgers

Gardner, Carton and Douglas
Issues: TAX
Rep By: Kathleen M. Nilles

Janus-Merritt Strategies, L.L.C.
Issues: GAM, TAX
Rep By: Scott P. Hoffman, Bethany Noble, Mark J. Robertson, J. Daniel Walsh

Nat'l Industrial Council

1331 Pennsylvania Ave. NW
North Lobby, Suite 600
Washington, DC 20004-1703
Tel: (202)637-3053
Fax: (202)637-3182

A federation of state manufacturers' and employers' ass'ns under the aegis of the Nat'l Ass'n of Manufacturers.

In-house, DC-area Employees

BUZBY, Barry: Exec. Dir., State Associations Group
STEWART, Mark: Exec. Director, Employer Association Group

Nat'l Industrial Sand Ass'n

4041 Powder Mill Rd.
Suite 402
Calverton, MD 20705
Tel: (301)595-5550
Fax: (301)595-3303

In-house, DC-area Employees

GLENN, Robert E.: President
HURLEY, Gerald: V. President

Nat'l Industrial Transportation League

1700 N. Moore St.
Suite 1900
Arlington, VA 22209-1904
Tel: (703)524-5011
Fax: (703)524-5017
Registered: LDA
Web: www.nitl.org
E-mail: info@nitl.org

Presents the viewpoint of the users of all modes of freight transportation.

Leg. Issues: TRA

In-house, DC-area Employees

EMMETT, Edward M.: President and Chief Operating Officer
GATTI, Peter: Director of Policy
LUHN, Kathy: Director, Government Affairs
RASTATTER, Edward: Director of Policy

Nat'l Industries for the Blind

1901 N. Beauregard St.
Suite 200
Alexandria, VA 22311-1727
Tel: (703)998-0770
Fax: (703)671-9053
Registered: LDA
Web: www.nib.org
E-mail: lburney@nib.org

Creates quality employment for people who are blind or visually impaired.

Leg. Issues: BUD, EDU, GOV, LBR

In-house, DC-area Employees

BEATTIE, Patricia: Director, Public Policy and Consumer Relations
BURNEY, Lou Ann: Director, Corporate Communications

Outside Counsel/Consultants

Jefferson Government Relations, L.L.C.
Issues: BUD, EDU, GOV, LBR
Rep By: Thomas R. Donnelly, Jr., Jeanne L. Morin

Nat'l Institute for Aerospace Studies and Services Inc.

Washington, DC
Leg. Issues: DEF

Outside Counsel/Consultants

Balzano Associates
Issues: DEF
Rep By: Michael P. Balzano, Jr., Ruthanne Goodman, Nancy Limauro, Janel Vermeulen

Nat'l Institute for Certification in Engineering Technologies

Alexandria, VA
Leg. Issues: GOV

Outside Counsel/Consultants

Halsey, Rains & Associates, LLC
Issues: GOV
Rep By: Steven C. Halsey, James Hubbard, Laurie D. Rains

Nat'l Institute for Citizen Education in the Law

Outside Counsel/Consultants

Mullenholz, Brimsek & Belair
Rep By: Robert R. Belair

Nat'l Institute for Health Care Management

1225 19th St. NW
Suite 710
Washington, DC 20036
Tel: (202)296-4426
Fax: (202)296-4319

Supports research and analysis of healthcare issues in order to assist consumers, healthcare professionals, government, its member companies and the healthcare industry in an effort to deliver high quality healthcare in a cost-effective manner to all residents of the U.S.

In-house, DC-area Employees

CHOCKLEY, Nancy: Exec. Director
KOTIF, Linda: Senior Director, Policy and Program Development

Nat'l Institute for Literacy

Washington, DC

Outside Counsel/Consultants

Widmeyer Communications, Inc.

Nat'l Institute for Public Policy

3031 Javier Rd.
Suite 300
Fairfax, VA 22031
Tel: (703)698-0563
Fax: (703)698-0566

In-house, DC-area Employees

PAYNE, Dr. Keith: President

Nat'l Institute for State Credit Union Examination

1655 N. Fort Myer Dr.
Suite 300
Arlington, VA 22209
Tel: (703)528-8351
Fax: (703)528-3248
Web: www.nascus.org
E-mail: offices@nascus.org

In-house, DC-area Employees

DUERR, Douglas: Chief Exec. Officer

Nat'l Institute for Water Resources

Amherst, MA
Leg. Issues: BUD, NAT

Outside Counsel/Consultants

Van Scoyoc Associates, Inc.
Issues: BUD, NAT
Rep By: Jan Schoonmaker, H. Stewart Van Scoyoc

Nat'l Institute of Building Sciences

1090 Vermont Ave. NW
Suite 700
Washington, DC 20005-4905
Tel: (202)289-7800
Fax: (202)289-1092
Web: www.nibs.org
E-mail: nibs@nibs.org

A public/private partnership authorized by Congress to improve the regulation of building construction in the U.S., facilitate the safe introduction of new and innovative technology in the building process, and disseminate performance criteria and other technical and regulatory information.

In-house, DC-area Employees

BRENNER, AIA, William A.: V. President
HARRIS, FAIA, David A.: President
HEIDER, Claret M.: V. President, BSC/MMC
KENNETT, Earle: V. President
LLOYD, John G.: V. President, Finance and Administration

Nat'l Institute of Certified Moving Consultants

1611 Duke St.
Alexandria, VA 22314
Tel: (703)683-7410
Fax: (703)683-7527
Web: www.promover.org
E-mail: amconf@amconf.org

In-house, DC-area Employees

JENNINGS, Patricia: V. President, Programs and Services

Nat'l Institute of Governmental Purchasing

151 Spring St.
Suite 300
Herndon, VA 20170
Tel: (703)736-8900
Fax: (703)736-9644
Web: www.nigp.org

A professional society founded in 1944 dedicated to raising the standards of public purchasing and materials management through education and technical development.

In-house, DC-area Employees

DEATHERAGE, Anne: Deputy Exec. V. President
GRIMM, CPPO, CPPB, Rick: Exec. V. President

Nat'l Institute of Oilseed Products

1101 15th St. NW
Suite 202
Washington, DC 20005
Tel: (202)785-8450
Fax: (202)223-9741
Web: www.oilseeds.com
E-mail: niop@assnhq.com

In-house, DC-area Employees

CRISTOL, Richard E.: Exec. Director

Outside Counsel/Consultants

The Kellen Company
Rep By: Richard E. Cristol

Nat'l Institute of Senior Centers

409 Third St. SW
Second Floor
Washington, DC 20024-6682
Tel: (202)479-6688
Web: www.ncoa.org

An organization of the Nat'l Council on the Aging. Established in 1970 to promote professional development of senior center professionals.

In-house, DC-area Employees

TODD, Constance: Director, Staff Advocate for Older Americans Legislation

Nat'l Institute of Senior Housing

409 Third St. SW
Second Floor
Washington, DC 20024-6682
Tel: (202)479-6693

A membership unit of the Nat'l Council on the Aging which addresses the growing need for independent housing adapted to the special requirements and interests of older Americans.

In-house, DC-area Employees

GOZONSKY, Moses

Nat'l Institute on Adult Daycare

409 Third St. SW
Second Floor
Washington, DC 20024-6682
Tel: (202)479-6690
Fax: (202)479-0735

An organization of the Nat'l Council on the Aging.

In-house, DC-area Employees

BAKER, Angela: Director

Nat'l Institute on Community-Based Long-Term Care

409 Third St. SW
Second Floor
Washington, DC 20024-6682
Tel: (202)479-6974
Fax: (202)479-0735

A membership unit of the Nat'l Council on the Aging.

In-house, DC-area Employees
MCCLENDON, Carol

Nat'l Institute on Financial Issues and Services for Elders

409 Third St. SW
Second Floor
Washington, DC 20024-6682
Web: www.ncoa.org
E-mail: info@ncoa.org
Tel: (202)479-1200
Fax: (202)479-0735

An interdisciplinary network of professionals and leaders in the field of financial services for elders, a constituent unit of the Nat'l Council on Aging. Seeks to educate financial service professionals, professionals in aging and the public about financial needs of older adults of all socio-economic levels. Contributes to the development of sound public policy related to financial needs of older adults.

In-house, DC-area Employees
FIRMAN, Ed.D., James P.
REINEMER, Michael: Director, Marketing and Communications

Nat'l Interfaith Coalition on Aging

409 Third St. SW
Second Floor
Washington, DC 20024-6682
Tel: (202)479-6689
Fax: (202)479-0735

A membership unit of the Nat'l Council on the Aging, including clergy, aging professionals with religious affiliations, congregations, chaplains, and national religious bodies.

In-house, DC-area Employees
GENTZER, Rick: Chairman

Nat'l Investor Relations Institute

8045 Leesburg Pike
Suite 600
Vienna, VA 22182
Web: www.niri.org
Tel: (703)506-3570
Fax: (703)506-3571

In-house, DC-area Employees
THOMPSON, Jr., Louis M.: President and Chief Exec. Officer

Nat'l IPA Coalition

Oakland, CA
Leg. Issues: HCR

Outside Counsel/Consultants

Shaw Pittman
Issues: HCR
Rep By: Bruce Fried

Nat'l Islamic Front Afghanistan

Peshawar, PAKISTAN

Outside Counsel/Consultants

Hayward Internat'l

Nat'l Italian American Foundation

1860 19th St. NW
Washington, DC 20009
Web: www.niaf.org
E-mail: info@niaf.org
Tel: (202)387-0600
Fax: (202)387-0800

In-house, DC-area Employees
O'CONNELL, Elizabeth: Director, Public Policy and Ethnic Affairs
ROTONDARO, Fred: Exec. Director

Outside Counsel/Consultants

Matz, Blancato & Associates, Inc.
Rep By: Robert B. Blancato

MV3 & Associates

Valente Lopatin & Schulze
Rep By: Mark Valente, III

Nat'l ITFS Ass'n

Detroit, MI
Leg. Issues: COM, EDU, FOR, TEC

Outside Counsel/Consultants

Dow, Lohnes & Albertson, PLLC
Issues: COM, EDU, FOR, TEC
Rep By: Todd D. Gray, Kenneth D. Salomon

Nat'l Jewish Democratic Council

777 N. Capitol St. NE
Suite 305
Washington, DC 20002
Web: www.njdc.org
E-mail: info@njdc.org
Tel: (202)216-9060
Fax: (202)216-9061

Promotes Jewish values in the Democratic Party and seeks greater Jewish participation in the Party.

Political Action Committee/s

Nat'l Jewish Democratic Council PAC

777 N. Capitol St. NE
Suite 305
Washington, DC 20002
Contact: Jason Silverberg
Tel: (202)216-9060
Fax: (202)216-9061

In-house, DC-area Employees
FORMAN, Ira N.: Exec. Director
HARRIS, David A.: Deputy Exec. Director
SILVERBERG, Jason: Political Director

Nat'l Jewish Medical and Research Center

Denver, CO
Leg. Issues: BUD

Outside Counsel/Consultants

Cassidy & Associates, Inc.
Issues: BUD
Rep By: Laura A. Neal, Sean O'Shea, Valerie Rogers Osborne

Nat'l Job Corps Ass'n

Alexandria, VA
Leg. Issues: ECN

Outside Counsel/Consultants

Leonard Resource Group
Issues: ECN

Nat'l Juice Products Ass'n

Tampa, FL
Leg. Issues: TRD

Outside Counsel/Consultants

Collier Shannon Scott, PLLC
Issues: TRD
Rep By: Kathleen Clark Kies, Robert W. Porter, Paul C. Rosenthal

Nat'l Kidney and Urologic Diseases Information Clearinghouse

Three Information Way
Bethesda, MD 20892-3580
Web: www.niddk.nih.gov
E-mail: nkudic@info.niddk.nih.gov
Tel: (301)654-4415
Fax: (301)907-8906

Provides educational materials and referrals regarding kidney and urologic diseases.

In-house, DC-area Employees
KRANZFELDER, Kathy: Project Officer

Nat'l Kidney Foundation

1522 K Street NW
Suite 825
Washington, DC 20005
Web: www.kidney.org
Tel: (202)216-9257
Fax: (202)216-9258
Registered: LDA

Heaquartered in New York, NY.

Leg. Issues: HCR, MED, MMM

In-house, DC-area Employees
CHIANCHIANO, Dolph: Director, Scientific and Public Policy
ZIMMERMAN, Troy: Government Relations Director

Nat'l Labor Relations Board Professional Ass'n

1099 14th St. NW
Suite 9120
Washington, DC 20570
Tel: (202)273-1749

A union of legal professionals employed at the National Labor Relations Board Headquarters in Washington.

Leg. Issues: LBR

In-house, DC-area Employees
ROSSEN, Leslie E.: President
SEDDELMEYER, David: Director, Legislative and Public Affairs

Nat'l Law Center on Homelessness and Poverty

1411 K St. NW
Suite 1400
Washington, DC 20005
Web: www.nlcph.org
E-mail: nlchp@nlchp.org
Tel: (202)638-2535
Fax: (202)628-2737

In-house, DC-area Employees
FOSCARINIS, Maria: Exec. Director
WEIR, Laurel: Policy Director

Nat'l Law Enforcement Council

888 16th St. NW
Suite 700
Washington, DC 20006-4103
Leg. Issues: LAW
Tel: (202)835-8020
Fax: (202)331-4291
Registered: LDA

In-house, DC-area Employees
BALDWIN, Donald: Exec. Director

Outside Counsel/Consultants

Donald Baldwin Associates
Issues: LAW
Rep By: Donald Baldwin

Nat'l Law Enforcement Officers Memorial Fund

605 E St. NW
Washington, DC 20004
Web: www.nleomf.com
Tel: (202)737-3400
Fax: (202)737-3405

Established and now oversees the Nat'l Law Enforcement Officers Memorial. Works to honor the service and sacrifice of America's law enforcement officers. Not a membership organization.

In-house, DC-area Employees
FLOYD, Craig W.: Chairman
LYONS-WYNNE, Lynn: Director, Public Liaison and Operations

Nat'l League of Cities

1301 Pennsylvania Ave. NW
Suite 550
Washington, DC 20004-1701
Web: www.nlc.org
E-mail: pa@nlc.org
Tel: (202)626-3000
Fax: (202)626-3043

Founded in 1924 and known until 1964 as the American Municipal Ass'n, the National League of Cities exists to represent the interests of its more than 1,500 member municipalities and 49 member state municipal leagues before the Federal Government.

Leg. Issues: COM, TEC

In-house, DC-area Employees
BECKER, Christine S.: Deputy Exec. Director
BORUT, Donald J.: Exec. Director
FLETCHER, Jeff: Director, Center for Public Affairs
KOCHEISEN, Carol: Senior Legislative Counsel
OTERO, Juan: Legislative Counsel
RIGSBY, Deborah: Legislative Counsel
WHITE, Melissa: Legislative Counsel
WHITMAN, Cameron: Director, Policy and Federal Relations

Outside Counsel/Consultants

Miller, Canfield, Paddock & Stone, P.L.C.
Issues: COM, TEC
Rep By: Tillman L. Lay

Nat'l League of Families of American Prisoners and Missing in Southeast Asia

1001 Connecticut Ave. NW
Suite 919
Washington, DC 20036
Web: www.pow-miafamilies.org
E-mail: info@pow-miafamilies.org
Tel: (202)223-6846
Fax: (202)785-9410

Seeks to obtain the release of all prisoners, the fullest possible accounting for the missing and repatriation of the remains of those who died in Southeast Asia.

In-house, DC-area Employees
GRIFFITHS, Ann Mills: Exec. Director

Nat'l League of Postmasters of the U.S.

1023 N. Royal St.
Alexandria, VA 22314-1569
Web: www.postmasters.org
E-mail: information@postmasters.org
Leg. Issues: BUD, GOV, HCR, INS, LBR, POS, RET
Tel: (703)548-5922
Fax: (703)836-8937

Political Action Committee/s

Nat'l League of Postmasters Political Action Committee

1023 N. Royal St.
Alexandria, VA 22314-1569
Contact: Joseph W. Cinadr
Tel: (703)548-5922
Fax: (703)836-8937

In-house, DC-area Employees
CINADR, Joseph W.: President
WEINBERG, Richard A.: Exec. Director

Nat'l Leased Housing Ass'n

1818 N St. NW
Suite 405
Washington, DC 20036
Web: www.hud.nhla/
E-mail: info@hudnlha.com
Tel: (202)785-8888
Fax: (202)785-2008
Registered: LDA

Represents more than 600 private and public organizations involved in government-related, low-income, multi-family rental housing.

Leg. Issues: HOU

In-house, DC-area Employees
MUHA, Denise B.: Exec. Director

Outside Counsel/Consultants

Nixon Peabody LLP
Issues: HOU
Rep By: Charles L. Edson, Stephen J. Wallace

Nat'l Legal & Policy Center

103 W. Broad St. Tel: (703)237-1970
Suite 620 Fax: (703)237-2090
Falls Church, VA 22046

A foundation to promote ethics in government.

In-house, DC-area Employees

BOEHM, Kenneth F.: Chairman

Nat'l Legal Aid and Defender Ass'n

1625 K St. NW Tel: (202)452-0620
Suite 800 Fax: (202)872-1031
Washington, DC 20006 Registered: LDA
Web: www.nlada.org
E-mail: info@nlada.org
Leg. Issues: BUD, LAW

In-house, DC-area Employees

CLARK, Julie: Director, Government Relations
LYONS, Clinton: Exec. Director
SAUNDERS, Donald M.: Director, Civil Division
WALLACE, H. Scott: Director, Defender Legal Services

Nat'l Legal Center for the Public Interest

1000 16th St. NW Tel: (202)296-1683
Suite 500 Fax: (202)293-2118
Washington, DC 20036
Web: www.nlcpi.org
E-mail: info@nlcpi.com

A nonpartisan, educational and public service foundation concerned with issues of public policy which relate to law or to the administration of justice. It concentrates its activities on providing the public and private sectors with timely information on key issues relating to the judiciary and the development of public policy through newsletters, monographs, conferences, executive briefings and special projects of national importance.

Leg. Issues: AGR, AUT, CAW, CHM, DEF, ECN, EDU, ENV, FIN, FUE, GOV, LBR, MIA, NAT, PHA, SCI, SMB, TOR, TRD

In-house, DC-area Employees

HUETER, Ernest B.: President
JACOBY, Irene: Senior V. President, Administration

Nat'l Liberty Museum

Philadelphia, PA
Leg. Issues: ECN, EDU, TOU, URB

Outside Counsel/Consultants

Doepken Keevican & Weiss
Issues: ECN, EDU, TOU, URB
Rep By: Clyde H. Slease, III

Nat'l Licensed Beverage Ass'n

20 S. Quaker Ln. Tel: (703)751-9730
Suite 230 Fax: (703)751-9748
Alexandria, VA 22314 Registered: LDA
Web: www.nlba.org
E-mail: nlba-mail@nlba.org

A national trade association of state associations, individual establishments, and industry related organizations dedicated to promoting and protecting the business, the image, and the future of licensed beverage establishments. Organized in 1950.

Leg. Issues: ADV, ALC, ART, BEV, CPT, CSP, FOO, GAM, IND, LBR, MON, SMB, TAX, TOB, TOU, TRA, TRD

Political Action Committee/s

Nat'l Licensed Beverage Ass'n Bar PAC
20 S. Quaker Ln. Tel: (703)751-9730
Suite 230 Fax: (703)751-9748
Alexandria, VA 22314

In-house, DC-area Employees

LEACH, Debra A.: Exec. Director

Outside Counsel/Consultants

R. J. Hudson Associates
Issues: ADV, ALC, ART, BEV, CPT, CSP, FOO, GAM, IND, LBR, MON, SMB, TAX, TOB, TOU, TRA
Rep By: David S. Germroth

Nat'l Lighting Bureau

1300 N. 17th St. Tel: (301)587-9572
Suite 1847 Fax: (301)589-2017
Rosslyn, VA 22209
Web: www.nlg.org
E-mail: info@nlb.com

In-house, DC-area Employees

PITSOR, Kyle: Exec. Director

Nat'l Lime Ass'n

200 N. Glebe Rd. Tel: (703)243-5463
Suite 800 Fax: (703)243-5489
Arlington, VA 22203 Registered: LDA
Web: www.lime.org
E-mail: natlime@lime.org

The trade association for U.S. and Canadian manufacturers of high calcium quicklime, dolomitic quicklime, and hydrated lime. Represents the interests of its members in Washington, provides input on standards and specifications for lime, and funds and manages research on current and new uses for lime.

Leg. Issues: ENV, GOV, NAT

In-house, DC-area Employees

MALES, Eric H.: Director, Regulatory Issues and Special Projects
PRILLAMAN, Hunter L.: Director, Government Affairs
SEEGER, Arline M.: Exec. Director

Nat'l Low Income Housing Coalition/LIHIS

1012 14th St. NW Tel: (202)662-1530
Suite 610 Fax: (202)393-1973
Washington, DC 20005
Web: www.nlihc.org

Established in 1974, The National Low Income Housing Coalition/LIHIS is dedicated solely to ending America's affordable housing crisis. NLIHC educates, organizes, and advocates to ensure decent, affordable housing within healthy neighborhoods for everyone. NLIHC provides up-to-date information, formulates policy, and educates the public on housing needs and the strategies for solutions.

Leg. Issues: HOU

In-house, DC-area Employees

CROWLEY, Sheila: President

Nat'l Lumber and Building Material Dealers Ass'n

40 Ivy St. SE Tel: (202)547-2230
Washington, DC 20003 Fax: (202)547-7640
Registered: LDA
Web: www.dealer.org

Represents 21 state and regional federated associations and 8,500 independent lumber and building material dealers before Congress, the White House and various federal agencies.

Leg. Issues: AGR, BAN, BNK, BUD, ENV, HCR, HOU, LBR, NAT, RES, SMB, TAX, TRD

Political Action Committee/s

Lumber Dealers Political Action Committee (LUDPAC)
40 Ivy St. SE Tel: (202)547-2230
Washington, DC 20003 Fax: (202)547-7640
Contact: Gary W. Donnelly

In-house, DC-area Employees

DONNELLY, Gary W.: President
HERTZOG, Linda: Director, Member Services
KEMPF, Kyle W.: Legislative Assistant
MORGAN, Jenna L.: Director, Government Affairs
WORDEN, Vicki: Director, Public Affairs

Outside Counsel/Consultants

London and Satagaj, Attorneys-at-Law
Rep By: John S. Satagaj

Nat'l Marine Life Center

Buzzards Bay, MA
Leg. Issues: ANI, ENV

Outside Counsel/Consultants

Sher & Blackwell
Issues: ANI, ENV
Rep By: Earl W. Comstock, Jeffrey R. Pike, Antilla E. Trotter, III

Nat'l Marine Manufacturers Ass'n

1819 L St. NW Tel: (202)861-1180
Suite 700 Fax: (202)861-1181
Washington, DC 20036 Registered: LDA

The Government Relations Office in Washington for the Chicago-based association. Reponsible for monitoring federal and state legislation and regulatory activity affecting its 1500 member companies who manufacture recreational boats and related marine products.

Leg. Issues: CPT, MAN, MAR

Political Action Committee/s

Nat'l Marine Manufacturers Ass'n PAC
1819 L St. NW Tel: (202)861-1180
Suite 700 Fax: (202)861-1181
Washington, DC 20036
Contact: John McKnight

NMMA Political Action Committee
1819 L St. NW Tel: (202)861-1180
Suite 700 Fax: (202)861-1181
Washington, DC 20036
Contact: Kelly Rote

In-house, DC-area Employees

BLACKISTONE, Mick: V. President, Government Relations
MCKNIGHT, John: Director, Environmental Relations
ROTE, Kelly: Director, Federal Government Relations

Outside Counsel/Consultants

Preston Gates Ellis & Rouvelas Meeds LLP
Issues: MAR
Rep By: Mark H. Ruge

Shaw Pittman
Issues: CPT
Rep By: Thomas J. Spulak

Nat'l Maritime Alliance

Woods Hole, MA

Outside Counsel/Consultants

Dyer Ellis & Joseph, P.C.
Rep By: Duncan C. Smith, III

Nat'l Maritime Safety Ass'n

2011 Pennsylvania Ave. NW Tel: (202)296-3005
Suite 301 Fax: (202)331-7479
Washington, DC 20006
E-mail: carroll@nmsa-usa.org

In-house, DC-area Employees

CARROLL, Jr., Charles T.: General Counsel

Outside Counsel/Consultants

Wilcox, Carroll & Froelich, PLLC
Rep By: Charles T. Carroll, Jr., F. Edwin Froelich, M.D.

Nat'l Marrow Donor Program

Minneapolis, MN Registered: LDA
Leg. Issues: BUD, HCR

Outside Counsel/Consultants

Patton Boggs, LLP
Issues: BUD, HCR
Rep By: Martha M. Kendrick, JoAnn V. Willis

Nat'l Materials Advisory Board

Washington, DC

Outside Counsel/Consultants

Wilson & Wilson

Nat'l Meat Ass'n

Oakland, CA
Leg. Issues: BUD, FOO

Outside Counsel/Consultants

Olsson, Frank and Weeda, P.C.
Issues: BUD, FOO
Rep By: John W. Bode, Susan P. Grymes, Karen Reis Harned, Stephen L. Lacey, Marshall L. Matz, Philip C. Olsson, Tyson Redpath, Ryan W. Stroschein

Nat'l Meat Canners Ass'n

1700 N. Moore St. Tel: (703)841-3680
Suite 1600 Fax: (703)527-0928
Arlington, VA 22209
Web: www.meatami.com
E-mail: nmca@meatami.com

Represents processors of commercially sterile meat and poultry products throughout the country. Members include companies of all sizes.

Leg. Issues: AGR, CSP, FOO, GOV, HCR

In-house, DC-area Employees

BOYLE, J. Patrick: Exec. Secretary
SHER, Jacky: Director, Administration

Nat'l Medical Ass'n

1012 10th St. NW Tel: (202)347-1895
Washington, DC 20001 Fax: (202)842-3293
Web: www.mnanet.org

Composed primarily of black physicians.

In-house, DC-area Employees

WILLIAMS, Rudolph M.: Exec. Director

Nat'l Medical Enterprises, Inc.

Santa Monica, CA

Outside Counsel/Consultants

Akin, Gump, Strauss, Hauer & Feld, L.L.P.

Nat'l Mental Health Ass'n

1021 Prince St.
Alexandria, VA 22314-2971
Tel: (703)684-7722
Fax: (703)684-5968
Registered: LDA
Web: www.nmha.org
E-mail: fedgovinfo@nmha.org
Leg. Issues: BUD, CIV, CSP, HCR, LAW, MMM, PHA, VET

In-house, DC-area Employees

ANDREW, Frances L.: Assistant Director, Legislative Affairs
BERONIO, Kirsten: Senior Director, Government Affairs
FAENZA, Michael M.: President and CEO
IBSON, Ralph: V. President, Government Affairs
KENYON, Allyson: Government Affairs Associate

Outside Counsel/Consultants

Powers Pyles Sutter & Verville, PC
Issues: BUD
Rep By: J. Michael Hall, Alyson M. Haywood

Nat'l Mentoring Partnership, Inc.

1400 I St. NW
Suite 850
Washington, DC 20005
Tel: (202)729-4360
Fax: (202)729-4341
Registered: LDA
Web: www.mentoring.org
E-mail: jwaller@mentoring.org

Convenes and staffs the Public Policy Council.

Leg. Issues: EDU, WEL

In-house, DC-area Employees

ANDERSON, Kristen: Project Manager, Government Relations
WALLER, James F.: V. President, Government Relations

Nat'l Migrant Head Start Ass'n

Washington, DC
Leg. Issues: EDU

Outside Counsel/Consultants

Robert A. Rapoza Associates
Issues: EDU
Rep By: Robert A. Rapoza

Nat'l Military Family Ass'n

6000 Stevenson Ave.
Suite 304
Alexandria, VA 22304-3526
Tel: (703)823-6632
Fax: (703)751-4857
Web: www.nmfa.org
E-mail: families@nmfa.org

Represents the interests of military family members and the active duty, reserve component, and retired personnel of seven uniformed services. Seeks to influence the development and implementation of policies that positively affect the quality of life for uniformed service families.

Leg. Issues: BUD, DEF, EDU, FAM, HCR, HOU, MED, MMM, PHA, RET, TAX, VET

In-house, DC-area Employees

RAEZER, Joyce: Associate Director, Government Affairs

Nat'l Military Intelligence Ass'n

9200 Centerway Rd.
Gaithersburg, MD 20879
Tel: (301)840-6642
Fax: (301)840-8502
Web: www.nmia.org
E-mail: zhi@nmia.org

Active and retired military and civilian intelligence personnel seeking to promote a stronger U. S. intelligence system through educational means. Publisher of American Intelligence Journal, the NMIA Newsletter, and NMIA in Cyberia.

Leg. Issues: AER, DEF, DIS, ENG, FOR, GOV

In-house, DC-area Employees

HAMBY, Zhi Marie: Exec. Director
THOMAS, Brig. Gen. Trent N.: President

Outside Counsel/Consultants

Real Trends
Rep By: Zhi Marie Hamby

Nat'l Milk Producers Federation

2101 Wilson Blvd.
Suite 400
Arlington, VA 22201
Tel: (703)243-6111
Fax: (703)841-9328
Registered: LDA
Web: www.nmpf.org
E-mail: nmpf@aol.com

A national association with membership composed of dairy cooperatives.

Leg. Issues: AGR, ANI, BUD, FOO, TAX, TRA, TRD

Political Action Committee/s

NMPF PAC
2101 Wilson Blvd.
Suite 400
Arlington, VA 22201
Tel: (703)243-6111
Fax: (703)841-9328
Contact: Roger D. Eldridge

In-house, DC-area Employees

ADAMS, John B.: Director, Animal Health and Farm Services
BALMER, Tom: Senior V. President
BARBER, Lindsay: Communications and Government Relations Assistant
BYRNE, Rob: V. President, Regulatory Affairs
CASTANEDA, Jaime: Senior Trade Analyst
CRYAN, Roger: Director, Economic Research
ELDRIDGE, Roger D.: V. President, Government Relations
GALEN, Christopher: V. President, Communications
ITLE, Carissa: Director, Environmental Progams
KOZAK, Jerome J.: Chief Exec. Officer
NICHOLS, Johnnie: Director, Technical Services
NUBERN, Chris: Director, Economic Research
RODRIGUEZ-SOLIS, Jose: Economics & Trade Analyst
VITALIANO, Dr. Peter: V. President, International Trade, Economics, and Market Research

Outside Counsel/Consultants

The Solomon Group, LLC
Issues: AGR, ANI, TAX, TRD
Rep By: Hon. Gerald B. H. Solomon, William R. Teator

Tuttle, Taylor & Heron
Issues: AGR
Rep By: Julian B. Tuttle

Nat'l Mining Ass'n

1130 17th St. NW
Washington, DC 20036-4677
Tel: (202)463-2625
Fax: (202)463-6152
Registered: LDA
Web: www.nma.org

Formed from the 1995 merger of the American Mining Congress and the Nat'l Coal Ass'n.

Leg. Issues: BUD, CAW, CSP, ENG, ENV, FOR, GOV, HCR, LAW, LBR, MAN, MAR, MON, NAT, RES, RRR, SMB, TAX, TRA, TRD, UTI, WAS

Political Action Committee/s

COALPAC
1130 17th St. NW
Washington, DC 20036-4677
Tel: (202)463-2645
Fax: (202)833-1965
Contact: Andrea L. Innes

MINEPAC
1130 17th St. NW
Washington, DC 20036-4677
Tel: (202)463-2645
Fax: (202)833-1965
Contact: Andrea L. Innes

In-house, DC-area Employees

ALTMEYER, Thomas H.: Senior V. President, Government Affairs
BENNETT, Karen: Director, Water and Waste
CARVER, Susan B.: V. President, Congressional Affairs
DUFFY, Michael F.: Deputy General Counsel
DWYER, Roderick T.: Deputy General Counsel
FENTON, Jr., G. F. "Ric": V. President, Congressional Affairs
FINKENBINDER, David O.: V. President, Lands Policy
FRISBY, Bradford V.: Assistant General Counsel
GABAUER, Peter: Deputy General Counsel
GERARD, Jack N.: President and Chief Exec. Officer
GERKIN, Daniel R.: Senior V. President Public and Constituent Relations
GRASSER, John L. C.: V. President, External Communications
HOLMES, Constance D.: Senior V. President, Policy Analysis
INNES, Andrea L.: V. President, Political Affairs
JACKSON, Bobby J.: V. President, Human Resources
JACOB, Anne Marie L.: Manager, Congressional Affairs
LEMA, Joseph E.: V. President, Manufacturers and Services Division
LONG, Robert S.: V. President, Government Affairs
PHELLEPS, Moya: V. President, International Trade
QUINN, Jr., Harold P.: Senior V. President, Legal and Regulatory Affairs and General Counsel
SHANAHAN, John: Director, Air Policy
SWEENEY, Katie: Associate General Counsel
WATZMAN, Bruce: V. President, Safety and Health
WILLIAMS, M. Darrell: AudioVisual Services

Outside Counsel/Consultants

McClure, Gerard & Neuenschwander, Inc.
Issues: BUD, ENV, NAT

Nat'l Environmental Strategies
Issues: BUD, CAW, ENV, NAT
Rep By: Marc I. Himmelstein

Nat'l Minority AIDS Council

1931 13th St. NW
Washington, DC 20009
Tel: (202)483-6622
Fax: (202)483-1135
Web: www.nmac.org

Membership includes minority community-based organizations.

Leg. Issues: HCR

In-house, DC-area Employees

LEON, Miguelina: Director, Government Relations and Public Policy

Nat'l Mitigation Bankers Ass'n

Bethesda, MD
Leg. Issues: CAW, ENV, NAT

Outside Counsel/Consultants

Oppenheimer Wolff & Donnelly LLP
Issues: CAW, ENV, NAT
Rep By: Margaret N. Strand

Nat'l Motor Freight Traffic Ass'n

2200 Mill Rd.
Alexandria, VA 22314
Tel: (703)838-1810
Fax: (703)683-1094
Web: www.erols.com/nmfta
E-mail: nmfta@erols.com

Publishes three tariffs and provides motor freight classification advice to and for members and the general public. Association members are motor common carriers of freight, specializing in less than truckload service.

Leg. Issues: TRU

In-house, DC-area Employees

FOLEY, Martin E.: Exec. Director

Nat'l Multi-Housing Council

1850 M St. NW
Suite 540
Washington, DC 20036
Tel: (202)974-2300
Fax: (202)775-0112
Registered: LDA
Web: www.nmhc.org
E-mail: info@nmhc.org

A trade association for multi-family housing owners, developers, builders, financiers, and managers.

Leg. Issues: BNK, CAW, CIV, ENV, HCR, HOU, TAX, TEC

Political Action Committee/s

Nat'l Multi Housing Council Political Action Committee
1850 M St. NW
Suite 540
Washington, DC 20036
Tel: (202)974-2300
Fax: (202)775-0112
Contact: James N. Arbury

In-house, DC-area Employees

ARBURY, James N.: V. President
DUTY, Kimberly D.: V. President, Communications
HARRIS, James "Jay": V. President, Property Management
LEE, Eileen C.: V. President, Environment
NICKSON, Ronald G.: V. President, Building Codes
OBRINSKY, Mark H.: V. President, Research and Chief Economist
RIDDLE, Clarine Nardi: Senior V. President

Outside Counsel/Consultants

Miller & Van Eaton, P.L.L.C.
Issues: TEC
Rep By: Matthew C. Ames, William Malone, Nicholas P. Miller

Washington Council Ernst & Young
Issues: HOU, TAX
Rep By: Doug Badger, Lauren Darling, John L. Doney, Jayne T. Fitzgerald, LaBrenda Garrett-Nelson, Gary J. Gasper, Bruce A. Gates, Nick Giordano, Cathy Koch, Robert J. Leonard, Richard Meltzer, Phillip D. Moseley, John D. Porter, Robert M. Rozen, Donna Steele-Flynn, Timothy J. Urban

Nat'l Museum of Women in the Arts

1250 New York Ave. NW
Washington, DC 20005
Tel: (202)783-5000
Fax: (202)393-3234
Web: www.nmwa.org

A non-profit, private museum for art by women.

Leg. Issues: ART

In-house, DC-area Employees

GREER, Ann: Director, Public Relations

Outside Counsel/Consultants

Chernikoff and Co.
Issues: ART
Rep By: Larry B. Chernikoff

Nat'l Music Publishers' Ass'n

New York, NY
Leg. Issues: CPT

Outside Counsel/Consultants

Griffin, Johnson, Dover & Stewart
Issues: CPT
Rep By: Patrick J. Griffin, David E. Johnson, Susan O. Mann

Paul, Weiss, Rifkind, Wharton & Garrison
Issues: CPT
Rep By: Carl W. Hampe

Nat'l Neighborhood Coalition

1875 Connecticut Ave. NW Tel: (202)408-8553
Suite 410 Fax: (202)408-8551
Washington, DC 20009
Web: www.neighborhoodcoalition.org
E-mail: nncnnc@erols.com

A membership association of national non-profit organizations that work with neighborhood groups. NHC also serves as an information clearinghouse on federal programs and national public policies.

Leg. Issues: BAN, ECN, FIN, HOU

In-house, DC-area Employees

WEISS, Betty: Exec. Director

Nat'l Neighborhood Housing Network

Anchorage, AK
Leg. Issues: HOU

Outside Counsel/Consultants

Robert A. Rapoza Associates
Issues: HOU
Rep By: Robert A. Rapoza

Nat'l Network for Youth

1319 F St. NW Tel: (202)783-7949
Suite 401 Fax: (202)783-7955
Washington, DC 20004
Web: www.nn4youth.org
E-mail: NN4Youth@worldnet.att.net

Represents over 1500 community-based agencies and organizations that serve youth in high-risk situations and their families.

In-house, DC-area Employees

HUGHES, Della: Exec. Director
ROLLIN, Mariam: Public Policy Director

Nat'l Network to End Domestic Violence

666 Pennsylvania Ave. SE Tel: (202)543-5566
Suite 303 Fax: (202)543-5626
Washington, DC 20003 Registered: LDA
Web: www.nnedv.org

A national organization representing state domestic violence coalitions.

Leg. Issues: FAM, INS, LAW, WEL

In-house, DC-area Employees

ROSENTHAL, Lynn: Exec. Director

Outside Counsel/Consultants

Mintz, Levin, Cohn, Ferris, Glovsky and Popeo, P.C.
Rep By: Fernando R. Laguarda

Nat'l Newspaper Ass'n

1010 N. Glebe Rd. Tel: (703)907-7900
Suite 450 Fax: (703)907-7901
Arlington, VA 22201
Web: www.nna.org
E-mail: info@nna.org

Represents over 4000 daily and non-daily newspapers with seminars, publications and government relations activities.

Leg. Issues: ADV, CON, CPT, GOV, LBR, POS, SCI, SMB, TAX

In-house, DC-area Employees

ALLEN, Kenneth B.: Exec. V. President and Chief Exec. Officer
BOONE, Senny: V. President and General Counsel
NELSON, Virginia: Communications Director

Nat'l Newspaper Publishers Ass'n

3200 13th St. NW Tel: (202)588-8764
Washington, DC 20010-2410 Fax: (202)588-5029
Web: www.nnpa.org
E-mail: nnpadc@nnpa.org

A trade association for African-American newpapers throughout the U.S. and the Virgin Islands.

Leg. Issues: ADV, ECN

In-house, DC-area Employees

JEALOUS, Benjamin: Exec. Director

Nat'l Nutritional Foods Ass'n

Newport Beach, CA
Leg. Issues: AGR, BUD, FOO, HCR, TOB

Outside Counsel/Consultants

Capitol Associates, Inc.
Issues: AGR, BUD, HCR, TOB
Rep By: Liz Gemski, Edward R. Long, Ph.D.

Edelman Public Relations Worldwide
Rep By: Daniel Puzo

Parry, Romani, DeConcini & Symms
Issues: FOO
Rep By: Edward H. Baxter, Hon. Dennis DeConcini, John M. Haddow, Scott D. Hatch, Shannon Davis Henderson, Jack W. Martin, Romano Romani, Linda Arey Skladany, Hon. Steven D. Symms

Sidley & Austin
Issues: FOO
Rep By: Alan C. Raul

Nat'l Ocean Industries Ass'n

1120 G St. NW Tel: (202)347-6900
Suite 900 Fax: (202)347-8650
Washington, DC 20005-3801 Registered: LDA
Web: www.noia.org
E-mail: noia@noia.org

Oil and gas companies, their suppliers and supporting firms, exploring and drilling in the outer continental shelf. Other companies engaged in shipbuilding, deep sea mining and other developers or users of ocean resources.

Leg. Issues: BUD, CAW, ENV, GOV, MAR, NAT

In-house, DC-area Employees

FRY, Tom: President
MICHELS, Tom: Director, Public Affairs
MORAN, Robert J.: Director, Government Affairs

Nat'l Oilheat Research Alliance (NORA)

A national association organized to promote the heat industry.

Leg. Issues: FUE

Outside Counsel/Consultants

Patton Boggs, LLP
Issues: FUE
Rep By: Thomas C. Downs, Elena Giberga, Edward J. Newberry, Elizabeth C. Vella

Nat'l Oilseed Processors Ass'n

1255 23rd St. NW Tel: (202)452-8040
Washington, DC 20037 Registered: LDA
E-mail: nopa@nopa.org
Leg. Issues: AGR, BUD, CHM, ENV, FOO, GOV, LBR, TAX, TRA, TRD

In-house, DC-area Employees

AILOR, David C.: Director, Regulatory Affairs
HOVERMALE, David J.: Director, Government and Public Relations
JOHNSON, Allen F.: President

Outside Counsel/Consultants

Dyer Ellis & Joseph, P.C.
Issues: ENV
Rep By: Laurie Crick Sahatjian, Duncan C. Smith, III, Jennifer M. Southwick, Jonathan K. Waldron, Sidney A. Wallace

Hauck and Associates
Rep By: David C. Ailor, Sheldon J. Hauck, Allen F. Johnson, David A. Saunders

Shaw Pittman
Issues: ENV
Rep By: David E. Menotti

Nat'l Organization for Associate Degree Nursing

11250 Roger Bacon Dr. Tel: (703)437-4377
Suite Eight Fax: (703)435-4390
Reston, VA 20190
Web: www.noadn.org/adnursing
E-mail: noadn@noadn.org

In-house, DC-area Employees

PRICE, CAE, Randall C.: Exec. Director

Outside Counsel/Consultants

Drohan Management Group
Rep By: Randall C. Price, CAE

Nat'l Organization for Competency Assurance

Washington, DC
Leg. Issues: LBR, SMB, VET

Outside Counsel/Consultants

The Plexus Consulting Group
Issues: LBR
Rep By: Yasmin Quiwzow

Smith, Bucklin and Associates, Inc.
Issues: SMB, VET
Rep By: Bonnie M. Aubin, Frank M. Moore, Stacey Moye

Nat'l Organization for the Reform of Marijuana Laws

1001 Connecticut Ave. NW Tel: (202)483-5500
Suite 710 Fax: (202)483-0057
Washington, DC 20036 Registered: LDA
Web: www.norml.org
E-mail: norml@norml.org

A non-profit lobby making marijuana legally available as a medicine for seriously ill Americans and decriminalizing the recreational use of marijuana by adults.

Leg. Issues: ALC, CIV, GOV

In-house, DC-area Employees

STROUP, R. Keith: Exec. Director

Nat'l Organization for Victim Assistance

1757 Park Rd. NW Tel: (202)232-6682
Washington, DC 20010 Fax: (202)462-2255
Web: www.try-nova.org
E-mail: nova@try-nova.org

A non-profit membership group providing education to victim assistance professionals and their allies, direct services to victims of crime and crisis, and advocacy for victims rights and services.

Leg. Issues: CON, DIS, LAW

In-house, DC-area Employees

STEIN, John Hollister: Deputy Director
YOUNG, Dr. Marlene: Exec. Director

Nat'l Organization for Women

733 15th St. NW 2nd Floor Tel: (202)628-8669
Washington, DC 20005 Fax: (202)785-8576
Web: www.now.org
E-mail: now@now.org

Seeks to insure the equal status and full participation of women in society.

Political Action Committee/s

Nat'l Organization for Women Political Action Committee (NOW Equality PAC)
733 15th St. NW 2nd Floor Tel: (202)628-8669
Washington, DC 20005 Fax: (202)785-8576
Contact: Karen Johnson

In-house, DC-area Employees

GANDY, Kim A.: Exec. V. President
IRELAND, Patricia: President
JOHNSON, Karen: V. President, Membership

Nat'l Organization of Black Law Enforcement Executives

4609 Pinecrest Office Park Dr. Tel: (703)658-1529
Suite F Fax: (703)658-9479
Second Floor
Alexandria, VA 22312
Web: www.noblenatl.org
E-mail: noble@noblenatl.org

Includes police chiefs, command-level officers, and others who support NOBLE's goals. Mission is to unify the considerable impact of black law enforcement officers on the problems of crime and delinquency in metropolitan areas.

In-house, DC-area Employees

FOSTER, Maurice: Chief Exec. Officer

Nat'l Organization of Social Security Claimants' Representatives

Midland Park, NJ Registered: LDA
Leg. Issues: GOV

Outside Counsel/Consultants

Bracewell & Patterson, L.L.P.

Winston & Strawn
Issues: GOV
Rep By: Hon. Beryl F. Anthony, Jr., Charles L. Kinney, Gregory K. Smith

Nat'l Organization on Disability

910 16th St. NW Tel: (202)293-5960
Suite 600 Fax: (202)293-7999
Washington, DC 20006
Web: www.nod.org

In-house, DC-area Employees

REICH, Alan A.: President

Nat'l Orthotics Manufacturers Ass'n

Washington, DC
Leg. Issues: HCR

Outside Counsel/Consultants

Latham & Watkins
Issues: HCR
Rep By: Edward Correia, Stuart Kurlander, Andrew Morton

The Legislative Strategies Group, LLC
Issues: HCR
Rep By: Martin B. Gold, Denise M. Henry, Steven M. Hilton, Larry E. Smith

Nat'l Osteoporosis Foundation

1232 22nd St. NW
Washington, DC 20037
Tel: (202)223-2226
Fax: (202)223-2237
Registered: LDA
Web: www.nof.org

National, nonprofit, voluntary health organization dedicated to reducing the widespread prevalence of osteoporosis through programs of research, education and advocacy. Membership consists of health care professionals, patients, academic institutions and the general public.

Leg. Issues: HCR

In-house, DC-area Employees

RAYMOND, Sandra C.: Exec. Director

Outside Counsel/Consultants

Evans & Black, Inc.
Issues: HCR
Rep By: Judy A. Black, Teresa J. Dyer, Rae Forker Evans

The Nat'l PAC

600 Pennsylvania Ave. SE
Washington, DC 20003
Tel: (202)879-7710
Fax: (202)879-7728

The nation's largest bipartisan, non-connected PAC dedicated to promoting strong U.S. support for the survival and security of Israel.

In-house, DC-area Employees

BROOKS, Charles D.: Exec. Director
JOSEPHSON, Marvin: Treasurer

Nat'l Paint and Coatings Ass'n

1500 Rhode Island Ave. NW
Washington, DC 20005-5597
Tel: (202)462-6272
Fax: (202)462-8549
Web: www.paint.org
E-mail: npca@paint.org
Leg. Issues: BUD, CAW, ENV, HCR, HOU, NAT, TOR

In-house, DC-area Employees

DOYLE, J. Andrew: President
GRAVES, Thomas J.: General Counsel
LLOYD, David: V. President, Government Affairs
SELL, Jim: Senior Counsel
SIDES, Stephen R.: V. President, Health and Safety

Outside Counsel/Consultants

Richard W. Bliss
Issues: ENV, TOR
Rep By: Pani Farkan

Holland & Knight LLP
Issues: CAW, ENV, HOU
Rep By: Jack M. Burkman, Mike Galano, Richard M. Gold, David C. Whitestone

McDermott, Will and Emery
Issues: BUD, HCR, HOU
Rep By: Neil Quinter

O'Connor & Hannan, L.L.P.
Issues: ENV, NAT
Rep By: Robert W. Barrie, Hon. Thomas J. Corcoran, George J. Mannina, Jr., Patrick E. O'Donnell

Winston & Strawn
Issues: ENV
Rep By: William N. Hall, Roger A. Keller, Jr.

Nat'l Parent Network on Disabilities

1130 17th St. NW
Suite 400
Washington, DC 20036
Tel: (202)463-2299
Fax: (202)463-9405
Registered: LDA
Web: www.npnd.org
E-mail: npnd@mindspring.com
Leg. Issues: FAM

In-house, DC-area Employees

SHEPARD, Linda: Exec. Director

Nat'l Park Foundation

1101 17th St. NW
Suite 1102
Washington, DC 20036
Tel: (202)785-4500
Fax: (202)785-3539
Web: www.nationalparks.org
E-mail: ask-npf@goparks.org

Chartered by Congress in 1967 as a private, nonprofit, philanthropic organization which seeks financial support from the private sector to support the National Park Service.

Leg. Issues: NAT

In-house, DC-area Employees

LARSON, Jennifer: Director, Public Relations
MADDY, Jim: President
NICOLL, Jill D.: Exec. V. President

Outside Counsel/Consultants

Crowell & Moring LLP
Issues: NAT
Rep By: Steven P. Quarles

Nat'l Park Hospitality Ass'n

Baltimore, MD
Registered: LDA

The NPHA is the national trade association of the men and women and their companies which provide lodging, food services, gifts and souvenirs, equipment rentals, transportation and other visitor services in units of the National Park System.

Leg. Issues: NAT, TAX, TOU

Outside Counsel/Consultants

The Argus Group, L.L.C.
Issues: TAX
Rep By: David R. Burton, Dan R. Mastromarco

Santini, Chartered
Issues: NAT, TOU
Rep By: Hon. James D. Santini

Nat'l Parking Ass'n

1112 16th St. NW
Suite 300
Washington, DC 20036
Tel: (202)296-4336
Fax: (202)331-8523
Registered: LDA

Political Action Committee/s

Nat'l Parking Ass'n Political Action Committee
1112 16th St. NW
Suite 300
Washington, DC 20036
Tel: (202)296-4336
Fax: (202)331-8523

In-house, DC-area Employees

KOCH, F. James: Legislative Director
O'DELL, Barbara: Exec. Director

Nat'l Parks Conservation Ass'n

1300 19th St. NW
Suite 300
Washington, DC 20036
Tel: (202)223-6722
Fax: (202)659-0650
Registered: LDA
Web: www.eparks.org
E-mail: npca@npca.org

A non-profit organization whose primary mission is protecting America's national parks and monuments and educating the public about the parks.

Leg. Issues: AVI, BUD, NAT

In-house, DC-area Employees

CHANDLER, William J.: V. President, Conservation Policy
COLLINS, Kevin: Visitor Experience
KEVICH, Fran
KIERNAN, Thomas C.: President
LOOMIS, Laura: Visitor Experience
VOORHEES, Philip: Senior Director, Park Funding and Management

Nat'l Partnership for Women and Families

1875 Connecticut Ave. NW
Suite 710
Washington, DC 20009
Tel: (202)986-2600
Fax: (202)986-2539
Registered: LDA
Web: www.nationalpartnership.org
E-mail: info@nationalpartnership.org

The National Partnership for Women & Families is a non-partisan, non-profit organization that promotes fairness in the workplace, quality healthcare, and policies that help women and men meet the dual demands of work and family. Working with business, government, unions, non-profit organizations, and the media, the National Partnership is a voice for fairness, source for solutions, and a force for change.

Leg. Issues: BNK, CIV, FAM, HCR, LBR, MMM, WEL

In-house, DC-area Employees

FRYE, Jocelyn C.: Director, Legal and Public Policy
LENHOFF, Donna R.: V. President and General Counsel
LICHTMAN, Judith L.: President
NESS, Debra L.: Exec. V. President
RUBINER, Laurie: V. President, Program and Policy
WEISS, Alice: Director, Health Policy

Outside Counsel/Consultants

Bass and Howes, Inc.
Issues: HCR, MMM
Rep By: Joanne M. Howes, Robyn Lipner

Nat'l Pasta Ass'n

Web: www.ilovepasta.org
E-mail: npa@ilovepasta.net

A trade ass'n representing U.S. pasta manufacturers and their related suppliers.

Outside Counsel/Consultants

Hogan & Hartson L.L.P.
Rep By: Gary Jay Kushner

Nat'l Patient Advocate Foundation

Newport News, VA
Leg. Issues: BUD, HCR, MED, MMM

Outside Counsel/Consultants

Bennett Turner & Coleman, LLP
Issues: BUD, HCR, MED, MMM
Rep By: Elizabeth Goss, Samuel D. Turner

Nat'l Pawnbrokers Ass'n

Dallas, TX
Leg. Issues: BNK, FIR

Outside Counsel/Consultants

Zuckerman Spaeder L.L.P.
Issues: BNK, FIR
Rep By: Ronald H. Weich

Nat'l Peace Foundation

1819 H St. NW
Suite 1200
Washington, DC 20006
Tel: (202)223-1770
Fax: (202)223-1718
Web: www.nationalpeace.org
E-mail: ntlpeace@aol.com

A private, nonpartisan, non-profit, membership organization whose mission is to build peace and conflict resolution.

In-house, DC-area Employees

LANSING, Kathleen: Deputy Director
STRICKLAND, Stephen P.: Chair of Board

Outside Counsel/Consultants

Alcalde & Fay
Rep By: Jennefer A. Hirshberg

Nat'l Peach Council

Columbia, SC
Registered: LDA
Leg. Issues: AGR, TRD

Outside Counsel/Consultants

O'Connor & Hannan, L.L.P.
Issues: AGR, TRD
Rep By: Hon. Thomas J. Corcoran, John M. Himmelberg

Nat'l Peanut Buying Point Ass'n

Tifton, GA
Leg. Issues: AGR

Outside Counsel/Consultants

Robert L. Redding
Issues: AGR
Rep By: Robert L. Redding, Jr.

Nat'l Pecan Shellers Ass'n

1101 15th St. NW
Suite 202
Washington, DC 20005
Tel: (202)785-3232
Fax: (202)223-9741

In-house, DC-area Employees

CRISTOL, Richard E.: Washington Representative

Outside Counsel/Consultants

The Kellen Company
Rep By: Richard E. Cristol

Nat'l Perinatal Ass'n

Tampa, FL

Outside Counsel/Consultants

McDermott, Will and Emery
Rep By: Wendy L. Krasner, Karen S. Sealander, Eric P. Zimmerman

Nat'l Pest Control Ass'n

8100 Oak St.
Dunn Loring, VA 22027
Tel: (703)573-8330
Fax: (703)573-4116
Registered: LDA
Web: www.pestworld.org
Leg. Issues: ENV, FOO

In-house, DC-area Employees

HARRINGTON, Eugene: Manager, Government Affairs
LEDERER, Jr., Robert F.: Exec. V. President
ROSENBERG, Robert: Director, Government Affairs

Outside Counsel/Consultants

Powell Tate

Nat'l Petrochemical Refiners Ass'n

1899 L St. NW
Suite 1000
Washington, DC 20036
Tel: (202)457-0480
Fax: (202)457-0486
Registered: LDA
Leg. Issues: CAW, CHM, ENG, ENV, FUE, TAX

In-house, DC-area Employees

ANTHONY, Betty: Director, Strategic Communications and Planning
CONNELLY, Elizabeth: Director of Administration
DEE, Norbert: Environmental Affairs Director

HAZLE, Jeffery: Director, Lubricants, Waxes, and Maintenance
HIGGINS, Terrence S.: Ass't Treasurer & Technical Director
HOGAN, Tim: Technical Analyst
KIRK, Sharon: Director, Congressional Affairs
KUTSKA, Helen M.: Director, Convention Services and Safety Programs
MCBRIDE, Maurice H.: Corporate Secretary & Attorney
PETERSEN, Bruce L.: Petrochemical Director
SLAUGHTER, Robert: Director, Public Policy
STERNFELS, Urvan R.: President
WHELAN, June M.: Director, Government Relations
WIGGLESWORTH, Tom: Environmental Analyst

Nat'l Petroleum Council

1625 K St. NW
Suite 600
Washington, DC 20006
Web: www.npc.org
E-mail: info@npc.org
Tel: (202)393-6100
Fax: (202)331-8539

Federal advisory committee to the Secretary of Energy on oil and natural gas matters.

In-house, DC-area Employees
BYRD, Carla Scali: Information Coordinator
GUY, IV, John H.: Deputy Exec. Director
NICHOLS, Marshall W.: Exec. Director

Nat'l Pharmaceutical Council

1894 Preston White Dr.
Reston, VA 20191
Web: www.npcnow.org
Tel: (703)620-6390
Fax: (703)476-0904

In-house, DC-area Employees
WILLIAMS, Karen: President

Nat'l Policy Ass'n

1424 16th St. NW
Suite 700
Washington, DC 20036
Web: www.npa1.org
E-mail: info@npa1.org
Tel: (202)265-7685
Fax: (202)797-5516

A non-profit, nonpartisan research organization that brings together key private sector leaders representing business, labor, agriculture and academia to focus on economic and social issues of mutual and national concern.

In-house, DC-area Employees
AUERBACH, James A.: Senior V. President
CRAWFORD, Steve: V. President
QUAINTON, Anthony C. E.: President and Chief Exec. Officer

Nat'l Pollution Prevention Roundtable

11 DuPont Circle NW
Suite 201
Washington, DC 20036
Tel: (202)466-7272
Fax: (202)466-7964

In-house, DC-area Employees
ROY, Natalie: Exec. Director

Nat'l Pork Producers Ass'n

Washington, DC

Outside Counsel/Consultants
The PMA Group
Rep By: Fred J. Clark, Kaylene Green, Paul J. Magliocchetti, Mark Rokala, Timothy K. Sanders, Dana Stewart

Nat'l Pork Producers Council

122 C St. NW
Suite 875
Washington, DC 20001
Web: www.nppc.org
Tel: (202)347-3600
Fax: (202)347-5265
Registered: LDA

An agricultural/pork industry trade association. Headquartered in Des Moines, IA.

Leg. Issues: AGR, ANI, CAW, ENV, FOO, TAX, TRD

In-house, DC-area Employees
BECKER, Leah: Government Relations Representative
COHEN, Steven: Director, Communications
FERRELL, Kirk: V. President, Public Policy
GIORDANO, Nick D.: International Trade Counsel
TANK, Alan: Chief Exec. Officer

Outside Counsel/Consultants
Capitolink, LLC
Issues: AGR, CAW, ENV
Rep By: Deborah M. Atwood, John H. Thorne, Ph.D.

Collier Shannon Scott, PLLC
Rep By: Paul C. Rosenthal

Crowell & Moring LLP
Rep By: Steven P. Quarles, Victor E. Schwartz, Ellen Steen

Nat'l Postal Mail Handlers Union

1101 Connecticut Ave. NW
Suite 500
Washington, DC 20036
Web: www.npmhu.org
Tel: (202)833-9095
Fax: (202)833-0008

Political Action Committee/s
Nat'l Postal Mail Handlers Union PAC
1101 Connecticut Ave. NW
Suite 500
Washington, DC 20036
Tel: (202)833-9095
Fax: (202)833-0008

In-house, DC-area Employees
GARDNER, Mark: National Secretary-Treasurer
QUINN, William H.: President

Nat'l Potato Council

Englewood, CO
Leg. Issues: AGR, CHM, FOO, TRD

Outside Counsel/Consultants
McDermott, Will and Emery
Issues: AGR, CHM, FOO, TRD
Rep By: Jerry C. Hill

Nat'l Potato Promotion Board

Denver, CO

Outside Counsel/Consultants
McDermott, Will and Emery
Rep By: Jerry C. Hill

Nat'l Power

London, UNITED KINGDOM
Leg. Issues: FOR, TRD

Outside Counsel/Consultants
BKSH & Associates
Issues: FOR, TRD
Rep By: John Kyte, Riva Levinson

Nat'l Press Foundation

1211 Connecticut Ave. NW
Suite 310
Washington, DC 20026
Web: www.natpress.org
E-mail: npf@natpress.org
Tel: (202)721-9100
Fax: (202)530-2855

Established in 1975. Provides grants, awards and continuing education to journalists, sponsors forums for policy-makers and the public, underwrites operations of the National Journalism Library for research in Washington, and assists minority youth towards careers in journalism. Also administers Washington Journalism Center conferences on public issues.

In-house, DC-area Employees
MEYERS, Bob: President

Outside Counsel/Consultants
Wilmer, Cutler & Pickering

Nat'l Prison Project

733 15th St. NW
Suite 620
Washington, DC 20005
E-mail: gotschnpp@aol.com
Tel: (202)393-4930
Fax: (202)393-4931

A project of the American Civil Liberties Union Foundation. Seeks to broaden prisoners' rights, improve overall prison conditions and develop alternatives to incarceration. Publishes a quarterly journal and other publications. Headquartered in New York, NY.

Leg. Issues: CIV

In-house, DC-area Employees
ALEXANDER, Elizabeth R.: Director

Outside Counsel/Consultants
Zuckerman Spaeder L.L.P.
Issues: CIV
Rep By: Ronald H. Weich

Nat'l Private Truck Council

66 Canal Center Plaza
Suite 600
Alexandria, VA 22314
Web: www.nptc.org
Tel: (703)683-1300
Fax: (703)683-1217
Registered: LDA

An association of companies which ship products they manufacture, distribute, or sell with their own truck fleets.

Leg. Issues: TRA, TRU

In-house, DC-area Employees
MLYNARCZYK, Matt: Director, Government Relations
PETTY, Gary F.: President and Chief Exec. Officer

Outside Counsel/Consultants
Zuckert, Scoutt and Rasenberger, L.L.P.
Issues: TRA
Rep By: Richard P. Schweitzer

Nat'l Pro-Life Alliance PAC

P.O. Box 4062
Merrifield, VA 22116
E-mail: roberthughes@erols.com
Leg. Issues: FAM

In-house, DC-area Employees
HUGHES, Robert: PAC Administrator

Nat'l Produce Production Inc.

Leg. Issues: AGR, BAN

Outside Counsel/Consultants
Preston Gates Ellis & Rouvelas Meeds LLP
Issues: AGR, BAN
Rep By: Werner W. Brandt, Hon. David Funderburk, Bruce J. Heiman, Ralph D. Nurnberger, Daniel Ritter, Emanuel L. Rouvelas, Steven R. "Rick" Valentine

Nat'l Propane Gas Ass'n

1101 17th St. NW
Suite 1004
Washington, DC 20036
Web: www.npga.org
Tel: (202)466-7200
Fax: (202)466-7205
Registered: LDA

Formerly (1989) Nat'l LP-Gas Ass'n. Headquartered in Lisle, IL.

Leg. Issues: CAW, ENG, ENV, FUE, TAX, TRA

Political Action Committee/s
PropanePAC
1101 17th St. NW
Suite 1004
Washington, DC 20036
Contact: Wilfred J. Otero
Tel: (202)466-7200
Fax: (202)466-7205

In-house, DC-area Employees
BONTEMPO, Lisa: Director, Legislative Affairs
OTERO, Wilfred J.: Political Affairs Coordinator
ROLDAN, Richard R.: V. President, Government Relations
SQUAIR, Philip A.: Director, Regulatory Affairs

Outside Counsel/Consultants
BKSH & Associates
Issues: ENV

McKenna & Cuneo, L.L.P.
Rep By: Chris Leason

Nat'l Prostate Cancer Coalition Co.

1158 15th St. NW
Washington, DC 20005
Web: www.4npcc.org
E-mail: Info@4npcc.org
Tel: (202)463-9455
Fax: (202)463-9456
Registered: LDA
Leg. Issues: BUD, HCR

In-house, DC-area Employees
ATKINS, M.D., Richard N.: Vice President and Chief Operating Officer
SCHWARTZ, William: President and Chief Exec. Officer

Outside Counsel/Consultants
Clark & Weinstock, Inc.
Issues: BUD, HCR
Rep By: Hon. Vic H. Fazio, Jr., Sandi Stuart, Hon. John Vincent "Vin" Weber

M & R Strategic Services
Rep By: William B. Wasserman

Nat'l Psoriasis Foundation

Portland, OR
Leg. Issues: HCR, MMM

Outside Counsel/Consultants
Powers Pyles Sutter & Verville, PC
Issues: HCR, MMM
Rep By: Judith Buckalew

Nat'l Public Radio

635 Massachusetts Ave. NW
Washington, DC 20001
Web: www.npr.org
Tel: (202)414-2000
Fax: (202)513-3329
Registered: LDA

A private, non-profit corporation established in 1970 to provide programming and representation for its member non-commercial radio stations.

Leg. Issues: BUD, COM, CPT, POS, TAX

In-house, DC-area Employees
JACKSON, Neal: General Counsel
KLOSE, Kevin: President and Chief Exec. Officer
LEWIS, Gregory A.: Associate General Counsel
WHITCOMB, James T.: National Affairs Associate

Nat'l Puerto Rican Coalition

1700 K St. NW
Suite 500
Washington, DC 20006
Web: www.bateylink.com
E-mail: nprc@aol.com

Tel: (202)223-3915
Fax: (202)429-2223

Organized in 1977, the Coalition seeks to further the social, economic, and political well-being of Puerto Ricans throughout the United States and Puerto Rico.

Leg. Issues: CIV, EDU, GOV, HCR, HOU, URB, VET, WEL

In-house, DC-area Employees

MIRABAL, Manuel: President

Nat'l Quality Health Council

Westerville, OH
Leg. Issues: HCR, MMM

Outside Counsel/Consultants

Jefferson Government Relations, L.L.C.
Issues: HCR, MMM
Rep By: John D. Desser, Thomas R. Donnelly, Jr.

Nat'l Railroad and Construction Maintenance Ass'n

Washington, DC
Web: www.nrcma.org
E-mail: info@nrcma.org
Leg. Issues: RRR, TRA

Outside Counsel/Consultants

Chambers, Conlon & Hartwell
Issues: RRR, TRA
Rep By: Ray B. Chambers, Keith O. Hartwell, Don Norden

Nat'l Railway Labor Conference

1901 L St. NW
Suite 500
Washington, DC 20036

Tel: (202)862-7200
Fax: (202)862-7230

In-house, DC-area Employees

ALLEN, Robert F.: Chairman
EVANS, Gail: Exec. Administrator

Nat'l Ready Mixed Concrete Ass'n

900 Spring St.
Silver Spring, MD 20910

Tel: (301)587-1400
Fax: (301)585-4219
Registered: LDA

Web: www.nrmca.org
E-mail: jluther@nrmca.org

Represents the ready mixed concrete industry.

Leg. Issues: CAW, ENV, GOV, LBR, MAN, NAT, ROD, SMB, TAX, TRA, TRU

Political Action Committee/s

CONCRETE PAC
900 Spring St.
Silver Spring, MD 20910
Contact: Jennifer LeFevre

Tel: (301)587-1400
Fax: (301)585-4219

In-house, DC-area Employees

GARBINI, Robert A.: President
LEFEVRE, Jennifer: Manager, Government Relations
LUTHER, Julie Renjilian: V. President, Government and Industry Relations

Nat'l Realty Committee

Washington, DC
Leg. Issues: TAX

Outside Counsel/Consultants

Foley & Lardner
Issues: TAX
Rep By: Jodi L. Hanson

Nat'l Recreation and Park Ass'n

22377 Belmont Ridge Rd.
Asburn, VA 20148

Tel: (703)858-0784
Fax: (703)858-0794

Web: www.activeparks.org
E-mail: info@nrpa.org

A non-profit service and educational organization dedicated to the wise use of leisure, conservation of natural and human resources, and improvement of park and recreation facilities and programs to provide wholesome and meaningful leisure opportunties for everyone.

In-house, DC-area Employees

ANDERSON, Van: Director, Professional Services
CORWIN, Michael: Director, Marketing and Communications
TICE, R. Dean: Exec. Director
TINDALL, Barry: Director, Public Policy

Nat'l Registry in Clinical Chemistry

815 15th St. NW
Suite 508
Washington, DC 20005
Web: www.members.aol.com/nrcc6/nrcc.htm
E-mail: nrcc6@aol.com

Tel: (202)393-7140
Fax: (202)393-4059

Certifies chemists who meet standards of education, experience, and examination.

In-house, DC-area Employees

SMITH, Ph.D., Gilbert E.: Exec. Director

Nat'l Rehabilitation Ass'n

633 S. Washington St.
Alexandria, VA 22314

Tel: (703)836-0850
Fax: (703)836-0848
Registered: LDA

Web: www.nationalrehab.org
E-mail: info@nationarehab.org

A member organization whose mission is providing opportunities through knowledge and diversity for professionals in the fields of rehabilitation for people with disabilities.

Leg. Issues: BUD, CIV, ECN, EDU, HCR, INS, LBR, MED, MMM

In-house, DC-area Employees

STEWART, Thomas G.: Director of Governmental Affairs
VAUGHAN, Michelle

Nat'l Rehabilitation Hospital

102 Irving St. NW
Washington, DC 20010-2949
Web: www.nrh.mhg.edu

Tel: (202)877-1000
Fax: (202)829-5180

NRH is a private, not-for-profit rehabilitation hospital providing comprehensive medical rehabilitation care. NRH also serves as an advocate for persons with disabilities.

Leg. Issues: HCR

In-house, DC-area Employees

ECKENHOFF, Edward A.: President and Chief Exec. Officer
ROCKWOOD, John: Director, Development

Outside Counsel/Consultants

Colex and Associates
Issues: HCR
Rep By: John P. Mack

Nat'l Rehabilitation Information Center

1010 Wayne Ave.
Suite 800
Silver Spring, MD 20910
Web: www.naric.com
E-mail: naricinfo@kra.com
Leg. Issues: EDU, HCR, MED

Tel: (301)562-2400
Fax: (301)562-2401

In-house, DC-area Employees

ODUM, Mark: Project Director

Nat'l Rehabilitation Political Action Committee

1213 29th St. NW
Washington, DC 20007

Tel: (202)333-5841
Fax: (202)333-5881

In-house, DC-area Employees

DUNCAN, Jack G.: Treasurer

Outside Counsel/Consultants

Duncan and Associates
Rep By: Jack G. Duncan

Nat'l Released Time Project

Falls Church, VA

Outside Counsel/Consultants

William J. Tobin and Associates

Nat'l Religious Broadcasters

7839 Ashton Ave.
Manassas, VA 20109

Tel: (703)330-7000
Fax: (703)330-7100

Web: www.nrb.org
E-mail: kstoll@nrb.org

Works to keep the airwaves open to religious broadcasters.

Leg. Issues: COM

In-house, DC-area Employees

GUSTAVSON, Dr. E. Brandt: President
STOLL, Karl: V. President, Communications

Outside Counsel/Consultants

Wiley, Rein & Fielding
Issues: COM
Rep By: Richard E. Wiley

Nat'l Religious Broadcasters, Music License Committee

Camarillo, CA
Leg. Issues: COM

Outside Counsel/Consultants

Alexander Strategy Group
Issues: COM

Wiley, Rein & Fielding
Rep By: Lawrence W. Secrest, III

Nat'l Religious Leadership Roundtable

1700 Kalorama Rd. NW
Washington, DC 20009-2624

Tel: (202)332-6483
Fax: (202)332-0207

An interfaith network of leaders from pro-GLBT faith, spiritual and religious organizations working in partnership with other justice-seeking groups to amplify the voice of pro-GLBT faith organizations in public discourse; promote understanding of and respect for pro-GLBT people with society and in communities of faith; promote understanding and respect within GLBT communities for a variety of faith paths and for religious liberty; and achieve commonly held goals which promote equality, spirituality and justice.

In-house, DC-area Employees

ELLIOT, David: Spokesperson

Nat'l Renal Administrators Ass'n

11250 Roger Bacon Dr.
Suite Eight
Reston, VA 20190
Leg. Issues: HCR, MMM

Tel: (703)437-4377
Fax: (703)435-4390

In-house, DC-area Employees

HOSKINS, Kathy: Deputy Director

Outside Counsel/Consultants

Congressional Consultants
Issues: HCR, MMM
Rep By: Gwen Gampel, Karen M. Late

Nat'l Renderers Ass'n

801 N. Fairfax St.
Suite 207
Alexandria, VA 22314
Web: www.renderers.org
E-mail: Renderers@nationalrenderers.com

Tel: (703)683-0155
Fax: (703)683-2626

Consults on issues of interest to the rendering industry, including domestic and international marketing, quality assurance, legislation. Also consults on relations with the FDA, USDA, and other government agencies.

In-house, DC-area Employees

COOK, Tom: President and Chief Exec. Officer

Nat'l Republican Congressional Committee

320 First St. SE
Washington, DC 20003

Tel: (202)479-7000
Fax: (202)863-0693

In-house, DC-area Employees

HISHTA, John: Exec. Director
MCELWAIN, Mike: Political Director
SECOR, Cathy: Director, Administration

Nat'l Republican Senatorial Committee

425 Second St. NE
Washington, DC 20002

Tel: (202)675-6000
Fax: (202)675-6058

A committee of Republican U.S. Senators organized for the election of Republicans to that body. Chairman is Sen. Mitch McConnell (R-KY).

In-house, DC-area Employees

BROOKS, Bob: Research Director
CATIGNANI, Linus: Finance Director
HUCKABY, Stan: Treasurer
LACIVITA, Chris: Political Director
LAW, Steven: Exec. Director
RAHAL, Ed: Director, Corporate Affairs
VOGEL, Alex: General Counsel

Nat'l Research Center for College and University Admissions

Lee's Summit, MO
Leg. Issues: EDU

Outside Counsel/Consultants

Pearson & Pipkin, Inc.

Widmeyer Communications, Inc.
Issues: EDU
Rep By: Kevin J. Bonderud

Nat'l Restaurant Ass'n

1200 17th St. NW
Washington, DC 20036-3097
Tel: (202)331-5900
Fax: (202)973-5373
Registered: LDA

Web: www.restaurant.org
E-mail: info@dineout.org

Represents foodservice operators and other interests of the industry with legislative, regulatory and public/consumer relations services. Also provides statistics and educational and training assistance through its Educational Foundation, located in Chicago.

Leg. Issues: AGR, BUD, CPT, FOO, HCR, IMM, LBR, SMB, TAX, TOB, TOU, TRA, TRD, UTI

Political Action Committee/s

Nat'l Restaurant Ass'n Political Action Committee

1200 17th St. NW
Washington, DC 20036-3097
Tel: (202)331-5900
Fax: (202)973-5373
Contact: Sean Bressett

In-house, DC-area Employees

ANDERSON, Steven C.: President and Chief Exec. Officer
BISKIN, Emery: Government Affairs Coordinator
BRESSETT, Sean: Director, Political Affairs
CULPEPPER, R. Lee: Senior V. President, Government Affairs and Public Policy
FLANAGAN, Brendan: Legislative Representative
GREEN, Rob J.: Director, Work Force Policy
GROVER, Steve: V. President, Regulatory Affairs
KILGORE, Peter: Senior V. President and General Counsel
MOUNT, Michael: Senior Manager, Media Relations
NOLT, Kristin: V. President, Media Relations
O'LEARY, Kathleen: Director, Tax Policy
PETROVA, Irina: Manager, Legislative Research Products
WESTBROOK, Gay: Legislative Representative
WILLIAMS, Ann: Manager, Political Affairs

Outside Counsel/Consultants

BKSH & Associates
Issues: CPT, FOO, HCR, TAX, TOB, TOU

Nat'l Retail Federation

325 Seventh St. NW
Suite 1100
Washington, DC 20004-2802
Tel: (202)783-7971
Fax: (202)737-2849
Registered: LDA

Web: www.nrf.com
Leg. Issues: APP, BAN, BNK, CPT, CSP, HCR, IND, LBR, MAR, POS, SMB, TAX, TEC, TRD, UTI

Political Action Committee/s

Nat'l Retail Federation Political Action Committee

325 Seventh St. NW
Suite 1100
Washington, DC 20004-2802
Tel: (202)783-7971
Fax: (202)737-2849
Contact: Steven J. Pfister

In-house, DC-area Employees

AUTOR, Erik: V. President, International Trade Counsel
CAHILL, D. Scott: V. President, Government and Industry Affairs
DUNCAN, Mallory B.: V. President and General Counsel
EPSTEIN, Michael: Manager, Communications
GATTI, Michael: V. President, Marketing and Public Relations
GILBERT, Donald M.: Senior V. President, Information Technology
GRAHAM, Katherine: Senior Director
HOTKA, M. Cathy: V. President, Information Technology
KNOBLOCH, Karen: Senior V. President, Membership
KOHUT, Carleen C.: Senior V. President
MANCE, Katherine T.: V. President, Research, Education and Community Affairs
MULLIN, Tracy: President and C.E.O.
PFISTER, Steven J.: Senior V. President, Government Relations
RIEHL, Maureen: V. President, State Industry Relations Counsel
RUCKER, Pamela: V. President, Public Relations
SCHEUER, Sarah: Manager, Media Relations
WHITAKER, Sarah: Director, Government Relations
WILD, Emily: Grassroots Coordinator

Outside Counsel/Consultants

Arthur Andersen LLP
Issues: TAX
Rep By: Rachelle Bernstein

Internat'l Business and Economic Research Corp.

Jenner & Block

Parry, Romani, DeConcini & Symms
Issues: BNK
Rep By: Edward H. Baxter, Hon. Dennis DeConcini, John M. Haddow, Scott D. Hatch, Shannon Davis Henderson, Jack W. Martin, Romano Romani, Linda Arey Skladany, Hon. Steven D. Symms

Patton Boggs, LLP
Rep By: Frank R. Samolis

The Trade Partnership
Issues: TRD
Rep By: Laura M. Baughman

Nat'l Review Magazine

New York, NY

Outside Counsel/Consultants

Policy Impact Communications

Nat'l Rifle Ass'n Institute for Legislative Action

11250 Waples Mill Rd.
Fairfax, VA 22030-7400
Tel: (703)267-1000
Fax: (703)267-3973
Registered: LDA

Web: www.nra.org

In-house, DC-area Employees

BAKER, James Jay: Exec. Director
CAROLINE, Glen: Director, Grassroots Office
COX, Christopher W.: Federal Liaison
CUNNINGHAM, Charles H.: Director, Federal Affairs
KOZUCH, Randy J.: Director, State and Local Affairs
LAMSON, Susan: Director, Conservation, Wildlife and Natural Resources Division
PARKERSON, William: Director, Research and Information
POWERS, Bill: Director, Public Relations and Communications
WILLIAMS, Michael E.: Federal Liaison

Outside Counsel/Consultants

Craig Shirley & Associates
Rep By: Diana L. Banister

Nat'l Rifle Ass'n of America

11250 Waples Mill Rd.
Fairfax, VA 22030-7400
Tel: (703)267-1000
Fax: (703)267-3918
Registered: LDA

Web: www.nra.org
E-mail: nra-contact@nra.org
Leg. Issues: CIV, FIR, LAW, NAT

Political Action Committee/s

Nat'l Rifle Ass'n Political Victory Fund

11250 Waples Mill Rd.
Fairfax, VA 22030-7400
Tel: (703)267-1000
Fax: (703)267-3918

In-house, DC-area Employees

COX, Christopher W.: Federal Liaison
CUNNINGHAM, Charles H.: Director, Federal Affairs
FRAZER, John C.: Federal Liaison
FREEMAN, Jeffrey B.: Federal Liaison
LAPIERRE, Jr., Wayne R.: Exec. V. President
OSBORNE, Jason M.: Federal Liaison
ROWE, Esq., Kirsten S.: Federal Liaison
WARNER, James H.: Assistant General Counsel
WILLIAMS, Michael E.: Federal Liaison

Outside Counsel/Consultants

Law Offices of Mark Barnes
Issues: FIR
Rep By: Mark J. Barnes, Tammy Begun

Hall, Green, Rupli, LLC
Issues: FIR
Rep By: John M. Green, G. Stewart Hall

Timmons and Co., Inc.
Issues: CIV, FIR, LAW
Rep By: Michael J. Bates, Douglas F. Bennett, Ellen B. Fitzgibbons, Bryce L. "Larry" Harlow, Timothy J. Keating, Tom C. Korologos, Richard J. Tarplin, William E. Timmons, Jr., William E. Timmons, Sr.

Nat'l Right to Life Committee

419 Seventh St. NW
Suite 500
Washington, DC 20004
Tel: (202)626-8800
Fax: (202)737-9189
Registered: LDA

Opposes abortion, infanticide and euthanasia.

Leg. Issues: ALC, BUD, CIV, CON, DEF, DOC, FAM, FOR, GOV, HCR, IND, INS, MED, MMM, PHA

Political Action Committee/s

Black Americans for Life PAC

419 Seventh St. NW
Suite 500
Washington, DC 20004
Tel: (202)626-8800
Fax: (202)737-9189
Contact: Amarie C. Natividad

Nat'l Right to Life Political Action Committee

419 Seventh St. NW
Suite 500
Washington, DC 20004
Tel: (202)626-8800
Fax: (202)737-9189
Contact: Carol Tobias

In-house, DC-area Employees

BALCH, Mary Spaulding: Director, State Legislative Department
BALCH, Thomas: Director, Medical Ethics Department
BOPP, Jr., James: Counsel
COLL, Patricia: Legislative Assistant
ECHEVARRIA, Laura: Director, Media Relations
FRANZ, Ph.D., Wanda: President
HOUGENS, Lori: Senior Congressional Liaison, Department of Medical Ethics
JOHNSON, Douglas D.: Legislative Director
NATIVIDAD, Amarie C.: Controller
NOLAN, Jennifer: Legislative Aide, Department of Medical Ethics
O'STEEN, Ph.D., David N.: Exec. Director
SHAUK, Amber: Secretary, Department of Medical Ethics
ST. MARTIN, Darla: Associate Exec. Director
TOBIAS, Carol: Director, Political Action Committee

Nat'l Right to Work Committee

8001 Braddock Rd.
Springfield, VA 22160
Tel: (703)321-9820
Fax: (703)321-7342
Registered: LDA

Established in 1955, NRWC is a single-purpose interest group opposing compulsory union membership. Has over 1.9 million supporters and a budget of about $8 million used in a nationwide educational lobbying program.

Leg. Issues: BUD, CIV, CON, LBR

Political Action Committee/s

State Employee Rights Campaign

8001 Braddock Rd.
Springfield, VA 22160
Tel: (703)321-9820
Fax: (703)321-7342
Contact: Mark A. Mix

In-house, DC-area Employees

CLAIR, Richard J.: Corporate Counsel
GREER, Stanley: Director, News and Information
LAJEUNESSE, Jr., Raymond J.: Attorney
LARSON, Reed E.: President
MIX, Mark A.: Senior V. President, Legislation
TOSTO, C. J.: Federal Legislative Liasion

Nat'l Right to Work Legal Defense Foundation

8001 Braddock Rd.
Springfield, VA 22160
Tel: (703)321-8510
Fax: (703)321-9319
Web: www.nrtw.org
E-mail: legal@nrtw.org

"Defending America's working men and women against the injustices of compulsory unionism." Works through the courts, providing free legal aid to workers suffering from abuses of compulsory unionism arrangements.

In-house, DC-area Employees

GLEASON, Stefan H.: V. President
LARSON, Reed E.: President
REED, Rex H.: Exec. V. President, Secretary and Legal Director

Nat'l Roofing Contractors Ass'n

324 Fourth St. NE
Washington, DC 20002
Tel: (202)546-7584
Fax: (202)546-9289
Registered: LDA

Web: www.nrca.net

Headquartered in Rosemont, IL.

Leg. Issues: BUD, GOV, LBR, SMB, TAX, TRU

Political Action Committee/s

ROOF PAC

324 Fourth St. NE
Washington, DC 20002
Tel: (202)546-7584
Fax: (202)546-9289
Contact: Craig S. Brightup

In-house, DC-area Employees

BRIGHTUP, Craig S.: Associate Exec. Director, Government Relations
GEHRING, Jennifer: Director, Federal Affairs
PRITCHETT, John M.: Manager, Public Affairs

Nat'l Rural Development & Finance Corp.

San Antonio, TX
Leg. Issues: BUD

Outside Counsel/Consultants

Robert A. Rapoza Associates
Issues: BUD
Rep By: Alison Feighan, Robert A. Rapoza

Nat'l Rural Development Ass'n

Washington, DC
Leg. Issues: BUD, ECN

Outside Counsel/Consultants

Romano & Associates, LLC
Issues: BUD, ECN
Rep By: John Romano

Nat'l Rural Electric Cooperative Ass'n

4301 Wilson Blvd.
Arlington, VA 22203-1860
Tel: (703)907-5500
Fax: (703)907-5516
Registered: LDA

Web: www.nreca.org
Leg. Issues: BUD, CAW, COM, ECN, ENG, ENV, HCR, LBR, NAT, POS, SCI, TAX, TEC, TRA, UTI, WEL

Political Action Committee/s

Action Committee for Rural Electrification

4301 Wilson Blvd. Tel: (703)907-5793
Arlington, VA 22203-1860 Fax: (703)907-5516
Contact: Robert M. Dawson

In-house, DC-area Employees

BOHANON, Chris: Representative, Lesgislative Affairs
CASE, Ted: Legislative Representative
CRONMILLER, Rae E.: Environmental Counsel
DAWSON, Robert M.: Director, Department Operations
ENGLISH, Hon. Glenn: Chief Exec. Officer
GLAZIER, Jonathan H.: Association Counsel
GREENHALGH, Ronald K.: Chief Engineer
HUMPHREY, Cliff: Legislative Representative
JORAY, Millie: Manager, Advocacy Tools Division
KEELTY, Lana: Legislative Representative
MCLENNAN, Robert "Mac": Senior Representative, Legislative Affairs
MILLER, Eleanor: Manager, Media and Public Relations
OLSON, Mattie: Director, Education and Training
PENRY, Charles D.: Legislative Representative
PETRY, Stephan: Legislative Director
RYAN, John: Senior Principal, Legislative Affairs
STONER, Dena G.: V. President, Government Relations
TILLMAN, Wallace F.: Director, Energy Policy
WHITMAN, Carol E.: Principal, Legislative Affairs
WYNN, Jr., H. Montee: Legislative Representative and Counsel

Outside Counsel/Consultants

Bergner Bockorny Castagnetti and Hawkins

Caplin & Drysdale, Chartered
Issues: LBR, TAX
Rep By: Kent A. Mason

George Kroloff & Associates

Van Ness Feldman, P.C.
Issues: ENG, ENV, NAT, TAX
Rep By: J. Curtis Rich

Nat'l Rural Health Ass'n

1320 19th St. NW Tel: (202)232-6200
Suite 350 Fax: (202)232-1133
Washington, DC 20036 Registered: LDA
Web: www.nrharural.org
E-mail: dc@nrharural.org

A national nonprofit membership organization headquartered in Kansas City, MO that provides leadership on rural health issues; through advocacy, communications, education, and research.

Leg. Issues: HCR, MMM, TAX

In-house, DC-area Employees

BRIGGS, Eli: Government Affiars Policy Specialist
MORGAN, Alan: V. President, Government Affairs and Policy

Nat'l Rural Housing Coalition

1250 I St. NW Tel: (202)393-5229
Suite 902 Fax: (202)393-3034
Washington, DC 20005 Registered: LDA
Web: www.rapoza.org/NRHC.html
E-mail: nrhc@webnrhc.org

An advocate for better housing and community facilities for low-income rural people.

Leg. Issues: BUD, CAW, HOU, WAS

In-house, DC-area Employees

RAPOZA, Robert A.: Legislative Director

Outside Counsel/Consultants

Robert A. Rapoza Associates
Issues: BUD, HOU
Rep By: Alison Feighan, Robert A. Rapoza

Nat'l Rural Letter Carriers' Ass'n

1630 Duke St. Tel: (703)684-5545
Alexandria, VA 22314 Fax: (703)548-8735
Registered: LDA
Web: www.nrlca.org
Leg. Issues: LBR

Political Action Committee/s

Nat'l Rural Letter Carriers' Ass'n Political Action Committee

1630 Duke St. Tel: (703)684-5545
Alexandria, VA 22314 Fax: (703)548-8735
Contact: Ken Parmelee

In-house, DC-area Employees

DAILING, Clifford D.: Secretary-Treasurer
FOLK, Cassie: Assistant Director, Government Affairs
PARMELEE, Ken: V. President, Governmental Affairs
SMITH, Steven R.: President

Nat'l Rural Telecom Ass'n

Blair, NE
Leg. Issues: AGR

Outside Counsel/Consultants

James Nicholas Ashmore & Associates
Issues: AGR
Rep By: James Nicholas Ashmore

The Hawthorn Group, L.C.

John F. O'Neal Law Offices
Issues: AGR
Rep By: John F. O'Neal

Nat'l Rural Water Ass'n

Duncan, OK
Leg. Issues: AGR, BUD, CAW, ENV

Outside Counsel/Consultants

Murray, Scheer, Montgomery, Tapia & O'Donnell
Issues: AGR, BUD, CAW, ENV
Rep By: Michael G. Keegan, John H. Montgomery

Nat'l Ryan White Title III (b) Coalition

Washington, DC

Outside Counsel/Consultants

The Sheridan Group
Rep By: Thomas F. Sheridan

Nat'l SAFE KIDS Campaign

1301 Pennsylvania Ave. NW Tel: (202)662-0600
Suite 1000 Fax: (202)393-2072
Washington, DC 20004
Web: www.safekids.org

The only nationwide organization dedicated to the prevention of childhood injuries, the leading killer of children in the U.S.

Leg. Issues: BUD

In-house, DC-area Employees

PAUL, Heather: Exec. Director

Outside Counsel/Consultants

Cassidy & Associates, Inc.
Issues: BUD
Rep By: Valerie Rogers Osborne, Mary E. Shields, Maureen Walsh

Nat'l Safety Council

1025 Connecticut Ave. NW Tel: (202)293-2270
Suite 1200 Fax: (202)293-0032
Washington, DC 20036
Web: www.nsc.org

A non-profit, non-governmental public service organization formed in 1913 and federally chartered by the U.S. Congress in 1953. Works to encourage the adoption of policies which will reduce unintentional deaths and injuries and preventable illnesses, on the job, on the highway, in the community at large, and in the area of environmental health.

In-house, DC-area Employees

HURLEY, Charles A.: Exec. Director, Public Affairs
WARD, Morris "Bud": Exec. Director, Environmental Health Center

Outside Counsel/Consultants

George Reagle
Rep By: George Reagle

Nat'l School Boards Ass'n

1680 Duke St. Tel: (703)838-6722
Alexandria, VA 22314-3407 Fax: (703)683-7590
Web: www.nsba.org

Represents the nation's 95,000 local school board members who determine policy for the more than 15,000 public school districts.

Leg. Issues: CPT

In-house, DC-area Employees

BLOM, Don: Assoc. Exec. Dir., Constituent Services, Publications, & Marketing
BRYANT, Dr. Anne L.: Exec. Director
DARDEN, Edwin: Senior Staff Attorney
FELTON, Reginald: Director, Federal Relations
FULLER, Daniel: Director, Federal Programs
MYER, Lori: Director, Federal Legislation
RESNICK, Michael A.: Assoc. Exec. Director, Advocacy and Issues Management
SEAMON, Harold P.: Deputy Exec. Director
UNDERWOOD, Julie: Assoc. Exec. Director and General Counsel
VILLANI, Joseph: Associate Exec. Director, Federation Member Services and Outreach

Outside Counsel/Consultants

Leslie Harris & Associates
Issues: CPT
Rep By: Leslie A. Harris

Hauser Group

Nat'l School Public Relations Ass'n

15948 Derwood Rd. Tel: (301)519-0496
Rockville, MD 20855 Fax: (301)519-0494
Web: www.nspra.org
E-mail: nspra@nspra.org

In-house, DC-area Employees

BAGIN, Rich D.: Exec. Director

Nat'l School Supply and Equipment Ass'n

8300 Colesville Rd. Tel: (301)495-0240
Suite 250 Fax: (301)495-3330
Silver Spring, MD 20910
Web: www.nssea.org
E-mail: nssea@nssea.com

In-house, DC-area Employees

HOLT, Timothy: C.E.O.
WATTS, Adrienne: Director, Marketing and Member Services

Nat'l School Transportation Ass'n

625 Slaters Ln. Tel: (703)684-3200
Suite 205 Fax: (703)684-3212
Alexandria, VA 22314
Web: www.schooltrans.com
E-mail: info@schooltrans.com

Fosters safe and efficient school bus transportation and education of its members in pupil transportation matters.

Leg. Issues: BUD, TAX, TRA

Political Action Committee/s

Nat'l School Transporation Ass'n Non-Partisan Transporation Action Committee

625 Slaters Ln. Tel: (703)684-3200
Suite 205 Fax: (703)684-3212
Alexandria, VA 22314

In-house, DC-area Employees

KULICK, Jeffery: Exec. Director

Outside Counsel/Consultants

BKSH & Associates
Issues: BUD, TAX, TRA

Nat'l Science Teachers Ass'n

1840 Wilson Blvd. Tel: (703)243-7100
Arlington, VA 22201 Fax: (703)243-7177
Web: www.nsta.org
E-mail: publicinfo@nsta.org
Leg. Issues: EDU

In-house, DC-area Employees

WHEELER, Gerald F.: Exec. Director

Outside Counsel/Consultants

Dean Blakey & Moskowitz
Issues: EDU
Rep By: Ellin J. Nolan

Nat'l Security Archive

The George Washington University Tel: (202)994-7000
Gelman Library, Suite 701 Fax: (202)994-7005
Washington, DC 20037
Web: www.gwu.edu/~nsarchiv
E-mail: nsarchiv@gwu.edu

A not-for-profit library, publisher and research organization. Maintains an archive of documents dealing with U.S. Government policy on foreign affairs, national security, and the Freedom of Information Act

In-house, DC-area Employees

BLANTON, Tom: Exec. Director
MARTIN, Kate: General Counsel

Nat'l Sediments Coalition

Washington, DC
Leg. Issues: CAW, ENV, WAS

Outside Counsel/Consultants

Swidler Berlin Shereff Friedman, LLP
Issues: CAW, ENV, WAS
Rep By: Keith N. Cole, Barry B. Direnfeld, Harold P. Goldfield, Charles H. Knauss

Nat'l Senior Citizens Law Center

1101 14th St. NW Tel: (202)289-6976
Suite 400 Fax: (202)289-7224
Washington, DC 20005
Web: www.nsclc.org
E-mail: nsclc@nsclc.org

Provides expert representation before agencies of government and the courts on behalf of the elderly poor.

In-house, DC-area Employees

MCINTYRE, Gerald: Acting Exec. Director

Nat'l Senior Service Corps Directors Ass'n

Leg. Issues: BUD, GOV

Outside Counsel/Consultants

Ledge Counsel
Issues: BUD, GOV

Nat'l Sheriffs' Ass'n

1450 Duke St. Tel: (703)836-7827
Alexandria, VA 22314-3490 Fax: (703)683-6541
Web: www.sheriffs.org
E-mail: nsamail@sheriffs.org
Leg. Issues: LAW

In-house, DC-area Employees

FAUST, Thomas N.: Exec. Director

Nat'l Shooting Sports Foundation Inc.

2987 Westhurst Lane Tel: (703)242-1690
Suite 110 Registered: LDA
Oakton, VA 22124
Web: www.nssf.org
Leg. Issues: FIR, NAT

In-house, DC-area Employees

CHAMBERS, James: V. President

Nat'l Silver Haired Congress

Springfield, IL

Outside Counsel/Consultants

Matz, Blancato & Associates, Inc.

Nat'l Ski Area Ass'n

Lakewood, CO
Leg. Issues: NAT

Outside Counsel/Consultants

Jack Ferguson Associates, Inc.
Issues: NAT
Rep By: Jack Ferguson

Nat'l Sleep Foundation

1522 K St. NW Tel: (202)347-3471
Suite 500 Fax: (202)347-3472
Washington, DC 20005
Web: www.sleepfoundation.org
E-mail: natsleep@erols.com
Leg. Issues: BUD, HCR, MED, TRA

In-house, DC-area Employees

GELULA, Richard: Exec. Director

Outside Counsel/Consultants

Sagamore Associates, Inc.
Issues: BUD, HCR, MED, TRA
Rep By: Dena S. Morris, David Nichols

Nat'l Small Business United

1156 15th St. NW Tel: (202)293-8830
Suite 1100 Fax: (202)872-8543
Washington, DC 20005 Registered: LDA
Web: www.nsbu.org
E-mail: nsbu@nsbu.org
Leg. Issues: BAN, CPT, ECN, ENV, HCR, LBR, SMB, TAX

Political Action Committee/s

Nat'l Small Business United PAC
1156 15th St. NW Tel: (202)293-8830
Suite 1100 Fax: (202)872-8543
Washington, DC 20005

In-house, DC-area Employees

DARIEN, Kristie L.: Manager, Government Affairs
DOZIER, Damon: Director, Government and Public Affairs
FLETCHER, Clinton: Government Affairs Coordinator
HEADINGTON, Edward: Manager, Media Affairs
MCCRACKEN, Todd: President

Nat'l Small Shipments Traffic Conference - NASSTRAC

499 S. Capitol St. SW Tel: (202)484-9188
Suite 604 Fax: (202)484-9189
Washington, DC 20003
E-mail: webmaster@nasstrac.org

In-house, DC-area Employees

PHILLIPS, Debra: Exec. Director

Nat'l Soc. of Accountants

1010 N. Fairfax St. Tel: (703)549-6400
Alexandria, VA 22314-1574 Fax: (703)549-2984
Registered: LDA
Web: www.nsacct.org

NSA is a non-profit organization of professionals who provide accounting, tax preparation, financial and estate planning, and management advisory services to an estimated 4 million individuals and business clients.

Political Action Committee/s

Nat'l Soc. of Public Accountants Political Action Committee
1010 N. Fairfax St. Tel: (703)549-6400
Alexandria, VA 22314-1574 Fax: (703)549-2984
Contact: Richard Fein

In-house, DC-area Employees

FEIN, Richard: Director, Federal Affairs and Taxation
MATHISEN, William: Exec. V. President
PHILLIPS, Bernard: Tax Manager

Nat'l Soc. of Black Engineers

1454 Duke St. Tel: (703)549-2207
Alexandria, VA 22314 Fax: (703)683-5312
Web: www.nsbe.org

An organization dedicated to increasing the participation of blacks in the fields of engineering and the engineering sciences.

In-house, DC-area Employees

LEZAMA, Michele: Exec. Director

Nat'l Soc. of Professional Engineers

1420 King St. Tel: (703)684-2800
Alexandria, VA 22314-2794 Fax: (703)836-4875
Registered: LDA
Web: www.nspe.org
E-mail: customer.service@nspe.org

Promotes the ethical, competent, and licensed practice of engineering, and works to enhance the professional, social, and economic well-being of its members.

Leg. Issues: AVI, BUD, CAW, DEF, ENV, GOV, HCR, HOU, INS, LBR, POS, RET, ROD, SCI, SMB, TAX, TEC, TRA, WAS

Political Action Committee/s

Nat'l Soc. of Professional Engineers Political Action Committee
1420 King St. Tel: (703)684-2800
Alexandria, VA 22314-2794 Fax: (703)836-4875
Contact: Brian Bauerle

In-house, DC-area Employees

BAUERLE, Brian: Manager, Congressional and Political Relations
BORY, Laurence D.: Director, Government Relations
LINDSAY, Linda P.: Manager, Congressional and State Relations
NATALE, Patrick: Exec. Director

Outside Counsel/Consultants

Edelman Public Relations Worldwide
Rep By: Julianne Tsapatsaris

Nat'l Soc. to Prevent Blindness

Schaumburg, IL

Outside Counsel/Consultants

Jenner & Block

Nat'l Soft Drink Ass'n

1101 16th St. NW Tel: (202)463-6732
Washington, DC 20036-4877 Fax: (202)463-8277
Registered: LDA
Web: www.nsda.org

A trade association.

Leg. Issues: AGR, BEV, FOO, LBR, TRD

Political Action Committee/s

Soft Drink PAC
1101 16th St. NW Tel: (202)463-6740
Washington, DC 20036-4877 Fax: (202)659-5349
Contact: Drew M. Davis

In-house, DC-area Employees

BALL, III, William L.: President
DAVIS, Drew M.: V. President, Federal Affairs
HIDEN, Barbara L.: Director, Federal Affairs
MCMANUS, William A.: Manager, Federal Affairs

Outside Counsel/Consultants

Bergner Bockorny Castagnetti and Hawkins
Issues: BEV
Rep By: Jeffrey T. Bergner, David A. Bockorny, David Castagnetti, Melissa Schulman
Fisher Consulting
Martin, Fisher & Associates, Inc.
Issues: AGR, BEV, FOO, LBR
Rep By: J. Paris Fisher, David O'B. Martin
Patton Boggs, LLP
Issues: TRD
Rep By: Darryl D. Nirenberg, Stuart M. Pape, Daniel E. Waltz
Winner & Associates

Nat'l Solid Wastes Management Ass'n

4301 Connecticut Ave. NW Tel: (202)244-4700
Washington, DC 20008 Fax: (202)966-4818
Web: www.envasns.org

In-house, DC-area Employees

MILLER, Chaz: Director, State Programs
PARKER, Bruce J.: Exec. V. President
REPA, Ph.D., Edward A.: Director, Environmental Programs

Nat'l Spa and Pool Institute

2111 Eisenhower Ave. Tel: (703)838-0083
Alexandria, VA 22314-4698 Fax: (703)549-0493
Registered: LDA
Web: www.nspi.org
E-mail: rgalvin@nspi.org

International trade association representing manufacturers, distributors, retailers, and contractors in the pool, spa, and hot tub industry. Also includes manufacturers, distributers, and retailers of pool/spa chemicals and equipment and pool service firms.

Leg. Issues: CSP, MAN, RES

In-house, DC-area Employees

CERGOL, Jack: Director, Communications
DIGIOVANNI, Carvin: Technical Director
GALVIN, Roger: Chief Exec. Officer
KARMOL, David L.: General Counsel and Director, Government Relations

Outside Counsel/Consultants

Richard W. Bliss
Issues: CSP, MAN, RES
Rep By: Pani Farkan

The Nat'l Space Grant Alliance

Bozeman, MT
Leg. Issues: AER, BUD, SCI

Outside Counsel/Consultants

Van Scoyoc Associates, Inc.
Issues: AER, BUD, SCI
Rep By: Carri Booth, Carolyn Fuller, H. Stewart Van Scoyoc

Nat'l Space Soc.

600 Pennsylvania Ave. SE Tel: (202)543-1900
Suite 201 Fax: (202)546-4189
Washington, DC 20003
Web: www.nss.org
E-mail: nsshq@nss.org

An organization of about 20,000 members which favors an active space exploration program.

Leg. Issues: AER, SCI

In-house, DC-area Employees

DASCH, Pat: Exec. Director

Nat'l Spiritual Assembly of the Baha'is of the United States

1320 19th St. NW Tel: (202)833-8990
Suite 701 Fax: (202)833-8988
Washington, DC 20036
E-mail: usnsa-oea@usbnc.org

A religious organization headquartered in Wilmette, IL.

Leg. Issues: ENV, FOR, IMM

In-house, DC-area Employees

COSBY, Kit: Director, Office of External Affairs
KAZEMZADEH, Dr. Firuz: Secretary, Office of External Affairs

Outside Counsel/Consultants

Gustafson Associates
Issues: FOR
Rep By: Robert C. Gustafson

The Nat'l Sports Center for the Disabled

Winter Park, CO

Outside Counsel/Consultants

McNamara & Associates
Rep By: Thomas J. McNamara

Nat'l Star Route Mail Contractors Ass'n

324 E. Capitol St. NE Tel: (202)543-1661
Washington, DC 20003-3897 Fax: (202)543-8863
Registered: LDA

Represents highway mail contractors.

Leg. Issues: POS

Political Action Committee/s

Nat'l Star Route Mail Contractors Political Action Committee

324 E. Capitol St. NE
Washington, DC 20003-3897
Contact: John V. "Skip" Maraney
Tel: (202)543-1661
Fax: (202)543-8863

In-house, DC-area Employees
MARANEY, John V. "Skip": Exec. Director

Nat'l Steel and Shipbuilding Co.

San Diego, CA
Registered: LDA

Outside Counsel/Consultants

Dyer Ellis & Joseph, P.C.
Rep By: James B. Ellis, II, Duncan C. Smith, III

Nat'l Steel Corp.

Mishawaka, IN
Registered: LDA
Leg. Issues: ENG, ENV, HCR, TAX, TRD

Outside Counsel/Consultants

Skadden, Arps, Slate, Meagher & Flom LLP
Issues: TRD
Rep By: Robert E. Lighthizer, John J. Mangan

John M. Stinson
Issues: ENG, ENV, HCR, TAX, TRD
Rep By: John M. Stinson

Nat'l Stone, Sand, and Gravel Ass'n

2101 Wilson Blvd.
Suite 100
Arlington, VA 22201
Tel: (703)525-8788
Registered: LDA

In-house, DC-area Employees
HAWKINS, III, Charles E.: V. President and Chief Exec. Officer

Nat'l Strategy Information Center

1730 Rhode Island Ave. NW
Suite 500
Washington, DC 20036
E-mail: nsic@ix.netcom.com
Tel: (202)429-0129
Fax: (202)659-5429

A nonprofit, nonpartisan education and research organization focused on non-traditional national security issues.

Leg. Issues: DEF, EDU, FOR, GOV, LAW

In-house, DC-area Employees
GODSON, Dr. Roy: President

Nat'l Stroke Ass'n

Englewood, CO
Leg. Issues: HCR, MED

Outside Counsel/Consultants

Patton Boggs, LLP
Issues: HCR, MED
Rep By: Penelope S. Farthing, Hon. Willis "Bill" D. Gradison, Florence W. Prioleau

Nat'l Structured Settlements Trade Ass'n

1420 16th St. NW
Suite 405
Washington, DC 20036
Web: www.nssta.com
Tel: (202)328-7460
Fax: (202)332-2301

Professional consultants who negotiate settlements in physical injury tort actions.

Leg. Issues: HCR, TAX

Political Action Committee/s

Nat'l Structured Settlements Trade Ass'n Political Action Committee
1420 16th St. NW
Suite 405
Washington, DC 20036
Contact: Randy Dyer, CAE
Tel: (202)328-7460
Fax: (202)332-2301

In-house, DC-area Employees
DYER, CAE, Randy

Outside Counsel/Consultants

Hogan & Hartson L.L.P.
Issues: HCR, TAX
Rep By: Nancy Granese, Hon. Robert H. Michel, John S. Stanton

TASC, Inc., Association Management
Rep By: Randy Dyer, CAE

Nat'l Student Speech Language Hearing Ass'n

10801 Rockville Pike
Rockville, MD 20852
Web: www.nsslha.org
Tel: (301)897-5700
Fax: (301)897-7350

Membership made up of undergraduate and graduate students in communications disorders. The above address is that of the American Speech-Language-Hearing Ass'n.

In-house, DC-area Employees
FLAHIVE, Lynn: Exec. Director

Nat'l Sunflower Ass'n

Bismarck, ND
Leg. Issues: AGR

Outside Counsel/Consultants

Gordley Associates
Issues: AGR
Rep By: John Gordley, Krysta Harden, Megan Marquet

Nat'l Tank Truck Carriers

2200 Mill Rd.
Suite 620
Alexandria, VA 22314
E-mail: nttc@juno.com
Tel: (703)838-1960
Fax: (703)684-5753
Registered: LDA

Political Action Committee/s

Nat'l Tank Truck Carriers Political Action Committee
2200 Mill Rd.
Suite 620
Alexandria, VA 22314
Contact: John Conley
Tel: (703)838-1960
Fax: (703)684-5753

In-house, DC-area Employees
CONLEY, John: V. President
HARVISON, Clifford J.: President

Nat'l Taxpayers Union

108 N. Alfred St.
Alexandria, VA 22314
Web: www.ntu.org
Tel: (703)683-5700
Fax: (703)683-5722
Registered: LDA

A non-partisan grassroots organization with 300,000 members that opposes wasteful spending and promotes tax cuts and a diminished bureaucracy. Established in 1969. Supports a constitutional amendment requiring a balanced budget and limited taxes. Rates members of Congress on their voting records on government spending.

Leg. Issues: AGR, BAN, BUD, CON, DEF, ECN, EDU, ENV, GOV, HCR, INS, LBR, MAR, MMM, RET, TAX, TOR, TRA, UTI, WEL

Political Action Committee/s

Nat'l Taxpayers Union Campaign Fund
108 N. Alfred St.
Alexandria, VA 22314
Contact: Alfred W. Cors, Jr.
Tel: (703)683-5700
Fax: (703)683-5722

In-house, DC-area Employees
BERTHOUD, John E.: President
CORS, Jr., Alfred W.: V. President, Government Affairs
DIRKSEN, Jeff: Director, Congressional Tracking
SCHLECHT, Eric V.: Director, Congressional Relations
SEPP, Peter J.: V. President, Communications
STANLEY, David M.: Chairman

Outside Counsel/Consultants

Citizen Strategies
Issues: BUD, ENV, GOV, INS, TAX
Rep By: David L. Keating

Nat'l Technical Systems

Acton, MA
Leg. Issues: CPI, CSP, LBR, TEC, TRD

Outside Counsel/Consultants

The M Companies
Issues: CPI, CSP, LBR, TEC, TRD
Rep By: Milton M. Bush, J.D., CAE

Nat'l Technological University

Fort Collins, CO

Outside Counsel/Consultants

Dow, Lohnes & Albertson, PLLC

Nat'l Telephone Cooperative Ass'n

4121 Wilson Blvd.
Tenth Floor
Arlington, VA 22203
Web: www.ntca.org
E-mail: publicrelations@ntca.org
Tel: (703)351-2000
Fax: (703)351-2001
Registered: LDA

Established in 1954. Represents both cooperative and commercial independent rural phone companies, many of which receive financing from the Rural Utility Service under the Department of Agriculture. Supports the Telephone Education Committee Organization.

Leg. Issues: BNK, BUD, COM, CON, CPT, FOR, GOV, INS, RET, SMB, TAX, TEC

Political Action Committee/s

Nat'l Telephone Cooperative Ass'n Telephone Education Committee Organization
4121 Wilson Blvd.
Tenth Floor
Arlington, VA 22203
Contact: Erin Templer
Tel: (703)351-2033
Fax: (703)351-2001

In-house, DC-area Employees
BLOOMFIELD, Shirley A.: V. President, Government Affairs and Association Services
BRIDGES, Jessica: Government Affairs Representative
BRUNNER, Michael E.: Exec. Vice President
GUILLORY, L. Marie: V. President, Legal and Industry
LOGAN, Tammie: Government Affairs Representative
NORTON, Marlee: Director, International Development
SLAFKY, Aaryn: Director, Communications
TAYLOR, Donna: Public Affairs Manager
TEMPLER, Erin: PAC Coordinator
WACKER, Thomas: Director, Government Affairs

Outside Counsel/Consultants

Collins & Company, Inc.
Issues: FOR
Rep By: James D. Bond, Richard L. Collins, Thomas A. Hooper, Shay D. Stautz

Nat'l Therapeutic Recreation Soc.

22377 Belmont Ridge Rd.
Ashburn, VA 20148-4501
Web: www.nrpa.org/branches/ntrs.html
E-mail: NTRSNRPA@aol.com
Tel: (703)858-0784
Fax: (703)858-0794

A branch of the Nat'l Recreation and Park Ass'n.

Leg. Issues: HCR

In-house, DC-area Employees
EPSTEIN, M.Ed.,CTRS, Rikki S.: Exec. Director

Nat'l Thoroughbred Racing Ass'n, Inc.

Louisville, KY
Leg. Issues: GAM, SCI, TAX

Outside Counsel/Consultants

Davis & Harman LLP
Issues: GAM, TAX
Rep By: Thomas A. Davis

The OB-C Group, LLC
Issues: GAM, SCI
Rep By: Thomas Keating, Kim F. McKernan, Charles J. Mellody, Patricia A. Nelson, Lawrence F. O'Brien, III, Linda E. Tarplin

Nat'l Tooling and Machining Ass'n

9300 Livingston Rd.
Fort Washington, MD 20744
Web: www.ntma.org
E-mail: john@ntma.org
Tel: (301)248-6200
Fax: (301)248-7104
Registered: LDA

An association of the precision tooling and machining industry. Represents 2,600 companies that manufacture precision machined parts, molds, dies, tools, and special machines.

Leg. Issues: SMB

Political Action Committee/s

Nat'l Tooling and Machining Ass'n Committee for a Strong Economy
9300 Livingston Rd.
Fort Washington, MD 20744
Contact: Louise Hall
Tel: (301)248-6200
Fax: (301)248-7104

In-house, DC-area Employees
COFFEY, Matthew B.: President and Chief Operating Officer
COX, Jr., John A.: Manager, Government Affairs
HALL, Louise: PAC Administrator
MEREDITH, John: Government Affairs Representative

Outside Counsel/Consultants

Webster, Chamberlain & Bean
Rep By: Alan P. Dye

Nat'l Tour Ass'n

Lexington, KY
Leg. Issues: TAX, TOU

Outside Counsel/Consultants

The Argus Group, L.L.C.
Issues: TAX, TOU
Rep By: David R. Burton, Dan R. Mastromarco

Santini, Chartered
Issues: TOU
Rep By: Hon. James D. Santini

Nat'l Trailer Dealers Ass'n

Fargo, ND

Outside Counsel/Consultants

Andrews Associates, Inc.
Rep By: Hon. Mark Andrews, Dr. Jacqueline Balk-Tusa

Nat'l Training Systems Ass'n

2111 Wilson Blvd.
Suite 400
Arlington, VA 22201
Web: www.trainingsystems
Tel: (703)522-1820
Fax: (703)243-1659

In-house, DC-area Employees
LEWIS, Fred: Exec. Director

Nat'l Treasury Employees Union

901 E St. NW
Suite 600
Washington, DC 20004
Tel: (202)783-4444
Fax: (202)783-4085
Registered: LDA

An independent labor union formed in 1948. Formerly (1973) Nat'l Ass'n of Internal Revenue Service Employees. Absorbed Nat'l Ass'n of Alcohol and Tobacco Tax Officers and Nat'l Customs Service Ass'n.

Leg. Issues: BUD, GOV, HCR, LBR, TAX

Political Action Committee/s

Nat'l Treasury Employees Union Political Action Committee (TEPAC)
901 E St. NW
Suite 600
Washington, DC 20004
Contact: Amanda R. Esquibel
Tel: (202)783-4444
Fax: (202)783-4085

In-house, DC-area Employees
ADKINS, Larry: Deputy General Counsel
ATKIN, Barbara: Deputy General Counsel
CASDEN, Carol: Assistant Counsel
ESQUIBEL, Amanda R.: Director, TEPAC
FERRIS, Frank: National Exec. V. President
GILMAN, Maureen: Director of Legislation
KELLEY, Colleen M.: National President
O'DUDEN, Gregory J.: General Counsel
SHAW, Susan: Deputy Director of Legislation
SHRIVER, Rob: Assistant Counsel
STET, Charlene A.: Legislative Field Operations Liaison
VORNDRAN, Kurt: Legislative Liaison
WALL, Jim: Legislative Liason
WYNNS, Pat: Associate General Counsel

Outside Counsel/Consultants

Ledge Counsel
Issues: GOV, LBR

Nat'l Truck Equipment Ass'n

1300 19th St. NW
Fifth Floor
Washington, DC 20036
Tel: (202)557-3500
Fax: (202)628-2011
Registered: LDA

Represents distributors and manufacturers of work-related trucks, truck bodies and equipment. Headquartered in Farmington Hills, MI.

Leg. Issues: ENV, LBR, ROD, SMB, TAX

Political Action Committee/s

Nat'l Truck Equipment Ass'n PAC (TREQPAC)
1300 19th St. NW
Fifth Floor
Washington, DC 20036
Contact: Michael E. Kastner
Tel: (202)628-2010
Fax: (202)628-2011

In-house, DC-area Employees
KASTNER, Michael E.: Director, Government Relations

Nat'l Trust for Historic Preservation

1785 Massachusetts Ave. NW
Washington, DC 20036
Web: www.nthp.org
Tel: (202)588-6000
Fax: (202)588-6059
Registered: LDA

The National Trust for Historic Preservation, chartered by Congress in 1949, is a private, nonprofit organization dedicated to protecting the irreplaceable. It fights to save historic buildings and the neighborhoods and landscapes they anchor. Through education and advocacy, the National Trust is revitalizing communities across the country and challenges citizens to create sensible plans for the future. It has six regional offices, 20 historic sites, and works with thousands of local community groups nationwide.

Leg. Issues: BUD, CON, GOV, HOU, NAT, POS, RES, ROD, TAX, TRA, URB

In-house, DC-area Employees
BEAUMONT, Constance E.: Director, State and Local Policy
BRINK, Peter: Senior V. President, Programs
COSTELLO, Daniel: Senior Program Associate
HIGGINS, Kathryn: V. President, Public Policy
KERR, Gordon: Director, Congressional Relations
MOE, Richard: President

Outside Counsel/Consultants

Covington & Burling
Issues: TAX
Rep By: Roderick A. DeArment

Nat'l Turfgrass Evaluation Program

Beltsville, MD
Leg. Issues: AGR

Outside Counsel/Consultants

McGuiness Norris & Williams, LLP
Issues: AGR
Rep By: William N. LaForge, Monte B. Lake

Nat'l Turkey Federation

1225 New York Ave. NW
Suite 400
Washington, DC 20005
Web: www.eatturkey.com
E-mail: info@turkeyfed.org
Tel: (202)898-0100
Fax: (202)898-0203
Registered: LDA

Represents the U.S. turkey industry before Congress and regulatory agencies, assists members in marketing and promotions, and provides educational opportunities for members.

Leg. Issues: AGR, ANI, BUD, CAW, FOO, LBR, MAR, TRD

Political Action Committee/s

Nat'l Turkey Federation Political Action Committee
1225 New York Ave. NW
Suite 400
Washington, DC 20005
Contact: Joel Brandenberger
Tel: (202)898-0100
Fax: (202)898-0203

In-house, DC-area Employees
BRANDENBERGER, Joel: V. President, Legislative Affairs
JOHNSON, Dr. Alice: V. President, Sciencitific and Regulatory Affairs
PROCTOR, Jr., Stuart E.: President and Chief Exec. Officer
ROSENBLATT, Sherrie: Director, Public Relations

Outside Counsel/Consultants

Capitolink, LLC
Issues: AGR, CAW
Rep By: John H. Thorne, Ph.D.

Nat'l U.S.-Arab Chamber of Commerce

1023 15th St. NW
Washington, DC 20005
Web: www.nusacc.org
Tel: (202)289-5920
Fax: (202)289-5938

Promotes business between the United States and the Arab world. The Chamber also has offices in Chicago, New York, Houston and an affiliate office in San Francisco.

In-house, DC-area Employees
HOLMES, Richard: President
SAMMAN, Mazhar: Exec. V. President

Nat'l Underground Railroad Freedom Center

Cincinnati, OH
Leg. Issues: BUD, EDU, NAT

Outside Counsel/Consultants

Williams & Jensen, P.C.
Issues: BUD, EDU, NAT
Rep By: William B. Canfield, J. Steven Hart, Robert J. Martinez, Anthony J. Roda

Nat'l Urban Coalition

2120 L St. NW
Suite 510
Washington, DC 20037
E-mail: nuc@tnt.org
Tel: (202)986-1460
Fax: (202)986-1468

Founded 1967. A network of 40 affiliate organizations around the country seeking private and government cooperation to help the poor, working class and minority populations of urban areas. Operates "Say YES to a Youngster's Future", an early education program for African-American and Latino children. Maintains interest in health, housing, economic development and other urban issues.

In-house, DC-area Employees
EDELIN, Ph.D., Ramona H.: President and Chief Exec. Officer
LINDBLOM, Louise: Director, Media Relations

Nat'l Urban League

1111 14th St. NW
Suite 1001
Washington, DC 20005
Tel: (202)898-1604
Fax: (202)408-1965

An inter-racial, non-profit, community service organization working to secure opportunities for African Americans and other minorities in every sector of American society.

In-house, DC-area Employees
SPRIGGS, William: Director, Research and Public Policy

Nat'l Utility Contractors Ass'n (NUCA)

4301 N. Fairfax Dr.
Suite 360
Arlington, VA 22203-1627
Web: www.nuca.com
Tel: (703)358-9300
Fax: (703)358-9307
Registered: LDA

Founded in 1964, NUCA represents 2,000 companies that build, repair, and maintain water, wastewater, gas, telecommunications, and electric systems.

Leg. Issues: BUD, CAW, ENV, FUE, LBR, ROD, SMB, TAX, TRA

Political Action Committee/s

Nat'l Utility Contractors Ass'n Legislative Information and Action Committee
4301 N. Fairfax Dr.
Suite 360
Arlington, VA 22203-1627
Tel: (703)358-9300
Fax: (703)358-9307

In-house, DC-area Employees
HILLMAN, A. William: Exec. V. President
MCCRUDDEN, III, Charles J.: Government Relations Representative
SMITH, Joseph: Government Relations Assistant
WAGNER, Pamela Hyde: Director, Education
WYMAN, Eben M.: Director of Government Relations

Outside Counsel/Consultants

Edmund C. Graber
Issues: CAW, TRA
Rep By: Edmund C. Graber

Nat'l Venture Capital Ass'n

1655 N. Fort Myer Dr.
Suite 850
Arlington, VA 22209
Web: www.nvca.org
Tel: (703)524-2549
Fax: (703)524-3940
Registered: LDA

Leg. Issues: ACC, CPT, ECN, FIN, IMM, MED, SCI, TAX, TOR

Political Action Committee/s

Nat'l Venture Capital Ass'n Political Action Committee
1655 N. Fort Myer Dr.
Suite 850
Arlington, VA 22209
Contact: Molly M. Myers
Tel: (703)524-2549
Fax: (703)524-3940

In-house, DC-area Employees
BROWNELL, Paul: V President, Legislative, Regulatory, and Entrepeneurial Affairs
HEESEN, Mark G.: President
MYERS, Molly M.: V. President, Administration and Program Development

Nat'l Veterans Foundation

Los Angeles, CA
Leg. Issues: VET

Outside Counsel/Consultants

Mehl, Griffin & Bartek Ltd.
Issues: VET
Rep By: Molly Griffin, Theodore J. Mehl

Nat'l Veterans Legal Services Program

2001 S St. NW
Suite 610
Washington, DC 20009
Web: www.nvlsp.org
E-mail: nvlsp@nvlsp.org
Tel: (202)265-8305
Fax: (202)328-0063

Represents veterans in a variety of legal cases. Particular emphasis is on the problems of Vietnam-era and Gulf War veterans, reform of Veterans Administration procedures, training of veterans advocates, publication of advocacy and self-help materials, the problems of veterans with less than honorable discharges and practice before the U.S. Court of Appeals for Veterans Claims.

Leg. Issues: VET

In-house, DC-area Employees
ADDLESTONE, David: Joint Exec. Director
STICHMAN, Barton: Joint Exec. Director

Nat'l Viatical Ass'n

1030 15th St. NW
Suite 870
Washington, DC 20005
Tel: (202)347-7361
Fax: (202)393-0336

In-house, DC-area Employees
COOPER, Valerie: Exec. Director

Outside Counsel/Consultants

The Kellen Company
Rep By: Valerie Cooper

Nat'l Vietnam and Gulf War Veterans Coalition, Inc.

3001 Veazey Terrace
716
Washington, DC 20008
Tel: (202)338-6882
Fax: (202)338-6950

A federation of approximately 105 veterans organizations devoted to the resolution of ten issues of concern to Vietnam and Gulf War veterans (e.g. live POWs, Agent Orange, judicial review of VA benefits decisions, Gulf War Syndrome benefits).

In-house, DC-area Employees
BENNETT, William T.: General Secretary
BURCH, Jr., J. Thomas: Chairman

Nat'l Vision Rehabilitation Cooperative

Outside Counsel/Consultants

Smith, Bucklin and Associates, Inc.
Rep By: Jill Rathbun

Nat'l Water Resources Ass'n

3800 N. Fairfax Dr.
Suite 4
Arlington, VA 22203
Tel: (703)524-1544
Fax: (703)524-1548
Registered: LDA
Web: www.nwra.org
E-mail: nwra@nwra.org

Represents 17 western states and their water concerns, specifically irrigated agriculture and municipal water supply issues relating to the Bureau of Reclamation.

Leg. Issues: CAW, ENV, NAT, UTI

In-house, DC-area Employees
ADAMS, Peter: Legislative Assistant
DONNELLY, Thomas F.: Exec. V. President
POLLY, Kris D.: Director, Government Relations

Nat'l Waterways Conference, Inc.

1130 17th St. NW
Washington, DC 20036-4676
Tel: (202)296-4415
Fax: (202)835-3861
Web: www.waterways.org
E-mail: hcook@waterways.org

A group of shippers, barge lines, shipyards, river valley associations, state water boards and port authorities working to promote a better understanding of the public value of the American waterways system.

Leg. Issues: BUD, MAR, NAT

In-house, DC-area Employees
COOK, Harry N.: President

Nat'l Weather Service Employees Organization

Washington, DC

NWSEO is dedicated to the interests of NWS and NESDIS employees.

Leg. Issues: SCI

Outside Counsel/Consultants
Kip Robinson
Issues: SCI
Rep By: Kip Robinson

Nat'l Welding Supply Ass'n

Philadelphia, PA

Outside Counsel/Consultants
Zuckert, Scoutt and Rasenberger, L.L.P.
Rep By: Richard P. Schweitzer

The Nat'l Wetlands Coalition

1050 Thomas Jefferson St. N.W
Seventh Floor
Washington, DC 20007
Tel: (202)298-1981
Fax: (202)338-2416
Registered: LDA
Web: www.thenwc.org
E-mail: nwc@vnf.com
Leg. Issues: CAW, ENV, NAT

In-house, DC-area Employees
SZABO, Robert G.: Exec. Director and Counsel

Outside Counsel/Consultants
Van Ness Feldman, P.C.
Issues: CAW, ENV, NAT
Rep By: Howard S. Bleichfeld, Paula J. Dietz, Robert G. Szabo

Nat'l Whistleblower Center

3238 P St. NW
Washington, DC 20007
Tel: (202)342-1902
Fax: (202)342-1904
Web: www.whistleblowers.org
E-mail: whistle@whistleblowers.org

The National Whistleblower Center advocates the protection of the environment, nuclear safety, and the strict enforcement of laws protecting the public welfare, the prevention of nuclear and environmental accidents, and the increased accountability of the government and private industry. The Center challenges attempts to retaliate against whistleblowers, alerts the public to the issues raised by whistleblowers, and initiates legal proceedings to expose a whistleblower's underlying concerns.

Leg. Issues: CAW, CIV, ENG, ENV, LAW, LBR, WAS

In-house, DC-area Employees
KOLESNIK, Kris: Exec. Director

Nat'l Wholesale Co., Inc.

Leg. Issues: BUD, CSP, GOV, POS, TAX, TEC

Outside Counsel/Consultants
Marshall A. Brachman
Issues: BUD, CSP, GOV, POS, TAX, TEC
Rep By: Marshall A. Brachman

Nat'l Wilderness Institute

P.O. Box 25766
Georgetown Station
Washington, DC 20007
Tel: (703)836-7404
Fax: (703)836-7405
Web: www.nwi.org

Dedicated to promoting sound science and common sense in the environmental arena.

In-house, DC-area Employees
GORDON, Jr., Robert E.: Director
STREETER, James R.: Director, Policy

Nat'l Wildlife Federation - Office of Federal and Internat'l Affairs

1400 16th St. NW
Suite 501
Washington, DC 20036-2266
Tel: (202)797-6800
Fax: (202)797-6646
Registered: LDA
Web: www.nwf.org

The nation's largest member-supported conservation education and advocacy organization. Founded in 1936, the Federation, its members and supporters, and affiliate organizations in 45 states and the Virgin Islands work to educate, inspire and assist individuals and organizations of diverse cultures to conserve wildlife and other natural resources while protecting the Earth's environment to promote a peaceful, equitable and sustainable future. Organization headquartered in Vienna, VA

Leg. Issues: BUD, CAW, ENV, NAT, RES

In-house, DC-area Employees
APPLEGATE, Jody: Project Manager
BRAMBLE, Barbara: Senior Director, International Affairs
CONRAD, David R.: Water Resources Specialist
FLOCKEN, Jeff: National Endangered Species Grassroots Coordinator
HALE, Malia
JOFFE, Paul L.: Associate Director, Advocacy
KOSTYACK, John F.: Counsel, Endangered Habitats
LESKY, Marcia: Population Policy Analyst
MCNITT, Ben: Senior Communications Manager
SHIMBERG, Steven J.: V. President, Office of Federal and International Affairs
SPENCER, Richard: Grassroots Coordinator, Water Issues
SUGAMELI, Glenn: Counsel, Takings/Private Property Rights
VAN PUTTEN, Mark: President and Chief Exec. Officer

Outside Counsel/Consultants
Conservation Strategies, LLC
Issues: CAW, NAT
Rep By: Richard Innes

Nat'l Wildlife Refuge Ass'n

1010 Wisconsin Ave.
Suite 200
Washington, DC 20007
Tel: (202)333-9075
Fax: (202)333-9077
Web: www.refugenet.org
E-mail: nwra@refugenet.org

Founded by wildlife refuge professionals, the NWRA is dedicated to the protection, perpetuation and expansion of the National Wildlife Refuge System. The Association was in a state of transition at the time this edition went to press. Further information on NWRA's personnel was unavailable at that time.

Leg. Issues: BUD

In-house, DC-area Employees
BOHLEN, Curtis: Chairman of the Board

Nat'l Women's Business Council

409 Third St. SW
Suite 210
Washington, DC 20024
Tel: (202)205-3850
Fax: (202)205-6825
Web: www.nwbc.gov

Established by the Women's Business Ownership Act of 1988, reauthorized and restructured in 1994 and 1997, to review the status of women business owners and make annual policy recommendations to the President and to Congress.

In-house, DC-area Employees
KING, Lynn: Deputy Director
MILLMAN, Amy: Exec. Director
PRESLEY, Gilda: Administrative Officer

Nat'l Women's Health Network

514 Tenth St. NW
Suite 400
Washington, DC 20004
Tel: (202)347-1140
Fax: (202)347-1168
Web: www.womenshealthnetwork.org

Founded in 1976 in Washington, DC to monitor federal health policy pertinent to women's health and to testify before Congress and Federal agencies. Members of the network are consumers, organizations and health centers. Sponsors the Women's Health Clearinghouse.

Leg. Issues: CSP, HCR

In-house, DC-area Employees
ALLINA, Amy: Program Director
PEARSON, Cindy: Exec. Director

Nat'l Women's History Museum

Alexandria, VA
Leg. Issues: BUD, EDU, RES

Outside Counsel/Consultants
Cash, Smith & Wages
Issues: BUD, EDU, RES
Rep By: Susan Jollie, Joan B. Wages

Nat'l Women's Law Center

11 Dupont Circle NW
Suite 800
Washington, DC 20036
Tel: (202)588-5180
Fax: (202)588-5185
Web: www.nwlc.org
E-mail: info@nwlc.org

A non-profit organization that has been working since 1972 to advance and protect women's legal rights. Focuses on major policy areas of importance to women and their families, such as tax reform, child support, employment, education, reproductive rights and health, child and adult dependent care, public assistance, and social security. Special attention is given to the concerns of low income women.

Leg. Issues: EDU, FAM, HCR, LBR, MMM, RET, SPO, WEL

In-house, DC-area Employees
ANNEXSTEIN, Leslie: Senior Counsel
APPELBAUM, Judith C.: V. President and Director, Employment Opportunities Program
CAMPBELL, Nancy Duff: Co-President
CHAUDHRY, Neena: Staff Counsel
ENTMACHER, Joan M.: V. President, Family Economic Security Program
FIRVIDA, Cristina Begona: Senior Counsel
GREENBERGER, Marcia D.: Co-President
LEVIN, Sharon: Senior Counsel
MEZEY, Jennifer: Fellow
MORRISON, Jill: Staff Counsel
ROBINSON, Kristin: V. President, Development
THOMAS, Frances: V. President and Director, Administration and Finance
WILLIAMS, Verna: V. President and Director, Educational Opportunities

Nat'l Women's Political Caucus

1630 Connecticut Ave. NW
Suite 201
Washington, DC 20009
Tel: (202)785-1100
Fax: (202)785-3605
Web: www.incacorp.com
E-mail: mailnwpc@aol.com

A national, bi-partisan grassroots organization dedicated to increasing the number of pro-choice women in elected and appointed office at all levels of government.

Political Action Committee/s
Nat'l Women's Political Caucus Campaign Support Committee
1630 Connecticut Ave. NW
Suite 201
Washington, DC 20009
Tel: (202)785-1100
Fax: (202)785-3605

In-house, DC-area Employees
KANTER, Beth: Political Director

Nat'l Writing Project

Berkeley, CA
Leg. Issues: BUD, EDU

Outside Counsel/Consultants
Dean Blakey & Moskowitz
Issues: BUD, EDU
Rep By: Ellin J. Nolan

Nat'l Yogurt Ass'n

2000 Corporate Ridge
Suite 1000
McLean, VA 22102
Tel: (703)821-0770
Fax: (703)821-1350
Registered: LDA

Leg. Issues: CSP, FOO, HCR

In-house, DC-area Employees
GARFIELD, Robert L.: V. President, Regulatory and Technical Affairs
SARASIN, CAE, Leslie G.: President

Outside Counsel/Consultants
Patton Boggs, LLP
Rep By: Stuart M. Pape

Nathan Associates Inc.

2101 Wilson Blvd.
Suite 1200
Arlington, VA 22201
Tel: (703)516-7700
Fax: (703)351-6162
Economic consultants.

In-house, DC-area Employees
BEYER, John C.: President

Nationwide Global

Columbus, OH

A financial services company.

Outside Counsel/Consultants

LeBoeuf, Lamb, Greene & MacRae L.L.P.
Rep By: A. Everette James

Nationwide Mutual Insurance Co.

1090 Vermont Ave. NW
Suite 800
Washington, DC 20005
Tel: (202)326-5242
Fax: (202)408-0241
Registered: LDA
Leg. Issues: ENV, HCR, INS, TAX

In-house, DC-area Employees

KRISTIANSEN, Lars B.: Representative, Legislative Affairs
ROUCH, Jeffrey D.: Director, Federal Relations

Outside Counsel/Consultants

Akin, Gump, Strauss, Hauer & Feld, L.L.P.
Issues: ENV, HCR, INS, TAX
Rep By: Donald C. Alexander, Sean G. D'Arcy

Native American Cultural & Educational Authority

Oklahoma City, OK
Leg. Issues: IND

Outside Counsel/Consultants

Murray, Scheer, Montgomery, Tapia & O'Donnell
Issues: IND
Rep By: John H. Montgomery

Native American Mohegans Inc.

Norwich, CT
Leg. Issues: IND

Outside Counsel/Consultants

McClure, Gerard & Neuenschwander, Inc.
Issues: IND
Rep By: Steven G. Barringer, Joseph T. Findaro, Matthew Iandoli, Nils W. Johnson, Hon. James A. McClure, Tod O. Neuenschwander

Native American Rights Fund

1712 N St. NW
Washington, DC 20036
Tel: (202)785-4166
Fax: (202)822-0068
Registered: FARA
Web: www.narf.org

Supports legal rights for Native Americans. Headquartered in Boulder, CO.

In-house, DC-area Employees

BABBY, Lorna K.: Managing Attorney

Outside Counsel/Consultants

Dunlap & Browder, Inc.
Rep By: Joseph B. Browder

Natomas

Leg. Issues: BUD, ENV, NAT

Outside Counsel/Consultants

The Ferguson Group, LLC
Issues: BUD, ENV, NAT
Rep By: W. Roger Gwinn

NATSO, Inc.

499 S. Capitol St. SW
Suite 502
Washington, DC 20003
Tel: (202)554-2510
Fax: (202)554-2520
Registered: LDA
Web: www.natso.com
E-mail: government@natso.com

Formerly the Nat'l Ass'n of Truck Stop Operators. Represents the nation's travel plazas and truck stops.

Leg. Issues: BUD, ENV, IND, ROD, TAX, TRA, TRU

Political Action Committee/s

NATSO Political Action Committee
499 S. Capitol St. SW
Suite 502
Washington, DC 20003
Tel: (202)554-2510
Fax: (202)554-2520
Contact: Scot E. Imus

In-house, DC-area Employees

ACRES, Amy A.: Director, Government Affairs
CLOWER, W. Dewey: President
IMUS, Scot E.: V. President, Government Affairs
JENKINS, Linda M.: Director, Government Affairs
LYNN, Jason M.: Director, Government Affairs
MULLINGS, Lisa J.: V. President, Communications

Outside Counsel/Consultants

Barnes & Thornburg
Issues: TAX, TRA
Rep By: Randolph J. Stayin

Natural Gas Supply Ass'n

805 15th St. NW
Suite 510
Washington, DC 20005
Tel: (202)326-9300
Fax: (202)326-9330
Registered: LDA
Web: www.ngsa.org

Chief lobbying organization for domestic natural gas producers of all sizes.

In-house, DC-area Employees

CRAMER, Laurie: Director, Communications
JAGTIANI, Patricia Wilson: Director, Regulatory Affairs
RESCH, Rhone: Director, Utility Regulation and Environmental Affairs
SHARP, John Hunter: V. President, Governmental Affairs and Counsel
ULREY, Peri: Senior Analyst

Natural Gas Vehicle Coalition

1100 Wilson Blvd.
Suite 850
Arlington, VA 22209
Tel: (703)527-3022
Fax: (703)527-3025
Registered: LDA
Web: www.ngvc.org
E-mail: rkolodziej@ngvc.org

Supports federal government programs which encourage the development of natural gas powered vehicles.

Leg. Issues: FUE

In-house, DC-area Employees

KERKHOVEN, Paul: Director, Government Relations
KOLODZIEJ, Richard: President

Outside Counsel/Consultants

The Accord Group
Issues: FUE
Rep By: Patrick H. Quinn

Natural History Museum of Los Angeles County

Los Angeles, CA
Leg. Issues: EDU, NAT

Outside Counsel/Consultants

Metcalf Federal Relations
Issues: EDU, NAT
Rep By: Anne Metcalf

Natural Resources Defense Council

1200 New York Ave. NW
Suite 400
Washington, DC 20005
Tel: (202)289-6868
Fax: (202)289-1060
Registered: LDA
Web: www.nrdc.org

A public interest law firm established in New York City in 1970 supported by about 400,000 dues paying members. Through education and appropriate litigation, NRDC works to preserve the nation's resources and environment for future generations.

Leg. Issues: BUD, CAW, GOV, RES, TRA, UTI

In-house, DC-area Employees

BENFIELD, Kaid: Senior Attorney
BUCCINO, Sharon: Senior Staff Attorney
CAMPAIGNE, Alyssondra: Legislative Director
CLUSEN, Chuck: Senior Policy Analyst
COCHRAN, Thomas B.: Senior Scientist
GREER, Linda: Senior Scientist
HAWKINS, David G.: Senior Attorney
LASHOF, Daniel A.: Senior Scientist
NORRIS, Robert S.: Senior Research Analyst
OLSON, Erik D.: Senior Attorney
SCHERR, S. Jacob: Senior Staff Attorney
STONER, Nancy: Senior Attorney
WEISS, Faith: Legislative Attorney
WETSTONE, Gregory S.: Director of Programs

Natural Technologies

New Rochelle, NY

Outside Counsel/Consultants

Garvey, Schubert & Barer
Rep By: Matthew R. Schneider

The Nature Conservancy

4245 N. Fairfax Dr.
Suite 100
Arlington, VA 20003-1606
Tel: (703)841-5300
Fax: (703)841-1283
Registered: LDA
Web: www.nature.org

An international nonprofit organization whose primary purpose is to protect ecologically significant natural areas and the life they shelter. Rescues threatened land and acquires outstanding unspoiled acres. Works with local, state, federal, and international governments to help identify and preserve rare species by protecting land.

Leg. Issues: AGR, ANI, BUD, CAW, ENG, ENV, GOV, NAT, RES, TAX

In-house, DC-area Employees

COON, Maggie: Director, Government Relations
EISENBERG, Jeff: Senior Policy Advisor, Agriculture
FAUSS, Gloria: Director, State Government Relations
HOOPER, Helen: Director, Congressional Affairs
HOWELL, Steve: Acting V. President and Chief Operating Officer
MCCORMICK, Steven J.: President
MCGOLDRICK, Jan: Senior Policy Advisor, EPA
MILLAN, William "Bill": Senior Policy Advisor, International
WILLIAMSON, David: Director, Communications

Outside Counsel/Consultants

Cassidy & Associates, Inc.
Rep By: Henry K. Giugni

Nature Islands, Inc.

Herndon, VA
Leg. Issues: FOR

Outside Counsel/Consultants

Gustafson Associates
Issues: FOR

Nature's Farm Products

Haywood, CA

Outside Counsel/Consultants

Porter, Wright, Morris & Arthur, LLP
Rep By: Bart S. Fisher

Naucalpan, Mexico, County of

Naucalpan de Juarez, MEXICO

Outside Counsel/Consultants

Akin, Gump, Strauss, Hauer & Feld, L.L.P.

NAV Canada

Ottawa, CANADA
Leg. Issues: AVI

Outside Counsel/Consultants

Michael E. Korens
Issues: AVI
Rep By: Michael E. Korens

Navajo Nation

1101 17th St. NW
Suite 250
Washington, DC 20036
Tel: (202)775-0393
Fax: (202)775-8075
Web: www.nnwo.org
Leg. Issues: AGR, BUD, EDU, IND, LAW, TAX

In-house, DC-area Employees

BROWN-YAZZIE, G. Michelle: Exec. Director

Outside Counsel/Consultants

Arent Fox Kintner Plotkin & Kahn, PLLC
Issues: AGR, BUD, EDU, IND, LAW, TAX
Rep By: Michael J. Kurman, Elliott I. Portnoy

Smith Law Firm
Issues: IND
Rep By: Gregory A. Smith

Navajo Nation Oil and Gas Co., Inc.

Window Rock, AZ
Leg. Issues: IND

Outside Counsel/Consultants

Nordhaus Haltom Taylor Taradash & Bladh LLP
Issues: IND
Rep By: Jill E. Grant

Navajo Refining Co.

Outside Counsel/Consultants

Patton Boggs, LLP

Naval Reserve Ass'n

1619 King St.
Alexandria, VA 22314-2793
Tel: (703)548-5800
Fax: (703)683-3647
Registered: LDA
Web: www.navy-reserve.org
E-mail: exec.dir@navy-reserve.org

The Naval Reserve Ass'n is a national and professional organization of officeer who have joined together to provide services to Naval Reserve Officers. The Association's major objective is to cooperate with the Naval Establishment in the solution of the many complex problems which arise in the administration of a Navy composed of both Regular career and Reserve personnel.

Leg. Issues: AVI, DEF, GOV, HCR, MAR, RET, VET

In-house, DC-area Employees

HALL, USN (Ret.), Rear Adm. Thomas F.: Exec. Director
HANSON, Marshall A.: Legislative Director
KEITH, Stephen T.: Deputy Exec. Director

NAVATEK Ship Design Hawaii

Outside Counsel/Consultants

R. J. Hudson Associates

NAVCOM Systems, Inc.

9815 Godwin Dr.
Manassas, VA 22111
Tel: (703)361-0884
Fax: (703)330-8967
Leg. Issues: AER, AVI, BUD, COM, CPI, DEF, GOV, MAN, POS, SMB, TAX, TEC, TOU, TRA, TRD, UNM

In-house, DC-area Employees

GARY, Sr., William H.: V. President, Business Development/Operations

Navigational Electronic Chart Systems Ass'n (NECSA)

Washington, DC
Leg. Issues: GOV, MAR

Outside Counsel/Consultants

John M. Palatiello & Associates
Issues: GOV, MAR
Rep By: John M. Palatiello

NAVSYS Corp.

Colorado Springs, CO

A manufacturer of navigation systems.

Leg. Issues: AER, BUD, DEF

Outside Counsel/Consultants

Ritter and Bourjaily, Inc.
Issues: AER, BUD, DEF
Rep By: Monte F. Bourjaily, III

Navy Joining Center

Columbus, OH
Leg. Issues: MAN

Outside Counsel/Consultants

Bettie McCarthy and Associates
Issues: MAN
Rep By: Elizabeth S. "Bettie" McCarthy

Navy League of the United States

2300 Wilson Blvd.
Arlington, VA 22201
Tel: (703)528-1775
Fax: (703)528-2333
Registered: LDA
Web: www.navyleague.org

Founded in 1902. A patriotic, educational civilian non-profit association that supports a strong defense establishment, especially the sea services, and a foreign policy consistent with maintaining America's security.

Leg. Issues: DEF, MAR, VET

In-house, DC-area Employees

FISHER, John R.: Nat'l President
GRAVES, Shannon: Director of Legislative Affairs
ROBINSON, Charles L.: Nat'l Exec. Director
THOMAS, David: Senior Director of Communications

NAWE: Advancing Women in Higher Education

1325 18th St. NW
Suite 210
Washington, DC 20036
Tel: (202)659-9330
Fax: (202)457-0946
Web: www.nawe.org
E-mail: webweaver@nawe.org

In-house, DC-area Employees

GANGONE, Ed.D., Lynn M.: Exec. Director

NBD Bank, N.A.

Detroit, MI

Outside Counsel/Consultants

Hughes Hubbard & Reed LLP

NCALL Research

Dover, DE

Outside Counsel/Consultants

Robert A. Rapoza Associates

NCI Coalition

Outside Counsel/Consultants

Podesta/Mattoon
Rep By: Ann Delory, Missi Tessier

NCR Corp.

1919 Pennsylvania Ave. NW
Suite 630
Washington, DC 20006-3411
Tel: (202)312-1110
Fax: (202)312-1115
Registered: LDA
Web: www.ncr.com
E-mail: loriann.bowman@ncr.com

Provider of information technology solutions, business knowledge systems and computers. Headquartered in Dayton, OH.

Leg. Issues: BAN, BUD, CPI, ENV, FIN, IMM, TAX, TRD

Political Action Committee/s

NCR Corp. Citizenship Fund
1919 Pennsylvania Ave. NW
Suite 630
Washington, DC 20006-3411
Tel: (202)312-1110
Fax: (202)312-1115
Contact: Philip D. Servidea

In-house, DC-area Employees

SERVIDEA, Philip D.: V. President, Government Affairs

Outside Counsel/Consultants

Cormac Group, LLP

Egle Associates
Issues: BUD, CPI
Rep By: Richard Egle

R. Duffy Wall and Associates
Issues: CPI, ENV, TRD
Rep By: Hon. Bill Brewster, Michael Bradley Enzi

NCRI - Southeast/NCRI - Chesapeake

Rosslyn, VA
Leg. Issues: AGR

Outside Counsel/Consultants

The GrayWell Group, Inc.
Issues: AGR
Rep By: Peter D. Caldwell

NCRIC, Inc.

Washington, DC

Formerly known as The Nat'l Capital Reciprocal Insurance Companies.

Leg. Issues: DOC, INS

Outside Counsel/Consultants

Betty Ann Kane & Co.
Issues: DOC, INS
Rep By: Betty Ann Kane

NCS Healthcare

Vancouver, WA
Leg. Issues: HCR

Outside Counsel/Consultants

Sher & Blackwell
Issues: HCR
Rep By: John W. Butler, Earl W. Comstock, Antilla E. Trotter, III

NCSJ: Advocates on Behalf of Jews in Russia, Ukraine, the Baltic States and Eurasia

1640 Rhode Island Ave. NW
Suite 501
Washington, DC 20036
Tel: (202)898-2500
Fax: (202)898-0822
Web: www.ncsj.org
E-mail: ncsj@ncsj.org

In-house, DC-area Employees

FRANKLIN, Shai: Director, Government Relations
LEVIN, Mark B.: Exec. Director, Washington Office

Nebraska Ethanol Board

Lincoln, NE

Outside Counsel/Consultants

Durante Associates
Rep By: Douglas A. Durante

Nebraska Public Power District

Columbus, NE
Leg. Issues: TEC

Outside Counsel/Consultants

Miller & Van Eaton, P.L.L.C.
Issues: TEC
Rep By: William Malone

Nebraska Wheat Board

Outside Counsel/Consultants

Gordley Associates
Rep By: John Gordley, Daryn McBeth

NEC USA, Inc.

Arlington, VA
Leg. Issues: TRD

Outside Counsel/Consultants

BKSH & Associates
Issues: TRD

Global Policy Group, Inc.

NEDA

Outside Counsel/Consultants

Alcalde & Fay
Rep By: Kevin J. Fay

NEDA/Resource Conservation and Recovery Act Project

1300 I St. NW
Suite 1000 West
Washington, DC 20005
Tel: (202)962-8531
Fax: (202)962-8542

A cross-industry coalition focusing on environmental issues under the Resource Conservation and Recovery Act and the Comprehensive Environmental Response, Compensation and Liability Act. Issues of primary interest include: nonhazardous waste management, recycling, pollution prevention, release reporting, waste transport, and remediation. Members include: AT&T, Chevron Corp., Dow Chemical, General Electric Co., IBM, Kaiser Aluminum and Chemical, Kimberly-Clark, OHM Corp, Phillips Petroleum, Procter & Gamble and Texaco.

Outside Counsel/Consultants

The Technical Group LLC

Negative Population Growth, Inc. (NPG)

1717 Massachusetts Ave. NW
Suite 101
Washington, DC 20009
Tel: (202)667-8950
Fax: (202)667-8953
Registered: LDA
Web: www.npg.org
E-mail: npg@org

NPG is a national nonprofit organization that educates the public about the harmful effects of U.S. overpopulation on our environment and quality of life; advocates smaller families and lower levels of immigration.

Leg. Issues: ENV, FAM, IMM, NAT, URB

In-house, DC-area Employees

STEIN, Sharon McCloe: Exec. Director

Negev Phosphates

Tel Aviv, ISRAEL

Outside Counsel/Consultants

Crowell & Moring LLP

Nehemiah Progressive Housing Development Corp.

Sacramento, CA
Leg. Issues: HOU

Outside Counsel/Consultants

Akin, Gump, Strauss, Hauer & Feld, L.L.P.
Issues: HOU
Rep By: J. David Carlin, Smith W. Davis, Frank J. Donatelli, Anthony Foti

Neighborhood Legal Services Program

701 Fourth St. NW
Washington, DC 20001
Tel: (202)682-2700
Fax: (202)682-0588

Provides free legal assistance to the indigent in the District of Columbia.

In-house, DC-area Employees

COOKE, Jr., Willie E.: Exec. Director

Neiman Marcus Group

Chestnut Hill, MA
Leg. Issues: APP

Outside Counsel/Consultants

Hale and Dorr LLP
Issues: APP
Rep By: Bonnie B. Byers, Gilbert B. Kaplan, Jay P. Urwitz

Nemacolin Mines Corp.

McMurray, PA

A subsidiary of Lykes Corp.

Outside Counsel/Consultants

Heenan, Althen & Roles
Rep By: Michael T. Heenan

NeoPharm, Inc.

Lake Forest, IL
Leg. Issues: PHA

Outside Counsel/Consultants

Smith Dawson & Andrews, Inc.
Issues: PHA
Rep By: Sherri Powar, James P. Smith

Nepal, Kingdom of

Kathmandu, NEPAL

Outside Counsel/Consultants

Washington World Group, Ltd.
Rep By: Edward J. von Kloberg, III

Nepal, Royal Embassy of

2131 Leroy Place NW Tel: (202)667-4550
Washington, DC 20008 Fax: (202)667-5534

Outside Counsel/Consultants

Washington World Group, Ltd.
Rep By: Edward J. von Kloberg, III

Nescrow.com Technologies

Mission, KS
Leg. Issues: CSP

Outside Counsel/Consultants

Wheat & Associates, Inc.
Issues: CSP
Rep By: Andrea Bevvino, Hon. Alan D. Wheat

Nestle USA, Inc.

1101 Pennsylvania Ave. NW Tel: (202)756-2299
Suite 600 Fax: (202)756-7556
Washington, DC 20004 Registered: LDA

A subsidiary of Nestle S.A. of Switzerland.

Leg. Issues: BEV, BUD, FOO, IMM, LBR, TRD

In-house, DC-area Employees

BRADBURY, Jr., John R.: Manager, Government Relations
HILSEN, Louise: Director, Government Relations

Outside Counsel/Consultants

Hogan & Hartson L.L.P.
Issues: BEV, FOO, IMM, LBR, TRD
Rep By: Jeanne S. Archibald, C. Michael Gilliland, Nancy Granese, William Michael House, Richard S. Silverman

Policy Directions, Inc.
Issues: BUD, FOO
Rep By: Steve Kopperud, Stephen Michael, Frankie L. Trull

Net Results, Inc.

Fairfax, VA
Leg. Issues: TEC, UTI

Outside Counsel/Consultants

The ILEX Group
Issues: TEC, UTI
Rep By: H. Hollister Cantus

NET-Political NewsTalk Network

717 Second St. NE Tel: (202)544-3200
Washington, DC 20002 Fax: (202)546-0182

A satellite television network which broadcasts populist programs.

In-house, DC-area Employees

SUTTON, Bob: Chief Exec. Officer
WEYRICH, Paul M.: President

NetCoalition.Com

1776 K Street NW Tel: (202)347-8099
Washington, DC 20006 Registered: LDA

An association of Internet companies including: EMusic.com, eBay, Yahoo!, theglobe.com, American Online, Lycos, DoubleClick, Amazon.com, Inktomi, and Excite@Home.

Leg. Issues: COM, CPI, CPT, CSP, LAW, SCI, TEC, TRD

In-house, DC-area Employees

EBERT, Daniel: Exec. Director

Outside Counsel/Consultants

Boesch & Co.
Issues: CPI
Rep By: Doyce A. Boesch

The Michael Lewan Co.
Issues: CPI, CPT, CSP
Rep By: Michael Lewan, Anne Saunders

McGuiness & Holch
Issues: COM, CPI
Rep By: Markham C. Erickson, Kevin S. McGuiness

Denny Miller McBee Associates
Issues: COM, CPI, CPT, SCI, TEC

Morrison & Foerster LLP
Issues: COM, CPI, CPT, LAW, SCI, TEC
Rep By: Jonathan Band

Piper Marbury Rudnick & Wolfe LLP
Issues: COM, CPI, CSP
Rep By: Emilio W. Cividanes, James J. Halpert, Heather Hamilton, Stuart P. Ingis, Katharine A. Pauley, Ronald L. Plesser

Wiley, Rein & Fielding
Issues: CPI, CPT
Rep By: Mimi W. Dawson

Netherlands Antilles, Government of

Curacao, NETHERLANDS ANTILLES

Outside Counsel/Consultants

O'Connor & Hannan, L.L.P.
Rep By: Patrick E. O'Donnell

Netherlands, Ministry of Foreign Affairs of the Government of

Amsterdam, NETHERLANDS

Outside Counsel/Consultants

Hoffman & Hoffman Public Relations

Netivation.com

Post Falls, ID
Leg. Issues: ADV, BUD, COM, CPI, SCI

Outside Counsel/Consultants

LaRocco & Associates
Issues: ADV, BUD, COM, CPI, SCI
Rep By: Hon. Lawrence P. LaRocco, Matthew LaRocco

Netscape Communications Corp.

Mountain View, CA Registered: LDA
Leg. Issues: COM, CPI, CPT, CSP, TRD

Outside Counsel/Consultants

MSP Strategic Communications, Inc.
Issues: COM, CPI, CPT, CSP
Rep By: Mitchell S. Pettit

Steptoe & Johnson LLP
Issues: TRD
Rep By: Stewart A. Baker, Paul R. Hurst, Peter Lichtenbaum

NetSchools

Atlanta, GA
Leg. Issues: COM, EDU

Outside Counsel/Consultants

Denny Miller McBee Associates
Issues: COM, EDU

Network Advertising Initiative

An ad hoc coalition whose membership includes 24/7 Media Inc., Adforce Inc., and Doubleclick Inc.

Outside Counsel/Consultants

Hogan & Hartson L.L.P.
Rep By: Christine A. Varney

Quinn Gillespie & Associates

Network Affiliated Stations Alliance

Leg. Issues: COM

Outside Counsel/Consultants

Covington & Burling
Issues: COM
Rep By: Gerard J. Waldron

Network in Solidarity with the People of Guatemala (NISGUA)

1830 Connecticut Ave. NW Tel: (202)518-7638
Washington, DC 20009 Fax: (202)223-8221
Web: www.nisgua.org
E-mail: nisgua@igc.org

An organization opposed to U.S. intervention in Guatemala. It is dedicated to building U.S. understanding of and support for the Guatemalan people's struggle for peace and justice.

Leg. Issues: FOR

In-house, DC-area Employees

DEAN, Heather: Exec. Director

NETWORK, A Nat'l Catholic Social Justice Lobby

801 Pennsylvania Ave. SE Tel: (202)547-5556
Suite 460 Fax: (202)547-5510
Washington, DC 20003 Registered: LDA
Web: www.networklobby.org
E-mail: network@networklobby.org

A national Catholic social justice lobby founded in 1971, with 11,000 members nationwide. Lobbies on issues such as global economic justice and securing just access to economic resources.

Leg. Issues: BUD, CIV, DEF, ECN, FOR, HCR, HOU, IMM, LBR, MMM, RET, TAX, TRA, WEL

In-house, DC-area Employees

CLARK, SSJ, Mary Elizabeth: Lobbyist
CURTIS, RSM, Anne: Lobbyist
NIEDRINGHAUS, Stephanie: Communications Coordinator
PINKERTON, CSJ, Catherine: Lobbyist
THORNTON, RSM, Kathy: Nat'l Coordinator

NeuLevel

Washington, DC

A database clearinghouse for the telecommunications and Internet industries.

Leg. Issues: CPI, SCI

Outside Counsel/Consultants

Greenberg Traurig, LLP
Issues: CPI, SCI
Rep By: Ronald L. Platt, Gary M. Shiffman

Neumann College

Aston, PA
Leg. Issues: BUD

Outside Counsel/Consultants

Cassidy & Associates, Inc.
Issues: BUD
Rep By: Michael Merola, Mary E. Shields, Lyllett Wentworth

Neurofibromatosis

Great Neck, NY

Outside Counsel/Consultants

Capitol Associates, Inc.
Rep By: Edward R. Long, Ph.D., Ronnie Kovner Tepp

Nevada Department of Transportation

Carson City, NV
Leg. Issues: TRA

Outside Counsel/Consultants

The Carmen Group
Issues: TRA
Rep By: James B. Young

Nevada Resort Ass'n

Las Vegas, NV
Leg. Issues: GAM

Outside Counsel/Consultants

Wayne Edward Mehl
Issues: GAM
Rep By: Wayne Edward Mehl

Nevada Test Site Development Corp.

Las Vegas, NV
Leg. Issues: ECN, ENG

Outside Counsel/Consultants

McClure, Gerard & Neuenschwander, Inc.
Issues: ECN, ENG
Rep By: Steven G. Barringer, Joseph T. Findaro, Matthew Iandoli, Nils W. Johnson, Hon. James A. McClure, Tod O. Neuenschwander

Nevada, Office of the Attorney General

Carson City, NV

Outside Counsel/Consultants

Duncan, Weinberg, Genzer & Pembroke, P.C.
Rep By: James F. Flug

Nevada, Washington Office of the State of

444 N. Capitol St.
Suite 209
Washington, DC 20001
E-mail: nevada@sso.org
Tel: (202)624-5405
Fax: (202)624-8181
Leg. Issues: TOU

In-house, DC-area Employees

PENNE, R. Leo: Director, DC Office
PIEPER, Michael: Director, DC Office

Outside Counsel/Consultants

Albertine Enterprises, Inc.
Issues: TOU
Rep By: James J. Albertine

New America Alliance

8201 Greensboro Dr.
Suite 300
McLean, VA 22102
Web: www.naaonline.org
E-mail: pavila@naaonline.org
Tel: (703)610-9000
Fax: (703)610-9005

Organization of American Latino business leaders united to promote the well being of the American Latino community with a focus on education, economic and political empowerment and strategic philanthropy.

Leg. Issues: ECN, EDU, IMM, SMB

In-house, DC-area Employees

AVILA, Pilar: Exec. V. President

Outside Counsel/Consultants

Ass'n Management Group
Rep By: Pilar Avila

New American Century PAC

Outside Counsel/Consultants

Bogart Associates Inc.

New American School

Arlington, VA
Leg. Issues: BUD, EDU

Outside Counsel/Consultants

Van Scoyoc Associates, Inc.
Issues: BUD, EDU
Rep By: Victor F. Klatt, III, Robert L. Knisely, H. Stewart Van Scoyoc

New California Life Holding, Inc.

Los Angeles, CA

Outside Counsel/Consultants

Akin, Gump, Strauss, Hauer & Feld, L.L.P.

New City Development

Outside Counsel/Consultants

Davidoff & Malito, LLP
Rep By: Kenneth C. Malito, Robert J. Malito, Stephen J. Slade

New College

Leg. Issues: EDU

Outside Counsel/Consultants

Russ Reid Co.
Issues: EDU
Rep By: Thomas C. Keller, Mark D. McIntyre

New Democrat Network

501 Capitol Ct. NE
Suite 200
Washington, DC 20002
Web: www.newdem.org
E-mail: info@newdem.org
Tel: (202)544-9200
Fax: (202)547-2929

A Political Action Committee that recruits, trains, promotes, and funds federal, state, and local candidates and supports New Democrat members of the House and Senate who advocate a new centrist, progressive approach to governing.

In-house, DC-area Employees

RIDDLE, Mark: Political Secretary
ROSENBERG, Simon: Founder and President
TEAGUE, Jeff: V. President, Development

New Directions for Policy

1015 18th St. NW
Suite 210
Washington, DC 20036
Web: www.ndpolicy.com
E-mail: tiltonjm@aol.com
Tel: (202)833-8877
Fax: (202)833-8932

In-house, DC-area Employees

MEYER, Jack A.: President

New Edge Networks

Vancouver, WA
Leg. Issues: COM, TAX

Outside Counsel/Consultants

Conkling, Fiskum & McCormick
Issues: COM, TAX
Rep By: Gary Conkling, David Fiskum, Daniel Jarman

New Energy and Industrial Technology Development Organization (NEDO)

2000 L St. NW
Suite 605
Washington, DC 20036
Tel: (202)822-9298
Fax: (202)822-9289

In-house, DC-area Employees

NAKANISHI, Hironori: Chief Representative

New England Aquarium

Boston, MA
Leg. Issues: MAR

Outside Counsel/Consultants

Glenn Roger Delaney
Issues: MAR
Rep By: Glenn Roger Delaney

New England Cable Television Ass'n

Braintree, MA

Outside Counsel/Consultants

Mintz, Levin, Cohn, Ferris, Glovsky and Popeo, P.C.
Rep By: Frank W. Lloyd

The New England Council, Inc.

331 Constitution Ave. NE
Washington, DC 20002
E-mail: newenglandcouncilDC@msn.com
Tel: (202)547-0048
Fax: (202)547-9149

A non-profit business association made up of the region's leading manufacturers, financial institutions, public utilities, service industries and colleges and universities. The council actively supports and promotes federal policies and legislation that enhance the business climate in the six-state area.

In-house, DC-area Employees

SAVAGE, Deirdre W.: V. President, Legislative Affairs

New England Deaconess Hospital

Boston, MA

Outside Counsel/Consultants

O'Neill, Athy & Casey, P.C.
Rep By: Martha L. Casey

New England Education Loan Marketing Corp. (Nellie Mae)

Braintree, MA

Outside Counsel/Consultants

Nixon Peabody LLP
Rep By: Stephen J. Wallace

New England Financial

Boston, MA
Formerly New England Life.

Leg. Issues: BAN, FIN, INS, RET, TAX

Outside Counsel/Consultants

Murray, Scheer, Montgomery, Tapia & O'Donnell
Issues: BAN, FIN, INS, RET, TAX
Rep By: Thomas R. Crawford, D. Michael Murray

New England Fuel Institute

Watertown, MA
Leg. Issues: FUE

Outside Counsel/Consultants

Verner, Liipfert, Bernhard, McPherson and Hand, Chartered
Issues: FUE
Rep By: Andrea J. Grant, Nancy A. Sheliga, John H. Zentay

New England Investment Co.

Boston, MA
Leg. Issues: FIN, TAX

Outside Counsel/Consultants

GLOBEMAC Associates
Issues: FIN, TAX
Rep By: Gordon D. MacKay

New England Life Insurance Co.

Boston, MA
Leg. Issues: BAN, FIN, INS, RET, TAX

Outside Counsel/Consultants

GLOBEMAC Associates
Issues: FIN, INS, TAX
Rep By: Gordon D. MacKay

Murray, Scheer, Montgomery, Tapia & O'Donnell
Issues: BAN, FIN, INS, RET, TAX
Rep By: Thomas R. Crawford, D. Michael Murray

New England Medical Center

Boston, MA

Outside Counsel/Consultants

O'Neill, Athy & Casey, P.C.
Rep By: Martha L. Casey, Christopher R. O'Neill

New England Mobile X-Ray

Stoughton, MA

Outside Counsel/Consultants

O'Connor & Hannan, L.L.P.
Rep By: Hon. Thomas J. Corcoran, Christina W. Fleps

New England Motor Rate Bureau

Burlington, MA

Outside Counsel/Consultants

Rea, Cross & Auchincloss
Rep By: Bryce Rea, Jr.

New England Organ Bank

Newton, MA

Outside Counsel/Consultants

Ropes & Gray
Rep By: Thomas M. Susman

New Haven, Connecticut, City of

Leg. Issues: RES

Outside Counsel/Consultants

Verner, Liipfert, Bernhard, McPherson and Hand, Chartered
Issues: RES
Rep By: Suzanne D. Cartwright, Denis J. Dwyer, William H. Minor, Neil T. Proto

New Jersey Department of Human Services

Trenton, NJ

Outside Counsel/Consultants

Covington & Burling

New Jersey Hospital Ass'n

536 First St. SE
Washington, DC 20003
Tel: (202)544-6259
Fax: (202)544-6141
Registered: LDA
Web: www.njha.com

Headquartered in New Jersey.

Leg. Issues: BUD, HCR, MMM

In-house, DC-area Employees

DILL, Bettina R.: Director, Federal Relations
LILLO, Peter J.: V. President, Government Relations

New Jersey Institute of Technology

Newark, NJ
Registered: LDA
Leg. Issues: AVI, DEF, ENV, TRA

Outside Counsel/Consultants

Cassidy & Associates, Inc.
Issues: AVI, DEF, ENV, TRA
Rep By: John A. Crumbliss, Gregory M. Gill, Christopher Lamond, Michael Merola, Brig. Gen. Terry Paul, USMC (Ret.), Blenda Pinto-Riddick, Gabor J. Rozsa

New Jersey Organ & Tissue Sharing Network

Springfield, NJ
Leg. Issues: MMM

Outside Counsel/Consultants

Health Policy Analysts
Issues: MMM
Rep By: G. Lawrence Atkins

New Jersey, State of

Trenton, NJ

Outside Counsel/Consultants

Rhoads Group

New Jersey, Washington Office of the State of

444 N. Capitol St. NW
Suite 201
Washington, DC 20001
Web: www.state.nj.us
Tel: (202)638-0631
Fax: (202)638-2296

The federal affairs office of the State of New Jersey.

In-house, DC-area Employees

CLARKE, Allison: Associate Director
GILES, Lance: Associate Director
WILSON, Linda E.: Acting Director

New Life Corp. of America

Brentwood, TN
Leg. Issues: FIN

Outside Counsel/Consultants

Mayer, Brown & Platt
Issues: FIN
Rep By: Timothy E. Keehan

New London Development Corp.

New London, CT
Leg. Issues: ECN

Outside Counsel/Consultants

Kutak Rock LLP
Issues: ECN
Rep By: Seth Kirshenberg, George R. Schlossberg, Barry P. Steinberg

New Majority Soc.

Washington, DC

A public policy group comprised of former Members of Congress and senior officials of the Reagan and Bush administrations dedicated to core Republican principles including limited government, expanded international trade, market-based solution to environmental regulation, and lower taxes.

Leg. Issues: GOV

Outside Counsel/Consultants

Valis Associates
Issues: GOV
Rep By: Jennifer Conti, Dana W. Hudson, Hon. Richard T. Schulze

New Media Strategies

Outside Counsel/Consultants

Saliba Action Strategies, LLC
Rep By: Khalil G. "Karl" Saliba

New Mexico Human Services Department

Santa Fe, NM

Outside Counsel/Consultants

Covington & Burling

New Mexico Indian Gaming Ass'n

Bernalillo, NM

Outside Counsel/Consultants

The Smith-Free Group

New Mexico State Land Office

Santa Fe, NM

Outside Counsel/Consultants

Elinor Schwartz
Rep By: Elinor Schwartz

New Mexico State Office of Research & Development

Las Cruces, NM
Leg. Issues: BUD, CPI, ECN, EDU, IND, MAN, SCI, TEC

Outside Counsel/Consultants

Meyers & Associates
Issues: BUD, CPI, ECN, EDU, IND, MAN, SCI, TEC
Rep By: Richard L. Meyers

New Mexico State University

Las Cruces, NM
Leg. Issues: BUD, EDU

Outside Counsel/Consultants

Meyers & Associates
Issues: BUD, EDU
Rep By: Larry D. Meyers, Richard L. Meyers

New Mexico State University, Department of Agriculture

Las Cruces, NM
Leg. Issues: AGR, BUD, EDU, NAT

Outside Counsel/Consultants

Meyers & Associates
Issues: AGR, BUD, EDU, NAT
Rep By: Richard L. Meyers

New Mexico State University, Department of Engineering

Las Cruces, NM
Leg. Issues: BUD, CAW, COM, DEF, DIS, EDU, ENG, ENV, MAN, SCI, TEC, WAS

Outside Counsel/Consultants

Meyers & Associates
Issues: BUD, CAW, COM, DEF, DIS, EDU, ENG, ENV, MAN, SCI, TEC, WAS
Rep By: Richard L. Meyers

New Mexico Tech

Socorro, NM
Leg. Issues: BUD, DEF

Outside Counsel/Consultants

The PMA Group
Issues: BUD, DEF
Rep By: Kaylene Green, Stephen Madey, Paul J. Magliocchetti, Charles Smith, Thomas Veltri, Sandra Welch

New Orleans Environmental Systems Foundation

Metarie, LA
Leg. Issues: EDU, ENV

Outside Counsel/Consultants

Washington Alliance Group, Inc.
Issues: EDU, ENV
Rep By: Bonnie Singer

New Orleans Internat'l Airport

New Orleans, LA
Leg. Issues: AVI, BUD, TRA

Outside Counsel/Consultants

Johnston & Associates, LLC
Issues: AVI, BUD, TRA
Rep By: Hon. J. Bennett Johnston, N. Hunter Johnston, W. Proctor Jones, Eric Tober

New Orleans, Louisiana, City of

Leg. Issues: BUD, DIS, ECN, ENG, ENV, URB

Outside Counsel/Consultants

Arent Fox Kintner Plotkin & Kahn, PLLC
Issues: BUD, DIS, ECN, ENV, URB
Rep By: Alison Kutler, Michael T. McNamara, Elliott I. Portnoy

Verner, Liipfert, Bernhard, McPherson and Hand, Chartered
Issues: ENG
Rep By: Paul E. Nordstrom, Glen J. Ortman, Sherry A. Quirk, Regina Speed-bost, Clinton A. Vince

New Orleans, Louisiana, Port of

Leg. Issues: BUD, DEF, MAR, TRA

Outside Counsel/Consultants

Jones, Walker, Waechter, Poitevent, Carrere & Denegre, L.L.P.
Issues: BUD, DEF, MAR, TRA
Rep By: John J. Jaskot, R. Christian Johnsen

The Livingston Group, LLC
Issues: BUD, MAR
Rep By: Melvin Goodweather, Richard Legendre, Hon. Robert L. Livingston, Jr., Richard L. Rodgers

New Orleans, Louisiana, Regional Transit Authority of

New Orleans, LA
Leg. Issues: BUD, TRA

Outside Counsel/Consultants

Adams and Reese LLP
Issues: BUD, TRA
Rep By: B. Jeffrey Brooks, Hon. James A. "Jimmy" Hayes, Andrea Wilkinson

Johnston & Associates, LLC
Issues: TRA
Rep By: Hon. J. Bennett Johnston, N. Hunter Johnston, Eric Tober

New Product Development Consortium

New York, NY

Outside Counsel/Consultants

Cannon Consultants, Inc.
Rep By: Charles A. Cannon

New Republican Majority Fund

201 N. Union St.
Suite 530
Alexandria, VA 22314
Tel: (703)299-6600
Fax: (703)548-5954

In-house, DC-area Employees

BOYLES, Bret K.: Exec. Director

New Sea Escape

Ft. Lauderdale, FL
Leg. Issues: TOU

Outside Counsel/Consultants

The MWW Group
Issues: TOU
Rep By: Jonathan B. Slade

New Skies Satellites N.V.

The Hague, NETHERLANDS
Leg. Issues: COM, TEC

Outside Counsel/Consultants

Higgins, McGovern & Smith, LLC
Issues: COM
Rep By: Patrick C. Koch

Lent Scrivner & Roth LLC
Issues: TEC
Rep By: Norman F. Lent, III, Hon. Norman F. Lent, Alan J. Roth, Michael S. Scrivner

New Starts Working Group

Leg. Issues: BUD, TRA

Outside Counsel/Consultants

Oppenheimer Wolff & Donnelly LLP
Issues: BUD, TRA

New Ways Ministry

4012 29th St.
Mt. Rainier, MD 20712
Web: www.newwaysministry.org
Tel: (301)277-5674
Fax: (301)864-8954

An educational and bridge-building ministry of reconciliation between the Catholic gay and lesbian community and the wider church.

In-house, DC-area Employees

DEBERNARDO, Francis: Exec. Director

New World Communications Group, Inc.

Marietta, GA

Outside Counsel/Consultants

Skadden, Arps, Slate, Meagher & Flom LLP

New York Bankers Ass'n

New York, NY
Leg. Issues: BAN

Outside Counsel/Consultants

Gibson, Dunn & Crutcher LLP
Issues: BAN
Rep By: Robert C. Eager, Cantwell Faulkner Muckenfuss, III, Victoria P. Rostow

New York Board of Trade

New York, NY
Leg. Issues: AGR, FIN

Outside Counsel/Consultants

Cadwalader, Wickersham & Taft
Issues: AGR, FIN
Rep By: Ellen S. Levinson

New York Botanical Garden

Bronx, NY
Leg. Issues: BUD

Outside Counsel/Consultants

Capitol Associates, Inc.
Issues: BUD
Rep By: Edward R. Long, Ph.D., Ronnie Kovner Tepp

New York City (Washington Office)

1301 Pennsylvania Ave. NW
Suite 350
Washington, DC 20004
Tel: (202)624-5900
Fax: (202)624-5926

Legislative interest involves all municipal issues and related matters.

New York City Board of Estimate

New York, NY

Outside Counsel/Consultants

Arnold & Porter
Rep By: Norman M. Sinel

New York City, New York, Council of

New York, NY
Leg. Issues: EDU, LBR, TRA

Outside Counsel/Consultants

The Ickes & Enright Group
Issues: EDU, LBR, TRA
Rep By: Janice Ann Enright, Harold M. Ickes

New York Clearing House Ass'n

New York, NY
Leg. Issues: FIN

Outside Counsel/Consultants

Sullivan & Cromwell
Issues: FIN
Rep By: Samuel R. Woodall, III

The New York Historical Soc.

New York, NY
Leg. Issues: EDU

Outside Counsel/Consultants

The Ickes & Enright Group
Issues: EDU
Rep By: Janice Ann Enright, Harold M. Ickes

New York Institute for Special Education

Bronx, NY
Leg. Issues: EDU

Outside Counsel/Consultants

Kerrigan & Associates, Inc.
Issues: EDU
Rep By: Michael J. Kerrigan

New York Institute of Technology

Islip, NY
Leg. Issues: BUD, EDU

Outside Counsel/Consultants

Preston Gates Ellis & Rouvelas Meeds LLP
Issues: BUD, EDU
Rep By: Amy Carlson

Washington Strategies, L.L.C.
Rep By: Jennifer Johnson Calvert, William P. Jarrell

New York Life Insurance Co.

1001 Pennsylvania Ave. NW
Suite 580 North
Washington, DC 20004-2505
Web: www.newyorklife.com
Tel: (202)783-1366
Fax: (202)393-2769
Registered: LDA

A seller of life insurance, annuities, and long term care insurance. Also provides asset management services. Headquartered in New York, NY.

Leg. Issues: BAN, FIN, HCR, INS, MMM, RET, TAX, TOR, TRD

In-house, DC-area Employees

COLGATE, Ms. Jessie M.: Senior V. President, Governmental Affairs
HAMRICK, Mary Moore: V. President, Government Relations
KRISTOFF, Sandra J.: Senior V. President
LEFRANCOIS, Ronald J.: V. President, Government Affairs
SANDER, Raymond J.: V. President, N.Y. Life International

Outside Counsel/Consultants

Crowell & Moring LLP

Mayer, Brown & Platt
Issues: TRD
Rep By: Scott Parven

Patton Boggs, LLP
Issues: BAN, INS, RET, TAX, TRD
Rep By: John F. Jonas

Timmons and Co., Inc.
Issues: FIN, INS, TAX, TRD
Rep By: Michael J. Bates, Douglas F. Bennett, Ellen B. Fitzgibbons, Bryce L. "Larry" Harlow, Timothy J. Keating, Tom C. Korologos, Richard J. Tarplin, William E. Timmons, Jr., William E. Timmons, Sr.

New York Life Internat'l Inc.

Washington, DC
Leg. Issues: TRD

Outside Counsel/Consultants

Crowell & Moring LLP
Issues: TRD
Rep By: Doral S. Cooper, Melissa Coyle, Garnett J. Sweeney

New York Mercantile Exchange

1331 Pennsylvania Ave. NW
Suite 550S
Washington, DC 20004
Tel: (202)662-8770
Fax: (202)662-8765
Registered: LDA

A commodities exchange headquartered in New York, NY.

Leg. Issues: CAW, CPT, ENG, FIN, TRD

In-house, DC-area Employees

DEWITT, Charlie: Government Affairs Associate
SEETIN, Mark: V. President, Government Affairs

Outside Counsel/Consultants

Sutherland Asbill & Brennan LLP
Rep By: Katherine P. Yarbrough

New York Metropolitan Transportation Authority

New York, NY
Leg. Issues: BUD, TRA

Outside Counsel/Consultants

Chambers, Conlon & Hartwell
Issues: TRA
Rep By: Don Norden

Smith Dawson & Andrews, Inc.
Issues: BUD, TRA
Rep By: Thomas C. Dawson

Vierra Associates, Inc.
Rep By: Dennis C. Vierra

New York Municipal Power Agency

Liverpool, NY
Leg. Issues: ENG, GOV

Outside Counsel/Consultants

Duncan, Weinberg, Genzer & Pembroke, P.C.
Issues: ENG, GOV
Rep By: Jeffrey C. Genzer, Thomas L. Rudebusch

New York Presbyterian Hospital - Cornell Medical Center

New York, NY

Outside Counsel/Consultants

Chambers Associates Inc.
Rep By: William A. Signer

Kelley, Drye & Warren LLP

New York Psychotherapy and Counseling Center

Queens Village, NY
Leg. Issues: MMM

Outside Counsel/Consultants

Davidoff & Malito, LLP
Issues: MMM
Rep By: Kenneth C. Malito, Robert J. Malito, Stephen J. Slade

New York Public Library

New York, NY
Leg. Issues: EDU

Outside Counsel/Consultants

Akin, Gump, Strauss, Hauer & Feld, L.L.P.
Issues: EDU
Rep By: Marlene M. Colucci, Smith W. Davis, Barney J. Skladany, Jr.

New York Roadway Improvement Coalition

Commack, NY
Leg. Issues: ROD

Outside Counsel/Consultants

The Carmen Group
Issues: ROD
Rep By: John Lagomarcino

New York State Ass'n of Health Care Providers

Albany, NY
Leg. Issues: INS, MMM
Registered: LDA

Outside Counsel/Consultants

Patton Boggs, LLP
Issues: INS, MMM
Rep By: John F. Jonas, Martha M. Kendrick, JoAnn V. Willis

New York State Democratic Committee

Albany, NY

Outside Counsel/Consultants

Issue Dynamics Inc.

New York State Department of Social Services

Albany, NY

Outside Counsel/Consultants

Covington & Burling

New York State Department of Transportation

Albany, NY
Leg. Issues: TRA

Outside Counsel/Consultants

Patton Boggs, LLP
Issues: TRA
Rep By: Anne Miano

New York State Health Facilities Ass'n

Albany, NY
Leg. Issues: MMM

Outside Counsel/Consultants

Akin, Gump, Strauss, Hauer & Feld, L.L.P.
Issues: MMM
Rep By: Smith W. Davis, Karen E. Goldmeier Green, Barney J. Skladany, Jr.

New York State Housing Finance Agency

New York, NY
Leg. Issues: HOU

Outside Counsel/Consultants

Nixon Peabody LLP
Issues: HOU
Rep By: Stephen J. Wallace

New York State Metropolitan Transportation Authority

New York, NY
Leg. Issues: TRA

Outside Counsel/Consultants

Patton Boggs, LLP
Issues: TRA
Rep By: Anne Miano

New York State Office of Federal Affairs

444 N. Capitol St. NW
Suite 301
Washington, DC 20001
Tel: (202)434-7100
Fax: (202)434-7110

Headquartered in New York, NY.

In-house, DC-area Employees

MAZZARELLA, James A.: Director
O'HARE, Kerry: Deputy Director

New York State Reliability Council

Albany, NY

Outside Counsel/Consultants

LeBoeuf, Lamb, Greene & MacRae L.L.P.
Rep By: L. Charles Landgraf

New York State Senate

444 N. Capitol St. NW
Suite 301
Washington, DC 20001
E-mail: axenfeld@senate.state.NY.US
Tel: (202)624-5880
Fax: (202)508-3850

Headquartered in Albany, NY.

In-house, DC-area Employees

AXENFELD-LANKFORD, Laurie: Exec. Director, Washington Office

New York State Thruway Authority

Albany, NY
Leg. Issues: TRA

Outside Counsel/Consultants

Patton Boggs, LLP
Issues: TRA
Rep By: Anne Miano

New York Stock Exchange

801 Pennsylvania Ave. NW
Suite 630
Washington, DC 20004-5878
Tel: (202)347-4300
Fax: (202)347-4370
Registered: LDA
Web: www.nyse.com

The New York Stock Exchange is a registered national securities exchange.

Leg. Issues: BAN, BNK, BUD, CPT, FIN, TAX, TEC

Political Action Committee/s

New York Stock Exchange Political Action Committee
801 Pennsylvania Ave. NW
Suite 630
Washington, DC 20004-5878
Tel: (202)347-4300
Fax: (202)347-4370
Contact: Doug Nappi

In-house, DC-area Employees

BLACKBURNE, Faith: Manager, Public Affairs
DAY, Harry F.: Counsel, Regulatory Affairs
EDGAR, Kevin R.: Special Counsel, Government Relations
MILLIGAN, Susan M.: Counsel, Government Relations
NAPPI, Doug: Vice President, Government Relations
SRODES, Cecile: Counsel, Legislative Affairs

Outside Counsel/Consultants

Ryan, Phillips, Utrecht & MacKinnon
Issues: FIN
Rep By: Rodney Hoppe, Jeffrey M. MacKinnon, Thomas M. Ryan, Joseph V. Vasapoli

Verner, Liipfert, Bernhard, McPherson and Hand, Chartered
Issues: CPT, FIN, TAX
Rep By: David B. Jacobsohn, John H. Zentay

The New York Structural Biology Center

New York, NY
Leg. Issues: BUD

Outside Counsel/Consultants

Downey McGrath Group, Inc.
Issues: BUD
Rep By: Elaine B. Acevedo, Hon. Thomas J. Downey, Jr., Hon. Raymond J. McGrath, John Peter Olinger

New York Trap Rock Co.

West Nyack, NY

Outside Counsel/Consultants

Heenan, Althen & Roles

New York University

New York, NY
Registered: LDA
Leg. Issues: AER, ALC, ANI, ART, AVI, BUD, CPT, DEF, EDU, ENG, ENV, FOR, HCR, IMM, MAR, MED, MMM, SCI, TAX, TEC, URB, VET

Outside Counsel/Consultants

Jorden Burt LLP
Issues: AER, ALC, ANI, ART, AVI, BUD, CPT, DEF, EDU, ENG, ENV, FOR, HCR, IMM, MAR, MED, MMM, SCI, TAX, TEC, URB, VET
Rep By: Patricia Branch, Alanna Dillon, Marna Gettleman, Marilyn Berry Thompson, Rebecca Tidman

New York University Medical Center

New York, NY
Leg. Issues: BUD, HCR, MED, MMM, TOB

Outside Counsel/Consultants

Capitol Associates, Inc.
Issues: BUD, HCR, MED, MMM, TOB
Rep By: Debra M. Hardy Havens, Edward R. Long, Ph.D., Ronnie Kovner Tepp

New York Waterways

Weehawken, NJ

Outside Counsel/Consultants

Sher & Blackwell
Rep By: Robert J. Blackwell, Sr., Jeffrey F. Lawrence, Jeffrey R. Pike

New York, State of

Albany, NY

Outside Counsel/Consultants

Royer & Babyak
Rep By: Michael T. Kinsella

New York/New Jersey Foreign Freight Forwarders and Brokers Ass'n, Inc.

Outside Counsel/Consultants

Rodriguez O'Donnell Fuerst Gonzalez & Williams
Rep By: Ashley W. Craig, Carlos Rodriguez

New Zealand Dairy Board

Wellington, NEW ZEALAND
Leg. Issues: AGR

Outside Counsel/Consultants

Blank Rome Comisky & McCauley, LLP
Rep By: Edward J. Farrell

Hogan & Hartson L.L.P.
Issues: AGR
Rep By: Humberto R. Pena

New Zealand Kiwifruit Marketing Board

Auckland, NEW ZEALAND
Leg. Issues: TRD

Outside Counsel/Consultants

Davis & Leiman, P.C.
Issues: TRD

The Newark Group

Cranford, NJ
Leg. Issues: ADV, CAW, ENG, ENV, FUE, GOV, MAN, TAX, WAS

Outside Counsel/Consultants

Colling Swift & Hynes
Issues: ADV, CAW, ENG, ENV, FUE, GOV, MAN, TAX, WAS
Rep By: Terese Colling, Pablo Collins, Robert J. Hynes, Jr., Hon. Allan B. Swift

Newark, California, City of

Outside Counsel/Consultants

Simon and Co., Inc.
Rep By: Heather Barber, Alex DeGood, Leonard S. Simon

Newark, New Jersey, City of

Leg. Issues: ALC, ART, AVI, BUD, CAW, ECN, EDU, ENV, GAM, HCR, HOU, IMM, LAW, LBR, MMM, NAT, POS, ROD, TAX, TEC, TRA, URB, WAS, WEL

Outside Counsel/Consultants

Jorden Burt LLP
Issues: ALC, ART, AVI, BUD, CAW, ECN, EDU, ENV, GAM, HCR, HOU, IMM, LAW, LBR, MMM, NAT, POS, ROD, TAX, TEC, TRA, URB, WAS, WEL
Rep By: Patricia Branch, Marna Gettleman, Marilyn Berry Thompson, Rebecca Tidman

Newbridge Networks

Kanata, CANADA

Outside Counsel/Consultants

J. LeBlanc Internat'l, LLC
Rep By: James L. LeBlanc

NewCity Communications, Inc.

Bridgeport, CT

Outside Counsel/Consultants

Kaye Scholer LLP
Rep By: Jason Shrinsky

Newell, Co.

Rockford, IL

Outside Counsel/Consultants

Sidley & Austin

Newhall Land and Farming Co.

Valencia, CA
Leg. Issues: TRA

Outside Counsel/Consultants

JSA-1, Inc.
Issues: TRA
Rep By: John S. Autry, William B. Barker

Newington-Cropsey Foundation

Hastings-on-Hudson, NY
Leg. Issues: ART

Outside Counsel/Consultants

Chwat and Company, Inc.
Issues: ART
Rep By: Scott Bizub, John Chwat, Derek Riker

Newman & Associates

Denver, CO
Leg. Issues: TAX

Outside Counsel/Consultants

Swidler Berlin Shereff Friedman, LLP
Issues: TAX
Rep By: Keith N. Cole, Barry B. Direnfeld, Brian W. Fitzgerald, Gary Gallant, William B. Glew, Jr., Harold P. Goldfield, Lester S. Hyman, Harold A. Levy

NewMarket Global Consulting Group

Washington, DC
Leg. Issues: FOR

Outside Counsel/Consultants

Collins & Company, Inc.
Issues: FOR
Rep By: James D. Bond, Richard L. Collins, Thomas A. Hooper, Shay D. Stautz

Newmont Mining Corp.

Houston, TX
Leg. Issues: BUD, ENV, NAT

Outside Counsel/Consultants

McClure, Gerard & Neuenschwander, Inc.
Issues: BUD, ENV, NAT
Rep By: Steven G. Barringer, Joseph T. Findaro, Matthew Iandoli, Nils W. Johnson, Hon. James A. McClure, Tod O. Neuenschwander

Newpark Resources/SOLOCO

Lafayette, LA
Leg. Issues: DEF, ENV, FUE

Outside Counsel/Consultants

James E. Guirard
Issues: DEF, ENV, FUE
Rep By: James E. Guirard, Jr.

Newport Group

Heathrow, FL
Leg. Issues: TAX

Outside Counsel/Consultants

Patton Boggs, LLP
Issues: TAX
Rep By: John F. Jonas

Newport News Shipbuilding Inc.

801 Pennsylvania Ave. NW
Suite 350
Washington, DC 20004
Tel: (202)783-1400
Fax: (202)783-1746
Registered: LDA
Web: www.nns.com
Leg. Issues: BUD, CAW, CPT, DEF, ENG, ENV, FOR, HCR, LBR, MAN, MAR, RET, SMB, TAX, TOR, TRD, WAS

Political Action Committee/s

Newport News Shipbuilding Political Action Committee (SHIPPAC)
801 Pennsylvania Ave. NW
Suite 350
Washington, DC 20004
Tel: (202)783-1400
Fax: (202)783-1746
Contact: D. Rick Wyatt

In-house, DC-area Employees

HENLEY, Tracey G.: Manager, PAC
RUPPERT, Carey D.: Director, Government Relations
SYERS, William A.: Director, Federal Relations
TUCKER, Patrick A.: V. President, Government Relations
WYATT, D. Rick: Treasurer, Newport News Shipbuilding Political Action Committee

Outside Counsel/Consultants

Alford & Associates
Issues: DEF
Rep By: Marty Alford

T. Edward Braswell
Issues: DEF
Rep By: T. Edward Braswell, Jr.

Commonwealth Consulting Corp.
Issues: DEF
Rep By: Christopher M. Lehman

The Direct Impact Co.

The OB-C Group, LLC
Issues: DEF
Rep By: Thomas Keating, Kim F. McKernan, Charles J. Mellody, Patricia A. Nelson, Lawrence F. O'Brien, III, Linda E. Tarplin

Verner, Liipfert, Bernhard, McPherson and Hand, Chartered
Issues: BUD, DEF
Rep By: Lloyd N. Hand

Newport News, Virginia, City of

Leg. Issues: ENV, IND

Outside Counsel/Consultants

Van Ness Feldman, P.C.
Issues: ENV, IND
Rep By: Richard G. Kozlowski, Thomas C. Roberts

Newport News, Virginia, Industrial Development Authority of the City of

Newport News, VA
Leg. Issues: DEF, TRA

Outside Counsel/Consultants

Madison Government Affairs
Issues: DEF, TRA
Rep By: Paul J. Hirsch, Jackson Kemper, III

News America Inc.

Washington, DC
Leg. Issues: COM, CPT

Outside Counsel/Consultants

Mayer, Brown & Platt
Issues: CPT
Rep By: Amb. Peter L. Scher

Podesta/Mattoon
Issues: COM, CPT
Rep By: Ann Delory, Kimberley Fritts, Anthony T. Podesta

News Corporation Ltd.

444 N. Capitol St. NW
Suite 740
Washington, DC 20001
Tel: (202)824-6500
Fax: (202)824-6510
Registered: LDA

Headquartered in Sydney, Australia. The parent company of Fox Inc. Lobbies on behalf of its subsidiaries, including: Fox Basic Cable, Fox Broadcasting Co., Fox Television Network, Harper Collins Publishing, News America Inc., and Twentieth Century Fox Film Corp.

Leg. Issues: ADV, ART, COM, CPT, TEC, TRD

Political Action Committee/s

FOXPAC
444 N. Capitol St. NW
Suite 740
Washington, DC 20001
Tel: (202)824-6500
Fax: (202)824-6510

In-house, DC-area Employees

LILLEY, Justin W.: V. President, Government Relations
MCGLOWAN, Angela: Director, Government Relations
O'CONNELL, Maureen A.: V. President, Regulatory and Government Relations
REGAN, Michael: Senior V. President, Government Affairs

Outside Counsel/Consultants

Baker & Hostetler LLP

Bergner Bockorny Castagnetti and Hawkins
Issues: ADV, ART, COM, CPT, TRD
Rep By: Jeffrey T. Bergner, David A. Bockorny, David Castagnetti, Melissa Schulman

Hogan & Hartson L.L.P.
Issues: CPT, TRD
Rep By: Raymond S. Calamaro, Mark S. McConnell, Hon. Robert H. Michel, Daniel B. Poneman

Skadden, Arps, Slate, Meagher & Flom LLP
Issues: TEC
Rep By: Ivan A. Schlager

The Washington Group
Rep By: Tripp Funderburk, Rita M. Lewis, G. John O'Hanlon, John D. Raffaelli, Tonya Saunders, Mark Schnabel, Richard Sullivan, Fowler West

Newsbank, Inc.

New Canaan, CT
Leg. Issues: GOV, MIA

Outside Counsel/Consultants

Kasten & Co.
Issues: GOV, MIA
Rep By: Robert W. Kasten, Jr., Frederick A. Ruth

Newsday

Melville, NY

Outside Counsel/Consultants

Hauser Group

NewsHunter.net, LLC

New York, NY
Leg. Issues: TEC

Outside Counsel/Consultants

Colling Swift & Hynes
Issues: TEC
Rep By: Terese Colling, Robert J. Hynes, Jr., Hon. Allan B. Swift

Newspaper Ass'n of America

529 14th St. NW
Suite 440
Washington, DC 20045-1402
Tel: (202)783-4697
Fax: (202)783-4699
Registered: LDA
Web: www.naa.org
Leg. Issues: ADV, COM, CPT, GOV, MIA, POS, TAX, TRD

In-house, DC-area Employees

BOYLE, Paul J.: V. President, Government Affairs
BRINKMANN, Robert J.: V. President and Counsel, Postal & Regulatory Affairs
BROWN, David S. J.: Senior V. President, Public Policy and General Counsel
HELMSLEY, E. Molly: Director, Government Affairs and Legislative Counsel
STURM, John F.: President and Chief Exec. Officer

Outside Counsel/Consultants

The Aker Partners Inc.
Issues: POS
Rep By: G. Colburn Aker

Baker, Donelson, Bearman & Caldwell, P.C.
Issues: POS
Rep By: J. Keith Kennedy, Charles R. Parkinson, John C. Tuck

Davidson & Company, Inc.
Issues: ADV, TAX
Rep By: James H. Davidson, Richard E. May, Stanley Sokul

Evans & Black, Inc.
Issues: POS
Rep By: Rae Forker Evans, Rafe Morrissey

Patton Boggs, LLP
Rep By: Thomas Hale Boggs, Jr., John F. Jonas

Podesta/Mattoon
Issues: CPT, GOV
Rep By: Claudia James

Wiley, Rein & Fielding
Issues: COM, POS
Rep By: James T. Bruce, III, Susan C. Buck, Mimi W. Dawson, Richard E. Wiley

Nexia Biotechnologies, Inc.

Plattsburgh, NY
Leg. Issues: SCI

Outside Counsel/Consultants

Commonwealth Group, Ltd.
Issues: SCI
Rep By: Christopher T. Cushing, Christopher J. Greeley

Nextel Communications, Inc.

2001 Edmund Halley Dr.
Reston, VA 20191
Tel: (703)433-4000
Registered: LDA
Web: www.nextel.com

In-house, DC-area Employees

FOOSANER, Robert

Outside Counsel/Consultants

Podesta/Mattoon
Rep By: Andrew C. Littman, Anthony T. Podesta

Stuntz, Davis & Staffier, P.C.

NextRX

Bothell, WA
Leg. Issues: HCR, PHA

Outside Counsel/Consultants

Sagamore Associates, Inc.
Issues: HCR, PHA
Rep By: Theodore W. Bristol, Frank S. Swain

Nextwave Telecom

1101 Pennsylvania Ave. NW
Suite 805
Washington, DC 20004
Tel: (202)347-2771
Fax: (202)347-2822
Registered: LDA
Web: www.nextwavetel.com

Washington office of a San Diego, CA-based company that builds and operates personal communications service networks.

Leg. Issues: COM, TEC

In-house, DC-area Employees

REGAN, Jr., Michael: Senior V. President, External Affairs

Outside Counsel/Consultants

Baker, Donelson, Bearman & Caldwell, P.C.
Issues: COM, TEC
Rep By: J. Keith Kennedy

Dewey Ballantine LLP
Issues: TEC
Rep By: David Leach

KPMG, LLP
Issues: TEC
Rep By: Linden C. Smith

Nez Perce Tribal Executive Committee

Lapwai, ID

Outside Counsel/Consultants

Dorsey & Whitney LLP
Rep By: Philip Baker-Shenk, David A. Bieging, Cindy Darcy, Sarah Ridley

NF Inc. - Mass Bay Area

Burlington, MA
Leg. Issues: BUD, HCR, TOB

Outside Counsel/Consultants

Capitol Associates, Inc.
Issues: BUD, HCR, TOB
Rep By: Edward R. Long, Ph.D., Ronnie Kovner Tepp

NFTC-FSC Coalition

Outside Counsel/Consultants

Miller & Chevalier, Chartered

Washington Council Ernst & Young

NHTSA

Outside Counsel/Consultants

Greer, Margolis, Mitchell, Burns & Associates
Rep By: David E. Mitchell, Will Taliaferro

NI Industries

Los Angeles, CA
Leg. Issues: DEF

Outside Counsel/Consultants

MARC Associates, Inc.
Issues: DEF
Rep By: Daniel C. Maldonado

Niagara Area Chamber of Commerce

Niagara Falls, NY
Leg. Issues: DEF

Outside Counsel/Consultants

Hyjek & Fix, Inc.
Issues: DEF
Rep By: Steven M. Hyjek, Irene D. Schecter, Karl H. Stegenga

Niagara Frontier Transportation Authority

Buffalo, NY
Leg. Issues: AVI, BUD, ROD, TRA

Outside Counsel/Consultants

Akin, Gump, Strauss, Hauer & Feld, L.L.P.
Issues: AVI, BUD, ROD, TRA
Rep By: Anthony Foti, Susan H. Lent, Hon. William L. Paxon

Niagara Mohawk Power Corp.

Syracuse, NY
Leg. Issues: BUD, CAW, TAX, TRA, UTI, WAS

Outside Counsel/Consultants

Swidler Berlin Shereff Friedman, LLP
Issues: BUD, CAW, TAX, TRA, UTI, WAS
Rep By: Barry B. Direnfeld, Brian W. Fitzgerald, Gary Gallant, William B. Glew, Jr., Harold P. Goldfield, Gary D. Slaiman

NICA Airline

Managua, NICARAGUA

Outside Counsel/Consultants

Mullenholz, Brimsek & Belair
Rep By: John R. Brimsek

Nicaraguan Foundation for Democracy and Development

Managua, NICARAGUA

Outside Counsel/Consultants

Washington World Group, Ltd.
Rep By: Edward J. von Kloberg, III

Niche Plan Sponsors, Inc.

Newport Beach, CA
Leg. Issues: RET, TAX

Outside Counsel/Consultants

Kehoe & Hambel
Issues: RET, TAX
Rep By: John Hambel, Danea M. Kehoe

Nicor, Inc.

Naperville, IL

Outside Counsel/Consultants

Mayer, Brown & Platt
Rep By: Penny L. Eastman

NICORE, Inc.

Tampa, FL
Leg. Issues: HCR

Outside Counsel/Consultants

Greenberg Traurig, LLP
Issues: HCR
Rep By: Ronald L. Platt

Niger, Government of the Republic of

Djamena, NIGER

Outside Counsel/Consultants

Washington World Group, Ltd.
Rep By: Edward J. von Kloberg, III

Nigeria, Embassy of the Federal Republic of

1333 16th St. NW
Washington, DC 20036
Tel: (202)986-8400
Fax: (202)986-8410

Outside Counsel/Consultants

Washington World Group, Ltd.
Rep By: Edward J. von Kloberg, III

Nigeria, Government of the Federal Republic of

Abuja, NIGERIA

Outside Counsel/Consultants

Barron-Birrell, Inc.

White & Case LLP

Nike, Inc.

507 Second St. NE
Washington, DC 20002
Tel: (202)543-6453
Fax: (202)544-6453
Registered: LDA

Web: www.nike.com
E-mail: brad.figel@nike.com

A retailer of footwear and apparel, headquartered in Beaverton, OR.

Leg. Issues: EDU, ENV, LBR, TRD

Political Action Committee/s

Nike, Inc. PAC
507 Second St. NE
Washington, DC 20002
Tel: (202)543-6453
Fax: (202)544-6453
Contact: Brad G. Figel

In-house, DC-area Employees

FIGEL, Brad G.: Director, Governmental Affairs and International Trade Counsel
PORTER, Orson: Deputy Director of Governmental Affairs

Niki Trading Co.

Leg. Issues: TRD

Outside Counsel/Consultants

Richard W. Bliss
Issues: TRD
Rep By: Pani Farkan

Nikon Corp.

Tokyo, JAPAN

Outside Counsel/Consultants

Hughes Hubbard & Reed LLP

Nilit America Corp.

Greensboro, NC

A nylon manufacturer.

Outside Counsel/Consultants

Arnold & Porter

Nilit Ltd.

Tel Aviv, ISRAEL

Outside Counsel/Consultants

Arnold & Porter

Nintendo of America, Inc.

Redmond, WA
Leg. Issues: CPT, TRD

Outside Counsel/Consultants

Arter & Hadden

SISCORP
Issues: CPT, TRD
Rep By: Donald F. Massey

Ninth Congressional District Republican Committee

Columbia, MO

Outside Counsel/Consultants

Sam Richardson
Rep By: Sam Richardson

Nippon Cargo Airlines

Tokyo, JAPAN

Outside Counsel/Consultants

Zuckert, Scoutt and Rasenberger, L.L.P.
Rep By: William H. Callaway, Jr., Charles J. Simpson, Jr., Rachel B. Trinder

Nippon Telegraph and Telephone Corp.

Tokyo, JAPAN
Leg. Issues: TEC

Outside Counsel/Consultants

Civic Service, Inc.
Issues: TEC
Rep By: Roy Pfautch, Michael W. Schick

Global USA, Inc.

Hogan & Hartson L.L.P.

Nippon Yusen Kaisha (NYK) Line

New York, NY
Leg. Issues: MAR

Outside Counsel/Consultants

Sher & Blackwell
Issues: MAR
Rep By: Robert J. Blackwell, Sr., Jeffrey F. Lawrence, Jeffrey R. Pike, Stanley O. Sher

Nisei Farmers League

Fresno, CA
Leg. Issues: AGR, CAW, TRA

Outside Counsel/Consultants

McGuiness Norris & Williams, LLP
Issues: AGR, CAW, TRA
Rep By: Timothy J. Bartl, William N. LaForge, Monte B. Lake

NISH - Creating Employment Opportunities for People with Severe Disabilities

2235 Cedar Ln.
Vienna, VA 22182
Tel: (703)560-6800
Fax: (703)849-8916
Registered: LDA

Web: www.nish.org

Formerly known as Nat'l Industries for the Severely Handicapped. Objective is to provide jobs for persons with severe diabilities by supplying prefessional and technical assistance to over 500 not-for-profit community rehabilitation programs interested in obtaining federal contracts under Public Law 92-28, the Javits-Wagner O'Day Act.

Leg. Issues: BUD, LBR, MMM, UNM

In-house, DC-area Employees

MCKINNON, Jr., Daniel W.: President
YOUNG, Tony: Director, Governmental Affairs

Outside Counsel/Consultants

J. C. Luman and Assoc.

Oppenheimer Wolff & Donnelly LLP
Issues: LBR
Rep By: Hon. Birch Bayh, Kevin O. Faley

NiSource Inc.

Merrillville, IN
Web: www.nisource.com
Leg. Issues: ENG, FUE, TAX

Outside Counsel/Consultants

Adams and Reese LLP
Issues: FUE, TAX
Rep By: Hon. James A. "Jimmy" Hayes

Akin, Gump, Strauss, Hauer & Feld, L.L.P.
Issues: ENG
Rep By: Barney J. Skladany, Jr., Henry A. Terhune

Nissan North America Inc.

196 Van Buren St.
Suite 450
Herndon, VA 20170
Tel: (703)456-2550
Fax: (703)456-2551
Registered: LDA

Web: www.nissan-na.com
Leg. Issues: AUT, BNK, CSP, FUE, MAN, TAX, TRD

In-house, DC-area Employees

AKIZUKI, Hoyato: Manager, Technical Affairs
FUJII, Noboru: Director, Technical Affairs
GRIFFIN, Luanne: Manager, Government Affairs
HANADA, Yuko: Analyst, Government Affairs
HINES, Terri: Manager, Corporate Communications

Outside Counsel/Consultants

Edelman Public Relations Worldwide
Rep By: Leslie Dach, Michael K. Deaver, Jere Sullivan

Hogan & Hartson L.L.P.
Issues: MAN
Rep By: James Chen, William Michael House, R. Latane Montague, Jeffrey W. Munk, Patrick M. Raher

Shutler and Low
Issues: AUT
Rep By: Roger C. Fairchild, Robert G. Kaler

Nissho-Iwai American Corp.

1825 K St. NW
Suite 1103
Washington, DC 20006
Tel: (202)429-0280
Fax: (202)429-0283

In-house, DC-area Employees

TADA, Yukio: General Manager

Nitrobenzene Ass'n

Washington, DC
Leg. Issues: CSP, MAN, WAS

Outside Counsel/Consultants

Hadley & McKenna
Issues: CSP, MAN, WAS
Rep By: Joseph E. Hadley, Jr.

NitroMed, Inc.

Bedford, MA
Leg. Issues: BUD, HCR, MED, MMM, PHA

Outside Counsel/Consultants

FoxKiser
Issues: BUD, HCR, MED, MMM, PHA
Rep By: Allan M. Fox, John Daniel Kiser, Diane E. Robertson

Nixon Center, The

1615 L St. NW
Suite 1250
Washington, DC 20036
Tel: (202)887-1000
Fax: (202)887-5222
Web: www.nixoncenter.org
E-mail: mail@nixoncenter.org

A non-partisan public policy institution committed to the analysis of policy challenges through the prism of American national interest.

Leg. Issues: DEF, FOR, FUE, TRD

In-house, DC-area Employees

KEMP, Geoffrey: Director, Regional Strategic Programs
RODMAN, Peter W.: Director, National Security Programs
SAUNDERS, Paul: Director
SIMES, Dimitri K.: President

NL Industries

6916 Wolf Run Shoals
Fairfax Station, VA 22039
Tel: (703)978-8038
Fax: (703)978-8039
Registered: LDA

Headquartered in Houston, TX.

Leg. Issues: CHM, CSP

Political Action Committee/s

NL Industries PAC
6916 Wolf Run Shoals
Fairfax Station, VA 22039
Tel: (703)978-8038
Fax: (703)978-8039
Contact: Karl J. Ottosen

In-house, DC-area Employees

OTTOSEN, Karl J.: PAC Contact

Outside Counsel/Consultants

Brownstein Hyatt & Farber, P.C.
Issues: CHM, CSP
Rep By: William T. Brack, Michael B. Levy

Ottosen and Associates
Rep By: Karl J. Ottosen

No-Wave, AB

Leg. Issues: CSP, TEC

Outside Counsel/Consultants

The Da Vinci Group
Issues: CSP, TEC

Noble Transoceanic Corp.

Washington, DC

Outside Counsel/Consultants

Johnson, Rogers & Clifton, L.L.P.

Noesis Inc.

Manassas, VA
Leg. Issues: AER, BUD, DEF, MAN, SCI

Outside Counsel/Consultants

The Legislative Strategies Group, LLC
Issues: DEF
Rep By: Melvin J. Littig, Grayson Winterling

Rooney Group Internat'l, Inc.
Issues: AER, BUD, DEF, MAN, SCI
Rep By: Jerry L. Kaffka, James W. Rooney

NoFire Technologies, Inc.

Bala Cynwyd, PA
Leg. Issues: DEF, SCI

Outside Counsel/Consultants

Commonwealth Consulting Corp.
Issues: SCI
Rep By: Christopher M. Lehman

The Gallagher Group, LLC
Issues: DEF
Rep By: James P. Gallagher

Nogales, Arizona, City of

Leg. Issues: ECN, ENV, IMM, LAW, URB

Outside Counsel/Consultants

Parry, Romani, DeConcini & Symms
Issues: ECN, ENV, IMM, LAW, URB
Rep By: Edward H. Baxter, Hon. Dennis DeConcini, John M. Haddow, Scott D. Hatch, Shannon Davis Henderson, Jack W. Martin, Romano Romani, Linda Arey Skladany, Hon. Steven D. Symms

Noise Reduction Technology Coalition

Washington, DC
Leg. Issues: AVI, ENV, TRD

Outside Counsel/Consultants

Sher & Blackwell
Issues: AVI, ENV, TRD
Rep By: Mark Atwood

NOKIA

1101 Connecticut Ave. NW
Suite 910
Washington, DC 20036
Tel: (202)887-1798
Fax: (202)887-0432
Registered: LDA

A manufacturer of cellular telephones.

Leg. Issues: TEC

In-house, DC-area Employees

COHEN, Cecily
FITZSIMON, Leo R.
PLUMMER, William B.: V. President, Government and Industry Affairs

Outside Counsel/Consultants

Meyers & Associates
Issues: TEC
Rep By: Larry D. Meyers, Richard L. Meyers

Verner, Liipfert, Bernhard, McPherson and Hand, Chartered
Issues: TEC
Rep By: John M. R. Kneuer, Lawrence R. Sidman

Nomura Internat'l plc

London, UNITED KINGDOM

A securities firm.

Leg. Issues: TEC

Outside Counsel/Consultants

Weil, Gotshal & Manges, LLP
Issues: TEC
Rep By: Joshua Janow, Robert C. Odle, Jr., Charles E. Roh, Jr., David Taylor, Larry I. Willis

Nomura Research Institute America, Inc.

601 13th St. NW
Suite 330 South
Washington, DC 20005
Web: www.nri.co.jp
Tel: (202)783-6013
Fax: (202)783-6005

An economic research institute.

In-house, DC-area Employees

YAMADA, Sawaaki: General Manager, Washington Office

Non Commissioned Officers Ass'n of the U.S.A.

225 N. Washington St.
Alexandria, VA 22314
Tel: (703)549-0311
Fax: (703)549-0245
Registered: LDA

Web: www.ncoausa.org
E-mail: legislat@ncoausa.org

A veteran/military association headquartered in San Antonio, TX.

Leg. Issues: BUD, DEF, VET

In-house, DC-area Employees

HARRINGTON, Alex J.: Director, Legislative Affairs
MIX, Robert R.
SCHNEIDER, Richard C.: Director, State and Veterans Affairs

Non-Bank Funds Transmitters Group

Includes CitiCorp Services; Comdata Network; Integrated Payment Systems; Interpayment Services; Thomas Cook, Inc.; Travelers Express Co.; and Western Union Financial Services.

Leg. Issues: FIN

Outside Counsel/Consultants

Howrey Simon Arnold & White
Issues: FIN
Rep By: Ezra C. Levine

Non-Ferrous Founders' Soc.

Des Plaines, IL
Leg. Issues: CAW, ENV, LBR

Outside Counsel/Consultants

Kinghorn & Associates, L.L.C.
Issues: CAW, ENV, LBR
Rep By: John W. Hilbert, II, Jeremy Scott

Noosack Indian Tribal council

Deming, WA

Outside Counsel/Consultants

SENSE, INC.
Rep By: C. Juliet Pittman

Norcal Waste Systems, Inc.

San Francisco, CA
Leg. Issues: ENV, TRU, WAS

Outside Counsel/Consultants

Baise + Miller, P.C.
Issues: ENV, TRU, WAS
Rep By: Eric P. Bock

Norchem Concrete Products Inc.

Hauppauge, NY
Leg. Issues: BUD, ROD

Outside Counsel/Consultants

Genesis Consulting Group, LLC
Issues: BUD, ROD
Rep By: Mark Benedict, Dana DeBeaumont

The Nordam Group

Tulsa, OK
Leg. Issues: AER, AVI, MAN

Outside Counsel/Consultants

Capitol Counsel Group, L.L.C.
Issues: AVI

Law Offices of Irene E. Howie
Issues: AER, MAN

Shaw Pittman
Issues: AVI
Rep By: J. E. Murdock, III

Nordstrom, Inc.

Seattle, WA
Leg. Issues: TAX

Outside Counsel/Consultants

William M. Diefenderfer
Issues: TAX
Rep By: William M. Diefenderfer, III

Ernst & Young LLP
Issues: TAX
Rep By: Lauren Darling, Patrick G. Heck, Phillip D. Moseley, Henry C. Ruempler, Donna Steele-Flynn

Kurzweil & Associates
Issues: TAX
Rep By: Jeffrey Kurzweil

Norfolk Southern Corp.

1500 K St. NW
Suite 375
Washington, DC 20005
Tel: (202)383-4166
Fax: (202)383-4018
Registered: LDA

Headquartered in Norfolk, VA.

Leg. Issues: BNK, BUD, CAW, ENV, FUE, HCR, LBR, MAR, RES, RET, ROD, RRR, TAX, TEC, TRA, TRU, WAS

In-house, DC-area Employees

ANTHONY, Steven J.: Assistant V. President
CORCORAN, John F.: Senior V. President, Public Affairs
MAESTRI, Bruno: V. President, Public Affairs

Outside Counsel/Consultants

Chambers, Conlon & Hartwell
Issues: RRR
Rep By: Ray B. Chambers, Jerome Conlon, Keith O. Hartwell, Don Norden

Dewey Ballantine LLP
Issues: RET, TAX
Rep By: Joseph K. Dowley

Hecht, Spencer & Associates
Issues: RRR, TAX, TRA
Rep By: Timothy P. Hecht, William H. Hecht, Franklin C. Phifer

James T. Molloy
Issues: RRR
Rep By: James T. Molloy

Bartley M. O'Hara
Issues: RRR, TAX, TRA
Rep By: Bartley M. O'Hara

Paul, Hastings, Janofsky & Walker LLP
Issues: BUD, RRR, TEC, TRA
Rep By: Ralph B. Everett

Valis Associates
Issues: RRR, TRA
Rep By: Jennifer Conti, Hon. Richard T. Schulze, Wayne H. Valis

Washington Consulting Alliance, Inc.
Issues: LBR, TRA
Rep By: Thomas L. Burgum

Whitten & Diamond
Issues: TRA
Rep By: Robert M. Diamond

Williams & Jensen, P.C.
Issues: RRR, TAX
Rep By: Robert E. Glennon, Jr., Karen Judd Lewis, John J. McMackin, Jr., Frank C. Vlossak, J. D. Williams

Winston & Strawn
Issues: RRR
Rep By: Hon. James H. Burnley, IV, Charles L. Kinney, Hon. John L. Napier, Joseph E. O'Leary, Douglas C. Richardson

Norfolk Southern Railroad

Washington, DC
Leg. Issues: RRR, TAX, TRD

Outside Counsel/Consultants

Hooper Owen & Winburn
Issues: RRR, TAX, TRD
Rep By: David Rudd, John P. Winburn

Norfolk, Virginia, City of

Leg. Issues: AVI, BUD, ECN, EDU, ENV, HOU, LAW, ROD, RRR, SMB, TAX, TRA, WEL

Outside Counsel/Consultants

Chambers Associates Inc.
Issues: BUD, ECN, EDU, ENV, HOU, LAW, ROD, RRR, SMB, TAX, TRA, WEL
Rep By: Janet A. Denton

Global Aviation Associates, Ltd.
Issues: AVI
Rep By: Jon F. Ash, Charles R. Chambers

Morrison & Foerster LLP
Issues: AVI
Rep By: G. Brian Busey

Norlight Telecommunications, Inc.

Brookfield, MI
Leg. Issues: TEC

Outside Counsel/Consultants

Greenberg Traurig, LLP
Issues: TEC
Rep By: Mitchell F. Brecher

Norsk Hydro

Outside Counsel/Consultants

Columbus Public Affairs

Nortel Networks

801 Pennsylvania Ave. NW
Suite 700
Washington, DC 20004
Tel: (202)347-4610
Fax: (202)508-3612
Registered: LDA

Web: www.nortelnetworks.com

Formerly known as Northern Telecom.

Leg. Issues: GOV, IMM, TAX, TEC, TRD

Political Action Committee/s

Nortel Networks Political Action Committee
801 Pennsylvania Ave. NW
Suite 700
Washington, DC 20004
Tel: (202)347-4610
Fax: (202)508-3612

In-house, DC-area Employees
CARTER-MAGUIRE, Melanie: V. President, Global Government Relations
FARMER, Greg: V. President, Government Relations - International Trade
GORDON, Mary S.: V. President, Government Relations - Congressional Affairs
PHILLIPS, Susan A.: Director, Global Government Relations, eCommerce Policy
STRASSBURGER, Raymond: Director, Government Relations - Telecommunications Policy

Outside Counsel/Consultants
Shaw Pittman
Rep By: Stephan E. Becker, Thomas J. Spulak, Andrew L. Woods

North American Ass'n of Food Equipment Manufacturers
Washington, DC
Leg. Issues: LBR

Outside Counsel/Consultants
Smith, Bucklin and Associates, Inc.
Issues: LBR
Rep By: Robert H. Wilbur

North American Bison Cooperative
New Rockford, ND

Outside Counsel/Consultants
Darby Enterprises

North American Brain Tumor Coalition
Des Plaines, IL
Leg. Issues: BUD, HCR, MED, MMM

Outside Counsel/Consultants
Bennett Turner & Coleman, LLP
Issues: BUD, HCR, MED, MMM
Rep By: Elizabeth Goss, Natasha Leskovsek, Kristi E. Schrode, Samuel D. Turner

North American Coal
Dallas, TX

Outside Counsel/Consultants
Valente Lopatin & Schulze
Rep By: Mark Valente, III

North American Communications Corp.
Biloxi, MS
Leg. Issues: BAN, BUD, CSP, LAW

Outside Counsel/Consultants
The Kamber Group
Issues: BAN, BUD, CSP, LAW
Rep By: Victor S. Kamber, Gavin McDonald

North American Datacom
Iuka, MS
Leg. Issues: TEC

Outside Counsel/Consultants
Cassidy & Associates, Inc.
Issues: TEC
Rep By: W. Campbell Kaufman, IV, Christopher Lamond

North American Die Casting Ass'n
Rosemont, IL
Leg. Issues: CAW

Outside Counsel/Consultants
Waterman & Associates
Issues: CAW
Rep By: Amy Lucas, Diana L. Waterman

North American Electric Reliability Council
Princeton, NJ
Leg. Issues: ENG, UTI

Outside Counsel/Consultants
Stuntz, Davis & Staffier, P.C.
Issues: ENG, UTI
Rep By: Linda Stuntz

North American Equipment Dealers Ass'n
1156 15th St. NW
Suite 302
Washington, DC 20005
Tel: (202)457-0825
Fax: (202)457-0864
Registered: LDA
Web: www.naeda.com
Leg. Issues: AGR, BNK, CAW, HCR, TAX, TRA, TRD

In-house, DC-area Employees
GAIBLER, Floyd D.: Legislative Director
WEGMEYER, Tyler: Manager, Government Affairs

North American Grain Export Ass'n, Inc.
1300 L St. NW
Suite 900
Washington, DC 20005
Tel: (202)682-4030
Fax: (202)682-4033
Registered: LDA
E-mail: info@naega.org

A not-for-profit trade association founded in 1912, whose purpose is to promote the commercial export of grain and oilseed trade from the United States. Membership includes private and public companies and farmer cooperatives involved in North American grain and seed trade.

Leg. Issues: AGR, MAR, TRD

In-house, DC-area Employees
MARTIN, Gary C.: President and Chief Exec. Officer
MILLER, W. Kirk: Director, International Programs and Regulatory Affairs

North American GSM Alliance, LLC
Chicago, IL
Leg. Issues: COM, TEC

Outside Counsel/Consultants
Harris, Wiltshire & Grannis LLP
Issues: COM, TEC
Rep By: Scott Blake Harris

Podesta/Mattoon
Issues: COM
Rep By: Claudia James

North American Industrial Hemp Council, Inc.
Madison, WI
Leg. Issues: AGR

Outside Counsel/Consultants
Shea & Gardner
Issues: AGR
Rep By: R. James Woolsey

North American Insulation Manufacturers Ass'n
44 Canal Center Plaza
Suite 310
Alexandria, VA 22314
Tel: (703)684-0084
Fax: (703)684-0427
Web: www.naima.org
E-mail: insulation@naima.org
Leg. Issues: ENG, TAX

In-house, DC-area Employees
MENTZER, Kenneth D.: President and Chief Exec. Officer

Outside Counsel/Consultants
Haake and Associates
Issues: ENG, TAX
Rep By: Timothy M. Haake, Nathan M. Olsen

North American Interstate Weather Modification Council
Austin, TX
Leg. Issues: SCI

Outside Counsel/Consultants
Richard L. Spees, Inc.
Issues: SCI
Rep By: Richard L. Spees

North American Meat Processors Ass'n
1910 Association Dr.
Reston, VA 20191-1547
Tel: (703)758-1900
Fax: (703)758-8001
Web: www.namp.com
E-mail: namp@ix.netcom.com
Leg. Issues: AGR, FOO, GOV

In-house, DC-area Employees
HOLMES, Marty: Exec. V. President

Outside Counsel/Consultants
Stanley J. Emerling
Issues: AGR, FOO, GOV
Rep By: Stanley J. Emerling

North American Millers' Ass'n
600 Maryland Ave. SW
Suite 305 West
Washington, DC 20024
Tel: (202)484-2200
Fax: (202)488-7416
Web: www.namamillers.org
E-mail: betsyfaga@aol.com

Represents the wheat, corn, and oat milling industries with government relations and public affairs activities.

Leg. Issues: AGR, CAW, ENV, FOO, TRD

In-house, DC-area Employees
BAIR, James A.: V. President
FAGA, Betsy: President

North American Natural Casing Ass'n
111 Park Place
Falls Church, VA 22046-4513
Tel: (703)533-0251
Fax: (703)241-5603
E-mail: nancahq@yahoo.com

In-house, DC-area Employees
BUZZERD, Jr., CAE, Harry W.: Senior Management Counsel
DENSTON, Susan: Account Executive
TYERYAR, CAE, Clay D.: Senior V. President

North American Retail Dealers Ass'n
Lombard, IL
Leg. Issues: BNK, CPT, LBR

Outside Counsel/Consultants
Goldberg & Associates, PLLC
Issues: BNK, CPT, LBR
Rep By: James M. Goldberg

North American Securities Administrators Ass'n (NASAA)
Ten G St. NE
Suite 710
Washington, DC 20002
Tel: (202)737-0900
Fax: (202)783-3571
Registered: LDA
Web: www.nasaa.org
E-mail: info@nasaa.org

NASAA is the national voice of securities agencies responsible for grass-roots protection and efficient capital formation.

Leg. Issues: BAN, FIN

In-house, DC-area Employees
BEAUCHAMP, Marc: Exec. Director
FISCHIONE, Deborah A.: Director of Policy
GRIFFIN, Royce: General Counsel

Outside Counsel/Consultants
Butera & Andrews
Issues: BAN
Rep By: James J. Butera, Frank Tillotson

North American Shipbuilding
Larose, LA
Leg. Issues: DEF, LBR, MAR

Outside Counsel/Consultants
Charlie McBride Associates, Inc.
Issues: DEF, LBR, MAR
Rep By: Charlie McBride

North American Soc. for Trenchless Technology
1655 N. Fort Myer Dr.
Suite 700
Arlington, VA 22209
Tel: (703)351-5252
Fax: (703)351-5261
Web: www.nastt.org
E-mail: dmartin@nastt.org

A technical society with mission to promote trenchless technology.

In-house, DC-area Employees
HEMPHILL, John: Deputy, Operations

North American Soc. of Pacing and Electrophysiology
2000 L St. NW
Suite 200
Washington, DC 20036
Tel: (202)416-1871
Fax: (202)416-1841
Registered: LDA
Web: www.naspe.org

An organization of physicians, scientists and allied professionals headquartered in Natick, Massachusetts. Specializes in the study and management of patients with cardiac arrthymias.

Leg. Issues: HCR

In-house, DC-area Employees
MELNICK, Amy: Director, Government Relations
NICKELSON, Daniel E.: Government Relations Liaison

North American Sports Management, Inc.
Winter Park, FL
Leg. Issues: GAM, IND

Outside Counsel/Consultants
Alcalde & Fay
Issues: IND
Rep By: Hon. Louis A. "Skip" Bafalis, Jim Davenport

Zane & Associates
Issues: GAM
Rep By: Curtis J. Zane

North American Steel Framing Alliance
Washington, DC
Leg. Issues: MAN

Outside Counsel/Consultants

Venable
Issues: MAN
Rep By: Brock R. Landry

North American Superhighway Coalition

Kansas City, MO
Leg. Issues: ECN, TRA

Outside Counsel/Consultants

Tate-LeMunyon, LLC
Issues: ECN, TRA
Rep By: Glenn B. LeMunyon, Dan C. Tate, Jr.

North American Technician Excellence

8201 Greensboro Dr.
Suite 300
McLean, VA 22102
Web: www.natex.org
Tel: (703)610-9000
Fax: (703)610-9005

Outside Counsel/Consultants

Ass'n Management Group
Rep By: Rex Boynton

North American Vaccine, Inc./AMVAX, Inc.

12103 Indian Creek Ct.
Beltsville, MD 20705
Tel: (301)419-8400
Fax: (301)419-0167

In-house, DC-area Employees
ABDUN-NABI, Daniel J.: Senior V. President

North American Venture Capital Ass'n

Arlington, VA

Outside Counsel/Consultants

The Direct Impact Co.

North Carolina Electric Membership Corp.

Raleigh, NC
Leg. Issues: BUD

Outside Counsel/Consultants

Womble Carlyle Sandridge & Rice, P.C.
Issues: BUD
Rep By: Debra Bryant, Donna Erat

North Carolina Global TransPark Authority

Raleigh, NC
Leg. Issues: AVI, BUD, TRA

Outside Counsel/Consultants

Shaw Pittman
Issues: AVI
Rep By: J. E. Murdock, III

Womble Carlyle Sandridge & Rice, P.C.
Issues: AVI, BUD, TRA
Rep By: Debra Bryant, Donna Erat, Kevin Darrow Jones

North Carolina Peanut Growers Ass'n

Nashville, NC
Leg. Issues: AGR, BUD, TRD

Outside Counsel/Consultants

Meyers & Associates
Issues: AGR, BUD, TRD
Rep By: Fran Boyd, Larry D. Meyers, Richard L. Meyers

North Carolina State Ports Authority

Wilmington, NC
Leg. Issues: BUD

Outside Counsel/Consultants

Womble Carlyle Sandridge & Rice, P.C.
Issues: BUD
Rep By: Debra Bryant

North Carolina, Hurricane Floyd Redevelopment Center of State of

Raleigh, NC
Leg. Issues: BUD, DIS

Outside Counsel/Consultants

Womble Carlyle Sandridge & Rice, P.C.
Issues: BUD, DIS
Rep By: Debra Bryant, Donna Erat

North Carolina, Washington Office of the State of

444 N. Capitol St. NW
Suite 332
Washington, DC 20001
Tel: (202)624-5830
Fax: (202)624-5836
Leg. Issues: AGR, ALC, AVI, BUD, CAW, COM, DIS, ECN, EDU, ENV, FAM, GOV, HCR, HOU, IND, LAW, MMM, NAT, ROD, RRR, TEC, TOB, TOU, TRA, TRD, URB, WAS, WEL

In-house, DC-area Employees
MCCLESKEY, James S.: Director, Washington Office

North Dakota State University

Fargo, ND
Leg. Issues: AGR, ANI, DEF, EDU, NAT, PHA, SCI, TRA

Outside Counsel/Consultants

Lee & Smith P.C.
Issues: AGR, ANI, DEF, EDU, NAT, PHA, SCI, TRA
Rep By: David B. Lee

North Dakota Wheat Commission

Bismarck, ND
Leg. Issues: AGR, TRD

Outside Counsel/Consultants

Robins, Kaplan, Miller & Ciresi L.L.P.
Issues: AGR, TRD
Rep By: Charles A. Hunnicutt

North Dakota, Department of Transportation of

Bismarck, ND

Outside Counsel/Consultants

John A. DeVierno
Rep By: John A. DeVierno

North Dakota, Governor's Office of the State of

Bismark, ND
Leg. Issues: AGR, BUD, ECN, EDU, GOV, NAT, TRA, TRD, UTI

Outside Counsel/Consultants

John G. "Toby" Burke
Issues: AGR, BUD, ECN, EDU, GOV, NAT, TRA, TRD, UTI
Rep By: John G. "Toby" Burke

North Metro Mayors Coalition

Brooklyn Park, MN
Leg. Issues: ROD, TRA

Outside Counsel/Consultants

Capital Partnerships (VA) Inc.
Issues: ROD, TRA
Rep By: Robin Angle, Kenneth W. Butler, Clay Gravely

North Miami Beach, Florida, City of

Leg. Issues: HOU, TRA

Outside Counsel/Consultants

Alcalde & Fay
Issues: HOU, TRA
Rep By: Hector Alcalde, Danielle McBeth

North Miami, Florida, City of

Outside Counsel/Consultants

Crowell & Moring LLP
Rep By: Steven P. Quarles

North of Ireland Free Trade Initiative

Londonberry, UNITED KINGDOM
Leg. Issues: TRD

Outside Counsel/Consultants

Carlyle Consulting
Issues: TRD
Rep By: Thomas C. Rodgers

North San Diego County Transit Development Board

San Diego, CA
Leg. Issues: BUD, DIS, TRA

Outside Counsel/Consultants

Honberger and Walters, Inc.
Issues: BUD, DIS, TRA
Rep By: Donald Gilchrest, Thomas P. Walters

North Shore Long Island Jewish Health System

Great Neck, NY
Leg. Issues: BUD

Outside Counsel/Consultants

Cassidy & Associates, Inc.
Issues: BUD
Rep By: Arthur D. Mason, Christine A. O'Connor, Diane Rinaldo, Hon. Martin A. Russo

North Slope Borough, Alaska

Barrow, AK
Leg. Issues: BUD, ECN, EDU, ENG, ENV, GOV, HCR, HOU, IND, MAR, NAT, POS, RES, TAX

Outside Counsel/Consultants

Van Ness Feldman, P.C.
Issues: BUD, ECN, EDU, ENG, ENV, GOV, HCR, HOU, IND, MAR, NAT, POS, RES, TAX
Rep By: Alan L. Mintz

North Topsail Beach, North Carolina, Town of

Leg. Issues: BUD, NAT

Outside Counsel/Consultants

Marlowe and Co.
Issues: BUD, NAT
Rep By: Howard Marlowe, Jeffrey Mazzella

Northcoast Communications, LLC

Bethpage, NY
Leg. Issues: TEC

Outside Counsel/Consultants

The Coursen Group
Issues: TEC
Rep By: Hon. Christopher D. Coursen

Northeast Entrepreneur Fund

Virginia, MN

Outside Counsel/Consultants

Robert A. Rapoza Associates
Rep By: Robert A. Rapoza

Northeast Illinois Regional Commuter Railroad Corp.

Chicago, IL
Leg. Issues: TRA

Outside Counsel/Consultants

The Carmen Group
Issues: TRA
Rep By: Gerald P. Carmen, David A. Keene, John Lagomarcino, James B. Young

Northeast Ohio Areawide Coordination Agency (NOACA)

Cleveland, OH
Leg. Issues: BUD, CAW, ENV, GOV, ROD, TRA

Outside Counsel/Consultants

Ainslie Associates
Issues: BUD, CAW, ENV, GOV, ROD, TRA
Rep By: Virginia J. Ainslie

Northeast Ohio Regional Sewer District

Cleveland, OH
Leg. Issues: CAW

Outside Counsel/Consultants

Ainslie Associates
Issues: CAW
Rep By: Virginia J. Ainslie

Squire, Sanders & Dempsey L.L.P.

Northeast Texas Electric Cooperative

Longview, TX
Leg. Issues: BUD, ENG, GOV, TAX, UTI

Outside Counsel/Consultants

Brickfield, Burchette, Ritts & Stone
Issues: BUD, ENG, GOV, TAX, UTI
Rep By: William H. Burchette, Colleen Newman, Christine C. Ryan

Northeast Utilities

701 Pennsylvania Ave. NW
Suite 300
Washington, DC 20004
Web: www.nu.com
Tel: (202)508-5301
Fax: (202)508-5304
Registered: LDA

An electric and gas utility company headquartered in Berlin, Connecticut.

Leg. Issues: CAW, ENG, ENV, LBR, NAT, TAX, TEC, WAS

Political Action Committee/s

NIEPAC
701 Pennsylvania Ave. NW
Suite 300
Washington, DC 20004
Tel: (202)508-5301
Fax: (202)508-5304

In-house, DC-area Employees
RAVITZ SMITH, Ruth: Director, Federal Governmental Affairs

Outside Counsel/Consultants

Bond & Company, Inc.
Issues: ENG
Rep By: Richard N. Bond

Northeast Ventures Corp.

Duluth, MN

Outside Counsel/Consultants

Robert A. Rapoza Associates
Rep By: Robert A. Rapoza

Northeast-Midwest Institute

218 D St. SE
Washington, DC 20003
Web: www.nemw.org
Tel: (202)544-5200
Fax: (202)544-0043

A nonprofit research and public education organization dedicated to the long-term economic vitality and environmental quality of the northeastern and midwestern states.

Leg. Issues: AGR, BUD, CAW, ECN, ENG, ENV, LBR, MAN, MAR, NAT, ROD, SCI, TRA, TRD, URB, UTI

In-house, DC-area Employees

MUNSON, Dick: Exec. Director

Northeastern University

Boston, MA
Leg. Issues: BUD, DEF, EDU

Outside Counsel/Consultants

Hale and Dorr LLP
Issues: EDU
Rep By: Jay P. Urwitz

O'Neill, Athy & Casey, P.C.
Issues: BUD, DEF, EDU
Rep By: Martha L. Casey, Christopher R. O'Neill

Northern Air Cargo

Anchorage, AK
Leg. Issues: TRA

Outside Counsel/Consultants

Jack Ferguson Associates, Inc.
Issues: TRA
Rep By: Jack Ferguson

Northern Border Pipeline Co.

Omaha, NE

Outside Counsel/Consultants

Wright & Talisman, P.C.
Rep By: Jeffrey G. DiSciullo

Northern California Power Agency

Roseville, CA

Cities of Alameda, Biggs, Gridley, Healdsburg, Lodi, Lompoc, Palo Alto, Redding, Roseville, Santa Clara and Ukiah, associated with the Plumas-Sierra Rural Electric Cooperative.

Leg. Issues: BUD, ENG

Outside Counsel/Consultants

The Ferguson Group, LLC
Issues: BUD
Rep By: W. Roger Gwinn

Kanner & Associates
Issues: ENG
Rep By: Martin B. Kanner

Morgan Meguire, LLC
Issues: ENG
Rep By: Scott Lindsay, Kyle G. Michel, Katie Parrott, C. Kyle Simpson, Deborah R. Sliz, Kiel Weaver

Spiegel & McDiarmid
Issues: ENG
Rep By: Lisa Dowden, Fran Francis, Robert C. McDiarmid

Northern Economic Initiatives Corp.

Marquette, MI

Outside Counsel/Consultants

Robert A. Rapoza Associates
Rep By: Robert A. Rapoza

Northern Essex Community College Foundation

Haverhill, MA
Leg. Issues: BUD

Outside Counsel/Consultants

Cassidy & Associates, Inc.
Issues: BUD
Rep By: Dennis M. Kedzior, Christopher Lamond, Jeffrey Lawrence

Northern Forest Alliance

Montpelier, VT
Leg. Issues: NAT

Outside Counsel/Consultants

Conservation Strategies, LLC
Issues: NAT

Northern Indiana Commuter Transportation District

Chesterton, IN

Outside Counsel/Consultants

Sagamore Associates, Inc.
Rep By: Dena S. Morris, David Nichols

Northern Indiana Public Service Co.

Hammond, IN
Leg. Issues: ENG, ENV, FUE, GOV, NAT, SCI, UTI

Outside Counsel/Consultants

Liebman & Associates, Inc.
Issues: ENG, ENV, FUE, GOV, NAT, SCI, UTI
Rep By: Murray Liebman

Northern Ireland, Government of

Belfast, IRELAND

Outside Counsel/Consultants

Morgan, Lewis & Bockius LLP

Northern Mariana Islands, Commonwealth of the

2121 R St. NW
Washington, DC 20008-1908
Tel: (202)673-5869
Fax: (202)673-5873
Registered: LDA

The constitutionally mandated office of the resident representative to the United States serving as the arm for the Government of the Northern Mariana Islands on all official matters relating to the federal government.

Leg. Issues: COM, SCI, TEC

In-house, DC-area Employees

BABAUTA, Juan N.: Resident Representative to the U.S.
BERDON, Trinidad T.: Fiscal Officer
KIYOSHI, Michael J.: Federal Programs Coordinator
MCDERMOTT, Rose: Federal Programs Coordinator
PANGELINAN, Edward: Special Assistant, Washington Representative
REYES, Paul: Assistant Fiscal Officer
SAURES, Emeterio: Federal Programs Coordinator
SWALBACH, Robert: Congressional Liaison
TAITANO, Francisco I.: Federal Programs Coordinator
TORRES, Peter A.: Federal Programs Coordinator

Outside Counsel/Consultants

Law Offices of Thomas K. Crowe
Issues: COM, SCI, TEC
Rep By: Thomas K. Crowe

Miller & Van Eaton, P.L.L.C.
Issues: TEC
Rep By: Betty Ann Kane, William Malone

Northern Michigan University

Leg. Issues: EDU

Outside Counsel/Consultants

Preston Gates Ellis & Rouvelas Meeds LLP
Issues: EDU
Rep By: Cindy O'Malley, Tim L. Peckinpaugh, Mark H. Ruge

Northern Textile Ass'n

Boston, MA
Leg. Issues: APP

Outside Counsel/Consultants

SRG & Associates
Issues: APP
Rep By: Augustine D. Tantillo

Northland Cranberries, Inc.

Wisconsin Rapids, WI
Leg. Issues: AGR

Outside Counsel/Consultants

Broydrick & Associates
Rep By: William Broydrick

Foley & Lardner
Issues: AGR
Rep By: Theodore H. Bornstein

Northland Holdings, Inc.

Seattle, WA
Leg. Issues: MAR

Outside Counsel/Consultants

Jack Ferguson Associates, Inc.
Issues: MAR
Rep By: Raga Elim, Jack Ferguson

Winston & Strawn
Issues: MAR
Rep By: H. Allen Black, III, Hon. James H. Burnley, IV, Lawrence I. Kiern, Thomas L. Mills, Joseph E. O'Leary, Constantine G. Papavizas, James T. Pitts, Douglas C. Richardson

NorthPoint Communications, Inc.

San Francisco, CA
Leg. Issues: COM, TEC

Outside Counsel/Consultants

Lawler, Metzger & Milkman, LLC
Issues: COM, TEC
Rep By: Ruth M. Milkman

Northpoint Technology, Ltd.

Portsmouth, NH

A communications engineering firm.

Leg. Issues: COM, TEC

Outside Counsel/Consultants

Akin, Gump, Strauss, Hauer & Feld, L.L.P.
Issues: TEC
Rep By: Barney J. Skladany, Jr., James R. Tucker, Jr.

American Continental Group, Inc.
Issues: COM
Rep By: Steve Colovas, Shawn H. Smeallie, Peter Terpeluk, Jr.

Podesta/Mattoon
Issues: COM
Rep By: Ann Delory, Kimberley Fritts, Claudia James, Kristen Leary

Preston Gates Ellis & Rouvelas Meeds LLP
Issues: TEC
Rep By: Lisa L. Friedlander, Hon. Lloyd Meeds, Martin L. Stern

Northrop Grumman Corp.

1000 Wilson Blvd.
Suite 2300
Arlington, VA 22209
Tel: (703)875-8400
Fax: (703)276-0711
Registered: LDA

Headquartered in Los Angeles, CA.

Leg. Issues: AER, BUD, DEF, ENG, ENV, MAN, MAR, TAX, TRA, TRD

In-house, DC-area Employees

HAMILTON, Larry: Director, Washington Public Affairs
HARPER, Diane: Manager, Legislative Affairs
HELM, Robert W.: Corporate V. President, Government Relations
KWALWASSER, Marsha
LAVRAKAS, Susan C.
MELTSNER, Jim: Manager, Legislative Affairs
MILLER, B. Parker: Manager, Legislative Affairs
O'TOOLE, Diane: Manager, Legislative Affairs
SUTTON, Steve: Manager, Legislative Affairs
WOODS, Jerry: Manager, Legislative Affairs

Outside Counsel/Consultants

American Systems Internat'l Corp.
Issues: DEF, MAN
Rep By: Robert D. McVey, William H. Skipper, Jr.

Morris J. Amitay, P.C.
Issues: DEF
Rep By: Morris J. Amitay

Bonner & Associates

John G. Campbell, Inc.
Issues: DEF
Rep By: John G. Campbell

Collins & Company, Inc.
Issues: DEF
Rep By: James D. Bond, Richard L. Collins, Thomas A. Hooper, Shay D. Stautz

Dyer Ellis & Joseph, P.C.
Issues: DEF
Rep By: Brian A. Bannon, James S. W. Drewry, Thomas M. Dyer, Duncan C. Smith, III, Jennifer M. Southwick

Ervin Technical Associates, Inc. (ETA)
Issues: AER, DEF
Rep By: Hon. Jack Edwards, James L. Ervin, Hon. Joseph M. McDade, Donald E. Richbourg

Gibson, Dunn & Crutcher LLP
Rep By: Hon. Meldon E. Levine, Alan A. Platt

Martin G. Hamberger & Associates
Issues: BUD, DEF
Rep By: Martin G. Hamberger

Johnston & Associates, LLC
Issues: BUD, DEF
Rep By: Hon. J. Bennett Johnston, N. Hunter Johnston, W. Proctor Jones, Eric Tober

Law Office of Zel E. Lipsen
Issues: AER, MAN
Rep By: Adam Emanuel, Zel E. Lipsen

Diane McRee Associates
Issues: BUD, DEF
Rep By: Diane B. McRee

Denny Miller McBee Associates
Issues: DEF

The Potomac Advocates
Issues: DEF
Rep By: Charles Scalera, Gary L. Sojka

Timmons and Co., Inc.
Issues: DEF, TAX, TRD
Rep By: Michael J. Bates, Douglas F. Bennett, Ellen B. Fitzgibbons, Bryce L. "Larry" Harlow, Timothy J. Keating, Tom C. Korologos, Richard J. Tarplin, William E. Timmons, Jr., William E. Timmons, Sr.

Donald E. Wilson Consulting
Issues: DEF

Northrop Marine

Sunnyvale, CA

Outside Counsel/Consultants

The PMA Group
Rep By: Kaylene Green, Gregory L. Hansen, Paul J. Magliocchetti

Northside Hospital

Leg. Issues: HCR, MMM

Outside Counsel/Consultants

McDermott, Will and Emery
Issues: HCR, MMM
Rep By: Wendy L. Krasner, Maggie A. Mitchell, Karen S. Sealander

Northside Savings Bank

Floral Park, NY

Outside Counsel/Consultants

McDermott, Will and Emery
Rep By: Wendy L. Krasner, Karen S. Sealander, Eric P. Zimmerman

Northstar Corridor Development Authority

Anoka, MN
Leg. Issues: BUD

Outside Counsel/Consultants

Mullenholz, Brimsek & Belair
Issues: BUD
Rep By: John R. Brimsek

Northwest Airlines, Inc.

901 15th St. NW
Suite 310
Washington, DC 20005
Tel: (202)842-3193
Fax: (202)289-6834
Registered: LDA
Leg. Issues: ADV, AVI, BUD, CAW, ECN, FIN, IMM, LBR, POS, TAX, TOU, TRA, TRD, WAS

In-house, DC-area Employees

BETHKE, Cecilia D.: Director, International and Bilateral Affairs
FOUSHEE, Ph.D., Clay: V. President, International and Regulatory Affairs
MISHKIN, David G.: V. President, International and Regulatory Affairs
MOLLURA, A. Dennis: Director, Corporate Communications
VEITH, Sally: Director, Government and Legislative Affairs

Outside Counsel/Consultants

Baker, Donelson, Bearman & Caldwell, P.C.
Issues: AVI
Rep By: Linda Hall Daschle, Albert B. Randall

Bergner Bockorny Castagnetti and Hawkins
Issues: AVI, BUD, LBR
Rep By: Jeffrey T. Bergner, David A. Bockorny, David Castagnetti, Melissa Schulman

The Carmen Group
Issues: AVI
Rep By: Ryan Adesnik, Gerald P. Carmen

Dewey Square Group
Issues: TRA, TRD
Rep By: Charles A. Baker, III, Jon Patrick Baskette, Charles Campion, Michael Whouley

Hohlt & Associates
Issues: AVI, ECN, LBR, TAX, TOU, TRA

Michael E. Korens
Issues: AVI
Rep By: Michael E. Korens

McDermott, Will and Emery
Issues: AVI, LBR
Rep By: Teresita Nolla

Powell Tate

Robertson, Monagle & Eastaugh
Rep By: Steven W. Silver

Robins, Kaplan, Miller & Ciresi L.L.P.
Issues: AVI
Rep By: Charles A. Hunnicutt

Sunrise Research Corp.
Issues: AVI
Rep By: Hon. Bob Packwood

Verner, Liipfert, Bernhard, McPherson and Hand, Chartered
Issues: AVI
Rep By: Hon. James J. Blanchard, Denis J. Dwyer, Rosemary B. Freeman, Lloyd N. Hand, Harry C. McPherson, John A. Merrigan, Steven R. Phillips, Russell E. Pommer, David A. Weiss

Northwest Aluminum Co.

The Dalles, OR
Leg. Issues: ENG

Outside Counsel/Consultants

Ball Janik, LLP
Issues: ENG
Rep By: Robert G. Hayes, Irene Ringwood

Northwest Ecosystem Alliance

Bellingham, WA
Leg. Issues: BUD

Outside Counsel/Consultants

R. Duffy Wall and Associates
Issues: BUD
Rep By: Hon. Rodney D. Chandler

Northwest Energy Efficiency Alliance

Portland, OR
Leg. Issues: ENG, TEC

Outside Counsel/Consultants

The Coursen Group
Issues: ENG, TEC
Rep By: Hon. Christopher D. Coursen

Northwest Forestry Ass'n

Portland, OR
Registered: LDA

Outside Counsel/Consultants

Crowell & Moring LLP
Rep By: Steven P. Quarles

Northwest Horticultural Council

Yakima, WA
Leg. Issues: AGR, TRD

Outside Counsel/Consultants

James Nicholas Ashmore & Associates
Issues: AGR, TRD
Rep By: James Nicholas Ashmore

Northwest Indian Fisheries Commission

Olympia, WA

Outside Counsel/Consultants

SENSE, INC.
Rep By: C. Juliet Pittman

Northwest Kidney Center/Northwest Organ Procurement Agency

Seattle, WA
An organ procurement organization.

Outside Counsel/Consultants

Davis Wright Tremaine LLP

Northwest Municipal Conference

Des Moines, IL
Leg. Issues: BUD, ENV, URB

Outside Counsel/Consultants

The Carmen Group
Issues: BUD, ENV, URB
Rep By: Mia O'Connell

Northwest Pipe Co.

Portland, OR
Leg. Issues: BUD

Outside Counsel/Consultants

John M. Stinson
Issues: BUD
Rep By: John M. Stinson

Northwest Pipeline Corp

Salt Lake City, UT

Outside Counsel/Consultants

Wright & Talisman, P.C.
Rep By: James T. McManus

Northwest Public Power Ass'n

Vancouver, WA
Leg. Issues: ENG

Outside Counsel/Consultants

Morgan Meguire, LLC
Issues: ENG
Rep By: Scott Lindsay, Kyle G. Michel, Katie Parrott, C. Kyle Simpson, Deborah R. Sliz, Kiel Weaver

Northwest Regional Education Laboratory

Portland, OR
Leg. Issues: BUD, EDU

Outside Counsel/Consultants

Capitol Associates, Inc.
Issues: BUD, EDU
Rep By: Edward R. Long, Ph.D., Julie P. Pawelczyk

Northwest Woodland Owners Council

Portland, OR
Leg. Issues: TAX

Outside Counsel/Consultants

Ball Janik, LLP
Issues: TAX
Rep By: James A. Beall, M. Victoria Cram

Northwestern Memorial Hospital

Chicago, IL
Leg. Issues: BUD, HCR, MMM, TOB

Outside Counsel/Consultants

Capitol Associates, Inc.
Issues: BUD, HCR, TOB
Rep By: Debra M. Hardy Havens, Edward R. Long, Ph.D., Ronnie Kovner Tepp

Capitol Health Group, LLC
Issues: HCR, MMM
Rep By: Michael D. Bromberg, Shawn Coughlin, Steven Jenning, Layna McConkey Peltier

Foley & Lardner
Issues: HCR
Rep By: Jodi L. Hanson

O'Neill, Athy & Casey, P.C.
Rep By: Andrew Athy, Jr., Martha L. Casey

Northwestern Michigan College

Traverse City, MI
Leg. Issues: BUD

Outside Counsel/Consultants

Preston Gates Ellis & Rouvelas Meeds LLP
Issues: BUD
Rep By: Mark H. Ruge

Northwestern Mutual Life Insurance Co.

8444 West Park Dr.
Suite 600
McLean, VA 22102
Tel: (703)269-6600
Fax: (703)288-9181
Registered: LDA
Leg. Issues: BAN, BNK, FIN, INS, RET, TAX, TOR

Political Action Committee/s

Northwestern Mutual Life Insurance Co. Federal PAC
8444 West Park Dr.
Suite 600
McLean, VA 22102
Tel: (202)296-1020
Fax: (202)296-5855
Contact: Frederic H. Sweet

In-house, DC-area Employees
SWEET, Frederic H.: Senior V. President and PAC Director

Outside Counsel/Consultants
Higgins, McGovern & Smith, LLC
Issues: FIN, INS, TAX, TOR
Rep By: Lawrence Higgins
Patton Boggs, LLP
Issues: BAN, BNK, FIN, INS, RET, TAX
Rep By: John F. Jonas
The Smith-Free Group
Issues: FIN
Rep By: James E. Smith

Northwestern Public Service
Huron, SD
Outside Counsel/Consultants
Wright & Talisman, P.C.
Rep By: Michael E. Small

Northwestern Steel and Wire Co.
Sterling, IL
Outside Counsel/Consultants
Wiley, Rein & Fielding
Rep By: Eileen P. Bradner, Sharon R. Fine, Hon. Jim Slattery

Northwestern University
Evanston, IL
Leg. Issues: BUD
Outside Counsel/Consultants
Cassidy & Associates, Inc.
Issues: BUD
Rep By: Michael Merola, Sean O'Shea, Hon. Martin A. Russo, Rachel Sotsky

Northwood Inc.
Center Line, MI
Leg. Issues: MMM
Outside Counsel/Consultants
Dennis M. Hertel & Associates
Issues: MMM
Rep By: Hon. Dennis M. Hertel

Norton Sound Health Corp.
Nome, AK
Leg. Issues: IND
Outside Counsel/Consultants
Hobbs, Straus, Dean and Walker, LLP
Issues: IND
Rep By: Carol L. Barbero, S. Bobo Dean, Marie Osceola-Branch, Jerry C. Straus, Geoffrey D. Strommer, F. Michael Willis

Norwalk, California, City of
Leg. Issues: BUD
Outside Counsel/Consultants
The Ferguson Group, LLC
Issues: BUD
Rep By: William Ferguson, Jr., W. Roger Gwinn, Charmayne Macon, Leslie Waters Mozingo, Ralph Webb

Norway, Government of the Kingdom of
Oslo, NORWAY
Outside Counsel/Consultants
Kessler & Associates Business Services, Inc.

Norwegian Cruise Line
Miami, FL
Leg. Issues: GAM, MAR
Outside Counsel/Consultants
Alcalde & Fay
Issues: GAM, MAR
Rep By: Hector Alcalde, Cynthia Colenda

Nossaman, Gunther, Knox & Elliott
San Francisco, CA
Leg. Issues: ENV, RES, TRA
Outside Counsel/Consultants
French & Company
Issues: ENV, RES, TRA
Rep By: Rebecca Dornbusch, Verrick O. French

Nottoway, Virginia, County of
Leg. Issues: BUD, ECN, EDU
Outside Counsel/Consultants
Madison Government Affairs
Issues: BUD, ECN, EDU
Rep By: Paul J. Hirsch, Myron M. Jacobson

Nova Southeastern University
Fort Lauderdale, FL
Leg. Issues: BUD, HCR, HOU
Outside Counsel/Consultants
Cartwright & Riley
Issues: BUD, HCR, HOU
Rep By: Russell S. Cartwright

Novartis Corp.
701 Pennsylvania Ave. NW
Suite 725
Washington, DC 20004
Tel: (202)638-7429
Fax: (202)628-4763
Registered: LDA
Web: www.novartis.com

Major Life Sciences company with businesses in pharmaceuticals, nutrition, and consumer health.

Leg. Issues: ANI, BUD, CAW, CHM, CPT, ENV, FOO, GOV, HCR, LBR, MMM, NAT, PHA, SCI, TAX, TRD, WAS

Political Action Committee/s
Novartis Employee Good Government Fund
701 Pennsylvania Ave. NW
Suite 725
Washington, DC 20004
Tel: (202)638-7429
Fax: (202)628-4763
Contact: Mary O'Reilly

In-house, DC-area Employees
BUMBAUGH, Deborah M.: Director, Federal Government Relations
CASSERLY, Dan: Director, Federal Government Relations
DRAKE, David P.: Director, Federal Government Relations
ELKIN, James R.: Exec. Director, Federal Government Relations
FRENCH, David: Director, Communications and Public Affairs
HALLER, Tracy: Director, Federal Government Relations
KING, Rachel K.: Senior V. President, Corporate Government Relations
LACEY, Jamie P.: Director, Communications and Public Affairs
O'REILLY, Mary: Manager, Legislative Affairs
ROSEN, Burt E.: V. President, Pharmaceutical Government Relations

Outside Counsel/Consultants
The Accord Group
Issues: CAW, ENV, FOO
Rep By: Robert F. Hurley
Arnold & Porter
Issues: MMM
Rep By: Grant Bagley
Bennett Turner & Coleman, LLP
C&M Internat'l, Ltd.
Issues: TRD
Rep By: Kathryn B. Clemans, Doral S. Cooper, Melissa Coyle
Kessler & Associates Business Services, Inc.
Issues: BUD, ENV, HCR, MMM, TAX, TRD
Rep By: Richard S. Kessler, Harry Sporidis
The Legislative Strategies Group, LLC
Muse & Associates
Issues: HCR, MMM
Rep By: Donald N. Muse
Ricchetti Inc.
R. Duffy Wall and Associates
Issues: HCR, SCI
Rep By: Hon. Bill Brewster, Ann Thomas G. Johnston
Williams & Jensen, P.C.
Issues: PHA
Rep By: George G. Olsen

Novartis Crop Protection
Greensboro, NC
Leg. Issues: AGR, CHM
Outside Counsel/Consultants
EOP Group, Inc.
Issues: AGR, CHM
Rep By: Jonathan Gledhill, Troy Hillier, Michael O'Bannon

Novartis Services, Inc.
701 Pennsylvania Ave. NW
Seventh Floor
Washington, DC 20004
Tel: (202)638-7429
Fax: (202)628-4763
Registered: LDA
Web: www.novartis.com
Leg. Issues: AGR, ENV, HCR, MED, TRD

In-house, DC-area Employees
BUMBAUGH, Deborah M.
CASSERLY, Dan: Director, Federal Government Relations
DRAKE, David P.
ELKIN, James R.
HALLER, Tracy
KING, Rachel K.

Novato, California, City of
Leg. Issues: DEF
Outside Counsel/Consultants
The Ferguson Group, LLC
Issues: DEF
Rep By: William Ferguson, Jr.

Novell, Inc.
2323 Horsepen Rd.
Suite 600
Herndon, VA 20171
Tel: (703)713-3500
Fax: (703)713-3555
Registered: LDA
Web: www.novell.com

A network software company.

Leg. Issues: CPI, CPT, FIN, FOR, IMM, LBR, MIA, SCI, TAX, TEC, TRD

In-house, DC-area Employees
BURTON, Jr., Daniel F.: V. President, Government Relations
SCHMIDT, Eric

Outside Counsel/Consultants
Arnold & Porter

NOW Solutions, Inc.
Santa Clara, CA
Leg. Issues: DEF, TRA
Outside Counsel/Consultants
Peter J. Rose
Issues: DEF, TRA
Rep By: Peter J. Rose

NPES, The Ass'n for Suppliers of Printing, Publishing, and Converting Technologies
1899 Preston White Dr.
Reston, VA 20191-4367
Tel: (703)264-7200
Fax: (703)620-0994
Registered: LDA
Web: www.npes.org
E-mail: npes@npes.org
Leg. Issues: CAW, CPT, CSP, ENV, LBR, TRD

In-house, DC-area Employees
DELMONTAGNE, Regis J.: President
HURLBURT, Carol J.: Director, Communications and Marketing
HURLEY, Michael W.: Director, International Trade
NUZZACO, Mark J.: Director, Government Affairs
PAULINO, Erin: Government Affairs Representative
SMYTHE, William K.: V. President

Outside Counsel/Consultants
Valis Associates
Issues: CSP, ENV, TRD
Rep By: Hon. Richard T. Schulze, Todd Tolson, Wayne H. Valis

nPower Advisors, LLC
San Francisco, CA
Leg. Issues: CPI, LBR, RET, SMB, TAX
Outside Counsel/Consultants
Buchanan Ingersoll, P.C.
Issues: CPI, LBR, RET, SMB, TAX
Rep By: Norma N. Sharara, Linda K. Shore

NRG Energy, Inc.
Minneapolis, MN
Leg. Issues: BUD, CAW, ENG, ENV, FOR, FUE, NAT, TAX, UTI
Outside Counsel/Consultants
EZ's Solutions, Inc.
Issues: BUD, CAW, ENG, ENV, FOR, FUE, NAT, TAX, UTI
Rep By: Elaine Ziemba

NSTAR
Boston, MA
Leg. Issues: UTI
Outside Counsel/Consultants
Walker F. Nolan
Issues: UTI
Rep By: Walker F. Nolan

NTS Development Corporation
Outside Counsel/Consultants
Columbus Public Affairs

NTS Mortgage Income Fund
Louisville, KY
Leg. Issues: BUD

Outside Counsel/Consultants

The Grizzle Company
Issues: BUD
Rep By: Richard A. Cantor, Charles L. Grizzle

NTT America

New York, NY
Leg. Issues: COM, TRD

Outside Counsel/Consultants

Hogan & Hartson L.L.P.
Issues: COM, TRD
Rep By: Lance D. Bultena, William Michael House, Jeffrey W. Munk, Joel S. Winnik

Paul Muroyama & Assoc.
Rep By: Paul Muroyama

Nu Skin Internat'l Inc.

Provo, UT
Leg. Issues: ADV, FOO

Outside Counsel/Consultants

Parry, Romani, DeConcini & Symms
Issues: ADV, FOO
Rep By: Edward H. Baxter, Hon. Dennis DeConcini, John M. Haddow, Scott D. Hatch, Shannon Davis Henderson, Jack W. Martin, Romano Romani, Linda Arey Skladany, Hon. Steven D. Symms

Nu Thena Systems, Inc.

McLean, VA
Leg. Issues: AER, BUD, DEF

Outside Counsel/Consultants

Ritter and Bourjaily, Inc.
Issues: AER, BUD, DEF
Rep By: Monte F. Bourjaily, III

Nucentrix Broadband Networks

Plano, TX

Outside Counsel/Consultants

Sher & Blackwell
Rep By: Earl W. Comstock, Jeffrey R. Pike

Nuclear Control Institute

1000 Connecticut Ave. NW
Suite 804
Washington, DC 20036
Tel: (202)822-8444
Fax: (202)452-0892
Registered: LDA
Web: www.nci.org/nci/
E-mail: nci@nci.org

A non-profit educational organization concerned with the proliferation of plutonium and highly-enriched uranium. Opposes the proliferation of sensitive nuclear technology, fissile materials, and reprocessing technology.

Leg. Issues: ENG

In-house, DC-area Employees

CLEMENTS, Tom: Exec. Director
LEVENTHAL, Paul: President

Nuclear Energy Institute

1776 I St. NW
Suite 400
Washington, DC 20006-3708
Tel: (202)739-8000
Fax: (202)785-4019
Registered: LDA
Web: www.nei.org
Leg. Issues: BUD, CAW, DEF, ECN, ENG, ENV, GOV, NAT, SCI, TAX, TRD, UTI, WAS

Political Action Committee/s

Nuclear Energy Institute Federal Political Action Committee
1776 I St. NW
Suite 400
Washington, DC 20006-3708
Tel: (202)739-8000
Fax: (202)785-4019
Contact: Ellie A. Shaw

In-house, DC-area Employees

BARBOUR, Leslie P.: Director, Legislative Programs
BEEDLE, Ralph: Senior V. President and Chief Nuclear Officer, Nuclear Generation
BISHOP, Robert W.: V. President, General Counsel, Secretary, and Treasurer
COLVIN, Joe F.: President and Chief Exec. Officer
FERTEL, Marvin: Senior V. President, Business Operations
HAGAN, James G.: Director, Legislative Programs
HOWARD, Angelina S.: Exec. V. President, Policy, Planning and External Affairs
KANE, John E.: V. President, Governmental Affairs
RICHARD, Michael T.: Director, Congressional Information Program
SHAW, Ellie A.: Governmental Affairs Coordinator
SLOMINSKI, Jerry: Director, Legislative Programs
WOLLERTON, Chinch V.: Senior Director, Legislative Programs

Outside Counsel/Consultants

The Advocacy Group
Issues: BUD, WAS
Rep By: John M. Nugent, Jr., George A. Ramonas

Alexander Strategy Group
Issues: ENG, WAS
Rep By: Edwin A. Buckham

Ray Billups
Issues: ENG
Rep By: Ray Billups

Bill Carney & Co.
Issues: BUD, ENG, WAS
Rep By: Hon. William Carney

EOP Group, Inc.
Issues: BUD, WAS
Rep By: Donald Gesseman, Joseph Hezir, Jan Mares, Corey McDaniel

Hohlt & Associates
Issues: BUD, ENG, TAX, WAS
Rep By: Richard F. Hohlt

Jefferson Consulting Group
Rep By: Robert J. Thompson

Johnston & Associates, LLC
Issues: BUD, ENG, GOV
Rep By: Hon. J. Bennett Johnston, N. Hunter Johnston, W. Proctor Jones, Eric Tober

O'Connor & Hannan, L.L.P.
Issues: ENG, ENV, GOV, SCI, UTI
Rep By: Roy C. Coffee

The Renkes Group, Ltd.
Issues: ENG
Rep By: Patrick Pettey, Gregg D. Renkes

Sagamore Associates, Inc.
Issues: BUD, ENG
Rep By: David Nichols, Doug Wasitis

The Smith-Free Group
Issues: ENG
Rep By: James C. Free, W. Timothy Locke, Alicia W. Smith

Michael L. Tiner
Issues: WAS
Rep By: Michael L. Tiner

Nuclear Information and Resource Service

1424 16th St. NW
Suite 404
Washington, DC 20036
Tel: (202)328-0002
Fax: (202)462-2183
Web: www.nirs.org
E-mail: nirsnet@nirs.org

A national clearinghouse for information on nuclear power and safe energy alternatives.

In-house, DC-area Employees

CAMPS, Kevin: Director, Radioactive Waste Project
GUNTER, Paul: Director, Reactor Watchdog Project
MARIOTTE, Michael: Exec. Director

Nuclear Threat Initiative

1747 Pennsylvania Ave. NW
7th Floor
Washington, DC 20006
Tel: (202)296-4810
Fax: (202)296-4811

Founded by Ted Turner and former Senator Sam Nunn (D-GA) to combat the threat of nuclear arms and other weapons of mass destruction.

In-house, DC-area Employees

ANDERSON, Brooke: V. President for Communications
HAMBURGER, Margaret: V. President for Biological Programs
HOLGATE, Laura: V. President for Russia
ROHLFING, Joan: Senior V. President for Operations

Nuevo Energy

Houston, TX
Leg. Issues: ENG

Outside Counsel/Consultants

Morgan Meguire, LLC
Issues: ENG
Rep By: Scott Lindsay, Kyle G. Michel, Katie Parrott, C. Kyle Simpson, Deborah R. Sliz, Kiel Weaver

NUI Environmental Group Inc.

Union, NJ

A gas distribution company.

Leg. Issues: BUD, ENV

Outside Counsel/Consultants

Chambers Associates Inc.
Issues: BUD, ENV
Rep By: Letitia Chambers

Nurses Organization of Veterans Affairs

Washington, DC
Web: www.vanurse.org
E-mail: nova@vanurse.org

Outside Counsel/Consultants

William S. Bergman Associates
Rep By: Deborah Beck

Nutra-Park

Outside Counsel/Consultants

The DCS Group

Nutrition Screening Initiative, The

A multi-disciplinary healthcare advocacy organization. Membership includes the American Academy of Family Physicians, the American Dietetic Ass'n and the Nat'l Council on the Aging.

Outside Counsel/Consultants

Greer, Margolis, Mitchell, Burns & Associates
Rep By: Alison Coleman, David A. Smith

Nuvotec

Richland, WA

Outside Counsel/Consultants

Chambers Associates Inc.

NxtWave Communications

Langhorne, PA
Leg. Issues: COM

Outside Counsel/Consultants

Verner, Liipfert, Bernhard, McPherson and Hand, Chartered
Issues: COM
Rep By: Sara W. Morris, David R. Siddall, Lawrence R. Sidman

NYK Bulkship, Inc.

New York, NY

Outside Counsel/Consultants

Oppenheimer Wolff & Donnelly LLP
Rep By: Harry W. Cladouhos, John H. Korns

Nylo-Flex Manufacturing Co., Inc.

Mobile, AL

Outside Counsel/Consultants

Max N. Berry Law Offices
Rep By: Max N. Berry

NYSCOPBA - New York State Correctional Officers & Police Benevolent Ass'n

Albany, NY
Leg. Issues: BUD, IMM, LAW, LBR

Outside Counsel/Consultants

Capitol Strategies
Issues: BUD, IMM, LAW
Rep By: Mary M. Tripp

Shannon M. Lahey Associates
Issues: LAW, LBR
Rep By: Shannon M. Lahey

O'Connor & Hannan, L.L.P.

1666 K St. NW
Suite 500
Washington, DC 20006-2803
Tel: (202)887-1400
Fax: (202)466-2198
Registered: LDA, FARA
Web: www.oconnorhannan.com
E-mail: oh@oconnorhannan.com
Leg. Issues: ENV

In-house, DC-area Employees

ADLER, Gary C.: Partner
ADLER, Robert M.: Partner
BARRIE, Robert W.: Senior Government Relations Advisor
BECK, Edward
COFFEE, Roy C.: Partner
CORCORAN, Hon. Thomas J.: Partner
DOMBO, Frederick T.: Associate
FAGRE, Danielle: Associate
FLEPS, Christina W.: Partner
HARMALA, Robert
HIMMELBERG, John M.: Partner
JENKINS, Timothy W.: Partner
KOENIGS, Craig A.: Associate
LEE, F. Gordon: Partner
MANNINA, Jr., George J.: Partner
MANTON, Hon. Thomas J.: Of Counsel
MELINCOFF, David R.: Partner
NICKERSON, William
O'CONNOR, Patrick J.: Senior Partner
O'DONNELL, Patrick E.: Partner
POTTER, J. Craig: Partner
PRESSLER, Hon. Larry: Partner
QUINN, Thomas H.: Partner
REED, III, Morgan W.: Legislative Consultant
SCHNEIDER, Thomas J.: Of Counsel

SPRINGER, David E.: Partner
SYMINGTON, Hon. James W.: Partner

Outside Counsel/Consultants

Symms, Lehn & Associates, Inc.
Issues: ENV

O'Gara-Hess & Eisenhardt

Fairfield, OH
Leg. Issues: DEF

Outside Counsel/Consultants

Boesch & Co.
Issues: DEF
Rep By: Doyce A. Boesch

O'Grady Peyton Internat'l

Boston, MA
Leg. Issues: IMM

Outside Counsel/Consultants

GPC Internat'l
Issues: IMM
Rep By: Bruce A. Morrison

O'Neill Properties Group

King of Prussia, PA

Outside Counsel/Consultants

Valente Lopatin & Schulze
Rep By: Mark Valente, III

John T. O'Rourke Law Offices

801 Pennsylvania Ave. NW
Fifth Floor
Washington, DC 20004
Tel: (202)662-4720
Fax: (202)662-4748
Registered: LDA
Leg. Issues: TAX

In-house, DC-area Employees

LAZARUS, Maggi A.: Associate
O'ROURKE, John T.: Principal

Outside Counsel/Consultants

Barents Group LLC
Issues: TAX
Rep By: David M. Skanderson, Linden C. Smith

George C. Tagg
Issues: TAX
Rep By: George C. Tagg

Oak Ridge, Tennessee, City of

Leg. Issues: ECN

Outside Counsel/Consultants

Kutak Rock LLP
Issues: ECN
Rep By: Seth Kirshenberg

Oakland Airport

Oakland, CA

Outside Counsel/Consultants

Pierre E. Murphy Law Offices

Oakland County Board of Supervisors

Pontiac, MI

Outside Counsel/Consultants

Government Relations, Inc.
Rep By: Thomas J. Bulger

Oakland, California, City of

Leg. Issues: DEF, EDU, ENV, TRA, WEL

Outside Counsel/Consultants

The Ferguson Group, LLC
Issues: DEF
Rep By: William Ferguson, Jr.

Greenberg Traurig, LLP
Issues: EDU, ENV, TRA, WEL
Rep By: Diane J. Blagman

Oakland, California, Port of

Leg. Issues: TRA

Outside Counsel/Consultants

Patton Boggs, LLP
Issues: TRA
Rep By: Philip A. Bangert

Oakland, Michigan, County of

Pontiac, MI
Leg. Issues: AVI, BUD, HOU, ROD, TRA

Outside Counsel/Consultants

Government Relations, Inc.
Issues: AVI, BUD, HOU, ROD, TRA
Rep By: Thomas J. Bulger, Mark H. Miller, John N. Young

Oakley, California, City of

Leg. Issues: LAW

Outside Counsel/Consultants

Simon and Co., Inc.
Issues: LAW
Rep By: Heather Barber, Alex DeGood, Leonard S. Simon

OAO Corp.

Greenbelt, MD
Leg. Issues: AER, DEF

Outside Counsel/Consultants

Cottone and Huggins Group
Issues: AER, DEF
Rep By: James B. Huggins

OBWEO

Hobart, OK
Leg. Issues: AGR

Outside Counsel/Consultants

Stephens Law Offices
Issues: AGR
Rep By: J. Gordon "Skip" Stephens, Jr.

Ocala, Florida, City of

Leg. Issues: GOV

Outside Counsel/Consultants

Duncan, Weinberg, Genzer & Pembroke, P.C.
Issues: GOV
Rep By: Janice L. Lower

Occidental Chemical Corporation

Dallas, TX

Outside Counsel/Consultants

Snavely, King, Majoros, O'Connor and Lee, Inc.
Rep By: Tom O'Connor

Occidental Internat'l Corporation

1717 Pennsylvania Ave. NW
Suite 400
Washington, DC 20006
Tel: (202)857-3000
Fax: (202)857-3030
Registered: LDA

The government affairs office of the parent company, Occidental Petroleum Corp. (see separate listing), headquartered in Los Angeles, CA.

Leg. Issues: CHM, ENG, ENV, FUE, GOV, TAX, TOR, TRD, UTI

Political Action Committee/s

OXYPAC

1717 Pennsylvania Ave. NW
Suite 400
Washington, DC 20006
Contact: Robert M. McGee
Tel: (202)857-3000
Fax: (202)857-3030

In-house, DC-area Employees

ARCHULETA, R. M. Julie: V. President, Government Affairs
COLLINS, William A.: Director, Health, Environment and Safety
DAVIS, Ian M.: V. President, International Affairs
HASSETT, Jace: Director, Legislative and Regulatory Affairs
MCGEE, Robert M.: President and Chief Exec. Officer
MCPHEE, Gerald T.: V. President, Federal Relations

Outside Counsel/Consultants

BKSH & Associates
Issues: GOV, TAX

Occidental Petroleum Corporation

1717 Pennsylvania Ave. NW
Suite 400
Washington, DC 20006
Tel: (202)857-3000
Fax: (202)857-3030

In-house, DC-area Employees

MCGEE, Robert M.: V. President

Oce-USA, Inc.

Chicago, IL
Leg. Issues: MAN

Outside Counsel/Consultants

Reed, Smith, LLP
Issues: MAN
Rep By: Marc Scheineson

Ocean Carriers Working Group

Washington, DC
Leg. Issues: MAR

Outside Counsel/Consultants

Sher & Blackwell
Issues: MAR
Rep By: John W. Butler, Marc J. Fink, Jeffrey R. Pike, Stanley O. Sher

Ocean County, NJ Utilities Authority

Leg. Issues: BUD, ENV, NAT, RES, TOU

Outside Counsel/Consultants

Reed, Smith, LLP
Issues: BUD, ENV, NAT, RES, TOU
Rep By: Christopher L. Rissetto

Ocean Futures Soc., Inc.

Santa Barbara, CA
Leg. Issues: ANI

Outside Counsel/Consultants

Perkins Coie LLP
Issues: ANI
Rep By: W. H. "Buzz" Fawcett

Ocean Isle Beach, North Carolina, Town of

Leg. Issues: BUD, NAT

Outside Counsel/Consultants

Marlowe and Co.
Issues: BUD, NAT
Rep By: Howard Marlowe, Jeffrey Mazzella

Ocean Services

Seattle, WA
Leg. Issues: MAR

Outside Counsel/Consultants

Zane & Associates
Issues: MAR
Rep By: Curtis J. Zane

Ocean Shipholding, Inc.

Houston, TX
Leg. Issues: TRA

Outside Counsel/Consultants

Robertson, Monagle & Eastaugh
Issues: TRA
Rep By: Bradley D. Gilman, Rick E. Marks

Ocean Spray Cranberries

Lakeville-Middleboro, MA
Leg. Issues: AGR, CAW, ENV, NAT

Outside Counsel/Consultants

Cassidy & Associates, Inc.
Issues: AGR, CAW, ENV, NAT
Rep By: Gerald S. J. Cassidy, John S. Doyle, Jr., Christy Carson Evans, Carl Franklin Godfrey, Jr., Mary Kate Kelly-Johnson, Arthur D. Mason, Daniel J. McNamara, Sean O'Shea, Louie Perry, James Rowan, Gabor J. Rozsa

Ocean Village Property Owners Ass'n, Inc.

Fort Pierce, FL
Leg. Issues: BUD, NAT

Outside Counsel/Consultants

Marlowe and Co.
Issues: BUD, NAT
Rep By: Howard Marlowe, Jeffrey Mazzella

Ocean World Lines, Inc.

Outside Counsel/Consultants

Rodriguez O'Donnell Fuerst Gonzalez & Williams
Rep By: Ashley W. Craig

Oceanside, California, City of

Leg. Issues: DEF, DIS, ECN, MAR, NAT, ROD

Outside Counsel/Consultants

The Ferguson Group, LLC
Issues: DEF, DIS, ECN, MAR, NAT, ROD
Rep By: William Ferguson, Jr., W. Roger Gwinn, Leslie Waters Mozingo

Ochsner Medical Institutions

New Orleans, LA
Registered: LDA
Leg. Issues: BUD, MED

Outside Counsel/Consultants

Van Scoyoc Associates, Inc.
Issues: BUD, MED
Rep By: Jan Schoonmaker, H. Stewart Van Scoyoc

OCI Wyoming
Green River, WY
Leg. Issues: LBR

Outside Counsel/Consultants

Patton Boggs, LLP
Issues: LBR
Rep By: Henry Chajet

Ocwen Federal Savings Bank
Outside Counsel/Consultants

Columbus Public Affairs

Oerlikon Aerospace, Inc.
Quebec, CANADA

A defense, communications, and electronics systems manufacturer.

Leg. Issues: DEF, TRD

Outside Counsel/Consultants

Verner, Liipfert, Bernhard, McPherson and Hand, Chartered
Issues: DEF, TRD
Rep By: Lloyd N. Hand

Office and Professional Employees Internat'l Union
1660 L St. NW
Suite 801
Washington, DC 20036
Tel: (202)393-4464
Fax: (202)347-0649
Leg. Issues: HCR

Political Action Committee/s

Voice of the Electorate (Office and Professional Employees Professional Internat'l Union)
1660 L St. NW
Suite 801
Washington, DC 20036
Tel: (202)393-4464
Fax: (202)347-0649
Contact: Gilles Beauregard

In-house, DC-area Employees

BEAUREGARD, Gilles: Secretary-Treasurer

Outside Counsel/Consultants

McGlotten & Jarvis
Issues: HCR
Rep By: Robert M. McGlotten

Office for the Advancement of Public Black Colleges
1307 New York Ave. NW
Suite 400
Washington, DC 20005
E-mail: paynej@nasulgc.org
Tel: (202)478-6049
Fax: (202)478-6046

In-house, DC-area Employees

PAYNE, Dr. N. Joyce: Director

Office of Hawaiian Affairs
Honolulu, HI
Leg. Issues: EDU, HCR, HOU

Outside Counsel/Consultants

Verner, Liipfert, Bernhard, McPherson and Hand, Chartered
Issues: EDU, HCR, HOU
Rep By: Denis J. Dwyer, Jenifer Martin

Office of Naval Research
Outside Counsel/Consultants

Alcalde & Fay
Rep By: J. B. Hancock

Office of the People's Counsel for the District of Columbia
1133 15th St. NW
Suite 500
Washington, DC 20005-2710
Tel: (202)727-3071
Fax: (202)727-1014

The statutorily created advocate for District of Columbia utility ratepayers.

In-house, DC-area Employees

NOEL, Elizabeth A.: People's Counsel

Official Artist Inc.
Beverly Hills, CA

A website design firm.

Outside Counsel/Consultants

Katten Muchin & Zavis
Rep By: Carol R. Van Cleef

Offshore Rig Museum, Inc.
Houston, TX
Leg. Issues: MAR

Outside Counsel/Consultants

Dyer Ellis & Joseph, P.C.
Issues: MAR
Rep By: Joan Bondareff, James S. W. Drewry, Duncan C. Smith, III, Jennifer M. Southwick

Ogden, Utah, City of
Leg. Issues: BUD

Outside Counsel/Consultants

Stites & Harbison
Issues: BUD
Rep By: Kenneth G. Lee

Oglala Lakota College
Kyle, SD
Leg. Issues: IND

Outside Counsel/Consultants

Sara Garland (and Associates)
Issues: IND
Rep By: Sara G. Garland

Oglala Sioux Tribe
Pine Ridge, SD
Leg. Issues: IND

Outside Counsel/Consultants

Morriset, Schlosser, Ayer & Jozwiak
Issues: IND
Rep By: Fran Ayer

Oglethorpe Power Corp.
Tucker, GA
Leg. Issues: ENG

Outside Counsel/Consultants

Verner, Liipfert, Bernhard, McPherson and Hand, Chartered
Issues: ENG
Rep By: David A. Fitzgerald, Sherry A. Quirk

Ohio Bureau of Employment Services
Columbus, OH
Leg. Issues: LBR

Outside Counsel/Consultants

Wise & Associates
Issues: LBR
Rep By: Dwayne Sattler

Ohio Cable Telecommunications Ass'n
Columbus, OH
Leg. Issues: COM

Outside Counsel/Consultants

Vorys, Sater, Seymour and Pease, LLP
Issues: COM

Ohio Hospital Ass'n
Columbus, OH
Leg. Issues: MMM

Outside Counsel/Consultants

Vinson & Elkins L.L.P.
Issues: MMM
Rep By: Larry A. Oday

Ohio Insurance Institute
Columbus, OH

Outside Counsel/Consultants

Vorys, Sater, Seymour and Pease, LLP

Ohio Municipal Electric Ass'n
Columbus, OH
Registered: LDA
Leg. Issues: ENG

Outside Counsel/Consultants

Kanner & Associates
Issues: ENG
Rep By: Martin B. Kanner

Spiegel & McDiarmid

Ohio Prosecuting Attorneys Ass'n
Columbus, OH

Outside Counsel/Consultants

Wright & Talisman, P.C.
Rep By: Scott M. DuBoff

Ohio River Valley Water Sanitation Commission
Cincinnati, OH
Leg. Issues: ENV

Outside Counsel/Consultants

Sagamore Associates, Inc.
Issues: ENV
Rep By: Julia P. Church, Doug Wasitis

Ohio Senate Republican Caucus
Columbus, OH

Outside Counsel/Consultants

Wilson Grand Communications
Rep By: Paul O. Wilson

Ohio State University
Columbus, OH
Leg. Issues: BUD

Outside Counsel/Consultants

Cassidy & Associates, Inc.
Issues: BUD
Rep By: Christy Carson Evans, Dennis M. Kedzior, Arthur D. Mason, Diane Rinaldo, Mary E. Shields, Rachel Sotsky

Ohio Supercomputing Center
Columbus, OH

Outside Counsel/Consultants

F.B.A.
Rep By: J. R. Kirkland

Ohio Wesleyan University
Delaware, OH
Leg. Issues: BUD

Outside Counsel/Consultants

Beacon Consulting Group, Inc.
Issues: BUD
Rep By: Katherine L. Halpin, Gordon P. MacDougall, Lisa A. Stewart

Ohio, Office of the Attorney General of the State of
Columbus, OH

Outside Counsel/Consultants

Duncan, Weinberg, Genzer & Pembroke, P.C.
Rep By: James F. Flug

Ohio, Washington Office of the State of
444 N. Capitol St. NW
Suite 546
Washington, DC 20001
Tel: (202)624-5844
Fax: (202)624-5847

In-house, DC-area Employees

GARVIN, June: Director

Oklahoma City, Oklahoma, City of
Leg. Issues: BUD, CAW, HOU, LAW, ROD, TAX, TRA

Outside Counsel/Consultants

Murray, Scheer, Montgomery, Tapia & O'Donnell
Issues: BUD, CAW, HOU, LAW, ROD, TAX, TRA
Rep By: John H. Montgomery

Oklahoma Department of Transportation
Oklahoma City, OK
Leg. Issues: ROD, TRA

Outside Counsel/Consultants

Alan Mauk Associates, Ltd.
Issues: ROD, TRA
Rep By: Alan R. Mauk

Oklahoma Gas and Electric Co.
Oklahoma City, OK
Leg. Issues: ENV, UTI

Outside Counsel/Consultants

Williams & Jensen, P.C.
Issues: ENV, UTI
Rep By: George D. Baker, David E. Franasiak, George G. Olsen

Oklahoma Indian Gaming Ass'n
Outside Counsel/Consultants

Ietan Consulting
Rep By: Wilson Pipestem, Larry Rosenthal

Oklahoma Natural Gas Co.
Tulsa, OK

Outside Counsel/Consultants
G. Frank West
Rep By: G. Frank West

Oklahoma State Medical Ass'n
Oklahoma City, OK
Leg. Issues: BUD, CAW, FAM, HCR, MMM, TOB

Outside Counsel/Consultants
Murray, Scheer, Montgomery, Tapia & O'Donnell
Issues: BUD, CAW, FAM, HCR, MMM, TOB
Rep By: John H. Montgomery

Oklahoma, State of
Oklahoma City, OK
Leg. Issues: BUD, GOV

Outside Counsel/Consultants
VSAdc.com
Issues: BUD, GOV
Rep By: J. R. Reskovac, H. Stewart Van Scoyoc

Olan Mills Inc.
Chattanooga, TN

Outside Counsel/Consultants
Wiley, Rein & Fielding

Old Dominion University
Norfolk, VA

Outside Counsel/Consultants
F.B.A.
Rep By: J. R. Kirkland

Old Harbor Native Corp.
Old Harbor, AK

Outside Counsel/Consultants
Birch, Horton, Bittner & Cherot
Rep By: Thomas L. Albert, Roy S. Jones, Jr.

Old Sturbridge Village
Sturbridge, MA
Leg. Issues: BUD

Outside Counsel/Consultants
Beacon Consulting Group, Inc.
Issues: BUD
Rep By: Katherine L. Halpin, Gordon P. MacDougall, Lisa A. Stewart

Oldcastle Materials Group
Washington, DC
Leg. Issues: ROD

Outside Counsel/Consultants
Van Scoyoc Associates, Inc.
Issues: ROD
Rep By: Steven O. Palmer, H. Stewart Van Scoyoc

Older Women's League
666 11th St. NW
Suite 700
Washington, DC 20001
Web: www.owl-national.org
Tel: (202)783-6686
Fax: (202)638-2356

Founded in 1980, OWL is a grass-roots organization focusing on issues and problems concerning mid-life older women through a D.C. national office and over 100 local chapters.

In-house, DC-area Employees
BRICELAND-BETTS, Deborah: Exec. Director
GOTWALS, Amy E.: Director, Public Policy
MAATZ, Lisa: Deputy Director of Program Affairs
SOLIS, Lupe: President

Olga Coal Co.
McMurray, PA
A subsidiary of Lykes Corp.

Outside Counsel/Consultants
Heenan, Althen & Roles

Olin Corp.
Norwalk, CT
Leg. Issues: CHM, FIR, MON

Outside Counsel/Consultants
Robert E. Smith
Issues: CHM, FIR, MON
Rep By: Robert E. Smith

Olin Corp.-Winchester Division
East Alton, IL

Outside Counsel/Consultants
Denny Miller McBee Associates

Olivenhain Municipal Water District
Encinitas, CA
Leg. Issues: BUD, NAT

Outside Counsel/Consultants
The Furman Group
Issues: BUD, NAT
Rep By: Thomas M. James

Olney Boys and Girls Club
Olney, MD
Leg. Issues: BUD

Outside Counsel/Consultants
Hogan & Hartson L.L.P.
Issues: BUD
Rep By: C. Michael Gilliland, Christine M. Warnke

Olsten Health Services
Melville, NY
Leg. Issues: BUD, HCR, MMM, VET

Outside Counsel/Consultants
Epstein Becker & Green, P.C.
Issues: BUD, HCR, MMM, VET
Rep By: Joyce A. Cowan, Elizabeth A. Lewis

Olympic Aid
Aurora, Ontario, CANADA
Leg. Issues: FOR, GOV

Outside Counsel/Consultants
Verner, Liipfert, Bernhard, McPherson and Hand, Chartered
Issues: FOR, GOV
Rep By: Rosemary B. Freeman, Ted Loud, John H. Zentay

Omaha Tribe of Nebraska
Macy, NE
Leg. Issues: IND, TOB

Outside Counsel/Consultants
Capital Consultants Corp.
Issues: IND, TOB
Rep By: Barry Hodgson, Michael David Kaiser

Oman, Sultanate of
Muscat, OMAN

Outside Counsel/Consultants
Patton Boggs, LLP

OMB Watch
1742 Connecticut Ave. NW
Washington, DC 20009-1146
Web: www.ombwatch.org
E-mail: ombwatch@ombwatch.org
Tel: (202)234-8494
Fax: (202)234-8584

A non-profit research and advocacy organization that monitors administrative governance issues, primarily those involving the White House Office of Management and Budget (OMB). Established to call greater attention to the power of OMB and to promote a more open and accountable government.

In-house, DC-area Employees
BASS, Dr. Gary D.: Exec. Director
MCDERMOTT, Patrice: Policy Analyst

Omega Air
Alexandria, VA
Leg. Issues: DEF

Outside Counsel/Consultants
The PMA Group
Issues: DEF
Rep By: William E. Berl, Kaylene Green, Stephen Madey, Paul J. Magliocchetti, Briggs Shade

Omega Oil Co.
Houston, TX
Develops oil drilling and production technology.
Leg. Issues: ENG, FUE, NAT, SCI

Outside Counsel/Consultants
Kaye Scholer LLP
Issues: FUE, NAT
Rep By: Christopher R. Brewster
Denny Miller McBee Associates
Issues: ENG, FUE, SCI

Omni Internat'l
Rockville, MD

Outside Counsel/Consultants
Williams & Connolly
Rep By: Brendan V. Sullivan, Jr.

Omnicare, Inc.
Leg. Issues: HCR, MMM

Outside Counsel/Consultants
Reed, Smith, LLP
Issues: HCR, MMM
Rep By: Phillips S. Peter

Omniflight Helicopters, Inc.
Dallas, TX
Leg. Issues: AVI, DEF, MED

Outside Counsel/Consultants
Potomac Strategies Internat'l LLC
Issues: AVI, DEF, MED
Rep By: James K. Wholey

OMNIPLEX World Services Corp.
McLean, VA
Leg. Issues: GOV, LBR, SMB

Outside Counsel/Consultants
Akin, Gump, Strauss, Hauer & Feld, L.L.P.
Issues: GOV, LBR, SMB
Rep By: David Geanacopoulos, Charles W. Johnson, IV, Barney J. Skladany, Jr.

Omnitech Robotics Inc.
Englewood, CO
Leg. Issues: DEF

Outside Counsel/Consultants
The Carmen Group
Issues: DEF
Rep By: John Lagomarcino

On-Line Investment Services
Jersey City, NJ
Leg. Issues: BAN

Outside Counsel/Consultants
Blank Rome Comisky & McCauley, LLP
Issues: BAN
Rep By: J. Caleb Boggs, III, David A. Norcross

OnCare, Inc.
San Bruno, CA
A physician management company.

Outside Counsel/Consultants
Arter & Hadden
Rep By: Daniel L. Cohen, Hon. Thomas G. Loeffler

Onconova Inc.
Princeton, NJ
Leg. Issues: BUD, DEF, MED

Outside Counsel/Consultants
Ritter and Bourjaily, Inc.
Issues: BUD, DEF, MED
Rep By: Monte F. Bourjaily, III

One Economy Corp.
Works to expand Internet use in inner-city communities by providing urban families with computers and teaching them basic online computer skills.
Leg. Issues: BUD, ECN, HOU, TEC

Outside Counsel/Consultants
Capitol Coalitions Inc.
Issues: BUD, ECN, HOU, TEC
Rep By: Amy R. Mehlman, Brett P. Scott, Jarvis C. Stewart

Onehealthbank.com
Cranbury, NJ
Leg. Issues: HCR, VET

Outside Counsel/Consultants
Brown & Associates
Issues: HCR, VET
Rep By: Jesse Brown, Shirley Carozza, Edward P. Scott

Oneida Indian Nation of New York
Vernon, NY
Leg. Issues: CPI, GAM, IND, TAX

Outside Counsel/Consultants

McGuiness & Holch
Issues: CPI, GAM, IND, TAX
Rep By: Markham C. Erickson, Niels C. Holch

Zuckerman Spaeder L.L.P.
Issues: IND
Rep By: William W. Taylor, III, Ronald H. Weich

Oneida Ltd.

Oneida, NY

Outside Counsel/Consultants

Collier Shannon Scott, PLLC
Rep By: Laurence J. Lasoff, Robert W. Porter

Oneida Tribe of Indians of Wisconsin

Leg. Issues: IND

Outside Counsel/Consultants

PACE-CAPSTONE
Issues: IND
Rep By: Scott C. Dacey

ONEOK Bushton Processing, LLC

Leg. Issues: FUE

Outside Counsel/Consultants

Duncan, Weinberg, Genzer & Pembroke, P.C.
Issues: FUE
Rep By: Kathleen L. Mazure

ONEOK Energy Marketing & Trading Co.

Leg. Issues: FUE

Outside Counsel/Consultants

Duncan, Weinberg, Genzer & Pembroke, P.C.
Issues: FUE
Rep By: Kathleen L. Mazure

ONEOK Field Services, Inc.

Leg. Issues: FUE

Outside Counsel/Consultants

Duncan, Weinberg, Genzer & Pembroke, P.C.
Issues: FUE
Rep By: Kathleen L. Mazure

ONEOK Gas Transportation, LLC

Leg. Issues: FUE

Outside Counsel/Consultants

Duncan, Weinberg, Genzer & Pembroke, P.C.
Issues: FUE
Rep By: Kathleen L. Mazure

ONEOK Midcontinent Market Center, Inc.

Leg. Issues: FUE

Outside Counsel/Consultants

Duncan, Weinberg, Genzer & Pembroke, P.C.
Issues: FUE
Rep By: Kathleen L. Mazure

ONEOK Midstream Gas Supply, LLC

Leg. Issues: FUE

Outside Counsel/Consultants

Duncan, Weinberg, Genzer & Pembroke, P.C.
Issues: FUE
Rep By: Kathleen L. Mazure

ONEOK OkTex Pipeline Co.

Leg. Issues: FUE

Outside Counsel/Consultants

Duncan, Weinberg, Genzer & Pembroke, P.C.
Issues: FUE
Rep By: Kathleen L. Mazure

ONEOK, Inc.

53 D St. SE
Washington, DC 20003-4017
Web: www.oneok.com
Tel: (202)488-8624

Engaged in oil and gas exploration, processing, storage, transmission and gas marketing. Headquartered in Tulsa, OK.

In-house, DC-area Employees

WEST, G. Frank: Manager, Government Affairs - Federal

Oneonta Trading Corp.

Wenatchee, WA
Leg. Issues: AGR, BUD, FOR, TRD

Outside Counsel/Consultants

James Nicholas Ashmore & Associates
Issues: AGR, BUD, FOR, TRD
Rep By: James Nicholas Ashmore

Online Privacy Alliance

Outside Counsel/Consultants

Hogan & Hartson L.L.P.
Rep By: Christine A. Varney

Ontario, Ministry of Economic Development and Trade

Ottawa, Ontario, CANADA

Outside Counsel/Consultants

Hogan & Hartson L.L.P.

Open Group Electronic Messaging Ass'n (EMA) Forum

San Jose, CA
Web: www.ema.org
E-mail: info@ema.org
Leg. Issues: COM, CPI, CPT, FIN, GOV, TEC

Outside Counsel/Consultants

Wiley, Rein & Fielding
Issues: COM, CPI, CPT, FIN, GOV, TEC
Rep By: James T. Bruce, III

openNET Coalition

Washington, DC
Leg. Issues: CPI, TEC

Outside Counsel/Consultants

Bond & Company, Inc.
Issues: CPI, TEC
Rep By: Richard N. Bond, Eileen Kean

Simon Strategies/Mindbeam
Issues: TEC
Rep By: Gregory C. Simon, Kristan Van Hook

Operation Lifesaver Inc.

1420 King St.
Suite 401
Alexandria, VA 22314
Web: www.oli.org
E-mail: general@oli.org
Tel: (703)739-0308
Fax: (703)519-8267

An active, continuing public education program designed to eliminate collisions, deaths, and injuries at roadway and train track intersections and on railroad rights-of-way. Sponsored cooperatively by government agencies, highway safety organizations, and the nation's railroads.

In-house, DC-area Employees

HALL, Gerri L.: President

Operation Right to Know

Gaithersburg, MD

Concerned with the posture of the U.S. government towards evidence supporting the existence of UFOs.

Leg. Issues: GOV

Outside Counsel/Consultants

Paradigm Research Group
Issues: GOV
Rep By: Stephen G. Bassett

Operations Security Professionals Soc.

9200 Centerway Rd.
Gaithersburg, MD 20879
Web: www.opsec.org
Tel: (301)840-6642
Fax: (301)840-8502
Leg. Issues: AER, COM, CPI, DEF, DIS, ENG, FIR, FOR, GOV, IMM, LAW, MIA, SCI, TEC, TRD

In-house, DC-area Employees

HAMBY, Zhi Marie: Exec. Director

Outside Counsel/Consultants

Real Trends
Rep By: Zhi Marie Hamby

Operative Plasterers' and Cement Masons' Internat'l Ass'n of the U.S. and Canada

14405 Laurel Pl.
Suite 300
Laurel, MD 20707
Web: www.opcmia.org
Tel: (301)470-4200
Fax: (301)470-2502

An international labor organization affiliated with AFL-CIO Represents plasterers and cement masons. Headquartered in Laurel, MD.

Political Action Committee/s

Plasterers' and Cement Masons' Action Committee
14405 Laurel Pl.
Suite 300
Laurel, MD 20707
Contact: John J. Dougherty
Tel: (301)470-4200
Fax: (301)470-2502

In-house, DC-area Employees

DOUGHERTY, John J.: General President

Operator Communications, Inc.

Leg. Issues: TEC

Outside Counsel/Consultants

Greenberg Traurig, LLP
Issues: TEC
Rep By: Mitchell F. Brecher

Opportunity Capital Corp.

Fremont, CA

A small business investment firm.

Leg. Issues: SMB

Outside Counsel/Consultants

Thelen Reid & Priest LLP
Issues: SMB
Rep By: Barry I. Berkoff, William A. Kirk, Jr., Richard Y. Roberts

Opportunity Internat'l

Oak Brook, IL
Leg. Issues: ECN

Outside Counsel/Consultants

Colling Swift & Hynes
Issues: ECN
Rep By: Terese Colling, Robert J. Hynes, Jr.

Opportunity Medical, Inc.

Highland Park, IL

Outside Counsel/Consultants

The PMA Group
Rep By: Kaylene Green, Patrick Hiu, Paul J. Magliocchetti, Sandra Welch

Optical Disc Corp.

Santa Fe Springs, CA
Leg. Issues: TRD

Outside Counsel/Consultants

Birch, Horton, Bittner & Cherot
Issues: TRD
Rep By: Thomas L. Albert, Ronald G. Birch

Optical Laboratories Ass'n

P.O. Box 2000
Merrifield, VA 22116-2000
Web: www.ola-labs.org
E-mail: olalabs@aol.com
Tel: (703)359-2830
Fax: (703)359-2834

In-house, DC-area Employees

DZIUBAN, Robert L.: Exec. Director
HIMELFARB, Phyllis R.: Manager, Membership and Communications

Optical Soc. of America

2010 Massachusetts Ave. NW
Washington, DC 20036
Web: www.osa.org
E-mail: info@osa.org
Tel: (202)223-8130
Fax: (202)223-1096
Registered: LDA

Organized to increase and diffuse the knowledge of optics and to promote the common interests of and encourage cooperation among scientists, designers and users of optical apparatus of all kinds.

Leg. Issues: BUD, EDU, MED, MIA, SCI, TEC

In-house, DC-area Employees

KLONOSKI, Grace: Strategic Marketing and Membership
PUGLISI, Matthew L.: Government Relations Manager
SCHIPANI, Meredith: Marketing Coordinator
THORNER, John: Exec. Director

Opticians Ass'n of America

7023 Little River Tnpk.
Suite 207
Annandale, VA 22003
Web: www.opticians.org
E-mail: oaa@opticians.org
Tel: (703)916-8856
Fax: (703)916-7966
Registered: LDA
Leg. Issues: CSP, HCR, MED, MMM, SMB, TRD

Political Action Committee/s

Opticians Committee for Political Education
7023 Little River Tnpk.
Suite 207
Annandale, VA 22003
Contact: Joyce M. Otto
Tel: (703)916-8856
Fax: (703)916-7966

In-house, DC-area Employees

OTTO, Joyce M.: Exec. Director

Outside Counsel/Consultants

Donald S. Dawson & Associates
Issues: TRD
Rep By: Donald S. Dawson

Optinel Systems

Outside Counsel/Consultants

Edelman Public Relations Worldwide
Rep By: Chuck Taylor

Option One Mortgage Corp.

Irvine, CA
Leg. Issues: BAN

Outside Counsel/Consultants

Butera & Andrews
Issues: BAN
Rep By: Cliff W. Andrews, Wright H. Andrews, Jr., James J. Butera, Philip S. Corwin, Frank Tillotson

Oracle Corp.

1667 K St. NW
Suite 640
Washington, DC 20006-1605
Tel: (202)835-7360
Fax: (202)467-4250
Registered: LDA
Web: www.oracle.com

A provider of database and application software. Also provides related consulting, support and training services.

Leg. Issues: BUD, CPI, CPT, CSP, DEF, FIN, GOV, IMM, LBR, SCI, TAX, TEC, TOR, TRD

Political Action Committee/s

Oracle Corp. PAC
1667 K St. NW
Suite 640
Washington, DC 20006-1605
Tel: (202)721-4807
Fax: (202)467-4250
Contact: Stacey Loeffler

In-house, DC-area Employees

ALHADEFF, Joseph: V. President
GLUECK, Kenneth: V. President, Government Affairs
LENFEST, Lauren: V. President, International Trade and Development
LOEFFLER, Stacey: Manager, Political Programs and Compliance
MCGEE, Kate: V. President, Corporate Affairs
PAVLOVIC, Dejan: Manager, Global Public Policy
VENTINO, Lucas: V. President, Global Trade Compliance

Outside Counsel/Consultants

Arthur Andersen LLP
Issues: TAX
Rep By: Rachelle Bernstein, Richard A. Gordon

Boesch & Co.
Issues: CPI, LBR, TAX, TEC
Rep By: Doyce A. Boesch

Brownstein Hyatt & Farber, P.C.
Issues: CPI
Rep By: William T. Brack, Thomas H. Hudson, Michael B. Levy

C&M Internat'l, Ltd.
Rep By: Kathryn B. Clemans, Doral S. Cooper

Collins & Company, Inc.
Issues: DEF
Rep By: James D. Bond, Scott Cassel, Richard L. Collins, Shay D. Stautz

Columbus Public Affairs

Jones, Walker, Waechter, Poitevent, Carrere & Denegre, L.L.P.
Issues: CPI
Rep By: Paul Cambon, John J. Jaskot, R. Christian Johnsen

The Michael Lewan Co.
Issues: TAX
Rep By: Michael Lewan, Anne Saunders

The Livingston Group, LLC

Manatt, Phelps & Phillips, LLP
Issues: BUD, CPI, GOV, TAX
Rep By: Luke Rose, Stephen M. Ryan, Robb Watters

Mayer, Brown & Platt
Issues: CPI
Rep By: Penny L. Eastman, Donald M. Falk, Mark H. Gitenstein, Jeffrey H. Lewis, Richard S. Williamson

R. Duffy Wall and Associates
Issues: TAX, TEC
Rep By: David C. Jory

Orange County Fire Authority

Orange, CA
Leg. Issues: GOV

Outside Counsel/Consultants

Peyser Associates, Inc.
Issues: GOV
Rep By: Thane Young

Orange County Sanitation Districts

Fountain Valley, CA
Leg. Issues: BUD, NAT

Outside Counsel/Consultants

ENS Resources, Inc.
Issues: BUD, NAT
Rep By: Eric Sapirstein

Orange County Transportation Authority

Orange, CA
Leg. Issues: ROD, TRA

Outside Counsel/Consultants

James F. McConnell
Issues: TRA
Rep By: James F. McConnell

Peyser Associates, Inc.
Issues: ROD, TRA
Rep By: Peter A. Peyser, Jr.

Richard L. Spees, Inc.
Issues: TRA
Rep By: Richard L. Spees

Orange County Water District

Fountain Valley, CA
Leg. Issues: BUD

Outside Counsel/Consultants

James F. McConnell
Issues: BUD
Rep By: James F. McConnell

Orange County, California

Outside Counsel/Consultants

Cormac Group, LLP

Orange Shipbuilding Co., Inc.

Orange, TX
Leg. Issues: DEF

Outside Counsel/Consultants

The PMA Group
Issues: DEF
Rep By: Kaylene Green, Gregory L. Hansen, Paul J. Magliocchetti

Orange, California, County of

Santa Ana, CA
Leg. Issues: DEF, TRA, URB

Outside Counsel/Consultants

Cassidy & Associates, Inc.
Rep By: Laurie J. Adler, Christy Carson Evans

Hill and Knowlton, Inc.
Issues: URB
Rep By: Fred DuVal, Gary G. Hymel, Jeffrey B. Trammell

James F. McConnell
Rep By: James F. McConnell

Rhoads Group
Rep By: Steven G. McKnight, Barry D. Rhoads

Spiegel & McDiarmid
Rep By: John J. Corbett, Jr.

Tate-LeMunyon, LLC
Issues: DEF, TRA
Rep By: Glenn B. LeMunyon

Orange, Florida, County of

Orlando, FL
Leg. Issues: ECN, GOV

Outside Counsel/Consultants

The Dutko Group, Inc.
Rep By: Ronald C. Kaufman

Kutak Rock LLP
Issues: ECN
Rep By: George R. Schlossberg

Richard L. Spees, Inc.
Issues: GOV
Rep By: Richard L. Spees

Orangeburg, New York, Town of

Outside Counsel/Consultants

Davidoff & Malito, LLP
Rep By: Stephen J. Slade

Orasure Technologies

Bethlehem, PA
Leg. Issues: BUD, MED

Outside Counsel/Consultants

Van Scoyoc Associates, Inc.
Issues: BUD, MED
Rep By: Steve E. Crane, Kevin F. Kelly, H. Stewart Van Scoyoc

OraVax, Inc.

Cambridge, MA
Leg. Issues: HCR

Outside Counsel/Consultants

Commonwealth Group, Ltd.
Issues: HCR
Rep By: Christopher T. Cushing, Christopher J. Greeley

Orbex Resources

Salem, KY

Outside Counsel/Consultants

Robert N. Pyle & Associates
Rep By: Alexis Hersh, Alison O'Neill, Robert N. Pyle

Orbital Resources, LLC

Bethesda, MD
Leg. Issues: AER, COM, TEC

Outside Counsel/Consultants

The ILEX Group
Issues: AER, COM, TEC
Rep By: H. Hollister Cantus

Orbital Sciences Corp.

21700 Atlantic Blvd.
Dulles, VA 20166
Tel: (703)406-5000
Fax: (703)406-5572
Registered: LDA
Web: www.orbital.com

A space technology company that designs, manufactures, operates and markets a broad range of space products and services.

Leg. Issues: AER, BUD, DEF, SCI, TEC, TRA, TRD

Political Action Committee/s

Orb PAC
21700 Atlantic Blvd.
Dulles, VA 20166
Tel: (703)406-5000
Fax: (703)406-5572
Contact: Barry Beneski

In-house, DC-area Employees

BENESKI, Barry
BITTERMAN, Mark E.: V. President, Government Relations
MYERS, Chris: Manager, Government Relations

Orbital Sciences Corp., Fairchild Defense Division

Germantown, MD
Leg. Issues: AER, CPI, DEF

Outside Counsel/Consultants

Potomac Strategies Internat'l LLC
Issues: AER, CPI, DEF
Rep By: C. Kenneth Allard, Robert J. Curran, Raymond F. DuBois, Jr.

ORBITZ

Chicago, IL
Leg. Issues: AVI, CPI, SCI, TRA

Outside Counsel/Consultants

Fleischman and Walsh, L.L.P.
Rep By: Louis H. Dupart, Krista Stark, John Wyma

Global Aviation Associates, Ltd.
Issues: AVI
Rep By: Jon F. Ash, Charles R. Chambers

Lawler, Metzger & Milkman, LLC
Issues: TRA
Rep By: Sante J. Esposito

The Wexler Group
Issues: AVI, CPI, SCI, TRA
Rep By: Adam Eisgrau, Timothy Hannegan, Patric G. Link, Patrick J. McCann, Dale W. Snape, Hon. Robert S. Walker, Anne Wexler

Winston & Strawn
Rep By: Hon. James H. Burnley, IV

Orcon Corp.

Union City, CA
Leg. Issues: AVI

Outside Counsel/Consultants

APCO Worldwide
Issues: AVI
Rep By: Hon. Don L. Bonker

Order Sons of Italy in America/Sons of Italy Foundation

219 E St. NE
Washington, DC 20002
Tel: (202)547-2900
Fax: (202)546-8168
Web: www.osia.com
E-mail: osianat@aol.com

Focuses on educational, philanthropic, cultural, and public policy issues.

In-house, DC-area Employees
PICCIGALLO, Ph.D., Philip R.: National Exec. Director and Chief Exec. Officer

Ordnance Development and Engineering Co. of Singapore

Singapore, SINGAPORE
Leg. Issues: DEF

Outside Counsel/Consultants
American Defense Internat'l, Inc.
Issues: DEF
Rep By: Michael Herson, Van D. Hipp, Jr., Dave Wilberding

Oregon Department of Transportation

Salem, OR
Leg. Issues: BUD, ROD, TRA

Outside Counsel/Consultants
Ball Janik, LLP
Issues: BUD, ROD, TRA
Rep By: James A. Beall, Michelle E. Giguere, Hal D. Hiemstra

Oregon Economic Development Department

Salem, OR
Leg. Issues: TRA

Outside Counsel/Consultants
Lindsay Hart Neil & Weigler
Issues: TRA
Rep By: Kathryn Beaubien, Peter Friedmann

Oregon Garden Foundation

Milwaukie, OR
Leg. Issues: BUD, ECN, EDU, NAT

Outside Counsel/Consultants
The Dutko Group, Inc.
Issues: BUD, ECN, EDU, NAT
Rep By: Gary J. Andres, Mark S. Irion, Kimberly M. Spaulding

Oregon Graduate Institute of Science and Technology

Beaverton, OR
Leg. Issues: BUD, CPI, EDU, SCI

Outside Counsel/Consultants
Conkling, Fiskum & McCormick
Issues: BUD, CPI, EDU, SCI
Rep By: Gary Conkling, Norm Eder, Daniel Jarman

Oregon Health Sciences University

Portland, OR
Leg. Issues: BUD

Outside Counsel/Consultants
Beacon Consulting Group, Inc.
Issues: BUD
Rep By: Jeffrey W. Henry, Gordon P. MacDougall, Lisa A. Stewart

Oregon Military Department

Salem, OR
Leg. Issues: DEF

Outside Counsel/Consultants
The Mike Waite Company
Issues: DEF
Rep By: Michael S. Waite

Oregon Utility Resource Coordination Ass'n (OURCA)

Portland, OR
Leg. Issues: ENG, NAT, UTI

Outside Counsel/Consultants
Kanner & Associates
Issues: ENG, NAT, UTI
Rep By: Martin B. Kanner

Oregon Water Resources Congress

Salem, OR
A trade group for water suppliers.
Leg. Issues: BUD, NAT

Outside Counsel/Consultants
Will and Carlson, Inc.
Issues: BUD, NAT
Rep By: Peter Carlson

Oregon Water Trust

Portland, OR
Leg. Issues: BUD

Outside Counsel/Consultants
John Freshman Associates, Inc.
Issues: BUD
Rep By: John D. Freshman, Lawrence P. Kast, Catherine B. Kiefer

Oregon, State of

Salem, OR

Outside Counsel/Consultants
Johnston & Associates, LLC
Rep By: Hon. J. Bennett Johnston

Organ Transplant Campaign

Outside Counsel/Consultants
The Dutko Group, Inc.

Organic Trade Ass'n

Greenfield, MA
Leg. Issues: AGR

Outside Counsel/Consultants
Resource Management Consultants, Inc.
Issues: AGR
Rep By: Robert J. Gray

Organization for Internat'l Investment

1901 Pennsylvania Ave. NW
Suite 807
Washington, DC 20006
Tel: (202)659-1903
Fax: (202)659-2293
Registered: LDA
Web: www.ofii.org

A Washington, DC-based ass'n representing the US subsidiaries of foreign parent companies. Member companies range from medium to large-sized enterprises. OFII is dedicated to ensuring that US subsidiaries receive nondiscriminatory treatment under US federal and state law.

Leg. Issues: GOV, TAX, TRD

In-house, DC-area Employees
MALAN, Todd M.: Exec. Director
MCLERNON, Nancy L.: Director, Economic & Legislative Affairs

Outside Counsel/Consultants
Miller & Chevalier, Chartered
Issues: TAX
Powell, Goldstein, Frazer & Murphy LLP
Issues: GOV, TRD
Rep By: Kelly Cameron, Michael E. Fine, Daniel M. Price

Organization for the Promotion and Advancement of Small Telecommunications Cos.

21 Dupont Circle NW
Suite 700
Washington, DC 20036
Tel: (202)659-5990
Fax: (202)659-4619
Registered: LDA
Web: www.opastco.org

The national trade association representing independently owned and operated telephone companies and cooperatives in rural America.

Leg. Issues: TEC

In-house, DC-area Employees
CAMARDO, Alison: Public Relations Coordinator
ERIKSON, Donald: Director, Legislative Relations
KELLEY-RIESETT, Kathleen: Director, Education
POLIKOFF, Stuart: Director, Government Relations
ROSE, John N.: President
SILVER, Martha K.: Director, Public Relations

Organization of Chinese Americans, Inc.

1001 Connecticut Ave. NW
Suite 601
Washington, DC 20036
Tel: (202)223-5500
Fax: (202)296-0540
Web: www.ocanatl.org
E-mail: oca@ocanatl.org

A national, non-profit, educational and civic organization of concerned Chinese Americans. Encourages active participation by Chinese Americans and Asian Americans in all areas of civic life. Has 41 local chapters in 24 states.

In-house, DC-area Employees
ONG, George: National President

Organization of Professional Employees of the U.S. Dep't of Agriculture (OPEDA)

P.O. Box 381
Washington, DC 20044
Tel: (202)720-4898
Fax: (202)720-6692
Web: www.usda.gov/opeda
E-mail: othompson@usda.gov

Purpose is to promote and support administrative and legislative issues of concern to federal employees and to conduct public service and awards programs to expand recognition of dedicated public service.

In-house, DC-area Employees
THOMPSON, Jr., Otis N.: Exec. Director

Orient Airlines Ass'n

Manila, PHILIPPINES

Outside Counsel/Consultants
Galland, Kharasch, Greenberg, Fellman & Swirsky, P.C.

Orient Overseas Container Line

Hong Kong, CHINA (PEOPLE'S REPUBLIC)

Outside Counsel/Consultants
Hill, Betts & Nash L.L.P.
Rep By: Brien E. Kehoe

Orincon Corp.

San Diego, CA
Leg. Issues: AVI, BUD, DEF, TRA

Outside Counsel/Consultants
Copeland, Lowery & Jacquez
Issues: AVI, BUD, DEF, TRA
Rep By: Jean Gingras Denton, Hon. William D. Lowery

Orion Air

Raleigh, NC

Outside Counsel/Consultants
Hewes, Gelband, Lambert & Dann, P.C.
Rep By: Stephen L. Gelband

Orkand Corp.

Leg. Issues: BUD

Outside Counsel/Consultants
MV3 & Associates
RTS Consulting
Valente Lopatin & Schulze
Issues: BUD
Rep By: Alan G. Lopatin, Richard T. Schulze, Jr., Mark Valente, III

Orlando Utilities Commission

Orlando, FL
Leg. Issues: ENG, GOV, UTI

Outside Counsel/Consultants
Duncan, Weinberg, Genzer & Pembroke, P.C.
Issues: ENG, GOV, UTI
Rep By: Richmond F. Allan, Wallace L. Duncan, James D. Pembroke

Orlando, Florida, City of

Leg. Issues: BUD, ECN

Outside Counsel/Consultants
Kutak Rock LLP
Issues: ECN
Rep By: Seth Kirshenberg, George R. Schlossberg, Barry P. Steinberg
Reed, Smith, LLP
Issues: BUD
Rep By: Christopher L. Rissetto

Orleans Levee District

New Orleans, LA
Leg. Issues: DIS

Outside Counsel/Consultants
The Palmer Group
Issues: DIS
Rep By: Clifford A. Palmer

Oromo Liberation Front

1810 Ninth St. NW
Washington, DC 20001
Tel: (202)462-5477
Fax: (202)332-7011
Registered: FARA

Presents the U.S. government and Congress with the OLF position and views on the political situation in Ethiopia.

In-house, DC-area Employees
GELETA, Abiyu: OLF Representative

Orphan Medical, Inc.
Minnetonka, MN
Leg. Issues: HCR, LAW, MED
Outside Counsel/Consultants
Policy Directions, Inc.
Issues: HCR, LAW, MED
Rep By: Kathleen "Kay" Holcombe, Stephen Michael, Frankie L. Trull

Ort's, Inc.
LaVale, MD
Outside Counsel/Consultants
Robert N. Pyle & Associates
Rep By: Robert N. Pyle

Ortho Concepts
Highland Heights, OH
Leg. Issues: MMM
Outside Counsel/Consultants
Haake and Associates
Issues: MMM
Rep By: Timothy M. Haake, Nathan M. Olsen

Ortho-McNeil Pharmaceutical Corp.
Raritan, NJ
Outside Counsel/Consultants
Edelman Public Relations Worldwide
Rep By: Peter Segall

Osceola, Florida, County of
Leg. Issues: ENV, TRA
Outside Counsel/Consultants
Alcalde & Fay
Issues: ENV, TRA
Rep By: Hon. Louis A. "Skip" Bafalis, Jim Davenport

Oscoda Management
Leg. Issues: TOU
Outside Counsel/Consultants
The Da Vinci Group
Issues: TOU

OSHA Reform Coalition
Outside Counsel/Consultants
RTS Consulting
Valente Lopatin & Schulze
Rep By: Richard T. Schulze, Jr.

Oshkosh Truck Corp.
1725 Jefferson Davis Hwy.
Suite 706
Arlington, VA 22202
Tel: (703)413-6200
Fax: (703)413-6384
Web: www.oshkoshtruck.com
E-mail: solutions@oshtruck.com
Headquartered in Oshkosh, WI.
Leg. Issues: BUD, DEF, FOR, MAN, SCI, TRU, WAS
In-house, DC-area Employees
FIELDING, F. C.: V. President, Government Operations
Outside Counsel/Consultants
Foley & Lardner
Issues: DEF
Rep By: Theodore H. Bornstein
McKenna & Cuneo, L.L.P.
Rep By: Del S. Dameron
Robison Internat'l, Inc.
Issues: BUD, DEF
Rep By: Richard B. Ladd, J. David Willson

OSI Systems, Inc.
Hawthorne, CA
Leg. Issues: LAW
Outside Counsel/Consultants
American Continental Group, Inc.
Issues: LAW
Rep By: John A. Cline, David A. Metzner, Shawn H. Smeallie

Osteoarthritis Research Soc. Internat'l
Outside Counsel/Consultants
Smith, Bucklin and Associates, Inc.

Osteopathic Health System of Texas
Forth Worth, TX
Leg. Issues: HCR
Outside Counsel/Consultants
Peter J. Rose
Issues: HCR
Rep By: Peter J. Rose

Ostex Internat'l Inc.
Seattle, WA
Leg. Issues: MMM
Outside Counsel/Consultants
Hale and Dorr LLP
Issues: MMM
Rep By: Barry J. Hurewitz, Jay P. Urwitz

Otter Tail Power Co.
Fergus Falls, MN
An electric utility.
Outside Counsel/Consultants
Troutman Sanders LLP
Rep By: Kevin C. Fitzgerald, William P. Marsan, Clifford S. Sikora

Ouachita Parish Police Jury
Ouachita Parish, LA
Leg. Issues: AVI, BUD, ECN, ROD, SMB, TRA, WAS
Outside Counsel/Consultants
Ross Atkins
Issues: AVI, BUD, ECN, ROD, SMB, TRA, WAS
Rep By: Ross Atkins

Ounalashka Corp.
Unalaska, AK
Leg. Issues: BUD, TAX
Outside Counsel/Consultants
Robertson, Monagle & Eastaugh
Issues: BUD, TAX
Rep By: Bradley D. Gilman, Rick E. Marks, Steven W. Silver

Our Lady of the Lake Regional Medical Center
Baton Rouge, LA
Leg. Issues: HCR
Outside Counsel/Consultants
Golin/Harris Internat'l
Issues: HCR
Rep By: C. Michael Fulton

Outback Steakhouse, Inc.
1775 Pennsylvania Ave. NW
Suite 1200
Washington, DC 20006
Tel: (202)463-7114
Fax: (202)463-7107
In-house, DC-area Employees
WHITESIDES, Allison: Director, Government Relations

Outdoor Advertising Ass'n of America
1850 M St. NW
Suite 1040
Washington, DC 20036
Tel: (202)833-5566
Fax: (202)833-1522
Registered: LDA
Web: www.oaaa.org
E-mail: info@oaaa.org
Leg. Issues: ADV, CON, ROD, TOB, TRA
Political Action Committee/s
Outdoor Advertising PAC
1850 M St. NW
Suite 1040
Washington, DC 20036
Tel: (202)833-5566
Fax: (202)833-1522
Contact: Nancy A. Odenthal
In-house, DC-area Employees
FLETCHER, Nancy J.: President and CEO
LAIBLE, Myron: V. President, Regulatory Affairs and Operations
ODENTHAL, Nancy A.: Manager, Legislative Services
Outside Counsel/Consultants
Ann Eppard Associates, Ltd.
Issues: TRA
Rep By: Julie Chlopecki, Ann Eppard, Karen Schechter
Rubin, Winston, Diercks, Harris & Cooke
Rep By: Eric M. Rubin

Outdoor Power Equipment Aftermarket Ass'n
Washington, DC
Web: www.opeaa.org
E-mail: opeaa@opeaa.org
Outside Counsel/Consultants
William S. Bergman Associates
Rep By: William S. Bergman, CAE

Outdoor Power Equipment Institute
341 S. Patrick St.
Alexandria, VA 22314
Tel: (703)549-7600
Fax: (703)549-7604
Web: www.opei.mow.org
E-mail: opei@opei.org
In-house, DC-area Employees
HARLEY, William: President and Chief Exec. Officer
Outside Counsel/Consultants
Collier Shannon Scott, PLLC
Rep By: Mark L. Austrian, William M. Guerry, Jr., Laurence J. Lasoff, Judith L. Oldham

Outdoor Recreation Coalition of America
Boulder, CO
Outside Counsel/Consultants
Hauser Group

Outpatient Ophthalmic Surgery Soc.
San Diego, CA
Leg. Issues: MMM
Political Action Committee/s
Outpatient Ophthalmic Surgery Soc. Political Action Comittee (OOSS PAC)
San Diego, CA
Outside Counsel/Consultants
McDermott, Will and Emery
Issues: MMM
Rep By: Michael A. Romansky, Eric P. Zimmerman

Ova Noss Family Partnership
Newport Beach, CA
Outside Counsel/Consultants
William E. Casselman, II
Rep By: William E. Casselman, II

Ovarian Cancer Nat'l Alliance
910 17th St. NW
Suite 413
Washington, DC 20006
Tel: (202)331-1332
Registered: LDA
Web: www.ovariancancer.org
E-mail: ocna@ovariancancer.org
Leg. Issues: BUD, HCR
In-house, DC-area Employees
KOLKER, Ann: Exec. Director
Outside Counsel/Consultants
Arent Fox Kintner Plotkin & Kahn, PLLC
Issues: BUD
Rep By: Katie Clarke, Douglas McCormack

Ovations/United Health Group
Vienna, VA
Leg. Issues: MMM
Outside Counsel/Consultants
Bergner Bockorny Castagnetti and Hawkins
Issues: MMM
Rep By: Jeffrey T. Bergner, David A. Bockorny, David Castagnetti, James W. Hawkins, Brenda Benjamin Reese, Melissa Schulman

Owens Corning
1401 K St. NW
Suite 702
Washington, DC 20005
Tel: (202)216-1080
Fax: (202)216-1081
Registered: LDA
Web: www.owenscorning.com
A manufacturer of building materials headquartered in Toledo, OH.
Leg. Issues: ENG, ENV, TAX, TOR
In-house, DC-area Employees
LIBONATI, John J.: Director, Government and Public Affairs
Outside Counsel/Consultants
Parry, Romani, DeConcini & Symms
Issues: TAX
Rep By: Edward H. Baxter, Hon. Dennis DeConcini, John M. Haddow, Scott D. Hatch, Shannon Davis Henderson, Jack W. Martin, Romano Romani, Linda Arey Skladany, Hon. Steven D. Symms
PriceWaterhouseCoopers
Issues: TAX
Rep By: Jim Carlisle, Kenneth J. Kies, Pat Raffaniello

Owens-Illinois, Inc.

1155 21st St. NW
Suite 310
Washington, DC 20036
Tel: (202)785-3559
Fax: (202)659-5249
Registered: LDA
Web: www.o-i.com
E-mail: danielsteen@owens-ill.com

Glass and plastic packaging manufacturer headquartered in Toledo, OH.

Leg. Issues: CSP, ENV, FOO, HCR, LBR, MAN, PHA, TAX, TOR, TRD

In-house, DC-area Employees

STEEN, Daniel K.: Director, Government Affairs/Washington Office

Outside Counsel/Consultants

Reed, Smith, LLP
Issues: MAN
Rep By: David C. Evans, Phillips S. Peter, C. Stevens Seale

Williams & Jensen, P.C.
Issues: CSP, TRD
Rep By: William B. Canfield, Robert E. Glennon, Jr., J. Steven Hart, Karen Judd Lewis, John J. McMackin, Jr., Anthony J. Roda, J. D. Williams

Owner-Operator Independent Drivers Ass'n, Inc.

Grain Valley, MO

A national organization representing small business truckers.

Leg. Issues: CSP, TEC, TRA

Political Action Committee/s

Owner-Operator Independent Drivers Ass'n Political Action Committee
Grain Valley, MO

Outside Counsel/Consultants

The Cullen Law Firm
Issues: CSP, TEC, TRA
Rep By: Paul D. Cullen, Sr.

Oxley

Branford, CT

Outside Counsel/Consultants

The PMA Group
Rep By: Kaylene Green, Paul J. Magliocchetti, Charles Smith

Oxnard Harbor District

Port Hueneme, CA
Leg. Issues: BUD, DEF, MAR, TRA

Outside Counsel/Consultants

Murray, Scheer, Montgomery, Tapia & O'Donnell
Issues: BUD, DEF, MAR, TRA
Rep By: John R. O'Donnell

Oxnard, California, City of

Leg. Issues: BUD, CAW, ECN, HOU, TRA

Outside Counsel/Consultants

Murray, Scheer, Montgomery, Tapia & O'Donnell
Issues: BUD, CAW, ECN, HOU, TRA
Rep By: John R. O'Donnell

OXY USA Inc.

Houston, TX
Leg. Issues: ENG

Outside Counsel/Consultants

Nat'l Environmental Strategies
Issues: ENG
Rep By: Marc I. Himmelstein

Oxygenated Fuels Ass'n

1300 N. 17th St.
Suite 1850
Arlington, VA 22209
Tel: (703)841-7100
Fax: (703)841-7720
Registered: LDA
Web: www.ofa.net

An international trade association established to advance the use of oxygenated fuel additives to improve the combustion performance of gasoline, thereby significantly reducing automotive tailpipe pollution.

Leg. Issues: CAW, ENG, ENV, FUE

In-house, DC-area Employees

LOCKHART, Robert F.: Director, Government Affairs
WIGGLESWORTH, Teresa N.: Exec. Director

Outside Counsel/Consultants

Barbour Griffith & Rogers, Inc.
Issues: CAW, FUE
Rep By: Haley Barbour, G. O. Lanny Griffith, Jr., Bill Himpler, Loren Monroe, Edward M. Rogers, Jr., Brent Thompson

Bracewell & Patterson, L.L.P.
Issues: ENV
Rep By: Hon. Edwin R. Bethune, Hon. Jim Chapman, Gene E. Godley, Marc C. Hebert, Charles L. Ingebretson, Michael L. Pate, Scott H. Segal, D. Michael Stroud, Jr.

Bob Moss Associates
Issues: ENG, ENV
Rep By: Bob Moss

Nat'l Environmental Strategies
Issues: CAW, FUE
Rep By: Marc I. Himmelstein, Richard D. Wilson

P & H Mining Equipment

Milwaukee, WI
Leg. Issues: CAW, ENV, NAT

Outside Counsel/Consultants

Stephens Law Offices
Issues: CAW, ENV, NAT

P & O Nedlloyd Ltd.

East Rutherford, NJ

Outside Counsel/Consultants

Hoppel, Mayer and Coleman

P2B Consulting

Outside Counsel/Consultants

The Dutko Group, Inc.

Pac Med Clinics

Seattle, WA
Leg. Issues: BUD, DEF, HCR

Outside Counsel/Consultants

Preston Gates Ellis & Rouvelas Meeds LLP
Issues: BUD, DEF, HCR
Rep By: Werner W. Brandt, Tim L. Peckinpaugh

PACAmerica Inc.

1719 Dogwood Dr.
Alexandria, VA 22302

A political action committee.

In-house, DC-area Employees

HOLTZMAN, Jill K.

PACCAR, Inc.

Bellevue, WA

A manufacturer of trucks.

Leg. Issues: AUT, CAW, ENV, HCR, MAN, ROD, TAX, TRA, TRD, TRU

Outside Counsel/Consultants

Kenneth F. Stinger
Issues: AUT, CAW, ENV, HCR, MAN, ROD, TAX, TRA, TRD, TRU
Rep By: Kenneth F. Stinger

Pacific 17

San Diego, CA
Leg. Issues: GOV

Outside Counsel/Consultants

Thelen Reid & Priest LLP
Issues: GOV
Rep By: William A. Kirk, Jr.

Pacific Basin Economic Council - U.S. Member Committee

1819 L St. NW
2nd Floor
Washington, DC 20036
Web: www.pbec.org/us
Tel: (202)293-1093
Fax: (202)289-1940

A private regional association of senior business leaders dedicated to the expansion of trade and investment in the Pacific.

In-house, DC-area Employees

ALLAN, L. Stuart: Director General
BODDE, Jr., William: Special Advisor

Pacific Capital Group, Inc.

Beverly Hills, CA
Leg. Issues: TRD

Outside Counsel/Consultants

Brownstein Hyatt & Farber, P.C.
Issues: TRD
Rep By: William T. Brack, Thomas H. Hudson, Michael B. Levy

Pacific Coast Cement

Ontario, CA
Leg. Issues: ENV, ROD, TRD

Outside Counsel/Consultants

Janus-Merritt Strategies, L.L.C.
Issues: ENV, ROD, TRD
Rep By: Mark J. Robertson, J. Daniel Walsh

Pacific Coast Council of Customs Brokers and Freight Forwarders Ass'n

San Francisco, CA
Leg. Issues: TRA

Outside Counsel/Consultants

Lindsay Hart Neil & Weigler
Issues: TRA
Rep By: Kathryn Beaubien, Peter Friedmann

Pacific Consolidated Industries

Santa Ana, CA
Leg. Issues: DEF

Outside Counsel/Consultants

American Defense Internat'l, Inc.
Issues: DEF
Rep By: Michael Herson, Van D. Hipp, Jr., Dave Wilberding

Pacific Dunlop, Ltd./Pacific Brands

North Melbourne, AUSTRALIA

Outside Counsel/Consultants

C&M Internat'l, Ltd.

Crowell & Moring LLP

The Pacific Forest Trust

Booneville, CA

Outside Counsel/Consultants

Baker, Donelson, Bearman & Caldwell, P.C.
Rep By: James D. Range

Pacific Life Insurance Co.

Newport Beach, CA
Leg. Issues: BAN, BUD, FIN, HCR, INS, RET, TAX

Outside Counsel/Consultants

Copeland, Lowery & Jacquez
Issues: BUD, FIN, HCR, TAX
Rep By: James M. Copeland, Jr.

Murray, Scheer, Montgomery, Tapia & O'Donnell
Issues: BAN, FIN, INS, RET, TAX
Rep By: Thomas R. Crawford, D. Michael Murray

Scribner, Hall & Thompson, LLP
Issues: TAX
Rep By: Susan J. Hotine, Thomas C. Thompson, Jr.

The Pacific Lumber Co.

Scotia, CA
Leg. Issues: NAT

Outside Counsel/Consultants

Patton Boggs, LLP
Issues: NAT
Rep By: Thomas Hale Boggs, Jr., Aubrey A. Rothrock, III

Pacific Marine

Honolulu, HI

A ship design and construction company.

Leg. Issues: DEF

Outside Counsel/Consultants

Collins & Company, Inc.
Issues: DEF
Rep By: James D. Bond, Richard L. Collins, Thomas A. Hooper, Shay D. Stautz

Pacific Maritime Ass'n

San Francisco, CA
Leg. Issues: LBR, MAR

Outside Counsel/Consultants

Robins, Kaplan, Miller & Ciresi L.L.P.
Issues: LBR, MAR
Rep By: Charles A. Hunnicutt, Harold E. Mesirow

Pacific Northwest Nat'l Laboratory

Richland, WA
Leg. Issues: DEF, ENV

Outside Counsel/Consultants

Mehl, Griffin & Bartek Ltd.
Issues: DEF, ENV
Rep By: Ronald J. Bartek, Molly Griffin, Theodore J. Mehl

Pacific Science Center

Seattle, WA
Leg. Issues: ECN, EDU

Outside Counsel/Consultants

Denny Miller McBee Associates
Issues: ECN, EDU

Pacific Seafood Processors Ass'n

1101 17th St. NW
Suite 609
Washington, DC 20036
Tel: (202)331-7736
Fax: (202)331-9686
Registered: LDA

A trade association headquartered in Seattle, WA. Specializes in government affairs.

Leg. Issues: FOO, MAR

In-house, DC-area Employees

PHELAN, Dennis J.: V. President

Outside Counsel/Consultants

O'Connor & Hannan, L.L.P.
Rep By: George J. Mannina, Jr.

Pacific Shipyards Internat'l, Hawaii

Outside Counsel/Consultants

R. J. Hudson Associates

Pacific States Marine Fisheries Commission

Gladstone, OR
Leg. Issues: BUD

Outside Counsel/Consultants

Robertson, Monagle & Eastaugh
Issues: BUD
Rep By: Bradley D. Gilman, Rick E. Marks

The Pacific Stock Exchange, Inc.

San Francisco, CA

Outside Counsel/Consultants

Vienna, Gregor & Associates
Rep By: Janet R. Gregor, Donald R. Marlais, Nancy L. Miller, Cheryl Vienna, David P. Vienna

Pacific Telecom, Inc.

Vancouver, WA

The telecommunications subsidiary of PacifiCorp.

Outside Counsel/Consultants

Birch, Horton, Bittner & Cherot
Rep By: William Bittner, Elisabeth H. Ross

Pacific Telesis

San Francisco, CA

Outside Counsel/Consultants

Bonner & Associates

Wiley, Rein & Fielding

Pacific Union College

Angwin, CA
Leg. Issues: BUD

Outside Counsel/Consultants

Edington, Peel & Associates, Inc.
Issues: BUD
Rep By: William H. Edington, Craig A. Meyers, Terry R. Peel

PacifiCare Health Systems

Santa Ana, CA
Registered: LDA
Leg. Issues: HCR, MMM

Outside Counsel/Consultants

The Direct Impact Co.

The Dutko Group, Inc.
Issues: HCR, MMM
Rep By: Gary J. Andres, Kimberly M. Spaulding

The Wexler Group
Issues: HCR
Rep By: Cynthia E. Berry, Jody A. Hoffman, Christine Maroulis, Dale W. Snape, Anne Wexler

PacifiCorp

Portland, OR
Registered: LDA
Leg. Issues: ENG, TRD

Outside Counsel/Consultants

Baker, Donelson, Bearman & Caldwell, P.C.
Issues: ENG, TRD
Rep By: J. Keith Kennedy, Francine Lamoriello

Packaging Machinery Manufacturers Institute

4350 N. Fairfax Dr.
Suite 600
Arlington, VA 22203
Tel: (703)243-8555
Fax: (703)243-8556
Web: www.packexpo.com
E-mail: pmmi@pmmi.org

In-house, DC-area Employees

CROSON, Matthew: Director, Communications
WELCOME, Jerry: V. President, Member Services
YUSKA, Charles D.: President

Outside Counsel/Consultants

Webster, Chamberlain & Bean
Rep By: Hugh K. Webster

PADCO, Inc.

Leg. Issues: FOR

Outside Counsel/Consultants

Collins & Company, Inc.
Issues: FOR
Rep By: James D. Bond, Richard L. Collins, Thomas A. Hooper, Shay D. Stautz

Paducah & Louisville Railroad

Paducah, IL
Leg. Issues: RRR

Outside Counsel/Consultants

Troutman Sanders LLP
Issues: RRR
Rep By: Sandra L. Brown, William P. Marsan, William A. Mullins, David C. Reeves

Pain Care Coalition

Washington, DC
Leg. Issues: HCR, MED, MMM

Outside Counsel/Consultants

Powers Pyles Sutter & Verville, PC
Issues: HCR, MED, MMM
Rep By: Robert J. Saner, II

PaineWebber Group, Inc.

1300 I St. NW
Suite 1050-E
Washington, DC 20005
Tel: (202)336-5085

Headquartered in New York, NY.

Leg. Issues: FIN

In-house, DC-area Employees

MAGRUDER, Coe: Senior V. President and District Manager, Washington

Outside Counsel/Consultants

Arnold & Porter
Issues: FIN
Rep By: Martha L. Cochran

Washington Council Ernst & Young
Rep By: Doug Badger, John L. Doney, Jayne T. Fitzgerald, LaBrenda Garrett-Nelson, Gary J. Gasper, Bruce A. Gates, Nick Giordano, Robert J. Leonard, Richard Meltzer, Robert M. Rozen, Timothy J. Urban

Painting and Decorating Contractors of America

3913 Old Lee Hwy.
Suite 33B
Fairfax, VA 22030
Tel: (703)359-0826
Fax: (703)359-2576
Web: www.pdca.org
Leg. Issues: ENV, SMB

Political Action Committee/s

Painting and Decorating Contractors and America PAC

3913 Old Lee Hwy.
Suite 33B
Fairfax, VA 22030
Tel: (703)359-0826
Fax: (703)359-2576
Contact: Mark Prysock

In-house, DC-area Employees

PRYSOCK, Mark: Director, Government Affairs; PAC Treasurer

Pakistan Internat'l Airlines

Karachi, PAKISTAN

Outside Counsel/Consultants

Zuckert, Scoutt and Rasenberger, L.L.P.
Rep By: Richard D. Mathias, Andrew R. Plump

Pakistan, Embassy of the Islamic Republic of

2315 Massachusetts Ave. NW
Washington, DC 20008
Tel: (202)939-6200
Fax: (202)387-0484
Web: www.pakistan-embassy.com
E-mail: parepwashington@erols.com

Outside Counsel/Consultants

Patton Boggs, LLP
Rep By: Katharine R. Boyce, John J. Deschauer, Jr.

Washington World Group, Ltd.
Rep By: Edward J. von Kloberg, III

Pakistan, Government of the Islamic Republic of

Islamabad, PAKISTAN
Leg. Issues: FOR

Outside Counsel/Consultants

Hooper Owen & Winburn
Issues: FOR
Rep By: Esperanza Gomez, Hon. Charles Wilson

Patton Boggs, LLP
Rep By: Lanny J. Davis

Mark A. Siegel & Associates

White & Case LLP

Pakistani-American Business Ass'n

Washington, DC

A non-profit trade association promoting business relations between Pakistan and the United States.

Outside Counsel/Consultants

Baker, Donelson, Bearman & Caldwell, P.C.
Rep By: Charles R. Johnston, Jr.

Palestinian Authority

Leg. Issues: FOR

Outside Counsel/Consultants

Bannerman and Associates, Inc.
Issues: FOR
Rep By: Edward G. Abington, M. Graeme Bannerman, W. Mark Habeeb, Anne Hingeley, William A. Miner, Valerie A. Schultz, Curt Silvers

Palm Beach, Florida, County of

West Palm Beach, FL
Leg. Issues: CAW, ECN, HOU, TRA

Outside Counsel/Consultants

U.S. Strategies Corp.
Issues: CAW, ECN, HOU, TRA
Rep By: Heidi Hanson

Palm Beach, Florida, Port of

Palm Beach, FL
Leg. Issues: ENV, TRA

Outside Counsel/Consultants

Alcalde & Fay
Issues: ENV, TRA
Rep By: Hon. Louis A. "Skip" Bafalis, Angela Plott

Palm Desert, California, City of

Leg. Issues: EDU

Outside Counsel/Consultants

Washington Alliance Group, Inc.
Issues: EDU
Rep By: Bonnie Singer

Palm Springs, California, City of

Leg. Issues: AVI, IND, RRR

Outside Counsel/Consultants

Alcalde & Fay
Issues: AVI, IND, RRR
Rep By: Mary Litton Fowler, Nancy Gibson Prowitt

Palmdale, California, City of

Leg. Issues: ROD, TRA

Outside Counsel/Consultants

Cassidy & Associates, Inc.
Issues: ROD, TRA
Rep By: Daniel J. McNamara, Gabor J. Rozsa, Lyllett Wentworth

Palmer Chiropractic University

Davenport, IA
Leg. Issues: EDU

Outside Counsel/Consultants

The Advocacy Group
Issues: EDU
Rep By: Robert E. Mills

Palmer Coking & Coal Co.

Black Diamond, WA

Outside Counsel/Consultants

Sam Richardson
Rep By: Sam Richardson

Palo Alto, California, City of

Leg. Issues: BUD, CAW, ECN, ENG, GOV, HOU, LAW, NAT, ROD, TRA, URB, UTI

Outside Counsel/Consultants

Duncan, Weinberg, Genzer & Pembroke, P.C.
Issues: ENG, GOV, UTI
Rep By: Wallace L. Duncan, James D. Pembroke

The Ferguson Group, LLC
Issues: BUD, CAW, ECN, HOU, LAW, NAT, ROD, TRA, URB
Rep By: Charmayne Macon

Pan American Health Organization

Washington, DC
Leg. Issues: BUD, FOR

Outside Counsel/Consultants

Edington, Peel & Associates, Inc.
Issues: BUD, FOR
Rep By: Terry R. Peel

Pan Pacific Pharmaceuticals

Providence, RI
Leg. Issues: HCR, IMM

Outside Counsel/Consultants

Jeffrey J. Kimbell & Associates
Issues: HCR, IMM

Pan-Alberta Gas Ltd.

Calgary, Alberta, CANADA

Outside Counsel/Consultants

Stuntz, Davis & Staffier, P.C.
Rep By: John R. Staffier

Panama Trans-Shipment Consortium

Washington, DC

Outside Counsel/Consultants

Akin, Gump, Strauss, Hauer & Feld, L.L.P.

Panama, Foreign Minister of the Republic of

Panama City, PANAMA

Outside Counsel/Consultants

Arnold & Porter

Panama, Government of the Republic of

Panama City, PANAMA

Outside Counsel/Consultants

Alcalde & Fay
Rep By: Hector Alcalde, Cynthia Colenda, Alana Weinstein

Arnold & Porter

Sidley & Austin

Washington World Group, Ltd.
Rep By: Edward J. von Kloberg, III

Panama, Public Service Regulatory Entity of the Government of the Republic of

Panama City, PANAMA

Outside Counsel/Consultants

Wilkinson, Barker and Knauer, LLP
Rep By: Leon T. Knauer

PanAmSat Corp.

1133 Connecticut Ave. NW
Suite 675
Washington, DC 20036
Web: www.panamsat.com
Tel: (202)223-3511
Fax: (202)861-4368
Registered: LDA

A satellite communications system headquartered in Greenwich, CT.

Leg. Issues: COM, TEC

In-house, DC-area Employees

GUDE, Kalbak: V. President, Government and Regulatory Affairs and Associate General Counsel

Outside Counsel/Consultants

Cormac Group, LLP
Issues: COM, TEC
Rep By: Patrick H. Williams

Jack Ferguson Associates, Inc.
Issues: COM, TEC
Rep By: Jack Ferguson

Goldberg, Godles, Wiener & Wright
Issues: COM, TEC
Rep By: Henry Goldberg

Holland & Knight LLP
Issues: COM, TEC
Rep By: Janet R. Studley

Hooper Owen & Winburn
Issues: TEC
Rep By: David Rudd, John P. Winburn

New Frontiers Communications Consulting
Issues: COM, TEC
Rep By: R. David Wilson

Pancyprian Ass'n of America

New York, NY
Leg. Issues: BUD, DEF, FOR

Outside Counsel/Consultants

Manatos & Manatos, Inc.
Issues: BUD, DEF, FOR
Rep By: Andrew E. Manatos, Mike A. Manatos

Panda Energy Internat'l

Dallas, TX
Leg. Issues: ENG, FOR, TRD

Outside Counsel/Consultants

Chadbourne and Parke LLP
Issues: TRD
Rep By: Keith Martin

Winston & Strawn
Issues: ENG, FOR
Rep By: Hon. Beryl F. Anthony, Jr., David W. Broome, Charles L. Kinney, Hon. John L. Napier, Douglas C. Richardson, John A. Waits, II

Paper Machine Clothing Council

Washington, DC

Outside Counsel/Consultants

Conlon, Frantz, Phelan & Pires
Rep By: David J. Frantz

Paper Recycling Coalition

Leg. Issues: ADV, CAW, ENG, ENV, FUE, GOV, MAN, TAX, WAS

Outside Counsel/Consultants

Colling Swift & Hynes
Issues: ADV, CAW, ENG, ENV, FUE, GOV, MAN, TAX, WAS
Rep By: Terese Colling, Pablo Collins, Robert J. Hynes, Jr., Hon. Allan B. Swift

Paper, Allied-Industrial, Chemical and Energy Workers Internat'l Union (PACE)

1155 15th St. NW
Suite 405
Washington, DC 20005
Tel: (202)293-7939
Fax: (202)293-7888
Registered: LDA

Formed by the 1999 merger of Oil, Chemical and Atomic Workers Internat'l Union and United Paperworkers Internat'l Union. A 330,000 member organization that addresses legislative issues of interest to organized labor. Headquartered in Nashville, TN.

Leg. Issues: LBR

In-house, DC-area Employees

STRADER, Lowell "Pete": Director, Citizenship-Legislative Department

Paperboard Packaging Council

201 N. Union St.
Suite 220
Alexandria, VA 22314
Web: www.ppcnet.org
E-mail: paperboardpackaging@ppcnet.org
Tel: (703)836-3300
Fax: (703)836-3290
Registered: LDA

In-house, DC-area Employees

BROWN, James: Director, Public Affairs

Pappas Telecasting Cos.

Visalia, CA

Outside Counsel/Consultants

Paul, Hastings, Janofsky & Walker LLP
Rep By: John Griffith Johnson, Jr.

Papua New Guinea, Embassy of

1779 Massachusetts Ave. NW
Suite 805
Washington, DC 20036
Web: www.pngembassy.org
E-mail: kunduwash@aol.com
Tel: (202)745-3680
Fax: (202)745-3679

Outside Counsel/Consultants

Washington World Group, Ltd.
Rep By: Edward J. von Kloberg, III

Par Pharmaceutical, Inc.

Spring Valley, NY

Outside Counsel/Consultants

Kleinfeld, Kaplan and Becker
Rep By: Alan H. Kaplan

Paradigm Support Corp.

Leg. Issues: HCR

Outside Counsel/Consultants

Lee Bechtel and Associates
Issues: HCR
Rep By: Lee Bechtel

Paradise Canyon Resort

Mesquite, NV
Leg. Issues: BUD, NAT

Outside Counsel/Consultants

The Furman Group
Issues: BUD, NAT
Rep By: K. Link Browder, Thomas M. James

Paradise Valley Hospital

Leg. Issues: BUD, ECN, HCR, MED

Outside Counsel/Consultants

Edington, Peel & Associates, Inc.
Issues: BUD, ECN, HCR, MED
Rep By: William H. Edington, Craig A. Meyers

Paraguay, Secretariat for Planning of the Republic of

Asuncion, PARAGUAY

Outside Counsel/Consultants

Patton Boggs, LLP

Paralyzed Veterans of America

801 18th St. NW
Washington, DC 20006
Tel: (202)872-1300
Fax: (202)416-7641
Registered: LDA

Leg. Issues: HCR, HOU, LBR, MED, SPO, TRA, VET

In-house, DC-area Employees

BOLLINGER, John: Deputy Exec. Director
CARSWELL, John: Associate Exec. Director, Health Policy
ENSINGER, Robert: Director, Communications
FOX, Sr., Joseph L.: National President
FULLER, Richard B.: National Legislation Director
GLOTFELTY, Rick: Associate Exec. Director, Veterans Benefits
HAGEL, Lawrence: General Counsel
MCCLOSKEY, Maureen A.: National Advocacy Director
MCLACHLAN, Jim: Associate Exec. Director, Development
ORTNER, Blake C.: Associate Legislative Director
PAGE, C. Lee: Associate Advocacy Director
PROKOP, Susan: Associate Advocacy Director
RABIN, Philip: Director of Communication
THOMAS, Harley: Associate Legislative Director
TUCKER, David M.: Senior Associate Legislative Director
VOLLMER, Douglas K.: Associate Exec. Director, Government Relations

Parametric Technology Corp.

Waltham, MA
Leg. Issues: CPI, DEF

Outside Counsel/Consultants

Hale and Dorr LLP
Issues: CPI, DEF
Rep By: Jay P. Urwitz

PARC Limited

Dublin, IRELAND

Outside Counsel/Consultants

Akin, Gump, Strauss, Hauer & Feld, L.L.P.

Parcel Shippers Ass'n

1211 Connecticut Ave. NW
Suite 610
Washington, DC 20036
Tel: (202)296-3690
Fax: (202)296-0343
Registered: LDA
Web: www.parcelshippers.org
E-mail: psaweb@erols.com

Works to keep parcel shipping rates down and services up.

Leg. Issues: BUD, GOV, POS

Political Action Committee/s

Parcel Shippers Ass'n Political Action Committee
1211 Connecticut Ave. NW
Suite 610
Washington, DC 20036
Tel: (202)296-3690
Fax: (202)296-0343
Contact: James Pierce Myers

In-house, DC-area Employees

MYERS, James Pierce: Exec. V. President

Pardee Construction Co.

Los Angeles, CA
Leg. Issues: TRA

Outside Counsel/Consultants

Richard L. Spees, Inc.
Issues: TRA
Rep By: Richard L. Spees

Parent Centers FYI

Lansing, MI
Leg. Issues: EDU

Outside Counsel/Consultants

Lockridge Grindal & Nauen, P.L.L.P.
Issues: EDU
Rep By: Dennis McGrann

Parents for Public Schools

Jackson, MS

A parent organization supporting public education.

Outside Counsel/Consultants

JMD Associates, Inc.
Rep By: David Bushnell

Parents Incorporated

Leg. Issues: HCR

Outside Counsel/Consultants

Zane & Associates
Issues: HCR
Rep By: Curtis J. Zane

Park Place

Chatham, NJ
Leg. Issues: GAM

Outside Counsel/Consultants

The MWW Group
Issues: GAM

Parker Drilling Co.

Tulsa, OK

Outside Counsel/Consultants

White & Case LLP
Rep By: Charles N. Brower

Parker Hannifin Corp.

Cleveland, OH

A manufacturer of motion control devices.

Leg. Issues: TRA

Outside Counsel/Consultants

Arent Fox Kintner Plotkin & Kahn, PLLC
Issues: TRA
Rep By: Lawrence F. Henneberger, Michael T. McNamara

Parker Jewish Geriatric Institute

New Hyde Park, NY

Outside Counsel/Consultants

Hogan & Hartson L.L.P.
Rep By: Nancy Granese, Jeffrey G. Schneider

Parkinson's Action Network

Santa Rosa, CA
Leg. Issues: BUD, MED, TOB

Outside Counsel/Consultants

Capitol Associates, Inc.
Issues: BUD, MED, TOB
Rep By: Liz Gemski, Edward R. Long, Ph.D.

Parkinson's Disease Foundation

New York, NY
Leg. Issues: HCR

Outside Counsel/Consultants

Liz Robbins Associates
Issues: HCR
Rep By: Liz Robbins

Parliamentary Human Rights Foundation

1615 L St. NW
Suite 900
Washington, DC 20036
Tel: (202)337-1022
Fax: (202)337-6678

A worldwide, voluntary, non-partisan, not-for-profit organization committed to the promotion of human rights. Works directly with parliamentarians to enhance understanding of the meaning and importance of human rights; offers training and technical assistance to human rights advocates, especially parliamentarians; calls attention to human rights abuses that violate internationally recognized standards; and nurtures constitutional democracy, the rule of law, and other protections of human rights.

In-house, DC-area Employees

BONKER, Hon. Don L.: President

Parsons Brinckerhoff Inc.

1401 K St. NW
Suite 701
Washington, DC 20005
Tel: (202)783-0241
Fax: (202)783-0229
Registered: LDA
Web: www.pbworld.com
E-mail: connor@pbworld.com

A civil engineering, planning, and construction management firm headquartered in New York, NY.

Leg. Issues: AVI, BAN, BUD, CAW, DEF, DIS, MAR, ROD, TEC, TRA

Political Action Committee/s

Parsons Brinckerhoff, Inc. PAC
1401 K St. NW
Suite 701
Washington, DC 20005
Tel: (202)783-0241
Fax: (202)783-0229
Contact: Catherine Connor

In-house, DC-area Employees

CONNOR, Catherine: V. President, Government Relations

Outside Counsel/Consultants

Thelen Reid & Priest LLP
Issues: BAN, DEF, DIS, TRA
Rep By: Barry I. Berkoff, William A. Kirk, Jr., Stephan M. Minikes, Richard Y. Roberts

Verner, Liipfert, Bernhard, McPherson and Hand, Chartered
Issues: TRA
Rep By: Denis J. Dwyer

Parsons Corp.

1133 15th St. NW
Suite 800
Washington, DC 20005
Fax: (202)775-6005
Web: www.parsons.com

Headquartered in Pasadena, CA. A group of companies providing planning, design and construction management services to state and local governments and federal and private clients in the fields of environment, oil and gas, transportation, power, telecommunications, and industrial engineering.

Leg. Issues: AVI, DEF, DOC, ENV, ROD, RRR, TAX, TEC, TRA, URB, WAS

Political Action Committee/s

PARPAC
1133 15th St. NW
Suite 800
Washington, DC 20005
Fax: (202)775-6005
Contact: Larry G. Shockley

In-house, DC-area Employees

BONDS, Andrew: V. President, Government Relations
SHOCKLEY, Larry G.: V. President, Government Relations
THRASH, James E.: Sr. V. President, Government Relations

Outside Counsel/Consultants

Hooper Owen & Winburn
Issues: TAX
Rep By: Steve Glaze, Lindsay D. Hooper, John P. Winburn

Participation 2000 Inc.

236 Massachusetts Ave. NE
Suite 206
Washington, DC 20002
Tel: (202)543-5540
Fax: (202)543-5547
Web: www.part2.org
E-mail: markhamsa@cs.com

A Democratic grassroots organization that recruits and trains young people to work on political campaigns.

In-house, DC-area Employees

MARKHAM, Susan A.: Exec. Director

Partido Accion Nacional (PAN)

Mexico City, MEXICO

Outside Counsel/Consultants

Anne V. Smith
Rep By: Anne V. Smith

Partido de la Liberacion Dominica

Outside Counsel/Consultants

Strategy Group Internat'l

Partners for Livable Communities

1429 21st St. NW
Second Floor
Washington, DC 20036
Tel: (202)887-5990
Fax: (202)466-4845

Formed in 1977 to work for the economic health and improvement of the quality of life of communities across the country.

In-house, DC-area Employees

MCNULTY, Robert H.: President

Partners Healthcare System, Inc.

Boston, MA
Leg. Issues: BUD, HCR, MED

Outside Counsel/Consultants

O'Neill, Athy & Casey, P.C.
Issues: BUD, HCR, MED
Rep By: Christopher R. O'Neill

Partners of the Americas

1424 K St. NW
Suite 700
Washington, DC 20005
Tel: (202)628-3300
Fax: (202)628-3306
Web: www.partners.net
E-mail: info@partners.poa.com

Network of professionals serving as community volunteers in Latin America, the Caribbean and the U.S.

Leg. Issues: DIS, FOR

In-house, DC-area Employees

BUTLER, Malcolm: President and Chief Exec. Officer

Partnership Defense Fund Trust

Portland, OR
Leg. Issues: TAX

Outside Counsel/Consultants

Gardner, Carton and Douglas
Issues: TAX
Rep By: Kathleen M. Nilles

Partnership for Advanced Technology in Housing (PATH)

Outside Counsel/Consultants

The Dutko Group, Inc.

Partnership for Better Schools

Cambridge, MA

Outside Counsel/Consultants

Cassidy & Associates, Inc.

Partnership for Caring

1620 Eye St. NW Suite 202
Washington, DC 20006
Tel: (202)296-8071
Fax: (202)296-8352
Registered: LDA
Web: www.partnershipforcaring.org
E-mail: pfc@partnershipforcaring.org

Provide information and assistance for finding living wills in the living will registry. Lobby on behalf of issues associated with end of life care.

Leg. Issues: FAM, HCR, MMM

In-house, DC-area Employees

KAPLAN, Karen: President

Outside Counsel/Consultants

Barksdale Ballard & Co., Inc.
Issues: FAM, HCR
Rep By: Nancy Reller

Witman Associates
Issues: HCR, MMM
Rep By: Ellen G. Witman

Partnership for Early Climate Action

Washington, DC
Leg. Issues: ENG, ENV, UTI

Outside Counsel/Consultants

Baker Botts, L.L.P.
Issues: ENG, ENV, UTI
Rep By: William M. Bumpers

Partnership for Organ Donation

Boston, MA

Outside Counsel/Consultants

The Observatory Group
Rep By: Nathaniel M. Semple

Partnership for Prevention

1233 20th St. NW
Suite 200
Washington, DC 20036
Web: www.prevent.org
Tel: (202)833-0009
Fax: (202)833-0113

A public health advocacy group.

In-house, DC-area Employees

COFFIELD, Ashley: Projects Manager
KNAB, Sarah T.: Projects Manager

Partnership for Recovery Coalition

Washington, DC
Leg. Issues: ALC, BUD, HCR, INS, TAX

Outside Counsel/Consultants

VSAdc.com
Issues: ALC, BUD, HCR, INS, TAX
Rep By: Carol A. McDaid

Pasadena, California, City of

Leg. Issues: HOU, LAW, TAX, TRA, URB

Outside Counsel/Consultants

Carolyn C. Chaney & Associates
Issues: HOU, LAW, TAX, TRA, URB
Rep By: Carolyn C. Chaney, Christopher F. Giglio

Pascua Yaqui Tribe of Arizona

Tucson, AZ

Outside Counsel/Consultants

Strategic Impact, Inc.
Rep By: Michael C. Jimenez, Patrick J. Mitchell

Passaic Valley Sewerage Commissioners

Newark, NJ
Leg. Issues: BUD, CAW

Outside Counsel/Consultants

Murray, Scheer, Montgomery, Tapia & O'Donnell
Issues: BUD, CAW
Rep By: Thomas R. Crawford, John H. Montgomery, D. Michael Murray, John R. O'Donnell

Passamaquoddy Tribe(s)(2)

Princeton/Perry, ME

Outside Counsel/Consultants

George Waters Consulting Service
Rep By: George Waters

Passenger Vessel Ass'n

1600 Wilson Blvd.
Suite 1000-A
Arlington, VA 22209
Tel: (703)807-0100
Fax: (703)807-0103
Registered: LDA
Web: www.passengervessel.com
E-mail: pva@vesselalliance.com

Represents the U.S.-flagged passenger vessel industry. Primary issues are safety and liability issues, Coast Guard regulations, and taxes and fees.

Leg. Issues: MAR

In-house, DC-area Employees

GROUNDWATER, John: Exec. Director
WELCH, Edmund B.: Legislative Director

Pastavilla Makarnacilik A.S.

Izmir, TURKEY
Leg. Issues: TRD

Outside Counsel/Consultants

Law Offices of David L. Simon
Issues: TRD
Rep By: David L. Simon

Pastificio Antonio Pallante

Caserta, ITALY
Leg. Issues: TRD

Outside Counsel/Consultants

Law Offices of David L. Simon
Issues: TRD
Rep By: David L. Simon

Pastificio Pagani

Rovato, ITALY
Leg. Issues: TRD

Outside Counsel/Consultants

Law Offices of David L. Simon
Issues: TRD
Rep By: David L. Simon

Patent Office Professional Ass'n

P.O. Box 15848
Arlington, VA 22215
Tel: (703)308-0818
Fax: (703)308-0818
Registered: LDA
Web: www.popa.org

An independent labor union representing all non-managerial professionals (other than trademark professionals) in the U.S. Patent and Trademark Office.

Leg. Issues: CPT, GOV, LBR

In-house, DC-area Employees

STERN, Ronald J.: President

Pathfinder Technology Inc.

Colorado Springs, CO
Leg. Issues: DEF

Outside Counsel/Consultants

The PMA Group
Issues: DEF
Rep By: Kaylene Green, Paul J. Magliocchetti, Briggs Shade, Thomas Veltri

Patient Access to Transplantation (PAT) Coalition

Washington, DC
Leg. Issues: BUD, HCR, MMM

Outside Counsel/Consultants

Patton Boggs, LLP
Issues: BUD, HCR, MMM
Rep By: John F. Jonas, Martha M. Kendrick, Elizabeth E. Ring, JoAnn V. Willis

Van Scoyoc Associates, Inc.
Issues: BUD, HCR, MMM
Rep By: Evan Knisely, H. Stewart Van Scoyoc

Patton Boggs, LLP

2550 M St. NW
Washington, DC 20037-1350
Tel: (202)457-6000
Fax: (202)457-6315
Registered: LDA, FARA
Web: www.pattonboggs.com
E-mail: info@pattonboggs.com
Leg. Issues: ADV, AGR, BUD, EDU, FOO, TAX, TRD

In-house, DC-area Employees

ABERNATHY, John
ADDISON, Daniel R.: Partner
ANDERSON, Todd: Associate
ANDREW, Anne Slaughter: Partner
ARBUCKLE, J. Gordon: Partner
AUSTIN, Jr., John: Of Counsel
BALTZAN, Elizabeth: Associate
BANGERT, Philip A.: Partner
BERNARD, Michelle D.: Partner
BESOZZI, Paul C.: Partner
BLOOMQUIST, Michael D.: Associate
BOGGS, Jr., Thomas Hale: Chair, Executive Committee
BOYCE, Katharine R.: Partner
BRAMS, Robert S.: Partner
BRAND, Joseph L.: Partner
BRIGHT, Bill: Legislative Specialist
BROWN, Michael A.: International Trade and Public Policy Specialist
BRUGGE, Parker: Partner
CAMP, John C.: Senior Counsel
CHAJET, Henry: Partner
CHORBA, Timothy A.: Partner
CHRISTIAN, Jr., James B.: Partner
COLE, Elliott H.: Partner
COWAN, Mark D.: Partner
CURTO, Michael A.: Partner
DAVINE, Amy C.: Associate
DAVIS, Geoffrey G.: Partner
DAVIS, Lanny J.: Partner
DESCHAUER, Jr., John J.: Partner
DILLEY, Dean M.: Partner
DINO, Michael: Policy Analyst
DOWNS, Thomas C.: Associate
DRIVER, Michael J.: Partner
DUNN, III, David E.: Partner
EICHBERG, Ross E.: Partner
FARBER, David J.: Partner
FARTHING, Penelope S.: Partner
FITHIAN, John F.: Partner
GARRETT, John C.: Defense Systems Consultant
GAVIN, Stephen Diaz: Partner
GIBERGA, Elena: Legislative Specialist
GIBSON, Shannon M.: Legislative Affairs Specialist
GINSBERG, Benjamin L.: Partner
GOLDSTEIN, Jennifer: Associate
GRADISON, Hon. Willis "Bill" D.: Senior Public Policy Counselor
GRIGG, Kenneth A.: Partner
HENDRIX, R. Brian: Associate
HETTINGER, Michael: Public Policy Counselor
HOOG, Michael: Associate
HOUGH, Clayton L.: Partner
JOHNSON, Hon. C. Donald "Don": Partner
JONAS, John F.: Partner
JONES, Robert C.: Partner
KAPLAN, Philip S.: Partner
KENDRICK, Martha M.: Partner
KIM, Harold: Associate
KLAUSNER, Joseph A.: Of Counsel
KOEHLER, Robert H.: Partner
KRACOV, Daniel A.: Partner
KUWANA, Eric A.: Partner
LABOSCHIN, Debra: Associate
LAUGHLIN, Hon. Greg H.: Of Counsel
LEE, III, Lansing B.: Of Counsel
LIEBMAN, Ronald S.: Partner
LOPINA, Brian C.: Of Counsel
MARANGI, Karen L.: Legislative Specialist
MARTIN, John C.: Partner
MASSA, III, Cliff: Partner
MATHIASCHECK, Susan: Partner
MAY, Timothy J.: Partner
MCDOWELL, G. Kendrick: Partner
MCGAHN, II, Donald F.: Associate
MEANS, Kathleen: Senior Health Policy Advisor
MEDEROS, Carolina L.: Transportation Consultant
MIANO, Anne: Counsel
MILLS, Timothy B.: Partner
MOOREHEAD, Donald V.: Partner
MORRIS, Jon Paul: Associate
MURRAY, Nancy A.: Of Counsel
NARDOTTI, Michael J.: Partner
NEWBERRY, Edward J.: Partner
NIRENBERG, Darryl D.: Partner
NORMAN, III, W. Caffey: Partner
O'DONNELL, Thomas P.: Of Counsel
O'HARA, Marie "Mimi": Legislative Affairs Specialist
OBERDORFER, John L.: Partner
PAPE, Stuart M.: Managing Partner
PEARLMAN, Donald H.: Partner
PETERS, Stephanie J.: Associate
PHILLIPS, Charles M.: Associate
PRIOLEAU, Florence W.: Partner
RABOY, David G.: Chief Economic Consultant
RANDLE, Russell V.: Partner
RASSMUSSEN, Garrett G.: Partner
REEDER, James A.: Partner
RING, Elizabeth E.: Associate
ROBERTSON, Peter D.: Partner
ROSENBERG, Andrew M.: Associate
ROTHROCK, III, Aubrey A.: Partner
RUBIN, Paul: Partner
SAMOLIS, Frank R.: Partner
SAVIT, Mark N.: Partner
SCHAENGOLD, Michael J.: Partner
SCHETTEWI, Jennifer B.: Associate
SCHMITZ, Joseph E.: Partner
SCHNEEBAUM, Steven M.: Partner
SCHUTZER, George J.: Partner
SHAW, John S.: Associate
SILER, Duane A.: Partner
SLATER, Rodney: Partner
SMITH, Jeffrey T.: Partner
SPOKES, Jennifer J.: Associate
STUART, III, James R.: Partner
TALISMAN, Charles E.: Partner
TAYLOR, Robert K.: Partner
THORNTON, Leslie T.: Partner, Public Policy
TODD, David C.: Partner
TRAPASSO, Joseph: Partner
TURNER, Jeffrey L.: Partner
TUTTLE, Alan A.: Partner
VANDERVER, Jr., Timothy A.: Partner
VANISON, Denise: Partner
VELLA, Elizabeth C.: Associate
VOGEL, John H.: Partner
WADE, J. Kirk: Partner
WALDEN, Gregory S.
WALTZ, Daniel E.: Partner
WILLIS, JoAnn V.: Senior Health Policy Advisor
WILSON, Paul A. J.: Partner
WISNER, Graham G.
WOOD, Benjamin
YAROWSKY, Jonathan R.: Partner

Outside Counsel/Consultants

Andrews Associates, Inc.
Issues: AGR, EDU, TAX
Rep By: Hon. Mark Andrews, Dr. Jacqueline Balk-Tusa

Hecht, Spencer & Associates
Issues: ADV, BUD, FOO, TAX, TRD
Rep By: William H. Hecht, Franklin C. Phifer

Millian Byers Associates, LLC
Rep By: Kenneth Y. Millian

Paucatuck Eastern Pequot Tribal Nation

North Stonington, CT
Leg. Issues: ECN, HOU, IND

Outside Counsel/Consultants

Chesapeake Enterprises, Inc.
Issues: IND
Rep By: J. John Fluharty, Scott W. Reed

Dorsey & Whitney LLP

Morriset, Schlosser, Ayer & Jozwiak
Issues: IND
Rep By: Fran Ayer, Jennifer P. Hughes

The Smith-Free Group
Issues: ECN, HOU
Rep By: James C. Free, Robert Hickmott, W. Timothy Locke, Alicia W. Smith

Paul Quinn College

Dallas, TX
Leg. Issues: EDU

Outside Counsel/Consultants

Dean Blakey & Moskowitz
Issues: EDU
Rep By: William A. Blakey

Paul, Hastings, Janofsky & Walker LLP

1299 Pennsylvania Ave. NW
Tenth Floor
Washington, DC 20004-2400
Tel: (202)508-9500
Fax: (202)508-9700
Registered: LDA, FARA
Web: www.phjw.com
E-mail: info@phjw.com
Leg. Issues: RET, TAX

Political Action Committee/s

Paul, Hastings, Janofsky and Walker Political Action Committee
1299 Pennsylvania Ave. NW
Tenth Floor
Washington, DC 20004-2400
Tel: (202)508-9500
Fax: (202)508-9700
Contact: Ralph B. Everett

In-house, DC-area Employees

BALL, Daniel R.: Associate
BARCELLA, Jr., E. Lawrence: Partner
BEHRE, Kirby D.: Partner
BURNS, David D.: Associate
COLE, Christopher A.: Associate
CROWE, Christine Marie: Associate
DAYANIM, Behnam: Associate
DICKSON, R. Bruce: Partner
ELLIOTT, E. Donald: Partner
EVERETT, Ralph B.: Partner
FARIA, Wendell M.: Of Counsel
FLICKER, Scott M.: Partner
HOPE, Judith Richards: Senior Counsel
JOHNSON, Jr., John Griffith: Partner
LIVELY, P. Susan: Associate
LOEB, G. Hamilton: Partner
NORTHROP, Carl W.: Partner
PATRIZIA, Charles A.: Partner
PERITO, Paul L.: Senior Counsel
PLOTKIN, Robert: Of Counsel
POERIO, J. Mark: Of Counsel
RYAN, Bruce D.: Partner
TOGNI, Patrick J.
WATCHMAN, Gregory R.: Of Counsel
YAMADA, Gerald H.: Of Counsel

Outside Counsel/Consultants

Caplin & Drysdale, Chartered
Issues: RET, TAX
Rep By: Kent A. Mason

Davis & Harman LLP
Issues: TAX
Rep By: Randolf H. Hardock

Paxson Communications Corp.

Clearwater, FL
Leg. Issues: COM, TEC

Outside Counsel/Consultants

Alcalde & Fay
Issues: COM, TEC
Rep By: Hector Alcalde, Jim Davenport, Vicki L. Iseman, Julie Patterson

Payless Shoe Source

Topeka, KS
A subsidiary of May Department Stores.
Leg. Issues: TRD

Outside Counsel/Consultants

Hogan & Hartson L.L.P.
Issues: TRD
Rep By: Irene Chang, Stephanie Henning, Warren H. Maruyama, Mark S. McConnell, Daniel B. Poneman

PC Strand Producers Coalition

Outside Counsel/Consultants

Collier Shannon Scott, PLLC
Rep By: Paul C. Rosenthal

PCS Health Systems, Inc.

Scottsdale, AZ
Leg. Issues: HCR

Outside Counsel/Consultants

Reed, Smith, LLP
Issues: HCR
Rep By: Phillips S. Peter, Marc Scheineson

PDA

7500 Old Georgetown Rd.
Suite 620
Bethesda, MD 20814
Tel: (301)986-0293
Fax: (301)986-0296
Web: www.pda.org
E-mail: info@pda.org
Education, training, and information exchange in pharmaceutical, science, and technology.
Leg. Issues: CHM, MAN, PHA, SCI

In-house, DC-area Employees

FRY, Edmund M.: President

PDI Ground Support Systems, Inc.

Cleveland, OH
Leg. Issues: DEF

Outside Counsel/Consultants

American Defense Internat'l, Inc.
Issues: DEF
Rep By: Michael Herson, Van D. Hipp, Jr., Dave Wilberding

PE Biosystems

Foster City, CA
Leg. Issues: BUD, CIV, CPI, LAW, SCI

Outside Counsel/Consultants

Smith Alling Lane, P.S.
Issues: BUD, CIV, CPI, LAW, SCI
Rep By: Lisa Hurst, Robert Mack, Michael McAleenan, Timothy Schellberg

The Peabody Group

St. Louis, MO
The nation's largest producer and marketer of coal.
Leg. Issues: ENG, IND, LBR, NAT, TAX

Outside Counsel/Consultants

The Willard Group
Issues: ENG, IND, LBR, NAT, TAX
Rep By: Daniel Scherder

Peace Action

1819 H St. NW
Suite 420
Washington, DC 20006-3603
Tel: (202)862-9740
Fax: (202)862-9762
Web: www.peace-action.org
Formerly known as SANE/FREEZE: Campaign for Global Security. A national membership organization working to develop public support for policies that will lead toward peace, including nuclear disarmament, reduced military spending and a non-interventionist foreign policy.
Leg. Issues: BUD, DEF

Political Action Committee/s

Peace Action PAC
1819 H St. NW
Suite 420
Washington, DC 20006-3603
Tel: (202)862-9740
Fax: (202)862-9762
Contact: Gordon Clark

In-house, DC-area Employees

CLARK, Gordon: Exec. Director

Peace Links

666 Eleventh St. NW
Suite 202
Washington, DC 20001
Tel: (202)783-7030
Fax: (202)783-7040
Web: www.peacelinkusa.org
E-mail: info@peacelink.org

In-house, DC-area Employees

MARKS, Deborah: Administrator
RUNKEL, Deedie: Director

Peachtree Settlement Funding

Norcross, GA
Leg. Issues: TAX

Outside Counsel/Consultants

Kelly and Associates, Inc.
Issues: TAX
Rep By: John A. Kelly

Peanut and Tree Nut Processors Ass'n

P.O. Box 59811
Potomac, MD 20859-9811
Tel: (301)365-2521
Fax: (301)365-7705
Web: www.ptnpa.org
E-mail: ptnpa@mindspring.com
The above address is that of American Trade and Professional Ass'n Management (see firm listing).

Political Action Committee/s

NUT PAC
P.O. Box 59811
Potomac, MD 20859-9811
Tel: (301)365-2521
Fax: (301)365-7705
Contact: Russell E. Barker

In-house, DC-area Employees

BARKER, Russell E.: President

Outside Counsel/Consultants

American Trade and Professional Ass'n Management
Rep By: Russell E. Barker

Pechanga Band of California Luiseno Indians

Temecula, CA
Leg. Issues: GAM, IND

Outside Counsel/Consultants

Patton Boggs, LLP
Issues: GAM, IND
Rep By: Katharine R. Boyce, Lanny J. Davis, Clayton L. Hough, Carolina L. Mederos, Jonathan R. Yarowsky

Pechanga Band of Luiseno Mission Indians

Outside Counsel/Consultants

Honberger and Walters, Inc.
Rep By: Donald Gilchrest, Roger F. Honberger, Thomas P. Walters

Pedestal

Washington, DC
Leg. Issues: BAN

Outside Counsel/Consultants

Butera & Andrews
Issues: BAN
Rep By: Cliff W. Andrews, Wright H. Andrews, Jr., James J. Butera, Frank Tillotson

Pediatricians for Children Inc.

601 13th St. NW
Suite 400 North
Washington, DC 20004
Tel: (202)347-8600
Fax: (202)393-6137
A political action committee.

In-house, DC-area Employees

NOYES, Elizabeth J.: Treasurer

Pediatrix Medical Group, Inc.

1610 Dewitt Avenue
Alexandria, VA 22301
Tel: (703)262-6434
Fax: (703)860-3187
Registered: LDA
Leg. Issues: HCR

In-house, DC-area Employees

JENKINS, Ellen D.: Director, Federal Affairs

Pedorthic Footwear Ass'n

Columbia, MD
Web: www.pedorthics.org
E-mail: janis@pedorthics.org
A not-for-profit organization representing professionals involved in the field of pedorthics..
Leg. Issues: HCR, MMM

Outside Counsel/Consultants

Arent Fox Kintner Plotkin & Kahn, PLLC
Issues: HCR, MMM
Rep By: Bill Applegate, Robert J. Waters

Peerless Petrochemicals, Inc.

Peneles, PR

Outside Counsel/Consultants

Bode & Grenier LLP
Rep By: William H. Bode

Pegasus Airwave

Boca Raton, FL
Leg. Issues: HCR, MMM

Outside Counsel/Consultants

Nusgart Consulting, LLC
Issues: HCR, MMM
Rep By: Marcia Nusgart

Pegasus Capital Advisors, L.P.

Cos Cob, CT
Leg. Issues: AER, FOR

Outside Counsel/Consultants

Akin, Gump, Strauss, Hauer & Feld, L.L.P.
Issues: AER, FOR
Rep By: Frank J. Donatelli, Elizabeth Hyman, S. Bruce Wilson

Pegasus Communications

New York, NY
Leg. Issues: TEC

Outside Counsel/Consultants

Dittus Communications
Rep By: Kristin Litterst, Jennifer Moire

Fierce and Isakowitz
Issues: TEC
Rep By: Kathryn Braden, Samantha Cook, Donald L. Fierce, Mark W. Isakowitz, Diane Moery

Shaw Pittman

Pegasus Management

Catonsville, MD
Leg. Issues: AVI

Outside Counsel/Consultants

AB Management Associates, Inc.
Issues: AVI
Rep By: Larry P. Barnett

PEI Electronics

Huntsville, AL
Leg. Issues: DEF

Outside Counsel/Consultants

Michael W. Adcock
Issues: DEF
Rep By: Michael W. Adcock

Patricia C. Kennedy
Issues: DEF
Rep By: Patricia C. Kennedy

Pelican Butte Corp.

Klamath Falls, OR
Leg. Issues: RES

Outside Counsel/Consultants

Manatt, Phelps & Phillips, LLP
Issues: RES
Rep By: Hon. Jack W. Buechner, June L. DeHart, James R. Jones, Jeff Kuhnreich, Jessica A. Wasserman

Pembroke Real Estate, Inc.

Boston, MA
Leg. Issues: RES

Outside Counsel/Consultants

The Carmen Group
Issues: RES
Rep By: Max Brown, Gerald P. Carmen, Diane Jemmott

Pemco Aviation Group, Inc.

Birmingham, AL
Leg. Issues: DEF

Outside Counsel/Consultants

Hurt, Norton & Associates
Issues: DEF
Rep By: Robert H. Hurt, Frank Norton, Helen C. Siracuse, William K. Takakoshi

Peninsula Airways, Inc.

Anchorage, AK

Outside Counsel/Consultants

Shaw Pittman
Rep By: Robert E. Cohn

Penn Mutual Life Insurance Co.

Philadelphia, PA

Outside Counsel/Consultants

Murray, Scheer, Montgomery, Tapia & O'Donnell
Rep By: Thomas R. Crawford, D. Michael Murray

Penn Yan, New York, Village of

Leg. Issues: GOV

Outside Counsel/Consultants

Duncan, Weinberg, Genzer & Pembroke, P.C.
Issues: GOV
Rep By: Richmond F. Allan, Jeffrey C. Genzer, Michael R. Postar

J. C. Penney Co., Inc.

1156 15th St. NW
Suite 502
Washington, DC 20005-1799
Tel: (202)862-4811
Fax: (202)862-4829
Registered: LDA

A retail organization headquartered in Plano, TX.

Leg. Issues: APP, BNK, HCR, LBR, POS, RET, TAX, TRA, TRD

Political Action Committee/s

PenneyPAC
1156 15th St. NW
Suite 502
Washington, DC 20005-1799
Contact: John Wirtz
Tel: (202)862-4811
Fax: (202)862-4829

In-house, DC-area Employees

DAVIS, Carrie: Administrative Manager, Government Relations
GILL, Rick: V. President and Director, Government Relations
MCELVANEY, Jason: Federal Government Relations Representative
PHILLIPS, Paula: Government Relations Specialist
WESLOW, Norman J.: Senior Government Relations Counsel
WIRTZ, John: Treasurer, PenneyPAC

Outside Counsel/Consultants

Hecht, Spencer & Associates
Issues: APP, LBR, TAX, TRA
Rep By: Timothy P. Hecht, William H. Hecht, Franklin C. Phifer

PennField Oil Co.

Omaha, NE
Leg. Issues: PHA

Outside Counsel/Consultants

Olsson, Frank and Weeda, P.C.
Issues: PHA
Rep By: John W. Bode, Susan P. Grymes, Karen Reis Harned, Stephen L. Lacey, Marshall L. Matz, Tyson Redpath, Ryan W. Stroschein, David F. Weeda

Pennington BioMedical Research Center

Baton Rouge, LA
Leg. Issues: AGR, BUD, DEF, EDU, ENG, FIN, NAT, TRA

Outside Counsel/Consultants

Adams and Reese LLP
Issues: AGR, BUD, DEF, EDU, ENG, FIN, NAT, TRA
Rep By: B. Jeffrey Brooks

Pennsylvania Economic Development Financing Authorities

Outside Counsel/Consultants

MV3 & Associates

Valente Lopatin & Schulze
Rep By: Mark Valente, III

Pennsylvania Higher Education Assistance Agency

Harrisburg, PA
Leg. Issues: BUD, EDU

Outside Counsel/Consultants

American Continental Group, Inc.
Issues: EDU
Rep By: Shawn H. Smeallie, Peter Terpeluk, Jr.

Capitol Associates, Inc.
Issues: BUD, EDU
Rep By: Edward R. Long, Ph.D., Julie P. Pawelczyk

Pennsylvania House

Lewisburg, PA

A manufacturer of furniture.

Outside Counsel/Consultants

O'Connor & Fierce Associates

Pennsylvania Nat'l Guard Ass'n

Camp Hill, PA
Leg. Issues: DEF, MAN

Outside Counsel/Consultants

American Systems Internat'l Corp.
Issues: DEF, MAN
Rep By: Robert D. McVey, William H. Skipper, Jr.

Pennsylvania Pharmaceutical Ass'n

Harrisburg, PA

Outside Counsel/Consultants

Chambers Associates Inc.

Pennsylvania Pyrotechnics Ass'n

Harrisburg, PA
Leg. Issues: TRA

Outside Counsel/Consultants

Ann Eppard Associates, Ltd.
Issues: TRA
Rep By: Julie Chlopecki, Ann Eppard

Pennsylvania Savings Ass'n Insurance Corp.

Camp Hill, PA

Outside Counsel/Consultants

Oppenheimer Wolff & Donnelly LLP

Pennsylvania Turnpike Commission

Harrisburg, PA
Leg. Issues: BUD

Outside Counsel/Consultants

Baker, Donelson, Bearman & Caldwell, P.C.
Issues: BUD
Rep By: Janet L. Powell

Ann Eppard Associates, Ltd.
Rep By: Julie Chlopecki, Ann Eppard

Pennsylvania, Washington Office of the Commonwealth of

444 N. Capitol St. NW
Suite 700
Washington, DC 20001
Tel: (202)624-7828
Fax: (202)624-7831

In-house, DC-area Employees

BOOTHBY, Clay: Associate Director
HALKIAS, Rebecca: Deputy Chief of Staff for Federal Affairs

Pennzoil-Quaker State Co.

Houston, TX
Leg. Issues: AUT, CAW, CSP, ENV, HCR, LBR, TAX, TRA, TRD

Outside Counsel/Consultants

Kathleen Winn & Associates, Inc.
Issues: AUT, CAW, CSP, ENV, HCR, LBR, TAX, TRA, TRD

Penobscot Indian Nation

Indian Island, ME

Outside Counsel/Consultants

Hall, Estill, Hardwick, Gable, Golden & Nelson
Rep By: Joseph R. Membrino

George Waters Consulting Service
Rep By: George Waters

PenRose Corp.

La Jolla, CA
Leg. Issues: RES

Outside Counsel/Consultants

Rothleder Associates, Inc.
Issues: RES

Pensacola Chamber of Commerce

Pensacola, FL
Leg. Issues: DEF

Outside Counsel/Consultants

Madison Government Affairs
Issues: DEF
Rep By: Paul J. Hirsch, Jackson Kemper, III

Pentachlorophenol Task Force

Washington, DC
Leg. Issues: CHM

Outside Counsel/Consultants

Patton Boggs, LLP
Issues: CHM
Rep By: Daniel R. Addison

People Advancing Christian Education (PACE)

119 C St. SE
Washington, DC 20003
Tel: (202)548-2563
Registered: LDA
Leg. Issues: EDU, FAM, REL, TAX

In-house, DC-area Employees

HUTCHESON, John
YOUNG, Jared G.

People For Montana

Outside Counsel/Consultants

Stevens Reed Curcio & Co.

People for the American Way

2000 M St. NW
Suite 400
Washington, DC 20036

Tel: (202)467-4999
Fax: (202)293-2672
Registered: LDA

A national non-profit, nonpartisan education organization founded in 1980 to promote First Amendment rights and democratic values. This 300,000 member organization focuses primarily on issues of church-state separation, religious liberty, free expression, civil rights and citizen responsibility.

Leg. Issues: ART, CIV, COM, CON, EDU, FAM, LAW, REL, TEC

Political Action Committee/s

People for the American Way Voters Alliance

2000 M St. NW
Suite 400
Washington, DC 20036

Tel: (202)467-4999
Fax: (202)293-2672

In-house, DC-area Employees

BLUM, Carol: V. President and Chief Operating Officer
COLEMAN, Nancy: Director, Media Relations
COLLINS, Mary Jean: National Field Director
FOSTER, Stephenie: Director, Public Policy
MINCBERG, Elliot M.: Exec. V. President and Director, Legal and General Counsel
MONTANINO, Deborah: Director, Development
NEAS, Ralph G.: President
OTTINGER, Larry: Senior Staff Attorney
SCHAFFER, Judith: Deputy Director
SCHOUMACHER, Stephanie: Senior V. President, Marketing Communications and Development

People for the Ethical Treatment of Animals

Norfolk, VA

Leg. Issues: ANI, CHM, ENV, HCR, SCI

Outside Counsel/Consultants

Shawn Coulson
Issues: ANI, CHM, ENV, HCR, SCI
Rep By: Hon. Ronald D. Coleman, William Wheeler

Peoples Bank

Bridgeport, CT

Leg. Issues: BAN, TAX

Outside Counsel/Consultants

Butera & Andrews
Issues: BAN, TAX
Rep By: Wright H. Andrews, Jr., James J. Butera

Peoria, Arizona, City of

Leg. Issues: EDU, ENV, LAW, RES, URB

Outside Counsel/Consultants

Parry, Romani, DeConcini & Symms
Issues: EDU, ENV, LAW, RES, URB
Rep By: Edward H. Baxter, Hon. Dennis DeConcini, John M. Haddow, Scott D. Hatch, Shannon Davis Henderson, Jack W. Martin, Romano Romani, Linda Arey Skladany, Hon. Steven D. Symms

Pepper Hamilton LLP

600 14th St. NW
Suite 500
Washington, DC 20005

Tel: (202)220-1200
Fax: (202)220-1665
Registered: LDA, FARA

In-house, DC-area Employees

CORTESE, Jr., Alfred W.: Partner
DORRIS, Gregory: Partner
EVANS, Jr., K. Stewart: Partner
RINKERMAN, Gary: Partner
SHEEHAN, Kenneth: Partner
TECKLER, Martin D.: Counsel

Outside Counsel/Consultants

MV3 & Associates

RTS Consulting

Valente Lopatin & Schulze
Rep By: Richard T. Schulze, Jr., Mark Valente, III

PepsiCo, Inc.

Purchase, NY
Registered: LDA

Leg. Issues: BEV, HCR, LBR, TAX, TRD

Outside Counsel/Consultants

American Continental Group, Inc.
Issues: BEV
Rep By: Steve Colovas, Shawn H. Smeallie, Peter Terpeluk, Jr.

Internat'l Business-Government Counsellors, Inc.
Rep By: John F. McDermid

Kilpatrick Stockton LLP
Rep By: Mark D. Wincek

McGuiness Norris & Williams, LLP
Issues: BEV
Rep By: William N. LaForge

Murray, Scheer, Montgomery, Tapia & O'Donnell
Issues: HCR, LBR, TAX, TRD
Rep By: Thomas R. Crawford, D. Michael Murray

Preston Gates Ellis & Rouvelas Meeds LLP
Rep By: Werner W. Brandt

Wilmer, Cutler & Pickering
Rep By: William J. Wilkins

Per Udsen

Grenaa, DENMARK

Defense equipment manufacturers.

Outside Counsel/Consultants

JGW Internat'l Ltd.
Rep By: Andrew M. Wilson, John G. Wilson

Perdue Farms Inc.

Salisbury, MD

Leg. Issues: BUD, LBR, TAX

Outside Counsel/Consultants

Kelly and Associates, Inc.
Issues: BUD, LBR, TAX
Rep By: John A. Kelly

Williams & Jensen, P.C.
Rep By: David E. Franasiak, Robert E. Glennon, Jr., J. Steven Hart, Anthony J. Roda

Performance Food Group Inc.

Richmond, VA

Outside Counsel/Consultants

Wells & Associates
Rep By: Milton T. Wells

Performing Animal Welfare Soc.

Galt, CA

Leg. Issues: ANI

Outside Counsel/Consultants

Sher & Blackwell
Issues: ANI
Rep By: Jeffrey R. Pike

Performing Arts Network of New Jersey

Trenton, NJ

Outside Counsel/Consultants

Bell, Boyd & Lloyd
Rep By: A. Thomas Carroccio

Periodical Management Group, Inc.

San Antonio, TX

Distributor of books and magazines.

Leg. Issues: DEF

Outside Counsel/Consultants

Marvin Leath Associates
Issues: DEF
Rep By: Hon. Marvin Leath

PerkinElmer Detection Systems

Woburn, MA

Provides a variety of scientific and technically-oriented products, custom equipment systems and related or specialized services to government and industrial customers.

Leg. Issues: AVI, LAW

Outside Counsel/Consultants

Akin, Gump, Strauss, Hauer & Feld, L.L.P.
Issues: AVI, LAW
Rep By: Sean G. D'Arcy, Smith W. Davis, Barney J. Skladany, Jr., Jose H. Villarreal

Perkins School for the Blind

Boston, MA

Leg. Issues: EDU

Outside Counsel/Consultants

Devillier Communications
Issues: EDU
Rep By: Barbara Lohman

Pernod Ricard

1225 I St. NW
Suite 500
Washington, DC 20005

Tel: (202)218-3525
Registered: LDA

A manufacturer and distributor of alcoholic and non-alcoholic beverages headquartered in Paris, France.

Leg. Issues: BEV, CPT, TRD

In-house, DC-area Employees

ORR, Mark: V. President, North American Affairs

Outside Counsel/Consultants

Dittus Communications
Rep By: Gloria S. Dittus, Shelton Jones, Kristin Litterst, Jennifer Moire

Hall, Green, Rupli, LLC
Issues: BEV
Rep By: John M. Green, G. Stewart Hall, Timothy R. Rupli

Powell, Goldstein, Frazer & Murphy LLP
Issues: TRD
Rep By: Daniel M. Price, Mark Traphagen

Perpetual Corp.

Washington, DC

Leg. Issues: TAX

Outside Counsel/Consultants

White & Case LLP
Issues: TAX
Rep By: William P. McClure

Perry Institute for Marine Science

West Palm Beach, FL

Leg. Issues: MAR, TAX

Outside Counsel/Consultants

O'Connor & Hannan, L.L.P.
Issues: MAR, TAX
Rep By: George J. Mannina, Jr.

Perry Tritech Inc.

Jupiter, FL

Leg. Issues: COM, DEF, TRD

Outside Counsel/Consultants

The MWW Group
Issues: COM, DEF, TRD
Rep By: Jonathan B. Slade

Verner, Liipfert, Bernhard, McPherson and Hand, Chartered
Issues: TRD
Rep By: Steven R. Phillips, Theresa M. Youngblood

Pershing Co. Water Conservation District of Nevada

Outside Counsel/Consultants

McClure, Gerard & Neuenschwander, Inc.
Rep By: Steven G. Barringer, Joseph T. Findaro, Matthew Iandoli, Nils W. Johnson, Hon. James A. McClure, Tod O. Neuenschwander

Pershing Division of DLJ Securities Corp.

Jersey City, NJ

Outside Counsel/Consultants

Rhoads Group

Personal Communications Industry Ass'n (PCIA)

500 Montgomery St.
Suite 700
Alexandria, VA 22314-1561

Tel: (703)739-0300
Fax: (703)836-1608
Registered: LDA

Web: www.pcia.com

Trade association representing wireless telecommunications industry companies before Congress, FCC, etc.

Leg. Issues: BUD, COM, TEC

Political Action Committee/s

PCIA PAC

500 Montgomery St.
Suite 700
Alexandria, VA 22314-1561

Tel: (703)739-0300
Fax: (703)836-1608

In-house, DC-area Employees

HOGGARTH, Robert: Senior V. President, Paging and Narrowband
KITCHEN, Jr., Emmett B. "Jay": President

Outside Counsel/Consultants

Paul, Hastings, Janofsky & Walker LLP
Issues: BUD, COM, TEC
Rep By: Ralph B. Everett

Townsend Solheim
Rep By: Linda T. Solheim

Wiley, Rein & Fielding
Issues: TEC
Rep By: Susan C. Buck, Mimi W. Dawson, Hon. Jim Slattery, Nancy J. Victory

Personal Watercraft Industry Ass'n

1819 L St. NW
Suite 700
Washington, DC 20036
Tel: (202)721-1621
Fax: (202)861-1181
Web: www.pwia.org
E-mail: stanfill@pwia.org

Affiliate of the National Marine Manufacturers Ass'n, (see seperate listing).

Leg. Issues: MAR, NAT, RES

In-house, DC-area Employees

FONTAINE, Monita W.: Exec. Director
STANFILL, Allison: Legislative Assistant

Outside Counsel/Consultants

Dittus Communications
Rep By: Alice Slater, Kristin Young

Preston Gates Ellis & Rouvelas Meeds LLP
Issues: MAR, NAT, RES
Rep By: Mark H. Ruge

Washington Strategies, L.L.C.
Rep By: Jennifer Johnson Calvert, William P. Jarrell

Peru, Government of the Republic of

Lima, PERU

Outside Counsel/Consultants

Patton Boggs, LLP

PESystems, Inc.

Fairfax, VA
Leg. Issues: DEF

Outside Counsel/Consultants

The Spectrum Group
Issues: DEF
Rep By: Paul E. McManus, James Rooney

PET Coalition

An association of medical imaging device manufacturers and distributors.

Leg. Issues: MMM

Outside Counsel/Consultants

Foley, Hoag & Eliot LLP
Issues: MMM
Rep By: Gare A. Smith

Pet Food Institute

Washington, DC
Web: www.petfoodinstitute.org

Represents 95% of the total dog and cat food tonnage produced in the U.S. Affiliate membership includes the leading suppliers of equipment, ingredients, packaging, and services to the pet food industry.

Outside Counsel/Consultants

Smith, Bucklin and Associates, Inc.
Rep By: Duane H. Ekedahl

Pet Industry Joint Advisory Council

1220 19th St. NW
Suite 400
Washington, DC 20036
Tel: (202)452-1525
Fax: (202)293-4377
Web: www.pijac.org
E-mail: info@pijac.org

A trade association working with organizations and business in the companion pet industry.

Leg. Issues: ANI, GOV, TRA

In-house, DC-area Employees

MEYERS, N. Marshall: Exec. V. President and General Counsel

Outside Counsel/Consultants

Meyers & Alterman
Rep By: N. Marshall Meyers

Peter White Coal Mining Co.

Bluefield, WV

A subsidiary of Belco Petroleum Corp.

Outside Counsel/Consultants

Heenan, Althen & Roles
Rep By: Michael T. Heenan

Petersburg, Alaska, City of

Leg. Issues: NAT, URB

Outside Counsel/Consultants

Robertson, Monagle & Eastaugh
Issues: NAT, URB
Rep By: Bradley D. Gilman, Rick E. Marks

Peterson Cos., Inc.

Fairfax, VA
Leg. Issues: TRA

Outside Counsel/Consultants

O'Malley, Miles, Nylen & Gilmore, P.A.
Issues: TRA
Rep By: John P. Davey, Andre J. Gingles, John P. McDonough

Verner, Liipfert, Bernhard, McPherson and Hand, Chartered
Issues: TRA
Rep By: Denis J. Dwyer, Lloyd N. Hand

Petro Star, Inc.

Anchorage, AK
Leg. Issues: DEF, ENG, ENV, FUE, RES, SMB, TAX

Outside Counsel/Consultants

Van Ness Feldman, P.C.
Issues: DEF, ENG, ENV, FUE, RES, SMB, TAX
Rep By: Howard J. Feldman, Alan L. Mintz, Thomas C. Roberts, Jonathon D. Simon

Petro-Canada

Oakville, CANADA
Leg. Issues: FUE

Outside Counsel/Consultants

Hill and Knowlton, Inc.
Issues: FUE
Rep By: Gary G. Hymel

Petrojam Ltd.

Kingston, JAMAICA

Outside Counsel/Consultants

Bode & Grenier LLP
Rep By: William H. Bode

Petroleum Heat and Power Co., Inc.

Stamford, CT
Leg. Issues: TRA

Outside Counsel/Consultants

Verner, Liipfert, Bernhard, McPherson and Hand, Chartered
Issues: TRA
Rep By: Gary J. Klein

Petroleum Helicopters

New Orleans, LA
Leg. Issues: AVI, TAX

Outside Counsel/Consultants

Jones, Walker, Waechter, Poitevent, Carrere & Denegre, L.L.P.
Issues: AVI, TAX
Rep By: John J. Jaskot, R. Christian Johnsen

Petroleum Marketers Ass'n of America

1901 N. Fort Myer Dr.
Suite 1200
Arlington, VA 22209-1604
Tel: (703)351-8000
Fax: (703)351-9160
Registered: LDA
Web: www.pmaa.org
E-mail: info@pmaa.org
Leg. Issues: BAN, ENV, FUE, GOV, ROD, TAX, TOB

Political Action Committee/s

Petroleum Marketers Ass'n of America Small Businessmen's Committee
1901 N. Fort Myer Dr.
Suite 1200
Arlington, VA 22209-1604
Tel: (703)351-8000
Fax: (703)351-9160
Contact: Sarah R. Dodge

In-house, DC-area Employees

DODGE, Sarah R.: Director, Legislative Affairs
YOUGH, Melissa I.: Counsel, Government Affairs

Outside Counsel/Consultants

Bassman, Mitchell & Alfano

Bergner Bockorny Castagnetti and Hawkins
Issues: BAN, ENV, FUE, GOV, ROD, TAX, TOB
Rep By: Jeffrey T. Bergner, David A. Bockorny, David Castagnetti, Melissa Schulman

PetrolRem, Inc.

Pittsburgh, PA
Leg. Issues: CAW, DEF, ENV, MAR, SCI

Outside Counsel/Consultants

Alcalde & Fay
Issues: ENV, MAR, SCI
Rep By: Hon. Louis A. "Skip" Bafalis, J. Michael Crye, Jim Davenport

The Evans Group, Ltd.
Issues: CAW
Rep By: Ferrell D. Carmine, Hon. Thomas B. Evans, Jr.

O'Brien, Klink & Associates
Issues: DEF, ENV, MAR
Rep By: David D. O'Brien, Shannon L. Scott

Petroport, Inc.

Houston, TX
Leg. Issues: NAT

Outside Counsel/Consultants

Verner, Liipfert, Bernhard, McPherson and Hand, Chartered
Issues: NAT
Rep By: Andrea J. Grant, Vicki E. Hart, John H. Zentay

Pew Center for Civic Journalism

Washington, DC

Outside Counsel/Consultants

Neuman and Co.
Rep By: Robert A. Neuman

Pew Center on Global Climate Change

2101 Wilson Blvd.
Suite 550
Arlington, VA 22201
Tel: (703)516-4146
Fax: (703)841-1422

In-house, DC-area Employees

CLAUSSEN, Eileen: President
DIRINGER, Elliot: Director, International Strategies

Pew Charitable Trust - Environmental Law & Policy Center of the Midwest

Chicago, IL

Outside Counsel/Consultants

Widmeyer Communications, Inc.

Pew Wilderness Center

122 C St. NW
Suite 240
Washington, DC 20001
Tel: (202)544-3691
Fax: (202)544-5197
Web: www.pewwildernesscenter.org

Provides assistance in media training, grassroots organizing, and campaign strategy to citizens' groups and organizations working for wilderness protection across the country

In-house, DC-area Employees

MATZ, Mike: Exec. Director
PERCY-MCDANIEL, Herma M.: Media Director
SCOTT, Doug: Policy Director

Pezold Management

Columbus, GA

Outside Counsel/Consultants

Shaw Pittman
Rep By: Dawn M. Sciarrino

Pfaltzgraff

New York, NY

A ceramicware manufacturer.

Outside Counsel/Consultants

Collier Shannon Scott, PLLC
Rep By: David A. Hartquist, Michael R. Kershow

Pfizer, Inc.

325 Seventh St. NW
Suite 1200
Washington, DC 20004-1007
Tel: (202)783-7070
Fax: (202)347-2044
Registered: LDA
Web: www.pfizer.com

A diversified, research-based health care company with businesses in pharmaceuticals, hospital products, animal health, consumer products, specialty chemicals, and specialty minerals. Headquartered in New York, NY. Acquired Warner-Lambert in 2000.

Leg. Issues: AGR, ANI, BUD, CPT, CSP, EDU, ENV, FOR, HCR, IMM, MED, MMM, PHA, RET, SCI, TAX, TOR, TOU, TRA, TRD

Political Action Committee/s

Pfizer PAC

325 Seventh St. NW
Suite 1200
Washington, DC 20004-1007
Contact: Catherine P. Bennett
Tel: (202)783-7070
Fax: (202)347-2044

In-house, DC-area Employees

BENNETT, Catherine P.: V. President, Federal Tax and Trade Legislation
BOLICK, Gary M.: Director, State Government Relations
BOWLER, M. Kenneth: V. President, Federal Government Relations
FINKELNBURG, Marjorie C.: Assistant Director, Government Relations
JUDGE, Dolly A.: Senior Director, Federal Relations
LAMARCA, Louis: Director, Federal Relations
MCCARTHY, Justin J.: Assistant Director, Government Relations

Outside Counsel/Consultants

Akin, Gump, Strauss, Hauer & Feld, L.L.P.
Issues: TRA, TRD
Rep By: Charles W. Johnson, IV, Susan H. Lent, Henry A. Terhune

Bennett Turner & Coleman, LLP

Brownstein Hyatt & Farber, P.C.
Issues: HCR
Rep By: William T. Brack, Michael B. Levy

Canfield & Associates, Inc.
Issues: MMM, TAX
Rep By: Roger Blauwet, April Boston, Anne C. Canfield

Capitol Health Group, LLC
Issues: HCR, MMM, PHA
Rep By: Michael D. Bromberg, Shawn Coughlin, Steven Jenning, Layna McConkey Peltier

Cassidy & Associates, Inc.

The Direct Impact Co.

Edelman Public Relations Worldwide

The Gorlin Group
Issues: TRD
Rep By: Jacques Gorlin

Hooper Owen & Winburn
Issues: PHA, TAX, TRA
Rep By: David Rudd, John P. Winburn

Jones, Day, Reavis & Pogue
Rep By: Raymond J. Wiacek

Kessler & Associates Business Services, Inc.
Issues: HCR, MMM, TAX, TRD
Rep By: Richard S. Kessler, James C. Musser

Lent Scrivner & Roth LLC
Issues: CSP, PHA, TRD
Rep By: Hon. Norman F. Lent, Norman F. Lent, III, Alan J. Roth, Michael S. Scrivner

David Nelson & Associates
Issues: HCR
Rep By: David W. Nelson

Parry, Romani, DeConcini & Symms
Issues: CPT, HCR, MED, MMM, TAX
Rep By: Edward H. Baxter, Hon. Dennis DeConcini, John M. Haddow, Scott D. Hatch, Shannon Davis Henderson, Jack W. Martin, Romano Romani, Linda Arey Skladany, Hon. Steven D. Symms

Ryan, Phillips, Utrecht & MacKinnon
Issues: ENV, HCR, MMM, PHA, TAX, TOU
Rep By: Rodney Hoppe, Jeffrey M. MacKinnon, William D. Phillips, Mark D. Planning, Thomas M. Ryan, Joseph V. Vasapoli

Washington Council Ernst & Young
Issues: HCR, TAX, TRD
Rep By: Doug Badger, Lauren Darling, John L. Doney, Jayne T. Fitzgerald, LaBrenda Garrett-Nelson, Gary J. Gasper, Bruce A. Gates, Nick Giordano, Cathy Koch, Robert J. Leonard, Richard Meltzer, Phillip D. Moseley, John D. Porter, Robert M. Rozen, Donna Steele-Flynn, Timothy J. Urban

Pfluger Enterprises LLC

Dallas, TX

A television services firm.

Leg. Issues: TEC, TRD

Outside Counsel/Consultants

George H. Denison
Issues: TEC, TRD
Rep By: George H. Denison

PG&E Corp.

700 11th St. NW
Suite 250
Washington, DC 20001
Tel: (202)638-3500
Fax: (202)638-3522
Registered: LDA

Web: www.pge-corp.com

Headquartered in San Francisco, CA.

Leg. Issues: ENG, ENV, TAX, UTI

In-house, DC-area Employees

CARTER, Rick: Manager, Federal Governmental Relations
HILL, Thomas M.: Manager, Federal Governmental Relations
KLINE, Steven L.: V. President, Federal Governmental and Regulatory Relations
PIDCOCK, Paulette C.: Director, Federal Governmental Relations
TOMCALA, Karen: Director, FERC Relations

Outside Counsel/Consultants

Akin, Gump, Strauss, Hauer & Feld, L.L.P.
Issues: ENG, TAX, UTI
Rep By: Joel Jankowsky, Robin M. Nuschler, Barney J. Skladany, Jr., Henry A. Terhune, Jose H. Villarreal

Troutman Sanders LLP
Issues: ENG
Rep By: Thomas C. Jensen, Bonnie Suchman, Dionne E. Thompson

PG&E Gas Transmission Northwest

Portland, OR

Outside Counsel/Consultants

Akin, Gump, Strauss, Hauer & Feld, L.L.P.
Rep By: Janet C. Boyd, Joel Jankowsky

PG&E Generating Co.

7500 Old Georgetown Rd.
Suite 1300
Bethesda, MD 20814-6161
Tel: (301)280-6800
Fax: (301)280-6900
Web: www.usgen.com
E-mail: jhawks@usgen.com

Formerly U.S. Generating Co. A developer, builder, owner, operator and manager of competitive power generation facilities.

Leg. Issues: CAW, ENG, ENV, UTI

In-house, DC-area Employees

HAWKS, John K.: V. President, Public Affairs and Government Relations
HURSTON, Pat: Corporate Communications Specialist

Outside Counsel/Consultants

Dickstein Shapiro Morin & Oshinsky LLP
Issues: CAW, ENG, ENV, UTI
Rep By: Sidney Dickstein, Larry F. Eisenstat, Hon. Wendell H. Ford, Elizabeth B. Haywood, Robert Mangas, Graham "Rusty" Mathews, Laurie McKay, Hon. Stanford E. Parris, Rebecah Moore Shepherd, Kenneth M. Simon, Laura Szabo, L. Andrew Zausner

PG&E Nat'l Energy Group

Bethesda, MD
Leg. Issues: ENG

Outside Counsel/Consultants

Foley & Lardner
Issues: ENG
Rep By: Theodore H. Bornstein, Jodi L. Hanson

The PGA Tour, Inc.

Ponte Vedra, FL
Registered: LDA
Leg. Issues: TAX

Outside Counsel/Consultants

Cassidy & Associates, Inc.
Issues: TAX
Rep By: Dan C. Tate, Sr., Maureen Walsh

Mark W. Goodin
Rep By: Mark W. Goodin

Verner, Liipfert, Bernhard, McPherson and Hand, Chartered
Issues: TAX
Rep By: Evan M. Migdail

Pharmaceutical Care Management Ass'n

2300 Ninth St. South
Suite 210
Arlington, VA 22204
Tel: (703)920-8480
Fax: (703)920-8491
Registered: LDA

Web: www.pcmanet.org
Leg. Issues: HCR

In-house, DC-area Employees

CHARLESTON, Suzanne E.: Director, Government Affairs
DONOHO, Patrick B.: V. President, Government Affairs and Public Policy
KONNOR, PharmMS, Delbert D.: President and Chief Exec. Officer

Pharmaceutical Products, Inc.

Boston, MA

Outside Counsel/Consultants

Peter S. Barash Associates, Inc.
Rep By: Peter S. Barash

Pharmaceutical Research and Manufacturers of America

1100 15th St. NW
Suite 900
Washington, DC 20005
Tel: (202)835-3400
Fax: (202)835-3414
Registered: LDA

Web: www.phrma.org

The Pharmaceutical Research and Manufacturers of America represents research-based pharmaceuticals that develop and produce prescription drugs and biological products in the United States.

Leg. Issues: BUD, CPT, CSP, DEF, HCR, MED, MMM, PHA, TAX, TRD, VET

Political Action Committee/s

Pharmaceutical Research and Manufacturers of America Better Government Committee

1100 15th St. NW
Suite 900
Washington, DC 20005
Contact: Anne Holmes
Tel: (202)835-3400
Fax: (202)835-3414

In-house, DC-area Employees

BANTHAM, Russel A.: Exec. V. President and General Counsel
COTTRELL, Jacqueline Dailey: Director, Public Affairs
CURRIE, Rodger: Assistant General Counsel
FINSTOM, Susan: Assistant V. President, International
GRAYSON, Mark: Senior Director, Communications
HERZFELD, Shannon S. S.: Senior V. President, International
HOLMER, Alan F.: President and Chief Exec. Officer
HOLMES, Anne: PAC Contact and Federal Affairs Coordinator
LUCAS, William L.: Associate V. President, State Government Affairs
LYNCH, Ann-Marie: V. President, Policy
MALMGREN, Kurt: Senior V. President, Government Affairs
MOLINEAUX, Christopher: V. President, Public Affairs
SAUL, Jr., Richard: Deputy V. President, International
SCHUMACHER, Edward: Senior Director, Policy
SPILKER, Dr. Bert A.: Senior V. President, Scientific and Regulatory Affairs
VAN HOOK, Matthew: Deputy General Counsel
WALL, Lori M.: Director, Public Policy
WALTERS, William: Assistant General Counsel
WOOLLETT, Ph.D., Gillian: Assistant V. President, Biologics and Biotechnology

Outside Counsel/Consultants

Alexander Strategy Group
Issues: MMM, PHA, TRD
Rep By: Edwin A. Buckham

Andreae, Vick & Associates, L.L.C.
Issues: TRD
Rep By: M. Christine Vick

Brown & Associates
Issues: VET
Rep By: Jesse Brown, Edward P. Scott

BSMG Worldwide

Clark & Weinstock, Inc.
Issues: HCR, MED, MMM
Rep By: Hon. Vic H. Fazio, Jr., Ed Kutler, Deirdre Stach, Sandi Stuart, Hon. John Vincent "Vin" Weber

Covington & Burling
Issues: HCR
Rep By: Peter Barton Hutt, Bruce N. Kuhlik

Creative Response Concepts

Davis & Harman LLP
Issues: HCR
Rep By: Richard S. Belas, Thomas A. Davis, Barbara Groves Mattox

The Gorlin Group
Issues: TRD
Rep By: Jacques Gorlin

Greenberg Traurig, LLP
Issues: HCR, MMM, PHA
Rep By: Howard J. Cohen

Health Policy Alternatives, Inc.
Issues: HCR
Rep By: Thomas Ault

Hogan & Hartson L.L.P.
Issues: TRD

Rep By: Jeanne S. Archibald, Donna A. Boswell, Irene Chang, Warren H. Maruyama, Beth L. Roberts, Ann Morgan Vickery

McKenna & Cuneo, L.L.P.

Gerald J. Mossinghoff
Rep By: Gerald J. Mossinghoff

Muse & Associates
Issues: HCR, MMM
Rep By: Donald N. Muse

Policy Directions, Inc.
Issues: HCR, MED, MMM
Rep By: Kathleen "Kay" Holcombe, Frankie L. Trull

Powell, Goldstein, Frazer & Murphy LLP
Issues: TRD
Rep By: Jeff Kushan

Saunders Consulting
Issues: HCR, TAX
Rep By: Albert C. Saunders

Skadden, Arps, Slate, Meagher & Flom LLP
Rep By: Roseann M. Cutrone, Fred T. Goldberg, Jr., Robert E. Lighthizer, Paul W. Oosterhuis

Stuntz, Davis & Staffier, P.C.
Issues: PHA
Rep By: Randall E. Davis

Tongour Simpson Holsclaw Green
Issues: PHA
Rep By: John Bradley "Brad" Holsclaw, Michael A. Tongour

Verner, Liipfert, Bernhard, McPherson and Hand, Chartered
Issues: HCR
Rep By: Hon. Daniel R. Coats, Vicki E. Hart, Michael E. O'Brien

Williams & Jensen, P.C.
Issues: CPT, CSP, HCR, MMM, PHA, TRD
Rep By: William B. Canfield, J. Steven Hart, George G. Olsen, Anthony J. Roda

Pharmacia Corp.

1455 F St. NW
Suite 450
Washington, DC 20004
Tel: (202)393-6040
Fax: (202)393-6050
Registered: LDA

Headquartered in Peapack, NJ. Formerly (2000) known as Pharmacia & Upjohn.. The company merged with Monsanto (see separate listing) in April of 2000.

Leg. Issues: ANI, BUD, CAW, CPT, ENV, HCR, MED, MMM, PHA, TAX, TRD, WAS

In-house, DC-area Employees

DONOGHUE BAXTER, Marguerite: Senior Director, Federal Government Affairs
GRAVES-MOORE, Pamela: Manager, Federal Government Affairs
GREISSING, Jr., Edward F.: V. President, Government Affairs
MORAN, Cynthia Root: Director, Government Affairs
MYERS, Jeff M.: Director, Government Affairs

Outside Counsel/Consultants

Alpine Group, Inc.
Issues: CPT, HCR, MED, MMM, PHA
Rep By: Dan Brouillette, James D. Massie, James Gregory Means, Rhod M. Shaw, Richard C. White, Sam White

The Duberstein Group, Inc.
Issues: ANI, CAW, ENV, HCR, MED, MMM, TAX
Rep By: John W. Angus, III, Michael S. Berman, Steven M. Champlin, Kenneth M. Duberstein, Henry M. Gandy, Daniel P. Meyer

John Freshman Associates, Inc.
Issues: ENV
Rep By: John D. Freshman, Lawrence P. Kast, Catherine B. Kiefer

Heidepriem & Mager, Inc.
Issues: HCR
Rep By: Karin Bolte, Pat Ford-Roegner, Christopher Gould, Nikki Heidepriem, Mimi Mager

Kessler & Associates Business Services, Inc.
Issues: BUD, ENV, HCR, TAX, WAS
Rep By: Howard Berman, Billy Lee Evans, Simon Gros, Richard S. Kessler, James C. Musser, Harry Sporidis

Mayer, Brown & Platt
Issues: HCR, TRD
Rep By: Amb. Peter L. Scher

Parry, Romani, DeConcini & Symms
Issues: CPT, HCR, MED, MMM
Rep By: Edward H. Baxter, Hon. Dennis DeConcini, John M. Haddow, Scott D. Hatch, Shannon Davis Henderson, Jack W. Martin, Romano Romani, Linda Arey Skladany, Hon. Steven D. Symms

Reed, Smith, LLP
Issues: HCR
Rep By: Marc Scheineson

Pharmanex

Simi Valley, CA
A diet supplement manufacturer.

Leg. Issues: FOO

Outside Counsel/Consultants

Patton Boggs, LLP
Issues: FOO
Rep By: Daniel A. Kracov, Stuart M. Pape

Pheasants Forever

St. Paul, MN
Leg. Issues: AGR

Outside Counsel/Consultants

Cashdollar-Jones & Co.
Issues: AGR
Rep By: Robert Cashdollar

Phelps Dodge Corp.

1420 New York Ave. NW
Suite 210
Washington, DC 20005
Tel: (202)789-1745
Fax: (202)371-1731
Registered: LDA

Leg. Issues: BUD, CAW, ENV, NAT, TAX

Political Action Committee/s

Phelps Dodge Employees Fund for Good Government
1420 New York Ave. NW
Suite 210
Washington, DC 20005
Contact: Linda D. Findlay
Tel: (202)789-1745
Fax: (202)371-1731

In-house, DC-area Employees

DAVIES, Kay: Manager, Government Relations
FINDLAY, Linda D.: V. President, Government Relations

Outside Counsel/Consultants

Winner & Associates

Philadelphia College of Osteopathic Medicine

Philadelphia, PA
Leg. Issues: BUD

Outside Counsel/Consultants

Cassidy & Associates, Inc.
Issues: BUD
Rep By: Douglass E. Bobbitt, Christopher Lamond

Philadelphia College of Textiles and Science

Philadelphia, PA
Leg. Issues: DEF, SCI

Outside Counsel/Consultants

Cassidy & Associates, Inc.
Issues: DEF, SCI
Rep By: Douglass E. Bobbitt, Carl Franklin Godfrey, Jr., Hon. Fred B. Rooney

Philadelphia Hospitality & Business Alliance

Outside Counsel/Consultants

R. J. Hudson Associates

Philadelphia Industrial Development Corp.

Philadelphia, PA
Leg. Issues: DEF, MAR, TRA

Outside Counsel/Consultants

Thelen Reid & Priest LLP
Issues: DEF, MAR, TRA
Rep By: Barry I. Berkoff, Richard J. Leidl, Stephan M. Minikes

Philadelphia Internat'l Airport

Philadelphia, PA
Leg. Issues: TRA

Outside Counsel/Consultants

Whitten & Diamond
Issues: TRA
Rep By: Robert M. Diamond, Regina M. Mellon

Philadelphia Regional Port Authority

Philadelphia, PA

Outside Counsel/Consultants

Hoppel, Mayer and Coleman

The Philadelphia Stock Exchange, Inc.

Philadelphia, PA

Outside Counsel/Consultants

Fulbright & Jaworski L.L.P.
Rep By: Peter V. B. Unger

Philadelphia University

Philedelphia, PA
Leg. Issues: BUD

Outside Counsel/Consultants

Cassidy & Associates, Inc.
Issues: BUD
Rep By: Douglass E. Bobbitt, Christine A. O'Connor, Blenda Pinto-Riddick

Philadelphia Zoo

Philadelphia, PA
Leg. Issues: ANI, BUD, ENV, TRA

Outside Counsel/Consultants

Metcalf Federal Relations
Issues: ANI, BUD, ENV, TRA
Rep By: Anne Metcalf, Amy Ford Sanders

Philadelphia, Pennsylvania, City of

Leg. Issues: CAW, ENV, HCR, HOU, LAW, ROD, TEC, TRA, WAS, WEL

Outside Counsel/Consultants

Peyser Associates, Inc.
Issues: CAW, ENV, HCR, HOU, LAW, ROD, TEC, TRA, WAS, WEL
Rep By: Thomas J. Howarth, Peter A. Peyser, Jr.

Thelen Reid & Priest LLP
Rep By: Barry I. Berkoff, Richard J. Leidl, Stephan M. Minikes

Whitten & Diamond
Issues: TRA
Rep By: Hon. Lucien Blackwell, Robert M. Diamond, Regina M. Mellon, Jamie L. Whitten

The Philanthropy Roundtable

1150 17th St. NW
Suite 503
Washington, DC 20036
Web: www.philanthropyroundtable.org
Tel: (202)822-8333
Fax: (202)822-8325

In-house, DC-area Employees

O'GARA, James F. X.: Exec. Director
WALTERS, John: President

Philip Morris Management Corp.

1341 G St. NW
Suite 900
Washington, DC 20005
Tel: (202)637-1500
Fax: (202)637-1505
Registered: LDA
Web: www.philipmorris.com
E-mail: Margaret.Gainer@pmmc.com

Philip Morris Management Corp. is the service organization for Philip Morris Companies, Inc. and its operating companies. Headquartered in New York, NY.

Leg. Issues: ADV, AGR, ALC, AVI, BEV, BNK, BUD, CAW, CDT, COM, CSP, DEF, ENV, FOO, FOR, GOV, HCR, LBR, MAN, MMM, RES, RET, SMB, TAX, TOB, TOR, TRA, TRD, WAS, WEL

In-house, DC-area Employees

BERNARD, Kristy: Legal Analyst
DONNER, Sally: Director, Federal Government Issues Planning and Research
FOLKERTS, Brian: Director, Government Affairs, Food
GIMBEL, Tod I.: District Director, East
HOEL, John: District Director, South
LATTANZIO, Ted: Director, Government Affairs Strategy and Development
LOMBARD, Tanya: Director, Government Affairs
MCKITTRICK, Beverly E.: Director, Government Affairs, Tobacco
MIHAS, Tracy: Manager, Client Services - Pmmc/Issues Planning and Research
NELSON, Jr., Donald M.: V. President, International Trade Relations
NORRIS, Frances M.: V. President, Government Affairs, Food
PERLMAN, Abigail: Director, Government Affairs
REED, Tom: Director, Government Affairs, Network Operations
REESE, Jr., Robert S.: Director, Government Affairs, Tobacco
ROBERTS, Peggy: Director, Corporate Communications
ROTHSTEIN, Amy: Senior Counsel, Corporate Affairs
SCOTT, Gregory R.: Director, Government Affairs, Tobacco
SCRUGGS, John F.: V. President, Government Affairs
SCULLY, Jr., Timothy H.: V. President, Beer
SMITH, Dan W.: Director, Government Affairs, Outreach
SORRELLS, John: Director, Media Relations
TURKER, Ejehan: Senior Legal Analyst
TURNER, Henry: V. President, State Government Affairs
WALSH, Molly: Director, Public Affairs - South
WESTFALL, Linda "Tuckie": Director, Government Affairs, Food

Outside Counsel/Consultants

BKSH & Associates
Issues: GOV, MAN, TAX, TOB

Griffin, Johnson, Dover & Stewart
Issues: BEV, FOO, TOB
Rep By: Walter J. "Joe" Stewart

Hall, Green, Rupli, LLC
Issues: FOO, TOB
Rep By: John M. Green, G. Stewart Hall

Hooper Owen & Winburn
Issues: TAX, TOB, TRA
Rep By: Lindsay D. Hooper, John P. Winburn

Kessler & Associates Business Services, Inc.
Issues: BEV, FOO, TOB
Rep By: Michael L. Bartlett, Billy Lee Evans, Richard S. Kessler, James C. Musser

The Paul Laxalt Group
Issues: BEV, FOO, TOB
Rep By: Hon. Paul D. Laxalt

Leonard and Co.
Issues: AGR
Rep By: Burleigh C. W. Leonard

Lesher & Russell, Inc.
Issues: AGR, BEV, FOO, TOB
Rep By: William G. Lesher, Randall M. Russell

McGlotten & Jarvis
Issues: BEV, FOO, TOB
Rep By: Robert M. McGlotten

James T. Molloy
Issues: BEV, FOO, TOB
Rep By: James T. Molloy

R. B. Murphy & Associates
Issues: BEV, FOO, TOB
Rep By: Rick Murphy

Olsson, Frank and Weeda, P.C.
Issues: BEV, FOO, TOB
Rep By: John W. Bode, Tyson Redpath, Ryan W. Stroschein

Jim Pasco & Associates
Issues: BEV, FOO, TOB
Rep By: James O. Pasco, Jr.

Susan S. Platt Consulting
Issues: AGR, ALC, BEV, BUD, FOO, TAX, TOB
Rep By: Susan S. Platt

Policy Directions, Inc.
Issues: BEV, FOO, TOB
Rep By: Kathleen "Kay" Holcombe

Ryan, Phillips, Utrecht & MacKinnon
Issues: BEV, FOO, TOB
Rep By: Rodney Hoppe, Jeffrey M. MacKinnon, Mark D. Planning, Thomas M. Ryan, Joseph V. Vasapoli

Swidler Berlin Shereff Friedman, LLP
Issues: BEV, FOO, TOB
Rep By: Gary D. Slaiman, Katherine R. Taylor

Tallon & Associates
Issues: BEV, FOO, TOB
Rep By: Hon. Robin Tallon

Michael L. Tiner
Issues: BEV, FOO, TOB
Rep By: Michael L. Tiner

Tuttle, Taylor & Heron
Issues: AGR
Rep By: Phillip L. Fraas

Philip Morris USA

New York, NY

Outside Counsel/Consultants

Covington & Burling

RTC Direct

Philipp Brothers Chemicals, Inc.

Fort Lee, NJ
Leg. Issues: AGR, CHM, ENV, PHA, TRD

Outside Counsel/Consultants

Downey McGrath Group, Inc.
Issues: AGR, CHM, ENV, PHA, TRD
Rep By: Hon. Thomas J. Downey, Jr., John Peter Olinger

Philippine Airlines

Manila, PHILIPPINES

Outside Counsel/Consultants

Zuckert, Scoutt and Rasenberger, L.L.P.
Rep By: Malcolm L. Benge

Philippine Sugar Alliance

Manila, PHILIPPINES

Outside Counsel/Consultants

Harry Kopp LLC
Rep By: Harry Kopp

Philippines Long Distance Telephone Co.

Makati City, PHILIPPINES

Outside Counsel/Consultants

BSMG Worldwide

Philippines, Department of Trade and Industry of the Republic of

Manila, PHILIPPINES

Outside Counsel/Consultants

C&M Internat'l, Ltd.

Patton Boggs, LLP
Rep By: Philip S. Kaplan

Philippines, Government of the Republic of

Manila, PHILIPPINES

Outside Counsel/Consultants

Patton Boggs, LLP

Philips Electronics North America Corp.

1300 I St. NW
Suite 1070 East
Washington, DC 20005
Tel: (202)962-8550
Fax: (202)962-8560
Registered: LDA
Web: www.philips.com

A diversified manufacturer of electrical and electronic components and equipment, consumer products and lighting headquartered in New York, NY.

Leg. Issues: COM, CON, ENG, ENV, MAN, MED, TAX, TRD, WAS

Political Action Committee/s

Philips Electronics North America Corp. Political Action Committee
1300 I St. NW
Suite 1070 East
Washington, DC 20005
Contact: Randall B. Moorhead
Tel: (202)962-8550
Fax: (202)962-8560

In-house, DC-area Employees

FRANCO, Patricia A.: Legislative and Regulatory Counsel
MOORHEAD, Randall B.: V. President, Government Affairs
MOSES, Indrani: Government Affairs Representative
PATTON, Thomas B.: V. President, Government Relations

Outside Counsel/Consultants

Verner, Liipfert, Bernhard, McPherson and Hand, Chartered
Issues: COM, MAN
Rep By: Sara W. Morris, David R. Siddall, Lawrence R. Sidman, David A. Weiss

The Phillips Collection

1600 21st St. NW
Washington, DC 20009-1090
Tel: (202)387-2151
Fax: (202)387-2436
Web: www.phillipscollection.org
E-mail: publicrelations@phillipscollection.org

A privately administered and publicly supported museum of 19th and 20th-century European and American art.

Leg. Issues: ART

In-house, DC-area Employees

CLINTON, Kate: Director, Development
COLOT, Thora S.R.: Director, Marketing and Business Operations
NAY, Mary Alice: Director, Corporate Membership
ROSSOTTI, Lynn: Director, Public Relations

Outside Counsel/Consultants

Chernikoff and Co.
Issues: ART
Rep By: Larry B. Chernikoff

Phillips Foods, Inc.

Baltimore, MD
Leg. Issues: TRD

Outside Counsel/Consultants

Akin, Gump, Strauss, Hauer & Feld, L.L.P.
Issues: TRD
Rep By: Warren E. Connelly, Barney J. Skladany, Jr., S. Bruce Wilson

Phillips Petroleum Co.

1776 I St. NW
Suite 700
Washington, DC 20006
Tel: (202)833-0907
Fax: (202)785-0639
Registered: LDA
Web: www.phillips66.com

Headquartered in Barlesville, OK.

Leg. Issues: BUD, CAW, CPT, CSP, ENV, FUE, GOV, HCR, IMM, MAN, NAT, REL, RET, RRR, TAX, TRA, TRD, TRU, UTI, WAS

In-house, DC-area Employees

DUNCAN, Don R.: Manager, Federal Relations
REAMY, Jeff: Environmental/Regulatory Affairs Coordinator
RUDD, Dana: Federal Relations Representative

Outside Counsel/Consultants

Baker, Donelson, Bearman & Caldwell, P.C.
Rep By: Francine Lamoriello, Joan M. McEntee, George Cranwell Montgomery

Phoenix Air Group, Inc.

Cartersville, GA
Leg. Issues: DEF

Outside Counsel/Consultants

Hurt, Norton & Associates
Issues: DEF
Rep By: Robert H. Hurt, Frank Norton

Phoenix Cardiovascular, Inc.

Leg. Issues: BUD, HCR

Outside Counsel/Consultants

Arent Fox Kintner Plotkin & Kahn, PLLC
Issues: BUD, HCR
Rep By: Douglas McCormack, William A. Sarraille

Phoenix Home Life Mutual Insurance Co.

Hartford, CT
Registered: LDA
Leg. Issues: BAN, TAX

Outside Counsel/Consultants

The Michael Lewan Co.
Issues: BAN, TAX
Rep By: Michael Lewan, Anne Saunders

Phoenix, Arizona, City of

Leg. Issues: BUD, CAW, ECN, EDU, ENV, HOU, LAW, NAT, ROD, TAX, TEC, TRA

Outside Counsel/Consultants

Cassidy & Associates, Inc.
Issues: CAW, ECN, NAT
Rep By: John A. Crumbliss, John S. Doyle, Jr., Christine A. O'Connor, Gabor J. Rozsa, Dan C. Tate, Sr.

Miller & Van Eaton, P.L.L.C.
Issues: TEC
Rep By: Joseph Van Eaton

Murray, Scheer, Montgomery, Tapia & O'Donnell
Issues: BUD, CAW, ECN, EDU, ENV, HOU, LAW, ROD, TAX, TRA
Rep By: John R. O'Donnell

Reed, Smith, LLP
Issues: BUD
Rep By: Christopher L. Rissetto

Photo Marketing Ass'n-Internat'l

Jackson, MI

Outside Counsel/Consultants

London and Satagaj, Attorneys-at-Law
Rep By: Sheldon I. London, John S. Satagaj

Photo Telesis

San Antonio, TX
Leg. Issues: DEF

Outside Counsel/Consultants

W. B. Driggers & Associates, Inc.
Issues: DEF
Rep By: W. B. Driggers

PhotoMEDEX

Radnor, PA

Outside Counsel/Consultants

MARC Associates, Inc.

PHP Healthcare Corp.

Reston, VA

Outside Counsel/Consultants

McDermott, Will and Emery
Rep By: Wendy L. Krasner

Physician Insurers Ass'n of America

2275 Research Blvd.
Suite 250
Rockville, MD 20850
Tel: (301)947-9000
Fax: (301)947-9090
Registered: LDA
Web: www.thepiaa.org
Leg. Issues: BUD, HCR, INS, MED, MMM, TAX

Political Action Committee/s

Physician Insurers PAC

2275 Research Blvd.
Suite 250
Rockville, MD 20850
Contact: Lawrence E. Smarr
Tel: (301)947-9000
Fax: (301)947-9090

In-house, DC-area Employees
BARTHOLOMEW, Lori A.: Director, Loss Prevention and Research
SMARR, Lawrence E.: President
WILSON, Bruce A.: Director, Government Relations

Outside Counsel/Consultants
Bracewell & Patterson, L.L.P.
Issues: HCR, INS, MED, TAX
Rep By: Hon. Edwin R. Bethune, Gene E. Godley, Marc C. Hebert

Physicians Ad hoc Coalition for Truth (PHACT)
Alexandria, VA
Leg. Issues: FAM, MED

Outside Counsel/Consultants
Tarne Powers & Associates
Issues: FAM, MED
Rep By: Michelle R. Powers, Gene Tarne

Physicians Committee for Responsible Medicine
5100 Wisconsin Ave. NW
Suite 404
Washington, DC 20016
Web: www.pcrm.org
E-mail: pcrm@pcrm.org
Tel: (202)686-2210
Fax: (202)686-2216

In-house, DC-area Employees
BARNARD, M.D., Neal D.: President

Physicians for Peace
Norfolk, VA

Outside Counsel/Consultants
Bain and Associates, Inc.

Physicians for Reproductive Choice and Health
New York, NY
Leg. Issues: FAM, HCR

Outside Counsel/Consultants
Bass and Howes, Inc.
Issues: FAM, HCR
Rep By: Kirsten Moore

Physicians for Social Responsibility
1875 Connecticut Ave.
Suite 1012
Washington, DC 20029
E-mail: psrnatl@psr.org
Tel: (202)898-0150
Fax: (202)898-0172

An alliance of physicians attempting to educate the government and the public about the medical consequences of nuclear war, environmental degradation, and societal violence, and about public policies which could limit those consequences.

In-house, DC-area Employees
MUSIL, Dr. Robert K.: Exec. Director
TILLER, Robert: Director, Security Programs

Piasecki Aircraft Corp.
Essington, PA
Leg. Issues: DEF

Outside Counsel/Consultants
Ikon Public Affairs
Issues: DEF

Pickands Mather and Co.
Cleveland, OH

Outside Counsel/Consultants
Bredhoff & Kaiser
Rep By: Elliot Bredhoff

Pickens Fuel Corp.
Seal Beach, CA
Leg. Issues: FUE

Outside Counsel/Consultants
The Laxalt Corp.
Issues: FUE
Rep By: Michelle D. Laxalt

Picker Internat'l
Highland Heights, OH

Outside Counsel/Consultants
Washington World Group, Ltd.
Rep By: Edward J. von Kloberg, III

Pickett, Virginia, Local Redevelopment Authority
Blackstone, VA

Outside Counsel/Consultants
Kutak Rock LLP
Rep By: Barry P. Steinberg

Pico Rivera, California, City of
Leg. Issues: BUD

Outside Counsel/Consultants
The Ferguson Group, LLC
Issues: BUD
Rep By: William Ferguson, Jr., Charmayne Macon

Piedmont Environmental Council
Charlottesville, VA
Registered: LDA
Leg. Issues: RES, TAX, TRA

Outside Counsel/Consultants
Murray, Scheer, Montgomery, Tapia & O'Donnell
Issues: RES, TAX, TRA
Rep By: Thomas R. Crawford, D. Michael Murray

Pier I Imports
Fort Worth, TX
Leg. Issues: TRD

Outside Counsel/Consultants
Williams & Jensen, P.C.
Issues: TRD
Rep By: Robert E. Glennon, Jr.

Pierce College
Philadelphia, PA
Leg. Issues: BUD

Outside Counsel/Consultants
Cassidy & Associates, Inc.
Issues: BUD
Rep By: Douglass E. Bobbitt, Gregory M. Gill

Pierce Transit
Tacoma, WA
Leg. Issues: BUD, TRA

Outside Counsel/Consultants
Simon and Co., Inc.
Issues: BUD, TRA
Rep By: Heather Barber, Alex DeGood, Leonard S. Simon

Pierce, Washington, County of
Leg. Issues: ENV, NAT

Outside Counsel/Consultants
Denny Miller McBee Associates
Issues: ENV, NAT

Pilgrim Airlines
New London, CT

Outside Counsel/Consultants
Hewes, Gelband, Lambert & Dann, P.C.
Rep By: Theodore I. Seamon

Pilgrim's Pride
Pittsburg, TX

Outside Counsel/Consultants
Williams & Jensen, P.C.
Rep By: Robert E. Glennon, Jr.

Piliero Mazza & Pargament
888 17th St. NW
Suite 1100
Washington, DC 20006
Web: www.pmplawfirm.com
E-mail: pmazza@pmplawfirm.com
Tel: (202)857-1000
Fax: (202)857-0200
Registered: LDA
Leg. Issues: IND, SMB

In-house, DC-area Employees
MAZZA, Pamela J.: Senior Partner

Outside Counsel/Consultants
Lydia Hofer & Associates
Issues: IND, SMB
Rep By: Lydia Hofer

Pilkington North America
Toledo, OH
Leg. Issues: AUT, ENG

Outside Counsel/Consultants
Sellery Associates, Inc.
Issues: AUT, ENG
Rep By: William C. Sellery, Jr.

Pilkington Thorn
Middlesex, UNITED KINGDOM
Leg. Issues: DEF

Outside Counsel/Consultants
Hyjek & Fix, Inc.
Issues: DEF
Rep By: Steven M. Hyjek, Karl H. Stegenga

Pillowtex Corp.
Dallas, TX
A home textile manufacturer.
Leg. Issues: TRD

Outside Counsel/Consultants
Podesta/Mattoon
Issues: TRD
Rep By: Timothy Powers

The Pillsbury Co.
Minneapolis, MN
Registered: LDA
Leg. Issues: AGR, BUD, FOO, TAX, TRD

Outside Counsel/Consultants
Haake and Associates
Issues: TAX, TRD
Rep By: Timothy M. Haake

Olsson, Frank and Weeda, P.C.
Issues: AGR, BUD, FOO
Rep By: John W. Bode, Richard L. Frank, Susan P. Grymes, Karen Reis Harned, Stephen L. Lacey, Marshall L. Matz, Tyson Redpath, Ryan W. Stroschein

Pilot Communications
Syracuse, NY

Outside Counsel/Consultants
Shaw Pittman

Pilots' Ass'n of the Bay and River Delaware
Philadelphia, PA
Leg. Issues: AVI, MAR

Outside Counsel/Consultants
Blank Rome Comisky & McCauley, LLP
Issues: AVI, MAR
Rep By: David A. Norcross

PIMCO Advisors, L.P.
Newport Beach, CA
Leg. Issues: TAX

Outside Counsel/Consultants
Murray, Scheer, Montgomery, Tapia & O'Donnell
Issues: TAX
Rep By: Thomas R. Crawford, D. Michael Murray

Pine Bluff Sand and Gravel Co.
Pine Bluff, AR
Leg. Issues: TRA

Outside Counsel/Consultants
Ann Eppard Associates, Ltd.
Issues: TRA
Rep By: Julie Chlopecki, Ann Eppard

Pinkering Corp.
Easton, MD
Leg. Issues: AVI

Outside Counsel/Consultants
Kimberly Consulting, LLC
Issues: AVI
Rep By: Richard H. Kimberly

Pinnacle West Capital Corp.
800 Connecticut Ave. NW
Suite 610
Washington, DC 20006
E-mail: robbieaiken@pinnacledc.com
Tel: (202)293-2655
Fax: (202)293-2666
Registered: LDA

A holding company headquartered in Phoenix, AZ. Subsidiaries include Arizona Public Service Co., SunCor Development, and El Dorado Investment.

Leg. Issues: BUD, CAW, ENG, ENV, TAX, TRA, UTI, WAS

Political Action Committee/s
Pinnacle West PAC
800 Connecticut Ave. NW
Suite 610
Washington, DC 20006
Contact: Robert S. Aiken
Tel: (202)293-2655
Fax: (202)293-2666

In-house, DC-area Employees
AIKEN, Robert S.: V. President, Federal Affairs

Outside Counsel/Consultants

The Renkes Group, Ltd.
Issues: ENG
Rep By: Gregg D. Renkes

Ryan, Phillips, Utrecht & MacKinnon

Thelen Reid & Priest LLP
Issues: TAX
Rep By: Howard A. Cooper

Weil, Gotshal & Manges, LLP

Pinon Community School Board

Pinon, AZ

Outside Counsel/Consultants

Hobbs, Straus, Dean and Walker, LLP
Rep By: Carol L. Barbero, Karen J. Funk, Aura Kanegis

Pinpoint Communications

Dallas, TX

Outside Counsel/Consultants

Arter & Hadden
Rep By: Hon. Thomas G. Loeffler

PinPoint Systems Internat'l, LLC

Westhampton Beach, NY
Leg. Issues: DEF

Outside Counsel/Consultants

The Van Fleet-Meredith Group
Issues: DEF
Rep By: M. Bruce Meredith, Paul F. Payette, Townsend A. Van Fleet

PINSA, S.A de CD

Mexico City, MEXICO
Leg. Issues: ENV, TRD

Outside Counsel/Consultants

Janus-Merritt Strategies, L.L.C.
Issues: ENV, TRD
Rep By: Mark J. Robertson

Pioneer Hi-Bred Internat'l, Inc.

601 Pennsylvania Ave. NW
North Bldg., Suite 325
Washington, DC 20004
Web: www.pioneer.com
Tel: (202)728-3613

A producer of farm seeds.

Leg. Issues: AGR

In-house, DC-area Employees

MANES, Julie: Washington Representative

Outside Counsel/Consultants

Whitten & Diamond
Issues: AGR
Rep By: Robert M. Diamond, Regina M. Mellon, Jamie L. Whitten

Pioneer of North America

Long Beach, CA
Leg. Issues: CPT

Outside Counsel/Consultants

Patton Boggs, LLP
Issues: CPT
Rep By: Thomas Hale Boggs, Jr., Brian C. Lopina, Jeffrey L. Turner

Pipe Tobacco Council, Inc.

1707 H St. NW
#800
Washington, DC 20006
Tel: (202)223-8204
Fax: (202)833-0379
Registered: LDA

Leg. Issues: TOB

In-house, DC-area Employees

SHARP, Norman F.: President

Outside Counsel/Consultants

Dickstein Shapiro Morin & Oshinsky LLP
Issues: TOB
Rep By: Henry C. Cashen, II, Hon. Wendell H. Ford, Elizabeth B. Haywood, Robert Mangas, Graham "Rusty" Mathews, Laurie McKay, Hon. Stanford E. Parris, Rebecah Moore Shepherd, L. Andrew Zausner

Piqua, Ohio, City of

Outside Counsel/Consultants

Spiegel & McDiarmid
Rep By: Kenneth A. Brown

Pitney Bowes, Inc.

409 12th St. SW
Suite 701
Washington, DC 20024-2191
Web: www.pb.com
Tel: (202)488-4464
Fax: (202)488-4396

Leg. Issues: CPT, POS

In-house, DC-area Employees

NASSEF, David: V. President, Federal Relations
ROJAS, Ernesto J.: Director, Regulatory Affairs

Outside Counsel/Consultants

Preston Gates Ellis & Rouvelas Meeds LLP
Issues: CPT, POS
Rep By: Werner W. Brandt, Amy Carlson, Bruce J. Heiman, Hon. Lloyd Meeds, Cindy O'Malley, Emanuel L. Rouvelas, W. Dennis Stephens, Steven R. "Rick" Valentine

Pittencrieff Communications, Inc.

Abilene, TX

Outside Counsel/Consultants

Gardner, Carton and Douglas

Pittsburgh, University of

Pittsburgh, PA
Leg. Issues: BUD

Outside Counsel/Consultants

Doepken Keevican & Weiss
Issues: BUD

The Pittston Co.

Glen Allen, VA
Leg. Issues: TAX

Outside Counsel/Consultants

Heenan, Althen & Roles

Williams & Jensen, P.C.
Issues: TAX
Rep By: J. Steven Hart, Karen Judd Lewis, Anthony J. Roda, David A. Starr

Pixtech, Inc.

Boise, ID
Leg. Issues: DEF

Outside Counsel/Consultants

Hale and Dorr LLP
Issues: DEF
Rep By: Bonnie B. Byers, Gilbert B. Kaplan

Pizza Hut, Inc.

Dallas, KS
Registered: LDA

Outside Counsel/Consultants

Covington & Burling
Rep By: Peter Barton Hutt

PJM Interconnection, L.L.C.

Norristown, PA

Outside Counsel/Consultants

Wright & Talisman, P.C.
Rep By: Robert H. Lamb, Barry S. Spector

PKC

Falls Church, VA
Leg. Issues: HCR

Outside Counsel/Consultants

The Spectrum Group
Issues: HCR
Rep By: Paul E. McManus, Gregory L. Sharp

Placer County Water Agency

Auburn, CA
Leg. Issues: BUD, ENV

Outside Counsel/Consultants

Impact Strategies
Issues: BUD, ENV
Rep By: Jeff Fedorchak

Placer Dome U.S. Inc.

San Francisco, CA
Leg. Issues: ENV, MON, NAT, TAX

Outside Counsel/Consultants

Crowell & Moring LLP
Issues: NAT
Rep By: Edward M. Green, R. Timothy McCrum, Steven P. Quarles

McClure, Gerard & Neuenschwander, Inc.
Issues: ENV, MON, NAT, TAX
Rep By: Steven G. Barringer, Joseph T. Findaro, Matthew Iandoli, Nils W. Johnson, Hon. James A. McClure, Tod O. Neuenschwander

Placer, California, County of

Auburn, CA
Leg. Issues: BUD

Outside Counsel/Consultants

Holland & Knight LLP
Issues: BUD
Rep By: Jack M. Burkman, Mike Galano, Richard M. Gold, P. J. Toker, David C. Whitestone

Placid Refining Co.

Dallas, TX
Leg. Issues: ENV, TAX

Outside Counsel/Consultants

Bracewell & Patterson, L.L.P.
Issues: ENV
Rep By: Hon. Edwin R. Bethune, Hon. Jim Chapman, Gene E. Godley, Marc C. Hebert, Charles L. Ingebretson, Michael L. Pate, Scott H. Segal, D. Michael Stroud, Jr.

PriceWaterhouseCoopers
Issues: TAX
Rep By: Jim Carlisle, Kenneth J. Kies, Bernard M. Shapiro

Plaintiffs Committee for TWA 800 and Swissair Air III Crashes

Outside Counsel/Consultants

Wise & Associates
Rep By: Dwayne Sattler, Nicholas P. Wise

Planar Systems, Inc.

Beaverton, OR
Leg. Issues: DEF

Outside Counsel/Consultants

Collier Shannon Scott, PLLC
Issues: DEF
Rep By: Robert W. Porter, Paul C. Rosenthal

PlanEcon Inc.

1111 14th St. NW
Suite 801
Washington, DC 20005
Web: www.planecon.com
E-mail: info@planecon.com
Tel: (202)898-0471
Fax: (202)898-0445

A consulting firm specializing in C.I.S. and Eastern European affairs.

In-house, DC-area Employees

CRANE, Dr. Keith: Research Director
VANOUS, Dr. Jan: President

Planet Electric

Van Nuys, CA
Leg. Issues: ENV

Outside Counsel/Consultants

Kessler & Associates Business Services, Inc.
Issues: ENV
Rep By: Michael L. Bartlett, Howard Berman, Billy Lee Evans, Richard S. Kessler

PlanetRx

South San Francisco, CA

Outside Counsel/Consultants

The Dutko Group, Inc.
Rep By: Gary J. Andres, Kimberly M. Spaulding

Planned Parenthood Federation of America

1780 Massachusetts Ave. NW
Washington, DC 20036
Tel: (202)785-3351
Fax: (202)293-4349
Registered: LDA
Web: www.plannedparenthood.org

Organization providing reproductive health care and advocacy concerning reproductive rights, prevention of unwanted pregnancies and women's health.

Leg. Issues: BUD, FAM, HCR

Political Action Committee/s

Planned Parenthood Action Fund Inc. PAC
1780 Massachusetts Ave. NW
Washington, DC 20036
Tel: (202)785-3351
Fax: (202)293-4349

In-house, DC-area Employees
CAREW, Nasserie: Media Relations
KORSMO, Chris: Director, Government Relations
LEU, Jodi: Associate, Government Relations
MILLER, Nina: Director, Planned Parenthood Action Fund, Inc. PAC
MOHACETTEZHPOUR, Shrine: Legislative Representative
TAYLOR, Amy J.: Legislative Representative
VIGUERIE, Kathryn: Legislative Representative

Planned Parenthood of America
New York, NY
Outside Counsel/Consultants
Arnold & Porter

Planning Systems, Inc.
McLean, VA
Leg. Issues: BUD, CPI, DEF
Outside Counsel/Consultants
Egle Associates
Issues: BUD, CPI
Rep By: Richard Egle
The PMA Group
Issues: DEF
Rep By: Daniel Cunningham, Sean Fogarty, Kaylene Green, Patrick Hiu, Paul J. Magliocchetti, Briggs Shade, Brian Thiel

Plano Molding Co.
Plano, IL
Outside Counsel/Consultants
O'Connor & Hannan, L.L.P.
Rep By: George J. Mannina, Jr.

Plano, Texas, City of
Leg. Issues: HOU, LAW, TRA, URB
Outside Counsel/Consultants
Barbara T. McCall Associates
Issues: HOU, LAW, TRA, URB
Rep By: Ralph Garboushian, Barbara T. McCall

Plaquemine, Louisiana, City of
Leg. Issues: ECN
Outside Counsel/Consultants
Adams and Reese LLP
Issues: ECN
Rep By: B. Jeffrey Brooks, Charlotte Collins

Plasma Protein Therapeutics Ass'n
1350 I St. NW
Suite 830
Washington, DC 20005
Tel: (202)789-3100
Fax: (202)789-4197
Web: www.plasmatherapeutics.org
E-mail: ppta@plasmatherapeutics.org
Leg. Issues: HCR
In-house, DC-area Employees
CHAMBLEE, Andrea: Director, Regulatory Affairs
LEVENSON, Meredith: Associate Director, Health Policy
SCHULTE, Linda: Director, Corporate Communications
Outside Counsel/Consultants
Dalrymple and Associates, L.L.C.
Rep By: Donald "Dack" Dalrymple
Hogan & Hartson L.L.P.
Issues: HCR
Rep By: C. Michael Gilliland, Helene C. Lasker, Christine M. Warnke

Plasma-Therm, Inc.
St. Petersburg, FL
Leg. Issues: DEF, MAN, SCI
Outside Counsel/Consultants
American Continental Group, Inc.
Issues: DEF, MAN, SCI
Rep By: Steve Colovas, David A. Metzner

Plastic Container Institute
Congers, NY
Outside Counsel/Consultants
Thompson, Hine and Flory LLP
Rep By: David H. Baker

Plastic Shipping Container Institute
Washington, DC
Outside Counsel/Consultants
Thompson, Hine and Flory LLP
Rep By: David H. Baker

Platinum Guild Internat'l
New York, NY
Leg. Issues: MON
Outside Counsel/Consultants
Verner, Liipfert, Bernhard, McPherson and Hand, Chartered
Issues: MON
Rep By: Martin Mendelsohn

Plattsburgh, New York, City of
Leg. Issues: ENG, GOV, UTI
Outside Counsel/Consultants
Duncan, Weinberg, Genzer & Pembroke, P.C.
Issues: ENG, GOV, UTI
Rep By: Jeffrey C. Genzer

Playa Vista
Los Angeles, CA
Leg. Issues: TRA
Outside Counsel/Consultants
Manatt, Phelps & Phillips, LLP
Issues: TRA
Rep By: Michael T. Brown, Hon. Jack W. Buechner, June L. DeHart, Jeff Kuhnreich

Playboy Enterprises, Inc.
Chicago, IL
Leg. Issues: GAM
Outside Counsel/Consultants
Greenberg Traurig, LLP
Issues: GAM
Rep By: Diane J. Blagman, Ronald L. Platt

Playtex Products, Inc.
Westport, CT
Leg. Issues: CPA
Outside Counsel/Consultants
Gibbons & Company, Inc.
Issues: CPA
Rep By: Clifford S. Gibbons, Hon. Sam M. Gibbons

Please Touch Museum, The Children's Museum of Philadelphia
Philadelphia, PA
Leg. Issues: ECN, EDU, TOU, URB
Outside Counsel/Consultants
Doepken Keevican & Weiss
Issues: ECN, EDU, TOU, URB
Rep By: Clyde H. Slease, III
Lackman & Associates, L.L.C.
Issues: EDU, URB
Rep By: Carey A. Lackman

PLO Mission
1717 K St. NW
Suite 407
Washington, DC 20036
Tel: (202)785-8394
Fax: (202)887-5337
Registered: FARA
E-mail: shamad9950@aol.com

Represents Palestinian interests at the League of Arab States in the United States.

In-house, DC-area Employees
HAMAD, Said: Deputy Chief of Mission
RAHMAN, Hasan Abdel: Director and Chief PLO Representative

Plum Creek Timber Co.
Seattle, WA
Leg. Issues: ENV, RES, TAX
Outside Counsel/Consultants
Nutter & Harris, Inc.
Issues: ENV, RES
Rep By: Robert L. Harris
PriceWaterhouseCoopers
Issues: TAX
Rep By: Jim Carlisle, Kirt C. Johnson, Kenneth J. Kies, Pat Raffaniello

Plumbing, Heating, Cooling Contractors-National Assoc.
180 S. Washington St.
P.O. Box 6808
Falls Church, VA 22040
Tel: (703)237-8100
Fax: (703)237-7442
Registered: LDA
Web: www.naphcc.org
E-mail: naphcc@naphcc.org

Dedicated to the promotion, advancement, education, and training of the industry.

Leg. Issues: CAW, CSP, ENV, LBR, SMB, TAX, TRA, UTI

Political Action Committee/s
Nat'l Ass'n of Plumbing-Heating-Cooling Contractors Political Action Committee
180 S. Washington St.
P.O. Box 6808
Falls Church, VA 22040
Tel: (703)237-8100
Fax: (703)237-7442
Contact: Lake Coulson
In-house, DC-area Employees
CASEY, D.L. "Ike": Exec. V. President
COULSON, Lake: Director, Government Relations

PMSC-Irby Steel
Gulfport, MS
Leg. Issues: MAN, TRA
Outside Counsel/Consultants
Forster & Associates
Issues: MAN, TRA
Rep By: Johann R. Forster

PMX Corp.
Outside Counsel/Consultants
Griffin, Johnson, Dover & Stewart

PNC Bank, N.A.
Pittsburgh, PA
Leg. Issues: FIN
Outside Counsel/Consultants
O'Connor & Fierce Associates
Rhoads Group
Issues: FIN
Rep By: Paul D. Behrends, Kathleen Ireland, Steven G. McKnight, B. Callan Nagle, Clifford R. Northup, Barry D. Rhoads, Thomas Worrall

PNH Associates
Pittsburgh, PA
Leg. Issues: MED
Outside Counsel/Consultants
Eckert Seamans Cherin & Mellott, LLC
Issues: MED
Rep By: LeRoy S. Zimmerman

Pocket Science, Inc.
Santa Clara, CA
Leg. Issues: COM
Outside Counsel/Consultants
Capitol Coalitions Inc.
Issues: COM
Rep By: Brett P. Scott

Podesta/Mattoon
1001 G St. NW
Suite 900 E
Washington, DC 20001-4545
Tel: (202)393-1010
Fax: (202)393-5510
Registered: LDA, FARA
Web: www.podesta.com/
E-mail: podesta@podesta.com
Leg. Issues: CAW, ENG
In-house, DC-area Employees
BROWN, Paul: Principal
DELORY, Ann: Associate
FRITTS, Kimberley: Principal
GELMAN, Matthew: Principal
JAMES, Claudia: President
LEARY, Kristen: Senior Associate
LITTMAN, Andrew C.: Principal
MADDOX, Lauren: Principal
MATTOON, Dan: Partner
MORRA, Elizabeth: Principal
PIANALTO, Antonella
PODESTA, Anthony T.: Chairman
POWERS, Timothy: Principal
ROTHSCHILD, Edwin S.: Associate
TESSIER, Missi: Principal
Outside Counsel/Consultants
NES, Inc.
Issues: CAW, ENG
Rep By: Richard Wilson

Point of Purchase Advertising Institute
Washington, DC
Web: www.popai.com
E-mail: kcurtis@popai.com
Leg. Issues: ADV, BEV, TOB
Outside Counsel/Consultants
Patton Boggs, LLP
Issues: ADV, BEV, TOB
Rep By: Thomas Hale Boggs, Jr., Penelope S. Farthing, John F. Fithian, Elena Giberga, Darryl D. Nirenberg, Thomas P. O'Donnell, James A. Reeder

Pointe Coupee Police Jury

New Roads, LA
Leg. Issues: COM, DIS

Outside Counsel/Consultants

Washington Consulting Alliance, Inc.
Issues: COM, DIS
Rep By: Thomas L. Burgum

The Points of Light Foundation

1400 I St. NW
Suite 800
Washington, DC 20005
Tel: (202)729-8000
Fax: (202)729-8100
Registered: LDA
Web: www.pointsoflight.org
E-mail: mstein@pointsoflight.org

Formed in 1990. The only national voluntary organization with the sole mission of stimulating and strengthening volunteer community service in addressing serious social problems.

In-house, DC-area Employees

BENTLEY, William: Senior V. President to Chief Exec. Officer
CRABBS, Raymond: Senior V. President
GOODWIN, Robert K.: President and Chief Exec. Officer

Pojoaque Pueblo

Leg. Issues: BUD, IND

Outside Counsel/Consultants

Manuel Lujan Associates
Issues: BUD, IND
Rep By: Lydia Hofer

Steptoe & Johnson LLP
Rep By: Thomas C. Collier, Jr.

Polar Air Cargo, Inc.

1201 Connecticut Ave. NW
Sixth Floor
Washington, DC 20036
Tel: (202)785-1995
Fax: (202)785-1694
Web: www.polaraircargo.com
E-mail: kevinbo@polaraircargo.com

International Air Freight Company headquartered in Long Beach, CA.

Leg. Issues: AVI, BUD, ENV, FOR, LBR, TAX, TRA, TRD

In-house, DC-area Employees

BORLAND, Kevin: Director of Government Affairs

Polaris Industries

Minneapolis, MN
Leg. Issues: CSP, MAN

Outside Counsel/Consultants

Albertine Enterprises, Inc.
Issues: CSP, MAN
Rep By: James J. Albertine, Dr. John M. Albertine

Polaroid Corp.

Cambridge, MA
Leg. Issues: TRD

Outside Counsel/Consultants

Barnes, Richardson and Colburn
Rep By: Matthew T. McGrath

Hogan & Hartson L.L.P.
Issues: TRD
Rep By: Jeanne S. Archibald

Internat'l Business-Government Counsellors, Inc.
Issues: TRD
Rep By: John F. McDermid

Police Executive Research Forum

1120 Connecticut Ave. NW
Suite 930
Washington, DC 20036
Tel: (202)466-7820
Fax: (202)466-7826
Web: www.policeforum.org
E-mail: perf@policeforum.org

Represents chief executives of large police departments. Dedicated to improving police practices through research, education, leadership and debate.

Leg. Issues: ALC, BUD, CIV, CON, FIR, LAW

In-house, DC-area Employees

PLOTKIN, Martha: Director, Communications and Legislative Affairs
WEXLER, Chuck: Exec. Director

Police Foundation

1201 Connecticut Ave. NW
Suite 200
Washington, DC 20036-2636
Tel: (202)833-1460
Fax: (202)659-9149
Web: www.policefoundation.org
E-mail: pfinfo@policefoundation.org

Non-profit research and technical assistance group dedicated to improving policing in America. Operates the National Center for the Study of Police and Civil Disorder, the Crime Mapping Laboratory, and the RAMS (Risk Analysis Management System), the QSI (Quality of Service Indicator), and the Institute for Integrity, Leadership, and Professionalism in Policing.

Leg. Issues: LAW

In-house, DC-area Employees

MALINA, Mary: Communications Director
WILLIAMS, Hubert: President

Policy Advantage

Denver, CO

Outside Counsel/Consultants

Capital Partnerships (VA) Inc.
Rep By: Robin Angle, Kenneth W. Butler, Clay Gravely

Policy and Taxation Group

Santa Ana, CA

Outside Counsel/Consultants

Schiff Hardin & Waite

Policy Development Group, Inc.

Phoenix, AZ
A public affairs firm.

Leg. Issues: AGR, RES

Outside Counsel/Consultants

Parry, Romani, DeConcini & Symms
Issues: AGR, RES
Rep By: Edward H. Baxter, Hon. Dennis DeConcini, John M. Haddow, Scott D. Hatch, Shannon Davis Henderson, Jack W. Martin, Romano Romani, Linda Arey Skladany, Hon. Steven D. Symms

Policy Group

1333 New Hampshire Ave. NW
Suite 400
Washington, DC 20036
Tel: (202)887-4000
Fax: (202)887-4288
A political action committee.

In-house, DC-area Employees

LASSMAN, Malcolm: Treasurer

Outside Counsel/Consultants

Akin, Gump, Strauss, Hauer & Feld, L.L.P.
Rep By: Malcolm Lassman

Polish-American Congress

1612 K St.
Suite 410
Washington, DC 20006
Tel: (202)296-6955
Fax: (202)835-1565

Interested in legislation and government action and practices affecting Americans of Polish origin and heritage. Headquartered in Chicago.

In-house, DC-area Employees

MISKIEWICZ, Sophia: Exec. Director, Legislative and Public Affairs

R. L. Polk & Co.

Detroit, MI

Outside Counsel/Consultants

Rogers & Wells

Polk County, Oregon

Dallas, OR
Leg. Issues: TRA

Outside Counsel/Consultants

Jamison and Sullivan, Inc.
Issues: TRA

Polk, Iowa, County of

Leg. Issues: BUD

Outside Counsel/Consultants

Sagamore Associates, Inc.
Issues: BUD
Rep By: Todd Atkinson, David U. Gogol

Polycistic Kidney Disease Foundation

Kansas City, MO
Leg. Issues: HCR

Outside Counsel/Consultants

Verner, Liipfert, Bernhard, McPherson and Hand, Chartered
Issues: HCR
Rep By: Hon. Daniel R. Coats, Vicki E. Hart

Polygon, Ltd.

Outside Counsel/Consultants

Berliner Corcoran & Rowe

Polyisocyanurate Insulation Manufacturers Ass'n

1331 F St. NW
Suite 975
Washington, DC 20004
Tel: (202)628-6558
Fax: (202)628-3856
Web: www.pima.org
E-mail: pima@pima.org
Leg. Issues: ENV, TAX

Political Action Committee/s

Polyisocyanurate Insulation Manufacturers Ass'n PAC

1331 F St. NW
Suite 975
Washington, DC 20004
Tel: (202)628-6558
Fax: (202)628-3856
Contact: Jared O. Blum

In-house, DC-area Employees

BLUM, Jared O.: President

Outside Counsel/Consultants

Hogan & Hartson L.L.P.
Issues: ENV, TAX
Rep By: Nancy Granese, William Michael House, Christine M. Warnke

White & Case LLP
Rep By: Robert D. Paul

PolyMedica Corp.

Woburn, MA
Leg. Issues: HCR, MMM

Outside Counsel/Consultants

The Paul Laxalt Group
Issues: HCR, MMM
Rep By: Hon. Paul D. Laxalt, Tom Loranger

Polynesian Airlines

Aisa, WESTERN SAMOA

Outside Counsel/Consultants

Squire, Sanders & Dempsey L.L.P.
Rep By: Robert D. Papkin, Edward W. Sauer

Polytec Group

Hong Kong, CHINA (PEOPLE'S REPUBLIC)
Leg. Issues: TRD

Outside Counsel/Consultants

Stephen F. Sims and Associates
Issues: TRD
Rep By: Stephen F. Sims

Polytechnic University

Brooklyn, NY
Leg. Issues: BUD

Outside Counsel/Consultants

Cassidy & Associates, Inc.
Issues: BUD
Rep By: Amos Hochstein, Scott D. MacConomy, Lyllett Wentworth

Joel Pomerene Hospital

Millersburg, OH
Leg. Issues: HCR

Outside Counsel/Consultants

Golin/Harris Internat'l
Issues: HCR
Rep By: C. Michael Fulton

Popcorn Board

Washington, DC
Registered: LDA

Outside Counsel/Consultants

McLeod, Watkinson & Miller
Rep By: Wayne R. Watkinson

Lois Pope Life Foundation

Outside Counsel/Consultants

Edelman Public Relations Worldwide
Rep By: Christine Kelly Cimko

Popejoy Construction Co.

Ulysses, KS

Outside Counsel/Consultants

Bryan Cave LLP

Population Action Internat'l

1300 19th St. NW
Second Floor
Washington, DC 20036
Web: www.populationaction.org
E-mail: pai@popact.org

Tel: (202)557-3400
Fax: (202)728-4177
Registered: LDA

A private, non-profit organization that seeks to increase political and financial support for effective population policies and programs grounded in individual rights. Founded in 1965, PAI advocates the expansion of voluntary family planning, related health services, educational, and economic opportunities for women. PAI also seeks to make clear the linkages between population, reproductive health, the environment, and health.

Leg. Issues: FOR

In-house, DC-area Employees

ALTROCCHI, Julia: Policy Analyst
BARTLETT, Terri L.: V. President, Public Policy and Strategic Initiatives
COEN, Amy: President
GARDNER-OUTLAW, Tom: Policy Analyst
LASHER, Craig: Senior Policy Analyst
MORENO, Lisa M.: Senior Legislative Policy Analyst
TURNBULL, Wendy: Legislative Representative

Outside Counsel/Consultants

Collins & Company, Inc.
Issues: FOR
Rep By: James D. Bond, Richard L. Collins, Thomas A. Hooper, Shay D. Stautz

Population Ass'n of America

8630 Fenton St.
Suite 722
Silver Spring, MD 20910
Web: www.popassoc.org
E-mail: info@popassoc.org

Tel: (301)565-6710
Fax: (301)565-7850

Founded in 1931 as a scientific and professional society dedicated to the research, study and analysis of demographic patterns, changes and projections for nations, regions and local areas.

Leg. Issues: SCI

In-house, DC-area Employees

DUDLEY, Stephanie D.: Exec. Director
HARRISON-CLARK, Anne: Public Affairs Consultant

Population Institute

107 Second St. NE
Washington, DC 20002
Web: www.populationinstitute.org
E-mail: web@populationinstitute.org

Tel: (202)544-3300
Fax: (202)544-0068

Dedicated to the achievement of a more equitable balance between the world's population, environment and resources. Informs and educates national and international leaders, journalists and the general public on international population issues.

Leg. Issues: ENV, FAM

In-house, DC-area Employees

BURDETT, Hal: Director, Public Information
FORNOS, Werner: President

Population Reference Bureau

1875 Connecticut Ave. NW
Suite 520
Washington, DC 20009
Web: www.prb.org
E-mail: popref@prb.org

Tel: (202)483-1100
Fax: (202)328-3937

Gathers, interprets and publishes information on population trends and their social, economic and environmental impact.

In-house, DC-area Employees

DONALDSON, Peter J.: President
YINGER, Nancy: Director, International Programs

Population Resource Center

1725 K St. NW
Suite 1102
Washington, DC 20006
Web: www.hometown.aol.com/popresctr/prc.html
E-mail: prc@prcdc.org

Tel: (202)467-5030
Fax: (202)467-5034

Established in 1975 as a non-profit, non-advocacy organization to inform and educate the government and public leaders on demographic trends that affect economic and social policies. Administrative headquarters are in Princeton, New Jersey.

In-house, DC-area Employees

THORNE, Nancy: Director, Washington Office

Porsche Cars North America, Inc.

Atlanta, GA
Leg. Issues: AUT, TAX

Outside Counsel/Consultants

Murray, Scheer, Montgomery, Tapia & O'Donnell
Issues: AUT, TAX
Rep By: Thomas R. Crawford, D. Michael Murray

Port Angeles, Washington, City of

Outside Counsel/Consultants

Preston Gates Ellis & Rouvelas Meeds LLP
Rep By: Tim L. Peckinpaugh

Port Authority of New York and New Jersey

1001 Connecticut Ave. NW
Suite 610
Washington, DC 20036
Web: www.panynj.gov
E-mail: pbea@panynj.gov

Tel: (202)887-5240
Fax: (202)887-0282

A bistate and public authority to provide regional transportation service and to promote and protect commerce in the NY-NJ metropolitan area.

Leg. Issues: AVI, GOV, ROD, RRR, TRA, TRU

In-house, DC-area Employees

BEA, Jr., Paul H.: Washington Representative, Director
JONES, James D. E.: Deputy Washington Representative
PATTERSON, Eliza: Legislative Representative

Outside Counsel/Consultants

LaRoe, Winn, Moerman & Donovan
Rep By: Paul M. Donovan

Port Hueneme, California, City of

Leg. Issues: BUD

Outside Counsel/Consultants

Murray, Scheer, Montgomery, Tapia & O'Donnell

E. Del Smith and Co.
Issues: BUD
Rep By: Margaret Allen, E. Del Smith

Port of Lake Charles

Lake Charles, LA
Leg. Issues: MAR, TRA

Outside Counsel/Consultants

Diane McRee Associates
Issues: MAR, TRA
Rep By: Diane B. McRee

Port of San Diego

San Diego, CA
Leg. Issues: AVI, MAR, TOU, TRA, TRU

Outside Counsel/Consultants

Carpi & Clay
Issues: AVI, MAR, TOU, TRA, TRU
Rep By: Kenneth A. Carpi

Honberger and Walters, Inc.
Rep By: Thomas P. Walters

Port of Tillamook Bay

Tillamook, OR
Leg. Issues: BUD

Outside Counsel/Consultants

Birch, Horton, Bittner & Cherot
Issues: BUD
Rep By: Thomas L. Albert, William Bittner

Verner, Liipfert, Bernhard, McPherson and Hand, Chartered
Issues: BUD
Rep By: Timothy M. Rutten, John H. Sterne, Jr.

Portable Power Equipment Manufacturers Ass'n

4330 East West Hwy.
Suite 310
Bethesda, MD 20814
Web: www.ppema.org
E-mail: ppemal@msn.com

Tel: (301)652-0774
Fax: (301)654-6138
Registered: LDA

In-house, DC-area Employees

HUTCHISON, Karen B.: V. President

Outside Counsel/Consultants

Dunaway & Cross
Rep By: Mac S. Dunaway

Portable Rechargeable Battery Ass'n

Atlanta, GA

Outside Counsel/Consultants

Howrey Simon Arnold & White
Rep By: George Kerchner, Saskia Mooney, Tracy Heinzman Smith, David B. Weinberg

Portals Development Associates L.P.

Washington, DC
Leg. Issues: RES, TRA

Outside Counsel/Consultants

Lawler, Metzger & Milkman, LLC
Issues: RES, TRA
Rep By: Sante J. Esposito, Gregory E. Lawler

Portland Cellular Partnership

Leg. Issues: COM

Outside Counsel/Consultants

O'Connor & Hannan, L.L.P.
Issues: COM
Rep By: Patrick E. O'Donnell, Thomas H. Quinn

Portland General Electric Co.

Portland, OR
Leg. Issues: UTI

Outside Counsel/Consultants

Vinson & Elkins L.L.P.
Issues: UTI
Rep By: Hon. Michael A. Andrews, Christopher M. Dawe

Portland Metro Regional Government

Portland, OR
Leg. Issues: WAS

Outside Counsel/Consultants

Wright & Talisman, P.C.
Issues: WAS
Rep By: Scott M. DuBoff

Portland Tri-Met

Portland, OR

Outside Counsel/Consultants

Peyser Associates, Inc.
Rep By: Peter A. Peyser, Jr.

Portland, Oregon, City of

Leg. Issues: BUD, CAW, ECN, ENV, GOV, HOU, LAW, NAT, TAX, TEC, TRA, URB

Outside Counsel/Consultants

Ball Janik, LLP
Issues: BUD, CAW, ECN, GOV, HOU, LAW, TAX, URB
Rep By: M. Victoria Cram

Miller & Van Eaton, P.L.L.C.
Issues: TEC
Rep By: Joseph Van Eaton

Simon and Co., Inc.
Issues: BUD, ENV, NAT, TRA
Rep By: Heather Barber, Alex DeGood, Leonard S. Simon

Portugal, Trade Commission of the Government of the Republic of

New York, NY

Outside Counsel/Consultants

Edelman Public Relations Worldwide
Rep By: Michael K. Deaver, Robert Rehg

Poseidon Resources Corp.

Stamford, CT

A water project development company.

Leg. Issues: ENV, WAS

Outside Counsel/Consultants

Dickstein Shapiro Morin & Oshinsky LLP
Rep By: Frederick M. Lowther, Bernard Nash, Hon. Stanford E. Parris, L. Andrew Zausner

ENS Resources, Inc.

Manatt, Phelps & Phillips, LLP
Issues: ENV, WAS
Rep By: Hon. Jack W. Buechner, James R. Jones

Potlatch Corp.

San Francisco, CA
Leg. Issues: CAW

Outside Counsel/Consultants

Wright & Talisman, P.C.
Issues: CAW
Rep By: Robert H. Lamb

The Potomac Advocates

321 D St. NE
Washington, DC 20002

Tel: (202)547-4192
Fax: (202)547-4674
Registered: LDA

Leg. Issues: AGR, DEF

In-house, DC-area Employees
RYAN, Patricia: Partner
SCALERA, Charles: Partner
SOJKA, Gary L.: Partner

Outside Counsel/Consultants
Pacquing Consulting Inc.
Issues: AGR, DEF
Rep By: Juliet Pacquing

Potomac Capital Investment Corp.

Washington, DC

Outside Counsel/Consultants
Shaw Pittman

Potomac Electric Power Co.

1900 Pennsylvania Ave. NW Tel: (202)872-2000
Washington, DC 20068 Registered: LDA
Leg. Issues: BUD, CAW, COM, DOC, ENG, ENV, FIN, GOV, HCR, LBR, NAT, RES, RRR, SMB, TAX, TRA, UTI

Political Action Committee/s
PEPCO Political Action Committee
1900 Pennsylvania Ave. NW Tel: (202)872-2000
Washington, DC 20068
Contact: James S. Potts

In-house, DC-area Employees
ELLIOTT, Kate: Senior Government Relations Representative
PERRY, Beverly: V. President, Government and Corporate Affairs
POTTS, James S.: V. President, Environmental
TORGERSON, William T.: Senior V. President and General Counsel, External Affairs
TRABUE, Ted: Manager, Government Relations - D.C.

Outside Counsel/Consultants
Balch & Bingham LLP
Issues: UTI
Rep By: Sean Cunningham, Fred Eames, Patrick J. McCormick, III

Ray Billups
Issues: ENG, UTI
Rep By: Ray Billups

Earle Palmer Brown Public Relations

Johnson Co.
Issues: COM, ENG, UTI

Potomac Heritage Partnership

Washington, DC
Leg. Issues: NAT, TOU

Outside Counsel/Consultants
Patton Boggs, LLP
Issues: NAT, TOU
Rep By: Parker Brugge, Thomas C. Downs

Potters Industries, Inc.

Parsippany, NJ
Leg. Issues: TRA

Outside Counsel/Consultants
Arthur E. Cameron
Issues: TRA
Rep By: Arthur E. Cameron, Sr.

Poverty and Race Research Action Council

3000 Connecticut Ave. NW Tel: (202)387-9887
Suite 200 Fax: (202)387-0764
Washington, DC 20008
Web: www.prrac.org
E-mail: info@prrac.org

Provides networking and communication between activists and researchers who work on race and poverty issues and provides grants for social science research on the intersection of race and poverty tied to an advocacy plan.

In-house, DC-area Employees
HARTMAN, Chester: President and Exec. Director

Powder Coating Institute

2121 Eisenhower Ave. Tel: (703)684-1770
Suite 401 Fax: (703)684-1771
Alexandria, VA 22314
Web: www.powdercoating.org
E-mail: pci-info@powdercoating.org

Represents the North American powder coating industry. Promotes powder coating technology and communicates the benefits of powder coating to manufacturers, consumers, and government.

In-house, DC-area Employees
BOCCHI, Gregory J.: Exec. Director
PALMER, Jeff: Director, Communications

Powell, Goldstein, Frazer & Murphy LLP

1001 Pennsylvania Ave. NW Tel: (202)347-0066
Suite 600 Fax: (202)624-7222
Washington, DC 20004 Registered: LDA, FARA
Web: www.pgfm.com
Leg. Issues: BUD

In-house, DC-area Employees
ABRAHAMS, Jessica: Partner
ALEXANDROV, Stanimir: Foreign Counsel
CAMERON, Kelly: Partner
CLARK, Alice Slayton: International Trade Analyst
COCO, Jr., Leo: Senior Policy Advisor
COLLINS, Charlotte: Of Counsel
DANIELS, Michael P.: Partner
DERRICK, Jr., Hon. Butler E.: Partner
DIGIULIAN, Maria: Associate
DRAZEK, Paul A.: Senior Policy Advisor
EFFGEN, Gretchen: Analyst
ELLIS, Neil: Partner
EYMAN, Barbara D. A.: Counsel
FINE, Michael E.: Partner
FISCHBECK, Kyra: Associate
FRIEDBACHER, Todd: Associate
FULLERTON, Lawrence R.: Partner
GAGE, Larry S.: Partner
GINSBURG, David: Senior Counsel
HAMMOND, David C.: Partner
HORTON, Katie: Senior Policy Advisor
HOWARD, Elizabeth Johns: Trade Policy Analyst
HUGE, Harry: Partner
JACOBS, Brenda A.: Partner
KAPPEL, Brett G.: Partner
KNAPP, John J.: Partner
KOFF, Alexander: Associate
KUSHAN, Jeff: Partner
LAZARUS, III, Simon: Partner
LUBAND, Charles: Associate
MCSHERRY, Carolyn: Analyst
PARVER, Alan K.: Managing Partner
PRICE, Daniel M.: Partner
QUAM, David C.: Associate
ROISTACHER, Charles H.: Partner
RUBIN, Leonard J.: Partner
SANDERS, Michael: Partner
SHAPIRO, Lisa: Analyst
SHOYER, Andrew: Partner
SKILLINGTON, G. Lee: Counsel
SLAFSKY, Ted: Coalition Manager
STRANNE, Steve K.: Partner
STRENIO, Andrew: Partner
SUCHMAN, Peter O.: Consultant
THORN, Craig A.: Senior Policy Advisor
TORRESEN, Jr., Robert: Partner
TRAPHAGEN, Mark: Partner
VON OEHSEN, William H. E.: Partner
WALDERS, Larry: Partner

Outside Counsel/Consultants
SLR Budget and Legislative Consulting
Issues: BUD

Power and Communications Contractors Ass'n

6301 Stevenson Ave. Tel: (703)823-1732
Suite One Fax: (703)823-5064
Alexandria, VA 22304
Web: www.pccaweb.org

In-house, DC-area Employees
STROTHER, Michael E.: Exec. V. President

Outside Counsel/Consultants
Strother & Hosking, Inc.
Rep By: Michael E. Strother

Power Distribution, Inc. (PDI)

Sandston, VA

A manufacturer of power distribution units.

Outside Counsel/Consultants
O'Connor & Fierce Associates

Power Mobility Coalition

Washington, DC

A coalition of health care medical equipment suppliers.

Leg. Issues: BUD, HCR

Outside Counsel/Consultants
Duane, Morris & Heckscher LLP
Issues: BUD, HCR
Rep By: Stephen M. Azia, Valerie J. Eastwood

Power Paragon Inc.

Anaheim, CA

Outside Counsel/Consultants
Thelen Reid & Priest LLP
Rep By: Barry I. Berkoff, Richard J. Leidl, Stephan M. Minikes

PowerGen

London, UNITED KINGDOM
Leg. Issues: ENG

Outside Counsel/Consultants
Lighthouse Energy Group LLC
Issues: ENG
Rep By: Tobyn J. Anderson, Merribel S. Ayres

Powerline Communications PAC

P.O. Box 150998
Alexandria, VA 22315

In-house, DC-area Employees
CAREY, USN (Ret.), Rr. Adm. James J.: Contact

Powerspan Corp.

New Durham, NH
Leg. Issues: ENG

Outside Counsel/Consultants
Lighthouse Energy Group LLC
Issues: ENG
Rep By: Tobyn J. Anderson, Merribel S. Ayres

Powerware

Raleigh, NC
Leg. Issues: AVI, GOV, TEC

Outside Counsel/Consultants
Albertine Enterprises, Inc.
Issues: AVI, GOV, TEC
Rep By: James J. Albertine, Dr. John M. Albertine

O'Connor & Fierce Associates
Rep By: Michael J. O'Connor

PPG Industries

Pittsburgh, PA Registered: LDA
Leg. Issues: TRD

Outside Counsel/Consultants
Baker & Hostetler LLP

Stewart and Stewart
Issues: TRD
Rep By: Alan M. Dunn, David S. Johanson, Terence P. Stewart

PPL

1331 Pennsylvania Ave. NW Tel: (202)662-8750
Suite 512 Fax: (202)662-8749
Washington, DC 20004 Registered: LDA

Formerly known as Pennsylvania Power and Light Co.

Leg. Issues: BUD, CAW, TAX, TRA, UTI, WAS

Political Action Committee/s
PPL People for Good Government
1331 Pennsylvania Ave. NW Tel: (202)662-8755
Suite 512 Fax: (202)662-8749
Washington, DC 20004
Contact: John S. Sparkman

In-house, DC-area Employees
PLAUSHIN, Nina: Manager, Federal Affairs
SPARKMAN, John S.: Director, Federal Public Affairs

Outside Counsel/Consultants
Internat'l Capital Strategies

Preston Gates Ellis & Rouvelas Meeds LLP
Rep By: Pamela J. Garvie, Tim L. Peckinpaugh, Emanuel L. Rouvelas, Steven R. "Rick" Valentine

Prairie Band of Potawatomi Indians

Mayetta, KS
Leg. Issues: IND

Outside Counsel/Consultants
Morriset, Schlosser, Ayer & Jozwiak
Issues: IND
Rep By: Fran Ayer

Prairie Wood Products

Prairie City, OR

Outside Counsel/Consultants
Jamison and Sullivan, Inc.
Rep By: Delos Cy Jamison, Jay R. Sullivan

Pratt & Whitney

1401 I St. NW
Suite 600
Washington, DC 20005-6523
Tel: (202)336-7430
Fax: (202)336-7421
Registered: LDA
Web: www.pratt-whitney.com
E-mail: summerm@corpdc.utc.com

A United Technologies company headquartered in Hartford, CT.

Leg. Issues: AVI

In-house, DC-area Employees

SUMMERS, Michael H.: Director, Washington Operations

Outside Counsel/Consultants

Commerce Consultants Internat'l Ltd.

Filler & Weller, P.C.
Issues: AVI

Praxair, Inc.

801 Pennsylvania Ave. NW
Suite 230
Washington, DC 20004
Tel: (202)393-0962
Fax: (202)347-1684
Registered: LDA
E-mail: Tom_Finnigan@Praxair.com

A producer of industrial gases and specialty coatings. Headquartered in Danbury, CT.

Leg. Issues: BUD, CPI, CPT, ENG, HCR, LBR, TAX, TRA, TRD

In-house, DC-area Employees

FINNIGAN, Thomas D.: Director, Government Relations

Pray, Walker, Jackman, Williamson & Marlar

Tulsa, OK

Outside Counsel/Consultants

Capitol Counsel Group, L.L.C.
Rep By: Warren Belmar

Precision Aerospace Corp.

Kirkland, WA
Leg. Issues: AVI, DEF

Outside Counsel/Consultants

Denny Miller McBee Associates
Issues: AVI, DEF

Precision Lift

Monarch, MT
Leg. Issues: DEF, MAN

Outside Counsel/Consultants

American Systems Internat'l Corp.
Issues: DEF, MAN
Rep By: Robert D. McVey, William H. Skipper, Jr.

Precision Medical

Northampton, PA
Leg. Issues: HCR, MMM

Outside Counsel/Consultants

Nusgart Consulting, LLC
Issues: HCR, MMM
Rep By: Marcia Nusgart

PrediWave

Fremont, CA
Leg. Issues: TEC

Outside Counsel/Consultants

Colling Swift & Hynes
Issues: TEC
Rep By: Terese Colling, Pablo Collins, Robert J. Hynes, Jr., Hon. Allan B. Swift

Premier Institute

Leg. Issues: ENV

Outside Counsel/Consultants

Ungaretti & Harris
Issues: ENV
Rep By: Joseph A. Cari, Jr.

Premier Parks, Inc.

Oklahoma City, OK
Leg. Issues: CSP, TOU

Outside Counsel/Consultants

Mercury Group
Issues: CSP, TOU

Premier, Inc.

444 N. Capitol St. NW
Suite 625
Washington, DC 20001
Tel: (202)393-0860
Fax: (202)393-0864
Registered: LDA

The Washington, DC office of a San Diego, CA-based company.

Leg. Issues: HCR

In-house, DC-area Employees

ALLINGER, Sharon: Federal Affairs Coordinator
REAGAN, Margaret: Director, Federal Affairs
SCOTT, James L.: Senior V. President

Premium Standard Farms

Kansas City, MO
Leg. Issues: AGR, CAW

Outside Counsel/Consultants

Bergner Bockorny Castagnetti and Hawkins
Issues: AGR
Rep By: Jeffrey T. Bergner, David A. Bockorny, David Castagnetti, James W. Hawkins, Brenda Benjamin Reese, Melissa Schulman

Capitolink, LLC
Issues: AGR, CAW
Rep By: Deborah M. Atwood, John H. Thorne, Ph.D.

Preneed Insurers Government Programs Coalition

Batesville, IN

A coalition of life insurance companies engaged in sales and marketing of funeral plans.

Leg. Issues: INS

Outside Counsel/Consultants

Patton Boggs, LLP
Issues: INS
Rep By: John F. Jonas, Martha M. Kendrick, Elizabeth E. Ring

Presbyterian Church (U.S.A.)

110 Maryland Ave. NE
Suite 104
Washington, DC 20002
Tel: (202)543-1126
Fax: (202)543-7755
E-mail: ga_washington_office@pcusa.org

In-house, DC-area Employees

IVORY, Elenora G.: Director, Washington Office

Preservation Action

1350 Connecticut Ave. NW
Suite 401
Washington, DC 20036
Tel: (202)659-0915
Fax: (202)659-0189
Registered: LDA
Web: www.preservationaction.org
E-mail: mail@preservationaction.org

Individuals and organizations concerned with historic preservation.

Leg. Issues: BUD, HOU, NAT, POS, RES, ROD, TAX, TOU, URB

In-house, DC-area Employees

MONTGOMERY, Susan West: President

A Presidential Classroom for Young Americans, Inc.

119 Oronoco St.
Alexandria, VA 22314-2015
Tel: (703)683-5400
Fax: (703)548-5728
Web: www.presidentialclassroom.org
E-mail: info@presidentialclassroom.org

The parent organization of national and international civic education opportunities for high school students. A private, non-profit, non-partisan education organization, Presidential Classroom has graduated more than 75,000 young leaders from its programs since 1969.

In-house, DC-area Employees

DIGIOIA, Lou: Manager, Congressional Affairs
GITTELMAN, Lynn: Director of Marketing
ROSICA, A. Joseph: Director, Communications
SCUDERI, Roy: Director, Finance and Administration
WICKLIFF, Jay: Exec. Director

Presidential Towers, Ltd.

Chicago, IL

An apartment owner.

Leg. Issues: HOU

Outside Counsel/Consultants

Coan & Lyons
Issues: HOU
Rep By: Carl A. S. Coan, Jr., Raymond K. James

Pressure Island

Menlo, CA

Outside Counsel/Consultants

Interface Inc.
Rep By: David C. Knapp

Preston Gates Ellis & Rouvelas Meeds LLP

1735 New York Ave. NW
Suite 500
Washington, DC 20006-4759
Tel: (202)628-1700
Fax: (202)331-1024
Registered: LDA, FARA
Web: www.prestongates.com
Leg. Issues: IND, POS, TOU

Political Action Committee/s

Preston Gates Ellis & Rouvelas Meeds LLP PAC
1735 New York Ave. NW
Suite 500
Washington, DC 20006-4759
Tel: (202)628-1700
Fax: (202)331-1024

In-house, DC-area Employees

BLANK, Jonathan: Managing Partner
BRANDT, Werner W.: Government Affairs Counselor
CAMPBELL, Gary: Associate
CARLSON, Amy: Partner
CONNER, Darrell: Government Affairs Counselor
CRAIN, Julie: Associate
DAVIS, Hon. Bob: Counselor
DIMOPOULOS, Arthur: Of Counsel
DORAN, Kelley P.: Associate
FLEMING, Elizabeth W.: Of Counsel
FRIEDLANDER, Lisa L.: Associate
FUNDERBURK, Hon. David: Government Affairs Counselor
GARVIE, Pamela J.: Partner
GEIGER, Susan B.: Partner
HEIMAN, Bruce J.: Partner
HOUCK, Caryn: Associate
HUTHER, Christopher S.: Partner
HUTSON, Harrison D.: Of Counsel
IVEY, Glenn: Partner
JACKSON, Kristie: Associate
KAPLAN, Donald A.: Partner
LONGSTRETH, John L.: Partner
MAGEE, Marybeth: Associate
MARKS, Jeffrey: Associate
MARSHALL, Rolf: Partner
MCCALMON, Brian K.: Associate
MEEDS, Hon. Lloyd: Of Counsel
MILLER, Eugene P.: Partner
MOSHER, Sol: Senior Advisor, Federal Affairs and International Trade
MYHRE, William N.: Partner
NURNBERGER, Ralph D.: Government Affairs Counselor
O'MALLEY, Cindy: Government Affairs Analyst
O'NEIL, Michael J.: Partner
PARK, Hong: Associate
PECKINPAUGH, Tim L.: Partner
PHILLIPS, Rosanne: Treasurer, Political Action Committee
RITTER, Daniel: Associate
RIZZO, Sandra: Of Counsel
ROMERO, Jorge: Associate
ROUVELAS, Emanuel L.: Chairman and Partner
RUGE, Mark H.: Partner
SABO, Melanie: Partner
SEE, Chad
SHOOK, William A.: Partner
STEPHENS, W. Dennis: Government Affairs Analyst
STERN, Martin L.: Partner
THOMAS, W. David: Associate
TROY, Megan: Associate
TUCKER, Lisa M.: Partner
VALENTINE, Steven R. "Rick": Of Counsel
WEISS, James R.: Partner

Outside Counsel/Consultants

Higgins, McGovern & Smith, LLC
Issues: TOU
Rep By: Carl M. Smith

James Pierce Myers
Issues: POS
Rep By: James Pierce Myers

Robertson, Monagle & Eastaugh
Issues: IND
Rep By: Steven W. Silver

Pretium S.C (Mexico)

Mexico City, MEXICO
Leg. Issues: ECN, FOR, TRD

Outside Counsel/Consultants

Janus-Merritt Strategies, L.L.C.
Issues: ECN, FOR, TRD
Rep By: Mark J. Robertson

Prevent Blindness America

Leg. Issues: BUD, HCR

Outside Counsel/Consultants

Arent Fox Kintner Plotkin & Kahn, PLLC
Issues: BUD, HCR
Rep By: Katie Clarke, Stacy Harbison, Douglas McCormack

Price Costco

Issaquah, WA
A retail/wholesale chain.

Outside Counsel/Consultants

EOP Group, Inc.
Rep By: Jonathan Gledhill, Michael O'Bannon

PriceWaterhouseCoopers

1301 K St. NW
Washington, DC 20005-3333
Tel: (202)414-1000
Fax: (202)414-1301
Registered: LDA
Leg. Issues: AVI, CPI, DEF, GOV, TRD

Political Action Committee/s

PriceWaterhouseCoopers Partners' Political Action Committee
1301 K St. NW
Washington, DC 20005-3333
Tel: (202)414-1000
Fax: (202)414-1301

In-house, DC-area Employees

ANGUS, Barbara: Partner
ANSON, Tim: Partner
BELL, Beverly E.: Director, Federal Government Affairs
CAMPBELL, Larry: Manager, Tax Policy
CARLISLE, Jim: Director
CARLSON, Donald G.: Director, National Tax Service
CHURCH, Elaine K.: Partner, Employee Benefits Services
HARMAN, John R.: Senior Manager, Tax Policy
JENNER, Gregory F.: Partner
JOHNSON, Kirt C.: Director
KIES, Kenneth J.: Managing Partner, Washington National Tax Service
LONGANO, Don R.: Partner
MCCONAGHY, Mark: Partner, Washington National Tax Service
MERRILL, Peter R.: Partner
NEWLAND, Dee E. "Ned": Manager, Tax Policy Economics
RAFFANIELLO, Pat: Managing Director
REPASS, David M.: Senior Manager
SCHOENFELD, Howard: Director
SHANAHAN, James R.: Partner
SHAPIRO, Bernard M.: Managing Partner
STARR, Sam: Partner
WELTMAN, Allen: Partner
WERTZ, Ken: Partner

Outside Counsel/Consultants

Bergson & Co.
Issues: DEF
Rep By: Paul C. Bergson

Chambers Associates Inc.
Rep By: Letitia Chambers

Dierman, Wortley, and Zola
Issues: GOV

GPC Internat'l
Issues: AVI
Rep By: John D. Cahill, Daniel K. Crann

Mayer, Brown & Platt
Issues: CPI, TRD
Rep By: Carol J. Bilzi, Brian T. Borders, Mark H. Gitenstein, Jeffrey H. Lewis, Charles A. Rothfeld

MV3 & Associates

Valente Lopatin & Schulze
Rep By: Mark Valente, III

Pride Africa

100 N. Pitt St.
Suite 202
Alexandria, VA 22314
Tel: (703)519-7778
Fax: (703)519-7557
E-mail: pride@africaonline.co.ke

A non-profit, international development agency registered in Washington, D.C. and headquartered in Nairobi, Kenya. Its major objective is to create a financial and information service network for small-scale entrepreneurs to increase incomes and employment and stimulate business growth across Africa.

In-house, DC-area Employees

CAMPAIGNE, Jonathan F.: Exec. Director
KESSLER, Lee: Director

Primavera Laboratories, Inc.

Rye, NY

Outside Counsel/Consultants

Garvey, Schubert & Barer
Rep By: Matthew R. Schneider

Prime Time 24

New York, NY
Leg. Issues: COM, CPT

Outside Counsel/Consultants

Powell Tate
Issues: COM, CPT

Primedia

Outside Counsel/Consultants

Widmeyer Communications, Inc.

Primerica, Inc.

New York, NY
Formerly known as the American Can Co.

Outside Counsel/Consultants

Balch & Bingham LLP

Prince George's, Maryland, County of

Upper Marlboro, MD
Leg. Issues: BUD, HOU, LAW, LBR, TEC, TRA, URB

Outside Counsel/Consultants

Arter & Hadden

Greenberg Traurig, LLP
Issues: BUD, HOU, LAW, LBR, TRA, URB
Rep By: Diane J. Blagman

Miller & Van Eaton, P.L.L.C.
Issues: TEC
Rep By: Nicholas P. Miller

Patton Boggs, LLP
Rep By: Michael A. Brown

Prince William County Service Authority

Leg. Issues: RES, UTI

Outside Counsel/Consultants

McGuireWoods L.L.P.
Issues: RES, UTI
Rep By: Hana Brilliant, Stephen A. Katsurinis, Jeffrey L. Schlagenhauf

Prince William County, Virginia

Prince William, VA
Leg. Issues: TRA

Outside Counsel/Consultants

Baker, Donelson, Bearman & Caldwell, P.C.
Issues: TRA
Rep By: Janet L. Powell

Prince William Sound Regional Citizen's Advisory Council

Anchorage, AK
Leg. Issues: BUD, ENV

Outside Counsel/Consultants

Birch, Horton, Bittner & Cherot
Issues: BUD, ENV
Rep By: Roy S. Jones, Jr.

Princess Cruise Lines

Los Angeles, CA
Leg. Issues: TOU

Outside Counsel/Consultants

The Renkes Group, Ltd.
Issues: TOU
Rep By: Gregg D. Renkes

Princess Tours

Seattle, WA
Leg. Issues: ENV, RES

Outside Counsel/Consultants

Van Ness Feldman, P.C.
Issues: ENV, RES
Rep By: Richard A. Agnew, Howard J. Feldman

Princeton University

444 N. Capitol St. NW
Suite 728
Washington, DC 20001
Tel: (202)639-8420
Fax: (202)639-8423

In-house, DC-area Employees

WELLS, Nan S.: Director, Office of Government Affairs

Principal Financial Group

1350 I St. NW
Suite 1030
Washington, DC 20005-3305
Tel: (202)682-1280
Fax: (202)682-1412
Registered: LDA
Web: www.principal.com

A leading provider of a wide range of financial products and services to businesses and individuals including retirement and asset management, life and health insurance, and mortgage banking. Headquartered in Des Moines, IA.

Leg. Issues: BNK, BUD, CIV, CPI, FIN, FOR, GOV, HCR, HOU, IMM, INS, LBR, MMM, RET, SMB, TAX, TRD

Political Action Committee/s

Principal Financial Group PRINPAC
1350 I St. NW
Suite 1030
Washington, DC 20005-3305
Tel: (202)682-1280
Fax: (202)682-1412
Contact: Stuart J. Brahs

In-house, DC-area Employees

BLUMER, Patti R.: Assistant Federal Legislative Director
BRAHS, Stuart J.: V. President, Federal Government Relations
FREDRICKSON, Debi: Compliance Analyst, Fed. Gov't Relations
RIDDLE, R. Lucia: V. President, Government Relations

Printing Industries of America

100 Daingerfield Rd.
Alexandria, VA 22314
Tel: (703)519-8100
Fax: (703)548-3227
Registered: LDA
Web: www.gain.net

An international graphic arts trade association federation of regional, state and city associations.

Leg. Issues: BUD, CAW, CPI, CPT, ENV, FOO, GOV, HCR, LBR, MAN, POS, RET, SMB, TAX, TOR, WAS

Political Action Committee/s

Printing Industries of America Political Action Committee (PrintPAC)
100 Daingerfield Rd.
Alexandria, VA 22314
Tel: (703)519-8100
Fax: (703)519-6481
Contact: Benjamin Y. Cooper

In-house, DC-area Employees

CHEEK, Felicia: Legislative Assistant
COOPER, Benjamin Y.: Senior V. President, Government Affairs
LECHNER, Wendy: Legislative Director
ROPER, Ray: President and Chief Exec. Officer

Outside Counsel/Consultants

Drinker Biddle & Reath LLP
Rep By: Michael J. Remington

McNamara & Associates
Issues: ENV, HCR, SMB, TAX
Rep By: Thomas J. McNamara

Ogletree Governmental Affairs, Inc.
Issues: LBR

Swidler Berlin Shereff Friedman, LLP
Issues: CAW
Rep By: Keith N. Cole

Priority Care

Leg. Issues: HCR

Outside Counsel/Consultants

Arent Fox Kintner Plotkin & Kahn, PLLC
Issues: HCR
Rep By: Stacy Harbison, Douglas McCormack, Connie A. Raffa

Prison Fellowship Ministries

P.O. Box 17500
Washington, DC 20041-0500
Tel: (703)478-0100
Fax: (703)834-3658
Web: www.pfm.org

In-house, DC-area Employees

COLSON, Charles W.: Chairman of the Board

Privacy Council

Outside Counsel/Consultants

Creative Response Concepts

PrivacyRight

San Mateo, CA
Leg. Issues: CPI, CSP, MIA

Outside Counsel/Consultants

Mercury Group
Issues: CPI, CSP, MIA

Private Care Ass'n, Inc.

Washington, DC
Leg. Issues: HCR, TAX

Outside Counsel/Consultants

Littler Mendelson, P.C.
Issues: HCR, TAX
Rep By: Russell A. Hollrah

Private Essential Access Community Hospitals (PEACH) Inc.

Sacramento, CA
Leg. Issues: BUD, HCR, MED, MMM

Outside Counsel/Consultants

DeBrunner and Associates, Inc.
Issues: BUD, HCR, MED, MMM
Rep By: Charles L. DeBrunner, Ellen J. Kugler, Kathryn D. Rooney

Private Fuels Storage, L.L.C.

La Crosse, WI
Leg. Issues: BUD, ENG

Outside Counsel/Consultants

McClure, Gerard & Neuenschwander, Inc.
Issues: BUD, ENG
Rep By: Steven G. Barringer, Joseph T. Findaro, Matthew Iandoli, Nils W. Johnson, Hon. James A. McClure, Tod O. Neuenschwander

Private Practice Section of the American Physical Therapy Ass'n

1710 Rhode Island Ave. NW
Suite 800
Washington, DC 20036
Tel: (202)457-1115
Fax: (202)457-9191
Registered: LDA
Web: www.ppsapta.org
E-mail: info@ppsapta.org
Leg. Issues: HCR, MMM, SMB

In-house, DC-area Employees

DUNNE, Joanne E.: Exec. Director

Outside Counsel/Consultants

Williams & Jensen, P.C.
Issues: HCR, MMM
Rep By: George G. Olsen

Pro Trade Group

A trade association.

Outside Counsel/Consultants

Aitken, Irvin, Lewin, Berlin, Vrooman & Cohn
Rep By: Bruce Aitken

Problem-Knowledge Coupler

Burlington, VT
Leg. Issues: VET

Outside Counsel/Consultants

Brown & Associates
Issues: VET
Rep By: Shirley Carozza, Edward P. Scott

Process Equipment Manufacturers' Ass'n

111 Park Place
Falls Church, VA 22046-4513
Tel: (703)538-1796
Fax: (703)241-5603
Web: www.pemanet.org
E-mail: pemahq@aol.com
Leg. Issues: GOV, TOR, TRD

In-house, DC-area Employees

BUZZERD, Jr., CAE, Harry W.: Exec. Director

Outside Counsel/Consultants

Ass'n and Soc. Management Internat'l Inc.

Barnes & Thornburg
Issues: GOV, TOR, TRD
Rep By: Randolph J. Stayin

Process Gas Consumers Group

Washington, DC
E-mail: egrenier@sablaw.com

An ad hoc group of gas consuming corporations including Alcan Aluminum, Alcoa, Arcadian, Bethlehem Steel, Carpenter Technology, Cone Mills, Corning Inc., Eaton Corp., Ford Motor Co., General Motors Corp, Owens-Corning Fiberglas Corp. Owens-Illinois, PPG, Grain Processing Inc., Reynolds Metals Co., The Timken Co. and Procter and Gamble.

Outside Counsel/Consultants

Sutherland Asbill & Brennan LLP

Processed Apples Institute

1101 15th St. NW
Suite 202
Washington, DC 20005
Tel: (202)785-3232
Fax: (202)223-9741

In-house, DC-area Employees

CRISTOL, Richard E.: Washington Representative

Outside Counsel/Consultants

The Kellen Company
Rep By: Richard E. Cristol

The Procter & Gamble Company

801 Pennsylvania Ave. NW
Suite 720
Washington, DC 20004-2604
Tel: (202)393-3400
Fax: (202)393-4606
Registered: LDA
Web: www.pg.com

Headquartered in Cincinnati, OH.

Leg. Issues: ALC, BUD, CPT, CSP, ENV, FOO, FOR, LAW, SCI, TAX, TEC, TRD

In-house, DC-area Employees

DUNCAN, Molly: Legislative Assistant
FAWCETT-HOOVER, Jane: V. President, National Government Relations
GENOVESI, Jacqueline: Legislative Assistant
MCCARTHY, James: Director, National Government Relations
MILLER, R. Scott: Director, National Government Relations

Outside Counsel/Consultants

Hills & Company, International Consultants
Issues: TRD
Rep By: Edward A. Casey, Robert Fisher, Carla A. Hills

Internat'l Business-Government Counsellors, Inc.
Issues: TRD
Rep By: John F. McDermid

Proctor Hospital

Peoria, IL
Leg. Issues: BUD

Outside Counsel/Consultants

Cassidy & Associates, Inc.
Issues: BUD
Rep By: Arthur D. Mason, Laura A. Neal, Diane Rinaldo

Prodigy

White Plains, NY

Outside Counsel/Consultants

Wiley, Rein & Fielding
Rep By: Susan C. Buck, Robert J. Butler, Bruce G. Joseph, Nancy J. Victory

Produce Marketing Ass'n

Newark, DE

Outside Counsel/Consultants

Keller and Heckman LLP
Rep By: Mel S. Drozen, Sheila A. Millar, Ralph A. Simmons

Product Liability Alliance, The

Washington, DC
E-mail: naw@nawd.org

A coalition of over 300 business interests lobbying for reform of product liability laws. Represented by the Nat'l Ass'n of Wholesaler-Distributors

Outside Counsel/Consultants

Crowell & Moring LLP
Rep By: Victor E. Schwartz

Product Liability Information Bureau

Outside Counsel/Consultants

Crowell & Moring LLP
Rep By: Victor E. Schwartz

Product Liability Prevention and Defense Group

111 Park Place
Falls Church, VA 22046
Tel: (703)538-1789
Fax: (703)241-5603

A coalition of capital goods machinery companies.

In-house, DC-area Employees

BUZZERD, Jr., CAE, Harry W.: Senior Management Counsel
TYERYAR, CAE, Clay D.: Exec. Director

Outside Counsel/Consultants

Ass'n and Soc. Management Internat'l Inc.
Rep By: Harry W. Buzzerd, Jr., CAE, Clay D. Tyeryar, CAE

Production Service & Sales District Council Pension Fund

Brooklyn, NY
Leg. Issues: LBR, RET, TAX

Outside Counsel/Consultants

Groom Law Group, Chartered
Issues: LBR, RET, TAX
Rep By: Jon W. Breyfogle, Gary M. Ford

Production Technology, Inc.

Arlington, VA
Leg. Issues: DEF

Outside Counsel/Consultants

Pacquing Consulting Inc.
Issues: DEF
Rep By: Juliet Pacquing

PROEXPORT

Bogota, COLOMBIA

Outside Counsel/Consultants

Powell, Goldstein, Frazer & Murphy LLP
Rep By: Alice Slayton Clark, Maria DiGiulian, Gretchen Effgen, Brenda A. Jacobs

Professional Airways Systems Specialists (AFL-CIO)

1150 17th St. NW
Suite 702
Washington, DC 20036
Tel: (202)293-7277
Fax: (202)293-7727
Registered: LDA
Web: www.passnational.org

Aviation Labor Union.

Leg. Issues: AVI, LBR, TRA

Political Action Committee/s

Professional Airways Systems Specialists - PASS PAC
1150 17th St. NW
Suite 702
Washington, DC 20036
Tel: (202)293-7277
Fax: (202)293-7727
Contact: Abby H. Bernstein

In-house, DC-area Employees

BERNSTEIN, Abby H.: Legislative Director
FANFALONE, Michael D.: National President

Professional Aviation Maintenance Ass'n

Washington, DC
Web: www.pama.org
E-mail: hq@pama.org
Leg. Issues: AVI, GOV, TRA

Outside Counsel/Consultants

Washington Aviation Group
Issues: AVI, GOV, TRA
Rep By: Arnolda Beaujuin, Chad Bierman, Jason Dickstein

Professional Bail Agents of the United States

Washington, DC
Web: www.pbus.com
E-mail: office@pbus.com
Leg. Issues: GOV, LAW, LBR

Outside Counsel/Consultants

Reed, Smith, LLP
Issues: GOV, LAW, LBR
Rep By: C. Stevens Seale

Professional Beauty Federation PAC

2550 M St. NW
Washington, DC 20037-1350
Tel: (703)527-7600
Fax: (703)527-8811

Works to promote and protect the professional beauty industry in government law and regulation.

Leg. Issues: EDU

In-house, DC-area Employees

SCHOENEMAN, Frank: PAC Contact

Outside Counsel/Consultants

Patton Boggs, LLP
Issues: EDU
Rep By: Brian C. Lopina

Professional Benefit Trust

Woodstock, IL
Leg. Issues: TAX

Outside Counsel/Consultants

Barbour Griffith & Rogers, Inc.
Issues: TAX
Rep By: Haley Barbour, G. O. Lanny Griffith, Jr., Bill Himpler, Loren Monroe, Edward M. Rogers, Jr.

Professional Engineering

Marrero, LA
Leg. Issues: BUD, DIS, ENV

Outside Counsel/Consultants

The Palmer Group
Issues: BUD, DIS, ENV
Rep By: Clifford A. Palmer

Professional Facilities Management

Providence, RI
Leg. Issues: ECN

Outside Counsel/Consultants

John C. Grzebien
Issues: ECN
Rep By: John C. Grzebien

Professional Managers Ass'n

P.O. Box 77235
National Capital Station
Washington, DC 20013
Tel: (202)874-1547
Fax: (202)874-1739
Web: www.promanager.org
E-mail: pmaoffice@aol.com

Represents more than 200,000 federal managers and management officials in the U.S. government.

Leg. Issues: BUD, DEF, GOV, RET, TAX, VET

In-house, DC-area Employees

MILLER, Hydi: Legislative/Communications Director

Professional Photographers of America

Atlanta, GA

Outside Counsel/Consultants

Wiley, Rein & Fielding

Professional Services Council

2101 Wilson Blvd.
Suite 750
Arlington, VA 22201
Tel: (703)875-8059
Fax: (703)875-8922
Registered: LDA
Web: www.pscouncil.org

Composed of associations and companies providing professional services to the government and private sector; members concerned with federal procurement and related issues.

Leg. Issues: ACC, AER, BUD, DEF, ECN, ENG, ENV, GOV, SCI, TRA

Political Action Committee/s

Professional Services Council PAC
2101 Wilson Blvd.
Suite 750
Arlington, VA 22201
Tel: (703)875-8059
Fax: (703)875-8922
Contact: Charles H. Cantus

In-house, DC-area Employees

CANTUS, Charles H.: V. President, Government Relations
MEYER, Lisa: V. President, Communications
SOLOWAY, Stan Z.: President

Outside Counsel/Consultants

Kirkland & Ellis
Rep By: James S. Hostetler

Profit Freight Systems/LEP

Atlanta, GA

Outside Counsel/Consultants

Galland, Kharasch, Greenberg, Fellman & Swirsky, P.C.

Profit Recovery Group Internat'l

Atlanta, GA
Leg. Issues: BUD, DEF

Outside Counsel/Consultants

Albers & Co.
Issues: BUD, DEF
Rep By: William E. Albers, Daniel B. Beardsley, M. Guy Rohling

Profit Sharing/401 (k) Council of America

601 13th St. NW
Suite 600 South
Washington, DC 20005-3807
Tel: (202)626-3634
Fax: (202)638-6635
Registered: LDA
Web: www.psca.org
E-mail: ferrigno@psca.org
Leg. Issues: RET, SMB, TAX

In-house, DC-area Employees

FERRIGNO, Edward: V. President, Washington Affairs
MURRAY, Samuel H.: V. President, Government Affairs

Outside Counsel/Consultants

White & Case LLP
Rep By: David A. Hildebrandt

Progeny Systems

Manassas, VA
Leg. Issues: DEF

Outside Counsel/Consultants

The Kemper Co.
Issues: DEF
Rep By: Jackson Kemper, Jr.

Progress Energy

801 Pennsylvania Ave. NW
Suite 250
Washington, DC 20004
Tel: (202)783-5530
Fax: (202)783-5569
Registered: LDA
Web: www.pgnmail.com

Formerly Carolina Power and Light Co and Florida Power Corp. Headquartered in Raleigh, NC.

Leg. Issues: CAW, ENG, TAX, UTI

In-house, DC-area Employees

CHOI, Caroline: Manager, Federal Regulatory Affairs
CRAMER, E. Sue: Manager, Federal Affairs
ROBERTS, David G.: Director, Public Affairs-Federal

Outside Counsel/Consultants

RFB, Inc.
Issues: CAW, ENG, UTI
Rep By: Raymond F. Bragg

Ryan, Phillips, Utrecht & MacKinnon
Issues: ENG, UTI
Rep By: Rodney Hoppe, Jeffrey M. MacKinnon, William D. Phillips, Mark D. Planning, Thomas M. Ryan, Joseph V. Vasapoli

Thelen Reid & Priest LLP
Issues: TAX
Rep By: David E. Jacobson

The Progress Freedom Foundation

1301 K St. NW
Suite 550E
Washington, DC 20005
Tel: (202)289-8928
Fax: (202)289-6079
Web: www.pff.org
E-mail: mail@pff.org

Studies the impact of the Digital Revolution and its implications for public policy.

Leg. Issues: COM, CPI, ENG, LBR, TEC

In-house, DC-area Employees

EISENACH, Jane Forston: Adjunct Fellow
EISENACH, Jeffrey A.: President, Senior Fellow and Co-Founder
KEYWORK, II, Ph.D., George A. "Jay": Chairman, Senior Fellow and Co-Founder
LENARD, Thomas: Senior Fellow and Director, Regulatory Studies
MCCOY, Garland T.: V. President, Development

Outside Counsel/Consultants

Shaw Pittman
Rep By: Jeffery L. Yablon

Progressive Nat'l Baptist Convention

601 50th St. NE
Washington, DC 20019
Tel: (202)396-0558
Fax: (202)398-4998
E-mail: info@pnbc.org

Founded in 1961 the Convention now represents over 1,000 churches. Affiliated with Nat'l Council of Churches and the World Council of Churches.

In-house, DC-area Employees

PITTS, Tyrone S.: General Secretary

Progressive Policy Institute

600 Pennsylvania Ave. SE
Suite 400
Washington, DC 20003
Tel: (202)547-0001
Fax: (202)544-5014
Web: www.ndol.org
E-mail: webmaster@dlcppi.org

A think tank affiliated with the Democratic Leadership Council and a project of the Third Way Foundation. Works to define and promote a new progressive politics for America in the 21st century.

Leg. Issues: BUD, DEF, ECN, EDU, ENV, FOR, GOV, HCR, SCI, TAX, TRD, URB, WEL

In-house, DC-area Employees

ALSTON, Charles C.: Exec. Director
ATKINSON, Robert: Director, Technology, Innovation and the New Economy Project
BOYLAN, Debbie: Director, Communications
COURT, Randolph: Technology Policy Analyst
HAM, Shane: Technology Policy Analyst
KIM, Anne: Director, Working Families Project
LEMIEUX, Jeff: Director, Economic Studies
MARSHALL, Will: President
MEAD, Sara: Policy Analyst, 21st Century Schools Project
MILT, Robert A.: Project Assistant
NIDER, Steven: Director, Foreign Policy and Defense Working Groups
ROTHERHAM, Andrew: Director, 21st Century Schools Project

Project ACTA

Leg. Issues: BUD, MAR

Outside Counsel/Consultants

Adams and Reese LLP
Issues: MAR
Rep By: D. Lee Forsgren

Project Funding Corp. (PFC)

Newport Beach, CA
Leg. Issues: HOU

Outside Counsel/Consultants

Nixon Peabody LLP
Issues: HOU
Rep By: Richard M. Price, Monica Hilton Sussman

The Project Leadership Committee, Lincoln Center for the Performing Arts

New York, NY
Leg. Issues: BUD, TAX

Outside Counsel/Consultants

Akin, Gump, Strauss, Hauer & Feld, L.L.P.
Issues: BUD, TAX
Rep By: Donald C. Alexander, Katherine D. Brodie, Smith W. Davis, Joel Jankowsky, Donald R. Pongrace

LeBoeuf, Lamb, Greene & MacRae L.L.P.
Issues: TAX
Rep By: D. Randall Benn, Peter Britell

Project Meal Foundation

Leg. Issues: HCR

Outside Counsel/Consultants

The Borden Group, Inc.
Issues: HCR
Rep By: Enid A. Borden

Project on Government Oversight, Inc.

666 11th St. NW
Suite 500
Washington, DC 20001
Tel: (202)347-1122
Fax: (202)347-1116
Web: www.pogo.org
E-mail: pogo@pogo.org

Investigates, exposes, and remedies waste, conflicts of interest, and other abuses in government operations.

In-house, DC-area Employees

BRIAN, Danielle: Exec. Director
DALEY, Beth: Public Affairs Director
MILLER, Eric: Defense Specialist

Project Return Foundation Inc.

New York, NY

A provider of housing and drug rehabilitation services for homeless persons.

Leg. Issues: HOU

Outside Counsel/Consultants

Davidoff & Malito, LLP
Issues: HOU
Rep By: Kenneth C. Malito, Stephen J. Slade

Project to Promote Competition and Innovation in the Digital Age

1133 Connecticut Ave. NW
Suite 1000
Washington, DC 20036

A coalition of high-tech companies.

Leg. Issues: CPI, CPT, CSP, LBR, SCI, TEC

In-house, DC-area Employees

PETTIT, Mitchell S.: Exec. Director

Outside Counsel/Consultants

The Duberstein Group, Inc.
Issues: CPI, CSP, LBR, SCI
Rep By: John W. Angus, III, Michael S. Berman, Steven M. Champlin, Kenneth M. Duberstein, Henry M. Gandy, Daniel P. Meyer

McGuiness & Holch
Issues: CPI, CSP, LBR, SCI
Rep By: Markham C. Erickson, Kevin S. McGuiness

MSP Strategic Communications, Inc.
Issues: CPI, CSP, LBR, SCI
Rep By: Mitchell S. Pettit

Parry, Romani, DeConcini & Symms
Issues: CPT, LBR, TEC
Rep By: Edward H. Baxter, Hon. Dennis DeConcini, John M. Haddow, Scott D. Hatch, Shannon Davis Henderson, Jack W. Martin, Romano Romani, Linda Arey Skladany, Hon. Steven D. Symms

Wise & Associates
Issues: LBR
Rep By: Nicholas P. Wise

Prologic

Fairmont, WV

Outside Counsel/Consultants

The PMA Group
Rep By: Kaylene Green, Paul J. Magliocchetti, Kelli Short, Thomas Veltri

PromPeru

Lima, PERU

Outside Counsel/Consultants

Chlopak, Leonard, Schechter and Associates
Rep By: Peter Schechter

Propane Consumers Coalition

Arlington, VA

Outside Counsel/Consultants

Koleda Childress & Co.
Rep By: James M. Childress

Propane Vehicle Council

1155 Connecticut Ave. NW
Suite 300
Washington, DC 20036
Tel: (202)530-0479
Fax: (202)223-0479
Registered: LDA
Web: www.propanegas.com
E-mail: jcolaneri@propanegas.com

A unit of the Nat'l Propane Gas Ass'n.

Leg. Issues: ENG, ENV, TAX

In-house, DC-area Employees

COLANERI, Joseph L.: Exec. Director

Outside Counsel/Consultants

Collier Shannon Scott, PLLC

The Propeller Club of the United States

3927 Old Lee Hwy.
Suite 101A
Fairfax, VA 22030
Tel: (703)691-2777
Fax: (703)691-4173
Web: www.propellerclubhq.com
E-mail: propclubhq@aol.com

Promotes and supports the American merchant marine in all its segments: ocean, inland waterways and on the Great Lakes; and the maritime industry generally. Consists of over 100 local clubs with 12,000 members in the U.S. and overseas.

In-house, DC-area Employees

GOEDHARD, Bart: Exec. V. President

Property Owners Remedy Alliance

Leg. Issues: CPT

Outside Counsel/Consultants

Meyer & Klipper, PLLC
Issues: CPT
Rep By: Michael R. Klipper, Christopher A. Mohr

Proprietary Industries Ass'n

Glendale, CA

Outside Counsel/Consultants

Bettie McCarthy and Associates
Rep By: Elizabeth S. "Bettie" McCarthy

Protective Life Insurance Co.

Birmingham, AL
Leg. Issues: HCR, INS

Outside Counsel/Consultants

Jay Grant & Associates
Issues: HCR, INS
Rep By: Jay B. Grant

Protein Technologies Internat'l

St. Louis, MO
Leg. Issues: TRD

Outside Counsel/Consultants

Hogan & Hartson L.L.P.
Issues: TRD
Rep By: Raymond S. Calamaro, Gary Jay Kushner

Proteus Co.

Chicago, IL
Leg. Issues: MAR, WAS

Outside Counsel/Consultants

Cassidy & Associates, Inc.
Issues: MAR, WAS
Rep By: John S. Doyle, Jr.

Providence City Arts for Youth, Inc.

Providence, RI
Leg. Issues: ART, ECN

Outside Counsel/Consultants

John C. Grzebien
Issues: ART, ECN
Rep By: John C. Grzebien

Providence Gas

Providence, RI

Outside Counsel/Consultants

Campbell Crane & Associates
Rep By: Jeanne M. Campbell

Providence Health System

Seattle, WA

Outside Counsel/Consultants

Davis Wright Tremaine LLP

Providence Performing Arts Center

Providence, RI
Leg. Issues: ART, ECN

Outside Counsel/Consultants

John C. Grzebien
Issues: ART, ECN
Rep By: John C. Grzebien

The Providence Plan

Providence, RI
Leg. Issues: ECN, ENC, URB

Outside Counsel/Consultants

GPC Internat'l
Issues: ECN, ENC, URB
Rep By: John D. Cahill, Daniel K. Crann, Suzanne Gemma

Providence Redevelopment Agency

Providence, RI
Leg. Issues: BUD, URB

Outside Counsel/Consultants

GPC Internat'l
Issues: BUD, URB
Rep By: John D. Cahill, Daniel K. Crann, Suzanne Gemma

Providence St. Vincent Medical Center

Portland, OR
Leg. Issues: DEF

Outside Counsel/Consultants

SISCORP
Issues: DEF
Rep By: Donald F. Massey

Provident Communications, Inc.

Dallas, TX

Outside Counsel/Consultants

Chambers Associates Inc.
Rep By: Letitia Chambers

Provideo Productions

Duluth, MN
Leg. Issues: TRA

Outside Counsel/Consultants

Lawler, Metzger & Milkman, LLC
Issues: TRA
Rep By: Sante J. Esposito, Gregory E. Lawler

Providian Financial Corp.

1155 Connecticut Ave. NW
Suite 500
Washington, DC 20036
Tel: (202)429-6606
Fax: (202)785-4868
Registered: LDA

Headquartered in San Francisco, CA

Leg. Issues: BAN, BNK

In-house, DC-area Employees

MCDERMOTT, Daniel J.: V. President, Government Relations

Outside Counsel/Consultants

Gibson, Dunn & Crutcher LLP
Rep By: Robert C. Eager

Province Healthcare, Inc.

Brentwood, TN
Leg. Issues: MMM

Outside Counsel/Consultants

Greenberg Traurig, LLP
Issues: MMM
Rep By: Howard J. Cohen, Rob Garagiola, Russell J. Mueller, Nancy E. Taylor, Timothy P. Trysla

Provo, Utah, City of

Leg. Issues: AVI, ECN, TRA, URB, UTI

Outside Counsel/Consultants

Jordan & Associates, Inc.
Issues: AVI, ECN, TRA, URB, UTI
Rep By: Patricia Jordan

Prowler Fisheries and Clipper Seafoods

Petersburg, AK
Leg. Issues: NAT

Outside Counsel/Consultants

Verner, Liipfert, Bernhard, McPherson and Hand, Chartered
Issues: NAT
Rep By: Steven R. Phillips, Timothy M. Rutten, John H. Sterne, Jr.

Prudential Insurance Co. of America

1140 Connecticut Ave. NW
Suite 510
Washington, DC 20036
Tel: (202)293-1676
Fax: (202)293-1658
Registered: LDA

An insurance company headquartered in Newark, New Jersey.

Leg. Issues: BAN, FIN, HCR, INS, TAX, TOR, TRD

In-house, DC-area Employees

BEGANS, Peter: V. President, Government Relations
O'HARA, Thomas G.: V. President, Government Relations
WACKERLE, Rex: V. President, Federal Government Relations
WALKER, Angela: Manager, Government Relations
WILLIAMS, Kaye F.: V. President, Government Relations

Outside Counsel/Consultants

American Continental Group, Inc.
Rep By: David A. Metzner, Shawn H. Smeallie, Peter Terpeluk, Jr.

Bergner Bockorny Castagnetti and Hawkins
Issues: INS, TAX

Gibson, Dunn & Crutcher LLP
Issues: BAN
Rep By: Robert C. Eager, Cantwell Faulkner Muckenfuss, III

Griffin & Associates
Issues: FIN, INS, TAX
Rep By: Janice B. Griffin

Peter Kinzler
Issues: FIN, INS, TAX, TOR, TRD
Rep By: Peter Kinzler

McDermott, Will and Emery
Issues: TAX
Rep By: Robert B. Harding

PriceWaterhouseCoopers

Prudential Securities, Inc.

Arlington, VA
Registered: LDA
Leg. Issues: GOV, MIA, TRD

Outside Counsel/Consultants

The Dutko Group, Inc.
Issues: GOV, MIA, TRD
Rep By: Gary J. Andres

PSC Systems

Rockville, MD

Outside Counsel/Consultants

The Coursen Group
Rep By: Hon. Christopher D. Coursen

PSE&G

One Massachusetts Ave. NW
Suite 710
Washington, DC 20001
Tel: (202)408-0800
Fax: (202)408-0214
Registered: LDA
Web: www.pseg.com
Leg. Issues: BUD, CAW, CPI, ENG, TAX, TRA

In-house, DC-area Employees

LUDECKE, Kristen: Manager, Governmental and Public Affairs
THOMPSON, Patricia L.: General Manager, Federal Affairs

Outside Counsel/Consultants

Governmental Strategies, Inc.

PSEKA, Internat'l Coordinating Committee, Justice for Cyprus

New York, NY

Outside Counsel/Consultants

Manatos & Manatos, Inc.
Rep By: Andrew E. Manatos, Mike A. Manatos

PSH Master L.P.I.

Columbus, OH

Outside Counsel/Consultants

Baker & Hostetler LLP
Rep By: William F. Conroy, Matthew J. Dolan, Steven A. Lotterer, David L. Marshall, Hon. Guy Vander Jagt

PSI

Andover, MA
Leg. Issues: DEF

Outside Counsel/Consultants

SISCORP
Issues: DEF
Rep By: Donald F. Massey

PSI Services Inc.

Bethesda, MD

Outside Counsel/Consultants

Powell, Goldstein, Frazer & Murphy LLP

PSINet Inc.

Herndon, VA
Leg. Issues: CPI, TEC

Outside Counsel/Consultants

Piper Marbury Rudnick & Wolfe LLP
Issues: CPI, TEC
Rep By: Alisa M. Bergman, James J. Halpert, Stuart P. Ingis, Paul W. Jamieson, Katharine A. Pauley, Ronald L. Plesser

Psychemedics Corp.

Cambridge, MA
Leg. Issues: ALC, LBR, SCI

Outside Counsel/Consultants

Global USA, Inc.
Issues: ALC, LBR, SCI
Rep By: George S. Kopp, Lottie H. Shackelford

Sills Associates
Issues: ALC, LBR, SCI
Rep By: Hilary Sills

Psychological Corp.

San Antonio, TX
Leg. Issues: EDU

Outside Counsel/Consultants

Hale and Dorr LLP
Issues: EDU
Rep By: Jay P. Urwitz

Public Advocate

5613 Leesburg Pike
Suite 17
Falls Church, VA 22041
Tel: (703)845-1808

A national non-partisan government watchdog and citizen action committee dedicated to limited government, a free market economy, a strong national defense and a reduced tax burden for Americans.

In-house, DC-area Employees

DELGAUDIO, Columbia Eugene: Exec. Director

Public Affairs Council

2033 K St. NW
Suite 700
Washington, DC 20006
Tel: (202)872-1790
Fax: (202)835-8343
Web: www.pac.org

A bi-partisan professional organization of corporate public affairs representatives established in 1954 as the Effective Citizens Organization. Associated with the Foundation for Public Affairs.

In-house, DC-area Employees

HAWKINSON, Brian P.: Director, Center for Public Affairs Management
PEDERSEN, Wes: Director, Communications and Public Relations
PINKHAM, Douglas G.: President

Public Agencies for Audit Reform

Calabasas, CA
Leg. Issues: BUD

Outside Counsel/Consultants

ENS Resources, Inc.
Issues: BUD
Rep By: Eric Sapirstein

Public Broadcasting Entities

Washington, DC
Leg. Issues: COM

Outside Counsel/Consultants

Verner, Liipfert, Bernhard, McPherson and Hand, Chartered
Issues: COM
Rep By: Vicki E. Hart, Lawrence R. Sidman

Public Broadcasting Service

1320 Braddock Pl.
Alexandria, VA 22314
Tel: (703)739-5000
Fax: (703)739-0775
Leg. Issues: BUD, COM, CPT, EDU, TEC

In-house, DC-area Employees

EPSTEIN, Tom: V. President, Communications and Public Relations, National Press Relations
FERENBACH, Gregory: Senior V. President and General Counsel
GOLDBERG, Dara: Director, Corporate Communications
MITCHELL, Pat: President
ROTENBERGER, Lesli: Senior V. President, Grand Management and Promotion Corporate Communication

Outside Counsel/Consultants

Convergence Services, Inc.
Issues: BUD, COM, EDU, TEC
Rep By: John M. Lawson

Covington & Burling
Issues: COM, CPT
Rep By: Joan L. Kutcher

Hauser Group

Public Campaign

1320 19th St. NW
Suite M-1
Washington, DC 20036
Tel: (202)293-0222
Fax: (202)293-0202
Registered: LDA
Web: www.publicampaign.org
Leg. Issues: GOV

In-house, DC-area Employees

ANDERSON, Susan L.: Washington Director
ETTLINGER, Michael P.: Deputy Director
LEIKEN, Brian: Sr. Outreach and Legislative Associate
NYHART, Nick: Exec. Director
SIFRY, Micah: Senior Analyst

Public Citizen, Inc.

1600 20th St. NW
Washington, DC 20009
Tel: (202)588-1000
Fax: (202)588-7799
Registered: LDA
Web: www.citizen.org

A national non-profit public interest group, founded by Ralph Nader in 1971, that advocates for consumer rights in the marketplace, safe products, a healthy environment and workplace, clean and safe energy sources, and corporate and government accountability.

Leg. Issues: ALC, AUT, BAN, BUD, CAW, CHM, CSP, ENG, FUE, GOV, HCR, INS, LAW, TOB, TRA, TRD, UTI

In-house, DC-area Employees

CLAYBROOK, Joan B.: President
HAUTER, Wenonah: Director, Critical Mass Energy Project
HIGLEY, Charlie: Senior Energy Policy Analyst
NADER, Ralph: Contact
VLADECK, David C.: Director, Public Citizen Litigation Group
WALLACH, Lori M.: Director, Global Trade
WEISSMAN, Steve
WOLFE, Sidney M.: Director, Public Citizen Health Research Group

Public Employee Retirement Systems of Colorado

Denver, CO

Outside Counsel/Consultants

McDermott, Will and Emery
Rep By: Maggie A. Mitchell

Public Employees for Environmental Responsibility (PEER)

2001 S St. NW
Suite 570
Washington, DC 20009
Tel: (202)265-7337
Fax: (202)265-4192
E-mail: info@peer.org

In-house, DC-area Employees

RUCH, Jeffrey: Exec. Director

Public Employees Roundtable

P.O. Box 75248
Washington, DC 20013-5248
Tel: (202)927-4926
Fax: (202)927-4920
Web: www.theroundtable.org
E-mail: info@theroundtable.org

A non-profit educational consortium of 37 professional and management associations with over one million members. Seeks to inform the public and lawmakers of the dedication and quality of the more than 20 million public employees serving this country. Forty federal, state and local government units hold associate membership.

In-house, DC-area Employees

BRATTON, Adam: Deputy Director, Operations
CONNELL, Marion Fitch: Exec. Director
KESTON, Joan: Chair

Outside Counsel/Consultants

Shaw, Bransford, Veilleux & Roth
Rep By: G. Jerry Shaw, Jr.

Public Financial Management

Philadelphia, PA
Leg. Issues: FIN

Outside Counsel/Consultants

American Continental Group, Inc.
Issues: FIN
Rep By: Peter Terpeluk, Jr.

Public Forum Institute

2300 M St. NW
Suite 900
Washington, DC 20037
Tel: (202)467-2774
Fax: (202)293-5717
Web: www.publicforuminstitute.com
E-mail: info@publicforuminstitute.com

An outcome-driven organization working to create the most effective means of advancing the exchange of information and ideas. Blends citizen engagement and the art and science of the public forum with professional conference planning, satellite and interactive meeting technologies, project team management, consumer and issue research, and public relations.

In-house, DC-area Employees

FRITZ, Alison: Vice President
LINDBERG, Roger: Exec. Director
MARICH, Mark: V. President
NEEL, Anne: Director
ORTMANS, Jonathan F.: President
ROSE, Jason: Director, Corporate Affairs

Public Generating Pool

Eugene, OR
Leg. Issues: ENV, NAT, UTI

Outside Counsel/Consultants

Van Ness Feldman, P.C.
Issues: ENV, NAT, UTI
Rep By: Gary D. Bachman, Robert Nordhaus

Public Health Foundation

1220 L St. NW
Suite 350
Washington, DC 20005
Tel: (202)898-5600
Fax: (202)898-5609
Web: www.phf.org
E-mail: rbialek@phf.org

Purpose is to strengthen and build capacity of national, state and local public health agencies and systems through applied research, training and technical assistance. Works closely with federal, state, and local health agencies. Focuses on community health planning and improvement, workforce development, and the effective use of data for policy making.

Leg. Issues: HCR

In-house, DC-area Employees

BIALEK, Ronald: President

Public Health Policy Advisory Board

Washington, DC
Leg. Issues: BUD, HCR, MED

Outside Counsel/Consultants

Mintz, Levin, Cohn, Ferris, Glovsky and Popeo, P.C.
Issues: BUD, HCR, MED
Rep By: Raymond D. Cotton

Public Hospital Pharmacy Coalition

Washington, DC
Leg. Issues: PHA

Outside Counsel/Consultants

Powell, Goldstein, Frazer & Murphy LLP
Issues: PHA
Rep By: Ted Slafsky, William H. E. von Oehsen

Public Housing Authorities Directors Ass'n

511 Capitol Ct. NE
Suite 200
Washington, DC 20002-4937
Tel: (202)546-5445
Fax: (202)546-2280
Registered: LDA
Web: www.phada.org
Leg. Issues: HOU

In-house, DC-area Employees

KAISER, Timothy G.: Exec. Director

Outside Counsel/Consultants

Coan & Lyons
Issues: HOU
Rep By: Carl A. S. Coan, Jr., Carl A. S. Coan, III, Raymond K. James

Public Interest Video Network

641 Fifth St. NE
Washington, DC 20002
Tel: (202)544-6040
Fax: (202)548-6002
Web: www.publicinterestvideo.com

A non-profit media center serving the communications needs of the public interest community and government agencies by providing media services such as organizational, educational and fund-raising videos; documentaries; public service announcements; and video news releases.

In-house, DC-area Employees
SLOBODOW, Arlen: Exec. Director

Public Lands Council

1301 Pennsylvania Ave. NW
Suite 300
Washington, DC 20004
Tel: (202)347-5355
Fax: (202)737-4086
Registered: LDA
Web: www.beef.org
E-mail: jcampbell@beef.org

A non-profit group that represents livestock operators who hold permits to graze livestock on public lands.

Leg. Issues: AGR, ENV

In-house, DC-area Employees
CAMPBELL, Jason: Exec. Director
KLUNDT, Scott: Associate Director

Public Policy Partners

Washington, DC
Leg. Issues: AVI

Outside Counsel/Consultants

Boesch & Co.
Issues: AVI
Rep By: Doyce A. Boesch

The Michael Lewan Co.
Issues: AVI
Rep By: Michael Lewan

Public Power Council

Portland, OR
Leg. Issues: ENG

Outside Counsel/Consultants

Kanner & Associates
Issues: ENG
Rep By: Martin B. Kanner

Public Properties Policy Ass'n

A coalition of developers who lease properties to the General Services Administration.

Outside Counsel/Consultants

Kilpatrick Stockton LLP
Rep By: Hon. Elliott H. Levitas

Public Risk Management Ass'n

1815 N. Fort Myer Dr.
Suite 1020
Arlington, VA 22209
Tel: (703)528-7701
Fax: (703)528-7966
Web: www.primacentral.org
E-mail: info@primacentral.org

Promotes effective risk management in the public interest as an essential component of administration.

In-house, DC-area Employees
HERT, James: Interim Exec. Director

Public Service Co. of Colorado

Denver, CO
Leg. Issues: ENG

Outside Counsel/Consultants

Hogan & Hartson L.L.P.
Issues: ENG
Rep By: Lance D. Bultena, William Michael House, Hon. Robert H. Michel, Jeffrey W. Munk, Patrick Nevins, Karol Lyn Newman

Public Service Co. of New Mexico

Albuquerque, NM
Leg. Issues: BUD, UTI

Outside Counsel/Consultants

Marcus G. Faust, P.C.
Issues: BUD, UTI
Rep By: Marcus G. Faust, Adrianne Firth

Public Service Research Council

320-D Maple Ave. East
Vienna, VA 22180
Tel: (703)242-3575
Fax: (703)242-3579
E-mail: publicsrc@erols.com

A citizens' lobby concerned with union-oriented issues. Opposes unionism and collective bargaining in public employment.

In-house, DC-area Employees
DENHOLM, David Y.: President

Public Service Research Foundation

320-D Maple Ave. East
Vienna, VA 22180
Tel: (703)242-3575
Fax: (703)242-3579
Web: www.psrf.org
E-mail: info@psrf.org

An education and research foundation concerned with the issue of public sector labor relations.

Leg. Issues: EDU, LBR

In-house, DC-area Employees
DENHOLM, David Y.: Washington Representative

Public Technology Inc.

1301 Pennsylvania Ave. NW
Suite 800
Washington, DC 20004
Tel: (202)626-2400
Fax: (202)626-2498

Represents the research, development and commercialization of technology in cities and counties in the U.S.

In-house, DC-area Employees
MCCLOUD, Thomas H.: Chief Operating Officer
TOREGAS, Costis: President

Public/Private Ventures

Philadelphia, PA
Leg. Issues: BUD, LAW

Outside Counsel/Consultants

Beacon Consulting Group, Inc.
Issues: BUD, LAW
Rep By: Jeffrey W. Henry, Gordon P. MacDougall, Lisa A. Stewart

Publicis Dialog

Seattle, WA

Outside Counsel/Consultants

George Kroloff & Associates

Pueblo de Conchiti

Conchiti, NM
An American Indian tribe.

Leg. Issues: IND

Outside Counsel/Consultants

Hobbs, Straus, Dean and Walker, LLP
Issues: IND
Rep By: Aura Kanegis, Jerry C. Straus

Pueblo of Acoma

Pueblo of Acoma, NM
Leg. Issues: IND

Outside Counsel/Consultants

Smith Law Firm
Issues: IND
Rep By: Gregory A. Smith

Pueblo of Laguna

Laguna, NM
An Indian tribal government.

Leg. Issues: IND

Outside Counsel/Consultants

Ducheneaux, Taylor & Associates, Inc.

Nordhaus Haltom Taylor Taradash & Bladh LLP
Issues: IND

Puerto Ricans for Civic Action

Mayaguez, PR
Leg. Issues: GOV

Outside Counsel/Consultants

The MWW Group
Issues: GOV
Rep By: Tracey Becker, Dana P. Bostic, Elizabeth A. Iadarola, Christine A. Pellerin, Jonathan B. Slade, Robert G. Sommer, Jeffery M. Walter

Puerto Rico Bankers Ass'n

San Juan, PR

Outside Counsel/Consultants

Drinker Biddle & Reath LLP
Rep By: Joaquin A. Marquez

Puerto Rico Chamber of Commerce

San Juan, PR

Outside Counsel/Consultants

Drinker Biddle & Reath LLP
Rep By: Joaquin A. Marquez

Puerto Rico Electric Power Authority

Leg. Issues: ENG

Outside Counsel/Consultants

Morgan Meguire, LLC
Issues: ENG
Rep By: Kyle G. Michel, C. Kyle Simpson, Deborah R. Sliz

Puerto Rico Federal Affairs Administration

1100 17th St. NW
Suite 800
Washington, DC 20036
Tel: (202)778-0710
Fax: (202)778-0721

An agency of the Executive Branch of the government of Puerto Rico. Represents the Governor of Puerto Rico in Washington.

Leg. Issues: BAN, GOV, HOU, TAX, WEL

In-house, DC-area Employees
APONTE, ESQ., Mari Carmen: Exec. Director

Puerto Rico Hospital Ass'n

Outside Counsel/Consultants

McDermott, Will and Emery

The Washington Group

Puerto Rico House of Representatives

Outside Counsel/Consultants

The Legacy Group
Rep By: Michael J. Govan

Puerto Rico Industrial Development Co.

Haton Rey, PR

Outside Counsel/Consultants

BKSH & Associates

Puerto Rico Manufacturers Ass'n

San Juan, PR

Outside Counsel/Consultants

Drinker Biddle & Reath LLP
Rep By: Joaquin A. Marquez

Puerto Rico Senate

San Juan, PR
Leg. Issues: AVI, ENV, GOV, TAX, TEC

Outside Counsel/Consultants

Alvarado & Gerken
Issues: AVI, TAX, TEC
Rep By: David A. Gerken

The MWW Group
Issues: ENV, GOV
Rep By: Jonathan B. Slade, Robert G. Sommer

Oldaker and Harris, LLP
Issues: GOV
Rep By: William C. Oldaker

Puerto Rico Telephone Co.

Caparra Heights, PR

Outside Counsel/Consultants

Snavely, King, Majoros, O'Connor and Lee, Inc.
Rep By: Michael Majoros

Puerto Rico U.S.A. Foundation

600 13th St. NW
Washington, DC 20005
Tel: (202)756-8213
Fax: (202)756-8087
Registered: LDA

Leg. Issues: TAX

In-house, DC-area Employees
HOLMES, Peter E.: Consultant

Puerto Rico, Attorney General of

Outside Counsel/Consultants

Morgan Meguire, LLC
Rep By: Kyle G. Michel

Puerto Rico, Commonwealth of

San Juan, PR
Leg. Issues: ECN, GOV, TAX, TRA

Outside Counsel/Consultants
BSMG Worldwide
Mark W. Goodin
Issues: ECN, GOV, TAX
Rep By: Mark W. Goodin
GPC Internat'l
Issues: TRA
Rep By: John D. Cahill, Peter G. Halpin, Carlos E. Iturregui, Andy Paven
McDermott, Will and Emery
Rep By: Neil Quinter
Winston & Strawn
Rep By: Hon. Beryl F. Anthony, Jr., Hon. James H. Burnley, IV, Peter N. Hiebert, Charles L. Kinney, John C. Kirtland, Michael J. McLaughlin, John D. McMickle, Francisco J. Pavia, Douglas C. Richardson, John A. Waits, II

Pulse Medical Instruments
Rockville, MD
Leg. Issues: DEF, TRA

Outside Counsel/Consultants
Preston Gates Ellis & Rouvelas Meeds LLP
Issues: DEF, TRA
Rep By: Pamela J. Garvie, Ralph D. Nurnberger

PulseTech Products Corp.
South Lake, TX
Leg. Issues: DEF, MAN

Outside Counsel/Consultants
American Systems Internat'l Corp.
Issues: DEF, MAN
Rep By: William H. Skipper, Jr.
Law Office of Zel E. Lipsen
Issues: DEF, MAN
Rep By: Zel E. Lipsen

Pulte Home Corp.
Bloomfield Hills, MI
Leg. Issues: BAN, TAX

Outside Counsel/Consultants
Miller & Chevalier, Chartered
Issues: BAN, TAX
Rep By: Leonard Bickwit, Jr.

Pump Service and Supply Co.
San Angelo, TX

Outside Counsel/Consultants
The Aegis Group, Ltd.
Rep By: A. Mario Castillo

The Purdue Frederick Co.
Norwalk, CT

Outside Counsel/Consultants
Chadbourne and Parke LLP
Rep By: Keith Martin

Purdue University
West Lafayette, IN
Leg. Issues: SCI

Outside Counsel/Consultants
Sagamore Associates, Inc.
Issues: SCI
Rep By: Doug Wasitis, Mark W. Weller

Pure Encapsulations, Inc.
Sudbury, MA
Leg. Issues: HCR, MMM, PHA

Outside Counsel/Consultants
Emord & Associates, P.C.
Issues: HCR, MMM, PHA
Rep By: Jonathan W. Emord, Eleanor A. Kolton, Claudia A. Lewis-Eng

Pure Energy Corp.
New York, NY
Leg. Issues: ENG

Outside Counsel/Consultants
Reed, Smith, LLP
Issues: ENG
Rep By: Phillips S. Peter

Pure Food Campaign
1660 L St. NW
Suite 216
Washington, DC 20036
Tel: (202)466-2823
Fax: (202)429-9602
A project of the Foundation on Economic Trends.

In-house, DC-area Employees
MARTINO, Laura: Chief of Staff

PURPA Reform Group
Washington, DC
Leg. Issues: UTI

Outside Counsel/Consultants
Thomas J. Dennis
Issues: UTI
Rep By: Thomas J. Dennis
Stuntz, Davis & Staffier, P.C.
Issues: UTI
Rep By: Randall E. Davis, Linda Stuntz

Put-in-Bay Boat Line Co.
Port Clinton, OH
Leg. Issues: TRA

Outside Counsel/Consultants
Dyer Ellis & Joseph, P.C.
Issues: TRA
Rep By: James S. W. Drewry, Lara Bernstein Mathews, Duncan C. Smith, III, Jennifer M. Southwick

Puyallup Tribe of Indians
Tacoma, WA
Leg. Issues: IND

Outside Counsel/Consultants
Sonosky, Chambers, Sachse & Endreson
Issues: IND
Rep By: Mary J. Pavel

PwC Contract Manufacturing Coalition
Washington, DC
Leg. Issues: TAX

Outside Counsel/Consultants
PriceWaterhouseCoopers
Issues: TAX
Rep By: Barbara Angus, Tim Anson, Kenneth J. Kies

PwC Leasing Coalition
Washington, DC
Leg. Issues: TAX

Outside Counsel/Consultants
PriceWaterhouseCoopers
Issues: TAX
Rep By: Barbara Angus, Jim Carlisle, Kenneth J. Kies

Pyrocap International Corp., Inc.
6551 Loisda Ct.
Suite 400
Springfield, VA 22150
Tel: (703)551-4452
Fax: (703)971-5892
Web: www.erols.com/pyrocap
E-mail: tedadams@pyrocap.net
Leg. Issues: SCI

In-house, DC-area Employees
ADAMS, III, Ted: President

Outside Counsel/Consultants
Foley Government and Public Affairs, Inc.
Issues: SCI
Rep By: Joseph P. Foley, Ralph J. Gervasio, Jr.

Q Systems, Inc.
Oak Ridge, TN
Leg. Issues: ENV

Outside Counsel/Consultants
Mehl, Griffin & Bartek Ltd.
Issues: ENV
Rep By: Ronald J. Bartek

Q-ZAB Coalition
Jackson, MS
Leg. Issues: ECN, EDU

Outside Counsel/Consultants
Adams and Reese LLP
Issues: ECN, EDU
Rep By: B. Jeffrey Brooks

Qatar, Embassy of
Washington, DC

Outside Counsel/Consultants
Patton Boggs, LLP

Qatar, Government of the State of
Doha, QATAR

Outside Counsel/Consultants
Patton Boggs, LLP
Rep By: David E. Dunn, III

QED Communications

Outside Counsel/Consultants
The Dutko Group, Inc.

QSP Inc.
Pleasantville, NY
Leg. Issues: EDU

Outside Counsel/Consultants
Patton Boggs, LLP
Issues: EDU
Rep By: Hon. Greg H. Laughlin, Darryl D. Nirenberg, Joseph Trapasso

QTEAM
Denver, CO
Leg. Issues: DEF

Outside Counsel/Consultants
Peter J. Rose
Issues: DEF
Rep By: Peter J. Rose

Quad City Development Group
Rock Island, IL
Leg. Issues: BUD, DEF, ECN

Outside Counsel/Consultants
Hurt, Norton & Associates
Issues: BUD, DEF, ECN
Rep By: Robert H. Hurt, Frank Norton, William K. Takakoshi

Quad Dimension
Leg. Issues: CPT

Outside Counsel/Consultants
Akin, Gump, Strauss, Hauer & Feld, L.L.P.
Issues: CPT
Rep By: J. David Carlin, Elizabeth Hyman, Barney J. Skladany, Jr.

Quad Pharmaceutical Inc.

Outside Counsel/Consultants
Kleinfeld, Kaplan and Becker
Rep By: Alan H. Kaplan

Qualcomm Inc.
2000 K St. NW
Suite 375
Washington, DC 20036
Tel: (202)263-0000
Fax: (202)263-0010
Registered: LDA
Web: www.qualcomm.com
Leg. Issues: TEC

In-house, DC-area Employees
NEIHARDT, Jonas: V. President, Government Affairs

Outside Counsel/Consultants
Powell, Goldstein, Frazer & Murphy LLP
Issues: TEC
Rep By: Kelly Cameron, Brett G. Kappel, Jeff Kushan, Simon Lazarus, III, David C. Quam, Andrew Shoyer

Qualimetrics, Inc.
Sacramento, CA
Leg. Issues: BUD, TRA

Outside Counsel/Consultants
Murray, Scheer, Montgomery, Tapia & O'Donnell
Issues: BUD, TRA
Rep By: Thomas R. Crawford, D. Michael Murray

Quality Research
Huntsville, AL
A high technology firm.

Outside Counsel/Consultants
Van Scoyoc Associates, Inc.

Qualtec, Inc.
Calverton, MD
Leg. Issues: DEF

Outside Counsel/Consultants
The Kemper Co.
Issues: DEF
Rep By: Jackson Kemper, Jr.

Quebec Lumber Manufacturers Ass'n
Quebec City, CANADA
Leg. Issues: FOR, GOV, IND, MAN, TRD

Outside Counsel/Consultants

Barnes & Thornburg
Issues: TRD
Rep By: Randolph J. Stayin

Sonnenschein, Nath & Rosenthal
Issues: FOR, GOV, IND, MAN, TRD
Rep By: Douglas E. Rosenthal

Quebec, Canada, Government of the Province of

Quebec City, CANADA

Outside Counsel/Consultants

Covington & Burling
Rep By: Harvey M. Applebaum

Pepper Hamilton LLP

Quebecor World (USA) Inc.

Greenwich, CT
Leg. Issues: ECN

Outside Counsel/Consultants

Arnold & Porter
Issues: ECN
Rep By: Martha L. Cochran

Quechan Indian Tribe

Yuma, AZ
Leg. Issues: IND

Outside Counsel/Consultants

Morriset, Schlosser, Ayer & Jozwiak
Issues: IND
Rep By: Fran Ayer, Jennifer P. Hughes

The Queen's Health System

Honolulu, HI

Outside Counsel/Consultants

Rhoads Group

Queens Borough Public Library

Jamaica, NY
Leg. Issues: BUD, CPT, TEC

Outside Counsel/Consultants

Davidoff & Malito, LLP
Issues: BUD, CPT, TEC
Rep By: Kenneth C. Malito, Stephen J. Slade

Queens County Bancorp Inc.

Flushing, NY
Leg. Issues: BAN

Outside Counsel/Consultants

Muldoon, Murphy & Faucette, LLP
Issues: BAN
Rep By: Joseph A. Muldoon, Sr.

Queensland Sugar, Ltd.

Sydney, AUSTRALIA
Leg. Issues: AGR

Outside Counsel/Consultants

Cleary, Gottlieb, Steen and Hamilton

Winston & Strawn
Issues: AGR
Rep By: Robert M. Bor, John A. Waits, II

Quest Diagnostics Inc.

815 Connecticut Ave. NW
Suite 330
Washington, DC 20006
Tel: (202)263-6260
Fax: (202)728-0338
Registered: LDA
E-mail: cusickk@questdiagnostics.com

A national clinical laboratory company headquartered in Teterboro, NJ.

Leg. Issues: HCR, MED, MMM

Political Action Committee/s

Quest Diagnostics Inc. Political Action Committee (Quest PAC)
815 Connecticut Ave. NW
Suite 330
Washington, DC 20006
Tel: (202)263-6260
Contact: Robin M. Sexton

In-house, DC-area Employees

CUSICK, Kristen: Director, Federal Affairs
SEXTON, Robin M.: Politcal Action Coordinator

Outside Counsel/Consultants

Colling Swift & Hynes
Issues: MED, MMM
Rep By: Terese Colling, Pablo Collins, Robert J. Hynes, Jr., Hon. Allan B. Swift

Quest Nevada, Inc.

Las Vegas, NY

Outside Counsel/Consultants

McClure, Gerard & Neuenschwander, Inc.
Rep By: Steven G. Barringer, Joseph T. Findaro, Matthew Iandoli, Nils W. Johnson, Hon. James A. McClure, Tod O. Neuenschwander

Questar Corp.

Salt Lake City, UT
Leg. Issues: FUE

Outside Counsel/Consultants

Sutherland Asbill & Brennan LLP

Robert K. Weidner
Issues: FUE
Rep By: Robert K. Weidner

Questar InfoComm Inc.

Salt Lake City, UT
Leg. Issues: TEC

Outside Counsel/Consultants

Greenberg Traurig, LLP
Issues: TEC
Rep By: Mitchell F. Brecher

Questcom

Portola, CA

Outside Counsel/Consultants

Dow, Lohnes & Albertson, PLLC
Rep By: Michael D. Hays

Questel-Orbit, Inc.

Leg. Issues: CPT

Outside Counsel/Consultants

Joseph L. Ebersole
Issues: CPT
Rep By: Joseph L. Ebersole

QuikWater

Outside Counsel/Consultants

Interface Inc.
Rep By: Albert B. Rosenbaum, III

Quinault Indian Nation

Taholah, WA
Leg. Issues: BUD, IND

Outside Counsel/Consultants

Dorsey & Whitney LLP
Issues: BUD, IND
Rep By: Philip Baker-Shenk, David A. Bieging, Virginia W. Boylan, Cindy Darcy, Sarah Ridley

SENSE, INC.
Rep By: C. Juliet Pittman

Quinnat Landing Hotel

Anchorage, AK
Leg. Issues: BUD, RES

Outside Counsel/Consultants

Birch, Horton, Bittner & Cherot
Issues: BUD, RES
Rep By: Thomas L. Albert, William Bittner, William P. Horn

Quintiles Transnational Corp.

Research Triangle Pk, NC
Leg. Issues: MED

Outside Counsel/Consultants

Washington Health Advocates
Issues: MED
Rep By: Lynn Morrison, Douglas Peddicord, Ph.D., Michele Sumilas

Qwest Communications

1020 19th St. NW
Washington, DC 20036
Tel: (202)429-3121
Fax: (202)293-0561
Registered: LDA
Web: www.qwest.com

A domestic and international long-distance telephone company headquartered in Denver, CO. Merged with US West in 2000.

Leg. Issues: COM, CPT, GAM, LAW, LBR, MED, TAX, TEC, TRD

In-house, DC-area Employees

BELVIN, Ms. Lauren "Pete": V. President, Federal Policy and Law
FIELDS, Drew: Exec. Director, Congressional Affairs
FLEMING, Roger T.: Exec. Director, Congressional Affairs
HANEY, Hance: Exec. Director, Regulatory Affairs
KUNKA, Jane: Director, Public Policy, Regulatory and Legislative Affairs
MASON, Nancy H.: Exec. Director, Congressional Relations
NEWMAN, Melissa: V. President, Regulatory Affairs

Outside Counsel/Consultants

Barbour Griffith & Rogers, Inc.
Issues: TEC
Rep By: Haley Barbour, G. O. Lanny Griffith, Jr., Loren Monroe, Edward M. Rogers, Jr.

Bergner Bockorny Castagnetti and Hawkins
Issues: TEC
Rep By: Jeffrey T. Bergner, David A. Bockorny, David Castagnetti, James W. Hawkins, Melissa Schulman

Commerce Consultants Internat'l Ltd.
Rep By: Laird Walker

Covington & Burling
Rep By: Roderick A. DeArment

Dewey Ballantine LLP
Rep By: Joseph K. Dowley

Hogan & Hartson L.L.P.
Issues: COM, TEC, TRD
Rep By: William Michael House, Hon. Robert H. Michel, Jeffrey W. Munk

Kelly and Associates, Inc.
Issues: LBR, TAX
Rep By: John A. Kelly

McSlarrow Consulting L.L.C.
Issues: TEC
Rep By: Alison McSlarrow

New Frontiers Communications Consulting
Issues: TEC
Rep By: R. David Wilson

Wiley, Rein & Fielding
Issues: TEC
Rep By: Susan C. Buck, Barbara G. Burchett

Williams & Jensen, P.C.
Issues: TEC
Rep By: Bertram W. Carp, J. Steven Hart, Karen Judd Lewis, John J. McMackin, Jr.

Wunder & Lilley
Issues: TEC
Rep By: Bernard J. Wunder, Jr.

R - Tech Veno

Outside Counsel/Consultants

Dittus Communications
Rep By: Jennifer Garfinkel, Chris McNamara

R&D Tax Credit Coalition

A coalition of high-technology companies concerned with the tax treatment of research and development expenses.

Leg. Issues: TAX

Outside Counsel/Consultants

Washington Council Ernst & Young
Issues: TAX
Rep By: Doug Badger, Lauren Darling, John L. Doney, Jayne T. Fitzgerald, LaBrenda Garrett-Nelson, Gary J. Gasper, Bruce A. Gates, Nick Giordano, Cathy Koch, Robert J. Leonard, Richard Meltzer, Phillip D. Moseley, John D. Porter, Robert M. Rozen, Donna Steele-Flynn, Timothy J. Urban

R&D Tax Regulation Group

Washington, DC
Leg. Issues: TAX

Outside Counsel/Consultants

Washington Council Ernst & Young
Issues: TAX
Rep By: Doug Badger, Lauren Darling, John L. Doney, Jayne T. Fitzgerald, LaBrenda Garrett-Nelson, Gary J. Gasper, Bruce A. Gates, Nick Giordano, Robert J. Leonard, Richard Meltzer, Phillip D. Moseley, John D. Porter, Robert M. Rozen, Donna Steele-Flynn, Timothy J. Urban

R. Duffy Wall and Associates

601 13th St. NW
Suite 410 South
Washington, DC 20005
Tel: (202)737-0100
Fax: (202)628-3965
Registered: LDA, FARA

Leg. Issues: EDU

Political Action Committee/s

R. Duffy Wall and Associates Inc. Political Action Committee
601 13th St. NW
Suite 410 South
Washington, DC 20005
Tel: (202)737-0100
Fax: (202)628-3965
Contact: Julia E. Chaney

In-house, DC-area Employees
BREWSTER, Hon. Bill: Chairman
CHANDLER, Hon. Rodney D.: President
CHANEY, Julia E.: V. President
COOPER, Stephen: Senior V. President
EMERICK, Kelli: V. President
EMERY, Rodney: V. President
ENZI, Michael Bradley: V. President
GREGORY, Jack: V. President
GRISSO, Michael E.: V. President
JACOB, Amy: V. President
JOHNSTON, Ann Thomas G.: V. President
JORY, David C.: Senior V. President
KRAUS, Angela: Assistant V. President
SCHUTE, Jr., William: Senior V. President
SWINDELLS, Grant: Senior Account Representative

Outside Counsel/Consultants
Timothy R. Rupli and Associates, Inc.
Issues: EDU
Rep By: Timothy R. Rupli

R.M.S. Titanic, Inc.
Atlanta, GA
Leg. Issues: MAR

Outside Counsel/Consultants
Robins, Kaplan, Miller & Ciresi L.L.P.
Issues: MAR
Rep By: Charles A. Hunnicutt, Harold E. Mesirow

R2 Technology, Inc.
Los Altos, CA
Leg. Issues: MED

Outside Counsel/Consultants
Heidepriem & Mager, Inc.
Issues: MED
Rep By: Karin Bolte, Nikki Heidepriem, Mimi Mager, Pat Ford Roegner

Racal Communications Inc.
Rockville, MD
Leg. Issues: DEF

Outside Counsel/Consultants
Manatt, Phelps & Phillips, LLP
Issues: DEF
Rep By: Mary Ann Gilleece, Jeff Kuhnreich

Radiant Aviation Services, Inc.
Leg. Issues: ENV

Outside Counsel/Consultants
Levine & Co.
Issues: ENV
Rep By: Ken Levine

Radio Shack Corp.
Fort Worth, TX
Registered: LDA
Leg. Issues: BNK, COM, TAX, TEC, TRD

Outside Counsel/Consultants
Drinker Biddle & Reath LLP
Issues: COM
Rep By: John W. Pettit

Marshall L. Lynam
Issues: BNK, TAX, TEC, TRD
Rep By: Marshall L. Lynam

Radio-Television News Directors Ass'n
1000 Connecticut Ave. NW
Suite 615
Washington, DC 20036-5302
Tel: (202)659-6510
Fax: (202)223-4007
Registered: LDA
Web: www.rtnda.org/rtnda/
E-mail: rtnda@rtnda.org

Serves the electronic news profession. Represents journalists in radio, television, broadcasting and cable, and emerging forms of electronic journalism.

Leg. Issues: COM, CON, MIA

In-house, DC-area Employees
COCHRAN, Barbara: President
STARK, Rosalind: Exec. Director
WELLE, Noreen: Director, Communications

Outside Counsel/Consultants
Wiley, Rein & Fielding
Issues: COM, MIA
Rep By: Kathleen A. Kirby

Radius, The Global Travel Co.
4330 East-West Hwy.
Suite 1100
Bethesda, MD 20814
Tel: (301)718-9500
Fax: (301)718-4290
Registered: LDA
Web: www.globaltravel.com

A travel management network operator.

Leg. Issues: AVI

Political Action Committee/s
WTT Inc. PAC (d.b.a. Woodside Travel Trust PAC)
4330 East-West Hwy.
Suite 1100
Bethesda, MD 20814
Tel: (301)718-9500
Fax: (301)718-4290

In-house, DC-area Employees
SIMON, Ethan Z.: V. President, Corporate Communications
SLAN, Allan G.: Exec. V. President

Outside Counsel/Consultants
Ungaretti & Harris
Issues: AVI
Rep By: Edward P. Faberman, Michelle M. Faust

Radix SA
Buenos Aires, ARGENTINA
Leg. Issues: TRD

Outside Counsel/Consultants
Davis & Leiman, P.C.
Issues: TRD

Rafael U.S.A., Inc.
4455 Connecticut Ave. NW
Suite B-400
Washington, DC 20008
Tel: (202)895-5290
Fax: (202)895-5298
Registered: FARA
E-mail: yitzhaki@ix.netcom.com
Leg. Issues: AER, AVI, GOV, LAW, MAR

In-house, DC-area Employees
YITZHAKI, Eliyahu: President and Chief Exec. Officer

Outside Counsel/Consultants
Teicher Consulting and Representation
Issues: AER, AVI, GOV, LAW, MAR
Rep By: Howard R. Teicher

RAG North America
Baltimore, MD
Leg. Issues: NAT, TAX

Outside Counsel/Consultants
Thomas D. Campbell & Assoc.
Issues: NAT, TAX
Rep By: Thomas D. Campbell

Rail Supply and Service Coalition
Washington, DC
Leg. Issues: RRR, TRA

Outside Counsel/Consultants
Chambers, Conlon & Hartwell
Issues: RRR, TRA
Rep By: Keith O. Hartwell, Don Norden

Railroad Retirement Tax Working Group
Leg. Issues: RET

Outside Counsel/Consultants
Dewey Ballantine LLP
Issues: RET
Rep By: Joseph K. Dowley, Basil W. Henderson, Andrew W. Kentz, John J. Salmon, James M. Wickett

Railroad Retirement Reform Working Group

Outside Counsel/Consultants
Deloitte & Touche LLP Nat'l Office - Washington
Rep By: Randall D. Weiss

Rails to Trails Conservancy
1100 17th St. NW
Tenth Floor
Washington, DC 20036
Tel: (202)331-9696
Fax: (202)331-9680
Registered: LDA

A nonprofit membership organization working with local conservation and recreation groups to preserve the national rail system for recreational use and in the interest of conservation.

Leg. Issues: NAT, TRA

In-house, DC-area Employees
FOWLER, Marianne W.: Senior V. President, Programs
LAUGHLIN, Keith: President

Railway Labor Executives' Ass'n
Washington, DC

Outside Counsel/Consultants
Highsaw, Mahoney & Clarke
Rep By: William G. Mahoney

Railway Progress Institute
700 N. Fairfax St.
Suite 601
Alexandria, VA 22314
Tel: (703)836-2332
Fax: (703)548-0058
Registered: LDA
Web: www.rpi.org
E-mail: rpi@rpi.org

The national trade association of the railway equipment and supply industry.

Leg. Issues: RRR, TRA

In-house, DC-area Employees
GAMACHE, Nicole B.: Assistant V. President
MATTHEWS, Robert A.: President
SIMPSON, Thomas D.: V. President

Rainbow/Push Coalition (National Bureau)
1002 Wisconsin Ave. NW
Washington, DC 20007
Tel: (202)333-5270
Fax: (202)728-1192
Web: www.rainbowpush.org
Leg. Issues: ECN

In-house, DC-area Employees
JACKSON, Sr., Rev. Jesse L.: President and Founder
LEONARD, Joe: Exec. Director
PEYTON, Keiana: Press Secretary

Outside Counsel/Consultants
Rubin, Winston, Diercks, Harris & Cooke
Rep By: Frederick D. Cooke, Jr.

Wheat & Associates, Inc.
Issues: ECN
Rep By: Hon. Alan D. Wheat

Rakisons, Ltd.
London, UNITED KINGDOM
Leg. Issues: GAM

Outside Counsel/Consultants
Greenberg Traurig, LLP
Issues: GAM
Rep By: Ronald L. Platt

Ralin Medical
Buffalo Grove, IL
A health care delivery system.

Outside Counsel/Consultants
Health Policy Group
Rep By: J. Michael Hudson

Ralston Purina Co.
1300 I St. NW
Suite 495-East Tower
Washington, DC 20005-3314
Tel: (202)289-2011
Fax: (202)289-2024
Registered: LDA
Leg. Issues: HCR, HOU, LBR, TAX, TRD

Political Action Committee/s
Ralston Purina Co. Committee for Good Government (RP-PAC)
1300 I St. NW
Suite 495-East Tower
Washington, DC 20005-3314
Tel: (202)289-2011
Fax: (202)289-2024
Contact: Claude D. Alexander

In-house, DC-area Employees
ALEXANDER, Claude D.: Director, Government Affairs
WIEDEMER, Anne Marie: Assistant Director, Government Affairs

Outside Counsel/Consultants
PriceWaterhouseCoopers
Issues: TAX
Rep By: Kenneth J. Kies, Don R. Longano

Ramgen Power Systems, Inc.
Bellevue, WA
Leg. Issues: ENG

Outside Counsel/Consultants
Denny Miller McBee Associates
Issues: ENG

Ramo Defense Systems, LLC
Nashville, TN
Leg. Issues: DEF

Outside Counsel/Consultants
Cassidy & Associates, Inc.
Issues: DEF
Rep By: Shawn Edwards, Christopher Lamond, Brig. Gen. Terry Paul, USMC (Ret.)

Ramsey, Minnesota, Board of Commissioners of the County of

St. Paul, MN
Leg. Issues: ENV, HCR, TOB, WAS, WEL

Outside Counsel/Consultants

Lockridge Grindal & Nauen, P.L.L.P.
Issues: ENV, HCR, TOB, WAS, WEL
Rep By: Dennis McGrann

Ranchers-Cattlemen Legal Action Fund

Columbus, MT
Leg. Issues: AGR, TRD

Outside Counsel/Consultants

Stewart and Stewart
Issues: AGR, TRD
Rep By: Alan M. Dunn, Amy S. Dwyer, David S. Johanson, Carl Moyer, Eric Salonen, Terence P. Stewart

Rancho Cucamonga, California, City of

Outside Counsel/Consultants

David Turch & Associates

Rancho Palos Verdes, California, City of

Leg. Issues: BUD

Outside Counsel/Consultants

E. Del Smith and Co.
Issues: BUD
Rep By: E. Del Smith

RAND Corp.

1200 S. Hayes St.
Arlington, VA 22202-5050
Tel: (703)413-1100
Fax: (703)413-8111
Registered: LDA
Web: www.rand.org

The Washington Office of a private, non-profit institution based in Santa Monica, CA. Helps improve policy and decision making through research and analysis.

In-house, DC-area Employees

HOFFMAN, Bruce: Director
KAGANOWICH, Gar: Director, Washington External Affairs
KIRBY, Sheila: Associate Director

Outside Counsel/Consultants

Winner & Associates

A. Philip Randolph Educational Fund

1444 I St. NW
Suite 300
Washington, DC 20005
E-mail: nhill@aprihq.org
Tel: (202)289-2774
Fax: (202)289-5289

In-house, DC-area Employees

HILL, Norman: President

A. Philip Randolph Institute

1444 I St. NW
Suite 300
Washington, DC 20005
E-mail: nhill@aphihq.org
Tel: (202)289-2774
Fax: (202)289-5289

Promotes increased participation by Blacks in national, state and local politics; trade and labor unions; and voter education and registration. Sponsors the A. Philip Randolph Educational Fund (see separate listing).

In-house, DC-area Employees

HILL, Norman: President

Random House

New York, NY

Outside Counsel/Consultants

Television Communicators
Rep By: Robert D. Wechter

Rapid Mat LLC

Leg. Issues: BUD, DEF, DIS

Outside Counsel/Consultants

Potomac Group
Issues: BUD, DEF, DIS
Rep By: Richard Y Hegg, Philip C. Karsting, G. Wayne Smith

Rapid Reporting, Inc.

Fort Worth, TX
Leg. Issues: TAX

Outside Counsel/Consultants

Peter J. Rose
Issues: TAX
Rep By: Peter J. Rose

RAPOCA Energy Co.

Bristol, VA
Leg. Issues: TAX

Outside Counsel/Consultants

J. Steven Griles & Associates
Issues: TAX
Rep By: J. Steven Griles

Raritan River Steel Co.

Outside Counsel/Consultants

Wiley, Rein & Fielding
Rep By: Charles O. Verrill, Jr.

Ratcliff Strategies

Washington, DC

Outside Counsel/Consultants

Dickstein Shapiro Morin & Oshinsky LLP
Rep By: Robert Mangas

Raufoss A/S, Defense Products Division

Raufoss, NORWAY
Leg. Issues: DEF

Outside Counsel/Consultants

Rooney Group Internat'l, Inc.
Issues: DEF
Rep By: James W. Rooney

Raychem Corp.

Menlo Park, CA

Outside Counsel/Consultants

Shaw Pittman

Raydon Corp.

Daytona Beach, FL
Leg. Issues: DEF, SCI

Outside Counsel/Consultants

Davis O'Connell, Inc.
Issues: DEF, SCI
Rep By: Lynda C. Davis, Ph.D., Terrence M. O'Connell

The Spectrum Group
Issues: DEF
Rep By: Lt. Gen. Augustus Cianciolo, USA (Ret.), Maj. Gen. Paul Fratarangelo, USMC (Ret.), Gregory L. Sharp

Raytheon Co.

1100 Wilson Blvd.
Suite 1500
Arlington, VA 22209
Tel: (703)841-5700
Registered: LDA

Headquartered in Lexington, MA.

Leg. Issues: AVI, BUD, CHM, COM, CSP, DEF, FIN, FOR, GOV, LBR, MAN, TAX, TRA, TRD

Political Action Committee/s

Raytheon PAC
1100 Wilson Blvd.
Suite 1500
Arlington, VA 22209
Contact: W. John Nichols
Tel: (703)841-5723
Fax: (703)841-5792

In-house, DC-area Employees

BEARD, Robin L.: President, Government Relations
HICKEY, James J.: Director, Congressional Relations, Army Programs
LEE, William J.: Director, Congressional Relations
MATTHEWS, III, David J.: Senior V. President, Congressional Relations
NICHOLS, W. John: V. President, Defense Programs and Congressional Relations
NIRENBERG, Lori H.: Director, Congressional Relations, Tax and Trade Issues
RAMIREZ, Lilia L.: Director, Congressional Relations, Navy Programs
WHITE, Toni D.: Senior Director, Government Relations

Outside Counsel/Consultants

American Systems Internat'l Corp.
Issues: DEF, MAN
Rep By: Robert D. McVey, William H. Skipper, Jr.

Arent Fox Kintner Plotkin & Kahn, PLLC
Issues: AVI, BUD, DEF, LBR, TAX, TRD
Rep By: Hon. Dale L. Bumpers, Hon. John C. Culver, Craig S. King, Michael T. McNamara, Todd Weiss

C. Baker Consulting Inc.
Issues: AVI, DEF, MAN
Rep By: Caleb Baker

Bracewell & Patterson, L.L.P.

Campbell Crane & Associates
Issues: TAX
Rep By: Jeanne M. Campbell, Daniel M. Crane

John G. Campbell, Inc.
Issues: DEF

W. B. Driggers & Associates, Inc.
Issues: DEF
Rep By: W. B. Driggers

Jones, Walker, Waechter, Poitevent, Carrere & Denegre, L.L.P.
Issues: BUD, DEF
Rep By: Paul Cambon, John J. Jaskot, R. Christian Johnsen, James Ogsbury

The Livingston Group, LLC
Issues: BUD, DEF
Rep By: Hon. Robert L. Livingston, Jr., J. Allen Martin, Richard L. Rodgers

The Montgomery Group
Rep By: Hon. G. V. "Sonny" Montgomery

The Potomac Advocates
Issues: DEF
Rep By: Gary L. Sojka

Verner, Liipfert, Bernhard, McPherson and Hand, Chartered
Issues: DEF
Rep By: John H. Zentay

Raytheon Missile Systems

Tucson, AZ
Leg. Issues: DEF

Outside Counsel/Consultants

American Defense Internat'l, Inc.
Issues: DEF
Rep By: Michael Herson, Van D. Hipp, Jr., Dave Wilberding

G.L. Merritt & Associates, Inc.
Issues: DEF
Rep By: Gordon L. Merritt

RCN Telecom Services Inc.

Princeton, NJ
Leg. Issues: TEC

Outside Counsel/Consultants

Swidler Berlin Shereff Friedman, LLP
Issues: TEC
Rep By: Gary D. Slaiman

RCRA Policy Forum

Washington, DC

Outside Counsel/Consultants

Clay Associates, Inc.

The Reader's Digest Ass'n

Pleasantville, NY
Leg. Issues: LBR, POS, TAX

Outside Counsel/Consultants

Davidson & Company, Inc.
Issues: LBR, TAX
Rep By: James H. Davidson, Richard E. May, Stanley Sokul

Dickstein Shapiro Morin & Oshinsky LLP
Issues: POS
Rep By: Elizabeth B. Haywood, Robert Mangas, Graham "Rusty" Mathews, Andrew P. Miller, Hon. Stanford E. Parris, Rebecah Moore Shepherd, L. Andrew Zausner

Reading Is Fundamental, Inc.

1825 Connecticut Ave. NW
Suite 400
Washington, DC 20009
Web: www.rif.org
Tel: (202)287-3220
Fax: (202)287-3196

In-house, DC-area Employees

TRUEHEART, William: President

Reading, Pennsylvania, City of

Outside Counsel/Consultants

Arnold & Porter

The Readnet Foundation

New York, NY
Leg. Issues: EDU

Outside Counsel/Consultants

Washington Alliance Group, Inc.
Issues: EDU
Rep By: Bonnie Singer

Real Access Alliance

Washington, DC
Leg. Issues: COM, RES, TEC

Outside Counsel/Consultants

Cooper, Carvin & Rosenthal
Issues: COM, RES
Rep By: Hamish Hume, Steven S. Rosenthal

Wallman Strategic Consulting, LLC
Issues: COM, TEC
Rep By: Brett Tarnutzer, Kathleen E. Wallman

Real Estate Capital Resources Ass'n

Washington, DC
Web: www.realworks.com/recra
E-mail: recra@realworks.com

Formerly known as Real Estate Capital Recovery Ass'n.

Outside Counsel/Consultants

Oppenheimer Wolff & Donnelly LLP
Rep By: Hon. Birch Bayh, Kevin O. Faley

Real Estate Roundtable

1420 New York Ave. NW
Suite 1100
Washington, DC 20005
Tel: (202)639-8400
Fax: (202)639-8442
Registered: LDA
Web: www.rer.org
E-mail: info@rer.org

The Real Estate Roundtable is the vehicle through which the nation's leading public and privately held real estate owners, advisors, builders, lenders and managers work together with the leadership of major national real estate trade organizations, on key tax, capital, credit, environmental, and technology issues in Washington DC..

Leg. Issues: BNK, CAW, ENV, FIN, HOU, NAT, RES, TAX, TEC, UTI

Political Action Committee/s

Real Estate Roundtable Political Action Committee, The (REALPAC)
1420 New York Ave. NW
Suite 1100
Washington, DC 20005
Tel: (202)639-8400
Fax: (202)639-8442
Contact: Jeffrey D. DeBoer

In-house, DC-area Employees

DEBOER, Jeffrey D.: President and Chief Operating Officer
JOWYK, Xenia: Director, Publications
PLATT, Roger: V. President and Counsel
RENNA, Stephen M.: V. President and Counsel
RODGERS, Jr., Clifton E.: V. President

Outside Counsel/Consultants

Covington & Burling
Rep By: John C. Dugan

Miller & Van Eaton, P.L.L.C.
Issues: TEC
Rep By: Matthew C. Ames, William Malone, Nicholas P. Miller

The Washington Group
Issues: RES, TAX
Rep By: Rita M. Lewis, G. John O'Hanlon, John D. Raffaelli, Mark Schnabel

Weil, Gotshal & Manges, LLP
Issues: ENV
Rep By: David B. Hird

Real Estate Services Providers Council

Washington, DC
Leg. Issues: BAN

Outside Counsel/Consultants

Foley & Lardner
Rep By: Jay N. Varon

Sue E. Johnson Associates
Issues: BAN
Rep By: Susan E. Johnson

Rebuild America's Schools

Washington, DC

An organization seeking federal financial aid for school construction.

Leg. Issues: EDU, TAX

Outside Counsel/Consultants

Federal Management Strategies, Inc.
Issues: EDU, TAX
Rep By: Robert P. Canavan

Reckitt & Colman Pharmaceuticals Inc.

Richmond, VA
Leg. Issues: ALC, ENV, HCR, MED

Outside Counsel/Consultants

Crowell & Moring LLP
Issues: ENV
Rep By: Nancy S. Bryson

Policy Directions, Inc.
Issues: ALC, HCR, MED
Rep By: Kathleen "Kay" Holcombe, Frankie L. Trull

Washington Liaison Group, LLC
Issues: ALC, HCR
Rep By: Gaston de Bearn, David M. Jenkins, II, Michael L. Reed

Reckitt Benckiser Professional

Wayne, NJ

Outside Counsel/Consultants

Interface Inc.
Rep By: Rudy R. Nessel

Recon/Optical, Inc.

Barrington, IL
Leg. Issues: BUD, DEF, FOR

Outside Counsel/Consultants

Stanfield Tindal, Inc.
Issues: BUD, DEF, FOR
Rep By: D'Anna Tindal

Recording for the Blind and Dyslexic, Inc.

Princeton, NJ
Registered: LDA

Provides audio and digital books, free of charge, to print-disabled students.

Leg. Issues: EDU

Outside Counsel/Consultants

Osborne A. Day
Rep By: Osborne A. Day

Van Scoyoc Associates, Inc.
Issues: EDU
Rep By: Robert L. Knisely, James W. Kohlmoos, H. Stewart Van Scoyoc, Noreene Wells

Recording Industry Ass'n of America

1330 Connecticut Ave. NW
Suite 300
Washington, DC 20036
Tel: (202)775-0101
Fax: (202)775-7253
Registered: LDA
Web: www.riaa.com

Founded in 1952, RIAA represents 90% of all legitimate recordings produced and sold in the U.S. Seeks legislative and regulatory action needed to maintain a healthy industry.

Leg. Issues: ART, BNK, CIV, COM, CPI, CPT, LAW, LBR, TAX, TEC

Political Action Committee/s

Recording Arts Political Action Committee
1330 Connecticut Ave. NW
Suite 300
Washington, DC 20036
Tel: (202)775-0101
Fax: (202)775-7253

In-house, DC-area Employees

ALLMAN, Kim: Director, Government Affairs
GLAZIER, Mitch: Senior V. President, Government Relations and Legislative Counsel
MARKS, Steven M.: Senior V. President, Business and Legal Affairs
ROSEN, Hilary B.: President and Chief Exec. Officer
SHERMAN, Cary: Senior Exec. V. President and General Counsel
TURKEWITZ, Neil: Exec. V. President, International
WEISS, Amy: Senior V. President, Communications

Outside Counsel/Consultants

Alpine Group, Inc.
Issues: CPI, CPT, LAW
Rep By: Dan Brouillette, Rhod M. Shaw

American Continental Group, Inc.
Issues: CPT, TEC
Rep By: Thaddeus E. Strom

The Dutko Group, Inc.

Podesta/Mattoon
Rep By: Ann Delory, Kimberley Fritts, Matthew Gelman, Claudia James, Andrew C. Littman, Anthony T. Podesta, Timothy Powers

Quinn Gillespie & Associates
Issues: ART, COM, CPT, LBR
Rep By: Edward W. Gillespie

Thelen Reid & Priest LLP
Issues: CPT
Rep By: William A. Kirk, Jr.

Washington Council Ernst & Young
Issues: ART, CIV, CPT, TAX
Rep By: Doug Badger, Lauren Darling, John L. Doney, Jayne T. Fitzgerald, LaBrenda Garrett-Nelson, Gary J. Gasper, Bruce A. Gates, Nick Giordano, Cathy Koch, Robert J. Leonard, Richard Meltzer, Phillip D. Moseley, John D. Porter, Robert M. Rozen, Donna Steele-Flynn, Timothy J. Urban

Williams & Jensen, P.C.
Issues: ART, BNK, CPT
Rep By: Bertram W. Carp, J. Steven Hart, Anthony J. Roda

Recovermat Technologies LLC

Bethesda, MD
Leg. Issues: WAS

Outside Counsel/Consultants

The Dutko Group, Inc.
Issues: WAS
Rep By: Mark S. Irion

Recovery Engineering, Inc.

Minneapolis, MN
Leg. Issues: DEF

Outside Counsel/Consultants

David Turch & Associates
Issues: DEF
Rep By: Marilyn E. Campbell, David N. M. Turch

RECRA

1250 Connecticut Ave. NW
Suite 700
Washington, DC 20005
Tel: (202)637-6667
Fax: (202)842-2869

Formerly Real Estate Capital Resources Ass'n.

Political Action Committee/s

RECRA Fund
1250 Connecticut Ave. NW
Suite 700
Washington, DC 20005
Tel: (202)637-6667
Fax: (202)842-2869
Contact: G. David Fensterheim

In-house, DC-area Employees

FENSTERHEIM, G. David: Exec. Director

Outside Counsel/Consultants

Fensterheim & Bean, P.C.
Rep By: Donald Bean, Jr., G. David Fensterheim

Recreation Vehicle Ass'n

Leg. Issues: AUT, MAN, TRA

Outside Counsel/Consultants

Arent Fox Kintner Plotkin & Kahn, PLLC
Issues: AUT, MAN, TRA
Rep By: Todd Weiss

Recreation Vehicle Dealers Ass'n of North America

3930 University Dr.
Fairfax, VA 22030-2515
Tel: (703)591-7130
Fax: (703)591-0734
Web: www.rvda.org
E-mail: info@rvda.org
Leg. Issues: AUT, CSP, TOU

In-house, DC-area Employees

INGRASSIA, Phil: Director, Communications
MOLINO, Mike: President
SHARN, Christy: Manager, State Communications

Outside Counsel/Consultants

Venable
Issues: AUT, CSP, TOU
Rep By: Brock R. Landry

Recreation Vehicle Industry Ass'n

P.O. Box 2999 Tel: (703)620-6003
Reston, VA 20191 Fax: (703)620-5071
Web: www.rvia.org

The national trade association for manufacturers of recreation vehicles and van conversions, industry suppliers, and service organizations.

Leg. Issues: TRA

In-house, DC-area Employees

BAKER, Bill: Director, Government Affairs
FARRELL, Dianne: V. President, Government Affairs
HUMPHREYS, David J.: President
KIRBY, Craig A.: V. President and General Counsel
LANDERS, Jay: Senior Director, Government Affairs
MORIAK, Susan: Assistant Director, Government Affairs
SCHMITT, Robert: Assistant General Counsel

Outside Counsel/Consultants

Sagamore Associates, Inc.
Issues: TRA
Rep By: Ann E. Cody, David U. Gogol, Mark W. Weller

Recreation Vehicle Rental Ass'n

3930 University Dr. Tel: (703)591-7130
Fairfax, VA 22030 Fax: (703)591-0734
Web: www.rvamerica.com/rvra/
E-mail: rvdanat@aol.com

In-house, DC-area Employees

MOLINO, Mike

Recreational Equipment Inc.

Kent, WA
Leg. Issues: RES

Outside Counsel/Consultants

Swidler Berlin Shereff Friedman, LLP
Issues: RES
Rep By: Keith N. Cole

Recreational Fishing Alliance

Outside Counsel/Consultants

Washington Strategies, L.L.C.
Rep By: Jennifer Johnson Calvert, William P. Jarrell

Red Lake Band of Chippewa Indians

Red Lake, MN
Leg. Issues: GAM, IND, TAX

Outside Counsel/Consultants

Dorsey & Whitney LLP
Issues: GAM, IND, TAX
Rep By: Philip Baker-Shenk, David A. Bieging, Virginia W. Boylan, Cindy Darcy, Mark Jarboe, Christopher Karns, Kevin J. Wadzinski

Holland & Knight LLP
Issues: IND
Rep By: Hon. Gerald E. Sikorski

Red River Trade Council

Crookston, MN
Leg. Issues: AGR, BUD, ECN, ROD, TEC, TRA

Outside Counsel/Consultants

Sara Garland (and Associates)
Issues: AGR, BUD, ECN, ROD, TEC, TRA
Rep By: Sara G. Garland

RedCreek Communications Inc.

Newark, CA
Leg. Issues: CPI

Outside Counsel/Consultants

Powell Tate
Issues: CPI

J. P. Redd Inc.

Salt Lake City, UT

Outside Counsel/Consultants

The Smith-Free Group

Vorys, Sater, Seymour and Pease, LLP
Rep By: Warren W. Glick

Redding, California, City of

Leg. Issues: URB

Outside Counsel/Consultants

Morgan Meguire, LLC
Issues: URB
Rep By: Scott Lindsay, Kyle G. Michel, Katie Parrott, C. Kyle Simpson, Deborah R. Sliz, Kiel Weaver

Redding, California, Electric Department of the City of

Leg. Issues: ENG, GOV, UTI

Outside Counsel/Consultants

Duncan, Weinberg, Genzer & Pembroke, P.C.
Issues: ENG, GOV, UTI
Rep By: Wallace L. Duncan, James D. Pembroke, Michael R. Postar

Redlands, California, City of

Redlands, CA
Leg. Issues: BUD, URB

Outside Counsel/Consultants

Copeland, Lowery & Jacquez
Issues: BUD, URB
Rep By: Hon. William D. Lowery, Jeffrey S. Shockey

Redstone

Denver, CO
Leg. Issues: ENG

Outside Counsel/Consultants

J. Steven Griles & Associates
Issues: ENG
Rep By: H. Spofford Canfield, IV, J. Steven Griles, John Northington

Redwood City, California, Port of

Leg. Issues: TRA

Outside Counsel/Consultants

Lindsay Hart Neil & Weigler
Issues: TRA
Rep By: Kathryn Beaubien, Peter Friedmann

Reebok Internat'l

Stoughton, MA
Leg. Issues: TRD

Political Action Committee/s

Reebok Internat'l Ltd. PAC
Stoughton, MA

Outside Counsel/Consultants

Lindsay Hart Neil & Weigler
Issues: TRD
Rep By: Kathryn Beaubien, Peter Friedmann

Reed-Elsevier Inc.

Newton, MA
Leg. Issues: CPT, MIA, TAX

Outside Counsel/Consultants

Proskauer Rose LLP
Issues: CPT, MIA
Rep By: Jon A. Baumgarten

Liz Robbins Associates
Rep By: Liz Robbins

Washington Council Ernst & Young
Issues: TAX
Rep By: Doug Badger, Lauren Darling, John L. Doney, Jayne T. Fitzgerald, LaBrenda Garrett-Nelson, Gary J. Gasper, Bruce A. Gates, Nick Giordano, Cathy Koch, Robert J. Leonard, Richard Meltzer, Phillip D. Moseley, John D. Porter, Robert M. Rozen, Donna Steele-Flynn, Timothy J. Urban

Christopher Reeve Paralysis Foundation

Springfield, NJ
Leg. Issues: BUD, HCR

Outside Counsel/Consultants

Akin, Gump, Strauss, Hauer & Feld, L.L.P.

Arent Fox Kintner Plotkin & Kahn, PLLC
Issues: BUD, HCR
Rep By: Hon. Dale L. Bumpers, Katie Clarke, Douglas McCormack, Robert J. Waters

Witeck * Combs Communications

Refined Sugars Inc.

Yonkers, NY
Leg. Issues: AGR

Outside Counsel/Consultants

Smith Martin & Boyette
Issues: AGR
Rep By: Van R. Boyette

The Refinishing Touch

Alpharetta, GA
Leg. Issues: DEF, GOV

Outside Counsel/Consultants

The Spectrum Group
Issues: DEF, GOV
Rep By: Lt. Gen. Augustus Cianciolo, USA (Ret.), Maj. Gen. Ray McCoy, USA (Ret.), Paul E. McManus, Gregory L. Sharp

Refugees Internat'l

1705 N St. NW Tel: (202)828-0110
Washington, DC 20036 Fax: (202)828-0819
Web: www.refugeesinternational.org
E-mail: ri@refintl.org

Works on behalf of refugees and displaced persons worldwide.

Leg. Issues: FOR

In-house, DC-area Employees

BACON, Kenneth H.: President

Regeneration Technologies Inc.

Alachua, FL
Leg. Issues: HCR

Outside Counsel/Consultants

Ketchum
Issues: HCR
Rep By: Samantha Lasky

Public Affairs Management, Inc.

Regents College

Albany, NY
Leg. Issues: BUD, EDU

Outside Counsel/Consultants

Van Scoyoc Associates, Inc.
Issues: BUD, EDU
Rep By: Steve E. Crane, Robert L. Knisely, James W. Kohlmoos, H. Stewart Van Scoyoc

ReGin Manufacturing Inc.

Fishers, IN
Leg. Issues: HCR, MMM

Outside Counsel/Consultants

Nusgart Consulting, LLC
Issues: HCR, MMM
Rep By: Marcia Nusgart

Regional Airline Ass'n

Washington, DC
Web: www.raa.org
E-mail: raa@dc.sba.com

Formerly known as the Commuter Airline Association of America.

Leg. Issues: AVI

Political Action Committee/s

Regional Airline Ass'n Political Action Committee
Washington, DC

Outside Counsel/Consultants

Crowell & Moring LLP

Smith, Bucklin and Associates, Inc.
Issues: AVI
Rep By: Faye A. Malarkey, Deborah C. McElroy

Regional Airport Authority of Louisville & Jefferson Co.

Louisville, KY
Leg. Issues: AVI, BUD, TRA

Outside Counsel/Consultants

Federal Access
Issues: AVI
Rep By: Timothy R. Cole

The Grizzle Company
Issues: BUD, TRA
Rep By: Richard A. Cantor, Charles L. Grizzle

Van Scoyoc Associates, Inc.
Issues: AVI, BUD
Rep By: Steven O. Palmer, Chad Schulken, H. Stewart Van Scoyoc

Regional Planning Commission

New Orleans, LA
Leg. Issues: AGR, AVI, BUD, ECN, ROD, TRA

Outside Counsel/Consultants

Johnston & Associates, LLC
Issues: AGR, AVI, BUD, ECN, ROD, TRA
Rep By: N. Hunter Johnston, W. Proctor Jones, Eric Tober

Regional Public Tansportation Authority

Phoenix, AZ
Leg. Issues: BUD, TRA

Outside Counsel/Consultants

Government Relations, Inc.
Issues: BUD, TRA
Rep By: Thomas J. Bulger, Mark H. Miller, John N. Young

Regional Railroads of America

Washington, DC

Outside Counsel/Consultants

Preston Gates Ellis & Rouvelas Meeds LLP

Regional Transit Authority

New Orleans, LA
Leg. Issues: BUD, TRA

Outside Counsel/Consultants

Adams and Reese LLP
Issues: BUD, TRA
Rep By: B. Jeffrey Brooks

Johnston & Associates, LLC
Issues: BUD, TRA
Rep By: Hon. J. Bennett Johnston, N. Hunter Johnston, Eric Tober

Regional Transportation Commission

Las Vegas, NV
Leg. Issues: BUD, TRA

Outside Counsel/Consultants

Marcus G. Faust, P.C.
Issues: BUD, TRA
Rep By: Marcus G. Faust, Adrianne Firth

Regional Transportation Commission of South Nevada

Las Vegas, NV
Leg. Issues: TRA

Outside Counsel/Consultants

Thompson Coburn LLP
Issues: TRA
Rep By: Hon. R. Lawrence Coughlin, Jane Sutter-Starke, G. Kent Woodman

Regions Financial Corp.

Birmingham, AL

Outside Counsel/Consultants

Alston & Bird LLP
Rep By: Frank M. Conner, III, Jonathan H. Talcott

Register.com

New York, NY
Leg. Issues: CPI, SCI, TEC

Outside Counsel/Consultants

Broad-Band Solutions
Issues: SCI
Rep By: Amy Hickox, Sage Rhodes

Susan Davis Internat'l
Issues: CPI, SCI, TEC
Rep By: Susan A. Davis

Regulatory Affairs Professionals Soc.

11300 Rockville Pike
Suite 1000
Rockville, MD 20852-3048
Tel: (301)770-2920
Fax: (301)770-2924
Web: www.raps.org
E-mail: raps@raps.org

In-house, DC-area Employees

KERAMIDAS, Sherry: Exec. Director

Regulatory Improvement Council

Washington, DC
Leg. Issues: ENV, GOV

Outside Counsel/Consultants

Valis Associates
Issues: ENV, GOV
Rep By: Todd Tolson, Wayne H. Valis

Rehabilitation Engineering and Assistive Technology Soc. of North America

Web: www.resna.org
E-mail: natloffice@resna.org

An interdisciplinary association of people with a common interest in technology and disability.

Outside Counsel/Consultants

Harles & Associates
Rep By: Charles Harles

Reheis, Inc.

Berkeley Heights, NJ

Outside Counsel/Consultants

Nutter & Harris, Inc.
Rep By: Jack O. Nutter

Reilly Industries

Indianapolis, IN
Leg. Issues: ENV

Outside Counsel/Consultants

Nat'l Environmental Strategies
Issues: ENV
Rep By: Marc I. Himmelstein

Reilly Mortgage Group Inc.

McLean, VA
Leg. Issues: HOU

Outside Counsel/Consultants

Nixon Peabody LLP
Issues: HOU
Rep By: Richard M. Price, Monica Hilton Sussman

Reinsurance Ass'n of America

1301 Pennsylvania Ave. NW
Suite 900
Washington, DC 20004
Tel: (202)638-3690
Fax: (202)638-0936
Registered: LDA
Web: www.reinsurance.org
E-mail: nutter@reinsurance.org
Leg. Issues: AVI, BAN, BNK, CPI, DIS, ENV, FIN, TAX

Political Action Committee/s

Reinsurance Association of America Political Action Committee
1301 Pennsylvania Ave. NW
Suite 900
Washington, DC 20004
Tel: (202)638-3690
Fax: (202)638-0936
Contact: Mary Seidel

In-house, DC-area Employees

HALL, Debra J.: V. President and General Counsel
LAFEVRE, Sandra L.: V. President and Assistant Secretary
NUTTER, Franklin W.: President
SEIDEL, Mary: Director, Federal Affairs

Outside Counsel/Consultants

Williams & Jensen, P.C.
Issues: BAN, BNK, DIS, FIN, TAX
Rep By: William B. Canfield, David E. Franasiak, Robert E. Glennon, Jr., David M. Landers, Jeffrey A. Tassey

Reiten Broadcasting, Inc.

Minot, ND

Outside Counsel/Consultants

Shaw Pittman

Reliant Energy, Inc.

801 Pennsylvania Ave. NW
Suite 620
Washington, DC 20004-2604
Tel: (202)783-7220
Fax: (202)783-8127
Registered: LDA

Headquartered in Houston, TX, Reliant Energy is the parent company of Houston Lighting & Power Co. and Reliant Energy Gas Transmission.

Leg. Issues: ENG, FUE, UTI

In-house, DC-area Employees

ALBRIGHT, Jr., C. H. "Bud": V. President, Federal Relations
GIBLIN, Christopher M.: Manager, Federal Relations
NICHOLS, Holly B.: Manager, Federal Relations

Outside Counsel/Consultants

Walker F. Nolan
Issues: ENG, UTI
Rep By: Walker F. Nolan

Religious Action Center of Reform Judaism

2027 Massachusetts Ave. NW
Washington, DC 20036
Tel: (202)387-2800
Fax: (202)667-9070
Web: www.rac.org
E-mail: rac@uahc.org

Purpose is to mobilize the Jewish community and to serve as its advocate in the nation's capital and its voice for social justice and religious liberty throughout the country.

In-house, DC-area Employees

PELAVIN, Mark: Associate Director
SAPERSTEIN, Rabbi David: Director

Religious Coalition for Reproductive Choice

1025 Vermont Ave. NW
Suite 1130
Washington, DC 20005-3516
Tel: (202)628-7700
Fax: (202)628-7716
Web: www.rcrc.org
E-mail: info@rcrc.org

An interfaith pro-choice coalition whose goal is to inform the media and the public that mainstream religions, such as United Methodist, Presbyterian, Jewish, United Church of Christ and others, support reproductive choice and oppose anti-abortion violence.

In-house, DC-area Employees

VEAZEY, Rev. Carlton W.: President and Chief Exec. Officer

Religious Technology Center

Los Angeles, CA
Leg. Issues: CIV, CPT, FOR

Outside Counsel/Consultants

Federal Legislative Associates, Inc.
Issues: CIV, CPT, FOR
Rep By: Stephen D. Amitay, David H. Miller

REM Engineering

Leg. Issues: SMB, VET

Outside Counsel/Consultants

Madison Government Affairs
Issues: SMB, VET
Rep By: Paul J. Hirsch, Myron M. Jacobson, Jackson Kemper, III

Remediation Financial, Inc.

Phoenix, AZ
Leg. Issues: CAW, ENV

Outside Counsel/Consultants

Kinghorn & Associates, L.L.C.
Issues: CAW, ENV
Rep By: Edward J. Kinghorn, Jr.

Renal Leadership Council

Torrance, CA
Leg. Issues: HCR, MMM

Political Action Committee/s

Renal Leadership Council Political Action Committee (RLC PAC).
Torrance, CA

Outside Counsel/Consultants

Congressional Consultants
Issues: HCR, MMM
Rep By: Gwen Gampel

Renal Physicians Ass'n

4701 Randolph Rd.
Suite 102
Rockville, MD 20852
Tel: (301)468-3515
Fax: (301)468-3511
Web: www.renalmd.org
E-mail: rpa@renalmd.org
Leg. Issues: HCR, INS, MED, MMM

In-house, DC-area Employees

BLASER, Robert: Director, Government Affairs
SINGER, Dale: Exec. Director

Outside Counsel/Consultants

Medical Advocacy Services, Inc.
Issues: HCR, MMM
Rep By: Robert Blaser, Holly Owen

RENEW (Republican Network to Elect Women)

Alexandria, VA
Web: www.users.aol.com/gorenew/
E-mail: repnetwork@aol.com

Identifies and provides training, financial support and technical assistance to Republican women candidates for local, state and federal office.

Outside Counsel/Consultants

Wiley, Rein & Fielding
Rep By: Jan W. Baran

Renew America

1200 18th St. NW
Suite 1100
Washington, DC 20036
Tel: (202)721-1545
Fax: (202)467-5780
Web: www.crest.org/renew_america
E-mail: renewamerica@counterpart.org

Non-profit environmental organization that collects, verifies and disseminates information on solutions to world environmental problems.

In-house, DC-area Employees

DAVIS, R. Mark: Exec. Director
SLAFER, Anna: Exec. Director

Renewable Energy Policy Project

Outside Counsel/Consultants

Duncan, Weinberg, Genzer & Pembroke, P.C.
Rep By: Jeffrey C. Genzer

Renewable Fuels Ass'n

One Massachusetts Ave. NW
Suite 820
Washington, DC 20001
Tel: (202)289-3835
Fax: (202)289-7519
Registered: LDA
Web: www.ethanolrfa.org
E-mail: info@ethanolrfa.org

The RFA represents the domestic ethanol industry, and promotes the increased production and use of fuel ethanol before Congress and federal agencies.

Leg. Issues: AGR, BUD, CAW, ENG, ENV, FUE, TAX

In-house, DC-area Employees
DINNEEN, Robert: V. President
GIGLIO, Mary: Director, Congressional and Public Affairs
VAUGHN, Eric: President

Outside Counsel/Consultants
Law Office of Edward D. Heffernan

Swidler Berlin Shereff Friedman, LLP
Issues: FUE, TAX
Rep By: Keith N. Cole, Barry B. Direnfeld, Gary D. Slaiman, Michael E. Ward

Valis Associates
Issues: FUE
Rep By: Hon. Dan Schaefer, Hon. Richard T. Schulze, Todd Tolson, Wayne H. Valis

Renewable Natural Resources Foundation

5430 Grosvenor Ln.
Bethesda, MD 20814
Tel: (301)493-9101
Fax: (301)493-6148
Web: www.rnrf.org
E-mail: info@rnrf.org

A consortium of 14 professional, scientific and educational societies concerned about conserving and replenishing renewable natural resources.

Leg. Issues: AGR, CAW, ENV, MAR, NAT

In-house, DC-area Employees
DAY, Robert D.: Exec. Director

Renewable Resources LLC

Leg. Issues: FIN, NAT

Outside Counsel/Consultants
Arent Fox Kintner Plotkin & Kahn, PLLC
Issues: FIN, NAT
Rep By: Hon. John C. Culver, Alison Kutler, Michael T. McNamara

Reno & Cavanaugh, PLLC

1250 I St. NW
Suite 900
Washington, DC 20005
Tel: (202)783-2800
Fax: (202)783-0550
Registered: LDA
Web: www.renocavanaugh.com
E-mail: lreno@renocavanaugh.com
Leg. Issues: BUD, HOU

In-house, DC-area Employees
CAVANAUGH, Gordon: Of Counsel
GENO, Sharon: Associate
GLASHEEN, Megan: Member
MCGOVERN, Julie S.: Associate
RENO, Lee P.: Member

Outside Counsel/Consultants
Van Scoyoc Associates, Inc.
Issues: BUD, HOU
Rep By: Steve E. Crane, Kevin F. Kelly, H. Stewart Van Scoyoc

Reno, Nevada, City of

Leg. Issues: BUD, URB

Outside Counsel/Consultants
Carolyn C. Chaney & Associates
Issues: URB
Rep By: Carolyn C. Chaney, Christopher F. Giglio

Manatt, Phelps & Phillips, LLP
Issues: BUD
Rep By: Michael T. Brown, June L. DeHart

Reno/Sparks Indian Colony

Reno, NV

Outside Counsel/Consultants
George Waters Consulting Service
Rep By: George Waters

Renova Inc.

New York, NY
Leg. Issues: TRD

Outside Counsel/Consultants
The Carmen Group
Issues: TRD
Rep By: Gerald P. Carmen, Jack Stevens

Rent-a-Center, Inc.

Plano, TX
Leg. Issues: BAN, CSP

Outside Counsel/Consultants
Brownstein Hyatt & Farber, P.C.
Issues: CSP
Rep By: Michael B. Levy

Butera & Andrews
Issues: BAN
Rep By: Wright H. Andrews, Jr., James J. Butera

Royer & Babyak
Issues: BAN
Rep By: Robert Stewart Royer

Renton, Washington, City of

Renton, WA
Leg. Issues: BUD, ECN

Outside Counsel/Consultants
The Petrizzo Group, Inc.
Issues: BUD, ECN
Rep By: Kara Kennedy, Thomas "T.J." Petrizzo

Repeal PUHCA Now Coalition

801 Pennsylvania Ave. NW
Washington, DC 20004
Tel: (202)628-0886
Fax: (202)628-1038
Registered: LDA
E-mail: fwendorf@csw.com
Leg. Issues: BAN, ENG, UTI

In-house, DC-area Employees
MENEZES, Mark W.: Director

Outside Counsel/Consultants
Bill Carney & Co.
Issues: BAN, ENG
Rep By: Jacqueline Carney, Hon. William Carney

Thomas J. Dennis
Issues: UTI
Rep By: Thomas J. Dennis

Repeal the Tax on Talking Coalition

Washington, DC
Leg. Issues: TAX

Outside Counsel/Consultants
Ernst & Young LLP
Issues: TAX
Rep By: Lauren Darling, Patrick G. Heck, Phillip D. Moseley, John D. Porter, Henry C. Ruempler, Donna Steele-Flynn

Reporters Committee for Freedom of the Press

1815 N. Fort Myer Dr.
Suite 900
Arlington, VA 22209
Tel: (703)807-2100
Fax: (703)807-2109
Web: www.rcfp.org/rcfp/
E-mail: rcfp@rcfp.org

Formed in 1970 as a national organization to obtain legal assistance and other support for members of the news media profession and in defense of the principles of freedom of the press.

In-house, DC-area Employees
DALGLISH, Lucy A.: Exec. Director
LESLIE, Gregg: Director, Legal Defense

Reproductive Health Technologies Project

1818 N St. NW
Suite 450
Washington, DC 20036
Tel: (202)530-2900
Fax: (202)530-2901
Web: www.rhtp.org
E-mail: RHTP@basshowes.com
Leg. Issues: BUD, HCR, MED

Outside Counsel/Consultants
Bass and Howes, Inc.
Issues: BUD, HCR, MED
Rep By: Kirsten Moore

Republic Industries, Inc.

Ft. Lauderdale, FL
Leg. Issues: TAX

Outside Counsel/Consultants
Wilmer, Cutler & Pickering
Issues: TAX
Rep By: Terrill A. Hyde, William J. Wilkins

Republic Nat'l Bank of New York

New York, NY

Outside Counsel/Consultants
Rogers & Wells

Television Communicators
Rep By: Robert D. Wechter

Republic Properties Corp.

1280 Maryland Ave. SW
Suite 280
Washington, DC 20024
Tel: (202)863-0300
Fax: (202)863-4049
Leg. Issues: RES

In-house, DC-area Employees
GRIGG, Steven A.: President

Outside Counsel/Consultants
Kilpatrick Stockton LLP
Issues: RES
Rep By: J. Christopher Brady, Hon. Elliott H. Levitas

Republic Services, Inc.

Fort Lauderdale, FL
Leg. Issues: ENV

Outside Counsel/Consultants
Baker & Hostetler LLP
Issues: ENV

Republican Governors Ass'n

310 First St. SE
Washington, DC 20003
Tel: (202)863-8587

In-house, DC-area Employees
FEDEWA, Kirsten A.: Director, Communications

Republican Jewish Coalition

415 Second St. NE
Washington, DC 20002
Tel: (202)547-7701
Fax: (202)544-2434
Registered: LDA
Web: www.rjchq.org
E-mail: rjc@rjchq.org

Composed of leading Jewish Republicans; seeking to enhance ties between the American Jewish community and Republican decision-makers in Washington and around the country.

Leg. Issues: ECN, EDU, FOR, GOV, TAX

In-house, DC-area Employees
BROOKS, Matthew: Exec. Director
DAROFF, William C.: Director of Congressional Affairs

Republican Leadership Coalition

Washington, DC
Leg. Issues: INS

Outside Counsel/Consultants
Chesapeake Enterprises, Inc.
Issues: INS
Rep By: Scott W. Reed

Republican Leadership Council

3222 M St. NW
Suite 501
Washington, DC 20007
Tel: (202)547-1700
Fax: (202)298-8787
Web: www.rlcnet.org

A political action committee.

In-house, DC-area Employees
MILLER, Mark L.: Exec. Director

Republican Main Street Partnership

1350 I St. NW
Suite 560
Washington, DC 20003
Tel: (202)682-3143
Fax: (202)682-3149
Web: www.republicanmainstreet.org
E-mail: sarahJQA@mindspring.com

In-house, DC-area Employees
RESNICK, Sarah Chamberlain: Exec. Director

Outside Counsel/Consultants
The Greystone Group (VA)
Rep By: Hon. Steve Gunderson

Republican Nat'l Committee

310 First St. SE
Washington, DC 20003
Tel: (202)863-8500
Fax: (202)863-8820
Web: www.rnc.org

In-house, DC-area Employees
JOSEFIAK, Thomas: Chief Counsel
MCSHERRY, Michael T.: Director, Government Affairs
SHEA, Beverly: Finance Director

Outside Counsel/Consultants
Stevens Reed Curcio & Co.

Wirthlin Worldwide

Republican Nat'l Hispanic Assembly of the U.S.

600 Pennsylvania Ave. SE
Suite 300
Washington, DC 20003
Web: www.rnha.org
E-mail: info@rnha.org
Tel: (202)544-6700
Fax: (202)544-6869

A chartered allied organization of the Republican Nat'l Committee, the Assembly works to get Hispanic Americans more involved in the American political process and to enlist their support for the GOP.

In-house, DC-area Employees
METELKO, Marta R.: Exec. Director
RIVERA, Jose: Chairman

Republicans for Choice

2760 Eisenhower Ave.
Suite 260
Alexandria, VA 22314
Web: www.republicansforchoice.com
E-mail: gop4choice@erols.com
Tel: (703)960-9882
Fax: (703)960-9885

An abortion rights political action committee.

Leg. Issues: HCR

In-house, DC-area Employees
STONE, Ann E. W.: Chairman

Republicans for Clean Air

Dallas, TX
Leg. Issues: CAW, UTI

Outside Counsel/Consultants
The Velasquez Group
Issues: CAW, UTI
Rep By: Jay Velasquez

Research & Development Laboratories

Culver City, CA
Leg. Issues: DEF, SCI

Outside Counsel/Consultants
Parry, Romani, DeConcini & Symms
Issues: DEF, SCI
Rep By: Edward H. Baxter, Hon. Dennis DeConcini, John M. Haddow, Scott D. Hatch, Shannon Davis Henderson, Jack W. Martin, Romano Romani, Linda Arey Skladany, Hon. Steven D. Symms

Research 2 Prevention

Washington, DC
Leg. Issues: BUD

Outside Counsel/Consultants
Arent Fox Kintner Plotkin & Kahn, PLLC
Issues: BUD
Rep By: Douglas McCormack, Robert J. Waters

Research Corp. Technology

Tucson, AZ
Leg. Issues: CPT

Outside Counsel/Consultants
Parry, Romani, DeConcini & Symms
Issues: CPT
Rep By: Edward H. Baxter, Hon. Dennis DeConcini, John M. Haddow, Scott D. Hatch, Shannon Davis Henderson, Jack W. Martin, Romano Romani, Linda Arey Skladany, Hon. Steven D. Symms

Research Foundation of the City University of New York

New York, NY
Leg. Issues: BUD

Outside Counsel/Consultants
Cassidy & Associates, Inc.
Issues: BUD
Rep By: W. Campbell Kaufman, IV, Christopher Lamond, Michael Merola, Barbara Sutton

Research Institute for Small & Emerging Business, Inc.

722 12th St. NW
Washington, DC 20005
Web: www.riseb.org
E-mail: info@riseb.org
Tel: (202)628-8382
Fax: (202)628-8392

Provides research on issues of interest to small and emerging businesses.

Leg. Issues: SMB

In-house, DC-area Employees
CARRION, Ana: Communications and Public Affairs Counsel
SCHULTZ, Mark: President and Chief Exec. Officer

Research Planning, Inc.

6400 Arlington Blvd.
Suite 1100
Falls Church, VA 22042
Web: www.rpihq.com
Tel: (703)237-8061
Fax: (703)237-8085

A small, minority-owned, professional services company, providing services to Federal, State, and local government agencies and several commercial firms. Services include emergency management/disaster preparedness, consequence and crisis management, policy doctrine and procedures development, and others.

Leg. Issues: DIS

In-house, DC-area Employees
LYON, III, Charles H.: Exec. V. President and V. President, Business Development
MADURO, Sr., Reynaldo P.: President
PETERSON, Grant C.: Senior V. President, Operations

Outside Counsel/Consultants
Winston & Strawn
Issues: DIS
Rep By: Hon. James H. Burnley, IV, Charles L. Kinney, Hon. John L. Napier, Douglas C. Richardson

Research Soc. on Alcoholism

Austin, TX
Leg. Issues: ALC, BUD, MED, TOB

Outside Counsel/Consultants
Capitol Associates, Inc.
Issues: ALC, BUD, MED, TOB
Rep By: Sara Milo, Julie Shroyer

Reserve Officers Ass'n of the U.S.

One Constitution Ave. NE
Washington, DC 20002
Tel: (202)479-2200
Fax: (202)479-0416
Registered: LDA

Leg. Issues: DEF

In-house, DC-area Employees
ANDERSON, USA (Ret), Lt. Col. Stephen P.: Legislative Counsel
EDENS, USAR (Ret.), Col. Frank A.: Director, Army Affairs
GILSTAD, USAFR(Ret.), Col. Claire: Director, Air Force Affairs
SPIEGEL, Jayson L.: Exec. Director

Resilient Floor Covering Ass'n

401 E. Jefferson St.
Suite 102
Rockville, MD 20850-1714
Web: www.rfci.com
E-mail: info@rfci.com
Tel: (301)340-8580
Fax: (301)340-7283

In-house, DC-area Employees
WIEGAND, Douglas: Managing Director

RESNA

1700 N. Moore St.
Suite 1540
Arlington, VA 22209
Web: www.resna.org
E-mail: natloffice@resna.org
Tel: (703)524-6686
Fax: (703)524-6630

Formerly the Ass'n for the Advancement of Rehabilitation Technology. An interdisciplinary association for the advancement of rehabilitation and assistive technologies. RESNA's membership ranges from rehabilitation professionals to providers and consumers. All members are dedicated to promoting the exchange of ideas and information for the advancement of assistive technology.

In-house, DC-area Employees
PENCAK, Lawrence: Exec. Director

Resources and Instruction for Staff Excellence, Inc.

Cincinnati, OH
Leg. Issues: BUD, COM, CPI, EDU, HCR, SCI, TAX, TEC, WEL

Outside Counsel/Consultants
Mark R. Cannon
Issues: BUD, COM, CPI, EDU, HCR, SCI, TAX, TEC, WEL
Rep By: Mark R. Cannon

Resources for the Future

1616 P St. NW
Washington, DC 20036
Web: www.rff.org
Tel: (202)328-5000
Fax: (202)939-3460

A non-profit organization established in 1952 to do independent research and educational work in natural resources and environmental quality.

In-house, DC-area Employees
KRUPNICK, Allen: Director, Quality of the Environment Division
PORTNEY, Paul R.: President
TAYLOR, Michael: Director, Center for Risk Management
TOMAN, Mike: Director, Energy and Natural Resources Division

Resources Trucking Inc.

North Bergen, NJ

Outside Counsel/Consultants
Hill, Betts & Nash L.L.P.
Rep By: Brien E. Kehoe

Respiratory Medication Providers Coalition

Lexington, KY
Leg. Issues: MMM, PHA

Outside Counsel/Consultants
McDermott, Will and Emery
Issues: MMM, PHA
Rep By: Robert B. Nicholas, Michael A. Romansky, Eric P. Zimmerman

Respironics

Pittsburgh, PA
Leg. Issues: HCR, MMM

Outside Counsel/Consultants
Nusgart Consulting, LLC
Issues: HCR, MMM
Rep By: Marcia Nusgart
Reed, Smith, LLP
Issues: HCR, MMM
Rep By: Phillips S. Peter

Restore America's Estuaries

Arlington, VA
Leg. Issues: CAW, ENV

Outside Counsel/Consultants
Ball Janik, LLP
Issues: ENV
Rep By: Robert G. Hayes, Hal D. Hiemstra
Conservation Strategies, LLC
Issues: CAW, ENV

RESULTS

440 First St. NW
Suite 450
Washington, DC 20001
Web: www.resultsusa.org
E-mail: results@resultsusa.org
Tel: (202)783-7100
Fax: (202)783-2818
Registered: LDA

Internat'l citizens lobby with over 150 groups in six countries working to create the political will to end hunger and poverty.

In-house, DC-area Employees
CARTER, Joanne: Legislative Director
MCMULLEN, Lynn: Exec. Director

Retail, Wholesale and Department Store Workers Union

New York, NY

Outside Counsel/Consultants
The Kamber Group
Rep By: Gavin McDonald

Retailers Bakery Ass'n

14239 Park Center Dr.
Laurel, MD 20707
Web: www.rbanet.com
E-mail: rba@rbanet.com
Tel: (301)725-2149
Fax: (301)725-2187

Represents the interests of in-store and retail bakeries in America.

In-house, DC-area Employees
HOUSTLE, Peter M.: Exec. V. President

The Retired Enlisted Ass'n

909 N. Washington St.
Suite 301
Alexandria, VA 22314
Tel: (703)684-1981
Fax: (703)548-4876
Registered: LDA

Leg. Issues: CON, DEF, MMM, TAX, VET

In-house, DC-area Employees
GARRETT, Steven: Legislative Assistant
HOLLEMAN, Deirdre Park: Deputy Legislative Director
OLANOFF, Mark: Legislative Director

The Retired Officers Ass'n (TROA)

201 N. Washington St.
Alexandria, VA 22314
Tel: (800)245-8762
Fax: (703)838-8173
Registered: LDA
Web: www.troa.org
E-mail: troa@troa.org

An independent, non-profit service organization of 400,000 members, with more than 460 local chapters in the U.S. and abroad. Represents active, reserve and retired personnel on Capitol Hill, and provides numerous other member services (retirement information, advice and assistance and post-retirement job placement).

Leg. Issues: DEF, GOV, MMM, TAX, VET

In-house, DC-area Employees
GIAIMO, USAF (Ret.), Col. Christopher J.: Director, Chapter Affairs
HARRIS, USAF (Ret.), Col. Marvin J.: Director, Public Relations
NELSON, USAF (Ret), Lt. Gen. Michael A.: President
STRICKLAND, USMC (Ret.), Maj. Joseph: Director, Administration
STROBRIDGE, USAF (Ret.), Col. Steven P.: Director, Government Relations
WYLIE, USN (Ret.), Capt. Peter C.: General Counsel and Secretary

Retiree Benefits Alliance

McLean, VA
Leg. Issues: TAX

Outside Counsel/Consultants

Institutional Labor Advisors
Issues: TAX
Rep By: William B. Cowen, Merritt J. Green, Gregory J. Ossi, David S. Smith, Jan W. Sturner

Retirement Income Coalition

Washington, DC
Leg. Issues: RET, TAX

Outside Counsel/Consultants

Covington & Burling
Issues: RET, TAX
Rep By: Roderick A. DeArment, John M. Vine

Retirement Industry Trust Ass'n

4424 Montgomery Ave.
Suite 102
Bethesda, MD 20814
Tel: (301)652-5066
Fax: (301)913-9146
E-mail: obryonco@aol.com
Leg. Issues: FIN, RET, TAX

In-house, DC-area Employees
O'BRYON, David S.: Exec. Director

Outside Counsel/Consultants

O'Bryon & Co.
Issues: FIN, RET, TAX
Rep By: David S. O'Bryon

Retlif Testing Laboratory, Inc.

Ronkonkoma, NY
Leg. Issues: COM, CPI, DEF, LBR, TEC, TRD

Outside Counsel/Consultants

The M Companies
Issues: COM, CPI, DEF, LBR, TEC, TRD
Rep By: Milton M. Bush, J.D., CAE

Retractable Technologies, Inc.

Little Elm, TX
Leg. Issues: CSP, HCR, MED

Outside Counsel/Consultants

Patton Boggs, LLP
Issues: CSP, HCR, MED
Rep By: Karen L. Marangi, Andrew M. Rosenberg, Jonathan R. Yarowsky

Return to Work Coalition

Spokane, WA

Outside Counsel/Consultants

Fleishman-Hillard, Inc

Reusable Industrial Packaging Ass'n

8401 Corporate Dr.
Suite 450
Landover, MD 20785
Tel: (301)577-3786
Fax: (301)577-6476
Registered: LDA
Web: www.reusablepackaging.org
E-mail: prankin@igc.org

Represents those involved in collecting, reconditioning, and recycling steel, plastic and other containers. Formerly the Nat'l Barrel and Drum Ass'n.

Leg. Issues: BUD, ENV, TRA, WAS

In-house, DC-area Employees
RANKIN, Paul W.: President

Outside Counsel/Consultants

Swidler Berlin Shereff Friedman, LLP
Issues: BUD, ENV
Rep By: Keith N. Cole, Brian W. Fitzgerald

Reusable Pallet and Container Coalition

Leg. Issues: DEF, ENV, TAX

Outside Counsel/Consultants

Arter & Hadden
Issues: ENV, TAX

E. Del Smith and Co.
Issues: DEF, ENV, TAX
Rep By: Margaret Allen, E. Del Smith

Reuters America Inc.

1333 H St. NW
Washington, DC 20005
Tel: (202)898-8300
Fax: (202)898-8383
Registered: LDA
Leg. Issues: COM, CPT, FIN, TEC, TRD

In-house, DC-area Employees
RICH, Peter D.: V. President, Government Relations

Outside Counsel/Consultants

Public Strategies Washington, Inc.
Issues: COM
Rep By: Joseph P. O'Neill

Williams & Jensen, P.C.
Issues: TEC
Rep By: Bertram W. Carp, J. Steven Hart, Anthony J. Roda, Tracy D. Taylor

Rexall Sundown

Boca Raton, FL
Leg. Issues: ADV, FOO

Outside Counsel/Consultants

Parry, Romani, DeConcini & Symms
Issues: ADV, FOO
Rep By: Edward H. Baxter, Hon. Dennis DeConcini, John M. Haddow, Scott D. Hatch, Shannon Davis Henderson, Jack W. Martin, Romano Romani, Linda Arey Skladany, Hon. Steven D. Symms

R. J. Reynolds Tobacco Co.

1201 F St. NW
Suite 1000
Washington, DC 20004-1077
Tel: (202)626-7200
Fax: (202)626-7208
Registered: LDA
Headquartered in Winston-Salem, NC.

Leg. Issues: AGR, TAX, TOB, TRD

In-house, DC-area Employees
FISH, John H.: V. President, Federal Government Affairs
FOREMAN, Donald D.: Director, Federal Government Affairs
GOMEZ, Humberto: Manager, Federal Government Affairs
JONES, Murray W.: Director, Federal Government Affairs

Outside Counsel/Consultants

JFS Group, Ltd.
Issues: TAX, TOB
Rep By: Jake Seher

McGuiness & Holch
Issues: TOB
Rep By: Kevin S. McGuiness

Potomac Group
Issues: TAX, TOB
Rep By: Richard Y Hegg, Philip C. Karsting, G. Wayne Smith

Shaw Pittman
Issues: TOB
Rep By: Thomas J. Spulak

Stuntz, Davis & Staffier, P.C.
Issues: TOB
Rep By: Randall E. Davis

Washington Council Ernst & Young
Issues: TAX, TOB, TRD
Rep By: Doug Badger, Lauren Darling, John L. Doney, Jayne T. Fitzgerald, LaBrenda Garrett-Nelson, Gary J. Gasper, Bruce A. Gates, Nick Giordano, Cathy Koch, Robert J. Leonard, Richard Meltzer, Phillip D. Moseley, John D. Porter, Robert M. Rozen, Donna Steele-Flynn, Timothy J. Urban

Williams & Connolly
Issues: TOB
Rep By: Richard M. Cooper, Philip Sechler

RGK Foundation

Austin, TX

Outside Counsel/Consultants

F.B.A.
Rep By: J. R. Kirkland

Rheem Water Heaters

Montgomery, AL

Outside Counsel/Consultants

Interface Inc.
Rep By: Robert G. Williams

Rheinmetall AG

Outside Counsel/Consultants

Edelman Public Relations Worldwide
Rep By: Christine Kelly Cimko

Rhode Island Resource Recovery Center

Johnston, RI
Leg. Issues: ENV, WAS

Outside Counsel/Consultants

Capitol City Group
Issues: ENV, WAS
Rep By: Gerald T. Harrington, John J. Hogan, Thomas P. Hogan, Christopher P. Vitale

Rhode Island School of Design

Providence, RI
Leg. Issues: BUD

Outside Counsel/Consultants

Cassidy & Associates, Inc.
Issues: BUD
Rep By: John A. Crumbliss, Christopher Lamond, Jeffrey Lawrence, Barbara Sutton

Rhodia, Inc.

Cranbury, NJ
Leg. Issues: CHM, TRD

Outside Counsel/Consultants

Preston Gates Ellis & Rouvelas Meeds LLP
Issues: CHM, TRD
Rep By: Mark H. Ruge

Rhone-Polenc Inc.

Research Triangle Pk, NC
Leg. Issues: CHM

Outside Counsel/Consultants

The Direct Impact Co.

Multinat'l Government Services, Inc.
Issues: CHM
Rep By: Brooks J. Bowen, Chuck Fromm, William G. Kelly, Eric Stas, Jim J. Tozzi

Rhythms NetConnections

Denver, CO
Leg. Issues: TEC

Outside Counsel/Consultants

Blumenfeld & Cohen
Rep By: Christy C. Kunin

Brownstein Hyatt & Farber, P.C.
Issues: TEC
Rep By: William T. Brack, Michael B. Levy, Andrew Spielman

Edelman Public Relations Worldwide
Rep By: Eric Hoffman, Chuck Taylor

Janus-Merritt Strategies, L.L.C.
Issues: TEC
Rep By: Scott P. Hoffman, Mark J. Robertson, J. Daniel Walsh

Rialto, California, City of

Leg. Issues: URB

Outside Counsel/Consultants

David Turch & Associates
Issues: URB
Rep By: Kevin D. Bosch, Marilyn E. Campbell, Henry Gallagher, David N. M. Turch

Rice Belt Warehouses

El Campo, TX
Leg. Issues: AGR, TRD

Outside Counsel/Consultants

Meyers & Associates
Issues: AGR, TRD
Rep By: Fran Boyd, Larry D. Meyers, Richard L. Meyers

Richardson Lawrie Associates

London, UNITED KINGDOM

Outside Counsel/Consultants

Gryphon Internat'l
Rep By: William L. Hoffman

Richardson Savings and Loan Ass'n

Richardson, TX

Outside Counsel/Consultants

Elias, Matz, Tiernan and Herrick

Richemont Internat'l Ltd.
London, UNITED KINGDOM
Leg. Issues: CSP

Outside Counsel/Consultants

Kent & O'Connor, Inc.
Issues: CSP
Rep By: Patrick C. O'Connor

Richmond, Virginia, City of
Leg. Issues: CAW

Outside Counsel/Consultants

McGuireWoods L.L.P.
Issues: CAW
Rep By: Hana Brilliant, F. Paul Calamita, Stephen A. Katsurinis, Hon. Lewis F. Payne, Jr., Jeffrey L. Schlagenhauf

Rickenbacker Port Authority
Columbus, OH
Leg. Issues: TRA

Outside Counsel/Consultants

Winston & Strawn
Issues: TRA
Rep By: Hon. James H. Burnley, IV, Douglas C. Richardson, John A. Waits, II

Riddle Technology, Inc.
Dallas, TX

Outside Counsel/Consultants

R. Duffy Wall and Associates

Riggs Bank, N.A.
Leg. Issues: BAN

Outside Counsel/Consultants

Akin, Gump, Strauss, Hauer & Feld, L.L.P.
Issues: BAN
Rep By: Smith W. Davis, Ado A. Machida

RIM
Englewood, CO

Outside Counsel/Consultants

Ikon Public Affairs
Rep By: Dominic Del Papa

Rineco Chemical Industries
Benton, AR

A chemical engineering company.

Leg. Issues: CHM, ENG

Outside Counsel/Consultants

The Advocacy Group
Issues: CHM, ENG
Rep By: John M. Nugent, Jr., George A. Ramonas

Rio Grande Valley Chamber of Commerce
Corpus Christi, TX
Leg. Issues: ECN

Outside Counsel/Consultants

Meyers & Associates
Issues: ECN
Rep By: Larry D. Meyers, Richard L. Meyers

Rio Grande Valley Irrigation
Corpus Christi, TX
Leg. Issues: BUD, GOV

Outside Counsel/Consultants

Meyers & Associates
Issues: BUD, GOV
Rep By: Larry D. Meyers

Rio Grande Valley Sugar Growers
1301 Pennsylvania Ave. NW
Suite 401
Washington, DC 20004-1729
Tel: (202)785-4070
Fax: (202)659-8581
Registered: LDA
E-mail: aselltexas@aol.com

Works to educate members of Congress and staff regarding sugar farming and U.S. policies and regulations affecting sugar farmers.

Leg. Issues: AGR

In-house, DC-area Employees

FREEMYER, Windsor: Washington Representative
SELL, Alisa M.: Washington Representative
YANCEY, Dalton: Washington Representative

Rio Grande Water Conservation District
Alamosa, CO
Leg. Issues: CAW, NAT

Outside Counsel/Consultants

Kogovsek & Associates
Issues: CAW, NAT
Rep By: Christine Ann Arbogast, Hon. Raymond P. Kogovsek

RioPort, Inc.
San Jose, CA

Outside Counsel/Consultants

Drinker Biddle & Reath LLP
Rep By: M. Howard Morse, Michael J. Remington

Ripon Educational Fund
Washington, DC

Outside Counsel/Consultants

Bogart Associates Inc.

Ripon Society
501 Capitol Ct. NE
Suite 300
Washington, DC 20002
Tel: (202)546-1292
Fax: (202)547-6560
Web: www.riponsociety.org
E-mail: info@riponsoc.org

A mainstream Republican public policy organization founded in 1964. Publishes the Ripon Forum, a journal of national politics and policy.

In-house, DC-area Employees

FRENZEL, Hon. Bill: President
HARJU, Lori: Exec. Director
ROBERTS, Ashleigh: Director of Communications

Outside Counsel/Consultants

Bogart Associates Inc.
Rep By: Jennifer Bogart
Kessler & Associates Business Services, Inc.
Rep By: Richard S. Kessler

RISE (Responsible Industry for a Sound Environment)
1156 15th St. NW
Suite 400
Washington, DC 20005
Tel: (202)872-3860
Fax: (202)463-0474
Registered: LDA
Web: www.acpa.org/rise

An association affiliated with the American Crop Protection Ass'n representing manufacturers, suppliers, and distributors of non-agricultural urban use pesticides.

Leg. Issues: ENV

In-house, DC-area Employees

JAMES, Allen: President

Risk and Insurance Management Soc., Inc. (RIMS)
New York, NY
Registered: LDA
Leg. Issues: ENV, FIN, HCR, INS

Outside Counsel/Consultants

McIntyre Law Firm, PLLC
Issues: ENV, FIN, HCR, INS
Rep By: Chrys D. Lemon, James T. McIntyre

Rite Aid Corp.
Harrisburg, PA
Leg. Issues: HCR

Outside Counsel/Consultants

Verner, Liipfert, Bernhard, McPherson and Hand, Chartered
Issues: HCR
Rep By: Matthew C. Bernstein, Andrew D. Eskin, Rosemary B. Freeman, Vicki E. Hart, Philip R. Hochberg, Jenifer Martin, John A. Merrigan, Sara W. Morris, Steven R. Phillips, Lawrence R. Sidman, John H. Zentay

Riverdeep Inc.
Leg. Issues: BUD, EDU

Outside Counsel/Consultants

Johnston & Associates, LLC
Issues: BUD, EDU
Rep By: Alex Flint, Hon. J. Bennett Johnston, N. Hunter Johnston, W. Proctor Jones, Eric Tober

Riverside Community College
Riverside, CA

Outside Counsel/Consultants

Mark S. Israel

Riverside County Schools
Riverside, CA
Leg. Issues: EDU

Outside Counsel/Consultants

Washington Alliance Group, Inc.
Issues: EDU
Rep By: Bonnie Singer

Riverside County Transportation Commission
Riverside, CA
Leg. Issues: TRA

Outside Counsel/Consultants

Cliff Madison Government Relations, Inc.
Issues: TRA
David Turch & Associates
Rep By: Marilyn E. Campbell, David N. M. Turch

Riverside County, California, Flood Control and Water Conservation District
Riverside, CA
Leg. Issues: BUD

Outside Counsel/Consultants

The Carmen Group
Issues: BUD
Rep By: Mia O'Connell

Riverside Habitat Acquisition, County of
Riverside, CA

Outside Counsel/Consultants

Copeland, Lowery & Jacquez
Rep By: Hon. William D. Lowery, Jeffrey S. Shockey

Riverside Medical Center
Kankakee, IL

Outside Counsel/Consultants

Cassidy & Associates, Inc.

Riverside South Planning Corp.
New York, NY
Leg. Issues: ROD

Outside Counsel/Consultants

The Carmen Group
Issues: ROD
Rep By: John Lagomarcino

Riverside Unified School District
Riverside, CA

Outside Counsel/Consultants

Mark S. Israel

Riverside, California, City of
Leg. Issues: ANI, BUD, ECN, FAM, HCR, HOU, TRA

Outside Counsel/Consultants

Copeland, Lowery & Jacquez
Issues: ANI, BUD, ECN, FAM, HCR, HOU, TRA
Rep By: Lynnette C. Jacquez

Riverside, California, County of
Leg. Issues: GOV

Outside Counsel/Consultants

Honberger and Walters, Inc.
Issues: GOV
Rep By: Greg Campbell, Donald Gilchrest, Thomas P. Walters

Riviera Beach, Florida, City of
Leg. Issues: ENV, TRA

Outside Counsel/Consultants

Alcalde & Fay
Issues: ENV, TRA
Rep By: Hon. Louis A. "Skip" Bafalis, Shantrel Brown, Jim Davenport, Danielle McBeth

RJR Co.
Winston Salem, NC
Leg. Issues: TOB

Outside Counsel/Consultants

Barbour Griffith & Rogers, Inc.
Issues: TOB
Rep By: Haley Barbour, G. O. Lanny Griffith, Jr., Loren Monroe, Edward M. Rogers, Jr.
McGuiness & Holch
Issues: TOB
Rep By: Kevin S. McGuiness

RJR Nabisco Holdings Co.
New York, NY
Outside Counsel/Consultants
Akin, Gump, Strauss, Hauer & Feld, L.L.P.
McDermott, Will and Emery
Rep By: Calvin P. Johnson, Stephen E. Wells, Jane E. Wilson
Williams & Connolly
Rep By: Richard M. Cooper

RKO General, Inc.
New York, NY
Outside Counsel/Consultants
Wilmer, Cutler & Pickering

RMI Titanium Co.
Niles, OH
Outside Counsel/Consultants
Wilmer, Cutler & Pickering
Rep By: John D. Greenwald, Leonard M. Shambon

RMS Disease Management Inc.
McGraw Park, IL
Leg. Issues: MMM
Outside Counsel/Consultants
Baker & Hostetler LLP
Issues: MMM
Rep By: Frederick H. Graefe, Kathleen M. Kerrigan

The Road Information Program (TRIP)
1726 M St. NW
Suite 401
Washington, DC 20036
Web: www.tripnet.org
E-mail: trip@tripnet.org
Tel: (202)466-6706
Fax: (202)785-4722

A private, non-profit highway transportation research organization.

In-house, DC-area Employees
WILKINS, William M.: Exec. Director

Roaring Fork Railroad Holding Authority
Aspen, CO
Leg. Issues: BUD, TRA
Outside Counsel/Consultants
BKSH & Associates
Issues: BUD, TRA

Liz Robbins Associates
441 New Jersey Ave. SE
Washington, DC 20003
Tel: (202)544-6093
Fax: (202)544-1465
Registered: LDA
E-mail: liz@lizrobbins.com
Leg. Issues: TAX
In-house, DC-area Employees
DERR, Sallie: Chief of Staff
ROBBINS, Liz: President
Outside Counsel/Consultants
Deloitte & Touche LLP Nat'l Office - Washington
Issues: TAX
Rep By: Mark Garay, C. Clinton Stretch

Robbins-Gioia, Inc.
Alexandria, VA
Leg. Issues: DEF
Outside Counsel/Consultants
Wayne Arny & Assoc.
Issues: DEF
Rep By: Wayne Arny, David D. O'Brien
David O'Brien and Associates
Issues: DEF
Rep By: David D. O'Brien, Shannon L. Scott

Robert Wood Johnson Foundation
Leg. Issues: FAM, HCR, RET
Outside Counsel/Consultants
Barksdale Ballard & Co., Inc.
Issues: FAM, HCR, RET
Rep By: Nancy Reller
Garrett Yu Hussein LLC

Robertson Aviation
Tempe, AZ
Leg. Issues: DEF
Outside Counsel/Consultants
The Spectrum Group
Issues: DEF
Rep By: Lt. Gen. Augustus Cianciolo, USA (Ret.), Paul E. McManus, Gregory L. Sharp

Robinson Terminal
Alexandria, VA
Leg. Issues: ROD
Outside Counsel/Consultants
Winston & Strawn
Issues: ROD
Rep By: Hon. James H. Burnley, IV, Joseph E. O'Leary

Robotic Industries Ass'n
Ann Arbor, MI
Outside Counsel/Consultants
Webster, Chamberlain & Bean
Rep By: Alan P. Dye

Robur Corp.
Evansville, IN
A manufacturer of heating ventilation and air conditioning equipment.
Leg. Issues: ENG
Outside Counsel/Consultants
Cascade Associates
Issues: ENG
Rep By: Jennifer A. Schafer

ROCCO, Inc.
Harrisonburg, VA
A poultry producer.
Outside Counsel/Consultants
Troutman Sanders Mays & Valentine L.L.P.

Roche Diagnostics
Indianapolis, IN
Outside Counsel/Consultants
Baker & Daniels
Rep By: Mark W. Weller

Rochester Institute of Technology
Rochester, NY
Leg. Issues: BUD
Outside Counsel/Consultants
Cassidy & Associates, Inc.
Issues: BUD
Rep By: Shawn Edwards, Judith M. Jacobson, Dennis M. Kedzior, Jeffrey Lawrence, Scott D. MacConomy, Blenda Pinto-Riddick

Rock Creek Psychiatric Hospital
Lemont, IL
Outside Counsel/Consultants
Parry, Romani, DeConcini & Symms

Rock of Ages Corp.
Barre, VT
Outside Counsel/Consultants
Patton Boggs, LLP
Rep By: Henry Chajet, David J. Farber

Rock Point Community School
Rock Point, AZ
Outside Counsel/Consultants
Hobbs, Straus, Dean and Walker, LLP
Rep By: Carol L. Barbero, Karen J. Funk, Aura Kanegis

Rock-Tenn Co.
Norcross, GA
Leg. Issues: ADV, CAW, ENG, ENV, FUE, GOV, MAN, TAX, WAS
Outside Counsel/Consultants
Colling Swift & Hynes
Issues: ADV, CAW, ENG, ENV, FUE, GOV, MAN, TAX, WAS
Rep By: Terese Colling, Pablo Collins, Robert J. Hynes, Jr., Hon. Allan B. Swift

Rockdale, Georgia, County of, Board of Commissioners of
Conyers, GA
Leg. Issues: CAW
Outside Counsel/Consultants
Holland & Knight LLP
Issues: CAW
Rep By: Jack M. Burkman, Mike Galano, Richard M. Gold, David C. Whitestone

Rocket Development Co.
Los Alamos, CA
Leg. Issues: AER, SCI
Outside Counsel/Consultants
The Wexler Group
Issues: AER, SCI
Rep By: Peter T. Holran, Hon. Robert S. Walker

Rocking K Development
Tucson, AZ
Outside Counsel/Consultants
Crowell & Moring LLP
Rep By: Steven P. Quarles

Rockville Centre, New York, Village of
Leg. Issues: ENG, ENV, GOV, UTI
Outside Counsel/Consultants
Duncan, Weinberg, Genzer & Pembroke, P.C.
Issues: ENG, ENV, GOV, UTI
Rep By: Richmond F. Allan, Jeffrey C. Genzer, Thomas L. Rudebusch

Rockwell Collins
Commonwealth Towers
1300 Wilson Blvd., Suite 200
Arlington, VA 22209-2307
Web: www.rockwell.com
Tel: (703)516-8230
Fax: (703)516-8294
Registered: LDA

An electronic controls, communications and displays company headquartered in Cedar Rapids, IA. Involved globally in avionics and communications, for both military and commercial markets.

Leg. Issues: AER, AVI, BUD, CPT, CSP, DEF, ENV, HCR, IMM, LBR, MAN, TAX, TRD

Political Action Committee/s
Rockwell Internat'l Corp. Good Government Committee
Commonwealth Towers
1300 Wilson Blvd., Suite 200
Arlington, VA 22209-2307
Contact: John A. Gonzalez
Tel: (703)516-8228
Fax: (703)516-8295

In-house, DC-area Employees
COGDELL, Martha L.: Director, Federal and State Government Relations
EICKHOFF, Bruce: Director, Department of Defense Marketing
GONZALEZ, John A.: Director, Congressional Relations - Government Programs
MCDONALD, Michael K.: V. President, Government Operations (Rockwell Collins)
SADLER, Linda C.: Director, Governmental and Regulatory Affairs
Outside Counsel/Consultants
Howrey Simon Arnold & White
Rep By: John DeQ. Briggs, III

Rocky Research
Outside Counsel/Consultants
Columbus Public Affairs

Rodale Press
Emmaus, PA
Leg. Issues: AGR, ENV, FOO
Outside Counsel/Consultants
McMahon and Associates
Issues: AGR, ENV, FOO
Rep By: Joseph E. McMahon

Roecker Engineering Co.
Plymouth, WI
Leg. Issues: BUD
Outside Counsel/Consultants
RFB, Inc.
Issues: BUD
Rep By: Raymond F. Bragg

Roger Williams Medical Center
Providence, RI
Leg. Issues: HCR
Outside Counsel/Consultants
GPC Internat'l
Issues: HCR
Rep By: John D. Cahill, Daniel K. Crann

Rohm and Haas Co.

1300 Wilson Blvd.
Suite 1220
Arlington, VA 22209
Tel: (703)741-5880
Fax: (703)741-5884
Registered: LDA
E-mail: mahgbh@rohmaas.com

A chemical manufacturing company headquartered in Philadelphia, PA.

Leg. Issues: CAW, CHM, CPT, CSP, ENG, ENV, HCR, MAR, RRR, TAX, TRD, WAS

In-house, DC-area Employees
HURWITZ, Geoffrey B.: Director, Federal and State Government Relations
WILLIAMS, Robin L.: Director, State Government Relations

ROHO, Inc.

Belleville, IL
Leg. Issues: HCR, MMM

Outside Counsel/Consultants
Nusgart Consulting, LLC
Issues: HCR, MMM
Rep By: Marcia Nusgart

Roizman & Cos.

Norristown, PA
Leg. Issues: HOU

Outside Counsel/Consultants
Patton Boggs, LLP
Issues: HOU
Rep By: Thomas P. O'Donnell, Joseph Trapasso

ROLITE, Inc.

Wayne, PA

Outside Counsel/Consultants
Wiley, Rein & Fielding

Rollerblade, Inc.

Minneapolis, MN
Leg. Issues: TRD

Outside Counsel/Consultants
Powell, Goldstein, Frazer & Murphy LLP
Issues: TRD
Rep By: Michael E. Fine, Robert Torresen, Jr.

Rollins Hudig Hall

Chicago, IL
Insurance brokers.

Outside Counsel/Consultants
Baker & Hostetler LLP
Rep By: Matthew J. Dolan, Steven A. Lotterer, Hon. Guy Vander Jagt

Rolls-Royce North America Inc.

14850 Conference Center Dr.
Suite 100
Chantilly, VA 20151-3831
Tel: (703)834-1700
Fax: (703)621-4989
Registered: LDA
Web: www.rollsroyce.com
E-mail: barry.new@rollsroyce.com

A power systems company operating in aerospace and industrial power markets. Produces a broad range of aero engines powering aircraft and helicopters for both commercial and military applications. Also provides industrial equipment for power generation, transmission and distribution, oil and gas, marine propulsion and materials handling. Headquartered in Chantilly, VA.

Leg. Issues: AER, AVI, BUD, DEF, ENG, MAR

Political Action Committee/s
Rolls-Royce North America PAC
14850 Conference Center Dr.
Suite 100
Chantilly, VA 20151-3831
Tel: (703)621-2850
Fax: (703)621-4989
Contact: Barry New

In-house, DC-area Employees
MILES, R. Jeffrey: Director, Technology Programs
NEW, Barry: Senior V. President, Government Relations
WORLEY, Michael: Director, Marine Programs

Romanian Orphans Connection, Inc.

Alexandria, VA

Outside Counsel/Consultants
Dublin Castle Group
Rep By: Maureen Flatley Hogan

Romyr Associates

Toronto, CANADA
Leg. Issues: GOV, MIA

Outside Counsel/Consultants
EMI Associates, Ltd.
Issues: GOV, MIA
Rep By: Eugene M. Iwanciw

Ronald Reagan Internat'l Center

Outside Counsel/Consultants
Dittus Communications
Rep By: Roni Singleton, Tim Sites

Roof Coatings Manufacturers Ass'n

4041 Powder Mill Rd.
Suite 104
Calverton, MD 20705
Tel: (301)348-2003
Fax: (301)348-2020
Web: www.roofcoatings.org
E-mail: russsnyder@roofcoatings.org
Leg. Issues: CAW, ENV, GOV

In-house, DC-area Employees
SNYDER, Russell K.: Exec. V. President

Outside Counsel/Consultants
The Kellen Company
Rep By: Russell K. Snyder
Venable
Issues: CAW, ENV, GOV
Rep By: Brock R. Landry

Theodore Roosevelt Conservation Alliance

Missoula, MT

Outside Counsel/Consultants
Outdoor Media, Inc.
Rep By: Tim Richardson

Roosevelt County Rural Electric Cooperative

Portales, NM

Outside Counsel/Consultants
Duncan, Weinberg, Genzer & Pembroke, P.C.
Rep By: Robert Weinberg

Roquette America

Leg. Issues: AGR, RRR, TRA, TRU

Outside Counsel/Consultants
Stephens Law Offices
Issues: AGR, RRR, TRA, TRU
Rep By: J. Gordon "Skip" Stephens, Jr.

Rosebud Sioux Tribal Council

Rosebud, SD
Leg. Issues: IND

Outside Counsel/Consultants
Ducheneaux, Taylor & Associates, Inc.
Issues: IND
Rep By: Peter S. Taylor

Rosemount, Inc.

Eden Prairie, MN

Outside Counsel/Consultants
Zuckert, Scoutt and Rasenberger, L.L.P.
Rep By: Rachel B. Trinder

Rosenbaum Trust

Chicago, IL
Leg. Issues: EDU

Outside Counsel/Consultants
The Wexler Group
Issues: EDU
Rep By: Peter T. Holran, Christine Maroulis, Hon. Robert S. Walker

Roseville, California, City of

Leg. Issues: CAW, ECN, ENV, IND, LAW, NAT, RES, ROD, RRR, TRA, URB

Outside Counsel/Consultants
The Ferguson Group, LLC
Issues: CAW, ECN, ENV, IND, LAW, NAT, RES, ROD, RRR, TRA, URB
Rep By: Mike Miller

Roslyn Bancorp Inc.

Roslyn, NY
Leg. Issues: BAN

Outside Counsel/Consultants
Muldoon, Murphy & Faucette, LLP
Issues: BAN
Rep By: Joseph A. Muldoon, Sr.

Ross Abbott Laboratories

Columbus, OH
Leg. Issues: MMM

Outside Counsel/Consultants
Bass and Howes, Inc.
Issues: MMM
Rep By: Rachel Laser, Robyn Lipner

Ross Stores, Inc.

Newark, CA
Leg. Issues: CSP, LBR

Outside Counsel/Consultants
Navarro Legislative & Regulatory Affairs
Issues: CSP, LBR

Ross University School of Medicine in Dominica

Roseau, DOMINICA
Leg. Issues: EDU, MMM

Outside Counsel/Consultants
The MWW Group
Issues: EDU, MMM
Rep By: Tracey Becker, Dana P. Bostic, Davon Gray, Jonathan B. Slade

Ross/Nutrition Screening Initiative

Outside Counsel/Consultants
Greer, Margolis, Mitchell, Burns & Associates
Rep By: David E. Mitchell, David A. Smith

Rotary Foundation

Evanston, IL
Assists Rotary Clubs with their community service programs.

Leg. Issues: BUD

Outside Counsel/Consultants
Capitol Associates, Inc.
Issues: BUD
Rep By: Liz Gemski, Edward R. Long, Ph.D.

Rotary Internat'l

Evanston, IL

Outside Counsel/Consultants
McDermott, Will and Emery

Rotary Rocket Co.

Redwood City, CA
Leg. Issues: AER

Outside Counsel/Consultants
LunaCorp, Inc.
Issues: AER
Rep By: Victoria Beckner, David Gump

RoTech Medical Corp.

Orlando, FL
Leg. Issues: MMM

Outside Counsel/Consultants
Arnold & Porter
Issues: MMM
Rep By: Grant Bagley

Rough Rock Community School

Chinle, AZ

Outside Counsel/Consultants
Hobbs, Straus, Dean and Walker, LLP
Rep By: Carol L. Barbero, Karen J. Funk, Aura Kanegis

The Rouse Company

Columbia, MD
A real estate development company specializing in shopping centers and planned communities.

Leg. Issues: FIN, HOU, TAX

Outside Counsel/Consultants
McKay Walker
Issues: TAX
Rep By: Lynda K. Walker
The OB-C Group, LLC
Issues: FIN, HOU, TAX
Rep By: Thomas Keating, Kim F. McKernan, Charles J. Mellody, Patricia A. Nelson, Lawrence F. O'Brien, III, Linda E. Tarplin

Roussel-UCLAF

Paris, FRANCE

Outside Counsel/Consultants
ENVIRON

Rowan Companies, Inc.
Houston, TX
Leg. Issues: GOV

Outside Counsel/Consultants
Sher & Blackwell
Issues: GOV
Rep By: Earl W. Comstock, Jeffrey F. Lawrence, Jeffrey R. Pike

Rowe Signal Media
Atlanta, GA
Leg. Issues: COM, GOV, MIA

Outside Counsel/Consultants
Scott Cohen
Issues: COM, GOV, MIA
Rep By: Scott Cohen

Roxanne Laboratories, Inc.
Ridgefield, CT
Leg. Issues: MMM

Outside Counsel/Consultants
Arnold & Porter
Issues: MMM
Rep By: Grant Bagley, Martha L. Cochran

Royal Brunei Airways
Bandar Seri Begawan, BRUNEI DARUSSALAM

Outside Counsel/Consultants
Zuckert, Scoutt and Rasenberger, L.L.P.
Rep By: Malcolm L. Benge, Charles J. Simpson, Jr.

Royal Caribbean Cruises, Ltd.
Miami, FL

Outside Counsel/Consultants
Winthrop, Stimson, Putnam & Roberts
Rep By: Donald A. Carr

Royal Dutch Shell Group
Amsterdam, NETHERLANDS

Outside Counsel/Consultants
Rogers & Wells

The Royal Jordanian Airline
New York, NY

Outside Counsel/Consultants
Baker & Hostetler LLP
Rep By: Joanne Young

Royal Netherlands, Embassy of the
Washington, DC

Outside Counsel/Consultants
Hill and Knowlton, Inc.
Rep By: Gary G. Hymel

Royal Norwegian Consulate General - New York
New York, NY

Outside Counsel/Consultants
Burson-Marsteller

Royal Ordnance North America, Inc.
Kingsport, TN
Leg. Issues: BUD, DEF

Outside Counsel/Consultants
Fishbein Associates, Inc.
Issues: BUD, DEF

Royal Wine Co.
Brooklyn, NY
Leg. Issues: TRD

Outside Counsel/Consultants
Manatt, Phelps & Phillips, LLP
Issues: TRD
Rep By: June L. DeHart, Donald S. Stein

RPM, Inc.
Cleveland, OH
Leg. Issues: LAW

Outside Counsel/Consultants
Wise & Associates
Issues: LAW
Rep By: Joshua Rubin, Nicholas P. Wise

RSA Security Inc.
Bedford, MA

Outside Counsel/Consultants
Preston Gates Ellis & Rouvelas Meeds LLP
Rep By: Amy Carlson, Bruce J. Heiman

RSR Corp.
Dallas, TX
Leg. Issues: ENV, TRA, TRD, WAS

Outside Counsel/Consultants
John M. Stinson
Issues: ENV
Rep By: John M. Stinson
The Technical Group LLC
Issues: ENV, TRA, TRD, WAS
Rep By: Michele Anders, Thomas D. Ovenden

RTCA, Inc.
1140 Connecticut Ave. NW
Suite 1020
Washington, DC 20036
Web: www.rtca.org
E-mail: dwatrous@rtca.org
Tel: (202)833-9339
Fax: (202)833-9434

A private, not-for-profit organization that addresses requirements and technical concepts for aviation. Produces recommended standards for the application of electronics technology to these topics. The recommendations developed by RTCA are often used as the basis for U.S. and international aviation policy decisions as well as for business decisions.

In-house, DC-area Employees
WATROUS, David S.: President

RTK Corp.
New Providence, NJ

Outside Counsel/Consultants
Crowell & Moring LLP
Rep By: Dana C. Contratto

The Ruan Companies
Des Moines, IA
Leg. Issues: TRA

Outside Counsel/Consultants
Redfern Resources
Issues: TRA
Rep By: Ed Redfern

Ruan Leasing Co.
Des Moines, IA
A truck leasing company.
Leg. Issues: TRU

Outside Counsel/Consultants
Chadbourne and Parke LLP
Issues: TRU
Rep By: Keith Martin

Rubber and Plastic Footwear Manufacturers Ass'n
Stuart, FL
Leg. Issues: TRD

Outside Counsel/Consultants
Mitchell J. Cooper
Issues: TRD
Rep By: Mitchell J. Cooper

Rubber Manufacturers Ass'n
1400 K St. NW
Suite 900
Washington, DC 20005
Tel: (202)682-4800
Fax: (202)682-4854
Registered: LDA
Web: www.rma.org
E-mail: info@rma.org
Leg. Issues: CAW, ENV, LBR, MAN, ROD, TAX, TRA, TRD, WAS

In-house, DC-area Employees
NORBERG, Tracey: Director, Environmental Affairs
SERUMGARD, John: Exec. V. President
SHEA, Donald B.: President and Chief Exec. Officer
WILSON, Ann: V. President, Government Affairs

Outside Counsel/Consultants
Clark & Weinstock, Inc.
Issues: TRA
Rep By: Hon. Vic H. Fazio, Jr., Sandi Stuart, Anne Urban, Hon. John Vincent "Vin" Weber
Fierce and Isakowitz
Rep By: Donald L. Fierce
Fleishman-Hillard, Inc

Rubie's Costume Co., Inc.
Richmond Hill, NY
Leg. Issues: TRD

Outside Counsel/Consultants
Adduci, Mastriani & Schaumberg, L.L.P.
Issues: TRD
Rep By: V. James Adduci, II, Michael L. Doane

Ruby Memorial Hospital
Morgantown, WV
Leg. Issues: BUD

Outside Counsel/Consultants
Golin/Harris Internat'l
Issues: BUD
Rep By: Carol C. Mitchell

Francis R. Ruddy Institute of Maritime Communications
New York, NY

Outside Counsel/Consultants
Wiley, Rein & Fielding
Rep By: Mimi W. Dawson

Rural Advancement Foundation Internat'l - USA
Pittsboro, NC
Leg. Issues: AGR

Outside Counsel/Consultants
Etka Consulting
Issues: AGR
Rep By: Steven D. Etka

Rural Coalition
1411 K St. NW
Suite 901
Washington, DC 20005
Web: www.ruralco.org
E-mail: ruralco@ruralco.org
Tel: (202)628-7160
Fax: (202)628-7165

A national alliance of diverse, grassroots, community-based organizations committed to just and sustainable development of rural areas. Current work includes cooperative market development, agriculture policy and civil rights, electronic networking, and environmental health research partnerships.

In-house, DC-area Employees
PICCIANO, Lorette: Exec. Director

Rural Community Assistance Corp.
Sacramento, CA
Leg. Issues: ECN

Outside Counsel/Consultants
Robert A. Rapoza Associates
Issues: ECN
Rep By: Robert A. Rapoza

Rural Community Insurance Co.
Sioux Falls, SD
Leg. Issues: AGR, BUD

Outside Counsel/Consultants
Vickers and Vickers
Issues: AGR, BUD
Rep By: Linda Vickers

Rural Health Network Coalition

Outside Counsel/Consultants
McDermott, Will and Emery
Rep By: Wendy L. Krasner, Eric P. Zimmerman

Rural Hospital Coalition

Outside Counsel/Consultants
Greenberg Traurig, LLP

Rural Public Lands County Council
Provo, UT
Leg. Issues: NAT

Outside Counsel/Consultants

Robert K. Weidner
Issues: NAT
Rep By: Robert K. Weidner

Rural Referral Centers Coalition

Leg. Issues: MMM

Outside Counsel/Consultants

McDermott, Will and Emery
Issues: MMM
Rep By: Calvin P. Johnson, Wendy L. Krasner, Karen S. Sealander, Eric P. Zimmerman

Rural States Federal Transportation Policy Development Group

Outside Counsel/Consultants

John A. DeVierno
Rep By: John A. DeVierno

Rural Telephone Finance Cooperative

2201 Cooperative Way
Herndon, VA 20171
Tel: (703)709-6700
Fax: (703)709-6780
Registered: LDA

Leg. Issues: ECN, FIN, TEC

In-house, DC-area Employees

CAPTAIN, Brad L.: Legislative Representative

Rush Presbyterian-St. Luke's Medical Center

Chicago, IL
Leg. Issues: BUD

Outside Counsel/Consultants

Arthur E. Cameron
Rep By: Arthur E. Cameron, Sr.

Cassidy & Associates, Inc.
Issues: BUD
Rep By: Sonya C. Clay, Michele Gioffre, Hon. Martin A. Russo, Barbara Sutton, Maureen Walsh

Frank Russell Co.

Tacoma, WA
Leg. Issues: FIN, RET, TAX, TRD

Outside Counsel/Consultants

The Petrizzo Group, Inc.
Issues: FIN, RET, TAX, TRD
Rep By: Kara Kennedy, Thomas "T.J." Petrizzo

Russell Corp.

Outside Counsel/Consultants

Bradley Arant Rose & White LLP

Rutgers University

New Brunswick, NJ
Leg. Issues: BUD, EDU, NAT, TRA

Outside Counsel/Consultants

Cavarocchi Ruscio Dennis Associates
Issues: BUD, EDU
Rep By: Lyle B. Dennis

Lawler, Metzger & Milkman, LLC
Issues: NAT, TRA
Rep By: Sante J. Esposito, Gregory E. Lawler

Ruth's Chris Steak House

Metairie, LA

Outside Counsel/Consultants

Earle Palmer Brown Public Relations

J. T. Rutherford & Associates

46 S. Glebe Rd.
Suite 202
Arlington, VA 22204
Tel: (703)920-8001
Registered: LDA

Leg. Issues: HCR, TRD

In-house, DC-area Employees

LAVANTY, Deanna D.: Senior Associate, Government Relations
LAVANTY, Donald F.: President
RUTHERFORD, J. T.: Founder

Outside Counsel/Consultants

Cooney & Associates, Inc.
Issues: HCR
Rep By: Patrick J. Cooney

The Willard Group
Issues: HCR, TRD
Rep By: John M. Falk

Rwanda, Government of the Republic of

Kigali, RWANDA

Outside Counsel/Consultants

Washington World Group, Ltd.
Rep By: Edward J. von Kloberg, III

Rx Vitamins, Inc.

Larchmont, NY
Leg. Issues: HCR, MMM, PHA

Outside Counsel/Consultants

Emord & Associates, P.C.
Issues: HCR, MMM, PHA
Rep By: Jonathan W. Emord, Eleanor A. Kolton, Claudia A. Lewis-Eng

Ryder System, Inc.

1900 M St. NW
Suite 700
Washington, DC 20036
Tel: (202)463-7090
Fax: (202)463-1830
Registered: LDA

Headquartered in Miami, FL.

Leg. Issues: CSP, HCR, LBR, RET, TAX, TOR, TRA, TRU

Political Action Committee/s

Ryder Employees Political Action Committee
1900 M St. NW
Suite 700
Washington, DC 20036
Contact: Kelly Shultz
Tel: (202)463-7090
Fax: (202)463-1830

In-house, DC-area Employees

COX, Frances K.: Legislative Representative
RICKARD, Lisa A.: Senior V. President, Government Relations
SHULTZ, Kelly: PAC Administrator

Outside Counsel/Consultants

Akin, Gump, Strauss, Hauer & Feld, L.L.P.
Issues: CSP, HCR, TAX
Rep By: Smith W. Davis, Barney J. Skladany, Jr.

G.R. Services
Issues: TRU
Rep By: Earl Eisenhart

Peyser Associates, Inc.
Issues: TRA
Rep By: Becky B. Weber

Reed, Smith, LLP
Issues: TOR, TRA, TRU
Rep By: C. Stevens Seale

S & B Infrastructure, Inc.

Houston, TX
Leg. Issues: DEF

Outside Counsel/Consultants

Bergson & Co.
Issues: DEF
Rep By: Paul C. Bergson

S-Corporation Ass'n

1501 M St. NW
Suite 700
Washington, DC 20005
Tel: (202)463-4381
Fax: (202)463-4394
Registered: LDA

Association of companies organized under the subchapters of the internal revenue code.

Leg. Issues: SMB, TAX

In-house, DC-area Employees

MULDER, Steven J.: V. President and Legislative Director
SILVERMAN, Stephanie E.: President and Chief Exec. Officer

Outside Counsel/Consultants

Manatt, Phelps & Phillips, LLP
Issues: SMB, TAX
Rep By: Steven J. Mulder, Stephanie E. Silverman

S-PAC

Outside Counsel/Consultants

RTS Consulting

Valente Lopatin & Schulze
Rep By: Richard T. Schulze, Jr.

S-TEC Sentry

Mineral Wells, TX
Leg. Issues: DEF

Outside Counsel/Consultants

Peter J. Rose
Issues: DEF
Rep By: Peter J. Rose

SI Corp.

Atlanta, GA
Leg. Issues: CPI

Outside Counsel/Consultants

Hogan & Hartson L.L.P.
Issues: CPI
Rep By: Lance D. Bultena, C. Michael Gilliland, William S. Haft, William Michael House

Saab AB

Linkoping, SWEDEN
Leg. Issues: DEF

Outside Counsel/Consultants

American Defense Internat'l, Inc.
Issues: DEF
Rep By: Michael Herson, Van D. Hipp, Jr., Dave Wilberding

SABIC Americas, Inc.

Houston, TX
Leg. Issues: CHM, FUE, MAN, TRD

Outside Counsel/Consultants

Miller & Chevalier, Chartered
Issues: TRD
Rep By: Leonard Bickwit, Jr., Homer E. Moyer, Jr.

The Wigglesworth Co.
Issues: CHM, FUE, MAN, TRD
Rep By: Teresa N. Wigglesworth

Sabolich Research & Development

Leg. Issues: BUD

Outside Counsel/Consultants

Arent Fox Kintner Plotkin & Kahn, PLLC
Issues: BUD
Rep By: Kendra Dimond, Stacy Harbison, Douglas McCormack

Sabre Inc.

1101 17th St. NW
Suite 602
Washington, DC 20036
Web: www.sabre.com
Tel: (202)467-8203
Fax: (202)467-8204
Registered: LDA

Travel technology company headquartered in Fort Worth, TX.

Leg. Issues: AVI, CPI, CSP, EDU, GOV, IMM, LBR, SCI, TAX, TOU, TRA, TRD

Political Action Committee/s

Sabre PAC
1101 17th St. NW
Suite 602
Washington, DC 20036
Tel: (202)467-8203
Fax: (202)467-8204

In-house, DC-area Employees

CHARENDOFF, Bruce J.: Senior V. President, Government Affairs and Associate General Counsel
GOODELL, Jeffrey: V. President, Government Affairs

Outside Counsel/Consultants

Boesch & Co.
Issues: TOU
Rep By: Doyce A. Boesch

Washington Resource Associates
Issues: CPI, EDU, GOV, LBR, TAX, TOU, TRA, TRD
Rep By: Christopher T. Long

Winthrop, Stimson, Putnam & Roberts
Rep By: Kenneth P. Quinn

Sabreliner Corp.

St. Louis, MO
Leg. Issues: AVI, DEF

Outside Counsel/Consultants

Susan Davis Internat'l
Issues: AVI
Rep By: Susan A. Davis

Manatt, Phelps & Phillips, LLP
Issues: DEF
Rep By: Mary Ann Gilleece, Jeff Kuhnreich

The PMA Group
Issues: AVI, DEF
Rep By: Kaylene Green, Joseph Littleton, Paul J. Magliocchetti

Sac & Fox Nation

Stroud, OK

Outside Counsel/Consultants

SENSE, INC.
Rep By: C. Juliet Pittman

SACO Defense

Saca, ME
Leg. Issues: DEF

Outside Counsel/Consultants

The PMA Group
Issues: DEF
Rep By: Kaylene Green, Paul J. Magliocchetti, Charles Smith, Mark Waclawski

Sacramento Area Council of Governments

Sacramento, CA
Leg. Issues: BUD

Outside Counsel/Consultants

The Ferguson Group, LLC
Issues: BUD
Rep By: Mike Miller

Sacramento Area Flood Control Agency

Sacramento, CA
Leg. Issues: BUD, DIS

Outside Counsel/Consultants

Cassidy & Associates, Inc.
Issues: BUD, DIS
Rep By: John A. Crumbliss, John S. Doyle, Jr., Christy Carson Evans, Gabor J. Rozsa, Hon. Martin A. Russo

Sacramento Housing and Redeveloping Agency

Sacramento, CA
Leg. Issues: BUD, HOU, URB

Outside Counsel/Consultants

Simon and Co., Inc.
Issues: BUD, HOU, URB
Rep By: Heather Barber, Alex DeGood, Leonard S. Simon

Sacramento Municipal Utility District

Sacramento, CA — Registered: LDA
Leg. Issues: ENG, UTI

Outside Counsel/Consultants

Morgan Meguire, LLC
Issues: ENG
Rep By: Katie Parrott, C. Kyle Simpson, Deborah R. Sliz

Van Ness Feldman, P.C.
Issues: ENG, UTI
Rep By: Suzanne C. Bacon, Michael A. Swiger

Sacramento, California, City of

Leg. Issues: BUD, TRA

Outside Counsel/Consultants

Clark & Weinstock, Inc.
Rep By: Hon. Vic H. Fazio, Jr.

Smith Dawson & Andrews, Inc.
Issues: BUD, TRA
Rep By: Thomas C. Dawson, James P. Smith

Sacramento, California, Department of Utilities of

Leg. Issues: BUD, ENV

Outside Counsel/Consultants

ENS Resources, Inc.
Issues: BUD
Rep By: Eric Sapirstein

John Freshman Associates, Inc.
Issues: BUD, ENV
Rep By: John D. Freshman, Lawrence P. Kast, Catherine B. Kiefer

Sacramento, California, Public Works Agency of the County of

Sacramento, CA
Leg. Issues: BUD, CAW, NAT, TRA

Outside Counsel/Consultants

ENS Resources, Inc.
Issues: BUD, NAT, TRA
Rep By: Eric Sapirstein

The Ferguson Group, LLC
Issues: BUD, CAW
Rep By: W. Roger Gwinn

Sacred Heart University

Leg. Issues: EDU

Outside Counsel/Consultants

Golin/Harris Internat'l
Issues: EDU
Rep By: C. Michael Fulton

Saf T Hammer

Scottsdale, AZ
Leg. Issues: FIR, LAW

Outside Counsel/Consultants

The Hoffman Group
Issues: FIR, LAW
Rep By: Gail H. Hoffman

Saf T Lok, Inc.

Tequesta, FL
Leg. Issues: BUD, CSP, FIR, LAW

Outside Counsel/Consultants

Nixon Peabody LLP
Issues: BUD, CSP, FIR, LAW
Rep By: Richard P. Stanton

Safari Club Internat'l

441-E Carlisle Dr.
Herndon, VA 20170-4802
Tel: (703)709-2293
Fax: (703)709-2296
Registered: LDA
E-mail: staff@sci-dc.org

Political Action Committee address is that of Ron C. Marlenee, an independent consultant.

Leg. Issues: ANI, LAW, NAT, RES

Political Action Committee/s

Safari Club Internat'l Political Action Committee
10192B Ashbrooke Ct.
Oakton, VA 22124
Tel: (703)938-3797

In-house, DC-area Employees

HAMANN, Jennifer: Legislative Assistant
MARKS, Ph.D., Stuart: Senior Scientist

Outside Counsel/Consultants

Ron C. Marlenee
Issues: ANI, RES
Rep By: Hon. Ron C. Marlenee

Safe Energy Communication Council

1717 Massachusetts Ave. NW
Suite 106
Washington, DC 20036
Web: www.safeenergy.org
E-mail: safeenergy@erols.com
Tel: (202)483-8491
Fax: (202)234-9194

A coalition of national public interest, media, environmental and safe energy groups that educates the public and media. Provides local, state and national organizations with technical assistance through media skills training and outreach strategies.

Leg. Issues: ENG, ENV, MIA, WAS

In-house, DC-area Employees

DENMAN, Scott: Exec. Director
GUNTER, Linda: Communications Director
SHERRY, Chris: Research Director

Safe Environment of America

Ludlow, MA
Leg. Issues: CHM, DEF, ENV, WAS

Outside Counsel/Consultants

The Solomon Group, LLC
Issues: CHM, DEF, ENV, WAS
Rep By: David M. Lonie, Lara Roholt Westdorp, Hon. Gerald B. H. Solomon

SAFE Foundation - NMD Project

Leg. Issues: DEF

Outside Counsel/Consultants

Ogletree Governmental Affairs, Inc.
Issues: DEF
Rep By: Harold P. Coxson

Safegate Internat'l AB

West Chester, PA
Leg. Issues: AVI, TRA

Outside Counsel/Consultants

Thompson Coburn LLP
Issues: AVI, TRA
Rep By: Hon. R. Lawrence Coughlin

Safeguard America's Family Enterprises

Washington, DC
Leg. Issues: TAX

Outside Counsel/Consultants

Andrews Associates, Inc.
Issues: TAX
Rep By: Hon. Mark Andrews, Dr. Jacqueline Balk-Tusa

Safer Foundation

Chicago, IL
Leg. Issues: BUD

Outside Counsel/Consultants

Beacon Consulting Group, Inc.
Issues: BUD
Rep By: Gordon P. MacDougall, Julie Debolt Moeller, Lisa A. Stewart

Safetran Systems Corp.

Louisville, KY
Leg. Issues: TRA

Outside Counsel/Consultants

Arthur E. Cameron
Issues: TRA
Rep By: Arthur E. Cameron, Sr.

Safety Harbor, Florida, City of

Leg. Issues: ROD, TRA

Outside Counsel/Consultants

The Carter Group
Issues: ROD, TRA
Rep By: Michael R. Carter

Safety Reasearch Center, Inc.

6106 MacArthur Blvd.
Suite 110
Bethesda, MD 20816
E-mail: src@cais.com
Tel: (301)263-0585
Fax: (301)263-0587
Registered: LDA
Leg. Issues: TRD, TRU

In-house, DC-area Employees

MCMAHON, Anthony J.: President

Outside Counsel/Consultants

The Potomac Research Group LLC
Issues: TRD
Rep By: G. Harris Jordan, Paul Welles Orr

Safety Storage Inc.

Hollister, CA

Outside Counsel/Consultants

American Systems Internat'l Corp.
Rep By: Robert D. McVey, William H. Skipper, Jr.

Safety Warning System, L.C.

Englewood, FL
Leg. Issues: TRA

Outside Counsel/Consultants

Edmund C. Graber
Issues: TRA
Rep By: Edmund C. Graber

Safety-Centered Solutions, Inc.

Leg. Issues: HCR

Outside Counsel/Consultants

GPC Internat'l
Issues: HCR
Rep By: John D. Cahill, Michael Day

Safety-Kleen Corp.

Columbia, SC — Registered: LDA
Leg. Issues: FUE, WAS

Outside Counsel/Consultants

BKSH & Associates
Issues: FUE, WAS
Rep By: Karen Chiccehitto, Jerry Klepner, John Kyte, Rebecca Sczudlo

Interface Inc.
Rep By: David C. Knapp, Brian Walsh

Safeway, Inc.

Pleasanton, CA
Leg. Issues: TAX

Outside Counsel/Consultants

Miller & Chevalier, Chartered
Issues: TAX
Rep By: Leonard Bickwit, Jr.

SafeWorks, LLC

Tukwila, WA
Leg. Issues: ECN

Outside Counsel/Consultants

John C. Grzebien
Issues: ECN
Rep By: John C. Grzebien

SAFT America Inc.

Cockeysville, MD
A battery research and development firm.

Leg. Issues: AER, DEF

Outside Counsel/Consultants
The Potomac Advocates
Issues: AER, DEF
Rep By: Charles Scalera, Gary L. Sojka

SAFT R&D Center
Cockeysville, MD
Outside Counsel/Consultants
The Potomac Advocates
Rep By: Charles Scalera, Gary L. Sojka

Sage Broadcasting Corp./SBC Technologies, Inc.
Hartford, CT
Outside Counsel/Consultants
Kaye Scholer LLP

Sagem Morpho
Tacoma, WA
Leg. Issues: BUD, CIV, CPI, DEF, ENG, GOV, IMM, LAW, SCI
Outside Counsel/Consultants
Smith Alling Lane, P.S.
Issues: BUD, CIV, CPI, DEF, ENG, GOV, IMM, LAW, SCI
Rep By: Lisa Hurst, Robert Mack, Michael McAleenan, Timothy Schellberg

Saginaw Chippewa Indian Tribe of Michigan
Mount Pleasant, MI
Leg. Issues: IND
Outside Counsel/Consultants
Morriset, Schlosser, Ayer & Jozwiak
Issues: IND
Rep By: Fran Ayer, Jennifer P. Hughes

SAIC
Washington, DC
Outside Counsel/Consultants
John G. Campbell, Inc.
Cormac Group, LLP

Saint Coletta of Greater Washington, Inc.
Alexandria, VA
Leg. Issues: BUD
Outside Counsel/Consultants
Cassidy & Associates, Inc.
Issues: BUD
Rep By: Dennis M. Kedzior, Mary E. Shields, Rachel Sotsky

Saint Joseph's Health Center Foundation, Inc.
Syracuse, NY
Leg. Issues: BUD
Outside Counsel/Consultants
Cassidy & Associates, Inc.
Issues: BUD
Rep By: Arthur D. Mason, Laura A. Neal

Saint-Gobain Corp.
Valley Forge, PA
Outside Counsel/Consultants
Haake and Associates
Rep By: Timothy M. Haake, Nathan M. Olsen

Sakura Bank Ltd.
Tokyo, JAPAN
Outside Counsel/Consultants
Jones, Day, Reavis & Pogue
Rep By: Michael Bradfield

Salamanca, New York, City Board of Public Utilities of
Leg. Issues: ENG, GOV
Outside Counsel/Consultants
Duncan, Weinberg, Genzer & Pembroke, P.C.
Issues: ENG, GOV
Rep By: Jeffrey C. Genzer, Tatjana M. Shonkwiler

Salazar Associates Internat'l, Inc.
Denver, CO
Leg. Issues: ENG
Outside Counsel/Consultants
Murray, Scheer, Montgomery, Tapia & O'Donnell
Issues: ENG
Rep By: Raul R. Tapia

Salem Communications Corp.
Camarillo, CA
Leg. Issues: COM
Outside Counsel/Consultants
Alexander Strategy Group
Issues: COM
Gallant Co.
Rep By: Karl Gallant

Salem, Oregon, City of
Leg. Issues: BUD
Outside Counsel/Consultants
Will and Carlson, Inc.
Issues: BUD
Rep By: Robert P. Will

Salesian Missions of the Salesian Soc.
New Rochelle, NY
Outside Counsel/Consultants
Vorys, Sater, Seymour and Pease, LLP

Salinas, California, City of
Leg. Issues: BUD, HOU, LAW, ROD, TAX, TRA
Outside Counsel/Consultants
Murray, Scheer, Montgomery, Tapia & O'Donnell
Issues: BUD, HOU, LAW, ROD, TAX, TRA
Rep By: John R. O'Donnell

Sallie Mae, Inc.
901 E St. NW
Fourth Floor
Washington, DC 20004
Tel: (202)969-8000
Fax: (202)969-8031
Registered: LDA
Leg. Issues: BNK, BUD, EDU, TAX, TEC
Political Action Committee/s
Sallie Mae, Inc. PAC
901 E St. NW
Fourth Floor
Washington, DC 20004
Contact: Chris Martin
Tel: (202)969-8026
Fax: (202)969-8031
In-house, DC-area Employees
CLARK, Peggy A.: Director, Government and Industry Relations
CLAY, Angie: Senior Assistant, Government Relations
DAVIS, Sarah P.: Director, Government Relations
DINAPOLI, Rose: V. President, Government and Industry Relations
DUCICH, Sarah E.: Director, Government and Industry Relations
KELER, Marianne M.: Senior V. President and General Counsel
MARTIN, Chris: Senior Government Relations Assistant
Outside Counsel/Consultants
Clark & Weinstock, Inc.
Issues: EDU
Rep By: Ed Kutler, Deirdre Stach, Hon. John Vincent "Vin" Weber
Hohlt & Associates
Issues: BNK, BUD, EDU, TAX
Rep By: Richard F. Hohlt
Jolly/Rissler, Inc.
Issues: BUD, EDU
Rep By: Thomas R. Jolly, Patricia F. Rissler
Kessler & Associates Business Services, Inc.
Issues: BNK, EDU, TAX, TEC
Rep By: Michael L. Bartlett, Richard S. Kessler

Salt Institute
700 N. Fairfax St.
Suite 600
Alexandria, VA 22314-2040
Web: www.saltinstitute.org
E-mail: info@saltinstitute.org
Tel: (703)549-4648
Fax: (703)548-2194

A non-profit association representing North American salt producers promoting better understanding of all aspects of salt production and use.

Leg. Issues: CHM, ENV, FOO, HCR, ROD, TRA
In-house, DC-area Employees
BERTRAM, Bruce M.: Technical Director
BRISCOE, III, Andrew: Director, Public Policy
HANNEMAN, Richard L.: President

Salt Lake City Olympic Organizing Committee
Salt Lake City, UT
Leg. Issues: BUD, CAW, CDT, EDU, ENG, ENV, HCR, HOU, IMM, LAW, MON, SPO, TEC, TRA, TRD
Outside Counsel/Consultants
Cambridge Systematics, Inc
Issues: BUD, TRA
Rep By: Michael P. Huerta
Copeland, Lowery & Jacquez
Issues: BUD, CAW, CDT, EDU, ENG, HCR, HOU, IMM, TRA
Rep By: Jean Gingras Denton, Hon. William D. Lowery
King & Spalding
Issues: BUD, LAW, MON, SPO, TRA, TRD
Rep By: Theodore M. Hester, Allison Kassir, Lisa K. Norton, William C. Talmadge
Patton Boggs, LLP
Issues: BUD, ENV, HOU, LAW, MON, SPO, TEC, TRA
Rep By: Joseph Trapasso

Salt Lake City, Utah, City of
Leg. Issues: BUD, ECN, ENV, HOU, TRA, URB
Outside Counsel/Consultants
Simon and Co., Inc.
Issues: BUD, ECN, ENV, HOU, TRA, URB
Rep By: Heather Barber, Alex DeGood, Leonard S. Simon

Salt River Pima Maricopa Indian Community
Scottsdale, AZ
Leg. Issues: RES
Outside Counsel/Consultants
Birch, Horton, Bittner & Cherot
Issues: RES
Rep By: William P. Horn, Roy S. Jones, Jr.

Salt River Project
214 Massachusetts Ave. NE
Suite 310
Washington, DC 20002
Tel: (202)546-8940
Registered: LDA

Provides water to the owners and occupants of lands within the Salt River reclamation district and produces electricity for use within the region. Headquartered in Phoenix, AZ.

Leg. Issues: BUD, ENG, ENV, IND, NAT, TAX, TRA, UTI
In-house, DC-area Employees
EASTMAN, Renee: Federal Affairs Manager
Outside Counsel/Consultants
The Hawthorn Group, L.C.
Rep By: Robert Bonitati
Verner, Liipfert, Bernhard, McPherson and Hand, Chartered
Issues: ENG
Rep By: Clinton A. Vince

Saltchuk Resources, Inc.
1000 Potomac St. NW
5th Floor
Washington, DC 20007
E-mail: alan@saltchuk.com
Tel: (202)944-1890
Fax: (202)944-1892
Registered: LDA

A holding company for maritime businesses headquartered in Seattle, WA.

Leg. Issues: MAR
Political Action Committee/s
Saltchuk Resources
1000 Potomac St. NW
5th Floor
Washington, DC 20007
Contact: Alan A. Butchman
Tel: (202)944-1890
Fax: (202)944-1892
In-house, DC-area Employees
BUTCHMAN, Alan A.: V. President for Government Relations and PAC Treasurer

Salton, Inc.
Mt. Prospect, IL
Leg. Issues: CSP
Outside Counsel/Consultants
Arent Fox Kintner Plotkin & Kahn, PLLC
Issues: CSP
Rep By: Georgia C. Ravitz, Ivan J. Wasserman
Patton Boggs, LLP
Issues: CSP
Rep By: Jennifer Goldstein, Daniel A. Kracov, Brian C. Lopina, Paul Rubin

Salvation Army
615 Slaters Ln.
Alexandria, VA 22313
Tel: (703)684-5500
Fax: (703)684-3478
In-house, DC-area Employees
HOOD, Cpt. George: Director of Public Affairs
JONES, Lt. Col. Tom: National Community Relations and Development Secretary

Sam Houston University
Huntsville, TX
Leg. Issues: EDU

Outside Counsel/Consultants

The Advocacy Group
Issues: EDU
Rep By: Robert E. Mills

Sam Rayburn G&T Electric Cooperative, Inc.
Longview, TX
Leg. Issues: BUD, ENG, GOV, TAX, UTI

Outside Counsel/Consultants

Brickfield, Burchette, Ritts & Stone
Issues: BUD, ENG, GOV, TAX, UTI
Rep By: William H. Burchette, Colleen Newman, Christine C. Ryan

SAMA Group of Ass'ns
225 Reinekers Ln.
Suite 625
Alexandria, VA 22314-2875
Tel: (703)836-1360
Fax: (703)836-6644
Registered: LDA

In-house, DC-area Employees

DUFF, Michael J.: Exec. Director, Analytical & Life Science Systems Ass'n

Sammons Enterprises, Inc.
Dallas, TX

Outside Counsel/Consultants

Arter & Hadden
Rep By: Daniel L. Cohen, Hon. Thomas G. Loeffler, Jon W. Plebani

SAMPCO Companies
Pittsfield, MA
Leg. Issues: URB

Outside Counsel/Consultants

The Washington Group
Issues: URB
Rep By: Tripp Funderburk, Rita M. Lewis, G. John O'Hanlon, John D. Raffaelli, Mark Schnabel, Richard Sullivan, Fowler West

Samsung Corp.
Seoul, KOREA
Leg. Issues: TRD

Outside Counsel/Consultants

Akin, Gump, Strauss, Hauer & Feld, L.L.P.
Issues: TRD
Rep By: Frank J. Donatelli

Samsung Heavy Industries Co., Ltd.
Seoul, KOREA
Leg. Issues: DEF

Outside Counsel/Consultants

O'Melveny and Myers LLP
Issues: DEF
Rep By: Donald T. Bliss, William T. Coleman, Jr., Hwan Kim, Kelly J. Riordan

Rooney Group Internat'l, Inc.
Issues: DEF

San Antonio City Public Service
San Antonio, TX

Outside Counsel/Consultants

Snavely, King, Majoros, O'Connor and Lee, Inc.

San Antonio Water System
San Antonio, TX

Outside Counsel/Consultants

Bracewell & Patterson, L.L.P.

San Antonio, Texas, City of
Leg. Issues: BUD, DEF, GOV, TRD

Outside Counsel/Consultants

Akin, Gump, Strauss, Hauer & Feld, L.L.P.
Issues: BUD, DEF, TRD
Rep By: Jose H. Villarreal

Arter & Hadden
Issues: GOV
Rep By: Hon. Thomas G. Loeffler, Jon W. Plebani

Hawkins, Delafield & Wood

San Bernardino Airport Authority
San Bernardino, CA
Leg. Issues: AVI

Outside Counsel/Consultants

David Turch & Associates
Issues: AVI
Rep By: Marilyn E. Campbell, David N. M. Turch

San Bernardino Associated Governments
San Bernardino, CA
Leg. Issues: TRA

Outside Counsel/Consultants

David Turch & Associates
Issues: TRA
Rep By: Kevin D. Bosch, Marilyn E. Campbell, David N. M. Turch

San Bernardino County Social Services Department
San Bernardino, CA
Leg. Issues: WEL

Outside Counsel/Consultants

Craig Associates
Issues: WEL
Rep By: Patricia J. Craig, Kathryn Dyjak, Leslie Sacks Gross

San Bernardino Valley Municipal Water District
San Bernardino, CA
Leg. Issues: BUD, CAW, ENV, REL

Outside Counsel/Consultants

Copeland, Lowery & Jacquez
Issues: BUD, CAW
Rep By: Jeffrey S. Shockey

Bartley M. O'Hara
Issues: BUD, REL
Rep By: Bartley M. O'Hara

Patton Boggs, LLP
Issues: ENV
Rep By: Daniel R. Addison, Thomas C. Downs, Russell V. Randle

Washington Consulting Alliance, Inc.
Issues: CAW, ENV
Rep By: Thomas L. Burgum

San Bernardino, California, City of

Outside Counsel/Consultants

Patton Boggs, LLP
Rep By: Daniel R. Addison, Thomas C. Downs, Russell V. Randle

David Turch & Associates

San Bernardino, California, County of
San Bernadino, CA
Leg. Issues: BUD, FAM, GOV, WEL

Outside Counsel/Consultants

Craig Associates
Issues: BUD, FAM, WEL
Rep By: Patricia J. Craig, Kathryn Dyjak

David Turch & Associates
Issues: GOV
Rep By: Kevin D. Bosch, Marilyn E. Campbell, Henry Gallagher, Victor Tambone, David N. M. Turch

San Carlos Irrigation and Drainage District
Coolidge, AZ
Leg. Issues: GOV, NAT

Outside Counsel/Consultants

John J. Rhodes
Issues: GOV, NAT
Rep By: Hon. John J. Rhodes, III

San Diego Ass'n of Governments
San Diego, CA

An association of local government entitities.

Leg. Issues: TRA

Outside Counsel/Consultants

Copeland, Lowery & Jacquez
Issues: TRA
Rep By: Jean Gingras Denton, Hon. William D. Lowery

San Diego County Water Authority
San Diego, CA
Leg. Issues: ENV, NAT

Outside Counsel/Consultants

Carpi & Clay
Issues: ENV, NAT
Rep By: Kenneth A. Carpi

San Diego Hospice Corp.
San Diego, CA
Leg. Issues: HCR

Outside Counsel/Consultants

Foley & Lardner
Issues: HCR
Rep By: Theodore H. Bornstein

San Diego Metropolitan Transit Development Board
Leg. Issues: BUD, RRR, TRA

Outside Counsel/Consultants

Honberger and Walters, Inc.
Issues: BUD, RRR, TRA
Rep By: Donald Gilchrest, Thomas P. Walters

San Diego Natural History Museum
San Diego, CA
Leg. Issues: BUD, SCI

Outside Counsel/Consultants

Carpi & Clay
Issues: BUD, SCI
Rep By: Kenneth A. Carpi

San Diego State University Foundation
San Diego, CA
Leg. Issues: AGR, BUD, DEF, EDU, ENV

Outside Counsel/Consultants

Copeland, Lowery & Jacquez
Issues: AGR, BUD, DEF, EDU, ENV
Rep By: Jean Gingras Denton, Hon. William D. Lowery

San Diego, California, City of
Leg. Issues: AVI, BUD, CAW, ECN, EDU, ENV, HCR, HOU, IMM, LBR, NAT, ROD, TAX, TRA, URB

Outside Counsel/Consultants

Copeland, Lowery & Jacquez
Issues: BUD, CAW, ECN, EDU, ENV, HCR, HOU, IMM, LBR, NAT, ROD, TAX, TRA, URB
Rep By: Jean Gingras Denton, Hon. William D. Lowery

The Ferguson Group, LLC
Issues: AVI
Rep By: William Ferguson, Jr.

San Diego, California, County of
Leg. Issues: GOV

Outside Counsel/Consultants

Honberger and Walters, Inc.
Issues: GOV
Rep By: Greg Campbell, Donald Gilchrest, Thomas P. Walters

San Diego, University of
San Diego, CA

Outside Counsel/Consultants

Cassidy & Associates, Inc.
Rep By: Carl Franklin Godfrey, Jr., Valerie Rogers Osborne, Maureen Walsh, Gerald Felix Warburg

San Dieguito School Transportation Cooperative
Encinitas, CA
Leg. Issues: EDU

Outside Counsel/Consultants

Federal Management Strategies, Inc.
Issues: EDU
Rep By: Robert P. Canavan

San Elijo Joint Powers Authority
Carlsbad, CA
Leg. Issues: BUD

Outside Counsel/Consultants

The Furman Group
Issues: BUD
Rep By: Thomas M. James

San Felipe Pueblo

Outside Counsel/Consultants

Steptoe & Johnson LLP
Rep By: Thomas C. Collier, Jr.

San Francisco AIDS Foundation
San Francisco, CA
Leg. Issues: BUD, HCR

Outside Counsel/Consultants

The Sheridan Group
Issues: BUD, HCR
Rep By: Thomas F. Sheridan

San Francisco Bar Pilots Ass'n

San Francisco, CA
Leg. Issues: MAR

Outside Counsel/Consultants

PACE-CAPSTONE
Issues: MAR
Rep By: James W. Wise

San Francisco Internat'l Airport

San Francisco, CA
Leg. Issues: AVI, BUD

Outside Counsel/Consultants

Smith Dawson & Andrews, Inc.
Issues: AVI, BUD
Rep By: Gregory B. Andrews, Thomas C. Dawson

San Francisco Wholesale Produce Ass'n

San Francisco, CA
Leg. Issues: DEF

Outside Counsel/Consultants

Wayne Arny & Assoc.
Issues: DEF
Rep By: Wayne Arny, David D. O'Brien

San Francisco, California, City and County of

Leg. Issues: AVI, BAN, BUD, ECN, HCR, HOU, LBR, TAX, TOB, TRA, WEL

Outside Counsel/Consultants

Downey McGrath Group, Inc.
Rep By: Hon. Thomas J. Downey, Jr.

MARC Associates, Inc.
Issues: BAN, BUD, ECN, HCR, HOU, LBR, TAX, TOB, TRA, WEL
Rep By: Edwin Allen, Cliff Madison, Daniel C. Maldonado, Eve O'Toole, Ellen Riker

Miller & Van Eaton, P.L.L.C.
Rep By: Nicholas P. Miller

Morrison & Foerster LLP
Issues: AVI
Rep By: G. Brian Busey

San Francisco, City of

Leg. Issues: ECN

Outside Counsel/Consultants

Kutak Rock LLP
Issues: ECN
Rep By: Seth Kirshenberg, George R. Schlossberg, Barry P. Steinberg

San Gabriel Basin Water Quality Authority

Covina, CA
Leg. Issues: BUD, CAW, ENV

Outside Counsel/Consultants

Akin, Gump, Strauss, Hauer & Feld, L.L.P.
Issues: CAW, ENV
Rep By: Susan H. Lent, David Quigley

The Furman Group
Issues: BUD
Rep By: Thomas M. James

San Gabriel Valley Water Ass'n

Azusa, CA
Leg. Issues: ENV

Outside Counsel/Consultants

Hicks-Richardson Associates
Issues: ENV
Rep By: Fred B. Hicks

San Jacinto, California, City of

Outside Counsel/Consultants

Mark S. Israel

San Joaquin Area Flood Agency

Stockton, CA
Leg. Issues: ENV, GOV

Outside Counsel/Consultants

Peyser Associates, Inc.
Issues: ENV, GOV
Rep By: Thane Young

San Joaquin Council of Governments

Stockton, CA
Leg. Issues: RES, TRA

Outside Counsel/Consultants

Copeland, Lowery & Jacquez
Issues: RES, TRA
Rep By: Jeffrey S. Shockey

San Joaquin Regional Rail Commission

Stockton, CA
Leg. Issues: TRA

Outside Counsel/Consultants

Copeland, Lowery & Jacquez
Issues: TRA
Rep By: Jeffrey S. Shockey

Dawson Mathis & Associates
Issues: TRA
Rep By: Hon. M. Dawson Mathis

San Joaquin Regional Transit District

Stockton, CA
Leg. Issues: TRA

Outside Counsel/Consultants

Peyser Associates, Inc.
Issues: TRA
Rep By: Thane Young

San Joaquin River Exchange Contractors Water Authority

Los Banos, CA
Leg. Issues: BUD, ENV

Outside Counsel/Consultants

Schramm, Williams & Associates, Inc.
Issues: BUD, ENV
Rep By: Nancy Williams

San Joaquin Valley Wide Air Pollution Study Agency

Fresno, CA
Leg. Issues: CAW

Outside Counsel/Consultants

McGuiness Norris & Williams, LLP
Issues: CAW
Rep By: William N. LaForge, Monte B. Lake

San Joaquin, California, County of

Stockton, CA
Leg. Issues: GOV

Outside Counsel/Consultants

Honberger and Walters, Inc.
Issues: GOV
Rep By: Greg Campbell, Donald Gilchrest, Thomas P. Walters

San Jose, California, City of

Leg. Issues: BUD, ENV, HOU, LAW, ROD, TRA

Outside Counsel/Consultants

Murray, Scheer, Montgomery, Tapia & O'Donnell
Issues: BUD, ENV, HOU, LAW, ROD, TRA
Rep By: John H. Montgomery

Shaw Pittman
Rep By: Robert E. Cohn, J. E. Murdock, III

San Juan Pueblo

Outside Counsel/Consultants

Steptoe & Johnson LLP
Rep By: Thomas C. Collier, Jr.

San Juan, Puerto Rico, City of

Leg. Issues: TRA

Outside Counsel/Consultants

The Roth Group
Issues: TRA
Rep By: Hon. Toby Roth, Sr.

San Leandro, California, City of

Leg. Issues: AVI, BUD, DIS, POS

Outside Counsel/Consultants

Simon and Co., Inc.
Issues: AVI, BUD, DIS, POS
Rep By: Heather Barber, Alex DeGood, Leonard S. Simon

San Luis Obispo, California, County of

San Luis Obispo, CA
Leg. Issues: BUD

Outside Counsel/Consultants

The Ferguson Group, LLC
Issues: BUD
Rep By: W. Roger Gwinn

San Miguel Valley Corp.

Outside Counsel/Consultants

Troutman Sanders Mays & Valentine L.L.P.

San Pasqual Band of Mission Indians

Valley Center, CA
Leg. Issues: IND

Outside Counsel/Consultants

Hall, Estill, Hardwick, Gable, Golden & Nelson
Issues: IND
Rep By: Joseph R. Membrino

San Tomo Group

Sacramento, CA

Outside Counsel/Consultants

Olsson, Frank and Weeda, P.C.
Rep By: John W. Bode, Richard L. Frank, Susan P. Grymes, Karen Reis Harned, Stephen L. Lacey, Marshall L. Matz, Tyson Redpath, Ryan W. Stroschein

Sand County Foundation

Madison, WI
Leg. Issues: ENG

Outside Counsel/Consultants

Foley & Lardner
Issues: ENG
Rep By: Theodore H. Bornstein

Sand Creek Descendants Trust

Anadarko, OK
Leg. Issues: IND

Outside Counsel/Consultants

Arter & Hadden
Issues: IND

The "Sandbagger" Corp.

Wauconda, IL
Leg. Issues: DEF, DIS

Outside Counsel/Consultants

Donald E. Wilson Consulting
Issues: DEF, DIS
Rep By: Donald E. Wilson

Sandia Pueblo

Bernallilo, NM
Leg. Issues: BUD, GAM, IND, NAT, TAX, TOU

Outside Counsel/Consultants

The Smith-Free Group
Issues: BUD, GAM, IND, NAT, TAX, TOU
Rep By: James C. Free, W. Timothy Locke, Alicia W. Smith

Steptoe & Johnson LLP
Rep By: Thomas C. Collier, Jr.

Sandy City, Utah, City of

Sandy City, UT
Leg. Issues: BAN

Outside Counsel/Consultants

The Dutko Group, Inc.
Issues: BAN
Rep By: Arthur H. Silverman, William Simmons

SangStat Medical Corp.

Menlo Park, CA
Leg. Issues: HCR, SCI

Outside Counsel/Consultants

Venable
Issues: HCR, SCI
Rep By: David G. Adams

Sanko Fisheries LLC

Lynnwood, WA

Outside Counsel/Consultants

Sher & Blackwell

Santa Ana Pueblo

Santa Ana, CA
Leg. Issues: IND

Outside Counsel/Consultants

Nordhaus Haltom Taylor Taradash & Bladh LLP
Issues: IND
Rep By: Jill E. Grant

Steptoe & Johnson LLP
Rep By: Thomas C. Collier, Jr.

Santa Ana River Flood Protection Agency

Santa Ana, CA
Leg. Issues: BUD

Outside Counsel/Consultants

James F. McConnell
Issues: BUD
Rep By: James F. McConnell

Santa Ana, California, City of

Leg. Issues: BUD, ECN, IMM, LAW, LBR, TRA

Outside Counsel/Consultants

The Ferguson Group, LLC
Issues: BUD, ECN, IMM, LAW, LBR, TRA
Rep By: William Ferguson, Jr., Leslie Waters Mozingo

Santa Barbara Electric Transit Institute

Santa Barbara, CA
Leg. Issues: BUD, TRA

Outside Counsel/Consultants

Copeland, Lowery & Jacquez
Issues: BUD, TRA
Rep By: Lynnette C. Jacquez

Santa Barbara Metropolitan Transit District

Santa Barbara, CA
Leg. Issues: BUD, TRA

Outside Counsel/Consultants

Copeland, Lowery & Jacquez
Issues: BUD, TRA
Rep By: Lynnette C. Jacquez

Santa Barbara Regional Health Authority

Goleta, CA
Leg. Issues: HCR, MMM

Outside Counsel/Consultants

Susan J. White & Associates
Issues: HCR, MMM
Rep By: Susan J. White

Santa Barbara, California, City of (Waterfront)

Leg. Issues: BUD

Outside Counsel/Consultants

E. Del Smith and Co.
Issues: BUD
Rep By: Margaret Allen, E. Del Smith

Santa Barbara, California, Public Works Department

Leg. Issues: BUD

Outside Counsel/Consultants

E. Del Smith and Co.
Issues: BUD
Rep By: Margaret Allen, E. Del Smith

Santa Clara Pueblo

Santa Clara, CA

Outside Counsel/Consultants

Steptoe & Johnson LLP
Rep By: Thomas C. Collier, Jr.

Santa Clara Valley Transportation Authority

San Jose, CA
Leg. Issues: BUD, ROD, TAX, TRA

Outside Counsel/Consultants

BKSH & Associates
Issues: BUD, ROD, TAX, TRA

Santa Clara Valley Water District

San Jose, CA
Leg. Issues: BUD

Outside Counsel/Consultants

The Carmen Group
Issues: BUD
Rep By: Mia O'Connell

Santa Clara, California, County of

Leg. Issues: BUD, ENV, GOV, HCR, HOU, IMM, WEL

Outside Counsel/Consultants

BKSH & Associates
Issues: BUD, ENV, GOV, HCR, HOU, IMM, WEL

Santa Clara, California, Electric Department of the City of

Leg. Issues: COM, ENG, GOV, UTI

Outside Counsel/Consultants

Duncan, Weinberg, Genzer & Pembroke, P.C.
Issues: COM, ENG, GOV, UTI
Rep By: Wallace L. Duncan, James D. Pembroke, Michael R. Postar

Santa Clarita, California, City of

Leg. Issues: BUD, ENV, GOV, HOU, NAT, ROD, TAX, TEC, TRA

Outside Counsel/Consultants

Jamison and Sullivan, Inc.
Issues: GOV, NAT

Murray, Scheer, Montgomery, Tapia & O'Donnell
Issues: BUD, ENV, HOU, ROD, TAX, TEC, TRA
Rep By: John H. Montgomery, John R. O'Donnell

Santa Cruz County Regional Transportation Commission

Santa Cruz, CA
Leg. Issues: TRA

Outside Counsel/Consultants

Carolyn C. Chaney & Associates
Issues: TRA
Rep By: Carolyn C. Chaney, Christopher F. Giglio

Santa Cruz Metropolitan Transit District

Santa Cruz, CA
Leg. Issues: TRA

Outside Counsel/Consultants

Carolyn C. Chaney & Associates
Issues: TRA
Rep By: Carolyn C. Chaney, Christopher F. Giglio

Santa Cruz Redevelopment Agency

Santa Cruz, CA
Oversees redevelopment efforts for the city of Santa Cruz.

Leg. Issues: URB

Outside Counsel/Consultants

Carolyn C. Chaney & Associates
Issues: URB
Rep By: Carolyn C. Chaney, Christopher F. Giglio

Santa Cruz Water and Power Districts Ass'n

Outside Counsel/Consultants

Strategic Impact, Inc.
Rep By: Michael C. Jimenez

Santa Cruz, California, County of

Leg. Issues: DIS

Outside Counsel/Consultants

Carolyn C. Chaney & Associates
Issues: DIS
Rep By: Carolyn C. Chaney, Christopher F. Giglio

Santa Cruz, California, Port of

Leg. Issues: BUD

Outside Counsel/Consultants

E. Del Smith and Co.
Issues: BUD
Rep By: Margaret Allen, E. Del Smith

Santa Fe Natural Tobacco Co.

Santa Fe, NM

Outside Counsel/Consultants

Long, Aldridge & Norman, LLP
Rep By: C. Randall Nuckolls

Santa Fe, New Mexico, County of

Santa Fe, NM
Leg. Issues: BUD, ENV, GOV

Outside Counsel/Consultants

Patrick M. Murphy & Associates
Issues: GOV
Rep By: Patrick M. Murphy

O'Connor & Hannan, L.L.P.
Issues: BUD, ENV
Rep By: Timothy W. Jenkins

Santa Monica, California, City of

Leg. Issues: BUD, TRA

Outside Counsel/Consultants

The Ferguson Group, LLC
Issues: BUD, TRA
Rep By: W. Roger Gwinn, Ralph Webb

Santa Rosa Memorial Hospital

Santa Rosa, CA
Leg. Issues: BUD, DIS, ECN, HCR, TEC

Outside Counsel/Consultants

Cassidy & Associates, Inc.
Issues: BUD, DIS, ECN, HCR, TEC
Rep By: Marie James, Valerie Rogers Osborne, Maureen Walsh, Gerald Felix Warburg

Santee Cooper (South Carolina Public Service Authority)

Monks Corner, SC

Outside Counsel/Consultants

Timothy X. Moore and Co.
Rep By: Timothy X. Moore

The Sanwa Bank , Ltd.

Tokyo, JAPAN
Leg. Issues: BAN

Outside Counsel/Consultants

Civic Service, Inc.
Issues: BAN
Rep By: Roy Pfautch, Michael W. Schick

Sanyo North American Corp.

New York, NY
Leg. Issues: CPT

Outside Counsel/Consultants

Patton Boggs, LLP
Issues: CPT
Rep By: Thomas Hale Boggs, Jr., Brian C. Lopina, Jeffrey L. Turner

SAP Public Services

Ronald Reagan Bldg.
Gray Tower
1300 Pennsylvania Ave. NW, Suite 500
Washington, DC 20004
Tel: (202)312-3500
Fax: (202)312-3501
Registered: LDA

A manufacturer of enterprise software.

Leg. Issues: CPI, CPT, DEF, GOV, IMM, SCI, TAX, TRD

In-house, DC-area Employees

CARSON, John: V. President, Federal Business Development
WERNER, Ulrich: V. President, Government Relations

Sappi Fine Paper NA

Boston, MA
Leg. Issues: CAW, ENV, LBR, MAN, NAT, TAX, TRA, TRD, WAS

Outside Counsel/Consultants

Smith & Harroff, Inc.
Issues: CAW, ENV, LBR, MAN, NAT, TAX, TRA, TRD, WAS
Rep By: Luke Popovich

Sara Lee Corp.

Chicago, IL
Leg. Issues: TAX

Outside Counsel/Consultants

BSMG Worldwide

The Duberstein Group, Inc.
Rep By: John W. Angus, III, Michael S. Berman, Steven M. Champlin, Kenneth M. Duberstein, Henry M. Gandy, Daniel P. Meyer

Kirkland & Ellis
Issues: TAX
Rep By: William S. Singer

KPMG, LLP
Issues: TAX
Rep By: Gail Galvan, Harry L. Gutman, Thomas A. Stout, Jr.

Skadden, Arps, Slate, Meagher & Flom LLP
Rep By: Robert E. Lighthizer

Sarasota, Florida, City of

Leg. Issues: BUD, CAW, NAT

Outside Counsel/Consultants

Holland & Knight LLP
Issues: CAW
Rep By: Jack M. Burkman, Richard M. Gold

Marlowe and Co.
Issues: BUD, NAT
Rep By: Howard Marlowe, Jeffrey Mazzella

Sarasota, Florida, County of

Leg. Issues: CAW

Outside Counsel/Consultants

Holland & Knight LLP
Issues: CAW
Rep By: Jack M. Burkman, Richard M. Gold, David C. Whitestone

Sargeant Marine, Inc.

Boca Raton, FL
Leg. Issues: MAR

Outside Counsel/Consultants

Sher & Blackwell
Issues: MAR
Rep By: Robert J. Blackwell, Sr., Earl W. Comstock, Jeffrey R. Pike, Antilla E. Trotter, III

Winthrop, Stimson, Putnam & Roberts
Rep By: William H. Espinosa

Sarnoff Corp.

Rosslyn, VA
Leg. Issues: DEF

Outside Counsel/Consultants

American Defense Internat'l, Inc.
Rep By: Michael Herson, Van D. Hipp, Jr., Dave Wilberding

Ervin Technical Associates, Inc. (ETA)
Issues: DEF
Rep By: William J. Andahazy, Hon. Jack Edwards, James L. Ervin

Potomac Strategies & Analysis, Inc.
Issues: DEF
Rep By: Peter C. Oleson

Verner, Liipfert, Bernhard, McPherson and Hand, Chartered
Issues: DEF
Rep By: Denis J. Dwyer, Lloyd N. Hand, Lawrence R. Sidman

SAT

San Diego, CA
Leg. Issues: DEF

Outside Counsel/Consultants

Alvarado & Gerken
Issues: DEF
Rep By: Susan E. Alvarado

SISCORP
Issues: DEF
Rep By: Donald F. Massey

SatCon Technology Corp.

Cambridge, MA
Leg. Issues: AUT, GOV

Outside Counsel/Consultants

Hale and Dorr LLP
Issues: AUT, GOV
Rep By: Jay P. Urwitz

Satellite Broadcasting and Communications Ass'n

225 Reinekers Ln.
Suite 600
Alexandria, VA 22314
Tel: (703)549-6990
Fax: (703)549-7640
Registered: LDA
Web: www.sbca.com
E-mail: info@sbca.org

Represents all segments of the satellite television industry. Committed to expanding the use of satellite technology for the delivery of video and broadband services.

Leg. Issues: CPT, TEC

Political Action Committee/s

Link-PAC
225 Reinekers Ln.
Suite 600
Alexandria, VA 22314
Contact: Andrew R. Paul
Tel: (703)549-6990
Fax: (703)549-7640

In-house, DC-area Employees

HEWITT, Charles C.: President
PAUL, Andrew R.: Senior V. President
WRIGHT, Andy: V. President, Government Affairs

Outside Counsel/Consultants

The Dutko Group, Inc.
Issues: CPT, TEC
Rep By: Kim Koontz Bayliss, Steve Perry, Juliette M. Raffensperger, Stephen Craig Sayle

SatoTravel

Leg. Issues: DEF

Outside Counsel/Consultants

The PMA Group
Issues: DEF
Rep By: Daniel Cunningham, Kaylene Green, Paul J. Magliocchetti, Mark Waclawski

Saudi Arabia, Government of

Riyadh, SAUDI ARABIA

Outside Counsel/Consultants

Akin, Gump, Strauss, Hauer & Feld, L.L.P.
Rep By: Richard B. Self, S. Bruce Wilson

Saudi Arabia, Ministry of Commerce

Riyadh, SAUDI ARABIA

Outside Counsel/Consultants

Akin, Gump, Strauss, Hauer & Feld, L.L.P.

Saudi Arabia, Royal Embassy of

601 New Hampshire Ave. NW
Washington, DC 20037
Tel: (202)342-3800
Fax: (202)337-3233
Web: www.saudiembassy.net
E-mail: info@saudiembassy.net

Outside Counsel/Consultants

Cassidy & Associates, Inc.
Rep By: Gerald S. J. Cassidy, Lawrence C. Grossman, Arthur D. Mason, Dan C. Tate, Sr., Gerald Felix Warburg

Dutton and Dutton, P.C.
Rep By: Frederick G. Dutton

Institutional Development Associates
Rep By: John A. Lucas, Jr.

Powell Tate
Rep By: Daniel L. Casey, Michael Gelb, Kathryn Waters Gest, Katherine C. Kolstad, Andrew Clark Miller, Jody Powell, Sheila B. Tate

Rhoads Group

Sault Ste. Marie Tribe of Chippewa Indians

Sault Ste. Marie, MI
Leg. Issues: BUD, GAM, IND

Outside Counsel/Consultants

Ryan, Phillips, Utrecht & MacKinnon
Issues: BUD, GAM, IND
Rep By: Rodney Hoppe, James C. Lamb, William D. Phillips, Mark D. Planning, Thomas M. Ryan, Joseph V. Vasapoli

Sault Ste. Marie, Michigan, City of

Outside Counsel/Consultants

Sonosky, Chambers, Sachse & Endreson
Rep By: William R. Perry

Savannah Airport Commission

Savannah, GA
Leg. Issues: AVI, DEF

Outside Counsel/Consultants

Hurt, Norton & Associates
Issues: AVI, DEF
Rep By: Robert H. Hurt, Frank Norton

Save America's Forests, Inc.

Four Library Ct. SE
Washington, DC 20003
Tel: (202)544-9219
Fax: (202)544-7462
Registered: LDA
Web: www.saveamericasforests.org
Leg. Issues: ENV

In-house, DC-area Employees

ROSS, Carl: Director

Outside Counsel/Consultants

Holland & Knight LLP
Issues: ENV
Rep By: Hon. Gerald E. Sikorski

Save America's Fossils for Everyone, Inc.

Dallas, TX
Leg. Issues: ENV, NAT

Outside Counsel/Consultants

Jan Campbell
Issues: ENV, NAT
Rep By: Jan Campbell

Save Barton Creek

Leg. Issues: ENV

Outside Counsel/Consultants

Patton Boggs, LLP
Issues: ENV
Rep By: Parker Brugge, John J. Deschauer, Jr., Thomas C. Downs, Michael J. Driver, Benjamin L. Ginsberg, John C. Martin, Carolina L. Mederos, Anne Miano, James A. Reeder, Paul A. J. Wilson

Save the Bay

Providence, RI

Concerned with the protection and preservation of Narragansett Bay.

Leg. Issues: ENV

Outside Counsel/Consultants

John C. Grzebien
Issues: ENV
Rep By: John C. Grzebien

Save the Greenback Coalition

Washington, DC
Leg. Issues: MON

Outside Counsel/Consultants

Foley & Lardner
Issues: MON
Rep By: Jerris Leonard, Russell Wapensky

Wells & Associates
Issues: MON
Rep By: Milton T. Wells

SAVI Technology

Sunnyvale, CA
Leg. Issues: DEF

Outside Counsel/Consultants

W. B. Driggers & Associates, Inc.
Issues: DEF
Rep By: W. B. Driggers

Savings Banks Life Insurance Fund

New York, NY
Leg. Issues: BAN, TAX

Outside Counsel/Consultants

Butera & Andrews
Issues: BAN, TAX
Rep By: Cliff W. Andrews, Wright H. Andrews, Jr., James J. Butera, Frank Tillotson

Savings Coalition of America

1300 Pennsylvania Ave. NW
Suite 700
Washington, DC 20024
Tel: (202)204-3004
Fax: (202)204-3026
Registered: LDA
Web: www.savingscoalition.org
E-mail: khamor@savingscoalition.org
Leg. Issues: TAX

In-house, DC-area Employees

HAMOR, Kathy V.: Exec. Director

SBC Communications Inc.

1401 I St. NW
Suite 1100
Washington, DC 20005
Tel: (202)326-8800
Fax: (202)408-4808
Registered: LDA
Web: www.sbc.com

The parent corporation of Southwestern Bell Telephone Co. Acquired Ameritech in 1999. Headquartered in San Antonio, TX.

Leg. Issues: COM, CPI, CPT, GOV, HCR, LAW, LBR, TAX, TEC, UTI

In-house, DC-area Employees

CONLEY, Karyne: Director, Federal Relations
DONOHO, Wendy L.: Exec. Director, Federal Relations
FINE, David: Assistant V. President, Government and International Relations
HEBERLEE, Brent: Exec. Director, Federal Relations
HILL-ARDOIN, Priscilla: Senior V. President-FCC
HOGAN, Gerald F.: Exec. Director, Federal Relations
LEATHERWOOD, Gloria Delgado: Exec. Director, National Constituency Relations
MCDOWELL, Marian E.: Director, Federal Relations
MCGIVERN, Timothy: Exec. Director, Federal Relations
MCKONE, Timothy P.: V. President, Congressional Affairs
SCOTT, Roxanne L.: Manager, Federal Relations
SMITH, Rodney A.: Exec. Director, Federal Relations

Outside Counsel/Consultants

Arter & Hadden
Rep By: Daniel L. Cohen, Hon. Thomas G. Loeffler, Jon W. Plebani

Chesapeake Enterprises, Inc.
Rep By: Scott W. Reed

Davis Manafort, Inc.
Issues: COM, TEC
Rep By: Richard H. Davis

Dewey Ballantine LLP
Rep By: David Leach

Fleischman and Walsh, L.L.P.
Rep By: Louis H. Dupart, Krista Stark, John Wyma

Fleishman-Hillard, Inc
Issues: TEC
Rep By: Paul W. Johnson, Frank Kauffman, Michael Mandigo

Global USA, Inc.
Issues: TEC
Rep By: Rosamond S. Brown, Dr. Bohdan Denysyk, George S. Kopp, Lottie H. Shackelford

Susan Molinari, L.L.P.
Rep By: Hon. Susan Molinari

The Kate Moss Company
Issues: TEC
Rep By: Kate Moss

Parry, Romani, DeConcini & Symms
Issues: LBR, TEC
Rep By: Edward H. Baxter, Hon. Dennis DeConcini, John M. Haddow, Scott D. Hatch, Shannon Davis Henderson, Jack W. Martin, Romano Romani, Linda Arey Skladany, Hon. Steven D. Symms

Paul, Hastings, Janofsky & Walker LLP
Issues: TEC
Rep By: Ralph B. Everett

Quinn Gillespie & Associates
Rep By: Edward W. Gillespie

Skadden, Arps, Slate, Meagher & Flom LLP
Rep By: Ivan A. Schlager

Tongour Simpson Holsclaw Green
Issues: TEC
Rep By: James F. Green, Michael A. Tongour

Twenty-First Century Group
Issues: TEC
Rep By: Hon. Jack M. Fields, Jr., Cynthia M. Wilkinson

Verner, Liipfert, Bernhard, McPherson and Hand, Chartered
Rep By: Jane Hickie, Ann W. Richards

SBREFA Coalition

Washington, DC
Leg. Issues: SMB

Outside Counsel/Consultants

Leonard Hurt Frost Lilly & Levin, PC
Issues: SMB
Rep By: Michael H. Levin

SCAN Health Plan

Long Beach, CA
Leg. Issues: HCR, MMM

Outside Counsel/Consultants

The Washington Group
Issues: HCR, MMM
Rep By: John D. Raffaelli, Tonya Saunders, Mark Schnabel

SCANA Corp.

Columbia, SC Registered: LDA
Leg. Issues: COM, ENG, TAX, TRA, UTI

Outside Counsel/Consultants

Balch & Bingham LLP
Issues: TRA, UTI
Rep By: Patrick J. McCormick, III, William F. Stiers

Johnson Co.
Issues: COM, ENG, TAX

Tongour Simpson Holsclaw Green
Issues: ENG
Rep By: John Bradley "Brad" Holsclaw, Michael A. Tongour

Scandinavian Airlines System (SAS)

Stockholm, SWEDEN

Outside Counsel/Consultants

White & Case LLP

SCC Communications Corp.

1225 I St. NW
Suite 500
Washington, DC 20005
Web: www.sccx.com
Tel: (202)312-2010
Fax: (202)785-2649

A provider of 911 services and information technology systems.

Leg. Issues: TEC

In-house, DC-area Employees

COHEN, Robert R.: Vice President, Government Relations
CORTESE FOXMAN, Melissa: V. President, Government Relations

Outside Counsel/Consultants

Paul, Hastings, Janofsky & Walker LLP
Issues: TEC
Rep By: Ralph B. Everett

Scenic America

801 Pennsylvania Ave. SE
Suite 300
Washington, DC 20003
Web: www.scenic.org
E-mail: scenic@scenic.org
Tel: (202)543-6200
Fax: (202)543-9130
Registered: LDA

A national non-profit membership organization dedicated to preserving the visual character of America's countrysides and communities. Provides education and assistance to Congress, federal agencies, states, local communities and individuals interested in controlling signs and creating scenic byways.

Leg. Issues: ENV, IND, NAT, RES, ROD, TRA, URB

In-house, DC-area Employees

MAGUIRE, Meg: President
PELIKAN, Thomas: Director of Policy

Scenic Hudson

Poughkeepsie, NY
Leg. Issues: CAW, ENV, NAT, WAS

Outside Counsel/Consultants

Ruth Frances Fleischer
Issues: CAW, ENV, NAT, WAS
Rep By: Ruth Frances Fleischer

Scepter Manufacturing Co. LTD

Scarborough, CANADA

Outside Counsel/Consultants

Rooney Group Internat'l, Inc.
Rep By: James W. Rooney

Schein Pharmaceutical, Inc.

Florham Park, NJ
Leg. Issues: MMM

Outside Counsel/Consultants

Congressional Consultants
Issues: MMM
Rep By: Gwen Gampel

Robert Schenk Internat'l Russia

Moscow, RUSSIA

Outside Counsel/Consultants

Gilbert A. Robinson, Inc.
Rep By: Gilbert A. Robinson

Schepens Eye Research Institute

Boston, MA
Leg. Issues: BUD

Outside Counsel/Consultants

O'Neill, Athy & Casey, P.C.
Issues: BUD
Rep By: Martha L. Casey

Paul Scherer & Co., LLP

New York, NY
Leg. Issues: LBR, TAX

Outside Counsel/Consultants

Davidson & Company, Inc.
Issues: LBR, TAX
Rep By: James H. Davidson, Richard E. May, Stanley Sokul

Schering A.G.

Outside Counsel/Consultants

The DCS Group

Schering Berlin Inc.

Cedar Knolls, NJ
Leg. Issues: MMM

Outside Counsel/Consultants

Baker & Hostetler LLP
Issues: MMM
Rep By: Frederick H. Graefe, Kathleen M. Kerrigan

Schering Corp.

Kenilworth, NJ

Outside Counsel/Consultants

Covington & Burling

Swidler Berlin Shereff Friedman, LLP
Rep By: Brian W. Fitzgerald, Gary Gallant, Lester S. Hyman, Gary D. Slaiman

Schering-Plough Corp.

Kenilworth, NJ
Leg. Issues: BUD, CPT, HCR, HLT, MED, MMM, PHA, TAX

Outside Counsel/Consultants

Clark & Weinstock, Inc.
Issues: BUD, CPT, HCR, MED, MMM, PHA, TAX
Rep By: Hon. Vic H. Fazio, Jr., Ed Kutler, Deirdre Stach, Sandi Stuart, Hon. John Vincent "Vin" Weber

Covington & Burling
Issues: CPT
Rep By: Ellen J. Flannery

Edelman Public Relations Worldwide
Rep By: Peter Segall

Levine & Co.
Issues: CPT, TAX
Rep By: Ken Levine

The Livingston Group, LLC
Issues: BUD, CPT, HCR
Rep By: Melvin Goodweather, Hon. Robert L. Livingston, Jr., J. Allen Martin, Richard L. Rodgers

Parry, Romani, DeConcini & Symms

Patton Boggs, LLP
Issues: HCR
Rep By: Hon. Willis "Bill" D. Gradison

PriceWaterhouseCoopers

Redfern Resources
Issues: HLT
Rep By: Ed Redfern

Weil, Gotshal & Manges, LLP
Issues: CPT
Rep By: Richard Ben-Veniste

Zeliff, Ireland, and Associates
Issues: BUD, CPT, HCR
Rep By: Hon. Andy Ireland, Hon. William H. Zeliff, Jr.

Schering-Plough Legislative Resources L.L.C.

1130 Connecticut Ave. NW
Suite 500
Washington, DC 20036
Web: www.sgp.com
Tel: (202)463-7372
Fax: (202)463-8809
Registered: LDA

Leg. Issues: BUD, CPT, HCR, MED, MMM, TAX, VET

In-house, DC-area Employees

EHRLICH, Paul C.: Congressional Relations Representative
LIVELY, Robert W.: Staff V. President, Congressional Relations

Outside Counsel/Consultants

Health Policy Analysts
Issues: HCR, MMM, VET
Rep By: G. Lawrence Atkins, Audrey Spolarich, Stephen G. Tilton

Schlumberger Technology Corp.

Houston, TX

Outside Counsel/Consultants

Preston Gates Ellis & Rouvelas Meeds LLP
Rep By: Tim L. Peckinpaugh

James E. Schneider, LLM Inc.

San Diego, CA
Leg. Issues: BAN, CAW, CIV, ECN, ENV, FIN, LBR, SMB, TAX

Outside Counsel/Consultants

Harry C. Alford & Associates, Inc.
Issues: BAN, CAW, CIV, ECN, ENV, FIN, LBR, SMB, TAX
Rep By: Harry C. Alford, Jr., Kermit R. Thomas

Schoenke & Associates

Outside Counsel/Consultants

Patton Boggs, LLP
Rep By: John F. Jonas

Scholastic, Inc.

New York, NY
Leg. Issues: ART, EDU, GOV, TAX, TEC

Outside Counsel/Consultants

American Continental Group, Inc.
Issues: EDU, GOV
Rep By: Shawn H. Smeallie

Liz Robbins Associates
Issues: ART, EDU, TAX, TEC
Rep By: Liz Robbins

School of Visual Arts

New York, NY
Leg. Issues: EDU

Outside Counsel/Consultants

Fern M. Lapidus
Issues: EDU
Rep By: Fern M. Lapidus

Schooner Capital Internat'l

Boston, MA

Outside Counsel/Consultants

Akin, Gump, Strauss, Hauer & Feld, L.L.P.

Schott Corp.

Yonkers, NY
Leg. Issues: DEF

Outside Counsel/Consultants

R. Wayne Sayer & Associates
Issues: DEF
Rep By: John Kania, William Morin, R. Wayne Sayer

W. Schulz GmbH

Krefeld, GERMANY
Leg. Issues: TRD

Outside Counsel/Consultants

Davis & Leiman, P.C.
Issues: TRD

Charles Schwab & Co., Inc.,

555 12th St. NW
Suite 740
Washington, DC 20004
Web: www.schwab.com
E-mail: frank.kelly@schwab.com
Tel: (202)638-3752
Registered: LDA

Headquartered in San Francisco, CA.

Leg. Issues: BAN, CPI, FIN, LBR, RET, TAX, TEC, TOR

In-house, DC-area Employees

FAMIGLIETTI, Kimberly M.: V. President, Government Affairs
KELLY, Frank: Senior V. President and Head of Government Affairs
TOWNSEND, Michael T.: V. President, Public Policy

Outside Counsel/Consultants

Bingham Dana LLP
Issues: FIN
Rep By: Neal E. Sullivan

Rhoads Group

Thelen Reid & Priest LLP
Issues: FIN
Rep By: Edward L. Pittman, Alan J. Reed, Richard Y. Roberts

Washington Council Ernst & Young
Issues: TAX
Rep By: Doug Badger, Lauren Darling, John L. Doney, Jayne T. Fitzgerald, LaBrenda Garrett-Nelson, Gary J. Gasper, Bruce A. Gates, Nick Giordano, Cathy Koch, Robert J. Leonard, Richard Meltzer, Phillip D. Moseley, John D. Porter, Robert M. Rozen, Donna Steele-Flynn, Timothy J. Urban

Schwab Fund for Charitable Giving

San Francisco, CA

Outside Counsel/Consultants

Morgan, Lewis & Bockius LLP

Schwan's Sales Enterprises

Marshall, MN
Leg. Issues: AGR, FUE, TAX

Outside Counsel/Consultants

Olsson, Frank and Weeda, P.C.
Issues: AGR, FUE, TAX
Rep By: John W. Bode, Susan P. Grymes, Karen Reis Harned, Dennis R. Johnson, Stephen L. Lacey, Marshall L. Matz, Tyson Redpath, Ryan W. Stroschein

Schweizer Aircraft Corp.

Elmira, NY
Leg. Issues: AVI, DEF

Outside Counsel/Consultants

The PMA Group
Issues: AVI, DEF
Rep By: Kaylene Green, Dr. John Lynch, Paul J. Magliocchetti, Kelli Short

SCI Systems, Inc.

1215 Jefferson Davis Hwy.
Suite 307
Arlington, VA 22202
Tel: (703)416-2211
Fax: (703)416-2213

In-house, DC-area Employees

GARRETT, Harley: Manager, Northeast Region

Science & Engineering Associates, Inc.

Metairie, LA
Leg. Issues: BUD, DEF, SCI

Outside Counsel/Consultants

Jones, Walker, Waechter, Poitevent, Carrere & Denegre, L.L.P.
Issues: BUD, DEF, SCI
Rep By: Paul Cambon, John J. Jaskot, R. Christian Johnsen

Murray, Scheer, Montgomery, Tapia & O'Donnell
Issues: BUD, DEF
Rep By: Thomas R. Crawford, D. Michael Murray, Mark Zelden

Science and Engineering Associates, Inc.

Albuquerque, NM
Leg. Issues: BUD, ENG, MAN, SCI

Outside Counsel/Consultants

Charlie McBride Associates, Inc.
Issues: BUD, ENG, MAN, SCI
Rep By: Charlie McBride

Science Applications Internat'l Corp. (SAIC)

2020 K St. NW
Suite 400
Washington, DC 20006
Tel: (202)530-8900
Fax: (202)530-5641
Registered: LDA
Web: www.saic.com

Leg. Issues: AER, APP, BUD, CPI, DEF, EDU, ENG, ENV, GOV, IMM, SCI, TEC, TRA, WAS

In-house, DC-area Employees

KILLEEN, John J.: Senior V. President, Government Affairs
ROSENBERG, R. A.: Exec. V. President, Washington Operations
THORPE, Kathryne M.: V. President, Government Affairs

Outside Counsel/Consultants

Birch, Horton, Bittner & Cherot
Issues: BUD
Rep By: Thomas L. Albert, Ronald G. Birch

Collins & Company, Inc.
Issues: DEF
Rep By: James D. Bond, Scott Cassel, Richard L. Collins, Shay D. Stautz

The Conaway Group LLC
Issues: DEF
Rep By: Lt. Gen. John B. Conaway, USAF (Ret.)

Copeland, Lowery & Jacquez
Issues: BUD, DEF, ENG, ENV
Rep By: Jean Gingras Denton, Hon. William D. Lowery

Cottone and Huggins Group
Issues: DEF, GOV
Rep By: James B. Huggins

Davis O'Connell, Inc.
Issues: DEF
Rep By: Lynda C. Davis, Ph.D., Terrence M. O'Connell

F.B.A.
Issues: CPI, EDU
Rep By: J. R. Kirkland

Haake and Associates
Issues: APP, DEF
Rep By: Timothy M. Haake, Nathan M. Olsen

The Kemper Co.
Issues: DEF
Rep By: Jackson Kemper, Jr.

Kerrigan & Associates, Inc.
Issues: SCI
Rep By: Michael J. Kerrigan

Charlie McBride Associates, Inc.
Issues: DEF, ENG, WAS
Rep By: Charlie McBride

Denny Miller McBee Associates
Issues: DEF

The PMA Group
Issues: CPI
Rep By: Kaylene Green, Paul J. Magliocchetti, Timothy K. Sanders

SISCORP
Issues: DEF
Rep By: Wendy Jordan, Donald F. Massey, Fran Shottes

Van Scoyoc Associates, Inc.
Issues: SCI
Rep By: Robert L. Knisely, H. Stewart Van Scoyoc

The Science Coalition

Leg. Issues: EDU

Outside Counsel/Consultants

Podesta/Mattoon
Issues: EDU

Science Leadership PAC

1225 I St. NW
Suite 810
Washington, DC 20005
Tel: (202)289-9800
Fax: (202)289-3588

In-house, DC-area Employees

MORE, Jeffery T.: PAC Administrator

Scientech Corp.

Washington, DC

An engineering consulting firm.

Leg. Issues: BUD, ENG, FOR

Outside Counsel/Consultants

EMI Associates, Ltd.
Issues: BUD, ENG, FOR
Rep By: Eugene M. Iwanciw

Scientific Fishery Systems, Inc.

Anchorage, AK
Leg. Issues: DEF, MAR

Outside Counsel/Consultants

The Kemper Co.
Issues: DEF, MAR
Rep By: Jackson Kemper, Jr.

Scientific Research Corp.

Atlanta, GA
Leg. Issues: DEF

Outside Counsel/Consultants

Hurt, Norton & Associates
Issues: DEF
Rep By: Robert H. Hurt, Frank Norton

Scientists Center for Animal Welfare

7833 Walker Dr.
Suite 410
Greenbelt, MD 20770
Web: www.scaw.com
E-mail: info@scaw.com
Tel: (301)345-3500
Fax: (301)345-3503

A non-profit organization of scientists and others concerned with the well-being of research animals.

In-house, DC-area Employees

KRULISCH, Lee: Exec. Director

Scot Pump

Cedarburg, WI

Outside Counsel/Consultants

Interface Inc.
Rep By: Robert G. Williams

Scott & White Hospital

Temple, TX
Leg. Issues: HCR

Outside Counsel/Consultants

Vinson & Elkins L.L.P.
Issues: HCR
Rep By: Larry A. Oday

Scottish Nat'l Party

Outside Counsel/Consultants

Porter, Wright, Morris & Arthur, LLP

Scottsdale, Arizona, City of

Leg. Issues: COM, LAW, RES, SCI, TAX, TRA, URB

Outside Counsel/Consultants

Carolyn C. Chaney & Associates
Issues: COM, LAW, RES, SCI, TAX, TRA, URB
Rep By: Carolyn C. Chaney, Christopher F. Giglio

Scram Technologies Inc.

Dunkirk, MD
Leg. Issues: BUD, DEF, SMB

Outside Counsel/Consultants

Ritter and Bourjaily, Inc.
Issues: BUD, DEF, SMB
Rep By: Monte F. Bourjaily, III

Screenprinting & Graphic Imaging Ass'n Internat'l

10015 Main St.
Fairfax, VA 22031-3489
Tel: (703)385-1335
Fax: (703)273-0456
Web: www.sgia.org
E-mail: sgia@sgia.org

Provides technical, educational, managerial, informational, governmental, research and safety services to members in the screen printing and graphic imaging industry.

Leg. Issues: CAW, ENV, WAS

In-house, DC-area Employees

CRAWFORD, Jr., John M.: President
JOFFE, Bruce: Director, Communication
KINTER, Marcia: V. President, Government Affairs
ROBERTSON, Michael: Exec. V. President

Outside Counsel/Consultants

Webster, Chamberlain & Bean
Rep By: Alan P. Dye

Scribe Communications, Inc.

King of Prussia, PA
Leg. Issues: BAN, FOR, TAX

Outside Counsel/Consultants

Janus-Merritt Strategies, L.L.C.
Issues: BAN, FOR, TAX
Rep By: Scott P. Hoffman, Bethany Noble, Mark J. Robertson, J. Daniel Walsh

Wilson & Wasserstein, Inc.
Issues: FOR
Rep By: Russell J. Wilson

Scripps League Newspaper, Inc.

Charlottesville, VA

Outside Counsel/Consultants

Wilmer, Cutler & Pickering

Scripps Research Institute

La Jolla, CA

Outside Counsel/Consultants

Arnold & Porter

Scull Law Firm, David L.

Bethesda, MD
Leg. Issues: TAX

Outside Counsel/Consultants

Dewey Ballantine LLP
Issues: TAX
Rep By: Andrew W. Kentz, James M. Wickett

Sea Bridge Internat'l LLC

McLean, VA
Leg. Issues: MAR

Outside Counsel/Consultants

William V. Brierre
Issues: MAR
Rep By: William V. Brierre, Jr.

Sea Containers America, Inc.

Washington, DC
Leg. Issues: MAR

Outside Counsel/Consultants

Jack Ferguson Associates, Inc.
Issues: MAR
Rep By: Raga Elim, Jack Ferguson

Sea Grant Ass'n

Charleston, SC
Leg. Issues: CAW, EDU, ENV, MAR, NAT, SCI

Outside Counsel/Consultants

Christopher A.G. Tulou
Issues: CAW, EDU, ENV, MAR, NAT, SCI
Rep By: Christopher A.G. Tulou

Sea Ventures Inc.

Hollywood, FL
Leg. Issues: MAR, TAX

Outside Counsel/Consultants

Dyer Ellis & Joseph, P.C.
Issues: MAR, TAX
Rep By: James S. W. Drewry, Thomas M. Dyer, Duncan C. Smith, III, Jennifer M. Southwick

Seaboard Corp.

818 Connecticut Ave. NW
Suite 801
Washington, DC 20006
Tel: (202)955-6111
Fax: (202)955-6118
Registered: LDA
E-mail: seabrd@aol.com
Leg. Issues: AGR, CAW, CDT, CSP, FOO, FOR, GOV, IMM, LBR, MAR, TAX, TRA, TRD

In-house, DC-area Employees

GORDON, Anthony: Government Affairs Assistant
MOSS, Ralph L.: Director, Government Affairs

Outside Counsel/Consultants

Steptoe & Johnson LLP

Seafarers Internat'l Union of North America

5201 Auth Way
Camp Springs, MD 20746
Tel: (301)899-0675
Fax: (301)899-7355
Registered: LDA
Web: www.seafarers.org
Leg. Issues: LBR, MAR, TRU

Political Action Committee/s

Seafarers Political Activity Donation (SPAD)
5201 Auth Way
Camp Springs, MD 20746
Tel: (301)899-0675
Fax: (301)899-7355
Contact: Terry Turner

In-house, DC-area Employees

SACCO, Michael: President
TURNER, Terry: Nat'l. Director, Political Action & Government Relations

Outside Counsel/Consultants

McGlotten & Jarvis
Issues: MAR
Rep By: Robert M. McGlotten

Potomac Group
Issues: LBR, MAR, TRU
Rep By: Richard Y Hegg, Philip C. Karsting, G. Wayne Smith

Seafarers Mobilization Action Research Team

Washington, DC
Leg. Issues: LBR, MAR

Outside Counsel/Consultants

Potomac Group
Issues: LBR, MAR
Rep By: Richard Y Hegg, Philip C. Karsting, G. Wayne Smith

Seafreeze

North Kingstown, RI
Leg. Issues: MAR

Outside Counsel/Consultants

Robertson, Monagle & Eastaugh
Issues: MAR
Rep By: Bradley D. Gilman, Rick E. Marks

Seal Beach, California, City of

Seal Beach, CA
Leg. Issues: DEF, RES

Outside Counsel/Consultants

Haake and Associates
Issues: RES
Rep By: Timothy M. Haake, Nathan M. Olsen

E. Del Smith and Co.
Issues: DEF
Rep By: E. Del Smith

Sealaska Corp.

Juneau, AK
Leg. Issues: BUD, ENV, IND, NAT, RES, TAX

Outside Counsel/Consultants

The Renkes Group, Ltd.
Issues: NAT
Rep By: Gregg D. Renkes

Van Ness Feldman, P.C.
Issues: BUD, ENV, IND, NAT, RES, TAX
Rep By: Howard S. Bleichfeld, Rebecca J. Boyd, Howard J. Feldman, Alan L. Mintz, Thomas C. Roberts

Seamans-Rome

Outside Counsel/Consultants

Cook and Associates
Rep By: Sheila E. Hixson

Search for Common Ground

1601 Connecticut Ave. NW
Suite 200
Washington, DC 20009
Tel: (202)265-4300
Fax: (202)232-6718
Web: www.sfcg.org
E-mail: search@sfcg.org

An independent, non-profit organization dedicated to finding workable solutions to divisive national and international problems. Programs aim to channel conflict toward constructive outcomes to build a more secure and peaceful world. Works to resolve conflict in the Middle East, Ukraine, Macedonia, Burundi, Indonesia, Angola, Turkey, Sierra Leone and the United States.

Leg. Issues: CIV, FOR, LBR

In-house, DC-area Employees

IDRISS, Shamil: C.O.O.
MARKS, John: President
MARKS, Susan Collin: Exec. V. President

SEARCH Group, Inc.

Sacramento, CA
A state criminal justice organization.
Leg. Issues: BUD, LAW

Outside Counsel/Consultants

Mullenholz, Brimsek & Belair
Issues: BUD, LAW
Rep By: Robert R. Belair, Susan C. Haller

Searchlight Victory Fund

818 Connecticut Ave. NW
#1100
Washington, DC 20006

Outside Counsel/Consultants

Oldaker and Harris, LLP
Rep By: William C. Oldaker

Sears, Roebuck and Co.

Hoffman Estates, IL
Registered: LDA
Leg. Issues: BNK, BUD, DEF, LBR, MAR, SCI, TAX, TRD

Outside Counsel/Consultants

The OB-C Group, LLC
Issues: BNK, BUD, DEF, LBR, MAR, SCI, TAX, TRD
Rep By: Thomas Keating, Kim F. McKernan, Charles J. Mellody, Patricia A. Nelson, Lawrence F. O'Brien, III, Linda E. Tarplin

Seaside, California, City of

Leg. Issues: ECN

Outside Counsel/Consultants

Kutak Rock LLP
Issues: ECN
Rep By: Rhonda Bond-Collins, Seth Kirshenberg, George R. Schlossberg, Barry P. Steinberg

Seattle City Light

Seattle, WA
Leg. Issues: ENG, TAX, UTI

Outside Counsel/Consultants

Van Ness Feldman, P.C.
Issues: ENG, TAX, UTI
Rep By: Richard A. Agnew

Seattle Housing Authority

Seattle, WA

Outside Counsel/Consultants

Preston Gates Ellis & Rouvelas Meeds LLP
Rep By: Tim L. Peckinpaugh

Seattle, Washington, City of

Leg. Issues: CAW, ENV, HCR, HOU, LAW, ROD, TEC, TRA, WAS, WEL

Outside Counsel/Consultants

Denny Miller McBee Associates

Peyser Associates, Inc.
Issues: CAW, ENV, HCR, HOU, LAW, ROD, TEC, TRA, WAS, WEL
Rep By: Thomas J. Howarth, Peter A. Peyser, Jr.

Seattle, Washington, Port of

Leg. Issues: AVI, MAR

Outside Counsel/Consultants

Preston Gates Ellis & Rouvelas Meeds LLP
Issues: AVI, MAR
Rep By: Jonathan Blank, Werner W. Brandt, John L. Longstreth, William N. Myhre, Tim L. Peckinpaugh, Emanuel L. Rouvelas, W. David Thomas

SEC Roundtable Group

Leg. Issues: UTI

Outside Counsel/Consultants

Thelen Reid & Priest LLP
Issues: UTI
Rep By: Richard Y. Roberts

Sechan Electronics

Lititz, PA
Leg. Issues: DEF

Outside Counsel/Consultants

The Wexler Group
Issues: DEF
Rep By: Peter T. Holran, Hon. Robert S. Walker

Secondary Materials and Recycled Textiles Ass'n

7910 Woodmont Ave.
Suite 1130
Bethesda, MD 20814
Web: www.smartasn.org
E-mail: smartasn@erols.com
Tel: (301)656-1077
Fax: (301)656-1079

Represents the interests of companies involved with used clothing, wiping cloths, fibers and textile recycling. Sponsors two conventions, a non-profit shippers association, and the Council for Textile Recycling.

Leg. Issues: APP, ENV, SMB

In-house, DC-area Employees

BRILL, Bernard D.: Exec. V. President

Secretaria de Agricultura, Granaderia y Desarrolo Rural (SAGAR)

Outside Counsel/Consultants

Manatt, Phelps & Phillips, LLP
Rep By: Susan M. Schmidt

Section 2039(e) Group

Outside Counsel/Consultants

McDermott, Will and Emery

Section 877 Coalition

Leg. Issues: TAX

Outside Counsel/Consultants

Alcalde & Fay
Issues: TAX
Rep By: Hector Alcalde, Hon. Louis A. "Skip" Bafalis

Secure Wrap, Inc.

Miami, FL
Leg. Issues: TOU, TRD, TRU

Outside Counsel/Consultants

Strategy Group Internat'l
Issues: TOU, TRD, TRU
Rep By: Emilio Gonzalez

Secured Access Portals, Inc.

Boca Raton, FL
Leg. Issues: CSP

Outside Counsel/Consultants

Janus-Merritt Strategies, L.L.C.
Issues: CSP
Rep By: Scott P. Hoffman, Bethany Noble, Mark J. Robertson

Securify

Palo Alto, CA

Outside Counsel/Consultants

American Continental Group, Inc.
Rep By: Steve Colovas, David A. Metzner

MSP Strategic Communications, Inc.
Rep By: Mitchell S. Pettit

Securities Industry Ass'n

1401 I St. NW
Suite 1000
Washington, DC 20005
Web: www.sia.com
Tel: (202)296-9410
Fax: (202)296-9775
Registered: LDA

Brings together the shared interests of nearly 800 securities firms, including investment banks, broker-dealers, and mutual fund companies. Co-headquartered in New York, NY.

Leg. Issues: BAN, BNK, BUD, CDT, CIV, COM, CPI, FIN, LBR, RET, TAX, TEC, TRD

Political Action Committee/s

Securities Industry Ass'n Political Action Committee

1401 I St. NW
Suite 1000
Washington, DC 20005
Tel: (202)296-9410
Fax: (202)296-9775

In-house, DC-area Employees

COSTANTINO, Jr., Lou A.: V. President, Congressional Relations
JUDGE, J. Steven: Senior V. President, Government Affairs
KASWELL, Stuart J.: Senior V. President and General Counsel
KRAMER, George R.: V. President and Associate General Counsel
LACKRITZ, Marc E.: President
LIESS, Liz A.: V. President and Director, Retirement Policy
MCCLANAHAN, Patricia: V. President, Director of Tax Policy
MICHAELIS, Dan V.: Assistant V. President, Corporate Communications
PARET, Jonathan R.: V. President and Legislative Counsel
RIVES, Elizabeth: V. President, Policy Analysis and Communications
ROBINSON, Rachel: V. President, Government Affairs
SPELLMAN, James D.: V. President and Director, Communication
STORRS, Josie: V. President, Congressional Relations

Outside Counsel/Consultants

Campbell Crane & Associates
Issues: BAN, TAX
Rep By: Jeanne M. Campbell, Daniel M. Crane

Cassidy & Associates, Inc.

Cleary, Gottlieb, Steen and Hamilton
Issues: FIN, TAX

The OB-C Group, LLC
Issues: FIN, TAX, TRD
Rep By: Thomas Keating, Kim F. McKernan, Charles J. Mellody, Patricia A. Nelson, Lawrence F. O'Brien, III, Linda E. Tarplin

John T. O'Rourke Law Offices
Issues: FIN
Rep By: John T. O'Rourke

Sullivan & Cromwell
Issues: FIN, TAX
Rep By: David P. Hariton

Washington Council Ernst & Young
Issues: RET, TAX
Rep By: Doug Badger, Lauren Darling, John L. Doney, Jayne T. Fitzgerald, LaBrenda Garrett-Nelson, Gary J. Gasper, Bruce A. Gates, Nick Giordano, Cathy Koch, Robert J. Leonard, Richard Meltzer, Phillip D. Moseley, John D. Porter, Robert M. Rozen, Donna Steele-Flynn, Timothy J. Urban

Securities Litigation Reform Coalition

San Francisco, CA

Outside Counsel/Consultants

Pillsbury Winthrop LLP

Securities Traders Ass'n

New York, NY

Outside Counsel/Consultants

Williams & Jensen, P.C.
Rep By: David E. Franasiak, J. Steven Hart, David A. Starr, Jeffrey A. Tassey

Security Capital Group

Santa Fe, NM
Leg. Issues: TAX

Outside Counsel/Consultants

Patton Boggs, LLP
Issues: TAX
Rep By: Benjamin L. Ginsberg, Donald V. Moorehead, Darryl D. Nirenberg, Aubrey A. Rothrock, III

Security Companies Organized for Legislative Action

A coalition of trade associations in the private security industry.

Leg. Issues: LAW, LBR

Outside Counsel/Consultants

Sellery Associates, Inc.
Issues: LAW, LBR
Rep By: Lawrence E. Sabbath, William C. Sellery, Jr.

Security Industry Ass'n

635 Slaters Ln.
Suite 110
Alexandria, VA 22314
Web: www.siaonline.org
E-mail: chase@siaonline.org
Tel: (703)683-2075
Fax: (703)683-2469
Leg. Issues: LAW

In-house, DC-area Employees

CHASE, Richard: Exec. Director

Outside Counsel/Consultants

Chwat and Company, Inc.
Issues: LAW
Rep By: Scott Bizub, John Chwat, Derek Riker

Security on Campus, Inc.

King of Prussia, PA
Leg. Issues: EDU, LAW

Outside Counsel/Consultants

Donald Baldwin Associates
Issues: EDU, LAW
Rep By: Donald Baldwin

Sedgwick James, Inc.

Memphis, TN

Outside Counsel/Consultants

Baker & Hostetler LLP
Rep By: Matthew J. Dolan, Steven A. Lotterer, Hon. Guy Vander Jagt

Seedco

New York, NY

A intermediary for housing and community development CDCs.

Leg. Issues: ECN, HOU, WEL

Outside Counsel/Consultants

Belew Law Firm
Issues: ECN, WEL
Rep By: Joy Carabasi Belew, M. Wendell Belew, Jr.

Patricia A. Taylor
Issues: HOU
Rep By: Patricia A. Taylor

Seemann Composites LLC

Gulfport, MS
Leg. Issues: DEF

Outside Counsel/Consultants

GHL Inc.
Issues: DEF
Rep By: Thomas R. Goldberg

SEFBO Pipeline Bridge, Inc.

Humble, TX
Leg. Issues: ENV, FUE, NAT

Outside Counsel/Consultants

The Dutko Group, Inc.
Issues: ENV, FUE, NAT
Rep By: Mark S. Irion

Seiko Epson Corp.

Nagono-Ken, JAPAN
Leg. Issues: CPT, TRD

Outside Counsel/Consultants

Morrison & Foerster LLP
Issues: CPT, TRD
Rep By: Jonathan Band, G. Brian Busey

Saunders and Company

Seldovia Native Ass'n, Inc.

Seldovia, AK

An American Indian tribe.

Outside Counsel/Consultants

Hobbs, Straus, Dean and Walker, LLP
Rep By: Carol L. Barbero, S. Bobo Dean, Karen J. Funk, Marie Osceola-Branch, Geoffrey D. Strommer

Self Help for Hard of Hearing People, Inc.

7910 Woodmont Ave.
Suite 1200
Bethesda, MD 20814
Web: www.shhh.org
E-mail: national@shhh.org
Tel: (301)657-2248
Fax: (301)913-9413

An international consumer organization of hard of hearing people, their relatives and friends. Dedicated to the well-being of people who do not hear well. Also have a (TTY) number, 301-657-2249.

Leg. Issues: GOV, HCR, TEC

In-house, DC-area Employees

BATTAT, Brenda: Deputy Exec. Director
CREAGAN, Timothy P.: Public Policy Program Coordinator
WILSON, Ph.D, Elizabeth J.: Exec. Director

Self-Insurance Institute of America, Inc.

1250 H St. NW
Suite 901
Washington, DC 20005
Tel: (202)463-8161
Fax: (202)463-8155
Registered: LDA

Headquartered in Santa Ana, CA.

Leg. Issues: HCR, INS, LBR

Political Action Committee/s

Self-Insurance Institute of America, Inc. PAC
1250 H St. NW
Suite 901
Washington, DC 20005
Contact: George Pantos

In-house, DC-area Employees

PANTOS, George: Contact

Outside Counsel/Consultants

Greenberg Traurig, LLP
Issues: HCR, INS
Rep By: Russell J. Mueller

Kinder & Associates, Inc.
Issues: HCR, LBR
Rep By: George Pantos, Ashley K. Williams

SEMATECH, Inc.

Austin, TX
A semiconductor manufacturing research consortium

Outside Counsel/Consultants

Dewey Ballantine LLP
Rep By: W. Clark McFadden, II

SEMCO

Port Huron, MI
Leg. Issues: FIN, TRA

Outside Counsel/Consultants

Thompson and Naughton, Inc.
Issues: FIN, TRA
Rep By: Kenneth W. Thompson

Semiconductor Equipment and Materials Internat'l

1401 K St. NW
Suite 601
Washington, DC 20005
Tel: (202)289-0440
Fax: (202)289-0441
Registered: LDA
Web: www.semi.org
E-mail: semidc@semi.org

Headquartered in San Jose, CA.

Leg. Issues: CPI, DEF, FIN, IMM, SCI, TAX, TRD

In-house, DC-area Employees

DOWLING, Jennifer Connell: Director, Public Policy
HADFIELD, Victoria: V. President, Public Policy

Outside Counsel/Consultants

Dewey Ballantine LLP
Rep By: Harry L. Clark

Semiconductor Industry Ass'n

San Jose, CA
Registered: LDA
Leg. Issues: BUD, IMM, TAX, TOR, TRD

Outside Counsel/Consultants

Dewey Ballantine LLP
Issues: BUD, IMM, TAX, TOR, TRD
Rep By: Margaret Angell, Kevin M. Dempsey, W. Clark McFadden, II, Alan W. Wolff

Seminole Tribe of Indians of Florida

Hollywood, FL
Leg. Issues: BUD, ENV, GAM, IND, TAX

Outside Counsel/Consultants

Hobbs, Straus, Dean and Walker, LLP
Issues: IND
Rep By: Carol L. Barbero, Karen J. Funk, Aura Kanegis, Marie Osceola-Branch, Michael L. Roy, Judith A. Shapiro, Jerry C. Straus, Joseph H. Webster

Jefferson Government Relations, L.L.C.
Issues: BUD, ENV, GAM, IND, TAX
Rep By: Jeanne L. Morin, Patricia A. Power, William A. Roberts

Sempra Energy

1001 G St. NW
Sixth Floor East
Washington, DC 20001-4545
Tel: (202)662-1700
Fax: (202)293-2887
Registered: LDA
Web: www.sempra.com

Formed by the merger of Pacific Enterprises and Enova Corp. in 1998. Headquartered in San Diego, CA.

Leg. Issues: ENG, FUE, UTI

In-house, DC-area Employees

FREER, David W.: Regional V. President, Federal Government Affairs
WILLIAMS, George P.: Director, Government Affairs

Outside Counsel/Consultants

The Direct Impact Co.

Hunton & Williams
Rep By: John J. Adams

O'Connor & Hannan, L.L.P.
Issues: ENG, FUE, UTI
Rep By: Roy C. Coffee

Seneca Resources Corporation

Houston, TX
Leg. Issues: BUD, NAT

Outside Counsel/Consultants

Alpine Group, Inc.
Issues: BUD, NAT
Rep By: Rhod M. Shaw, Monica Skopec

Senegal, Government of the Republic of

Dakar, SENEGAL

Outside Counsel/Consultants

Washington World Group, Ltd.
Rep By: Edward J. von Kloberg, III

Senior Army Reserve Commanders Ass'n

7000 Millwood Rd.
Bethesda, MD 20817
Tel: (301)229-1550
Fax: (301)229-4905
E-mail: helsm@rca.org

Represents the leadership of the Army Reserve, as a professional association, in Washington, D.C., to help assure that the USAR receives appropriate missions and resources to support national defense at the lowest possible cost.

In-house, DC-area Employees

HELM, Brig. Gen. Lewis M.: Executive Director

Senior Executives Ass'n

P.O. Box 44808
Washington, DC 20026-4808
Tel: (202)927-7000
Fax: (202)927-5192
Web: www.seniorexecs.com
E-mail: seniorexec@aol.com

Works to advance professionalism of federal government executive-level career employees and to advocate their interests.

Leg. Issues: GOV

In-house, DC-area Employees

BONOSARO, Carol A.: President
DRIVER, Bryan: Director, Communications
SHAW, Jr., G. Jerry: General Counsel

Outside Counsel/Consultants

Shaw, Bransford, Veilleux & Roth
Issues: GOV
Rep By: G. Jerry Shaw, Jr., Katherine E. Swiencki

Sense Technologies, Inc.

Omaha, NE
Leg. Issues: AUT, TRA

Outside Counsel/Consultants

Bacino & Associates
Issues: AUT, TRA
Rep By: Geoff Bacino

Sensis Corp.

Dewitt, NY
Leg. Issues: SCI, TRA

Outside Counsel/Consultants

Richard L. Spees, Inc.
Issues: SCI, TRA
Rep By: Richard L. Spees

Sensor Oil and Gas Co.

Oklahoma City, OK
Leg. Issues: ENG

Outside Counsel/Consultants

Duncan, Weinberg, Genzer & Pembroke, P.C.
Issues: ENG
Rep By: Richmond F. Allan

Sensor Research and Development Corp.

Orono, ME
Leg. Issues: CAW, DEF, DIS, ENV, FOO, MED

Outside Counsel/Consultants

Commonwealth Consulting Corp.
Issues: DEF, ENV

GHL Inc.
Issues: CAW, DEF, DIS, FOO, MED
Rep By: Thomas R. Goldberg

Sensor Technologies and Systems Inc.

Scottsdale, AZ
An engineering, science, research and development company.

Leg. Issues: DEF, LAW

Outside Counsel/Consultants

The Carter Group
Issues: DEF, LAW
Rep By: Michael R. Carter

Sentara Norfolk General Hospital

Norfolk, VA

Outside Counsel/Consultants

Williams & Connolly

The Sentencing Project

514 10th St. NW
Suite 1000
Washington, DC 20005
Tel: (202)628-0871
Fax: (202)628-1091
Web: www.sentencingproject.org
E-mail: staff@sentencingproject.org

An organization established to reduce over-reliance upon jails and prisons through greater use of alternatives to incarceration and to increase the public's understanding of sentencing and the criminal justice system.

In-house, DC-area Employees

MAUER, Marc: Assistant Director
YOUNG, Malcolm C.: Exec. Director

Separation Technologies

Needham, MA
Leg. Issues: ENG, FIN

Outside Counsel/Consultants

Sher & Blackwell
Issues: ENG, FIN
Rep By: Earl W. Comstock, Jeffrey R. Pike

Sepracor, Inc.

Marlborough, MA
Leg. Issues: CPT, HCR, MED, SCI

Outside Counsel/Consultants

Cassidy & Associates, Inc.

Jeffrey J. Kimbell & Associates
Issues: CPT, HCR, MED, SCI
Rep By: Jeffrey J. Kimbell

SePRO Corp.

Carmel, IN
Leg. Issues: AGR, BUD, CAW, ENV

Outside Counsel/Consultants

Capitolink, LLC
Issues: AGR, BUD, CAW, ENV
Rep By: Thomas R. Hebert, John H. Thorne, Ph.D.

Sequent Computer Systems

Beaverton, OR

Outside Counsel/Consultants

Skadden, Arps, Slate, Meagher & Flom LLP
Rep By: Roseann M. Cutrone

Sequoia Ventures

San Francisco, CA
Leg. Issues: TAX

Outside Counsel/Consultants

Akin, Gump, Strauss, Hauer & Feld, L.L.P.
Issues: TAX

Serono Laboratories, Inc.

1700 Rockville Pike
Suite 210
Rockville, MD 20852
Tel: (301)770-2597
Fax: (301)770-2589
Registered: LDA
Web: www.serono.com
Leg. Issues: CPT, EDU, HCR, MED, MMM, PHA

In-house, DC-area Employees

RUGGIERI, Nicholas L.: V. President, Government Affairs

Outside Counsel/Consultants

Akin, Gump, Strauss, Hauer & Feld, L.L.P.
Issues: HCR, MED
Rep By: Karen E. Goldmeier Green, Gary A. Heimberg, Barney J. Skladany, Jr., Daniel L. Spiegel, S. Bruce Wilson

Bennett Turner & Coleman, LLP
Issues: CPT, MED, MMM
Rep By: Alan R. Bennett, Bruce Manheim, Michael D. Petty

Heidepriem & Mager, Inc.
Issues: EDU, HCR, MED
Rep By: Christopher Gould, Nikki Heidepriem

Latham & Watkins
Issues: PHA
Rep By: Nicholas W. Allard, Edward Correia, John R. Manthei

Washington Liaison Group, LLC
Issues: EDU, HCR, MED
Rep By: Gaston de Bearn, David M. Jenkins, II, Michael L. Reed

Service Corp. Internat'l

Houston, TX
Leg. Issues: BUD, LBR, TAX

Outside Counsel/Consultants

Miller & Chevalier, Chartered
Issues: TAX

Don Wallace Associates, Inc.
Issues: BUD, LBR
Rep By: John Gilliland, Donald L. Wallace, Jr.

Service Employees Internat'l Union

1313 L St. NW
Washington, DC 20005
Tel: (202)898-3200
Fax: (202)898-3304
Registered: LDA
Web: www.workingfamilies.com

With over one million members, SEIU represents private and public sector workers from diverse industries, including health, building service, office work, industy, education, transportation, social service, and others.

Leg. Issues: BUD, CPI, EDU, GOV, HCR, IMM, LBR, MMM, UNM, URB, WEL

Political Action Committee/s

Service Employees Internat'l Union COPE Political Action Committee
1313 L St. NW
Washington, DC 20005
Tel: (202)898-3200
Fax: (202)898-3304

In-house, DC-area Employees

BORWEGEN, B. William: Director, Health and Safety
FORD, Patricia: Exec. V. President
GOLUBOCK, Carol: Attorney
HOWLEY, John: Director, Public Policy
MCDONALD, Ingrid: Senior Policy Analyst
REGAN, Carol: Director, Health Policy
ROBERTS, George D.: Director, Legislative Department
STERN, Andrew: President

Outside Counsel/Consultants

Bond & Company, Inc.
Rep By: Richard N. Bond, Eileen Kean, Andy Madden

The Ickes & Enright Group
Issues: BUD, HCR, IMM, LBR, MMM
Rep By: Janice Ann Enright, Harold M. Ickes

Service Station Dealers of America and Allied Trades

9420 Annapolis Rd.
Suite 307
Lanham, MD 20706
Tel: (301)577-4956
Fax: (301)731-0039
Web: www.ssda-at.org
E-mail: ssda-at@mindspring.com

Political Action Committee/s

Service Station Dealers of America Political Action Committee
9420 Annapolis Rd.
Suite 307
Lanham, MD 20706
Tel: (301)577-4956
Fax: (301)731-0039
Contact: Kathleen Stokes

In-house, DC-area Employees

LITTLEFIELD, Amy: Director, Federal Government Relations
LITTLEFIELD, Roy E.: Exec. V. President
STOKES, Kathleen: Assistant to the Exec. V. President and PAC Contact

Servicios Aereos de Honduras (SAHSA)

Tegucigalpa, HONDURAS

Outside Counsel/Consultants

Squire, Sanders & Dempsey L.L.P.
Rep By: Robert D. Papkin

Servicios Corporativos Cintra SA de CV

Mexico City, MEXICO

Outside Counsel/Consultants

Manatt, Phelps & Phillips, LLP
Rep By: Irwin P. Altschuler, Abbe David Lowell

Servo Corp. of America

Westbury, NY
Leg. Issues: TRD

Outside Counsel/Consultants

Jefferson Consulting Group
Issues: TRD
Rep By: Robert J. Thompson

SESAC, Inc.

Nashville, TN
Leg. Issues: ART, CPT

Outside Counsel/Consultants

Manatt, Phelps & Phillips, LLP
Issues: ART, CPT
Rep By: Robert J. Kabel, Susan M. Schmidt

Sesame Workshop

New York, NY
Leg. Issues: COM, FOR

Outside Counsel/Consultants

Sara Garland (and Associates)
Issues: COM, FOR
Rep By: Rachel A. Emmons, Sara G. Garland

Seton Hill College

Greensburg, PA
Leg. Issues: BUD, DEF, EDU, FOR

Outside Counsel/Consultants

The Peterson Group
Issues: BUD, DEF, EDU, FOR
Rep By: William P. Sears

Seven Seas Petroleum USA Inc.

Houston, TX
Leg. Issues: ENG

Outside Counsel/Consultants

Morgan Meguire, LLC
Issues: ENG
Rep By: Kyle G. Michel, C. Kyle Simpson, Deborah R. Sliz, Kiel Weaver

Severance Trust Executive Program

Woodbridge, CT
Leg. Issues: TAX

Outside Counsel/Consultants

Greenberg Traurig, LLP
Issues: TAX
Rep By: Russell J. Mueller

Seward, Alaska, City of

Leg. Issues: BUD, URB

Outside Counsel/Consultants

Robertson, Monagle & Eastaugh
Issues: BUD
Rep By: Bradley D. Gilman, Rick E. Marks, Steven W. Silver

Zane & Associates
Issues: URB
Rep By: Curtis J. Zane

Sewerage and Water Board of New Orleans

New Orleans, LA
Leg. Issues: BUD, CAW, HOU, URB

Outside Counsel/Consultants

Johnston & Associates, LLC
Issues: BUD, CAW, HOU, URB
Rep By: N. Hunter Johnston, W. Proctor Jones, Eric Tober

Jones, Walker, Waechter, Poitevent, Carrere & Denegre, L.L.P.
Issues: BUD, CAW
Rep By: Paul Cambon, John J. Jaskot, R. Christian Johnsen

SFX Broadcasting

New York, NY

Outside Counsel/Consultants

Shaw Pittman

SGS Government Programs, Inc.

New York, NY

A subsidiary of Societe Generale de Surveillance S.A. of Geneva, Switzerland, a trade inspection firm.

Outside Counsel/Consultants

Shea & Gardner
Rep By: John D. Aldock, Patrick M. Hanlon

SGS North America, Inc.

Parsippany, NJ

An international inspection service; affiliated with Societe Generale de Surveillance.

Outside Counsel/Consultants

Shea & Gardner
Rep By: John D. Aldock, Patrick M. Hanlon

Shake-A-Leg

Miami, FL
Leg. Issues: BUD, SPO

Outside Counsel/Consultants

Sagamore Associates, Inc.
Issues: BUD, SPO
Rep By: Ann E. Cody, David U. Gogol

The Shakespeare Theatre

Washington, DC

Not-for-profit theater specializing in classical dramatic works of literature.

Leg. Issues: ART

Outside Counsel/Consultants

Chernikoff and Co.
Issues: ART
Rep By: Larry B. Chernikoff

Shaklee Corp.

San Francisco, CA

Involved in the sale of dietary supplements.

Leg. Issues: FOR, TRD

Outside Counsel/Consultants

Powell, Goldstein, Frazer & Murphy LLP
Issues: FOR, TRD
Rep By: Daniel M. Price, Andrew Shoyer

Shakopee Business Council

Prior Lake, MN

Outside Counsel/Consultants

Chesapeake Enterprises, Inc.
Rep By: Scott W. Reed

Shakopee Mdewakanton Sioux Tribe

Prior Lake, MN
Leg. Issues: BUD, GAM, GOV, IND, TAX

Outside Counsel/Consultants

Chesapeake Enterprises, Inc.
Issues: GOV, IND, TAX
Rep By: J. John Fluharty

Dorsey & Whitney LLP
Issues: BUD, GAM, TAX
Rep By: Philip Baker-Shenk, David A. Bieging, Virginia W. Boylan, Cindy Darcy, Mark Jarboe, Sarah Ridley, Kevin J. Wadzinski

Steptoe & Johnson LLP
Rep By: Thomas C. Collier, Jr.

Swidler Berlin Shereff Friedman, LLP
Rep By: James Hamilton

Share Our Strength

733 15th St. NW
Suite 640
Washington, DC 20005
Tel: (202)393-2925
Fax: (202)347-5868
Web: www.strength.org

An anti-hunger and anti-poverty organization working nationally and internationally.

In-house, DC-area Employees

OSBORNE, Arison: Director, Public Relations
ROGAN, Maura Walsh: Deputy Director, Public Relations
SHORE, Bill: Exec. Director

Outside Counsel/Consultants

Winthrop, Stimson, Putnam & Roberts

Shared Legal Capability for Intellectual Property

Washington, DC
Leg. Issues: COM, CPT

Outside Counsel/Consultants

Lutzker & Lutzker LLP
Issues: COM, CPT
Rep By: Arnold P. Lutzker

The Sharing Network

Springfield, NJ
Leg. Issues: HCR

Outside Counsel/Consultants

McNamara & Associates
Issues: HCR
Rep By: Thomas J. McNamara

Sharon Tube Co.

Sharon, PA
Leg. Issues: TRA

Outside Counsel/Consultants

Schagrin Associates
Issues: TRA
Rep By: Roger B. Schagrin

Sharp Electronics Corp.

Mahwah, NJ
Leg. Issues: CPT

Outside Counsel/Consultants

Patton Boggs, LLP
Issues: CPT
Rep By: Thomas Hale Boggs, Jr., Brian C. Lopina, Jeffrey L. Turner

D. E. Shaw & Co.

New York, NY

An investment management services company.

Leg. Issues: FIN

Outside Counsel/Consultants

Commonwealth Group, Ltd.
Issues: FIN
Rep By: Bradley D. Belt

Shaw Group

Leg. Issues: MAN, TRD

Outside Counsel/Consultants

Brownstein Hyatt & Farber, P.C.
Issues: MAN, TRD
Rep By: Thomas H. Hudson

Shea & Gardner

1800 Massachusetts Ave. NW
Washington, DC 20036
Tel: (202)828-2000
Fax: (202)828-2195
Registered: LDA, FARA

In-house, DC-area Employees

ALDOCK, John D.: Partner and Chair, Executive Committee
BASSECHES, Robert T.: Partner
COOK, David B.: Partner
GOODMAN, Collette C.
HANLON, Patrick M.: Partner
HANLON, William R.: Partner
RICH, John Townsend: Partner
WOOLSEY, R. James: Partner

Outside Counsel/Consultants

Chambers Associates Inc.
Rep By: Letitia Chambers, Mary S. Lyman

Shea's Performing Arts Center

Buffalo, NY
Leg. Issues: ART, ECN

Outside Counsel/Consultants

John C. Grzebien
Issues: ART, ECN
Rep By: John C. Grzebien

Sheep Ranch Rancheria

Tracy, CA
Leg. Issues: GAM, IND

Outside Counsel/Consultants

The State Affairs Co.
Issues: GAM, IND
Rep By: Bonnie L. Chafe, Carol Smith

Sheesley Construction Corp.

Johnstown, PA

Outside Counsel/Consultants

Sam Richardson
Rep By: Sam Richardson

Sheet Metal and Air Conditioning Contractors' Nat'l Ass'n

305 Fourth St. NE
Washington, DC 20002
Tel: (202)547-8202
Fax: (202)547-8810
Registered: LDA
Web: www.smacna.org
E-mail: info@smacna.org
Leg. Issues: BUD, GOV, HCR, LBR, RES, SMB

Political Action Committee/s

Sheet Metal and Air Conditioning Contractors' Nat'l Ass'n Political Action Committee (SMAC PAC)
305 Fourth St. NE
Washington, DC 20002
Tel: (202)547-8202
Fax: (202)547-8810
Contact: Dana S. Thompson

In-house, DC-area Employees

KOLBE, Jr., Stanley E.: Director, Legislation
THOMPSON, Dana S.: Director, Political Affairs

Sheet Metal Workers' Internat'l Ass'n

1750 New York Ave. NW
Sixth Floor
Washington, DC 20006
Tel: (202)783-5880
Fax: (202)662-0895
Registered: LDA
Web: www.smwia.org
Leg. Issues: BUD, CAW, EDU, LBR, ROD, TAX, TRD, UTI, WAS

Political Action Committee/s

Sheet Metal Workers' Internat'l Ass'n Political Action League
1750 New York Ave. NW
Sixth Floor
Washington, DC 20006
Tel: (202)783-5880
Fax: (202)662-0895
Contact: Vincent A. Panvini

In-house, DC-area Employees

BUCHANAN, Don: Director, Railroad and Shipyard Workers
PANVINI, Vincent A.: Director, Legislative Department
SULLIVAN, Michael J.: General President
ZLOTOPOLSKI, Alfred T.: General Secretary-Treasurer

Outside Counsel/Consultants

The Kamber Group
Rep By: Steven A. Johnson, Victor S. Kamber

Shelby, Tennessee, County of

Memphis, TN
Leg. Issues: EDU, GOV, HCR, LAW, MMM

Outside Counsel/Consultants

Hyjek & Fix, Inc.
Issues: EDU, GOV, LAW
Rep By: Donald J. Fix, Steven M. Hyjek, Karl H. Stegenga

Susan J. White & Associates
Issues: HCR, MMM
Rep By: Susan J. White

Sheldahl, Inc.

Northfield, MN

Outside Counsel/Consultants

R. Wayne Sayer & Associates
Rep By: R. Wayne Sayer

Shell Oil Co.

1401 I St. NW
Suite 1030
Washington, DC 20005
Tel: (202)466-1405
Fax: (202)466-1498
Registered: LDA

Owned by Royal Dutch Shell.

Leg. Issues: CAW, CHM, CSP, ENV, FOR, FUE, GOV, LBR, NAT, TAX, TRA, TRD

In-house, DC-area Employees

RICH, Jr., James E.: Washington Representative
WARD, Stephen E.: V. President, Government Affairs

Outside Counsel/Consultants

Bracewell & Patterson, L.L.P.
Issues: ENV

Morgan Meguire, LLC
Rep By: Kyle G. Michel, C. Kyle Simpson

Patton Boggs, LLP
Issues: FUE
Rep By: Thomas Hale Boggs, Jr., Donald V. Moorehead

Shaw Pittman
Issues: LBR

Shelters, Inc.

Arlington, VA
Leg. Issues: DIS

Outside Counsel/Consultants

Rooney Group Internat'l, Inc.
Issues: DIS
Rep By: James W. Rooney

Shenandoah Valley

Outside Counsel/Consultants

Nat'l Strategies Inc.
Rep By: David K. Aylward, Marsha Scherr

Shepherd Oil Co.

Jennings, LA

Outside Counsel/Consultants

Bode & Grenier LLP
Rep By: William H. Bode

Sherburne, New York, Village of

Leg. Issues: UTI

Outside Counsel/Consultants

Duncan, Weinberg, Genzer & Pembroke, P.C.
Issues: UTI
Rep By: Jeffrey C. Genzer

Sheriff Jefferson Parrish, Louisiana

Metairie, LA
Leg. Issues: BUD, LAW

Outside Counsel/Consultants

Patton Boggs, LLP
Issues: BUD, LAW
Rep By: Robert C. Jones, Elizabeth C. Vella

City of Sherrill, New York

Sherrill, NY

Outside Counsel/Consultants

Duncan, Weinberg, Genzer & Pembroke, P.C.
Rep By: Jeffrey C. Genzer

Sherritt Internat'l

Toronto, CANADA
Leg. Issues: IMM, TRD

Outside Counsel/Consultants

Contango LLC
Issues: IMM, TRD
Rep By: Candice Shy Hooper

Sherwin Williams Co.

Cleveland, OH
Leg. Issues: CSP, HCR, INS, TAX

Outside Counsel/Consultants

Cassidy & Associates, Inc.
Issues: CSP, HCR
Rep By: Mary Kate Kelly-Johnson, Arthur D. Mason, Blenda Pinto-Riddick, Hon. Martin A. Russo, Dan C. Tate, Sr., Gerald Felix Warburg

Murray, Scheer, Montgomery, Tapia & O'Donnell
Issues: INS, TAX
Rep By: Thomas R. Crawford, D. Michael Murray

Shieldalloy Metallurgical Corp.

Newfield, NJ
Leg. Issues: ENV

Outside Counsel/Consultants

Baker & Hostetler LLP
Issues: ENV

Harris Ellsworth & Levin
Rep By: Cheryl N. Ellsworth

Shipbuilders Council of America

1600 Wilson Blvd.
Suite 1000
Arlington, VA 22209
Tel: (703)351-6734
Fax: (703)351-6736
Registered: LDA
Web: www.shipbuilders.org
Leg. Issues: BUD, CAW, DEF, ENV, LBR, TRA, TRD

In-house, DC-area Employees

MCCLUER, Jess P.: Manager, Government and Administrative Affairs
WALKER, Allen: President

Shiprock Alternative Schools, Inc.

Shiprock, AZ
Leg. Issues: IND

Outside Counsel/Consultants

Hobbs, Straus, Dean and Walker, LLP
Issues: IND
Rep By: Carol L. Barbero, Karen J. Funk, Lisa F. Ryan

Shipston Group, LTD

Nassau, BAHAMAS
Leg. Issues: TAX

Outside Counsel/Consultants

Hooper Owen & Winburn
Issues: TAX
Rep By: Hon. Charles Wilson

Shivwitz Band of the Paiute Indian Tribe of Utah

Santa Clara, UT
Leg. Issues: IND

Outside Counsel/Consultants

The Wexler Group
Issues: IND
Rep By: Dale W. Snape

Shoalwater Bay Indian Tribe

Tokeland, WA
Leg. Issues: IND

Outside Counsel/Consultants

Hobbs, Straus, Dean and Walker, LLP
Issues: IND
Rep By: Carol L. Barbero, S. Bobo Dean, Karen J. Funk, Craig A. Jacobson, Aura Kanegis, Marie Osceola-Branch, Starla K. Roels, Geoffrey D. Strommer, Joseph H. Webster

Shorebank Corp.

Chicago, IL
Leg. Issues: ECN

Outside Counsel/Consultants

Robert A. Rapoza Associates
Issues: ECN
Rep By: Robert A. Rapoza

Short Brothers (USA), Inc.

1023 15th St. NW
Suite 1000
Washington, DC 20005-2602
Tel: (202)414-8980
Fax: (202)789-0076
Registered: LDA

A subsidiary of Bombardier Aerospace (see separate listing).

Leg. Issues: AER, DEF

In-house, DC-area Employees

BROOKS, A. Oakley: President

Shorts Missile Systems

Belfast, UNITED KINGDOM
Leg. Issues: DEF

Outside Counsel/Consultants

Hyjek & Fix, Inc.
Issues: DEF
Rep By: Steven M. Hyjek, Irene D. Schecter

Shoshone-Bannock Tribes of the Fort Hall Indian Reservation

Fort Hall, ID

Outside Counsel/Consultants

Sonosky, Chambers, Sachse & Endreson
Rep By: William R. Perry

Showell Farms Inc.

Showell, MD

Outside Counsel/Consultants

Kelly and Associates, Inc.
Rep By: John A. Kelly

Shreveport, Louisiana, City of

Leg. Issues: BUD, TRA, URB

Outside Counsel/Consultants

Patton Boggs, LLP
Issues: BUD, TRA, URB
Rep By: Carolina L. Mederos, Edward J. Newberry

Shriner-Midland Co.

6432 Quincy Pl.
Falls Church, VA 22042
Tel: (703)237-8135
Fax: (703)533-9103
E-mail: shrinermidland@aol.com

Specializes in management strategies, systems, and economic analysis for public policy issues including regulation, trade, and taxation.

Leg. Issues: AER, AVI, ECN, TAX

In-house, DC-area Employees

MICHAELSON, Leslie: Manager, Association Research and Economics
SHRINER, Robert D.: Managing Partner

Shriners Hospital for Children

Tampa, FL
Leg. Issues: CSP, HCR

Outside Counsel/Consultants

Campbell Crane & Associates
Issues: CSP, HCR
Rep By: Jeanne M. Campbell, Daniel M. Crane

Shubert Organization Inc.

New York, NY
Leg. Issues: ART, TAX

Outside Counsel/Consultants

Murray, Scheer, Montgomery, Tapia & O'Donnell
Issues: ART, TAX
Rep By: Thomas R. Crawford, D. Michael Murray

Shurberg Broadcasting of Hartford Inc.

Hartford, CT

Outside Counsel/Consultants

Bechtel & Cole
Rep By: Harry F. Cole

Sibley Memorial Hospital

Washington, DC
Leg. Issues: DOC

Outside Counsel/Consultants

Shaw Pittman
Issues: DOC
Rep By: Thomas J. Spulak

Sickle Cell Disease Ass'n of America

Culver City, CA
Leg. Issues: BUD, HCR

Outside Counsel/Consultants

Van Scoyoc Associates, Inc.
Issues: BUD, HCR
Rep By: Anita R. Estell, Kimberly Johnson, H. Stewart Van Scoyoc

SICPA Industries of America, Inc.

Springfield, VA
Leg. Issues: BAN

Outside Counsel/Consultants

Robert L. Redding
Issues: BAN
Rep By: Robert L. Redding, Jr.

Sidem International Ltd.

London, UNITED KINGDOM
Leg. Issues: TRD

Outside Counsel/Consultants

TerraCom-Strategic Communications
Issues: TRD
Rep By: Felix R. Sanchez

Siderar S.A.I.C.

Buenos Aires, ARGENTINA

Outside Counsel/Consultants

White & Case LLP
Rep By: David P. Houlihan

Siderca Corp.

Buenos Aires, ARGENTINA

Outside Counsel/Consultants

White & Case LLP
Rep By: David P. Houlihan

Siderurgica del Orinoco (Sidor), C.A.

Caracas, VENEZUELA

Outside Counsel/Consultants

White & Case LLP
Rep By: David P. Houlihan

Siemens Corp.

701 Pennsylvania Ave. NW
Suite 720
Washington, DC 20004
Tel: (202)434-4800
Fax: (202)347-4015
Registered: LDA

Headquartered in New York, NY.

Leg. Issues: MAN, TRD

Political Action Committee/s

Siemens Corp. PAC
701 Pennsylvania Ave. NW
Suite 720
Washington, DC 20004
Tel: (202)434-4800
Fax: (202)347-4015
Contact: John Chestnut

In-house, DC-area Employees

CHESTNUT, John: PAC Contact
ESHERICK, Mark
KERR, Eleanor
MIKEL, John: Director, Legislative Affairs
SHERMAN, Patricia A.
TODD, Doug
WARD, Gregg: V. President, Government Relations

Outside Counsel/Consultants

American Continental Group, Inc.
Rep By: David A. Metzner, Shawn H. Smeallie, Peter Terpeluk, Jr.
Ricchetti Inc.

Siemens Transportation Systems, Inc.

701 Pennsylvania Ave. NW
Suite 720
Washington, DC 20004
Tel: (202)434-4821
Fax: (202)737-5403
E-mail: sandy.bushue@sts.siemens.com
Leg. Issues: TRA

In-house, DC-area Employees

BUSHUE, Sandy: Director, Government Affairs

Outside Counsel/Consultants

Foley & Lardner
Issues: TRA
Rep By: Donald M. Itzkoff

Siemens Westinghouse Power Corporation

701 Pennsylvania Ave. NW
Suite 720
Washington, DC 20004
Tel: (202)434-4818
Fax: (202)347-4015
E-mail: andrew.robart@swpc.siemens.com

Manufacturer of combustion gas and steam electric turbines and generators. Also develops solid oxide fuel cells. Headquartered in Orlando, FL.

Leg. Issues: BUD, CAW, ENG, FIN, FUE, NAT, SCI

In-house, DC-area Employees

ROBART, Andrew W.: Manager, Government Relations

Sierra Club

408 C St. NE
Washington, DC 20002
Tel: (202)547-1141
Fax: (202)547-6009
Registered: LDA
Web: www.sierraclub.org

Mission of the organization is to explore, enjoy and protect the wild places of the earth; to practice and promote the responsible use of the earth's ecosystems and resources; to educate and enlist humanity to protect and restore the quality of the natural and human environment; and to use all lawful means to carry out these objectives. Headquartered in San Francisco, CA.

Leg. Issues: AGR, BUD, CAW, ENG, ENV, FAM, FUE, HCR, RES, WAS

Political Action Committee/s

Sierra Club Political Committee
408 C St. NE
Washington, DC 20002
Tel: (202)547-1141
Fax: (202)547-6009

In-house, DC-area Employees

BECKER, Daniel F.: Director, Global Warming and Energy Program
BINGAMAN, Jr., Robert L.: National Field Director
COSGROVE, Sean: Associate Representative, Land Protection
GRIFFIN, Melanie: Director, Land Protection Program
HOPKINS, Ed: Director, Environmental Quality Program
LOVAAS, Deron: Associate Representative
MANSKOPF, Dirk: Conservation Assistant, Environmental Quality
MATTISON, Allen: Director, Media Relations
MESNIKOFF, Ann: Associate Representative, Global Warming and Energy
MILLS, Stephen: Director, International Program
NEWMAN, Michael: National Political Representative
PIERCE, Melinda: Washington Representative, Land Protection Program
QUERAL, Alejandro: Associate Representative
SEASE, Debbie: Legislative Director
SELIGMAN, Daniel: Senior Trade Fellow, International Program
WHITE, Deanna: Deputy, Political Director
WOLFE, Dana: Associate Representative, Land Protection

Sierra Health Services

Las Vegas, NV

Outside Counsel/Consultants

The Direct Impact Co.

Sierra Madre, California, City of

Leg. Issues: BUD, CAW, ENV, LAW, NAT, ROD, TRA, URB

Outside Counsel/Consultants

The Ferguson Group, LLC
Issues: BUD, CAW, ENV, LAW, NAT, ROD, TRA, URB
Rep By: William Ferguson, Jr., Trent Lehman

Sierra Military Health Services, Inc.
Leg. Issues: DEF

Outside Counsel/Consultants

Hurt, Norton & Associates
Issues: DEF
Rep By: Robert H. Hurt, Frank Norton, Helen C. Siracuse, William K. Takakoshi

Patton Boggs, LLP
Issues: DEF
Rep By: Thomas Hale Boggs, Jr., John J. Deschauer, Jr., Shannon M. Gibson, Robert H. Koehler, Stuart M. Pape, Florence W. Prioleau

Sierra Nevada Corp.
Sparks, NV
Leg. Issues: DEF, TRD

Outside Counsel/Consultants

John G. Campbell, Inc.
Issues: DEF

The Carter Group
Issues: DEF, TRD
Rep By: Michael R. Carter

Sierra Pacific Industries
Redding, CA
Leg. Issues: BUD, TAX

Outside Counsel/Consultants

Washington Council Ernst & Young
Issues: BUD, TAX
Rep By: Doug Badger, John L. Doney, Jayne T. Fitzgerald, LaBrenda Garrett-Nelson, Gary J. Gasper, Bruce A. Gates, Nick Giordano, Robert J. Leonard, Richard Meltzer, Robert M. Rozen, Timothy J. Urban

Sierra Pacific Resources
Reno, NV
Leg. Issues: BUD, UTI

Outside Counsel/Consultants

Marcus G. Faust, P.C.
Issues: BUD, UTI
Rep By: Marcus G. Faust, Adrianne Firth

The Paul Laxalt Group
Issues: UTI
Rep By: Hon. Paul D. Laxalt, Tom Loranger

Sierra Technologies Inc.
Buffalo, NY
Leg. Issues: AER, DEF

Outside Counsel/Consultants

Lawrence Ryan Internat'l, Inc.
Issues: AER, DEF

SIG Arms
Exeter, NH
Leg. Issues: FIR

Outside Counsel/Consultants

Zeliff, Ireland, and Associates
Issues: FIR
Rep By: Hon. William H. Zeliff, Jr.

SIGCOM, Inc.
Greensboro, NC
Leg. Issues: DEF, ROD, SCI, TEC

Outside Counsel/Consultants

James E. Guirard
Issues: ROD, SCI, TEC
Rep By: James E. Guirard, Jr.

The PMA Group
Issues: DEF
Rep By: Daniel Cunningham, Daniel E. Fleming, Paul J. Magliocchetti, Brian Thiel, Mark Waclawski, Sandra Welch

Sigma-Tau Pharmaceuticals, Inc.
Web: www.sigmatau.com
E-mail: info@sigmatau

Outside Counsel/Consultants

Fleishman-Hillard, Inc

Signal Behavioral Health Network
Denver, CO
Leg. Issues: ALC, BUD, HCR, MMM, WEL

Outside Counsel/Consultants

Kogovsek & Associates
Issues: ALC, BUD, HCR, MMM, WEL
Rep By: Christine Ann Arbogast, Hon. Raymond P. Kogovsek

Sikorsky Aircraft Corp.
Stratford, CT

Outside Counsel/Consultants

Baker, Donelson, Bearman & Caldwell, P.C.
Rep By: George Cranwell Montgomery

Siletz Tribal Council
Siletz, OR
Leg. Issues: IND

Outside Counsel/Consultants

Ducheneaux, Taylor & Associates, Inc.
Issues: IND
Rep By: Franklin D. Ducheneaux

Silicon Graphics/SGI
E-mail: jimgov@sgi.com

A high performance computer systems manufacturing service.

Leg. Issues: CPI, CPT, GOV, MIA, SCI, TAX, TRD

Outside Counsel/Consultants

The Advocacy Group
Issues: CPI
Rep By: George A. Ramonas

Silicon Valley Group
San Jose, CA
Leg. Issues: BUD, DEF, SCI

Outside Counsel/Consultants

R. Wayne Sayer & Associates
Issues: BUD, DEF, SCI
Rep By: John Kania, William Morin, R. Wayne Sayer

Silver Group, Inc.
San Francisco, CA

Outside Counsel/Consultants

Covington & Burling

Silver King Communications
St. Petersburg, FL

Outside Counsel/Consultants

Skadden, Arps, Slate, Meagher & Flom LLP
Rep By: John C. Quale

Silver Users Ass'n
1730 M St. NW
Suite 911
Washington, DC 20036-4505
E-mail: office1730@aol.com
Tel: (202)785-3050

Founded in 1947, the Silver Users Ass'n represents the interests of companies that make, sell or distribute products of which silver forms an essential part and exists to keep its members informed on all developments affecting the use and availability of this metal. The Ass'n takes action when necessary to ensure the ready availability of silver to the industry.

Leg. Issues: BAN, CAW, CDT, CHM, DEF, ENV, FIN, GOV, LBR, MAN, MED, MON, NAT, SMB, TRD, WAS

In-house, DC-area Employees

FRANKLAND, Jr., Walter L.: Exec. V. President

Silver, Freedman & Taff
Washington, DC
Leg. Issues: BAN

Outside Counsel/Consultants

Butera & Andrews
Issues: BAN
Rep By: Cliff W. Andrews, Wright H. Andrews, Jr., James J. Butera, Frank Tillotson

Silverline Technologies, Inc.
Piscataway, NJ
Leg. Issues: BUD

Outside Counsel/Consultants

Preston Gates Ellis & Rouvelas Meeds LLP
Issues: BUD
Rep By: Ralph D. Nurnberger

Simark Trading Co., Inc.
Washington, DC

Outside Counsel/Consultants

Johnson, Rogers & Clifton, L.L.P.

Simon & Schuster Inc.
New York, NY

Outside Counsel/Consultants

Television Communicators
Rep By: Robert D. Wechter

Simpson Investment Co.
Seattle, WA
Leg. Issues: ENV

Outside Counsel/Consultants

Richard L. Barnes
Rep By: Richard L. Barnes

Preston Gates Ellis & Rouvelas Meeds LLP
Issues: ENV

Simula, Inc.
Phoenix, AZ
Registered: LDA

Designs and manufactures crash safety and energy absorption systems and devices.

Leg. Issues: AUT, AVI, BUD, CSP, DEF, RRR, TRA

Outside Counsel/Consultants

Dorfman & O'Neal, Inc.
Issues: AUT, AVI, CSP, RRR, TRA
Rep By: Ira H. Dorfman

Robison Internat'l, Inc.
Issues: BUD, DEF, TRA
Rep By: Stephen A. Evered, J. David Willson

The Spectrum Group
Issues: DEF
Rep By: Lt. Gen. Augustus Cianciolo, USA (Ret.), Lt. Gen. John B "Skip" Hall, Jr., USAF(Ret.), Paul E. McManus, James Rooney, Gregory L. Sharp

Sinclair Broadcast Group, Inc.
Cockeysville, MD
Leg. Issues: COM

Outside Counsel/Consultants

Shaw Pittman
Issues: COM
Rep By: Martin R. Leader

Singapore Technologies Automotive
Singapore, SINGAPORE
Leg. Issues: BUD, DEF, TRD

Outside Counsel/Consultants

GMA Internat'l
Issues: BUD, DEF, TRD
Rep By: Edward C. O'Connor

Singapore Technologies, Inc.
Singapore, SINGAPORE
Leg. Issues: MAN

Outside Counsel/Consultants

Greenberg Traurig, LLP
Issues: MAN
Rep By: Joseph Reeder

Singapore Trade Development Board

Outside Counsel/Consultants

Powell, Goldstein, Frazer & Murphy LLP

Singapore, Embassy of the Republic of
3501 International Place NW
Washington, DC 20008
Tel: (202)537-3100
Fax: (202)537-0876
Web: www.mfa.gov.sg/washington
E-mail: singemb@bellatlantic.net
Leg. Issues: FOR

Outside Counsel/Consultants

Powell, Goldstein, Frazer & Murphy LLP

T. Dean Reed Co.

White & Case LLP
Rep By: William J. Clinton, Walter J. Spak

Singapore, Government of the Republic of
Singapore, SINGAPORE

Outside Counsel/Consultants

APCO Worldwide

White & Case LLP
Rep By: William J. Clinton, Walter J. Spak

Singer Asset Management Co., L.L.C.
New York, NY
Leg. Issues: TAX

Outside Counsel/Consultants

Greenberg Traurig, LLP
Issues: TAX
Rep By: Ronald L. Platt

Singer Assett Finance, Inc.

New York, NY
Leg. Issues: TAX

Outside Counsel/Consultants

Kelly and Associates, Inc.
Issues: TAX
Rep By: John A. Kelly

The Singer Group

Outside Counsel/Consultants

Verner, Liipfert, Bernhard, McPherson and Hand, Chartered
Rep By: Lawrence E. Levinson

Single Stick

Phoenix, AZ
Leg. Issues: TOB

Outside Counsel/Consultants

Manatt, Phelps & Phillips, LLP
Issues: TOB
Rep By: Hon. Jack W. Buechner

SINTEF Telecom and Informatics

Trondheim, NORWAY
A research institution.

Leg. Issues: DEF

Outside Counsel/Consultants

American Defense Internat'l, Inc.
Issues: DEF
Rep By: Michael Herson, Van D. Hipp, Jr., Dave Wilberding

Sippican, Inc.

Marion, MA
Leg. Issues: DEF

Outside Counsel/Consultants

John G. Campbell, Inc.
Issues: DEF

Bob Davis & Associates
Issues: DEF
Rep By: Hon. Robert W. Davis

Sirius Satellite Radio, Inc.

New York, NY
Leg. Issues: ART, COM, CPT

Outside Counsel/Consultants

The Paul Laxalt Group
Issues: ART, COM, CPT
Rep By: Hon. Paul D. Laxalt, Tom Loranger

Siscorp

Derry, NH
Leg. Issues: EDU, ENV, MED, SCI

Outside Counsel/Consultants

The Advocacy Group
Issues: EDU, ENV, MED, SCI
Rep By: Robert E. Mills

Sisseton-Wahpoton Sioux Indian Tribe

Agency Village, SD
Leg. Issues: BUD, HCR, IND

Outside Counsel/Consultants

Romano & Associates, LLC
Issues: BUD, HCR, IND
Rep By: John Romano

Sister Cities Internat'l

Alexandria, VA
Leg. Issues: FOR, GOV, URB

Outside Counsel/Consultants

Bentley, Adams, Hargett, Riley and Co., Inc.
Issues: GOV, URB
Rep By: Frederick A. Biestek, Jr., Michael Hargett, H. McGuire Riley, John Rosamond

Capital Consultants Corp.
Issues: FOR
Rep By: Michael David Kaiser

Sisters of Charity of Leavenworth Health Services

Billings, MT
Leg. Issues: HCR, MED, MMM

Outside Counsel/Consultants

Van Ness Feldman, P.C.
Issues: HCR, MED, MMM
Rep By: J. Curtis Rich

Sisters of Charity of the Incarnate Word

Houston, TX
Leg. Issues: DEF

Outside Counsel/Consultants

Advantage Associates, Inc.
Issues: DEF
Rep By: Hon. Bill Sarpalius

Sisters of Providence Health Systems

Seattle, WA
Leg. Issues: BUD, HCR, IMM, INS, MMM, TAX, WEL

Outside Counsel/Consultants

Conkling, Fiskum & McCormick
Issues: BUD, HCR, IMM, INS, MMM, TAX, WEL
Rep By: Gary Conkling, Daniel Jarman

Site Inc.

Lexington, KY

Outside Counsel/Consultants

Verner, Liipfert, Bernhard, McPherson and Hand, Chartered
Rep By: Linda M. Weinberg

Sithe Energies

New York, NY

Outside Counsel/Consultants

Chadbourne and Parke LLP
Rep By: Keith Martin

Jefferson-Waterman Internat'l, LLC
Rep By: Ann B. Wrobleski

SiTV

Outside Counsel/Consultants

Podesta/Mattoon
Rep By: Ann Delory, Kimberley Fritts, Matthew Gelman, Claudia James, Andrew C. Littman

Six Agency Committee

Glendale, CA
Leg. Issues: BUD, IND, NAT

Outside Counsel/Consultants

Will and Carlson, Inc.
Issues: BUD, IND, NAT
Rep By: Peter Carlson, Robert P. Will

Skadden, Arps, Slate, Meagher & Flom LLP

1440 New York Ave. NW
Washington, DC 20005
Tel: (202)371-7000
Fax: (202)393-5760
Registered: LDA, FARA

Web: www.skadden.com
Leg. Issues: ENV, TAX

Political Action Committee/s

Skadden Arps Political Action Committee
1440 New York Ave. NW
Washington, DC 20005
Tel: (202)371-7000
Fax: (202)393-5760
Contact: Lynn R. Coleman

In-house, DC-area Employees

BARNETTE, Curtis: Of Counsel
BENNETT, Robert S.: Partner
BERLIN, Kenneth: Partner
BRUSCA, Richard L.: Partner
COLEMAN, Lynn R.: Partner
CUTRONE, Roseann M.: Counsel
ESTES, III, John N.: Partner
FLYNN, Brian: Legislative Consultant
GOLDBERG, Jr., Fred T.: Partner
GOLDMAN, Leslie J.: Partner
GROSS, Kenneth A.: Partner
HAMILTON, Stephen W.: Partner
HECHT, Jim: Partner
HOUGH, Jessica A.
LIGHTHIZER, Robert E.: Partner
LOSEY, James A.: Associate
MANGAN, John J.: Partner
NAEVE, Clifford M.: Partner
OOSTERHUIS, Paul W.: Partner
QUALE, John C.: Partner
SCHERMAN, William S.: Partner
SCHLAGER, Ivan A.
STEPTOE, Mary Lou: Partner
SWEET, Jr., William J.: Partner
WEIMER, Brian D.: Associate

Outside Counsel/Consultants

GPC Internat'l
Issues: ENV
Rep By: Roger S. Berry, John D. Cahill, Michael Day

Washington Council Ernst & Young
Issues: TAX
Rep By: Doug Badger, Lauren Darling, John L. Doney, Jayne T. Fitzgerald, LaBrenda Garrett-Nelson, Gary J. Gasper, Bruce A. Gates, Nick Giordano, Robert J. Leonard, Richard Meltzer, Phillip D. Moseley, John D. Porter, Robert M. Rozen, Donna Steele-Flynn, Timothy J. Urban

SKF USA, Inc.

King of Prussia, PA
Leg. Issues: AER, DEF, TRD

Outside Counsel/Consultants

Ervin Technical Associates, Inc. (ETA)
Issues: AER, DEF, TRD
Rep By: James L. Ervin

Skills USA-VICA

P.O. Box 3000
Leesburg, VA 20177
Tel: (703)777-8810
Fax: (703)777-8999
Web: www.skillsusa.org
E-mail: anyinfo@skillsusa.org

Formerly the Vocational Industrial Clubs of America. A non-profit association for career and technical education students.

In-house, DC-area Employees

HOLDSWORTH, Thomas W.: Director, Communications and Public Affairs
LAWRENCE, Timothy W.: Exec. Director

Outside Counsel/Consultants

Webster, Chamberlain & Bean

Skipps Cutting

Villanueva Cortes, HONDURAS
An apparel manufacturer.

Leg. Issues: APP, TRD

Outside Counsel/Consultants

Sandler, Travis & Rosenberg, P.A.
Issues: APP, TRD
Rep By: Nicole Bivens Collinson, Chandri Navarro-Bowman, Ron Sorini

SKW Chemicals, Inc.

Marietta, GA
Leg. Issues: TRD

Outside Counsel/Consultants

Winthrop, Stimson, Putnam & Roberts
Issues: TRD
Rep By: William L. Matthews, C. Christopher Parlin, Christopher R. Wall

SkyBridge, LLC

Bethesda, MD
Leg. Issues: COM, TEC

Outside Counsel/Consultants

The Dutko Group, Inc.
Issues: COM, TEC
Rep By: Kim Koontz Bayliss, Louis Lehrman, Steve Perry, Juliette M. Raffensperger, Stephen Craig Sayle

Paul, Weiss, Rifkind, Wharton & Garrison
Issues: COM
Rep By: Jeffrey H. Olson, Phillip L. Spector

Skyhook Technologies, Inc.

Draper, UT
Leg. Issues: DEF, MAN

Outside Counsel/Consultants

Peduzzi Associates, Ltd.
Issues: DEF, MAN
Rep By: Paul E. Elliott, Joseph L. Ferreira, C. V. Meadows, Lawrence P. Peduzzi, Ronald A. Putnam

Skytruck, Inc.

Clearwater, FL

Outside Counsel/Consultants

Johnson, Rogers & Clifton, L.L.P.

SKYWATCH Internat'l

Leanosa, TX
Leg. Issues: GOV

Outside Counsel/Consultants

Paradigm Research Group
Issues: GOV

Sleep Products Safety Council
Alexandria, VA
Leg. Issues: CSP

Outside Counsel/Consultants

Sparber and Associates
Issues: CSP
Rep By: Peter G. Sparber, Karen Suhr

Slim Fast Foods Co.
West Palm Beach, FL

Manufacturer of diet foods and supplements.

Leg. Issues: ADV, FOO

Outside Counsel/Consultants

Holland & Knight LLP
Issues: ADV, FOO
Rep By: Hon. Gerald E. Sikorski

SLM Holding Corp.
Reston, VA
Leg. Issues: EDU

Outside Counsel/Consultants

Downey McGrath Group, Inc.
Issues: EDU
Rep By: Nancy Donaldson, Hon. Thomas J. Downey, Jr., Hon. Raymond J. McGrath, Michael R. Wessel

Sloan Valve Co.
Franklin Park, IL

Outside Counsel/Consultants

Howrey Simon Arnold & White

Slovak Information Agency
Bratislava, SLOVAKIA

Outside Counsel/Consultants

Washington World Group, Ltd.
Rep By: Edward J. von Kloberg, III

Slovakia, Government of
Bratislava, SLOVAKIA

Outside Counsel/Consultants

Law Office of Paige E. Reffe
Rep By: Paige E. Reffe

Slovenia, Republic of
Ljubljana, SLOVENIA

Outside Counsel/Consultants

Washington World Group, Ltd.
Rep By: Edward J. von Kloberg, III

SM&A
Vienna, VA
Leg. Issues: DEF, LAW

Outside Counsel/Consultants

Madison Government Affairs
Issues: DEF, LAW
Rep By: Paul J. Hirsch, Myron M. Jacobson, Jackson Kemper, III

Small Business Council of America
4800 Hampden Ln.
Seventh Floor
Bethesda, MD 20814
Tel: (301)656-7603
Fax: (301)654-7354
Registered: LDA
Web: www.sbca.net
Leg. Issues: LBR, RET, SMB, TAX

In-house, DC-area Employees

CALIMAFDE, Paula A.: Chairman
CROW, David T.: Legislative Consultant

Outside Counsel/Consultants

Paley Rothman Goldstein Rosenberg & Cooper
Issues: LBR, RET, SMB, TAX
Rep By: Paula A. Calimafde

Small Business Exporters Ass'n
Washington, DC

Outside Counsel/Consultants

The Morrison Group, Inc.
Rep By: James W. Morrison, Ph.D.

Small Business Regulatory Council
Washington, DC
Leg. Issues: ECN, SMB, TAX

Outside Counsel/Consultants

The Argus Group, L.L.C.
Issues: ECN, SMB, TAX

Small Business Survival Committee
1920 L St. NW
Suite 200
Washington, DC 20036
Tel: (202)785-0238
Fax: (202)822-8118
Registered: LDA
Web: www.sbsc.org
E-mail: dgbowser@sbsc.org

A non profit nonpartisan grassroots lobbying organization fighting against the growing burden of taxes and regulations on small business and individuals.

Leg. Issues: GOV, LBR, SMB

In-house, DC-area Employees

BOWSER, David G.: V. President
KEATING, Raymond I.: Chief Economist
KERRIGAN, Karen: Chairman

Outside Counsel/Consultants

Thompson & Thompson
Issues: GOV, LBR
Rep By: David L. Thompson

Small Property Owners Ass'n of America
Cambridge, MA

Outside Counsel/Consultants

Dublin Castle Group
Rep By: Maureen Flatley Hogan

Smartforce
Redwood City, CA
Leg. Issues: BUD

Outside Counsel/Consultants

Cassidy & Associates, Inc.
Issues: BUD
Rep By: John A. Crumbliss, Shawn Edwards, Amos Hochstein, W. Campbell Kaufman, IV, Maureen Walsh

Smith & Nephew, Inc.
Largo, FL
Leg. Issues: HCR, MMM

Outside Counsel/Consultants

Nusgart Consulting, LLC
Issues: HCR, MMM
Rep By: Marcia Nusgart

Smith & Wesson
Springfield, MA
Leg. Issues: SCI

Outside Counsel/Consultants

Capitol Partners
Issues: SCI
Rep By: William Cunningham, Jonathan M. Orloff

Smith Barney Harris Upham & Co.
New York, NY

Outside Counsel/Consultants

Kutak Rock LLP

Williams & Jensen, P.C.
Rep By: John J. McMackin, Jr.

The Charles E. Smith Companies
Arlington, VA
Leg. Issues: BUD, RES, TAX

Outside Counsel/Consultants

Hecht, Spencer & Associates
Issues: BUD, RES, TAX
Rep By: Timothy P. Hecht, William H. Hecht, Franklin C. Phifer

Patton Boggs, LLP
Issues: RES
Rep By: Thomas Hale Boggs, Jr., John J. Deschauer, Jr., Brian C. Lopina, Edward J. Newberry

Smith Dawson & Andrews, Inc.
1000 Connecticut Ave. NW
Suite 302
Washington, DC 20036
Tel: (202)835-0740
Fax: (202)775-8526
Registered: LDA, FARA
Web: www.sda-inc.com
Leg. Issues: ACC, ART

In-house, DC-area Employees

ANDREWS, Gregory B.
BAILEY, Kirk
DAWSON, Thomas C.
GAINES, Robert A.
LUGO, Ramon Luis
POWAR, Sherri
RILEY, Susan Mary
SMITH, James P.
WARNER, Ray

Outside Counsel/Consultants

O'Connor & Hannan, L.L.P.
Issues: ACC, ART
Rep By: Hon. Thomas J. Corcoran

Smith Development, LLC
Manteno, IL
Leg. Issues: RES

Outside Counsel/Consultants

Greenberg Traurig, LLP
Issues: RES
Rep By: Diane J. Blagman, Gregory McDonald, Ronald L. Platt

The Smith, Korach, Hayet, Haynie Partnership
Miami, FL
Leg. Issues: DEF, VET

Outside Counsel/Consultants

Law Offices of James L. Kane
Issues: DEF, VET
Rep By: James L. Kane, Jr.

Smithfield Foods Inc.
Smithfield, VA
Leg. Issues: AGR, CAW

Outside Counsel/Consultants

Capitolink, LLC
Issues: AGR, CAW
Rep By: Deborah M. Atwood, John H. Thorne, Ph.D.

McGuireWoods L.L.P.
Issues: AGR
Rep By: Stephen A. Katsurinis, Hon. Lewis F. Payne, Jr., Jeffrey L. Schlagenhauf

Williams & Jensen, P.C.
Rep By: William B. Canfield, Bertram W. Carp, J. Steven Hart, Anthony J. Roda

SmithKline Beecham Consumer Healthcare, LLP
Pittsburgh, PA
Leg. Issues: ADV, CPT, MED

Outside Counsel/Consultants

Bennett Turner & Coleman, LLP
Issues: ADV, CPT, MED
Rep By: Alan R. Bennett, Jayne P. Bultena, Michael D. Petty

Smiths Aerospace
1225 Jefferson Davis Hwy.
Suite 1100
Arlington, VA 22202
Tel: (703)416-9400
Fax: (703)416-9404
Web: www.smiths-group.com
E-mail: geluz-pat@si.com

Formerly known as Smiths Industries - Aerospace & Defense Systems Inc. Headquartered in London, England.

In-house, DC-area Employees

CARNEY, Ginger: Director, International Trade Controls
DONOVAN, George J.: V. President, Government Relations

Smiths Industries Aerospace and Defense Systems
Grand Rapids, MI
Leg. Issues: DEF

Outside Counsel/Consultants

American Defense Internat'l, Inc.
Issues: DEF
Rep By: Michael Herson, Van D. Hipp, Jr., Dave Wilberding

Smithsonian Institution
1000 Jefferson Dr. SW
Suite T360
Washington, DC 20560
Tel: (202)357-2962
Fax: (202)786-2274
Web: www.si.edu/newstar.htm

In-house, DC-area Employees

PAYNE, Nell: Director, Government Relations
REIDY, Maura: Senior Government Relations Specialist

Smokeless Tobacco Council
1627 K St. NW
Suite 700
Washington, DC 20006
Tel: (202)452-1252
Fax: (202)452-0118
Registered: LDA
Leg. Issues: ADV, TAX, TOB

Political Action Committee/s

Smokeless Tobacco Council Political Action Committee

1627 K St. NW
Suite 700
Washington, DC 20006
Contact: Robert Y. Maples
Tel: (202)452-1252
Fax: (202)452-0118

In-house, DC-area Employees

BLILEY, Christopher P.: Director, Government Relations
LEEPER, John E.: Senior Director, Government Relations
MAPLES, Robert Y.: President
MOCK, Mary: V. President, Secretary and Treasurer

Outside Counsel/Consultants

Dickstein Shapiro Morin & Oshinsky LLP
Issues: TOB
Rep By: Henry C. Cashen, II, Hon. Wendell H. Ford, Elizabeth B. Haywood, Robert Mangas, Graham "Rusty" Mathews, Laurie McKay, Hon. Stanford E. Parris, Rebecah Moore Shepherd, L. Andrew Zausner

Smokers Pneumoconiosis Council

Vienna, VA
Leg. Issues: TAX

Outside Counsel/Consultants

Thomas D. Campbell & Assoc.
Issues: TAX
Rep By: Thomas D. Campbell

SMS Corp.

Malvern, PA
Leg. Issues: HCR, VET

Outside Counsel/Consultants

Albertine Enterprises, Inc.
Issues: HCR, VET
Rep By: James J. Albertine

Smurfit Stone Container Corp.

Clayton, MO
Leg. Issues: ADV, CAW, ENG, ENV, FUE, GOV, MAN, TAX, WAS

Outside Counsel/Consultants

Colling Swift & Hynes
Issues: ADV, CAW, ENG, ENV, FUE, GOV, MAN, TAX, WAS
Rep By: Terese Colling, Pablo Collins, Robert J. Hynes, Jr., Hon. Allan B. Swift

Snack Food Ass'n

1711 King St.
Suite One
Alexandria, VA 22314
Tel: (703)836-4500
Fax: (703)836-8262
Registered: LDA
Web: www.sfa.org
E-mail: sfa@sfa.org
Leg. Issues: BUD, ENV, FOO, TRA, TRD, TRU, UTI

Political Action Committee/s

SnackPAC
1711 King St.
Suite One
Alexandria, VA 22314
Contact: Katherine Northup
Tel: (703)836-4500
Fax: (703)836-8262

In-house, DC-area Employees

MCCARTHY, James A.: President and Chief Exec. Officer
NORTHUP, Katherine: Government Relations Representative
SEILER, Elizabeth Avery: Sr. V. President, Government and Public Affairs
WILKES, Ann P.: V. President, Communications

Outside Counsel/Consultants

G.R. Services
Issues: TRU
Rep By: Earl Eisenhart

Snake River Sugar Co.

Ogden, UT
Leg. Issues: AGR, TAX

Outside Counsel/Consultants

Symms, Lehn & Associates, Inc.
Issues: AGR, TAX

Soap and Detergent Ass'n

1500 K St. NW
Suite 300
Washington, DC 20005
Tel: (202)347-2900
Fax: (202)347-4110
Registered: LDA
Web: www.cleaning101.com
E-mail: info@sdahq.org
Leg. Issues: ENV

In-house, DC-area Employees

GRIESING, Dennis: V. President, Government Affairs
SANSONI, Brian T.: V. President, Communication and Education

Outside Counsel/Consultants

Hogan & Hartson L.L.P.
Issues: ENV
Rep By: James Chen, Warren H. Maruyama, Humberto R. Pena

Soave Enterprises

Outside Counsel/Consultants

The Da Vinci Group
Rep By: Mark R. Smith

Soboba Band of Mission Indians

San Jacinto, CA
Leg. Issues: IND

Outside Counsel/Consultants

The State Affairs Co.
Issues: IND
Rep By: Bonnie L. Chafe

Soc. for American Archaeology

900 Second St. NE
Suite 12
Washington, DC 20002-3557
Tel: (202)789-8200
Fax: (202)789-0284
Registered: LDA
Web: www.saa.org
E-mail: headquarters@saa.org
Leg. Issues: BUD, IND

In-house, DC-area Employees

BRIMSEK, Tobi: Exec. Director
CRAIB, Donald F.: Manager, Government Affairs and Counsel

Soc. for Animal Protective Legislation

P.O. Box 3719
Georgetown Station
Washington, DC 20007
Tel: (202)337-2334
Fax: (202)338-9478
Registered: LDA
Web: www.saplonline.org

Interested in furthering legislation favoring humane treatment of all animals.

Leg. Issues: ANI

In-house, DC-area Employees

BEMELMANS, Madeleine: President
GLEIBER, John: Exec. Secretary
LISS, Cathy: Legislative Director
ROBERTS, Adam M.: Legislative Assistant
STEVENS, Christine: Secretary

Soc. for Excellence in Eyecare

Tarpon Springs, FL
Leg. Issues: HCR

Outside Counsel/Consultants

Arent Fox Kintner Plotkin & Kahn, PLLC
Issues: HCR
Rep By: Jeff Peters, Alan E. Reider, Allison Shuren

Soc. for Human Resource Management

1800 Duke St.
Alexandria, VA 22314
Tel: (703)548-3440
Fax: (703)836-0367
Registered: LDA
Web: www.shrm.org
E-mail: shrm@shrm.org

An organization dedicated to excellence in human resource management. Includes more than 93,000 individuals working for a cross-section of employers, from smaller family operations to large, multi-national corporations.

Leg. Issues: BAN, LBR

In-house, DC-area Employees

COMPTON, Kathron: Director, Public Affairs
DRINAN, Helen: President and Chief Exec. Officer
JACKSON BELLINGER, Julia: Manager, Tax Benefits Regulation and Legislation
MEISINGER, SPHR, Susan R.: Chief Operating Officer
PIERCE, Sarah: Legislative Representative
ROBBIN, Elizabeth: Employment Regulation and Legislation
ZEPPELIN, Deron: Director, Governmental Affairs

Outside Counsel/Consultants

Butera & Andrews
Issues: BAN
Rep By: Cliff W. Andrews, Wright H. Andrews, Jr., James J. Butera, Frank Tillotson

Working for the Future, LLC
Rep By: Deanna R. Gelak

Soc. for In Vitro Biology

9315 Largo Dr. West
Suite 255
Largo, MD 20774
Tel: (301)324-5054
Fax: (301)324-5057
Web: www.sivb.org
E-mail: sivb@sivb.org

Provides an interdisciplinary forum for the exchange of ideas, learning, and teaching about basic and applied problems of cellular and developmental biology. The research interests of the association emphasize in vitro cell culture systems. Members are scientists, students, technicians, administrators and executives from academia, government and industry.

Leg. Issues: SCI

In-house, DC-area Employees

ELLIS, Marietta: Managing Director

Soc. for Industrial & Applied Mathematics

Philadelphia, PA
Leg. Issues: BUD, EDU, IMM, SCI

Outside Counsel/Consultants

Lewis-Burke Associates
Issues: BUD, EDU, IMM, SCI
Rep By: April L. Burke, Mark Marin

Soc. for Marketing Professional Services

99 Canal Center Plaza
Suite 250
Alexandria, VA 22314
Tel: (703)549-6117
Fax: (703)549-2498
Web: www.smps.org
E-mail: info@smps.org
Leg. Issues: EDU, RES

In-house, DC-area Employees

WORTH, Ronald D.: Exec. V. President

Soc. for Mucosal Immunology

Bethesda, MD
Leg. Issues: HCR, MED

Outside Counsel/Consultants

PAI Management Corp.
Issues: HCR, MED
Rep By: Norman E. Wallis, Ph.D.

Soc. for Neuroscience

11 Dupont Circle NW
Suite 500
Washington, DC 20036
Tel: (202)462-6688
Fax: (202)234-9770
Registered: LDA
Web: www.sfn.org
E-mail: info@sfn.org

An interdisciplinary organization to enhance information exchange. The membership of 28,000 includes clinicians, research scientists and students.

Leg. Issues: BUD, MED

In-house, DC-area Employees

BEANG, Nancy: Exec. Director
WAINIK, Allison: Manager, Governmental and Public Affairs

Outside Counsel/Consultants

Policy Directions, Inc.
Issues: BUD, MED
Rep By: Stephen Michael, Frankie L. Trull

Soc. for Occupational and Environmental Health

McLean, VA
Web: www.soeh.org
E-mail: soeh@degnon.org

Serves as a forum for the presentation of scientific data and the exchange of information among occupational and environmental health professionals in government, industry, labor, and academia with the aim of reducing the risks of occupational and environmental hazards.

Outside Counsel/Consultants

Degnon Associates, Inc.

Soc. for Pediatric Pathology

McLean, VA
Web: www.spponline.org
E-mail: socpedpath@degnon.org

Outside Counsel/Consultants

Degnon Associates, Inc.

Soc. for Research Administration

Outside Counsel/Consultants

The Plexus Consulting Group

Soc. for Risk Analysis

McLean, VA
Web: www.sra.org
E-mail: sraburkmgt@aol.com

Outside Counsel/Consultants

Burk & Associates
Rep By: Richard J. Burk, Jr.

Soc. for Technical Communication

901 N. Stuart St.
Suite 904
Arlington, VA 22203-1822
Tel: (703)522-4114
Fax: (703)522-2075
Web: www.stc-va.org
E-mail: stc@stc-va.org

In-house, DC-area Employees

STOLGITIS, William C.: Exec. Director and Counsel

Soc. for Vascular Surgery

Leg. Issues: HCR, MMM

Outside Counsel/Consultants

Arent Fox Kintner Plotkin & Kahn, PLLC
Issues: HCR, MMM
Rep By: Stacy Harbison, William A. Sarraille, Allison Shuren

Soc. for Women's Health Research

1828 L St. NW
Suite 625
Washington, DC 20036
Tel: (202)223-8224
Fax: (202)833-3472
Web: www.womens-health.org
E-mail: information@womens-health.org
Leg. Issues: BUD, HCR, MED

In-house, DC-area Employees

BIEGEL, Roberta: Director, Government Relations
BOLLT, Anita: Deputy Director
GREENBERGER, M.S.W., Phyllis M.: President and Chief Exec. Officer
KAPLAN, Melissa: Government Relations Assistant
LIPTAK, Elisabeth: Communications Director
MARTS, Sherry: Scientific Director
PARRISH, Linda Jo: Development Director

Outside Counsel/Consultants

Cavarocchi Ruscio Dennis Associates
Issues: BUD, HCR, MED
Rep By: Elizabeth Bartheld, Lyle B. Dennis

SPECTRUM Science Public Relations, Inc.
Issues: HCR, MED
Rep By: John J. Seng

Soc. of American Florists

1601 Duke St.
Alexandria, VA 22314-3406
Tel: (703)836-8700
Fax: (703)836-8705
Registered: LDA
Web: www.safnow.org

The Society of American Florists (SAF) is the national trade association that represents and supports the floral industry. Its members are growers, wholesalers, retailers, importers, manufacturers, suppliers, educators, students, and allied organizations.

Leg. Issues: AGR, HCR, IMM, LBR, SMB, TRA, TRD

Political Action Committee/s

Soc. of American Florists Political Action Committee
1601 Duke St.
Alexandria, VA 22314-3406
Tel: (703)836-8700
Fax: (703)836-8705
Contact: Chris Brown

In-house, DC-area Employees

BROWN, Chris: Manager of Political and Legislative Outreach
GRUENBURG, Drew: Senior V. President, Government Relations
LITTLE, Jeanne: Director, Government Relations
SCHMALE, Lin: Senior Director, Government Relations

Outside Counsel/Consultants

Jenner & Block

Soc. of American Foresters

5400 Grosvenor Ln.
Bethesda, MD 20814-2198
Tel: (301)897-8720
Fax: (301)897-3690
Web: www.safnet.org
E-mail: safweb@safnet.org

The mission of the Society of American Foresters is to advance the science, education, technology, and practice of forestry; to enhance the competency of its members; to establish standards of professional excellence; and to use the knowledge, skills, and conservation ethic of the profession to ensure the continued health and use of forest ecosystems and the present and future availability of forest resources to benefit society.

Leg. Issues: NAT

In-house, DC-area Employees

BANZHAF, William H.: Exec. V. President
GARDNER, Lori B.: Director, Communications and Member Services
GHANNAM, Jeff: Director, Media Relations
GOERGEN, Michael: Director, Forest Policy

Soc. of Automotive Engineers (SAE Internat'l)

2000 L St. NW
Suite 200
Washington, DC 20036
Tel: (202)416-1649
Fax: (202)416-1618
Web: www.sae.org
E-mail: DouglasR@SAE.org

In-house, DC-area Employees

READ, Douglas E.: Manager, Washington Office

Soc. of Cardiovascular and Interventional Radiology

10201 Lee Hwy.
Suite 500
Fairfax, VA 22030
Tel: (703)691-1805
Fax: (703)691-1855
Web: www.scvir.org
E-mail: info@scvir.org

Political Action Committee/s

Soc. of Cardiovascular and Interventional Radiology Political Action Committee
10201 Lee Hwy.
Suite 500
Fairfax, VA 22030
Tel: (703)691-1805
Fax: (703)691-1855
Contact: Tricia McClenny

In-house, DC-area Employees

MCCLENNY, Tricia: Assistant Exec. Director
POMERANTZ, Paul: Exec. Director

Soc. of Competitive Intelligence Professionals

1700 Diagonal Rd.
Suite 600
Alexandria, VA 22314-2866
Tel: (703)739-0696
Fax: (703)739-2524
Web: www.scip.org
E-mail: info@scip.org

A non-profit organization of individuals who evaluate competitors and competitive situations and associate to improve their skills.

In-house, DC-area Employees

BRECHT, Paul: Deputy Director and Chief Financial Officer
WEBER, William: Exec. Director

Soc. of Consumer Affairs Professionals in Business

801 N. Fairfax St.
Suite 404
Alexandria, VA 22314-1757
Tel: (703)519-3700
Fax: (703)549-4886
Web: www.socap.org
E-mail: socap@socap.org
Leg. Issues: CSP

In-house, DC-area Employees

GARCIA, CAE, Lou: Exec. Director

Soc. of Diagnostic Medical Sonographers

Leg. Issues: HCR, MMM

Outside Counsel/Consultants

Arent Fox Kintner Plotkin & Kahn, PLLC
Issues: HCR, MMM
Rep By: Stacy Harbison, William A. Sarraille, Allison Shuren

Soc. of General Internal Medicine

2501 M St. NW
Suite 575
Washington, DC 20037
Tel: (202)887-5150
Fax: (202)887-5405
Registered: LDA
Web: www.sgim.org
E-mail: karlsond@sgim.org
Leg. Issues: BUD, HCR, MED, VET

In-house, DC-area Employees

KARLSON, Ph.D., David: Exec. Director

Outside Counsel/Consultants

Medical Advocacy Services, Inc.
Issues: BUD, HCR, MED, VET
Rep By: Robert Blaser

Soc. of Glass and Ceramic Decorators

4340 East-West Hwy.
Bethesda, MD 20814
Tel: (301)951-3933
Fax: (301)951-3801
Web: www.sgcd.org
E-mail: sgcd@sgcd.org

In-house, DC-area Employees

BOPT, Andrew: Exec. Director

Outside Counsel/Consultants

Zuckert, Scoutt and Rasenberger, L.L.P.
Rep By: James A. Calderwood

Soc. of Gyneocologic Oncologists

Chicago, IL
Leg. Issues: BUD, HCR, MED, MMM

Outside Counsel/Consultants

Smith, Bucklin and Associates, Inc.
Issues: BUD, HCR, MED, MMM
Rep By: Jill Rathbun

Soc. of Independent Gasoline Marketers of America

11911 Freedom Dr.
Suite 590
Reston, VA 20190
Tel: (703)709-7000
Fax: (703)709-7007
Web: www.sigma.org
Leg. Issues: BAN, ENV, LBR, TAX, TOB

Political Action Committee/s

Soc. of Independent Gasoline Marketers Political Action Committee
11911 Freedom Dr.
Suite 590
Reston, VA 20190
Tel: (703)709-7000
Fax: (703)709-7007

In-house, DC-area Employees

DOYLE, Kenneth A.: Exec. V. President

Outside Counsel/Consultants

Collier Shannon Scott, PLLC
Issues: BAN, ENV, LBR, TAX, TOB
Rep By: R. Timothy Columbus, Kathleen Clark Kies, Jeffrey L. Leiter, Gregory M. Scott, Dana S. Wood

Soc. of Industrial and Office Realtors

700 11th St. NW
Suite 510
Washington, DC 20001-4511
Tel: (202)737-1150
Fax: (202)737-8796
Web: www.sior.com

Affiliated with the Nat'l Ass'n of Realtors.

Leg. Issues: RES

In-house, DC-area Employees

HINTON, Pamela J.: Exec. V. President

Soc. of Maternal-Fetal Medicine

Outside Counsel/Consultants

Smith, Bucklin and Associates, Inc.
Rep By: Jill Rathbun

Soc. of Nat'l Ass'n Publications

Vienna, VA
Web: www.snaponline.org
E-mail: info@snaponline.org

Outside Counsel/Consultants

Ass'n Management Bureau
Rep By: Laura Skoff

Soc. of Nuclear Medicine

1850 Samuel Morse Dr.
Reston, VA 20198
Tel: (703)708-9000
Fax: (703)708-9015
Registered: LDA
Web: www.snm.org
E-mail: kmaynard@snm.org

A multi-disciplinary organization of more than 16,000 physicians, physicists, chemists, radiopharmacists, technologists and others interested in the diagnostic, therapeutic and investigational uses of nuclear medicine. Founded in 1954.

Leg. Issues: ENG, HCR, MED, MMM, WAS

Political Action Committee/s

Soc. of Nuclear Medicine PAC
1850 Samuel Morse Dr.
Reston, VA 20198
Tel: (703)708-9000
Fax: (703)708-9020
Contact: William J. Bertera

In-house, DC-area Employees

BERTERA, William J.: Exec. Director
UFFELMAN, William: Director, Public Policy

Outside Counsel/Consultants

Mintz, Levin, Cohn, Ferris, Glovsky and Popeo, P.C.
Rep By: Alvin J. Lorman

Soc. of Professional Benefit Administrators

Two Wisconsin Circle
Suite 670
Chevy Chase, MD 20815-7003
Tel: (301)718-7722
Fax: (301)718-9440
Web: www.users.erols.com/spba

The national association of employee benefit Third Party Administration firms (TPAs).

Leg. Issues: GOV, HCR, INS, LBR, RET

In-house, DC-area Employees

HUNT, Jr., Frederick D.: President
LEIGHT, Elizabeth Ysla: Director, Government Relations
LENNAN, Anne C.: V. President and Director of Federal Affairs

Outside Counsel/Consultants

Hunt Management Systems
Issues: GOV, HCR, INS, LBR, RET
Rep By: Frederick D. Hunt, Jr., Elizabeth Ysla Leight, Anne C. Lennan

Soc. of Professional Journalists

Greencastle, IN

Outside Counsel/Consultants

Baker & Hostetler LLP
Rep By: Robert Lystad, Bruce W. Sanford

Soc. of Research Administrators

Web: www.sra.rams.com
E-mail: sra@dc.sba.com

Outside Counsel/Consultants

Smith, Bucklin and Associates, Inc.
Rep By: Jeff McFarland

Soc. of Teachers of Family Medicine

2021 Massachusetts Ave. NW
Washington, DC 20036
Tel: (202)986-3309
Fax: (202)232-9044
Registered: LDA
Web: www.stfm.org
E-mail: oafmdc@stfm.org

Headquartered in Leewood, KS.

Leg. Issues: HCR, MED, MMM

In-house, DC-area Employees

WITTENBERG, Hope R.: Director, Government Relations

Soc. of the Plastics Industry

1801 K St. NW
Suite 600K
Washington, DC 20006
Tel: (202)974-5200
Fax: (202)296-7005
Registered: LDA
Web: www.plasticsindustry.org
Leg. Issues: CAW, ENV, GOV, TOR

Political Action Committee/s

Society of the Plastics Industry PAC (PlasticPAC)
1801 K St. NW
Suite 600K
Washington, DC 20006
Tel: (202)974-5204
Fax: (202)296-7218
Contact: Debi Q. Richardson

In-house, DC-area Employees

ANDERSON, Lori M.: Director, Economic and International Trade Affairs
DILLS, Jennifer: Strategic Planning Officer
DUNCAN, Donald K.: President
FREEMAN, Jr., Lewis R.: Chief Lobbyist and Senior Gov't Affairs Fellow
HEALEY, Maureen: Chief State and Regulatory Affairs Officer
LIMBACH, Bonnie M.: Chief Communications Officer
RICHARDSON, Debi Q.: Assistant Director, Safety, Health and State Affairs

Outside Counsel/Consultants

Valis Associates
Issues: CAW, ENV, TOR
Rep By: Todd Tolson, Wayne H. Valis

Soc. of Thoracic Surgeons

Washington, DC
Registered: LDA
Leg. Issues: HCR, MED, MMM

Political Action Committee/s

Soc. of Thoracic Surgeons Political Action Committee
Washington, DC

Outside Counsel/Consultants

Capitol Health Group, LLC
Issues: HCR, MMM
Rep By: Michael D. Bromberg, Shawn Coughlin, Steven Jenning, Layna McConkey Peltier

Davidoff & Malito, LLP
Issues: MMM
Rep By: Kenneth C. Malito, Robert J. Malito, Stephen J. Slade

Fleishman-Hillard, Inc
Rep By: William Black

The Plexus Consulting Group
Issues: HCR, MED, MMM
Rep By: Yasmin Quiwzow

Smith, Bucklin and Associates, Inc.
Issues: HCR, MMM
Rep By: Corinne Colgan, Robert H. Wilbur

Soc. of Toxicology

1767 Business Center Dr.
Suite 302
Reston, VA 20190
Tel: (703)438-3115
Fax: (703)438-3113
Web: www.toxicology.org
E-mail: sothq@toxicology.org

Dedicated to developing knowledge that improves the health and safety of living beings and protects their environment.

Leg. Issues: ANI, BUD, CAW, ENV, HCR, MED, SCI, TOB

In-house, DC-area Employees

MCCOY, Michael: Director, Public Affairs

Outside Counsel/Consultants

Ass'n Innovation and Management, Inc.
Rep By: Shawn D. Lamb

Capitol Associates, Inc.
Issues: BUD, CAW, ENV, MED, TOB
Rep By: Sara Milo

Soc. of Vascular Technology

4601 Presidents Dr.
Suite 260
Lanham, MD 20706-4365
Tel: (301)459-7550
Fax: (301)459-5651
Web: www.svtnet.org
E-mail: info@svtnet.org

A non-profit 501(c)(3) professional society.

Leg. Issues: HCR, LBR, MMM

In-house, DC-area Employees

STONE, Suzanne: Exec. Director

Outside Counsel/Consultants

Arent Fox Kintner Plotkin & Kahn, PLLC
Issues: HCR, MMM
Rep By: Stacy Harbison, William A. Sarraille, Allison Shuren

Soccer Industry Council of America

c/o Sporting Goods Manufacturers Ass'n
1625 K St. NW, Suite 900
Washington, DC 20006-1604
Tel: (202)775-1762
Fax: (202)296-7462
Registered: LDA
Web: www.sportlink.com
E-mail: tomsgma@aol.com

In-house, DC-area Employees

COVE, Thomas J.

Societe Air France

Roissey, FRANCE
Leg. Issues: TRA

Outside Counsel/Consultants

Silverberg, Goldman & Bikoff, LLP
Issues: TRA
Rep By: Michael Goldman

Societe Generale de Surveillance Holding S.A.

Geneva, SWITZERLAND

An international inspection service, particularly in import-export trade.

Leg. Issues: TRD

Outside Counsel/Consultants

Shea & Gardner
Issues: TRD
Rep By: John D. Aldock, Patrick M. Hanlon

Societe Nationale d'Etude et Construction de Moteurs d'Aviation (SNECMA)

Melun Cedex, FRANCE
Leg. Issues: DEF

Outside Counsel/Consultants

Meredith Concept Group, Inc.
Issues: DEF
Rep By: Sandra K. Meredith

Sodak Gaming Inc.

Rapid City, SD
Leg. Issues: GAM, IND

Outside Counsel/Consultants

Lydia Hofer & Associates
Issues: GAM

Jana McKeag
Issues: GAM, IND
Rep By: Jana McKeag

Sodexho Marriott Services, Inc.

Gaithersburg, MD
Leg. Issues: DEF, FOO, TAX

Political Action Committee/s

Sodexho Marriott Services Inc. PAC
Gaithersburg, MD

Outside Counsel/Consultants

Clark & Weinstock, Inc.
Issues: DEF
Rep By: Hon. Vic H. Fazio, Jr., Sandi Stuart, Hon. John Vincent "Vin" Weber

Kurzweil & Associates
Issues: FOO, TAX
Rep By: Jeffrey Kurzweil

Soft Telesis Inc.

Seoul, KOREA
Leg. Issues: TEC

Outside Counsel/Consultants

The Washington Group
Issues: TEC

Software & Information Industry Ass'n (SIIA)

1730 M St. NW
Suite 700
Washington, DC 20036-4510
Tel: (202)452-1600
Fax: (202)223-8756
Registered: LDA
Web: www.siia.net

A trade association for companies in the software and information industries.

Leg. Issues: BUD, CPI, EDU, FIN, GOV, IMM, LBR, TAX, TEC, TRD

Political Action Committee/s

SIIA Political Action Committee
1730 M St. NW
Suite 700
Washington, DC 20036-4510
Tel: (202)452-1600
Fax: (202)223-8756
Contact: Kenneth A. Wasch

In-house, DC-area Employees

BOHANNON, Mark
BOWERS, Steve: Director, Public Relations
GEORGE, Melinda: Director, Education Policy
HALL, Lauren: Exec. V. President
KUPFERSCHMID, Keith: Intellectual Property Counsel
LEDUC, David: Manager, Public Policy
SCHNEIDERMAN, Mark: Manager, Federal Education Policy
WASCH, Kenneth A.: President

Software Finance and Tax Executives Council

Leg. Issues: TAX

Outside Counsel/Consultants

R. Duffy Wall and Associates
Issues: TAX
Rep By: David C. Jory

Software Productivity Consortium

Herndon, VA
Leg. Issues: BUD, CPI

Outside Counsel/Consultants

Cavarocchi Ruscio Dennis Associates
Issues: BUD, CPI
Rep By: Nicholas G. Cavarocchi, Domenic R. Ruscio

Griffin, Johnson, Dover & Stewart
Issues: BUD, CPI
Rep By: G. Jack Dover

Sojourners

2401 15th St. NW
Washington, DC 20009
Tel: (202)328-8842
Fax: (202)328-8757
Web: www.sojo.net
E-mail: sojourners@sojourners.com

An organization of ecumenical Christians consisting of a national network combining faith and action and a bi-monthly magazine which examines issues of faith, politics and culture. Seeks to connect individuals and groups working locally for change.

In-house, DC-area Employees

WALLIS, Jim: Editor-in-Chief

SOL Source Technologies, Inc.

Boulder, CO
Leg. Issues: ADV, FOO

Outside Counsel/Consultants

Parry, Romani, DeConcini & Symms
Issues: ADV, FOO
Rep By: Edward H. Baxter, Hon. Dennis DeConcini, John M. Haddow, Scott D. Hatch, Shannon Davis Henderson, Jack W. Martin, Romano Romani, Linda Arey Skladany, Hon. Steven D. Symms

Solana Beach, California, City of

Leg. Issues: BUD, NAT

Outside Counsel/Consultants

Marlowe and Co.
Issues: BUD, NAT
Rep By: Howard Marlowe, Jeffrey Mazzella

Solar Electric Light Co.

Chevy Chase, MD
Leg. Issues: ENG

Outside Counsel/Consultants

Duncan, Weinberg, Genzer & Pembroke, P.C.
Issues: ENG
Rep By: Jeffrey C. Genzer

Solar Energy Industries Ass'n (SEIA)

1616 H St. NW
Suite 800
Washington, DC 20006-4999
Tel: (202)628-7979
Fax: (202)628-7779
Registered: LDA
Web: www.seia.org
E-mail: solarsklar@aol.com
Leg. Issues: ENG, ENV

In-house, DC-area Employees

HAMER, Glenn: Exec. Director

Outside Counsel/Consultants

Duncan, Weinberg, Genzer & Pembroke, P.C.
Issues: ENG
Rep By: Jeffrey C. Genzer

The Stella Group, Ltd.
Issues: ENG, ENV
Rep By: Stella Sklar

Solar Energy Research and Education Foundation

1616 H St. NW
Eighth Floor
Washington, DC 20006-4999
Tel: (202)628-7979
Fax: (202)628-7779

A 501(c)(3) educational organization developing a museum in Washington (the Center for Renewable Energy and Sustainable Technology) featuring interactive, CD-ROM-based, computer technology.

Leg. Issues: EDU, ENG

In-house, DC-area Employees

LAPAS, Linda: Exec. Director

Outside Counsel/Consultants

Duncan, Weinberg, Genzer & Pembroke, P.C.
Issues: EDU, ENG
Rep By: Jeffrey C. Genzer, Tatjana M. Shonkwiler

Solectron

Milipitas, CA

Outside Counsel/Consultants

Dewey Ballantine LLP

Powell Tate

Solex Environmental Systems, Inc.

Houston, TX
Leg. Issues: ENG, ENV

Outside Counsel/Consultants

Bracewell & Patterson, L.L.P.
Issues: ENG, ENV
Rep By: Hon. Edwin R. Bethune, Hon. Jim Chapman, Gene E. Godley, Marc C. Hebert, Charles L. Ingebretson, Michael L. Pate, Scott H. Segal, D. Michael Stroud, Jr.

Solid Waste Agency of Northern Cook County

Des Plaines, IL
Leg. Issues: CAW, WAS

Outside Counsel/Consultants

O'Connor & Hannan, L.L.P.
Issues: CAW, WAS
Rep By: Hon. Thomas J. Corcoran, George J. Mannina, Jr.

Solid Waste Ass'n of North America

1100 Wayne Ave.
Suite 700
Silver Spring, MD 20907-7219
Tel: (301)585-2898
Fax: (301)589-7068
Web: www.swana.org
E-mail: info@swana.org

Non-profit association of municipal solid waste management professionals. Primary membership are employees of local government and local government agencies. Objectives are to increase professionalism in the field and to represent membership interests.

Leg. Issues: TAX, WAS

In-house, DC-area Employees

SKINNER, Ph.D., John H.: Exec. Director and Chief Exec. Officer

Outside Counsel/Consultants

Baise + Miller, P.C.
Issues: TAX
Rep By: Eric P. Bock

Solid Waste Authority of Central Ohio

Grove City, OH

Outside Counsel/Consultants

Wright & Talisman, P.C.
Rep By: Scott M. DuBoff, Robert H. Lamb

Solipsys Corp.

Laurel, MD
Leg. Issues: DEF

Outside Counsel/Consultants

Collins & Company, Inc.
Issues: DEF
Rep By: James D. Bond, Scott Cassel, Richard L. Collins, Shay D. Stautz

Solo Cup Co.

Highland Park, IL

Outside Counsel/Consultants

McDermott, Will and Emery

Solus Research, Inc.

Indianapolis, IN
Leg. Issues: FOO, MED

Outside Counsel/Consultants

Reed, Smith, LLP
Issues: FOO, MED
Rep By: Marc Scheineson

Solutia Inc.

1776 I St. NW
Suite 1030
Washington, DC 20006
Tel: (202)822-1690
Fax: (202)822-1693
Registered: LDA
Web: www.solutia.com

A manufacturer of specialty chemical products headquartered in St. Louis, MO.

Leg. Issues: AUT, CAW, CHM, DIS, ENG, ENV, GOV, HOU, INS, LAW, NAT, RRR, TRA, TRD, TRU, URB, WAS

Political Action Committee/s

Solutia Citizenship Fund
1776 I St. NW
Suite 1030
Washington, DC 20006
Contact: Glenn S. Ruskin
Tel: (202)822-1690
Fax: (202)822-1693

In-house, DC-area Employees

JENNINGS, Allison: Government Affairs Specialist
RUSKIN, Glenn S.: V. President, Public Affairs
WILSON, Greg: Director, Federal Affairs

Solvay Minerals

Green River, WY
Leg. Issues: LBR

Outside Counsel/Consultants

Patton Boggs, LLP
Issues: LBR
Rep By: Henry Chajet

Solvay, New York, Village of

Solvay, NY

Outside Counsel/Consultants

Duncan, Weinberg, Genzer & Pembroke, P.C.
Rep By: Jeffrey C. Genzer

Somach, Simmons & Dunn

Sacramento, CA
Leg. Issues: BUD, NAT

Outside Counsel/Consultants

The Ferguson Group, LLC
Issues: BUD, NAT
Rep By: W. Roger Gwinn, Greg Wang

Somerset Pharmaceuticals

Tampa, FL

Outside Counsel/Consultants

C. McClain Haddow & Associates
Rep By: C. McClain Haddow

Somerville Housing Group

Cambridge, MA
Leg. Issues: BUD

Outside Counsel/Consultants

Holland & Knight LLP
Issues: BUD
Rep By: Robert Hunt Bradner, Jack M. Burkman, Mike Galano, Michael Gillis, Richard M. Gold, Douglas J. Patton, P. J. Toker, Beth Viola

Sonetech Corp.

Bedford, NH
Leg. Issues: AER, DEF

Outside Counsel/Consultants

The Kemper Co.
Issues: AER, DEF
Rep By: Jackson Kemper, Jr.

Songwriters Guild of America

Weehawken, NJ
Leg. Issues: ART, CPT

Outside Counsel/Consultants

The Cuneo Law Group, P.C.
Issues: ART, CPT
Rep By: James J. Schweitzer

Sonoma County Water Agency

Santa Rosa, CA
Leg. Issues: BUD, ENV

Outside Counsel/Consultants

Alcalde & Fay
Issues: ENV
Rep By: Jason Lee, Paul Schlesinger

Van Ness Feldman, P.C.
Issues: BUD
Rep By: Nancy Macan McNally, Robert G. Szabo

Sonoma, California, County of

Santa Rosa, CA
Leg. Issues: ECN, TRA

Outside Counsel/Consultants

Alcalde & Fay
Issues: ECN, TRA
Rep By: Jason Lee, Paul Schlesinger

Sonomedica, Inc.

Vienna, VA
Leg. Issues: HCR

Outside Counsel/Consultants

RPH & Associates, L.L.C.
Issues: HCR

Sonomish, Washington, County of

Everett, WA
Leg. Issues: ENV, NAT

Outside Counsel/Consultants

Denny Miller McBee Associates
Issues: ENV, NAT

SonoSite

Bothell, WA
Leg. Issues: BUD, EDU, HCR

Outside Counsel/Consultants

Smith, Bucklin and Associates, Inc.
Issues: BUD, EDU, HCR
Rep By: Jill Rathbun

Sony Corp.

Tokyo, JAPAN
Leg. Issues: CPT

Outside Counsel/Consultants

Debevoise and Plimpton
Issues: CPT
Rep By: Jeffrey P. Cunard

Wilmer, Cutler & Pickering

Sony Corp. of America
New York, NY
Outside Counsel/Consultants
Willkie Farr & Gallagher
Rep By: Christopher A. Dunn

Sony Electronics, Inc.
1200 G. St. NW
Suite 800
Washington, DC 20005
Tel: (202)434-8994
Fax: (202)783-4513
Registered: LDA
Web: www.sony.com
E-mail: christina.tellalian@am.sony.com
Leg. Issues: AVI, BUD, COM, CPT, FOR, IMM, SCI, TEC, TRD

In-house, DC-area Employees
TELLALIAN, Christina: Sr. Manager, Public and Government Affairs
WIGINTON, Joel: V. President, Government Affairs.

Outside Counsel/Consultants
Patton Boggs, LLP
Issues: CPT
Rep By: Thomas Hale Boggs, Jr., Brian C. Lopina, Jeffrey L. Turner

Sony Music Entertainment Inc.
New York, NY
Leg. Issues: BNK, CPT, TRD
Outside Counsel/Consultants
Jim Pasco & Associates
Issues: CPT
Rep By: James O. Pasco, Jr.
The Smith-Free Group
Issues: BNK, CPT, TRD
Rep By: James C. Free, W. Timothy Locke, Alicia W. Smith

Sony Pictures Entertainment Inc.
Culver City, CA
Leg. Issues: CPT, IMM, TRD
Outside Counsel/Consultants
The Smith-Free Group
Issues: CPT, IMM, TRD
Rep By: James C. Free, W. Timothy Locke, Alicia W. Smith

Sony Trans Com
Irvine, CA
Leg. Issues: AVI
Outside Counsel/Consultants
Teicher Consulting and Representation
Issues: AVI
Rep By: Howard R. Teicher

Soo Line Railroad, Inc.
Minneapolis, MN
Leg. Issues: BUD, ENV, IMM, RRR, TAX, TRU, WAS
Outside Counsel/Consultants
Mullenholz, Brimsek & Belair
Issues: BUD, ENV, IMM, RRR, TAX, TRU, WAS
Rep By: John R. Brimsek

Sorptive Minerals Institute
Washington, DC
Registered: LDA
E-mail: lcoogan@navista.net
Outside Counsel/Consultants
Strat@Comm (Strategic Communications Counselors)

SOS Interpreting Ltd.
New York, NY
Leg. Issues: LAW
Outside Counsel/Consultants
Davidoff & Malito, LLP
Issues: LAW
Rep By: Kenneth C. Malito, Robert J. Malito, Stephen J. Slade

Sotheby's Holdings Inc.
New York, NY
Leg. Issues: ART, TAX
Outside Counsel/Consultants
Covington & Burling
Issues: ART, TAX
Rep By: Roderick A. DeArment, David R. Grace

Sound Transit
Washington, DC
Leg. Issues: TRA
Outside Counsel/Consultants
Peyser Associates, Inc.
Issues: TRA
Rep By: Thomas J. Howarth, Peter A. Peyser, Jr., Becky B. Weber

South Africa Foundation
Parktown, SOUTH AFRICA
Outside Counsel/Consultants
C/R Internat'l, L.L.C

South Africa, Embassy of the Republic of
Washington, DC
Outside Counsel/Consultants
Issue Dynamics Inc.

South African Airways
Johannesburg, SOUTH AFRICA
Outside Counsel/Consultants
Zuckert, Scoutt and Rasenberger, L.L.P.
Rep By: Frank J. Costello

South African Government/World Bank
Johannesburg, SOUTH AFRICA
Leg. Issues: DEF, FOR, GOV, RES
Outside Counsel/Consultants
Capital Consultants Corp.
Issues: DEF, FOR, GOV, RES
Rep By: Michael David Kaiser

South African Sugar Ass'n
Durban, SOUTH AFRICA
Registered: FARA
Leg. Issues: TRD
Outside Counsel/Consultants
Tuttle, Taylor & Heron
Issues: TRD
Rep By: Phillip L. Fraas

South Atlantic-TransAndes Economic Committee
Buenos Aires, ARGENTINA
Outside Counsel/Consultants
MacKenzie McCheyne, Inc.

South Bend, Indiana, City of
Leg. Issues: URB
Outside Counsel/Consultants
Sagamore Associates, Inc.
Issues: URB
Rep By: Dena S. Morris

South Carolina Department of Transportation
Columbia, SC
Leg. Issues: TRA
Outside Counsel/Consultants
Winston & Strawn
Issues: TRA
Rep By: Roger A. Keller, Jr., Hon. John L. Napier

South Carolina Nat'l Guard Ass'n
Columbia, SC
Leg. Issues: DEF, MAN
Outside Counsel/Consultants
American Systems Internat'l Corp.
Issues: DEF, MAN

South Carolina Public Railways
Charleston, SC
Leg. Issues: BUD, RRR
Outside Counsel/Consultants
The Laurin Baker Group
Issues: BUD, RRR
Rep By: Laurin M. Baker

South Carolina Public Service Authority
Columbia, SC
Leg. Issues: ENG, UTI
Outside Counsel/Consultants
Timothy X. Moore and Co.
Issues: ENG, UTI
Rep By: Timothy X. Moore

South Carolina Research Authority
Columbia, SC
Leg. Issues: DEF, TRA
Outside Counsel/Consultants
Kinghorn & Associates, L.L.C.
Issues: DEF, TRA
Rep By: John W. Hilbert, II, Edward J. Kinghorn, Jr., Jeremy Scott

South Carolina Technology Alliance
Charleston, SC
Outside Counsel/Consultants
Kinghorn & Associates, L.L.C.
Rep By: Edward J. Kinghorn, Jr., Jeremy Scott

South Carolina, Washington Office of the State of
444 N. Capitol St. NW
Suite 203
Washington, DC 20001
Tel: (202)624-7784
Fax: (202)624-7800
In-house, DC-area Employees
TECKLENBURG, Michael: Director, Washington Office of the Governor

South Coast Air Quality Management District
Diamond Bar, CA
Outside Counsel/Consultants
Patton Boggs, LLP

South Dakota, Department of Transportation of
Pierre, SD
Outside Counsel/Consultants
John A. DeVierno
Rep By: John A. DeVierno

South Dakota, Office of the Attorney General of the State of
Pierre, SD
Outside Counsel/Consultants
Duncan, Weinberg, Genzer & Pembroke, P.C.
Rep By: James F. Flug

South Gate, California, City of
Leg. Issues: GOV
Outside Counsel/Consultants
Joe Velasquez & Associates
Issues: GOV
Rep By: Joe Velasquez

South Jersey Regional Council of Carpenters
Gloucester, NJ
Outside Counsel/Consultants
Krivit & Krivit, P.C.

South Louisiana, Port of
LaPlace, LA
Leg. Issues: BUD
Outside Counsel/Consultants
Adams and Reese LLP
Issues: BUD
Rep By: B. Jeffrey Brooks, Hon. James A. "Jimmy" Hayes, Andrea Wilkinson

South Mississippi Electric Power Ass'n
Hattiesburg, MS
Leg. Issues: ENG, UTI
Outside Counsel/Consultants
Duncan, Weinberg, Genzer & Pembroke, P.C.
Issues: ENG, UTI
Rep By: Robert Weinberg

South Salt Lake, Utah, City of
South Salt Lake, UT
Leg. Issues: URB
Outside Counsel/Consultants
Jordan & Associates, Inc.
Issues: URB
Rep By: Patricia Jordan

South Tahoe Public Utility District
South Lake Tahoe, CA
Leg. Issues: BUD, CAW, ENV

Outside Counsel/Consultants

ENS Resources, Inc.
Issues: BUD
Rep By: Eric Sapirstein

Impact Strategies
Issues: BUD, CAW, ENV

South West Florida Enterprises, Inc.

Miami, FL

Outside Counsel/Consultants

Arter & Hadden
Rep By: W. James Jonas, III, Hon. Thomas G. Loeffler

Southcoast Health System

New Bedford, MA
Leg. Issues: BUD, HCR, MED, MMM

Outside Counsel/Consultants

DeBrunner and Associates, Inc.
Issues: BUD, HCR, MED, MMM
Rep By: Charles L. DeBrunner, Ellen J. Kugler, Kathryn D. Rooney

Southdown, Inc.

Houston, TX
Leg. Issues: ENV, NAT, RES

Outside Counsel/Consultants

Bracewell & Patterson, L.L.P.
Issues: ENV
Rep By: Gene E. Godley, Marc C. Hebert, Michael L. Pate, Scott H. Segal

Podesta/Mattoon

Vinson & Elkins L.L.P.
Issues: NAT, RES
Rep By: Hon. Michael A. Andrews

Southeast Alaska Regional Health Corp. (SEARHC)

Juneau, AK
Leg. Issues: HCR, IND

Outside Counsel/Consultants

Preston Gates Ellis & Rouvelas Meeds LLP
Issues: HCR, IND
Rep By: Werner W. Brandt, Darrell Conner, Susan B. Geiger, Hon. Lloyd Meeds

Southeast Alaska Seiners Ass'n

Juneau, AK
Leg. Issues: MAR

Outside Counsel/Consultants

O'Connor & Hannan, L.L.P.
Issues: MAR
Rep By: Robert W. Barrie, George J. Mannina, Jr., Patrick J. O'Connor

Southeast Asia Resource Action Center (SEARAC)

1628 16th St. NW
Third Floor
Washington, DC 20009-3099
Web: www.searac.org
Tel: (202)667-4690
Fax: (202)667-6449

In-house, DC-area Employees

YANG, KaYing: Exec. Director

Southeast Business Partnership

Denver, CO
Leg. Issues: TRA

Outside Counsel/Consultants

Capital Partnerships (VA) Inc.
Issues: TRA
Rep By: Robin Angle, Kenneth W. Butler, Clay Gravely

Southeast Conference

Juneau, AK
Leg. Issues: UTI

Outside Counsel/Consultants

Robertson, Monagle & Eastaugh
Issues: UTI
Rep By: Steven W. Silver

Southeast Dairy Farmer Ass'n

Leg. Issues: AGR, ENV, FOO

Outside Counsel/Consultants

The Garrison Group
Issues: AGR, ENV, FOO
Rep By: Charles Garrison

Resource Management Consultants, Inc.
Issues: AGR
Rep By: Robert J. Gray

Southeast Missouri State University

Cape Girardeau, MO
Leg. Issues: EDU

Outside Counsel/Consultants

Golin/Harris Internat'l
Issues: EDU
Rep By: C. Michael Fulton

Southeast Water Coalition

Pico Rivera, CA
Leg. Issues: BUD, CAW, ENV

Outside Counsel/Consultants

The Ferguson Group, LLC
Issues: BUD, CAW, ENV
Rep By: W. Roger Gwinn, Ralph Webb

Southeastern Federal Power Customers, Inc.

Montgomery, AL
Leg. Issues: ENG

Outside Counsel/Consultants

Verner, Liipfert, Bernhard, McPherson and Hand, Chartered
Issues: ENG
Rep By: David A. Fitzgerald, Sherry A. Quirk, John H. Sterne, Jr., Clinton A. Vince, John H. Zentay

Southeastern Legal Foundation

Atlanta, GA

Outside Counsel/Consultants

Craig Shirley & Associates
Rep By: Jenny Kefauver, Craig P. Shirley

Southeastern Louisiana University

Harahan, LA
Leg. Issues: BUD

Outside Counsel/Consultants

Adams and Reese LLP
Issues: BUD
Rep By: B. Jeffrey Brooks

Southeastern Michigan Council of Government

Detroit, MI
Leg. Issues: ENV, IMM, RRR, TAX, TRA

Outside Counsel/Consultants

Dykema Gossett PLLC
Issues: ENV, IMM, RRR, TAX, TRA
Rep By: David K. Arthur, Nancy R. Barbour

Southeastern Pennsylvania Consortium for Higher Education

Philadelphia, PA
Leg. Issues: BUD

Outside Counsel/Consultants

Cassidy & Associates, Inc.
Issues: BUD
Rep By: Michael Merola, Hon. Fred B. Rooney, Mary E. Shields

Southeastern Pennsylvania Transit Authority

Philadelphia, PA
Leg. Issues: TRA

Outside Counsel/Consultants

American Continental Group, Inc.
Issues: TRA
Rep By: John A. Cline, Peter Terpeluk, Jr.

Peyser Associates, Inc.
Issues: TRA
Rep By: Thomas J. Howarth, Peter A. Peyser, Jr., Becky B. Weber

Southeastern Universities Research Ass'n

Outside Counsel/Consultants

Jorden Burt LLP

Powers Pyles Sutter & Verville, PC
Rep By: J. Michael Hall

Southern Air Transport

Columbus, OH

Outside Counsel/Consultants

Pierre E. Murphy Law Offices
Rep By: Pierre E. Murphy

Southern Ass'n of Forestry Economics

Baconton, GA
Leg. Issues: AGR

Outside Counsel/Consultants

Shaw Pittman
Issues: AGR
Rep By: Anita K. Epstein, Claudia Hrvatin, Thomas J. Spulak, Andrew L. Woods

Southern Auto Sales, Inc.

East Windsor, CT

Outside Counsel/Consultants

Mark W. Goodin
Rep By: Mark W. Goodin

Southern California Ass'n of Governments

Los Angeles, CA
Leg. Issues: ROD, TRA

Outside Counsel/Consultants

Murray, Scheer, Montgomery, Tapia & O'Donnell
Issues: ROD, TRA
Rep By: Thomas R. Crawford, John H. Montgomery, D. Michael Murray, John R. O'Donnell, Raul R. Tapia

Southern California Organ Procurement Consortium

Los Angeles, CA
Leg. Issues: HCR

Outside Counsel/Consultants

Gibson, Dunn & Crutcher LLP
Issues: HCR
Rep By: Alan A. Platt

Southern California Public Power Authority

Pasadena, CA
Leg. Issues: ENG, GOV, UTI

Outside Counsel/Consultants

Duncan, Weinberg, Genzer & Pembroke, P.C.
Issues: ENG, GOV, UTI
Rep By: Richmond F. Allan, Wallace L. Duncan, James D. Pembroke, Michael R. Postar

Morgan Meguire, LLC
Issues: ENG
Rep By: Scott Lindsay, Kyle G. Michel, Katie Parrott, C. Kyle Simpson, Deborah R. Sliz, Kiel Weaver

Southern California Regional Rail Authority

Los Angeles, CA
Leg. Issues: TRA

Outside Counsel/Consultants

David Turch & Associates
Issues: TRA
Rep By: Marilyn E. Campbell, David N. M. Turch

Southern Co.

1130 Connecticut Ave. NW
Suite 830
Washington, DC 20036
Tel: (202)261-5000
Fax: (202)296-7937
Registered: LDA

Parent company of Alabama Power, Georgia Power, Gulf Power, Mississippi Power, Savannah Electric, and Southern Nuclear. Southern Company supplies electricity to 3.9 million customers in the southeastern United States. Headquartered in Atlanta, GA.

Leg. Issues: BUD, ENG, ENV, UTI, WAS

In-house, DC-area Employees

ASHER, Anne W.: Manager, Administrative and Special Projects
CREWS, Mark: Director, Federal Regulatory Affairs
FINLEY, Elise K.: Manager, Federal Legislative Affairs
LASS, Conrad: Manager, Federal Legislative Affairs
LAWRENCE, H. Adam: Director, Federal Legislative Affairs
MCCOOL, Jr., James M.: Director, Federal Legislative Affairs
MILLER, Joseph "Buzz": V. President, Government Relations
RIITH, Michael: Manager, Federal Legislative Affairs
WOLAK, Jeanne Hicks: Director, Federal Legislative Affairs

Outside Counsel/Consultants

Balch & Bingham LLP
Issues: UTI
Rep By: Patrick J. McCormick, III

Barbour Griffith & Rogers, Inc.
Issues: ENV, UTI
Rep By: Haley Barbour, Carl Biersack, G. O. Lanny Griffith, Jr., Bill Himpler, Loren Monroe, Edward M. Rogers, Jr., Brent Thompson

Dittus Communications
Rep By: Gloria S. Dittus

Dorsey & Whitney LLP
Issues: ENV
Rep By: George Sugiyama

The Hawthorn Group, L.C.
Rep By: John Ashford

The Renkes Group, Ltd.
Issues: ENG
Rep By: Gregg D. Renkes

Ryan, Phillips, Utrecht & MacKinnon
Issues: ENG, WAS
Rep By: Rodney Hoppe, Jeffrey M. MacKinnon, William D. Phillips, Thomas M. Ryan, Joseph V. Vasapoli

The Smith-Free Group
Issues: BUD, UTI
Rep By: James C. Free, W. Timothy Locke, Alicia W. Smith

Troutman Sanders LLP
Issues: ENG
Rep By: Kevin C. Fitzgerald, William P. Marsan, Clifford S. Sikora, Bonnie Suchman

Southern Coalition for Advanced Transportation

Atlanta, GA
Leg. Issues: BUD

Outside Counsel/Consultants

Holland & Knight LLP
Issues: BUD
Rep By: Richard M. Gold, David C. Whitestone

Southern Generation

Birmingham, AL

Outside Counsel/Consultants

The Hawthorn Group, L.C.
Rep By: John Ashford

Southern Governors Ass'n

444 N. Capitol St. NW — Tel: (202)624-5897
Suite 200 — Fax: (202)624-7797
Washington, DC 20001
Web: www.southerngovernors.org
E-mail: sga@sso.org

Represents governors of 16 southern and border states, the U.S. Virgin Islands, and Puerto Rico on state, regional, and federal policy issues reflecting the South.

In-house, DC-area Employees

FINLEY, Catherine: Policy Analyst
KUBIAK, Greg: Senior Policy and Program Manager
OSBORNE, Beth: Policy Analyst
SCHNEIDER, Elizabeth G.: Exec. Director

Southern Illinois University

Carbondale, IL
Leg. Issues: AGR, TRA

Outside Counsel/Consultants

Winston & Strawn
Issues: AGR, TRA
Rep By: Douglas C. Richardson

Southern Maryland Electric Cooperative, Inc.

Hughesville, MD
Leg. Issues: ENG, UTI

Outside Counsel/Consultants

Duncan, Weinberg, Genzer & Pembroke, P.C.
Issues: ENG, UTI
Rep By: Robert Weinberg

Southern Maryland Navy Alliance, Inc.

Hollywood, MD

Involved in research, development and acquisition of defense equipment.

Outside Counsel/Consultants

Rhoads Group

Southern Methodist University

Dallas, TX

Outside Counsel/Consultants

Hogan & Hartson L.L.P.
Rep By: C. Michael Gilliland, William Michael House, Sharon McBride, Jeffrey W. Munk

Southern Research Institute

Birmingham, AL
Leg. Issues: ENG, MED

Outside Counsel/Consultants

Hall, Green, Rupli, LLC
Issues: ENG, MED
Rep By: John M. Green, G. Stewart Hall

Southern Tier Cement Committee

Washington, DC

Members include Alamo Cement Co., Ash Grove Cement Co., Blue Circle Cement, Calaveras Cement Co., Florida Crushed Stone, Florida Rock Industries, Giant Cement Co., Kaiser Cement Corp., Lafarge Corp., Lone Star Industries, Medusa Corp., Nat'l Cement Co., North Texas Cement Co., Phoenix Cement Co., Riverside Cement Co., RMC Lonestar, Southdown, Tarmac America, Texas Industries, Texas-Lehigh Cement Co., Arizona Portland Cement, California Portland Cement, Lehigh Portland Cement Co., and RC Cement Co., Inc.

Leg. Issues: TRA

Outside Counsel/Consultants

King & Spalding
Issues: TRA
Rep By: Carol Brewer, Joseph W. Dorn, Theodore M. Hester, Michael P. Mabile

Southern Utah Wilderness Alliance

122 C St. NW — Tel: (202)546-2215
Suite 240 — Fax: (202)544-5197
Washington, DC 20001
Leg. Issues: NAT, RES

In-house, DC-area Employees

HAMMOND, Keith
MCHARG, Herb
THOMAS, Liz

Southern Ute Indian Tribe

Ignacio, CO
Leg. Issues: AGR, BUD, CAW, ENG, FUE, GAM, HOU, IND, NAT, TAX

Outside Counsel/Consultants

Kogovsek & Associates
Issues: AGR, BUD, CAW, ENG, FUE, GAM, HOU, IND, NAT, TAX
Rep By: Christine Ann Arbogast, Hon. Raymond P. Kogovsek

Southwest Airlines

1250 I St. NW — Tel: (202)682-4532
Suite 1110 DGA 4GA
Washington, DC 20005

Headquartered in Dallas, TX.

Leg. Issues: AVI

In-house, DC-area Employees

CRUSE, Kelly: Coordinator, Government Affairs

Outside Counsel/Consultants

Public Strategies Washington, Inc.
Issues: AVI
Rep By: Joseph P. O'Neill, Paul M. Snyder

Southwest Border Technology Project

Tucson, AZ

Outside Counsel/Consultants

Strategic Impact, Inc.
Rep By: Michael C. Jimenez, Patrick J. Mitchell

Southwest Peanut Growers

Gorman, TX

Manages peanut marketing.

Leg. Issues: AGR, BUD, TRD

Outside Counsel/Consultants

Meyers & Associates
Issues: AGR, BUD, TRD
Rep By: Fran Boyd, Larry D. Meyers, Richard L. Meyers

Southwest Peanut PAC

Washington, DC

Outside Counsel/Consultants

Meyers & Associates
Rep By: Larry D. Meyers

Southwest Power Pool

Little Rock, AR

Outside Counsel/Consultants

Wright & Talisman, P.C.
Rep By: Michael E. Small

Southwest Texas State University

San Marcos, TX
Leg. Issues: EDU

Outside Counsel/Consultants

The Advocacy Group
Issues: EDU
Rep By: Robert E. Mills

Southwest Water Conservation District of Colorado

Durango, CO

Outside Counsel/Consultants

Will and Carlson, Inc.
Rep By: Peter Carlson, Robert P. Will

Southwestern Bell Corp., Media Ventures

Rockville, MD

Outside Counsel/Consultants

Potomac Incorporated

Southwestern Electric Cooperative, Inc.

Greenville, IL
Leg. Issues: ENG, UTI

Outside Counsel/Consultants

Duncan, Weinberg, Genzer & Pembroke, P.C.
Issues: ENG, UTI
Rep By: Michael R. Postar

Southwestern Public Service Co.

Amarillo, TX — Registered: LDA

Outside Counsel/Consultants

Wright & Talisman, P.C.
Rep By: Alan J. Statman

Southwestern Water Conservation District

Durango, CO
Leg. Issues: AGR, BUD, NAT

Outside Counsel/Consultants

Kogovsek & Associates
Issues: AGR, BUD, NAT
Rep By: Christine Ann Arbogast, Hon. Raymond P. Kogovsek

Southwire, Inc.

Carrollton, GA
Leg. Issues: BUD, ENV, TAX, TRD

Outside Counsel/Consultants

Alpine Group, Inc.
Issues: BUD, ENV, TAX, TRD
Rep By: James D. Massie

Blank Rome Comisky & McCauley, LLP
Rep By: George C. Myers, Jr., Victor M. Wigman

Sovereign Bank

Boston, MA
Leg. Issues: FIN

Outside Counsel/Consultants

GPC Internat'l
Issues: FIN
Rep By: John D. Cahill

Soy Protein Council

Washington, DC
Web: www.spcouncil.org

Members are processors and distributors of vegetable proteins and their products, for use and consumption in human food.

Outside Counsel/Consultants

Hauck and Associates
Rep By: Sheldon J. Hauck, David A. Saunders

Space Access

Palmdale, CA
Leg. Issues: AER, AVI, BUD, COM, FIN, GOV, TRA

Outside Counsel/Consultants

Meyers & Associates
Issues: AER, AVI, BUD, COM, FIN, GOV, TRA
Rep By: Larry D. Meyers, Richard L. Meyers

Space Dynamics Laboratory

Logan, UT
Leg. Issues: AER, BUD, DEF, ENV, SCI

Outside Counsel/Consultants

Lee & Smith P.C.
Issues: DEF
Rep By: David B. Lee, C. William Smith

Kay Allan Morrell, Attorney-at-Law
Issues: AER, BUD, DEF, ENV, SCI
Rep By: Kay Allan Morrell

Space Explorers Inc.

DePere, WI
Leg. Issues: EDU, SCI

Outside Counsel/Consultants

Van Scoyoc Associates, Inc.
Issues: EDU, SCI
Rep By: Steve E. Crane, Kevin F. Kelly, H. Stewart Van Scoyoc

Space Grant Coalition

Leg. Issues: BUD

Outside Counsel/Consultants

Van Scoyoc Associates, Inc.
Issues: BUD
Rep By: Carolyn Fuller

Space Imaging, Inc.

Thornton, CO
Leg. Issues: AER, BUD, FOR, SCI

Outside Counsel/Consultants

McClure, Gerard & Neuenschwander, Inc.
Issues: AER, BUD, FOR, SCI
Rep By: Steven G. Barringer, Joseph T. Findaro, Matthew Iandoli, Nils W. Johnson, Hon. James A. McClure, Tod O. Neuenschwander

Space Mark

Colorado Springs, CO
Leg. Issues: BUD

Outside Counsel/Consultants

Birch, Horton, Bittner & Cherot
Issues: BUD
Rep By: Thomas L. Albert, Ronald G. Birch

Space Media

Washington, DC
Leg. Issues: EDU, SCI

Outside Counsel/Consultants

Dierman, Wortley, and Zola
Issues: EDU, SCI

Space Station Associates

Outside Counsel/Consultants

The Plexus Consulting Group
Rep By: Fred H. Hutchison

Space Transportation Ass'n

2800 Shirlington Rd.
Suite 405
Arlington, VA 22206
Tel: (703)671-4116
Fax: (703)931-6432
Registered: LDA
Web: www.spacetransportation.org
E-mail: sta4space@aol.com

Represents the interests of people and organizations who intend to develop, build, operate and use space transportation vehicles and systems to provide reliable economical, safe and routine access to space for government and private users.

In-house, DC-area Employees

MCCOY, Ty: Chairman
ROGERS, Thomas F.: Chief Scientist
STALLMER, Eric W.: President

SpaceData Internat'l

Miami, FL
Leg. Issues: COM, SCI, TEC

Outside Counsel/Consultants

The Dutko Group, Inc.
Issues: COM, SCI, TEC
Rep By: Kim Koontz Bayliss, Louis Lehrman, Steve Perry, Juliette M. Raffensperger, Stephen Craig Sayle

Paul, Weiss, Rifkind, Wharton & Garrison
Issues: TEC
Rep By: Carl W. Hampe

SPACEHAB, Inc.

300 D St. SW
Suite 814
Washington, DC 20024
Tel: (202)488-3500
Fax: (202)488-1300
Web: www.spacehab.com

Specializes in commercial space services.

Leg. Issues: AER, BUD, SCI, TRD

In-house, DC-area Employees

RYAN, Maureen: Director, Government Relations

Outside Counsel/Consultants

Tighe, Patton, Tabackman & Babbin
Issues: SCI
Rep By: Brent S. Franzel

Spacelabs Medical Inc.

Redmond, WA
Leg. Issues: CPI, DEF, HCR, MED, SCI, VET

Outside Counsel/Consultants

Potomac Strategies Internat'l LLC
Issues: CPI, DEF, HCR, MED, SCI, VET
Rep By: Raymond F. DuBois, Jr., Cynthia Trutanic, James K. Wholey

Spaceport Florida Authority

Cocoa Beach, FL
Leg. Issues: AER, TAX

Outside Counsel/Consultants

Holland & Knight LLP
Issues: AER, TAX
Rep By: Harold R. Bucholtz

Spanish Broadcasting System, Inc.

New York, NY
Leg. Issues: COM, TAX

Outside Counsel/Consultants

Kaye Scholer LLP
Issues: COM, TAX
Rep By: Christopher R. Brewster

Sparton Electronics, Florida, Inc.

De Leon Springs, FL
Leg. Issues: DEF

Outside Counsel/Consultants

Alford & Associates
Issues: DEF
Rep By: Marty Alford

Spatial Integrated Systems

Rockville, MD
Leg. Issues: DEF

Outside Counsel/Consultants

The PMA Group
Issues: DEF
Rep By: William E. Berl, Kaylene Green, Patrick Hiu, Paul J. Magliocchetti

Spatial Technologies Industry Ass'n

Washington, DC
Leg. Issues: SCI

Outside Counsel/Consultants

The Potomac Research Group LLC
Issues: SCI
Rep By: G. Harris Jordan, Paul Welles Orr

Spaulding Rehabilitation Hospital

Boston, MA
Leg. Issues: HCR, MMM

Outside Counsel/Consultants

O'Neill, Athy & Casey, P.C.
Issues: HCR, MMM
Rep By: Martha L. Casey

SPD Technologies

Philadelphia, PA
Leg. Issues: DEF, TRA

Outside Counsel/Consultants

Thelen Reid & Priest LLP
Issues: DEF, TRA
Rep By: Barry I. Berkoff, Richard J. Leidl, Stephan M. Minikes

Speak Out! USA

228 Seventh St. SE
Washington, DC 20003
Tel: (202)543-4357
Fax: (202)547-9312

A non-profit association to empower and give voice to American citizens. Its focus is on opinion, statistical, market, and public policy research. Produces reports and documentary films.

In-house, DC-area Employees

ERB TULLY, Valerie: Managing Director, Public Relations

SpeakOut.com

1225 I St. NW
Suite 400
Washington, DC 20005
Tel: (202)777-3100
Web: www.speakout.com
E-mail: christy@speakout.com

In-house, DC-area Employees

VESTAL, Christine: V. President, Content and Editor-in-Chief

Special Committee for Workplace Product Liability Reform

Leg. Issues: TOR, TRD

Outside Counsel/Consultants

Barnes & Thornburg
Issues: TOR, TRD
Rep By: Randolph J. Stayin

Special Libraries Ass'n

1700 18th St. NW
Washington, DC 20009
Tel: (202)234-4700
Fax: (202)265-9317
Registered: LDA
Web: www.sla.org
E-mail: sla@sla.org
Leg. Issues: CPT, GOV, LBR, TAX, TOR

In-house, DC-area Employees

BENDER, Ph.D., David R.: Exec. Director
CASEY, Robert "Fred": Assistant Exec. Director, Program and Strategic Development
CROSBY, IV, John H.: Director, Public Communications

Outside Counsel/Consultants

Venable
Issues: CPT, GOV, LBR, TAX, TOR
Rep By: Jeffrey S. Tenenbaum

Special Olympics, Inc.

1325 G St. NW
Suite 500
Washington, DC 20005
Tel: (202)628-3630
Fax: (202)628-0067
Web: www.specialolympics.org
E-mail: SOImail@aol.com

A not-for-profit international sports organization for people with mental retardation.

In-house, DC-area Employees

ELLIOTT, Kimberly A.: Sr. Advisor to the President
SHRIVER, Ph.D., Timothy P.: President and Chief Exec. Officer
TURRENTINE, J. Drake: General Counsel

Outside Counsel/Consultants

Williams & Connolly
Rep By: Gregory B. Craig

Special Vehicle Coalition

Washington, DC
Leg. Issues: TRA

Outside Counsel/Consultants

Thompson Coburn LLP
Issues: TRA
Rep By: Warren L. Dean

Specialized Carriers and Rigging Ass'n

2750 Prosperity Ave.
Suite 620
Fairfax, VA 22031-4312
Tel: (703)698-0291
Fax: (703)698-0297
Web: www.scranet.org
E-mail: info@scranet.org
Leg. Issues: ENG, GOV, LBR, ROD, TRA, TRU

In-house, DC-area Employees

BRYMER, N. Eugene: Exec. V. President
DANDREA, Joel: V. President
O'QUINN, Beth: V. President

Specialized Technical Services, Inc.

Beavercreek, OH

Outside Counsel/Consultants

The Carter Group
Rep By: Michael R. Carter, Scott D. McClean

Specialty Equipment Market Ass'n

1317 F St. NW
Suite 500
Washington, DC 20004
Web: www.sema.org
Tel: (202)783-6007
Fax: (202)783-6024

A trade association for manufacturers, distributors and retailers of specialty and performance automotive equipment. Headquartered in Diamond Bar, CA.

Leg. Issues: CAW, TRA

In-house, DC-area Employees

CAUDILL, Brian: Outreach and Public Affairs Director
MCDONALD, Stephen: Director, Government and Technical Affairs
SPENCER, Linda M.: Director, International and Government Relations

Specialty Steel Industry of North America

Washington, DC
Web: www.ssina.com
Leg. Issues: DEF, TRA

Outside Counsel/Consultants

Collier Shannon Scott, PLLC
Issues: DEF, TRA
Rep By: David A. Hartquist, Lauren R. Howard, Laurence J. Lasoff, Robert W. Porter

Specialty Tubing Group

An association composed of U.S. producers of specialty steel pipe and tubing products and their suppliers. Focuses on international trading issues.

Outside Counsel/Consultants

Collier Shannon Scott, PLLC
Rep By: Jeffrey S. Beckington, David A. Hartquist, Robert W. Porter

Spectrum Astro, Inc.

Gilbert, AZ
Leg. Issues: AER, DEF, GOV, SCI

Outside Counsel/Consultants

Birch, Horton, Bittner & Cherot
Issues: AER
Rep By: William Bittner

Cottone and Huggins Group
Issues: AER, DEF, GOV
Rep By: James B. Huggins

R. V. Davis and Associates
Issues: AER
Rep By: Robert V. Davis, J. William Foster

R. G. Flippo and Associates, Inc.
Issues: AER, DEF
Rep By: Hon. Ronnie G. Flippo

Law Offices of Pamela L. Meredith
Issues: DEF, SCI
Rep By: Pamela L. Meredith

Spectrum Consulting, Inc.

Logan, UT

Outside Counsel/Consultants

Winston & Strawn
Rep By: David W. Broome, John A. Waits, II

Spectrum Health Care Resources, Inc.

Colorado Springs, CO
Leg. Issues: BUD, DEF, HCR

Outside Counsel/Consultants

Astra Solutions, LLC
Issues: BUD, DEF, HCR
Rep By: Donna L. Hoffmeier

Speedway Motorsports

Outside Counsel/Consultants

Edelman Public Relations Worldwide
Rep By: Neal Flieger

Spelman College

Atlanta, GA
Leg. Issues: BUD, EDU

Outside Counsel/Consultants

Van Scoyoc Associates, Inc.
Issues: BUD, EDU
Rep By: Anita R. Estell, H. Stewart Van Scoyoc

Sperry Marine Inc.

Charlottesville, VA
Leg. Issues: DEF

Outside Counsel/Consultants

Brown and Company, Inc.
Issues: DEF
Rep By: Cynthia L. Brown, Hugh N. "Rusty" Johnson, Frank W. Losey

Spiegel Inc.

Downers Grove, IL
Leg. Issues: APP, BAN, TRD

Outside Counsel/Consultants

Flack Associates
Issues: APP, BAN, TRD
Rep By: Susan Garber Flack

Spina Bifida Ass'n of America

4590 MacArthur Blvd. NW
Suite 250
Washington, DC 20007
Tel: (202)944-3285
Fax: (202)944-3295
Registered: LDA
Web: www.sbaa.org
E-mail: sbaa@sbaa.org
Leg. Issues: BUD, EDU, HCR, VET

In-house, DC-area Employees

BROWNSTEIN, Cindy: Chief Exec. Officer
CARLIN, Roberta S.

Spirit Airlines

Outside Counsel/Consultants

Holland & Knight LLP
Rep By: Jack M. Burkman, Michael Gillis, Jim J. Marquez, Hon. Gerald E. Sikorski

Spokane Area Chamber of Commerce

Spokane, WA
Leg. Issues: BUD, CSP, DEF, DIS, ECN, MED, MMM, RES

Outside Counsel/Consultants

LaRocco & Associates
Issues: BUD, CSP, DEF, DIS, ECN, MED, MMM, RES
Rep By: Hon. Lawrence P. LaRocco, Matthew LaRocco

Spokane Regional Solid Waste System

Spokane, WA

Outside Counsel/Consultants

Wright & Talisman, P.C.
Rep By: Scott M. DuBoff

Spokane Tribe

Wellpinit, WA
Leg. Issues: TAX

Outside Counsel/Consultants

Dorsey & Whitney LLP
Issues: TAX
Rep By: Philip Baker-Shenk, David A. Bieging, Virginia W. Boylan, Cindy Darcy, Sarah Ridley, Kevin J. Wadzinski

Spokane, Washington, City of

Spokane, WA
Leg. Issues: ROD

Outside Counsel/Consultants

Perkins Coie LLP
Issues: ROD
Rep By: W. H. "Buzz" Fawcett

Sporting Arms and Ammunition Manufacturers' Institute, Inc.

2987 Westhurst Lane
Suite 110
Oakton, VA 22124
Web: www.saami.org
Tel: (703)242-1690
Registered: LDA
Leg. Issues: FIR, NAT

In-house, DC-area Employees

CHAMBERS, James: Exec. Director

Sporting Goods Manufacturers Ass'n

1150 17th St. NW
Suite 407
Washington, DC 20036
Tel: (202)775-1762
Fax: (202)296-7462
Registered: LDA
Web: www.sportlink.com

A trade association representng the sporting goods industry.

Leg. Issues: APP, BUD, EDU, LBR, NAT, RES, SPO, TAX, TOR, TRD

In-house, DC-area Employees

COVE, Thomas J.: V. President, Government Relations

Sports Apparel Products Council

c/o Sporting Goods Manufacturers Ass'n
1150 17th St. NW, Suite 407
Washington, DC 20036-1604
Web: www.sportlink.com
E-mail: tomsgma@aol.com
Tel: (202)775-1762
Fax: (202)296-7462
Registered: LDA

In-house, DC-area Employees

COVE, Thomas J.

Sports Corp., Ltd.

Chicago, IL
Leg. Issues: SPO, URB

Outside Counsel/Consultants

Capital Consultants Corp.
Issues: SPO, URB
Rep By: Seth Barnhard, Michael David Kaiser

Sports Lawyers Ass'n

11250 Roger Bacon Dr.
Suite Eight
Reston, VA 20190
Web: www.sportslaw.org/sla
E-mail: sla@sportslaw.org
Tel: (703)437-4377
Fax: (703)435-4390

In-house, DC-area Employees

DROHAN, CAE, William M.: Exec. Director

Outside Counsel/Consultants

Drohan Management Group
Rep By: William M. Drohan, CAE, Richard A. Guggolz

Sportsmen's Legal Defense Fund

Affiliated with the Wildlife Legislative Fund of America (see separate listing). Represents the legislative interests of hunters.

Outside Counsel/Consultants

Birch, Horton, Bittner & Cherot
Rep By: William P. Horn

Spot Image Corp.

Reston, VA

Outside Counsel/Consultants

The Potomac Advocates
Rep By: Charles Scalera, Gary L. Sojka

Spring Hill Camps

Evart, MI
Leg. Issues: TAX

Outside Counsel/Consultants

Sagamore Associates, Inc.
Issues: TAX
Rep By: David U. Gogol, Frank S. Swain

Springettsbury, Pennsylvania, Township of

Leg. Issues: BUD, ENV, NAT, RES, TOU

Outside Counsel/Consultants

Reed, Smith, LLP
Issues: BUD, ENV, NAT, RES, TOU
Rep By: Christopher L. Rissetto

Springfield, Massachusetts, City of

Leg. Issues: BUD, HCR

Outside Counsel/Consultants

Philip W. Johnston Associates
Issues: BUD, HCR
Rep By: Philip W. Johnston, Merrill E. Warschoff

Springfield, Missouri, City Utilities of

Leg. Issues: ENG

Outside Counsel/Consultants

Morgan Meguire, LLC
Issues: ENG
Rep By: Scott Lindsay, Kyle G. Michel, Katie Parrott, C. Kyle Simpson, Deborah R. Sliz, Kiel Weaver

Springfield, Oregon, City of

Leg. Issues: BUD, CAW

Outside Counsel/Consultants

Smith Dawson & Andrews, Inc.
Issues: BUD, CAW
Rep By: Sherri Powar, James P. Smith

Springfield, Oregon, School District #19

Leg. Issues: EDU

Outside Counsel/Consultants

Smith Dawson & Andrews, Inc.
Issues: EDU
Rep By: Gregory B. Andrews, Kirk Bailey, Thomas C. Dawson, Sherri Powar, James P. Smith

Springs Industries, Inc.

1225 I St. NW
Suite 500
Washington, DC 20005
Tel: (202)682-4711
Fax: (202)682-4591
Registered: LDA
E-mail: susan.lord@springs.com

Headquartered in Fort Mill, SC.

Leg. Issues: APP, CSP, EDU, ENV, HCR, IMM, LBR, MAN, TAX, TRD, UNM, WAS

In-house, DC-area Employees

LORD, Susan B.: V. President, Federal Government Relations

Sprint Corp.

401 Ninth St. NW
Suite 400
Washington, DC 20004
Tel: (202)585-1900
Fax: (202)585-1899
Registered: LDA

Headquartered in Kansas City, MO.

Leg. Issues: BUD, DOC, GOV, LBR, TAX, TEC, TRD

In-house, DC-area Employees

BARLOON, William J.: Director, Government Affairs
KEITHLEY, Jay: V. President, Federal Regulatory-LTD
KESTENBAUM, Leon M.: V. President, Federal Regulatory - LDD
KILGORE, Gregory: Director, Government Affairs
LANCETTI, Luisa: V. President, Federal Regulatory - PCS
MCCANN, Vonya B.: Senior V. President, Federal External Affairs
MURPHY, Sara Hope: Assistant V. President, Government Affairs
O'NEILL, William S.: Director, Government Affairs

Outside Counsel/Consultants

The Dutko Group, Inc.
Issues: BUD, LBR, TAX, TEC
Rep By: Gary J. Andres, Kimberly M. Spaulding

Betty Ann Kane & Co.
Issues: DOC, TEC
Rep By: Betty Ann Kane

Willkie Farr & Gallagher
Issues: GOV, TEC
Rep By: Sue D. Blumenfeld, Russell L. Smith

SQM North America Corp.

Atlanta, GA

A fertilizer marketing firm.

Outside Counsel/Consultants

Capitolink, LLC

Square 3942 Associates Limited Partnership

Potomac, MD
Leg. Issues: DOC, GOV, RES, WAS

Outside Counsel/Consultants

Carmen & Muss, P.L.L.C.
Issues: DOC, GOV, RES, WAS
Rep By: Melinda L. Carmen

Squaxin Island Indian Tribe

Shelton, WA

Outside Counsel/Consultants

SENSE, INC.
Rep By: C. Juliet Pittman

E. R. Squibb and Sons, Inc.

Princeton, NJ

A subsidiary of Bristol-Myers Squibb Co.

Outside Counsel/Consultants

Kleinfeld, Kaplan and Becker
Rep By: Kinsey S. Reagan, Peter O. Safir

SRI Internat'l

Menlo Park, CA
Leg. Issues: DEF

Outside Counsel/Consultants

The Conaway Group LLC
Issues: DEF
Rep By: Lt. Gen. John B. Conaway, USAF (Ret.)

The Potomac Advocates
Issues: DEF
Rep By: Charles Scalera, Gary L. Sojka

The Spectrum Group
Rep By: Gregory L. Sharp

Srpska, Government of the Republic of

Banjaluka, SRPSKA

Outside Counsel/Consultants

PBN Company
Rep By: Paul Nathanson

SRT Group

Miami, FL
Leg. Issues: BUD, ENG, SCI

Outside Counsel/Consultants

Charlie McBride Associates, Inc.
Issues: BUD, ENG, SCI
Rep By: Charlie McBride

SSI Services, Inc.

Bridgeville, PA

Outside Counsel/Consultants

O'Connor & Fierce Associates

St. Augustine Beach, Florida, City of

Leg. Issues: BUD, NAT

Outside Counsel/Consultants

Marlowe and Co.
Issues: BUD, NAT
Rep By: Howard Marlowe, Jeffrey Mazzella

St. Augustine College

Raleigh, NC
Leg. Issues: EDU

Outside Counsel/Consultants

Dean Blakey & Moskowitz
Issues: EDU
Rep By: William A. Blakey

St. Barnabas Healthcare System

Toms River, NJ
Leg. Issues: MMM

Outside Counsel/Consultants

Akin, Gump, Strauss, Hauer & Feld, L.L.P.
Issues: MMM
Rep By: Anthony Foti, Gary A. Heimberg, Jorge J. Lopez, Jr., David B. Palmer, Hon. William L. Paxon, Barney J. Skladany, Jr.

St. Benedictine Hospital

Kingston, NY

Outside Counsel/Consultants

Wilson, Elser, Moskowitz, Edelman & Dicker LLP

St. Bernard Port, Harbor and Terminal District

Chalmette, LA
Leg. Issues: MAR

Outside Counsel/Consultants

Colex and Associates
Issues: MAR
Rep By: John P. Mack

St. Bernard's Hospital

Chicago, IL
Leg. Issues: HCR, IMM, INS, MED, MMM

Outside Counsel/Consultants

Akin, Gump, Strauss, Hauer & Feld, L.L.P.
Issues: HCR, IMM, INS, MED, MMM
Rep By: James R. Tucker, Jr.

St. Cloud, Minnesota, City of

Leg. Issues: URB

Outside Counsel/Consultants

David Turch & Associates
Issues: URB
Rep By: Kevin D. Bosch, Marilyn E. Campbell, Victor Tambone, David N. M. Turch

St. Croix Chippewa Indians of Wisconsin

Hertel, WI
Leg. Issues: GAM, IND

Outside Counsel/Consultants

O'Connor & Hannan, L.L.P.
Issues: GAM, IND
Rep By: Roy C. Coffee, Hon. Thomas J. Corcoran, Patrick J. O'Connor

Sonosky, Chambers, Sachse & Endreson
Rep By: William R. Perry

St. Elizabeth's Medical Center

Boston, MA
Leg. Issues: HCR

Outside Counsel/Consultants

Monfort & Wolfe
Issues: HCR
Rep By: Charles A. Monfort

St. Francis Hospital

Poughkeepsie, NY

Outside Counsel/Consultants

R. Duffy Wall and Associates

St. Gabriel, Louisiana, Town of

St. Gabriel, LA
Leg. Issues: BUD

Outside Counsel/Consultants

Jones, Walker, Waechter, Poitevent, Carrere & Denegre, L.L.P.
Issues: BUD
Rep By: John J. Jaskot, R. Christian Johnsen

St. George Island Traditional Council

St. George Island, AK
Leg. Issues: IND

Outside Counsel/Consultants

Dorsey & Whitney LLP
Issues: IND
Rep By: Philip Baker-Shenk, David A. Bieging, Christopher Karns, Kevin J. Wadzinski

St. George Tanaq

Anchorage, AK
Leg. Issues: RES

Outside Counsel/Consultants

Birch, Horton, Bittner & Cherot
Issues: RES
Rep By: William Bittner

St. George's University School of Medicine

Bay Shore, NY
Leg. Issues: HCR

Outside Counsel/Consultants

Health and Medicine Counsel of Washington
Issues: HCR
Rep By: Dale P. Dirks, Susie Dobert

The St. Joe Co.

Leg. Issues: APP, AVI

Outside Counsel/Consultants

Hogan & Hartson L.L.P.
Issues: APP, AVI
Rep By: C. Michael Gilliland, William Michael House

St. Joseph University

Philadelphia, PA
Leg. Issues: EDU

Outside Counsel/Consultants

Whitten & Diamond
Issues: EDU
Rep By: Robert M. Diamond, Jamie L. Whitten

St. Jude Medical, Inc.

St. Paul, MN
Leg. Issues: HCR, MAN, MED, MMM, SCI

Outside Counsel/Consultants

McKenna & Cuneo, L.L.P.
Issues: MAN, MED, MMM

Public Policy Partners, LLC
Issues: HCR, MMM, SCI
Rep By: Hon. David Durenberger, Daniel Waldmann, Jeffrey Weekly

St. Lawrence Seaway Pilots Ass'n

Cape Vincent, NY
Leg. Issues: MAR

Outside Counsel/Consultants

Preston Gates Ellis & Rouvelas Meeds LLP
Issues: MAR
Rep By: Mark H. Ruge

St. Louis Airport Authority

St. Louis, MO
Leg. Issues: AVI

Outside Counsel/Consultants

Bracy Williams & Co.
Issues: AVI
Rep By: Terrence L. Bracy, James P. Brown, Laura L. Madden

Spiegel & McDiarmid
Rep By: John J. Corbett, Jr.

St. Louis Metropolitan Sewer District

St. Louis, MO
Leg. Issues: UTI

Outside Counsel/Consultants

Bracy Williams & Co.
Issues: UTI
Rep By: Terrence L. Bracy, James P. Brown, Laura L. Madden

St. Louis Office of Cable Television

St. Louis, MO
Leg. Issues: TEC

Outside Counsel/Consultants

Miller & Van Eaton, P.L.L.C.
Issues: TEC
Rep By: Nicholas P. Miller

St. Louis Regional Education and Public Television Commission

St. Louis, MO

Outside Counsel/Consultants

Dow, Lohnes & Albertson, PLLC
Rep By: Todd D. Gray, Kenneth D. Salomon

St. Louis University, School of Public Health

St. Louis, MO
Leg. Issues: BUD, DIS, HCR

Outside Counsel/Consultants

Powers Pyles Sutter & Verville, PC
Issues: BUD, DIS, HCR
Rep By: Judith Buckalew

St. Louis, Minnesota, Board of Commissioners of the County

Duluth, MN
Leg. Issues: HCR, TAX, TRA

Outside Counsel/Consultants

Lockridge Grindal & Nauen, P.L.L.P.
Issues: HCR, TAX, TRA
Rep By: Dennis McGrann

St. Louis, Minnesota, Social Services Department of the County of

Duluth, MN

Outside Counsel/Consultants

Craig Associates
Rep By: Patricia J. Craig

St. Louis, Missouri, City of

Leg. Issues: ECN, ENV, GOV, HCR, HOU, TRA, URB

Outside Counsel/Consultants

Bracy Williams & Co.
Issues: GOV
Rep By: James P. Brown

Clay and Associates
Issues: ECN, ENV, GOV, HCR, HOU, TRA, URB
Rep By: Michelle C. Clay

St. Louis/Lake Counties Regional Rail Authority

Virginia, MN
Leg. Issues: BUD, FUE, RRR, TRA

Outside Counsel/Consultants

Lockridge Grindal & Nauen, P.L.L.P.
Issues: BUD, FUE, RRR, TRA
Rep By: John D. Burton, Amy Johnson, Dennis McGrann

St. Lucie, Florida, County of

Fort Pierce, FL
Leg. Issues: BUD, NAT

Outside Counsel/Consultants

Marlowe and Co.
Issues: BUD, NAT
Rep By: Howard Marlowe, Jeffrey Mazzella

St. Mary's Hospital

Huntington, WV
Leg. Issues: HCR

Outside Counsel/Consultants

Golin/Harris Internat'l
Issues: HCR
Rep By: Carol C. Mitchell

St. Matthew's University School of Medicine

San Pedro Town, BELIZE
Leg. Issues: EDU

Outside Counsel/Consultants

Dow, Lohnes & Albertson, PLLC
Issues: EDU
Rep By: Jonathan Glass, Michael B. Goldstein, Kenneth D. Salomon

St. Paul Cos.

St. Paul, MN Registered: LDA
Leg. Issues: HCR

Outside Counsel/Consultants

Mayer, Brown & Platt
Issues: HCR
Rep By: Jeffrey H. Lewis, Carolyn P. Osolinik

St. Paul, Alaska, City of

Leg. Issues: BUD, ECN, ENV, FOR, FUE, IND, MAR, NAT, URB

Outside Counsel/Consultants

Schmeltzer, Aptaker & Shepard, P.C.
Issues: BUD, ECN, ENV, FOR, FUE, IND, MAR, NAT, URB
Rep By: C. Mateo Paz-Soldan, J. Anthony Smith

St. Paul, Minnesota, City of

Leg. Issues: ENV, TRA

Outside Counsel/Consultants

Lockridge Grindal & Nauen, P.L.L.P.
Issues: ENV, TRA
Rep By: Dennis McGrann

St. Peter's Medical Center

New Brunswick, NJ
Leg. Issues: HCR, MMM

Outside Counsel/Consultants

McDermott, Will and Emery
Issues: HCR, MMM
Rep By: Wendy L. Krasner, Maggie A. Mitchell, Karen S. Sealander

St. Petersburg Community College

St. Petersburg, FL
Leg. Issues: DEF, EDU

Outside Counsel/Consultants

Davis O'Connell, Inc.
Issues: DEF, EDU
Rep By: Lynda C. Davis, Ph.D., Terrence M. O'Connell

St. Regis Mohawk Tribe

Hogansburg, NY
An American Indian tribe.

Leg. Issues: IND

Outside Counsel/Consultants

Hobbs, Straus, Dean and Walker, LLP
Issues: IND
Rep By: Carol L. Barbero, S. Bobo Dean, Karen J. Funk

St. Thomas/St. John Chamber of Commerce, Inc.

St. Thomas, VI
Leg. Issues: TRD

Outside Counsel/Consultants

Donald S. Dawson & Associates
Issues: TRD
Rep By: Donald S. Dawson

St. Vincent Catholic Medical Centers

New York, NY
Leg. Issues: HOU, IMM, MMM

Outside Counsel/Consultants

Davidoff & Malito, LLP
Issues: HOU, IMM, MMM
Rep By: Kenneth C. Malito, Stephen J. Slade

R. Duffy Wall and Associates

Stable Value Investments Ass'n

2121 K St. NW Tel: (202)261-6530
Suite 800
Washington, DC 20037

In-house, DC-area Employees
MITCHELL, Gina: President

Staff Builders, Inc.

Lake Success, NY
Leg. Issues: BNK, GOV, HCR, MMM

Outside Counsel/Consultants

Hogan & Hartson L.L.P.
Issues: BNK, GOV, HCR, MMM
Rep By: Nancy Granese, Jeffrey G. Schneider

Stafford, Virginia, County of

Leg. Issues: TRA

Outside Counsel/Consultants

The Carmen Group
Issues: TRA
Rep By: John Hassell, Diane Jemmott, John Lagomarcino

A. E. Staley Manufacturing Co.

Decatur, IL

Outside Counsel/Consultants

Akin, Gump, Strauss, Hauer & Feld, L.L.P.

Stamford Hospital

Stamford, CT
Leg. Issues: MMM

Outside Counsel/Consultants

McDermott, Will and Emery
Issues: MMM
Rep By: Eric P. Zimmerman

Stamford, Connecticut, City of

Outside Counsel/Consultants

Spiegel & McDiarmid

Stamps.com

Santa Monica, CA
Leg. Issues: POS

Outside Counsel/Consultants

Akin, Gump, Strauss, Hauer & Feld, L.L.P.
Issues: POS
Rep By: David Geanacopoulos, Daniel L. Spiegel, Robin Weisman

Standard & Poor's Corp.

New York, NY

Outside Counsel/Consultants

Thelen Reid & Priest LLP
Rep By: Richard Y. Roberts

Widmeyer Communications, Inc.

Standard Chartered Bank

New York, NY
Leg. Issues: FIN

Outside Counsel/Consultants

Global Policy Group, Inc.
Issues: FIN
Rep By: Douglas J. Bergner

Standing Rock Sioux Tribe

Fort Yates, ND
Leg. Issues: BUD, IND

Outside Counsel/Consultants

Sonosky, Chambers, Sachse & Endreson
Issues: BUD, IND
Rep By: Mary J. Pavel, William R. Perry

Stanford Financial Group

Leg. Issues: FIN, TEC

Outside Counsel/Consultants

Greenberg Traurig, LLP
Issues: TEC

Verner, Liipfert, Bernhard, McPherson and Hand, Chartered
Issues: FIN
Rep By: Lawrence E. Levinson, Harry C. McPherson

The Stanley Works

New Britain, CT
Leg. Issues: MAN, TOR, TRD

Outside Counsel/Consultants

Ablondi, Foster, Sobin & Davidow, P.C.
Issues: TRD
Rep By: Richard H. Abbey

Skadden, Arps, Slate, Meagher & Flom LLP
Issues: TRD
Rep By: Brian Flynn

William F. Whitsitt Policy and Government Affairs
Issues: MAN, TOR, TRD
Rep By: William F. Whitsitt

Stanly County Airport Authority

New London, CT
Leg. Issues: AVI, DEF, DIS

Outside Counsel/Consultants

The PMA Group
Issues: AVI, DEF, DIS
Rep By: Daniel Cunningham, Kaylene Green, Paul J. Magliocchetti, Brian Thiel, Mark Waclawski

Stanton & Associates

1747 Pennsylvania Ave. NW
Suite 105
Washington, DC 20006
Tel: (202)467-4333
Fax: (202)467-4353
Registered: LDA

In-house, DC-area Employees

STANTON, Hon. James V.: Principal

Outside Counsel/Consultants

James T. Molloy
Rep By: James T. Molloy

Staples, Inc.

Framingham, MA
Leg. Issues: TAX

Outside Counsel/Consultants

Verner, Liipfert, Bernhard, McPherson and Hand, Chartered
Issues: TAX
Rep By: Denis J. Dwyer, Vicki E. Hart, Noelle M. Hawley, John H. Zentay

Star Systems

Reston, VA
Leg. Issues: BAN, FIN

Outside Counsel/Consultants

The Smith-Free Group
Issues: BAN, FIN
Rep By: Doyle Bartlett, James E. Smith

Star Tobacco & Pharmaceuticals Inc.

Petersburg, VA
Leg. Issues: TOB

Outside Counsel/Consultants

Paul, Hastings, Janofsky & Walker LLP
Issues: TOB
Rep By: Paul L. Perito

Starnet Communications Internat'l

St. John's, ANTIGUA AND BARBUDA
Leg. Issues: CPI, GAM

Outside Counsel/Consultants

Greenberg Traurig, LLP
Issues: CPI, GAM
Rep By: James F. Miller, Ronald L. Platt, Shana Tesler, Timothy P. Trysla

Starrett City Associates

New York, NY

A multi-family residential developer.

Leg. Issues: HOU

Outside Counsel/Consultants

Nixon Peabody LLP
Rep By: Stephen J. Wallace

Powell, Goldstein, Frazer & Murphy LLP
Issues: HOU
Rep By: John J. Knapp

Starrett Corp.

Leg. Issues: HOU

Outside Counsel/Consultants

Swidler Berlin Shereff Friedman, LLP
Issues: HOU
Rep By: Harold A. Levy

Starwood Hotels & Resorts Worldwide, Inc.

White Plains, WA
Leg. Issues: TAX, TOU

Outside Counsel/Consultants

The Carmen Group
Issues: TOU
Rep By: Ryan Adesnik, David M. Carmen

Greenberg Traurig, LLP
Issues: TAX
Rep By: James F. Miller

Starwood Lodging/Starwood Capital Group, L.P.

Greenwich, CT
Leg. Issues: RES, TAX

Outside Counsel/Consultants

Verner, Liipfert, Bernhard, McPherson and Hand, Chartered
Issues: RES, TAX
Rep By: Berl Bernhard, Virginia R. Boggs, Vicki E. Hart, Brenda G. Meister, Martin Mendelsohn, John A. Merrigan

State and Territorial Air Pollution Program Administrators

444 N. Capitol St. NW
Suite 307
Washington, DC 20001
Web: www.4cleanair.org
Tel: (202)624-7864
Fax: (202)624-7863

A national association of state and territorial air pollution control officials.

Leg. Issues: ENV

In-house, DC-area Employees

BECKER, S. William: Exec. Director

State Farm Insurance Cos.

1710 Rhode Island Ave. NW
Suite 700
Washington, DC 20036-3007
Web: www.statefarm.com
Tel: (202)466-5208
Fax: (202)263-4435
Registered: LDA

Headquartered in Bloomington, IL.

Leg. Issues: AUT, BAN, CSP, DIS, FIN, GOV, HCR, INS, TOR, TRD, TRU

In-house, DC-area Employees

DILLARD, Regina K.: Federal Affairs Counsel
MANESS, Alan D.: Federal Affairs Director and Counsel
RUIZ, Art: Director, Federal Affairs

Outside Counsel/Consultants

Arnold & Porter
Issues: AUT, CSP, DIS, FIN, HCR, INS
Rep By: Martha L. Cochran, James F. Fitzpatrick, Nancy L. Perkins, Stanford G. Ross

State Government Affairs Council

1255 23rd St. NW
Suite 200
Washington, DC 20037-1174
Web: www.sgac.org
E-mail: stategov@sgac.org
Tel: (202)728-0500
Fax: (202)833-3636

A coalition of corporations and associations seeking to improve the governmental process at the state level and promote better understanding between private industry and state governments. Includes 120 multi-national corporations and national trade associations.

In-house, DC-area Employees

CUMMINGS, Kelly: Director of Operations and Member Services
LOUDY, Elizabeth A.: Exec. Director

Outside Counsel/Consultants

Hauck and Associates
Rep By: Kelly Cummings, Elizabeth A. Loudy

O'Connor & Hannan, L.L.P.
Rep By: Timothy W. Jenkins

State Guard Ass'n of the U.S.

P.O. Box 206
Lothian, MD 20711
Web: www.sgaus.org
E-mail: hquarter@sgaus.org
Tel: (301)261-9099
Fax: (301)261-9099

Advocates a viable state militia system, i.e. home guards.

Leg. Issues: LAW

In-house, DC-area Employees

MCHENRY, Paul T.: Exec. Director

State Legislative Policy Institute

P.O. Box 42442
Washington, DC 20015
E-mail: slpi@aol.com
Tel: (202)494-7991

Organization of state legislators and labor unions focusing on working family and economic policy, fair census and redistricting policies, and election reform.

Leg. Issues: GOV, LBR

In-house, DC-area Employees

WICE, Jeffrey M.: Counsel

State Street Bank and Trust Co.

Boston, MA
Leg. Issues: BAN, FIN, RET

Outside Counsel/Consultants

Barbour Griffith & Rogers, Inc.
Issues: RET
Rep By: Haley Barbour, G. O. Lanny Griffith, Jr., Edward M. Rogers, Jr., Brent Thompson

O'Connor & Hannan, L.L.P.
Issues: BAN, FIN, RET
Rep By: Edward Beck, Danielle Fagre, Timothy W. Jenkins, Thomas H. Quinn

State Street Development Co. of Boston

Boston, MA

An apartment building management firm.

Leg. Issues: HOU

Outside Counsel/Consultants

Coan & Lyons
Issues: HOU
Rep By: Carl A. S. Coan, Jr., Raymond K. James

State Universities Retirement System of Illinois Pension Fund

Champaign, IL

Outside Counsel/Consultants

Skadden, Arps, Slate, Meagher & Flom LLP
Rep By: Lynn R. Coleman

State University of New York (SUNY)

Leg. Issues: BUD

Outside Counsel/Consultants

Arent Fox Kintner Plotkin & Kahn, PLLC
Issues: BUD
Rep By: Stacy Harbison, Douglas McCormack

State University of New York at Albany

Albany, NY
Registered: LDA
Leg. Issues: BUD, EDU

Outside Counsel/Consultants

Akin, Gump, Strauss, Hauer & Feld, L.L.P.

Policy Directions, Inc.
Issues: BUD, EDU
Rep By: Stephen Michael, Frankie L. Trull

States Ratification Committee

Alexandria, VA
Leg. Issues: AGR, GOV, TRD

Outside Counsel/Consultants

The Solomon Group, LLC
Issues: AGR, GOV, TRD
Rep By: Hon. Gerald B. H. Solomon, William R. Teator

Statoil Energy

Outside Counsel/Consultants

Dittus Communications
Rep By: Trudi Boyd, Gloria S. Dittus, Jeffrey Eshelman

Statute of Repose Coalition (SORC)

Washington, DC

Outside Counsel/Consultants

Campbell Crane & Associates

Steam Generator Coalition

Washington, DC
Leg. Issues: TRD

Outside Counsel/Consultants

PriceWaterhouseCoopers
Issues: TRD
Rep By: Kirt C. Johnson, Pat Raffaniello

The Steel Alliance

1707 L St. NW
Suite 650
Washington, DC 20036
Web: www.thenewsteel.org
Tel: (202)955-5777
Fax: (202)955-4549

In-house, DC-area Employees
BLUMENTHAL, Holly: Manager, Communications
STEPHENSON, Mark: Exec. Director

Outside Counsel/Consultants
Porter/Novelli
Rep By: Donald H. Cady
Wirthlin Worldwide

Steel Manufacturers Ass'n

1730 Rhode Island Ave. NW
Suite 907
Washington, DC 20036-3101
Web: www.steelnet.org
E-mail: danjczek@steelnet.org
Tel: (202)296-1515
Fax: (202)296-2506
Registered: LDA

A trade group of 59 companies, including 48 U.S. steel companies, seven Canadian and four Mexican. U.S. members account for about 50% of U.S. steel production.

Leg. Issues: CAW, EDU, ENG, ENV, GOV, LBR, MAN, TRA, TRD, WAS

In-house, DC-area Employees
DANJCZEK, Thomas A.: President
DEELY, Carol: Manager, Member Services
STUART, Eric J.: Manager, Committee Affairs

Outside Counsel/Consultants
Brickfield, Burchette, Ritts & Stone
Issues: ENG
Rep By: James Brew
Collier Shannon Scott, PLLC
Issues: ENV
Rep By: John L. Wittenborn, Dana S. Wood
Wiley, Rein & Fielding

Steel Recycling Institute

1667 K St. NW
Suite 460
Washington, DC 20006
Web: www.recycle-steel.org
Tel: (202)496-9686
Registered: LDA

Affiliated with the American Iron and Steel Institute (see separate listing). Works to ensure the continuing development of the steel recycling infrastructure and to educate the solid waste management industry, government, business, and the consumer about the environment. Headquarted in Pittsburgh, PA.

Leg. Issues: ENV

In-house, DC-area Employees
FOLEY, Walter J. "Chip": Director, Government Relations - Recycling

Steel Service Center Institute

1403 King St.
Alexandria, VA 22314
Web: www.ssci.org
E-mail: sscigov@aol.com
Tel: (703)535-1093
Fax: (703)535-1094
Registered: LDA

The Steel Service Center Institute is a Chicago based international trade association which primarily serves steel distributors.

Leg. Issues: BNK, IMM, TAX, TOR, TRD

Political Action Committee/s
Steel Service Center Institute PAC
1403 King St.
Alexandria, VA 22314
Contact: Nicole LaPorte
Tel: (703)535-1093
Fax: (703)535-1094

In-house, DC-area Employees
CARRAGHER, Robert J.: V. President, Governmental Affairs
LAPORTE, Nicole: Manager, Governmental Affairs

Outside Counsel/Consultants
Internat'l Advisory Services Group Ltd.
Issues: TRD
Rep By: Charles H. Blum

Steel Shipping Container Institute

Washington, DC
Web: www.steelcontainers.com
E-mail: ssci@steelcontainers.com

Outside Counsel/Consultants
The Technical Group LLC

Stelco Inc.

Hamilton, CANADA

Outside Counsel/Consultants
Dow, Lohnes & Albertson, PLLC
Rep By: Kenneth D. Salomon

Stepan Co.

Outside Counsel/Consultants
Ungaretti & Harris
Rep By: Joseph A. Cari, Jr., Michelle M. Faust

Stephens Group, Inc.

Little Rock, AK
Leg. Issues: BAN, FIN, TAX

Outside Counsel/Consultants
Hooper Owen & Winburn
Issues: TAX
Rep By: Steve Glaze
O'Connor & Hannan, L.L.P.
Issues: FIN
Rep By: Hon. Larry Pressler
Bill Simpson & Associates
Issues: BAN, TAX
Rep By: William G. Simpson

Stephens, Cross, Ihlenfeld and Boring, Inc.

Washington, DC
Leg. Issues: GOV

Outside Counsel/Consultants
J. Arthur Weber & Associates
Issues: GOV
Rep By: Joseph A. Weber

SteriGenics Internat'l

Corona, CA

Outside Counsel/Consultants
Olsson, Frank and Weeda, P.C.
Rep By: John W. Bode, Susan P. Grymes, Karen Reis Harned, Stephen L. Lacey, Marshall L. Matz, Tyson Redpath, Ryan W. Stroschein

SterilMed, Inc.

Minneapolis, MN
Leg. Issues: MED

Outside Counsel/Consultants
Congressional Consultants
Issues: MED
Rep By: Gwen Gampel, Karen M. Late

Sterling Chemical Co.

Houston, TX
Leg. Issues: ENV, TAX, TRD, WAS

Outside Counsel/Consultants
Bracewell & Patterson, L.L.P.
Issues: ENV, TAX, TRD, WAS
Rep By: Gene E. Godley, Marc C. Hebert, Michael L. Pate, Scott H. Segal

Sterling Internat'l Consultants, Inc.

Chestnut Ridge, NY
Leg. Issues: APP, BUD, FOR

Outside Counsel/Consultants
Steptoe & Johnson LLP
Issues: APP, BUD, FOR
Rep By: Sheldon E. Hochberg, Edward J. Krauland, Richard R. Verma

Stetson University

Deland, FL

Outside Counsel/Consultants
F.B.A.
Rep By: J. R. Kirkland

Stevens Institute of Technology

Hoboken, NJ
Leg. Issues: DEF, ECN

Outside Counsel/Consultants
Alcalde & Fay
Issues: DEF, ECN
Rep By: Hon. Louis A. "Skip" Bafalis, Jim Davenport

Stewart & Stevenson Services, Inc.

Sealy, TX
Registered: LDA
Leg. Issues: AVI, DEF, MAN, TAX, TRD

Outside Counsel/Consultants
C. Baker Consulting Inc.
Issues: AVI, DEF, MAN
Rep By: Caleb Baker
Cambridge Internat'l, Inc.
Issues: DEF
Rep By: Justus P. White
Michael Chase Associates, LTD
Issues: DEF
Rep By: Michael T. Chase
Manatt, Phelps & Phillips, LLP
Issues: DEF
Rep By: Mary Ann Gilleece, Jeff Kuhnreich
Verner, Liipfert, Bernhard, McPherson and Hand, Chartered
Issues: DEF, TAX, TRD
Rep By: Virginia R. Boggs, Lloyd N. Hand, Brenda G. Meister, Steven R. Phillips

Stewart & Stevenson Tactical Vehicle Systems, LP

Outside Counsel/Consultants
Edelman Public Relations Worldwide
Rep By: Christine Kelly Cimko

Stewart Enterprises, Inc.

Metairie, LA
Leg. Issues: CSP

Outside Counsel/Consultants
Jones, Walker, Waechter, Poitevent, Carrere & Denegre, L.L.P.
Issues: CSP
Rep By: Paul Cambon, John J. Jaskot, R. Christian Johnsen, James Ogsbury
The Livingston Group, LLC
Issues: CSP
Rep By: Melvin Goodweather, Richard Legendre, Hon. Robert L. Livingston, Jr., J. Allen Martin, Richard L. Rodgers

Stidd Systems, Inc.

Greenport, NY
Leg. Issues: DEF

Outside Counsel/Consultants
American Defense Internat'l, Inc.
Issues: DEF
Rep By: Michael Herson, Van D. Hipp, Jr., Bonnie Shindelman, Dave Wilberding

Stillman College

Tuscaloosa, AL
Leg. Issues: EDU, HCR, TEC, URB

Outside Counsel/Consultants
Sally L. Albright
Issues: EDU, HCR, TEC, URB
Rep By: Sally L. Albright

Stilman Advanced Strategies

Dever, CO
Leg. Issues: AVI, DEF

Outside Counsel/Consultants
The Carter Group
Issues: AVI, DEF
Rep By: Michael R. Carter

Stilwell Financial Inc.

Kansas City, MO
Leg. Issues: FIN, TAX, TRA

Outside Counsel/Consultants
Hooper Owen & Winburn
Issues: TAX, TRA
Rep By: Lindsay D. Hooper
Sydney Probst
Issues: FIN
Rep By: Sydney Probst

Stine Seed Co.

Leg. Issues: AGR

Outside Counsel/Consultants
Redfern Resources
Issues: AGR
Rep By: Ed Redfern

Stirling Energy Systems

Outside Counsel/Consultants
McClure, Gerard & Neuenschwander, Inc.
Rep By: Steven G. Barringer, Joseph T. Findaro, Matthew Iandoli, Nils W. Johnson, Hon. James A. McClure, Tod O. Neuenschwander

Stock Co. Information Group

Washington, DC
Leg. Issues: TAX

Outside Counsel/Consultants

Davis & Harman LLP
Issues: TAX
Rep By: John T. Adney, Richard S. Belas, Thomas A. Davis, William B. Harman, Jr., Barbara Groves Mattox, Janis K. McClintock

Stockbridge-Munsee Community Band of Mohican Indians

Bowler, WI
Leg. Issues: BUD, IND, TAX

Outside Counsel/Consultants

Dorsey & Whitney LLP
Issues: BUD, IND, TAX
Rep By: Philip Baker-Shenk, David A. Bieging, Virginia W. Boylan, Cindy Darcy, Sarah Ridley, Kevin J. Wadzinski

Stockton East Water District

Stockton, CA
Leg. Issues: NAT

Outside Counsel/Consultants

Boesch & Co.
Issues: NAT
Rep By: Doyce A. Boesch

Stockton, California, Port of

Stockton, CA
Leg. Issues: DEF

Outside Counsel/Consultants

E. Del Smith and Co.
Issues: DEF
Rep By: E. Del Smith

Stockton, City of

Leg. Issues: ECN, ENV, GOV, WEL

Outside Counsel/Consultants

Peyser Associates, Inc.
Issues: ECN, ENV, GOV, WEL
Rep By: Thane Young

Stoll Stoll Berne Lokting & Shlachter, P.C.

Portland, OR
Leg. Issues: AVI, FOR, TOU, TRA

Outside Counsel/Consultants

Dow, Lohnes & Albertson, PLLC
Issues: AVI, FOR, TOU, TRA
Rep By: Michael D. Hays, Kenneth D. Salomon

Stone and Webster Engineering Corp.

900 19th St. NW
Suite 600
Washington, DC 20006-2105
Tel: (202)261-1900
Fax: (202)261-1949
Registered: LDA
Web: www.stoneweb.com

A subsidiary of Stone and Webster, Inc.

Leg. Issues: ENG, ENV, TRA, WAS

Political Action Committee/s

Stone and Webster Inc. Political Action Committee
900 19th St. NW
Suite 600
Washington, DC 20006-2105
Tel: (202)261-1900
Fax: (202)261-1949
Contact: Stephen M. Marlo

In-house, DC-area Employees

MARLO, Stephen M.: Manager, Washington Operations

Outside Counsel/Consultants

Preston Gates Ellis & Rouvelas Meeds LLP
Issues: ENG, ENV
Rep By: Cindy O'Malley, Tim L. Peckinpaugh, W. Dennis Stephens

Stone Investments, Inc.

Dallas, TX
Leg. Issues: CPI, CPT, GAM, HCR, IND, LAW

Outside Counsel/Consultants

Jefferson Consulting Group
Issues: CPI, CPT, GAM, HCR, IND, LAW
Rep By: Robert J. Thompson

Stony Brook Foundation

Stony Brook, NY
Leg. Issues: EDU, HCR

Outside Counsel/Consultants

American Continental Group, Inc.
Issues: EDU, HCR
Rep By: Steve Colovas, David A. Metzner, Shawn H. Smeallie

Stop It Now!

Haydenville, MA
Leg. Issues: FAM, HCR

Outside Counsel/Consultants

The Ferguson Group, LLC
Issues: FAM, HCR
Rep By: William Ferguson, Jr., Ron Hamm

Stop MFN for China '96 Coalition

Outside Counsel/Consultants

Creative Response Concepts

Storage Technology Corp.

700 13th St. NW
Suite 260
Washington, DC 20005
Tel: (202)347-4060
Fax: (202)347-3892
Registered: LDA
Web: www.storagetek.com

Headquartered in Louisville, CO.

Leg. Issues: CPI, CPT, FIN, GOV, HCR, IMM, SCI, TAX, TRD

Political Action Committee/s

Storage Technology Corp. Political Action Committee
700 13th St. NW
Suite 260
Washington, DC 20005
Tel: (202)347-4060
Fax: (202)347-3892

In-house, DC-area Employees

CALLINICOS, Sean: Manager, Government Relations

Outside Counsel/Consultants

Morrison & Foerster LLP
Issues: CPI, GOV
Rep By: Jonathan Band

Storck U.S.A.

Chicago, IL
Leg. Issues: TRD

Outside Counsel/Consultants

Baker & McKenzie
Issues: TRD
Rep By: Susan G. Braden, Teresa A. Gleason, Kevin M. O'Brien

Straddle Rules Tax Group

Washington, DC
Leg. Issues: TAX

Outside Counsel/Consultants

Washington Council Ernst & Young
Issues: TAX
Rep By: Doug Badger, Lauren Darling, John L. Doney, Jayne T. Fitzgerald, LaBrenda Garrett-Nelson, Gary J. Gasper, Bruce A. Gates, Nick Giordano, Robert J. Leonard, Richard Meltzer, Phillip D. Moseley, John D. Porter, Robert M. Rozen, Donna Steele-Flynn, Timothy J. Urban

Straight Talk America

Outside Counsel/Consultants

Stevens Reed Curcio & Co.

Stratcor

Danbury, CT

Outside Counsel/Consultants

Robert N. Pyle & Associates
Rep By: Robert N. Pyle

Strategic Minerals Corp.

Danbury, CT
Leg. Issues: DEF, TRD

Outside Counsel/Consultants

deKieffer & Horgan
Issues: TRD
Rep By: Donald E. deKieffer

Robert N. Pyle & Associates
Issues: DEF
Rep By: Alexis Hersh, Alison O'Neill, Robert N. Pyle

Stratus Systems Inc.

New Orleans, LA
Leg. Issues: DEF

Outside Counsel/Consultants

American Defense Internat'l, Inc.
Issues: DEF
Rep By: Michael Herson, Van D. Hipp, Jr., Dave Wilberding

Streampipe.com

Outside Counsel/Consultants

Columbus Public Affairs

Street Law Inc.

1600 K St. NW
Suite 602
Washington, DC 20006-2801
Tel: (202)293-0088
Fax: (202)293-0089
Web: www.streetlaw.org
E-mail: clearinghouse@streetlaw.org
Leg. Issues: BUD

In-house, DC-area Employees

O'BRIEN, Edward L.: Exec. Director

Outside Counsel/Consultants

Hauser Group

Mullenholz, Brimsek & Belair
Issues: BUD
Rep By: Robert R. Belair, Susan C. Haller

Strictly Business Software System

Huntington, WV
Leg. Issues: GOV

Outside Counsel/Consultants

Cottone and Huggins Group
Issues: GOV
Rep By: James B. Huggins

Stroh Brewing Co.

Detroit, MI

Outside Counsel/Consultants

McDermott, Will and Emery
Rep By: Jerry C. Hill, Maggie A. Mitchell, T. Raymond Williams

Student Loan Finance Corp.

Aberdeen, SD
Leg. Issues: BAN, EDU, FIN

Outside Counsel/Consultants

The Spectrum Group
Issues: BAN, EDU, FIN
Rep By: Cheryl Kandaras Chapman, P.E., Gregory L. Sharp

Student Loan Funding Corp.

Cincinnati, OH
Leg. Issues: BUD, EDU, GOV

Outside Counsel/Consultants

Dean Blakey & Moskowitz
Issues: BUD, EDU
Rep By: John E. Dean

O'Connor & Hannan, L.L.P.
Issues: EDU, GOV
Rep By: Hon. Thomas J. Corcoran, Patrick E. O'Donnell, Thomas H. Quinn, Thomas J. Schneider, Hon. James W. Symington

Student Loan Servicing Alliance

Lombard, IL

Outside Counsel/Consultants

Patricia Sullivan
Rep By: Patricia Sullivan

Student Press Law Center

1815 N. Fort Myer Dr.
Suite 900
Arlington, VA 22209-1817
Tel: (703)807-1904
Fax: (703)807-2109
Web: www.splc.org
E-mail: splc@splc.org

Provides free legal advice to student newspapers and publications around the country, for both colleges and high schools.

In-house, DC-area Employees

GOODMAN, Mark: Exec. Director
HIESTAND, Mike: Staff Attorney

Julien J. Studley, Inc.

Washington, DC
Leg. Issues: RES

Outside Counsel/Consultants

Kilpatrick Stockton LLP
Issues: RES
Rep By: Richard Barnett, J. Christopher Brady, Neil I. Levy

Study Circles

Outside Counsel/Consultants

Hauser Group

Stuyvesant Dredging Co.

Metairie, LA
Leg. Issues: MAR

Outside Counsel/Consultants

Sher & Blackwell
Issues: MAR
Rep By: Earl W. Comstock, Jeffrey F. Lawrence, Jeffrey R. Pike

Styrene Information and Research Center

Arlington, VA

A special purpose group of the Soc. of the Plastics Industry.

Leg. Issues: ENV, MAN

Outside Counsel/Consultants

John Adams Associates Inc.
Rep By: A. John Adams

Parry, Romani, DeConcini & Symms
Issues: ENV, MAN
Rep By: Edward H. Baxter, Hon. Dennis DeConcini, John M. Haddow, Scott D. Hatch, Shannon Davis Henderson, Jack W. Martin, Romano Romani, Linda Arey Skladany, Hon. Steven D. Symms

Sub-Zero Freezer Co. Inc.

Madison, WI
Leg. Issues: ENG, ENV

Outside Counsel/Consultants

Foley & Lardner
Issues: ENG, ENV
Rep By: Theodore H. Bornstein

Subaru of America

Cherry Hill, NJ
Leg. Issues: CAW, TRD

Outside Counsel/Consultants

Cassidy & Associates, Inc.
Issues: CAW, TRD
Rep By: Douglass E. Bobbitt, Christy Carson Evans, Arthur D. Mason, Michael Merola, Dan C. Tate, Sr.

Subaru-Isuzu Automotive, Inc.

Lafayette, IN

Outside Counsel/Consultants

Willkie Farr & Gallagher
Rep By: Kenneth J. Pierce

Suburban Mobility Authority for Regional Transportation

Detroit, MI
Leg. Issues: BUD, TRA

Outside Counsel/Consultants

Government Relations, Inc.
Issues: BUD, TRA
Rep By: Thomas J. Bulger, Mark H. Miller, John N. Young

Sudden Infant Death Syndrome Alliance

Baltimore, MD
Leg. Issues: BUD

Outside Counsel/Consultants

Health and Medicine Counsel of Washington
Issues: BUD
Rep By: Staci Sigman Dennison, Dale P. Dirks

Suffolk, New York, County of

Smithtown, NY
Leg. Issues: AGR, ECN, TRA, WEL

Outside Counsel/Consultants

Pamela Ray-Strunk and Associates
Issues: AGR, ECN, TRA, WEL
Rep By: Pamela Ray-Strunk

Sugar Ass'n, Inc.

1101 15th St. NW
Suite 600
Washington, DC 20005
Tel: (202)785-1122
Fax: (202)785-5019
Registered: LDA
Web: www.sugar.org
E-mail: sugar@sugar.org

Represents processors and refiners of beet and cane sugar. Funds research and conducts public communications programs on the role of sugar in nutrition.

Leg. Issues: FOO

In-house, DC-area Employees

BAKER, Dr. Charles W.: V. President, Scientific Affairs
ELDER, Dick: Director, Public Relations
JERNIGAN, Bryan: Director, Communications
KEELOR, Dr. Richard: President and Chief Exec. Officer
OVERTON, Alica A.: V. President and Treasurer
PLANT, Michelle Sutton: Director, Public Policy

Sugar Cane Growers Cooperative of Florida

Belle Glade, FL
Leg. Issues: ENV, NAT, RES

Outside Counsel/Consultants

Dawson & Associates, Inc.
Issues: ENV, NAT, RES
Rep By: Robert K. Dawson, Jonathan P. Deason, Ph.D., Edward Dickey, Ph.D., Lester Edelman, Lt. Gen. Vald Heiberg, Hon. John Myers, Lt. Gen. Arthur E. Williams, USA (Ret.)

Sugiyama Chain Co., Ltd.

Iruma-Shi, JAPAN
Leg. Issues: TRD

Outside Counsel/Consultants

Davis & Leiman, P.C.
Issues: TRD

Suiza Foods Corp.

Dallas, TX
Registered: LDA
Leg. Issues: AGR, FOO, LBR

Outside Counsel/Consultants

Swidler Berlin Shereff Friedman, LLP
Issues: AGR, FOO, LBR
Rep By: Paul T. Denis, Barry B. Direnfeld, Brian W. Fitzgerald, Harold P. Goldfield, Gary D. Slaiman, Katherine R. Taylor

Thelen Reid & Priest LLP
Issues: AGR
Rep By: Barry I. Berkoff, William A. Kirk, Jr., Stephan M. Minikes, Nancy K. West

Sullivan & Cromwell

1701 Pennsylvania Ave. NW
Suite 800
Washington, DC 20006
Tel: (202)956-7500
Fax: (202)293-6330
Registered: LDA

Leg. Issues: BAN, FIN

In-house, DC-area Employees

COHEN, H. Rodgin: Partner
CRAFT, Jr., Robert H.: Managing Partner
HARITON, David P.: Partner
LIBOW, Daryl: Partner
MCCALL, D. Mark: Of Counsel
PFEIFFER, Margaret K.: Partner
RAISLER, Kenneth M.: Partner
SIMMONS, Rebecca J.: Partner
WILLIAMSON, Edwin D.: Partner
WISEMAN, Michael: Partner
WOODALL, III, Samuel R.: Government Affairs Specialist

Outside Counsel/Consultants

Chambers Associates Inc.
Rep By: Letitia Chambers

Parry, Romani, DeConcini & Symms
Issues: BAN, FIN

Sumitomo Chemical Co., Ltd.

Osaka, JAPAN

Outside Counsel/Consultants

McKenna & Cuneo, L.L.P.
Rep By: Joseph F. Dennin

Sumitomo Corp. of America

800 Connecticut Ave. NW
Suite 1000
Washington, DC 20006
Tel: (202)785-9210
Fax: (202)861-0690
Leg. Issues: TRD

In-house, DC-area Employees

KAMESAKI, Mutsuya: Director, Business Development
TFURUMI, Kunio: General Manager

Outside Counsel/Consultants

Jefferson-Waterman Internat'l, LLC
Issues: TRD
Rep By: Daniel J. O'Neill

Summary Agency, Ltd.

Outside Counsel/Consultants

Rodriguez O'Donnell Fuerst Gonzalez & Williams
Rep By: Carlos Rodriguez

Summit Health Institute for Research and Education

440 First St. NW
Suite 430
Washington, DC 20001
E-mail: shire@shireinc.org
Tel: (202)371-0277
Fax: (202)371-0460

In-house, DC-area Employees

PEROT, Ruth: Exec. Director

Summit Technology

Waltham, MA
Leg. Issues: MED

Outside Counsel/Consultants

Cassidy & Associates, Inc.
Issues: MED
Rep By: Jeffrey Lawrence, Laura A. Neal, Barbara Sutton

Sumner, Tennessee, Resource Authority of the County of

Gallatin, TN

Outside Counsel/Consultants

Wright & Talisman, P.C.
Rep By: Scott M. DuBoff

Sun Diamond Growers, Inc.

Pleasanton, CA
Leg. Issues: AGR

Outside Counsel/Consultants

Haley and Associates
Issues: AGR
Rep By: Daniel D. Haley

Sun Healthcare Group, Inc.

1401 I Street NW Suite 520
Washington, DC 20005
Tel: (202)842-2003
Fax: (202)682-4008
Registered: LDA
Web: www.sunh.com

Headquartered in Albuquerque, NM.

Leg. Issues: BUD, HCR, MMM, PHA

In-house, DC-area Employees

ROBILLARD, Marda J.: Senior V. President, Government Relations

Outside Counsel/Consultants

Chesapeake Enterprises, Inc.
Issues: HCR
Rep By: Scott W. Reed

The Washington Group
Issues: HCR, MMM

Sun Innovations, Inc.

Milton, WA
Leg. Issues: SMB, TAX

Outside Counsel/Consultants

Evergreen Associates, Ltd.
Issues: SMB, TAX
Rep By: Robert M. Brooks

Sun Jet Internat'l, Inc.

Largo, FL

Outside Counsel/Consultants

Pierre E. Murphy Law Offices
Rep By: Pierre E. Murphy

Sun Microsystems

1300 I St. NW
Suite 420 East
Washington, DC 20005
Tel: (202)326-7520
Fax: (202)326-7525
Registered: LDA
Web: www.sun.com

Headquartered in Palo Alto, CA.

Leg. Issues: CPI, EDU, GOV, LBR, SCI, TAX, TRD

In-house, DC-area Employees

HANKIN, Christopher G.: Director, Federal Affairs
SACHS, Lowell: Manager, Federal Affairs
SMITH, Robert: Federal Affairs Representative

Outside Counsel/Consultants

F.B.A.
Issues: CPI, SCI
Rep By: J. R. Kirkland

Robert Rarog
Issues: CPI, TRD
Rep By: Robert Rarog

Washington Resource Associates
Issues: CPI, EDU, GOV, LBR, TAX, TRD
Rep By: Christopher T. Long

Sun Outdoor Advertising
Tacoma, WA
Outside Counsel/Consultants
Preston Gates Ellis & Rouvelas Meeds LLP
Rep By: John L. Longstreth, James R. Weiss

Sun Pacific Internat'l
Tucson, AZ
Leg. Issues: AVI
Outside Counsel/Consultants
Sher & Blackwell
Issues: AVI
Rep By: Mark Atwood

Sunbelt Cement
Houston, TX
Leg. Issues: ENV, ROD, TRD
Outside Counsel/Consultants
Janus-Merritt Strategies, L.L.C.
Issues: ENV, ROD, TRD
Rep By: Mark J. Robertson, J. Daniel Walsh

SunCor Development Co.
Phoenix, AR
Leg. Issues: ENV
Outside Counsel/Consultants
The Renkes Group, Ltd.
Issues: ENV
Rep By: Patrick Pettey

SunCruz Casino
A Florida-based floating casino operation.
Outside Counsel/Consultants
Greenberg Traurig, LLP
Rep By: Jack Abramoff, Anthony C. Rudy

Sunkist Growers, Inc.
50 F St. NW
Suite 1100
Washington, DC 20001
Tel: (202)879-0256
Fax: (202)628-8233
Registered: LDA
Leg. Issues: AGR, BUD, ENG, ENV, FOO, INS, NAT, SMB, TAX, TRD
Political Action Committee/s
Sunkist Federal PAC
50 F St. NW
Suite 1100
Washington, DC 20001
Tel: (202)879-0256
Fax: (202)628-8233
In-house, DC-area Employees
QUARLES, W. Kam: Assistant Director
Outside Counsel/Consultants
Tuttle, Taylor & Heron
Issues: AGR
Rep By: Julian B. Heron, Jr.

Sunmar Shipping, Inc.
Washington, DC
Outside Counsel/Consultants
Preston Gates Ellis & Rouvelas Meeds LLP
Rep By: William N. Myhre

Sunoco, Inc.
1130 Connecticut Ave. NW
Suite 710
Washington, DC 20036
Web: www.sunocoinc.com
Tel: (202)628-1010
Fax: (202)628-1041
Registered: LDA
Headquartered in Philadelphia, PA.
Leg. Issues: ENV, TAX
In-house, DC-area Employees
KNOLL, Albert B.: Senior Legislative Representative
WYLIE, Thomas L.: V. President, Federal Government Relations
Outside Counsel/Consultants
McKay Walker
Issues: TAX
Rep By: Lynda K. Walker
Nat'l Environmental Strategies
Issues: ENV
Rep By: Marc I. Himmelstein
Wright & Talisman, P.C.
Rep By: Robert H. Lamb

Sunrider Internat'l
Torrance, CA
Outside Counsel/Consultants
Commerce Consultants Internat'l Ltd.
Rep By: Richard Richards

Sunrise Assisted Living
Arlington, VA
Leg. Issues: HCR
Outside Counsel/Consultants
The Carmen Group
Issues: HCR
Rep By: Ryan Adesnik, Diane Jemmott

Sunrise Medical
Longmont, CO
Leg. Issues: HCR, MMM
Outside Counsel/Consultants
Nusgart Consulting, LLC
Issues: HCR, MMM
Rep By: Marcia Nusgart
Reed, Smith, LLP
Issues: MMM
Rep By: Phillips S. Peter

Sunset Properties, Inc.
Salina, KS
Leg. Issues: AGR, BUD, GOV
Outside Counsel/Consultants
Westerly Group
Issues: AGR, BUD, GOV
Rep By: Sarah Brown, Kirk L. Clinkenbeard

Sunstone Behavioral Health
Nashville, TN
Leg. Issues: MMM
Outside Counsel/Consultants
MARC Associates, Inc.
Issues: MMM
Rep By: Randolph B. Fenninger

SunSweet Growers, Inc.
Yuba City, CA
Leg. Issues: AGR, TRD
Outside Counsel/Consultants
Haley and Associates
Issues: AGR, TRD
Rep By: Daniel D. Haley

SunTrust Banks, Inc.
Atlanta, GA
Leg. Issues: BAN
Outside Counsel/Consultants
Katten Muchin & Zavis
Issues: BAN
Rep By: Carol R. Van Cleef

SUNY Empire State College
Saratoga Springs, NY
Leg. Issues: DEF, EDU
Outside Counsel/Consultants
The Solomon Group, LLC
Issues: DEF, EDU
Rep By: Hon. Gerald B. H. Solomon, William R. Teator

Suomi College
Hancock, MI
Leg. Issues: EDU
Outside Counsel/Consultants
Robert A. Rapoza Associates
Issues: EDU
Rep By: Robert A. Rapoza, Deidre Swesnik

Super Reachback Coalition
Leg. Issues: LBR, TAX
Outside Counsel/Consultants
Symms, Lehn & Associates, Inc.
Issues: LBR, TAX

Superfund Action Alliance
Arlington, VA
Leg. Issues: ENV, SCI, WAS
Outside Counsel/Consultants
ADA Consulting Services
Issues: ENV, SCI, WAS
Rep By: Alicia A. Dugan

Superfund Action Coalition
Arlington, VA
A coalition whose mission is to amend CERCLA by doing away with its retroactive and strict liability provisions as they pertain to non-willful polluters prior to 1986.
Outside Counsel/Consultants
Bode & Grenier LLP
Rep By: William H. Bode

Superfund Reform '95
A coalition of about 1300 trade associations and companies seeking changes in the 1980 superfund law. Members include: American Internat'l Group, Alcan Aluminum, Texaco, the Reinsurance Ass'n of America and the Grocery Manufacturers of America, among others.
Outside Counsel/Consultants
Nat'l Strategies Inc.
Rep By: David K. Aylward
Williams & Jensen, P.C.
Rep By: George D. Baker

Superior Bank, FSB
Oak Terrace, IL
Leg. Issues: BAN, HOU, TAX
Outside Counsel/Consultants
Butera & Andrews
Issues: BAN, HOU, TAX
Rep By: Cliff W. Andrews, Wright H. Andrews, Jr., James J. Butera, Frank Tillotson

Superpharm Corp.
Bay Shore, NY
Outside Counsel/Consultants
Wilmer, Cutler & Pickering

Supra Telecom & Information Systems, Inc.
Miami, FL
Leg. Issues: TEC
Outside Counsel/Consultants
Patton Boggs, LLP
Issues: TEC
Rep By: Paul C. Besozzi, John F. Fithian

Surety Ass'n of America
1101 Connecticut Ave. NW
Suite 800
Washington, DC 20036
Web: www.surety.org
E-mail: information@surety.org
Tel: (202)463-0600
Fax: (202)463-0606
Registered: LDA
The Surety Ass'n of America (SAA) is a voluntary, non-profit, unincorporated association of companies engaged in the business of suretyship. The SAA represents almost 700 surety companies which collectively underwrite the overwhelming majority of fidelity and surety bonds written in the United States, as well as eight foreign affiliates. The SAA is licensed as a rating or advisory organization by all state insurance departments, except that of Texas, and as a statistical agent for the reporting of surety experience.
Leg. Issues: INS
In-house, DC-area Employees
DUKE, Robert J.: Director, Underwriting
GALLAGHER, Edward G.: General Counsel
HAMBY, Martha R.: V. President
SCHUBERT, Lynn M.: President

Surety Information Office
5225 Wisconsin Ave. NW
Suite 600
Washington, DC 20015-2014
Web: www.sio.org
E-mail: sio@sio.org
Tel: (202)686-7463
Fax: (202)686-3656
Formed in January 1993 to disseminate information about the benefits of contract surety bonding in both public and private construction. Supported by the Nat'l Ass'n of Surety Bond Producers and the Surety Ass'n of America.
Leg. Issues: INS
In-house, DC-area Employees
GRANT, Jason D.: Manager, Communications Programs
MCINTYRE, Marla: Exec. Director

Surface Transportation Policy Project
1100 17th St. NW
Suite Ten
Washington, DC 20036
Web: www.transact.org
E-mail: stpp@transact.org
Tel: (202)466-2636
Fax: (202)466-2247
In-house, DC-area Employees
BURWELL, David: President/Chief Exec. Officer
KIENITZ, Roy: Exec. Director

SurfControl

Outside Counsel/Consultants

Dittus Communications
Rep By: Gloria S. Dittus, Karine Elsen, Cynthia Giorgio, Erin Mitchell, Jennifer Moire, Tim Sites

SurfWatch

Outside Counsel/Consultants

Dittus Communications
Rep By: Debra Cabral, Gloria S. Dittus

Suriname, Government of the Republic of

Paramaribo, SURINAME

Outside Counsel/Consultants

Washington World Group, Ltd.
Rep By: Edward J. von Kloberg, III

White & Case LLP

Survival Inc.

Seattle, WA
Leg. Issues: DEF

Outside Counsel/Consultants

Denny Miller McBee Associates
Issues: DEF

Surviving Selma

Outside Counsel/Consultants

Dittus Communications
Rep By: Jeffrey Eshelman, Cynthia Giorgio, Chris McNamara, Tim Sites

Susan B. Anthony List

Alexandria, VA
Leg. Issues: FAM

Outside Counsel/Consultants

Tarne Powers & Associates
Issues: FAM
Rep By: Michelle R. Powers

Susanville Indian Rancheria

Shingle Springs, CA
An American Indian tribe.

Leg. Issues: IND

Outside Counsel/Consultants

Hobbs, Straus, Dean and Walker, LLP
Issues: IND
Rep By: S. Bobo Dean, Karen J. Funk, Marie Osceola-Branch, Michael L. Roy, Judith A. Shapiro, Geoffrey D. Strommer, Joseph H. Webster

Susquehanna Health System

Williamsport, PA
Leg. Issues: BUD, HCR, MED, MMM

Outside Counsel/Consultants

Capitol Associates, Inc.
Issues: BUD
Rep By: Edward R. Long, Ph.D., Julie P. Pawelczyk

DeBrunner and Associates, Inc.
Issues: BUD, HCR, MED, MMM
Rep By: Charles L. DeBrunner, Wendy W. Herr, Ellen J. Kugler, Kathryn D. Rooney

Susquehanna Investment Group

Bala Cynwyd, PA
Leg. Issues: FIN

Outside Counsel/Consultants

Fontheim Partners, PC
Issues: FIN
Rep By: Eric Biel, Kenneth I. Levinson

Sutter, California, County of

Yuba City, CA
Leg. Issues: BUD, ENV

Outside Counsel/Consultants

The Ferguson Group, LLC
Issues: BUD, ENV
Rep By: W. Roger Gwinn

Sutton & Sutton Solicitors

London, UNITED KINGDOM
Leg. Issues: BUD

Outside Counsel/Consultants

Baker & Hostetler LLP
Issues: BUD
Rep By: Mark A. Cymrot, Steven A. Lotterer, Hon. Guy Vander Jagt

Svenska Petroleum Exploration AB

Stockholm, SWEDEN
Leg. Issues: FOR, FUE, TRD

Outside Counsel/Consultants

Akin, Gump, Strauss, Hauer & Feld, L.L.P.
Issues: FOR, FUE, TRD
Rep By: Steven R. Ross, Edward L. Rubinoff

SVS, Inc.

Albuquerque, NM

Outside Counsel/Consultants

The PMA Group
Rep By: Kaylene Green, Joseph Littleton, Stephen Madey, Paul J. Magliocchetti

Swan Creek River Confederated Ojibbwa Tribes of Michigan

Saginaw, MI
Leg. Issues: IND

Outside Counsel/Consultants

Patton Boggs, LLP
Issues: IND
Rep By: Thomas Hale Boggs, Jr., Katharine R. Boyce, Harold Kim

SWATH Ocean Systems, Inc.

Chula Vista, CA
Leg. Issues: DEF

Outside Counsel/Consultants

Cassidy & Associates, Inc.
Issues: DEF
Rep By: Shawn Edwards, Brig. Gen. Terry Paul, USMC (Ret.), Rear Admiral G. Dennis Vaughan, (Ret.)

Rhoads Group
Issues: DEF
Rep By: Paul D. Behrends, Kathleen Ireland, Steven G. McKnight, Clifford R. Northup, Barry D. Rhoads, Elizabeth R. Sharpstene, Thomas Worrall

Swaziland Sugar Ass'n

Mabane, SWAZILAND
Leg. Issues: TAX, TRD

Outside Counsel/Consultants

Murray, Scheer, Montgomery, Tapia & O'Donnell
Issues: TAX, TRD
Rep By: Thomas R. Crawford, D. Michael Murray

Swaziland, Embassy of the Kingdom of

3400 International Dr. NW
Suite 3M
Washington, DC 20008
Tel: (202)362-6683
Fax: (202)244-8059
E-mail: swaziland@compuserv.com

Outside Counsel/Consultants

Washington World Group, Ltd.
Rep By: Edward J. von Kloberg, III

Swaziland, Kingdom of

Mabane, SWAZILAND
Leg. Issues: ECN

Outside Counsel/Consultants

Africa Global Partners
Issues: ECN
Rep By: Mimi Nedelcovych

Swedish Match

A manufacturer of smokeless tobacco.

Leg. Issues: FOO, HCR, TOB

Outside Counsel/Consultants

Alpine Group, Inc.
Issues: FOO, HCR, TOB
Rep By: Dan Brouillette, James Gregory Means

Sweetener Users Ass'n

3231 Valley Lane
Falls Church, VA 22044
Tel: (703)532-9360
Fax: (703)532-9361

In-house, DC-area Employees

HAMMER, Thomas A.: President

Outside Counsel/Consultants

Hammer & Co.
Rep By: Thomas A. Hammer

Sweetwater Authority

Chula Vista, CA
Leg. Issues: BUD

Outside Counsel/Consultants

Honberger and Walters, Inc.
Issues: BUD
Rep By: Donald Gilchrest, Thomas P. Walters

Swidler Berlin Shereff Friedman, LLP

3000 K St. NW
Suite 300
Washington, DC 20007
Tel: (202)424-7500
Fax: (202)424-7643
Registered: LDA, FARA
Web: www.swidlaw.com
Leg. Issues: BUD, CAW, ENV, GOV

Political Action Committee/s

Swidler & Berlin Political Action Committee
3000 K St. NW
Suite 300
Washington, DC 20007
Tel: (202)424-7500
Fax: (202)424-7643

In-house, DC-area Employees

BARNES, Peter: Member
BERLIN, Edward: Chairman
BLAU, Russell M.: Partner
COLE, Keith N.: Partner
COOPER, Kathy: Associate
DEBRY, Kristine: Associate
DELORENZO, James
DENIS, Paul T.
DIRENFELD, Barry B.: Managing Partner
ERNST, Martin C.
FITZGERALD, Brian W.: Partner
GALLAGHER, Lynn M.: Counsel
GALLANT, Gary: Associate
GLEW, Jr., William B.: Counsel
GOLDFIELD, Harold P.: Senior Partner
HAMILTON, James: Partner
HYMAN, Lester S.: Senior Counsel
JAFFE, Kenneth G.: Partner
KIDDOO, Jean L.: Partner
KNAUSS, Charles H.: Partner
LEVY, Harold A.: Of Counsel
LIPMAN, Andrew D.: Partner
LORE, Kenneth G.: Partner
MARSHALL, Jr., Thurgood: Partner
MILLER, Leonard A.: Partner
POPKIN, Richard A.: Partner
SCHANER, Kenneth I.: Partner
SLAIMAN, Gary D.: Partner
SPOONER, Nancy K.: Partner
STEINWURTZEL, Robert N.: Partner
TAYLOR, Katherine R.: Associate
VALENTE, Thomas
WANG, Catherine: Member
WARD, Michael E.: Counsel
WHITEHEAD, Priscilla A.: Partner
WIGMORE, Michael B.: Associate
WILHEIM, William B.: Associate
ZENER, Robert V.

Outside Counsel/Consultants

LPI Consulting, Inc.
Issues: BUD, CAW, ENV, GOV
Rep By: Teresa Gorman

SwimWithTheSharks.com

101 North Carolina St. SE
Suite 401
Washington, DC 20003
Tel: (202)543-8331
Fax: (202)543-4225
Web: www.swimwiththesharks.com
E-mail: john@swimwiththesharks.com

A business and political consulting firm; area of expertise in trade issues, mainly between US and Mexico.

In-house, DC-area Employees

KOCOL, John M.: Chief Exec. Officer

Swinomish Tribal Community

LaConner, WA

Outside Counsel/Consultants

SENSE, INC.
Rep By: C. Juliet Pittman

SWIPCO, U.S.

Washington, DC
Provides third-party procurement services and preshipment inspection and auditing.

Leg. Issues: FOR, GOV

Outside Counsel/Consultants

Manatt, Phelps & Phillips, LLP
Issues: FOR, GOV
Rep By: Hon. Jack W. Buechner, June L. DeHart, Eric Farnsworth, Robert J. Kabel, Jeff Kuhnreich, Susan M. Schmidt, Jessica A. Wasserman

Murray & Murray
Issues: GOV

Swisher Internat'l Inc.
Jacksonville, FL
A manufacturer of cigars and smokeless tobacco products.
Leg. Issues: TOB
Outside Counsel/Consultants
Bergson & Co.
Issues: TOB
Rep By: Paul C. Bergson

Swiss Bank Corp.
Basel, SWITZERLAND
Leg. Issues: BAN
Outside Counsel/Consultants
Wilmer, Cutler & Pickering
Issues: BAN
Rep By: Lloyd N. Cutler, Roger M. Witten

Swiss Bankers Ass'n
Leg. Issues: BAN
Outside Counsel/Consultants
Wilmer, Cutler & Pickering
Issues: BAN
Rep By: Lloyd N. Cutler

Swiss Investors Protection Ass'n
Geneva, SWITZERLAND
Leg. Issues: BAN, BUD, FIN, TAX
Outside Counsel/Consultants
Andrew F. Quinlan
Issues: BAN, BUD, FIN, TAX
Rep By: Andrew F. Quinlan

Swiss Munition Enterprise
Thune, SWITZERLAND
A defense contractor.
Leg. Issues: DEF
Outside Counsel/Consultants
American Defense Internat'l, Inc.
Issues: DEF
Rep By: Van D. Hipp, Jr., Dave Wilberding

Swiss Ordnance Enterprise
Thune, SWITZERLAND
Outside Counsel/Consultants
Global Marketing and Development Solutions
Rep By: Ronald L. Carlberg

Swissair
Zurich, SWITZERLAND
Leg. Issues: AVI
Outside Counsel/Consultants
Global Aviation Associates, Ltd.
Issues: AVI
Rep By: Jon F. Ash, Charles R. Chambers

Switzerland, Economic Development, State of Vaud
Lausanne, SWITZERLAND
Leg. Issues: ECN
Outside Counsel/Consultants
Global Communicators
Issues: ECN
Rep By: Katherine M. Christie, James W. Harff, Kristine E. Heine

SWL Communications LLC
Boston, MA
Leg. Issues: TEC
Outside Counsel/Consultants
GPC Internat'l
Issues: TEC

Swope Parkway Health Center
Kansas City, MO
Leg. Issues: BUD, ECN, HCR
Outside Counsel/Consultants
Sara Garland (and Associates)
Issues: BUD, ECN, HCR
Rep By: Rachel A. Emmons, Sara G. Garland

Sycuan Band of Mission Indians
El Cajon, CA
Outside Counsel/Consultants
SENSE, INC.
Rep By: C. Juliet Pittman

Symbol Technologies, Inc.
Holtsville, NY
A manufacturer and marketer of bar code-based data capture systems.
Outside Counsel/Consultants
Collier Shannon Scott, PLLC
Rep By: John B. Brew, Kathleen Clark Kies, Laurence J. Lasoff, Paul C. Rosenthal, Dana S. Wood

Synapse
Leg. Issues: BAN, POS
Outside Counsel/Consultants
The MWW Group
Issues: BAN, POS
Rep By: Tracey Becker, Jonathan B. Slade, Robert G. Sommer

Syngenta
Outside Counsel/Consultants
Alpine Group, Inc.

Synkinetics, Inc.
Lowell, MA
Outside Counsel/Consultants
Commonwealth Group, Ltd.

Synovus Financial Corp.
Columbus, GA
A banking and credit card processing company.
Outside Counsel/Consultants
Covington & Burling
Rep By: John C. Dugan

Syntex (USA) Inc.
Palo Alto, CA
Outside Counsel/Consultants
Covington & Burling
Rep By: Roderick A. DeArment

Synthetic Genetics
Long Beach, CA
Outside Counsel/Consultants
Washington Consulting Alliance, Inc.

Synthetic Organic Chemical Manufacturers Ass'n
1850 M St. NW
Suite 700
Washington, DC 20036
Web: www.socma.com
Tel: (202)721-4100
Fax: (202)296-8548
Registered: LDA

SOCMA is a trade association representing batch and custom chemical manufacturers, a highly innovative, entrepreneurial and customer-driven sector of the chemical industry.
Leg. Issues: CAW, CHM, DIS, ENV, GOV, LBR, MAN, SCI, SMB, TAX, TRA, TRD, WAS
In-house, DC-area Employees
FORDING, Jr., Edmund H.: President
GUNNULFSEN, Jeffrey: Manager, Government Affairs
HEYL, Michael S.: Manager, Government Relations
MORRIS, Carolyn Covey: V. President, Public and Government Affairs
NEWTON, Vanessa: Manager, Communications

Syntroleum Corp.
Tulsa, OK
Leg. Issues: DEF, FUE
Outside Counsel/Consultants
American Defense Internat'l, Inc.
Issues: DEF
Rep By: Michael Herson, Van D. Hipp, Jr., Dave Wilberding
Patton Boggs, LLP
Issues: FUE
Rep By: John C. Garrett, Jeffrey T. Smith

Synzyme Technologies, Inc.
Irvine, CA
Leg. Issues: DEF, ENG, HCR, MED
Outside Counsel/Consultants
Berkshire Inc.
Issues: DEF, ENG, HCR, MED
Rep By: Michael T. Kelley

Syquest Technology, Inc.
Fremont, CA
Outside Counsel/Consultants
Wiley, Rein & Fielding
Rep By: Charles O. Verrill, Jr.

Syracuse University
Syracuse, NY
Leg. Issues: BUD, CPT, EDU, SCI, TAX
Outside Counsel/Consultants
Lewis-Burke Associates
Issues: BUD, CPT, EDU, SCI, TAX
Rep By: Rachel Brown, April L. Burke

System & Computer Technology Corp.
Outside Counsel/Consultants
Valente Lopatin & Schulze
Rep By: Susan Feeney, Richard T. Schulze, Jr., Mark Valente, III

System Planning Corp.
Arlington, VA
Leg. Issues: DEF
Outside Counsel/Consultants
The Spectrum Group
Issues: DEF

Systematics
Little Rock, AR
Outside Counsel/Consultants
Jones, Day, Reavis & Pogue

Systems Simulation Solutions Inc.
Alexandria, VA
A computer simulation and modeling company.
Leg. Issues: AER, DEF
Outside Counsel/Consultants
Madison Government Affairs
Issues: AER, DEF
Rep By: Paul J. Hirsch, Jackson Kemper, III

Szlavik, Hogan & Miller
Washington, DC
Outside Counsel/Consultants
Janus-Merritt Strategies, L.L.C.
Rep By: Bethany Noble

T & N Industries
Southfield, MI
Leg. Issues: AUT, HCR, MAN
Outside Counsel/Consultants
Bloomfield Associates, Inc.
Issues: AUT, HCR, MAN
Rep By: Douglas M. Bloomfield

T.W.Y. Co., Ltd.
Seoul, KOREA
Leg. Issues: DEF, FOR, IMM
Outside Counsel/Consultants
R. J. Hudson Associates
Issues: DEF, FOR, IMM

TACA de Honduras
Tegucigalpa, HONDURAS
Outside Counsel/Consultants
Mullenholz, Brimsek & Belair
Rep By: John R. Brimsek

TACA Internat'l Airlines
San Salvador, EL SALVADOR
Outside Counsel/Consultants
Mullenholz, Brimsek & Belair
Rep By: John R. Brimsek

Taco Bell Corp.
Irvine, CA
Registered: LDA
Leg. Issues: FOO
Outside Counsel/Consultants
Hogan & Hartson L.L.P.
Issues: FOO
Rep By: Humberto R. Pena

Tacoma, Washington, City of

Leg. Issues: BUD, ENG, ENV, HOU, NAT, TAX, TEC, URB, UTI

Outside Counsel/Consultants

Miller & Van Eaton, P.L.L.C.
Issues: TEC
Rep By: Joseph Van Eaton

Simon and Co., Inc.
Issues: BUD, HOU, TAX, URB
Rep By: Heather Barber, Alex DeGood, Leonard S. Simon

Van Ness Feldman, P.C.
Issues: ENG, ENV, NAT, UTI
Rep By: Gary D. Bachman, Thomas C. Roberts, Michael A. Swiger

Tacoma, Washington, Port of

Tacoma, WA
Leg. Issues: MAR, TAX, TRA, TRD

Outside Counsel/Consultants

Denny Miller McBee Associates
Issues: MAR, TRA, TRD

Preston Gates Ellis & Rouvelas Meeds LLP
Issues: MAR, TAX
Rep By: Jonathan Blank, Mark H. Ruge

Tacoma, Washington, Public Utilities Department of

Tacoma, WA
Leg. Issues: UTI

Outside Counsel/Consultants

Simon and Co., Inc.
Issues: UTI
Rep By: Heather Barber, Alex DeGood, Leonard S. Simon

TAESA (Transportes Aereos Ejecutivos, S.A. de C.V.)

Mexico City, MEXICO

Outside Counsel/Consultants

Pierre E. Murphy Law Offices

Tai Ji Men Qigong Academy

Leg. Issues: FOR

Outside Counsel/Consultants

Pro Advance Inc.
Issues: FOR
Rep By: Andrew J. Garlikov

Tailored Clothing Ass'n

1155 21st St. NW
Suite 300
Washington, DC 20036
Tel: (202)659-8201

Below address is that of the firm Williams & Jensen, P.C.

Leg. Issues: APP, TRD

Political Action Committee/s

Clothing Industry & Workers PAC
1155 21st St. NW
Suite 300
Washington, DC 20036
Tel: (202)659-8201
Contact: J. Steven Hart

In-house, DC-area Employees

HART, J. Steven: PAC Director
MCCARLIE, Christine C.: Exec. Director

Outside Counsel/Consultants

Sandler, Travis & Rosenberg, P.A.
Issues: APP, TRD
Rep By: Nicole Bivens Collinson, Philip Gallas, Chandri Navarro-Bowman, Susan Renton

Williams & Jensen, P.C.
Issues: APP, TRD
Rep By: J. Steven Hart, David A. Starr

Taipei Economic and Cultural Representative Office in the United States

4201 Wisconsin Ave. NW
Washington, DC 20016-2137
Tel: (202)895-1800
Fax: (202)966-0825

Represents the interests of Taiwan in the United States.

Leg. Issues: FOR, TRD

In-house, DC-area Employees

CHEN, C.J.: Representative

Outside Counsel/Consultants

Bergner Bockorny Castagnetti and Hawkins
Rep By: Jeffrey T. Bergner, David A. Bockorny, David Castagnetti, Melissa Schulman

Global USA, Inc.
Issues: FOR
Rep By: Rosamond S. Brown, George S. Kopp

Heller & Rosenblatt

O'Connor & Hannan, L.L.P.
Rep By: Patrick E. O'Donnell, Thomas H. Quinn

The Solomon Group, LLC
Issues: FOR, TRD
Rep By: David M. Lonie, Hon. Gerald B. H. Solomon

Symms, Lehn & Associates, Inc.
Issues: FOR

Wasserman and Associates
Rep By: Gary Wasserman

Taiwan Power Co.

Taipei, CHINA (TAIWAN)

Outside Counsel/Consultants

Shaw Pittman

Taiwan Research Institute

Taipei, CHINA (TAIWAN)

Outside Counsel/Consultants

Cassidy & Associates, Inc.
Rep By: James Rowan, Hon. Martin A. Russo, Gerald Felix Warburg

Rhoads Group

Taiwan Studies Institute

Taipei, CHINA (TAIWAN)
Leg. Issues: DEF, FOR, TRD

Outside Counsel/Consultants

Cassidy & Associates, Inc.
Issues: DEF, FOR, TRD
Rep By: Gerald S. J. Cassidy, Amos Hochstein, Hon. Martin A. Russo, Maureen Walsh, Gerald Felix Warburg, Stephen Whitaker

Powell Tate
Issues: DEF, FOR, TRD
Rep By: Laurence I. Barrett, Barbara L. Francis, Kathryn Waters Gest, Katherine C. Kolstad

Rhoads Group
Issues: DEF, FOR, TRD
Rep By: Paul D. Behrends, Kathleen Ireland, Steven G. McKnight, Clifford R. Northup, Barry D. Rhoads, Elizabeth R. Sharpstene

Taiwan, Directorate General of Telecommunications

Taipei, CHINA (TAIWAN)

Outside Counsel/Consultants

Severance Internat'l, Inc.

Taiwan, Government of

Taipei, CHINA (TAIWAN)

Outside Counsel/Consultants

Verner, Liipfert, Bernhard, McPherson and Hand, Chartered

Take Back the House

300 N. Lee St.
Suite 500
Alexandria, VA 2214

A political action committee.

In-house, DC-area Employees

HODGDON, S. A.: PAC Administrator

Take The Field, Inc.

New York, NY
Leg. Issues: BUD, ENV, SPO

Outside Counsel/Consultants

Gottehrer and Co.
Issues: BUD, SPO
Rep By: Barry Gottehrer

Liz Robbins Associates
Issues: ENV
Rep By: Liz Robbins

Talgo

Seattle, WA
Leg. Issues: RRR

Outside Counsel/Consultants

Colling Swift & Hynes
Issues: RRR
Rep By: Terese Colling, Pablo Collins, Robert J. Hynes, Jr., Hon. Allan B. Swift

Talladega College

Talladega, AL
Leg. Issues: BUD, EDU

Outside Counsel/Consultants

Dean Blakey & Moskowitz
Issues: BUD, EDU
Rep By: William A. Blakey

Tallahassee, Florida, City of

Leg. Issues: GOV, TEC

Outside Counsel/Consultants

Miller & Van Eaton, P.L.L.C.
Issues: TEC
Rep By: Joseph Van Eaton

Richard L. Spees, Inc.
Issues: GOV
Rep By: Richard L. Spees

Tambrands, Inc.

White Plains, NY

Outside Counsel/Consultants

Arnold & Porter

Tampa Bay Performing Arts Center

Tampa, FL
Leg. Issues: ECN

Outside Counsel/Consultants

John C. Grzebien
Issues: ECN
Rep By: John C. Grzebien

Tampa Port Authority

Tampa, FL
Leg. Issues: TRA

Outside Counsel/Consultants

Alcalde & Fay
Issues: TRA
Rep By: Hector Alcalde, J. Michael Crye, Lois Moore

Tampa, Florida, City of

Leg. Issues: HOU, TRA

Outside Counsel/Consultants

Alcalde & Fay
Issues: HOU, TRA
Rep By: Hector Alcalde, Kathy Jurado Munoz

TAMSA

Mexico City, MEXICO

Outside Counsel/Consultants

White & Case LLP
Rep By: David P. Houlihan

Tan Holdings Corp.

Lower Base Saipan, GU

Outside Counsel/Consultants

Preston Gates Ellis & Rouvelas Meeds LLP
Rep By: Ralph D. Nurnberger

Tanadgusix Corp.

St. Paul Island, AK
Leg. Issues: BUD

Outside Counsel/Consultants

Birch, Horton, Bittner & Cherot
Issues: BUD
Rep By: Thomas L. Albert, William P. Horn

Tanimura & Antle, Inc.

Salinas, CA
Leg. Issues: AGR, TAX

Outside Counsel/Consultants

Haake and Associates
Issues: AGR, TAX
Rep By: Timothy M. Haake, Nathan M. Olsen

Tanners Countervailing Duty Coalition

Outside Counsel/Consultants

Collier Shannon Scott, PLLC
Rep By: Lauren R. Howard

Tanzania, Office of the Foreign Minister of the United Republic of

Dar es Salaam, TANZANIA

Outside Counsel/Consultants

Washington World Group, Ltd.
Rep By: Edward J. von Kloberg, III

Taos Pueblo

Taos, NM

Outside Counsel/Consultants

Steptoe & Johnson LLP
Rep By: Thomas C. Collier, Jr.

TAP/Air Portugal

Newark, NJ
Leg. Issues: AVI

Outside Counsel/Consultants

Bristol Group, Inc.
Issues: AVI
Rep By: Paul G. Afonso, Daniel G. Papadopoulos

TAPS Renewal Task Force

Los Angeles, CA
Leg. Issues: ENV, FUE, NAT, RES

Outside Counsel/Consultants

Steptoe & Johnson LLP
Issues: ENV, FUE, NAT, RES
Rep By: Thomas C. Collier, Jr., John J. Duffy, Robert Jordan, Cynthia Taub

Target Corp.

Minneapolis, MN
Leg. Issues: APP, HCR, TRD

Outside Counsel/Consultants

Flack Associates
Issues: APP, HCR, TRD
Rep By: Susan Garber Flack

Tarrant Regional Water District

Fort Worth, TX
Leg. Issues: AGR, ENV

Outside Counsel/Consultants

Hicks-Richardson Associates
Issues: AGR, ENV
Rep By: Carol A. Hicks, Fred B. Hicks

Tarzana Treatment Center

Tarzana, CA
Leg. Issues: HCR

Outside Counsel/Consultants

Berliner, Candon & Jimison
Issues: HCR
Rep By: Carla Kish, Burt Margolin

TASC, Inc.

Arlington, VA
Professional and technical services.

Outside Counsel/Consultants

Albertine Enterprises, Inc.
Rep By: James J. Albertine, Dr. John M. Albertine

Tatarstan, Republic of

Kazan, RUSSIA

Outside Counsel/Consultants

Murray, Scheer, Montgomery, Tapia & O'Donnell
Rep By: D. Michael Murray

Tate and Lyle North American Sugars Inc.

New York, NY — Registered: LDA
Leg. Issues: AGR, FOO, TRD

Outside Counsel/Consultants

Preston Gates Ellis & Rouvelas Meeds LLP
Issues: AGR, FOO, TRD
Rep By: Werner W. Brandt, Bruce J. Heiman, Sol Mosher, W. Dennis Stephens

Tax Action Group

Washington, DC
Leg. Issues: TAX

Outside Counsel/Consultants

Valis Associates
Issues: TAX
Rep By: Hon. Richard T. Schulze, Todd Tolson, Wayne H. Valis

Tax Analysis

Arlington, VA
Leg. Issues: MIA, TAX

Outside Counsel/Consultants

Cornish F. Hitchcock
Issues: MIA, TAX
Rep By: Cornish F. Hitchcock

Tax Executives Institute, Inc.

1200 G St. NW
Suite 300
Washington, DC 20005
Tel: (202)638-5601
Fax: (202)638-5607
Web: www.tei.org
E-mail: mmurphy@tei.org

A professional association of about 5,000 tax executives from the 2,700 largest corporations in North America.

Leg. Issues: TAX

In-house, DC-area Employees

FAHEY, Mary L.: Tax Counsel
MCCORMALLY, Timothy J.: General Counsel and Director, Tax Affairs
MURPHY, Michael J.: Exec. Director
RASMUSSEN, Jeffery P.: Tax Counsel

Tax Fairness Coalition

Washington, DC
Leg. Issues: BUD, TAX

Outside Counsel/Consultants

Skadden, Arps, Slate, Meagher & Flom LLP
Issues: TAX
Rep By: Fred T. Goldberg, Jr.

Washington Council Ernst & Young
Issues: BUD, TAX
Rep By: Doug Badger, Lauren Darling, John L. Doney, Jayne T. Fitzgerald, LaBrenda Garrett-Nelson, Gary J. Gasper, Bruce A. Gates, Nick Giordano, Cathy Koch, Robert J. Leonard, Richard Meltzer, Phillip D. Moseley, John D. Porter, Robert M. Rozen, Donna Steele-Flynn, Timothy J. Urban

Tax Foundation, Inc.

1250 H St. NW
Suite 750
Washington, DC 20005
Tel: (202)783-2760
Fax: (202)783-6868
Web: www.taxfoundation.org
E-mail: tf@taxfoundation.org

A non-profit research and education organization founded in 1937 concerned with national, state and local fiscal policies and activities.

Leg. Issues: TAX

In-house, DC-area Employees

AHERN, Bill: Director, Communications
FLEENOR, Patrick: Chief Economist
HODGE, Scott A.: Exec. Director
MOODY, Scott: Economist

Tax Information Group

Lincoln, NE

A coalition of small to mid-size mutual life insurance companies.

Leg. Issues: TAX

Outside Counsel/Consultants

Wilmer, Cutler & Pickering
Issues: TAX

Tax Policy Coalition

Leg. Issues: TAX

Outside Counsel/Consultants

Ernst & Young LLP
Issues: TAX
Rep By: Lauren Darling, Patrick G. Heck, Phillip D. Moseley, Henry C. Ruempler, Donna Steele-Flynn

Tax/Shelter Coalition

Outside Counsel/Consultants

Washington Council Ernst & Young
Rep By: Doug Badger, John L. Doney, Jayne T. Fitzgerald, LaBrenda Garrett-Nelson, Gary J. Gasper, Bruce A. Gates, Nick Giordano, Robert J. Leonard, Richard Meltzer, Robert M. Rozen, Timothy J. Urban

Taxicab, Limousine and Paratransit Ass'n

3849 Farragut Ave.
Kensington, MD 20895
Tel: (301)946-5701
Fax: (301)946-4641
Web: www.tlpa.org
E-mail: info@tlpa.org

Represents the owners and managers of private, for-hire ground transportation fleets (taxis, limousines, airport shuttles, paratransit, and non-emergency medical).

Leg. Issues: COM, LBR, TAX, TRA

Political Action Committee/s

Internat'l Taxicab and Livery Ass'n Political Action Committee
3849 Farragut Ave.
Kensington, MD 20895
Tel: (301)946-5701
Fax: (301)946-4641
Contact: Alfred LaGasse

In-house, DC-area Employees

LAGASSE, Alfred: Exec. V. President

Outside Counsel/Consultants

Arter & Hadden
Issues: COM
Rep By: William K. Keane

Capital Partnerships (VA) Inc.
Issues: TRA
Rep By: Robin Angle, Kenneth W. Butler, Clay Gravely

Thompson Coburn LLP
Issues: TRA
Rep By: Edward J. Gill, Jr.

Webster, Chamberlain & Bean
Issues: LBR
Rep By: Arthur Herold, Charles M. Watkins

Taxpayer Assets Project

P.O. Box 19367
Washington, DC 20036
Tel: (202)387-8030
Fax: (202)234-5176

Advocates greater public access to government computer databases.

In-house, DC-area Employees

LOVE, James P.: Director

Taxpayers Against Fraud, The False Claims Legal Center

1220 19th St. NW
Suite 501
Washington, DC 20036
Tel: (202)296-4826
Fax: (202)296-4838
Registered: LDA
Web: www.taf.org

Taxpayers Against Fraud, The False Claims Act Legal Center (TAF) is a non-profit public interest organization dedicated to combating fraud against the federal goverment through the promotion of the False Claims Act (FCA). TAF's mission is both activist and educational.

Leg. Issues: DEF, GOV, LAW, MMM

In-house, DC-area Employees

MOORMAN, Jim: President/C.E.O.

Outside Counsel/Consultants

BSMG Worldwide

The Cuneo Law Group, P.C.
Issues: DEF, GOV, LAW, MMM
Rep By: Jonathan W. Cuneo, Michael G. Lenett, James J. Schweitzer

Medicaid Policy, L.L.C.
Issues: MMM
Rep By: Andrew G. Schneider

Parry, Romani, DeConcini & Symms
Issues: GOV, LAW
Rep By: Edward H. Baxter, Hon. Dennis DeConcini, John M. Haddow, Scott D. Hatch, Shannon Davis Henderson, Jack W. Martin, Romano Romani, Linda Arey Skladany, Hon. Steven D. Symms

Twenty-First Century Group
Issues: GOV
Rep By: Hon. Jack M. Fields, Jr., Cynthia M. Wilkinson

Williams & Jensen, P.C.
Issues: DEF
Rep By: Karen Judd Lewis

Taylor Packing Co., Inc.

Wyalusing, PA
Leg. Issues: AGR

Outside Counsel/Consultants

Hogan & Hartson L.L.P.
Issues: AGR
Rep By: Gary Jay Kushner, Kyra A. Todd

TCF Financial Corp.

Minneapolis, MN
A savings and loan holding company.

Leg. Issues: BAN, BNK

Outside Counsel/Consultants
The Advocacy Group
Issues: BAN, BNK
Rep By: Jon L. Boisclair

TCI

Leg. Issues: TEC

Outside Counsel/Consultants
Jones, Day, Reavis & Pogue
Skadden, Arps, Slate, Meagher & Flom LLP
Rep By: John C. Quale

TCOM, L.P.

Columbia, MD
Leg. Issues: AER, AVI, DEF

Outside Counsel/Consultants
Advantage Associates, Inc.
Issues: AER, AVI, DEF
Rep By: Hon. Bill Sarpalius, Hon. Robin Tallon
Parry, Romani, DeConcini & Symms
Rep By: Edward H. Baxter, Hon. Dennis DeConcini, John M. Haddow, Scott D. Hatch, Shannon Davis Henderson, Jack W. Martin, Romano Romani, Linda Arey Skladany, Hon. Steven D. Symms

TCS

Outside Counsel/Consultants
Dittus Communications
Rep By: Tom Conway, Jeffrey Eshelman, Tim Sites

TD Waterhouse Group

New York, NY
Leg. Issues: FIN

Outside Counsel/Consultants
JFS Group, Ltd.
Issues: FIN

TDS Telecommunications

Madison, WI
Leg. Issues: TEC

Outside Counsel/Consultants
Foley & Lardner
Issues: TEC
Rep By: Theodore H. Bornstein

TDX Village Corp.

St. Paul Island, AK
Leg. Issues: IND

Outside Counsel/Consultants
Zane & Associates
Issues: IND
Rep By: Curtis J. Zane

Tea Ass'n of the U.S.A., Inc.

New York, NY

Outside Counsel/Consultants
Keller and Heckman LLP
Rep By: Wayne V. Black, Martha E. Marrapese

Teach for America

New York, NY
Leg. Issues: BUD, EDU

Outside Counsel/Consultants
Van Scoyoc Associates, Inc.
Issues: BUD, EDU
Rep By: Victor F. Klatt, III, Robert L. Knisely, James W. Kohlmoos, H. Stewart Van Scoyoc

Team Santa Rosa Economic Development Council

Santa Rosa County, FL
Leg. Issues: DEF, ECN

Outside Counsel/Consultants
Madison Government Affairs
Issues: DEF, ECN
Rep By: Paul J. Hirsch, Jackson Kemper, III

Team Stratford

Bridgeport, CT
Leg. Issues: ECN

Outside Counsel/Consultants
Kutak Rock LLP
Issues: ECN
Rep By: Seth Kirshenberg, George R. Schlossberg, Barry P. Steinberg

TECHHEALTH.COM

Tampa, FL
Leg. Issues: BUD, DEF, HCR

Outside Counsel/Consultants
Arent Fox Kintner Plotkin & Kahn, PLLC
Issues: BUD, DEF, HCR
Rep By: Douglas McCormack, Robert J. Waters

Techneglas, Inc.

Columbus, OH
Leg. Issues: TRD

Outside Counsel/Consultants
Reed, Smith, LLP
Issues: TRD
Rep By: Phillips S. Peter

Technology Integration Group

A computer services provider.

Leg. Issues: GOV

Outside Counsel/Consultants
Adams and Reese LLP
Issues: GOV
Rep By: Hon. James A. "Jimmy" Hayes, Beverly E. Jones

Technology Network

Palo Alto, CA

A collection of present and previous executives of high technology companies wishing to enhance their role in education reform and to contain shareholder lawsuits.

Leg. Issues: CPI, IMM, TAX, TRD

Outside Counsel/Consultants
Mayer, Brown & Platt
Issues: CPI
Rep By: Brian T. Borders, Kim Marie Boylan, Mark H. Gitenstein, Jeffrey H. Lewis, Charles A. Rothfeld
Quinn Gillespie & Associates
Issues: IMM, TAX, TRD
Rep By: Bruce H. Andrews, Edward W. Gillespie, David Lugar, John M. "Jack" Quinn

Technology Systems, Inc.

Wiscasset, ME
Leg. Issues: DEF, SCI

Outside Counsel/Consultants
The Kemper Co.
Issues: DEF, SCI
Rep By: Jackson Kemper, Jr.

Techsnabexport, A.O.

Moscow, RUSSIA
Leg. Issues: ENG

Outside Counsel/Consultants
White & Case LLP
Issues: ENG
Rep By: Carolyn B. Lamm, Frank Panopoulos

TECO Energy, Inc.

Tampa, FL Registered: LDA
Leg. Issues: ENG, FUE, NAT, TAX, TRA, TRD, UTI

Outside Counsel/Consultants
Gallagher, Boland and Meiburger
Issues: ENG, FUE, NAT, TRA, UTI
Rep By: Peter C. Lesch
Greenberg Traurig, LLP
Issues: ENG, TAX, TRD
Hecht, Spencer & Associates
Issues: TRA, UTI
Rep By: Timothy P. Hecht, William H. Hecht, Franklin C. Phifer
Hooper Owen & Winburn
Issues: ENG, TAX, UTI
Rep By: Lindsay D. Hooper, Daryl H. Owen

TECO Transport Corp.

TAmpa, FL
Leg. Issues: AGR, MAR, TAX

Outside Counsel/Consultants
Schnader Harrison Segal & Lewis LLP
Issues: AGR, MAR, TAX

Tecumseh Products Co.

New Holstein, WI
Leg. Issues: CAW, ENV, MAN

Outside Counsel/Consultants
Van Ness Feldman, P.C.
Issues: CAW, ENV, MAN
Rep By: Nancy Macan McNally, Richard A. Penna

Tejon Ranch Co.

Lebec, CA

Outside Counsel/Consultants
Wright & Talisman, P.C.
Rep By: Michael J. Thompson

The Tekamah Corp.

Rockville, MD
Leg. Issues: DEF

Outside Counsel/Consultants
Impact Strategies
Issues: DEF
Rep By: Jeff Fedorchak

TEKSID/Fiat U.S.A.

Farmington Hill, MI

Outside Counsel/Consultants
Porter, Wright, Morris & Arthur, LLP
Rep By: Leslie Alan Glick

TELACU

Los Angeles, CA
Leg. Issues: ECN

Outside Counsel/Consultants
MARC Associates, Inc.
Rep By: Daniel C. Maldonado, Eve O'Toole, Shannon Penberthy
Moss McGee Bradley & Foley
Issues: ECN
Rep By: Leander J. Foley, III
Robert A. Rapoza Associates
Rep By: Robert A. Rapoza

Telacu Carpenter

Irvine, CA

A community development corporate venture.

Outside Counsel/Consultants
Moss McGee Bradley & Foley
Rep By: Leander J. Foley, III

Telcordia Technologies, Inc.

2020 K St. NW Tel: (202)776-5464
Suite 400 Fax: (202)776-5424
Washington, DC 20006
Web: www.telcordia.com

Headquartered in Morristown, NJ.

Leg. Issues: TEC

In-house, DC-area Employees
ANDERSON, Heidi: Director, Government Affairs
KNAPP, Michael: Exec. Director, Federal and State Regulatory Relations
RIMO, Tricia: V. President, Government Affairs, SAIC

Outside Counsel/Consultants
Halprin, Temple, Goodman & Maher
Issues: TEC
Rep By: Joel H. Bernstein, Riley K. Temple

Telecommunications Industry Ass'n

2500 Wilson Blvd. Tel: (703)907-7700
Suite 300 Fax: (703)907-7727
Arlington, VA 22201 Registered: LDA
Web: www.tiaonline.org
E-mail: tia@tia.eia.org

A full-service national trade organization of more than 1000 large and small companies which provide communications and information technology products, materials, systems, distribution services and professional services to the United States and countries around the world.

Leg. Issues: TEC, TRD

In-house, DC-area Employees
AMSELLE, Anna: V. President, Finance
ANDERSON, Judith: Staff Director, International Standards
BART, Daniel L.: Sr. V. President, Standards and Special Projects
BELT, Bill: Director, Technical Regulatory Affairs
BOSWELL, Mary Beth: Director, Emerging Technology Markets
BRADSHAW, Mary: V. President, Global Enterprise Marketing Development
BREDEN, Roberta: Director, Technical and Regulatory Affairs
CHALDEN, Jack: General Manager, Trade Shows
CLARK, Todd: Director, Trade Show Marketing

FLANIGAN, Matthew J.: President
GRACE, Sharon: Director, Marketing Communications Services
HAYLER, Susan: Director, Standards Development & Promotion
INGRAM, Marc: Director, GetCommStuff.com
JANOSKO, A.J.: Director, Trade Show Operations
KECK, Christine: Director, Global Services Provider Relations
KHLOPIN, Derek: Director, Law and Public Policy
KIM, Christina: Controller
KIPREOS, Thanos: Senior Director, Global Standards and Technology
KRYS, Susan: Director, Trade Show Exhibitor Sales & Marketing
KURTZMAN, Andrew: Managing Director, GetCommStuff.com
LESSO, Maryann: Associate V. President, Member Relations
LEUCK, Jason: Director, Latin America Programs
MAHLE, Darlene: Director, Human Resources
MILEVA, Rali: Director, Public Relations
NELSON, Eric: V. President, Global Network Marketing
RIME, Monique: Director, Global Enterprise Market Development
ROSENBLATT, Gerry: Director, Technical and Regulatory Affairs
SEIFFERT, Grant E.: V. President, External Affairs and Global Policy
SMITH, David: Webmaster & Director, Internet Development
WATERS, Mary Piper: Executive Assistant to the President
WIELAND, Henry: V. President, Marketing Services

Outside Counsel/Consultants

Cormac Group, LLP

Twenty-First Century Group
Issues: TEC
Rep By: Hon. Jack M. Fields, Jr., Cynthia M. Wilkinson

Valis Associates
Issues: TEC, TRD
Rep By: Jennifer Conti, Hon. Richard T. Schulze, Wayne H. Valis

Willkie Farr & Gallagher
Issues: TEC
Rep By: Philip L. Verveer

Telecorp PCS Inc.

Arlington, VA
Leg. Issues: TEC

Outside Counsel/Consultants

McDermott, Will and Emery
Issues: TEC
Rep By: Calvin P. Johnson, Neil Quinter

O'Connor & Hannan, L.L.P.
Rep By: Morgan W. Reed, III, David E. Springer

Teledesic Corp.

1730 Rhode Island Ave. NW
Suite 1000
Washington, DC 20036
Tel: (202)721-0960
Fax: (202)296-8953
Registered: LDA
Web: www.teledesic.com
E-mail: larry@teledesic.com
Leg. Issues: COM, SCI, TEC

In-house, DC-area Employees

HUTCHINGS, Suzanne: Regulatory Counsel
WILLIAMS, Lawrence H.: V. President, International and Government Affairs

Outside Counsel/Consultants

Downey McGrath Group, Inc.
Issues: SCI, TEC
Rep By: Hon. Thomas J. Downey, Jr.

Teledyne Controls, Inc.

Los Angeles, CA
Leg. Issues: AVI, GOV

Outside Counsel/Consultants

Crowell & Moring LLP
Issues: GOV
Rep By: Karen Hastie Williams

The PMA Group
Issues: AVI
Rep By: Kaylene Green, Dr. John Lynch, Paul J. Magliocchetti

Teledyne, Inc.

Los Angeles, CA

Outside Counsel/Consultants

Ivins, Phillips & Barker

Teledyne-Commodore, LLC

Huntsville, AL
Leg. Issues: DEF

Outside Counsel/Consultants

King & Spalding
Issues: DEF
Rep By: Theodore M. Hester

TeleFlex Canada, Ltd.

Richmond, CANADA
Leg. Issues: DEF

Outside Counsel/Consultants

The PMA Group
Issues: DEF
Rep By: Daniel Cunningham, Kaylene Green, Paul J. Magliocchetti, Charles Smith, Mark Waclawski

Telefonos de Mexico

Cuauhtemoc, MEXICO
Leg. Issues: TEC

Outside Counsel/Consultants

Fleishman-Hillard, Inc
Issues: TEC
Rep By: Michael Mandigo

Telegate, Inc.

Arlington, VA
Leg. Issues: TEC

Outside Counsel/Consultants

RMA Internat'l, Inc.
Issues: TEC
Rep By: Otto J. Reich

Teleglobe Communications Corp.

11480 Commerce Park Dr.
Reston, VA 20191
Tel: (703)755-2000
Fax: (703)755-2623
Registered: LDA
Web: www.teleglobe.com

A global telecommunications company offering carriers, switchless resellers, Internet Service Providers, television broadcasters and multinational corporations telecommunications services on a domestic and global basis. A subsidiary of Canada's Teleglobe Inc. Currently has more than 500 employees in the D.C. area.

Leg. Issues: TEC

In-house, DC-area Employees

ENNS, Bill: V. President, Corporate Development and Regulatory Affairs
RYAN, Russ: Manager, Marketing and Corporate Communications
TIEVSKY, Charles A.: Assistant V. President, Regulatory Affairs

Telephone Operators Caucus

Washington, DC
Leg. Issues: ADV, ART, BUD, COM, CPT, MIA

Outside Counsel/Consultants

Wiley, Rein & Fielding
Issues: ADV, ART, BUD, COM, CPT, MIA
Rep By: Mary Jo Manning

Teletech Teleservices, Inc.

Denver, CO
Leg. Issues: TAX

Outside Counsel/Consultants

Brownstein Hyatt & Farber, P.C.
Issues: TAX
Rep By: William T. Brack, Thomas H. Hudson, Michael B. Levy

Health Policy Group
Rep By: J. Michael Hudson

Television Ass'n of Programmers Latin America (TAP Latin America)

Laurel, MD
Leg. Issues: COM, TRD

Outside Counsel/Consultants

Mintz, Levin, Cohn, Ferris, Glovsky and Popeo, P.C.
Issues: COM, TRD
Rep By: Frank W. Lloyd

Teligent, Inc.

8065 Leesburg Pike
Suite 400
Vienna, VA 22182
Tel: (703)762-5100
Fax: (703)762-5200
Registered: LDA
Web: www.teligent.com
Leg. Issues: COM, GOV, MIA, TEC

In-house, DC-area Employees

MEENAHAN, Kathleen

Outside Counsel/Consultants

Cormac Group, LLP

Greener and Hook, LLC
Issues: COM, GOV, MIA, TEC

Patton Boggs, LLP
Issues: COM, TEC
Rep By: Thomas Hale Boggs, Jr.

Podesta/Mattoon
Rep By: Kimberley Fritts, Claudia James, Anthony T. Podesta, Timothy Powers

Widmeyer Communications, Inc.

Temecula, California, City of

Leg. Issues: URB

Outside Counsel/Consultants

David Turch & Associates
Issues: URB
Rep By: Kevin D. Bosch, Marilyn E. Campbell, David N. M. Turch

Tempe, Arizona, City of

Leg. Issues: ECN

Outside Counsel/Consultants

The Advocacy Group
Issues: ECN
Rep By: George A. Ramonas

Temple University

Philadelphia, PA
Leg. Issues: EDU, HCR

Outside Counsel/Consultants

Federal Management Strategies, Inc.
Issues: EDU
Rep By: Robert P. Canavan

Whitten & Diamond
Issues: EDU, HCR
Rep By: Robert M. Diamond, Regina M. Mellon, Jamie L. Whitten

Temple University Health System

Philadelphia, PA
Leg. Issues: BUD, HCR, MED, MMM

Outside Counsel/Consultants

O'Neill, Athy & Casey, P.C.
Issues: BUD, HCR, MED, MMM
Rep By: Martha L. Casey, John Knapp

Tempur-Medical Inc.

Lexington, KY
Leg. Issues: HCR, MMM

Outside Counsel/Consultants

Nusgart Consulting, LLC
Issues: HCR, MMM
Rep By: Marcia Nusgart

Temsco Helicopter, Inc.

Ketchikan, AK
Leg. Issues: TRA

Outside Counsel/Consultants

Robertson, Monagle & Eastaugh
Issues: TRA
Rep By: Steven W. Silver

Tennessee Valley Authority - Washington Office

One Massachusetts Ave. NW
Suite 300
Washington, DC 20001
Tel: (202)898-2999
Fax: (202)898-2998
Web: www.tva.gov

A U.S. government owned corporation headquartered in Knoxville, TN that manages the Tennessee River for flood control, navigation and recreation and supplies the energy needs for Tennessee and portions of Alabama, Georgia, Kentucky, Mississippi, North Carolina and Virginia.

In-house, DC-area Employees

NIELSON, Scott K.: Representative
PABLO, Jeanette: Manager
WITHROW, David: V. President, Government Relations

Tennessee Valley Public Power Ass'n

Chattanooga, TN
Leg. Issues: ENG

Outside Counsel/Consultants

Morgan Meguire, LLC
Issues: ENG
Rep By: Scott Lindsay, Kyle G. Michel, Katie Parrott, C. Kyle Simpson, Deborah R. Sliz, Kiel Weaver

Tensiodyne Scientific Corp.

West Los Angeles, CA
Leg. Issues: AER, BUD, DEF, TRA

Outside Counsel/Consultants

Gibson, Dunn & Crutcher LLP
Issues: DEF
Rep By: Alan A. Platt

Ikon Public Affairs
Issues: DEF

Craig Snyder & Associates
Issues: AER, BUD, DEF, TRA
Rep By: Craig Snyder

Tensor Technologies, Inc.

Madison, AL
Leg. Issues: AVI, TRA

Outside Counsel/Consultants

R. G. Flippo and Associates, Inc.
Issues: AVI, TRA
Rep By: Hon. Ronnie G. Flippo, Vicki P. Wallace

Tequity

Corte Madera, CA
Leg. Issues: BUD, COM, EDU, TEC

Outside Counsel/Consultants

Convergence Services, Inc.
Issues: BUD, COM, EDU, TEC
Rep By: John M. Lawson

The Teratology Soc.

Reston, VA
Web: www.teratology.org
E-mail: tshq@teratology.org

Outside Counsel/Consultants

Ass'n Innovation and Management, Inc.
Rep By: Tonia Masson

Terra Chemicals Internat'l

Sioux City, IA

Outside Counsel/Consultants

McDermott, Will and Emery

TerraPoint

The Woodlands, TX
Leg. Issues: BUD

Outside Counsel/Consultants

Hooper Owen & Winburn
Issues: BUD
Rep By: Lindsay D. Hooper

Terrene Institute

Four Herbert St.
Alexandria, VA 22305
Tel: (703)548-5473
Fax: (703)548-6299
Web: www.terrene.org
E-mail: terrinst@aol.com

A non-profit organization that links the corporate with the governmental and academic worlds to improve the environment.

In-house, DC-area Employees

TAGGART, Judith F.: Exec. V. President

Tesoro Petroleum Corp.

San Antonio, TX

Outside Counsel/Consultants

Arter & Hadden
Rep By: W. James Jonas, III, Hon. Thomas G. Loeffler

Wright & Talisman, P.C.
Rep By: Robert H. Benna

Tesuque Pueblo

Outside Counsel/Consultants

Steptoe & Johnson LLP
Rep By: Thomas C. Collier, Jr.

Tetra Tech

Pasadena, CA
Leg. Issues: DEF

Outside Counsel/Consultants

The Spectrum Group
Issues: DEF
Rep By: Cheryl Kandaras Chapman, P.E., Lt. Gen. Augustus Cianciolo, USA (Ret.), Maj. Gen. Paul Fratarangelo, USMC (Ret.), RAdm. James B. Hinkle, USN (Ret.), Paul E. McManus

Tetrahydrofuran Task Force

1850 M St. NW
Suite 700
Washington, DC 20036
Tel: (202)721-4145
Fax: (202)296-8120
E-mail: rick.opatick@socma.com

A trade association for producers of tetrahydrofuran.

Leg. Issues: CSP, MAN, WAS

In-house, DC-area Employees

KORDOSKI, Ph.D, Edward W.: Exec. Director

Outside Counsel/Consultants

Hadley & McKenna
Issues: CSP, MAN, WAS
Rep By: Joseph E. Hadley, Jr.

Tett Enterprises

901 New Jersey Ave. NW
Washington, DC 20001-1133
Tel: (202)326-9170
Registered: LDA
E-mail: latett@yahoo.com
Leg. Issues: APP, ECN, IND, MAN, SMB, TRD, URB, WEL

In-house, DC-area Employees

TETT, Lois: Consultant

TEVA Pharmaceuticals

Outside Counsel/Consultants

Columbus Public Affairs

Tex-La Electric Cooperative of Texas

Nacogdoches, TX
Leg. Issues: BUD, ENG, GOV, TAX, UTI

Outside Counsel/Consultants

Brickfield, Burchette, Ritts & Stone
Issues: BUD, ENG, GOV, TAX, UTI
Rep By: William H. Burchette, Colleen Newman, Christine C. Ryan

Tex-USA Fund

607 14th St. NW
Suite 800
Washington, DC 20004

A political action committee

In-house, DC-area Employees

MILLS, T. J.: Contact

Texaco Group Inc.

1050 17th St. NW
Suite 500
Washington, DC 20036
Tel: (202)331-1427
Fax: (202)785-4702
Registered: LDA
Leg. Issues: BUD, CAW, CIV, ENG, ENV, GOV, HCR, LAW, LBR, MAN, NAT, RES, TAX, TRA, TRD, UTI

In-house, DC-area Employees

BRESNICK, William O.: Senior Environmental Representative
KOSTIW, Michael V.: General Manager, International Relations
PRUITT, James C.: V. President, Government Relations
RIVERS, Phillip W.: Senior Government Relations Representative
WASHINGTON, Gregory J.: Senior Government Relations Representative

Outside Counsel/Consultants

Holland & Knight LLP
Issues: ENG, ENV, LBR
Rep By: Joanna S. Han, Michael R. Hatcher, Jeffrey P. Hildebrant, Weldon H. Latham

Nat'l Environmental Strategies

Shaw Pittman
Issues: CIV, ENV, LAW
Rep By: Rodolfo Fuentes

Williams & Jensen, P.C.
Issues: CAW, ENV, TAX
Rep By: George D. Baker, William B. Canfield, David E. Franasiak, Robert E. Glennon, Jr., J. Steven Hart

Texas A&M Engineering Experiment Station

College Station, TX
Leg. Issues: ENG

Outside Counsel/Consultants

Morgan Meguire, LLC
Issues: ENG
Rep By: Ramola Musante, Dawn Schrepel, C. Kyle Simpson

Texas A&M Research Foundation

College Station, TX
Leg. Issues: AGR, BUD, CAW, DEF, DIS, EDU, ENG, ENV, FUE, HCR, HOU, LAW, MAR, ROD, TAX, TRA, TRD

Outside Counsel/Consultants

Meyers & Associates
Issues: AGR, BUD, CAW, DEF, DIS, EDU, ENG, ENV, FUE, HCR, HOU, LAW, MAR, ROD, TAX, TRA, TRD
Rep By: Shelley Wilson Dodd, Larry D. Meyers

Texas Chiropractic College

Pasadena, CA
Leg. Issues: EDU, MED

Outside Counsel/Consultants

The Advocacy Group
Issues: EDU, MED
Rep By: Robert E. Mills

Texas Cities Legislative Coalition (TCLC)

Washington, DC
Registered: LDA

Works to protect and advance the officially adopted interests of the cities of Austin, Dallas, Denton, Lubbock and Plano in relation to the legislative and executive branches of the federal government.

Outside Counsel/Consultants

Barbara T. McCall Associates
Rep By: Barbara T. McCall

Texas College

Tyler, TX
Leg. Issues: EDU

Outside Counsel/Consultants

Dean Blakey & Moskowitz
Issues: EDU
Rep By: William A. Blakey

Texas Corn Producers Board

Dimmit, TX

Outside Counsel/Consultants

Durante Associates
Rep By: Douglas A. Durante

Texas Freedom Fund

P.O. Box 6136
Alexandria, VA 22306
Tel: (703)360-8386
Fax: (703)619-1122

In-house, DC-area Employees

GILLESPIE, Cathy: Exec. Director
MACKINNON, Jeff: Treasurer

Texas Gas Transmission Corp.

Owensboro, KY

Outside Counsel/Consultants

Wright & Talisman, P.C.

Texas Health Resources

Irving, TX
Leg. Issues: CSP, HCR, INS, MMM, PHA, TAX

Outside Counsel/Consultants

VSAdc.com
Issues: CSP, HCR, INS, MMM, PHA, TAX
Rep By: Carol A. McDaid, H. Stewart Van Scoyoc

Texas Instruments

1455 Pennsylvania Ave. NW
Suite 375
Washington, DC 20004
Tel: (202)628-3133
Fax: (202)628-2980
Registered: LDA
Web: www.ti.com

A global semiconductor company. Designs and supplies digital signal processing solutions. Headquartered in Dallas, TX, the company's businesses also include materials and controls, educational and productivity solutions, and digital imaging. Maintains manufacturing or sales operations in more than 25 countries.

Leg. Issues: BUD, CPI, GOV, HCR, IMM, LBR, MON, TAX, TEC, TRD

In-house, DC-area Employees

BOIDOCK, John K.: V. President, Government Relations
COLLINS, Paula: Director, Government Relations-Human Relations and Education
JOHNSON, Cynthia K.: Director, Government Relations-International Trade
LARSON, Daniel M.: Director, Government and Media Relations

Texas Manufactured Housing Ass'n

Austin, TX
Leg. Issues: HOU

Outside Counsel/Consultants

Akin, Gump, Strauss, Hauer & Feld, L.L.P.
Issues: HOU
Rep By: Marlene M. Colucci, Smith W. Davis, Joel Jankowsky, Michael S. Mandel, Barney J. Skladany, Jr., Jose H. Villarreal

Verner, Liipfert, Bernhard, McPherson and Hand, Chartered
Issues: HOU
Rep By: Jane Hickie, Ann W. Richards

The Texas Medical Center

Houston, TX

Outside Counsel/Consultants

Akin, Gump, Strauss, Hauer & Feld, L.L.P.
Rep By: Sylvia A. de Leon

Texas Municipal Power Agency

Denton, TX
Leg. Issues: ENG

Outside Counsel/Consultants

The Washington Group
Issues: ENG
Rep By: William J. Burke, Tripp Funderburk, Rita M. Lewis, G. John O'Hanlon, John D. Raffaelli, Tonya Saunders, Mark Schnabel

Texas NF Foundation

Dallas, TX
Web: www.texasnf.org
E-mail: Texasnf@aol.com
Leg. Issues: BUD, HCR, TOB

Outside Counsel/Consultants

Capitol Associates, Inc.
Issues: BUD, HCR, TOB
Rep By: Edward R. Long, Ph.D., Ronnie Kovner Tepp

Texas Pacific Group

Fort Worth, TX
Leg. Issues: BUD, TAX

Outside Counsel/Consultants

Williams & Jensen, P.C.
Issues: BUD, TAX
Rep By: Robert E. Glennon, Jr., George G. Olsen

Texas Petrochemicals Corp.

Houston, TX
Leg. Issues: ENV

Outside Counsel/Consultants

Bracewell & Patterson, L.L.P.
Issues: ENV
Rep By: Hon. Edwin R. Bethune, Hon. Jim Chapman, Gene E. Godley, Marc C. Hebert, Charles L. Ingebretson, Michael L. Pate, Scott H. Segal, D. Michael Stroud, Jr.

Texas Savings and Community Bankers

Austin, TX
Leg. Issues: BAN, HOU

Outside Counsel/Consultants

Butera & Andrews
Issues: BAN, HOU
Rep By: Cliff W. Andrews, Wright H. Andrews, Jr., James J. Butera, Frank Tillotson

Texas Tech University System

Lubbock, TX
Leg. Issues: BUD

Outside Counsel/Consultants

Cassidy & Associates, Inc.
Issues: BUD
Rep By: Carl Franklin Godfrey, Jr., Dennis M. Kedzior, Jeffrey Lawrence, Daniel J. McNamara, Valerie Rogers Osborne, Blenda Pinto-Riddick

Texas Veterans Land Board

Austin, TX

Outside Counsel/Consultants

Vinson & Elkins L.L.P.
Rep By: Charles L. Almond

The Texas Wind Power Co.

Austin, TX
Leg. Issues: ENG

Outside Counsel/Consultants

Capitol Counsel Group, L.L.C.
Issues: ENG

Texas Windstorm Insurance Ass'n

Austin, TX
Leg. Issues: BUD, TAX

Outside Counsel/Consultants

Bracewell & Patterson, L.L.P.
Issues: BUD, TAX
Rep By: Hon. Edwin R. Bethune, Hon. Jim Chapman, Gene E. Godley, Marc C. Hebert, Charles L. Ingebretson, Michael L. Pate, Scott H. Segal, D. Michael Stroud, Jr.

Texas, Office of State-Federal Relations of the State of

122 C St. NW
Suite 200
Washington, DC 20001
Tel: (202)638-3927
Fax: (202)628-1943
Web: www.offr.state.tx.us

In-house, DC-area Employees

RICH, Laurie M.: Exec. Director

The Textile Museum

2320 S St. NW
Washington, DC 20008
Tel: (202)667-0441
Fax: (202)483-0994
Web: www.textilemuseum.org
E-mail: info@textilemuseum.org

Dedicated to furthering the understanding of mankind's creative achievements in the textile arts. Committed to serving as a center of excellence in scholarly research, conservation, interpretation, and exhibition of textiles.

Leg. Issues: ART

In-house, DC-area Employees

NEUBAUER, Julia: Public Information Assistant

Outside Counsel/Consultants

Chernikoff and Co.
Issues: ART
Rep By: Larry B. Chernikoff

Textile Rental Services Ass'n of America

1120 Connecticut Ave. NW
Suite 1060
Washington, DC 20036
Tel: (202)833-6395
Fax: (202)833-0018
Registered: LDA
Web: www.trsa.org
Leg. Issues: CAW

In-house, DC-area Employees

FATH, Marie: Director, Government Affairs

Outside Counsel/Consultants

Galland, Kharasch, Greenberg, Fellman & Swirsky, P.C.

Textile/Clothing Technology Center

Cary, NC
Leg. Issues: APP

Outside Counsel/Consultants

SRG & Associates
Issues: APP
Rep By: Augustine D. Tantillo

Textron Inc.

1101 Pennsylvania Ave. NW
Suite 400
Washington, DC 20004-2504
Tel: (202)637-3800
Fax: (202)637-3860
Registered: LDA

Headquarters are in Providence, RI.

Leg. Issues: AUT, AVI, BAN, DEF, MAN, TAX, TRA, TRD

In-house, DC-area Employees

HOWELL, Mary L.: Exec. V. President, Government, Internat'l Investor Relations & Corp. Commun.
KOZICHAROW, Eugene: Exec. Director, Public Affairs
ROWLAND, Robert O.: Director, Congressional Relations
SMITH, Richard F.: V. President, Congressional Affairs
STEWART, Marise R.: Director, Government Affairs
THOMAS, Gordon M.: Director, Government Affairs
WHITEHURST, Calvert S.: Manager, Government Affairs

Outside Counsel/Consultants

Collins & Company, Inc.
Issues: DEF
Rep By: Richard L. Collins

Marvin Leath Associates
Issues: DEF
Rep By: Hon. Marvin Leath

The PMA Group
Issues: DEF
Rep By: Daniel Cunningham, Daniel E. Fleming, Kaylene Green, Paul J. Magliocchetti, Briggs Shade, Thomas Veltri

SISCORP
Issues: DEF
Rep By: Wendy Jordan, Fran Shottes

Francis J. Sullivan Associates
Issues: DEF
Rep By: Francis J. Sullivan

Textron Systems Division

Wilmington, MA
Defense contractors.

Leg. Issues: DEF

Outside Counsel/Consultants

Collins & Company, Inc.
Issues: DEF
Rep By: James D. Bond, Richard L. Collins, Thomas A. Hooper, Shay D. Stautz

Texuna Internat'l USA Ltd.

Woodbridge, NJ

Outside Counsel/Consultants

Vorys, Sater, Seymour and Pease, LLP
Rep By: Warren W. Glick

Tg Soda Ash

Granger, WY
Leg. Issues: LBR

Outside Counsel/Consultants

Patton Boggs, LLP
Issues: LBR
Rep By: Henry Chajet

THA: An Ass'n of Hospitals and Health Systems

1747 Pennsylvania Ave. NW
Suite 1200
Washington, DC 20006
Tel: (202)775-0600
Registered: LDA

Above address is that of the firm Foley, Hoag & Eliot, LLP (see separate listing). Maria Beatrice Grauce acts on behalf of THA as a federal relations representative

Leg. Issues: HCR, MMM

Outside Counsel/Consultants

Foley, Hoag & Eliot LLP
Issues: HCR, MMM
Rep By: Marie Beatrice Grause

Thai Gypsum Products Co., Ltd.

Bangkok, THAILAND

Outside Counsel/Consultants

Commerce Consultants Internat'l Ltd.
Rep By: Steve Richards

Thailand, Department of Foreign Trade of

Bangkok, THAILAND

Outside Counsel/Consultants

St. Maxens & Company
Rep By: Thomas F. St. Maxens, II

White & Case LLP
Rep By: William J. Clinton, Walter J. Spak

Thales

99 Canal Center Plaza
Suite 450
Alexandria, VA 22314
Tel: (703)838-9685
Fax: (703)838-1688
Registered: FARA
Web: www.thomson-csf-uf.com

Formerly Thomson-CSF Inc.

Leg. Issues: AER, DEF

In-house, DC-area Employees

GAYAT, Francois: Chairman and Chief Exec. Officer

Outside Counsel/Consultants

BKSH & Associates
Issues: AER, DEF

Thelen Reid & Priest LLP

701 Pennsylvania Ave. NW
Suite 800
Washington, DC 20004
Tel: (202)508-4000
Fax: (202)508-4321
Registered: LDA, FARA
Web: www.thelenreid.com
Leg. Issues: AVI, BUD, ENG, TAX, TRA, UTI

Political Action Committee/s

Thelen Reid & Priest L.L.P. Political Action Committee
701 Pennsylvania Ave. NW
Suite 800
Washington, DC 20004
Tel: (202)508-4010
Fax: (202)508-4321
Contact: Stephan M. Minikes

In-house, DC-area Employees

BERKOFF, Barry I.: Legislative Representative
COOPER, Howard A.: Partner
DACEK, Raymond F.: Of Counsel
ENGLISH, Jr., Charles M.: Partner
ESTEVEZ, Mareza I.
EVENS, Mark F.: Partner
GOODWIN, Lee M.: Partner
HALL, III, Robert T.: Partner

HONIGMAN, Steven S.: Partner
JACOBSON, David E.: Partner
KIRK, Jr., William A.: Partner
LEIDL, Richard J.: Partner
MINIKES, Stephan M.: Partner
MITCHELL, James K.: Partner
PITTMAN, Edward L.: Of Counsel
PRAKASH, Ambari: Associate
REED, Alan J.: Associate-Business & Finance
ROBERTS, Richard Y.: Partner
SCHAEFGEN, John R.: Partner
WEISENFELD, David J.
WEST, Nancy K.: Senior Legislative Representative
YOVIENE, Wendy M.: Associate

Outside Counsel/Consultants

Ann Eppard Associates, Ltd.
Issues: AVI, BUD, TRA
Rep By: Julie Chlopecki, Ann Eppard

Ernst & Young LLP
Issues: ENG, TAX, UTI
Rep By: Tom S. Nuebig

Thera Matrix

Pontiac, MI
Leg. Issues: HCR

Outside Counsel/Consultants

Jack H. McDonald
Issues: HCR
Rep By: Hon. Jack H. McDonald

Theragenics Corp.

Norcross, GA
Leg. Issues: ENG, GOV

Outside Counsel/Consultants

Powell, Goldstein, Frazer & Murphy LLP
Issues: ENG, GOV
Rep By: Hon. Butler E. Derrick, Jr.

Thermal Energy Systems, Inc.

San Diego, CA

Outside Counsel/Consultants

Wilson & Wilson

Thermedics Detection, Inc.

Chelmsford, MA
Leg. Issues: GOV

Outside Counsel/Consultants

Hale and Dorr LLP
Issues: GOV
Rep By: Jay P. Urwitz

Thermo EcoTek Corp.

Waltham, MA
Leg. Issues: EBG, ENV, TAX

Outside Counsel/Consultants

Manatt, Phelps & Phillips, LLP
Issues: EBG, ENV, TAX
Rep By: Hon. Jack W. Buechner

ThermoEnergy Corp.

Little Rock, AR
Leg. Issues: CAW, ENV

Outside Counsel/Consultants

Washington Consulting Alliance, Inc.
Issues: CAW, ENV
Rep By: Thomas L. Burgum

ThermoTrex Corp.

San Diego, CA

Outside Counsel/Consultants

SISCORP
Rep By: Wendy Jordan, Robert Meissner, Fran Shottes

Thiokol Propulsion

1735 Jefferson Davis Hwy.
Suite 1001
Arlington, VA 22202-3461
Tel: (703)413-6300
Fax: (703)413-6316
Registered: LDA
Web: www.thiokol.com

Headquartered in Brigham City, UT.

Leg. Issues: AER, DEF, TAX, TRA

Political Action Committee/s

Thiokol. PAC
1735 Jefferson Davis Hwy.
Suite 1001
Arlington, VA 22202-3461
Tel: (703)413-6300
Fax: (703)413-6316
Contact: John Canatsey

In-house, DC-area Employees

CANATSEY, John: Director, Legislative Liaison (Defense)
HENINGER, Lynn W.: Director, Legislative Liaison (Space)
MCCOY, Tidal W.: V. President, Government Relations

Thomas Group Internat'l

Dallas, TX
Leg. Issues: DEF, ECN, GOV

Outside Counsel/Consultants

The Eagles Group
Issues: DEF, ECN, GOV
Rep By: Terence Costello

Thomas Jefferson Equal Tax Soc.

1469 Spring Vale Ave.
McLean, VA 22101
Tel: (703)356-5800
Fax: (703)893-7945
Web: www.miketecton.com

In-house, DC-area Employees

TECTON, Mike: President

Thomas Jefferson University

Philadelphia, PA
Leg. Issues: BUD, DEF, HCR, MED

Outside Counsel/Consultants

Schroth & Associates
Issues: BUD, DEF, HCR, MED
Rep By: Craig Snyder

Thomas Jefferson University Hospital

Philadelphia, PA
Leg. Issues: BUD, HCR, MED, MMM

Outside Counsel/Consultants

Capitol Associates, Inc.
Issues: BUD
Rep By: Edward R. Long, Ph.D., Julie P. Pawelczyk

DeBrunner and Associates, Inc.
Issues: BUD, HCR, MED, MMM
Rep By: Charles L. DeBrunner, Ellen J. Kugler, Kathryn D. Rooney

Thomas Pink, Inc.

Leg. Issues: TRD

Outside Counsel/Consultants

Butterfield Carter & Associates
Issues: TRD
Rep By: R. Ian Butterfield, Gavin J. Carter

Thompson Creek Metals Co.

Englewood, CO

A mineral production company.

Leg. Issues: NAT, TAX

Outside Counsel/Consultants

Thomas D. Campbell & Assoc.
Issues: NAT, TAX
Rep By: Thomas D. Campbell

Thompson Lighting Protection Inc.

St. Paul, MN
Leg. Issues: GOV, SCI, SMB

Outside Counsel/Consultants

Foley Government and Public Affairs, Inc.
Issues: GOV, SCI, SMB
Rep By: Joseph P. Foley, Paul C. Lavery

Thompson Publishing, Inc.

Washington, DC
Leg. Issues: EDU

Outside Counsel/Consultants

Dewey Ballantine LLP
Rep By: Andrew W. Kentz, John J. Salmon

Holland & Knight LLP
Issues: EDU
Rep By: Douglas J. Patton

Van Scoyoc Associates, Inc.

Thomson Consumer Electronics, Inc.

Washington, DC
Registered: LDA
Leg. Issues: COM, MAN, TRD

Outside Counsel/Consultants

Verner, Liipfert, Bernhard, McPherson and Hand, Chartered
Issues: COM, MAN, TRD
Rep By: Hon. James J. Blanchard, Vicki E. Hart, Philip R. Hochberg, John M. R. Kneuer, Sara W. Morris, David R. Siddall, Lawrence R. Sidman, David A. Weiss

The Thomson Corp.

Stamford, CT
Leg. Issues: CPT

Outside Counsel/Consultants

Liz Robbins Associates
Issues: CPT
Rep By: Liz Robbins

Thorn Microwave Devices

Middix, UNITED KINGDOM

Outside Counsel/Consultants

O'Connor & Fierce Associates
Rep By: Michael J. O'Connor

Three Affiliated Tribes of Fort Berthold Reservation

New Town, ND
Leg. Issues: BUD, ENV, IND, NAT

Outside Counsel/Consultants

Hobbs, Straus, Dean and Walker, LLP
Rep By: Karen J. Funk, Michael L. Roy, Hans Walker, Jr.

Moss McGee Bradley & Foley
Issues: IND
Rep By: Leander J. Foley, III

Van Ness Feldman, P.C.
Issues: BUD, ENV, IND, NAT
Rep By: Patricia J. Beneke, Daniel S. Press, J. Curtis Rich, Steven Richardson

Thunderbird, The American Graduate School of Internat'l Management

Glendale, AZ
Leg. Issues: BUD

Outside Counsel/Consultants

Arter & Hadden
Issues: BUD
Rep By: Daniel L. Cohen

Thurmont, Maryland, Town of

Leg. Issues: GOV

Outside Counsel/Consultants

Duncan, Weinberg, Genzer & Pembroke, P.C.
Issues: GOV
Rep By: Janice L. Lower

TI Group Inc.

Abington, UNITED KINGDOM

An aircraft component manufacturer.

Leg. Issues: DEF, EDU

Outside Counsel/Consultants

Dyer Ellis & Joseph, P.C.
Issues: DEF
Rep By: Brian A. Bannon, Joseph O. Click, Laurie Crick Sahatjian, Thomas M. Dyer, Wayne A. Keup, Margaret Dillenburg Rifka, Duncan C. Smith, III

Washington Alliance Group, Inc.
Issues: EDU
Rep By: Bonnie Singer

TIAA-CREF

555 12th St. NW
Suite 700 South
Washington, DC 20004
Tel: (202)637-0090
Fax: (202)637-8950
Registered: LDA
Web: www.tiaa-cref.org

Manages nationwide pension system for educational institutions.

Leg. Issues: BAN, FIN, INS, RET, TAX

In-house, DC-area Employees

OAKLEY, Diane: V. President, Government Relations
STANGES, Milly Crawford

Outside Counsel/Consultants

The OB-C Group, LLC
Issues: TAX
Rep By: Thomas Keating, Kim F. McKernan, Charles J. Mellody, Patricia A. Nelson, Lawrence F. O'Brien, III, Linda E. Tarplin

Tichenor and Associates

Louisville, KY
Leg. Issues: DEF, GOV

Outside Counsel/Consultants

Holland & Knight LLP
Issues: DEF, GOV
Rep By: Robert Hunt Bradner, Jack M. Burkman

Ticketmaster
Los Angeles, CA
A computerized ticketing service.
Leg. Issues: ART, TOU
Outside Counsel/Consultants
Evans & Black, Inc.
Issues: ART, TOU
Rep By: Judy A. Black, Teresa J. Dyer, Rafe Morrissey

Tiffany & Co.
New York, NY
Leg. Issues: CSP, TRD
Outside Counsel/Consultants
Cassidy & Associates, Inc.
Issues: CSP, TRD
Rep By: Douglass E. Bobbitt, Christy Carson Evans, Gregory M. Gill, Lindsay Lawrence, Stephen Whitaker

Tiger Fund
New York, NY
Leg. Issues: CDT
Outside Counsel/Consultants
Chesapeake Enterprises, Inc.
Issues: CDT
Rep By: J. John Fluharty

Tilda Rice
Rainham Essex, UNITED KINGDOM
Outside Counsel/Consultants
Max N. Berry Law Offices

Tile Contractors Ass'n of America
11501 Georgia Ave., Suite 203
Wheaton, MD 20902
Tel: (301)949-5995
Fax: (301)949-8373
Web: www.tcaainc.org
E-mail: tcaa@realweb.com
In-house, DC-area Employees
WALSH, Helen: Exec. Director

Tillamook County Creamery Ass'n
Tillamook, OR
Leg. Issues: AGR
Outside Counsel/Consultants
Thelen Reid & Priest LLP
Issues: AGR
Rep By: Charles M. English, Jr., Wendy M. Yoviene

Timbisha Shoshone Tribe
Oakland, CA
Outside Counsel/Consultants
Ducheneaux, Taylor & Associates, Inc.
Rep By: Peter S. Taylor

Time Domain Corp.
1666 K St. NW
Suite 250
Washington, DC 20006
Tel: (202)835-3016
Fax: (202)835-3008
Web: www.timedomain.com
Leg. Issues: COM, DEF, ENG, SCI, TEC, TRA
In-house, DC-area Employees
ROSS, Jeff: V. President, Corporate Development and Strategy
WEBB, III, USA, Col. William L.: Senior V. President
Outside Counsel/Consultants
American Defense Internat'l, Inc.
Issues: DEF
Rep By: Michael Herson, Van D. Hipp, Jr., Dave Wilberding
Ashby and Associates
Rep By: R. Barry Ashby
Harris, Wiltshire & Grannis LLP
Issues: COM, TEC
Rep By: Scott Blake Harris
Patton Boggs, LLP
Issues: ENG, SCI, TEC
Rep By: Paul C. Besozzi, Thomas Hale Boggs, Jr., Jonathan R. Yarowsky
Simon Strategies/Mindbeam
Issues: TEC
Rep By: Gregory C. Simon, Kristan Van Hook
Van Scoyoc Associates, Inc.
Issues: SCI, TRA
Rep By: Ray Cole, H. Stewart Van Scoyoc
Wiley, Rein & Fielding
Issues: TEC
Rep By: Susan C. Buck, Mimi W. Dawson, Mary Jo Manning

Time Warner Telecom Inc.
Stamford, CT
Leg. Issues: TEC
Outside Counsel/Consultants
Cormac Group, LLP
Greenberg Traurig, LLP
Issues: TEC
Rep By: Mitchell F. Brecher

Timet-Titantium Metals Corp.
Denver, CO
Leg. Issues: TRD
Outside Counsel/Consultants
Brownstein Hyatt & Farber, P.C.
Issues: TRD
Rep By: William T. Brack, Michael B. Levy

Timex Corp.
Waterbury, CT
Outside Counsel/Consultants
Howrey Simon Arnold & White
Rep By: Stuart H. Harris

The Timken Co.
Canton, OH
Leg. Issues: BAN, BUD, ENV, HCR, LBR, TRD, UTI
Outside Counsel/Consultants
Downey McGrath Group, Inc.
Issues: TRD
Rep By: Delanne Bernier, Michael R. Wessel
Genesis Consulting Group, LLC
Issues: BAN, BUD, ENV, HCR, LBR, TRD
Rep By: Mark Benedict, Dana DeBeaumont
Impact Strategies
Issues: HCR, LBR, TRD, UTI
Rep By: Shannon Doyle, Jeff Fedorchak
Stewart and Stewart
Issues: TRD
Rep By: Alan M. Dunn, Amy S. Dwyer, David S. Johanson, Carl Moyer, Terence P. Stewart

Tip Tax Coalition
Mount Pocono, PA
Leg. Issues: TAX
Outside Counsel/Consultants
Patton Boggs, LLP
Issues: TAX
Rep By: Clayton L. Hough, Brian C. Lopina, George J. Schutzer

Tire Ass'n of North America
11921 Freedom Dr.
Suite 550
Reston, VA 20190
Tel: (703)736-8082
Fax: (703)904-4339
Registered: LDA
Web: www.tana.net
E-mail: info@tana.net
Formerly known as Nat'l Tire Dealers and Retreaders Ass'n.
Leg. Issues: AUT, BUD, CAW, CSP, ENV, HCR, LBR, MAN, ROD, SMB, TAX, TRA, TRD, TRU
In-house, DC-area Employees
KOGEL, Ross: Exec. V. President
MACDICKEN, Becky: Director of Government Affairs

Tire Industry Safety Council
1400 K St. NW
Ninth Floor
Washington, DC 20005
Tel: (202)783-1022
Fax: (202)682-4854
Web: www.tisc.org
E-mail: kristen@tmn.com
TISC can be contacted via the internet through the Rubber Manufactures (see seperate listing) website at www.rma.org.
In-house, DC-area Employees
ZEILINSKI, Dan: Director

Tishman Construction Corp. of Washington D.C.
Washington, DC
Leg. Issues: GOV
Outside Counsel/Consultants
GPC Internat'l
Issues: GOV
Rep By: Daniel K. Crann

Titan Corp.
400 Virginia Ave. SW
Suite C-150
Washington, DC 20024
Tel: (202)488-9740
Registered: LDA
Web: www.titan.com
Leg. Issues: AVI, BUD, DEF, FOO, GOV
In-house, DC-area Employees
DRESSENDORFER, John: V. President, Government Relations
Outside Counsel/Consultants
Haake and Associates
Rep By: Timothy M. Haake, Nathan M. Olsen
The PMA Group
Rep By: William E. Berl, Sean Fogarty, Kaylene Green, Gregory L. Hansen, Paul J. Magliocchetti, Timothy K. Sanders

Titan Scan
San Diego, CA
Leg. Issues: AGR, FOO
Outside Counsel/Consultants
Olsson, Frank and Weeda, P.C.
Issues: AGR, FOO
Rep By: John W. Bode, Susan P. Grymes, Karen Reis Harned, Stephen L. Lacey, Marshall L. Matz, Tyson Redpath, Ryan W. Stroschein

Titanium Metals Corp.
Denver, CO
Leg. Issues: DEF
Outside Counsel/Consultants
The Spectrum Group
Issues: DEF
Rep By: Lt. Gen. Augustus Cianciolo, USA (Ret.), Adm. Wesley McDonald, USN (Ret.), Gregory L. Sharp

Title I Home Improvement Lenders Ass'n
1625 Massachusetts Ave. NW
Suite 601
Washington, DC 20036
Tel: (202)328-9171
Fax: (202)265-4435
Registered: LDA
Web: www.hila.com
Political Action Committee/s
The HIL PAC
1625 Massachusetts Ave. NW
Suite 601
Washington, DC 20036
Tel: (202)328-9171
Fax: (202)265-4435
Contact: Peter H. Bell
In-house, DC-area Employees
BELL, Peter H.: Exec. Director

The Title XI Coalition
Arlington, VA
Leg. Issues: BUD, MAR
Outside Counsel/Consultants
Preston Gates Ellis & Rouvelas Meeds LLP
Issues: BUD, MAR
Rep By: Darrell Conner, Mark H. Ruge

TJTC Recovery Project Coalition
Washington, DC
Leg. Issues: TAX
Outside Counsel/Consultants
Greenberg Traurig, LLP
Issues: TAX
Rep By: Ronald L. Platt
McDermott, Will and Emery
Rep By: Calvin P. Johnson

TMC Technologies
Fairmont, WV
Leg. Issues: GOV
Outside Counsel/Consultants
Cottone and Huggins Group
Issues: GOV
Rep By: James B. Huggins

TMC, Inc.
Babylon, NY
Outside Counsel/Consultants
Chambers Associates Inc.
Rep By: William A. Signer

TMS Consulting, LLC
Montgomery, AL
Outside Counsel/Consultants
Bradley Arant Rose & White LLP

Tobacco Fairness Coalition
Wilson, NC
Leg. Issues: TAX, TOB, TRD
Outside Counsel/Consultants
Miller & Co.
Issues: TAX, TOB, TRD
Rep By: Richard W. Miller

Tobacco Industry Labor Management Committee
Washington, DC
Outside Counsel/Consultants
Thompson, Hine and Flory LLP
Rep By: David H. Baker

Tobacco Industry Testing Laboratory, Inc.
Rockville, MD
Outside Counsel/Consultants
Thompson, Hine and Flory LLP
Rep By: David H. Baker

Tobacco Quota Warehouse Alliance
Washington, DC
Leg. Issues: AGR
Outside Counsel/Consultants
Robert L. Redding
Issues: AGR
Rep By: Robert L. Redding, Jr.

Todd Shipyards Inc.
Seattle, WA
Leg. Issues: DEF, TRA
Outside Counsel/Consultants
Denny Miller McBee Associates
Issues: DEF, TRA

Todhunter Internat'l, Inc.
West Palm Beach, FL
Leg. Issues: ENV, TAX
Outside Counsel/Consultants
The Dutko Group, Inc.
Issues: ENV, TAX
Rep By: Arthur H. Silverman, William Simmons

Togo, Embassy of the Republic of
Washington, DC
Outside Counsel/Consultants
Bruce Fein
Rep By: Bruce Fein

Togo, Government of the Republic of
Lome, TOGO
Outside Counsel/Consultants
Washington World Group, Ltd.
Rep By: Edward J. von Kloberg, III

Tohono O'Odham Nation
Sells, AZ
Leg. Issues: IND
Outside Counsel/Consultants
Ducheneaux, Taylor & Associates, Inc.
Issues: IND
Rep By: Franklin D. Ducheneaux
Oldaker and Harris, LLP
Rep By: William C. Oldaker

The Tokyo Electric Power Company, Inc.
1901 L St. NW
Suite 720
Washington, DC 20036
Tel: (202)457-0790
Fax: (202)457-0810

A Japanese utility whose Washington office is primarily engaged in research.

In-house, DC-area Employees
FURUYA, Toshihiko: General Manager and Director
SUZUKI, Hitoshi: Deputy General Manager
Outside Counsel/Consultants
Washington Policy & Analysis, Inc.
Rep By: Scott L. Campbell, William F. Martin

Toledo Edison Co.
Toledo, OH
Outside Counsel/Consultants
Shaw Pittman
Rep By: Jay E. Silberg

Tolmex
Monterrey, MEXICO
Leg. Issues: ENV, ROD, TRD
Outside Counsel/Consultants
Janus-Merritt Strategies, L.L.C.
Issues: ENV, ROD, TRD
Rep By: Mark J. Robertson

Tooele, Utah, City of
Leg. Issues: BUD
Outside Counsel/Consultants
The Furman Group
Issues: BUD
Rep By: K. Link Browder, Thomas M. James

Toolex USA, Inc.
Leg. Issues: TRD
Outside Counsel/Consultants
Collier Shannon Scott, PLLC
Issues: TRD
Rep By: John B. Brew, Kathleen Clark Kies, Robert W. Porter

Torchmark Corp.
Birmingham, AL
Registered: LDA
Leg. Issues: HCR, INS, MMM, PHA, ROD, TAX
Outside Counsel/Consultants
Deloitte & Touche LLP Nat'l Office - Washington
Issues: TAX
Rep By: Gregory Stephenson, Randall D. Weiss
VSAdc.com
Issues: HCR, INS, MMM, PHA, ROD, TAX
Rep By: Carol A. McDaid, H. Stewart Van Scoyoc

The Toro Co.
Minneapolis, MN
Outside Counsel/Consultants
Dunaway & Cross
Rep By: Mac S. Dunaway
Thompson, Hine and Flory LLP
Rep By: Gilbert B. Lessenco

Torrington Co.
Torrington, CT
Leg. Issues: DEF, TRD
Outside Counsel/Consultants
Greenberg Traurig, LLP
Issues: DEF, TRD
Rep By: Diane J. Blagman, Howard A. Vine
Stewart and Stewart
Issues: TRD
Rep By: Geert M. De Prest, Alan M. Dunn, David S. Johanson, Carl Moyer

Tort Reform Institute
Washington, DC
Leg. Issues: DOC, TOR
Outside Counsel/Consultants
Betty Ann Kane & Co.
Issues: DOC, TOR
Rep By: Betty Ann Kane

Tosco Corp.
Stamford, CT
Leg. Issues: CAW, ENV, FUE
Outside Counsel/Consultants
Bastianelli, Brown & Kelley
Issues: FUE
Rep By: Marcus W. Sisk
Kessler & Associates Business Services, Inc.
Issues: CAW, ENV
Rep By: Howard Berman, Harry Sporidis

Toshiba Consumer Products, Inc.
Wayne, NJ
Leg. Issues: CPT
Outside Counsel/Consultants
Patton Boggs, LLP
Issues: CPT
Rep By: Thomas Hale Boggs, Jr., Brian C. Lopina, Jeffrey L. Turner

Toshiba Corp.
Tokyo, JAPAN
Outside Counsel/Consultants
White & Case LLP
Rep By: David P. Houlihan

Toto USA, Inc.
Morrow, GA
Leg. Issues: ENG, NAT
Outside Counsel/Consultants
Potomac Resources, Inc.
Issues: ENG, NAT
Rep By: Edward R. Osann

Touch America
Butte, MT
Leg. Issues: TEC
Outside Counsel/Consultants
Jamison and Sullivan, Inc.
Issues: TEC

Tougaloo College
Tougaloo, MS
Outside Counsel/Consultants
Cassidy & Associates, Inc.
Rep By: Gregory M. Gill

Tourette Syndrome Ass'n, Inc.
Bayside, NY
Leg. Issues: HCR, MMM
Outside Counsel/Consultants
Powers Pyles Sutter & Verville, PC
Issues: HCR, MMM
Rep By: Judith Buckalew

Tourist Railroad Ass'n, Inc.
Denver, CO
Outside Counsel/Consultants
Anderson and Pendleton, C.A.
Rep By: Francis G. McKenna

Touro College
Vallejo, CA
Leg. Issues: EDU
Outside Counsel/Consultants
Russ Reid Co.
Issues: EDU
Rep By: Thomas C. Keller, Mark D. McIntyre

Touro Law Center
Huntington, NY
Leg. Issues: BUD
Outside Counsel/Consultants
Pamela Ray-Strunk and Associates
Issues: BUD
Rep By: Pamela Ray-Strunk

Tower Air, Inc.
New York, NY
Outside Counsel/Consultants
Hewes, Gelband, Lambert & Dann, P.C.
Rep By: Stephen L. Gelband

Town of Fort Sheridan Co., LLC
Chicago, IL
Outside Counsel/Consultants
Bryan Cave LLP
Rep By: Hon. Alan J. Dixon

Toxicology Forum
1575 I St. NW
Suite 325
Washington, DC 20005
Web: www.toxforum.org
E-mail: toxforum@clark.net
Tel: (202)659-0030
Fax: (202)789-0905

Mediates public discussion of crucial scientific and regulatory issues.

In-house, DC-area Employees
SHUBIK, Philippe: President

Toy Manufacturers of America
New York, NY
Leg. Issues: CSP, TRD
Outside Counsel/Consultants
Internat'l Business and Economic Research Corp.
Denny Miller McBee Associates
Issues: CSP, TRD
Sharretts, Paley, Carter and Blauvelt
Issues: TRD
Rep By: Duncan A. Nixon

Toyota Motor Corp.

Toyota City, JAPAN
Leg. Issues: AUT

Outside Counsel/Consultants

Capital Strategies Group, Inc.
Issues: AUT
Rep By: Tammi Hayes

Squire, Sanders & Dempsey L.L.P.
Rep By: Ritchie T. Thomas

Toyota Motor Manufacturing North America

Georgetown, KY
Registered: LDA
Leg. Issues: CAW, ENV, MAN

Outside Counsel/Consultants

Shutler and Low
Rep By: Roger C. Fairchild

Van Ness Feldman, P.C.
Issues: CAW, ENV, MAN
Rep By: Richard A. Penna, Robert G. Szabo

Toyota Motor North America, U.S.A., Inc.

1850 M St. NW
Suite 600
Washington, DC 20036
Tel: (202)775-1700
Fax: (202)822-0928
Registered: LDA
Web: www.toyota.com
Leg. Issues: AUT, BNK, CAW, CSP, ENG, ENV, FUE, HCR, MAN, SCI, TAX, TRD

In-house, DC-area Employees

BAMFORD, Gil: V. President, Government Affairs
ING, Charles E.: Director, Government Affairs
QUIST, Earl C.: Director, Industry Affairs
VOSS, Martha: Washington Public Relations Manager

Outside Counsel/Consultants

Alpine Group, Inc.
Issues: AUT, ENV, FUE
Rep By: Rhod M. Shaw, Monica Skopec

Hogan & Hartson L.L.P.
Issues: MAN, TRD
Rep By: Jeanne S. Archibald, Raymond S. Calamaro, William Michael House

Kendall and Associates
Issues: CSP
Rep By: William T. Kendall

Van Ness Feldman, P.C.
Issues: CAW, CSP, ENG, SCI
Rep By: Howard J. Feldman, Richard A. Penna, Robert G. Szabo

Toyota Technical Center U.S.A. Inc.

Ann Arbor, MI
Leg. Issues: AUT

Outside Counsel/Consultants

Shutler and Low
Issues: AUT
Rep By: Roger C. Fairchild, Robert G. Kaler

Tracer ES&T Inc.

San Marcos, CA

Outside Counsel/Consultants

Ashby and Associates
Rep By: R. Barry Ashby

Tracer Research Corporation

Tucson, AZ

Outside Counsel/Consultants

Nat'l Environmental Strategies

Trade Ass'n Liaison Council

c/o Valis Associates
1700 Pennsylvania Ave. NW, Suite 950
Washington, DC 20006
E-mail: valis@erols.com
Tel: (202)393-5055
Fax: (202)393-0120
Registered: LDA

A group of executives of some 40 leading business and industrial trade associations. This address listed is that of the Valis Associates. Please contact Wayne Valis, the Exec. Director, for further information about the Trade Ass'n Liaison Council.

Leg. Issues: GOV

In-house, DC-area Employees

HUDSON, Dana W.: Coordinator
SHARKEY, III, Andrew G.: Chairman
VALIS, Wayne H.: Exec. Director

Outside Counsel/Consultants

Valis Associates
Issues: GOV
Rep By: Dana W. Hudson, Wayne H. Valis

Trade Exchange of America

Oak Park, MI

Outside Counsel/Consultants

Royer & Babyak
Rep By: Robert Stewart Royer

Trade Show Exhibitors Ass'n

5501 Backlick Rd.
Suite 105
Springfield, VA 22151
Web: www.tsea.org
E-mail: tsea@tsea.org
Tel: (703)941-3725
Fax: (703)941-8275

In-house, DC-area Employees

BANDY, Michael J.: President

Trading Cove Associates

Outside Counsel/Consultants

Dorsey & Whitney LLP
Rep By: David A. Bieging, Virginia W. Boylan

Traditional Values Coalition

139 C St. SE
Washington, DC 20003
Tel: (202)547-8570
Fax: (202)546-6403
Registered: LDA
Web: www.traditionalvalues.org
E-mail: tvcwashdc@traditionalvalues.org

A grass-roots Christian lobby headquartered in Anaheim, CA. Promotes religious liberties and a Christian perspective on sexuality and other social issues. Serves as an information clearinghouse for churchgoers nationwide.

Leg. Issues: BNK, BUD, CON, CPI, DEF, EDU, FAM, FOR, GAM, GOV, HCR, IMM, LAW, LBR, REL, SCI, TAX, TOB

In-house, DC-area Employees

MOORE, Christy: Director, Communications
SHELDON, Rev. Louis P.: Chairman
SHELDON-LAFFERTY, Andrea A.: Exec. Director, Government Relations

Traffic.com

Wayne, PA
Leg. Issues: COM, CPI, DIS, ECN, ROD, SCI, TRA

Outside Counsel/Consultants

The Da Vinci Group
Issues: CPI, TRA

Ann Eppard Associates, Ltd.
Issues: COM, SCI, TRA
Rep By: Julie Chlopecki, Ann Eppard

Simon Strategies/Mindbeam
Issues: CPI, DIS, ECN, ROD, TRA
Rep By: Ann P. Morton, Gregory C. Simon, Christopher Ulrich, Kristan Van Hook

Winston & Strawn
Rep By: Hon. James H. Burnley, IV

Trailer Marine Transport Corp.

Outside Counsel/Consultants

Rodriguez O'Donnell Fuerst Gonzalez & Williams
Rep By: Carlos Rodriguez

Trajen, Inc.

Bryan, TX
Leg. Issues: AVI, DEF, FUE, GOV, SMB, TRA, TRU

Outside Counsel/Consultants

Baker Botts, L.L.P.
Issues: AVI, DEF, FUE, GOV, SMB, TRA, TRU
Rep By: Jeffrey Stonerock

Trans Ocean Leasing Corp.

New York, NY

Outside Counsel/Consultants

Wilmer, Cutler & Pickering
Rep By: Ronald J. Greene

Trans Union Corp.

Chicago, IL
Leg. Issues: BAN, FIN

Outside Counsel/Consultants

The Kate Moss Company
Issues: BAN, FIN
Rep By: Kate Moss

Trans World Airlines, Inc.

900 19th St. NW
Suite 350
Washington, DC 20006
Tel: (202)457-4760
Fax: (202)457-4767
Registered: LDA
Web: www.twa.com

Headquartered in St. Louis, MO.

Leg. Issues: AVI, IMM, TAX, TRA

Political Action Committee/s

Trans World Airlines PAC
900 19th St. NW
Suite 350
Washington, DC 20006
Contact: Norma H. Kaehler
Tel: (202)457-4762
Fax: (202)457-4767

In-house, DC-area Employees

ASTE, George: Staff V. President, International Affairs
KAEHLER, Norma H.: V. President, Government Affairs

Outside Counsel/Consultants

Davidoff & Malito, LLP
Issues: AVI
Rep By: Robert J. Malito, Stephen J. Slade

Podesta/Mattoon
Issues: TRA
Rep By: Ann Delory, Matthew Gelman, Kristen Leary, Antonella Pianalto, Anthony T. Podesta

Trans World Assurance Co.

San Mateo, CA
Leg. Issues: INS

Outside Counsel/Consultants

Baker & Hostetler LLP
Issues: INS
Rep By: Frederick H. Graefe, Christopher T. Stephen

Trans-Ona S.A.M.C.I.F.

Buenos Aires, ARGENTINA
Leg. Issues: MAR

Outside Counsel/Consultants

TransNat'l Business Development Corp.
Issues: MAR
Rep By: Peter J. Levine

TransAfrica Forum

1744 R St. NW
Washington, DC 20009
Tel: (202)797-2301
Fax: (202)797-2382
Web: www.transafricaforum.org
E-mail: transforum@igc.org

Founded in 1977 as the first black foreign policy lobby in this country. Seeks to inform and organize popular opinion in support of a more progressive U.S. foreign policy toward the nations of Africa and the Caribbean and toward peoples of African descent throughout the world.

In-house, DC-area Employees

ROBINSON, Randall: President

TransAlta Corp.

Calgary, CANADA
Leg. Issues: ENG, ENV

Outside Counsel/Consultants

Van Ness Feldman, P.C.
Issues: ENG, ENV
Rep By: Richard A. Agnew

Transamerica Corp.

San Francisco, CA

Outside Counsel/Consultants

Scribner, Hall & Thompson, LLP
Rep By: Susan J. Hotine, Thomas C. Thompson, Jr.

Transamerica Financial Services Co.

Los Angeles, CA

Outside Counsel/Consultants

Akin, Gump, Strauss, Hauer & Feld, L.L.P.
Rep By: Janet C. Boyd, Joel Jankowsky, Michael S. Mandel, Steven R. Ross

Transamerica Occidental Life Insurance Co.

Los Angeles, CA

Outside Counsel/Consultants

Akin, Gump, Strauss, Hauer & Feld, L.L.P.
Rep By: Marlene M. Colucci, Smith W. Davis, Steven R. Ross

The Transatlantic Business Dialogue

c/o PricewaterhouseCoopers LLP
1900 K St. NW, Suite 900
Washington, DC 20009
Web: www.tabd.com
Tel: (202)822-4769
Fax: (202)822-5640

Below address, phone and fax is that of the firm PricewaterhouseCoopers LLP (see separate listing).

In-house, DC-area Employees

SCHROETER, Lisa: Exec. Director
WELTMAN, Allen: Chair, Steering Committee
WERNER, Jeff: Director

TransAtlantic Lines - Iceland ehf

Gardabaer, ICELAND
Leg. Issues: DEF

Outside Counsel/Consultants

Dyer Ellis & Joseph, P.C.
Issues: DEF
Rep By: Brian A. Bannon, James S. W. Drewry, Duncan C. Smith, III

Transconex, Inc.

Miami, FL

Outside Counsel/Consultants

Denning & Wohlstetter

Transconsortia

Denver, CO
Leg. Issues: ENG, FUE

Outside Counsel/Consultants

Mary-Rose Szoka de Valladares
Issues: ENG, FUE
Rep By: Mary-Rose Szoka de Valladares

Transcontinental Gas Pipeline Corp.

Houston, TX

Outside Counsel/Consultants

Wright & Talisman, P.C.
Rep By: Gregory Grady

Transhumance Holding Co., Inc.

Davis, CA
Leg. Issues: FOO, TRD

Outside Counsel/Consultants

Olsson, Frank and Weeda, P.C.
Issues: FOO, TRD
Rep By: John W. Bode, David L. Durkin, Susan P. Grymes, Karen Reis Harned, Stephen L. Lacey, Marshall L. Matz, Philip C. Olsson, Tyson Redpath, Ryan W. Stroschein

Transit Mixed Concrete Co.

Leg. Issues: RES

Outside Counsel/Consultants

RFB, Inc.
Issues: RES
Rep By: Raymond F. Bragg

Transkaryotic Therapies Inc.

Cambridge, MA
Leg. Issues: CPT

Outside Counsel/Consultants

Swidler Berlin Shereff Friedman, LLP
Issues: CPT
Rep By: Barry B. Direnfeld, Brian W. Fitzgerald, Gary Gallant, Harold P. Goldfield

Transmission Access Policy Study Group

Sun Prairie, WI

An ad hoc group formed to address concerns regarding the restructuring of the electric utlity industry.

Leg. Issues: ENG

Outside Counsel/Consultants

Morgan Meguire, LLC
Issues: ENG
Rep By: Scott Lindsay, Kyle G. Michel, Katie Parrott, C. Kyle Simpson, Deborah R. Sliz, Kiel Weaver

Spiegel & McDiarmid
Issues: ENG
Rep By: Cindy S. Bogorad, Robert C. McDiarmid

Transmission Agency of Northern California

Sacramento, CA
Leg. Issues: ENG, UTI

Outside Counsel/Consultants

Duncan, Weinberg, Genzer & Pembroke, P.C.
Issues: ENG, UTI
Rep By: Wallace L. Duncan, James D. Pembroke, Michael R. Postar

TransNat'l Business Development Corp.

Potomac, MD
Leg. Issues: MAR

Outside Counsel/Consultants

Alvarado & Gerken
Issues: MAR
Rep By: Susan E. Alvarado, David A. Gerken

Transnat'l Development Consortium

4200 Cathedral Ave. NW
Suite 715
Washington, DC 20016
E-mail: lane_miller@hotmail.com
Leg. Issues: AER, BAN, CPI, DEF, ECN, FIN, FOR, GOV, MAN, SMB, TEC, TRD

In-house, DC-area Employees

MILLER, Lane F.: Principal, International Investement/Trade and Strategic Alliances

TransOceanic Shipping

New Orleans, LA
Leg. Issues: TRA, TRD

Outside Counsel/Consultants

Jones, Walker, Waechter, Poitevent, Carrere & Denegre, L.L.P.
Issues: TRA
Rep By: John J. Jaskot, R. Christian Johnsen

Washington Council Ernst & Young
Issues: TRD
Rep By: Doug Badger, John L. Doney, Jayne T. Fitzgerald, LaBrenda Garrett-Nelson, Gary J. Gasper, Bruce A. Gates, Nick Giordano, Robert J. Leonard, Richard Meltzer, Robert M. Rozen, Timothy J. Urban

Transpacific Stabilization Agreement

San Francisco, CA
Leg. Issues: MAR

Outside Counsel/Consultants

Preston Gates Ellis & Rouvelas Meeds LLP
Issues: MAR
Rep By: Darrell Conner, John L. Longstreth, Mark H. Ruge

Sher & Blackwell
Issues: MAR
Rep By: Marc J. Fink, Stanley O. Sher

TRANSPO

South Bend, IN

Outside Counsel/Consultants

Sagamore Associates, Inc.
Rep By: Dena S. Morris, David Nichols

Transport Workers Union of America, AFL-CIO

New York, NY
Leg. Issues: LBR, TRA

Outside Counsel/Consultants

O'Donnell, Schwartz & Anderson, P.C.
Issues: LBR, TRA
Rep By: Arthur M. Luby

Transportation Corridor Agencies

Irvine, CA
Leg. Issues: ENV, TRA

Outside Counsel/Consultants

The Ferguson Group, LLC
Issues: ENV, TRA
Rep By: William Ferguson, Jr., W. Roger Gwinn, Mike Miller

McConnell/Ferguson Group
Rep By: William Ferguson, Jr., James F. McConnell

Transportation District Commission of Hampton Roads

Norfolk, VA
Leg. Issues: TRA

Outside Counsel/Consultants

Holland & Knight LLP
Issues: TRA

Transportation Institute

5201 Auth Way
Fifth Floor
Camp Springs, MD 20746
Web: www.trans-inst.org
E-mail: info@trans-inst.org
Tel: (301)423-3335
Fax: (301)423-0634
Registered: LDA

A trade association of U.S.-flag shipping, towing and dredging companies. Carries out research and education on a broad range of martime transportation issues: oil tankers, foreign and domestic shipping trades, barges and tugboat operations on the Great Lakes and inland waterways.

Leg. Issues: MAR, TAX, TRA, TRD

In-house, DC-area Employees

EVANS, Lawrence H.: Director, Domestic Marine Affairs
HENRY, James L.: Chairman and President
SNOW, Gerard C.: Director, Government Affairs

Outside Counsel/Consultants

Baker & Hostetler LLP
Issues: TAX
Rep By: William F. Conroy, Matthew J. Dolan, Frederick H. Graefe, Steven A. Lotterer, David L. Marshall, Hon. Guy Vander Jagt

William V. Brierre
Issues: MAR
Rep By: William V. Brierre, Jr.

The Duberstein Group, Inc.
Issues: MAR
Rep By: John W. Angus, III, Michael S. Berman, Steven M. Champlin, Kenneth M. Duberstein, Henry M. Gandy, Daniel P. Meyer

Potomac Group
Issues: MAR
Rep By: Richard Y Hegg, Philip C. Karsting, G. Wayne Smith

Preston Gates Ellis & Rouvelas Meeds LLP
Issues: MAR, TRD
Rep By: Darrell Conner, Susan B. Geiger, Bruce J. Heiman, John L. Longstreth, Rolf Marshall, William N. Myhre, Emanuel L. Rouvelas, Mark H. Ruge

Robertson, Monagle & Eastaugh
Issues: TRA
Rep By: Bradley D. Gilman, Rick E. Marks

Transportation Intermediaries Ass'n

3601 Eisenhower Ave.
Suite 110
Alexandria, VA 22304-6439
Web: www.tianet.org
E-mail: info@tianet.org
Tel: (703)329-1894
Fax: (703)329-1898
Registered: LDA

An education and policy organization for North American transportation intermediaries.

Leg. Issues: TRA, TRU

Political Action Committee/s

TIAPAC
3601 Eisenhower Ave.
Suite 110
Alexandria, VA 22304-6439
Contact: Edward L. Mortimer
Tel: (703)329-1895
Fax: (703)329-1898

In-house, DC-area Employees

MORTIMER, Edward L.: Director, Government Affairs
SMYTHE, Leigh H.: Manager, Communications
VOLTMANN, Robert A.: Exec. Director and Chief Exec. Officer

Transportation Maritima Mexicana

Leg. Issues: ALC

Outside Counsel/Consultants

Verner, Liipfert, Bernhard, McPherson and Hand, Chartered
Issues: ALC
Rep By: Lawrence E. Levinson, John A. Merrigan

Transportation Reform Alliance

Washington, DC

A coalition of rail, air, bus, maritime and surface transportation companies and associations, plus shippers and public interest groups, advocating transportation deregulation, competitiveness and safety.

Leg. Issues: TRA

Outside Counsel/Consultants

Valis Associates
Issues: TRA
Rep By: Jennifer Conti, Hon. Richard T. Schulze, Wayne H. Valis

Transportation-Communications Internat'l Union

Three Research Place
Rockville, MD 20850
Tel: (301)948-4910
Fax: (301)948-1369
Registered: LDA
Web: www.tcunion.org
Leg. Issues: HCR, LBR, RET, RRR, TRA

Political Action Committee/s

Responsible Citizen's Political League
Three Research Place
Rockville, MD 20850
Tel: (301)948-4910
Fax: (301)330-7673
Contact: Anthony Padilla

In-house, DC-area Employees

BOSHER, L.E.: International Secretary/Treasurer
PADILLA, Anthony: Assistant National Legislative Director
RANDOLPH, Jr., Howard W.: International V. President and National Legislative Director
SCARDELLETTI, Robert A.: International President

Transportes Aereos Mercantiles Panamericanos

Miami, FL

Outside Counsel/Consultants

Winthrop, Stimson, Putnam & Roberts
Rep By: Robert Reed Gray

Transrapid Internat'l

Leg. Issues: TRA

Outside Counsel/Consultants

Kilpatrick Stockton LLP
Issues: TRA
Rep By: J. Christopher Brady, Neil I. Levy

Transtracheal Systems

Englewood, CO
Leg. Issues: HCR, MMM

Outside Counsel/Consultants

GRQ, Inc.
Issues: HCR, MMM
Rep By: Patricia Booth, Phillip Porte

TRAUX Engineering

San Diego, CA
Leg. Issues: SCI

Outside Counsel/Consultants

Van Scoyoc Associates, Inc.
Issues: SCI
Rep By: Thomas L. Lankford, H. Stewart Van Scoyoc

Travel Business Roundtable

Washington, DC
Leg. Issues: TAX, TOU

Outside Counsel/Consultants

BKSH & Associates
Issues: TAX, TOU

Travel Council for Fair Competition

Washington, DC
Leg. Issues: TAX

Outside Counsel/Consultants

The Argus Group, L.L.C.
Issues: TAX
Rep By: David R. Burton, Dan R. Mastromarco

Travel Industry Ass'n of America

1100 New York Ave. NW
Suite 450
Washington, DC 20005
Tel: (202)408-8422
Fax: (202)408-1255
Registered: LDA
Web: www.tia.org

A national, non-profit association representing all components of the travel industry.

Leg. Issues: TOU

In-house, DC-area Employees

HUGHES, Meredith: Manager, Legislative Affairs
KOEHL, Dexter: V. President, Public Relations and Communications
NORMAN, William S.: President and Chief Exec. Officer
WANDER, Elyse: Senior V. President, Government and Public Affairs
WEBSTER, Rick: Director, Government Affairs

Outside Counsel/Consultants

Patton Boggs, LLP
Issues: TOU
Rep By: Thomas Hale Boggs, Jr., Thomas C. Downs, Edward J. Newberry, Jeffrey L. Turner, Elizabeth C. Vella

Travelers Express Co., Inc.

Minneapolis, MN

Outside Counsel/Consultants

Mary Vihstadt
Rep By: Mary Vihstadt

Travelocity.com

1101 17th St. NW
Suite 602
Washington, DC 20036
Tel: (202)467-8203
Fax: (202)467-8204
Registered: LDA
Web: www.travelocity.com

Internet travel agency headquartered in Fort Worth, TX.

Leg. Issues: AVI, CPI, CSP, EDU, GOV, IMM, LBR, SCI, TAX, TOU, TRA, TRD

Political Action Committee/s

Travelocity.com PAC
1101 17th St. NW
Suite 602
Washington, DC 20036
Tel: (202)467-8203
Fax: (202)467-8204

In-house, DC-area Employees

CHARENDOFF, Bruce J.: Senior V. President, Government Affairs
GOODELL, Jeffrey: V. President, Government Affairs

Outside Counsel/Consultants

Jay Grant & Associates
Issues: AVI
Rep By: Jay B. Grant, David M. Olive

TREA Senior Citizens League (TSCL)

909 N. Washington St.
Suite 300
Alexandria, VA 22314
Tel: (703)548-5568
Fax: (703)684-3258
Registered: LDA
E-mail: tscl4@erols.com

Assists members and supporters in educating senior citizens about their rights and freedoms. Also works to protect and defend senior citizens' benefits.

Leg. Issues: CON, DEF, HOU, MMM, PHA, RET, TAX

Political Action Committee/s

TREA Senior Citizens League PAC (TSCL PAC)
909 N. Washington St.
Suite 300
Alexandria, VA 22314
Tel: (703)548-5568
Fax: (703)684-3258
Contact: Katherine M. Angiolillo

In-house, DC-area Employees

ANGIOLILLO, Katherine M.: Deputy Legislative Director
PLUMER, Michael W.: Deputy Legislative Director
RIVERA, Nelson: Administrative Director
TORSCH, USNR, Cdr. Virginia: Legislative Director

Trex Enterprises

San Diego, CA

Outside Counsel/Consultants

Collins & Company, Inc.
Rep By: James D. Bond, Richard L. Collins, Thomas A. Hooper, Shay D. Stautz

The PMA Group
Rep By: Kaylene Green, Patrick Hiu, Paul J. Magliocchetti, Thomas Veltri

TRI Capital Corp.

San Francisco, CA
Leg. Issues: HOU

Outside Counsel/Consultants

Nixon Peabody LLP
Issues: HOU
Rep By: Richard M. Price, Monica Hilton Sussman

Tri Nat'l Aviation

Clearwater, FL

Outside Counsel/Consultants

Johnson, Rogers & Clifton, L.L.P.

Tri Path Inc.

Redmond, WA

A manufacturer of medical devices.

Leg. Issues: GOV, HCR, MMM

Outside Counsel/Consultants

GRQ, Inc.
Issues: GOV, HCR, MMM
Rep By: Patricia Booth, Phillip Porte

Tri West Healthcare Alliance

Phoenix, AZ

Outside Counsel/Consultants

Defense Health Advisors, Inc.
Rep By: Charlotte L. Tsoucalas

The Tri-Alliance of Rehabilitation Professionals

10801 Rockville Pike
Rockville, MD 20852
Tel: (301)897-5700
Fax: (301)897-7356
Web: www.asha.org
E-mail: irc@asha.org

A coalition composed of the American Physical Therapy Ass'n, the American Occupational Therapy Ass'n and the American Speech, Language and Hearing Ass'n.

Leg. Issues: MMM

In-house, DC-area Employees

SPAHR, Frederick T.: Contact

Outside Counsel/Consultants

Muse & Associates
Issues: MMM
Rep By: Donald N. Muse, Gregory A. Portner, MPA

Tri-City Industrial Development Council

Kennewick, WA
Registered: LDA
Leg. Issues: BUD, WAS

Outside Counsel/Consultants

Preston Gates Ellis & Rouvelas Meeds LLP
Issues: BUD, WAS
Rep By: Tim L. Peckinpaugh

Tri-City Regional Port District

Granite City, IL
Leg. Issues: TRA

Outside Counsel/Consultants

The Spectrum Group
Issues: TRA
Rep By: Joan Bondareff, Lt. Gen. Augustus Cianciolo, USA (Ret.), Lt. Gen. Jerome H. Granrud, USA (Ret.), Dr. John Lynch, Gregory L. Sharp

Tri-County Alliance

Barnwell, SC
Leg. Issues: ECN

Outside Counsel/Consultants

Kinghorn & Associates, L.L.C.
Issues: ECN
Rep By: John W. Hilbert, II, Edward J. Kinghorn, Jr., Jeremy Scott

Tri-County Commuter Rail Authority

Pompano Beach, FL
Leg. Issues: TRA

Outside Counsel/Consultants

American Continental Group, Inc.
Issues: TRA
Rep By: John A. Cline, Shawn H. Smeallie

Tri-County Metropolitan Transportation District of Oregon

Portland, OR

Outside Counsel/Consultants

Holland & Knight LLP

TRI-MET Tri-County Metropolitan Transportation

Washington, DC
Leg. Issues: TRA

Outside Counsel/Consultants

Peyser Associates, Inc.
Issues: TRA
Rep By: Peter A. Peyser, Jr.

Triad Design Group

Oklahoma City, OK
Leg. Issues: TRA

Outside Counsel/Consultants

Colex and Associates
Issues: TRA
Rep By: John P. Mack

Trial Lawyers for Public Justice, P.C.

1717 Massachusetts Ave. NW
Suite 800
Washington, DC 20036
Tel: (202)797-8600
Fax: (202)232-7203
Web: www.tlpj.org
E-mail: tlpj@tlpj.org

A national public interest law firm which brings major damage and other precedent-setting civil lawsuits against corporations and the government over health, safety, environmental, civil rights, consumer and other public policy issues.

In-house, DC-area Employees
BLAND, Paul: Staff Attorney
BRUECKNER, Leslie: Staff Attorney
HECKER, James: Environmental Attorney
KIMMEL, Adele: Staff Attorney

Triathlon Broadcasting

San Diego, CA
Outside Counsel/Consultants
Shaw Pittman

Tribal Alliance of Northern California

Sacramento, CA
Outside Counsel/Consultants
Arter & Hadden
Rep By: Hon. Thomas G. Loeffler

Tribal Ass'n on Solid Waste and Emergency Response (TASWER)

1001 Connecticut Ave. NW
Suite 400
Washington, DC 20036
Web: www.taswer.org
Tel: (202)331-8084
Fax: (202)331-8068

Conducts research and influences policy for tribal environmental protection.

Leg. Issues: ENV, IND, WAS

In-house, DC-area Employees
TAYLOR, Heather: Government Relations
TOMHAVE, Jeff: Exec. Director

TRIBASA

Mexico City, MEXICO
Outside Counsel/Consultants
Pierre E. Murphy Law Offices

Tribune Co.

1722 I St. NW
Suite 400
Washington, DC 20006
Tel: (202)775-7750
Fax: (202)223-3844
Registered: LDA
Web: www.tribune.com
E-mail: ssheehan@tribune.com
Leg. Issues: ADV, ART, COM, CPT, MIA, SPO

In-house, DC-area Employees
SHEEHAN, Shaun M.: V. President, Washington

Outside Counsel/Consultants
Dewey Ballantine LLP
Rep By: Joseph K. Dowley, Andrew W. Kentz
Patton Boggs, LLP
Issues: ART, CPT, MIA
Rep By: Clayton L. Hough

Tricap Management Corp.

Los Angeles, CA
Leg. Issues: HOU, URB
Outside Counsel/Consultants
Kimberly Consulting, LLC
Issues: HOU, URB
Rep By: Richard H. Kimberly

Tricon Global Restaurants Inc.

Louisville, KY
Leg. Issues: FOO, LBR, TAX
Outside Counsel/Consultants
Fierce and Isakowitz
Issues: FOO, LBR, TAX
Rep By: Kathryn Braden, Samantha Cook, Donald L. Fierce, Mark W. Isakowitz, Diane Moery
Murray, Scheer, Montgomery, Tapia & O'Donnell
Issues: TAX
Rep By: Thomas R. Crawford, D. Michael Murray

Trident Seafood Corp.

Seattle, WA
Leg. Issues: FOO, MAR
Outside Counsel/Consultants
Glenn Roger Delaney
Issues: FOO, MAR
Rep By: Glenn Roger Delaney
EOP Group, Inc.
Rep By: Michael O'Bannon
O'Connor & Hannan, L.L.P.
Rep By: Gary C. Adler, George J. Mannina, Jr.
Robertson, Monagle & Eastaugh
Issues: MAR
Rep By: Bradley D. Gilman, Rick E. Marks

Trident Systems Inc.

Fairfax, VA
Leg. Issues: DEF
Outside Counsel/Consultants
Higgins, McGovern & Smith, LLC
Issues: DEF
Rep By: Carl M. Smith

Trifinery, Inc.

Houston, TX
Leg. Issues: FUE
Outside Counsel/Consultants
American Continental Group, Inc.
Issues: FUE
Rep By: John A. Cline, David A. Metzner, Shawn H. Smeallie

Trigen Energy Corp.

White Plains, NY
Leg. Issues: ENG
Outside Counsel/Consultants
Troutman Sanders LLP
Issues: ENG
Rep By: Thomas C. Jensen, William P. Marsan, Bonnie Suchman, Dionne E. Thompson

Trigon Healthcare Inc.

Richmond, VA
Leg. Issues: LBR
Outside Counsel/Consultants
McGuireWoods L.L.P.
Issues: LBR
Rep By: Stephen A. Katsurinis, Hon. Lewis F. Payne, Jr.

Trimble Navigation, Ltd.

Sunnyvale, CA
Develops and manufactures products related to the global positioning system.
Leg. Issues: BUD, TEC
Outside Counsel/Consultants
Birch, Horton, Bittner & Cherot
Issues: BUD
Rep By: Thomas L. Albert, William Bittner
Capitol Coalitions Inc.
Issues: TEC
Rep By: Brett P. Scott

Trinidad and Tobago, Embassy of the Republic of

1708 Massachusetts Ave. NW
Washington, DC 20036
Outside Counsel/Consultants
Washington World Group, Ltd.
Rep By: Edward J. von Kloberg, III

Trinidad and Tobago, Government of

Port-of-Spain, TRINIDAD & TOBAGO
Outside Counsel/Consultants
Steptoe & Johnson LLP
Rep By: Mark A. Moran

Trinity Health

Farmington Hills, MI
Leg. Issues: BUD, HCR
Outside Counsel/Consultants
Cassidy & Associates, Inc.
Issues: BUD
Rep By: W. Campbell Kaufman, IV, Blenda Pinto-Riddick
Jones, Day, Reavis & Pogue
Issues: HCR
Rep By: Teresa A. Brooks

Trinity Partners, Inc.

Jacksonville, FL
Leg. Issues: ENV, RES
Outside Counsel/Consultants
Capital Consultants Corp.
Issues: ENV, RES
Rep By: Seth Barnhard, Michael David Kaiser

Trinity Public Utilities District

Weaverville, CA
Leg. Issues: ENG, GOV
Outside Counsel/Consultants
Duncan, Weinberg, Genzer & Pembroke, P.C.
Issues: ENG, GOV
Rep By: Jeffrey C. Genzer, James D. Pembroke

Triosyn Corp.

South Burlington, VT
Leg. Issues: DEF
Outside Counsel/Consultants
The PMA Group
Issues: DEF
Rep By: Kaylene Green, Patrick Hiu, Paul J. Magliocchetti, Brian Thiel, Sandra Welch

Tripoli Rocketry Ass'n

Orem, UT
Leg. Issues: CHM, CSP, SCI
Outside Counsel/Consultants
BKSH & Associates
Issues: CHM, CSP, SCI
Rep By: John Kyte

TriWest Healthcare Alliance, Inc.

Phoenix, AZ
Leg. Issues: DEF, HCR, MMM, VET
Outside Counsel/Consultants
Grisso Consulting
Rep By: Michael E. Grisso
Public Policy Partners, LLC
Issues: DEF, HCR, MMM, VET
Rep By: Hon. David Durenberger
R. Duffy Wall and Associates

Trizec Hahn Corp.

Toronto, CANADA
Leg. Issues: RES, TAX
Outside Counsel/Consultants
Hooper Owen & Winburn
Issues: RES, TAX
Rep By: Lindsay D. Hooper

Tropical Shipping and Construction Co.

Rivera Beach, FL
Outside Counsel/Consultants
Hoppel, Mayer and Coleman
Rep By: Paul D. Coleman, Neal Michael Mayer

Trout Unlimited

1500 Wilson Blvd.
Suite 310
Arlington, VA 22209
Tel: (703)522-0200
Fax: (703)284-9400
Registered: LDA
Web: www.tu.org
E-mail: trout@tu.org

Specializes in cold water conservation.

Leg. Issues: NAT

In-house, DC-area Employees
GAUVIN, Charles F.: President and Chief Exec. Officer
MOYER, Steven N.: V. President, Conservation Program

Troy State University - Montgomery

Montgomery, AL
Leg. Issues: BUD, EDU
Outside Counsel/Consultants
R. G. Flippo and Associates, Inc.
Issues: BUD, EDU
Rep By: Hon. Ronnie G. Flippo, Vicki P. Wallace

Truck Manufacturers Ass'n

1225 New York Ave. NW
Suite 300
Washington, DC 20005
Tel: (202)638-7825
Fax: (202)737-3742
Web: www.mema.org/tma/tma.html
E-mail: tma_bill@ix.netcom.com

Represents U.S. and Canadian manufacturers of medium- and heavy-duty trucks. Coordinates dialogue, research, and technical information exchange between the industry and the governmental entities that regulate the industry.

Leg. Issues: TRA, TRU

In-house, DC-area Employees
LEASURE, Jr., William A.: Exec. Director

Truck Mixer Manufacturers Bureau

900 Spring St.
Silver Spring, MD 20910
Tel: (301)587-1400
Fax: (301)587-1605
Web: www.nrmca.org

The TMMB is the trade organization for the manufacturers of truck mounted concrete mixers and agitators.

In-house, DC-area Employees
GARBINI, Robert A.: Exec. Secretary
MAHER, Nicole R.: Bureau Administrator

Truck Renting and Leasing Ass'n

1725 Duke St.
Suite 600
Alexandria, VA 22314-3457
Tel: (703)299-9120
Fax: (703)299-9115
Registered: LDA
Web: www.TRALA.org
E-mail: mpayne@trala.org
Leg. Issues: CAW, ENV, INS, TAX, TOR, TRA, TRU

In-house, DC-area Employees
LYNCH, John: Manager, Government Affairs
PAYNE, J. Michael: President and Chief Exec. Officer
VROOM, Peter J.: Exec. V. President

Outside Counsel/Consultants
Legislative Solutions
Issues: CAW, INS, TAX, TOR, TRA, TRU
Rep By: Daniel J. Fleming

Zuckert, Scoutt and Rasenberger, L.L.P.
Issues: TRU
Rep By: Richard P. Schweitzer

Truck Trailer Manufacturers Ass'n

1020 Princess St.
Alexandria, VA 22314
Tel: (703)549-3010
Fax: (703)549-3014

A trade association representing commercial trailer manufacturers and their suppliers.

Leg. Issues: TRA, TRU

In-house, DC-area Employees
BOWLING, Richard P.: President

Truckee Donner Electric Power Utility District

Truckee, CA
Leg. Issues: ENG

Outside Counsel/Consultants
Morgan Meguire, LLC
Issues: ENG
Rep By: Kyle G. Michel, C. Kyle Simpson, Deborah R. Sliz, Kiel Weaver

Truckload Carriers Ass'n

2200 Mill Rd.
Third Floor
Alexandria, VA 22314
Tel: (703)838-1950
Fax: (703)836-6610
Web: www.truckload.org
E-mail: tca@truckload.org

Formerly known as the Interstate Truckload Carriers Conference, the association was formed in 1938 through a merger of the Common Carrier Conference-Irregular Route and the Contract Carrier Conference. Tailored exclusively to the needs of truckload carrier executives.

Leg. Issues: FUE, ROD

In-house, DC-area Employees
HIRSCH, Robert: President
ROTHSTEIN, Robert G.: General Counsel

TruePosition Inc.

King of Prussia, PA
Registered: LDA
Leg. Issues: TEC

Outside Counsel/Consultants
Nat'l Strategies Inc.
Issues: TEC
Rep By: David K. Aylward

Timmons and Co., Inc.
Issues: TEC
Rep By: Michael J. Bates, Douglas F. Bennett, Ellen B. Fitzgibbons, Bryce L. "Larry" Harlow, Timothy J. Keating, Tom C. Korologos, Richard J. Tarplin, William E. Timmons, Jr., William E. Timmons, Sr.

Truman Scholarship Foundation, Harry S

712 Jackson Place NW
Washington, DC 20006
Tel: (202)395-4831
Fax: (202)395-6995
Web: www.truman.gov
E-mail: staff@truman.gov

Established as the official federal memorial to honor the 33rd President of the United States. Awards scholarships to rising seniors in pursuit of a career in government or public service. Activities of the Foundation are funded by a special trust in the U.S. Treasury.

In-house, DC-area Employees
BLAIR, Louis H.: Exec. Secretary

The Trump Organization

New York, NY
Leg. Issues: GAM, MAR, TAX

Outside Counsel/Consultants
Dyer Ellis & Joseph, P.C.
Issues: MAR, TAX
Rep By: Laurie Crick Sahatjian, Thomas M. Dyer, Jeanne Marie Grasso, Lara Bernstein Mathews, Duncan C. Smith, III, Jennifer M. Southwick, Jonathan K. Waldron

Ikon Public Affairs
Issues: GAM
Rep By: Roger J. Stone

Trust for Public Land

666 Pennsylvania Ave. SE
Suite 401
Washington, DC 20003
Tel: (202)543-7552
Fax: (202)544-4723
Registered: LDA
Web: www.tpl.org/tpl

A national non-profit land conservation organization that works with government agencies and communities to protect natural, recreational, historic, and other resource lands for public use and enjoyment.

Leg. Issues: BUD, NAT, RES, TRA

In-house, DC-area Employees
DECOSTER, Katherine B.: Assistant Director
FRONT, Alan: Senior V. President
KANE, Lesley: V. President, Legislative Affairs

Outside Counsel/Consultants
Crowell & Moring LLP

TRW Inc.

1001 19th St. North
Suite 800
Arlington, VA 22209-3901
Tel: (703)276-5100
Fax: (703)276-5057
Registered: LDA
Web: www.trw.com

Headquartered in Cleveland, OH.

Leg. Issues: AER, AUT, AVI, BUD, CPI, CSP, DEF, ENV, FUE, GOV, HCR, IMM, LBR, SCI, TAX, TEC, TRD, WAS

Political Action Committee/s
TRW Good Government Fund
1001 19th St. North
Suite 800
Arlington, VA 22209-3901
Contact: Lauren M. Heller
Tel: (703)276-5086
Fax: (703)276-5057

In-house, DC-area Employees
CARTER, John R.: V. President, Government Relations, Defense and National Security Programs
ESPERNE, Jeanine: Director, Government Relations-Defense and Nat'l Security Programs
GALIHER-OTT, Kathleen: Director, Government Relations
HALES, Shirley I.: Director, Government Relations
HELLER, Lauren M.: Manager, Government Relations
HULL, Brenda J.: Director, Government Relations, Defense and National Security Programs
KLEIN, Scott: Manager, Government Relations
MCMAHON, Kevin P.: Director, Government Relations
ODEEN, Phil: Exec. V. President, Washington Operations
PERKINS, Peter: Director, Government Relations-Defense and Nat'l Security Programs

Outside Counsel/Consultants
The Advocacy Group
Issues: ENV
Rep By: John M. Nugent, Jr., George A. Ramonas

Peter S. Barash Associates, Inc.
Rep By: Peter S. Barash

LegisLaw
Issues: TAX
Rep By: Linda A. Woolley, Esq.

Multinat'l Government Services, Inc.
Issues: AUT, GOV
Rep By: Bruce Levinson, Jim J. Tozzi

MultiState Associates

The Spectrum Group
Issues: DEF
Rep By: Gail Dady, RAdm. James B. Hinkle, USN (Ret.), James Rooney

TRW Space and Electronics Group

Redondo Beach, CA
Leg. Issues: DEF

Outside Counsel/Consultants
Morris J. Amitay, P.C.
Issues: DEF
Rep By: Morris J. Amitay

TRW Systems Integration Group

Fairfax, VA

Outside Counsel/Consultants
Durante Associates
Rep By: Raymond W. Durante

TSG Ventures Inc.

Stamford, CT
Leg. Issues: SMB

Outside Counsel/Consultants
Thelen Reid & Priest LLP
Issues: SMB
Rep By: William A. Kirk, Jr.

TTX Co.

Chicago, IL

A rail car pooling and leasing company.

Leg. Issues: RRR, TRA

Outside Counsel/Consultants
Williams & Jensen, P.C.
Issues: RRR, TRA
Rep By: Karen Judd Lewis, John J. McMackin, Jr., Anthony J. Roda

Tubos de Acero de Mexico, S.A.

Mexico City, MEXICO

Outside Counsel/Consultants
Paul, Hastings, Janofsky & Walker LLP
Rep By: G. Hamilton Loeb

Tucson, Arizona, City of

Leg. Issues: GOV, TEC

Outside Counsel/Consultants
Bracy Williams & Co.
Issues: GOV
Rep By: Michael M. Bracy, Terrence L. Bracy, James P. Brown, Laura L. Madden, Tracy P. Tucker, Susan J. Williams

Miller & Van Eaton, P.L.L.C.
Issues: TEC
Rep By: William Malone, Joseph Van Eaton

Tufts University

Medford, MA

Outside Counsel/Consultants
The Dutko Group, Inc.

Tufts University School of Veterinary Medicine

North Grafton, MA

Outside Counsel/Consultants
Cassidy & Associates, Inc.
Rep By: Carl Franklin Godfrey, Jr.

Tukwila, Washington, City of

Leg. Issues: BUD

Outside Counsel/Consultants
Ball Janik, LLP
Issues: BUD
Rep By: James A. Beall, Michelle E. Giguere, Hal D. Hiemstra

Tulalip Tribes

Marysville, WA

An Indian tribal government.

Leg. Issues: ENV, GAM, IND

Outside Counsel/Consultants
Ducheneaux, Taylor & Associates, Inc.
Issues: IND
Rep By: Franklin D. Ducheneaux

Hecht, Spencer & Associates
Issues: ENV, GAM, IND
Rep By: Timothy P. Hecht, William H. Hecht, Franklin C. Phifer

Tulane University

New Orleans, LA
Leg. Issues: BUD, DEF, EDU, ENG, ENV, HOU, MED, MMM, SCI, TRA, URB

Outside Counsel/Consultants

Barbour Griffith & Rogers, Inc.
Issues: EDU
Rep By: Haley Barbour, Scott Barnhart, G. O. Lanny Griffith, Jr., Loren Monroe

Johnston & Associates, LLC
Issues: BUD, ENG, ENV, HOU, TRA, URB
Rep By: Hon. J. Bennett Johnston, N. Hunter Johnston, W. Proctor Jones, Eric Tober

Jones, Walker, Waechter, Poitevent, Carrere & Denegre, L.L.P.
Issues: BUD, EDU
Rep By: Paul Cambon, John J. Jaskot, R. Christian Johnsen

Royer & Babyak
Rep By: Paul Nelson

Van Scoyoc Associates, Inc.
Issues: BUD, DEF, EDU, MED, MMM, SCI
Rep By: Jan Schoonmaker, H. Stewart Van Scoyoc

Tulare, California, County of

Leg. Issues: ECN, LAW, ROD

Outside Counsel/Consultants

Alcalde & Fay
Issues: ECN, LAW, ROD
Rep By: Paul Schlesinger, Tim Stroud

Tule River Tribal Council

Porterville, CA
Leg. Issues: IND, TAX

Outside Counsel/Consultants

Carlyle Consulting
Issues: IND, TAX
Rep By: Thomas C. Rodgers

Tulsa Airport Authority

Tulsa, OK
Leg. Issues: AER, AVI, BUD, GOV

Outside Counsel/Consultants

VSAdc.com
Issues: AER, AVI, BUD, GOV
Rep By: J. R. Reskovac

Tulsa, Oklahoma, City of

Leg. Issues: TEC

Outside Counsel/Consultants

Miller & Van Eaton, P.L.L.C.
Issues: TEC
Rep By: Matthew C. Ames

Tumalo Irrigation District

Bend, OR
Leg. Issues: UTI

Outside Counsel/Consultants

Will and Carlson, Inc.
Issues: UTI

Tunica Biloxi Indians of Louisiana

Marksville, LA
Leg. Issues: BUD, ECN, ENV, GAM, HOU, IND, TAX, TOU

Outside Counsel/Consultants

Johnston & Associates, LLC
Issues: BUD, ECN, ENV, GAM, HOU, IND, TAX, TOU
Rep By: Hon. J. Bennett Johnston, N. Hunter Johnston, W. Proctor Jones, Eric Tober

Tunisia, Embassy of the Republic of

1515 Massachusetts Ave. NW
Washington, DC 20005
Tel: (202)862-1850
Fax: (202)862-1858

Outside Counsel/Consultants

White & Case LLP

Tunisian Agency for External Communication

Tunis, TUNISIA

Outside Counsel/Consultants

Afridi & Angell LLP

Tupperware Corp.

Orlando, FL
Leg. Issues: TAX

Outside Counsel/Consultants

PriceWaterhouseCoopers
Issues: TAX
Rep By: Barbara Angus, Kenneth J. Kies

Turbine Controls, Inc.

Bloomfield, CT
Leg. Issues: DEF

Outside Counsel/Consultants

Mehl, Griffin & Bartek Ltd.
Issues: DEF
Rep By: Molly Griffin, Theodore J. Mehl

Turfgrass Producers Internat'l

Rolling Meadows, IL
Leg. Issues: AGR, IMM

Outside Counsel/Consultants

McGuiness Norris & Williams, LLP
Issues: AGR, IMM
Rep By: William N. LaForge, Monte B. Lake

Turkey, Central Bank of

Ankara, TURKEY

Outside Counsel/Consultants

Hoffman & Hoffman Public Relations

Turkey, Embassy of the Republic of

2525 Massachusetts Ave. NW
Washington, DC 20008
Tel: (202)612-6700
Fax: (202)659-0744
Web: www.turkey.org
E-mail: info@turkey.org

Outside Counsel/Consultants

The Solomon Group, LLC
Rep By: Hon. Gerald B. H. Solomon

Turkey, Government of the Republic of

Ankara, TURKEY
Leg. Issues: FOR, TRD

Outside Counsel/Consultants

Arnold & Porter

IMPACT, LLC

Jones, Walker, Waechter, Poitevent, Carrere & Denegre, L.L.P.

The Livingston Group, LLC

Law Offices of David L. Simon
Issues: TRD
Rep By: David L. Simon

The Solomon Group, LLC
Issues: FOR, TRD
Rep By: Dana Bauer, David M. Lonie, Hon. Gerald B. H. Solomon

Turkish Airlines

Istanbul, TURKEY

Outside Counsel/Consultants

Zuckert, Scoutt and Rasenberger, L.L.P.
Rep By: Charles J. Simpson, Jr.

Turkish Industrialists and Businessmen's Ass'n (TUSIAD)

1250 24th St. NW
Suite 300
Washington, DC 20037
Tel: (202)776-7770
Fax: (202)776-2771
Registered: LDA
Web: www.tusiad-us.org
Leg. Issues: ECN, FIN, FOR, FUE, GOV, MAN, TOU, TRD

In-house, DC-area Employees

AKYUZ, Abdullah: President

Outside Counsel/Consultants

IMPACT, LLC
Issues: ECN, FOR, FUE, TOU, TRD
Rep By: Arzu Tuncata-Tarimcilar

Turkish Republic of Northern Cyprus, Embassy of

1667 K St. NW
Suite 690
Washington, DC 20006
Tel: (202)887-6198
Fax: (202)467-0685
Registered: FARA
Web: www.trncwashdc.org
E-mail: KKTC@erols.com

Represents the Turkish Republic of Northern Cyprus in the U.S.

Leg. Issues: FOR

In-house, DC-area Employees

ERDENGIZ, Ahmet: Representative
GUCLU, Damla: First Secretary

Turks Air Limited

Providenciales, TURKS & CAICOS ISLANDS

Outside Counsel/Consultants

Pierre E. Murphy Law Offices

Turlock Irrigation District

Turlock, CA

Outside Counsel/Consultants

Birch, Horton, Bittner & Cherot
Rep By: William P. Horn

Turtle Mountain Community College

Belcourt, ND
Leg. Issues: BUD

Outside Counsel/Consultants

Sara Garland (and Associates)
Issues: BUD
Rep By: Sara G. Garland

Tuskegee University, Office of

Federal Relations Office
11 Dupont Circle NW, Suite 220
Washington, DC 20036
Tel: (202)863-9384
Fax: (202)863-9388
Registered: LDA
E-mail: fron@erols.com

Traditionally black university located in Tuskegee, AL.

In-house, DC-area Employees

SMITH, Willa H.: Director

Tustin, California, City of

Leg. Issues: ECN

Outside Counsel/Consultants

Kutak Rock LLP
Issues: ECN
Rep By: Rhonda Bond-Collins, Seth Kirshenberg, George R. Schlossberg

TV Azteca

Mexico City, MEXICO

Outside Counsel/Consultants

Pierre E. Murphy Law Offices

TV Guide, Inc.

Tulsa, OK
Leg. Issues: CDT, CPT, TEC

Outside Counsel/Consultants

The Dutko Group, Inc.
Issues: CDT, CPT, TEC
Rep By: Kim Koontz Bayliss, Steve Perry, Juliette M. Raffensperger, Stephen Craig Sayle

TV Radio Now Corp. (i Crave TV)

Toronto, CANADA
Leg. Issues: COM

Outside Counsel/Consultants

Federal Legislative Associates, Inc.
Issues: COM
Rep By: Stephen D. Amitay, David H. Miller

TVA Watch

700 13th St. NW
Suite 950
Washington, DC 20005
Tel: (202)434-8918
Fax: (202)638-5129

An ad hoc industry group seeking to influence legislation revising the Tennessee Valley Authority Act. Members include: Duke Power Co., Entergy Corp.., SCANA Corp., Illinova Corp., and LG&E Kentucky Utilities.

Leg. Issues: BUD, ENG, ENV, GOV, UTI

Outside Counsel/Consultants

Alpine Group, Inc.
Issues: BUD, ENG, UTI
Rep By: James Gregory Means

Balch & Bingham LLP
Issues: ENG, ENV, UTI
Rep By: Sean Cunningham, Fred Eames, Patrick J. McCormick, III

Greg Copeland
Issues: UTI
Rep By: Greg Copeland

Redland Energy Group
Issues: ENG, GOV, UTI
Rep By: John A. Howes

TVX Mineral Hill Mine

Gardiner, MT

Outside Counsel/Consultants

Robertson, Monagle & Eastaugh

Twentynine Palms Band of Mission Indians

Coachella, CA
Leg. Issues: IND

Outside Counsel/Consultants

The State Affairs Co.
Issues: IND
Rep By: Bonnie L. Chafe

Twentynine Palms Water District

Twentynine Palms, CA
Leg. Issues: UTI

Outside Counsel/Consultants

Peyser Associates, Inc.
Issues: UTI
Rep By: Peter A. Peyser, Jr., Thane Young

Twin Laboratories, Inc.

Hauppauge, NY

Outside Counsel/Consultants

Parry, Romani, DeConcini & Symms

TWK

Kaiserslautern, GERMANY

Outside Counsel/Consultants

Markcorp Inc.
Rep By: Michael Clark

TXU Business Services

600 Pennsylvania Ave. NW
Suite 200
North Bldg.
Washington, DC 20004
Tel: (202)628-1020
Fax: (202)628-1007
Registered: LDA

Formerly Texas Utilities Services, Inc. Headquartered in Dallas, TX.

Leg. Issues: ENG, ENV, FUE, NAT, TAX, TEC, UTI, WAS

In-house, DC-area Employees

KRECHTING, John: Manager, Federal Regulatory Affairs
LYNCH, David: Governmental Affairs Manager
SCRIVNER, Kerrill K.: V. President, Governmental Affairs

Outside Counsel/Consultants

Walker F. Nolan
Issues: ENG, UTI
Rep By: Walker F. Nolan

O'Neill, Athy & Casey, P.C.
Issues: ENG, ENV, FUE, NAT, TAX, TEC, UTI, WAS
Rep By: Andrew Athy, Jr., Christopher R. O'Neill

Ryan, Phillips, Utrecht & MacKinnon
Issues: UTI, WAS
Rep By: Rodney Hoppe, Jeffrey M. MacKinnon, William D. Phillips, Mark D. Planning, Thomas M. Ryan, Joseph V. Vasapoli

Tongour Simpson Holsclaw Green
Issues: UTI
Rep By: John Bradley "Brad" Holsclaw, Michael A. Tongour

Washington Council Ernst & Young
Issues: TAX, UTI
Rep By: Doug Badger, Lauren Darling, John L. Doney, Jayne T. Fitzgerald, LaBrenda Garrett-Nelson, Gary J. Gasper, Bruce A. Gates, Nick Giordano, Cathy Koch, Robert J. Leonard, Richard Meltzer, Phillip D. Moseley, John D. Porter, Robert M. Rozen, Donna Steele-Flynn, Timothy J. Urban

TXU Inc.

Leg. Issues: UTI

Outside Counsel/Consultants

Tongour Simpson Holsclaw Green
Issues: UTI
Rep By: Michael A. Tongour

Tyco Internat'l (US), Inc.

122 C St. NW
Suite 520
Washington, DC 20001
Tel: (202)393-5100
Fax: (202)393-5110
Registered: LDA

Acquired Mallinckrodt Inc. in October of 2000. Headquartered in Exeter, NH.

Leg. Issues: CAW, ENV, MAN, MED, MMM, TAX, TEC, TRD

In-house, DC-area Employees

BUNNING, Susan: Manager, Public Affairs Tyco Healthcare
CONNORS, Kathleen: Office Administrator
POLGAR, Thomas C.: Senior V. President, Public Affairs

Outside Counsel/Consultants

The Advocacy Group
Issues: MED
Rep By: Robert J. Dotchin

Tyson Foods, Inc.

Springdale, AR
Leg. Issues: ENV, FOO

Outside Counsel/Consultants

Arent Fox Kintner Plotkin & Kahn, PLLC
Issues: ENV, FOO
Rep By: Hon. Dale L. Bumpers, Mary Hope Davis, Michael T. McNamara, Todd Weiss

Tyson's Governmental Sales, LLC

Vienna, VA
Leg. Issues: AUT, BUD, DEF, FUE, MAN

Outside Counsel/Consultants

O'Connor & Hannan, L.L.P.
Issues: AUT, BUD, DEF, FUE, MAN
Rep By: Hon. Thomas J. Corcoran, Frederick T. Dombo, Danielle Fagre, Patrick E. O'Donnell

U.S. Apparel Industry Council

Miami, FL

Outside Counsel/Consultants

Sandler, Travis & Rosenberg, P.A.
Rep By: Ronald W. Gerdes, Chandri Navarro-Bowman, Thomas G. Travis

U.S. Apple Ass'n

6707 Old Dominion Dr.
Suite 320
McLean, VA 22101
Web: www.usapple.org
E-mail: usapple@usapple.org
Tel: (703)442-8850
Fax: (703)790-0845

A trade association representing the U.S. apple industry, from the grower through the retailer. Membership comprises two categories: state and regional organizations representing growers; and individual companies.

Leg. Issues: AGR

Political Action Committee/s

U.S. Apple Ass'n PAC
6707 Old Dominion Dr.
Suite 320
McLean, VA 22101
Contact: Kraig R. Naasz
Tel: (703)442-8850
Fax: (703)790-0845

In-house, DC-area Employees

CRANNEY, Jr., James R.: V. President, Industry Services
NAASZ, Kraig R.: President and Chief Exec. Officer
PIMM, Harriet: Manager, Communications
STEWART DALY, Julia: Director, Public Relations

Outside Counsel/Consultants

McDermott, Will and Emery
Issues: AGR
Rep By: Edward M. Ruckert

U.S. Ass'n of Former Members of Congress

233 Pennsylvania Ave. SE
Suite 200
Washington, DC 20003-1107
Web: www.usafmc.org
E-mail: usafmc@mindspring.com
Tel: (202)543-8676
Fax: (202)543-7145

A nonpartisan, non-profit, educational, research, and social organization with approximately 600 members. The organization was founded in 1970 and has been chartered by Congress. Promotes improved public understanding of the role of Congress as a unique institution as well as the importance of representative democracy as a system of government, both domestically and internationally.

In-house, DC-area Employees

BUECHNER, Hon. Jack W.: Treasurer
ERLENBORN, Hon. John N.: President
LAROCCO, Hon. Lawrence P.: V. President
MCHUGH, Hon. Matthew F.: Past President
REED, Linda A.: Exec. Director
SLATTERY, Hon. Jim: Secretary

U.S. Ass'n of Importers of Textiles and Apparel

New York, NY
Web: www.usaita.com
E-mail: quota@aol.com
Registered: LDA

Represents the fashion industry, including designers, manufacturers, importers, retailers, and related service industries.

Leg. Issues: TRD

Outside Counsel/Consultants

Powell, Goldstein, Frazer & Murphy LLP
Issues: TRD
Rep By: Brenda A. Jacobs

U.S. Banknote Corp.

New York, NY

Outside Counsel/Consultants

Wiley, Rein & Fielding
Rep By: Fred F. Fielding

U.S. Basic Skills

505 Hampton Park Blvd.
Suite D
Capitol Heights, MD 20743
Web: www.usbasics.org
Tel: (301)324-3966
Fax: (301)324-3969

Sales/support of the U.S. Basic Skills Learning System (Comprehensive Competencies Program), a K-12 and functional, multimedia learning system.

Leg. Issues: EDU

In-house, DC-area Employees

CLUNE, Dennis M.: Chief Operating Officer

U.S. Borax, Inc.

Valencia, CA

Outside Counsel/Consultants

Jack Ferguson Associates, Inc.
Rep By: Jack Ferguson

U.S. Border Control

8180 Greensboro Dr.
Suite 1070
McLean, VA 22102
Web: www.usbc.org
E-mail: staff@usbc.org
Tel: (703)356-6568
Registered: LDA

Lobbies for the reform of border and immigration policies.

Leg. Issues: IMM, TRD

In-house, DC-area Employees

NELSON, Edward I.: President

U.S. Business Alliance for Customs Modernization

Escondido, CA
Leg. Issues: TRD

Outside Counsel/Consultants

Gibson, Dunn & Crutcher LLP
Issues: TRD
Rep By: Judith A. Lee

U.S. Canola Ass'n

Washington, DC
Leg. Issues: AGR

Outside Counsel/Consultants

Gordley Associates
Issues: AGR
Rep By: John Gordley, Megan Marquet, Daryn McBeth

U.S. Catholic Conference

3211 Fourth St. NE
Washington, DC 20017
Web: www.nccp.uscc.org
Tel: (202)541-3000

In-house, DC-area Employees

GRINCEWICH, Katherine C.: Assistant General Counsel
MONIHAN, Frank: Exec. Director, Office of Government Liason

U.S. Central Credit Union

Overland Park, KS

Outside Counsel/Consultants

O'Connor & Hannan, L.L.P.
Rep By: Roy C. Coffee, Thomas H. Quinn

U.S. Chamber Institute for Legal Reform

1615 H St. NW
Washington, DC 20062
Tel: (202)463-5724
Fax: (202)463-5302
Registered: LDA
Web: www.uschamber.com

Leg. Issues: BUD, CON, CPI, CSP, FIR, GOV, HCR, INS, TAX, TOB, TOR

In-house, DC-area Employees

COLE, Tom: Consultant
WOOTTON, James: President

Outside Counsel/Consultants

Morgan, Lewis & Bockius LLP
Issues: TOR

U.S. Chamber Task Force on Punitive Damages

Washington, DC
Leg. Issues: TAX

Outside Counsel/Consultants

Miller & Chevalier, Chartered
Issues: TAX
Rep By: Leonard Bickwit, Jr., Lawrence B. Gibbs

U.S. Citrus Science Council

Santa Paula, CA
Leg. Issues: AGR, BUD, TRD

Outside Counsel/Consultants

Schramm, Williams & Associates, Inc.
Issues: AGR, BUD, TRD
Rep By: Anita Brown, Gabriele Ludwig, Robert Schramm, Nancy Williams

U.S. Clay Producers Traffic Ass'n

Iselin, NJ
Leg. Issues: TRA

Outside Counsel/Consultants

G.W. Fauth & Associates Inc.
Issues: TRA
Rep By: Gerald W. Fauth, III

U.S. Colombia Business Partnership

Washington, DC
Leg. Issues: FOR

Outside Counsel/Consultants

Andreae, Vick & Associates, L.L.C.
Issues: FOR
Rep By: Charles N. Andreae, III, William Burlew

U.S. Contract Tower Ass'n

Alexandria, VA

Outside Counsel/Consultants

AB Management Associates, Inc.
Rep By: Larry P. Barnett

U.S. Disabled Athletes Fund

Atlanta, GA
Leg. Issues: EDU, HCR

Outside Counsel/Consultants

Sagamore Associates, Inc.
Issues: EDU, HCR
Rep By: Dena S. Morris

U.S. Display Consortium

San Jose, CA
Leg. Issues: DEF

Outside Counsel/Consultants

Hyjek & Fix, Inc.
Issues: DEF
Rep By: Donald J. Fix, Steven M. Hyjek, Karl H. Stegenga

U.S. English, Inc.

1747 Pennsylvania Ave. NW
Suite 1100
Washington, DC 20006
Web: www.us-english.org
Tel: (202)833-0100
Fax: (202)833-0108
Registered: LDA

A nonprofit, nonpartisan citizens action group seeking to make English the official language of government at all levels. Established in 1983.

Leg. Issues: BUD, CIV, EDU, GOV, LBR, NAT, TAX

In-house, DC-area Employees

BENNETT, Todd: Government Relations Representative
BLACK, Will: Director, Membership Development
MUJICA, Mauro E.: Chairman of the Board/Chief Exec. Officer
SCHULTZ, Tim: Director, Communications

U.S. Family Network

1300 Pennsylvania Ave. NW
Suite 700
Washington, DC 20004
E-mail: usfn@juno.com
Registered: LDA
Leg. Issues: CIV, ECN, EDU, FAM, GOV, HCR, TAX, WEL

In-house, DC-area Employees

ALBANEZE, Roger D.
GAMBRELL, Brooke
MILLS, Robert G.: Exec. Director

U.S. Federation of Small Businesses, Inc.

Albany, NY

Political Action Committee/s

Small Biz PAC
Albany, NY

Outside Counsel/Consultants

Ottosen and Associates
Rep By: Karl J. Ottosen

U.S. Fencing Ass'n

Colorado Springs, CO
Leg. Issues: SPO

Outside Counsel/Consultants

Wilson & Wasserstein, Inc.
Issues: SPO
Rep By: Russell J. Wilson

U.S. Figure Skating Ass'n

Colorado Springs, CO
Leg. Issues: SPO

Outside Counsel/Consultants

Paul, Hastings, Janofsky & Walker LLP
Issues: SPO
Rep By: Ralph B. Everett, G. Hamilton Loeb

U.S. Filter

Palm Desert, CA
Leg. Issues: CAW, ENV, URB

Outside Counsel/Consultants

Alpine Group, Inc.
Issues: CAW, ENV, URB
Rep By: Dan Brouillette, James D. Massie, James Gregory Means

Boesch & Co.
Issues: CAW
Rep By: Doyce A. Boesch

U.S. Fittings Group

Outside Counsel/Consultants

McKenna & Cuneo, L.L.P.
Rep By: Peter Buck Feller

U.S. Fund for UNICEF

1775 K St. NW
Suite 360
Washington, DC 20006
Web: www.unicefusa.org
Tel: (202)296-4242
Fax: (202)296-4060
Registered: LDA

Headquartered in New York, NY.

Leg. Issues: BUD, FOR

In-house, DC-area Employees

METTIMANO, Joseph J.: Assistant Director
MORIARTY, Kevin: Legislative Coordinator and Program Manager
RENDON, Martin Stephen: V. President, Public Policy and Advocacy

Outside Counsel/Consultants

Edington, Peel & Associates, Inc.
Issues: BUD, FOR
Rep By: Terry R. Peel

U.S. Grains Council

1400 K St. NW
Suite 1200
Washington, DC 20005
Web: www.grains.org
E-mail: grains@grains.org
Tel: (202)789-0789
Fax: (202)898-0522

A private, non-profit organization that develops and expands export markets for U.S. produced feed grains and co-products through a network of 12 international offices.

In-house, DC-area Employees

HOBBIE, Kenneth: President

U.S. Gypsum Co.

Chicago, IL
Leg. Issues: CSP

Outside Counsel/Consultants

Morgan, Lewis & Bockius LLP
Issues: CSP

U.S. Healthcare

Blue Bell, PA
Leg. Issues: HCR

Outside Counsel/Consultants

Blank Rome Comisky & McCauley, LLP
Issues: HCR
Rep By: David A. Norcross

U.S. Hispanic Chamber of Commerce

2175 K St. NW
Suite 100
Washington, DC 20036
Web: www.ushcc.com
E-mail: ushcc@ushcc.com
Tel: (202)842-1212
Fax: (202)842-3221

Promotes Hispanic economic interests. Represents a national and international business network dedicated to the development of Hispanic enterprises. Advocates for over 1.4 million Hispanic-owned firms in the United States and Puerto Rico.

Leg. Issues: SMB, TRD

In-house, DC-area Employees

HERRERA, George: President and Chief Exec. Officer
LISBOA-FARRON, Elizabeth: Chair

U.S. Immigrant Investor Ass'n

1107 Massachusetts Ave. NW
Washington, DC 20005
A political action committee.

In-house, DC-area Employees

CHAN, May S.: PAC Administrator

U.S. Interactive

Houston, TX
Leg. Issues: COM, SCI, TEC

Outside Counsel/Consultants

Ryan, Phillips, Utrecht & MacKinnon
Issues: COM, SCI, TEC
Rep By: Rodney Hoppe, Jeffrey M. MacKinnon, William D. Phillips, Thomas M. Ryan, Joseph V. Vasapoli

U.S. Internet Council

Washington, DC
Web: www.usiia.org
E-mail: info@usiia.org
Leg. Issues: TAX, TEC

Outside Counsel/Consultants

Sally L. Albright
Issues: TAX, TEC
Rep By: Sally L. Albright

U.S. Investigations Services

Annandale, PA
Leg. Issues: BUD

Outside Counsel/Consultants

Arnold & Porter
Issues: BUD
Rep By: Martha L. Cochran

U.S. Marine Corp.

New Orleans, LA
A defense shipbuilding company.

Leg. Issues: DEF

Outside Counsel/Consultants

Robertson, Monagle & Eastaugh
Issues: DEF
Rep By: Bradley D. Gilman, Rick E. Marks

U.S. Mink Export Development Council

Carrollton, PA
Leg. Issues: AGR, BUD, TRD

Outside Counsel/Consultants

McDermott, Will and Emery
Issues: AGR, BUD, TRD
Rep By: Carolyn B. Gleason, Jerry C. Hill

U.S. Mint

Washington, DC

Outside Counsel/Consultants

Hill and Knowlton, Inc.
Rep By: Steve Kramer, David MacKay

U.S. Oil and Gas Ass'n

801 Pennsylvania Ave. NW
Suite 840
Washington, DC 20004-2615
Tel: (202)638-4400
Fax: (202)638-5967
Registered: LDA
Leg. Issues: BNK, BUD, CAW, ECN, ENG, ENV, FUE, GOV, MAR, NAT

Political Action Committee/s

Mid-Continent Oil and Gas Political Action Committee (MID PAC)
801 Pennsylvania Ave. NW
Suite 840
Washington, DC 20004-2615
Contact: Albert L. Modiano
Tel: (202)638-4400
Fax: (202)638-5967

In-house, DC-area Employees

GIBBENS, Wayne: President
MODIANO, Albert L.: V. President

Outside Counsel/Consultants

The Livingston Group, LLC
Issues: BUD, ENG, FUE
Rep By: Hon. Robert L. Livingston, Jr., J. Allen Martin

U.S. Olympic Committee

1150 18th St. NW
Suite 300
Washington, DC 20036
Tel: (202)466-3399
Fax: (202)466-5068

Headquartered in Colorado Springs, CO.

Leg. Issues: SPO

In-house, DC-area Employees

BULL, Stephen B.: Director, Government Relations

Outside Counsel/Consultants

Sagamore Associates, Inc.
Issues: SPO
Rep By: Ann E. Cody, David U. Gogol, Dena S. Morris

U.S. Oncology

Houston, TX
Leg. Issues: HCR, MED, MMM

Outside Counsel/Consultants

McSlarrow Consulting L.L.C.
Issues: HCR, MMM
Rep By: Alison McSlarrow

Policy Directions, Inc.
Issues: HCR, MED, MMM
Rep By: Kathleen "Kay" Holcombe, Stephen Michael, Frankie L. Trull

Washington Council Ernst & Young
Issues: HCR, MED, MMM
Rep By: Doug Badger, Lauren Darling, John L. Doney, Jayne T. Fitzgerald, LaBrenda Garrett-Nelson, Gary J. Gasper, Bruce A. Gates, Nick Giordano, Cathy Koch, Robert J. Leonard, Richard Meltzer, Phillip D. Moseley, John D. Porter, Robert M. Rozen, Donna Steele-Flynn, Timothy J. Urban

U.S. Overseas Cooperative Development

4301 Wilson Blvd.
Suite 1017
Arlington, VA 22203
Tel: (703)907-5667
Fax: (703)907-5519
Registered: LDA
E-mail: ted.weihe@nreca.org
Leg. Issues: FOR

In-house, DC-area Employees

WEIHE, Theodore Frederick: Exec. Director

U.S. Postal Service

Washington, DC
Leg. Issues: ENV, WAS

Outside Counsel/Consultants

Goodstein & Associates
Issues: ENV, WAS
Rep By: Richard F. Goodstein

U.S. Public Interest Research Group

218 D St. SE
Second Floor
Washington, DC 20003
Tel: (202)546-9707
Fax: (202)546-2461
Registered: LDA
Web: www.pirg.org/uspirg
E-mail: uspirg@pirg.org

The national lobbying office for state public interest research groups, i.e., non-profit, non-partisan consumer and environmental advocacy organizations. Funded by citizen contributions.

Leg. Issues: BAN, BNK, BUD, CAW, CHM, CSP, EDU, ENG, ENV, FIN, FOO, FUE, GOV, HCR, NAT, RES, TOB, TRD, UTI, WAS

In-house, DC-area Employees

AURILIO, Anna: Staff Scientist
COPE, Grant: Staff Attorney
FRISHBERG, Ivan: Higher Education Project Director
HUTCHINS, Julia: Democracy Advocate
KARPINSKI, Gene: Exec. Director
MIERZWINSKI, Edmund: Consumer Program Director
SHULTZ, Lexi: Staff Attorney
SITTENFELD, Tiernan: Staff Attorney
WEINTRAUB, Rachel: Staff Attorney

U.S. Rice Producers Ass'n

Arlington, VA

Outside Counsel/Consultants

The PMA Group
Rep By: Fred J. Clark, Kaylene Green, Paul J. Magliocchetti, Mark Rokala

U.S. Senate Federal Credit Union

Outside Counsel/Consultants

Edelman Public Relations Worldwide
Rep By: Bob Knott

U.S. Space & Rocket Center

Huntsville, AL
Leg. Issues: EDU, TOU

Outside Counsel/Consultants

Hall, Green, Rupli, LLC
Issues: EDU, TOU
Rep By: John M. Green, G. Stewart Hall

U.S. Steel

Pittsburgh, PA
Leg. Issues: ENV

Outside Counsel/Consultants

Sparber and Associates
Issues: ENV
Rep By: Peter O'Rourke, Peter G. Sparber

U.S. Term Limits

10 G St. NE
Suite 410
Washington, DC 20002
Tel: (202)379-3000
Fax: (202)379-3010
Web: www.termlimits.org
E-mail: admin@ustermlimits.org

A grassroots organization supporting term limits at the local, state and Congressional levels.

Leg. Issues: CON, GOV

In-house, DC-area Employees

JACOB, Paul: National Director

U.S. Tour Operators Ass'n

Outside Counsel/Consultants

Downey McGrath Group, Inc.

U.S. Trade Law Study Group

Outside Counsel/Consultants

Nat'l Grass Roots & Communications

U.S. Wheat Associates, Inc.

1620 I St. NW
Suite 801
Washington, DC 20006
Tel: (202)463-0999
Fax: (202)785-1052
Web: www.uswheat.org
E-mail: info@uswheat.org

The foreign market development organization of the U.S. wheat industry. Headquartered in Washington, with 15 overseas offices in Asia, Africa, Europe, Central and South America, and Russia. Also maintains a west coast office in Portland, OR.

In-house, DC-area Employees

TRACY, Alan T.: President

U.S. Wireless Data, Inc.

New York, NY
Leg. Issues: SMB

Outside Counsel/Consultants

The Smith-Free Group
Issues: SMB
Rep By: Doyle Bartlett, James C. Free, Robert Hickmott, W. Timothy Locke, Alicia W. Smith

U.S.-ASEAN Business Council Inc.

1101 17th St. NW
Suite 411
Washington, DC 20036
Tel: (202)289-1911
Fax: (202)289-0519
Web: www.us-asean.org
E-mail: mail@usasean.org

Committed to expanding U.S. business presence in countries belonging to the Ass'n of Southeast Asian Nations (ASEAN) through support of policies that assist U.S. companies in identifying and competing for business opportunities.

In-house, DC-area Employees

BOWER, Ernest Z.: President

U.S.-Azerbaijan Council, Inc.

Washington, DC

Outside Counsel/Consultants

Baker, Donelson, Bearman & Caldwell, P.C.
Rep By: Charles R. Johnston, Jr.

U.S.-Canadian Caucus of Mayors

Leg. Issues: TOU, TRD

Outside Counsel/Consultants

The Aegis Group, Ltd.
Issues: TOU, TRD
Rep By: A. Mario Castillo

U.S.-China Business Council

1818 N St. NW
Suite 200
Washington, DC 20036
Tel: (202)429-0340
Fax: (202)775-2476
Web: www.uschina.org
E-mail: info@uschina.org

Established in May, 1973. A private non-profit, dues-supported organization of 300 companies. Established to assist American companies in doing business with China.

In-house, DC-area Employees

KAPP, Robert A.: President

U.S.-Cuba Business Council

5315 Lee Hwy.
Suite B
Arlington, VA 22207
Tel: (703)241-0038
Fax: (703)241-0548
Web: www.uscubacouncil.com
E-mail: uscubabiz@aol.com

In-house, DC-area Employees

COX, Thomas E.: President

U.S.-Mongolia Business Council, Inc.

1015 Duke St.
Alexandria, VA 22314-3551
Tel: (703)549-8444
Fax: (703)549-6526
Web: www.usmongolia.org
E-mail: usmbc@us-mongolia.org

A non-profit membership association of American and Canadian companies and organizations interested, active, or invested in Mongolia. Works with both the U.S. and Mongolian governments to promote and advance North American business interests in Mongolia.

In-house, DC-area Employees

KENNY, G. Michael: Exec. Director
SAUNDERS, Steven R.: President

Outside Counsel/Consultants

Saunders and Company

U.S.-Russia Business Council

1701 Pennsylvania Ave. NW
Suite 520
Washington, DC 20006
Tel: (202)739-9180
Fax: (202)659-5920
Web: www.usrbc.org

A non-profit membership organization of American firms founded in 1993. Its mission is to develop and expand U.S. private-sector trade and investment in Russia, in the interest of both nations.

In-house, DC-area Employees

JONES, Jeffrey: Program Manager
LAWSON, Eugene K.: President

U.S.-Turkish Business Council of DEIK

Istanbul, TURKEY
Leg. Issues: FOR, TRD

Outside Counsel/Consultants

Caspian Group
Issues: FOR, TRD
Rep By: Lydia Borland

U.S.-Turkmenistan Business Council

805 15th St. NW
Suite 500
Washington, DC 20005
Tel: (202)682-0534
Fax: (202)371-6601

A non-profit association of U.S. companies seeking to increase their business activities in Turkmenistan. Founded in 1997.

In-house, DC-area Employees

CHAMBERS, Letitia: Interim Exec. Director

Outside Counsel/Consultants

Chambers Associates Inc.

U.S./Mexico Border Counties Coalition

San Diego, CA
Leg. Issues: BUD

Outside Counsel/Consultants

Carpi & Clay
Issues: BUD
Rep By: Kenneth A. Carpi

UBS Warburg

New York, NY
Leg. Issues: BAN, CPI, FIN, HCR

Outside Counsel/Consultants

McDermott, Will and Emery
Rep By: Neil Quinter

O'Connor & Hannan, L.L.P.
Issues: BAN, CPI, FIN
Rep By: Roy C. Coffee, Frederick T. Dombo, Danielle Fagre, Timothy W. Jenkins, William Nickerson, Thomas H. Quinn

U.S. Strategies Corp.
Issues: HCR
Rep By: Gary F. Capistrant, Steven E. Carey, Brad Traverse

UDV North America, Inc.

1301 K St. NW
Suite 1000 East
Washington, DC 20005
Tel: (202)715-1105
Fax: (202)715-1114
Registered: LDA
Web: www.diageo.com
Leg. Issues: ADV, ALC, BEV, CAW, DEF, LBR, TAX, TRD

In-house, DC-area Employees

BERTMAN, Mike: Director, Federal and International Affairs
PANZER, Carolyn: Senior V. President, Public Policy

Outside Counsel/Consultants

Bergner Bockorny Castagnetti and Hawkins
Issues: BEV, LBR, TAX
Rep By: Jeffrey T. Bergner, David A. Bockorny, David Castagnetti, James W. Hawkins

Powell Tate

UDV/Heublein, Inc.

E-mail: foxlobby@aol.com
Leg. Issues: ADV, ALC, BEV, CPT, FOO, TAX, TRD

Outside Counsel/Consultants

JBC Internat'l
Issues: TRD
Rep By: Jeannie M. Boone, James B. Clawson

Uganda, Embassy of the Republic of

5911 16th St. NW
Washington, DC 20011
Tel: (202)726-7100
Fax: (202)726-1727
Web: www.ugandaweb.com/ugembassy
E-mail: ugembassy@aol.com
Leg. Issues: FOR

Outside Counsel/Consultants

Foley, Hoag & Eliot LLP
Issues: FOR
Rep By: Traci D. Humes, Paul S. Reichler

Uganda, Government of the Republic of

Kampala, UGANDA
Leg. Issues: FOR

Outside Counsel/Consultants

Foley, Hoag & Eliot LLP
Issues: FOR
Rep By: Traci D. Humes, Paul S. Reichler

UGI Utilities, Inc.

Valley Forge, PA
Leg. Issues: ENV

Outside Counsel/Consultants

Morgan, Lewis & Bockius LLP
Issues: ENV
Rep By: John E. Daniel

UKR Investments, Inc.

Outside Counsel/Consultants

Edelman Public Relations Worldwide
Rep By: Christine Kelly Cimko

Ukraine, Government of

Kiev, UKRAINE
Leg. Issues: FOR

Outside Counsel/Consultants

APCO Worldwide
Issues: FOR
Rep By: Hon. Don L. Bonker, Deborah L. Louison

Ukraine, Ministries of Industy, Foreign Economic Relations, and Foreign Affairs of the Government of

Kiev, UKRAINE

Outside Counsel/Consultants

Aitken, Irvin, Lewin, Berlin, Vrooman & Cohn

Ukrainian Nat'l Ass'n, Inc.

Parsippany, NJ
Leg. Issues: BUD, FOR

Outside Counsel/Consultants

EMI Associates, Ltd.
Issues: BUD, FOR
Rep By: Eugene M. Iwanciw

Ulster Unionist Party

Belfast, IRELAND
Registered: FARA
E-mail: uupna@ix.netcom.com

Outside Counsel/Consultants

AWS Services
Rep By: Anne W. Smith

Ultracard, Inc.

Campbell, CA
Leg. Issues: DEF

Outside Counsel/Consultants

Cassidy & Associates, Inc.
Issues: DEF
Rep By: John A. Crumbliss, Brig. Gen. Terry Paul, USMC (Ret.)

Ultraprise.com

Dulles, VA
Leg. Issues: BAN, SCI

Outside Counsel/Consultants

GPC Internat'l
Issues: BAN, SCI
Rep By: Bruce A. Morrison

Ultratech Stepper Inc.

San Jose, CA
A manufacturer of semiconductor manufacturing equipment.
Leg. Issues: CPI, SCI

Outside Counsel/Consultants

RBG Associates
Issues: CPI, SCI
Rep By: Richard B. Griffin, Jr.

Umatilla Irrigation Districts Coordinating Committee

Hermiston, OR

Outside Counsel/Consultants

Jamison and Sullivan, Inc.

Umatilla Water Users

Hermiston, OR

Outside Counsel/Consultants

Jamison and Sullivan, Inc.
Rep By: Delos Cy Jamison, Jay R. Sullivan

UMonitor.com

Leg. Issues: BAN, SCI

Outside Counsel/Consultants

Hoover Partners
Issues: BAN, SCI
Rep By: Kimberly Hoover

Unalaska, Alaska, City of

Leg. Issues: ECN

Outside Counsel/Consultants

Robertson, Monagle & Eastaugh
Issues: ECN
Rep By: Bradley D. Gilman, Rick E. Marks

Underwriters Digital Research, Inc.

New York, NY
Leg. Issues: CON, CPI, CSP

Outside Counsel/Consultants

Curson Koopersmith Partners, Inc.
Issues: CON, CPI, CSP
Rep By: Jeffrey M. Koopersmith, Theodore B. Koopersmith

Underwriters Laboratories Inc.

1850 M St. NW
Suite 1000
Washington, DC 20036
Tel: (202)296-7840
Fax: (202)872-1576
Web: www.ul.com

In-house, DC-area Employees

GILLERMAN, Gordon: Manager, Governmental Affairs

Unideal Navitankers

Kifissia, GREECE
Leg. Issues: MAR

Outside Counsel/Consultants

The Evans Group, Ltd.
Issues: MAR
Rep By: Geryld B. Christianson, Hon. Thomas B. Evans, Jr.

Uniden Corp.

Fort Worth, TX
Leg. Issues: TEC

Outside Counsel/Consultants

Akin, Gump, Strauss, Hauer & Feld, L.L.P.
Issues: TEC
Rep By: Marlene M. Colucci, David Geanacopoulos, Barney J. Skladany, Jr.

Skadden, Arps, Slate, Meagher & Flom LLP

UNIFI, Inc.

Raleigh, NC
Leg. Issues: CAW, TAX

Outside Counsel/Consultants

Albertine Enterprises, Inc.
Issues: CAW, TAX
Rep By: James J. Albertine, Dr. John M. Albertine

Unified Industries, Inc.

Springfield, VA
Leg. Issues: BUD, DEF, GOV, SCI, SMB

Outside Counsel/Consultants

Foley Government and Public Affairs, Inc.
Issues: BUD, DEF, GOV, SCI, SMB
Rep By: Joseph P. Foley

Unified Voice (Interior Designers)

A result of the merger of the Council of Federal Interior Designers, the Institute of Business Designers, the Internat'l Soc. of Interior Designers, the Institute of Store Planners and the Interior Design Educators Council.

Outside Counsel/Consultants

TASC, Inc., Association Management
Rep By: Randy Dyer, CAE

Unifinancial Internat'l, Inc.

Arlington, VA

Outside Counsel/Consultants

Patton Boggs, LLP
Rep By: Daniel R. Addison

Uniform and Textile Service Ass'n

1300 N. 17th St.
Suite 750
Arlington, VA 22209
Tel: (703)247-2600
Fax: (703)841-4750
Registered: LDA
Web: www.utsa.com
E-mail: info@utsa.com
Leg. Issues: CAW, LBR, WAS

In-house, DC-area Employees

DOLBEARE, Mary Anne: Director, Government, Public Affairs and Marketing
DUNLAP, David D.: Director, Environmental and Regulatory Affairs
HOBSON, David F.: President and Chief Exec. Officer
KOEPPER, Ken: Director, Communications

Uniformed Services Dental Alliance

San Antonio, TX
Leg. Issues: DEF, HCR

Outside Counsel/Consultants

Advantage Associates, Inc.
Issues: DEF, HCR
Rep By: Hon. Robert D. McEwen, Hon. Bill Sarpalius, Hon. Robin Tallon

Uniformed Services Family Health Plan

Outside Counsel/Consultants

Dittus Communications
Rep By: Debra Cabral, Jennifer Garfinkel, Chris McNamara

UniGroup, Inc.

Fenton, MO
A transportation services company.
Leg. Issues: BAN, BNK, TRA, TRU

Outside Counsel/Consultants

Arent Fox Kintner Plotkin & Kahn, PLLC
Issues: BAN

Thompson Coburn LLP
Issues: BNK, TRA, TRU
Rep By: Michael G. Roberts

Zuckert, Scoutt and Rasenberger, L.L.P.
Issues: TRA
Rep By: James A. Calderwood

Unilever N.V.

Rotterdam, NETHERLANDS

Outside Counsel/Consultants

Greenberg Traurig, LLP
Rep By: Howard A. Vine

Unilever United States, Inc.

816 Connecticut Ave. NW
Seventh Floor
Washington, DC 20006-2705
Tel: (202)828-1010
Fax: (202)828-4550
Registered: LDA
Web: www.unilever.com

Specializes in consumer products (household, personal care, consmetics and fragrances) and headquartered in New York, NY.

Leg. Issues: AGR, BUD, CDT, CPI, CSP, DEF, ENV, FOO, LAW, TAX, TRD, UTI

In-house, DC-area Employees

BECK, Lauren E.: Legislative Representative
LANGAN, Thomas P.: Manager, Government Affairs
LUSTIG, David Vernon: Director, Government Relations

Outside Counsel/Consultants

Greenberg Traurig, LLP
Issues: BUD, ENV, FOO, TRD
Rep By: Diane J. Blagman, Howard A. Vine

Parry, Romani, DeConcini & Symms
Issues: AGR, CSP, DEF, ENV, FOO, TRD
Rep By: Edward H. Baxter, Hon. Dennis DeConcini, John M. Haddow, Scott D. Hatch, Shannon Davis Henderson, Jack W. Martin, Romano Romani, Linda Arey Skladany, Hon. Steven D. Symms

Union Bank of Switzerland

Zurich, SWITZERLAND
Leg. Issues: BAN

Outside Counsel/Consultants

Wilmer, Cutler & Pickering
Issues: BAN
Rep By: Lloyd N. Cutler, Roger M. Witten

Union City, New Jersey, City of

Outside Counsel/Consultants

Krivit & Krivit, P.C.

Union Hospital

Terre Haute, IN
Leg. Issues: AGR, BUD, HCR

Outside Counsel/Consultants

Sagamore Associates, Inc.
Issues: AGR, BUD, HCR
Rep By: Julia P. Church, David Nichols, Mark W. Weller

Union Institute - Office for Social Responsibility, The

1710 Rhode Island Ave. NW
Suite 1100
Washington, DC 20036
Tel: (202)496-1630
Fax: (202)496-1635
Web: www.tui.edu
E-mail: mrosenman@tui.edu

Applied research unit of The Union Institute, a national university. Headquartered in Cincinnati, OH.

In-house, DC-area Employees

ROSENMAN, Ph.D., Mark: V. President

The Union Labor Life Insurance Co.

111 Massachusetts Ave. NW
Washington, DC 20001
Tel: (202)682-0900
Fax: (202)682-6784
Registered: LDA
Web: www.ullico.com
E-mail: epacheco@ullicolaw.com

Political Action Committee/s

ULLIPAC

111 Massachusetts Ave. NW
Washington, DC 20001
Tel: (202)682-0900
Fax: (202)682-6784
Contact: Joseph A. Carabillo

In-house, DC-area Employees

BARROW, Erin: Senior Legal Assistant
CARABILLO, Joseph A.: V. President and Chief Legal Officer
GEORGINE, Robert A.: President, Chairman, and Chief Exec. Officer

Union of Concerned Scientists

1707 H St. NW
Suite 600
Washington, DC 20006-3919
Tel: (202)223-6133
Fax: (202)223-6162
Registered: LDA
Web: www.ucsusa.org
E-mail: ucs@ucsusa.org

Promotes arms control, strategic arms limitation talks, balanced sustainable energy policies, reduced reliance on nuclear power, sustainable agriculture practices, and progressive U.S. policies on global environmental issues such as climate change, biodiversity, and ozone depletion.

Leg. Issues: AGR, DEF, ENG, TRA

In-house, DC-area Employees

COLLINA, Thomas: Director, Global Security Program
DEAN, Jonathan: Advisor, Global Security Issues
HAYES, Richard: Media Director
LOCHBAUM, David A.: Nuclear Safety Engineer
MELLON, Margaret: Director, Food and Environment
MEYER, Alden: Director, Government Relations
RISSLER, Jane: Senior Scientist, Food and Environment
RITTER, Lloyd: Policy Coordinator, Climate Change
ROBINSON, Michelle: Senior Advocate for Clean Vehicles
SUNDERGILL, Ron: Washington Representative for Clean Energy
WINDLE, Phyllis: Senior Scientist, Global Environment Program
YOUNG, Stephen: Washington Representative, Senior Analyst

Union of Councils for Soviet Jews

1819 H St. NW
Suite 230
Washington, DC 20006
Tel: (202)775-9770
Fax: (202)775-9776
Web: www.fsumonitor.com
E-mail: ucsj@ucsj.com

The headquarters office for twelve "Soviet Jewry" member councils in the U.S. and for eight human rights bureaus in the former Soviet Union. Work is in defense of human rights of citizens of the former Soviet states, towards the rule of law, and in opposition to antisemitism.

Leg. Issues: CIV, FOR, GOV, IMM

In-house, DC-area Employees

NAFTALIN, Micah: National Director

Union of Needletrades, Industrial, and Textile Employees (UNITE)

888 16th St. NW
Suite 303
Washington, DC 20006
Tel: (202)347-7417
Fax: (202)347-0708
Registered: LDA
Web: www.unitedunion.org
E-mail: ahoffman@unitedunion.org

Headquartered in New York, NY.

Leg. Issues: BNK, CIV, DEF, FOR, GOV, HCR, IMM, LBR, TAX, TRD, UNM, WEL

Political Action Committee/s

Union of Needletrades, Industrial, and Textile Employees PAC

888 16th St. NW
Suite 303
Washington, DC 20006
Tel: (202)347-7417
Fax: (202)347-0708
Contact: Ann F. Hoffman

In-house, DC-area Employees

HOFFMAN, Ann F.: Associate Legislative Director

Union Pacific

600 13th St. NW
Suite 340
Washington, DC 20005
Tel: (202)662-0100
Fax: (202)662-0199
Registered: LDA

Leg. Issues: BNK, BUD, ENG, ENV, HCR, NAT, RRR, TAX, TRA, TRD, TRU

Political Action Committee/s

Union Pacific Fund for Effective Government

600 13th St. NW
Suite 340
Washington, DC 20005
Tel: (202)662-0100
Fax: (202)662-0199
Contact: Mary E. McAuliffe

In-house, DC-area Employees

ANDRES, Susan Auther: Director, Washington Affairs - Transportation
BATEMAN, Jr., Joseph R.: Senior Assistant V. President, Government Affairs
MANESS, Katherine W.: Director, Washington Affairs - Political
MCAULIFFE, Mary E.: V. President, External Relations
ROCK, Michael A.: Assistant V. President, External Affairs

Outside Counsel/Consultants

Covington & Burling

Dewey Ballantine LLP
Issues: BNK, TAX, TRA
Rep By: Andrew W. Kentz, John J. Salmon, James M. Wickett

The Dutko Group, Inc.
Issues: TRA
Rep By: Gary J. Andres, Kimberly M. Spaulding

Dykema Gossett PLLC
Issues: RRR
Rep By: Charles R. Bernardini

Ann Eppard Associates, Ltd.
Issues: RRR
Rep By: Julie Chlopecki, Ann Eppard, Karen Schechter

Paul, Hastings, Janofsky & Walker LLP
Issues: BUD, RRR, TAX
Rep By: Ralph B. Everett

Potomac Group
Issues: RRR, TAX, TRU
Rep By: Richard Y Hegg, Philip C. Karsting, G. Wayne Smith

Powell, Goldstein, Frazer & Murphy LLP
Rep By: Hon. Butler E. Derrick, Jr.

Skadden, Arps, Slate, Meagher & Flom LLP
Issues: TRA, TRD
Rep By: Ivan A. Schlager

Timmons and Co., Inc.
Issues: NAT, RRR, TAX
Rep By: Michael J. Bates, Douglas F. Bennett, Ellen B. Fitzgibbons, Bryce L. "Larry" Harlow, Timothy J. Keating, Tom C. Korologos, Richard J. Tarplin, William E. Timmons, Jr., William E. Timmons, Sr.

Zane & Associates
Issues: RRR
Rep By: Curtis J. Zane

Union Pacific Railroad Co.

Omaha, NE
Leg. Issues: TRA

Outside Counsel/Consultants

James T. Molloy
Rep By: James T. Molloy

Patton Boggs, LLP
Issues: TRA
Rep By: Thomas Hale Boggs, Jr., Lanny J. Davis, Robert C. Jones, Hon. Greg H. Laughlin

Union Sanitary District

Fremont, CA
Leg. Issues: BUD, NAT

Outside Counsel/Consultants

ENS Resources, Inc.
Issues: BUD, NAT
Rep By: Eric Sapirstein

Union Switch and Signal, Inc.

Pittsburgh, PA
Leg. Issues: TRA

Outside Counsel/Consultants

Tongour Simpson Holsclaw Green
Issues: TRA
Rep By: Michael A. Tongour

UNIPAC Service Corp.

Aurora, CO
Registered: LDA

A servicer of guaranteed student loans.

Leg. Issues: BUD, EDU, TAX

Outside Counsel/Consultants

Dean Blakey & Moskowitz
Issues: BUD, EDU, TAX
Rep By: John E. Dean

Uniroyal Chemical Co., Inc.

Geismar, LA
Leg. Issues: TRD

Outside Counsel/Consultants

Howrey Simon Arnold & White
Rep By: John DeQ. Briggs, III

JBC Internat'l
Issues: TRD
Rep By: James B. Clawson, Michael Eads, George M. "Matt" Mattingley, Jr.

Uniroyal Technology Corp.

Sarasota, FL

A manufacturing and technology company.

Outside Counsel/Consultants

Greenberg Traurig, LLP
Rep By: Diane J. Blagman, Peter M. Gillon, Ronald W. Kleinman, Nancy E. Taylor, Howard A. Vine

UniServe Inc.

Pittsburgh, PA
Leg. Issues: TRA

Outside Counsel/Consultants

Jeffrey M. Anders
Issues: TRA
Rep By: Jeffrey M. Anders

Unisite, Inc.

Richardson, TX
Leg. Issues: TEC

Outside Counsel/Consultants

The Laxalt Corp.
Issues: TEC
Rep By: Michelle D. Laxalt

Unisys Corp.

1901 Pennsylvania Ave. NW
Suite 302
Washington, DC 20006
Tel: (202)293-7720
Fax: (202)293-7757
Registered: LDA

Provides advanced computer-based information systems, networks and services to domestic and international commercial and government markets.

Leg. Issues: BUD, CPI, CPT, DEF, GOV, IMM, MED, SCI, TAX, TRD

Political Action Committee/s

Unisys Corp. Employess PAC
8008 Westpark Dr.
McLean, VA 22102

In-house, DC-area Employees

HOYDYSH, Dan: Director, Washington Office

Outside Counsel/Consultants

Adams and Reese LLP
Issues: DEF, MED
Rep By: B. Jeffrey Brooks, Andrea Wilkinson

Holland & Knight LLP
Issues: GOV
Rep By: Hon. Gerald E. Sikorski

Manatt, Phelps & Phillips, LLP
Issues: BUD, CPI, DEF, GOV
Rep By: Stephen M. Ryan, Robb Watters

Unitarian Universalist Ass'n of Congregations

2026 P St. NW
Suite Three
Washington, DC 20036-6944
Tel: (202)296-4672
Fax: (202)296-4673
Web: www.uua.org
E-mail: uuawo@uua.org

A public policy and legislative advocacy office dealing with issue education and skill building on behalf of the association headquartered in Boston, MA.

Leg. Issues: CIV

In-house, DC-area Employees

CAVENAUGH, Rob: Legislative Director, Washington Office
RILEY, Rev. Meg A.: Director, Washington Office

Unitech Services Group, Inc.

Leg. Issues: ENG, ENV, WAS

Outside Counsel/Consultants

Morgan, Lewis & Bockius LLP
Issues: ENG, ENV, WAS
Rep By: John E. Daniel

United Airlines

1025 Connecticut Ave. NW
Suite 1210
Washington, DC 20036
Tel: (202)296-1950
Fax: (202)296-2873
Registered: LDA
Web: www.ual.com

Headquartered in Chicago, IL.

Leg. Issues: AVI, BUD, ENV, IMM, LBR, TAX, TOU, TRA, TRD

Political Action Committee/s

UAPAC
1025 Connecticut Ave. NW
Suite 1210
Washington, DC 20036
Tel: (202)296-1712
Fax: (202)296-2873
Contact: John Buscher

In-house, DC-area Employees

ANDERSON, Mark R.: Senior Director, Federal Affairs
BUSCHER, John: Director, Public Affairs, Eastern Region
CHIU, Sandra L.: Director, International Affairs
LONGMUIR, Shelley A.: Senior V. President, International, Regulatory, and Governmental Affairs
MORRISEY, Stephen J.: Director, Governmental Affairs
SOLOMON, Irica: Manager, Legislative Affairs

Outside Counsel/Consultants

Brand & Frulla, P.C.
Issues: AVI, LBR, TOU, TRA
Rep By: David E. Frulla, Andrew D. Herman

The Duberstein Group, Inc.
Issues: AVI, ENV, TAX
Rep By: John W. Angus, III, Michael S. Berman, Steven M. Champlin, Kenneth M. Duberstein, Henry M. Gandy, Daniel P. Meyer

Ann Eppard Associates, Ltd.
Issues: AVI, TRA
Rep By: Julie Chlopecki, Ann Eppard, Karen Schechter

Jack Ferguson Associates, Inc.
Issues: AVI, TRA
Rep By: Jack Ferguson

Heidepriem & Mager, Inc.
Issues: AVI
Rep By: Christopher Gould, Nikki Heidepriem, Mimi Mager

Holland & Knight LLP
Issues: AVI, BUD, TRA
Rep By: Richard M. Gold, Hon. Gerald E. Sikorski, Janet R. Studley, David C. Whitestone

Hooper Owen & Winburn
Rep By: David Rudd

The Ickes & Enright Group
Issues: AVI
Rep By: Janice Ann Enright, Harold M. Ickes

Michael E. Korens
Issues: AVI
Rep By: Michael E. Korens

Mayer, Brown & Platt
Issues: TRA, TRD
Rep By: Amb. Peter L. Scher

Patton Boggs, LLP
Issues: AVI, LBR
Rep By: Thomas Hale Boggs, Jr., Hon. Greg H. Laughlin, Jonathan R. Yarowsky

R. Duffy Wall and Associates

Wilmer, Cutler & Pickering

United Arab Emirates, Government of

Abu Dhabi, UNITED ARAB EMIRATES

Outside Counsel/Consultants

Verner, Liipfert, Bernhard, McPherson and Hand, Chartered

United Ass'n of Journeymen and Apprentices of the Plumbing and Pipe Fitting Industry of the U.S. and Canada

901 Massachusetts Ave. NW
Washington, DC 20001
Tel: (202)628-5823
Fax: (202)628-5024
Registered: LDA
Web: www.ua.org
Leg. Issues: LBR

Political Action Committee/s

United Ass'n Political Education Committee
901 Massachusetts Ave. NW
Washington, DC 20001
Tel: (202)628-5823
Fax: (202)628-5024
Contact: Luckie L. McClintock

In-house, DC-area Employees

GARDNER, C. Randal: Assistant General President
LAMM, William C.: (Local 602)
MADDALONI, Martin J.: General President
MCCLINTOCK, Luckie L.: Director, Political and Legislative Affairs
RHOTEN, William C.: Director, Department of Safety and Health

United Asset Management Corp.

Boston, MA
Leg. Issues: TAX

Outside Counsel/Consultants

Steptoe & Johnson LLP
Issues: TAX
Rep By: Mark J. Silverman

United Automobile, Aerospace and Agricultural Implement Workers of America (UAW)

1350 I St. NW
Suite 510
Washington, DC 20005
Tel: (202)828-8500
Fax: (202)293-3457
Registered: LDA

Leg. Issues: AER, AGR, AUT, BAN, BNK, BUD, CIV, COM, CON, CSP, DEF, EDU, FAM, GOV, HCR, HOU, IMM, LBR, MMM, RET, TAX, TRD, TRU, UNM, VET, WEL

Political Action Committee/s

United Automobile Workers PAC
1350 I St. NW
Suite 510
Washington, DC 20005
Tel: (202)828-8500
Fax: (202)293-3457
Contact: Alan V. Reuther

In-house, DC-area Employees

BECKMAN, Steve: Assistant Director, Governmental and International Affairs
CHRISTENSEN, John: International Representative
REUTHER, Alan V.: Legislative Director
ROULEAU, Mary: Deputy Legislative Director
SOMSON, Barbara: Deputy Legislative Director
STILLMAN, Don: Director, Government and International Affairs
TATE, Eula M.: Legislative Representative
YOKICH, Stephen P.: President

United Biscuit

Mt. Laurel, NJ
Leg. Issues: TRD

Outside Counsel/Consultants

Murray, Scheer, Montgomery, Tapia & O'Donnell
Issues: TRD
Rep By: Thomas R. Crawford, D. Michael Murray

United Brotherhood of Carpenters and Joiners of America

Web: www.necarpenters.org
Leg. Issues: LBR, NAT, RET, TAX, TRA, WAS

Outside Counsel/Consultants

Bond & Company, Inc.
Issues: LBR
Rep By: Richard N. Bond, Eileen Kean

Downey McGrath Group, Inc.
Issues: RET, TAX
Rep By: Nancy Donaldson, Hon. Thomas J. Downey, Jr., Hon. Raymond J. McGrath

United California Savings Bank

Anaheim, CA

Outside Counsel/Consultants

Dave Evans Associates
Rep By: Hon. Dave Evans

United Catcher Boats

Seattle, WA
Leg. Issues: MAR

Outside Counsel/Consultants

Sher & Blackwell
Issues: MAR
Rep By: Earl W. Comstock, Jeffrey R. Pike

United Cement Corp.

Carefree, AZ

Outside Counsel/Consultants

Dunlap & Browder, Inc.
Rep By: Joseph B. Browder, Louise C. Dunlap

United Cerebral Palsy Ass'n

1660 L St. NW
Suite 700
Washington, DC 20036
Tel: (202)776-0406
Fax: (202)776-0414
Registered: LDA
Web: www.ucp.org
E-mail: ucpnatl@ucp.org

Seeks to improve the quality of life for persons with cerebral palsy and related disabilities and their families.

Leg. Issues: BUD, EDU, GOV, INS, MMM, TEC, UNM, WEL

In-house, DC-area Employees

COOK, Michelle: Policy Legal Counsel

United Church of Christ Justice and Witness Ministry

110 Maryland Ave. NE
Suite 207
Washington, DC 20002
Tel: (202)543-1517
Fax: (202)543-5994
Web: www.ucc.org

Committed to empowering efforts to shape public policy based on the values of the church. The OCIS Washington office provides leadership, resources, and organizing strategies for United Church of Christ members engaged in legislative advocacy. Headquartered in Cleveland, OH.

Leg. Issues: CIV, FAM, GAM, HOU, WEL

In-house, DC-area Employees

CONOVER, Rev. Patrick: Legislative Director
SORENSEN, Sandra: Associate, Communications & Media Advocacy
STIEF, Rev. Ron: Director

United Cities Gas Co.

Brentwood, TN

Outside Counsel/Consultants

Crowell & Moring LLP
Rep By: Harold J. Heltzer

United Companies Financial Corp.

Baton Rouge, LA

Outside Counsel/Consultants

Long Law Firm
Rep By: C. Kris Kirkpatrick

United Concordia Companies, Inc.

Harrisburg, PA
Leg. Issues: DEF, HCR, INS

Outside Counsel/Consultants

Astra Solutions, LLC
Issues: DEF, HCR, INS
Rep By: Donna L. Hoffmeier

United Dairy Industry Ass'n

Rosemont, IL

Outside Counsel/Consultants

McLeod, Watkinson & Miller
Rep By: Wayne R. Watkinson

United Defense, L.P.

1525 Wilson Blvd.
Suite 700
Arlington, VA 22209
Tel: (703)312-6100
Fax: (703)312-6196
Registered: LDA

A manufacturer of armored combat vehicles and weapons delivery systems for American and allied armed forces.

Leg. Issues: BUD, DEF, FOR, GOV, TRD

Political Action Committee/s

United Defense Employees PAC
1525 Wilson Blvd.
Suite 700
Arlington, VA 22209
Contact: John A. Mullett
Tel: (703)312-6100
Fax: (703)312-6196

In-house, DC-area Employees

MULLETT, John A.: V. President, Government Affairs
RABAUT, Thomas W.: President and Chief Exec. Offficer
WAGNER, Dennis A.: V. President, Business Development and Domestic Marketing

Outside Counsel/Consultants

Ervin Technical Associates, Inc. (ETA)
Issues: DEF
Rep By: William J. Andahazy, Hon. Jack Edwards, James L. Ervin, Donald E. Richbourg

Martin, Fisher & Associates, Inc.
Issues: BUD, DEF
Rep By: J. Paris Fisher, David O'B. Martin

Mayer, Brown & Platt
Issues: DEF
Rep By: Mark H. Gitenstein, Miriam R. Nemetz, Carolyn P. Osolinik

Patton Boggs, LLP
Rep By: Katharine R. Boyce, John J. Deschauer, Jr.

Robison Internat'l, Inc.
Issues: BUD, DEF
Rep By: Sandra A. Gilbert, Richard B. Ladd

Ungaretti & Harris
Issues: GOV
Rep By: Sheri Bucher, Joseph A. Cari, Jr., Page Faulk, Chuck Konigsberg

The Van Fleet-Meredith Group
Issues: DEF
Rep By: M. Bruce Meredith, Paul F. Payette, Townsend A. Van Fleet

Verner, Liipfert, Bernhard, McPherson and Hand, Chartered
Issues: DEF
Rep By: Hon. Daniel R. Coats, Michael E. O'Brien, Steven R. Phillips

Wilmer, Cutler & Pickering
Issues: DEF, FOR, TRD
Rep By: Leonard M. Shambon

United Development Corp.

Columbia, SC

Outside Counsel/Consultants

McDermott, Will and Emery

United Distribution Cos.

New York, NY
Leg. Issues: BUD, CSP

Outside Counsel/Consultants

Markey and Associates
Issues: BUD, CSP
Rep By: Patricia E. Markey

United Egg Ass'n

Decatur, GA

Trade association of manufacturers of egg products (liquid, dry and frozen) for use in further processed products.

Leg. Issues: AGR, BUD, CAW, FOO, MAN, TRD, WEL

Outside Counsel/Consultants

McLeod, Watkinson & Miller
Issues: AGR, BUD, CAW, FOO, MAN, TRD, WEL
Rep By: Robert R. Green, Michael R. McLeod, Laura L. Phelps

United Egg Producers

Atlanta, GA

The largest federation of regional cooperatives in the egg industry.

Leg. Issues: AGR, BUD, CAW, FOO, MAN, TRD, WEL

Outside Counsel/Consultants

Capitolink, LLC
Issues: AGR, CAW
Rep By: John H. Thorne, Ph.D.

McLeod, Watkinson & Miller
Issues: AGR, BUD, CAW, FOO, MAN, TRD, WEL
Rep By: Robert R. Green, Michael R. McLeod, Laura L. Phelps

United Electrical Workers of America

1800 Diagonal Rd.
Suite 600
Alexandria, VA 22314
Tel: (703)684-3123
Fax: (703)519-8982
Registered: LDA
Web: www.ranknfile-ue.org
Leg. Issues: LBR

In-house, DC-area Employees

TOWNSEND, Chris: Political Director

United Fidelity Life Insurance

Kansas City, MO

Outside Counsel/Consultants

Baker & Hostetler LLP

United Food and Commercial Workers Internat'l Union

1775 K St. NW
Washington, DC 20006
Tel: (202)223-3111
Fax: (202)466-1562
Registered: LDA
Web: www.ufcw.org
Leg. Issues: AGR, APP, BUD, CSP, FOO, GOV, HCR, IMM, LBR, UNM

Political Action Committee/s

Active Ballot Club
1775 K St. NW
Washington, DC 20006
Contact: Joseph T. Hansen
Tel: (202)223-3111
Fax: (202)466-1562

In-house, DC-area Employees

DENIER, Greg: Assistant to the President
DORITY, Douglas H.: International President
DUNPHY, David: Assistant to the Director, Legislative and Political Affairs
FUNK, Robert E.: General Counsel
HANSEN, Joseph T.: International Secretary and Treasurer
HAROLD-FOSTER, Toni: Lobbyist
SCARCELLI, Pat: Director, Legislative and Political Affairs
WILSON, Michael J.: Chief Lobbyist

United Fresh Fruit and Vegetable Ass'n

727 N. Washington St.
Alexandria, VA 22314
Tel: (703)836-3410
Fax: (703)836-2049
Registered: LDA
Web: www.uffva.org
E-mail: united@uffva.org
Leg. Issues: AGR, BUD, ENV, FOO, HCR, LBR, TAX, TRD, WEL

Political Action Committee/s

FreshPAC
727 N. Washington St.
Alexandria, VA 22314
Contact: Diane L. Cullo
Tel: (703)836-3410
Fax: (703)836-2049

In-house, DC-area Employees

CULLO, Diane L.: Director of Public Affairs and Communications; PAC Contact
GUENTHER, Robert L.: V. President, Government Public Affairs
STENZEL, Thomas E.: President and C.E.O.

Outside Counsel/Consultants

Olsson, Frank and Weeda, P.C.
Issues: AGR, BUD, FOO
Rep By: John W. Bode, David L. Durkin, Susan P. Grymes, Karen Reis Harned, Stephen L. Lacey, Marshall L. Matz, Michael J. O'Flaherty, Tyson Redpath, Ryan W. Stroschein

United Gamefowl Breeders Ass'n, Inc.

Danville, OH
Leg. Issues: AGR

Outside Counsel/Consultants

Johnston & Associates, LLC
Issues: AGR
Rep By: Hon. J. Bennett Johnston, Eric Tober

Meyers & Associates

United Health Group

1225 New York Ave. NW
Suite 475
Washington, DC 20005
Tel: (202)371-1303
Fax: (202)371-5569
Registered: LDA

Headquartered in Minnetonka, MN.

Leg. Issues: HCR, MMM

Political Action Committee/s

United Health PAC
1225 New York Ave. NW
Suite 475
Washington, DC 20005
Contact: Manuela Boehm
Tel: (202)371-1303
Fax: (202)371-5569

In-house, DC-area Employees

BOEHM, Manuela: PAC Contact
GEMEINHARDT, Elise A.: V. President, Federal Affairs

Outside Counsel/Consultants

Barbour Griffith & Rogers, Inc.
Issues: HCR, MMM
Rep By: Haley Barbour, G. O. Lanny Griffith, Jr., Loren Monroe

Verner, Liipfert, Bernhard, McPherson and Hand, Chartered
Issues: HCR, MMM
Rep By: John A. Merrigan

United Healthcare

Minnetonka, MN
Leg. Issues: HCR

Outside Counsel/Consultants

Greenberg Traurig, LLP
Issues: HCR
Rep By: James F. Miller

United Hellenic American Congress

Chicago, IL
Registered: LDA
Leg. Issues: BUD, DEF, FOR

Outside Counsel/Consultants

Manatos & Manatos, Inc.
Issues: BUD, DEF, FOR
Rep By: Andrew E. Manatos, Mike A. Manatos

United Homeowners Ass'n

655 15th St. NW
Suite 460
Washington, DC 20005
Tel: (202)408-8842
Fax: (202)408-8156
Web: www.uha.org
E-mail: aclark@uha.org

A national, non-profit homeowners association created to promote and preserve homeownership and to represent the interests of America's 65 million homeowners. Provides consumer advice, newsletters and discounts on products and services.

In-house, DC-area Employees

CLARK, Jordan: President

Outside Counsel/Consultants

J. C. Luman and Assoc.

United Jewish Communities, Inc.

1700 K St. NW
Suite 1150
Washington, DC 20006
Tel: (202)785-5900
Fax: (202)785-4937
Registered: LDA
Web: www.ujcdc.org

Assists 200 Jewish federations to keep informed of federal programs and to apply for and obtain appropriate federal assistance for their programs.

Leg. Issues: IMM, TAX

In-house, DC-area Employees

AVIV, Diana: V. President, Public Policy and Director, Human Services and Social Policy
DROGOSZ, Kayla: Public Affairs Associate
GOLDBERG, Robert: Senior Legislative Associate

GREENBERG, Frankee: Deputy Director, Human Services and Social Policy Pillar
HAILPERN, Nancy: Director, Washington Mission Programs
KLINE, Stephan: Director, Legislative Affairs
KRAVETZ, Lauri: Legislative Assistant
KREMSNER, Sarah: Legislative Assistant
MARKOWITZ, Jennie: Legislative Assistant
MILLER, Yvette A.: Director, Public and Community Affairs

Outside Counsel/Consultants

Baker & Hostetler LLP
Issues: TAX
Rep By: Edward J. Beckwith, Matthew J. Dolan

The DCS Group

Witman Associates
Issues: IMM
Rep By: Ellen G. Witman

United Kingdom, Government of

London, UNITED KINGDOM

Outside Counsel/Consultants

Holland & Knight LLP

Morgan, Lewis & Bockius LLP

United Lao Congress for Democracy

Menomie, WI
Leg. Issues: DEF, FOR, TRD, VET

Outside Counsel/Consultants

Philip S. Smith & Associates, Inc.
Issues: DEF, FOR, TRD, VET
Rep By: Philip S. Smith

United Methodist Church General Board of Church and Society

100 Maryland Ave. NE
Suite 300
Washington, DC 20002
Web: www.umc-gbcs.org
E-mail: gbcs@umc-gbcs.org
Tel: (202)488-5600
Fax: (202)488-5619

The international public policy program board of the United Methodist Church.

Leg. Issues: AGR, ALC, ANI, APP, ART, AUT, BAN, BUD, CAW, CHM, CIV, COM, CON, CSP, DEF, DOC, ECN, EDU, ENG, ENV, FAM, FIR, FOO, FOR, FUE, GAM, GOV, HCR, HOU, IMM, IND, LAW, LBR, MAN, MED, MMM, NAT, RET, SCI, TOB, TRD, UNM, URB, WAS, WEL

In-house, DC-area Employees

WINKLER, James: General Secretary

United Mine Workers of America

8315 Lee Hwy.
Fairfax, VA 22031
Tel: (703)208-7200
Fax: (703)208-7132
Registered: LDA
Web: www.umwa.org
E-mail: general@umwa.org
Leg. Issues: CAW, ENV, HCR, LBR

Political Action Committee/s

Coal Miners Political Action Committee
8315 Lee Hwy.
Fairfax, VA 22031
Tel: (703)208-7200
Fax: (703)208-7132
Contact: Bill Banig

In-house, DC-area Employees

BANIG, Bill: Director, Government Affairs
BUCKNER, Michael W.: Research Director
CRANDALL, Grant: General Counsel
JONES, Jerry D.: V. President
ROBERTS, Cecil E.: President
TARLEY, Carlo: Secretary-Treasurer

Outside Counsel/Consultants

McGlotten & Jarvis
Issues: ENV, HCR
Rep By: John T. Jarvis

United Motorcoach Ass'n

113 S. West St.
Fourth Floor
Alexandria, VA 22314
Web: www.uma.org
E-mail: info@uma.org
Tel: (703)838-2929
Fax: (703)838-2950

A trade association established in 1971 representing over 800 bus companies in the United States.

Leg. Issues: AUT, CAW, ENV, MAN, ROD, SMB, TAX, TOU, TRA

In-house, DC-area Employees

LITTLER, Charles N.
PARRA, Victor S.
SPRAGUE, Stephen G.: Chief Operating Officer

Outside Counsel/Consultants

The Argus Group, L.L.C.
Issues: TAX, TOU
Rep By: David R. Burton, Dan R. Mastromarco

United Nations Ass'n of the U.S.A.

1779 Massachusetts Ave. NW
Suite 610
Washington, DC 20036
Web: www.unausa.org
Tel: (202)462-3446
Registered: LDA
Leg. Issues: FOR

In-house, DC-area Employees

DIMOFF, Steven A.: V. President, Washington Office
LUERS, William H.: Chairman and President

United Nations Development Programme

Outside Counsel/Consultants

Valente Lopatin & Schulze
Rep By: Alan G. Lopatin, Richard T. Schulze, Jr., Mark Valente, III

United Negro College Fund, Inc.

1444 I St. NW
Suite 500
Washington, DC 20005
Web: www.uncf.ocr
Tel: (202)737-8631
Fax: (202)737-8651
Registered: LDA

Provides access to higher education headquartered in Fairfax, VA.

Leg. Issues: BUD, EDU

In-house, DC-area Employees

ATKINSON, Leslie: Director, Government Affairs

Outside Counsel/Consultants

Dean Blakey & Moskowitz
Issues: BUD, EDU
Rep By: William A. Blakey

United Network for Organ Sharing

Richmond, VA
Leg. Issues: BUD, HCR

Outside Counsel/Consultants

BKSH & Associates
Issues: BUD, HCR

United Pan-Europe Communications, NV

Amsterdam, NETHERLANDS
Leg. Issues: COM, FOR, TEC, TRD

Outside Counsel/Consultants

New Frontiers Communications Consulting
Issues: COM, FOR, TEC, TRD
Rep By: R. David Wilson

Ryan, Phillips, Utrecht & MacKinnon
Issues: TEC
Rep By: Rodney Hoppe, Jeffrey M. MacKinnon, William D. Phillips, Mark D. Planning, Thomas M. Ryan, Joseph V. Vasapoli

Verner, Liipfert, Bernhard, McPherson and Hand, Chartered
Issues: FOR, TEC, TRD
Rep By: Steven R. Phillips

United Parcel Service

316 Pennsylvania Ave. SE
Suite 300
Washington, DC 20003
Web: www.ups.com
Tel: (202)675-4220
Fax: (202)675-4230
Registered: LDA
Leg. Issues: AVI, BUD, CAW, ENG, ENV, FIN, HCR, INS, LBR, POS, RRR, TAX, TEC, TRA, TRD, TRU, WAS

In-house, DC-area Employees

BERGMAN, Bob: V. President, Public Affairs
CHURCHILL, Kenneth: V. President, Public Affairs
DUBOIS, Marcel: Manager, Public Affairs
ENVALL, Kirsten: Manager, Public Affairs
FOSTER, Ron: V. President, Public Affairs
JACKSON, Selina: Manager, Public Affairs
LEWIS, Nicholas: Manager, Public Affairs
OKUN, Steven R.: Manager, Public Affairs
SEGAL, Tad: Director, Public Relations
SHELBY, Sheryl W.: Manager, Public Affairs
WASHINGTON, Sheryl Webber: V. President, Public Affairs
WELLMAN, Jr., Arnold F.: Corporate V. President, Domestic/Internat'l Public Affairs
WINTERS, Harry M.: V. President, Public Affairs

Outside Counsel/Consultants

Arter & Hadden

Bradley Arant Rose & White LLP
Issues: TAX

Collier Shannon Scott, PLLC

Earle Palmer Brown Public Relations
Issues: POS, TRU

Federal Access
Issues: AVI, POS
Rep By: Timothy R. Cole

Hogan & Hartson L.L.P.
Issues: TRD
Rep By: Jeanne S. Archibald, Raymond S. Calamaro, Philip Larson

Dawson Mathis & Associates
Issues: POS, TAX
Rep By: Hon. M. Dawson Mathis

Mayer, Brown & Platt
Issues: TRA, TRD
Rep By: Amb. Peter L. Scher

The OB-C Group, LLC
Issues: LBR, POS, TRD
Rep By: Thomas Keating, Kim F. McKernan, Charles J. Mellody, Patricia A. Nelson, Lawrence F. O'Brien, III, Linda E. Tarplin

Bartley M. O'Hara
Issues: POS, RRR, TAX, TRA
Rep By: Bartley M. O'Hara

Policy Consulting Services
Issues: CAW, ENG, FIN, POS
Rep By: Paul C. Smith

PriceWaterhouseCoopers
Issues: TAX
Rep By: Barbara Angus, Jim Carlisle, Kenneth J. Kies, Pat Raffaniello

Ross & Hardies
Issues: TRD

Wayne Schley
Issues: POS
Rep By: Wayne Schley

Widmeyer Communications, Inc.

Wiley, Rein & Fielding
Rep By: Fred F. Fielding

United Payors and United Providers

Rockville, MD
Leg. Issues: HCR

Outside Counsel/Consultants

MV3 & Associates

Valente Lopatin & Schulze
Issues: HCR
Rep By: Alan G. Lopatin, Richard T. Schulze, Jr., Mark Valente, III

United Pilots Political Action Committee

Chicago, IL

Outside Counsel/Consultants

Committee Management Associates
Rep By: Michael de Blois

United Seniors Ass'n

3900 Jermantown Rd.
Suite 450
Fairfax, VA 22030
Web: www.unitedseniors.org
E-mail: usa@unitedseniors.org
Tel: (703)359-6500
Fax: (703)359-6510
Registered: LDA

The United Seniors Ass'n is composed of over 680,000 members nationwide and is the leading conservative seniors organization dedicated to ensuring the retirement security of all Americans.

Leg. Issues: BUD, GOV, HCR, MMM, RET, TAX

In-house, DC-area Employees

BOULTER, Hon. Beau: Legislative Counsel
JARVIS, Charles W.: President
MAHONEY, Mary: Director, Government Relations

Outside Counsel/Consultants

Beau Boulter
Rep By: Hon. Beau Boulter

The Carmen Group
Issues: GOV
Rep By: David A. Keene

United Service Organization

Washington, DC
Leg. Issues: BUD, DEF

Outside Counsel/Consultants

Cassidy & Associates, Inc.
Issues: BUD, DEF
Rep By: Shawn Edwards, Lawrence C. Grossman, Dennis M. Kedzior, Arthur D. Mason, Brig. Gen. Terry Paul, USMC (Ret.), Hon. Martin A. Russo, Dan C. Tate, Sr.

United Soybean Board

Creve Coeur, MO

Outside Counsel/Consultants

The Eddie Mahe Company

McLeod, Watkinson & Miller
Rep By: Wayne R. Watkinson

United Space Alliance

Houston, TX
Leg. Issues: AER

Outside Counsel/Consultants

Cassidy & Associates, Inc.
Issues: AER
Rep By: Laurie J. Adler, Jeffrey Lawrence, Arthur D. Mason, Brig. Gen. Terry Paul, USMC (Ret.), Marnie Russ, Hon. Martin A. Russo

R. V. Davis and Associates
Issues: AER
Rep By: J. William Foster

Rhoads Group

United Special Transport Air Resources, LLC (USTAR)

Leg. Issues: AVI, DEF, TRA

Outside Counsel/Consultants

Jones, Walker, Waechter, Poitevent, Carrere & Denegre, L.L.P.
Issues: AVI, DEF, TRA
Rep By: Paul Cambon, John J. Jaskot, R. Christian Johnsen

United States Air Tour Ass'n

4041 Powder Mill Rd.
Suite 201
Calverton, MD 20705
Tel: (301)931-8770
Fax: (301)931-8774
Registered: LDA
Web: www.usata.com
E-mail: stevebassett@usata.com
Leg. Issues: TOU

In-house, DC-area Employees

BASSETT, Steve: President

Outside Counsel/Consultants

Santini, Chartered
Issues: TOU
Rep By: Hon. James D. Santini

United States Beet Sugar Ass'n

1156 15th St. NW
Suite 1019
Washington, DC 20005
Tel: (202)296-4820
Registered: LDA
Leg. Issues: AGR, TRD

Political Action Committee/s

Beet Sugar Political Action Committee
1156 15th St. NW
Suite 1019
Washington, DC 20005
Tel: (202)296-4820
Contact: Desiree Franklin

In-house, DC-area Employees

FRANKLIN, Desiree: PAC Contact
JOHNSON, Jr., James W. M.: President

Outside Counsel/Consultants

Ablondi, Foster, Sobin & Davidow, P.C.
Rep By: F. David Foster

Howrey Simon Arnold & White
Rep By: John F. Bruce

United States Business and Industry Council

910 16th St. NW
Suite 300
Washington, DC 20006
Tel: (202)728-1980
Fax: (202)728-1981
Registered: LDA
Web: www.usbusiness.org
E-mail: council@usbusiness.org

Supported by 1500 conservative business leaders. Priority issues are economic growth, smaller government, a national interest trade policy, deficit reduction through non-defense spending restraint, regulatory reform and a high standard of living for all Americans.

Leg. Issues: AGR, APP, AUT, BUD, CAW, CIV, CPT, DEF, ECN, ENV, FOR, GOV, HCR, IMM, INS, LBR, MAN, RES, SMB, TAX, TRD

In-house, DC-area Employees

KEARNS, Kevin L.: President
WALTON CROUCH, Laura: V. President

United States Cane Sugar Refiners' Ass'n

1730 Rhode Island Ave. NW
Suite 608
Washington, DC 20036
Tel: (202)331-1458
Fax: (202)785-5110
Registered: LDA
E-mail: uscsra@worldnet.att.net
Leg. Issues: AGR, TRD

In-house, DC-area Employees

KOMINUS, Nicholas: President

Outside Counsel/Consultants

Edington, Peel & Associates, Inc.
Rep By: William H. Edington

The Potomac Research Group LLC
Issues: AGR, TRD
Rep By: G. Harris Jordan, Paul Welles Orr

United States Catholic Conference

3211 Fourth St. NE
Washington, DC 20017
Tel: (202)541-3000
Fax: (202)541-3322
Web: www.nccbuscc.org

In-house, DC-area Employees

CANAN, G. Patrick: Associate Director, Government Liaison
CARR, John: Secretary, Social Development and World Peace
CHOPKO, Mark E.: General Counsel
DAVIS, Rev. William F.: Assistant Secretary, Catholic Schools and Public Policy
FAY, Msgr. William: General Secretary
FRANKEN, Mark: Exec. Director, Migration and Refugee Services
GALLAGHER, Mark J.: Associate Director, Government Liaison
HALLORAN, Deirdre: Associate General Counsel
HILL, Micheal: Associate Director, Government Liaison
LIEKWEG, John A.: Associate General Counsel
MANISCALCO, Msgr. Francis J.: Director, Communications
MONAHAN, Frank: Director, Office of Government Liaison

Outside Counsel/Consultants

Williams & Connolly

United States Catholic Office of Bishops/Secretariat for Hispanic Affairs

3211 Fourth St. NE
Washington, DC 20017
Tel: (202)541-3150
Fax: (202)722-8717

Established in 1945 to represent the interests of Catholic Hispanics.

In-house, DC-area Employees

CRUZ, Ronaldo: Director

United States Cellular Corp.

Chicago, IL

Outside Counsel/Consultants

Sidley & Austin
Rep By: Michael A. Nemeroff

United States Coast Guard Chief Petty Officers Ass'n

5520 G Hempstead Way
Springfield, VA 22151
Tel: (703)941-0395
Fax: (703)941-0397
E-mail: cgcpoa@aol.com
Leg. Issues: BUD, DEF, EDU, FAM, GOV, HCR, MMM, PHA, POS, RET, TAX, VET

In-house, DC-area Employees

SCARAMASTRO, T. R.: Exec. Director

United States Committee for Refugees

1717 Massachusetts Ave. NW
Suite 200
Washington, DC 20036
Tel: (202)347-3507
Fax: (202)347-3418
Registered: LDA
Web: www.irsa_uscr.org

A public information and advocacy program of the Immigration and Refugee Service of America. Established in 1958; encourages the American public to participate actively in efforts to assist the world's refugees.

In-house, DC-area Employees

DRUMTRA, Jeff: Africa Policy Analyst
FRELICK, Bill: Director, Policy
RUIZ, Hiram A.: Senior Policy Analyst
WINTER, Roger: Exec. Director

United States Conference of Mayors

1620 I St. NW
Suite 400
Washington, DC 20006
Tel: (202)293-7330
Fax: (202)293-2352
Web: www.usmayors.org

A non-partisan national organization of city governments established in 1933 as a national forum through which the country's larger cities express their concerns and work to meet the needs of urban America. Members are mayors of cities with populations over 30,000.

Leg. Issues: URB

In-house, DC-area Employees

COCHRAN, J. Thomas: Exec. Director
MCCARTY, Kevin: Assistant Exec. Director
SOMERS, Edward: Assistant Exec. Director

Outside Counsel/Consultants

Baker & Hostetler LLP
Issues: URB

United States Council for Internat'l Business

1030 15th St. NW
Suite 800
Washington, DC 20005
Tel: (202)371-1316
Fax: (202)371-8249
E-mail: scanner@uscib-dc.org

Established in 1945 with headquarters in New York City, the Council represents the interests and expresses the positions of U.S. business on a broad range of international trade, finance and investment related issues. Advocates advantages of private enterprise and a free market economy. Members are corporations, associations and law and consulting firms interested in international trade. Represents U.S. business in Washington; and, as the organization that consults with the major intergovernmental bodies influencing international business, in the Business and Industry Advisory Committee to the OECD, in the ILO as the U.S. member of the International Organization of Employers, and as a member of the International Chamber of Commerce, it consults with various U.N. agencies.

In-house, DC-area Employees

CANNER, Stephen: V. President, Investment Policy
DEAL, Timothy: Senior V. President, Washington Office
FOTI, Suzanne: Manager, Biotechnology and Agriculture
GAVIN, III, Joseph G.: V. President, Trade Policy

Outside Counsel/Consultants

McGuiness Norris & Williams, LLP
Rep By: Edward E. Potter

United States Education Finance Corp.

Miami, FL
Leg. Issues: EDU

Outside Counsel/Consultants

The MWW Group
Issues: EDU
Rep By: Tracey Becker, Dana P. Bostic, Davon Gray, Christine A. Pellerin, Jonathan B. Slade

United States Energy Ass'n

1300 Pennsylvania Ave. NW
Suite 550
Mailbox 142
Washington, DC 20004-3022
Tel: (202)312-1230
Fax: (202)682-1682
Web: www.usea.org

Seeks to develop and promote sound, objective policy positions on energy issues, drawing on the views of all sectors of the energy community and presenting findings and conclusions to the federal government, the media and the public.

Leg. Issues: ENG, ENV, FOR, FUE, NAT, SCI, UTI

In-house, DC-area Employees

WORTHINGTON, Barry K.: Exec. Director

United States Enrichment Corp.

Bethesda, MD
Leg. Issues: ENG, TRD

Outside Counsel/Consultants

Patton Boggs, LLP
Issues: TRD
Rep By: Thomas P. O'Donnell, James A. Reeder, Frank R. Samolis

Rhoads Group
Issues: ENG
Rep By: Paul D. Behrends, Kathleen Ireland, Steven G. McKnight, Clifford R. Northup, Barry D. Rhoads, Elizabeth R. Sharpstene, Thomas Worrall

United States Marine Repair

Norfolk, VA
Leg. Issues: BUD, DEF

Outside Counsel/Consultants

Washington Resource Associates
Issues: BUD, DEF
Rep By: Christopher T. Long

United States Maritime Coalition

Leg. Issues: MAR

Outside Counsel/Consultants

Preston Gates Ellis & Rouvelas Meeds LLP
Issues: MAR
Rep By: Werner W. Brandt, Darrell Conner, Pamela J. Garvie, Susan B. Geiger, Bruce J. Heiman, John L. Longstreth, Rolf Marshall, Hon. Lloyd Meeds, Sol Mosher, William N. Myhre, Tim L. Peckinpaugh, Daniel Ritter, Emanuel L. Rouvelas, Mark H. Ruge, W. Dennis Stephens

United States Nat'l Committee for Pacific Economic Cooperation

1819 L St. NW
Second Floor
Washington, DC 20036
Web: www.pecc.org
E-mail: uspecc@pecc.org
Tel: (202)293-3995
Fax: (202)293-1402

Established in 1984 by Secretary of State George Shultz. Comprised of senior U.S. business, government and education leaders who advise the government on U.S.-Pacific Basin economic issues. Acts as an official observer to APEC.

In-house, DC-area Employees

BORTHWICK, Mark: Exec. Director

United States Navy Memorial Foundation

701 Pennsylvania Ave. NW
Suite 123
Washington, DC 20004
Web: www.lonesailor.org
E-mail: ahoy@lonesailor.org
Tel: (202)737-2300
Fax: (202)737-2308

In-house, DC-area Employees

MCKINNEY, USN (Ret.), Rear Adm. Henry C.: President and Chief Exec. Officer

United States Pan Asian American Chamber of Commerce

1329 18th St. NW
Washington, DC 20036
Web: www.uspaacc.org
E-mail: uspaacc@his.com
Tel: (202)296-5221
Fax: (202)296-5225

A national non-profit organization representing Asian American and other businesses and professionals. Provides members with a wide variety of educational, information and advocacy programs.

In-house, DC-area Employees

ALLEN, Susan Au: President

United States Parachute Ass'n

1440 Duke St.
Alexandria, VA 22314
Web: www.uspa.org
E-mail: uspa@uspa.org
Tel: (703)836-3495
Fax: (703)836-2843
Registered: LDA

A not-for-profit membership association dedicated to the promotion of safe skydiving and the support of those who enjoy it.

Leg. Issues: AVI, SPO

In-house, DC-area Employees

BAGLEY, Larry K.: Deputy Exec. Director
NEEDELS, Christopher: Exec. Director
SCOTT, Edward M.: Director, Government Affairs and Group Membership

United States Pharmacopeia

1261 Twinbrook Pkwy.
Rockville, MD 20852
Web: www.usp.org
Tel: (301)881-0666
Fax: (301)816-8148
Leg. Issues: MED

In-house, DC-area Employees

BORDEN, Sherrie: Director, Professional and Public Affairs

Outside Counsel/Consultants

Zuckerman Spaeder L.L.P.
Issues: MED
Rep By: Charles Angulo, Ronald H. Weich

United States Pharmacopeial Convention

12601 Twinbrook Pkwy.
Rockville, MD 20852
Web: www.usp.org
Tel: (301)881-0666

A not-for-profit, volunteer-based, private organization that establishes legally-recognized standards of identity, quality, strength, purity, packaging, and labeling of medicines and other health care technologies, and develops authoritative information for their appropriate use.

In-house, DC-area Employees

VALENTINO, Dr. Joseph G.: Senior V. President, Secretary, and General Counsel
WILLIAMS, Roger L.: Exec. V. President

United States Student Ass'n

1413 K St. NW
Tenth Floor
Washington, DC 20005
Web: www.essential.org/ussa
E-mail: ussa@essential.org
Tel: (202)347-8772
Fax: (202)393-5886
Registered: LDA

The largest student membership organization in the country. Priority concerns include creation of a quality, universally accessible system of higher education, protection of civil and constitutional rights, and the development of statewide coalitions and local student organizations.

Leg. Issues: CIV, EDU

In-house, DC-area Employees

BARBOUR, Corye: Legislative Director
BEATTY, Julia: V. President
FISCHER, Alison: President

United States Sugar Corp.

Clewiston, FL
Leg. Issues: AGR, BUD, CAW, NAT, RES

Outside Counsel/Consultants

Davis & Harman LLP
Issues: AGR
Rep By: Thomas A. Davis

Hogan & Hartson L.L.P.
Issues: AGR
Rep By: Humberto R. Pena

Hunton & Williams
Issues: BUD, CAW, NAT, RES
Rep By: Virginia S. Albrecht

United States Telecom Ass'n

1401 H St. NW
Suite 600
Washington, DC 20005-2136
Web: www.usta.org
Tel: (202)326-7300
Fax: (202)326-7333
Registered: LDA
Leg. Issues: CAW, COM, CPI, CPT, GOV, HCR, LAW, TAX, TEC

Political Action Committee/s

United States Telephone Political Action Committee
1401 H St. NW
Suite 600
Washington, DC 20005-2136
Tel: (202)326-7300
Fax: (202)326-7333

In-house, DC-area Employees

BATES, William C.: Director, Government Relations
BOLGER, David A.: V. President, Communications
BROWN, Dale: V. President, Mid-Sized Companies
CARPENTER, Elaine: Chief of Staff
CLINTON, Larry: V. President, Large Company Affairs
COHEN, David B.: V. President, Small Company Affairs
DUNKEL, Bob: Director, Government Relations
GREEN, Paul: V. President, Development and Marketing
HAHN, Mary: V. President, Administration
KENT, Linda: Associate General Counsel
LYTLE, Gary R.: Interim President and Chief Exec. Officer
RUBIN, Michael: V. President, Government Relations
SARJEANT, Larry: V. President, Legal and Regulatory Affairs
ZIEGLER, Alyson: Director, Legislative Affairs and Counsel

Outside Counsel/Consultants

Dewey Ballantine LLP
Issues: TAX
Rep By: Joseph K. Dowley

Hall, Green, Rupli, LLC
Issues: TEC
Rep By: John M. Green, G. Stewart Hall

Public Strategies, Inc.
Rep By: Wallace J. Henderson

Tongour Simpson Holsclaw Green
Issues: TEC
Rep By: Michael A. Tongour

Wunder & Lilley
Issues: COM, CPI, GOV, TAX, TEC
Rep By: Bernard J. Wunder, Jr.

United States Tuna Foundation

1101 17th St. NW
Suite 609
Washington, DC 20036
Tel: (202)857-0610
Fax: (202)331-9686
Registered: LDA

The trade association of the U.S. tuna fishing industry. Headquartered in San Diego, CA.

Leg. Issues: FOO, MAR, NAT

In-house, DC-area Employees

BURNEY, David G.: Exec. Director
THOMAS, Randi: National Representative

Outside Counsel/Consultants

Diane McRee Associates
Issues: MAR
Rep By: Diane B. McRee

United States Windpower, Inc.

Livermore, CA

Outside Counsel/Consultants

Edwin T. C. Ing
Rep By: Edwin T. C. Ing

United States-China Chamber of Commerce

St. Louis, MO

Outside Counsel/Consultants

White & Case LLP

United States-Mexico Chamber of Commerce

1300 Pennsylvania Ave. NW
Suite 270
Ronald Reagan Internat'l Trade Bldg.
Washington, DC 20004-3021
Web: www.usmcoc.org
Tel: (202)371-8680
Fax: (202)371-8686

In-house, DC-area Employees

ZAPANTA, Albert C.: President

The United States-New Zealand Council

1801 F St. NW
Washington, DC 20006
Web: www.usnzcouncil.org
E-mail: info@usnzcouncil.org
Tel: (202)842-0772
Fax: (202)842-0749

Fosters business, political and cultural relations between the U.S. and New Zealand.

In-house, DC-area Employees

KANE, Kevin: Exec. Director

United Steelworkers of America

1150 17th St. NW
Suite 300
Washington, DC 20036
Web: www.usofa.org
Tel: (202)778-4384
Fax: (202)293-5308
Registered: LDA
Leg. Issues: CSP, ECN, ENG, GOV, HCR, INS, LBR, NAT, TAX, TRD

Political Action Committee/s

United Steelworkers of America PAC
1150 17th St. NW
Suite 300
Washington, DC 20036
Contact: William J. Klinefelter
Tel: (202)778-4384
Fax: (202)293-5308

In-house, DC-area Employees

FRANCISCO, Stephen R.: Legislative Representative
GERARD, Leo: President
HUBBARD, Gary L.: Director, Public Affairs
KLINEFELTER, William J.: Legislative and Political Director

Outside Counsel/Consultants

Downey McGrath Group, Inc.
Issues: ECN, LBR, TRD
Rep By: Michael R. Wessel

United Student Aid Group

Indianapolis, IN

Outside Counsel/Consultants

Wiley, Rein & Fielding

United Technologies Carrier

Syracuse, NY

Outside Counsel/Consultants

Squire, Sanders & Dempsey L.L.P.
Rep By: Edward A. Geltman

United Technologies Corp.

1401 I St. NW
Suite 600
Washington, DC 20005
Tel: (202)336-7400
Fax: (202)336-7530
Registered: LDA

Headquartered in Hartford, CT.

Leg. Issues: AER, AVI, BUD, CAW, DEF, ENG, ENV, FOR, GOV, SCI, TAX, TRA, TRD

Political Action Committee/s

United Technologies Corp. PAC
1401 I St. NW
Suite 600
Washington, DC 20005
Contact: Isabel Corte-Real
Tel: (202)336-7400
Fax: (202)336-7529

In-house, DC-area Employees

BAYER, Judith: Director, Environmental Government Affairs
BEAUCHAMP, Rene: V. President, Government Business Development
COLLINS, Eva: Government Affairs Representative
CORTE-REAL, Isabel: PAC Administrator

HARKIN, Ruth R.: Senior V. President, International Affairs and Government Relations
HUMPHRIES, John M.: Congressional Relations Representative
KAGDIS, J. A.: Comanche Market Director
KOPECKY, Sr., John: Director, Space and Aero Propulsion Programs
MCKEON, Kit: Director, OSD Requirements
PAULSON, Kristin E.: Manager, Congressional Affairs
PEACE, Chris: Congressional Relations Representative
POLLARD, Jr., Albert W.: Director, Internat'l Business Development
PREISS, Jeremy: Chief International Trade Counsel
RISSEEUW, Hugh: Director, Navy Programs
ROBERT, III, Wade H.: V. President, Government Relations
SELIGMAN, Scott D.: Director, Public Relations
WALSH, Susan M.: Director, Commercial and International Programs

Outside Counsel/Consultants

Baker, Donelson, Bearman & Caldwell, P.C.
Issues: AVI
Rep By: Linda Hall Daschle

Crowell & Moring LLP
Rep By: Brian C. Elmer, W. Stanfield Johnson, Karen Hastie Williams

Griffin, Johnson, Dover & Stewart
Issues: DEF, TRD
Rep By: William C. Danvers, G. Jack Dover, Patrick J. Griffin, Keith Heard, David E. Johnson, Susan O. Mann, Walter J. "Joe" Stewart, Leonard Swinehart

Mayer, Brown & Platt
Issues: DEF
Rep By: Mark H. Gitenstein, Miriam R. Nemetz, Carolyn P. Osolinik

Patton Boggs, LLP
Issues: ENV
Rep By: Thomas C. Downs, Russell V. Randle

United Telecom Council

1140 Connecticut Ave. NW
Suite 1140
Washington, DC 20036
Web: www.utc.org
Tel: (202)872-0030
Fax: (202)872-1331
Registered: LDA

A trade association representing telecommunications interests of utilities, pipelines, and other critical infrastructure companies.

Leg. Issues: TEC

In-house, DC-area Employees
DUCKENFIELD, Pace: Associate Counsel
KILBOURNE, Brett: Associate Counsel
LYON, Jill: V. President and General Counsel
MORONEY, William: President/Chief Operating Exec.
PARKS, Prudence

United Transportation Union

304 Pennsylvania Ave. SE
Washington, DC 20003
Tel: (202)543-7714
Fax: (202)543-0015
Registered: LDA
Web: www.utu.org
E-mail: nldutu@aol.com
Leg. Issues: BUD, LBR, RRR, TRA

Political Action Committee/s

United Transportation Union PAC
304 Pennsylvania Ave. SE
Washington, DC 20003
Tel: (202)543-7714
Fax: (202)543-0015
Contact: James M. Brunkenhoefer

In-house, DC-area Employees
BELDEN, Scott: Chief of Staff
BRUNKENHOEFER, James M.: National Legislative Director

United Tribes Technical College

Bismark, ND

A two-year vocational education college.

Outside Counsel/Consultants

Hobbs, Straus, Dean and Walker, LLP
Rep By: Karen J. Funk

United Union of Roofers, Waterproofers and Allied Workers

1660 L St. NW
Suite 800
Washington, DC 20036
Tel: (202)463-7663
Fax: (202)463-6906
Web: www.unionroofers.com
E-mail: roofers@unionroofers.com

In-house, DC-area Employees
KRUSE, Earl J.: International President

United Van Lines, Inc.

Fenton, MO

Outside Counsel/Consultants

Zuckert, Scoutt and Rasenberger, L.L.P.
Rep By: James A. Calderwood

United Water Services

Outside Counsel/Consultants

The Dutko Group, Inc.

UNIVEC

Farmingdale, NY

Outside Counsel/Consultants

Matz, Blancato & Associates, Inc.
Rep By: Robert B. Blancato

Universal Systems and Technology Inc.

Outside Counsel/Consultants

Shaw Pittman
Rep By: John E. Jensen

Universal Systems, Inc.

Chantilly, VA
Leg. Issues: AVI, BUD, DEF

Outside Counsel/Consultants

Van Scoyoc Associates, Inc.
Issues: AVI, BUD, DEF
Rep By: Thomas L. Lankford, Steven O. Palmer, H. Stewart Van Scoyoc

Universal Wireless Communications Consortium

Bellevue, WA
Leg. Issues: FOR, SCI, TEC, TRD

Outside Counsel/Consultants

Law Offices of Michael R. Gardner, P.C.
Issues: FOR, SCI, TEC, TRD
Rep By: Michael R. Gardner

Universities Research Ass'n

Washington, DC
Leg. Issues: BUD, CPT, EDU, ENG, GOV, SCI, TAX

Outside Counsel/Consultants

Lewis-Burke Associates
Issues: BUD, CPT, EDU, ENG, GOV, SCI, TAX
Rep By: Rachel Brown, April L. Burke, Mark A. Burnham, Mark Marin

University College Dublin

Dublin, IRELAND
Leg. Issues: EDU

Outside Counsel/Consultants

Hale and Dorr LLP
Issues: EDU
Rep By: Jay P. Urwitz

University Continuing Education Ass'n

One Dupont Circle NW
Suite 615
Washington, DC 20036-1168
Web: www.nucea.edu
E-mail: postmaster@nucea.edu
Tel: (202)659-3130
Fax: (202)785-0374

A non-profit member organization representing over 425 accredited degree-granting colleges and universities which provide continuing higher education opportunities to part-time students.

Leg. Issues: CPT, EDU, LBR, WEL

In-house, DC-area Employees
GWYNN, Peter: Director, Government Relations and Program Development
KOHL, Kay J.: Exec. Director

University Corp. for Atmospheric Research

Boulder, CO
Leg. Issues: BUD, CPT, IMM, SCI

Outside Counsel/Consultants

Lewis-Burke Associates
Issues: BUD, CPT, IMM, SCI
Rep By: Rachel Brown, April L. Burke, Mark A. Burnham

University Emergency Medicine Foundation

Providence, RI
Leg. Issues: HCR

Outside Counsel/Consultants

The PMA Group
Issues: HCR
Rep By: Kaylene Green, Patrick Hiu, Paul J. Magliocchetti, Dana Stewart, Brian Thiel

University Health Associates, Inc.

Morgantown, WV
Leg. Issues: EDU, ENV

Outside Counsel/Consultants

Golin/Harris Internat'l
Issues: EDU, ENV
Rep By: C. Michael Fulton

University Health System of New Jersey

Trenton, NJ

Outside Counsel/Consultants

Jorden Burt LLP

University Heights Science Park

Newark, NJ
Leg. Issues: ECN, SCI, URB

Outside Counsel/Consultants

Charlie McBride Associates, Inc.
Issues: ECN, SCI, URB
Rep By: Charlie McBride

University Medical Associates

Charleston, SC
Leg. Issues: BUD, HCR

Outside Counsel/Consultants

Patton Boggs, LLP
Issues: BUD, HCR
Rep By: John F. Jonas, Martha M. Kendrick, Elizabeth E. Ring, JoAnn V. Willis

University Medical Center of Southern Nevada

Las Vegas, NV
Leg. Issues: HCR

Outside Counsel/Consultants

Cassidy & Associates, Inc.
Issues: HCR
Rep By: Lawrence C. Grossman, Christopher Lamond

University of Akron

Akron, OH
Leg. Issues: EDU

Outside Counsel/Consultants

F.B.A.
Issues: EDU
Rep By: J. R. Kirkland

O'Connor & Hannan, L.L.P.
Rep By: F. Gordon Lee, Patrick E. O'Donnell

University of Alabama - Huntsville

Huntsville, AL
Leg. Issues: EDU

Outside Counsel/Consultants

Hall, Green, Rupli, LLC
Issues: EDU
Rep By: John M. Green, G. Stewart Hall

University of Alabama System

Tuscaloosa, AL
Leg. Issues: BUD, EDU, MED, SCI

Outside Counsel/Consultants

Michael W. Adcock
Rep By: Michael W. Adcock

Van Scoyoc Associates, Inc.
Issues: BUD, EDU, MED, SCI
Rep By: Michael W. Adcock, Ray Cole, H. Stewart Van Scoyoc

University of Alaska

Anchorage, AK
Leg. Issues: BUD, EDU, RES

Outside Counsel/Consultants

Birch, Horton, Bittner & Cherot
Issues: BUD, RES
Rep By: Thomas L. Albert, Ronald G. Birch, William P. Horn

F.B.A.
Issues: EDU
Rep By: J. R. Kirkland

University of Arizona

Tuscon, AZ
Leg. Issues: BUD

Outside Counsel/Consultants
Van Scoyoc Associates, Inc.
Issues: BUD
Rep By: Kevin F. Kelly

University of California at Irvine Advanced Power and Energy Program

Irvine, CA
Leg. Issues: APP

Outside Counsel/Consultants
MARC Associates, Inc.
Issues: APP
Rep By: Cliff Madison, Daniel C. Maldonado, Eve O'Toole

University of California at Los Angeles

Los Angeles, CA
Leg. Issues: DIS

Outside Counsel/Consultants
Winston & Strawn
Issues: DIS
Rep By: Hon. Beryl F. Anthony, Jr., Peter N. Hiebert

University of California at Riverside

Riverside, CA
Leg. Issues: EDU

Outside Counsel/Consultants
Washington Alliance Group, Inc.
Issues: EDU
Rep By: Bonnie Singer

University of California, Office of Federal Government Relations

1523 New Hampshire Ave. NW
Washington, DC 20036
Tel: (202)588-0002
Fax: (202)785-2669
Registered: LDA
Web: www.ucop.edu
Leg. Issues: AGR, BUD, CPT, DEF, EDU, ENG, ENV, HCR, IMM, MED, MMM, SCI, TAX

In-house, DC-area Employees
BANNAN, Kathryn: Federal Government Relations Specialist
GOURLAY, Diana: Legislative Director
HAMILTON, John: Legislative Director
MATHIAS, Sarah Avellar: Senior Consultant
PETERSON, Matt: Senior Legislative Analyst
POULAKIDAS, Jennifer: Legislative Director
SCHOMER, Christie: Legislative Analyst
SUDDUTH, A. Scott: Assistant V. President

University of Central Florida

Orlando, FL

Outside Counsel/Consultants
The Advocacy Group
Rep By: Robert E. Mills

University of Cincinnati

Cincinnati, OH
Leg. Issues: BUD, CPT, EDU, HCR, IMM, MED, SCI, TAX

Outside Counsel/Consultants
Lewis-Burke Associates
Issues: BUD, CPT, EDU, HCR, IMM, MED, SCI, TAX
Rep By: Rachel Brown, April L. Burke, Mark A. Burnham

University of Colorado, Office of the President

Boulder, CO
Leg. Issues: BUD, ECN, EDU, IND

Outside Counsel/Consultants
Law Office of Paige E. Reffe
Issues: BUD, ECN, EDU, IND
Rep By: Paige E. Reffe

University of Connecticut

Storrs, CT
Leg. Issues: BUD, EDU

Outside Counsel/Consultants
Van Scoyoc Associates, Inc.
Issues: BUD, EDU
Rep By: Steve E. Crane, Kevin F. Kelly

University of Dubuque

Dubuque, IA
Leg. Issues: BUD

Outside Counsel/Consultants
Cassidy & Associates, Inc.
Issues: BUD
Rep By: Douglass E. Bobbitt, Carl Franklin Godfrey, Jr., Laura A. Neal

University of Findlay

Findlay, OH
Leg. Issues: BUD, DIS, HCR

Outside Counsel/Consultants
Powers Pyles Sutter & Verville, PC
Issues: BUD, DIS, HCR
Rep By: Judith Buckalew

University of Florida Health Science Center

Gainesville, FL
Leg. Issues: AGR, BUD, HCR

Outside Counsel/Consultants
Powers Pyles Sutter & Verville, PC
Issues: AGR, BUD, HCR
Rep By: J. Michael Hall, Alyson M. Haywood

University of Georgia

Athens, GA
Leg. Issues: BUD, EDU

Outside Counsel/Consultants
Long, Aldridge & Norman, LLP
Issues: BUD, EDU
Rep By: C. Randall Nuckolls, Patrick C. Turner

University of Georgia - College of Agricultural and Environmental Sciences

Athens, GA

Outside Counsel/Consultants
Robert L. Redding
Rep By: Robert L. Redding, Jr.

University of Hawaii

Leg. Issues: BUD

Outside Counsel/Consultants
Cassidy & Associates, Inc.
Issues: BUD
Rep By: Shawn Edwards, Jeffrey Lawrence

University of Houston

Houston, TX
Leg. Issues: EDU

Outside Counsel/Consultants
The Advocacy Group
Issues: EDU
Rep By: Robert J. Dotchin, George A. Ramonas

University of Idaho

Moscow, ID
Leg. Issues: BUD

Outside Counsel/Consultants
Van Scoyoc Associates, Inc.
Issues: BUD
Rep By: Carolyn Fuller, H. Stewart Van Scoyoc

University of Louisville

Louisville, KY
Leg. Issues: BUD, EDU

Outside Counsel/Consultants
Dean Blakey & Moskowitz
Issues: BUD, EDU
Rep By: William A. Blakey

The Grizzle Company
Issues: BUD
Rep By: Richard A. Cantor, Charles L. Grizzle

University of Massachusetts

Amherst, MA
Registered: LDA
Leg. Issues: DEF, FOO

Outside Counsel/Consultants
Campbell Crane & Associates
Issues: DEF, FOO
Rep By: Jeanne M. Campbell, Daniel M. Crane

University of Massachusetts Memorial Health System

Worcester, MA
Leg. Issues: BUD

Outside Counsel/Consultants
Cassidy & Associates, Inc.
Issues: BUD
Rep By: Marie James, Mary Kate Kelly-Johnson, Sean O'Shea, Hon. Martin A. Russo, Barbara Sutton

University of Medicine and Dentistry of New Jersey

Newark, NJ
Registered: LDA
Leg. Issues: AER, ALC, ANI, ART, AVI, BUD, CPT, DEF, EDU, ENG, ENV, FOR, HCR, IMM, MAR, MED, MMM, SCI, TAX, TEC, URB, VET

Outside Counsel/Consultants
Jorden Burt LLP
Issues: AER, ALC, ANI, ART, AVI, BUD, CPT, DEF, EDU, ENG, ENV, FOR, HCR, IMM, MAR, MED, MMM, SCI, TAX, TEC, URB, VET
Rep By: Patricia Branch, Alanna Dillon, Marna Gettleman, Marilyn Berry Thompson, Rebecca Tidman

University of Medicine and Dentistry of New Jersey - School of Health Related Professionals

Leg. Issues: BUD, HCR

Outside Counsel/Consultants
Arent Fox Kintner Plotkin & Kahn, PLLC
Issues: BUD, HCR
Rep By: Douglas McCormack, William A. Sarraille

University of Miami

Coral Gables, FL
Registered: LDA
Leg. Issues: AER, ALC, ANI, ART, AVI, BUD, CPT, DEF, ECN, EDU, ENG, ENV, FOR, GOV, HCR, IMM, MAR, MED, MMM, SCI, TAX, TEC, URB, VET

Outside Counsel/Consultants
Jefferson Government Relations, L.L.C.
Issues: EDU
Rep By: William A. Roberts

Jorden Burt LLP
Issues: AER, ALC, ANI, ART, AVI, BUD, CPT, DEF, ECN, EDU, ENG, ENV, FOR, HCR, IMM, MAR, MED, MMM, SCI, TAX, TEC, URB, VET
Rep By: Alanna Dillon, Marna Gettleman, Marilyn Berry Thompson, Rebecca Tidman

McGuireWoods L.L.P.
Issues: EDU
Rep By: Joseph H. Bogosian, Stephen A. Katsurinis, Jeffrey L. Schlagenhauf

Policy Impact Communications
Issues: EDU, GOV

University of Michigan Medical Center

Ann Arbor, MI
Leg. Issues: MED

Outside Counsel/Consultants
Verner, Liipfert, Bernhard, McPherson and Hand, Chartered
Issues: MED
Rep By: Rosemary B. Freeman, Vicki E. Hart, Jenifer Martin

University of Mississippi

University, MS
Leg. Issues: EDU

Outside Counsel/Consultants
Barbour Griffith & Rogers, Inc.
Issues: EDU
Rep By: Haley Barbour, Scott Barnhart, G. O. Lanny Griffith, Jr., Loren Monroe

University of Mississippi Medical Center

Jackson, MS
Leg. Issues: EDU

Outside Counsel/Consultants
Barbour Griffith & Rogers, Inc.
Issues: EDU
Rep By: Haley Barbour, G. O. Lanny Griffith, Jr., Loren Monroe

University of Missouri

Columbia, MO
Leg. Issues: BUD, SCI, TRA

Outside Counsel/Consultants
Van Scoyoc Associates, Inc.
Issues: BUD, SCI, TRA
Rep By: Steve E. Crane, Kevin F. Kelly

University of Nebraska

Lincoln, NE
Leg. Issues: BUD, EDU, MED, SCI

Outside Counsel/Consultants
Van Scoyoc Associates, Inc.
Issues: BUD, EDU, MED, SCI
Rep By: Carri Booth, Carolyn Fuller, Evan Knisely, H. Stewart Van Scoyoc

University of Nevada - Las Vegas

Las Vegas, NV
Leg. Issues: BUD, EDU

Outside Counsel/Consultants

Alcalde & Fay
Issues: EDU
Rep By: Hon. James H. Bilbray, Kathy Jurado Munoz

Cassidy & Associates, Inc.
Issues: BUD
Rep By: Lawrence C. Grossman, Christopher Lamond

F.B.A.
Issues: EDU
Rep By: J. R. Kirkland

University of Nevada - Reno

Reno, NV
Leg. Issues: EDU

Outside Counsel/Consultants

Richard L. Spees, Inc.
Issues: EDU
Rep By: Richard L. Spees

University of New Orleans

New Orleans, LA
Leg. Issues: BUD, ENV

Outside Counsel/Consultants

Johnston & Associates, LLC
Issues: BUD, ENV
Rep By: Hon. J. Bennett Johnston, N. Hunter Johnston, W. Proctor Jones, Eric Tober

University of New Orleans Foundation

New Orleans, LA
Leg. Issues: BUD, EDU

Outside Counsel/Consultants

Jones, Walker, Waechter, Poitevent, Carrere & Denegre, L.L.P.
Issues: BUD, EDU
Rep By: Paul Cambon, John J. Jaskot, R. Christian Johnsen

Van Scoyoc Associates, Inc.
Issues: BUD
Rep By: Carolyn Fuller, Buzz Hawley, Kevin F. Kelly, John C. "Jay" Stone, H. Stewart Van Scoyoc

University of North Carolina at Chapel Hill

Chapel Hill, NC
Leg. Issues: BUD, EDU, MED, SCI

Outside Counsel/Consultants

Van Scoyoc Associates, Inc.
Issues: BUD, EDU, MED, SCI
Rep By: Jane Bobbitt, Carri Booth, Carolyn Fuller, Keith Morrison, H. Stewart Van Scoyoc

University of North Carolina at Greensboro

Greensboro, NC
Leg. Issues: AGR, BUD, EDU, FAM

Outside Counsel/Consultants

Meyers & Associates
Issues: AGR, BUD, EDU, FAM
Rep By: Shelley Wilson Dodd, Larry D. Meyers, Richard L. Meyers

University of North Dakota

Grand Forks, ND
Leg. Issues: AER, AGR, AVI, BUD, EDU, ENG, ENV, HCR

Outside Counsel/Consultants

Sara Garland (and Associates)
Issues: AER, AGR, AVI, BUD, EDU, ENG, ENV, HCR
Rep By: Sara G. Garland

University of Notre Dame

South Bend, IN
Leg. Issues: BUD, EDU

Outside Counsel/Consultants

Van Scoyoc Associates, Inc.
Issues: BUD, EDU
Rep By: H. Stewart Van Scoyoc

University of Oklahoma

2301 S. Jefferson Davis Hwy.
Buchanan Mall
Arlington, VA 22202
E-mail: OUinDC@aol.com
Tel: (703)418-4800
Fax: (703)418-2730

Headquartered in Norman, OK.

Leg. Issues: EDU

In-house, DC-area Employees

ALLGOOD, Annette Y.: Operations Manager

Outside Counsel/Consultants

Boesch & Co.
Issues: EDU
Rep By: Doyce A. Boesch

Suzie Brewster & Associates
Rep By: Suzie Brewster

Jack Ferguson Associates, Inc.
Issues: EDU
Rep By: Jack Ferguson

University of Oregon

Eugene, OR
Registered: LDA
Leg. Issues: BUD, DEF, SCI

Outside Counsel/Consultants

Cascade Associates
Issues: BUD, DEF, SCI
Rep By: Jennifer A. Schafer

University of Pennsylvania/School of Dental Medicine

Philadelphia, PA
Leg. Issues: BUD, HCR, TOB

Outside Counsel/Consultants

Capitol Associates, Inc.
Issues: BUD, HCR, TOB
Rep By: Edward R. Long, Ph.D., Ronnie Kovner Tepp

University of Phoenix

Phoenix, AZ
Leg. Issues: BUD, EDU

Outside Counsel/Consultants

Rooney Group Internat'l, Inc.
Issues: EDU

Van Scoyoc Associates, Inc.
Issues: BUD, EDU
Rep By: Victor F. Klatt, III, Robert L. Knisely, H. Stewart Van Scoyoc

University of Pittsburgh Medical Center (UPMC)

Pittsburgh, PA
Leg. Issues: BUD

Outside Counsel/Consultants

Cassidy & Associates, Inc.
Issues: BUD
Rep By: Michael Merola, Valerie Rogers Osborne, Maureen Walsh

Rhoads Group

University of Puerto Rico

San Juan, PR
Registered: LDA
Leg. Issues: BUD

Outside Counsel/Consultants

Cassidy & Associates, Inc.
Issues: BUD
Rep By: Carl Franklin Godfrey, Jr., Dennis M. Kedzior, Blenda Pinto-Riddick

Dow, Lohnes & Albertson, PLLC
Rep By: Todd D. Gray, Kenneth D. Salomon

University of Redlands

Redlands, CA
Leg. Issues: BUD, EDU, SCI

Outside Counsel/Consultants

Copeland, Lowery & Jacquez
Issues: BUD, EDU, SCI
Rep By: Jeffrey S. Shockey

University of San Diego

San Diego, CA
Leg. Issues: BUD

Outside Counsel/Consultants

Cassidy & Associates, Inc.
Issues: BUD
Rep By: Valerie Rogers Osborne, Gerald Felix Warburg

University of San Francisco

Leg. Issues: BUD

Outside Counsel/Consultants

Cassidy & Associates, Inc.
Issues: BUD
Rep By: Blenda Pinto-Riddick, Mary E. Shields, Gerald Felix Warburg

University of South Alabama

Mobile, AL
Leg. Issues: EDU

Outside Counsel/Consultants

Hall, Green, Rupli, LLC
Issues: EDU
Rep By: John M. Green, G. Stewart Hall

University of South Carolina

Leg. Issues: SCI

Outside Counsel/Consultants

The Eagles Group
Issues: SCI
Rep By: Terence Costello

University of South Florida Research Foundation

Tampa, FL
Leg. Issues: DIS, EDU, HCR, MAR, MED

Outside Counsel/Consultants

JCP Associates
Issues: DIS, EDU, HCR, MAR, MED
Rep By: James C. Pirius

University of Southern California

Los Angeles, CA
Web: www.usc.edu
Leg. Issues: BUD, CPT, EDU, IMM, MED, SCI, TAX

Outside Counsel/Consultants

Lewis-Burke Associates
Issues: BUD, CPT, EDU, IMM, MED, SCI, TAX
Rep By: Rachel Brown, April L. Burke, Mark A. Burnham

University of Southern Mississippi

Hattiesburg, MS
Leg. Issues: ENV, MAR

Outside Counsel/Consultants

Barbour Griffith & Rogers, Inc.
Issues: ENV, MAR
Rep By: G. O. Lanny Griffith, Jr., James H. Johnson, Loren Monroe

University of Southwestern Louisiana

Lafayette, LA
Leg. Issues: AGR, APP, BUD, EDU, ENG, ENV, GOV, NAT, SCI

Outside Counsel/Consultants

Johnston & Associates, LLC
Issues: AGR, APP, BUD, EDU, ENG, ENV, GOV, NAT, SCI
Rep By: Hon. J. Bennett Johnston, N. Hunter Johnston, Eric Tober

University of Tennessee

Knoxville, TN

Outside Counsel/Consultants

Cottone and Huggins Group
Rep By: James B. Huggins

University of Texas

Austin, TX
Leg. Issues: EDU

Outside Counsel/Consultants

Timothy R. Rupli and Associates, Inc.
Issues: EDU
Rep By: Timothy R. Rupli

University of Texas - Houston Health Science Center

Houston, TX
Leg. Issues: BUD, HCR, TEC

Outside Counsel/Consultants

Vinson & Elkins L.L.P.
Issues: BUD, HCR, TEC
Rep By: Hon. Michael A. Andrews

University of Texas Health Systems

Austin, TX

Outside Counsel/Consultants

Health Policy Group
Rep By: J. Michael Hudson

University of Texas Office of Federal Relations

1901 Pennsylvania Ave. NW
Suite 700
Washington, DC 20006
Tel: (202)955-9091
Fax: (202)955-9039

In-house, DC-area Employees

DALE, Shana L.: Assistant V. Chancellor for Federal Relations
FRANZ, Mark A.: V. Chancellor for Federal Relations

University of Tulsa
Tulsa, OK
Leg. Issues: AER, ALC, ANI, ART, AVI, BUD, CPT, DEF, EDU, ENG, ENV, FOR, HCR, IMM, MAR, MED, MMM, SCI, TAX, TEC, URB, VET

Outside Counsel/Consultants

Jorden Burt LLP
Issues: AER, ALC, ANI, ART, AVI, BUD, CPT, DEF, EDU, ENG, ENV, FOR, HCR, IMM, MAR, MED, MMM, SCI, TAX, TEC, URB, VET
Rep By: Patricia Branch, Alanna Dillon, Marna Gettleman, Marilyn Berry Thompson, Rebecca Tidman

University of Utah
Salt Lake City, UT
Leg. Issues: BUD, EDU

Outside Counsel/Consultants

Timmons and Co., Inc.
Issues: BUD, EDU
Rep By: Michael J. Bates, Douglas F. Bennett, Ellen B. Fitzgibbons, Bryce L. "Larry" Harlow, Timothy J. Keating, Tom C. Korologos, Richard J. Tarplin, William E. Timmons, Jr., William E. Timmons, Sr.

University of Vermont
Burlington, VT
Leg. Issues: BUD, EDU

Outside Counsel/Consultants

Dean Blakey & Moskowitz
Issues: BUD, EDU
Rep By: Ellin J. Nolan

F.B.A.
Issues: EDU
Rep By: J. R. Kirkland

University of Virginia
Charlottesville, VA
Leg. Issues: AER, ALC, ANI, ART, AVI, BUD, CPT, DEF, ECN, EDU, ENG, ENV, FOR, HCR, IMM, MAR, MED, MMM, SCI, TAX, TEC, URB, VET

Outside Counsel/Consultants

Jorden Burt LLP
Issues: AER, ALC, ANI, ART, AVI, BUD, CPT, DEF, ECN, EDU, ENG, ENV, FOR, HCR, IMM, MAR, MED, MMM, SCI, TAX, TEC, URB, VET
Rep By: Patricia Branch, Alanna Dillon, Marna Gettleman, Marilyn Berry Thompson, Rebecca Tidman

University of Washington
444 N. Capitol St. NW
Suite 418
Washington, DC 20001
Tel: (202)624-1420
Fax: (202)624-1429
Registered: LDA

A research university headquartered in Seattle, WA.

Leg. Issues: BUD, CPI, CPT, EDU, ENG, HCR, IMM, MED, MMM, SCI, TAX, TEC

In-house, DC-area Employees

PERRY, Barbara F.: Assistant V. President, University Relations/Director Federal Relations

University of West Florida
Pensacola, FL
Leg. Issues: EDU, ENV

Outside Counsel/Consultants

Madison Government Affairs
Issues: EDU, ENV
Rep By: Paul J. Hirsch, Myron M. Jacobson, Jackson Kemper, III

University Science Alliance

Outside Counsel/Consultants

Chlopak, Leonard, Schechter and Associates
Rep By: Robert A. Chlopak

University System of Maryland
3300 Metzerott Rd.
Adelphi, MD 20783-1690
Tel: (202)488-6800
Fax: (202)488-7064
Registered: LDA

Web: www.usmh.usmd.edu
E-mail: psweet@usmh.usmd.edu

Statewide system of public colleges, universities and research institutions.

Leg. Issues: AGR, BUD, CPT, DEF, EDU, HCR, IMM, MED, SCI, SPO, TAX

In-house, DC-area Employees

SWEET, Paul: Associate V. Chancellor for Research Policy and Federal Relations

University Technology Park

Outside Counsel/Consultants

Washington Strategies, L.L.C.
Rep By: Jennifer Johnson Calvert, William P. Jarrell

University Village Ass'n/Near West Side Conservation Community Council
Chicago, IL

Outside Counsel/Consultants

J/T Group
Rep By: Robert E. Juliano

Univision Television Group Inc.
Los Angeles, CA

Outside Counsel/Consultants

Shaw Pittman

Univision Television Network
Los Angeles, CA

Outside Counsel/Consultants

Shaw Pittman

UNOCAL Corp.
1150 Connecticut Ave. NW
Suite 1025
Washington, DC 20036
Tel: (202)367-2760
Fax: (202)367-2790
Registered: LDA

Energy corp. headquartered in El Segundo, CA.

Leg. Issues: CAW, ENV, FOR, FUE, GOV, HCR, NAT, RET, ROF, SCI, TAX, TRD, UTI

Political Action Committee/s

Union Oil (UNOCAL) Political Awareness Fund
1150 Connecticut Ave. NW
Suite 1025
Washington, DC 20036
Tel: (202)367-2774
Fax: (202)367-2790
Contact: John L. Rafuse

In-house, DC-area Employees

HUDSON, Laura C.: Federal and International Affairs
ICHORD, J. William: General Manager and V. President, Washington Office
PHELPS, Francie: Federal and International Affairs
RAFUSE, John L.: Federal and International Affairs

Outside Counsel/Consultants

Timmons and Co., Inc.
Issues: ROF, TAX, TRD
Rep By: Michael J. Bates, Douglas F. Bennett, Ellen B. Fitzgibbons, Bryce L. "Larry" Harlow, Timothy J. Keating, Tom C. Korologos, Richard J. Tarplin, William E. Timmons, Jr., William E. Timmons, Sr.

Van Scoyoc Associates, Inc.
Issues: CAW
Rep By: Kevin F. Kelly, H. Stewart Van Scoyoc

Wilmer, Cutler & Pickering
Rep By: Paul J. Mode, Jr.

UNR Asbestos-Disease Trust
North Aurora, IL

Outside Counsel/Consultants

Hughes Hubbard & Reed LLP

UNUM/Provident Corp.
601 Pennsylvania Ave. NW
South Bldg., Suite 900
Washington, DC 20004
Tel: (202)434-8190
Fax: (202)347-1909
Registered: LDA

A group of insurance companies. Formed by the merger of UNUM Corp. and Provident Companies, Inc.

Leg. Issues: BUD, CSP, FAM, FIN, INS, LBR, RET, TAX, TRD

In-house, DC-area Employees

COOK, Sandy: V. President, Federal Relations

Outside Counsel/Consultants

Jorden Burt LLP

Julia J. Norrell & Associates
Issues: BUD, CSP, FAM, FIN, INS, LBR, RET, TAX, TRD
Rep By: Julia J. Norrell

Upland, California, City of
Leg. Issues: DEF, GOV, HOU, RES, ROD, TRA

Outside Counsel/Consultants

Foley Government and Public Affairs, Inc.
Issues: GOV, HOU, RES, ROD
Rep By: Joseph P. Foley

Smith Dawson & Andrews, Inc.
Issues: DEF, TRA
Rep By: Robert A. Gaines

UPMC Health System
Pittsburgh, PA
Leg. Issues: HCR

Outside Counsel/Consultants

The Dutko Group, Inc.
Issues: HCR
Rep By: Arthur H. Silverman, William Simmons

UPMC Presbyterian

Outside Counsel/Consultants

Hogan & Hartson L.L.P.
Rep By: Isabel P. Dunst, Nancy Granese, Hon. Robert H. Michel

Upper Klamath Water Users
Fort Klamath, OR
Leg. Issues: IND, NAT

Outside Counsel/Consultants

Jamison and Sullivan, Inc.
Issues: IND, NAT
Rep By: Delos Cy Jamison, Jay R. Sullivan

Upper Midwest Coalition
Madison, WI
Leg. Issues: AGR

Outside Counsel/Consultants

Thelen Reid & Priest LLP
Issues: AGR
Rep By: Charles M. English, Jr., Wendy M. Yoviene

Upper Midwest Dairy Coalition
Madison, WI
Leg. Issues: AGR

Outside Counsel/Consultants

Etka Consulting
Issues: AGR
Rep By: Steven D. Etka

Ober, Kaler, Grimes & Shriver

Upper San Gabriel Municipal Water District
El Monte, CA
Leg. Issues: BUD

Outside Counsel/Consultants

The Furman Group
Issues: BUD
Rep By: Thomas M. James

Upper Sioux Indian Community
Granite Falls, MN
Leg. Issues: GAM, IND

Outside Counsel/Consultants

O'Connor & Hannan, L.L.P.
Issues: GAM, IND
Rep By: Hon. Thomas J. Corcoran, J. Craig Potter

Upper Yampa Water Conservancy District
Steamboat Springs, CO
Leg. Issues: AGR, BUD, NAT

Outside Counsel/Consultants

Kogovsek & Associates
Issues: AGR, BUD, NAT

Uranium Producers of America
Santa Fe, NM
Leg. Issues: BUD

Outside Counsel/Consultants

EOP Group, Inc.
Issues: BUD
Rep By: Joseph Hezir, Richard Irby

Urban Health Care Coalition of Pennsylvania
Harrisburg, PA
Leg. Issues: HCR, MMM

Outside Counsel/Consultants

Capitol Associates, Inc.
Issues: HCR, MMM
Rep By: William A. Finerfrock, Debra M. Hardy Havens

The Urban Institute
2100 M St. NW
Washington, DC 20037
Tel: (202)833-7200
Fax: (202)429-0687
Web: www.urban.org.
E-mail: paffairs@ui.urban.org.

A non-partisan, non-profit policy research and educational organization to study social and economic problems confronting the nation. Cooperates with federal agencies, states, cities and the private sector.

In-house, DC-area Employees

ACS, Gregory P.: Senior Research Associate
BORIS, Elizabeth: Director, Center on Nonprofits and Philanthropy
BROWN, Susan M.: Director, Public Affairs
BURT, Martha R.: Director, Social Services Research
COURRIER, Kathleen: V. President, Communications
FIX, Michael E.: Director, Immigrant Policy Research
GIBSON, James O.: Consultant
GRANT, H. Morton: V. President, Controller and Treasurer
HANNAWAY, Jane: Director, Education Policy Center
HARRELL, Adele: Director, Program on Law and Behavior
HATRY, Harry P.: Director, State and Local Government Research
HOLAHAN, John F.: Director, Health Policy Center
KINGSLEY, G. Thomas: Senior Fellow
KONDRATAS, Anna: Deputy Director, Assessing the New Federalism Project
LERMAN, Robert: Director, Human Resources Policy Center
MOON, Marilyn: Senior Fellow
NICHOLS, Len: Principal Research Associate, Health Policy Center
PASSEL, Jeffrey S.: Director, Immigration Policy Research
PENNER, Dr. Rudolph G.: Senior Fellow
PETERSON, George E.: Senior Fellow
SMITH NIGHTINGALE, Demetra: Director, Welfare and Training Research
SONENSTEIN, Freya Lund: Director, Population Studies Center
STEUERLE, C. Eugene: Senior Fellow
TELGARSKY, Jeffrey P.: Director, International Activities Center
THOMPSON, Lawrence H.: Senior Fellow
TURNER, Margery A.: Director, Metrolpolitan Housing and Community Policy Center
WEIL, Alan: Director, Assessing the New Federalism Project
WEINER, Joshua M.: Principal Research Associate, Health Policy Center
ZEDLEWSKI, Sheila R.: Director, Income and Benefits Policy Center
ZUCKERMAN, Stephen: Principal Research Associate, Health Policy Center

Urban Land Institute

1025 Thomas Jefferson St. NW
Suite 500 W
Washington, DC 20007-5201
Web: www.uli.org
Tel: (202)624-7000
Fax: (202)624-7140

The Urban Land Institute is a nonprofit educational and research institute that is supported and directed by its members. Its mission is to provide responsible leadership in the use of land in order to enhance the total environment. Established in 1936, the Institute today has nearly 13,000 members and associates representing the entire spectrum of the land use and development disciplines.

In-house, DC-area Employees

CUMMINS, Cheryl C.: Exec. V. President and Chief Operating Officer
GOLDSMITH, Marta: V. President, Policy and Practice
LEVITT, Rachelle: Senior V. President, Policy and Practice
MULVIHILL, David: Director, Information Services
OLIVERI, Ann: Senior V. President, Leadership and Outreach
ROSAN, Richard: President

Urenco, Inc.

2600 Virginia Ave. NW
Suite 610
Washington, DC 20037
Tel: (202)337-6644
Fax: (202)337-2421
Registered: FARA

A subsidiary of Urenco Ltd. of the United Kingdom.

In-house, DC-area Employees

LENNY, Peter L.: President/Chief Exec. Officer/Director

Urologix, Inc.

Minneapolis, MN
Leg. Issues: MMM

Outside Counsel/Consultants

MARC Associates, Inc.
Rep By: Bernard Patashnik

Public Policy Partners, LLC
Issues: MMM
Rep By: Hon. David Durenberger, Daniel Waldmann, Jeffrey Weekly

UroMedica Corp.

Los Angeles, CA
Leg. Issues: MMM

Outside Counsel/Consultants

Holland & Knight LLP
Issues: MMM
Rep By: Keith D. Lind

US Acqua Sonics Corp.

Atlanta, GA
Leg. Issues: CAW, ENG

Outside Counsel/Consultants

Smith, Hinaman & Associates
Issues: CAW, ENG
Rep By: Randy Hinaman, Don Smith

US Airways

Crystal Park Four
2345 Crystal Dr.
Arlington, VA 22227
Web: www.usairways.com
Tel: (703)872-5100
Fax: (703)872-5134
Registered: LDA
Leg. Issues: AVI, BUD, LBR, TAX, TRA

Political Action Committee/s

US Airways Political Action Committee
Crystal Park Four
2345 Crystal Dr.
Arlington, VA 22227
Contact: J. Ronald Reeves
Tel: (703)872-5111
Fax: (703)872-5109

In-house, DC-area Employees

CASTELVETER, David A.: Director, Public Relations
MURRAY, Rosemary Griffin: Director, Government Affairs
REEVES, J. Ronald: V. President, Government Affairs
WEINTRAUB, Richard M.: Senior Director, Public Relations and Press Spokesman

Outside Counsel/Consultants

Manatt, Phelps & Phillips, LLP
Issues: AVI
Rep By: Hon. Jack W. Buechner, Robert J. Kabel

O'Melveny and Myers LLP
Issues: AVI, LBR, TRA
Rep By: Donald T. Bliss, Joel Stephen Burton, William T. Coleman, Jr., Ronald A. Klain, Kelly J. Riordan

Patton Boggs, LLP
Rep By: Thomas Hale Boggs, Jr., Penelope S. Farthing, Donald V. Moorehead

RTC Direct

Skadden, Arps, Slate, Meagher & Flom LLP
Issues: AVI
Rep By: Curtis Barnette, Ivan A. Schlager

Swidler Berlin Shereff Friedman, LLP
Issues: TRA
Rep By: Gary D. Slaiman, Katherine R. Taylor

US Bancorp

Minneapolis, MN
Leg. Issues: BAN, CSP, FIN, GOV

Outside Counsel/Consultants

The Carmen Group
Issues: BAN, CSP, FIN, GOV
Rep By: Hon. Beau Boulter, Gerald P. Carmen, David A. Keene

US JVC Corp.

Wayne, NJ
Leg. Issues: TRD

Outside Counsel/Consultants

St. Maxens & Company
Issues: TRD
Rep By: Thomas F. St. Maxens, II

US Steel Group

Pittsburgh, PA
Leg. Issues: TRD

Outside Counsel/Consultants

Skadden, Arps, Slate, Meagher & Flom LLP
Issues: TRD
Rep By: Robert E. Lighthizer

US-Asia Institute

232 E. Capitol St. NE
Washington, DC 20003
Web: www.usasiainstitute.com
E-mail: usasia1@aol.com
Tel: (202)544-3181
Fax: (202)543-1748

The US-Asia Institute, established in 1979, is a national nonprofit, nonpartisan organization which focuses on strengthening economic cooperation, communication, and cultural exchange between the United States and countries of Asia. The headquarters are located in Washington with members including Asians, Americans of Asian decent, and those with an interest in Asia from the business, community, academic, governmental, and quasi-governmental sectors.

Leg. Issues: FOR, TRD

In-house, DC-area Employees

KEE, Esther G.: Secretary/Treasurer
KONOSHIMA, Joji: President and Trustee

US-ROC (Taiwan) Business Council

1700 N. Moore St.
Suite 1703
Arlington, VA 22209
Web: www.us-roc.org
E-mail: council@usa-roc.org
Tel: (703)465-2930
Fax: (703)465-2937

Supports American business interests in Taiwan and acts as an information clearinghouse.

In-house, DC-area Employees

HAMMOND-CHAMBERS, Rupert: President

USA Biomass Power Producers Alliance

Sacramento, CA
Leg. Issues: BUD, ENV, TAX

Outside Counsel/Consultants

The Renkes Group, Ltd.
Issues: ENV, TAX
Rep By: Patrick Pettey, Gregg D. Renkes

Washington Council Ernst & Young
Issues: BUD, TAX
Rep By: Doug Badger, Lauren Darling, John L. Doney, Jayne T. Fitzgerald, LaBrenda Garrett-Nelson, Gary J. Gasper, Bruce A. Gates, Nick Giordano, Cathy Koch, Robert J. Leonard, Richard Meltzer, Phillip D. Moseley, John D. Porter, Robert M. Rozen, Donna Steele-Flynn, Timothy J. Urban

USA Funds, Inc.

2000 L St. NW
Suite 402
Washington, DC 20036
Web: www.usafunds.org
Tel: (202)466-4306
Fax: (202)223-0145
Registered: LDA

A provider of financial, information, and management service to those pursuing, providing, and promoting higher education. Headquartered in Indianapolis, IN.

Leg. Issues: EDU

In-house, DC-area Employees

COWEN, Lee: V. President, Government Relations
MUILENBURG, Terry L.: Senior V. President, Government and Industry Relations

USA Networks

New York, NY

Outside Counsel/Consultants

Venable
Rep By: Ian D. Volner

USA Rice Federation

4301 N. Fairfax Dr.
Suite 305
Arlington, VA 22203-1616
Web: www.usarice.com
Tel: (703)351-8161
Fax: (703)351-8162
Registered: LDA
Leg. Issues: AGR, ENV

Political Action Committee/s

USA Rice Federation PAC
4301 N. Fairfax Dr.
Suite 305
Arlington, VA 22203-1616
Tel: (703)351-8161
Fax: (703)351-8162

In-house, DC-area Employees

TERPSTRA, Ellen: President/Chief Exec. Officer

Outside Counsel/Consultants

Lesher & Russell, Inc.
Issues: AGR
Rep By: William G. Lesher, Randall M. Russell

Winston & Strawn
Issues: AGR, ENV
Rep By: Robert M. Bor

USA WORKS!

Sandston, VA
Leg. Issues: LBR

Outside Counsel/Consultants

Moss McGee Bradley & Foley
Issues: LBR
Rep By: David A. Bradley, Leander J. Foley, III

USA/Scientific Plastics Inc.

Ocala, FL

Outside Counsel/Consultants

Howrey Simon Arnold & White
Rep By: Michael A. Hertzberg

USAA - United Services Automobile Ass'n

1455 F St. NW
Suite 420
Washington, DC 20004
Tel: (202)628-6442
Fax: (202)628-6537
Registered: LDA

Provider of financial services and insurance products for military personnel and their dependents. Headquartered in San Antonio, TX.

Leg. Issues: BAN, CSP, ENV, FIN, HCR, INS, LBR, TAX, TOR

Political Action Committee/s

USAA Group PAC
1455 F St. NW
Suite 420
Washington, DC 20004
Tel: (202)628-6442
Fax: (202)628-6537
Contact: Christopher C. Seeger

In-house, DC-area Employees

CALLANAN, Susan W.: Assistant V. President, Federal Legislative Affairs
PERROS, Georgette: Federal Affairs Associate
RANKIN, Al: Senior V. President and Chief Communications Officer
SEEGER, Christopher C.: V. President/Federal Legislative Affairs

Outside Counsel/Consultants

Arter & Hadden
Crowell & Moring LLP
Issues: CSP, INS
Rep By: Mark A. Behrens, Victor E. Schwartz
Ernst & Young LLP
Foley & Lardner
Issues: TAX
Rep By: R. Lee Christie, Jodi L. Hanson, Richard F. Riley, Jr.
Williams & Jensen, P.C.
Issues: FIN, TAX
Rep By: George D. Baker, Philip E. Bechtel, Robert E. Glennon, Jr., David M. Landers, Karen Judd Lewis, Jeffrey A. Tassey, J. D. Williams

USEC, Inc.

6903 Rockledge Dr.
Bethesda, MD 20817
Tel: (301)564-3200
Fax: (301)564-3201
Registered: LDA
Web: www.usec.com

Formerly United States Enrichment Corp.

Leg. Issues: BUD, ENG, FOR, LBR, TRD

Political Action Committee/s

USEC Inc. PAC
6903 Rockledge Dr.
Bethesda, MD 20817
Tel: (301)564-3200
Fax: (301)564-3201
Contact: Gary G. Ellsworth

In-house, DC-area Employees

BROWN, Russell R.
ELLSWORTH, Gary G.: Contact, Political Action Committee
STUCKLE, Elizabeth: Director, Corporate Communications
TIMBERS, Jr., William H.: President and Chief Exec. Officer

Outside Counsel/Consultants

Johnston & Associates, LLC
Issues: ENG
Rep By: Alex Flint, Hon. J. Bennett Johnston, W. Proctor Jones
Quinn Gillespie & Associates
Issues: BUD, ENG
Rep By: Bruce H. Andrews, Edward W. Gillespie, David Lugar
Steptoe & Johnson LLP
Rep By: Richard O. Cunningham

USF Surface Preparation

Houston, TX

Outside Counsel/Consultants

Interface Inc.
Rep By: David C. Knapp, Robert G. Williams

USFHP Conference Group

Washington, DC
Leg. Issues: BUD, DEF, HCR, TRA

Outside Counsel/Consultants

Federal Health Strategies, Inc.
Issues: BUD, DEF, HCR, TRA
Rep By: Norbert M. Meister
Preston Gates Ellis & Rouvelas Meeds LLP
Issues: BUD, DEF, HCR
Rep By: Cindy O'Malley, Tim L. Peckinpaugh

USPA & IRA

Fort Worth, TX
Leg. Issues: BAN

Outside Counsel/Consultants

Butera & Andrews
Issues: BAN
Rep By: Cliff W. Andrews, Wright H. Andrews, Jr., James J. Butera, Frank Tillotson

USPCI, Inc.

Houston, TX

Outside Counsel/Consultants

Arter & Hadden

USS Wisconsin Foundation

Norfolk, VA
Leg. Issues: ECN, EDU

Outside Counsel/Consultants

Madison Government Affairs
Issues: ECN, EDU
Rep By: Paul J. Hirsch, Myron M. Jacobson, Jackson Kemper, III

UST Public Affairs, Inc.

1331 F St. NW
Suite 450
Washington, DC 20004
Tel: (202)638-6890
Fax: (202)220-3619
Registered: LDA

Also serves as federal government relations office for subsidiaries, U.S. Smokeless Tobacco Co., Internat'l Wine & Spirits Ltd., and UST Enterprises Inc. Headquartered in Greenwich, CT.

Leg. Issues: AGR, BEV, BUD, CSP, HCR, TAX, TOB

Political Action Committee/s

UST Executives Administrators and Managers Political Action Committee (USTeamPAC)
1331 F St. NW
Suite 450
Washington, DC 20004
Tel: (202)638-6890
Fax: (202)220-3619
Contact: Todd A. Walker

In-house, DC-area Employees

WALKER, Todd A.: V. President, Federal Government Relations

Outside Counsel/Consultants

The Advocacy Group
Issues: BEV, TAX, TOB
Rep By: Robert J. Dotchin
BKSH & Associates
Issues: TOB
Rep By: Mark Disler, Katherine Friess, James C. Healey
Bracewell & Patterson, L.L.P.
Issues: AGR, BUD, CSP, HCR, TAX, TOB
Rep By: Hon. Jim Chapman, Charles L. Ingebretson, Michael L. Pate
Gottehrer and Co.
Issues: TAX, TOB
Rep By: Barry Gottehrer
Hall, Green, Rupli, LLC
Issues: TOB
Rep By: John M. Green
O'Connor & Hannan, L.L.P.
Issues: BEV, TAX, TOB
Rep By: Thomas H. Quinn

USX Corp.

1101 Pennsylvania Ave. NW
Suite 510
Washington, DC 20004
Tel: (202)783-6333
Fax: (202)783-6309
Registered: LDA
Web: www.usx.com

Headquartered in Pittsburgh, PA.

Leg. Issues: AUT, BUD, CAW, ENG, ENV, FOR, FUE, HCR, LBR, NAT, RET, TAX, TRA, TRD, WAS

Political Action Committee/s

USX Corporation Political Action Committee
1101 Pennsylvania Ave. NW
Suite 510
Washington, DC 20004
Tel: (202)783-6315
Fax: (202)783-6309
Contact: Marilyn A. Harris, Ph.D.

In-house, DC-area Employees

FREER, Paula D.: Manager, Governmental Affairs
HARRIS, Ph.D., Marilyn A.: General Manager, Federal Government Affairs
RICHARDS, Patricia M.: Manager, Governmental Affairs
SALMON, Scott: Manager, Government Affairs
STRAUB, Terrence D.: V. President, Public Affairs

Outside Counsel/Consultants

Campbell Crane & Associates
Issues: RET, TAX
Rep By: Jeanne M. Campbell, Daniel M. Crane
The Duberstein Group, Inc.
Issues: FOR, FUE
Rep By: John W. Angus, III, Michael S. Berman, Steven M. Champlin, Kenneth M. Duberstein, Henry M. Gandy, Daniel P. Meyer
Frank Fenton
Issues: ENV, TAX, TRA, TRD
Rep By: Frank Fenton
Garvey, Schubert & Barer
Issues: FOR, HCR
Rep By: Richard A. Wegman
O'Neill, Athy & Casey, P.C.
Issues: ENV, HCR, TAX, TRD
Rep By: Andrew Athy, Jr., Christopher R. O'Neill
Reed, Smith, LLP
Issues: FUE
Rep By: Phillips S. Peter, C. Stevens Seale

Utah Department of Transportation

Salt Lake City, UT
Leg. Issues: TRA

Outside Counsel/Consultants

The Carmen Group
Issues: TRA
Rep By: James B. Young

Utah Natural Products Alliance

Salt Lake City, UT
Leg. Issues: FOO

Outside Counsel/Consultants

Parry, Romani, DeConcini & Symms
Issues: FOO
Rep By: Edward H. Baxter, Hon. Dennis DeConcini, John M. Haddow, Scott D. Hatch, Shannon Davis Henderson, Jack W. Martin, Romano Romani, Linda Arey Skladany, Hon. Steven D. Symms

Utah State University

Logan, UT
Registered: LDA
Leg. Issues: AER, AGR, ANI, BUD, DEF, EDU, ENV, LAW, NAT, RES, SCI, TRA

Outside Counsel/Consultants

Lee & Smith P.C.
Issues: AGR, ANI, DEF, EDU, LAW, NAT, RES, SCI, TRA
Rep By: David B. Lee, C. William Smith
Kay Allan Morrell, Attorney-at-Law
Issues: AER, AGR, ANI, BUD, DEF, EDU, ENV, NAT, SCI, TRA
Rep By: Kay Allan Morrell

Utah Transit Authority

Salt Lake City, UT
Leg. Issues: TRA

Outside Counsel/Consultants

Charles H. Graves & Associates
Issues: TRA
Rep By: Charles H. Graves

Utah, State of

400 N. Capitol St. NW
Suite 388
Washington, DC 20001
Tel: (202)624-7704
Fax: (202)624-7707

In-house, DC-area Employees

NEUMANN, Joanne Snow: Director, Washington Office

UTAM, Inc.

Outside Counsel/Consultants

Wiley, Rein & Fielding
Rep By: Mimi W. Dawson

Ute Mountain Ute Indian Tribe

Towaoc, CO
Leg. Issues: AGR, BUD, CAW, ENG, FUE, GAM, HOU, IND, NAT, TAX

Outside Counsel/Consultants

Kogovsek & Associates
Issues: AGR, BUD, CAW, ENG, FUE, GAM, HOU, IND, NAT, TAX
Rep By: Christine Ann Arbogast, Hon. Raymond P. Kogovsek

Utica Cutlery Inc.

Utica, NY

Outside Counsel/Consultants

Collier Shannon Scott, PLLC

UtiliCorp United, Inc.

Kansas City, MO
Leg. Issues: TAX, UTI

Outside Counsel/Consultants

Arthur Andersen LLP
Issues: TAX
Rep By: Rachelle Bernstein, Harrison J. Cohen, Weston J. Coulam, Richard A. Gordon, Carol Doran Klein

Wiley, Rein & Fielding
Issues: UTI
Rep By: James T. Bruce, III, Barbara G. Burchett, Mimi W. Dawson

Utility Air Regulatory Group

Washington, DC

An ad hoc group of utility companies, the Edison Electric Institute and the Nat'l Rural Electric Cooperative Ass'n formed to represent the utility industry's views on regulations concerning air quality standards.

Outside Counsel/Consultants

Hunton & Williams
Rep By: Henry V. Nickel

Utility Decommissioning Tax Group

Washington, DC Registered: LDA
Leg. Issues: TAX

Outside Counsel/Consultants

Thelen Reid & Priest LLP
Issues: TAX

Utility Solid Waste Activities Group

Washington, DC
Leg. Issues: WAS

Outside Counsel/Consultants

Piper Marbury Rudnick & Wolfe LLP
Issues: WAS
Rep By: Jeffrey F. Liss, William R. Weissman

Utility Workers Union of America

815 16th St. NW
Washington, DC 20006
Web: www.uwua.org
Tel: (202)347-8105
Fax: (202)347-4872

A labor organization.

Leg. Issues: HCR, LBR, UTI

Political Action Committee/s

Utility Workers of America Political Contributions Committee
815 16th St. NW
Washington, DC 20006
Contact: Gary M. Ruffner
Tel: (202)347-8105
Fax: (202)347-4872

In-house, DC-area Employees

RUFFNER, Gary M.: National Secretary/Treasurer
WIGHTMAN, Donald E.: President

UWC - Strategic Services on Unemployment and Workers' Compensation

1201 New York Ave. NW
Suite 750
Washington, DC 20005
Web: www.uwcstrategy.org
E-mail: oxfelde@uwcstrategy.org
Tel: (202)682-1515
Fax: (202)842-2556
Registered: LDA

Formerly (1997) UBA. Works on behalf of business to control the costs of unemployment and workers' compensation programs. Seeks to limit federal government involvement in such programs, preferring state systems as a means of ensuring reasonable benefits at less cost.

Leg. Issues: LBR

In-house, DC-area Employees

OXFELD, Eric J.: President
SAMPSON, Vincent T.: Associate Legislative Counsel

Uwohali, Inc.

Huntsville, AL
Leg. Issues: DEF

Outside Counsel/Consultants

Michael W. Adcock
Issues: DEF
Rep By: Michael W. Adcock

Uzbekistan, Government of the Republic of

Tashkent, UZBEKISTAN

Outside Counsel/Consultants

White & Case LLP
Rep By: Carolyn B. Lamm

V-ONE Corp.

Germantown, MD
Leg. Issues: CPI, DEF, HCR, MED

Outside Counsel/Consultants

Potomac Strategies Internat'l LLC
Issues: CPI, DEF, HCR, MED
Rep By: Cynthia Trutanic

Vacuum Insulation Ass'n

Leg. Issues: ENG, FOO, MED

Outside Counsel/Consultants

Inter-Associates, Inc.
Issues: ENG, FOO, MED
Rep By: William H. Werst, Jr.

Vail Associates

Vail, CO

Outside Counsel/Consultants

Brownstein Hyatt & Farber, P.C.
Rep By: William T. Brack, Michael B. Levy

Valencia Community College

Orlando, FL
Leg. Issues: EDU

Outside Counsel/Consultants

Davis O'Connell, Inc.
Issues: EDU
Rep By: Lynda C. Davis, Ph.D.

Valent U.S.A. Corp.

2033 K St. NW
Suite 850
Washington, DC 20006
Tel: (202)872-4688
Fax: (202)872-4689

An agricultural chemicals company headquartered in Walnut Creek, CA.

Leg. Issues: AGR, CHM

In-house, DC-area Employees

FAY, Dan: Manager, Federal Registration and Regulatory Affairs
MAURER, Eric J.: Manager, Federal Registration

Valentec Systems, Inc.

Mt. Arlington, NJ
Leg. Issues: BUD, DEF

Outside Counsel/Consultants

Fishbein Associates, Inc.
Issues: BUD, DEF

Valero Energy Corp.

San Antonio, TX
Leg. Issues: ENV, TAX, TRD

Outside Counsel/Consultants

Bracewell & Patterson, L.L.P.
Issues: ENV, TAX, TRD
Rep By: Gene E. Godley, Marc C. Hebert, Michael L. Pate, Scott H. Segal

Valhi, Inc.

Dallas, TX

Outside Counsel/Consultants

Ottosen and Associates
Rep By: Karl J. Ottosen

Valio Finnish Co-operative Dairies Ass'n

Helsinki, FINLAND

Outside Counsel/Consultants

Max N. Berry Law Offices
Rep By: Max N. Berry

Valley Children's Hospital

Madera, CA
Leg. Issues: HCR

Outside Counsel/Consultants

Patton Boggs, LLP
Issues: HCR
Rep By: Hon. Willis "Bill" D. Gradison, Martha M. Kendrick, Edward J. Newberry

Valley Fig Growers

Fresno, CA
Leg. Issues: AGR, TRD

Outside Counsel/Consultants

Haley and Associates
Issues: AGR, TRD
Rep By: Daniel D. Haley

Valley Forge Flag Co.

Great Neck, NY
Leg. Issues: GOV

Outside Counsel/Consultants

Blank Rome Comisky & McCauley, LLP
Issues: GOV
Rep By: Rebecca F. South

The Tierney Group
Rep By: Chriss H. Winston

Valley Hope Ass'n

Norton, KS
Leg. Issues: ALC, BUD, HCR, INS, TAX

Outside Counsel/Consultants

VSAdc.com
Issues: ALC, BUD, HCR, INS, TAX
Rep By: Carol A. McDaid

Valley Hospital Foundation

Paramus, NJ
Leg. Issues: BUD

Outside Counsel/Consultants

Cassidy & Associates, Inc.
Issues: BUD
Rep By: John A. Crumbliss, W. Campbell Kaufman, IV, Dennis M. Kedzior, Michael Merola

Valley Pride Pack

Washington, DC
Leg. Issues: AGR, FOO

Outside Counsel/Consultants

Lockridge Grindal & Nauen, P.L.L.P.
Issues: AGR, FOO
Rep By: John D. Burton, Dennis McGrann

Value Options Health Care Inc.

Norfolk, VA
Leg. Issues: HCR

Outside Counsel/Consultants

Denison, Scott Associates
Issues: HCR

ValueVision Internat'l, Inc.

Minneapolis,.MN

Outside Counsel/Consultants

Wilmer, Cutler & Pickering
Rep By: William R. Richardson, Jr.

Valve Manufacturers Ass'n of America

1050 17th St. NW
Suite 280
Washington, DC 20036
Web: www.vma.org
E-mail: vma@vma.org
Tel: (202)331-8105
Fax: (202)296-0378
Registered: LDA

Trade association representing U.S. and Canadian manufacturers of industrial valves and actuators.

Leg. Issues: CAW, CPT, ENG, ENV, FOR, FUE, MAN, TRD

In-house, DC-area Employees

SANDLER, William: President

Outside Counsel/Consultants

Collier Shannon Scott, PLLC
Issues: CAW, CPT, ENG, ENV, FOR, MAN, TRD
Rep By: David A. Hartquist

Van Ommeren Shipping (USA), Inc.

Stamford, CT
Leg. Issues: MAR

Outside Counsel/Consultants

Winston & Strawn
Issues: MAR
Rep By: Thomas L. Mills, Constantine G. Papavizas

Van Scoyoc Associates, Inc.

1420 New York Ave. NW
Suite 1050
Washington, DC 20005
Tel: (202)638-1950
Fax: (202)638-7714
Registered: LDA, FARA

Leg. Issues: BUD, EDU, FOR, MED, MMM, SCI, TRA

In-house, DC-area Employees

ADCOCK, Michael W.
ANDERSON, Jason
BOBBITT, Jane
BOOTH, Carri: Legislative Assistant
CARTER, W. Minor: Of Counsel
COLE, Ray: Associate V. President
CRANE, Steve E.: Legislative Associate
DOHONEY, James
ESTELL, Anita R.: V. President

FULLER, Carolyn: V. President
GRIMM, Paul: V. President
HAWLEY, Buzz: Legislative Counsel
IARROBINO, Paul
JOHNSON, Kimberly: Legislative Counsel
KELLY, Kevin F.: V. President
KLATT, III, Victor F.
KNISELY, Evan: Legislative Assistant
KNISELY, Robert L.
KOHLMOOS, James W.: V. President
LANKFORD, Thomas L.: V. President
MALOW, Jessica: Legislative Assistant
MORRISON, Keith: Special Assistant to the President, Legislative Assistant
PALMER, Steven O.: V. President
PORTERFIELD, Lendell: Economist and Legislative Analyst
RUHE, Shirley L.: Of Counsel
SCHOONMAKER, Jan: V. President
SCHULKEN, Chad: Legislative Assistant
SPEAR, Scott
STONE, John C. "Jay": V. President
THOMSON, Jasper: Legislative Assistant
TRINCA, Jeffrey S.: V. President
VAN SCOYOC, H. Stewart: President
WELLS, Noreene: Program Assistant

Outside Counsel/Consultants

Michael W. Adcock
Issues: BUD, EDU, FOR, MED, MMM, SCI, TRA
Rep By: Michael W. Adcock

Vance Development Authority

Enid, OK
Leg. Issues: AER, BUD, DEF

Outside Counsel/Consultants

VSAdc.com
Issues: AER, BUD, DEF
Rep By: J. R. Reskovac, H. Stewart Van Scoyoc

Vanderbilt University

122 C St. NW
Suite 310
Washington, DC 20001
Tel: (202)824-6680
Fax: (202)393-6288
Leg. Issues: EDU, HCR, MMM, SCI

In-house, DC-area Employees

BASS, Mel: Director, Federal Relations, Vanderbilt University Medical Center
VINCENT, Geoffrey H.: Director, Federal Relations

Vanderbilt University Medical Center

Nashville, TN
Leg. Issues: HCR

Outside Counsel/Consultants

Verner, Liipfert, Bernhard, McPherson and Hand, Chartered
Issues: HCR
Rep By: Vicki E. Hart

The Vandervort Group, LLC

Leg. Issues: BUD, EDU, HCR, TEC

Outside Counsel/Consultants

The Solomon Group, LLC
Issues: BUD, EDU, HCR, TEC
Rep By: Hon. Gerald B. H. Solomon, William R. Teator

Vandium Industry Coalition

Outside Counsel/Consultants

Genesis Consulting Group, LLC
Rep By: Mark Benedict, Dana DeBeaumont

Vanguard Airlines, Inc.

Kansas City, MO
Leg. Issues: AVI

Outside Counsel/Consultants

Shaw Pittman
Issues: AVI
Rep By: Robert E. Cohn, Sheryl R. Israel

Vanguard Charitable Endowment Program

Malvern, PA
Leg. Issues: TAX

Outside Counsel/Consultants

Morgan, Lewis & Bockius LLP
Issues: TAX
Rep By: Celia Roady

PriceWaterhouseCoopers
Issues: TAX
Rep By: Howard Schoenfeld

Vanguard Medical Concepts, Inc.

Lakeland, FL
Leg. Issues: MED

Outside Counsel/Consultants

Congressional Consultants
Issues: MED
Rep By: Gwen Gampel, Karen M. Late

Vanguard Research, Inc.

Fairfax, VA
Leg. Issues: ENV

Outside Counsel/Consultants

American Continental Group, Inc.
Issues: ENV
Rep By: David A. Metzner

Vanguard University

Costa Mesa, CA
Leg. Issues: EDU

Outside Counsel/Consultants

Russ Reid Co.
Issues: EDU
Rep By: Thomas C. Keller, Mark D. McIntyre

The Vantage Group, Inc.

Boston, MA
Leg. Issues: POS

Outside Counsel/Consultants

Williams & Jensen, P.C.
Issues: POS
Rep By: William B. Canfield, Anthony J. Roda

Vantage Point Network, LLC

Fort Collins, CO
Leg. Issues: AGR, CAW, CPI

Outside Counsel/Consultants

Capitolink, LLC
Issues: AGR, CAW, CPI
Rep By: Thomas R. Hebert, John H. Thorne, Ph.D.

Variable Annuity Life Insurance Co.

Houston, TX
Leg. Issues: LBR, TAX

Outside Counsel/Consultants

Caplin & Drysdale, Chartered
Issues: LBR, TAX
Rep By: Kent A. Mason

Cassidy & Associates, Inc.

VASP Airlines

San Paolo, BRAZIL

Outside Counsel/Consultants

Squire, Sanders & Dempsey L.L.P.
Rep By: Robert D. Papkin, Edward W. Sauer

Vector Research, Inc.

Ann Arbor, MI
Leg. Issues: DEF, HCR

Outside Counsel/Consultants

Defense Health Advisors, Inc.
Issues: DEF
Rep By: Charlotte L. Tsoucalas

Health Policy Group
Issues: HCR
Rep By: J. Michael Hudson

Velazquez Victory Fund-Federal

P.O. Box 70101
Washington, DC 20024
Tel: (301)947-0278
Fax: (301)947-1531

In-house, DC-area Employees

WINPISINGER, Vickie L.

Venetian Casino Resort, LLC

Las Vegas, NV
Leg. Issues: AVI, COM, ENG, ENV, GAM, TAX, TRA, WAS

Outside Counsel/Consultants

Patton Boggs, LLP
Issues: AVI, COM, ENG, ENV, GAM, TAX, TRA, WAS
Rep By: Donald V. Moorehead

Venezuela, Bolivarian Republic of

Caracas, VENEZUELA

Outside Counsel/Consultants

Arnold & Porter

Venice Gathering System, L.L.C.

Outside Counsel/Consultants

Wright & Talisman, P.C.
Rep By: Jeffrey G. DiSciullo

Venice, Florida, City of

Venice, FL
Leg. Issues: BUD, NAT

Outside Counsel/Consultants

Marlowe and Co.
Issues: BUD, NAT
Rep By: Howard Marlowe, Jeffrey Mazzella

Ventura County Citizens Against Radar Emissions (VCCARE)

Ojai, CA
Leg. Issues: BUD

Outside Counsel/Consultants

Patton Boggs, LLP
Issues: BUD
Rep By: Thomas Hale Boggs, Jr., Elena Giberga, Clayton L. Hough, Lansing B. Lee, III, Edward J. Newberry

Ventura County Community-Navy Action Partnership

Ventura, CA
A local government economic development coalition.
Leg. Issues: BUD, DEF

Outside Counsel/Consultants

Copeland, Lowery & Jacquez
Issues: BUD, DEF
Rep By: Lynnette C. Jacquez

The Ventura Group

Washington, DC

Outside Counsel/Consultants

Ashby and Associates
Rep By: R. Barry Ashby

Ventura Port District

Ventura, CA
Leg. Issues: BUD

Outside Counsel/Consultants

Baker, Donelson, Bearman & Caldwell, P.C.
Issues: BUD
Rep By: J. Keith Kennedy

Ventura, California, County of

Leg. Issues: GOV

Outside Counsel/Consultants

Honberger and Walters, Inc.
Issues: GOV
Rep By: Greg Campbell, Donald Gilchrest, Thomas P. Walters

Venture Catalysts

Outside Counsel/Consultants

Jana McKeag
Rep By: Jana McKeag

Veridian Corp.

1200 S. Hay St.
Suite 1100
Arlington, VA 22202
Tel: (703)575-3100
Fax: (703)575-3200
Leg. Issues: AER, DEF, GOV, LAW, SCI, TRA

Political Action Committee/s

Veridian Inc. Employees Political Action Committee (Veridian-PAC)
1200 S. Hay St.
Suite 1100
Arlington, VA 22202
Tel: (703)575-3170
Fax: (703)575-3233
Contact: Phyllis Seidler

In-house, DC-area Employees

HOWE, Jr., Jerald S.: Senior V. President and General Counsel
SEIDLER, Phyllis: Assistant Secretary

Outside Counsel/Consultants

The Carter Group
Issues: AER, DEF, LAW
Rep By: Michael R. Carter

The Potomac Advocates
Issues: DEF
Rep By: Charles Scalera, Gary L. Sojka

Veridian Engineering

Buffalo, NY
Leg. Issues: BUD, TRA

Outside Counsel/Consultants

Van Scoyoc Associates, Inc.
Issues: BUD, TRA
Rep By: Ray Cole, Steven O. Palmer, Chad Schulken, H. Stewart Van Scoyoc

VeriSign/Network Solutions, Inc.

505 Huntmar Park Dr.
Herndon, VA 20170
Tel: (703)742-0400
Registered: LDA
Leg. Issues: COM, CPI, CPT, MIA, SCI, TEC

Political Action Committee/s

Internet Leadership PAC
505 Huntmar Park Dr.
Herndon, VA 20170
Tel: (703)742-0400
Contact: Shane Tews

In-house, DC-area Employees

AISENBERG, Michael A.: Director of Public Policy
COCHETTI, Roger J.
ROOSA, Christopher: PAC Administrator
RUTT, James: Chief Exec. Officer
SAPIRO, Miriam: Director, International Policy
TEWS, Shane: Director, Public Policy

Outside Counsel/Consultants

Capitol Coalitions Inc.
Issues: TEC
Rep By: Brett P. Scott

Dittus Communications
Rep By: Tom Conway, Gloria S. Dittus, Shelton Jones, Kristin Litterst

The Dutko Group, Inc.
Issues: COM, CPT, TEC
Rep By: Kim Koontz Bayliss, Louis Lehrman, Steve Perry, Juliette M. Raffensperger, Stephen Craig Sayle

Wilmer, Cutler & Pickering
Issues: CPI, CPT, MIA, SCI, TEC
Rep By: Lloyd N. Cutler

Veritas Communications

Ottawa, CANADA

Outside Counsel/Consultants

J. LeBlanc Internat'l, LLC
Rep By: James L. LeBlanc

Veritect

Reston, VA
Leg. Issues: CSP

Outside Counsel/Consultants

The Carter Group
Issues: CSP
Rep By: Michael R. Carter

Verizon Communications

1300 I St. NW
Suite 400 West
Washington, DC 20005
Tel: (202)515-2400
Fax: (202)336-7921
Registered: LDA
Web: www.verizon.com

A national-global voice/data/wireless/information services provider. Formed from the merger of Bell Atlantic and GTE.

Leg. Issues: COM, HCR, LBR, TAX, TEC, TRD

Political Action Committee/s

Verizon Political Action Committee
1300 I St. NW
Suite 400 West
Washington, DC 20005
Tel: (202)515-2440
Fax: (202)336-7920
Contact: Pamela Powers

In-house, DC-area Employees

BARR, William P.: Exec. V. President and General Counsel
BISHOP, Robert D.: Director, Media Relations
BOLAND, Michael: Senior V. President, Federal Legislative Affairs
BUTTA, Susan Cavender: Director, Public Affairs
CABRAL, Victor G.: Exec. Director, International Policy and Regulatory Affairs (The Americas)
CORBETT-SANDERS, Karen: V. President, International Policy and Regulatory Affairs
DILLOW, Frank W.: V. President, Federal Government Relations
EVANS, Gordon R.: V. President, Federal Regulatory
EVE, Eric: Assistant V. President, Federal Government Relations
GASTON, Patrick G.: Exec. Director, Strategic Alliances
GLAVES, Dennis: V. President, Federal Government Relations
GOODMAN, John: Assistant General Counsel
GOULD, Geoffrey C.: Senior V. President, State Government Relations
GUMPER, Frank J.: V. President, Public Policy Development
HOEWING, C. Lincoln "Link": Assistant V. President, Internet
MCCLOSKEY, Colleen A.: Senior V. President, Regulatory Planning
MCLERNON, Kevin: Director, Federal Government Affairs
MEKELBURG, Andrew: Assistant V. President, Federal Government Relations
MOTT, Roger: V. President, Federal Government Relations
MULLET, Mark S.: V. President, Federal Government Relations
POWERS, Pamela: Exec. Director, Political Operations
RICHESON, Darlene: Assistant V. President, Federal Government Relations
SENN, W. Edward: V. President, Federal Government Relations
TAUKE, Hon. Thomas J.: Senior V. President, Public Policy and External Affairs
TROY, Michael H.: V. President, Federal Government Relations
WESTNER, Joe: Assistant V. President, Federal Government Relations
YOUNG, III, Edward D.: Senior V. President, Federal and International Public Policy
ZANOWIC, Kathleen: Assistant V. President, Federal Government Relations

Outside Counsel/Consultants

American Continental Group, Inc.
Issues: TEC
Rep By: Thaddeus E. Strom

Arthur Andersen LLP

Baker & Hostetler LLP
Issues: TEC
Rep By: Frederick H. Graefe, Richard H. Hauser

Bonner & Associates

Collier Shannon Scott, PLLC
Rep By: Doris O. Matsui

Covington & Burling
Issues: TAX
Rep By: Roderick A. DeArment

Law Offices of Kevin G. Curtin
Issues: TEC
Rep By: Kevin G. Curtin

Dewey Ballantine LLP
Rep By: Joseph K. Dowley

Edelman Public Relations Worldwide
Rep By: Neal Flieger

Fleischman and Walsh, L.L.P.

Robert Garcia and Associates, Inc
Rep By: Hon. Robert Garcia

Greener and Hook, LLC

Halprin, Temple, Goodman & Maher
Issues: TEC
Rep By: Joel H. Bernstein, Riley K. Temple

Leslie Harris & Associates
Issues: TEC
Rep By: Jill Bond, Leslie A. Harris

Issue Dynamics Inc.

Manatt, Phelps & Phillips, LLP
Issues: COM, TEC
Rep By: William P. Cook, Erik V. Huey, James R. Jones, John L. Ray

McGuireWoods L.L.P.
Issues: TEC
Rep By: Stephen A. Katsurinis, Jeffrey L. Schlagenhauf

MSP Strategic Communications, Inc.
Rep By: Mitchell S. Pettit

New Frontiers Communications Consulting
Issues: TEC
Rep By: R. David Wilson

O'Connor & Hannan, L.L.P.
Issues: TEC
Rep By: Hon. Larry Pressler

O'Melveny and Myers LLP
Issues: LBR, TEC
Rep By: Arthur B. Culvahouse, Jr.

Quinn Gillespie & Associates

Rhoads Group

Twenty-First Century Group
Issues: TEC
Rep By: Hon. Jack M. Fields, Jr., Cynthia M. Wilkinson

The Udwin Group
Issues: TEC
Rep By: Gerald E. Udwin

Verner, Liipfert, Bernhard, McPherson and Hand, Chartered
Issues: TEC
Rep By: Lawrence R. Sidman

R. Duffy Wall and Associates
Issues: COM, HCR, TAX, TEC, TRD
Rep By: Hon. Bill Brewster, David C. Jory

Verizon Pennsylvania Inc.

1300 I St. NW
Room 400
Washington, DC 20005
Tel: (202)515-2562
Registered: LDA
Web: www.verizon.com

A telephone operating company of Verizon Communications Inc. Headquartered in Philadelphia, PA.

In-house, DC-area Employees

WESTNER, Joe: Director, Federal Relations (Washington)

Verizon Washington, DC, Inc.

1710 H St. NW
Ninth Floor
Washington, DC 20006
Tel: (202)392-1021
Fax: (202)392-1759
Registered: LDA
Web: www.verizon.com

An operating company of Verizon Communications Inc, headquartered in New York, NY.

Political Action Committee/s

Verizon Federal PAC
1710 H St. NW
Ninth Floor
Washington, DC 20006
Tel: (202)392-1021
Fax: (202)392-1759

In-house, DC-area Employees

CLARK, Kenneth: Director, External Affairs
JOHNS, Marie C.: President and Chief Exec. Officer
LEWIS, Catherine: Senior Specialist, Media Relations

Outside Counsel/Consultants

Leftwich & Douglas
Rep By: Natalie O. Ludoway

Skadden, Arps, Slate, Meagher & Flom LLP

Verizon Wireless

1300 I St. NW
Suite 400 West
Washington, DC 20005
Tel: (202)515-2400
Fax: (202)589-3750
Registered: LDA
Web: www.verizonwireless.com

Formerly Bell Atlantic Mobile. Headquartered in New York, NY.

Leg. Issues: BUD, COM, CPT, NAT, TAX, TEC

In-house, DC-area Employees

AZARE, Monica
SCOTT, John H.
WOOLLEY, Howard: V. President, Federal Relations

Outside Counsel/Consultants

The DCS Group

McClure, Gerard & Neuenschwander, Inc.
Issues: BUD, NAT, TEC
Rep By: Steven G. Barringer, Joseph T. Findaro, Matthew Iandoli, Nils W. Johnson, Hon. James A. McClure, Tod O. Neuenschwander

Wiley, Rein & Fielding
Issues: BUD, COM, CPT, TAX, TEC
Rep By: Mimi W. Dawson, Sharon R. Fine, Peter Krug, Mary Jo Manning, Lane McIntosh, Robert L. Pettit

Verner, Liipfert, Bernhard, McPherson and Hand, Chartered

901 15th St. NW
Suite 700
Washington, DC 20005-2301
Tel: (202)371-6000
Fax: (202)371-6279
Registered: LDA, FARA
Web: www.verner.com
E-mail: verner@verner.com
Leg. Issues: AER, AVI, CPT, ECN, FIN, FUE, GOV, HCR, HOU, PHA, POS, TAX, TEC, TOB, TRD

Political Action Committee/s

Verner, Liipfert, Bernhard, McPherson and Hand PAC
901 15th St. NW
Suite 700
Washington, DC 20005-2301
Tel: (202)371-6000
Fax: (202)371-6279

In-house, DC-area Employees

BERG, Michael D.: Member of Firm
BERNHARD, Berl: Co-Founder
BERNSTEIN, Matthew C.: Member of Firm
BLANCHARD, Hon. James J.: Member of Firm
BOGGS, Virginia R.: Associate
BROOM, R. Stuart: Member of Firm
BROWN, Jamie E.
CARTWRIGHT, Suzanne D.: Director, Legislative Affairs
COATS, Hon. Daniel R.: Special Counsel
COE, Jo-Anne: Strategic Planner
DARNEILLE, III, Hopewell H.: Member of Firm
DOLE, Hon. Robert J.: Special Counsel
DUNCAN, III, Lawrence: Associate
DWYER, Denis J.: Dir., Legislation and Federal Affairs
ESKIN, Andrew D.: Member of Firm
EVANS, William C.: Member of Firm
FITZGERALD, David A.: Associate
FREEMAN, Rosemary B.: Director, Public Affairs
FREILICH, Harold I.: Member of Firm
GARON, Richard J.: Senior Advisor, International Relations

GRANT, Andrea J.: Member of Firm
GROSSMAN, Marla P.: Member of Firm
HAND, Lloyd N.: Member of Firm
HARRIS, Marshall F.
HART, Vicki E.: Director, Legislation and Federal Affairs
HAWLEY, Noelle M.: Associate
HICKIE, Jane: Member of Firm
HOCHBERG, Philip R.: Of Counsel
JACOBSOHN, David B.: Of Counsel
JOHNSON, Stephen R.: Associate
KELLER, Thomas J.: Member of Firm
KLEIN, Gary J.: Member of Firm
KNEUER, John M. R.
KRAMER, William D.: Member of Firm
LEGRO, Stanley W.: Of Counsel
LEVINSON, Lawrence E.: Member of Firm
LOUD, Ted: Public Relations Coordinator
LUTZ, Martin T.: Member of Firm
MACKINNON, Douglas M.: Director, Communications to the Office of Hon. Robert J. Dole
MANSON, III, Joseph L.: Member of Firm
MARTIN, Jenifer: Associate
MCDONALD, Hon. Jack H.: Consultant
MCGRATH, Edward J.: Member of Firm
MCPHERSON, Harry C.: Member of Firm
MEISTER, Brenda G.: Member of Firm
MENDELSOHN, Martin: Member of Firm
MERRIGAN, John A.: Member of Firm
MIETUS, John R.: Member of Firm
MIGDAIL, Evan M.: Member of Firm
MINOR, William H.: Associate
MITCHELL, Hon. George J.: Special Counsel
MIZOGUCHI, Brian A.: Member of Firm
MORRIS, Sara W.: Telecommunications Consultant
NATALIE, Ronald B.: Member of Firm
NEILSON, Mikol S.: Of Counsel
NORDSTROM, Paul E.: Member of Firm
O'BRIEN, Michael E.: Legislative Consultant
ORTMAN, Glen J.: Member of Firm
PHILLIPS, Steven R.: Member of Firm
PICARD, B. Donovan: Shareholder
PICKUP, James A.: Associate
POMMER, Russell E.: Member of Firm
PROTO, Neil T.: Member of Firm
QUIRK, Sherry A.: Member of Firm
RICHARDS, Ann W.: Senior Advisor
ROBERTS, Michael J.: Member of Firm
RUTTEN, Timothy M.: Associate
SANCHEZ, Ignacio E.
SHAKOW, Susannah W.: Associate
SHELIGA, Nancy A.: Legislative Assistant
SIDDALL, David R.: Member of Firm
SIDMAN, Lawrence R.: Member of Firm
SPEED-BOST, Regina: Of Counsel
STERNE, Jr., John H.: Of Counsel
SWANSTROM, Deborah A.: Member of Firm
TEMKIN, Susan O.: Member of Firm
VINCE, Clinton A.: Member of Firm
WEINBERG, Linda M.: Member of Firm
WEISS, David A.: Director, Trade Policy
WERNER, Eric T.: Member of Firm
YOUNGBLOOD, Theresa M.: Associate
ZEITLER, William A.: Member of Firm
ZENTAY, John H.: Member of Firm

Outside Counsel/Consultants

Barents Group LLC
Issues: TOB
Rep By: David M. Skanderson, Linden C. Smith

Jack H. McDonald
Issues: AER, AVI, CPT, ECN, FIN, FUE, HCR, HOU, PHA, POS, TAX, TEC, TOB, TRD
Rep By: Hon. Jack H. McDonald

Robertson, Monagle & Eastaugh
Issues: GOV
Rep By: Bradley D. Gilman, Rick E. Marks, Steven W. Silver

Vernon, California, City of

Leg. Issues: IMM

Outside Counsel/Consultants

Whitten & Diamond
Issues: IMM
Rep By: Robert M. Diamond, Jamie L. Whitten

Vero Beach, Florida, City of

Leg. Issues: AVI

Outside Counsel/Consultants

AB Management Associates, Inc.
Issues: AVI
Rep By: Larry P. Barnett

Vertical Flight Foundation

217 N. Washington St.
Alexandria, VA 22314
Tel: (703)684-6777
Fax: (703)739-9279
Web: www.vtol.org
E-mail: ahs703@aol.com

In-house, DC-area Employees

FLATER, M. E. Rhett

Vertical Net, Inc.

Outside Counsel/Consultants

Verner, Liipfert, Bernhard, McPherson and Hand, Chartered
Rep By: John A. Merrigan

Vertis Neuroscience

St. Louis, MO
Leg. Issues: MED, MMM

Outside Counsel/Consultants

Public Policy Partners, LLC
Issues: MED, MMM
Rep By: Hon. David Durenberger, Daniel Waldmann, Jeffrey Weekly

Very Special Arts

1300 Connecticut Ave. NW
Suite 700
Washington, DC 20036
Tel: (202)628-2800
Fax: (202)737-0725
Web: www.vsarts.org

Creates learning opportunities through the arts for people with disabilities, especially children and youth.

Leg. Issues: BUD, EDU

In-house, DC-area Employees

KEMP, John D.: President and Chief Exec. Officer
MACKINNON, Jessie: V. President, Communications

Outside Counsel/Consultants

Dean Blakey & Moskowitz
Issues: BUD, EDU
Rep By: Ellin J. Nolan

H. D. Vest Financial Service

Irving, TX
Registered: LDA

Outside Counsel/Consultants

Preston Gates Ellis & Rouvelas Meeds LLP
Rep By: Tim L. Peckinpaugh

Vest Inc.

Los Angeles, CA
Leg. Issues: TRA

Outside Counsel/Consultants

Schagrin Associates
Issues: TRA
Rep By: Tamara L. Browne, Roger B. Schagrin

Vestal Group of Companies

Istanbul, TURKEY
Leg. Issues: APP

Outside Counsel/Consultants

Arnold & Porter
Issues: APP
Rep By: Nancy L. Perkins

Veterans of Foreign Wars of the U.S.

200 Maryland Ave. NE
Washington, DC 20002
Tel: (202)543-2239
Fax: (202)543-6719
Registered: LDA

Offers services to veterans. Headquartered in Kansas City, MO.

Leg. Issues: VET

Political Action Committee/s

VFW-Political Action Committee, Inc.

200 Maryland Ave. NE
Washington, DC 20002
Tel: (202)543-2239
Fax: (202)543-6719

In-house, DC-area Employees

CARNEY, Jack: PAC, Contact
CULLINAN, Dennis M.: Director, National Legislative Service
DANIELS, Sidney: Deputy Director, National Legislative Services/Action Code
JUARBE, Jr., Frederico: Director, National Veterans Service
MANHAN, Robert D.: Assistant Director, National Legislative Service
SMITH, William G.: Director, Public Affairs
WALLACE, Robert E.: Exec. Director

VHA Inc.

1200 New Hampshire Ave. NW
Suite 410
Washington, DC 20036
Tel: (202)721-8100
Fax: (202)721-8105
Registered: LDA
Web: www.vha.com
Leg. Issues: HCR, TAX

Political Action Committee/s

Voluntary Hospitals of America Political Action Committee

1200 New Hampshire Ave. NW
Suite 410
Washington, DC 20036
Tel: (202)721-8100
Fax: (202)721-8105
Contact: Edward Goodman

In-house, DC-area Employees

BOURQUE, Daniel P.: Group Senior V. President
CURRY, Page: Government Relations Representative
GOODMAN, Edward: V. President, Public Policy

Outside Counsel/Consultants

Gardner, Carton and Douglas
Issues: TAX
Rep By: Kathleen M. Nilles

Shaw Pittman

Viacom Inc.

1501 M St. NW
Suite 1100
Washington, DC 20005
Tel: (202)785-7300
Fax: (202)785-6360
Registered: LDA
Web: www.viacom.com

An entertainment and publishing company. The operations of Viacom include Blockbuster, CBS Television, CBS Television Stations Division, Black Entertainment Television, MTV Networks, Simon and Schuster Publishing, television stattions and movie screens in 12 countries. Viacom holds a half interest in Comedy Central and UPN. Parent company is National Amusements, Inc., which operates approximately 1,100 screens in the United States, the United Kingdom and South America.

Leg. Issues: COM, CPT, TEC

Political Action Committee/s

Viacom Political Action Committee

1501 M St. NW
Suite 1100
Washington, DC 20005
Tel: (202)785-7300
Fax: (202)785-6360
Contact: Patrick W. Archer

In-house, DC-area Employees

ARCHER, Patrick W.: Legislative Assistant
FERRELL, DeDe: V. President, Government Affairs
FRESE, Elizabeth Norris: Office Manager, Government Affairs
LUCEY, Anne C.: V. President, Regulatory Affairs
MACKINNON, Gail G.: V. President of Government Affairs
MELTON, Carol: Senior V. President, Government Affairs

Outside Counsel/Consultants

McMahon and Associates

O'Neill, Athy & Casey, P.C.
Issues: TEC
Rep By: Andrew Athy, Jr., Christopher R. O'Neill

Quinn Gillespie & Associates

VIASA

Caracas, VENEZUELA

Outside Counsel/Consultants

Squire, Sanders & Dempsey L.L.P.
Rep By: Robert D. Papkin, Edward W. Sauer

ViaSat, Inc.

Carlsbad, CA
Leg. Issues: AER, BUD, DEF, SCI

Outside Counsel/Consultants

Ritter and Bourjaily, Inc.
Issues: AER, BUD, DEF, SCI
Rep By: Monte F. Bourjaily, III

Viatel, Inc.

2000 Pennsylvania Ave. NW
Suite 500
Washington, DC 20006
Tel: (202)887-1574
Registered: LDA
Leg. Issues: TEC, TRD

In-house, DC-area Employees

GINSBURG, Mindy: V. President, Regulatory Affairs

Viatical Ass'n of America

Washington, DC

Outside Counsel/Consultants

Smith, Bucklin and Associates, Inc.
Rep By: William E. Kelley

Viaticus, Inc.

Chicago, IL
Leg. Issues: TAX

Outside Counsel/Consultants

Washington Council Ernst & Young
Issues: TAX
Rep By: Doug Badger, Lauren Darling, John L. Doney, Jayne T. Fitzgerald, LaBrenda Garrett-Nelson, Gary J. Gasper, Bruce A. Gates, Nick Giordano, Cathy Koch, Robert J. Leonard, Richard Meltzer, Phillip D. Moseley, John D. Porter, Robert M. Rozen, Donna Steele-Flynn, Timothy J. Urban

ViaTronix

Stoneybrook, NY
Leg. Issues: HCR

Outside Counsel/Consultants

Ervin Technical Associates, Inc. (ETA)
Issues: HCR
Rep By: Hon. Joseph M. McDade

Victims of Communism Memorial Foundation

Washington, DC
Leg. Issues: FOR

Outside Counsel/Consultants

George H. Denison
Issues: FOR
Rep By: George H. Denison

Victims Rights PAC

1400 16th St. NW
Suite 330
Washington, DC 20036
Tel: (202)462-8800
Fax: (202)265-6564

In-house, DC-area Employees

BROWN, Charles G.

City of Victorville Redevelopment Agency

Victorville, CA
Leg. Issues: AVI, BUD, DEF, TRA

Outside Counsel/Consultants

Copeland, Lowery & Jacquez
Issues: AVI, BUD, DEF, TRA
Rep By: Jeffrey S. Shockey

Victorville, California, City of

Leg. Issues: BUD, TRA

Outside Counsel/Consultants

E. Del Smith and Co.
Issues: BUD, TRA
Rep By: Margaret Allen, E. Del Smith

Victory Wholesale Grocers Inc.

Springboro, OH
Leg. Issues: CPT

Outside Counsel/Consultants

Stephen F. Sims and Associates
Issues: CPT
Rep By: Stephen F. Sims

Vidalia Onion Business Council

Vidalia, GA
Leg. Issues: AGR

Outside Counsel/Consultants

Robert L. Redding
Issues: AGR
Rep By: Robert L. Redding, Jr.

Video Network Communications

Portsmouth, NH
Leg. Issues: DEF

Outside Counsel/Consultants

Ervin Technical Associates, Inc. (ETA)
Issues: DEF
Rep By: William J. Andahazy, Hon. Jack Edwards, James L. Ervin

Viejas Band of Kumeyaay Indians

Alpine, CA
Leg. Issues: GAM, IND

Outside Counsel/Consultants

Janus-Merritt Strategies, L.L.C.
Issues: GAM, IND
Rep By: Thomas W. Brierton, Scott P. Hoffman, Omar Nashashibi, Bethany Noble, Mark J. Robertson, J. Daniel Walsh

SENSE, INC.
Issues: GAM, IND
Rep By: C. Juliet Pittman

Vietnam Veterans of America Foundation

2001 S St. NW
Suite 740
Washington, DC 20009
Web: www.vvaf.org
Tel: (202)483-9222
Registered: LDA

A provider of humanitarian assistance to victims of war. Focuses primarily on landmine victims.

Leg. Issues: DEF, FOR, LAW, VET

In-house, DC-area Employees

LOGE, Peter
MCKENNA, Tiffany: Director

Outside Counsel/Consultants

Jefferson-Waterman Internat'l, LLC
Issues: FOR
Rep By: Col. Richard L. Klass, USAF (Ret.)

Zuckerman Spaeder L.L.P.
Issues: LAW
Rep By: Charles Angulo, Ronald H. Weich

Vietnam Veterans of America, Inc.

8605 Cameron St.
Suite 400
Silver Spring, MD 20910
Web: www.vva.org
Tel: (301)585-4000
Fax: (301)585-0519
Registered: LDA

A national service organization with over 500 chapters and 52,000 members. Focuses on issues related to the Vietnam experience and Vietnam veterans.

In-house, DC-area Employees

DUGGINS, George C.: President
WEIDMAN, Rick: Director, Government Relations
WILSON, Monty: National Service Representative

View PAC

Outside Counsel/Consultants

Bogart Associates Inc.

Village Enterprises

New York, NY

Outside Counsel/Consultants

Peter S. Barash Associates, Inc.
Rep By: Peter S. Barash

Village of Kiryas Joel

Monroe, NY
Leg. Issues: MED

Outside Counsel/Consultants

Russ Reid Co.
Issues: MED
Rep By: Thomas C. Keller, Mark D. McIntyre, Jovita Wenner

Villanova University

Villanova, PA

Outside Counsel/Consultants

Cassidy & Associates, Inc.
Rep By: Gerald S. J. Cassidy, Shawn Edwards, Daniel J. McNamara, Blenda Pinto-Riddick

The Vinegar Institute

1101 15th St. NW
Suite 202
Washington, DC 20005
Tel: (202)785-3232
Fax: (202)223-9741

In-house, DC-area Employees

CRISTOL, Richard E.: Washington Representative

Outside Counsel/Consultants

The Kellen Company
Rep By: Richard E. Cristol

Vinifera Wine Growers Ass'n

P.O. Box 10045
Alexandria, VA 22310
E-mail: thewinexchange@aol.com
Tel: (703)922-7049
Fax: (703)922-0617

A non-profit wine education and advocacy association.

Leg. Issues: ALC, BEV, CSP, TRD

In-house, DC-area Employees

MURCHIE, Gordon W.: President

Vinyl Institute

Morristown, NJ
Web: www.vinyl-info.org
Leg. Issues: CHM, CSP, HCR

Outside Counsel/Consultants

Jefferson Government Relations, L.L.C.
Issues: CHM, CSP, HCR
Rep By: Thomas R. Donnelly, Jr., Robert D. McArver, Jr., Patricia A. Power, Randal P. Schumacher

Violence Policy Center

1140 19th St. NW
Suite 600
Washington, DC 20036
Web: www.vpc.org
E-mail: mail@vpc.org
Tel: (202)822-8200
Fax: (202)822-8205
Registered: LDA

A non-profit educational foundation that conducts research on firearms violence and works to reduce gun death and injury in America.

Leg. Issues: FIR, TOR

In-house, DC-area Employees

BROCK, Karen: Health Policy Analyst
DIAZ, Tom: Senior Policy Analyst
FISHER, Lynn: Communications Assistant
LANGLEY, Marty: Policy Analyst
RAND, Kristen: Legislative Director
SELIGMAN, Naomi: Communications Director
STENZEL, Aimee: Publications Coordinator
SUDBAY, Joe: Public Policy Director
SUGARMANN, Josh: Exec. Director

Virgin Atlantic Airways

Crawley, UNITED KINGDOM
Leg. Issues: TRA

Outside Counsel/Consultants

The Hawthorn Group, L.C.

Levine & Co.
Issues: TRA
Rep By: Ken Levine

Virgin Islands Watch and Jewelry Manufacturers Ass'n

Outside Counsel/Consultants

Winston & Strawn
Rep By: Edward F. Gerwin, Jr., Peter N. Hiebert

Virgin Islands, Government of the

Charlotte Amalie, VI
Leg. Issues: BUD, DIS, GOV, TAX, TRD

Outside Counsel/Consultants

The Dutko Group, Inc.

Winston & Strawn
Issues: BUD, DIS, GOV, TAX, TRD
Rep By: Peter N. Hiebert, Charles L. Kinney, John C. Kirtland, John D. McMickle, John A. Waits, II

Virgin Islands, Office of the Governor

444 N. Capitol St. NW
Suite 305
Washington, DC 20001
Tel: (202)624-3562
Fax: (202)624-3594

The Washington office of the U.S. Virgin Islands.

In-house, DC-area Employees

CORBIN, Dr. Carlyle: Representative, External Affairs

Virgin Valley Water District

Mesquite, NV
Leg. Issues: BUD

Outside Counsel/Consultants

The Furman Group
Issues: BUD
Rep By: K. Link Browder, Thomas M. James

Virginia Baseball Club

6420 Grovedale Dr.
Alexandria, VA 22310
Tel: (703)971-1732
Fax: (703)971-5327

An investor group formed to bring major league baseball to Northern Virginia.

In-house, DC-area Employees

COLLINS, III, William L.: Chairman and Chief Executive Officer
URBANSKI, Lynn C.: Corporate Secretary, Public Affairs

Virginia Beach, Virginia, City of

Leg. Issues: ENV, TRA, TRD

Outside Counsel/Consultants

Alcalde & Fay
Issues: ENV, TRA, TRD
Rep By: Mary Litton Fowler, Angela Plott, Nancy Gibson Prowitt

Virginia Center for Innovative Technology

Leg. Issues: SCI

Outside Counsel/Consultants

The Wexler Group
Issues: SCI
Rep By: Adam Eisgrau, Patric G. Link, Hon. Robert S. Walker

Virginia Commonwealth Trading Co.

Virginia Beach, VA
Leg. Issues: CPT

Outside Counsel/Consultants

Verner, Liipfert, Bernhard, McPherson and Hand, Chartered
Issues: CPT
Rep By: Lloyd N. Hand, Noelle M. Hawley, James A. Pickup, Linda M. Weinberg, David A. Weiss

Virginia Commonwealth University
Richmond, VA
Leg. Issues: BUD, EDU, HCR, IMM, SCI, TAX

Outside Counsel/Consultants

Lewis-Burke Associates
Issues: BUD, EDU, HCR, IMM, SCI, TAX
Rep By: Rachel Brown, April L. Burke, Mark A. Burnham, Michael Ledford

Virginia Liaison Office
444 N. Capitol St. NW
Suite 214
Washington, DC 20001
Tel: (202)783-1769
Fax: (202)783-7687

In-house, DC-area Employees
FREEMAN, III, Joseph E.: Director, Virginia Liaison Office
HIVLEY, Dawn: Special Assistant, State/Federal Relations
TAYLOR, Duane: Special Assistant, State/Federal Relations

Virginia Living Museum
Newport News, VA
Leg. Issues: ANI, BUD, ECN, EDU, ENV, NAT, SCI

Outside Counsel/Consultants

Madison Government Affairs
Issues: ANI, BUD, ECN, EDU, ENV, NAT, SCI
Rep By: Paul J. Hirsch, Myron M. Jacobson

Virginia Peanut Growers Ass'n
Capron, VA
Manages peanut marketing.

Leg. Issues: AGR, BUD, TRD

Outside Counsel/Consultants

Meyers & Associates
Issues: AGR, BUD, TRD
Rep By: Fran Boyd, Larry D. Meyers, Richard L. Meyers

Virginia Polytechnic Institute and State University
Blacksburg, VA
Leg. Issues: BUD, EDU

Outside Counsel/Consultants

Van Scoyoc Associates, Inc.
Issues: BUD, EDU
Rep By: Paul Grimm, Buzz Hawley, Paul Iarrobino, H. Stewart Van Scoyoc

Virginia Tech Intellectual Properties, Inc.
Blacksburg, VA
Leg. Issues: BUD, COM, EDU, SCI, TRA

Outside Counsel/Consultants

Van Scoyoc Associates, Inc.
Issues: BUD, COM, EDU, SCI, TRA
Rep By: Jan Schoonmaker, H. Stewart Van Scoyoc

Virginia Wineries Ass'n
P.O. Box 31342
Alexandria, VA 22310
E-mail: thewinexchange@aol.com
Tel: (703)922-7049
Fax: (703)922-0617

A non-profit trade association representing Viriginia wineries; promotes quality wine production, marketing and consumer education.

Leg. Issues: AGR, ALC, BEV, CSP, TRD

In-house, DC-area Employees
MURCHIE, Gordon W.: Exec. Director

Virginia-Carolina's Peanut Political Action Committee
412 First St. SE
Suite One
Washington, DC 20003
Tel: (202)484-2773
Fax: (202)484-0770

In-house, DC-area Employees
MEYERS, Larry D.: Treasurer

Outside Counsel/Consultants

Meyers & Associates
Rep By: Larry D. Meyers

Virologic, Inc.
South San Francisco, CA
Leg. Issues: HCR

Outside Counsel/Consultants

Holland & Knight LLP
Issues: HCR
Rep By: Jeffrey F. Boothe

Virtual Drug Development
Brentwood, TN
Leg. Issues: DEF

Outside Counsel/Consultants

American Defense Internat'l, Inc.
Issues: DEF
Rep By: Michael Herson, Van D. Hipp, Jr., Dave Wilberding

Virtual Impact Productions
Longwood, FL
Leg. Issues: DEF

Outside Counsel/Consultants

American Defense Internat'l, Inc.
Issues: DEF
Rep By: Michael Herson, Van D. Hipp, Jr., Dave Wilberding

Virtual Medical Group
Morrisville, NC
Leg. Issues: HCR

Outside Counsel/Consultants

McMillan, Hill & Associates
Issues: HCR

VISA U.S.A., Inc.
2121 K St. NW
Suite 700
Washington, DC 20037
Tel: (202)296-9230
Fax: (202)862-5498
Registered: LDA
Leg. Issues: BAN, BNK, CPT, CSP, FIN, HCR, IMM, SCI, TAX

In-house, DC-area Employees
BENTZ, Rhonda: Director, Public Affairs
LAYMAN, Thomas: Senior V. President
MACCARTHY, Mark: Senior V. President for Public Policy
MUSKETT, Margarete: Exec. Assistant
SMITH, W. Lamar: Senior V. President, Government Relations
TOWNE, Robert: V. President

Outside Counsel/Consultants

Creative Response Concepts

Morrison & Foerster LLP
Issues: BAN, BNK, CPT, CSP, FIN, SCI, TAX
Rep By: L. Richard Fischer, Thomas C. McCormick

O'Connor & Hannan, L.L.P.
Issues: BAN, BNK, FIN, TAX
Rep By: Roy C. Coffee, Hon. Thomas J. Corcoran, Danielle Fagre, Timothy W. Jenkins, Patrick E. O'Donnell, Thomas H. Quinn

The Smith-Free Group
Issues: BNK
Rep By: James C. Free, W. Timothy Locke, James E. Smith

Timmons and Co., Inc.
Issues: BAN
Rep By: Michael J. Bates, Douglas F. Bennett, Ellen B. Fitzgibbons, Bryce L. "Larry" Harlow, Timothy J. Keating, Tom C. Korologos, Richard J. Tarplin, William E. Timmons, Sr., William E. Timmons, Jr.

The Velasquez Group
Issues: BAN
Rep By: Jay Velasquez

Verner, Liipfert, Bernhard, McPherson and Hand, Chartered
Issues: CPT, FIN, HCR, IMM, TAX
Rep By: Andrew D. Eskin, Vicki E. Hart, Jenifer Martin, John A. Merrigan, Theresa M. Youngblood

The Wexler Group
Issues: BAN, CPT, CSP, HCR
Rep By: Cynthia E. Berry, Jody A. Hoffman

Visalia, California, City of
Leg. Issues: GOV, ROD, TRD

Outside Counsel/Consultants

Jefferson Government Relations, L.L.C.
Issues: GOV, ROD, TRD
Rep By: William A. Roberts, Daniel J. Sheehan

Vishay Intertechnologies, Inc.
Malvern, PA

Outside Counsel/Consultants

Porter, Wright, Morris & Arthur, LLP
Rep By: Leslie Alan Glick

Visible Genetics
Suwanee, GA
Leg. Issues: HCR, MED, MMM

Outside Counsel/Consultants

Policy Directions, Inc.
Issues: HCR, MED, MMM
Rep By: Kathleen "Kay" Holcombe, Stephen Michael, Frankie L. Trull

VISICU
Baltimore, MD
Leg. Issues: DEF

Outside Counsel/Consultants

American Defense Internat'l, Inc.
Issues: DEF
Rep By: Michael Herson, Van D. Hipp, Jr., Dave Wilberding

Vision Council of America
1700 Diagonal Rd.
Suite 500
Alexandria, VA 22314
Web: www.visionsite.org
E-mail: vca@visionsite.org
Tel: (703)548-4560
Fax: (703)548-4580

In-house, DC-area Employees
THOMAS, William C.: Exec. V. President/Chief Exec. Officer
WILSON, William J.: Director, Public Relations

Vision Systems Internat'l
San Jose, CA

Outside Counsel/Consultants

American Systems Internat'l Corp.
Rep By: Robert D. McVey, William H. Skipper, Jr.

Vision Technologies, Inc.
Rogers, AR
Leg. Issues: AVI, COM, CPI, MAN, SCI, SMB, TEC

Outside Counsel/Consultants

Jay Grant & Associates
Issues: AVI, COM, CPI, MAN, SCI, SMB, TEC
Rep By: David M. Olive

Visitalk.com
Phoenix, AZ
Leg. Issues: SCI

Outside Counsel/Consultants

Capital Strategies Group, Inc.
Issues: SCI
Rep By: Tammi Hayes

Visiting Nurse Service of New York
New York, NY
Leg. Issues: HCR, MED

Outside Counsel/Consultants

The GrayWell Group, Inc.
Issues: HCR

VSAdc.com
Issues: HCR, MED
Rep By: Carol A. McDaid, H. Stewart Van Scoyoc

Visiting Nurses Health System
Atlanta, GA
Leg. Issues: HCR

Outside Counsel/Consultants

Hurt, Norton & Associates
Issues: HCR
Rep By: Robert H. Hurt, Frank Norton

Visually Impaired Data Processors Internat'l
1155 15th St. NW
Suite 1004
Washington, DC 20005
Web: www.acb.org
E-mail: info@acb.org
Tel: (202)467-5081
Fax: (202)467-5085

An affiliate of the American Council of the Blind.

In-house, DC-area Employees
CRAWFORD, Charles
EDWARDS, Paul: President

Visually Impaired Veterans of America
1155 15th St. NW
Suite 1004
Washington, DC 20005
Web: www.acb.org
Tel: (202)467-5081
Fax: (202)467-5085

In-house, DC-area Employees
DOWLAND, David: President

Vitarine Pharmaceuticals Inc.

Outside Counsel/Consultants

Kleinfeld, Kaplan and Becker
Rep By: Alan H. Kaplan

Vitas Healthcare Corp.

555 13th St. NW
Suite Three East
Washington, DC 20004
Tel: (202)637-7228
Fax: (202)637-8715
Web: www.vitas.com
E-mail: tom@vitas.com

Headquartered in Miami, FL.

Leg. Issues: HCR, MMM

In-house, DC-area Employees
KOUTSOUMPAS, J. Thomas: V. President, Public Affairs

Outside Counsel/Consultants

Holland & Knight LLP
Issues: HCR, MMM
Rep By: Janet R. Studley

Verner, Liipfert, Bernhard, McPherson and Hand, Chartered
Issues: HCR, MMM
Rep By: Vicki E. Hart

ViTel Net

Vienna, VA
Leg. Issues: DEF

Outside Counsel/Consultants

American Defense Internat'l, Inc.
Issues: DEF
Rep By: Michael Herson, Van D. Hipp, Jr., Dave Wilberding

Vitol, S.A., Inc.

Houston, TX

A petroleum trading company.

Outside Counsel/Consultants

Collier Shannon Scott, PLLC
Rep By: Kathleen Clark Kies, Gregory M. Scott, Michael D. Sherman

Vivendi Universal

1401 I St. NW
Suite 1220
Washington, DC 20005
Tel: (202)898-6400
Fax: (202)898-6454
Registered: LDA

Headquartered in Paris, France.

Leg. Issues: ADV, ART, BEV, CAW, CPT, DEF, FIN, TAX, TOU, TRA, TRD

In-house, DC-area Employees
BENDALL, Jennifer L.: Senior Federal Lobbyist
CAPLAN, Bennett: Director, Policy Development
CHELLI, Marie: Director, Public Policy
GERSON, Matthew T.: V. President, Entertainment Public Policy
GODLOWSKI, Matt: Manager, Public Policy
HELLER, Stephen: Associate, Government Affairs

Outside Counsel/Consultants

Clark & Weinstock, Inc.
Issues: TOU
Rep By: Hon. Vic H. Fazio, Jr., Sandi Stuart, Hon. John Vincent "Vin" Weber

Fontheim Internat'l, LLC
Issues: FIN, TRD
Rep By: Claude G. B. Fontheim, Kenneth I. Levinson

Janus-Merritt Strategies, L.L.C.
Issues: ADV, ART, BEV, CPT, TAX
Rep By: Scott P. Hoffman, Bethany Noble, Mark J. Robertson, J. Daniel Walsh

Podesta/Mattoon
Rep By: Ann Delory, Kimberley Fritts, Matthew Gelman, Claudia James, Andrew C. Littman, Anthony T. Podesta

VIVRA

Burlingame, CA

Outside Counsel/Consultants

McDermott, Will and Emery
Rep By: Calvin P. Johnson, Michael A. Romansky, Eric P. Zimmerman

VLOC

New Port Richey, FL
Leg. Issues: DEF

Outside Counsel/Consultants

SISCORP
Issues: DEF
Rep By: Robert Meissner

Vocus Government Relations

4325 Forbes Blvd.
Lanham, MD 20706
Tel: (301)459-2590
Fax: (301)459-2827
Web: www.vocus.com
E-mail: info@vocus.com

Provides web-based solutions for government relations, public relations, and investor relations.

In-house, DC-area Employees
WILLIAMS, Wade S.: Director, Government Affairs

Voest Alpine Steel

New York, NY

Outside Counsel/Consultants

Barnes, Richardson and Colburn
Rep By: Gunter Von Conrad

Voices, Inc.

Beverly Hills, CA
Leg. Issues: ADV

Outside Counsel/Consultants

Mattox Woolfolk, LLC
Issues: ADV
Rep By: Richard B. Mattox, Deya Smith, Gregory Willis, Brian P. Woolfolk

VoiceStream Wireless Corp.

Leg. Issues: GOV, TEC, TRD

Outside Counsel/Consultants

Baker, Donelson, Bearman & Caldwell, P.C.
Issues: TEC
Rep By: Hon. Howard H. Baker, Jr., J. Keith Kennedy, John C. Tuck

Cassidy & Associates, Inc.
Issues: TEC, TRD
Rep By: John A. Crumbliss, Christy Carson Evans, Lawrence C. Grossman, W. Campbell Kaufman, IV, Mary Kate Kelly-Johnson, Arthur D. Mason, Michael Merola, Hon. Martin A. Russo, Dan C. Tate, Sr.

Harris, Wiltshire & Grannis LLP
Issues: TEC
Rep By: Karen Gulick, Scott Blake Harris, John T. Nakahata

Preston Gates Ellis & Rouvelas Meeds LLP
Issues: TEC
Rep By: Werner W. Brandt, Hon. David Funderburk, Pamela J. Garvie, Hon. Lloyd Meeds, Sol Mosher, Ralph D. Nurnberger, Michael J. O'Neil, Tim L. Peckinpaugh, Emanuel L. Rouvelas, Mark H. Ruge, Chad See, W. Dennis Stephens, W. David Thomas, Steven R. "Rick" Valentine

Ryan, Phillips, Utrecht & MacKinnon
Issues: GOV, TEC
Rep By: Rodney Hoppe, Jeffrey M. MacKinnon, William D. Phillips, Mark D. Planning, Thomas M. Ryan, Joseph V. Vasapoli

Townsend Solheim
Issues: TEC
Rep By: Linda T. Solheim

Voith Hydro, Inc.

876 N. Greenbrier St.
Arlington, VA 22205-1221
Tel: (703)741-0776
Fax: (703)741-0749
Registered: LDA
E-mail: rthor@erols.com

Concerned with the sale, financing, and export of hydraulic turbines for electric power generation.

Leg. Issues: BAN

In-house, DC-area Employees
THORESEN, Robert: Consultant

Volkswagen of America, Inc.

1300 Pennsylvania Ave. NW
Suite 860
Washington, DC 20004
Tel: (202)842-5800
Fax: (202)842-8612
Registered: LDA

Specializes in the importation and distribution of automobiles. Headquartered in Auburn Hills, MI.

Leg. Issues: AUT

In-house, DC-area Employees
KENNEBECK, Joseph W.: Director, Government Affairs
LEAHY, W. Christopher: Manager, Government Relations
SMITH, S. Marijke: Government Relations Assistant

Volkswagen, AG

Wolfsburg, GERMANY
Leg. Issues: AUT, CAW, CSP, ENV, TRA, TRD

Outside Counsel/Consultants

Akin, Gump, Strauss, Hauer & Feld, L.L.P.
Issues: AUT, CAW, CSP, ENV, TRA, TRD
Rep By: David Geanacopoulos, Daniel L. Spiegel, S. Bruce Wilson

Vollmer Public Relations

Houston, TX

Outside Counsel/Consultants

Cassidy & Associates, Inc.
Rep By: W. Campbell Kaufman, IV

Volunteer Trustees of Not-for-Profit Hospitals

818 18th St. NW
Suite 410
Washington, DC 20006
Tel: (202)659-0338
Fax: (202)659-0116
Registered: LDA
Web: www.volunteertrustees.org
E-mail: vt@sprintmail.com

A national association of not-for-profit, hospital and health system governing boards.

In-house, DC-area Employees
MILLER, Linda B.: President

Volunteers in Technical Assistance

1600 Wilson Blvd.
Suite 710
Arlington, VA 22209
Tel: (703)276-1800
Fax: (703)243-1865
Web: www.vita.org
E-mail: vita@vita.org

In-house, DC-area Employees
SCHARFFENBERGER, George: President

Volusia, Florida, County of

Deland, FL
Leg. Issues: AVI, BUD, NAT, TRA

Outside Counsel/Consultants

Jefferson Government Relations, L.L.C.
Issues: AVI, BUD, NAT, TRA
Rep By: Patricia A. Power, William A. Roberts, Daniel J. Sheehan

Voorhees College

Denmark, SC
Leg. Issues: BUD, EDU, WEL

Outside Counsel/Consultants

Dean Blakey & Moskowitz
Issues: BUD, EDU, WEL
Rep By: William A. Blakey

Vornado Inc.

Saddle Brook, NJ

A real estate investment trust.

Leg. Issues: RES, TAX

Outside Counsel/Consultants

Williams & Jensen, P.C.
Issues: RES, TAX
Rep By: Robert E. Glennon, Jr.

Vortec Corp.

Collegeville, PA
Leg. Issues: ENG

Outside Counsel/Consultants

Hartke & Hartke
Issues: ENG
Rep By: Vance Hartke, Wayne Hartke

Vortex, Inc.

Ft. Collins, CO
Leg. Issues: DEF

Outside Counsel/Consultants

The Carter Group
Issues: DEF
Rep By: Michael R. Carter, Scott D. McClean

Votainer Consolidation Service

New York, NY

Outside Counsel/Consultants

Rodriguez O'Donnell Fuerst Gonzalez & Williams
Rep By: Carlos Rodriguez

Voters For Choice

1010 Wisconsin Ave. NW
Suite 410
Washington, DC 20007
Tel: (202)944-5080
Fax: (202)944-5081
E-mail: voters4c@earthlink.net

An organization to provide financial and technical support to political candidates who favor a woman's right to have a safe and legal abortion. Registered as a political action committee with the Federal Election Commission. VFC, operating on the state, local, and federal levels, is the largest independent pro-choice political action committee.

In-house, DC-area Employees
BRITELL, Maureen: Exec. Director
COLLINS, Mary Jean: Treasurer
KIEHL, Kristina: Democratic Chair
STEINEM, Gloria: President

Vredenburg

Reston, VA
Leg. Issues: DEF

Outside Counsel/Consultants
John G. Campbell, Inc.
Issues: DEF
Rep By: John G. Campbell

Vulcan Chemicals

1101 30th St. NW
Suite 500
Washington, DC 20007
Tel: (202)293-0635
Fax: (202)659-3119
Registered: LDA

In-house, DC-area Employees
WILKINSON, E. John: Director, Government Affairs

Outside Counsel/Consultants
Millian Byers Associates, LLC
Shaw Pittman
Rep By: Thomas J. Spulak

Vulcan Materials Co.

Birmingham, AL
Registered: LDA
Leg. Issues: CHM, NAT, ROD

Outside Counsel/Consultants
Bradley Arant Rose & White LLP
Issues: NAT, ROD
Hogan & Hartson L.L.P.
Issues: CHM, NAT
Rep By: C. Michael Gilliland, William Michael House, Warren H. Maruyama, Jeffrey W. Munk, Christine M. Warnke
Patton Boggs, LLP
Rep By: George J. Schutzer

Vulcan Northwest Inc.

Bellevue, WA

Outside Counsel/Consultants
The Petrizzo Group, Inc.
Rep By: Kara Kennedy, Thomas "T.J." Petrizzo

WABCO

Walnut Creek, CA

Outside Counsel/Consultants
Preston Gates Ellis & Rouvelas Meeds LLP
Rep By: Brian K. McCalmon, James R. Weiss

Wabtec Corp.

Wilmerding, PA
A manufacturer of freight and passenger railroad brakes, draft gear, doors and end-of-train units.

Leg. Issues: RRR

Outside Counsel/Consultants
RBG Associates
Issues: RRR
Rep By: Richard B. Griffin, Jr.

Wackenhut Corrections Corp.

Coral Gables, FL
Leg. Issues: DOC, LAW

Outside Counsel/Consultants
The Da Vinci Group
Issues: DOC, LAW
Rep By: Mark R. Smith

Wackenhut Services, Inc.

Palm Beach, FL
Leg. Issues: ENG, LAW

Outside Counsel/Consultants
Van Scoyoc Associates, Inc.
Issues: ENG, LAW
Rep By: Paul Grimm, Buzz Hawley, John C. "Jay" Stone, H. Stewart Van Scoyoc

Waddell & Reed Financial, Inc.

Shawnee Mission, KS
Leg. Issues: FIN

Outside Counsel/Consultants
R. Duffy Wall and Associates
Issues: FIN
Rep By: Hon. Bill Brewster, David C. Jory

Waesche, Sheinbaum, and O'Regan

New York, NY
Leg. Issues: ENV, GOV, TRA

Outside Counsel/Consultants
Ernest J. Corrado
Issues: ENV, GOV, TRA
Rep By: Ernest J. Corrado

Waggoner Engineering, Inc.

Jackson, MS
Leg. Issues: ECN, ENC, ENV, TRA

Outside Counsel/Consultants
Winston & Strawn
Issues: ECN, ENC, ENV, TRA
Rep By: John C. Kirtland, John A. Waits, II

Wake, North Carolina, County of

Leg. Issues: BUD, CAW, ENV, HCR, HOU, LAW, MMM, NAT, TRA, URB, WEL

Outside Counsel/Consultants
The Ferguson Group, LLC
Issues: BUD, CAW, ENV, HCR, HOU, LAW, MMM, NAT, TRA, URB, WEL
Rep By: W. Roger Gwinn

Wakota Bridge Coalition

St. Paul, MN
Leg. Issues: ROD

Outside Counsel/Consultants
Lockridge Grindal & Nauen, P.L.L.P.
Issues: ROD
Rep By: Dennis McGrann

Wal-Mart Stores, Inc.

1201 New York Ave. NW
Suite 200
Washington, DC 20005-3917
Tel: (202)962-4991
Fax: (202)962-4846
Headquartered in Bentonville, AR.

Leg. Issues: TAX

In-house, DC-area Employees
LEZY, Norm G.: V. President, Federal and International Government Relations

Outside Counsel/Consultants
Miller & Chevalier, Chartered
Issues: TAX
Rep By: Leonard Bickwit, Jr.
Patton Boggs, LLP
Stevens Reed Curcio & Co.

Walgreen Co.

Deerfield, IL
Leg. Issues: HCR

Outside Counsel/Consultants
Potomac Group
Issues: HCR
Rep By: Richard Y Hegg, Philip C. Karsting, G. Wayne Smith

Walker Digital Corp.

Stamford, CT
A telecommunications firm.

Leg. Issues: GAM

Outside Counsel/Consultants
Akin, Gump, Strauss, Hauer & Feld, L.L.P.
Powell, Goldstein, Frazer & Murphy LLP
Issues: GAM
Rep By: Hon. Butler E. Derrick, Jr., Brett G. Kappel, Simon Lazarus, III, David C. Quam

Walker River Paiute Tribe

Schurz, NV

Outside Counsel/Consultants
George Waters Consulting Service
Rep By: George Waters

Arthur T. Walker

Kittanning, PA
A natural resources development company.

Outside Counsel/Consultants
Akin, Gump, Strauss, Hauer & Feld, L.L.P.

Wall Street Journal

New York, NY

Outside Counsel/Consultants
Snavely, King, Majoros, O'Connor and Lee, Inc.
Rep By: Charles W. King

Wallcovering Ass'n

Chicago, IL
Leg. Issues: CHM, MAN

Outside Counsel/Consultants
The Plexus Consulting Group
Issues: CHM, MAN
Rep By: Fred H. Hutchison

Walmer Dollhouses, Inc.

Alexandria, VA

Outside Counsel/Consultants
Vorys, Sater, Seymour and Pease, LLP
Rep By: James K. Alford

Walsh Enterprises Internat'l

Seattle, WA
Leg. Issues: BUD, FOR

Outside Counsel/Consultants
Sagamore Associates, Inc.
Issues: BUD, FOR
Rep By: Theodore W. Bristol, David U. Gogol

Walton Enterprises

Bentonville, AR
Leg. Issues: BAN, EDU, TAX

Outside Counsel/Consultants
Patton Boggs, LLP
Issues: BAN, EDU, TAX
Rep By: Thomas Hale Boggs, Jr., Donald V. Moorehead, Aubrey A. Rothrock, III

Wam!Net

Eagan, MN
Leg. Issues: SCI

Outside Counsel/Consultants
Patton Boggs, LLP
Issues: SCI
Rep By: Michael J. Driver

Wang Laboratories Inc.

Lowell, MA
Leg. Issues: GOV

Outside Counsel/Consultants
Hale and Dorr LLP
Issues: GOV
Rep By: Jay P. Urwitz

Warburg, Pincus & Co., Inc., E. M.

New York, NY
Leg. Issues: BUD, TAX

Outside Counsel/Consultants
Liz Robbins Associates
Issues: BUD, TAX
Rep By: Liz Robbins
Wilmer, Cutler & Pickering

Wards Cove Packing Co.

Seattle, WA

Outside Counsel/Consultants
O'Connor & Hannan, L.L.P.
Rep By: George J. Mannina, Jr.

Warland Investment Co.

Santa Monica, CA
Leg. Issues: DEF, RES

Outside Counsel/Consultants
Hogan & Hartson L.L.P.
Issues: DEF, RES
Rep By: David J. Hensler, John S. Jenkins, Jeffrey W. Munk

Warnaco, Inc.

801 Pennsylvania Ave. NW
Suite 640
Washington, DC 20004
E-mail: mgale@warnaco.com
Tel: (202)737-3800
Fax: (202)393-1004
Headquartered in New York, NY.

Leg. Issues: LBR, TAX, TRD

In-house, DC-area Employees
GALE, Michael R.: V. President, International Trade and Government Relations

Wartsila Diesel, Inc.

Annapolis, MD

Outside Counsel/Consultants

Akin, Gump, Strauss, Hauer & Feld, L.L.P.
Rep By: Gary A. Heimberg, Charles W. Johnson, IV, Barney J. Skladany, Jr.

Wasatch Front Regional Council

Bountiful, UT
Leg. Issues: BUD

Outside Counsel/Consultants

The Wexler Group
Issues: BUD
Rep By: Patrick J. McCann

Washington and Jefferson College

Washington, PA
Leg. Issues: BUD, ECN, EDU, SCI

Outside Counsel/Consultants

Davis O'Connell, Inc.
Issues: BUD, ECN, EDU, SCI
Rep By: Lynda C. Davis, Ph.D., Terrence M. O'Connell

Washington Area Lawyers for the Arts

815 15th St. NW
Suite 900
Washington, DC 20005
Web: www.thewala.org
E-mail: executivedirector@thewala.org
Tel: (202)393-2826
Fax: (202)393-4444

Provides free legal assistance and business information to low income artists and arts groups. Mediation services are offered for arts related disputes on a low sliding scale fee basis. Also provides education programs on arts and business related subjects. Arts related publications and a research library are available to the public.

In-house, DC-area Employees
MALLOY, John Davis: Director of Legal Services

Washington Ass'n of Sheriffs and Police Chiefs

Olympia, WA
Leg. Issues: BUD, LAW

Outside Counsel/Consultants

Smith Alling Lane, P.S.
Issues: BUD, LAW
Rep By: Lisa Hurst, Robert Mack, Michael McAleenan, Timothy Schellberg

The Washington Ballet

Washington, DC
Registered: LDA

Founded in 1976 by Artistic Director Emeritus Mary Day, The Washington Ballet is the professional resident company affiliated with the Washington School of Ballet. Presents a diversified repertoire of classical and contemporary ballets by both celebrated and emerging choreographers. Presents a full season each year at the Kennedy Center. Presents The Nutcracker at the Warner Theatre and George Mason University's Center for the Arts. Also tours nationally and internationally.

Leg. Issues: ART

Outside Counsel/Consultants

Chernikoff and Co.
Issues: ART
Rep By: Larry B. Chernikoff

Washington Business Group on Health

50 F St. NW
Suite 600
Washington, DC 20001
E-mail: wbgh@wbgh.org
Tel: (202)628-9320
Fax: (202)628-9244

A national non-profit organization devoted exclusively to the analysis of health policy and related worksite issues from the perspective of large employers. Business Group members, typically Fortune 500 and large public sector employers, provide health coverage for more than 30 million U.S. workers, retirees, and their families.

In-house, DC-area Employees
ENGLAND, M.D., Mary Jane: President
KING, Kathleen: V. President

Washington Citizens for World Trade

Olympia, WA
Leg. Issues: AGR
Registered: LDA

Outside Counsel/Consultants

Wiley, Rein & Fielding
Issues: AGR
Rep By: Sharon R. Fine, Hon. Jim Slattery

Washington Construction Co.

Outside Counsel/Consultants

Snavely, King, Majoros, O'Connor and Lee, Inc.
Rep By: Tom O'Connor

Washington Consulting Group

6707 Democracy Blvd.
Suite 1010
Bethesda, MD 20817
Web: www.washcg.com
Tel: (301)656-2330
Fax: (301)656-1324
Leg. Issues: AVI, ENG, TRA, TRD

In-house, DC-area Employees
CHAPELLI, Jr., Armando C.: President and Chief Exec. Officer

Outside Counsel/Consultants

Capitol Capital Group
Issues: AVI, TRA, TRD
Rep By: Michael J. Jones, Peter Mai

Van Scoyoc Associates, Inc.
Issues: AVI, ENG, TRA
Rep By: Buzz Hawley, Kevin F. Kelly, John C. "Jay" Stone, H. Stewart Van Scoyoc

Washington Council of Agencies

1001 Connecticut Ave. NW
Suite 925
Washington, DC 20036
Web: www.wcamonprofits.org
E-mail: wca@wcamonprofits.org
Tel: (202)457-0540
Fax: (202)457-0549

A coalition of non-profit organizations.

Leg. Issues: DOC, TAX

In-house, DC-area Employees
JOHNSON, Betsy: Exec. Director

Washington County, Oregon, Land Use and Transportation of

Hillsboro, OR
Leg. Issues: TRA

Outside Counsel/Consultants

Verner, Liipfert, Bernhard, McPherson and Hand, Chartered
Issues: TRA
Rep By: Timothy M. Rutten

Washington D.C. Convention and Visitors Ass'n

1212 New York Ave. NW
Sixth Floor
Washington, DC 20005-3992
Web: www.washington.org
Tel: (202)789-7000
Fax: (202)789-7037

In-house, DC-area Employees
DICKERSON, Cindy: President

Washington Discussion Group

c/o American Cotton Shippers Ass'n
1725 K St. NW, Suite 1404
Washington, DC 20006
Tel: (202)296-7116
Fax: (202)659-5322

An informal organization of prominent Washington area lobbyists, lawyers and corporate and association government relations officers.

In-house, DC-area Employees
GILLEN, Neal P.: Secretary-Treasurer

Washington Ethical Soc.

7750 16th St. NW
Washington, DC 20012
E-mail: wes@ethicalsociety.org
Tel: (202)882-6650
Fax: (202)829-1354

A humanistic, educational and religious community seeking to improve the quality of life through the cultivation of ethical character and a more ethical society. Member of the American Ethical Union. The Society supports projects for peace, human rights, ecology and the abolition of hunger.

In-house, DC-area Employees
MONTAGNA, Donald: Senior Leader

Washington Flyer Taxi Drivers Ass'n, Inc.

Alexandria, VA
Leg. Issues: CIV, IMM, LBR, TRA

Outside Counsel/Consultants

Nealon & Moran, L.L.P.
Issues: CIV, IMM, LBR, TRA
Rep By: Brian J. Moran

Washington Gas

1100 H St. NW
Washington, DC 20080
Tel: (202)624-6033
Fax: (202)624-6621
Registered: LDA
Web: www.washgas.com
E-mail: dhope@washgas.com
Leg. Issues: BUD, CAW, ENG, ENV, LBR, TRA, UTI, WEL

Political Action Committee/s

Washington Gas Federal PAC
1100 H St. NW
Washington, DC 20080
Contact: Doreen C. Hope
Tel: (202)624-6033
Fax: (202)624-6221

In-house, DC-area Employees
HOPE, Doreen C.: Director, Federal Affairs
SIMS, Roberta: V. President, Corporate Relations

Washington Group Internat'l

1900 M St. NW
5th Floor
Washington, DC 20036
Web: www.wgint.com
Tel: (202)638-6355
Fax: (202)638-1419
Registered: LDA

An international engineering and construction firm; headquartered in Boise, ID.

Leg. Issues: BUD, ENG, FOR, TRA, WAS

Political Action Committee/s

Washington Group International PAC
1900 M St. NW
5th Floor
Washington, DC 20036
Contact: Betty L. Rendin
Tel: (202)638-6355
Fax: (202)638-1419

In-house, DC-area Employees
RENDIN, Betty L.: Treasurer, Washington Group Internat'l PAC

Outside Counsel/Consultants

The Smith-Free Group
Issues: ENG
Rep By: James C. Free, Robert Hickmott, W. Timothy Locke

Verner, Liipfert, Bernhard, McPherson and Hand, Chartered
Issues: ENG, FOR
Rep By: Berl Bernhard, Marshall F. Harris, Douglas M. MacKinnon, Edward J. McGrath, Harry C. McPherson, Michael E. O'Brien, James A. Pickup

Washington Hospital Center

Washington, DC

Outside Counsel/Consultants

Widmeyer Communications, Inc.

Washington Independent Writers

733 15th St. NW
Suite 220
The Woodward Bldg.
Washington, DC 20005
Web: www.washwriter.org
E-mail: washwriter@aol.com
Tel: (202)347-4973
Fax: (202)628-0298

A membership organization for 2,500 freelance writers.

In-house, DC-area Employees
CHAPIN, Isolde: Exec. Director

Washington Infrastructure Services, Inc.

Arlington, VA
Leg. Issues: ROD, RRR, TRA

Outside Counsel/Consultants

The ILEX Group
Issues: ROD, RRR, TRA
Rep By: H. Hollister Cantus

Washington Institute for Near East Policy

1828 L St. NW
Suite 1050
Washington, DC 20036
Web: www.washingtoninstitute.org
E-mail: info@washingtoninstitute.org
Tel: (202)452-0650
Fax: (202)223-5364

A think tank.

In-house, DC-area Employees
EISENSTADT, Michael: Military Affairs Fellow
MAKOVSKY, David: Senior Fellow
ROSS, Dennis B.: Counselor and Distinguished Fellow
SATLOFF, Robert: Exec. Director

Washington Kurdish Institute

605 G St. SW
Washington, DC 20024
Web: www.kurd.org/kurd
E-mail: wki@kurd.org
Tel: (202)484-0140
Fax: (202)484-0142

Works for research, advocacy, and education on issues of concern to Kurdish people worldwide.

In-house, DC-area Employees
AMITAY, Michael P.: Exec. Director

Washington Legal Clinic for the Homeless

1800 Massachusetts Ave. NW
Washington, DC 20036
E-mail: washlch@erols.com
Tel: (202)872-1494
Fax: (202)872-1932

In-house, DC-area Employees
FUGERE, Patricia M.: Director

Washington Legal Foundation

2009 Massachusetts Ave. NW
Washington, DC 20036
Web: www.wlf.org
E-mail: root@wlf.org
Tel: (202)588-0302
Fax: (202)588-0371

Supports free market principles, limited and accountable government, individual rights, business civil liberties, and judicial and lawyer ethics.

In-house, DC-area Employees
KAMENAR, Paul D.: Senior Exec. Counsel
LAMMI, Glenn G.: Chief Counsel, Legal Studies Division
LARCHER, Constance C.: Exec. Director and President
POPEO, Daniel J.: Chairman and General Counsel
SAMP, Richard A.: Chief Counsel

Washington Metropolitan Area Transit Authority

600 Fifth St. NW
Washington, DC 20001
E-mail: dlipman@wmata.com
Tel: (202)962-1003
Fax: (202)962-2466

Specializes in rail and bus transportation.

Leg. Issues: BUD, DOC, TAX, TRA

In-house, DC-area Employees
LIPMAN, Deborah Swartz: Director, Government and Community Relations

Outside Counsel/Consultants
BKSH & Associates
Issues: BUD, DOC, TAX, TRA

Washington Mutual Bank

Seattle, WA
Headquartered in Seattle, WA.

Leg. Issues: BAN, BUD, FIN, HOU, INS, TAX

Outside Counsel/Consultants
Gibson, Dunn & Crutcher LLP
Issues: BAN
Rep By: Robert C. Eager, Cantwell Faulkner Muckenfuss, III
Hohlt & Associates
Issues: BAN, BUD, FIN, HOU, INS, TAX
Rep By: Richard F. Hohlt
The Smith-Free Group
Issues: BAN, FIN
Rep By: James C. Free, James E. Smith

Washington Office on Africa

212 E. Capitol St.
Washington, DC 20003
Tel: (202)547-7503
Fax: (202)547-7505
Registered: LDA
Web: www.woaafrica.org
E-mail: woa@igc.org

An advocacy movement organization seeking to articulate and promote a just American policy toward Africa. Monitors Congressional legislation and executive policies and actions and issues action alerts to advance progressive legislation and policy.

In-house, DC-area Employees
SPENCER, Leon: Exec. Director

Washington Office on Latin American

1630 Connecticut Ave. NW
Washington, DC 20009
Web: www.wola.org
E-mail: wola@wola.org
Tel: (202)797-2171
Fax: (202)797-2172

Founded in 1974 by a coalition of religious and civic leaders, WOLA promotes human rights, democracy and equitable economic development in Latin America and the Caribbean. It facilitates dialogue between governmental and non-governmental actors, monitors the impact of policies and programs of governments and international organizations, and promotes alternatives through reporting, education, training, and advocacy.

Leg. Issues: DEF, FOR

In-house, DC-area Employees
SPENCER, William A.: Deputy Director
VICKERS, George: Exec. Director

The Washington Opera

Washington, DC
Web: www.DC-OPERA.org
Leg. Issues: ART

Outside Counsel/Consultants
Chernikoff and Co.
Issues: ART
Rep By: Larry B. Chernikoff
The Dutko Group, Inc.
Issues: ART
Rep By: Arthur H. Silverman, William Simmons

Washington Pacific Publications, Inc.

Leg. Issues: MIA

Outside Counsel/Consultants
Pacific Islands Washington Office
Issues: MIA
Rep By: Fred Radewagen

Washington Parking Ass'n

Washington, DC
Leg. Issues: TRA

Outside Counsel/Consultants
Lowe & Associates, Ltd.
Issues: TRA
Rep By: George H. Lowe, Jr.

Washington Performing Arts Society

Washington, DC
Leg. Issues: ART

Outside Counsel/Consultants
Chernikoff and Co.
Issues: ART
Rep By: Larry B. Chernikoff

Washington Political Action Committee

444 N. Capitol St. NW
Suite 712
Washington, DC 20001
Tel: (202)347-5859
Fax: (202)393-7006

A pro-Israel political action committee.

In-house, DC-area Employees
AMITAY, Morris J.: Treasurer/Administrator

Outside Counsel/Consultants
Morris J. Amitay, P.C.
Rep By: Morris J. Amitay

The Washington Post Co.

1150 15th St. NW
Washington, DC 20071
Tel: (202)334-6000
Fax: (202)334-4536
Leg. Issues: LBR, TAX, TEC

In-house, DC-area Employees
BUTLER, Patrick: V. President, Corporate Offices
CALDERON, Rima: Director, Corporate Communications
KNIGHT, Guyon H.: V. President, Corporate Communications
RODRIGUEZ, Virginia O.: Public Relations Director
WILSON, Theresa: Manager, Risk

Outside Counsel/Consultants
Baker, Donelson, Bearman & Caldwell, P.C.
Issues: LBR
Rep By: J. Keith Kennedy, Charles R. Parkinson, John C. Tuck
The Coursen Group
Issues: TEC
Rep By: Hon. Christopher D. Coursen
Covington & Burling
Issues: LBR
Rep By: Roderick A. DeArment
Davidson & Company, Inc.
Issues: LBR, TAX
Rep By: James H. Davidson, Richard E. May, Stanley Sokul

Washington Public Utility Districts Ass'n

Seattle, WA
Leg. Issues: ENG

Outside Counsel/Consultants
Morgan Meguire, LLC
Issues: ENG
Rep By: Scott Lindsay, Kyle G. Michel, Katie Parrott, C. Kyle Simpson, Deborah R. Sliz, Kiel Weaver

Washington Real Estate Investment Trust

6110 Executive Blvd.
Suite 800
Rockville, MD 20852-3927
Web: www.washreit.com
Tel: (301)984-9400
Fax: (301)984-9610

A self-administered, equity real estate investment trust investing in income-producing properties in the greater Washington-Baltimore region.

In-house, DC-area Employees
CRONIN, Edmund B.: President and Chief Executive Officer
FINGER, Larry E.: Senior V. President and Chief Financial Officer
FRANKLIN, Laura M.: V. President and Chief Accounting Officer

Washington Regional Transplant Consortium

8110 Gatehouse Rd.
Suite 101 West
Falls Church, VA 22042
Tel: (703)641-0100
Fax: (703)641-0211

In-house, DC-area Employees
BRIGHAM, Lori: Exec. Director

Outside Counsel/Consultants
Baker & Hostetler LLP
Rep By: Frederick H. Graefe

Washington Researchers

1655 N. Fort Meyer Dr.
Suite 800
Arlington, VA 22209
Web: www.washingtonresearchers.com
E-mail: research@researchers.com
Tel: (703)312-6004
Fax: (703)527-4586

A business research/competitive intelligence firm. Provides publishing and consulting services and seminars.

In-house, DC-area Employees
HOUSE, Doug: President

Washington Soccer Partners

Herndon, VA
Leg. Issues: IMM

Outside Counsel/Consultants
Thelen Reid & Priest LLP
Issues: IMM
Rep By: Barry I. Berkoff, Mareza I. Estevez, Richard J. Leidl, Nancy K. West

Washington Sports & Entertainment, L.P.

601 F St. NW
Washington, DC 20004
Tel: (202)661-5000
Fax: (202)661-5108
Leg. Issues: ECN, TAX

In-house, DC-area Employees
HOLLAND, Judith: V. President, Community Relations
MORELAND, Rick: V. President, Corporate Marketing
WILLIAMS, Matthew: V. President, Communications

Outside Counsel/Consultants
The Carmen Group
Issues: ECN, TAX
Rep By: Ryan Adesnik, Gerald P. Carmen, Diane Jemmott

Washington State Hospital Ass'n

Seattle, WA

Outside Counsel/Consultants
Preston Gates Ellis & Rouvelas Meeds LLP
Rep By: Hon. Lloyd Meeds

Washington State Impact Aid Ass'n

Wapato, WA
Leg. Issues: EDU

Outside Counsel/Consultants
Evergreen Associates, Ltd.
Issues: EDU
Rep By: Robert M. Brooks, Marcus M. Riccelli

Washington Technical Professional Forum (WTPF)

112 Elden St.
Unit J
Herndon, VA 20170
Tel: (703)709-8299
Fax: (703)709-1036

In-house, DC-area Employees
CAMPBELL, Nancy A.: Membership Coordinator
GOLD, Josh: Deputy Director

Washington Workshops

3222 N St. NW
Suite 340
Washington, DC 20007
Tel: (202)965-3434
Fax: (202)965-1018
Leg. Issues: EDU

In-house, DC-area Employees
SIEVERS, Sharon: President

Outside Counsel/Consultants

Alcalde & Fay
Issues: EDU
Rep By: Danielle McBeth, Lois Moore

Washington, Department of Information of the State of

Olympia, WA
Leg. Issues: COM

Outside Counsel/Consultants

Reed, Smith, LLP
Issues: COM
Rep By: Judith L. Harris, Phillips S. Peter

Washington, Department of Transportation of the State of

Olympia, WA — Registered: LDA
Leg. Issues: MAR, ROD, RRR, TRA

Outside Counsel/Consultants

Denny Miller McBee Associates
Issues: MAR, ROD, RRR, TRA

Washington, Minnesota, County of

Stillwater, MN

Outside Counsel/Consultants

Lockridge Grindal & Nauen, P.L.L.P.
Rep By: Dennis McGrann

Washington, State of

Olympia, WA

Outside Counsel/Consultants

Johnston & Associates, LLC
Rep By: Hon. J. Bennett Johnston

Washoe County

Reno, NV
Leg. Issues: BUD, ENV, NAT

Outside Counsel/Consultants

The Ferguson Group, LLC
Issues: BUD, ENV, NAT
Rep By: W. Roger Gwinn

Washoe County Regional Transportation Commission

Reno, NV
Leg. Issues: TRA

Outside Counsel/Consultants

Charles H. Graves & Associates
Issues: TRA
Rep By: Charles H. Graves

Washoe Tribe of Nevada and California

Gardnerville, NV

Outside Counsel/Consultants

George Waters Consulting Service
Rep By: George Waters

Wasilla, Alaska, City of

Wasilla, AK
Leg. Issues: URB

Outside Counsel/Consultants

Robertson, Monagle & Eastaugh
Issues: URB
Rep By: Steven W. Silver

Waste Control Specialists, Inc.

Pasadena, TX

A waste disposal company.

Leg. Issues: ENG, ENV, GOV, TAX, WAS

Outside Counsel/Consultants

Arnold & Porter
Issues: WAS
Rep By: Martha L. Cochran

BKSH & Associates
Issues: ENG, ENV, GOV, WAS

Egan & Associates
Issues: WAS

Hooper Owen & Winburn
Issues: TAX, WAS
Rep By: Daryl H. Owen

Waste Management, Inc.

601 Pennsylvania Ave. NW
Suite 300
The North Bldg.
Washington, DC 20004
Tel: (202)628-3500
Fax: (202)628-0400
Registered: LDA

Formerly known as WMX Technologies, Inc. Headquartered in Houston, TX.

Leg. Issues: ENG, ENV, TAX, TRU, WAS

Political Action Committee/s

Waste Management Employees Better Government Fund

601 Pennsylvania Ave. NW
Suite 300
The North Bldg.
Washington, DC 20004
Contact: Kimberley A. Engle
Tel: (202)628-3500
Fax: (202)628-0400

In-house, DC-area Employees
BRIGGUM, Sue M.: Director, Environmental Affairs
EISENBUD, Robert: Director, Legislative Affairs
ENGLE, Kimberley A.: Manager, Government Affairs
KARDELL, Lisa R.: Manager, Government Affairs
SKERNOLIS, Edmund J.: Director, Regulatory Affairs
STALVEY, Allan: V. President, Government Affairs

Outside Counsel/Consultants

James E. Boland
Issues: ENV, TAX, WAS
Rep By: James E. Boland, Jr.

Hooper Owen & Winburn
Issues: TAX, WAS
Rep By: Steve Glaze

George C. Tagg
Issues: TAX, WAS
Rep By: George C. Tagg

Waste Policy Institute

12850 Middlebrook Rd.
Suite 205
Germantown, MD 20874
Web: www.wpi.org
Tel: (301)528-1960

In-house, DC-area Employees
ROGERS, Richard H.: Senior Manager, Communications
WILCZYNSKI, Ed: Operations Manager

Water and Wastewater Equipment Manufacturers Ass'n

P.O. Box 17402 Dulles Internat'l Airport
Washington, DC 20041
Web: www.wwema.org
E-mail: wwema@erols.com
Tel: (703)444-1777
Fax: (703)444-1779

Leg. Issues: ENV

In-house, DC-area Employees
KRISTOF, Dawn C.: President

Outside Counsel/Consultants

Barnes & Thornburg
Issues: ENV
Rep By: Randolph J. Stayin

Water Environment Federation

601 Wythe St.
Alexandria, VA 22314-1994
Web: www.wef.org
E-mail: webfeedback@wef.org
Tel: (703)684-2400
Fax: (703)684-2492

A non-profit, technical organization whose objective is to preserve and enhance the global water environment.

Leg. Issues: CAW, ENV, UTI, WAS

In-house, DC-area Employees
BENSON, Jack: Deputy Exec. Director, Marketing Business Development
BLATT, Nancy L.: Director, Public Information
BROWN, Quincalee: Exec. Director
GRAY, Albert C.: Deputy Exec. Director - Technical
O'NEILL, Eileen: Director, Technical and Educational Services
RICKER, Timothy: Deputy Exec. Director, Administration
SULLIVAN, James K.: Manager, Legislative Affairs
WILLIAMS, Timothy: Director, Government Affairs

Water Environment Research Foundation

601 Wythe St.
Alexandria, VA 22314-1994
Tel: (703)684-2400
Fax: (703)684-2492

Leg. Issues: BUD, ENV

In-house, DC-area Employees
REINHARDT, Glenn: Exec. Director

Outside Counsel/Consultants

LeBoeuf, Lamb, Greene & MacRae L.L.P.
Issues: BUD, ENV
Rep By: D. Randall Benn, LaJuana S. Wilcher

Water Infrastructure Network

Washington, DC
Leg. Issues: CAW

Outside Counsel/Consultants

The Accord Group
Issues: CAW
Rep By: Robert F. Hurley, Jeffery T. More

Water Quality 2000

601 Wythe St.
Alexandria, VA 22314-1994
Tel: (703)684-2400
Fax: (703)684-2475

In-house, DC-area Employees
WILLIAMS, Timothy: Contact

Water Quality Insurance Syndicate

New York, NY
Leg. Issues: ENV

Outside Counsel/Consultants

Thacher Proffitt & Wood
Issues: ENV
Rep By: Barbara D. Burke

Water Replenishment District of Southern California

Cerritos, CA
Leg. Issues: BUD, ENV, NAT

Outside Counsel/Consultants

Carpi & Clay
Issues: ENV, NAT
Rep By: Kenneth A. Carpi

Murray, Scheer, Montgomery, Tapia & O'Donnell
Issues: BUD
Rep By: John R. O'Donnell, Raul R. Tapia

Water Systems Council

Glen Ellyn, IL
Leg. Issues: AGR, BUD, ENV, MAN

Outside Counsel/Consultants

Holland & Knight LLP
Issues: AGR, BUD, ENV, MAN
Rep By: Mike Galano, Richard M. Gold

WateReuse Ass'n

Arlington, VA
Leg. Issues: BUD

Outside Counsel/Consultants

ENS Resources, Inc.
Issues: BUD
Rep By: Eric Sapirstein

Waterman Steamship Co.

1000 16th St. NW
Suite 305
Washington, DC 20036
Tel: (202)659-3804
Fax: (202)296-1980
Registered: LDA

Leg. Issues: MAR

In-house, DC-area Employees
LEYH, J. Robert: Senior V. President, Government Relations

Waterworks Internat'l, Inc.

Woburn, MA
Leg. Issues: ENV, FUE, SCI

Outside Counsel/Consultants

Charlie McBride Associates, Inc.
Issues: ENV, FUE, SCI
Rep By: Charlie McBride

Watson Energy

Metarie, LA
Leg. Issues: ENG

Outside Counsel/Consultants

Potomac Group
Issues: ENG
Rep By: Richard Y Hegg, Philip C. Karsting, G. Wayne Smith

Watson Pharmaceuticals, Inc.

Corona, CT

Outside Counsel/Consultants

Parry, Romani, DeConcini & Symms

The Watson Wyatt Worldwide Co.

1717 H St. NW
Washington, DC 20006

In-house, DC-area Employees
HALEY, John: Chief Exec. Officer

Watsonville, California, City of
Leg. Issues: BUD
Outside Counsel/Consultants
The Furman Group
Issues: BUD
Rep By: Thomas M. James

Watts Health Foundation
Los Angeles, CA
Outside Counsel/Consultants
Epstein Becker & Green, P.C.
Rep By: Joyce A. Cowan

Wausau Insurance Cos.
Wausau, WI
Leg. Issues: ENV, HCR, INS, TAX
Outside Counsel/Consultants
Akin, Gump, Strauss, Hauer & Feld, L.L.P.
Issues: ENV, HCR, INS, TAX
Rep By: Donald C. Alexander, Sean G. D'Arcy

WAVE, Inc.
525 School St. SW
Suite 500
Washington, DC 20024
Tel: (202)484-0103
Fax: (202)488-7595
E-mail: wave4kids@aol.com

A national youth employment, education and training organization for youth and youth professionals.

In-house, DC-area Employees
BROWN, Jr., Lawrence C.: President
FOX, David: Chairman

Waveband, Inc.
Torrance, CA
An aviation technology company.
Outside Counsel/Consultants
Ashby and Associates
Rep By: R. Barry Ashby

Waves States Ratification Committee
Leg. Issues: AGR
Outside Counsel/Consultants
Resource Management Consultants, Inc.
Issues: AGR
Rep By: Robert J. Gray

Wayland Academy
Beaver Dam, WI
Leg. Issues: BUD, EDU
Outside Counsel/Consultants
Kimberly Consulting, LLC
Issues: BUD, EDU
Rep By: Richard H. Kimberly

Wayne State University
499 S. Capitol St. SW
Suite 508
Washington, DC 20003
Tel: (202)488-7267
Fax: (202)488-7269
Registered: LDA
E-mail: craig.piercy@wayne.edu
Leg. Issues: BUD, EDU, SCI
In-house, DC-area Employees
PIERCY, Craig: Assistant V. President, Federal Affairs

Wayne, Michigan, County of
Detroit, MI
Leg. Issues: TRA, URB
Outside Counsel/Consultants
Patton Boggs, LLP
Issues: TRA, URB
Rep By: Michael A. Brown, Parker Brugge, John F. Fithian, Martha M. Kendrick, Carolina L. Mederos

Ways to Work
Milwaukee, WI
Leg. Issues: BUD, WEL
Outside Counsel/Consultants
Sagamore Associates, Inc.
Issues: BUD, WEL
Rep By: Todd Atkinson, David U. Gogol

WBFF
Baltimore, MD
Outside Counsel/Consultants
Shaw Pittman

Weather Channel
Atlanta, GA
Leg. Issues: BUD, COM, SCI
Outside Counsel/Consultants
Long, Aldridge & Norman, LLP
Issues: BUD, COM, SCI
Rep By: C. Randall Nuckolls, Patrick C. Turner

Weather Risk Management Ass'n
1030 15th St. NW
Suite 870
Washington, DC 20005
Tel: (202)298-2818
Fax: (202)393-0336
In-house, DC-area Employees
COOPER, Valerie: Exec. Director
Outside Counsel/Consultants
The Kellen Company
Rep By: Valerie Cooper

Del E. Webb Corp.
Phoenix, AZ
Leg. Issues: NAT
Outside Counsel/Consultants
Crowell & Moring LLP
Issues: NAT
Rep By: Steven P. Quarles

J. Arthur Weber & Associates
1140 23rd St. NW
Suite 806
Washington, DC 20037
Tel: (202)293-7187
Fax: (202)872-1150
Registered: LDA
Leg. Issues: GOV
In-house, DC-area Employees
WEBER, Joseph A.: President
Outside Counsel/Consultants
Stephens, Cross, Ihlenfeld & Boring, Inc.
Issues: GOV

WebMD
Atlanta, GA
Leg. Issues: CPI, HCR
Outside Counsel/Consultants
Hogan & Hartson L.L.P.
Issues: CPI, HCR
Rep By: Lance D. Bultena, C. Michael Gilliland, William S. Haft
Patrick M. Murphy & Associates
Issues: CPI
Rep By: Patrick M. Murphy

webwasher.com
Leg. Issues: CPI
Outside Counsel/Consultants
Arent Fox Kintner Plotkin & Kahn, PLLC
Issues: CPI
Rep By: Alison Kutler, Michael T. McNamara

Wegmans Food Markets, Inc.
Rochester, NY
A food retailer.
Leg. Issues: TAX
Outside Counsel/Consultants
Patton Boggs, LLP
Issues: TAX
Rep By: Donald V. Moorehead, Aubrey A. Rothrock, III

Weider Nutritional Group
Salt Lake City, UT
Leg. Issues: FOO, HCR, MMM, PHA
Outside Counsel/Consultants
Emord & Associates, P.C.
Issues: HCR, MMM, PHA
Rep By: Jonathan W. Emord, Eleanor A. Kolton, Claudia A. Lewis-Eng
Patton Boggs, LLP
Issues: FOO
Rep By: Brian C. Lopina

Weidlinger Associates, Inc.
New York, NY
Leg. Issues: DEF
Outside Counsel/Consultants
The PMA Group
Issues: DEF
Rep By: Kaylene Green, Stephen Madey, Paul J. Magliocchetti

Weidmann Associates
Outside Counsel/Consultants
Hauser Group

Weight Watchers Internat'l, Inc.
Jericho, NY
Outside Counsel/Consultants
Howrey Simon Arnold & White
Liz Robbins Associates

Weinberg Investments, Inc.
Sioux City, IA
Leg. Issues: HOU
Outside Counsel/Consultants
Coan & Lyons
Issues: HOU
Rep By: Carl A. S. Coan, Jr., Raymond K. James

Weirton Steel Corp.
Weirton, WV
Leg. Issues: TRA, TRD
Outside Counsel/Consultants
Schagrin Associates
Issues: TRA, TRD
Rep By: Tamara L. Browne, Roger B. Schagrin

Simon Weisenthal Center/Museum of Tolerance
Los Angeles, CA
Outside Counsel/Consultants
Verner, Liipfert, Bernhard, McPherson and Hand, Chartered
Rep By: Martin Mendelsohn

Welch's Foods, Inc.
Westfield, NY
Leg. Issues: CAW, ENV, FOO, TRD
Outside Counsel/Consultants
Davidoff & Malito, LLP
Issues: ENV, TRD
Rep By: Kenneth C. Malito, Robert J. Malito, Stephen J. Slade
McDermott, Will and Emery
Rep By: Carolyn B. Gleason
Nixon Peabody LLP
Issues: CAW, ENV
Rep By: Richard P. Stanton
Robert N. Pyle & Associates
Issues: FOO
Rep By: Alexis Hersh, Alison O'Neill, Robert N. Pyle

Welcon, Inc.
Providence, RI
Leg. Issues: ENV
Outside Counsel/Consultants
Bracewell & Patterson, L.L.P.
Issues: ENV
Rep By: Hon. Edwin R. Bethune, Hon. Jim Chapman, Gene E. Godley, Marc C. Hebert, Charles L. Ingebretson, Michael L. Pate, Scott H. Segal, D. Michael Stroud, Jr.

Weld-It Trucks
Los Angeles, CA
Outside Counsel/Consultants
Interface Inc.
Rep By: Albert B. Rosenbaum, III

Welfare to Work Partnership
1250 Connecticut Ave. NW
Suite 610
Washington, DC 20036
Tel: (202)955-3005
Fax: (202)955-1087
Web: www.welfaretowork.org
E-mail: info@welfaretowork.org

A national, nonpartisan, nonprofit effort of the business community to help move people on public assistance to jobs in the private sector.

Leg. Issues: WEL
In-house, DC-area Employees
CARROLL, Rodney: President and Chief Exec. Officer
EVANS, Eric: V. President, Communications
FRIEDMAN, Dorian: V. President, Policy and Planning

KEAST, Robert: Director, Policy
KHARFEN, Michael: Chief Operating Officer

Outside Counsel/Consultants

Saliba Action Strategies, LLC
Issues: WEL

Wellesley College

Outside Counsel/Consultants

Widmeyer Communications, Inc.

The Wellness Plan

Detroit, MI
Leg. Issues: HCR

Outside Counsel/Consultants

Dykema Gossett PLLC
Issues: HCR
Rep By: David K. Arthur, Nancy R. Barbour

WellPoint Health Networks/Blue Cross of California/UNICARE

1455 Pennsylvania Ave. NW
Suite 575
Washington, DC 20004
Web: www.wellpoint.com
Tel: (202)638-4076
Fax: (202)638-1096
Registered: LDA

Headquartered in Thousand Oaks, CA.

Leg. Issues: BUD, GOV, HCR, LBR, MMM, TAX

In-house, DC-area Employees

BASS, Kristin: Director, Federal Affairs
DOYLE, Theresa: Director, Federal Affairs
HEAD, Bill: Manager, Legislative Affairs
MORRISON, Andrew F.
STEFFLE, Jerry

Outside Counsel/Consultants

The Direct Impact Co.

Greenberg Traurig, LLP
Rep By: James F. Miller

The OB-C Group, LLC
Issues: BUD, HCR, TAX
Rep By: Thomas Keating, Kim F. McKernan, Charles J. Mellody, Patricia A. Nelson, Lawrence F. O'Brien, III, Linda E. Tarplin

Wells Fargo Bank, N.A.

San Francisco, CA
Leg. Issues: BAN

Outside Counsel/Consultants

Bryan Cave LLP
Rep By: Stanley J. Marcuss

Davis Polk & Wardwell
Issues: BAN
Rep By: Theodore A. Doremus, Jr.

Theodore A. Doremus, Jr.
Rep By: Theodore A. Doremus, Jr.

Wells Manufacturing Co.

Skokie, IL

Outside Counsel/Consultants

McDermott, Will and Emery

Wellton-Mohawk Irrigation and Drainage District

Leg. Issues: BUD, ENG, NAT

Outside Counsel/Consultants

McClure, Gerard & Neuenschwander, Inc.
Issues: BUD, ENG, NAT
Rep By: Steven G. Barringer, Joseph T. Findaro, Matthew Iandoli, Nils W. Johnson, Hon. James A. McClure, Tod O. Neuenschwander

Wendella Sightseeing Boats Inc.

Chicago, IL
Leg. Issues: TRA

Outside Counsel/Consultants

Dyer Ellis & Joseph, P.C.
Issues: TRA
Rep By: James S. W. Drewry, Lara Bernstein Mathews, Duncan C. Smith, III, Jennifer M. Southwick

Wendy's Internat'l, Inc.

Dublin, OH
Leg. Issues: LBR, TAX

Outside Counsel/Consultants

Lathrop & Gage, L.C.
Issues: LBR, TAX
Rep By: W. Peyton George

SEDERHOLM Public Affairs, Inc.
Rep By: Pamela Sederholm

J. G. Wentworth

Philadelphia, PA
Leg. Issues: TAX

Outside Counsel/Consultants

Reed, Smith, LLP
Issues: TAX
Rep By: Phillips S. Peter

WESCAM

Flamborough, CANADA
Leg. Issues: AER, BUD, MAR, MIA

Outside Counsel/Consultants

Teicher Consulting and Representation
Issues: AER, BUD, MAR, MIA
Rep By: Howard R. Teicher

West African Friends

Porto-Novo, BENIN

Outside Counsel/Consultants

Wilson & Wasserstein, Inc.
Rep By: Glen D. Wasserstein, Russell J. Wilson

West Basin Municipal Water District

Carson, CA
Leg. Issues: BUD

Outside Counsel/Consultants

The Furman Group
Issues: BUD
Rep By: Thomas M. James

West Chester University

Outside Counsel/Consultants

Washington Strategies, L.L.C.
Rep By: Jennifer Johnson Calvert, William P. Jarrell

West Coast Refuse and Recycling Coalition

Salem, OR
Leg. Issues: ENV, TRU, WAS

Outside Counsel/Consultants

Baise + Miller, P.C.
Issues: ENV, TRU, WAS
Rep By: Eric P. Bock

West Group

Eagan, MN
Registered: LDA
Leg. Issues: MIA

Outside Counsel/Consultants

Cordia Cos.
Rep By: Louis J. Cordia

Holland & Knight LLP
Issues: MIA
Rep By: Jack M. Burkman, Hon. Gerald E. Sikorski

West Hills Community College District

Coalinga, CA
Leg. Issues: EDU

Outside Counsel/Consultants

The Furman Group
Issues: EDU
Rep By: Thomas M. James

West Jefferson Levee District

Marrero, LA
Leg. Issues: DIS

Outside Counsel/Consultants

The Palmer Group
Issues: DIS
Rep By: Clifford A. Palmer

West Jordan, Utah, City of

Leg. Issues: CAW, ECN

Outside Counsel/Consultants

Murray, Scheer, Montgomery, Tapia & O'Donnell
Issues: CAW, ECN
Rep By: John H. Montgomery, John R. O'Donnell

West Lafayette, Indiana, City of

Leg. Issues: BUD, HOU, TRA

Outside Counsel/Consultants

Sagamore Associates, Inc.
Issues: BUD, HOU, TRA
Rep By: Doug Wasitis

West Pac Vessel Owners Ass'n

San Diego, CA

Outside Counsel/Consultants

Davis Wright Tremaine LLP

West Palm Beach, Florida, City of

Leg. Issues: CAW

Outside Counsel/Consultants

Holland & Knight LLP
Issues: CAW
Rep By: Jack M. Burkman, Richard M. Gold, David C. Whitestone

West Valley City, Utah

Leg. Issues: BUD, TRA

Outside Counsel/Consultants

The Ferguson Group, LLC
Issues: BUD, TRA
Rep By: W. Roger Gwinn, Leslie Waters Mozingo

West Virginia State Rail Authority

Charleston, WV

Outside Counsel/Consultants

Anderson and Pendleton, C.A.
Rep By: Francis G. McKenna

West Virginia University Center on Aging

Morgantown, WV

Outside Counsel/Consultants

Matz, Blancato & Associates, Inc.
Rep By: Robert B. Blancato

West Virginia University Hospitals, Inc.

Morgantown, WV

Outside Counsel/Consultants

Golin/Harris Internat'l
Rep By: Carol C. Mitchell

West Virginia, Office of the Attorney General of the State of

Charleston, WV

Outside Counsel/Consultants

Duncan, Weinberg, Genzer & Pembroke, P.C.
Rep By: James F. Flug

West*Group Management LLC

McLean, VA
Leg. Issues: RES

Outside Counsel/Consultants

Holland & Knight LLP
Issues: RES
Rep By: David C. Whitestone

Westar Group, Inc.

Washington, DC
Leg. Issues: TRD

Outside Counsel/Consultants

Akin, Gump, Strauss, Hauer & Feld, L.L.P.
Issues: TRD
Rep By: Smith W. Davis, William J. Farah, Barney J. Skladany, Jr., S. Bruce Wilson

Westcare Foundation, Inc.

Las Vegas, NV
Leg. Issues: BUD

Outside Counsel/Consultants

Beacon Consulting Group, Inc.
Issues: BUD
Rep By: Gordon P. MacDougall, Lisa A. Stewart, Kyndel Turvaville

Western Ag Resources Inc.

Leg. Issues: AGR, TRD

Outside Counsel/Consultants

James Nicholas Ashmore & Associates
Issues: AGR, TRD
Rep By: James Nicholas Ashmore

Western Alliance of Farmworker Advocates, Inc. (WAFA)

Santa Rose, CA
Leg. Issues: AGR

Outside Counsel/Consultants

Moss McGee Bradley & Foley
Issues: AGR
Rep By: Leander J. Foley, III

Western Coal Traffic League

Washington, DC
An association of western coal shippers.

Leg. Issues: RRR

Political Action Committee/s

Western Coal Traffic League Political Action Committee
Washington, DC

Outside Counsel/Consultants

Slover & Loftus
Issues: RRR
Rep By: John H. LeSeur, Christopher A. Mills, Peter A. Pfohl

Western Coalition of Arid States

San Jacinto, CA
Leg. Issues: BUD, ENV

Outside Counsel/Consultants

Will and Carlson, Inc.
Issues: BUD, ENV
Rep By: Peter Carlson, Robert P. Will

Western Coalition Political Action Committee

Washington, DC

Outside Counsel/Consultants

Williams & Jensen, P.C.
Rep By: Anthony J. Roda

Western Development

Washington, DC
Leg. Issues: RES

Outside Counsel/Consultants

The Carmen Group
Issues: RES
Rep By: Ryan Adesnik, Diane Jemmott

Western Financial/Westcorp Inc.

Irvine, CA
Leg. Issues: BAN, FIN

Outside Counsel/Consultants

Steptoe & Johnson LLP
Issues: BAN, FIN
Rep By: John T. Collins

Western Gas Resources

Denver, CO
Leg. Issues: FUE

Outside Counsel/Consultants

NES, Inc.
Issues: FUE

Western Governors Ass'n

Denver, CO
Leg. Issues: HCR

Outside Counsel/Consultants

The Dutko Group, Inc.
Issues: HCR
Rep By: Arthur H. Silverman, William Simmons

Western Governors University

Salt Lake City, UT
Leg. Issues: HCR

Outside Counsel/Consultants

The Dutko Group, Inc.
Issues: HCR
Rep By: Arthur H. Silverman, William Simmons

Western Great Lakes Pilots Ass'n

Superior, WI
Leg. Issues: MAR

Outside Counsel/Consultants

Preston Gates Ellis & Rouvelas Meeds LLP
Issues: MAR
Rep By: John L. Longstreth, Mark H. Ruge

Western Growers Ass'n

Newport Beach, CA
Leg. Issues: AGR, BUD, ENV, FOO, IMM, TAX, TRD

Outside Counsel/Consultants

Schramm, Williams & Associates, Inc.
Issues: AGR, BUD, ENV, FOO, IMM, TAX, TRD
Rep By: Anita Brown, Gabriele Ludwig, Duane L. Musser, Robert Schramm, Nancy Williams

Western Growers Insurance Services

Newport Beach, CA
Leg. Issues: HCR

Outside Counsel/Consultants

Schramm, Williams & Associates, Inc.
Issues: HCR
Rep By: Duane L. Musser, Robert Schramm

Western Interconnection Coordination Forum

Salt Lake City, UT
Leg. Issues: ENG, UTI

Outside Counsel/Consultants

Stuntz, Davis & Staffier, P.C.
Issues: ENG, UTI
Rep By: Linda Stuntz

Western Interstate Region

440 First St. NW — Tel: (202)942-4234
Eighth Floor — Fax: (202)942-4281
Washington, DC 20001
Web: www.naco.org/affils/wir
E-mail: pbeddoe@naco.org

Affiliated with the Nat'l Ass'n of Counties. Above address is that of the Nat'l Ass'n of Counties. Dedicated to the promotion of Western interests within NACo., including public land issues, community stability and economic development, and the promotion of the traditional Western way of life. Membership consists of fifteen Western states.

In-house, DC-area Employees

BEDDOE, Paul V.: Contact

Western Kentucky University

Bowling Green, KY
Leg. Issues: BUD

Outside Counsel/Consultants

Stites & Harbison
Issues: BUD
Rep By: Kenneth G. Lee

Western League of Savings Institutions

1301 Pennsylvania Ave. NW — Tel: (202)737-5113
Suite 500 — Fax: (202)737-6017
Washington, DC 20004 — Registered: LDA
Web: www.westernleague.org
E-mail: WLSIinWDC@aol.com

A trade association representing California, Arizona, and Nevada savings and loans. Headquartered in Los Angeles, CA.

Leg. Issues: BAN

Political Action Committee/s

FEDPAC
1301 Pennsylvania Ave. NW — Tel: (202)737-5113
Suite 500 — Fax: (202)737-6017
Washington, DC 20004
Contact: Louis H. Nevins

In-house, DC-area Employees

NEVINS, Louis H.: President

Western Michigan University

Kalamazoo, MI
Leg. Issues: BUD

Outside Counsel/Consultants

Capitol Associates, Inc.
Issues: BUD
Rep By: Edward R. Long, Ph.D., Julie P. Pawelczyk, Julie Shroyer

Western Pacific Economic Council

Outside Counsel/Consultants

Greenberg Traurig, LLP
Rep By: Jack Abramoff

Western Peanut Growers Ass'n

Seminole, TX
Leg. Issues: AGR

Outside Counsel/Consultants

Winston & Strawn
Issues: AGR
Rep By: Robert M. Bor, John A. Waits, II

Western Pioneer, Inc.

Seattle, WA
A shipping company.

Outside Counsel/Consultants

Davis Wright Tremaine LLP

Western Pistachio Ass'n

Leg. Issues: AGR, BUD, ENV

Outside Counsel/Consultants

Schramm, Williams & Associates, Inc.
Issues: AGR, BUD, ENV
Rep By: Duane L. Musser, Robert Schramm, Nancy Williams

Western Range Ass'n

Citrus Heights, CA
Leg. Issues: AGR, IMM, NAT

Outside Counsel/Consultants

McGuiness Norris & Williams, LLP
Issues: AGR, IMM, NAT
Rep By: James S. Holt

Western Research Institute

Laramie, WY
An environmental research institute.

Leg. Issues: BUD, TRA

Outside Counsel/Consultants

ENS Resources, Inc.
Issues: BUD, TRA
Rep By: Eric Sapirstein

Western Resources

Topeka, KS
Leg. Issues: ENG

Outside Counsel/Consultants

Westerly Group
Issues: ENG
Rep By: Sarah Brown, Kirk L. Clinkenbeard

Western States Land Commissioners Ass'n

Outside Counsel/Consultants

Elinor Schwartz
Rep By: Elinor Schwartz

Western States Petroleum Ass'n

Glendale, CA
Leg. Issues: ENV

Outside Counsel/Consultants

McGuiness Norris & Williams, LLP
Issues: ENV
Rep By: William N. LaForge, Monte B. Lake

Western States Tourism Policy Council

Carson City, NV
Leg. Issues: TOU

Outside Counsel/Consultants

Albertine Enterprises, Inc.
Issues: TOU
Rep By: Aubrey C. King

Western Systems Coordinating Council

Salt Lake City, UT

Outside Counsel/Consultants

Wright & Talisman, P.C.
Rep By: Michael E. Small

Western Systems Power Pool

Phoenix, AZ

Outside Counsel/Consultants

Wright & Talisman, P.C.
Rep By: Michael E. Small

Western Tube & Conduit Co.

Long Beach, CA
Leg. Issues: TRA

Outside Counsel/Consultants

Schagrin Associates
Issues: TRA
Rep By: Roger B. Schagrin

Western United Dairymen
Modesto, CA
Outside Counsel/Consultants
Tuttle, Taylor & Heron
Rep By: Phillip L. Fraas

Western Urban Water Coalition
Leg. Issues: NAT
Outside Counsel/Consultants
Perkins Coie LLP
Issues: NAT
Rep By: Guy R. Martin

Western Wireless Internat'l
Bellevue, WA
Leg. Issues: FOR, TEC, TRD
Outside Counsel/Consultants
Hogan & Hartson L.L.P.
Issues: TEC
Rep By: Michele Farquhar, Christine M. Warnke
Jefferson-Waterman Internat'l, LLC
Issues: FOR, TRD
Rep By: Ann B. Wrobleski

Westex Inc.
Chicago, IL
A manufacturer of flame resistant clothing.
Outside Counsel/Consultants
Bryan Cave LLP
Rep By: Hon. Alan J. Dixon

Westfield America, Inc.
Los Angeles, CA
Leg. Issues: RES, TAX
Outside Counsel/Consultants
The Washington Group
Issues: RES, TAX
Rep By: Richard Sullivan

Westfield Companies
Westfield Center, OH
Outside Counsel/Consultants
Akin, Gump, Strauss, Hauer & Feld, L.L.P.

Westfield Corp.
Los Angeles, CA
Outside Counsel/Consultants
Susan Davis Internat'l

Westhill Partners
New York, NY
Leg. Issues: UTI
Outside Counsel/Consultants
Forscey & Stinson, PLLC
Issues: UTI
Rep By: Michael A. Forscey

Westinghouse
Washington, DC
Leg. Issues: WAS
Outside Counsel/Consultants
Campbell Crane & Associates
Rep By: Jeanne M. Campbell
Patton Boggs, LLP
Issues: WAS
Rep By: Michael J. Driver

Westinghouse Electric Co.
1900 M St. NW
Suite 500
Washington, DC 20036
Tel: (202)945-6400
Fax: (202)945-6404
Registered: LDA
Headquartered in Pittsburgh, PA.
Leg. Issues: ENG, TRD
Political Action Committee/s
Westinghouse Employees Political Participation Program
1900 M St. NW
Suite 500
Washington, DC 20036
Contact: Robert R. Zoglman
Tel: (202)945-6400
Fax: (202)945-6404
In-house, DC-area Employees
KIRST, Michael E.: Director, Government and International Affairs
ZOGLMAN, Robert R.: V. President, Government and International Affairs

Outside Counsel/Consultants
F.B.A.
Rep By: J. R. Kirkland
Hurt, Norton & Associates
Issues: TRD
Rep By: Robert H. Hurt, Frank Norton, Katharine Calhoun Wood

Westinghouse Government Services Group
Washington, DC
Leg. Issues: BUD, ENG, ENV, WAS
Outside Counsel/Consultants
The Advocacy Group
Rep By: John M. Nugent, Jr.
Capitol Coalitions Inc.
Issues: WAS
Rep By: Amy R. Mehlman, Brett P. Scott, Jarvis C. Stewart
Martin G. Hamberger & Associates
Issues: ENG, ENV, WAS
Rep By: Martin G. Hamberger, Brian M. Tynan
Johnston & Associates, LLC
Issues: BUD, ENV
Rep By: Alex Flint, W. Proctor Jones
The Smith-Free Group
Issues: ENG
Rep By: James C. Free, Robert Hickmott, W. Timothy Locke

Westlands Water District
Fresno, CA
Leg. Issues: BUD, ENV, NAT
Outside Counsel/Consultants
McClure, Gerard & Neuenschwander, Inc.
Issues: BUD, ENV, NAT
Rep By: Steven G. Barringer, Joseph T. Findaro, Matthew Iandoli, Nils W. Johnson, Hon. James A. McClure, Tod O. Neuenschwander

Westminster College
Salt Lake City, UT
Outside Counsel/Consultants
Cassidy & Associates, Inc.
Rep By: Carl Franklin Godfrey, Jr.

Westminster, California, City of
Leg. Issues: ENV, GOV
Outside Counsel/Consultants
Peyser Associates, Inc.
Issues: ENV, GOV
Rep By: Thane Young

Westmoreland Coal Co.
Colorado Springs, CO
Leg. Issues: ENV, NAT, UTI
Outside Counsel/Consultants
Jefferson Government Relations, L.L.C.
Issues: ENV, NAT, UTI
Rep By: Thomas R. Donnelly, Jr., Katherine M. Krauser, Randal P. Schumacher, Daniel J. Sheehan

Roy F. Weston, Inc.
West Chester, PA
Leg. Issues: BUD, DEF, ENV
Outside Counsel/Consultants
Madison Government Affairs
Issues: BUD, ENV
Rep By: Paul J. Hirsch, Myron M. Jacobson
Whitten & Diamond
Issues: DEF, ENV
Rep By: Robert M. Diamond, Jamie L. Whitten

WESTVACO
New York, NY
Registered: LDA
A paper products manufacturer.
Leg. Issues: RET
Outside Counsel/Consultants
Covington & Burling
Issues: RET
Rep By: Roderick A. DeArment

WETA
P.O. Box 2626
Washington, DC 20013
Tel: (703)998-2600
Fax: (703)998-3401
Web: www.weta.com
Leg. Issues: EDU, TEC
In-house, DC-area Employees
COHEN, Arthur: Senior V. President for Radio
STEWART, Mary: Director, Corporate Communications

Outside Counsel/Consultants
Convergence Services, Inc.
Issues: EDU, TEC
Rep By: John M. Lawson

Weyerhaeuser Co.
1100 Connecticut Ave. NW
Suite 530
Washington, DC 20036
Tel: (202)293-7222
Fax: (202)293-2955
Registered: LDA
Leg. Issues: CAW, ENG, ENV, HCR, IMM, NAT, TAX, TRA, TRD
In-house, DC-area Employees
BENSON, III, Frederick S.: V. President, Federal and International Affairs
PORTER, Julia: Manager, Government Affairs
RISNER, Gary D.: Manager, Federal Regulatory Affairs
SCHLEGEL, Paul: Senior Federal Affairs Manager
Outside Counsel/Consultants
William M. Diefenderfer
Issues: TAX
Rep By: William M. Diefenderfer, III
Perkins Coie LLP
Issues: NAT
Rep By: Guy R. Martin
Van Scoyoc Associates, Inc.
Issues: TAX
Rep By: H. Stewart Van Scoyoc

WFMJ-TV
Youngstown, OH
Outside Counsel/Consultants
Shaw Pittman

WGBO-TV
Joliet, IL
Outside Counsel/Consultants
Shaw Pittman

Wheat Export Trade Education Committee
415 Second St. NE
Suite 300
Washington, DC 20002
Tel: (202)547-2004
Fax: (202)546-2638
Registered: FARA
E-mail: wetec@uswheat.org
Leg. Issues: AGR, BUD, FOO, FOR, MAR, RRR, SCI, TRA, TRD, TRU
In-house, DC-area Employees
SPANGLER, Barbara R.: Exec. Director
Outside Counsel/Consultants
Mayer, Brown & Platt
Issues: TRD
Rep By: Michael W. Punke

Wheat First Butcher Singer
Richmond, VA
Outside Counsel/Consultants
The Legislative Strategies Group, LLC

Wheat Foods Council
Englewood, CO
Outside Counsel/Consultants
Fleishman-Hillard, Inc
Rep By: Jim Mulhern

Wheat Gluten Industry Council
Atchison, KS
Leg. Issues: TRD
Outside Counsel/Consultants
Barnes & Thornburg
Issues: TRD
Rep By: John R. Edgell, Randolph J. Stayin, Jeffrey L. Taylor
Wiley, Rein & Fielding
Issues: TRD
Rep By: Hon. Jim Slattery

Wheatland Tube Co.
Wheatland, PA
Leg. Issues: TRA
Outside Counsel/Consultants
Schagrin Associates
Issues: TRA
Rep By: Tamara L. Browne, Roger B. Schagrin

Wheelabrator Environmental Systems, Inc.
Hampton, NH
Outside Counsel/Consultants
Akin, Gump, Strauss, Hauer & Feld, L.L.P.

Wheelabrator-Cleanwater Systems-BioGro Division

Annapolis, MD

Outside Counsel/Consultants

Solutions Group
Rep By: Robert Burgess, John F. Herrity

Wheelchairs for the World Foundation

Danville, CA

Outside Counsel/Consultants

Cassidy & Associates, Inc.
Rep By: Douglass E. Bobbitt, Carl Franklin Godfrey, Jr., Amos Hochstein

Wheeling & Lake Erie Railway Co.

Brewster, OH
Leg. Issues: RRR

Outside Counsel/Consultants

Murray, Scheer, Montgomery, Tapia & O'Donnell
Issues: RRR
Rep By: Thomas R. Crawford, D. Michael Murray

Wheeling Pittsburgh Steel Corp.

Leg. Issues: MAN, TRD

Outside Counsel/Consultants

Patton Boggs, LLP
Issues: MAN, TRD
Rep By: John J. Deschauer, Jr., Elena Giberga, Frank R. Samolis

Wheeling, West Virginia, City of

Leg. Issues: CAW

Outside Counsel/Consultants

McGuireWoods L.L.P.
Issues: CAW
Rep By: Joseph H. Bogosian, F. Paul Calamita, Stephen A. Katsurinis, Hon. Lewis F. Payne, Jr., Jeffrey L. Schlagenhauf

Wheelock College

Boston, MA
Leg. Issues: EDU

Outside Counsel/Consultants

Hale and Dorr LLP
Issues: EDU
Rep By: Jay P. Urwitz

Whirlpool Corp.

St. Joseph, MI — Registered: LDA

Outside Counsel/Consultants

Arter & Hadden
Rep By: Hon. Thomas G. Loeffler

White Knight Broadcasting

Lafayette, LA

Outside Counsel/Consultants

Shaw Pittman

White Mountain Apache Tribe

Whiteriver, AZ
Leg. Issues: ECN, ENV, GAM, IND, TOU

Outside Counsel/Consultants

Neuman and Co.
Issues: ECN, ENV, GAM, IND, TOU
Rep By: Robert A. Neuman

White Pigeon Paper Co.

Elgin, IL
Leg. Issues: ADV, CAW, ENG, ENV, FUE, GOV, MAN, TAX, WAS

Outside Counsel/Consultants

Colling Swift & Hynes
Issues: ADV, CAW, ENG, ENV, FUE, GOV, MAN, TAX, WAS
Rep By: Terese Colling, Pablo Collins, Robert J. Hynes, Jr., Hon. Allan B. Swift

Whitman-Walker Clinic

1407 S St. NW
Washington, DC 20009
Tel: (202)797-3500
Fax: (202)797-3504
Web: www.wwc.org

In-house, DC-area Employees

FLEGEL, Laura: Legal Director

R. C. Whitner and Associates, Inc.

1800 N. Kent St.
Suite 1104
Arlington, VA 22209
Tel: (703)243-1400
Fax: (703)525-0626
Registered: LDA
E-mail: whitner@erols.com
Leg. Issues: DEF

In-house, DC-area Employees

WHITNER, R. C.: President

Outside Counsel/Consultants

R. H. White Public Affairs Consulting
Issues: DEF
Rep By: Richard H. White

Whittier, California, City of

Leg. Issues: UTI

Outside Counsel/Consultants

Ball Janik, LLP
Issues: UTI
Rep By: M. Victoria Cram

Wholesale Nursery Growers of America

1250 I St. NW
Suite 500
Washington, DC 20005
Tel: (202)789-2900
Fax: (202)789-1893
Registered: LDA
Leg. Issues: AGR, IMM, LBR

In-house, DC-area Employees

DOLIBOIS, Robert: Exec. V. President
GALSTER, Geoff: Administrator

Outside Counsel/Consultants

McGuiness Norris & Williams, LLP
Issues: LBR
Rep By: Monte B. Lake

Wholesale Telecommunications Corp.

Coral Gables, FL
Leg. Issues: TEC

Outside Counsel/Consultants

Greenberg Traurig, LLP
Issues: TEC
Rep By: Mitchell F. Brecher

Wi-LAN, Inc.

Alberta, CANADA
Leg. Issues: COM, CPI, TEC

Outside Counsel/Consultants

David O'Brien and Associates
Issues: COM, CPI, TEC
Rep By: David D. O'Brien, Shannon L. Scott

Wickland Oil Co.

Sacramento, CA
Leg. Issues: TAX

Outside Counsel/Consultants

Collier Shannon Scott, PLLC
Issues: TAX
Rep By: Kathleen Clark Kies, Michael D. Sherman

Widener University

Chester, PA
Leg. Issues: BUD

Outside Counsel/Consultants

Cassidy & Associates, Inc.
Issues: BUD
Rep By: Douglass E. Bobbitt, Christy Carson Evans, Maureen Walsh

Washington Strategies, L.L.C.
Rep By: Jennifer Johnson Calvert, William P. Jarrell

Wider Opportunities for Women

815 15th St. NW
Suite 916
Washington, DC 20005
Tel: (202)638-3143
Fax: (202)638-4885
Web: www.wowonline.org
E-mail: info@wowonline.org

A private non-profit organization that works to ensure economic independence and equality of opportunity for women. Works at the local, state and national levels to increase public awareness of women's employment and economic needs; design, test and share innovative program and policy approaches to meeting women's employment needs; and expand women's employment options and earnings potential.

Wien Air Alaska

Anchorage, AK

Outside Counsel/Consultants

Hewes, Gelband, Lambert & Dann, P.C.
Rep By: Theodore I. Seamon

Wiland-Bell Productions

Leg. Issues: ART, HCR

Outside Counsel/Consultants

Barksdale Ballard & Co., Inc.
Issues: ART, HCR
Rep By: D. Michael Ballard

Wilberforce University

Wilberforce, OH
Leg. Issues: BUD, EDU

Outside Counsel/Consultants

Dean Blakey & Moskowitz
Issues: BUD, EDU
Rep By: William A. Blakey

Wild Alabama

Moulton, AL
Leg. Issues: NAT, RES

Outside Counsel/Consultants

Patton Boggs, LLP
Issues: NAT, RES
Rep By: Michael D. Bloomquist, Amy C. Davine, Lanny J. Davis, Susan Mathiascheck, Peter D. Robertson

Wild Bird Feeding Institute

Leg. Issues: AGR, NAT, RES, TAX

Outside Counsel/Consultants

Gordley Associates
Issues: AGR, NAT, RES, TAX
Rep By: John Gordley

The Wilderness Soc.

1615 M St. NW
Washington, DC 20036
Tel: (202)833-2300
Fax: (202)429-3958
Registered: LDA
Web: www.wilderness.org

A national, non-profit citizens' organization with a membership of about 350,000 that works to save endangered wildlands and ensure wise management of natural resources.

Leg. Issues: BUD

In-house, DC-area Employees

ALBERSWERTH, Dave: Director, BLM Program
BARRY, Don: Exec. V. President
FENNELL, Rosalyn: Director, Nat'l Parks
FRANCIS, Michael A.: Director, National Forests Program
GREENBURG, Jerry: V. President, Communications
GUNN, Susan H.: Director, Budget and Appropriations
HILL, Yvette: Policy Associate
LANCE, Linda: V. President, Public Policy
MEADOWS, III, William H.: President
WALTMAN, James R.: Director, Refuges and Wildlife Program

Wildlife Advocacy Project

Outside Counsel/Consultants

Meyer & Glitzenstein

Wildlife Conservation and Zoos PAC

818 Connecticut Ave. NW
Suite 1007
Washington, DC 20006

In-house, DC-area Employees

SMITH, Christopher H.

Wildlife Forever

Eden Prairie, MN
Leg. Issues: ENV

Outside Counsel/Consultants

Outdoor Media, Inc.
Issues: ENV
Rep By: Tim Richardson

Wildlife Habitat Council

1010 Wayne Ave.
Suite 920
Silver Spring, MD 20910
Tel: (301)588-8994
Fax: (301)588-4629
Web: www.wildlifehc.org/wildlifehc
E-mail: Whc@wildlifehc.org

Works to increase the amount of quality wildlife habitat on corporate, private and public lands.

Leg. Issues: CAW, ENV, NAT

In-house, DC-area Employees
HOWARD, Bill: President
KAUFFMAN, Vanessa C.: Director of Marketing and Communications

Wildlife Legislative Fund of America

1155 Connecticut Ave. NW
Suite 1200
Washington, DC 20036
Tel: (202)862-8364
Fax: (202)659-1027

An association of sportsmen-conservation organizations established to protect the heritage of the American sportman to hunt, fish and trap. Through its associated organizations the Fund represents an aggregate membership of more than 1.5 million sportsmen-conservationists. Headquartered in Columbus, OH.

Leg. Issues: ANI, NAT

In-house, DC-area Employees
HORN, William P.: Washington Counsel

Outside Counsel/Consultants
Birch, Horton, Bittner & Cherot
Issues: ANI, NAT
Rep By: Thomas L. Albert, Douglas S. Burdin, Julia Gustafson, William P. Horn

Wildlife Management Institute

1101 14th St. NW
Suite 801
Washington, DC 20005
Web: www.wildlifemgmt.org/wmi
Tel: (202)371-1808
Fax: (202)408-5059

Programs of the Institute have been in existence under various names since 1911. Incorporated in New York in 1946. Purpose is to advance sound management of natural resources, especially wildlife.

In-house, DC-area Employees
MCCABE, Richard E.: V. President
SPARROWE, Rollin D.: President

The Wildlife Soc.

5410 Grosvenor Ln.
Bethesda, MD 20814
Web: www.wildlife.org/index
E-mail: tws@wildlife.org
Tel: (301)897-9770
Fax: (301)530-2471

An international organization of professionals and scholars engaged in wildlife research, management, and education. Dedicated to sound stewardship of wildlife resources and environments upon which wildlife and humans depend. Promotes excellence in wildlife stewardship through science and education.

Leg. Issues: NAT

In-house, DC-area Employees
FRANKLIN, Thomas M.: Director, Wildlife Policy
HODGDON, Harry E.: Exec. Director

Wiley, Rein & Fielding

1776 K St. NW
Washington, DC 20006
Tel: (202)719-7000
Fax: (202)719-7049
Registered: LDA

Web: www.wrf.com
Leg. Issues: TAX, UTI

In-house, DC-area Employees
BARAN, Jan W.: Partner
BAYES, James R.: Partner
BODORFF, Richard
BOONE, Jr., Robert E.: Of Counsel
BRADNER, Eileen P.: Partner
BROWN, Tyrone: Of Counsel
BRUCE, III, James T.: Partner
BRUNNER, Thomas W.: Partner
BUCK, Susan C.: Government Affairs Consultant
BURCHETT, Barbara G.: Government Affairs Consultant
BUTLER, Robert J.: Partner
DAWSON, Mimi W.: Government Affairs Consultant
DESILVA, Eric W.: Partner
FIELDING, Fred F.: Partner
FINE, Sharon R.
GREGG, Donna C.: Partner
HODGES, John A.: Partner
JOHNSEN, Wayne D.: Partner
JOSEPH, Bruce G.: Partner
KAMP, John
KIRBY, Kathleen A.: Counsel
KIRBY, Thomas W.: Partner
KRUG, Peter
KRULWICH, Andrew S.: Partner
LAHAM, Carol: Partner
LEWIS, Michael A.: Consultant
MANNING, Mary Jo: Counsel
MCINTOSH, Lane
NAHRA, Kirk J.: Partner
O'CONNELL, Pete: Of Counsel
PETTIT, Robert L.: Partner
POTTER, Trevor: Partner
PRICE, Alan H.: Partner
REIN, Bert W.: Partner
REYNOLDS, III, John B.: Partner
ROSS, Peter: Partner
SECREST, III, Lawrence W.: Partner
SENKOWSKI, R. Michael: Partner
SHIELDS, Peter D.: Partner
SLATTERY, Hon. Jim: Partner
TROY, Daniel E.: Partner
VERRILL, Jr., Charles O.: Partner
VICTORY, Nancy J.: Partner
VOGT, Gregory J.: Partner
WALLACE, Jr., James H.: Partner
WILEY, Richard E.: Partner

Outside Counsel/Consultants
F/P Research Associates
Issues: TAX, UTI
Rep By: Ronald Crawford

Wilke, Fleury, Hoffelt, Gould & Birney, LLP

Sacramento, CA
Leg. Issues: ENV

Outside Counsel/Consultants
McGuiness Norris & Williams, LLP
Issues: ENV
Rep By: William N. LaForge

Wilkie Farr & Gallagher

Washington, DC
Leg. Issues: TRD

Outside Counsel/Consultants
Chlopak, Leonard, Schechter and Associates
Issues: TRD
Rep By: Tiffany Gagliardi, Maria Christina Gonzalez-Noguera, Charles G. Leonard, Peter Schechter

Washington Council Ernst & Young
Issues: TRD
Rep By: Doug Badger, Lauren Darling, John L. Doney, Jayne T. Fitzgerald, LaBrenda Garrett-Nelson, Gary J. Gasper, Bruce A. Gates, Nick Giordano, Cathy Koch, Robert J. Leonard, Richard Meltzer, Phillip D. Moseley, John D. Porter, Robert M. Rozen, Donna Steele-Flynn, Timothy J. Urban

William Tyndale College

Farmington Hills, MI
Leg. Issues: EDU

Outside Counsel/Consultants
Russ Reid Co.
Issues: EDU
Rep By: Thomas C. Keller, Mark D. McIntyre, Jovita Wenner

The Williams Companies

1627 I St. NW
Suite 900
Washington, DC 20006
Tel: (202)833-8994
Fax: (202)835-0707
Registered: LDA

Subsidiaries also represented include Williams Field Services, Williams Pipe Line Co., Williams Natural Gas Co., Northwest Pipe Line Co, Williams Communications Group, Transcontintental Pipeline and Texas Gas Transmission.

Leg. Issues: CAW, COM, ENV, TAX, TRA, UTI

In-house, DC-area Employees
EMLING, Gretchen: Manager, Government Affairs
JACKSON, Glenn F.: Director, Government Affairs
LAWRENCE, Deborah B.: V. President, Government Affairs

Outside Counsel/Consultants
BKSH & Associates
Issues: CAW, ENV

Collier Shannon Scott, PLLC

McClure, Gerard & Neuenschwander, Inc.
Rep By: Steven G. Barringer, Joseph T. Findaro, Matthew Iandoli, Nils W. Johnson, Hon. James A. McClure, Tod O. Neuenschwander

White & Case LLP
Rep By: Linda E. Carlisle, J. Roger Mentz

Williams Field Services

Tulsa, OK

Outside Counsel/Consultants
Wright & Talisman, P.C.
Rep By: James T. McManus

Williams Pipelines Central, Inc.

Tulsa, OK

Outside Counsel/Consultants
Wright & Talisman, P.C.
Rep By: Gregory Grady

The Williamson Group

Rockville, MD

Outside Counsel/Consultants
Hargett Consulting
Rep By: Jack Hargett

Williamsport, Maryland, Town of

Leg. Issues: GOV

Outside Counsel/Consultants
Duncan, Weinberg, Genzer & Pembroke, P.C.
Issues: GOV
Rep By: Janice L. Lower

Wilmer, Cutler & Pickering

2445 M St. NW
Washington, DC 20037-1420
Tel: (202)663-6000
Fax: (202)663-6363
Registered: LDA, FARA

Web: www.wilmer.com
E-mail: law@wilmer.com
Leg. Issues: TEC

In-house, DC-area Employees
BECKER, Brandon: Partner
BERMAN, Bruce M.: Partner
CAMPBELL, James S.: Partner
CASS, Richard W.: Partner
CASSIDY, Jr., Robert C.: Partner
CHARYTAN, Lynn: Partner
CHESTON, Sheila C.
CLAYTON, Carol: Associate
COLLINS, J. Barclay: Associate
COX, J. Edward: Commercial Analyst
CUTLER, Lloyd N.: Partner
DUNNE, Steven M.: Associate
GRAY, C. Boyden: Partner
GREENE, Ronald J.: Partner
GREENWALD, John D.: Partner
HARWOOD, Jr., John H.: Partner
HOYT, Robert F.: Associate
HUT, Stephen
HYDE, Terrill A.: Partner
JETTON, Jr., C. Loring: Partner
KING, Neil J.: Partner
KOLASKY, Jr., William J.: Partner
LAKE, Jr., F. David: Partner
LAKE, William T.: Partner
LANG, Jeffrey M.: Partner
LEE, Yoon-Young: Partner
LEVY, Charles S.: Partner
MANLEY, Jeffrey: Partner
MELTZER, Ronald I.: Associate
MODE, Jr., Paul J.: Partner
NURICK, Lester: Counsel
OLSON, Thomas P.: Partner
PAYTON, John: Partner
PERLSTEIN, William J.: Partner
PETERSON, Cathleen: Partner
PHYTHYON, Daniel
PICKER, Colin: Associate
PICKERING, John H.: Senior Counsel
PRIBBLE, Robert: Legislative Specialist
RABINOVITZ, Bruce: Partner
RICHARDSON, Jr., William R.: Partner
SHAMBON, Leonard M.: Counsel
SHERBURNE, Jane C.: Partner
SMYTHE, Marianne K.: Partner
SQUIRE, Daniel H.: Partner
STOEPPELWERTH, Ali M.: Associate
TRENOR, John A.: Associate
VOLLMER, Andrew N.: Partner
WILKINS, William J.: Partner
WILSON, Gary D.: Partner
WITTEN, Roger M.: Partner
WRATHALL, James R.: Partner

Outside Counsel/Consultants
Griffin, Johnson, Dover & Stewart
Issues: TEC
Rep By: William C. Danvers, G. Jack Dover, Patrick J. Griffin, Keith Heard, David E. Johnson, Susan O. Mann, Walter J. "Joe" Stewart, Leonard Swinehart

The OB-C Group, LLC
Issues: TEC
Rep By: Thomas Keating, Kim F. McKernan, Charles J. Mellody, Patricia A. Nelson, Lawrence F. O'Brien, III, Linda E. Tarplin

Wilmington Savings Fund Society

Wilmington, DE
Leg. Issues: BAN, BNK, BUD, ECN, FIN, HOU, TAX

Outside Counsel/Consultants
Hohlt & Associates
Issues: BAN, BNK, BUD, ECN, FIN, HOU, TAX
Rep By: Richard F. Hohlt

Wilson Composites Group

Folsom, CA
Leg. Issues: DEF

Outside Counsel/Consultants

GHL Inc.
Issues: DEF
Rep By: Thomas R. Goldberg

Window Covering Manufacturers Ass'n

4041 Powder Mill Rd.
Suite 104
Calverton, MD 20705
Tel: (301)348-2005
Fax: (301)348-2020

In-house, DC-area Employees

SNYDER, Russell K.: Washington Representative

Outside Counsel/Consultants

The Kellen Company
Rep By: Russell K. Snyder

Window Covering Safety Council

4041 Powder Mill Rd.
Suite 104
Calverton, MD 20705
Tel: (202)348-2005
Fax: (202)348-2020

In-house, DC-area Employees

SNYDER, Russell K.: Washington Representative

Outside Counsel/Consultants

The Kellen Company
Rep By: Russell K. Snyder

Windsock Research

Dallas, TX

Outside Counsel/Consultants

The Campo Group, Ltd.
Rep By: Terry T. Campo

Windsor Group

Outside Counsel/Consultants

Edelman Public Relations Worldwide
Rep By: Bob Knott

Wine and Spirits Wholesalers of America

805 15th St. NW
Suite 430
Washington, DC 20005
Tel: (202)371-9792
Fax: (202)789-2405
Registered: LDA
Web: www.wswa.org
E-mail: juanita.duggan@wswa.org
Leg. Issues: ADV, ALC, BEV, CSP, GOV, HCR, TAX, TRD, TRU

Political Action Committee/s

Wine and Spirits Wholesalers of America Political Action Committee
805 15th St. NW
Suite 430
Washington, DC 20005
Tel: (202)371-9792
Fax: (202)789-2405
Contact: Rae Ann Bevington

In-house, DC-area Employees

BEVINGTON, Rae Ann: Director, Political Affairs
DUGGAN, Juanita D.: Chief Exec. Officer and Exec. V. President
ENGLAND, Peggy P.: V. President, Public Affairs and Communications
GEGG, Joseph C.: Senior V. President
JOHNSON, Mike: Director, Government Relations
SLOANE, David: V. President, Federal Government Relations
WOLF, Craig: General Counsel

Outside Counsel/Consultants

Griffin, Johnson, Dover & Stewart
Issues: ADV, ALC, BEV
Rep By: William C. Danvers, G. Jack Dover, Patrick J. Griffin, Keith Heard, David E. Johnson, Susan O. Mann, Walter J. "Joe" Stewart, Leonard Swinehart

Hooper Owen & Winburn
Issues: TAX
Rep By: Steve Glaze, Lindsay D. Hooper, John P. Winburn

McGuiness & Holch
Issues: BEV
Rep By: Markham C. Erickson, Kevin S. McGuiness

Strat@Comm (Strategic Communications Counselors)
Issues: ALC, BEV, CSP, GOV, HCR, TRD, TRU
Rep By: Elinore Boeke

Wine Institute

601 13th St. NW
Suite 580 South
Washington, DC 20005
Tel: (202)408-0870
Fax: (202)371-0061
Registered: LDA
E-mail: robertpkoch@aol.com

Headquartered in San Francisco, CA.

Leg. Issues: ALC, BEV, BUD, CON, HCR, LAW, TAX, TRD

In-house, DC-area Employees

KOCH, Robert P.: Senior V. President

Outside Counsel/Consultants

JBC Internat'l
Issues: TRD
Rep By: Jeannie M. Boone, James B. Clawson, George M. "Matt" Mattingley, Jr.

Morgan, Lewis & Bockius LLP
Issues: ALC, BEV, CON, LAW

Winegrape Growers of America

Sacramento, CA
Leg. Issues: BUD, TRD

Outside Counsel/Consultants

Schramm, Williams & Associates, Inc.
Issues: BUD, TRD
Rep By: Anita Brown, Robert Schramm, Nancy Williams

The Wing Group

Aspen, CO

Outside Counsel/Consultants

Skadden, Arps, Slate, Meagher & Flom LLP
Rep By: Lynn R. Coleman

Winnebago Tribe of Nebraska

Winnebago, NE
Leg. Issues: BUD

Outside Counsel/Consultants

Dorsey & Whitney LLP
Issues: BUD
Rep By: Philip Baker-Shenk, David A. Bieging, Virginia W. Boylan, Cindy Darcy, Sarah Ridley

Winner Internat'l

Sharon, PA

A manufacturer of anti-theft devices.

Outside Counsel/Consultants

Collier Shannon Scott, PLLC
Rep By: Michael J. Coursey

Winslow Press

Del Ray Beach, FL
Leg. Issues: EDU, TAX

Outside Counsel/Consultants

Ervin Technical Associates, Inc. (ETA)
Issues: EDU, TAX
Rep By: Hon. Joseph M. McDade

Winstar Communications, Inc.

1615 L St. NW
Suite 1260
Washington, DC 20036
Tel: (202)367-7600
Fax: (202)659-1931
Registered: LDA
Leg. Issues: COM, CPI, GOV, TEC

In-house, DC-area Employees

MERBETH, Russell: V. President, State Regulatory Affairs
MURRAY, David T.: Director, Government Affairs
OHLSON, Barry: Counsel
SANDRI, Jr., Joseph M.: V. President and Regulatory Counsel

Outside Counsel/Consultants

The Dutko Group, Inc.
Issues: COM, GOV, TEC
Rep By: Kim Koontz Bayliss, Louis Lehrman, Steve Perry, Juliette M. Raffensperger, Stephen Craig Sayle

Greenberg Traurig, LLP
Issues: TEC

Harris, Wiltshire & Grannis LLP
Issues: COM, TEC
Rep By: Scott Blake Harris

Sher & Blackwell
Issues: GOV, TEC
Rep By: Earl W. Comstock, Jeffrey R. Pike

WinStar Internat'l

New York, NY
Leg. Issues: TEC

Outside Counsel/Consultants

The Washington Group
Issues: TEC
Rep By: Kevin D. Allen, G. John O'Hanlon, John D. Raffaelli, Richard Sullivan

Winstar Petroleum

Petersburg, AK
Leg. Issues: ENG

Outside Counsel/Consultants

Verner, Liipfert, Bernhard, McPherson and Hand, Chartered
Issues: ENG
Rep By: Andrew D. Eskin, Steven R. Phillips

Harry Winston Research Foundation

New York, NY

Outside Counsel/Consultants

Garvey, Schubert & Barer
Rep By: Matthew R. Schneider

The Winterthur Group

Geneva, SWITZERLAND
Leg. Issues: BAN

Outside Counsel/Consultants

Barbour Griffith & Rogers, Inc.
Issues: BAN
Rep By: G. O. Lanny Griffith, Jr., Loren Monroe

Wire Reinforcement Institute

Washington, DC

Outside Counsel/Consultants

Howe, Anderson & Steyer, P.C.
Rep By: James E. Anderson

Wireless Communications Ass'n

1140 Connecticut Ave. NW
Suite 810
Washington, DC 20036
Tel: (202)452-7823
Fax: (202)452-0041
Web: www.wcai.com
E-mail: communication@wcai.com

Represents wireless cable operators and vendors.

Leg. Issues: COM, CPT, TAX

In-house, DC-area Employees

KREIG, Andrew T.: President

Outside Counsel/Consultants

Latham & Watkins
Issues: COM, CPT, TAX
Rep By: Nicholas W. Allard

Wilkinson, Barker and Knauer, LLP
Rep By: Jonathan V. Cohen, Robert Primosch, Paul J. Sinderbrand

The Wireless Communications Council

Outside Counsel/Consultants

Baker & Hostetler LLP
Rep By: Frederick H. Graefe, Hon. Guy Vander Jagt

Wireless Information Networks Forum (WinForum)

Washington, DC

Outside Counsel/Consultants

Smith, Bucklin and Associates, Inc.
Rep By: Anna Darin

Wireless Location Industry Ass'n

Leg. Issues: TEC

Outside Counsel/Consultants

Berliner, Candon & Jimison
Issues: TEC
Rep By: John W. Jimison, Carla Kish

CLARION Management Resources, Inc.
Rep By: Christopher Bailey, Carole M. Rogin

Wireless Technology Research, L.L.C.

Studies the potential health effects of wireless technologies. All inquiries should be directed through the organization, rather than through outside counsel.

Leg. Issues: HCR, MED

Outside Counsel/Consultants

Townsend Solheim
Issues: HCR, MED
Rep By: Linda T. Solheim

Wisconsin Central Transportation Corp.

Rosemont, IL
Leg. Issues: RRR

Outside Counsel/Consultants

Murray, Scheer, Montgomery, Tapia & O'Donnell
Issues: RRR
Rep By: Thomas R. Crawford, D. Michael Murray

Wisconsin Energy Corp.

Milwaukee, WI
Registered: LDA

Headquartered in Milwaukee, WI.

Leg. Issues: CAW, ENG, ENV, FUE, GOV, UTI, WAS

Outside Counsel/Consultants

Broydrick & Associates
Issues: CAW, ENG, FUE, UTI, WAS
Rep By: William Broydrick, Bill Viney

Troutman Sanders LLP
Issues: ENG, ENV, GOV, UTI
Rep By: Thomas C. Jensen, Clifford S. Sikora, Bonnie Suchman

Wisconsin Gas Co.

Milwaukee, WI
Leg. Issues: ENG, ENV, UTI

Outside Counsel/Consultants

Foley & Lardner
Issues: ENG, ENV, UTI
Rep By: Theodore H. Bornstein

Wisconsin Public Service Corp.

Green Bay, WI
Leg. Issues: ENG

Outside Counsel/Consultants

The Carmen Group
Issues: ENG
Rep By: Mel Cottone, David A. Keene

Wisconsin, Office of the Attorney General of the State of

Madison, WI

Outside Counsel/Consultants

Duncan, Weinberg, Genzer & Pembroke, P.C.
Rep By: James F. Flug

Wisconsin, Washington Office of the State of

444 N. Capitol St. NW
Suite 613
Washington, DC 20001
Web: www.state.wi.us
Tel: (202)624-5870
Fax: (202)624-5871

In-house, DC-area Employees

BAAB, Schuyler J.: Director, Washington Office

Wittenburg University

Springfield, OH
Leg. Issues: BUD, EDU

Outside Counsel/Consultants

Sagamore Associates, Inc.
Issues: BUD, EDU
Rep By: Todd Atkinson, Doug Wasitis

WLTV

Miami, FL

Outside Counsel/Consultants

Shaw Pittman

WMF/Huntoon, Paige Associates Ltd.

Edison, NJ
Leg. Issues: HOU

Outside Counsel/Consultants

Nixon Peabody LLP
Issues: HOU
Rep By: Richard M. Price, Monica Hilton Sussman

WNHT

Concord, NH

Outside Counsel/Consultants

Sutherland Asbill & Brennan LLP

WNVT/WNVC

Falls Church, VA
Leg. Issues: BUD, COM, EDU, TEC

Outside Counsel/Consultants

Convergence Services, Inc.
Issues: BUD, COM, EDU, TEC
Rep By: John M. Lawson

Wocom Commodities Limited

Hong Kong, CHINA (PEOPLE'S REPUBLIC)

Outside Counsel/Consultants

Sidley & Austin

Wolf Creek Nuclear Operating Corp.

Burlington, KS

A joint venture of Kansas City Power & Light Co., Kansas Gas & Electric Co. and Kansas Electric Power Cooperative, Inc.

Outside Counsel/Consultants

Shaw Pittman
Rep By: Jay E. Silberg

Wolf Springs Ranches, Inc.

Westcliffe, CO
Leg. Issues: AVI, DEF, NAT

Outside Counsel/Consultants

Kogovsek & Associates
Issues: AVI, DEF, NAT
Rep By: Christine Ann Arbogast, Hon. Raymond P. Kogovsek

Woman's Nat'l Democratic Club

1526 New Hampshire Ave. NW
Washington, DC 20036
Tel: (202)232-7363
Fax: (202)986-2791

The WNDC is an educational, political, cultural and social organization for Democrats.

In-house, DC-area Employees

MOONEY, Kathy: General Manager

Women and Infants' Hospital

Providence, RI
Leg. Issues: HCR, MMM

Outside Counsel/Consultants

McDermott, Will and Emery
Issues: HCR, MMM
Rep By: Wendy L. Krasner, Maggie A. Mitchell, Karen S. Sealander

Women Business Owners Corp. Inc.

Palos Verdes, CA

A trade association of women business owners. Seeks to increase affirmative action opportunities for women-owned firms.

Outside Counsel/Consultants

Crowell & Moring LLP
Rep By: Karen Hastie Williams

Women for Tax Reform

Washington, DC

Outside Counsel/Consultants

Creative Response Concepts

Women in Community Service

1900 N. Beauregard St.
Suite 103
Alexandria, VA 22311
Web: www.wics.org
E-mail: WICSNatl@wics.org
Tel: (703)671-0500
Fax: (703)671-4489

A national nonprofit organization founded in 1964, WICS promotes self-reliance and economic independence to reduce the number of young women and youth living in poverty. WICS addresses issues surrounding employment, job training, welfare reform, poverty, and cultural diversity. They provide support services, mentoring, and workforce preparation programs nationwide.

In-house, DC-area Employees

LENDSEY, Jacquelyn L.: President/CEO

Women in Government Relations, Inc.

1029 Vermont Ave. NW
Suite 510
Washington, DC 20005-3527
Web: www.wgr.org
E-mail: infowgr@earthlink.net
Tel: (703)971-9205
Fax: (703)971-6997

An organization of about 800 women/men with government relations/public affairs responsibilities in corporations, trade associations, law firms, government agencies and public interest groups.

In-house, DC-area Employees

BARDACH, Emily: Director
HUGHES, Phyllis E.: President

Women Officials in NACo

440 First St. NW
Eighth Floor
Washington, DC 20001
Tel: (202)942-4228
Fax: (202)737-0480

A forum and communications network representing women in county government.

Leg. Issues: AGR, ALC, ART, CAW, CIV, ECN, EDU, ENV, FAM, HCR, HOU, LAW, LBR, MIA, MMM, RET, SCI, SMB, TAX, TEC, TOB, TRA, TRD, URB, UTI, WAS, WEL

In-house, DC-area Employees

CRAYTON, Christina

Women's Action for New Directions (WAND)/Women Legislators' Lobby (WILL)

110 Maryland Ave. NE
Suite 205
Washington, DC 20002
E-mail: wand@wand.org
Tel: (202)543-8505
Fax: (202)675-6469
Registered: LDA

A national women's organization working to empower women to act politically to reduce violence and militarism, and to redirect federal resources to meet human and environmental needs. The Women Legislators' Lobby (WILL) is a program of WAND which organizes female state legislators in all 50 states to lobby on behalf of this agenda. Supports women running for Congress.

Political Action Committee/s

WILL PAC
110 Maryland Ave. NE
Suite 205
Washington, DC 20002
Tel: (202)543-8505
Fax: (202)675-6469

In-house, DC-area Employees

OBER, Ann: WILL Washington Director
ROBSON, Kimberly: Director, Policy and Programs

Women's Campaign Fund

734 15th St. NW
Suite 500
Washington, DC 20005
Web: www.wcfonline.org
Tel: (202)393-8164
Fax: (202)393-0649

Provides financial and technical support to pro-choice women candidates from all parties for public office.

In-house, DC-area Employees

HENRI, Erica: Political Director
MEDALIE, Susan: Exec. Director

Women's College Coalition

125 Michigan Ave. NE
Suite 340
Washington, DC 20017
Web: www.womenscolleges.org
Tel: (202)234-0443
Fax: (202)234-0445

A public information effort on behalf of women's colleges and women's higher education. Sponsors research on women in higher education.

In-house, DC-area Employees

SEBRECHTS, Jadwiga S.: President

Women's Hospital

Baton Rouge, LA
Leg. Issues: HCR, MMM

Outside Counsel/Consultants

McDermott, Will and Emery
Issues: HCR, MMM
Rep By: Wendy L. Krasner, Maggie A. Mitchell, Karen S. Sealander

Women's Hospital of Greensboro

Greensboro, NC
Leg. Issues: HCR, MMM

Outside Counsel/Consultants

McDermott, Will and Emery
Issues: HCR, MMM
Rep By: Wendy L. Krasner, Maggie A. Mitchell, Karen S. Sealander

Women's Information Network

1800 R St. NW
Suite C-4
Washington, DC 20009
Web: www.winonline.org
E-mail: info@winonline.org
Tel: (202)347-2827
Fax: (202)347-1418

A professional, political and social network dedicated to empowering women through career opportunities and networking, with a tradition of pro-choice Democratic support.

In-house, DC-area Employees

HABERMAN-GOMEZ, Amy: Chairperson

Women's Policy, Inc.

409 12th St. SW
Suite 310
Washington, DC 20024
Web: www.womenspolicy.org
E-mail: webmaster@womenspolicy.org
Tel: (202)554-2323
Fax: (202)554-2346

A non-partisan, non-profit organization that conducts legislative analysis and provides information on congressional actions affecting women and families.

Leg. Issues: CIV, EDU, GOV, HCR, LAW, MMM, SMB

In-house, DC-area Employees

HALL, Cynthia A.: President
LEARY, Mary Anne: Exec. Director

Women's Pro-Israel Nat'l Political Action Committee (Win PaC)

2020 Pennsylvania Ave. NW
Suite 275
Washington, DC 20006
Tel: (202)296-2946

In-house, DC-area Employees

ULLMAN, Joyce: Treasurer

Women's Research and Education Institute

1750 New York Ave. NW
Suite 350
Washington, DC 20006
Web: www.wrei.org
E-mail: wrei@wrei.org
Tel: (202)628-0444
Fax: (202)628-0458

Conducts research on women's equity issues. Publishes reports on issues relevant to current legislation. Administers Congressional Fellowship Program on Women and Public Policy.

In-house, DC-area Employees

MANNING, USN (Ret.), Capt. Lory: Director, Women in Military Project
MEARS, Rachel: Director, Women's Fellowship Program
SCANLAN, Susan: President

Women's Sports Foundation

New York, NY
Leg. Issues: SPO

Outside Counsel/Consultants

Bracy Williams & Co.
Issues: SPO
Rep By: Linda Doorfee Flaherty, Susan J. Williams

Wood Corp.

Metairie, LA
Leg. Issues: TRD

Outside Counsel/Consultants

Harris Ellsworth & Levin
Issues: TRD
Rep By: Hon. Herbert E. Harris, II, Jeffrey S. Levin

Wood Machinery Manufacturers of America

Philadelphia, PA

Outside Counsel/Consultants

London and Satagaj, Attorneys-at-Law
Rep By: Sheldon I. London, John S. Satagaj

Wood Products Indoor Air Consortium

Washington, DC
Leg. Issues: ENV

Outside Counsel/Consultants

Venable
Issues: ENV
Rep By: Brock R. Landry

Woodbury County, Iowa

Sioux City, IA
Leg. Issues: CAW, ENV, GOV

Outside Counsel/Consultants

Redfern Resources
Issues: CAW, ENV, GOV
Rep By: Ed Redfern

Woodfin Suite Hotels

San Diego, CA
Leg. Issues: TOU

Outside Counsel/Consultants

Verner, Liipfert, Bernhard, McPherson and Hand, Chartered
Issues: TOU
Rep By: Lawrence E. Levinson

Woodland, California, City of

Woodland, CA
Leg. Issues: ENV, GOV

Outside Counsel/Consultants

Peyser Associates, Inc.
Issues: ENV, GOV
Rep By: Thane Young

Woodmont Corporation

Fort Worth, TX
Leg. Issues: CAW, ENV, GOV, RES

Outside Counsel/Consultants

Akin, Gump, Strauss, Hauer & Feld, L.L.P.
Issues: CAW, ENV, GOV, RES
Rep By: David Geanacopoulos, Charles W. Johnson, IV

Woodmont, LLC

Outside Counsel/Consultants

BKSH & Associates

Woods Hole Oceanographic Institution

Woods Hole, MA
Leg. Issues: SCI

Outside Counsel/Consultants

Hill and Knowlton, Inc.
Rep By: Neil Dhillon, Gary G. Hymel, Frank Mankiewicz

E. Del Smith and Co.
Issues: SCI
Rep By: Margaret Allen, E. Del Smith

Woods Hole Steamship Authority

Woods Hole, MA
Leg. Issues: MAR

Outside Counsel/Consultants

Sher & Blackwell
Issues: MAR
Rep By: Earl W. Comstock, Jeffrey R. Pike

Wool Fiber, Yarn Fabric Coalition

Washington, DC
Leg. Issues: APP, TRD

Outside Counsel/Consultants

Meyers & Associates
Issues: APP, TRD
Rep By: Fran Boyd, Larry D. Meyers, Richard L. Meyers

Word Chiropractic Alliance

Outside Counsel/Consultants

Albertine Enterprises, Inc.
Rep By: James J. Albertine

The Work Colleges

Carlinville, IL
Leg. Issues: BUD, EDU

Outside Counsel/Consultants

Dean Blakey & Moskowitz
Issues: BUD, EDU
Rep By: William A. Blakey

Work Opportunity Tax Credit Coalition

Falls Church, VA

An ad hoc coalition advocating expansion of the Federal Work Opportunity Tax Credit.

Outside Counsel/Consultants

Paul Suplizio Associates
Rep By: Paul E. Suplizio

Working Today

New York, NY

Outside Counsel/Consultants

Hauser Group

Workplaces Against Salting Abuse

1300 N. 17th St.
Eighth Floor
Arlington, VA 22209
Tel: (703)812-2000
Fax: (703)812-8201
Registered: LDA

In-house, DC-area Employees

SPENCER, William B.: Contact

World Council of Hellenes

Chicago, IL

Outside Counsel/Consultants

Manatos & Manatos, Inc.

World Duty Free Americas, Inc.

Ridgefield, CT
Leg. Issues: TOU, TRD

Outside Counsel/Consultants

The Aegis Group, Ltd.
Issues: TOU, TRD
Rep By: A. Mario Castillo

World Federalist Ass'n

420 Seventh St. SE
Washington, DC 20003
Web: www.wfa.org
E-mail: wfa@wfa.org
Tel: (202)546-3950
Fax: (202)546-3749

A globally oriented organization which asserts that peace can best be achieved through the creation and enforcement of world law.

Leg. Issues: FOR

In-house, DC-area Employees

ANDERSON, Hon. John B.: Exec. Director
FLEMING, Tony: Director, Media Relations
GRUBOR, Justina: Director, Partners Program
HAMILTON, Heather: ICC Project Director
HOFFMAN, Scott: Field Director
KNIGHT, Aaron: Chief of Staff
THOMPSON, Liz L.: Director, Development
WOLLERY, Chuck: Issues Director

World Federation for Mental Health

1021 Prince St.
Alexandria, VA 22314
Web: www.wfmh.com
E-mail: wfmh@erols.com
Tel: (703)838-7544
Fax: (703)519-7648

In-house, DC-area Employees

HUNTER, Richard C.: Deputy Secretary General

World Federation of Free Latvians

Outside Counsel/Consultants

Downey McGrath Group, Inc.

World Floor Covering Ass'n

Anaheim, CA
Leg. Issues: ENV, SMB, TAX

Outside Counsel/Consultants

Collier Shannon Scott, PLLC
Issues: ENV, SMB, TAX
Rep By: R. Timothy Columbus, Scott A. Sinder

World Food Prize

Des Moines, IA
Leg. Issues: SCI

Outside Counsel/Consultants

Redfern Resources
Issues: SCI
Rep By: Ed Redfern

World Government of World Citizens

1012 14th St. NW
Suite 1106
Washington, DC 20005
Web: www.worldgovernment.org
E-mail: info@worldservice.org
Tel: (202)638-2662
Fax: (202)638-0638

A world citizen government founded in 1953 to implement worldwide legal observance of human rights.

Leg. Issues: CIV, CON, EDU, ENV, FOR, GOV, IMM, TOU

In-house, DC-area Employees

DAVIS, Garry: World Coordinator
GALLUP, David: President, Administration

World Health Organization

Geneva, SWITZERLAND

Outside Counsel/Consultants

Chlopak, Leonard, Schechter and Associates
Rep By: Peter Schechter, Kelly Sullivan

World Hunger Education Service

P.O. Box 29056
Washington, DC 20017
Web: www.worldhunger.org
E-mail: hungerno@aol.com
Tel: (202)269-6322
Fax: (202)269-6322

Informs people about world hunger and poverty in the U.S.

Leg. Issues: FOR

In-house, DC-area Employees

VANDERSLICE, Lane: Managing Editor, Hunger Notes

World Institute on Disability

Oakland, CA

Outside Counsel/Consultants

Issue Dynamics Inc.

World Jewish Congress

New York, NY

Outside Counsel/Consultants

Bloomfield Associates, Inc.
Rep By: Douglas M. Bloomfield

RTC Direct

World Jurist Ass'n of the World Peace Through Law Center

1000 Connecticut Ave. NW
Suite 202
Washington, DC 20036
Web: www.worldjurist.org
E-mail: wja@worldjurist.org
Tel: (202)466-5428
Fax: (202)452-8540

A non-profit organization established under the auspices of the American Bar Ass'n in 1963. Seeks peaceful international relations under a rule of law. Holds biennial international conference/and publishes the newsletter, The World Jurist.

In-house, DC-area Employees

HENNEBERRY, Margaretha M.: Exec. V. President
MONACO, Daniel J.: President

World Learning Inc.

1015 15th St. NW
Suite 750
Washington, DC 20005
Web: www.worldlearning.org
Tel: (202)408-5420
Fax: (202)408-5397
Registered: LDA

Runs international education, exchange, and development programs. Works to promote intercultural understanding and global development. Headquartered in Brattleboro, VT.

Leg. Issues: BUD, FOR

In-house, DC-area Employees

EGLINTON, Stephanie J.: Government Relations Coordinator

World Resources Institute

Ten G St. NE
Suite 800
Washington, DC 20002
Tel: (202)729-7600
Fax: (202)729-7610

An independent, non-profit organization. WRI's research studies aim to generate accurate information about global resources and environmental conditions, analyze emerging issues, and develop creative responses to both problems and opportunities. Brings the insights of scientific research, economic analysis, and practical experience to political, business and other leaders around the world through publication of books, reports, and papers, and frequently sponsors briefings and conferences. Materials also provide the print and broadcast media with new perspectives and information.

Leg. Issues: AGR, CAW, ENG, ENV, FUE, NAT, SCI

In-house, DC-area Employees

AMOR, Adlai: Director, Media Relations
ARNOLD, Matthew: Chief Operating Officer and Senior V. President, Operations
BEANE, Marjorie: Secretary-Treasurer
JANETOS, Anthony: Senior V. President, Programs
LASH, Jonathan: President
RUCKELSHAUS, William D.: Chairman, Board of Directors

World Service Authority

1012 14th St. NW
Suite 1106
Washington, DC 20005
Web: www.worldservice.org
E-mail: info@worldservice.org
Tel: (202)638-2662
Fax: (202)638-0638

The administrative branch of the World Government of World Citizens. Issues documents based on articles in the Universal Declaration of Human Rights. Provides legal assistance, legal tools and human rights education to individuals suffering from human rights violations throughout the world. Maintains an Internet newsletter, WORLD CITIZEN NEWS, on its web site.

Leg. Issues: CIV, CON, EDU, ENV, GOV, IMM, LAW, TOU

In-house, DC-area Employees

DAVIS, Garry: Political Consultant
GALLUP, David: President

World Shipping Council

1015 15th St. NW
Suite 450
Washington, DC 20005
Tel: (202)589-1230
Registered: LDA
Leg. Issues: LBR, MAR, TAX, TRA, TRU

In-house, DC-area Employees

KJAER, Lars: V. President
KOCH, Christopher L.: President and Chief Exec. Officer
O'HARE, Don: V. President

World Sports Exchange

St. John's, ANTIGUA AND BARBUDA
Leg. Issues: GAM

Outside Counsel/Consultants

Bacino & Associates
Issues: GAM
Rep By: Geoff Bacino

World Wide Energy Group

Honolulu, HI

Outside Counsel/Consultants

Durante Associates
Rep By: Douglas A. Durante

World Wide Packets

Spokane, WA

Outside Counsel/Consultants

R. Duffy Wall and Associates

World Wide Technology

Outside Counsel/Consultants

Alcalde & Fay
Rep By: Rodney A. Coleman

World Wildlife Fund

1250 24th St. NW
Washington, DC 20037
Web: www.worldwildlife.org
Tel: (202)293-4800
Fax: (202)293-9211
Registered: LDA

Organization has three major objectives: protecting natural areas and wildlife populations, promoting sustainable use of natural resources, and promoting efficient resouce use and reducing pollution. Part of a network of 28 WWF national organizations coordinated by an international secretariat in Gland, Switzerland, it is the world's leading international organization working to maintain the earth's resources.

Leg. Issues: ANI, BUD, CAW, ENV, MAR, NAT, RES

In-house, DC-area Employees

ACKERLY, Margaret: General Counsel
COLBORN, Theo: Senior Scientist
FITZHUGH, Estrellita Jones
FULLER, Kathryn S.: President
LEAPE, James P.: V. President
LIPPMAN, Tom: V. President, Public Affairs
REILLY, William K.: Chairman of the Board
SNODGRASS, Randall: Director, Congressional Relations
WILLIAMS, Christopher: Program Officer, U.S. Program
YEAGER, Brooks: V. President, Global Threats

Outside Counsel/Consultants

Baker, Donelson, Bearman & Caldwell, P.C.
Issues: ENV
Rep By: James D. Range

Conservation Strategies, LLC
Issues: CAW, NAT

Law Office of C. Deming Cowles
Issues: ENV, MAR, NAT
Rep By: C. Deming Cowles

Winthrop, Stimson, Putnam & Roberts
Rep By: Donald A. Carr

World Wrestling Federation Entertainment Inc.

Stamford, CT

Outside Counsel/Consultants

The Carmen Group
Rep By: Bob Burkett, David A. Keene

Worldlink Logistics Inc.

Cherry Hill, NJ

Outside Counsel/Consultants

Galland, Kharasch, Greenberg, Fellman & Swirsky, P.C.
Rep By: David P. Street

WorldSpace Corp.

2400 N St. NW
Washington, DC 20037
Web: www.worldspace.com
E-mail: info@worldspace.com
Tel: (202)969-6000
Fax: (202)969-6001
Registered: LDA

Satellite communications company.

Leg. Issues: COM, TEC

In-house, DC-area Employees

SAMARA, Noah A.: Chief Exec. Officer

Outside Counsel/Consultants

Scribe Consulting & Communications
Rep By: Joseph J. Szlavik

Technology, Entertainment and Communications (TEC) Law Group
Issues: TEC
Rep By: Talib I. Karim, Rosalind Parker

Worldwatch Institute

1776 Massachusetts Ave. NW
Washington, DC 20036
Web: www.worldwatch.org
E-mail: worldwatch@worldwatch.org
Tel: (202)452-1999
Fax: (202)296-7365

A research body established in 1974 to alert the public and policymakers to global environmental problems. Publishes State of the World, an annual assessment of global environmental issues and emerging trends, a bi-monthly magazine, World Watch, the Environmental Alert series of books, Worldwatch Papers, a database computer disk, and Vital Signs, an annual look at environmentally related trends.

Leg. Issues: LBR, TAX

In-house, DC-area Employees

FLAVIN, Christopher: President

Worldwide Aviation Services, Ltd.

Miami, FL

Outside Counsel/Consultants

Pierre E. Murphy Law Offices
Rep By: Pierre E. Murphy

Worldwide E-Commerce Fraud Prevention Network

Outside Counsel/Consultants

The DCS Group

WorldWide Minerals Ltd.

Toronto, CANADA
Leg. Issues: TRD

Outside Counsel/Consultants

The Evans Group, Ltd.
Issues: TRD
Rep By: Geryld B. Christianson, Hon. Thomas B. Evans, Jr.

Worldwide Printing Thermographers Ass'n

1030 15th St. NW
Suite 870
Washington, DC 20005
Tel: (202)393-1780
Fax: (202)393-0336

In-house, DC-area Employees

COOPER, Valerie: Exec. Director

Outside Counsel/Consultants

The Kellen Company
Rep By: Valerie Cooper

WOTC Project

Washington, DC
Leg. Issues: TAX

Outside Counsel/Consultants

Greenberg Traurig, LLP
Issues: TAX
Rep By: Ronald L. Platt

McDermott, Will and Emery
Rep By: Calvin P. Johnson

Wound Ostomy Continence Nurses

Costa Mesa, CA
Leg. Issues: HCR, MMM

Outside Counsel/Consultants

Smith Dawson & Andrews, Inc.
Issues: HCR, MMM
Rep By: Gregory B. Andrews, Sherri Powar

WPC Brands, Inc.

Jackson, WI
Leg. Issues: CHM

Outside Counsel/Consultants

The Grizzle Company
Issues: CHM
Rep By: Richard A. Cantor, Charles L. Grizzle

WPTT-TV

Pittsburgh, PA

Outside Counsel/Consultants

Shaw Pittman

WPXT

Portland, ME

Outside Counsel/Consultants

Drinker Biddle & Reath LLP
Rep By: John P. Bankson, Jr.

Wrangell, Alaska, City of

Leg. Issues: URB

Outside Counsel/Consultants

Robertson, Monagle & Eastaugh
Issues: URB
Rep By: Bradley D. Gilman, Rick E. Marks

Wright, Lindsey & Jennings

Little Rock, AR
Leg. Issues: BAN, TAX

Outside Counsel/Consultants

Gottehrer and Co.
Issues: BAN, TAX
Rep By: Barry Gottehrer

Wm. Wrigley Jr. Co.

Chicago, IL
Leg. Issues: TRD

Outside Counsel/Consultants

Baker & McKenzie
Issues: TRD
Rep By: Teresa A. Gleason, Kevin M. O'Brien

Writers Guild of America

Hollywood, CA
Leg. Issues: CPT

Outside Counsel/Consultants

Margaret Cone
Issues: CPT
Rep By: Margaret Cone

Writing Instrument Manufacturers Ass'n

Moorestown, NJ

Outside Counsel/Consultants

Thompson, Hine and Flory LLP
Rep By: David H. Baker

WSYT

Syracuse, NY

Outside Counsel/Consultants

Sutherland Asbill & Brennan LLP

WTTE

Columbus, OH

Outside Counsel/Consultants

Shaw Pittman

WXTV

Paterson, NJ

Outside Counsel/Consultants

Shaw Pittman

Wyandotte Tribe of Oklahoma

Wyandotte, OK
Leg. Issues: IND

Outside Counsel/Consultants

Zane & Associates
Issues: IND
Rep By: Curtis J. Zane

The Wyatt Co.

Washington, DC

Outside Counsel/Consultants

Crowell & Moring LLP
Rep By: Harold J. Heltzer, Karen Hastie Williams

Wyeth-Ayerst Laboratories

Radnor, PA — Registered: LDA
Leg. Issues: BUD, MMM, PHA

Outside Counsel/Consultants

Barnes, Richardson and Colburn
Rep By: Ansis M. Helmanis

The Direct Impact Co.

Heidepriem & Mager, Inc.
Issues: PHA
Rep By: Karin Bolte, Mimi Mager

Holland & Knight LLP
Issues: BUD
Rep By: Steven H. Wright

The Wexler Group
Issues: MMM
Rep By: Cynthia E. Berry, Jody A. Hoffman, Christine Maroulis, Erika Moritsugu, Dale W. Snape

Wyeth-Ayerst Pharmaceuticals

Radnor, PA
Leg. Issues: BUD, HCR, MMM

Outside Counsel/Consultants

Arnold & Porter
Issues: MMM
Rep By: Grant Bagley

Holland & Knight LLP
Issues: BUD, HCR
Rep By: Robert Hunt Bradner, Michael Gillis, Richard M. Gold, Steven H. Wright

Wyoming, Department of Transportation of

Cheyenne, WY

Outside Counsel/Consultants

John A. DeVierno
Rep By: John A. DeVierno

Wyoming, Office of the Attorney General of the State of

Cheyenne, WY

Outside Counsel/Consultants

Duncan, Weinberg, Genzer & Pembroke, P.C.
Rep By: James F. Flug

X-PAC

3509 Connecticut Ave. NW — Tel: (202)387-3848
Suite 175
Washington, DC 20008-2400
Web: www.x-pac.org
E-mail: xpac2000@email.com

A political action committee. Supports federal candidates who favor progressive Social Security reform. Also seeks to raise political awareness among younger Americans.

Leg. Issues: BUD, FIN, RET

In-house, DC-area Employees

PANETTA, Michael J.: Exec. Director

X.L. Insurance Co.

Hamilton, BERMUDA

Outside Counsel/Consultants

Bernstein Law Firm, PLLC
Rep By: George K. Bernstein, Robert B. Shapiro

Xcel Energy, Inc.

801 Pennsylvania Ave. NW — Tel: (202)783-5505
Suite 212 — Fax: (202)783-6873
Washington, DC 20004 — Registered: LDA
Web: www.xcelenergy.com

Formed by the merger of New Century Energies and Northern States Power Co. in 2000. An electric utility providing service to business and residential customers. Headquartered in Minneapolis, MN.

Leg. Issues: BUD, CAW, ENG, FUE, UTI, WAS

In-house, DC-area Employees

O'DONNELL, John A.: Director, Federal Public Affairs

Outside Counsel/Consultants

Johnston & Associates, LLC
Issues: BUD, ENG
Rep By: Alex Flint, Hon. J. Bennett Johnston, W. Proctor Jones

The Smith-Free Group
Issues: ENG
Rep By: James C. Free, Robert Hickmott

XCEL Medical Pharmacy, Ltd.

Woodland Hills, CA
Leg. Issues: HCR, MMM, PHA

Outside Counsel/Consultants

Emord & Associates, P.C.
Issues: HCR, MMM, PHA
Rep By: Jonathan W. Emord, Eleanor A. Kolton, Claudia A. Lewis-Eng

Xcellsis Corp.

Poway, CA
Leg. Issues: BUD, DEF, TRA

Outside Counsel/Consultants

Van Scoyoc Associates, Inc.
Issues: BUD, DEF, TRA
Rep By: Ray Cole, Thomas L. Lankford, Steven O. Palmer

Xerox Corp.

1401 H St. NW — Tel: (202)414-1200
Suite 200 — Fax: (202)414-1217
Washington, DC 20005 — Registered: LDA

A designer, engineer, developer, manufacturer, marketer and servicer of document processing products and systems headquartered in Rochester, NY.

Leg. Issues: BUD, CPI, CPT, ECN, ENV, GOV, HCR, IMM, LBR, MAN, SCI, TAX, TEC, TRD

Political Action Committee/s

Team Xerox PAC
1401 H St. NW — Tel: (202)414-1200
Suite 200 — Fax: (202)414-1217
Washington, DC 20005

In-house, DC-area Employees

CAHN, Michele L.: Manager, Domestic Government Policy
FARREN, J. Michael: Corporate V. President, External Affairs
KLEIN, Kenneth H.: Director, International External Affairs

Outside Counsel/Consultants

The National Group, LLP
Rep By: Vincent M. Versage

Xeta Internat'l Corp.

Alexandria, VA
Leg. Issues: DEF

Outside Counsel/Consultants

American Defense Internat'l, Inc.
Issues: DEF
Rep By: Michael Herson, Van D. Hipp, Jr., Dave Wilberding

XL Capital Ltd

Hamilton,
Leg. Issues: TAX

Outside Counsel/Consultants

Vinson & Elkins L.L.P.
Issues: TAX
Rep By: John E. Chapoton, Christine L. Vaughn

XM Satellite Radio, Inc.

Reston, VA
Leg. Issues: COM

Outside Counsel/Consultants

The Wexler Group
Issues: COM
Rep By: Adam Eisgrau

XO Communications

Washington, DC
Leg. Issues: TEC

Outside Counsel/Consultants

Cormac Group, LLP

The Dutko Group, Inc.
Issues: TEC
Rep By: Kim Koontz Bayliss, Louis Lehrman, Steve Perry, Juliette M. Raffensperger, Stephen Craig Sayle

Xybernaut

Fairfax, VA
Leg. Issues: COM

Outside Counsel/Consultants

E. Del Smith and Co.
Issues: COM
Rep By: E. Del Smith

Yahoo!

2000 Pennsylvania Ave NW — Tel: (202)887-6932
Washington, DC 20006 — Registered: LDA
Leg. Issues: COM, CPI, CPT

In-house, DC-area Employees

SCHEIBEL, John

Outside Counsel/Consultants

Morrison & Foerster LLP
Issues: CPI
Rep By: Jonathan Band

Yakima, Washington, City of

Leg. Issues: TRA

Outside Counsel/Consultants

Manatt, Phelps & Phillips, LLP
Issues: TRA
Rep By: Hon. Jack W. Buechner, June L. DeHart, Jeff Kuhnreich

Yale Materials Handling Corp.

Flemington, NJ

Outside Counsel/Consultants

Thompson, Hine and Flory LLP
Rep By: Mark Roy Sandstrom

Yamaha Motor Corp. U.S.A.

Cypress, CA
Leg. Issues: CSP

Outside Counsel/Consultants

Willkie Farr & Gallagher
Issues: CSP
Rep By: David P. Murray, Russell L. Smith

Wilmer, Cutler & Pickering
Rep By: Robert C. Cassidy, Jr.

Yankton Sioux Tribe

Marty, SD
Leg. Issues: IND

Outside Counsel/Consultants

Greenberg Traurig, LLP
Issues: IND
Rep By: Brian J. Drapeaux, Ronald L. Platt

The Washington Group
Issues: IND
Rep By: Rita M. Lewis, G. John O'Hanlon, John D. Raffaelli, Tonya Saunders

W. G. Yates & Sons Construction Co.

Philadelphia, MS
Leg. Issues: RES

Outside Counsel/Consultants

David F. Godfrey
Issues: RES
Rep By: David F. Godfrey

Yates County Cable TV Committee

Penn Yan, NY
Leg. Issues: COM, GOV, UTI

Outside Counsel/Consultants

Duncan, Weinberg, Genzer & Pembroke, P.C.
Issues: COM, GOV, UTI
Rep By: Michael R. Postar

Yavapai-Prescott Indian Tribe

Prescott, AZ

Outside Counsel/Consultants

Steptoe & Johnson LLP

Yazoo County, Mississippi Port Commission

Yazoo City, MS
Leg. Issues: BUD

Outside Counsel/Consultants

Barbour Griffith & Rogers, Inc.
Issues: BUD
Rep By: Haley Barbour, G. O. Lanny Griffith, Jr., Edward M. Rogers, Jr.

Yellow Corp.

Kansas City, MO — Registered: LDA
Leg. Issues: LBR, MAR, TAX, TRU

Outside Counsel/Consultants

Winston & Strawn
Issues: LBR, MAR, TAX, TRU
Rep By: David W. Broome, Hon. James H. Burnley, IV, Charles L. Kinney, Michael J. McLaughlin, John D. McMickle, Joseph E. O'Leary, Douglas C. Richardson, Gregory K. Smith, John A. Waits, II

Yellow Pages Publishers Ass'n

Troy, MI
Leg. Issues: ADV, TAX, TEC

Outside Counsel/Consultants

Davidson & Company, Inc.
Issues: ADV, TAX
Rep By: James H. Davidson, Richard E. May, Stanley Sokul

Halprin, Temple, Goodman & Maher
Issues: TEC
Rep By: Joel H. Bernstein, Albert Halprin

Yemen, Government of

Sanaa, YEMEN

Outside Counsel/Consultants

Verner, Liipfert, Bernhard, McPherson and Hand, Chartered
Rep By: B. Donovan Picard

Yeshiva of South Shore

Hewlett, NY

A developer of education programs for disable persons.

Outside Counsel/Consultants

Russ Reid Co.

Yipes Transmission, Inc.

San Francisco, CA
Leg. Issues: TEC

Outside Counsel/Consultants

Greenberg Traurig, LLP
Issues: TEC
Rep By: Mitchell F. Brecher

YMCA of Metropolitan Washington

1112 16th St. NW
Suite 720
Washington, DC 20036
Web: www.ymcawashdc.org
Tel: (202)232-6700
Fax: (202)797-4486

In-house, DC-area Employees

BALLANGEE, Judy: Senior V. President, Communications
REESE-HAWKINS, Angie: President and Chief Exec. Officer

YMCA of the USA Public Policy Office

1701 K St. NW
Suite 903
Washington, DC 20006
Web: www.ymca.net
Tel: (202)835-9043
Fax: (202)835-9030
Registered: LDA
Leg. Issues: BUD, URB, WEL

In-house, DC-area Employees

CAMPBELL, Thomas R.: Assistant Director
DURBIN, Eden Fisher: Director, Public Policy

York County Solid Waste Authority

York, PA

Outside Counsel/Consultants

Wright & Talisman, P.C.
Rep By: Scott M. DuBoff

Yosemite Nat'l Institute

Outside Counsel/Consultants

Powers Pyles Sutter & Verville, PC
Rep By: Judith Buckalew

YouBet.com

Los Angeles, CA
Leg. Issues: CPI, GAM

Outside Counsel/Consultants

Foley & Lardner
Issues: CPI, GAM
Rep By: Jodi L. Hanson, Jerris Leonard

GPC Internat'l
Issues: GAM
Rep By: John D. Cahill, Peter G. Halpin

Young America's Foundation

110 Elden St.
Suite A
Herndon, VA 20170
Web: www.yaf.org
E-mail: yaf@yaf.org
Tel: (703)318-9608
Fax: (703)318-9122

In-house, DC-area Employees

ROBINSON, Ron: President

Outside Counsel/Consultants

Pearson & Pipkin, Inc.
Rep By: Ronald W. Pearson

Young Astronaut Council

1308 19th St. NW
Washington, DC 20036
Web: www.yac.org
E-mail: youngastronaut@aol.com
Tel: (202)682-1984
Fax: (202)244-4800

Mission is to encourage student interest and skills in math, science, and related fields. Sponsors a national education program for children ages 5-14.

In-house, DC-area Employees

BLALOCK, Cecelia: V. President

Young Brothers Development (USA), Inc.

Miami, FL

Outside Counsel/Consultants

Commerce Consultants Internat'l Ltd.
Rep By: Richard Richards

W. F. Young Inc.

Springfield, MA

Outside Counsel/Consultants

Wiley, Rein & Fielding

Young Republican Hispanic Ass'n

Outside Counsel/Consultants

Bogart Associates Inc.

Young Republican Nat'l Federation, Inc.

600 Pennsylvania Ave. SE
Suite 302
Washington, DC 20003
Web: www.yrock.com
E-mail: yrnfinc@yrock.com
Tel: (202)608-1417
Fax: (202)608-1430

An allied organization of the Republican Nat'l Committee. Provides a vehicle for its approximately 150,000 members from all states and territories of the United States, 40 years of age and under, to learn about, and become involved in, the Republican Party.

In-house, DC-area Employees

BENKIE, DeeDee: Co-Chairman
MCCARTHY, Kevin: Chairman
VERNON, Robert M.: Exec. Director

Youngstown Mines Corp.

McMurray, PA

A subsidiary of Lykes Corp.

Outside Counsel/Consultants

Heenan, Althen & Roles
Rep By: Michael T. Heenan

Youngstown-Warren Regional Chamber

Youngstown, OH
Leg. Issues: BUD, CAW, ENV, ROD, TRD

Outside Counsel/Consultants

Ainslie Associates
Issues: BUD, CAW, ENV, ROD, TRD
Rep By: Virginia J. Ainslie

Yours.com

Outside Counsel/Consultants

Dittus Communications
Rep By: Gloria S. Dittus

Youth For Understanding Internat'l Exchange

3501 Newark St. NW
Washington, DC 20016
Web: www.youthforunderstanding.org
Tel: (202)966-6800
Fax: (202)895-1104

Seeks to promote international understanding and cultural diversity through homestay-based youth exchange programs.

Leg. Issues: EDU

In-house, DC-area Employees

COWAL, Sally Grooms: President
O'CONNOR, Thomas: V. President, Public Affairs, Develpoment and Planning

Youth Guidance of Chicago

Chicago, IL
Leg. Issues: EDU

Outside Counsel/Consultants

JCP Associates
Issues: EDU
Rep By: James C. Pirius

Youth Policy Institute

1320 Fenwick Lane
Suite 506
Silver Spring, MD 20910
E-mail: corpsnet@mnsinc.com
Tel: (301)585-0580
Fax: (301)585-0584

In-house, DC-area Employees

HACKETT, David L.: Exec. Director

Youth Service America

1101 15th St. NW
Suite 200
Washington, DC 20005-5002
Web: www.servenet.org
E-mail: info@ysa.org
Tel: (202)296-2992
Fax: (202)296-4030

Establishes and promotes youth service programs providing opportunities for youth, ages five to twenty-five, to become involved in volunteer service activities.

In-house, DC-area Employees

CULBERTSON, Steven A.: Chief Exec. Officer
OTTMAN, Kathryn Jo: V. President of Development

Youthbuild, USA
Belmont, MA
Provides housing development and youth job training.
Leg. Issues: BUD
Outside Counsel/Consultants
Robert A. Rapoza Associates
Issues: BUD
Rep By: Robert A. Rapoza

Youyang
Kyunggi-Do, KOREA
Leg. Issues: DEF
Outside Counsel/Consultants
American Defense Internat'l, Inc.
Issues: DEF
Rep By: Michael Herson, Van D. Hipp, Jr., Dave Wilberding

Ysleta Del Sur Pueblo
El Paso, TX
Leg. Issues: IND
Outside Counsel/Consultants
Piliero Mazza & Pargament
Issues: IND
Rep By: Pamela J. Mazza

The Yucel Group
Istanbul, TURKEY
Leg. Issues: TRD
Outside Counsel/Consultants
Law Offices of David L. Simon
Issues: TRD
Rep By: David L. Simon

Yukon City, Oklahoma, City of
Outside Counsel/Consultants
Alan Mauk Associates, Ltd.
Rep By: Alan R. Mauk

Yukon Pacific
Anchorage, AK
Leg. Issues: ENG, ENV, FUE, NAT
Outside Counsel/Consultants
Birch, Horton, Bittner & Cherot
Issues: NAT
Rep By: Thomas L. Albert, Ronald G. Birch, William P. Horn
Gardner, Carton and Douglas
Issues: ENV
Rep By: Patrick Rock
The Paul Laxalt Group
Issues: FUE
Rep By: Hon. Paul D. Laxalt, Tom Loranger
Charlie McBride Associates, Inc.
Issues: ENG
Rep By: Charlie McBride

Yukon-Kuskokwim Health Corp.
Bethel, AK
Leg. Issues: BUD, IND
Outside Counsel/Consultants
Sonosky, Chambers, Sachse & Endreson
Issues: BUD, IND
Rep By: Mary J. Pavel, William R. Perry

Yuma, Arizona, City of
Leg. Issues: BUD
Outside Counsel/Consultants
The Ferguson Group, LLC
Issues: BUD
Rep By: William Ferguson, Jr.

YWCA of the USA
Leg. Issues: ALC, BUD, SPO, URB, WEL
Outside Counsel/Consultants
Bracy Williams & Co.
Issues: SPO
Rep By: Linda Doorfee Flaherty, Susan J. Williams

Z Spanish Network
Sacramento, CA
Outside Counsel/Consultants
Shaw Pittman

Z-Tel Communications Inc.
Tampa, FL
Leg. Issues: TEC
Outside Counsel/Consultants
Adams and Reese LLP
Issues: TEC
Rep By: Hon. James A. "Jimmy" Hayes

Zachery Taylor Parkway Commission
Norwood, LA
Leg. Issues: TAX, TRA
Outside Counsel/Consultants
Adams and Reese LLP
Issues: TAX, TRA
Rep By: B. Jeffrey Brooks, Hon. James A. "Jimmy" Hayes

H. B. Zachry
San Antonio, TX
Outside Counsel/Consultants
Arter & Hadden
Rep By: Daniel L. Cohen, Hon. Thomas G. Loeffler, Jon W. Plebani

Zaire, Office of the President of the Republic of
Kinshasa, ZAIRE
Outside Counsel/Consultants
Washington World Group, Ltd.
Rep By: Edward J. von Kloberg, III

Zamorano
Tegucigalpa, HONDURAS
Leg. Issues: AGR, BUD, FOR
Outside Counsel/Consultants
Kimberly Consulting, LLC
Issues: AGR, BUD, FOR
Rep By: Richard H. Kimberly

ZapMe! Corp.
San Ramon, CA
Leg. Issues: EDU, TEC
Outside Counsel/Consultants
Van Scoyoc Associates, Inc.
Issues: EDU, TEC
Rep By: James W. Kohlmoos, H. Stewart Van Scoyoc

ZapWorld.com
Sebastopol, CA
Leg. Issues: CSP, TRA
Outside Counsel/Consultants
Lawler, Metzger & Milkman, LLC
Issues: CSP, TRA
Rep By: Sante J. Esposito

Nidal Z. Zayed and Associates
Chicago, IL
Leg. Issues: COM, GOV
Outside Counsel/Consultants
O'Connor & Hannan, L.L.P.
Issues: COM, GOV
Rep By: Robert W. Barrie, Hon. Thomas J. Corcoran, Timothy W. Jenkins, Patrick J. O'Connor, Patrick E. O'Donnell

Zeigler Coal Holding Co.
Fairview Heights, IL
Outside Counsel/Consultants
Covington & Burling
Rep By: Roderick A. DeArment, Ronald A. Pearlman

Zenith Electronics Corp.
Glenview, IL
Leg. Issues: COM
Outside Counsel/Consultants
Law Offices of Kevin G. Curtin
Issues: COM
Rep By: Kevin G. Curtin
Frederick L. Ikenson, P.C.
Rep By: Frederick L. Ikenson

Zenware Solutions, Inc.
Leg. Issues: AER
Outside Counsel/Consultants
R. V. Davis and Associates
Issues: AER
Rep By: Robert V. Davis, J. William Foster

Zero Population Growth, Inc.
1400 16th St. NW
Suite 320
Washington, DC 20036
Tel: (202)332-2200
Fax: (202)332-2302
Registered: LDA
Web: www.zpg.org
E-mail: info@zpg.org
Works to achieve a sustainable balance of population, resources, and the environment in the U.S. and worldwide.
Leg. Issues: ENV, FAM, FOR, HCR
In-house, DC-area Employees
CLINE, Tim: Director, Communications
DALEY, Mark: Press Officer
DIXON, Brian E.: Director, Government Relations
SEAGER, John: Exec. Director
SMITH, Heather L.: Senior Legislative Associate

ZERO TO THREE/Nat'l Center for Infants, Toddlers, and Families
734 15th St. NW
Suite 1000
Washington, DC 20005
Tel: (202)638-1144
Fax: (202)638-0851
Web: www.zerotothree.org
E-mail: 0to3@zerotothree.org
A national non-profit organization devoted to the healthy development of infants, toddlers and families.
Leg. Issues: EDU, FAM, HCR
In-house, DC-area Employees
MELMED, Matthew E.: Exec. Director

Ziff Investors Partnership
New York, NY
Leg. Issues: BUD, TAX
Outside Counsel/Consultants
Washington Council Ernst & Young
Issues: BUD, TAX
Rep By: Doug Badger, Lauren Darling, John L. Doney, Jayne T. Fitzgerald, LaBrenda Garrett-Nelson, Gary J. Gasper, Bruce A. Gates, Nick Giordano, Cathy Koch, Robert J. Leonard, Richard Meltzer, Phillip D. Moseley, John D. Porter, Robert M. Rozen, Donna Steele-Flynn, Timothy J. Urban

Zimbabwe, Republic of
Harare, ZIMBABWE
Leg. Issues: FOR
Outside Counsel/Consultants
Cohen and Woods Internat'l, Inc.
Rep By: Herman J. Cohen, James L. Woods
George H. Denison
Issues: FOR
Rep By: George H. Denison

Zinc Corp. of America
Monaca, PA
Leg. Issues: DEF, ENV
Outside Counsel/Consultants
O'Brien, Klink & Associates
Issues: DEF, ENV
Rep By: David D. O'Brien, Shannon L. Scott

Zions Bank Co.
Salt Lake City, UT
Leg. Issues: BAN
Outside Counsel/Consultants
Marshall A. Brachman
Issues: BAN
Rep By: Marshall A. Brachman

Zions First Nat'l Bank
Salt Lake City, UT
Leg. Issues: BAN
Outside Counsel/Consultants
Sullivan & Cromwell
Issues: BAN
Rep By: Samuel R. Woodall, III

Zirconia Sales America
Marietta, GA
Leg. Issues: WAS
Outside Counsel/Consultants
EOP Group, Inc.
Issues: WAS
Rep By: Joseph Hezir, Corey McDaniel, Michael O'Bannon

Zirconium Environmental Committee (ZEC)

Leg. Issues: ENV

Outside Counsel/Consultants

Kilpatrick Stockton LLP
Issues: ENV
Rep By: J. Christopher Brady, J. Vance Hughes, Charles Simmons

Zone Therapeutics, Inc.

College Park, MD
Leg. Issues: BUD, GOV, MED, PHA, SCI

Outside Counsel/Consultants

Foley Government and Public Affairs, Inc.
Issues: BUD, GOV, MED, PHA, SCI
Rep By: Joseph P. Foley

Zuckert, Scoutt and Rasenberger, L.L.P.

888 17th St. NW
Suite 600
Washington, DC 20006-3959
Tel: (202)298-8660
Fax: (202)342-0683
Registered: LDA, FARA

Leg. Issues: AVI, TEC, TOU, TRA

In-house, DC-area Employees

ALLEN, Richard A.: Partner
BENGE, Malcolm L.: Partner
CALDERWOOD, James A.: Partner
CALLAWAY, Jr., William H.: Partner
COSTELLO, Frank J.: Partner
KISSICK, Ralph L.: Partner
MATHIAS, Richard D.: Partner
PERA, Lonnie E.: Partner
PLUMP, Andrew R.
SCHOELLHAMER, Paul E.: Partner and Director, Government Affairs
SCHWEITZER, Richard P.: Partner
SIMPSON, Jr., Charles J.: Partner
TRINDER, Rachel B.: Partner
YINGLING, Monique E.: Partner

Outside Counsel/Consultants

Lawler, Metzger & Milkman, LLC
Issues: AVI, TRA
Rep By: Sante J. Esposito

Van Scoyoc Associates, Inc.
Issues: TEC, TOU
Rep By: Steven O. Palmer, Chad Schulken, H. Stewart Van Scoyoc

Zurich Financial Group

Zurich, SWITZERLAND
Registered: LDA

Represents the federal legislative interests of its member companies who underwrite property/casualty insurance, life insurance, reinsurance, and manage personal institutional financial assets. Parent company is Zurich Insurance Co. of Zurich, Switzerland.

Leg. Issues: AUT, BNK, BUD, CPI, ENV, FIN, FOR, GOV, IMM, INS, RET, SCI, TAX, TOB

Outside Counsel/Consultants

Brenda R. Viehe-Naess
Issues: INS, TAX
Rep By: Brenda R. Viehe-Naess

Zurich Financial Services Group

Zurich, SWITZERLAND

A provider of environmental liability insurance.

Outside Counsel/Consultants

The Accord Group
Rep By: Jeffery T. More

Zurich U.S. Specialties

Zurich, SWITZERLAND
Leg. Issues: AGR, ENV, INS, RES, WAS

Outside Counsel/Consultants

The Accord Group
Issues: AGR, ENV, INS, RES, WAS
Rep By: Jeffery T. More

2001 Washington Representatives

Executive Branch - Legislative Offices

Listed on the following pages are the primary persons responsible for legislative and congressional relations within the White House and the major departments and agencies of the federal government. The Executive Branch offices in which these people work are divided into three groups: The Executive Office of the President, Federal Departments, and Administrative Agencies. The people listed are, in effect, lobbyists for the Administration in its dealings with Congress. Their inclusion is intended to give the researcher a more complete record of the advocacy community in Washington.

Executive Office of the President

Executive Office of the President - Council on Environmental Quality

722 Jackson Place NW
Washington, DC 20503-0002
Tel: (202)395-5750
Fax: (202)456-6546
Web: www.whitehouse.gov/cep

Legislative/Congressional Affairs Personnel

JABLOW, Judy W., Associate Director for Congressional Relations

Executive Office of the President - Nat'l Security Council

1600 Pennsylvania Ave. NW
Room 375
Washington, DC 20500
Tel: (202)456-9171
Fax: (202)456-9170

Legislative/Congressional Affairs Personnel

ANDRICOS, Mike, Director, Legislative Affairs

Executive Office of the President - Office of Management and Budget

Eisenhower Exec. Office Bldg.
725 17th St., N.W.
Washington, DC 20503
Tel: (202)395-4790
Fax: (202)395-3888
Web: www.whitehouse.gov/OMB

Legislative/Congressional Affairs Personnel

DUY, Jennifer, Confidential Assistant

GORE, Elizabeth, Special Assistant for Policy and Legislation

KIEFFER, Charles, Acting Associate Director, Legislative Affairs

LIVINGSTON, Burk, Legislative Assistant

PELLETIER, Eric, Associate Director, Legislative Affairs

ZEGERS, Ted, Special Assistant for Policy and Legislation

ZWEIG, Lisa, Legislative Analyst

Executive Office of the President - Office of Nat'l Drug Control Policy

750 17th St. NW
Washington, DC 20503
Tel: (202)395-6655
Fax: (202)395-6708
Web: www.whitehousedrugpolicy.gov

Legislative/Congressional Affairs Personnel

AMIDZICH, Gail, Assistant Director, Office of Legislative Affairs

MANATT, Michelle A., Director, Office of Legislative Affairs

Executive Office of the President - Office of the Vice President

Old Executive Office Bldg.
Room 276
Washington, DC 20501
Tel: (202)456-6774
Fax: (202)456-1606

Legislative/Congressional Affairs Personnel

ALLGOOD, Lauren, Exec. Assistant for Legislative Affairs

DORN, Nancy P., Assistant to the V. President for Legislative Affairs

RUHLEN, Stephen S., Deputy Assistant to the V. President for Legislative Affairs (House)

WOLFF, Candi, Deputy Assistant to the V. President for Legislative Affairs (House)

Executive Office of the President - The White House

1600 Pennsylvania Ave. NW
Washington, DC 20500
Tel: (202)456-2230
Fax: (202)456-1806
Web: www.whitehouse.gov

Legislative/Congressional Affairs Personnel

CALIO, Nicholas E., Assistant to the President and Director for Legislative Affairs

CHADWICK, Kirsten A., Special Assistant to the President for Legislative Affairs, House Liaison Office

CICCONE, Christine M., Special Assistant to the President for Legislative Affairs, Senate Liaison Office

CONKLIN, Brian C., Special Assistant to the President for Legislative Affairs, House Liaison Office

CONWAY, Michael

DAVIE, Jill, Legislative Correspondent, House Liaison Office

GREGORY, Ginger, Exec. Assistant to the Director of Legislative Affairs

HOBBS, David W., Deputy Assistant to the President for Legislative Affairs/House Liaison

HOWARD, Jack, Deputy Assistant to the President and Deputy Director for Legislative Affairs

JEFFCOAT, Scott, Legislative Assistant, House Liaison Office

JOHNSTON, Megan, Exec. Assistant to the Deputy Director for Legislation

KENIRY, Daniel J., Special Assistant to the President for Legislative Affairs, House Liaison Office

LEHMAN, Dirksen, Special Assistant to the President for Legislative Affairs, Senate Liaison Office

LITTERST, R. Nelson, Special Assistant to the President for Legislative Affairs, House Liaison Office

MCCARTHY, Daniel, Staff Assistant for Correspondence, House Liaison Office

MCNITT, Townsend L., Special Assistant to the President for Legislative Affairs, Senate Liaison Office

OJAKLI, Ziad S., Deputy Assistant to the President for Legislative Affairs, Senate Liaison Office

ROWAN, Peter, Special Assistant to the President for Legislative Affairs, House Liaison Office

SISCO, John, Legislative Correspondent

Executive Office of the President - US Trade Representative

600 17th St. NW
Room 113
Washington, DC 20508
Tel: (202)395-6951
Fax: (202)395-3911
Web: www.ustr.gov

Legislative/Congressional Affairs Personnel

VERONEAU, John K., U.S. Trade Representative for Congressional Affairs

Federal Departments

Department of Agriculture

1400 Independence Ave. SW
Washington, DC 20250
Tel: (202)720-7095
Fax: (202)720-8077

Legislative/Congressional Affairs Personnel

WORSHAM, Wanda, Acting Assistant Secretary for Congressional Relations

Department of Agriculture - Agricultural Marketing Service

1400 Independence Ave. SW
Room 3510 South Bldg.
Washington, DC 20250
Web: www.ams.usda.gov
Tel: (202)720-3203
Fax: (202)720-8477

Legislative/Congressional Affairs Personnel

SARCONE, Christine, Legislative Staff Director

Department of Agriculture - Agricultural Research Service

1400 Independence Ave. SW
Washington, DC 20250
Web: www.ars.usda.gov
Tel: (202)720-3656

Legislative/Congressional Affairs Personnel

TARKINGTON, Marshall, Senior Legislative Analyst

Department of Agriculture - Animal and Plant Health Inspection Service

1400 Independence Ave. SW
Stop 3407, Room 1147, South Bldg.
Washington, DC 20250
Web: www.aphis.usda.gov
Tel: (202)720-2511
Fax: (202)720-3982

Legislative/Congressional Affairs Personnel

HODGE, Debbie A., Management Analyst, Legislative and Public Affairs
LLOYD, Elizabeth J., Legislative Analyst
MCAULEY, Sue S., Assistant to the Director for Legislative Affairs
QUARLES, Lynn T., Deputy Director, Legislative and Public Affairs

Department of Agriculture - Farm Service Agency

1400 Independence Ave. SW
Room 3013 South
Washington, DC 20250
Web: www.fsa.usda.gov
Tel: (202)720-3865
Fax: (202)720-9105

Legislative/Congressional Affairs Personnel

MITCHELL, Larry, Deputy Administrator for Farm Programs

Department of Agriculture - Food and Nutrition Service

Office of Govermental Affairs
3101 Park Center Dr.
Alexandria, VA 22302
Web: www.fns.usda.gov/fns
Tel: (703)305-2281
Fax: (703)305-2312

Legislative/Congressional Affairs Personnel

BEARD, Bob, Legislative Specialist
CARPINO, Christine, Acting Deputy Director, Communications and Governmental Affairs
IPPOLITO, Frank, Director, Governmental Affairs Staff
STANSFIELD, Carol, Legislative Specialist

Department of Agriculture - Food Safety and Inspection Service

1400 Independence Ave. SW
Washington, DC 20250
Web: www.fsis.usda.gov
Tel: (202)720-3897
Fax: (202)720-5704

Legislative/Congressional Affairs Personnel

CHURCH, Christopher, Deputy Director, Congressional and Public Affairs Staff
ELBERTSON, Marianne, Constituent Affairs Specialist, Congressional and Public Affairs Staff
GASTON, Beth, Chief Press Officer, Congressional and Public Affairs Staff
SWACINA, Linda M., Director, Congressional and Public Affairs Staff

Department of Agriculture - Foreign Agricultural Service

1400 Independence Ave. SW
Room 5065 South
Washington, DC 20250
Web: www.usda.gov/fas
Tel: (202)720-6829
Fax: (202)720-8097

Legislative/Congressional Affairs Personnel

MCCLURE, Sharon, Acting Director, Legislative Affairs Staff

Department of Agriculture - Forest Service

201 14th St. SW
Fifth Floor SW
Washington, DC 20250
E-mail: la/wo@fs.fed.us
Web: www.fs.fed.us
Tel: (202)205-1216
Fax: (202)205-1225

Legislative/Congressional Affairs Personnel

BARNES, Saundra L., Staff Assistant, Programs and Legislation
CONTEE, Yvette, Staff Assistant, Legislative Affairs Staff
DAVIS, Mary, Deputy Director, Legislative Affairs Staff
DE COSTER, Timothy P., Director, Legislative Affairs Staff
PHILLIPS, Randall G., Deputy Chief, Programs and Legislation

Department of Agriculture - Natural Resources Conservation Service

12th and Independence Ave. SW
Room 5121, South Bldg.
Washington, DC 20250
Web: www.nrcs.usda.gov
Tel: (202)720-2771
Fax: (202)690-0854

Legislative/Congressional Affairs Personnel

ALVAREZ, Sharyn, Legislative Research Specialist
CARLSON, Eric, Legislative Specialist
MCKALIP, Douglas J., Acting Director, Legislative Affairs

Department of Agriculture - Research, Education, and Economics Mission Area

14th and Independence Ave. SW
Stop 2280
Washington, DC 20250-2280
Web: www.reeusda.gov
Tel: (202)720-4465
Fax: (202)720-6882

Legislative/Congressional Affairs Personnel

CASULA, Pat, Legislative Analyst
RODRIGUEZ, Gladys, Director, Legislative Office

Department of Agriculture - Rural Utilities Service

1400 Independence Ave. SW
Room 4051, South Bldg.
Washington, DC 20250
Web: www.usda.gov/rus/home/home.htm
Tel: (202)720-1255
Fax: (202)205-9219

Legislative/Congressional Affairs Personnel

CRAIN, Claiborn H., Legislative and Public Affairs Advisor

Department of Air Force

1160 Air Force Pentagon
Washington, DC 20330-1160
Web: www.safll.hq.af.mil
Tel: (703)697-8153
Fax: (703)697-2001

Legislative/Congressional Affairs Personnel

ANDERSON, Col. Michael, Chief, Programs and Legislation Division, Legislative Liaison
BLACKMAN, Maj. Brenda, Exec. Officer, Legislative Liaison
BRAUN, Col. Gil, Chief, Weapons System Liaison Division, Legislative Liaison
BUNCE, Col. Pete, Chief, House Liaison Office, Legislative Liaison
COOK, SM Sgt. J. J., Deputy Exec. Officer, Legislative Liaison
ESTY, Sandi, Chief, Air Operations Officer, Legislative Liaison
GIVHAN, Lt. Col. Walter, Chief, Congressional Action Division, Legislative Liaison
KOENIG, Col. Lyle, Senate Liaison, Legislative Liaison
MOSELEY, Maj. Gen. T. Michael, Director, Legislative Liaison
WASHABAUGH, Col. Mark, Chief, Congressional Inquiry Division, Legislative Liaison
WOOD, Brig. Gen. Steve, Deputy Director, Legislative Liaison

Department of Army

The Pentagon
Room 2C631
Washington, DC 20310-1600
Tel: (703)695-6368
Fax: (703)697-3847

Legislative/Congressional Affairs Personnel

ANDERSON, LTC (P) Dave, Exec. Officer
FAGAN, Janet, Acting Chief, Congressional Inquiry Division, Legislative Liaison
LENNOX, Jr., Maj. Gen. William J., Chief, Legislative Liaison
LEWIS, Col. Dennis, Chief, Programs Division, Legislative Liaison
PETERSON, Col. Tim, Chief, Senate Liaison Division, Legislative Liaison
RIOPEL, Maj. Sue, Assistant Exec. Officer, Legislative Liaison
TAYLOR, Brig. Gen. Joe, Deputy Chief, Legislative Liaison
TRIMBLE, Col. Dan, Chief, Investigations and Legislation Division, Legislative Liaison
TURNER, Col. Abe, Chief, House Liaison Division, Legislative Liaison
WINCHESTER, Robert J., Special Assistant for Legislative Affairs, Legislative Liaison

Department of Army - U.S. Army Corps of Engineers

441 G St. NW
Room 3F05
Washington, DC 20314-1000
Web: www.usace.mil
Tel: (202)761-1059
Fax: (202)761-8843

Legislative/Congressional Affairs Personnel

RAUSCH, James P., Chief, Office of Congressional Affairs

Department of Commerce

14th and Constitution Ave. NW
Washington, DC 20230
Web: www.doc.gov
Tel: (202)482-3663
Fax: (202)482-4420

Legislative/Congressional Affairs Personnel

BECKER, Brenda L., Assistant Secretary for Legislative and Intergovernmental Affairs (Nominated)
MARTIN, Catherine J., Director, White House Liaison Office
WOOLF, Karen Swanson, Assistant Secretary and Deputy Assistant Secretary, Legislation

Department of Commerce - Bureau of Export Administration

14th and Constitution Ave. NW
Washington, DC 20230
Web: www.bxa.doc.gov
Tel: (202)482-0097
Fax: (202)482-4665

Legislative/Congressional Affairs Personnel

COTTILLI, Eugene J., Public Affairs Specialist, Office of Congressional, Public and Intergovernmental Affairs

Department of Commerce - Bureau of the Census

4700 Silver Hill Rd. 0002
Washington, DC 20233-0002
Tel: (301)457-2495
Fax: (301)457-1782

Legislative/Congressional Affairs Personnel

PARVIS, Cathy C., Administrative Contact

Department of Commerce - Economic Development Administration

14th and Constitution Ave. NW
Room 7814A
Washington, DC 20230
Web: www.doc.gov/eda/
Tel: (202)482-2309
Fax: (202)501-4828

Legislative/Congressional Affairs Personnel

ATWOOD, John B., Communications and Congressional Liaison Specialist
BOWDEN, Delores, Communications and Congressional Liaison Assistant
EARMAN, Barbara, Communications and Congressional Liaison Specialist
JONES, Vera M., Communications and Congressional Liaison Assistant
LITTLE, Linda A., Communications and Congressional Liaison Specialist
MONTGOMERY, Gwen, Communications and Congressional Liaison Specialist
MONTGOMERY, Margaret, Communications and Congressional Liaison Assistant
PODOLSKE, Lewis R., Acting Director, Office of Communications and Congressional Liaison

Department of Commerce - Inspector General

14th and Constitution Ave. NW
Room 7898C
Washington, DC 20230
Web: www.oig.doc.gov

Tel: (202)482-3052
Fax: (202)482-0567

Legislative/Congressional Affairs Personnel

RICKENBACH, Jessica J., Legislative and Intergovernmental Affairs Officer

Department of Commerce - Internat'l Trade Administration

14th and Constitution Ave. NW
Room 3434
Washington, DC 20230
Web: www.ita.doc.gov

Tel: (202)482-3015
Fax: (202)482-0900

Legislative/Congressional Affairs Personnel

NAAS, Penelope, Acting Director, Office of Legislative and Intergovernmental Affairs

Department of Commerce - Nat'l Institute of Standards and Technology

Administration Bldg.
Room A1109
Quince Orchard & Clopper Rds.
Gaithersburg, MD 20899-1002
Web: www.nist.gov

Tel: (301)975-3080
Fax: (301)926-2569

Legislative/Congressional Affairs Personnel

HINES, Verna B., Director, Congressional and Legislative Affairs
KIMBALL, Kevin, Senior Legislative Analyst

Department of Commerce - Nat'l Marine Fisheries Service

8484 Georgia Ave.
Room 215
Silver Spring, MD 20910
Web: www.nmfs.noaa.gov

Tel: (301)427-2014

Legislative/Congressional Affairs Personnel

SCHAEFER, Richard H., Chief, Intergovernmental and Recreational Fisheries Staff

Department of Commerce - Nat'l Telecommunications and Information Administration

1401 Constitution Ave. NW
Room 4898
Washington, DC 20230
Web: www.ntia.doc.gov

Tel: (202)482-1551
Fax: (202)482-1635

Legislative/Congressional Affairs Personnel

GUTTUSO, Joseph, Acting Director, Office of Congressional Affairs

Department of Commerce - Nat'l Weather Service

14th and Constitution Ave. NW
Room 5221
Washington, DC 20230
Web: www.rdc.noaa.gov

Tel: (202)482-4981
Fax: (202)482-4960

Legislative/Congressional Affairs Personnel

SCHUFREIDER, Jim, Legislative Affairs Specialist

Department of Commerce - United States Patent and Trademark Office

c/o Asst Secy & Commissioner Patents and Trademarks
Washington, DC 20231
Web: www.uspto.gov

Tel: (703)305-8600
Fax: (703)305-8664

Legislative/Congressional Affairs Personnel

COOKSEY, Janie, Congressional Liaison
STOLL, Robert L., Administrator, Legislative and International Affairs Office

Department of Defense

1300 Defense Pentagon
Washington, DC 20301-1300
Web: www.defenselink.mil

Tel: (703)697-6210
Fax: (703)693-5530

Legislative/Congressional Affairs Personnel

CLARK, USAF, Col. Leo, Special Assistant for Space, C3I & Special Operations, Office of Legislative Liaison
CURRY, USA, Col. Don, Director, House Affairs, Office of Legislative Liaison
FRASER, USN, Cdr. James, Director, Senate Affairs, Office of Legislative Affairs
GONZALEZ, USAF, Lt. Col. Fernando, Special Assistant for Personnel Policy, Office of Legislative Liaison
KING, USA, Lt. Col. Greg, Special Assistant for Guard & Reserve Affairs, Logistics, Readiness, Office of Legislative Liaison
MILLER, USN, Cdr. Chip, Special Assistant for Research, Testing & Evaluation, Office of Legislative Liaison
MOORE, Powel A., Assistant Secretary for Legislative Affairs (Nominated)
SMYTHE, USMC, Col. Ana, Military Assistant, Office of Legislative Affairs
STARK, USA, Col. Richard, Special Assistant for Energy, Healthcare Policy, Legal Issues, Office of Legislative Liaison
WIMPLE, USAF, Lt. Col. Robert, Special Assistant for C3I Weapons Systems, Acquisition and Policy, Office of Legislative Liaison

Department of Defense - Chairman, Joint Chiefs of Staff

The Pentagon
Room 2E837
Washington, DC 20318-9999
E-mail: webbwl@js.pentagon.mil
Web: www.defenselink.mil/pubs/almanac/joint_staff.html

Tel: (703)614-1777
Fax: (703)697-3083

Legislative/Congressional Affairs Personnel

ZELLER, USN, Capt. Randall, Legislative Assistant

Department of Defense - Defense Information Systems Agency

701 S. Court House Rd.
Room 4320
Arlington, VA 22204-2199
Web: www.disa.mil/disahomesjs.html

Tel: (703)607-6700
Fax: (703)607-4081

Legislative/Congressional Affairs Personnel

MILLER, Russell C., Chief, Congressional Affairs

Department of Defense - Defense Logistics Agency

8725 John J. Kingman Rd.
Suite 2533
Ft. Belvoir, VA 22060-6221
Web: www.dla.mil

Tel: (703)767-6200
Fax: (703)767-6312

Legislative/Congressional Affairs Personnel

GLOVER, Rebecca, Congressional Affairs Specialist
ROMAN, Jeanette, Congressional Affairs Specialist
WILLIAMS, Joyce, Chief, Congressional Affairs Division

Department of Defense - Defense Security Cooperation Agency

1111 Jefferson Davis Hwy.
Arlington, VA 22202-4306

Tel: (703)604-6617
Fax: (703)604-6542

Legislative/Congressional Affairs Personnel

MURRAY, Vanessa Allen, Director, Legislation and Planning

Department of Defense - Defense Security Service

1340 Braddock Place
Sixth Floor
Alexandria, VA 22314-1651
Web: www.dss.mil

Tel: (703)325-9471

Legislative/Congressional Affairs Personnel

CLUBB, Caryl L., Chief, Office of Congressional and Public Affairs

Department of Defense - Defense Threat Reduction Agency

8725 John T. Kingman Rd.
Ft. Belvoir, VA 22060-6201
Web: www.dtra.mil

Tel: (703)810-4941
Fax: (703)810-4534

Legislative/Congressional Affairs Personnel

SUBKO, Jeffrey B., Chief, Congressional Liaison Office and Chief, Legislative Affairs Office

Department of Defense - Nat'l Imagery and Mapping Agency

4600 Sangamore Rd.
Bethesda, MD 20816-5003
Web: www.nima.mil

Tel: (301)227-5800

Legislative/Congressional Affairs Personnel

WILLIAMS, Michelle, Director, Congressional Affairs Office

Department of Education

400 Maryland Ave. SW
Washington, DC 20202-3100
Web: www.ed.gov

Tel: (202)401-0020
Fax: (202)401-1438

Legislative/Congressional Affairs Personnel

LINDER, Diana, Legislative Specialist

Department of Energy

1000 Independence Ave. S.W.
Washington, DC 20585-0800
Web: www.ci.doe.gov

Tel: (202)586-2777
Fax: (202)586-7246

Legislative/Congressional Affairs Personnel

CHUMBRIS, Nicholas A., Director, Congressional Liaison

Department of Energy - Federal Energy Regulatory Commission

888 First St. NW
Washington, DC 20426
Web: www.ferc.fed.us

Tel: (202)208-0004
Fax: (202)208-2106

Legislative/Congressional Affairs Personnel

CHAMBLEE, Don A., Acting Director (Senate Liaison), Congressional, Intergovernmental, and Public Affairs
CONNORS, Carol, Deputy Director (House Liaison), Congressional, Intergovernmental, and Public Affairs

Department of Health and Human Services

Hubert H. Humphrey Bldg.
200 Independence Ave. SW
Washington, DC 20201
Web: www.os.dhhs.gov

Tel: (202)690-7627
Fax: (202)690-7380

Legislative/Congressional Affairs Personnel

BUTLER, Beatrice L., Staff Assistant, Congressional Liaison
CALVIN, Diana, Chief, Legislative Reference Unit
JOYCE, Cynthia, Correspondence Specialist, Congressional Liaison
WALLACE, Sondra S., Associate General Counsel, Legislation Division
WHITAKER, Scott, Assistant Secretary for Legislation (Nominated)

Department of Health and Human Services - Administration for Children and Families

370 L'Enfant Promenade S.W.
Fifth Floor
Washington, DC 20447
Web: www.acf.dhhs.gov

Tel: (202)401-9223
Fax: (202)401-4562

Legislative/Congressional Affairs Personnel

COHEN, Mary, Director, Legislative and Regulatory Affairs Division
MOCKO, Madeline, Director, Office of Legislative Affairs and Budget

Department of Health and Human Services - Center for Biologics Evaluation and Research

1401 Rockville Pike
Suite 200 North
Rockville, MD 20852-1448
Web: www.fda.gov/cber/cberftp.html

Tel: (301)827-2000
Fax: (301)827-3843

Legislative/Congressional Affairs Personnel

BINKLEY, Joanne, Congressional and Public Affairs Division

Department of Health and Human Services - Center for Medicaid and State Operations

200 Independence Ave. SW
Room 337D
Washington, DC 20201

Tel: (202)690-8501

Legislative/Congressional Affairs Personnel

FENTON, Rick, Acting Director, Intergovernmental and Tribal Affairs Group

Department of Health and Human Services - Food and Drug Administration

Parklawn Bldg. 15-57
5600 Fishers Ln.
Rockville, MD 20857
Web: www.fda.gov/
Tel: (301)827-3793
Fax: (301)827-2567

Legislative/Congressional Affairs Personnel

PLAISIER, Melinda K., Associate Commissioner for Legislative Affairs

Department of Health and Human Services - Health Care Financing Administration

200 Independence Ave. SW
Room 341H
Washington, DC 20201
Web: www.hcfa.gov
Tel: (202)690-5960
Fax: (202)690-8168

Legislative/Congressional Affairs Personnel

BOULANGER, Jennifer, Director, Medicare Part A Analysis Group
COLEMAN, Kathryn, Director, Hearings and Policy Presentation Group
HICKMAN, Peter, Director, Medicare Part B Analysis Group
JOHNSON, Don, Deputy Director, Office of Legislation
KESS, Linda E., Exec. Officer, Office of Legislation
RUDOWITZ, Robin, Director, Medicare Analysis Group
TALLEY, Carleen, Director, Congressional Affairs Group

Department of Health and Human Services - Health Resources and Services Administration

Parklawn Bldg.
5600 Fishers Ln.
Rockville, MD 20857
Web: www.hrsa.gov
Tel: (301)443-2460
Fax: (301)443-9270

Legislative/Congressional Affairs Personnel

NANNIS, Paul N., Director, Office of Planning, Evaluation and Legislation
STROUP, Patricia, Director, Legislation Division, Office of Planning, Evaluation and Legislation
VAN NOSTRAND, Lyman, Deputy Director, Office of Planning, Evaluation and Legislation

Department of Health and Human Services - Indian Health Service

5600 Fishers Ln.
Room 6-05
Rockville, MD 20857
Web: www.ihs.gov
Tel: (301)443-7261
Fax: (301)443-4794

Legislative/Congressional Affairs Personnel

MAHSETKY, Michael D., Director, Legislative Affairs

Department of Health and Human Services - Nat'l Center for Health Statistics

6525 Belcrest Rd.
Room 1120
Hyattsville, MD 20782
Web: www.nchs.cdc.gov/nchs
Tel: (301)458-4100
Fax: (301)458-4021

Legislative/Congressional Affairs Personnel

HUNTER, Edward L., Associate Director for Planning, Budget, and Legislation

Department of Health and Human Services - Nat'l Institutes of Health

9000 Rockville Pike
Bldg. One, Room 244
Bethesda, MD 20892
Web: www.nih.gov
Tel: (301)496-3471
Fax: (301)496-0840

Legislative/Congressional Affairs Personnel

CORBETT, Linwood, Legislative Analyst
DARIOTIS, Dina, Legislative Analyst
FLAMBERG, Gemma, Legislative Analyst
GRAY, Roz, Deputy Director, Office of Legislative Policy and Analysis
HANSBERGER, Patricia B., Legislative Analyst
HIGGINS, Lauren, Legislative Analyst
HOUSER, Anne, Legislative Analyst
LEVARIO, Andrea, Legislative Analyst
SMOLONSKY, Marc, Associate Director, Office of Legislative Policy and Analysis

Department of Health and Human Services - Substance Abuse and Mental Health Services Administration

5600 Fishers Ln.
Room 12C-15
Rockville, MD 20857
E-mail: info@samhsa.gov
Web: www.samhsa.gov
Tel: (301)443-4640
Fax: (301)443-1450

Legislative/Congressional Affairs Personnel

FAHA, Joseph D., Director, Division of Legislative and External Affairs

Department of Housing and Urban Development

451 Seventh St. SW
Washington, DC 20410
Web: www.hud.gov
Tel: (202)708-0005
Fax: (202)708-3794

Legislative/Congressional Affairs Personnel

HODGES, Paulette J., Assistant to the Deputy Assistant Secretary, Office of Congressional Relations
SCHIMMEL, Jo Ann P., Intergovernmental Relations Information Management Specialist, Office of Intergovernmental Relations
VACCARELLA, Frank J., Senior Intergovernmental Relations Officer
WHEELER, Shelva, Administrative Officer, Congressional and Intergovernmental Relations

Department of Interior

1849 C St. NW
Washington, DC 20240
Web: www.doi.gov/ocl
Tel: (202)208-7693
Fax: (202)208-7619

Legislative/Congressional Affairs Personnel

APPLER, Nancy, Congressional Services Specialist, Office of Congressional and Legislative Affairs
CARDINALE, Richard T., Assistant Legislative Counsel
FREEMAN-SIMMONS, Shayla, Acting Director, Office of Congressional and Legislative Affairs
HARRISON, Nancy F., Chief, Legislative Service Branch, Office of Legislative Counsel
HYDE, Sharon, Assistant to the Director, Office of Congressional and Legislative Affairs
JONES, Michael, Special Assistant to the Director, Office of Congressional and Legislative Affairs
LYDER, Jane M., Legislative Counsel
PEAKE, Suzanne, Staff Assistant to the Director, Office of Congressional and Legislative Affairs

Department of Interior - Bureau of Indian Affairs

18th and C Sts. NW
MS-4559-MIB
Washington, DC 20240
Web: www.doi.gov/bia/clahome
Tel: (202)208-5706
Fax: (202)208-4623

Legislative/Congressional Affairs Personnel

CHEEK, Jacquelyn M., Director, Office of Congressional and Legislative Affairs

Department of Interior - Bureau of Land Management

1620 L St. NW
Room 401
Washington, DC 20036
Web: www.blm.gov
Tel: (202)452-7726
Fax: (202)452-0346

Legislative/Congressional Affairs Personnel

DANNA, Tony, Legislative Affairs Group Manager
SLATER, Karen, Intergovernmental Affairs Manager

Department of Interior - Bureau of Reclamation

1849 C St. NW
Room 7639
Washington, DC 20240
Web: www.usbr.gov
Tel: (202)513-0565
Fax: (202)513-0304

Legislative/Congressional Affairs Personnel

SONKEN, Lori J., Chief, Congressional and Legislative Affairs Group

Department of Interior - Fish and Wildlife Service

1849 C St. NW
Washington, DC 20240
Web: www.fws.gov
Tel: (202)208-5403
Fax: (202)208-7059

Legislative/Congressional Affairs Personnel

ALT, Nicole, Legislative Specialist
BOWMAN, Randy, Senior Legislative Specialist
COLEMAN, Brenda, Legislative Specialist
HATHAWAY, Julia, Legislative Specialist
HOBBS, Douglas, Legislative Specialist
KODIS, Martin, Legislative Specialist
PITTS, Alexandra, Chief, Division of Congressional and Legislative Affairs

Department of Interior - Nat'l Park Service

18th and C Sts. NW
Room 3210
Washington, DC 20240
Web: www.nps.gov
Tel: (202)208-5656
Fax: (202)208-5683

Legislative/Congressional Affairs Personnel

HELLMANN, Donald J., Acting Assistant Director, Legislative and Congressional Affairs

Department of Interior - Office of Insular Affairs

1849 C St. NW
MS: 4319
Washington, DC 20240
Web: www.doi.gov/oia
Tel: (202)208-4754
Fax: (202)501-7759

Legislative/Congressional Affairs Personnel

SANDER, Stephen, Staff Assistant, Legislative Affairs

Department of Justice

950 Pennsylvania Ave. NW
Washington, DC 20530
Web: www.usdoj.gov
Tel: (202)514-2141
Fax: (202)514-4482

Legislative/Congressional Affairs Personnel

BRYANT, Daniel J., Assistant Attorney General for Legislative Affairs (Nominated)
WALTER, Sheryl, Acting Assistant Attorney General for Legislative Affairs

Department of Justice - Antitrust Division

601 D St. NW
Room 10120
Washington, DC 20530
E-mail: antitrust@justice.usdoj.gov
Web: www.usdoj.gov
Tel: (202)514-2497
Fax: (202)514-9082

Legislative/Congressional Affairs Personnel

CARLETON, Brenda F., Chief Legislative Unit, Legal Policy Section

Department of Justice - Criminal Division

Patrick Henry Bldg.
601 D St., N.W., Room 6917
Washington, DC 20530
Tel: (202)514-3062
Fax: (202)514-9412

Legislative/Congressional Affairs Personnel

WROBLEWSKI, Jonathan J., Acting Director, Office of Policy and Legislation

Department of Justice - Drug Enforcement Administration

700 Army Navy Dr.
Arlington, VA 22202
Web: www.usdoj.gov/dea
Tel: (202)307-7363
Fax: (202)307-4778

Legislative/Congressional Affairs Personnel

SHAW, Catherine H., Chief, Office of Congressional and Public Affairs
TERESI, Toni P., Chief, Congressional Affairs Section, Office of Congressional and Public Affairs

Department of Justice - Environment and Natural Resources Division

Patrick Henry Bldg.
601 D St. NW, Room 8022
Washington, DC 20004
Web: www.usdoj.gov/enrd
Tel: (202)514-2586
Fax: (202)616-3362

Legislative/Congressional Affairs Personnel

MILIUS, Pauline H., Chief, Policy Legislation and Special Litigation Section

Department of Justice - Federal Bureau of Investigation

935 Pennsylvania Ave. NW
Washington, DC 20530-0001
Web: www.fbi.gov
Tel: (202)324-2727
Fax: (202)324-6490

Legislative/Congressional Affairs Personnel
COLLINGWOOD, John E., Assistant Director, Office of Public and Congressional Affairs

Department of Justice - Federal Bureau of Prisons

320 First St. NW
Washington, DC 20534
Tel: (202)514-9663
Fax: (202)514-5935
Web: www.bop.gov

Legislative/Congressional Affairs Personnel
GARRETT, Judith Simon, Chief, Office of Congressional Affairs

Department of Justice - Immigration and Naturalization Service

425 I St. NW
Room 7030
Washington, DC 20536
Tel: (202)514-5231
Fax: (202)514-1117
Web: www.ins.usdoj.gov

Legislative/Congressional Affairs Personnel
RATLIFF, Gerri L., Acting Director, Office of Congressional Relations
TAYLOR, Sarah, Director, Congressional Legislation Branch

Department of Justice - Office of Justice Programs

810 Seventh St. NW
Washington, DC 20531
Tel: (202)307-0703
Fax: (202)514-5958
E-mail: askocpa@ojp.usdoj.gov
Web: www.ojp.usdoj.gov/ocpa

Legislative/Congressional Affairs Personnel
KENDRICK, Glenda, Associate Deputy Director, Office of Congressional and Public Affairs
KRAMER, Harri J., Director, Office of Congressional and Public Affairs
RIZZUTO, Chris, Deputy Director, Office of Congressional and Public Affairs

Department of Justice - Tax Division

950 Pennsylvania Ave. NW
Room 4645
Washington, DC 20530
Tel: (202)307-6419
Fax: (202)305-0660

Legislative/Congressional Affairs Personnel
CSONTOS, Stephen J., Senior Legislative Counsel, Office of Legislation and Policy

Department of Justice - United States Marshals Service

600 Army-Navy Dr.
Arlington, VA 22202
Tel: (202)307-9220
Fax: (202)307-5228
Web: www.usdoj.gov/marshals

Legislative/Congressional Affairs Personnel
FOOSHE, Alexis, Legislative Affairs Specialist

Department of Labor

200 Constitution Ave. NW
Room S-1325
Washington, DC 20210
Tel: (202)693-4600
Fax: (202)693-4642
Web: www.dol.gov

Legislative/Congressional Affairs Personnel
BAYLYFF, Chris, Legislative Assistant, Office of Congressional and Intergovernmental Affairs
DANIELS, Joycelyn J., Administrative Officer, Office of Congressional and Intergovernmental Affairs
IVENSON, Christine, Assistant Secretary, Office of Congressional and Intergovernmental Affairs
MARONEY, Kevin, Acting Assistant Secretary for Congressional and Intergovernmental Affairs
TIDWELL, Claudette, Staff Assistant, Office of Congressional and Intergovernmental Affairs
WILLIAMS, Janice, Staff Assistant, Office of Congressional Intergovernmental Affairs

Department of Labor - Mine Safety and Health Administration

Ballston Tower #3
4015 Wilson Blvd.
Arlington, VA 22203
Tel: (703)235-1392
Fax: (703)235-4369
Web: www.msha.gov

Legislative/Congressional Affairs Personnel
MILANESE, Sylvia E., Congressional Liaison, Office of Congressional and Legislative Affairs

Department of Labor - Office of Workforce Security

200 Constitution Ave. NW
Washington, DC 20210
Tel: (202)693-3038
Fax: (202)693-3229

Legislative/Congressional Affairs Personnel
HILDEBRAND, Jerry, Chief, Division of Legislation
WEBB, Lynne, Federal Legislation Team

Department of Labor - Solicitor

200 Constitution Ave. NW
Washington, DC 20210
Tel: (202)219-8201
Fax: (202)501-2583
Web: www.dol.gov/sol

Legislative/Congressional Affairs Personnel
COHEN, Bruce, Deputy Associate Solicitor, Legislative and Legal Counsel
LESSER, William C., Legislative Communications Counsel
SHAPIRO, Robert A., Associate Solicitor, Legislative and Legal Counsel

Department of Navy

The Pentagon
Washington, DC 20350-1300
Tel: (703)697-7146
Fax: (703)614-7089
Web: www.navy.mil

Legislative/Congressional Affairs Personnel
BAGGETT, Capt. Joseph E., Director, Legislation, Legislative Affairs
BROWN, Capt. Will A., Director, Navy Programs, Office of Legislative Affairs
DENKLER, Capt. J. Michael, House Liaison Principal Deputy, Office of Legislative Affairs
DUNNE, Capt. Patrick W., Deputy Chief, Legislative Affairs
ERSKINE, Lt. Cdr. James M., Director, Management Division, Office of Legislative Affairs
GEIST, Brenda S., Director, Congressional Travel Division, Office of Legislative Affairs
GRADY, Cmdr. Chris, Exec. Assistant, Office of Legislative Affairs
HENNEY, Cmdr. Fred, Director, Public Affairs and Contract Notifications Division, Legislative Affairs
ROUGHEAD, Rear Adm Gary, Chief, Office of Legislative Affairs
SHUFORD, Capt. Jacob, Senate Liaison Principal Deputy, Office of Legislative Affairs

Department of Navy - Chief of Naval Operations Office

The Pentagon
Washington, DC 20350-2000
Tel: (703)697-7146

Legislative/Congressional Affairs Personnel
DAWSON, Jr., Rear Adm J. Cutler, Special Assistant, Legislative Support
MORIN, Cmdr. C. N., Assistant for Legal and Legislative Matters

Department of Navy - United States Marine Corps

The Pentagon
4C678
Washington, DC 20350
Tel: (703)614-3382
Fax: (703)614-5964
Web: www.usmc.mil

Legislative/Congressional Affairs Personnel
CASSIDY, Col. B., Senate Liaison Officer
CORWIN, Brig. Gen. Tony L., Legislative Director, Office of the Legislative Assistant to the Commandant
FLEMING, Col. Dan G., Deputy to the Legislative Director, Office of the Legislative Assistant to the Commandant
REGNER, Col. M., House Liaison Officer

Department of State - Bureau of Legislative Affairs

2201 C St. NW
Washington, DC 20520-7261
Tel: (202)647-4204
Fax: (202)647-2762
Web: www.state.gov/s/h

Legislative/Congressional Affairs Personnel
CARTER, John T., Administrative Services, Office of Legislative Operations
FAULKNER, Tamara, International Crime, Counter Narcotics & Legal Affairs Legislative Management Officer
GUEST, Michael, Deputy Assistant Secretary - Regional Political Affairs
KAKESAKO, Susan, Legislative Management Officer
KRHOUINK, Kimberly, Special Assistant, Congressional Affairs
LANDE, Jim, Legislative Management Officer
LODGE, Terri, Arms Control and Political-Military Issues Legislative Management Officer
MCILVAINE, Steve, African Affairs Legislative Management Officer
NORMAN, Marcia, Director, Office of Legislative Operations
NUSSBAUM, Jonathan, Consular, Population & Refugees Affairs Legislative Management Officer
RAETHER, Carl, Legislative Management Officer
REED, Roxanne, Congressional Inquiries Chief
REICH, Thomas, Balkans, Europe & NATO Affairs Legislative Management Officer
STEPANCHUK, John, European & Newly Independent States Affairs Legislative Management Officer
TREJO, Maria, Western Hemisphere Affairs Legislative Management Officer

Department of State - Non-Proliferation Bureau

2201 C St. NW
Washington, DC 20520
Tel: (202)736-4242
Fax: (202)736-4250
Web: www.state.gov/t/np

Legislative/Congressional Affairs Personnel
KESSLER, J. Christian, Director, Office of Congressional and Public Affairs

Department of Transportation

400 Seventh St. SW
MS: 10100
Washington, DC 20590
Tel: (202)366-4687
Fax: (202)366-7153
E-mail: dotlegislation@ost.dot.gov
Web: www.dot.gov

Legislative/Congressional Affairs Personnel
BLUMENTHAL, Patricia, Assistant, Legislative Reference
DECELL, Jane, Deputy Assistant General Counsel, Office of Legislation
FRAZIER, Mike, Assistant Secretary for Governmental Affairs
HERLIHY, Thomas W., Assistant General Counsel, Office of Legislation

Department of Transportation - Federal Aviation Administration

800 Independence Ave. SW
Room 921 D
Washington, DC 20591
Tel: (202)267-3217
Fax: (202)267-5194

Legislative/Congressional Affairs Personnel
WALSH, Mary, Assistant Chief Counsel for Legislation
ZOELLER, Thomas E., Deputy Assistant Chief Counsel for Legislation

Department of Transportation - Federal Highway Administration

400 Seventh St. SW
Room 3318
Washington, DC 20590
Tel: (202)366-0761
Fax: (202)366-7696
Web: www.fhwa.dot.gov

Legislative/Congressional Affairs Personnel
BINDER, Susan J., Director, Office of Legislative and Strategic Planning
COLE, Mary, Staff Assistant, Office of Legislative and Strategic Planning
COMEAU, Cliff, Highway Needs and Investment, Office of Legislative and Strategic Planning
WEISS, Mike, Legislative Analyst, Office of Legislative and Strategic Planning

Department of Transportation - Federal Transit Administration

400 Seventh St. SW
Room 9316
Washington, DC 20590
Tel: (202)366-4011
Fax: (202)366-3809
Web: www.fta.dot.gov

Legislative/Congressional Affairs Personnel
MARISTCH, Rita, Assistant Chief Counsel for Legislative and Regulatory Affairs

Department of Transportation - Maritime Administration

400 Seventh St. SW
7206 F
Washington, DC 20590
Tel: (202)366-1707
Fax: (202)366-3890
Web: www.marad.dot.gov

Legislative/Congressional Affairs Personnel

GURLAND, Christine Slowikowski, Director, Office of Congressional and Public Affairs

Department of Transportation - Surface Transportation Board

The Mercury Bldg.
1925 K St. NW
Washington, DC 20423-0001
Tel: (202)565-1594
Fax: (202)565-9016
Web: www.stb.dot.gov

Legislative/Congressional Affairs Personnel

BEITER, Nancy R., Attorney/Advisor, Congressional and Public Services

KING, Dan G., Director, Congressional and Public Services

SAINT-LOUIS, Rudolph A., Attorney/Advisor, Congressional and Public Services

WATSON, A. Dennis, Associate Director, Congressional and Public Services

Department of Transportation - United States Coast Guard

400 Seventh St. SW
Suite 10402
Washington, DC 20590
Tel: (202)366-4280
Fax: (202)366-7124
Web: www.uscg.mil

Legislative/Congressional Affairs Personnel

CONAWAY, Cdr. Brian R., Deputy Chief, Congressional Affairs Staff, Office of Government and Public Affairs

EBLE, Nancy, Legislative Analyst, Congressional Affairs Staff, Office of Government and Public Affairs

GOULD, Lt. Cdr. Austin, Government Liaison, Congressional Affairs Staff, Office of Governmental and Congressional Affairs

PAPP, Capt. Robert J., Chief, Congressional Affairs Staff, Office of Government and Public Affairs

POULIN, Cmdr. Steven, Chief, Legislative Liaison Staff

RICHEY, Cdr. Thomas, Chief, Senate Liaison Staff, Congressional Relations Staff, Office of Government and Public Affairs

SCHULTZ, Cdr. Karl, House Liaison Staff, Congressional Affairs Staff, Office of Government and Public Affairs

Department of Treasury

1500 Pennsylvania Ave. NW
Washington, DC 20220
Tel: (202)622-1900
Fax: (202)622-0534
Web: www.treas.gov

Legislative/Congressional Affairs Personnel

BEST, Amy, Special Assistant to the Assistant Secretary

CAMERON, Jr., Arthur E., Deputy Assistant Secretary (Appropriations and Management)

DUNCAN, John M., Assistant Secretary, Office of Legislative Affairs

GRAYSON, Cherry, Legislative Assistant

HARRIS BERRY, Gail, Legislative Research Assistant

JONES, Janet L., Scheduling Coordinator to the Assistant Secretary, Office of Legislative Affairs

KEELER, Tim, Deputy to the Assistant Secretary (International)

O'DONNELL, Katie, Special Assistant to the Assistant Secretary, Office of Legislative Affairs

POWELL, Linda L., Administrative Officer, Office of Legislative Affairs

QUINN, Katie, Deputy Assistant Secretary (Enforcement)

SMITH, Amy, Deputy Assistant Secretary (Banking and Finance)

STARKS, Ora D., Congressional Inquiries Analyst, Office of Legislative Affairs

SU, Peter, Special Assistant, Office of Legislative Affairs

YOUNG, James T., Deputy Assistant Secretary (Tax and Budget)

Department of Treasury - Bureau of Alcohol, Tobacco and Firearms

650 Massachusetts Ave. NW
Room 8150
Washington, DC 20226
Tel: (202)927-8490
Fax: (202)927-8863
E-mail: legislativeaffairs@atfhq.atf.treas.gov
Web: www.atf.treas.gov

Legislative/Congressional Affairs Personnel

RADEN, Lewis P., Executive Assistant, Legislative Affairs

Department of Treasury - Comptroller of the Currency

250 E St. SW
Washington, DC 20219
Tel: (202)874-4840
Fax: (202)874-5305
Web: www.occ.treas.gov

Legislative/Congressional Affairs Personnel

MCFARLANE, Carolyn Z., Director, Congressional Liaison

SOLOMON, Karen, Director, Legislative and Regulatory Activities, Office of Chief Counsel

Department of Treasury - Financial Management Service

Liberty Center
401 14th St. SW
Washington, DC 20227
Tel: (202)874-6760
Fax: (202)874-7016
Web: www.fms.treas.gov/news/index.html

Legislative/Congressional Affairs Personnel

LONG, Michael, Legislative and Public Affairs Specialist

LONGNECKER, Tom, Legislative Affairs Specialist

MCHALE, Alvina M., Director, Legislative and Public Affairs Office

WEBER, Marty, Legislative Specialist/FOIA Disclosure Officer

Department of Treasury - Internal Revenue Service

1111 Constitution Ave. NW
Washington, DC 20224
Tel: (202)622-3720
Fax: (202)622-4733
E-mail: floyd.williams@.irs.gov
Web: www.irs.ustreas.gov

Legislative/Congressional Affairs Personnel

DASH, Mary L., Branch Chief, Congressional Correspondence

OURSLER, Leonard, Branch Chief, Congressional Affairs

RAY, Paula, Congressional Inquiries

TOBER, Karen, Congressional Inquiries

VINCENT, Duane, Acting Branch Chief Legislation and Reports

WILLIAMS, Floyd L., National Director for Legislative Affairs

Department of Treasury - Office of Thrift Supervision

1700 G St. NW
Fifth Floor
Washington, DC 20552
Tel: (202)906-6445
Fax: (202)906-6518
Web: www.access.gpo.gov/ots

Legislative/Congressional Affairs Personnel

DAKIN, Deborah, Deputy Chief Counsel for Regulations and Legislation

Department of Treasury - Tax Policy

1500 Pennsylvania Ave. NW
Washington, DC 20220
Tel: (202)622-0050
Fax: (202)622-0646
Web: www.treas.gov/taxpolicy

Legislative/Congressional Affairs Personnel

EPSTEIN, Louise, Associate Tax Legislative Counsel

HANSON, Robert, Deputy Tax Legislative Counsel for Regulatory Affairs

KAUFMAN, Beth, Associate Tax Legislative Counsel

MIKRUT, Joseph M., Tax Legislative Counsel

PARCELL, John, Acting Deputy Tax Legislative Counsel

Department of Treasury - United States Customs Service

1300 Pennsylvania Ave. NW
Room 6.4A
Washington, DC 20229
Tel: (202)927-1760
Fax: (202)927-2152
Web: www.customs.treas.gov

Legislative/Congressional Affairs Personnel

QUINN, Richard, Acting Assistant Commissioner, Congressional Affairs

Department of Treasury - United States Secret Service

950 H St. NW
Room 8350
Washington, DC 20001
Tel: (202)406-5676
Fax: (202)406-5740
Web: www.treas.gov/usss

Legislative/Congressional Affairs Personnel

BURKE, Douglas J., Assistant Special Agent-in-Charge, Congressional Affairs

CROWLEY, Katherine C., Special Agent in Charge, Congressional Affairs

IRVING, Paul D., Deputy Assistant Director, Congressional Affairs

Department of Veterans Affairs

810 Vermont Ave. NW
Washington, DC 20420
Tel: (202)273-5611
Fax: (202)273-6792
Web: www.va.gov/oca

Legislative/Congressional Affairs Personnel

ALLEN, Christopher, Legislative Affairs Officer

ARMSTRONG, Richard, House Liaison Representative

BITTINGER, Deborah, Congressional Relations Officer

BUFFINGTON, Bill, Director, Legislative Affairs

COVINGTON, Patricia, Senate Liaison Officer

DEMBLING, Doug, Congressional Relations Officer

DOWNS, Paul, House Liaison Officer

ERGER, Nurit, Director, Congressional Relations

GIBBIN, Holly, Legislative Analyst

GREENBERG, Kenneth, Director, Congressional Reports and Correspondence

HARRIS, Renee, Legislative Analyst

JENSEN, Alexa, Congressional Relations Officer

JURVELIN, Linda E., Assistant Director, Congressional Liaison Services

LIKEL, Charles, Congressional Relations Officer

MARTY, Elizabeth, Legislative Affairs Officer

MAYO, Philip R., Director, Congressional Liaison Services

MUGG, Pamela, House Liaison Representative

RIGGIN, Philip, Deputy Assistant Secretary, Congressional Affairs

STACK, Mary Kay, Congressional Relations Officer

THOMAS, Rosalind, Legislative Affairs Officer

VANZANDT, Jim, GAO Liaison

WEINER, Stuart, Senate Liaison Representative

WILSON, Thomas, Special Assistant

Department of Veterans Affairs - Veterans Health Administration

810 Vermont Ave. NW
Room 8151
Washington, DC 20420
Tel: (202)273-5789
Fax: (202)273-6161
Web: www.va.gov/About_VA/orgs/vha

Legislative/Congressional Affairs Personnel

RAMSEY, William, Director, Legislative Programs

Administrative Agencies

Agency for Internat'l Development

Ronald Reagan Bldg.
1300 Pennsylvania Ave. NW
Washington, DC 20523
Web: www.usaid.gov
Tel: (202)712-4300
Fax: (202)216-3237

Legislative/Congressional Affairs Personnel

BALTIMORE, Elizabeth, Legislative Program Specialist, Congressional Liaison Division
BENNETT, Barbara, Legislative Program Specialist, Congressional Liaison Division
COOK, Bette, Legislative Program Specialist, Congressional Liaison Division
DETTER, Brian, Legislative Program Specialist, Congressional Liaison Division
HOOD, Elouise, Congressional Correspondence/Documents Legislation Program Specialist
JENKINS, Dana, Administrative Officer, Bureau for Legislative and Public Affairs
MORRIS, Kathy, Congressional Notifications Legislative Program Specialist, Bureau of Legislative and Public Affairs
RAYBURN, Dorothy, Legislative Program Specialist, Congressional Liaison Division
SANFUENTES, Vince, Legislative Program Specialist, Congressional Liaison Division
SHELTON, Todd, Legislative Program Specialist, Congressional Liaison Division
TUCKER, Cynthia, Senior Administrative Officer, Bureau for Legislative and Public Affairs

Appalachian Regional Commission

1666 Connecticut Ave. NW
Suite 700
Washington, DC 20235-0001
E-mail: crea@arc.gov
Web: www.arc.gov
Tel: (202)884-7660
Fax: (202)884-7693

Legislative/Congressional Affairs Personnel

LAND, Guy, Special Counsel and Director, Congressional Affairs

Broadcasting Board of Governors

Wilbur G. Cohen Bldg.
330 Independence Ave. SW, Room 3360
Washington, DC 20547
Tel: (202)401-3736
Fax: (202)401-6605

Legislative/Congressional Affairs Personnel

ANDROSS, Susan, Congressional and External Affairs Coordinator
RICKMAN, Gregg, Congressional Outreach

Central Intelligence Agency

At the time this edition went to press, the position of Director, Congressional Affairs was vacant. No further information was available at that time.

CIA Headquarters
Washington, DC 20505
Web: www.cia.gov
Tel: (703)482-6121
Fax: (703)482-5841

Chemical Safety and Hazard Investigation Board

2175 K St. NW
Suite 400
Washington, DC 20037-1809
Web: www.chemsafety.gov
Tel: (202)261-7600
Fax: (202)261-7650

Legislative/Congressional Affairs Personnel

COGAN, Phillip S., Deputy Director, Congressional and Public Affairs
WAGER, Robert J., Director, Office of Congressional and Public Affairs

Commission on Civil Rights

624 Ninth St. NW
Washington, DC 20425
Web: www.usccr.gov
Tel: (202)376-8317
Fax: (202)376-8315

Legislative/Congressional Affairs Personnel

ALTON, Kimberly, Interim Contact

Commodity Futures Trading Commission

Three LaFayette Centre
1155 21st St. NW
Washington, DC 20581
Web: www.cftc.gov
Tel: (202)418-5075
Fax: (202)418-5542

Legislative/Congressional Affairs Personnel

GREENWOOD, Jr., Allen Beau, Director, Office of Legislative and Intergovernmental Affairs
LESLIE, J. Douglass, Acting Senior Counsel, Office of Legislative and Intergovernmental Affairs

Consumer Product Safety Commission

4330 East-West Hwy.
Room 720
Bethesda, MD 20207
Web: www.cpsc.gov
Tel: (301)504-0515
Fax: (301)504-0016

Legislative/Congressional Affairs Personnel

O'LEARY, Maureen, Director, Office of Congressional Relations

Corporation for Nat'l Service

1201 New York Ave. NW
Washington, DC 20525
Web: www.nationalservice.org
Tel: (202)606-5000
Fax: (202)208-4214

Legislative/Congressional Affairs Personnel

AVERY, Kevin, Director, Congressional and Intergovernmental Relations

Environmental Protection Agency

Ariel Rios Federal Bldg.
(1301-MC)
1200 Pennsylvania Ave. NW
Washington, DC 20460
Web: www.epa.gov
Tel: (202)564-5200
Fax: (202)501-1519

Legislative/Congressional Affairs Personnel

ASTON, Michele, Air/Pesticides Team Leader, Office of Congressional and Intergovernmental Relations
FLORY, Mark, State/Local Team Leader, Office of Congressional and Intergovernmental Affairs
HAGGINS, Marrietta, Staff Assistant, Congressional and Intergovernmental Affairs
HILLER, Michelle A., Acting Deputy Associate Administrator for State/Local Relations
JONES, Clara, Staff Assistant, Congressional and Intergovernmental Relations
KRENIK, Edward, Associate Administrator for Congressional and Intergovernmental Relations
LUND, Lisa C., Deputy Associate Administrator for Congressional and Intergovernmental Relations
MCKEEVER, Michele, Waste and Superfund Team Leader, Office of Congressional and Intergovernmental Relations
REEDER, John E., Deputy Associate Administrator, Congressional Affairs
ROESCH, Shawana, Water Team Leader, Office of Congressional and Intergovernmental Relations
STEVENS, Mark E., Senior Advisor for Congressional Oversight
SYKES, Kathy, Appropriations/Enforcement Team Leader, Office of Congressional and Intergovernmental Affairs
TAITT, Julie, Director, Information Management Division, Office of Congressional and Intergovernmental Relations
WILSON, Steven, NEPPS/Compliance Team Leader, Office of Congressional and Intergovernmental Relations

Equal Employment Opportunity Commission

1801 L St. NW
Washington, DC 20507
Web: www.eeoc.gov
Tel: (202)663-4900
Fax: (202)663-4912

Legislative/Congressional Affairs Personnel

ANDERSON, Sylvia, Assistant Director, Legislative Affairs
HARRISON, Sabrina, Congressional Liaison Assistant
KENDRICK, Ethel, Congressional Liaison Specialist
TORCIVIA, Regina, Congressional Liaison Specialist
YERGAN-WILLIS, Renae, Congressional Liaison Specialist

Export-Import Bank

811 Vermont Ave. NW
Washington, DC 20571
Web: www.exim.gov
Tel: (202)565-3230
Fax: (202)565-3236

Legislative/Congressional Affairs Personnel

BERRY, Marsha, V. President, Congressional and External Affairs
HELLERT, William E., Deputy Vice President, Congressional and External Affairs
HOUSER, Susan, Senior Congressional Analyst
THOMPSON, Beverly K., Senior Legislative Analyst
WELLIG, Deborah A., Senior Legislative Analyst

Farm Credit Administration

1501 Farm Credit Dr.
McLean, VA 22102-5090
E-mail: info-line@fca.gov
Web: www.fca.gov
Tel: (703)883-4056
Fax: (703)790-3260

Legislative/Congressional Affairs Personnel

DECELL, III, Hal C., Director, Office of Congressional and Public Affairs
MCBETH, Mark, Assistant Director for Congressional and Public Affairs
QUINN, Christine D., Assistant Director of Congressional and Public Affairs

Federal Communications Commission

445 12th St. NW
Washington, DC 20554
Tel: (202)418-1900
Fax: (202)418-2806

Legislative/Congressional Affairs Personnel

ATKINSON, Diane, Congressional Liaison Specialist
BALAGUER, James, Legislative Analyst
BERNSTEIN, Jon, Attorney/Advisor, Legislative and Intergovernmental Affairs
CHAPMAN, Connie, Legislative Analyst
ERBACH, Donald C., Senior Advisor, Legislative and Intergovernmental Affairs
HENDRICKSON, Florence, Staff Assistant, Legislative and Intergovermental Affairs
KLITZMAN, Stephen H., Associate Director, Legislative and Intergovernmental Affairs
MEDLEY, Joy, Legislative Analyst
PENDER, Jill, Attorney/Advisor, Legislative and Intergovernmental Affairs
PETTY, Monica, Special Assistant, Legislative and Intergovernmental Affairs

Federal Deposit Insurance Corp.

550 17th St. NW
Washington, DC 20429-9990
Web: www.fdic.gov
Tel: (202)898-7055
Fax: (202)898-3745

Legislative/Congressional Affairs Personnel

BAGGAGE, Mable T., Administrative Officer, Office of Legislative Affairs
COOPER, Evelyn, Legislative Information Assistant, Office of Legislative Affairs
GOODMAN, Alice C., Director, Office of Legislative Affairs
SPITLER, Eric J., Deputy Director, Office of Legislative Affairs

Federal Election Commission

999 E St. NW
Room 933
Washington, DC 20463
Web: www.fec.gov
Tel: (202)694-1000
Fax: (202)219-2338

Legislative/Congressional Affairs Personnel

VANBRAKLE, Christina H., Congressional Affairs Officer

Federal Emergency Management Agency

Federal Center Plaza
500 C St. SW
Washington, DC 20472
Web: www.fema.gov
Tel: (202)646-4500
Fax: (202)646-2531

Legislative/Congressional Affairs Personnel

BRADDOCK, Richard, Acting Director, Office of Intergovernmental Affairs
MCCARTHY, Francis, Acting Deputy Director, Office of Congressional and Legislative Affairs

Federal Housing Finance Board

1777 F St. NW
Washington, DC 20006
Web: www.fhfb.gov
Tel: (202)408-2998
Fax: (202)408-2947

Legislative/Congressional Affairs Personnel

HUDAK, Stephen P., Acting Director, Office of Congressional Affairs

Federal Maritime Commission

800 N. Capitol St. NW
Room 1018
Washington, DC 20573
Web: www.fmc.gov
Tel: (202)523-5740
Fax: (202)523-5738

Legislative/Congressional Affairs Personnel

LARSON, Amy, Legislative Counsel

Federal Reserve System

20th and C Sts. NW
Washington, DC 20551
Tel: (202)452-3456
Fax: (202)452-2611

Legislative/Congressional Affairs Personnel
HAMBLEY, Winthrop D., Deputy Congressional Liaison
LOPEZ, John H., Congressional Liaison Assistant
WERNEKE, Diane E., Special Assistant to the Board, Congressional Liaison
WINN, Donald J., Assistant to the Board, Congressional Liaison

Federal Trade Commission

600 Pennsylvania Ave. NW
Washington, DC 20580
Web: www.ftc.gov
Tel: (202)326-2468
Fax: (202)326-3585

Legislative/Congressional Affairs Personnel
KANDO-PINEDA, Carol A., Legislative Counsel, Office of Congressional Relations
THOMAS, David R., Director, Office of Congressional Relations

General Services Administration

1800 F St. NW
Washington, DC 20405
Web: www.gsa.gov
Tel: (202)501-0563
Fax: (202)219-5742

Legislative/Congressional Affairs Personnel
BELL, Glynis L., Acting Associate Administrator, Congressional and Intergovernmental Affairs
JACKSON, Brian, Special Assistant, Congressional and Intergovernmental Affairs
SHORT, Brenda A., Congressional Liaison

Institute for Museum and Library Services

1100 Pennsylvania Ave. NW
Room 510
Washington, DC 20506
E-mail: imlsinfo@imls.gov
Web: www.imls.gov
Tel: (202)606-8339
Fax: (202)606-8591

Legislative/Congressional Affairs Personnel
BITTNER, Mamie, Director, Public and Legislative Affairs
PEDROSO, Margo, Congressional Affairs Specialist

Internat'l Trade Commission

500 E St. SW
Washington, DC 20436
E-mail: ncarman@usitc.gov
Web: www.usitc.gov
Tel: (202)205-3151
Fax: (202)205-2139

Legislative/Congressional Affairs Personnel
CARMAN, Nancy M., Congressional Relations Officer

Merit Systems Protection Board

1615 M St.
N.W.
Washington, DC 20419
Web: www.mspb.gov
Tel: (202)653-7171
Fax: (202)653-7130

Legislative/Congressional Affairs Personnel
WILCOTS, Rosalyn L., Legislative Counsel

Nat'l Aeronautics and Space Administration

300 E St. SW
Washington, DC 20546
Web: www.hq.nasa.gov
Tel: (202)358-1948
Fax: (202)358-4340

Legislative/Congressional Affairs Personnel
CHERRY, Barbara F., Director, Liaison Division, Office of Legislative Affairs
FOREHAND, Lon, Legislative Affairs Specialist
KERWIN, Mary D., Acting Associate Administrator, Legislative Affairs
KIEFFER, Margaret, Legislative Affairs Specialist
PAVLIK, Margaret C., Congressional Correspondence Unit
ROTHMAN, Helen, Director, Congressional Inquiries Division
STEHMER, Karl H., Legislation
TRACY, Anne M., Administrative Officer, Office of Legislative Affairs

Nat'l Credit Union Administration

1775 Duke St.
Alexandria, VA 22314-3428
E-mail: pacamail@ncua.gov
Web: www.ncua.gov
Tel: (703)518-6330
Fax: (703)518-6409

Legislative/Congressional Affairs Personnel
LOFTUS, Robert E., Director, Office of Public and Congressional Affairs

Nat'l Endowment for the Arts

1100 Pennsylvania Ave. NW
Room 524
Washington, DC 20506
Web: http://arts.endow.gov
Tel: (202)682-5434
Fax: (202)682-5638

Legislative/Congressional Affairs Personnel
KIRBY, Michael, Deputy Director, Congressional and White House Liaison
WOODRUFF, Richard P., Director, Congressional and White House Liaison

Nat'l Endowment for the Humanities

1100 Pennsylvania Ave. NW
Washington, DC 20506
Web: www.neh.gov
Tel: (202)606-8328
Fax: (202)606-8588

Legislative/Congressional Affairs Personnel
ROBERTS, John W., Deputy Chairman

Nat'l Indian Gaming Commission

1441 L St. NW
Ninth Floor
Washington, DC 20005
Web: www.nigc.gov
Tel: (202)632-7003
Fax: (202)632-7066

Legislative/Congressional Affairs Personnel
NAYBACK, Kyle T., Director, Congressional and Public Affairs

Nat'l Science Foundation

4201 Wilson Blvd.
Arlington, VA 22230
Web: www.nsf.gov/od/lpa/start.htm
Tel: (703)292-8070
Fax: (703)292-9089

Legislative/Congressional Affairs Personnel
MACKLLIN, Sheila
PEARCE, Karen H., Legislative Policy Analyst
STONNER, David M., Head, Congressional Affairs Section

Nat'l Transportation Safety Board

490 East L'Enfant Plaza SW
Sixth Floor
Washington, DC 20594
Web: www.ntsb.gov
Tel: (202)314-6121
Fax: (202)314-6122

Legislative/Congressional Affairs Personnel
SCOTT, Betty, Deputy Director, Government Affairs, Office of Government, Public and Family Affairs

Nuclear Regulatory Commission

One White Flint North Bldg.
11555 Rockville Pike
Rockville, MD 20852
Web: www.nrc.gov
Tel: (301)415-1776
Fax: (301)415-8571

Legislative/Congressional Affairs Personnel
PORTNER, Linda E., Associate Director/Assistant to the Chairman for Congressional Communications
RATHBUN, Dennis K., Director, Office of Congressional Affairs

Office of Personnel Management

Theodore Roosevelt Federal Bldg.
1900 E St. NW
Washington, DC 20415
E-mail: cbsmith@opm.gov
Web: www.opm.gov
Tel: (202)606-1300
Fax: (202)606-1344

Legislative/Congressional Affairs Personnel
CHISOLM-KING, Janet, Congressional Relations Officer
GIVENS, Veronica I., Legislative Analyst
HOKE, Robert J., Deputy Director, Office of Congressional Relations
LUSKEY, Charlene E., Chief, Congressional Liaison
WOLF, Harry A., Chief, Legislative Analysis Office

Overseas Private Investment Corp.

1100 New York Ave. NW
12th Floor
Washington, DC 20527
Web: www.opic.gov
Tel: (202)336-8417
Fax: (202)336-7949

Legislative/Congressional Affairs Personnel
FREDERICK, Jeannie P., Congressional Assistant
HORANBURG, Richard C., Director, Congressional Affairs

Peace Corps

1111 20th St. NW
Washington, DC 20526
Web: www.peacecorps.gov
Tel: (202)692-2244
Fax: (202)692-2101

Legislative/Congressional Affairs Personnel
NOTMAN, Liz, Deputy Director, Congressional Relations
PALMIERI, Suzanne, Director, Congressional Relations

Railroad Retirement Board

1310 G St. NW
Suite 500
Washington, DC 20005-3004
Web: www.rrb.gov
Tel: (202)272-7742
Fax: (202)272-7728

Legislative/Congressional Affairs Personnel
STANLEY, Margaret A., Director, Office of Legislative Affairs

Securities and Exchange Commission

450 Fifth St. NW
Washington, DC 20549
Web: www.sec.gov
Tel: (202)942-0010
Fax: (202)942-9650

Legislative/Congressional Affairs Personnel
ARONSON, Tracey, Director
CARTER, Casey M., Deputy Director, Office of Congressional and Intergovernmental Affairs
FREEMAN, Sharon K., Legislative Assistant
KIERNAN, Peter S., Legislative Counsel
LEVINE, Estee S., Director, Office of Congressional and Intergovernmental Affairs

Selective Service System

1515 Wilson Blvd.
Fourth Floor
Arlington, VA 22209-2425
Web: www.sss.gov
Tel: (703)605-4100
Fax: (703)605-4133

Legislative/Congressional Affairs Personnel
BRODSKY, Lewis C., Director, Office of Public and Congressional Affairs

Small Business Administration

409 Third St. SW
Suite 7900
Washington, DC 20416
Web: www.sbaonline.sba.gov
Tel: (202)205-6700
Fax: (202)205-7374

Legislative/Congressional Affairs Personnel
ASHLEY-ROGERS, Rhonda, Program Specialist, Office of Congressional and Legislative Affairs
COOPER, Tiffani D., Congressional Relations Specialist
DEANE, Lorraine P., Legislative Affairs Specialist
HALL, Mardel, Staff Assistant, Legislative Affairs
HERNANDEZ, Mary, Congressional Relations Specialist
HONTZ, Karen, Legislative Affairs Specialist
LAVERDY, Marina, Legislative Affairs Specialist
PEYTON, Ramona E., Congressional Relations Specialist
SNOOK, Sheldon, Legislative Affairs Specialist

Social Security Administration-Office of Legislation and Congressional Affairs

500 E St. SW
Eighth Floor
Washington, DC 20254-0001
Web: www.ssa.gov
Tel: (202)358-6030
Fax: (202)358-6074

Legislative/Congressional Affairs Personnel
DALY, William, Social Insurance Program Advisor, Office of Legislative and Congressional Affairs
GARRO, Dianne B., Assistant Deputy Commissioner for Legislative and Congressional Affairs
O'DONNELL, James, Social Insurance Program Advisor, Office of Legislative and Congressional Affairs
PHILLIPS, Webster, Associate Commissioner for Legislative and Congressional Affairs

Trade and Development Agency

1621 N. Kent St.
Suite 300
Arlington, VA 22209-2131
Web: www.tda.gov
Tel: (703)875-4357
Fax: (703)875-4009

Legislative/Congressional Affairs Personnel
YESIN, Erol, Legislative/Public Affairs Support

United States Office of Special Counsel

1730 M St. NW
Suite 300
Washington, DC 20036-4505
Web: www.osc.gov

Tel: (202)653-2253
Fax: (202)653-5151

Legislative/Congressional Affairs Personnel

MCFARLAND, Jane J., Director, Office of Legislative and Public Affairs

United States Postal Service

475 L'Enfant Plaza SW
Washington, DC 20260
Web: www.usps.gov

Tel: (202)268-2506
Fax: (202)268-2503

Legislative/Congressional Affairs Personnel

CONWAY, Anthony C., Government Relations Manager
CURRIER, Ken, Government Relations Manager
EDWARDS, Thomas J., Manager, Government Liaison
GORDON, Stephen, Public Policy Planning and Analysis
KENDALL, Deborah A., Manager, Policy/Strategy
KING, Mitch, Government Relations Manager
MICOCCI, John, Public Policy Programs
SIMPSON, MaryAnn, Government Relations Manager
WILLHITE, Deborah K., Senior V. President, Government Relations

2001 Washington Representatives

The People

The following pages contain an alphabetical listing of the individuals who work for the various firms, clients and government offices in the three preceding sections. Please note that because this directory focuses on the advocacy community in the nation's capital, only individuals who spend the majority of their time in the Washington, DC area and have an office here have been included. These 17,000 individuals are loosely termed "lobbyists", regardless of their registration status under FARA or LDA, because they serve as advocates for the interests of their clients or employers.

AAMOTH, Robert

1200 19th St. NW
Suite 500
Washington, DC 20036
Tel: (202)955-9600
Fax: (202)955-9792

Employers
Kelley, Drye & Warren LLP (Of Counsel)

AARON, Henry J.

1775 Massachusetts Ave. NW
Washington, DC 20036-2188
Tel: (202)797-6000
Fax: (202)797-6004
Former Assistant Secretary for Planning and Evaluation, Department of Health, Education and Welfare; former Chairman, Advisory Council on Social Security.

Employers
The Brookings Institution (Senior Fellow, Economic Studies)

AARON, Rebecca

509 C St. NE
Washington, DC 20002
Tel: (202)546-3800
Fax: (202)544-6771
Former Education Director, President's Commission on White House Fellowships, during the Clinton administration. Former Aide to Rep. Harold Ford Jr. (D-TN).

Employers
Capitol Coalitions Inc. (Manager, Congressional Affairs)

ABAJIAN, Peter

122 C St. NW
Suite 350
Washington, DC 20001
Tel: (202)393-3434
Fax: (202)638-4904
Registered: LDA
EMail: pabajian@pacbell.net

Employers
Armenian Assembly of America (Director, Western Region Office)

ABBEY, Richard H.

1150 18th St. NW
Ninth Floor
Washington, DC 20036
Tel: (202)296-3355
Fax: (202)296-3922
Registered: LDA
EMail: rabbey@ablondifoster.com
Chief Counsel (1980-85), Deputy Chief Counsel (1977-80), and Assistant Chief Counsel (1972-77), U.S. Customs Service.

Employers
Ablondi, Foster, Sobin & Davidow, P.C. (Partner)

Clients Represented
On Behalf of Ablondi, Foster, Sobin & Davidow, P.C.
The Stanley Works

ABBOTT, Ande M.

2722 Merrilee Dr.
Suite 360
Fairfax, VA 22031
Tel: (703)560-1493
Fax: (703)560-2584
Registered: LDA

Employers
Internat'l Brotherhood of Boilermakers, Iron Shipbuilders, Blacksmiths, Forgers and Helpers (Assistant to the International President)

ABBOUD, Jeffrey S.

P.O. Box 1408
Great Falls, VA 22066
Tel: (703)623-1927
Fax: (703)536-1927
Registered: LDA
Former Legislative Assistant to Sen. Edward Zorinsky (D-NE). Former Legislative Assistant to Sen. David Karnes (R-NE).

Employers
Technology Advocates, Inc. (Principal)

Clients Represented
On Behalf of Technology Advocates, Inc.
Fuel Cell Power Ass'n
Gas Turbine Ass'n, Inc.

ABBOUD, Meggan

1200 Wilson Blvd.
Arlington, VA 22209
Tel: (703)465-3045
Registered: LDA

Employers
The Boeing Co. (Director, Constituent Relations)

ABDULLAH, Khalil

444 N. Capitol St. NW
Suite 622
Washington, DC 20001
Tel: (202)624-5457
Fax: (202)508-3826

Employers
Nat'l Black Caucus of State Legislators (Exec. Director)

ABDUN-NABI, Daniel J.

12103 Indian Creek Ct.
Beltsville, MD 20705
Tel: (301)419-8500
Fax: (301)419-0167

Employers
North American Vaccine, Inc./AMVAX, Inc. (Senior V. President)

ABEGG, Heidi

1747 Pennsylvania Ave. NW
Suite 1000
Washington, DC 20006
Tel: (202)785-9500
Fax: (202)835-0243

Employers
Webster, Chamberlain & Bean (Associate)

ABENANTE, Paul

1350 I St. NW
Suite 1290
Washington, DC 20005
Tel: (202)789-0300
Fax: (202)898-1164
Registered: LDA

Employers
American Bakers Ass'n (President and Chief Exec. Officer)

ABERNATHY, John

2550 M St. NW
Washington, DC 20037-1350
Tel: (202)457-6000
Fax: (202)457-6315

Employers
Patton Boggs, LLP

ABERNETHY, Charles

1025 Connecticut Ave. NW
Suite 501
Washington, DC 20036
Tel: (202)828-6816
Fax: (202)828-6849
EMail: charles.abernethy@gencorp.com

Employers
GenCorp (Manager, Automotive, Export, Administration)

ABERNETHY, David S.

625 Indiana Ave. NW Suite 200
Washington, DC 20004
Tel: (202)393-0660
Fax: (202)393-0533
Registered: LDA
EMail: dsahip@erols.com

Employers
HIP Health Plans (Senior V. President, Public Policy and Regulatory Affairs)

ABERNETHY, Stacey Colleen

700 13th St. NW
Suite 1000
Washington, DC 20005
Tel: (202)347-6633
Fax: (202)347-8713
Registered: FARA

Employers
Powell Tate (V. President and Deputy Director of Research)

Clients Represented

On Behalf of Powell Tate
Brita GmbH

ABIDOS, Christy

1133 21st St. NW
Suite 700
Washington, DC 20036
EMail: cabidos@janus-merritt.com
Tel: (202)887-6900
Fax: (202)887-6970

Employers
Janus-Merritt Strategies, L.L.C. (Office Manager, Assistant Managing Partner)

ABINGTON, Edward G.

888 16th St. NW
Washington, DC 20006
Tel: (202)835-8177
Fax: (202)835-8161
Registered: LDA, FARA
U.S. Counsel General (Jerusalem), Department of State, 1993-97.

Employers
Bannerman and Associates, Inc.

Clients Represented

On Behalf of Bannerman and Associates, Inc.
Palestinian Authority

ABLE, Jr., Edward H.

1575 I St. NW
Suite 400
Washington, DC 20005
Tel: (202)289-1818
Fax: (202)289-6578

Employers
American Ass'n of Museums (President and Chief Exec. Officer)

ABLER, Ronald F.

1710 16th St. NW
Washington, DC 20009-3198
EMail: gaia@aag.org
Tel: (202)234-1450
Fax: (202)234-2744

Employers
Ass'n of American Geographers (Exec. Director)

ABLETT, Joan

122 C St. NW
Suite 350
Washington, DC 20001
EMail: jablett@aaainc.org
Tel: (202)393-3434
Fax: (202)638-4904

Employers
Armenian Assembly of America (Director, Public Affairs)

ABLONDI, Italo H.

1150 18th St. NW
Ninth Floor
Washington, DC 20036
EMail: iablondi@ablondifoster.com
Tel: (202)296-3355
Fax: (202)296-3922
U.S. International Trade Commission, 1975-78. Commissioner, U.S. Tariff Commission, 1972-74.

Employers
Ablondi, Foster, Sobin & Davidow, P.C. (Senior Partner)

ABLOTT, Vance

1250 N. Pitt St.
Alexandria, VA 22314
EMail: vablott@challenger.org
Tel: (703)683-9740
Fax: (703)683-7546

Employers
Challenger Center for Space Science Education (President)

ABNEE, Conn

701 Pennsylvania Ave. NW
Third Floor
Washington, DC 20004
Tel: (202)508-5500
Fax: (202)508-5222

Employers
Geothermal Heat Pump Consortium (Exec. Director)

ABNEY, D.V.M., Pamela

1101 Vermont Ave. NW
Suite 710
Washington, DC 20005-3521
Tel: (202)789-0007
Fax: (202)842-4360
Registered: LDA

Employers
American Veterinary Medical Ass'n (Assistant Director, Government Relations)

ABOLT, Russ

501 Wythe St.
Alexandria, VA 22314
Tel: (703)683-8371
Fax: (703)683-4503

Employers
Internat'l Sleep Products Ass'n (Exec. V. President)

ABOOD, Sheila

600 Maryland Ave. SW
Suite 100 West
Washington, DC 20024-2571
Tel: (202)651-7093
Fax: (202)651-7001
Registered: LDA

Employers
American Nurses Ass'n (Associate Director, Federal Government Relations)

ABRAHAM, Fred

1301 Pennsylvania Ave. NW
Suite 402
Washington, DC 20004
Tel: (202)347-1530
Fax: (202)347-1533
Registered: LDA

Employers
Ducks Unlimited Inc. (Director, Conservation Policy)

ABRAHAM, Rick

2100 Reston Pkwy.
Suite 400
Reston, VA 20191-1218
EMail: abraham@asmc.org
Tel: (703)758-7790
Fax: (703)758-7787

Employers
Ass'n of Sales & Marketing Companies (President, ASMC Foodservice)

ABRAHAMS, Jessica

1001 Pennsylvania Ave. NW
Suite 600
Washington, DC 20004
Tel: (202)347-0066
Fax: (202)624-7222
Registered: FARA

Employers
Powell, Goldstein, Frazer & Murphy LLP (Partner)

ABRAM, Jonathan

555 13th St. NW
Washington, DC 20004-1109
Tel: (202)637-5600
Fax: (202)637-5910

Employers
Hogan & Hartson L.L.P.

Clients Represented

On Behalf of Hogan & Hartson L.L.P.
Nat'l College Access Network

ABRAMOFF, Jack

800 Connecticut Ave. NW
Suite 500
Washington, DC 20006
Tel: (202)331-3103
Fax: (202)331-3101

Employers
Greenberg Traurig, LLP (Senior Director, Government Affairs)

Clients Represented

On Behalf of Greenberg Traurig, LLP
Channel One Network
Chitimacha Tribe of Louisiana
Choctaw Indians, Mississippi Band of
Coushatta Tribe of Louisiana
SunCruz Casino
Western Pacific Economic Council

ABRAMOWITZ, Mort

1755 Massachusetts Ave. NW
Suite 400
Washington, DC 20036
EMail: abramowitz@tcf.org
Tel: (202)387-0400
Fax: (202)483-9430

Employers
The Century Foundation (Senior Fellow)

ABRAMOWITZ, Sheppie

1612 K St. NW
Suite 700
Washington, DC 20006
Tel: (202)822-0043
Fax: (202)822-0089
Registered: LDA

Employers
Internat'l Rescue Committee Inc. (Special Advisor)

ABRAMS, Elliott

1015 15th St. NW
Suite 900
Washington, DC 20005
EMail: ethics@eppc.org
Tel: (202)682-1200
Fax: (202)408-0632

Employers
Ethics and Public Policy Center (President)

ABRAMS, Fern

1400 I St. NW
Suite 540
Washington, DC 20005-2208
EMail: fabrams@ipc.org
Tel: (202)638-6219
Fax: (202)638-0145

Employers
IPC Washington Office (Director, Environmental Policy)

ABRAMS, Jacqueline M.

1051 N. George Mason Dr.
Arlington, VA 22205
EMail: jacabr@aol.com
Tel: (703)276-0949
Fax: (703)527-3269

Employers
American Citizens Abroad (Director)

ABRAMS, Matthew J.

1220 19th St. NW
Suite 400
Washington, DC 20036
Tel: (202)822-0707
Fax: (202)822-0714
Registered: LDA, FARA

Employers
CANAMCO (The Canadian-American Company) (President)

Clients Represented

On Behalf of CANAMCO (The Canadian-American Company)
Aerospace Industries Ass'n of Canada

ABRAMS, Robert G.

1299 Pennsylvania Ave. NW
Washington, DC 20004-2402
EMail: abramsr@howrey.com
Tel: (202)783-0800
Fax: (202)383-6610
Law Clerk to Judge William E. Doyle, U.S. Court of Appeals, Tenth Circuit, 1972-73.

Employers
Howrey Simon Arnold & White (Partner)

Clients Represented

On Behalf of Howrey Simon Arnold & White
Exxon Co., U.S.A.

ABRAMSON, Stanley H.

1050 Connecticut Ave. NW
Washington, DC 20036-5339
Tel: (202)857-6000
Fax: (202)857-6395
Registered: LDA
Former Associate General Counsel in Charge of Pesticides and Toxic Substances, Environmental Protection Agency.

Employers
Arent Fox Kintner Plotkin & Kahn, PLLC (Member)

Clients Represented

On Behalf of Arent Fox Kintner Plotkin & Kahn, PLLC
Biotechnology Industry Organization

ABROMSON, Ellen Jane

7315 Wisconsin Ave.
Bethesda, MD 20814
Tel: (301)280-1000
Fax: (301)280-1031

Employers
Acacia Life Insurance Co. (Second V. President, Associate Counsel and Government Relations Representative)

ABUZAAKOUK, Aly R.

1212 New York Ave. NW
Suite 400
Washington, DC 20005
EMail: director@amconline.org
Tel: (202)789-2262
Fax: (202)789-2550

Employers
American Muslim Council (Exec. Director)

ACEVEDO, Elaine B.

1225 I St. NW
Suite 350
Washington, DC 20005
Tel: (202)789-1110
Fax: (202)789-1116
Registered: LDA
EMail: eacevedo@dmggroup.com

Employers
Downey McGrath Group, Inc. (V. President)

Clients Represented
On Behalf of Downey McGrath Group, Inc.
Chevron, U.S.A.
Fantasma Networks, Inc.
The New York Structural Biology Center

ACKERLY, John

1825 K St. NW
Suite 520
Washington, DC 20006
Tel: (202)785-1515
Fax: (202)785-4343

Employers
Internat'l Campaign for Tibet (President)

ACKERLY, Margaret

1250 24th St. NW
Washington, DC 20037
Tel: (202)293-4800
Fax: (202)293-9211

Employers
World Wildlife Fund (General Counsel)

ACKERMAN, Karen

815 16th St. NW
Washington, DC 20006
Tel: (202)637-5000
Fax: (202)637-5058

Employers
AFL-CIO (American Federation of Labor and Congress of Industrial Organizations) (Staff Director, Political Department)

ACKERMAN, Kenneth

1400 16th St. NW
Suite 400
Washington, DC 20036-2220
EMail: kackerman@ofwlaw.com
Tel: (202)518-6379
Fax: (202)234-3583
Administrator, Risk Management Agency, Department of Agriculture, 1993-2000. Also worked for the Commodity Futures Trading Commission and on the staffs of the Senate Committee on Governmental Affairs and the Senate Committee on Agriculture.

Employers
Olsson, Frank and Weeda, P.C. (Of Counsel)

ACKERMANN, Leroy L.

P.O. Box 17265
Washington, DC 20041
Tel: (703)478-2228
Fax: (703)742-8471
EMail: llackermann@jps.net

Employers
American Soc. of Appraisers (PAC Administrator)

ACKLEY, Steve

913 King St.
Alexandria, VA 22314
Tel: (703)549-9592
Fax: (703)549-9601
EMail: bain@bainpr.com

Employers
Bain and Associates, Inc. (Senior V. President)

ACORD, Heather

333 John Carlyle St.
Suite 200
Alexandria, VA 22314
Tel: (703)548-3118
Fax: (703)548-3119

Employers
Associated General Contractors of America (Assistant Director, Public Affairs)

ACOSTA, Renee

66 Canal Center Plaza
Suite 310
Alexandria, VA 22314
Tel: (703)548-2200
Fax: (703)548-7684

Employers
Internat'l Service Agencies (President)

ACOTT, Mike

5100 Forbes Blvd.
Suite 200
Lanham, MD 20706
Tel: (301)731-4748
Fax: (301)731-4621

Employers
Nat'l Asphalt Pavement Ass'n (President)

ACQUARD, Charles A.

8300 Colesville Rd.
Suite 101
Silver Spring, MD 20910
EMail: cacquard@erols.com
Tel: (301)589-6313
Fax: (301)589-6380

Employers
Nat'l Ass'n of State Utility Consumer Advocates (NASUCA) (Exec. Director)

ACQUINO, Edward

1220 L St. NW
Washington, DC 20005
Tel: (202)682-8000
Fax: (202)682-8232
Registered: LDA

Employers
American Petroleum Institute (Senior Tax Accountant)

ACRES, Amy A.

499 S. Capitol St. SW
Suite 502
Washington, DC 20003
EMail: aacres@natso.com
Tel: (202)554-2510
Fax: (202)554-2520

Employers
NATSO, Inc. (Director, Government Affairs)

ACS, Gregory P.

2100 M St. NW
Washington, DC 20037
Tel: (202)833-7200
Fax: (202)429-0687

Employers
The Urban Institute (Senior Research Associate)

ADAIR, Marshall P.

2101 E St. NW
Washington, DC 20037
Tel: (202)338-4045
Fax: (202)338-6820
EMail: pres@afsa.org

Employers
American Foreign Service Ass'n (President)

ADAMS, A. John

655 National Press Bldg.
Washington, DC 20045
Tel: (202)737-8400
Fax: (202)737-8406
Registered: FARA
EMail: jadams@johnadams.com
Director, Office of Public Affairs, Executive Office of the President (Price Commission), 1971-73.

Employers
John Adams Associates Inc. (President)

Clients Represented
On Behalf of John Adams Associates Inc.
Council for LAB/LAS Environmental Research (CLER)
Environmental Industry Council
King Communications Corp.
Styrene Information and Research Center

ADAMS, Cecelia

1615 H St. NW
Washington, DC 20062-2000
Tel: (202)463-5600
Fax: (202)887-3430
Registered: LDA

Employers
Chamber of Commerce of the U.S.A. (Director, Congressional and Public Affairs)

ADAMS, Danny E.

1200 19th St. NW
Suite 500
Washington, DC 20036
EMail: dadams@kelleydrye.com
Tel: (202)955-9600
Fax: (202)955-9792
Special Assistant to the Chief, Common Carrier Bureau, Federal Communications Commission, 1975-78.

Employers
Kelley, Drye & Warren LLP (Partner)

ADAMS, David G.

1201 New York Ave. NW
Suite 1000
Washington, DC 20005
Tel: (202)216-8014
Fax: (202)962-8300
Registered: LDA
EMail: dgadams@venable.com

Employers
Venable (Partner)

Clients Represented
On Behalf of Venable
Cell Tech
Ergo Science Corp.
Merck & Co.
Molecular BioSystems, Inc.
SangStat Medical Corp.

ADAMS, Gina

300 Maryland Ave. NE
Washington, DC 20002
Tel: (202)546-1631
Fax: (202)546-3309
Registered: LDA

Employers
FedEx Corp. (Staff V. President, Government Affairs)

ADAMS, Jane A.

601 13th St. NW
Suite 200 North
Washington, DC 20005
Tel: (202)682-9462
Registered: LDA

Employers
BASF Corporation (Manager, State Government Relations)

ADAMS, Jane M.

1400 I St. NW
Suite 530
Washington, DC 20005
Tel: (202)371-9746
Fax: (202)371-2760
Registered: LDA

Employers
Juvenile Diabetes Foundation Internat'l (Associate Director, Public Affairs and Government Relations)

ADAMS, John B.

2101 Wilson Blvd.
Suite 400
Arlington, VA 22201
EMail: jadams@nmpf.org
Tel: (703)243-6111
Fax: (703)841-9328

Employers
Nat'l Milk Producers Federation (Director, Animal Health and Farm Services)

ADAMS, John J.

1900 K St. NW
Washington, DC 20006-1109
Tel: (202)955-1500
Fax: (202)778-2201
Registered: LDA, FARA
EMail: jadams@hunton.com

Employers
Hunton & Williams (Senior Counsel)

Clients Represented
On Behalf of Hunton & Williams
Almont Shipping Terminals
Edison Electric Institute
Sempra Energy

ADAMS, Kenneth L.

2101 L St. NW
Washington, DC 20037-1526
Tel: (202)785-9700
Fax: (202)887-0689
Registered: LDA
EMail: adamsk@dsmo.com
Legislative Assistant to Rep. Abner J. Mikva (D-IL), 1970-72.

Employers
Dickstein Shapiro Morin & Oshinsky LLP (Partner)

Clients Represented
On Behalf of Dickstein Shapiro Morin & Oshinsky LLP
Exxon Valdez Oil Spill Litigation Plaintiffs

ADAMS, Matthew T.

600 13th St. NW
Washington, DC 20005-3096
Tel: (202)756-8301
Fax: (202)756-8087
EMail: madams@mwe.com
Office of Tax Legislative Counsel, Treasury Department, 1967-69.

Employers
McDermott, Will and Emery (Counsel)

ADAMS, Nick

900 19th St. NW
Suite 300
Washington, DC 20006
Tel: (202)862-5100
Fax: (202)862-5164

Employers
The Aluminum Ass'n (Director, Statistics and Economics)

ADAMS, Peter

3800 N. Fairfax Dr.
Suite 4
Arlington, VA 22203
Tel: (703)524-1544
Fax: (703)524-1548
Registered: LDA
EMail: padams@nwra.org

Employers
Nat'l Water Resources Ass'n (Legislative Assistant)

ADAMS, III, Ted

6551 Loisda Ct.
Suite 400
Springfield, VA 22150
Tel: (703)551-4452
Fax: (703)971-5892
EMail: tedadams@pyrocap.net

Employers
Pyrocap International Corp., Inc. (President)

ADAMS-TAYLOR, Sharon

1801 N. Moore St.
Arlington, VA 22209
Tel: (703)528-0700
Fax: (703)528-2146
EMail: sadams@aasa.org

Employers
American Ass'n of School Administrators (Director, Children's Initiatives)

ADAMSON, Terrence

1145 17th St. NW
Washington, DC 20036
Tel: (202)857-7000
Fax: (202)775-6141

Employers
Nat'l Geographic Soc. (Senior V. President, Law, Business and Government)

ADCOCK, Daniel C.

606 N. Washington St.
Alexandria, VA 22314
Tel: (703)838-7760
Fax: (703)838-7782
Registered: LDA

Employers
Nat'l Ass'n of Retired Federal Employees (Assistant Director, Legislation)

ADCOCK, Michael W.

1420 New York Ave. NW
Suite 1050
Washington, DC 20005
Tel: (202)638-1950
Fax: (202)638-7714
Registered: LDA
Administrative Assistant to Rep. Bud Cramer (D-AL), 1991-96. Press Secretary-Legislative Assistant to Rep. Ronnie Flippo (D-AL), 1983-91.

Employers
Self-employed as an independent consultant.
Van Scoyoc Associates, Inc.

Clients Represented
As an independent consultant
Cooper Green Hospital
Intergraph Corp. Federal Systems Division
Jefferson State Community College
PEI Electronics
University of Alabama System
Uwohali, Inc.
Van Scoyoc Associates, Inc.
On Behalf of Van Scoyoc Associates, Inc.
DGME Fairness Initiative
University of Alabama System

ADDISON, Angela M.

1050 Thomas Jefferson St. NW
Seventh Floor
Washington, DC 20007
Tel: (202)298-1800
Fax: (202)338-2416
EMail: AMA@vnf.com

Employers
Van Ness Feldman, P.C. (Associate)

ADDISON, Daniel R.

2550 M St. NW
Washington, DC 20037-1350
Tel: (202)457-6000
Fax: (202)457-6315
Registered: LDA
EMail: daddison@pattonboggs.com
Special Counselor, Office of the General Counsel, Nat'l Oceanic and Atmospheric Administration, Department of Commerce, 1989-93. Special Assistant to Senator Pete Wilson (R-CA), 1987-88. Former Special Counselor for Natural Resources, Department of Commerce. Former Acting Associate Administrator for Industry and Congressional Affairs, General Services Administration.

Employers
Patton Boggs, LLP (Partner)

Clients Represented
On Behalf of Patton Boggs, LLP
Greenwood Village, Colorado, City of
Nat'l Center for Manufacturing Sciences
Pentachlorophenol Task Force
San Bernardino Valley Municipal Water District
San Bernardino, California, City of
Unifinancial Internat'l, Inc.

ADDLESTONE, David

2001 S St. NW
Suite 610
Washington, DC 20009
Tel: (202)265-8305
Fax: (202)328-0063
EMail: david_addlestone@nvlsp.org

Employers
Nat'l Veterans Legal Services Program (Joint Exec. Director)

ADDUCI, II, V. James

1200 17th St. NW
Fifth Floor
Washington, DC 20036
Tel: (202)467-6300
Fax: (202)466-2006
Registered: LDA
Attorney, U.S. International Trade Commission, 1975-77.

Employers
Adduci, Mastriani & Schaumberg, L.L.P. (Partner)

Clients Represented
On Behalf of Adduci, Mastriani & Schaumberg, L.L.P.
Rubie's Costume Co., Inc.

ADESNIK, Ryan

1299 Pennsylvania Ave. NW
Suite 800 West
Washington, DC 20004
Tel: (202)785-0500
Fax: (202)785-5277
Registered: LDA
EMail: adesnikr@carmengroup.com
Former Senior Legislative Aide to Rep. Benjamin Gilman (R-NY).

Employers
The Carmen Group (V. President)
LMRC, Inc. (Chief of Staff)

Clients Represented
On Behalf of The Carmen Group
ADVO, Inc.
Dillard University
GELCO Information Network GSD, Inc.
Illinois Department of Transportation
Major Medicaid Hospital Coalition
Northwest Airlines, Inc.
Starwood Hotels & Resorts Worldwide, Inc.
Sunrise Assisted Living
Washington Sports & Entertainment, L.P.
Western Development

ADKINS, Amanda

122 C St. NW
Suite 505
Washington, DC 20001
Tel: (202)484-2282
Fax: (202)783-3306

Employers
GOPAC (Political Director)

ADKINS, Genesee

1666 K St. NW
Washington, DC 20006
Tel: (202)296-4700
Fax: (202)496-4324
EMail: gadkins@apt.com

Employers
American Public Transportation Ass'n (Government Relations Policy Specialist)

ADKINS, Larry

901 E St. NW
Suite 600
Washington, DC 20004
Tel: (202)783-4444
Fax: (202)783-4085

Employers
Nat'l Treasury Employees Union (Deputy General Counsel)

ADKINS, Richard Brian

1250 I St. NW
Suite 200
Washington, DC 20005
Tel: (202)737-8888
Fax: (202)638-4922

Employers
Information Technology Industry Council (Government Relations Counsel)

ADLER, Allan R.

50 F St. NW
Fourth Floor
Washington, DC 20001-1564
Tel: (202)220-4544
Fax: (202)347-3690
Registered: LDA
EMail: adler@publishers.org

Employers
Ass'n of American Publishers (V. President, Legal and Government Affairs)

ADLER, Gary C.

1666 K St. NW
Suite 500
Washington, DC 20006-2803
Tel: (202)887-1400
Fax: (202)466-2198
Registered: LDA

Employers
O'Connor & Hannan, L.L.P. (Partner)

Clients Represented
On Behalf of O'Connor & Hannan, L.L.P.
Nat'l Ass'n of Ticket Brokers
Trident Seafood Corp.

ADLER, Laurie J.

700 13th St. NW
Suite 400
Washington, DC 20005
Tel: (202)347-0773
Fax: (202)347-0785

Employers
Cassidy & Associates, Inc. (V. President)

Clients Represented
On Behalf of Cassidy & Associates, Inc.
Alenia Aerospazig
The BOSE Corp.
Jewish Family Service Ass'n of Cleveland
Liberty Science Center
Orange, California, County of
United Space Alliance

ADLER, Prudence

21 Dupont Circle NW
Suite 800
Washington, DC 20036
EMail: prue@arl.org

Tel: (202)296-2296
Fax: (202)872-0884
Registered: LDA

Employers
Ass'n of Research Libraries (Assistant Exec. Director, Federal Relations and Information Policy)

ADLER, Robert M.

1666 K St. NW
Suite 500
Washington, DC 20006-2803

Tel: (202)887-1400
Fax: (202)466-2198

Special Assistant to the Attorney General (1976-77) and Trial Attorney, Tax Division (1968-74), Department of Justice.

Employers
O'Connor & Hannan, L.L.P. (Partner)

Clients Represented
On Behalf of O'Connor & Hannan, L.L.P.
Kendall-Jackson Winery

ADLER, Wendy

1225 I St. NW
Suite 1100
Washington, DC 20005

Tel: (202)898-0792
Fax: (202)371-9615

Employers
Handgun Control, Inc. (Director, Law Enforcement Relations)

ADNEY, John T.

1455 Pennsylvania Ave. NW
Suite 1200
Washington, DC 20004

Tel: (202)347-2230
Fax: (202)393-3310
Registered: LDA

Law Clerk to Judge Marion T. Bennett (1976-77) and Law Clerk, Trial Division (1975-76), U.S. Claims Court.

Employers
Davis & Harman LLP (Partner)

Clients Represented
On Behalf of Davis & Harman LLP
Aegon USA
Stock Co. Information Group

AERY, Shaila

1199 N. Fairfax St.
Suite 1000
Alexandria, VA 22314
EMail: saery@hawthorngroup.com

Tel: (703)299-4499
Fax: (703)299-4488

Chief of Staff to Senator Barbara Mikulski (D-MD), 1996-99.

Employers
The Hawthorn Group, L.C. (President and Chief Operating Officer)

AFONSO, Paul G.

1900 L St. NW
Suite 407
Washington, DC 20036

Tel: (202)293-3454
Fax: (202)393-3455
Registered: LDA

Employers
Bristol Group, Inc. (General Counsel)

Clients Represented
On Behalf of Bristol Group, Inc.
Boston Edison Co.
TAP/Air Portugal

AFTERGOOD, Steven

307 Massachusetts Ave. NE
Washington, DC 20002
EMail: saftergood@igc.org

Tel: (202)675-1012
Fax: (202)675-1010

Employers
Federation of American Scientists (Project Director, Government Secrecy Project)

AGNEW, Richard A.

1050 Thomas Jefferson St. NW
Seventh Floor
Washington, DC 20007

Tel: (202)298-1800
Fax: (202)338-2416
Registered: LDA

Employers
Van Ness Feldman, P.C.

Clients Represented
On Behalf of Van Ness Feldman, P.C.
Bellingham, Washington, City of
Princess Tours
Seattle City Light
TransAlta Corp.

AGUTO, Danielle

1717 K St. NW
Suite 507
Washington, DC 20036
EMail: daguto@ftna.com

Tel: (202)822-2058
Fax: (202)822-2099
Registered: LDA

Employers
France Telecom North America (V. President and General Counsel)

AHEARN, Patrick

1029 N. Royal St.
Suite 400
Alexandria, VA 22314
EMail: pahearn@directimpact.com

Tel: (703)684-1245
Fax: (703)684-1249

Employers
The Direct Impact Co. (V. President, Field Operations)

AHERN, Bill

1250 H St. NW
Suite 750
Washington, DC 20005
EMail: ahern@taxfoundations.org

Tel: (202)783-2760
Fax: (202)783-6868

Employers
Tax Foundation, Inc. (Director, Communications)

AHERN, Catherine A.

1225 New York Ave. NW
Suite 450
Washington, DC 20005
EMail: arc@funoutdoors.com

Tel: (202)682-9530
Fax: (202)682-9529

Employers
American Recreation Coalition (V. President, Member Services)

AHMED, Ph.D., Karim

1725 K St. NW
Suite 212
Washington, DC 20006
EMail: info@cnie.org

Tel: (202)530-5810
Ext: 210
Fax: (202)628-4311

Employers
Nat'l Council for Science and the Environment (Secretary/Treasurer)

AHMED, Sarah

1250 Fourth St. SW
Suite WG-1
Washington, DC 20024

Tel: (202)863-2951
Fax: (202)863-2952

Employers
Council for the Nat'l Interest (Program Assistant)

AHN, Jin

1155 15th St. NW
Suite 811
Washington, DC 20005

Tel: (202)775-8130
Fax: (202)223-2662

Employers
Persimmon Group Inc. (President)

Clients Represented
On Behalf of Persimmon Group Inc.
Kia Motors Corp.

AHNEN, Stephen

325 Seventh St. NW
Washington, DC 20004

Tel: (202)638-1100
Fax: (202)626-2345

Employers
American Hospital Ass'n (V. President, Special Assistant to the President)

AIKEN, Robert S.

800 Connecticut Ave. NW
Suite 610
Washington, DC 20006

Tel: (202)293-2655
Fax: (202)293-2666
Registered: LDA

Employers
Arizona Public Service Co. (V. President, Public Affairs)
Pinnacle West Capital Corp. (V. President, Federal Affairs)

AIKEN-O'NEILL, Patricia

1015 18th St. NW
Suite 1010
Washington, DC 20036
EMail: sightebaa@aol.com

Tel: (202)775-4999
Fax: (202)429-6036

Employers
Eye Bank Ass'n of America (President and Chief Exec. Officer)

AIKENS, Joan D.

1000 16th St. NW
Suite 500
Washington, DC 20036

Tel: (202)293-2231
Fax: (202)293-2118
Registered: LDA

Employers
Public Affairs Management, Inc. (Managing Director)

AILOR, David C.

1255 23rd St. NW
Suite 200
Washington, DC 20037-1174
EMail: dailor@hauck.com

Tel: (202)452-8100
Fax: (202)833-3636

Employers
Hauck and Associates (V. President, Regulatory Affairs)
Nat'l Oilseed Processors Ass'n (Director, Regulatory Affairs)

Clients Represented
On Behalf of Hauck and Associates
American Coke and Coal Chemicals Institute
Nat'l Oilseed Processors Ass'n

AINSLIE, Virginia J.

3812 N. Sixth Rd.
Arlington, VA 22203

Tel: (703)527-5404
Fax: (703)243-9251
Registered: LDA

Employers
Ainslie Associates (President)

Clients Represented
On Behalf of Ainslie Associates
Cleveland Advanced Manufacturing Program
Cleveland Clinic Foundation
Cleveland State University - College of Urban Affairs
Northeast Ohio Areawide Coordination Agency (NOACA)
Northeast Ohio Regional Sewer District
Youngstown-Warren Regional Chamber

AISENBERG, Michael A.

505 Huntmar Park Dr.
Herndon, VA 20170

Tel: (703)742-0400
Registered: LDA

Employers
VeriSign/Network Solutions, Inc. (Director of Public Policy)

AISTARS, Sandra M.

1615 L St. NW
Suite 700
Washington, DC 20036-5610
EMail: sandra.aistars@weil.com

Tel: (202)682-7000
Fax: (202)857-0939
Registered: LDA

Employers
Weil, Gotshal & Manges, LLP (Associate)

Clients Represented
On Behalf of Weil, Gotshal & Manges, LLP
Copyright Clearance Center, Inc.
Empire Blue Cross and Blue Shield
InterTrust, Inc.
Matsushita Electric Corp. of America

AITKEN, Bruce

666 11th St. NW
Suite 315
Washington, DC 20001
EMail: 75031.241@compuserve.com

Tel: (202)331-8045
Fax: (202)331-8191
Registered: LDA, FARA

Employers
Aitken, Irvin, Lewin, Berlin, Vrooman & Cohn (Partner)

Clients Represented

On Behalf of Aitken, Irvin, Lewin, Berlin, Vrooman & Cohn

Colgate Palmolive
Hyundai Motor Co.
Pro Trade Group

AITKEN, Herve H.

908 King St.
Suite 300
Alexandria, VA 22314
EMail: haaitken@law.com
Tel: (703)836-9400
Fax: (703)836-9410

Employers

Thiemann Aitken Vohra & Rutledge, L.L.C. (Member)

Clients Represented

On Behalf of Thiemann Aitken Vohra & Rutledge, L.L.C.

Midwest Motor Express, Inc.

AITKEN, Michael P.

1233 20th St. NW
Suite 301
Washington, DC 20036-1250
Tel: (202)429-0311
Fax: (202)429-0149

Employers

College and University Professional Ass'n for Human Resources (Associate Exec. Director, Government and External Relations)

AKER, G. Colburn

2000 K St. NW
Suite 801
Washington, DC 20006
EMail: aker@akerpartners.com
Tel: (202)789-2424
Fax: (202)789-1818

Executive Assistant to Senator John C. Culver (D-IA), 1973-77.

Employers

The Aker Partners Inc. (Managing Partner)

Clients Represented

On Behalf of The Aker Partners Inc.

Ass'n of Clinical Research Professionals
Ephedra Education Council
Moore Medical Corp.
Newspaper Ass'n of America

AKHTER, M.D., Mohammed N.

800 I St. NW
Washington, DC 20001
Tel: (202)777-2510
Fax: (202)777-2534

Employers

American Public Health Ass'n (Exec. Director)

AKIZUKI, Hoyato

196 Van Buren St.
Suite 450
Herndon, VA 20170
Tel: (703)456-2557
Fax: (703)456-2551

Employers

Nissan North America Inc. (Manager, Technical Affairs)

AKMAN, Jerome P.

1050 Connecticut Ave. NW
Washington, DC 20036-5339
Tel: (202)857-6000
Fax: (202)857-6395

Employers

Arent Fox Kintner Plotkin & Kahn, PLLC (Member)

Clients Represented

On Behalf of Arent Fox Kintner Plotkin & Kahn, PLLC

Valmet Corp.

AKWEI, Adotei

600 Pennsylvania Ave. SE
Fifth Floor
Washington, DC 20003
Tel: (202)544-0200
Fax: (202)546-7142
Registered: LDA

Employers

Amnesty Internat'l U.S.A. (Advocacy Director for Africa)

AKYUZ, Abdullah

1250 24th St. NW
Suite 300
Washington, DC 20037
Tel: (202)776-7770
Registered: LDA

Employers

Turkish Industrialists and Businessmen's Ass'n (TUSIAD) (President)

AL-MTWALI, Mounthir

1100 17th St. NW
Suite 602
Washington, DC 20036
Tel: (202)265-3219
Fax: (202)331-1525
Registered: FARA

Employers

League of Arab States/Arab Information Center (Information Officer)

ALBANEZE, Roger D.

1300 Pennsylvania Ave. NW
Suite 700
Washington, DC 20004
Registered: LDA

Employers

U.S. Family Network

ALBERS, William E.

1911 N. Ft. Myer Dr.
Suite 707
Arlington, VA 22209
EMail: balbers@alberscom.com
Tel: (703)358-9100
Fax: (703)358-9106
Registered: LDA

Employers

Albers & Co. (President)

Clients Represented

On Behalf of Albers & Co.

Infiltrator Systems, Inc.
Eli Lilly and Co.
May Department Stores Co.
Profit Recovery Group Internat'l

ALBERSWERTH, Dave

1615 M St. NW
Washington, DC 20036
EMail: dave_alberswerth@tws.org
Tel: (202)833-2300
Fax: (202)429-3945
Registered: LDA

Employers

The Wilderness Soc. (Director, BLM Program)

ALBERT, Sarah

1734 N St. NW
Washington, DC 20036-2990
Tel: (202)347-3168
Ext: 140
Fax: (202)835-0246

Employers

General Federation of Women's Clubs (Public Policy Director)

ALBERT, Stacey Stern

1300 I St. NW
Suite 900 East
Washington, DC 20005
EMail: stacey.albert@compaq.com
Tel: (202)962-3830
Fax: (202)962-3838
Registered: LDA

Employers

Compaq Computer Corp. (Sr. Counsel, Government Affairs)

ALBERT, Thomas L.

1155 Connecticut Ave. NW
Suite 1200
Washington, DC 20036
EMail: talbert@dc.bhb.com
Tel: (202)659-5800
Fax: (202)659-1027
Registered: LDA

Employers

Birch, Horton, Bittner & Cherot (Member)

Clients Represented

On Behalf of Birch, Horton, Bittner & Cherot

Alaska Professional Hunters Ass'n
Aleut Corp.
Anchorage, Alaska, Municipality of
Clearwater Environmental, Inc.
Council Tree Communications, L.L.C.
CSX Corp.
Digital Matrix Corp.
DuPont
Fairbanks, Alaska, North Star Borough of
Feld Entertainment Inc.
ICRC Energy, Inc.
Old Harbor Native Corp.
Optical Disc Corp.
Port of Tillamook Bay
Quinnat Landing Hotel
Science Applications Internat'l Corp. (SAIC)
Space Mark
Tanadgusix Corp.
Trimble Navigation, Ltd.
University of Alaska
Wildlife Legislative Fund of America
Yukon Pacific

ALBERTINE, James J.

1156 15th St. NW
Suite 505
Washington, DC 20005
Tel: (202)659-2979
Fax: (202)659-3020
Registered: LDA

Former Legislative Aide to Rep. Gene Andrew Maguire (D-NJ) and Rep. Raymond Lederer (D-PA).

Employers

Albertine Enterprises, Inc. (Partner)
American Ass'n of Entrepreneurs (Contact, Political Action Committee)
American League of Lobbyists (President)

Clients Represented

On Behalf of Albertine Enterprises, Inc.

American Ass'n of Entrepreneurs
Ass'n of School Business Officials Internat'l
Coleman Aerospace Co.
Employers Council on Flexible Compensation
Energy Absorption Systems, Inc.
Greater Washington Soc. of Ass'n Executives
Health Data Exchange Corp.
Internat'l Snowmobile Manufacturers Ass'n
Nevada, Washington Office of the State of
Polaris Industries
Powerware
SMS Corp.
TASC, Inc.
UNIFI, Inc.
Word Chiropractic Alliance

ALBERTINE, Dr. John M.

1156 15th St. NW
Suite 505
Washington, DC 20005
Tel: (202)659-2979
Fax: (202)659-3020
Registered: LDA

Former Legislative Aide to Sen. Lloyd Bentsen (D-TX).

Employers

Albertine Enterprises, Inc. (Chairman)

Clients Represented

On Behalf of Albertine Enterprises, Inc.

American Ass'n of Entrepreneurs
Coleman Aerospace Co.
Energy Absorption Systems, Inc.
Internat'l Snowmobile Manufacturers Ass'n
Jam Shoe Concepts, Inc.
Polaris Industries
Powerware
TASC, Inc.
UNIFI, Inc.

ALBERTS, Dr. Bruce

2101 Constitution Ave. NW
Washington, DC 20418
Tel: (202)334-2000
Fax: (202)334-1684

Employers

Nat'l Academy of Sciences (President)

ALBIZO, Joel

1250 I St. NW
Suite 500
Washington, DC 20005
EMail: jalbizo@anla.org
Tel: (202)789-2900
Fax: (202)789-1893

Employers

American Nursery and Landscape Ass'n (Senior Director, Membership and Marketing)

ALBRECHT, Virginia S.

1900 K St. NW
Washington, DC 20006-1109
Tel: (202)955-1500
Fax: (202)778-2201
Registered: LDA

Law Clerk to Judge John P. Weise, U.S. Court of Claims, Trial Division, 1981-82.

Employers

The Foundation for Environmental and Economic Progress (Director, Government Affairs and General Counsel)

Hunton & Williams (Partner)

Clients Represented

On Behalf of Hunton & Williams

The Foundation for Environmental and Economic Progress

The Irvine Co.

Mills Corporation

United States Sugar Corp.

ALBRIGHT, Jr., C. H. "Bud"

801 Pennsylvania Ave. NW
Suite 620
Washington, DC 20004-2604
Tel: (202)783-7220
Fax: (202)783-8127
Registered: LDA
EMail: bud_albright@reliantenergy.com

Employers

Reliant Energy, Inc. (V. President, Federal Relations)

ALBRIGHT, David H.

236 Massachusetts Ave. NE
Suite 500
Washington, DC 20002
Tel: (202)547-3633
Fax: (202)547-3634

Member of the Openess Advisory Panel of the Secretary of Energy Advisory Board, U.S. Department of Energy, 1996-Present. Former consultant to the Congressional Research Service.

Employers

Institute for Science and Internat'l Security (President)

ALBRIGHT, Sally L.

507 G St. SW
Washington, DC 20024
Tel: (202)421-4555
Fax: (202)546-0506
Registered: LDA

Former Senior Legislative Assistant to Rep. Earl F. Hilliard (D-AL). Served as Staff Assistant to Senator Richard Shelby (D-AL).

Employers

Self-employed as an independent consultant.

Clients Represented

As an independent consultant

Gallery Watch

Stillman College

U.S. Internet Council

ALCADE, Nancy

1341 G St. NW
Suite 200
Washington, DC 20005
Tel: (202)347-5990
Fax: (202)347-5941
EMail: nalcade@clj.com

Employers

Copeland, Lowery & Jacquez (Legislative Associate)

ALCALDE, Hector

2111 Wilson Blvd.
Eighth Floor
Arlington, VA 22201-3058
Tel: (703)841-0626
Fax: (703)243-2874
Registered: LDA
EMail: halcalde@alcalde-fay.com

Chief of Staff to Rep. Sam Gibbons (D-FL), 1962-73.

Employers

Alcalde & Fay (Founder/Senior Partner)

Clients Represented

On Behalf of Alcalde & Fay

American Maglev Technology Inc.
AMFM, Inc.
Bay County, Florida
Cargill, Inc.
Carnival Foundation
Clearwater, Florida, City of
CNF Transportation, Inc.
Computer Sciences Corp.
Cruise Industry Charitable Foundation
Dallas, Texas, City of
Glencairn, Ltd.
Hillsborough, Florida, County of
Hispanic Broadcasting Inc.
Internat'l Council of Cruise Lines
Jacksonville, Florida, Port Authority of the City of
Jovan Broadcasting
Miami-Dade, Florida, County of
Mitretek Systems
North Miami Beach, Florida, City of
Norwegian Cruise Line
Panama, Government of the Republic of
Paxson Communications Corp.
Section 877 Coalition
Tampa Port Authority
Tampa, Florida, City of
Telemundo

ALCALDE, Richard

1212 New York Ave. NW
Suite 350
Washington, DC 20005
Tel: (202)842-5077
Fax: (202)842-5010
Registered: LDA

Employers

Hall, Green, Rupli, LLC (Associate)

ALCRE, Jennifer

1225 I St. NW
Suite 350
Washington, DC 20005
Tel: (202)789-1110
Fax: (202)789-1116

Employers

Downey McGrath Group, Inc.

ALDEN, John

555 12th St. NW
Suite 950N
Washington, DC 20004
Tel: (202)371-2220
Fax: (202)371-1497

Employers

Freedom Technologies, Inc. (V. President)

ALDERFER, Kenneth

1333 New Hampshire Ave. NW
Suite 400
Washington, DC 20036
Tel: (202)887-4000
Fax: (202)887-4288

Employers

Akin, Gump, Strauss, Hauer & Feld, L.L.P. (Senior Counsel)

Clients Represented

On Behalf of Akin, Gump, Strauss, Hauer & Feld, L.L.P.

Fremont Group, Inc.

ALDOCK, John D.

1800 Massachusetts Ave. NW
Washington, DC 20036
Tel: (202)828-2000
Fax: (202)828-2195
Registered: LDA, FARA

Assistant U.S. Attorney for the District of Columbia, Department of Justice, 1968-71. Law Clerk to Judge Luther W. Youngdahl, U.S. District Court for the District of Columbia, 1967-68.

Employers

Shea & Gardner (Partner and Chair, Executive Committee)

Clients Represented

On Behalf of Shea & Gardner

Center for Claims Resolution
SGS Government Programs, Inc.
SGS North America, Inc.
Societe Generale de Surveillance Holding S.A.

ALDRICH, Stephanie

1310 G St. NW
12th Floor
Washington, DC 20005
Tel: (202)626-4780
Fax: (202)626-4833
Registered: LDA

Employers

Blue Cross Blue Shield Ass'n (Senior Policy Consultant II)

ALEMAIN, Alan C.

440 R St. NW
Washington, DC 20001
Tel: (202)462-3614
Fax: (202)387-1034

Employers

Africare (Director, Anglophone East and West Africa Region)

ALEXANDER, Barry

1227 25th St. NW
Suite 700
Washington, DC 20037
Tel: (202)861-0900
Fax: (202)296-2882
Registered: LDA

Employers

Epstein Becker & Green, P.C. (Associate)

ALEXANDER, Claude D.

1300 I St. NW
Suite 495-East Tower
Washington, DC 20005-3314
Tel: (202)289-2011
Fax: (202)289-2024
Registered: LDA

Employers

Ralston Purina Co. (Director, Government Affairs)

ALEXANDER, Deborah

2027 Massachusetts Ave. NW
Washington, DC 20036
Tel: (202)332-4001
Fax: (202)387-3434
EMail: washrep@ajcongress.org

Employers

American Jewish Congress (Special Assistant, Government and Public Affairs)

ALEXANDER, Donald C.

1333 New Hampshire Ave. NW
Suite 400
Washington, DC 20036
Tel: (202)887-4000
Fax: (202)887-4288
Registered: LDA

Chairman, Internal Revenue Service Exempt Organizations Advisory Group, 1987-89. Commissioner, Coal Leasing Commission, Department of Interior, 1983-84. Member, Commission on Federal Paperwork, 1975-77. Commissioner, Internal Revenue Service, Department of Treasury 1973-77.

Employers

Akin, Gump, Strauss, Hauer & Feld, L.L.P. (Partner)

Clients Represented

On Behalf of Akin, Gump, Strauss, Hauer & Feld, L.L.P.

Air Transport Ass'n of America
Alliance of American Insurers
American Financial Group
ANCOR
Bear, Stearns and Co.
Bechtel Group, Inc.
Cummins Engine Co.
EMC Corp.
Johnson & Johnson, Inc.
Municipal Financial Consultants Inc.
Nationwide Mutual Insurance Co.
The Project Leadership Committee, Lincoln Center for the Performing Arts
Wausau Insurance Cos.

ALEXANDER, Donna K.

1399 New York Ave. NW
Eighth Floor
Washington, DC 20005-4711
Tel: (202)434-8400
Fax: (202)434-8456
Registered: LDA
EMail: dalexander@bondmarkets.com

Chief Counsel to Rep. Alex McMillan (R-NC), 1987-91. Served on Staff to Rep. Howard Coble (R-NC), 1985-87. Department of Justice, 1983-85. Served on Staff to Rep. W. Eugene Johnston III (R-NC), 1981-83.

Employers

The Bond Market Ass'n (V. President)

ALEXANDER, Elizabeth R.

733 15th St. NW
Suite 620
Washington, DC 20005
Tel: (202)393-4930
Fax: (202)393-4931

Employers

Nat'l Prison Project (Director)

ALEXANDER, LaVerne

1025 Connecticut Ave. NW
Suite 309
Washington, DC 20036
Tel: (202)659-3780
Fax: (202)331-8065
Registered: LDA

Employers
Girl Scouts of the U.S.A. - Washington Office (Director, Government Relations)

ALEXANDER, Mary K.

1620 L St. NW
Suite 1150
Washington, DC 20036
Tel: (202)223-2575
Fax: (202)223-2614
Registered: LDA

Employers
Matsushita Electric Corp. of America (Assistant General Manager, Government and Public Affairs)

ALEXANDER, Nick

1100 Connecticut Ave. NW
Suite 430
Washington, DC 20036
EMail: alexander@ific.org
Tel: (202)296-6540
Fax: (202)296-6547

Employers
Internat'l Food Information Council (Director, Media Relations)

ALEXANDER, Maj. Gen. Richard C.

One Massachusetts Ave. NW
Washington, DC 20001
Tel: (202)789-0031
Fax: (202)682-9358

Employers
Nat'l Guard Ass'n of the U.S. (Exec. Director)

ALEXANDER, Stephen

1250 H St. NW
Suite 800
Washington, DC 20005
Tel: (202)857-3400
Fax: (202)857-3401
Registered: LDA

Employers
Eastman Kodak Co. (Director, Technology and Environmental Affairs)

ALEXANDER, Jr., Hon. William V. "Bill"

908 Pennsylvania Ave. SE
Washington, DC 20003
Tel: (202)544-5666
Fax: (202)544-4647
Registered: LDA
EMail: balexander@advantage-dc.com
Member, U.S. House of Representatives (D-AK), 1969-93.

Employers
Advantage Associates, Inc. (Associate)

ALEXANDROV, Stanimir

1001 Pennsylvania Ave. NW
Suite 600
Washington, DC 20004
EMail: salexand@pgfm.com
Tel: (202)347-0066
Fax: (202)624-7222

Employers
Powell, Goldstein, Frazer & Murphy LLP (Foreign Counsel)

ALFELDA, Margaret A.

633 Pennsylvania Ave. NW
Sixth Floor
Washington, DC 20004
Tel: (202)783-7959
Fax: (202)783-1489

Employers
Nat'l Grid USA (Office Manager)

ALFORD, Brenda

P.O. Box 13858
Silver Spring, MD 20911-0858
Tel: (301)585-8051

Employers
American Ass'n of Black Women Entrepreneurs Corp. (Founding National President)

ALFORD, Jr., Harry C.

1350 Connecticut Ave. NW
Suite 825
Washington, DC 20036
Tel: (202)466-6888
Fax: (202)466-4918
Registered: LDA

Employers
Harry C. Alford & Associates, Inc.

Clients Represented
On Behalf of Harry C. Alford & Associates, Inc.
James E. Schneider, LLM Inc.

ALFORD, James K.

1828 L St. NW
Eleventh Floor
Washington, DC 20036-5109
EMail: alforji@vssp.com
Tel: (202)467-8801
Fax: (202)467-8900

Employers
Vorys, Sater, Seymour and Pease, LLP (Counsel)

Clients Represented
On Behalf of Vorys, Sater, Seymour and Pease, LLP
Advanced Material Resources, Inc.
The Consulting Center
Indotrade, Inc.
Motorists Insurance Cos.
Walmer Dollhouses, Inc.

ALFORD, Marty

3207 Chichester Lane
Fairfax, VA 22301
Tel: (703)204-2867
Fax: (703)204-2867
Registered: LDA

Employers
Alford & Associates

Clients Represented
On Behalf of Alford & Associates
Aeromet, Inc.
Air Cruisers, Inc.
Go! Systems, Inc.
W. L. Gore & Associates
Lockheed Martin Aeronautical Systems Co.
Newport News Shipbuilding Inc.
Sparton Electronics, Florida, Inc.

ALFORD, Ralph

3207 Chichester Lane
Fairfax, VA 22301
Tel: (703)204-2867
Fax: (703)204-2867
Registered: LDA

Employers
Alford & Associates (President)

Clients Represented
On Behalf of Alford & Associates
Marine Sonic Technology

ALHADEFF, Joseph

1667 K St. NW
Suite 640
Washington, DC 20006-1605
EMail: joseph.alhadeff@oracle.com
Tel: (202)721-4816
Fax: (202)467-4250
Registered: LDA

Employers
Oracle Corp. (V. President)

ALIFERIS, Scott

1401 H St. NW
Suite 900
Washington, DC 20005
Tel: (202)326-5526
Fax: (202)326-5595
Registered: LDA

Employers
Alliance of Automobile Manufacturers, Inc. (Manager, Government Affairs)

ALIN, Michael

608 Massachusetts Ave. NE
Washington, DC 20002
Tel: (202)546-3480
Fax: (202)546-3240

Employers
American Soc. of Interior Designers (Exec. Director)

ALKER, Joan Christina

1334 G St. NW
Suite 300
Washington, DC 20005-3169
Tel: (202)628-3030
Fax: (202)347-2417
Registered: LDA

Employers
Families U.S.A. Foundation (Deputy Director, Government Affairs)

ALLAN, L. Stuart

1819 L St. NW
2nd Floor
Washington, DC 20036
EMail: sallan@pbecus.org
Tel: (202)293-1093
Fax: (202)289-1940

Employers
Pacific Basin Economic Council - U.S. Member Committee (Director General)

ALLAN, Richmond F.

1615 M St. NW
Suite 800
Washington, DC 20036-3203
EMail: rfa@dwgp.com
Tel: (202)467-6370
Fax: (202)467-6379
Deputy Solicitor (1968) and Associate Solicitor (1965-67), Indian Affairs, Department of the Interior. Trial Attorney (1965) and Assistant U.S. Attorney, District of Montana (1961-64), Department of Justice. Law Clerk to Judge W. Pope, U.S. Court of Appeals, Ninth Circuit, 1958-59.

Employers
Duncan, Weinberg, Genzer & Pembroke, P.C. (Principal)

Clients Represented
On Behalf of Duncan, Weinberg, Genzer & Pembroke, P.C.
Basin Electric Power Cooperative
Bergen, New York, Village of
Boonville, New York, Village of
Freeport, New York, Electric Department of the Village of
Greenport, New York, Village Electric Department of
Jamestown, New York, Board of Public Utilities
Massena, New York, Town of
Orlando Utilities Commission
Penn Yan, New York, Village of
Rockville Centre, New York, Village of
Sensor Oil and Gas Co.
Southern California Public Power Authority

ALLARD, C. Kenneth

1717 Pennsylvania Ave. NW
12th Floor
Washington, DC 20006
EMail: allardck@aol.com
Tel: (202)416-0150
Registered: LDA
Dean of Students, National War College, 1993-94. Special Assistant to the Chief of Staff, Department of the Army, 1987-90.

Employers
Potomac Strategies Internat'l LLC (V. President)

Clients Represented
On Behalf of Potomac Strategies Internat'l LLC
Orbital Sciences Corp., Fairchild Defense Division

ALLARD, Nicholas W.

555 11th St. NW
Suite 1000
Washington, DC 20004
Tel: (202)637-2286
Fax: (202)637-2201
Registered: LDA
Administrative Assistant and Chief of Staff to Senator Daniel Patrick Moynihan (D-NY), 1986-87. Minority Staff Counsel and Legal Counsel to Senator Edward Kennedy (D-MA), 1984-86. Law Clerk to Judge Patricia M. Wald, U.S. Court of Appeals for the District of Columbia, 1980-81, and to Chief Judge Robert F. Peckham, U.S. District Court for the Northern District of California, 1979-80.

Employers
Latham & Watkins (Partner)

Clients Represented
On Behalf of Latham & Watkins
American Public Communications Council
General Cigar Holdings, Inc.
Independent Telephone and Telecommunications Alliance
Leap Wireless Internat'l
Serono Laboratories, Inc.
Wireless Communications Ass'n

ALLEGRETTI, Thomas A.

1600 Wilson Blvd.
Suite 1000
Arlington, VA 22209
Tel: (703)841-9300
Fax: (703)841-0389
Registered: LDA

Employers
American Waterways Operators (President)

ALLEN, Alexis B.

1250 I St. NW
Suite 1200
Washington, DC 20005-3924
Tel: (202)371-8544
Fax: (202)371-8470

Employers
Aerospace Industries Ass'n of America (Director, Communications)

ALLEN, Barbara

440 First St. NW
Third Floor
Washington, DC 20001-2085
Tel: (202)638-2952
Fax: (202)638-4004
Registered: LDA

Employers
Child Welfare League of America (Senior Policy Analyst)

ALLEN, Carla C.

1730 K St. NW
Suite 910
Washington, DC 20006
Tel: (202)463-1400
Fax: (202)463-6199

Employers
Institute for Research on the Economics of Taxation (IRET) (V. President, Communications)

ALLEN, Christopher

810 Vermont Ave. NW
Washington, DC 20420
Tel: (202)273-9419
Fax: (202)273-9988

Employers
Department of Veterans Affairs (Legislative Affairs Officer)

ALLEN, Edward L.

1990 M St. NW
Suite 400
Washington, DC 20036
EMail: coalgovpro@aol.com
Tel: (202)331-0975
Fax: (202)822-9788

Employers
Coalition for Government Procurement (Exec. Director)

ALLEN, Edwin

1101 17th St. NW
Suite 803
Washington, DC 20036
Tel: (202)833-0007
Fax: (202)833-0086
Registered: LDA
Former Minority Counsel, House Committee on Energy and Commerce.

Employers
MARC Associates, Inc. (Senior Counsel)

Clients Represented
On Behalf of MARC Associates, Inc.
AdvaMed
American Soc. of Nuclear Cardiology
Boehringer Ingelheim Pharmaceuticals, Inc.
Cerebral Palsy Council
Federation of State Medical Boards of the U.S.
L.A. Care Health Plan
Massachusetts Medical Device Industry Council
San Francisco, California, City and County of

ALLEN, Ernest

699 Prince St.
Alexandria, VA 22314-3175
Tel: (703)235-3900
Fax: (703)274-2222

Employers
Nat'l Center for Missing and Exploited Children (President)

ALLEN, Fletcher

1776 I St. NW
Suite 1000
Washington, DC 20006
Tel: (202)785-4888
Fax: (202)457-6597
Registered: LDA

Employers
BP Amoco Corp. (Director, Government Affairs)

ALLEN, Jeremy W.

1875 I St. NW
12th Floor
Washington, DC 20006
Tel: (202)466-6550
Fax: (202)785-1756
Registered: LDA
EMail: jallen@ppsv.com
Former Legislative Fellow to Rep. Michael Bilirakis (R-FL).

Employers
Powers Pyles Sutter & Verville, PC (Legislative Director)

Clients Represented
On Behalf of Powers Pyles Sutter & Verville, PC
American Medical Rehabilitation Providers Ass'n

ALLEN, Kenneth B.

1010 N. Glebe Rd.
Suite 450
Arlington, VA 22201
EMail: kallen@nna.org
Tel: (703)907-7900
Fax: (703)907-7901

Employers
Nat'l Newspaper Ass'n (Exec. V. President and Chief Exec. Officer)

ALLEN, Kevin D.

1401 K St. NW
Suite 400
Washington, DC 20005
Tel: (202)789-2111
Fax: (202)789-4883
Registered: LDA, FARA
EMail: kallen@thewashingtongroup.com

Employers
The Washington Group (Senior V. President)

Clients Represented
On Behalf of The Washington Group
Korea Information & Communication, Ltd.
Microsoft Corp.
WinStar Internat'l

ALLEN, Lisa

1010 Wisconsin Ave. NW
Ninth Floor
Washington, DC 20007
EMail: lallen@gmabrands.com
Tel: (202)337-9400
Fax: (202)337-4508

Employers
Grocery Manufacturers of America (Director, Member Communications)

ALLEN, Margaret

1130 Connecticut Ave. NW
Suite 650
Washington, DC 20036
Tel: (202)822-8300
Fax: (202)832-8315
Registered: LDA

Employers
E. Del Smith and Co. (Legislative Director)

Clients Represented
On Behalf of E. Del Smith and Co.
Anaheim, California, City of
Anaheim, California, Public Utilities of the City of
Apple Valley, California, City of
Barstow, California, City of
Bioelectromagnetics Soc.
California Independent Petroleum Ass'n
Chino Hills, California, City of
Contra Costa, California, Tenants of the County of
Corte Madera, California, Town of
Downey, California, Economic Development of the City of
Hesperia, California, City of
Laguna Beach, California, City of
Long Beach Naval Shipyard Employees Ass'n
Long Beach Water Department
Long Beach, California, City of
Long Beach, California, Port of
Los Angeles, California, County of
Morro Bay, California, City of
Nat'l Independent Private Schools Ass'n
Port Hueneme, California, City of
Reusable Pallet and Container Coalition
Santa Barbara, California, City of (Waterfront)
Santa Barbara, California, Public Works Department
Santa Cruz, California, Port of
Victorville, California, City of
Woods Hole Oceanographic Institution

ALLEN, Marjorie D.

1625 L St. NW
Washington, DC 20036-5687
Tel: (202)429-1184
Fax: (202)223-3413
Registered: LDA
EMail: mallen@afscme.org

Employers
American Federation of State, County and Municipal Employees (Legislative Affairs Specialist)

ALLEN, Mark

1199 N. Fairfax St.
Suite 400
Alexandria, VA 22314
EMail: mark_allen@marketstrategies.com
Tel: (703)535-8505
Fax: (703)535-8517

Employers
Market Strategies Inc. (Washington Partner)

ALLEN, MaryLee

25 E St. NW
Washington, DC 20001
Tel: (202)628-8787
Fax: (202)662-3550
Registered: LDA

Employers
Children's Defense Fund (Director, Child Welfare and Mental Health)

ALLEN, Meghan

1025 Connecticut Ave. NW
Suite 501
Washington, DC 20036
EMail: meghan.allen@gencorp.com
Tel: (202)828-6800
Fax: (202)828-6849

Employers
GenCorp (Manager, Congressional Relations)

ALLEN, Michael

1101 15th St. NW
Suite 1212
Washington, DC 20005
Tel: (202)467-5730
Ext: 17
Fax: (202)223-0409
Registered: LDA
EMail: michaela@bazelon.org

Employers
Bazelon Center for Mental Health Law, Judge David L. (Staff Attorney, Housing Issues)

ALLEN, Nicole

701 Pennsylvania Ave. NW
Suite 750
Washington, DC 20004
Tel: (202)783-4400
Fax: (202)783-4410
Registered: LDA
EMail: ciab@ciab.com

Employers
The Council of Insurance Agents & Brokers (Director, State Affairs)

ALLEN, Pamela J.

122 C St. NW
Suite 540
Washington, DC 20001
Tel: (202)628-1558
Fax: (202)628-1601
Registered: LDA
EMail: pallen@namic.org

Employers
Nat'l Ass'n of Mutual Insurance Companies (V. President, Federal Affairs)

ALLEN, Richard A.

888 17th St. NW
Suite 600
Washington, DC 20006-3959
Tel: (202)298-8660
Fax: (202)342-0683
Registered: LDA
EMail: raallen@zsrlaw.com
General Counsel, Interstate Commerce Commission, 1979-82. Assistant to the Solicitor General, Department of Justice, 1976-79. Law Clerk to Judge Carl McGowan, U.S. Court of Appeals, District of Columbia Circuit, 1971.

Employers
Zuckert, Scoutt and Rasenberger, L.L.P. (Partner)

ALLEN, Robert F.

1901 L St. NW
Suite 500
Washington, DC 20036
Tel: (202)862-7200
Fax: (202)862-7230

Employers
Nat'l Railway Labor Conference (Chairman)

ALLEN, Susan Au

1329 18th St. NW
Washington, DC 20036
Tel: (202)296-5221
Fax: (202)296-5225

Employers
United States Pan Asian American Chamber of Commerce (President)

ALLEN, William A.

1090 Vermont Ave. NW
Suite 1100
Washington, DC 20005-4961
Tel: (202)789-3500
Fax: (202)789-6390

Employers
Joint Center for Political and Economic Studies (V. President for Development)

ALLGOOD, Annette Y.

2301 S. Jefferson Davis Hwy.
Buchanan Mall
Arlington, VA 22202
EMail: OUinDC@aol.com
Tel: (703)418-4800
Fax: (703)418-2730

Employers
University of Oklahoma (Operations Manager)

ALLGOOD, Lauren

Old Executive Office Bldg.
Room 276
Washington, DC 20501
Tel: (202)456-6647
Fax: (202)456-1606

Employers
Executive Office of the President - Office of the Vice President (Exec. Assistant for Legislative Affairs)

ALLINA, Amy

514 Tenth St. NW
Suite 400
Washington, DC 20004
Tel: (202)347-1140
Fax: (202)347-1168

Employers
Nat'l Women's Health Network (Program Director)

ALLINGER, Sharon

444 N. Capitol St. NW
Suite 625
Washington, DC 20001
Tel: (202)393-0860
Fax: (202)393-0864
Registered: LDA

Employers
Premier, Inc. (Federal Affairs Coordinator)

ALLIS, Stephen

2001 M St. NW
Washington, DC 20036
Tel: (202)467-3000
Fax: (202)533-8500
Registered: LDA

Employers
KPMG, LLP (Partner)

ALLISON, Kathy

8201 Greensboro Dr.
Suite 300
McLean, VA 22102
Tel: (703)610-9000
Fax: (703)610-9005

Employers
Ass'n Management Group

Clients Represented
On Behalf of Ass'n Management Group
Nat'l Ass'n of Retail Collection Attorneys

ALLISON, Richard G.

9650 Rockville Pike
Bethesda, MD 20814
EMail: allisonr@asns.faseb.org
Tel: (301)530-7050
Fax: (301)571-1892

Employers
American Soc. for Nutritional Sciences (Exec. Officer)

ALLMAN, Kim

1330 Connecticut Ave. NW
Suite 300
Washington, DC 20036
Tel: (202)775-0101
Fax: (202)775-7253

Employers
Recording Industry Ass'n of America (Director, Government Affairs)

ALLMAN, Tracey

600 Pennsylvania Ave. SE
Suite 330
Washington, DC 20003
Tel: (202)544-9815
Fax: (202)544-9816

Employers
American Ass'n of Political Consultants (Exec. Director)

ALLNUT, Bob

1615 L St. NW
Suite 900
Washington, DC 20036
EMail: ballnut@apcoworldwide.com
Tel: (202)778-1000
Fax: (202)466-6002

Employers
APCO Worldwide (Senior Counselor)

ALMEIDA, Paul E.

815 16th St. NW
Washington, DC 20006
Tel: (202)638-0320
Fax: (202)628-4379
Registered: LDA

Employers
AFL-CIO - Professional Employees Department (President)

ALMEIDA, Raymond A.

50 F St. NW
Suite 500
Washington, DC 20001
EMail: ralmeida@bread.org
Tel: (301)608-2400
Fax: (301)608-2401
Registered: LDA

Employers
Bread for the World (International Analyst)

ALMGREN, Kenneth D.

1771 N St. NW
Washington, DC 20036-2891
Tel: (202)429-5304
Fax: (202)429-3931

Employers
Nat'l Ass'n of Broadcasters (Exec. V. President and Chief Financial Officer)

ALMOND, Ben G.

1818 N St. NW
Eighth Floor
Washington, DC 20036
Tel: (202)293-1707

Employers
Cingular Wireless (Regulatory Affairs)

ALMOND, Charles L.

1455 Pennsylvania Ave. NW
Suite 700
Washington, DC 20004-1008
Tel: (202)639-6500
Fax: (202)639-6604
Registered: LDA

Employers
Vinson & Elkins L.L.P. (Partner)

Clients Represented
On Behalf of Vinson & Elkins L.L.P.
Greater Texas Student Loan Corp.
Texas Veterans Land Board

ALMSTEDT, Kermit W.

555 13th St. NW
Suite 500 West
Washington, DC 20004
EMail: kalmstedt@omm.com
Tel: (202)383-5300
Fax: (202)383-5414
Legislative Assistant to Senator John C. Danforth (R-MO), 1977-81. Trial Attorney, Antitrust Division, Department of Justice, 1970-71.

Employers
O'Melveny and Myers LLP (Partner)

ALMY, David W.

1200 18th St. NW
Suite 400
Washington, DC 20036-2506
EMail: dalmy@nbaa.org
Tel: (202)783-9000
Fax: (202)331-8364

Employers
Nat'l Business Aviation Ass'n (V. President, Strategic Program)

ALONGE, Shauna E.

1001 Pennsylvania Ave. NW
Suite 1100
Washington, DC 20004-2595
Tel: (202)624-2500
Fax: (202)628-5116
Attorney-Advisor, Department of the Navy, 1979-86.

Employers
Crowell & Moring LLP (Partner)

ALPERSTEIN, Brian

2121 K St. NW
Suite 800
Washington, DC 20037
Tel: (202)261-3520
Fax: (202)261-3523
Registered: LDA

Employers
Lasa, Monroig & Veve (Partner)

Clients Represented
On Behalf of Lasa, Monroig & Veve
Mendez University System, Ana G.

ALSOP, Ryan

1130 Connecticut Ave. NW
Suite 650
Washington, DC 20036
Tel: (202)822-8300
Fax: (202)822-8315
Registered: LDA

Employers
E. Del Smith and Co.

Clients Represented
On Behalf of E. Del Smith and Co.
Aquarium of the Pacific

ALSTON, Charles C.

600 Pennsylvania Ave. SE
Suite 400
Washington, DC 20003
EMail: calston@dlcppi.org
Tel: (202)546-0007
Fax: (202)544-5002

Employers
Democratic Leadership Council (Exec. Director)
Progressive Policy Institute (Exec. Director)

ALT, Kurt

P.O. Box 2789
Reston, VA 20195-0789
Tel: (703)435-2900
Fax: (703)435-2537

Employers
Hardwood Plywood and Veneer Ass'n (Director, Environmental Policy and Veneer Member Services)

ALT, Nicole

1849 C St. NW
Washington, DC 20240
Tel: (202)208-5403
Fax: (202)208-7059

Employers
Department of Interior - Fish and Wildlife Service (Legislative Specialist)

ALTAU, Karl S.

400 Hurley Ave.
Rockville, MD 20850
Tel: (301)340-1954
Fax: (301)309-1406
Registered: LDA

Employers
Joint Baltic American Nat'l Committee, Inc. (Managing Director)

ALTERMAN, Stephen A.

1220 19th St. NW
Suite 400
Washington, DC 20036
Tel: (202)466-8270
Fax: (202)293-4377
Chief, Legal Division, Bureau of Enforcement (1974-75) and Attorney (1968-73), Civil Aeronautics Board.

Employers
Meyers & Alterman (Partner)

ALTHEN, William I.

1110 Vermont Ave. NW
Suite 400
Washington, DC 20005
EMail: walthen@harlaw.com
Tel: (202)887-0800
Fax: (202)775-8518

Employers
Heenan, Althen & Roles (Partner)

Clients Represented
On Behalf of Heenan, Althen & Roles
American League of Lobbyists

ALTMAN, E. T.

P.O. Box 2789
Reston, VA 20195-0789
Tel: (703)435-2900
Fax: (703)435-2537

Employers
Hardwood Plywood and Veneer Ass'n (President)

ALTMAN, Emily

1300 I St. NW
12th Floor
Washington, DC 20005
Tel: (202)326-3980
Fax: (202)326-3981
Registered: LDA

Employers
Morgan Stanley Dean Witter & Co. (Principal, International Government Relations)

ALTMAN, Jeffrey P.

1900 K St. NW
Washington, DC 20006
Tel: (202)496-7500
Fax: (202)496-7756
EMail: jeff_altman@mckennacuneo.com

Employers
McKenna & Cuneo, L.L.P. (Partner)

Clients Represented

On Behalf of McKenna & Cuneo, L.L.P.
American Soc. of Clinical Pathologists

ALTMEYER, Thomas H.

1130 17th St. NW
Washington, DC 20036-4677
Tel: (202)463-2653
Fax: (202)833-1965
Registered: LDA
EMail: taltmeyer@nma.org

Employers
Nat'l Mining Ass'n (Senior V. President, Government Affairs)

ALTON, Kimberly

624 Ninth St. NW
Washington, DC 20425
Tel: (202)376-8317
Fax: (202)376-8315

Employers
Commission on Civil Rights (Interim Contact)

ALTROCCHI, Julia

1300 19th St. NW
Second Floor
Washington, DC 20036
Tel: (202)557-3400
Fax: (202)728-4177
Registered: LDA

Employers
Population Action Internat'l (Policy Analyst)

ALTSCHUL, Michael E.

1250 Connecticut Ave. NW
Suite 800
Washington, DC 20036
Tel: (202)785-0081
Fax: (202)785-0721
Registered: LDA
EMail: maltschul@ctia.org

Employers
Cellular Telecommunications and Internet Ass'n (Sr. V. President)

ALTSCHULER, Irwin P.

1501 M St. NW
Suite 700
Washington, DC 20005-1702
Tel: (202)463-4300
Fax: (202)463-4394
Registered: LDA, FARA
EMail: ialtschuler@manatt.com

Employers
Manatt, Phelps & Phillips, LLP (Partner)

Clients Represented

On Behalf of Manatt, Phelps & Phillips, LLP
Asociacion Columbiana de Exportadores de Flores (ASOCOLFLORES)
CEMEX Central, S.A. de C.V.
Servicios Corporativos Cintra SA de CV

ALUISE, Timothy J.

1050 17th St. NW
Suite 900
Washington, DC 20036
Tel: (202)466-5300
Fax: (202)466-5508
Registered: LDA
Assistant Clerk, U.S. Supreme Court, 1979.

Employers
Hessel and Aluise, P.C. (Principal)

Clients Represented

On Behalf of Hessel and Aluise, P.C.
Nat'l Cooperative Bank

ALUISI, Toni

1211 Connecticut Ave. NW
Suite 608
Washington, DC 20036
Tel: (202)496-1000
Fax: (202)496-1300
EMail: taluisi@qorvis.com

Employers
Qorvis Communications (Director)

ALVARADO, Audrey

1900 L St. NW
Suite 605
Washington, DC 20036
Tel: (202)467-6262
Fax: (202)467-6261

Employers
Nat'l Council of Nonprofit Ass'ns (Exec. Director)

ALVARADO, Susan E.

300 Third St. NE
Suite 204
Washington, DC 20002
Tel: (202)544-0003
Fax: (202)544-6635
Registered: LDA
Former Governor, U.S. Postal Service. Assistant for Legislative Affairs to the Vice President, The White House, 1980-83. Legislative Assistant to Senator Ted Stevens (R-AK), 1976-80.

Employers
Alvarado & Gerken (Partner)

Clients Represented

On Behalf of Alvarado & Gerken
Grumman Olson
Mas-Hamilton Group
MCI WorldCom Corp.
SAT
TransNat'l Business Development Corp.

ALVAREZ, Debra

601 E St. NW
Washington, DC 20049
Tel: (202)434-3800
Fax: (202)434-6477
Registered: LDA

Employers
AARP (American Ass'n of Retired Persons) (Legislative Specialist)

ALVAREZ, Diego

1301 Pennsylvania Ave. NW
Suite 400
Washington, DC 20004
Tel: (202)347-0915
Fax: (202)347-0919
EMail: dalvarez@cla.ci.la.ca.us

Employers
Los Angeles, California, Washington Office of the City of (Legislative Representative)

ALVAREZ, Sharyn

12th and Independence Ave. SW
Room 5121, South Bldg.
Washington, DC 20250
Tel: (202)720-2771
Fax: (202)690-0854

Employers
Department of Agriculture - Natural Resources Conservation Service (Legislative Research Specialist)

AMADOR, Angelo

1717 K St. NW
Suite 311
Washington, DC 20036
Tel: (202)293-2828
Fax: (202)293-2849
Registered: LDA

Employers
Mexican-American Legal Defense and Educational Fund (Policy Analyst)

AMBACH, Gordon M.

One Massachusetts Ave. NW
Suite 700
Washington, DC 20001-1431
Tel: (202)408-5505
Fax: (202)408-8072

Employers
Council of Chief State School Officers (Exec. Director)

AMBERSON, Michele

2000 K St. NW
Suite 801
Washington, DC 20006
Tel: (202)789-2424
Fax: (202)789-1818
EMail: amberson@akerpartners.com
Former Press Officer, Environmental Protection Agency and Department of Health and Human Services, during the Clinton administration. Also worked for V. President Gore.

Employers
The Aker Partners Inc. (Associate Partner)

AMBROSE, John

1133 15th St. NW
Suite 300
Washington, DC 20005
Tel: (202)452-0109
Fax: (202)223-2329
Registered: LDA
EMail: jambrose@aamft.org

Employers
American Ass'n for Marriage and Family Therapy (Director, Legal and Government Affairs)

AMERINE, David R.

1501 M St. NW
Suite 700
Washington, DC 20005-1702
Tel: (202)463-4300
Fax: (202)463-4394
EMail: damerine@manatt.com
Attorney, Office of General Counsel, Department of Commerce, 1980-81. Attorney, Office of Regulations and Rulings, U.S. Customs Service, Department of the Treasury, 1978-79.

Employers
Manatt, Phelps & Phillips, LLP (Partner)

AMES, Matthew C.

1155 Connecticut Ave. NW
Suite 1000
Washington, DC 20036-4306
Tel: (202)785-0600
Fax: (202)785-1234
EMail: mames@millervaneaton.com

Employers
Miller & Van Eaton, P.L.L.C. (Director)

Clients Represented

On Behalf of Miller & Van Eaton, P.L.L.C.
Building Owners and Managers Ass'n Internat'l
Nat'l Apartment Ass'n
Nat'l Multi-Housing Council
Real Estate Roundtable
Tulsa, Oklahoma, City of

AMES, Robert G.

1201 New York Ave. NW
Suite 1000
Washington, DC 20005
Tel: (202)962-4840
Fax: (202)962-8300
EMail: rgames@venable.com

Employers
Venable (Partner)

AMIDZICH, Gail

750 17th St. NW
Room 819
Washington, DC 20503
Tel: (202)395-5595
Fax: (202)395-6708

Employers
Executive Office of the President - Office of Nat'l Drug Control Policy (Assistant Director, Office of Legislative Affairs)

AMITAY, Michael P.

605 G St. SW
Washington, DC 20024
Tel: (202)484-0140
Fax: (202)484-0142

Employers
Washington Kurdish Institute (Exec. Director)

AMITAY, Morris J.

444 N. Capitol St. NW
Suite 712
Washington, DC 20001
Tel: (202)347-6613
Fax: (202)393-7006
Registered: LDA
Director, American-Israel Public Affairs Committee, 1975-80. Former Senior Legislative Aide to Senator Abraham Ribicoff (D-CT), 1970-74. Foreign Service Officer, Department of State, 1962-69.

Employers
Morris J. Amitay, P.C. (President)
Jewish Institute for Nat'l Security Affairs (V. Chair)
Washington Political Action Committee (Treasurer/Administrator)

Clients Represented

On Behalf of Morris J. Amitay, P.C.
Advantage Healthplan Inc.
Israel Aircraft Industries, Ltd.
Lau Technologies
Northrop Grumman Corp.
TRW Space and Electronics Group
Washington Political Action Committee

AMITAY, Stephen D.

444 N. Capitol St. NW
Suite 712
Washington, DC 20001
Tel: (202)347-6613
Fax: (202)393-7006
Registered: LDA
Staff member, Defense Technology Security Administration, Department of Defense, 1992. Professional Staff Member, Subcommittee on General Service and Federalism, Senate Governmental Affairs Committee, 1987-90.

Employers
Morris J. Amitay, P.C. (Of Counsel)
Federal Legislative Associates, Inc. (Associate)

Clients Represented

On Behalf of Morris J. Amitay, P.C.
Advantage Healthplan Inc.

On Behalf of Federal Legislative Associates, Inc.
Commercial Finance Ass'n
Document Authentification System
FIRSTPLUS Financial Group Inc.
PenOp Inc.
Religious Technology Center
TV Radio Now Corp. (i Crave TV)

AMO, Dylan

1111 19th St. NW
Suite 800
Washington, DC 20036
Tel: (202)463-2779
Fax: (202)463-2424

Employers
American Forest & Paper Ass'n (PAC Manager)

AMOR, Adlai

Ten G St. NE
Suite 800
Washington, DC 20002
Tel: (202)729-7736
Fax: (202)729-7610

Employers
World Resources Institute (Director, Media Relations)

AMSELLE, Anna

2500 Wilson Blvd.
Suite 300
Arlington, VA 22201
EMail: aamselle@tia.eia.org
Tel: (703)907-7732
Fax: (703)907-7727

Employers
Telecommunications Industry Ass'n (V. President, Finance)

AMTETTI, Rosemary I.

4121 Wilson Blvd.
11th Floor
Arlington, VA 22203
Tel: (703)258-0000
Fax: (703)258-0001

Employers
Craver, Mathews, Smith and Co. (President)

AMUNDSON, Jan S.

1331 Pennsylvania Ave. NW
Sixth Floor
Washington, DC 20004-1790
EMail: jamundson@nam.org
Tel: (202)637-3059
Fax: (202)637-3024

Employers
Nat'l Ass'n of Manufacturers (V. President, Law Department and General Counsel)

AMUNDSON, Sara Jane

227 Massachusetts Ave. NE
Suite 100
Washington, DC 20002
EMail: info@ddal.org
Tel: (202)546-1761
Fax: (202)546-2193

Employers
Doris Day Animal League (Deputy Director)

ANABLE, David

1616 H St. NW
Third Floor
Washington, DC 20006
Tel: (202)737-3700
Fax: (202)737-0530

Employers
Internat'l Center for Journalists (President)

ANAYA, Bill

1350 I St. NW
Suite 400
Washington, DC 20005-3306
Tel: (202)371-6900
Fax: (202)842-3578
Registered: LDA

Employers
Motorola, Inc. (Manager, Federal Legislative Relations)

ANDAHAZY, William J.

106 North Carolina Ave. SE
Washington, DC 20003
Tel: (202)863-0001
Fax: (202)863-0096
Registered: LDA

Employers
Ervin Technical Associates, Inc. (ETA)

Clients Represented

On Behalf of Ervin Technical Associates, Inc. (ETA)
ACS Defense, Inc.
Computer Coalition for Responsible Exports
Ingalls Shipbuilding
Lister Bolt & Chain Co.
Lockheed Martin Corp.
Sarnoff Corp.
Science Applications Internat'l Corp. (SAIC)
United Defense, L.P.
Video Network Communications

ANDERS, Christopher

122 Maryland Ave. NE
Washington, DC 20002
Tel: (202)544-1681
Fax: (202)546-0738

Employers
American Civil Liberties Union (Legislative Counsel, Gay and Lesbian Issues)

ANDERS, Jeffrey M.

1615 L St. NW
Suite 650
Washington, DC 20036
Tel: (202)659-0979
Fax: (202)659-3010
Registered: LDA

Employers
Self-employed as an independent consultant.

Clients Represented

As an independent consultant
Cephalon, Inc.
UniServe Inc.

ANDERS, Michele

1300 I St. NW
Suite 1000 West
Washington, DC 20005
EMail: mander@rcra.com
Tel: (202)962-8531
Fax: (202)962-8542
Registered: LDA

Employers
The Technical Group LLC (Senior Consultant)

Clients Represented

On Behalf of The Technical Group LLC
RSR Corp.

ANDERSON, Anthony A.

700 14th St. NW
Suite 900
Washington, DC 20005
Tel: (202)508-1000
Fax: (202)508-1010
Registered: LDA

Attorney Advisor, Legislation and Regulations Division, Office of the Chief Counsel, Urban Mass Transportation Administration, 1980-84.

Employers
Thompson Coburn LLP (Partner)

ANDERSON, Bill

1750 New York Ave. NW
Washington, DC 20006
EMail: banderson@ibpat.org
Tel: (202)637-0738
Fax: (202)637-0755
Registered: LDA

Employers
Internat'l Union of Painters and Allied Trades (Assistant to the General President)

ANDERSON, Brenda G.

601 Pennsylvania Ave. NW
Suite 540
North Bldg.
Washington, DC 20004
EMail: bgfleming@ashland.com
Tel: (202)223-8290
Fax: (202)293-2913
Registered: LDA

Employers
Ashland Inc. (Washington Representative)

ANDERSON, Brian

555 13th St. NW
Suite 500 West
Washington, DC 20004
EMail: banderson@omm.com
Tel: (202)383-5300
Fax: (202)383-5414
Registered: LDA

Employers
O'Melveny and Myers LLP (Partner)

ANDERSON, Brooke

1747 Pennsylvania Ave. NW
7th Floor
Washington, DC 20006
Tel: (202)296-4810
Fax: (202)296-4811

Formerly served in the National Security Council and the Department of Energy.

Employers
Nuclear Threat Initiative (V. President for Communications)

ANDERSON, Bryan D.

800 Connecticut Ave. NW
Suite 711
Washington, DC 20006
EMail: bryananderson@na.ko.com
Tel: (202)973-2663
Fax: (202)466-2262
Registered: LDA

Employers
The Coca-Cola Company (Director, Government Relations)

ANDERSON, Byron E.

1101 Pennsylvania Ave. NW
Suite 515
Washington, DC 20004
Tel: (202)628-4600
Fax: (202)628-5410
Registered: LDA

Aide to Senator William Armstrong (R-CO), 1978-80 and to Rep. Stanford Parris (R-VA), 1981-85.

Employers
American General Corp. (Sr. V. President, Government Affairs)

ANDERSON, Caroline

600 Maryland Ave. SW
Suite 800
Washington, DC 20024
Tel: (202)484-3600
Fax: (202)484-3604
Registered: LDA

Employers
American Farm Bureau Federation (Director, Dairy Livestock, Poultry, and Aquaculture)

ANDERSON, Corinne

5422 Second St. NW
Washington, DC 20011
Tel: (202)723-8182
Fax: (202)723-8182

Employers
Nat'l Federation of Democratic Women (President)

ANDERSON, Curtis M.

1156 15th St. NW
Suite 1020
Washington, DC 20005
EMail: curtis@nasda-hq.org
Tel: (202)296-9680
Fax: (202)296-9686

Secretary to the Board, Farm Credit Administration, 1990-94; Attorney-Advisor, Department of the Interior, 1988-90.

Employers
Nat'l Ass'n of State Departments of Agriculture (Chief Financial Officer)

ANDERSON, Darryl J.

1300 L St. NW
Suite 1200
Washington, DC 20005-4178
Tel: (202)898-1707
Fax: (202)682-9276

Counsel, Senate Committee on Labor and Human Resources, 1977-82. Law Clerk to Judge Wade H. McCree, Jr., U.S. Court of Appeals, Sixth Circuit, 1970-72.

Employers
O'Donnell, Schwartz & Anderson, P.C. (President)

Clients Represented

On Behalf of O'Donnell, Schwartz & Anderson, P.C.
American Postal Workers Union

ANDERSON, LTC (P) Dave

The Pentagon
Room 2C631
Washington, DC 20310-1600
Tel: (703)695-3524
Fax: (703)614-7599

Employers
Department of Army (Exec. Officer)

ANDERSON, Heidi

2020 K St. NW
Suite 400
Washington, DC 20006
EMail: handerso@telcordia.com
Tel: (202)776-5464
Fax: (202)776-5424

Employers
Telcordia Technologies, Inc. (Director, Government Affairs)

ANDERSON, Jr., James A.

1725 K St. NW
Suite 300
Washington, DC 20006
Tel: (202)872-0885
Fax: (202)296-5940
Registered: LDA

Employers
Nat'l Ass'n of Wholesaler-Distributors (V. President, Government Relations)

ANDERSON, James E.

1747 Pennsylvania Ave. NW
Suite 1050
Washington, DC 20006
EMail: janderson@haspc.com
Tel: (202)296-5680
Fax: (202)331-8049

Assistant U.S. Attorney for the District of Maryland (1970-76) and Special Agent, Federal Bureau of Investigation (1967-70), Department of Justice.

Employers
Howe, Anderson & Steyer, P.C. (Partner)

Clients Represented

On Behalf of Howe, Anderson & Steyer, P.C.
Greater Washington Soc. of Ass'n Executives
Wire Reinforcement Institute

ANDERSON, Jason

1420 New York Ave. NW
Suite 1050
Washington, DC 20005
Tel: (202)638-1950
Fax: (202)638-7714
Registered: LDA

Employers
Van Scoyoc Associates, Inc.

Clients Represented

On Behalf of Van Scoyoc Associates, Inc.
Glankler Brown, PLLC

ANDERSON, Jeannette

1500 King St.
Suite 301
Alexandria, VA 22314-2730
EMail: janderson@peanutsusa.com
Tel: (703)838-9500
Fax: (703)838-9089

Employers
American Peanut Council (President)

ANDERSON, Jeffrey

1331 Pennsylvania Ave. NW
Suite 1300 North
Washington, DC 20004
EMail: jeff.anderson@eds.com
Tel: (202)637-6724
Fax: (202)637-6759

Employers
EDS Corp. (Director, International Relations)

ANDERSON, Dr. John A.

1333 H St. NW
West Tower
Eighth Floor
Washington, DC 20005
EMail: elcon@elcon.org
Tel: (202)682-1390
Fax: (202)289-6370
Registered: LDA

Employers
Electricity Consumers Resource Council (ELCON) (Exec. Director)

ANDERSON, Hon. John B.

420 Seventh St. SE
Washington, DC 20003
Tel: (202)546-3950
Fax: (202)546-3749

Member, U.S. House of Representatives (R-IL), 1961-1981.

Employers
The Center for Voting and Democracy (President)
World Federalist Ass'n (Exec. Director)

ANDERSON, Judith

2500 Wilson Blvd.
Suite 300
Arlington, VA 22201
EMail: janderson@tia.eia.org
Tel: (703)907-7551
Fax: (703)907-7727

Employers
Telecommunications Industry Ass'n (Staff Director, International Standards)

ANDERSON, Karen

701 Pennsylvania Ave. NW
Suite 600
Washington, DC 20004
Tel: (202)624-1246
Fax: (202)624-1298
Registered: LDA
EMail: kanderson@lanlaw.com

Congressional Liaison, Region 2 Office, Environmental Protection Agency, 1997-98. Regional Coordinator, Office of Political Affairs, Exec. Office of the President, The White House, 1993-95.

Employers
Long, Aldridge & Norman, LLP (Public Policy Advisor)

Clients Represented

On Behalf of Long, Aldridge & Norman, LLP
AFLAC, Inc.
BellSouth Corp.
Biotechnology Industry Organization
Monsanto Co.

ANDERSON, Kathryn L.

1700 Pennsylvania Ave. NW
Suite 500
Washington, DC 20006-4771
Tel: (202)393-6200
Fax: (202)639-8808
Registered: LDA
EMail: kathy.anderson@mutualofomaha.com

Employers
Mutual of Omaha Insurance Companies (Manager, Federal Government Affairs)

ANDERSON, Kevin D.

1120 20th St. NW
Suite 725
Washington, DC 20007
Tel: (202)822-9822
Fax: (202)822-9808
Registered: LDA

Employers
Nat'l Club Ass'n (V. President, Legal and Government Relations)

ANDERSON, Kristen

1400 I St. NW
Suite 850
Washington, DC 20005
EMail: kanderson@mentoring.org
Tel: (202)729-4373
Fax: (202)729-4341

Employers
Nat'l Mentoring Partnership, Inc. (Project Manager, Government Relations)

ANDERSON, Larry

815 16th St. NW
Washington, DC 20006
Tel: (202)637-5000
Fax: (202)637-5058

Employers
AFL-CIO (American Federation of Labor and Congress of Industrial Organizations) (Director, Support Services)

ANDERSON, Lori M.

1801 K St. NW
Suite 600K
Washington, DC 20006
Tel: (202)371-5281
Fax: (202)296-7218
Registered: LDA

Employers
Soc. of the Plastics Industry (Director, Economic and International Trade Affairs)

ANDERSON, M. Jean

1615 L St. NW
Suite 700
Washington, DC 20036-5610
Tel: (202)682-7000
Fax: (202)857-0939
Registered: LDA
EMail: jean.anderson@weil.cm

Chief Counsel for International Trade (1986-88) and Senior Trade Advisor and Special Counsel to the Undersecretary for International Trade (1982-86), Department of Commerce.

Employers
Weil, Gotshal & Manges, LLP (Partner)

ANDERSON, Mahlon G.

12600 Fair Lakes Circle
Fairfax, VA 22033-4904
Tel: (703)222-4100
Fax: (703)802-8621

Employers
AAA MidAtlantic (Director, Public and Government Relations)

ANDERSON, Mark A.

815 16th St. NW
Washington, DC 20006
Tel: (202)737-7200
Fax: (202)737-7208

Employers
AFL-CIO - Food and Allied Service Trades Department (President)

ANDERSON, Mark I.

1225 I St. NW
Suite 601
Washington, DC 20005
EMail: markanderson@hillintl.com
Tel: (202)408-3000
Fax: (202)408-3058

Employers
Hill Internat'l, Inc. (Senior V. President)

ANDERSON, Mark R.

1025 Connecticut Ave. NW
Suite 1210
Washington, DC 20036
Tel: (202)296-1950
Fax: (202)296-2873
Registered: LDA

Employers
United Airlines (Senior Director, Federal Affairs)

ANDERSON, Col. Michael

1160 Air Force Pentagon
Room 5D927
Washington, DC 20330-1160
Tel: (703)697-7950

Employers
Department of Air Force (Chief, Programs and Legislation Division, Legislative Liaison)

ANDERSON, Pamela Jo

1050 Thomas Jefferson St. NW
Seventh Floor
Washington, DC 20007
EMail: pja@vnf.com
Tel: (202)298-1800
Fax: (202)338-2416

Employers
Van Ness Feldman, P.C. (Member)

ANDERSON, Philmore B.

1001 Pennsylvania Ave. NW
Washington, DC 20004-2599
Tel: (202)624-2000
Fax: (202)624-2319
Registered: LDA

Employers
American Council of Life Insurers (V. President, Federal Relations)

ANDERSON, Rebecca L.

1155 21st St. NW
Suite 300
Washington, DC 20036
Tel: (202)659-8201
Fax: (202)659-5249
Registered: LDA

Administrative Assistant, White House Office of Legislative Affairs, 1988-92; Administrative Assistant, White House Legislative Affairs Senate, 1986-88.

Employers
Williams & Jensen, P.C. (Director, Government Affairs)

Clients Represented

On Behalf of Williams & Jensen, P.C.
Aegon USA
American Share Insurance
Internat'l Ass'n of Amusement Parks and Attractions

ANDERSON, Rennie

1101 14th St. NW
Suite 1400
Washington, DC 20005
Tel: (202)682-9400
Fax: (202)682-1331

Employers
Defenders of Wildlife (International Associate)

ANDERSON, Richard F.

6035 Burke Centre Pkwy.
Suite 360
Burke, VA 22015
Tel: (703)250-9042
Fax: (703)239-9042
Registered: LDA

Employers
Council of Industrial Boiler Owners (CIBO)

ANDERSON, Serena

1300 I St. NW
Suite 470 East
Washington, DC 20005
EMail: sanderson@amgen.com
Tel: (202)354-6100
Fax: (202)289-7448

Employers
Amgen (Associate Director, Public Policy)

ANDERSON, Stanton D.

2121 K St. NW
Suite 650
Washington, DC 20037
Tel: (202)296-2400
Fax: (202)296-2409
Registered: LDA, FARA
Deputy Assistant Secretary, Department of State, 1973-75. Staff Assistant to the President, Executive Office of the President, The White House, 1971-73.

Employers
Global USA, Inc. (Chairman)
McDermott, Will and Emery (Partner)

Clients Represented
On Behalf of McDermott, Will and Emery
Electronic Industries Ass'n of Japan
Government Development Bank of Puerto Rico

ANDERSON, USA (Ret), Lt. Col. Stephen P.

One Constitution Ave. NE
Washington, DC 20002
EMail: sanderson@roa.org
Tel: (202)479-2200
Fax: (202)479-0416
Registered: LDA

Employers
Reserve Officers Ass'n of the U.S. (Legislative Counsel)

ANDERSON, Steven C.

1200 17th St. NW
Washington, DC 20036-3097
Tel: (202)331-5900
Fax: (202)973-5373

Employers
Nat'l Restaurant Ass'n (President and Chief Exec. Officer)

ANDERSON, Susan L.

1320 19th St. NW
Suite M-1
Washington, DC 20036
Tel: (202)293-0222
Fax: (202)293-0202
Registered: LDA

Employers
Public Campaign (Washington Director)

ANDERSON, Sylvia

1801 L St. NW
MS: 9317
Washington, DC 20507
Tel: (202)663-4900
Fax: (202)663-4912

Employers
Equal Employment Opportunity Commission (Assistant Director, Legislative Affairs)

ANDERSON, Terje

1413 K St. NW
Seventh Floor
Washington, DC 20005-3442
EMail: tanderson@napwa.org
Tel: (202)898-0414
Fax: (202)898-0435
Registered: LDA

Employers
Nat'l Ass'n of People with AIDS, Inc. (Exec. Director)

ANDERSON, Tobyn J.

1200 18th St. NW
Suite 850
Washington, DC 20036
EMail: tanderson@lighthouse-energy.com
Tel: (202)822-2000
Fax: (202)822-2156
Registered: LDA
Legislative Assistant and Legislative Director to Senator Kent Conrad (D-ND), 1987-91.

Employers
Lighthouse Energy Group LLC (V. President)

Clients Represented
On Behalf of Lighthouse Energy Group LLC
Alliance Pipeline, L.P.
Ballard Power Systems
The Beacon Group Energy Funds
Calpine Corp.
Coleman Powermate
PowerGen
Powerspan Corp.

ANDERSON, Todd

2550 M St. NW
Washington, DC 20037-1350
Tel: (202)457-6000
Fax: (202)457-6315
Registered: LDA

Employers
Patton Boggs, LLP (Associate)

Clients Represented
On Behalf of Patton Boggs, LLP
Clayton College of Natural Health
Crane Co.

ANDERSON, Van

22377 Belmont Ridge Rd.
Asburn, VA 20148
EMail: vanderson@nrpa.org
Tel: (703)858-0784
Fax: (703)858-0794

Employers
Nat'l Recreation and Park Ass'n (Director, Professional Services)

ANDERSON, II, William A.

1400 L St. NW
Washington, DC 20005-3502
Tel: (202)371-5986
Fax: (202)371-5950
Registered: LDA

Employers
Winston & Strawn (Partner, Environmental Practice)

Clients Represented
On Behalf of Winston & Strawn
Murphy Oil U.S.A.

ANDREAE, III, Charles N.

1250 I St. NW
Suite 1105
Washington, DC 20005
EMail: chip@avallc.com
Tel: (202)682-5151
Fax: (202)682-2185
Legislative Assistant (1977-80) and Executive Assistant (1980-80) to Senator Richard Lugar (R-IN). Administrative Assistant to Senator Richard Lugar (R-IN), 1984-89. Staff Member, Senate Select Committee on Intelligence, 1981-84.

Employers
Andreae, Vick & Associates, L.L.C. (Partner)

Clients Represented
On Behalf of Andreae, Vick & Associates, L.L.C.
U.S. Colombia Business Partnership

ANDRES, Gary J.

412 First St. SE
Suite 100
Washington, DC 20003
EMail: gandres@dutkogroup.com
Tel: (202)484-4884
Fax: (202)484-0109
Registered: LDA
Deputy Assistant to the President for Legislative Affairs, The White House, 1989-93. Former Legislative Assistant to Rep. Carlos Moorhead (R-CA) and to Rep. Tom Corcoran (R-IL).

Employers
The Dutko Group, Inc. (Senior Managing Partner)

Clients Represented
On Behalf of The Dutko Group, Inc.
Accenture
Alcatel USA
America's Community Bankers
Distilled Spirits Council of the United States, Inc.
FedEx Corp.
Food Distributors Internat'l (NAWGA-IFDA)
Household Internat'l, Inc.
Nat'l Ground Water Ass'n
Oregon Garden Foundation
PacifiCare Health Systems
PlanetRx
Prudential Securities, Inc.
Sprint Corp.
Union Pacific

ANDRES, Susan Auther

600 13th St. NW
Suite 340
Washington, DC 20005
Tel: (202)662-0100
Fax: (202)662-0199
Registered: LDA

Employers
Union Pacific (Director, Washington Affairs - Transportation)

ANDREW, Anne Slaughter

2550 M St. NW
Washington, DC 20037-1350
Tel: (202)457-6000
Fax: (202)457-6315

Employers
Patton Boggs, LLP (Partner)

ANDREW, Frances L.

1021 Prince St.
Alexandria, VA 22314-2971
EMail: fandrew@nmha@org
Tel: (703)684-7722
Fax: (703)684-5968
Registered: LDA

Employers
Nat'l Mental Health Ass'n (Assistant Director, Legislative Affairs)

ANDREWS, Beverly

1725 Jefferson Davis Hwy.
Crystal Square 2, Suite 300
Arlington, VA 22202
Tel: (703)413-5600
Fax: (703)413-5617

Employers
Lockheed Martin Corp. (Director, International Relations and Trade)

ANDREWS, Bruce H.

1133 Connecticut Ave. NW
Fifth Floor
Washington, DC 20036
Tel: (202)457-1110
Fax: (202)457-1130
Registered: LDA
Former Legislative Director, Rep. Tim Holden (D-PA).

Employers
Quinn Gillespie & Associates (Associate)

Clients Represented
On Behalf of Quinn Gillespie & Associates
American Hospital Ass'n
Instinet
LVMH Moet Hennessy Louis Vuitton S.A.
Technology Network
USEC, Inc.

ANDREWS, Cliff W.

1301 Pennsylvania Ave. NW
Suite 500
Washington, DC 20004
EMail: candrews@butera-andrews.com
Tel: (202)347-6875
Fax: (202)347-6876
Registered: LDA
Staff Assistant to Sen. Harry Reid (D-NV), 1996.

Employers
Butera & Andrews (Legislative Director)

Clients Represented
On Behalf of Butera & Andrews
Advanta Corp.
American Council of State Savings Supervisors
Bluebonnet Savings Bank
Charter One
Citizens Bank
Coalition to Amend the Financial Information Privacy Act (CAFPA)
Committee to Preserve Aspen
Community Banks Ass'n of New York State
Community Preservation Corp.
Countrywide Mortgage Corp.
Derivatives Net, Inc.
Dime Savings Bank of New York
Federal Home Loan Bank of Boston
Federal Home Loan Bank of Topeka
Federation for American Immigration Reform (FAIR)
FM Watch
FRANMAC/Taco Pac
Independence Bank
Internat'l Swaps and Derivatives Dealers Ass'n
Luse Lehman Gorman Pomerenk & Schick, P.C.
Nat'l Home Equity Mortgage Ass'n
Option One Mortgage Corp.
Pedestal
Savings Banks Life Insurance Fund
Silver, Freedman & Taff
Soc. for Human Resource Management
Superior Bank, FSB
Texas Savings and Community Bankers
USPA & IRA

ANDREWS, Gregory B.

1000 Connecticut Ave. NW
Suite 302
Washington, DC 20036
EMail: Grega@sda-inc.com
Tel: (202)835-0740
Fax: (202)775-8526
Registered: LDA, FARA

Employers
Smith Dawson & Andrews, Inc.

Clients Represented
On Behalf of Smith Dawson & Andrews, Inc.
Alston & Bird, LLP
Ceiba, Puerto Rico, City of
Certified Automotive Parts Ass'n
George Washington University, Office of Government Relations
Georgia Municipal Gas Ass'n
Georgia, State of
Hillwood Development Corp.
Japan, Embassy of
Litton Advanced Systems
Litton Systems, Inc.
Mothers Against Drunk Driving (MADD)
San Francisco Internat'l Airport
Springfield, Oregon, School District #19
Wound Ostomy Continence Nurses

ANDREWS, James H.

1150 18th St. NW
Suite 200
Washington, DC 20036
Tel: (202)223-0820
Fax: (202)223-2385
Registered: LDA

Employers
Kellogg Brown and Root (V. President)

ANDREWS, Hon. Mark

2550 M St. NW
Suite 250
Washington, DC 20037
Tel: (202)457-5671
Fax: (202)785-0480
Registered: LDA
Member, U.S Senate (R-ND), 1981-87. Member, U.S. House of Representatives, 1963-81.

Employers
Andrews Associates, Inc. (Chairman)

Clients Represented
On Behalf of Andrews Associates, Inc.
Mars, Inc.
Nat'l Trailer Dealers Ass'n
Patton Boggs, LLP
Safeguard America's Family Enterprises

ANDREWS, Hon. Michael A.

1455 Pennsylvania Ave. NW
Suite 700
Washington, DC 20004-1008
Tel: (202)639-6500
Fax: (202)639-6604
Registered: LDA
EMail: mandrews@velaw.com
Member, House of Representatives (D-TX), 1983-94. Law Clerk, U.S. District Court for the Southern District of Texas, 1971-72.

Employers
Vinson & Elkins L.L.P. (Partner)

Clients Represented
On Behalf of Vinson & Elkins L.L.P.
7-Eleven, Inc.
Kansas City Southern Industries
Lincoln Property Co.
Nat'l Ass'n of Settlement Purchasers
Portland General Electric Co.
Southdown, Inc.
Texas A&M University System
University of Texas - Houston Health Science Center

ANDREWS, Nicole

1341 G St. NW
Suite 1100
Washington, DC 20005
Tel: (202)393-2260
Fax: (202)393-0712

Employers
Infotech Strategies, Inc. (Account Supervisor)

ANDREWS, Sarah

1718 Connecticut Ave. NW
Suite 200
Washington, DC 20009
Tel: (202)483-1140
Fax: (202)483-1248

Employers
Electronic Privacy Information Center (Policy Analyst)

ANDREWS, Jr., Wright H.

1301 Pennsylvania Ave. NW
Suite 500
Washington, DC 20004
Tel: (202)347-6875
Fax: (202)628-4426
Registered: LDA
EMail: wandrews@butera-andrews.com
Chief Legislative Assistant to Senator Sam Nunn (D-GA), 1973-75.

Employers
Butera & Andrews (Partner)

Clients Represented
On Behalf of Butera & Andrews
Advanta Corp.
British Nuclear Fuels plc
Charter One
Citizens Bank
Coalition to Amend the Financial Information Privacy Act (CAFPA)
Committee to Preserve Aspen
Community Banks Ass'n of New York State
Derivatives Net, Inc.
Dime Savings Bank of New York
Federal Home Loan Bank of Boston
Federal Home Loan Bank of Topeka
Federation for American Immigration Reform (FAIR)
FM Watch
FRANMAC/Taco Pac
Independence Bank
Internat'l Swaps and Derivatives Dealers Ass'n
Luse Lehman Gorman Pomerenk & Schick, P.C.
Nat'l Home Equity Mortgage Ass'n
Option One Mortgage Corp.
Pedestal
Peoples Bank
Rent-a-Center, Inc.
Savings Banks Life Insurance Fund
Silver, Freedman & Taff
Soc. for Human Resource Management
Superior Bank, FSB
Texas Savings and Community Bankers
USPA & IRA

ANDRICOS, Mike

1600 Pennsylvania Ave. NW
Room 375
Washington, DC 20500
Tel: (202)456-9171
Fax: (202)456-9170

Employers
Executive Office of the President - Nat'l Security Council (Director, Legislative Affairs)

ANDRINGA, Dr. Robert C.

321 Eighth St. NE
Washington, DC 20002
Tel: (202)546-8713
Fax: (202)546-8913
EMail: randringa@cccu.org

Employers
Council for Christian College and Universities (President)

ANDROSS, Susan

Wilbur G. Cohen Bldg.
330 Independence Ave. SW, Room 3360
Washington, DC 20547
Tel: (202)401-3736
Fax: (202)401-6605

Employers
Broadcasting Board of Governors (Congressional and External Affairs Coordinator)

ANDRUKITIS, Barbara C.

50 E St. SE
Washington, DC 20003
Tel: (202)546-2600
Fax: (202)484-1979
Registered: LDA

Employers
Kendall and Associates (President)

ANENBERG, Scott A.

2300 N St. NW
Washington, DC 20037-1128
Tel: (202)663-8000
Fax: (202)663-8007
Registered: LDA
EMail: scott.anenbert@shawpittman.com

Employers
Shaw Pittman (Partner)

Clients Represented
On Behalf of Shaw Pittman
Ass'n of Banks of Israel
Bank Leumi le-Israel B.M.
Chevy Chase Bank, F.S.B.

ANGAROLA, Christina

600 New Hampshire Ave. NW
Suite 601
Washington, DC 20037
Tel: (202)333-7400
Fax: (202)333-1638

Employers
Hill and Knowlton, Inc.

Clients Represented
On Behalf of Hill and Knowlton, Inc.
Motorola, Inc.

ANGEL, Usbaldo

1710 Rhode Island Ave. NW
Tenth Floor
Washington, DC 20036
EMail: uangel@rofgw.com
Tel: (202)973-2989
Fax: (202)293-3307

Employers
Rodriguez O'Donnell Fuerst Gonzalez & Williams (Associate)

ANGELIER, Amy

1300 N. 17th St.
Eighth Floor
Arlington, VA 22209
Tel: (703)812-2000
Fax: (703)812-8202
Registered: LDA
EMail: angelier@abc.org

Employers
Coalition to Repeal the Davis-Bacon Act (Washington Representative)

ANGELL, Margaret

1775 Pennsylvania Ave. NW
Suite 200
Washington, DC 20006
Tel: (202)862-1000
Fax: (202)862-1093
Registered: LDA

Employers
Dewey Ballantine LLP (Semiconductor Policy Specialist)

Clients Represented
On Behalf of Dewey Ballantine LLP
Semiconductor Industry Ass'n

ANGELL, Phillip S.

1250 24th St. NW
Suite 300
Washington, DC 20037
Tel: (703)326-8221
Fax: (202)466-6249

Employers
HearingRoom.com (Chairman)

ANGIOLILLO, Katherine M.

909 N. Washington St.
Suite 300
Alexandria, VA 22314
Tel: (703)548-5568
Fax: (703)684-3258
Registered: LDA

Employers
TREA Senior Citizens League (TSCL) (Deputy Legislative Director)

ANGLE, Robin

11350 Random Hills Rd.
Suite 800
Fairfax, VA 22030
Tel: (703)620-1365
Fax: (703)620-4709
Registered: LDA
EMail: rangle@cpiva.com

Employers
Capital Partnerships (VA) Inc. (Associate)

Clients Represented
On Behalf of Capital Partnerships (VA) Inc.
Anoka County Regional Railroad Authority
Denver, Colorado, City and County of
Douglas, Colorado, County of
Friedlob, Sanderson, Raskin, Paulson, Toutillott
North Metro Mayors Coalition
Policy Advantage
Southeast Business Partnership
Taxicab, Limousine and Paratransit Ass'n

ANGLE, Stephen

1455 Pennsylvania Ave. NW
Suite 700
Washington, DC 20004-1008
Tel: (202)639-6500
Fax: (202)639-6604
Former Assistant General Counsel, Federal Energy Regulatory Commission, Department of Energy.

Employers
Vinson & Elkins L.L.P. (Partner)

ANGULO, Charles

1201 Connecticut Ave. NW
Suite 600
Washington, DC 20036
Tel: (202)778-1800
Fax: (202)822-8106
Registered: LDA

Employers
Zuckerman Spaeder L.L.P.

Clients Represented

On Behalf of Zuckerman Spaeder L.L.P.
Amity, Inc.
United States Pharmacopeia
Vietnam Veterans of America Foundation

ANGUS, Barbara

1301 K St. NW
Washington, DC 20005-3333
Tel: (202)414-1000
Fax: (202)414-1301
Registered: LDA
EMail: barbara.angus@us.pwcglobal.com

Employers
PriceWaterhouseCoopers (Partner)

Clients Represented

On Behalf of PriceWaterhouseCoopers
American Council of Life Insurers
Contract Manufacturing Coalition
Goldman, Sachs and Co.
Interest Allocation Coalition
PwC Contract Manufacturing Coalition
PwC Leasing Coalition
Tupperware Corp.
United Parcel Service

ANGUS, III, John W.

2100 Pennsylvania Ave. NW
Suite 500
Washington, DC 20037
Tel: (202)728-1100
Fax: (202)728-1123
Registered: LDA

Employers
The Duberstein Group, Inc. (Senior V. President and General Counsel)

Clients Represented

On Behalf of The Duberstein Group, Inc.
Amerada Hess Corp.
American Apparel & Footwear Ass'n
American Ass'n of Health Plans (AAHP)
American Council of Life Insurers
American Gaming Ass'n
The American Water Works Co.
AOL Time Warner
The Business Roundtable
Comcast Corp.
Conoco Inc.
CSX Corp.
Direct Marketing Ass'n, Inc.
Dow Corning Corp.
Fannie Mae
General Motors Corp.
Goldman, Sachs and Co.
Nat'l Cable Television Ass'n
Pharmacia Corp.
Project to Promote Competition and Innovation in the Digital Age
Sara Lee Corp.
Transportation Institute
United Airlines
USX Corp.

ANNEXSTEIN, Leslie

11 Dupont Circle NW
Suite 800
Washington, DC 20036
Tel: (202)588-5180
Fax: (202)588-5185

Employers
Nat'l Women's Law Center (Senior Counsel)

ANSELL, Damon

1920 L St. NW
Suite 200
Washington, DC 20036
Tel: (202)785-0266
Fax: (202)785-0261
Registered: LDA
EMail: dansell@atr-dc.org

Employers
Americans for Tax Reform (V. President, Policy)

ANSELL, David L.

1001 Pennsylvania Ave. NW
Suite 800
Washington, DC 20004-2505
Tel: (202)639-7000
Fax: (202)639-7008
EMail: david_ansell@ffhsj.com

Employers
Fried, Frank, Harris, Shriver & Jacobson (Partner)

ANSON, Tim

1301 K St. NW
Washington, DC 20005-3333
Tel: (202)414-1000
Fax: (202)414-1301
Registered: LDA
EMail: tim.anson@us.pwcglobal.com

Employers
PriceWaterhouseCoopers (Partner)

Clients Represented

On Behalf of PriceWaterhouseCoopers
Bank of America
Contract Manufacturing Coalition
PwC Contract Manufacturing Coalition

ANTHES, Matthew D.

2111 Wilson Blvd.
Suite 1200
Arlington, VA 22201
Tel: (703)522-1845
Fax: (703)351-6634
EMail: manthes@columbuspublicaffairs.com
Served in the Office of Political Affairs, the White House.

Employers
Columbus Public Affairs (Senior Associate)

ANTHONY, Jr., Hon. Beryl F.

1400 L St. NW
Washington, DC 20005-3502
Tel: (202)371-5754
Fax: (202)371-5950
Registered: LDA
EMail: banthony@winston.com
Member, U.S. House of Representatives (D-AR), 1978-93.

Employers
Winston & Strawn (Partner and Director, Legislative and Regulatory Practice)

Clients Represented

On Behalf of Winston & Strawn
AirCell, Inc.
Barr Laboratories
Cooper Tire and Rubber Co.
Corning Inc.
Eastern Band of Cherokee Indians
The ESOP (Employee Stock Ownership Plan) Ass'n
Federal Judges Ass'n
Federal Magistrate Judges Ass'n
Internat'l Council of Shopping Centers
Lockheed Martin Corp.
Motor Coach Industries, Inc.
Murphy Oil U.S.A.
Nat'l Geographic Soc.
Nat'l Organization of Social Security Claimants' Representatives
Panda Energy Internat'l
Puerto Rico, Commonwealth of
University of California at Los Angeles

ANTHONY, Betty

1899 L St. NW
Suite 1000
Washington, DC 20036
Tel: (202)457-0480
Fax: (202)457-0486
Registered: LDA
EMail: betty_anthony@npradc.org

Employers
Nat'l Petrochemical Refiners Ass'n (Director, Strategic Communications and Planning)

ANTHONY, Calvin J.

205 Daingerfield Rd.
Alexandria, VA 22314
Tel: (703)683-8200
Fax: (703)683-3619
Registered: LDA

Employers
Nat'l Community Pharmacists Ass'n (Exec. V. President)

ANTHONY, Edwin

701 Pennsylvania Ave. NW
Washington, DC 20004-2696
Tel: (202)508-5520
Fax: (202)508-5360

Employers
Edison Electric Institute (V. President, Member Relations and Corporate Secretary)

ANTHONY, Steven J.

1500 K St. NW
Suite 375
Washington, DC 20005
Tel: (202)383-4432
Fax: (202)383-4018
Registered: LDA

Employers
Norfolk Southern Corp. (Assistant V. President)

ANTHONY, Virginia Q.

3615 Wisconsin Ave. NW
Washington, DC 20016
Tel: (202)966-7300
Fax: (202)966-2891
EMail: vqanthony@aacap.org

Employers
American Academy of Child and Adolescent Psychiatry (Exec. Director)

ANTLEY, Corinne M.

1200 New Hampshire Ave. NW
Suite 800
Washington, DC 20036-6802
Tel: (202)776-2000
Fax: (202)776-2222
EMail: cantley@dlalaw.com

Employers
Dow, Lohnes & Albertson, PLLC (Member)

ANTONE, IV, Thomas M.

701 Pennsylvania Ave. NW
Suite 900
Washington, DC 20004-2608
Tel: (202)434-7300
Fax: (202)434-7400
Registered: LDA
EMail: tantone@mintz.com
Executive Secretary for Health (1982-83) and Assistant Secretary for Health Legislation (1980-82), Department of Health and Human Service.

Employers
Mintz, Levin, Cohn, Ferris, Glovsky and Popeo, P.C. (Partner)

ANZOATEGUI, Carlos

17413 Collier Way
Poolesville, MD 20837
Tel: (301)605-0501
Fax: (301)605-0503
Registered: FARA

Employers
Committee on Human Rights for the People of Nicaragua (Chairman)
Potomac Consulting Group (Managing Partner)

Clients Represented

On Behalf of Potomac Consulting Group
Committee on Human Rights for the People of Nicaragua

APATOFF, Adam S.

666 11th St. NW
Suite 315
Washington, DC 20001
Tel: (202)331-8045
Fax: (202)331-8191
Registered: LDA

Employers
Aitken, Irvin, Lewin, Berlin, Vrooman & Cohn (Associate)

Clients Represented

On Behalf of Aitken, Irvin, Lewin, Berlin, Vrooman & Cohn
Colgate Palmolive

APONTE, Ana

8630 Fenton St.
Suite 126
Silver Spring, MD 20910
Tel: (202)628-3952
Fax: (301)588-0011

Employers
Nat'l Coalition of Black Meeting Planners (President)

APONTE, ESQ., Mari Carmen

1100 17th St. NW
Suite 800
Washington, DC 20036
Tel: (202)778-0710
Fax: (202)778-0721

Employers
Puerto Rico Federal Affairs Administration (Exec. Director)

APPELBAUM, Eileen

1660 L St. NW
Suite 1200
Washington, DC 20036
Tel: (202)775-8810
Fax: (202)775-0819
EMail: epi@epinet.org

Employers
Economic Policy Institute (Associate Research Director)

APPELBAUM, Judith C.

11 Dupont Circle NW
Suite 800
Washington, DC 20036
Tel: (202)588-5180
Fax: (202)588-5185
EMail: jappelbaum@nwlc.org

Employers
Nat'l Women's Law Center (V. President and Director, Employment Opportunities Program)

APPLE, Dr. Martin A.

1155 16th St. NW
Suite 1017
Washington, DC 20036
Tel: (202)872-4452
Fax: (202)872-4079

Employers
Council of Scientific Society Presidents (President)

APPLEBAUM, Harvey M.

1201 Pennsylvania Ave. NW
Washington, DC 20004-2401
EMail: happlebaum@cov.com
Tel: (202)662-6000
Fax: (202)662-6291

Employers
Covington & Burling (Partner)

Clients Represented

On Behalf of Covington & Burling
AT&T
British Columbia, Canada, Government of the Province of
Canon USA, Inc.
Chambre Syndicale des Producteurs d'Aciers Fins et Speciaux
Domtar, Inc.
Exxon Co., U.S.A.
Quebec, Canada, Government of the Province of

APPLEBAUM, Rhona

1350 I St. NW
Suite 300
Washington, DC 20005
Tel: (202)639-5900
Fax: (202)639-5932
Registered: LDA

Employers
Nat'l Food Processors Ass'n (Exec. V. President, Scientific and Regulatory Affairs)

APPLEGATE, Bill

1050 Connecticut Ave. NW
Washington, DC 20036-5339
Tel: (202)857-6000
Fax: (202)857-6395
Registered: LDA

Employers
American Soc. of Transplantation (Director, Government Relations)
Arent Fox Kintner Plotkin & Kahn, PLLC (Government Relations Director)

Clients Represented

On Behalf of Arent Fox Kintner Plotkin & Kahn, PLLC
American Ass'n of Bioanalysts
American Ass'n of Occupational Health Nurses
American College of Nurse Practitioners
American Soc. of Transplantation
Ass'n of Pain Management Anesthesiologist
Assisted Living Federation of America
Eastman Kodak Co.
France Telecom America do Sul Ltda.
Mercy Hospital of Des Moines, Iowa
Molina Medical Centers
Pedorthic Footwear Ass'n

APPLEGATE, David

4220 King St.
Alexandria, VA 22302-1502
EMail: govt@agiweb.org
Tel: (703)379-2480
Fax: (703)379-7563
Registered: LDA

Employers
American Geological Institute (Director, Government Affairs)

APPLEGATE, Jody

1400 16th St. NW
Suite 501
Washington, DC 20036-2266
Tel: (202)797-6800
Fax: (202)797-6646
Registered: LDA

Employers
Nat'l Wildlife Federation - Office of Federal and Internat'l Affairs (Project Manager)

APPLER, Nancy

1849 C St. NW
Room 6254
Washington, DC 20240
EMail: nancy_appler@ios.doi.gov
Tel: (202)208-7693
Fax: (202)208-7619

Employers
Department of Interior (Congressional Services Specialist, Office of Congressional and Legislative Affairs)

AQUILINE, Matthew S.

821 15th St. NW
Washington, DC 20005
Tel: (202)383-3913
Fax: (202)383-3122

Employers
Internat'l Council of Employers of Bricklayers and Allied Craftsmen (Exec. Director)

ARAUJO, Jaeleen K.

1050 Thomas Jefferson St. NW
Seventh Floor
Washington, DC 20007
EMail: JKA@vnf.com
Tel: (202)298-1800
Fax: (202)338-2416

Employers
Van Ness Feldman, P.C. (Associate)

ARBOGAST, Christine Ann

1001 Pennsylvania Ave. NW
Suite 760 North
Washington, DC 20004
Tel: (202)661-7060
Fax: (202)661-7066
Registered: LDA
Former aide to Rep. Ray Kogovsek (D-CO).

Employers
Kogovsek & Associates (V. President)

Clients Represented

On Behalf of Kogovsek & Associates
The Legislative Strategies Group, LLC
Rio Grande Water Conservation District
Signal Behavioral Health Network
Southern Ute Indian Tribe
Southwestern Water Conservation District
Ute Mountain Ute Indian Tribe
Wolf Springs Ranches, Inc.

ARBUCKLE, J. Gordon

2550 M St. NW
Washington, DC 20037-1350
Tel: (202)457-6000
Fax: (202)457-6315
Registered: LDA, FARA
EMail: garbuckle@pattonboggs.com

Employers
Patton Boggs, LLP (Partner)

Clients Represented

On Behalf of Patton Boggs, LLP
Nat'l Center for Manufacturing Sciences

ARBURY, James N.

1850 M St. NW
Suite 540
Washington, DC 20036
EMail: jarbury@nmhc.org
Tel: (202)974-2300
Fax: (202)775-0112
Registered: LDA
Former Administrative Assistant to Senator Donald W. Riegle, (D-MI).

Employers
Nat'l Multi-Housing Council (V. President)

ARCENEAUX, Michael N.

1717 K St. NW
Suite 801
Washington, DC 20036
EMail: michaela@amwa.net
Tel: (202)331-2820
Fax: (202)785-1845
Registered: LDA
Legal Assistant to Senator John Breaux (D-LA), 1994-95.

Employers
Ass'n of Metropolitan Water Agencies (Director, Legislative and Public Affairs)

ARCHER, Patrick W.

1501 M St. NW
Suite 1100
Washington, DC 20005
Tel: (202)785-7300
Fax: (202)785-6360

Employers
Viacom Inc. (Legislative Assistant)

ARCHEY, William T.

601 Pennsylvania Ave. NW
Suite 600
North Bldg.
Washington, DC 20004
Tel: (202)682-9110
Fax: (202)682-9111
Registered: LDA

Employers
American Electronics Ass'n (President and Chief Exec. Officer)

ARCHIBALD, Jeanne S.

555 13th St. NW
Washington, DC 20004-1109
Tel: (202)637-5740
Fax: (202)637-5910
Registered: LDA, FARA
EMail: jsarchibald@hhlaw.com
General Counsel (1990-93), Deputy General Counsel (1988-90), and Deputy Assistant General Counsel, International Affairs (1986-88), Department of the Treasury. Associate General Counsel, Office of the U.S. Trade Representative, 1980-86. Professional Staff Member, Subcommittee on Trade, House Ways and Means Committee, 1975-80.

Employers
Hogan & Hartson L.L.P. (Managing Partner, Practice Administration)

Clients Represented

On Behalf of Hogan & Hartson L.L.P.
Danaher Corp.
Grocery Manufacturers of America
Michelin North America
Nestle USA, Inc.
Pharmaceutical Research and Manufacturers of America
Polaroid Corp.
Toyota Motor North America, U.S.A., Inc.
United Parcel Service

ARCHULETA, Mark

888 16th St. NW
Suite 305
Washington, DC 20006
EMail: archuleta@bipac.org
Tel: (202)833-1880
Fax: (202)833-2338

Employers
Business-Industry Political Action Committee (Director, Finance and Administration)

ARCHULETA, R. M. Julie

1717 Pennsylvania Ave. NW
Suite 400
Washington, DC 20006
Tel: (202)857-3023
Fax: (202)857-3014
Registered: LDA

Employers
Occidental Internat'l Corporation (V. President, Government Affairs)

ARCURI, Jeff

1100 Wayne Ave.
Suite 1100
Silver Spring, MD 20910
Tel: (301)587-8202
Fax: (301)587-2711

Employers
Ass'n for Information and Image Management Internat'l (V. President, Marketing and Meetings)

ARD, Jean

5845 Richmond Hwy.
Suite 630
Alexandria, VA 22303-1870
Tel: (301)960-1100
Registered: LDA

Employers
Leukemia & Lymphoma Soc. (V. President, Government Affairs)

ARDOUNY, Bryan

122 C St. NW
Suite 350
Washington, DC 20001
EMail: bryan@aaainc.org
Tel: (202)393-3434
Fax: (202)638-4904

Employers
Armenian Assembly of America (Director, Government Relations)

ARFSTROM, Kari

1801 N. Moore St.
Arlington, VA 22209
EMail: karfstrom@aasa.org
Tel: (703)528-0700
Fax: (703)528-2146

Employers
American Ass'n of School Administrators (Project Director, Rural/Small Schools)

ARGUST, Marcia F.

636 I St. NW
Washington, DC 20001-3736
Tel: (202)898-2444
Fax: (202)898-1185
Registered: LDA

Former Legislative Assistant to Rep. Sherwood L. Boehlert (R-NY).

Employers

American Soc. of Landscape Architects (Director, Public and Government Affairs)

ARLINGTON, John G.

1130 Connecticut Ave. NW
Suite 1000
Washington, DC 20036
Tel: (202)828-7100
Fax: (202)293-1219
Registered: LDA
EMail: jarlington@aiadc.org

Employers

American Insurance Ass'n (Assistant V. President, Federal Affairs)

ARMACOST, Michael H.

1775 Massachusetts Ave. NW
Washington, DC 20036-2188
Tel: (202)797-6000
Fax: (202)797-6004

Ambassador to Japan, 1989-93; Under Secretary of State for Political Affairs, Department of State, 1984-89; Ambassador to the Philippines, 1982-84.

Employers

The Brookings Institution (President)

ARMISTEAD, Rex

1275 Pennsylvania Ave. NW
Tenth Floor
Washington, DC 20004
Tel: (202)347-1434
Fax: (202)347-1534
Registered: LDA

Deputy Under Secretary (1982-84) and Special Assistant to the Secretary (1981-82), Department of Agriculture.

Employers

Johnson Co.

Clients Represented

On Behalf of Johnson Co.

DATRON, Inc.

ARMSTRONG, Edward

1150 Connecticut Ave. NW
Suite 201
Washington, DC 20036
Tel: (202)955-6200
Fax: (202)955-6215
EMail: earmstrong@gcwdc.com

Employers

Goddard Claussen (V. President)

ARMSTRONG, CAE, Elizabeth B.

111 Park Place
Falls Church, VA 22046-4513
Tel: (703)533-0251
Fax: (703)241-5603

Employers

American Paper Machinery Ass'n (Exec. Director)
Ass'n and Soc. Management Internat'l Inc. (Senior V. President)
Internat'l Ass'n of Emergency Managers (Exec. Director)
Nat'l Ass'n of State EMS Directors (Exec. Director)

Clients Represented

On Behalf of Ass'n and Soc. Management Internat'l Inc.

American Paper Machinery Ass'n
Internat'l Ass'n of Emergency Managers
Nat'l Ass'n of State EMS Directors

ARMSTRONG, Jan M.

1225 I St. NW
Suite 500
Washington, DC 20005-3914
Tel: (202)682-4778
Fax: (301)770-2416
EMail: jmarmstro@aol.com

Employers

Armstrong Associates, Inc. (President)

Clients Represented

On Behalf of Armstrong Associates, Inc.

Avis, Inc.
HealthFEST of Maryland, Inc.

ARMSTRONG, Julie

1250 Connecticut Ave. NW
Suite 800
Washington, DC 20036
Tel: (202)785-0081
Fax: (202)776-0540
Registered: LDA
EMail: jarmstrong@ctia.org

Employers

Cellular Telecommunications and Internet Ass'n (Manager, Congressional Affairs)

ARMSTRONG, Philip C.

6400 Goldsboro Rd.
Suite 500
Bethesda, MD 20817
Tel: (301)263-2312
Fax: (301)263-2269
EMail: parmstro@epb.com

Acting Deputy Assistant Secretary for Public Affairs, Department of Education, 1984-85. Special Assistant to the Assistant Secretary for Health Affairs (1982-84) and Special Assistant to the Assistant Secretary for Public Affairs (1981-82), Department of Defense.

Employers

Earle Palmer Brown Public Relations (Partner, Managing Director)

ARMSTRONG, R. Scott

2620 Quebec St. NW
Washington, DC 20008-1221
Tel: (202)364-1100
Fax: (202)364-2438
EMail: sarmst@cni.org

Senior Investigator for the Select Committee on Presidential Campaign Activities, U.S. Senate, 1973-74.

Employers

Information Trust (Exec. Director)

ARMSTRONG, Richard

Rayburn House Office Bldg.
Room B328
Washington, DC 20515
Tel: (202)225-2280
Fax: (202)453-5225

Employers

Department of Veterans Affairs (House Liaison Representative)

ARMSTRONG-DAILEY, Ann

2202 Mount Vernon Ave.
Suite 3C
Alexandria, VA 22301
Tel: (703)684-0330
Fax: (703)684-0226

Employers

Children's Hospice Internat'l (Founding Director)

ARNDORFER, Kay

1629 K St. NW
Suite 200
Washington, DC 20006-1629
Tel: (202)777-7575
Fax: (202)777-7577

Employers

The Advocacy Institute (Director, Tobacco Control Project)

ARNETT, Angela

1001 Pennsylvania Ave. NW
Washington, DC 20004-2599
Tel: (202)624-2000
Fax: (202)624-2319
Registered: LDA

Employers

American Council of Life Insurers (Senior Counsel)

ARNOLD, Andrew

300 Independence Ave. SE
Washington, DC 20003
Tel: (202)546-5611

Employers

Liberty Lobby (Editor)

ARNOLD, Jeffrey D.

440 First St. NW
Eighth Floor
Washington, DC 20001
Tel: (202)942-4286
Fax: (202)942-4281
EMail: jarnold@naco.org

Employers

Nat'l Ass'n of Counties (Deputy Legislative Director)

ARNOLD, John

1200 G St. NW
Suite 400
Washington, DC 20005
Tel: (202)783-8700
Fax: (202)783-8750
Registered: LDA

Employers

AdvaMed (Director, e-Communications)

ARNOLD, Mary

1120 20th St. NW
Suite 1000
Washington, DC 20036
Tel: (202)457-3810
Fax: (202)457-2571
EMail: marnold@att.com

Employers

AT&T (V. President, Congressional Affairs)

ARNOLD, Matthew

Ten G St. NE
Suite 800
Washington, DC 20002
Tel: (202)729-7600
Fax: (202)729-7610

Employers

World Resources Institute (Chief Operating Officer and Senior V. President, Operations)

ARNOLD, Shannon

2300 N St. NW
Washington, DC 20037-1128
Tel: (202)663-8000
Fax: (202)663-8007
Registered: LDA
EMail: shannon.arnold@shawpittman.com

Employers

Shaw Pittman (Associate)

Clients Represented

On Behalf of Shaw Pittman

Medicare Cost Contractors Alliance

ARNOLD, Thomas K.

6043 Shaffer Dr.
Alexandria, VA 22310
Tel: (703)660-6311
Fax: (703)660-2328
Registered: LDA

Assistant Counsel, Subcommittee on Oversight, House Ways and Means Committee, 1987-95. Senior Counsel, Office of General Counsel, General Accounting Office, 1984-87. Assistant Counsel, Office of General Counsel, Department of the Navy, 1978-84.

Employers

Self-employed as an independent consultant.

Clients Represented

As an independent consultant

American Network of Community Options and Resources (ANCOR)

ARNSBARGER, Linda A.

2000 Pennsylvania Ave. NW
Suite 5500
Washington, DC 20006
Tel: (202)887-1500
Fax: (202)887-0763
Registered: LDA
EMail: larnsbarger@mofo.com

Law Clerk to Judge Kenneth W. Starr, U.S. Court of Appeals, District of Columbia Circuit, 1985-86.

Employers

Morrison & Foerster LLP (Of Counsel)

ARNWINE, Barbara R.

1401 New York Ave. NW
Suite 400
Washington, DC 20005
Tel: (202)662-8600
Fax: (202)638-0482
EMail: barnwine@lawyerscomm.org

Employers

Lawyers' Committee for Civil Rights Under Law (Exec. Director)

ARNY, Wayne

2600 Virginia Ave. NW
Suite 600
Washington, DC 20037
Tel: (202)338-6650
Fax: (202)338-5950
Registered: LDA

Served in the U.S. Navy, 1960-81; Senate Armed Services Committee staff, 1981-84; Department of the Navy, 1984-86; Office of Management and Budget, 1986-89.

Employers

Wayne Arny & Assoc. (President)
David O'Brien and Associates (Partner)

Clients Represented

On Behalf of Wayne Arny & Assoc.

American Logistics Infrastructure Improvement Consortium
John Crane-LIPS, Inc.
Cruising America Coalition
DRS Technologies, Inc.
The Environmental Co., Inc.
Guam Internat'l Airport Authority
Jered Industries, Inc.
The Kinetics Group
MacGregor
Robbins-Gioia, Inc.
San Francisco Wholesale Produce Ass'n

On Behalf of David O'Brien and Associates

John Crane-LIPS, Inc.
DRS

ARON, David E.

600 13th St. NW
Washington, DC 20005-3096
Tel: (202)756-8221
Fax: (202)756-8087
EMail: daron@mwe.com
Former Special Counsel to the Director of Division of Trading and Markets, Commodity Futures Trading Commission.

Employers
McDermott, Will and Emery (Associate)

ARON, Leon

1150 17th St. NW
Washington, DC 20036
Tel: (202)862-5800
Fax: (202)862-7177
EMail: laron@aei.org

Employers
American Enterprise Institute for Public Policy Research (Resident Scholar)

ARON, Nan

11 Dupont Circle NW
Second Floor
Washington, DC 20036
Tel: (202)822-6070
Fax: (202)822-6068
Registered: LDA
EMail: naron@afj.org

Employers
Alliance for Justice (President)

ARONOW, Geoffrey

555 12th St. NW
Washington, DC 20004-1206
Tel: (202)942-5000
Fax: (202)942-5999
EMail: Geoffrey_Aronow@aporter.com
Former Director of Enforcement, Commodity Futures Trading Commission.

Employers
Arnold & Porter (Partner)

ARONS, Dave

2040 S St. NW
Washington, DC 20009
Tel: (202)387-5072
Fax: (202)387-5149
Registered: LDA

Employers
Charity Lobbying in the Public Interest (Co-Director)

ARONSON, Tracey

450 Fifth St. NW
Washington, DC 20549
Tel: (202)942-0010
Fax: (202)942-9650

Employers
Securities and Exchange Commission (Director)

ARQUIT, Kevin J.

607 14th St. NW
Washington, DC 20005
Tel: (202)434-0700
Fax: (202)912-6000
EMail: arquitny@rw.com
General Counsel, 1988-89, and Director, Bureau of Competition, 1989-92, Federal Trade Commission.

Employers
Rogers & Wells (Partner)

Clients Represented

On Behalf of Rogers & Wells

Major League Baseball Players Ass'n

ART, Andrew B.

1050 Thomas Jefferson St. NW
Seventh Floor
Washington, DC 20007
Tel: (202)298-1800
Fax: (202)338-2416
EMail: ABA@vnf.com

Employers
Van Ness Feldman, P.C. (Associate)

ARTEAGA, Roland

805 15th St. NW
Washington, DC 20005-2207
Tel: (202)682-5993
Fax: (202)682-9054
EMail: dcucl@cuna.com

Employers
Defense Credit Union Council (President and Chief Exec. Officer)

ARTHUR, David K.

1300 I St. NW
Suite 300 West
Washington, DC 20005
Tel: (202)522-8600
Fax: (202)522-8669
Registered: LDA
Former Legislative Assistant to Rep. John Conyers, Jr. (D-MI).

Employers
Dykema Gossett PLLC (Legislative Associate)

Clients Represented

On Behalf of Dykema Gossett PLLC

Arvin Meritor Automotive
Comerica, Inc.
Detroit Public Schools
Detroit, Michigan, City of
Great Lakes Corporate Resources
Michigan Insurance Federation
Southeastern Michigan Council of Government
The Wellness Plan

ARTHURS, Jean

4023 25th Rd. North
Arlington, VA 22207
Tel: (703)527-4565
Fax: (703)527-3881

Employers
Nat'l Ass'n of Military Widows (Legislative Liaison-President)

ARZT, Leonard

7910 Woodmont Ave.
Suite 1303
Bethesda, MD 20814
Tel: (301)913-9360
Fax: (301)913-0372

Employers
Nat'l Ass'n for Proton Therapy (Exec. Director)

ASH, Jon F.

1800 K St. NW
Suite 1104
Washington, DC 20006
Tel: (202)457-0212
Fax: (202)833-3183
Registered: FARA
EMail: jfa@ga2online.com

Employers
Global Aviation Associates, Ltd. (Managing Director)

Clients Represented

On Behalf of Global Aviation Associates, Ltd.

Ass'n of Asia Pacific Airlines
Austrian Airlines
Dallas/Fort Worth Internat'l Airport Board
Las Vegas/McCarran Internat'l Airport
Memphis-Shelby County Airport Authority
Norfolk, Virginia, City of
ORBITZ
Swissair

ASHBY, R. Barry

1350 I St. NW
Suite 1240
Washington, DC 20005
Tel: (202)296-3840
Fax: (202)682-0146
EMail: rbashby@aol.com

Employers
Ashby and Associates (President)

Clients Represented

On Behalf of Ashby and Associates

Business News Publishing Co.
Composite Innovations, Inc.
Imaging Technologies Inc.
Intelligent Optical Systems, Inc.
The Lared Group
Time Domain Corp.
Tracer ES&T Inc.
The Ventura Group
Waveband, Inc.

ASHE, Glenn M.

1421 Prince St.
Suite 200
Alexandria, VA 22314
Tel: (703)519-0801
Fax: (703)519-1898
Registered: LDA

Employers
American Bureau of Shipping (Director)

ASHER, Anne W.

1130 Connecticut Ave. NW
Suite 830
Washington, DC 20036
Tel: (202)261-5000
Fax: (202)296-7937

Employers
Southern Co. (Manager, Administrative and Special Projects)

ASHFORD, Deborah

555 13th St. NW
Washington, DC 20004-1109
Tel: (202)637-5600
Fax: (202)637-5910

Employers
Hogan & Hartson L.L.P.

Clients Represented

On Behalf of Hogan & Hartson L.L.P.

Direct Selling Ass'n

ASHFORD, John

1199 N. Fairfax St.
Suite 1000
Alexandria, VA 22314
Tel: (703)299-4499
Fax: (703)299-4488
EMail: jashford@hawthorngroup.com

Employers
The Hawthorn Group, L.C. (Chairman and Chief Exec. Officer)

Clients Represented

On Behalf of The Hawthorn Group, L.C.

Southern Co.
Southern Generation

ASHLEY-ROGERS, Rhonda

409 Third St. SW
Suite 7900
Washington, DC 20416
Tel: (202)205-6700
Fax: (202)205-7374
EMail: rhonda.ashley1@sba.gov

Employers
Small Business Administration (Program Specialist, Office of Congressional and Legislative Affairs)

ASHMORE, James Nicholas

1156 15th St. NW
Suite 315
Washington, DC 20005-1704
Tel: (202)452-1003
Fax: (202)452-1311
Registered: LDA
EMail: jnashmore@erols.com
Former Senior Aide to Rep. Thomas S. Foley (D-WA).

Employers
James Nicholas Ashmore & Associates (President)

Clients Represented

On Behalf of James Nicholas Ashmore & Associates

American Crop Protection Ass'n
Battelle
Battelle Memorial Institute
The Boeing Co.
Gardena Alfalfa Growers Ass'n
Nat'l Rural Telecom Ass'n
Northwest Horticultural Council
Oneonta Trading Corp.
Western Ag Resources Inc.

ASKEW, Todd

1101 Vermont Ave. NW
12th Floor
Washington, DC 20005-3583

Tel: (202)789-7462
Fax: (202)789-7485
Registered: LDA

Employers
American Medical Ass'n (Assistant Director, Congressional Affairs)

ASKIN, Jonathan

888 17th St. NW
Suite 900
Washington, DC 20006
EMail: jaskin@alts.org

Tel: (202)969-2587
Fax: (202)969-2581
Registered: LDA

Employers
Ass'n for Local Telecommunications Services (General Counsel)

ASMONGA, Donald D.

1225 I St. NW
Suite 500
Washington, DC 20005
EMail: don.asmonga@ahima.org

Tel: (202)218-3535
Fax: (202)682-0078
Registered: LDA

Employers
American Health Information Management Ass'n (Manager, Government Relations)

ASNANI, Rick

1201 15th St. NW
Washington, DC 20005-2800

Tel: (202)822-0470
Fax: (202)822-0572
Registered: LDA

Employers
Nat'l Ass'n of Home Builders of the U.S. (Senior Political Field Director)

ASPRAY, Dr. William

1100 17th St. NW
Suite 507
Washington, DC 20036
EMail: info@cra.org

Tel: (202)234-2111
Fax: (202)667-1066

Employers
Computing Research Ass'n (Exec. Director)

ASTE, George

900 19th St. NW
Suite 350
Washington, DC 20006

Tel: (202)457-4754
Fax: (202)457-4767
Registered: LDA

Employers
Trans World Airlines, Inc. (Staff V. President, International Affairs)

ASTON, Michele

Ariel Rios Federal Bldg.
(1301-MC)
1200 Pennsylvania Ave. NW
3rd Floor
Washington, DC 20460
EMail: aston.michele@epa.gov

Tel: (202)564-6988
Fax: (202)501-1550

Employers
Environmental Protection Agency (Air/Pesticides Team Leader, Office of Congressional and Intergovernmental Relations)

ATAGI, Patrick S.

1156 15th St. NW
Suite 1020
Washington, DC 20005
EMail: patrick@nasda-hq.org

Tel: (202)296-9680
Fax: (202)296-9686

Employers
Nat'l Ass'n of State Departments of Agriculture (Manager, Legislative and Regulatory Affairs)

ATCITTY, Shenan R.

2099 Pennsylvania Ave. NW
Suite 100
Washington, DC 20006
EMail: sratcitt@hklaw.com

Tel: (202)955-3000
Fax: (202)955-5564

Employers
Holland & Knight LLP

ATERNO, Kathy

4455 Connecticut Ave. NW
Suite A300
Washington, DC 20008
EMail: katerno@cleanwater.org

Tel: (202)895-0420
Fax: (202)895-0438

Employers
Clean Water Action (Managing Director)

ATHY, Jr., Andrew

1310 19th St. NW
Washington, DC 20036

Tel: (202)466-6555
Fax: (202)466-6596
Registered: LDA, FARA

Counsel, House Committee on Interstate and Foreign Commerce, 1977-81. Attorney, Office of General Counsel, Federal Election Commission, 1976-77.

Employers
O'Neill, Athy & Casey, P.C. (Partner)

Clients Represented
On Behalf of O'Neill, Athy & Casey, P.C.
AT&T
Glass Packaging Institute
Harvard University Washington Office
Industry Union Glass Container Promotion Program
JM Family Enterprises
Lehman Brothers
Marathon Oil Co.
Northwestern Memorial Hospital
TXU Business Services
USX Corp.
Viacom Inc.

ATKIN, Barbara

901 E St. NW
Suite 600
Washington, DC 20004

Tel: (202)783-4444
Fax: (202)783-4085

Employers
Nat'l Treasury Employees Union (Deputy General Counsel)

ATKINS, G. Lawrence

1350 I St. NW
Suite 870
Washington, DC 20005

Tel: (202)638-0550
Fax: (202)737-1947
Registered: LDA

Former Republican Staff Director, Senate Committee on Aging.

Employers
Health Policy Analysts (President)
Managed Care Compliance Solutions, Inc. (Principal)

Clients Represented
On Behalf of Health Policy Analysts
Corporate Health Care Coalition
Employer Health Care Innovation Project
New Jersey Organ & Tissue Sharing Network
Schering-Plough Legislative Resources L.L.C.

ATKINS, M.D., Richard N.

1158 15th St. NW
Washington, DC 20005
EMail: Atkins@4npcc.org

Tel: (202)463-9455
Fax: (202)463-9456
Registered: LDA

Employers
Nat'l Prostate Cancer Coalition Co. (Vice President and Chief Operating Officer)

ATKINS, Ross

216 Justice Ct. NE
Suite A
Washington, DC 20006

Tel: (202)547-7721
Fax: (202)547-7835

Projects Director to Senator Mary Landrieu (D-LA), 1997-98. Staff aide to Senator J. Bennett Johnston (D-LA), 1986-93.

Employers
Self-employed as an independent consultant.
Connectcuba (Managing Director)

Clients Represented
As an independent consultant
Connectcuba
Monroe, Louisiana, Chamber of Commerce of the City of
Monroe, Louisiana, City of
Ouachita Parish Police Jury

ATKINSON, Alan R.

1620 I St. NW
Suite 615
Washington, DC 20006
EMail: alan@moinc.com

Tel: (202)463-8493
Fax: (202)463-8497
Registered: LDA

Employers
JBC Internat'l (Trade Analyst)
Management Options, Inc.

Clients Represented
On Behalf of JBC Internat'l
Joint Industry Group (JIG)
On Behalf of Management Options, Inc.
American Teleservices Ass'n

ATKINSON, Diane

445 12th St. NW
Room 8-C404
Washington, DC 20554

Tel: (202)418-1900
Fax: (202)418-2806

Employers
Federal Communications Commission (Congressional Liaison Specialist)

ATKINSON, Frank B.

1050 Connecticut Ave. NW
Suite 1200
Washington, DC 20036
EMail: fbatkins@mwbb.com

Tel: (202)857-1700
Fax: (202)857-1737
Registered: LDA

Department of Justice, 1982-88.

Employers
McGuireWoods L.L.P. (Chairman, Executive Committee, McGuire Woods Consulting, LLC)

Clients Represented
On Behalf of McGuireWoods L.L.P.
CSX Corp.
Eastman Chemical Co.
Families of Anthoniessen, Bekaert, Eyskens, Van den Heede, and Vermander

ATKINSON, Jay

1825 Connecticut Ave. NW
Fifth Floor
Washington, DC 20009
EMail: jay.atkinson@widmeyer.com

Tel: (202)667-0901
Fax: (202)667-0902

Employers
Widmeyer Communications, Inc. (Chief Financial Officer)

ATKINSON, Jeannie M.

1221 Massachusetts Ave. NW
Washington, DC 20005

Tel: (202)772-4348
Fax: (202)772-4409

Employers
Catholic Charities Immigration Legal Services (Program Administrator)

ATKINSON, Leslie

1444 I St. NW
Suite 500
Washington, DC 20005
EMail: latkinso@uncf.org

Tel: (202)737-8631
Fax: (202)737-8651
Registered: LDA

Former Chief of Staff to Rep. Louis Stokes (D-OH). Also served as Associate Staff, House Committee on Appropriations.

Employers
United Negro College Fund, Inc. (Director, Government Affairs)

ATKINSON, Robert

600 Pennsylvania Ave. SE
Suite 400
Washington, DC 20003
EMail: ratkinson@dlcppi.org

Tel: (202)608-1239
Fax: (202)544-5014

Employers
Progressive Policy Institute (Director, Technology, Innovation and the New Economy Project)

ATKINSON, Todd

805 15th St. NW
Suite 700
Washington, DC 20005
EMail: htatkins@bakerd.com

Tel: (202)312-7400
Fax: (202)312-7441
Registered: LDA

Employers
Sagamore Associates, Inc. (V. President)

Clients Represented

On Behalf of Sagamore Associates, Inc.

Allegheny County, Pennsylvania, Housing Authority
Geothermal Heat Pump Consortium
Historic Landmarks Foundation of Indiana
Polk, Iowa, County of
Ways to Work
Wittenburg University

ATTAWAY, Fritz E.

1600 I St. NW
Washington, DC 20006
Tel: (202)293-1966
Fax: (202)296-7410
Registered: LDA

Employers

Motion Picture Ass'n of America (Senior V. President, Government Relations and General Counsel)

ATWATER, Frank G.

606 N. Washington St.
Alexandria, VA 22314
Tel: (703)838-7760
Fax: (703)838-7782
Registered: LDA

Employers

Nat'l Ass'n of Retired Federal Employees (President)

ATWELL, Meredith

600 14th Street NW
Suite 750
Washington, DC 20005
Tel: (202)220-0400
Fax: (202)220-0401

Employers

COVAD Communications Co. (Director, Legislative Affairs)

ATWELL, Robert

1215 Jefferson Davis Hwy.
Suite 1004
Arlington, VA 22202
EMail: atwell@drs.com
Tel: (703)416-8000
Fax: (703)416-8010

Employers

DRS Technologies, Inc. (V. President, Army Programs)

ATWOOD, Deborah M.

1156 15th St. NW
Suite 400
Washington, DC 20005
EMail: datwood@capitolink.com
Tel: (202)427-7800
Fax: (202)296-0833
Registered: LDA

Former Deputy Associate Administrator for Congressional and Legislative Affairs, Environmental Protection Agency.

Employers

Capitolink, LLC (Senior Associate)

Clients Represented

On Behalf of Capitolink, LLC

Nat'l Ass'n of Conservation Districts
Nat'l Pork Producers Council
Premium Standard Farms
Smithfield Foods Inc.

ATWOOD, James R.

1201 Pennsylvania Ave. NW
Washington, DC 20004-2401
EMail: jatwood@cov.com
Tel: (202)662-6000
Fax: (202)662-6291

Deputy Legal Advisor (1979-80) and Deputy Assistant Secretary, Economic and Business Affairs (1978-79), Department of State. Law Clerk to Chief Justice Warren E. Burger, U.S. Supreme Court, 1970-71. Law Clerk to Judge Shirley M. Hufstedler, U.S. Court of Appeals, Ninth Circuit, 1969-70.

Employers

Covington & Burling (Partner)

ATWOOD, John B.

14th and Constitution Ave. NW
Room 7814A
Washington, DC 20230
Tel: (202)482-2309
Fax: (202)501-4828

Employers

Department of Commerce - Economic Development Administration (Communications and Congressional Liaison Specialist)

ATWOOD, Mark

1850 M St. NW
Suite 900
Washington, DC 20036
Tel: (202)463-2500
Fax: (202)463-4950
Registered: LDA

Employers

Sher & Blackwell (Partner)

Clients Represented

On Behalf of Sher & Blackwell

AeroRepublica, S.A.
Casino Express Airlines
Chapman Freeborn America
Custom Air Transport
Japan Internat'l Transport Institute
Kalitta Air, L.L.C.
M K Airlines
Noise Reduction Technology Coalition
Sun Pacific Internat'l

AUBIN, Bonnie M.

2025 M St. NW
Suite 800
Washington, DC 20036
EMail: bonnie_aubin@dc.sba.com
Tel: (202)367-2100
Fax: (202)367-1200
Registered: LDA

Employers

Smith, Bucklin and Associates, Inc.

Clients Represented

On Behalf of Smith, Bucklin and Associates, Inc.

Nat'l Organization for Competency Assurance

AUER, Kenneth E.

50 F St. NW
Suite 900
Washington, DC 20001
EMail: auer@fccouncil.com
Tel: (202)879-0843
Fax: (202)626-8718
Registered: LDA

Employers

Farm Credit Council (C.E.O.)

AUERBACH, James A.

1424 16th St. NW
Suite 700
Washington, DC 20036
EMail: npajim@npa1.org
Tel: (202)884-7627
Fax: (202)797-5516

Employers

Nat'l Policy Ass'n (Senior V. President)

AUERBACH, Randy

918 F St. NW
Washington, DC 20004-1400
Tel: (202)216-2400
Fax: (202)371-9449

Employers

American Immigration Lawyers Ass'n (Director, Publications)

AUGLIS, Linda M.

1100 S. Washington St.
First Floor
Alexandria, VA 22314-4494
Tel: (703)683-4300
Fax: (703)683-8965
Registered: LDA

Employers

Nat'l Beer Wholesalers Ass'n (Director, Political Affairs)

AULAKH, Dr. Gurmit Singh

1901 Pennsylvania Ave. NW
Suite 802
Washington, DC 20006
Tel: (202)833-3262
Fax: (202)452-9161
Registered: FARA

Employers

Khalistan, Council of (President)

AULT, USN (Ret.), Capt. Frank W.

2009 N. 14th St.
Suite 300
Arlington, VA 22201
Tel: (703)527-3065
Fax: (703)528-4229
Registered: LDA

Employers

American Retirees Ass'n (Exec. Director)

AULT, Thomas

444 N. Capitol St. NW
Suite 821
Washington, DC 20001
Tel: (202)737-3390
Fax: (202)628-3607

Employers

Health Policy Alternatives, Inc. (Principal)

Clients Represented

On Behalf of Health Policy Alternatives, Inc.

AdvaMed
American Hospital Ass'n
Federation of American Hospitals
Johnson & Johnson, Inc.
Medtronic, Inc.
Pharmaceutical Research and Manufacturers of America

AURILIO, Anna

218 D St. SE
Second Floor
Washington, DC 20003
Tel: (202)546-9707
Fax: (202)546-2461
Registered: LDA

Employers

U.S. Public Interest Research Group (Staff Scientist)

AUSTELL, Theodore "Ted"

1200 Wilson Blvd.
Arlington, VA 22209-1989
Tel: (703)465-3555
Fax: (703)465-3001

Employers

The Boeing Co. (V. President, International Policy)

AUSTIN, Brian E.

807 Maine Ave. SW
Washington, DC 20024
Tel: (202)554-3501
Fax: (202)554-3581

Employers

Disabled American Veterans (Associate National Service Director)

AUSTIN, Joe

2111 Wilson Blvd.
Eighth Floor
Arlington, VA 22201-3058
EMail: austin@alcalde-fay.com
Tel: (703)841-0626
Fax: (703)243-2874

Employers

Alcalde & Fay (Partner)

AUSTIN, Jr., John

2550 M St. NW
Washington, DC 20037-1350
Tel: (202)457-6000
Fax: (202)457-6315

Former Trial Attorney, Department of Interior.

Employers

Patton Boggs, LLP (Of Counsel)

AUSTIN, K. Sabrina

1101 Vermont Ave. NW
Suite 400
Washington, DC 20005
EMail: austin@dbmlaw.com
Tel: (202)289-3900
Fax: (202)371-0197
Registered: LDA

Employers

Dean Blakey & Moskowitz (Senior Associate)

Clients Represented

On Behalf of Dean Blakey & Moskowitz

Diversified Collection Services, Inc.

AUSTRIAN, Mark L.

3050 K St. NW
Washington, DC 20007
EMail: maustrian@colliershannon.com
Tel: (202)342-8400
Fax: (202)342-8451

Law Clerk to Judge Orrin G. Judd, U.S. District Court for the Eastern District of New York, 1970-71.

Employers

Collier Shannon Scott, PLLC (Member)

Clients Represented

On Behalf of Collier Shannon Scott, PLLC

Outdoor Power Equipment Institute

AUTERY, C. Reuben

2107 Wilson Blvd.
Suite 600
Arlington, VA 22201
Tel: (703)525-7060
Fax: (703)525-6790

Employers

Gas Appliance Manufacturers Ass'n (President)

AUTON, Garland

1600 20th St. NW
Washington, DC 20009-1001
Tel: (202)588-7780
Fax: (202)588-7798

Employers
Buyers Up (Program Manager)

AUTOR, Erik

325 Seventh St. NW
Suite 1100
Washington, DC 20004-2802
Tel: (202)783-7971
Fax: (202)737-2849
Registered: LDA

Employers
Nat'l Retail Federation (V. President, International Trade Counsel)

AUTRY, David E.

807 Maine Ave. SW
Washington, DC 20024
Tel: (202)554-3501
Fax: (202)554-3581

Employers
Disabled American Veterans (Deputy National Director, Communications)

AUTRY, John S.

1133 Connecticut Ave. NW
Suite 1010
Washington, DC 20036
Tel: (202)775-2360
Fax: (202)775-2364
Registered: LDA

Employers
JSA-1, Inc. (President and Chief Exec. Officer)

Clients Represented

On Behalf of JSA-1, Inc.
Newhall Land and Farming Co.

AUXIER, Gary

1801 K St. NW
Suite 1000L
Washington, DC 20006
EMail: gary_auxier@washbm.com
Tel: (202)530-0400
Fax: (202)530-4500

Employers
Burson-Marsteller (Managing Director, Public Affairs)

AUZUNNE, Adrienne

8300 Colesville Rd.
Suite 750
Silver Spring, MD 20910
Tel: (301)585-1855
Fax: (301)585-1866

Employers
Nat'l Burglar and Fire Alarm Ass'n (Director, Government Relations)

AVAKIAN, Michael

5211 Port Royal Rd.
Suite 103
Springfield, VA 22151
Tel: (703)321-9180
Fax: (703)321-9325

Employers
Center on Nat'l Labor Policy (General Counsel)

AVERY, Kevin

1201 New York Ave. NW
Washington, DC 20525
Tel: (202)606-5000
Ext: 473
Fax: (202)208-4214

Employers
Corporation for Nat'l Service (Director, Congressional and Intergovernmental Relations)

AVILA, Pilar

8201 Greensboro Dr.
Suite 300
McLean, VA 22102
Tel: (703)610-9000
Fax: (703)610-9005

Employers
Ass'n Management Group
New America Alliance (Exec. V. President)

Clients Represented

On Behalf of Ass'n Management Group
New America Alliance

AVIV, Diana

1700 K St. NW
Suite 1150
Washington, DC 20006
EMail: diana.aviv@ujc.org
Tel: (202)736-5868
Fax: (202)785-4937
Registered: LDA

Employers
United Jewish Communities, Inc. (V. President, Public Policy and Director, Human Services and Social Policy)

AXENFELD-LANKFORD, Laurie

444 N. Capitol St. NW
Suite 301
Washington, DC 20001
EMail: axenfeld@senate.state.NY.US
Tel: (202)624-5880
Fax: (202)508-3850

Employers
New York State Senate (Exec. Director, Washington Office)

AXTELL, Robert

1775 Massachusetts Ave. NW
Washington, DC 20036-2188
Tel: (202)797-6000
Fax: (202)797-6004

Employers
The Brookings Institution (Fellow, Economic Studies)

AYER, Fran

1730 Rhode Island Ave. NW
Suite 209
Washington, DC 20036-3120
Tel: (202)331-8690
Fax: (202)331-8738
Registered: LDA

Employers
Morriset, Schlosser, Ayer & Jozwiak (Attorney)

Clients Represented

On Behalf of Morriset, Schlosser, Ayer & Jozwiak
Alaska Eskimo Whaling Commission
Bay Mills Indian Community
Kake, Alaska, Organized Village of
Oglala Sioux Tribe
Paucatuck Eastern Pequot Tribal Nation
Prairie Band of Potawatomi Indians
Quechan Indian Tribe
Saginaw Chippewa Indian Tribe of Michigan

AYERS, Carolyn S.

1325 G St. NW
Suite 700
Washington, DC 20005
EMail: cayers@ahi.org
Tel: (202)637-2440
Fax: (202)393-1667

Employers
Animal Health Institute (V. President, Administration and Finance)

AYERS, Stephanie

P.O. Box 19367
Washington, DC 20036
Tel: (202)588-1000
Fax: (202)588-7795

Employers
Freedom of Information Clearinghouse (Contact)

AYLWARD, David K.

888 17th St. NW
12th Floor
Washington, DC 20006
Tel: (202)429-8744
Fax: (202)296-2962
Registered: LDA

Former Chief Counsel and Staff Director, Subcommittee on Telecommunications, Consumer Protection and Finance, House Committee on Commerce.

Employers
Nat'l Strategies Inc. (President)

Clients Represented

On Behalf of Nat'l Strategies Inc.
American Trucking Ass'ns
ATX Technologies
Cellular Telecommunications and Internet Ass'n
The Comcare Alliance
General Reinsurance Corp.
Marconi
Maricopa, Arizona, County of
The McGuffey Project
Shenandoah Valley
Superfund Reform '95
TruePosition Inc.

AYLWARD, Rayna

1560 Wilson Blvd.
Suite 1175
Arlington, VA 22209
Tel: (703)276-3519
Fax: (703)276-8168

Employers
Mitsubishi Electric & Electronics, USA (Exec. Director, Mitsubishi Electric America Foundation)

AYRES, Larry F.

1317 I St. NW
Suite 300 W
Washington, DC 20005
Tel: (202)522-8606
Fax: (202)522-8669
Registered: LDA

Employers
The Atlantic Group, Public Affairs, Inc. (President)

Clients Represented

On Behalf of The Atlantic Group, Public Affairs, Inc.
Carwell Products, Inc.
Compuware Corp.
Dykema Gossett
Barbara A. Karmanos Cancer Institute
Malden Mills Industries, Inc.

AYRES, Merribel S.

1200 18th St. NW
Suite 850
Washington, DC 20036
EMail: mayres@lighthouse-energy.com
Tel: (202)822-2000
Fax: (202)822-2156
Registered: LDA

Employers
Lighthouse Energy Group LLC (President)

Clients Represented

On Behalf of Lighthouse Energy Group LLC
Alliance Pipeline, L.P.
Ballard Power Systems
The Beacon Group Energy Funds
Calpine Corp.
Coleman Powermate
PowerGen
Powerspan Corp.

AZARE, Monica

1300 I St. NW
Suite 400 West
Washington, DC 20005
Tel: (202)515-2400
Fax: (202)589-3750
Registered: LDA

Employers
Verizon Wireless

AZIA, Stephen M.

1667 K St. NW
Suite 700
Washington, DC 20006
Tel: (202)776-7800
Fax: (202)776-7801
Registered: LDA

Employers
Duane, Morris & Heckscher LLP

Clients Represented

On Behalf of Duane, Morris & Heckscher LLP
Power Mobility Coalition

BAAB, Schuyler J.

444 N. Capitol St. NW
Suite 613
Washington, DC 20001
Tel: (202)624-5870
Fax: (202)624-5871

Employers
Wisconsin, Washington Office of the State of (Director, Washington Office)

BABAUTA, Juan N.

2121 R St. NW
Washington, DC 20008-1908
Tel: (202)673-5869
Fax: (202)673-5873
Registered: LDA

Employers
Northern Mariana Islands, Commonwealth of the (Resident Representative to the U.S.)

BABBITT, Bruce E.

555 11th St. NW
Suite 1000
Washington, DC 20004
Tel: (202)637-2200
Fax: (202)637-2201

Secretary, Department of the Interior, 1993-2001.

Employers
Latham & Watkins (Of Counsel)

BABBY, Lorna K.

1712 N St. NW
Washington, DC 20036
EMail: babby@narf.org
Tel: (202)785-4166
Fax: (202)822-0068

Employers
Native American Rights Fund (Managing Attorney)

BABER, Patti Jo

P.O. Box 30005
Alexandria, VA 22310
Tel: (703)960-3011
Fax: (703)960-4070

Employers
American League of Lobbyists (Exec. Director)

BABIARZ, Linda

431 18th St. NW
Washington, DC 20006
Tel: (202)639-3125
Fax: (202)639-6116
EMail: babiarzl@usa.redcross.org

Employers
American Red Cross (Analyst)

BABICS CHASE, Catherine C.

750 First St. NE
Suite 901
Washington, DC 20002
Tel: (202)408-1711
Fax: (202)408-1699
EMail: cbchase@saferoads.org

Employers
Advocates for Highway and Auto Safety (Director, State Affairs)

BABYAK, Gregory R.

925 15th St. NW
Fifth Floor
Washington, DC 20006
Tel: (202)296-0784
Fax: (202)293-2768
Registered: LDA
EMail: gbabyak@royerandbabyak.com
Former Chief of Staff to Rep. James Scheuer (D-NY).

Employers
Royer & Babyak (Partner)

Clients Represented
On Behalf of Royer & Babyak
Bloomberg L.P.
Contact Lens Institute
Genentech, Inc.

BACA, USA (Ret.), Lt. Gen Edward

11 Canal Center Plaza
Suite 103
Alexandria, VA 22314
Tel: (703)683-4222
Fax: (703)683-0645
Registered: LDA
Chief National Guard Bureau, 1994-98.

Employers
The Spectrum Group

BACAK, Jr., Walter W.

225 Reinekers Lane
Suite 590
Alexandria, VA 22314
Tel: (703)683-6100
Fax: (703)683-6122
EMail: ata@atanet.org

Employers
American Translators Ass'n (Exec. Director)

BACCHUS, Julie

2011 Pennsylvania Ave. NW
Suite 800
Washington, DC 20006
Tel: (202)835-0437
Fax: (202)835-0442

Employers
Medical Advocacy Services, Inc. (Government Affairs Representative)

BACH, Dianne

7910 Woodmont Ave.
Suite 700
Bethesda, MD 20814
Tel: (301)654-2055
Fax: (301)654-5920

Employers
American Gastroenterological Ass'n (V. President, Communications and Marketing)

BACHELLER, Burt P.

1200 Wilson Blvd.
Arlington, VA 22209-1989
Tel: (703)465-3546
Fax: (703)465-3038

Employers
The Boeing Co. (Director, International Programs)

BACHENHEIMER, Cara

1227 25th St. NW
Suite 700
Washington, DC 20037
Tel: (202)861-0900
Fax: (202)296-2882
Registered: LDA

Employers
Epstein Becker & Green, P.C. (Senior Counsel)

BACHINGER, Mary

2501 M St. NW
Suite 400
Washington, DC 20037
Tel: (202)861-2500
Fax: (202)861-2583

Employers
Nat'l Ass'n of College and University Business Officers (Senior Policy Analyst)

BACHMAN, Gary D.

1050 Thomas Jefferson St. NW
Seventh Floor
Washington, DC 20007
Tel: (202)298-1800
Fax: (202)338-2416
Registered: LDA
EMail: gdb@unf.com

Employers
Van Ness Feldman, P.C. (Member)

Clients Represented
On Behalf of Van Ness Feldman, P.C.
Public Generating Pool
Tacoma, Washington, City of

BACHMAN, Jr., Kenneth L.

2000 Pennsylvania Ave. NW
Washington, DC 20006
Tel: (202)974-1500
Fax: (202)974-1999
Registered: LDA, FARA
Law Clerk to Judge Irving Ben Cooper, U.S. District Court for the Southern District of New York, 1968-70.

Employers
Cleary, Gottlieb, Steen and Hamilton (Partner)

Clients Represented
On Behalf of Cleary, Gottlieb, Steen and Hamilton
Asahi Glass Co.
Kuwait, Government of

BACHNER, John P.

8811 Colesville Rd.
Suite G 106
Silver Spring, MD 20910
Tel: (301)589-9121
Fax: (301)589-2017

Employers
Bachner Communications, Inc. (President)

Clients Represented
On Behalf of Bachner Communications, Inc.
ASFE

BACHRACH, Eve E.

1150 Connecticut Ave. NW
12th Floor
Washington, DC 20036
Tel: (202)429-9260
Fax: (202)223-6835

Employers
Consumer Healthcare Products Ass'n (Senior V. President, General Counsel and Secretary)

BACINO, Geoff

112 Southwest St.
Alexandria, VA 22314
Tel: (703)549-8454
Fax: (703)836-5255
Registered: LDA
EMail: Bacino1@aol.com

Employers
Bacino & Associates (President)

Clients Represented
On Behalf of Bacino & Associates
Liberty Check Printers
Sense Technologies, Inc.
World Sports Exchange

BACK, Kelli D.

1800 K St. NW
Suite 720
Washington, DC 20006
Tel: (202)457-6633
Fax: (202)457-6636
Registered: LDA

Employers
Law Offices of Mark S. Joffe (Attorney)

Clients Represented
On Behalf of Law Offices of Mark S. Joffe
Medicare Cost Contractors Alliance

BACKUS, Jeremy

430 S. Capitol St. SE
Washington, DC 20003
Tel: (202)863-8000
Fax: (202)863-8174

Employers
Democratic Nat'l Committee (Press Secretary)

BACO, Luis E.

600 13th St. NW
Washington, DC 20005-3096
Tel: (202)756-8095
Fax: (202)756-8087
Registered: LDA
EMail: lbaco@mwe.com
Legislative Director and Deputy Chief of Staff to Rep. Carlos Romero-Barcelo, 1993-97.

Employers
McDermott, Will and Emery (Attorney at Law)

Clients Represented
On Behalf of McDermott, Will and Emery
Government Development Bank of Puerto Rico

BACON, Amy E.

1900 Duke St.
Suite 200
Alexandria, VA 22314
Tel: (703)299-1050
Fax: (703)299-1044
Registered: LDA
EMail: bacona@asco.org

Employers
American Soc. of Clinical Oncology (Legislative Specialist)

BACON, Joel

601 Madison
Suite 400
Alexandria, VA 22314
Tel: (703)824-0500
Fax: (703)820-1395

Employers
AAAE-ACI (Director, Legislative Affairs)

BACON, Kenneth H.

1705 N St. NW
Washington, DC 20036
Tel: (202)828-0110
Fax: (202)828-0819
Assistant Secretary of Defense, Public Affairs, 1994-2001.

Employers
Refugees Internat'l (President)

BACON, Suzanne C.

1050 Thomas Jefferson St. NW
Seventh Floor
Washington, DC 20007
Tel: (202)298-1800
Fax: (202)338-2416
Registered: LDA
Former Legislative Assistant to Senator Dirk Kempthorne (R-ID).

Employers
Van Ness Feldman, P.C. (Associate Director, Gov't Issues)

Clients Represented
On Behalf of Van Ness Feldman, P.C.
Sacramento Municipal Utility District

BADAMI, Scott M.

700 13th St. NW
Suite 700
Washington, DC 20005-3960
Tel: (202)508-6000
Fax: (202)508-6200
EMail: smbadami@bryancave.com
Legislative Director and Press Secretary to Rep. Ike Skelton (D-MO), 1984-88.

Employers
Bryan Cave LLP (Counsel)

BADER, Anne C.

1701 K St. NW
Suite 1100
Washington, DC 20006
Tel: (202)223-7940
Fax: (202)223-7947

Employers
The Fund for Peace (V. President, Development and Communications)

BADGER, Doug

1150 17th St. NW
Suite 601
Washington, DC 20036
Tel: (202)293-7474
Fax: (202)293-8811
Registered: LDA
Former Chief of Staff to Senator Don Nickles (R-OK).

Employers
Washington Council Ernst & Young (Partner)

Clients Represented

On Behalf of Washington Council Ernst & Young

Aetna Inc.
Aetna Life & Casualty Co.
Allen & Co.
American Express Co.
American Insurance Ass'n
American Staffing Ass'n
Anheuser-Busch Cos., Inc.
Antitrust Coalition for Consumer Choice in Health Care
Apartment Investment and Management Co.
Ass'n of American Railroads
Ass'n of Home Appliance Manufacturers
AT&T
AT&T Capital Corp.
Aventis Pharmaceuticals, Inc.
Baxter Healthcare Corp.
BHC Communications, Inc.
Bulmer Holding PLC, H. P.
Cash Balance Coalition
Citigroup
Coalition for Fairness in Defense Exports
Coalition to Preserve Tracking Stock
ComEd
The Connell Co.
Deferral Group
Directors Guild of America
Doris Duke Charitable Foundation
Eaton Vance Management Co.
Eden Financial Corp.
The Enterprise Foundation
Fannie Mae
FedEx Corp.
Ford Motor Co.
GE Capital Assurance
General Electric Co.
General Motors Corp.
Global Competitiveness Coalition
Grasslands Water District
Group Health, Inc.
Haz-X Support Services Corp.
HEREIU
Gilbert P. Hyatt, Inventor
Investment Co. Institute
Large Public Power Council
Local Initiatives Support Corp.
Lockheed Martin Corp.
MacAndrews & Forbes Holdings, Inc.
Marsh & McLennan Cos.
MCG Northwest, Inc.
McLane Co.
Merrill Lynch & Co., Inc.
Metropolitan Banking Group
Microsoft Corp.
Mutual of Omaha Insurance Companies
Nat'l Ass'n for State Farm Agents
Nat'l Ass'n of Professional Employer Organizations
Nat'l Ass'n of Real Estate Investment Trusts
Nat'l Ass'n of State Farm Agents
Nat'l Cable Television Ass'n
Nat'l Defined Contribution Council
Nat'l Foreign Trade Council, Inc.
Nat'l Multi-Housing Council
PaineWebber Group, Inc.
Pfizer, Inc.
R&D Tax Credit Coalition
R&D Tax Regulation Group
Recording Industry Ass'n of America
Reed-Elsevier Inc.
R. J. Reynolds Tobacco Co.
Charles Schwab & Co., Inc.,
Securities Industry Ass'n
Sierra Pacific Industries
Skadden, Arps, Slate, Meagher & Flom LLP
Straddle Rules Tax Group
Tax Fairness Coalition
Tax/Shelter Coalition
TransOceanic Shipping
TU Services
TXU Business Services
U.S. Oncology
USA Biomass Power Producers Alliance
Viaticus, Inc.
Wilkie Farr & Gallagher
Ziff Investors Partnership

BAEBLER, Paul

1200 G St. NW
Suite 510
Washington, DC 20005
EMail: paul@csa-dc.org
Tel: (202)347-0600
Fax: (202)347-0608

Employers
Contract Services Ass'n of America (Director, Membership Services)

BAER, Don

7700 Wisconsin Ave.
Bethesda, MD 20814
Tel: (301)986-1999
Fax: (301)986-5998

Employers
Discovery Communications, Inc. (Exec. V. President, Strategies)

BAER, Teresa D.

555 11th St. NW
Suite 1000
Washington, DC 20004
Tel: (202)637-2200
Fax: (202)637-2201
Registered: LDA
Judicial Clerk to Judge Anthony M. Kennedy, U.S. Court of Appeals, Ninth Circuit, 1985-86.

Employers
Latham & Watkins (Counsel)

BAER, Wendy J.

4214 King St. West
Alexandria, VA 22302
Tel: (703)820-6696
Fax: (703)820-8550

Employers
IWPA - The Internat'l Wood Products Ass'n (Exec. Vice President)

BAER, William E.

1800 M St. NW
Washington, DC 20036
Tel: (202)467-7000
Fax: (202)467-7176
Registered: LDA
EMail: wbaer@morganlewis.com

Employers
Morgan, Lewis & Bockius LLP

Clients Represented

On Behalf of Morgan, Lewis & Bockius LLP

Credit Suisse First Boston Corp.

BAER, William J.

555 12th St. NW
Washington, DC 20004-1206
Tel: (202)942-5000
Fax: (202)942-5999
EMail: William_Baer@aporter.com
Director, Bureau of Competition, Federal Trade Commission, 1995-99. Also held the positions Trial Attorney, Assistant to the Director of Bureau of Consumer Protection, Attorney Advisor to the Chairman, Assistant General Counsel, and Director of Congressional Relations, all at the Federal Trade Commission.

Employers
Arnold & Porter (Partner)

BAFALIS, Hon. Louis A. "Skip"

2111 Wilson Blvd.
Eighth Floor
Arlington, VA 22201-3058
Tel: (703)841-0626
Fax: (703)243-2874
Registered: LDA
EMail: bafalis@alcalde-fay.com
Member, U.S. House of Representatives (R-FL), 1973-83.

Employers
Alcalde & Fay (Partner)

Clients Represented

On Behalf of Alcalde & Fay

Bay County, Florida
Boca Raton, Florida, City of
Deerfield Beach, Florida, City of
Internat'l Council of Cruise Lines
Mitretek Systems
North American Sports Management, Inc.
Osceola, Florida, County of
Palm Beach, Florida, Port of
PetrolRem, Inc.
Riviera Beach, Florida, City of
Section 877 Coalition
Stevens Institute of Technology

BAFFER, Barbara

1634 I St. NW
Suite 600
Washington, DC 20006-4083
Tel: (202)783-2200
Fax: (202)783-2206
Registered: LDA

Employers
Ericsson Inc. (Director, Public Affairs and Regulation)

BAGGAGE, Mable T.

550 17th St. NW
MS: 6066
Washington, DC 20429-9990
Tel: (202)898-6982
Fax: (202)898-3745

Employers
Federal Deposit Insurance Corp. (Administrative Officer, Office of Legislative Affairs)

BAGGETT, Capt. Joseph E.

The Pentagon
MS: 5C800
Washington, DC 20350-1300
EMail: baggett.joe@hq.navy.mil
Tel: (703)695-5276
Fax: (703)614-7089

Employers
Department of Navy (Director, Legislation, Legislative Affairs)

BAGIN, Rich D.

15948 Derwood Rd.
Rockville, MD 20855
EMail: nspra@nspra.org
Tel: (301)519-0496
Fax: (301)519-0494

Employers
Nat'l School Public Relations Ass'n (Exec. Director)

BAGLEY, Grant

555 12th St. NW
Washington, DC 20004-1206
Tel: (202)942-5000
Fax: (202)942-5999
Registered: LDA
EMail: Grant_Bagley@aporter.com
Former Director of the Coverage and Analysis Group, Office of Clinical Standards and Quality, Health Care Financing Administration, Department of Health and Human Services.

Employers
Arnold & Porter (Partner)

Clients Represented

On Behalf of Arnold & Porter

Mentor Corp.
Novartis Corp.
RoTech Medical Corp.
Roxanne Laboratories, Inc.
Wyeth-Ayerst Pharmaceuticals

BAGLEY, John F.

901 D St. SW
Suite 900
Washington, DC 20024
EMail: Jack.Bagley@Battelle.org
Tel: (202)479-0500
Registered: LDA

Employers
Battelle Memorial Institute (V. President, External Relations)

BAGLEY, Larry K.

1440 Duke St.
Alexandria, VA 22314
EMail: LBagley@uspa.org
Tel: (703)836-3495
Fax: (703)836-2843

Employers
United States Parachute Ass'n (Deputy Exec. Director)

BAGLIEN, Brent A.

1627 I St. NW
Suite 950
Washington, DC 20006
Tel: (202)223-5115
Fax: (202)223-5118
Registered: LDA

Employers
ConAgra Foods, Inc. (V. President, Government Affairs)

BAHIN, Charlotte M.

900 19th St. NW
Suite 400
Washington, DC 20006
Tel: (202)857-3100
Fax: (202)296-8716
Registered: LDA

Employers
America's Community Bankers (Regulatory Counsel)

BAHR, Morton

501 Third St. NW
Washington, DC 20001-2797
Tel: (202)434-1100
Fax: (202)434-1139

Employers
Communications Workers of America (President)

BAHRET, Mary Ellen

1201 F St. NW
Suite 200
Washington, DC 20004
Tel: (202)554-9000
Fax: (202)554-0496
Registered: LDA

Former Legislative Assistant and Deputy Press Secretary to Senator Larry E. Craig (R-ID).

Employers
Nat'l Federation of Independent Business (Manager, Legislative Affairs/Senate)

BAILEY, Arthur L.

1330 Connecticut Ave. NW
Washington, DC 20036-1795
Tel: (202)429-3000
Fax: (202)429-3902
EMail: abailey@steptoe.com

Trial Attorney, Appellate Section, Taxation Division, Department of Justice, 1972-77. Tax Law Specialist, Exempt Organizations Branch, Internal Revenue Service, 1969-72.

Employers
Steptoe & Johnson LLP (Partner)

BAILEY, Christopher

515 King St.
Suite 420
Alexandria, VA 22314-3103
Tel: (703)684-5570
Fax: (703)684-6048

Employers
CLARION Management Resources, Inc.

Clients Represented
On Behalf of CLARION Management Resources, Inc.
Wireless Location Industry Ass'n

BAILEY, Jr., Harold G.

1000 Potomac St. NW
Suite 500
Washington, DC 20007
Tel: (202)965-7880
Fax: (202)965-1729
Registered: LDA, FARA
EMail: bbailey@gsblaw.com

Employers
Garvey, Schubert & Barer (Partner)

Clients Represented
On Behalf of Garvey, Schubert & Barer
Bolsa Chica Land Trust

BAILEY, Jeanne

1401 New York Ave. NW
Suite 640
Washington, DC 20005
Tel: (202)628-8303
Fax: (202)628-2846

Employers
American Water Works Ass'n (Regulatory Engineer)

BAILEY, Kirk

1000 Connecticut Ave. NW
Suite 302
Washington, DC 20036
Tel: (202)835-0740
Fax: (202)775-8526
Registered: LDA

Employers
Smith Dawson & Andrews, Inc.

Clients Represented
On Behalf of Smith Dawson & Andrews, Inc.
Kansas City Area Transportation Authority
Mothers Against Drunk Driving (MADD)
Springfield, Oregon, School District #19

BAILEY, Melissa

1050 Connecticut Ave. NW
Washington, DC 20036-5339
Tel: (202)857-6000
Fax: (202)857-6395

Employers
Arent Fox Kintner Plotkin & Kahn, PLLC (Associate)

BAILEY, Norman A.

1311 Dolly Madison Blvd.
Suite 2A
McLean, VA 22101
Tel: (703)506-0779
Fax: (703)506-8085
EMail: normanabailey@aol.com

Former Staff Member, Nat'l Security Council during the Reagan Administration.

Employers
Norman A. Bailey, Inc. (President)

Clients Represented
On Behalf of Norman A. Bailey, Inc.
The AES Corp.
Bank of Tokyo-Mitsubishi
Inter-Nation Capital Management
Madeira Development Co.

BAILEY, Pamela G.

1200 G St. NW
Suite 400
Washington, DC 20005
Tel: (202)783-8700
Fax: (202)783-8750

Employers
AdvaMed (President)

BAILEY, Paul

701 Pennsylvania Ave. NW
Washington, DC 20004-2696
Tel: (202)508-5640
Fax: (202)508-5150

Employers
Edison Electric Institute (V. President, Environmental)

BAILEY, R. Lane

2300 Clarendon Blvd.
Suite 610
Arlington, VA 22201-3367
Tel: (703)351-5666
Fax: (703)351-5667
EMail: lbailey@golinharris.com

Administrative Assistant (1988-98), State Director (1984-88), and Special Assistant (1977-84) to Senator John D. Rockefeller IV (D-WV).

Employers
Golin/Harris Internat'l (Managing Director)

BAIME, David S.

One Dupont Circle NW
Suite 410
Washington, DC 20036
Tel: (202)728-0200
Ext: 224
Fax: (202)833-2467
Registered: LDA
EMail: dbaime@aacc.nche.edu

Employers
American Ass'n of Community Colleges (Director, Government Relations)

BAIN, C. Jackson

913 King St.
Alexandria, VA 22314
Tel: (703)549-9592
Fax: (703)549-9601
EMail: bain@bainpr.com

Employers
Bain and Associates, Inc. (Chairman)

Clients Represented
On Behalf of Bain and Associates, Inc.
Biotechnology Industry Organization

BAIN, Sandra Kyle

913 King St.
Alexandria, VA 22314
Tel: (703)549-9592
Fax: (703)549-9601
EMail: bain@bainpr.com

Employers
Bain and Associates, Inc. (President)

BAINE, Kevin T.

725 12th St. NW
Washington, DC 20005
Tel: (202)434-5000
Fax: (202)434-5029

Employers
Williams & Connolly (Partner)

BAIR, James A.

600 Maryland Ave. SW
Suite 305 West
Washington, DC 20024
Tel: (202)484-2200
Ext: 107
Fax: (202)488-7416
EMail: jabair@aol.com

Employers
North American Millers' Ass'n (V. President)

BAIRD, Bruce A.

1201 Pennsylvania Ave. NW
Washington, DC 20004-2401
Tel: (202)662-6000
Fax: (202)662-6291
EMail: bbaird@cov.com

Assistant Attorney, Southern District of New York, 1980-89. Law Clerk, Second Circuit, Court of Appeals, 1976-77. Special Assistant to the Deputy Attorney General, 1975-76.

Employers
Covington & Burling (Partner)

BAISE, Gary H.

1020 19th St. NW
Suite 400
Washington, DC 20036
Tel: (202)331-9100
Fax: (202)331-9060
Registered: LDA

Acting Deputy Attorney General (1974), Associate Deputy Attorney General (1973-74), and Trial Attorney (1969-70); Department of Justice. Director, Office of Legislation (1971-73) and Assistant to the Administrator (1970-71), Environmental Protection Agency.

Employers
Baise + Miller, P.C. (Partner)

Clients Represented
On Behalf of Baise + Miller, P.C.
Food Distributors Internat'l (NAWGA-IFDA)
Nat'l Ass'n of Wheat Growers

BAISH, Mary Alice

E.B. Williams Law Library
Georgetown University Law Center
111 G St. NW
Washington, DC 20001-1417
Tel: (202)662-9200
Fax: (202)662-9202
Registered: LDA
EMail: baish@law.georgetown.edu

Employers
American Ass'n of Law Libraries (Associate Washington Affairs Representative)

BAJER, Ed

1015 15th St. NW
Suite 802
Washington, DC 20005
Tel: (202)347-7474
Fax: (202)898-0068
EMail: ebajer@acec.org

Employers
American Consulting Engineers Council (Director, Energy and Interprofessional Programs)

BAKER, Allison A.

The Willard Office Bldg.
1455 Pennsylvania Ave. NW
Washington, DC 20004
Tel: (202)783-6000
Fax: (202)783-4171

Employers
Gibbons & Company, Inc.

BAKER, Rabbi Andrew

1156 15th St. NW
Suite 1201
Washington, DC 20005
Tel: (202)785-4200
Fax: (202)785-4115

Employers
American Jewish Committee (Director, European Affairs)

BAKER, Angela

409 Third St. SW
Second Floor
Washington, DC 20024-6682
Tel: (202)479-6690
Fax: (202)479-0735

Employers
Nat'l Institute on Adult Daycare (Director)

BAKER, Benjamin

3208 Park View Rd.
Chevy Chase, MD 20815
Tel: (301)951-3345
Fax: (301)951-1846

Employers
Eversole Associates (Associate)

BAKER, Bill

P.O. Box 2999
Reston, VA 20191
Tel: (703)620-6003
Ext: 313
Fax: (703)620-5071
EMail: bbaker@rvia.org

Employers
Recreation Vehicle Industry Ass'n (Director, Government Affairs)

BAKER, Brett

2011 Pennsylvania Ave. NW
Suite 800
Washington, DC 20006-1808
Tel: (202)261-4533
Fax: (202)835-0443
Registered: LDA
EMail: bbaker@mail.acponline.org

Employers
American College of Physicians-American Soc. of Internal Medicine (ACP-ASIM) (Associate, Third Party Relations and Regulatory Affairs)

BAKER, Caleb

901 15th Street NW
Washington, DC 20005
Tel: (202)371-6329
Fax: (202)312-3011
Registered: LDA

Employers
C. Baker Consulting Inc. (President)

Clients Represented

On Behalf of C. Baker Consulting Inc.
Allison Transmission Division, General Motors Corp.
General Dynamics Corp.
Honeywell Internat'l, Inc.
Raytheon Co.
Stewart & Stevenson Services, Inc.

BAKER, III, Charles A.

1001 G St. NW
Suite 300 East
Washington, DC 20001
Tel: (202)638-5616
Fax: (202)638-5612
Registered: LDA
EMail: cbaker@deweysquare.com

Employers
Dewey Square Group (Partner)

Clients Represented

On Behalf of Dewey Square Group
Northwest Airlines, Inc.

BAKER, Dr. Charles W.

1101 15th St. NW
Suite 600
Washington, DC 20005
Tel: (202)785-1122
Ext: 12
Fax: (202)785-5019

Employers
Sugar Ass'n, Inc. (V. President, Scientific Affairs)

BAKER, David H.

1920 N St. NW
Washington, DC 20036
Tel: (202)973-2709
Fax: (202)331-8330
EMail: dbaker@thf.com

Employers
Thompson, Hine and Flory LLP (Partner)

Clients Represented

On Behalf of Thompson, Hine and Flory LLP
Alliance for Responsible Cuba Policy
American Pyrotechnics Ass'n
Asphalt Emulsion Manufacturers Ass'n
Asphalt Recycling and Reclaiming Ass'n
Bridgeport and Port Jefferson Steamboat Co.
Lighter Ass'n, Inc.
Nat'l Council For Fireworks Safety
Plastic Container Institute
Plastic Shipping Container Institute
Tobacco Industry Labor Management Committee
Tobacco Industry Testing Laboratory, Inc.
Writing Instrument Manufacturers Ass'n

BAKER, Edwin "Ted" W.

P.O. Box 17265
Washington, DC 20041
Tel: (703)478-2228
Fax: (703)742-8471
EMail: tbaker@appraisers.org

Employers
American Soc. of Appraisers (Exec. V. President)

BAKER, Emily A.

1015 15th St. NW
Suite 802
Washington, DC 20005
Tel: (202)347-7474
Fax: (202)898-0076
EMail: ebaker@acec.org

Employers
American Consulting Engineers Council (Deputy Director, Environmental Programs/EBAC)
Environmental Business Action Coalition (Deputy Exec. Director)

BAKER, George D.

1155 21st St. NW
Suite 300
Washington, DC 20036
Tel: (202)659-8201
Fax: (202)659-5249
Registered: LDA
EMail: gdbaker@wms-jen.com
Former Attorney, Office of Hearings and Appeals, Department of Energy.

Employers
Williams & Jensen, P.C. (Partner)

Clients Represented

On Behalf of Williams & Jensen, P.C.
Ad Hoc Coalition of Commercial and Investment Banks
Bass Enterprises Production Co.
CIGNA Corp.
Colonial Pipeline Co.
Estee Lauder, Inc.
Eurex Deutschland
KSL Development Corp.
Oklahoma Gas and Electric Co.
Superfund Reform '95
Texaco Group Inc.
USAA - United Services Automobile Ass'n

BAKER, Gerald E.

1625 Massachusetts Ave. NW
Washington, DC 20036
Tel: (202)797-4039
Fax: (202)797-4030
Registered: LDA

Employers
Air Line Pilots Ass'n Internat'l (Senior Legislative Representative)

BAKER, Gwen

3138 N. Tenth St.
Arlington, VA 22201
Tel: (703)522-4770
Fax: (703)522-0594

Employers
Nat'l Ass'n of Federal Credit Unions (Director, Regulatory Affairs and Federal Regulatory Counsel)

BAKER, Jr., Hon. Howard H.

801 Pennsylvania Ave. NW
Suite 800
Washington, DC 20004
Tel: (202)508-3400
Fax: (202)508-3402
Registered: LDA, FARA
EMail: hbaker@bdbc.com
Chief of Staff to the President, The White House, 1987-88. Member, U.S. Senate (R-TN), 1966-85. (Served as Senate Majority Leader, 1981-85, and Senate Minority Leader, 1977-81.)

Employers
Baker, Donelson, Bearman & Caldwell, P.C. (Shareholder)

Clients Represented

On Behalf of Baker, Donelson, Bearman & Caldwell, P.C.
Deutsche Telekom, Inc.
Loral Space and Communications, Ltd.
VoiceStream Wireless Corp.

BAKER, III, James A.

1001 Pennsylvania Ave. NW
Suite 220 South
Washington, DC 20004
Tel: (202)347-2626
Fax: (202)347-1818
Former Secretary of State and White House Chief of Staff.

Employers
The Carlyle Group (Senior Counselor)

BAKER, IV, James A.

1299 Pennsylvania Ave. NW
Suite 1300 West
Washington, DC 20004-2400
Tel: (202)639-7700
Fax: (202)639-7890
Registered: LDA
Counsel to the Majority Leader, U.S. Senate, 1982-85.

Employers
Baker Botts, L.L.P. (Partner)

Clients Represented

On Behalf of Baker Botts, L.L.P.
Aventis Pharmaceutical Products
Harris, Texas, Metropolitan Transit Authority of
Mickey Leland Nat'l Urban Air Toxics Research Center

BAKER, James Jay

11250 Waples Mill Rd.
Fairfax, VA 22030-7400
Tel: (703)267-1000
Fax: (703)267-3973
Registered: LDA

Employers
Nat'l Rifle Ass'n Institute for Legislative Action (Exec. Director)

BAKER, Jules Evan

1424 16th St. NW
Suite 102
Washington, DC 20036
Tel: (202)328-2191
Fax: (202)265-6682

Employers
Nat'l Ass'n for Human Development (President)

BAKER, Laurin M.

526 Bellvue Pl.
Alexandria, VA 22314-1408
Tel: (703)548-5545
Fax: (703)548-1339

Employers
The Laurin Baker Group (President)

Clients Represented

On Behalf of The Laurin Baker Group
Illinois Tool Works
Industrial Fasteners Institute
Kinghorn & Associates, L.L.C.
South Carolina Public Railways

BAKER, Mark

400 N. Capitol St. NW
Suite 363
Washington, DC 20001
Tel: (202)783-0280
Fax: (202)737-4518
Former Legislative Director and Legal Counsel, Senator Conrad Burns (R-MT); Chief of Staff, Rep. Rick Hill (R-MT).

Employers
Denny Miller McBee Associates (Of Counsel)

BAKER, Mark

1250 I St. NW
Suite 400
Washington, DC 20005-3998
Tel: (202)628-3544
Fax: (202)682-8888
EMail: mbaker@discus.org

Employers
Distilled Spirits Council of the United States, Inc. (V. President, International Trade)

BAKER, Maxine B.

8200 Jones Branch Dr.
McLean, VA 22102
Tel: (703)903-2362
Fax: (703)903-4270

Employers
Federal Home Loan Mortgage Corp. (Freddie Mac) (President and CEO of Foundation and V. President of Community Relations)

BAKER, P. Jean

601 Pennsylvania Ave. NW
Suite 700
Washington, DC 20004-2676
Tel: (202)737-0392
Fax: (202)737-9099
EMail: bakerj@adr.org

Employers
American Arbitration Ass'n (V. President, Government Programs)

BAKER, Pauline H.

1701 K St. NW
Suite 1100
Washington, DC 20006
Tel: (202)223-7940
Fax: (202)223-7947
EMail: pbaker@fundforpeace.org

Employers
The Fund for Peace (President)

BAKER, Robin

600 New Hampshire Ave. NW
Suite 601
Washington, DC 20037
Tel: (202)333-7400
Fax: (202)333-1638

Employers
Hill and Knowlton, Inc. (Managing Director)

BAKER, Stewart A.

1330 Connecticut Ave. NW
Washington, DC 20036-1795
Tel: (202)429-3000
Fax: (202)429-3902
EMail: sbaker@steptoe.com

General Counsel, National Security Agency, 1992-94. Deputy General Counsel and Special Assistant, Department of Education, 1979-81. Law Clerk to Justice John Paul Stevens, U.S. Supreme Court, 1977-78, and to Chief Judge Frank M. Coffin, U.S. Court of Appeals, First Circuit, 1976-77.

Employers
Steptoe & Johnson LLP (Partner)

Clients Represented
On Behalf of Steptoe & Johnson LLP
Motorola, Inc.
Netscape Communications Corp.

BAKER, Willie

P.O. Box 66268
Washington, DC 20035-6268
Tel: (202)429-1203
Fax: (202)429-1102

Employers
Coalition of Black Trade Unionists (Exec. V. President)

BAKER-SHENK, Philip

1001 Pennsylvania Ave. NW
Suite 300S
Washington, DC 20004
Tel: (202)824-8800
Fax: (202)824-8990
Registered: LDA
EMail: bakershenk.philip@dorseylaw.com

Former Majority General Counsel, Senate Committee on Indian Affairs.

Employers
Dorsey & Whitney LLP (Partner)

Clients Represented
On Behalf of Dorsey & Whitney LLP
Aleutian Pribilof Islands Community Development Ass'n
Bristol Bay Native Corp.
Central Council of Tlingit and Haida Indian Tribes of Alaska
Cow Creek Umpqua Tribe of Oregon
Cuyapaipe Band of Mission Indians
Delaware Tribe of Indians
Grand Traverse Band of Chippewa and Ottawa Indians
Hoopa Valley Tribal Council
Jamestown-S'Klallam Indian Tribe
Little River Band of Ottawa Indians
Nez Perce Tribal Executive Committee
Pascua Yaqui Tribe of Arizona
Quinault Indian Nation
Red Lake Band of Chippewa Indians
Saginaw Chippewa Indian Tribe of Michigan
Shakopee Mdewakanton Sioux Tribe
Spokane Tribe
St. George Island Traditional Council
Stockbridge-Munsee Community Band of Mohican Indians
Winnebago Tribe of Nebraska

BALAGUER, James

445 12th St. NW
Room 8-C445
Washington, DC 20554
Tel: (202)418-1900
Fax: (202)418-2806

Employers
Federal Communications Commission (Legislative Analyst)

BALCERZAK, Steven

1350 I St. NW
Suite 870
Washington, DC 20005
Tel: (202)638-0550
Fax: (202)737-1947

Employers
Managed Care Compliance Solutions, Inc. (Principal)

BALCH, M.D., Charles

1900 Duke St.
Suite 200
Alexandria, VA 22314
Tel: (703)299-1050
Fax: (703)299-1044

Employers
American Soc. of Clinical Oncology (Exec. V. President and Chief Exec. Officer)

BALCH, Mary Spaulding

419 Seventh St. NW
Suite 500
Washington, DC 20004
Tel: (202)626-8800
Fax: (202)737-9189

Employers
Nat'l Right to Life Committee (Director, State Legislative Department)

BALCH, Thomas

419 Seventh St. NW
Suite 500
Washington, DC 20004
Tel: (202)626-8800
Fax: (202)737-9189
Registered: LDA

Employers
Nat'l Right to Life Committee (Director, Medical Ethics Department)

BALDWIN, MPH, Barbara

4405 East-West Hwy.
Suite 405
Bethesda, MD 20814-9139
Tel: (301)913-9517
Fax: (301)913-9520
EMail: run@americanrunning.org

Employers
American Running and Fitness Ass'n (Director, Information Services)

BALDWIN, Donald

888 16th St. NW
Suite 700
Washington, DC 20006-4103
Tel: (202)835-8020
Fax: (202)331-4291
Registered: LDA

Chairman (1986) and Member (1981-86), National Institute of Justice Advisory Board. White House Assistant; Administrative Assistant to Members of Congress.

Employers
Donald Baldwin Associates (President)
Nat'l Law Enforcement Council (Exec. Director)

Clients Represented
On Behalf of Donald Baldwin Associates
Citizens for Law and Order
Federal Criminal Investigators Ass'n
Nat'l Law Enforcement Council
Security on Campus, Inc.

BALDWIN, Jana V. T.

600 13th St. NW
Washington, DC 20005-3096
Tel: (202)756-8191
Fax: (202)756-8087
EMail: jbaldwin@mwe.com

Employers
McDermott, Will and Emery (Partner)

BALILES, Gerald L.

1900 K St. NW
Washington, DC 20006-1109
Tel: (202)955-1500
Fax: (202)778-2201
Registered: LDA
EMail: gbaliles@hunton.com

Employers
Hunton & Williams (Partner)

Clients Represented
On Behalf of Hunton & Williams
Coalition for a Global Standard on Aviation Noise

BALIS, Stanley W.

1140 19th St. NW
Suite 700
Washington, DC 20036
Tel: (202)296-2960
Fax: (202)296-0166

Assistant Director for Oil and Gas Pipeline and Producer Enforcement, Federal Energy Regulatory Commission, 1978-79.

Employers
Miller, Balis and O'Neil, P.C. (Principal)

Clients Represented
On Behalf of Miller, Balis and O'Neil, P.C.
American Public Gas Ass'n

BALK-TUSA, Dr. Jacqueline

2550 M St. NW
Suite 250
Washington, DC 20037
Tel: (202)457-5671
Fax: (202)785-0480
Registered: LDA

Employers
Andrews Associates, Inc. (President)

Clients Represented
On Behalf of Andrews Associates, Inc.
Mars, Inc.
Nat'l Trailer Dealers Ass'n
Patton Boggs, LLP
Safeguard America's Family Enterprises

BALL, Andrea

1629 K St. NW
Suite 1100
Washington, DC 20006
Tel: (202)785-6710
Fax: (202)331-4212
EMail: anjball@aol.com

Employers
Agri/Washington (Accounts Director)

Clients Represented
On Behalf of Agri/Washington
American Ass'n of Grain Inspection and Weighing Agencies
Apple Processors Ass'n
Canadian-American Business Council

BALL, Daniel R.

1299 Pennsylvania Ave. NW
Tenth Floor
Washington, DC 20004-2400
Tel: (202)508-9500
Fax: (202)508-9700
EMail: danielball@paulhastings.com

Attorney-Advisor, Federal Communications Commission, 1994-97. Legislative Assistant, Senate Committee on the Budget, 1994.

Employers
Paul, Hastings, Janofsky & Walker LLP (Associate)

BALL, Markham

2099 Pennsylvania Ave. NW
Suite 100
Washington, DC 20006
Tel: (202)955-3000
Fax: (202)955-5564
Registered: LDA
EMail: mball@hklaw.com

General Counsel, Agency for International Development, 1977-79; Staff Director, Peace Corps, 1966-67; Assistant General Counsel, Office of Economic Opportunity, and General Counsel, VISTA, 1964-66.

Employers
Holland & Knight LLP (Partner)

Clients Represented
On Behalf of Holland & Knight LLP
Seacoast Power LLC

BALL, Will N.

818 Connecticut Ave. NW
Suite 600
Washington, DC 20006-2702
Tel: (202)466-0670
Fax: (202)466-0684
Registered: LDA

Employers
Caterpillar Inc. (Washington Manager, Government Affairs)

BALL, III, William L.

1101 16th St. NW
Washington, DC 20036-4877
Tel: (202)463-6733
Fax: (202)463-8172
Registered: LDA

Employers
Nat'l Soft Drink Ass'n (President)

BALLANGEE, Judy

1112 16th St. NW
Suite 720
Washington, DC 20036
Tel: (202)232-6700
Fax: (202)797-4486

Employers
YMCA of Metropolitan Washington (Senior V. President, Communications)

BALLARD, D. Michael

1951 Kidwell Dr.
Suite 205
Vienna, VA 22182
Tel: (703)827-8771
Fax: (703)827-0783
EMail: mballard@bballard.com

Director, Communications, U.S. Postal Service, 1973-84. Legislative Assistant and Press Secretary to Rep. Clement J. Zablocki (D-WI), 1968-70.

Employers
Barksdale Ballard & Co., Inc. (President and General Manager)

Clients Represented

On Behalf of Barksdale Ballard & Co., Inc.
Wiland-Bell Productions

BALLEN, Debra T.

1130 Connecticut Ave. NW
Suite 1000
Washington, DC 20036
EMail: dballen@aiadc.org
Tel: (202)828-7100
Fax: (202)293-1219

Employers
American Insurance Ass'n (Senior V. President, Policy Development/Research)

BALLEN, Robert G.

1990 M St. NW
Suite 500
Washington, DC 20036
Tel: (202)776-0700
Fax: (202)776-0720
Registered: LDA
Member, Legal Division, Federal Reserve Board, 1981-85.

Employers
Schwartz & Ballen (Partner)

Clients Represented

On Behalf of Schwartz & Ballen
American Council of Life Insurers
American Insurance Ass'n

BALLENTINE, James

1120 Connecticut Ave. NW
Washington, DC 20036
Tel: (202)663-5000
Fax: (202)828-7541
Registered: LDA

Employers
American Bankers Ass'n (Director, Center for Community Development)

BALMER, Tom

2101 Wilson Blvd.
Suite 400
Arlington, VA 22201
EMail: tbalmer@nmpf.org
Tel: (703)243-6111
Fax: (703)841-9328

Employers
Nat'l Milk Producers Federation (Senior V. President)

BALTIMORE, Elizabeth

Ronald Reagan Bldg.
1300 Pennsylvania Ave. NW
MS: 6.10A
Washington, DC 20523
Tel: (202)712-4300
Fax: (202)216-3036

Employers
Agency for Internat'l Development (Legislative Program Specialist, Congressional Liaison Division)

BALTZAN, Elizabeth

2550 M St. NW
Washington, DC 20037-1350
Tel: (202)457-6000
Fax: (202)457-6315
Registered: LDA

Employers
Patton Boggs, LLP (Associate)

Clients Represented

On Behalf of Patton Boggs, LLP
DFS Group Ltd.

BALZ, Frank

1025 Connecticut Ave. NW
Suite 700
Washington, DC 20036
Tel: (202)785-8866
Fax: (202)835-0003

Employers
Nat'l Ass'n of Independent Colleges and Universities (V. President, Research and Policy Analysis)

BALZANO, Christopher

1730 N. Lynn St.
Suite 504
Arlington, VA 22209
Tel: (703)276-1412
Fax: (703)276-1415
Registered: LDA

Employers
Balzano Associates

Clients Represented

On Behalf of Balzano Associates
The Business Roundtable

BALZANO, Jr., Michael P.

1730 N. Lynn St.
Suite 504
Arlington, VA 22209
Tel: (703)276-1412
Fax: (703)276-1415
Registered: LDA

Employers
Balzano Associates (President)

Clients Represented

On Behalf of Balzano Associates
Boeing Defense and Space Group
The Business Roundtable
Lockheed Martin Corp.
Nat'l Institute for Aerospace Studies and Services Inc.

BAMFORD, Gil

1850 M St. NW
Suite 600
Washington, DC 20036
Tel: (202)775-1700
Fax: (202)822-0928
Registered: LDA

Employers
Toyota Motor North America, U.S.A., Inc. (V. President, Government Affairs)

BANCROFT, David B.

1015 15th St. NW
Suite 802
Washington, DC 20005
EMail: dbancroft@acec.org
Tel: (202)347-7474
Fax: (202)898-0068

Employers
American Consulting Engineers Council (Director, Environmental Programs/EBAC)

BANCROFT, Virginia D.

1331 Pennsylvania Ave. NW
Suite 1300 North
Washington, DC 20004
EMail: gina.bancroft@eds.com
Tel: (202)637-6702
Fax: (202)637-6759
Registered: LDA

Employers
EDS Corp. (Director, Global Government Affairs)

BAND, Jonathan

2000 Pennsylvania Ave. NW
Suite 5500
Washington, DC 20006
EMail: jband@mofo.com
Tel: (202)887-1555
Fax: (202)887-0763
Registered: LDA, FARA

Employers
Morrison & Foerster LLP (Partner)

Clients Represented

On Behalf of Morrison & Foerster LLP
American Library Ass'n
eBay Inc.
Fujitsu Limited
NetCoalition.Com
Seiko Epson Corp.
Storage Technology Corp.
Yahoo!

BANDOW, Doug

1000 Massachusetts Ave. NW
Washington, DC 20001
Tel: (202)842-0200
Fax: (202)842-3490

Employers
Cato Institute (Senior Fellow)

BANDY, Michael J.

5501 Backlick Rd.
Suite 105
Springfield, VA 22151
EMail: mbandy@tsea.org
Tel: (703)941-3725
Fax: (703)941-8275

Employers
Trade Show Exhibitors Ass'n (President)

BANG-JENSEN, Nina

740 15th St. NW
Washington, DC 20005
Tel: (202)662-1595
Fax: (202)662-1597

Employers
Coalition for Internat'l Justice (Exec. Director)

BANGERT, Philip A.

2550 M St. NW
Washington, DC 20037-1350
Tel: (202)457-6000
Fax: (202)457-6315
Registered: LDA
EMail: pbangert@pattonboggs.com

Employers
Patton Boggs, LLP (Partner)

Clients Represented

On Behalf of Patton Boggs, LLP
APL Limited
Denver Regional Transportation District
Dredging Contractors of America
H.A.H. of Wisconsin L.P.
LA 1 Coalition
Lancaster, California, City of
LOOP, Inc.
Midcoast Interstate Transmission, Inc.
Oakland, California, Port of

BANIG, Bill

8315 Lee Hwy.
Fairfax, VA 22031
Tel: (703)208-7200
Fax: (703)208-7132
Registered: LDA
EMail: bbanig@umwa.org

Employers
United Mine Workers of America (Director, Government Affairs)

BANISTER, Diana L.

122 S. Patrick St.
Alexandria, VA 22314
EMail: diana@craigshirley.com
Tel: (703)739-5920
Fax: (703)739-5924

Employers
Craig Shirley & Associates (V. President)

Clients Represented

On Behalf of Craig Shirley & Associates
Nat'l Rifle Ass'n Institute for Legislative Action

BANKES, Joel

444 N. Capitol St. NW
Suite 414
Washington, DC 20001
Tel: (202)624-8180
Fax: (202)624-8828

Employers
Nat'l Child Support Enforcement Ass'n (Exec. Director)

BANKS, James

555 13th St. NW
Washington, DC 20004-1109
Tel: (202)637-5802
Fax: (202)637-5910
Registered: LDA
EMail: jtbanks@hhlaw.com

Employers
Hogan & Hartson L.L.P. (Partner)

Clients Represented

On Behalf of Hogan & Hartson L.L.P.
Fishable Waters Coalition
InterAmerica's Group LLC

BANKS, Pamela F.

3900 Wisconsin Ave. NW
Washington, DC 20016
Tel: (202)752-7000
Fax: (202)752-6099

Employers
Fannie Mae (V. President, Regulatory Compliance)

BANKSON, Jr., John P.

1500 K St.
Suite 1100
Washington, DC 20005
EMail: john_bankson@dbr.com
Tel: (202)842-8800
Fax: (202)842-8465

Employers
Drinker Biddle & Reath LLP (Of Counsel)

Clients Represented

On Behalf of Drinker Biddle & Reath LLP
KJVI
KKVI
KTTY
WPXT

BANKUS, G. Kent

3190 Fairview Park Dr.
Falls Church, VA 22042
Tel: (703)876-3498
Fax: (703)876-3125
Registered: LDA

Employers

General Dynamics Corp. (V. President, Government Relations)

BANNAN, Kathryn

1523 New Hampshire Ave. NW
Washington, DC 20036
Tel: (202)588-0002
Fax: (202)785-2669
Registered: LDA
EMail: kathryn.bannan@ucop.edu

Employers

University of California, Office of Federal Government Relations (Federal Government Relations Specialist)

BANNERMAN, M. Graeme

888 16th St. NW
Washington, DC 20006
Tel: (202)835-8177
Fax: (202)835-8161
Registered: LDA, FARA

Former Staff Director, Senate Foreign Relations Committee.

Employers

Bannerman and Associates, Inc. (President)

Clients Represented

On Behalf of Bannerman and Associates, Inc.

Assurance Technology Corp.
Egypt, Government of the Arab Republic of
El Salvador, Embassy of the Republic of
Internat'l College
Lebanese American University
Palestinian Authority

BANNON, Brian A.

600 New Hampshire Ave. NW
11th Floor
Washington, DC 20037
Tel: (202)944-3000
Fax: (202)944-3068
Registered: LDA
EMail: bab@dejlaw.com

Employers

Dyer Ellis & Joseph, P.C. (Partner)

Clients Represented

On Behalf of Dyer Ellis & Joseph, P.C.

Alaska Ship and Drydock, Inc.
Avondale Industries, Inc.
John Crane-LIPS, Inc.
DaimlerChrysler Corp.
Electronic Design Inc.
Northrop Grumman Corp.
TI Group Inc.
TransAtlantic Lines - Iceland ehf

BANTHAM, Russel A.

1100 15th St. NW
Suite 900
Washington, DC 20005
Tel: (202)835-3400
Fax: (202)835-3414
Registered: LDA

Employers

Pharmaceutical Research and Manufacturers of America (Exec. V. President and General Counsel)

BANTON, Linda W.

1001 Pennsylvania Ave. NW
Suite 700 South
Washington, DC 20004
Tel: (202)662-2682
Fax: (202)662-2624
Registered: LDA

Employers

Honeywell Internat'l, Inc. (V. President, Aerospace Government Relations)

BANZHAF, III, John F.

2013 H St. NW
Washington, DC 20006
Tel: (202)659-4310
Fax: (202)833-3921

Employers

Action on Smoking and Health (Exec. Director and Chief Counsel)

BANZHAF, William H.

5400 Grosvenor Ln.
Bethesda, MD 20814-2198
Tel: (301)897-8720
Fax: (301)897-3690
EMail: banzhafb@safnet.org

Employers

Soc. of American Foresters (Exec. V. President)

BAPTISTA, Samuel J.

1300 I St. NW
12th Floor
Washington, DC 20005
Tel: (202)326-3993
Fax: (202)326-3981

Employers

Morgan Stanley Dean Witter & Co. (Managing Director, Government Affairs)

BARAGAR, Emory W.

1200 Wilson Blvd.
Arlington, VA 22209
Tel: (703)465-3684
Fax: (703)465-3040
Registered: LDA

Employers

The Boeing Co. (V. President, Government Relations Operations)

BARALD, Patricia A.

1201 Pennsylvania Ave. NW
Washington, DC 20004-2401
Tel: (202)662-6000
Fax: (202)662-6291
EMail: pbarald@cov.com

Employers

Covington & Burling (Partner)

BARAN, Jan W.

1776 K St. NW
Washington, DC 20006
Tel: (202)719-7000
Fax: (202)719-7049

Former Member, President's Commission on Federal Ethics Law Reform, 1989; Executive Assistant to the Chairman, Federal Election Commission, 1977-79.

Employers

Wiley, Rein & Fielding (Partner)

Clients Represented

On Behalf of Wiley, Rein & Fielding

RENEW (Republican Network to Elect Women)

BARAN, Mark

1120 Connecticut Ave. NW
Washington, DC 20036
Tel: (202)663-5000
Fax: (202)828-4548
Registered: LDA

Employers

American Bankers Ass'n (Senior Tax Counsel)

BARASH, Peter S.

1440 New York Ave. NW
Suite 400
Washington, DC 20005
Tel: (202)466-2221
Fax: (202)466-4455
Registered: LDA

Former Staff Director for the Commerce, Consumer and Monetary Affairs Subcommittee, U.S. House of Representatives.

Employers

Peter S. Barash Associates, Inc. (President)

Clients Represented

On Behalf of Peter S. Barash Associates, Inc.

American Soc. of Appraisers
CLT Appraisal Services, Inc.
Council of Appraisal and Property Professional Societies
Guest and Associates
Joint Venture Partners
Morris Communications
Pharmaceutical Products, Inc.
TRW Inc.
Village Enterprises

BARBER, Heather

1660 L St. NW
Suite 1050
Washington, DC 20036
Tel: (202)659-2229
Fax: (202)659-5234
Registered: LDA
EMail: HB1simonco@aol.com

Employers

Simon and Co., Inc. (Director, Federal Affairs)

Clients Represented

On Behalf of Simon and Co., Inc.

AC Transit
Alameda Corridor Transportation Authority
American Water Works Ass'n
Carmel, Indiana, City of
Citrus Heights, California, City of
Easter Seals
Fresno, California, City of
Madison, Wisconsin, City of
Newark, California, City of
Oakley, California, City of
Pierce Transit
Portland, Oregon, City of
Sacramento Housing and Redeveloping Agency
Salt Lake City, Utah, City of
San Leandro, California, City of
Tacoma, Washington, City of
Tacoma, Washington, Public Utilities Department of

BARBER, Lindsay

2101 Wilson Blvd.
Suite 400
Arlington, VA 22201
Tel: (703)243-6111
Fax: (703)841-9328
EMail: lbarber@nmpf.org

Employers

Nat'l Milk Producers Federation (Communications and Government Relations Assistant)

BARBER, Randy

1705 DeSales St. NW
Washington, DC 20036
Tel: (202)775-9072
Fax: (202)775-9074

Employers

Center for Economic Organizing (Director)

BARBERO, Carol L.

2120 L St. NW
Suite 700
Washington, DC 20037
Tel: (202)822-8282
Fax: (202)296-8834
Registered: LDA

Employers

Hobbs, Straus, Dean and Walker, LLP (Partner)

Clients Represented

On Behalf of Hobbs, Straus, Dean and Walker, LLP

Alamo Navajo School Board
Black Mesa Community School Board
Bristol Bay Area Health Corp.
Choctaw Indians, Mississippi Band of
Metlakatla Indian Community
Miccosukee Tribe of Indians of Florida
Norton Sound Health Corp.
Pinon Community School Board
Rock Point Community School
Rough Rock Community School
Seldovia Native Ass'n, Inc.
Seminole Tribe of Indians of Florida
Shiprock Alternative Schools, Inc.
Shoalwater Bay Indian Tribe
St. Regis Mohawk Tribe

BARBOUR, Corye

1413 K St. NW
Tenth Floor
Washington, DC 20005
Tel: (202)347-8772
Fax: (202)393-5886
Registered: LDA

Employers

United States Student Ass'n (Legislative Director)

BARBOUR, Haley

1275 Pennsylvania Ave. NW
Tenth Floor
Washington, DC 20004
Tel: (202)333-4936
Fax: (202)833-9392
Registered: LDA

Director, Office of Political Affairs, The White House, 1985-87.

Employers

Barbour Griffith & Rogers, Inc. (Chairman and Chief Exec. Officer)

Clients Represented

On Behalf of Barbour Griffith & Rogers, Inc.

Air Transport Ass'n of America
Alliance for Quality Nursing Home Care
American Maritime Congress
American Trucking Ass'ns
Amgen
Artists Coalition
Bay Harbor Management, L.C.
BellSouth Telecommunications, Inc.
Better World Campaign
Bristol-Myers Squibb Co.
Broadcast Music Inc. (BMI)
Brown and Williamson Tobacco Corp.
Camp Dresser and McKee, Inc.
Canadian Nat'l Railway Co.
Citizens for Jobs and the Economy
DaimlerChrysler Corp.
Delta Air Lines
Education Networks of America
FM Watch
GCG Partners
GlaxoSmithKline
Illinois State Board of Education
INTELSAT - Internat'l Telecommunications Satellite Organization
Lockheed Martin Corp.
LVMH Moet Hennessy Louis Vuitton S.A.
Lyondell Chemical Co.
MassMutual Financial Group
Microsoft Corp.
Oxygenated Fuels Ass'n
Professional Benefit Trust
Qwest Communications
RJR Co.
Southern Co.
State Street Bank and Trust Co.
Tulane University
United Health Group
University of Mississippi
University of Mississippi Medical Center
Yazoo County, Mississippi Port Commission

BARBOUR, Leslie P.

1776 I St. NW
Suite 400
Washington, DC 20006-3708
Tel: (202)739-8000
Fax: (202)785-4019
Registered: LDA

Employers

Nuclear Energy Institute (Director, Legislative Programs)

BARBOUR, Nancy R.

1300 I St. NW
Suite 300 West
Washington, DC 20005
Tel: (202)522-8600
Fax: (202)522-8669
Registered: LDA

Legislative Director (1981-85) and Legislative Assistant (1965-69) to Rep. William Ford (D-MI), 1981-85. Legislative Assistant to Rep. Herb Harris (D-VA), 1975-80.

Employers

Dykema Gossett PLLC (Director, Federal Government Affairs)

Clients Represented

On Behalf of Dykema Gossett PLLC

Arvin Meritor Automotive
Calhoun County Community Development
Citizen's Committee to Save the Federal Center
Comerica, Inc.
Detroit Public Schools
Detroit, Michigan, City of
Ferris State University
Great Lakes Corporate Resources
Manulife USA
Southeastern Michigan Council of Government
The Wellness Plan

BARCELLA, Jr., E. Lawrence

1299 Pennsylvania Ave. NW
Tenth Floor
Washington, DC 20004-2400
Tel: (202)508-9500
Fax: (202)508-9700
EMail: larrybarcella@paulhastings.com

Chief Counsel, House October Surprise Task Force, 1992-93. Assistant U.S. Attorney for the District of Columbia, Department of Justice, 1970-86.

Employers

Paul, Hastings, Janofsky & Walker LLP (Partner)

BARCLAY, Betsy

1101 Pennsylvania Ave. NW
Sixth Floor
Washington, DC 20004
Tel: (202)756-7750
Fax: (202)756-7545
Registered: LDA
EMail: bbarclay@etrade.com

Aide to Senator Robert Taft Jr., (R-OH), 1972-76. Staff Member, Committee on Commerce, U.S. Senate, 1976-80.

Employers

E*TRADE Group, Inc. (V. President of Government Affairs)

BARCLAY, Charles

4212 King St.
Alexandria, VA 22312
Tel: (703)824-0500
Fax: (703)820-1395
Registered: LDA

Employers

American Ass'n of Airport Executives (President)

BARDACH, Emily

1029 Vermont Ave. NW
Suite 510
Washington, DC 20005-3527
Tel: (703)971-9205
Fax: (703)971-6997

Employers

Women in Government Relations, Inc. (Director)

BARDIN, David J.

1050 Connecticut Ave. NW
Washington, DC 20036-5339
Tel: (202)857-6000
Fax: (202)857-6395
Registered: LDA

Trial Attorney, 1958-65, Assistant General Counsel, 1965-67, and Deputy General Counsel 1967-69, Federal Power Commission. Deputy Administrator, Federal Energy Administration, 1977. Administrator of the Economic Regulatory Administration, Department of Energy, 1977-79.

Employers

Arent Fox Kintner Plotkin & Kahn, PLLC (Of-Counsel)

BARETT, Jaia

21 Dupont Circle NW
Suite 800
Washington, DC 20036
Tel: (202)296-2296
Fax: (202)872-0884
EMail: jaia@arl.org

Employers

Ass'n of Research Libraries (Deputy Exec. Director)

BARFIELD, Claude E.

1150 17th St. NW
Washington, DC 20036
Tel: (202)862-5800
Fax: (202)862-7177
EMail: cbarfield@aei.org

Employers

American Enterprise Institute for Public Policy Research (Resident Scholar and Director, Science and Technology Policy Studies)

BARGANIER, III, Brooks C.

8116 Arlington Blvd. Suite 901
Falls Church, VA 22042

Employers

Citizens for a Republican Majority

BARIS, David H.

4701 Sangamore Rd.
Suite P15
Bethesda, MD 20816
Tel: (301)263-9841
Fax: (301)229-2443

Employers

American Ass'n of Bank Directors (Exec. Director and General Counsel)

BARKER, Alec D.

1245 35th St. NW
Washington, DC 20007

Employers

1245 Foundation

BARKER, Robert H.

1150 17th St. NW
Suite 310
Washington, DC 20036
Tel: (202)296-6508
Fax: (202)296-3052

Employers

American Fiber Manufacturers Ass'n (V. President)

BARKER, Rosina B.

1700 Pennsylvania Ave. NW
Suite 600
Washington, DC 20006
Tel: (202)393-7600
Fax: (202)393-7601
Registered: LDA

Employers

Ivins, Phillips & Barker (Associate)

BARKER, Russell E.

P.O. Box 59811
Potomac, MD 20859-9811
Tel: (301)365-2521
Fax: (301)365-7705
Registered: LDA, FARA

Employers

American Trade and Professional Ass'n Management (President)
Peanut and Tree Nut Processors Ass'n (President)

Clients Represented

On Behalf of American Trade and Professional Ass'n Management

Peanut and Tree Nut Processors Ass'n

BARKER, William B.

1133 Connecticut Ave. NW
Suite 1010
Washington, DC 20036
Tel: (202)775-2360
Fax: (202)775-2364
Registered: LDA

Employers

JSA-1, Inc. (Senior Associate)

Clients Represented

On Behalf of JSA-1, Inc.

Newhall Land and Farming Co.

BARKLIND, Sharla M.

1101 Vermont Ave. NW
Suite 200
Washington, DC 20005
Tel: (202)898-2200
Fax: (202)898-2213

Senior Legislative Assistant to Rep. Paul E. Kanjorski (D-PA), 1999-2000, and former Legislative Assistant to Rep. Karen McCarthy (D-MO)

Employers

Nat'l Ass'n of Regulatory Utility Commissioners (Assistant General Counsel)

BARLOON, William J.

401 Ninth St. NW
Suite 400
Washington, DC 20004
Tel: (202)585-1928
Fax: (202)585-1898
Registered: LDA

Employers

Sprint Corp. (Director, Government Affairs)

BARNA, Elisabeth A.

499 S. Capitol St. SW
Suite 502A
Washington, DC 20003
Tel: (202)554-3060
Fax: (202)554-3160
EMail: ebarna@motor-freight.com

Employers

Motor Freight Carriers Ass'n (Director, Communications)

BARNARD, M.D., Neal D.

5100 Wisconsin Ave. NW
Suite 404
Washington, DC 20016
Tel: (202)686-2210
Fax: (202)686-2216

Employers

Physicians Committee for Responsible Medicine (President)

BARNES, Clifford E.

1227 25th St. NW
Suite 700
Washington, DC 20037
Tel: (202)861-0900
Fax: (202)296-2882
Registered: LDA
EMail: cbarnes@ebglaw.com

Employers

Epstein Becker & Green, P.C. (Member)

BARNES, Donald M.

1919 Pennsylvania Ave. NW
Suite 600
Washington, DC 20006-3404
Tel: (202)326-1500
Fax: (202)326-1555

Employers

Jenkens & Gilchrist (Managing Shareholder)

Clients Represented

On Behalf of Jenkens & Gilchrist

American Amusement Machine Ass'n

BARNES, Gary L.

515 King St.
Suite 420
Alexandria, VA 22314-3103
Tel: (703)684-6681
Fax: (703)684-6048

Employers
Internat'l Soc. of Hospitality Consultants (President)

BARNES, Gordon

1111 19th St. NW
Suite 800
Washington, DC 20036
Tel: (202)463-2700
Fax: (202)463-2785
Registered: LDA

Employers
American Forest & Paper Ass'n (Manager, Grassroots)

BARNES, John D.

1350 I St. NW
Suite 880
Washington, DC 20005
Tel: (202)842-3555
Fax: (202)842-4355

Employers
American Academy of Dermatology (Associate Exec. Director, Government Affairs and Health Policy)

BARNES, Johnny

1400 20th St. NW
Suite 119
Washington, DC 20036
Tel: (202)457-0800
Fax: (202)452-1868

Employers
American Civil Liberties Union of the Nat'l Capital Area (Exec. Director)

BARNES, Joseph L.

125 N. West St.
Alexandria, VA 22314-2754
Tel: (703)683-1400
Fax: (703)549-6610
Registered: LDA

Employers
Fleet Reserve Ass'n (Director, Legislative Programs)

BARNES, Lori Weaver

99 Canal Center Plaza
Suite 500
Alexandria, VA 22314-1538
EMail: lori@aiada.org
Tel: (703)519-7800
Fax: (703)519-7810

Employers
American Internat'l Automobile Dealers Ass'n (Manager, Public Relations)

BARNES, Mark J.

1350 I St. NW
Suite 1255
Washington, DC 20005
Tel: (202)626-0089
Fax: (202)626-0088
Registered: LDA
EMail: markb17@aol.com
Counsel to the Secretary for Drug Abuse Policy, Office of the Secretary, Department of Health and Human Services, 1989-93. Associate Director, Administration Group, Office of Personnel Management, 1988-89. Deputy General Counsel, Office of General Counsel, Office of Personnel Management, 1986-87. Chief Counsel to Senator Ted Stevens (R-AK), 1981-84.

Employers
Law Offices of Mark Barnes (Attorney)

Clients Represented

On Behalf of Law Offices of Mark Barnes
Briklee Trading Co.
Cash America Internat'l
Century Internat'l Arms
Firearms Importers Roundtable Trade Group
Intrac Arms Internat'l LLC
Lew Horton Distributing Co.
Mossberg Group, LLC
Nat'l Ass'n of Arms Shows
Nat'l Pawnbrokers Ass'n
Nat'l Rifle Ass'n of America

BARNES, Hon. Michael D.

1225 I St. NW
Suite 1100
Washington, DC 20005
Tel: (202)289-7319
Fax: (202)408-1851

Employers
The Center to Prevent Handgun Violence (President)
Handgun Control, Inc. (President)

BARNES, Peter

3000 K St. NW
Suite 300
Washington, DC 20007
Tel: (202)424-7500
Fax: (202)424-7643
Registered: LDA

Employers
Swidler Berlin Shereff Friedman, LLP (Member)

Clients Represented

On Behalf of Swidler Berlin Shereff Friedman, LLP
WRD Venture/NWD Venture

BARNES, Richard L.

5335 Wisconsin Ave. NW
Suite 440
Washington, DC 20015
Tel: (202)895-1513
Fax: (301)320-7565
Registered: LDA
Professional Staff Member, House Government Operations Committee, 1977-79.

Employers
Self-employed as an independent consultant.

Clients Represented

As an independent consultant
Simpson Investment Co.

BARNES, Saundra L.

201 14th St. SW
Fifth Floor SW
Washington, DC 20250
EMail: sbarnes01@fs.fed.us
Tel: (202)205-1607
Fax: (202)205-0936

Employers
Department of Agriculture - Forest Service (Staff Assistant, Programs and Legislation)

BARNET, Richard J.

733 15th St. NW
Suite 1020
Washington, DC 20005
Tel: (202)234-9382
Fax: (202)387-7915

Employers
Institute for Policy Studies (Distinguished Fellow)

BARNETT, Larry P.

6123 Lundy Pl.
Burke, VA 22015
Tel: (703)455-2332
Fax: (703)455-4894
Registered: LDA

Employers
AB Management Associates, Inc. (President)

Clients Represented

On Behalf of AB Management Associates, Inc.
AAAE-ACI
Diversified Internat'l Sciences Corp.
Megapulse, Inc.
Pegasus Management
U.S. Contract Tower Ass'n
Vero Beach, Florida, City of

BARNETT, Richard

700 13th St. NW
Suite 800
Washington, DC 20005
Tel: (202)508-5800
Fax: (202)508-5858
Former Senior Professional Staff Member, House Committee on Transportation and Infrastructure for 18 years. Former Associate Administrator, General Services Administration for 5 years. Former Chief of Staff, Government Printing Office for 4 years.

Employers
Kilpatrick Stockton LLP (Director, Government Relations)

Clients Represented

On Behalf of Kilpatrick Stockton LLP
American Realty Advisors
Capitol Concerts, Inc.
Julien J. Studley, Inc.

BARNETT, Robert B.

725 12th St. NW
Washington, DC 20005
Tel: (202)434-5000
Fax: (202)434-5029
Legislative Assistant to Senator Walter F. Mondale (D-MN), 1973-75. Law Clerk to Justice Byron R. White, U.S. Supreme Court, 1972-73, and to Judge John Minor Wisdom, U.S. Court of Appeals, Fifth Circuit, 1971-72.

Employers
Williams & Connolly (Partner)

Clients Represented

On Behalf of Williams & Connolly
Chamber of Independent Gas Stations of Argentina

BARNETT, Robert E.

2000 M St. NW
Suite 740
Washington, DC 20036-3313
Tel: (202)463-6040
Fax: (202)785-5209
Registered: LDA
Former Chairman, Federal Deposit Insurance Corporation.

Employers
Barnett & Sivon, P.C. (Partner)

Clients Represented

On Behalf of Barnett & Sivon, P.C.
Citigroup
Community Financial Services Ass'n
The Financial Services Roundtable

BARNETT, Thomas O.

1201 Pennsylvania Ave. NW
Washington, DC 20004-2401
Tel: (202)662-6000
Fax: (202)662-6291
EMail: tbarnett@cov.com
Law Clerk to Judge Harrison Winter, U.S. Court of Appeals for the Fourth Circuit, 1989-90.

Employers
Covington & Burling (Partner)

Clients Represented

On Behalf of Covington & Burling
Canon USA, Inc.
Canon, Inc.

BARNETTE, Curtis

1440 New York Ave. NW
Washington, DC 20005
Tel: (202)371-7000
Fax: (202)393-5760
Registered: LDA
Member President's Trade Advisory Committee, 1989-97.

Employers
Skadden, Arps, Slate, Meagher & Flom LLP (Of Counsel)

Clients Represented

On Behalf of Skadden, Arps, Slate, Meagher & Flom LLP
US Airways

BARNETTE, Marcia L.

228 Seventh St. SE
Washington, DC 20003-4306
Tel: (202)547-7424
Fax: (202)547-9559

Employers
Home Care Aide Ass'n of America (Contact)

BARNHARD, Seth

750 First St. NE
9th Floor
Washington, DC 20002
Tel: (202)745-2900
Fax: (202)745-2901

Employers
Capital Consultants Corp. (V. President)

Clients Represented

On Behalf of Capital Consultants Corp.
Cherokee Investment Partners, LLC
Dolce Internat'l
Sports Corp., Ltd.
Trinity Partners, Inc.

BARNHART, Scott

1275 Pennsylvania Ave. NW
Tenth Floor
Washington, DC 20004
Tel: (202)333-4936
Fax: (202)833-9392
Registered: LDA
Former Deputy Administrative Assistant to Senator Connie Mack (R-FL).

Employers
Barbour Griffith & Rogers, Inc. (Of Counsel)

Clients Represented

On Behalf of Barbour Griffith & Rogers, Inc.
DaimlerChrysler Corp.
Illinois State Board of Education
Tulane University
University of Mississippi

BARNICLE, Timothy M.

700 11th St. NW
Suite 750
Washington, DC 20001
EMail: tbarnicle@ncee.org
Tel: (202)783-3668
Fax: (202)783-3672

Employers

Nat'l Center on Education and the Economy (Director, Workforce Services)

BARON, Kevin

1776 Massachusetts Ave. NW
Suite 620
Washington, DC 20036
EMail: kb@alliance-exchange.org
Tel: (202)293-6141
Fax: (202)293-6144
Registered: LDA

Employers

Alliance for Internat'l Educational and Cultural Exchange, The (Policy Specialist)

BAROODY, Michael E.

1331 Pennsylvania Ave. NW
Sixth Floor
Washington, DC 20004-1790
Tel: (202)637-3120
Fax: (202)637-3182
Registered: LDA

Assistant Secretary for Policy, Department of Labor, during the Reagan and first Bush administrations.

Employers

Nat'l Ass'n of Manufacturers (Exec. V. President)

BARR, Terry N.

50 F St. NW
Suite 900
Washington, DC 20001
EMail: tbarr@ncfc.org
Tel: (202)626-8700
Fax: (202)626-8722
Registered: LDA

Employers

Nat'l Council of Farmer Cooperatives (Chief Economist and V. President, Agriculture and Trade Policy)

BARR, William P.

1300 I St. NW
Suite 400 West
Washington, DC 20005
Tel: (202)336-7900
Fax: (202)336-7921

Attorney General, Department of Justice, 1991-93.

Employers

Verizon Communications (Exec. V. President and General Counsel)

BARRACK, David W.

112 Elden St.
Unit J
Herndon, VA 20170
Tel: (703)709-8299
Fax: (703)709-1036

Employers

American Edged Products Manufacturers Ass'n (Exec. Director)
Barrack Ass'n Management (Owner/President)
Nat'l Ass'n of Metal Finishers (Exec. Director)
Nat'l Ass'n of Public Insurance Adjusters (Exec. Director)

Clients Represented

On Behalf of Barrack Ass'n Management

American Edged Products Manufacturers Ass'n
Nat'l Ass'n of Metal Finishers
Nat'l Ass'n of Public Insurance Adjusters

BARRETO, Jr., Julio

630 I St. NW
Washington, DC 20001-3736
Tel: (202)289-3500
Fax: (202)289-8181

Employers

Nat'l Ass'n of Housing and Redevelopment Officials (Director, Legislative and Program Development)

BARRETT, Gina

1426 21st St. NW
Suite 200
Washington, DC 20036
Tel: (202)429-9370
Fax: (202)833-1129

Employers

Greater Washington Soc. of Ass'n Executives (Director, Public Affairs)

BARRETT, Jim

1660 L St. NW
Suite 1200
Washington, DC 20036
EMail: epi@epinet.org
Tel: (202)775-8810
Fax: (202)775-0819

Employers

Economic Policy Institute (Economist)

BARRETT, Laurence I.

700 13th St. NW
Suite 1000
Washington, DC 20005
Tel: (202)347-6633
Fax: (202)347-8713
Registered: LDA, FARA

Employers

Powell Tate (V. President)

Clients Represented

On Behalf of Powell Tate

Taiwan Studies Institute

BARRETT, Jr., Michael F.

700 13th St. NW
Suite 350
Washington, DC 20005
Tel: (202)637-0040
Fax: (202)637-0041
Registered: LDA

Chief Counsel and Staff Director, Oversight and Investigations Subcommittee, House Energy and Commerce Committee, 1981-91. Legislative Counsel, Energy and Power Subcommittee, House Interstate and Foreign Commerce Committee, 1975-81. Legislative Counsel, Special Subcommittee on Investigations, House Committee on Interstate and Foreign Commerce, 1970-75. Trial Attorney, Securities and Exchange Commission, 1967-70. Trial Attorney, Federal Trade Commission, 1962-66.

Employers

Self-employed as an independent consultant.
Rhoads Group (Of Counsel)

Clients Represented

As an independent consultant

Alyeska Pipeline Service Co.
Citigroup
Lockheed Martin Corp.

BARRETT, Michelle

1300 N. 17th St.
Eighth Floor
Rosslyn, VA 22209-3801
EMail: barrett@abc.org
Tel: (703)812-2000
Fax: (703)812-8202
Registered: LDA

Employers

Associated Builders and Contractors (Regional Field Representative)

BARRETT, William H.

600 13th St. NW
Washington, DC 20005-3096
EMail: wbarrett@mwe.com
Tel: (202)756-8070
Fax: (202)756-8087

Employers

McDermott, Will and Emery (Partner)

Clients Represented

On Behalf of McDermott, Will and Emery

Lockheed Martin Corp.

BARRIE, Robert W.

1666 K St. NW
Suite 500
Washington, DC 20006-2803
Tel: (202)887-1400
Fax: (202)466-2198
Registered: LDA

Employers

O'Connor & Hannan, L.L.P. (Senior Government Relations Advisor)

Clients Represented

On Behalf of O'Connor & Hannan, L.L.P.

Allergan, Inc.
American Forest & Paper Ass'n
ATOFINA Chemicals, Inc.
CommSource Internat'l, Inc.
Exxon Mobil Corp.
FMC Corp.
General Electric Co.
Georgia-Pacific Corp.
P. H. Glatfelter
Montrose Chemical Co.
Nat'l Paint and Coatings Ass'n
Southeast Alaska Seiners Ass'n
Nidal Z. Zayed and Associates

BARRINGER, Steven G.

201 Maryland Ave. NE
Washington, DC 20002
EMail: steve@mgninc.com
Tel: (202)543-7200
Fax: (202)543-0616
Registered: LDA

Staff Attorney and Special Assistant to the Solicitor, Office of Solicitor, Department of Interior, 1983-86.

Employers

McClure, Gerard & Neuenschwander, Inc. (Principal)

Clients Represented

On Behalf of McClure, Gerard & Neuenschwander, Inc.

American Gaming Ass'n
Barrick Goldstrike Mines, Inc.
Boise State University
Brush Wellman, Inc.
Coachella Valley Water District
Echo Bay Mining
Family Farm Alliance (Project Transfer Council)
Harquehala Irrigation District
Hecla Mining Co.
Helli USA Airways
Henderson, Nevada, City of
Howard Hughes Corp.
Idaho Power Co.
Independence Mining Co., Inc.
Internat'l Bottled Water Ass'n
Nat'l Endangered Species Act Reform Coalition
Native American Mohegans Inc.
Nevada Test Site Development Corp.
Newmont Mining Corp.
Pershing Co. Water Conservation District of Nevada
Placer Dome U.S. Inc.
Private Fuels Storage, L.L.C.
Quest Nevada, Inc.
Space Imaging, Inc.
Stirling Energy Systems
Verizon Wireless
Wellton-Mohawk Irrigation and Drainage District
Westlands Water District
The Williams Companies

BARRINGER, William H.

Three Lafayette Center
1155 21st St. NW
Washington, DC 20036-3384
Tel: (202)328-8000
Fax: (202)887-8979
Registered: LDA

Employers

Willkie Farr & Gallagher (Partner)

Clients Represented

On Behalf of Willkie Farr & Gallagher

Fuji Heavy Industries Ltd.
Fuji Photo Film U.S.A., Inc.
Japan Iron and Steel Exporters Ass'n
Meat and Livestock Australia

BARRON, Blaine A.

1299 Pennsylvania Ave. NW
Suite 1100 West
Washington, DC 20004-2407
Tel: (202)637-4000
Fax: (202)637-4006

Employers

General Electric Co. (Manager, Financial Analysis and Regulatory Operations)

BARRON, David H.

1101 30th St. NW
Suite 500
Washington, DC 20007
Tel: (202)338-5393
Fax: (202)338-5391

Employers

Barron-Birrell, Inc. (Chairman)

Clients Represented

On Behalf of Barron-Birrell, Inc.

Liberia, Office of the President of the Republic of

BARRON, Katie M.

1341 G St. NW
Suite 1100
Washington, DC 20005
Tel: (202)585-0230
Fax: (202)393-0712

Employers

Infotech Strategies, Inc. (Senior Director, Communications)

BARROW, Craig S.

1776 I St. NW
Suite 1050
Washington, DC 20006
Tel: (202)429-3438
Fax: (202)429-3467
Registered: LDA

Employers
Dow AgroSciences (Leader, Science Policy and Regulatory Affairs)

BARROW, Erin

111 Massachusetts Ave. NW
Washington, DC 20001
Tel: (202)682-6971
Fax: (202)682-6784
EMail: ebarrow@ullicolaw.com

Employers
The Union Labor Life Insurance Co. (Senior Legal Assistant)

BARROW, Larry

6039 Riddle Walk
Alexandria, VA 22302

Employers
Mandela Group

BARROWS, David

1225 I St. NW
Suite 500
Washington, DC 20005
Tel: (202)312-2005
Fax: (202)289-8683
Registered: LDA
EMail: dawsonassociates@worldnet.att.net

Employers
Dawson & Associates, Inc. (Senior Advisor)

Clients Represented

On Behalf of Dawson & Associates, Inc.
AgriPartners

BARROWS, John

7801 Norfolk Ave.
Bethesda, MD 20814
Tel: (301)986-1830
Fax: (301)986-1876

Employers
Internat'l Eye Foundation/Soc. of Eye Surgeons (Director of Programs)

BARRY, Albert P.

1213 Jefferson Davis Hwy.
Suite 802
Arlington, VA 22202-4304
Tel: (703)412-4170
Fax: (703)416-4820
Registered: LDA
EMail: barry@aaicorp.com
Deputy Assistant Secretary, Department of Defense, 1981-85. Legislative Director, U.S. Senate, 1979-81. Officer, U.S. Marine Corps, 1958-79.

Employers
AAI Corp. (V. President, Washington Operations)

BARRY, Don

1615 M St. NW
Washington, DC 20036
Tel: (202)833-2300
Fax: (202)429-3958
Registered: LDA
EMail: don_barry@tws.org
Former Assistant Secretary for Fish and Wildlife and Parks, Department of the Interior.

Employers
The Wilderness Soc. (Exec. V. President)

BARRY, Lisa B.

1101 Connecticut Ave. NW
Suite 400
Washington, DC 20036-4303
Tel: (202)530-7878
Fax: (202)530-7879

Employers
AOL Time Warner (V. President, International Public Policy)

BARRY, Michael

1307 New York Ave. NW
Suite 200
Washington, DC 20005
Tel: (202)466-2044
Fax: (202)466-2662
EMail: mab@acpm.org

Employers
American College of Preventive Medicine (Director, Public Affairs)

BARRY, Paul

1200 G St. NW
Suite 400
Washington, DC 20005
Tel: (202)783-8700
Fax: (202)783-8750

Employers
AdvaMed (Associate V. President, Global Strategy and Analysis)

BARRY, Richard A.

7979 Old Georgetown Rd.
Suite 500
Bethesda, MD 20814
Tel: (301)986-9700
Fax: (301)986-9795
EMail: richard.barry@ascouncil.org

Employers
Adhesive and Sealant Council (President)

BARSA, John D.

1250 I St. NW
Suite 1200
Washington, DC 20005-3924
Tel: (202)371-8532
Fax: (202)371-8470
Registered: LDA

Employers
Aerospace Industries Ass'n of America (Manager, Legislative Affairs)

BARSH, Jr., Harry E.

700 13th St. NW
Suite 400
Washington, DC 20005
Tel: (202)347-0773
Fax: (202)347-0785
Registered: LDA
EMail: hbarsh@cassidy.com

Employers
Cassidy & Associates, Inc. (Senior Consultant)

Clients Represented

On Behalf of Cassidy & Associates, Inc.
American Superconductor Corp.

BARSKY, David A.

1850 M St. NW
Suite 400
Washington, DC 20036
Tel: (202)293-8200
Fax: (202)872-0145
Registered: LDA

Employers
Krooth & Altman (Partner)

Clients Represented

On Behalf of Krooth & Altman
Healthcare Financing Study Group

BARSTOW, Scott

5999 Stevenson Ave.
Alexandria, VA 22304-3300
Tel: (703)823-9800
Ext: 234
Fax: (703)823-0252
Registered: LDA
EMail: sbarstow@counseling.org

Employers
American Counseling Ass'n (Director, Public Policy and Legislation)

BART, Daniel L.

2500 Wilson Blvd.
Suite 300
Arlington, VA 22201
Tel: (703)907-7703
Fax: (703)907-7727
Registered: LDA
EMail: dbart@tia.eia.org

Employers
Telecommunications Industry Ass'n (Sr. V. President, Standards and Special Projects)

BARTEK, Ronald J.

2001 Jefferson Davis Hwy.
Suite 209
Arlington, VA 22202
Tel: (703)413-0090
Fax: (703)413-4467
Registered: LDA
EMail: rbartek@mehlgriffinbartek.com
Professional Staff, House Armed Services Committee, 1989-95. Delegation Member for INF Treaty Negotiations and Deputy for Verification for CFE Treaty (1985-89) and NATO Action Officer (1984-85), Bureau of Political and Military Affairs, Department of State. Professional Member, Arms Control Intelligence Staff, Central Intelligence Agency, 1978-84. U.S. Army, 1966-70.

Employers
Mehl, Griffin & Bartek Ltd. (V. President)

Clients Represented

On Behalf of Mehl, Griffin & Bartek Ltd.
Battelle Memorial Institute
Chandler Evans Control Systems
D3 Internat'l Energy, LLC
El Camino Resources, Ltd.
Exide Corp.
Friedrich's Ataxia Research Alliance
Motorola Space and Systems Technology Group
Pacific Northwest Nat'l Laboratory
Q Systems, Inc.

BARTH, Richard C.

1350 I St. NW
Suite 400
Washington, DC 20005-3306
Tel: (202)371-6900
Fax: (202)842-3578
Registered: LDA

Employers
Motorola, Inc. (V. President and Director, Telecommunications Strategy and Regulation)

BARTH, Roger V.

1801 K St. NW
Suite 1205L
Washington, DC 20006
Tel: (202)452-7373
Fax: (202)452-7333

Employers
Self-employed as an independent consultant.

BARTHELD, Elizabeth

317 Massachusetts Ave. NE
Suite 200
Washington, DC 20002
Tel: (202)546-4732
Fax: (202)546-1257
Registered: LDA

Employers
Cavarocchi Ruscio Dennis Associates

Clients Represented

On Behalf of Cavarocchi Ruscio Dennis Associates
Soc. for Women's Health Research

BARTHOLOMEW, Lori A.

2275 Research Blvd.
Suite 250
Rockville, MD 20850
Tel: (301)947-9000
Fax: (301)947-9090
Registered: LDA

Employers
Physician Insurers Ass'n of America (Director, Loss Prevention and Research)

BARTL, Timothy J.

1015 15th St. NW
Suite 1200
Washington, DC 20005
Tel: (202)789-8600
Fax: (202)789-1708
Registered: LDA
EMail: tbartl@mnwlaw.net
Legislative Director to Rep. Steve Gunderson (R-WI), 1993-96.

Employers
McGuiness Norris & Williams, LLP (Associate)

Clients Represented

On Behalf of McGuiness Norris & Williams, LLP
Labor Policy Ass'n (LPA)
Nat'l Council of Agricultural Employers
Nisei Farmers League

BARTLETT, Bruce

655 15th St. NW Suite 375
Washington, DC 20005
Tel: (202)421-7784
Fax: (202)421-7785
EMail: brucebarlett@compuserve.com

Employers
Nat'l Center for Policy Analysis (Senior Fellow)

BARTLETT, Doyle

1401 K St. NW
12th Floor
Washington, DC 20005
Tel: (202)393-4760
Fax: (202)393-3516
Registered: LDA
Former Chief of Staff to Rep. Bill McCollum (R-FL)

Employers
The Smith-Free Group (Senior V. President)

Clients Represented

On Behalf of The Smith-Free Group
Star Systems
U.S. Wireless Data, Inc.

BARTLETT, J.D., Melissa

1422 Duke St.
Alexandria, VA 22314
Tel: (703)838-0033
Fax: (703)548-1890
Registered: LDA

Employers
American Medical Group Ass'n (Legislative Counsel)

BARTLETT, Michael L.

210 Seventh St. SE
Washington, DC 20003
Tel: (202)547-6808
Fax: (202)546-5425
Registered: LDA
EMail: mlbartlet@aol.com
Professional Staff Member, House Budget Committee, 1993-97.

Employers
Kessler & Associates Business Services, Inc. (Senior Legislative Associate/Director, Corporate Communications)

Clients Represented
On Behalf of Kessler & Associates Business Services, Inc.
Amgen
Burlington Northern Santa Fe Railway
Dunn-Edwards Corp.
Exelon Corp.
Grocery Manufacturers of America
Mercy Health System of Northwest Arkasas
Nat'l Ass'n of Securities Dealers, Inc. (NASD)
Philip Morris Management Corp.
Planet Electric
Sallie Mae, Inc.

BARTLETT, Patricia L.

601 13th St. NW
Suite 300
Washington, DC 20005
Tel: (202)756-3671
Fax: (202)347-1420

Employers
Georgia Institute of Technology (Director, Federal Relations)

BARTLETT, Steve

805 15th St. NW
Suite 600
Washington, DC 20005
Tel: (202)289-4322
Fax: (202)289-1903
Registered: LDA

Employers
The Financial Services Roundtable (President)

BARTLETT, Terri L.

1300 19th St. NW
Second Floor
Washington, DC 20036
Tel: (202)557-3400
Fax: (202)728-4177
Registered: LDA

Employers
Population Action Internat'l (V. President, Public Policy and Strategic Initiatives)

BARTOLINI, Mark Ryan

1612 K St. NW
Suite 700
Washington, DC 20006
Tel: (202)822-0043
Fax: (202)822-0089
Registered: LDA

Employers
Internat'l Rescue Committee Inc. (V. President, Government Relations)

BARTRAM, Darin

1050 Connecticut Ave. NW
Suite 1100
Washington, DC 20036-5304
Tel: (202)861-1500
Fax: (202)861-1790

Employers
Baker & Hostetler LLP

Clients Represented
On Behalf of Baker & Hostetler LLP
Croatia, Republic of

BARUAH, Smita

1717 Massachusetts Ave. NW
Suite 701
Washington, DC 20036
Tel: (202)667-8227
Fax: (202)667-8236

Employers
InterAction (Legislative Assistant)

BARWIG, Andrew

1600 K St. NW
Suite 601
Washington, DC 20006
EMail: abarwig@aaiusa.org
Tel: (202)429-9210
Fax: (202)429-9214

Employers
Arab American Institute (Communications Director)

BARZANI, Farhad

1015 18th St. NW
Suite 704
Washington, DC 20036
Tel: (202)331-9505
Fax: (202)331-9506

Employers
Kurdistan Democratic Party - Iraq (Representative)

BARZIER, Marilyn

4340 East-West Hwy.
Suite 402
Bethesda, MD 20814
Tel: (301)657-0270
Fax: (301)657-0275

Employers
Nat'l Ass'n of School Psychologists (Deputy Exec. Director)

BASILE, Jo-Anne R.

1250 Connecticut Ave. NW
Suite 800
Washington, DC 20036
Tel: (202)785-0081
Fax: (202)785-0721
Registered: LDA
EMail: jbasile@ctia.org

Employers
Cellular Telecommunications and Internet Ass'n (V. President, External and Industry Relations)

BASILE, Michael D.

1200 New Hampshire Ave. NW
Suite 800
Washington, DC 20036-6802
EMail: mbasile@dlalaw.com
Tel: (202)776-2000
Fax: (202)776-2222

Employers
Dow, Lohnes & Albertson, PLLC (Member)

BASKERVILLE, Anthony

807 Maine Ave. SW
Washington, DC 20024
Tel: (202)554-3501
Fax: (202)554-3581

Employers
Disabled American Veterans (Deputy National Service Director, Employment)

BASKETTE, Jon Patrick

1001 G St. NW
Suite 300 East
Washington, DC 20001
Tel: (202)638-5616
Fax: (202)638-5612
Registered: LDA
EMail: jbaskette@deweysquare.com

Employers
Dewey Square Group (Principal)

Clients Represented
On Behalf of Dewey Square Group
Northwest Airlines, Inc.

BASKIN, Maurice

1201 New York Ave. NW
Suite 1000
Washington, DC 20005
EMail: mbaskin@venable.com
Tel: (202)962-4823
Fax: (202)962-8300

Employers
Venable (Partner)

Clients Represented
On Behalf of Venable
Associated Builders and Contractors

BASS, Dr. Gary D.

1742 Connecticut Ave. NW
Washington, DC 20009-1146
Tel: (202)234-8494
Fax: (202)234-8584
EMail: bassg@rtk.net

Employers
OMB Watch (Exec. Director)

BASS, I. Scott

1722 I St. NW
Washington, DC 20006
Tel: (202)736-8000
Fax: (202)736-8711

Employers
Sidley & Austin (Partner)

BASS, III, Kenneth C.

1201 New York Ave. NW
Suite 1000
Washington, DC 20005
EMail: kcbass@venable.com
Tel: (202)962-4890
Fax: (202)962-8300
Counsel for Intelligence Policy, Department of Justice, 1979-81. Law clerk to Justice Hugo Black, U.S. Supreme Court, 1969-70.

Employers
Venable (Partner)

BASS, Kristin

1455 Pennsylvania Ave. NW
Suite 575
Washington, DC 20004
EMail: kristin.bass@wellpoint.com
Tel: (202)638-4076
Fax: (202)638-1096

Employers
WellPoint Health Networks/Blue Cross of California/UNICARE (Director, Federal Affairs)

BASS, Linda

6400 Goldsboro Rd.
Suite 500
Bethesda, MD 20817
EMail: lbass@epb.com
Tel: (301)263-2241
Fax: (301)263-2269

Employers
Earle Palmer Brown Public Relations (Account Director, EPB PR)

BASS, Marie

1818 N St. NW
Suite 450
Washington, DC 20036
Tel: (202)530-2900
Fax: (202)530-2901
Registered: LDA
EMail: mbass@basshowes.com

Employers
Bass and Howes, Inc. (Principal)

BASS, Mel

122 C St. NW
Suite 310
Washington, DC 20001
EMail: mel.bass@vanderbilt.edu
Tel: (202)824-6682
Fax: (202)393-6288

Employers
Vanderbilt University (Director, Federal Relations, Vanderbilt University Medical Center)

BASS-CORS, Sandy

119 Oronoco St.
Suite 300
Alexandria, VA 22314-2015
Tel: (703)519-7555
Fax: (703)519-7747
Registered: LDA
EMail: sandy@careauto.org

Employers
Coalition for Auto Repair Equality (CARE) (Exec. Director)

BASSECHES, Robert T.

1800 Massachusetts Ave. NW
Washington, DC 20036
Tel: (202)828-2000
Fax: (202)828-2195
Law Clerk to Justice Hugo L. Black, U.S. Supreme Court, 1959, and Judge David L. Bazelon, U.S. Court of Appeals, District of Columbia Circuit, 1958-59.

Employers
Shea & Gardner (Partner)

Clients Represented
On Behalf of Shea & Gardner
APL Limited

BASSETT, Patrick F.

1620 L St. NW
Suite 1100
Washington, DC 20036-5605
Tel: (202)973-9700
Fax: (202)973-9790

Employers
Nat'l Ass'n of Independent Schools (President)

BASSETT, Stephen G.

4938 Hampden Ln.
Suite 161
Bethesda, MD 20814
Tel: (301)564-1820
Fax: (301)564-4066
Registered: LDA
EMail: paradigmrg@aol.com

Employers
Paradigm Research Group (Consultant)

Clients Represented
On Behalf of Paradigm Research Group
Center for the Study of Extraterrestrial Intelligence
The Enterprise Mission
Hickman Report
Operation Right to Know

BASSETT, Steve

4041 Powder Mill Rd.
Suite 201
Calverton, MD 20705
Tel: (301)931-8770
Fax: (301)931-8774
Registered: LDA
EMail: stevebassett@usata.com

Employers
United States Air Tour Ass'n (President)

BASTARACHE, Gerald

400 Virginia Ave. SW
Suite 800
Washington, DC 20024-2370
Tel: (202)484-4847
Fax: (202)484-3483

Employers
Intelligent Transportation Soc. of America (Director, Communications)

BATEMAN, Jr., Joseph R.

600 13th St. NW
Suite 340
Washington, DC 20005
Tel: (202)662-0100
Fax: (202)662-0199
Registered: LDA

Employers
Union Pacific (Senior Assistant V. President, Government Affairs)

BATEMAN, Marguerite

1401 H St. NW
12th Floor
Washington, DC 20005-2148
Tel: (202)326-5800
Fax: (202)326-5827
Registered: LDA

Employers
Investment Co. Institute (Associate Counsel)

BATEMAN, Paul W.

1112 16th St. NW
Suite 240
Washington, DC 20036
Tel: (202)835-0185
Fax: (202)835-0155
Deputy Assistant to the President for Management, The White House, 1989-92. Deputy Treasurer, Department of the Treasury, 1985-88. Deputy Assistant Secretary for Economic Development, Department of Commerce, 1982-85. Staff Assistant, The White House, 1981-82.

Employers
The Gold and Silver Institute (President)
Klein & Saks, Inc. (President)

Clients Represented
On Behalf of Klein & Saks, Inc.
The Gold and Silver Institute

BATES, Douglas P.

1001 Pennsylvania Ave. NW
Washington, DC 20004-2599
Tel: (202)624-2000
Fax: (202)624-2319
Registered: LDA

Employers
American Council of Life Insurers (Assistant V. President, Tax)

BATES, Gardner

2001 L St. NW
Suite 506
Washington, DC 20036-4919
Tel: (202)775-2790
Fax: (202)223-7225

Employers
Chlorine Institute (Director, Public & Member Communications)

BATES, John D.

655 15th St. NW
Suite 900
Washington, DC 20005-5701
Tel: (202)626-5800
Fax: (202)628-0858
EMail: jbates@milchev.com
Former Director, Civil Division, United States Attorney's Office.

Employers
Miller & Chevalier, Chartered (Member)

BATES, Michael J.

1850 K St. NW
Suite 850
Washington, DC 20006
Tel: (202)331-1760
Fax: (202)822-9376
Registered: LDA
Former Counsel, House Committee on Energy and Commerce. Former Legislative Director to Rep. Edward Madigan (R-IL).

Employers
Timmons and Co., Inc. (V. President and General Counsel)

Clients Represented
On Behalf of Timmons and Co., Inc.
American Council of Life Insurers
American Petroleum Institute
American Soc. of Anesthesiologists
Anheuser-Busch Cos., Inc.
Asbestos Working Group
AT&T
Bay Harbor Management, L.C.
Bristol-Myers Squibb Co.
Cox Enterprises Inc.
DaimlerChrysler Corp.
Farallon Capital Management
Federal Home Loan Mortgage Corp. (Freddie Mac)
Micron Technology, Inc.
Napster, Inc.
Nat'l Rifle Ass'n of America
New York Life Insurance Co.
Northrop Grumman Corp.
TruePosition Inc.
Union Pacific
University of Utah
UNOCAL Corp.
VISA U.S.A., Inc.

BATES, Richard M.

1150 17th St. NW
Suite 400
Washington, DC 20036
Tel: (202)222-4700
Fax: (202)222-4799
Former Administrative Assistant to Rep. Beryl Anthony (D-AR) and former Executive Director, Democratic Congressional Campaign Committee.

Employers
The Walt Disney Co. (V. President, Government Relations)

BATES, William C.

1401 H St. NW
Suite 600
Washington, DC 20005-2136
Tel: (202)326-7300
Fax: (202)326-7333
Registered: LDA

Employers
United States Telecom Ass'n (Director, Government Relations)

BATSON, Russell B.

1120 Connecticut Ave. NW
Suite 1080
Washington, DC 20036
Tel: (202)466-7362
Fax: (202)429-4915
Registered: LDA

Employers
American Furniture Manufacturers Ass'n (V. President, Government Affairs)

BATTAT, Brenda

7910 Woodmont Ave.
Suite 1200
Bethesda, MD 20814
Tel: (301)657-2248
Fax: (301)913-9413

Employers
Self Help for Hard of Hearing People, Inc. (Deputy Exec. Director)

BAUER, Anne Watson

17904 Georgia Ave.
Suite 215
Olney, MD 20832-2277
Tel: (301)570-2111
Fax: (301)570-2212
EMail: aceied@aol.com

Employers
Ass'n for Childhood Education Internat'l (Editor/Director of Publications)

BAUER, Dana

801 Pennsylvania Ave. NW
Suite 750
Washington, DC 20004
Tel: (202)628-3750
Fax: (202)624-0659
Registered: FARA
EMail: danabauerdc@aol.com
Deputy Director, Office of Southern European Affairs, Department of State, 1997-99. Intelligence Officer, Central Intelligence Agency, 1993-97. Senior Analyst, Defense Intelligence Agency, Department of Defense, 1980-93.

Employers
The Solomon Group, LLC (Associate)

Clients Represented
On Behalf of The Solomon Group, LLC
Turkey, Government of the Republic of

BAUER, David

1010 Massachusetts Ave. NW
Washington, DC 20001
Tel: (202)289-4434
Fax: (202)289-4435
Registered: LDA

Employers
American Road and Transportation Builders Ass'n (ARTBA) (Director, Policy)

BAUER, Julie

1455 Pennsylvania Ave. NW
Suite 1225
Washington, DC 20004
Tel: (202)783-1190
Fax: (202)347-5835
Registered: LDA

Employers
Chicago Board of Trade (Director, Government Relations)

BAUER, Robert F.

607 14th St. NW
Suite 700
Washington, DC 20005-2011
Tel: (202)628-6600
Fax: (202)434-1690

Employers
Perkins Coie LLP (Managing Partner)

BAUERLE, Brian

1420 King St.
Alexandria, VA 22314-2794
Tel: (703)684-2800
Fax: (703)836-4875

Employers
Nat'l Soc. of Professional Engineers (Manager, Congressional and Political Relations)

BAUGHMAN, Laura M.

1775 Pennsylvania Ave. NW
Suite 1250
Washington, DC 20006
Tel: (202)347-1041
Fax: (202)628-0669
Registered: LDA
EMail: baughman@tradepartnership.com

Employers
The Trade Partnership (President)

Clients Represented
On Behalf of The Trade Partnership
The Business Roundtable
Coalition for GSP
Council of the Americas
Nat'l Retail Federation

BAUM, Mark W.

2100 Reston Pkwy.
Suite 400
Reston, VA 20191-1218
Tel: (703)758-7790
Fax: (703)758-7787
EMail: baum@asmc.org

Employers
Ass'n of Sales & Marketing Companies (President)

BAUMAN, Barbara

2000 L St. NW
Suite 805
Washington, DC 20036
Tel: (202)293-7513
Fax: (202)293-2697
Registered: LDA

Employers
Electric Power Research Institute (Director, Washington Office)

BAUMAN, Barry H.

1140 Connecticut Ave.
Suite 503
Washington, DC 20036

Tel: (202)429-0045
Fax: (202)429-6982
Registered: LDA

Employers
Lawyers for Civil Justice (Exec. Director)

BAUMAN, Carlea

1701 N. Beauregard St.
Alexandria, VA 22311

Tel: (703)549-1500
Ext: 2060
Fax: (703)549-8748
Registered: LDA

EMail: cbauman@diabetes.org

Employers
American Diabetes Ass'n (Director, Grassroots Advocacy)

BAUMANN, Henry L.

1771 N St. NW
Washington, DC 20036-2891

Tel: (202)429-5430
Fax: (202)775-3526
Registered: LDA

Employers
Nat'l Ass'n of Broadcasters (Exec. V. President, Law and Regulatory Policy)

BAUMBUSCH, Peter L.

1050 Connecticut Ave. NW
Washington, DC 20036-5306
EMail: pbaumbusch@gdclaw.com

Tel: (202)955-8500
Fax: (202)467-0539

Employers
Gibson, Dunn & Crutcher LLP (Partner)

BAUMGARTEN, Jon A.

1233 20th St. NW
Suite 800
Washington, DC 20036-2396
EMail: JABaumgarten@prokauer.com
General Counsel, U.S. Copyright Office, 1976-79.

Tel: (202)416-6800
Fax: (202)416-6899
Registered: LDA

Employers
Proskauer Rose LLP (Partner)

Clients Represented
On Behalf of Proskauer Rose LLP
Reed-Elsevier Inc.

BAUMGARTNER, Lisa

2120 L St. NW
Suite 400
Washington, DC 20037

Tel: (202)223-9541
Fax: (202)223-9579

Employers
M & R Strategic Services (Senior V. President)

BAUR, Donald C.

607 14th St. NW
Suite 700
Washington, DC 20005-2011
General Counsel, U.S. Marine Mammal Commission, 1984-87. Attorney, Office of the Solicitor, Department of the Interior, 1979-84.

Tel: (202)628-6600
Fax: (202)434-1690
Registered: LDA

Employers
Perkins Coie LLP (Partner)

BAVINGER, III, William F.

700 13th St. NW
Suite 700
Washington, DC 20005-3960
EMail: wfbavinger@bryancave.com
Assistant General Counsel (1975-76) and Staff Attorney (1974-75), Securities and Exchange Commission. Law Clerk to Judge Wade H. McCree, U.S. Court of Appeals, Sixth Circuit, 1968-69.

Tel: (202)508-6000
Fax: (202)508-6200

Employers
Bryan Cave LLP (Partner)

BAWDEN, Ben

8503 Pelham Rd.
Bethesda, MD 20817

Tel: (301)564-9708
Fax: (301)564-9706
Registered: LDA

Employers
Direct Impact, LLC

Clients Represented
On Behalf of Direct Impact, LLC
California, State of, Attorney General's Office

BAXT, Leonard J.

1200 New Hampshire Ave. NW
Suite 800
Washington, DC 20036-6802
EMail: lbaxt@dlalaw.com

Tel: (202)776-2000
Fax: (202)776-2222

Employers
Dow, Lohnes & Albertson, PLLC (Member)

BAXTER, Edward H.

233 Constitution Ave. NE
Washington, DC 20002

Tel: (202)547-4000
Fax: (202)543-5044
Registered: LDA

EMail: ehbaxter@aol.com
Former Chief Counsel and Staff Director, Subcommittee on Patents, Copyrights and Trademarks, Senate Committee on the Judiciary, and Former Counsel, Senate Committee on the Judiciary.

Employers
Parry, Romani, DeConcini & Symms (V. President, Government Relations)

Clients Represented
On Behalf of Parry, Romani, DeConcini & Symms
AIDS Healthcare Foundation
Andrx Pharmaceutical Corp.
Armstrong World Industries, Inc.
Asphalt Systems, Inc.
Aventis Pharmaceutical Products
Avondale, Arizona, City of
Bank of New York
Bristol-Myers Squibb Co.
Coalition Against Database Piracy
Composites Fabricators Ass'n
Ferraro, USA
Formosan Ass'n for Public Affairs
GAF Corp.
GlaxoSmithKline
Herbalife Internat'l, Inc.
Hoechst Marion Roussel Deutschland GmbH
Inter-Cal Corp.
Katten Muchin & Zavis
Motion Picture Ass'n of America
Nat'l Air Cargo, Inc.
Nat'l Nutritional Foods Ass'n
Nat'l Retail Federation
Nogales, Arizona, City of
Nu Skin Internat'l Inc.
Owens Corning
Peoria, Arizona, City of
Pfizer, Inc.
Pharmacia Corp.
Pharmanex
Policy Development Group, Inc.
Project to Promote Competition and Innovation in the Digital Age
Research & Development Laboratories
Research Corp. Technology
Rexall Sundown
SBC Communications Inc.
SOL Source Technologies, Inc.
Styrene Information and Research Center
Taxpayers Against Fraud, The False Claims Legal Center
TCOM, L.P.
Unilever United States, Inc.
Utah Natural Products Alliance

BAXTER, Thomas A.

2300 N St. NW
Washington, DC 20037-1128
EMail: thomas.baxter@shawpittman.com
Special Assistant for Litigation, Price Commission and Cost of Living Council, Executive Office of the President, The White House, 1972-73.

Tel: (202)663-8000
Fax: (202)663-8007

Employers
Shaw Pittman (Partner)

BAYER, Judith

1401 I St. NW
Suite 600
Washington, DC 20005
EMail: bayerj@corpdc.utc.com

Tel: (202)336-7400
Fax: (202)336-7447
Registered: LDA

Employers
United Technologies Corp. (Director, Environmental Government Affairs)

BAYES, James R.

1776 K St. NW
Washington, DC 20006

Tel: (202)719-7000
Fax: (202)719-7049
Registered: LDA

Employers
Wiley, Rein & Fielding (Partner)

Clients Represented
On Behalf of Wiley, Rein & Fielding
A. H. Belo Corp.

BAYH, Hon. Birch

1620 L St. NW
Suite 600
Washington, DC 20036
EMail: bbayh@oppenheimer.com
Member, U.S. Senate (D-IN), 1963-81

Tel: (202)312-8000
Fax: (202)312-8100
Registered: LDA, FARA

Employers
Oppenheimer Wolff & Donnelly LLP (Partner)

Clients Represented
On Behalf of Oppenheimer Wolff & Donnelly LLP
Association des Constructeurs Europeens de Motocycles
Bio-Vascular, Inc.
CBI Industries
ComEd
Cook Group
Crown Butte Mines, Inc.
ICN Pharmaceuticals, Inc.
Illinois Tool Works
Nat'l Basketball Ass'n
NISH - Creating Employment Opportunities for People with Severe Disabilities
Real Estate Capital Resources Ass'n

BAYLISS, Kim Koontz

412 First St. SE
Suite 100
Washington, DC 20003
EMail: kbayliss@dutkogroup.com
Legislative Assistant and Legislative Director to Rep. Mike Synar (D-OK), 1983-92.

Tel: (202)484-4884
Fax: (202)484-0109
Registered: LDA

Employers
The Dutko Group, Inc. (Partner)

Clients Represented
On Behalf of The Dutko Group, Inc.
Alcatel USA
ASCENT (Ass'n of Community Enterprises)
Ass'n for Competitive Technology
AT&T
AT&T Wireless Services, Inc.
Cable & Wireless, Inc.
Competitive Telecommunications Ass'n (COMPTEL)
European Telecommunications Standards Institute (ETSI)
EXCEL Communications Inc.
Satellite Broadcasting and Communications Ass'n
SkyBridge, LLC
SpaceData Internat'l
TV Guide, Inc.
VeriSign/Network Solutions, Inc.
Winstar Communications, Inc.
XO Communications

BAYLOR, Gregory S.

4208 Evergreen Ln.
Suite 222
Annandale, VA 22003

Tel: (703)642-1070
Ext: 3502
Fax: (703)642-1075
Registered: LDA

EMail: GBaylor@clsnet.org

Employers
Christian Legal Soc. (Associate Director, Center for Law and Religious Freedom)

BAYLYFF, Chris

200 Constitution Ave. NW
Room S-1325
Washington, DC 20210
EMail: baylyff-chris@dol.gov

Tel: (202)693-4600
Fax: (202)693-4642

Employers
Department of Labor (Legislative Assistant, Office of Congressional and Intergovernmental Affairs)

BEA, Jr., Paul H.

1001 Connecticut Ave. NW
Suite 610
Washington, DC 20036
EMail: pbea@panynj.gov
Tel: (202)887-5240
Fax: (202)887-0282

Legislative Assistant to Edward J. Patten (D-NJ), 1972-78.

Employers

Port Authority of New York and New Jersey (Washington Representative, Director)

BEACH, Dr. Bert B.

12501 Old Columbia Pike
Silver Spring, MD 20904-6600
EMail: 74617,2745@compuserve.com
Tel: (301)680-6683
Fax: (301)680-6695

Employers

Internat'l Religious Liberty Ass'n (V. President)

BEACH, William

214 Massachusetts Ave. NE
Washington, DC 20002
Tel: (202)546-4400
Fax: (202)546-8328

Employers

Heritage Foundation (Director, Center for Data Analysis)

BEAL, Lisa S.

Ten G St. NE
Suite 700
Washington, DC 20002
Tel: (202)216-5900
Fax: (202)216-0876

Employers

Interstate Natural Gas Ass'n of America (Director, Environmental Affairs)

BEALE, Joanne Elden

1875 I St. NW
Suite 1000
Washington, DC 20006
EMail: jbeale@chausa.org
Tel: (202)296-3993
Fax: (202)296-3997
Registered: LDA

Employers

Catholic Health Ass'n of the United States (Co-Director, Sponsor Services)

BEALL, James A.

1455 F St. NW
Suite 225
Washington, DC 20005
Tel: (202)638-3307
Fax: (202)783-6947
Registered: LDA

Professional Staff, House Committee on Ways and Means, 1979-80. Legislative Coordinator for Rep. Al Ullman (D-OR), 1977-78. Attorney-Advisor, Department of the Interior, 1976-77.

Employers

Ball Janik, LLP (D.C. Office Managing Partner)

Clients Represented

On Behalf of Ball Janik, LLP

Cascade General, Inc.
City University
Clackamas, Oregon, County of
Clatsop Community College
Concentrex
Greenbrier Companies
Guardian Marine Internat'l LLC
Hood River, Oregon, Port of
Northwest Woodland Owners Council
Oregon Department of Transportation
Schnitzer Steel Industries, Inc.
Tukwila, Washington, City of
U.S. Forest Capital

BEALL, Ph.D., Robert J.

6931 Arlington Rd.
Suite 200
Bethesda, MD 20814
Tel: (301)951-4422
Fax: (301)951-6378

Employers

Cystic Fibrosis Foundation (President/Chief Exec. Officer)

BEALL, Thomas

1901 L St. NW
Suite 300
Washington, DC 20036
EMail: tom.beall@dc.ogilvypr.com
Tel: (202)466-7590
Fax: (202)296-3727

Employers

Ogilvy Public Relations Worldwide (Managing Director, Global Health and Medical Practice)

BEAMER BOHNERT, Suzanne C.

707 N. Saint Asaph St.
Alexandria, VA 22314
EMail: suzy@signs.org
Tel: (703)836-4012
Fax: (703)836-8353

Employers

Internat'l Sign Ass'n (V. President, Government Relations and Public Affairs)

BEAN, Jr., Donald

1250 Connecticut Ave. NW
Suite 700
Washington, DC 20005
Tel: (202)637-6667
Fax: (202)842-2869

Employers

Fensterheim & Bean, P.C. (Partner)

Clients Represented

On Behalf of Fensterheim & Bean, P.C.

RECRA

BEAN, Michael

1875 Connecticut Ave. NW
Suite 1016
Washington, DC 20009
Tel: (202)387-3500
Fax: (202)319-8590

Employers

Environmental Defense Fund (Chairman, Wildlife Program)

BEANE, Marjorie

Ten G St. NE
Suite 800
Washington, DC 20002
Tel: (202)729-7600
Fax: (202)729-7610

Employers

World Resources Institute (Secretary-Treasurer)

BEANG, Nancy

11 Dupont Circle NW
Suite 500
Washington, DC 20036
Tel: (202)462-6688
Fax: (202)234-9770
Registered: LDA

Employers

Soc. for Neuroscience (Exec. Director)

BEARD, Bob

Office of Govermental Affairs
3101 Park Center Dr.
Room 806
Alexandria, VA 22302
EMail: bob_beard@fns.usda.gov
Tel: (703)305-2010
Fax: (703)305-2312

Employers

Department of Agriculture - Food and Nutrition Service (Legislative Specialist)

BEARD, Dan

1901 Pennsylvania Ave. NW
Suite 1100
Washington, DC 20006
Tel: (202)861-2242
Fax: (202)861-4290

Employers

Nat'l Audubon Soc. (Senior V. President, Public Policy)

BEARD, Michael K.

1023 15th St. NW
Suite 600
Washington, DC 20005
EMail: csgv@csgv.org
Tel: (202)408-0061
Registered: LDA

Employers

Coalition to Stop Gun Violence (President and Chief Exec. Officer)

BEARD, Robin L.

1100 Wilson Blvd.
Suite 1500
Arlington, VA 22209
EMail: robin_l_beard@raytheon.com
Tel: (703)841-5724
Fax: (703)841-5793

Employers

Raytheon Co. (President, Government Relations)

BEARDSLEY, Daniel B.

1911 N. Ft. Myer Dr.
Suite 707
Arlington, VA 22209
EMail: dbeardsley@alberscom.com
Tel: (703)358-9100
Fax: (703)358-9106
Registered: LDA

Served for 15 years with the Environmental Protection Agency.

Employers

Albers & Co. (Managing Partner)

Clients Represented

On Behalf of Albers & Co.

Infiltrator Systems, Inc.
Eli Lilly and Co.
Profit Recovery Group Internat'l

BEARDSLEY, Kate C.

919 18th St. NW
Suite 600
Washington, DC 20006
Tel: (202)736-3615
Fax: (202)736-3608
Registered: LDA

Deputy Director, U.S. Regulatory Council, 1979-80. Special Counsel to the Executive Associate Director, Office of Management and Budget, 1976-79.

Employers

Buc & Beardsley (Partner)

Clients Represented

On Behalf of Buc & Beardsley

CryoLife, Inc.

BEARSE, Michael

905 16th St. NW
Washington, DC 20006
Tel: (202)737-8320
Fax: (202)737-2754

Employers

Laborers' Internat'l Union of North America (General Counsel)

BEASHER, Mark

2819 Winchester Way
Falls Church, VA 22042
Tel: (703)532-4256
Fax: (703)532-4976
Registered: LDA

Employers

Argo Public Enterprise (Beasher)

Clients Represented

On Behalf of Argo Public Enterprise

Diversified Collection Services, Inc.

BEASLEY, Vicky

555 11th St. NW
Suite 1000
Washington, DC 20004
Tel: (202)637-2200
Fax: (202)637-2201
Registered: LDA

Employers

Latham & Watkins

Clients Represented

On Behalf of Latham & Watkins

American Public Communications Council

BEATSON, Nora

1399 New York Ave. NW
Suite 900
Washington, DC 20005
Tel: (202)585-5818
Fax: (202)585-5820

Employers

American Internat'l Group, Inc. (Associate Director, Government Affairs)

BEATTIE, Patricia

1901 N. Beauregard St.
Suite 200
Alexandria, VA 22311-1727
EMail: pbeattie@nib.org
Tel: (703)998-0770
Fax: (703)671-9053
Registered: LDA

Employers

Nat'l Industries for the Blind (Director, Public Policy and Consumer Relations)

BEATTY, Julia

1413 K St. NW
Tenth Floor
Washington, DC 20005
Tel: (202)347-8772
Fax: (202)393-5886

Employers

United States Student Ass'n (V. President)

BEATY, Elizabeth
1595 Spring Hill Rd.
Suite 330
Vienna, VA 22182
Tel: (703)506-3260
Fax: (703)506-3266

Employers
Ass'n Management Bureau

Clients Represented
On Behalf of Ass'n Management Bureau
Nat'l Ass'n of Telecommunications Officers and Advisors

BEAUBIEN, Kathryn
1275 Pennsylvania Ave. NW
Ninth Floor
Washington, DC 20004
Tel: (202)467-8383
Fax: (202)467-8381
Registered: LDA

Employers
Lindsay Hart Neil & Weigler (Regulatory Manager)

Clients Represented
On Behalf of Lindsay Hart Neil & Weigler
Agriculture Ocean Transportation Coalition
Coalition of New England Companies for Trade
Maritime Fire and Safety Ass'n
Oregon Economic Development Department
Pacific Coast Council of Customs Brokers and Freight Forwarders Ass'n
Redwood City, California, Port of
Reebok Internat'l

BEAUCHAMP, Marc
Ten G St. NE
Suite 710
Washington, DC 20002
Tel: (202)737-0900
Fax: (202)783-3571

Employers
North American Securities Administrators Ass'n (NASAA) (Exec. Director)

BEAUCHAMP, Rene
1401 I St. NW
Suite 600
Washington, DC 20005
Tel: (202)336-7400
Fax: (202)336-7527

Employers
United Technologies Corp. (V. President, Government Business Development)

BEAUJUIN, Arnolda
1707 H St. NW
Suite 703
Washington, DC 20006
Tel: (202)478-5425
Registered: LDA

Employers
Washington Aviation Group

Clients Represented
On Behalf of Washington Aviation Group
Aircraft Electronics Ass'n
Airline Suppliers Ass'n
Professional Aviation Maintenance Ass'n

BEAUMONT, Constance E.
1785 Massachusetts Ave. NW
Washington, DC 20036
Tel: (202)588-6000
Fax: (202)588-6059

Employers
Nat'l Trust for Historic Preservation (Director, State and Local Policy)

BEAUMONT, Dina
501 Third St. NW
Washington, DC 20001-2797
Tel: (202)434-1100
Fax: (202)434-1318

Employers
Communications Workers of America (Exec. Assistant to the President)

BEAUMONT, Guy D.
123 N. Henry St.
Alexandria, VA 22314-2903
Tel: (703)684-0416
Fax: (703)684-3280
EMail: gbeaumont@theacos.com

Employers
American College of Osteopathic Surgeons (Exec. Director)

BEAUMONT, Nancy Perkin
1111 N. Fairfax St.
Alexandria, VA 22314
Tel: (703)684-2782
Fax: (703)684-7343

Employers
American Physical Therapy Ass'n (Senior V. President, Communications Div.)

BEAUREGARD, Gilles
1660 L St. NW
Suite 801
Washington, DC 20036
Tel: (202)393-4464
Fax: (202)347-0649

Employers
Office and Professional Employees Internat'l Union (Secretary-Treasurer)

BECCHI, Rosemary D.
1666 K St. NW
Suite 800
Washington, DC 20006
Tel: (202)481-7000
Fax: (202)862-7098
Registered: LDA

Employers
Arthur Andersen LLP (Manager)

Clients Represented
On Behalf of Arthur Andersen LLP
Eagle-Picher Personal Injury Settlement Trust

BECHTEL, Gene A.
1901 L St. NW
Suite 250
Washington, DC 20036
Tel: (202)833-4190
Fax: (202)833-3084

Employers
Bechtel & Cole (Board Chair and Principal)

Clients Represented
On Behalf of Bechtel & Cole
Advanced Cordless Technologies, Inc.

BECHTEL, Lee
8506 Sundale Dr.
Silver Spring, MD 20910
Tel: (301)588-2822
Fax: (301)588-2822
Registered: LDA

Employers
Lee Bechtel and Associates (Principal)

Clients Represented
On Behalf of Lee Bechtel and Associates
American Ass'n of Naturopathic Physicians
American Soc. of Extra-Corporeal Technology
EquiMed Corp.
Paradigm Support Corp.

BECHTEL, Philip E.
1155 21st St. NW
Suite 300
Washington, DC 20036
Tel: (202)659-8201
Fax: (202)659-5249
EMail: pebechtel@wms-jen.com
Chief Counsel (1997-98) and Deputy Staff Director (1995-96), Senate Committee on Banking, Housing and Urban Affairs. Legislative Director and General Counsel to Senator Alfonse M. D'Amato (R-NY), 1990-95. Supervisory Trial Attorney, Enforcement, Federal Energy Regulatory Commission, 1987-90. Director, Division of Administration Litigation (1981-87) and Attorney, Office of General Counsel (1975-81), Consumer Product Safety Commission.

Employers
Williams & Jensen, P.C. (Partner)

Clients Represented
On Behalf of Williams & Jensen, P.C.
Credit Suisse First Boston Corp.
First Union Corp.
Internat'l Ass'n of Amusement Parks and Attractions
USAA - United Services Automobile Ass'n

BECK, Andy
8400 W. Park Dr.
McLean, VA 22102
Tel: (703)821-7000

Employers
Nat'l Automobile Dealers Ass'n (Director of Government Communications)

BECK, Deborah
1726 M St. NW
Suite 1101
Washington, DC 20036
Tel: (202)452-1520
Fax: (202)833-1577
EMail: dib@wsba.com

Employers
William S. Bergman Associates (V. President)

Clients Represented
On Behalf of William S. Bergman Associates
Nat'l Ass'n of Lottery Purchasers
Nurses Organization of Veterans Affairs

BECK, Edward
1666 K St. NW
Suite 500
Washington, DC 20006-2803
Tel: (202)887-1400
Fax: (202)466-2198
Registered: LDA

Employers
O'Connor & Hannan, L.L.P.

Clients Represented
On Behalf of O'Connor & Hannan, L.L.P.
Bank of America
State Street Bank and Trust Co.

BECK, Jennifer
236 Massachusetts Ave. NE
Suite 203
Washington, DC 20002-5702
Tel: (202)543-7780
Fax: (202)546-3266

Employers
American Humane Ass'n (Policy Analyst)

BECK, Lauren E.
816 Connecticut Ave. NW
Seventh Floor
Washington, DC 20006-2705
Tel: (202)828-1010
Fax: (202)828-4550
Registered: LDA
EMail: lauren.beck@unilever.com

Employers
Unilever United States, Inc. (Legislative Representative)

BECK, Peter M.
1101 Vermont Ave. NW
Suite 401
Washington, DC 20005
Tel: (202)371-0690
Fax: (202)371-0692
Registered: FARA
EMail: pmb@keia.org

Employers
Korea Economic Institute of America (Director, Research and Academic Affairs)

BECK, Rob
7910 Woodmont Ave.
Suite 300
Bethesda, MD 20814-3015
Tel: (301)657-0881
Fax: (301)657-0869
EMail: rbeck@autism-soc.org

Employers
Autism Soc. of America, Inc. (Exec. Director)

BECKER, Brandon
2445 M St. NW
Washington, DC 20037-1420
Tel: (202)663-6000
Fax: (202)663-6363
EMail: bbecker@wilmer.com
Special Advisor to the Chairman for International Derivatives (1995-96) and Director, Division of Market Regulation (1993-95), Securities and Exchange Commission.

Employers
Wilmer, Cutler & Pickering (Partner)

BECKER, Brenda L.
14th and Constitution Ave. NW
Room 5421
Washington, DC 20230
Tel: (202)482-3663
Fax: (202)482-4420

Employers
Department of Commerce (Assistant Secretary for Legislative and Intergovernmental Affairs (Nominated))

BECKER, Christine S.
1301 Pennsylvania Ave. NW
Suite 550
Washington, DC 20004-1701
Tel: (202)626-3017
Fax: (202)626-3043
EMail: becker@nlc.org

Employers
Nat'l League of Cities (Deputy Exec. Director)

BECKER, Daniel F.

408 C St. NE
Washington, DC 20002
Tel: (202)547-1141
Fax: (202)547-6009
Registered: LDA

Employers
Sierra Club (Director, Global Warming and Energy Program)

BECKER, Darby M. R.

1400 K St. NW
Suite 801
Washington, DC 20005-2485
Tel: (202)393-1500
Fax: (202)842-4063
Registered: LDA

Employers
General Aviation Manufacturers Ass'n (General Counsel)

BECKER, Evelyn

555 13th St. NW
Suite 500 West
Washington, DC 20004
Tel: (202)383-5300
Fax: (202)383-5414
Registered: LDA
EMail: ebecker@omm.com

Employers
O'Melveny and Myers LLP (Special Counsel)

BECKER, Fred R.

3138 N. Tenth St.
Arlington, VA 22201
Tel: (703)522-4770
Fax: (703)522-0594

Employers
Nat'l Ass'n of Federal Credit Unions (President)

BECKER, Jeffrey G.

122 C St. NW
Suite 750
Washington, DC 20001-2109
Tel: (202)737-2337
Fax: (202)737-7004
Registered: LDA

Employers
Beer Institute (President)

BECKER, Leah

122 C St. NW
Suite 875
Washington, DC 20001
Tel: (202)347-3600
Fax: (202)347-5265
Registered: LDA

Employers
Nat'l Pork Producers Council (Government Relations Representative)

BECKER, Linda M.

1401 H St. NW
Suite 700
Washington, DC 20005
Tel: (202)414-6757
Fax: (202)414-6736

Employers
DaimlerChrysler Corp. (Senior Manager, Public Policy and Communications)

BECKER, Mila

601 E St. NW
Washington, DC 20049
Tel: (202)434-3770
Fax: (202)434-3758
Registered: LDA

Employers
AARP (American Ass'n of Retired Persons) (Legislative Representative)

BECKER, S. William

444 N. Capitol St. NW
Suite 307
Washington, DC 20001
Tel: (202)624-7864
Fax: (202)624-7863

Employers
Ass'n of Local Air Pollution Control Officials (Exec. Director)
State and Territorial Air Pollution Program Administrators (Exec. Director)

BECKER, Scott

1211 Connecticut Ave. NW
Suite 608
Washington, DC 20036
EMail: sbecker@astphld.org
Tel: (202)822-5227
Fax: (202)887-5098

Employers
Ass'n of State and Territorial Public Health Laboratory Directors (Exec. Director)

BECKER, Stephan E.

2300 N St. NW
Washington, DC 20037-1128
Tel: (202)663-8000
Fax: (202)663-8007
Registered: LDA
EMail: stephan.becker@shawpittman.com

Employers
Shaw Pittman (Partner)

Clients Represented
On Behalf of Shaw Pittman
Nortel Networks

BECKER, Tracey

1747 Pennsylvania Ave. NW
Suite 1150
Washington, DC 20006
Tel: (202)296-6222
Fax: (202)296-4507
Former Legislative Assistant to Senator Joseph Biden Jr. (D-DE).

Employers
The MWW Group (Federal Affairs Representative)

Clients Represented
On Behalf of The MWW Group
Bacardi-Martini, USA, Inc.
Domino's Pizza
Internat'l Distance Learning
Puerto Ricans for Civic Action
Ross University School of Medicine in Dominica
Synapse
United States Education Finance Corp.

BECKINGTON, Jeffrey S.

3050 K St. NW
Washington, DC 20007
Tel: (202)342-8400
Fax: (202)342-8451
Registered: LDA
EMail: jbecking@colliershannon.com

Employers
Collier Shannon Scott, PLLC (Member)

Clients Represented
On Behalf of Collier Shannon Scott, PLLC
COMPACT
Copper and Brass Fabricators Council
Damascus Tubular Products
Miller Co.
Specialty Tubing Group

BECKMAN, Steve

1350 I St. NW
Suite 510
Washington, DC 20005
Tel: (202)828-8500
Fax: (202)293-3457
Registered: LDA

Employers
United Automobile, Aerospace and Agricultural Implement Workers of America (UAW) (Assistant Director, Governmental and International Affairs)

BECKMANN, David

50 F St. NW
Suite 500
Washington, DC 20001
EMail: dbeckmann@bread.org
Tel: (301)608-2400
Fax: (301)608-2401

Employers
Bread for the World (President)

BECKNER, Paul N.

1250 H St. NW
Suite 700
Washington, DC 20005-3908
EMail: Beckner@cse.org
Tel: (202)783-3870
Fax: (202)783-4687

Employers
Citizens for a Sound Economy (President)

BECKNER, Victoria

4350 N. Fairfax Dr.
Suite 900
Arlington, VA 22203
Tel: (703)207-4500
Registered: LDA

Employers
LunaCorp, Inc. (Director of External Affairs)

Clients Represented
On Behalf of LunaCorp, Inc.
Rotary Rocket Co.

BECKNER, William M.

7910 Woodmont Ave.
Suite 800
Bethesda, MD 20814
EMail: ncrp@ncrp.com
Tel: (301)657-2652
Fax: (301)907-8768

Employers
Nat'l Council on Radiation Protection and Measurement (Exec. Director)

BECKWITH, David

1724 Massachusetts Ave. NW
Washington, DC 20036-1969
Tel: (202)775-3629
Fax: (202)775-3695

Employers
Nat'l Cable Television Ass'n (V. President, Communications)

BECKWITH, Edward J.

1050 Connecticut Ave. NW
Suite 1100
Washington, DC 20036-5304
Tel: (202)861-1500
Fax: (202)861-1790
Registered: LDA

Employers
Baker & Hostetler LLP

Clients Represented
On Behalf of Baker & Hostetler LLP
United Jewish Communities, Inc.

BECKWITH, Lyle

1605 King St.
Alexandria, VA 22314-2792
Tel: (703)684-3600
Fax: (703)836-4564
Registered: LDA
EMail: lbeckwith@cstorecentral.com

Employers
Nat'l Ass'n of Convenience Stores (Director, Government Relations)

BEDARD, Robert

408 Third St. SE
Washington, DC 20003
Tel: (202)546-1821
Fax: (202)543-2405

Employers
Artists Rights Today (ART PAC) (Treasurer)

BEDDOE, Paul V.

440 First St. NW
Eighth Floor
Washington, DC 20001
EMail: pbeddoe@naco.org
Tel: (202)942-4234
Fax: (202)942-4281

Employers
Western Interstate Region (Contact)

BEDDOW, David T.

555 13th St. NW
Suite 500 West
Washington, DC 20004
Tel: (202)383-5300
Fax: (202)383-5414
Registered: LDA
EMail: dbeddow@omm.com

Employers
O'Melveny and Myers LLP (Partner)

Clients Represented
On Behalf of O'Melveny and Myers LLP
Advanced Micro Devices

BEDDOW, Tom F.

1101 15th St. NW
Suite 1100
Washington, DC 20005
EMail: tfbeddow@mmm.com
Tel: (202)331-6948
Fax: (202)331-2805

Employers
Minnesota Mining and Manufacturing Co. (3M Co.) (V. President, Public Affairs and Government Affairs)

BEDELL, Anthony

1250 I St. NW
Suite 500
Washington, DC 20005
Tel: (202)789-2900
Ext: 3005
Fax: (202)789-1893
EMail: abedell@anla.org

Employers
American Nursery and Landscape Ass'n (Director, Government Relations)

BEDELL, Robert P.

6001 Haverhill Ct.
Springfield, VA 22152
Tel: (703)644-7973
Administrator, Office of Federal Procurement Policy (1986-88); Deputy Administrator, Office of Information and Regulatory Affairs (1983-86); Deputy General Counsel (1978-83); and Assistant General Counsel (1973-78), Office of Management and Budget. Trial Attorney, Office of the Army Chief Attorney, 1971-73.

Employers
RPB Co.

Clients Represented
On Behalf of RPB Co.
Dun & Bradstreet

BEDLIN, Howard

409 Third St. SW
Second Floor
Washington, DC 20024
Tel: (202)479-1200
Fax: (202)479-0735
Registered: LDA

Employers
Nat'l Coalition of Consumer Organizations on Aging (Contact)
Nat'l Council on the Aging (V. President, Policy and Advocacy)

BEDNASH, Geraldine

One Dupont Circle NW
Suite 530
Washington, DC 20036
Tel: (202)463-6930
Ext: 222
Fax: (202)785-8320
EMail: pbednash@aacn.nche.edu

Employers
American Ass'n of Colleges of Nursing (Exec. Director)

BEEBE, Cora

1401 K St. NW
Suite 900
Washington, DC 20005
Tel: (202)626-8550
Fax: (202)626-8578
Registered: LDA

Employers
Jefferson Consulting Group (V. President)

Clients Represented
On Behalf of Jefferson Consulting Group
Franklin Covey

BEEDLE, Ralph

1776 I St. NW
Suite 400
Washington, DC 20006-3708
Tel: (202)739-8000
Fax: (202)785-4019

Employers
Nuclear Energy Institute (Senior V. President and Chief Nuclear Officer, Nuclear Generation)

BEEKS, Kenneth

1717 Pennsylvania Ave. NW
Suite 350
Washington, DC 20006
Tel: (202)296-2125
Fax: (202)296-2490
EMail: kbeeks@bens.org

Employers
Business Executives for Nat'l Security (V. President, Policy)

BEEMER, Jennifer

810 First St. NE
Suite 510
Washington, DC 20002
Tel: (202)289-5440
Fax: (202)289-3707
EMail: jbeemer@gypsum.org

Employers
Gypsum Ass'n (Director, Government Regulatory Affairs)

BEERS, Donald O.

555 12th St. NW
Washington, DC 20004-1206
Tel: (202)942-5000
Fax: (202)942-5999
Registered: LDA
EMail: Donald_Beers@aporter.com
Associate Chief Counsel for Drugs (1984-85), Associate Chief Counsel for Enforcement (1978-85), and Attorney, Office of Chief Counsel (1975-85), Food and Drug Administration. Law Clerk to Judge Milton Pollack, Southern District of New York, 1974-75.

Employers
Arnold & Porter (Partner)

BEETHAM, Mary Beth

1101 14th St. NW
Suite 1400
Washington, DC 20005
Tel: (202)682-9400
Fax: (202)682-1331
Registered: LDA
EMail: mbeetham@defenders.org

Employers
Defenders of Wildlife (Director, Legislative Affairs)

BEGANS, Peter

1140 Connecticut Ave. NW
Suite 510
Washington, DC 20036
Tel: (202)293-1355
Fax: (202)293-1658
Registered: LDA
EMail: peter.begans@prudential.com

Employers
Prudential Insurance Co. of America (V. President, Government Relations)

BEGLEY, Dennis F.

2175 K St. NW
Suite 350
Washington, DC 20037-1845
Tel: (202)659-5700
Fax: (202)659-5711

Employers
Reddy, Begley, & McCormick, LLP (Managing Partner)

Clients Represented
On Behalf of Reddy, Begley, & McCormick, LLP
Asterisk Communications
GHB Broadcasting Corp.
KTTW-TV and KTTM-TV

BEGUN, Tammy

1350 I St. NW
Suite 1255
Washington, DC 20005
Tel: (202)626-0089
Fax: (202)626-0088
Registered: LDA

Employers
Law Offices of Mark Barnes (Attorney)

Clients Represented
On Behalf of Law Offices of Mark Barnes
Briklee Trading Co.
Cash America Internat'l
Firearms Importers Roundtable Trade Group
Lew Horton Distributing Co.
Nat'l Ass'n of Arms Shows
Nat'l Pawnbrokers Ass'n
Nat'l Rifle Ass'n of America

BEHAN, William M.

1808 I St. NW
Eighth Floor
Washington, DC 20006
Tel: (202)223-4817
Fax: (202)296-0011
Registered: LDA

Employers
Deere & Co. (Director, Federal Government Affairs)

BEHNKE, Carl D.

701 Pennsylvania Ave. NW
Washington, DC 20004-2696
Tel: (202)508-5232
Fax: (202)508-5186

Employers
Edison Electric Institute (V. President, Human Resources and Corporate Services)

BEHRE, Kirby D.

1299 Pennsylvania Ave. NW
Tenth Floor
Washington, DC 20004-2400
Tel: (202)508-9500
Fax: (202)508-9700
EMail: kirbybehre@paulhastings.com
Assistant U.S. Attorney for the District of Columbia, Department of Justice, 1989-95.

Employers
Paul, Hastings, Janofsky & Walker LLP (Partner)

BEHRENDS, Paul D.

700 13th St. NW
Suite 350
Washington, DC 20005
Tel: (202)637-0040
Fax: (202)637-0041
Registered: LDA, FARA
Senior Advisor for International Relations and National Security Affairs to Rep. Dana Rohrabacher (R-CA), 1990-97. Legislative Director, House Republican Task Force on the Balkan Crisis, 1992-95.

Employers
Rhoads Group (V. President)

Clients Represented
On Behalf of Rhoads Group
AAAE-ACI
Airports Council Internat'l - North America
American Management Systems
Dick Corp.
The Justice Project, Inc.
PNC Bank, N.A.
SWATH Ocean Systems, Inc.
Taiwan Studies Institute
United States Enrichment Corp.

BEHRENS, Mark A.

1001 Pennsylvania Ave. NW
Suite 1100
Washington, DC 20004-2595
Tel: (202)624-2500
Fax: (202)628-5116
Registered: LDA

Employers
Crowell & Moring LLP (Partner)

Clients Represented
On Behalf of Crowell & Moring LLP
American Ass'n of Health Plans (AAHP)
American Tort Reform Ass'n
Bridgestone/Firestone, Inc.
Guidant Corp.
Nat'l Ass'n of Wholesaler-Distributors
USAA - United Services Automobile Ass'n

BEIGHTOL, David J.

400 N. Capitol St. NW
Suite 590
Washington, DC 20001
Tel: (202)393-3224
Fax: (202)393-7718
EMail: david.j.beightol@jci.com
Former Aide to the President for Intergovernmental Affairs, The White House, during Bush I administration.

Employers
Johnson Controls, Inc. (Director, Government Affairs)

BEISNER, John H.

555 13th St. NW
Suite 500 West
Washington, DC 20004
Tel: (202)383-5300
Fax: (202)383-5414
Registered: LDA
EMail: jbeisner@omm.com

Employers
O'Melveny and Myers LLP (Partner)

Clients Represented
On Behalf of O'Melveny and Myers LLP
Civil Justice Reform Group

BEITER, Nancy R.

The Mercury Bldg.
1925 K St. NW
Room 847
Washington, DC 20423-0001
Tel: (202)565-1592
Fax: (202)565-9016
EMail: beitern@stb.dot.gov
Attorney, Office of Public Assistance, Interstate Commerce Commission, 1988-95.

Employers
Department of Transportation - Surface Transportation Board (Attorney/Advisor, Congressional and Public Services)

BELAIR, Robert R.

1150 Connecticut Ave. NW
Suite 700
Washington, DC 20036
Tel: (202)296-8000
Fax: (202)296-8803
Registered: LDA, FARA
EMail: bobbelair@aol.com
Attorney, Federal Trade Commission, 1973-75. Acting General Counsel, Committee on Privacy, Office of the President, 1975-76.

Employers
Mullenholz, Brimsek & Belair (Partner)

Clients Represented
On Behalf of Mullenholz, Brimsek & Belair
Center for Civic Education
ChoicePoint
The Coalition on Motor Vehicle Privacy
Constitutional Rights Foundation
Equifax Inc.
First Data Corp./Telecheck
Nat'l Institute for Citizen Education in the Law
SEARCH Group, Inc.
Street Law Inc.

BELAS, Richard S.

1455 Pennsylvania Ave. NW
Suite 1200
Washington, DC 20004
Tel: (202)347-2230
Fax: (202)393-3310
Registered: LDA
Chief Counsel to Senate Majority Leader Robert J. Dole (R-KS), 1985-89. Deputy Chief Counsel (1983-84), Majority Tax Counsel (1981-83) and Minority Tax Counsel (1980-81), Senate Finance Committee.

Employers
Davis & Harman LLP (Partner)

Clients Represented
On Behalf of Davis & Harman LLP
Ad Hoc Life/Non-life Consolidation Group
Aegon USA
Allstate Insurance Co.
American General Life Insurance Co.
American Investors Life Insurance
Bethlehem Steel Corp.
Boston Capital
CIGNA Corp.
Committee of Annuity Insurers
Florida Power and Light Co.
General Aviation Manufacturers Ass'n
Lincoln Nat'l Corp.
Louisiana Workers' Compensation Corporation
Nat'l Business Aviation Ass'n
Nat'l Cattleman's Beef Ass'n
Pharmaceutical Research and Manufacturers of America
Stock Co. Information Group
Worldspan, L.P.

BELDEN, Joe

1025 Vermont Ave. NW
Suite 606
Washington, DC 20005
EMail: HAC@ruralhome.org
Tel: (202)842-8600
Fax: (202)347-3441

Employers
Housing Assistance Council (Deputy Exec. Director)

BELDEN, Roy S.

1200 New Hampshire Ave. NW
Washington, DC 20036
Tel: (202)974-5600
Fax: (202)974-5602
EMail: roy.belden@chadbourne.com
Staff Assistant to Senator John Heinz (R-PA), 1985-86. Legislative Assistant to Rep. Toby Roth (R-WI), 1986-90.

Employers
Chadbourne and Parke LLP

BELDEN, Scott

304 Pennsylvania Ave. SE
Washington, DC 20003
EMail: utsldutu@aol.com
Tel: (202)543-7714
Fax: (202)543-0015

Employers
United Transportation Union (Chief of Staff)

BELESS, Dr. Donald W.

1725 Duke St.
Suite 500
Alexandria, VA 22314
EMail: info@cswe.org
Tel: (703)683-8080
Fax: (703)683-8099

Employers
Council on Social Work Education (Exec. Director)

BELEW, Joe D.

1000 Wilson Blvd.
Suite 2500
Arlington, VA 22209-3908
EMail: jbelew@cbanet.org
Tel: (703)276-1750
Fax: (703)528-1290
Registered: LDA

Employers
Consumer Bankers Ass'n (President)

BELEW, Joy Carabasi

1150 Connecticut Ave. NW
Suite 900
Washington, DC 20036-4104
EMail: jbelew@belewlaw.com
Tel: (202)862-4348
Fax: (202)862-4130
Registered: LDA
Former Deputy Director, Congressional and Legislative Affairs, Interstate Commerce Commission. Former Congressional Relations Officer, Department of Transportation.

Employers
Belew Law Firm (Director, Government Relations)

Clients Represented
On Behalf of Belew Law Firm
BAE SYSTEMS North America
Government Employees Hospital Ass'n
Seedco

BELEW, Jr., M. Wendell

1150 Connecticut Ave. NW
Suite 900
Washington, DC 20036-4104
EMail: wbelew@belewlaw.com
Tel: (202)862-4348
Fax: (202)862-4130
Registered: LDA
Chief Counsel, House Budget Committee, 1976-86.

Employers
Belew Law Firm (President)

Clients Represented
On Behalf of Belew Law Firm
BAE SYSTEMS North America
Government Employees Hospital Ass'n
Seedco

BELFORD, Kevin B.

400 N. Capitol St. NW
Washington, DC 20001
EMail: kbelford@aga.org
Tel: (202)824-7000
Fax: (202)824-7115

Employers
American Gas Ass'n (General Counsel)

BELKIN, Edward

600 New Hampshire Ave. NW
Suite 601
Washington, DC 20037
EMail: ebelkin@hillandknowlton.com
Tel: (202)333-7400
Fax: (202)333-1638
Former Director of Communications for Senator David Durenberger (R-MN).

Employers
Hill and Knowlton, Inc. (Sr. Managing Director, Sr. Counselor Media Relations)

BELKNAP, Katherine

8630 Fenton St.
Suite 930
Silver Spring, MD 20910
EMail: belknap@macroint.com
Tel: (301)608-8998
Fax: (301)608-8958

Employers
ABLEDATA (Project Director)

BELL, Ann

611 Second St. NE
Washington, DC 20002
EMail: abell@IMAPS.org
Tel: (202)548-4001
Fax: (202)548-6115

Employers
Internat'l Microelectronics and Packaging Soc. - IMAPS (Manager, Corporate Relations)

BELL, Beverly E.

1900 K St. NW
Suite 900
Washington, DC 20006
Tel: (202)822-4000
Fax: (202)822-5800
Registered: LDA

Employers
PriceWaterhouseCoopers (Director, Federal Government Affairs)

BELL, Christopher

1722 I St. NW
Washington, DC 20006
Tel: (202)736-8000
Fax: (202)736-8711
Registered: LDA
EMail: cbell@sidley.com
Law Clerk to Judge Philip Pratt, U.S. District Court, Eastern District of Michigan, 1985-87

Employers
Sidley & Austin (Partner)

Clients Represented
On Behalf of Sidley & Austin
Appleton Papers, Inc.

BELL, Denise

1350 I St. NW
Suite 590
Washington, DC 20005
EMail: dbell@cap.org
Tel: (202)354-7106
Fax: (202)354-7155
Registered: LDA

Employers
College of American Pathologists (Director, Government Affairs)

BELL, Glynis L.

1800 F St. NW
MS: 6105
Washington, DC 20405
EMail: glynis.bell@gsa.gov
Tel: (202)501-0563
Fax: (202)219-5742

Employers
General Services Administration (Acting Associate Administrator, Congressional and Intergovernmental Affairs)

BELL, Jackie D.

1120 G St. NW
Suite 1050
Washington, DC 20005
Tel: (202)347-4446
Registered: LDA

Employers
Georgia-Pacific Corp. (Director, Federal Government Affairs)

BELL, Mariam

P.O. Box 16069
Washington, DC 20041-6069
Tel: (703)904-7312
Fax: (703)478-9679

Employers
Justice Fellowship (National Director, Federal Affairs)

BELL, Peter H.

1625 Massachusetts Ave. NW
Suite 601
Washington, DC 20036-2244
Tel: (202)939-1750
Fax: (202)265-4435
Registered: LDA

Employers
Nat'l Housing and Rehabilitation Ass'n (Exec. Director)
Title I Home Improvement Lenders Ass'n (Exec. Director)

BELL, Vikki

P.O. Box 3228
Arlington, VA 22203
Tel: (703)525-5067
Registered: LDA

Employers
Self-employed as an independent consultant.

Clients Represented
As an independent consultant
Canberra Packard BioScience

BELL, William C.

1701 Pennsylvania Ave. NW
Suite 500
Washington, DC 20006
Tel: (202)861-0666
Fax: (202)861-0437

Employers
Mitsui and Co. (U.S.A.), Inc. (International Projects Manager)

BELLAMY, Lorenzo

1100 Connecticut Ave. NW
Suite 1000
Washington, DC 20036
Tel: (202)785-5222
Fax: (202)785-5224
Registered: LDA

Employers
The Bellamy Law Firm, P.C. (Owner)

Clients Represented
On Behalf of The Bellamy Law Firm, P.C.
Chevron, U.S.A.

BELLINI, Christopher J.

1050 Connecticut Ave. NW
Washington, DC 20036-5306
EMail: cbellini@gdclaw.com
Tel: (202)955-8500
Fax: (202)467-0539
Attorney, Federal Reserve Board, 1989-94.

Employers
Gibson, Dunn & Crutcher LLP (Partner)

Clients Represented
On Behalf of Gibson, Dunn & Crutcher LLP
Investment Co. Institute

BELLIS, James P.

1120 20th St. NW
Suite 520 South
Washington, DC 20036
Tel: (202)296-1883
Fax: (202)296-1430
Registered: LDA

Employers
Ass'n of Nat'l Advertisers (Manager, Government Relations)

BELMAN, Murray J.

1909 K St. NW
Suite 600
Washington, DC 20006-1167
Tel: (202)585-6900
Fax: (202)585-6969
Deputy Legal Advisor (1967-69), Assistant Legal Advisor for Economic Affairs (1965-67), and Attorney/Advisor (1961-65), all at the Department of State.

Employers
Thompson Coburn LLP (Partner)

BELMAR, Warren

1201 New York Ave. NW
Suite 1000
Washington, DC 20005
Tel: (202)216-8524
Fax: (202)962-8300
Registered: LDA
Attorney, Office of Legal Counsel, Department of Justice, 1967-69. Law Clerk, U.S. Court of Appeals, District of Columbia Circuit, 1966-67.

Employers
Capitol Counsel Group, L.L.C. (Managing Partner)

Clients Represented
On Behalf of Capitol Counsel Group, L.L.C.
Boys and Girls Clubs of Greater Washington
Crown Central Petroleum Corp.
Federal Home Loan Bank of Dallas
Houston Galveston Area Council
M.B. Consultants, Inc.
Pray, Walker, Jackman, Williamson & Marlar

BELMONT, CAE, Barbara S.

700 S. Washington St.
Suite 300
Alexandria, VA 22314
Tel: (703)739-3900
Fax: (703)739-3915

Employers
American School Food Service Ass'n (Exec. Director)

BELSCHNER, Shanna

Three Bethesda Metro Center
Suite 1100
Bethesda, MD 20814
EMail: sjb@necanet.org
Tel: (301)657-3110
Fax: (301)215-4500
Registered: LDA

Employers
Nat'l Electrical Contractors Ass'n

BELT, Bill

1300 Pennsylvania Ave. NW
Suite 350
Washington, DC 20044
EMail: bbelt@tia.eia.org
Tel: (202)383-1482
Fax: (202)383-1495

Employers
Telecommunications Industry Ass'n (Director, Technical Regulatory Affairs)

BELT, Bradley D.

1001 Pennsylvania Ave. NW
Suite 450 North
Washington, DC 20004
Tel: (202)789-4040
Fax: (202)789-4242
Registered: LDA
Legislative Director and General Counsel to Senator John McCain (R-AZ), 1993-94. Minority Chief Counsel, Subcommittee on Securities, Senate Committee on Banking, Housing and Urban Affairs, 1988-93. Counsel to Commissioner Charles Cox (1987-88), Special Counsel, Office of Tender Offers (1985-87), and Attorney/Advisor, Corporate Finance (1984-85), all with the Securities and Exchange Commission. Financial Analyst, Federal Reserve, 1980-81.

Employers
Commonwealth Group, Ltd. (Managing Director)

Clients Represented
On Behalf of Commonwealth Group, Ltd.
Enron Corp.
Massachusetts Turnpike Authority
D. E. Shaw & Co.

BELVIN, Ms. Lauren "Pete"

1020 19th St. NW
Washington, DC 20036
Tel: (202)429-3121
Fax: (202)293-0561

Employers
Qwest Communications (V. President, Federal Policy and Law)

BEMELMANS, Madeleine

P.O. Box 3719
Georgetown Station
Washington, DC 20007
EMail: awi@awionline.org
Tel: (202)337-2334
Fax: (202)338-9478

Employers
Soc. for Animal Protective Legislation (President)

BEN-DAVID, Lenny

1714 N St. NW
Washington, DC 20036
Tel: (202)462-8990
Fax: (202)462-8995

Employers
Consult (Managing Director)

BEN-VENISTE, Richard

1615 L St. NW
Suite 700
Washington, DC 20036-5610
EMail: richard.ben-veniste@weil.com
Tel: (202)682-7000
Fax: (202)857-0939
Registered: LDA

Employers
Weil, Gotshal & Manges, LLP (Partner)

Clients Represented
On Behalf of Weil, Gotshal & Manges, LLP
Schering-Plough Corp.

BENDALL, Jennifer L.

1401 I St. NW
Suite 1220
Washington, DC 20005
Tel: (202)898-6400
Fax: (202)898-6454
Former aide to Senator Richard Shelby (D-AL).

Employers
Vivendi Universal (Senior Federal Lobbyist)

BENDER, Ph.D., David R.

1700 18th St. NW
Washington, DC 20009
EMail: david-b@sla.org
Tel: (202)234-4700
Fax: (202)265-9317
Registered: LDA

Employers
Special Libraries Ass'n (Exec. Director)

BENDER, Raymond G.

1200 New Hampshire Ave. NW
Suite 800
Washington, DC 20036-6802
EMail: rbender@dlalaw.com
Tel: (202)776-2000
Fax: (202)776-2222

Employers
Dow, Lohnes & Albertson, PLLC (Member)

BENEDICK, Richard E.

1725 K St. NW
Suite 212
Washington, DC 20006
EMail: info@cnie.org
Tel: (202)530-5810
Fax: (202)628-4311

Employers
Nat'l Council for Science and the Environment (President)

BENEDICT, Mark

P.O. Box 322
McLean, VA 22101
Tel: (703)444-2153
Fax: (703)444-6158
Registered: LDA

Employers
Genesis Consulting Group, LLC (President)

Clients Represented
On Behalf of Genesis Consulting Group, LLC
Elkem Materials Inc.
FED Corp.
Integrated Skilled Care of Ohio
Lennox Internat'l
Lumber Fair Trade Group
Norchem Concrete Products Inc.
The Timken Co.
Vandium Industry Coalition

BENEDICT, Scott N.

2000 Pennsylvania Ave. NW
Washington, DC 20006
Tel: (202)974-1500
Fax: (202)974-1999
Registered: LDA, FARA

Employers
Cleary, Gottlieb, Steen and Hamilton (Special Counsel)

BENEKE, Patricia J.

1050 Thomas Jefferson St. NW
Seventh Floor
Washington, DC 20007
Tel: (202)298-1800
Fax: (202)338-2416
Registered: LDA
Former Assistant Secretary for Water and Science, Department of the Interior.

Employers
Van Ness Feldman, P.C. (Member)

Clients Represented
On Behalf of Van Ness Feldman, P.C.
Iowa, Dept. of Natural Resources of State of
Three Affiliated Tribes of Fort Berthold Reservation

BENESKI, Barry

21700 Atlantic Blvd.
Dulles, VA 20166
Tel: (703)406-5000
Fax: (703)406-5572

Employers
Orbital Sciences Corp.

BENFIELD, James C.

601 13th St. NW
Suite 900 South
Washington, DC 20005
EMail: jcbenfield@aol.com
Tel: (202)783-5588
Fax: (202)783-5595
Registered: LDA

Employers
Bracy Williams & Co.

Clients Represented
On Behalf of Bracy Williams & Co.
Business Alliance for Internat'l Economic Development
The Coin Coalition
Michigan Consolidated Gas Co.

BENFIELD, Kaid

1200 New York Ave. NW
Suite 400
Washington, DC 20005
Tel: (202)289-6868
Fax: (202)289-1060

Employers
Natural Resources Defense Council (Senior Attorney)

BENGE, Malcolm L.

888 17th St. NW
Suite 600
Washington, DC 20006-3959
EMail: mlbenge@zsrlaw.com
Tel: (202)298-8660
Fax: (202)342-0683

Employers
Zuckert, Scoutt and Rasenberger, L.L.P. (Partner)

Clients Represented
On Behalf of Zuckert, Scoutt and Rasenberger, L.L.P.
Airtours Internat'l
Eva Airways Corp.
Kenya Airways
Korean Air Lines
Philippine Airlines
Royal Brunei Airways

BENGSTON, Kay

122 C St. NW
Suite 125
Washington, DC 20001
EMail: kay.bengston@ecunet.org
Tel: (202)783-7507
Fax: (202)783-7502

Employers
Lutheran Office for Governmental Affairs/Evangelical Lutheran Church in America (Assistant Director)

BENITEZ, Juan Carlos

701 Pennsylvania Ave. NW
Suite 600
Washington, DC 20004
Tel: (202)624-1200
Fax: (202)624-1298

Employers
Long, Aldridge & Norman, LLP (Of Counsel)

BENJAMIN, Maynard H.

300 N. Washington St.
Suite 500
Alexandria, VA 22314-2530
Tel: (703)739-2200
Fax: (703)739-2209
Registered: LDA

Employers
Envelope Manufacturers Ass'n of America (President)

BENJAMIN, Thomas

1029 N. Royal St.
Suite 400
Alexandria, VA 22314
EMail: TBenjamin@directimpact.com
Tel: (703)684-1245
Fax: (703)684-1249

Employers
The Direct Impact Co. (V. President)

BENKIE, DeeDee

600 Pennsylvania Ave. SE
Suite 302
Washington, DC 20003
Tel: (202)608-1417
Fax: (202)608-1430

Employers
Young Republican Nat'l Federation, Inc. (Co-Chairman)

BENKIN, Isaac D.

1133 Connecticut Ave. NW
Suite 1200
Washington, DC 20036
Tel: (202)775-9800
Fax: (202)833-8491

Administrative Law Judge, Federal Power Commission and Federal Energy Regulatory Commission, 1974-90. Assistant Chief Counsel and Attorney/Advisor, Office of Chief Counsel, Federal Highway Administration, Department of Transportation, 1967-74. Trial Attorney, Civil Division, Department of Justice, 1964-67. Law Clerk to Judge Samuel Whitaker, U.S. Court of Claims, 1963-64.

Employers
Winthrop, Stimson, Putnam & Roberts (Partner)

BENN, D. Randall

1875 Connecticut Ave. NW
Suite 1200
Washington, DC 20009-5728
EMail: dbenn@llgm.com
Tel: (202)986-8047
Fax: (202)986-8102
Registered: LDA

Attorney-Advisor to the Assistant Administrator for Water, Environmental Protection Agency, 1991-93.

Employers
LeBoeuf, Lamb, Greene & MacRae L.L.P. (Partner)

Clients Represented

On Behalf of LeBoeuf, Lamb, Greene & MacRae L.L.P.
Ass'n of Metropolitan Sewerage Agencies
Houston, Texas, Department of Public Works & Engineering of the City of
Jazz at Lincoln Center Inc.
Lloyd's of London
The Project Leadership Committee, Lincoln Center for the Performing Arts
Water Environment Research Foundation

BENNA, Robert H.

1200 G St. NW
Suite 600
Washington, DC 20005-3802
EMail: benna@wrightlaw.com
Tel: (202)393-1200
Fax: (202)393-1240

Technical Assistant, Office of Administrative Law Judges, Federal Energy Regulatory Commission, 1976-83. Staff Witness and Engineer, Bureau of Natural Gas, Federal Power Commission, 1971-76.

Employers
Wright & Talisman, P.C.

Clients Represented

On Behalf of Wright & Talisman, P.C.
Tesoro Petroleum Corp.

BENNER, Mara

625 Slaters Ln.
Suite 200
Alexandria, VA 22314-1171
EMail: marab@aahomecare.org
Tel: (703)836-6263
Fax: (703)836-6730
Registered: LDA

Employers
American Ass'n for Homecare (V. President, Government Relations)

BENNETT, Alan R.

1900 K St. NW
Suite 750
Washington, DC 20006
Tel: (202)833-4500
Fax: (202)833-2859
Registered: LDA

Employers
Bennett Turner & Coleman, LLP (Partner)

Clients Represented

On Behalf of Bennett Turner & Coleman, LLP
Bristol-Myers Squibb Co.
Serono Laboratories, Inc.
SmithKline Beecham Consumer Healthcare, LLP

BENNETT, Alexander E.

555 12th St. NW
Washington, DC 20004-1206
EMail: Alexander_Bennett@aporter.com
Tel: (202)942-5000
Fax: (202)942-5999

Employers
Arnold & Porter (Partner)

BENNETT, B. Timothy

601 Pennsylvania Ave. NW
Suite 600
North Bldg.
Washington, DC 20004
Tel: (202)682-9110
Fax: (202)682-9111
Registered: LDA

Employers
American Electronics Ass'n (Senior V. President, International)

BENNETT, Barbara

Ronald Reagan Bldg.
1300 Pennsylvania Ave. NW
MS: 6.10A
Washington, DC 20523
EMail: babennett@usaid.gov
Tel: (202)712-4300
Fax: (202)216-3036

Employers
Agency for Internat'l Development (Legislative Program Specialist, Congressional Liaison Division)

BENNETT, Blair A.

80 F St. NW
Suite 804
Washington, DC 20001
Tel: (202)347-3042
Fax: (202)347-3046

Employers
Fraioli/Siggins

BENNETT, Catherine P.

325 Seventh St. NW
Suite 1200
Washington, DC 20004-1007
Tel: (202)783-7070
Fax: (202)347-2044
Registered: LDA

Employers
Pfizer, Inc. (V. President, Federal Tax and Trade Legislation)

BENNETT, Douglas F.

1850 K St. NW
Suite 850
Washington, DC 20006
Tel: (202)331-1760
Fax: (202)822-9376
Registered: LDA

Majority Counsel (1995) and Minority Counsel (1989-95), House Committee on Energy and Commerce.

Employers
Timmons and Co., Inc. (Exec. V. President)

Clients Represented

On Behalf of Timmons and Co., Inc.
American Council of Life Insurers
American Petroleum Institute
American Soc. of Anesthesiologists
Anheuser-Busch Cos., Inc.
Asbestos Working Group
AT&T
Bay Harbor Management, L.C.
Bristol-Myers Squibb Co.
Cox Enterprises Inc.
DaimlerChrysler Corp.
Farallon Capital Management
Federal Home Loan Mortgage Corp. (Freddie Mac)
Micron Technology, Inc.
Napster, Inc.
Nat'l Rifle Ass'n of America
New York Life Insurance Co.
Northrop Grumman Corp.
TruePosition Inc.
Union Pacific
University of Utah
UNOCAL Corp.
VISA U.S.A., Inc.

BENNETT, John J.

1111 N. Fairfax St.
Alexandria, VA 22314
Tel: (703)684-2782
Fax: (703)684-7343

Employers
American Physical Therapy Ass'n (General Counsel)

BENNETT, Karen

1130 17th St. NW
Washington, DC 20036-4677
Tel: (202)463-3240
Fax: (202)463-3257
Registered: LDA

Employers
Nat'l Mining Ass'n (Director, Water and Waste)

BENNETT, Kimberly

1920 L St. NW
Washington, DC 20036
EMail: kbennett@kamber.com
Tel: (202)223-8700
Fax: (202)659-5559

Employers
The Kamber Group (Senior Account Exec.)

Clients Represented

On Behalf of The Kamber Group
D.C. Lottery

BENNETT, Raymond T.

2805 Washington Ave.
Chevy Chase, MD 20815
Tel: (301)588-8461
Fax: (301)495-6362

Employers
Tuvin Associates (Associate)

Clients Represented

On Behalf of Tuvin Associates
Motion Picture and Television Fund

BENNETT, Renee

1615 L St. NW
Suite 450
Washington, DC 20036
EMail: renee_bennett@globalcrossing.com
Tel: (202)872-0063
Registered: LDA

Employers
Global Crossing North America, Inc. (Manager, Federal Legislative and Regulatory Affairs)

BENNETT, Robert S.

1440 New York Ave. NW
Washington, DC 20005
Tel: (202)371-7000
Fax: (202)393-5760

Law Clerk to Judge Howard F. Corcoran, U.S. District Court for the District of Columbia, 1965-67.

Employers
Skadden, Arps, Slate, Meagher & Flom LLP (Partner)

Clients Represented

On Behalf of Skadden, Arps, Slate, Meagher & Flom LLP
Georgia, Government of the Republic of

BENNETT, Todd

1747 Pennsylvania Ave. NW
Suite 1100
Washington, DC 20006
Tel: (202)833-0100
Fax: (202)833-0108
Registered: LDA

Employers
U.S. English, Inc. (Government Relations Representative)

BENNETT, William J.

214 Massachusetts Ave. NE
Washington, DC 20002
Tel: (202)546-4400
Fax: (202)546-8328

Employers
Heritage Foundation (Distinguished Fellow, Cultural Policy Studies)

BENNETT, William T.

3001 Veazey Terrace
716
Washington, DC 20008
Tel: (202)338-6882
Fax: (202)338-6950

Employers
Nat'l Vietnam and Gulf War Veterans Coalition, Inc. (General Secretary)

BENNEWITH, Alex

700 13th St. NW
Suite 400
Washington, DC 20005
EMail: abennewith@cassidy.com
Tel: (202)347-0773
Fax: (202)347-0785

Employers
Cassidy & Associates, Inc. (Account Executive)

BENOIT, Michael R.

1225 I St. NW
Suite 300
Washington, DC 20005
Tel: (202)789-1945
Fax: (202)408-9392
Registered: LDA

Employers
Cement Kiln Recycling Coalition (Exec. Director)

BENSON, III, Frederick S.

1100 Connecticut Ave. NW
Suite 530
Washington, DC 20036
Tel: (202)293-7222
Fax: (202)293-2955
Registered: LDA

Employers
Weyerhaeuser Co. (V. President, Federal and International Affairs)

BENSON, Jack

601 Wythe St.
Alexandria, VA 22314-1994
Tel: (703)684-2400
Fax: (703)684-2492

Employers
Water Environment Federation (Deputy Exec. Director, Marketing Business Development)

BENSON, James S.

1200 G St. NW
Suite 400
Washington, DC 20005
Tel: (202)783-8700
Fax: (202)783-8750
Registered: LDA

Employers
AdvaMed (Exec. V. President, Technology and Regulatory Affairs)

BENTLEY, David

1775 Pennsylvania Ave. NW
Suite 200
Washington, DC 20006
Tel: (202)862-1000
Fax: (202)862-1093
Registered: LDA

Employers
Dewey Ballantine LLP (Associate)

BENTLEY, James

325 Seventh St. NW
Washington, DC 20004
Tel: (202)638-1100
Fax: (202)626-4630
Registered: LDA

Employers
American Hospital Ass'n (Senior V. President, Strategic Policy Planning)

BENTLEY, William

1400 I St. NW
Suite 800
Washington, DC 20005
EMail: wbentley@pointsoflight.org
Tel: (202)729-8000
Fax: (202)729-8100

Employers
The Points of Light Foundation (Senior V. President to Chief Exec. Officer)

BENTO, Michael

1901 L St. NW
Suite 300
Washington, DC 20036
EMail: mike.bento@dc.ogilvypr.com
Tel: (202)466-7590
Fax: (202)775-8169

Employers
Ogilvy Public Relations Worldwide (Senior V. President)

BENTZ, Rhonda

2121 K St. NW
Suite 700
Washington, DC 20037
Tel: (202)296-9230
Fax: (202)862-5498

Employers
VISA U.S.A., Inc. (Director, Public Affairs)

BENZ, Steven T.

455 Spring Park Pl.
Suite 200
Herndon, VA 20170
Tel: (703)326-5600
Fax: (703)326-5660

Employers
Marine Spill Response Corporation (President)

BERDON, Trinidad T.

2121 R St. NW
Washington, DC 20008-1908
EMail: tberdon@aol.com
Tel: (202)673-5869
Fax: (202)673-5873

Employers
Northern Mariana Islands, Commonwealth of the (Fiscal Officer)

BERDUT, Caridad

1200 17th St. NW
Fifth Floor
Washington, DC 20036
Tel: (202)467-6300
Fax: (202)466-2006
Former Attorney/Advisor and Acting Chief, Intellectual Property Branch, U.S. Customs Service, Department of Treasury.

Employers
Adduci, Mastriani & Schaumberg, L.L.P.

BEREJKA, Marc

21 Dupont Circle NW
Fifth Floor
Washington, DC 20036
Tel: (202)263-5900
Fax: (202)263-5901
Registered: LDA

Employers
Microsoft Corp. (Senior Attorney)

BERG, Brother Joseph

1731 King St.
Suite 200
Alexandria, VA 22314
EMail: jberg@catholiccharitiesusa.org
Tel: (703)549-1390
Fax: (703)549-1656

Employers
Catholic Charities USA (Director for Leadership/Mission)

BERG, Michael D.

901 15th St. NW
Suite 700
Washington, DC 20005-2301
Tel: (202)371-6000
Fax: (202)371-6279

Employers
Verner, Liipfert, Bernhard, McPherson and Hand, Chartered (Member of Firm)

Clients Represented

On Behalf of Verner, Liipfert, Bernhard, McPherson and Hand, Chartered
Qwest Communications

BERGAN, Tim N.

1015 18th St. NW
Suite 1100
Washington, DC 20036-5725
EMail: tbergan@csbsdc.org
Tel: (202)728-5725
Fax: (202)296-1928
Registered: LDA

Employers
Conference of State Bank Supervisors (Senior V. President, Internat'l)

BERGENHOLTZ, Stephen

1200 Wilson Blvd.
Arlington, VA 22209
Tel: (703)465-3008

Employers
The Boeing Co. (Legal Counsel)

BERGER, Amy F.

800 Connecticut Ave. NW
Suite 500
Washington, DC 20006
Tel: (202)331-3103
Fax: (202)331-3101

Employers
Greenberg Traurig, LLP

BERGER, Paul S.

555 12th St. NW
Washington, DC 20004-1206
EMail: Paul_Berger@aporter.com
Tel: (202)942-5000
Fax: (202)942-5999
Registered: FARA

Employers
Arnold & Porter (Partner)

Clients Represented

On Behalf of Arnold & Porter
Israel, Economic Mission of the Government of the State of

BERGIN, Tim

1201 Pennsylvania Ave. NW
P.O. Box 407
Washington, DC 20044-0407
Tel: (202)626-6600
Fax: (202)626-6780

Employers
Squire, Sanders & Dempsey L.L.P. (Partner)

Clients Represented

On Behalf of Squire, Sanders & Dempsey L.L.P.
McGraw-Hill Cos., The

BERGMAN, Allan I.

105 N. Alfred St.
Alexandria, VA 22314
Tel: (703)236-6000
Fax: (703)236-6001

Employers
Brain Injury Ass'n (President and Chief Exec. Officer)

BERGMAN, Bob

316 Pennsylvania Ave. SE
Suite 300
Washington, DC 20003
Tel: (202)675-3354
Fax: (202)675-4230
Registered: LDA

Employers
United Parcel Service (V. President, Public Affairs)

BERGMAN, David

1133 15th St. NW
Suite 300
Washington, DC 20005
EMail: dbergman@aamft.org
Tel: (202)452-0109
Fax: (202)223-2329
Registered: LDA

Employers
American Ass'n for Marriage and Family Therapy (Manager, Government Affairs)

BERGMAN, CAE, William S.

1726 M St. NW
Suite 1101
Washington, DC 20036
EMail: wsb@wsba.com
Tel: (202)452-1520
Fax: (202)833-1577

Employers
William S. Bergman Associates (President)

Clients Represented

On Behalf of William S. Bergman Associates

Nat'l Ass'n of Lottery Purchasers
Outdoor Power Equipment Aftermarket Ass'n

BERGMANN, Robert

1627 I St. NW
Suite 550
Washington, DC 20006
Tel: (202)659-4777
Fax: (202)659-4779
Registered: LDA, FARA

Employers

Representative of German Industry and Trade

Clients Represented

On Behalf of Representative of German Industry and Trade

Ass'n of German Chambers of Industry & Commerce (DIHT)
Federation of German Industries (BDI)

BERGNER, Douglas J.

1101 16th St. NW
Washington, DC 20036
Tel: (202)496-1550
Fax: (202)496-1552
Registered: LDA, FARA

Employers

Global Policy Group, Inc. (President)

Clients Represented

On Behalf of Global Policy Group, Inc.

E.ON North America, Inc.
Standard Chartered Bank

BERGNER, Jeffrey T.

1101 16th St. NW
Suite 500
Washington, DC 20036
Tel: (202)659-9111
Fax: (202)659-6387
Registered: LDA, FARA

Staff Director, Senate Foreign Relations Committee, 1985-86. Administrative Assistant (1983-84), Legislative Director (1981-82), and Legislative Assistant (1978-80) to Senator Richard Lugar (R-IN).

Employers

Bergner Bockorny Castagnetti and Hawkins (President)

Clients Represented

On Behalf of Bergner Bockorny Castagnetti and Hawkins

AdvaMed
Agilent Technologies
American Bankers Ass'n
American Hospital Ass'n
Biogen, Inc.
The Boeing Co.
Bristol-Myers Squibb Co.
Business Executives for Nat'l Security
Cerner Corp.
Chicago Board Options Exchange
Computer Coalition for Responsible Exports
Dell Computer Corp.
Elanco Animal Health
Everglades Defense Council
First Health Group Corp.
GlaxoSmithKline
Hewlett-Packard Co.
Lucent Technologies
Medtronic, Inc.
Monsanto Co.
Nat'l Ass'n of Real Estate Investment Trusts
Nat'l Soft Drink Ass'n
News Corporation Ltd.
Northwest Airlines, Inc.
Ovations/United Health Group
Petroleum Marketers Ass'n of America
Philip Morris Management Corp.
Premium Standard Farms
Qwest Communications
Taipei Economic and Cultural Representative Office in the United States
UDV North America, Inc.

BERGSON, Paul C.

190 Falcon Ridge Rd.
Great Falls, VA 22066
Tel: (703)757-9270
Fax: (703)757-9275
Registered: LDA
EMail: brgmstr@erols.com

Served in the Energy Research and Development Administration, 1975-77. Major General, U.S. Army Reserve.

Employers

Bergson & Co. (Principal)

Clients Represented

On Behalf of Bergson & Co.

General Dynamics Corp.
PriceWaterhouseCoopers
S & B Infrastructure, Inc.
Swisher Internat'l Inc.

BERGSTEN, C. Fred

11 Dupont Circle NW
Suite 620
Washington, DC 20036
Tel: (202)328-9000
Fax: (202)328-5432

Employers

Institute for Internat'l Economics (Director)

BERISH, Jim

900 17th St. NW
Suite 1100
Washington, DC 20006
Tel: (202)884-7014
Fax: (202)884-7070
Registered: LDA
EMail: jim_berish@hp.com

Employers

Hewlett-Packard Co. (Manager, Federal Procurement Policy)

BERKELEY, III, Alfred R.

1735 K St. NW
11th Floor
Washington, DC 20006
Tel: (202)496-2500

Employers

NASDAQ Stock Market (President)

BERKOFF, Barry I.

701 Pennsylvania Ave. NW
Suite 800
Washington, DC 20004
Tel: (202)508-4131
Fax: (202)508-4321
Registered: LDA
EMail: bberkoff@thelenreid.com

Employers

Thelen Reid & Priest LLP (Legislative Representative)

Clients Represented

On Behalf of Thelen Reid & Priest LLP

Abilene Industrial Foundation, Inc.
Airport Minority Advisory Council
Airports Council Internat'l - North America
Capital Region Airport Commission
Corpus Christi Port Authority
Denver, Colorado, City of
DRS Precision Echo Inc.
DRS Technologies, Inc.
L.B. Foster Co.
J & B Management Co.
The Jewelers' Security Alliance
MCA Inc.
Metro Machine Corp. of Virginia
Metro Machine of Pennsylvania, Inc.
Metroplex Corp.
Opportunity Capital Corp.
Parsons Brinckerhoff Inc.
Philadelphia Industrial Development Corp.
Philadelphia, Pennsylvania, City of
Power Paragon Inc.
SPD Technologies
Suiza Foods Corp.
Washington Soccer Partners

BERKOFF, Todd S.

1747 Pennsylvania Ave. NW
Suite 1150
Washington, DC 20006
Tel: (202)557-2970
Fax: (202)296-4507

Employers

The MWW Group (Legislative Associate)

Clients Represented

On Behalf of The MWW Group

Detroit Medical Center
GAF Corp.
Green County Health Care, Inc.

BERKOWITZ, Herbert

214 Massachusetts Ave. NE
Washington, DC 20002
Tel: (202)546-4400
Fax: (202)546-8328

Employers

Heritage Foundation (V. President, Public Relations)

BERL, William E.

1755 Jefferson Davis Hwy.
Suite 1107
Arlington, VA 22202
Tel: (703)415-0344
Fax: (703)415-0182
Registered: LDA

Employers

The PMA Group (Associate)

Clients Represented

On Behalf of The PMA Group

Caterpillar Inc.
Coronado, California, City of
IMSSCO Inc.
Marconi Communications Federal
Omega Air
Spatial Integrated Systems
Titan Corp.

BERLIN, Edward

3000 K St. NW
Suite 300
Washington, DC 20007
Tel: (202)424-7500
Fax: (202)424-7643

Assistant General Counsel, Federal Power Commission, 1966-69. Attorney, Civil Division, Appellate Section, Department of Justice, 1961-66.

Employers

Swidler Berlin Shereff Friedman, LLP (Chairman)

BERLIN, Kenneth

1440 New York Ave. NW
Washington, DC 20005
Tel: (202)371-7000
Fax: (202)393-5760

Employers

Skadden, Arps, Slate, Meagher & Flom LLP (Partner)

BERLINER, Roger A.

1225 19th St. NW
Suite 800
Washington, DC 20036
Tel: (202)955-6067
Fax: (202)293-0307
Registered: LDA, FARA

Consultant, House Committee on Energy and Commerce, 1981. Director, Division of Congressional Liaison, Federal Energy Regulatory Commission, 1980. Legislative Director (1979) and Legislative Assistant (1977-78) to Senator Howard Metzenbaum (D-OH). Legislative Analyst, House Democratic Study Group, 1975-76. Special Assistant to Rep. Thomas Luken (D-OH), 1973.

Employers

Berliner, Candon & Jimison (Partner)

Clients Represented

On Behalf of Berliner, Candon & Jimison

Guam, Territory of
Los Angeles, California, County of

BERLS, Tatiana G.

1615 L St. NW
Suite 900
Washington, DC 20036
Tel: (202)778-1000
Fax: (202)466-6002
EMail: tberls@apcoworldwide.com

Employers

APCO Worldwide (V. President and Managing Director, Russia/CIS Services)

BERLYN, Debra R.

1156 15th St. NW
Suite 520
Washington, DC 20005
Tel: (202)835-0202
Fax: (202)835-1132

Employers

Competition Policy Institute (Exec. Director)

BERMAN, Bruce M.

2445 M St. NW
Washington, DC 20037-1420
Tel: (202)663-6000
Fax: (202)663-6363
EMail: bberman@wilmer.com

Former Law Clerk to Judge Walter K. Stapleton, U.S. District Court for the District of Delaware.

Employers

Wilmer, Cutler & Pickering (Partner)

Clients Represented

On Behalf of Wilmer, Cutler & Pickering

Howard, Meedles, Tammen & Bergendoff

BERMAN, Daniel M.

1275 Pennsylvania Ave. NW
Washington, DC 20004-2415
Tel: (202)383-0100
Fax: (202)637-3593

Employers
Sutherland Asbill & Brennan LLP (Partner)

Clients Represented
On Behalf of Sutherland Asbill & Brennan LLP
W. C. Bradley Co.
Encyclopaedia Britannica, Inc.

BERMAN, Ellen

2000 L St. NW
Suite 802
Washington, DC 20036
EMail: eberm@aol.com
Tel: (202)659-0404
Fax: (202)659-0407

Employers
Consumer Energy Council of America Research Foundation (President)

BERMAN, Howard

210 Seventh St. SE
Washington, DC 20003
Tel: (202)547-6808
Fax: (202)546-5425
Registered: LDA
Former Deputy Director, Criminal Enforcement Counsel Division, Environmental Protection Agency.

Employers
Kessler & Associates Business Services, Inc. (Senior V. President, Environmental Counsel)

Clients Represented
On Behalf of Kessler & Associates Business Services, Inc.
Dunn-Edwards Corp.
Pharmacia Corp.
Planet Electric
Tosco Corp.

BERMAN, Jeffrey G.

1400 L St. NW
Washington, DC 20005-3502
Tel: (202)371-5979
Fax: (202)371-5950
Registered: LDA
EMail: jberman@winston.com
Former Counsel to Senate Committee on Government Affairs. Former Senior Advisor to House Minority Leader Richard Gephardt (D-MO).

Employers
Winston & Strawn (Partner, Corporate Practice)

Clients Represented
On Behalf of Winston & Strawn
AirCell, Inc.

BERMAN, Jerry

1634 I St. NW
Suite 1100
Washington, DC 20006-4003
EMail: jberman@cdt.org
Tel: (202)637-9800
Fax: (202)637-0968

Employers
Center for Democracy and Technology (Exec. Director)

BERMAN, Marshall

1500 K St. NW
Suite 850
Washington, DC 20005
EMail: berman@compete.org
Tel: (202)682-4292
Fax: (202)682-5150

Employers
Council on Competitiveness (Exec. Director-Internet Learning Network)

BERMAN, Michael S.

2100 Pennsylvania Ave. NW
Suite 500
Washington, DC 20037
Tel: (202)728-1100
Fax: (202)728-1123
Registered: LDA
Former aide to V. President Walter Mondale.

Employers
The Duberstein Group, Inc. (President)

Clients Represented
On Behalf of The Duberstein Group, Inc.
Amerada Hess Corp.
American Apparel & Footwear Ass'n
American Ass'n of Health Plans (AAHP)
American Council of Life Insurers
American Gaming Ass'n
The American Water Works Co.
AOL Time Warner
The Business Roundtable
Comcast Corp.
Conoco Inc.
CSX Corp.
Direct Marketing Ass'n, Inc.
Dow Corning Corp.
Fannie Mae
General Motors Corp.
Goldman, Sachs and Co.
Marathon Oil Co.
Nat'l Cable Television Ass'n
Pharmacia Corp.
Project to Promote Competition and Innovation in the Digital Age
Sara Lee Corp.
Transportation Institute
United Airlines
USX Corp.

BERMAN, Paul J.

1201 Pennsylvania Ave. NW
Washington, DC 20004-2401
EMail: pberman@cov.com
Tel: (202)662-6000
Fax: (202)662-6291

Employers
Covington & Burling (Partner)

Clients Represented
On Behalf of Covington & Burling
Anchorage Telephone Utility

BERMAN, Richard B.

1775 Pennsylvania Ave. NW
Suite 1200
Washington, DC 20006
EMail: rberman@new-reality.com
Tel: (202)463-7100
Fax: (202)463-7107
Registered: LDA

Employers
Berman and Company (President)

Clients Represented
On Behalf of Berman and Company
American Beverage Institute
Employment Policies Institute Foundation

BERMAN, Dr. Robin Ely

11140 Rockville Pike
Suite 101
Rockville, MD 20852
EMail: ngf@gaucherdisease.org
Tel: (301)816-1515
Fax: (301)816-1516

Employers
Nat'l Gaucher Foundation (Medical Director/President and Chief Exec. Officer)

BERMAN, Wayne

1800 K St. NW
Suite 1124
Washington, DC 20006
Tel: (202)833-4923
Fax: (202)223-8036
Registered: LDA
EMail: bermanent@aol.com
Former Assistant Secretary for Policy, Department of Commerce during the Bush I administration.

Employers
Berman Enterprises (Managing Director)

Clients Represented
On Behalf of Berman Enterprises
Flo-Sun Sugar
Greater New York Hospital Ass'n

BERMINGHAM, Maya

1800 M St. NW
Washington, DC 20036
Tel: (202)467-7076
Fax: (202)467-7176
Registered: LDA
EMail: mbermingham@morganlewis.com

Employers
Morgan, Lewis & Bockius LLP (Associate)

Clients Represented
On Behalf of Morgan, Lewis & Bockius LLP
Cord Blood Registry, Inc.

BERNA, Rachel

1341 Connecticut Ave. NW
Third Floor
Washington, DC 20036
Tel: (202)862-3900
Fax: (202)862-5500

Employers
Scribe Consulting & Communications (Research and Project Manager)

BERNARD, Kristy

1341 G St. NW
Suite 900
Washington, DC 20005
Tel: (202)637-1595
Fax: (202)637-1581

Employers
Philip Morris Management Corp. (Legal Analyst)

BERNARD, Michelle D.

2550 M St. NW
Washington, DC 20037-1350
Tel: (202)457-6000
Fax: (202)457-6315
Registered: LDA
EMail: mbernard@pattonboggs.com

Employers
Patton Boggs, LLP (Partner)

BERNARD, Sandy

1111 16th St. NW
Washington, DC 20036-4873
Tel: (202)785-7788
Fax: (202)466-7637

Employers
American Ass'n of University Women (President)

BERNARDINI, Charles R.

1300 I St. NW
Suite 300 West
Washington, DC 20005
Tel: (202)522-8600
Fax: (202)522-8669
Registered: LDA

Employers
Dykema Gossett PLLC (Of Counsel)

Clients Represented
On Behalf of Dykema Gossett PLLC
Union Pacific

BERNHARD, Berl

901 15th St. NW
Suite 700
Washington, DC 20005-2301
Tel: (202)371-6000
Fax: (202)371-6279
Registered: LDA
Senior Advisor to the Secretary, Department of State, 1980-81. Director (1961-63), Deputy Director (1959-60), and Supervisory General Attorney (1959), U.S. Commission on Civil Rights. Law Clerk to Judge Luther W. Youngdahl, U.S. District Court for the District of Columbia, 1954-56.

Employers
Verner, Liipfert, Bernhard, McPherson and Hand, Chartered (Co-Founder)

Clients Represented
On Behalf of Verner, Liipfert, Bernhard, McPherson and Hand, Chartered
Accenture
American Financial Group
ArianeSpace, Inc.
Cyprus, Government of the Republic of
The Walt Disney Co.
India, Government of the Republic of
Microsoft Corp.
Qwest Communications
RJR Nabisco Holdings Co.
Starwood Lodging/Starwood Capital Group, L.P.
Washington Group Internat'l

BERNHARD, Mary E.

1300 Wilson Blvd.
Arlington, VA 22209
Tel: (703)741-5910
Fax: (703)741-6098
Registered: LDA
EMail: mary_bernhard@americanchemistry.com

Employers
American Chemistry Council (Director)

BERNHARDS, John

1200 G St. NW
Suite 500
Washington, DC 20005
EMail: jbern@atis.org
Tel: (202)628-6380
Fax: (202)393-5453

Employers
Alliance for Telecommunications Industry Solutions (Director, Public Relations)

BERNHARDT, Pamela Fandel

1341 G St. NW
Suite 1100
Washington, DC 20005
Tel: (202)585-0220
Fax: (202)393-0712

Employers
Infotech Strategies, Inc. (V. President, Finance)

BERNIER, Delanne

1225 I St. NW
Suite 350
Washington, DC 20005
EMail: dbernier@dmggroup.com
Tel: (202)789-1110
Fax: (202)789-1116
Registered: LDA

Employers
Downey McGrath Group, Inc. (V. President)

Clients Represented

On Behalf of Downey McGrath Group, Inc.
American Soc. of Anesthesiologists
The Timken Co.

BERNSTEIN, Abby H.

1150 17th St. NW
Suite 702
Washington, DC 20036
Tel: (202)293-7277
Fax: (202)293-7727
Registered: LDA

Employers
Professional Airways Systems Specialists (AFL-CIO) (Legislative Director)

BERNSTEIN, Caryl S.

1730 K St. NW
Washington, DC 20006
Tel: (202)452-8010
Fax: (202)296-2065
Registered: FARA
Former Vice President, Insurance, Overseas Private Investment Corp.

Employers
Bernstein Law Firm, PLLC (Parnter)

BERNSTEIN, David

1156 15th St. NW
Suite 1201
Washington, DC 20005
Tel: (202)785-4200
Fax: (202)785-4115

Employers
American Jewish Committee (Director, Washington Chapter)

BERNSTEIN, George K.

1730 K St. NW
Washington, DC 20006
EMail: gkblaw@aol.com
Tel: (202)452-8010
Fax: (202)296-2065
Registered: FARA
Interstate Land Sales Administrator, Office of Interstate Land Sales Registration (1972-74) and Federal Insurance Administrator, Federal Insurance Administration (1969-74), Department of Housing and Urban Development.

Employers
Bernstein Law Firm, PLLC (Partner)

Clients Represented

On Behalf of Bernstein Law Firm, PLLC
X.L. Insurance Co.

BERNSTEIN, James S.

9650 Rockville Pike
Bethesda, MD 20814-3995
Tel: (301)530-7060
Fax: (301)530-7061

Employers
American Soc. for Pharmacology and Experimental Therapeutics (Director, Public Affairs)

BERNSTEIN, Jared

1660 L St. NW
Suite 1200
Washington, DC 20036
EMail: epi@epinet.org
Tel: (202)775-8810
Fax: (202)775-0819

Employers
Economic Policy Institute (Economist)

BERNSTEIN, Joel H.

555 12th St. NW
Suite 950 North
Washington, DC 20004
Tel: (202)371-9100
Fax: (202)371-1497
Registered: LDA
Legislative Counsel to Rep. Don Ritter (R-PA), 1990-92.

Employers
Halprin, Temple, Goodman & Maher (Partner)

Clients Represented

On Behalf of Halprin, Temple, Goodman & Maher
Automated Credit Exchange
Telcordia Technologies, Inc.
Verizon Communications
Yellow Pages Publishers Ass'n

BERNSTEIN, Jon

445 12th St. NW
Room 8-C458
Washington, DC 20554
Tel: (202)418-1900
Fax: (202)418-2806

Employers
Federal Communications Commission (Attorney/Advisor, Legislative and Intergovernmental Affairs)

BERNSTEIN, Matthew C.

901 15th St. NW
Suite 700
Washington, DC 20005-2301
EMail: mcbernstein@verner.com
Tel: (202)371-6000
Fax: (202)371-6279
Registered: LDA
Legislative Assistant to Senator Howard Metzenbaum (D-OH), 1987;1988-89. Professional Staff Member, House Banking Committee, 1987-88. Former Staff Director, Senate Steel Caucus.

Employers
Verner, Liipfert, Bernhard, McPherson and Hand, Chartered (Member of Firm)

Clients Represented

On Behalf of Verner, Liipfert, Bernhard, McPherson and Hand, Chartered
Bacardi-Martini, USA, Inc.
Biovail Corp. Internat'l
Citigroup
Home Warranty Coalition
Lockheed Martin Tactical Systems
Merrill Lynch & Co., Inc.
Rite Aid Corp.
RJR Nabisco Holdings Co.

BERNSTEIN, Michael L.

555 12th St. NW
Washington, DC 20004-1206
EMail: Michael_Bernstein@aporter.com
Tel: (202)942-5000
Fax: (202)942-5999
Law Clerk to Judge Judith N. Keep, U.S. District Court, Southern District of California, 1989-90.

Employers
Arnold & Porter (Partner)

BERNSTEIN, Mitch H.

1050 Thomas Jefferson St. NW
Seventh Floor
Washington, DC 20007
EMail: mhb@vnf.com
Tel: (202)298-1800
Fax: (202)338-2416
Registered: LDA

Employers
Van Ness Feldman, P.C. (Member)

BERNSTEIN, Rachelle

1666 K St. NW
Suite 800
Washington, DC 20006
Tel: (202)481-7000
Fax: (202)862-7098
Registered: LDA

Employers
Arthur Andersen LLP (Tax Partner, Office of Federal Tax Services)

Clients Represented

On Behalf of Arthur Andersen LLP
AutoNation, Inc.
Coalition for the Fair Taxation of Business Transactions
Coalition on Royalties Taxation
Eagle-Picher Personal Injury Settlement Trust
Hybrid Branch Coalition
Microsoft Corp.
Nat'l Ass'n of Investors Corporation (NAIC)
Nat'l Retail Federation
Oracle Corp.
UtiliCorp United, Inc.

BERNSTEIN, Ph.D., Robert

1101 15th St. NW
Suite 1212
Washington, DC 20005
EMail: robertb@bazelon.org
Tel: (202)467-5730
Ext: 25
Fax: (202)223-0409

Employers
Bazelon Center for Mental Health Law, Judge David L. (Exec. Director)

BERNSTEIN, Roger D.

1300 Wilson Blvd.
Suite 800
Arlington, VA 22209
Tel: (703)253-0700
Fax: (703)253-0701

Employers
American Plastics Council (V. President, Government Affairs)

BERNTHAL, Eric L.

555 11th St. NW
Suite 1000
Washington, DC 20004
Tel: (202)637-2200
Fax: (202)637-2201
Law Clerk to Judge Ruggero J. Aldisert, U.S. Court of Appeals, Third Circuit, 1970-72.

Employers
Latham & Watkins (Managing Partner)

BERONIO, Kirsten

1021 Prince St.
Alexandria, VA 22314-2971
EMail: kberonio@nmha.org
Tel: (703)684-7722
Fax: (703)684-5968
Registered: LDA

Employers
Nat'l Mental Health Ass'n (Senior Director, Government Affairs)

BERRY, Ann

1350 I St. NW
Suite 590
Washington, DC 20005
EMail: aberry@cap.org
Tel: (202)354-7103
Fax: (202)354-7155

Employers
College of American Pathologists (Manager, Political Development)

BERRY, Cynthia E.

1317 F St. NW
Suite 600
Washington, DC 20004
EMail: berry@wexlergroup.com
Tel: (202)638-2121
Fax: (202)638-7045
Registered: LDA

Employers
The Wexler Group (Principal/General Counsel)

Clients Represented

On Behalf of The Wexler Group
Blue Cross and Blue Shield of California
Immunex Corp.
IMS Health Inc.
MENC: The Nat'l Ass'n for Music Education
Nat'l Ass'n of Music Merchants
Orange County Public Schools
PacifiCare Health Systems
VISA U.S.A., Inc.
Wyeth-Ayerst Laboratories

BERRY, J. Daniel

1301 K St. NW
Suite 800 East
Washington, DC 20005
EMail: dberry@ropesgray.com
Tel: (202)626-3900
Fax: (202)626-3961
Associate General Counsel for Grants, Contracts and General Law (1987-88) and Assistant General Counsel for Superfund (1983-87), Environmental Protection Agency.

Employers
Ropes & Gray (Partner)

BERRY, J. Patrick

1299 Pennsylvania Ave. NW
Suite 1300 West
Washington, DC 20004-2400
Tel: (202)639-7700
Fax: (202)639-7890
Registered: LDA
Counsel, Senate Committee on Energy and Natural Resources, 1975-77.

Employers
Baker Botts, L.L.P. (Partner)

Clients Represented

On Behalf of Baker Botts, L.L.P.

IT Group, Inc.

BERRY, Marsha

811 Vermont Ave. NW
Washington, DC 20571
Tel: (202)565-3230
Fax: (202)565-3236

Employers

Export-Import Bank (V. President, Congressional and External Affairs)

BERRY, Max N.

3213 O St. NW
Washington, DC 20007
Tel: (202)298-6134
Fax: (202)333-3348
Registered: LDA, FARA

Attorney, Office of the Chief Counsel, Bureau of Customs, Department of the Treasury, 1963-1967. Captain, International Affairs Division, Office of the Judge Advocate General, Department of the Army, 1960-63.

Employers

Max N. Berry Law Offices (Attorney-at-Law)

Clients Represented

On Behalf of Max N. Berry Law Offices

American Importers and Exporters/Meat Products Group
Ass'n of Chocolate, Biscuit and Confectionery Industries of the EEC
Atalanta Corp.
AVEBE America, Inc.
Centre National Interprofessionel de L'Economie Laitiere (French Dairy Ass'n)
Committee to Assure the Availability of Casein
Florida Department of Citrus
Gallard-Schlesinger Chemical Manufacturing Corp.
Gist Brocades
Junex Enterprises
Nylo-Flex Manufacturing Co., Inc.
Valio Finnish Co-operative Dairies Ass'n

BERRY, Maya

1600 K St. NW
Suite 601
Washington, DC 20006
EMail: mberry@aaiusa.org
Tel: (202)429-9210
Fax: (202)429-9214

Employers

Arab American Institute (Government Relations Director)

BERRY, Roger S.

1120 Connecticut Ave. NW
Suite 1100
Washington, DC 20036
Tel: (202)861-5899
Fax: (202)861-5795
Registered: LDA

Employers

GPC Internat'l

Clients Represented

On Behalf of GPC Internat'l

Skadden, Arps, Slate, Meagher & Flom LLP

BERRY, Steven K.

1250 Connecticut Ave. NW
Suite 800
Washington, DC 20036
Tel: (202)785-0081
Fax: (202)776-0540
Registered: LDA

Employers

Cellular Telecommunications and Internet Ass'n (Senior V. President, Congressional Affairs)

BERRY, Willard M.

1333 H St. NW
Suite 630
Washington, DC 20004
EMail: wberry@eabc.org
Tel: (202)347-9292
Fax: (202)628-5498
Registered: LDA

Employers

European-American Business Council (President)

BERSHERS, Kristine

214 Massachusetts Ave. NE
Washington, DC 20002
Tel: (202)546-4400
Fax: (202)546-8328

Employers

Heritage Foundation (Media Relations Manager)

BERTERA, William J.

1850 Samuel Morse Dr.
Reston, VA 20198
EMail: wbertera@snm.org
Tel: (703)708-9000
Ext: 1240
Fax: (703)708-9020

Employers

Soc. of Nuclear Medicine (Exec. Director)

BERTHOUD, John E.

108 N. Alfred St.
Alexandria, VA 22314
Tel: (703)683-5700
Fax: (703)683-5722
Registered: LDA

Employers

Nat'l Taxpayers Union (President)

BERTHOUD, Maria

412 First St. SE
Suite 300
Washington, DC 20003
Tel: (202)863-7000
Fax: (202)863-7015
Registered: LDA

Employers

Independent Insurance Agents of America, Inc. (V. President, Federal Government Affairs)

BERTMAN, Mike

1301 K St. NW
Suite 1000 East
Washington, DC 20005
Tel: (202)715-1105
Fax: (202)715-1114
Registered: LDA

Employers

UDV North America, Inc. (Director, Federal and International Affairs)

BERTRAM, Bruce M.

700 N. Fairfax St.
Suite 600
Alexandria, VA 22314-2040
EMail: bert@saltinstitute.org
Tel: (703)549-4648
Fax: (703)548-2194

Employers

Salt Institute (Technical Director)

BESHAROV, Douglas J.

1150 17th St. NW
Washington, DC 20036
EMail: dbesharov@aei.org
Tel: (202)862-5800
Fax: (202)862-7177

Employers

American Enterprise Institute for Public Policy Research (Resident Scholar)

BESOZZI, Paul C.

2550 M St. NW
Washington, DC 20037-1350
EMail: pbesozzi@pattonboggs.com
Tel: (202)457-6000
Fax: (202)457-6315
Registered: LDA, FARA

General Counsel and Minority Counsel, Senate Committee on Armed Services, 1980-84.

Employers

Patton Boggs, LLP (Partner)

Clients Represented

On Behalf of Patton Boggs, LLP

Commco, L.L.C.
Supra Telecom & Information Systems, Inc.
Time Domain Corp.

BESSER, Marla

1701 K St. NW
Suite 200
Washington, DC 20006-1503
EMail: mbesser@alliance1.org
Tel: (202)223-3447
Fax: (202)331-7476

Employers

Alliance for Children and Families (Policy Analyst)

BESSETTE, Robert D.

6035 Burke Centre Pkwy.
Suite 360
Burke, VA 22015
EMail: bessette@cibo.org
Tel: (703)250-9042
Fax: (703)239-9042
Registered: LDA

Employers

Council of Industrial Boiler Owners (CIBO) (President)

BESSLING, Stacey

14750 Sweitzer Ln.
Suite 100
Laurel, MD 20707-5906
EMail: sbessling@aium.org
Tel: (301)498-4100
Fax: (301)498-4450

Employers

American Institute of Ultrasound in Medicine (Public Relations Coordinator)

BEST, Amy

1500 Pennsylvania Ave. NW
Room 3030MT
Washington, DC 20220
Tel: (202)622-1970
Fax: (202)622-0534

Employers

Department of Treasury (Special Assistant to the Assistant Secretary)

BETHKE, Cecilia D.

901 15th St. NW
Suite 310
WAS 1150
Washington, DC 20005
Tel: (202)842-3193
Fax: (202)289-6834
Registered: LDA

Employers

Northwest Airlines, Inc. (Director, International and Bilateral Affairs)

BETHUNE, Hon. Edwin R.

2000 K St. NW
Suite 500
Washington, DC 20006-1872
Tel: (202)828-5852
Fax: (202)223-1225
Registered: LDA

Member, U.S. House of Representatives (R-AR), 1979-85.

Employers

Bracewell & Patterson, L.L.P. (Partner)

Clients Represented

On Behalf of Bracewell & Patterson, L.L.P.

Air Conditioning Contractors of America
Alltel Corporation
American Chemistry Council
Council of Industrial Boiler Owners (CIBO)
Envirocare of Utah, Inc.
FBI Agents Ass'n
Gary-Williams Energy Corp.
Houston, Texas, Port Authority of the City of
Huntsman Corp.
Oxygenated Fuels Ass'n
Physician Insurers Ass'n of America
Placid Refining Co.
Solex Environmental Systems, Inc.
Texas Petrochemicals Corp.
Texas Windstorm Insurance Ass'n
Welcon, Inc.

BETKE, Todd W.

1615 L St. NW
Suite 700
Washington, DC 20036-5610
EMail: todd.betke@weil.com
Tel: (202)682-7000
Fax: (202)857-0939
Registered: LDA

Employers

Weil, Gotshal & Manges, LLP (Associate)

BETZ, Cathy Clark

1444 I St. NW
Suite 410
Washington, DC 20005
EMail: cbetz@robertbetz.com
Tel: (202)347-1990
Fax: (202)628-2310
Registered: LDA

Employers

Robert Betz Associates, Inc. (Exec. Health Counsel)

Clients Represented

On Behalf of Robert Betz Associates, Inc.

Council of Surgical Specialty Facilities and Institutes

BETZ, Robert B.

1444 I St. NW
Suite 410
Washington, DC 20005
EMail: rbetz@robertbetz.com
Tel: (202)347-1990
Fax: (202)628-2310
Registered: LDA

Employers

Robert Betz Associates, Inc. (President)

Clients Represented

On Behalf of Robert Betz Associates, Inc.

American Ass'n of Eye and Ear Hospitals
Council of Surgical Specialty Facilities and Institutes
Health Industry Group Purchasing Ass'n

BETZLER, Mary Roddy

10314 Nolan Dr.
Rockville, MD 20850
Tel: (301)762-7102
Fax: (301)762-3955

Employers

Irish American Democrats (Political Director)

BEVELS, Terry D.

1317 F St. NW
Suite 400
Washington, DC 20004
Tel: (202)737-5110
Fax: (202)737-6721
Registered: LDA
EMail: tbevels@aol.com

Staff Assistant, Professional Staff, House Committee on Appropriations, 1980-86. Budget and Program Analyst, Office of the Secretary, Department of Agriculture, 1971-80.

Employers

Terry Bevels Consulting

Clients Represented

On Behalf of Terry Bevels Consulting

Chatham Area Transit Authority
Columbia University
Internat'l Center for Clubhouse Development
Joslin Diabetes Center

BEVERIDGE, III, Albert J.

1350 I St. NW
Suite 700
Washington, DC 20005
Tel: (202)789-6000
Fax: (202)789-6190

Attorney, Tax Division, Department of Justice, 1965-1968.

Employers

Beveridge & Diamond, P.C. (Partner)

BEVILL, Hon. Tom

1225 I St. NW
Suite 500
Washington, DC 20005
Tel: (202)312-2005
Fax: (202)289-8683
Registered: LDA
EMail: dawsonassociates@worldnet.att.net

Member U.S. House of Representatives (D-AL), 1967-97.

Employers

Dawson & Associates, Inc. (Senior Advisor)

Clients Represented

On Behalf of Dawson & Associates, Inc.

Anglogold Americas, Inc.
Great Lakes Dredge & Dock

BEVINGTON, Rae Ann

805 15th St. NW
Suite 430
Washington, DC 20005
Tel: (202)371-9792
Fax: (202)789-2405
EMail: RaeAnn.Bevington@wswa.org

Employers

Wine and Spirits Wholesalers of America (Director, Political Affairs)

BEVVINO, Andrea

1201 S. Eads St.
Suite Two
Arlington, VA 22202
Tel: (703)271-8773
Fax: (703)271-9594
Registered: LDA
EMail: abevvino@wheatgr.com

Employers

Wheat & Associates, Inc. (Director, Government Relations)

Clients Represented

On Behalf of Wheat & Associates, Inc.

Airgas, Inc.
The Century Council
GE Capital Mortgage Insurance Co. (GEMICO)
Nescrow.com Technologies

BEY, Barbara

1001 Pennsylvania Ave. NW
Washington, DC 20004-2599
Tel: (202)624-2000
Fax: (202)624-2319

Employers

American Council of Life Insurers (Senior V. President, Public Affairs and Publishing)

BEYE, Mamadou

1401 I St. NW
Suite 1200
Washington, DC 20005-2225
Tel: (202)408-5812
Fax: (202)408-5842
Registered: LDA
EMail: mbey@chevron.com

Employers

The Chevron Companies (International Relations Representative)

BEYER, Alisa

600 New Hampshire Ave. NW
Suite 601
Washington, DC 20037
Tel: (202)333-7400
Fax: (202)333-1638

Employers

Hill and Knowlton, Inc. (Practice Leader)

BEYER, John C.

2101 Wilson Blvd.
Suite 1200
Arlington, VA 22201
Tel: (703)516-7700
Fax: (703)351-6162

Employers

Nathan Associates Inc. (President)

BEZOLD, Ph.D., Clement

100 N. Pitt St.
Suite 235
Alexandria, VA 22314-3134
Tel: (703)684-5880
Fax: (703)684-0640
EMail: cbezold@altfutures.com

Employers

Institute for Alternative Futures (President)

BHARGAVA, Deepak

1000 Wisconsin Ave. NW
Washington, DC 20007
Tel: (202)342-0567
Fax: (202)333-5462
EMail: bhargavad@commchange.org

Employers

Center for Community Change (Director, Public Policy)
Nat'l Campaign for Jobs and Income Support (Contact)

BIALEK, Ronald

1220 L St. NW
Suite 350
Washington, DC 20005
Tel: (202)898-5600
Ext: 3005
Fax: (202)898-5609
EMail: rbialek@phf.org

Employers

Public Health Foundation (President)

BIANCHI, Maria

8201 Greensboro Dr.
Suite 300
McLean, VA 22102
Tel: (703)610-9000
Fax: (703)610-9005

Employers

Ass'n Management Group

Clients Represented

On Behalf of Ass'n Management Group

Nat'l Ass'n of Naturopathic Physicians

BIANCHI, Melissa

555 13th St. NW
Washington, DC 20004-1109
Tel: (202)637-3653
Fax: (202)637-5910
Registered: LDA
EMail: mbianchi@hhlaw.com

Employers

Hogan & Hartson L.L.P. (Associate)

BICKEL, Lori A.

1275 K St. NW
Suite 1212
Washington, DC 20005
Tel: (703)787-0000
Fax: (202)312-5005
Registered: LDA

Employers

Healthcare Distribution Management Ass'n (Associate Director, Regulatory Affairs)

BICKWIT, Jr., Leonard

655 15th St. NW
Suite 900
Washington, DC 20005-5701
Tel: (202)626-5800
Fax: (202)628-0858
Registered: LDA, FARA
EMail: lbickwit@milchev.com

General Counsel, Nuclear Regulatory Commission, 1979-83. Chief Legislative Assistant to Senator John Glenn (D-OH), 1975-79. Counsel, Subcommittee on the Environment, Senate Commerce Committee, 1969-74.

Employers

Miller & Chevalier, Chartered (Member)

Clients Represented

On Behalf of Miller & Chevalier, Chartered

Ass'n of Financial Services Holding Companies
Blue Cross and Blue Shield of California
Boston Edison Co.
H. E. Butt Grocery Co.
Chevy Chase Bank, F.S.B.
Envirocare of Utah, Inc.
Exxon Mobil Corp.
Framatome, S.A.
Ernest & Julio Gallo Winery
Mutual of America
Pulte Home Corp.
SABIC Americas, Inc.
Safeway, Inc.
U.S. Chamber Task Force on Punitive Damages
Wal-Mart Stores, Inc.

BIDDLE, Timothy M.

1001 Pennsylvania Ave. NW
Suite 1100
Washington, DC 20004-2595
Tel: (202)624-2500
Fax: (202)628-5116
Registered: LDA

Employers

Crowell & Moring LLP (Partner)

Clients Represented

On Behalf of Crowell & Moring LLP

Helicopter Ass'n Internat'l

BIDDLE, CAE, Walter

1300 N. 17th St.
Suite 1847
Rosslyn, VA 22209
Tel: (703)841-3211
Fax: (703)841-3311

Employers

Nat'l Electrical Safety Foundation (Exec. Director)

BIDEN, Hunter

818 Connecticut Ave. NW
Suite 1100
Washington, DC 20006
Tel: (202)728-1010
Fax: (202)728-4044

Employers

The National Group, LLP (Partner)

BIDERMAN, David

4301 Connecticut Ave. NW
Suite 300
Washington, DC 20008
Tel: (202)244-4700
Fax: (202)966-4818

Employers

Environmental Industry Ass'ns (General Counsel)

BIEBER, Sander M.

1775 I St. NW
Washington, DC 20006
Tel: (202)261-3308
Fax: (202)261-3333
EMail: sander.bieber@dechert.com

Employers

Dechert (Partner)

BIECHMAN, John C.

1110 N. Glebe Rd.
Suite 210
Arlington, VA 22201
Tel: (703)516-4346
Fax: (703)516-4350

Employers

Nat'l Fire Protection Ass'n (V. President, Government Affairs)

BIEGEL, Roberta

1828 L St. NW
Suite 625
Washington, DC 20036
Tel: (202)496-5007
Fax: (202)833-3472
EMail: roberta@womens-health.org

Employers
Soc. for Women's Health Research (Director, Government Relations)

BIEGING, David A.

1001 Pennsylvania Ave. NW
Suite 300S
Washington, DC 20004
Tel: (202)824-8800
Fax: (202)824-8990
Registered: LDA
EMail: beiging.dave@dorseylaw.com
Administrative Assistant to Rep. Martin O. Sabo (D-MN), 1979-87. Special Assistant to the Vice President, The White House, 1977-78. Legislative Assistant to Senator Walter F. Mondale (D-MN), 1975-76.

Employers
Dorsey & Whitney LLP (Partner)

Clients Represented

On Behalf of Dorsey & Whitney LLP
Aleutian Pribilof Islands Community Development Ass'n
Ass'n of Internat'l Automobile Manufacturers
Bristol Bay Native Corp.
Central Council of Tlingit and Haida Indian Tribes of Alaska
Cow Creek Umpqua Tribe of Oregon
Cuyapaipe Band of Mission Indians
Delaware Tribe of Indians
Diamond Game Enterprises, Inc.
Excelsior Gaming, Inc.
Grand Traverse Band of Chippewa and Ottawa Indians
Hoopa Valley Tribal Council
Jamestown-S'Klallam Indian Tribe
Las Vegas Paiute Tribe
Little River Band of Ottawa Indians
Lower Elwaha S'Klallam Tribe
Minneapolis-St. Paul Metropolitan Council
Nez Perce Tribal Executive Committee
Pascua Yaqui Tribe of Arizona
Quinault Indian Nation
Red Lake Band of Chippewa Indians
Shakopee Mdewakanton Sioux Tribe
Spokane Tribe
St. George Island Traditional Council
Stockbridge-Munsee Community Band of Mohican Indians
Trading Cove Associates
Winnebago Tribe of Nebraska

BIEL, Eric

601 13th St. NW
Suite 1100
Washington, DC 20005
Tel: (202)429-2217
Fax: (202)296-8727
Registered: LDA
Deputy Under Secretary of Commerce for Trade Policy/Acting Director, Office of Policy and Strategic Planning, U.S. Department of Commerce, and Counselor to the Secretariat, 1998-2000.

Employers
Fontheim Partners, PC

Clients Represented

On Behalf of Fontheim Partners, PC
Susquehanna Investment Group

BIERLY, Ph.D., Eugene W.

2000 Florida Ave. NW
Washington, DC 20009
Tel: (202)777-7506
Fax: (202)328-0566
EMail: ebierly@agu.org

Employers
American Geophysical Union (Senior Scientist)

BIERMAN, Chad

1707 H St. NW
Suite 703
Washington, DC 20006
Tel: (202)478-5425
Registered: LDA

Employers
Washington Aviation Group

Clients Represented

On Behalf of Washington Aviation Group
Aircraft Electronics Ass'n
Airline Suppliers Ass'n
Professional Aviation Maintenance Ass'n

BIERMAN, Everett E.

1801 K St. NW
Washington, DC 20006
Tel: (202)775-7100
Fax: (202)857-0172
Registered: LDA
Former U.S. Ambassador and former Minority Staff Director, House Foreign Affairs Committee.

Employers
Arter & Hadden (Consultant)

BIERMAN, James N.

3000 K St. NW
Suite 500
Washington, DC 20007-5109
Tel: (202)672-5300
Fax: (202)672-5399
EMail: jbierman@foleylaw.com
Member Civil Rights Reviewing Authority, Department of Health, Education and Welfare, 1979-80.

Employers
Foley & Lardner (Partner-in-Charge)

BIERMAN, John

2121 K St. NW
Suite 701
Washington, DC 20037
Tel: (202)452-0952
Fax: (202)452-0959
EMail: jack@baft.org

Employers
Bankers' Ass'n for Finance and Trade (Director, Communication and Issues Management)

BIERON, Brian

1775 I St. NW
Suite 700
Washington, DC 20006
Tel: (202)261-4000
Fax: (202)261-4001
Policy Director, House Rules Committee, 1998-2001. Legislative Assistant to Rep. David Dreier (R-CA), 1993-98. Former Legislative Director to Rep. Bob McEwen (R-OH).

Employers
Clark & Weinstock, Inc.

BIERSACK, Carl

1275 Pennsylvania Ave. NW
Tenth Floor
Washington, DC 20004
Tel: (202)333-4936
Fax: (202)833-9392
Registered: LDA
Former Legislative Director to Senator Trent Lott (R-MS).

Employers
Barbour Griffith & Rogers, Inc. (Director, Government Affairs)

Clients Represented

On Behalf of Barbour Griffith & Rogers, Inc.
Air Transport Ass'n of America
American Maritime Congress
Ass'n of Oil Pipelines
Bay Harbor Management, L.C.
Canadian Nat'l Railway Co.
Citizens for Jobs and the Economy
Delta Air Lines
INTELSAT - Internat'l Telecommunications Satellite Organization
Lockheed Martin Corp.
Lyondell Chemical Co.
Southern Co.

BIESTEK, Jr., Frederick A.

120 S. Payne St.
Alexandria, VA 22314
Tel: (703)684-7300
Fax: (703)684-7302
Registered: LDA
EMail: fbiestek@bahrinc.com
Member of Senator Joe Lieberman's personal staff, 1996-98. Army Legislative Liaison Officer, 1995-96. Served in the Army, 1976-98.

Employers
Bentley, Adams, Hargett, Riley and Co., Inc. (Deputy Director, Government Relations)

Clients Represented

On Behalf of Bentley, Adams, Hargett, Riley and Co., Inc.
InWork Technologies
Munitions Industrial Base Task Force
Sister Cities Internat'l

BIGGERT, Adrienne

1129 20th St. NW
Suite 600
Washington, DC 20036-3421
Tel: (202)778-3200
Fax: (202)778-8479
Registered: LDA
EMail: abiggert@aahp.org

Employers
American Ass'n of Health Plans (AAHP) (Washington Representative)

BIKOFF, James

1101 30th St. NW
Suite 120
Washington, DC 20007
Tel: (202)944-3301
Fax: (202)944-3306

Employers
Silverberg, Goldman & Bikoff, LLP (Partner)

BILBRAY, Hon. James H.

2111 Wilson Blvd.
Eighth Floor
Arlington, VA 22201-3058
Tel: (703)841-0626
Fax: (703)243-2874
Registered: LDA
EMail: bilbray@alcalde-fay.com
Member, U.S. House of Representatives (D-NV), 1987-94.

Employers
Alcalde & Fay (Partner)

Clients Represented

On Behalf of Alcalde & Fay
American Magline Group
Arcata Associates, Inc.
Las Vegas Convention and Visitors Authority
University of Nevada - Las Vegas

BILCHIK, Shay

440 First St. NW
Third Floor
Washington, DC 20001-2085
Tel: (202)638-2952
Fax: (202)638-4004

Employers
Child Welfare League of America (Exec. Director)

BILLER, Moe

1300 L St. NW
Washington, DC 20005
Tel: (202)842-4246
Fax: (202)842-4297
Registered: LDA

Employers
American Postal Workers Union (President)

BILLET, Steven

1120 20th St. NW
Suite 1000
Washington, DC 20036
Registered: LDA

Employers
Concert USA

BILLINGS, Leon G.

1625 K St. NW
Suite 790
Washington, DC 20006
Tel: (202)293-7800
Fax: (202)293-7808
Registered: LDA
Executive Assistant to Secretary of State Edmund Muskie, Department of State, 1980-81. Administrative Assistant to Senator Edmund S. Muskie (D-ME), 1978-80. Staff Director, Environmental Pollution Subcommittee, Senate Committee on Public Works, 1966-78.

Employers
Leon G. Billings, Inc. (President)

Clients Represented

On Behalf of Leon G. Billings, Inc.
Downey McGrath Group, Inc.
Industry Urban-Development Agency
Lincoln Pulp and Paper Co.

BILLINGS, Paul

1726 M St. NW
Suite 902
Washington, DC 20036
Tel: (202)785-3355
Fax: (202)452-1805

Employers
American Lung Ass'n (Assistant Director, Government Relations)

BILLINGS, Shannon

1401 H St. NW
12th Floor
Washington, DC 20005-2148
Tel: (202)326-5892
Fax: (202)326-5899

Employers
Investment Co. Institute (Director, Political Affairs)

BILLINGSLEY, M. Scott

122 S. Royal St.
Alexandria, VA 22314-3328
Tel: (703)838-0373
Fax: (703)838-1698
Registered: LDA

Employers
Cordia Cos. (Counsel)

BILLUPS, Karen K.

1776 I St. NW
Suite 275
Washington, DC 20006
Tel: (202)530-7300
Fax: (202)530-7350
Registered: LDA

Employers
Entergy Services, Inc. (Director, Federal Affairs and Washington Counsel)

BILLUPS, Ray

306 N. Columbus St.
Alexandria, VA 22314
Tel: (202)255-5787
Registered: LDA

Employers
Self-employed as an independent consultant.

Clients Represented
As an independent consultant
Edison Electric Institute
Nuclear Energy Institute
Potomac Electric Power Co.

BILLY, David B.

1750 New York Ave. NW
Washington, DC 20006
Tel: (202)737-8484
Fax: (202)737-8418
Registered: LDA

Employers
Internat'l Ass'n of Fire Fighters (Political Action Director)

BILOWITH, Karen

1400 I St. NW
Suite 1220
Washington, DC 20005
Tel: (202)408-4848
Fax: (202)408-1818

Employers
Nat'l AIDS Fund (Program Officer)

BILZI, Carol J.

1909 K St. NW
Washington, DC 20006
Tel: (202)263-3000
Fax: (202)263-3300
Registered: LDA
EMail: cbilzi@mayerbrown.com

Employers
Mayer, Brown & Platt (Counsel)

Clients Represented
On Behalf of Mayer, Brown & Platt
Accenture
Ernst & Young LLP
General Electric Co.
KPMG, LLP
PriceWaterhouseCoopers

BINDEMAN, CPCU, ARP, Deborah

1825 K St. NW
Suite 703
Washington, DC 20006
EMail: dbindeman@iso.com
Tel: (202)466-2800
Fax: (202)466-2090

Employers
Insurance Services Office, Inc. (Senior Federal Affairs Representative)

BINDER, Sarah

1775 Massachusetts Ave. NW
Washington, DC 20036-2188
Tel: (202)797-6000
Fax: (202)797-6004
Press Secretary and Legislative Aide to Rep. Lee H. Hamilton (D-IN), 1986-90.

Employers
The Brookings Institution (Senior Fellow, Government Studies)

BINDER, Susan J.

400 Seventh St. SW
Room 3318
Washington, DC 20590
EMail: susan.binder@thwa.dot.gov
Tel: (202)366-9208
Fax: (202)366-7696

Employers
Department of Transportation - Federal Highway Administration (Director, Office of Legislative and Strategic Planning)

BINGAMAN, Jr., Robert L.

408 C St. NE
Washington, DC 20002
Tel: (202)547-1141
Fax: (202)547-6009
Registered: LDA

Employers
Sierra Club (National Field Director)

BINKLEY, Joanne

1401 Rockville Pike
Suite 200 North
Rockville, MD 20852-1448
Tel: (301)827-2000
Fax: (301)827-3843

Employers
Department of Health and Human Services - Center for Biologics Evaluation and Research (Congressional and Public Affairs Division)

BINZ, Ronald J.

1156 15th St. NW
Suite 520
Washington, DC 20005
Tel: (202)835-0202
Fax: (202)835-1132

Employers
Competition Policy Institute (President and Policy Director)

BINZEL, Peggy K.

1724 Massachusetts Ave. NW
Washington, DC 20036-1969
Tel: (202)775-3550
Fax: (202)775-3695

Employers
Nat'l Cable Television Ass'n (Exec. V. President)

BINZEL, William P.

1401 I St. NW
Suite 240
Washington, DC 20005
Tel: (202)414-8002
Fax: (202)414-8010
Registered: LDA
EMail: william_binzel@mastercard.com

Employers
MasterCard Internat'l (V. President, Public Affairs)

BIRCH, Bryan

1219 Prince St.
Alexandria, VA 22314
Tel: (703)519-3846
Fax: (703)519-3849
Registered: LDA
EMail: eangus@eangus.org

Employers
Enlisted Ass'n of the Nat'l Guard of the United States (Office Administrator)

BIRCH, Elizabeth M.

919 18th St. NW
Suite 800
Washington, DC 20006
Tel: (202)628-4160
Fax: (202)347-5323
Registered: LDA

Employers
Human Rights Campaign Fund (Exec. Director)

BIRCH, Ronald G.

1155 Connecticut Ave. NW
Suite 1200
Washington, DC 20036
Tel: (202)659-5800
Fax: (202)659-1027
Registered: LDA
EMail: rbirch@dc.bhb.com
Administrative Aide to Senator Ted Stevens (R-AK), 1968-71.

Employers
Birch, Horton, Bittner & Cherot (President and Shareholder)

Clients Represented
On Behalf of Birch, Horton, Bittner & Cherot
Aleut Corp.
American Public Transportation Ass'n
Ass'n of American Railroads
CSX Corp.
Digital Matrix Corp.
Fairbanks, Alaska, North Star Borough of
ICRC Energy, Inc.
Marotta Scientific Controls, Inc.
Optical Disc Corp.
Science Applications Internat'l Corp. (SAIC)
Space Mark
University of Alaska
Yukon Pacific

BIRCH, Thomas L.

733 15th St. NW
Suite 938
Washington, DC 20005
Tel: (202)347-3666
Registered: LDA

Employers
Self-employed as an independent consultant.

Clients Represented
As an independent consultant
Nat'l Assembly of State Arts Agencies
Nat'l Child Abuse Coalition

BIRD, Eugene

1250 Fourth St. SW
Suite WG-1
Washington, DC 20024
EMail: count@igc.apc.org
Tel: (202)863-2951
Fax: (202)863-2952

Employers
Council for the Nat'l Interest (President)

BIRD, Mary E.

901 N. Stuart St.
Suite 900
Arlington, VA 22203
Tel: (703)527-7600
Ext: 38
Fax: (703)527-8811
Registered: LDA

Employers
Nat'l Accrediting Commission of Cosmetology Arts & Sciences, Inc. (Director, Government Relations and Legal Dept.)

BIRD, Michael

444 N. Capitol St. NW
Suite 515
Washington, DC 20001
Tel: (202)624-5400
Fax: (202)737-1069

Employers
Nat'l Conference of State Legislatures (Federal Affairs Counsel)

BIRD, Robert S.

601 Pennsylvania Ave. NW
Suite 420
North Bldg.
Washington, DC 20004
Tel: (202)737-8200
Fax: (202)638-4914
Registered: LDA

Employers
General Mills (Director, Washington Office)

BIRD, Ronald E.

1015 15th St. NW
Suite 1200
Washington, DC 20005
EMail: rbird@epf.org
Tel: (202)789-8685
Fax: (202)789-8684

Employers
Employment Policy Foundation (Chief Economist)
McGuiness Norris & Williams, LLP (Chief Economist)

BIRDSALL, Cheryl C.

555 New Jersey Ave. NW
Washington, DC 20001
Tel: (202)393-5693
Fax: (202)879-4402
Registered: LDA

Employers
American Federation of Teachers (Associate Director, Legislation)

BIRKEL, Richard C.

801 Buchanan St. NE
Washington, DC 20017
Tel: (202)529-7600
Fax: (202)529-2028

Employers
Kennedy Institute, Lt. Joseph P. (President and Chief Exec. Officer)

BIRKHOFER, William J.

413 New York Ave. SE
Washington, DC 20003
Tel: (202)543-3866
Fax: (202)168-0
Registered: LDA
EMail: bill.birkhofer@jacobs.com

Employers
Jacobs Engineering Group Inc. (V. President and Director, Government Affairs)

BIRNKRANT, Henry J.

601 Pennsylvania Ave. NW
11th Floor, North Bldg.
Washington, DC 20004-2601
EMail: hbirnkrant@alston.com
Tel: (202)756-3300
Fax: (202)756-3333

Employers
Alston & Bird LLP (Partner)

Clients Represented
On Behalf of Alston & Bird LLP
Matsushita Electric Corp. of America

BIRNS, Laurence R.

1444 I St. NW
Suite 211
Washington, DC 20005
EMail: coha@coha.org
Tel: (202)216-9261
Fax: (202)216-9193

Employers
Council on Hemispheric Affairs (Director)

BIRO, Ladd K.

1331 Pennsylvania Ave. NW
Sixth Floor
Washington, DC 20004-1790
Tel: (202)637-3191
Fax: (202)637-3182

Employers
Nat'l Ass'n of Manufacturers (Senior V. President, Marketing, Member Communications and Services)

BIROS, Mark J.

1233 20th St. NW
Suite 800
Washington, DC 20036-2396
EMail: MBiros@proskauer.com
Tel: (202)416-6800
Fax: (202)416-6899
Assistant U.S. Attorney, District of Columbia, Department of Justice, 1977-88. Assistant Counsel, Senate Select Committee on Presidential Campaign Activities, 1973-74.

Employers
Proskauer Rose LLP (Partner)

BIRRELL, Jeffrey C.

1101 30th St. NW
Suite 500
Washington, DC 20007
Tel: (202)338-5393
Fax: (202)338-5391

Employers
Barron-Birrell, Inc. (President and Chief Exec. Officer)

Clients Represented
On Behalf of Barron-Birrell, Inc.
Liberia, Office of the President of the Republic of

BISACQUINO, Thomas J.

2201 Cooperative Way
Third Floor
Herndon, VA 22071
EMail: bisacquino@naiop.org
Tel: (703)904-7100
Fax: (703)904-7942
Registered: LDA

Employers
Nat'l Ass'n of Industrial and Office Properties (President)

BISCHOFF, Carol Ann

1900 M St. NW
Suite 800
Washington, DC 20036-3508
EMail: cbischoff@comptel.org
Tel: (202)296-6650
Fax: (202)296-7585
Registered: LDA

Employers
Competitive Telecommunications Ass'n (COMPTEL) (Exec. V. President and General Counsel)

BISHOP, Frank

1414 Prince St.
Suite 200
Alexandria, VA 22314
EMail: info@naseo.org
Tel: (703)299-8800
Fax: (703)299-6208

Employers
Nat'l Ass'n of State Energy Officials (Exec. Director)

BISHOP, James

924 G St. NW
Washington, DC 20001
EMail: bishopj@catholiccharitiesdc.org
Tel: (202)772-4398
Fax: (202)772-4402

Employers
Catholic Charities Archdiocesan Legal Network (Program Administrator)

BISHOP, Mason

444 N. Capitol St. NW
Suite 142
Washington, DC 20001
Tel: (202)431-8020
Fax: (202)434-8033

Employers
Nat'l Ass'n of State Workforce Agencies (Director, Legislation and Marketing)

BISHOP, Robert D.

1300 I St. NW
Suite 400 West
Washington, DC 20005
Tel: (202)515-2516
Fax: (202)336-7926

Employers
Verizon Communications (Director, Media Relations)

BISHOP, Robert W.

1776 I St. NW
Suite 400
Washington, DC 20006-3708
Tel: (202)739-8000
Fax: (202)785-4019

Employers
Nuclear Energy Institute (V. President, General Counsel, Secretary, and Treasurer)

BISHOP, Susan

2215 Constitution Ave. NW
Washington, DC 20037-2985
Tel: (202)628-4410
Fax: (202)783-2351

Employers
American Pharmaceutical Ass'n (PAC Contact)

BISHOP, Terri

425 Second St. NW
Washington, DC 20001
Tel: (202)393-4409
Fax: (202)783-3254

Employers
Community for Creative Non-Violence (President and Co-Spokesperson)

BISKIN, Emery

1200 17th St. NW
Washington, DC 20036-3097
Tel: (202)331-5915
Fax: (202)973-5373

Employers
Nat'l Restaurant Ass'n (Government Affairs Coordinator)

BISSEN, Robert

1615 L St. NW
Suite 900
Washington, DC 20036
EMail: rbissen@apcoworldwide.com
Tel: (202)778-1000
Fax: (202)466-6002
Registered: LDA, FARA

Employers
APCO Worldwide (V. President, Government Relations)

BITTERMAN, Mark E.

21700 Atlantic Blvd.
Dulles, VA 20166
EMail: bitterman.mark@orbital.com
Tel: (703)406-5523
Fax: (703)406-5572
Registered: LDA

Employers
Orbital Sciences Corp. (V. President, Government Relations)

BITTINGER, Deborah

810 Vermont Ave. NW
Room 516
Washington, DC 20420
Tel: (202)273-5615
Fax: (202)273-6791

Employers
Department of Veterans Affairs (Congressional Relations Officer)

BITTMAN, Robert

601 13th St. NW
Suite 600 South
Washington, DC 20005
Tel: (202)626-3600
Fax: (202)639-9355

Employers
White & Case LLP

BITTNER, Mamie

1100 Pennsylvania Ave. NW
Room 510
Washington, DC 20506
EMail: mbittner@imls.gov
Tel: (202)606-8339
Fax: (202)606-8591

Employers
Institute for Museum and Library Services (Director, Public and Legislative Affairs)

BITTNER, William

1155 Connecticut Ave. NW
Suite 1200
Washington, DC 20036
Tel: (202)659-5800
Fax: (202)659-1027
Registered: LDA

Employers
Birch, Horton, Bittner & Cherot (Shareholder)

Clients Represented
On Behalf of Birch, Horton, Bittner & Cherot
Alaska Aerospace
Alaska Communications Systems, Inc.
Council Tree Communications, L.L.C.
Pacific Telecom, Inc.
Port of Tillamook Bay
Quinnat Landing Hotel
Spectrum Astro, Inc.
St. George Tanaq
Trimble Navigation, Ltd.

BIXBY, Robert

1819 H St. NW
Suite 800
Washington, DC 20006
EMail: concord@concordcoalition.org
Tel: (202)467-6222
Fax: (202)467-6333

Employers
Concord Coalition (Exec. Director)

BIZUB, Scott

635 Slaters Lane
Suite 140
Alexandria, VA 22314
EMail: Scott.Bizub@chwatco.com
Tel: (703)684-7703
Fax: (703)684-7594
Registered: LDA

Employers
Chwat and Company, Inc. (Director, Government Relations)

Clients Represented
On Behalf of Chwat and Company, Inc.
AccuWeather
Nat'l Ass'n of Assistant United States Attorneys
Newington-Cropsey Foundation
Security Industry Ass'n

BJORKLUND, Laura

1016 16th St. NW
Suite 300
Washington, DC 20036
Tel: (202)862-4400
Fax: (202)862-4432

Employers
Nat'l Federation of Federal Employees (Business Representative)

BJORNSON, Ms. Gerrie

1825 I St. NW
Suite 400
Washington, DC 20006
EMail: GBJORNSON@corp.bfg.com
Tel: (202)429-2060
Fax: (202)331-9501
Registered: LDA

Employers
B. F. Goodrich Co. (V. President, Government Relations)

BLAAUW, Coen

552 Seventh St. SE
Washington, DC 20003
Tel: (202)547-3686
Fax: (202)543-7891

Employers
Formosan Ass'n for Public Affairs (Exec. Director)

BLACK, Jr., Charles R.

1801 K St. NW
Suite 901-L
Washington, DC 20006
EMail: Charlie_Black@bm.com
Tel: (202)530-0500
Fax: (202)530-4800
Registered: LDA
Former Senior Advisor to the President, The White House, during the Reagan and Bush I administrations. Former Political Consultant to Senators Jesse Helms (R-NC), Robert

Dole (R-KS), Phil Gramm (R-TX), and Dave Durenberger (R-MN).

Employers
BKSH & Associates (President and Chief Exec. Officer)

Clients Represented
On Behalf of BKSH & Associates
Lumenos
M-Unit
J. P. Morgan Chase & Co.

BLACK, Clifford
60 Massachusetts Ave. NE
Washington, DC 20002
Tel: (202)906-3860
Fax: (202)906-3306

Employers
AMTRAK (Nat'l Rail Passenger Corp.) (Director, Special Projects)

BLACK, Edward J.
666 11th St. NW
Suite 600
Washington, DC 20001
EMail: eblack@ccianet.org
Tel: (202)783-0070
Fax: (202)783-0534
Registered: LDA
Served as Deputy to Assistant Secretary of Congressional Affairs, Department of Commerce; Administrative Assistant to Rep. John LaFalce (D-NY); Congressional Liaison to Secretary Henry Kissinger, Department of State; Legislative Director to Rep. Louis Stokes (D-OH).

Employers
Computer and Communications Industry Ass'n (CCIA) (President, Chief Exec. Officer, and Treasurer)

BLACK, III, H. Allen
1400 L St. NW
Washington, DC 20005-3502
Tel: (202)371-5700
Fax: (202)371-5950

Employers
Winston & Strawn

Clients Represented
On Behalf of Winston & Strawn
Northland Holdings, Inc.

BLACK, Joseph A.
1101 30th St. NW
Suite 300
Washington, DC 20007
Tel: (202)944-8600
Fax: (202)944-8611

Employers
The Cullen Law Firm (Partner)

BLACK, Joseph P. H.
1111 N. Fairfax St.
Alexandria, VA 22314
Tel: (703)684-2782
Fax: (703)684-7343

Employers
American Physical Therapy Ass'n (Senior V. President, Education)

BLACK, Judy A.
1615 L St. NW
Suite 1220
Washington, DC 20036-5610
EMail: jblack@winstarmail.com
Tel: (202)659-0946
Fax: (202)659-4972
Registered: LDA

Employers
American Council of Young Political Leaders (President)
Evans & Black, Inc. (Principal)

Clients Represented
On Behalf of Evans & Black, Inc.
Brinker Internat'l
Girl Scouts of the U.S.A. - Washington Office
Hallmark Cards, Inc.
Internat'l Council of Shopping Centers
Nat'l Osteoporosis Foundation
Ticketmaster

BLACK, Wayne V.
1001 G St. NW
Suite 500 West
Washington, DC 20001
EMail: black@khlaw.com
Tel: (202)434-4100
Fax: (202)434-4646

Employers
Keller and Heckman LLP (Partner)

Clients Represented
On Behalf of Keller and Heckman LLP
Tea Ass'n of the U.S.A., Inc.

BLACK, Will
1747 Pennsylvania Ave. NW
Suite 1100
Washington, DC 20006
Tel: (202)833-0100
Fax: (202)833-0108

Employers
U.S. English, Inc. (Director, Membership Development)

BLACK, William
1615 L St. NW
Suite 1000
Washington, DC 20036
EMail: blackb@fleishman.com
Tel: (202)659-0330
Fax: (202)223-8199
Registered: LDA
Former Chief of Staff Rep. Steny Hoyer (D-MD).

Employers
Fleishman-Hillard, Inc (Senior V. President)

Clients Represented
On Behalf of Fleishman-Hillard, Inc
American Ambulance Ass'n
Kahl Pownall Advocates
Soc. of Thoracic Surgeons

BLACKBURN-MORENO, Ronald
1444 I St. NW
Suite 800
Washington, DC 20005
Tel: (202)835-3600
Fax: (202)835-3613

Employers
ASPIRA Ass'n, Inc. (President)

BLACKBURNE, Faith
801 Pennsylvania Ave. NW
Suite 630
Washington, DC 20004-5878
EMail: fblackburne@nyse.com
Tel: (202)347-4300
Fax: (202)347-4370

Employers
New York Stock Exchange (Manager, Public Affairs)

BLACKISTONE, Mick
1819 L St. NW
Suite 700
Washington, DC 20036
EMail: mblackistone@nmma.org
Tel: (202)861-1180
Fax: (202)861-1181
Registered: LDA
Confidential Assistant to the Commissioner, Public Buildings Service, General Services Administration, 1970-77. Press Secretary to Senator Richard Schweiker (R-PA), 1969-70

Employers
Nat'l Marine Manufacturers Ass'n (V. President, Government Relations)

BLACKLOW, Roger
905 16th St. NW
Washington, DC 20006
Tel: (202)737-8320
Fax: (202)737-2754
Registered: LDA

Employers
Laborers' Internat'l Union of North America (National Political Coordinator)

BLACKMAN, Maj. Brenda
1160 Air Force Pentagon
Room 4D927
Washington, DC 20330-1160
EMail: brenda.blackman@pentagon.af.mil
Tel: (703)697-4142
Fax: (703)697-2001

Employers
Department of Air Force (Exec. Officer, Legislative Liaison)

BLACKWELDER, Brent
1025 Vermont Ave. NW
Third Floor
Washington, DC 20005
EMail: bblackwelder@foe.org
Tel: (202)783-7400
Ext: 284
Fax: (202)783-0444
Registered: LDA

Employers
Friends of the Earth (President)

BLACKWELL, Lisa E.
1735 New York Ave. NW
Washington, DC 20006
EMail: lblackwell@aia.org
Tel: (202)626-7300
Fax: (202)626-7365

Employers
The American Institute of Architects (Managing Director, Government Affairs)

BLACKWELL, Hon. Lucien
1725 DeSales St. NW
Suite 800
Washington, DC 20036
Tel: (202)659-6542
Fax: (202)659-5730
Registered: LDA
Former Member, U.S. House of Representatives (D-PA), 1991-94.

Employers
Whitten & Diamond

Clients Represented
On Behalf of Whitten & Diamond
Philadelphia, Pennsylvania, City of

BLACKWELL, Sr., Robert J.
1850 M St. NW
Suite 900
Washington, DC 20036
Tel: (202)463-2500
Fax: (202)463-4950
Registered: LDA, FARA
Assistant Secretary for Maritime Affairs, Department of Commerce, 1972-79.

Employers
Sher & Blackwell (Partner)

Clients Represented
On Behalf of Sher & Blackwell
Maersk Inc.
New York Waterways
Nippon Yusen Kaisha (NYK) Line
Sargeant Marine, Inc.

BLACKWELL, Ron
815 16th St. NW
Washington, DC 20006
Tel: (202)637-5000
Fax: (202)637-5058

Employers
AFL-CIO (American Federation of Labor and Congress of Industrial Organizations) (Director, Corporate Affairs)

BLAGMAN, Diane J.
800 Connecticut Ave. NW
Suite 500
Washington, DC 20006
EMail: blagmand@gtlaw.com
Tel: (202)331-3121
Fax: (202)331-3101
Registered: LDA
Chief of Staff (1988-93) and Legislative Assistant (1993-85) to Rep. Bob Carr (D-MI). Legislative Assistant and Federal Grants Coordinator to Rep. Peter Peyser (D-NY).

Employers
Greenberg Traurig, LLP (Director, Legislative and Regulatory Affairs)

Clients Represented
On Behalf of Greenberg Traurig, LLP
Bexar Metropolitan Water District
Bowman Internat'l Corp.
Cambridge Management Inc.
Cellar Door Amphitheaters
Claire's Stores, Inc.
Deloitte Consulting
Florida Department of Agriculture and Consumer Services
Healtheon/Web MD
Miami, Florida, City of
Miami-Dade, Florida, County of
Mount Vernon, City of
Nat'l Ass'n of Community Health Centers
Nat'l Ass'n of Computer Consultant Businesses
Nat'l Center for Genome Research
Oakland, California, City of
Playboy Enterprises, Inc.
Prince George's, Maryland, County of
Smith Development, LLC
Torrington Co.
Unilever United States, Inc.
Uniroyal Technology Corp.

BLAIR, Alice K.
431 18th St. NW
Washington, DC 20006
EMail: blaira@usa.redcross.org
Tel: (202)639-3125
Fax: (202)639-6116
Registered: LDA

Employers
American Red Cross (Manager, State Relations and Grass Roots Advocacy)

BLAIR, Bruce G.

1779 Massachusetts Ave. NW Tel: (202)332-0600
Suite 615 Fax: (202)462-4559
Washington, DC 20036

Employers
Center for Defense Information (President)

BLAIR, Louis H.

712 Jackson Place NW Tel: (202)395-4831
Washington, DC 20006 Fax: (202)395-6995
EMail: staff@truman.gov

Employers
Truman Scholarship Foundation, Harry S (Exec. Secretary)

BLAIR, Margaret

1775 Massachusetts Ave. NW Tel: (202)797-6000
Washington, DC 20036-2188 Fax: (202)797-6004

Employers
The Brookings Institution (Non-Resident Senior Fellow, Economic Studies)

BLAIR, Michele

1300 I St. NW Tel: (202)962-3830
Suite 900 East Fax: (202)962-3838
Washington, DC 20005 Registered: LDA
EMail: michele.blair@compaq.com

Employers
Compaq Computer Corp. (Manager, Government Affairs)

BLAKE, Jonathan D.

1201 Pennsylvania Ave. NW Tel: (202)662-6000
Washington, DC 20004-2401 Fax: (202)662-6291
EMail: jblake@cov.com

Employers
Covington & Burling (Partner)

Clients Represented

On Behalf of Covington & Burling
Ass'n for Maximum Service Television, Inc.

BLAKE, Linda

1000 Vermont Ave. NW Tel: (202)371-2830
12th Floor Fax: (202)371-0424
Washington, DC 20005

Employers
Americans for the Arts (Director, Marketing and Public Relations)

BLAKELY, Ed

99 Canal Center Plaza Tel: (703)683-8512
Suite 200 Fax: (703)683-4622
Alexandria, VA 22314

Employers
Smith & Harroff, Inc. (V. President)

BLAKELY, Regina

2200 Mill Rd. Tel: (703)838-1977
Alexandria, VA 22314 Fax: (703)548-1841

Employers
American Trucking Ass'ns (Senior V. President, Stategic and Litigation Communication)

BLAKEY, William A.

1101 Vermont Ave. NW Tel: (202)289-3900
Suite 400 Fax: (202)371-0197
Washington, DC 20005 Registered: LDA
EMail: bblakey@dbmlaw.com
Staff Director, Senate Subcommittee on Employment and Productivity, Committee on Labor and Human Resources, 1987-89. Legislative Aide to Senator Paul Simon (D-IL), 1981-87.

Employers
Dean Blakey & Moskowitz (Partner)

Clients Represented

On Behalf of Dean Blakey & Moskowitz
Bethune-Cookman College
Bowie State University
Chicago State University
Claflin College
Clark Atlanta University
Council for Opportunity in Education
DeVry, Inc.
HBCU/PAC
Knoxville College
Mendez University System, Ana G.
Minority Males Consortium
Paul Quinn College
St. Augustine College
Talladega College
Texas College
United Negro College Fund, Inc.
University of Louisville
Voorhees College
Wilberforce University
The Work Colleges

BLALOCK, Cecelia

1308 19th St. NW Tel: (202)682-1984
Washington, DC 20036 Fax: (202)244-4800
EMail: yaci@aol.com

Employers
Young Astronaut Council (V. President)

BLANCATO, Robert B.

1101 Vermont Ave. NW Tel: (202)789-0470
Suite 1001 Fax: (202)682-3984
Washington, DC 20005 Registered: LDA
EMail: msbrb@erols.com
Executive Director, White House Conference on Aging, 1993-96.

Employers
Matz, Blancato & Associates, Inc. (President)

Clients Represented

On Behalf of Matz, Blancato & Associates, Inc.
AFLAC, Inc.
Americans for Long Term Care Security
City Meals on Wheels USA
Council of Senior Centers and Services of New York City, Inc.
Nat'l Ethnic Coalition of Organizations
Nat'l Italian American Foundation
UNIVEC
West Virginia University Center on Aging

BLANCHARD, Hon. James J.

901 15th St. NW Tel: (202)371-6000
Suite 700 Fax: (202)371-6279
Washington, DC 20005-2301 Registered: LDA
Ambassador to Canada, Department of State, 1993-96. Member, U.S. House of Representatives (D-MI), 1975-83.

Employers
Verner, Liipfert, Bernhard, McPherson and Hand, Chartered (Member of Firm)

Clients Represented

On Behalf of Verner, Liipfert, Bernhard, McPherson and Hand, Chartered
Alliance Pipeline, L.P.
Biovail Corp. Internat'l
CanWest
Federal Home Loan Bank of Indianapolis
Kasten Chase Applied Research Limited
Northwest Airlines, Inc.
Thomson Consumer Electronics, Inc.

BLANCHARD, Judith A.

1401 I St. NW Tel: (202)408-5831
Suite 1200 Fax: (202)408-5845
Washington, DC 20005-2225
EMail: jubl@chevron.com

Employers
The Chevron Companies (Federal Relation Manager)

BLANCHFIELD, John

1120 Connecticut Ave. NW Tel: (202)663-5000
Washington, DC 20036 Fax: (202)828-4548
Registered: LDA

Employers
American Bankers Ass'n (Director, Center for Agricultural and Rural Banking)

BLAND, Paul

1717 Massachusetts Ave. NW Tel: (202)797-8600
Suite 800 Fax: (202)232-7203
Washington, DC 20036
EMail: pbland@tlpj.org

Employers
Trial Lawyers for Public Justice, P.C. (Staff Attorney)

BLANEY, III, Harry C.

AFSA Bldg. Tel: (202)944-5519
2101 E St. NW Fax: (202)338-6820
Washington, DC 20037
EMail: colead@afsa.org

Employers
Coalition for American Leadership Abroad/American Foreign Affairs Organizations, Inc. (President)

BLANEY, Nancy

1755 Massachusetts Ave. NW Tel: (202)232-5020
Suite 418 Fax: (202)797-8947
Washington, DC 20036 Registered: LDA
EMail: nblaney@erols.com

Employers
American Soc. for the Prevention of Cruelty to Animals National Legislative Office (Director, National Legislative Office)

BLANK, Helen

25 E St. NW Tel: (202)628-8787
Washington, DC 20001 Fax: (202)662-3560
Registered: LDA

Employers
Children's Defense Fund (Director, Child Care)

BLANK, Jonathan

1735 New York Ave. NW Tel: (202)628-1700
Suite 500 Fax: (202)331-1024
Washington, DC 20006-4759 Registered: LDA

Employers
Preston Gates Ellis & Rouvelas Meeds LLP (Managing Partner)

Clients Represented

On Behalf of Preston Gates Ellis & Rouvelas Meeds LLP
Amgen
Capitol Cargo Internat'l Airlines, Inc.
Chitimacha Tribe of Louisiana
Greater Orlando Aviation Authority
Marine Transport Corp.
Maryland Department of Transportation
Maryland, Aviation Administration of the State of
Orange, California, County of
Seattle, Washington, Port of
Starwood Hotels & Resorts Worldwide, Inc.
Tacoma, Washington, Port of

BLANKENBURG, Daniel W.

1201 F St. NW Tel: (202)554-9000
Suite 200 Fax: (202)554-0496
Washington, DC 20004
Former Legislative Assistant to Rep. Thomas W. Ewing (R-IL). Former Legislative Director to Rep. John M. Shimkus, (R-IL). Former Staff Member to Rep. Donald A. Manzullo, (R-IL).

Employers
Nat'l Federation of Independent Business (Manager, Government Relations)

BLANKLEY, Tony

1909 K St. NW Tel: (202)973-5800
Fourth Floor Fax: (202)973-5858
Washington, DC 20006
Former Press Secretary to Speaker of the House, Rep. Newt Gingrich (R-GA).

Employers
Porter/Novelli (Of Counsel)

BLANTON, USAF (Ret), Lt. Gen. Charles C.

909 N. Washington St. Tel: (703)549-4455
Alexandria, VA 22314 Fax: (703)706-5961

Employers
Armed Forces Benefit Ass'n (President)

BLANTON, Tom

The George Washington University
Gelman Library, Suite 701
Washington, DC 20037
Tel: (202)994-7000
Fax: (202)994-7005

Employers
Nat'l Security Archive (Exec. Director)

BLASER, Robert

2011 Pennsylvania Ave. NW
Suite 800
Washington, DC 20006-1808
Tel: (202)261-4500
Fax: (202)835-0443
Registered: LDA

Employers
American College of Physicians-American Soc. of Internal Medicine (ACP-ASIM) (Senior Associate, Congressional Relations)
Medical Advocacy Services, Inc. (Director)
Renal Physicians Ass'n (Director, Government Affairs)

Clients Represented

On Behalf of Medical Advocacy Services, Inc.
American Ass'n of Clinical Endocrinologists
American College of Rheumatology
Renal Physicians Ass'n
Soc. of General Internal Medicine

BLASEY, III, Ralph G.

1050 Connecticut Ave. NW
Suite 1100
Washington, DC 20036-5304
Tel: (202)861-1500
Fax: (202)861-1790
Registered: LDA

Employers
Baker & Hostetler LLP

BLASINSKY, Mary

1201 F St. NW
Suite 200
Washington, DC 20004
Tel: (202)554-9000
Fax: (202)554-0496

Employers
Nat'l Federation of Independent Business (Chief of Staff)

BLATT, Nancy L.

601 Wythe St.
Alexandria, VA 22314-1994
EMail: nblatt@wef.org
Tel: (703)684-2400
Fax: (703)684-2492

Employers
Water Environment Federation (Director, Public Information)

BLATTER, Victoria

601 Pennsylvania Ave. NW
Suite 1200
North Bldg.
Washington, DC 20036
Tel: (202)638-4170
Fax: (202)638-3670

Employers
Merck & Co. (Director, Federal Policy and Government Relations)

BLAU, Robert T.

1133 21st St. NW
Suite 900
Washington, DC 20036
EMail: robert.blau@bellsouth.com
Tel: (202)463-4100
Fax: (202)463-4631
Registered: LDA

Employers
BellSouth Corp. (V. President, Exec. and Federal Regulatory Affairs)

BLAU, Russell M.

3000 K St. NW
Suite 300
Washington, DC 20007
Tel: (202)424-7500
Fax: (202)424-7643
Registered: LDA

Employers
Swidler Berlin Shereff Friedman, LLP (Partner)

BLAUL, William

8111 Gatehouse Rd.
Falls Church, VA 22042-1203
EMail: blaulb@usa.redcross.org

Employers
American Red Cross (V. President, Communications and Marketing)

BLAUNSTEIN, Phyllis

1825 Connecticut Ave. NW
Fifth Floor
Washington, DC 20009
EMail: phyllis.blaunstein@widmeyer.com
Tel: (202)667-0901
Fax: (202)667-0902

Employers
Widmeyer Communications, Inc. (Senior Counsel)

BLAUWET, Roger

801 Pennsylvania Ave. NW
Suite 625
Washington, DC 20004
Tel: (202)661-2100
Fax: (202)661-2101
Registered: LDA
Former Tax Counsel to Senator Max Baucus (D-MT).

Employers
Canfield & Associates, Inc. (Principal)

Clients Represented

On Behalf of Canfield & Associates, Inc.
Air Transport Ass'n of America
American Home Products Corp.
Ass'n of Financial Guaranty Insurers
Consumer Mortgage Coalition
GE Commercial Real Estate & Financial Services
Merck & Co.
Mutual of Omaha Insurance Companies
Pfizer, Inc.

BLAZEY, Leon

1200 G St. NW
Suite 800
Washington, DC 20005
Tel: (202)434-8759
Fax: (301)365-2864

Employers
The Accountants Coalition (Exec. Director)

BLEICHER, Samuel A.

1140 Connecticut Ave. NW
Suite 1212
Washington, DC 20036
EMail: sbleicher@milesstockbridge.com
Tel: (202)434-8100
Fax: (202)737-0097
Registered: LDA
Deputy General Counsel and Senior Executive, National Oceanic and Atmospheric Administration, Department of Commerce, 1977-81.

Employers
Miles & Stockbridge, P.C. (Principal)

Clients Represented

On Behalf of Miles & Stockbridge, P.C.
Black & Decker Corp., The
Elmer Larson, Inc.

BLEICHFELD, Howard S.

1050 Thomas Jefferson St. NW
Seventh Floor
Washington, DC 20007
EMail: hsb@vnf.com
Tel: (202)298-1800
Fax: (202)338-2416
Registered: LDA

Employers
Van Ness Feldman, P.C. (Of Counsel)

Clients Represented

On Behalf of Van Ness Feldman, P.C.
Methanex Inc.
The Nat'l Wetlands Coalition
Sealaska Corp.

BLEIER, Lisa

1120 Connecticut Ave. NW
Washington, DC 20036
Tel: (202)663-5000
Fax: (202)828-4548
Registered: LDA

Employers
American Bankers Ass'n (Senior Counsel)

BLILEY, Christopher P.

1627 K St. NW
Suite 700
Washington, DC 20006
Tel: (202)452-1252
Ext: 22
Fax: (202)452-0118
Registered: LDA

Employers
Smokeless Tobacco Council (Director, Government Relations)

BLILEY, Jr., Hon. Thomas J.

3050 K St. NW
Washington, DC 20007
Tel: (202)342-8646
Fax: (202)342-8451
Member, U.S. House of Representatives (R-VA), 1981-2000.

Employers
Collier Shannon Scott, PLLC (Senior Advisor, Gov't Relations and Public Pol.)

BLINKEN, Alan J.

1333 New Hampshire Ave. NW
Suite 400
Washington, DC 20036
Tel: (202)887-4000
Fax: (202)887-4288
Ambassador to Belgium, Department of State, 1993-98.

Employers
Akin, Gump, Strauss, Hauer & Feld, L.L.P. (Senior Advisor)

BLISS, Donald T.

555 13th St. NW
Suite 500 West
Washington, DC 20004
EMail: dbliss@omm.com
Tel: (202)383-5300
Fax: (202)383-5414
Registered: LDA
Acting General Counsel, Department of Transportation, 1976-77. Deputy General Counsel, Department of Transportation, 1975-77. Chief Policy Coordinator, Agency for Internat'l Development, 1974-75. Special Assistant to the Administrator, Environmental Protection Agency, 1973-74. Assistant to the Secretary and Executive Secretary, Department of Health, Education, and Welfare, 1969-73. Peace Corps Volunteer Lawyer, 1966-68.

Employers
O'Melveny and Myers LLP (Partner)

Clients Represented

On Behalf of O'Melveny and Myers LLP
CIGNA Corp.
Samsung Heavy Industries Co., Ltd.
US Airways

BLISS, John S.

1620 L St. NW
Suite 1210
Washington, DC 20036
Tel: (202)955-6062
Fax: (202)955-6070
Minority Chief Counsel, Subcommittee on the Constitution (1993) and Minority Chief Counsel, Subcommittee on Technology and the Law and Subcommittee on Juvenile Crime (1991-92), Committee on the Judiciary, U.S. Senate.

Employers
Higgins, McGovern & Smith, LLC (Partner)

Clients Represented

On Behalf of Higgins, McGovern & Smith, LLC
Coalition Against Product Tampering

BLISS, Mary Ellen

601 E St. NW
Washington, DC 20049
Tel: (202)434-3770
Fax: (202)434-6477
Registered: LDA

Employers
AARP (American Ass'n of Retired Persons) (Director, Federal Affairs, Economic Issues)

BLISS, Richard W.

1079 Papermill Ct. NW
Washington, DC 20007
Tel: (202)337-6008
Fax: (202)337-6193
Registered: LDA

Employers
Richard W. Bliss

BLOCH, Nancy J.

814 Thayer Ave.
Suite 250
Silver Spring, MD 20910
Tel: (301)587-1788
Fax: (301)587-1791

Employers
Nat'l Ass'n of the Deaf (Exec. Director)

BLOCH, Ronald

600 13th St. NW
Washington, DC 20005-3096
EMail: rbloch@mwe.com
Tel: (202)756-8012
Fax: (202)756-8087
Legal Director to Commissioner Mary Gardiner Jones; Senior Trial Attorney, Bureau of Competition; Assistant Director, Bureau of Competition, all at Federal Trade Commission.

Employers
McDermott, Will and Emery (Counsel)

BLOCK, Barbara
Three Lafayette Center
1155 21st St. NW
Washington, DC 20036-3384
Tel: (202)328-8000
Fax: (202)887-8979
Registered: LDA

Employers
Willkie Farr & Gallagher (Senior Legislative Analyst)

Clients Represented
On Behalf of Willkie Farr & Gallagher
Hamilton, Rabinovitz & Alschuler

BLOCK, Jeffrey
805 15th St. NW
Suite 300
Washington, DC 20005-2207
Tel: (202)682-4200
Fax: (202)682-9054
Registered: LDA

Employers
Credit Union Nat'l Ass'n, Inc.

BLOCK, John R.
201 Park Washington Ct.
Falls Church, VA 22046-4621
Tel: (703)532-9400
Fax: (703)538-4673
Registered: LDA
EMail: johnb@fdi.org

Employers
Food Distributors Internat'l (NAWGA-IFDA) (President)

BLOCK, Richard A. "Chip"
2001 Jefferson Davis Hwy.
Suite 209
Arlington, VA 22202
Tel: (703)413-0090
Fax: (703)413-4467
EMail: cblock@mehlgriffinbartek.com

Employers
Mehl, Griffin & Bartek Ltd. (V. President, Business Development and Technology)

BLOCKER, Andy
1101 17th St. NW
Suite 600
Washington, DC 20036
Tel: (202)496-5644
Fax: (202)496-5660
Registered: LDA
EMail: andy.blocker@aa.com

Employers
American Airlines (Managing Director)

BLOCKER, David
211 N. Union St.
Suite 250
Alexandria, VA 22314
Tel: (703)299-9100
Fax: (703)299-9110
EMail: dblocker@dmfgroup.com

Employers
Davis Manafort, Inc. (Director, Legislative Research)

BLOCKER, Rene
444 N. Capitol St. NW
Suite 425
Washington, DC 20001
Tel: (202)624-8699
Fax: (202)624-8819
EMail: rblocker@mtc.gov

Employers
Multistate Tax Commission (Deputy Director)

BLOCKLIN, Peter
1120 Connecticut Ave. NW
Washington, DC 20036
Tel: (202)663-5000
Fax: (202)828-4548
Registered: LDA

Employers
American Bankers Ass'n (Senior, Federal Legislative Representative-Senate Manager)

BLOCKSTEIN, Ph.D., David E.
1725 K St. NW
Suite 212
Washington, DC 20006
Tel: (202)530-5810
Ext: 205
Fax: (202)628-4311
EMail: info@cnie.org

Employers
Nat'l Council for Science and the Environment (Senior Scientist)

BLOM, Don
1680 Duke St.
Alexandria, VA 22314-3407
Tel: (703)838-6722
Fax: (703)683-7590

Employers
Nat'l School Boards Ass'n (Assoc. Exec. Dir., Constituent Services, Publications, & Marketing)

BLOOD, Rebecca
2301 M St. NW
Washington, DC 20037-1484
Tel: (202)467-2929
Fax: (202)467-2910
Registered: LDA
EMail: rblood@APPAnet.org

Employers
American Public Power Ass'n (Senior Government Relations Representative)

BLOOM, Colleen C.
2519 Connecticut Ave. NW
Washington, DC 20008-1520
Tel: (202)783-2242
Fax: (202)783-2255

Employers
American Ass'n of Homes and Services for the Aging (Housing Policy Analyst)

BLOOM, Daniel John
500 N. Washington St.
Alexandria, VA 22314
Tel: (703)551-2108
Fax: (703)551-2109
Executive Assistant to the Administrator, Small Business Administration, 1989-91. Legislative Director to Rep. F. James Sensenbrenner, Jr. (R-WI), 1985-89.

Employers
Blue Ridge Internat'l Group, L.L.C. (Managing Principal)

BLOOM, David I.
1909 K St. NW
Washington, DC 20006
Tel: (202)263-3000
Fax: (202)263-3300
Registered: LDA
EMail: dbloom@mayerbrown.com

Employers
Mayer, Brown & Platt (Partner)

BLOOM, John L.
225 N. Manchester St.
Arlington, VA 22203
Tel: (703)276-6710
Fax: (703)276-6711
Registered: LDA

Employers
Self-employed as an independent consultant.

Clients Represented
As an independent consultant
American Cancer Soc.

BLOOM, Lauren M.
1100 17th St. NW
Seventh Floor
Washington, DC 20036
Tel: (202)223-8196
Fax: (202)872-1948
Registered: LDA

Employers
American Academy of Actuaries (General Counsel/Director, Professionalism)

BLOOMBERG, Mary Beth
1029 N. Royal St.
Suite 400
Alexandria, VA 22314
Tel: (703)684-1245
Fax: (703)684-1249
EMail: MBloomberg@directimpact.com

Employers
The Direct Impact Co. (Principal)

Clients Represented
On Behalf of The Direct Impact Co.
Nat'l Family Planning and Reproductive Health Ass'n

BLOOMFIELD, Douglas M.
13712 Wagon Way
Silver Spring, MD 20906
Tel: (301)460-3285
Fax: (301)460-4187
Registered: LDA
Held staff positions, U.S. Congress, 1971-80.

Employers
Bloomfield Associates, Inc. (President)

Clients Represented
On Behalf of Bloomfield Associates, Inc.
Kazakhstan 21st Century Foundation
T & N Industries
World Jewish Congress

BLOOMFIELD, Mark A.
1750 K St. NW
Suite 400
Washington, DC 20006-2300
Tel: (202)293-5811
Fax: (202)785-8165
Registered: LDA
EMail: MarkBloom@aol.com

Employers
American Council for Capital Formation (President)

BLOOMFIELD, Shirley A.
4121 Wilson Blvd.
Tenth Floor
Arlington, VA 22203
Tel: (703)351-2044
Fax: (703)351-2001
Registered: LDA
EMail: sbloomfield@ntca.org

Employers
Nat'l Telephone Cooperative Ass'n (V. President, Government Affairs and Association Services)

BLOOMQUIST, Michael D.
2550 M St. NW
Washington, DC 20037-1350
Tel: (202)457-6000
Fax: (202)457-6315
Registered: LDA
Former Member, Office of the Solicitor, Department of the Interior.

Employers
Patton Boggs, LLP (Associate)

Clients Represented
On Behalf of Patton Boggs, LLP
Wild Alabama

BLOUIN, Robert
1200 18th St. NW
Suite 400
Washington, DC 20036-2506
Tel: (202)783-9000
Fax: (202)331-8364

Employers
Nat'l Business Aviation Ass'n (Senior V. President, Operations)

BLOUNT, John
818 Connecticut Ave. NW
Suite 1100
Washington, DC 20006
Tel: (202)728-1010
Fax: (202)728-4044
Registered: LDA
Legislative Assistant to Rep. Bill Emerson (R-MO), 1980-83. Legislative Assistant to Rep. George William Whitehurst (R-VA), 1978-80.

Employers
The National Group, LLP (Partner)

Clients Represented
On Behalf of The National Group, LLP
Adventist Health System/Sunbelt, Inc.
Biotechnology Industry Organization
Bituminous Coal Operators Ass'n
Delta Air Lines

BLOWE, Felita
1015 15th St. NW
Suite 1100
Washington, DC 20005
Tel: (202)488-7000
Fax: (202)488-0806
Registered: LDA
EMail: fblowe@cwfa.org

Employers
Concerned Women for America (Legislative Coordinator)

BLUE, Christina
8484 Georgia Ave.
Suite 700
Silver Spring, MD 20910
Tel: (301)608-1552
Fax: (301)608-1557

Employers
Biscuit and Cracker Manufacturers Ass'n (Director, Government Relations)

BLUE, Chuck
1111 19th St. NW
Suite 403
Washington, DC 20036
Tel: (202)296-2237
Fax: (202)296-1151
EMail: cblue@aaes.org

Employers
American Ass'n of Engineering Societies (Director, Communications and Public Awareness)

BLUHM, Christopher

P.O. Box 31220
4720 Montgomery Ln.
Bethesda, MD 20824-1220
Tel: (301)652-2682
Fax: (301)652-7711

Employers
American Occupational Therapy Ass'n, Inc. (Assoc. Exec. Director for Business Operations Office)

BLUM, Carol

2000 M St. NW
Suite 400
Washington, DC 20036
Tel: (202)467-4999
Fax: (202)293-2672

Employers
People for the American Way (V. President and Chief Operating Officer)

BLUM, Charles H.

1707 L St. NW
Suite 725
Washington, DC 20036
Tel: (202)296-6625
Fax: (202)659-3904
Registered: LDA
EMail: iasg@erols.com
Assistant Trade Representative (1983-88), Deputy Assistant Trade Representative (1981-83), Director, Steel Trade Policy (1980-81), all in the office of the U.S. Trade Representative. Foreign Service Officer, Department of State, 1971-80.

Employers
Internat'l Advisory Services Group Ltd. (President)

Clients Represented

On Behalf of Internat'l Advisory Services Group Ltd.
European Confederation of Iron and Steel Industries (EUROFER)
Steel Service Center Institute

BLUM, Jared O.

1331 F St. NW
Suite 975
Washington, DC 20004
EMail: job@pima.org
Tel: (202)628-6558
Fax: (202)628-3856

Employers
Polyisocyanurate Insulation Manufacturers Ass'n (President)

BLUM, Jennifer L.

1500 K St.
Suite 1100
Washington, DC 20005
Tel: (202)842-8800
Fax: (202)842-8465
Registered: LDA

Employers
Drinker Biddle & Reath LLP

Clients Represented

On Behalf of Drinker Biddle & Reath LLP
The Hearst Corp.

BLUM, Maureen

1717 Pennsylvania Ave. NW
Suite 200
Washington, DC 20006
EMail: mblum@ij.org
Tel: (202)955-1300
Fax: (202)955-1329

Employers
Institute for Justice (Director, Outreach Programs)

BLUMA, Stephanie

1501 M St. NW
Suite 600
Washington, DC 20005-1710
Tel: (202)739-0200
Fax: (202)659-8287

Employers
BSMG Worldwide (Senior Associate)

BLUMENFELD, Sue D.

Three Lafayette Center
1155 21st St. NW
Washington, DC 20036-3384
Tel: (202)328-8000
Fax: (202)887-8979
Special Assistant to the Chief, Common Carrier Bureau, Federal Communications Commission, 1979-81. Attorney, Bureau of Competition, Federal Trade Commission, 1977-79.

Employers
Willkie Farr & Gallagher (Partner)

Clients Represented

On Behalf of Willkie Farr & Gallagher
Riverhead Community Development Agency
Sprint Corp.

BLUMENTHAL, Holly

1707 L St. NW
Suite 650
Washington, DC 20036
Tel: (202)955-5777
Fax: (202)955-4549

Employers
The Steel Alliance (Manager, Communications)

BLUMENTHAL, Patricia

400 Seventh St. SW
MS: 10100
Washington, DC 20590
Tel: (202)366-4687
Fax: (202)366-7153

Employers
Department of Transportation (Assistant, Legislative Reference)

BLUMER, Patti R.

1350 I St. NW
Suite 1030
Washington, DC 20005-3305
Tel: (202)682-1280
Fax: (202)682-1412
Registered: LDA
EMail: blumer.patti@principal.com

Employers
Principal Financial Group (Assistant Federal Legislative Director)

BOARDMAN, Ellen O.

4748 Wisconsin Ave. NW
Washington, DC 20016
Tel: (202)362-0041

Employers
O'Donoghue & O'Donoghue

BOAZ, David D.

1000 Massachusetts Ave. NW
Washington, DC 20001
Tel: (202)842-0200
Fax: (202)842-3490

Employers
Cato Institute (Exec. V. President)

BOBBITT, Douglass E.

700 13th St. NW
Suite 400
Washington, DC 20005
Tel: (202)347-0773
Fax: (202)347-0785
Registered: LDA, FARA
EMail: dbobbitt@cassidy.com
Office of Commissioner of Customs and Office of the Secretary of the Treasury, 1984-90. Associate Staff Member, House Committee on Appropriations, 1975-81; Minority Staff, 1981-84.

Employers
Cassidy & Associates, Inc. (Senior V. President)

Clients Represented

On Behalf of Cassidy & Associates, Inc.
Crane & Co.
D'Youville College
Forum Health
Immaculata College
Internat'l Snowmobile Manufacturers Ass'n
Philadelphia College of Osteopathic Medicine
Philadelphia College of Textiles and Science
Philadelphia University
Pierce College
Subaru of America
Tiffany & Co.
University of Dubuque
Wheelchairs for the World Foundation
Widener University

BOBBITT, Jane

1420 New York Ave. NW
Suite 1050
Washington, DC 20005
Tel: (202)638-1950
Fax: (202)638-7714
Registered: LDA

Employers
Van Scoyoc Associates, Inc.

Clients Represented

On Behalf of Van Scoyoc Associates, Inc.
University of North Carolina at Chapel Hill

BOCCHI, Gregory J.

2121 Eisenhower Ave.
Suite 401
Alexandria, VA 22314
Tel: (703)684-1770
Fax: (703)684-1771

Employers
Powder Coating Institute (Exec. Director)

BOCCHINO, Carmella A.

1129 20th St. NW
Suite 600
Washington, DC 20036-3421
EMail: cbocchino@aahp.org
Tel: (202)778-3200
Fax: (202)778-8479
Registered: LDA

Employers
American Ass'n of Health Plans (AAHP) (Medical Director)

BOCK, Eric P.

1020 19th St. NW
Suite 400
Washington, DC 20036
Tel: (202)331-9100
Fax: (202)331-9060
Registered: LDA

Employers
Baise + Miller, P.C. (Partner)

Clients Represented

On Behalf of Baise + Miller, P.C.
California Refuse Removal Council
Ice Ban America, Inc.
Martinizing Environmental Group
Norcal Waste Systems, Inc.
Solid Waste Ass'n of North America
West Coast Refuse and Recycling Coalition

BOCKORNY, David A.

1101 16th St. NW
Suite 500
Washington, DC 20036
Tel: (202)659-9111
Fax: (202)659-6387
Registered: LDA, FARA
Special Assistant to the President for Legislative Affairs, The White House, during the Reagan administration.

Employers
Bergner Bockorny Castagnetti and Hawkins (Chairman)

Clients Represented

On Behalf of Bergner Bockorny Castagnetti and Hawkins
AdvaMed
Agilent Technologies
American Bankers Ass'n
American Hospital Ass'n
Biogen, Inc.
The Boeing Co.
Bristol-Myers Squibb Co.
Business Executives for Nat'l Security
Cerner Corp.
Chicago Board Options Exchange
Computer Coalition for Responsible Exports
Dell Computer Corp.
Elanco Animal Health
Everglades Defense Council
First Health Group Corp.
GlaxoSmithKline
Hewlett-Packard Co.
Lucent Technologies
Medtronic, Inc.
Monsanto Co.
Nat'l Ass'n of Real Estate Investment Trusts
Nat'l Soft Drink Ass'n
News Corporation Ltd.
Northwest Airlines, Inc.
Ovations/United Health Group
Petroleum Marketers Ass'n of America
Philip Morris Management Corp.
Premium Standard Farms
Qwest Communications
Taipei Economic and Cultural Representative Office in the United States
UDV North America, Inc.

BODAKEN, Michael

1101 30th St. NW
Suite 400
Washington, DC 20007
EMail: mbodaken@nhtinc.org
Tel: (202)333-8931
Fax: (202)833-1031
Registered: LDA

Employers
Nat'l Housing Trust (President)

BODDE, Jr., William

1819 L St. NW
2nd Floor
Washington, DC 20036
EMail: billbodde@aol.com
Tel: (202)293-1093
Fax: (202)289-1940

Employers
Pacific Basin Economic Council - U.S. Member Committee (Special Advisor)

Clients Represented
On Behalf of Bode & Grenier LLP
The Environmental Business Ass'n
Independent Terminal Operators Ass'n
Mount Airy Refining Co.
Peerless Petrochemicals, Inc.
Petrojam Ltd.
Shepherd Oil Co.
Superfund Action Coalition

BODDIE, Judith Ann

701 Pennsylvania Ave. NW
Washington, DC 20004-2696
Tel: (202)508-5469
Fax: (202)508-5403
Registered: LDA

Employers
Edison Electric Institute (Senior Governmental Affairs Representative)

BODE, Holly A.

1801 K St. NW
Suite 901-L
Washington, DC 20006
EMail: holly_bode@bm.com
Tel: (202)530-0500
Fax: (202)530-4800
Registered: LDA

Special Assistant to the Deputy Assistant Secretary for Legislation (Health), Office of the Assistant Secretary for Legislation, Department of Health and Human Services, 1994-99. Health Care Advisor to Rep. Sander Levin (D-MI), 1993-94. Staff Member, Senate Special Committee on Aging, 1986-93.

Employers
BKSH & Associates (Director)

BODE, John W.

1400 16th St. NW
Suite 400
Washington, DC 20036-2220
EMail: jbode@ofwlaw.com
Tel: (202)518-6323
Fax: (202)234-1560
Registered: LDA

Assistant Secretary for Food and Consumer Services, Department of Agriculture, 1985-89.

Employers
Olsson, Frank and Weeda, P.C. (Principal)

Clients Represented
On Behalf of Olsson, Frank and Weeda, P.C.
Adheris, Inc.
American Academy of Audiology
American Commodity Distribution Ass'n
American School Food Service Ass'n
Ass'n of Medical Device Reprocessors
Aventis Pasteur
Beef Products, Inc.
California Canning Peach Ass'n
Chocolate Manufacturers Ass'n of the U.S.A.
Duramed Pharmaceuticals, Inc.
Food Distributors Internat'l (NAWGA-IFDA)
General Mills
Gentrac Inc.
Health Resource Publishing Co.
Institute of Food Technologists
Kraft Foods, Inc.
Lower Brule Sioux Tribe
Mead Johnson Nutritional Group
Nat'l Ass'n of Margarine Manufacturers
Nat'l Ass'n of Pharmaceutical Manufacturers
Nat'l Coalition of Food Importers Ass'n
Nat'l Confectioners Ass'n
Nat'l Food Processors Ass'n
Nat'l Frozen Pizza Institute
Nat'l Meat Ass'n
PennField Oil Co.
Philip Morris Management Corp.
The Pillsbury Co.
San Tomo Group
Schwan's Sales Enterprises
SteriGenics Internat'l
Titan Scan
Transhumance Holding Co., Inc.
United Fresh Fruit and Vegetable Ass'n
Urner Barry Publications, Inc.

BODE, William H.

1150 Connecticut Ave. NW
Suite 900
Washington, DC 20036-4182
Tel: (202)828-4100
Fax: (202)828-4130

Employers
Bode & Grenier LLP (Partner)
The Environmental Business Ass'n (President)

BODNER, James M.

600 13th St. NW
Suite 640
Washington, DC 20005-3096
EMail: jmb@cohengroup.net
Tel: (202)756-8500
Fax: (202)756-8510

Deputy Under Secretary for Policy, U.S. Department of Defense, 1997-2001.

Employers
The Cohen Group (Senior V. President)

BODORFF, Richard

1776 K St. NW
Washington, DC 20006
Tel: (202)719-7000
Fax: (202)719-7049
Registered: LDA

Employers
Wiley, Rein & Fielding

Clients Represented
On Behalf of Wiley, Rein & Fielding
Hearst-Argyle Television, Inc.

BOEHM, Kenneth F.

103 W. Broad St.
Suite 620
Falls Church, VA 22046
Tel: (703)237-1970
Fax: (703)237-2090

Employers
Nat'l Legal & Policy Center (Chairman)

BOEHM, Manuela

1225 New York Ave. NW
Suite 475
Washington, DC 20005
Tel: (202)371-1303
Fax: (202)371-5569

Employers
United Health Group (PAC Contact)

BOEKE, Elinore

818 Connecticut Ave. NW
Second Floor
Washington, DC 20006
EMail: eboeke@stratacomm.net
Tel: (202)289-2001
Fax: (202)289-1327

Employers
Strat@Comm (Strategic Communications Counselors) (Account Executive)

Clients Represented
On Behalf of Strat@Comm (Strategic Communications Counselors)
Wine and Spirits Wholesalers of America

BOESCH, Doyce A.

1001 Pennsylvania Ave. NW
Suite 850 North
Washington, DC 20004
EMail: doyceboesch@aol.com
Tel: (202)347-2222
Fax: (202)347-4242
Registered: LDA

Former Chief of Staff to Senator Don Nickles (R-OK).

Employers
Boesch & Co. (President)

Clients Represented
On Behalf of Boesch & Co.
AT&T
The Business Roundtable
Children's Health Fund
Huron Hospital
Integris Health Systems
NetCoalition.Com
O'Gara-Hess & Eisenhardt
Oracle Corp.
Public Policy Partners
Sabre Inc.
Stockton East Water District
U.S. Filter
University of Oklahoma

BOFFA, John

733 15th St. NW
Suite 500
Washington, DC 20005
Tel: (202)466-6977
Fax: (202)637-9825
Registered: FARA

Employers
Boffa & Associates, Inc. (President)

Clients Represented
On Behalf of Boffa & Associates, Inc.
Internet Internat'l Trade Council

BOGART, Jennifer

1200 Trinity Dr.
Alexandria, VA 22314
Tel: (703)823-8674
Fax: (703)823-2628

Employers
Bogart Associates Inc. (President)

Clients Represented
On Behalf of Bogart Associates Inc.
Ripon Society

BOGER, William H.

1120 20th St. NW
Suite 800
Washington, DC 20036
Tel: (202)778-6150
Fax: (202)778-6155
Registered: LDA

Employers
Bingham Dana LLP

Clients Represented
On Behalf of Bingham Dana LLP
Fleet Financial Group, Inc.
FleetBoston Financial

BOGGS, Brent

Ten G St. NE
Suite 480
Washington, DC 20002
Tel: (202)347-7936
Fax: (202)347-5237

Employers
Brotherhood of Locomotive Engineers (PAC Contact)

BOGGS, George R.

One Dupont Circle NW
Suite 410
Washington, DC 20036
EMail: gboggs@aacc.nche.edu
Tel: (202)728-0200
Fax: (202)833-2467

Employers
American Ass'n of Community Colleges (President)

BOGGS, III, J. Caleb

900 17th St. NW
Suite 1000
Washington, DC 20006
EMail: boggs@blankrome.com
Tel: (202)530-7475
Fax: (202)530-7476
Registered: LDA

Republican Counsel, Senate Committee on Governmental Affairs, 1991-95. Staff Counsel, Senate Permanent Subcommittee on Investigations, 1991.

Employers
Blank Rome Comisky & McCauley, LLP (Of Counsel)

Clients Represented
On Behalf of Blank Rome Comisky & McCauley, LLP
Countrywide Home Loans, Inc.
Federal Nat'l Payables, Inc.
The Nat'l Foundation for Teaching Entrepreneurship
On-Line Investment Services

BOGGS, Larry A.

1299 Pennsylvania Ave. NW
Suite 1100 West
Washington, DC 20004-2407
Tel: (202)637-4000
Fax: (202)637-4006
Registered: LDA

Employers
General Electric Co. (Counsel, Environmental, Legislative and Regulatory Affairs)

BOGGS, Michael D.

905 16th St. NW
Washington, DC 20006
Tel: (202)737-8320
Fax: (202)737-2754

Employers
Laborers' Internat'l Union of North America (Director, International Affairs)

BOGGS, Jr., Thomas Hale

2550 M St. NW
Washington, DC 20037-1350
Tel: (202)457-6000
Fax: (202)457-6315
Registered: LDA, FARA
EMail: tboggs@pattonboggs.com
Coordinator, National Defense Executive Reserve, Executive Office of the President, The White House, 1965-66. Economist, Joint Economic Committee, 1961-65.

Employers
Patton Boggs, LLP (Chair, Executive Committee)

Clients Represented

On Behalf of Patton Boggs, LLP
Aera Energy LLC
African Coalition for Trade, Inc.
Alcatel
American Advertising Federation
American Ass'n of Advertising Agencies
American Trans Air
AOL Time Warner
Ass'n of Nat'l Advertisers
Ass'n of Trial Lawyers of America
BNFL, Inc.
Bristol-Myers Squibb Co.
Commco, L.L.C.
L. P. Conwood Co.
DFS Group Ltd.
Direct Marketing Ass'n, Inc.
Dole Food Co.
Elf Aquitine
European Energy Company Coalition
FM Watch
H.A.H. of Wisconsin L.P.
Hitachi Home Electronics, Inc.
Internat'l Swaps and Derivatives Dealers Ass'n
Magazine Publishers of America
Mars, Inc.
Matsushita Electric Corp. of America
MCI WorldCom Corp.
Midcoast Interstate Transmission, Inc.
Mitsubishi Electronics America (Consumer Electronics Group)
Nat'l Automatic Merchandising Ass'n
Nat'l Cable Television Ass'n
Nat'l Center for Manufacturing Sciences
Newspaper Ass'n of America
Outdoor Advertising Ass'n of America
The Pacific Lumber Co.
Pioneer of North America
Point of Purchase Advertising Institute
Sanyo North American Corp.
Sharp Electronics Corp.
Shell Oil Co.
Sierra Military Health Services, Inc.
The Charles E. Smith Companies
Sony Electronics, Inc.
Swan Creek River Confederated Ojibbwa Tribes of Michigan
Teligent, Inc.
Time Domain Corp.
Toshiba Consumer Products, Inc.
Travel Industry Ass'n of America
Union Pacific Railroad Co.
United Airlines
US Airways
Ventura County Citizens Against Radar Emissions (VCCARE)
Walton Enterprises
WQED Pittsburgh

BOGGS, Virginia R.

901 15th St. NW
Suite 700
Washington, DC 20005-2301
Tel: (202)371-6000
Fax: (202)371-6279
Registered: LDA

Employers
Verner, Liipfert, Bernhard, McPherson and Hand, Chartered (Associate)

Clients Represented

On Behalf of Verner, Liipfert, Bernhard, McPherson and Hand, Chartered
Bacardi-Martini, USA, Inc.
Merrill Lynch & Co., Inc.
Starwood Lodging/Starwood Capital Group, L.P.
Stewart & Stevenson Services, Inc.

BOGORAD, Cindy S.

1350 New York Ave. NW
Suite 1100
Washington, DC 20005-4798
Tel: (202)879-4000
Fax: (202)393-2866
Registered: LDA
EMail: bogoradc@spiegelmcd.com

Employers
Spiegel & McDiarmid (Partner)

Clients Represented

On Behalf of Spiegel & McDiarmid
Transmission Access Policy Study Group

BOGOSIAN, Joseph H.

1050 Connecticut Ave. NW
Suite 1200
Washington, DC 20036
Tel: (202)857-1700
Fax: (202)857-1737
Registered: LDA, FARA
EMail: jhbogosi@mwcllc.com
Former Staff Member, International Relations Committee, U.S. House of Representatives and Legislative Aide to Rep. James J. Howard (D-NJ).

Employers
McGuireWoods L.L.P. (V. President, McGuire Woods Consulting, LLC)

Clients Represented

On Behalf of McGuireWoods L.L.P.
Allegiance Healthcare Corp.
Center for Governmental Studies of the University of Virginia
CSX Corp.
Fibrowatt, Inc.
Financial Services Council
Huntington Sanitary Board
Korea, Embassy of
University of Miami
Wheeling, West Virginia, City of

BOGREN, Scott

1341 G St. NW
Tenth Floor
Washington, DC 20005
Tel: (202)628-1480
Fax: (202)737-9197
EMail: bogren@ctaa.org

Employers
Community Transportation Ass'n of America (Associate Director, Communications)

BOHANNON, Mark

1730 M St. NW
Suite 700
Washington, DC 20036-4510
Tel: (202)452-1600
Fax: (202)223-8756
Registered: LDA

Employers
Software & Information Industry Ass'n (SIIA)

BOHANON, Chris

4301 Wilson Blvd.
Arlington, VA 22203--186
Tel: (703)907-5829
Fax: (703)907-5516
Registered: LDA
EMail: chris.bohanon@nreca.org

Employers
Nat'l Rural Electric Cooperative Ass'n (Representative, Lesgislative Affairs)

BOHLEN, Curtis

1010 Wisconsin Ave.
Suite 200
Washington, DC 20007
Tel: (202)333-9075
Fax: (202)333-9077

Employers
Nat'l Wildlife Refuge Ass'n (Chairman of the Board)

BOHLEN, Larry

1025 Vermont Ave. NW
Third Floor
Washington, DC 20005
Tel: (202)783-7400
Ext: 251
Fax: (202)783-0444
EMail: lbohlen@foe.org

Employers
Friends of the Earth (Director, Community Health and Environmental Programs)

BOHLKE, Gary

1667 K St. NW
Suite 700
Washington, DC 20006
Tel: (202)776-7800
Fax: (202)776-7801
EMail: glbohlke@duanemorris.com
Associate General Counsel, Office of the General Counsel, Farm Credit Administration, 1988-91. Assistant Solicitor and Senior Attorney, Office of the Solicitor, Department of the Interior, 1974-88. Attorney-Advisor, Office of the General Counsel, Corps of Engineers, Department of the Army, Department of Defense, 1972-74.

Employers
Duane, Morris & Heckscher LLP (Partner)

BOHN, Donald W.

1350 I St. NW
Suite 1210
Washington, DC 20005-3305
Tel: (202)589-1016
Fax: (202)589-1001
Registered: LDA

Employers
Johnson & Johnson, Inc. (Exec. Director, Federal Affairs and Reimbursement)

BOIAGIAN, Mindi

1201 F St. NW
Suite 200
Washington, DC 20004
Tel: (202)554-9000
Fax: (202)554-0496

Employers
Nat'l Federation of Independent Business (Director, Media Communications)

BOIDOCK, John K.

1455 Pennsylvania Ave. NW
Suite 375
M/S 4072
Washington, DC 20004
Tel: (202)628-3133
Fax: (202)628-2980
Registered: LDA
EMail: jboidock@ti.com

Employers
Texas Instruments (V. President, Government Relations)

BOISCLAIR, Jon L.

1350 I St. NW
Suite 680
Washington, DC 20005-3305
Tel: (202)393-4841
Fax: (202)393-5596
EMail: bosco@advocacy.com

Employers
The Advocacy Group

Clients Represented

On Behalf of The Advocacy Group
Consumer Electronics Ass'n
Detroit Internat'l Bridge Co./The Ambassador Bridge
Minnesota Life Insurance Co.
TCF Financial Corp.

BOISTURE, Robert A.

One Thomas Circle NW
Suite 1100
Washington, DC 20005
Tel: (202)862-5070
Fax: (202)429-3301
Registered: LDA
EMail: rab@capdale.com

Employers
Caplin & Drysdale, Chartered (Member)

Clients Represented

On Behalf of Caplin & Drysdale, Chartered
Council on Foundations
Independent Sector

BOK, Derek

1250 Connecticut Ave. NW
Washington, DC 20036
Tel: (202)833-1200
Fax: (202)659-3716

Employers
Common Cause (Chairman)

BOKAT, Stephen A.

1615 H St. NW
Washington, DC 20062-2000
Tel: (202)463-5337
Fax: (202)463-5346
EMail: sbokat@uschamber.com

Employers
Chamber of Commerce of the U.S.A. (V. President and General Counsel)

BOLAND, Christopher T.

1023 15th St. NW
Suite 900
Washington, DC 20005-2602
Tel: (202)289-7200
Fax: (202)289-7698
EMail: cboland@gbmdc.com
Staff Director, Senate Committee on Atomic Energy; Counsel-Staff Director, Joint Congressional Committee on Atomic Energy, 1945-47.

Employers
Gallagher, Boland and Meiburger (Senior Counsel)

BOLAND, Jr., James E.

1155 Connecticut Ave. NW
Suite 300
Washington, DC 20036
Tel: (202)467-8507
Fax: (202)544-7467
Registered: LDA

Former General Counsel, Senate Banking, Housing and Urban Affairs Committee.

Employers
Self-employed as an independent consultant.

Clients Represented
As an independent consultant
Compaq Computer Corp.
Federal Home Loan Mortgage Corp. (Freddie Mac)
The Limited Inc.
Morgan Stanley Dean Witter & Co.
Waste Management, Inc.

BOLAND, Michael

1300 I St. NW
Suite 400 West
Washington, DC 20005
Tel: (202)515-2400
Fax: (202)336-7921

Chief Counsel and Floor Assistant to the House Republican Whip, Rep. Trent Lott (R-MS), 1985-87. Senior Counsel, House Energy and Commerce Committee, 1978-84.

Employers
Verizon Communications (Senior V. President, Federal Legislative Affairs)

BOLDEN, Darwin K.

1725 Jefferson Davis Hwy.
Crystal Square 2, Suite 300
Arlington, VA 22202
Tel: (703)413-5600
Fax: (703)413-5613

Employers
Lockheed Martin Corp. (Government Relations Representative)

BOLEN, Edward M.

1400 K St. NW
Suite 801
Washington, DC 20005-2485
Tel: (202)393-1500
Fax: (202)842-4063
Registered: LDA

Employers
General Aviation Manufacturers Ass'n (President)

BOLES, Anita Lacy

801 Pennsylvania Ave. NW
Suite 230
Washington, DC 20004
EMail: abole@bradleyarant.com
Tel: (202)393-7173
Fax: (202)347-1684
Registered: LDA

Former Chief of Staff and Chief Information Officer, Merit Systems Protection Board, 1993-2000; Chief of Staff, Rep. Ben Erdreich (D-AL), 1983-93.

Employers
Bradley Arant Rose & White LLP (Director, Government Affairs)

BOLGER, David A.

1401 H St. NW
Suite 600
Washington, DC 20005-2136
Tel: (202)326-7300
Fax: (202)326-7333

Employers
United States Telecom Ass'n (V. President, Communications)

BOLGER, Glen

277 S. Washington St.
Suite 320
Alexandria, VA 22314
EMail: gbolger@pos.org
Tel: (703)836-7655
Fax: (703)836-8117

Employers
Public Opinion Strategies (Partner)

Clients Represented
On Behalf of Public Opinion Strategies
Cellular Telecommunications and Internet Ass'n

BOLICK, Clint

1717 Pennsylvania Ave. NW
Suite 200
Washington, DC 20006
EMail: cbolick@ij.org
Tel: (202)955-1300
Fax: (202)955-1329

Employers
Institute for Justice (V. President and Director, Litigation)

BOLICK, Gary M.

325 Seventh St. NW
Suite 1200
Washington, DC 20004-1007
Tel: (202)783-7070
Fax: (202)347-2044

Employers
Pfizer, Inc. (Director, State Government Relations)

BOLLINGER, John

801 18th St. NW
Washington, DC 20006
Tel: (202)872-1300
Fax: (202)785-4452

Employers
Paralyzed Veterans of America (Deputy Exec. Director)

BOLLON, Vincent J.

1750 New York Ave. NW
Washington, DC 20006
Tel: (202)737-8484
Fax: (202)737-8418

Employers
Internat'l Ass'n of Fire Fighters (General Secretary-Treasurer)

BOLLT, Anita

1828 L St. NW
Suite 625
Washington, DC 20036
EMail: anita@womens-health.org
Tel: (202)496-5005
Fax: (202)833-3472

Employers
Soc. for Women's Health Research (Deputy Director)

BOLTE, Karin

888 17th St. NW
Suite 800
Washington, DC 20006
EMail: kbolte@heimag.com
Tel: (202)822-8060
Fax: (202)822-9088
Registered: LDA

Employers
Heidepriem & Mager, Inc. (Associate)

Clients Represented
On Behalf of Heidepriem & Mager, Inc.
American Home Products Corp.
Cytyc Corp.
Pharmacia Corp.
R2 Technology, Inc.
Wyeth-Ayerst Laboratories

BOLTON, John R.

1150 17th St. NW
Washington, DC 20036
EMail: jbolton@aei.org
Tel: (202)862-5800
Fax: (202)862-7177

Employers
American Enterprise Institute for Public Policy Research (Senior V. President)

BOMAR, Ernest

4900-B S. 31st St.
Arlington, VA 22206
Tel: (703)820-7400
Fax: (703)931-4520

Employers
Ass'n and Government Relations Management, Inc. (V. President)

BOMAR, Nora

6903 Rockledge Dr.
Suite 730
Bethesda, MD 20817
Tel: (301)272-2320
Fax: (301)272-2369

Employers
EMC Corp. (Manager, Government Affairs)

BOMBERG, Neil

440 First St. NW
Eighth Floor
Washington, DC 20001
EMail: nbomberg@naco.org
Tel: (202)942-4205
Fax: (202)942-4281

Employers
Nat'l Ass'n of Counties (Associate Legislative Director, Employment and Training)
Nat'l Ass'n of County Training and Employment Professionals (Contact)

BONAR, Jennifer

2001 M St. NW
Washington, DC 20036
Tel: (202)467-3000
Fax: (202)533-8500
Registered: LDA

Employers
KPMG, LLP

Clients Represented
On Behalf of KPMG, LLP
The KPMG FSC Coalition
Nat'l Council of Farmer Cooperatives

BOND, Brian

1012 14th St. NW
Suite 1000
Washington, DC 20005
EMail: victoryf@aol.com
Tel: (202)842-8679
Fax: (202)289-3863

Employers
Gay and Lesbian Victory Fund (Exec. Director)

BOND, Dennis

1750 New York Ave. NW
Washington, DC 20006
Tel: (202)637-0700
Fax: (202)637-0771
Registered: LDA

Employers
Internat'l Union of Painters and Allied Trades

BOND, Irene R.

801 Pennsylvania Ave.
Suite 650
Washington, DC 20004
EMail: irene.r.bond@aezp.com
Tel: (202)624-0761
Fax: (202)624-0775

Employers
American Express Co. (Manager, Government Affairs)

BOND, James D.

2111 Wilson Blvd.
Suite 700
Arlington, VA 22201
Tel: (703)351-5058
Fax: (703)522-1738
Registered: LDA

Clerk, Senate Committee on Appropriations, 1972-97.

Employers
Collins & Company, Inc. (Exec. V. President)

Clients Represented
On Behalf of Collins & Company, Inc.
The Boeing Co.
Citizens Network for Foreign Affairs (CNFA)
Derry Investment Initiatives
EarthData Holdings
Hawaii Economic Development Alliance, State of
Internat'l Agriculture and Rural Development Group
Internat'l Fund for Agricultural Development
Loral Space and Communications, Ltd.
Mari-Flite Ferries, Inc.
Marquette University
Nat'l Telephone Cooperative Ass'n
NewMarket Global Consulting Group
Northrop Grumman Corp.
Oracle Corp.
Pacific Marine
PADCO, Inc.
Population Action Internat'l
Science Applications Internat'l Corp. (SAIC)
Solipsys Corp.
Textron Systems Division
Trex Enterprises

BOND, Jill

2120 L St. NW
Suite 400
Washington, DC 20037
EMail: jbond@lharris.com
Tel: (202)478-6185
Fax: (202)478-6171
Registered: LDA

Employers
Leslie Harris & Associates (Managing Director and V. President, Strategic Initiatives)

Clients Represented
On Behalf of Leslie Harris & Associates
AOL Time Warner
EdLinc
Leadership Conference on Civil Rights
Verizon Communications

BOND, Langhorne M.

1615 L St. NW
Suite 1200
Washington, DC 20036
Tel: (202)466-6300
Fax: (202)463-0678

Employers
Bell, Boyd & Lloyd (Of Counsel)

BOND, Phil

900 17th St. NW
Suite 1100
Washington, DC 20006
EMail: phil_bond@hp.com
Tel: (202)884-7041
Fax: (202)884-7070
Registered: LDA

Employers
Hewlett-Packard Co. (Director, Federal Public Policy)

BOND, Richard N.

919 Prince St.
Alexandria, VA 22314
Tel: (703)684-6098
Fax: (703)684-7138
Registered: LDA
Former Deputy Chief of Staff to the V. President, The White House, during the Reagan administration.

Employers
Bond & Company, Inc. (Chairman)

Clients Represented
On Behalf of Bond & Company, Inc.
The Century Council
Hackensack University Medical Center Foundation
HCR-Manor Care, Inc.
Northeast Utilities
openNET Coalition
Service Employees Internat'l Union
United Brotherhood of Carpenters and Joiners of America

BOND-COLLINS, Rhonda

1101 Connecticut Ave. NW
Suite 1000
Washington, DC 20036
Tel: (202)828-2400
Fax: (202)828-2488
Registered: LDA

Employers
Kutak Rock LLP

Clients Represented
On Behalf of Kutak Rock LLP
Alameda, California, City of
Highland Park, Illinois, City of Highwood Local Redevelopment Authority and the City of
Seaside, California, City of
Tustin, California, City of

BONDAREFF, Joan

600 New Hampshire Ave. NW
11th Floor
Washington, DC 20037
Tel: (202)944-3000
Fax: (202)944-3068
Registered: LDA
Former Chief Counsel and Acting Deputy Administrator, Maritime Administration, Department of Transportation. Former Senior Counsel, House Committee on Merchant Marine and Fisheries.

Employers
Dyer Ellis & Joseph, P.C. (Counsel)
The Spectrum Group (Transportation Principal)

Clients Represented
On Behalf of Dyer Ellis & Joseph, P.C.
FastShip, Inc.
Offshore Rig Museum, Inc.
On Behalf of The Spectrum Group
ADSI Inc.
Everett, Washington, Port of
Nat'l Health Care Access Coalition
Tri-City Regional Port District

BONDERUD, Kevin J.

1825 Connecticut Ave. NW
Fifth Floor
Washington, DC 20009
EMail: kevin.bonderud@widmeyer.com
Tel: (202)667-0901
Fax: (202)667-0902
Press Secretary to Rep. Martin Sabo (D-MN), 1981-90.

Employers
Widmeyer Communications, Inc. (Senior V. President/Group Director)

Clients Represented
On Behalf of Widmeyer Communications, Inc.
Education Communications, Inc.
Kids in the Know
Nat'l Research Center for College and University Admissions

BONDS, Andrew

1133 15th St. NW
Suite 800
Washington, DC 20005
Fax: (202)775-6005

Employers
Parsons Corp. (V. President, Government Relations)

BONFIGLIO, Barbara Wixon

1155 21st St. NW
Suite 300
Washington, DC 20036
EMail: bwbonfiglio@wms-jen.com
Tel: (202)659-8201
Fax: (202)659-5249
Registered: LDA
Former Hearing Examiner, Board of Contract Appeals, Army Corps of Engineers.

Employers
Arena PAC (Treasurer)
Common Sense Common Solutions PAC
Williams & Jensen, P.C. (Partner)

Clients Represented
On Behalf of Williams & Jensen, P.C.
Arena PAC
Human Rights Campaign

BONFINI, Jeremy

1634 I St. NW
Suite 300
Washington, DC 20006
Tel: (202)626-4393
Fax: (202)628-2525

Employers
Intel Corp. (Government Relations Manager)

BONGIORNO, Phillip

1350 I St. NW
Suite 590
Washington, DC 20005
EMail: pbongio@cap.org
Tel: (202)354-7113
Fax: (202)354-7155

Employers
College of American Pathologists (Policy Analyst, Professional Affairs)

BONILLA, Manuel E.

1101 Vermont Ave. NW
Suite 606
Washington, DC 20005
EMail: m.bonilla@asawash.org
Tel: (202)289-2222
Fax: (202)371-0384
Registered: LDA

Employers
American Soc. of Anesthesiologists (Associate Director, Federal)

BONITATI, Robert

1199 N. Fairfax St.
Suite 1000
Alexandria, VA 22314
EMail: rbonitati@hawthorngroup.com
Tel: (703)299-4499
Fax: (703)299-4488

Employers
The Hawthorn Group, L.C. (Senior V. President)

Clients Represented
On Behalf of The Hawthorn Group, L.C.
Salt River Project

BONITT, John E.

555 12th St. NW
Suite 650
Washington, DC 20004-1205
Tel: (202)393-7950
Fax: (202)393-7960
Registered: LDA

Employers
Eli Lilly and Co. (Director, Federal Affairs)

BONK, Kathy

1200 New York Ave. NW
Suite 300
Washington, DC 20005
EMail: kbonk@ccmc.org
Tel: (202)326-8700
Fax: (202)682-2154

Employers
Communications Consortium (President and Chief Exec. Officer)

BONKER, Hon. Don L.

1615 L St. NW
Suite 900
Washington, DC 20036
EMail: dbonker@apcoworldwide.com
Tel: (202)778-1000
Fax: (202)466-6002
Registered: LDA, FARA
Member, House of Representatives (D-WA), 1975-89.

Employers
APCO Worldwide (Exec. V. President)
Internat'l Management and Development Institute (President and Chief Exec. Officer)
Parliamentary Human Rights Foundation (President)

Clients Represented
On Behalf of APCO Worldwide
COSCO Americas Inc.
Holy Land Trust
India, Government of the Republic of
Most Group Limited
Orcon Corp.
Ukraine, Government of

BONNER, Jack

1101 17th St. NW
Eighth Floor
Washington, DC 20036
Tel: (202)463-8880
Fax: (202)833-3584
Executive Assistant and Press Secretary to Senator John Heinz (R-PA), 1979-82.

Employers
Bonner & Associates (President)

BONNER, Mary Pat

729 15th St. NW
Third Floor
Washington, DC 20005
Tel: (202)737-5877
Fax: (202)737-6061

Employers
Bonner Group, Inc. (President)

BONNER, Sandy Cohen

1101 17th St. NW
Eighth Floor
Washington, DC 20036
Tel: (202)463-8880
Fax: (202)833-3584
Former Legislative Assistant to Senator John Heinz (R-PA), 1982-84; Attorney, Office of Special Counsel, U.S. Merit Systems Protection Board, 1979-80.

Employers
Bonner & Associates (General Counsel)

BONOSARO, Carol A.

P.O. Box 44808
Washington, DC 20026-4808
Tel: (202)927-7000
Fax: (202)927-5192

Employers
Senior Executives Ass'n (President)

BONTEMPO, Lisa

1101 17th St. NW
Suite 1004
Washington, DC 20036
EMail: lbontempo@dc.npga.org
Tel: (202)466-7200
Fax: (202)466-7205
Registered: LDA

Employers
Nat'l Propane Gas Ass'n (Director, Legislative Affairs)

BOOHER, Jr., C. William

11 Canal Center Plaza
Suite 110
Alexandria, VA 22314
Tel: (703)548-0280
Registered: LDA
Deputy Assistant Secretary, Technology Policy, Department of Commerce, 1991-98.

Employers
Booher & Associates (Principal)

Clients Represented
On Behalf of Booher & Associates
Foundation for Veterans' Health Care
Nat'l Ass'n of VA Physicians and Dentists

BOOKBINDER, Ronald B.

1050 17th St. NW
Suite 410
Washington, DC 20036
Tel: (202)296-8537
Fax: (202)872-1212
Registered: LDA

Employers
Japan Automobile Manufacturers Ass'n (Director, Government Affairs)

BOONE, Jeannie M.

1620 I St. NW
Suite 615
Washington, DC 20006
Tel: (202)463-8493
Fax: (202)463-8497
Registered: LDA
EMail: jboone@moinc.com

Office of Europe and the Mediterranean, Office of the United States Trade Representative, Executive Office of the President, The White House, 1996-97.

Employers
JBC Internat'l (Exec. Administrator)

Clients Represented

On Behalf of JBC Internat'l
California Ass'n of Winegrape Growers
DIAGEO
UDV/Heublein, Inc.
Wine Institute

BOONE, Linda

333 1/2 Pennsylvania Ave. SE
Washington, DC 20003-1148
Tel: (202)546-1969
Fax: (202)546-2063
Registered: LDA

Employers
Nat'l Coalition for Homeless Veterans (Exec. Director)

BOONE, Jr., Robert E.

1776 K St. NW
Washington, DC 20006
Tel: (202)719-7000
Fax: (202)719-7049

Employers
Wiley, Rein & Fielding (Of Counsel)

BOONE, Senny

1010 N. Glebe Rd.
Suite 450
Arlington, VA 22201
Tel: (703)907-7900
Fax: (703)907-7901
EMail: sboone@nna.org

Employers
Nat'l Newspaper Ass'n (V. President and General Counsel)

BOOS, Michael

4101 Chain Bridge Rd.
Suite 312
Fairfax, VA 22030
Tel: (703)352-4788
Fax: (703)591-2505

Employers
Citizens United (V. President)

BOOTH, Carri

1420 New York Ave. NW
Suite 1050
Washington, DC 20005
Tel: (202)638-1950
Fax: (202)638-7714
Registered: LDA

Former Deputy Legislative Assistant to Senator Conrad Burns (R-MT).

Employers
Van Scoyoc Associates, Inc. (Legislative Assistant)

Clients Represented

On Behalf of Van Scoyoc Associates, Inc.
Montana State University
The Nat'l Space Grant Alliance
University of Nebraska
University of North Carolina at Chapel Hill

BOOTH, Patricia

5454 Wisconsin Ave.
Suite 1270
Chevy Chase, MD 20815
Tel: (301)718-0202
Fax: (301)718-2976
Registered: LDA
EMail: pbooth@erols.com

Served with the Health Care Financing Administration, Department of Health and Human Services, for 18 years.

Employers
GRQ, Inc. (Principal)

Clients Represented

On Behalf of GRQ, Inc.
American Ass'n of Cardiovascular and Pulmonary Rehabilitation
American College of Chest Physicians
HCR-Manor Care, Inc.
Mallinckrodt-Nellcor Puritan Bennett
Nat'l Ass'n for Medical Direction of Respiratory Care
Transtracheal Systems
Tri Path Inc.

BOOTHBY, Clay

444 N. Capitol St. NW
Suite 700
Washington, DC 20001
Tel: (202)624-7828
Fax: (202)624-7831

Employers
Pennsylvania, Washington Office of the Commonwealth of (Associate Director)

BOOTHE, Jeffrey F.

2099 Pennsylvania Ave. NW
Suite 100
Washington, DC 20006
Tel: (202)955-3000
Fax: (202)955-5564
Registered: LDA
EMail: jboothe@hklaw.com

Professional Staff Member, Senate Appropriations Committee, 1982-87. Legislative Assistant to Senator Mark O. Hatfield (R-OR), 1978-82.

Employers
Holland & Knight LLP (Partner)

Clients Represented

On Behalf of Holland & Knight LLP
Virologic, Inc.

BOOZER, Lyndon K.

1133 21st St. NW
Suite 900
Washington, DC 20036
Tel: (202)463-4100
Fax: (202)463-4196
Registered: LDA
EMail: lyndon.boozer@bellsouth.com

Employers
BellSouth Corp. (Exec. Director, Federal Relations)

BOPP, Jr., James

419 Seventh St. NW
Suite 500
Washington, DC 20004
Tel: (202)626-8800
Fax: (202)737-9189

Employers
Nat'l Right to Life Committee (Counsel)

BOPT, Andrew

4340 East-West Hwy.
Bethesda, MD 20814
Tel: (301)951-3933
Fax: (301)951-3801
EMail: abopt@sgcd.org

Employers
Soc. of Glass and Ceramic Decorators (Exec. Director)

BOR, Robert M.

1400 L St. NW
Washington, DC 20005-3502
Tel: (202)371-5730
Fax: (202)371-5950
Registered: LDA
EMail: rbor@winston.com

Chief Counsel, House Committee on Agriculture, 1975-85. Division Director, Office of General Counsel (1968-75) Assistant Division Director, Supervisory Attorney and Attorney/Advisor, Office of General Counsel (1953-68 and 1948-51), all at the Department of Agriculture. Attorney/Advisor, Office of Price Stabilization, 1951-53.

Employers
Winston & Strawn (Of Counsel, Legislative and Regulatory Practice)

Clients Represented

On Behalf of Winston & Strawn
American Honey Producers Ass'n
Cheese Importers Ass'n of America
Liberty Maritime Co.
Queensland Sugar, Ltd.
USA Rice Federation
Western Peanut Growers Ass'n

BORDEN, Enid A.

1414 Prince St.
Suite 302
Alexandria, VA 22314
Tel: (703)548-3692
Fax: (703)548-8024
EMail: enid@tbg.dgsys.com

Director of Public Affairs (Reg. II), Department of Health and Human Services, 1981-83. Director of Public Affairs (OHDS), Department of Health and Human Services, 1983-86. Deputy Commissioner for Policy and External Affairs, Social Security Administration, 1986-88.

Employers
The Borden Group, Inc. (President)

Clients Represented

On Behalf of The Borden Group, Inc.
Project Meal Foundation

BORDEN, Sherrie

1261 Twinbrook Pkwy.
Rockville, MD 20852
Tel: (301)881-0666
Fax: (301)816-8148
EMail: slb@usp.org

Employers
United States Pharmacopeia (Director, Professional and Public Affairs)

BORDERS, Brian T.

1909 K St. NW
Washington, DC 20006
Tel: (202)263-3000
Fax: (202)263-3300
Registered: LDA
EMail: bborders@mayerbrown.com

Employers
Mayer, Brown & Platt (Counsel)

Clients Represented

On Behalf of Mayer, Brown & Platt
Accenture
Ass'n of Publicly Traded Companies
KPMG, LLP
PriceWaterhouseCoopers
Technology Network

BORGER, Henry A.

2101 Constitution Ave. NW
Washington, DC 20418
Tel: (202)334-3378
Fax: (202)334-3370

Employers
Federal Facilities Council (Exec. Secretary)

BORGHESANI, Jr., William H.

1001 G St. NW
Suite 500 West
Washington, DC 20001
Tel: (202)434-4100
Fax: (202)434-4646
EMail: borghesani@khlaw.com

Attorney/Advisor, Federal Communications Commission, 1957-58.

Employers
Keller and Heckman LLP (Partner)

BORGHESE, Phyllis

1200 G St. NW
Suite 800
Washington, DC 20005-8707
Tel: (202)434-8778
Fax: (202)434-8703

Employers
Nat'l Ass'n of Tax Practitioners (Government Affairs Representative)

BORIS, Elizabeth

2100 M St. NW
Washington, DC 20037
Tel: (202)833-7200
Fax: (202)429-0687

Employers
The Urban Institute (Director, Center on Nonprofits and Philanthropy)

BORK, Robert H.

1150 17th St. NW
Washington, DC 20036
Tel: (202)862-5800
Fax: (202)862-7177
EMail: rbork@aei.org

Employers
American Enterprise Institute for Public Policy Research (John M. Olin Scholar in Legal Studies)

BORKON, Lynn L.

1640 King St.
P.O. Box 1443
Alexandria, VA 22313
Tel: (703)683-8170
Fax: (703)543-2383
Registered: LDA
EMail: lborkon@astd.org
Former Communications Director, Rep. Nicholas Smith (R-MI) and Office of the Chief Administrative Officer, U.S. House of Representatives.

Employers
American Soc. for Training and Development (Government Relations Associate)

BORLAND, Kevin

1201 Connecticut Ave. NW
Sixth Floor
Washington, DC 20036
Tel: (202)785-1995
Fax: (202)785-1694
EMail: kevibo@polaraircargo.com
Legislative Director to Rep. John Shadegg (R-AZ), 1995. Press Secretary and Legislative Assistant to Rep. Dan Miller (R-FL), 1993-94. Legislative Assistant to Rep. John J. Rhodes (R-AZ), 1991-92.

Employers
Polar Air Cargo, Inc. (Director of Government Affairs)

BORLAND, Lydia

1455 F St. NW
Suite 225
Washington, DC 20005
Tel: (202)624-0016
Fax: (202)783-6947
Registered: LDA
EMail: lborland@erols.com

Employers
Caspian Group

Clients Represented
On Behalf of Caspian Group
U.S.-Turkish Business Council of DEIK

BORN, Brooksley

555 12th St. NW
Washington, DC 20004-1206
Tel: (202)942-5832
Fax: (202)942-5999
EMail: brooksley_born@aporter.com
Chairperson, Commodity Futures Trading Commission, 1996-99.

Employers
Arnold & Porter (Partner)

BORNSTEIN, Theodore H.

3000 K St. NW
Suite 500
Washington, DC 20007-5109
Tel: (202)672-5300
Fax: (202)672-5399
Registered: LDA
EMail: tbornstein@foleylaw.com
Chief of Staff, Senator Herbert Kohl (D-WI), 1993-97; Director, Reinvestment Task Force, Department of Defense, 1993; Administrative Assistant and Legislative Director, Rep. Les Aspin (D-WI), 1987-93.

Employers
Foley & Lardner (Partner)

Clients Represented
On Behalf of Foley & Lardner
Aurora Health Care, Inc.
CMC/Heartland Partnership
Liquid Metal Technologies
Milwaukee, City of
Northland Cranberries, Inc.
Oshkosh Truck Corp.
PG&E Nat'l Energy Group
San Diego Hospice Corp.
Sand County Foundation
Sub-Zero Freezer Co. Inc.
TDS Telecommunications
Wisconsin Gas Co.

BOROUGHS, Lizbet

1400 K St. NW
Washington, DC 20005
Tel: (202)682-6000
Fax: (202)682-6850

Employers
American Psychiatric Ass'n (Associate Director, Government Relations)

BORRA, RD, Susan

1100 Connecticut Ave. NW
Suite 430
Washington, DC 20036
Tel: (202)296-6540
Fax: (202)296-6547
EMail: borra@ific.org

Employers
Internat'l Food Information Council (Senior V. President, Director of Nutrition)

BORRELLI, Alice

1120 20th St. NW
Suite 1000
Washington, DC 20036
Tel: (202)457-2124
Fax: (202)457-2571
Registered: LDA
EMail: aborrelli@att.com

Employers
AT&T (Director, Federal Government Affairs)

BORTHWICK, Mark

1819 L St. NW
Second Floor
Washington, DC 20036
Tel: (202)293-3995
Fax: (202)293-1402

Employers
United States Nat'l Committee for Pacific Economic Cooperation (Exec. Director)

BORUT, Donald J.

1301 Pennsylvania Ave. NW
Suite 550
Washington, DC 20004-1701
Tel: (202)626-3010
Fax: (202)626-3143
EMail: borut@nlc.org

Employers
Nat'l League of Cities (Exec. Director)

BORWEGEN, B. William

1313 L St. NW
Washington, DC 20005
Tel: (202)898-3200
Fax: (202)898-3304
Registered: LDA

Employers
Service Employees Internat'l Union (Director, Health and Safety)

BORY, Laurence D.

1420 King St.
Alexandria, VA 22314-2794
Tel: (703)684-2874
Fax: (703)836-4875
Registered: LDA
EMail: lbory@nspe.org

Employers
Nat'l Soc. of Professional Engineers (Director, Government Relations)

BORYSOWICZ, Mary Ann

1900 Association Dr.
Reston, VA 20191-1599
Tel: (703)476-3450
Fax: (703)476-4566

Employers
Nat'l Ass'n for Girls and Women in Sport (Exec. Director)

BOSAK, KathyAnn

440 First St. NW
Eighth Floor
Washington, DC 20001
Tel: (202)942-4206
Fax: (202)737-0480
EMail: kbosak@naco.org

Employers
Nat'l Ass'n of Counties (Director, Finance and Administration)

BOSCH, David D.

1667 K St. NW
Suite 1200
Washington, DC 20006
Tel: (202)223-7750
Fax: (202)223-7756

Employers
Aramco Services Co. (Director, Washington Office)

BOSCH, Kevin D.

517 Second St. NE
Washington, DC 20002
Tel: (202)543-3744
Fax: (202)543-3509
Registered: LDA

Employers
David Turch & Associates (Associate)

Clients Represented
On Behalf of David Turch & Associates
Rialto, California, City of
San Bernardino Associated Governments
San Bernardino, California, County of
St. Cloud, Minnesota, City of
Temecula, California, City of

BOSCO, Cassandra

1200 18th St. NW
Suite 400
Washington, DC 20036-2506
Tel: (202)783-9000
Fax: (202)331-8364
EMail: cbosco@nbaa.org

Employers
Nat'l Business Aviation Ass'n (Director, Public Relations)

BOSGRAAF, Kimberly

1201 F St. NW
Suite 200
Washington, DC 20004
Tel: (202)554-9000
Fax: (202)554-0496

Employers
Nat'l Federation of Independent Business (Counsel, Regulatory Policy)

BOSHARA, Ray

777 N. Capitol St. NE
Suite 410
Washington, DC 20002
Tel: (202)408-9788
Fax: (202)408-9793
Registered: LDA
EMail: ray@cfeb.org

Employers
Corporation for Enterprise Development (Policy Director)

BOSHER, L.E.

Three Research Place
Rockville, MD 20850
Tel: (301)948-4910
Fax: (301)948-1369

Employers
Transportation-Communications Internat'l Union (International Secretary/Treasurer)

BOSITIS, David A.

1090 Vermont Ave. NW
Suite 1100
Washington, DC 20005-4961
Tel: (202)789-3500
Fax: (202)789-6390

Employers
Joint Center for Political and Economic Studies (Senior Research Associate)

BOSLEY, John J.

1700 K St. NW
13th Floor
Washington, DC 20006-0011
Tel: (202)457-0710
Fax: (202)269-9352

Employers
Metropolitan Washington Council of Governments (General Counsel)
Nat'l Ass'n of Regional Councils (Legal Counsel)

BOSLEY, Scott

11690B Sunrise Valley Dr.
Reston, VA 20191
Tel: (703)453-1122
Fax: (703)453-1133

Employers
American Soc. of Newspaper Editors (Exec. Director)

BOSMANS, Denise M.

12884 Harbor Dr.
Woodside, VA 20192
Tel: (703)490-6777
Fax: (703)492-4404
EMail: dbosmans@nasda.com

Employers
Nat'l Ass'n of State Development Agencies (Director, Membership Services)

BOSS, Terry D.

Ten G St. NE
Suite 700
Washington, DC 20002
Tel: (202)216-5900
Fax: (202)216-0876

Employers
Interstate Natural Gas Ass'n of America (V. President, Environment, Safety and Operations)

BOSSMAN, David A.

1501 Wilson Blvd.
Suite 1100
Arlington, VA 22209-3199
EMail: dbossman@afia.org
Tel: (703)524-0810
Fax: (703)524-1921

Employers
American Feed Industry Ass'n (President)

BOSTIC, Dana P.

1747 Pennsylvania Ave. NW
Suite 1150
Washington, DC 20006
Tel: (202)296-6222
Fax: (202)296-4507
Registered: LDA
EMail: dbostic@mww.com
Former Legislative Assistant to Senator James M. Jeffers (R-VT), Senate Committee on Health, Education, Labor and Pensions.

Employers
The MWW Group (Deputy Director, Federal Affairs)

Clients Represented
On Behalf of The MWW Group
Bacardi-Martini, USA, Inc.
Cuban American Nat'l Foundation/Cuban American Foundation
Detroit Medical Center
Domino's Pizza
Green County Health Care, Inc.
Internat'l Distance Learning
Little Havana Activities and Nutrition Centers
Nat'l Ass'n of Community Health Centers
Puerto Ricans for Civic Action
Ross University School of Medicine in Dominica
United States Education Finance Corp.

BOSTON, April

801 Pennsylvania Ave. NW
Suite 625
Washington, DC 20004
Tel: (202)661-2100
Fax: (202)661-2101
Registered: LDA

Employers
Canfield & Associates, Inc. (Director, Government Affairs)

Clients Represented
On Behalf of Canfield & Associates, Inc.
Air Transport Ass'n of America
American Home Products Corp.
Ass'n of Financial Guaranty Insurers
Consumer Mortgage Coalition
GE Commercial Real Estate & Financial Services
Merck & Co.
Pfizer, Inc.

BOSTON, Dan

801 Pennsylvania Ave. NW
Suite 245
Washington, DC 20004-2604
Tel: (202)624-1522
Fax: (202)737-6462
Registered: LDA
EMail: dboston@americashospitals.com
Majority Staff Counsel, House Committee on Commerce, 1997-99.

Employers
Federation of American Hospitals (Assistant V. President, Legislation and Public Affairs)

BOSTON, Dennis

Ten G St. NE
Suite 440
Washington, DC 20002
Tel: (202)628-5935
Fax: (202)347-3548
Registered: LDA

Employers
Brotherhood of Railroad Signalmen (V. President)

BOSTON, Robert

518 C St. NE
Washington, DC 20002
Tel: (202)466-3234
Fax: (202)466-2587

Employers
Americans United for Separation of Church and State (Assistant Director, Communications)

BOSWELL, Donna A.

555 13th St. NW
Washington, DC 20004-1109
Tel: (202)637-5814
Fax: (202)637-5910
Registered: LDA
EMail: daboswell@hhlaw.com

Employers
Hogan & Hartson L.L.P. (Partner)

Clients Represented
On Behalf of Hogan & Hartson L.L.P.
DNA Sciences, Inc.
Genentech, Inc.
Pharmaceutical Research and Manufacturers of America

BOSWELL, Mary Beth

2500 Wilson Blvd.
Suite 300
Arlington, VA 22201
Tel: (703)907-7736
Fax: (703)907-7727

Employers
Telecommunications Industry Ass'n (Director, Emerging Technology Markets)

BOSWORTH, Barry P.

1775 Massachusetts Ave. NW
Washington, DC 20036-2188
Tel: (202)797-6000
Fax: (202)797-6004
Director, Council on Wage and Price Stability, 1977-79; Staff Economist, President's Council of Economic Advisers, 1968-69.

Employers
The Brookings Institution (Senior Fellow, Economic Studies)

BOUCHER JAMESON, Jennifer

1300 N. 17th St.
Eighth Floor
Rosslyn, VA 22209-3801
Tel: (703)812-2000
Fax: (703)812-8202
Registered: LDA
EMail: boucher@abc.org

Employers
Associated Builders and Contractors (Director, Legislative Affairs)
Coalition to Repeal the Davis-Bacon Act (Legislative Director)

BOUDREAU, Martha L.

1615 L St. NW
Suite 1000
Washington, DC 20036
Tel: (202)659-0330
Fax: (202)296-1775
Registered: FARA
EMail: boudream@fleishma.com
Former Staff member to Rep. David E. Bonoir (D-MI).

Employers
Fleishman-Hillard, Inc (Senior V. President and Partner)

BOUDREAU, Paul

1001 Pennsylvania Ave. NW
Suite 700 South
Washington, DC 20004
Tel: (202)662-2650
Fax: (202)662-2674
Registered: LDA

Employers
Honeywell Internat'l, Inc.

BOUDRIAS, Claude P.

1300 Wilson Blvd.
Arlington, VA 22209
Tel: (703)741-5915
Fax: (703)741-6097
Registered: LDA
EMail: claude_boudrais@americanchemistry.com

Employers
American Chemistry Council (Director)

BOULANGER, Jennifer

200 Independence Ave. SW
Room 341H
Washington, DC 20201
Tel: (202)690-5705
Fax: (202)690-8168

Employers
Department of Health and Human Services - Health Care Financing Administration (Director, Medicare Part A Analysis Group)

BOULET, Jr., James

8001 Forbes Pl.
Suite 109
Springfield, VA 22151
Tel: (703)321-8818
Fax: (703)321-8408
Registered: LDA

Employers
English First, Inc. (Exec. Director)

BOULTER, Hon. Beau

1299 Pennsylvania Ave. NW
Suite 800 West
Washington, DC 20004
Tel: (202)785-0500
Fax: (202)785-5277
Registered: LDA
Member, House of Representatives (R-TX), 1985-89.

Employers
Self-employed as an independent consultant.
The Carmen Group (Senior Associate)
LMRC, Inc. (Senior Associate)
United Seniors Ass'n (Legislative Counsel)

Clients Represented
As an independent consultant
United Seniors Ass'n
On Behalf of The Carmen Group
Hyundai Space & Aircraft Co., Ltd.
Illinois Department of Transportation
US Bancorp

BOURJAILY, III, Monte F.

218 S. Fairfax St.
Alexandria, VA 22314
Tel: (703)549-2322
Fax: (703)519-8275
Registered: LDA
EMail: mboujaily@aol.com

Employers
Ritter and Bourjaily, Inc. (President)

Clients Represented
On Behalf of Ritter and Bourjaily, Inc.
Microcosm, Inc.
NanoDynamics, Inc.
NAVSYS Corp.
Nu Thena Systems, Inc.
Onconova Inc.
Scram Technologies Inc.
ViaSat, Inc.

BOURNE, Laura L.

655 15th St. NW
Washington, DC 20005-5701
Tel: (202)220-0631
Fax: (202)220-0873
Registered: LDA
EMail: lbourne@fmi.org

Employers
Food Marketing Institute (Director, Government Relations)

BOURQUE, Daniel P.

1200 New Hampshire Ave. NW
Suite 410
Washington, DC 20036
EMail: dbourque@vha.com
Tel: (202)721-8100
Fax: (202)721-8105

Employers
VHA Inc. (Group Senior V. President)

BOWARD, Gary

214 Massachusetts Ave. NE
Washington, DC 20002
Tel: (202)546-4400
Fax: (202)546-8328

Employers
Heritage Foundation (Chief of Staff and Assistant to the President)

BOWDEN, Delores

14th and Constitution Ave. NW
Room 7814A
Washington, DC 20230
Tel: (202)482-2309
Fax: (202)501-4828

Employers
Department of Commerce - Economic Development Administration (Communications and Congressional Liaison Assistant)

BOWEN, Brooks J.

11 Dupont Circle NW
Suite 700
Washington, DC 20036
Tel: (202)293-5886
Fax: (202)939-6969
Registered: LDA

Employers
Multinat'l Government Services, Inc.

Clients Represented
On Behalf of Multinat'l Government Services, Inc.
Cellular Telecommunications and Internet Ass'n
General Tire, Inc.
Goodyear Tire and Rubber Co.
Rhone-Polenc Inc.

BOWEN, Vincent

601 13th St. NW
Suite 600 South
Washington, DC 20005
EMail: bowenvi@washdc.whitecase.com
Tel: (202)626-3600
Fax: (202)639-9355

Employers
White & Case LLP (Associate)

BOWENS, Jacqueline D.

111 Michigan Ave. NW
Washington, DC 20010
Tel: (202)884-4933
Fax: (202)884-5988
EMail: jbowens@cnmc.org

Employers
Children's Nat'l Medical Center (V. President, Government and Public Affairs)

BOWER, Ernest Z.

1101 17th St. NW
Suite 411
Washington, DC 20036
Tel: (202)289-1911
Fax: (202)289-0519

Employers
U.S.-ASEAN Business Council Inc. (President)

BOWERS, Jr., John

1101 17th St. NW
Suite 400
Washington, DC 20036
Tel: (202)955-6304
Fax: (202)955-6048

Employers
Internat'l Longshoremen's Ass'n (Legislative Director)

BOWERS, Michael

1133 15th St. NW
Suite 300
Washington, DC 20005
Tel: (202)452-0109
Fax: (202)223-2329
Registered: LDA
EMail: mbowers@aamft.org

Employers
American Ass'n for Marriage and Family Therapy (Exec. Director)

BOWERS, Steve

1730 M St. NW
Suite 700
Washington, DC 20036-4510
Tel: (202)452-1600
Fax: (202)223-8756

Employers
Software & Information Industry Ass'n (SIIA) (Director, Public Relations)

BOWLAND, Amy R.

415 Second St. NE
Suite 300
Washington, DC 20002-4993
Tel: (202)547-7800
Fax: (202)546-2638

Employers
Nat'l Ass'n of Wheat Growers (Director, Communications)

BOWLDEN, Taylor R.

1776 Massachusetts Ave. NW
Suite 500
Washington, DC 20036
Tel: (202)857-1200
Fax: (202)857-1220
Registered: LDA

Employers
American Highway Users Alliance (V. President, Policy and Government Affairs)

BOWLER, M. Kenneth

325 Seventh St. NW
Suite 1200
Washington, DC 20004-1007
Tel: (202)783-7070
Fax: (202)347-2044
Registered: LDA

Employers
Pfizer, Inc. (V. President, Federal Government Relations)

BOWLER, III, R. T. E.

2341 Jefferson Davis Hwy.
Suite 1100
Arlington, VA 22202
Tel: (703)418-0808
Fax: (703)418-0811

Employers
Bath Iron Works Corp. (Director, Washington Operations)

BOWLING, Richard P.

1020 Princess St.
Alexandria, VA 22314
Tel: (703)549-3010
Fax: (703)549-3014

Employers
Truck Trailer Manufacturers Ass'n (President)

BOWMAN, Bobbi

11690B Sunrise Valley Dr.
Reston, VA 20191
Tel: (703)453-1122
Fax: (703)453-1133

Employers
American Soc. of Newspaper Editors (Diversity Director)

BOWMAN, Heather

2500 Wilson Blvd.
Arlington, VA 22201-3834
Tel: (703)907-7582
Fax: (703)907-7501
Registered: LDA
EMail: hbowman@eia.org

Employers
Electronic Industries Alliance (Manager, Environmental Issues)

BOWMAN, Karlyn H.

1150 17th St. NW
Washington, DC 20036
Tel: (202)862-5800
Fax: (202)862-7177
EMail: kbowman@aei.org

Employers
American Enterprise Institute for Public Policy Research (Resident Fellow)

BOWMAN, Margaret

1025 Vermont Ave.
Suite 720
Washington, DC 20005
Tel: (202)347-7550
Fax: (202)347-9240
Registered: LDA
EMail: amrivers@amrivers.org

Employers
American Rivers (Director, Hydropower Programs)

BOWMAN, Michael

801 G St. NW
Washington, DC 20001
Tel: (202)393-2100
Fax: (202)393-2134
Registered: LDA

Employers
Family Research Council, Inc. (V. President, Government Relations)

BOWMAN, Michael

1215 Jefferson Davis Hwy.
Suite 1004
Arlington, VA 22202
Tel: (703)416-8000
Fax: (703)416-8010
Registered: LDA
EMail: mike_bowman@drs.com

Employers
DRS Technologies, Inc. (Sr. V. President, Washington Operations)

BOWMAN, Randy

1849 C St. NW
Washington, DC 20240
Tel: (202)208-5403
Fax: (202)208-6965

Employers
Department of Interior - Fish and Wildlife Service (Senior Legislative Specialist)

BOWSER, David G.

1920 L St. NW
Suite 200
Washington, DC 20036
Tel: (202)785-0238
Fax: (202)822-8118
EMail: dgbowser@sbsc.org

Employers
Small Business Survival Committee (V. President)

BOXALL, Jr., James A.

9111 Old Georgetown Rd.
Bethesda, MD 20814-1699
Tel: (301)493-2360
Fax: (301)493-2376
EMail: boxall@asnc.org

Employers
American Soc. of Nuclear Cardiology (Director, Health Policy)

BOYCE, Katharine R.

2550 M St. NW
Washington, DC 20037-1350
Tel: (202)457-6000
Fax: (202)457-6315
Registered: LDA, FARA
EMail: kboyce@pattonboggs.com

Legislative Assistant and Press Secretary to Rep. Brock Adams (D-WA), 1973-77. Legislative Aide to Rep. James G. O'Hara (D-MI), 1972-73.

Employers
Patton Boggs, LLP (Partner)

Clients Represented

On Behalf of Patton Boggs, LLP
American Committee for Peace and Justice in South Asia
H.A.H. of Wisconsin L.P.
Intercultural Cancer Council
Kickapoo Tribe of Oklahoma
Pakistan, Embassy of the Islamic Republic of
Pechanga Band of California Luiseno Indians
Swan Creek River Confederated Ojibbwa Tribes of Michigan
United Defense, L.P.

BOYD, Dennis W.

8621 Silver Oak Ct.
Springfield, VA 22153
Tel: (800)403-3374
Fax: (703)455-8282
Registered: LDA

Former senior executive with the Appalachian Regional Commission and the Federal Emergency Management Agency, 1980-87.

Employers
Financial Programs, Inc. (Exec. Director)
Nat'l Ass'n of Assistant United States Attorneys (Exec. Director)

Clients Represented

On Behalf of Financial Programs, Inc.
Nat'l Ass'n of Assistant United States Attorneys

BOYD, Evelyn Y.

1350 I St. NW
Suite 400
Washington, DC 20005-3306
Tel: (202)371-6900
Fax: (202)842-3578
Registered: LDA

Employers
Motorola, Inc. (Director, International Trade Relations (Latin America))

BOYD, Fran

412 First St. SE
Suite One
Washington, DC 20003
Tel: (202)484-2773
Fax: (202)484-0770
Registered: LDA

Formerly with the Farm Credit Administration, Department of Agriculture.

Employers
American Sheep Industry Ass'n (Contact, RAMSPAC)
Meyers & Associates (V. President)

Clients Represented

On Behalf of Meyers & Associates
American Beekeeping Federation
American Sheep Industry Ass'n
Canadian River Municipal Water Authority
Council for Agricultural Science and Technology
Irrigation Projects Reauthorization Council
Minor Use, Minor Species Coalition
Nat'l Ass'n for Agricultural Stewardship
North Carolina Peanut Growers Ass'n
Rice Belt Warehouses
Southwest Peanut Growers
Virginia Peanut Growers Ass'n
Wool Fiber, Yarn Fabric Coalition

BOYD, Janet C.

1333 New Hampshire Ave. NW
Suite 400
Washington, DC 20036
Tel: (202)887-4000
Fax: (202)887-4288
Registered: LDA

Employers
Akin, Gump, Strauss, Hauer & Feld, L.L.P. (Partner)

Clients Represented

On Behalf of Akin, Gump, Strauss, Hauer & Feld, L.L.P.

American Airlines
ANCOR
AOL Time Warner
Barrick Goldstrike Mines, Inc.
Bear, Stearns and Co.
The Carlyle Group
Cummins Engine Co.
First Nationwide Bank
PG&E Gas Transmission Northwest
Transamerica Financial Services Co.

BOYD, Rebecca J.

1050 Thomas Jefferson St. NW
Seventh Floor
Washington, DC 20007
EMail: rjb@vnf.com
Tel: (202)298-1800
Fax: (202)338-2416

Employers

Van Ness Feldman, P.C. (Associate)

Clients Represented

On Behalf of Van Ness Feldman, P.C.

Sealaska Corp.

BOYD, Sandra

1331 Pennsylvania Ave. NW
Sixth Floor
Washington, DC 20004-1790
EMail: sboyd@nam.org
Tel: (202)637-3000
Fax: (202)637-3182

Employers

Nat'l Ass'n of Manufacturers (Assistant V. President, Employment Policy)

BOYD, Susan

1794 Columbia Rd. NW
Washington, DC 20009
Tel: (202)328-8160
Fax: (202)387-3378

Employers

Concern, Inc. (Exec. Director)

BOYD, Thomas M.

601 Pennsylvania Ave. NW
11th Floor, North Bldg.
Washington, DC 20004-2601
Tel: (202)756-3372
Fax: (202)756-3333
Registered: LDA
EMail: tboyd@alston.com

Director, Office of Policy Development, Department of Justice, (1989-1991); Assistant Attorney General, Office of Legislative Affairs (1988-89); Deputy Assistant General, Office of Legislative Affairs (1986-88); and Attorney Advisor (1974-76); Department of Justice. Former Republican Counsel, House Committee on the Judiciary.

Employers

Alston & Bird LLP (Partner)

Clients Represented

On Behalf of Alston & Bird LLP

Advanced Glassfiber Yarns
AFLAC, Inc.
The Assurant Group
CarsDirect.com
General Electric Co.
Morgan Stanley Dean Witter & Co.
Nat'l Coalition on E-Commerce and Privacy

BOYD, Trudi

1150 17th St. NW
Suite 701
Washington, DC 20036
EMail: trudib@dittus.com
Tel: (202)775-1401
Fax: (202)775-1404

Chief of Staff (1987-92) and Director of Communications (1985-87) for Rep. Larry Combest (R-TX).

Employers

Dittus Communications (V. President, Media Relations)

Clients Represented

On Behalf of Dittus Communications

American Business for Legal Immigration
Bizee.com
Digital Focus
Editorial Information Network
Magazine Publishers of America
Statoil Energy

BOYER, Philip B.

421 Aviation Way
Frederick, MD 21701
Tel: (301)695-2020
Fax: (301)695-2375
Registered: LDA

EMail: phil.boyer@aopa.org

Employers

Aircraft Owners and Pilots Ass'n (President)

BOYETTE, Van R.

915 15th St. NW
Suite 800
Washington, DC 20005
Tel: (202)347-2980
Fax: (202)347-2992
Registered: LDA

EMail: VanDesk@aol.com

Legislative Counsel to Senator Russell B. Long (D-LA), 1977-81.

Employers

Smith Martin & Boyette (Partner)

Clients Represented

On Behalf of Smith Martin & Boyette

Florida Crystals Corp.
Montana Land Reliance
Refined Sugars Inc.

BOYKIN, C.D.

601 Pennsylvania Ave. NW
Suite 325, North Bldg.
Washington, DC 20004
Tel: (202)728-3600
Fax: (202)728-3649
Registered: LDA

Employers

DuPont (Manager, Government Affairs)

BOYKIN, Curtis A.

1401 New York Ave.
Suite 600
Washington, DC 20005
Tel: (202)434-9100

Employers

Leftwich & Douglas

BOYLAN, Debbie

600 Pennsylvania Ave. SE
Suite 400
Washington, DC 20003
Tel: (202)547-0001
Fax: (202)546-0628
EMail: dboylan@dlcppi.org

Employers

Progressive Policy Institute (Director, Communications)

BOYLAN, Kim Marie

1909 K St. NW
Washington, DC 20006
Tel: (202)263-3000
Fax: (202)263-3300
Registered: LDA

Employers

Mayer, Brown & Platt (Partner)

Clients Represented

On Behalf of Mayer, Brown & Platt

Technology Network

BOYLAN, Virginia W.

1001 Pennsylvania Ave. NW
Suite 300S
Washington, DC 20004
Tel: (202)824-8800
Fax: (202)824-8990
Registered: LDA

EMail: boylan.virginia@dorseylaw.com

Deputy Staff Director, Senior Counsel, Minority Counsel, and Staff Attorney, Senate Select Committee on Indian Affairs, 1979-93. Legislative Assistant to Rep. John Melcher (D-MT), 1971-77.

Employers

Dorsey & Whitney LLP (Partner)

Clients Represented

On Behalf of Dorsey & Whitney LLP

Aleutian Pribilof Islands Community Development Ass'n
Bay Mills Indian Community
Bristol Bay Native Corp.
Central Council of Tlingit and Haida Indian Tribes of Alaska
Cow Creek Umpqua Tribe of Oregon
Cuyapaipe Band of Mission Indians
Delaware Tribe of Indians
Diamond Game Enterprises, Inc.
Gaming Management Internat'l II, Ltd.
Grand Traverse Band of Chippewa and Ottawa Indians
Little River Band of Ottawa Indians
Lower Elwaha S'Klallam Tribe
Pascua Yaqui Tribe of Arizona
Quinault Indian Nation
Red Lake Band of Chippewa Indians
Saginaw Chippewa Indian Tribe of Michigan
Shakopee Mdewakanton Sioux Tribe
Spokane Tribe
Stockbridge-Munsee Community Band of Mohican Indians
Trading Cove Associates
Winnebago Tribe of Nebraska

BOYLE, D.V.M., Dale D.

1101 Vermont Ave. NW
Suite 710
Washington, DC 20005-6308
EMail: nafv@erols.com
Tel: (202)289-6334
Fax: (202)842-4360

Employers

Nat'l Ass'n of Federal Veterinarians (Executive V. President)

BOYLE, J. Patrick

1700 N. Moore St.
Suite 1600
Arlington, VA 22209
Tel: (703)841-2400
Fax: (703)527-0938
Registered: LDA

Administrator, Agricultural Marketing Service, Department of Agriculture, 1986-89. Former aide to Senator Pete Wilson (R-CA).

Employers

American Meat Institute (President and Chief Exec. Officer)
Nat'l Meat Canners Ass'n (Exec. Secretary)

BOYLE, Joy Bates

1615 L St. NW
Suite 1000
Washington, DC 20036
Tel: (202)659-0330
Fax: (202)223-8199
Registered: LDA

EMail: boylej@fleishman.com

Former Staff member to Rep. Jerry Lewis (R-CA).

Employers

Fleishman-Hillard, Inc (V. President)

Clients Represented

On Behalf of Fleishman-Hillard, Inc

Jacobs Engineering Group Inc.

BOYLE, Kevin Charles

555 11th St. NW
Suite 1000
Washington, DC 20004
Tel: (202)637-2200
Fax: (202)637-2201

Employers

Latham & Watkins (Partner)

BOYLE, Paul J.

529 14th St. NW
Suite 440
Washington, DC 20045-1402
Tel: (202)783-4697
Fax: (202)783-4699
Registered: LDA

EMail: boylp@naa.org

Employers

Newspaper Ass'n of America (V. President, Government Affairs)

BOYLES, Bret K.

201 N. Union St.
Suite 530
Alexandria, VA 22314
Tel: (703)299-6600
Fax: (703)548-5954

Employers

New Republican Majority Fund (Exec. Director)

BOYNTON, Rex

8201 Greensboro Dr.
Suite 300
McLean, VA 22102
EMail: rboynton@amg-inc.com
Tel: (703)610-9000
Fax: (703)610-9005

Employers
Ass'n Management Group

Clients Represented
On Behalf of Ass'n Management Group
North American Technician Excellence

BOZEK, C. Richard

701 Pennsylvania Ave. NW
Washington, DC 20004-2696
Tel: (202)508-5641
Fax: (202)508-5150
Registered: LDA

Employers
Edison Electric Institute (Manager, Environmental Programs)

BOZELL, L. Brent

325 S. Patrick St.
Alexandria, VA 22314
Tel: (703)683-9733
Fax: (703)683-9736

Employers
Media Research Center (President)

BRAATEN, Kaye

440 First St. NW
Eighth Floor
Washington, DC 20001
EMail: kbraaten@naco.org
Tel: (202)942-4291
Fax: (202)393-2630

Employers
Nat'l Ass'n of Counties (Representative, County Services)

BRACHMAN, Marshall A.

444 Carbery Place NE
Washington, DC 20002
Tel: (202)365-1018
Fax: (202)544-1760
Registered: LDA

Employers
Self-employed as an independent consultant.

Clients Represented
As an independent consultant
Adams County, Colorado
Allied Marketing
Arizona Mail Order Co.
Camelbak Products, Inc.
Diamond Ventures
Direct Marketing Ass'n, Inc.
Edmund Scientific Co.
Interface Inc.
Lockheed Martin Aeronautical Systems Co.
Nat'l Wholesale Co., Inc.
Zions Bank Co.

BRACK, William T.

1615 L St. NW
Suite 450
Washington, DC 20036
Tel: (202)296-7353
Fax: (202)296-7009
Registered: LDA
Chief of Staff to Senator Hank Brown (R-CO), 1991-95.

Employers
Brownstein Hyatt & Farber, P.C.

Clients Represented
On Behalf of Brownstein Hyatt & Farber, P.C.
American Salvage Pool Ass'n
Apollo Advisors
AT&T Broadband & Internet Service
Colorado Credit Union Systems
Express One Internat'l Inc.
First Data Corp./Telecheck
Global Crossing North America, Inc.
Liggett Group, Inc.
Mariner Post Acute Network
Nat'l Cable Television Ass'n
NL Industries
Oracle Corp.
Pacific Capital Group, Inc.
Pfizer, Inc.
Rhythms NetConnections
Teletech Teleservices, Inc.
Timet-Titantium Metals Corp.
Vail Associates

BRACKEN, Ann

1025 Connecticut Ave. NW
Suite 200
Washington, DC 20036
EMail: bracken@acca.com
Tel: (202)293-4103
Fax: (202)293-4701

Employers
American Corporate Counsel Ass'n (V. President)

BRACKETT, Rick

219 N. Washington St.
Alexandria, VA 22314
Tel: (703)836-7990
Fax: (703)836-9739

Employers
Peduzzi Associates, Ltd. (Associate)

BRACY, Michael M.

601 13th St. NW
Suite 900 South
Washington, DC 20005
Tel: (202)783-5588
Fax: (202)783-5595
Registered: LDA
EMail: mmbracy@bracywilliams.com

Employers
Bracy Williams & Co.
Low Power Radio Coalition (Exec. Director)

Clients Represented
On Behalf of Bracy Williams & Co.
Atlanta, Georgia, City of
Daishowa America Co., Ltd.
Michigan Consolidated Gas Co.
Tucson, Arizona, City of

BRACY, Terrence L.

601 13th St. NW
Suite 900 South
Washington, DC 20005
Tel: (202)783-5588
Fax: (202)783-5595
Registered: LDA
EMail: tlbracy@aol.com
Former Assistant Secretary for Congressional and Governmental Affairs, Department of Transportation.

Employers
Bracy Williams & Co. (Chief Exec. Officer)

Clients Represented
On Behalf of Bracy Williams & Co.
Allied Pilots Ass'n
Atlanta, Georgia, City of
Bi-State Development Agency
Business Alliance for Internat'l Economic Development
Daishowa America Co., Ltd.
Fort Worth Transportation Authority
Fort Worth, Texas, City of
Foundation for Integrated Medicine
Michigan Consolidated Gas Co.
St. Louis Airport Authority
St. Louis Metropolitan Sewer District
Tucson, Arizona, City of

BRAD, Johnson

1667 K St. NW
Suite 700
Washington, DC 20006
Tel: (202)776-7800
Fax: (202)776-7801
Registered: LDA
EMail: bcjohnson@duanemorris.com

Employers
Duane, Morris & Heckscher LLP (Partner)

Clients Represented
On Behalf of Duane, Morris & Heckscher LLP
Mortgage Bankers Ass'n of America

BRADBURY, Anne

1300 N. 17th St.
Eighth Floor
Rosslyn, VA 22209-3801
Tel: (703)812-2000
Fax: (703)812-8202
Registered: LDA
EMail: bradbury@abc.org

Employers
Associated Builders and Contractors (Director, Work Place Policy)

BRADBURY, Jr., John R.

1101 Pennsylvania Ave. NW
Suite 600
Washington, DC 20004
Tel: (202)756-2299
Fax: (202)756-7556
Registered: LDA

Employers
Nestle USA, Inc. (Manager, Government Relations)

BRADDOCK, Richard

Federal Center Plaza
500 C St. SW
Washington, DC 20472
Tel: (202)646-4500
Fax: (202)646-2531

Employers
Federal Emergency Management Agency (Acting Director, Office of Intergovernmental Affairs)

BRADDON, Cynthia H.

1200 G St. NW
Suite 900
Washington, DC 20005-3802
Tel: (202)383-2000
Fax: (202)383-3718
Registered: LDA

Employers
McGraw-Hill Cos., The (V. President, Washington Affairs)

BRADEN, E. Mark

1050 Connecticut Ave. NW
Suite 1100
Washington, DC 20036-5304
Tel: (202)861-1500
Fax: (202)861-1790
Registered: LDA
EMail: Mbraden@baker-hostetler.com

Employers
Baker & Hostetler LLP (Partner)

Clients Represented
On Behalf of Baker & Hostetler LLP
American Resort Development Ass'n
Moose Internat'l Inc.

BRADEN, Kathryn

600 New Hampshire Ave. NW
Tenth Floor
Washington, DC 20037
Tel: (202)333-8667
Fax: (202)298-9109
Registered: LDA
EMail: katiebraden@erols.com
Former Legislative Assistant to Senator Bill Frist (R-TN).

Employers
Fierce and Isakowitz (Senior Associate)

Clients Represented
On Behalf of Fierce and Isakowitz
American Ass'n of Nurse Anesthetists
American Gaming Ass'n
DuPont
Federation of American Hospitals
Generic Pharmaceutical Ass'n
Health Insurance Ass'n of America
Liberty Maritime Co.
MCI WorldCom Corp.
Pegasus Communications
Tricon Global Restaurants Inc.

BRADEN, Susan G.

815 Connecticut Ave. NW
Suite 900
Washington, DC 20006-4078
Tel: (202)452-7000
Fax: (202)452-7073
Registered: LDA
EMail: susan.g.braden@bakernet.com
Special Counsel to the Chairman (1984-85) and Senior Attorney to the Commissioner and Acting Chairman (1980-83), Federal Trade Commission. Senior Trial Attorney, Antitrust Division, Energy Section (1978-80) and Cleveland Field Office (1973-78), Department of Justice.

Employers
Baker & McKenzie (Of Counsel)

Clients Represented
On Behalf of Baker & McKenzie
Drives Inc.
Gulf State Steel Inc.
Storck U.S.A.

BRADFIELD, Daniel

2000 L St. NW
Suite 300
Washington, DC 20036-0646
Tel: (202)835-8800
Fax: (202)835-8879
Registered: LDA

Employers
Ketchum (Vice President and Group Manager; Director, Grassroots Communications)

BRADFIELD, Michael

51 Louisiana Ave. NW
Washington, DC 20001
Tel: (202)879-3939
Fax: (202)626-1700
Registered: FARA
EMail: mbradfield@jonesday.com
General Counsel to the Board of Governors, Federal Reserve System, 1981-89. General Counsel for International Affairs

(1967-75) and Attorney (1962-67), Department of the Treasury.

Employers
Jones, Day, Reavis & Pogue (Partner)

Clients Represented
On Behalf of Jones, Day, Reavis & Pogue
Sakura Bank Ltd.

BRADFORD, Martina L.

900 19th St. NW
Suite 700
Washington, DC 20006
Tel: (202)530-7000
Fax: (202)530-7104
Registered: LDA

Employers
Lucent Technologies (Corporate V. President, Public Affairs)

BRADLEY, Cynthia P.

1625 L St. NW
Washington, DC 20036-5687
Tel: (202)429-1196
Fax: (202)223-2413
Registered: LDA
EMail: cbradley@afscme.org

Employers
American Federation of State, County and Municipal Employees (Legislative Affairs Specialist)

BRADLEY, David A.

810 1st St. NW
Washington, DC 20002
Tel: (202)842-2092
Fax: (202)842-2095
Registered: LDA

Employers
Moss McGee Bradley & Foley (Partner)
Nat'l Community Action Foundation (Exec. Director)

Clients Represented
On Behalf of Moss McGee Bradley & Foley
Kake Tribal Corp.
Nat'l Community Action Foundation
USA WORKS!

BRADLEY, Leigh A.

2099 Pennsylvania Ave. NW
Suite 100
Washington, DC 20006
Tel: (202)955-3000
Fax: (202)955-5564
EMail: labradley@hklaw.com

Employers
Holland & Knight LLP

BRADLEY, Lynne E.

1301 Pennsylvania Ave. NW
Suite 403
Washington, DC 20004
Tel: (202)628-8410
Fax: (202)628-8419
Registered: LDA
EMail: leb@alawash.org

Employers
American Library Ass'n (Director, Government Relations)

BRADNER, Eileen P.

1776 K St. NW
Washington, DC 20006
Tel: (202)719-7000
Fax: (202)719-7049
Registered: LDA

Employers
Wiley, Rein & Fielding (Partner)

Clients Represented
On Behalf of Wiley, Rein & Fielding
Birmingham Steel Corp.
Club Car, Inc.
Co-Steel Raritan
Connecticut Steel Corp.
Georgetown Industries
Keystone Consolidated Industries, Inc.
Northwestern Steel and Wire Co.

BRADNER, Robert Hunt

2099 Pennsylvania Ave. NW
Suite 100
Washington, DC 20006
Tel: (202)955-3000
Fax: (202)955-5564
Registered: LDA
EMail: rbradner@hklaw.com
Former Administrative Assistant and Counsel (1995-2000), Chief of Staff (1990-93), Legislative Director (1987-90), and Legislative Assistant (1985-87) to Rep. John Porter (R-IL).

Employers
Holland & Knight LLP (Senior Counsel)

Clients Represented
On Behalf of Holland & Knight LLP
American Chemistry Council
Bridgestone/Firestone, Inc.
Illinois Primary Health Care Ass'n
Somerville Housing Group
Tichenor and Associates
Wyeth-Ayerst Pharmaceuticals

BRADSHAW, Mary

2500 Wilson Blvd.
Suite 300
Arlington, VA 22201-3834
Tel: (703)907-7700
Fax: (703)907-7727
EMail: mbradshaw@mmta.org

Employers
Multi Media Telecommunications Ass'n (MMTA) (President)
Telecommunications Industry Ass'n (V. President, Global Enterprise Marketing Development)

BRADSHAW, Richard

2111 Wilson Blvd.
Suite 1200
Arlington, VA 22201
Tel: (703)522-1845
Fax: (703)351-6634
EMail: rbradshaw@columbuspublicaffairs.com
Former Special Assistant for Energy Resource Policy, Department of Energy and former Foreign Service Officer, Department of State.

Employers
Columbus Public Affairs (V. President)

BRADY, Betsy

1120 20th St. NW
Suite 1000
Washington, DC 20036
Tel: (202)457-3824
Fax: (202)457-2571
Registered: LDA
EMail: betbrady@att.com

Employers
AT&T (V. President, Federal Government Affairs)

BRADY, Cathleen

1001 Pennsylvania Ave. NW
Washington, DC 20004-2599
Tel: (202)624-2000
Fax: (202)624-2319
Registered: LDA

Employers
American Council of Life Insurers (Senior Counsel)

BRADY, Hugh S.

1133 21st St. NW
Suite 900
Washington, DC 20036
Tel: (202)463-4100
Fax: (202)463-4196
Registered: LDA
EMail: hugh.brady@bellsouth.com

Employers
BellSouth Corp. (Exec. Director, Legislative Affairs)

BRADY, J. Christopher

700 13th St. NW
Suite 800
Washington, DC 20005
Tel: (202)508-5800
Fax: (202)508-5858
Registered: LDA
Associate Administrator for Policy and Analysis (1991-92) and Acting Associate Administrator for Congressional Affairs (1986-89), General Services Administration. Legislative Director for Senator John Warner (R-VA), 1986-98. Legislative Assistant/Legislative Director for Rep. Thomas J. Bliley (R-VA), 1981-85.

Employers
Kilpatrick Stockton LLP (Director, Legislative Affairs)

Clients Represented
On Behalf of Kilpatrick Stockton LLP
American Realty Advisors
Atlanta, Georgia, City of
The Freedom Forum
Hoffman Management, Inc.
Republic Properties Corp.
Julien J. Studley, Inc.
Transrapid Internat'l
Zirconium Environmental Committee (ZEC)

BRADY, John

1029 N. Royal St.
Suite 400
Alexandria, VA 22314
Tel: (703)684-1245
Fax: (703)684-1249
EMail: JBrady@directimpact.com

Employers
The Direct Impact Co. (Chairman and Chief Exec. Officer)

BRADY, Richard A.

1201 Pennsylvania Ave. NW
Washington, DC 20004-2401
Tel: (202)662-6000
Fax: (202)662-6291
EMail: rbrady@cov.com

Employers
Covington & Burling (Partner)

BRADY, Robert P.

555 13th St. NW
Washington, DC 20004-1109
Tel: (202)637-6969
Fax: (202)637-5910
Registered: LDA
EMail: rpbrady@hhlaw.com
Executive Assistant to the Commissioner (1981-83), Associate Chief Counsel, Bureau of Foods, (1980-81), Associate Chief Counsel for Enforcement and for Biologics (1976-80), Office of the Chief Counsel, Food and Drug Administration.

Employers
Hogan & Hartson L.L.P. (Partner)

Clients Represented
On Behalf of Hogan & Hartson L.L.P.
DNA Sciences, Inc.

BRADY, Sarah

1225 I St. NW
Suite 1100
Washington, DC 20005
Tel: (202)289-7319
Fax: (202)408-1851

Employers
The Center to Prevent Handgun Violence (Chair)
Handgun Control, Inc. (Chair)

BRAGG, Raymond F.

3315 Cummings Ln.
Chevy Chase, MD 20815
Tel: (301)913-9012
Fax: (301)913-9041
Registered: LDA
Exec. Secretary to Senator Herman E. Talmadge (D-GA), 1973-78.

Employers
RFB, Inc. (President)

Clients Represented
On Behalf of RFB, Inc.
Circle K Convenience Stores
Dale Service Corp.
Progress Energy
Roecker Engineering Co.
Transit Mixed Concrete Co.
Valero Energy Corp.

BRAHMS, Thomas W.

1099 14th St. NW
Suite 300 West
Washington, DC 20005-3438
Tel: (202)289-0222
Fax: (202)289-7722

Employers
Institute of Transportation Engineers (Exec. Director)

BRAHS, Stuart J.

1350 I St. NW
Suite 1030
Washington, DC 20005-3305
Tel: (202)682-1280
Fax: (202)682-1412
Registered: LDA
EMail: brahs.stuart@principal.com
Former Legislative Director to Senator Abe Ribicoff (D-CT). Served as Senior Legislative Assistant to Rep. Steve Solarz (D-NY) and Rep. Richard Ottinger (D-NY). Former Administrative Assistant to Rep. Herman Badillo (D-NY). Former Operations Officer, Latin American Programs Division, Peace Corps.

Employers
Principal Financial Group (V. President, Federal Government Relations)

BRAILOV, Marc

601 Pennsylvania Ave. NW
Suite 600
North Bldg.
Washington, DC 20004
Tel: (202)682-9110
Fax: (202)682-9111

Employers
American Electronics Ass'n (Director, Communications)

BRAMBLE, Barbara

1400 16th St. NW
Suite 501
Washington, DC 20036-2266
EMail: bramble@nwf.org
Tel: (202)797-6800
Fax: (202)797-5486
Registered: LDA

Employers
Nat'l Wildlife Federation - Office of Federal and Internat'l Affairs (Senior Director, International Affairs)

BRAMS, Robert S.

2550 M St. NW
Washington, DC 20037-1350
EMail: rbrams@pattonboggs.com
Tel: (202)457-6000
Fax: (202)457-6315
Registered: LDA

Employers
Patton Boggs, LLP (Partner)

BRANAND, Robert

Four E St. SE
Washington, DC 20003
Tel: (202)546-4100
Registered: LDA

Employers
Robert Branand Internat'l (Principal)

BRANCH, L. Maurice

1133 15th St. NW
Suite 640
Washington, DC 20005
EMail: maurice@ala-national.org
Tel: (202)466-2520
Fax: (202)296-4419

Employers
American Logistics Ass'n (V. President, Operations)

BRANCH, Patricia

1025 Thomas Jefferson St. NW
Suite 400 East
Washington, DC 20007-0805
Tel: (202)965-8100
Fax: (202)965-6403
Registered: LDA

Employers
Jorden Burt LLP (Legislative Coordinator)

Clients Represented

On Behalf of Jorden Burt LLP
American Museum of Natural History
Assurant Group
Atlantic Health Systems
The Colonial Williamsburg Foundation
Florida State University System
Gainesville Regional Utilities
Gainesville, Florida, City of
Lovelace Respiratory Research Institute
Miami Beach, Florida, City of
New York University
Newark, New Jersey, City of
University of Medicine and Dentistry of New Jersey
University of Tulsa
University of Virginia

BRAND, Betsy

1836 Jefferson Place NW
Washington, DC 20036
Tel: (202)775-9731
Fax: (202)775-9733

Employers
American Youth Policy Forum (Co-director)

BRAND, Joseph L.

2550 M St. NW
Washington, DC 20037-1350
EMail: jbrand@pattonboggs.com
Tel: (202)457-6000
Fax: (202)457-6315
Registered: FARA

Employers
Patton Boggs, LLP (Partner)

BRAND, Stanley M.

923 15th St. NW
Washington, DC 20005
EMail: sbrand@brand-frulla.com
Tel: (202)662-9700
Fax: (202)737-7565
General Counsel to the Clerk of the U.S. House of Representatives, 1976-83. Attorney/Advisor, Investment Management Division, Securities and Exchange Commission, 1974-76. Legislative Assistant to House Majority Leader, Rep. Thomas P. O'Neill (D-MA), 1971-74.

Employers
Brand & Frulla, P.C. (Partner)

BRANDENBERGER, Joel

1225 New York Ave. NW
Suite 400
Washington, DC 20005
Tel: (202)898-0100
Fax: (202)898-0203
Registered: LDA

Employers
Nat'l Turkey Federation (V. President, Legislative Affairs)

BRANDON, Barry W.

1333 New Hampshire Ave. NW
Suite 400
Washington, DC 20036
Tel: (202)887-4000
Fax: (202)887-4288
Former Chief of Staff and former General Counsel, National Indian Gaming Commission. Also served as Deputy Director, Office on Indian Water Rights, Department of Interior and as Senior Trial Attorney, Department of Justice.

Employers
Akin, Gump, Strauss, Hauer & Feld, L.L.P. (Senior Counsel)

BRANDON, Douglas

1150 Connecticut Ave. NW
Fourth Floor
Washington, DC 20036-4104
Tel: (202)223-9222
Fax: (202)223-9095

Employers
AT&T Wireless Services, Inc. (V. President, External Affairs and Law)

BRANDON, Robert M.

1730 Rhode Island Ave. NW
Suite 712
Washington, DC 20036
Tel: (202)331-1550
Fax: (202)331-1663
Registered: LDA

Employers
Robert M. Brandon and Associates (President)

Clients Represented

On Behalf of Robert M. Brandon and Associates
A Greater Washington
Best Health Care Inc.
Electric Consumers Alliance
Localisation Industry Standards Ass'n
Lottery.com
Nat'l Ass'n for Public Interest Law (NAPIL)

BRANDT, Irene M.

555 12th St. NW
Suite 650
Washington, DC 20004-1205
Tel: (202)393-7950
Fax: (202)393-7960

Employers
Eli Lilly and Co. (Senior Government Affairs Associate)

BRANDT, Werner W.

1735 New York Ave. NW
Suite 500
Washington, DC 20006-4759
Tel: (202)628-1700
Fax: (202)331-1024
Registered: LDA
Seargeant-at-Arms, U.S. House of Representatives, 1992-95. Executive Assistant (1989-92), Assistant (1981-89) and Legislative Assistant (1972-81) to Rep. Thomas S. Foley (D-WA). Foreign Service Officer, Department of State, 1972-81.

Employers
Preston Gates Ellis & Rouvelas Meeds LLP (Government Affairs Counselor)

Clients Represented

On Behalf of Preston Gates Ellis & Rouvelas Meeds LLP
Akzo Nobel Chemicals, Inc.
Burlington Northern Santa Fe Railway
Chitimacha Tribe of Louisiana
eLottery, Inc.
Future of Puerto Rico Inc.
Grant County P.U.D., Washington
Magazine Publishers of America
Microsoft Corp.
Nat'l Center for Economic Freedom, Inc.
Nat'l Produce Production Inc.
Pac Med Clinics
PepsiCo, Inc.
Pitney Bowes, Inc.
Prime Time 24
Seattle, Washington, Port of
Southeast Alaska Regional Health Corp. (SEARHC)
Tate and Lyle North American Sugars Inc.
United States Maritime Coalition
VoiceStream Wireless Corp.

BRANNIGAN, Rosalind

1575 I St. NW
Suite 210
Washington, DC 20005
Tel: (202)663-6090
Fax: (202)414-6199

Employers
Drug Strategies (Senior V. President, Strategic Planning)

BRANSFORD, William L.

1100 Connecticut Ave. NW
Suite 900
Washington, DC 20036-4101
Tel: (202)463-8400
Fax: (202)833-8082
Attorney, Office of the Chief Counsel, Internal Revenue Service (1981-83) and Attorney-Advisory, Office of the Chief Counsel, Bureau of Public Debt (1978-81), Department of the Treasury.

Employers
Shaw, Bransford, Veilleux & Roth (Partner)

BRANTLEY, Chris J.

1828 L St. NW
Suite 1202
Washington, DC 20036-5104
EMail: c.brantley@ieee.org
Tel: (202)785-0017
Fax: (202)785-0835
Registered: LDA

Employers
Institute of Electrical and Electronics Engineers, Inc. (Director, Government Relations and Operations)

BRASHARES, William C.

701 Pennsylvania Ave. NW
Suite 900
Washington, DC 20004-2608
Tel: (202)434-7300
Fax: (202)434-7400

Employers
Mintz, Levin, Cohn, Ferris, Glovsky and Popeo, P.C. (Partner)

BRASWELL, Jr., T. Edward

1800 N. Kent St.
Suite 907
Arlington, VA 22209
Tel: (703)528-0840
Fax: (703)524-1005
Registered: LDA

Employers
Self-employed as an independent consultant.

Clients Represented

As an independent consultant
Newport News Shipbuilding Inc.

BRATTON, Adam

P.O. Box 75248
Washington, DC 20013-5248
EMail: abratton@theroundtable.org
Tel: (202)927-4921
Fax: (202)927-4920

Employers
Public Employees Roundtable (Deputy Director, Operations)

BRAUN, Col. Gil

1160 Air Force Pentagon
Room 4D961
Washington, DC 20330-1160
Tel: (703)697-6711
Fax: (703)697-2001

Employers
Department of Air Force (Chief, Weapons System Liaison Division, Legislative Liaison)

BRAUN, Kathleen G.

1220 L St. NW
Washington, DC 20005
Tel: (202)682-8000
Fax: (202)682-8232
Former Aide to Senator George Voinovich (R-OH).

Employers
American Petroleum Institute (Federal Relations Representative)

BRAUNSTEIN, Richard L.

1200 New Hampshire Ave. NW
Suite 800
Washington, DC 20036-6802
EMail: rbraunstein@dlalaw.com
Tel: (202)776-2000
Fax: (202)776-2222

Employers
Dow, Lohnes & Albertson, PLLC (Member)

BRAUNSTEIN, Roy

1300 L St. NW
Washington, DC 20005
Tel: (202)842-4200
Fax: (202)682-2528
Registered: LDA
EMail: rbraunstein@apwu.org

Employers
American Postal Workers Union (Legislative Director)

BRAXTON, Melissa

1501 Lee Hwy.
Arlington, VA 22209-1198
Tel: (703)247-5800
Fax: (703)247-5853
EMail: mbraxton@afa.org

Employers
Air Force Ass'n (Manager, News and Information)

BRAY, Charles W.

1451 Dolley Madison Blvd.
McLean, VA 22101-3850
Tel: (703)761-2600
Fax: (703)761-4334

Employers
Internat'l Ass'n of Food Industry Suppliers (President)

BRAY, Janet

200 Orchard Ridge Dr.
Suite 302
Gaithersburg, MD 20878
Tel: (301)212-9608
Fax: (301)990-1611
Registered: LDA
EMail: jbray@naea.org

Employers
Nat'l Ass'n of Enrolled Agents (Exec. V. President)

BRAY, Kellie

400 N. Washington St.
Alexandria, VA 22314-9980
Tel: (703)836-9340
Fax: (703)836-1279
Registered: LDA
EMail: kelliebr@pianet.org

Employers
Nat'l Ass'n of Professional Insurance Agents (Director, Political Affairs)

BRAZIEL, Rob

8400 W. Park Dr.
McLean, VA 22102
Tel: (703)547-5500
Registered: LDA

Employers
Nat'l Automobile Dealers Ass'n (Legislative Counsel)

BRAZIL, Noel

1505 Prince St.
Suite 300
Alexandria, VA 22314
Tel: (703)739-9200
Fax: (703)739-9497
Registered: LDA

Employers
American Optometric Ass'n (Manager, Political Action Committee)

BREAKS, Katherine M.

2001 M St. NW
Washington, DC 20036
Tel: (202)467-3000
Fax: (202)533-8500
Registered: LDA

Employers
KPMG, LLP (Associate)

Clients Represented
On Behalf of KPMG, LLP
Apple Computer, Inc.
The KPMG FSC Coalition

BREAM, Joseph R.

1815 N. Fort Myer Dr.
Suite 500
Arlington, VA 22209-1805
Tel: (703)527-0226
Fax: (703)527-0229

Employers
Nat'l Aeronautic Ass'n of the U.S.A. (Treasurer)

BRECHER, Mitchell F.

800 Connecticut Ave. NW
Suite 500
Washington, DC 20006
Tel: (202)331-3152
Fax: (202)261-0152
EMail: brecherm@gtlaw.com
Former Attorney/Advisor, Federal Communications Commission.

Employers
Greenberg Traurig, LLP (Shareholder)

Clients Represented
On Behalf of Greenberg Traurig, LLP
Arbinet
e.spire Communications, Inc.
GeoPhone, LLC
Internat'l Telecom Ltd.
LDMI Telecommunications, Inc.
Norlight Telecommunications, Inc.
Operator Communications, Inc.
Questar InfoComm Inc.
Time Warner Telecom Inc.
Wholesale Telecommunications Corp.
Yipes Transmission, Inc.

BRECHER, Richard

1350 I St. NW
Suite 400
Washington, DC 20005-3306
Tel: (202)371-6900
Fax: (202)842-3578
Registered: LDA

Employers
Motorola, Inc. (Director, International Trade Relations (Asia))

BRECHT, Paul

1700 Diagonal Rd.
Suite 600
Alexandria, VA 22314-2866
Tel: (703)739-0696
Fax: (703)739-2524

Employers
Soc. of Competitive Intelligence Professionals (Deputy Director and Chief Financial Officer)

BRECK, Richard

611 Second St. NE
Washington, DC 20002
Tel: (202)548-4001
Fax: (202)548-6115
EMail: rbreck@imaps.org

Employers
Internat'l Microelectronics and Packaging Soc. - IMAPS (Exec. Director)

BREDEN, Roberta

2500 Wilson Blvd.
Suite 300
Arlington, VA 22201
Tel: (703)907-7705
Fax: (703)907-7727
Registered: LDA
EMail: rbreden@tia.eia.org

Employers
Telecommunications Industry Ass'n (Director, Technical and Regulatory Affairs)

BREDHOFF, Elliot

1000 Connecticut Ave. NW
Suite 1300
Washington, DC 20036
Tel: (202)842-2600
Fax: (202)842-1888

Employers
Bredhoff & Kaiser (Senior Counsel)

Clients Represented
On Behalf of Bredhoff & Kaiser
Pickands Mather and Co.

BREEDLOVE, Adrienne M.

1385 Piccard Dr.
Rockville, MD 20850-4340
Tel: (301)869-5800
Fax: (301)990-9690
EMail: abreedlove@mcaa.org

Employers
Mechanical Contractors Ass'n of America (Associate Director, MSCA)

BREEDLOVE, Carolyn

1201 16th St. NW
Washington, DC 20036
Tel: (202)833-4000
Registered: LDA

Employers
Nat'l Education Ass'n of the U.S. (Senior Professional Associate, Government Relations)

BREINDEL, Barry

1025 Connecticut Ave. NW
Suite 501
Washington, DC 20036
Tel: (202)828-6865
Fax: (202)828-6849

Employers
GenCorp (Director, BMD and Technology (Aerojet))

BREITFELD, Julie S.

1020 19th St. NW
Suite 850
Washington, DC 20036
Tel: (202)452-9100
Fax: (202)452-9555
Registered: FARA
EMail: julie.breitfeld@usa.telekom.de

Employers
Deutsche Telekom, Inc. (Senior Manager, Regulatory and Govt. Affairs)

BREMER, Charles V.

1130 Connecticut Ave. NW
Suite 1200
Washington, DC 20036-3954
Tel: (202)862-0500
Fax: (202)862-0570

Employers
American Textile Manufacturers Institute (Director, International Trade)

BREMER, Heather H.

P.O. Box 25366
Washington, DC 20007-8366
Tel: (202)337-3185
Registered: LDA
EMail: capitolrep@aol.com

Employers
Washington Healthcare Representatives (President)

Clients Represented
On Behalf of Washington Healthcare Representatives
Allergan, Inc.
Cochlear Corp.
Metra Biosystems, Inc.

BRENNAN, Barry

1421 Prince St.
Alexandria, VA 22314-2814
Tel: (703)836-9200
Fax: (703)548-8204
EMail: brennanb@mfsanet.org

Employers
Mailing & Fulfillment Services Ass'n (Director, Postal Affairs)

BRENNAN, Janis H.

1747 Pennsylvania Ave. NW
Suite 1200
Washington, DC 20006
Tel: (202)223-1200
Fax: (202)785-6687
Registered: LDA, FARA
EMail: jhbrennan@fhe.com

Employers
Foley, Hoag & Eliot LLP (Partner)

BRENNAN, Maria E.

1595 Spring Hill Rd.
Suite 330
Vienna, VA 22182
Tel: (703)506-3260
Fax: (703)506-3266

Employers
Ass'n Management Bureau

Clients Represented
On Behalf of Ass'n Management Bureau
Ass'n of Female Exhibit Contractors and Event Organizers

BRENNER, Daniel L.

1724 Massachusetts Ave. NW
Washington, DC 20036-1969
Tel: (202)775-3550
Fax: (202)775-3603
Registered: LDA

Employers
Nat'l Cable Television Ass'n (Senior V. President, Law and Regulatory Policy)

BRENNER, Kyd D.

1001 Pennsylvania Ave. NW
Suite 600 North
Washington, DC 20004
Tel: (202)661-7098
Fax: (202)661-7093
EMail: kbrenner@dtbassociates.com

Employers
DTB Associates, LLP (Partner)

BRENNER, AIA, William A.

1090 Vermont Ave. NW
Suite 700
Washington, DC 20005-4905
Tel: (202)289-7800
Fax: (202)289-1092
EMail: bbrenner@nibs.org

Employers
Nat'l Institute of Building Sciences (V. President)

BRENT, Richard

818 Connecticut Ave. NW
Suite 600
Washington, DC 20006-2702
Tel: (202)466-0676
Fax: (202)466-0684
Registered: LDA

Employers
Caterpillar Inc. (Washington Manager, Solar)

BRESNICK, William O.

1050 17th St. NW
Suite 500
Washington, DC 20036
Tel: (202)331-1427
Fax: (202)785-4702
Registered: LDA

Employers
Texaco Group Inc. (Senior Environmental Representative)

BRESSER, Gregory A.

5413-C Backlick Rd.
Springfield, VA 22151
Tel: (703)354-2140
Fax: (703)642-2054
EMail: info@purpleheart.org

Employers
Military Order of the Purple Heart of the U.S.A. (Nat'l Service Director)

BRESSETT, Sean

1200 17th St. NW
Washington, DC 20036-3097
Tel: (202)331-5900
Fax: (202)973-5373

Employers
Nat'l Restaurant Ass'n (Director, Political Affairs)

BREUER, Lanny A.

1201 Pennsylvania Ave. NW
Washington, DC 20004-2401
Tel: (202)662-6000
Fax: (202)662-6291
EMail: lbreuer@cov.com
Special Counsel to the President, The White House, 1997-99.

Employers
Covington & Burling (Partner)

BREW, James

1025 Thomas Jefferson St. NW
Eighth Floor, West Tower
Washington, DC 20007
Tel: (202)342-0800
Fax: (202)342-0807
Registered: LDA
EMail: jbrew@bbrslaw.com

Employers
Brickfield, Burchette, Ritts & Stone (Partner)

Clients Represented

On Behalf of Brickfield, Burchette, Ritts & Stone
Steel Manufacturers Ass'n

BREW, John B.

3050 K St. NW
Washington, DC 20007
Tel: (202)342-8400
Fax: (202)342-8451
Registered: LDA
EMail: jbrew@colliershannon.com

Employers
Collier Shannon Scott, PLLC (Member)

Clients Represented

On Behalf of Collier Shannon Scott, PLLC
American Flange Producers Marking Coalition
Symbol Technologies, Inc.
Toolex USA, Inc.

BREWER, Carol

1730 Pennsylvania Ave. NW
Suite 1200
Washington, DC 20006-4706
Tel: (202)737-0500
Fax: (202)626-3737
Registered: LDA

Employers
King & Spalding (International Trade Specialist)

Clients Represented

On Behalf of King & Spalding
Southern Tier Cement Committee

BREWER, Elisa

412 First St. SE
Suite 12
Washington, DC 20003
Tel: (202)484-8400
Fax: (202)484-8408

Employers
American Ass'n of Nurse Anesthetists (Political Action Coordinator)

BREWER, Michael F.

1200 New Hampshire Ave. NW
Suite 445
Washington, DC 20036
Tel: (202)822-8882
Fax: (202)822-8822
Registered: LDA
EMail: mfbrewer@worldnet.att.net

Employers
Brewer Consulting Group, Inc. (President)

Clients Represented

On Behalf of Brewer Consulting Group, Inc.
ACNielsen Corp.

BREWSTER, Hon. Bill

601 13th St. NW
Suite 410 South
Washington, DC 20005
Tel: (202)737-0100
Fax: (202)628-3965
Registered: LDA
Member, U.S. House of Representatives (D-OK), 1991-96.

Employers
R. Duffy Wall and Associates (Chairman)

Clients Represented

On Behalf of R. Duffy Wall and Associates
American Gas Ass'n
Beretta U.S.A. Corp.
CIGNA Corp.
Entergy Services, Inc.
Fleishman-Hillard, Inc
Home Care Ass'n of New York State
Metropolitan Mortgage and Securities, Inc.
Nat'l Ass'n of Counties
NCR Corp.
Novartis Corp.
Verizon Communications
Waddell & Reed Financial, Inc.

BREWSTER, Brad

1200 G St. NW
Suite 800
Washington, DC 20005
Tel: (202)434-8768
Fax: (202)434-8707

Employers
Winning Strategies Washington, D.C., LLC

BREWSTER, Christopher R.

The McPherson Bldg.
901 15th St. NW, Suite 1100
Washington, DC 20005
Tel: (202)682-3535
Fax: (202)682-3580
Registered: LDA
EMail: cbrewster@kayesscholer.com
Associate Director for Marketing Practices, Bureau of Consumer Protection, Federal Trade Commission, 1982-84. Legislative Assistant to Senator John Danforth (R-MO). Counsel, Senate Committee on Government Affairs, 1977-82.

Employers
Kaye Scholer LLP (Counsel)

Clients Represented

On Behalf of Kaye Scholer LLP
BNFL, Inc.
Korean Semiconductor Industry Ass'n
Malrite Communications Group, Inc.
J. P. Morgan Chase & Co.
Omega Oil Co.
Spanish Broadcasting System, Inc.

BREWSTER, Suzie

451 New Jersey Ave. SE
Washington, DC 20003
Tel: (202)544-6363
Fax: (202)544-3219
Registered: LDA, FARA

Employers
Suzie Brewster & Associates (President)

Clients Represented

On Behalf of Suzie Brewster & Associates
Collier Shannon Scott, PLLC
University of Oklahoma

BREYFOGLE, Jon W.

1701 Pennsylvania Ave. NW
Suite 1200
Washington, DC 20006
Tel: (202)857-0620
Fax: (202)659-4503
Registered: LDA
EMail: jwb@groom.com
Senior Legislative Officer, Office of Congressional Affairs, Department of Labor, 1989-92. Policy Analyst, Office of Management and Budget, Executive Office of the President, The White House, 1985-87.

Employers
Groom Law Group, Chartered (Partner)

Clients Represented

On Behalf of Groom Law Group, Chartered
American Benefits Council
American Council of Life Insurers
Blue Cross Blue Shield Ass'n
Buffalo Carpenters Pension Fund
Production Service & Sales District Council Pension Fund
Prudential Insurance Co. of America
Wachovia Bank, N.A.

BRIAN, Danielle

666 11th St. NW
Suite 500
Washington, DC 20001
Tel: (202)347-1122
Fax: (202)347-1116

Employers
Project on Government Oversight, Inc. (Exec. Director)

BRICELAND-BETTS, Deborah

666 11th St. NW
Suite 700
Washington, DC 20001
Tel: (202)783-6686
Fax: (202)638-2356

Employers
Older Women's League (Exec. Director)

BRICELAND-BETTS, Timothy

440 First St. NW
Third Floor
Washington, DC 20001-2085
Tel: (202)638-2952
Fax: (202)638-4004
Registered: LDA

Employers
Child Welfare League of America (Senior Policy Analyst)

BRICKELL, Beatrice A.

1707 L St. NW
Suite 725
Washington, DC 20036
Tel: (202)223-4433
Fax: (202)659-3904
EMail: customs@sharretts-paley

Employers
Sharretts, Paley, Carter and Blauvelt

BRICKFIELD, Peter J. P.

1025 Thomas Jefferson St. NW
Eighth Floor, West Tower
Washington, DC 20007
Tel: (202)342-0800
Fax: (202)342-0807

Employers
Brickfield, Burchette, Ritts & Stone (Partner)

BRIDENBAUGH, Thomas D.

1401 New York Ave.
Suite 600
Washington, DC 20005
Tel: (202)434-9100
Registered: LDA

Employers
Leftwich & Douglas

BRIDGES, Jessica

4121 Wilson Blvd.
Tenth Floor
Arlington, VA 22203
Tel: (703)351-2000
Registered: LDA
EMail: jbridges@ntca.org

Employers
Nat'l Telephone Cooperative Ass'n (Government Affairs Representative)

BRIDGMAN, Jim

1801 18th St. NW
Suite 9-2
Washington, DC 20009
Tel: (202)833-4668
Fax: (202)234-9536

Employers
Alliance for Nuclear Accountability (Program Director)

BRIEN, Michael

1776 I St. NW
Suite 1000
Washington, DC 20006
Tel: (202)785-4888
Fax: (202)457-6597
Registered: LDA

Employers
BP Amoco Corp. (PAC Administrator)

BRIER, M. William

701 Pennsylvania Ave. NW
Washington, DC 20004-2696
Tel: (202)508-5300
Fax: (202)508-5759
Registered: LDA

Employers
Edison Electric Institute (V. President, Communication)

BRIERRE, Jr., William V.

1101 Connecticut Ave. NW
Suite 900
Washington, DC 20036
Tel: (202)296-7787
Fax: (202)296-7780
Registered: LDA

Employers
Self-employed as an independent consultant.

Clients Represented
As an independent consultant
Ad Hoc Maritime Coalition
General Electric Co.
Labor Management Maritime Committee, Inc.
Maersk Inc.
Maritime Institute for Research and Industrial Development
Sea Bridge Internat'l LLC
Transportation Institute

BRIERTON, Thomas W.

1133 21st St. NW
Suite 700
Washington, DC 20036
Tel: (202)887-6900
Fax: (202)887-6970
Registered: LDA
EMail: tbrierton@janus-merritt.com
Former Deputy Staff Director, Subcommittee on the Census, U.S. House of Representatives. Senior Policy Coordinator, 1997-98, Legislative Assistant 1995-96, to Rep. J. Dennis Hastert, (R-IL).

Employers
Janus-Merritt Strategies, L.L.C. (Principal)

Clients Represented
On Behalf of Janus-Merritt Strategies, L.L.C.
Napster, Inc.
Viejas Band of Kumeyaay Indians

BRIESE, Garry L.

4025 Fair Ridge Dr.
Fairfax, VA 22033-2868
Tel: (703)273-0911
Fax: (703)273-9363

Employers
Internat'l Ass'n of Fire Chiefs (Exec. Director)

BRIGGS, Alan L.

1201 Pennsylvania Ave. NW
P.O. Box 407
Washington, DC 20044-0407
Tel: (202)626-6600
Fax: (202)626-6780
Registered: FARA
EMail: abriggs@ssd.com

Employers
Squire, Sanders & Dempsey L.L.P. (Managing Partner)

BRIGGS, Eli

1320 19th St. NW
Suite 350
Washington, DC 20036
Tel: (202)232-6200
Fax: (202)232-1133
Registered: LDA
EMail: dc@nrharural.org

Employers
Nat'l Rural Health Ass'n (Government Affiars Policy Specialist)

BRIGGS, III, John DeQ.

1299 Pennsylvania Ave. NW
Washington, DC 20004-2402
Tel: (202)783-0800
Fax: (202)383-6610
Registered: LDA
EMail: briggsj@howrey.com
Law Clerk to Judge Frank J. Murray, U.S. District Court for the District of Massachusetts, 1972-73.

Employers
Howrey Simon Arnold & White (Partner)

Clients Represented
On Behalf of Howrey Simon Arnold & White
Rockwell Collins
Uniroyal Chemical Co., Inc.

BRIGGS, Tom

1775 I St. NW
Suite 800
Washington, DC 20006
Tel: (202)466-9169
Fax: (202)828-3372
EMail: tom.briggs@enron.com

Employers
Enron Corp. (V. President, Government Affairs)

BRIGGUM, Sue M.

601 Pennsylvania Ave. NW
Suite 300
The North Bldg.
Washington, DC 20004
Tel: (202)628-3500
Fax: (202)628-0400
Registered: LDA

Employers
Waste Management, Inc. (Director, Environmental Affairs)

BRIGHAM, Lori

8110 Gatehouse Rd.
Suite 101 West
Falls Church, VA 22042
Tel: (703)641-0100
Fax: (703)641-0211

Employers
Washington Regional Transplant Consortium (Exec. Director)

BRIGHT, Bill

2550 M St. NW
Washington, DC 20037-1350
Tel: (202)457-6000
Fax: (202)457-6315
Former Minority Research Director, Committee on the Judiciary, U.S. House of Representatives.

Employers
Patton Boggs, LLP (Legislative Specialist)

Clients Represented
On Behalf of Patton Boggs, LLP
EchoStar Communications Corp.

BRIGHTUP, Craig S.

324 Fourth St. NE
Washington, DC 20002
Tel: (202)546-7584
Fax: (202)546-9289
Registered: LDA
EMail: cbrightup@nrca.net

Employers
Nat'l Roofing Contractors Ass'n (Associate Exec. Director, Government Relations)

BRIGNER, Sharon

Ten G St. NE
Suite 600
Washington, DC 20002-4215
Tel: (202)216-0420
Fax: (202)216-0446
EMail: brigners@ncpssm.org

Employers
Nat'l Committee to Preserve Social Security and Medicare (Senior Policy Analyst)

BRILL, Bernard D.

7910 Woodmont Ave.
Suite 1130
Bethesda, MD 20814
Tel: (301)656-1077
Fax: (301)656-1079

Employers
Secondary Materials and Recycled Textiles Ass'n (Exec. V. President)

BRILL, II, Richard Budd

1525 Wilson Blvd.
Suite 600
Arlington, VA 22209
Tel: (703)527-1670
Fax: (703)527-5477
Registered: LDA

Employers
Jellinek, Schwartz & Connolly (Research Assistant)

BRILLIANT, Hana

1050 Connecticut Ave. NW
Suite 1200
Washington, DC 20036
Tel: (202)857-1700
Fax: (202)857-1737
Registered: LDA

Employers
McGuireWoods L.L.P.

Clients Represented
On Behalf of McGuireWoods L.L.P.
Alexandria, Virginia, Sanitation Authority of the City of
CSO Partnership
Lynchburg, Virginia, City of
Prince William County Service Authority
Richmond, Virginia, City of

BRILLIANT, Myron A.

1615 H St. NW
Washington, DC 20062-2000
Tel: (202)463-5460
Fax: (202)463-3173
Registered: LDA
EMail: mbrilliant@uschamber.com

Employers
Chamber of Commerce of the U.S.A. (Manager, Asia)

BRIMSEK, John R.

1150 Connecticut Ave. NW
Suite 700
Washington, DC 20036
Tel: (202)296-8000
Fax: (202)296-8803
Registered: LDA, FARA
EMail: jrb@mbblawyers.com
Appropriations and Legislative Counsel to Rep. Martin Sabo (D-MN), 1983-89. Attorney and Deputy Chief Counsel, General Services Administration Board of Appeals, 1979-83. Legislative Assistant to Senator Wendell Anderson (D-MN), 1977-78.

Employers
Mullenholz, Brimsek & Belair (Partner)

Clients Represented
On Behalf of Mullenholz, Brimsek & Belair
Aviateca Airline
The Coalition on Motor Vehicle Privacy
Copa Airline
Delaware and Hudson Railroad
Fergus Falls, Minnesota, City of
NICA Airline
Northstar Corridor Development Authority
Soo Line Railroad, Inc.
TACA de Honduras
TACA Internat'l Airlines

BRIMSEK, Tobi

900 Second St. NE
Suite 12
Washington, DC 20002-3557
Tel: (202)789-8200
Fax: (202)789-0284
EMail: tobi_brimsek@saa.org

Employers
Soc. for American Archaeology (Exec. Director)

BRINK, Peter

1785 Massachusetts Ave. NW
Washington, DC 20036
Tel: (202)588-6000
Fax: (202)588-6059

Employers
Nat'l Trust for Historic Preservation (Senior V. President, Programs)

BRINKMAN, Karen

555 11th St. NW
Suite 1000
Washington, DC 20004
Tel: (202)637-2200
Fax: (202)637-2201
Registered: LDA

Employers
Latham & Watkins

Clients Represented
On Behalf of Latham & Watkins
Independent Telephone and Telecommunications Alliance

BRINKMANN, Robert J.

529 14th St. NW
Suite 440
Washington, DC 20045-1402
Tel: (202)783-4697
Fax: (202)783-4699
Registered: LDA
EMail: brinb@naa.org

Employers
Newspaper Ass'n of America (V. President and Counsel, Postal & Regulatory Affairs)

BRINTNALL, Michael A.

1120 G St. NW
Suite 730
Washington, DC 20005
EMail: brintnal@naspaa.org
Tel: (202)628-8965
Fax: (202)626-4978

Employers
Nat'l Ass'n of Schools of Public Affairs and Administration (Exec. Director)

BRINTZENHOFE, Nicola

1029 N. Royal St.
Suite 400
Alexandria, VA 22314
EMail: nbrintzenhofe@directimpact.com
Tel: (703)684-1245
Fax: (703)684-1249

Employers
The Direct Impact Co. (Chief Financial Officer)

BRISCOE, III, Andrew

700 N. Fairfax St.
Suite 600
Alexandria, VA 22314-2040
EMail: briscoe_andy@saltinstitute.org
Tel: (703)549-4648
Fax: (703)548-2194

Employers
Salt Institute (Director, Public Policy)

BRISCUSO, Raymond

1625 K St. NW
Suite 1100
Washington, DC 20006-1604
EMail: rbriscuso@bio.org
Tel: (202)857-0244
Fax: (202)857-0237

Employers
Biotechnology Industry Organization (Exec. Director)

BRISTOL, Theodore W.

805 15th St. NW
Suite 700
Washington, DC 20005
Tel: (202)223-0964
Fax: (202)312-7441
Registered: LDA
EMail: twbristo@bakerd.com
Former Legislative Director to Rep. Norman Dicks (D-WA). Former Legislative Director, Legislative Assistant, to Rep. Don Baker (D-WA). Former Legislative Staff Member for Sen Frank Lautenberg, (D-NJ). Former Assistant to Senator Richard Stone (D-FL)

Employers
Sagamore Associates, Inc. (Senior V. President)

Clients Represented
On Behalf of Sagamore Associates, Inc.
2001 World Police and Fire Games
Fort Wayne, Indiana, City of
Geothermal Heat Pump Consortium
Medford, Oregon, City of
NextRX
Walsh Enterprises Internat'l

BRITAIN, Robert G.

1300 N. 17th St.
Suite 1847
Rosslyn, VA 22209
Tel: (703)841-3241
Fax: (703)841-3341
Registered: LDA
EMail: bob_britain@nema.org
Served with Food and Drug Administration, 1962-85.

Employers
Nat'l Electrical Manufacturers Ass'n (V. President, Medical Products)

BRITELL, Maureen

1010 Wisconsin Ave. NW
Suite 410
Washington, DC 20007
Tel: (202)944-5080
Fax: (202)944-5081

Employers
Voters For Choice (Exec. Director)

BRITELL, Peter

1875 Connecticut Ave. NW
Suite 1200
Washington, DC 20009-5728
Tel: (202)986-8000
Fax: (202)986-8102
Registered: LDA

Employers
LeBoeuf, Lamb, Greene & MacRae L.L.P.

Clients Represented
On Behalf of LeBoeuf, Lamb, Greene & MacRae L.L.P.
The Project Leadership Committee, Lincoln Center for the Performing Arts

BRITTO, Karen

601 Pennsylvania Ave. NW
Suite 350
North Bldg.
Washington, DC 20004
EMail: brittok@dteenergy.com
Tel: (202)347-8420
Fax: (202)347-8423
Registered: LDA

Employers
Detroit Edison Co. (Washington Representative)

BROADBENT, Nan

1200 New York Ave. NW
Washington, DC 20005
Tel: (202)326-6400
Fax: (202)371-9526

Employers
American Ass'n for the Advancement of Science (Director of Communications)

BROADSTONE, James M.

1023 15th St. NW
Suite 900
Washington, DC 20005-2602
EMail: jbroadstone@gbmdc.com
Tel: (202)289-7200
Fax: (202)289-7698
Staff Attorney, Federal Power Commission, 1972-73.

Employers
Gallagher, Boland and Meiburger (Partner)

Clients Represented
On Behalf of Gallagher, Boland and Meiburger
Gas Research Institute

BROAS, Timothy M.

1400 L St. NW
Washington, DC 20005-3502
EMail: tbroas@winston.com
Tel: (202)371-5750
Fax: (202)371-5950

Employers
Winston & Strawn (Partner)

Clients Represented
On Behalf of Winston & Strawn
American General Financial Group

BROBECK, Stephen

1424 16th St. NW
Suite 604
Washington, DC 20036
EMail: sbrobeck@essential.org
Tel: (202)387-6121
Fax: (202)265-7989

Employers
Consumer Federation of America (Exec. Director)

BROCK, Karen

1140 19th St. NW
Suite 600
Washington, DC 20036
Tel: (202)822-8200
Fax: (202)822-8205

Employers
Violence Policy Center (Health Policy Analyst)

BROCK, Thomas H.

1233 20th St. NW
Suite 800
Washington, DC 20036-2396
EMail: TBrock@proskauer.com
Tel: (202)416-6800
Fax: (202)416-6899

Employers
Proskauer Rose LLP (Senior Counsel)

BROCKMEYER, Michael F.

1200 19th St. NW
Washington, DC 20036-2430
Tel: (202)861-3907
Fax: (202)223-2085
Registered: LDA
EMail: michael.brockmeyer@piperrudnick.com

Employers
Piper Marbury Rudnick & Wolfe LLP (Partner)

Clients Represented
On Behalf of Piper Marbury Rudnick & Wolfe LLP
Lexis-Nexis

BROCKWAY, David

2001 M St. NW
Washington, DC 20036
Tel: (202)467-3000
Fax: (202)533-8500
Former Chief of Staff and Deputy of Chief of Staff, Joint Committee on Taxation, U.S. Congress.

Employers
KPMG, LLP

BRODERICK, Kelly

1100 New York Ave. NW
Suite 1050
Washington, DC 20005
Tel: (202)842-1645
Fax: (202)842-0850

Employers
American Bus Ass'n (Legislative Assistant)

BRODIE, Katherine D.

1333 New Hampshire Ave. NW
Suite 400
Washington, DC 20036
Tel: (202)887-4000
Fax: (202)887-4288
Registered: LDA

Employers
Akin, Gump, Strauss, Hauer & Feld, L.L.P.

Clients Represented
On Behalf of Akin, Gump, Strauss, Hauer & Feld, L.L.P.
Banro American Resources Inc.
Dow Jones & Co., Inc.
Gila River Indian Community
Poongsan Corporation
The Project Leadership Committee, Lincoln Center for the Performing Arts

BRODSKY, Art

2100 Pennsylvania Ave. NW
Suite 535
Washington, DC 20037
Tel: (202)822-1700
Fax: (202)822-1919
Director of Communications, National Telecommunications and Information Administration, Department of Commerce, 2000-01.

Employers
Simon Strategies/Mindbeam (Senior V. President)

BRODSKY, Lewis C.

1515 Wilson Blvd.
Fourth Floor
Arlington, VA 22209-2425
EMail: lbrodsky@sss.gov
Tel: (703)605-4100
Fax: (703)605-4106
Assistant Director for Public Affairs, Selective Service System, 1986-95. Public Affairs Director, U.S. Army Reserve, 1982-86. Information Director, Department of Agriculture, 1980-82. Public Affairs Officer, U.S. Army Reserve, 1972-80.

Employers
Selective Service System (Director, Office of Public and Congressional Affairs)

BRODSKY, Marc H.

One Physics Ellipse
College Park, MD 20740-3843
EMail: brodsky@aip.org
Tel: (301)209-3131
Fax: (301)209-0843

Employers
American Institute of Physics (Exec. Director and Chief Exec. Officer)

BRODY, Mimi A.

2100 L St. NW
Washington, DC 20037
Tel: (202)452-1100
Fax: (202)778-6132

Employers
Humane Soc. of the United States (Director, Federal Legislation)

BROFF, Nancy B.

Ten G St. NE
Suite 750
Washington, DC 20002-4213
Tel: (202)336-6700
Fax: (202)336-6828
Registered: LDA
EMail: NancyB@career.org

Employers
Career College Ass'n (General Counsel)

BROGEN, Stephen

51 Louisiana Ave. NW
Washington, DC 20001
Tel: (202)879-3939
Fax: (202)626-1700

Employers
Jones, Day, Reavis & Pogue

BROMBERG, Michael D.

1100 New York Ave. NW
Suite 200M
Washington, DC 20005
Tel: (202)367-0440
Fax: (202)367-0470
Registered: LDA
EMail: mike@caphg.com
Legislative Assistant and Administrative Assistant to Rep. Herbert Tenzer (D-NY), 1966-69.

Employers
Capitol Health Group, LLC (Chairman)

Clients Represented

On Behalf of Capitol Health Group, LLC
Abbott Laboratories
Beverly Enterprises
Bristol-Myers Squibb Co.
Express Scripts Inc.
Greater New York Hospital Ass'n
Healthcare Leadership Council
Humana Inc.
Johnson & Johnson, Inc.
Medassets.com
Nat'l Ass'n of Psychiatric Health Systems
Northwestern Memorial Hospital
Pfizer, Inc.
Soc. of Thoracic Surgeons

BROMME, Jeffrey S.

555 12th St. NW
Washington, DC 20004-1206
Tel: (202)942-5000
Fax: (202)942-5999
EMail: Jeffrey_Bromme@aporter.com
Former General Counsel, Consumer Product Safety Commission.

Employers
Arnold & Porter (Partner)

BROOK, Douglas A.

1155 Connecticut Ave. NW
Suite 502
Washington, DC 20036
Tel: (202)872-5522
Fax: (202)872-5521
Registered: LDA

Employers
The LTV Corp. (V. President, Government Affairs)

BROOKHART, Sarah

1010 Vermont Ave. NW
Suite 1100
Washington, DC 20005-4907
Tel: (202)783-2077
Fax: (202)783-2083

Employers
American Psychological Soc. (Director, Policy and Communications)

BROOKS, A. Oakley

1023 15th St. NW
Suite 1000
Washington, DC 20005-2602
Tel: (202)414-8980
Fax: (202)789-0076
Registered: LDA

Employers
Short Brothers (USA), Inc. (President)

BROOKS, Andrea

80 F St. NW
Washington, DC 20001
Tel: (202)639-6419
Fax: (202)639-6441

Employers
American Federation of Government Employees (AFL-CIO) (Director, Womens/Fair Practices Dept.)

BROOKS, B. Jeffrey

409 Ninth St. NW
Suite 610 South
Washington, DC 20004
Tel: (202)737-3234
Fax: (202)737-0264
Registered: LDA
EMail: BrooksBJ@arlaw.com
Chief Counsel (1995-97) and State Director (1994-95) to Rep. Richard Baker (R-LA). Former Judicial Law Clerk to the Hon. Elizabeth Pickett, Chief Judge, U.S. District Court, Eleventh District.

Employers
Adams and Reese LLP (Partner-in-Charge, Washington Office)

Clients Represented

On Behalf of Adams and Reese LLP
Baton Rouge, Louisiana, City of
Coastal Impact Assistance & Reinvestment
Coweta County (Georgia) School Board
GE Capital Corp.
Iberville Parish
Interregional Associates
Jefferson Parish Council
Lafayette Airport Commission
Louisiana Credit Union Ass'n
Louisiana Internat'l Group
Louisiana State University
Loyola University
New Orleans, Louisiana, Regional Transit Authority of
Pennington BioMedical Research Center
Plaquemine, Louisiana, City of
Q-ZAB Coalition
Regional Transit Authority
South Louisiana, Port of
Southeastern Louisiana University
Swiftships
Textron Marine and Land
Unisys Corp.
Zachery Taylor Parkway Commission

BROOKS, Bob

425 Second St. NE
Washington, DC 20002
Tel: (202)675-6000
Fax: (202)675-6058

Employers
Nat'l Republican Senatorial Committee (Research Director)

BROOKS, Brian

555 13th St. NW
Suite 500 West
Washington, DC 20004
Tel: (202)383-5300
Fax: (202)383-5414
Registered: LDA
EMail: bbrooks@omm.com

Employers
O'Melveny and Myers LLP (Associate)

Clients Represented

On Behalf of O'Melveny and Myers LLP
Lockheed Martin Corp.

BROOKS, Charles D.

600 Pennsylvania Ave. SE
Washington, DC 20003
Tel: (202)879-7710
Fax: (202)879-7728

Employers
The Nat'l PAC (Exec. Director)

BROOKS, Mary E.

1730 M St. NW
Suite 1000
Washington, DC 20036
Tel: (202)429-1965
Fax: (202)429-0854
Registered: LDA

Employers
League of Women Voters of the United States (Senior Lobbyist)

BROOKS, Matthew

415 Second St. NE
Washington, DC 20002
Tel: (202)547-7701
Fax: (202)544-2434
EMail: rjc@rjchq.org

Employers
Republican Jewish Coalition (Exec. Director)

BROOKS, Michelle

1255 23rd St. NW
Washington, DC 20037
Tel: (202)955-0002
Fax: (202)835-1144

Employers
Council of Federal Home Loan Banks (V. President, Government Relations)

BROOKS, Robert M.

206 G St. NE
Washington, DC 20002
Tel: (202)543-3383
Fax: (202)544-7716
Registered: LDA

Employers
Evergreen Associates, Ltd.

Clients Represented

On Behalf of Evergreen Associates, Ltd.
Central Kitsap School District
Choctaw Nation of Oklahoma
Clover Park School District
Medical Lake School District
Military Impacted School Districts Ass'n
Sun Innovations, Inc.
Washington State Impact Aid Ass'n

BROOKS, Sharon D.

1400 16th St. NW
Suite 400
Washington, DC 20036-2220
Tel: (202)518-6360
Fax: (202)234-0399
EMail: sbrooks@ofwlaw.com

Employers
Olsson, Frank and Weeda, P.C. (Associate)

BROOKS, Steve

430 First St. SE
Washington, DC 20003
Tel: (202)544-6245
Fax: (202)675-6568
Registered: LDA

Employers
American Trucking Ass'ns (Counselor to the Senior V. President and Director, Political & External Affairs)

BROOKS, Teresa A.

51 Louisiana Ave. NW
Washington, DC 20001
Tel: (202)879-3939
Fax: (202)626-1700
Registered: LDA
EMail: tabrooks@jonesday.com

Employers
Jones, Day, Reavis & Pogue (Partner)

Clients Represented

On Behalf of Jones, Day, Reavis & Pogue
Trinity Health

BROOKS, Tricia

426 C St. NE
Washington, DC 20002
Tel: (202)544-1880
Fax: (202)543-2565
Registered: LDA
EMail: tb@capitolassociates.com

Employers
Capitol Associates, Inc. (Associate)

Clients Represented

On Behalf of Capitol Associates, Inc.
Cell Therapeutics Inc.
FDA-NIH Council
Joint Council of Allergy, Asthma and Immunology

BROOM, R. Stuart

901 15th St. NW
Suite 700
Washington, DC 20005-2301
Tel: (202)371-6000
Fax: (202)371-6279
EMail: rsbroom@verner.com

Employers
Verner, Liipfert, Bernhard, McPherson and Hand, Chartered (Member of Firm)

Clients Represented

On Behalf of Verner, Liipfert, Bernhard, McPherson and Hand, Chartered
General Motors Corp.

BROOME, David W.

1400 L St. NW
Washington, DC 20005-3502
Tel: (202)371-5802
Fax: (202)371-5950
Registered: LDA
EMail: dbroome@winston.com

Employers
Winston & Strawn (Political Advisor)

Clients Represented

On Behalf of Winston & Strawn
Panda Energy Internat'l
Spectrum Consulting, Inc.
Yellow Corp.

BROONER, Mary E.

1350 I St. NW
Suite 400
Washington, DC 20005-3306
Tel: (202)371-6900
Fax: (202)842-3578
Registered: LDA

Employers
Motorola, Inc. (Director, Telecommunications Strategy and Regulation)

BRORSEN, Les

1225 Connecticut Ave. NW
Washington, DC 20036
Tel: (202)327-5968
Fax: (202)327-8863
Registered: LDA
EMail: les.brorsen@ey.com
Chief of Staff (1990-97), Legislative Director (1989-90), Field Representative (1987-89), and Legislative Assistant (1984-87), to Senator Don Nickles (R-OK).

Employers
Ernst & Young LLP (National Director, Government Relations)

BROSCH, Kevin

1001 Pennsylvania Ave. NW
Suite 600 North
Washington, DC 20004
Tel: (202)661-7097
Fax: (202)661-7093
EMail: kbrosch@dtbassociates.com
Special Advisor on International Trade, Senate Committee on Agriculture Nutrition and Forestry, 1999-2000. Special Senior Trade Advisor to the Director of Trade Policy, Foreign Agricultural Service (1998-99) and Deputy Assistant General Counsel for International Trade, Office of the General Counsel (1989-98), Department of Agriculture.

Employers
DTB Associates, LLP (Partner)

BROUGH, Wayne

1250 H St. NW
Suite 700
Washington, DC 20005-3908
Tel: (202)783-3870
Fax: (202)783-4687
EMail: wbrough@cse.org

Employers
Citizens for a Sound Economy (Chief Economist)

BROUILLETTE, Dan

660 Pennsylvania Ave. SE
Suite 201
Washington, DC 20003
Tel: (202)548-2312
Fax: (202)547-4658
Registered: LDA
Former Legislative Director to Rep. W. J. "Billy" Tauzin (R-LA), 1989-96

Employers
Alpine Group, Inc. (Partner)

Clients Represented
On Behalf of Alpine Group, Inc.
Arthur Andersen LLP
BP Amoco Corp.
Business Software Alliance
Lockheed Martin Global Telecommunications
Pharmacia Corp.
Recording Industry Ass'n of America
Swedish Match
U.S. Filter

BROWDER, Joseph B.

418 Tenth St. SE
Washington, DC 20003
Tel: (202)546-3720
Fax: (202)546-5557
Registered: LDA
EMail: dandb@intr.net
Special Assistant to the Assistant Secretary for Land and Water, Department of the Interior 1977-80. Director, Energy & Environment, Carter-Mondale Presidential Transition Planning, 1976.

Employers
Dunlap & Browder, Inc. (Partner)

Clients Represented
On Behalf of Dunlap & Browder, Inc.
Bones Brothers Ranch
Clean Air Campaign
Izaak Walton League of America (Mangrove and Florida Keys Chapters)
Klamath Tribes
Native American Rights Fund
United Cement Corp.

BROWDER, K. Link

1401 K St. NW
Suite 450
Washington, DC 20005
Tel: (202)737-0700
Fax: (202)737-0455
Registered: LDA
EMail: klbrowder@furmangroup.com

Employers
The Furman Group (Associate)

Clients Represented
On Behalf of The Furman Group
California Water Service Co.
Fallon, Nevada, City of
Mesquite Resort Ass'n
Mesquite, Nevada, City of
Moapa Valley Water District
Paradise Canyon Resort
Tooele, Utah, City of
Virgin Valley Water District

BROWDER, Marliss

325 Seventh St. NW
Suite 1250
Washington, DC 20004
Tel: (202)347-8193
Fax: (202)347-9304
EMail: mbrowder@kemperinsurance.com
Former staff, Sen. Mitch McConnell (R-KY). Majority staff, House Committee on Banking and Financial Services.

Employers
Kemper Insurance Cos. (Senior Federal Relations Specialist)

BROWER, Charles N.

601 13th St. NW
Suite 600 South
Washington, DC 20005
Tel: (202)626-3600
Fax: (202)639-9355
EMail: browech@washdc.whitecase.com
Deputy Special Counselor to the President, The White House, 1987. Acting Legal Advisor (1973) and Deputy Legal Advisor (1971-72), Assistant Legal Advisor for European Affairs (1969-71), Department of State.

Employers
White & Case LLP (Partner)

Clients Represented
On Behalf of White & Case LLP
Parker Drilling Co.

BROWN, Anita

517 C St. NE
Washington, DC 20002
Tel: (202)543-4455
Fax: (202)543-4586
Registered: LDA
Staff Assistant for Trade, House Committee on Agriculture, 1974-95.

Employers
Schramm, Williams & Associates, Inc.

Clients Represented
On Behalf of Schramm, Williams & Associates, Inc.
California Asparagus Commission
California Ass'n of Winegrape Growers
California Pistachio Commission
Dole Food Co.
Lana'i Co.
U.S. Citrus Science Council
Western Growers Ass'n
Winegrape Growers of America

BROWN, Annemarie

1025 Connecticut Ave. NW
Suite 910
Washington, DC 20036
Tel: (202)467-5088

Employers
Mazda North America Operations (Government Affairs Representative)

BROWN, Brenda

700 11th St. NW
Washington, DC 20001-4507
Tel: (202)383-1099
Fax: (202)383-7540
Registered: LDA
EMail: bbrown@realtors.org

Employers
Nat'l Ass'n of Realtors (Housing Policy Representative)

BROWN, Charles G.

1400 16th St. NW
Suite 330
Washington, DC 20036
Tel: (202)462-8800
Fax: (202)265-6564

Employers
Victims Rights PAC

BROWN, Chris

1601 Duke St.
Alexandria, VA 22314-3406
Tel: (703)836-8700
Fax: (703)836-8705

Employers
Soc. of American Florists (Manager of Political and Legislative Outreach)

BROWN, Cynthia A.

1640 Wisconsin Ave. NW
Washington, DC 20007
Tel: (202)337-2701
Fax: (202)337-4271
Registered: LDA
EMail: cbrown@facs.org

Employers
American College of Surgeons (Interim Director, Health Policy and Advocacy Department)

BROWN, Cynthia L.

600 Pennsylvania Ave. SE
Suite 304
Washington, DC 20003
Tel: (202)544-9614
Fax: (202)544-9618
Registered: LDA

Employers
American Shipbuilding Ass'n (President)
Brown and Company, Inc. (President)

Clients Represented
On Behalf of Brown and Company, Inc.
American Defense Internat'l, Inc.
American Shipbuilding Ass'n
Bird-Johnson Co.
Merant PVCS
Sperry Marine Inc.

BROWN, Dale

1401 H St. NW
Suite 600
Washington, DC 20005-2136
Tel: (202)326-7300
Fax: (202)326-7333

Employers
United States Telecom Ass'n (V. President, Mid-Sized Companies)

BROWN, David C.

400 Seventh St. NW
Fourth Floor
Washington, DC 20004
Tel: (202)347-7500
Fax: (202)347-7501
Registered: LDA

Employers
Exelon Corp. (V. President, Congressional Affairs)

BROWN, David N.

1201 Pennsylvania Ave. NW
Washington, DC 20004-2401
Tel: (202)662-6000
Fax: (202)662-6291
EMail: dbrown@cov.com

Employers
Covington & Burling (Partner)

BROWN, David S. J.

529 14th St. NW
Suite 440
Washington, DC 20045-1402
Tel: (202)783-4697
Fax: (202)783-4699
Registered: LDA
EMail: browd@naa.org

Employers
Newspaper Ass'n of America (Senior V. President, Public Policy and General Counsel)

BROWN, Felicien "Fish"

1875 I St. NW
Suite 1000
Washington, DC 20006
Tel: (202)296-3993
Fax: (202)296-3997
Registered: LDA
EMail: fbrown@chausa.org

Employers
Catholic Health Ass'n of the United States (Director, Public Policy)

BROWN, J. Noah

1740 N St. NW
Washington, DC 20036
Tel: (202)775-4667
Fax: (202)223-1297
Registered: LDA
EMail: nbrown@acct.org

Employers
Ass'n of Community College Trustees (Director, Public Policy)

BROWN, James

201 N. Union St.
Suite 220
Alexandria, VA 22314
Tel: (703)836-3300
Fax: (703)836-3290

Employers
Paperboard Packaging Council (Director, Public Affairs)

BROWN, James A.

444 N. Capitol St. NW
Suite 401
Washington, DC 20001
EMail: JBrown@CSG.org
Tel: (202)624-5460
Fax: (202)624-5452
Counsel to the Chair, Federal Election Commission, 1992-1997. Counsel to Senator Governmental Affairs Committee, 1997-1998.

Employers
Council of State Governments (Director, Washington Office and General Counsel)

BROWN, James P.

601 13th St. NW
Suite 900 South
Washington, DC 20005
EMail: jbrowndc@aol.com
Tel: (202)783-5588
Fax: (202)783-5595
Registered: LDA

Employers
Bracy Williams & Co. (V. President)

Clients Represented

On Behalf of Bracy Williams & Co.
Atlanta, Georgia, City of
Bi-State Development Agency
Fort Worth Transportation Authority
Fort Worth, Texas, City of
Foundation for Integrated Medicine
Lambert-St. Louis Internat'l Airport
Nassif & Associates
St. Louis Airport Authority
St. Louis Metropolitan Sewer District
St. Louis, Missouri, City of
Tucson, Arizona, City of

BROWN, Jamie E.

901 15th St. NW
Suite 700
Washington, DC 20005-2301
Tel: (202)371-6000
Fax: (202)371-6279
Registered: LDA
Former Legislative Counsel to Senator Connie Mack (R-FL)

Employers
Verner, Liipfert, Bernhard, McPherson and Hand, Chartered

Clients Represented

On Behalf of Verner, Liipfert, Bernhard, McPherson and Hand, Chartered
Equal Justice Coalition
Magna Entertainment Corp.

BROWN, Jesse

11 Canal Center Plaza
Suite 103
Alexandria, VA 20005
Tel: (703)683-6990
Fax: (703)683-0645
Registered: LDA
Secretary of Veterans Affairs, Clinton Administration, 1993-97

Employers
Brown & Associates

Clients Represented

On Behalf of Brown & Associates
Onehealthbank.com
Pharmaceutical Research and Manufacturers of America

BROWN, Ken

1611 N. Kent St.
Suite 901
Arlington, VA 22209
Tel: (703)351-4969
Fax: (703)351-0090

Employers
Alexis de Tocqueville Institution (President)

BROWN, Kenneth A.

1350 New York Ave. NW
Suite 1100
Washington, DC 20005-4798
EMail: brown@spiegelmcd.com
Tel: (202)879-4000
Fax: (202)393-2866
Registered: LDA
Legislative Aide to Rep. Bill D. Gradison (R-OH), 1977-78.

Employers
Spiegel & McDiarmid (Public Affairs Director)

Clients Represented

On Behalf of Spiegel & McDiarmid
Piqua, Ohio, City of

BROWN, Jr., Lawrence C.

525 School St. SW
Suite 500
Washington, DC 20024
EMail: wave4kids@aol.com
Tel: (202)484-0103
Fax: (202)488-7595

Employers
WAVE, Inc. (President)

BROWN, Lori J.

1875 I St. NW
Suite 1050
Washington, DC 20006-5409
Tel: (202)331-8585
Fax: (202)331-2032

Employers
Scribner, Hall & Thompson, LLP (Partner)

BROWN, Marjorie Eilertsen

2300 Clarendon Blvd.
Suite 610
Arlington, VA 22201-3367
EMail: mbrown@golinharris.com
Tel: (703)351-5666
Fax: (703)351-5667

Employers
Golin/Harris Internat'l (Senior V. President)

BROWN, Mark B.

122 C St. NW
Suite 125
Washington, DC 20001
EMail: mark.brown@ecunet.org
Tel: (202)783-7507
Fax: (202)783-7502

Employers
Lutheran Office for Governmental Affairs/Evangelical Lutheran Church in America (Assistant Director)

BROWN, Mary L.

1133 19th St. NW
Washington, DC 20036
EMail: mary.brown@wcom.com
Tel: (202)887-2551
Fax: (202)887-3304

Employers
MCI WorldCom Corp. (V. President, Federation Regulations)

BROWN, Max

1299 Pennsylvania Ave. NW
Suite 800 West
Washington, DC 20004
Tel: (202)785-0500
Fax: (202)785-5277
Registered: LDA

Employers
The Carmen Group (Exec. V. President and Chief Operating Officer)

Clients Represented

On Behalf of The Carmen Group
Pembroke Real Estate, Inc.

BROWN, Michael A.

2550 M St. NW
Washington, DC 20037-1350
EMail: mbrown@pattonboggs.com
Tel: (202)457-6000
Fax: (202)457-6315
Registered: LDA

Employers
Patton Boggs, LLP (International Trade and Public Policy Specialist)

Clients Represented

On Behalf of Patton Boggs, LLP
American Trans Air
Azurix
Detroit, Michigan, Public School System of the County of
GovWorks.com
Midcoast Interstate Transmission, Inc.
Prince George's, Maryland, County of
Wayne, Michigan, County of

BROWN, Michael J.

801 Pennsylvania Ave. NW
Suite 730
Washington, DC 20004
Tel: (202)638-0026
Fax: (202)638-7787
Registered: LDA
Press Secretary, U.S. Mint, Treasury Department, 1981-89.

Employers
Barrick Goldstrike Mines, Inc. (V. President, U.S. Public Affairs)

BROWN, Michael J.

1700 N. Moore St.
Suite 1600
Arlington, VA 22209
Tel: (703)841-2400
Fax: (703)527-0938
Registered: LDA

Employers
American Meat Institute (V. President, Legislative Affairs)

BROWN, Michael T.

1501 M St. NW
Suite 700
Washington, DC 20005-1702
EMail: mbrown@manatt.com
Tel: (202)463-4300
Fax: (202)463-4394
Registered: LDA, FARA

Employers
Manatt, Phelps & Phillips, LLP (Associate)

Clients Represented

On Behalf of Manatt, Phelps & Phillips, LLP
AIS, Inc.
Congo, Republic of
DAG Petroleum
Kean Tracers, Inc.
Keller Equity Group, Inc.
Playa Vista
Reno, Nevada, City of

BROWN, II, Omer F.

1010 Vermont Ave. NW
Suite 810
Washington, DC 20005
Tel: (202)783-9100
Fax: (202)783-9103
Registered: LDA

Employers
Harmon & Wilmot, L.L.P. (Partner)

Clients Represented

On Behalf of Harmon & Wilmot, L.L.P.
Contractors Internat'l Group on Nuclear Liability
Energy Contractors Price-Anderson Group

BROWN, Paul

1001 G St. NW
Suite 900 E
Washington, DC 20001-4545
Tel: (202)393-1010
Fax: (202)393-5510
Former Floor Assistant to Senator Tom Daschle (D-SD).

Employers
Podesta/Mattoon (Principal)

BROWN, Peg

412 First St. SE
Suite 100
Washington, DC 20003
Tel: (202)484-4884
Fax: (202)484-0109

Employers
The Dutko Group, Inc.

Clients Represented

On Behalf of The Dutko Group, Inc.
Carpet and Rug Institute
Coalition to Advance Sustainable Technology
Level 3 Communications LLC

BROWN, Quincalee

601 Wythe St.
Alexandria, VA 22314-1994
EMail: qbrown@wef.org
Tel: (703)684-2400
Fax: (703)684-2492

Employers
Water Environment Federation (Exec. Director)

BROWN, Rachel

1233 20th St. NW
Suite 610
Washington, DC 20036
Tel: (202)466-4111
Fax: (202)466-4123
Registered: LDA
EMail: rachel_brown@lewis-burke.org

Employers
Lewis-Burke Associates (Government Relations Assistant)

Clients Represented
On Behalf of Lewis-Burke Associates
Ass'n of Independent Research Institutes
Associated Universities Inc.
Syracuse University
Universities Research Ass'n
University Corp. for Atmospheric Research
University of Cincinnati
University of Southern California
Virginia Commonwealth University

BROWN, Richard N.

1016 16th St. NW
Suite 300
Washington, DC 20036
Tel: (202)862-4400
Fax: (202)862-4432

Employers
Nat'l Federation of Federal Employees (National President)

BROWN, Rick

1220 L St. NW
Washington, DC 20005
Tel: (202)682-8432
Fax: (202)682-8294
Registered: LDA

Employers
American Petroleum Institute (Senior Manager, Federal Agencies)

BROWN, Robert M.

2001 M St. NW
Washington, DC 20036
Tel: (202)467-3000
Fax: (202)533-8500
Registered: LDA

Employers
KPMG, LLP

Clients Represented
On Behalf of KPMG, LLP
The INDOPCO Coalition

BROWN, Robert M.

51 Louisiana Ave. NW
Washington, DC 20001
Tel: (202)879-3939
Fax: (202)626-1700
Registered: FARA
EMail: rmbrown@jonesday.com
Liaison to the Senate for the Department of the Army, 1981-86. Special Assistant to Senator Charles Mathias (R-MD), 1986.

Employers
Jones, Day, Reavis & Pogue (Government Affairs Representative)

BROWN, Ronald G.

100 Indiana Ave. NW
Washington, DC 20001
Tel: (202)393-4695
Fax: (202)737-1540

Employers
Nat'l Ass'n of Letter Carriers of the United States of America (V. President)

BROWN, Rosamond S.

2121 K St. NW
Suite 650
Washington, DC 20037
Tel: (202)296-2400
Fax: (202)296-2409
Registered: LDA, FARA
EMail: Rosamond@GlobalUSAinc.com
Former Legislative Assistant to Rep. Beryl Anthony Jr. (D-AR), Ways & Means Committee.

Employers
Global USA, Inc. (V. President)

Clients Represented
On Behalf of Global USA, Inc.
Dade, Florida, County of
Hyundai Motor Co.
Jacksonville Electric Authority
SBC Communications Inc.
Taipei Economic and Cultural Representative Office in the United States

BROWN, Russell R.

6903 Rockledge Dr.
Bethesda, MD 20817
Tel: (301)564-3200
Fax: (301)564-3201

Employers
USEC, Inc.

BROWN, Jr., S. M. Henry

1776 I St. NW
Suite 275
Washington, DC 20006
Tel: (202)530-7300
Fax: (202)530-7350
Registered: LDA

Employers
Entergy Services, Inc. (V. President, Governmental Affairs)

BROWN, Sandra L.

401 Ninth St. NW
Suite 1000
Washington, DC 20004
Tel: (202)274-2959
Fax: (202)274-2994
Registered: LDA
Attorney, Counsel's Office, The White House, 1996. Attorney/Advisor, Interstate Commerce Commission, 1995. Legislative Assistant to Rep. Eric D. Fingerhud (D-OH), 1993-95.

Employers
Troutman Sanders LLP (Associate)

Clients Represented
On Behalf of Troutman Sanders LLP
Kansas City Southern Industries
Paducah & Louisville Railroad

BROWN, Sarah

P.O. Box 2204
Washington, DC 20013
Tel: (202)628-9774
Fax: (202)628-9776
Registered: LDA
EMail: sbrown@slbrown.com

Employers
Westerly Group (Senior Associate)

Clients Represented
On Behalf of Westerly Group
Microcosm, Inc.
Sunset Properties, Inc.
Western Resources

BROWN, Shantrel

2111 Wilson Blvd.
Eighth Floor
Arlington, VA 22201-3058
Tel: (703)841-0626
Fax: (703)243-2874
Registered: LDA

Employers
Alcalde & Fay

Clients Represented
On Behalf of Alcalde & Fay
Deerfield Beach, Florida, City of
Jovan Broadcasting
Riviera Beach, Florida, City of

BROWN, Sharie

3000 K St. NW
Suite 500
Washington, DC 20007-5109
Tel: (202)672-5300
Fax: (202)672-5399
EMail: sbrown@foleylaw.com

Employers
Foley & Lardner (Partner)

BROWN, Stan

555 13th St. NW
Washington, DC 20004-1109
Tel: (202)637-5600
Fax: (202)637-5910

Employers
Hogan & Hartson L.L.P.

Clients Represented
On Behalf of Hogan & Hartson L.L.P.
Dana Corp.

BROWN, Stephen H.

412 First St. SE
Suite 100
Washington, DC 20003
Tel: (202)484-4884
Fax: (202)484-0109
Political Advisor to House Minority Leader, Rep. Richard A. Gephardt (D-MO), 2000-2001.

Employers
The Dutko Group, Inc. (V. President)

BROWN, Susan M.

2100 M St. NW
Washington, DC 20037
Tel: (202)261-5702
Fax: (202)429-0687
EMail: paffairs@ui.urban.org

Employers
The Urban Institute (Director, Public Affairs)

BROWN, Theresa Cardinal

918 F St. NW
Washington, DC 20004-1400
Tel: (202)216-2400
Fax: (202)371-9449
Registered: LDA
EMail: tbrown@aila.org

Employers
American Immigration Lawyers Ass'n (Associate Director, Advocacy)

BROWN, Tyrone

1776 K St. NW
Washington, DC 20006
Tel: (202)719-7000
Fax: (202)719-7049
Commissioner, Federal Communications Commission, 1977-81. Staff Director, Subcommittee on Intergovernmental Relations, Senate Committee on Governmental Affairs, 1970-71. Law Clerk to Chief Justice Earl Warren, U.S. Supreme Court, 1967-68.

Employers
Wiley, Rein & Fielding (Of Counsel)

BROWN, Capt. Will A.

The Pentagon
MS: 5C840
Washington, DC 20350-1300
Tel: (703)693-2919
Fax: (703)693-0656
EMail: brown.will@hq.navy.mil

Employers
Department of Navy (Director, Navy Programs, Office of Legislative Affairs)

BROWN-YAZZIE, G. Michelle

1101 17th St. NW
Suite 250
Washington, DC 20036
Tel: (202)775-0393
Fax: (202)775-8075

Employers
Navajo Nation (Exec. Director)

BROWNE, Crystal M.

1015 15th St. NW
Suite 802
Washington, DC 20005
Tel: (202)347-7474
Fax: (202)898-0068
EMail: cbrowne@acec.org

Employers
American Consulting Engineers Council (Administrative Assistant, Government Affairs)

BROWNE, Maureen

1200 17th St. NW
Fifth Floor
Washington, DC 20036
Tel: (202)467-6300
Fax: (202)466-2006

Employers
Adduci, Mastriani & Schaumberg, L.L.P. (Associate)

BROWNE, Tamara L.

1100 15th St. NW
Suite 700
Washington, DC 20005
Tel: (202)223-1700
Fax: (202)429-2522
Registered: LDA
EMail: schagrin@erols.com
Legislative Assistant (1985) and Legislative Director (1985-88) for Rep. Peter Visclosky (D-IN).

Employers
Schagrin Associates (Director, Governmental Affairs)

Clients Represented

On Behalf of Schagrin Associates

Alliant Techsystems, Inc.
Bitrek Corp.
Committee on Pipe and Tube Imports
Geneva Steel Co.
Hannibal Industries
IPSCO Tubulars, Inc.
LTV Copperweld
Maverick Tube Corp.
Vest Inc.
Weirton Steel Corp.
Wheatland Tube Co.

BROWNE, Thomas J.

1301 Pennsylvania Ave. NW
Suite 1100
Washington, DC 20004-1707
Tel: (202)626-4000
Fax: (202)639-0658
Registered: LDA

Employers

Air Transport Ass'n of America (Managing Director, Aviation Infrastructure)

BROWNELL, Arthur W.

1932 Relda Ct.
Falls Church, VA 22043
Tel: (703)536-9352
Fax: (703)536-8176
Registered: LDA

Employers

Self-employed as an independent consultant.

Clients Represented

As an independent consultant

Council of Industrial Boiler Owners (CIBO)

BROWNELL, F. William

1900 K St. NW
Washington, DC 20006-1109
Tel: (202)955-1500
Fax: (202)778-2201
Registered: LDA

Employers

Hunton & Williams (Partner)

Clients Represented

On Behalf of Hunton & Williams

American Road and Transportation Builders Ass'n (ARTBA)
Clean Air Regulatory Information Group
Edison Electric Institute

BROWNELL, Paul

1655 N. Fort Myer Dr.
Suite 850
Arlington, VA 22209
Tel: (703)524-2549
Fax: (703)524-3940
Registered: LDA

Employers

Nat'l Venture Capital Ass'n (V President, Legislative, Regulatory, and Entrepeneurial Affairs)

BROWNLEE, D.H.

1025 Connecticut Ave. NW
Suite 501
Washington, DC 20036
EMail: don.brownlee@aerojet.com
Tel: (202)828-6826
Fax: (202)828-6849

Employers

GenCorp (Director, Tactical Weapons and Systems (Aerojet))

BROWNLEE, John T.

800 Connecticut Ave. NW
Suite 711
Washington, DC 20006
EMail: jbrownlee@na.ko.com
Tel: (202)973-2667
Fax: (202)466-2262

Employers

The Coca-Cola Company (Manager, Government Relations)

BROWNSTEIN, Cindy

4590 MacArthur Blvd. NW
Suite 250
Washington, DC 20007
Tel: (202)944-3285
Fax: (202)944-3295

Employers

Spina Bifida Ass'n of America (Chief Exec. Officer)

BROYDRICK, William

444 N. Capitol St. NW
Suite 837
Washington, DC 20001
EMail: billb@broydrick.com
Tel: (202)637-0637
Fax: (202)544-5321
Registered: LDA

Employers

Broydrick & Associates (President)

Clients Represented

On Behalf of Broydrick & Associates

Barr Laboratories
Bell Ambulance
Blood Center of Southeastern Wisconsin
Children's Hospital of Wisconsin
Direct Supply
Innovative Resource Group
Mount Sinai Hospital
Nat'l Ass'n of Children's Hospitals Inc.
Northland Cranberries, Inc.
Wisconsin Energy Corp.

BRUBAKER, Joel

801 Pennsylvania Ave. NW
Suite 310
Washington, DC 20004
Tel: (202)434-8150
Fax: (202)434-8156
Registered: LDA

Employers

GPU, Inc. (Federal Affairs Representative)

BRUCE, Carol Elder

1747 Pennsylvania Ave. NW
Suite 300
Washington, DC 20006
Tel: (202)293-0398
Fax: (202)393-0363

Employers

Tighe, Patton, Tabackman & Babbin (Partner)

BRUCE, E. Edward

1201 Pennsylvania Ave. NW
Washington, DC 20004-2401
EMail: ebruce@cov.com
Tel: (202)662-6000
Fax: (202)662-6291

Law Clerk to Justice Potter Stewart, U.S. Supreme Court, 1966-67.

Employers

Covington & Burling (Partner)

BRUCE, III, James T.

1776 K St. NW
Washington, DC 20006
Tel: (202)719-7000
Fax: (202)719-7049
Registered: LDA

Former Senior Counsel, Senate Committee on Energy and Natural Resources, 1977-89; Counsel, Senate Committee on Aeronautical and Space Sciences, 1975-77.

Employers

Wiley, Rein & Fielding (Partner)

Clients Represented

On Behalf of Wiley, Rein & Fielding

Advanced Integrated Technology, Inc.
ARINC, Inc.
Columbia University
Earth, Energy & Environment
The Edison Project
Newspaper Ass'n of America
Open Group Electronic Messaging Ass'n (EMA) Forum
UtiliCorp United, Inc.

BRUCE, John F.

1299 Pennsylvania Ave. NW
Washington, DC 20004-2402
EMail: brucej@howrey.com
Tel: (202)783-0800
Fax: (202)383-6610

Law Clerk to Judge Walter M. Bastian, U.S. Court of Appeals for the District of Columbia, 1966-67.

Employers

Howrey Simon Arnold & White (Partner)

Clients Represented

On Behalf of Howrey Simon Arnold & White

American Portland Cement Alliance
Liberty Corp.
United States Beet Sugar Ass'n

BRUCE, Teresa

1901 L St. NW
Suite 300
Washington, DC 20036
EMail: teresa.bruce@dc.ogilvypr.com
Tel: (202)466-7590
Fax: (202)466-7598

Employers

Ogilvy Public Relations Worldwide (V. President)

BRUCE, Virnell A.

1200 Wilson Blvd.
Arlington, VA 22209-1989
Tel: (703)465-3250
Fax: (703)465-3032

Employers

The Boeing Co. (V. President, Communications)

BRUDERLE, Thomas P.

2000 N. 14th St.
Suite 450
Arlington, VA 22201
Tel: (703)276-3805
Fax: (703)841-7797
Registered: LDA

Employers

Nat'l Ass'n of Health Underwriters (Director, Congressional Affairs)

BRUECKNER, Leslie

1717 Massachusetts Ave. NW
Suite 800
Washington, DC 20036
EMail: lbrueckner@tlpj.org
Tel: (202)797-8600
Fax: (202)232-7203

Employers

Trial Lawyers for Public Justice, P.C. (Staff Attorney)

BRUENING, Paula

1634 I St. NW
Suite 1100
Washington, DC 20006-4003
EMail: pbruening@cdt.org
Tel: (202)637-9800
Fax: (202)637-0968

Employers

Center for Democracy and Technology (Staff Counsel)

BRUETT, Cameron

1627 I St. NW
Suite 950
Washington, DC 20006
Tel: (202)223-5115
Fax: (202)223-5118

Employers

ConAgra Foods, Inc. (Government Affairs Analyst)

BRUGGE, Parker

2550 M St. NW
Washington, DC 20037-1350
Tel: (202)457-6000
Fax: (202)457-6315
Registered: LDA
EMail: pbrugge@pattonboggs.com

Counsel to the Assistant Administrator for Solid Waste and Emergency Response, Environmental Protection Agency, 1993-97. Clerk to Judge Edward Smith, U.S. Court of Appeals for the Federal Circuit, 1988-89

Employers

Patton Boggs, LLP (Partner)

Clients Represented

On Behalf of Patton Boggs, LLP

American Soc. of Safety Engineers
Austin, Texas, City of
AutoNation, Inc.
Chesapeake Bay Foundation
W. R. Grace & Co.
Houston, Texas, City of
Magnificent Research Inc.
Potomac Heritage Partnership
Save Barton Creek
Wayne, Michigan, County of

BRUGGEN, Hilary

1211 Connecticut Ave. NW
Suite 608
Washington, DC 20036
EMail: hbruggen@qorvis.com
Tel: (703)744-7800
Fax: (703)744-7840

Employers

Qorvis Communications (Managing Director)

BRUINOOGE, Suanna

1900 Duke St.
Suite 200
Alexandria, VA 22314
Tel: (703)299-1050
Fax: (703)299-1044

Senior Health Policy Advisor (1999-2000) and Legislative Assistant (1997-98) to Rep. Nancy Johnson (R-CT). Legislative Assistant to Rep. Vernon J. Ehlers (R-MI), 1994-96.

Employers
American Soc. of Clinical Oncology (Senior Policy Analyst)

BRUNE, Louis

1608 K St. NW
Washington, DC 20006
Tel: (202)861-2700
Fax: (202)861-2786
Registered: LDA

Employers
American Legion (Legislative Grassroots Coordinator)

BRUNER, Cheryl

1301 K St. NW
Suite 1200 West
Washington, DC 20005
Tel: (202)515-4031
Fax: (202)515-5078
Registered: LDA
EMail: cheryl_bruner@lotus.com

Employers
Lotus Development Corp. (Senior Director, Public Policy and Government Affairs)

BRUNKENHOEFER, James M.

304 Pennsylvania Ave. SE
Washington, DC 20003
Tel: (202)543-7714
Fax: (202)543-0015
Registered: LDA
EMail: utsldutu@aol.com

Employers
United Transportation Union (National Legislative Director)

BRUNNER, Jan M.

1400 16th St. NW
Suite 400
Washington, DC 20036-2220
Tel: (202)518-6380
Fax: (202)234-3550
EMail: jbrunner@ofwlaw.com

Employers
Olsson, Frank and Weeda, P.C. (Associate)

BRUNNER, Michael E.

4121 Wilson Blvd.
Tenth Floor
Arlington, VA 22203
Tel: (703)351-2000
Fax: (703)351-2001
Registered: LDA
EMail: mbrunner@ntca.org

Employers
Nat'l Telephone Cooperative Ass'n (Exec. Vice President)

BRUNNER, Thomas W.

1776 K St. NW
Washington, DC 20006
Tel: (202)719-7000
Fax: (202)719-7049

Employers
Wiley, Rein & Fielding (Partner)

BRUNO, Joseph A.

1730 M St. NW
Suite 911
Washington, DC 20036
Tel: (202)966-6321
Registered: LDA

Employers
Associated Industries of Massachusetts (Senior V. President, Federal Relations)

BRUNO, William B.

2519 Connecticut Ave. NW
Washington, DC 20008-1520
Tel: (202)783-2242
Fax: (202)783-2255
Registered: LDA

Employers
American Ass'n of Homes and Services for the Aging (Director, Congressional Affairs)
Mental and Addictive Disorders Appropriations Coalition (Associate Director)

BRUNS, Kevin T.

2000 L St. NW
Suite 300
Washington, DC 20036-0646
Tel: (202)835-8800
Fax: (202)835-8879
Former Counsel and Press Secretary, House Committee on Economic and Educational Opportunities. Former Deputy General Counsel, House Committee on Post Office and Civil Service. Aide and Committee Counsel to Senator John Glenn (D-OH), 1986-91.

Employers
Ketchum (V. President and Group Manager, Public Affairs)

BRUSCA, Richard L.

1440 New York Ave. NW
Washington, DC 20005
Tel: (202)371-7000
Fax: (202)393-5760

Employers
Skadden, Arps, Slate, Meagher & Flom LLP (Partner)

BRUSE, J. Charles

888 16th St. NW
Suite 700
Washington, DC 20006
Tel: (202)835-8126
Fax: (202)835-8227
Registered: LDA

Employers
Allstate Insurance Co. (V. President and Assistant General Counsel)

BRUSER, Lawrence

1701 Pennsylvania Ave. NW
Suite 500
Washington, DC 20006
Tel: (202)861-0665
Fax: (202)861-0437

Employers
Mitsui and Co. (U.S.A.), Inc. (Deputy General Manager, and Director, Government Affairs)

BRUSKIN, Gene L.

815 16th St. NW
Washington, DC 20006
Tel: (202)737-7200
Fax: (202)737-7208

Employers
AFL-CIO - Food and Allied Service Trades Department (Secretary-Treasurer)

BRUSTEIN, Michael

3105 South St. NW
Washington, DC 20007
Tel: (202)965-3652
Fax: (202)965-8913
Registered: LDA
EMail: mbrustein@bruman.com

Employers
Brustein & Manasevit (Managing Partner)

Clients Represented

On Behalf of Brustein & Manasevit
California Department of Education

BRYAN, Jacalyn L.

1275 K St. NW
Suite 800
Washington, DC 20005
Tel: (202)371-9090
Fax: (202)371-9797
Registered: LDA

Employers
Ass'n of State and Territorial Health Officials (Deputy Director for Policy & Programs)

BRYANT, Dr. Anne L.

1680 Duke St.
Alexandria, VA 22314-3407
Tel: (703)838-6722
Fax: (703)683-7590

Employers
Nat'l School Boards Ass'n (Exec. Director)

BRYANT, Chris

1300 I St. NW
Suite 1000 West
Washington, DC 20005
Tel: (202)962-8531
Fax: (202)962-8542
EMail: cbryant@rcra.com

Employers
The Technical Group LLC (President)

Clients Represented

On Behalf of The Technical Group LLC
Kimberly-Clark Corp.

BRYANT, Daniel J.

950 Pennsylvania Ave. NW
Washington, DC 20530
Tel: (202)514-2141
Fax: (202)514-4482

Employers
Department of Justice (Assistant Attorney General for Legislative Affairs (Nominated))

BRYANT, David

1201 16th St. NW
Washington, DC 20036
Tel: (202)833-4000
Registered: LDA

Employers
Nat'l Education Ass'n of the U.S. (Senior Professional Associate)

BRYANT, Debra

1120 19th St. NW
Eighth Floor
Washington, DC 20036
Tel: (202)467-6900
Fax: (202)467-6910
Registered: LDA
EMail: debryant@wcsr.com

Employers
Womble Carlyle Sandridge & Rice, P.C. (Director, Federal Government Relations)

Clients Represented

On Behalf of Womble Carlyle Sandridge & Rice, P.C.
North Carolina Electric Membership Corp.
North Carolina Global TransPark Authority
North Carolina State Ports Authority
North Carolina, Hurricane Floyd Redevelopment Center of State of

BRYANT, Kathy J.

700 N. Fairfax St.
Suite 306
Alexandria, VA 22314
Tel: (703)836-8808
Fax: (703)459-0976
Registered: LDA
EMail: fasa@fasa.org

Employers
Federated Ambulatory Surgery Ass'n (Exec. Director)

BRYANT, Ralph C.

1775 Massachusetts Ave. NW
Washington, DC 20036-2188
Tel: (202)797-6000
Fax: (202)797-6004
Former Director, Division of International Finance, Federal Reserve Board; former Lead International Economic, Federal Open Market Committee; Consultant, Congressional Budget Office, Federal Reserve, International Monetary Fund, Department of Treasury, and World Bank.

Employers
The Brookings Institution (Senior Fellow, Economic Studies)

BRYANT, Sr., M.D.,, Thomas E.

1555 Connecticut Ave. NW
Suite 200
Washington, DC 20036
Tel: (202)462-9600
Fax: (202)462-9043

Employers
Aspirin Foundation of America, Inc. (President)
Non-Profit Management Associates, Inc. (Chairman)

Clients Represented

On Behalf of Non-Profit Management Associates, Inc.
Aspirin Foundation of America, Inc.

BRYEN, Shoshana

1717 K St. NW
Suite 800
Washington, DC 20006
Tel: (202)833-0020
Fax: (202)296-6452
EMail: sbryen@jinsa.org

Employers
Jewish Institute for Nat'l Security Affairs (Special Projects Director)

BRYMER, N. Eugene

2750 Prosperity Ave.
Suite 620
Fairfax, VA 22031-4312
Tel: (703)698-0291
Fax: (703)698-0297

Employers
Specialized Carriers and Rigging Ass'n (Exec. V. President)

BRYSON, Judy

440 R St. NW
Washington, DC 20001
Tel: (202)462-3614
Fax: (202)387-1034

Employers
Africare (Director, Food for Development)

BRYSON, Nancy S.

1001 Pennsylvania Ave. NW
Suite 1100
Washington, DC 20004-2595
Tel: (202)624-2500
Fax: (202)628-5116
Registered: LDA

Trial Attorney, Lands Division, Department of Justice, 1979-84. Appellate Attorney, Department of Labor, 1975-79.

Employers
Crowell & Moring LLP (Partner)

Clients Represented
On Behalf of Crowell & Moring LLP
Cosmetic, Toiletry and Fragrance Ass'n
Reckitt & Colman Pharmaceuticals Inc.

BUCCIERO, Jr., Michael

1001 G St. NW
Suite 400 East
Washington, DC 20001
Tel: (202)638-3730
Fax: (202)638-3516
Registered: LDA
EMail: mbucciero@peyser.com

Former Assistant Secretary, Intergovernmental Relations, Department of Housing and Urban Development

Employers
Peyser Associates, Inc.

Clients Represented
On Behalf of Peyser Associates, Inc.
Federal Home Loan Bank of Seattle
Macon, City of
Monroe Center, LLC

BUCCINO, Sharon

1200 New York Ave. NW
Suite 400
Washington, DC 20005
Tel: (202)289-6868
Fax: (202)289-1060

Employers
Natural Resources Defense Council (Senior Staff Attorney)

BUCHAN, Philip

444 N. Capitol St. NW
Suite 359
Washington, DC 20001
Tel: (202)624-5442
Fax: (202)624-8189

Employers
Iowa, Washington Office of the State of (Director, Washington Office)

BUCHANAN, Don

1750 New York Ave. NW
Sixth Floor
Washington, DC 20006
Tel: (202)783-5880
Fax: (202)662-0896

Employers
Sheet Metal Workers' Internat'l Ass'n (Director, Railroad and Shipyard Workers)

BUCHER, Sheri

1500 K St. NW
Suite 250
Washington, DC 20005-1714
Tel: (202)639-7508
Fax: (202)639-7505
Registered: LDA
EMail: sbucher@uhlaw.com

Assistant to Senator Charles S. Robb (D-VA), 1995-96.

Employers
Ungaretti & Harris (Legislative Director)

Clients Represented
On Behalf of Ungaretti & Harris
Allegiance Healthcare Corp.
Cardinal Health Inc.
Computer Communications Industry of America
Medical Research Laboratories
United Defense, L.P.

BUCHHOLZ, Mary Beth

1808 Swann St. NW
Washington, DC 20009
Tel: (202)462-7288
Fax: (202)483-1964
Registered: LDA

Employers
The Sheridan Group (Senior Legislative Associate)

Clients Represented
On Behalf of The Sheridan Group
Chronic Fatigue and Immune Dysfunction Syndrome Ass'n of America
Fenton Communications

BUCHMAN, Ellen

1111 16th St. NW
Washington, DC 20036-4873
Tel: (202)785-7704
Fax: (202)466-7618
EMail: buchman@aauw.org

Employers
American Ass'n of University Women (Field Director)

BUCHOLTZ, Harold R.

2099 Pennsylvania Ave. NW
Suite 100
Washington, DC 20006
Tel: (202)955-3000
Fax: (202)955-5564
Registered: LDA
EMail: hbucholt@hklaw.com

Attorney, Interpretative Division, Office of Chief Counsel, Internal Revenue Service, 1976-81.

Employers
Holland & Knight LLP (Partner)

Clients Represented
On Behalf of Holland & Knight LLP
Florida Gas Utility
Spaceport Florida Authority

BUCHOVECKY, John J.

1050 Thomas Jefferson St. NW
Seventh Floor
Washington, DC 20007
Tel: (202)298-1800
Fax: (202)338-2416
Registered: FARA
EMail: jjb@vnf.com

Employers
Van Ness Feldman, P.C. (Member)

BUCHSBAUM, Michael

P.O. Box 1804
Department 599
Washington, DC 20013
Tel: (301)341-4100
Fax: (301)618-4967

Employers
Giant Food Inc. (V. President, General Counsel)

BUCK, Susan C.

1776 K St. NW
Washington, DC 20006
Tel: (202)719-7000
Fax: (202)719-7049
Registered: LDA

Employers
Wiley, Rein & Fielding (Government Affairs Consultant)

Clients Represented
On Behalf of Wiley, Rein & Fielding
A. H. Belo Corp.
Columbia University
Gannett Co., Inc.
Hearst-Argyle Television, Inc.
MassMutual Financial Group
Newspaper Ass'n of America
Personal Communications Industry Ass'n (PCIA)
Prodigy
Qwest Communications
SnapTrack
Time Domain Corp.

BUCKALEW, Judith

1875 I St. NW
12th Floor
Washington, DC 20006
Tel: (202)466-6550
Fax: (202)785-1756
Registered: LDA
EMail: jbuckalew@ppsv.com

Senior Policy and Legislative Advisor to Senator Kay Bailey Hutchison (R-TX) and Senator Lauch Faircloth (R-NC), 1996-99. Special Assistant to the President, The White House, 1983-85. Legislative Assistant to Senator J. Danforth Quayle (R-IN), 1980-83.

Employers
Powers Pyles Sutter & Verville, PC (Director, Public Policy and Legislation)

Clients Represented
On Behalf of Powers Pyles Sutter & Verville, PC
American Academy of Neurology
Bon Secours Charity Health System
Hooper, Lundy and Bookman
InterTribal Bison Cooperative
Nat'l Ass'n of Victims of Transfusion-associated HIV
Nat'l Psoriasis Foundation
St. Louis University, School of Public Health
Tourette Syndrome Ass'n, Inc.
University of Findlay
Yosemite Nat'l Institute

BUCKHAM, Edwin A.

P.O. Box 5711
Arlington, VA 22205
Tel: (202)543-5136
Fax: (202)543-5266
Registered: LDA

Former aide to Rep. Tom DeLay (R-TX).

Employers
Alexander Strategy Group

Clients Represented
On Behalf of Alexander Strategy Group
Enron Corp.
Nuclear Energy Institute
Pharmaceutical Research and Manufacturers of America

BUCKLEY, Jane

2425 18th St. NW
Washington, DC 20009-2096
Tel: (202)232-4108
Fax: (202)332-0463

Employers
Institute for Local Self-Reliance (Director)

BUCKLEY, Jean

1912 Association Dr.
Reston, VA 20191-1591
Tel: (703)860-3334
Fax: (703)758-0749

Employers
Future Business Leaders of America - Phi Beta Lambda (President and Chief Exec. Officer)

BUCKLEY, Jeremiah S.

1717 Pennsylvania Ave. NW
Washington, DC 20006
Tel: (202)974-1000
Fax: (202)331-9330
Registered: LDA
EMail: jbuckley@gph.com

Minority Staff Director (1977-79) and Minority Counsel, Subcommittee on Housing (1973-77), Senate Committee on Banking, Housing and Urban Affairs. Assistant Counsel, House Committee on Government Operations, 1971-73.

Employers
Goodwin, Procter & Hoar LLP

Clients Represented
On Behalf of Goodwin, Procter & Hoar LLP
Electronic Financial Services Council
Massachusetts Bankers Ass'n

BUCKLEY, Richard

555 12th St. NW
Suite 650
Washington, DC 20004-1205
Tel: (202)393-7950
Fax: (202)393-7960

Employers
Eli Lilly and Co. (Manager, Federal Affairs)

BUCKLEY, William

1211 Connecticut Ave. NW
Suite 608
Washington, DC 20036
Tel: (202)496-1000
Fax: (202)496-1300
EMail: bbuckley@qorvis.com

Employers
Qorvis Communications (Managing Director)

BUCKNER, Michael W.

8315 Lee Hwy.
Fairfax, VA 22031
Tel: (703)208-7200
Fax: (703)208-7132
EMail: mbuckner@umwa.org

Employers
United Mine Workers of America (Research Director)

BUCKS, Dan R.

444 N. Capitol St. NW
Suite 425
Washington, DC 20001
Tel: (202)624-8699
Fax: (202)624-8819
EMail: mtc@mtc.gov

Employers
Multistate Tax Commission (Exec. Director)

BUCKSTEAD, John

1100 17th St. NW
Suite 500
Washington, DC 20036
Tel: (202)265-7546
Fax: (202)265-8850
EMail: jb@nacaa.org

Employers
Nat'l Ass'n of Community Action Agencies (Exec. Director)

BUDASHEWITZ, Philip

1140 Connecticut Ave. NW
Suite 350
Washington, DC 20036
Tel: (202)872-7800
Fax: (202)872-7808
Registered: LDA

Employers
Elan Pharmaceutical Research Corp.

BUDDE, Bernadette A.

888 16th St. NW
Suite 305
Washington, DC 20006
EMail: budde@bipac.org
Tel: (202)833-1880
Fax: (202)833-2338

Employers
Business-Industry Political Action Committee (Senior V. President)

BUDETTI, Maureen R.

1025 Connecticut Ave. NW
Suite 700
Washington, DC 20036
Tel: (202)785-8866
Fax: (202)835-0003
Registered: LDA

Employers
Nat'l Ass'n of Independent Colleges and Universities (Director, Legislative Affairs for Student Aid Policy)

BUDWAY, Robert R.

1625 Massachusetts Ave. NW
Suite 500
Washington, DC 20036
Tel: (202)232-4677
Fax: (202)232-5756
Registered: LDA

Employers
Can Manufacturers Institute (President and General Counsel)

BUECHNER, Hon. Jack W.

1501 M St. NW
Suite 700
Washington, DC 20005-1702
Tel: (202)463-4300
Fax: (202)463-4394
Registered: LDA, FARA
EMail: jbuechner@manatt.com
Member, U.S. House of Representatives (R-MO), 1987-91 (served as Deputy Minority Whip, 1989-91).

Employers
Manatt, Phelps & Phillips, LLP (Partner)
U.S. Ass'n of Former Members of Congress (Treasurer)

Clients Represented
On Behalf of Manatt, Phelps & Phillips, LLP
AIS, Inc.
Asociacion Columbiana de Exportadores de Flores (ASOCOLFLORES)
Bolivia, Embassy of
Catellus Development Corp.
CEMEX Central, S.A. de C.V.
Coalition for Global Perspectives
Employee-Owned S Corporations of America
Intuit, Inc.
Kean Tracers, Inc.
Keller Equity Group, Inc.
Mexico, Embassy of
Mitsubishi Motors America, Inc.
Pelican Butte Corp.
Playa Vista
Poseidon Resources Corp.
Single Stick
SWIPCO, U.S.
Thermo EcoTek Corp.
US Airways
Yakima, Washington, City of

BUECHNER, William

1010 Massachusetts Ave. NW
Washington, DC 20001
Tel: (202)289-4434
Fax: (202)289-4435
Registered: LDA

Employers
American Road and Transportation Builders Ass'n (ARTBA) (V. President, Economics and Research; Manager, Education and Research)

BUENTE, Jr., David T.

1722 I St. NW
Washington, DC 20006
Tel: (202)736-8000
Fax: (202)736-8711
Registered: LDA
EMail: dbuente@sidley.com
Chief, Environmental Enforcement Division (1985-90) and Attorney, Environmental and Natural Resources Division (1979-85), Department of Justice. Office of the Solicitor, Department of the Interior, 1978-79.

Employers
Sidley & Austin (Partner)

Clients Represented
On Behalf of Sidley & Austin
American Petroleum Institute
Appleton Papers, Inc.
ARCO Coal Co.
General Electric Co.

BUERMEYER, Nancy

919 18th St. NW
Suite 800
Washington, DC 20006
Tel: (202)628-4160
Fax: (202)347-5323
Registered: LDA

Employers
Human Rights Campaign Fund (Deputy Director, Legislation)

BUFF, Bill

1776 Massachusetts Ave. NW
Suite 500
Washington, DC 20036
Tel: (202)857-1200
Fax: (202)857-1220
Registered: LDA

Employers
American Highway Users Alliance (Director, Communications and Government Affairs)

BUFFENBARGER, R. Thomas

9000 Machinists Pl.
Upper Marlboro, MD 20772-2687
Tel: (301)967-4500
Fax: (301)967-4588

Employers
Internat'l Ass'n of Machinists and Aerospace Workers (President)

BUFFINGTON, Bill

810 Vermont Ave. NW
Room 515F
Washington, DC 20420
Tel: (202)224-9419
Fax: (202)273-9988

Employers
Department of Veterans Affairs (Director, Legislative Affairs)

BUFFINGTON, Cynthia

1385 Piccard Dr.
Rockville, MD 20850-4340
EMail: cbuffington@mcaa.org
Tel: (301)869-5800
Fax: (301)990-9690

Employers
Mechanical Contractors Ass'n of America (Exec. Director, Strategic Events Management)

BUFFON, Charles E.

1201 Pennsylvania Ave. NW
Washington, DC 20004-2401
Tel: (202)662-6000
Fax: (202)662-6291
Registered: LDA
EMail: cbuffon@cov.com

Employers
Covington & Burling (Partner)

BUGEL, James

1818 N St. NW
Eighth Floor
Washington, DC 20036
Tel: (202)293-1707

Employers
Cingular Wireless

BUGGS, Jesse

601 Pennsylvania Ave. NW
Suite 900
Washington, DC 20004
Tel: (202)547-3566
Fax: (202)639-8238

Employers
Cottone and Huggins Group (Senior V. President, Engineering and Environmental Systems)

BUIS, Tom

400 N. Capitol St. NW
Suite 790
Washington, DC 20001
Tel: (202)554-1600
Fax: (202)554-1654
Registered: LDA

Employers
Nat'l Farmers Union (Farmers Educational & Co-operative Union of America) (V. President, Government Relations)

BULAWKA, Bohdan

1350 I St. NW
Suite 400
Washington, DC 20005-3306
Tel: (202)371-6900
Fax: (202)842-3578
Registered: LDA

Employers
Motorola, Inc. (V. President and Director, ITU Global Strategy)

BULCAO, Douglas W.

1130 Connecticut Ave. NW
Suite 1200
Washington, DC 20036-3954
Tel: (202)862-0500
Fax: (202)862-0537
Registered: LDA

Employers
American Textile Manufacturers Institute (Deputy Exec. V. President; Director, Government Relations Division)

BULGER, M.D., Roger J.

1400 16th St. NW
Suite 720
Washington, DC 20036
Tel: (202)265-9600
Fax: (202)265-7514

Employers
Ass'n of Academic Health Centers (President)

BULGER, Thomas J.

1050 17th St. NW
Suite 510
Washington, DC 20036
EMail: TBulger825@aol.com
Tel: (202)775-0079
Fax: (202)785-0477
Registered: LDA

Employers
Government Relations, Inc. (President)

Clients Represented
On Behalf of Government Relations, Inc.
Aldaron Inc.
Ass'n for Commuter Transportation
Capital Area Transit Authority
Community Transit
Fairfax, Virginia, County of
Friends of ITS/ITS America
Gateway Cities
High Speed Ground Transportation Ass'n
Intelligent Transportation Soc. of America
Mass Transit Authority
Metropolitan Transportation Commission
Monroe, New York, County of
Oakland County Board of Supervisors
Oakland, Michigan, County of
Regional Public Tansportation Authority
Suburban Mobility Authority for Regional Transportation

BULL, Stephen B.

1150 18th St. NW
Suite 300
Washington, DC 20036
Tel: (202)466-3399
Fax: (202)466-5068

Employers
U.S. Olympic Committee (Director, Government Relations)

BULLARD, Edward M.

1401 I St. NW
Suite 600
Washington, DC 20005
Tel: (202)336-7468
Fax: (202)336-7518
Registered: LDA

Employers
Hamilton Sundstrand (Director, Washington Operations)

BULLARD, Shawn

440 First St. NW
Eighth Floor
Washington, DC 20001
EMail: sbullard@naco.org
Tel: (202)393-6226
Fax: (202)393-2630

Employers
Nat'l Ass'n of Counties (Associate Legislative Director, Large Urban County Caucus)

BULOW, Kay

500 N. Washington St.
Alexandria, VA 22314
Tel: (703)551-2108
Fax: (703)551-2109
Deputy Administrator, Small Business Administration, 1989-90. Assistant Secretary for Management and Budget, Department of Commerce, 1981-88.

Employers
Blue Ridge Internat'l Group, L.L.C. (Managing Principal)

BULTENA, Jayne P.

1900 K St. NW
Suite 750
Washington, DC 20006
Tel: (202)833-4500
Fax: (202)833-2859
Registered: LDA

Employers
Bennett Turner & Coleman, LLP (Partner)

Clients Represented
On Behalf of Bennett Turner & Coleman, LLP
SmithKline Beecham Consumer Healthcare, LLP

BULTENA, Lance D.

555 13th St. NW
Washington, DC 20004-1109
Tel: (202)637-5587
Fax: (202)637-5910
Registered: LDA
EMail: ldbultena@hhlaw.com
Former Counsel, Subcommittee on Consumer Affairs, Foreign Commerce and Tourism, Senate Commerce Committee.

Employers
Hogan & Hartson L.L.P. (Partner)

Clients Represented
On Behalf of Hogan & Hartson L.L.P.
BrokerTek Global, L.L.C.
DNA Sciences, Inc.
eBay Inc.
Grocery Manufacturers of America
Koch Industries, Inc.
NTT America
Public Service Co. of Colorado
S1 Corp.
WebMD

BULTMAN, Brig. Gen. Roger

435 N. Lee St.
Alexandria, VA 22314
Tel: (703)683-4911
Fax: (703)683-4501
EMail: mwwhq@aol.com

Employers
Military Order of the World Wars (Chief of Staff)

BUMANIS, Al

8455 Colesville Rd.
Suite 1000
Silver Spring, MD 20910-3392
Tel: (301)589-3300
Fax: (301)589-5175
EMail: bumanis@musictherapy.org

Employers
American Music Therapy Ass'n (Director, Conferences and Communications)

BUMBAUGH, Deborah M.

701 Pennsylvania Ave. NW
Suite 725
Washington, DC 20004
Tel: (202)638-7429
Fax: (202)628-4763
Registered: LDA

Employers
Novartis Corp. (Director, Federal Government Relations)
Novartis Services, Inc.

BUMGARNER, Carrie L.

1200 G St. NW
Suite 600
Washington, DC 20005-3802
Tel: (202)393-1200
Fax: (202)393-1240
EMail: bumgarner@wrightlaw.com
Advisor, Office of Acquisition Policy, General Services Administration, 1988.

Employers
Wright & Talisman, P.C.

BUMPERS, Hon. Dale L.

1050 Connecticut Ave. NW
Washington, DC 20036-5339
Tel: (202)857-8951
Fax: (202)857-6395
Registered: LDA
EMail: bumperd@arentfox.com
Member, U.S. Senate (D-AR), 1975-99.

Employers
Arent Fox Kintner Plotkin & Kahn, PLLC (Member)

Clients Represented
On Behalf of Arent Fox Kintner Plotkin & Kahn, PLLC
Acxiom Corp.
American Airlines
American Public Power Ass'n
Raytheon Co.
Christopher Reeve Paralysis Foundation
Tyson Foods, Inc.

BUMPERS, William M.

1299 Pennsylvania Ave. NW
Suite 1300 West
Washington, DC 20004-2400
Tel: (202)639-7700
Fax: (202)639-7890

Employers
Baker Botts, L.L.P. (Partner)

Clients Represented
On Behalf of Baker Botts, L.L.P.
Entergy Corp.
Partnership for Early Climate Action

BUNCE, Col. Pete

Rayburn House Office Bldg.
Room B322
Washington, DC 20515-6854
Tel: (202)685-4531
Fax: (202)685-5782

Employers
Department of Air Force (Chief, House Liaison Office, Legislative Liaison)

BUNNING, Susan

122 C St. NW
Suite 520
Washington, DC 20001
Tel: (202)393-5100
Fax: (202)393-5110
Registered: LDA

Employers
Tyco Internat'l (US), Inc. (Manager, Public Affairs Tyco Healthcare)

BUNTING, Kate

1625 K St. NW
Suite 500
Washington, DC 20006
Tel: (202)223-2277
Fax: (202)296-8695
Registered: LDA
EMail: bunting@dc.care.org

Employers
CARE (Cooperative for Assistance and Relief Everywhere) (Director, Public Policy Initiatives)

BUNTON, Jeannie

401 Ninth St.
Second Floor
Washington, DC 20004-2037
Tel: (202)879-9600
Fax: (202)879-9700

Employers
Corporation for Public Broadcasting (Director, Communications)

BURCH, Jr., Charles F.

601 13th St. NW
Suite 710 North
Washington, DC 20005
Tel: (202)628-3936
Fax: (202)628-3949
EMail: cfb@arianespace-inc.com

Employers
ArianeSpace, Inc. (V. President, Sales)

BURCH, Christine C.

1301 Pennsylvania Ave. NW
Suite 950
Washington, DC 20004
Tel: (202)585-0100
Fax: (202)585-0101
Registered: LDA
Senate Labor Committee, 1976-80. Staff Member for Senator Edward M. Kennedy (D-MA), 1969-76.

Employers
Nat'l Ass'n of Public Hospitals and Health Systems (Exec. Director)

BURCH, Jr., J. Thomas

3001 Veazey Terrace
716
Washington, DC 20008
Tel: (202)338-6882
Fax: (202)338-6950
Major, Department of the Army, Department of Defense, 1966-74.

Employers
Nat'l Vietnam and Gulf War Veterans Coalition, Inc. (Chairman)

BURCHAM, Jr., John B.

5101 River Rd.
Suite 108
Bethesda, MD 20816
Tel: (301)656-1494
Fax: (301)656-7539
EMail: nabr@narbonline.org

Employers
Nat'l Ass'n of Beverage Retailers (Exec. Director)

BURCHETT, Barbara G.

1776 K St. NW
Washington, DC 20006
Tel: (202)719-7000
Fax: (202)719-7049
Registered: LDA

Employers
Wiley, Rein & Fielding (Government Affairs Consultant)

Clients Represented
On Behalf of Wiley, Rein & Fielding
ARINC, Inc.
Qwest Communications
UtiliCorp United, Inc.

BURCHETTE, William H.

1025 Thomas Jefferson St. NW
Eighth Floor, West Tower
Washington, DC 20007
Tel: (202)342-0800
Fax: (202)342-0807
Registered: LDA
EMail: wburchette@bbrslaw.com

Employers
Brickfield, Burchette, Ritts & Stone (Partner)

Clients Represented
On Behalf of Brickfield, Burchette, Ritts & Stone
East Texas Electric Cooperative
Northeast Texas Electric Cooperative
Sam Rayburn G&T Electric Cooperative, Inc.
Tex-La Electric Cooperative of Texas

BURDETT, Hal

107 Second St. NE
Washington, DC 20002
Tel: (202)544-3300
Fax: (202)544-0068
EMail: hburdett@populationinstitute.org

Employers
Population Institute (Director, Public Information)

BURDETT, Stacy

1100 Connecticut Ave. NW
Suite 1020
Washington, DC 20036
Tel: (202)452-8320
Fax: (202)296-2371
Registered: LDA

Employers
Anti-Defamation League (Associate Director)

BURDIN, Douglas S.

1155 Connecticut Ave. NW
Suite 1200
Washington, DC 20036
Tel: (202)659-5800
Fax: (202)659-1027
Registered: LDA
EMail: dburdin@dc.bhb.com

Employers
Birch, Horton, Bittner & Cherot (Member)

Clients Represented
On Behalf of Birch, Horton, Bittner & Cherot
Alaska State Snowmobile Ass'n
Blue Ribbon Coalition
Internat'l Snowmobile Manufacturers Ass'n
Wildlife Legislative Fund of America

BUREAU, Lisa C.

1200 New Hampshire Ave. NW
Suite 800
Washington, DC 20036-6802
Tel: (202)776-2000
Fax: (202)776-2222
EMail: lbureau@dlalaw.com

Employers
Dow, Lohnes & Albertson, PLLC (Member)

BURGA, Tim

Ten G St. NE
Suite 750
Washington, DC 20002-4213
Tel: (202)336-6700
Fax: (202)336-6828
EMail: TimB@career.org

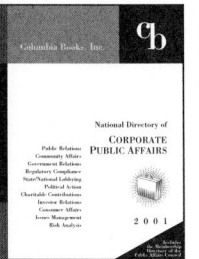

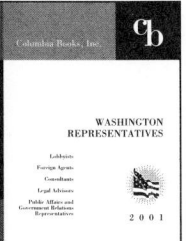

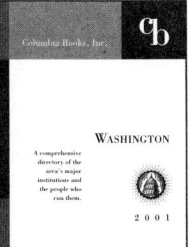

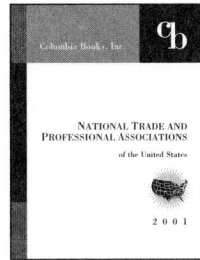

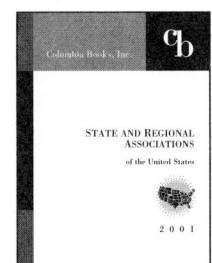

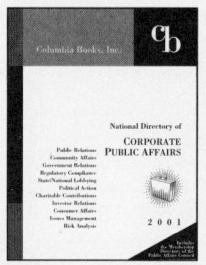

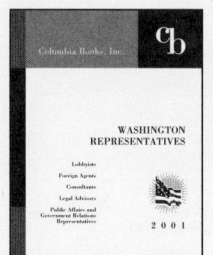

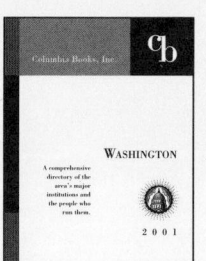

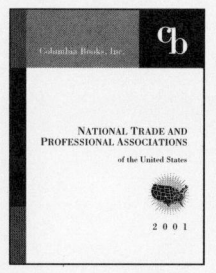

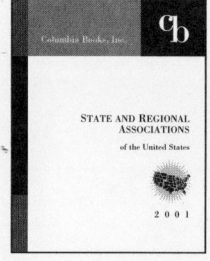

Employers
Career College Ass'n (Political Director)

BURGASSER, Jessica

1350 I St. NW
Suite 1255
Washington, DC 20005
Tel: (202)626-0089
Fax: (202)626-0088
Registered: LDA

Employers
Law Offices of Mark Barnes

Clients Represented
On Behalf of Law Offices of Mark Barnes
Intrac Arms Internat'l LLC

BURGER, Ben

305 Cameron St.
Alexandria, VA 22314
EMail: bburger@srcmedia.com
Tel: (703)683-8326
Fax: (703)683-8826

Employers
Stevens Reed Curcio & Co. (Senior V. President)

BURGER, George

700 13th St. NW
Suite 1000
Washington, DC 20005
Tel: (202)347-6633
Fax: (202)347-8713
Registered: LDA

Employers
Powell Tate (Principal)

BURGER, James M.

1200 New Hampshire Ave. NW
Suite 800
Washington, DC 20036-6802
EMail: jburger@dlalaw.com
Tel: (202)776-2000
Fax: (202)776-2222

Employers
Dow, Lohnes & Albertson, PLLC (Member)

BURGER, Sarah Greene

1424 16th St. NW
Suite 202
Washington, DC 20036
Tel: (202)332-2275
Fax: (202)332-2949

Employers
Nat'l Citizens Coalition for Nursing Home Reform (Interim Exec. Director)

BURGER, Susan

1201 15th St. NW
Washington, DC 20005-2800
Tel: (202)822-0470
Fax: (202)822-0572

Employers
Nat'l Ass'n of Home Builders of the U.S. (Director, Finance and Operations)

BURGESS, Cathy L.

1350 I St. NW
Suite 870
Washington, DC 20005
Tel: (202)638-2945
Fax: (202)737-1947
Registered: LDA

Employers
Burgess Consulting (President)

BURGESS, Robert

10335 Democracy Ln.
Fairfax, VA 22030
Tel: (703)352-0225
Fax: (703)352-8894
Registered: LDA

Employers
Solutions Group (V. President)

Clients Represented
On Behalf of Solutions Group
Wheelabrator-Cleanwater Systems-BioGro Division

BURGESS-SMITH, Leslie

1701 Clarendon Blvd.
Arlington, VA 22209
Tel: (703)276-8800
Fax: (703)243-2593
Registered: LDA

Employers
American Chiropractic Ass'n (Director, Political Action Committee)

BURGIO, Patti

1828 L St. NW
Suite 906
Washington, DC 20036
Tel: (202)785-3756
Fax: (202)429-9417
Registered: LDA

Employers
American Soc. of Mechanical Engineers

BURGOYNE, Robert A.

801 Pennsylvania Ave. NW
Washington, DC 20004-2604
EMail: rburgoyne@fulbright.com
Tel: (202)662-4513
Fax: (202)662-4643

Employers
Fulbright & Jaworski L.L.P. (Partner)

BURGUM, Thomas L.

421 New Jersey Ave. SE
Washington, DC 20003
Tel: (703)318-7169
Registered: LDA

Employers
Washington Consulting Alliance, Inc. (V. President, Legislative Affairs)

Clients Represented
On Behalf of Washington Consulting Alliance, Inc.
American Agriculture Movement, Inc.
Data Dynamics
EnerTech Industries Inc.
Heartland Communications & Management Inc.
Immune Complex Corp.
Metrocall Inc.
Norfolk Southern Corp.
Pointe Coupee Police Jury
San Bernardino Valley Municipal Water District
ThermoEnergy Corp.

BURK, Jr., Richard J.

1313 Dolly Madison Blvd.
Suite 402
McLean, VA 22101
Tel: (703)790-1745
Fax: (703)790-2672

Employers
Burk & Associates (President)

Clients Represented
On Behalf of Burk & Associates
American Board of Health Physics
Health Physics Soc.
Soc. for Risk Analysis

BURKE, Ann Marie

2300 N St. NW
Washington, DC 20037-1128
EMail: ann-marie.burke@shawpittman.com
Tel: (202)663-8638
Fax: (202)663-8007
Former Professional Staff Member, House Committee on Government Operations. Former Legislative Assistant to Rep. Major Owens (D-NY)

Employers
Shaw Pittman (Associate)

BURKE, April L.

1233 20th St. NW
Suite 610
Washington, DC 20036
EMail: april@lewis-burke.org
Tel: (202)466-4111
Fax: (202)466-4123
Registered: LDA
Attorney, Office of Legislative Counsel, U.S. Senate, 1978-80.

Employers
Lewis-Burke Associates (Principal)

Clients Represented
On Behalf of Lewis-Burke Associates
Ass'n of Independent Research Institutes
Associated Universities Inc.
California Institute of Technology
Soc. for Industrial & Applied Mathematics
Syracuse University
Universities Research Ass'n
University Corp. for Atmospheric Research
University of Cincinnati
University of Southern California
Virginia Commonwealth University

BURKE, Barbara D.

1700 Pennsylvania Ave. NW
Suite 800
Washington, DC 20006
EMail: bburke@thacherproffitt.com
Tel: (202)347-8400
Fax: (202)347-6238
Registered: LDA

Employers
Thacher Proffitt & Wood (Legislative/Regulatory Consultant)

Clients Represented
On Behalf of Thacher Proffitt & Wood
Water Quality Insurance Syndicate

BURKE, Brian E.

2099 Pennsylvania Ave. NW
Suite 100
Washington, DC 20006
EMail: beburke@hklaw.com
Tel: (202)955-3000
Fax: (202)955-5564

Employers
Holland & Knight LLP (Senior Counsel)

BURKE, Diane B.

1625 L St. NW
Washington, DC 20036-5687
EMail: dburke@afscme.org
Tel: (202)429-1193
Fax: (202)223-3413
Registered: LDA

Employers
American Federation of State, County and Municipal Employees (Assistant Director)

BURKE, Douglas J.

950 H St. NW
Room 8350
Washington, DC 20001
Tel: (202)406-5676
Fax: (202)406-5740

Employers
Department of Treasury - United States Secret Service (Assistant Special Agent-in-Charge, Congressional Affairs)

BURKE, Edmund W.

1330 Connecticut Ave. NW
Washington, DC 20036-1795
Tel: (202)429-3000
Fax: (202)429-3902

Employers
Steptoe & Johnson LLP (Partner)

BURKE, George A.

1750 New York Ave. NW
Washington, DC 20006
Tel: (202)737-8484
Fax: (202)737-8418
Registered: LDA

Employers
Internat'l Ass'n of Fire Fighters (Assistant to the General President, Communications)

BURKE, John G. "Toby"

400 N. Capitol St. NW
Suite 585
Washington, DC 20001
Tel: (202)347-6607
Fax: (202)393-7718
Registered: LDA

Employers
Self-employed as an independent consultant.

Clients Represented
As an independent consultant
North Dakota, Governor's Office of the State of

BURKE, John R.

1550 Wilson Blvd.
Suite 701
Arlington, VA 22209
Tel: (703)527-7505
Fax: (703)527-7512

Employers
Foodservice & Packaging Institute, Inc. (President)

BURKE, Kevin J.

2021 Massachusetts Ave. NW
Washington, DC 20036
Tel: (202)232-9033
Fax: (202)232-9044

Employers
American Academy of Family Physicians (Director, Washington Office)

BURKE, Kevin M.

201 Park Washington Ct.
Falls Church, VA 22046-4621
EMail: kevin@fdi.org
Tel: (703)532-9400
Fax: (703)538-4673
Registered: LDA

Employers
Food Distributors Internat'l (NAWGA-IFDA) (V. President, Government Relations)

BURKE, R. Brian

1742 N St. NW
Washington, DC 20036
Tel: (202)223-0957
Fax: (202)429-9574
Attorney, U.S. Customs Service, Department of Treasury, 1977-81.

Employers
Rode & Qualey

Clients Represented
On Behalf of Rode & Qualey
Greyfab (Bangladesh) Ltd.

BURKE, Richard J.

601 13th St. NW
Suite 600 South
Washington, DC 20005
Tel: (202)626-3600
Fax: (202)639-9355
EMail: burkeri@washdc.whitecase.com

Employers
White & Case LLP (Associate)

BURKE, Robert E.

1775 I St. NW
Suite 520
Washington, DC 20006
Tel: (202)496-0200
Fax: (202)496-0201
EMail: bobburke@muse-associates.com
Senior Health Policy Advisor, General Accounting Office, 1987-89.

Employers
Muse & Associates (V. President)

BURKE, Sharon

600 Pennsylvania Ave. SE
Fifth Floor
Washington, DC 20003
Tel: (202)544-0200
Fax: (202)546-7142

Employers
Amnesty Internat'l U.S.A. (Advocacy Director for Middle East and North Africa)

BURKE, William J.

1401 K St. NW
Suite 400
Washington, DC 20005
Tel: (202)789-2111
Fax: (202)789-4883
Registered: LDA
EMail: bburke@thewashingtongroup.com
Legislative Director for Rep. Patrick Kennedy (D-R.I.) 1994-2000

Employers
The Washington Group (Director, Legislative Affairs)

Clients Represented
On Behalf of The Washington Group
American Hospital Ass'n
IVAX Corp.
Korea Information & Communication, Ltd.
Microsoft Corp.
Texas Municipal Power Agency

BURKETT, Bob

1299 Pennsylvania Ave. NW
Suite 800 West
Washington, DC 20004
Tel: (202)785-0500
Fax: (202)785-5277

Employers
The Carmen Group (Senior Consultant)

Clients Represented
On Behalf of The Carmen Group
World Wrestling Federation Entertainment Inc.

BURKHARDT, Patricia

P.O. Box 65111
Washington, DC 20037

Employers
American College of Nurse-Midwives (PAC Administrator)

BURKMAN, Jack M.

2099 Pennsylvania Ave. NW
Suite 100
Washington, DC 20006
Tel: (202)457-7053
Fax: (202)955-5564
Registered: LDA
EMail: jburkman@hklaw.com
Former Legislative Counsel to Rep. Rick Lazio (R-NY).

Employers
Holland & Knight LLP (Associate)

Clients Represented
On Behalf of Holland & Knight LLP
American Chemistry Council
Benova, Inc.
Bridgestone/Firestone, Inc.
Consortium for Plant Biotechnology Research
DuPont
FMC Corp.
S.C. Johnson and Son, Inc.
Murphy Oil U.S.A.
Nassau County Health Care Corp.
Nat'l Paint and Coatings Ass'n
Placer, California, County of
Rockdale, Georgia, County of, Board of Commissioners of
Sarasota, Florida, City of
Sarasota, Florida, County of
Seacoast Power LLC
Somerville Housing Group
Spirit Airlines
Tichenor and Associates
West Group
West Palm Beach, Florida, City of

BURLEW, William

1250 I St. NW
Suite 1105
Washington, DC 20005
Tel: (202)682-5151
Fax: (202)682-2185
Registered: LDA

Employers
Andreae, Vick & Associates, L.L.C.

Clients Represented
On Behalf of Andreae, Vick & Associates, L.L.C.
U.S. Colombia Business Partnership

BURLING, William

1101 Connecticut Ave. NW
Suite 1200
Washington, DC 20036
Tel: (202)298-8107
Fax: (202)298-8108
EMail: frabur@aol.com

Employers
Franklin & Burling (Partner)

BURMAN, Allan V.

1401 K St. NW
Suite 900
Washington, DC 20005
Tel: (202)626-8550
Fax: (202)626-8578
Former Senior Advisor to the Deputy Director and Administrator for Federal Procurement Policy, Office of Management and Budget.

Employers
Jefferson Consulting Group (President, Jefferson Solutions, LLC)

BURNES, Jr., John

1050 Thomas Jefferson St. NW
Seventh Floor
Washington, DC 20007
Tel: (202)298-1800
Fax: (202)338-2416
EMail: jhb@vnf.com
Staff Attorney, Criminal Division, Appellate Section, Department of Justice, 1976-78. Staff Attorney, Office of the Solicitor, Federal Power Commission, 1972-76.

Employers
Van Ness Feldman, P.C. (Member)

BURNET, Lining

910 17th St. NW
Fifth Floor
Washington, DC 20006
Tel: (202)466-3800
Fax: (202)466-3801

Employers
American Legislative Exchange Council (Director, Programs)

BURNETT, Bill B.

901 N. Washington St.
Suite 600
Alexandria, VA 22314
Tel: (703)741-7686
Fax: (703)741-7698

Employers
NAADAC, The Ass'n for Addiction Professionals (President)

BURNETT, Helen

808 17th St. NW
Suite 600
Washington, DC 20006
Tel: (202)466-7800
Fax: (202)887-0905

Employers
Ruder Finn Washington (Senior V. President)

BURNETT, Jefferson

1620 L St. NW
Suite 1100
Washington, DC 20036-5605
Tel: (202)973-9700
Fax: (202)973-9790

Employers
Nat'l Ass'n of Independent Schools (Director, Government Relations)

BURNETT, Laird

1700 K St. NW
Suite 601
Washington, DC 20006
Tel: (202)296-6207
Fax: (202)296-4067

Employers
Kaiser Permanente (Senior Legislative Representative)

BURNEY, David G.

1101 17th St. NW
Suite 609
Washington, DC 20036
Tel: (202)857-0610
Fax: (202)331-9686
Registered: LDA

Employers
United States Tuna Foundation (Exec. Director)

BURNEY, Lou Ann

1901 N. Beauregard St.
Suite 200
Alexandria, VA 22311-1727
Tel: (703)998-0770
Fax: (703)671-9053
EMail: lburney@nib.org

Employers
Nat'l Industries for the Blind (Director, Corporate Communications)

BURNHAM, Mark A.

1233 20th St. NW
Suite 610
Washington, DC 20036
Tel: (202)466-4111
Fax: (202)466-4123
Registered: LDA
EMail: mark_burnham@lewis-burke.org

Employers
Lewis-Burke Associates (Government Relations Assistant)

Clients Represented
On Behalf of Lewis-Burke Associates
Associated Universities Inc.
California Institute of Technology
Universities Research Ass'n
University Corp. for Atmospheric Research
University of Cincinnati
University of Southern California
Virginia Commonwealth University

BURNIM, Ira A.

1101 15th St. NW
Suite 1212
Washington, DC 20005
Tel: (202)467-5730
Ext: 29
Fax: (202)223-0409

Employers
Bazelon Center for Mental Health Law, Judge David L. (Legal Director)

BURNLEY, IV, Hon. James H.

1400 L St. NW
Washington, DC 20005-3502
Tel: (202)371-5718
Fax: (202)371-5950
Registered: LDA
EMail: jburnley@winston.com
Secretary (1987-89), Deputy Secretary (1983-87), and General Counsel (1983), Department of Transportation. Associate Deputy Attorney General, Department of Justice, 1982-83.

Employers
Winston & Strawn (Partner, Transportation Practice)

Clients Represented

On Behalf of Winston & Strawn

Abilene, Texas, City of
American Airlines
Barr Laboratories
Certified Airline Passenger Services, LLC
Columbia Ventures, LLC
Cooper Tire and Rubber Co.
DMJM + Harris
EyeTicket Corp.
Federal Home Loan Bank of New York
Liberty Maritime Co.
Marinette Marine Corp.
Motor Coach Industries, Inc.
Norfolk Southern Corp.
Northland Holdings, Inc.
ORBITZ
Puerto Rico, Commonwealth of
Research Planning, Inc.
Rickenbacker Port Authority
Robinson Terminal
Traffic.com
Yellow Corp.

BURNS, Anne Davis

1600 Wilson Blvd.
Suite 1000
Arlington, VA 22209
Tel: (703)841-9300
Fax: (703)841-0389

Employers
American Waterways Operators (Director, Public Affairs)

BURNS, Annie

1010 Wisconsin Ave. NW
Suite 800
Washington, DC 20007
Tel: (202)338-8700
Fax: (202)338-2334

Employers
Greer, Margolis, Mitchell, Burns & Associates (Partner)

BURNS, Brian R.

1300 I St. NW
Suite 520 West
Washington, DC 20005-3314
Tel: (202)408-0090
Fax: (202)408-1750
Registered: LDA

Employers
Hoffmann-La Roche Inc. (Director, Federal Government Affairs)

BURNS, David D.

1299 Pennsylvania Ave. NW
Tenth Floor
Washington, DC 20004-2400
EMail: davidburns@paulhastings.com
Tel: (202)508-9500
Fax: (202)508-9700

Employers
Paul, Hastings, Janofsky & Walker LLP (Associate)

BURNS, Hugh P.

6801 Rockledge Dr.
Bethesda, MD 20817
Tel: (301)897-6308
Fax: (301)897-6252

Employers
Lockheed Martin Corp. (Director, Marketing Communications)

BURNS, Joseph P.

8201 Corporate Dr.
Suite 410
Landover, MD 20785-2229
EMail: hcss@erols.com
Tel: (301)731-4701
Fax: (301)731-8286

Employers
Healthcare Council of the Nat'l Capital Area (President and Chief Exec. Officer)

BURNS, C.A.E., Nancy A.

5904 Richmond Hwy.
Suite 408
Alexandria, VA 22303
Tel: (703)329-8500
Fax: (703)329-0155

Employers
Color Marketing Group (Exec. Director)

BURNS, Patrick A.

1250 H St. NW
Suite 700
Washington, DC 20005-3908
EMail: Burns@cse.org
Tel: (202)783-3870
Fax: (202)783-4687

Employers
Citizens for a Sound Economy (Director, Environmental Policy)

BURNS, Robert

1150 18th St. NW
Ninth Floor
Washington, DC 20036
Tel: (202)296-3355
Fax: (202)296-3922

Employers
Ablondi, Foster, Sobin & Davidow, P.C. (Partner)

BURNS, Sascha M.

227 Massachusetts Ave. NE
Suite One
Washington, DC 20002
EMail: burns@tongoursimpson.com
Former Aide to Senator San Nunn (D-GA)
Tel: (202)544-7600
Fax: (202)544-6770

Employers
Tongour Simpson Holsclaw Green (V. President, Government Relations)

Clients Represented

On Behalf of Tongour Simpson Holsclaw Green

Ass'n for Advanced Life Underwriting
Corning Inc.

BURNS, Steve

1775 I St. NW
Suite 800
Washington, DC 20006
EMail: sburns@enron.com
Tel: (202)466-9166
Fax: (202)828-3372

Employers
Enron Corp. (Director, Federal Government Affairs)

BURNS, Thaddeus

1333 New Hampshire Ave. NW
Suite 400
Washington, DC 20036
Tel: (202)887-4000
Fax: (202)887-4288
Registered: LDA

Employers
Akin, Gump, Strauss, Hauer & Feld, L.L.P.

Clients Represented

On Behalf of Akin, Gump, Strauss, Hauer & Feld, L.L.P.

Human Genome Sciences Inc.

BURR, Geoff

1300 N. 17th St.
Eighth Floor
Arlington, VA 22209
EMail: burr@abc.org
Tel: (703)812-2000
Fax: (703)812-8202
Registered: LDA

Employers
Coalition to Repeal the Davis-Bacon Act (Legal Assistant)

BURRIDGE, James L.

5102 Yuma St. NW
Washington, DC 20016
Tel: (202)686-0262
Fax: (202)956-5235

Employers
Burridge Associates

Clients Represented

On Behalf of Burridge Associates

FMC Corp.

BURRUS, William

1300 L St. NW
Washington, DC 20005
Tel: (202)842-4246
Fax: (202)842-4297

Employers
American Postal Workers Union (Exec. V. President)

BURSTEIN, Diane B.

1724 Massachusetts Ave. NW
Washington, DC 20036-1969
Tel: (202)775-3550
Fax: (202)775-3603
Registered: LDA

Employers
Nat'l Cable Television Ass'n (Deputy General Counsel)

BURT, Christine

1000 Thomas Jefferson St. NW
Suite 515
Washington, DC 20007
Tel: (202)342-8086
Fax: (202)342-9063

Employers
Leather Industries of America (Coordinator, Membership)

BURT, Martha R.

2100 M St. NW
Washington, DC 20037
Tel: (202)833-7200
Fax: (202)429-0687

Employers
The Urban Institute (Director, Social Services Research)

BURT, Robert N.

1615 L St. NW
Suite 1100
Washington, DC 20036-5610
Tel: (202)872-1260
Fax: (202)466-3509

Employers
The Business Roundtable (Chairman)

BURTLESS, Gary

1775 Massachusetts Ave. NW
Washington, DC 20036-2188
Economist, Department of Labor (1979-81) and Department of Health, Education, and Welfare (1977-79).
Tel: (202)797-6000
Fax: (202)797-6004

Employers
The Brookings Institution (Senior Fellow, Economic Studies)

BURTON, Alan J.

1133 15th St. NW
Suite 640
Washington, DC 20005
EMail: alanb@ala-national.org
Tel: (202)466-2520
Ext: 3014
Fax: (202)296-4419

Employers
American Logistics Ass'n (President)

BURTON, B. Kent

3211 Jermantown Rd.
Suite 300
Fairfax, VA 22030
EMail: kburton@covantaenergy.com
Assistant Secretary, Department of Commerce, 1984-1989.
Tel: (703)246-0833
Fax: (703)246-0808
Registered: LDA

Employers
Covanta Energy Corporation (Senior V. President, Policy and International Business Relations)

BURTON, Jr., Daniel F.

2323 Horsepen Rd.
Suite 600
Herndon, VA 20171
EMail: DFBurton@Novell.com
Tel: (703)713-3500
Fax: (703)713-3555
Registered: LDA

Employers
Novell, Inc. (V. President, Government Relations)

BURTON, David R.

333 N. Fairfax St.
Suite 302
Alexandria, VA 22314
EMail: drbargus@aol.com
Tel: (703)548-5868
Fax: (703)548-5869
Registered: LDA

Employers
The Argus Group, L.L.C. (Partner)

Clients Represented

On Behalf of The Argus Group, L.L.C.

America Outdoors
American Soc. of Travel Agents
Americans for Fair Taxation
Nat'l Park Hospitality Ass'n
Nat'l Tour Ass'n
Travel Council for Fair Competition
United Motorcoach Ass'n

BURTON, Joanna

1090 Vermont Ave. NW
Suite 510
Washington, DC 20005
Tel: (202)414-0140
Fax: (202)544-3525
Registered: LDA

Employers
American Osteopathic Ass'n (PAC Director)

BURTON, Joel Stephen

555 13th St. NW
Suite 500 West
Washington, DC 20004
Tel: (202)383-5300
Fax: (202)383-5414
Registered: LDA
EMail: jburton@omm.com

Employers

O'Melveny and Myers LLP (Of Counsel)

Clients Represented

On Behalf of O'Melveny and Myers LLP

US Airways

BURTON, John D.

601 Pennsylvania Ave. NW
South Bldg., Suite 900
Washington, DC 20004
Tel: (202)434-8163
Fax: (202)639-8238
Registered: LDA
EMail: jdburton@locklaw.com

Employers

Lockridge Grindal & Nauen, P.L.L.P. (Specialist, Federal Relations)

Clients Represented

On Behalf of Lockridge Grindal & Nauen, P.L.L.P.

Joint Powers Board
St. Louis/Lake Counties Regional Rail Authority
Valley Pride Pack

BURTON, Larry D.

1776 I St. NW
Suite 1000
Washington, DC 20006
Tel: (202)785-4888
Fax: (202)457-6597
Registered: LDA

Employers

BP Amoco Corp. (V. President, Federal Government Affairs)

BURTSCHI, Mark

1420 New York Ave. NW
Suite 200
Washington, DC 20005
Tel: (202)682-9250
Fax: (202)682-1533
Registered: LDA
EMail: mark.burtschi@goodyear.com

Employers

Goodyear Tire and Rubber Co. (Director, Federal and State Affairs)

BURTT, Andrew

8000 Towers Crescent Dr.
Suite 680
Vienna, VA 22182
Tel: (703)821-5002
Fax: (703)821-3795
EMail: help@meatnz.com

Employers

Meat New Zealand (Regional Manager, North America)

BURWELL, David

1100 17th St. NW
Suite Ten
Washington, DC 20036
Tel: (202)466-2636
Fax: (202)466-2247

Employers

Surface Transportation Policy Project (President/Chief Exec. Officer)

BURWELL, Frances G.

910 17th St. NW
Tenth Floor
Washington, DC 20006
Tel: (202)778-4970
Fax: (202)463-7241
EMail: fburwell@acus.org

Employers

Atlantic Council of the United States (Director, Transatlantic Relations Program)

BUSCHER, John

1025 Connecticut Ave. NW
Suite 1210
Washington, DC 20036
Tel: (202)296-1712
Fax: (202)296-2873
Registered: LDA

Employers

United Airlines (Director, Public Affairs, Eastern Region)

BUSEY, G. Brian

2000 Pennsylvania Ave. NW
Suite 5500
Washington, DC 20006
Tel: (202)887-1500
Fax: (202)887-0763
Registered: LDA
EMail: gbusey@mofo.com
Law Clerk to Judge John H. Pratt, U.S. District Court for the District of Columbia, 1982-83.

Employers

Morrison & Foerster LLP (Partner)

Clients Represented

On Behalf of Morrison & Foerster LLP

Denver, Colorado, City of
Norfolk, Virginia, City of
San Francisco, California, City and County of
Seiko Epson Corp.

BUSH, Barbara

1220 L St. NW
Washington, DC 20005
Tel: (202)682-8462
Fax: (202)682-8232

Employers

American Petroleum Institute (Taxation Associate Director)

BUSH, Charlotte

3601E Chain Bridge Rd.
Fairfax, VA 22030
Tel: (703)218-1955
Fax: (703)218-1960

Employers

Federation of Government Information Processing Councils (Manager, Operations)

BUSH, Derek

2000 Pennsylvania Ave. NW
Washington, DC 20006
Tel: (202)974-1500
Fax: (202)974-1999
Registered: LDA

Employers

Cleary, Gottlieb, Steen and Hamilton (Associate)

BUSH, J.D., CAE, Milton M.

3942 N. Upland St.
Arlington, VA 22207
Tel: (703)533-9539
Fax: (703)533-1612
Registered: LDA
EMail: themcos@aol.com

Employers

Internat'l Federation of Inspection Agencies, North American Committee (Exec. Director)
The M Companies (Principal)

Clients Represented

On Behalf of The M Companies

Entela, Inc.
Internat'l Federation of Inspection Agencies, North American Committee
Nat'l Technical Systems
Retlif Testing Laboratory, Inc.

BUSHMAN, Jesse

1717 Pennsylvania Ave. NW
Suite 600
Washington, DC 20006
Tel: (202)293-3450
Fax: (202)293-2787

Employers

Medical Group Management Ass'n (Field Representative)

BUSHNELL, David

4600 N. Park Ave.
Suite 101
Chevy Chase, MD 20815
Tel: (301)654-8316
Fax: (301)654-8336
Registered: LDA
EMail: dbjmdassoc@aol.com

Employers

JMD Associates, Inc. (Managing Director)

Clients Represented

On Behalf of JMD Associates, Inc.

Engelhard Corp.
Parents for Public Schools

BUSHUE, Sandy

701 Pennsylvania Ave. NW
Suite 720
Washington, DC 20004
Tel: (202)434-4821
Fax: (202)737-5403
Registered: LDA
EMail: sandy.bushue@sts.siemens.com

Employers

Siemens Transportation Systems, Inc. (Director, Government Affairs)

BUTCHMAN, Alan A.

1000 Potomac St. NW
5th Floor
Washington, DC 20007
Tel: (202)944-1890
Fax: (202)944-1892
Registered: LDA
EMail: alan@saltchuk.com

Employers

Saltchuk Resources, Inc. (V. President for Government Relations and PAC Treasurer)

BUTERA, James J.

1301 Pennsylvania Ave. NW
Suite 500
Washington, DC 20004
Tel: (202)347-6875
Fax: (202)347-6876
Registered: LDA
EMail: jbutera@butera-andrews.com

Employers

Butera & Andrews (Partner)

Clients Represented

On Behalf of Butera & Andrews

Advanta Corp.
American Council of State Savings Supervisors
Bluebonnet Savings Bank
British Nuclear Fuels plc
Charter One
Citizens Bank
Coalition to Amend the Financial Information Privacy Act (CAFPA)
Committee to Preserve Aspen
Community Banks Ass'n of New York State
Community Preservation Corp.
Countrywide Mortgage Corp.
Derivatives Net, Inc.
Dime Savings Bank of New York
Federal Home Loan Bank of Boston
Federal Home Loan Bank of Topeka
FM Watch
FRANMAC/Taco Pac
Independence Bank
Internat'l Swaps and Derivatives Dealers Ass'n
Luse Lehman Gorman Pomerenk & Schick, P.C.
Nat'l Home Equity Mortgage Ass'n
North American Securities Administrators Ass'n (NASAA)
Option One Mortgage Corp.
Pedestal
Peoples Bank
Rent-a-Center, Inc.
Savings Banks Life Insurance Fund
Silver, Freedman & Taff
Soc. for Human Resource Management
Superior Bank, FSB
Texas Savings and Community Bankers
USPA & IRA

BUTLER, Beatrice L.

Hubert H. Humphrey Bldg.
200 Independence Ave. SW
Room 406G
Washington, DC 20201
Tel: (202)690-7644
Fax: (202)690-7380
EMail: bbutler@os.dhhs.gov

Employers

Department of Health and Human Services (Staff Assistant, Congressional Liaison)

BUTLER, Benjamin H.

5535 Hempstead Way
Springfield, VA 22151
Tel: (703)750-1342
Fax: (703)354-4380
EMail: naus@ix.netcom.com

Employers

Nat'l Ass'n for Uniformed Services (Associate Legislative Counsel)

BUTLER, John W.

1850 M St. NW
Suite 900
Washington, DC 20036
Tel: (202)463-2500
Fax: (202)463-4950
Registered: LDA

Employers

Sher & Blackwell (Partner)

Clients Represented

On Behalf of Sher & Blackwell

Internat'l Brotherhood of Teamsters
NCS Healthcare
Ocean Carriers Working Group

BUTLER, Kenneth W.

11350 Random Hills Rd.
Suite 800
Fairfax, VA 22030
Tel: (703)620-4914
Fax: (703)620-4709
Registered: LDA
EMail: kwbutler@erols.com
Associate Administrator, Federal Transit Administration, Department of Transportation, 1984-87.

Employers
Capital Partnerships (VA) Inc. (Senior Principal)

Clients Represented
On Behalf of Capital Partnerships (VA) Inc.
Anoka County Regional Railroad Authority
Denver, Colorado, City and County of
Douglas, Colorado, County of
Friedlob, Sanderson, Raskin, Paulson, Toutillott
North Metro Mayors Coalition
Policy Advantage
Southeast Business Partnership
Taxicab, Limousine and Paratransit Ass'n

BUTLER, Malcolm

1424 K St. NW
Suite 700
Washington, DC 20005
EMail: mb@partners.net
Tel: (202)628-3300
Fax: (202)628-3306

Employers
Partners of the Americas (President and Chief Exec. Officer)

BUTLER, Patrick

1150 15th St. NW
Washington, DC 20071
EMail: butlerp@washpost.com
Tel: (202)334-6000
Fax: (202)334-6664

Employers
The Washington Post Co. (V. President, Corporate Offices)

BUTLER, Robert J.

1776 K St. NW
Washington, DC 20006
Tel: (202)719-7000
Fax: (202)719-7049

Employers
Wiley, Rein & Fielding (Partner)

Clients Represented
On Behalf of Wiley, Rein & Fielding
Prodigy

BUTLER, Stuart M.

214 Massachusetts Ave. NE
Washington, DC 20002
Tel: (202)546-4400
Fax: (202)546-8328

Employers
Heritage Foundation (V. President, Domestic and Economic Policy Studies)

BUTLER, Sydney J.

8403 Colesville Rd.
Suite 710
Silver Spring, MD 20910
Tel: (301)562-0777
Fax: (301)562-0888
Registered: LDA
EMail: sbutler@aza.org

Employers
American Zoo and Aquarium Ass'n (Exec. Director)

BUTLER, Tara A.

1735 New York Ave. NW
Washington, DC 20006
Tel: (202)626-7300
Fax: (202)626-7365
Registered: LDA
EMail: tbutler@aia.org

Employers
The American Institute of Architects (Legislative Analyst, Federal Affairs)

BUTNER, Blain B.

1200 New Hampshire Ave. NW
Suite 800
Washington, DC 20036-6802
Tel: (202)776-2000
Fax: (202)776-2222
Registered: LDA
EMail: bbutner@dlalaw.com
Former Staff Member, U.S. Senate Committee on Governmental Affairs.

Employers
Dow, Lohnes & Albertson, PLLC (Member)

BUTSAVAGE, Carey R.

1920 L St. NW
Suite 510
Washington, DC 20036
Tel: (202)861-9700
Fax: (202)861-9711
Staff Attorney, National Labor Relations Board, 1976-79.

Employers
Butsavage & Associates, P.C. (President)
Labor for America PAC (Treasurer)

Clients Represented
On Behalf of Butsavage & Associates, P.C.
Labor for America PAC

BUTTA, Susan Cavender

1300 I St. NW
Suite 400 West
Washington, DC 20005
Tel: (202)515-2515
Fax: (202)336-7926

Employers
Verizon Communications (Director, Public Affairs)

BUTTERFIELD, Jeanne A.

918 F St. NW
Washington, DC 20004-1400
Tel: (202)216-2400
Fax: (202)371-9449
Registered: LDA
EMail: jbutterfield@aila.org

Employers
American Immigration Lawyers Ass'n (Exec. Director)

BUTTERFIELD, Kristin

1120 Connecticut Ave. NW
Washington, DC 20036
Tel: (202)663-5212
Fax: (202)828-4548
Registered: LDA

Employers
American Bankers Ass'n (Associate Director, Grassroots)

BUTTERFIELD, R. Ian

1010 Pennsylvania Ave. SE
Washington, DC 20003
Tel: (202)544-7845
Fax: (202)544-7847
Registered: LDA, FARA
EMail: ib@bcanda.com
Staff Member, Senate Committee on Government Affairs, 1983-95.

Employers
Butterfield Carter & Associates (Principal)

Clients Represented
On Behalf of Butterfield Carter & Associates
Institute of Cetacean Research
Japan, Embassy of
Thomas Pink, Inc.

BUTTERFIELD, William

1615 L St. NW
Suite 1200
Washington, DC 20036
Tel: (202)466-6300
Fax: (202)463-0678

Employers
Bell, Boyd & Lloyd

BUTTS, Donna M.

1222 C St. NW
#820
Washington, DC 20001
Tel: (202)638-1263
Fax: (202)638-7555

Employers
Generations United (Exec. Director)

BUXTON, C. Michael

1455 Pennsylvania Ave. NW
Suite 700
Washington, DC 20004-1008
Tel: (202)639-6500
Fax: (202)639-6604
Law Clerk to Justice William H. Rehnquist, U.S. Supreme Court, 1973-74. Special Assistant U.S. Attorney for the District of Columbia (1972) and Attorney-Advisor, Office of Legal Counsel (1971-73), Department of Justice.

Employers
Vinson & Elkins L.L.P. (Partner)

BUYERS, Rhonda

11140 Rockville Pike
Suite 101
Rockville, MD 20852
EMail: rlbuyers@aol.com
Tel: (301)816-1515
Fax: (301)816-1516

Employers
Nat'l Gaucher Foundation (Exec. Director)

BUZBY, Barry

1331 Pennsylvania Ave. NW
North Lobby, Suite 600
Washington, DC 20004-1703
Tel: (202)637-3053
Fax: (202)637-3182

Employers
Nat'l Industrial Council (Exec. Dir., State Associations Group)

BUZZERD, Jr., CAE, Harry W.

111 Park Place
Falls Church, VA 22046-4513
Tel: (703)533-0251
Fax: (703)241-5603

Employers
American Textile Machinery Ass'n (Exec. V. President)
Ass'n and Soc. Management Internat'l Inc. (President)
North American Natural Casing Ass'n (Senior Management Counsel)
Process Equipment Manufacturers' Ass'n (Exec. Director)
Product Liability Prevention and Defense Group (Senior Management Counsel)

Clients Represented
On Behalf of Ass'n and Soc. Management Internat'l Inc.
Product Liability Prevention and Defense Group

BYARS, Dottie

440 First St. NW
Eighth Floor
Washington, DC 20001
EMail: dbyars@naco.org
Tel: (202)942-4208
Fax: (202)393-2630

Employers
Nat'l Ass'n of Counties (State Association Liaison)
Nat'l Council of County Ass'n Executives (Contact)

BYARS, Napoleon

1501 Lee Hwy.
Arlington, VA 22209-1198
Tel: (703)247-5800
Fax: (703)247-5853
EMail: nbyars@afa.org

Employers
Air Force Ass'n (Director, Policy and Communications)

BYER, Eric

4226 King St.
Alexandria, VA 22302-1507
Tel: (703)845-9000
Fax: (703)845-8176
Registered: LDA
EMail: ebyer@nata-online.org

Employers
Nat'l Air Transportation Ass'n (Government Specialist)

BYERLY, Christi

7401 Wisconsin Ave.
Suite 500
Bethesda, MD 20814
Tel: (301)986-8585
Fax: (301)652-5690

Employers
COGEMA, Inc. (Communications Manager)

BYERS, Bonnie B.

1455 Pennsylvania Ave. NW
Suite 1000
Washington, DC 20004
Tel: (202)942-8400
Fax: (202)942-8484
Registered: LDA
EMail: bonnie.byers@haledorr.com
Economist, International Trade Administration, Department of Commerce, 1983-86.

Employers
Hale and Dorr LLP (Trade Economist)

Clients Represented
On Behalf of Hale and Dorr LLP
Blyth Industries, Inc.
Micron Technology, Inc.
Neiman Marcus Group
Pixtech, Inc.

BYERS, H. James

1090 Vermont Ave. NW
Third Floor
Washington, DC 20005
EMail: hbyers@milbya.com
Tel: (202)842-5000
Fax: (202)789-4293

Employers
Millian Byers Associates, LLC (President)

Clients Represented
On Behalf of Millian Byers Associates, LLC
American Chemistry Council
C F Industries, Inc.
Chlorine Chemistry Council
Federal Strategies Group
Hager Sharp Inc.

BYERS, Jacqueline
440 First St. NW
Eighth Floor
Washington, DC 20001
EMail: jbyers@naco.org
Tel: (202)942-4285
Fax: (202)737-0480

Employers
Nat'l Ass'n of Counties (Director, Research)

BYLER, J. Daryl
110 Maryland Ave. NE
Suite 502
Washington, DC 20002
EMail: J._Daryl_Byler@mcc.org
Tel: (202)544-6564
Fax: (202)544-2820

Employers
Mennonite Central Committee Washington Office (Director)

BYNUM, Judith Kloss
738 Ninth St. SE
Washington, DC 20003
Tel: (202)246-2140
Registered: LDA

Employers
JKB Communications (Owner)

Clients Represented
On Behalf of JKB Communications
Academy of General Dentistry

BYNUM, Marjorie
1401 Wilson Blvd.
Suite 1100
Arlington, VA 22209
Tel: (703)522-5055
Fax: (703)525-2279
Registered: LDA

Employers
Information Technology Ass'n of America (ITAA)

BYRD, Carla Scali
1625 K St. NW
Suite 600
Washington, DC 20006
EMail: cbyrd@npc.org
Tel: (202)393-6100
Fax: (202)331-8539

Employers
Nat'l Petroleum Council (Information Coordinator)

BYRD, Janell M.
1444 I St. NW
Tenth Floor
Washington, DC 20005
Tel: (202)682-1300
Fax: (202)682-1312

Employers
NAACP Legal Defense and Educational Fund, Inc. (Director, Washington Office)

BYRD, Ricardo
1651 Fuller St. NW
Washington, DC 20009
Tel: (202)332-7766
Fax: (202)332-2314

Employers
Nat'l Ass'n of Neighborhoods (Exec. Director)

BYRD KEENAN, CAE, Barbara
225 Reinekers Lane
Suite 300
Alexandria, VA 22314
EMail: bkeenan@caionline.org
Tel: (703)548-8600
Fax: (703)684-1581

Employers
Community Ass'ns Institute (CAI) (President)

BYRNE, John J.
1120 Connecticut Ave. NW
Washington, DC 20036
Tel: (202)663-5000
Fax: (202)828-5052
Registered: LDA

Employers
American Bankers Ass'n (Senior Counsel and Compliance Manager)

BYRNE, Rob
2101 Wilson Blvd.
Suite 400
Arlington, VA 22201
EMail: rbyrne@nmpf.org
Tel: (703)243-6111
Fax: (703)841-9328

Employers
Nat'l Milk Producers Federation (V. President, Regulatory Affairs)

BYRNES, David
2600 Virginia Ave. NW
Suite 600
Washington, DC 20037
EMail: byrnesdw@hotmail.com
Tel: (202)338-6550
Fax: (202)338-5950

Employers
O'Brien, Klink & Associates (Associate)

BYRNES, John T.
1200 New Hampshire Ave. NW
Suite 800
Washington, DC 20036-6802
EMail: jbyrnes@dlalaw.com
Tel: (202)776-2000
Fax: (202)776-2222

Employers
Dow, Lohnes & Albertson, PLLC (Member)

BYRON, James E.
122 C St. NW
Suite 650
Washington, DC 20001
Tel: (202)639-8300
Fax: (202)639-5038

Employers
Nat'l Committee for an Effective Congress (Treasurer)

CABANISS, John
1001 19th St. North
Suite 1200
Arlington, VA 22209
EMail: jcabaniss@aiam.org
Tel: (703)525-7788
Fax: (703)525-8817

Employers
Ass'n of Internat'l Automobile Manufacturers (Director, Government and Energy)

CABELLY, Robert J.
1150 17th St. NW
Suite 406
Washington, DC 20036
Tel: (202)261-2840
Fax: (202)861-6490
Registered: FARA

Formerly held positions at the State Department and the White House.

Employers
C/R Internat'l, L.L.C (Managing Member)

CABRAL, Debra
1150 17th St. NW
Suite 701
Washington, DC 20036
EMail: debrac@dittus.com
Tel: (202)775-1401
Fax: (202)775-1404

Special Assistant to House Speaker Thomas P. O'Neill Jr. (D-MA), 1980-87. Assistant Clerk, House Select Committee to Investigate Covert Arms Transactions with Iran, 1987-88.

Employers
Dittus Communications (Exec. V. President)

Clients Represented
On Behalf of Dittus Communications
Citigroup
Community Financial Services Ass'n
Magazine Publishers of America
Nat'l Alliance Against Blacklisting
Nat'l Cooperative Business Ass'n
SurfWatch
Uniformed Services Family Health Plan

CABRAL, Sam A.
1421 Prince St.
Suite 400
Alexandria, VA 22314
Tel: (703)549-7473
Fax: (703)683-9048

Employers
Internat'l Union of Police Ass'ns (President)

CABRAL, Victor G.
1300 I St. NW
Suite 400 West
Washington, DC 20005
Tel: (202)515-2435
Fax: (202)289-7983

Employers
Verizon Communications (Exec. Director, International Policy and Regulatory Affairs (The Americas))

CABRERA, Sherri
2101 Wilson Blvd.
Suite 610
Arlington, VA 22201
Tel: (703)558-0400
Fax: (703)558-0401
Registered: LDA

Staff member, Committee on Science, 1989-94, Committee on Small Business, 1987-89, U.S. House of Representatives.

Employers
Manufactured Housing Institute (Director, Government Affairs)

CADE, Marilyn
1120 20th St. NW
Suite 1000
Washington, DC 20036
EMail: mcade@att.com
Tel: (202)457-2106
Fax: (202)457-2571
Registered: LDA

Employers
AT&T (Director, Federal Government Affairs)

CADY, Donald H.
1909 K St. NW
Fourth Floor
Washington, DC 20006
Tel: (202)973-5800
Fax: (202)973-5858

Employers
Porter/Novelli (Partner)

Clients Represented
On Behalf of Porter/Novelli
The Steel Alliance

CADY, John R.
1350 I St. NW
Suite 300
Washington, DC 20005
Tel: (202)639-5900
Fax: (202)639-5932
Registered: LDA

Employers
Nat'l Food Processors Ass'n (President)

CAFRUNY, Madalyn B.
2301 M St. NW
Washington, DC 20037-1484
EMail: mcafruny@APPAnet.org
Tel: (202)467-2952
Fax: (202)467-2910

Employers
American Public Power Ass'n (Director, Public Communications)

CAGE, Kenneth L.
600 13th St. NW
Washington, DC 20005-3096
EMail: kcage@mwe.com
Tel: (202)756-8000
Fax: (202)756-8087

Former Patent Attorney, Atomic Energy Commission; Deputy Patent Counsel, Department of Energy; Group Director, Patent and Trademark Office.

Employers
McDermott, Will and Emery (Partner)

CAGGIANO, Paul J.
1990 M St. NW
Suite 400
Washington, DC 20036
EMail: coalgovpro@aol.com
Tel: (202)331-0975
Fax: (202)822-9788

Employers
Coalition for Government Procurement (President)

CAHILL, D. Scott
325 Seventh St. NW
Suite 1100
Washington, DC 20004-2802
Tel: (202)783-7971
Fax: (202)737-2849
Registered: LDA

Employers
Nat'l Retail Federation (V. President, Government and Industry Affairs)

CAHILL, John D.

1120 Connecticut Ave. NW
Suite 1100
Washington, DC 20036
Tel: (202)861-5899
Fax: (202)861-5795
Registered: LDA
EMail: jcahill@gpcusa.com
Staff member, Office of the Speaker, U.S. House of Representatives, 1978-80.

Employers
GPC Internat'l (Senior V. President)

Clients Represented
On Behalf of GPC Internat'l
Alcan Aluminum Corp.
Bechtel/Parsons Brinkeroff Joint Venture
Boardman, Ohio, Township of
Country Hen
Fidelity Investments Co.
Hanover Capital Partners Ltd.
Ion Track Instruments
Legal Seafood
Massachusetts Port Authority
Nellie Mae
PriceWaterhouseCoopers
The Providence Plan
Providence Redevelopment Agency
Puerto Rico, Commonwealth of
Roger Williams Medical Center
Safety-Centered Solutions, Inc.
Skadden, Arps, Slate, Meagher & Flom LLP
Sovereign Bank
Starnet Corp.
Stone and Webster Engineering Corp.
YouBet.com

CAHILL, Judith

100 N. Pitt
Suite 400
Alexandria, VA 22314
Tel: (703)683-8416
Fax: (703)683-8417

Employers
Academy of Managed Care Pharmacy (Exec. Director)

CAHILL, Kenneth

2001 M St. NW
Fourth Floor
Washington, DC 20036
Tel: (202)533-5660
Fax: (202)533-8580
Registered: LDA

Employers
Barents Group LLC (Healthcare)

CAHILL, Leslie C.

601 13th St. NW
Suite 570 South
Washington, DC 20005-3807
Tel: (202)638-3128
Fax: (202)638-3171
EMail: lcahill@amseed.org

Employers
American Seed Trade Ass'n (V. President, Government Affairs)

CAHN, Michele L.

1401 H St. NW
Suite 200
Washington, DC 20005
Tel: (202)414-1288
Fax: (202)414-1217
Registered: LDA

Employers
Xerox Corp. (Manager, Domestic Government Policy)

CAIN, Morrison G.

1700 N. Moore St.
Suite 2250
Arlington, VA 22209
Tel: (703)841-2300
Fax: (703)841-1183
Registered: LDA
EMail: mcain@imra.org

Employers
Internat'l Mass Retailers Ass'n (Senior V. President, Government Affairs)

CAINE, Christopher G.

1301 K St. NW
Suite 1200-West Tower
Washington, DC 20005-3307
Tel: (202)515-5800
Fax: (202)515-5113
Registered: LDA
EMail: ccaine@us.ibm.com

Employers
Internat'l Business Machines Corp. (V. President, Governmental Programs)

CALABIA, Ted

1000 Connecticut Ave. NW
Suite 304
Washington, DC 20036
Tel: (202)296-4484
Fax: (202)293-3060

Employers
Masaoka & Associates, Inc. (Associate)

CALAMARO, Raymond S.

555 13th St. NW
Washington, DC 20004-1109
Tel: (202)637-5720
Fax: (202)637-5910
Registered: LDA
EMail: rscalamaro@hhlaw.com
Team Leader, Clinton-Gore Transition Team, 1992-93. Deputy Assistant U.S. Attorney General, Department of Justice, 1977-79, Carter-Mondale Transition Team, 1976-77. Legislative Director for Senator Gaylord A. Nelson (D-WI), 1973-75.

Employers
Hogan & Hartson L.L.P. (Partner)

Clients Represented
On Behalf of Hogan & Hartson L.L.P.
Biopure Corp.
DNA Sciences, Inc.
Grocery Manufacturers of America
Integra Life Sciences
Kensey Nash Corp.
News Corporation Ltd.
Protein Technologies Internat'l
Toyota Motor North America, U.S.A., Inc.
United Parcel Service

CALAMITA, F. Paul

1050 Connecticut Ave. NW
Suite 1200
Washington, DC 20036
Tel: (202)857-1700
Fax: (202)857-1737
Registered: LDA
EMail: fpcalami@mwbb.com

Employers
McGuireWoods L.L.P. (Partner)

Clients Represented
On Behalf of McGuireWoods L.L.P.
CSO Partnership
Lynchburg, Virginia, City of
Richmond, Virginia, City of
Wheeling, West Virginia, City of

CALANDRO, Tony

1310 G St. NW
12th Floor
Washington, DC 20005
Tel: (202)626-4780
Fax: (202)626-4833

Employers
Blue Cross Blue Shield Ass'n (Director, Grassroots Program)

CALDEIRA, Victoria

800 Connecticut Ave. NW
Suite 1100
Washington, DC 20006
Tel: (202)416-4168
Fax: (202)296-7177
Registered: LDA
EMail: victoria_caldeira@baxter.com

Employers
Baxter Healthcare Corp. (Director, Federal Legislative Affairs)

CALDERON, Rima

1150 15th St. NW
Washington, DC 20071
Tel: (202)334-6000
Fax: (202)334-4536
EMail: calderonr@washpost.com

Employers
The Washington Post Co. (Director, Corporate Communications)

CALDERWOOD, James A.

888 17th St. NW
Suite 600
Washington, DC 20006-3959
Tel: (202)298-8660
Fax: (202)342-0683
Registered: LDA
EMail: jacalderwood@zsrlaw.com
Senior Trial Attorney, Antitrust Division, Department of Justice, 1970-78.

Employers
Zuckert, Scoutt and Rasenberger, L.L.P. (Partner)

Clients Represented
On Behalf of Zuckert, Scoutt and Rasenberger, L.L.P.
Soc. of Glass and Ceramic Decorators
UniGroup, Inc.
United Van Lines, Inc.

CALDWELL, Alan

4025 Fair Ridge Dr.
Fairfax, VA 22033-2868
Tel: (703)273-0911
Fax: (703)273-9363
Registered: LDA
EMail: govrels@ichiefs.org

Employers
Internat'l Ass'n of Fire Chiefs (Director, Government Relations)

CALDWELL, Barry H.

2001 Pennsylvania Ave. NW
Suite 350
Washington, DC 20006-1825
Tel: (202)296-7174
Fax: (202)296-2521
Registered: LDA
EMail: barry.caldwell@cigna.com
Former Chief of Staff to Senator Arlen Spector, (R-PA)

Employers
CIGNA Corp. (V. President, Government Relations)

CALDWELL, Bret

25 Louisiana Ave. NW
Washington, DC 20001-2198
Tel: (202)624-6911
Fax: (202)624-6918

Employers
Internat'l Brotherhood of Teamsters (Government Affairs Dept.)

CALDWELL, Peter D.

205 S. Whiting St.
Suite 308
Alexandria, VA 22304
Tel: (703)751-8022
Fax: (703)751-5735
Registered: LDA
Legislative Counsel to Senator James M. Jeffords (R-VT), 1989-94. Special Counsel, Office of the Comptroller of the Currency, Department of Treasury, 1978-79.

Employers
The GrayWell Group, Inc. (President)

Clients Represented
On Behalf of The GrayWell Group, Inc.
Horizon Organic Dairy, Inc.
Nat'l Cooperative Business Ass'n
NCRI - Southeast/NCRI - Chesapeake

CALFEE, John

1150 17th St. NW
Washington, DC 20036
Tel: (202)862-5800
Fax: (202)862-7177
EMail: calfeej@aei.org

Employers
American Enterprise Institute for Public Policy Research (Resident Scholar)

CALHOUN, John A.

1000 Connecticut Ave. NW
13th Floor
Washington, DC 20036
Tel: (202)466-6272
Fax: (202)785-1595
EMail: jack@ncpc.org

Employers
Nat'l Crime Prevention Council (President and C.E.O.)

CALI, Leonard J.

1120 20th St. NW
Suite 1000
Washington, DC 20036
Tel: (202)457-3810
Fax: (202)457-2571
EMail: lcali@att.com

Employers
AT&T (V. President and Director, Federal Regulatory Affairs)

CALIFF, Lee H.

1909 K St. NW
Suite 500
Washington, DC 20006-1101
Tel: (202)956-5306
Fax: (202)956-5305

Employers
Alcoa Inc. (Manager, Government Affairs)

CALIMAFDE, Paula A.

4800 Hampden Ln.
Seventh Floor
One Bethesda Center
Bethesda, MD 20814-2922
Tel: (301)656-7603
Fax: (301)654-7354
Registered: LDA

Employers
Paley Rothman Goldstein Rosenberg & Cooper
Small Business Council of America (Chairman)

Clients Represented
On Behalf of Paley Rothman Goldstein Rosenberg & Cooper
Small Business Council of America

CALIO, Nicholas E.

1600 Pennsylvania Ave. NW
2nd Fl, W. Wing
Washington, DC 20500
Tel: (202)456-2230
Fax: (202)456-6220
Assistant to the President for Legislative Affairs, The White House (1992) and Deputy Assistant to the President for House Legislative Affairs (1989-91), Executive Office of the President, The White House.

Employers
Executive Office of the President - The White House (Assistant to the President and Director for Legislative Affairs)

CALKINS, Barbara J.

1660 L St. NW
Suite 208
Washington, DC 20036
EMail: bjc@atpm.org
Tel: (202)463-0550
Fax: (202)463-0555

Employers
Ass'n of Teachers of Preventive Medicine (Exec. Director)

CALKINS, Charles L.

125 N. West St.
Alexandria, VA 22314-2754
Tel: (703)683-1400
Fax: (703)549-6610
Registered: LDA

Employers
Fleet Reserve Ass'n (National Exec. Secretary)

CALL, Michael

2001 Pennsylvania Ave. NW
Suite 700
Washington, DC 20006
EMail: michaelcall@micusa.com
Tel: (202)331-7301
Fax: (202)331-7277

Employers
Mitsubishi Internat'l Corp. (V. President, Deputy General Manager)

CALLAHAN, Debra J.

1920 L St. NW
Suite 800
Washington, DC 20036
EMail: lcv@lcv.org
Tel: (202)785-8683
Fax: (202)835-0491
Registered: LDA

Employers
League of Conservation Voters (President)

CALLAHAN, Jenifer L.

600 Pennsylvania Ave. SE
Suite 400
Washington, DC 20003
EMail: jcallahan@dlcppi.org
Tel: (202)546-0007
Fax: (202)544-5002

Employers
Democratic Leadership Council (Director, Office of the President)

CALLAHAN, John J.

1120 20th St. NW
Suite 700 North
Washington, DC 20036-3406
Tel: (202)973-1200
Fax: (202)973-1212

Employers
Hall, Estill, Hardwick, Gable, Golden & Nelson (Associate)

CALLAHAN, Kateri A.

701 Pennsylvania Ave. NW
Third Floor
Washington, DC 20004
Tel: (202)508-5995
Fax: (202)508-5924
Registered: LDA

Employers
The Electric Vehicle Ass'n of the Americas (EVAA) (Exec. Director)

CALLAHAN, Michael

513 Capitol Ct. NE
Suite 300
Washington, DC 20002
Tel: (202)546-0100
Fax: (202)547-0936

Employers
Congressional Management Foundation (IT Analyst)

CALLAN, James

1005 E St. SE
Washington, DC 20003
EMail: jcallan@agaviation.org
Tel: (202)546-5722
Fax: (202)546-5726
Registered: LDA
Worked for Rep. Benjamin A. Gilman (R-NY), 1980.

Employers
Nat'l Agricultural Aviation Ass'n (Exec. Director)

CALLANAN, Susan W.

1455 F St. NW
Suite 420
Washington, DC 20004
Tel: (202)628-6442
Fax: (202)628-6537
Registered: LDA

Employers
USAA - United Services Automobile Ass'n (Assistant V. President, Federal Legislative Affairs)

CALLAS, George

2001 M St. NW
Washington, DC 20036
Tel: (202)467-3000
Fax: (202)533-8500

Employers
KPMG, LLP

Clients Represented
On Behalf of KPMG, LLP
The KPMG FSC Coalition

CALLAWAY, Robbie

600 Jefferson Plaza
Suite 401
Rockville, MD 20852
EMail: rcallaway@bgca.org
Tel: (301)251-6676
Fax: (301)294-3052

Employers
Boys and Girls Clubs of America (Senior V. President)

CALLAWAY, Jr., William H.

888 17th St. NW
Suite 600
Washington, DC 20006-3959
EMail: whcallaway@zsrlaw.com
Tel: (202)298-8660
Fax: (202)342-0683

Employers
Zuckert, Scoutt and Rasenberger, L.L.P. (Partner)

Clients Represented
On Behalf of Zuckert, Scoutt and Rasenberger, L.L.P.
Air Afrique
All Nippon Airways Co.
Challenge Air Cargo
Korean Air Lines
Nippon Cargo Airlines

CALLETT, David P.

1333 New Hampshire Ave. NW
Suite 400
Washington, DC 20036
Tel: (202)887-4000
Fax: (202)887-4288

Employers
Akin, Gump, Strauss, Hauer & Feld, L.L.P. (Partner)

Clients Represented
On Behalf of Akin, Gump, Strauss, Hauer & Feld, L.L.P.
Exxon Mobil Corp.

CALLINICOS, Sean

700 13th St. NW
Suite 260
Washington, DC 20005
Tel: (202)347-4060
Fax: (202)347-3892
Former General Counsel to Senator Lauch Faircloth (R-NC). Law Clerk, U.S. District Court for Wilmington, North Carolina, 1989-91.

Employers
Storage Technology Corp. (Manager, Government Relations)

CALLIS, Dianne B.

3133 Mount Vernon Ave.
Alexandria, VA 22305
EMail: dcallis@napsweb.org
Tel: (703)684-0180
Fax: (703)684-0071

Employers
Nat'l Ass'n of Personnel Services (President)

CALLWOOD, Kevin

1401 K St. NW
Tenth Floor
Washington, DC 20005
Tel: (202)216-2200
Fax: (202)216-2999
Former Deputy Assistant Secretary of State for African Affairs, Department of State and former Vice President, Overseas Private Investment Corp.

Employers
Jefferson-Waterman Internat'l, LLC (Exec. V. President)

CALNAN, Jacqueline

908 King St.
Suite 201
Alexandria, VA 22314-3121
EMail: AMP@Amprogress.org
Tel: (703)836-9595
Fax: (703)836-9594

Employers
Americans for Medical Progress (President)

CALOMIRIS, Charles

1150 17th St. NW
Washington, DC 20036
EMail: ccalomiris@aei.org
Tel: (202)862-5800
Fax: (202)862-7177

Employers
American Enterprise Institute for Public Policy Research (Visiting Scholar)

CALPIN, Patrick

955 L'Enfant Plaza SW
Suite 5300
Washington, DC 20024
Tel: (202)554-1650
Fax: (202)488-3542

Employers
Honda North America, Inc. (Analyst, Government Relations)

CALVERT, E. Bruce

1444 I Street NW
Suite 400
Washington, DC 20005
EMail: bcalvert@ilta.org
Tel: (202)659-2301
Fax: (202)466-4166

Employers
Independent Liquid Terminals Ass'n (Director, Administration)

CALVERT, Jennifer Johnson

2300 Clarendon Blvd.
Suite 401
Arlington, VA 22201
EMail: jenniferc@washingtonstrategies.com
Tel: (703)516-4787
Fax: (703)522-2628
Registered: LDA
Former Legislative Assistant to Rep. Joel Hefley (R-CO). Former Aide, Senator Alan Simpson (R-WY)

Employers
Washington Strategies, L.L.C.

Clients Represented
On Behalf of Washington Strategies, L.L.C.
Ballard, Spahr, Andrews & Ingersoll LLP
Corning Inc.
Internat'l Longevity Center
Maersk Inc.
New York Institute of Technology
Personal Watercraft Industry Ass'n
Recreational Fishing Alliance
University Technology Park
West Chester University
Widener University

CALVIN, Diana

Hubert H. Humphrey Bldg.
200 Independence Ave. SW
Room 435G
Washington, DC 20201
EMail: dcalvin@os.dhhs.gov
Tel: (202)690-7750
Fax: (202)690-7309

Employers
Department of Health and Human Services (Chief, Legislative Reference Unit)

CAMARDO, Alison

21 Dupont Circle NW
Suite 700
Washington, DC 20036
EMail: aec@opastco.org
Tel: (202)659-5990
Fax: (202)659-4619

Employers
Organization for the Promotion and Advancement of Small Telecommunications Cos. (Public Relations Coordinator)

CAMBELL, Glenn

1730 Pennsylvania Ave. NW
Suite 1200
Washington, DC 20006-4706
Tel: (202)737-0500
Fax: (202)626-3737

Employers
King & Spalding

Clients Represented

On Behalf of King & Spalding
The Egg Factory, LLC

CAMBON, Paul

499 S. Capitol St. SW
Suite 600
Washington, DC 20003
Tel: (202)828-8363
Fax: (202)828-6907
Registered: LDA
EMail: pcambon@joneswalker.com
Former Legislative Director to Rep. Bob Livingston (R-LA).

Employers
Jones, Walker, Waechter, Poitevent, Carrere & Denegre, L.L.P. (Director of Government Affairs)

Clients Represented

On Behalf of Jones, Walker, Waechter, Poitevent, Carrere & Denegre, L.L.P.
ACS Government Solutions Group
American Ass'n of Nurse Anesthetists
The Audubon Institute
Avondale Industries, Inc.
Bailey Link
Baton Rouge, Louisiana, City of
Boys Town USA
Broward, Florida, County of
Burk-Kleinpeter, Inc.
Columbus General, L.L.C.
Committee of Unsecured Creditors
General Category Tuna Ass'n
General Electric Co.
Imedia.IT, Inc.
Ingram Barge Company
Internat'l Technology Resources, Inc.
Jacobus Tenbroek Memorial Fund
JRL Enterprises
LA Center for the Blind
Lockheed Martin Global Telecommunications
Martinez and Curtis
Mesa, Arizona, City of
Oracle Corp.
Peoplesoft USA, Inc.
Raytheon Co.
Science & Engineering Associates, Inc.
Sewerage and Water Board of New Orleans
Stewart Enterprises, Inc.
Tulane University
United Special Transport Air Resources, LLC (USTAR)
University of New Orleans Foundation

CAMERA, CAE, Gaylen Millard

2025 M St. NW
Suite 800
Washington, DC 20036
Tel: (202)367-2100
Fax: (202)367-1200

Employers
Smith, Bucklin and Associates, Inc. (V. President, Health and Sciences)

CAMERON, Sr., Arthur E.

225 C St. NE
Suite A
Washington, DC 20002
Tel: (202)543-7275
Fax: (703)759-2248
Registered: LDA
An attorney. Employee, U.S. House of Representatives, 1950-68. Associate Counsel, Select Congressional Committee on Crime, 1969-70.

Employers
Self-employed as an independent consultant.

Clients Represented

As an independent consultant
Minnesota Mining and Manufacturing Co. (3M Co.)
Minnesota Mining and Manufacturing Co. (Traffic Control Materials Division)
Potters Industries, Inc.
Rush Presbyterian-St. Luke's Medical Center
Safetran Systems Corp.

CAMERON, Jr., Arthur E.

1500 Pennsylvania Ave. NW
Room 3025M
Washington, DC 20220
Tel: (202)622-1940
Fax: (202)622-0534

Employers
Department of Treasury (Deputy Assistant Secretary (Appropriations and Management))

CAMERON, Brad

4115 Wisconsin Ave. NW
Suite 211
Washington, DC 20016
EMail: brad@ngrc.com
Tel: (202)966-0440
Fax: (202)966-3336
Former Legislative Director for Rep. Steve Gunderson (R-WI).

Employers
Nat'l Grass Roots & Communications (Chief Exec. Officer)

CAMERON, Bruce P.

1725 17th St. NW
Suite 109
Washington, DC 20009
Tel: (202)667-9563
Fax: (202)332-6544
Registered: LDA, FARA

Employers
Bruce P. Cameron & Associates (Lobbyist)

Clients Represented

On Behalf of Bruce P. Cameron & Associates
Mozambique, Government of the Republic of

CAMERON, Donald B.

The McPherson Bldg.
901 15th St. NW, Suite 1100
Washington, DC 20005
Tel: (202)682-3500
Fax: (202)682-3580
Registered: LDA

Employers
Kaye Scholer LLP

Clients Represented

On Behalf of Kaye Scholer LLP
Korean Iron and Steel Ass'n

CAMERON, Kelly

1001 Pennsylvania Ave. NW
Suite 600
Washington, DC 20004
Tel: (202)347-0066
Fax: (202)624-7222
Registered: LDA
EMail: kcameron@pgfm.com
Senior Attorney, International Bureau and Principal Negotiator (1994-97); Legal Assistant to the Chief, Common Carrier Bureau (1993-94); and Attorney, Common Carrier Bureau (1983-93), all at the Federal Communications Commission.

Employers
Powell, Goldstein, Frazer & Murphy LLP (Partner)

Clients Represented

On Behalf of Powell, Goldstein, Frazer & Murphy LLP
Cegetel, S.A.
EUTELSAT
Inmarsat
Organization for Internat'l Investment
Qualcomm Inc.

CAMERON, Richard

555 11th St. NW
Suite 1000
Washington, DC 20004
Tel: (202)637-2200
Fax: (202)637-2201
Registered: LDA

Employers
Latham & Watkins

Clients Represented

On Behalf of Latham & Watkins
Independent Telephone and Telecommunications Alliance

CAMERON, Scott J.

2121 K St. NW
Suite 800
Washington, DC 20037
EMail: scameron@us.chep.com
Tel: (202)261-6518
Registered: LDA

Employers
Chep USA (Director, Government and Regulatory Affairs)

CAMM, Nancy Holcombe

1000 Wilson Blvd.
Suite 2500
Arlington, VA 22209-3908
EMail: ncamm@cbanet.org
Tel: (703)276-1750
Fax: (703)528-1290
Registered: LDA

Employers
Consumer Bankers Ass'n (Manager, Congressional Affairs)

CAMMER, Paul A.

P.O. Box 68
Fairfax, VA 22039
EMail: cammer@iamdigex.net
Tel: (703)802-3416
Fax: (703)631-8340

Employers
Business Council on Indoor Air (President)
Cammer and Associates (President)

Clients Represented

On Behalf of Cammer and Associates
Business Council on Indoor Air
Japan Industrial Conference for Ozone Layer Protection

CAMMER, Sandra S.

P.O. Box 68
Fairfax, VA 22039
EMail: cammer@iamdigex.net
Tel: (703)802-3416
Fax: (703)631-8340

Employers
Cammer and Associates (V. President and Secretary)

CAMMISA, Mike

1001 19th St. North
Suite 1200
Arlington, VA 22209
EMail: mcammisa@aiam.org
Tel: (703)525-7788
Fax: (703)525-8817

Employers
Ass'n of Internat'l Automobile Manufacturers (Director, Safety)

CAMP, John C.

2550 M St. NW
Washington, DC 20037-1350
Tel: (202)457-6000
Fax: (202)457-6315
Registered: FARA
EMail: jcamp@pattonboggs.com

Employers
Patton Boggs, LLP (Senior Counsel)

CAMP, Larry E.

11495 Commerce Park Dr.
Reston, VA 20191-1507
Tel: (703)620-4880
Fax: (703)476-8522
Registered: LDA

Employers
Internat'l Registries, Inc.

Clients Represented

On Behalf of Internat'l Registries, Inc.
Marshall Islands, Republic of the

CAMPAGNA, Shannon

1100 S. Washington St.
First Floor
Alexandria, VA 22314-4494
EMail: scampagna@nbwa.org
Tel: (703)683-4300
Fax: (703)683-8965
Registered: LDA

Employers
Nat'l Beer Wholesalers Ass'n (Washington Representative)

CAMPAIGNE, Alyssondra

1200 New York Ave. NW
Suite 400
Washington, DC 20005
Tel: (202)289-6868
Fax: (202)289-1060
Registered: LDA

Employers
Natural Resources Defense Council (Legislative Director)

CAMPAIGNE, Jonathan F.

100 N. Pitt St.
Suite 202
Alexandria, VA 22314
Tel: (703)519-7778
Fax: (703)519-7557

Employers
Pride Africa (Exec. Director)

CAMPBELL, Angela J.

600 New Jersey Ave. NW
Suite 312
Washington, DC 20001
Tel: (202)662-9535
Fax: (202)662-9634

Employers
Citizens Communications Center (Associate Director)

CAMPBELL, Bernie

1101 17th St. NW
Suite 203
Washington, DC 20036
Tel: (202)496-0280

Employers
The Accountability Project (Exec. Director)

CAMPBELL, Bonnie

1050 Connecticut Ave. NW
Washington, DC 20036-5339
Tel: (202)857-6000
Fax: (202)857-6395
Worked for Department of Justice.

Employers
Arent Fox Kintner Plotkin & Kahn, PLLC (Counsel)

CAMPBELL, C. Thomas

1776 I St. NW
Suite 1050
Washington, DC 20006
Tel: (202)429-3438
Fax: (202)429-3467
Registered: LDA

Employers
Dow AgroSciences (Manager, Federal Government Relations)

CAMPBELL, Candace

9912 Georgetown Pike
Suite D-2
Great Falls, VA 22066
Tel: (703)759-0662
Fax: (703)759-6711
Registered: LDA

Employers
American Preventive Medical Ass'n (Exec. Director)

CAMPBELL, Jr., Hon. Carroll A.

1001 Pennsylvania Ave. NW
Washington, DC 20004-2599
Tel: (202)624-2000
Fax: (202)624-2319

Employers
American Council of Life Insurers (President and Chief Exec. Officer)

CAMPBELL, Chad

819 Seventh St. NW
Washington, DC 20001
Tel: (202)833-8940
Fax: (202)833-8945
Registered: LDA

Employers
EOP Group, Inc.

Clients Represented
On Behalf of EOP Group, Inc.
Gas Research Institute

CAMPBELL, David A.

1900 M St. NW
Suite 500
Washington, DC 20036
Tel: (202)785-2635
Fax: (202)785-4037
Registered: LDA

Employers
BNFL, Inc. (Manager, Corporate External Affairs)

CAMPBELL, Debbie

One Dupont Circle NW
Suite 530
Washington, DC 20036
Tel: (202)463-6930
Ext: 224
Fax: (202)785-8320
EMail: dcampbell@aacn.nche.edu

Employers
American Ass'n of Colleges of Nursing (Director, Government Affairs)

CAMPBELL, F. Hamer

1738 Elton Rd.
Suite 200
Silver Spring, MD 20903
Tel: (301)445-5400
Fax: (301)445-5499

Employers
Maryland Nat'l Capitol Building Ass'n (Director, Government Affairs and Senior Legislative Representative)

CAMPBELL, Gary

1735 New York Ave. NW
Suite 500
Washington, DC 20006-4759
Tel: (202)628-1700
Fax: (202)331-1024

Employers
Preston Gates Ellis & Rouvelas Meeds LLP (Associate)

CAMPBELL, Greg

440 First St. NW
Suite 430
Washington, DC 20001
Tel: (202)737-7523
Fax: (202)737-6788
Registered: LDA

Employers
Honberger and Walters, Inc. (Associate)

Clients Represented
On Behalf of Honberger and Walters, Inc.
Monterey Salinas Transit
Riverside, California, County of
San Diego, California, County of
San Joaquin, California, County of
Ventura, California, County of

CAMPBELL, Jr., James I.

8610 Hidden Hill Lane
Potomac, MD 20854
Tel: (301)983-2538
Registered: LDA
EMail: jcampbell@jcampbell.com

Employers
Office of James I. Campbell (Principal)

CAMPBELL, James S.

2445 M St. NW
Washington, DC 20037-1420
Tel: (202)663-6000
Fax: (202)663-6363
Registered: FARA
EMail: jcampbell@wilmer.com
Counsel, Office of the Secretary, Department of Housing and Urban Development, 1977-78. Special Assistant, Antitrust Division, Department of Justice, 1967-68. Law Clerk to Justice William O. Douglas, U.S. Supreme Court, 1964.

Employers
Wilmer, Cutler & Pickering (Partner)

CAMPBELL, Jan

411 Independence Ave. SE
Washington, DC 20003
Tel: (202)546-6733
Fax: (202)546-6732
Registered: LDA

Employers
Self-employed as an independent consultant.

Clients Represented
As an independent consultant
Save America's Fossils for Everyone, Inc.

CAMPBELL, Jason

1301 Pennsylvania Ave. NW
Suite 300
Washington, DC 20004
Tel: (202)347-0228
Fax: (202)638-0607

Employers
Nat'l Cattleman's Beef Ass'n (Director, Public Lands)
Public Lands Council (Exec. Director)

CAMPBELL, Jeanne M.

1010 Pennsylvania Ave. SE
Washington, DC 20003
Tel: (202)546-4991
Fax: (202)544-7926
Registered: LDA
EMail: campcran@aol.com
Legislative Director and Press Secretary to Rep. Margaret Heckler (R-MA), 1980. Staff Assistant to Rep. Dan Rostenkowski (D-IL), 1978.

Employers
Campbell Crane & Associates (President and Chief Exec. Officer)

Clients Represented
On Behalf of Campbell Crane & Associates
American Ass'n of Advertising Agencies
The Ass'n For Manufacturing Technology (AMT)
Celanese Government Relations Office
The Chubb Corp.
Citigroup
Massachusetts Water Resources Authority
Merck & Co.
Providence Gas
Raytheon Co.
Securities Industry Ass'n
Shriners Hospital for Children
University of Massachusetts
USX Corp.
Westinghouse

CAMPBELL, Jeffrey

1300 I St. NW
Suite 900 East
Washington, DC 20005
Tel: (202)962-3830
Fax: (202)962-3838
Registered: LDA
EMail: jeff.campbell@compaq.com

Employers
Compaq Computer Corp. (Director, Federal Government Affairs)

CAMPBELL, John D.

2200 Clarendon Blvd.
Suite 1202
Arlington, VA 22201
Tel: (703)284-5400
Fax: (703)284-5449

Employers
Ball Aerospace & Technologies Corp. (Manager, Legislative Affairs)

CAMPBELL, John G.

9300-D Old Keene Mill Rd.
Burke, VA 22015
Tel: (703)455-8885
Fax: (703)440-9208
Registered: LDA

Employers
John G. Campbell, Inc. (President)

Clients Represented
On Behalf of John G. Campbell, Inc.
Computer Sciences Corp.
IT Group, Inc.
Northrop Grumman Corp.
Vredenburg

CAMPBELL, Larry

1301 K St. NW
Washington, DC 20005-3333
Tel: (202)414-1000
Fax: (202)414-1301
Registered: LDA
EMail: larry.campbell@us.pwcglobal.com
Press Secretary/Legislative Aide to Rep. William Coyne (D-PA), 1990-95. Legislative Aide to Rep. Ronnie Flippo (D-AL), 1986-90.

Employers
PriceWaterhouseCoopers (Manager, Tax Policy)

CAMPBELL, Marilyn E.

517 Second St. NE
Washington, DC 20002
Tel: (202)543-3744
Fax: (202)543-3509
Registered: LDA

Employers
David Turch & Associates (Chief Operating Officer)

Clients Represented
On Behalf of David Turch & Associates
Digital Biometrics, Inc.
Dyno Nobel, Inc.
Recovery Engineering, Inc.
Rialto, California, City of
Riverside County Transportation Commission
San Bernardino Airport Authority
San Bernardino Associated Governments
San Bernardino, California, County of
Southern California Regional Rail Authority
St. Cloud, Minnesota, City of
Temecula, California, City of

CAMPBELL, Melanie L.

1629 K St. NW
Suite 801
Washington, DC 20006

Tel: (202)659-4929
Fax: (202)659-5025

Employers
Nat'l Coalition on Black Civic Participation, Inc. (Exec. Director)

CAMPBELL, Michael D.

655 15th St. NW
Suite 900
Washington, DC 20005-5701

Tel: (202)626-5800
Fax: (202)628-0858

Employers
Miller & Chevalier, Chartered (Exec. Director)

CAMPBELL, Michael W.

1250 I St. NW
Suite 804
Washington, DC 20005
EMail: Michael.Campbell@phwilm.zeneca.com

Tel: (202)289-2570
Fax: (202)289-2580

Employers
AstraZeneca Inc. (Federal Government Affairs Assistant)

CAMPBELL, Nancy A.

112 Elden St.
Unit J
Herndon, VA 20170

Tel: (703)709-8299
Fax: (703)709-1036

Employers
Barrack Ass'n Management (Account Manager)
Nat'l Ass'n of Metal Finishers (Membership Coordinator)
Washington Technical Professional Forum (WTPF) (Membership Coordinator)

CAMPBELL, Nancy Duff

11 Dupont Circle NW
Suite 800
Washington, DC 20036
EMail: info@nwlc.org

Tel: (202)588-5180
Fax: (202)588-5185

Employers
Nat'l Women's Law Center (Co-President)

CAMPBELL, Randy

1000 Connecticut Ave. NW
Suite 1001
Washington, DC 20036
EMail: rcampbell@naftz.org

Tel: (202)331-1950
Fax: (202)331-1994

Employers
Nat'l Ass'n of Foreign Trade Zones (Exec. Director)

CAMPBELL, Sabrina V.

801 Pennsylvania Ave. NW
Suite 214
Washington, DC 20004

Tel: (202)628-1645
Fax: (202)628-4276
Registered: LDA

Employers
American Electric Power Co. (Director, Federal Agency Relations)

CAMPBELL, Scott L.

1025 Thomas Jefferson St. NW
Suite 411 West
Washington, DC 20007

Tel: (202)965-1161
Fax: (202)965-1177
Registered: LDA, FARA

Employers
Washington Policy & Analysis, Inc. (President)

Clients Represented

On Behalf of Washington Policy & Analysis, Inc.
The Tokyo Electric Power Company, Inc.

CAMPBELL, Stephen F.

5430 Grosvenor Lane
Suite 130
Bethesda, MD 20814-2142

Tel: (301)564-1623
Fax: (301)564-0588

Employers
Commercial Vehicle Safety Alliance (Exec. Director)

CAMPBELL, Stuart P.

1120 Connecticut Ave. NW
Suite 910
Washington, DC 20006
EMail: SPCAMPBELL@chn.org

Tel: (202)223-2532
Fax: (202)223-2538

Employers
Coalition on Human Needs (Exec. Director)

CAMPBELL, Thomas D.

517 Queen St.
Alexandria, VA 22314

Tel: (703)683-0773
Registered: LDA

Employers
Thomas D. Campbell & Assoc. (President)

Clients Represented

On Behalf of Thomas D. Campbell & Assoc.
RAG North America
Smokers Pneumonoconiosis Council
Thompson Creek Metals Co.

CAMPBELL, Thomas R.

1701 K St. NW
Suite 903
Washington, DC 20006

Tel: (202)835-9043
Fax: (202)835-9030
Registered: LDA

Employers
YMCA of the USA Public Policy Office (Assistant Director)

CAMPBELL, W. Douglas

1776 K St. NW
Suite 300
Washington, DC 20006

Tel: (202)530-5505
Fax: (202)719-7270
Registered: LDA

Employers
Self-employed as an independent consultant.

Clients Represented

As an independent consultant
AOL Time Warner

CAMPI, Jim

1331 H St. NW
Suite 1001
Washington, DC 20005
EMail: jcampi@civilwar.org

Tel: (202)367-1861
Ext: 205

Employers
The Civil War Preservation Trust (Director, Communications)

CAMPION, Charles

1001 G St. NW
Suite 300 East
Washington, DC 20001
EMail: ccampion@deweysquare.com

Tel: (202)638-5616
Fax: (202)638-5612

Employers
Dewey Square Group (Partner)

Clients Represented

On Behalf of Dewey Square Group
Northwest Airlines, Inc.

CAMPO, Terry T.

1730 K St. NW
Suite 1100
Washington, DC 20006

Tel: (202)466-2819
Fax: (202)466-3535

Special Assistant and Chief of Staff and General Counsel, Department of Commerce, 1985-87. Counsel, Senate Judiciary Committee, 1983-85.

Employers
The Campo Group, Ltd. (President)

Clients Represented

On Behalf of The Campo Group, Ltd.
S. A. Campo
Chicago Global, Ltd.
Crystal Group
Farrell & Campo
Windsock Research

CAMPS, Kevin

1424 16th St. NW
Suite 404
Washington, DC 20036

Tel: (202)328-0002
Fax: (202)462-2183

Employers
Nuclear Information and Resource Service (Director, Radioactive Waste Project)

CANAN, G. Patrick

3211 Fourth St. NE
Washington, DC 20017

Tel: (202)541-3140
Fax: (202)541-3313

Employers
United States Catholic Conference (Associate Director, Government Liaison)

CANAN, Linda

1625 L St. NW
Washington, DC 20036-5687

Tel: (202)429-1198
Fax: (202)429-1197

Employers
American Federation of State, County and Municipal Employees (Assistant Director, Political Action)

CANATSEY, John

1735 Jefferson Davis Hwy.
Suite 1001
Arlington, VA 22202-3461

Tel: (703)413-6300
Fax: (703)413-6316
Registered: LDA

Employers
Thiokol Propulsion (Director, Legislative Liaison (Defense))

CANAVAN, Colin

1300 Wilson Blvd.
Arlington, VA 22209
EMail: colin_canavan@americanchemistry.com

Tel: (703)741-5000
Fax: (703)741-6000

Employers
American Chemistry Council (Coordinator, Federal Relations)

CANAVAN, Robert P.

1440 N St. NW
Suite 1016
Washington, DC 20005

Tel: (202)462-5911
Fax: (202)588-8094
Registered: LDA

Employers
Federal Management Strategies, Inc. (Consultant)

Clients Represented

On Behalf of Federal Management Strategies, Inc.
CAL-FED
Federal Advocacy for California Education
Forest Counties Schools Coalition
Nat'l Education Ass'n of the U.S.
Nat'l Forest Counties School Coalition
Rebuild America's Schools
San Dieguito School Transportation Cooperative
Temple University

CANDLER, Linda

1901 N. Fort Myer Dr.
Suite 700
Arlington, VA 22209
EMail: lcandler@nfi.org

Tel: (703)524-8884
Fax: (703)524-4619

Employers
Nat'l Fisheries Institute (V. President, Communications)

CANDON, Mary Eva

1225 19th St. NW
Suite 800
Washington, DC 20036

Tel: (202)955-6067
Fax: (202)293-0307
Registered: LDA

Employers
Berliner, Candon & Jimison (Partner)
Guam, Washington Office of the Governor (Counsel)

Clients Represented

On Behalf of Berliner, Candon & Jimison
Guam, Territory of

CANFIELD, Anne C.

801 Pennsylvania Ave. NW
Suite 625
Washington, DC 20004

Tel: (202)661-2100
Fax: (202)661-2101
Registered: LDA

Employers
Canfield & Associates, Inc. (President)
Consumer Mortgage Coalition (Exec. Director)

Clients Represented

On Behalf of Canfield & Associates, Inc.

Air Transport Ass'n of America
American Home Products Corp.
Ass'n of Financial Guaranty Insurers
Consumer Mortgage Coalition
GE Commercial Real Estate & Financial Services
Merck & Co.
Mutual of Omaha Insurance Companies
Pfizer, Inc.

CANFIELD, IV, H. Spofford

2600 Virginia Ave. NW
Suite 600
Washington, DC 20037
Tel: (202)333-2524
Fax: (202)338-5950
Registered: LDA

Government service in the Nixon, Ford, Reagan and Bush I administrations, including service at the Department of the Interior, and the Interstate Commerce Commission, and in various positions with the U.S. Senate and with Vice Presidents Agnew, Ford and Rockefeller.

Employers

J. Steven Griles & Associates

Clients Represented

On Behalf of J. Steven Griles & Associates

Redstone

CANFIELD, William B.

1155 21st St. NW
Suite 300
Washington, DC 20036
Tel: (202)659-8201
Fax: (202)659-5249
Registered: LDA
EMail: wbcanfield@wms-jen.com

Staff Director and Counsel, Senate Republican Conference, 1991-93. Chief Counsel, National Republican Senatorial Campaign Committee, 1989-91. Republican Chief Counsel, Senate Committee on Rules, 1987-89. Counsel, Senate Committee on Ethics, 1978-86. Counsel to Librarian, Library of Congress, 1976-78. Counsel, Committee of House Administration, 1975-76.

Employers

Williams & Jensen, P.C. (Partner)

Clients Represented

On Behalf of Williams & Jensen, P.C.

Ad Hoc Coalition of Commercial and Investment Banks
Bass Enterprises Production Co.
The Church Alliance
Dunn-Padre, Inc.
HP Global Workplaces, Inc.
Nat'l Underground Railroad Freedom Center
Owens-Illinois, Inc.
Pharmaceutical Research and Manufacturers of America
Reinsurance Ass'n of America
Smithfield Foods Inc.
Texaco Group Inc.
The Vantage Group, Inc.

CANIS, Jonathan

1200 19th St. NW
Suite 500
Washington, DC 20036
Tel: (202)955-9600
Fax: (202)955-9792

Employers

Kelley, Drye & Warren LLP (Partner)

CANNER, Stephen

1030 15th St. NW
Suite 800
Washington, DC 20005
Tel: (202)371-1316
Fax: (202)371-8249

Employers

United States Council for Internat'l Business (V. President, Investment Policy)

CANNON, Bruce

2120 L St. NW
Suite 305
Washington, DC 20037
Tel: (202)659-4620
Fax: (202)659-0500

Employers

Internat'l Bridge, Tunnel and Turnpike Ass'n (Director, Public Affairs)

CANNON, Charles A.

1300 Pennsylvania Ave. NW
Suite 700
Washington, DC 20004
Tel: (202)204-3040
Fax: (202)204-3041
Registered: LDA
EMail: chacannon@aol.com

Employers

Cannon Consultants, Inc. (President)

Clients Represented

On Behalf of Cannon Consultants, Inc.

Allboxesdirect
ISL Inc.
Land Mine Detection Systems, Inc.
N-VIRO Internat'l Corp.
Nat'l Audubon Soc.
New Product Development Consortium

CANNON, Dean H.

1350 I St. NW
Suite 700
Washington, DC 20005
Tel: (202)789-6000
Fax: (202)789-6190

Employers

Beveridge & Diamond, P.C.

CANNON, Mark R.

1335 Murray Downs Way
Reston, VA 20194
Tel: (703)787-9277
Registered: LDA

Employers

Self-employed as an independent consultant.

Clients Represented

As an independent consultant

Resources and Instruction for Staff Excellence, Inc.

CANOVA, Diane M.

1150 Connecticut Ave. NW
Suite 810
Washington, DC 20036
Tel: (202)785-7900
Fax: (202)785-7950
Registered: LDA
EMail: diane@heart.org

Employers

American Heart Ass'n (V. President, Advocacy)

CANSLER, Tim

600 Maryland Ave. SW
Suite 800
Washington, DC 20024
Tel: (202)484-3600
Fax: (202)484-3604
Registered: LDA

Employers

American Farm Bureau Federation (Director, Commodities and Rural Development)

CANTER, Mark A.

1001 Pennsylvania Ave. NW
Washington, DC 20004-2599
Tel: (202)624-2000
Fax: (202)624-2319

Employers

American Council of Life Insurers (Senior Counsel)

CANTOR, L. Michael

1250 24th St. NW
Suite 300
Washington, DC 20037
Tel: (202)835-1617
Registered: LDA

Employers

Maritime Investment Corp. (Managing Director)

CANTOR, Richard A.

1400 16th St. NW
Suite 400
Washington, DC 20036
Tel: (202)234-2101
Fax: (202)234-1614
Registered: LDA

Deputy Associate Administrator for Regional Operations and State/Local Relations, Environmental Protection Agency, 1991-92. Attorney-Advisor, Federal Transit Administration, Department of Transportation, 1988-91.

Employers

The Grizzle Company (President)

Clients Represented

On Behalf of The Grizzle Company

al group Lonza
Ashland Inc.
ENTEK Corp.
GSE Systems, Inc.
Internat'l Council of Shopping Centers
ManTech Internat'l
Mas-Hamilton Group
NTS Mortgage Income Fund
Regional Airport Authority of Louisville & Jefferson Co.
University of Louisville
WPC Brands, Inc.

CANTOR-WEINBERG, Julie

1310 G St. NW
Suite 770
Washington, DC 20005
Tel: (202)508-0800
Fax: (202)508-0818

Employers

Guidant Corp. (Manager, Government Affairs)

CANTREL, Jr., Francis J.

1133 19th St. NW
Washington, DC 20036
Tel: (202)887-3112
Fax: (202)887-3123
Registered: LDA
EMail: frank.cantrel@wcom.com

Employers

MCI WorldCom Corp. (Director, Government Relations)

CANTRELL, Jean

1200 New Hampshire Ave. NW
Suite 440
Washington, DC 20036
Tel: (202)463-2154
Fax: (202)463-2163
Registered: LDA
EMail: cantrellj@dnb.com

Employers

Dun & Bradstreet (Exec. Director, Government Affairs)

CANTUS, Charles H.

2101 Wilson Blvd.
Suite 750
Arlington, VA 22201
Tel: (703)875-8059
Fax: (703)875-8922
Registered: LDA
EMail: cantus@pscouncil.org

Employers

Professional Services Council (V. President, Government Relations)

CANTUS, H. Hollister

1173 Huntover Ct.
Suite 200
McLean, VA 22102
Tel: (703)760-7873
Fax: (703)356-4519

Former Associate Administrator, National Aeronautics and Space Administration, 1987-89. Director of Congressional Relations, Energy Reserch and Development Agency, 1977-79. Deputy Assistant Secretary, Department of Defense, 1974-75. Professional Staff Member, House Armed Services Committee, 1970-74.

Employers

Alcalde & Fay (Partner, Aerospace and Technology)
The ILEX Group (President and Chief Exec. Officer)

Clients Represented

On Behalf of The ILEX Group

Applied Knowledge Group
Digital Commerce Corp.
European Aeronautics, Defence and Space, Inc.
Net Results, Inc.
Orbital Resources, LLC
Washington Infrastructure Services, Inc.

CAPISTRANT, Gary F.

1055 N. Fairfax St.
Suite 201
Alexandria, VA 22314-3563
Tel: (703)739-7999
Fax: (703)739-7995
Registered: LDA

Employers

U.S. Strategies Corp. (Senior V. President, Health)

Clients Represented

On Behalf of U.S. Strategies Corp.

Acute Long Term Hospital Ass'n
Healthsouth Corp.
Home Access Health
Integrated Health Services, Inc.
IVAX Corp.
Nat'l Ass'n of Community Health Centers
UBS Warburg

CAPLAN, Bennett

1401 I St. NW
Suite 1220
Washington, DC 20005
Tel: (202)898-6400
Fax: (202)898-6454
Registered: LDA

Employers

Vivendi Universal (Director, Policy Development)

CAPON, Ross

900 Second St. NE
Suite 308
Washington, DC 20002-3557
EMail: narp@narprail.org
Tel: (202)408-8362
Fax: (202)408-8287
Registered: LDA

Employers
Nat'l Ass'n of Railroad Passengers (Exec. Director)

CAPTAIN, Brad L.

2201 Cooperative Way
Herndon, VA 20171
Tel: (703)709-6700
Fax: (703)709-6780
Registered: LDA

Employers
Rural Telephone Finance Cooperative (Legislative Representative)

CAPUANO, Donald J.

4748 Wisconsin Ave. NW
Washington, DC 20016
Tel: (202)362-0041

Employers
O'Donoghue & O'Donoghue

CAPUTO, Annie

400 Seventh St. NW
Fourth Floor
Washington, DC 20004
Tel: (202)347-7500
Fax: (202)347-7501

Employers
ComEd (Strategic Issues Communicator)
Exelon Corp. (Manager, Congressional Affairs)

CARABILLO, Joseph A.

111 Massachusetts Ave. NW
Washington, DC 20001
EMail: jcarabillo@ullicolaw.com
Tel: (202)682-0900
Fax: (202)682-6784
Registered: LDA

Employers
The Union Labor Life Insurance Co. (V. President and Chief Legal Officer)

CARD, Bradford

412 First St. SE
Suite 100
Washington, DC 20003
Tel: (202)484-4884
Fax: (202)484-0109
Former Chief of Staff for Rep. John Sweeney (R-NY).

Employers
The Dutko Group, Inc. (V. President)

CARD, Noel R.

1100 17th St. NW
Seventh Floor
Washington, DC 20036
EMail: 74672.3550@compuserve.com
Tel: (202)223-8196
Fax: (202)872-1948

Employers
American Academy of Actuaries (Director, Communications)

CARDAMONE, Thomas

110 Maryland Ave. NE
Suite 201
Washington, DC 20002
EMail: cardamone@clw.org
Tel: (202)546-0795
Fax: (202)546-5142
Registered: LDA

Employers
Council for a Livable World Education Fund (Director, Conventional Arms Transfers Project and Editor, Arms Trade News)

CARDINALE, Richard T.

1849 C St. NW
Room 6245
Washington, DC 20240
EMail: richard_cardinale@ios.doi.gov
Tel: (202)208-4547
Fax: (202)208-7619

Employers
Department of Interior (Assistant Legislative Counsel)

CARDMAN, Denise A.

740 15th St. NW
Ninth Floor
Washington, DC 20005
Tel: (202)662-1761
Fax: (202)662-1762
Registered: LDA

Employers
American Bar Ass'n (Senior Legislative Counsel)

CARELLI, Frank

1016 16th St. NW
Suite 300
Washington, DC 20036
Tel: (202)862-4400
Fax: (202)862-4432
Registered: LDA

Employers
Internat'l Ass'n of Machinists and Aerospace Workers (Assistant Legislative Director)
Nat'l Federation of Federal Employees (Legislative Liaison)

CAREW, Nasserie

1780 Massachusetts Ave. NW
Washington, DC 20036
Tel: (202)785-3351
Fax: (202)293-4349

Employers
Planned Parenthood Federation of America (Media Relations)

CAREY, Arlene P.

119 N. Henry St.
Third Floor
Alexandria, VA 22314-2903
EMail: careynealon@aol.com
Tel: (703)921-9111
Fax: (703)836-8009

Employers
CAREY/NEALON & Associates, L.L.C. (Exec. Director)

CAREY, USN (Ret.), Rr. Adm. James J.

119 N. Henry St.
Third Floor
Alexandria, VA 22314-2903
EMail: DefenseNet@aol.com
Tel: (703)921-9111
Fax: (703)836-8009
Registered: LDA

Employers
CAREY/NEALON & Associates, L.L.C. (Chairman)
Internet Security, Privacy & Self-Regulation PAC (PAC Administrator)
Media Fusion L.L.C.
Powerline Communications PAC (Contact)

Clients Represented

On Behalf of CAREY/NEALON & Associates, L.L.C.
Amtech Internat'l
Media Fusion L.L.C.

CAREY, Kate H.

1620 L St. NW
Suite 800
Washington, DC 20036-5617
Tel: (202)659-3575
Fax: (202)659-1026
Registered: LDA

Employers
Metropolitan Life Insurance Co. (V. President, Government Relations)

CAREY, Mary G.

1150 17th St. NW
Suite 400
Washington, DC 20036
Tel: (202)222-4700
Fax: (202)222-4799

Employers
The Walt Disney Co. (Manager)

CAREY, Steven E.

1055 N. Fairfax St.
Suite 201
Alexandria, VA 22314-3563
Tel: (703)739-7999
Fax: (703)739-7995
Registered: LDA
Legislative Director to Senator Tim Hutchinson (R-AR), 1998-2000. Also served as Assistant to Rep. Carl Pursell (R-MI) and as Legislative Director to Rep. Jay W. Dickey (R-AR) and Rep. Harold Rogers (R-KY).

Employers
U.S. Strategies Corp. (V. President, Legislative Affairs)

Clients Represented

On Behalf of U.S. Strategies Corp.
American Institute for Public Safety
American Nursery and Landscape Ass'n
Ash Britt
Harrah's Entertainment, Inc.
Healthsouth Corp.
Integrated Health Services, Inc.
JRL Enterprises
Nat'l Ass'n of Community Health Centers
UBS Warburg

CARI, Jr., Joseph A.

1500 K St. NW
Suite 250
Washington, DC 20005-1714
EMail: jacari@uhlaw.com
Tel: (202)639-7510
Fax: (202)639-7505
Registered: LDA
Special Assistant Attorney General, Department of Justice, 1986-87. Special Counsel, Drug Enforcement Caucus, Senate Judiciary Committee, 1986-87. Legislative Assistant to Rep. Marty Russo (D-IL), 1974-75.

Employers
Ungaretti & Harris (Partner)

Clients Represented

On Behalf of Ungaretti & Harris
Allegiance Healthcare Corp.
Computer Communications Industry of America
ComScore
Premier Institute
Stepan Co.
United Defense, L.P.

CARINO, Jr., Maurice E.

1667 K St. NW
Suite 550
Washington, DC 20006
EMail: mcarino156@aol.com
Tel: (202)775-6211
Fax: (202)775-6221
Registered: LDA

Employers
Bethlehem Steel Corp. (V. President, Federal Government Affairs)

CARL, Carlton

1050 31st St. NW
Washington, DC 20007
Tel: (202)965-3500
Fax: (202)342-5484

Employers
Ass'n of Trial Lawyers of America (Director, Media Relations)

CARLBERG, Ronald L.

2121 Eisenhower
Suite 600
Alexandria, VA 22314
EMail: carlbergr@gmdsinc.com
Tel: (703)299-6649
Fax: (703)299-9213
Registered: FARA
Former Director, International Acquisition Office, Department of Defense.

Employers
Global Marketing and Development Solutions (Exec. V. President)

Clients Represented

On Behalf of Global Marketing and Development Solutions
Swiss Ordnance Enterprise

CARLETON, Brenda F.

601 D St. NW
Room 10120
Washington, DC 20530
Tel: (202)514-2497
Fax: (202)514-9082

Employers
Department of Justice - Antitrust Division (Chief Legislative Unit, Legal Policy Section)

CARLEY, Dr. David

700 13th St. NW
Suite 400
Washington, DC 20005
EMail: dcarley@cassidy.com
Tel: (202)347-0773
Fax: (202)347-0785
Registered: LDA

Employers
Cassidy & Associates, Inc. (Senior Consultant)

CARLEY, Wayne W.

12030 Sunrise Valley Dr.
Suite 110
Reston, VA 20191-3409
EMail: wcarley@aol.com
Tel: (703)264-9696
Fax: (703)264-7778

Employers
Nat'l Ass'n of Biology Teachers (Exec. Director)

CARLILE, Jane

1350 I St. NW
Suite 590
Washington, DC 20005
EMail: jcarlile@cap.org
Tel: (202)354-7111
Fax: (202)354-7155
Registered: LDA

Employers
College of American Pathologists (Assistant Director, Professional Affairs)

CARLIN, J. David

1333 New Hampshire Ave. NW
Suite 400
Washington, DC 20036
Tel: (202)887-4000
Fax: (202)887-4288
Registered: LDA

Assistant Secretary for Congressional Relations, Department of Agriculture 1996-98.

Employers
Akin, Gump, Strauss, Hauer & Feld, L.L.P. (Partner)

Clients Represented
On Behalf of Akin, Gump, Strauss, Hauer & Feld, L.L.P.
American Family Enterprises
Bridgestone/Firestone, Inc.
Competitive Consumer Lending Coalition
Farm Credit Bank of Texas
Fontana Union Water Co.
Knoll Pharmaceutical Co.
Nehemiah Progressive Housing Development Corp.
Quad Dimension

CARLIN, Roberta S.

4590 MacArthur Blvd. NW
Suite 250
Washington, DC 20007
Tel: (202)944-3285
Fax: (202)944-3295
Registered: LDA

Employers
Spina Bifida Ass'n of America

CARLISLE, Jim

1301 K St. NW
Washington, DC 20005-3333
Tel: (202)414-1000
Fax: (202)414-1301
Registered: LDA
EMail: jim.carlisle@us.pwcglobal.com

Employers
PriceWaterhouseCoopers (Director)

Clients Represented
On Behalf of PriceWaterhouseCoopers
Alliance Capital Management LP
American Council of Life Insurers
Automobile Manufacturers R&D Coalition
Bank of America
Blue Cross Blue Shield Ass'n
Clark/Bardes, Inc.
Coalition for Fair Tax Credits
Coalition of Corporate Taxpayers
Electronic Commerce Tax Study Group
General Motors Corp.
Owens Corning
Placid Refining Co.
Plum Creek Timber Co.
PwC Leasing Coalition
United Parcel Service

CARLISLE, Linda E.

601 13th St. NW
Suite 600 South
Washington, DC 20005
Tel: (202)626-3666
Fax: (202)639-9355
Registered: LDA
EMail: lcarlisle@whitecase.com

Special Assistant to the Assistant Secretary for Tax Policy, 1985-87. Attorney-Adviser, Department of the Treasury, 1984-85.

Employers
White & Case LLP (Partner)

Clients Represented
On Behalf of White & Case LLP
Alticor, Inc.
Employee-Owned S Corporations of America
Liberty Check Printers
Mercedes-Benz of North America, Inc.
Methanex Inc.
The Williams Companies

CARLSON, Amy

1735 New York Ave. NW
Suite 500
Washington, DC 20006-4759
Tel: (202)628-1700
Fax: (202)331-1024
Registered: LDA

Employers
Preston Gates Ellis & Rouvelas Meeds LLP (Partner)

Clients Represented
On Behalf of Preston Gates Ellis & Rouvelas Meeds LLP
Americans for Computer Privacy
Business Software Alliance
New York Institute of Technology
Orange, California, County of
Pitney Bowes, Inc.
Prime Time 24
RSA Security Inc.

CARLSON, Don F.

7901 Westpark Dr.
McLean, VA 22102-4206
Tel: (703)893-2900
Fax: (703)893-1151

Employers
The Ass'n For Manufacturing Technology (AMT) (President)

CARLSON, Donald G.

1301 K St. NW
Washington, DC 20005-3333
Tel: (202)414-1000
Fax: (202)414-1301

Aide to Reps. Bill Archer (R-TX), 1971-2001; Donald W. Riegle, Jr. (R-MI), 1967; and James Harvey (R-MI), 1967-70. Also served in the U.S Marine Corps Reserve.

Employers
PriceWaterhouseCoopers (Director, National Tax Service)

CARLSON, Eric

12th and Independence Ave. SW
Room 5121, South Bldg.
Washington, DC 20250
Tel: (202)720-2771
Fax: (202)690-0854

Employers
Department of Agriculture - Natural Resources Conservation Service (Legislative Specialist)

CARLSON, George N.

1666 K St. NW
Suite 800
Washington, DC 20006
Tel: (202)481-7000
Fax: (202)862-7098

Former Director, Office of Tax Analysis, Department of Treasury.

Employers
Arthur Andersen LLP (Partner, Office of Federal Tax Services)

CARLSON, Peter

1015 18th St. NW
Suite 600
Washington, DC 20036
Tel: (202)429-4344
Fax: (202)429-4342
Registered: LDA

Employers
Will and Carlson, Inc.

Clients Represented
On Behalf of Will and Carlson, Inc.
Animas-La Plata Water Conservancy District
Clark County Regional Flood Control District
Eastern Municipal Water District
Garrison Diversion Conservancy District
Kennedy/Jenks Consultants
The Metropolitan Water District of Southern California
Oregon Water Resources Congress
Six Agency Committee
Southern Ute Indian Tribe
Southwest Water Conservation District of Colorado
Western Coalition of Arid States

CARLSTROM, Jr., Robert E.

7800 Stable Way
Potomac, MD 20854
Tel: (301)767-5949
Fax: (301)983-5681
Registered: LDA

Employers
Self-employed as an independent consultant.

Clients Represented
As an independent consultant
The Doe Run Co.
Human Capital Resources
Internat'l Lead Zinc Research Organization, Inc. (ILZRO)

CARLTON, Nancy M.

601 Pennsylvania Ave. NW
Suite 1200
North Bldg.
Washington, DC 20036
Tel: (202)638-4170
Fax: (202)638-3670
Registered: LDA

Employers
Merck & Co. (Exec. Director, Federal Policy and Government Relations)

CARLUCCI, Frank C.

1001 Pennsylvania Ave. NW
Suite 220 South
Washington, DC 20004
Tel: (202)347-2626
Fax: (202)347-1818

Employers
The Carlyle Group (Chairman)

CARMAN, Nancy M.

500 E St. SW
MS: 716C
Washington, DC 20436
Tel: (202)205-3151
Fax: (202)205-2139
EMail: ncarman@usitc.gov

Former Professional Staff Member, House Committee on Foreign Affairs.

Employers
Internat'l Trade Commission (Congressional Relations Officer)

CARMEN, David M.

1299 Pennsylvania Ave. NW
Suite 800 West
Washington, DC 20004
Tel: (202)785-0500
Fax: (202)785-5277
Registered: LDA, FARA
EMail: carmend@carmengroup.com

Employers
The Carmen Group (President and Chief Exec. Officer)
LMRC, Inc. (President and Chief Exec. Officer)

Clients Represented
On Behalf of The Carmen Group
ADVO, Inc.
Air Transport Ass'n of America
Dillard University
GELCO Information Network GSD, Inc.
Illinois Department of Transportation
MedStar Health
Starwood Hotels & Resorts Worldwide, Inc.

CARMEN, Gerald P.

1299 Pennsylvania Ave. NW
Suite 800 West
Washington, DC 20004
Tel: (202)785-0500
Fax: (202)785-5277
Registered: LDA

Employers
The Carmen Group (V. Chairman)
LMRC, Inc. (V. Chairman)

Clients Represented
On Behalf of The Carmen Group
Air Transport Ass'n of America
American Gas Ass'n
Hyundai Space & Aircraft Co., Ltd.
Major Medicaid Hospital Coalition
Northeast Illinois Regional Commuter Railroad Corp.
Northwest Airlines, Inc.
Pembroke Real Estate, Inc.
Renova Inc.
US Bancorp
Washington Sports & Entertainment, L.P.

CARMEN, Melinda L.

1901 Pennsylvania Ave. NW
Suite 300
Washington, DC 20006
Tel: (202)728-1001
Fax: (202)728-4055
Registered: LDA

Deputy General Counsel, Department of Energy, 1983-86. Director of Investigations, Import Administration, Department of Commerce, 1981-83. Legislative Director to Senator Gordon Humphrey (R-NH), 1979-81.

Employers
Carmen & Muss, P.L.L.C. (Member)

Clients Represented
On Behalf of Carmen & Muss, P.L.L.C.
DM Electronics Recycling Corporation
Square 3942 Associates Limited Partnership

CARMI, Vicky I.

3114 Circle Hill Rd.
Alexandria, VA 22305-1606
Tel: (703)548-1234
Fax: (703)548-6216
EMail: info@itctrade.com

Employers
Internat'l Trade Council (Director, Research)

CARMINE, Ferrell D.

700 13th St. NW
Suite 950
Washington, DC 20005
Tel: (202)333-8777
Fax: (202)333-8722
Registered: LDA
EMail: dcarmine@earthlink.net

Trademark Attorney, U.S. Patent and Trademark Office, Department of Commerce, 1991-2000. Acting Director of Public Affairs, Office of Consumer Affairs, The White House, 1990-91. Special Assistant, Office of Vocational and Adult Education, Department of Education, 1986-90. Director of Public Affairs, Region III, Department of Housing and Urban Development, 1984-86.

Employers
The Evans Group, Ltd. (Senior V. President)

Clients Represented
On Behalf of The Evans Group, Ltd.
PetrolRem, Inc.

CARNEAL, Garry

1275 K St. NW
Suite 1100
Washington, DC 20005
Tel: (202)216-9010

Employers
American Accreditation Healthcare Commission/URAC (President)

CARNEAL, George V.

555 13th St. NW
Washington, DC 20004-1109
Tel: (202)637-5600
Fax: (202)637-5910

Employers
Hogan & Hartson L.L.P. (Director, Transportation Practice Group)

Clients Represented
On Behalf of Hogan & Hartson L.L.P.
El Toro Reuse Planning Authority

CARNEVALE, Anthony P.

1800 K St. NW
Suite 900
Washington, DC 20006
Tel: (202)659-0616
Fax: (202)887-0875

Employers
Educational Testing Service (V. President for Public Leadership)

CARNEVALE, V.M.D., Richard A.

1325 G St. NW
Suite 700
Washington, DC 20005
Tel: (202)637-2440
Fax: (202)393-1667
EMail: rcarnevale@ahi.org

Employers
Animal Health Institute (V. President, Regulatory, Scientific, and International Affairs)

CARNEY, Ginger

1225 Jefferson Davis Hwy.
Suite 1100
Arlington, VA 22202
Tel: (703)416-9400
Fax: (703)416-9404
EMail: carney-ginger@si.com

Employers
Smiths Aerospace (Director, International Trade Controls)

CARNEY, Jack

200 Maryland Ave. NE
Washington, DC 20002
Tel: (202)543-2239
Fax: (202)543-6719

Employers
Veterans of Foreign Wars of the U.S. (PAC, Contact)

CARNEY, Jacqueline

523 Seventh St. SE
Washington, DC 20003
Tel: (202)543-5237
Fax: (202)543-5269
EMail: jackie@billcarneyco.com

Employers
Bill Carney & Co. (V. President)

Clients Represented
On Behalf of Bill Carney & Co.
Clean Energy Group
COGEMA, Inc.
Edison Electric Institute
Repeal PUHCA Now Coalition

CARNEY, John

1015 15th St. NW
Suite 802
Washington, DC 20005
Tel: (202)347-7474
Fax: (202)898-0068
Registered: LDA
EMail: jcarney@acec.org

Employers
American Consulting Engineers Council (Director, Transportation and Infrastructure)

CARNEY, Hon. William

523 Seventh St. SE
Washington, DC 20003
Tel: (202)543-5237
Fax: (202)543-5269
Registered: LDA
EMail: bill@billcarneyco.com

Former Member of Congress, U.S. House of Representatives (R-NY), 1979-86.

Employers
Bill Carney & Co. (President)

Clients Represented
On Behalf of Bill Carney & Co.
Clean Energy Group
COGEMA, Inc.
Edison Electric Institute
Lockheed Martin Naval Electronics Surveillance Systems
Nuclear Energy Institute
Repeal PUHCA Now Coalition

CARNEY-TALLEY, Sandra

1250 I St. NW
Suite 1200
Washington, DC 20005-3924
Tel: (202)371-8503
Fax: (202)371-8470

Employers
Aerospace Industries Ass'n of America (Assistant V. President, Policy and Planning)

CAROLINE, Glen

11250 Waples Mill Rd.
Fairfax, VA 22030-7400
Tel: (703)267-1000
Fax: (703)267-3918

Employers
Nat'l Rifle Ass'n Institute for Legislative Action (Director, Grassroots Office)

CAROLLA, Bob

Colonial Place Three
2107 Wilson Blvd., Suite 300
Arlington, VA 22201-3042
Tel: (703)524-7600
Fax: (703)524-9094

Employers
Nat'l Alliance for the Mentally Ill (Director, Communications)

CAROZZA, Michael C.

655 15th St. NW
Suite 300
Washington, DC 20005
Tel: (202)783-0900
Fax: (202)783-2308
Registered: LDA
EMail: michael.carozza@bms.com

Employers
Bristol-Myers Squibb Co. (Vice President, Federal Relations)

CAROZZA, Shirley

11 Canal Center Plaza
Suite 103
Alexandria, VA 20005
Tel: (703)683-6990
Fax: (703)683-0645
Registered: LDA

Employers
Brown & Associates

Clients Represented
On Behalf of Brown & Associates
Onehealthbank.com
Problem-Knowledge Coupler

CARP, Bertram W.

1155 21st St. NW
Suite 300
Washington, DC 20036
Tel: (202)659-8201
Fax: (202)659-5249
Registered: LDA
EMail: bwcarp@wms-jen.com

Deputy Assistant to the President for Domestic Affairs and Policy, The White House, 1977-81. Legislative Counsel to Senator Walter F. Mondale (D-MN), 1970-77. Attorney, Office of the General Counsel, Department of Health, Education and Welfare, 1969-70.

Employers
Williams & Jensen, P.C. (Partner)

Clients Represented
On Behalf of Williams & Jensen, P.C.
AOL Time Warner
The Coca-Cola Company
Fannie Mae
Gateway, Inc.
Internat'l Ass'n of Amusement Parks and Attractions
Nat'l Cable Television Ass'n
Qwest Communications
Recording Industry Ass'n of America
Reuters America Inc.
Smithfield Foods Inc.

CARPENTER, Elaine

1401 H St. NW
Suite 600
Washington, DC 20005-2136
Tel: (202)326-7300
Fax: (202)326-7333

Employers
United States Telecom Ass'n (Chief of Staff)

CARPENTER, Jr., Jot D.

1120 20th St. NW
Suite 1000
Washington, DC 20036
Tel: (202)457-3810
Fax: (202)457-2571
Registered: LDA
EMail: jdcjr@att.com

Former Aide to Rep. Michael G. Oxley (R-OH).

Employers
AT&T (V. President, Congressional Affairs)

CARPENTER, Pilar Maria

1101 30th St. NW
Suite 500
Washington, DC 20007
Tel: (202)625-4880
Fax: (202)625-4881

Employers
Greenwich Capital Markets, Inc. (Policy Analyst, Legal and External Affairs)

CARPENTER, Robert R.

1530 Wilson Blvd.
Suite 210
Arlington, VA 22209
Tel: (703)358-2890
Fax: (703)358-9786
Registered: LDA
EMail: RRCarpenter@celanese.com

Employers
Celanese Government Relations Office (Director, State and Federal Affairs)

CARPENTER, Ted Galen

1000 Massachusetts Ave. NW
Washington, DC 20001
Tel: (202)842-0200
Fax: (202)842-3490

Employers
Cato Institute (V. President, Defense and Foreign Policy Studies)

CARPENTIER, Patrick

601 Pennsylvania Ave. NW
Suite 900
Washington, DC 20004
Tel: (202)547-3566
Fax: (202)639-8238

Employers
Cottone and Huggins Group (V. President, International Security)

CARPI, Kenneth A.

1130 Connecticut Ave. NW
Suite 650
Washington, DC 20036
Tel: (202)822-8300
Fax: (202)822-8315
Registered: LDA

Employers
Carpi & Clay (Partner)
E. Del Smith and Co.

Clients Represented
On Behalf of Carpi & Clay
California Children's Hospital Ass'n
El Centro Regional Medical Center
Encinitas, California, City of
Hertz Corp.
Hollis-Eden Pharmaceuticals, Inc.
Mount High Hosiery, Ltd.
Port of San Diego
San Diego County Water Authority
San Diego Natural History Museum
U.S./Mexico Border Counties Coalition
Water Replenishment District of Southern California

On Behalf of E. Del Smith and Co.
California-American Water Co.
Hollis-Eden Pharmaceuticals, Inc.

CARPINELLI, Stephen

1401 K St. NW
Tenth Floor
Washington, DC 20005
Tel: (202)216-2200
Fax: (202)216-2999

Employers
Jefferson-Waterman Internat'l, LLC (Director)

CARPINO, Christine

Office of Govermental Affairs
3101 Park Center Dr.
Room 805
Alexandria, VA 22302
EMail: christine.carpino@fns.usda.gov
Tel: (703)305-2039
Fax: (703)305-2312

Employers
Department of Agriculture - Food and Nutrition Service (Acting Deputy Director, Communications and Governmental Affairs)

CARR, Alice J.

4843 27th Rd. South
Arlington, VA 22206-1301
Tel: (703)998-8700
Fax: (703)998-1896
Registered: LDA

Employers
Federal Access (Secretary-Treasurer)

CARR, Courtenay

1620 I St. NW
Suite 615
Washington, DC 20006
EMail: ccarr@moinc.com
Tel: (202)463-8493
Fax: (202)463-8497
Registered: LDA
Program Assistant, Veterans Administration, 1996.

Employers
JBC Internat'l (Trade Analyst)

Clients Represented
On Behalf of JBC Internat'l
Coalition for Intellectual Property Rights (CIPR)

CARR, Donald A.

1133 Connecticut Ave. NW
Suite 1200
Washington, DC 20036
Tel: (202)775-9800
Fax: (202)833-8491
Acting Assistant Attorney General (1989) and Counselor to the Assistant Attorney General (1987-89), Land and Natural Resources Division, and Chief, Wildlife and Marine Resources Section (1983-88), all at the Department of Justice.

Employers
Winthrop, Stimson, Putnam & Roberts (Managing Partner)

Clients Represented
On Behalf of Winthrop, Stimson, Putnam & Roberts
Royal Caribbean Cruises, Ltd.
World Wildlife Fund

CARR, Douglas

1200 18th St. NW
Suite 400
Washington, DC 20036-2506
Tel: (202)783-9000
Fax: (202)331-8364

Employers
Nat'l Business Aviation Ass'n (Director, Government Affairs manager)

CARR, James H.

4000 Wisconsin Ave. NW
Washington, DC 20016
Tel: (202)274-8060

Employers
Fannie Mae (Senior V. President, Policy, Research, Evaluation & Training, Fannie Mae Foundation)

CARR, John

3211 Fourth St. NE
Washington, DC 20017
Tel: (202)541-3180
Fax: (202)541-3339

Employers
United States Catholic Conference (Secretary, Social Development and World Peace)

CARR, John

1325 Massachusetts Ave. NW
Washington, DC 20005
Tel: (202)628-5451
Fax: (202)628-5767

Employers
Nat'l Air Traffic Controllers Ass'n (President)

CARR, Lisa

1501 M St. NW
Suite 600
Washington, DC 20005-1710
Tel: (202)739-0200
Fax: (202)659-8287
Former Legislative Director to Rep. John Conyers, Jr. (D-MI)

Employers
BSMG Worldwide (Senior Associate)

CARR, Martin

2000 N. 14th St.
Suite 450
Arlington, VA 22201
EMail: mcarr@nahu.org
Tel: (703)276-3816
Fax: (703)841-7797

Employers
Nat'l Ass'n of Health Underwriters (Manager, Communications)

CARRAGHER, Robert J.

1403 King St.
Alexandria, VA 22314
Tel: (703)535-1093
Fax: (703)535-1094
Registered: LDA
EMail: bcarragher@ssci.org
Legislative Assistant/Correspondent to Senator Sam Nunn (D-GA), 1978-80.

Employers
Steel Service Center Institute (V. President, Governmental Affairs)

CARRIER, Elizabeth

1301 Pennsylvania Ave. NW
Suite 950
Washington, DC 20004
EMail: bcarrier@naph.org
Tel: (202)585-0100
Fax: (202)585-0101

Employers
Nat'l Ass'n of Public Hospitals and Health Systems (V. President, Managed Care)

CARRINGTON, Glenn

1666 K St. NW
Suite 800
Washington, DC 20006
Tel: (202)481-7000
Fax: (202)862-7098
Registered: LDA

Employers
Arthur Andersen LLP (Partner)

Clients Represented
On Behalf of Arthur Andersen LLP
AutoNation, Inc.
Eagle-Picher Personal Injury Settlement Trust

CARRION, Ana

722 12th St. NW
Washington, DC 20005
Tel: (202)628-8382
Fax: (202)628-8392

Employers
Research Institute for Small & Emerging Business, Inc. (Communications and Public Affairs Counsel)

CARROCCIO, A. Thomas

1615 L St. NW
Suite 1200
Washington, DC 20036
Tel: (202)466-6300
Fax: (202)463-0678

Employers
Bell, Boyd & Lloyd (Partner)

Clients Represented
On Behalf of Bell, Boyd & Lloyd
KJAZ-FM
Performing Arts Network of New Jersey

CARROLL, Bruce

1350 I St. NW
Suite 1210
Washington, DC 20005-3305
Tel: (202)589-1000
Ext: 1011
Fax: (202)589-1001

Employers
Johnson & Johnson, Inc. (Manager, Federal Affairs)

CARROLL, Jr., Charles T.

2011 Pennsylvania Ave. NW
Suite 301
Washington, DC 20006
EMail: carroll@nmsa-usa.org
Tel: (202)296-2810
Fax: (202)331-7479
Counsel, Senate Committee on Labor and Human Resources, 1988-89. Counsel, Senate Labor Subcommittee, 1981-87.

Employers
Nat'l Ass'n of Waterfront Employers (General Counsel)
Nat'l Maritime Safety Ass'n (General Counsel)
Wilcox, Carroll & Froelich, PLLC (Partner)

Clients Represented
On Behalf of Wilcox, Carroll & Froelich, PLLC
Nat'l Ass'n of Waterfront Employers
Nat'l Maritime Safety Ass'n
Shell Oil Co.

CARROLL, David W.

12950 Worldgate Dr.
Suite 500
Herndon, VA 20170
Tel: (703)480-3600
Fax: (703)796-2214
Registered: LDA

Employers
Lafarge Corp. (V. President, Environment, Health and Safety and Public Affairs)

CARROLL, USN (Ret.), Rear Adm. Eugene

1779 Massachusetts Ave. NW
Suite 615
Washington, DC 20036
Tel: (202)332-0600
Fax: (202)462-4559

Employers
Center for Defense Information (Deputy Director)

CARROLL, Kenneth

1776 I St. NW
Suite 275
Washington, DC 20006
Tel: (202)530-7300
Fax: (202)530-7350
Registered: LDA

Employers
Entergy Services, Inc. (Director, Federal Tax and Environmental Legislative Policy and Strategy)

CARROLL, Phil

526 King St.
Suite 511
Alexandria, VA 22314
EMail: phil.carroll@nahma.org
Tel: (703)683-8630
Fax: (703)683-8634
Registered: LDA

Employers
Nat'l Affordable Housing Management Ass'n (President)

CARROLL, Rodney

1250 Connecticut Ave. NW
Suite 610
Washington, DC 20036
Tel: (202)955-3005
Fax: (202)955-1087

Employers
Welfare to Work Partnership (President and Chief Exec. Officer)

CARROLL, William H.

1300 I St. NW
Suite 300 West
Washington, DC 20005
Tel: (202)522-8600
Fax: (202)522-8669
General Counsel, Ballistic Missile Defense Organization, Department of Defense, 1985-94. Special Assistant for Contracting Integrity (1985) and Associate Counsel, Contracts (1976-84), Defense Logistics Agency, Department of Defense. Assistant Counsel, Department of Navy, 1971-75.

Employers
Dykema Gossett PLLC (Of Counsel)

CARSON, John

Ronald Reagan Bldg.
Gray Tower
1300 Pennsylvania Ave. NW, Suite 500
Washington, DC 20004
Tel: (202)312-3500
Fax: (202)312-3501
Registered: LDA

Employers
SAP Public Services (V. President, Federal Business Development)

CARSON, Peter

1901 L St. NW
Suite 300
Washington, DC 20036

Tel: (202)466-7590
Fax: (202)466-7598
Registered: LDA

Employers
Ogilvy Public Relations Worldwide (Senior V. President)

CARSON, Richard

1233 20th St. NW
Suite 402
Washington, DC 20036-2330
EMail: richard@aafa.org

Tel: (800)727-8462
Fax: (202)466-8940

Employers
Asthma and Allergy Foundation of America (Director, Public Policy)

CARSWELL, John

801 18th St. NW
Washington, DC 20006

Tel: (202)872-1300
Fax: (202)785-4452

Employers
Paralyzed Veterans of America (Associate Exec. Director, Health Policy)

CARTER, Casey M.

450 Fifth St. NW
Room 6103
Washington, DC 20549

Tel: (202)942-0010
Fax: (202)942-9650

Employers
Securities and Exchange Commission (Deputy Director, Office of Congressional and Intergovernmental Affairs)

CARTER, Gavin J.

1010 Pennsylvania Ave. SE
Washington, DC 20003

Tel: (202)544-7845
Fax: (202)544-7847
Registered: FARA

EMail: gc@bcanda.com

Employers
Butterfield Carter & Associates (Principal)

Clients Represented

On Behalf of Butterfield Carter & Associates
Institute of Cetacean Research
Japan, Embassy of
Thomas Pink, Inc.

CARTER, Dr. Gene R.

1703 N. Beauregard St.
Alexandria, VA 22311-1714
EMail: gcarter@ascd.org

Tel: (703)575-5600
Fax: (703)575-5400

Employers
Ass'n for Supervision and Curriculum Development (Exec. Director)

CARTER, Joanne

440 First St. NW
Suite 450
Washington, DC 20001

Tel: (202)783-7100
Fax: (202)783-2818
Registered: LDA

EMail: carter@resultsusa.org

Employers
RESULTS (Legislative Director)

CARTER, John R.

1001 19th St. North
Suite 800
Arlington, VA 22209-3901

Tel: (703)276-5120
Fax: (703)276-5119
Registered: LDA

EMail: jack.carter@trw.com

Employers
TRW Inc. (V. President, Government Relations, Defense and National Security Programs)

CARTER, John T.

2201 C St. NW
Room 7260
Washington, DC 20520-7261

Tel: (202)647-2067
Fax: (202)647-2762

Employers
Department of State - Bureau of Legislative Affairs (Administrative Services, Office of Legislative Operations)

CARTER, Michael R.

1301 K St. NW
Suite 900
East Tower
Washington, DC 20005

Tel: (202)408-8007
Fax: (202)408-8719
Registered: LDA

EMail: mike.carter@thecartergroup-dc.com
Served as Legislative Liaison, The White House Military Office, Department of the Air Force, Department of Defense.

Employers
The Carter Group (Principal)

Clients Represented

On Behalf of The Carter Group
Advanced Technology Systems
Airborne Tactical Advantage Co.
Military Order of the Purple Heart of the U.S.A.
Safety Harbor, Florida, City of
Sensor Technologies and Systems Inc.
Sierra Nevada Corp.
Specialized Technical Services, Inc.
Stilman Advanced Strategies
Veridian Corp.
Veritect
Vortex, Inc.

CARTER, Rick

700 11th St. NW
Suite 250
Washington, DC 20001

Tel: (202)638-3503
Fax: (202)638-3522
Registered: LDA

EMail: rick.carter@pge-corp.com

Employers
PG&E Corp. (Manager, Federal Governmental Relations)

CARTER, Thomas L.

1301 K St. NW
Suite 900
East Tower
Washington, DC 20005

Tel: (202)408-8007
Fax: (202)408-8719

Former Military Advisor to the Director of Legislative Affairs, Department of the Air Force and Deputy Assistant Secretary for Legislative Affairs (1989-90), Department of Defense. Assistant to Senator Robert J. Dole (R-KS), 1986-89. Air Force Aide, Exec. Office of the President, The White House, 1984-86.

Employers
The Carter Group

CARTER, W. Minor

1420 New York Ave. NW
Suite 1050
Washington, DC 20005
EMail: mcarter@vsadc.com

Tel: (202)638-1950
Fax: (202)638-7714

Employers
Van Scoyoc Associates, Inc. (Of Counsel)

CARTER-MAGUIRE, Melanie

801 Pennsylvania Ave. NW
Suite 700
Washington, DC 20004
EMail: cmaguire@nortelnetworks.com

Tel: (202)347-4610
Fax: (202)508-3612

Employers
Nortel Networks (V. President, Global Government Relations)

CARTWRIGHT, Julia

699 Prince St.
Alexandria, VA 22314-3175

Tel: (703)235-3900
Fax: (703)274-2222

Employers
Nat'l Center for Missing and Exploited Children (Legislative Counsel)

CARTWRIGHT, Russell S.

1140 Connecticut Ave.
Suite 502
Washington, DC 20036

Tel: (202)293-9101
Fax: (202)293-9111
Registered: LDA

EMail: rcartwright@teamer.com

Employers
Cartwright & Riley (Principal)

Clients Represented

On Behalf of Cartwright & Riley
Anthem, Inc.
GTECH Corp.
Kentucky, Commonwealth of
Nova Southeastern University

CARTWRIGHT, Suzanne D.

901 15th St. NW
Suite 700
Washington, DC 20005-2301

Tel: (202)371-6000
Fax: (202)371-6279
Registered: LDA

Legislative Assistant to Rep. Jim Moody (D-WI), 1983-85.

Employers
Verner, Liipfert, Bernhard, McPherson and Hand, Chartered (Director, Legislative Affairs)

Clients Represented

On Behalf of Verner, Liipfert, Bernhard, McPherson and Hand, Chartered
Bombardier Transportation/Bombardier Transit Corporation
G.E. Harris Harmon
Heritage Development
Merle Hay Mall Limited Partners
New Haven, Connecticut, City of

CARTY, Lee

1101 15th St. NW
Suite 1212
Washington, DC 20005

Tel: (202)467-5730
Ext: 21
Fax: (202)223-0409

EMail: leec@bazelon.org

Employers
Bazelon Center for Mental Health Law, Judge David L. (Director, Publications and Communications)

CARUSO, George C.

526 King St.
Suite 511
Alexandria, VA 22314

Tel: (703)683-8630
Fax: (703)683-8634
Registered: LDA

EMail: george.caruso@nahma.org

Employers
Nat'l Affordable Housing Management Ass'n (Exec. Director)

CARVER, Susan B.

1130 17th St. NW
Washington, DC 20036-4677

Tel: (202)463-2650
Fax: (202)833-1965
Registered: LDA

EMail: scarver@nma.org

Employers
Nat'l Mining Ass'n (V. President, Congressional Affairs)

CARVIN, Margaret L.

1101 Vermont Ave. NW
12th Floor
Washington, DC 20005-3583

Tel: (202)789-7458
Fax: (202)789-7485
Registered: LDA

Employers
American Medical Ass'n (Assistant Director, Congressional Affairs)

CARVIN, Michael A.

1500 K St. NW
Suite 200
Washington, DC 20005

Tel: (202)220-9600
Fax: (202)220-9601

Deputy Assistant Attorney General, Office of Legal Counsel, U.S. Department of Justice, 1987-88. Deputy Assistant Attorney General, Civil Rights Division, Department of Justice, 1985-87.

Employers
Cooper, Carvin & Rosenthal (Partner)

CARY, Matthew J.

1000 Vermont Ave. NW
Suite 700
Washington, DC 20005

Tel: (202)408-0808
Fax: (202)408-0876

Clinton/Gore Transition Team, Transportation Cluster Group, Office of the Secretary, Department of Transportation, 1993.

Employers
Susan Davis Internat'l (Senior Associate)

CASDEN, Carol

901 E St. NW
Suite 600
Washington, DC 20004

Tel: (202)783-4444
Fax: (202)783-4085

Employers
Nat'l Treasury Employees Union (Assistant Counsel)

CASE, David

734 15th St. NW
Suite 720
Washington, DC 20005
Tel: (202)783-0870
Fax: (202)737-2038
Registered: LDA

Employers
Environmental Technology Council (Exec. Director)

CASE, III, Frank H.

2600 Virginia Ave. NW
Suite 1000
Washington, DC 20037-1905
Tel: (202)333-8800
Fax: (202)337-6065
Registered: LDA

Employers
Schmeltzer, Aptaker & Shepard, P.C. (Partner)

CASE, Dr. Larry D.

1410 King St.
Suite 400
Alexandria, VA 22314
EMail: larry_case@ffa.org
Tel: (703)838-5889
Fax: (703)838-5888

Employers
Nat'l FFA Organization (National Advisor and Chief Exec. Officer)

CASE, Ted

4301 Wilson Blvd.
Arlington, VA 22203-1860
Tel: (703)907-5834
Fax: (703)907-5516
Registered: LDA
EMail: ted.case@nreca.org

Employers
Nat'l Rural Electric Cooperative Ass'n (Legislative Representative)

CASEY, Cecelia M.

333 John Carlyle St.
Suite 200
Alexandria, VA 22314
EMail: caseyc@agc.org
Tel: (703)837-5435

Employers
Associated General Contractors of America (Legislative Assistant, Congressional Relations)

CASEY, D.L. "Ike"

180 S. Washington St.
P.O. Box 6808
Falls Church, VA 22040
Tel: (703)237-8100
Fax: (703)237-7442

Employers
Plumbing, Heating, Cooling Contractors- National Assoc. (Exec. V. President)

CASEY, Daniel L.

700 13th St. NW
Suite 1000
Washington, DC 20005
Tel: (202)347-6633
Fax: (202)347-8713
Registered: FARA

Employers
Powell Tate (Senior V. President, Director of Research)

Clients Represented
On Behalf of Powell Tate
Saudi Arabia, Royal Embassy of

CASEY, Diane M.

900 19th St. NW
Suite 400
Washington, DC 20006
Tel: (202)857-3100
Fax: (202)296-8716

Employers
America's Community Bankers (President and Chief Exec. Officer)

CASEY, Edward A.

1200 19th St. NW
Suite 201
Washington, DC 20036-2065
Tel: (202)822-4700
Fax: (202)822-4710
Former Deputy Assistant Secretary for Inter-American Affairs, Department of State.

Employers
Hills & Company, International Consultants (Managing Director)

Clients Represented
On Behalf of Hills & Company, International Consultants
The Procter & Gamble Company

CASEY, Eric

1421 Prince St.
Alexandria, VA 22314-2814
EMail: wecasey@mfsanet.org
Tel: (703)836-9200
Fax: (703)548-8204

Employers
Mailing & Fulfillment Services Ass'n (Director, Marketing)

CASEY, Gregory S.

888 16th St. NW
Suite 305
Washington, DC 20006
Tel: (202)833-1880
Fax: (202)833-2338

Employers
Business-Industry Political Action Committee (President and Chief Exec. Officer)

CASEY, James L.

1301 Pennsylvania Ave. NW
Suite 1100
Washington, DC 20004-1707
Tel: (202)626-4000
Fax: (202)626-4139

Employers
Air Transport Ass'n of America (V. President and Deputy General Counsel)

CASEY, Joanne F.

7501 Greenway Center Dr.
S-720
Greenbelt, MD 20770-6705
EMail: iana@intermodal.org
Tel: (301)982-3400
Fax: (301)982-4815

Employers
Intermodal Ass'n of North America (President)

CASEY, Kevin

499 S. Capitol St. SW
Suite 405
Washington, DC 20003
Tel: (202)863-1292
Fax: (202)863-1104
Registered: LDA

Employers
Harvard University Washington Office (Director, Federal/State Government Relations)

CASEY, Lee A.

1050 Connecticut Ave. NW
Suite 1100
Washington, DC 20036-5304
Tel: (202)861-1500
Fax: (202)861-1790
Office of Legal Counsel (1992-93) and Office of Legal Policy (1986-90), Department of Justice. Law Clerk to Chief Judge Alex Kozinski, U.S. Claims Court, 1984-85.

Employers
Baker & Hostetler LLP

Clients Represented
On Behalf of Baker & Hostetler LLP
Croatia, Republic of

CASEY, Martha L.

1310 19th St. NW
Washington, DC 20036
Tel: (202)466-6555
Fax: (202)466-6596
Registered: LDA, FARA
Counsel to Rep. Brian Donnelly (D-MA), 1982-87. Legislative Assistant to Rep. Joseph Early (D-MA), 1977-79.

Employers
O'Neill, Athy & Casey, P.C. (Partner)

Clients Represented
On Behalf of O'Neill, Athy & Casey, P.C.
Beth Israel/Deaconess Medical Center
Boston Museum of Science
Coalition of Boston Teaching Hospitals
Harvard University Washington Office
Massachusetts General/Brigham and Women's Hospital
McLean Hospital
New England Deaconess Hospital
New England Medical Center
Northeastern University
Northwestern Memorial Hospital
Schepens Eye Research Institute
Spaulding Rehabilitation Hospital
Temple University Health System

CASEY, Robert "Fred"

1700 18th St. NW
Washington, DC 20009
Tel: (202)234-4700
Fax: (202)265-9317
Registered: LDA
EMail: fred@sla.org

Employers
Special Libraries Ass'n (Assistant Exec. Director, Program and Strategic Development)

CASHDOLLAR, Robert

1629 K St. NW
Suite 1100
Washington, DC 20006
Tel: (202)728-4058
Fax: (202)466-5283
Registered: LDA

Employers
Cashdollar-Jones & Co. (President)

Clients Represented
On Behalf of Cashdollar-Jones & Co.
American Bankers Ass'n
Nat'l Farmers Organization
Pheasants Forever

CASHDOLLAR, Winthrop

1201 F St. NW
Suite 500
Washington, DC 20004
Tel: (202)824-1600
Fax: (202)824-1651
Registered: LDA

Employers
Health Insurance Ass'n of America

CASHEN, II, Henry C.

2101 L St. NW
Washington, DC 20037-1526
Tel: (202)785-9700
Fax: (202)887-0689
Registered: LDA, FARA
EMail: cashenh@dsmo.com
Deputy Assistant to the President (1971-73) and Deputy Counsel to the President (1969-70), The White House.

Employers
Dickstein Shapiro Morin & Oshinsky LLP (Partner)

Clients Represented
On Behalf of Dickstein Shapiro Morin & Oshinsky LLP
American Greyhound Track Operators Ass'n
Cigar Ass'n of America
First USA Bank
Harbour Group Industries, Inc.
Incentive Federation Sweepstakes Trust Fund
Internat'l Brotherhood of Teamsters
Lorillard Tobacco Co.
Nat'l Ass'n of Chain Drug Stores
Pipe Tobacco Council, Inc.
Smokeless Tobacco Council

CASHEN, Kathleen

444 N. Capitol St. NW
Suite 142
Washington, DC 20001
Tel: (202)431-8020
Fax: (202)434-8033

Employers
Nat'l Ass'n of State Workforce Agencies (Employment and Training Director)

CASILLAS, Conwey

1155 15th St. NW
Suite 801
Washington, DC 20005
Tel: (202)466-8621
Fax: (202)466-8643
Registered: LDA

Employers
Education Finance Council (Director, Communications and Membership Services)

CASKIE, Allen R.

1001 Pennsylvania Ave. NW
Washington, DC 20004-2599
Tel: (202)624-2000
Fax: (202)624-2319
Registered: LDA

Employers
American Council of Life Insurers (Chief Counsel, Federal Relations)

CASNER, Bruce M.

1332 Independence Ave. SE
Washington, DC 20003-2365
Tel: (202)543-4600
Former Congressional Staff member.

Employers
Morgan Casner Associates, Inc. (President)

CASS, Richard W.

2445 M St. NW
Washington, DC 20037-1420
Tel: (202)663-6000
Fax: (202)663-6363
Registered: FARA
EMail: rcass@wilmer.com
Former Law Clerk to Judge William H. Timbers, U.S. Court of Appeals, Second Circuit.

Employers
Wilmer, Cutler & Pickering (Partner)

Clients Represented

On Behalf of Wilmer, Cutler & Pickering
Dallas Cowboys

CASSAT, Peter C.

1200 New Hampshire Ave. NW
Suite 800
Washington, DC 20036-6802
Tel: (202)776-2000
Fax: (202)776-2222
EMail: pcassat@dlalaw.com

Employers
Dow, Lohnes & Albertson, PLLC (Member)

CASSE, Daniel

1030 15th St. NW
Suite 1100
Washington, DC 20005
Tel: (202)783-4600
Fax: (202)783-4601
Special Assistant to the President for Cabinet Affairs, 1990-93. Special Assistant to the Director of National Drug Control Policy, 1989-90.

Employers
White House Writers Group (Senior Director)

CASSEDY, Joan Walsh

1629 K St. NW
Suite 400
Washington, DC 20006
Tel: (202)887-5872
Ext: 202
Fax: (202)887-0021
EMail: jcassedy@acil.org

Employers
American Council of Independent Laboratories (Exec. Director)

CASSEL, Scott

2111 Wilson Blvd.
Suite 700
Arlington, VA 22201
Tel: (703)351-5058
Fax: (703)522-1738
Registered: LDA

Employers
Collins & Company, Inc.

Clients Represented

On Behalf of Collins & Company, Inc.
Derry Investment Initiatives
Mari-Flite Ferries, Inc.
Oracle Corp.
Science Applications Internat'l Corp. (SAIC)
Solipsys Corp.

CASSELMAN, II, William E.

P.O. Box 156
Aldie, VA 20105-0156
Tel: (703)551-2108
Fax: (703)327-3116
Registered: LDA
Counsel to the President (1974-75) and Legal Counsel to the Vice President (1973-74), The White House. General Counsel, General Services Administration, 1971-73. Deputy Special Assistant to the President for Congressional Relations, The White House, 1969-71. Legislative Assistant to Rep. Robert McClory (R-IL), 1965-69.

Employers
Blue Ridge Internat'l Group, L.L.C. (Managing Principal)
Self-employed as an independent consultant.

Clients Represented

As an independent consultant
Agency-Internat'l, Ltd.
Federal Systems Group, Inc.
Ova Noss Family Partnership

CASSERLY, Dan

701 Pennsylvania Ave. NW
Suite 725
Washington, DC 20004
Tel: (202)638-7429
Fax: (202)628-4763
Registered: LDA

Employers
Novartis Corp. (Director, Federal Government Relations)
Novartis Services, Inc. (Director, Federal Government Relations)

CASSERLY, James L.

701 Pennsylvania Ave. NW
Suite 900
Washington, DC 20004-2608
Tel: (202)434-7300
Fax: (202)434-7400
Former Senior Advisor to the Commissioner, Federal Communications Commission.

Employers
Mintz, Levin, Cohn, Ferris, Glovsky and Popeo, P.C. (Partner)

Clients Represented

On Behalf of Mintz, Levin, Cohn, Ferris, Glovsky and Popeo, P.C.
Comcast Corp.

CASSERLY, Michael

1301 Pennsylvania Ave. NW
Suite 702
Washington, DC 20004
Tel: (202)393-2427
Fax: (202)393-2400
EMail: mcasserly@cgcr.org

Employers
Council of the Great City Schools (Exec. Director)

CASSIDY, Col. B.

Russell Senate Office Bldg.
Room 182
Washington, DC 20510
Tel: (202)685-6009

Employers
Department of Navy - United States Marine Corps (Senate Liaison Officer)

CASSIDY, Gerald S. J.

700 13th St. NW
Suite 400
Washington, DC 20005
Tel: (202)347-0773
Fax: (202)347-0785
Registered: LDA, FARA
EMail: gcassidy@cassidy.com
General Counsel, Senate Select Committee on Nutrition and Human Needs, (1969-73) and (1974-75).

Employers
Cassidy & Associates, Inc. (Chairman and C.E.O., Cassidy Companies, Inc.)

Clients Represented

On Behalf of Cassidy & Associates, Inc.
Boston College
Boston University
E Lottery
Ocean Spray Cranberries
Saudi Arabia, Royal Embassy of
Taiwan Studies Institute
Villanova University

CASSIDY, Lee M.

1111 19th St. NW
11th Floor
Washington, DC 20036
Tel: (202)628-4380
Fax: (202)628-4383
EMail: nonprofitfederation@the-dma.org

Employers
Direct Marketing Ass'n Nonprofit Federation (Exec. Director)

CASSIDY, Paige

1120 20th St. NW
Suite 1000
Washington, DC 20036
Tel: (202)457-3839
Fax: (202)457-2571
Registered: LDA
EMail: cassidy@att.com

Employers
AT&T (V. President, Congressional Affairs)

CASSIDY, Philip E.

888 17th St. NW
Suite 506
Washington, DC 20006
Tel: (202)298-7650
Fax: (202)785-0296

Employers
The Business Council (Exec. Director)

CASSIDY, Jr., Robert C.

2445 M St. NW
Washington, DC 20037-1420
Tel: (202)663-6000
Fax: (202)663-6363
Registered: LDA
EMail: rcassidy@wilmer.com
General Counsel, Office of the U.S. Trade Representative, Executive Office of the President, The White House, 1979-81. International Trade Counsel, Senate Committee on Finance, 1975-79.

Employers
Wilmer, Cutler & Pickering (Partner)

Clients Represented

On Behalf of Wilmer, Cutler & Pickering
ITT World Directories, Inc.
Yamaha Motor Corp. U.S.A.

CASSIDY, Susan Booth

555 12th St. NW
Washington, DC 20004-1206
Tel: (202)942-5000
Fax: (202)942-5999
EMail: Susan_Cassidy@aporter.com

Employers
Arnold & Porter (Partner)

CASSO, Mark A.

1101 17th St. NW
Suite 608
Washington, DC 20036
Tel: (202)466-6777
Fax: (202)466-6767
Registered: LDA
EMail: mcasso@cirt.org

Employers
Construction Industry Round Table, Inc. (President)

CASSON, Joseph E.

1233 20th St. NW
Suite 800
Washington, DC 20036-2396
Tel: (202)416-6800
Fax: (202)416-6899
EMail: JCasson@proskauer.com

Employers
Proskauer Rose LLP (Partner)

CASTAGNETTI, David

1101 16th St. NW
Suite 500
Washington, DC 20036
Tel: (202)659-9111
Fax: (202)659-6387
Registered: LDA
Former Chief of Staff to Senator Max Baucus (D-MT). Former Chief of Staff to Rep. Norman Y. Mineta (D-CA). Senior Staff Member, Rep. Ed Markey, (D-MA)

Employers
Bergner Bockorny Castagnetti and Hawkins (Principal)

Clients Represented

On Behalf of Bergner Bockorny Castagnetti and Hawkins
AdvaMed
Agilent Technologies
American Bankers Ass'n
American Hospital Ass'n
Biogen, Inc.
The Boeing Co.
Bristol-Myers Squibb Co.
Business Executives for Nat'l Security
Cerner Corp.
Chicago Board Options Exchange
Computer Coalition for Responsible Exports
Dell Computer Corp.
Elanco Animal Health
Everglades Defense Council
First Health Group Corp.
GlaxoSmithKline
Hewlett-Packard Co.
Lucent Technologies
Medtronic, Inc.
Monsanto Co.
Nat'l Ass'n of Real Estate Investment Trusts
Nat'l Soft Drink Ass'n
News Corporation Ltd.
Northwest Airlines, Inc.
Ovations/United Health Group
Petroleum Marketers Ass'n of America
Philip Morris Management Corp.
Premium Standard Farms
Qwest Communications
Taipei Economic and Cultural Representative Office in the United States
UDV North America, Inc.

CASTANEDA, Jaime

2101 Wilson Blvd.
Suite 400
Arlington, VA 22201
Tel: (703)243-6111
Fax: (703)841-9328
EMail: jcastaneda@nmpf.org

Employers
Nat'l Milk Producers Federation (Senior Trade Analyst)

CASTEEL, Jr., Carroll K.

1133 19th St. NW
Washington, DC 20036
Tel: (202)887-3830
Fax: (202)736-6880
EMail: ck.chp.casteel@wcom.com

Employers
MCI WorldCom Corp. (V. President, State Regulatory Affairs and Governmental Affairs)

CASTELVETER, David A.

Crystal Park Four
2345 Crystal Dr.
Arlington, VA 22227
Tel: (703)872-5100
Fax: (703)872-5134
EMail: david_castelveter@usairways.com

Employers
US Airways (Director, Public Relations)

CASTILLO, A. Mario

2472 Belmont Rd. NW
Washington, DC 20008
Tel: (202)518-9590
Fax: (202)518-9592
Registered: LDA, FARA

Special Assistant to Commissioner, Equal Employment Opportunity Commission, 1973-77. Chief of Staff, House Committee on Agriculture.

Employers
The Aegis Group, Ltd. (President)

Clients Represented
On Behalf of The Aegis Group, Ltd.
Dairy Trade Advisory Council
The Dairy Trade Coalition
Pump Service and Supply Co.
U.S.-Canadian Caucus of Mayors
World Duty Free Americas, Inc.

CASTLE, Tess

1200 G St. NW
Suite 400
Washington, DC 20005
Tel: (202)783-8700
Fax: (202)783-8750
Registered: LDA

Employers
AdvaMed (Associate V. President, Technical and Regulatory Affairs)

CASTRO, Dr. Oswaldo

2121 Georgia Ave. NW
Washington, DC 20059
Tel: (202)806-7930
Fax: (202)806-4517

Employers
Center for Sickle Cell Disease (Director)

CASULA, Pat

14th and Independence Ave. SW
Stop 2280
Washington, DC 20250-2280
Tel: (202)720-4465
Fax: (202)720-6882

Employers
Department of Agriculture - Research, Education, and Economics Mission Area (Legislative Analyst)

CASWELL, Taylor

325 Seventh St. NW
Suite 1225
Washington, DC 20004
Tel: (202)737-1445
Registered: LDA

Employers
Farmers Insurance Group (Director, Federal Affairs)

CATALDO, Carol

1725 Duke St.
Suite 600
Alexandria, VA 22314-3457
Tel: (703)549-0124
Fax: (703)299-9115
EMail: cataldo2@ix.netcom.com

Employers
Carol Cataldo & Associates (President)

Clients Represented
On Behalf of Carol Cataldo & Associates
Commission of Accredited Truck Driving Schools (CATDS)

CATANGUI, Raul G.

400 Virginia Ave. SW
Suite 800
Washington, DC 20024-2370
Tel: (202)484-4847
Fax: (202)484-3483
Registered: LDA
EMail: rcatangui@itsa.org

Former Legislative Assistant to Rep. Patsy T. Mink (D-HI).

Employers
Intelligent Transportation Soc. of America (Legislative and Regulatory Counsel)

CATANIA, David A.

1333 New Hampshire Ave. NW
Suite 400
Washington, DC 20036
Tel: (202)887-4000
Fax: (202)887-4288

Employers
Akin, Gump, Strauss, Hauer & Feld, L.L.P. (Associate)

CATE, George M.

503 Carlisle Dr.
Suite 125
Herndon, VA 20170
Tel: (703)435-8556
Fax: (703)435-0056
EMail: gcate@amsect.org

Employers
American Soc. of Extra-Corporeal Technology (Exec. Director)

CATHCART, Chris

1913 I St. NW
Washington, DC 20006
Tel: (202)872-8110
Fax: (202)872-8114
Registered: LDA
EMail: ccathcart@csma.org

Employers
Consumer Specialties Products Ass'n (President)

CATIGNANI, Linus

425 Second St. NE
Washington, DC 20002
Tel: (202)675-6000
Fax: (202)675-6058

Employers
Nat'l Republican Senatorial Committee (Finance Director)

CATON, Cary K.

888 17th St. NW
12th Floor
Washington, DC 20006
Tel: (202)429-8744
Fax: (202)296-2962

Employers
Nat'l Strategies Inc. (V. President)

CATTANEO, John M.

The Willard Office Bldg.
1455 Pennsylvania Ave. NW
Washington, DC 20004
Tel: (202)783-6000
Fax: (202)783-4171
Registered: LDA
EMail: jcattaneo@his.com

Employers
Gibbons & Company, Inc.

Clients Represented
On Behalf of Gibbons & Company, Inc.
ETREMA Products, Inc./Edge Technologies

CATTANEO, Joseph J.

515 King St.
Suite 420
Alexandria, VA 22314-3103
Tel: (703)684-5570
Fax: (703)684-6048
EMail: jcattaneo@clarionmr.com

Employers
CLARION Management Resources, Inc. (Director of Marketing and Public Relations)
Glass Packaging Institute (President)

Clients Represented
On Behalf of CLARION Management Resources, Inc.
Glass Packaging Institute

CATTO, Amb. Henry E.

910 17th St. NW
Tenth Floor
Washington, DC 20006
Tel: (202)463-7226
Fax: (202)463-7241

Employers
Atlantic Council of the United States (Chairman)

CAUDILL, Brian

1317 F St. NW
Suite 500
Washington, DC 20004
Tel: (202)783-6007
Fax: (202)783-6024
EMail: brianc@sema.org

Employers
Specialty Equipment Market Ass'n (Outreach and Public Affairs Director)

CAUSEY, Dawn

1120 Connecticut Ave. NW
Washington, DC 20036
Tel: (202)663-5000
Fax: (202)828-5051
Registered: LDA

Employers
American Bankers Ass'n (Director, Financial Institution Affairs, and Counsel)

CAVANAGH, John

733 15th St. NW
Suite 1020
Washington, DC 20005
Tel: (202)234-9382
Fax: (202)387-7915

Employers
Institute for Policy Studies (Co-Director)

CAVANAUGH, Gordon

1250 I St. NW
Suite 900
Washington, DC 20005
Tel: (202)783-2800
Fax: (202)783-0550
Registered: LDA
EMail: gcavanaugh@renocavanaugh.com

Administrator, Farmers Home Administration, Department of Agriculture, 1977-81. Exec. Director, Housing Assistance Council, 1971-76.

Employers
Reno & Cavanaugh, PLLC (Of Counsel)

Clients Represented
On Behalf of Reno & Cavanaugh, PLLC
Council of Large Public Housing Authorities

CAVANAUGH, J. Michael

2099 Pennsylvania Ave. NW
Suite 100
Washington, DC 20006
Tel: (202)955-3000
Fax: (202)955-5564
EMail: mcavanau@hklaw.com

Great Lakes Regional Counsel (1976-77) and Office of General Counsel (1974-77), Maritime Administration, Department of Transportation.

Employers
Holland & Knight LLP (Partner)

CAVANAUGH, Philip T.

1401 I St. NW
Suite 1200
Washington, DC 20005-2225
Tel: (202)408-5800
Fax: (202)408-5845
Registered: LDA
EMail: ptca@chevron.com

Employers
The Chevron Companies (V. President, Government Relations)
Chevron, U.S.A. (General Manager)

CAVANEY, Byron "Red"

1220 L St. NW
Washington, DC 20005
Tel: (202)682-8000
Fax: (202)682-8232
Registered: LDA

Deputy Assistant to the President for Public Liaison, Executive Office of the President, The White House, 1981-83. Also served as Aide to Presidents Richard Nixon and Gerald Ford.

Employers
American Petroleum Institute (President)

CAVAROCCHI, Nicholas G.

317 Massachusetts Ave. NE
Suite 200
Washington, DC 20002
Tel: (202)546-4732
Fax: (202)546-1257
Registered: LDA
EMail: ncavarocchi@dc-crd.com

Professional Staff Member, House Committee on Appropriations, 1974-79. Budget Officer, Health Service and Mental Health Administration (1970-71) and Grants Management Officer, National Institutes of Health (1964-69), Department of Health and Human Services.

Employers
Cavarocchi Ruscio Dennis Associates (Senior Partner)

Clients Represented

On Behalf of Cavarocchi Ruscio Dennis Associates
American Ass'n for Dental Research
American Ass'n of Public Health Dentistry
American Indian Higher Education Consortium
American Soc. of General Surgeons
American Soc. of Pediatric Nephrology
Boys Town Nat'l Research Hospital
Delta Dental Plans Ass'n
Nat'l Coalition for Osteoporosis and Related Bone Diseases
Software Productivity Consortium

CAVARRETTA, Joseph

2101 Wilson Blvd.
Suite 1002
Arlington, VA 22201
Tel: (703)841-1751
Fax: (703)841-1860
EMail: jcavarretta@retailing.org

Employers
Electronic Retailing Ass'n (V. President, Membership)

CAVE, Bob

11094-D Lee Hwy.
Suite 102
Fairfax, VA 22030
Tel: (703)352-3890
Fax: (703)352-1271
EMail: bcave@apga.org

Employers
American Public Gas Ass'n (Exec. Director)

CAVENAUGH, Rob

2026 P St. NW
Suite Three
Washington, DC 20036-6944
Tel: (202)296-4672
Fax: (202)296-4673
EMail: rcavenaugh@uua.org

Employers
Unitarian Universalist Ass'n of Congregations (Legislative Director, Washington Office)

CAVENDISH, Elizabeth

1156 15th St. NW
Suite 700
Washington, DC 20005
Tel: (202)973-3000
Fax: (202)973-3096
Registered: LDA
EMail: ecavendish@naral.org

Legal Advisor, Office of Legal Counsel (1993-95) and Trial Attorney (1989-93), Department of Justice.

Employers
Nat'l Abortion and Reproductive Rights Action League (V. President, Legal Director and General Counsel)

CAVINS, Mary Jane

1101 17th St. NW
Suite 300
Washington, DC 20036
Tel: (202)331-1770
Fax: (202)331-1969

Employers
Cosmetic, Toiletry and Fragrance Ass'n (V. President, Legislative Services)

CAYO, Carol

1401 Wilson Blvd.
Suite 1100
Arlington, VA 22209
Tel: (703)522-5055
Fax: (703)525-2279
Registered: LDA
EMail: ccayo@itaa.org

Employers
Information Technology Ass'n of America (ITAA) (Director, Government Affairs-Taxation Policy)

CEBALLOS, Kelly L.

1730 M St. NW
Suite 1000
Washington, DC 20036
Tel: (202)429-1965
Fax: (202)429-4343
EMail: kceballos@lwv.org

Employers
League of Women Voters of the United States (Senior Director, Communications)

CEBULA, Andrew V.

421 Aviation Way
Frederick, MD 21701
Tel: (301)695-2000
Fax: (301)695-2375
Registered: LDA
EMail: andy.cebula@aopa.org

Employers
Aircraft Owners and Pilots Ass'n (V. President, Government and Technical Affairs)

CECCHETTI, Ann

10420 Green Acres Dr.
Silver Spring, MD 20903
Tel: (301)434-2002
Fax: (301)434-2002

Employers
Self-employed as an independent consultant.

Clients Represented

As an independent consultant
Battelle

CECH, Ph.D., Thomas R.

4000 Jones Bridge Rd.
Chevy Chase, MD 20815-6789
Tel: (301)215-8855
Fax: (301)215-8863

Employers
Howard Hughes Medical Institute (President)

CELLA, Glenn R.

P.O. Box 33457
Washington, DC 20033
Tel: (202)628-0933
Fax: (202)296-7374
EMail: gcella@shippers.org

Employers
American Institute for Shippers' Ass'ns (Exec. Director)

CELLI, Bernard

1717 K St. NW
Suite 507
Washington, DC 20036
Tel: (202)822-2056
Fax: (202)822-2099
EMail: bcelli@ftna.com

Employers
France Telecom North America (Associate, Regulatory and Policy Affairs)

CERASALE, Gerald E.

1111 19th St. NW
Suite 1100
Washington, DC 20036
Tel: (202)861-2423
Fax: (202)955-0085
Registered: LDA
EMail: jerrycerasale@the-dma.org

Employers
Direct Marketing Ass'n, Inc. (Sr. V. President, Governmental Affairs)

CERGOL, Jack

2111 Eisenhower Ave.
Alexandria, VA 22314-4698
Tel: (703)838-0083
Fax: (703)549-0493
EMail: jcergol.nspi.org

Employers
Nat'l Spa and Pool Institute (Director, Communications)

CERISANO, John C.

1310 G St. NW
12th Floor
Washington, DC 20005
Tel: (202)626-4780
Fax: (202)626-4833
Registered: LDA

Employers
Blue Cross Blue Shield Ass'n (Director, Congressional Relations)

CERONE, Christopher

1200 G St. NW
Suite 400
Washington, DC 20005
Tel: (202)783-8700
Fax: (202)783-8750

Employers
AdvaMed (Director, Global Strategy and Analysis)

CERTNER, David

601 E St. NW
Washington, DC 20049
Tel: (202)434-3760
Registered: LDA

Employers
AARP (American Ass'n of Retired Persons) (Senior Coordinator, Federal Affairs)

CHACON, Ruth W.

1825 Connecticut Ave. NW
Fifth Floor
Washington, DC 20009
Tel: (202)667-0901
Fax: (202)667-0902
EMail: ruth.chacon@widmeyer.com

Employers
Widmeyer Communications, Inc. (Senior Counsel)

CHADWICK, Kirsten A.

1600 Pennsylvania Ave. NW
112 E. Wing
Washington, DC 20500
Tel: (202)456-6620
Fax: (202)456-2604

Executive Assistant, Office of Legislative Affairs, The White House, during the Bush I administration.

Employers
Executive Office of the President - The White House (Special Assistant to the President for Legislative Affairs, House Liaison Office)

CHAFE, Bonnie L.

1600 Wilson Blvd.
Suite 205
Arlington, VA 22209
Tel: (703)358-8600
Fax: (703)358-8885
Registered: LDA

Employers
The State Affairs Co.

Clients Represented

On Behalf of The State Affairs Co.
Elk Valley Rancheria
Hopland Band of Pomo Indians
Sheep Ranch Rancheria
Soboba Band of Mission Indians
Twentynine Palms Band of Mission Indians

CHAGNON, Joseph

1729 21st St. NW
Washington, DC 20009-1101
Tel: (202)986-4209
Fax: (202)986-4211

Employers
American Federation of School Administrators (Treasurer)

CHAJET, Henry

2550 M St. NW
Washington, DC 20037-1350
Tel: (202)457-6000
Fax: (202)457-6315
Registered: LDA
EMail: hchajet@pattonboggs.com

Employers
Patton Boggs, LLP (Partner)

Clients Represented

On Behalf of Patton Boggs, LLP
AKZO Aramid Products Inc.
Coalition to Preserve Mine Safety Standards
FMC Wyoming Corp.
General Chemical Corp.
Homestake Mining
Martin Marietta Aggregates
Methane Awareness Resource Group
Morton Internat'l
OCI Wyoming
Rock of Ages Corp.
Solvay Minerals
Tg Soda Ash

CHALDEN, Jack

2500 Wilson Blvd.
Suite 300
Arlington, VA 22201
Tel: (703)907-7744
Fax: (703)907-7727
EMail: jchalden@tia.eia.org

Employers
Telecommunications Industry Ass'n (General Manager, Trade Shows)

CHALMERS, Walton M.

555 13th St. NW
Suite 1010 East
Washington, DC 20004
Tel: (202)637-6500
Fax: (202)637-6507
Registered: LDA

Employers
American Gaming Ass'n (V. President)

CHAMBERLAIN, Paul F.

1330 Connecticut Ave. NW
Suite 210
Washington, DC 20036-1704
EMail: pchamberlain@itta.com
Tel: (202)828-2614
Fax: (202)828-2617

Employers
Internat'l Technology & Trade Associates, Inc. (ITTA, Inc.) (V. President)

CHAMBERLIN, Susan E.

1000 Massachusetts Ave. NW
Washington, DC 20001
Tel: (202)842-0200
Fax: (202)842-3490

Employers
Cato Institute (Director, External Affairs)

CHAMBERS, Charles R.

1800 K St. NW
Suite 1104
Washington, DC 20006
EMail: crc@ga2online.com
Tel: (202)457-0212
Fax: (202)833-3183

Employers
Global Aviation Associates, Ltd. (Senior V. President)

Clients Represented

On Behalf of Global Aviation Associates, Ltd.
Ass'n of Asia Pacific Airlines
Austrian Airlines
Dallas/Fort Worth Internat'l Airport Board
Las Vegas/McCarran Internat'l Airport
Memphis-Shelby County Airport Authority
Norfolk, Virginia, City of
ORBITZ
Swissair

CHAMBERS, James

2987 Westhurst Lane
Suite 110
Oakton, VA 22124
Registered: LDA

Employers
Nat'l Shooting Sports Foundation Inc. (V. President)
Sporting Arms and Ammunition Manufacturers' Institute, Inc. (Exec. Director)

CHAMBERS, Letitia

805 15th St. NW
Suite 500
Washington, DC 20005
Tel: (202)371-9770
Fax: (202)371-6601
Registered: LDA
EMail: lchambers@chambersinc.com
U.S. Representative to the United Nations General Assembly, 1996. Chief Budget Advisor, Clinton/Gore Transition, 1992-93. Former Staff Director, Senate Committee on Labor and Human Resources. Minority Staff Director, Senate Special Committee on Aging, 1978. Former Senior Budget and Policy Analyst, Senate Budget Committee.

Employers
American Arts Alliance (Treasurer)
Chambers Associates Inc. (President)
Coalition of Publicly Traded Partnerships (President)
U.S.-Turkmenistan Business Council (Interim Exec. Director)

Clients Represented

On Behalf of Chambers Associates Inc.
American Arts Alliance
Castaic Lakewater Agency
Coalition of Publicly Traded Partnerships
Crown American Properties
Defenders of Wildlife
Francotyp-Postalia
High River Limited Partnership
Nat'l Congress of American Indians
NUI Environmental Group Inc.
PriceWaterhouseCoopers
Provident Communications, Inc.
Shea & Gardner
Sullivan & Cromwell

CHAMBERS, Ray B.

122 C St. NW
Suite 850
Washington, DC 20001
Tel: (202)638-7790
Fax: (202)638-1045
Registered: LDA
EMail: ray.chambers@cchinc.com
Director, Congressional Relations, Department of Transportation, 1973-75. Deputy Assistant Secretary for Field Administration, Department of Health, Education and Welfare, 1971-73. Administrative Assistant to Rep. Phil Ruppe (R-MI), 1967-71.

Employers
Chambers, Conlon & Hartwell (Chairman)

Clients Represented

On Behalf of Chambers, Conlon & Hartwell
American Short Line and Regional Railroad Ass'n
Delaware Otsego System
Florida East Coast Industries Inc.
Nat'l Railroad and Construction Maintenance Ass'n
Norfolk Southern Corp.

CHAMBERS, Reid Peyton

1250 I St. NW
Suite 1000
Washington, DC 20005
Tel: (202)682-0240
Fax: (202)682-0249
Associate Solicitor, Department of the Interior, 1973-76.

Employers
Sonosky, Chambers, Sachse & Endreson (Partner)

Clients Represented

On Behalf of Sonosky, Chambers, Sachse & Endreson
Great Lakes Indian Fish and Wildlife Commission
Hopi Indian Tribe

CHAMBLEE, Andrea

1350 I St. NW
Suite 830
Washington, DC 20005
EMail: achamblee@pptaglobal.org
Tel: (202)789-3100
Fax: (202)789-4197

Employers
Plasma Protein Therapeutics Ass'n (Director, Regulatory Affairs)

CHAMBLEE, Don A.

888 First St. NW
MS: 11 H-15
Washington, DC 20426
Tel: (202)208-0870
Fax: (202)208-2106

Employers
Department of Energy - Federal Energy Regulatory Commission (Acting Director (Senate Liaison), Congressional, Intergovernmental, and Public Affairs)

CHAMEIDES, Steven B.

3000 K St. NW
Suite 500
Washington, DC 20007-5109
EMail: schameides@foleylaw.com
Tel: (202)672-5300
Fax: (202)672-5399

Employers
Foley & Lardner (Partner)

CHAMPINE, Christopher

1101 14th St. NW
Suite 1400
Washington, DC 20005
EMail: cchampine@defenders.org
Tel: (202)682-9400
Fax: (202)682-1331

Employers
Defenders of Wildlife (Grassroots Coordinator)

CHAMPION, Thomas J.

633 Pennsylvania Ave. NW
Sixth Floor
Washington, DC 20004
Tel: (202)783-9020
Fax: (202)783-1489
Registered: LDA
EMail: championt@coned.com

Employers
Consolidated Edison Co. of New York (Manager, Federal Government Relations)

CHAMPLIN, Steven M.

2100 Pennsylvania Ave. NW
Suite 500
Washington, DC 20037
Tel: (202)728-1100
Fax: (202)728-1123
Registered: LDA
Exec. Director, House Democratic Caucus, 1991-93. Exec. Floor Assistant to the House Majority Whip, 1987-91. Legislative Director and Administrative Assistant to Rep. David Bonior (D-MI), 1981-86.

Employers
The Duberstein Group, Inc. (V. President)

Clients Represented

On Behalf of The Duberstein Group, Inc.
Amerada Hess Corp.
American Apparel & Footwear Ass'n
American Ass'n of Health Plans (AAHP)
American Council of Life Insurers
American Gaming Ass'n
The American Water Works Co.
AOL Time Warner
The Business Roundtable
Comcast Corp.
Conoco Inc.
CSX Corp.
Direct Marketing Ass'n, Inc.
Dow Corning Corp.
Fannie Mae
General Motors Corp.
Goldman, Sachs and Co.
Nat'l Cable Television Ass'n
Pharmacia Corp.
Project to Promote Competition and Innovation in the Digital Age
Sara Lee Corp.
Transportation Institute
United Airlines
USX Corp.

CHAN, May S.

1107 Massachusetts Ave. NW
Washington, DC 20005

Employers
U.S. Immigrant Investor Ass'n (PAC Administrator)

CHANDLER, Kathleen K.

601 Pennsylvania Ave. NW
South Bldg., Suite 900
Washington, DC 20004
Tel: (202)434-8163
Fax: (202)639-8238

Employers
Lockridge Grindal & Nauen, P.L.L.P.

CHANDLER, CAE, Linda C.

1575 I St. NW
Washington, DC 20005-1103
EMail: lchandler@asaenet.org
Tel: (202)626-2700
Fax: (202)371-8825

Employers
American Soc. of Ass'n Executives (Exec. V. President)

CHANDLER, Hon. Rodney D.

601 13th St. NW
Suite 410 South
Washington, DC 20005
Tel: (202)737-0100
Fax: (202)628-3965
Registered: LDA
Member, U.S. House of Representatives (R-WA), 1983-93.

Employers
R. Duffy Wall and Associates (President)

Clients Represented

On Behalf of R. Duffy Wall and Associates
American Internat'l Group, Inc.
Fleishman-Hillard, Inc
Home Care Ass'n of New York State
Metropolitan Mortgage and Securities, Inc.
Nat'l Ass'n of Counties
Northwest Ecosystem Alliance

CHANDLER, William J.

1300 19th St. NW
Suite 300
Washington, DC 20036
Tel: (202)223-6722
Fax: (202)659-0650
Registered: LDA

Employers
Nat'l Parks Conservation Ass'n (V. President, Conservation Policy)

CHANEY, Carolyn C.

1401 K St. NW
Suite 700
Washington, DC 20005
Tel: (202)842-4930
Fax: (202)842-5051
Registered: LDA
EMail: chaney@capitaledge.com

Employers
Carolyn C. Chaney & Associates (President)

Clients Represented

On Behalf of Carolyn C. Chaney & Associates

Beaumont, Texas, City of
Farmers Branch, Texas, City of
Lincoln, Nebraska, City of
Pasadena, California, City of
Reno, Nevada, City of
Santa Cruz County Regional Transportation Commission
Santa Cruz Metropolitan Transit District
Santa Cruz Redevelopment Agency
Santa Cruz, California, County of
Scottsdale, Arizona, City of

CHANEY, Julia E.

601 13th St. NW
Suite 410 South
Washington, DC 20005
Tel: (202)737-0100
Fax: (202)628-3965

Employers
R. Duffy Wall and Associates (V. President)

Clients Represented

On Behalf of R. Duffy Wall and Associates

American Gas Ass'n
Nat'l Ass'n of Counties

CHANEY, Pete

1385 Piccard Dr.
Rockville, MD 20850-4340
Tel: (301)869-5800
Fax: (301)990-9690
Registered: LDA
EMail: pchaney@mcaa.org

Employers
Mechanical Contractors Ass'n of America (Director Safety and Health)

CHANG, Audrey

3000 K St. NW
Suite 300
Washington, DC 20007
Tel: (202)295-8787
Fax: (202)295-8799

Employers
The Harbour Group (Director)

CHANG, Irene

555 13th St. NW
Washington, DC 20004-1109
Tel: (202)637-6413
Fax: (202)637-5910
Registered: LDA
EMail: ifchang@hhlaw.com

Employers
Hogan & Hartson L.L.P. (Associate)

Clients Represented

On Behalf of Hogan & Hartson L.L.P.

Payless Shoe Source
Pharmaceutical Research and Manufacturers of America

CHANOW, Murray S.

3138 N. Tenth St.
Arlington, VA 22201
Tel: (703)522-4770
Fax: (703)522-0594
Registered: LDA

Employers
Nat'l Ass'n of Federal Credit Unions (Senior, Legislative Representative)

CHAPEL, Christopher

801 Pennsylvania Ave. NW
Suite 220
Washington, DC 20004-2604
Tel: (202)347-7082
Fax: (202)347-7076

Employers
Florida Power and Light Co. (Manager, Governmental Affairs, Washington Office)

CHAPELLI, Jr., Armando C.

6707 Democracy Blvd.
Suite 1010
Bethesda, MD 20817
Tel: (301)656-2330
Fax: (301)656-1324

Employers
Washington Consulting Group (President and Chief Exec. Officer)

CHAPIN, Christopher K.

1250 24th St. NW
Suite 300
Washington, DC 20037
Tel: (703)326-8219
Fax: (202)466-6249

Employers
HearingRoom.com (Senior V. President)

CHAPIN, Isolde

733 15th St. NW
Suite 220
The Woodward Bldg.
Washington, DC 20005
Tel: (202)347-4973
Fax: (202)628-0298

Employers
Washington Independent Writers (Exec. Director)

CHAPMAN, Bob

701 Pennsylvania Ave. NW
Suite 650
Washington, DC 20004
EMail: bob.chapman@cancer.org
Tel: (202)661-5705
Fax: (202)661-5750

Employers
American Cancer Soc. (Director, Operations)

CHAPMAN, P.E., Cheryl Kandaras

11 Canal Center Plaza
Suite 103
Alexandria, VA 22314
Tel: (703)683-4222
Fax: (703)683-0645
Registered: LDA

Former Principal Deputy Assistant Secretary for Installations and the Environment, Department of the Navy.

Employers
The Spectrum Group

Clients Represented

On Behalf of The Spectrum Group

Student Loan Finance Corp.
Tetra Tech

CHAPMAN, Connie

445 12th St. NW
Room 8-C425
Washington, DC 20554
Tel: (202)418-1900
Fax: (202)418-2806

Employers
Federal Communications Commission (Legislative Analyst)

CHAPMAN, Hon. Jim

2000 K St. NW
Suite 500
Washington, DC 20006-1872
Tel: (202)828-5833
Fax: (202)223-1225
Registered: LDA
EMail: jchapman@bracepatt.com

Member, U.S. House of Representatives (D-TX), 1985-97.

Employers
Bracewell & Patterson, L.L.P. (Partner)

Clients Represented

On Behalf of Bracewell & Patterson, L.L.P.

Alltel Corporation
Council of Industrial Boiler Owners (CIBO)
Envirocare of Utah, Inc.
FBI Agents Ass'n
Gary-Williams Energy Corp.
Houston, Texas, Port Authority of the City of
Huntsman Corp.
Oxygenated Fuels Ass'n
Placid Refining Co.
Solex Environmental Systems, Inc.
Texas Petrochemicals Corp.
Texas Windstorm Insurance Ass'n
UST Public Affairs, Inc.
Welcon, Inc.

CHAPMAN, John

7700 Leesburg Pike
Suite 421
Falls Church, VA 22043
Tel: (703)847-2677
Fax: (703)556-6485

Employers
Law Enforcement Alliance of America (President)

CHAPMAN, Kelly G.

444 N. Capitol St. NW
Suite 729
Washington, DC 20001
Tel: (202)585-4200
Fax: (202)737-3874
Registered: LDA
EMail: kelly_chapman@dom.com

Employers
Dominion Resources, Inc. (Manager, Federal Policy)

CHAPMAN, Nancy

1723 U St. NW
Washington, DC 20009
Tel: (202)659-1858
Fax: (202)387-5553
Registered: LDA

Professional Staff, House Agriculture Committee, 1981-85.

Employers
N. Chapman Associates (President)

Clients Represented

On Behalf of N. Chapman Associates

Apple Processors Ass'n
Mycogen Corp.

CHAPOTON, John E.

1455 Pennsylvania Ave. NW
Suite 700
Washington, DC 20004-1008
Tel: (202)639-6500
Fax: (202)639-6604
Registered: LDA

Assistant Secretary for Tax Policy (1981-84) and Tax Legislative Counsel (1970-72), Department of the Treasury.

Employers
Vinson & Elkins L.L.P. (Partner)

Clients Represented

On Behalf of Vinson & Elkins L.L.P.

Cheyne Walk Trust
Kansas City Southern Industries
Nat'l Ass'n of Settlement Purchasers
XL Capital Ltd

CHAPPELEAR-MARSHALL, Patsy

1700 K St. NW
13th Floor
Washington, DC 20006-0011
Tel: (202)457-0710
Ext: 11
Fax: (202)269-9352
EMail: chappel@narc.org

Employers
Nat'l Ass'n of Regional Councils (Director of Operations)

CHARENDOFF, Bruce J.

1101 17th St. NW
Suite 602
Washington, DC 20036
EMail: bruce.charendoff@sabre.com
Tel: (202)467-8203
Fax: (202)467-8204

Employers
Sabre Inc. (Senior V. President, Government Affairs and Associate General Counsel)
Travelocity.com (Senior V. President, Government Affairs)

CHARLES, Michael

1015 15th St. NW
Suite 600
Washington, DC 20005
Tel: (202)789-2200
Fax: (202)289-6797
Registered: LDA
EMail: mcharles@dc.asce.org

Employers
American Soc. of Civil Engineers (Senior Manager, Government Relations)

CHARLES, Robert B.

8503 Pelham Rd.
Bethesda, MD 20817
Tel: (301)564-9708
Fax: (301)564-9706
Registered: LDA

Employers
Direct Impact, LLC (President)

Clients Represented

On Behalf of Direct Impact, LLC

California, State of, Attorney General's Office
D.A.R.E. America

CHARLESTON, Suzanne E.

2300 Ninth St. South
Suite 210
Arlington, VA 22204
Tel: (703)920-8480
Fax: (703)920-8491
Registered: LDA

Employers
Pharmaceutical Care Management Ass'n (Director, Government Affairs)

CHARMATZ, Marc

814 Thayer Ave.
Suite 250
Silver Spring, MD 20910
Tel: (301)587-7732
Fax: (301)587-0234

Employers
Nat'l Ass'n of the Deaf (Counsel)

CHARNER, Ivan

1825 Connecticut Ave. NW
Seventh Floor
Washington, DC 20009
EMail: icharner@aed.org
Tel: (202)884-8186
Fax: (202)884-8422

Employers
Academy for Educational Development - Nat'l Institute for Work and Learning (V. President and Director)

CHARNOFF, Gerald

2300 N St. NW
Washington, DC 20037-1128
Tel: (202)663-8000
Fax: (202)663-8007
EMail: gerald.charnoff@shawpittman.com
Assistant to the Director, Division of Licensing and Regulation (1960) and Office of General Counsel (1957-60), Atomic Energy Commission.

Employers
Shaw Pittman (Partner)

Clients Represented
On Behalf of Shaw Pittman
Dresdner Bank AG
MATEK

CHARROW, Robert

1001 Pennsylvania Ave. NW
Suite 1100
Washington, DC 20004-2595
Tel: (202)624-2500
Fax: (202)628-5116

Employers
Crowell & Moring LLP (Partner)

CHARYK, William R.

1050 Connecticut Ave. NW
Washington, DC 20036-5339
Tel: (202)857-6000
Fax: (202)857-6395

Employers
Arent Fox Kintner Plotkin & Kahn, PLLC (Member)

CHARYTAN, Lynn

2445 M St. NW
Washington, DC 20037-1420
Tel: (202)663-6000
Fax: (202)663-6363
Registered: LDA

Employers
Wilmer, Cutler & Pickering (Partner)

CHASE, Bob

1201 16th St. NW
Washington, DC 20036
Tel: (202)833-4000

Employers
Nat'l Education Ass'n of the U.S. (President)

CHASE, JoAnn

1301 Connecticut Ave. NW
Suite 200
Washington, DC 20036
EMail: jchase@erols.com
Tel: (202)466-7767
Fax: (202)466-7797

Employers
Nat'l Congress of American Indians (Exec. Director)

CHASE, Matthew

400 N. Capitol St. NW
Suite 390
Washington, DC 20001
Tel: (202)624-7806
Fax: (202)624-8813

Employers
Nat'l Ass'n of Development Organizations (Deputy Director, Legislative Affairs)

CHASE, Michael T.

601 Madison St.
Suite 200
Alexandria, VA 22314
Tel: (703)765-4147
Fax: (703)765-4148
Registered: LDA

Employers
Michael Chase Associates, LTD (President)

Clients Represented
On Behalf of Michael Chase Associates, LTD
Allison Transmission Division, General Motors Corp.
American Systems Internat'l Corp.
Carwell Products, Inc.
Stewart & Stevenson Services, Inc.

CHASE, Mike

555 11th St. NW
Suite 750
Washington, DC 20005
Tel: (202)637-3506
Fax: (202)637-3504

Employers
El Paso Corporation (Manager, Federal Agency Affairs)

CHASE, Richard

635 Slaters Ln.
Suite 110
Alexandria, VA 22314
EMail: chase@siaonline.org
Tel: (703)683-2075
Fax: (703)683-2469

Employers
Security Industry Ass'n (Exec. Director)

CHASIA, James

555 12th St. NW
Suite 950N
Washington, DC 20004
Tel: (202)371-2220
Fax: (202)371-1497

Employers
Freedom Technologies, Inc. (Director, Strategic Analysis)

CHASKES, Deborah

8045 Leesburg Pike
Suite 650
Vienna, VA 22182
Tel: (703)506-3555
Fax: (703)506-3556

Employers
AmeriChoice Health Services, Inc. (V. President and Deputy General Counsel)

CHASON, Anna

1875 I St. NW
Suite 600
Washington, DC 20006
EMail: achason@nareit.com
Tel: (202)739-9400
Fax: (202)739-9401

Employers
Nat'l Ass'n of Real Estate Investment Trusts (Public Affairs Counsel)

CHATMAN, Priscilla

Ten G St. NE
Suite 600
Washington, DC 20002-4215
Tel: (202)216-0420
Fax: (202)216-0446
Registered: LDA

Employers
Nat'l Committee to Preserve Social Security and Medicare (Senior Policy Analyst)

CHATTMAN, Ray

1801 Alexander Bell Dr.
Suite 500
Reston, VA 20191
Tel: (703)264-7500
Fax: (703)264-7551

Employers
American Institute of Aeronautics and Astronautics (Foundation Director)

CHAUDET, Stephen E.

1725 Jefferson Davis Hwy.
Crystal Square 2, Suite 300
Arlington, VA 22202
EMail: steve_e_chaudet@lmco.com
Tel: (703)413-5996
Fax: (703)413-5846

Employers
Lockheed Martin Corp. (V. President, State and Local Government Affairs and PAC)

CHAUDHRY, Neena

11 Dupont Circle NW
Suite 800
Washington, DC 20036
EMail: nchaudhry@nwlc.org
Tel: (202)588-5180
Fax: (202)588-5185

Employers
Nat'l Women's Law Center (Staff Counsel)

CHAVEZ-THOMPSON, Linda

815 16th St. NW
Washington, DC 20006
Tel: (202)637-5000
Fax: (202)637-5058

Employers
AFL-CIO (American Federation of Labor and Congress of Industrial Organizations) (Exec. V. President)

CHEEK, Felicia

100 Daingerfield Rd.
Alexandria, VA 22314
Tel: (703)519-8100
Fax: (703)548-3227
Registered: LDA
EMail: fcheek@printing.org

Employers
Printing Industries of America (Legislative Assistant)

CHEEK, Jacquelyn M.

18th and C Sts. NW
MS-4559-MIB
Washington, DC 20240
EMail: jackiecheek@bia.gov
Tel: (202)208-5706
Fax: (202)208-4623

Employers
Department of Interior - Bureau of Indian Affairs (Director, Office of Congressional and Legislative Affairs)

CHEEK, John

700 N. Fairfax St.
Suite 210
Alexandria, VA 22314
Tel: (703)838-2870
Fax: (703)838-1620

Employers
Nat'l Indian Education Ass'n (Exec. Director)

CHELLI, Marie

1401 I St. NW
Suite 1220
Washington, DC 20005
Tel: (202)898-6400
Fax: (202)898-6454

Employers
Vivendi Universal (Director, Public Policy)

CHEN, C.J.

4201 Wisconsin Ave. NW
Washington, DC 20016-2137
Tel: (202)895-1800
Fax: (202)966-0825

Employers
Taipei Economic and Cultural Representative Office in the United States (Representative)

CHEN, James

555 13th St. NW
Washington, DC 20004-1109
Tel: (202)637-5713
Fax: (202)637-5910
Registered: LDA
EMail: jcchen@hhlaw.com
Attorney/Advisor, Office of Regulatory Enforcement, Toxics and Pesticides Enforcement Division (1994-96) and Attorney/Advisor, Office of Regulatory Enforcement, RCRA Division (1991-94), Environmental Protection Agency.

Employers
Hogan & Hartson L.L.P. (Associate)

Clients Represented
On Behalf of Hogan & Hartson L.L.P.
Nissan North America Inc.
Soap and Detergent Ass'n

CHEN, Jennifer C.

600 13th St. NW
Washington, DC 20005-3096
Tel: (202)756-8396
Fax: (202)756-8087
EMail: jchen@mwe.com
Former Patent Examiner, Patent and Trademark Office.

Employers
McDermott, Will and Emery (Associate)

CHEN, Kenneth

1300 I St. NW
Suite 470 East
Washington, DC 20005
Tel: (202)354-6100
Fax: (202)289-7448

Employers
Amgen (Director, Public Policy)

CHENEY, Lynne V.

1150 17th St. NW
Washington, DC 20036
EMail: lcheney@aei.org
Tel: (202)862-5800
Fax: (202)862-7177

Employers
American Enterprise Institute for Public Policy Research (Senior Fellow)

CHERIAN, Ph.D., Joy

1030 15th St. NW
Washington, DC 20005-1503
EMail: jcci@erols.com
Tel: (202)842-1030
Fax: (202)842-1225
Commissioner, U.S. Equal Employment Opportunity Commission (EEOC), 1987-93.

Employers
J. Cherian Consultants, Inc. (President)

CHERICO, Holly

4200 Wilson Blvd.
Suite 800
Arlington, VA 22203-1838
EMail: hcherico@cbbb.bbb.org
Tel: (703)276-0100
Fax: (703)525-8277

Employers
Council of Better Business Bureaus (V.President, Public Relations and Communications)

CHERNEY, Colburn T.

1301 K St. NW
Suite 800 East
Washington, DC 20005
EMail: ccherney@ropesgray.com
Tel: (202)626-3900
Fax: (202)626-3961
Associate General Counsel for Water (1983-86) and Assistant General Counsel for Superfund (1981-83), Environmental Protection Agency.

Employers
Ropes & Gray (Partner)

CHERNIKOFF, Larry B.

1320 18th St. NW
Suite 100
Washington, DC 20036
Tel: (202)223-9280
Fax: (202)223-6608
Registered: LDA
Formerly worked for the National Endowment for the Arts.

Employers
Chernikoff and Co. (President)

Clients Represented

On Behalf of Chernikoff and Co.
American Architectural Foundation
Arena Stage
Capital Children's Museum
The Choral Arts Soc. of Washington
The Corcoran Gallery of Art
Directors Guild of America
Federal City Council
Folger Shakespeare Library
Ford's Theatre
Heritage Preservation
Independent Television Service
Meridian Internat'l Center
Thelonius Monk Institute of Jazz
Nat'l Building Museum
Nat'l Museum of Women in the Arts
The Phillips Collection
The Shakespeare Theatre
The Textile Museum
The Washington Ballet
The Washington Opera
Washington Performing Arts Society

CHEROW, Evelyn

10801 Rockville Pike
Rockville, MD 20852
Tel: (301)897-5700
Fax: (301)571-0457
Registered: LDA

Employers
American Speech, Language, and Hearing Ass'n (Director, Audiology Division)

CHERRY, Barbara F.

300 E St. SW
Room 9L33
Washington, DC 20546
EMail: bcherry@hq.nasa.gov
Tel: (202)358-1948
Fax: (202)358-4340

Employers
Nat'l Aeronautics and Space Administration (Director, Liaison Division, Office of Legislative Affairs)

CHERRY, Edward T.

1667 K St. NW
Suite 460
Washington, DC 20006
EMail: ed_cherry@fmc.com
Tel: (202)956-5218
Fax: (202)956-5235
Registered: LDA

Employers
FMC Corp. (Director, Regulatory Affairs)

CHERRY, Jan E.

1301 Pennsylvania Ave. NW
Suite 1050
Washington, DC 20004
Tel: (202)942-9840
Fax: (202)942-9847

Employers
Constellation Energy Group (Federal Relations Assistant)

CHESCAVAGE, Dorsey

1401 K St. NW
Suite 900
Washington, DC 20005
Tel: (202)626-8550
Fax: (202)626-8578
Registered: LDA

Employers
Jefferson Consulting Group (Director)

Clients Represented

On Behalf of Jefferson Consulting Group
First Consulting Group
Franklin Covey
M.D. - I.P.A.

CHESSEN, James

1120 Connecticut Ave. NW
Washington, DC 20036
Tel: (202)663-5000
Fax: (202)828-4547
Registered: LDA

Employers
American Bankers Ass'n (Chief Economist and Group Director)

CHESSON, Jack

444 N. Capitol St. NW
Suite 701
Washington, DC 20001
EMail: JChesson@naic.org
Tel: (202)624-7790
Fax: (202)624-8579

Employers
Nat'l Ass'n of Insurance Commissioners (Senior Legislative Counsel)

CHESTER, Jr., George M.

1201 Pennsylvania Ave. NW
Washington, DC 20004-2401
EMail: gchester@cov.com
Tel: (202)662-6000
Fax: (202)662-6291
Law Clerk to Judge Tamm, U.S. Court of Appeals for the District of Columbia Circuit, 1976-77. Lieutenant, U.S. Navy, 1970-72.

Employers
Covington & Burling (Partner)

Clients Represented

On Behalf of Covington & Burling
The Ass'n For Manufacturing Technology (AMT)

CHESTNUT, John

701 Pennsylvania Ave. NW
Suite 720
Washington, DC 20004
Tel: (202)434-4800
Fax: (202)347-4015

Employers
Siemens Corp. (PAC Contact)

CHESTON, Sheila C.

2445 M St. NW
Washington, DC 20037-1420
Tel: (202)663-6000
Fax: (202)663-6363
Registered: LDA

Employers
Wilmer, Cutler & Pickering

Clients Represented

On Behalf of Wilmer, Cutler & Pickering
American Civil Liberties Union

CHETTLE, J. Anne

1010 Massachusetts Ave. NW
Washington, DC 20001
Tel: (202)789-8107
Fax: (202)789-8109
Registered: LDA

Employers
High Speed Ground Transportation Ass'n (Director, Public Affairs)

CHETTLE, John H.

1050 Connecticut Ave. NW
Washington, DC 20036-5366
EMail: jchettle@flks.com
Tel: (202)672-5300
Fax: (202)672-5399

Employers
Freedman, Levy, Kroll & Simonds (Partner)

Clients Represented

On Behalf of Freedman, Levy, Kroll & Simonds
Medical University of Southern Africa

CHEUNG, Joanna

1520 18th St. NW
Washington, DC 20036
Tel: (202)331-8947
Fax: (202)331-8958

Employers
Hong Kong Economic and Trade Office (Trade Officer)

CHIANCHIANO, Dolph

1522 K Street NW
Suite 825
Washington, DC 20005
Tel: (202)216-9257
Fax: (202)216-9258
Registered: LDA

Employers
Nat'l Kidney Foundation (Director, Scientific and Public Policy)

CHIAPPETTA, Christina Ott

1617 Duke St.
Alexandria, VA 22314
EMail: cchiap@ipma-hr.org
Tel: (703)549-7100
Fax: (703)684-0948

Employers
Internat'l Personnel Management Ass'n (Director, Government Affairs)

CHICCEHITTO, Karen

1801 K St. NW
Suite 901-L
Washington, DC 20006
EMail: karen_chiccehitto@bm.com
Tel: (202)530-0500
Fax: (202)530-4800
Registered: LDA, FARA
Former Senior Policy Analyst, Assistant to the Chief of Staff, and Director of Administration to Speaker of the House, Rep. Newt Gingrich (R-GA). Senior Legislative Assistant to Rep. Jim Kolbe (R-AZ), 1991-93.

Employers
BKSH & Associates (Director)

Clients Represented

On Behalf of BKSH & Associates
M-Unit
J. P. Morgan Chase & Co.
Safety-Kleen Corp.

CHIDESTER, Becky

1055 Thomas Jefferson St. NW
Suite 500
Washington, DC 20007
Tel: (202)625-2111
Fax: (202)424-7900

Employers
RTC Direct (President)

CHILCOTT, Susan

1307 New York Ave.
Fifth Floor
Washington, DC 20005-4701
EMail: chilcotts@aascu.org
Tel: (202)293-7070
Fax: (202)296-5819

Employers
American Ass'n of State Colleges and Universities (Director, Communications)

CHILDERS, John B.

One Dupont Circle NW
Suite 200
Washington, DC 20036-1131
Tel: (202)331-8080
Fax: (202)331-7925

Employers
Consortium of Universities of the Washington Metropolitan Area (President and Chief Exec. Officer)

CHILDRESS, James M.

1110 N. Glebe Rd.
Suite 610
Arlington, VA 22201
EMail: jchildress@kcihq.com
Tel: (703)276-0600
Fax: (703)276-7662

Employers
Koleda Childress & Co. (Principal)

Clients Represented

On Behalf of Koleda Childress & Co.
Eastman Chemical Co.
Gasification Technologies Council
Propane Consumers Coalition

CHILDRESS, Martina

600 Pennsylvania Ave. SE
Suite 400
Washington, DC 20003
EMail: mchildress@dlcppi.org
Tel: (202)546-0007
Fax: (202)544-5002

Employers
Democratic Leadership Council (Office Manager and Intern Coordinator)

CHILDS, Blair G.

2121 K St. NW
Suite 800
Washington, DC 20007
EMail: bchilds@strategicadvocacy.com
Tel: (202)261-6539
Fax: (202)261-6541
Registered: LDA

Employers
Alliance for Affordable Services (Washington Representative)
The Strategic Advocacy Group (President)

Clients Represented

On Behalf of The Strategic Advocacy Group
Alliance for Affordable Services
American Small Businesses Ass'n
Americans for Financial Security

CHILDS, Stephanie

900 19th St. NW
Suite 700
Washington, DC 20006
Tel: (202)530-7065
Fax: (202)530-7007
Registered: LDA
Nominations Counsel, Senate Judiciary Committee, 1990; Special Assistant to Director, Office of Drug Control Policy, in Bush I administration, 1991-92.

Employers
Lucent Technologies (Director, Global Public Affairs)

CHIN, Yee Wah

701 Pennsylvania Ave. NW
Suite 900
Washington, DC 20004-2608
EMail: ywchin@mintz.com
Tel: (202)434-7300
Fax: (202)434-7400

Employers
Mintz, Levin, Cohn, Ferris, Glovsky and Popeo, P.C. (Of Counsel)

CHIPPS, Katie B.

701 Pennsylvania Ave. NW
Third Floor
Washington, DC 20004
Tel: (202)508-5995
Fax: (202)508-5924
Registered: LDA

Employers
The Electric Vehicle Ass'n of the Americas (EVAA) (Public Policy Associate)

CHISOLM-KING, Janet

Theodore Roosevelt Federal Bldg.
1900 E St. NW
MS: 5H30
Washington, DC 20415
Tel: (202)606-1300
Fax: (202)606-1344

Employers
Office of Personnel Management (Congressional Relations Officer)

CHIU, David S.

633 Pennsylvania Ave. NW
Fourth Floor
Washington, DC 20004
Tel: (202)783-5910
Fax: (202)783-5911
Former Aide to Senator Paul Simon (D-IL). Former Counsel, Subcommittee on the Constitution, Senate Committee on the Judiciary. Served as Federal Law Clerk to Judge James Browning, U.S. Court of Appeals, Ninth Circuit.

Employers
Grassroots Enterprise, Inc. (Co-Founder and V. President, Political Services and Business Development)

CHIU, Johnny C.

1150 18th St. NW
Ninth Floor
Washington, DC 20036
EMail: jchiu@ablondifoster.com
Tel: (202)296-3355
Fax: (202)296-3922
Registered: FARA

Employers
Ablondi, Foster, Sobin & Davidow, P.C. (Associate)

CHIU, Sandra L.

1025 Connecticut Ave. NW
Suite 1210
Washington, DC 20036
Tel: (202)296-2370
Fax: (202)296-2873

Employers
United Airlines (Director, International Affairs)

CHLOPAK, Robert A.

1850 M St. NW
Suite 550
Washington, DC 20036
Tel: (202)289-5900
Fax: (202)289-4141
Registered: LDA, FARA

Employers
Chlopak, Leonard, Schechter and Associates (President)

Clients Represented

On Behalf of Chlopak, Leonard, Schechter and Associates
Intuit, Inc.
University Science Alliance

CHLOPECKI, Julie

211 N. Union St.
Suite 100
Alexandria, VA 22314
Tel: (703)739-2545
Fax: (703)739-2718
Registered: LDA

Employers
Ann Eppard Associates, Ltd. (Transportation Specialist)

Clients Represented

On Behalf of Ann Eppard Associates, Ltd.
Air Transport Ass'n of America
Air-21 Coalition
Amadeus Global Travel Distribution SA
American Beverage Institute
American Maritime Officers Service
Anthony Timberlands, Inc.
Boucher & James
Calspan University of Buffalo Research Center
COMARCO Wireless Technology
Dade County Board of Commissioners
Daniel, Mann, Johnson & Mendenhall
Day & Zimmermann, Inc.
Delta Development Group, Inc.
FedEx Corp.
George Zamias Developers
Harlingen Area Chamber of Commerce
Indiana County Development Corp.
Jefferson Government Relations, L.L.C.
Outdoor Advertising Ass'n of America
Pennsylvania Pyrotechnics Ass'n
Pennsylvania Turnpike Commission
Pine Bluff Sand and Gravel Co.
Thelen Reid & Priest LLP
Traffic.com
Union Pacific
United Airlines

CHOCKLEY, Nancy

1225 19th St. NW
Suite 710
Washington, DC 20036
Tel: (202)296-4426
Fax: (202)296-4319

Employers
Nat'l Institute for Health Care Management (Exec. Director)

CHOI, Caroline

801 Pennsylvania Ave. NW
Suite 250
Washington, DC 20004
EMail: caroline.choi@pgnmail.com
Tel: (202)783-5530
Fax: (202)783-5569
Registered: LDA

Employers
Progress Energy (Manager, Federal Regulatory Affairs)

CHOPKO, Mark E.

3211 Fourth St. NE
Washington, DC 20017
Tel: (202)541-3300
Fax: (202)541-3337
Attorney and Senior Attorney, Nuclear Regulatory Commission, 1977-84.

Employers
Nat'l Conference of Catholic Bishops, Secretariat for Pro-Life Activities
United States Catholic Conference (General Counsel)

CHOQUETTE, William

4330 East-West Hwy.
Suite 314
Bethesda, MD 20814
Tel: (301)718-8860
Fax: (301)718-8862

Employers
Gilbane Building Co. (V. President and Washington Contact)

CHORBA, Timothy A.

2550 M St. NW
Washington, DC 20037-1350
EMail: tchorba@pattonboggs.com
Tel: (202)457-6060
Fax: (202)457-6315
Registered: LDA

Employers
Patton Boggs, LLP (Partner)

CHORLINS, Marjorie

1350 I St. NW
Suite 400
Washington, DC 20005-3306
Tel: (202)371-6900
Fax: (202)842-3578

Employers
Motorola, Inc. (Director, International Trade & Corporate Relations)

CHOSLOWSKY, V. S.

P.O. Box 19001
Washington, DC 20036-9001
Tel: (202)331-1363

Employers
Commercial Associates Incorporated (Managing Director)

CHOTIN, Elizabeth E.

1730 Rhode Island Ave. NW
Suite 409
Washington, DC 20036
Tel: (202)293-6883
Fax: (202)293-1753

Employers
American Committee for the Weizmann Institute of Science (Director, Government Relations)

CHOULDJIAN, Elizabeth S.

888 17th St. NW
Suite 904
Washington, DC 20006
Tel: (202)775-1918
Fax: (202)775-1918

Employers
Armenian Nat'l Committee of America (Director, Communications)

CHRISTENSEN, Eric

445-B Carlisle Dr.
Herndon, VA 20170
Tel: (703)689-2370

Employers
Landmark Legal Foundation Center for Civil Rights (V. President, Development and Communications)

CHRISTENSEN, John

1350 I St. NW
Suite 510
Washington, DC 20005
Tel: (202)828-8500
Fax: (202)293-3457

Employers
United Automobile, Aerospace and Agricultural Implement Workers of America (UAW) (International Representative)

CHRISTENSON, Arne L.

3900 Wisconsin Ave. NW
Washington, DC 20016
Tel: (202)752-7000
Fax: (202)752-6099
Former aide to Speaker of the House, Rep. Newt Gingrich (R-GA).

Employers
Fannie Mae (Senior V. President, Regulatory Policy)

CHRISTIAN, Betty Jo

1330 Connecticut Ave. NW
Washington, DC 20036-1795
Tel: (202)429-8113
Fax: (202)429-3902
V. Chairman (1976-78), Commissioner (1976-79) Associate General Counsel (1971-76) and Attorney (1961-68), all at the Interstate Commerce Commission. Trial Attorney, Department of Labor, 1968-70.

Employers
Steptoe & Johnson LLP (Partner)

CHRISTIAN, Ernest S.

800 Connecticut Ave. NW
Suite 705
Washington, DC 20006-2717
Tel: (202)898-2090
Fax: (202)898-2086
Former worked for the Department of the Treasury.

Employers
Ernest S. Christian

CHRISTIAN, Jr., James B.

2550 M St. NW
Washington, DC 20037-1350
Tel: (202)457-6000
Fax: (202)457-6315
Registered: LDA
EMail: jchristian@pattonboggs.com
Legislative Counsel and Professional Staff Member, Senate Appropriations Committee, 1974-77.

Employers
Patton Boggs, LLP (Partner)

Clients Represented

On Behalf of Patton Boggs, LLP
Barringer Technologies
College Savings Bank
Condor-Pacific Industries
L. P. Conwood Co.
Corning Inc.
Alan Hilburg & Associates
James Hardie Building Products Inc.
LOOP, Inc.
MCI WorldCom Corp.

CHRISTIANSON, Geryld B.

700 13th St. NW
Suite 950
Washington, DC 20005
Tel: (202)333-8777
Fax: (202)333-8722
Registered: LDA, FARA
EMail: gchristianson@theevansgroupltd.com
Staff Director, Senate Committee on Foreign Relations, 1987-95. Minority Staff Director, Senate Committee on Foreign Relations, 1981-87. Foreign Relations Specialist to Rep. Claiborne Pell (D-RI), 1975-80. Foreign Service Officer, Department of State, 1958-75. Served in the U.S. Army Reserve, 1957-63.

Employers
The Evans Group, Ltd. (Senior Counselor)

Clients Represented

On Behalf of The Evans Group, Ltd.
Kazakhstan 21st Century Foundation
Naigai, Inc.
Unideal Navitankers
WorldWide Minerals Ltd.

CHRISTIE, Katherine M.

901 15th St. NW
Suite 370
Washington, DC 20005
Tel: (202)371-9600
Fax: (202)371-0808
Registered: FARA
Former Senior Press Officer, National Endowment for the Arts.

Employers
Global Communicators (President)

Clients Represented

On Behalf of Global Communicators
Switzerland, Economic Development, State of Vaud

CHRISTIE, R. Lee

888 16th St. NW
7th Floor
Washington, DC 20006-4103
Tel: (202)835-8000
Fax: (202)835-8136
Registered: LDA

Employers
Foley & Lardner (Partner)

Clients Represented

On Behalf of Foley & Lardner
USAA - United Services Automobile Ass'n

CHRISTMAN, Keith A.

1300 Wilson Blvd.
Arlington, VA 22209
Tel: (703)741-5935
Fax: (703)741-6935
Registered: LDA
EMail: keith_christman@cmahq.com

Employers
Chlorine Chemistry Council (Director, Disinfection and Government Relations)

CHRISTOFFERSEN, Nils

1400 16th St. NW
Suite 210
Washington, DC 20036
EMail: nilsatart@aol.com
Tel: (202)939-3421
Fax: (202)939-3420

Employers
Africa Resources Trust USA (Director)

CHRISTOPH FRIEDMAN, Jessica

1050 Thomas Jefferson St. NW
Seventh Floor
Washington, DC 20007
EMail: jcf@vnf.com
Tel: (202)298-1800
Fax: (202)338-2416

Employers
Van Ness Feldman, P.C. (Associate)

CHRISTY, Jr., David S.

1133 Connecticut Ave. NW
Suite 1200
Washington, DC 20036
Tel: (202)775-9800
Fax: (202)833-8491
Registered: LDA, FARA

Employers
Winthrop, Stimson, Putnam & Roberts (Associate)

Clients Represented

On Behalf of Winthrop, Stimson, Putnam & Roberts
Korean Semiconductor Industry Ass'n

CHUMBRIS, Nicholas A.

1000 Independence Ave. SW
Room 8G-026
Washington, DC 20585-0863
EMail: nick.chumbris@hq.doe.gov
Tel: (202)586-2777
Fax: (202)586-7246

Employers
Department of Energy (Director, Congressional Liaison)

CHURCH, Christopher

1400 Independence Ave. SW
Room 1175-S
Washington, DC 20250
Tel: (202)720-9113
Fax: (202)720-5704

Employers
Department of Agriculture - Food Safety and Inspection Service (Deputy Director, Congressional and Public Affairs Staff)

CHURCH, Elaine K.

1301 K St. NW
Washington, DC 20005-3333
Tel: (202)414-1000
Fax: (202)414-1301
Registered: LDA

Employers
PriceWaterhouseCoopers (Partner, Employee Benefits Services)

CHURCH, Julia P.

805 15th St. NW
Suite 700
Washington, DC 20005
EMail: jpchurch@bakerd.com
Tel: (202)312-7400
Fax: (202)312-7441

Employers
Sagamore Associates, Inc. (V. President)

Clients Represented

On Behalf of Sagamore Associates, Inc.
2001 World Police and Fire Games
Huntingdon College
Ohio River Valley Water Sanitation Commission
Union Hospital

CHURCH, Lynne H.

1401 New York Ave. NW
11th Floor
Washington, DC 20005
Tel: (202)628-8200
Fax: (202)628-8260
Registered: LDA
EMail: epsa@mindspring.com

Employers
Electric Power Supply Ass'n (President)

CHURCHILL, Christine M.

The Willard Office Bldg.
1455 Pennsylvania Ave. NW
Washington, DC 20004
Tel: (202)783-6000
Fax: (202)783-4171
Registered: LDA
Former aide to Rep. Phil Crane (R-IL).

Employers
Gibbons & Company, Inc.

CHURCHILL, Kenneth

316 Pennsylvania Ave. SE
Suite 300
Washington, DC 20003
Tel: (202)675-4259
Fax: (202)675-4230
Registered: LDA

Employers
United Parcel Service (V. President, Public Affairs)

CHWAT, John

635 Slaters Lane
Suite 140
Alexandria, VA 22314
Tel: (703)684-7703
Fax: (703)684-7594
Registered: LDA, FARA
EMail: John.Chwat@chwatco.com
Former Legislative Assistant to Rep. Sy Halpern (R-NY), 1971-73. Member, Senate Labor and Public Welfare Committee Minority Staff, 1973. U.S. Department of Agriculture, Congressional Relations, 1973-74. Congressional Research Service, Library of Congress, 1974-76. Administrative Assistant to Rep. John Breckenridge (D-KY), 1976-78. Administrative Assistant to Rep. Bill Boner (D-TN), 1978-80.

Employers
Chwat and Company, Inc. (President)

Clients Represented

On Behalf of Chwat and Company, Inc.
AccuWeather
American Friends of the Czech Republic
American Radio Relay League
BCI, Inc.
Center for Regulatory Effectiveness
Federal Physicians Ass'n
Nat'l Ass'n of Assistant United States Attorneys
Newington-Cropsey Foundation
Security Industry Ass'n

CIANCIOLO, USA (Ret.), Lt. Gen. Augustus

11 Canal Center Plaza
Suite 103
Alexandria, VA 22314
Tel: (703)683-4222
Fax: (703)683-0645
Registered: LDA
Former Military Deputy to the Assistant Secretary for Research, Development and Acquisition, Department of the Army.

Employers
The Spectrum Group

Clients Represented

On Behalf of The Spectrum Group
KPMG, LLP
Raydon Corp.
The Refinishing Touch
Robertson Aviation
Simula, Inc.
Tetra Tech
Titanium Metals Corp.
Tri-City Regional Port District

CIANFRANI, Andrea

1575 I St. NW
Washington, DC 20005-1103
Tel: (202)626-2831
Fax: (202)371-1673
Registered: LDA
EMail: acianfrani@asaenet.org

Employers
American Soc. of Ass'n Executives (PAC Manager)

CICCONE, Christine M.

1600 Pennsylvania Ave. NW
107 E. Wing
Washington, DC 20500
Tel: (202)456-6493
Fax: (202)456-2604

Employers
Executive Office of the President - The White House (Special Assistant to the President for Legislative Affairs, Senate Liaison Office)

CICCONI, James W.

1120 20th St. NW
Suite 1000
Washington, DC 20036
Tel: (202)457-3810
Fax: (202)457-2571
Registered: LDA

Assistant to the President and Deputy Chief of Staff (1989-90) and Special Assistant to the President and Special Assistant to the Chief of Staff (1981-85), Executive Office of the President, The White House. Transition Staff Member (1988-89) and General Counsel (1980-81), Department of State.

Employers
AT&T (General Counsel and Exec. V. President, Law and Government Affairs)

CIMKO, Christine Kelly

1875 I St. NW
Suite 900
Washington, DC 20005
Tel: (202)371-0200
Fax: (202)371-2858

Former Director, Communications to the Senate Armed Services Committee under Senator Strom Thurmond (R-SC).

Employers
Edelman Public Relations Worldwide (V. President, Image and Events)

Clients Represented

On Behalf of Edelman Public Relations Worldwide
The Conference Board
Disabled Veterens' LIFE Memorial Foundation Inc.
Fuji Photo Film U.S.A., Inc.
Lois Pope Life Foundation
Rheinmetall AG
Stewart & Stevenson Tactical Vehicle Systems, LP
UKR Investments, Inc.

CINADR, Joseph W.

1023 N. Royal St.
Alexandria, VA 22314-1569
Tel: (703)548-5922
Fax: (703)836-8937
EMail: jcinadr@postmasters.org

Employers
Nat'l League of Postmasters of the U.S. (President)

CINNAMOND, Bill

666 11th St. NW
Suite 600
Washington, DC 20001
Tel: (202)783-0070
Fax: (202)783-0534
EMail: wcinnamo@ccianet.org

Served as Legislative Assistant to Senator Mike Gravel (D-AK) and Director of Legislative and Public Affairs, Office of Special Counsel.

Employers
Computer and Communications Industry Ass'n (CCIA) (Staff Counsel)

CIOCCI, Linda Church

One Massachusetts Ave. NW
Suite 850
Washington, DC 20001
Tel: (202)682-1700
Fax: (202)682-9478
Registered: LDA
EMail: linda@hydro.org

Employers
Nat'l Hydropower Ass'n (Exec. Director)

CIORLETTI, Julia

1101 Vermont Ave. NW
12th Floor
Washington, DC 20005-3583
Tel: (202)789-7427
Fax: (202)789-7401
Registered: LDA

Employers
American Medical Ass'n (Assistant Director of Congressional Affairs)

CIPOLLA, Frank

800 N. Capitol St. NW
Suite 250
Washington, DC 20002
Tel: (202)682-4010
Fax: (202)682-1119
EMail: fcipolla@napwash.org

Employers
Nat'l Academy of Public Administration (Director, Center for HRM)

CIRINCIONE, Joseph

1779 Massachusetts Ave. NW
Washington, DC 20036
Tel: (202)483-7600
Fax: (202)483-1840
EMail: jcirincione@ceip.org

Employers
Carnegie Endowment for Internat'l Peace (Senior Associate)

CIRRINCIONE, Jane Dunn

2301 M St. NW
Washington, DC 20037-1484
Tel: (202)467-2974
Fax: (202)467-2910
EMail: jcirrincione@APPAnet.org

Employers
American Public Power Ass'n (Senior Government Relations Representative)

CISNEROS, Adrienne Laura

700 13th St. NW
Suite 1000
Washington, DC 20005
Tel: (202)347-6633
Fax: (202)347-8713
Registered: FARA

Employers
Powell Tate (Manager, Media Relations)

CIVIDANES, Emilio W.

1200 19th St. NW
Washington, DC 20036-2430
Tel: (202)861-3911
Fax: (202)223-2085
Registered: LDA
EMail: emilio.cividanes@piperrudnick.com

Former Counsel, Technology and the Law Subcommittee, Senate Committee on the Judiciary

Employers
Piper Marbury Rudnick & Wolfe LLP (Of Counsel)

Clients Represented

On Behalf of Piper Marbury Rudnick & Wolfe LLP
AOL Time Warner
Commercial Internet Exchange Ass'n
Direct Marketing Ass'n, Inc.
Individual Reference Services Group
Lexis-Nexis
NetCoalition.Com

CIVILETTI, Benjamin R.

1201 New York Ave. NW
Suite 1000
Washington, DC 20005
Tel: (202)962-4843
Fax: (202)962-8300
EMail: brciviletti@venable.com

Attorney General (1979-81), Deputy Attorney General (1978-79), Assistant Attorney General, Criminal Division (1977-78), and Assistant U.S. Attorney (1962-64), all at the Department of Justice. Law Clerk to Judge W. Calvin Chestnut, U.S. District Court for the District of Maryland, 1961-62.

Employers
Venable (Partner)

CIZIK, Richard

1001 Connecticut Ave. NW
Suite 522
Washington, DC 20036
Tel: (202)789-1011
Fax: (202)842-0392
EMail: rcizik@nae.net

Employers
Nat'l Ass'n of Evangelicals (V. President, Governmental Affairs)

CLADOUHOS, Harry W.

1620 L St. NW
Suite 600
Washington, DC 20036
Tel: (202)312-8000
Fax: (202)312-8100
Registered: LDA
EMail: hcladouhos@owdlaw.com

Senior Trial Attorney, Trial Section, Antitrust Division, Department of Justice, 1957-69.

Employers
Oppenheimer Wolff & Donnelly LLP (Partner)

Clients Represented

On Behalf of Oppenheimer Wolff & Donnelly LLP
Association des Constructeurs Europeens de Motocycles
MGF Industries Inc.
NYK Bulkship, Inc.

CLAFFEY, Terri G.

1133 19th St. NW
Washington, DC 20036
Tel: (202)887-2607
Fax: (202)887-3123
Registered: LDA
EMail: terri.claffey@wcom.com

Employers
MCI WorldCom Corp. (Senior Policy Advisor, Government Relations)

CLAGETT, Brice M.

1201 Pennsylvania Ave. NW
Washington, DC 20004-2401
Tel: (202)662-6000
Fax: (202)662-6291
EMail: bclagett@cov.com

Consultant, Working Group on Investment, Advisory Committee on International Economic Policy, Department of State. Legal Advisor, Transition Team for the President-Elect, Department of State, 1981. Former Secretary, Committee on Rule Making, Administration Conference of the United States.

Employers
Covington & Burling (Partner)

CLAIR, Richard J.

8001 Braddock Rd.
Springfield, VA 22160
Tel: (703)321-9820
Fax: (703)321-7342
Registered: LDA

Employers
Nat'l Right to Work Committee (Corporate Counsel)

CLAMAN, Kimberly

1401 Wilson Blvd.
Suite 1100
Arlington, VA 22209
Tel: (703)522-5055
Fax: (703)525-2279
Registered: LDA
EMail: kclaman@itaa.org

Employers
Information Technology Ass'n of America (ITAA) (V. President, Global Affairs)

CLANCY, Felicity Feather

1701 Clarendon Blvd.
Arlington, VA 22209
Tel: (703)276-8800
Fax: (703)243-2593

Employers
American Chiropractic Ass'n (V. President, Communications)

CLANCY, Jayne

1625 L St. NW
Washington, DC 20036-5687
Tel: (202)429-5094
Fax: (202)223-3413
Registered: LDA
EMail: jclancy@afscme.org

Employers
American Federation of State, County and Municipal Employees (Legislative Representative)

CLANCY, Michael W.

2099 Pennsylvania Ave. NW
Suite 100
Washington, DC 20006
Tel: (202)955-3000
Fax: (202)955-5564
Registered: LDA
EMail: mclancy@hklaw.com

Employers
Holland & Knight LLP (Partner)

CLANCY, Patrick J.

1850 M St. NW
Suite 400
Washington, DC 20036
Tel: (202)293-8200
Fax: (202)872-0145
Registered: LDA

Employers
Krooth & Altman (Partner)

Clients Represented

On Behalf of Krooth & Altman
District of Columbia Hospital Ass'n
Healthcare Financing Study Group

CLAPP, Philip E.

1200 18th St. NW
Washington, DC 20036
EMail: peclapp@environet.org
Tel: (202)887-8800
Fax: (202)887-8877

Employers
Nat'l Environmental Trust (President)

CLARK, Alice Slayton

1001 Pennsylvania Ave. NW
Suite 600
Washington, DC 20004
EMail: asclark@pgfm.com
Tel: (202)347-0066
Fax: (202)624-7222
Registered: LDA, FARA
Legislative Assistant (1991-93) and Legislative Correspondent (1987-89) in the House of Representatives.

Employers
Powell, Goldstein, Frazer & Murphy LLP (International Trade Analyst)

Clients Represented
On Behalf of Powell, Goldstein, Frazer & Murphy LLP
Carpet Export Promotion Council
China, Embassy of the People's Republic of
DuPont
The DuPont Pharmaceutical Co.
Footwear Distributors and Retailers of America
Hong Kong Trade Development Council
PROEXPORT

CLARK, Dr. Andrew M.

1828 L St. NW
Suite 906
Washington, DC 20036-5104
Tel: (202)775-5966
Fax: (202)429-9417

Employers
Marine Technology Soc. (President)

CLARK, Beth

1630 Connecticut Ave. NW
Third Floor
Washington, DC 20009
EMail: antarctica@igc.org
Tel: (202)234-2480
Fax: (202)234-2482

Employers
The Antarctica Project (Director)

CLARK, Carol J.

1211 Connecticut Ave. NW
Suite 608
Washington, DC 20036
EMail: cclark@astphld.org
Tel: (202)822-5227
Fax: (202)887-5098

Employers
Ass'n of State and Territorial Public Health Laboratory Directors (Director, Administration)

CLARK, Donald J.

9650 Rockville Pike
Room 3300
Bethesda, MD 20814-3998
Tel: (301)530-7110
Fax: (301)571-1863

Employers
American Soc. for Clinical Nutrition (Exec. Officer)

CLARK, Ph.D., Elizabeth

750 First St. NE
Suite 700
Washington, DC 20002
Tel: (202)408-8600
Fax: (202)336-8311

Employers
Nat'l Ass'n of Social Workers (Exec. Director)

CLARK, Ernest

1629 K St. NW
Suite 602
Washington, DC 20006
Tel: (202)785-4477
Fax: (202)785-1244

Employers
Nat'l Ass'n of Real Estate Brokers (President and Chief Exec. Officer)

CLARK, Fred J.

1755 Jefferson Davis Hwy.
Suite 1107
Arlington, VA 22202
Tel: (703)415-0344
Fax: (703)415-0182
Registered: LDA

Employers
The PMA Group (Associate)

Clients Represented
On Behalf of The PMA Group
Cheese of Choice Coalition
Chicago Mercantile Exchange
CoBank, ACB
Florida Sugar Cane League, Inc.
General Mills
Generic Pharmaceutical Ass'n
Nat'l Ass'n of RC&D Councils
Nat'l Ass'n of Resource Conservation
Nat'l Cattleman's Beef Ass'n
Nat'l Pork Producers Ass'n
U.S. Rice Producers Ass'n

CLARK, Gordon

1819 H St. NW
Suite 420
Washington, DC 20006-3603
EMail: gclark@peace-action.org
Tel: (202)862-9740
Fax: (202)862-9762

Employers
Peace Action (Exec. Director)

CLARK, Harry L.

1775 Pennsylvania Ave. NW
Suite 200
Washington, DC 20006
Tel: (202)862-1000
Fax: (202)862-1093
Registered: LDA

Employers
Dewey Ballantine LLP (Counsel)

Clients Represented
On Behalf of Dewey Ballantine LLP
Semiconductor Equipment and Materials Internat'l

CLARK, Harry W.

1775 I St. NW
Suite 700
Washington, DC 20006
Tel: (202)261-4000
Fax: (202)261-4001

Employers
Clark & Weinstock, Inc. (Managing Partner)

CLARK, J. R.

441 Fourth St. NW
Room 1010
Washington, DC 20001
Tel: (202)727-6265
Fax: (202)727-6895

Employers
District of Columbia Office of Intergovernmental Relations (Deputy Director)

CLARK, Jack

1615 H St. NW
Washington, DC 20062-2000
Tel: (202)659-6000
Fax: (202)463-5836

Employers
Chamber of Commerce of the U.S.A. (Director, Congressional and Public Affairs)

CLARK, James F.

2300 Clarendon Blvd.
Suite 1010
Arlington, VA 22201
Tel: (703)527-4414
Fax: (703)527-0421
Registered: LDA

Employers
Robertson, Monagle & Eastaugh

Clients Represented
On Behalf of Robertson, Monagle & Eastaugh
Alaska Forest Ass'n
Alaska Pulp Corp.
Echo Bay Mining
The Glacier Bay Group
Gustavus Electric Co.

CLARK, John S.

501 Third St. NW
Washington, DC 20001-2797
EMail: jclark@cwa-union.org
Tel: (202)434-1254
Fax: (202)434-1426

Employers
Nat'l Ass'n of Broadcast Employees and Technicians-Communications Workers of America, AFL-CIO (NABET-CWA) (Sector President)

CLARK, Jordan

655 15th St. NW
Suite 460
Washington, DC 20005
Tel: (202)408-8842
Fax: (202)408-8156

Employers
United Homeowners Ass'n (President)

CLARK, Julia A.

8630 Fenton St.
Suite 400
Silver Spring, MD 20910-3803
EMail: clark.julia@worldnet.att.net
Tel: (301)565-9016
Fax: (301)565-0018
Registered: LDA

Employers
Internat'l Federation of Professional and Technical Engineers (General Counsel)

CLARK, Julia Penny

1000 Connecticut Ave. NW
Suite 1300
Washington, DC 20036
Tel: (202)842-2600
Fax: (202)842-1888
Member, Committee on Admissions and Grievances, U.S. Court of Appeals for the District of Columbia Circuit, 1990-96.

Employers
Bredhoff & Kaiser (Partner)

CLARK, Julie

1625 K St. NW
Suite 800
Washington, DC 20006
EMail: govrelations@nlada.org
Tel: (202)452-0620
Fax: (202)872-1031
Registered: LDA

Employers
Nat'l Legal Aid and Defender Ass'n (Director, Government Relations)

CLARK, Kenneth

1710 H St. NW
Tenth Floor
Washington, DC 20006
EMail: kenneth.e.clark@verizon.com
Tel: (202)392-1444
Fax: (202)659-4948

Employers
Verizon Washington, DC, Inc. (Director, External Affairs)

CLARK, USAF, Col. Leo

1300 Defense Pentagon
Washington, DC 20301-1300
Tel: (703)697-6210
Fax: (703)693-5530

Employers
Department of Defense (Special Assistant for Space, C3I & Special Operations, Office of Legislative Liaison)

CLARK, Louis

1612 K St. NW
Suite 400
Washington, DC 20006
Tel: (202)408-0034
Fax: (202)408-9855

Employers
Government Accountability Project (GAP) (Exec. Director)

CLARK, SSJ, Mary Elizabeth

801 Pennsylvania Ave. SE
Suite 460
Washington, DC 20003
EMail: network@networklobby.org
Tel: (202)547-5556
Fax: (202)547-5510
Registered: LDA

Employers
NETWORK, A Nat'l Catholic Social Justice Lobby (Lobbyist)

CLARK, Michael

1615 H St. NW
Washington, DC 20062-2000
Tel: (202)659-6000
Fax: (202)463-5836

Employers
Chamber of Commerce of the U.S.A. (Exec. Director of the U.S.-India Business Council (USIBC))

CLARK, Michael

1201 Pennsylvania Ave. NW
Suite 300
Washington, DC 20004
Tel: (202)661-4642
Fax: (202)661-4699
Registered: LDA

Employers
Markcorp Inc. (President)

Clients Represented

On Behalf of Markcorp Inc.

Edenspace Systems Corp.
TWK

CLARK, Paul S.

600 New Hampshire Ave. NW
Suite 601
Washington, DC 20037
Tel: (202)333-7400
Fax: (202)333-1638

Spokesperson, Governmental Affairs Committee, U.S. Senate, 1995-98. Director, Communications, Office of Personnel Management, The White House, during the Bush I administration.

Employers

Hill and Knowlton, Inc. (Senior Managing Director, Director of Media Relations)

Clients Represented

On Behalf of Hill and Knowlton, Inc.

Motorola, Inc.

CLARK, Paul T.

1200 G St. NW
Suite 350
Washington, DC 20005
Tel: (202)737-8833
Fax: (202)737-5184
Registered: LDA
EMail: clark@sewkis.com

Legislative Assistant to Rep. Mark W. Hannaford (D-CA), 1976-77.

Employers

Seward & Kissel, LLP (Partner)

Clients Represented

On Behalf of Seward & Kissel, LLP

Merrill Lynch & Co., Inc.

CLARK, Peggy A.

901 E St. NW
Fourth Floor
Washington, DC 20004
Tel: (202)969-8000
Fax: (202)969-8031
Registered: LDA
EMail: peggy.clark@slma.com

Employers

Sallie Mae, Inc. (Director, Government and Industry Relations)

CLARK, Peggy E.

One Dupont Circle NW Suite 700
Washington, DC 20036-1113
Tel: (202)736-5800
Fax: (202)467-0790

Employers

Aspen Institute (Exec. V. President, Policy Programs)

CLARK, Sheila

600 Pennsylvania Ave. SE
Suite 310
Washington, DC 20003
Tel: (202)543-9311
Fax: (202)543-9743
Registered: LDA

Employers

Nat'l Black Women's Health Project (Policy Associate)

CLARK, Thomas R.

919 18th St. NW
Suite 200
Washington, DC 20006
Tel: (202)872-7700
Fax: (202)872-7713
Registered: LDA
EMail: tom_clark@farmermac.com

Counsel, Senate Committee on Agriculture, Nutrition and Forestry, 1981-84, 1987-89; Agricultural Marketing Service (1984-87) and Office of General Counsel (1973-81), Department of Agriculture.

Employers

Federal Agricultural Mortgage Corp. (Farmer Mac) (V. President, Corporate Relations)

CLARK, Todd

2500 Wilson Blvd.
Suite 300
Arlington, VA 22201
Tel: (703)907-7498
Fax: (703)907-7727
EMail: tclark@tia.eia.org

Employers

Telecommunications Industry Ass'n (Director, Trade Show Marketing)

CLARK-SULLIVAN, Esq., Carla

1300 I St. NW
Suite 1090
East Tower
Washington, DC 20005-3314
Tel: (202)962-8690
Fax: (202)962-8699

Employers

American Institute of Chemical Engineers (Legislative Affairs)

CLARKE, Allison

444 N. Capitol St. NW
Suite 201
Washington, DC 20001
Tel: (202)638-0631
Fax: (202)638-2296

Employers

New Jersey, Washington Office of the State of (Associate Director)

CLARKE, Catherine

10801 Rockville Pike
Rockville, MD 20852
Tel: (301)897-5700
Ext: 4182
Fax: (301)571-0457
Registered: LDA

Employers

American Speech, Language, and Hearing Ass'n (Director, Federal Legislation Branch)

CLARKE, Harry

8405 Greensboro Dr.
Suite 100
McLean, VA 22102
Tel: (301)214-6400
Fax: (301)214-6430

Employers

BMC Software (General Manager, Federal Operations)

CLARKE, James B.

700 11th St. NW
Washington, DC 20001-4507
Tel: (202)383-7535
Fax: (202)383-7540
EMail: jclarke@realtors.org

Employers

Nat'l Ass'n of Realtors (Political Representative)

CLARKE, James L.

1575 I St. NW
Washington, DC 20005-1103
Tel: (202)626-2703
Fax: (202)371-1673
Registered: LDA
EMail: jclarke@asaenet.org

Employers

American Soc. of Ass'n Executives (Senior V. President, Public Policy)

CLARKE, Jeanne

1050 17th St. NW
Suite 300
Washington, DC 20036
Tel: (202)296-3390
Fax: (202)296-3399

Employers

Apartment and Office Building Ass'n of Metropolitan Washington (Director, Finance and Membership)

CLARKE, Jr., John O.

1050 17th St. NW
Suite 590
Washington, DC 20036
Tel: (202)296-8500
Fax: (202)296-7143

Employers

Highsaw, Mahoney & Clarke (Partner)

CLARKE, Jonathan G.

1220 16th St. NW
Washington, DC 20036
Tel: (202)659-4608
Fax: (202)785-5178
Registered: LDA

Employers

American Hellenic Institute Public Affairs Committee (Public Affairs Consultant)

CLARKE, Katie

1050 Connecticut Ave. NW
Washington, DC 20036-5339
Tel: (202)857-6000
Fax: (202)857-6395
Registered: LDA

Employers

Arent Fox Kintner Plotkin & Kahn, PLLC (Government Relations Director)

Clients Represented

On Behalf of Arent Fox Kintner Plotkin & Kahn, PLLC

American Academy of Orthotists and Prosthetists
Amputee Coalition
Arthritis Foundation
Bassett Healthcare
Education and Training Resources
Magnitude Information Systems
Ovarian Cancer Nat'l Alliance
Prevent Blindness America
Christopher Reeve Paralysis Foundation

CLARKE, Peggy A.

555 13th St. NW
Suite 500 West
Washington, DC 20004
Tel: (202)383-5300
Fax: (202)383-5414
Registered: LDA
EMail: pclarke@omm.com

Employers

O'Melveny and Myers LLP (Special Counsel)

Clients Represented

On Behalf of O'Melveny and Myers LLP

Coalition for Truth in Environmental Marketing Information, Inc.

CLARKE, Robert L.

2000 K St. NW
Suite 500
Washington, DC 20006-1872
Tel: (202)828-5800
Fax: (202)223-1225

Comptroller of the Currency, Department of Treasury, 1985-92.

Employers

Bracewell & Patterson, L.L.P. (Partner)

CLARKE, Jr., Tim

1902 Association Dr.
Reston, VA 20190
Tel: (703)620-6600
Ext: 207
Fax: (703)620-5873
Registered: LDA

Employers

American Medical Student Ass'n (Director of Public Relations)

CLARKE, Victoria "Torrie"

600 New Hampshire Ave. NW
Suite 601
Washington, DC 20037
Tel: (202)333-7400
Fax: (202)333-1638

Former Assistant to the U.S. Trade Representative, Office of the U.S. Trade Representative, Executive Office of the President, The White House during the Bush I administration. Press Secretary to Senator John McCain (R-AZ), 1988-89. Press Secretary to Rep. McCain, 1984-88. Executive Assistant, Office of Legal Policy, Department of Justice, 1982. Press Aide, Office of the Vice President, The White House, 1981-82.

Employers

Hill and Knowlton, Inc. (General Manager)

CLAUDY, Lynn

1771 N St. NW
Washington, DC 20036-2891
Tel: (202)429-5340
Fax: (202)775-4981

Employers

Nat'l Ass'n of Broadcasters (Senior V. President, Science and Technology)

CLAUSSEN, Eileen

2101 Wilson Blvd.
Suite 550
Arlington, VA 22201
Tel: (703)516-4146
Fax: (703)841-1422

Former Assistant Secretary for Oceans and International Environmental and Scientific Affairs, Department of State.

Employers

Pew Center on Global Climate Change (President)

CLAWSON, James B.

1620 I St. NW
Suite 615
Washington, DC 20006
Tel: (202)463-8493
Fax: (202)463-8497
Registered: LDA

Assistant Secretary General, Customs Cooperation Council, 1977-81. Deputy Assistant Secretary, Office of Enforcement, Operations and Tariff Affairs, Department of the Treasury, 1973-76. White House Policy Council, 1969-72.

Employers
JBC Internat'l (Chief Exec. Officer)
Joint Industry Group (JIG) (Secretariat)
Management Options, Inc.

Clients Represented

On Behalf of JBC Internat'l
Allen-Bradley
The BOSE Corp.
California Ass'n of Winegrape Growers
Coalition for Intellectual Property Rights (CIPR)
DIAGEO
Joint Industry Group (JIG)
Meridian Worldwide
UDV/Heublein, Inc.
Uniroyal Chemical Co., Inc.
Wine Institute

On Behalf of Management Options, Inc.
American Teleservices Ass'n

CLAWSON, Jason B.

1620 I St. NW
Suite 615
Washington, DC 20006
Tel: (202)463-8493
Fax: (202)463-8497
Registered: LDA
EMail: jason@moinc.com

Employers
JBC Internat'l (President and Chief of Staff)
Management Options, Inc.

Clients Represented

On Behalf of JBC Internat'l
Joint Industry Group (JIG)

On Behalf of Management Options, Inc.
American Teleservices Ass'n

CLAY, Angie

901 E St. NW
Fourth Floor
Washington, DC 20004
Tel: (202)969-8023
Fax: (202)969-8030

Employers
Sallie Mae, Inc. (Senior Assistant, Government Relations)

CLAY, Don R.

655 15th St. NW
Suite 445
Washington, DC 20005
EMail: clayd@kochind.com
Tel: (202)737-1977

Employers
Koch Industries, Inc. (Director, Environmental and Regulatory Affairs)

CLAY, Michelle C.

12116 Kerwood Rd.
Silver Spring, MD 20904
Tel: (301)622-5472
Fax: (301)622-5140
Registered: LDA
EMail: mcclay217@aol.com

Employers
Clay and Associates (President)

Clients Represented

On Behalf of Clay and Associates
Lambert-St. Louis Internat'l Airport
St. Louis, Missouri, City of

CLAY, Sonya C.

700 13th St. NW
Suite 400
Washington, DC 20005
Tel: (202)347-0773
Fax: (202)347-0785
Registered: LDA
EMail: sclay@cassidy.com
Former Legislative Director and Deputy Chief of Staff to Rep. Barbara Lee (D-CA). Former Staff Member to Reps. Steny Hoyer (D-MD), Jose E. Serrano (D-NY) and Glen Browder (D-AL).

Employers
Cassidy & Associates, Inc. (Associate)

Clients Represented

On Behalf of Cassidy & Associates, Inc.
Barry University
El Segundo, California, City of
Jewish Family Service Ass'n of Cleveland
Rush Presbyterian-St. Luke's Medical Center

CLAYBROOK, Joan B.

1600 20th St. NW
Washington, DC 20009
Tel: (202)588-1000
Fax: (202)588-7799
Registered: LDA

Employers
Public Citizen, Inc. (President)

CLAYTON, Carol

2445 M St. NW
Washington, DC 20037-1420
Tel: (202)663-6000
Fax: (202)663-6363
Registered: LDA
EMail: cclayton@wilmer.com

Employers
Wilmer, Cutler & Pickering (Associate)

CLAYTON, Jack

P.O. Box 1222
Sterling, VA 20167
Tel: (703)379-9188

Employers
Council of Volunteer Americans (V. President)

CLAYTON, Joseph

1825 Connecticut Ave. NW
Fifth Floor
Washington, DC 20009
EMail: joseph.clayton@widmeyer.com
Tel: (202)667-0901
Fax: (202)667-0902
Former aide to Senator Alan Dixon (D-IL).

Employers
Widmeyer Communications, Inc. (President and Chief Operating Officer)

CLAYTON, Kenneth J.

1120 Connecticut Ave. NW
Washington, DC 20036
Tel: (202)663-5000
Fax: (202)828-4548
Registered: LDA

Employers
American Bankers Ass'n (Chief Legislative Counsel)

CLEARY, Carrie

1050 17th St. NW
Suite 701
Washington, DC 20036
Tel: (202)289-5850
Registered: LDA

Employers
Nat'l Campaign for Hearing Health (Deputy Director)

CLEARY, Patrick J.

1331 Pennsylvania Ave. NW
Sixth Floor
Washington, DC 20004-1790
Tel: (202)637-3131
Fax: (202)637-3182
Registered: LDA
EMail: pcleary@nam.org

Employers
Nat'l Ass'n of Manufacturers (V. President, Human Resources Policy)

CLEARY, Peter

1010 Wisconsin Ave. NW
Ninth Floor
Washington, DC 20007
Tel: (202)337-9400
Fax: (202)337-4508

Employers
Grocery Manufacturers of America (Manager, Public Policy Communications)

CLEMANS, Kathryn B.

1001 Pennsylvania Ave. NW
Suite 1275
Washington, DC 20004
Tel: (202)624-2895
Fax: (202)628-5116
Registered: LDA

Employers
C&M Internat'l, Ltd. (Director)

Clients Represented

On Behalf of C&M Internat'l, Ltd.
Novartis Corp.
Oracle Corp.

CLEMENTS, Bill

1299 Pennsylvania Ave. NW
Suite 1100 West
Washington, DC 20004-2407
Tel: (202)637-4000
Fax: (202)637-4300
Registered: LDA

Employers
General Electric Co. (Senior Manager, International Trade Regulation)

CLEMENTS, Ronald

701 Pennsylvania Ave. NW
Washington, DC 20004-2696
Tel: (202)508-5471
Fax: (202)508-5403
Registered: LDA

Employers
Edison Electric Institute (Director, Governmental Affairs)

CLEMENTS, Tom

1000 Connecticut Ave. NW
Suite 804
Washington, DC 20036
EMail: clements@nci.org
Tel: (202)822-8444
Fax: (202)452-0892

Employers
Nuclear Control Institute (Exec. Director)

CLEMMER, Elizabeth

601 E St. NW
Washington, DC 20049
Tel: (202)434-3910
Fax: (202)434-6402
EMail: eclemmer@aarp.org

Employers
AARP (American Ass'n of Retired Persons) (Associate Director, Public Policy Institute)

CLERIHUE, Randy J.

1000 Massachusetts Ave. NW
Washington, DC 20001
Tel: (202)842-0200
Fax: (202)842-3490

Employers
Cato Institute (Director, Public Affairs)

CLEVELAND, Nancy

9455 Silver King Ct.
Fairfax, VA 22031
Tel: (703)385-7133
Fax: (703)385-7137

Employers
LC Technologies (Medical Coordinator)

CLICK, Joseph O.

600 New Hampshire Ave. NW
11th Floor
Washington, DC 20037
Tel: (202)944-3000
Fax: (202)944-3068
Registered: LDA, FARA
EMail: joc@dejlaw.com

Employers
Dyer Ellis & Joseph, P.C. (Partner)

Clients Represented

On Behalf of Dyer Ellis & Joseph, P.C.
China Shipping (Group) Co.
TI Group Inc.

CLIMER, Jerome F.

316 Pennsylvania Ave. SE
Suite 403
Washington, DC 20003
EMail: change_leader@conginst.org
Tel: (202)547-4600
Fax: (202)547-3556

Employers
Congressional Institute, Inc. (President)

CLIMO, Beth L.

1120 Connecticut Ave. NW
Washington, DC 20036
Tel: (202)663-5000
Fax: (202)828-4546
Registered: LDA

Employers
American Bankers Ass'n (Exec. Director, ABA Securities Association and ABA Insurance Association)

CLINE, John A.

2099 Pennsylvania Ave. NW
Suite 850
Washington, DC 20006
Tel: (202)419-2500
Fax: (202)419-2510
Registered: LDA
EMail: cline@accgrep.com
Former Associate Administrator, Federal Transit Administration; Director, Office of Congressional Affairs, Department of Transportation; and Special Assistant to the President for Intergovernmental Affairs, The White House during the Bush I administration.

Employers
American Continental Group, Inc. (Consultant, Government Relations)

Clients Represented

On Behalf of American Continental Group, Inc.
Ass'n of American Railroads
Coalition for Travel Industry Parity
Colorado Intermountain Fixed Guideway Authority
Los Angeles County Metropolitan Transportation Authority
Martin Color-Fi
OSI Systems, Inc.
Southeastern Pennsylvania Transit Authority
Tri-County Commuter Rail Authority
Trifinery, Inc.

CLINE, Michael P.

1219 Prince St.
Alexandria, VA 22314
Tel: (703)519-3846
Fax: (703)519-3849
Registered: LDA
EMail: eangus@eangus.org

Employers
Enlisted Ass'n of the Nat'l Guard of the United States (Exec. Director/Chief Exec. Officer)
The Military Coalition (Co-Chairman)

CLINE, Tim

1400 16th St. NW
Suite 320
Washington, DC 20036
Tel: (202)332-2200
Fax: (202)332-2302

Employers
Zero Population Growth, Inc. (Director, Communications)

CLINKENBEARD, Kirk L.

P.O. Box 2204
Washington, DC 20013
Tel: (202)628-9774
Fax: (202)628-9776
Registered: LDA

Employers
Westerly Group (President)

Clients Represented

On Behalf of Westerly Group
Microcosm, Inc.
Sunset Properties, Inc.
Western Resources

CLINTON, Kate

1600 21st St. NW
Washington, DC 20009-1090
Tel: (202)387-2151
Fax: (202)387-2436

Employers
The Phillips Collection (Director, Development)

CLINTON, Larry

1401 H St. NW
Suite 600
Washington, DC 20005-2136
Tel: (202)326-7300
Fax: (202)326-7333
EMail: Lclinton@usta.org

Employers
United States Telecom Ass'n (V. President, Large Company Affairs)

CLINTON, Walter

1350 Connecticut Ave. NW
Suite 1102
Washington, DC 20036
Tel: (202)223-4747
Fax: (202)223-4245
EMail: wallyc@ccicorporate.com

Employers
The Clinton Group (President)

CLINTON, William J.

601 13th St. NW
Suite 600 South
Washington, DC 20005
Tel: (202)626-3600
Fax: (202)639-9355
EMail: clintwi@washdc.whitecase.com

Employers
White & Case LLP (Partner)

Clients Represented

On Behalf of White & Case LLP
Malaysia Ministry of Trade
Singapore, Embassy of the Republic of
Singapore, Government of the Republic of
Thailand, Department of Foreign Trade of

CLOHERTY, William M.

3211 Tennyson St. NW
Washington, DC 20015-2429
Tel: (202)966-0732
Fax: (202)363-1801
Registered: LDA

Staff Member, Office of the U.S. Trade Representative, Exec. Office of the President, The White House, 1979.

Employers
Boston University
Self-employed as an independent consultant.

Clients Represented

As an independent consultant
Alliance for the Prudent Use of Antibiotics (APUA)
Atom Sciences, Inc.
Burstein Laboratories, Inc.
First Scientific Corp.
Incyte Pharmaceuticals, Inc.
Lackawanna Junior College
Nat'l Bureau of Asian Research

CLOUD, Deborah

2519 Connecticut Ave. NW
Washington, DC 20008-1520
Tel: (202)783-2242
Fax: (202)783-2255

Employers
American Ass'n of Homes and Services for the Aging (V. President, Communications)

CLOUD, Stephen J.

1220 L St. NW
Washington, DC 20005
Tel: (202)682-8413
Fax: (202)682-8232
Registered: LDA

Employers
American Petroleum Institute (Legislative Research Manager)

CLOW, Byron B.

6731 Whittier Ave.
Suite C-100
McLean, VA 22101
Tel: (703)442-8888
Fax: (703)821-1824
EMail: ima@bellatlantic.net

Employers
Internat'l Magnesium Ass'n (Exec. V. President)

CLOWER, W. Dewey

1199 N. Fairfax St.
Suite 801
Alexandria, VA 22314
Tel: (703)549-2100
Fax: (703)684-4525
Registered: LDA

Employers
NATSO, Inc. (President)

CLUBB, Caryl L.

1340 Braddock Place
Sixth Floor
Alexandria, VA 22314-1651
Tel: (703)325-9471

Employers
Department of Defense - Defense Security Service (Chief, Office of Congressional and Public Affairs)

CLUNE, Dennis M.

505 Hampton Park Blvd.
Suite D
Capitol Heights, MD 20743
Tel: (301)324-3966
Fax: (301)324-3969
EMail: den@usbasics.org

Employers
U.S. Basic Skills (Chief Operating Officer)

CLUSEN, Chuck

1200 New York Ave. NW
Suite 400
Washington, DC 20005
Tel: (202)289-6868
Fax: (202)289-1060

Employers
Natural Resources Defense Council (Senior Policy Analyst)

COAN, Jr., Carl A. S.

1100 Connecticut Ave. NW
Suite 1000
Washington, DC 20036
Tel: (202)728-1070
Fax: (202)293-2448
Registered: LDA

Assistant General Counsel (1968-69) and Attorney (1958-69), Department of Housing and Urban Development.

Employers
Coan & Lyons (Partner)

Clients Represented

On Behalf of Coan & Lyons
Akron Tower Housing Partnership
Coalition for Affordable Housing Preservation
Hempstead, New York, Village of
Presidential Towers, Ltd.
Public Housing Authorities Directors Ass'n
State Street Development Co. of Boston
Weinberg Investments, Inc.

COAN, III, Carl A. S.

1100 Connecticut Ave. NW
Suite 1000
Washington, DC 20036
Tel: (202)728-1070
Fax: (202)293-2448
Registered: LDA

Employers
Coan & Lyons (Partner)

Clients Represented

On Behalf of Coan & Lyons
Public Housing Authorities Directors Ass'n

COATES, Jr., Vincent J.

1730 M St. NW
Suite 911
Washington, DC 20036
Tel: (202)293-4762
Fax: (202)659-5760
Registered: LDA

Employers
Kimmitt, Coates & McCarthy (President)

Clients Represented

On Behalf of Kimmitt, Coates & McCarthy
Absaroka Trust
Alliant Techsystems, Inc.
MSE, Inc.

COATS, Hon. Daniel R.

901 15th St. NW
Suite 700
Washington, DC 20005-2301
Tel: (202)371-6000
Fax: (202)371-6279
Registered: LDA
EMail: drcoats@verner.com

Member, U.S. Senate (R-IN), 1989-99. Member, U.S. House of Representatives (R-IN), 1981-89.

Employers
Verner, Liipfert, Bernhard, McPherson and Hand, Chartered (Special Counsel)

Clients Represented

On Behalf of Verner, Liipfert, Bernhard, McPherson and Hand, Chartered
Amgen
Nat'l Heritage Foundation
Pharmaceutical Research and Manufacturers of America
Polycistic Kidney Disease Foundation
United Defense, L.P.

COBB, Antoine P.

401 Ninth St. NW
Suite 1000
Washington, DC 20004
Tel: (202)274-2906
Fax: (202)274-2994
Registered: LDA

Employers
Troutman Sanders LLP (Associate)

COBB, Robert

1199 N. Fairfax St.
Suite 1000
Alexandria, VA 22314
Tel: (703)299-4499
Fax: (703)299-4488
EMail: bcobb@hawthorngroup.com

Employers
The Hawthorn Group, L.C. (Managing Principal, Hawthorn Southeast)

COBB, Ty

555 13th St. NW
Washington, DC 20004-1109
Tel: (202)637-5600
Fax: (202)637-5910

Employers
Hogan & Hartson L.L.P.

Clients Represented

On Behalf of Hogan & Hartson L.L.P.
Medtronic, Inc.

COBERT, Ronald N.

1730 M St. NW
Suite 400
Washington, DC 20036
Tel: (202)296-2900
Fax: (202)296-1370

Employers
American Institute for Shippers' Ass'ns (General Counsel)
Grove, Jaskiewicz, and Cobert (Partner)

Clients Represented
On Behalf of Grove, Jaskiewicz, and Cobert
American Institute for Shippers' Ass'ns

COBURN, David H.

1330 Connecticut Ave. NW
Washington, DC 20036-1795
Tel: (202)429-3000
Fax: (202)429-3902
Registered: LDA

Employers
Steptoe & Johnson LLP (Partner)

Clients Represented
On Behalf of Steptoe & Johnson LLP
Coach USA

COCHETTI, Roger J.

505 Huntmar Park Dr.
Herndon, VA 20170
Tel: (703)742-0400
Registered: LDA

Employers
VeriSign/Network Solutions, Inc.

COCHRAN, Barbara

1000 Connecticut Ave. NW
Suite 615
Washington, DC 20036-5302
Tel: (202)659-6510
Fax: (202)223-4007
Registered: LDA
EMail: barbarac@rtnda.org

Employers
Radio-Television News Directors Ass'n (President)

COCHRAN, J. Thomas

1620 I St. NW
Suite 400
Washington, DC 20006
Tel: (202)293-7330
Fax: (202)293-2352

Employers
United States Conference of Mayors (Exec. Director)

COCHRAN, Martha L.

555 12th St. NW
Washington, DC 20004-1206
Tel: (202)942-5228
Fax: (202)942-5999
Registered: LDA
EMail: Martha_Cochran@aporter.com
Chief Counsel and Staff Director, Subcommittee on Securities, Senate Committee on Banking, Housing and Urban Affairs, 1989-94. Legislative Director and Senior Domestic Policy Advisor to Senator Christopher Dodd (D-CT), 1987-89. Senior Finance Counsel, Subcommittee on Telecommunications, Consumer Protection and Finance, House Committee on Energy and Commerce, 1981-87. Attorney and Special Counsel, Division of Enforcement, Securities and Exchange Commission, 1975-81.

Employers
Arnold & Porter (Partner)

Clients Represented
On Behalf of Arnold & Porter
Bruce Vladek
Consolidated Administration and Security Services, Inc.
First Savings Bank, F.S.B.
Greenwich Capital Markets, Inc.
Metropolitan Mortgage and Securities, Inc.
PaineWebber Group, Inc.
Quebecor World (USA) Inc.
Roxanne Laboratories, Inc.
State Farm Insurance Cos.
U.S. Investigations Services
Waste Control Specialists, Inc.

COCHRAN, Thomas B.

1200 New York Ave. NW
Suite 400
Washington, DC 20005
Tel: (202)289-6868
Fax: (202)289-1060

Employers
Natural Resources Defense Council (Senior Scientist)

COCO, Jr., Leo

1001 Pennsylvania Ave. NW
Suite 600
Washington, DC 20004
Tel: (202)347-0066
Fax: (202)624-7222
Former Deputy Assistant Secretary for Intergovernmental and Corporate Affairs, Department of Education. Chief of Staff to Rep. Lloyd Doggett (D-TX), 1995-99. Floor Assistant to the Chief Deputy Whip, Rep. Butler Derrick (D-SC), 1991-95. Staff Director, Subcommittee on Legislative Process, House Committee on Rules and Administrative Assistant to Rep. Derrick, 1985-91. Special Assistant to Rlep. Gillis Long (D-LA), 1977-84.

Employers
Powell, Goldstein, Frazer & Murphy LLP (Senior Policy Advisor)

CODD, Bernard P.

600 13th St. NW
Washington, DC 20005-3096
Tel: (202)756-8000
Fax: (202)756-8087
EMail: bcodd@mwe.com
Patent Examiner, Patent and Trademark Office, 1993-2000.

Employers
McDermott, Will and Emery (Associate)

CODDING, Faye

122 C St. NW
Suite 125
Washington, DC 20001
Tel: (202)783-7507
Fax: (202)783-7502
EMail: faye.codding@ecunet.org

Employers
Lutheran Office for Governmental Affairs/Evangelical Lutheran Church in America (Assistant Director)

CODDING, Fred H.

10382 Main St.
Suite 200
P.O. Box 280
Fairfax, VA 22030
Tel: (703)591-1870
Fax: (703)591-1895

Employers
Nat'l Ass'n of Miscellaneous, Ornamental and Architectural Products Contractors
Nat'l Ass'n of Reinforcing Steel Contractors (Exec. Director and General Counsel)

CODY, Ann E.

805 15th St. NW
Suite 700
Washington, DC 20005
Tel: (202)312-7400
Fax: (202)312-7441
Registered: LDA
EMail: aecody@bakerd.com

Employers
Sagamore Associates, Inc. (V. President)

Clients Represented
On Behalf of Sagamore Associates, Inc.
Indianapolis Neighborhood Housing Partnership
Recreation Vehicle Industry Ass'n
Shake-A-Leg
U.S. Olympic Committee

CODY, Ph.D., George T.

2213 M St. NW
Third Floor
Washington, DC 20037
Tel: (202)223-9333
Fax: (202)223-1399

Employers
American Task Force for Lebanon (Exec. Director)

COE, Bonnie L.

910 17th St. NW
Tenth Floor
Washington, DC 20006
Tel: (202)778-4999
Fax: (202)463-7241
EMail: blcoe@acus.org

Employers
Atlantic Council of the United States (Director, Atlantic-Pacific Interrelationships Program)

COE, Jo-Anne

901 15th St. NW
Suite 700
Washington, DC 20005-2301
Tel: (202)371-6000
Fax: (202)371-6279
Registered: FARA

Employers
Verner, Liipfert, Bernhard, McPherson and Hand, Chartered (Strategic Planner)

COEN, Amy

1300 19th St. NW
Second Floor
Washington, DC 20036
Tel: (202)557-3400
Fax: (202)728-4177

Employers
Population Action Internat'l (President)

COFER, Jr., Williston B.

4001 Pine Brook Rd.
Alexandria, VA 22310
Tel: (703)960-2331
Fax: (703)960-4611
Registered: LDA
EMail: wilcofer@erols.com
Senior Professional Staff Member (1992-93) and Professional Staff Member (1977-92), Subcommittee on Readiness, House Committee on Armed Services. Team Leader, House Committee on Appropriations, 1974-77. Auditor, General Accounting Office, 1965-74.

Employers
Will Cofer Associates (President)

Clients Represented
On Behalf of Will Cofer Associates
Gino Morena Enterprises

COFFEE, Roy C.

1666 K St. NW
Suite 500
Washington, DC 20006-2803
Tel: (202)887-1400
Fax: (202)466-2198
Registered: LDA

Employers
O'Connor & Hannan, L.L.P. (Partner)

Clients Represented
On Behalf of O'Connor & Hannan, L.L.P.
Amgen
Associated Credit Bureaus, Inc.
BellSouth Corp.
California Tax Credit Allocation Committee
Celera Genomics
Nuclear Energy Institute
Sempra Energy
St. Croix Chippewa Indians of Wisconsin
U.S. Central Credit Union
UBS Warburg
VISA U.S.A., Inc.

COFFEY, Jr., Alan F.

1800 M. St. NW
Washington, DC 20004
Tel: (202)467-7873
Registered: LDA
Staff Director and General Counsel (1995-97) and Minority Chief Counsel (1983-95), House Judiciary Committee. Deputy General Counsel, Department of Housing and Urban Development, 1981-83. Minority Counsel, Subcommittee on Administrative Law and Government Relations, House Judiciary Committee, 1974-81. Legislative Assistant to Rep. Hamilton Fish (R-NY), 1970-74. Assistant for Congressional Relations (1969-70) and Program Analyst (1967-68), Department of Housing and Urban Development.

Employers
Self-employed as an independent consultant.

Clients Represented
As an independent consultant
American Insurance Ass'n

COFFEY, Matthew B.

9300 Livingston Rd.
Fort Washington, MD 20744
Tel: (301)248-6200
Fax: (301)248-7104
EMail: matt@ntma.org

Employers
Nat'l Tooling and Machining Ass'n (President and Chief Operating Officer)

COFFEY, Nancy

2000 L St. NW
Suite 300
Washington, DC 20036-0646
Tel: (202)835-8800
Fax: (202)835-8879
EMail: nancy.coffey@ketchum.com
Former Deputy Assistant Secretary, Public Affiars, Department of Labor during the Clinton administration and Director, Communications to Sen. Howard M. Metzenbaum (D-OH).

Employers
Ketchum (Senior V. President, Media Relations)

COFFEY, Tiffany

1016 16th St. NW
Suite 300
Washington, DC 20036
Tel: (202)862-4400
Fax: (202)862-4432

Employers
Nat'l Federation of Federal Employees (Dir. of Publications & Public Relations)

COFFIELD, Ashley

1233 20th St. NW
Suite 200
Washington, DC 20036
Tel: (202)833-0009
Fax: (202)833-0113

Employers
Partnership for Prevention (Projects Manager)

COFFIN, Jane

1120 20th St. NW
Suite 1000
Washington, DC 20036
Tel: (202)457-2280
Fax: (202)457-2571

Employers
AT&T (Director, International Affairs)

COGAN, Phillip S.

2175 K St. NW
Suite 400
Washington, DC 20037-1809
EMail: phil.cogan@csb.gov
Tel: (202)261-7650
Fax: (202)261-7650

Employers
Chemical Safety and Hazard Investigation Board (Deputy Director, Congressional and Public Affairs)

COGDELL, Martha L.

Commonwealth Towers
1300 Wilson Blvd., Suite 200
Arlington, VA 22209-2307
EMail: mlcogdel@collins.rockwell.com
Tel: (703)516-8227
Fax: (703)516-8295
Registered: LDA

Employers
Rockwell Collins (Director, Federal and State Government Relations)

COHEN, Abba

1730 Rhode Island Ave. NW
Suite 504
Washington, DC 20036
Tel: (202)835-0414
Fax: (202)835-0424

Employers
Agudath Israel of America (Director and Counsel, Washington Office)

COHEN, Ariel

214 Massachusetts Ave. NE
Washington, DC 20002
Tel: (202)546-4400
Fax: (202)546-8328

Employers
Heritage Foundation (Senior Policy Analyst, Russian and Eurasion Affairs)

COHEN, Arthur

P.O. Box 2626
Washington, DC 20013
Tel: (703)998-2600
Fax: (703)998-3401

Employers
WETA (Senior V. President for Radio)

COHEN, Barry E.

1001 Pennsylvania Ave. NW
Suite 1100
Washington, DC 20004-2595
Tel: (202)624-2500
Fax: (202)628-5116
Registered: FARA

Served in the Office of the Assistant General Counsel for International Affairs, Department of Defense, 1971-73.

Employers
Crowell & Moring LLP (Partner)

Clients Represented
On Behalf of Crowell & Moring LLP
The Feldspar Corp.

COHEN, Bob

1401 Wilson Blvd.
Suite 1100
Arlington, VA 22209
EMail: bcohen@itaa.org
Tel: (703)522-5055
Fax: (703)525-2279

Employers
Information Technology Ass'n of America (ITAA) (Senior V. President, Communications)

COHEN, Bruce

200 Constitution Ave. NW
Washington, DC 20210
Tel: (202)219-8101
Fax: (202)501-2583

Employers
Department of Labor - Solicitor (Deputy Associate Solicitor, Legislative and Legal Counsel)

COHEN, Calman J.

1211 Connecticut Ave. NW
Suite 801
Washington, DC 20036
Tel: (202)659-5147
Fax: (202)659-1347
Registered: LDA

Employers
Emergency Committee for American Trade (President)

COHEN, Catherine Grealy

1101 Vermont Ave. NW
Suite 700
Washington, DC 20005
EMail: cgcohen@aaodc.org
Tel: (202)737-6662
Fax: (202)737-7061
Registered: LDA

Employers
American Academy of Ophthamology - Office of Federal Affairs (V. President, Governmental Affairs Division)

COHEN, Cecily

1101 Connecticut Ave. NW
Suite 910
Washington, DC 20036
Tel: (202)887-1798
Fax: (202)887-0432
Registered: LDA

Employers
NOKIA

COHEN, Dan

1050 31st St. NW
Washington, DC 20007
Tel: (202)965-3500
Fax: (202)342-5484
Registered: LDA

Employers
Ass'n of Trial Lawyers of America (Director, National Affairs)

COHEN, Daniel L.

1801 K St. NW
Washington, DC 20006
EMail: dcohen@arterhadden.com
Tel: (202)775-7100
Fax: (202)857-0172
Registered: LDA, FARA

Employers
Arter & Hadden (Principal)

Clients Represented
On Behalf of Arter & Hadden
American Koyo Corp.
Americans for Fair Taxation
Ass'n for Responsible Thermal Treatment
Billing Concepts, Inc.
BKK Corp.
Cellular Telecommunications and Internet Ass'n
Centerior Energy Corp.
Circus Circus Enterprises, Inc.
Citigroup
Edison Electric Institute
Envirocare of Utah, Inc.
Federated Investors, Inc.
HCA Healthcare Corp.
Hicks, Muse, Tate & Furst
LCOR, Inc.
Metabolife
OnCare, Inc.
Sammons Enterprises, Inc.
SBC Communications Inc.
Thunderbird, The American Graduate School of Internat'l Management
H. B. Zachry

COHEN, Daniel M.

317 Massachusetts Ave. NE
Suite 300
Washington, DC 20002
Tel: (202)789-3960
Fax: (202)789-1813

Employers
The Cuneo Law Group, P.C. (Attorney)

COHEN, David

1629 K St. NW
Suite 200
Washington, DC 20006-1629
EMail: info@advocacy.org
Tel: (202)777-7575
Fax: (202)777-7577

Employers
The Advocacy Institute (Co-Director)

COHEN, David B.

1401 H St. NW
Suite 600
Washington, DC 20005-2136
EMail: dcohen@usta.org
Tel: (202)326-7300
Fax: (202)326-7333

Employers
United States Telecom Ass'n (V. President, Small Company Affairs)

COHEN, David S.

1055 Thomas Jefferson St. NW
Suite 504
Washington, DC 20007
EMail: dcohen@cohenmohr.com
Tel: (202)342-2550
Fax: (202)342-6147
Registered: LDA

Employers
Cohen Mohr LLP (Partner)

Clients Represented
On Behalf of Cohen Mohr LLP
Computer and Communications Industry Ass'n (CCIA)

COHEN, Edward

955 L'Enfant Plaza SW
Suite 5300
Washington, DC 20024
Tel: (202)554-1650
Fax: (202)488-3542

Employers
Honda North America, Inc. (V. President, Govt. and Industry Relations)

COHEN, Edwin S.

1201 Pennsylvania Ave. NW
Washington, DC 20004-2401
EMail: ecohen@cov.com
Tel: (202)662-6000
Fax: (202)662-6291

Under Secretary (1972-73) and Assistant Secretary (1969-1972), Department of Treasury. Member, Advisory Group to the Commissioner, Internal Revenue Service, Department of Treasury, 1967-68. Staff member and Counsel, Advisory Group on Corporate Taxes, Ways and Means Committee, U.S. House of Representatives, 1956-58.

Employers
Covington & Burling (Senior Counsel)

COHEN, George H.

1000 Connecticut Ave. NW
Suite 1300
Washington, DC 20036
Tel: (202)842-2600
Fax: (202)842-1888

Appellate Court Litigation Attorney (1963-66) and Attorney-Advisor (1960-63), National Labor Relations Board.

Employers
Bredhoff & Kaiser (Partner)

Clients Represented
On Behalf of Bredhoff & Kaiser
Major League Baseball Players Ass'n

COHEN, Gerry

1825 Connecticut Ave. NW
Fifth Floor
Washington, DC 20009
Tel: (202)667-0901
Fax: (202)667-0902

Employers
Widmeyer Communications, Inc. (Senior Counsel)

COHEN, H. Rodgin

1701 Pennsylvania Ave. NW
Suite 800
Washington, DC 20006
Tel: (202)956-7500
Fax: (202)293-6330
Registered: LDA

Employers
Sullivan & Cromwell (Partner)

Clients Represented
On Behalf of Sullivan & Cromwell
First Union Corp.
Goldman, Sachs and Co.
Morgan Guaranty Trust Co.

COHEN, Harrison J.

1666 K St. NW
Suite 800
Washington, DC 20006
Tel: (202)481-7000
Fax: (202)862-7098
Registered: LDA

Employers
Arthur Andersen LLP (National Director)

Clients Represented

On Behalf of Arthur Andersen LLP
UtiliCorp United, Inc.

COHEN, Herman J.

1621 N. Kent St.
Suite 1619
Arlington, VA 22209
Tel: (703)516-9510
Fax: (703)516-4547
Registered: LDA, FARA
EMail: ambcohen@cohenandwoods.com
Former Assistant Secretary for Africa, Department of State.

Employers
Cohen and Woods Internat'l, Inc. (President)
Denison, Scott and Cohen (Partner)

Clients Represented

On Behalf of Cohen and Woods Internat'l, Inc.
Angola, Government of the Republic of
Burkina Faso, Government of
Zimbabwe, Republic of

On Behalf of Denison, Scott and Cohen
The Friends of Democratic Congo

COHEN, Howard J.

800 Connecticut Ave. NW
Suite 500
Washington, DC 20006
Tel: (202)331-3103
Fax: (202)331-3101
Registered: LDA
EMail: cohenh@gtlaw.com
Counsel, House Committee on Commerce, 1988-99.

Employers
Greenberg Traurig, LLP (Shareholder)

Clients Represented

On Behalf of Greenberg Traurig, LLP
American Ass'n of Health Plans (AAHP)
American Soc. of Anesthesiologists
Amgen
Baxter Healthcare Corp.
Community Health Systems, Inc.
Deloitte Consulting
Fresenius Medical Care North America
Healtheon/Web MD
Humana Inc.
LifePoint Hospitals, Inc.
Merck & Co.
Nat'l Ass'n of Community Health Centers
Nat'l Center for Genome Research
Pharmaceutical Research and Manufacturers of America
PHP Healthcare Corp.
Province Healthcare, Inc.

COHEN, Irving P.

1920 N St. NW
Washington, DC 20036
Tel: (202)331-8800
Fax: (202)331-8330
EMail: icohen@thf.com

Employers
Thompson, Hine and Flory LLP (Partner)

COHEN, Irwin

801 Pennsylvania Ave. NW
Washington, DC 20004-2604
Tel: (202)662-4679
Fax: (202)662-4643
EMail: icohen@fulbright.com
Attorney Advisor to the Administrator and Deputy Director of Program Integrity, Health Care Financing Administration, Department of Health and Human Services, 1982-85. Member Health Care Financing Administratiion, 1968-82. Agent, Internal Revenue Service, Department of the Treasury, 1963-68.

Employers
Fulbright & Jaworski L.L.P. (Partner)

COHEN, Jacqueline

1128 16th St. NW
Washington, DC 20036-4802
Tel: (202)463-2124
Fax: (202)467-0559
Registered: LDA
EMail: jackiec@awmanet.org
Legislative Assistant to Senator Arlen Specter (R-PA), 1981-82. Legislative Assistant to Senator Jacob K. Javits (R-NY), 1969-80.

Employers
American Wholesale Marketers Ass'n (V. President, Government and Industry Affairs)

COHEN, Jay Gordon

1333 New Hampshire Ave. NW
Suite 400
Washington, DC 20036
Tel: (202)887-4000
Fax: (202)887-4288
EMail: jcohen@akingump.com

Employers
Akin, Gump, Strauss, Hauer & Feld, L.L.P. (Partner)

COHEN, Jeffrey E.

801 Pennsylvania Ave. NW
Suite 245
Washington, DC 20004-2604
Tel: (202)624-1520
Fax: (202)737-6462
Registered: LDA
EMail: jcohen@americashospitals.com
Senior Legislative Assistant to Rep. Karen Thurman (D-FL), 1995-2000.

Employers
Federation of American Hospitals (Assistant V. President, Legislation)

COHEN, John L.

801 Pennsylvania Ave. NW
Suite 310
Washington, DC 20004
Tel: (202)434-8150
Fax: (202)434-8156
Registered: LDA

Employers
GPU, Inc. (Manager, Government Affairs)

COHEN, Jonathan A.

1625 Massachusetts Ave. NW
Washington, DC 20036
Tel: (202)797-4033
Fax: (202)797-4030

Employers
Air Line Pilots Ass'n Internat'l (Director, Legal Department)

COHEN, Jonathan V.

2300 N St. NW
Suite 700
Washington, DC 20037-1128
Tel: (202)783-4141
Fax: (202)783-5851
EMail: joncohen@wbklaw.com
Former Associate Chief, Wireless Telecommunications Bureau, Assistant Chief, Mass Media Bureau, Senior Counsel, Office of Pans and Policy, and Special Assistant to the Chairman, all at the Federal Communications Commission. Assistant Counsel to the President, The White House, during the Clinton administration.

Employers
Wilkinson, Barker and Knauer, LLP (Partner)

Clients Represented

On Behalf of Wilkinson, Barker and Knauer, LLP
Wireless Communications Ass'n

COHEN, M.D., Jordan J.

2450 N St. NW
Washington, DC 20037-1126
Tel: (202)828-0400
Fax: (202)828-1125

Employers
Ass'n of American Medical Colleges (President)

COHEN, Laurence J.

1125 15th St. NW
Suite 801
Washington, DC 20005
Tel: (202)785-9300
Fax: (202)775-1950
Alternate Member, Chairman's Task Force (1976-77) and Legal Assistant and Supervising Attorney (1964-67), National Labor Relations Board.

Employers
Sherman, Dunn, Cohen, Leifer & Yellig, P.C. (Partner)

Clients Represented

On Behalf of Sherman, Dunn, Cohen, Leifer & Yellig, P.C.
Internat'l Brotherhood of Electrical Workers

COHEN, Mary

370 L'Enfant Promenade SW
Fifth Floor
Washington, DC 20447
Tel: (202)401-5175
Fax: (202)401-4562
EMail: mcohen@acf.dhhs.gov

Employers
Department of Health and Human Services - Administration for Children and Families (Director, Legislative and Regulatory Affairs Division)

COHEN, N. Jerold

1275 Pennsylvania Ave. NW
Washington, DC 20004-2415
Tel: (202)383-0100
Fax: (202)637-3593

Employers
Sutherland Asbill & Brennan LLP (Partner)

COHEN, Neal M.

1615 L St. NW
Suite 900
Washington, DC 20036
Tel: (202)778-1000
Fax: (202)466-6002
EMail: ncohen@apcoworldwide.com

Employers
APCO Worldwide (Exec. V. President and Managing Director, APCO US)

COHEN, Rick

2001 S St. NW
Suite 620
Washington, DC 20009
Tel: (202)387-9177
Fax: (202)332-5084

Employers
Nat'l Committee for Responsive Philanthropy (President)

COHEN, Rita D.

1211 Connecticut Ave. NW
Suite 610
Washington, DC 20036
Tel: (202)296-7277
Fax: (202)296-0343
Registered: LDA

Employers
Magazine Publishers of America (Senior V. President, Legislative and Regulatory Policy)

COHEN, Robert R.

1225 I St. NW
Suite 500
Washington, DC 20005
Tel: (202)312-2010
Fax: (202)785-2649

Employers
SCC Communications Corp. (Vice President, Government Relations)

COHEN, Roberta

1775 Massachusetts Ave. NW
Washington, DC 20036-2188
Tel: (202)797-6000
Fax: (202)797-6004
Public Member, U.S. Delegation to United Nations Commission on Human Rights, 1998; former Deputy Assistant Secretary for Human Rights and Senior Advisor to U.S. Delegation to United Nations, Department of State.

Employers
The Brookings Institution (Guest Scholar, Foreign Policy Studies)

COHEN, Roger

1301 Pennsylvania Ave. NW
Suite 1100
Washington, DC 20004-1707
Tel: (202)626-4000
Fax: (202)628-0707

Employers
Air Transport Ass'n of America (Managing Director, State Government Affairs)

COHEN, Scott

1801 N. Herndon St.
Arlington, VA 22201-5209
Tel: (703)527-0425
Fax: (703)524-2665
Former Foreign Affairs Advisor to Senator Charles H. Percy (R-IL); former Spokesman and Staff Director, Senate Foreign Relations Committee; and former officer, Central Intelligence Agency.

Employers
Self-employed as an independent consultant.

Clients Represented

As an independent consultant
Federation of American Scientists
Rowe Signal Media

COHEN, Sharon L.

1625 K St. NW
Suite 1100
Washington, DC 20006-1604
Tel: (202)857-0244
Fax: (202)857-0237
Registered: LDA

Employers
Biotechnology Industry Organization (V. President for Health Policy)

COHEN, Stephen P.

1775 Massachusetts Ave. NW
Washington, DC 20036-2188
Tel: (202)797-6000
Fax: (202)797-6004
Member, Policy Planning Staff, Department of State, 1985-87.

Employers
The Brookings Institution (Senior Fellow, Foreign Policy Studies)

COHEN, Steven

122 C St. NW
Suite 875
Washington, DC 20001
Tel: (202)347-3600
Fax: (202)347-5265

Employers
Nat'l Pork Producers Council (Director, Communications)

COHEN, Steven A.

1901 L St. NW
Suite 300
Washington, DC 20036
Tel: (202)466-7590
Fax: (202)466-7598
EMail: steve.cohen@dc.ogilvypr.com
Deputy Assistant Secretary for Public Affairs and Director, Strategic Planning, Department of Housing and Urban Development, 1999. Deputy Director of Communications, Office of the First Lady, Executive Office of the President, The White House, 1996-98. Special Assistant to the Director of Communications, Office of the Chief of Staff, Executive Office of the President, The White House, 1993-95.

Employers
Ogilvy Public Relations Worldwide (V. President)

Clients Represented

On Behalf of Ogilvy Public Relations Worldwide
INTELSAT - Internat'l Telecommunications Satellite Organization

COHEN, Susan A.

1120 Connecticut Ave. NW
Suite 460
Washington, DC 20036
Tel: (202)296-4012
Fax: (202)223-5756
Registered: LDA

Employers
The Alan Guttmacher Institute (Senior Public Policy Associate)

COHEN, Thomas W.

1701 K St. NW
Suite 800
Washington, DC 20006
Tel: (202)835-8979
Fax: (202)833-9536
Registered: LDA

Employers
Davison, Cohen & Co. (President)

Clients Represented

On Behalf of Davison, Cohen & Co.
Ass'n for Local Telecommunications Services
Corning Inc.

COHEN, Tod

555 13th St. NW
Suite 300
Washington, DC 20004
Tel: (202)637-5981
Fax: (202)637-5940
Registered: LDA
EMail: tcohen@ebay.com
Former aide to Reps. Jim Moody (D-WI) and Wayne Owens (D-UT).

Employers
eBay Inc. (Director of Government Affairs)

COHEN, Hon. William S.

600 13th St. NW
Suite 640
Washington, DC 20005-3096
Tel: (202)756-8500
Fax: (202)756-8510
EMail: wsc@cohengroup.net
Secretary, Department of Defense, 1997-2001. Member, U.S. Senate (R-ME), 1979-97. Member, U.S. House of Representatives (R-ME), 1973-79

Employers
The Cohen Group (Chairman and Chief Exec. Officer)

COHN, Robert E.

2300 N St. NW
Washington, DC 20037-1128
Tel: (202)663-8000
Fax: (202)663-8007
Registered: LDA, FARA
EMail: robert.cohn@shawpittman.com
Executive Assistant to the Chairman and Board Members (1976-77) and Senior Trial Attorney (1970-76), Civil Aeronautics Board.

Employers
Shaw Pittman (Partner)

Clients Represented

On Behalf of Shaw Pittman
Air Foyle, Ltd.
Big Sky Airlines
Delta Air Lines
Hawaii, State of
Kansas City, Missouri, City of
Midway Airlines Corp.
Nat'l Air Transportation Ass'n
Peninsula Airways, Inc.
San Jose, California, City of
Vanguard Airlines, Inc.

COIA, Arthur A.

905 16th St. NW
Washington, DC 20006
Tel: (202)737-8320
Fax: (202)737-2754

Employers
Laborers' Internat'l Union of North America (General President)

COKER, Mary

601 Pennsylvania Ave. NW
Suite 900
Washington, DC 20004
Tel: (202)547-3566
Fax: (202)639-8238

Employers
Cottone and Huggins Group (V. President, Public Relations)

COLANERI, Joseph L.

1155 Connecticut Ave. NW
Suite 300
Washington, DC 20036
Tel: (202)530-0479
Fax: (202)223-0479
Registered: LDA

Employers
Propane Vehicle Council (Exec. Director)

COLATRIANO, Vincent

1500 K St. NW
Suite 200
Washington, DC 20005
Tel: (202)220-9600
Fax: (202)220-9601

Employers
Cooper, Carvin & Rosenthal (Partner)

COLBERT, James

1717 K St. NW
Suite 800
Washington, DC 20006
Tel: (202)833-0020
Fax: (202)296-6452
EMail: jcolbert@jinsa.org

Employers
Jewish Institute for Nat'l Security Affairs (Communications Director)

COLBORN, Theo

1250 24th St. NW
Washington, DC 20037
Tel: (202)293-4800
Fax: (202)293-9211

Employers
World Wildlife Fund (Senior Scientist)

COLBURN, Cork

3190 Fairview Park Dr.
Falls Church, VA 22042
Tel: (703)876-3034
Fax: (703)876-3600
Registered: LDA

Employers
General Dynamics Corp. (Staff V. President, Congressional Relations)

COLE, Christopher A.

1299 Pennsylvania Ave. NW
Tenth Floor
Washington, DC 20004-2400
Tel: (202)508-9500
Fax: (202)508-9700
EMail: christophercole@paulhastings.com

Employers
Paul, Hastings, Janofsky & Walker LLP (Associate)

COLE, Elliott H.

2550 M St. NW
Washington, DC 20037-1350
Tel: (202)457-6000
Fax: (202)457-6315
Registered: FARA
EMail: ecole@pattonboggs.com

Employers
Patton Boggs, LLP (Partner)

COLE, Harry F.

1901 L St. NW
Suite 250
Washington, DC 20036
Tel: (202)833-4190
Fax: (202)833-3084

Employers
Bechtel & Cole (Principal)

Clients Represented

On Behalf of Bechtel & Cole
Shurberg Broadcasting of Hartford Inc.

COLE, James M.

700 13th St. NW
Suite 700
Washington, DC 20005-3960
Tel: (202)508-6000
Fax: (202)508-6200
EMail: jmcole@bryancave.com
Former Special Counsel, House Committee on Standards of Official Conduct. Chief of Staff, Office of the Special Counsel to the Attorney General (1992); Deputy Chief (1989-92) and Trial Attorney (1980-89), Public Integrity Section, Criminal Division; and Trial Attorney, Attorney General's Honor Graduate Program, Criminal Division (1979-80), all at the Department of Justice.

Employers
Bryan Cave LLP (Partner)

COLE, Keith N.

3000 K St. NW
Suite 300
Washington, DC 20007
Tel: (202)424-7500
Fax: (202)424-7643
Registered: LDA
Former Counsel, U.S. Senate Small Business Committee.

Employers
Swidler Berlin Shereff Friedman, LLP (Partner)

Clients Represented

On Behalf of Swidler Berlin Shereff Friedman, LLP
California Independent System Operator
Florida Power and Light Co.
Intersil Corp.
Marconi plc
Nat'l Sediments Coalition
Newman & Associates
Printing Industries of America
Recreational Equipment Inc.
Renewable Fuels Ass'n
Reusable Industrial Packaging Ass'n
Samsung Heavy Industries Co., Ltd.

COLE, Kenneth W.

1660 L St. NW
Fourth Floor
Washington, DC 20036
Tel: (202)775-5092
Fax: (202)775-5095

Employers
General Motors Corp. (V. President, Government Relations)

COLE, Lisa

440 First St. NW
Eighth Floor
Washington, DC 20001
Tel: (202)942-4270
Fax: (202)393-2630
EMail: lcole@naco.org

Employers
Nat'l Ass'n of Counties (Director, NACO Services)

COLE, Mary

400 Seventh St. SW
Room 3318
Washington, DC 20590
Tel: (202)366-9208
Fax: (202)366-7696
EMail: mary.cole@thwa.dot.gov

Employers
Department of Transportation - Federal Highway Administration (Staff Assistant, Office of Legislative and Strategic Planning)

COLE, Ray

1420 New York Ave. NW
Suite 1050
Washington, DC 20005
Tel: (202)638-1950
Fax: (202)638-7714
Registered: LDA

Former District Representative to Senator Richard C. Shelby (R-AL).

Employers
Van Scoyoc Associates, Inc. (Associate V. President)

Clients Represented

On Behalf of Van Scoyoc Associates, Inc.
Alabama, Department of Transportation of the State of
Alabama Water and Wastewater Institute, Inc.
Brain Trauma Foundation
FedEx Corp.
Glankler Brown, PLLC
Jefferson County Commission
Los Angeles County Metropolitan Transportation Authority
MilTec
Montgomery Airport Authority
Montgomery, Alabama, Chamber of Commerce of
Time Domain Corp.
University of Alabama System
Veridian Engineering
Xcellsis Corp.

COLE, Robert E.

655 15th St. NW
Suite 200
Washington, DC 20005
Tel: (202)638-2020
Fax: (202)638-1991
Registered: LDA

Employers
Kaiser Aluminum & Chemical Corp. (V. President, Government Affairs)

COLE, Robert T.

601 Pennsylvania Ave. NW
11th Floor, North Bldg.
Washington, DC 20004-2601
Tel: (202)756-3306
Fax: (202)756-3333
Registered: LDA
EMail: rcole@alston.com

International Tax counsel, U.S. Treasury Department, 1971-73.

Employers
Alston & Bird LLP (Partner)

Clients Represented

On Behalf of Alston & Bird LLP
Matsushita Electric Corp. of America
Nat'l Foreign Trade Council, Inc.

COLE, Steven J.

4200 Wilson Blvd.
Suite 800
Arlington, VA 22203-1838
Tel: (703)276-0100
Fax: (703)525-8277
Registered: LDA
EMail: scole@cbbb.bbb.org

Employers
Council of Better Business Bureaus (Senior V. President and General Counsel)

COLE, Steven R.

1700 K St. NW
Suite 601
Washington, DC 20006
Tel: (202)296-1314
Fax: (202)296-4067

Employers
Kaiser Permanente (Director of Public Policy)

COLE, Timothy R.

4843 27th Rd. South
Arlington, VA 22206-1301
Tel: (703)998-8700
Fax: (703)998-1896
Registered: LDA

Formerly served in the Federal Aviation Administration, Department of Transportation.

Employers
Federal Access (President)

Clients Represented

On Behalf of Federal Access
Regional Airport Authority of Louisville & Jefferson Co.
United Parcel Service

COLE, Tom

1615 H St. NW
Washington, DC 20062
Tel: (202)463-5724
Fax: (202)463-5302

Employers
U.S. Chamber Institute for Legal Reform (Consultant)

COLEMAN, Alison

1010 Wisconsin Ave. NW
Suite 800
Washington, DC 20007
Tel: (202)338-8700
Fax: (202)338-2334

Employers
Greer, Margolis, Mitchell, Burns & Associates (Associate)

Clients Represented

On Behalf of Greer, Margolis, Mitchell, Burns & Associates
Nutrition Screening Initiative, The

COLEMAN, Brenda

1849 C St. NW
Washington, DC 20240
Tel: (202)208-5403
Fax: (202)208-6965

Employers
Department of Interior - Fish and Wildlife Service (Legislative Specialist)

COLEMAN, Devon

1101 17th St. NW
Suite 803
Washington, DC 20036
Tel: (202)833-0007
Fax: (202)833-0086

Employers
MARC Associates, Inc.

COLEMAN, Dorothy

1331 Pennsylvania Ave. NW
Sixth Floor
Washington, DC 20004-1790
Tel: (202)637-3073
Fax: (202)637-3182
EMail: dcoleman@nam.org

Employers
Nat'l Ass'n of Manufacturers (V. President, Tax Policy)

COLEMAN, Hon. E. Thomas

601 13th St. NW
Suite 200 North
Washington, DC 20005
Tel: (202)682-9462
Registered: LDA

Member, U.S. House of Representatives (R-MO), 1976-93.

Employers
BASF Corporation (V. President, Government Relations)

COLEMAN, Franklin L.

1250 I St. NW
Suite 400
Washington, DC 20005-3998
Tel: (202)628-3544
Fax: (202)682-8888
Registered: LDA
EMail: fcoleman@discus.org

Employers
Distilled Spirits Council of the United States, Inc. (Senior V. President, Public Affairs and Communications)

COLEMAN, Kathryn

200 Independence Ave. SW
Room 341H
Washington, DC 20201
Tel: (202)690-6277
Fax: (202)690-8168

Employers
Department of Health and Human Services - Health Care Financing Administration (Director, Hearings and Policy Presentation Group)

COLEMAN, Lynn R.

1440 New York Ave. NW
Washington, DC 20005
Tel: (202)371-7000
Fax: (202)393-5760
Registered: LDA

Deputy Secretary (1980-81) and General Counsel (1978-80), Department of Energy. Law Clerk to Judge John R. Brown, U.S. Court of Appeals, Fifth Circuit, 1964-65.

Employers
Skadden, Arps, Slate, Meagher & Flom LLP (Partner)

Clients Represented

On Behalf of Skadden, Arps, Slate, Meagher & Flom LLP
Consolidated Freightways Corp.
State Universities Retirement System of Illinois Pension Fund
The Wing Group

COLEMAN, Nancy

2000 M St. NW
Suite 400
Washington, DC 20036
Tel: (202)467-4999
Fax: (202)293-2672

Employers
People for the American Way (Director, Media Relations)

COLEMAN, Paul D.

1000 Connecticut Ave. NW
Suite 400
Washington, DC 20036
Tel: (202)296-5460
Fax: (202)296-5463

Employers
Hoppel, Mayer and Coleman (Partner)

Clients Represented

On Behalf of Hoppel, Mayer and Coleman
Tropical Shipping and Construction Co.

COLEMAN, Rodney A.

2111 Wilson Blvd.
Eighth Floor
Arlington, VA 22201-3058
Tel: (703)841-0626
Fax: (703)243-2874
Registered: LDA
EMail: coleman@alcalde-fay.com

Assistant Secretary for Manpower, Reserve Affairs, Installations and Environment, Department of the Air Force, 1994-98. White House Fellow and Special Assistant to the Secretary, Department of the Interior, 1971-72.

Employers
Alcalde & Fay (Partner)

Clients Represented

On Behalf of Alcalde & Fay
Arcata Associates, Inc.
Hillsborough, Florida, County of
Mitretek Systems
World Wide Technology

COLEMAN, Ronald D.

1430 Spring Hill Rd.
Suite 500
McLean, VA 22102
Tel: (703)556-7778
Fax: (703)448-6692

Employers
Internat'l Televent Inc. (Chairman & Chief Exec. Officer)

COLEMAN, Hon. Ronald D.

1850 M St. NW
Suite 280
Washington, DC 20036
Tel: (202)331-7900
Fax: (202)331-0726
Registered: LDA

Member, U.S. House of Representatives (D-TX), 1983-97. Captain, Department of the Army, Department of Defense, 1967.

Employers
Shawn Coulson (Partner)

Clients Represented

On Behalf of Shawn Coulson
Domes Internat'l, Inc.
People for the Ethical Treatment of Animals

COLEMAN, Terry S.

1900 K St. NW
Suite 750
Washington, DC 20006
Tel: (202)833-4500
Fax: (202)833-2859
Registered: LDA

Employers
Bennett Turner & Coleman, LLP (Partner)

Clients Represented

On Behalf of Bennett Turner & Coleman, LLP
American Soc. of Clinical Oncology

COLEMAN, Jr., William T.

555 13th St. NW
Suite 500 West
Washington, DC 20004
Tel: (202)383-5300
Fax: (202)383-5414
Registered: LDA
EMail: wcoleman@omm.com

Secretary, Department of Transportation, 1975-77.

Employers
O'Melveny and Myers LLP (Senior Partner)

Clients Represented

On Behalf of O'Melveny and Myers LLP

CIGNA Corp.
Samsung Heavy Industries Co., Ltd.
US Airways

COLENDA, Cynthia

2111 Wilson Blvd.
Eighth Floor
Arlington, VA 22201-3058
Tel: (703)841-0626
Fax: (703)243-2874
Registered: LDA

Employers

Alcalde & Fay

Clients Represented

On Behalf of Alcalde & Fay

Cruise Industry Charitable Foundation
Miami Heat
Norwegian Cruise Line
Panama, Government of the Republic of

COLER, Kate

655 15th St. NW
Washington, DC 20005-5701
Tel: (202)220-0633
Fax: (202)220-0873
Registered: LDA
EMail: kcoler@fmi.org

Employers

Food Marketing Institute (Director, Government Relations)

COLFORD, Chris

600 New Hampshire Ave. NW
Suite 601
Washington, DC 20037
EMail: ccolford@hillandknowlton.com
Tel: (202)333-7400
Fax: (202)333-1638

Employers

Hill and Knowlton, Inc. (Managing Director)

COLGAN, Corinne

2025 M St. NW
Suite 800
Washington, DC 20036
EMail: corinne_colgan@dc.sba.com
Tel: (202)367-2100
Fax: (202)367-1200

Employers

Smith, Bucklin and Associates, Inc.

Clients Represented

On Behalf of Smith, Bucklin and Associates, Inc.

Soc. of Thoracic Surgeons

COLGATE, Ms. Jessie M.

1001 Pennsylvania Ave. NW
Suite 580 North
Washington, DC 20004-2505
Tel: (202)783-4484
Fax: (202)393-2769
Registered: LDA

Employers

New York Life Insurance Co. (Senior V. President, Governmental Affairs)

COLGATE, Stephen

1200 19th St. NW
Washington, DC 20036-2430
Tel: (202)861-3900
Fax: (202)223-2085
Former Assistant Attorney General for Administration, Department of Justice.

Employers

Piper Marbury Rudnick & Wolfe LLP (Exec. Director)

COLKER, Ed.D., Laura J.

1332 Independence Ave. SE
Washington, DC 20003-2365
Tel: (202)543-4600

Employers

Morgan Casner Associates, Inc. (Senior Associate)

COLL, Patricia

419 Seventh St. NW
Suite 500
Washington, DC 20004
Tel: (202)626-8820
Fax: (202)347-3668
Registered: LDA

Employers

Nat'l Right to Life Committee (Legislative Assistant)

COLLADO, Emilio G.

P.O. Box 464
Washington, DC 20044-0464
Registered: LDA

Employers

American Watch Ass'n (Treasurer, Political Action Committee)
Coalition to Preserve the Integrity of American Trademarks (Exec. Director)
Collado Associates, Inc. (President)

Clients Represented

On Behalf of Collado Associates, Inc.

American Watch Ass'n
Coalition to Preserve the Integrity of American Trademarks

COLLELI, Ralph

1220 L St. NW
Washington, DC 20005
Tel: (202)682-8000
Fax: (202)682-8232
Registered: LDA

Employers

American Petroleum Institute (Senior Attorney)

COLLENDER, Stanley

1615 L St. NW
Suite 1000
Washington, DC 20036
EMail: collends@fleishman.com
Tel: (202)659-0330
Fax: (202)296-6119

Employers

Fleishman-Hillard, Inc (Senior V. President)

COLLETON, Maura

1211 Connecticut Ave. NW
Suite 608
Washington, DC 20036
EMail: mcolleton@qorvis.com
Tel: (202)496-1000
Fax: (202)496-1300

Employers

Qorvis Communications (Director)

COLLETT, Anne

633 Pennsylvania Ave. NW
Fourth Floor
Washington, DC 20004
Tel: (202)783-2596
Fax: (202)628-5379
Registered: LDA, FARA
EMail: acollett@psw-inc.com
Legislative Assistant to Senator Carol Moseley-Braun (D-IL), 1994-98. Legislative Assistant to Senator Alan Dixon (D-IL), 1990-93.

Employers

Public Strategies Washington, Inc.

Clients Represented

On Behalf of Public Strategies Washington, Inc.

Greater El Paso Chamber of Commerce
Mexico, Secretaria de Comercio y Fomento Industrial (SECOFI)

COLLIER, James A. "Jay"

99 Canal Center Plaza
Suite 500
Alexandria, VA 22314-1538
EMail: jay@aiada.org
Tel: (703)519-7800
Fax: (703)519-7810

Employers

American Internat'l Automobile Dealers Ass'n (General Manager, AIADA Services)

COLLIER, Jennifer

236 Massachusetts Ave. NE
Suite 505
Washington, DC 20002
EMail: jcollier@lac-dc.org
Tel: (202)544-5478
Fax: (202)544-5712

Employers

Legal Action Center of the City of New York, Inc. (Director, National Policy)

COLLIER, Jr., Thomas C.

1330 Connecticut Ave. NW
Washington, DC 20036-1795
Tel: (202)429-3000
Fax: (202)429-3902
Registered: LDA
Chief of Staff and Chief Operating Officer, Department of the Interior, 1993-95. Deputy Assistant Secretary for Regulatory Functions and Interstate Land Sales Administrator (1980-81) and Special Assistant to the General Counsel (1979-80), Department of Housing and Urban Development. Law Clerk to Judge Charles Clark, U.S. Court of Appeals, Fifth Circuit, 1975-76.

Employers

Steptoe & Johnson LLP (Partner)

Clients Represented

On Behalf of Steptoe & Johnson LLP

Acoma Pueblo
Isleta Pueblo
Jicarilla Apache Tribe
Mesalero Apache Tribe
Nambe Pueblo
Pojoaque Pueblo
San Felipe Pueblo
San Juan Pueblo
Sandia Pueblo
Santa Ana Pueblo
Santa Clara Pueblo
Shakopee Mdewakanton Sioux Tribe
Taos Pueblo
TAPS Renewal Task Force
Tesuque Pueblo

COLLINA, Thomas

1707 H St. NW
Suite 600
Washington, DC 20006-3919
Tel: (202)223-6133
Fax: (202)223-6162
Registered: LDA

Employers

Union of Concerned Scientists (Director, Global Security Program)

COLLING, Terese

1331 F St. NW
Suite 800
Washington, DC 20004
Tel: (202)347-8000
Fax: (202)347-8920
Registered: LDA
EMail: colling@csandh.com

Employers

Colling Swift & Hynes (Principal)

Clients Represented

On Behalf of Colling Swift & Hynes

Frank Beam and Co.
Caraustar
Chuck & Rock Adventure Productions, Inc.
Garden State Paper Co., Inc.
Greenman Technologies Inc.
Media General, Inc.
The Newark Group
NewsHunter.net, LLC
Opportunity Internat'l
Paper Recycling Coalition
PrediWave
Quest Diagnostics Inc.
Rock-Tenn Co.
Smurfit Stone Container Corp.
Talgo
White Pigeon Paper Co.

COLLINGWOOD, John E.

935 Pennsylvania Ave. NW
Washington, DC 20530-0001
Tel: (202)324-2727
Fax: (202)324-6490

Employers

Department of Justice - Federal Bureau of Investigation (Assistant Director, Office of Public and Congressional Affairs)

COLLINS, Arthur R.

1825 I Street NW
Suite 400
Washington, DC 20006
Tel: (202)429-2732
Fax: (202)429-6834
Registered: LDA
EMail: artc@pubpriv.com

Employers

Public Private Partnership

Clients Represented

On Behalf of Public Private Partnership

Brown and Williamson Tobacco Corp.
Lorillard Tobacco Co.

COLLINS, Bryan

1666 K St. NW
Suite 800
Washington, DC 20006
Tel: (202)481-7000
Fax: (202)862-7098
Registered: LDA

Employers

Arthur Andersen LLP (Partner)

Clients Represented

On Behalf of Arthur Andersen LLP

AutoNation, Inc.

COLLINS, Charlotte

1001 Pennsylvania Ave. NW
Suite 600
Washington, DC 20004
Tel: (202)347-0066
Fax: (202)624-7222
Registered: LDA
EMail: ccollins@pgfm.com

Legislative correspondent to Rep. Richard H. Baker (R-LA), 1999-2000.

Employers

Adams and Reese LLP (Legislative Assistant)
Powell, Goldstein, Frazer & Murphy LLP (Of Counsel)

Clients Represented

On Behalf of Adams and Reese LLP

Baton Rouge, Louisiana, City of
Plaquemine, Louisiana, City of

On Behalf of Powell, Goldstein, Frazer & Murphy LLP

Nat'l Ass'n of Public Hospitals and Health Systems

COLLINS, Daniel

555 11th St. NW
Suite 750
Washington, DC 20005
Tel: (202)637-3506
Fax: (202)637-3504

Employers

El Paso Corporation (V. President and Associate General Counsel)

COLLINS, Dyann

1001 Connecticut Ave. NW
Suite 1250
Washington, DC 20036
Tel: (202)331-1010
Fax: (202)331-0640

Employers

Competitive Enterprise Institute (Assistant Editor)

COLLINS, Eva

1401 I St. NW
Suite 600
Washington, DC 20005
Tel: (202)336-7400
Fax: (202)336-7529
Registered: LDA

Employers

United Technologies Corp. (Government Affairs Representative)

COLLINS, Gerald

1731 King St.
Suite 200
Alexandria, VA 22314
Tel: (703)549-1390
Fax: (703)549-1656
EMail: gcollins@catholiccharitiesusa.org

Employers

Catholic Charities USA (Director of Disaster Response)

COLLINS, J. Barclay

2445 M St. NW
Washington, DC 20037-1420
Tel: (202)663-6000
Fax: (202)663-6363
Registered: LDA

Employers

Wilmer, Cutler & Pickering (Associate)

Clients Represented

On Behalf of Wilmer, Cutler & Pickering

IATA U.S. Frequent Flyer Tax Interest Group

COLLINS, Jeremiah C.

725 12th St. NW
Washington, DC 20005
Tel: (202)434-5000
Fax: (202)434-5029

Employers

Williams & Connolly (Partner)

COLLINS, John T.

1330 Connecticut Ave. NW
Washington, DC 20036-1795
Tel: (202)429-3000
Fax: (202)429-3902
Registered: LDA
EMail: jcollins@steptoe.com

General Counsel (1982-85) and Counsel (1977-82), Senate Committee on Banking, Housing and Urban Affairs. Senior Attorney, Federal Reserve Board, 1975-77. Attorney, Securities and Exchange Commission, 1972-75.

Employers

Steptoe & Johnson LLP (Partner)

Clients Represented

On Behalf of Steptoe & Johnson LLP

Bear, Stearns and Co.
Federal Home Loan Bank of San Francisco
Institute of Internat'l Bankers
Western Financial/Westcorp Inc.

COLLINS, Kevin

1300 19th St. NW
Suite 300
Washington, DC 20036
Tel: (202)223-6722
Fax: (202)659-0650
Registered: LDA

Employers

Nat'l Parks Conservation Ass'n (Visitor Experience)

COLLINS, Mary Jean

1010 Wisconsin Ave. NW
Suite 410
Washington, DC 20007
Tel: (202)944-5080
Fax: (202)944-5081

Employers

People for the American Way (National Field Director)
Voters For Choice (Treasurer)

COLLINS, Michael

2407 15th St. NW
Suite 406
Washington, DC 20009
Tel: (202)248-0305

Employers

House Majority Fund

COLLINS, Michael

1050 Connecticut Ave. NW
Washington, DC 20036-5306
Tel: (202)955-8500
Fax: (202)467-0539
Registered: LDA

Employers

Gibson, Dunn & Crutcher LLP

Clients Represented

On Behalf of Gibson, Dunn & Crutcher LLP

CNF Transportation, Inc.

COLLINS, Mike

700 13th St. NW
Suite 1000
Washington, DC 20005
Tel: (202)347-6633
Fax: (202)347-8713

Former Communications Director at the House Commerce Committee for Chairman Tom Bliley (R-VA), 1995-97.

Employers

Powell Tate (Exec. V. President)

COLLINS, Molly

325 Seventh St. NW
Washington, DC 20004
Tel: (202)638-1100
Fax: (202)626-4626
Registered: LDA

Employers

American Hospital Ass'n (Senior Associate Director, Public Policy Development)

COLLINS, Pablo

1331 F St. NW
Suite 800
Washington, DC 20004
Tel: (202)347-8000
Fax: (202)347-8920
Registered: LDA
EMail: collins@csandh.com

Legislative Director (1987-89) and Administrative Assistant (1989-91) to Rep. Bill Richardson (D-NM). Legislative Assistant to Rep. E. (Kika) de la Garza (D-TX), 1979-85.

Employers

Colling Swift & Hynes (Senior Associate)

Clients Represented

On Behalf of Colling Swift & Hynes

Caraustar
Chuck & Rock Adventure Productions, Inc.
Garden State Paper Co., Inc.
Greenman Technologies Inc.
Media General, Inc.
The Newark Group
Paper Recycling Coalition
PrediWave
Quest Diagnostics Inc.
Rock-Tenn Co.
Smurfit Stone Container Corp.
Talgo
White Pigeon Paper Co.

COLLINS, Paula

1455 Pennsylvania Ave. NW
Suite 375
M/S 4072
Washington, DC 20004
Tel: (202)628-3133
Fax: (202)628-2980
Registered: LDA
EMail: pcollins@ti.com

Employers

Texas Instruments (Director, Government Relations-Human Relations and Education)

COLLINS, Richard L.

2111 Wilson Blvd.
Suite 700
Arlington, VA 22201
Tel: (703)351-5057
Fax: (703)522-1738
Registered: LDA

Clerk, Subcommittee on Defense, Senate Committee on Appropriations, 1973-75. Served in the U.S. Army, 1963-66.

Employers

Collins & Company, Inc. (President)

Clients Represented

On Behalf of Collins & Company, Inc.

The Boeing Co.
Citizens Network for Foreign Affairs (CNFA)
Derry Investment Initiatives
EarthData Holdings
Hawaii Economic Development Alliance, State of
Internat'l Agriculture and Rural Development Group
Internat'l Fund for Agricultural Development
Loral Space and Communications, Ltd.
Mari-Flite Ferries, Inc.
Marquette University
Nat'l Telephone Cooperative Ass'n
NewMarket Global Consulting Group
Northrop Grumman Corp.
Oracle Corp.
Pacific Marine
PADCO, Inc.
Population Action Internat'l
Science Applications Internat'l Corp. (SAIC)
Solipsys Corp.
Textron Inc.
Textron Systems Division
Trex Enterprises

COLLINS, Susan M.

1775 Massachusetts Ave. NW
Washington, DC 20036-2188
Tel: (202)797-6000
Fax: (202)797-6004

Senior Staff Economist, President's Council of Economic Advisers, 1989-90.

Employers

The Brookings Institution (Senior Fellow, Economic Studies)

COLLINS, T. Bryon

Healy Hall
Third Floor
Box 571243
37th & O Sts. NW
Washington, DC 20057
Tel: (202)687-3455
Fax: (202)687-1656

Employers

Georgetown University (Senior Counselor, Federal Relations)

COLLINS, William A.

1717 Pennsylvania Ave. NW
Suite 400
Washington, DC 20006
Tel: (202)857-3000
Fax: (202)857-3030

Employers

Occidental Internat'l Corporation (Director, Health, Environment and Safety)

COLLINS, III, William L.

6420 Grovedale Dr.
Alexandria, VA 22310
Tel: (703)971-1732
Fax: (703)971-5327

Employers
Virginia Baseball Club (Chairman and Chief Executive Officer)

COLLINS CHADWICK, Ann

1555 King St.
Alexandria, VA 22314
EMail: staff@aafcs.org
Tel: (703)706-4600
Fax: (703)706-4663

Employers
American Ass'n of Family and Consumer Sciences (Director)

COLLINSON, Nicole Bivens

1300 Pennsylvania Ave. NW
Suite 400
Ronald Reagan Bldg.
Washington, DC 20004
EMail: nbc@strtrade.com
Tel: (202)638-2230
Fax: (202)638-2236
Registered: LDA

Former Assistant Chief Textile Negotiator, Office of the U.S. Trade Representative, Executive Office of the President. Former Country Analyst, Department of Commerce.

Employers
Sandler, Travis & Rosenberg, P.A. (Director, International Trade)

Clients Represented

On Behalf of Sandler, Travis & Rosenberg, P.A.
American Apparel & Footwear Ass'n
American Textile Co.
Cambodia, Ministry of Commerce, Royal Kingdom of
Confederation of Garment Exporters of the Philippines
The Hosiery Ass'n
Intradeco
Nilit America Corp.
Skipps Cutting
Sri Lanka Apparel Exporters Ass'n
Tailored Clothing Ass'n

COLLISHAW, Karen

9111 Old Georgetown Rd.
Bethesda, MD 20814
EMail: kcollish@acc.org
Tel: (301)897-2692
Fax: (301)897-8757
Registered: LDA

Employers
American College of Cardiology (Associate Exec. V. President, Advocacy)

COLMAN, Jeffrey

440 First St. NW
Suite 600
Washington, DC 20001
Tel: (202)639-5200
Registered: LDA

Employers
American Israel Public Affairs Committee (Legislative Liaison/Lobbyist)

COLMAN, Kim

1101 Vermont Ave. NW
Suite 700
Washington, DC 20005
EMail: kcolman@aaodc.org
Tel: (202)737-6662
Fax: (202)737-7061
Registered: LDA

Employers
American Academy of Ophthamology - Office of Federal Affairs (Manager Reimbursement Policy)

COLOMBARO, Geri J.

1301 K St. NW
Suite 1200-West Tower
Washington, DC 20005-3307
EMail: cjcolom@us.ibm.com
Tel: (202)515-5003
Fax: (202)515-5055
Registered: LDA

Employers
Internat'l Business Machines Corp. (Program Director, Public Affairs, Human Resources)

COLOT, Thora S.R.

1600 21st St. NW
Washington, DC 20009-1090
EMail: tcolot@phillipscollection.org
Tel: (202)387-2151
Ext: 240
Fax: (202)387-2436

Employers
The Phillips Collection (Director, Marketing and Business Operations)

COLOVAS, Steve

2099 Pennsylvania Ave. NW
Suite 850
Washington, DC 20006
EMail: Colovas@acgrep.com
Tel: (202)419-2500
Fax: (202)419-2510
Registered: LDA

Special Assistant, Department of the Treasury, 1991-92. Deputy Assistant Secretary, Department of State, 1989-90. Special Assistant, Office of Management and Budget, Executive Office of the President, 1988.

Employers
American Continental Group, Inc. (Director)

Clients Represented

On Behalf of American Continental Group, Inc.
Coalition for Travel Industry Parity
EEI
Fisher Imaging
Northpoint Technology, Ltd.
PepsiCo, Inc.
Plasma-Therm, Inc.
Securify
Stony Brook Foundation

COLPITTS, Cindy

1350 I St. NW
Suite 1255
Washington, DC 20005
Tel: (202)626-0089
Fax: (202)626-0088
Registered: LDA

Employers
Law Offices of Mark Barnes

Clients Represented

On Behalf of Law Offices of Mark Barnes
Intrac Arms Internat'l LLC
Mossberg Group, LLC

COLSON, Charles W.

P.O. Box 17500
Washington, DC 20041-0500
Tel: (703)478-0100
Fax: (703)834-3658

Employers
Prison Fellowship Ministries (Chairman of the Board)

COLTHARP, James R.

2001 Pennsylvania Ave. NW
Suite 500
Washington, DC 20006
EMail: jim_coltharp@comcast.com
Tel: (202)638-5678
Fax: (202)466-7718
Registered: LDA

Employers
Comcast Corp. (Senior Director, Public Policy)

COLTON, David

1401 Wilson Blvd.
Suite 1100
Arlington, VA 22209
EMail: dcolton@itaa.org
Tel: (703)522-5055
Fax: (703)525-2279
Registered: LDA

Employers
Information Technology Ass'n of America (ITAA) (V. President, Strategic Initiatives)

COLUCCI, Marlene M.

1333 New Hampshire Ave. NW
Suite 400
Washington, DC 20036
Tel: (202)887-4000
Fax: (202)887-4288
Registered: LDA

Employers
Akin, Gump, Strauss, Hauer & Feld, L.L.P. (Senior Counsel)

Clients Represented

On Behalf of Akin, Gump, Strauss, Hauer & Feld, L.L.P.
American Amateur Karate Federation
American Consulting Engineers Council
American Legion
AT&T
Bombardier, Inc.
Citizen's Educational Foundation
Construction Industry Round Table, Inc.
Educational Foundation for Citizenship and Statehood Project
First Nationwide Bank
Granite Broadcasting Co.
Susan G. Komen Breast Cancer Foundation
New York Public Library
Texas Manufactured Housing Ass'n
Transamerica Occidental Life Insurance Co.
Uniden Corp.

COLUMBUS, R. Timothy

3050 K St. NW
Washington, DC 20007
EMail: tcolumbu@colliershannon.com
Tel: (202)342-8555
Fax: (202)342-8451
Registered: LDA, FARA

Employers
Collier Shannon Scott, PLLC (Member)

Clients Represented

On Behalf of Collier Shannon Scott, PLLC
CARFAX, Inc.
Fannie Mae
Lion Oil Co.
Nat'l Ass'n of Convenience Stores
Soc. of Independent Gasoline Marketers of America
World Floor Covering Ass'n

COLVILLE, Mary

1015 15th St. NW
Suite 930
Washington, DC 20005
Tel: (202)296-2622
Fax: (202)293-4005
Registered: LDA

Employers
Nat'l Chicken Council (Director, Government Relations)

COLVIN, Joe F.

1776 I St. NW
Suite 400
Washington, DC 20006-3708
Tel: (202)739-8000
Fax: (202)785-4019

Employers
Nuclear Energy Institute (President and Chief Exec. Officer)

COMBS, Ann L.

1001 Pennsylvania Ave. NW
Washington, DC 20004-2599
Tel: (202)624-2000
Fax: (202)624-2319
Registered: LDA

Employers
American Council of Life Insurers (V. President and Chief Counsel, Retirement and Pensions)

COMBS, Roberta

499 S. Capitol St. SW
Suite 615
Washington, DC 20003
Tel: (202)479-6900
Fax: (202)479-4260

Employers
Christian Coalition of America (Exec. V. President)

COMBS, Wesley I.

2120 L St. NW
Suite 850
Washington, DC 20037
EMail: wcombs@witeckcombs.com
Tel: (202)887-0500
Fax: (202)887-5633

Employers
Witeck * Combs Communications (President)

COMEAU, Cliff

400 Seventh St. SW
Room 3318
Washington, DC 20590
EMail: cliff.comeau@thwa.dot.gov
Tel: (202)366-4051
Fax: (202)366-7696

Employers
Department of Transportation - Federal Highway Administration (Highway Needs and Investment, Office of Legislative and Strategic Planning)

COMEDY, Yolanda

1301 K St. NW
Suite 1200-West Tower
Washington, DC 20005-3307
EMail: ycomedy@us.ibm.com
Tel: (202)515-5013

Employers
Internat'l Business Machines Corp. (Corporate Community Relations Manager)

COMER, Douglas B.

1634 I St. NW
Suite 300
Washington, DC 20006
Tel: (202)626-4385
Fax: (202)628-2525
Registered: LDA

Employers
Intel Corp. (Director, Legal Affairs)

COMER, Edward H.

701 Pennsylvania Ave. NW
Washington, DC 20004-2696
Tel: (202)508-5615
Fax: (202)508-5673
Registered: LDA

Employers
Edison Electric Institute (V. President, General Counsel)

COMINI, Laura

P.O. Box 65153
Washington, DC 20035

Employers
Nat'l Federation of Democratic Women (Treasurer, PAC)

COMPTON, Kathron

1800 Duke St.
Alexandria, VA 22314
EMail: kcompton@shrm.org
Tel: (703)548-3440
Fax: (703)836-0367

Employers
Soc. for Human Resource Management (Director, Public Affairs)

COMSTOCK, Earl W.

1850 M St. NW
Suite 900
Washington, DC 20036
Tel: (202)463-2500
Fax: (202)463-4950
Registered: LDA
Legislative Director to Senator Ted Stevens (R-AK), 1991-96. Staff member, Committee on Commerce, Science and Transportation, U.S. Senate, 1988-91.

Employers
Sher & Blackwell (Partner)

Clients Represented

On Behalf of Sher & Blackwell
ASCENT (Ass'n of Community Enterprises)
AUPS/Mo Hussain
Dolphin Safe/Fair Trade Campaign
Fair Fisheries Coalition
Focal Communications
Humane Soc. of the United States
Icicle Seafoods, Inc.
Internat'l Fund for Animal Welfare
Level 3 Communications LLC
Mindspring
Nat'l Marine Life Center
NCS Healthcare
Nucentrix Broadband Networks
PanAmSat Corp.
Rowan Companies, Inc.
Sargeant Marine, Inc.
Separation Technologies
Stuyvesant Dredging Co.
United Catcher Boats
Winstar Communications, Inc.
Woods Hole Steamship Authority

CONAWAY, Cdr. Brian R.

400 Seventh St. SW
Suite 10402
Washington, DC 20590
EMail: bconaway@comdit.uscg.mil
Tel: (202)366-4280
Fax: (202)366-7124

Employers
Department of Transportation - United States Coast Guard (Deputy Chief, Congressional Affairs Staff, Office of Government and Public Affairs)

CONAWAY, John B.

1150 Connecticut Ave. NW
Suite 700
Washington, DC 20036
Tel: (202)296-8000
Fax: (202)296-8803
Registered: LDA

Employers
Mullenholz, Brimsek & Belair

Clients Represented

On Behalf of Mullenholz, Brimsek & Belair
Center for Civic Education
Constitutional Rights Foundation

CONAWAY, USAF (Ret.), Lt. Gen. John B.

11 Canal Center Plaza
Suite 103
Alexandria, VA 22314
Tel: (703)683-4222
Fax: (703)683-0645
Registered: LDA
Chief, National Guard Bureau, 1990-1993.

Employers
The Conaway Group LLC (President)
The Spectrum Group

Clients Represented

On Behalf of The Conaway Group LLC
Accenture
AGS Defense, Inc.
Comtel Secure Fiber Telecommunications, Inc.
DFI Internat'l
EDS Corp.
Essential Technologies, Inc.
General Dynamics Corp.
Gulfstream Aerospace Corp.
Lockheed Martin Corp.
Mountain Top Technologies, Inc.
Science Applications Internat'l Corp. (SAIC)
SRI Internat'l
United States Business Interiors

CONDEELIS, Mary

2121 K St. NW
Suite 701
Washington, DC 20037
EMail: mary@baft.org
Tel: (202)452-0952
Fax: (202)452-0959
Registered: LDA

Employers
Bankers' Ass'n for Finance and Trade (Exec. Director)

CONDON, Leonard W.

1700 N. Moore St.
Suite 1600
Arlington, VA 22209
Tel: (703)841-2400
Fax: (703)527-0938
Registered: LDA

Employers
American Meat Institute (V. President, International Trade)

CONDON, Mark

601 13th St. NW
Suite 570 South
Washington, DC 20005-3807
EMail: mcondon@amseed.org
Tel: (202)638-3128
Fax: (202)638-3171

Employers
American Seed Trade Ass'n (V. President of International Marketing)

CONDREY, Jr., Bailey L.

800 Connecticut Ave. NW
Suite 620
Washington, DC 20006
EMail: bcondrey@methanol.org
Tel: (202)467-5050
Fax: (202)331-9055

Employers
American Methanol Institute (Director, Communications)

CONE, Margaret

1620 I St. NW
Suite 520
Washington, DC 20006
Tel: (202)265-3988
Fax: (202)833-4849
Registered: LDA

Employers
Self-employed as an independent consultant.

Clients Represented

As an independent consultant
Artists Coalition
Writers Guild of America

CONKLIN, Brian C.

1600 Pennsylvania Ave. NW
112 E. Wing
Washington, DC 20500
Tel: (202)456-6620
Fax: (202)456-2604
Legislative Director, Office of Rep. Sonny Bono (R-CA), 1995-96.

Employers
Executive Office of the President - The White House (Special Assistant to the President for Legislative Affairs, House Liaison Office)

CONKLING, Gary

1275 K St. NW
Suite 810
Washington, DC 20005
EMail: garyc@cfmpdx.com
Tel: (202)408-2100
Fax: (202)408-2115
Registered: LDA

Employers
Conkling, Fiskum & McCormick (President)

Clients Represented

On Behalf of Conkling, Fiskum & McCormick
Electro Scientific Industries, Inc.
Industrial Customers of Northwest Utilities
Mentor Graphics Corp.
New Edge Networks
Oregon Graduate Institute of Science and Technology
Sisters of Providence Health Systems

CONKO, Gregory

1001 Connecticut Ave. NW
Suite 1250
Washington, DC 20036
Tel: (202)331-1010
Fax: (202)331-0640

Employers
Competitive Enterprise Institute (Director of Food Safety Policy)

CONLAN, Jr., Robert J.

1722 I St. NW
Washington, DC 20006
EMail: rconlan@sidley.com
Tel: (202)736-8000
Fax: (202)736-8711

Employers
Sidley & Austin (Partner)

CONLEY, Jeffrey B.

818 Connecticut Ave. NW
Second Floor
Washington, DC 20006
EMail: jconley@stratacomm.net
Tel: (202)289-2001
Fax: (202)289-1327
Registered: LDA

Employers
Strat@Comm (Strategic Communications Counselors) (Principal)

CONLEY, John

2200 Mill Rd.
Suite 620
Alexandria, VA 22314
EMail: nttc@juno.com
Tel: (703)838-1960
Fax: (703)684-5753

Employers
Nat'l Tank Truck Carriers (V. President)

CONLEY, Karyne

1401 I St. NW
Suite 1100
Washington, DC 20005
Tel: (202)326-8865
Fax: (202)408-4796

Employers
SBC Communications Inc. (Director, Federal Relations)

CONLON, Jerome

122 C St. NW
Suite 850
Washington, DC 20001
EMail: jerry.conlon@cchinc.com
Tel: (202)638-7790
Fax: (202)638-1045
Registered: LDA

Employers
Chambers, Conlon & Hartwell (Senior Partner)

Clients Represented

On Behalf of Chambers, Conlon & Hartwell
The False Claims Act Legal Center
Florida East Coast Industries Inc.
Norfolk Southern Corp.
Union Pacific

CONLON, Michael J.

1818 N St. NW
Suite 700
Washington, DC 20036
Tel: (202)331-7050
Fax: (202)331-9306
Registered: LDA
EMail: mjc@cfpllaw.com

Employers
Conlon, Frantz, Phelan & Pires (Partner)
Heavy Vehicle Maintenance Group (President)

Clients Represented
On Behalf of Conlon, Frantz, Phelan & Pires
Automotive Engine Rebuilders Ass'n
Automotive Parts Rebuilders Ass'n
Automotive Refrigeration Products Institute
Heavy Vehicle Maintenance Group
Internat'l Mobile Air Conditioning Ass'n

CONN, Joseph L.

518 C St. NE
Washington, DC 20002
Tel: (202)466-3234
Fax: (202)466-2587

Employers
Americans United for Separation of Church and State (Managing Editor, Church and State Magazine)

CONNALLY, James

4701 Sangamore Rd.
Suite N100
Bethesda, MD 20816-2508
Tel: (301)229-5800
Fax: (301)229-5045
Registered: LDA

Employers
Burdeshaw Associates, Ltd. (Associate)

Clients Represented
On Behalf of Burdeshaw Associates, Ltd.
Martin-Baker Aircraft Co., Ltd.

CONNAUGHTON, James

1722 I St. NW
Washington, DC 20006
Tel: (202)736-8000
Fax: (202)736-8711
Registered: LDA

Employers
Sidley & Austin (Partner)

Clients Represented
On Behalf of Sidley & Austin
ARCO Coal Co.
General Electric Co.

CONNAUGHTON, Jeffrey J.

1133 Connecticut Ave. NW
Fifth Floor
Washington, DC 20036
Tel: (202)457-1110
Fax: (202)457-1130
Registered: LDA

Employers
Quinn Gillespie & Associates (Principal)

Clients Represented
On Behalf of Quinn Gillespie & Associates
The Chubb Corp.
Instinet
Metropolitan Life Insurance Co.

CONNAUGHTON, Sean T.

401 Ninth St. NW
Suite 1000
Washington, DC 20004
Tel: (202)274-2871
Fax: (202)654-5646
Registered: LDA, FARA
EMail: sean.connaughton@troutmansanders.com
Office of Marine Safety and Environmental Protection, Coast Guard, 1983-86; Department of Transportation, 1986-88.

Employers
Troutman Sanders LLP (Of Counsel)

CONNAUGHTON, Thomas A.

625 Slaters Ln.
Suite 200
Alexandria, VA 22314-1171
Tel: (703)836-6263
Fax: (703)836-6730
EMail: thomasc@aahomecare.org

Employers
American Ass'n for Homecare (Chief Exec. Officer)

CONNELL, Karen

2100 Reston Pkwy.
Suite 400
Reston, VA 20191-1218
Tel: (703)758-7790
Fax: (703)758-7787
EMail: connell@asmc.org

Employers
Ass'n of Sales & Marketing Companies (Exec. V. President)

CONNELL, Marion Fitch

P.O. Box 75248
Washington, DC 20013-5248
Tel: (202)927-4926
Fax: (202)927-4920

Employers
Public Employees Roundtable (Exec. Director)

CONNELLY, D. Barry

1090 Vermont Ave. NW
Suite 200
Washington, DC 20005-4905
Tel: (202)371-0910
Fax: (202)371-0134
Registered: LDA

Employers
Associated Credit Bureaus, Inc. (President)

CONNELLY, Elizabeth

1899 L St. NW
Suite 1000
Washington, DC 20036
Tel: (202)457-0480
Fax: (202)457-0486
EMail: liz_connelly@npradc.org

Employers
Nat'l Petrochemical Refiners Ass'n (Director of Administration)

CONNELLY, Jeanne K.

1200 18th St. NW
Suite 850
Washington, DC 20036
Tel: (202)822-2000
Fax: (202)822-2156
Registered: LDA
EMail: jconnelly@calpine.com
Former Staff Member, Senate Committee on Labor and Human Resources.

Employers
Calpine Corp. (V. President, Federal Relations)

CONNELLY, Warren E.

1333 New Hampshire Ave. NW
Suite 400
Washington, DC 20036
Tel: (202)887-4000
Fax: (202)887-4288

Employers
Akin, Gump, Strauss, Hauer & Feld, L.L.P. (Partner)

Clients Represented
On Behalf of Akin, Gump, Strauss, Hauer & Feld, L.L.P.
Fujitsu Limited
Phillips Foods, Inc.

CONNER, Charles F.

1701 Pennsylvania Ave. NW
Suite 950
Washington, DC 20006
Tel: (202)331-1634
Fax: (202)331-2054
Registered: LDA
EMail: cconner@corn.org

Employers
Corn Refiners Ass'n, Inc. (President)

CONNER, Darrell

1735 New York Ave. NW
Suite 500
Washington, DC 20006-4759
Tel: (202)628-1700
Fax: (202)331-1024
Registered: LDA

Employers
Preston Gates Ellis & Rouvelas Meeds LLP (Government Affairs Counselor)

Clients Represented
On Behalf of Preston Gates Ellis & Rouvelas Meeds LLP
American Classic Voyages Co.
Ivarans Rederiasa
Southeast Alaska Regional Health Corp. (SEARHC)
The Title XI Coalition
Transpacific Stabilization Agreement
Transportation Institute
United States Maritime Coalition

CONNER, III, Frank M.

601 Pennsylvania Ave. NW
11th Floor, North Bldg.
Washington, DC 20004-2601
Tel: (202)756-3300
Fax: (202)756-3333

Employers
Alston & Bird LLP

Clients Represented
On Behalf of Alston & Bird LLP
Regions Financial Corp.

CONNERTON, Robert J.

1401 New York Ave. NW
Tenth Floor
Washington, DC 20005-2102
Tel: (202)737-1900
Fax: (202)659-3458
EMail: rconnerton@connerton-ray.com

Employers
Connerton & Ray (Partner)

CONNERTON, Terese M.

1401 New York Ave. NW
Tenth Floor
Washington, DC 20005-2102
Tel: (202)737-1900
Fax: (202)659-3458
EMail: tconnerton@connerton-ray.com
Special Litigation Division, Solicitor's Office, Department of Labor, 1984-86.

Employers
Connerton & Ray (Partner)

CONNOLLY, Annemargaret

1615 L St. NW
Suite 700
Washington, DC 20036-5610
Tel: (202)682-7000
Fax: (202)857-0939
Registered: LDA
EMail: annemargaret.connolly@weil.com

Employers
Weil, Gotshal & Manges, LLP (Partner)

Clients Represented
On Behalf of Weil, Gotshal & Manges, LLP
GAF Corp.

CONNOLLY, Gerald E.

2111 Wilson Blvd.
Suite 1200
Arlington, VA 22201
Tel: (703)522-1845
Fax: (703)351-6634
EMail: gconnolly@columbuspublicaffairs.com
Former Senior Professional Staff Member, Senate Committee on Foreign Relations.

Employers
Columbus Public Affairs (Exec. V. President)

CONNOLLY, Peter C.

219 N. Washington St.
Alexandria, VA 22314
Tel: (703)836-7990
Fax: (703)836-9739

Employers
Peduzzi Associates, Ltd. (Associate)

CONNOLLY, Peter M.

2099 Pennsylvania Ave. NW
Suite 100
Washington, DC 20006
Tel: (202)955-3000
Fax: (202)955-5564
EMail: pconnoll@hklaw.com
Legislative Counsel to Senator Gaylord A. Nelson (D-WI), 1978-80.

Employers
Holland & Knight LLP (Partner)

CONNOR, Catherine

1401 K St. NW
Suite 701
Washington, DC 20005
Tel: (202)783-0241
Fax: (202)783-0229
Registered: LDA
EMail: connor@pbworld.com
Served in the U.S. Department of Transportation.

Employers
Parsons Brinckerhoff Inc. (V. President, Government Relations)

CONNOR, Christopher

1199 N. Fairfax St.
Suite 425
Alexandria, VA 22314
Tel: (703)548-8621
Fax: (703)236-1949

Employers
Leadership PAC 2002

CONNOR, G. Brent

1801 K St. NW
Washington, DC 20006
Tel: (202)775-0725
Fax: (202)223-8604

Employers
Robins, Kaplan, Miller & Ciresi L.L.P. (Associate)

CONNOR, Kenneth L.

801 G St. NW
Washington, DC 20001
Tel: (202)393-2100
Fax: (202)393-2134

Employers
American Renewal (President)
Family Research Council, Inc. (President)

CONNORS, Carol

888 First St. NW
MS: 11 H-20
Washington, DC 20426
Tel: (202)208-0870
Fax: (202)208-2106

Employers
Department of Energy - Federal Energy Regulatory Commission (Deputy Director (House Liaison), Congressional, Intergovernmental, and Public Affairs)

CONNORS, John P.

1201 New York Ave. NW
Suite 600
Washington, DC 20005-3931
Tel: (202)289-3121
Fax: (202)289-3185
Registered: LDA
EMail: jconnors@ahma.com

Employers
American Hotel and Lodging Ass'n (Exec. V. President, Governmental Affairs)

CONNORS, Kathleen

122 C St. NW
Suite 520
Washington, DC 20001
Tel: (202)393-5100
Fax: (202)393-5110

Employers
Tyco Internat'l (US), Inc. (Office Administrator)

CONNORTON, John V.

601 13th St. NW
Suite 800 North
Washington, DC 20005
Tel: (202)682-1480
Fax: (202)682-1497
Registered: LDA

Employers
Hawkins, Delafield & Wood (Partner)

Clients Represented

On Behalf of Hawkins, Delafield & Wood
Mortgage Bankers Ass'n of America

CONOVER, Rev. Patrick

110 Maryland Ave. NE
Suite 207
Washington, DC 20002
EMail: conoverp@ucc.org
Tel: (202)543-1517
Fax: (202)543-5994

Employers
United Church of Christ Justice and Witness Ministry (Legislative Director)

CONRAD, Andrew

1775 Pennsylvania Ave. NW
Suite 200
Washington, DC 20006
Tel: (202)862-1000
Fax: (202)862-1093
Registered: LDA

Employers
Dewey Ballantine LLP (Associate)

Clients Represented

On Behalf of Dewey Ballantine LLP
AFLAC, Inc.

CONRAD, David R.

1400 16th St. NW
Suite 501
Washington, DC 20036-2266
Tel: (202)797-6800
Fax: (202)797-6646
Registered: LDA
EMail: conrad@nwf.org

Employers
Nat'l Wildlife Federation - Office of Federal and Internat'l Affairs (Water Resources Specialist)

CONRAD, Jr., Deacon Joseph M.

1200 Varnum St. NE
Washington, DC 20017
Tel: (202)529-6480
Fax: (202)526-1262

Employers
Nat'l Catholic Conference for Interracial Justice (Exec. Director)

CONRAD, Kathy P.

1401 K St. NW
Suite 900
Washington, DC 20005
Tel: (202)626-8550
Fax: (202)626-8578
Registered: LDA

Employers
Jefferson Consulting Group (V. President)

Clients Represented

On Behalf of Jefferson Consulting Group
Apple Computer, Inc.
First Consulting Group
Franklin Covey

CONRAD, Robin S.

1615 H St. NW
Washington, DC 20062-2000
EMail: rconrad@uschamber.com
Tel: (202)463-5337
Fax: (202)463-5346

Employers
Chamber of Commerce of the U.S.A. (V. President, National Chamber Litigation Center)

CONRAD, Shawn D.

501 Wythe St.
Alexandria, VA 22314
Tel: (703)683-8371
Fax: (703)683-4503

Employers
Internat'l Sleep Products Ass'n (V. President, Government Relations and Issues Management)

CONROY, M.D., Robert M.

11 Canal Center Plaza
Suite 110
Alexandria, VA 22314
Tel: (703)548-0280
Fax: (703)683-7939

Employers
Nat'l Ass'n of VA Physicians and Dentists (President)

CONROY, William F.

1050 Connecticut Ave. NW
Suite 1100
Washington, DC 20036-5304
Tel: (202)861-1500
Fax: (202)861-1790
Registered: LDA, FARA
EMail: wconroy@baker-hostetler.com

Employers
Baker & Hostetler LLP (Partner)

Clients Represented

On Behalf of Baker & Hostetler LLP
American Electric Power Co.
American Resort Development Ass'n
Cafaro Co.
The Chubb Corp.
Citigroup
The Council of Insurance Agents & Brokers
Edison Electric Institute
Flexi-Van Leasing
Florida Residential and Casualty Joint Underwriting Ass'n
Florida Windstorm Underwriting Ass'n
Forest City Ratner Companies
KeyCorp, Inc.
Marsh & McLennan Cos.
Nat'l Ass'n of Real Estate Investment Trusts
PSH Master L.P.I.
Transportation Institute

CONSTANTINE, III, George E.

1575 I St. NW
Washington, DC 20005-1103
Tel: (202)626-2818
Fax: (202)371-1673
Registered: LDA
EMail: gconstantine@asaenet.org

Employers
American Soc. of Ass'n Executives (Staff Counsel)

CONTEE, Yvette

201 14th St. SW
Fifth Floor SW
Washington, DC 20250
EMail: yvette.contee@fs.fed.us
Tel: (202)205-1030
Fax: (202)205-1225

Employers
Department of Agriculture - Forest Service (Staff Assistant, Legislative Affairs Staff)

CONTI, Heather

1250 I St. NW
Suite 500
Washington, DC 20005
Tel: (202)789-2900
Ext: 3006
Fax: (202)789-1893
EMail: hconti@anla.org

Employers
American Nursery and Landscape Ass'n (Govt. Relations Coordinator and PAC Contact)

CONTI, Jennifer

1700 Pennsylvania Ave. NW
Suite 950
Washington, DC 20006
Tel: (202)393-5055
Fax: (202)393-0120
Registered: LDA
EMail: jconti@erols.com
Formerly served in the Antitrust Division, Department of Justice.

Employers
Valis Associates (Senior Account Exec.)

Clients Represented

On Behalf of Valis Associates
American Consulting Engineers Council
Ass'n of American Railroads
CH2M Hill
Joint Southeast Public Improvement Council
New Majority Soc.
Norfolk Southern Corp.
Telecommunications Industry Ass'n
Transportation Reform Alliance

CONTRATTO, Dana C.

1001 Pennsylvania Ave. NW
Suite 1100
Washington, DC 20004-2595
Tel: (202)624-2500
Fax: (202)628-5116
Registered: LDA
Law Clerk to Chief Judge Tamm (1974-75) and Court Law Clerk (1973-74), U.S. Court of Appeals for the District of Columbia Circuit.

Employers
Crowell & Moring LLP (Partner)

Clients Represented

On Behalf of Crowell & Moring LLP
Associated Gas Distributors
KeySpan Energy
Knoxville Utilities Board
Lehn & Fink Products Group
Memphis Light, Gas and Water Division
RTK Corp.

CONWAY, Anthony C.

475 L'Enfant Plaza SW
MS: 10707
Washington, DC 20260
Tel: (202)268-3748

Employers
United States Postal Service (Government Relations Manager)

CONWAY, Daniel

One Massachusetts Ave. NW
Suite 350
Washington, DC 20001
Tel: (202)408-8123
Ext: 112
Fax: (202)296-7683
Registered: LDA
EMail: dconway@chubb.com

Employers
The Chubb Corp. (Senior V. President)

CONWAY, Janice E.

3050 K St. NW
Washington, DC 20007
Tel: (202)342-8806
Fax: (202)342-8451
Registered: LDA, FARA
EMail: jconway@colliershannon.com

Employers
Collier Shannon Scott, PLLC (Government Relations Advisor)

Clients Represented

On Behalf of Collier Shannon Scott, PLLC
Bicycle Manufacturers Ass'n of America

CONWAY, Michael

1600 Pennsylvania Ave. NW
Washington, DC 20500
Tel: (202)456-2230
Fax: (202)456-1806

Employers
Executive Office of the President - The White House

CONWAY, Tom

1150 17th St. NW
Suite 701
Washington, DC 20036
EMail: tomc@dittus.com
Tel: (202)775-1401
Fax: (202)775-1404

Employers
Dittus Communications (Senior V. President)

Clients Represented

On Behalf of Dittus Communications
Business Software Alliance
Comptel
Digital Focus
Hess
Intel Corp.
Internat'l Limousine
Microsoft Corp.
TCS
VeriSign/Network Solutions, Inc.

COOK, Bette

Ronald Reagan Bldg.
1300 Pennsylvania Ave. NW
MS: 6.10A
Washington, DC 20523
EMail: bcook@usaid.gov
Tel: (202)712-4300
Fax: (202)216-3036

Employers
Agency for Internat'l Development (Legislative Program Specialist, Congressional Liaison Division)

COOK, David B.

1800 Massachusetts Ave. NW
Washington, DC 20036
Tel: (202)828-2000
Fax: (202)828-2195
Attorney, Office of the General Counsel, Council on Environmental Quality, Executive Office of the President, The White House, 1972-75. Law Clerk to Judge Carl McGowan, U.S. Court of Appeals, District of Columbia Circuit, 1971-72.

Employers
Shea & Gardner (Partner)

COOK, G. Mark

555 11th St. NW
Suite 750
Washington, DC 20005
Tel: (202)637-3506
Fax: (202)637-3504

Employers
El Paso Corporation (Associate General Counsel, Pipelines)

COOK, Harry N.

1130 17th St. NW
Washington, DC 20036-4676
EMail: hcook@waterways.org
Tel: (202)296-4415
Fax: (202)835-3861

Employers
Nat'l Waterways Conference, Inc. (President)

COOK, SM Sgt. J. J.

1160 Air Force Pentagon
Room 4D927
Washington, DC 20330-1160
Tel: (703)697-2650
Fax: (703)697-2001

Employers
Department of Air Force (Deputy Exec. Officer, Legislative Liaison)

COOK, Janine

600 13th St. NW
Washington, DC 20005-3096
EMail: jcook@mwe.com
Tel: (202)756-8000
Fax: (202)756-8087
Attorney, Office of Associate Chief Counsel, Internal Revenue Service, 1995-99.

Employers
McDermott, Will and Emery (Partner)

COOK, Jennifer

444 N. Capitol St. NW
Suite 701
Washington, DC 20001
EMail: JCook@naic.org
Tel: (202)624-7790
Fax: (202)624-8579

Employers
Nat'l Ass'n of Insurance Commissioners (Assistant Counsel, Health Policy)

COOK, Judith Wise

801 Pennsylvania Ave. NW
Suite 725
Washington, DC 20004
EMail: judy.cook@aventis.com
Tel: (202)628-0500
Fax: (202)682-0538
Registered: LDA

Employers
Aventis Pharmaceuticals, Inc. (Director, Health Policy and Biotechnology Programs)

COOK, Kenneth A.

1718 Connecticut Ave. NW
Suite 600
Washington, DC 20009
Tel: (202)667-6982
Fax: (202)232-2592

Employers
Environmental Working Group (President)

COOK, Michelle

1660 L St. NW
Suite 700
Washington, DC 20036
EMail: mcook@ucpa.org
Tel: (202)776-0406
Fax: (202)776-0414
Registered: LDA

Employers
United Cerebral Palsy Ass'n (Policy Legal Counsel)

COOK, Peter L.

1725 K St. NW
Suite 1212
Washington, DC 20006
Tel: (202)833-8383
Fax: (202)331-7442
Registered: LDA

Employers
Nat'l Ass'n of Water Companies (Exec. Director)

COOK, Samantha

600 New Hampshire Ave. NW
Tenth Floor
Washington, DC 20037
Tel: (202)333-8667
Fax: (202)298-9109
Former Senior Legislative Assistant to Rep. Roy Blunt (R-MO).

Employers
Fierce and Isakowitz

Clients Represented

On Behalf of Fierce and Isakowitz
American Ass'n of Nurse Anesthetists
Credit Union Nat'l Ass'n, Inc.
DuPont
Edison Internat'l
Federation of American Hospitals
Generic Pharmaceutical Ass'n
Health Insurance Ass'n of America
MCI WorldCom Corp.
Pegasus Communications
Tricon Global Restaurants Inc.

COOK, Sandy

601 Pennsylvania Ave. NW
South Bldg., Suite 900
Washington, DC 20004
Tel: (202)434-8190
Fax: (202)347-1909
Registered: LDA

Employers
UNUM/Provident Corp. (V. President, Federal Relations)

COOK, Steve

700 11th St. NW
Washington, DC 20001-4507
EMail: scook@realtors.org
Tel: (202)383-1014
Fax: (202)383-7540
Registered: LDA

Employers
Nat'l Ass'n of Realtors (V. President, Public Affairs)

COOK, Timothy

One Thomas Circle NW
Suite 400
Washington, DC 20005
Tel: (202)659-8111
Fax: (202)659-9216

Employers
Independent Community Bankers of America (Senior Editor)

COOK, Tom

801 N. Fairfax St.
Suite 207
Alexandria, VA 22314
EMail: tcook@nationalrenderers.com
Tel: (703)683-4983
Fax: (703)683-2626

Employers
Nat'l Renderers Ass'n (President and Chief Exec. Officer)

COOK, William P.

1501 M St. NW
Suite 700
Washington, DC 20005-1702
EMail: wcook@manatt.com
Tel: (202)463-4300
Fax: (202)463-4394
Registered: LDA
U.S. Attorney's Office, 1991-92. General Counsel of Immigration & Naturalization Service, 1989-90. Civil and Criminal Division, Department of Justice, 1984-87.

Employers
Manatt, Phelps & Phillips, LLP (Partner)

Clients Represented

On Behalf of Manatt, Phelps & Phillips, LLP
AIS, Inc.
Verizon Communications

COOKE, Jr., Edmund D.

1400 L St. NW
Washington, DC 20005-3502
EMail: ecooke@winston.com
Tel: (202)371-5796
Fax: (202)371-5950
Registered: LDA
Former Attorney, Appellate Court Division, National Labor Relations Board; Attorney, Equal Employment Opportunity Commission; Counsel, House Committee on Education and Labor; Counsel, House Committee on Administration; Chief Legislative Assistant to Rep. Harold Washington (D-IL); and Counsel Subcommittee on Employment Opportunity, House Committee on Education and Labor. Captain, U.S. Air Force, 1966-70.

Employers
Winston & Strawn (Partner, Employment Relations Practice)

COOKE, Jr., Frederick D.

1155 Connecticut Ave.
Sixth Floor
Washington, DC 20036
Tel: (202)861-0870
Fax: (202)429-0657
Former Corporation Counsel for the District of Columbia, 1987-89.

Employers
Rubin, Winston, Diercks, Harris & Cooke (Partner)

Clients Represented

On Behalf of Rubin, Winston, Diercks, Harris & Cooke
Rainbow/Push Coalition (National Bureau)

COOKE, Jr., Willie E.

701 Fourth St. NW
Washington, DC 20001
Tel: (202)682-2700
Fax: (202)682-0588

Employers
Neighborhood Legal Services Program (Exec. Director)

COOKSEY, Janie

c/o Asst Secy & Commissioner Patents and Trademarks
Washington, DC 20231
Tel: (703)305-9310
Fax: (703)305-8885

Employers
Department of Commerce - United States Patent and Trademark Office (Congressional Liaison)

COON, Charli

214 Massachusetts Ave. NE
Washington, DC 20002
Tel: (202)546-4400
Fax: (202)546-8328

Employers
Heritage Foundation (Senior Policy Analyst, Energy and Environment)

COON, Maggie

4245 N. Fairfax Dr.
Suite 100
Arlington, VA 20003-1606
EMail: mcoon@tnc.org
Tel: (703)841-5315
Fax: (703)841-1283

Employers
The Nature Conservancy (Director, Government Relations)

COONEY, Brian

2101 Wilson Blvd.
Suite 610
Arlington, VA 22201
Tel: (703)558-0400
Fax: (703)558-0401
Registered: LDA

Employers
Manufactured Housing Institute (V. President, Government Affairs)

COONEY, Edward

229 1/2 Pennsylvania Ave. SE
Washington, DC 20003
Tel: (202)547-7022
Fax: (202)547-7575

Employers
Congressional Hunger Center (Exec. Director)

COONEY, Emily

One Massachusetts Ave. NW
Suite 333
Washington, DC 20001
EMail: ecooney@cnponline.org
Tel: (202)682-1800
Fax: (202)682-1818

Employers
Center for Nat'l Policy (Events Coordinator)

COONEY, Nelson J.

11490 Commerce Park Dr.
Reston, VA 20191-1525
EMail: cooney@bia.org
Tel: (703)620-0010
Fax: (703)620-3928

Employers
Brick Industry Ass'n (President)

COONEY, Patrick J.

3910 Keller Ave.
Alexandria, VA 22302
EMail: patrick_cooney@msn.com
Tel: (703)933-0020
Registered: LDA

Employers
Cooney & Associates, Inc. (President)

Clients Represented

On Behalf of Cooney & Associates, Inc.
American College of Nurse-Midwives
American Physical Therapy Ass'n
Nat'l Ass'n of Chain Drug Stores
J. T. Rutherford & Associates

COONEY, Philip

1220 L St. NW
Washington, DC 20005
Tel: (202)682-8000
Fax: (202)682-8232
Registered: LDA

Employers
American Petroleum Institute (Senior Attorney)

COONS, Barbara

600 New Hampshire Ave. NW
Suite 601
Washington, DC 20037
EMail: bcoons@hillandknowlton.com
Tel: (202)333-7400
Fax: (202)333-1638
Registered: FARA
Former Education Liaison Specialist, Library of Congress.

Employers
Hill and Knowlton, Inc. (Senior Managing Director, U.S. Director Research Services)

COOPER, B. Jay

1615 L St. NW
Suite 900
Washington, DC 20036
Tel: (202)778-1000
Fax: (202)466-6002

Employers
APCO Worldwide (Senior V. President)

COOPER, Benjamin S.

1101 Vermont Ave. NW
Suite 604
Washington, DC 20005-3521
EMail: bcooper@aopl.org
Tel: (202)408-7970
Fax: (202)408-7983
Registered: LDA

Employers
Ass'n of Oil Pipelines (Exec. Director)

COOPER, Benjamin Y.

100 Daingerfield Rd.
Alexandria, VA 22314
EMail: bcooper@printing.org
Tel: (703)519-8100
Fax: (703)519-6481
Registered: LDA

Employers
Printing Industries of America (Senior V. President, Government Affairs)

COOPER, Caroline G.

1101 Vermont Ave. NW
Suite 401
Washington, DC 20005
EMail: cgc@keia.org
Tel: (202)371-0690
Fax: (202)371-0692
Registered: FARA

Employers
Korea Economic Institute of America (Director, Congressional Affairs)

COOPER, Charles J.

1500 K St. NW
Suite 200
Washington, DC 20005
Tel: (202)220-9600
Fax: (202)220-9601
Assistant Attorney General, Office of Legal Counsel (1985-88), Deputy Assistant Attorney General, Civil Rights Division (1982-85) and Special Assistant to the Assistant Attorney General, Civil Rights Division (1981-82), Department of Justice.

Employers
Cooper, Carvin & Rosenthal (Partner)

COOPER, Christine M.

1015 15th St. NW
Suite 1200
Washington, DC 20005
EMail: ccooper@mnwlaw.net
Tel: (202)789-8600
Fax: (202)789-1708

Employers
McGuiness Norris & Williams, LLP (Partner)

COOPER, Donna

440 First St. NW
Suite 410
Washington, DC 20001
Tel: (202)347-6953
Fax: (202)393-6596

Employers
Nat'l Ass'n of Black County Officials (Exec. Director)

COOPER, Doral S.

1001 Pennsylvania Ave. NW
Suite 1100
Washington, DC 20004-2595
EMail: dcooper@cromor.com
Tel: (202)624-2895
Fax: (202)628-5116
Registered: LDA
Former Assistant U.S. Trade Representative, Office of the United States Trade Representative, Executive Office of the President, The White House. Former Economist, Division of International Finance, Board of Governors, Federal Reserve System.

Employers
C&M Internat'l, Ltd. (President)
Crowell & Moring LLP (President, C & M International)

Clients Represented

On Behalf of C&M Internat'l, Ltd.
Avon Products, Inc.
DNA Plant Technology Corp.
The Limited Inc.
Novartis Corp.
Oracle Corp.

On Behalf of Crowell & Moring LLP
New York Life Internat'l Inc.

COOPER, Evelyn

550 17th St. NW
MS: 6078
Washington, DC 20429-9990
Tel: (202)898-6983
Fax: (202)898-3745

Employers
Federal Deposit Insurance Corp. (Legislative Information Assistant, Office of Legislative Affairs)

COOPER, Howard A.

701 Pennsylvania Ave. NW
Suite 800
Washington, DC 20004
EMail: hcooper@thelenreid.com
Tel: (202)508-4301
Fax: (202)508-4321
Registered: LDA

Employers
Thelen Reid & Priest LLP (Partner)

Clients Represented

On Behalf of Thelen Reid & Priest LLP
Edison Electric Institute
Pinnacle West Capital Corp.

COOPER, J. Michael

700 13th St. NW
Suite 700
Washington, DC 20005-3960
EMail: jmcooper@bryancave.com
Tel: (202)508-6000
Fax: (202)508-6200
Law Clerk to Judge Arlin M. Adams, U.S. Court of Appeals, Third Circuit, 1973-74.

Employers
Bryan Cave LLP (Partner)

COOPER, Josephine

1401 H St. NW
Suite 900
Washington, DC 20005
Tel: (202)326-5591
Fax: (202)326-5595

Employers
Alliance of Automobile Manufacturers, Inc. (President and Chief Exec. Officer)

COOPER, Joshua

1891 Preston White Dr.
Reston, VA 20191-9312
Tel: (703)648-8900
Fax: (703)262-9312

Employers
American College of Radiology (Director, Congressional Relations)

COOPER, Kathy

3000 K St. NW
Suite 300
Washington, DC 20007
Tel: (202)424-7500
Fax: (202)424-7643
Registered: LDA

Employers
Swidler Berlin Shereff Friedman, LLP (Associate)

COOPER, Mark N.

504 Highgate Terrace
Silver Spring, MD 20904
EMail: markcooper@aol.com
Tel: (301)384-2204
Fax: (301)236-0519
Registered: LDA

Employers
Consumer Federation of America (Research Director)

COOPER, Mitchell J.

1001 Connecticut Ave. NW
Washington, DC 20036
Tel: (202)331-1858
Fax: (202)331-1850
Registered: LDA

Employers
Self-employed as an independent consultant.

Clients Represented

As an independent consultant
Rubber and Plastic Footwear Manufacturers Ass'n

COOPER, R. Clarke

499 S. Capitol St. SW
Suite 417
Washington, DC 20003
Tel: (202)554-9494
Fax: (202)554-9454
Registered: LDA

Employers
Miccosukee Tribe of Indians of Florida (Director, Government Affairs)

COOPER, Ranny

1501 M St. NW
Suite 600
Washington, DC 20005-1710
EMail: rcooper@bsmg.com
Tel: (202)739-0200
Fax: (202)659-8287

Employers
BSMG Worldwide (Partner)

COOPER, Richard M.

725 12th St. NW
Washington, DC 20005
Tel: (202)434-5000
Fax: (202)434-5029
Registered: LDA

Chief Counsel, Food and Drug Administration, 1977-79. Senior Member, Office of Energy Policy, Executive Office of the President, The White House, 1977. Law Clerk to Justice William J. Brennan, U.S. Supreme Court, 1969-70.

Employers
Williams & Connolly (Partner)

Clients Represented
On Behalf of Williams & Connolly
IVAX Corp.
R. J. Reynolds Tobacco Co.
RJR Nabisco Holdings Co.

COOPER, Roger B.

400 N. Capitol St. NW
Washington, DC 20001
Tel: (202)824-7120
Fax: (202)824-7092
Registered: LDA
EMail: rcooper@aga.org

Employers
American Gas Ass'n (Exec. V. President, Policy and Analysis)

COOPER, Scott

900 17th St. NW
Suite 1100
Washington, DC 20006
Tel: (202)884-7036
Fax: (202)884-7070
Registered: LDA
EMail: scott_cooper2@hp.com

Employers
Hewlett-Packard Co. (Manager, Technology Policy)

COOPER, Stephen

601 13th St. NW
Suite 410 South
Washington, DC 20005
Tel: (202)737-0100
Fax: (202)628-3965
Registered: LDA

Employers
R. Duffy Wall and Associates (Senior V. President)

Clients Represented
On Behalf of R. Duffy Wall and Associates
American Ambulance Ass'n
Home Care Ass'n of New York State

COOPER, Thomas E.

1299 Pennsylvania Ave. NW
Suite 1100 West
Washington, DC 20004-2407
Tel: (202)637-4000
Fax: (202)637-4412

Employers
General Electric Co. (V. President, Aerospace Technology)

COOPER, Tiffani D.

409 Third St. SW
Suite 7900
Washington, DC 20416
EMail: tiffani.cooper@sba.gov
Tel: (202)205-6700
Fax: (202)205-7374

Employers
Small Business Administration (Congressional Relations Specialist)

COOPER, Valerie

1030 15th St. NW
Suite 870
Washington, DC 20005
EMail: vcooper@kellenco.com
Tel: (202)393-1780
Fax: (202)393-0336

Employers
The Kellen Company (Senior Account Executive)
Nat'l Viatical Ass'n (Exec. Director)
Weather Risk Management Ass'n (Exec. Director)
Worldwide Printing Thermographers Ass'n (Exec. Director)

Clients Represented
On Behalf of The Kellen Company
Nat'l Viatical Ass'n
Weather Risk Management Ass'n
Worldwide Printing Thermographers Ass'n

COOPER, Yurika S.

1401 K St. NW
Tenth Floor
Washington, DC 20005
Tel: (202)416-1720
Fax: (202)416-1719
Registered: LDA

Employers
Wilson & Wasserstein, Inc.

Clients Represented
On Behalf of Wilson & Wasserstein, Inc.
Bangladeshi-American Friendship Soc. of New York

COOPERMAN, Leonard

1150 18th St. NW
Ninth Floor
Washington, DC 20036
Tel: (202)296-3355
Fax: (202)296-3922

Employers
Ablondi, Foster, Sobin & Davidow, P.C. (Associate)

COOPERMAN, Richard M.

1000 16th St. NW
Suite 400
Washington, DC 20036
Tel: (202)785-0550
Fax: (202)785-0210
Registered: FARA
EMail: cfmincdc@aol.com

Employers
Counselors For Management, Inc. (Founder, Managing Director)

COORSH, Richard

1201 F St. NW
Suite 500
Washington, DC 20004
EMail: rcoorsh@hiaa.org
Tel: (202)824-1787
Fax: (202)824-1614

Employers
Health Insurance Ass'n of America (V. President, Communications)

COPAKEN, Richard D.

1201 Pennsylvania Ave. NW
Washington, DC 20004-2401
Tel: (202)662-6000
Fax: (202)662-6291
EMail: rcopaken@cov.com

Lead U.S. Counsel to the Commonwealth of Puerto Rico, 1981-89 and to the Republic of the Marshall Islands. Fellow, The White House, 1966-67.

Employers
Covington & Burling (Partner)

COPE, Grant

218 D St. SE
Second Floor
Washington, DC 20003
Tel: (202)546-9707
Fax: (202)546-2461
Registered: LDA

Employers
U.S. Public Interest Research Group (Staff Attorney)

COPE, Robert L.

1730 M St. NW
Suite 400
Washington, DC 20036
Tel: (202)296-2900
Fax: (202)296-1370

Employers
Grove, Jaskiewicz, and Cobert (Partner)

COPELAND, Greg

2110 Yale Dr.
Alexandria, VA 22307
Tel: (703)768-3780
Fax: (703)765-8308
Registered: LDA

Employers
Self-employed as an independent consultant.

Clients Represented
As an independent consultant
TVA Watch

COPELAND, Jr., James M.

1341 G St. NW
Suite 200
Washington, DC 20005
Tel: (202)347-5990
Fax: (202)347-5941
Registered: LDA
EMail: copeland@clj.com

Deputy Assistant to the President for Congressional Relations, The White House, 1978-80. Director, Congressional Relations, Federal Home Loan Bank Board, 1977. Former Administrative Assistant to Rep. Pete Stark (D-CA), 1973-77.

Employers
Copeland, Lowery & Jacquez (Partner)

Clients Represented
On Behalf of Copeland, Lowery & Jacquez
Alameda, California, County of
Bay Area Rapid Transit District
Berkeley, California, City of
Deerfield Senior Services
Internation Securities Exchange
Pacific Life Insurance Co.

COPLE, III, William J.

1350 I St. NW
Ninth Floor
Washington, DC 20005-3304
Tel: (202)898-5800
Fax: (202)682-1639

Special Assistant U.S. Attorney for the Eastern District of Virginia, Department of Justice, 1984-85. Chief Trial Counsel, U.S. Army Engineer Center, Fort Belvoir, Virginia, 1983-84. Office of General Counsel, Office of the Secretary, Department of Defense, 1980-83. Captain, U.S. Army, 1980-85.

Employers
Spriggs & Hollingsworth (Partner)

CORBETT, Jr., John J.

1350 New York Ave. NW
Suite 1100
Washington, DC 20005-4798
Tel: (202)879-4000
Fax: (202)393-2866
Registered: LDA
EMail: corbettj@spiegelmcd.com

Employers
Spiegel & McDiarmid (Partner)

Clients Represented
On Behalf of Spiegel & McDiarmid
CADDO Lake Institute
Des Moines Community School District
Lehigh-Northhampton Airport Authority
Minneapolis-St. Paul Metropolitan Airports Commission
Orange, California, County of
St. Louis Airport Authority

CORBETT, Linwood

9000 Rockville Pike
Bldg. One, Room 244
Bethesda, MD 20892
EMail: corbettl@od.nih.gov
Tel: (301)496-3471
Fax: (301)496-0840

Employers
Department of Health and Human Services - Nat'l Institutes of Health (Legislative Analyst)

CORBETT-SANDERS, Karen

1300 I St. NW
Suite 400 West
Washington, DC 20005
Tel: (202)515-2430
Fax: (202)289-7983

Employers
Verizon Communications (V. President, International Policy and Regulatory Affairs)

CORBIN, Dr. Carlyle

444 N. Capitol St. NW
Suite 305
Washington, DC 20001
Tel: (202)624-3562
Fax: (202)624-3594

Employers
Virgin Islands, Office of the Governor (Representative, External Affairs)

CORCORAN, John F.

1500 K St. NW
Suite 375
Washington, DC 20005
Tel: (202)383-4551
Fax: (202)383-4018
Registered: LDA

Employers
Norfolk Southern Corp. (Senior V. President, Public Affairs)

CORCORAN, Kevin P.

2000 N. 14th St.
Suite 450
Arlington, VA 22201

Tel: (703)276-0220
Fax: (703)841-7797

Employers
Nat'l Ass'n of Health Underwriters (Exec. V. President)

CORCORAN, Lisa

1299 Pennsylvania Ave. NW
Suite 800 West
Washington, DC 20004

Tel: (202)785-0500
Fax: (202)785-5277
Registered: LDA

Employers
The Carmen Group (Program Director)

CORCORAN, Melissa

910 16th St. NW
Suite 402
Washington, DC 20006

Tel: (202)775-0084
Fax: (202)775-0784

Employers
Milliken and Co. (Legislative Assistant)

CORCORAN, Hon. Thomas J.

1666 K St. NW
Suite 500
Washington, DC 20006-2803

Tel: (202)887-1400
Fax: (202)466-2198
Registered: LDA, FARA

Member, U.S. House of Representatives (R-IL), 1977-85.

Employers
O'Connor & Hannan, L.L.P. (Partner)

Clients Represented

On Behalf of O'Connor & Hannan, L.L.P.

Allergan, Inc.
American Forest & Paper Ass'n
American Free Trade Ass'n
ATOFINA Chemicals, Inc.
Bear, Stearns and Co.
Brooks Tropicals, Inc.
Exxon Mobil Corp.
FMC Corp.
General Electric Co.
Georgia-Pacific Corp.
P. H. Glatfelter
Healthcare Financing Study Group
JSG Trading Co.
KEECO
Kendall-Jackson Winery
Kurdistan Democratic Party USA
Lockheed Martin Corp.
Montrose Chemical Co.
M. A. Mortenson Co.
Mortgage Bankers Ass'n of America
Nat'l Paint and Coatings Ass'n
Nat'l Peach Council
New England Mobile X-Ray
Smith Dawson & Andrews, Inc.
Solid Waste Agency of Northern Cook County
St. Croix Chippewa Indians of Wisconsin
Student Loan Funding Corp.
Tyson's Governmental Sales, LLC
Upper Sioux Indian Community
VISA U.S.A., Inc.
Nidal Z. Zayed and Associates

CORDARO, John B.

1875 I St. NW
Suite 400
Washington, DC 20006
EMail: cordaro@crnusa.org

Tel: (202)872-1488
Fax: (202)872-9594
Registered: LDA

Employers
Council for Responsible Nutrition (President and Chief Exec. Officer)

CORDIA, Liz

122 S. Royal St.
Alexandria, VA 22314-3328
EMail: liz@cordia.com

Tel: (703)838-0373
Fax: (703)838-1698

White House Presidential Personnel, 1985-86.

Employers
Cordia Cos. (V. President)

CORDIA, Louis J.

122 S. Royal St.
Alexandria, VA 22314-3328
EMail: lou@cordia.com

Tel: (703)838-0373
Fax: (703)838-1698

Served on the House Republican Research Committee, 1975-77. Served with the Environmental Protection Agency, 1981-83.

Employers
Cordia Cos. (President and Chief Exec. Officer)

Clients Represented

On Behalf of Cordia Cos.

West Group

CORLEY, Jr., William Brooks

P.O. Box 3070
Merrifield, VA 22116
EMail: mc@mcleague

Tel: (703)207-9588
Fax: (703)207-0047

Employers
Marine Corps League (Exec. Director)

CORMIER, Kristin

444 N. Capitol St. NW
Suite 401
Washington, DC 20001
EMail: kcormier@csg.org

Tel: (202)624-5460
Fax: (202)624-5452

Employers
Council of State Governments (Policy and Legislation Director)

CORN-REVERE, Robert

555 13th St. NW
Washington, DC 20004-1109

Tel: (202)637-5600
Fax: (202)637-5910

Employers
Hogan & Hartson L.L.P.

CORNELISON, Joseph

1333 New Hampshire Ave. NW
Suite 400
Washington, DC 20036

Tel: (202)887-4000
Fax: (202)887-4288

Employers
Akin, Gump, Strauss, Hauer & Feld, L.L.P. (Senior Counsel)

CORNISH, Jill

7910 Woodmont Ave.
Suite 1150
Bethesda, MD 20814-3062
EMail: jill@associationtrends.com

Tel: (301)652-8666
Fax: (301)656-8654

Employers
Association Trends (Publisher)

CORNISH, Pat

2012 Massachusetts Ave. NW
Washington, DC 20036

Tel: (202)293-1100
Fax: (202)861-0298

Employers
Business and Professional Women/USA (National President)

CORONEL, Susan

1201 F St. NW
Suite 500
Washington, DC 20004

Tel: (202)824-1600
Fax: (202)824-1651
Registered: LDA

Employers
Health Insurance Ass'n of America

CORR, Christopher F.

601 13th St. NW
Suite 600 South
Washington, DC 20005

Tel: (202)626-3600
Fax: (202)639-9355

Employers
White & Case LLP (Partner)

CORR, William V.

1707 L St. NW
Suite 800
Washington, DC 20036

Tel: (202)296-5469
Fax: (202)296-5427
Registered: LDA

Employers
Campaign for Tobacco-Free Kids (Exec. V. President)

CORRADO, Ernest J.

1801 K St. NW
Suite 1200
Washington, DC 20006

Tel: (202)736-2784
Fax: (202)223-8604
Registered: LDA

Staff Director and General Counsel, House Committee on Merchant Marine and Fisheries, 1968-79. Office of General Counsel, National Labor Relations Board 1963-67. Office of the Solicitor, Department of Labor, 1958-65.

Employers
Self-employed as an independent consultant.

Clients Represented

As an independent consultant

Bourgas Intermodal Feasability Study
Waesche, Sheinbaum, and O'Regan

CORRAO, Joe

1635 Prince St.
Alexandria, VA 22314-3406

Tel: (703)683-4646
Fax: (703)683-4745
Registered: LDA

Employers
Helicopter Ass'n Internat'l (Director, Regulations)

CORREIA, Edward

555 11th St. NW
Suite 1000
Washington, DC 20004

Tel: (202)637-2200
Fax: (202)637-2201
Registered: LDA

Employers
Latham & Watkins

Clients Represented

On Behalf of Latham & Watkins

ElderCare Companies
Nat'l Orthotics Manufacturers Ass'n
Serono Laboratories, Inc.

CORRIE, Quentin R.

12600 Fair Lakes Circle
Suite 220
Fairfax, VA 22033

Tel: (703)222-2200
Fax: (703)222-0321

Employers
Anderson and Corrie (Partner)

Clients Represented

On Behalf of Anderson and Corrie

AAA MidAtlantic

CORRIGAN, Angela

1401 I St. NW
Suite 240
Washington, DC 20005
EMail: angela_corrigan@mastercard.com

Tel: (202)414-8001
Fax: (202)414-8010

Employers
MasterCard Internat'l (Legislative Assistant)

CORRIGAN, Richard L.

1250 H St. NW
Suite 575
Washington, DC 20005

Tel: (202)393-2426
Fax: (202)783-8410

Employers
CH2M Hill (Senior V. President, Governmental Affairs)
Design Professionals Coalition (V. Chairman)

CORRIGAN, Susan

333 N. Fairfax St.
Suite 100
Alexandria, VA 22314
EMail: ProductDonations@GiftsInKind.org

Tel: (703)836-2121
Fax: (703)549-1481
Registered: LDA

Employers
Gifts In Kind Internat'l (President and Chief Exec. Officer)

CORRY, Martin C.

601 E St. NW
Washington, DC 20049

Tel: (202)434-3750
Fax: (202)434-3758
Registered: LDA

Employers
AARP (American Ass'n of Retired Persons) (Director, Federal Affairs)

CORS, Jr., Alfred W.

108 N. Alfred St.
Alexandria, VA 22314
Tel: (703)683-5700
Fax: (703)683-5722
Registered: LDA

Employers
Nat'l Taxpayers Union (V. President, Government Affairs)

CORSO, Anthony R.

1333 New Hampshire Ave. NW
Suite 400
Washington, DC 20036
EMail: acorso@akingump.com
Tel: (202)887-4000
Fax: (202)887-4288

Employers
Akin, Gump, Strauss, Hauer & Feld, L.L.P. (Senior Advisor)

CORTE-REAL, Isabel

1401 I St. NW
Suite 600
Washington, DC 20005
Tel: (202)336-7400
Fax: (202)336-7529

Employers
United Technologies Corp. (PAC Administrator)

CORTESE, Jr., Alfred W.

600 14th St. NW
Fifth Floor
Washington, DC 20005
EMail: awc@corteseplic.com
Tel: (202)637-9696
Fax: (202)637-9797
Registered: LDA

Assistant Executive Director, Federal Trade Commission, 1971-73.

Employers
Cortese PLLC (Manager)
Pepper Hamilton LLP (Partner)

Clients Represented
On Behalf of Cortese PLLC
American Competitiveness Institute
Florida Department of Children & Families
General Motors Corp.

CORTESE FOXMAN, Melissa

1225 I St. NW
Suite 500
Washington, DC 20005
Tel: (202)312-2010
Fax: (202)785-2649

Employers
SCC Communications Corp. (V. President, Government Relations)

CORTINA, Thomas A.

2111 Wilson Blvd.
Eighth Floor
Arlington, VA 22201-3058
EMail: cortina@alcalde-fay.com
Tel: (703)841-0626
Fax: (703)243-2874

Employers
Alcalde & Fay (Partner)
Halon Alternatives Research Corp.

Clients Represented
On Behalf of Alcalde & Fay
Earthshell Container Corp.
Great Lakes Chemical Corp.
Halon Alternatives Research Corp.
Intel Corp.
Internat'l Climate Change Partnership

CORWIN, Michael

22377 Belmont Ridge Rd.
Asburn, VA 20148
EMail: mcorwin@nrpa.org
Tel: (703)858-0784
Fax: (703)858-0794

Employers
Nat'l Recreation and Park Ass'n (Director, Marketing and Communications)

CORWIN, Philip S.

1301 Pennsylvania Ave. NW
Suite 500
Washington, DC 20004
Tel: (202)347-6875
Fax: (202)347-6876
Registered: LDA

Legislative Assistant to Senator Harrison Williams (D-NJ), 1980-81. Professional Staff Member, Senate Committee on Aging, 1976-79.

Employers
Butera & Andrews

Clients Represented
On Behalf of Butera & Andrews
American Bankers Ass'n
Commercial Finance Ass'n
Option One Mortgage Corp.

CORWIN, Brig. Gen. Tony L.

The Pentagon
4C678
Washington, DC 20350
Tel: (703)614-1686
Fax: (703)614-5964

Employers
Department of Navy - United States Marine Corps (Legislative Director, Office of the Legislative Assistant to the Commandant)

COSBY, Kit

1320 19th St. NW
Suite 701
Washington, DC 20036
Tel: (202)833-8990
Fax: (202)833-8988

Employers
Nat'l Spiritual Assembly of the Baha'is of the United States (Director, Office of External Affairs)

COSENTINO, Victor J.

1055 Thomas Jefferson St. NW
Suite 601
Washington, DC 20007
Tel: (202)337-8000
Fax: (202)265-9363
Registered: FARA

Employers
Finkelstein, Thompson & Loughran (Associate)

Clients Represented
On Behalf of Finkelstein, Thompson & Loughran
Canadian Broadcasting Corp.

COSGRIFF, Lawrence E.

1200 G St. NW
Suite 800
Washington, DC 20005
Tel: (202)331-1424
Fax: (202)775-8427
Registered: LDA

Employers
APL Limited (V. President, Government Affairs)

COSGROVE, Sean

408 C St. NE
Washington, DC 20002
Tel: (202)547-1141
Fax: (202)547-6009

Employers
Sierra Club (Associate Representative, Land Protection)

COSGROVE, Timothy

1201 Pennsylvania Ave. NW
P.O. Box 407
Washington, DC 20044-0407
Tel: (202)626-6600
Fax: (202)626-6780

Employers
Squire, Sanders & Dempsey L.L.P.

Clients Represented
On Behalf of Squire, Sanders & Dempsey L.L.P.
Cleveland Clinic Foundation

COSTABILE, Mary R.

1301 Pennsylvania Ave. NW
Suite 403
Washington, DC 20004
EMail: mrc@alawash.org
Tel: (202)628-8410
Fax: (202)628-8419
Registered: LDA

Employers
American Library Ass'n (Associate Director)

COSTANTINO, Jr., Lou A.

1401 I St. NW
Suite 1000
Washington, DC 20005
EMail: lcostantino@sia.com
Tel: (202)296-9410
Fax: (202)296-9775
Registered: LDA

Employers
Securities Industry Ass'n (V. President, Congressional Relations)

COSTELLO, Ann S.

1101 Pennsylvania Ave. NW
Suite 900
Washington, DC 20004
Tel: (202)637-3700
Fax: (202)637-3773

Employers
Goldman, Sachs and Co. (V. President)

COSTELLO, Daniel

1785 Massachusetts Ave. NW
Washington, DC 20036
Tel: (202)588-6000
Fax: (202)588-6059
Registered: LDA

Employers
Nat'l Trust for Historic Preservation (Senior Program Associate)

COSTELLO, Frank J.

888 17th St. NW
Suite 600
Washington, DC 20006-3959
EMail: fjcostello@zsrlaw.com
Tel: (202)298-8660
Fax: (202)342-0683

Employers
Zuckert, Scoutt and Rasenberger, L.L.P. (Partner)

Clients Represented
On Behalf of Zuckert, Scoutt and Rasenberger, L.L.P.
Martinair Holland
Nat'l Business Aviation Ass'n
South African Airways

COSTELLO, John H.

1111 19th St. NW
Suite 900
Washington, DC 20036
EMail: jcostello@cnfa.org
Tel: (202)296-3920
Fax: (202)296-3948

Employers
Citizens Network for Foreign Affairs (CNFA) (President)

COSTELLO, Lisa

1201 New York Ave. NW
Suite 600
Washington, DC 20005-3931
Tel: (202)289-3100
Fax: (202)289-3199

Former Staff Assistant to Rep. Bob Smith (R-NH).

Employers
American Hotel and Lodging Ass'n (PAC Director)

COSTELLO, Terence

499 S. Capitol St. SW
Suite 518
Washington, DC 20003
Tel: (202)484-0082
Fax: (202)484-5696
Registered: LDA

Former Professional Staff Member, House Armed Services Committee.

Employers
The Eagles Group (President)

Clients Represented
On Behalf of The Eagles Group
Diamond Head Financial Group
Edmund Scientific Co.
Export Management Services, Inc.
Mainwave Technologies
Thomas Group Internat'l
University of South Carolina

COSTER, John M.

P.O. Box 1417-D49
Alexandria, VA 22313-1417
Tel: (703)549-3001
Fax: (703)549-0771

Employers
Nat'l Ass'n of Chain Drug Stores (V. President, Federal and State Programs)

COSTIN, Sara

600 New Hampshire Ave. NW
Suite 601
Washington, DC 20037
Tel: (202)333-7400
Fax: (202)333-1638

Employers
Hill and Knowlton, Inc. (Managing Director)

COSTON, William D.

1201 New York Ave. NW
Suite 1000
Washington, DC 20005
EMail: adcoston@venable.com
Tel: (202)962-4813
Fax: (202)962-8300

Employers
Venable (Partner)

Clients Represented

On Behalf of Venable

Information Technology Industry Council

COTTER, Deborah

750 First St. NE
Washington, DC 20002-4242
Tel: (202)336-5500
Fax: (202)336-6069
Registered: LDA

Employers

American Psychological Ass'n (Legislative Assistant, Public Interest Policy)

COTTER, Lisa M.

1801 K St. NW
Suite 901-L
Washington, DC 20006
EMail: Lisa_Cotter@bm.com
Tel: (202)530-0500
Fax: (202)530-4800
Registered: LDA, FARA

Employers

BKSH & Associates (Director)

Clients Represented

On Behalf of BKSH & Associates

Advertising Company ART-ERIA
Jigawa, Nigerian State of

COTTILLI, Eugene J.

14th and Constitution Ave. NW
Room 3897
Washington, DC 20230
Tel: (202)482-2721
Fax: (202)482-2421

Employers

Department of Commerce - Bureau of Export Administration (Public Affairs Specialist, Office of Congressional, Public and Intergovernmental Affairs)

COTTON, Raymond D.

701 Pennsylvania Ave. NW
Suite 900
Washington, DC 20004-2608
EMail: rcotton@mintz.com
Tel: (202)434-7300
Fax: (202)434-7400
Registered: FARA

Special Assistant to the Secretary (1971-73) and Attorney/Advisor, Office of General Counsel (1969-70), Department of Health, Education and Welfare.

Employers

Mintz, Levin, Cohn, Ferris, Glovsky and Popeo, P.C. (Partner)

Clients Represented

On Behalf of Mintz, Levin, Cohn, Ferris, Glovsky and Popeo, P.C.

American College of Chest Physicians
Ass'n of Governing Boards of Universities and Colleges
California State University Institute
CVS, Inc.
George Washington University, Office of Government Relations
Mariner Post Acute Network
Medical College of Virginia, Dept. of Neurology, Office of the Chairman
Michigan Technological University
Monmouth University
Morehouse School of Medicine
Public Health Policy Advisory Board

COTTONE, Mel

1299 Pennsylvania Ave. NW
Suite 800 West
Washington, DC 20004
Tel: (202)785-0500
Fax: (202)785-5277
Registered: LDA

Assistant to Senator Robert F. Kennedy (D-NY), 1968. Staff Assistant, The White House, 1961-64.

Employers

The Carmen Group
Cottone and Huggins Group (Chairman)

Clients Represented

On Behalf of The Carmen Group

Wisconsin Public Service Corp.

On Behalf of Cottone and Huggins Group

Alliant Energy

COTTRELL, Jacqueline Dailey

1100 15th St. NW
Suite 900
Washington, DC 20005
Tel: (202)835-3400
Fax: (202)835-3414

Employers

Pharmaceutical Research and Manufacturers of America (Director, Public Affairs)

COUCH, Linda

2519 Connecticut Ave. NW
Washington, DC 20008-1520
Tel: (202)783-2242
Fax: (202)783-2255
Registered: LDA

Employers

American Ass'n of Homes and Services for the Aging (Associate Director)

COUFAL, Barbara

1625 L St. NW
Washington, DC 20036-5687
EMail: bcoufal@afscme.org
Tel: (202)429-5006
Fax: (202)223-3413
Registered: LDA

Employers

American Federation of State, County and Municipal Employees (Legislative Affairs Specialist)

COUGHLIN, Jeffrey R.

2501 M St. NW
Suite 550
Washington, DC 20037-1308
EMail: coughlin@im.org
Tel: (202)861-7700
Fax: (202)861-9731
Registered: LDA

Employers

Ass'n of Professors of Medicine (Legislative Associate)

COUGHLIN, Hon. R. Lawrence

700 14th St. NW
Suite 900
Washington, DC 20005
Tel: (202)508-1000
Fax: (202)508-1010
Registered: LDA

Member, U.S. House of Representatives (R-PA), 1969-93.

Employers

Thompson Coburn LLP (Partner)

Clients Represented

On Behalf of Thompson Coburn LLP

American Trucking Ass'ns
CEMEX USA
Los Angeles County Metropolitan Transportation Authority
Massachusetts Bay Transportation Authority
Metropolitan Atlanta Rapid Transit Authority
Regional Transportation Commission of South Nevada
Safegate Internat'l AB

COUGHLIN, Shawn

1100 New York Ave. NW
Suite 200M
Washington, DC 20005
EMail: shawn@caphg.com
Tel: (202)367-0440
Fax: (202)367-0470
Registered: LDA

Professional Staff Member, Subcommittee on Health, House Ways and Means Committee, 1995-96. Senior Health Policy Advisor to Rep. Nancy Johnson (R-CT), 1994-95. Legislative Assistant to Rep. Fred Grandy (R-IA), 1991-94.

Employers

Capitol Health Group, LLC (Principal)

Clients Represented

On Behalf of Capitol Health Group, LLC

Abbott Laboratories
Beverly Enterprises
Bristol-Myers Squibb Co.
Express Scripts Inc.
Greater New York Hospital Ass'n
Healthcare Leadership Council
Humana Inc.
Johnson & Johnson, Inc.
Medassets.com
Nat'l Ass'n of Psychiatric Health Systems
Northwestern Memorial Hospital
Pfizer, Inc.
Soc. of Thoracic Surgeons

COULAM, Weston J.

1666 K St. NW
Suite 800
Washington, DC 20006
Tel: (202)481-7000
Fax: (202)862-7098
Registered: LDA

Former Legislative Assistant to Senator Orrin G. Hatch (R-UT).

Employers

Arthur Andersen LLP (Manager)

Clients Represented

On Behalf of Arthur Andersen LLP

Coalition for the Fair Taxation of Business Transactions
Coalition to Preserve Employee Ownership of S Corporation
Eagle-Picher Personal Injury Settlement Trust
Hybrid Branch Coalition
Nat'l Ass'n of Investors Corporation (NAIC)
UtiliCorp United, Inc.

COULOMBE, Mary

1111 19th St. NW
Suite 800
Washington, DC 20036
Tel: (202)463-2700
Fax: (202)463-2785
Registered: LDA

Employers

American Forest & Paper Ass'n (Director, Timber Access and Supply)

COULSON, Lake

180 S. Washington St.
P.O. Box 6808
Falls Church, VA 22040
Tel: (703)237-8100
Fax: (703)237-7442
Registered: LDA

Employers

Plumbing, Heating, Cooling Contractors- National Assoc. (Director, Government Relations)

COUPER, William

730 15th St. NW
Fifth Floor
Washington, DC 20005
EMail: william.couper@bankof america.com
Tel: (202)624-1006
Fax: (202)624-7979

Employers

Bank of America (President)

COURPRON, Henri

198 Van Buren St.
Herndon, VA 20170
Tel: (703)834-3400
Fax: (703)834-3340

Employers

Airbus Industrie of North America, Inc. (President & Chief Operating Officer)

COURRIER, Kathleen

2100 M St. NW
Washington, DC 20037
Tel: (202)833-7200
Fax: (202)429-0687

Employers

The Urban Institute (V. President, Communications)

COURSEN, Hon. Christopher D.

1133 Connecticut Ave. NW
Suite 900
Washington, DC 20036
Tel: (202)775-0880
Fax: (202)872-9372
Registered: LDA

Has served as Chairman to the Advisory Board for Cuba Broadcasting, Exec. Office of the President, The White House. Majority Communications Counsel, Senate Committee on Commerce, Science, and Transportation, 1980-83.

Employers

The Coursen Group (President)

Clients Represented

On Behalf of The Coursen Group

Cablevision Systems Corp.
Medium-Sized Cable Operators Group
Northcoast Communications, LLC
Northwest Energy Efficiency Alliance
PSC Systems
The Washington Post Co.

COURSEY, Michael J.

3050 K St. NW
Washington, DC 20007
EMail: mcoursey@colliershannon.com
Tel: (202)342-8400
Fax: (202)342-8451
Registered: LDA

Deputy Assistant Secretary for Investigations (1988-89) and Director, Office of Investigations (1986-88), International Trade Administration, Department of Commerce.

Employers

Collier Shannon Scott, PLLC (Member)

Clients Represented

On Behalf of Collier Shannon Scott, PLLC

American Beekeeping Federation
American Honey Producers Ass'n
Coalition for Fair Atlantic Salmon Trade
Fair Atlantic Salmon Trade
Flexel, Inc.
Fresh Garlic Producer Ass'n
Winner Internat'l

COURT, Randolph

600 Pennsylvania Ave. SE
Suite 400
Washington, DC 20003
EMail: rcourt@dlcppi.org
Tel: (202)547-0001
Fax: (202)544-5014

Employers

Progressive Policy Institute (Technology Policy Analyst)

COURTIEN, William A.

1750 New York Ave. NW
Washington, DC 20006
Tel: (202)637-0700
Fax: (202)637-0771
Registered: LDA

Employers

Internat'l Union of Painters and Allied Trades (Exec. Assistant to the General President)

COURTNEY, Jim

1620 I St. NW
Suite 800
Washington, DC 20006
Tel: (202)833-9070
Fax: (202)833-9612

Employers

Generic Pharmaceutical Ass'n (Director, Communications)

COURTNEY, Kurt

1133 21st St. NW
Suite 700
Washington, DC 20036
EMail: wckmc12@aol.com
Tel: (202)887-6900
Fax: (202)887-6970

Employers

Janus-Merritt Strategies, L.L.C. (Assistant, Research Director)

COURTNEY, Rob

1634 I St. NW
Suite 1100
Washington, DC 20006-4003
EMail: rob@cdt.org
Tel: (202)637-9800
Fax: (202)637-0968

Employers

Center for Democracy and Technology (Policy Analyst)

COUSINO, Janelle

888 17th St. NW
Suite 800
Washington, DC 20006
Tel: (202)296-7010
Fax: (202)296-9374

Employers

Martin & Glantz LLC (V. President)

COVAIS, Ron

1725 Jefferson Davis Hwy.
Crystal Square 2, Suite 300
Arlington, VA 22202
Tel: (703)413-5600
Fax: (703)413-5617

Employers

Lockheed Martin Corp. (V. President, The Americas)

COVALL, Mark

325 Seventh St. NW
Suite 625
Washington, DC 20004-2802
EMail: execdir@naphs.org
Tel: (202)393-6700
Ext: 16
Fax: (202)783-6041
Registered: LDA

Employers

Nat'l Ass'n of Psychiatric Health Systems (Exec. Director)

COVE, Thomas J.

1150 17th St. NW
Suite 407
Washington, DC 20036
EMail: tomsgma@aol.com
Tel: (202)775-1762
Fax: (202)296-7462
Registered: LDA

Staff member, Drug Enforcement Administration, Department of Justice, 1985-91. Office of Sergeant at Arms, U.S. Senate, 1979-85.

Employers

Athletic Footwear Ass'n (V. President, Government Relations)
Billiard and Bowling Institute of America
Soccer Industry Council of America
Sporting Goods Manufacturers Ass'n (V. President, Government Relations)
Sports Apparel Products Council

COVELL, Andrea M.

One GEICO Plaza
Washington, DC 20076-0001
Tel: (301)986-3000

Employers

GEICO Corp. (V. President and Legislative Counsel)

COVERT, Rick

919 18th St. NW
Suite 300
Washington, DC 20006
Tel: (202)296-5544
Fax: (202)223-0321
Registered: LDA

Employers

American Financial Services Ass'n (V. President, State Government Affairs)

COVINGTON, Patricia

Hart Senate Office Bldg.
Room 321
Washington, DC 20510
Tel: (202)224-5351
Fax: (202)453-5218

Employers

Department of Veterans Affairs (Senate Liaison Officer)

COWAL, Sally Grooms

3501 Newark St. NW
Washington, DC 20016
EMail: cowal@us.yfu.org
Tel: (202)966-6800
Fax: (202)895-1104

Employers

Youth For Understanding Internat'l Exchange (President)

COWAN, Cameron

Washington Harbour
3050 K St. NW, Suite 200
Washington, DC 20007
Tel: (202)339-8400
Fax: (202)339-8500

Employers

Orrick Herrington & Sutcliffe LLP (Managing Partner)

COWAN, Frank

1625 L St. NW
Washington, DC 20036
Tel: (202)429-1111
Fax: (202)429-1102

Employers

American Federation of State, County and Municipal Employees (Assistant to the President)

COWAN, Glenn

1401 I St. NW
Suite 220
Washington, DC 20005
Tel: (202)216-8910
Fax: (202)216-8901

Employers

Public Strategies, Inc. (Managing Director)

COWAN, Joyce A.

1227 25th St. NW
Suite 700
Washington, DC 20037
Tel: (202)861-0900
Fax: (202)296-2882
Registered: LDA

Employers

Epstein Becker & Green, P.C. (Associate)

Clients Represented

On Behalf of Epstein Becker & Green, P.C.

AmSurg Corp.
Emergency Department Practice Management Ass'n (EDPMA)
Fallon Community Health Plan
Federation of American Hospitals
Nat'l Anti-Vivisection Soc.
Nat'l Funeral Directors Ass'n
Olsten Health Services
Watts Health Foundation

COWAN, Mark D.

2550 M St. NW
Washington, DC 20037-1350
Tel: (202)457-6000
Fax: (202)457-6315
Registered: LDA

Chief of Staff and Counselor (1982-84) and Deputy Assistant Secretary, Occupational Safety and Health Administration (1981-82), Commissioner, National Commission on Employment Policy, 1990-92. Department of Labor. Former Counsel, House Committee on Standards of Official Conduct. Former Operations Officer and Assistant Legislative Counsel, Central Intelligence Agency.

Employers

Patton Boggs, LLP (Partner)

Clients Represented

On Behalf of Patton Boggs, LLP

Internet Safety Ass'n

COWARD, Nicholas F.

815 Connecticut Ave. NW
Suite 900
Washington, DC 20006-4078
Tel: (202)452-7000
Fax: (202)452-7073

Employers

Baker & McKenzie (Managing Partner)

COWDEN, Dick

4717 Girton Ave.
Shady Side, MD 20764
Tel: (202)466-2687
Fax: (202)318-1103

Employers

American Ass'n of Enterprise Zones (Exec. Director)

COWDRY, M.D., Rex

Colonial Place Three
2107 Wilson Blvd., Suite 300
Arlington, VA 22201-3042
Tel: (703)524-7600
Fax: (703)524-9094
Registered: LDA

Employers

Nat'l Alliance for the Mentally Ill (Deputy Exec. Director, Research)

COWEN, Lee

2000 L St. NW
Suite 402
Washington, DC 20036
EMail: lcowen@usafunds.org
Tel: (202)466-4306
Fax: (202)223-0145
Registered: LDA

Employers

USA Funds, Inc. (V. President, Government Relations)

COWEN, William B.

1497 Chain Bridge Rd.
Suite 300
McLean, VA 22101
EMail: wcowen@ilalaw.com
Tel: (703)893-7071
Fax: (703)893-8020
Registered: LDA

Employers

Institutional Labor Advisors (Member of Firm)

Clients Represented

On Behalf of Institutional Labor Advisors

Retiree Benefits Alliance

COWLES, C. Deming

316 South Carolina Ave. SE
Washington, DC 20003
Tel: (202)544-9660
Fax: (202)544-9661
Registered: LDA

Employers

Law Office of C. Deming Cowles (Owner)

Clients Represented

On Behalf of Law Office of C. Deming Cowles

Elim, Alaska, City of
World Wildlife Fund

COX, Christopher W.

11250 Waples Mill Rd.
Fairfax, VA 22030-7400
Tel: (202)651-2567
Fax: (202)651-2577
Registered: LDA

Employers
Nat'l Rifle Ass'n Institute for Legislative Action (Federal Liaison)
Nat'l Rifle Ass'n of America (Federal Liaison)

COX, Craig

345 S. Patrick St.
Alexandria, VA 22314
Tel: (703)836-3654
Fax: (703)836-6086
Registered: LDA

Employers
Bob Lawrence & Associates (Senior Associate)

Clients Represented
On Behalf of Bob Lawrence & Associates
Minnesota Mining and Manufacturing Co. (3M Co.)

COX, Cynthia K.

1133 21st St. NW
Suite 900
Washington, DC 20036
EMail: cox.cynthia@bsc.bls.com
Tel: (202)463-4100
Fax: (202)463-4196
Registered: LDA

Employers
BellSouth Corp. (Exec. Director, Federal and State Relations)

COX, Douglas

1050 Connecticut Ave. NW
Washington, DC 20036-5306
EMail: dcox@gdclaw.com
Tel: (202)955-8500
Fax: (202)467-0539
Former Deputy Assistant Attorney General, Office of Legal Counsel, Department of Justice.

Employers
Gibson, Dunn & Crutcher LLP (Partner)

COX, Frances K.

1900 M St. NW
Suite 700
Washington, DC 20036
Tel: (202)463-7090
Fax: (202)463-1830
Registered: LDA

Employers
Ryder System, Inc. (Legislative Representative)

COX, III, George E.

1101 Vermont Ave. NW
12th Floor
Washington, DC 20005-3583
Tel: (202)789-7412
Fax: (202)789-7485
Registered: LDA

Employers
American Medical Ass'n (Senior Washington Counsel, Division of Legislative Counsel)

COX, J. Edward

2445 M St. NW
Washington, DC 20037-1420
Tel: (202)663-6000
Fax: (202)663-6363
Registered: FARA

Employers
Wilmer, Cutler & Pickering (Commercial Analyst)

COX, Jr., John A.

9300 Livingston Rd.
Fort Washington, MD 20744
EMail: john@ntma.org
Tel: (301)248-6200
Fax: (301)248-7104
Registered: LDA

Employers
Nat'l Tooling and Machining Ass'n (Manager, Government Affairs)

COX, CAE, John B.

2107 Wilson Blvd.
Suite 700
Arlington, VA 22201-3042
Tel: (703)243-2800
Fax: (703)243-9650

Employers
American Ass'n of Pharmaceutical Scientists (Exec. Director)

COX, John H.

1620 I St. NW
Suite 925
Washington, DC 20006
Tel: (202)293-5800
Fax: (202)463-8998
Press Secretary to Senator Jeff Sessions (R-AL), 1997-2000. Press Assistant to Speaker of the House, Rep. Newt Gingrich (R-GA), 1995-97.

Employers
The Roberts Group (Director, Government Relations)

COX, Joseph J.

1730 M St. NW
Suite 407
Washington, DC 20036
EMail: jcox@knowships.org
Tel: (202)775-4399
Fax: (202)659-3795
Registered: LDA

Employers
Chamber of Shipping of America (President)

COX, Kay

555 12th St. NW
Suite 1230
Washington, DC 20004
Tel: (202)783-1115
Fax: (202)783-5411

Employers
Beverly Enterprises (V. President, Federal Government Relations)

COX, Lisa

1225 New York Ave. NW
Suite 250
Washington, DC 20005-6156
Tel: (202)347-4450
Fax: (202)347-4453
Registered: LDA

Employers
American Soc. of Clinical Pathologists (Manager, Congressional and Regulatory Affairs)

COX, Rebecca G.

1350 I St. NW
Suite 1250
Washington, DC 20005
EMail: rcox01@coair.com
Tel: (202)289-6060
Fax: (202)289-1546
Registered: LDA
Formerly served in the Department of Transportation during the Reagan administration.

Employers
Continental Airlines Inc. (V. President, Government Affairs)

COX, Samuel W.

9200 Rockville Pike
Bethesda, MD 20814-3896
EMail: scox@goodwill.org
Tel: (301)530-6500
Fax: (301)530-1516

Employers
Goodwill Industries Internat'l, Inc. (Exec. V. President and Chief Operating Officer)

COX, Thomas E.

5315 Lee Hwy.
Suite B
Arlington, VA 22207
Tel: (703)241-0038
Fax: (703)241-0548

Employers
U.S.-Cuba Business Council (President)

COX, William M.

666 11th St. NW
Suite 600
Washington, DC 20001
EMail: wcox@ccianet.org
Tel: (202)783-0070
Fax: (202)783-0534
Served as Administrative Director, House Committee on International Relations. Former Administrative Assistant, House Committee on Foreign Affairs. Served as Systems Administrator to Rep. Lee H. Hamilton (D-IN).

Employers
Computer and Communications Industry Ass'n (CCIA) (Director, Operations)

COXSON, Harold P.

2400 N St. NW
Fifth Floor
Washington, DC 20037
Tel: (202)728-1164
Fax: (202)728-2992
Registered: LDA
Appellate Attorney, Office of the Solicitor, Department of Labor, 1972-74.

Employers
Ogletree Governmental Affairs, Inc. (Principal)

Clients Represented
On Behalf of Ogletree Governmental Affairs, Inc.
Alliance to Keep Americans Working
Americans for Better Borders
Council on Labor Law Equality
First Tuesday Group
Nat'l Alliance Against Blacklisting
SAFE Foundation - NMD Project

COYLE, Carmela

325 Seventh St. NW
Washington, DC 20004
Tel: (202)638-1100
Fax: (202)626-2670
Registered: LDA

Employers
American Hospital Ass'n (Senior V. President, Policy)

COYLE, Melissa

1001 Pennsylvania Ave. NW
Suite 1100
Washington, DC 20004-2595
EMail: mcoyle@cromor.com
Tel: (202)624-2938
Fax: (202)628-5116
Registered: LDA
Former Chief Negotiator on Tariffs and Market Access Issues, Office of the United States Trade Representative, Executive Office of the President, The White House. Former Director, Office of Mexico, Department of Commerce. Former Staff Trade Expert, House Ways and Means Committee and National Security Council

Employers
C&M Internat'l, Ltd. (Director)
Crowell & Moring LLP (Director, C & M International)

Clients Represented
On Behalf of C&M Internat'l, Ltd.
Avon Products, Inc.
DNA Plant Technology Corp.
Novartis Corp.
On Behalf of Crowell & Moring LLP
New York Life Internat'l Inc.

COYNE, Glenn

1776 Massachusetts Ave. NW
Suite 400
Washington, DC 20036
Tel: (202)872-0611
Fax: (202)872-0643

Employers
American Institute of Certified Planners (Director)

COYNE, III, Hon. James K.

4226 King St.
Alexandria, VA 22302-1507
EMail: JKC@nata-online.org
Tel: (703)845-9000
Fax: (703)845-8176
Registered: LDA
Member, U.S. House of Representatives (R-PA), 1981-83.

Employers
Nat'l Air Transportation Ass'n (President)

CRABBS, Raymond

1400 I St. NW
Suite 800
Washington, DC 20005
EMail: rcrabbs@pointsoflight.org
Tel: (202)729-8000
Fax: (202)729-8100

Employers
The Points of Light Foundation (Senior V. President)

CRABILL, Donald E.

1225 I St. NW
Suite 500
Washington, DC 20005
EMail: dawsonassociates@worldnet.att.net
Tel: (202)312-2005
Fax: (202)289-8683
Registered: LDA
Former Deputy Associate Director, Natural Resources, Office of Management and Budget, Executive Office of the President.

Employers
Dawson & Associates, Inc. (Senior Advisor)

Clients Represented
On Behalf of Dawson & Associates, Inc.
Anglogold Americas, Inc.
Chemical Land Holdings, Inc.

CRAFT, Jr., Robert H.

1701 Pennsylvania Ave. NW
Suite 800
Washington, DC 20006
Tel: (202)956-7500
Fax: (202)293-6330

Exec. Assistant to Chairman, Securities and Exchange Commission, 1976. Special Assistant to Under Secretary, Department of State, 1974-76.

Employers
Sullivan & Cromwell (Managing Partner)

CRAFTON, Ph.D., Christine G.

1350 I St. NW
Suite 400
Washington, DC 20005-3306
Tel: (202)371-6900
Fax: (202)842-3578

Employers
Motorola, Inc. (V. President and Director, Broadband Regulatory Policy)

CRAIB, Donald F.

900 Second St. NE
Suite 12
Washington, DC 20002-3557
EMail: donald_craib@saa.org
Tel: (202)789-8200
Fax: (202)789-0284
Registered: LDA

Employers
Soc. for American Archaeology (Manager, Government Affairs and Counsel)

CRAIG, Ashley W.

1710 Rhode Island Ave. NW
Tenth Floor
Washington, DC 20036
EMail: acraig@rofgw.com
Tel: (202)973-2981
Fax: (202)293-3307
Registered: LDA

Employers
Rodriguez O'Donnell Fuerst Gonzalez & Williams (Associate)

Clients Represented

On Behalf of Rodriguez O'Donnell Fuerst Gonzalez & Williams
Coalition for Fair Play in Ocean Shipping
New York/New Jersey Foreign Freight Forwarders and Brokers Ass'n, Inc.
Ocean World Lines, Inc.

CRAIG, Bruce

400 A St. SE
Washington, DC 20003
EMail: rbcraig3@juno.com
Tel: (202)544-2422
Ext: 116
Fax: (202)544-8307

Formerly at Nat'l Park Service, Department of the Interior.

Employers
Nat'l Coordinating Committee for the Promotion of History (Director)

CRAIG, Daniel

1724 Massachusetts Ave. NW
Washington, DC 20036-1969
Tel: (202)775-3550
Fax: (202)775-3671
Registered: LDA

Employers
Nat'l Cable Television Ass'n (Director, Legislative Policy)

CRAIG, Gregory B.

725 12th St. NW
Washington, DC 20005
Tel: (202)434-5000
Fax: (202)434-5029

Senior Advisor on Foreign Policy and Defense to Senator Edward M. Kennedy (D-MA), 1984-88.

Employers
Williams & Connolly (Partner)

Clients Represented

On Behalf of Williams & Connolly
Haiti, Chamber of Commerce of the Republic of
Special Olympics, Inc.

CRAIG, Patricia J.

1001 Connecticut Ave. NW
Suite 507
Washington, DC 20036
Tel: (202)466-0001
Fax: (202)466-0002
Registered: LDA

Employers
Craig Associates (President)

Clients Represented

On Behalf of Craig Associates
County Welfare Directors Ass'n of California
Dakota, Minnesota, County of
San Bernardino County Social Services Department
San Bernardino, California, County of
St. Louis, Minnesota, Social Services Department of the County of

CRAIGHEAD, Alison S.

1120 Connecticut Ave. NW
Suite 480
Washington, DC 20036-3989
Tel: (202)775-8277
Fax: (202)775-8284

Employers
American Dietetic Ass'n (Manager, Government and Political Affairs)

CRAIN, Claiborn H.

1400 Independence Ave. SW
Room 4051, South Bldg.
Washington, DC 20250
EMail: ccrain@rus.usda.gov
Tel: (202)720-1255
Fax: (202)720-1725

Employers
Department of Agriculture - Rural Utilities Service (Legislative and Public Affairs Advisor)

CRAIN, Julie

1735 New York Ave. NW
Suite 500
Washington, DC 20006-4759
Tel: (202)628-1700
Fax: (202)331-1024

Employers
Preston Gates Ellis & Rouvelas Meeds LLP (Associate)

CRAINE, Brenda L.

1101 Vermont Ave. NW
12th Floor
Washington, DC 20005-3583
Tel: (202)789-7447
Fax: (202)789-7401

Employers
American Medical Ass'n (Assistant Director, Division of Media and Information Services)

CRAM, M. Victoria

1455 F St. NW
Suite 225
Washington, DC 20005
Tel: (202)638-3307
Fax: (202)783-6947
Registered: LDA

Staff Assistant to Rep. John Seiberling (D-OH), 1978-79.

Employers
Ball Janik, LLP (Government Relations Consultant)

Clients Represented

On Behalf of Ball Janik, LLP
Bellevue, Washington, City of
Greenbrier Companies
Hermiston, Oregon, City of
Las Vegas, Nevada, City of
Modesto, California, City of
Northwest Woodland Owners Council
Portland, Oregon, City of
Whittier, California, City of

CRAMER, E. Sue

801 Pennsylvania Ave. NW
Suite 250
Washington, DC 20004
EMail: e-sue.cramer@fpc.com
Tel: (202)783-5560
Fax: (202)783-5569
Registered: LDA

Employers
Progress Energy (Manager, Federal Affairs)

CRAMER, Laurie

805 15th St. NW
Suite 510
Washington, DC 20005
EMail: lcramer@ngsa.org
Tel: (202)326-9300
Fax: (202)326-9330

Employers
Natural Gas Supply Ass'n (Director, Communications)

CRAMER, Wendy Rice

1808 I St. NW
Eighth Floor
Washington, DC 20006
Tel: (202)223-4817
Fax: (202)296-0011

Employers
Deere & Co. (Manager, Federal Government Affairs)

CRAMPTON, Ann F.

655 National Press Bldg.
Washington, DC 20045
EMail: acrampton@johnadams.com
Tel: (202)737-8400
Fax: (202)737-8406

Employers
John Adams Associates Inc. (V. President and Director, Administration)

CRANDALL, Derrick A.

1225 New York Ave. NW
Suite 450
Washington, DC 20005
EMail: arc@funoutdoors.com
Tel: (202)682-9530
Fax: (202)682-9529

Employers
American League of Anglers and Boaters (Contact)
American Recreation Coalition (President)

CRANDALL, Grant

8315 Lee Hwy.
Fairfax, VA 22031
Tel: (703)208-7200
Fax: (703)208-7132

Employers
United Mine Workers of America (General Counsel)

CRANDALL, Kathy

1801 18th St. NW
Suite 9-2
Washington, DC 20009
Tel: (202)833-4668
Fax: (202)234-9536

Employers
Alliance for Nuclear Accountability (Program Associate)

CRANDALL, Robert W.

1775 Massachusetts Ave. NW
Washington, DC 20036-2188
Tel: (202)797-6000
Fax: (202)797-6004

Former Acting Deputy and Assistant Director, Council on Wage and Price Stability.

Employers
The Brookings Institution (Senior Fellow, Economic Studies)

CRANE, Brent

1615 L St. NW
Suite 900
Washington, DC 20036
EMail: craneimdi@aol.com
Tel: (202)337-1022
Fax: (202)337-6678

Employers
Internat'l Management and Development Institute (Director, Programs and Publications)

CRANE, Daniel M.

1010 Pennsylvania Ave. SE
Washington, DC 20003
Tel: (202)546-4991
Fax: (202)544-7926
Registered: LDA

Served as Legislative Director for Rep. John LaFalce (D-NY) and Senator Daniel Patrick Moynihan (D-NY). Former Tax Counsel to Rep. Frank Guarini (D-NJ), 1991.

Employers
Campbell Crane & Associates

Clients Represented

On Behalf of Campbell Crane & Associates
American Ass'n of Advertising Agencies
Celanese Government Relations Office
The Chubb Corp.
Citigroup
Massachusetts Water Resources Authority
Merck & Co.
Raytheon Co.
Securities Industry Ass'n
Shriners Hospital for Children
University of Massachusetts
USX Corp.

CRANE, Edward H.

1000 Massachusetts Ave. NW
Washington, DC 20001
Tel: (202)842-0200
Fax: (202)842-3490

Employers
Cato Institute (President and Chief Exec. Officer)

CRANE, Dr. Keith

1111 14th St. NW
Suite 801
Washington, DC 20005
Tel: (202)898-0471
Fax: (202)898-0445

Employers
PlanEcon Inc. (Research Director)

CRANE, Martin J.

1125 15th St. NW
Suite 801
Washington, DC 20005
Tel: (202)785-9300
Fax: (202)775-1950

Employers
Sherman, Dunn, Cohen, Leifer & Yellig, P.C.

CRANE, Rhonda

1120 20th St. NW
Suite 1000
Washington, DC 20036
EMail: rcrane@att.com
Tel: (202)457-2402
Fax: (202)457-2571

Employers
AT&T (Director, International Public Affairs)

CRANE, Stacey L.

1029 Vermont Ave. NW
Suite 710
Washington, DC 20005
Tel: (202)737-0660
Fax: (202)737-0662

Employers
Municipal Treasurers Ass'n of the United States and Canada (Exec. Director)

CRANE, Stephen C.

950 N. Washington St.
Alexandria, VA 22314-1552
Tel: (703)836-2272
Fax: (703)684-1924

Employers
American Academy of Physician Assistants (Exec. V. President)

CRANE, Steve E.

1420 New York Ave. NW
Suite 1050
Washington, DC 20005
Tel: (202)638-1950
Fax: (202)638-1928
Registered: LDA

Employers
Van Scoyoc Associates, Inc. (Legislative Associate)

Clients Represented

On Behalf of Van Scoyoc Associates, Inc.
APG Army Alliance
Arista Knowledge Systems, Inc.
Ass'n of Schools of Public Health
Ass'n of Universities for Research in Astronomy, Inc.
Baltimore, Maryland, City of
Bethesda Academy for the Performing Arts
Board on Human Sciences
Computer Data Systems, Inc.
Computer Sciences Corp.
Johns Hopkins School of Hygiene and Public Health
Johns Hopkins University-Applied Physics Lab
Lehigh University
Morgan State University
Mount Sinai School of Medicine
NASA Aeronautics Support Team
Nat'l Ass'n for Equal Opportunity in Higher Education
Orasure Technologies
Regents College
Reno & Cavanaugh, PLLC
Space Explorers Inc.
University of Connecticut
University of Missouri

CRANER, Lorne W.

1212 New York Ave. NW
Suite 900
Washington, DC 20005
Tel: (202)408-9450
Fax: (202)408-9462

Employers
Internat'l Republican Institute (President)

CRANFORD, Sharon H.

200 Orchard Ridge Dr.
Suite 302
Gaithersburg, MD 20878
EMail: scranford@naea.org
Tel: (301)212-9608
Fax: (301)990-1611
Registered: LDA

Employers
Nat'l Ass'n of Enrolled Agents (Director, Public Policy and External Relations)

CRANN, Daniel K.

1120 Connecticut Ave. NW
Suite 1100
Washington, DC 20036
EMail: dcrann@gpcusa.com
Tel: (202)861-5899
Fax: (202)861-5795
Registered: LDA

Senior Legislative Assistant to Rep. Peter Blute (R-MA), 1995-97.

Employers
GPC Internat'l (Director of Federal Relations)

Clients Represented

On Behalf of GPC Internat'l
Boardman, Ohio, Township of
Fidelity Investments Co.
Ion Track Instruments
Massachusetts Port Authority
Nellie Mae
PriceWaterhouseCoopers
The Providence Plan
Providence Redevelopment Agency
Roger Williams Medical Center
Tishman Construction Corp. of Washington D.C.

CRANNEY, Jr., James R.

6707 Old Dominion Dr.
Suite 320
McLean, VA 22101
EMail: jcranney@usapple.org
Tel: (703)442-8850
Fax: (703)790-0845

Employers
U.S. Apple Ass'n (V. President, Industry Services)

CRANWELL, George E.

4113 Lee Hwy.
Arlington, VA 22207
Tel: (703)522-2255
Fax: (703)522-0765

Employers
Cranwell & O'Connell (Partner)

Clients Represented

On Behalf of Cranwell & O'Connell
American Soc. for Photogrammetry and Remote Sensing
Arlington Educational Ass'n Retirement Housing Corp.
Ass'n of Teacher Educators
Internat'l Council on Education for Teaching
Internat'l Geographic Information Foundation

CRAVEN, Donald B.

1333 New Hampshire Ave. NW
Suite 400
Washington, DC 20036
Tel: (202)887-4000
Fax: (202)887-4288

Associate Assistant Administrator and Acting Assistant Administrator, Federal Energy Administration, 1974-75. Trial Attorney, Tax Division, Department of Justice, 1968-73.

Employers
Akin, Gump, Strauss, Hauer & Feld, L.L.P. (Partner)

CRAVER, Roger M.

4121 Wilson Blvd.
11th Floor
Arlington, VA 22203
Tel: (703)258-0000
Fax: (703)258-0001

Employers
Craver, Mathews, Smith and Co. (Chairman)

CRAWFORD, Brian

1300 N. 17th St.
Eighth Floor
Arlington, VA 22209
EMail: crawford@abc.org
Tel: (703)812-2000
Fax: (703)812-8202
Registered: LDA

Employers
Coalition to Repeal the Davis-Bacon Act (Washington Representative)

CRAWFORD, Charles

1155 15th St. NW
Suite 1004
Washington, DC 20005
EMail: ccrawford@acb.org
Tel: (202)467-5081
Fax: (202)467-5085

Employers
American Council of the Blind (Exec. Director)
Library Users of America
Nat'l Ass'n of Blind Teachers
Visually Impaired Data Processors Internat'l

CRAWFORD, Christopher L.

6764 Old McLean Village Dr.
McLean, VA 22101
Tel: (703)748-2575

Employers
Nat'l Ass'n of Development Companies (Exec. Director)

CRAWFORD, Jr., John M.

10015 Main St.
Fairfax, VA 22031-3489
EMail: sgia@sgia.org
Tel: (703)385-1335
Fax: (703)273-0456

Employers
Screenprinting & Graphic Imaging Ass'n Internat'l (President)

CRAWFORD, Michael

919 18th St. NW
Suite 800
Washington, DC 20006
Tel: (202)628-4160
Fax: (202)347-5323

Employers
Human Rights Campaign Fund (Western Field Organizer)

CRAWFORD, Rebecca B.

1725 K St. NW
Suite 1404
Washington, DC 20006
Tel: (202)296-7116
Fax: (202)659-5322
Registered: LDA

Employers
American Cotton Shippers Ass'n

CRAWFORD, Richard C.

801 Pennsylvania Ave. NW
North Bldg., Suite 252
Washington, DC 20004-2604
Tel: (202)737-4444
Fax: (202)737-0951
Registered: LDA

Employers
Coors Brewing Company (Director, Federal Government Affairs)

CRAWFORD, Richard L. "Dick"

1725 DeSales St. NW
Suite 802
Washington, DC 20036
EMail: dick.crawford@mcd.com
Tel: (202)887-8900
Fax: (202)887-8907
Registered: LDA

Employers
McDonald's Corp. (Senior Director, Government Relations)

CRAWFORD, Ronald

1700 K St. NW
Suite 1000
Washington, DC 20006
Tel: (202)296-5505
Fax: (202)296-6140
Registered: LDA

Employers
F/P Research Associates (President)

Clients Represented

On Behalf of F/P Research Associates
American Bus Ass'n
Nat'l Cable Television Ass'n
Wiley, Rein & Fielding

CRAWFORD, Steve

1424 16th St. NW
Suite 700
Washington, DC 20036
EMail: scrawford@npa1.org
Tel: (202)265-7685
Fax: (202)797-5516

Employers
Nat'l Policy Ass'n (V. President)

CRAWFORD, Thomas R.

1200 New Hampshire Ave NW
Suite 430
Washington, DC 20036
EMail: trcrawford@aol.com
Tel: (202)955-3030
Fax: (202)955-1147
Registered: LDA

Employers
Murray, Scheer, Montgomery, Tapia & O'Donnell (Legislative Director)

Clients Represented

On Behalf of Murray, Scheer, Montgomery, Tapia & O'Donnell

Allmerica Financial
California State Assembly - Committee on Rules
Cleveland Cliffs Iron Co.
Equitable Assurance Soc. of the United States
The Equitable Cos.
Iron Ore Ass'n
Lafayette Consolidated Government
Metropolitan Life Insurance Co.
Mine Safety Appliances
MONY Life Insurance Co.
Nat'l Council of Coal Lessors
New England Financial
New England Life Insurance Co.
Pacific Life Insurance Co.
Passaic Valley Sewerage Commissioners
Penn Mutual Life Insurance Co.
PepsiCo, Inc.
Piedmont Environmental Council
PIMCO Advisors, L.P.
Porsche Cars North America, Inc.
Qualimetrics, Inc.
Science & Engineering Associates, Inc.
Sherwin Williams Co.
Shubert Organization Inc.
Southern California Ass'n of Governments
Swaziland Sugar Ass'n
Tricon Global Restaurants Inc.
United Biscuit
Wheeling & Lake Erie Railway Co.
Wisconsin Central Transportation Corp.

CRAWFORD, Tim

1700 K St. NW
Suite 1000
Washington, DC 20006
Tel: (202)296-5505
Fax: (202)296-6140

Employers

F/P Research Associates (V. President)

CRAWLEY, Penny

919 18th St. NW
Tenth Floor
Washington, DC 20006
Tel: (202)263-2900
Fax: (202)263-2960

Employers

Issue Dynamics Inc. (Senior Consultant, Grassroots Organizing Team)

CRAYBAS, Marisa

700 13th St. NW
Suite 400
Washington, DC 20005
Tel: (202)347-0773
Fax: (202)347-0785
EMail: mcraybas@cassidy.com

Former Intern for Domestic Policy, The White House, Executive Office of the President.

Employers

Cassidy & Associates, Inc. (Account Executive)

CRAYTON, Christina

440 First St. NW
Eighth Floor
Washington, DC 20001
Tel: (202)942-4228
Fax: (202)737-0480

Employers

Women Officials in NACo

CREAGAN, Timothy P.

7910 Woodmont Ave.
Suite 1200
Bethesda, MD 20814
Tel: (301)657-2248
Fax: (301)913-9413

Employers

Self Help for Hard of Hearing People, Inc. (Public Policy Program Coordinator)

CREECH, Catherine L.

655 15th St. NW
Suite 900
Washington, DC 20005-5701
Tel: (202)626-5800
Fax: (202)628-0858
EMail: ccreech@milchev.com

Attorney/Advisor, Office of Tax Policy, Department of the Treasury, 1991-94.

Employers

Miller & Chevalier, Chartered (Member)

CREGAN, James R.

1211 Connecticut Ave. NW
Suite 610
Washington, DC 20036
Tel: (202)296-7277
Fax: (202)296-0343
Registered: LDA

Employers

Magazine Publishers of America (Exec. V. President, Government Affairs)

CREIGHTON, Richard C.

1225 I St. NW
Suite 300
Washington, DC 20005
Tel: (202)408-9494
Fax: (202)408-0877
Registered: LDA

Employers

American Portland Cement Alliance (President)

CRERAR, Ken A.

701 Pennsylvania Ave. NW
Suite 750
Washington, DC 20004
Tel: (202)783-4400
Fax: (202)783-4410
Registered: LDA
EMail: ciab@ciab.com

Employers

The Council of Insurance Agents & Brokers (President and Chief Exec. Officer)

CRESCENZO, Raymond T.

1090 Vermont Ave. NW
Suite 200
Washington, DC 20005-4905
Tel: (202)371-0910
Fax: (202)371-0134
Registered: LDA

Employers

Associated Credit Bureaus, Inc. (V. President, Industry Relations)

CRESSY, Peter H.

1250 I St. NW
Suite 400
Washington, DC 20005-3998
Tel: (202)628-3544
Fax: (202)682-8888
EMail: pcressy@discus.org

Employers

Distilled Spirits Council of the United States, Inc. (President and Chief Exec. Officer)

CREWS, Clyde Wayne

1000 Massachusetts Ave. NW
Washington, DC 20001
Tel: (202)842-0200
Fax: (202)842-3490

Employers

Cato Institute (Director, Technology Studies)

CREWS, Mark

1130 Connecticut Ave. NW
Suite 830
Washington, DC 20036
Tel: (202)261-5000
Fax: (202)296-7937

Employers

Southern Co. (Director, Federal Regulatory Affairs)

CRIBBEN, Mark V.

2121 K Street NW
Suite 325
Washington, DC 20037
Tel: (202)728-0610
Fax: (202)728-0617
EMail: mcribben@acep.org

Employers

American College of Emergency Physicians (Political Action Director)

CRICK SAHATJIAN, Laurie

600 New Hampshire Ave. NW
11th Floor
Washington, DC 20037
Tel: (202)944-3000
Fax: (202)944-3068
Registered: LDA
EMail: lcs@dejlaw.com

Employers

Dyer Ellis & Joseph, P.C. (Partner)

Clients Represented

On Behalf of Dyer Ellis & Joseph, P.C.

American Coke and Coal Chemicals Institute
BLNG, Inc.
Browning Transport Management
FastShip, Inc.
Glass Packaging Institute
Hvide Marine Inc.
Marine Spill Response Corporation
Nat'l Oilseed Processors Ass'n
TI Group Inc.
The Trump Organization

CRIGLER, John

1000 Potomac St. NW
Suite 500
Washington, DC 20007
Tel: (202)965-7880
Fax: (202)965-1729

Employers

Garvey, Schubert & Barer (Partner)

CRIPPS, Corrie

500 E. Street SW
Suite 920
Washington, DC 20024
Tel: (202)479-4050
Fax: (202)484-1312
Registered: LDA
EMail: corrie.cripps@aopa.org

Employers

Aircraft Owners and Pilots Ass'n (Legislative Representative)

CRISTOL, Richard E.

1101 15th St. NW
Suite 202
Washington, DC 20005
Tel: (202)785-3232
Fax: (202)223-9741
EMail: rcristol@kellencompany.com

Employers

Ass'n for Dressings and Sauces (President)
Ass'n of Fund-Raising Distributors and Suppliers (Washington Representative)
Calorie Control Council (Washington Representative)
Exhibit Designers and Producers Ass'n (Washington Representative)
Food Update Foundation (Exec. Director)
Healthcare Convention and Exhibitors Ass'n (Washington Representative)
Internat'l Food Additives Council (Washington Representative)
Internat'l Formula Council (Exec. V. President)
Internat'l Jelly and Preserve Ass'n (Washington Representative)
The Kellen Company (Exec. V. President)
Lignin Institute (Washington Representative)
Nat'l Ass'n of Margarine Manufacturers (President)
Nat'l Institute of Oilseed Products (Exec. Director)
Nat'l Pecan Shellers Ass'n (Washington Representative)
Processed Apples Institute (Washington Representative)
The Vinegar Institute (Washington Representative)

Clients Represented

On Behalf of The Kellen Company

Ass'n for Dressings and Sauces
Ass'n of Fund-Raising Distributors and Suppliers
Calorie Control Council
Exhibit Designers and Producers Ass'n
Food Update Foundation
Healthcare Convention and Exhibitors Ass'n
Internat'l Food Additives Council
Internat'l Formula Council
Internat'l Jelly and Preserve Ass'n
Lignin Institute
Nat'l Ass'n of Margarine Manufacturers
Nat'l Institute of Oilseed Products
Nat'l Pecan Shellers Ass'n
Processed Apples Institute
The Vinegar Institute

CRITZ, Anna

One Dupont Circle NW
Suite 340
Washington, DC 20036-1170
Tel: (202)223-2318
Fax: (202)293-2223
EMail: critza@act.org

Employers

ACT, Inc. (Director)

CROCKER, Michael

1215 Jefferson Davis Hwy.
Suite 1004
Arlington, VA 22202
Tel: (703)416-8000
Fax: (703)416-8010
EMail: mdcrocker@drs.com

Employers

DRS Technologies, Inc. (V. President, Navy Programs)

CROCKER, Thomas E.

601 Pennsylvania Ave. NW
11th Floor, North Bldg.
Washington, DC 20004-2601
Tel: (202)756-3318
Fax: (202)756-3333
Registered: LDA
EMail: tcrocker@alston.com
Foreign Service Officer, Department of State, 1976-1981.

Employers
Alston & Bird LLP (Partner)

Clients Represented
On Behalf of Alston & Bird LLP
General Electric Co.

CROCKETT, Elizabeth Schmidtlein

1730 Pennsylvania Ave. NW
Suite 1200
Washington, DC 20006-4706
Tel: (202)737-0500
Fax: (202)626-3737

Employers
King & Spalding (Associate)

CROMARTIE, Michael

1015 15th St. NW
Suite 900
Washington, DC 20005
EMail: ethics@eppc.org
Tel: (202)682-1200
Fax: (202)408-0632

Employers
Ethics and Public Policy Center (V. President)

CRONIN, Edmund B.

6110 Executive Blvd.
Suite 800
Rockville, MD 20852-3927
EMail: lcronin@washreit.com
Tel: (301)984-9400
Fax: (301)984-9610

Employers
Washington Real Estate Investment Trust (President and Chief Executive Officer)

CRONIN, Jeff

1250 Connecticut Ave. NW
Washington, DC 20036
Tel: (202)833-1200
Fax: (202)659-3716

Employers
Common Cause (Press Secretary)

CRONIN, Kevin

900 19th St. NW
Suite 250
Washington, DC 20006
Tel: (202)682-2345
Fax: (202)218-7730

Employers
Internat'l Insurance Council (President)

CRONMILLER, Rae E.

4301 Wilson Blvd.
Arlington, VA 22203-1860
Tel: (703)907-5791
Fax: (703)907-5517
Registered: LDA
EMail: rae.cronmiller@nreca.org

Employers
Nat'l Rural Electric Cooperative Ass'n (Environmental Counsel)

CROOKS, Edwin W.

1015 15th St. NW
Suite 700
Washington, DC 20005-2605
Tel: (202)828-5200
Fax: (202)785-2645

Employers
Bechtel Group, Inc. (V. President and Development and Finance Manager (Bechtel Enterprises))

CROPPER, Cabell

444 N. Capitol St. NW
Suite 618
Washington, DC 20001
EMail: info@ncja.org
Tel: (202)624-1440
Fax: (202)508-3859

Employers
Nat'l Criminal Justice Ass'n (Exec. Director)

CROSBY, Harriett

1601 Connecticut Ave. NW
Suite 301
Washington, DC 20009
EMail: hcrosby@isar.org
Tel: (202)387-3034
Fax: (202)667-3291

Employers
ISAR, Initiative for Social Action and Renewal in Eurasia (President)

CROSBY, IV, John H.

1700 18th St. NW
Washington, DC 20009
Tel: (202)234-4700
Fax: (202)265-9317
Registered: LDA
EMail: john-c@sla.org

Employers
Special Libraries Ass'n (Director, Public Communications)

CROSBY, Mary

3615 Wisconsin Ave. NW
Washington, DC 20016
Tel: (202)966-7300
Fax: (202)966-1944
Registered: LDA
EMail: mcrosby@aacap.org

Employers
American Academy of Child and Adolescent Psychiatry (Director, Government Affairs/Deputy Exec. Director)

CROSBY, Jr., William D.

801 Pennsylvania Ave. NW
Suite 750
Washington, DC 20004
Tel: (202)628-3750
Fax: (202)624-0659
Registered: LDA
EMail: billcrosby@solomongroup.com
Chief Counsel (1995-99) and Republican Chief Counsel (1972-95), House Rules Committee. Served in the U.S. Navy, 1968-71.

Employers
The Solomon Group, LLC (V. President and Chief Operating Officer)

Clients Represented
On Behalf of The Solomon Group, LLC
Alliance for American Innovation, Inc.
Clough, Harbour & Associates LLP
General Electric Co.
"K" Line America, Inc.

CROSER, M. Doreen

444 N. Capitol St. NW
Suite 846
Washington, DC 20001-1512
EMail: dcroser@aamr.org
Tel: (202)387-1968
Fax: (202)387-2193

Employers
American Ass'n on Mental Retardation (Exec. Director)

CROSON, Matthew

4350 N. Fairfax Dr.
Suite 600
Arlington, VA 22203
Tel: (703)243-8555
Fax: (703)243-8556

Employers
Packaging Machinery Manufacturers Institute (Director, Communications)

CROSS, Aaron W.

1301 K St. NW
Suite 1200-West Tower
Washington, DC 20005-3307
Tel: (202)515-5091
Fax: (202)515-5078
Registered: LDA
EMail: across@us.ibm.com

Employers
Internat'l Business Machines Corp. (Public Policy Program Director)

CROSS, Christopher T.

1319 F St. NW
Suite 900
Washington, DC 20004-1152
EMail: info@c-b-e.org
Tel: (202)347-4171
Fax: (202)347-5047

Employers
Council for Basic Education (President)

CROSS, Jordan

1801 N. Moore St.
Arlington, VA 22209
Tel: (703)528-0700
Fax: (703)528-2146
EMail: jcross@aasa.org

Employers
American Ass'n of School Administrators (Legislative Specialist)

CROSS, Mary

555 New Jersey Ave. NW
Washington, DC 20001
Tel: (202)393-6370
Fax: (202)879-4402
Registered: LDA

Employers
American Federation of Teachers (Associate Director, Legislative Affairs)

CROTTEAU, Craig A.

1401 K St. NW
Suite 801
Washington, DC 20005
Tel: (202)682-1147
Fax: (202)682-1171
Registered: LDA

Employers
IT Group, Inc. (V. President, Government Affairs)

CROUSE, Michael J.

1750 New York Ave. NW
Washington, DC 20006
Tel: (202)737-8484
Fax: (202)737-8418

Employers
Internat'l Ass'n of Fire Fighters (Chief of Staff)

CROW, David T.

4800 Hampden Ln.
Seventh Floor
Bethesda, MD 20814
Tel: (301)656-7603
Fax: (301)654-7354
Registered: LDA
EMail: dcrow@dclrs.com
Special Assistant to the Chief of Staff of the Secretary (1985-86) and Staff Member (1981-85), Department of Agriculture. Former Special Assistant to Rep. E. Thomas Coleman (R-MO).

Employers
Small Business Council of America (Legislative Consultant)

CROWDERS, Charles E.

1450 G St. NW
Suite 500
Washington, DC 20005
Registered: LDA

Employers
Auyua Inc.

CROWE, Christine Marie

1299 Pennsylvania Ave. NW
Tenth Floor
Washington, DC 20004-2400
EMail: christinecrowe@paulhastings.com
Tel: (202)508-9500
Fax: (202)508-9700
Law Clerk, Office of Thrift Supervision, Department of Treasury, 1991-92. Law Clerk, Office of the Pardon Attorney, Department of Justice, 1990-91.

Employers
Paul, Hastings, Janofsky & Walker LLP (Associate)

CROWE, David A.

1201 15th St. NW
Washington, DC 20005-2800
Tel: (202)822-0200
Fax: (202)822-0572

Employers
Nat'l Ass'n of Home Builders of the U.S. (Staff V. President, Housing Policy)

CROWE, Thomas K.

2300 M St. NW
Suite 800
Washington, DC 20037
Tel: (202)973-2890
Fax: (202)973-2891
Registered: LDA
EMail: tkcrowe@bellatlantic.net

Employers
Law Offices of Thomas K. Crowe

Clients Represented
On Behalf of Law Offices of Thomas K. Crowe
Northern Mariana Islands, Commonwealth of the

CROWLEY, Daniel F. C.

1735 K St. NW
Washington, DC 20006-1506
Tel: (202)728-6989
Fax: (202)728-8419
EMail: dan.crowley@nasd.com

Employers
Nat'l Ass'n of Securities Dealers, Inc. (NASD) (V. President, Governmental Affairs)

CROWLEY, Katherine C.

950 H St. NW
Room 8350
Washington, DC 20001
EMail: kcrowley@usss.treas.gov
Tel: (202)406-5676
Fax: (202)406-5740

Employers
Department of Treasury - United States Secret Service (Special Agent in Charge, Congressional Affairs)

CROWLEY, Sheila

1012 14th St. NW
Suite 610
Washington, DC 20005
EMail: info@nlihc.org
Tel: (202)662-1530
Fax: (202)393-1973
Congressional Fellow to the Minority Staff, Subcommittee on Housing Opportunity and Community Development, Senate Committee on Banking, Housing and Urban Affairs, 1997.

Employers
Nat'l Low Income Housing Coalition/LIHIS (President)

CROWN, Michele F.

1400 16th St. NW
Suite 400
Washington, DC 20036-2220
EMail: mcrown@ofwlaw.com
Tel: (202)518-6316
Fax: (202)234-0399

Employers
Olsson, Frank and Weeda, P.C. (Of Counsel)

CRUM, Janis

1333 New Hampshire Ave. NW
Suite 400
Washington, DC 20036
Tel: (202)887-4000
Fax: (202)887-4288
Former Counsel to the Chairman, Federal Communications Commission.

Employers
Akin, Gump, Strauss, Hauer & Feld, L.L.P. (Associate)

CRUM, John

1155 16th St. NW
Washington, DC 20036
EMail: j_crum@acs.org
Tel: (202)872-4534
Fax: (202)872-6055

Employers
American Chemical Soc. (Exec. Director)

CRUMBLISS, John A.

700 13th St. NW
Suite 400
Washington, DC 20005
EMail: jcrumbliss@cassidy.com
Tel: (202)347-0773
Fax: (202)347-0785
Registered: LDA

Employers
Cassidy & Associates, Inc. (Account Executive)

Clients Represented
On Behalf of Cassidy & Associates, Inc.
Lorain County Community College
New Jersey Institute of Technology
Phoenix, Arizona, City of
Rhode Island School of Design
Sacramento Area Flood Control Agency
Smartforce
Ultracard, Inc.
Valley Hospital Foundation
VoiceStream Wireless Corp.

CRUMLEY, James

1650 Tysons Blvd.
Suite 1700
McLean, VA 22201
Tel: (703)790-6300
Fax: (703)790-6365
Registered: LDA

Employers
ITT Industries (V. President, Government Relations)

CRUMP, CMP, CAE, John

1225 11th St. NW
Washington, DC 20001
EMail: nationalba@aol.com
Tel: (202)842-3900
Fax: (202)289-6170

Employers
Nat'l Bar Ass'n (Exec. Director)
Nat'l Coalition of Black Meeting Planners (Chairman)

CRUSE, Kelly

1250 I St. NW
Suite 1110 DGA 4GA
Washington, DC 20005
Tel: (202)682-4530

Employers
Southwest Airlines (Coordinator, Government Affairs)

CRUZ, Ronaldo

3211 Fourth St. NE
Washington, DC 20017
Tel: (202)541-3150
Fax: (202)722-8717

Employers
United States Catholic Office of Bishops/Secretariat for Hispanic Affairs (Director)

CRYAN, Roger

2101 Wilson Blvd.
Suite 400
Arlington, VA 22201
EMail: rcryan@nmpf.org
Tel: (703)243-6111
Fax: (703)841-9328

Employers
Nat'l Milk Producers Federation (Director, Economic Research)

CRYAN, Thomas M.

1666 K St. NW
Suite 800
Washington, DC 20006
Tel: (202)481-7000
Fax: (202)862-7098
Registered: LDA

Employers
Arthur Andersen LLP (Principal)

CRYE, J. Michael

2111 Wilson Blvd.
Eighth Floor
Arlington, VA 22201-3058
EMail: crye@alcalde-fay.com
Tel: (703)841-0626
Fax: (703)243-2874
Registered: LDA

Employers
Alcalde & Fay (Partner)
Internat'l Council of Cruise Lines (President)

Clients Represented
On Behalf of Alcalde & Fay
Internat'l Council of Cruise Lines
PetrolRem, Inc.
Tampa Port Authority

CSONTOS, Stephen J.

950 Pennsylvania Ave. NW
Room 4645
Washington, DC 20530
Tel: (202)307-6419
Fax: (202)305-0660

Employers
Department of Justice - Tax Division (Senior Legislative Counsel, Office of Legislation and Policy)

CUERVO, Asela M.

625 Slaters Ln.
Suite 200
Alexandria, VA 22314-1171
EMail: aselac@aahomecare.org
Tel: (703)836-6263
Fax: (703)836-6730
Registered: LDA

Employers
American Ass'n for Homecare (V. President, Legal and Government Affairs)

CULBERTSON, Eliza

600 Pennsylvania Ave. SE
Suite 400
Washington, DC 20003
EMail: eculbertson@dlcppi.org
Tel: (202)546-0007
Fax: (202)546-0628

Employers
Democratic Leadership Council (Director, Information Systems)

CULBERTSON, Steven A.

1101 15th St. NW
Suite 200
Washington, DC 20005-5002
EMail: culbs@ysa.org
Tel: (202)296-2992
Fax: (202)296-4030

Employers
Youth Service America (Chief Exec. Officer)

CULKIN, Jr., Charles W.

2208 Mount Vernon Ave.
Alexandria, VA 22301-1314
Tel: (703)684-6931
Fax: (703)548-9367

Employers
Ass'n of Government Accountants (Exec. Director)

CULLEEN, Lawrence E.

555 12th St. NW
Washington, DC 20004-1206
EMail: Lawrence_Culleen@aporter.com
Tel: (202)942-5000
Fax: (202)942-5999
Former Chief of Staff to the Assistant Administrator for Prevention, Pesticides and Toxic Substances, Environmental Protection Agency.

Employers
Arnold & Porter (Special Counsel)

CULLEN, Elizabeth

750 First St. NE
Washington, DC 20002-4242
Tel: (202)336-5500
Fax: (202)336-6069
Registered: LDA

Employers
American Psychological Ass'n (Director, Congressional Affairs)

CULLEN, Geoffrey

1625 Massachusetts Ave. NW
Suite 500
Washington, DC 20036
Tel: (202)232-4677
Fax: (202)232-5756

Employers
Can Manufacturers Institute (Director, Government Relations)

CULLEN, Katie

1401 H St. NW
Suite 220
Washington, DC 20005
Tel: (202)467-6240
Fax: (202)467-6225
Registered: LDA

Employers
Integrated Waste Services Ass'n (V. President, Media Relations and Legislative Affairs)

CULLEN, Maura

1140 Connecticut Ave.
Suite 502
Washington, DC 20036
Tel: (202)293-9101
Fax: (202)293-9111
Registered: LDA

Employers
Cartwright & Riley (Partner)

Clients Represented
On Behalf of Cartwright & Riley
Anthem, Inc.
Kentucky, Commonwealth of

CULLEN, Sr., Paul D.

1101 30th St. NW
Suite 300
Washington, DC 20007
Tel: (202)944-8600
Fax: (202)944-8611
Registered: LDA
Trial Attorney, Civil Division, Department of Justice, 1970-72.

Employers
The Cullen Law Firm (Partner)

Clients Represented
On Behalf of The Cullen Law Firm
Owner-Operator Independent Drivers Ass'n, Inc.

CULLINAN, Dennis M.

200 Maryland Ave. NE
Washington, DC 20002
EMail: dcullinan@vfwdc.org
Tel: (202)543-2239
Fax: (202)543-0961
Registered: LDA

Employers
Veterans of Foreign Wars of the U.S. (Director, National Legislative Service)

CULLO, Diane L.

727 N. Washington St.
Alexandria, VA 22314
Tel: (703)836-3410
Fax: (703)836-2049

Employers
United Fresh Fruit and Vegetable Ass'n (Director of Public Affairs and Communications; PAC Contact)

CULPEPPER, R. Lee

1200 17th St. NW
Washington, DC 20036-3097
Tel: (202)331-5900
Fax: (202)973-5373
Registered: LDA
EMail: lculpepper@dineout.org

Employers
Coalition for Job Opportunities (Contact)
Nat'l Restaurant Ass'n (Senior V. President, Government Affairs and Public Policy)

CULVAHOUSE, Jr., Arthur B.

555 13th St. NW
Suite 500 West
Washington, DC 20004
Tel: (202)383-5300
Fax: (202)383-5414
Registered: LDA
EMail: aculvahouse@omm.com
Counsel to the President, The White House, 1987-89. Chief Legislative Assistant to Senator Howard H. Baker, Jr. (R-TN), 1973-76.

Employers
O'Melveny and Myers LLP (Partner)

Clients Represented
On Behalf of O'Melveny and Myers LLP
Advanced Micro Devices
Civil Justice Reform Group
Verizon Communications

CULVER, Hon. John C.

1050 Connecticut Ave. NW
Washington, DC 20036-5339
Tel: (202)857-6000
Fax: (202)857-6395
Registered: LDA
Member, U.S. House of Representatives (D-IA), 1965-75. Member, U.S. Senate (D-IA), 1975-81.

Employers
Arent Fox Kintner Plotkin & Kahn, PLLC (Member)

Clients Represented
On Behalf of Arent Fox Kintner Plotkin & Kahn, PLLC
Biomedical Research Institute
Fannie Mae
Raytheon Co.
Renewable Resources LLC

CUMMINGS, Cassandra

1400 I St. NW
Suite 540
Washington, DC 20005-2208
Tel: (202)638-6219
Fax: (202)638-0145
EMail: cassandracummings@ipc.org

Employers
IPC Washington Office (Government Coordinator)

CUMMINGS, Kelly

1255 23rd St. NW
Suite 200
Washington, DC 20037-1174
Tel: (202)452-8100
Fax: (202)833-3636

Employers
Hauck and Associates
State Government Affairs Council (Director of Operations and Member Services)

Clients Represented
On Behalf of Hauck and Associates
State Government Affairs Council

CUMMINGS, Marc D.

1341 G St. NW
Suite 1100
Washington, DC 20005
Tel: (202)393-2260
Fax: (202)393-0712

Employers
Infotech Strategies, Inc. (Director, E-Government and E-Business)

CUMMINGS, Philip T.

1225 I St. NW
Suite 810
Washington, DC 20005
Tel: (202)289-9800
Fax: (202)289-3588
Registered: LDA
EMail: pcummings@theaccordgroup.com
Chief Counsel (1987-88, 1977-80), Minority Counsel (1981-86), and Counsel (1970-76), Senate Committee on Environment and Public Works.

Employers
The Accord Group (Principal and PAC Contact)

Clients Represented
On Behalf of The Accord Group
Clean Water Act Reauthorization Coalition
General Electric Co.

CUMMINS, Cheryl C.

1025 Thomas Jefferson St. NW
Suite 500 W
Washington, DC 20007-5201
Tel: (202)624-7000
Fax: (202)624-7140
EMail: ccummins@uli.org

Employers
Urban Land Institute (Exec. V. President and Chief Operating Officer)

CUMMINS, James

1920 L St. NW
Washington, DC 20036
Tel: (202)223-8700
Fax: (202)659-5559
EMail: jcummins@kamber.com

Employers
The Kamber Group (V. President, Senior Producer)

CUNARD, Jeffrey P.

555 13th St. NW
1100 East
Washington, DC 20004-1179
Tel: (202)383-8000
Fax: (202)383-8118
Registered: FARA
EMail: jpcunard@debevoise.com
Law Clerk to Judge William Matthew Byrne, Jr., U.S. District Court for Central District of Columbia, 1980-81.

Employers
Debevoise and Plimpton (Partner)

Clients Represented
On Behalf of Debevoise and Plimpton
Sony Corp.

CUNEO, Garrett

1701 Clarendon Blvd.
Arlington, VA 22209
Tel: (703)276-8800
Fax: (703)243-2593
Registered: LDA

Employers
American Chiropractic Ass'n (Exec. V. President)

CUNEO, Jonathan W.

317 Massachusetts Ave. NE
Suite 300
Washington, DC 20002
Tel: (202)789-3960
Fax: (202)789-1813
Registered: LDA
Counsel, Subcommittee on Monopolies and Commercial Law, House Judiciary Committee, 1981-86. Attorney, Office of the General Counsel, Federal Trade Commission, 1978-81. Law Clerk to Judge Edward A. Tamm, U.S. Court of Appeals for the District of Columbia Circuit, 1977-78.

Employers
The Cuneo Law Group, P.C.

Clients Represented
On Behalf of The Cuneo Law Group, P.C.
Committee to Support the Antitrust Laws
Nat'l Ass'n of Securities and Commercial Law Attorneys
Taxpayers Against Fraud, The False Claims Legal Center

CUNNINGHAM, Carl

2011 Pennsylvania Ave. NW
Suite 800
Washington, DC 20006-1808
Tel: (202)261-4500
Ext: 259
Fax: (202)835-0443
EMail: asimprokop@mem.po.com

Employers
American College of Physicians-American Soc. of Internal Medicine (ACP-ASIM) (Director, Competitiveness Advisory Services)

CUNNINGHAM, Charles H.

11250 Waples Mill Rd.
Fairfax, VA 22030-7400
Tel: (202)651-2570
Fax: (202)651-2577
Registered: LDA

Employers
Nat'l Rifle Ass'n Institute for Legislative Action (Director, Federal Affairs)
Nat'l Rifle Ass'n of America (Director, Federal Affairs)

CUNNINGHAM, Charles V.

3797 Dade Dr.
Annandale, VA 22003
Tel: (703)204-2366
Fax: (703)204-2367
Registered: LDA
EMail: ccunningham@cox.rr.com
Director, Fibers Analysis Division, Agricultural, Stabilization and Conservation Service, Department of Agriculture, 1962-92.

Employers
Charles V. Cunningham & Assoc. (President)

Clients Represented
On Behalf of Charles V. Cunningham & Assoc.
Dunavant Enterprises
Hohenberg Brothers, Co.

CUNNINGHAM, Daniel

1755 Jefferson Davis Hwy.
Suite 1107
Arlington, VA 22202
Tel: (703)415-0344
Fax: (703)415-0182
Registered: LDA

Employers
The PMA Group (Associate)

Clients Represented
On Behalf of The PMA Group
AAI Corp.
Battelle
Biocontrol Technology, Inc.
Cartwright Electronics
Concurrent Technologies Corp.
CRYPTEK Secure Communications, LLC
Dynacom Industries
Electro-Radiation Inc.
Gentex Corp.
Guild Associates
L-3 Communications Corp.
MIC Industries, Inc.
Microvision, Inc.
MTS Systems Inc.
Planning Systems, Inc.
SatoTravel
SIGCOM, Inc.
Stanly County Airport Authority
TeleFlex Canada, Ltd.
Textron Inc.

CUNNINGHAM, Don

1801 K St. NW
Suite 1000L
Washington, DC 20006
Tel: (202)530-0400
Fax: (202)530-4500
EMail: don_cunningham@washbm.com

Employers
Burson-Marsteller (Managing Director, Media Practice)

CUNNINGHAM, Richard O.

1330 Connecticut Ave. NW
Washington, DC 20036-1795
Tel: (202)429-6434
Fax: (202)429-3902

Employers
Steptoe & Johnson LLP (Partner)

Clients Represented
On Behalf of Steptoe & Johnson LLP
USEC, Inc.

CUNNINGHAM, Sean

1275 Pennsylvania Ave. NW
Tenth Floor
Washington, DC 20004
Tel: (202)347-6000
Fax: (202)347-6001
Registered: LDA

Employers
Balch & Bingham LLP (Attorney)

Clients Represented
On Behalf of Balch & Bingham LLP
FirstEnergy Co.
informal coalition
Potomac Electric Power Co.
TVA Watch

CUNNINGHAM, Sherri

410 First St. SE
Third Floor
Washington, DC 20003
Tel: (202)484-2776
Fax: (202)484-7016
EMail: scunningham@dcsgroup.com

Employers
The DCS Group (Group Director)

CUNNINGHAM, Susan O.

401 Ninth St. NW
Suite 900
Washington, DC 20004
Tel: (202)585-8734
Fax: (202)585-8080
EMail: scunningham@nixonpeabody.com

Employers
Nixon Peabody LLP (Partner)

CUNNINGHAM, William

601 Pennsylvania Ave. NW
Suite 900 South
Washington, DC 20004
Tel: (202)220-3181
Registered: LDA
Deputy Staff Director, Senate Banking Committee, 1989-91. Former Adminstrative Assistant to Rep. Joe Kennedy (D-MA).

Employers
Capitol Partners (Principal)

Clients Represented
On Behalf of Capitol Partners
Biochemics
Biogen, Inc.
Biomatrix
Cambridge Redevelopment Authority
Concord Family and Adolescent Services
Emmanuel College
FLIR Systems, Inc.
Marsh USA, Inc.
Smith & Wesson

CUNNINGHAM, William J.

555 New Jersey Ave. NW
Washington, DC 20001
Tel: (202)393-6301
Fax: (202)879-4402
Registered: LDA

Employers
American Federation of Teachers (Associate Director, Legislative Affairs)

CUPPERNULL, Carolyn M.

1615 L St. NW
Suite 650
Washington, DC 20036
Tel: (202)626-8547
Fax: (202)626-8581
EMail: cmcupp@jeffersongr.com

Employers
Jefferson Government Relations, L.L.C. (Principal and Chief Administrative Officer)

CUPPETT, Ted

1320 Fenwick Ln.
Suite 100
Silver Spring, MD 20910
Tel: (301)588-1454
Fax: (301)588-4732

Employers
American Federation of Home Care Providers (President)

CURCIO, Paul

305 Cameron St.
Alexandria, VA 22314
Tel: (703)683-8326
Fax: (703)683-8826
EMail: pcurcio@srcmedia.com

Employers
Stevens Reed Curcio & Co. (Partner)

CURLIN, Peggy

1400 16th St. NW
Suite 100
Washington, DC 20036
Tel: (202)667-1142
Fax: (202)332-4496
EMail: curlin@cedpa.org

Employers
Centre for Development and Population Activities (President)

CURRAN, Frank P.

7315 Wisconsin Ave.
Suite 1250W
Bethesda, MD 20814
Tel: (301)907-2862
Fax: (301)907-2864
Registered: LDA

Employers
Ass'n for Financial Professionals, Inc. (V. President, Government Relations and Technical Services)

CURRAN, Robert J.

1717 Pennsylvania Ave. NW
12th Floor
Washington, DC 20006
Tel: (202)416-0150
Registered: LDA
EMail: bobcurran@cs.net

Employers
Potomac Strategies Internat'l LLC (V. President)

Clients Represented
On Behalf of Potomac Strategies Internat'l LLC
Command Systems Inc.
Orbital Sciences Corp., Fairchild Defense Division

CURRIE, Rodger

1100 15th St. NW
Suite 900
Washington, DC 20005
Tel: (202)835-3400
Fax: (202)835-3414
Former Staff Member, House Committee on Ways and Means.

Employers
Pharmaceutical Research and Manufacturers of America (Assistant General Counsel)

CURRIER, Ken

475 L'Enfant Plaza SW
MS: 10917
Washington, DC 20260
Tel: (202)268-3616

Employers
United States Postal Service (Government Relations Manager)

CURRIS, Constantine

1307 New York Ave.
Fifth Floor
Washington, DC 20005-4701
Tel: (202)478-4647
Fax: (202)478-1511
EMail: currisc@aascu.org

Employers
American Ass'n of State Colleges and Universities (President)

CURRY, Anne McGhee

655 15th St. NW
Washington, DC 20005-5701
Tel: (202)220-0623
Fax: (202)220-0873
Registered: LDA
EMail: acurry@fmi.org

Employers
Food Marketing Institute (V. President, Legislative and Political Affairs)

CURRY, USA, Col. Don

1300 Defense Pentagon
Room 3D919
Washington, DC 20301-1300
Tel: (703)695-4132
Fax: (703)695-5860

Employers
Department of Defense (Director, House Affairs, Office of Legislative Liaison)

CURRY, John J.

1891 Preston White Dr.
Reston, VA 20191-9312
Tel: (703)648-8900
Fax: (703)262-9312

Employers
American College of Radiology (Exec. Director)

CURRY, Page

1200 New Hampshire Ave. NW
Suite 410
Washington, DC 20036
Tel: (202)721-8100
Fax: (202)721-8105
Registered: LDA
EMail: pcurry@vha.com

Employers
VHA Inc. (Government Relations Representative)

CURTIN, Kevin G.

700 13th St. NW
Suite 500
Washington, DC 20005
Tel: (202)508-6017
Fax: (202)508-6111
Registered: LDA
Chief Counsel and Staff Director (1989-96), Senior Counsel (1987-89) and Legislative Counsel (1976-87), Senate Committee on Commerce, Science and Transportation.

Employers
Law Offices of Kevin G. Curtin

Clients Represented
On Behalf of Law Offices of Kevin G. Curtin
Air Transport Ass'n of America
Anheuser-Busch Cos., Inc.
CSX Corp.
Maersk Inc.
Nat'l Center for Tobacco-Free Kids
Verizon Communications
Zenith Electronics Corp.

CURTIS, RSM, Anne

801 Pennsylvania Ave. SE
Suite 460
Washington, DC 20003
Tel: (202)547-5556
Fax: (202)547-5510
Registered: LDA
EMail: network@networklobby.org

Employers
NETWORK, A Nat'l Catholic Social Justice Lobby (Lobbyist)

CURTIS, Chris

2980 Fairview Park Dr.
Suite 1400
Falls Church, VA 22042
Tel: (703)289-7800
Registered: LDA

Employers
Capital One Financial Corp. (Associate General Counsel)

CURTIS, Dina

900 19th St. NW
Suite 400
Washington, DC 20006
Tel: (202)628-5624
Fax: (202)296-8716
Registered: LDA

Employers
American League of Financial Institutions (President)

CURTIS, Garry

1090 Vermont Ave. NW
Third Floor
Washington, DC 20005
Tel: (202)842-3600
Fax: (202)842-4032

Employers
Hager Sharp Inc. (Senior V. President)

CURTIS, Jody

1828 L St. NW
Suite 300
Washington, DC 20036
Tel: (202)466-6512
Fax: (202)785-3926

Employers
Council on Foundations (Managing Editor, "Foundation News and Commentary")

CURTIS, Kevin

1200 18th St. NW
Washington, DC 20036
Tel: (202)887-8800
Fax: (202)887-8877
Registered: LDA
EMail: kcurtis@environet.org

Employers
Nat'l Environmental Trust (V. President, Government Affairs)

CURTIS, Lynn A.

1660 L St. NW
Suite 200
Washington, DC 20036
Tel: (202)429-0440
Fax: (202)452-0164

Employers
Milton S. Eisenhower Foundation (President)

CURTIS, Tom

1401 New York Ave. NW
Suite 640
Washington, DC 20005
Tel: (202)628-8303
Fax: (202)628-2846
EMail: tcurtis@awwa.org

Employers
American Water Works Ass'n (Deputy Exec. Director)

CURTISS, Catherine

1775 I St. NW
Suite 600
Washington, DC 20006-2401
Tel: (202)721-4600
Fax: (202)721-4646

Employers
Hughes Hubbard & Reed LLP (Partner)

Clients Represented

On Behalf of Hughes Hubbard & Reed LLP

Canada, Government of
Ecuador, Government of the Republic of

CURTISS, James R.

1400 L St. NW
Washington, DC 20005-3502
Tel: (202)371-5751
Fax: (202)371-5950
Registered: LDA
EMail: jcurtiss@winston.com

Member, Nuclear Regulatory Commission, 1988-93. Former Counsel and Staff Director, Senate Environment and Public Works Subcommittee on Nuclear Regulation.

Employers

Winston & Strawn (Partner, Energy Practice)

Clients Represented

On Behalf of Winston & Strawn

CAMECO Corp.

CURTO, Michael A.

2550 M St. NW
Washington, DC 20037-1350
Tel: (202)457-6000
Fax: (202)457-6315
Registered: LDA
EMail: mcurto@pattonboggs.com

Employers

Patton Boggs, LLP (Partner)

Clients Represented

On Behalf of Patton Boggs, LLP

Mars, Inc.

CURZON, Elliott R.

1775 I St. NW
Washington, DC 20006
Tel: (202)261-3341
Fax: (202)261-3333
EMail: elliott.curzon@dechert.com

Employers

Dechert (Counsel)

CUSHING, Christopher T.

1001 Pennsylvania Ave. NW
Suite 450 North
Washington, DC 20004
Tel: (202)789-4040
Fax: (202)789-4242
Registered: LDA

Employers

Commonwealth Group, Ltd. (President)

Clients Represented

On Behalf of Commonwealth Group, Ltd.

American Management Services, Inc.
CTC Corp.
EXECUTONE Information Systems, Inc.
Maricopa, Arizona, County of
Massachusetts Turnpike Authority
Nexia Biotechnologies, Inc.
OraVax, Inc.

CUSHING, Mark L.

1666 K St. NW
Suite 1200
Washington, DC 20005
Tel: (202)833-9200
Fax: (202)293-5939

Employers

Winstead, Sechrest & Minick, P.C. (Of Counsel)

CUSICK, Kristen

815 Connecticut Ave. NW
Suite 330
Washington, DC 20006
Tel: (202)263-6263
Fax: (202)728-0338
Registered: LDA
EMail: cusickk@questdiagnostics.com

Employers

Quest Diagnostics Inc. (Director, Federal Affairs)

CUSTER, Jr., B. Scott

2300 N St. NW
Washington, DC 20037-1128
Tel: (202)663-8000
Fax: (202)663-8007
EMail: scott.custer@shawpittman.com

Executive Assistant to the Deputy Secretary, Department of State.

Employers

Shaw Pittman (Partner)

Clients Represented

On Behalf of Shaw Pittman

Air Foyle, Ltd.

CUTLER, Eliot R.

1333 New Hampshire Ave. NW
Suite 400
Washington, DC 20036
Tel: (202)887-4000
Fax: (202)887-4288
Registered: LDA

Employers

Akin, Gump, Strauss, Hauer & Feld, L.L.P. (Partner)

CUTLER, Jay B.

1400 K St. NW
Washington, DC 20005
Tel: (202)682-6060
Fax: (202)682-6850
Registered: LDA

Employers

American Psychiatric Ass'n (Director, Government Relations/Special Counsel)

CUTLER, Lloyd N.

2445 M St. NW
Washington, DC 20037-1420
Tel: (202)663-6000
Fax: (202)663-6363
Registered: LDA
EMail: lcutler@wilmer.com

Counsel to the President, The White House, 1994 and 1979-80. Former Law Clerk to Judge Charles Clark, U.S. Court of Appeals, Second Circuit.

Employers

Wilmer, Cutler & Pickering (Partner)

Clients Represented

On Behalf of Wilmer, Cutler & Pickering

Deutsche Telekom, Inc.
Loral Space and Communications, Ltd.
Swiss Bank Corp.
Swiss Bankers Ass'n
Union Bank of Switzerland
VeriSign/Network Solutions, Inc.

CUTLER, Lynn G.

2099 Pennsylvania Ave. NW
Suite 100
Washington, DC 20006
Tel: (202)955-3000
Fax: (202)955-5564
EMail: lgcutler@hklaw.com

Employers

Holland & Knight LLP (Senior Public Affairs Advisor)

CUTLER, Michael E.

1201 Pennsylvania Ave. NW
Washington, DC 20004-2401
Tel: (202)662-6000
Fax: (202)662-6291
EMail: mcutler@cov.com

Law Clerk to Judge Arlin M. Adams, U.S. Court of Appeals, Third Circuit, 1981-82.

Employers

Covington & Burling (Partner)

Clients Represented

On Behalf of Covington & Burling

Columbia Capital Corp.

CUTLER, Walter L.

1630 Crescent Pl. NW
Washington, DC 20009-4099
Tel: (202)667-6800
Fax: (202)667-1475

Employers

Meridian Internat'l Center (President)

CUTRONE, Roseann M.

1440 New York Ave. NW
Washington, DC 20005
Tel: (202)371-7000
Fax: (202)393-5760
Registered: LDA

Employers

Skadden, Arps, Slate, Meagher & Flom LLP (Counsel)

Clients Represented

On Behalf of Skadden, Arps, Slate, Meagher & Flom LLP

American Electronics Ass'n
Clark/Bardes, Inc.
Fidelity Charitable Gift Fund
Fort Howard Corp.
MCI WorldCom Corp.
Pharmaceutical Research and Manufacturers of America
Sequent Computer Systems

CUTTINO, Phyllis

1301 Connecticut Ave. NW
Suite 700
Washington, DC 20036
Tel: (202)462-4900
Fax: (202)462-2686
Registered: LDA

Employers

Better World Campaign (V. President, Public Affairs)

CYMROT, Mark A.

1050 Connecticut Ave. NW
Suite 1100
Washington, DC 20036-5304
Tel: (202)861-1500
Fax: (202)861-1790
Registered: LDA

Employers

Baker & Hostetler LLP

Clients Represented

On Behalf of Baker & Hostetler LLP

Sutton & Sutton Solicitors

CYNKAR, Robert J.

1500 K St. NW
Suite 200
Washington, DC 20005
Tel: (202)220-9600
Fax: (202)220-9601

Deputy Assistant Attorney General, Civil Division, Department of Justice, 1985-88. Special Assistant to the Attorney General, Department of Justice, 1985. Assistant U.S. Attorney, Eastern District of Virginia, Department of Justice, 1981-83. General Counsel, Subcommittee on Regulatory Reform, Senate Judiciary Committee, 1979-81. Minority Counsel, Subcommittee on Improvements in Judicial Machinery, Senate Judiciary Committee, 1979-81.

Employers

Cooper, Carvin & Rosenthal (Partner)

CYS, Richard L.

1500 K St. NW
Suite 450
Washington, DC 20005
Tel: (202)508-6600
Fax: (202)508-6699

Employers

Davis Wright Tremaine LLP (Partner)

CZEPLUCH, Ralf W. K.

P.O. Box 338
McLean, VA 22101
Tel: (703)827-8855
Registered: LDA

Employers

Self-employed as an independent consultant.

Clients Represented

As an independent consultant

Edison Electric Institute

CZWARTACKI, John

1875 I St. NW
Suite 540
Washington, DC 20006
Tel: (202)822-0655
Fax: (202)822-2022
EMail: cz@greenerandhook.com

Press Secretary to Senate Majority Leader Trent Lott (R-MS), 1998-2000. Communications Director to Rep. L. William Paxon (R-NY), 1997-98. Press Secretary, House Republican Conference, 1994-96. Press Secretary to Rep. John Boehner (R-OH), 1992-94. Spokesperson, Department of Housing and Urban Development 1989-92.

Employers

Greener and Hook, LLC (Partner)

D'AGOSTINO, Bruce

7918 Jones Branch Dr.
Suite 540
McLean, VA 22102-3307
Tel: (703)356-2622
Fax: (703)356-6388
EMail: bdagostino@cmaanet.org

Employers

Construction Management Ass'n of America (Exec. Director)

D'ARCY, Sean G.

1333 New Hampshire Ave. NW
Suite 400
Washington, DC 20036
Tel: (202)887-4000
Fax: (202)887-4288
Registered: LDA

Former tax aide to Rep. Don Pease (D-OH).

Employers

Akin, Gump, Strauss, Hauer & Feld, L.L.P. (Partner)

Clients Represented

On Behalf of Akin, Gump, Strauss, Hauer & Feld, L.L.P.

Alliance of American Insurers
American Airlines
APKINDO
Bear, Stearns and Co.
Bechtel Group, Inc.
The Boeing Co.
Citizen's Educational Foundation
Educational Foundation for Citizenship and Statehood Project
EMC Corp.
Fremont Group, Inc.
Heard Goggan Blair & Williams
Liberty Mutual Insurance Group
Nationwide Mutual Insurance Co.
PerkinElmer Detection Systems
Wausau Insurance Cos.

D'ESPOSITO, Julian

1909 K St. NW
Washington, DC 20006
Tel: (202)263-3000
Fax: (202)263-3300

Employers

Mayer, Brown & Platt

Clients Represented

On Behalf of Mayer, Brown & Platt

Illinois, State of

D'ESPOSITO, Stephen

1612 K St. NW
Suite 808
Washington, DC 20006
Tel: (202)887-1872
Fax: (202)887-1875

Employers

Mineral Policy Center (President)

D'ORAZIO, Triana R.

1717 K St. NW
Suite 311
Washington, DC 20036
Tel: (202)293-2828
Fax: (202)293-2849

Employers

Mexican-American Legal Defense and Educational Fund (Public Affairs Coordinator)

D'SOUZA, Dinesh

1150 17th St. NW
Washington, DC 20036
Tel: (202)862-5800
Fax: (202)862-7177
EMail: ddsouza@aei.org

Employers

American Enterprise Institute for Public Policy Research (John Olin Research Fellow)

D'ZURILLA, June

1101 15th St. NW
Suite 1100
Washington, DC 20005
Tel: (202)331-6950
Fax: (202)331-2805
Registered: LDA
EMail: jsdzurilla@mmm.com

Employers

Minnesota Mining and Manufacturing Co. (3M Co.) (Manager, Government Relations)

DAALDER, Ivo H.

1775 Massachusetts Ave. NW
Washington, DC 20036-2188
Tel: (202)797-6000
Fax: (202)797-6004

Former Member, Study Group of U.S. Commission on National Security/21st Century; Director for European Affairs, National Security Council, 1996-96.

Employers

The Brookings Institution (Visiting Fellow, Foreign Policy Studies)

DABAGHI, William K.

1801 K St. NW
Washington, DC 20006
Tel: (202)775-7100
Fax: (202)857-0172
Registered: LDA, FARA
EMail: wdabaghi@arterhadden.com

Director, Office of Congressional Affairs, Office of the Secretary, Department of Transportation, 1982-83. Attorney, Office of General Counsel, Small Business Administration, 1974-76.

Employers

Arter & Hadden (Partner)

Clients Represented

On Behalf of Arter & Hadden

Canadian Broiler Hatching Egg Marketing Agency
Canadian Chicken Marketing Agency
Canadian Egg Marketing Agency
Canadian Turkey Marketing Agency
Houston Clearing House Ass'n

DABROWSKI, Ray

12501 Old Columbia Pike
Silver Spring, MD 20904
Tel: (301)680-6300
Fax: (301)680-6312
EMail: 73064.104@compuserve.com

Employers

General Conference of Seventh-day Adventists (Director, Communication)

DABSON, Brian

777 N. Capitol St. NE
Suite 410
Washington, DC 20002
Tel: (202)408-9788
Fax: (202)408-9793
Registered: LDA
EMail: BrianD@cfeb.org

Employers

Corporation for Enterprise Development (President)

DACEK, Raymond F.

701 Pennsylvania Ave. NW
Suite 800
Washington, DC 20004
Tel: (202)508-4100
Fax: (202)508-4321
Registered: LDA
EMail: rdacek@thelenreid.com

Employers

Thelen Reid & Priest LLP (Of Counsel)

Clients Represented

On Behalf of Thelen Reid & Priest LLP

Edison Electric Institute

DACEY, Scott C.

300 N. Lee St.
Suite 500
Alexandria, VA 22314
Tel: (703)518-8600
Fax: (703)518-8611
Registered: LDA

Chief of Staff, National Indian Gaming Commission, 1998-99.

Employers

PACE-CAPSTONE (Partner)

Clients Represented

On Behalf of PACE-CAPSTONE

Agua Caliente Band of Cahuilla Indians
Barona Band of Mission Indians
Colorado River Indian Tribes
Kern, California, County of
Morongo Band of Mission Indians
Multimedia Games, Inc.
Oneida Tribe of Indians of Wisconsin

DACH, Leslie

1875 I St. NW
Suite 900
Washington, DC 20005
Tel: (202)371-0200
Fax: (202)371-2858
Registered: FARA

Special Assistant to Chairman, Senate Agriculture Committee, 1987.

Employers

Edelman Public Relations Worldwide (V. Chairman)

Clients Represented

On Behalf of Edelman Public Relations Worldwide

American Health Care Ass'n
Bacardi Ltd.
Nissan North America Inc.

DADE, Michael

200 Orchard Ridge Dr.
Suite 302
Gaithersburg, MD 20878
Tel: (301)212-9608
Fax: (301)990-1611
Registered: LDA
EMail: mdade@naea.org

Employers

Nat'l Ass'n of Enrolled Agents (Legislative Assistant)

DADISMAN, Ellen C.

1828 L St. NW
Suite 300
Washington, DC 20036
Tel: (202)466-6512

Employers

Council on Foundations (V. President, Government and Media Relations)

DADY, Gail

11 Canal Center Plaza
Suite 103
Alexandria, VA 22314
Tel: (703)683-4222
Fax: (703)683-0645
Registered: LDA

Employers

The Spectrum Group

Clients Represented

On Behalf of The Spectrum Group

TRW Inc.

DAFFRON, Thomas

1800 K St. NW
Suite 1010
Washington, DC 20006
Tel: (202)296-5030
Fax: (202)296-4750

Chief of Staff to Senator Fred Thompson (R-TN), 1994-98 and Chief of Staff to Senator William Cohen (R-ME), 1973-90.

Employers

American Defense Internat'l, Inc.

Clients Represented

On Behalf of American Defense Internat'l, Inc.

Internat'l Trade Resources Group
Marine Desalination Systems LLC

DAHL, Bob

1100 Connecticut Ave. NW
Suite 330
Washington, DC 20036
Tel: (202)955-9001
Fax: (202)861-6065

Employers

Fair Government Foundation (President)

DAHL, Elizabeth

50 F St. NW
Suite 110
Washington, DC 20001
Tel: (202)662-4240
Fax: (202)662-4241

Employers

Constitution Project (Deputy Director)

DAHLJELM, Harvey

1650 Tysons Blvd.
Suite 1700
McLean, VA 22102
Tel: (703)790-6300
Fax: (703)790-6365

Employers

ITT Industries Defense (Director, Air Force and Space Programs)

DAHLLOF, Steven J.

1901 L St. NW
Suite 300
Washington, DC 20036
Tel: (202)466-7590
Fax: (202)775-8169
EMail: steve.dahllof@dc.ogilvypr.com

Employers

Ogilvy Public Relations Worldwide (Managing Director, Washington Office)

Clients Represented

On Behalf of Ogilvy Public Relations Worldwide

The American Floral Marketing Council

DAIGNEAULT, Michael G.

1747 Pennsylvania Ave. NW
Suite 400
Washington, DC 20006
EMail: michael@ethics.org
Tel: (202)737-2258
Fax: (202)737-2227
Registered: LDA

Employers
Ethics Resource Center Inc. (President)

DAILEY, Brian

1725 Jefferson Davis Hwy.
Crystal Square 2, Suite 300
Arlington, VA 22202
Tel: (703)413-5601
Fax: (703)413-5617

Employers
Lockheed Martin Corp. (V. President, Washington Operations)

DAILING, Clifford D.

1630 Duke St.
Alexandria, VA 22314
Tel: (703)684-5545
Fax: (703)548-8735

Employers
Nat'l Rural Letter Carriers' Ass'n (Secretary-Treasurer)

DAKIN, Deborah

1700 G St. NW
Fifth Floor
Washington, DC 20552
EMail: deborah.dakin@ots.treas.gov
Tel: (202)906-6445
Fax: (202)906-6518

Employers
Department of Treasury - Office of Thrift Supervision (Deputy Chief Counsel for Regulations and Legislation)

DALE, Shana L.

1901 Pennsylvania Ave. NW
Suite 700
Washington, DC 20006
Tel: (202)955-9091
Fax: (202)955-9039

Employers
University of Texas Office of Federal Relations (Assistant V. Chancellor for Federal Relations)

DALESSANDRI, Ruth

1731 King St.
Suite 200
Alexandria, VA 22314
EMail: rdalessandri@catholiccharitiesusa.org
Tel: (703)549-1390
Fax: (703)549-1656

Employers
Catholic Charities USA (V. President, Social Service)

DALEY, Beth

666 11th St. NW
Suite 500
Washington, DC 20001
EMail: beth@pogo.org
Tel: (202)347-1122
Fax: (202)347-1116

Employers
Project on Government Oversight, Inc. (Public Affairs Director)

DALEY, Mark

1400 16th St. NW
Suite 320
Washington, DC 20036
Tel: (202)332-2200
Fax: (202)332-2302

Employers
Zero Population Growth, Inc. (Press Officer)

DALEY, Steve

1909 K St. NW
Fourth Floor
Washington, DC 20006
Tel: (202)973-5800
Fax: (202)973-5858

Employers
Porter/Novelli (Senior V. President)

DALGLISH, Lucy A.

1815 N. Fort Myer Dr.
Suite 900
Arlington, VA 22209
Tel: (703)809-2100
Fax: (703)807-2109

Employers
Reporters Committee for Freedom of the Press (Exec. Director)

DALLUGE, Charles D.

1201 Connecticut Ave. NW
Tenth Floor
Washington, DC 20036
Tel: (202)861-4600
Fax: (202)872-8530

Employers
Leo A. Daly Co. (V. President and Managing Principal)

DALRYMPLE, Donald "Dack"

1926 N St. NW
Third Floor
Washington, DC 20036
EMail: dackdal@erols.com
Tel: (202)833-1043
Fax: (202)833-0370
Registered: LDA

Counsel, House Subcommittee on Health and the Environment, Committee on Energy and Commerce, 1974-79; Legislative Assistant to Rep. Paul Rogers (D-FL), 1970, 1973-74.

Employers
Dalrymple and Associates, L.L.C. (Managing Director and Principal)

Clients Represented
On Behalf of Dalrymple and Associates, L.L.C.
Aventis Pasteur
BD
BioPort Corp.
Biotechnology Industry Organization
Centocor, Inc.
Edelman Public Relations Worldwide
Plasma Protein Therapeutics Ass'n

DALSTON, Ph.D., FAC, Jeptha W.

730 11th St. NW
Fourth Floor
Washington, DC 20001-4510
EMail: jdalston@aupha.org
Tel: (202)638-1448
Ext: 116
Fax: (202)638-3429

Employers
Ass'n of University Programs in Health Administration (President and Chief Exec. Officer)

DALY, Abbe

350 John Carlyle St.
Suite 200
Alexandria, VA 22314
EMail: adaly@opoffice.org
Tel: (703)836-7114
Ext: 3049
Fax: (703)836-0838

Employers
American Board for Certification in Orthotics and Prosthetics, Inc. (ABC) (Director, Marketing)

DALY, Brendan

1225 I St. NW
Suite 1100
Washington, DC 20005
Tel: (202)898-0792
Fax: (202)371-9615

Employers
Handgun Control, Inc. (Director, Communications)

DALY, John Jay

4515 Willard Ave.
Suite 1903
Chevy Chase, MD 20815-3614
EMail: johndaly@erols.com
Tel: (301)656-2510
Fax: (301)656-8069

Employers
Daly Communications (President)

DALY, Joseph P.

5101 Wisconsin Ave. NW
Washington, DC 20016
Tel: (202)362-0840
Fax: (202)966-9409
Registered: LDA

Attorney, Legal Advisory Services Division, Comptroller of the Currency, Department of the Treasury, 1982-85.

Employers
Muldoon, Murphy & Faucette, LLP (Partner)

DALY, Nancy Riese

12500 Fair Lakes Circle
Suite 375
Fairfax, VA 22033
Tel: (703)502-1550
Fax: (703)502-7852
Registered: LDA

Employers
American Soc. for Therapeutic Radiology and Oncology (Director, Government Relations)

DALY, Sharon M.

1731 King St.
Suite 200
Alexandria, VA 22314
EMail: sdaly@catholiccharitiesusa.org
Tel: (703)549-1390
Fax: (703)549-6280

Employers
Catholic Charities USA (V. President, Social Policy)

DALY, Thomas R.

9302 Lee Hwy.
Fairfax, VA 22031-1215
EMail: tdaly@ofplaw.com
Tel: (703)218-2110
Fax: (703)218-2160
Registered: LDA

Employers
Odin, Feldman, & Pittleman, P.C. (Attorney)

Clients Represented
On Behalf of Odin, Feldman, & Pittleman, P.C.
American Chiropractic Ass'n

DALY, William

500 E St. SW
Eighth Floor
Room 811
Washington, DC 20254-0001
Tel: (202)358-6032
Fax: (202)358-6074

Employers
Social Security Administration-Office of Legislation and Congressional Affairs (Social Insurance Program Advisor, Office of Legislative and Congressional Affairs)

DAMERON, Del S.

1900 K St. NW
Washington, DC 20006
EMail: del_dameron@mckennacuneo.com
Tel: (202)496-7500
Fax: (202)496-7756

Employers
McKenna & Cuneo, L.L.P. (Managing Partner)

Clients Represented
On Behalf of McKenna & Cuneo, L.L.P.
Oshkosh Truck Corp.

DAMGARD, John M.

2001 Pennsylvania Ave. NW
Suite 600
Washington, DC 20006-1807
Tel: (202)466-5460
Fax: (202)296-3184
Registered: LDA

Employers
Futures Industry Ass'n (President)

DANA, Charles

50 F St. NW
Suite 900
Washington, DC 20001
EMail: dana@fccouncil.com
Tel: (202)879-0848
Fax: (202)626-8718
Registered: LDA

Employers
Farm Credit Council (General Counsel)

DANAS, Andrew M.

1730 M St. NW
Suite 400
Washington, DC 20036
Tel: (202)296-2900
Fax: (202)296-1370

Employers
Grove, Jaskiewicz, and Cobert (Partner)

DANCE, Glenn E.

1666 K St. NW
Suite 800
Washington, DC 20006
Tel: (202)481-7000
Fax: (202)862-7098
Registered: LDA

Employers
Arthur Andersen LLP (Partner)

Clients Represented
On Behalf of Arthur Andersen LLP
Nat'l Ass'n of Investors Corporation (NAIC)

DANDREA, Joel

2750 Prosperity Ave.
Suite 620
Fairfax, VA 22031-4312
Tel: (703)698-0291
Fax: (703)698-0297

Employers
Specialized Carriers and Rigging Ass'n (V. President)

DANEKER, Michael

555 12th St. NW
Washington, DC 20004-1206
Tel: (202)942-5000
Fax: (202)942-5999
EMail: Michael_Daneker@aporter.com

Employers
Arnold & Porter (Partner)

DANFORTH, Hon. John C.

700 13th St. NW
Suite 700
Washington, DC 20005-3960
Tel: (202)508-6000
Fax: (202)508-6200
Registered: LDA
EMail: jcdanforth@bryancave.com
Member, U.S. Senate (R-MO), 1976-95.

Employers
Bryan Cave LLP (Partner)

DANIEL, III, Aubrey M.

725 12th St. NW
Washington, DC 20005
Tel: (202)434-5000
Fax: (202)434-5029

Employers
Williams & Connolly (Partner)

Clients Represented
On Behalf of Williams & Connolly
Archer Daniels Midland Co.
General Motors Corp.
Internat'l Truck and Engine Corp.

DANIEL, David A.

1155 16th St. NW
Washington, DC 20036
Tel: (202)872-4600
Fax: (202)872-4615
EMail: d_daniel@acs.org

Employers
American Chemical Soc. (Assistant Exec. Director and Chief Administrative Officer)

DANIEL, John E.

1800 M St. NW
Washington, DC 20036
Tel: (202)467-7437
Fax: (202)467-7176
Registered: LDA
EMail: jedaniel@morganlewis.com
Former Chief of Staff, Environmental Protection Agency.

Employers
Morgan, Lewis & Bockius LLP (Of Counsel)

Clients Represented
On Behalf of Morgan, Lewis & Bockius LLP
UGI Utilities, Inc.
Unitech Services Group, Inc.

DANIEL, L. Maurice

600 New Hampshire Ave. NW
11th Floor
Washington, DC 20037
Tel: (202)944-3000
Fax: (202)944-3068
Former Director of Political Affairs, Office of the Vice President, Executive Office of the President, The White House, during the Clinton administration.

Employers
Dyer Ellis & Joseph, P.C. (Senior Government Affairs Advisor)

Clients Represented
On Behalf of Dyer Ellis & Joseph, P.C.
BLNG, Inc.

DANIELS, Joycelyn J.

200 Constitution Ave. NW
Room S-1325
Washington, DC 20210
Tel: (202)693-4600
Fax: (202)693-4642
EMail: daniels-joycelyn@dol.gov

Employers
Department of Labor (Administrative Officer, Office of Congressional and Intergovernmental Affairs)

DANIELS, Michael P.

1001 Pennsylvania Ave. NW
Suite 600
Washington, DC 20004
Tel: (202)347-0066
Fax: (202)624-7222
Registered: LDA

Employers
Powell, Goldstein, Frazer & Murphy LLP (Partner)

Clients Represented
On Behalf of Powell, Goldstein, Frazer & Murphy LLP
Footwear Distributors and Retailers of America
Hong Kong Trade Development Council

DANIELS, Rhonda

1220 L St. NW
Suite 500
Washington, DC 20005
Tel: (202)371-6700
Fax: (202)289-8544
EMail: rdaniels@arda.org

Employers
American Resort Development Ass'n (Corporate Counsel)

DANIELS, Sidney

200 Maryland Ave. NE
Washington, DC 20002
Tel: (202)543-2239
Fax: (202)543-0961
Registered: LDA
EMail: sdaniels@vfwdc.org

Employers
Veterans of Foreign Wars of the U.S. (Deputy Director, National Legislative Services/Action Code)

DANIELSON, David S.

1505 Prince St.
Suite 300
Alexandria, VA 22314
Tel: (703)739-9200
Fax: (703)739-9497
Registered: LDA

Employers
American Optometric Ass'n (Deputy Director, Government Relations)

DANIELSON, Jack

1111 19th St. NW
Suite 800
Washington, DC 20036
Tel: (202)463-2700
Fax: (202)463-2785

Employers
American Forest & Paper Ass'n (Director, Congressional Affairs)

DANIELSON, Nancy

400 N. Capitol St. NW
Suite 790
Washington, DC 20001
Tel: (202)554-1600
Fax: (202)554-1654
Registered: LDA

Employers
Nat'l Farmers Union (Farmers Educational & Co-operative Union of America) (Senior Policy Analyst)

DANISH, Kyle W.

1050 Thomas Jefferson St. NW
Seventh Floor
Washington, DC 20007
Tel: (202)298-1800
Fax: (202)338-2416
EMail: KWD@vnf.com

Employers
Van Ness Feldman, P.C. (Associate)

DANJCZEK, Thomas A.

1730 Rhode Island Ave. NW
Suite 907
Washington, DC 20036-3101
Tel: (202)296-1515
Fax: (202)296-2506
Registered: LDA

Employers
Steel Manufacturers Ass'n (President)

DANNA, Tony

1620 L St. NW
Room 401
Washington, DC 20036
Tel: (202)452-7726
Fax: (202)452-0346

Employers
Department of Interior - Bureau of Land Management (Legislative Affairs Group Manager)

DANNAHEY, Mary

50 S. Picket St.
Suite 110
Alexandria, VA 22304-7206
Tel: (703)823-7234
Fax: (703)823-7237

Employers
Composite Can and Tube Institute (Associate Manager, Meetings, Publications and Programs)

DANNENFELDT, Paula

1816 Jefferson Place NW
Washington, DC 20036
Tel: (202)833-2672
Fax: (202)833-4657
Registered: LDA
EMail: pdannenfeldt@amsa-cleanwater.org

Employers
Ass'n of Metropolitan Sewerage Agencies (Deputy Exec. Director)

DANNENFELSER, Martin J.

801 G St. NW
Washington, DC 20001
Tel: (202)393-2100
Fax: (202)393-2134
Registered: LDA

Employers
Family Research Council, Inc. (V. President, Public Affairs)

DANNER, Donald "Dan"

1201 F St. NW
Suite 200
Washington, DC 20004
Tel: (202)554-9000
Fax: (202)484-1566
Registered: LDA
Former Special Assistant to the President and Deputy Director, Office of Public Liaison, The White House, during the Reagan administration.

Employers
Nat'l Federation of Independent Business (Senior V. President, Federal Public Policy)

DANSKY, Becky

1629 K St. NW
Suite 1010
Washington, DC 20006
Tel: (202)466-3311
Fax: (202)466-3435

Employers
Leadership Conference on Civil Rights (Research Assistant)

DANVERS, William C.

1300 Connecticut Ave. NW
Suite 600
Washington, DC 20036
Tel: (202)775-8116
Fax: (202)223-0358
Registered: LDA
Former Senior Director of Legislative Affairs, National Security Council. Former Legislative Assistant to Senator Joseph Lieberman (D-CT). Former Subcommittee Staff Director, House Banking Committee

Employers
Griffin, Johnson, Dover & Stewart (Lobbyist)

Clients Represented
On Behalf of Griffin, Johnson, Dover & Stewart
American Agrisurance
American Fish Spotters Ass'n
Avue Technologies
Dell Computer Corp.
Deloitte Consulting
Directors Guild of America
Fannie Mae
The Justice Project, Inc.
Local Initiatives Support Corp.
United Technologies Corp.
Wilmer, Cutler & Pickering
Wine and Spirits Wholesalers of America

DAOUST, Josee

1700 N. Moore St.
Suite 1600
Arlington, VA 22209
Tel: (703)841-2400
Fax: (703)527-0938

Employers
American Meat Institute (Manager, Public Affairs)

DARBOUZE, Farrah

409 12th St. SW
P.O. Box 96920
Washington, DC 20090-6920
Tel: (202)863-2509
Fax: (202)488-3985
Registered: LDA
EMail: fdarbouze@acog.org

Employers
American College of Obstetricians and Gynecologists (Legislative Assistant)

DARBY, Paul B.

5030 Gardner Dr.
Alexandria, VA 22304
Tel: (703)567-1000
Fax: (703)567-1022
Registered: LDA

EMail: pbdarby@home.com
Assistant to the Secretay of Agriculture, 1976-80.

Employers
Darby Enterprises (President)

DARCY, Cindy

1001 Pennsylvania Ave. NW
Suite 300S
Washington, DC 20004
Tel: (202)824-8800
Fax: (202)824-8990
Registered: LDA
EMail: darcy.cindy@dorseylaw.com

Employers
Dorsey & Whitney LLP (Legislative Director)

Clients Represented

On Behalf of Dorsey & Whitney LLP
Aleutian Pribilof Islands Community Development Ass'n
Bristol Bay Native Corp.
Central Council of Tlingit and Haida Indian Tribes of Alaska
Cow Creek Umpqua Tribe of Oregon
Cuyapaipe Band of Mission Indians
Delaware Tribe of Indians
Grand Traverse Band of Chippewa and Ottawa Indians
Hoopa Valley Tribal Council
Little River Band of Ottawa Indians
Lower Elwaha S'Klallam Tribe
Nez Perce Tribal Executive Committee
Pascua Yaqui Tribe of Arizona
Quinault Indian Nation
Red Lake Band of Chippewa Indians
Shakopee Mdewakanton Sioux Tribe
Spokane Tribe
Stockbridge-Munsee Community Band of Mohican Indians
Winnebago Tribe of Nebraska

DARDEN, Edwin

1680 Duke St.
Alexandria, VA 22314-3407
Tel: (703)838-6722
Fax: (703)683-7590

Employers
Nat'l School Boards Ass'n (Senior Staff Attorney)

DARDEN, Hon. George "Buddy"

701 Pennsylvania Ave. NW
Suite 600
Washington, DC 20004
Tel: (202)624-1213
Fax: (202)624-1298
Registered: LDA
EMail: gdarden@lanlaw.com
Member, U.S. House of Representatives (D-GA), 1983-95.

Employers
Long, Aldridge & Norman, LLP (Partner)

Clients Represented

On Behalf of Long, Aldridge & Norman, LLP
AFLAC, Inc.
Lockheed Martin Aeronautical Systems Co.

DARIEN, Kristie L.

1156 15th St. NW
Suite 1100
Washington, DC 20005
Tel: (202)293-8830
Fax: (202)872-8543
Registered: LDA

Employers
Nat'l Small Business United (Manager, Government Affairs)

DARIN, Anna

2025 M St. NW
Suite 800
Washington, DC 20036
Tel: (202)367-2100
Fax: (202)367-1200

Employers
American Ass'n for Adult and Continuing Education (Association Manager)
Smith, Bucklin and Associates, Inc.

Clients Represented

On Behalf of Smith, Bucklin and Associates, Inc.
Council of Development Finance Agencies
Wireless Information Networks Forum (WinForum)

DARIOTIS, Dina

9000 Rockville Pike
Bldg. One, Room 244
Bethesda, MD 20892
Tel: (301)496-3471
Fax: (301)496-0840

EMail: dariotid@od.nih.gov

Employers

Department of Health and Human Services - Nat'l Institutes of Health (Legislative Analyst)

DARLAND, Dallas L.

1201 16th St. NW
Washington, DC 20036
Tel: (202)822-7840
Fax: (202)822-7779

Employers

Nat'l Foundation for the Improvement of Education (Director, Institutional Advancement)

DARLING, Colleen

1200 18th St. NW
Second Floor
Washington, DC 20036
Tel: (202)467-6100
Fax: (202)467-6101
Registered: LDA

EMail: colleen@independentsector.org

Employers

Independent Sector (Writer/Researcher, Office of the President)

DARLING, Erin Lewis

701 Pennsylvania Ave. NW
Suite 900
Washington, DC 20004-2608
Tel: (202)434-7300
Fax: (202)434-7400
Registered: LDA

EMail: edarling@mintz.com

Employers

Mintz, Levin, Cohn, Ferris, Glovsky and Popeo, P.C. (Associate)

Clients Represented

On Behalf of Mintz, Levin, Cohn, Ferris, Glovsky and Popeo, P.C.

CVS, Inc.

Medical College of Virginia, Dept. of Neurology, Office of the Chairman

DARLING, Lauren

1225 Connecticut Ave. NW
Washington, DC 20036
Tel: (202)327-7749
Fax: (202)327-6719
Registered: LDA

EMail: lauren.darling@ey.com

Employers

Ernst & Young LLP (Senior Manager)

Washington Council Ernst & Young (Senior Manager)

Clients Represented

On Behalf of Ernst & Young LLP

E-Commerce Coalition

Edison Electric Institute

General Ore Internat'l Corp. Ltd.

INCOL 2000

Interest Netting Coalition

Koch Industries, Inc.

MassMutual Financial Group

Nordstrom, Inc.

Repeal the Tax on Talking Coalition

Tax Policy Coalition

On Behalf of Washington Council Ernst & Young
Aetna Life & Casualty Co.
American Insurance Ass'n
American Staffing Ass'n
Anheuser-Busch Cos., Inc.
Antitrust Coalition for Consumer Choice in Health Care
Apartment Investment and Management Co.
Ass'n of Home Appliance Manufacturers
AT&T
Aventis Pharmaceuticals, Inc.
Baxter Healthcare Corp.
BHC Communications, Inc.
Bulmer Holding PLC, H. P.
Cash Balance Coalition
Citigroup
Coalition for Fairness in Defense Exports
Coalition to Preserve Tracking Stock
ComEd
The Connell Co.
Deferral Group
Directors Guild of America
Doris Duke Charitable Foundation
Eaton Vance Management Co.
Eden Financial Corp.
The Enterprise Foundation
Fannie Mae
FedEx Corp.
Ford Motor Co.
General Electric Co.
Global Competitiveness Coalition
Grasslands Water District
Group Health, Inc.
HEREIU
Gilbert P. Hyatt, Inventor
Investment Co. Institute
Large Public Power Council
Local Initiatives Support Corp.
MacAndrews & Forbes Holdings, Inc.
Marsh & McLennan Cos.
MCG Northwest, Inc.
McLane Co.
Merrill Lynch & Co., Inc.
Metropolitan Banking Group
Nat'l Ass'n for State Farm Agents
Nat'l Ass'n of Professional Employer Organizations
Nat'l Ass'n of Real Estate Investment Trusts
Nat'l Defined Contribution Council
Nat'l Foreign Trade Council, Inc.
Nat'l Multi-Housing Council
Pfizer, Inc.
R&D Tax Credit Coalition
R&D Tax Regulation Group
Recording Industry Ass'n of America
Reed-Elsevier Inc.
R. J. Reynolds Tobacco Co.
Charles Schwab & Co., Inc.,
Securities Industry Ass'n
Skadden, Arps, Slate, Meagher & Flom LLP
Straddle Rules Tax Group
Tax Fairness Coalition
TXU Business Services
U.S. Oncology
USA Biomass Power Producers Alliance
Viaticus, Inc.
Wilkie Farr & Gallagher
Ziff Investors Partnership

DARMAN, Richard G.

1001 Pennsylvania Ave. NW
Suite 220 South
Washington, DC 20004
Tel: (202)347-2626
Fax: (202)347-1818

Employers
The Carlyle Group (Senior Advisor)

DARNEILLE, III, Hopewell H.

901 15th St. NW
Suite 700
Washington, DC 20005-2301
Tel: (202)371-6000
Fax: (202)371-6279
Registered: LDA
Law Clerk to Chief Judge Edward S. Northrop, U.S. District Court for the District of Maryland, 1974-75.

Employers
Verner, Liipfert, Bernhard, McPherson and Hand, Chartered (Member of Firm)

DAROFF, William C.

415 Second St. NE
Washington, DC 20002
Tel: (202)547-7701
Fax: (202)544-2434
Registered: LDA
EMail: wdaroff@rjchq.org
Aide to Rep. Jack Kemp (D-NY), 1986-88; Special Assistant, Department of Energy, 1989-90.

Employers
Republican Jewish Coalition (Director of Congressional Affairs)

DARR, Anne

1360 Beverly Rd.
Suite 201
McLean, VA 22101
Tel: (703)448-1000
Fax: (703)790-3460

Employers
DeHart and Darr Associates, Inc.

DARR, Linda Bauer

1100 New York Ave. NW
Suite 1050
Washington, DC 20005
Tel: (202)842-1645
Fax: (202)842-0850

Employers
American Bus Ass'n (V. President, Policy and External Affairs)

DARROW, Alan

4226 King St.
Alexandria, VA 22302-1507
EMail: adarrow@nata-online.org
Tel: (703)845-9000
Fax: (703)845-8176

Employers
Nat'l Air Transportation Ass'n (V. President)

DARROW, Diane L.

8201 Greensboro Dr.
Suite 300
McLean, VA 22102
Tel: (703)610-9000
Fax: (703)610-9005

Employers
Ass'n Management Group
Nat'l Ass'n of Retail Collection Attorneys (Exec. Director)

Clients Represented

On Behalf of Ass'n Management Group
Nat'l Ass'n of Retail Collection Attorneys

DASCH, Ms. Pat

600 Pennsylvania Ave. SE
Suite 201
Washington, DC 20003
EMail: nssdasch@nss.org
Tel: (202)543-1900
Fax: (202)546-4189

Employers
Nat'l Space Soc. (Exec. Director)

DASCHLE, Linda Hall

801 Pennsylvania Ave. NW
Suite 800
Washington, DC 20004
EMail: ldaschle@bdbc.com
Tel: (202)508-3477
Fax: (202)508-3402
Registered: LDA

Deputy Administrator, Federal Aviation Administration, Department of Transportation, 1993-97. Director, Office of Congressional, Community and Consumer Affairs, Civil Aeronautics Board, 1980-84.

Employers
Baker, Donelson, Bearman & Caldwell, P.C. (Senior Public Policy Advisor)

Clients Represented

On Behalf of Baker, Donelson, Bearman & Caldwell, P.C.
AAAE-ACI
American Airlines
American Concrete Pavement Ass'n (ACPA)
The Boeing Co.
Cleveland, City of/Cleveland Hopkins Internat'l Airport
L-3 Communications Corp.
Lockheed Martin Air Traffic Management
Loral Space and Communications, Ltd.
Northwest Airlines, Inc.
United Technologies Corp.

DASH, Mary L.

1111 Constitution Ave. NW
Room 3236
Washington, DC 20224
EMail: mary.l.dash@irs.gov
Tel: (202)622-3736
Fax: (202)622-3048

Employers
Department of Treasury - Internal Revenue Service (Branch Chief, Congressional Correspondence)

DAUE, Janice

3900 Wisconsin Ave. NW
Washington, DC 20016
Tel: (202)752-2131
Fax: (202)752-6099

Employers
Fannie Mae (V. President, Public Affairs)

DAUKSZ, Edward

1650 Tysons Blvd.
Suite 1700
McLean, VA 22102
Tel: (703)790-6300
Fax: (703)790-6365
Registered: LDA

Employers
ITT Industries Defense (Director, Army and Marine Corps Programs)

DAUPHINE, Jonathan D.

601 E St. NW
A6-560
Washington, DC 20049
Tel: (202)434-3744
Fax: (202)434-6403

Employers
Long Term Care Campaign (Exec. Director)

DAVENPORT, Jim

2111 Wilson Blvd.
Eighth Floor
Arlington, VA 22201-3058
EMail: davenport@alcalde-fay.com
Tel: (703)841-0626
Fax: (703)243-2874
Registered: LDA

Former Legislative Assistant, Rep. Gerald B. Solomon (R-NY)

Employers
Alcalde & Fay (Associate)

Clients Represented

On Behalf of Alcalde & Fay
AMFM, Inc.
Bay County, Florida
Boca Raton, Florida, City of
Christian Network, Inc.
Computer Sciences Corp.
Deerfield Beach, Florida, City of
Glencairn, Ltd.
Hispanic Broadcasting Inc.
Jovan Broadcasting
Mitretek Systems
North American Sports Management, Inc.
Osceola, Florida, County of
Paxson Communications Corp.
PetrolRem, Inc.
Riviera Beach, Florida, City of
Stevens Institute of Technology
Telemundo

DAVEY, John P.

11785 Beltsville Dr.
Tenth Floor
Calverton, MD 20705
Tel: (301)572-7900
Fax: (301)572-6655
Registered: LDA

Employers
O'Malley, Miles, Nylen & Gilmore, P.A. (Managing Partner)

Clients Represented

On Behalf of O'Malley, Miles, Nylen & Gilmore, P.A.
Peterson Cos., Inc.

DAVID, John

1771 N St. NW
Washington, DC 20036-2891
Tel: (202)429-5305
Fax: (202)775-3523

Employers
Nat'l Ass'n of Broadcasters (Exec. V. President, Radio)

DAVIDSON, Alan

1634 I St. NW
Suite 1100
Washington, DC 20006-4003
EMail: abt@cdt.org
Tel: (202)637-9800
Fax: (202)637-0968

Employers
Center for Democracy and Technology (Staff Counsel)

DAVIDSON, Daryl

3401 Columbia Pike
Suite 400
Arlington, VA 22204
Tel: (703)920-2720
Fax: (703)920-2889

Employers
Ass'n for Unmanned Vehicle Systems International (Exec. Director)

DAVIDSON, Douglas

1300 I St. NW
12th Floor
Washington, DC 20005
Tel: (202)326-3980
Fax: (202)326-3981

Employers
Morgan Stanley Dean Witter & Co. (Chairman, Morgan Stanley Dean Witter PAC)

DAVIDSON, Howard

740 15th St. NW
Washington, DC 20005
Tel: (202)662-1720
Fax: (202)662-1755

Employers
ABA Center on Children and the Law (Director)

DAVIDSON, James H.

1101 Pennsylvania Ave. NW
Suite 810
The Evening Star Building
Washington, DC 20004
EMail: jhd@davidsondc.com
Tel: (202)638-1101
Fax: (202)638-1102
Registered: LDA

Chief Counsel and Staff Director, U.S. Senate Judiciary Subcommittee on Administrative Practice and Procedure, 1979-81. Chief Counsel, U.S. Senate Governmental Affairs Subcommittee on Intergovernmental Relations, 1974-79. Special Assistant to Senator Stuart Symington (D-MO), 1971-74.

Employers
Davidson & Company, Inc. (Principal)

Clients Represented

On Behalf of Davidson & Company, Inc.
Advertising Tax Coalition
American Advertising Federation
American Ass'n for Homecare
American Ass'n of Advertising Agencies
AOL Time Warner
Apria Healthcare Group
Ass'n of Nat'l Advertisers
The Business Roundtable
Corporation for Enterprise Development
Direct Marketing Ass'n, Inc.
eBay Inc.
Ellicott Internat'l
Federal Home Loan Mortgage Corp. (Freddie Mac)
Grocery Manufacturers of America
The Hearst Corp.
Independent Contractor Coalition
Magazine Publishers of America
Nat'l Ass'n of Broadcasters
Newspaper Ass'n of America
The Reader's Digest Ass'n
Paul Scherer & Co., LLP
The Washington Post Co.
Yellow Pages Publishers Ass'n

DAVIDSON, Jennifer A.

1140 19th St. NW
Suite 900
Washington, DC 20036
EMail: jdavidson@kkblaw.com
Tel: (202)223-5120
Fax: (202)223-5619

Employers
Kleinfeld, Kaplan and Becker (Associate)

DAVIDSON, Richard

325 Seventh St. NW
Washington, DC 20004
Tel: (202)638-1100
Fax: (202)626-2345
Registered: LDA

Employers
American Hospital Ass'n (President)

DAVIDSON, Seth A.

1400 16th St. NW
Suite 600
Washington, DC 20036
EMail: sdavidson@fw-law.com
Tel: (202)939-7900
Fax: (202)745-0916
Registered: LDA

Employers
Fleischman and Walsh, L.L.P. (Partner)

Clients Represented

On Behalf of Fleischman and Walsh, L.L.P.
mp3.com
Nat'l Cable Television Ass'n

DAVIE, Jill

1600 Pennsylvania Ave. NW
102 E. Wing
Washington, DC 20500
Tel: (202)456-5677
Fax: (202)456-2256

Employers
Executive Office of the President - The White House (Legislative Correspondent, House Liaison Office)

DAVIES, Catherine

1101 14th St. NW Tel: (202)682-9400
Suite 1400 Fax: (202)682-1331
Washington, DC 20005
EMail: kdavies@defenders.org

Employers
Defenders of Wildlife (Manager, Publications)

DAVIES, Dionne

1120 Connecticut Ave. NW Tel: (202)663-5000
Washington, DC 20036 Fax: (202)828-4548
Registered: LDA

Employers
American Bankers Ass'n (Senior Federal Legislative Representative)

DAVIES, Kay

1420 New York Ave. NW Tel: (202)789-1745
Suite 210 Fax: (202)371-1731
Washington, DC 20005

Employers
Phelps Dodge Corp. (Manager, Government Relations)

DAVIES, Ms. Terry

607 14th St. NW Tel: (202)347-1501
Suite 800 Fax: (202)347-1521
Washington, DC 20005 Registered: LDA
EMail: Terry.Davies@LPCorp.com

Employers
Louisiana Pacific Corp. (Corporate Manager, Government Relations)

DAVINE, Amy C.

2550 M St. NW Tel: (202)457-5667
Washington, DC 20037-1350 Fax: (202)457-6315
Registered: LDA
EMail: adavine@pattonboggs.com

Employers
Patton Boggs, LLP (Associate)

Clients Represented
On Behalf of Patton Boggs, LLP
Dictaphone Corp.
Wild Alabama

DAVIS, Bill

4350 N. Fairfax Dr. Tel: (703)528-1902
Suite 640 Fax: (703)528-3546
Arlington, VA 22203-1620
EMail: bdavis@aaanet.org

Employers
American Anthropological Ass'n (Exec. Director)

DAVIS, Hon. Bob

1735 New York Ave. NW Tel: (202)628-1700
Suite 500 Fax: (202)331-1024
Washington, DC 20006-4759 Registered: LDA
Member, U.S. House of Representatives (R-MI), 1979-93.

Employers
Preston Gates Ellis & Rouvelas Meeds LLP (Counselor)

DAVIS, Carrie

1156 15th St. NW Tel: (202)862-4813
Suite 502 Fax: (202)862-4829
Washington, DC 20005-1799
EMail: cbdavis@jcpenney.com

Employers
J. C. Penney Co., Inc. (Administrative Manager, Government Relations)

DAVIS, Charlie

763-A Delaware Ave. SW
Washington, DC 20024

Employers
Conservative Republican Network (PAC Administrator)

DAVIS, Christopher L.

1101 17th St. NW Tel: (202)775-9750
Suite 703 Fax: (202)331-8446
Washington, DC 20036
Special Assistant to the President for Congressional Liaison (1979-80) and Management Associate, Office of Management and Budget (1977-78), Executive Office of the President, The White House.

Employers
Institute for Certified Investment Management Consultants (Exec. Director)
Investment Program Ass'n (President)
Money Management Institute (Exec. Director)

DAVIS, III, Delacroix "Del"

1317 F St. NW Tel: (202)737-1800
Suite 200 Fax: (202)737-2485
Washington, DC 20004 Registered: LDA
Former Minority Staff Assistant, Subcommittee on VA-HUD, Subcommittee on the Interior, and Subcommittee on Agriculture; Majority Staff Assistant, Subcommittee on Defense; and Majority Staff Director, Subcommittee on Transportation; all with the House Committee on Appropriations

Employers
Edington, Peel & Associates, Inc. (Associate)

DAVIS, Don

409 Third St. SW Tel: (202)479-6632
Second Floor Fax: (202)479-6664
Washington, DC 20024-6682

Employers
Nat'l Ass'n of Older Worker Employment Services (V. President)

DAVIS, Drew M.

1101 16th St. NW Tel: (202)463-6740
Washington, DC 20036-4877 Fax: (202)659-5349
Registered: LDA

Employers
Nat'l Soft Drink Ass'n (V. President, Federal Affairs)

DAVIS, Edwin H.

1250 Connecticut Ave. NW Tel: (202)833-1200
Washington, DC 20036 Fax: (202)659-3716
Registered: LDA

Employers
Common Cause (Associate Director, Issues Development)

DAVIS, Fred G.

701 Pennsylvania Ave. NW Tel: (202)508-5477
Washington, DC 20004-2696 Fax: (202)508-5403
Registered: LDA

Employers
Edison Electric Institute (Director, Governmental Affairs)

DAVIS, Garry

1012 14th St. NW Tel: (202)638-2662
Suite 1106 Fax: (202)638-0638
Washington, DC 20005

Employers
World Government of World Citizens (World Coordinator)
World Service Authority (Political Consultant)

DAVIS, Geoffrey G.

2550 M St. NW Tel: (202)457-6000
Washington, DC 20037-1350 Fax: (202)457-6315
Registered: FARA
EMail: gdavis@pattonboggs.com

Employers
Patton Boggs, LLP (Partner)

DAVIS, Ian M.

1717 Pennsylvania Ave. NW Tel: (202)857-3000
Suite 400 Fax: (202)857-3030
Washington, DC 20006 Registered: LDA

Employers
Occidental Internat'l Corporation (V. President, International Affairs)

DAVIS, USAF (Ret.), Gen. J. B.

11 Canal Center Plaza Tel: (703)683-4222
Suite 103 Fax: (703)683-0645
Alexandria, VA 22314 Registered: LDA
Former Chief of Staff, Supreme Headquarters, North Atlantic Treaty Organization and Commander, U.S. Forces in Japan, U.S. Air Force.

Employers
The Spectrum Group

Clients Represented
On Behalf of The Spectrum Group
AAI Corp.
ADSI Inc.
Barksdale Foward
KPMG, LLP

DAVIS, Jim

80 F St. NW Tel: (202)639-6419
Washington, DC 20001 Fax: (202)639-6441

Employers
American Federation of Government Employees (AFL-CIO) (National Secretary-Treasurer)

DAVIS, Kamer

1901 L St. NW Tel: (202)466-7590
Suite 300 Fax: (202)833-2471
Washington, DC 20036
EMail: kamer.davis@dc.ogilvypr.com

Employers
Ogilvy Public Relations Worldwide (Senior V. President, Internet Marketing)

DAVIS, Kimberly

1725 DeSales St. NW Tel: (202)429-5609
Suite 600 Fax: (202)872-0619
Washington, DC 20036

Employers
Center for Marine Conservation

DAVIS, Lanny J.

2550 M St. NW Tel: (202)457-6000
Washington, DC 20037-1350 Fax: (202)457-6315
Registered: LDA, FARA
EMail: ldavis@pattonboggs.com
Special Counsel to the President, Executive Office of the President, The White House, 1996-98.

Employers
Patton Boggs, LLP (Partner)

Clients Represented
On Behalf of Patton Boggs, LLP
American Committee for Peace and Justice in South Asia
Beauty and Barber Supply Industries, Inc.
Crane Co.
Dictaphone Corp.
Pakistan, Government of the Islamic Republic of
Pechanga Band of California Luiseno Indians
Union Pacific Railroad Co.
Wild Alabama
WQED Pittsburgh

DAVIS, Lisa

Ten G St. NE Tel: (202)216-0420
Suite 600 Fax: (202)216-0446
Washington, DC 20002-4215 Registered: LDA

Employers
Nat'l Committee to Preserve Social Security and Medicare (Senior Policy Analyst)

DAVIS, Lizanne H.

1667 K St. NW Tel: (202)956-5211
Suite 460 Fax: (202)956-5235
Washington, DC 20006 Registered: LDA
EMail: lizanne_davis@fmc.com

Employers
FMC Corp. (Director, Government Affairs)

DAVIS, Ph.D., Lynda C.

444 N. Capitol St.
Suite 841
Washington, DC 20001
Tel: (202)638-5333
Fax: (202)638-5335
Registered: LDA
EMail: ldavis@davisoconnell.com
Former Aide, Office of Management and Budget, Executive Office of the President, the White House. Former Aide, Senate Budget and Appropriations Committees.

Employers
Davis O'Connell, Inc. (President)

Clients Represented
On Behalf of Davis O'Connell, Inc.
CompTIA
Constellation Technology Corp.
Contra Costa Community College District
Episcopal AIDS Ministry
Florida Community College of Jacksonville
Florida Department of Education
Illinois Community College Board
LifeLink Foundation
Los Angeles Community College District
Raydon Corp.
Science Applications Internat'l Corp. (SAIC)
St. Petersburg Community College
Valencia Community College
Washington and Jefferson College

DAVIS, Lynne

2450 N St. NW
Washington, DC 20037-1126
Tel: (202)828-0526
Fax: (202)862-6218
Registered: LDA

Employers
Ass'n of American Medical Colleges (Director, Health Care Legislative Affairs)

DAVIS, Marianne

1401 K St. NW
Suite 600
Washington, DC 20005
Tel: (202)835-9898
Fax: (202)853-9893

Employers
ASCENT (Ass'n of Community Enterprises) (Manager, Conference Services)

DAVIS, Mark

7203 Ludwood Ct.
Alexandria, VA 22306
Tel: (703)768-4484
Fax: (703)765-6739
Registered: LDA
Former Congressional Liaison, Federal Election Commission and former Staff Member, House Ethics Committee.

Employers
Riggs Government Relations Consulting LLC

Clients Represented
On Behalf of Riggs Government Relations Consulting LLC
Edupoint.com

DAVIS, Mark D.

5108 34th St. NW
Washington, DC 20008
Tel: (202)296-4790
Fax: (202)296-4791
EMail: DLTrade@aol.com

Employers
Davis & Leiman, P.C. (Attorney)

DAVIS, Mark W.

1030 15th St. NW
Suite 1100
Washington, DC 20005
Tel: (202)783-4600
Fax: (202)783-4601
Former Speechwriter for the President, 1989-91. Former Speechwriter for the Cabinet during the Reagan Administration.

Employers
White House Writers Group (Senior Director)

DAVIS, Mary

201 14th St. SW
Fifth Floor SW
Washington, DC 20250
Tel: (202)205-1583
Fax: (202)205-1225
EMail: mary.davis@fs.fed.us

Employers
Department of Agriculture - Forest Service (Deputy Director, Legislative Affairs Staff)

DAVIS, Mary E.

5818 Bradley Blvd.
Bethesda, MD 20814
Tel: (301)229-5999
Registered: LDA

Employers
Self-employed as an independent consultant.

Clients Represented
As an independent consultant
Interstate Natural Gas Ass'n of America

DAVIS, Mary Hope

1050 Connecticut Ave. NW
Washington, DC 20036-5339
Tel: (202)857-6000
Fax: (202)857-6395
Registered: LDA
Former Chief of Staff, Sen. Dale Bumpers (D-AR).

Employers
Arent Fox Kintner Plotkin & Kahn, PLLC (Government Relations Director)

Clients Represented
On Behalf of Arent Fox Kintner Plotkin & Kahn, PLLC
American Public Power Ass'n
Tyson Foods, Inc.

DAVIS, Michael G.

1900 Association Dr.
Reston, VA 20191-1598
Tel: (703)476-3400
Fax: (703)476-9527
EMail: evp@aahperd.org

Employers
American Alliance for Health, Physical Education, Recreation and Dance (Exec. V. President)

DAVIS, R. Mark

1200 18th St. NW
Suite 1100
Washington, DC 20036
Tel: (202)721-1545
Fax: (202)467-5780

Employers
Renew America (Exec. Director)

DAVIS, Randall E.

1275 Pennsylvania Ave. NW
Ninth Floor
Washington, DC 20004
Tel: (202)662-6790
Fax: (202)624-0866
Registered: LDA
EMail: rdavis@sdsatty.com

Employers
Stuntz, Davis & Staffier, P.C. (President)

Clients Represented
On Behalf of Stuntz, Davis & Staffier, P.C.
Alliance for Competitive Electricity
Bridgestone/Firestone, Inc.
Los Angeles, California, County of
Pharmaceutical Research and Manufacturers of America
PURPA Reform Group
R. J. Reynolds Tobacco Co.

DAVIS, Randall P. K.

1448 Duke St.
Alexandria, VA 22314
Tel: (703)836-4800
Fax: (703)836-4801
Registered: LDA
EMail: rdavis@iaapa.org

Employers
Internat'l Ass'n of Amusement Parks and Attractions (V. President, Government Relations)

DAVIS, Rebecca

499 S. Capitol St. SW
Suite 600
Washington, DC 20003
Tel: (202)554-1222
Fax: (202)554-1230
Registered: LDA
EMail: dwawashdc@aol.com

Employers
Don Wallace Associates, Inc.

Clients Represented
On Behalf of Don Wallace Associates, Inc.
Cotton Warehouse Ass'n of America

DAVIS, Richard H.

211 N. Union St.
Suite 250
Alexandria, VA 22314
Tel: (703)299-9100
Fax: (703)299-9110
Registered: LDA
EMail: rdavis@dmfgroup.com
Former Associate Director, Office of Cabinet Affairs, The White House during the Reagan administration.

Employers
Davis Manafort, Inc. (Managing Partner)

Clients Represented
On Behalf of Davis Manafort, Inc.
GTECH Corp.
SBC Communications Inc.

DAVIS, Richard S.

1350 I St. NW
Suite 700
Washington, DC 20005
Tel: (202)789-6000
Fax: (202)789-6190
Law Clerk to Judge H. Emory Widener, Jr., U.S. Court of Appeals, Fourth Circuit, 1980-81.

Employers
Beveridge & Diamond, P.C. (Partner)

DAVIS, Robert P.

1909 K St. NW
Washington, DC 20006
Tel: (202)263-3000
Fax: (202)263-3300
Registered: LDA
EMail: rdavis@mayerbrown.com
Solicitor, U.S. Department of Labor, 1989-91. Chief of Staff to Secretary of Transportation, 1983-85.

Employers
Mayer, Brown & Platt (Partner)

DAVIS, Robert R.

900 19th St. NW
Suite 400
Washington, DC 20006
Tel: (202)857-3100
Fax: (202)296-8716
Registered: LDA

Employers
America's Community Bankers (Director, Government Relations)

DAVIS, Robert V.

499 S. Capitol St. SW
Suite 504
Washington, DC 20003
Tel: (202)554-3626
Fax: (202)554-1961
Registered: LDA
Former Deputy Undersecretary, Department of Defense.

Employers
R. V. Davis and Associates (Principal)

Clients Represented
On Behalf of R. V. Davis and Associates
Ball Aerospace & Technology Corp.
Insyte Corp.
Motorola Space and Systems Technology Group
Spectrum Astro, Inc.
Zenware Solutions, Inc.

DAVIS, Hon. Robert W.

2361 Jefferson Davis Hwy.
Suite 506
Arlington, VA 22202
Tel: (703)418-1410
Fax: (703)418-6882
Registered: LDA, FARA
Member, U.S. House of Representatives (R-MI), 1979-93.

Employers
Bob Davis & Associates (President)

Clients Represented
On Behalf of Bob Davis & Associates
American Science and Engineering, Inc.
Atlantic States Marine Fisheries Commission
British Aerospace
Casa Aircraft USA, Inc.
Environmental Research and Education Foundation
Fel Corp.
Frequency Engineering Laboratories
Marquette General Hospital
The Modernization Forum
Sippican, Inc.

DAVIS, Sarah P.

901 E St. NW
Fourth Floor
Washington, DC 20004
Tel: (202)969-8020
Fax: (202)969-8030
Registered: LDA
EMail: sara.davis@slma.com

Employers
Sallie Mae, Inc. (Director, Government Relations)

DAVIS, Sheila

1301 Pennsylvania Ave. NW
Suite 1030
Washington, DC 20004
Tel: (202)824-0402
Fax: (202)824-0418

Employers
Cinergy Corp. (Manager, Federal Government Affairs)

DAVIS, Sidney

8300 Greensboro Dr.
Suite 750
McLean, VA 22102
Tel: (703)790-8466
Fax: (703)790-8631

Employers
American Academy of Audiology (Communications Director)

DAVIS, Smith W.

1333 New Hampshire Ave. NW
Suite 400
Washington, DC 20036
Tel: (202)887-4000
Fax: (202)887-4288
Registered: LDA

Counsel, Subcommittee on Crime, House Judiciary Committee, 1978-79. Clerk, U.S. District Court, District of Columbia, 1977-78.

Employers
Akin, Gump, Strauss, Hauer & Feld, L.L.P. (Partner)

Clients Represented

On Behalf of Akin, Gump, Strauss, Hauer & Feld, L.L.P.
American Airlines
American Express Co.
Competitive Consumer Lending Coalition
Dow Jones & Co., Inc.
EMC Corp.
Exxon Mobil Corp.
Gila River Indian Community
Granite Broadcasting Co.
L.L. Capital Partners, Inc.
Mortgage Insurance Companies of America
Motion Picture Ass'n of America
Nehemiah Progressive Housing Development Corp.
New York Public Library
New York State Health Facilities Ass'n
PerkinElmer Detection Systems
The Project Leadership Committee, Lincoln Center for the Performing Arts
Riggs Bank, N.A.
Ryder System, Inc.
Texas Manufactured Housing Ass'n
Transamerica Occidental Life Insurance Co.
Westar Group, Inc.

DAVIS, Steven M.

905 16th St. NW
Washington, DC 20006
Tel: (202)783-3545
Fax: (202)347-1721
Registered: LDA

Employers
Laborers-Employers Cooperation & Education Trust (Marketing Representative)

DAVIS, Susan A.

1000 Vermont Ave. NW
Suite 700
Washington, DC 20005
Tel: (202)408-0808
Fax: (202)408-0876
Registered: LDA, FARA

Employers
Susan Davis Internat'l (Chairman)

Clients Represented

On Behalf of Susan Davis Internat'l
Internet Council of Registrars
Register.com
Sabreliner Corp.

DAVIS, Thomas A.

1455 Pennsylvania Ave. NW
Suite 1200
Washington, DC 20004
Tel: (202)347-2230
Fax: (202)393-3310
Registered: LDA

Office of the Chief Counsel, Internal Revenue Service, 1966-70. Captain, U.S. Army Reserve, Active Duty, 1964-66.

Employers
Davis & Harman LLP (Partner)

Clients Represented

On Behalf of Davis & Harman LLP
Allstate Insurance Co.
American General Life Insurance Co.
American Horse Council, Inc.
Armco Inc.
Bethlehem Steel Corp.
Cellular Telecommunications and Internet Ass'n
Chicago Board of Trade
Committee of Annuity Insurers
Florida Power and Light Co.
Nat'l Cattleman's Beef Ass'n
Nat'l Thoroughbred Racing Ass'n, Inc.
Pharmaceutical Research and Manufacturers of America
Stock Co. Information Group
United States Sugar Corp.

DAVIS, Timothy S.

801 Pennsylvania Ave.
Suite 650
Washington, DC 20004
Tel: (202)624-0761
Fax: (202)624-0775
Registered: LDA
EMail: tim.davis@aexp.com

Employers
American Express Co. (Senior V. President, Government Affairs)

DAVIS, Rev. William F.

3211 Fourth St. NE
Washington, DC 20017
Tel: (202)541-3148
Fax: (202)541-3390

Employers
United States Catholic Conference (Assistant Secretary, Catholic Schools and Public Policy)

DAVITIAN, S. Leigh

1321 Duke St.
Alexandria, VA 22314-3563
Tel: (703)739-1300
Fax: (703)739-1321
Registered: LDA
EMail: Ldavitian@ascp.com

Employers
American Soc. of Consultant Pharmacists (Director, Government Affairs)

DAWE, Christopher M.

1455 Pennsylvania Ave. NW
Suite 700
Washington, DC 20004-1008
Tel: (202)639-6500
Fax: (202)639-6604
Registered: LDA
EMail: cdawe@velaw.com

Employers
Vinson & Elkins L.L.P. (Associate)

Clients Represented

On Behalf of Vinson & Elkins L.L.P.
Portland General Electric Co.

DAWSON, Albert R.

805 15th St. NW
Suite 700
Washington, DC 20005
Tel: (202)312-7440
Fax: (202)312-7460
EMail: ardawson@bakerd.com

Employers
Baker & Daniels (Partner)

DAWSON, Donald S.

1133 Connecticut Ave. NW
Tenth Floor
Washington, DC 20036
Tel: (202)775-2370
Fax: (202)833-8491
Registered: LDA

Administrative Assistant to the President, The White House, 1947-53. Administrative Assistant to the Federal Loan Administrator, 1939-43.

Employers
Donald S. Dawson & Associates (Attorney)

Clients Represented

On Behalf of Donald S. Dawson & Associates
Leo A. Daly Co.
Opticians Ass'n of America
St. Thomas/St. John Chamber of Commerce, Inc.

DAWSON, Jr., Rear Adm J. Cutler

The Pentagon
MS: 5C760
Washington, DC 20350-2000
Tel: (703)697-7146
EMail: dawson.cutler@hq.navy.mil

Employers
Department of Navy - Chief of Naval Operations Office (Special Assistant, Legislative Support)

DAWSON, Mimi W.

1776 K St. NW
Washington, DC 20006
Tel: (202)719-7000
Fax: (202)719-7049
Registered: LDA

Former Deputy Secretary of Transportation, 1987-89; and Commissioner, Federal Communications Commission, 1981-87.

Employers
Wiley, Rein & Fielding (Government Affairs Consultant)

Clients Represented

On Behalf of Wiley, Rein & Fielding
ARINC, Inc.
A. H. Belo Corp.
Engage Technologies
Gannett Co., Inc.
Hearst-Argyle Television, Inc.
INTELSAT - Internat'l Telecommunications Satellite Organization
Mobile Telecommunications Technologies Corp.
Motorola, Inc.
NetCoalition.Com
Newspaper Ass'n of America
Personal Communications Industry Ass'n (PCIA)
Francis R. Ruddy Institute of Maritime Communications
Time Domain Corp.
UTAM, Inc.
UtiliCorp United, Inc.
Verizon Wireless

DAWSON, Rhett B.

1250 I St. NW
Suite 200
Washington, DC 20005
Tel: (202)737-8888
Fax: (202)638-4922
Registered: LDA

Employers
Information Technology Industry Council (President)

DAWSON, Robert K.

1225 I St. NW
Suite 500
Washington, DC 20005
Tel: (202)312-2005
Fax: (202)289-8683
Registered: LDA
EMail: dawsonassociates@worldnet.att.net

Associate Director, Office of Management and Budget, 1987-89. Assistant Secretary for Civil Works (1984-87) and Deputy Assistant Secretary for Civil Works (1981-84), Department of the Army. Administrator, House Transportation and Infrastructure Committee, 1974-81. Legislative Director for Rep. Jack Edwards (R-AL), 1972-74.

Employers
Dawson & Associates, Inc. (President)

Clients Represented

On Behalf of Dawson & Associates, Inc.
AgriPartners
Chemical Land Holdings, Inc.
Florida Citrus Mutual
Florida Farm Bureau
Florida Sugar Cane League, Inc.
Great Lakes Dredge & Dock
Sugar Cane Growers Cooperative of Florida

DAWSON, Robert M.

4301 Wilson Blvd.
Arlington, VA 22203-1860
Tel: (703)907-5793
Fax: (703)907-5516
EMail: bob.dawson@nreca.org

Employers
Nat'l Rural Electric Cooperative Ass'n (Director, Department Operations)

DAWSON, Thomas C.

1000 Connecticut Ave. NW
Suite 302
Washington, DC 20036
Tel: (202)835-0740
Fax: (202)775-8526
Registered: LDA
EMail: tomd@sda-inc.com

Employers
Smith Dawson & Andrews, Inc.

Clients Represented

On Behalf of Smith Dawson & Andrews, Inc.

Alston & Bird, LLP
Certified Automotive Parts Ass'n
Georgia Municipal Gas Ass'n
Georgia, State of
Hillwood Development Corp.
Kansas City Area Transportation Authority
Lane Transit District
Litton Advanced Systems
Litton Systems, Inc.
Mothers Against Drunk Driving (MADD)
New York Metropolitan Transportation Authority
Sacramento, California, City of
San Francisco Internat'l Airport
Springfield, Oregon, School District #19

DAWSON, Tom

214 Massachusetts Ave. NE
Washington, DC 20002
Tel: (202)546-4400
Fax: (202)546-8328

Employers
Heritage Foundation (Educational Affairs Fellow)

DAWSON, Tom H.

1725 DeSales St. NW
Suite 800
Washington, DC 20036
Tel: (202)659-6546
Fax: (202)659-5730

Employers
Whitten & Diamond (Consultant)

DAY, Brenda T.

1401 H St. NW
Suite 700
Washington, DC 20005
Tel: (202)414-6714
Fax: (202)414-6743
Registered: LDA

Employers
DaimlerChrysler Corp. (Director, Congressional Affairs)

DAY, Harry F.

801 Pennsylvania Ave. NW
Suite 630
Washington, DC 20004-5878
Tel: (202)347-4300
Fax: (202)347-4370
Registered: LDA
EMail: hday@nyse.com

Employers
New York Stock Exchange (Counsel, Regulatory Affairs)

DAY, Osborne A.

2000 P St. NW
Suite 510
Washington, DC 20036
Tel: (202)466-6789
Fax: (202)296-3862
Registered: LDA

Employers
Self-employed as an independent consultant.

Clients Represented

As an independent consultant

Recording for the Blind and Dyslexic, Inc.

DAY, Robert D.

5430 Grosvenor Ln.
Bethesda, MD 20814
Tel: (301)493-9101
Fax: (301)493-6148
EMail: info@rnrf.org

Employers
Renewable Natural Resources Foundation (Exec. Director)

DAYANIM, Behnam

1299 Pennsylvania Ave. NW
Tenth Floor
Washington, DC 20004-2400
Tel: (202)508-9500
Fax: (202)508-9700
Registered: LDA
EMail: bdayanim@paulhastings.com
Law Clerk to Judge Frank A. Kaufman, U.S. District Court for the District of Maryland, 1993-94.

Employers
Paul, Hastings, Janofsky & Walker LLP (Associate)

Clients Represented

On Behalf of Paul, Hastings, Janofsky & Walker LLP

Amdahl Corp.
CFSBdirect Inc.
The Marine and Fire Insurance Ass'n of Japan, Inc.

DE ALESSI, Michael

1001 Connecticut Ave. NW
Suite 1250
Washington, DC 20036
Tel: (202)331-1010
Fax: (202)331-0640

Employers
Competitive Enterprise Institute (Director of Center for Private Conservation)

DE BEARN, Gaston

8000 Towers Crescent Dr.
Suite 1350
Tysons Corner, VA 22182
Tel: (703)760-7888
Fax: (703)753-2932
Registered: LDA
EMail: gdebxiv@erols.com
Staff, Senate Committee on Government Operations, 1957-60.

Employers
Washington Liaison Group, LLC (President)

Clients Represented

On Behalf of Washington Liaison Group, LLC

Reckitt & Colman Pharmaceuticals Inc.
Serono Laboratories, Inc.

DE BERNARDO, Mark A.

1225 I St. NW
Suite 1000
Washington, DC 20005-3914
Tel: (202)842-7400
Fax: (202)842-0022

Employers
Institute for a Drug-Free Workplace (Exec. Director)

DE BLOIS, Michael

P.O. Box 7564
Arlington, VA 22207-7564
Tel: (703)241-1741
Fax: (703)241-1939

Employers
Committee Management Associates (Director)

Clients Represented

On Behalf of Committee Management Associates

Nat'l Ass'n of Independent Insurers
United Pilots Political Action Committee

DE COSTER, Timothy P.

201 14th St. SW
Fifth Floor SW
Washington, DC 20250
Tel: (202)205-1216
Fax: (202)205-1225
EMail: tim.decoster@fs.fed.us
Minority Consultant (1995), Staff Director, Subcommittee on Livestock (1993-95), and Staff Director, Subcommittee on Forests, Family Farms and Energy (1987-93), House Committee on Agriculture. Legislative Director (1985-87) and Legislative Assistant (1981-84) to Rep. Harold L. Volkmer (D-MO).

Employers
Department of Agriculture - Forest Service (Director, Legislative Affairs Staff)

DE GRAMONT, Jacqueline

655 15th St. NW
Suite 900
Washington, DC 20005-5701
Tel: (202)626-5800
Fax: (202)628-0858
Registered: LDA
EMail: jdegramont@milchev.com

Employers
Miller & Chevalier, Chartered (Associate)

DE JONGH, Allison

1801 Alexander Bell Dr.
Suite 500
Reston, VA 20191
Tel: (703)264-7500
Fax: (703)264-7551
Registered: LDA

Employers
American Institute of Aeronautics and Astronautics (Government Relations Representative)

DE LA CRUZ, Peter L.

1001 G St. NW
Suite 500 West
Washington, DC 20001
Tel: (202)434-4100
Fax: (202)434-4646
EMail: delacruz@khlaw.com
Trial Attorney, Antitrust Division, U.S. Department of Justice, 1976-80.

Employers
Keller and Heckman LLP (Partner)

DE LEON, Sylvia A.

1333 New Hampshire Ave. NW
Suite 400
Washington, DC 20036
Tel: (202)887-4000
Fax: (202)887-4288
Registered: LDA
EMail: sdeleon@akingump.com
Member, Task Force on the White House Conference on Travel and Tourism, 1995. Coordinator of Transportation Issues, Presidential Transition Team, 1993. Presidential Appointee to the National Commission to Ensure a Strong Competitive Airline Industry, 1993.

Employers
Akin, Gump, Strauss, Hauer & Feld, L.L.P. (Partner)

Clients Represented

On Behalf of Akin, Gump, Strauss, Hauer & Feld, L.L.P.

American Airlines
American Express Co.
Frederic R. Harris, Inc.
Harris, Texas, Metropolitan Transit Authority of
The Texas Medical Center

DE MARTINEZ, Julie Warner

1701 Clarendon Blvd.
Arlington, VA 22209
Tel: (703)276-8800
Fax: (703)243-2593

Employers
American Chiropractic Ass'n (V. President, Member Services)

DE MATTIES, Catalan

1400 I St. NW
Suite 1220
Washington, DC 20005
Tel: (202)408-4848
Fax: (202)408-1818

Employers
Nat'l AIDS Fund (Director, Development)

DE POSADA, Robert

101 1/2 S. Union St.
Alexandria, VA 22314
Tel: (703)684-5100
Fax: (703)684-5424
Registered: LDA

Employers
Smith Fairfield, Inc.

DE POY, Sandra

1220 L St. NW
Suite 500
Washington, DC 20005
Tel: (202)371-6700
Fax: (202)289-8544
Registered: LDA
EMail: sdepoy@arda.org

Employers
American Resort Development Ass'n (Director, Federal Relations and ARDA PAC)

DE PREST, Geert M.

2100 M St. NW
Suite 200
Washington, DC 20037
Tel: (202)785-4185
Fax: (202)466-1286
EMail: gdeprest@stewartlaw.com

Employers
Stewart and Stewart (Partner)

Clients Represented

On Behalf of Stewart and Stewart

Floral Trade Council
Torrington Co.

DEAL, David

1220 L St. NW
Washington, DC 20005
Tel: (202)682-8000
Fax: (202)682-8232
Registered: LDA

Employers
American Petroleum Institute (Managing Attorney)

DEAL, Martha P.

315 S. Patrick St.
Alexandria, VA 22314-3501
Tel: (703)836-9300
Fax: (703)836-9303
EMail: office@mdna.org

Employers
Machinery Dealers Nat'l Ass'n (Exec. V. President)

DEAL, Timothy

1030 15th St. NW
Suite 800
Washington, DC 20005
EMail: tdeal@uscib-dc.org
Tel: (202)371-1316
Fax: (202)371-8249

Employers
United States Council for Internat'l Business (Senior V. President, Washington Office)

DEALY, Brendan

1225 I St. NW
Suite 1100
Washington, DC 20005
Tel: (202)289-7319
Fax: (202)408-1851

Employers
The Center to Prevent Handgun Violence (Director, Communications)

DEAN, Carol A.

10201 Lee Hwy.
Suite 225
Fairfax, VA 22030
Tel: (703)359-7090
Fax: (703)352-0493
Registered: LDA

Employers
Building Service Contractors Ass'n Internat'l (Exec. V. President)

DEAN, Heather

1830 Connecticut Ave. NW
Washington, DC 20009
Tel: (202)518-7638
Fax: (202)223-8221

Employers
Network in Solidarity with the People of Guatemala (NISGUA) (Exec. Director)

DEAN, John E.

1101 Vermont Ave. NW
Suite 400
Washington, DC 20005
Tel: (202)289-3900
Fax: (202)371-0197
Registered: LDA
EMail: deandbm@dbmlaw.com
Assistant Counsel, House Committee on Education and Labor, 1983-85.

Employers
Dean Blakey & Moskowitz (Managing Partner)

Clients Represented

On Behalf of Dean Blakey & Moskowitz
Chase Manhattan Bank
Chela Financial
Consumer Bankers Ass'n
Diversified Collection Services, Inc.
Fair Share Coalition
Management Concepts, Inc.
Student Loan Funding Corp.
UNIPAC Service Corp.

DEAN, Jonathan

1707 H St. NW
Suite 600
Washington, DC 20006-3919
Tel: (202)223-6133
Fax: (202)223-6162

Employers
Union of Concerned Scientists (Advisor, Global Security Issues)

DEAN, Lisa

717 Second St. NE
Washington, DC 20002
EMail: Ldean@freecongress.org
Tel: (202)204-5303
Fax: (202)543-5605

Employers
Free Congress Research and Education Foundation (V. President, Technology Policy)

DEAN, Maggie

2400 N St. NW
Fifth Floor
Washington, DC 20037
Tel: (202)728-1164
Fax: (202)728-2992

Employers
Ogletree Governmental Affairs, Inc. (Principal)

Clients Represented

On Behalf of Ogletree Governmental Affairs, Inc.
Eka Chemicals
Nat'l Alliance Against Blacklisting

DEAN, Michael

1250 Connecticut Ave. NW
Suite 800
Washington, DC 20036
Tel: (202)785-0081
Fax: (202)785-0721

Employers
Cellular Telecommunications and Internet Ass'n (PAC Contact)

DEAN, Roberta

1275 K St. NW
Suite 1212
Washington, DC 20005
Tel: (703)787-0000
Fax: (202)312-5005
Registered: LDA

Employers
Healthcare Distribution Management Ass'n (Associate Director, Congressional Affairs)

DEAN, S. Bobo

2120 L St. NW
Suite 700
Washington, DC 20037
Tel: (202)822-8282
Fax: (202)296-8834
Registered: LDA

Employers
Hobbs, Straus, Dean and Walker, LLP (Partner)

Clients Represented

On Behalf of Hobbs, Straus, Dean and Walker, LLP
Alamo Navajo School Board
Alaska Native Health Board
Bristol Bay Area Health Corp.
Choctaw Indians, Mississippi Band of
Menominee Indian Tribe
Metlakatla Indian Community
Miccosukee Tribe of Indians of Florida
Norton Sound Health Corp.
Seldovia Native Ass'n, Inc.
Shoalwater Bay Indian Tribe
St. Regis Mohawk Tribe
Susanville Indian Rancheria

DEAN, Virginia

1120 Connecticut Ave. NW
Washington, DC 20036
Tel: (202)663-5000
Fax: (202)663-7578

Employers
American Bankers Ass'n (Exec. Director, Communications)

DEAN, Warren L.

1909 K St. NW
Suite 600
Washington, DC 20006-1167
Tel: (202)585-6900
Fax: (202)585-6969
Registered: LDA

Employers
Thompson Coburn LLP (Partner)

Clients Represented

On Behalf of Thompson Coburn LLP
Air Transport Ass'n of America
General Ore Internat'l Corp. Ltd.
Special Vehicle Coalition

DEANE, James G.

1101 14th St. NW
Suite 1400
Washington, DC 20005
EMail: jdeane@defenders.org
Tel: (202)682-9400
Fax: (202)682-1331

Employers
Defenders of Wildlife (V. President, Publications)

DEANE, Lorraine P.

409 Third St. SW
Suite 7900
Washington, DC 20416
EMail: lorraine.deane@sba.gov
Tel: (202)205-6700
Fax: (202)205-7374

Employers
Small Business Administration (Legislative Affairs Specialist)

DEANNA, Jennifer S.

601 Pennsylvania Ave. NW
Suite 350
North Bldg.
Washington, DC 20004
EMail: deannaj@dteenergy.com
Tel: (202)347-8420
Fax: (202)347-8423
Registered: LDA

Employers
Detroit Edison Co. (Legislative Assistant)

DEARMENT, Roderick A.

1201 Pennsylvania Ave. NW
Washington, DC 20004-2401
Tel: (202)662-5900
Fax: (202)662-6291
Registered: LDA
EMail: rdearment@cov.com
Deputy Secretary, Department of Labor, 1989-91. Chief of Staff to Senate Majority Leader Robert Dole (R-KS), 1985-86. Chief Counsel and Staff Director (1983-85), Deputy Chief Counsel (1981-82) and Deputy Chief Minority Counsel (1979-81), Senate Committee on Finance

Employers
Covington & Burling (Partner)

Clients Represented

On Behalf of Covington & Burling
American Ass'n of Oral and Maxillofacial Surgeons
American Council on Education
American Watch Ass'n
Ass'n of American Medical Colleges
Attorneys' Liability Assurance Soc. Inc.
The Business Roundtable
Christie's Inc.
Coalition of Boston Teaching Hospitals
Federal Home Loan Mortgage Corp. (Freddie Mac)
General Electric Co.
Land Trust Alliance
Nat'l Trust for Historic Preservation
Qwest Communications
Retirement Income Coalition
Sotheby's Holdings Inc.
Syntex (USA) Inc.
Verizon Communications
The Washington Post Co.
WESTVACO
Zeigler Coal Holding Co.

DEARYBURY, Sheila

1909 K St. NW
Washington, DC 20006
Tel: (202)263-3000
Fax: (202)263-3300
Registered: LDA
EMail: sdearybury@mayerbrown.com
Counsel, House Armed Services Committee, 1998-99. Staff Attorney, Sentencing Commission, 1993-94.

Employers
Mayer, Brown & Platt (Associate)

Clients Represented

On Behalf of Mayer, Brown & Platt
General Dynamics Corp.

DEASON, Ph.D., Jonathan P.

1010 Massachusetts Ave. NW
Washington, DC 20001
Tel: (202)289-4434
Fax: (202)289-4435
Registered: LDA
Director, Office of Environmental Policy and Compliance, Department of the Interior, 1989-94.

Employers
American Road and Transportation Builders Ass'n (ARTBA) (Environmental Consultant)
Dawson & Associates, Inc. (Senior Advisor)

Clients Represented

On Behalf of Dawson & Associates, Inc.
AgriPartners
Anglogold Americas, Inc.
Chemical Land Holdings, Inc.
Florida Citrus Mutual
Florida Farm Bureau
Florida Sugar Cane League, Inc.
Sugar Cane Growers Cooperative of Florida

DEATHERAGE, Anne

151 Spring St.
Suite 300
Herndon, VA 20170
EMail: adeatherage@nigp.org
Tel: (703)736-8900
Ext: 238
Fax: (703)736-9644

Employers
Nat'l Institute of Governmental Purchasing (Deputy Exec. V. President)

DEAVER, Carolyn J.

1101 17th St. NW
Suite 300
Washington, DC 20036
Tel: (202)331-1770
Fax: (202)331-1969

Employers
Cosmetic, Toiletry and Fragrance Ass'n (V. President, Foundation)

DEAVER, Michael K.

1875 I St. NW
Suite 900
Washington, DC 20005
Tel: (202)371-0200
Fax: (202)371-2858
Registered: LDA, FARA

Former Deputy Chief of Staff to the President, The White House during the Reagan Administration.

Employers

Edelman Public Relations Worldwide (V. Chairman, International Relations)

Clients Represented

On Behalf of Edelman Public Relations Worldwide

AT&T
Bacardi Ltd.
Church of Jesus Christ of Latter Day Saints
Fuji Photo Film U.S.A., Inc.
Microsoft Corp.
Nat'l Ass'n of Broadcasters
Nissan North America Inc.
Portugal, Trade Commission of the Government of the Republic of

DEBEAUMONT, Dana

P.O. Box 322
McLean, VA 22101
Tel: (703)444-2153
Fax: (703)444-6158
Registered: LDA

Employers

Genesis Consulting Group, LLC (Director, Communications)

Clients Represented

On Behalf of Genesis Consulting Group, LLC

Elkem Materials Inc.
FED Corp.
Integrated Skilled Care of Ohio
Lennox Internat'l
Norchem Concrete Products Inc.
The Timken Co.
Vandium Industry Coalition

DEBERNARDO, Francis

4012 29th St.
Mt. Rainier, MD 20712
Tel: (301)277-5674
Fax: (301)864-8954

Employers

New Ways Ministry (Exec. Director)

DEBEVOISE, II, Eli Whitney

555 12th St. NW
Washington, DC 20004-1206
Tel: (202)942-5000
Fax: (202)942-5999
EMail: Whitney_Debevoise@aporter.com

Law Clerk to Judge William J. Holloway, Jr., U.S. Court of Appeals, Tenth Circuit, 1978-79.

Employers

Arnold & Porter (Partner)

DEBOER, Jeffrey D.

1420 New York Ave. NW
Suite 1100
Washington, DC 20005
Tel: (202)639-8400
Fax: (202)639-8442
Registered: LDA
EMail: jdeboer@rer.org

Employers

Real Estate Roundtable (President and Chief Operating Officer)

DEBOISSIERE, Alex

1301 Pennsylvania Ave. NW
Suite 1030
Washington, DC 20004
Tel: (202)824-0402
Fax: (202)824-0418
Registered: LDA

Employers

Cinergy Corp. (Manager, Federal Regulatory Affairs)

DEBOLT, Don J.

1350 New York Ave. NW
Suite 900
Washington, DC 20005
Tel: (202)628-8000
Fax: (202)628-0812

Employers

Internat'l Franchise Ass'n (President)

DEBRUNNER, Charles L.

Ten Pidgeon Hill Dr.
Suite 150
Sterling, VA 20165
Tel: (703)444-4091
Fax: (703)444-3029
Registered: LDA
EMail: charlie@debrunnerandassociates.com

Employers

DeBrunner and Associates, Inc. (President)

Clients Represented

On Behalf of DeBrunner and Associates, Inc.

Albert Einstein Medical Center
Catholic Healthcare West
Health Quest
Nat'l Ass'n of Urban Hospitals
Private Essential Access Community Hospitals (PEACH) Inc.
Southcoast Health System
Susquehanna Health System
Thomas Jefferson University Hospital

DEBRY, Kristine

3000 K St. NW
Suite 300
Washington, DC 20007
Tel: (202)424-7500
Fax: (202)424-7643
Registered: LDA

Speechwriter, Office of the Secretary, Department of Health and Human Services, 1992-94.

Employers

Swidler Berlin Shereff Friedman, LLP (Associate)

Clients Represented

On Behalf of Swidler Berlin Shereff Friedman, LLP

Coalition to Ensure Responsible Billing
Frontier Communications Corp.
ICG Communications, Inc.
Marconi plc

DEBUS, Tim

727 N. Washington St.
Alexandria, VA 22314
Tel: (540)314-3214
Fax: (703)836-2049

Employers

Internat'l Banana Ass'n (V. President)

DEBUTTS, Thomas M.

1133 Connecticut Ave. NW
Suite 1200
Washington, DC 20036
Tel: (202)775-9800
Fax: (202)833-8491
Registered: FARA

Director, Exporter Assistance Staff (1988-89) and Assistant to the Director, Office of Export Licensing (1984-88), Bureau of Export Administration, Department of Commerce.

Employers

Winthrop, Stimson, Putnam & Roberts (Associate)

DECAIN, Ann

801 Pennsylvania Ave. NW
Suite 730
Washington, DC 20004
Tel: (202)756-2432
Fax: (202)756-2433
Registered: LDA
EMail: DeCain@howdc.com

Employers

Hooper Owen & Winburn (Senior Legislative Specialist)

DECAPRIO, Robert

1101 15th St. NW
Suite 202
Washington, DC 20005
Tel: (202)785-3232
Fax: (202)223-9741
EMail: rdecaprio@kellencompany.com

Employers

The Kellen Company (Account Executive)
Messenger Courier Ass'n of the Americas (Exec. Director)

Clients Represented

On Behalf of The Kellen Company

Messenger Courier Ass'n of the Americas

DECARLO, Jacqueline

4350 N. Fairfax Dr.
Suite 410
Arlington, VA 22203
Tel: (703)528-4141
Ext: 130
Fax: (703)528-4145
EMail: decarlo@afop.org

Employers

Ass'n of Farmworker Opportunity Programs (Senior Manager, AmeriCorps Program)

DECELL, III, Hal C.

1501 Farm Credit Dr.
MS: 4120
McLean, VA 22102-5090
Tel: (703)883-4056
Fax: (703)790-3260

Employers

Farm Credit Administration (Director, Office of Congressional and Public Affairs)

DECELL, Jane

400 Seventh St. SW
MS: 10100
Washington, DC 20590
Tel: (202)366-4687
Fax: (202)366-7153

Employers

Department of Transportation (Deputy Assistant General Counsel, Office of Legislation)

DECELLE, Arthur J.

122 C St. NW
Suite 750
Washington, DC 20001-2109
Tel: (202)737-2337
Fax: (202)737-7004

Employers

Beer Institute (Exec. V. President and General Counsel)

DECHAINE, Dr. James

1733 King St.
Alexandria, VA 22314
Tel: (703)549-7464
Fax: (703)549-6980

Employers

Legislative Solutions (Partner)

Clients Represented

On Behalf of Legislative Solutions

Allied Charities of Minnesota
American Trucking Ass'ns

DECKER, Carolyn Lee

805 15th St. NW
Suite 700
Washington, DC 20005
Tel: (202)312-7400
Fax: (202)312-7441
EMail: caleedec@bakerd.com

Employers

Sagamore Associates, Inc. (V. President)

DECKER, Curtis

900 Second St. NE
Suite 211
Washington, DC 20002
Tel: (202)408-9514
Fax: (202)408-9520
Registered: LDA

Employers

Nat'l Ass'n of Protection and Advocacy Systems (NAPAS) (Exec. Director)

DECKER, Larry

700 13th St. NW
Suite 700
Washington, DC 20005-5922
Tel: (202)508-6364
Fax: (202)508-6330

Employers

H & R Block, Inc. (Legislative Assistant)

DECKER, Michael B.

1399 New York Ave. NW
Eighth Floor
Washington, DC 20005-4711
Tel: (202)434-8400
Fax: (202)434-8456
Registered: LDA
EMail: mdecker@bondmarkets.com

Employers

The Bond Market Ass'n (V. President, Research and Policy Analysis)

DECONCINI, Hon. Dennis

233 Constitution Ave. NE
Washington, DC 20002
Tel: (202)547-4000
Fax: (202)543-5044
Registered: LDA
EMail: prandd@aol.com

Member, U.S. Senate (D-AZ), 1977-95.

Employers

Compex Corp.
Parry, Romani, DeConcini & Symms (Partner)

Clients Represented

On Behalf of Parry, Romani, DeConcini & Symms

AIDS Healthcare Foundation
Andrx Pharmaceutical Corp.
Armstrong World Industries, Inc.
Asphalt Systems, Inc.
Aventis Pharmaceutical Products
Avondale, Arizona, City of
Bank of New York
Bristol-Myers Squibb Co.
Coalition Against Database Piracy
Composites Fabricators Ass'n
Ferraro, USA
Formosan Ass'n for Public Affairs
GAF Corp.
GlaxoSmithKline
Herbalife Internat'l, Inc.
Hoechst Marion Roussel Deutschland GmbH
Inter-Cal Corp.
Katten Muchin & Zavis
Motion Picture Ass'n of America
Nat'l Air Cargo, Inc.
Nat'l Nutritional Foods Ass'n
Nat'l Retail Federation
Nogales, Arizona, City of
Nu Skin Internat'l Inc.
Owens Corning
Peoria, Arizona, City of
Pfizer, Inc.
Pharmacia Corp.
Pharmanex
Policy Development Group, Inc.
Project to Promote Competition and Innovation in the Digital Age
Research & Development Laboratories
Research Corp. Technology
Rexall Sundown
SBC Communications Inc.
SOL Source Technologies, Inc.
Styrene Information and Research Center
Taxpayers Against Fraud, The False Claims Legal Center
TCOM, L.P.
Unilever United States, Inc.
Utah Natural Products Alliance

DECOSTER, Katherine B.

666 Pennsylvania Ave. SE
Suite 401
Washington, DC 20003
Tel: (202)543-7552
Fax: (202)544-4723
Registered: LDA

Employers
Trust for Public Land (Assistant Director)

DEE, Norbert

1899 L St. NW
Suite 1000
Washington, DC 20036
EMail: norbert_dee@npradc.org
Tel: (202)457-0480
Fax: (202)457-0486
Registered: LDA

Employers
Nat'l Petrochemical Refiners Ass'n (Environmental Affairs Director)

DEEDS, Ted

7700 Leesburg Pike
Suite 421
Falls Church, VA 22043
Tel: (703)847-2677
Fax: (703)556-6485

Employers
Law Enforcement Alliance of America (Director, Operations)

DEELEY, George

1615 H St. NW
Washington, DC 20062-2000
Tel: (202)659-6000
Fax: (202)463-5836

Employers
Chamber of Commerce of the U.S.A. (Assistant Director, Europe, International Division)

DEELY, Carol

1730 Rhode Island Ave. NW
Suite 907
Washington, DC 20036-3101
Tel: (202)296-1515
Fax: (202)296-2506

Employers
Steel Manufacturers Ass'n (Manager, Member Services)

DEEM, Richard A.

1101 Vermont Ave. NW
12th Floor
Washington, DC 20005-3583
Tel: (202)789-7413
Fax: (202)789-7581
Registered: LDA

Employers
American Medical Ass'n (V. President, Government Affairs)

DEERE, William R.

500 E St. SW
Suite 250
Washington, DC 20024
EMail: bill.deere@aopa.org
Tel: (202)479-4050
Fax: (202)484-1312
Registered: LDA

Employers
Aircraft Owners and Pilots Ass'n (V. President and Exec. Director, AOPA Legislative Affairs)

DEETS, Horace B.

601 E St. NW
Washington, DC 20049
Tel: (202)434-2300
Fax: (202)434-2320
Registered: LDA

Employers
AARP (American Ass'n of Retired Persons) (Exec. Director)

DEFIFE, Susan

1250 24th St. NW
Suite 300
Washington, DC 20037
Tel: (703)326-8224
Fax: (202)466-6249

Employers
HearingRoom.com (President)

DEFORE, Ron

818 Connecticut Ave. NW
Second Floor
Washington, DC 20006
EMail: rdefore@stratacomm.net
Tel: (202)289-2001
Fax: (202)289-1327
Registered: LDA

Former Deputy Assistant Secretary for Public Affairs; former Director of Public and Consumer Affairs, National Highway Traffic Safety Administration, Department of Transportation; Former Public Affairs Director, The Peace Corps.

Employers
Strat@Comm (Strategic Communications Counselors) (Principal)

Clients Represented

On Behalf of Strat@Comm (Strategic Communications Counselors)

Americans for Responsible Alcohol Access
Continental Teves

DEFRANCIS, Suzanne

1909 K St. NW
Fourth Floor
Washington, DC 20006
Tel: (202)973-5800
Fax: (202)973-5858
Registered: LDA

Employers
Porter/Novelli (Senior V. President, Public Affairs)

DEFREHN, Randy G.

815 16th St. NW
Washington, DC 20006
EMail: rdefrehn@nccmp.org
Tel: (202)737-5315
Fax: (202)737-1308
Registered: LDA

Employers
Nat'l Coordinating Committee for Multiemployer Plans (Exec. Director)

DEGIUSTI, Paul

1200 G St. NW
Suite 900
Washington, DC 20005-3802
Tel: (202)383-3700
Fax: (202)383-3718
Registered: LDA

Employers
McGraw-Hill Cos., The (Director, Washington Affairs)

DEGNON, CAE, George K.

6728 Old McLean Village Dr.
McLean, VA 22101
Tel: (703)556-9222
Fax: (703)556-8729

Employers
Degnon Associates, Inc. (President)

Clients Represented

On Behalf of Degnon Associates, Inc.

Academy for Eating Disorders

DEGNON, Laura

6728 Old McLean Village Dr.
McLean, VA 22101
Tel: (703)556-9222
Fax: (703)556-8729

Employers
Degnon Associates, Inc. (V. President)

Clients Represented

On Behalf of Degnon Associates, Inc.

American Psychosomatic Soc.

DEGNON, Marge

6728 Old McLean Village Dr.
McLean, VA 22101
Tel: (703)556-9222
Fax: (703)556-8729

Employers
Degnon Associates, Inc. (V. President)

Clients Represented

On Behalf of Degnon Associates, Inc.

Ambulatory Pediatric Ass'n

DEGONIA, Mary Elise

1915 17th St. NW
Washington, DC 20009
Tel: (202)265-5276
Fax: (202)234-2108
Registered: LDA

Employers
Capitol Perspectives (President)

Clients Represented

On Behalf of Capitol Perspectives

Alternative Schools Network
Jobs for Youth
Nat'l Council of La Raza

DEGOOD, Alex

1660 L St. NW
Suite 1050
Washington, DC 20036
EMail: ad1simonco@aol.com
Tel: (202)659-2229
Fax: (202)659-5234
Registered: LDA

Employers
Simon and Co., Inc. (Director, Congressional Affairs)

Clients Represented

On Behalf of Simon and Co., Inc.

AC Transit
Alameda Corridor Transportation Authority
American Water Works Ass'n
Carmel, Indiana, City of
Citrus Heights, California, City of
Easter Seals
Fresno, California, City of
Madison, Wisconsin, City of
Newark, California, City of
Oakley, California, City of
Pierce Transit
Portland, Oregon, City of
Sacramento Housing and Redeveloping Agency
Salt Lake City, Utah, City of
San Leandro, California, City of
Tacoma, Washington, City of
Tacoma, Washington, Public Utilities Department of

DEHART, June L.

1501 M St. NW
Suite 700
Washington, DC 20005-1702
EMail: jdehart@manatt.com
Tel: (202)463-4300
Fax: (202)463-4394
Registered: LDA, FARA

Chief Counsel, Subcommittee on Energy, Nuclear Proliferation and Government Processes, Senate Committee on Governmental Affairs, 1985-87. Legislative Counsel to Senator Thad Cochran (R-MS), 1981-85.

Employers
Manatt, Phelps & Phillips, LLP (Partner)

Clients Represented

On Behalf of Manatt, Phelps & Phillips, LLP

Alameda Corridor Transportation Authority
Asociacion Columbiana de Exportadores de Flores (ASOCOLFLORES)
BellSouth Corp.
Catellus Development Corp.
CEMEX Central, S.A. de C.V.
Congo, Republic of
Keller Equity Group, Inc.
Pelican Butte Corp.
Playa Vista
Reno, Nevada, City of
Royal Wine Co.
SWIPCO, U.S.
Yakima, Washington, City of

DEIER, David

122 C St. NW
Suite 505
Washington, DC 20001
Tel: (202)484-2282
Fax: (202)783-3306

Employers
GOPAC (Chairman)

DEITZ, William T.

1717 K St. NW
Suite 500
Washington, DC 20006
Tel: (202)466-9000
Fax: (202)466-9009
Registered: LDA

Former Administrative Assistant to Rep. Frank Thompson, Jr. (D-NJ) and Special Counsel to the House of Representatives Public Works and Transportation Committee.

Employers
Palumbo & Cerrell, Inc. (V. President, Legislative and Regulatory Affairs)

Clients Represented

On Behalf of Palumbo & Cerrell, Inc.

American Soc. of Composers, Authors and Publishers
American Trans Air
HT Medical
Los Angeles, California, Metropolitan Transit Authority of

DEITZER, Harry J.

2302 Horse Pen Rd.
Herndon, VA 20171-3499
EMail: hdeitzer@ncma.org
Tel: (703)713-1900
Fax: (703)713-1910

Employers
Nat'l Concrete Masonry Ass'n (Director, Marketing)

DEJARNETTE, Jr., Edmund T.

1900 K St. NW
Washington, DC 20006-1109
Tel: (202)955-1500
Fax: (202)778-2201
Registered: LDA

Employers
Hunton & Williams (Counsel)

DEKIEFFER, Donald E.

729 15th St. NW
Suite 800
Washington, DC 20005
EMail: ddekieffer@dhlaw.com
Tel: (202)783-6900
Fax: (202)783-6909
Registered: LDA

Employers
deKieffer & Horgan (Partner)

Clients Represented

On Behalf of deKieffer & Horgan

Strategic Minerals Corp.

DEL PAPA, Dominic

1101 30th St. NW
Suite 220
Washington, DC 20007
Tel: (202)337-6600
Fax: (202)337-6660
Registered: LDA

Employers
Ikon Public Affairs (Principal)

Clients Represented

On Behalf of Ikon Public Affairs

Denver Children's Hospital
RIM

DEL POLITO, Gene A.

1901 N. Fort Myer Dr.
Suite 401
Arlington, VA 22209-1609
EMail: genedp@postcom.org
Tel: (703)524-0096
Fax: (703)524-1871
Registered: LDA

Employers
Ass'n for Postal Commerce (President)

DEL ROSARIO, Gerald J.

444 N. Capitol St. NW
Suite 428
Washington, DC 20001
Tel: (202)624-1478
Fax: (202)624-1475

Legislative Assistant to Rep. George Brown, Jr. (D-CA), 1992-96.

Employers
Viohl and Associates, Inc.

Clients Represented

On Behalf of Viohl and Associates, Inc.

Indiana, Office of the Governor of the State of
Ivy Tech State College

DELANEY, Bill

7910 Science Application Court
Vienna, VA 22182
EMail: william.j.delaney@saic.com
Tel: (703)676-1100
Fax: (703)903-1525

Employers
Boeing Information Services (President)

DELANEY, Glenn Roger

601 Pennsylvania Ave. NW
Suite 900
Washington, DC 20004
Tel: (202)434-8220
Fax: (202)639-8817
Registered: LDA

Employers
Self-employed as an independent consultant.

Clients Represented

As an independent consultant

Blue Water Fishermen's Ass'n
Internat'l Ass'n of Fish and Wildlife Agencies
Louisiana Department of Wildlife and Fisheries - Fur and Refuse Division
New England Aquarium
Trident Seafood Corp.

DELANEY, John J.

1150 17th St. NW
Suite 302
Washington, DC 20036
Tel: (202)293-8510
Fax: (202)293-8513
Registered: LDA

Employers
Linowes and Blocher LLP (Partner)

DELANEY, Shawn

819 Seventh St. NW
Washington, DC 20001
Tel: (202)833-8940
Fax: (202)833-8945
Registered: LDA

Employers
EOP Group, Inc.

Clients Represented

On Behalf of EOP Group, Inc.

FMC Corp.

DELANEY, Wilma

1776 I St. NW
Suite 1050
Washington, DC 20006
Tel: (202)429-3420
Fax: (202)429-3467
Registered: LDA

Employers
The Dow Chemical Co. (V. President, Federal and State Government Affairs)

DELAPLANE, James

1212 New York Ave. NW
Suite 1250
Washington, DC 20005-3987
Tel: (202)289-6700
Fax: (202)289-4582
Registered: LDA

Employers
American Benefits Council (V. President, Retirement Policy)

DELBRIDGE, USA (Ret.), Maj. Gen. Norman G.

11 Canal Center Plaza
Suite 103
Alexandria, VA 22314
Tel: (703)683-4222
Fax: (703)683-0645
Registered: LDA

Employers
The Spectrum Group

DELEE, Debra

1815 H St. NW
Suite 920
Washington, DC 20006
EMail: APNDC@peacenow.org
Tel: (202)728-1893
Fax: (202)728-1895

Employers
Americans for Peace Now (President and Chief Exec. Officer)

DELGADO, Ph.D., Jane L.

1501 16th St. NW
Washington, DC 20036-1401
Tel: (202)387-5000
Fax: (202)265-8027

Employers
Nat'l Alliance for Hispanic Health (President and Chief Exec. Officer)

DELGADO, Jeanne

700 11th St. NW
Washington, DC 20001-4507
EMail: afletcher@realtors.org
Tel: (202)383-1079
Fax: (202)383-7540
Registered: LDA

Employers
Nat'l Ass'n of Realtors (Business Issues Policy Representative)

DELGADO VOTAW, Carmen

1701 K St. NW
Suite 200
Washington, DC 20006-1503
EMail: cvotaw@alliance1.org
Tel: (202)223-3447
Fax: (202)331-7476

Employers
Alliance for Children and Families (Senior V. President, Public Policy)

DELGANDIO, Frank

Park Center
107 E. Holly Ave., Suite 11
Sterling, VA 20164
Tel: (703)430-9668
Fax: (703)450-1745

Employers
Internat'l Soc. of Air Safety Investigators (President)

DELGAUDIO, Columbia Eugene

5613 Leesburg Pike
Suite 17
Falls Church, VA 22041
Tel: (703)845-1808

Employers
Public Advocate (Exec. Director)

DELINE, Donald A.

1150 18th St. NW
Suite 200
Washington, DC 20036
EMail: don.deline@halliburton.com
Tel: (202)223-0820
Fax: (202)223-2385
Registered: LDA

General Counsel (1994-97) and Republican Counsel (1993-94), Senate Committee on Armed Services. Legislative Counsel to the Secretary, Department of Defense, 1990-93 and 1978-81.

Employers
Halliburton/Brown & Root (Director, Government Affairs)

DELK, Mitchell

1101 Pennsylvania Ave. NW
Suite 950
Washington, DC 20004
Tel: (202)434-8600
Fax: (202)434-8626
Registered: LDA

Employers
Federal Home Loan Mortgage Corp. (Freddie Mac) (V. President, Government Relations)

DELLINGER, Kent

955 L'Enfant Plaza SW
Suite 5300
Washington, DC 20024
Tel: (202)554-1650
Fax: (202)488-3542

Employers
Honda North America, Inc. (Manager, Government Relations)

DELLINGER, III, Walter E.

555 13th St. NW
Suite 500 West
Washington, DC 20004
Tel: (202)383-5300
Fax: (202)383-5414
EMail: wdellinger@omm.com
Former Head, Office of Legal Counsel, Department of Justice.

Employers
O'Melveny and Myers LLP (Partner)

Clients Represented
On Behalf of O'Melveny and Myers LLP
Coalition for Asbestos Resolution

DELMONTAGNE, Regis J.

1899 Preston White Dr.
Reston, VA 20191-4367
Tel: (703)264-7200
Fax: (703)620-0994
EMail: rdelmont@npes.org

Employers
NPES, The Ass'n for Suppliers of Printing, Publishing, and Converting Technologies (President)

DELOGU, Nancy N.

1225 I St. NW
Suite 1000
Washington, DC 20005-3914
Tel: (202)842-7400
Fax: (202)842-0022

Employers
Institute for a Drug-Free Workplace (Counsel)

DELONG, James V.

1001 Connecticut Ave. NW
Suite 1250
Washington, DC 20036
Tel: (202)331-1010
Fax: (202)331-0640

Employers
Competitive Enterprise Institute (Senior Fellow)

DELORENZO, James

3000 K St. NW
Suite 300
Washington, DC 20007
Tel: (202)424-7500
Fax: (202)424-7643
Registered: LDA

Employers
Swidler Berlin Shereff Friedman, LLP

Clients Represented
On Behalf of Swidler Berlin Shereff Friedman, LLP
BroadSpan Communications, Inc.
Dairy.com
Napster, Inc.

DELORY, Ann

1001 G St. NW
Suite 900 E
Washington, DC 20001-4545
Tel: (202)393-1010
Fax: (202)393-5510
Registered: LDA
EMail: delory@podesta.com
Former Executive Assistant to the Secretary, Department of Labor, during the Clinton administration and Legislative Aide to Senator Edward M. Kennedy (D-MA).

Employers
Podesta/Mattoon (Associate)

Clients Represented
On Behalf of Podesta/Mattoon
American Psychological Ass'n
AOL Time Warner
Aventis CropScience
Celera Genomics
Chiquita Brands Internat'l, Inc.
GE Power Systems
Motion Picture Ass'n of America
Nat'l Ass'n of Broadcasters
Nat'l Food Processors Ass'n
NCI Coalition
News America Inc.
Northpoint Technology, Ltd.
Recording Industry Ass'n of America
SiTV
Trans World Airlines, Inc.
Vivendi Universal

DELPONTE, Paul

1100 Connecticut Ave. NW
12th Floor
Washington, DC 20036
Tel: (202)452-6500
Fax: (202)452-6502

Employers
IssueSphere (Partner)

DELUCA, Gina

529 14th St. NW
Suite 655
Washington, DC 20045
Tel: (202)737-0171
Fax: (202)737-8406

Employers
Council for LAB/LAS Environmental Research (CLER) (Associate)

DEMAREST, Jr., William F.

600 14th St. NW
Washington, DC 20005
Tel: (202)783-8400
Fax: (202)783-4211
Registered: LDA

Employers
Shook, Hardy & Bacon LLP (Partner)

Clients Represented
On Behalf of Shook, Hardy & Bacon LLP
Molecular Separations Inc.

DEMATTEO, Carl S.

600 Maryland Ave. SW
Suite 800
Washington, DC 20024
Tel: (202)484-3600
Fax: (202)484-3604
Registered: LDA

Employers
American Farm Bureau Federation (Director, Political Education)

DEMBLING, Doug

810 Vermont Ave. NW
Room 514
Washington, DC 20420
Tel: (202)273-5615
Fax: (202)273-6791

Employers
Department of Veterans Affairs (Congressional Relations Officer)

DEMCZUK, Bernard

714 21st St. NW
Third Floor
Washington, DC 20052
Tel: (202)994-9132
Fax: (202)994-1229

Employers
George Washington University, Office of Government Relations (Assistant V. President, Government Relations)

DEMENT, Polly

1090 Vermont Ave. NW
Third Floor
Washington, DC 20005
Tel: (202)842-3600
Fax: (202)842-4032
Former Communications Director, Bipartisan Commission on Entitlement and Tax Reform and earlier with the Congressional-Presidential Nat'l Commission on Children.

Employers
Hager Sharp Inc. (Senior Communications Counselor)

DEMEO, Marisa J.

1717 K St. NW
Suite 311
Washington, DC 20036
Tel: (202)293-2828
Fax: (202)293-2849
Registered: LDA

Employers
Mexican-American Legal Defense and Educational Fund (Regional Counsel)

DEMING, John L.

1825 I St. NW
Suite 400
Washington, DC 20006
Tel: (202)857-5200
Fax: (202)857-5219

Employers
Ciba Specialty Chemicals Corp. (V. President, Government Affairs)

DEMPSEY, Jim

1634 I St. NW
Suite 1100
Washington, DC 20006-4003
Tel: (202)637-9800
Fax: (202)637-0968

Employers
Center for Democracy and Technology (Senior Staff Counsel)
Digital Privacy and Security Working Group (Contact)

DEMPSEY, Kevin M.

1775 Pennsylvania Ave. NW
Suite 200
Washington, DC 20006
Tel: (202)862-1000
Fax: (202)862-1093
Registered: LDA
Minority Counsel, Subcommittee on Foreign Commerce and Tourism, Senate Committee on Commerce, Science and Transportation, 1992-94. Counsel on International Trade and Banking to Senator John C. Danforth (R-MO), 1990-92. Minority Counsel, Senate Committee on Commerce, Science and Transportation, 1989-90.

Employers
Dewey Ballantine LLP (Partner)

Clients Represented
On Behalf of Dewey Ballantine LLP
American Forest & Paper Ass'n
Coalition for Fair Lumber Imports
Semiconductor Industry Ass'n

DEMSKE, Amy

444 N. Capitol St. NW
Suite 837
Washington, DC 20001
Tel: (202)637-0637
Fax: (202)544-5321
Registered: LDA
EMail: ademske@boydrick.com

Employers
Broydrick & Associates (Director, Washington Office and Partner)

Clients Represented
On Behalf of Broydrick & Associates
Bell Ambulance
Blood Center of Southeastern Wisconsin
Children's Hospital of Wisconsin
Direct Supply
Extendicare Health Services Inc.
Innovative Resource Group
Loyola University Health System
Mount Sinai Hospital
Nat'l Ass'n of Children's Hospitals Inc.

DEMULLE, Fran

1726 M St. NW
Suite 902
Washington, DC 20036
Tel: (202)785-3355
Fax: (202)452-1805

Employers
American Lung Ass'n (Director, Washington Office and Government Relations)

DENEZZA, Eugene

4701 Sangamore Rd.
Suite N100
Bethesda, MD 20816-2508
Tel: (301)229-5800
Fax: (301)229-5045
Registered: LDA

Employers
Burdeshaw Associates, Ltd. (Associate)

DENHOLM, David Y.

320-D Maple Ave. East
Vienna, VA 22180
Tel: (703)242-3575
Fax: (703)242-3579

Employers
Americans Against Union Control of Government
Public Service Research Council (President)
Public Service Research Foundation (Washington Representative)

DENIER, Greg

1775 K St. NW
Washington, DC 20006
Tel: (202)223-3111
Fax: (202)466-1562

Employers
United Food and Commercial Workers Internat'l Union (Assistant to the President)

DENIS, Paul T.

3000 K St. NW
Suite 300
Washington, DC 20007

Tel: (202)424-7500
Fax: (202)424-7643
Registered: LDA

Employers

Swidler Berlin Shereff Friedman, LLP

Clients Represented

On Behalf of Swidler Berlin Shereff Friedman, LLP

Dairy.com
Suiza Foods Corp.

DENISON, George H.

Eight E St. SE
Washington, DC 20003

Tel: (202)543-4172
Fax: (202)546-6294
Registered: LDA, FARA

Former Aide to Senator Barry Goldwater (R-AZ). Minority Counsel, Senate Labor Committee, 1962-65. Legislative Assistant to Robert Griffin, Aide to President Gerald Ford, 1976-77.

Employers

Self-employed as an independent consultant.
Denison, Scott and Cohen (Partner)
Denison, Scott Associates (Partner)
Washington Public Affairs Group

Clients Represented

As an independent consultant

Bangor Internat'l Airport
Congo, Democratic Republic of the
Federation of Electric Power Cos. of Japan
Mail 2000, Inc.
Mauritania, Government of the Islamic Republic of
Med Images, Inc.
Pfluger Enterprises LLC
Victims of Communism Memorial Foundation
Zimbabwe, Republic of

On Behalf of Denison, Scott and Cohen

The Friends of Democratic Congo

On Behalf of Denison, Scott Associates

Bristol-Myers Squibb Co.

DENIT, Jeffery D.

1701 Pennsylvania Ave. NW
Suite 1200
Washington, DC 20006
EMail: info@clayassociates.com

Tel: (202)861-0160
Fax: (202)861-3101

Deputy Director, Office of Solid Waste, 1985-93; Director, Effluent Guidelines Division, Office of Water 1981-85, Environmental Protection Agency. From 1970-80 held several other positions in EPA and its predecessor agency, Federal Water Pollution Control Administration.

Employers

Clay Associates, Inc. (V. President and Technical Director)

DENKLER, Capt. J. Michael

Rayburn House Office Bldg.
Room B324

Washington, DC 20515
EMail: denkler.mike@hq.navy.mil

Tel: (202)225-7808
Fax: (202)685-6077

Employers

Department of Navy (House Liaison Principal Deputy, Office of Legislative Affairs)

DENMAN, Scott

1717 Massachusetts Ave. NW
Suite 106
Washington, DC 20036

EMail: sdenman@erols.com

Tel: (202)483-8491
Ext: 14
Fax: (202)234-9194

Employers

Safe Energy Communication Council (Exec. Director)

DENNE, Eileen E.

1010 Duke St.
Alexandria, VA 22314-3589

Tel: (703)684-5700
Fax: (703)684-6321

Employers

American Ass'n of Port Authorities (Director, Public Relations)

DENNETT, Diana

1129 20th St. NW
Suite 600
Washington, DC 20036-3421
EMail: ddennett@aahp.org

Tel: (202)778-3200
Fax: (202)778-8479
Registered: LDA

Employers

American Ass'n of Health Plans (AAHP) (Exec. V. President)

DENNETT, Paul W.

1212 New York Ave. NW
Suite 1250
Washington, DC 20005-3987

Tel: (202)289-6700
Fax: (202)289-4582
Registered: LDA

Employers

American Benefits Council (V. President, Health Policy)

DENNIN, Joseph F.

1900 K St. NW
Washington, DC 20006

Tel: (202)496-7500
Fax: (202)496-7756
Registered: FARA

EMail: joseph_dennin@mckennacuneo.com

Assistant Secretary for International Economic Policy (1984-86), Deputy Assistant Secretary for Africa, the Near East and South Asia (1982-84), and Deputy Assistant Secretary for Finance, Investment and Services (1981-82), all at the Department of Commerce. Deputy Associate Attorney General, Department of Justice, 1979-81. Director of Operations, International Trade Commission, 1978-79. Staff Assistant to the President, The White House, 1976-78. Counsel, Senate Select Committee on Intelligence, 1975-76.

Employers

McKenna & Cuneo, L.L.P. (Partner)

Clients Represented

On Behalf of McKenna & Cuneo, L.L.P.

Sumitomo Chemical Co., Ltd.

DENNIS, Darlene C.

P.O. Box 31220
4720 Montgomery Ln.
Bethesda, MD 20824-1220

Tel: (301)652-2682
Fax: (301)652-7711

Employers

American Occupational Therapy Ass'n, Inc. (Political Action Administrator)

DENNIS, Lyle B.

317 Massachusetts Ave. NE
Suite 200
Washington, DC 20002

Tel: (202)546-4732
Fax: (202)546-1257
Registered: LDA

EMail: ldennis@dc-crd.com

Administrative Assistant to Rep. Bernard J. Dwyer (D-NJ), 1981-93

Employers

Cavarocchi Ruscio Dennis Associates (Partner)

Clients Represented

On Behalf of Cavarocchi Ruscio Dennis Associates

American Ass'n for the Study of Liver Diseases
Ass'n of University Programs in Health Administration
Cooley's Anemia Foundation
Council of Colleges of Acupuncture and Oriental Medicine
The Genome Action Coalition
The Jeffrey Modell Foundation
Rutgers University
Soc. for Women's Health Research

DENNIS, Patrick

700 11th St. NW
Washington, DC 20001-4507
EMail: pdennis@realtors.org

Tel: (202)383-1245
Fax: (202)383-7540

Employers

Nat'l Ass'n of Realtors (Political Representative)

DENNIS, Sandra J. P.

1800 M St. NW
Washington, DC 20036

Tel: (202)467-7009
Fax: (202)467-7176
Registered: LDA

EMail: sdennis@morganlewis.com

Employers

Morgan, Lewis & Bockius LLP (Partner)

DENNIS, Thomas J.

209 Tenth St. SE
Washington, DC 20003

Tel: (202)543-4541
Fax: (202)543-4457
Registered: LDA

Employers

Self-employed as an independent consultant.

Clients Represented

As an independent consultant

ARCO Products Co.
Edison Electric Institute
Energy East Management Corp.
PURPA Reform Group
Repeal PUHCA Now Coalition

DENNIS, Warren L.

1233 20th St. NW
Suite 800
Washington, DC 20036-2396
EMail: WDennis@proskauer.com

Tel: (202)416-6800
Fax: (202)416-6899

Trial Attorney, Honors Law Program, Civil Rights Division, Department of Justice, 1972-77.

Employers

Proskauer Rose LLP (Partner)

DENNISON, Staci Sigman

507 Capitol Ct. NE
Suite 200
Washington, DC 20002

Tel: (202)544-7499
Fax: (202)546-7105
Registered: LDA

Employers

Health and Medicine Counsel of Washington (Administrative Assistant)

Clients Represented

On Behalf of Health and Medicine Counsel of Washington

American Academy of Family Physicians
American Ass'n of Pharmaceutical Scientists
American Lung Ass'n
American Soc. of Clinical Pathologists
American Thoracic Soc.
Ass'n of Minority Health Profession Schools
Digestive Disease Nat'l Coalition
Dystonia Medical Research Foundation
Sudden Infant Death Syndrome Alliance

DENO, Stanford

2111 Wilson Blvd.
Eighth Floor
Arlington, VA 22201

Tel: (703)296-8463
Fax: (703)522-3811
Registered: LDA

Employers

Internat'l Council of Cruise Lines (Director, Technical Operations)

DENSON, Jennifer

1666 Connecticut Ave. NW
Suite 400
Washington, DC 20009

Tel: (202)328-7004
Fax: (202)387-3447
Registered: LDA

Employers

Federation for American Immigration Reform (FAIR) (Associate Director)

DENSTON, Susan

111 Park Place
Falls Church, VA 22046-4513

Tel: (703)533-0251
Fax: (703)241-5603

Employers

Ass'n and Soc. Management Internat'l Inc. (Account Executive)
North American Natural Casing Ass'n (Account Executive)

DENT, Linda

3138 N. Tenth St.
Arlington, VA 22201

Tel: (703)522-4770
Fax: (703)522-0594

Employers

Nat'l Ass'n of Federal Credit Unions (Director, Regulatory Compliance)

DENTON, Janet A.

805 15th St. NW
Suite 500
Washington, DC 20005
EMail: denton@chambersinc.com

Tel: (202)371-9770
Fax: (202)371-6601
Registered: LDA

Employers
American Arts Alliance (Director)
Chambers Associates Inc. (Senior V. President)

Clients Represented
On Behalf of Chambers Associates Inc.
American Arts Alliance
Nat'l Healthy Start Ass'n
Norfolk, Virginia, City of

DENTON, Jean Gingras

1341 G St. NW Tel: (202)347-5990
Suite 200 Fax: (202)347-5941
Washington, DC 20005 Registered: LDA
EMail: jdenton@clj.com
Senior Legislative Aide to Rep. Bill Lowery (R-CA), 1987-92.

Employers
Copeland, Lowery & Jacquez (Partner)

Clients Represented
On Behalf of Copeland, Lowery & Jacquez
Bay Area Rapid Transit District
Digital System Resources, Inc.
Orincon Corp.
Salt Lake City Olympic Organizing Committee
San Diego Ass'n of Governments
San Diego State University Foundation
San Diego, California, City of
Science Applications Internat'l Corp. (SAIC)

DENTON, Jeremy W.

1110 N. Glebe Rd. Tel: (703)528-5115
Suite 500 Fax: (703)524-1074
Arlington, VA 22201-5720

Employers
Industrial Telecommunications Ass'n, Inc. (Director, Government Affairs)

DENTON, Neal

1211 Connecticut Ave. NW Tel: (202)462-5132
Suite 620 Fax: (202)462-0423
Washington, DC 20036-2701 Registered: LDA
EMail: alliance@nonprofitmailers.org

Employers
Alliance of Nonprofit Mailers (Exec. Director)

DENYSYK, Dr. Bohdan

2121 K St. NW Tel: (202)296-2400
Suite 650 Fax: (202)296-2409
Washington, DC 20037 Registered: LDA, FARA
EMail: Bo@GlobalUSAinc.com
Regional Political Director, Republican National Committee, 1980. Presidential Transition Personnel, 1981. Deputy Assistant Secretary for Export Administration, Department of Commerce, 1981-84. White House Awards Commission, 1985.

Employers
Global USA, Inc. (President and Chief Exec. Officer)

Clients Represented
On Behalf of Global USA, Inc.
All Nippon Airways Co.
Japan Federation of Construction Contractors, Inc.
Komatsu Ltd.
Kyocera Corp.
Loral Space and Communications, Ltd.
Mazak Corp. & Mazak Sales and Service, Inc.
SBC Communications Inc.

DEPOY, Martin L.

1875 I St. NW Tel: (202)739-9400
Suite 600 Fax: (202)739-9401
Washington, DC 20006 Registered: LDA
EMail: mdepoy@nareit.com

Employers
Nat'l Ass'n of Real Estate Investment Trusts (V. President, Government Relations)

DERDERIAN, J.D.

1620 L St. NW Tel: (202)721-9134
Suite 1210 Fax: (202)955-6070
Washington, DC 20036

Employers
Cormac Group, LLP

DEREUTER, William R.

1455 Pennsylvania Ave. NW Tel: (202)661-7100
Suite 950 Fax: (202)661-7110
Washington, DC 20004-1087 Registered: LDA

Employers
Merrill Lynch & Co., Inc. (V. President, Government Relations)

DERKS, Paula

1707 H St. NW Tel: (202)478-5425
Suite 703 Registered: LDA
Washington, DC 20006

Employers
Washington Aviation Group

Clients Represented
On Behalf of Washington Aviation Group
Aircraft Electronics Ass'n

DEROCCO, Emily S.

444 N. Capitol St. NW Tel: (202)431-8020
Suite 142 Fax: (202)434-8033
Washington, DC 20001

Employers
Nat'l Ass'n of State Workforce Agencies (Exec. Director)

DERR, Sallie

441 New Jersey Ave. SE Tel: (202)544-6093
Washington, DC 20003 Fax: (202)544-1465

Employers
Liz Robbins Associates (Chief of Staff)

DERRICK, Jr., Hon. Butler E.

1001 Pennsylvania Ave. NW Tel: (202)624-7213
Suite 600 Fax: (202)624-7222
Washington, DC 20004 Registered: LDA
EMail: bderrick@pgfm.com
Member, U.S. House of Representatives, (D-SC), 1975-94. Former Deputy Majority Whip, and Former Vice Chairman, House Rules Committee

Employers
Powell, Goldstein, Frazer & Murphy LLP (Partner)

Clients Represented
On Behalf of Powell, Goldstein, Frazer & Murphy LLP
Cargill, Inc.
Concurrent Technologies Corp.
Fluor Corp.
Kinetic Biosystems Inc.
Theragenics Corp.
Union Pacific
Walker Digital Corp.

DESANTIS, Victor J.

601 13th St. NW Tel: (202)626-3600
Suite 600 South Fax: (202)639-9355
Washington, DC 20005
EMail: desanvi@washdc.whitecase.com

Employers
White & Case LLP (Partner)

DESARNO, Judith M.

1627 K St. NW 12th Floor Tel: (202)293-3114
Washington, DC 20006 Fax: (202)293-1990
Registered: LDA
EMail: jdesarno@nfprha.org

Employers
Nat'l Family Planning and Reproductive Health Ass'n (President)

DESCHAUER, Jr., John J.

2550 M St. NW Tel: (202)457-6000
Washington, DC 20037-1350 Fax: (202)457-6315
Registered: LDA, FARA
EMail: jdeschauer@pattonboggs.com
Director of Senate Affairs, Department of Defense, 1990-94. Legislative Counsel, Office of the Secretary, Department of the Navy, 1988-90.

Employers
Patton Boggs, LLP (Partner)

Clients Represented
On Behalf of Patton Boggs, LLP
Air Force Memorial Foundation
Augusta-Richmond, Georgia, County of
Coalition for Electronic Commerce
Crane Co.
Dimensions Internat'l
IIT Research Institute
MCI WorldCom Corp.
Nat'l Center for Manufacturing Sciences
Pakistan, Embassy of the Islamic Republic of
Save Barton Creek
Sierra Military Health Services, Inc.
The Charles E. Smith Companies
United Defense, L.P.
Wheeling Pittsburgh Steel Corp.

DESETA, Anne

601 13th St. NW Tel: (202)682-9462
Suite 200 North
Washington, DC 20005

Employers
BASF Corporation (Manager, Grassroots Program)

DESHIELDS, Vangie

1299 Pennsylvania Ave. NW Tel: (202)785-0500
Suite 800 West Fax: (202)785-5277
Washington, DC 20004 Registered: LDA

Employers
The Carmen Group

DESHLER, Kirsten Zimmer

712 S. Adams St. Tel: (703)486-9555
Arlington, VA 22204 Fax: (703)486-1666
Registered: LDA
EMail: kzdeshler@aol.com
Legislative Assistant to Rep. Richard H. Lehman (D-CA), 1989-93. Staff Assistant, Subcommittee on Postsecondary Education, Training, and Life-Long Learning, House Committee on Education and the Workforce, 1987-89.

Employers
The Zimmer Deshler Group (President)

DESIDERIO, Duane J.

1150 17th St. NW Tel: (202)293-8510
Suite 302 Fax: (202)293-8513
Washington, DC 20036 Registered: LDA

Employers
Linowes and Blocher LLP (Associate)

DESILVA, Eric W.

1776 K St. NW Tel: (202)719-7000
Washington, DC 20006 Fax: (202)719-7049

Employers
Wiley, Rein & Fielding (Partner)

DESMOND, James M.

1725 Jefferson Davis Hwy. Tel: (703)413-5600
Crystal Square 2, Suite 300 Fax: (703)413-5617
Arlington, VA 22202 Registered: LDA

Employers
Lockheed Martin Corp. (V. President, Energy Sector Legislation)

DESSER, John D.

1615 L St. NW Tel: (202)626-8238
Suite 650 Fax: (202)626-8593
Washington, DC 20036 Registered: LDA
EMail: desser@jeffersongr.com
Former Chief Health Policy Advisor to Rep. Jon Kyl (R-AZ), 1993-94. Former Health Policy Aide to Senator John McCain (R-AZ), 1990-93.

Employers
Jefferson Government Relations, L.L.C. (V. President)

Clients Represented
On Behalf of Jefferson Government Relations, L.L.C.
Bass Hotels and Resorts, Inc.
Cummins-Allison Corp.
eHealth Insurance Services, Inc.
Iredell Memorial Hospital
Nat'l Quality Health Council

DETLEFSEN, Clay

1250 H St. NW
Suite 900
Washington, DC 20005

Tel: (202)737-4332
Fax: (202)331-7820
Registered: LDA

Employers
Internat'l Dairy Foods Ass'n (Director, Environmental and Worker Safety Issues)

DETMER, Kyra Lee

1101 Connecticut Ave. NW
Suite 401
Washington, DC 20036

Tel: (202)296-7513
Fax: (202)296-7514
Registered: LDA

Employers
The Hartford (Director, Federal Affairs)

DETTER, Brian

Ronald Reagan Bldg.
1300 Pennsylvania Ave. NW
MS: 6.10A
Washington, DC 20523

Tel: (202)712-4300
Fax: (202)216-3036

Employers
Agency for Internat'l Development (Legislative Program Specialist, Congressional Liaison Division)

DETTKE, Dr. Dieter

1155 15th St. NW
Suite 1100
Washington, DC 20005

Tel: (202)331-1819
Fax: (202)331-1837

Employers
Friedrich Ebert Foundation (Exec. Director, Washington Office)

DETTMANN, Charles E.

50 F St. NW
Suite 4101
Washington, DC 20001

Tel: (202)639-2200
Fax: (202)639-2930

Employers
Ass'n of American Railroads (Exec. V. President, Safety and Operations)

DEUTSCH, Jo Ellen

1275 K St. NW
Fifth Floor
Washington, DC 20005
EMail: jdeutsch@afanet.org

Tel: (202)712-9799
Fax: (202)712-9792
Registered: LDA

Employers
Ass'n of Flight Attendants (Director, Government Affairs)

DEUTSCH, Kenneth

919 18th St. NW
Tenth Floor
Washington, DC 20006

Tel: (202)263-2900
Fax: (202)263-2960

Employers
Issue Dynamics Inc. (Senior V. President)

DEUTSCH, Richard

1140 Connecticut Ave. NW
Suite 1050
Washington, DC 20036

Tel: (202)331-5790
Fax: (202)331-9334

Employers
American Health Quality Ass'n (Director, Communications)

DEVEREUX, Erik

P.O. Box 18766
Washington, DC 20036-1876
EMail: appam@ui.urban.org

Tel: (202)261-5788
Fax: (202)223-1149

Employers
Ass'n for Public Policy Analysis and Management (Exec. Director)

DEVIERNO, John A.

818 Connecticut Ave. NW
Suite 1100
Washington, DC 20006

Tel: (202)496-3459
Fax: (202)728-4044
Registered: LDA

Attorney, Office of General Counsel, Department of Transportation, 1977-81.

Employers
Self-employed as an independent consultant.
The National Group, LLP (Partner)

Clients Represented
As an independent consultant
CSX Corp.
Idaho, Department of Transportation of the State of
Montana, Department of Transportation of the State of
North Dakota, Department of Transportation of
Rural States Federal Transportation Policy Development Group
South Dakota, Department of Transportation of
Wyoming, Department of Transportation of

DEVILLIER, Linda

1899 L St. NW
Suite 200
Washington, DC 20036

Tel: (202)833-8121
Fax: (202)833-8155

Employers
Devillier Communications (President)

Clients Represented
On Behalf of Devillier Communications
Lockheed Martin Corp.

DEVINE, Danny

2121 K St. NW
Suite 600
Washington, DC 20037-2121

Tel: (202)659-0670
Fax: (202)775-6312

Employers
Employee Benefit Research Institute (Director, Public Relations)

DEVINE, Thomas A.

2141 Wisconsin Ave. NW
Suite H
Washington, DC 20007

Tel: (202)337-9600
Fax: (202)337-9620
Registered: LDA

Employers
Strategic Choices, Inc.

Clients Represented
On Behalf of Strategic Choices, Inc.
Colombian Coffee Federation

DEVINE, Thomas M.

1612 K St. NW
Suite 400
Washington, DC 20006

Tel: (202)408-0034
Fax: (202)408-9855

Employers
Government Accountability Project (GAP) (Legal Director)

DEVINE, Thomas R.

888 Sixteenth St. NW
Seventh Floor
Washington, DC 20006-4103

Tel: (202)835-8096
Fax: (202)835-8136
Registered: LDA, FARA

Legislative Staff, Office of the Chief Counsel, Federal Aviation Administration, Department of Transportation, 1979-85.

Employers
Foley & Lardner (Partner)

Clients Represented
On Behalf of Foley & Lardner
AAAE-ACI

DEVINSKY, Paul

600 13th St. NW
Washington, DC 20005-3096
EMail: pdevinsky@mwe.com

Tel: (202)756-8369
Fax: (202)756-8087

Former Patent Counsel, Department of Energy; Patent Examiner, Patent and Trademark Office.

Employers
McDermott, Will and Emery (Partner)

DEVORE, P. Cameron

1500 K St. NW
Suite 450
Washington, DC 20005

Tel: (202)508-6600
Fax: (202)508-6699
Registered: LDA

Employers
Davis Wright Tremaine LLP (Partner)

Clients Represented
On Behalf of Davis Wright Tremaine LLP
Ass'n of Nat'l Advertisers

DEWEY, Robert

1101 14th St. NW
Suite 1400
Washington, DC 20005
EMail: rdewey@defenders.org

Tel: (202)682-9400
Fax: (202)682-1331
Registered: LDA

Employers
Defenders of Wildlife (V. President, Government Relations and External Affairs)

DEWHIRST, Mary

1350 Connecticut Ave. NW
Suite 200
Washington, DC 20036
EMail: mary@apts.org

Tel: (202)887-1700
Fax: (202)293-2422
Registered: LDA

Employers
Ass'n of America's Public Television Stations (V. President, Government Relations)

DEWITT, Charles B.

8150 Leesburg Pike
Suite 900
Vienna, VA 22182

Tel: (703)760-8866
Fax: (703)760-8870
Registered: LDA

Employers
Lafayette Group, Inc. (Partner)

DEWITT, Charlie

1331 Pennsylvania Ave. NW
Suite 550S
Washington, DC 20004
EMail: nymex4@unidial.com

Tel: (202)662-8771
Fax: (202)662-8765
Registered: LDA

Employers
New York Mercantile Exchange (Government Affairs Associate)

DEWITT, Stephen Wright

1904 Association Dr.
Reston, VA 20191

Tel: (703)860-0200
Fax: (703)476-5432
Registered: LDA

Employers
Nat'l Ass'n of Secondary School Principals (Director, Federal Relations)

DEWITT, Timothy

555 12th St. NW
Washington, DC 20004-1206
EMail: Timothy_Dewitt@aporter.com

Tel: (202)942-5000
Fax: (202)942-5999

Employers
Arnold & Porter (Partner)

DEXTER, Jennifer

700 13th St. NW
Suite 200
Washington, DC 20005
EMail: jdexter@opa.easter-seals.org

Tel: (202)347-3066
Fax: (202)737-7914
Registered: LDA

Employers
Easter Seals (Senior Government Relations Specialist)

DEZENHALL, Eric

1130 Connecticut Ave. NW
Suite 600
Washington, DC 20036

Tel: (202)296-0263
Fax: (202)452-9371
Registered: FARA

Employers
Nichols-Dezenhall Communication Management Group, Ltd. (President)

DHILLON, Neil

600 New Hampshire Ave. NW
Suite 601
Washington, DC 20037

Tel: (202)333-7400
Fax: (202)333-1638
Registered: LDA

Employers
Hill and Knowlton, Inc. (Managing Director)

Clients Represented

On Behalf of Hill and Knowlton, Inc.

Ford Motor Co.
Woods Hole Oceanographic Institution

DIAMOND, Henry L.

1350 I St. NW
Suite 700
Washington, DC 20005
Tel: (202)789-6000
Fax: (202)789-6190

Chairman (1973-76) and Member (1972-73), President's Advisory Commission on Environmental Quality. Assistant to the U.S. Attorney General, Department of Justice, 1962.

Employers

Beveridge & Diamond, P.C. (Partner)

Clients Represented

On Behalf of Beveridge & Diamond, P.C.

Gateway Visitor Center Corp.

DIAMOND, Richard

1330 Connecticut Ave. NW
Washington, DC 20036-1795
Tel: (202)429-3000
Fax: (202)429-3902
Registered: FARA
EMail: rdiamond@steptoe.com

Law Clerk to Chief Justice Warren E. Burger, U.S. Supreme Court, 1972-73, and to Judge Stanley A. Weigel, U.S. District Court for the Northern District of California, 1971-72.

Employers

Steptoe & Johnson LLP (Of Counsel)

DIAMOND, Robert M.

1725 DeSales St. NW
Suite 800
Washington, DC 20036
Tel: (202)659-6540
Fax: (202)659-5730
Registered: LDA

Administrative Assistant and Tax Counsel to Rep. Don Bailey (D-PA), 1980-82 and to Rep. Ray Lederer (D-PA), 1977-80.

Employers

Whitten & Diamond (Member)

Clients Represented

On Behalf of Whitten & Diamond

Bombardier, Inc.
Can Manufacturers Institute
Gas Technology Institute
Lehigh Coal & Navigation Co.
Mountain Top Technologies, Inc.
Norfolk Southern Corp.
Philadelphia Internat'l Airport
Philadelphia, Pennsylvania, City of
Pioneer Hi-Bred Internat'l, Inc.
St. Joseph University
Temple University
Vernon, California, City of
Roy F. Weston, Inc.

DIAZ, Steven A.

1300 I St. NW
Suite 300 West
Washington, DC 20005
Tel: (202)522-8600
Fax: (202)522-8669
Registered: LDA

Employers

Dykema Gossett PLLC (Member)

DIAZ, Tom

1140 19th St. NW
Suite 600
Washington, DC 20036
Tel: (202)822-8200
Fax: (202)822-8205

Employers

Violence Policy Center (Senior Policy Analyst)

DIBBER, Barbara

505 Huntmar Park Dr.
Suite 210
Herndon, VA 20170
Tel: (703)437-0100
Fax: (703)481-3596

Employers

Nat'l Conference of States on Building Codes and Standards (Communications Specialist)

DICKE, Stephen P.

1875 I St. NW
Suite 1050
Washington, DC 20006-5409
Tel: (202)331-8585
Fax: (202)331-2032

Employers

Scribner, Hall & Thompson, LLP (Partner)

DICKENS, William T.

1775 Massachusetts Ave. NW
Washington, DC 20036-2188
Tel: (202)797-6000
Fax: (202)797-6004

Former Senior Economist, President's Council of Economic Advisers.

Employers

The Brookings Institution (Senior Fellow, Economic Studies)

DICKERSON, Cindy

1212 New York Ave. NW
Sixth Floor
Washington, DC 20005-3992
Tel: (202)789-7000
Fax: (202)789-7037

Employers

Washington D.C. Convention and Visitors Ass'n (President)

DICKERSON, Shawn

1255 22nd St. NW
Fourth Floor
Washington, DC 20037
Tel: (202)715-1300
Fax: (202)463-7190

Employers

CAIS Internet (Administrative Assistant for Legal Counsel)

DICKEY, Ph.D., Edward

1225 I St. NW
Suite 500
Washington, DC 20005
Tel: (202)312-2005
Fax: (202)289-8683
Registered: LDA
EMail: dawsonassociates@worldnet.att.net

Former Deputy Assistant Secretary, Office of the Assistant Secretary of the Army for Civil Works and former Chief of the Planning Division, U.S. Army Corps of Engineers, Department of the Army.

Employers

Dawson & Associates, Inc. (Senior Advisor)

Clients Represented

On Behalf of Dawson & Associates, Inc.

Chemical Land Holdings, Inc.
Florida Citrus Mutual
Florida Farm Bureau
Florida Sugar Cane League, Inc.
Sugar Cane Growers Cooperative of Florida

DICKEY, Jr., Ph.D., John S.

2000 Florida Ave. NW
Washington, DC 20009
EMail: jdickey@agu.org
Tel: (202)777-7505
Fax: (202)328-0566

Employers

American Geophysical Union (Director, Outreach and Research Support)

DICKINSON, Hon. Bill

908 Pennsylvania Ave. SE
Washington, DC 20003
Tel: (202)544-5666
Fax: (202)544-4647

Member, U.S. House of Representatives (R-AL), 1965-93.

Employers

Advantage Associates, Inc. (Partner)

DICKINSON, Elaine

880 S. Pickett St.
Alexandria, VA 22304
Tel: (703)461-2864
Fax: (703)461-2845
Registered: LDA
EMail: edickinson@boatus.com

Employers

Boat Owners Ass'n of The United States (BOAT/U.S.) (Assistant V. President)

DICKINSON, Dr. Gloria

7961 Eastern Ave.
Silver Spring, MD 20910
Tel: (301)587-5900
Fax: (301)587-5915

Employers

Ass'n for the Study of Afro-American Life and History (President)

DICKSON, David

1725 DeSales St. NW
Suite 600
Washington, DC 20036
Tel: (202)429-5609
Fax: (202)872-0619

Employers

Center for Marine Conservation

DICKSON, Ellen

1350 I St. NW
Suite 1000
Washington, DC 20005
EMail: edickson@ford.com
Tel: (202)962-5383
Fax: (202)962-5417

Employers

Ford Motor Co. (Manager, Washington Communications)

DICKSON, R. Bruce

1299 Pennsylvania Ave. NW
Tenth Floor
Washington, DC 20004-2400
EMail: rbrucedickson@paulhastings.com
Tel: (202)508-9500
Fax: (202)508-9700

Employers

Paul, Hastings, Janofsky & Walker LLP (Partner)

Clients Represented

On Behalf of Paul, Hastings, Janofsky & Walker LLP

Aspirin Foundation of America, Inc.
Big Dog Sportswear
Bristol-Myers Squibb Co.
Chlorobenzene Producers Ass'n
Meyer Pharmaceuticals

DICKSTEIN, Jason

1707 H St. NW
Suite 703
Washington, DC 20006
Tel: (202)478-5425
Registered: LDA

Employers

Washington Aviation Group (President)

Clients Represented

On Behalf of Washington Aviation Group

Aircraft Electronics Ass'n
Airline Suppliers Ass'n
Professional Aviation Maintenance Ass'n

DICKSTEIN, Sidney

2101 L St. NW
Washington, DC 20037-1526
EMail: dicksteins@dsmo.com
Tel: (202)785-9700
Fax: (202)887-0689

Employers

Dickstein Shapiro Morin & Oshinsky LLP (Senior Counsel)

Clients Represented

On Behalf of Dickstein Shapiro Morin & Oshinsky LLP

PG&E Generating Co.

DICONTI, Michael A.

1615 L St. NW
Suite 1100
Washington, DC 20036-5610
Tel: (202)872-1260
Fax: (202)466-3509

Employers

The Business Roundtable (Director, Administration)

DIDION, Catherine J.

1200 New York Ave. NW
Suite 650
Washington, DC 20005
EMail: awis@awis.org
Tel: (202)326-8940
Fax: (202)326-8960

Employers

Ass'n for Women in Science (Exec. Director)

DIEFENDERFER, III, William M.

P.O. Box 1040
Great Falls, VA 22066
Tel: (703)759-0822
Fax: (703)438-3126
Registered: LDA

Employers

Self-employed as an independent consultant.

Clients Represented

As an independent consultant

Nordstrom, Inc.
Weyerhaeuser Co.

DIEGEL, Rick

1125 15th St. NW
Washington, DC 20005
Tel: (202)728-6046
Fax: (202)728-6144
Registered: LDA

Employers
Internat'l Brotherhood of Electrical Workers (Political/Legislative Director)

DIERCKS, Walter E.

1155 Connecticut Ave.
Sixth Floor
Washington, DC 20036
Tel: (202)861-0870
Fax: (202)429-0657
Deputy Assistant Director (1976-77) and Staff Attorney (1972-76), Bureau of Consumer Protection, Federal Trade Commission.

Employers
Rubin, Winston, Diercks, Harris & Cooke (Partner)

DIERLAM, Bryan

1301 Pennsylvania Ave. NW
Suite 300
Washington, DC 20004
Tel: (202)347-0228
Fax: (202)638-0607

Employers
Nat'l Cattleman's Beef Ass'n (Associate Director, Agriculture Policy)

DIETER, Richard

1320 18th St. NW
Fifth Floor
Washington, DC 20036
Tel: (202)293-6970
Fax: (202)822-4787
EMail: rdieter@essential.org

Employers
Death Penalty Information Center (Exec. Director)

DIETRICH, Deborah F.

1220 19th St. NW
Washington, DC 20036
Tel: (202)775-0436
Fax: (202)775-0061
Registered: LDA
EMail: ddietrich@amchp.org

Employers
Ass'n of Maternal and Child Health Programs (AMCHP) (Director, Legislative Affairs)

DIETZ, Paula J.

1050 Thomas Jefferson St. NW
Seventh Floor
Washington, DC 20007
Tel: (202)298-1800
Fax: (202)338-2416
Registered: LDA
EMail: PJD@vnf.com

Employers
Van Ness Feldman, P.C. (Associate Director, Governmental Issues)

Clients Represented
On Behalf of Van Ness Feldman, P.C.
Coal Utilization Research Council
The Nat'l Wetlands Coalition

DIGENOVA, Joseph E.

901 15th St. NW
Suite 430
Washington, DC 20005
Tel: (202)289-7701
Fax: (202)289-7706
Registered: LDA
Special Counsel, House Education and the Workforce Committee, 1998. U.S. Attorney (1983-88) and Principal Assistant U.S. Attorney (1982-83) for the District of Columbia, Department of Justice. Staff Director and Chief Counsel, Senate Rules Committee, 1981-82. Administrative Assistant and Legislative Counsel to Senator Charles Mathias (R-MD), 1979-81. Counsel, Senate Judiciary Committee, 1978. Counsel, Subcommittee on the District of Columbia, Senate Committee on Governmental Affairs, 1976. Counsel on Intelligence Matters to the Attorney General, Department of Justice, 1976-77. Counsel, Senate Select Committee on Intelligence, 1975-76.

Employers
diGenova & Toensing (Partner)

Clients Represented
On Behalf of diGenova & Toensing
American Hospital Ass'n

DIGGES, Jr., Robert

2200 Mill Rd.
Alexandria, VA 22314
Tel: (703)838-1889
Fax: (703)683-3226

Employers
American Trucking Ass'ns (V. President and Director, Litigation Center)

DIGGS, Carol

1875 I St. NW
Suite 900
Washington, DC 20005
Tel: (202)371-0200
Fax: (202)371-2858
Registered: FARA

Employers
Edelman Public Relations Worldwide (V. President)

Clients Represented
On Behalf of Edelman Public Relations Worldwide
American Plastics Council
Motorcycle Industry Council

DIGGS, Charles

10801 Rockville Pike
Rockville, MD 20852
Tel: (301)897-5700
Ext: 4151
Fax: (301)897-7356
Registered: LDA
EMail: cdiggs@asha.org

Employers
American Speech, Language, and Hearing Ass'n (Manager, Government Relations)

DIGIACINTO, Jacqui

1350 Beverly Rd.
Suite 108
McLean, VA 22101
Tel: (703)748-0400
Fax: (703)748-0402
EMail: jacquidigiacinto@patientadvocacy.org

Employers
Center for Patient Advocacy (Program Coordinator)

DIGIOIA, Lou

119 Oronoco St.
Alexandria, VA 22314-2015
Tel: (703)683-5400
Fax: (703)548-5728
EMail: ldigioia@presidentialclassroom.org

Employers
A Presidential Classroom for Young Americans, Inc. (Manager, Congressional Affairs)

DIGIOVANNI, Carvin

2111 Eisenhower Ave.
Alexandria, VA 22314-4698
Tel: (703)838-0083
Fax: (703)549-0493
EMail: cdigiovanni@nspi.org

Employers
Nat'l Spa and Pool Institute (Technical Director)

DIGIULIAN, Maria

1001 Pennsylvania Ave. NW
Suite 600
Washington, DC 20004
Tel: (202)347-0066
Fax: (202)624-7222
Registered: LDA, FARA
EMail: mdigiuli@pgfm.com
Graduate Fellow, House Foreign Affairs Committee, 1992.

Employers
Powell, Goldstein, Frazer & Murphy LLP (Associate)

Clients Represented
On Behalf of Powell, Goldstein, Frazer & Murphy LLP
China, Embassy of the People's Republic of
Footwear Distributors and Retailers of America
Hong Kong Trade Development Council
PROEXPORT

DILAPI, Christine

1350 I St. NW
Suite 400
Washington, DC 20005-3306
Tel: (202)371-6900
Fax: (202)842-3578

Employers
Motorola, Inc. (Senior Engineer, Satellite Regulatory Affairs)

DILL, Bettina R.

536 First St. SE
Washington, DC 20003
Tel: (202)544-6259
Fax: (202)544-6141
Registered: LDA

Employers
New Jersey Hospital Ass'n (Director, Federal Relations)

DILLARD, Regina K.

1710 Rhode Island Ave. NW
Suite 700
Washington, DC 20036-3007
Tel: (202)466-5208
Fax: (202)263-4435
Registered: LDA

Employers
State Farm Insurance Cos. (Federal Affairs Counsel)

DILLEHAY, J. Whayne

1616 H St. NW
Third Floor
Washington, DC 20006
Tel: (202)737-3700
Fax: (202)737-0530

Employers
Internat'l Center for Journalists (V. President)

DILLEY, Dean M.

2550 M St. NW
Washington, DC 20037-1350
Tel: (202)457-6000
Fax: (202)457-6315
Registered: LDA, FARA
EMail: ddilley@pattonboggs.com
Associate Counsel, Office of the General Counsel, Department of the Air Force, 1980-84.

Employers
Patton Boggs, LLP (Partner)

DILLON, Alanna

1025 Thomas Jefferson St. NW
Suite 400 East
Washington, DC 20007-0805
Tel: (202)965-8115
Fax: (202)965-6403
Registered: LDA

Employers
Jorden Burt LLP (Legislative Coordinator)

Clients Represented
On Behalf of Jorden Burt LLP
American Museum of Natural History
Atlantic Health Systems
The Colonial Williamsburg Foundation
Florida State University System
Gainesville Regional Utilities
Lovelace Respiratory Research Institute
New York University
University of Medicine and Dentistry of New Jersey
University of Miami
University of Tulsa
University of Virginia

DILLON, Ben

1201 15th St. NW
Third Floor
Washington, DC 20005
Tel: (202)857-4722
Fax: (202)857-4799
Registered: LDA
EMail: bdillon@ipaa.org

Employers
Independent Petroleum Ass'n of America (V. President, Public Resources)

DILLOW, Frank W.

1300 I St. NW
Suite 400 West
Washington, DC 20005
Tel: (202)515-2557
Fax: (202)336-7921

Employers
Verizon Communications (V. President, Federal Government Relations)

DILLS, Jennifer

1801 K St. NW
Suite 600K
Washington, DC 20006
Tel: (202)974-5212
Fax: (202)296-7355

Employers
Soc. of the Plastics Industry (Strategic Planning Officer)

DILWORTH, Tom

1775 Pennsylvania Ave. NW
Suite 1200
Washington, DC 20006
Tel: (202)463-7100
Fax: (202)463-7107

Employers
Berman and Company (V. President, Operations)

DIMARTINO, Rita

1120 20th St. NW
Suite 1000
Washington, DC 20036
Tel: (202)457-2406
Fax: (202)457-2571
Registered: LDA
EMail: dmartino@att.com

Employers
AT&T (Director, Federal Government Affairs)

DIMOFF, Steven A.

1779 Massachusetts Ave. NW
Suite 610
Washington, DC 20036
Tel: (202)462-3446
Registered: LDA

Employers
United Nations Ass'n of the U.S.A. (V. President, Washington Office)

DIMOND, Kendra

1050 Connecticut Ave. NW
Washington, DC 20036-5339
Tel: (202)857-6000
Fax: (202)857-6395
Worked for Department of Health and Human Services.

Employers
Arent Fox Kintner Plotkin & Kahn, PLLC (Member)

Clients Represented

On Behalf of Arent Fox Kintner Plotkin & Kahn, PLLC
Sabolich Research & Development

DIMOPOULOS, Arthur

1735 New York Ave. NW
Suite 500
Washington, DC 20006-4759
Tel: (202)628-1700
Fax: (202)331-1024
Registered: LDA

Employers
Preston Gates Ellis & Rouvelas Meeds LLP (Of Counsel)

Clients Represented

On Behalf of Preston Gates Ellis & Rouvelas Meeds LLP
KB Holdings

DIMOS, John

805 15th St. NW
Suite 300
Washington, DC 20005-2207
Tel: (202)682-4200
Fax: (202)682-9054
Registered: LDA

Employers
Credit Union Nat'l Ass'n, Inc. (Manager, Senate Legislative Affairs)

DINAN, Donald R.

1120 20th St. NW
Suite 700 North
Washington, DC 20036-3406
Tel: (202)973-1200
Fax: (202)973-1212

Employers
Hall, Estill, Hardwick, Gable, Golden & Nelson (Partner)

DINAPOLI, Rose

901 E St. NW
Fourth Floor
Washington, DC 20004
Tel: (202)969-8020
Fax: (202)969-8030
Registered: LDA
EMail: rose.dinapoli@slma.com

Employers
Sallie Mae, Inc. (V. President, Government and Industry Relations)

DINEEN, Michael F.

325 Seventh St. NW
Suite 1250
Washington, DC 20004
Tel: (202)347-8193
Fax: (202)347-9304
Registered: LDA
Administrative Assistant to Rep. Dan Kuykendall (R-TN), 1970-74, and Rep. Matthew J. Rinaldo (R-NJ), 1974-75.

Employers
Kemper Insurance Cos. (V. President, Legislative Affairs)
Lumbermens Mutual Casualty Co.

DINEGAR, James C.

1735 New York Ave. NW
Washington, DC 20006
Tel: (202)626-7300
Fax: (202)626-7365
EMail: jdinegar@aia.org

Employers
The American Institute of Architects (Chief Operating Officer)

DINERSTEIN, Paula N.

1615 M St. NW
Suite 800
Washington, DC 20036-3203
Tel: (202)467-6370
Fax: (202)467-6379
EMail: pnd@dwgp.com

Employers
Duncan, Weinberg, Genzer & Pembroke, P.C. (Of Counsel)

DINES, Richard J.

1401 New York Ave. NW
Suite 1100
Washington, DC 20005
Tel: (202)638-6222
Fax: (202)628-6726
Registered: LDA

Employers
Nat'l Cooperative Business Ass'n (Director of Cooperative Business Development)

DINGES, IV, Charles V.

1015 15th St. NW
Suite 600
Washington, DC 20005
Tel: (202)789-2200
Fax: (202)289-6797
Registered: LDA
EMail: cdinges@dc.asce.org

Employers
American Soc. of Civil Engineers (Managing Director, Communications and Government Relations)

DINNEEN, Robert

One Massachusetts Ave. NW
Suite 820
Washington, DC 20001
Tel: (202)289-3835
Fax: (202)289-7519
Registered: LDA
EMail: ethanolrfa@aol.com

Employers
Renewable Fuels Ass'n (V. President)

DINO, Michael

2550 M St. NW
Washington, DC 20037-1350
Tel: (202)457-6000
Fax: (202)457-6315
Registered: LDA

Employers
Patton Boggs, LLP (Policy Analyst)

Clients Represented

On Behalf of Patton Boggs, LLP
Greenwood Village, Colorado, City of

DINSMORE, Alan M.

820 First St. NE
Suite 400
Washington, DC 20002
Tel: (202)408-8171
Fax: (202)289-7880
Registered: LDA
EMail: adinsmore@afb.net

Employers
American Foundation for the Blind - Governmental Relations Group (Senior Governmental Relations Representative)

DION, Deborah

815 16th St. NW
Washington, DC 20006
Tel: (202)637-5000
Fax: (202)637-5058

Employers
AFL-CIO (American Federation of Labor and Congress of Industrial Organizations) (Outreach Specialist)

DIONNE, E.J.

1775 Massachusetts Ave. NW
Washington, DC 20036-2188
Tel: (202)797-6000
Fax: (202)797-6004

Employers
The Brookings Institution (Senior Fellow, Government Studies)

DIPASQUALE, Frank

1825 Samuel Morse Dr.
Reston, VA 20190
Tel: (703)437-5300
Fax: (703)437-7768
EMail: fdipasquale@nationalgrocers.org

Employers
Nat'l Grocers Ass'n (Senior V. President)

DIRENFELD, Barry B.

3000 K St. NW
Suite 300
Washington, DC 20007
Tel: (202)424-7500
Fax: (202)424-7643
Registered: LDA, FARA
Former Chief Legislative Counsel, Senator Howard Metzenbaum, (D-OH). Former Chief Counsel and Staff Director, Senate Judiciary Committee, Subcommittee on Antitrust, Monopolies, and Business

Employers
Swidler Berlin Shereff Friedman, LLP (Managing Partner)

Clients Represented

On Behalf of Swidler Berlin Shereff Friedman, LLP
American Bakers Ass'n
Artichoke Enterprises, Inc.
Aventis Pharmaceuticals, Inc.
California Independent System Operator
Dairy.com
Florida Power and Light Co.
General Electric Co.
Hyundai Semiconductor America, Inc.
Matsushita Electric Corp. of America
Merrill Lynch & Co., Inc.
Microsoft Corp.
Napster, Inc.
Nat'l Ass'n of Chain Drug Stores
Nat'l Housing and Rehabilitation Ass'n
Nat'l Sediments Coalition
Newman & Associates
Niagara Mohawk Power Corp.
Renewable Fuels Ass'n
Samsung Heavy Industries Co., Ltd.
Suiza Foods Corp.
Transkaryotic Therapies Inc.
WRD Venture/NWD Venture

DIRIENZO, Michael

1112 16th St. NW
Suite 240
Washington, DC 20036
Tel: (202)835-0952
Fax: (202)835-0155
Registered: LDA

Employers
American Zinc Ass'n (Director, Public Affairs)
Klein & Saks, Inc.

Clients Represented

On Behalf of Klein & Saks, Inc.
The Gold and Silver Institute

DIRINGER, Elliot

2101 Wilson Blvd.
Suite 550
Arlington, VA 22201
Tel: (703)516-4146
Fax: (703)841-1422
Former Deputy Press Secretary to the President (2000) and former Director of Communications, Executive Office of the President, The White House.

Employers
Pew Center on Global Climate Change (Director, International Strategies)

DIRKS, Dale P.

507 Capitol Ct. NE
Suite 200
Washington, DC 20002
Tel: (202)544-7499
Fax: (202)546-7105
Registered: LDA
EMail: ddirks@aol.com

Employers
Health and Medicine Counsel of Washington (President)

Clients Represented

On Behalf of Health and Medicine Counsel of Washington
American Academy of Family Physicians
American Ass'n of Pharmaceutical Scientists
American Lung Ass'n
American Soc. of Clinical Pathologists
American Thoracic Soc.
Ass'n of Academic Health Sciences Library Directors
Ass'n of Minority Health Profession Schools
Coalition of Positive Outcomes in Pregnancy
Crohn's and Colitis Foundation of America
Digestive Disease Nat'l Coalition
Dystonia Medical Research Foundation
ESA, Inc.
Immune Deficiency Foundation, Inc.
Medical Library Ass'n/Ass'n of Academic Health Sciences Library Directors
St. George's University School of Medicine
Sudden Infant Death Syndrome Alliance

DIRKSEN, Jeff

108 N. Alfred St.
Alexandria, VA 22314
Tel: (703)683-5700
Fax: (703)683-5722

Employers
Nat'l Taxpayers Union (Director, Congressional Tracking)

DISCIULLO, Jeffrey G.

1200 G St. NW
Suite 600
Washington, DC 20005-3802
EMail: disciullo@wrightlaw.com
Tel: (202)393-1200
Fax: (202)393-1240

Employers
Wright & Talisman, P.C.

Clients Represented
On Behalf of Wright & Talisman, P.C.
Columbia Gas Transmission Corp.
Columbia Gulf Transmission Corp.
Northern Border Pipeline Co.
Venice Gathering System, L.L.C.

DISLER, Mark

1801 K St. NW
Suite 901-L
Washington, DC 20006
EMail: mark_disler@bm.com
Tel: (202)530-0500
Fax: (202)530-4800
Registered: LDA, FARA
Former Chief Counsel, Senate Committee on the Judiciary. Former Special Assistant to the General Counsel, Department of Education. Also served as General Counsel, U.S. Commission on Civil Rights and as Deputy Assistant Attorney General for Civil Rights, Department of Justice.

Employers
BKSH & Associates (Director)

Clients Represented
On Behalf of BKSH & Associates
Accenture
UST Public Affairs, Inc.

DITLOW, Clarence M.

1825 Connecticut Ave. NW
Suite 330
Washington, DC 20009
Tel: (202)328-7700
Fax: (202)387-0140

Employers
Center for Auto Safety (Exec. Director)

DITTO, Joy

2301 M St. NW
Washington, DC 20037-1484
Tel: (202)467-2900
Fax: (202)467-2910

Employers
American Public Power Ass'n (Government Relations)

DITTUS, Gloria S.

1150 17th St. NW
Suite 701
Washington, DC 20036
EMail: gloriad@dittus.com
Tel: (202)775-1401
Fax: (202)775-1404
Staff Aide to Senator Donald Stewart (D-AL), 1978-80.

Employers
Dittus Communications (President and Chief Exec. Officer)

Clients Represented
On Behalf of Dittus Communications
Alabama Power
American Business for Legal Immigration
Americans for Computer Privacy
Business Software Alliance
CapNet
Comptel
Dell Computer Corp.
DoubleClick
Editorial Information Network
FM Watch
Kraft Foods, Inc.
Legend Airlines
Pernod Ricard
Southern Co.
Statoil Energy
SurfControl
SurfWatch
VeriSign/Network Solutions, Inc.
Yours.com

DIUGOS, Barbara

1299 Pennsylvania Ave. NW
Suite 800 West
Washington, DC 20004
Tel: (202)785-0500
Fax: (202)785-5277
Registered: LDA

Employers
The Carmen Group

Clients Represented
On Behalf of The Carmen Group
Hyundai Space & Aircraft Co., Ltd.

DIVENERE, Lucia

409 12th St. SW
P.O. Box 96920
Washington, DC 20090-6920
EMail: ldivenere@acog.org
Tel: (202)863-2510
Fax: (202)488-3985
Registered: LDA

Employers
American College of Obstetricians and Gynecologists (Manager, Federal Government Relations)

DIXON, Hon. Alan J.

700 13th St. NW
Suite 700
Washington, DC 20005-3960
EMail: ajdixon@bryancave.com
Tel: (202)508-6000
Fax: (202)508-6200
Registered: LDA
Member, U.S. Senate (D-IL), 1981-93.

Employers
Bryan Cave LLP (Partner)

Clients Represented
On Behalf of Bryan Cave LLP
American Council of State Savings Supervisors
Business Computer Training Institute
Chicago Mercantile Exchange
Electronics Consultants Inc.
Glenview, Illinois, Village of
Highland Park, Illinois, City of Highwood Local Redevelopment Authority and the City of
Highwood, Illinois, City of
Town of Fort Sheridan Co., LLC
Westex Inc.

DIXON, Brian E.

1400 16th St. NW
Suite 320
Washington, DC 20036
Tel: (202)332-2200
Fax: (202)332-2302
Registered: LDA

Employers
Zero Population Growth, Inc. (Director, Government Relations)

DIXON, Doris L.

One Dupont Circle NW
Suite 310
Washington, DC 20036
EMail: ddixon@ncaa.org
Tel: (202)293-3050
Fax: (202)293-3075
Registered: LDA

Employers
Nat'l Collegiate Athletic Ass'n (Director, Federal Relations)

DIXON, Jill

401 F St. NW
Washington, DC 20001
Tel: (202)272-2448
Fax: (202)272-2564

Employers
Nat'l Building Museum (Director, Public Affairs)

DOANE, E. David

1444 I Street NW
Suite 400
Washington, DC 20005
EMail: ddoane@ilta.org
Tel: (202)842-9200
Fax: (202)326-8660

Employers
Independent Liquid Terminals Ass'n (V. President)

DOANE, Michael L.

1200 17th St. NW
Fifth Floor
Washington, DC 20036
Tel: (202)467-6300
Fax: (202)466-2006
Registered: LDA

Employers
Adduci, Mastriani & Schaumberg, L.L.P. (Associate)

Clients Represented
On Behalf of Adduci, Mastriani & Schaumberg, L.L.P.
Rubie's Costume Co., Inc.

DOBERT, Susie

507 Capitol Ct. NE
Suite 200
Washington, DC 20002
Tel: (202)544-7499
Fax: (202)546-7105

Employers
Health and Medicine Counsel of Washington (Legislative Assistant)

Clients Represented
On Behalf of Health and Medicine Counsel of Washington
Ass'n of Minority Health Profession Schools
Digestive Disease Nat'l Coalition
St. George's University School of Medicine

DOBRIANSKY, Larisa

1333 New Hampshire Ave. NW
Suite 400
Washington, DC 20036
Tel: (202)887-4000
Fax: (202)887-4288

Employers
Akin, Gump, Strauss, Hauer & Feld, L.L.P.

Clients Represented
On Behalf of Akin, Gump, Strauss, Hauer & Feld, L.L.P.
Mitsubishi Corp.

DOBRIANSKY, Paula

1779 Massachusetts Ave. NW
Suite 710
Washington, DC 20036
Tel: (202)518-3400
Fax: (202)986-2984

Employers
Council on Foreign Relations (V. President/Washington Director)

DOBSON, Sharon

515 King St.
Suite 420
Alexandria, VA 22314
EMail: SDobson@Clarionmr.com
Tel: (703)836-2090
Fax: (703)684-6048

Employers
American Institute of Chemists (Exec. Director)
American Institute of Chemists Foundation (Contact)

DOCANTO, Licy

701 Pennsylvania Ave. NW
Suite 650
Washington, DC 20004
EMail: licy.docanto@cancer.org
Tel: (202)661-5718
Fax: (202)661-5750
Registered: LDA

Employers
American Cancer Soc. (Manager, Special Populations/Medically Underserved)

DOCKSAI, Ph.D., Ronald F.

1275 Pennsylvania Ave. NW
Suite 801
Washington, DC 20004
Tel: (202)737-8900
Fax: (202)737-8909
Registered: LDA

Employers
Bayer Corp. (V. President, Federal Government Relations)

DODD, Shelley Wilson

412 First St. SE
Suite One
Washington, DC 20003
EMail: swdodd@aol.com
Tel: (202)484-2773
Fax: (202)484-0770
Registered: LDA

Employers
Meyers & Associates (Senior Associate, Higher Education)

Clients Represented
On Behalf of Meyers & Associates
Coalition for Maritime Education
Texas A&M Research Foundation
University of North Carolina at Greensboro

DODDRIDGE, Kathy

1201 15th St. NW
Washington, DC 20005-2800
Tel: (202)822-0470
Fax: (202)822-0572
Registered: LDA

Employers

Nat'l Ass'n of Home Builders of the U.S. (Staff V. President, Legislative Affairs)

DODGE, Bill

1700 K St. NW
13th Floor
Washington, DC 20006-0011
EMail: dodge@narc.org
Tel: (202)457-0710
Fax: (202)269-9352

Employers

Nat'l Ass'n of Regional Councils (Exec. Director)

DODGE, Garen E.

1225 I St. NW
Suite 1000
Washington, DC 20005-3914
Tel: (202)842-7400
Fax: (202)842-0022

Employers

Institute for a Drug-Free Workplace (Assistant Director)

DODGE, Sarah R.

1901 N. Fort Myer Dr.
Suite 1200
Arlington, VA 22209-1604
Tel: (703)351-8000
Fax: (703)351-9160
Registered: LDA

Former Legislative Assistant, Reps. Robert Michel (R-IL), and Andrew Ireland, (R-FL)

Employers

Petroleum Marketers Ass'n of America (Director, Legislative Affairs)

DODGEN, Ph.D., Dan

750 First St. NE
Washington, DC 20002-4242
Tel: (202)336-5500
Fax: (202)336-6069
Registered: LDA

Employers

American Psychological Ass'n (Senior Legislative and Federal Affairs Officer)

DODSON, Andrew C.

1100 S. Washington St.
First Floor
Alexandria, VA 22314-4494
EMail: adodson@nbwa.org
Tel: (703)683-4300
Fax: (703)683-8965
Registered: LDA

Employers

Nat'l Beer Wholesalers Ass'n (Washington Representative)

DODSON, Kathy

1650 King St.
Suite 500
Alexandria, VA 22314
EMail: kdodson@aopanet.org
Tel: (703)836-7116
Fax: (703)836-0838
Registered: LDA

Employers

American Orthotic and Prosthetic Ass'n (Director, Government Relations)

DODSON, Melissa

1201 F St. NW
Suite 500
Washington, DC 20004
Tel: (202)824-1600
Fax: (202)824-1651
Registered: LDA

Employers

Health Insurance Ass'n of America (Federal Legislative Director)

DOGGETT, Jon

600 Maryland Ave. SW
Suite 800
Washington, DC 20024
Tel: (202)484-3600
Fax: (202)484-3604
Registered: LDA

Employers

American Farm Bureau Federation (Senior Director, Natural Resources and Energy)

DOHERTY, Eileen

1030 15th St. NW
Suite 1100
Washington, DC 20005
Tel: (202)783-4600
Fax: (202)783-4601

Director, Communications, Nat'l Telecommunications and Information Administration, Department of Commerce, 1988-92. Associate Director, Office of Private Initiatives, The White House, 1984-88.

Employers

White House Writers Group (Senior Director)

DOHERTY, Robert B.

2011 Pennsylvania Ave. NW
Suite 800
Washington, DC 20006-1808
EMail: rdoherty@mail.acponline.org
Tel: (202)261-4530
Fax: (202)835-0443
Registered: LDA

Employers

American College of Physicians-American Soc. of Internal Medicine (ACP-ASIM) (Senior V. President, Division of Governmental Affairs and Public Policy)

DOHONEY, James

1420 New York Ave. NW
Suite 1050
Washington, DC 20005
Tel: (202)638-1950
Fax: (202)638-7714
Registered: LDA

Former Legislative Assistant to Senator Robert C. Smith (R-NH).

Employers

Van Scoyoc Associates, Inc.

DOLAN, Jr., Charles H.

2000 L St. NW
Suite 300
Washington, DC 20036-0646
Tel: (202)835-8800
Fax: (202)835-8879

Former V. Chairman, U.S. Advisory Commission on Public Diplomacy, United States Information Agency; Special Assistant to the Ambassador, U.S. Mission to Ireland, Department of State; and Legislative Assistant to Rep. Joseph Early (D-MA).

Employers

Ketchum (Senior V. President)

DOLAN, Edward

555 13th St. NW
Washington, DC 20004-1109
EMail: ecdolan@hhlaw.com
Tel: (202)637-5677
Fax: (202)637-5910
Registered: LDA

Law Clerk, Drug Enforcement Administration (1978) and Staff Assistant (1977), Department of Justice.

Employers

Hogan & Hartson L.L.P. (Partner)

DOLAN, Matthew J.

1050 Connecticut Ave. NW
Suite 1100
Washington, DC 20036-5304
EMail: Mdolan@baker-hostetler.com
Tel: (202)861-1500
Fax: (202)861-1790
Registered: LDA

Former Legislative Assistant to Senator Dave Durenberger (R-MN).

Employers

Baker & Hostetler LLP (Partner)

Clients Represented

On Behalf of Baker & Hostetler LLP

American Electric Power Co.
American Football Coaches Ass'n
American Resort Development Ass'n
Blue Cross and Blue Shield of Ohio
Bristol-Myers Squibb Co.
Cafaro Co.
The Chubb Corp.
Citigroup
The Council of Insurance Agents & Brokers
D. H. Blair Investment Banking Corp.
Eagle-Picher Personal Injury Settlement Trust
Edison Electric Institute
Federation of American Hospitals
Flexi-Van Leasing
Florida Residential and Casualty Joint Underwriting Ass'n
Florida Windstorm Underwriting Ass'n
Forest City Ratner Companies
Froedtert Memorial Lutheran Hospital
KeyCorp, Inc.
Loeb & Loeb
Marsh & McLennan Cos.
Medical Mutual of Ohio
Moose Internat'l Inc.
Motion Picture Ass'n of America
Nat'l Ass'n of Optometrics and Opticians
Nat'l Ass'n of Real Estate Investment Trusts
PSH Master L.P.I.
Rollins Hudig Hall
Sedgwick James, Inc.
Transportation Institute
United Jewish Communities, Inc.

DOLBEARE, Mary Anne

1300 N. 17th St.
Suite 750
Arlington, VA 22209
EMail: dolbeare@utsa.com
Tel: (703)247-2600
Fax: (703)841-4750
Registered: LDA

Employers

Uniform and Textile Service Ass'n (Director, Government, Public Affairs and Marketing)

DOLE, Gregory S.

1200 Wilson Blvd.
Arlington, VA 22209-1989
Tel: (703)465-3500
Fax: (703)465-3001

Employers

The Boeing Co. (Director, Commercial Trade Policy)

DOLE, Hon. Robert J.

901 15th St. NW
Suite 700
Washington, DC 20005-2301
EMail: rjdole@verner.com
Tel: (202)371-6000
Fax: (202)371-6279

Member, U.S. Senate (1969-96) and House of Representatives (1961-69) (R-KS). Senate Republican Leader, 1985-96. Chairman, Republican National Committee, 1971-74

Employers

Verner, Liipfert, Bernhard, McPherson and Hand, Chartered (Special Counsel)

DOLIBOIS, Robert

1250 I St. NW
Suite 500
Washington, DC 20005
EMail: rdolibois@anla.org
Tel: (202)789-2900
Ext: 3007
Fax: (202)789-1893

Employers

American Nursery and Landscape Ass'n (Exec. V. President)
Garden Centers of America (Exec. V. President)
Horticultural Research Institute (Exec. V. President)
Nat'l Ass'n of Plant Patent Owners (Exec. V. President)
Wholesale Nursery Growers of America (Exec. V. President)

DOLIM, Barbara

1385 Piccard Dr.
Rockville, MD 20850-4340
EMail: bdolim@mcaa.org
Tel: (301)869-5800
Fax: (301)990-9690

Employers

Mechanical Contractors Ass'n of America (Exec. Director, MSCA)

DOLLINGER, Bill

2000 P St. NW
Suite 415
Washington, DC 20036
EMail: foa@igc.apc.org
Tel: (202)296-2172
Fax: (202)296-2190

Employers
Committee for Humane Legislation (Washington Representative)

DOLLINGER, Stephen

1220 L St. NW
Washington, DC 20005
Tel: (202)682-8000
Fax: (202)682-8232
Registered: LDA

Employers
American Petroleum Institute (Senior Tax Attorney)

DOMBI, William

228 Seventh St. SE
Washington, DC 20003-4306
Tel: (202)547-7424
Fax: (202)547-3540
Registered: LDA

Employers
Nat'l Ass'n for Home Care (Director, Center for Health Care Law)

DOMBO, Frederick T.

1666 K St. NW
Suite 500
Washington, DC 20006-2803
Tel: (202)887-1400
Fax: (202)466-2198
Registered: LDA
Former Counsel, Rep. Michael Forbes (D-NY).

Employers
O'Connor & Hannan, L.L.P. (Associate)

Clients Represented
On Behalf of O'Connor & Hannan, L.L.P.
American Free Trade Ass'n
California Debt Limit Allocation Committee
CompTIA
Kendall-Jackson Winery
Kurdistan Democratic Party USA
Tyson's Governmental Sales, LLC
UBS Warburg

DOMENICK, Julie

1401 H St. NW
12th Floor
Washington, DC 20005-2148
Tel: (202)326-5890
Fax: (202)326-5899
Registered: LDA

Employers
Investment Co. Institute (Exec. V. President)

DOMINY, Charles E.

1150 18th St. NW
Suite 200
Washington, DC 20036
Tel: (202)223-0820
Fax: (202)223-2385
Registered: LDA
EMail: chuck.dominy@halliburton.com

Employers
Halliburton/Brown & Root (V. President, Government Affairs)

DONAHUE, George

1275 K St. NW
Fifth Floor
Washington, DC 20005
Tel: (202)712-9799
EMail: gdonahue@afanet.org

Employers
Ass'n of Flight Attendants (V. President)

DONAHUE, Kathleen

1660 Internat'l Dr.
Suite 600
McLean, VA 22102
Tel: (703)734-4334
Fax: (703)734-4340

Employers
Troutman Sanders Mays & Valentine L.L.P. (Of Counsel)

DONALDSON, Anita

1250 H St. NW
Suite 700
Washington, DC 20005-3908
Tel: (202)783-3870
Fax: (202)783-4687
EMail: donaldson@cse.org

Employers
Citizens for a Sound Economy (Director, Public Affairs)

DONALDSON, Ph.D., Gerald

750 First St. NE
Suite 901
Washington, DC 20002
Tel: (202)408-1711
Fax: (202)408-1699
EMail: jdonaldson@saferoads.org

Employers
Advocates for Highway and Auto Safety (Senior Research Director)

DONALDSON, Nancy

1225 I St. NW
Suite 350
Washington, DC 20005
Tel: (202)789-1110
Fax: (202)789-1116
Registered: LDA
EMail: ndonaldson@dmggroup.com

Employers
Downey McGrath Group, Inc. (V. President)

Clients Represented
On Behalf of Downey McGrath Group, Inc.
American Management Systems
Chevron, U.S.A.
The Limited Inc.
Merck & Co.
SLM Holding Corp.
United Brotherhood of Carpenters and Joiners of America

DONALDSON, Peter J.

1875 Connecticut Ave. NW
Suite 520
Washington, DC 20009
Tel: (202)483-1100
Fax: (202)328-3937
EMail: pjdonaldson@prb.org

Employers
Population Reference Bureau (President)

DONALDSON, Richard C.

1676 International Dr.
McLean, VA 22102
Tel: (703)790-7900
Fax: (703)821-2397
Registered: LDA
EMail: richard.donaldson@shawpittman.com

Employers
Shaw Pittman (Partner)

DONATELLI, Frank J.

1333 New Hampshire Ave. NW
Suite 400
Washington, DC 20036
Tel: (202)887-4000
Fax: (202)887-4288
Registered: LDA
Political Director (1987-89) and Deputy Assistant to the President, Office of Public Liaison (1983-85), The White House. Administrator, Agency for International Development, 1983-84.

Employers
Akin, Gump, Strauss, Hauer & Feld, L.L.P. (Partner)

Clients Represented
On Behalf of Akin, Gump, Strauss, Hauer & Feld, L.L.P.
American Legion
Bear, Stearns and Co.
British Columbia, Canada, Government of the Province of
L.L. Capital Partners, Inc.
Nat'l Basketball Ass'n
Nat'l Hockey League
Nehemiah Progressive Housing Development Corp.
Pegasus Capital Advisors, L.P.
Samsung Corp.

DONEGAN, Jr., Thomas J.

1101 17th St. NW
Suite 300
Washington, DC 20036
Tel: (202)331-1770
Fax: (202)331-1969

Employers
Cosmetic, Toiletry and Fragrance Ass'n (V. President, Legal and General Counsel)

DONESKI, Donna

1010 Wayne Ave.
Suite 770
Silver Spring, MD 20910
Tel: (301)650-9127
Fax: (301)565-9670
Registered: LDA

Employers
Nat'l Coalition for Cancer Survivorship (Director, Marketing and Communications)

DONEY, John L.

1150 17th St. NW
Suite 601
Washington, DC 20036
Tel: (202)293-7474
Fax: (202)293-8811
Registered: LDA
Former Assistant Secretary for the Majority of the U.S. Senate.

Employers
Washington Council Ernst & Young (Senior Manager)

Clients Represented
On Behalf of Washington Council Ernst & Young
Aetna Inc.
Aetna Life & Casualty Co.
Allegiance Healthcare Corp.
Allen & Co.
American Express Co.
American Insurance Ass'n
American Staffing Ass'n
Anheuser-Busch Cos., Inc.
Antitrust Coalition for Consumer Choice in Health Care
Apartment Investment and Management Co.
Ass'n of American Railroads
Ass'n of Home Appliance Manufacturers
AT&T
AT&T Capital Corp.
Avco Financial Services
Aventis Pharmaceuticals, Inc.
Baxter Healthcare Corp.
BHC Communications, Inc.
Bulmer Holding PLC, H. P.
Cash Balance Coalition
Chamber of Shipping of America
Citigroup
Coalition for Fairness in Defense Exports
Coalition to Preserve Tracking Stock
ComEd
The Connell Co.
Deferral Group
Directors Guild of America
Doris Duke Charitable Foundation
Eaton Vance Management Co.
Eden Financial Corp.
The Enterprise Foundation
Fannie Mae
FedEx Corp.
Ford Motor Co.
GE Capital Assurance
General Electric Co.
General Motors Corp.
Global Competitiveness Coalition
Grasslands Water District
Group Health, Inc.
Haz-X Support Services Corp.
HEREIU
Gilbert P. Hyatt, Inventor
Investment Co. Institute
Large Public Power Council
Local Initiatives Support Corp.
Lockheed Martin Corp.
MacAndrews & Forbes Holdings, Inc.
Marsh & McLennan Cos.
MCG Northwest, Inc.
McLane Co.
Merrill Lynch & Co., Inc.
Metropolitan Banking Group
Microsoft Corp.
Nat'l Ass'n for State Farm Agents
Nat'l Ass'n of Professional Employer Organizations
Nat'l Ass'n of Real Estate Investment Trusts
Nat'l Defined Contribution Council
Nat'l Foreign Trade Council, Inc.
Nat'l Multi-Housing Council
PaineWebber Group, Inc.
Pfizer, Inc.
R&D Tax Credit Coalition
R&D Tax Regulation Group
Recording Industry Ass'n of America
Reed-Elsevier Inc.
R. J. Reynolds Tobacco Co.
Charles Schwab & Co., Inc.,
Securities Industry Ass'n
Sierra Pacific Industries
Skadden, Arps, Slate, Meagher & Flom LLP
Straddle Rules Tax Group
Tax Fairness Coalition
Tax/Shelter Coalition
TransOceanic Shipping
TU Services
TXU Business Services
U.S. Oncology
USA Biomass Power Producers Alliance
Viaticus, Inc.
Wilkie Farr & Gallagher
Ziff Investors Partnership

DONNELLAN, Christopher M.

317 S. Patrick St.
Alexandria, VA 22314
Tel: (703)519-0300
Fax: (703)519-0311
Registered: LDA
Legislative assistant to Rep. Richard Neal (D-MA), 1991-95.

Employers
Internat'l Brotherhood of Police Officers
Law Enforcement Steering Committee
Nat'l Ass'n of Government Employees (Legislative Director)

DONNELLAN, Kevin J.

601 E St. NW
Washington, DC 20049
Tel: (202)434-3705
Fax: (202)434-3714
Registered: LDA

Employers
AARP (American Ass'n of Retired Persons) (Director, Grassroots Advocacy)

DONNELLAN, Rebecca A.

1200 19th St. NW
Suite 210
Washington, DC 20036
Tel: (202)452-0900
Fax: (202)452-0930
Registered: LDA
EMail: rdonnellan@dilworthlaw.com
Trial Lawyer, Environment and Natural Resources Division, Department of Justice, 1978-91. Special Assistant to the Assistant Administrator for Policy and Planning, National Oceanic and Atmopheric Administration, Department of Commerce, 1977-78.

Employers
Dilworth Paxson, LLP (Partner)

Clients Represented
On Behalf of Dilworth Paxson, LLP
Alaska Federation of Natives
Bethel Native Corp.

DONNELLI, Maury

219 N. Washington St.
Alexandria, VA 22314
Tel: (703)836-7990
Fax: (703)836-9739

Employers
Peduzzi Associates, Ltd. (Associate)

DONNELLY, Gary W.

40 Ivy St. SE
Washington, DC 20003
Tel: (202)547-2230
Fax: (202)547-7640
Registered: LDA
EMail: gary@dealer.org

Employers
Nat'l Lumber and Building Material Dealers Ass'n (President)

DONNELLY, Mary Adele

1725 DeSales St. NW
Suite 600
Washington, DC 20036
Tel: (202)429-5609
Fax: (202)872-0619

Employers
Center for Marine Conservation

DONNELLY, Patrick J.

1776 I St. NW
Suite 1050
Washington, DC 20006
Tel: (202)429-3438
Fax: (202)429-3467
Registered: LDA

Employers
Dow AgroSciences (Global Leader, Government and Public Relations)

DONNELLY, Thomas F.

3800 N. Fairfax Dr.
Suite 4
Arlington, VA 22203
Tel: (703)524-1544
Fax: (703)524-1548
Registered: LDA
EMail: tdonnelly@nwra.org

Employers
Nat'l Water Resources Ass'n (Exec. V. President)

DONNELLY, Jr., Thomas R.

1615 L St. NW
Suite 650
Washington, DC 20036
Tel: (202)626-8508
Fax: (202)626-8593
Registered: LDA
EMail: tom_donnelly@jeffersongr.com
Former Special Assistant to the President, The White House, 1983-85. Assistant Secretary for Legislation, Department of Health and Human Services, 1981-83.

Employers
Jefferson Government Relations, L.L.C. (Principal and V. Chairman)

Clients Represented
On Behalf of Jefferson Government Relations, L.L.C.
Bass Hotels and Resorts, Inc.
Cummins-Allison Corp.
eHealth Insurance Services, Inc.
Iredell Memorial Hospital
Nat'l Industries for the Blind
Nat'l Quality Health Council
Vinyl Institute
Westmoreland Coal Co.

DONNER, Sally

1341 G St. NW
Suite 900
Washington, DC 20005
Tel: (202)637-1580
Fax: (202)637-1537

Employers
Philip Morris Management Corp. (Director, Federal Government Issues Planning and Research)

DONOGHUE BAXTER, Marguerite

1455 F St. NW
Suite 450
Washington, DC 20004
Tel: (202)393-6040
Fax: (202)393-6050
Registered: LDA
Assistant, AIDS Program/Policy Coordinator (1985-88) and Clinical Nurse Specialist, National Cancer Institute (1982-85), National Institutes of Health, Department of Health and Human Services.

Employers
Pharmacia Corp. (Senior Director, Federal Government Affairs)

DONOHO, Patrick B.

2300 Ninth St. South
Suite 210
Arlington, VA 22204
Tel: (703)920-8480
Fax: (703)920-8491
Registered: LDA

Employers
Pharmaceutical Care Management Ass'n (V. President, Government Affairs and Public Policy)

DONOHO, Wendy L.

1401 I St. NW
Suite 1100
Washington, DC 20005
Tel: (202)326-8814
Fax: (202)408-8717
Registered: LDA

Employers
SBC Communications Inc. (Exec. Director, Federal Relations)

DONOHOE, David A.

1333 New Hampshire Ave. NW
Suite 400
Washington, DC 20036
Tel: (202)887-4000
Fax: (202)887-4288

Employers
Akin, Gump, Strauss, Hauer & Feld, L.L.P. (Partner)

DONOHUE, Thomas J.

1615 H St. NW
Washington, DC 20062-2000
Tel: (202)659-6000
Fax: (202)463-5836
Former Deputy Assistant Postmaster General, during the Reagan and Bush I Administrations.

Employers
Chamber of Commerce of the U.S.A. (President and Chief Exec. Officer)

DONOVAN, Charles

801 G St. NW
Washington, DC 20001
Tel: (202)393-2100
Fax: (202)393-2134

Employers
Family Research Council, Inc. (Exec. V. President)

DONOVAN, David L.

1320 19th St. NW
Suite 300
Washington, DC 20036
Tel: (202)887-1970
Fax: (202)887-0950
Registered: LDA

Employers
Ass'n of Local Television Stations (V. President, Legal and Legislative Affairs)

DONOVAN, George J.

1225 Jefferson Davis Hwy.
Suite 1100
Arlington, VA 22202
Tel: (703)416-9400
Fax: (703)416-9404

Employers
Smiths Aerospace (V. President, Government Relations)

DONOVAN, Paul M.

3900 Highwood Court NW
Washington, DC 20007
Tel: (202)298-8100
Fax: (202)298-8200

Employers
LaRoe, Winn, Moerman & Donovan (Partner)

Clients Represented
On Behalf of LaRoe, Winn, Moerman & Donovan
Chlorine Institute
Port Authority of New York and New Jersey

DONOVAN, William J.

3138 N. Tenth St.
Arlington, VA 22201
Tel: (703)522-4770
Fax: (703)524-0594
Registered: LDA

Employers
Nat'l Ass'n of Federal Credit Unions (Senior V. President and General Counsel)

DOOLEY, Barbara A.

1301 K Street NW
Suite 325
Washington, DC 20005
EMail: dooley@cix.org
Tel: (703)709-8200
Fax: (703)709-5249

Employers
Commercial Internet Exchange Ass'n (President)

DOOLEY, Cathleen M.

1350 I St. NW
Suite 1210
Washington, DC 20005-3305
Tel: (202)589-1000
Ext: 1008
Fax: (202)589-1001

Employers
Johnson & Johnson, Inc. (Director, Federal Affairs)

DOOLEY, Edward

4301 N. Fairfax Dr.
Suite 425
Arlington, VA 22203
EMail: edooley@ari.org
Tel: (703)524-8800
Fax: (703)528-3816

Employers
Air-Conditioning and Refrigeration Institute (V. President, Communication and Education)

DORAN, Kelley P.

1735 New York Ave. NW
Suite 500
Washington, DC 20006-4759
Tel: (202)628-1700
Fax: (202)331-1024

Employers
Preston Gates Ellis & Rouvelas Meeds LLP (Associate)

DORAN, Michael

One Thomas Circle NW
Suite 1100
Washington, DC 20005
Tel: (202)862-5021
Fax: (202)429-3301
Registered: LDA
EMail: mtd@capdale.com
Office of the Benefits Tax Counsel, Department of the Treasury.

Employers
Caplin & Drysdale, Chartered (Member)

DOREMUS, Jr., Theodore A.

1300 I St. NW
Suite 1000 East
Washington, DC 20005
Tel: (202)962-7160
Fax: (202)962-7111
Registered: LDA
General Counsel, Minority Staff, House Committee on Banking, Finance and Urban Affairs, 1975-79. Senior Branch Attorney, Securities and Exchange Commission, 1970-75.

Employers
Davis Polk & Wardwell (Of Counsel)
Self-employed as an independent consultant.

Clients Represented
On Behalf of Davis Polk & Wardwell
Brown Brothers Harriman & Co.
Wells Fargo Bank, N.A.
As an independent consultant
The Financial Services Roundtable
Wells Fargo Bank, N.A.

DORFMAN, Ira H.

915 15th St. NW
Suite 600
Washington, DC 20005-2302
Tel: (202)393-8444
Ext: 104
Fax: (202)393-8666
Registered: LDA
EMail: idorfman@dorfmanoneal.com
Professional Staff Member, Senate Energy and Natural Resources Committee, 1979-81.

Employers
Dorfman & O'Neal, Inc. (President)

Clients Represented
On Behalf of Dorfman & O'Neal, Inc.
American Honda Motor Co., Inc.
FuelMaker Corp.
Simula, Inc.

DORGAN, Kimberly O.

1001 Pennsylvania Ave. NW
Washington, DC 20004-2599
Tel: (202)624-2000
Fax: (202)624-2319
Registered: LDA

Employers
American Council of Life Insurers (Deputy V. President, Federal Relations)

DORITY, Douglas H.

1775 K St. NW
Washington, DC 20006
Tel: (202)223-3111
Fax: (202)466-1562

Employers
United Food and Commercial Workers Internat'l Union (International President)

DORN, James A.

1000 Massachusetts Ave. NW
Washington, DC 20001
Tel: (202)842-0200
Fax: (202)842-3490

Employers
Cato Institute (V. President, Academic Affairs)

DORN, Joseph W.

1730 Pennsylvania Ave. NW
Suite 1200
Washington, DC 20006-4706
Tel: (202)737-0500
Fax: (202)626-3737
Registered: LDA

Employers
King & Spalding (Partner)

Clients Represented
On Behalf of King & Spalding
Southern Tier Cement Committee

DORN, Nancy P.

Old Executive Office Bldg.
Room 276
Washington, DC 20501
Tel: (202)456-6774
Fax: (202)456-1606
Former Assistant Secretary of the Army (Civil Works), 1991-93. Former Special Assistant to President Reagan, 1988-89; and to President Bush, 1988-90.

Employers
Executive Office of the President - Office of the Vice President (Assistant to the V. President for Legislative Affairs)

DORNBUSCH, Rebecca

601 13th St. NW
Suite 370 South
Washington, DC 20005
Tel: (202)783-7272
Fax: (202)783-4345
Registered: LDA

Employers
French & Company (V. President)

Clients Represented
On Behalf of French & Company
Encapco Technologies, LLC
Information Spectrum Inc.
Internat'l Biometric Industry Ass'n
Levine-Fricke Restoration Corp.
Nossaman, Gunther, Knox & Elliott

DORRANCE, Jr., Samuel R.

1718 Connecticut Ave. NW
Suite 300
Washington, DC 20009
Tel: (202)232-7933
Fax: (202)234-1328

Employers
Center for Resource Economics (Director, Marketing)

DORRIS, Gregory

600 14th St. NW
Suite 500
Washington, DC 20005
Tel: (202)220-1200
Fax: (202)220-1665

Employers
Pepper Hamilton LLP (Partner)

DORSEY, Deborah Wood

1301 Pennsylvania Ave. NW
Suite 400
Washington, DC 20004
EMail: dwdorsey@cla.ci.la.ca.us
Tel: (202)347-0915
Fax: (202)347-0919

Employers
Los Angeles, California, Washington Office of the City of (Legislative Representative)

DORSEY, Laura

6540 Arlington Blvd.
Falls Church, VA 22042
EMail: laura@irrigation.org
Tel: (703)536-7080
Fax: (703)536-7019

Employers
Irrigation Ass'n (Director, Communications)

DORT, II, Dean R.

1808 I St. NW
Eighth Floor
Washington, DC 20006
Tel: (202)223-4817
Fax: (202)296-0011
Registered: LDA

Employers
Deere & Co. (V. President, International)

DORT, Terrie M.

325 Seventh St. NW
Suite 1100
Washington, DC 20004
Tel: (202)626-8183
Fax: (202)626-8185
Registered: LDA

Employers
Nat'l Council of Chain Restaurants (President)

DOSS, Joseph

1700 Diagonal Rd.
Suite 650
Alexandria, VA 22314
EMail: jdoss@bottledwater.org
Tel: (703)683-5213
Fax: (703)683-4074

Employers
Internat'l Bottled Water Ass'n (President)

DOSWELL, W. Carter

1101 Pennsylvania Ave. NW
Suite 900
Washington, DC 20004
Tel: (202)637-3700
Fax: (202)637-3773

Employers
Goldman, Sachs and Co. (V. President)

DOTCHIN, Robert J.

1350 I St. NW
Suite 680
Washington, DC 20005-3305
Tel: (202)393-4841
Fax: (202)393-5596
Registered: LDA
EMail: robert@advocacy.com
Legislative Assistant to Senator Lowell Weicker (R-CT), 1973-76. Republican Staff Director, Senate Small Business Committee, 1977-88.

Employers
The Advocacy Group

Clients Represented
On Behalf of The Advocacy Group
American Institute for Foreign Studies
Consumer Electronics Ass'n
Long Island University
Nat'l Ass'n of Small Business Investment Companies
Tyco Internat'l (US), Inc.
University of Houston
UST Public Affairs, Inc.

DOUBRAVA, Richard

1301 Pennsylvania Ave. NW
Suite 1100
Washington, DC 20004-1707
Tel: (202)626-4000
Fax: (202)626-4208

Employers
Air Transport Ass'n of America (Managing Director, Security)

DOUCET, Shane

1201 F St. NW
Suite 200
Washington, DC 20004
Tel: (202)554-9000
Fax: (202)554-0496

Employers
Nat'l Federation of Independent Business (Manager, Legislative Affairs)

DOUGHERTY, Brian J.

1155 16th St. NW
Washington, DC 20036
Tel: (202)872-4600
Fax: (202)872-4615
Registered: LDA

Employers
American Chemical Soc.

DOUGHERTY, Ellen A.

122 C St. NW
Suite 510
Washington, DC 20001
EMail: dougherty@dc.ncga.com
Tel: (202)628-7001
Fax: (202)628-1933

Employers
Nat'l Corn Growers Ass'n (Director, Washington Communications)

DOUGHERTY, John J.

14405 Laurel Pl.
Suite 300
Laurel, MD 20707
Tel: (301)470-4200
Fax: (301)470-2502

Employers
Operative Plasterers' and Cement Masons' Internat'l Ass'n of the U.S. and Canada (General President)

DOUGHERTY, Joseph

214 Massachusetts Ave. NE
Washington, DC 20002
Tel: (202)608-6143
Fax: (202)546-8328

Employers
Heritage Foundation (Public Relations Associate)

DOUGLAS, Frederick A.

1401 New York Ave.
Suite 600
Washington, DC 20005
Tel: (202)434-9100
Registered: LDA

Employers
Leftwich & Douglas (Parnter)

DOUGLAS, John L.

601 Pennsylvania Ave. NW
11th Floor, North Bldg.
Washington, DC 20004-2601
Tel: (202)756-7880
Fax: (202)756-3333
Registered: LDA
EMail: jdouglas@alston.com

Employers
Alston & Bird LLP (Partner)

DOUGLAS, Susan

1300 Spring St.
Suite 500
Silver Spring, MD 20910
EMail: Suedouglas@aol.com
Tel: (301)589-6372
Fax: (301)588-0854

Employers
Nat'l Fenestration Rating Council (Administrator)

DOUGLASS, Adele

236 Massachusetts Ave. NE
Suite 203
Washington, DC 20002-5702
Tel: (202)543-7780
Fax: (202)546-3266
Registered: LDA

Employers
American Humane Ass'n (Director, Washington Office)

DOUGLASS, Hugh M.

1615 L St. NW
Suite 650
Washington, DC 20036
EMail: hugh_douglass@jeffersongr.com
Tel: (202)626-8241
Fax: (202)626-8581

Employers
Jefferson Government Relations, L.L.C. (V. President and Chief Financial Officer)

DOUGLASS, USAF (Ret.), Brig. Gen. John W.

1250 I St. NW
Suite 1200
Washington, DC 20005-3924
Tel: (202)371-8500
Fax: (202)371-8470

Employers
Aerospace Industries Ass'n of America (President and Chief Exec. Officer)

DOUGLASS, Mary

1319 F St. NW
Suite 604
Washington, DC 20004
EMail: mdouglass@ajli.org
Tel: (202)393-3364
Fax: (202)393-4517

Employers
Ass'n of Junior Leagues, Internat'l (Senior Associate/Meetings Manager)

DOVE, Randolph V.

1331 Pennsylvania Ave. NW
Suite 1300 North
Washington, DC 20004
EMail: randy.dove@eds.com
Tel: (202)637-6728
Fax: (202)637-6759
Registered: LDA

Employers
EDS Corp. (Exec. Director, Government Relations)

DOVE, Stephen

2200 Mill Rd.
Alexandria, VA 22314
Tel: (703)838-1880
Fax: (703)548-1841

Employers
American Trucking Ass'ns (Manager, Legislative Affairs)

DOVER, Agnes

555 13th St. NW
Washington, DC 20004-1109
Tel: (202)637-5975
Fax: (202)637-5910
Registered: LDA
EMail: apdover@hhlaw.com
Deputy General Counsel for Procurement and Intellectual Property, Department of Energy, 1993-96.

Employers
Hogan & Hartson L.L.P. (Partner)

DOVER, G. Jack

1300 Connecticut Ave. NW
Suite 600
Washington, DC 20036
Tel: (202)775-8116
Fax: (202)223-0358
Registered: LDA, FARA
Former Legislative Aide to Rep. Dennis Eckert (D-OH) and Senator John Glenn (D-OH) and Domestic Policy Staff, The White House, during the Carter Administration.

Employers
Griffin, Johnson, Dover & Stewart (Lobbyist)

Clients Represented

On Behalf of Griffin, Johnson, Dover & Stewart
Alaska Communications Systems, Inc.
American Agrisurance
American Fish Spotters Ass'n
American Petroleum Institute
American Soc. of Anesthesiologists
Avue Technologies
Computer Coalition for Responsible Exports
Council of Smaller Enterprises
Dell Computer Corp.
Deloitte Consulting
Delta Dental Plans Ass'n
Directors Guild of America
Fannie Mae
Hong Kong Economic and Trade Office
Independent Telephone and Telecommunications Alliance
The Justice Project, Inc.
Local Initiatives Support Corp.
Monsanto Co.
Software Productivity Consortium
United Technologies Corp.
Wilmer, Cutler & Pickering
Wine and Spirits Wholesalers of America

DOWD, John W.

1333 New Hampshire Ave. NW
Suite 400
Washington, DC 20036
Tel: (202)887-4000
Fax: (202)887-4288
Chief, Organized Crime Strike Force (1974-78), Prosecutor, Organized Crime and Racketeering Section, Criminal Division (1972-74), and Attorney, Tax Division (1969-70), Department of Justice.

Employers
Akin, Gump, Strauss, Hauer & Feld, L.L.P. (Partner)

DOWDEN, Lisa

1350 New York Ave. NW
Suite 1100
Washington, DC 20005-4798
EMail: dowdenl@spiegelmcd.com
Tel: (202)879-4000
Fax: (202)393-2866
Registered: LDA

Employers
Spiegel & McDiarmid (Partner)

Clients Represented

On Behalf of Spiegel & McDiarmid
Northern California Power Agency

DOWELL, Jill

1350 I St. NW
Suite 400
Washington, DC 20005-3306
Tel: (202)371-6875
Fax: (202)842-3578
Registered: LDA

Employers
Motorola, Inc. (Manager, Federal Legislative Relations)

DOWLAND, David

1155 15th St. NW
Suite 1004
Washington, DC 20005
Tel: (202)467-5081
Fax: (202)467-5085

Employers
Visually Impaired Veterans of America (President)

DOWLEY, Joseph K.

1775 Pennsylvania Ave. NW
Suite 200
Washington, DC 20006
Tel: (202)862-1034
Fax: (202)862-1093
Registered: LDA
EMail: jdowley@deweyballantine.com
Chief Counsel (1985-87) and Assistant Chief Counsel (1980-84), House Committee on Ways and Means. Administrative Assistant to Rep. Dan Rostenkowski (D-IL), 1976-81.

Employers
Dewey Ballantine LLP (Partner)

Clients Represented

On Behalf of Dewey Ballantine LLP
AFLAC, Inc.
Norfolk Southern Corp.
Northwestern Memorial Hospital
Qwest Communications
Railroad Retirement Tax Working Group
Tribune Co.
United States Telecom Ass'n
Verizon Communications

DOWLING, Jennifer Connell

1401 K St. NW
Suite 601
Washington, DC 20005
EMail: jconnell-dowling@semi.org
Tel: (202)289-0440
Fax: (202)289-0441
Registered: LDA

Employers
Semiconductor Equipment and Materials Internat'l (Director, Public Policy)

DOWLING, S. Colin

1101 Pennsylvania Ave. NW
Suite 1000
Washington, DC 20004
EMail: dowling@citi.com
Tel: (202)879-6837
Fax: (202)508-4511
Registered: LDA

Employers
Citigroup (Sr. V. President and Dir., State Government Affairs)

DOWNEY, Arthur T.

816 Connecticut Ave. NW
Second Floor
Washington, DC 20006-2705
EMail: art.downey@bakerhughes.com
Tel: (202)785-8093
Fax: (202)785-4509
Registered: LDA

Employers
Baker Hughes Incorporated (V. President, Government Affairs)

DOWNEY, Jr., Hon. Thomas J.

1225 I St. NW
Suite 350
Washington, DC 20005
EMail: tdowney@dmggroup.com
Tel: (202)789-1110
Fax: (202)789-1116
Registered: LDA
Member, U.S. House of Representatives (D-NY), 1975-93.

Employers
Downey McGrath Group, Inc. (Chairman)

Clients Represented

On Behalf of Downey McGrath Group, Inc.
American Foundation for AIDS Research
American Management Systems
American Soc. of Anesthesiologists
AOL Time Warner
The Boeing Co.
Breakthrough Technologies Institute
Chevron, U.S.A.
Dental Recycling North America
DoubleClick
DuPont
Energy Efficiency Systems, Inc.
Fannie Mae
Fantasma Networks, Inc.
Fuji Photo Film U.S.A., Inc.
Healthcare Ass'n of New York State
Kalkines, Arky, Zall and Bernstein
The Limited Inc.
Merck & Co.
Metropolitan Life Insurance Co.
Microsoft Corp.
Nat'l Cable Television Ass'n
The New York Structural Biology Center
Philipp Brothers Chemicals, Inc.
San Francisco, California, City and County of
SLM Holding Corp.
St. John's University
Teledesic Corp.
United Brotherhood of Carpenters and Joiners of America

DOWNING, Winifred

1155 15th St. NW
Suite 1004
Washington, DC 20005
Tel: (202)467-5081
Fax: (202)467-5085

Employers
Library Users of America (President)

DOWNS, Anthony

1775 Massachusetts Ave. NW
Washington, DC 20036-2188
Tel: (202)797-6000
Fax: (202)797-6004

Employers
The Brookings Institution (Senior Fellow, Economic Studies)

DOWNS, Paul

Rayburn House Office Bldg.
B328
Washington, DC 20515
Tel: (202)225-2280
Fax: (202)453-5225

Employers
Department of Veterans Affairs (House Liaison Officer)

DOWNS, Thomas C.

2550 M St. NW
Washington, DC 20037-1350
Tel: (202)457-6000
Fax: (202)457-6315
Registered: LDA
EMail: tdowns@pattonboggs.com
Chief of Staff and Legislative Director to Rep. George Hochbrueckner (D-NY), 1987-95 Legislative Assistant to Rep. Martin Olav-Sabo (D-MN), 1985-87

Employers
Patton Boggs, LLP (Associate)

Clients Represented

On Behalf of Patton Boggs, LLP
BNFL, Inc.
Frederick Douglass Gardens, Inc.
Jacksonville, Florida, City of
Nat'l Ass'n of Uniform Manufacturers and Distributors
Nat'l Oilheat Research Alliance (NORA)
Potomac Heritage Partnership
San Bernardino Valley Municipal Water District
San Bernardino, California, City of
Save Barton Creek
Travel Industry Ass'n of America
United Technologies Corp.

DOYLE, Elizabeth Z.

1414 Prince St.
Suite 302
Alexandria, VA 22314
Tel: (703)548-3692
Fax: (703)548-8024
Former Deputy Under Secretary for Intergovernmental Affairs, Department of Labor; former Director of Public Liaison, Interagency Council on the Homeless; former Director of Intergovernmental Affairs, Region II, Department of Health and Human Services.

Employers
The Borden Group, Inc. (Account Executive)

DOYLE, J. Andrew

1500 Rhode Island Ave. NW
Washington, DC 20005-5597
Tel: (202)462-6272
Fax: (202)462-8549

Employers
Nat'l Paint and Coatings Ass'n (President)

DOYLE, Jr., John S.

700 13th St. NW
Suite 400
Washington, DC 20005
Tel: (202)347-0773
Fax: (202)347-0785
Registered: LDA
EMail: jdoyle@cassidy.com
Former Chief of Staff, House Committee on Public Works and Transportation; Chief Counsel, House Committee on Science, Space and Technology; Chief of Staff to Rep. James A. Hayes (D-LA); Minority Counsel for Water, House Committee on Public Works and Transportation; and Principal Deputy Assistant Secretary and Acting Assistant Secretary of the Army (Civil Works) during the Reagan and Bush I administrations.

Employers
Cassidy & Associates, Inc. (Senior V. President)

Clients Represented

On Behalf of Cassidy & Associates, Inc.
Abtech Industries
El Segundo, California, City of
Maersk Inc.
Ocean Spray Cranberries
Phoenix, Arizona, City of
Proteus Co.
Sacramento Area Flood Control Agency

DOYLE, Kenneth A.

11911 Freedom Dr.
Suite 590
Reston, VA 20190
Tel: (703)709-7000
Fax: (703)709-7007

Employers
Soc. of Independent Gasoline Marketers of America (Exec. V. President)

DOYLE, Shannon

3927 Old Lee Hwy.
Suite 102
Fairfax, VA 22030
Tel: (703)503-4000
Registered: LDA
EMail: shannon.doyle@impact-strategies.com
Legislative Assistant to Rep. Bill Zeliff (R-NH), 1994-96.

Employers
Impact Strategies (Legislative Director)

Clients Represented

On Behalf of Impact Strategies
R. R. Donnelley & Sons
Environmental Commonsense Coalition
The Timken Co.

DOYLE, Stephen P.

440 Maple Ave. East
Suite 201
Vienna, VA 22188
Tel: (703)242-4670
Fax: (703)242-4675
Registered: LDA

Employers
Alarm Industry Communications Committee (Exec. V. President)
Central Station Alarm Ass'n (Exec. V. President)

DOYLE, Theresa

1455 Pennsylvania Ave. NW
Suite 575
Washington, DC 20004
Tel: (202)638-4076
Fax: (202)638-1096
Registered: LDA

Employers
WellPoint Health Networks/Blue Cross of California/UNICARE (Director, Federal Affairs)

DOYNE, Karen

2000 L St. NW
Suite 300
Washington, DC 20036-0646
Tel: (202)835-8800
Fax: (202)835-8879
EMail: karen.doyne@ketchum.com
Former Press Secretary to Senator David Durenberger (R-MN).

Employers
Ketchum (Director, Litigation Communications)

DOZIER, Damon

1156 15th St. NW
Suite 1100
Washington, DC 20005
Tel: (202)293-8830
Fax: (202)872-8543
Former Legislative Assistant, Senate Committee on Small Business.

Employers
Nat'l Small Business United (Director, Government and Public Affairs)

DRAGGON, Robert O.

1015 15th St. NW
Suite 700
Washington, DC 20005-2605
Tel: (202)828-5200
Fax: (202)785-2645

Employers
Bechtel Group, Inc. (Assistant Managing Director (Bechtel Enterprises))

DRAGONETTI, John J.

4220 King St.
Alexandria, VA 22302-1502
Tel: (703)379-2480
Fax: (703)379-7563
Registered: LDA
EMail: dragon@agiweb.org

Employers
American Geological Institute (Senior Advisor, Government Affairs)

DRAKE, David P.

701 Pennsylvania Ave. NW
Suite 725
Washington, DC 20004
Tel: (202)638-7429
Fax: (202)628-4763
Registered: LDA

Employers
Novartis Corp. (Director, Federal Government Relations)
Novartis Services, Inc.

DRAKE, Stuart A. C.

655 15th St. NW
Suite 1200
Washington, DC 20005
Tel: (202)879-5000
Fax: (202)879-5200
Registered: LDA

Employers
Kirkland & Ellis (Partner)

Clients Represented

On Behalf of Kirkland & Ellis
General Motors Corp.

DRAPEAUX, Brian J.

800 Connecticut Ave. NW
Suite 500
Washington, DC 20006
Tel: (202)331-3108
Fax: (202)331-3101
EMail: drapeauxb@gtlaw.com
Legislative Assistant for Native American Affairs to Senator Thomas Daschle (D-SD), 1997-99.

Employers
Greenberg Traurig, LLP (Assistant Director, Government Affairs)

Clients Represented

On Behalf of Greenberg Traurig, LLP
Yankton Sioux Tribe

DRAZEK, Paul A.

1001 Pennsylvania Ave. NW
Suite 600
Washington, DC 20004
Tel: (202)347-0066
Fax: (202)624-7222
EMail: pdrazek@pgfm.com
Former Special Assistant to the Secretary, Department of Agriculture, during the Clinton Administration. Also served as Trade Policy and Marketing Specialist, Foreign Agricultural Service, Department of Agriculture.

Employers
DTB Associates, LLP (Partner)
Powell, Goldstein, Frazer & Murphy LLP (Senior Policy Advisor)

Clients Represented

On Behalf of Powell, Goldstein, Frazer & Murphy LLP
Monsanto Co.

DREHER, Robert

401 Ninth St. NW
Suite 1000
Washington, DC 20004
Tel: (202)274-2851
Fax: (202)274-2994
Deputy General Counsel, Environmental Protection Agency, 1996-2000.

Employers
Troutman Sanders LLP (Of Counsel)

DRELLOW, Pam

1310 G St. NW
12th Floor
Washington, DC 20005
Tel: (202)626-4780
Fax: (202)626-4833

Employers
Blue Cross Blue Shield Ass'n (Managing Director, Public Affairs)

DRESSENDORFER, John

400 Virginia Ave. SW
Suite C-150
Washington, DC 20024
Tel: (202)488-9740
Ext: 108
Registered: LDA

Employers
Titan Corp. (V. President, Government Relations)

DREWRY, James S. W.

600 New Hampshire Ave. NW
11th Floor
Washington, DC 20037
Tel: (202)944-3000
Fax: (202)944-3068
Registered: LDA, FARA
EMail: jsd@dejlaw.com
Democratic General Counsel, Senate Commerce Committee, 1994-99. Legislative Counsel, Senate Commerce Committee, 1987-1994. Senior Democratic Counsel for Oceans and Atmosphere, Senate Commerce Committee, 1980-1987. Served in the Nat'l Oceanic and Atmospheric Administration, Department of Commerce, 1975-80.

Employers
Dyer Ellis & Joseph, P.C. (Partner)

Clients Represented

On Behalf of Dyer Ellis & Joseph, P.C.
Bender Shipbuilding & Repair Co., Inc.
BLNG, Inc.
China Shipping (Group) Co.
John Crane-LIPS, Inc.
Cross Sound Ferry Services, Inc.
FastShip, Inc.
Friede Goldman Halter
Fruit Shippers Ltd.
Heerema Marine Contractors Nederland B.V.
Hornblower Marine Services, Inc.
Hvide Marine Inc.
Northrop Grumman Corp.
Offshore Rig Museum, Inc.
Put-in-Bay Boat Line Co.
Sea Ventures Inc.
TransAtlantic Lines - Iceland ehf
Wendella Sightseeing Boats Inc.

DRIESLER, Marty

1390 Chain Bridge Rd.
Suite 47
McLean, VA 22102
Tel: (703)448-6989
Fax: (703)448-3323
EMail: Marty54@erols.com
Chief of Staff to Rep. Harold Rogers (R-KY), 1981-92.

Employers
Issues Management Ass'n (V. President)

DRIESLER, Stephen D.

1390 Chain Bridge Rd.
Suite 47
McLean, VA 22102
Tel: (703)448-6989
Fax: (703)448-3323
Registered: LDA
EMail: Sdries@erols.com
Chief of Staff to Rep. Larry J. Hopkins (R-KY), 1979-82.

Employers
Issues Management Ass'n (President)

DRIESSEN, J. Kenneth

10560 Arrowhead Dr.
Fairfax, VA 22030
Tel: (703)385-0700
Fax: (703)385-4637

Employers
MRJ Technology Solutions (Chief Exec. Officer)

DRIGGERS, W. B.

9616 Burke View Ave.
Burke, VA 22015
Tel: (703)250-1852
Fax: (703)250-1857
Registered: LDA
EMail: wbdassoc1@aol.com
Retired Colonel, Department of the Air Force.

Employers
W. B. Driggers & Associates, Inc. (President)

Clients Represented
On Behalf of W. B. Driggers & Associates, Inc.
A. D. Butler and Associates, Inc.
Karta Technologies Inc.
Madison Government Affairs
Photo Telesis
Raytheon Co.
SAVI Technology

DRIGGS, Kathi

1733 King St.
Alexandria, VA 22314
Tel: (703)739-9500
Fax: (703)739-0124
EMail: driggsk@cmaa.org

Employers
Club Managers Ass'n of America (V. President)

DRINAN, Helen

1800 Duke St.
Alexandria, VA 22314
Tel: (703)548-3440
Fax: (703)836-0367

Employers
Soc. for Human Resource Management (President and Chief Exec. Officer)

DRISCOLL, Kevin J.

740 15th St. NW
Ninth Floor
Washington, DC 20005
Tel: (202)662-1766
Fax: (202)662-1762
Registered: LDA

Employers
American Bar Ass'n (Senior Legislative Counsel)

DRISCOLL, Timothy

815 15th St. NW
Washington, DC 20005
Tel: (202)783-3788
Fax: (202)393-0219
Registered: LDA

Employers
Internat'l Union of Bricklayers and Allied Craftsworkers (Program Assistant, Government Relations)

DRIVER, Bryan

P.O. Box 44808
Washington, DC 20026-4808
Tel: (202)927-7000
Fax: (202)927-5192

Employers
Senior Executives Ass'n (Director, Communications)

DRIVER, Michael J.

2550 M St. NW
Washington, DC 20037-1350
Tel: (202)457-6000
Fax: (202)457-6315
Registered: LDA
EMail: mdriver@pattonboggs.com

Employers
Patton Boggs, LLP (Partner)

Clients Represented
On Behalf of Patton Boggs, LLP
Austin, Texas, City of
BNFL, Inc.
Broe Companies, Inc.
Greenwood Village, Colorado, City of
Save Barton Creek
Wam!Net
Westinghouse

DROGOSZ, Kayla

1700 K St. NW
Suite 1150
Washington, DC 20006
EMail: kayla.drogosz@ujc.org
Tel: (202)736-5882
Fax: (202)785-4937

Employers
United Jewish Communities, Inc. (Public Affairs Associate)

DROHAN, CAE, William M.

11250 Roger Bacon Dr.
Suite Eight
Reston, VA 20190
EMail: dmg@drohanmgmt.com
Tel: (703)437-4377
Fax: (703)435-4390

Employers
Drohan Management Group (President)
Sports Lawyers Ass'n (Exec. Director)

Clients Represented
On Behalf of Drohan Management Group
Sports Lawyers Ass'n

DROZEN, Mel S.

1001 G St. NW
Suite 500 West
Washington, DC 20001
EMail: drozen@khlaw.com
Tel: (202)434-4100
Fax: (202)434-4646

Employers
Keller and Heckman LLP (Partner)

Clients Represented
On Behalf of Keller and Heckman LLP
Produce Marketing Ass'n

DRUMMER, Robert G.

1611 Duke St.
Alexandria, VA 22314
Tel: (703)683-7410
Fax: (703)683-7527
Registered: LDA

Employers
American Moving and Storage Ass'n (V. President, Government Affairs and General Counsel)

DRUMTRA, Jeff

1717 Massachusetts Ave. NW
Suite 200
Washington, DC 20036
Tel: (202)347-3507
Fax: (202)347-3418
Registered: LDA
EMail: jeff.drutra@irsa-uscr.org

Employers
United States Committee for Refugees (Africa Policy Analyst)

DRY, Lisa J.

1625 K St. NW
Suite 1100
Washington, DC 20006-1604
EMail: ldry@bio.org
Tel: (202)857-0244
Fax: (202)857-0237

Employers
Biotechnology Industry Organization (Director, Communication)

DU MELLE, Fran

1726 M St. NW
Suite 902
Washington, DC 20036
Tel: (202)785-3355
Fax: (202)452-1805
Registered: LDA

Employers
American Thoracic Soc. (Exec. V. President)

DU PONT, Hon. Pete

655 15th St. NW Suite 375
Washington, DC 20005
Tel: (202)628-6671
Fax: (202)628-6474

Employers
Nat'l Center for Policy Analysis (Policy Chairman)

DUBECK, John B.

1001 G St. NW
Suite 500 West
Washington, DC 20001
EMail: dubeck@khlaw.com
Tel: (202)434-4100
Fax: (202)434-4646

Employers
Keller and Heckman LLP (Partner)

DUBENSKY, Mitch

1111 19th St. NW
Suite 800
Washington, DC 20036
Tel: (202)463-2700
Fax: (202)463-2785
Registered: LDA
EMail: mitch_dubensky@afandpa.org

Employers
American Forest & Paper Ass'n (Director, Forest and Wetlands)

DUBERSTEIN, Kenneth M.

2100 Pennsylvania Ave. NW
Suite 500
Washington, DC 20037
Tel: (202)728-1100
Fax: (202)728-1123
Registered: LDA
Deputy Chief and Chief of Staff (1987-89), Assistant to the President for Legislative Affairs (1981-83) and Deputy Assistant to the President for Legislative Affairs (1981), The White House. Deputy Under Secretary, Department of Labor, 1976-77. Director, Congressional and Intergovernmental Affairs, General Services Administration, 1972-76. Research Assistant to Senator Jacob Javits (R-NY), 1965-67.

Employers
The Duberstein Group, Inc. (Chairman and Chief Exec. Officer)

Clients Represented
On Behalf of The Duberstein Group, Inc.
Amerada Hess Corp.
American Apparel & Footwear Ass'n
American Ass'n of Health Plans (AAHP)
American Council of Life Insurers
American Gaming Ass'n
The American Water Works Co.
AOL Time Warner
The Business Roundtable
Comcast Corp.
Conoco Inc.
CSX Corp.
Direct Marketing Ass'n, Inc.
Dow Corning Corp.
Fannie Mae
General Motors Corp.
Goldman, Sachs and Co.
Marathon Oil Co.
Nat'l Cable Television Ass'n
Pharmacia Corp.
Project to Promote Competition and Innovation in the Digital Age
Sara Lee Corp.
Transportation Institute
United Airlines
USX Corp.

DUBOFF, Scott M.

1200 G St. NW
Suite 600
Washington, DC 20005-3802
Tel: (202)393-1200
Fax: (202)393-1240
Registered: LDA
EMail: duboff@wrightlaw.com
Attorney, Office of the Solicitor (1975-77) and Attorney, Office of the General Counsel (1973-75), Federal Power Commission.

Employers
Wright & Talisman, P.C.

Clients Represented
On Behalf of Wright & Talisman, P.C.
Atlantic County Utilities Authority
Bristol Resource Recovery Facility Operating Committee
Delaware, Pennsylvania, Solid Waste Authority of the County of
Greater Detroit Resource Recovery Authority
Housatonic Resources Recovery Authority
Huntsville, Alabama, Solid Waste Disposal Authority of the City of
Indianapolis, Indiana, City of
Marion County Solid Waste Management
Montgomery County, Ohio/Montgomery County Solid Waste District
Ohio Prosecuting Attorneys Ass'n
Portland Metro Regional Government
Solid Waste Authority of Central Ohio
Spokane Regional Solid Waste System
Sumner, Tennessee, Resource Authority of the County of
York County Solid Waste Authority

DUBOIS, Marcel

316 Pennsylvania Ave. SE
Suite 300
Washington, DC 20003
Tel: (202)675-4237
Fax: (202)675-4230
Registered: LDA

Employers
United Parcel Service (Manager, Public Affairs)

DUBOIS, Jr., Raymond F.

1717 Pennsylvania Ave. NW
12th Floor
Washington, DC 20006
EMail: raydubois@aol.com
Tel: (202)416-0150
Registered: LDA

Deputy Under Secretary, Department of the Army, 1976-77. Staff Assistant to the Secretary, Department of Defense, 1973-75. Research Assistant to Senator Charles H. Percy (R-IL), 1967.

Employers
Potomac Strategies Internat'l LLC (President)

Clients Represented
On Behalf of Potomac Strategies Internat'l LLC
Ass'n of the United States Army
Command Systems Inc.
GEO Centers, Inc.
Member-Link Systems, Inc.
memorize.com
Orbital Sciences Corp., Fairchild Defense Division
Spacelabs Medical Inc.

DUBUC, Carroll E.

2200 Wilson Blvd.
Suite 800
Arlington, VA 22201
Tel: (703)525-2260
Fax: (703)525-2489

Employers
Cohen, Gettings & Dunham, PC (Of Counsel)

Clients Represented
On Behalf of Cohen, Gettings & Dunham, PC
Air China Internat'l Corp., Ltd.
China Eastern Airlines

DUCHENEAUX, Franklin D.

303 Massachusetts Ave. NE
Washington, DC 20002
Tel: (202)544-1353
Fax: (202)544-0620
Registered: LDA
EMail: dtanet@aol.com

Former Special Counsel, House of Representatives Interior and Insular Affairs Committee.

Employers
Ducheneaux, Taylor & Associates, Inc. (Partner)

Clients Represented
On Behalf of Ducheneaux, Taylor & Associates, Inc.
The Ashley Group
Grand Traverse Band of Chippewa and Ottawa Indians
Leech Lake Tribal Council
Minnesota Indian Gaming Ass'n
Siletz Tribal Council
Tohono O'Odham Nation
Tulalip Tribes

DUCHENSE, Steve

1501 M St. NW
Suite 600
Washington, DC 20005-1710
EMail: sduchens@bsmg.com
Tel: (202)739-0200
Fax: (202)659-8287

Employers
BSMG Worldwide (Managing Director)

DUCICH, Sarah E.

901 E St. NW
Fourth Floor
Washington, DC 20004
EMail: sarah.ducich@slma.com
Tel: (202)969-8020
Fax: (202)969-8031

Employers
Sallie Mae, Inc. (Director, Government and Industry Relations)

DUCKENFIELD, Pace

1140 Connecticut Ave. NW
Suite 1140
Washington, DC 20036
EMail: pduckenf@utc.org
Tel: (202)872-0030
Fax: (202)872-1331
Registered: LDA

Employers
United Telecom Council (Associate Counsel)

DUDDY, Marianne T.

1500 Massachusetts Ave. NW
Suite 11
Washington, DC 20005
EMail: mtduddy@aol.com
Tel: (202)861-0017
Fax: (202)429-9808

Employers
Dignity/USA (Exec. Director)

DUDLEY, Jane

1025 Connecticut Ave. NW
Suite 400
Washington, DC 20036
Tel: (202)659-6800
Fax: (202)331-0573
Registered: LDA

Employers
Whiteford, Taylor & Preston (Director, Governmental Affairs)

DUDLEY, Stephanie D.

8630 Fenton St.
Suite 722
Silver Spring, MD 20910
EMail: stephanie@popassoc.org
Tel: (301)565-6710
Fax: (301)565-7850

Employers
Population Ass'n of America (Exec. Director)

DUDZINSKY, Jr., William S.

1200 New Hampshire Ave. NW
Suite 800
Washington, DC 20036-6802
EMail: wdudzinsky@dlalaw.com
Tel: (202)776-2000
Fax: (202)776-2222

Employers
Dow, Lohnes & Albertson, PLLC (Member)

DUERR, Douglas

1655 N. Fort Myer Dr.
Suite 300
Arlington, VA 22209
Tel: (703)528-8351
Fax: (703)528-3248
Registered: LDA

Employers
Credit Union Council of the Nat'l Ass'n of State Credit Union Supervisors (President and Chief Exec. Officer)
Nat'l Ass'n of State Credit Union Supervisors (President and Chief Exec. Officer)
Nat'l Institute for State Credit Union Examination (Chief Exec. Officer)

DUESTERBERG, Thomas J.

1525 Wilson Blvd.
Suite 900
Arlington, VA 22209
EMail: tduesterberg@mapi.net
Tel: (703)841-9000
Fax: (703)841-9514

Former Chief of Staff to Rep. Christopher Cox (R-CA); Assistant Secretary for International Economic Policy, Department of Commerce; Chief of Staff to Senator Dan Quayle (R-IN).

Employers
Manufacturers Alliance/MAPI Inc. (President and Chief Exec. Officer)

DUFF, Daniel

1666 K St. NW
Washington, DC 20006
Tel: (202)296-4700
Fax: (202)496-4324
Registered: LDA
EMail: dduff@apta.com

Employers
American Public Transportation Ass'n (Chief Counsel and V. President, Government Affairs)

DUFF, Diane C.

1920 N St. NW
Suite 800
Washington, DC 20036
Tel: (202)216-9270
Fax: (202)216-9662
Registered: LDA
EMail: diane@railcompetition.org

Employers
Alliance for Rail Competition (Exec. Director)

DUFF, James C.

801 Pennsylvania Ave. NW
Suite 800
Washington, DC 20004
Tel: (202)508-3400
Fax: (202)508-3402

Administrative Assistant to Chief Justice William H. Rehnquist and Chief of Staff, U.S. Supreme Court, 1996-2000. Legislative Staff to Senator Robert Taft, Jr. (R-OH), 1975.

Employers
Baker, Donelson, Bearman & Caldwell, P.C.

DUFF, Michael J.

225 Reinekers Ln.
Suite 625
Alexandria, VA 22314-2875
EMail: mduff@alssa.org
Tel: (703)836-1360
Fax: (703)836-6644
Registered: LDA

Staff Member, Subcommittee on Investigations, House Interstate and Foreign Commerce Committee, 1971.

Employers
Analytical and Life Science Systems Ass'n (Exec. Director)
SAMA Group of Ass'ns (Exec. Director, Analytical & Life Science Systems Ass'n)

DUFFIELD, Barbara

1012 14th St. NW
Suite 600
Washington, DC 20005-3471
EMail: info@nationalhomeless.org
Tel: (202)737-6444
Fax: (202)737-6445

Employers
Nat'l Coalition for the Homeless (Director, Education)

DUFFY, John J.

1330 Connecticut Ave. NW
Washington, DC 20036-1795
Tel: (202)429-3000
Fax: (202)429-3902
Registered: LDA
EMail: jduffy@steptoe.com

Counselor to the Secretary, Department of the Interior, 1993-96.

Employers
Steptoe & Johnson LLP (Of Counsel)

Clients Represented
On Behalf of Steptoe & Johnson LLP
Agua Caliente Band of Cahuilla Indians
Mashpee Wampanoag Indian Tribal Council, Inc.
TAPS Renewal Task Force

DUFFY, Michael F.

1130 17th St. NW
Washington, DC 20036-4677
Tel: (202)463-2612
Fax: (202)463-3257
Registered: LDA
EMail: mduffy@nma.org

Employers
Nat'l Mining Ass'n (Deputy General Counsel)

DUFFY, Richard M.

1750 New York Ave. NW
Washington, DC 20006
Tel: (202)737-8484
Fax: (202)737-8418
Registered: LDA

Employers
Internat'l Ass'n of Fire Fighters (Assistant to the General President, Occupational Safety & Health)

DUFFY, Stephen C.

310 S. Henry St.
Alexandria, VA 22314
Tel: (703)299-9291
Fax: (703)299-8898

Employers
American Academy of Facial Plastic and Reconstructive Surgery (Exec. V. President)

DUGAN, Alicia A.

25461 Carberry Dr.
South Riding, VA 20152
Tel: (703)327-0598
Fax: (703)327-9477
Registered: LDA

Employers
ADA Consulting Services (President)

Clients Represented
On Behalf of ADA Consulting Services
Air Quality Standards Coalition
Superfund Action Alliance

DUGAN, John C.

1201 Pennsylvania Ave. NW
Washington, DC 20004-2401
Tel: (202)662-6000
Fax: (202)662-6291
Registered: LDA
EMail: jdugan@cov.com

Assistant Secretary for Domestic Finance (1992-93) and Deputy Assistant Secretary, Financial Institutions Policy (1989-92), Department of Treasury. Minority General Counsel (1987-89) and Staff Counsel (1985-87), Committee on Banking, Housing and Urban Affairs, U.S. Senate.

Employers
Covington & Burling (Partner)

Clients Represented

On Behalf of Covington & Burling
American Bankers Ass'n
Brown Brothers Harriman & Co.
Mountain West Savings Bank, F.S.B.
Real Estate Roundtable
Synovus Financial Corp.

DUGAN, Jr., Dr. John V.

1730 M St. NW
Suite 911
Washington, DC 20036
Tel: (202)293-6116
Fax: (202)293-7444
Registered: LDA
EMail: jackdugan@earthlink.net

Employers
Self-employed as an independent consultant.

Clients Represented

As an independent consultant
American Institute of Chemical Engineers
Battelle

DUGAN, Tom

1010 Massachusetts Ave. NW
Suite 210
Washington, DC 20001
Tel: (202)371-1153
Fax: (202)371-1032

Employers
George Waters Consulting Service (Staff Attorney)

DUGAS, Denise L.

1090 Vermont Ave. NW
Suite 1100
Washington, DC 20005-4961
Tel: (202)789-3500
Fax: (202)789-6391

Employers
Joint Center for Political and Economic Studies (V. President, Communications & Marketing)

DUGGAN, Brian

1225 New York Ave. NW
Suite 300
Washington, DC 20005
Tel: (202)393-6362
Fax: (202)737-3742
Registered: LDA

Employers
Motor and Equipment Manufacturers Ass'n (Director, Internat'l Programs)

DUGGAN, Joseph P.

410 First St. SE
Third Floor
Washington, DC 20003
Tel: (202)484-2776
Fax: (202)484-7016
Registered: LDA
EMail: jduggan@dcsgroup.com
Communication and Policy Director, Commerce Committee, U.S. Senate, 1994-95. Budget and Economics Advisor to Rep. Christopher Cox (R-CA), 1993-94. Speech writer to the President, Exec. Office of the President, The White House, 1991-92. Various positions in the Department of State, 1986-91 and 1981-85.

Employers
The DCS Group (Senior V. President)

DUGGAN, Juanita D.

805 15th St. NW
Suite 430
Washington, DC 20005
Tel: (202)371-9792
Fax: (202)789-2405
Registered: LDA
EMail: juanita.duggan@wswa.org

Employers
Wine and Spirits Wholesalers of America (Chief Exec. Officer and Exec. V. President)

DUGGINS, George C.

8605 Cameron St.
Suite 400
Silver Spring, MD 20910
Tel: (301)585-4000
Fax: (301)585-0519

Employers
Vietnam Veterans of America, Inc. (President)

DUJACK, Steve

1616 P St. NW
Suite 200
Washington, DC 20036
Tel: (202)939-3800
Fax: (202)939-3868

Employers
Environmental Law Institute (Director, Communications)

DUKE, Emily

1001 Connecticut Ave. NW
Suite 1250
Washington, DC 20036
Tel: (202)331-1010
Fax: (202)331-0640

Employers
Competitive Enterprise Institute (Director of Development)

DUKE, Robert J.

1101 Connecticut Ave. NW
Suite 800
Washington, DC 20036
Tel: (202)463-0600
Fax: (202)463-0606

Employers
Surety Ass'n of America (Director, Underwriting)

DULK-JACOBS, Valerie

1625 K St. NW
Suite 210
Washington, DC 20006
Tel: (202)785-5980
Fax: (202)785-5969
Registered: LDA
EMail: adaction@ix.netcom.com

Employers
Americans for Democratic Action (Special Assistant to the Director)

DUMOULIN, John

2011 Pennsylvania Ave. NW
Suite 800
Washington, DC 20006-1808
Tel: (202)261-4535
Fax: (202)835-0443
Registered: LDA
EMail: jdumoulin@mail.acponline.org

Employers
American College of Physicians-American Soc. of Internal Medicine (ACP-ASIM) (Director, Managed Care and Regulatory Affairs)

DUNAWAY, Mac S.

1700 K St. NW
Suite 800
Washington, DC 20006
Tel: (202)862-9700
Fax: (202)862-9710
Registered: LDA
EMail: duncross@msn.com

Employers
Dunaway & Cross (Managing Partner)

Clients Represented

On Behalf of Dunaway & Cross
Aerospace Industries Ass'n of America
American Electric Power Co.
Crown Controls Corp.
Goodman Manufacturing Co., L.P.
Industrial Truck Ass'n
Portable Power Equipment Manufacturers Ass'n
The Toro Co.

DUNCAN, Andy

1700 Diagonal Rd.
Suite 300
Alexandria, VA 22314
Tel: (703)837-1500
Fax: (703)525-5762
Registered: LDA

Employers
Nat'l Hospice & Palliative Care Organization (Manager, Government Relations)

DUNCAN, Bonnie

Three Bethesda Metro Center
Suite 1100
Bethesda, MD 20814
EMail: bnd@necanet.org
Tel: (301)657-3110
Fax: (301)215-4500

Employers
Nat'l Electrical Contractors Ass'n (Director, Communications)

DUNCAN, Charles

2121 K St. NW
Suite 650
Washington, DC 20037
Tel: (202)296-2400
Fax: (202)296-2409
Registered: LDA

Employers
Global USA, Inc.

Clients Represented

On Behalf of Global USA, Inc.
DRC, Inc.

DUNCAN, Don R.

1776 I St. NW
Suite 700
Washington, DC 20006
Tel: (202)833-0907
Fax: (202)785-0639
Registered: LDA

Employers
Phillips Petroleum Co. (Manager, Federal Relations)

DUNCAN, Donald K.

1801 K St. NW
Suite 600K
Washington, DC 20006
Tel: (202)974-5200
Fax: (202)296-7005

Employers
Soc. of the Plastics Industry (President)

DUNCAN, Duane S.

3900 Wisconsin Ave. NW
Washington, DC 20016
Tel: (202)752-7000
Fax: (202)752-6099
Registered: LDA

Employers
Fannie Mae (V. President, Government and Industry Relations)

DUNCAN, Harley T.

444 N. Capitol St. NW
Suite 348
Washington, DC 20001
EMail: duncan.fta@taxx.geis.com
Tel: (202)624-5890
Fax: (202)624-7888

Employers
Federation of Tax Administrators (Exec. Director)

DUNCAN, Jacci

1595 Spring Hill Road
Suite 330, Tysons Corner
Vienna, VA 22182
Tel: (703)506-3290
Fax: (703)506-3266

Employers
American Women in Radio and Television (Exec. Director)
Ass'n Management Bureau

DUNCAN, Jack G.

1213 29th St. NW
Washington, DC 20007
Tel: (202)333-5841
Fax: (202)333-5881
Counsel and Staff Director, House Subcommittee on Select Education, 1969-79; Legislative Assistant, Social and Rehabilitative Service, Dept. of Health, Education and Welfare, 1968-69; Chief Legislative Officer, Rehabilitation Services Administration, HEW, 1967-68; Attorney, Foreign Claims Settlement Commission, Department of State, 1964-67.

Employers
Ass'n of Independent Colleges of Art and Design (Legislative Counsel)
Duncan and Associates (President)
Nat'l Rehabilitation Political Action Committee (Treasurer)

Clients Represented

On Behalf of Duncan and Associates
American Citizens for the Arts Political Action Committee
American Network of Community Options and Resources (ANCOR)
American Rehab Action
Ass'n of Independent Colleges of Art and Design
Conference of Educational Administrators of Schools and Programs for the Deaf
Convention of American Instructors of the Deaf
Council of State Administrators of Vocational Rehabilitation
Nat'l Council of State Agencies for the Blind
Nat'l Council on Rehabilitation Education
Nat'l Rehabilitation Political Action Committee

DUNCAN, Janell Mayo

1666 Connecticut Ave. NW
Suite 310
Washington, DC 20009
Tel: (202)462-6262
Fax: (202)265-9548
Registered: LDA
EMail: duncja@consumer.org

Employers
Consumers Union of the United States (Legislative Counsel)

DUNCAN, John M.

1500 Pennsylvania Ave. NW
Room 3025MT
Washington, DC 20220
Tel: (202)622-1900
Fax: (202)622-0534

Employers
Department of Treasury (Assistant Secretary, Office of Legislative Affairs)

DUNCAN, Josh

80 F St. NW
Suite 804
Washington, DC 20001
Tel: (202)347-3042
Fax: (202)347-3046

Employers
Fraioli/Siggins

DUNCAN, III, Lawrence

901 15th St. NW
Suite 700
Washington, DC 20005-2301
Tel: (202)371-6000
Fax: (202)371-6279
Registered: LDA
EMail: lduncan@verner.com

Employers
Verner, Liipfert, Bernhard, McPherson and Hand, Chartered (Associate)

Clients Represented

On Behalf of Verner, Liipfert, Bernhard, McPherson and Hand, Chartered
The Walt Disney Co.

DUNCAN, Mallory B.

325 Seventh St. NW
Suite 1100
Washington, DC 20004-2802
Tel: (202)783-7971
Fax: (202)737-2849
Registered: LDA

Employers
Nat'l Retail Federation (V. President and General Counsel)

DUNCAN, Molly

801 Pennsylvania Ave. NW
Suite 720
Washington, DC 20004-2604
Tel: (202)393-3400
Fax: (202)393-4606
Registered: LDA

Employers
The Procter & Gamble Company (Legislative Assistant)

DUNCAN, Monica

1825 I St. NW
Suite 400
Washington, DC 20006
Tel: (202)408-7052
Fax: (202)682-3084
Registered: FARA

Employers
Ross-Robinson & Associates (Legislative Assistant)

Clients Represented

On Behalf of Ross-Robinson & Associates
Caribbean Banana Exporters Ass'n
Haiti, Office of the President of the Republic of

DUNCAN, Wallace L.

1615 M St. NW
Suite 800
Washington, DC 20036-3203
Tel: (202)467-6370
Fax: (202)467-6379
EMail: wld@dwgp.com
Special Assistant to the Solicitor, Department of the Interior, 1962-1965.

Employers
Duncan, Weinberg, Genzer & Pembroke, P.C. (President)

Clients Represented

On Behalf of Duncan, Weinberg, Genzer & Pembroke, P.C.
College Station, Texas, City of
M-S-R Public Power Agency
Massena, New York, Town of
The Metropolitan Water District of Southern California
Modesto/Turlock Irrigation District
Municipal Electric Utilities Ass'n of New York State
Orlando Utilities Commission
Palo Alto, California, City of
Redding, California, Electric Department of the City of
Santa Clara, California, Electric Department of the City of
Southern California Public Power Authority
Transmission Agency of Northern California

DUNCAN, Will

P.O. Box 66268
Washington, DC 20035-6268
Tel: (202)429-1203
Fax: (202)429-1102

Employers
Coalition of Black Trade Unionists (Special Assistant)

DUNCAN, William C.

1050 17th St. NW
Suite 410
Washington, DC 20036
Tel: (202)296-8537
Fax: (202)872-1212
Registered: LDA

Employers
Japan Automobile Manufacturers Ass'n (General Director, Washington Office)

DUNGAN, Arthur E.

2001 L St. NW
Suite 506
Washington, DC 20036-4919
Tel: (202)775-2790
Fax: (202)223-7225

Employers
Chlorine Institute (V. Pres., Safety, Health & Environment)

DUNGY, Gwendolyn J.

1875 Connecticut Ave. NW
Suite 418
Washington, DC 20009-5728
Tel: (202)265-7500
Fax: (202)797-1157

Employers
Nat'l Ass'n of Student Personnel Administrators (Exec. Director)

DUNHAM, D.V.M., Bernadette M.

1101 Vermont Ave. NW
Suite 710
Washington, DC 20005-3521
Tel: (202)789-0007
Fax: (202)842-4360
Registered: LDA

Employers
American Veterinary Medical Ass'n (Assistant Director, Government Relations)

DUNHAM, J. Mark

133 H. St. NW
Suite 600
Washington, DC 20005
Tel: (202)737-2670
Fax: (202)347-4285
EMail: jdunham@nationalhealthmuseum.org

Employers
Nat'l Health Museum (Acting Director)

DUNKEL, Bob

1401 H St. NW
Suite 600
Washington, DC 20005-2136
Tel: (202)326-7300
Fax: (202)326-7333
Registered: LDA

Employers
United States Telecom Ass'n (Director, Government Relations)

DUNKELBERGER, Jr., H. Edward

1201 Pennsylvania Ave. NW
Washington, DC 20004-2401
Tel: (202)662-6000
Fax: (202)662-6291
Registered: LDA
EMail: hdunkelberger@cov.com

Employers
Covington & Burling (Partner)

Clients Represented

On Behalf of Covington & Burling
Internat'l Dairy Foods Ass'n
Milk Industry Foundation

DUNLAP, David D.

1300 N. 17th St.
Suite 750
Arlington, VA 22209
Tel: (703)247-2600
Fax: (703)841-4750
Registered: LDA
EMail: dunlap@utsa.com

Employers
Uniform and Textile Service Ass'n (Director, Environmental and Regulatory Affairs)

DUNLAP, Louise C.

418 Tenth St. SE
Washington, DC 20003
Tel: (202)546-3720
Fax: (202)546-5557
Registered: LDA
EMail: dandb@intr.net

Employers
Dunlap & Browder, Inc. (Partner)

Clients Represented

On Behalf of Dunlap & Browder, Inc.
ARCADIS/California Energy Commission
Bones Brothers Ranch
Clean Air Campaign
United Cement Corp.

DUNLOP, Becky Norton

214 Massachusetts Ave. NE
Washington, DC 20002
Tel: (202)546-4400
Fax: (202)546-8328

Employers
Heritage Foundation (V. President, External Affairs)

DUNLOP, George S.

2816 S. Joyce St.
Arlington, VA 22202
Tel: (703)684-7228
Fax: (703)684-2981
Registered: LDA
Administrative Aide to Senator Jesse Helms (R-NC), 1995 and 1973-79. Staff Director, Senate Committee on Agriculture, Nutrition and Forestry, 1979-86. Assistant Secretary, Natural Resources and Environment, Department of Agriculture, 1986-89. Rifleman, United States Marine Corps, 1966-68.

Employers
Century Communications, Inc. (V. President)

Clients Represented

On Behalf of Century Communications, Inc.
Citizens Network for Foreign Affairs (CNFA)

DUNLOP, Susan

815 16th St. NW
Washington, DC 20006
Tel: (202)637-5316
Fax: (202)637-5058
EMail: 70521,25@compuserve.com

Employers
AFL-CIO (American Federation of Labor and Congress of Industrial Organizations) (Assistant to the Exec. V. President)

DUNN, Alan M.

2100 M St. NW
Suite 200
Washington, DC 20037
Tel: (202)785-4185
Fax: (202)466-1286
Registered: LDA
EMail: adunn@stewartlaw.com

Employers
Stewart and Stewart (Partner)

Clients Represented

On Behalf of Stewart and Stewart
Dierman, Wortley, and Zola
Libbey, Inc.
PPG Industries
Ranchers-Cattlemen Legal Action Fund
The Timken Co.
Torrington Co.

DUNN, Aura Kenny

110 S. Union St.
Suite 250
Alexandria, VA 22314
Tel: (703)548-1975 Ext: 14
Fax: (703)548-0726
Registered: LDA
EMail: adunn@convg.com
Professional Staff Member, Senate Committee on Appropriations, Subcommittee on Labor, Health and Human Services 1999-2000. Legislative Assistant to Senator Arlen Specter (R-PA), 1997-98. Legislative Assistant to Rep. Jack Quinn (R-NY), 1995-97.

Employers
Convergence Services, Inc. (Director, Federal Policy)

DUNN, Christopher A.

Three Lafayette Center
1155 21st St. NW
Washington, DC 20036-3384
Tel: (202)328-8000
Fax: (202)887-8979
Law Clerk to Chief Judge Wilson Cowen, U.S. Court of Appeals, Federal Circuit, 1976-77, and for the Trial Division, U.S. Court of Claims, 1975-76.

Employers
Willkie Farr & Gallagher (Partner)

Clients Represented
On Behalf of Willkie Farr & Gallagher
Branco Peres Citrus, S.A.
Continuous Color Coat, Ltd.
Sony Corp. of America

DUNN, III, David E.
2550 M St. NW
Washington, DC 20037-1350
Tel: (202)457-6000
Fax: (202)457-6315
Registered: LDA, FARA
EMail: ddunn@pattonboggs.com

Employers
Patton Boggs, LLP (Partner)

Clients Represented
On Behalf of Patton Boggs, LLP
Mars, Inc.
Qatar, Government of the State of

DUNN, Jr., H. Stewart
1700 Pennsylvania Ave. NW
Suite 600
Washington, DC 20006
Tel: (202)393-7600
Fax: (202)393-7601
Registered: LDA

Employers
Ivins, Phillips & Barker (Partner)

DUNN, Jean B.
1717 Massachusetts Ave. NW
Suite 503
Washington, DC 20036
Tel: (202)328-3136
Fax: (202)939-3166

Employers
Nat'l Democratic Institute for Internat'l Affairs (V. President)

DUNN, Jeffrey A.
1201 New York Ave. NW
Suite 1000
Washington, DC 20005
EMail: jadunn@venable.com
Tel: (202)962-4870
Fax: (202)962-8300

Employers
Venable (Partner)

DUNN, Loretta L.
1200 Wilson Blvd.
Arlington, VA 22209-1989
Tel: (703)465-3282
Fax: (703)465-3341
Registered: LDA

Employers
The Boeing Co.

DUNN, Mari Lee
1750 K St. NW
Suite 400
Washington, DC 20006-2300
EMail: dunnml@aol.com
Tel: (202)293-5811
Fax: (202)785-8165
Registered: LDA

Employers
American Council for Capital Formation (Senior V. President)

DUNN, Mary Mitchell
805 15th St. NW
Suite 300
Washington, DC 20005-2207
Tel: (202)682-4200
Fax: (202)682-9054
Registered: LDA

Employers
Credit Union Nat'l Ass'n, Inc. (Senior V. President and Associate General Counsel, Regulatory Advocacy)

DUNN, Dr. Michael
1761 N St. NW
Washington, DC 20036-2882
EMail: editor@mideasti.org
Tel: (202)785-1141
Fax: (202)331-8861

Employers
Middle East Institute (Editor, Middle East Journal)

DUNNE, Joanne E.
1710 Rhode Island Ave. NW
Suite 800
Washington, DC 20036
Tel: (202)457-1115
Fax: (202)457-9191
Registered: LDA

Employers
American Physical Therapy Ass'n (Exec. Director, Private Practice Section)
Private Practice Section of the American Physical Therapy Ass'n (Exec. Director)

DUNNE, Capt. Patrick W.
The Pentagon
MS: 5C760
Washington, DC 20350-1300
EMail: dunne.patrick@hq.navy.mil
Tel: (703)697-7146
Fax: (703)614-7089

Employers
Department of Navy (Deputy Chief, Legislative Affairs)

DUNNE, Steven M.
2445 M St. NW
Washington, DC 20037-1420
Tel: (202)663-6000
Fax: (202)663-6363
Registered: FARA

Employers
Wilmer, Cutler & Pickering (Associate)

DUNNING, Margaret Suzor
1825 Connecticut Ave. NW
Fifth Floor
Washington, DC 20009
EMail: margaret.dunning@widmeyer.com
Tel: (202)667-0901
Fax: (202)667-0902

Employers
Widmeyer Communications, Inc. (Senior V. President/Group Director)

DUNPHY, David
1775 K St. NW
Washington, DC 20006
Tel: (202)223-3111
Fax: (202)466-1562

Employers
United Food and Commercial Workers Internat'l Union (Assistant to the Director, Legislative and Political Affairs)

DUNST, Isabel P.
555 13th St. NW
Washington, DC 20004-1109
EMail: ipdunst@hhlaw.com
Tel: (202)637-5818
Fax: (202)637-5910
Registered: LDA

Deputy General Counsel (1987-90), Associate General Counsel (1979-87), and Staff Attorney, Public Health Division, Office of the General Counsel (1971-79), Department of Health and Human Services.

Employers
Hogan & Hartson L.L.P. (Partner)

Clients Represented
On Behalf of Hogan & Hartson L.L.P.
UPMC Presbyterian

DUNTON, Holly S.
601 Pennsylvania Ave. NW
Suite 540
North Bldg.
Washington, DC 20004
EMail: hsdunton@ashland.com
Tel: (202)223-8290
Fax: (202)293-2913
Registered: LDA

Employers
Ashland Inc. (Public Affairs Coordinator)

DUPART, Louis H.
1400 16th St. NW
Suite 600
Washington, DC 20036
Tel: (202)939-7900
Fax: (202)745-0916
Registered: LDA

Majority Chief Counsel and Staff Director, Subommittee on Antitrust, Business Rights and Competition, Senate Judiciary Committee 1997-98. Chief Counsel on Intelligence, House Permanent Select Committee on Intelligence, 1988-97.

Employers
Fleischman and Walsh, L.L.P. (Partner)

Clients Represented
On Behalf of Fleischman and Walsh, L.L.P.
ACTA Technology
American Airlines
AOL Time Warner
Currenex
EWA Land Information Group, Inc.
Farallon Capital Management
Forest Cities
Guardian Industries Corp.
Indigo
Katten Muchin & Zavis
Midway Airlines Corp.
mp3.com
ORBITZ
Sabre Inc.
SBC Communications Inc.

DUPREE, Jr., Robert F.
1130 Connecticut Ave. NW
Suite 1200
Washington, DC 20036-3954
Tel: (202)862-0500
Fax: (202)862-0537
Registered: LDA

Employers
American Textile Manufacturers Institute (Associate Director, Government Relations)

DURAN, Ingrid
504 C St. NE
Washington, DC 20002
Tel: (202)543-1771
Fax: (202)546-2143

Employers
Congressional Hispanic Caucus Institute (CHCI) (Exec. Director)

DURANTE, Douglas A.
1925 N. Lynn St.
Suite 725
Arlington, VA 22209
Tel: (703)276-8444
Fax: (703)276-8447
Registered: LDA

Department of Energy, 1981-82. Director of Public Affairs, Nat'l Alcohol Fuels Commission, 1979-81.

Employers
Durante Associates (V. President)

Clients Represented
On Behalf of Durante Associates
ARK Energy, Inc.
Clean Fuels Development Coalition
Energy Pacific, Inc.
Information Resources, Inc.
Nebraska Ethanol Board
Texas Corn Producers Board
World Wide Energy Group

DURANTE, Raymond W.
1925 N. Lynn St.
Suite 725
Arlington, VA 22209
Tel: (703)276-8444
Fax: (703)276-8447

Former Special Projects Manager, Presidential Exchange Program, Department of Interior.

Employers
Durante Associates (President)

Clients Represented
On Behalf of Durante Associates
TRW Systems Integration Group

DURBIN, Eden Fisher
1701 K St. NW
Suite 903
Washington, DC 20006
Tel: (202)835-9043
Fax: (202)835-9030
Registered: LDA

Employers
YMCA of the USA Public Policy Office (Director, Public Policy)

DURBIN, Margaret
1001 Pennsylvania Ave. NW
Washington, DC 20004-2599
Tel: (202)624-2000
Fax: (202)624-2319
Registered: LDA

Employers
American Council of Life Insurers (Senior Counsel and Director, Federal Relations)

DURBIN, Martin J.

1300 Wilson Blvd.
Suite 800
Arlington, VA 22209
EMail: fedgov@ameriplas.org
Tel: (703)253-0700
Fax: (703)253-0701
Registered: LDA

Employers
American Plastics Council (Director, Federal and International Affairs)

DURENBERGER, Hon. David

1001 Pennsylvania Ave. NW
Suite 850 North
Washington, DC 20004-2505
EMail: ddurenberger@policypartners.com
Tel: (202)661-3580
Fax: (202)737-4242
Registered: LDA
Member, U.S. Senate (R-MN), 1978-95.

Employers
Public Policy Partners, LLC (President)

Clients Represented
On Behalf of Public Policy Partners, LLC
Express Scripts Inc.
Johnson & Johnson, Inc.
Minneapolis-St. Paul Metropolitan Airports Commission
St. Jude Medical, Inc.
TriWest Healthcare Alliance, Inc.
Urologix, Inc.
Vertis Neuroscience

DURKAY, James

1225 I St. NW
Suite 500
Washington, DC 20005
Tel: (202)312-2005
Fax: (202)289-8683
Registered: LDA

Employers
Dawson & Associates, Inc. (Senior Advisor)

Clients Represented
On Behalf of Dawson & Associates, Inc.
Chemical Land Holdings, Inc.
Great Lakes Dredge & Dock

DURKEE, David

10401 Connecticut Ave.
Kensington, MD 20895
Tel: (301)933-8600
Fax: (301)946-8452

Employers
Bakery, Confectionery and Tobacco Workers Internat'l Union (Secretary-Treasurer)

DURKIN, David L.

1400 16th St. NW
Suite 400
Washington, DC 20036-2220
EMail: ddurkin@ofwlaw.com
Tel: (202)518-6313
Fax: (202)234-3550
Registered: LDA
Law Clerk to Judge Jaime Pieras, Jr., U.S. District Court for the District of Puerto Rico, 1986-88.

Employers
Olsson, Frank and Weeda, P.C. (Principal)

Clients Represented
On Behalf of Olsson, Frank and Weeda, P.C.
Transhumance Holding Co., Inc.
United Fresh Fruit and Vegetable Ass'n

DURLING, James P.

Three Lafayette Center
1155 21st St. NW
Washington, DC 20036-3384
Tel: (202)328-8000
Fax: (202)887-8979

Employers
Willkie Farr & Gallagher (Partner)

Clients Represented
On Behalf of Willkie Farr & Gallagher
Hyundai Electronics Industries Co., LTD
Japan Iron and Steel Exporters Ass'n
Matsushita Electric Industrial Co., Ltd.

DUROCHER, Cort

1801 Alexander Bell Dr.
Suite 500
Reston, VA 20191
Tel: (703)264-7500
Fax: (703)264-7551

Employers
American Institute of Aeronautics and Astronautics (Exec. Director)

DURST, Michael

1730 Pennsylvania Ave. NW
Suite 1200
Washington, DC 20006-4706
Tel: (202)737-0500
Fax: (202)626-3737

Employers
King & Spalding (Partner)

DUSCHA, Lloyd

1225 I St. NW
Suite 500
Washington, DC 20005
Tel: (202)312-2005
Fax: (202)289-8683
Registered: LDA

Employers
Dawson & Associates, Inc. (Senior Advisor)

DUTILH, Katherine M.

910 16th St. NW
Suite 402
Washington, DC 20006
Tel: (202)775-0084
Fax: (202)775-0784
Registered: LDA

Employers
Milliken and Co. (Legislative Assistant)

DUTTON, Frederick G.

5017 Tilden St. NW
Washington, DC 20016
Tel: (202)686-3500
Fax: (202)966-6621
Registered: FARA
Special Assistant to the President, 1961-1962. Assistant Secretary of State for Congressional Relations, 1962-1964.

Employers
Dutton and Dutton, P.C. (Partner/President)

Clients Represented
On Behalf of Dutton and Dutton, P.C.
Saudi Arabia, Royal Embassy of

DUTY, Kimberly D.

1850 M St. NW
Suite 540
Washington, DC 20036
Tel: (202)974-2300
Fax: (202)775-0112

Employers
Nat'l Multi-Housing Council (V. President, Communications)

DUVAL, Fred

600 New Hampshire Ave. NW
Suite 601
Washington, DC 20037
Tel: (202)333-7400
Fax: (202)333-1638
Registered: LDA
Former Deputy Assistant to the President and Deputy Director, Intergovernmental Affairs, Intergovernmental Affairs Office, Executive Office of the President, The White House, during the Clinton Administration.

Employers
Hill and Knowlton, Inc. (Sr. Counselor, Public Affairs and Government Relations)

Clients Represented
On Behalf of Hill and Knowlton, Inc.
Eurapair International, Inc.
Orange, California, County of

DUVALL, Henry

1301 Pennsylvania Ave. NW
Suite 702
Washington, DC 20004
Tel: (202)393-2427
Fax: (202)393-2400

Employers
Council of the Great City Schools (Director, Communications)

DUY, Jennifer

Eisenhower Exec. Office Bldg.
725 17th St. NW
Washington, DC 20503
Tel: (202)395-4790
Fax: (202)395-3888

Employers
Executive Office of the President - Office of Management and Budget (Confidential Assistant)

DWYER, Amy S.

2100 M St. NW
Suite 200
Washington, DC 20037
EMail: adwyer@stewartlaw.com
Tel: (202)785-4185
Fax: (202)466-1286
Registered: LDA

Employers
Stewart and Stewart (Of Counsel)

Clients Represented
On Behalf of Stewart and Stewart
Floral Trade Council
Ranchers-Cattlemen Legal Action Fund
The Timken Co.

DWYER, Daniel R.

1140 19th St. NW
Suite 900
Washington, DC 20036
EMail: ddwyer@kkblaw.com
Tel: (202)223-5120
Fax: (202)223-5619

Employers
Kleinfeld, Kaplan and Becker (Partner)

DWYER, Denis J.

901 15th St. NW
Suite 700
Washington, DC 20005-2301
EMail: djdwyer@verner.com
Tel: (202)371-6000
Fax: (202)371-6279
Registered: LDA, FARA

Employers
Verner, Liipfert, Bernhard, McPherson and Hand, Chartered (Dir., Legislation and Federal Affairs)

Clients Represented
On Behalf of Verner, Liipfert, Bernhard, McPherson and Hand, Chartered
Bombardier Transportation/Bombardier Transit Corporation
Capital Metropolitan Transportation Authority
The Walt Disney Co.
George Washington University, Office of Government Relations
Goldman, Sachs and Co.
G.E. Harris Harmon
Lockheed Martin Corp.
Merle Hay Mall Limited Partners
New Haven, Connecticut, City of
Northwest Airlines, Inc.
Office of Hawaiian Affairs
Parsons Brinckerhoff Inc.
Peterson Cos., Inc.
Sarnoff Corp.
Staples, Inc.

DWYER, Roderick T.

1130 17th St. NW
Washington, DC 20036-4677
EMail: rdwyer@nma.org
Tel: (202)463-9782
Fax: (202)463-3257
Registered: LDA

Employers
Nat'l Mining Ass'n (Deputy General Counsel)

DYE, Alan P.

1747 Pennsylvania Ave. NW
Suite 1000
Washington, DC 20006
Tel: (202)785-9500
Fax: (202)835-0243
Attorney/Advisor to Judge Austin Hoyt, U.S. Tax Court, 1973-75.

Employers
Webster, Chamberlain & Bean (Partner)

Clients Represented
On Behalf of Webster, Chamberlain & Bean
Nat'l Center for Homeopathy
Nat'l Tooling and Machining Ass'n
Robotic Industries Ass'n
Screenprinting & Graphic Imaging Ass'n Internat'l

DYE, Stuart S.

2099 Pennsylvania Ave. NW
Suite 100
Washington, DC 20006
EMail: sdye@hklaw.com
Tel: (202)955-3000
Fax: (202)955-5564
Registered: LDA, FARA
Special Assistant on Law of the Sea Matters, International Law Division, Office of the Judge Advocate General (1965-66) and Secretary, Navy Staff, Deep Submergence Systems Review Group, Office of Legislative Affairs (1963-64), Department of the Navy.

Employers
Holland & Knight LLP (Partner)

DYER, Barbara

1509 22nd St. NW
Washington, DC 20037-1073
Tel: (202)457-0588
Ext: 502
Fax: (202)296-1098

Employers
The Hitachi Foundation (President and Chief Exec. Officer)

DYER, Joseph J.

815 Connecticut Ave. NW
Suite 500
Washington, DC 20006-4004
Tel: (202)463-2400
Fax: (202)828-5393

Employers
Seyfarth, Shaw, Fairweather & Geraldson (Partner)

DYER, Michael J.

5550 Friendship Blvd.
Suite 310
Chevy Chase, MD 20815-7231
EMail: mdyer@aacom.org
Tel: (301)968-4151
Fax: (301)968-4185
Registered: LDA

Employers
American Ass'n of Colleges of Osteopathic Medicine (V. President, Government Relations)

DYER, CAE, Randy

1420 16th St. NW
Suite 405
Washington, DC 20036
Tel: (202)328-7460
Fax: (202)332-2301

Employers
Nat'l Structured Settlements Trade Ass'n
TASC, Inc., Association Management (Exec. V. President)

Clients Represented

On Behalf of TASC, Inc., Association Management
Early Learning Years Institute
Internat'l Electronic Article Surveillance Manufacturers
Nat'l Structured Settlements Trade Ass'n
Unified Voice (Interior Designers)

DYER, Teresa J.

1615 L St. NW
Suite 1220
Washington, DC 20036-5610
EMail: tjdyer@winstarmail.com
Tel: (202)659-0946
Fax: (202)659-4972
Registered: LDA

Employers
Evans & Black, Inc. (Director, Government Affairs)

Clients Represented

On Behalf of Evans & Black, Inc.
Girl Scouts of the U.S.A. - Washington Office
Internat'l Council of Shopping Centers
Komen Breast Cancer Foundation, The Susan G.
Nat'l Osteoporosis Foundation
Ticketmaster

DYER, Thomas M.

600 New Hampshire Ave. NW
11th Floor
Washington, DC 20037
EMail: tmd@dejlaw.com
Tel: (202)944-3054
Fax: (202)944-3068
Registered: LDA, FARA

Employers
Dyer Ellis & Joseph, P.C. (Partner)

Clients Represented

On Behalf of Dyer Ellis & Joseph, P.C.
Avondale Industries, Inc.
BLNG, Inc.
China Shipping (Group) Co.
Clipper Cruise Line
FastShip, Inc.
Fruit Shippers Ltd.
Heerema Marine Contractors Nederland B.V.
Hvide Marine Inc.
Kvaerner Shipholding, Inc.
Kvaerner Philadelphia Shipyard Inc.
Northrop Grumman Corp.
Sea Ventures Inc.
TI Group Inc.
The Trump Organization

DYJAK, Kathryn

1001 Connecticut Ave. NW
Suite 507
Washington, DC 20036
Tel: (202)466-0001
Fax: (202)466-0002

Employers
Craig Associates (V. President)

Clients Represented

On Behalf of Craig Associates
County Welfare Directors Ass'n of California
Dakota, Minnesota, County of
San Bernardino County Social Services Department
San Bernardino, California, County of

DYKE, Charles W.

1330 Connecticut Ave. NW
Suite 210
Washington, DC 20036-1704
EMail: cdyke@itta.com
Tel: (202)828-2614
Fax: (202)828-2617

Employers
Internat'l Technology & Trade Associates, Inc. (ITTA, Inc.) (Chairman, C.E.O.)

DYKES, Michael

600 13th St. NW
Suite 660
Washington, DC 20005
Tel: (202)783-2460
Fax: (202)783-2468
Registered: LDA

Employers
Monsanto Co. (V. President, Government Affairs)

DYM, Herbert

1201 Pennsylvania Ave. NW
Washington, DC 20004-2401
EMail: hdym@cov.com
Tel: (202)662-6000
Fax: (202)662-6291

Employers
Covington & Burling (Partner)

DYSART, Mark

1010 Massachusetts Ave. NW
Washington, DC 20001
Tel: (202)789-8107
Fax: (202)789-8109
Registered: LDA

Employers
High Speed Ground Transportation Ass'n (President)

DZIUBAN, Robert L.

P.O. Box 2000
Merrifield, VA 22116-2000
Tel: (703)359-2830
Fax: (703)359-2834

Employers
Optical Laboratories Ass'n (Exec. Director)

EADS, Michael

1620 I St. NW
Suite 615
Washington, DC 20006
EMail: eads@moinc.com
Tel: (202)463-8493
Fax: (202)463-8497
Registered: LDA

Employers
JBC Internat'l (V. President)

Clients Represented

On Behalf of JBC Internat'l
Uniroyal Chemical Co., Inc.

EADS, Timur

6903 Rockledge Dr.
Suite 730
Bethesda, MD 20817
EMail: eads_timur@emc.com
Tel: (301)272-2836
Fax: (301)272-2369
Registered: LDA

Employers
EMC Corp. (Director of Government Affairs)

EAGER, Robert C.

1050 Connecticut Ave. NW
Washington, DC 20036-5306
EMail: reager@gdclaw.com
Tel: (202)955-8500
Fax: (202)467-0539
Registered: LDA

Employers
Gibson, Dunn & Crutcher LLP (Partner)

Clients Represented

On Behalf of Gibson, Dunn & Crutcher LLP
California Federal Bank
Dollar Bank
New York Bankers Ass'n
Providian Financial Corp.
Prudential Insurance Co. of America
Washington Mutual Bank

EAGLE, Jacqueline H.

1400 16th St. NW
Suite 400
Washington, DC 20036-2220
EMail: jeagle@ofwlaw.com
Tel: (202)518-6358
Fax: (202)234-3537

Employers
Olsson, Frank and Weeda, P.C. (Of Counsel)

EAGLE, Lindsay

1250 I St. NW
Suite 500
Washington, DC 20005
EMail: leagle@anla.org
Tel: (202)789-2900
Ext: 3012
Fax: (202)789-1893

Employers
American Nursery and Landscape Ass'n (Director of Communications)

EAGLEBURGER, Lawrence S.

801 Pennsylvania Ave. NW
Suite 800
Washington, DC 20004
Tel: (202)508-3400
Fax: (202)508-3402
Registered: FARA

Secretary (1992-93) and Deputy Secretary (1989-92), Department of State.

Employers
Baker, Donelson, Bearman & Caldwell, P.C. (Senior Foreign Policy Advisor)

EAMES, Fred

1275 Pennsylvania Ave. NW
Tenth Floor
Washington, DC 20004
Tel: (202)347-6000
Fax: (202)347-6001
Registered: LDA

Counsel to Chairman Mike Oxley (R-OH), House Committee on Commerce, 1995-98. Legislative Director and Legislative Aide to Rep. Paul Gillmor (R-OH), 1989-95.

Employers
Balch & Bingham LLP (Partner)

Clients Represented

On Behalf of Balch & Bingham LLP
FirstEnergy Co.
informal coalition
Potomac Electric Power Co.
TVA Watch

EARL, Tony

750 First St. NE
Suite 940
Washington, DC 20002
Tel: (202)408-9260
Fax: (202)408-8896

Employers
Center for Clean Air Policy (Chairman)

EARLEY, Penelope

1307 New York Ave. NW
Suite 300
Washington, DC 20005-4701
Tel: (202)293-2450
Fax: (202)457-8095
Registered: LDA

Employers
American Ass'n of Colleges for Teacher Education (V. President, Government Relations)

EARLY, A. Blakeman

2212 Glasgow Rd.
Alexandria, VA 22307
Tel: (703)765-1031
Fax: (703)765-1031
Registered: LDA

Employers
Self-employed as an independent consultant.

Clients Represented

As an independent consultant
American Lung Ass'n

EARLY, Kerry P.

1120 Connecticut Ave. NW
Washington, DC 20036
Tel: (202)663-5000
Fax: (202)663-5212
Registered: LDA

Employers
American Bankers Ass'n (Associate Director, Washington Information)

EARMAN, Barbara

14th and Constitution Ave. NW
Room 7814A
Washington, DC 20230
Tel: (202)482-2309
Fax: (202)501-4828

Employers
Department of Commerce - Economic Development Administration (Communications and Congressional Liaison Specialist)

EAST, Dr. Bill

1800 Diagonal Rd.
Suite 320
Alexandria, VA 22314
EMail: east@nasdse.org
Tel: (703)519-3800
Fax: (703)519-3808

Employers
Nat'l Ass'n of State Directors of Special Education (Exec. Director)

EAST, Emelie

400 N. Capitol St. NW
Suite 363
Washington, DC 20001
Tel: (202)783-0280
Fax: (202)737-4518
Registered: LDA
Former Professional Staff, Senate Appropriations Committee. Former Staff Assistant to Rep. Norm Dicks (D-WA).

Employers
Denny Miller McBee Associates (V. President)

EASTERLING, Barbara J.

501 Third St. NW
Washington, DC 20001-2797
Tel: (202)434-1100
Fax: (202)434-1481

Employers
Communications Workers of America (Secretary-Treasurer)

EASTMAN, Michael J.

1015 15th St. NW
Suite 1200
Washington, DC 20005
Tel: (202)789-8600
Fax: (202)789-1708

Employers
Labor Policy Ass'n (LPA) (Director of Government Relations)
McGuiness Norris & Williams, LLP (Associate)

Clients Represented

On Behalf of McGuiness Norris & Williams, LLP
Labor Policy Ass'n (LPA)

EASTMAN, Penny L.

1909 K St. NW
Washington, DC 20006
Tel: (202)263-3000
Fax: (202)263-3300
Registered: LDA
Deputy Administrator, Maritime Administration, Department of Transportation, 1989-92. Deputy Assistant Secretary, Bureau of International Organizations Affairs, Department of State, 1988-89. Deputy Press Secretary, Department of the Interior, 1987-88. Office of Congressional Relations, Department of Commerce, 1983-85. Office of Intergovernmental Affairs, The White House, 1981-83. Staff, U.S. House of Representatives, 1975-78.

Employers
Mayer, Brown & Platt (Legislative Director)

Clients Represented

On Behalf of Mayer, Brown & Platt
Ace Ltd.
Bertelsmann AG
Chicago Stock Exchange, Inc.
ED&F Man Inc.
Federal Home Loan Bank of Chicago
Nicor, Inc.
Oracle Corp.

EASTMAN, Renee

214 Massachusetts Ave. NE
Suite 310
Washington, DC 20002
Tel: (202)546-8940
Registered: LDA

Employers
Salt River Project (Federal Affairs Manager)

EASTON, Jr., John J.

701 Pennsylvania Ave. NW
Washington, DC 20004-2696
Tel: (202)508-5633
Fax: (202)508-5360

Employers
Edison Electric Institute (V. President, International Programs)

EASTWOOD, Valerie J.

1667 K St. NW
Suite 700
Washington, DC 20006
Tel: (202)776-7800
Fax: (202)776-7801
Registered: LDA

Employers
Duane, Morris & Heckscher LLP

Clients Represented

On Behalf of Duane, Morris & Heckscher LLP
Power Mobility Coalition

EATON, Charles H. S.

3190 Fairview Park Dr.
Falls Church, VA 22042
Tel: (703)876-3735
Fax: (703)876-3600
Registered: LDA

Employers
General Dynamics Corp. (Manager, Government Relations)

EBELL, Myron

1001 Connecticut Ave. NW
Suite 1250
Washington, DC 20036
Tel: (202)331-1010
Fax: (202)331-0640

Employers
Competitive Enterprise Institute (Director Global Warming and International Environmental Policy)

EBERHART, Gary

400 N. Washington St.
Alexandria, VA 22314-9980
EMail: garyeb@pianet.org
Tel: (703)836-9340
Fax: (703)836-1279

Employers
Nat'l Ass'n of Professional Insurance Agents (Exec. V. President)

EBERLE, Bruce W.

1420 Spring Hill Rd.
Suite 490
McLean, VA 22102
EMail: beberle@eberle1.com
Tel: (703)821-1550
Fax: (703)821-0920

Employers
Bruce W. Eberle & Assoc., Inc. (Chairman, Board of Directors)

EBERLY, Brenda L.

201 Maryland Ave. NE
Washington, DC 20002
EMail: bleberly@imcglobal.com
Tel: (202)543-8700
Fax: (202)543-1562
Registered: LDA

Employers
IMC Global Inc. (Manager, Government Affairs)

EBERSOLE, Joseph L.

2101 Connecticut Ave. NW
Suite 63
Washington, DC 20008-1760
Tel: (202)265-9447
Fax: (202)265-7126
Registered: LDA

Employers
Self-employed as an independent consultant.

Clients Represented

As an independent consultant
Coalition for Patent Information Dissemination
Derwent, Inc.
Dialoge Corp.
IFI Claims Services
Lexis-Nexis
MicroPatent, LLC
Questel-Orbit, Inc.

EBERSPACHER, Jack

415 Second St. NE
Suite 300
Washington, DC 20002-4993
Tel: (202)547-7800
Fax: (202)546-2638

Employers
Nat'l Ass'n of Wheat Growers (Chief Exec. Officer)

EBERSTADT, Nicholas N.

1150 17th St. NW
Washington, DC 20036
EMail: eberstadt@aei.org
Tel: (202)862-5800
Fax: (202)862-7177

Employers
American Enterprise Institute for Public Policy Research (Visiting Scholar)

EBERT, Daniel

1776 K Street NW
Washington, DC 20006
Tel: (202)719-3379
Registered: LDA

Employers
NetCoalition.Com (Exec. Director)

EBLE, Nancy

400 Seventh St. SW
Suite 10402
Washington, DC 20590
EMail: neble@comdit.uscg.mil
Tel: (202)366-0008
Fax: (202)366-7124

Employers
Department of Transportation - United States Coast Guard (Legislative Analyst, Congressional Affairs Staff, Office of Government and Public Affairs)

ECCLES, Robert N.

555 13th St. NW
Suite 500 West
Washington, DC 20004
EMail: reccles@omm.com
Tel: (202)383-5300
Fax: (202)383-5414
Associate Solicitor (1982-88), Deputy Associate solicitor (1980-82), and Trial Attorney (1977-80), Department of Labor. Trial Attorney, Department of Justice, 1972-77.

Employers
O'Melveny and Myers LLP (Partner)

ECHEVARRIA, Laura

419 Seventh St. NW
Suite 500
Washington, DC 20004
Tel: (202)626-8800
Fax: (202)737-9189

Employers
Nat'l Right to Life Committee (Director, Media Relations)

ECKART, Brad

600 Maryland Ave. SW
Suite 800
Washington, DC 20024
Tel: (202)484-3600
Fax: (202)484-3604
Registered: LDA

Employers
American Farm Bureau Federation (Deputy Director, Washington Office and Legislative Services)

ECKELS, Timothy J.

1875 I St. NW
Suite 1000
Washington, DC 20006
EMail: teckels@chusa.org
Tel: (202)296-3993
Fax: (202)296-3997
Registered: LDA

Employers
Catholic Health Ass'n of the United States (Senior V. President)

ECKENHOFF, Edward A.

102 Irving St. NW
Washington, DC 20010-2949
Tel: (202)877-1776
Fax: (202)829-5180

Employers
Nat'l Rehabilitation Hospital (President and Chief Exec. Officer)

ECKERLY, Susan

1201 F St. NW
Suite 200
Washington, DC 20004
Tel: (202)554-9000
Fax: (202)484-1566
Registered: LDA

Employers
Nat'l Federation of Independent Business (Director, Federal Public Policy/Senate)

ECKERT, Doug

801 Pennsylvania Ave. NW
Suite 230
Washington, DC 20004
Tel: (202)393-7150
Fax: (202)347-1684
Registered: LDA
EMail: deckert@bradleyarant.com
Senior Legislative Aide to Senator Trent Lott (R-MS), 1987-89.

Employers
Bradley Arant Rose & White LLP (Partner)

ECKL, Chris

2301 M St. NW
Washington, DC 20037-1484
Tel: (202)467-2924
Fax: (202)467-2910
Registered: LDA
EMail: ceckl@APPAnet.org

Employers
American Public Power Ass'n (Government Relations Representative)

ECKLAND, William S.

1722 I St. NW
Washington, DC 20006
Tel: (202)736-8000
Fax: (202)736-8711
EMail: wesckland@sidley.com

Employers
Sidley & Austin (Partner)

ECKMAN, Richard

One Dupont Circle NW
Suite 320
Washington, DC 20036
Tel: (202)466-7230
Fax: (202)466-7238

Employers
Council of Independent Colleges (President)

EDDINGTON, Robin

733 15th St. NW
Suite 540
Washington, DC 20005
Tel: (202)628-8866
Fax: (202)628-9800
EMail: reddington@ncrc.org

Employers
Nat'l Community Reinvestment Coalition (Director, Legislative and Regulatory Affairs)

EDDY, Tammy

1201 15th St. NW
Washington, DC 20005-2800
Tel: (202)822-0470
Fax: (202)822-0572
Registered: LDA

Employers
Nat'l Ass'n of Home Builders of the U.S. (Staff V. President, Congressional Affairs)

EDELIN, Ph.D., Ramona H.

2120 L St. NW
Suite 510
Washington, DC 20037
Tel: (202)986-1460
Fax: (202)986-1468

Employers
Congressional Black Caucus Foundation (Exec. Director)
Nat'l Urban Coalition (President and Chief Exec. Officer)

EDELMAN, Doreen M.

801 Pennsylvania Ave. NW
Suite 800
Washington, DC 20004
Tel: (202)508-3400
Fax: (202)508-3402
EMail: dme@bdbc.com

Employers
Baker, Donelson, Bearman & Caldwell, P.C. (Of Counsel)

Clients Represented

On Behalf of Baker, Donelson, Bearman & Caldwell, P.C.
American-Turkish Council
Burger King Corp.
E-Tech
Howard Energy Internat'l

EDELMAN, Lester

1225 I St. NW
Suite 500
Washington, DC 20005
Tel: (202)312-2005
Fax: (202)289-8683
Registered: LDA
EMail: dawsonassociates@worldnet.att.net
Former Chief Counsel, U.S. Army Corps of Engineers, Department of the Army. Former Counsel, House Committee on Transportation and Infrastructure.

Employers
Dawson & Associates, Inc. (Senior Counsel and Senior Advisor)

Clients Represented

On Behalf of Dawson & Associates, Inc.
Florida Citrus Mutual
Florida Sugar Cane League, Inc.
Great Lakes Dredge & Dock
Sugar Cane Growers Cooperative of Florida

EDELMAN, Marian Wright

25 E St. NW
Washington, DC 20001
Tel: (202)628-8787
Fax: (202)662-3510

Employers
Children's Defense Fund (President)

EDELSON, Howard J.

1016 16th St. NW
Fifth Floor
Washington, DC 20036
Tel: (202)293-5794
Fax: (202)223-6178
Registered: LDA

Employers
Consumers Energy Co. (Director, Regional State Governmental Affairs)

EDENS, USAR (Ret.), Col. Frank A.

One Constitution Ave. NE
Washington, DC 20002
Tel: (202)479-2200
Fax: (202)479-0416
Registered: LDA

Employers
Reserve Officers Ass'n of the U.S. (Director, Army Affairs)

EDER, Norm

1275 K St. NW
Suite 810
Washington, DC 20005
Tel: (202)408-2100
Fax: (202)408-2115
Registered: LDA
EMail: norme@cfmpdx.com

Employers
Conkling, Fiskum & McCormick (Partner)

Clients Represented

On Behalf of Conkling, Fiskum & McCormick
Electro Scientific Industries, Inc.
Industrial Customers of Northwest Utilities
Oregon Graduate Institute of Science and Technology

EDGAR, Elizabeth

Colonial Place Three
2107 Wilson Blvd., Suite 300
Arlington, VA 22201-3042
Tel: (703)524-7600
Fax: (703)524-9094
Registered: LDA

Employers
Nat'l Alliance for the Mentally Ill (Director, State Health Care)

EDGAR, Kevin R.

801 Pennsylvania Ave. NW
Suite 630
Washington, DC 20004-5878
Tel: (202)347-4300
Fax: (202)347-4370
Registered: LDA
EMail: kedgar@nyse.com

Employers
New York Stock Exchange (Special Counsel, Government Relations)

EDGAR, William C.

700 13th St. NW
Suite 700
Washington, DC 20005-3960
Tel: (202)508-6000
Fax: (202)508-6200
EMail: wcedgar@bryancave.com

Employers
Bryan Cave LLP (Partner)

EDGE, Joe D.

1500 K St.
Suite 1100
Washington, DC 20005
Tel: (202)842-8800
Fax: (202)842-8465
EMail: joe_edge@dbr.com
Trial Attorney, Common Carrier Bureau, Federal Communications Commission, 1974-75.

Employers
Drinker Biddle & Reath LLP (Partner)

Clients Represented

On Behalf of Drinker Biddle & Reath LLP
General Communications, Inc.

EDGELL, John R.

1401 I St. NW
Suite 500
Washington, DC 20005
Tel: (202)289-1313
Fax: (202)289-1330
EMail: john.edgell@btlaw.com
Chief of Staff and Press Secretary to Rep. Dennis Kucinich (D-OH), 1997-01. Legislative Director to Rep. Joseph P. Kennedy (D-MA), 1995-96. Legislative Director to Rep. Bill Luther (D-MN), 1995. Professional Staff, Government Operations Subcommittee on Information, Justice, Transportation and Agriculture, U.S. House of Representatives, 1994-95. Special Assistant, Office of the Secretary and the Economic Development Administration, U.S. Department of Commerce, 1993-94. Legislative Assistant to Rep. Fortney Hillman "Pete" Stark, Jr. (D-CA), 1987-93. Staff Assistant to Rep. Thomas A. Daschle (D-SD), 1985-86. Staff Assistant to Senator William "Bill" Bradley (D-NJ), 1979.

Employers
Barnes & Thornburg (Partner)

Clients Represented

On Behalf of Barnes & Thornburg
Wheat Gluten Industry Council

EDIE, John A.

1828 L St. NW
Suite 300
Washington, DC 20036
Tel: (202)466-6512
Fax: (202)785-3926

Employers
Council on Foundations (Senior V. President and General Counsel)

EDINGTON, William H.

1317 F St. NW
Suite 200
Washington, DC 20004
Tel: (202)737-1800
Fax: (202)737-2485
Registered: LDA
Former Staff Member, House Committee on Appropriations and former Management Specialist, Department of Treasury.

Employers
Edington, Peel & Associates, Inc. (Principal)

Clients Represented

On Behalf of Edington, Peel & Associates, Inc.
American Board of Trial Advocates
Arrowhead Regional Medical Center
Firearms Training Systems, Inc.
Florida State University
Kettering Medical Center
Lockheed Martin Corp.
Metropolitan Atlanta Rapid Transit Authority
Pacific Union College
Paradise Valley Hospital
United States Cane Sugar Refiners' Ass'n

EDMONDSON, Jr., Joseph

3000 K St. NW
Suite 500
Washington, DC 20007-5109
Tel: (202)672-5300
Fax: (202)672-5399
EMail: jedmondson@foleylaw.com

Employers
Foley & Lardner (Partner)

EDSON, Charles L.

401 Ninth St. NW
Suite 900
Washington, DC 20004
Tel: (202)585-8788
Fax: (202)585-8080
Registered: LDA
EMail: cedson@nixonpeabody.com
Chief, Public Housing Section, Office of General Counsel, Department of Housing and Urban Development, 1968-70.

Employers
Nixon Peabody LLP (Partner)

Clients Represented

On Behalf of Nixon Peabody LLP

Affordable Housing Tax Credit Coalition
Council for Affordable and Rural Housing
Edward A. Fish Associates
Institute for Responsible Housing Preservation
Light Associates
MetroPlains Development, Inc.
Nat'l Leased Housing Ass'n

EDWARDS, J. Brad

1001 Pennsylvania Ave. NW
Washington, DC 20004-2599
Tel: (202)624-2000
Fax: (202)624-2319
Registered: LDA

Employers

American Council of Life Insurers (Director, Political Affairs and Federal Relations)

EDWARDS, Ph.D., J. David

4646 40th St. NW
Washington, DC 20016
Tel: (202)966-8477
Fax: (202)966-8310

Employers

Joint Nat'l Committee for Languages (Exec. Director)
Nat'l Council for Languages and Internat'l Studies (Exec. Director)

EDWARDS, Hon. Jack

106 North Carolina Ave. SE
Washington, DC 20003
Tel: (202)863-0001
Fax: (202)863-0096
Registered: LDA
Member, U.S. House of Representatives (R-AL), 1965-85.

Employers

Ervin Technical Associates, Inc. (ETA)

Clients Represented

On Behalf of Ervin Technical Associates, Inc. (ETA)

Computer Coalition for Responsible Exports
General Dynamics Corp.
Ingalls Shipbuilding
Kaiser-Hill Co., L.L.C.
Kaman Diversified Technologies Corp.
Lister Bolt & Chain Co.
Lockheed Martin Corp.
Martins Point Health Care
Northrop Grumman Corp.
Sarnoff Corp.
United Defense, L.P.
Video Network Communications

EDWARDS, James R.

900 17th St. NW
Suite 600
Washington, DC 20006
Tel: (202)452-8700
Fax: (202)296-9561

Employers

Healthcare Leadership Council (Communications Manager)

EDWARDS, Jill

925 15th St. NW
5th Floor
Washington, DC 20005
Tel: (202)342-9610
Fax: (202)342-0650

Employers

Kelly and Associates, Inc. (Associate)

EDWARDS, Laura Saul

1350 I St. NW
Suite 880
Washington, DC 20005
EMail: ledwards@aad.org
Tel: (202)842-3555
Fax: (202)842-4355

Employers

American Academy of Dermatology (Assistant Director, Federal Affairs)

EDWARDS, Macon T.

600 Pennsylvania Ave. SE
Suite 320
Washington, DC 20003
EMail: medwards@themec.com
Tel: (202)969-8110
Fax: (202)969-7036
Registered: LDA

Employers

The Macon Edwards Co. (President)

Clients Represented

On Behalf of The Macon Edwards Co.

American Soc. of Farm Managers and Rural Appraisers
American Sugar Cane League of the U.S.A.
Coalition for Crop Insurance Improvement
Capital Equipment Legislative Coalition
First South Production Credit Ass'n
Gildan Activewear
Supima Ass'n of America

EDWARDS, III, Martin E.

Ten G St. NE
Suite 700
Washington, DC 20002
Tel: (202)216-5900
Fax: (202)216-0875
Registered: LDA

Employers

Interstate Natural Gas Ass'n of America (Director, Legislative Affairs)

EDWARDS, Missy

1401 K St. NW
Suite 400
Washington, DC 20005
Tel: (202)789-2111
Fax: (202)789-4883

Employers

The Washington Group (Senior V. President)

EDWARDS, Paul

1155 15th St. NW
Suite 1004
Washington, DC 20005
Tel: (202)467-5081
Fax: (202)467-5085

Employers

Visually Impaired Data Processors Internat'l (President)

EDWARDS, Shawn

700 13th St. NW
Suite 400
Washington, DC 20005
EMail: sedwards@cassidy.com
Tel: (202)347-0773
Fax: (202)347-0785
Registered: LDA
Former Staff for Senator John Warner (R-VA). Former Staff Assistant, Senate Armed Services Committee. Former Intern, office of Senator Strom Thurmond (R-SC).

Employers

Cassidy & Associates, Inc. (Account Exec.)

Clients Represented

On Behalf of Cassidy & Associates, Inc.

Abtech Industries
The Boeing Co.
CMS Defense Systems, Inc.
General Dynamics Corp.
Lockheed Martin Corp.
M2 Technologies Inc.
Ramo Defense Systems, LLC
Rochester Institute of Technology
Smartforce
SWATH Ocean Systems, Inc.
United Service Organization
University of Hawaii
Villanova University

EDWARDS, Thomas J.

475 L'Enfant Plaza SW
MS: 10837
Washington, DC 20260
Tel: (202)268-2353
Fax: (202)268-3775

Employers

United States Postal Service (Manager, Government Liaison)

EDWARDS, Tony M.

1875 I St. NW
Suite 600
Washington, DC 20006
EMail: tedwads@nareit.com
Tel: (202)739-9400
Fax: (202)739-9401
Registered: LDA

Employers

Nat'l Ass'n of Real Estate Investment Trusts (Senior V. President and General Counsel)

EDWARDSON, Bryan B.

1101 15th St. NW
Suite 1000
Washington, DC 20005
EMail: bryan_edwardson@cargill.com
Tel: (202)530-8160
Registered: LDA

Employers

Cargill, Inc. (Director, Public Policy)

EFFGEN, Gretchen

1001 Pennsylvania Ave. NW
Suite 600
Washington, DC 20004
Tel: (202)347-0066
Fax: (202)624-7222

Employers

Powell, Goldstein, Frazer & Murphy LLP (Analyst)

Clients Represented

On Behalf of Powell, Goldstein, Frazer & Murphy LLP

China, Embassy of the People's Republic of
Hong Kong Trade Development Council
PROEXPORT

EFRUS, Robert G.

2111 Wilson Blvd.
Suite 1200
Arlington, VA 22201
EMail: refrus@columbuspublicaffairs.com
Tel: (703)522-1845
Fax: (703)351-6634
Former Legislative Assistant to Senator Paul Trible (R-VA).

Employers

Columbus Public Affairs (Senior V. President)

EGAN, Irene M.

3211 Jermantown Rd.
Suite 300
Fairfax, VA 22030
EMail: iegan@covantaenergy.com
Tel: (703)246-0830
Fax: (703)246-0808

Employers

Covanta Energy Corporation (Community and Government Affairs Representative)

EGAN, Jr., James C.

607 14th St. NW
Washington, DC 20005
EMail: eganjc@rw.com
Tel: (202)434-0700
Fax: (202)912-6000
Director of Litigation (1990-94) and Assistant Director of Litigation (1979-90), Bureau of Competition, Federal Trade Commission.

Employers

Rogers & Wells (Counsel)

EGAN, Joseph R.

1500 K St. NW
Suite 200
Washington, DC 20005
Tel: (202)220-9610
Fax: (202)220-9608
Registered: LDA

Employers

Egan & Associates (Chairman)

Clients Represented

On Behalf of Egan & Associates

ABB Combustion Engineering Nuclear Power

EGAN, Michael J.

1275 Pennsylvania Ave. NW
Washington, DC 20004-2415
Tel: (202)383-0100
Fax: (202)637-3593

Employers

Sutherland Asbill & Brennan LLP (Of Counsel)

EGE, Stephen M.

734 15th St. NW
12th Floor
Washington, DC 20005
Tel: (202)347-0300
Fax: (202)347-2172
Assistant to the Chairman, Federal Home Loan Bank Board, 1977-79.

Employers

Elias, Matz, Tiernan and Herrick (Partner)

EGER, Charles L.

1350 I St. NW
Suite 400
Washington, DC 20005-3306
Tel: (202)371-6900
Fax: (202)842-3578
Registered: LDA

Employers

Motorola, Inc. (Director, Regulatory Affairs)

EGGERS, Susan

401 Ninth St. NW
Suite 900
Washington, DC 20004
Tel: (202)585-8000
Fax: (202)585-8080

Employers
Nixon Peabody LLP (Associate)

EGLE, Richard

1625 Beulah Rd.
Vienna, VA 22182
Tel: (703)319-2276
Fax: (703)319-2283
Registered: LDA
EMail: egle@erols.com

Employers
Egle Associates (Principal Owner)

Clients Represented

On Behalf of Egle Associates
NCR Corp.
Planning Systems, Inc.

EGLINTON, Stephanie J.

1015 15th St. NW
Suite 750
Washington, DC 20005
Tel: (202)408-5420
Fax: (202)408-5397
Registered: LDA

Employers
World Learning Inc. (Government Relations Coordinator)

EGNER, David

1130 Connecticut Ave. NW
Suite 600
Washington, DC 20036
Tel: (202)296-0263
Fax: (202)452-9371
Former Director, Office of Public Affairs, Department of Housing and Urban Development.

Employers
Nichols-Dezenhall Communication Management Group, Ltd. (V. President)

EHRENHAFT, Peter D.

1150 18th St. NW
Ninth Floor
Washington, DC 20036
Tel: (202)296-3355
Fax: (202)296-3922
EMail: pehrenhaft@ablondifoster.com
Deputy Assistant Secretary and Special Counsel for Tariff Affairs, Department of the Treasury, 1977-79. Senior Law Clerk to Chief Justice Earl Warren, U.S. Supreme Court, 1961-62. Motions Law Clerk, U.S. Court of Appeals for the District of Columbia Circuit, 1957-48.

Employers
Ablondi, Foster, Sobin & Davidow, P.C. (Partner)

EHRGOOD, Jr., Thomas A.

1300 I St. NW
Suite 900 East
Washington, DC 20005
Tel: (202)962-3828
Fax: (202)962-3838
Registered: LDA
EMail: ehrgood@compaq.com

Employers
Compaq Computer Corp. (Director, International Government Counsel)

EHRLICH, Paul C.

1130 Connecticut Ave. NW
Suite 500
Washington, DC 20036
Tel: (202)463-7372
Fax: (202)463-8809
Registered: LDA

Employers
Schering-Plough Legislative Resources L.L.C. (Congressional Relations Representative)

EHRLICH, Stacy L.

1140 19th St. NW
Suite 900
Washington, DC 20036
Tel: (202)223-5120
Fax: (202)223-5619
EMail: sehrlich@kkblaw.com
Former Clerk to Judge Alexander Denson, U.S. District Court for the Eastern District of North Carolina.

Employers
Kleinfeld, Kaplan and Becker (Partner)

EHUDIN, Marc L.

1213 Jefferson Davis Hwy.
Suite 802
Arlington, VA 22202-4304
Tel: (703)412-4170
Fax: (703)416-4820
Registered: LDA
EMail: ehudin@aaicorp.com
Senior Legislative Assistant to Rep. Frank Tejeda (D-TX), 1993-96. Field Representative to Rep. Beverly Byron (D-MD), 1989-92.

Employers
AAI Corp. (Director, Legislative Affairs)

EICHBERG, Ross E.

2550 M St. NW
Washington, DC 20037-1350
Tel: (202)457-6000
Fax: (202)457-6315
Registered: LDA, FARA
EMail: reichberg@pattonboggs.com

Employers
Patton Boggs, LLP (Partner)

EICHER, Jill A.

1100 Duke Street
Alexandria, VA 22314
Tel: (703)548-8538
Fax: (703)548-8499
Registered: LDA
EMail: eicher@aarc.org

Employers
American Ass'n for Respiratory Care (Director, Government Affairs)

EICKHOFF, Bruce

Commonwealth Towers
1300 Wilson Blvd., Suite 200
Arlington, VA 22209-2307
Tel: (703)516-8218
Fax: (703)516-8298
EMail: beeickof@collins.rockwell.com

Employers
Rockwell Collins (Director, Department of Defense Marketing)

EIDE, Peter J.

c/o Chamber of Commerce of the U.S.
1615 H St. NW
Washington, DC 20062-2000
Tel: (202)463-5507
Fax: (202)463-5901
Registered: LDA

Employers
Chamber of Commerce of the U.S.A. (Manager, Labor Law)
Nat'l Alliance Against Blacklisting (Contact)

EIDEN, Matt

1615 H St. NW
Washington, DC 20062
Tel: (202)463-5500
Fax: (202)463-3129

Employers
Nat'l Chamber Foundation (Program Coordinator)

EILBOTT, Eli D.

1615 M St. NW
Suite 800
Washington, DC 20036-3203
Tel: (202)467-6370
Fax: (202)467-6379
EMail: ede@dwgp.com

Employers
Duncan, Weinberg, Genzer & Pembroke, P.C. (Principal)

EIRAS, Anna

214 Massachusetts Ave. NE
Washington, DC 20002
Tel: (202)546-4400
Fax: (202)546-8328

Employers
Heritage Foundation (Policy Analyst, Trade and Latin America)

EIRING, Gene P.

1301 K St. NW
Suite 900
East Tower
Washington, DC 20005
Tel: (202)408-8007
Fax: (202)408-8704
Former Military Advisor, U.S. Embassy in Peru and Country Director on International Affairs, U.S. Air Force.

Employers
The Carter Group

EISELSBERG, David

2121 K St. NW
Suite 650
Washington, DC 20037
Tel: (202)296-2400
Fax: (202)296-2409
EMail: David@GlobalUSAinc.com

Employers
Global USA, Inc. (Director, Research)

EISEN, Jonathan B.

201 Park Washington Ct.
Falls Church, VA 22046-4621
Tel: (703)532-9400
Fax: (703)538-4673
Registered: LDA
EMail: jone@fdi.org

Employers
Food Distributors Internat'l (NAWGA-IFDA) (Director, Government Relations)

EISENACH, Jane Forston

1301 K St. NW
Suite 550E
Washington, DC 20005
Tel: (202)289-8929
Fax: (202)289-6079

Employers
The Progress Freedom Foundation (Adjunct Fellow)

EISENACH, Jeffrey A.

1301 K St. NW
Suite 550E
Washington, DC 20005
Tel: (202)289-8928
Fax: (202)289-6079
EMail: jeisenach@pff.org

Employers
The Progress Freedom Foundation (President, Senior Fellow and Co-Founder)

EISENBERG, Jeff

4245 N. Fairfax Dr.
Suite 100
Arlington, VA 20003-1606
Tel: (703)841-3675
Fax: (703)841-7400
Registered: LDA

Employers
The Nature Conservancy (Senior Policy Advisor, Agriculture)

EISENBERG, Susan

227 Massachusetts Ave. NE
Suite 303
Washington, DC 20002
Tel: (202)543-7032
Fax: (202)543-7062

Employers
American Federation for Medical Research (Exec. Director)

EISENBUD, Robert

601 Pennsylvania Ave. NW
Suite 300
The North Bldg.
Washington, DC 20004
Tel: (202)628-3500
Fax: (202)628-0400
Registered: LDA

Employers
Waste Management, Inc. (Director, Legislative Affairs)

EISENHART, Earl

1100 New York Ave. NW
Suite 580
Washington, DC 20005
Tel: (202)898-1050
Fax: (202)789-4006
Registered: LDA
EMail: ebeisnht@aol.com

Employers
G.R. Services (President)

Clients Represented

On Behalf of G.R. Services
American Bakers Ass'n
Intermodal Ass'n of North America
Ryder System, Inc.
Snack Food Ass'n

EISENLA, Kristofer

2100 Pennsylvania Ave. NW
Suite 535
Washington, DC 20037
Tel: (202)822-1700
Fax: (202)822-1919

Employers
Simon Strategies/Mindbeam (Communications Specialist)

EISENSTADT, Michael

1828 L St. NW
Suite 1050
Washington, DC 20036
Tel: (202)452-0650
Ext: 206
Fax: (202)223-5364
EMail: michaele@washingtoninstitute.org

Employers
Washington Institute for Near East Policy (Military Affairs Fellow)

EISENSTAT, David H.

1333 New Hampshire Ave. NW
Suite 400
Washington, DC 20036
Tel: (202)887-4000
Fax: (202)887-4288

Employers
Akin, Gump, Strauss, Hauer & Feld, L.L.P. (Partner)

EISENSTAT, Larry F.

2101 L St. NW
Washington, DC 20037-1526
Tel: (202)785-9700
Fax: (202)887-0689
EMail: EisenstatL@dsmo.com

Employers
Dickstein Shapiro Morin & Oshinsky LLP (Partner)

Clients Represented

On Behalf of Dickstein Shapiro Morin & Oshinsky LLP
PG&E Generating Co.

EISGRAU, Adam

1317 F St. NW
Suite 600
Washington, DC 20004
Tel: (202)638-2121
Fax: (202)638-7045
Registered: LDA
EMail: eisgrau@wexlergroup.com

Employers
The Wexler Group (Principal/Director)

Clients Represented

On Behalf of The Wexler Group
American Mobile Satellite Corp.
Digital Media Ass'n
ORBITZ
Virginia Center for Innovative Technology
XM Satellite Radio, Inc.

EISNER, David

22000 AOL Way
Dulles, VA 20166
Tel: (703)448-8700
Fax: (703)265-2803
EMail: Daveisner@aol.com

Employers
AOL Time Warner (V. President, Corporate Communications)

EITER, Steve

1299 Pennsylvania Ave. NW
Suite 800 West
Washington, DC 20004
Tel: (202)785-0500
Fax: (202)785-5277
Registered: LDA

Employers
The Carmen Group (Creative Director)

EIZENSTADT, Stuart E.

1201 Pennsylvania Ave. NW
Washington, DC 20004-2401
Tel: (202)662-6000
Fax: (202)662-6291
Undersecretary for Economic, Business and Agricultural Affairs, Department of State, 1997-2001. Undersecretary for International Trade, Department of Commerce, 1996-97. U.S. Ambassador to the European Union (Brussels, Belgium), Department of State, 1993-96. Assistant to the President for Domestic Affairs and Policy and Executive Director, Domestic Policy Staff, Executive Office of the President, The White House, 1977-81. Director, Policy Planning and Analysis, Carter/Mondale Transition Planning Group, 1976-77. Law Clerk to Judge Newell Edenfield, U.S. District Court for the Northern District of Georgia, 1968-70. Staff Member, The White House, 1967-68.

Employers
Covington & Burling

EKEDAHL, Duane H.

2025 M St. NW
Suite 800
Washington, DC 20036
Tel: (202)367-2100
Fax: (202)367-1200
EMail: duane_ekedahl@dc.sba.com

Employers
Smith, Bucklin and Associates, Inc.

Clients Represented

On Behalf of Smith, Bucklin and Associates, Inc.
Pet Food Institute

ELAM, Mark R.

1001 Pennsylvania Ave. NW
Washington, DC 20004-2599
Tel: (202)624-2000
Fax: (202)624-2319

Employers
American Council of Life Insurers (Exec. V. President, Government Relations and Chief Operating Officer)

ELBERTSON, Marianne

1400 Independence Ave. SW
Room 1180-S
Washington, DC 20250
Tel: (202)720-8594
Fax: (202)720-5704

Employers
Department of Agriculture - Food Safety and Inspection Service (Constituent Affairs Specialist, Congressional and Public Affairs Staff)

ELDER, Albert

900 19th St. NW
Suite 400
Washington, DC 20006
Tel: (202)857-3100
Fax: (202)296-8716
Registered: LDA

Employers
America's Community Bankers (Government Relations)

ELDER, Dick

1101 15th St. NW
Suite 600
Washington, DC 20005
Tel: (202)785-1122
Fax: (202)785-5019

Employers
Sugar Ass'n, Inc. (Director, Public Relations)

ELDRED, John S.

1001 G St. NW
Suite 500 West
Washington, DC 20001
Tel: (202)434-4100
Fax: (202)434-4646
EMail: eldred@khlaw.com
Trial Attorney, Food and Drug Administration, 1970-75.

Employers
Keller and Heckman LLP (Partner)

ELDRIDGE, Roger D.

2101 Wilson Blvd.
Suite 400
Arlington, VA 22201
Tel: (703)243-6111
Fax: (703)841-9328
Registered: LDA
EMail: reldridge@nmpf.org

Employers
Nat'l Milk Producers Federation (V. President, Government Relations)

ELIM, Raga

203 Maryland Ave. NE
Washington, DC 20002
Tel: (202)544-6655
Fax: (202)544-5763
Registered: LDA

Employers
Jack Ferguson Associates, Inc.

Clients Represented

On Behalf of Jack Ferguson Associates, Inc.
Northland Holdings, Inc.
Sea Containers America, Inc.

ELKIN, James R.

701 Pennsylvania Ave. NW
Suite 725
Washington, DC 20004
Tel: (202)638-7429
Fax: (202)628-4763
Registered: LDA

Employers
Novartis Corp. (Exec. Director, Federal Government Relations)
Novartis Services, Inc.

ELLENBERGER, James N.

815 16th St. NW
Washington, DC 20006
Tel: (202)637-5000
Fax: (202)637-5058

Employers
AFL-CIO (American Federation of Labor and Congress of Industrial Organizations) (Assistant Director, Occupational Safety & Health Department)

ELLER, Jeff

1401 I St. NW
Suite 220
Washington, DC 20005
Tel: (202)216-8910
Fax: (202)216-8901
Registered: LDA
Deputy Assistant and Director of Media Affairs, Executive Office of the President, The White House, 1993-94.

Employers
Public Strategies, Inc.

Clients Represented

On Behalf of Public Strategies, Inc.
Bridgestone/Firestone, Inc.

ELLETT, E. Tazewell

555 13th St. NW
Washington, DC 20004-1109
Tel: (202)637-8644
Fax: (202)637-5910
Registered: LDA
EMail: etellett@hhlaw.com
Chief Counsel (1985-88) and Special Counsel to the Administrator (1984), Federal Aviation Administration, Department of Transportation. Special Assistant to Member Donald D. Engen, National Transportation Safety Board, 1982-84.

Employers
Hogan & Hartson L.L.P. (Partner)

Clients Represented

On Behalf of Hogan & Hartson L.L.P.
Air Transport Ass'n of America
Executive Jet
GE Capital Aviation Services
Lee County Port Authority

ELLICOTT, John L.

1201 Pennsylvania Ave. NW
Washington, DC 20004-2401
Tel: (202)662-6000
Fax: (202)662-6291
EMail: jellicott@cov.com
Office of the Judge Advocate General, U.S. Navy, 1955-58.

Employers
Covington & Burling (Senior Counsel)

ELLINGSWORTH, Rosalind K.

1916 N. Daniel St.
Arlington, VA 22201
Tel: (703)524-0630
Fax: (202)778-2201
Registered: LDA

Employers
Self-employed as an independent consultant.

Clients Represented

As an independent consultant
Coalition for a Global Standard on Aviation Noise

ELLIOT, David

1700 Kalorama Rd.
Suite 101
Washington, DC 20009-2702
Tel: (202)332-6483
Fax: (202)332-0207

Employers
Nat'l Gay and Lesbian Task Force (Director, Public Information)
Nat'l Religious Leadership Roundtable (Spokesperson)

ELLIOT, Kimberly Ann

11 Dupont Circle NW
Suite 620
Washington, DC 20036
Tel: (202)328-9000
Fax: (202)328-5432
EMail: kelliot@iie.com

Employers
Institute for Internat'l Economics (Research Fellow)

ELLIOT, Warren

601 13th St. NW
Suite 370 South
Washington, DC 20005
Tel: (202)783-7272
Fax: (202)783-4345

Employers
French & Company (Of Counsel)

ELLIOTT, E. Donald

1299 Pennsylvania Ave. NW
Tenth Floor
Washington, DC 20004-2400
Tel: (202)508-9500
Fax: (202)508-9700
EMail: edonaldelliott@paulhastings.com
Former General Counsel, Environmental Protection Agency. Law Clerk to Judge David Bazelon, U.S. Court of Appeals,

District of Columbia Circuit, 1975-76, and to Judge Gerhard Gesell, U.S. District Court for the District of Columbia, 1974-75.

Employers
Paul, Hastings, Janofsky & Walker LLP (Partner)

Clients Represented
On Behalf of Paul, Hastings, Janofsky & Walker LLP
Coalition for Truth in Environmental Marketing Information, Inc.
FirstEnergy Co.

ELLIOTT, Kate
1900 Pennsylvania Ave. NW
Washington, DC 20068
Tel: (202)331-6708
Registered: LDA

Employers
Potomac Electric Power Co. (Senior Government Relations Representative)

ELLIOTT, Kimberly A.
1325 G St. NW
Suite 500
Washington, DC 20005
EMail: ellkso@aol.com
Tel: (202)824-0210
Fax: (202)628-0067

Employers
Special Olympics, Inc. (Sr. Advisor to the President)

ELLIOTT, Kinn
1101 Vermont Ave. NW
12th Floor
Washington, DC 20005-3583
Tel: (202)789-7461
Fax: (202)789-7485

Employers
American Medical Ass'n (Director, Political and Grassroots Membership)

ELLIOTT, M. Diane
421 New Jersey Ave. SE
Washington, DC 20003
Tel: (202)547-5696
Fax: (202)547-5697

Employers
American Ass'n of Private Railroad Car Owners, Inc. (Exec. Director)

ELLIOTT, Paul E.
219 N. Washington St.
Alexandria, VA 22314
Tel: (703)836-7990
Fax: (703)836-9739
Registered: LDA
EMail: paul.elliott@pal-aerospace.com

Employers
Peduzzi Associates, Ltd. (Associate)

Clients Represented
On Behalf of Peduzzi Associates, Ltd.
DRS - EOSG
Integrated Medical Systems
Lord Corp.
Marconi Flight Systems, Inc.
Skyhook Technologies, Inc.

ELLIOTT, Robert F.
1201 New York Ave. NW
Suite 600
Washington, DC 20005-3931
EMail: relliott@ahma.com
Tel: (202)289-3190
Fax: (202)289-3185

Employers
American Hotel and Lodging Ass'n (Director, Regulatory Affairs)

ELLIS, Allison
1155 Connecticut Ave. NW
Suite 1200
Washington, DC 20036
EMail: AEllis@dc-bhb.com
Tel: (202)659-5800
Fax: (202)659-1027
Registered: LDA

Employers
Birch, Horton, Bittner & Cherot (Associate)

ELLIS, Andrew K.
1200 Wilson Blvd.
Arlington, VA 22209-1989
Tel: (703)465-3500
Fax: (703)465-3001

Employers
The Boeing Co. (V. President, Government Relations (Aircraft and Missles Group))

ELLIS, Ellen Wilkins
325 Seventh St.
Suite 1225
Washington, DC 20004
Tel: (202)737-0440
Fax: (202)628-2313
Registered: LDA

Employers
MassMutual Financial Group (Second V. President, Government Relations)

ELLIS, II, James B.
600 New Hampshire Ave. NW
11th Floor
Washington, DC 20037
EMail: jbe@dejlaw.com
Tel: (202)944-3051
Fax: (202)944-3068
Registered: LDA
Special Assistant to the Secretary, Department of Transportation, 1980-82.

Employers
Dyer Ellis & Joseph, P.C. (Partner)

Clients Represented
On Behalf of Dyer Ellis & Joseph, P.C.
Avondale Industries, Inc.
Bender Shipbuilding & Repair Co., Inc.
FastShip, Inc.
Heerema Marine Contractors Nederland B.V.
Hvide Marine Inc.
Intermare Navigation SA
Kvaerner Shipholding, Inc.
Kvaerner Philadelphia Shipyard Inc.
Nat'l Steel and Shipbuilding Co.

ELLIS, James W.
P.O. Box 5711
Arlington, VA 22205
Tel: (202)543-5136
Fax: (202)543-5266
Registered: LDA

Employers
Alexander Strategy Group (V. President)

ELLIS, Marietta
9315 Largo Dr. West
Suite 255
Largo, MD 20774
EMail: sivb@sivb.org
Tel: (301)324-5054
Fax: (301)324-5057

Employers
Soc. for In Vitro Biology (Managing Director)

ELLIS, Neil
1001 Pennsylvania Ave. NW
Suite 600
Washington, DC 20004
Tel: (202)347-0066
Fax: (202)624-7222

Employers
Powell, Goldstein, Frazer & Murphy LLP (Partner)

Clients Represented
On Behalf of Powell, Goldstein, Frazer & Murphy LLP
Joint Stock Company Severstal

ELLIS, Ryan
3124 N. Tenth St.
Arlington, VA 22201
EMail: rellis@govreform.org
Tel: (703)243-7400
Fax: (703)243-7403

Employers
Council for Government Reform (Director, Government Relations)

ELLIS, William T.
3000 K St. NW
Suite 500
Washington, DC 20007-5109
EMail: wellis@foleylaw.com
Tel: (202)672-5300
Fax: (202)672-5399

Employers
Foley & Lardner (Partner)

ELLISON, Mark C.
9306 Old Keene Mill Rd.
Burke, VA 22015
Tel: (703)455-3600
Fax: (703)455-3603

Employers
Hardy & Ellison, P.C. (V. President)

Clients Represented
On Behalf of Hardy & Ellison, P.C.
Consumer Satellite Systems, Inc.

ELLMAN, Eric J.
1090 Vermont Ave. NW
Suite 200
Washington, DC 20005-4905
Tel: (202)371-0910
Fax: (202)371-0134
Registered: LDA

Employers
Associated Credit Bureaus, Inc. (Senior Manager, State Government Relations)

ELLROD, III, Frederick E.
1155 Connecticut Ave. NW
Suite 1000
Washington, DC 20036-4306
Tel: (202)785-0600
Fax: (202)785-1234

Employers
Miller & Van Eaton, P.L.L.C. (Director)

Clients Represented
On Behalf of Miller & Van Eaton, P.L.L.C.
Henrico County, Virginia

ELLSWORTH, Cheryl N.
The Watergate
Suite 1113
2600 Virginia Ave. NW
Washington, DC 20037-1905
Tel: (202)337-8338
Fax: (202)337-6685

Employers
Harris Ellsworth & Levin (Partner)

Clients Represented
On Behalf of Harris Ellsworth & Levin
Ass'n of Food Industries, Inc.
Committee of Domestic Steel Wire Rope and Specialty Cable Manufacturers
Shieldalloy Metallurgical Corp.

ELLSWORTH, Gary G.
6903 Rockledge Dr.
Bethesda, MD 20817
Tel: (301)564-3200
Fax: (301)564-3201

Employers
USEC, Inc. (Contact, Political Action Committee)

ELMENDORF, Edward M.
1307 New York Ave.
Fifth Floor
Washington, DC 20005-4701
EMail: elmendorfe@aascu.org
Tel: (202)478-4651
Fax: (202)296-5819

Employers
American Ass'n of State Colleges and Universities (V. President, Government Relations)

ELMENDORF, Fritz M.
1000 Wilson Blvd.
Suite 2500
Arlington, VA 22209-3908
EMail: felmendorf@cbanet.org
Tel: (703)276-1750
Fax: (703)528-1290

Employers
Consumer Bankers Ass'n (V. President, Communications and Public Relations)

ELMER, Brian C.
1001 Pennsylvania Ave. NW
Suite 1100
Washington, DC 20004-2595
EMail: belmer@cromor.com
Tel: (202)624-2500
Fax: (202)628-5116
Law Clerk to Chief Judges Miller and Bazelon, U.S. Court of Appeals for the District of Columbia Circuit, 1962-64.

Employers
Crowell & Moring LLP (Partner)

Clients Represented
On Behalf of Crowell & Moring LLP
Nashua Corp.
United Technologies Corp.

ELSBREE, Amy
60 Massachusetts Ave. NE
Washington, DC 20002
Tel: (202)906-3884
Fax: (202)906-3175

Employers
AMTRAK (Nat'l Rail Passenger Corp.) (Senior Director, Government Affairs)

ELSEN, Karine

1150 17th St. NW
Suite 701
Washington, DC 20036
EMail: karine.elsen@dittus.com

Tel: (202)775-1401
Fax: (202)775-1404

Employers
Dittus Communications (Assistant V. President)

Clients Represented
On Behalf of Dittus Communications
eLink
SurfControl

ELWELL, Robert G.

818 Connecticut Ave. NW
Suite 1200
Washington, DC 20006

Tel: (202)872-8181
Fax: (202)872-8696

Employers
Internat'l Business-Government Counsellors, Inc. (V. President and Special Advisor)

ELWOOD, Thomas W.

1730 M St. NW
Suite 500
Washington, DC 20036

Tel: (202)293-4848
Fax: (202)293-4852

Employers
Ass'n of Schools of Allied Health Professions (Exec. Director)

ELY, Bert

P.O. Box 21010
Alexandria, VA 22320

Tel: (703)836-4101
Fax: (703)836-1403
Registered: LDA

EMail: bert@ely-co.com

Employers
Ely & Co., Inc. (President)

Clients Represented
On Behalf of Ely & Co., Inc.
Ass'n of Bank Couriers

ELY, Jr., Clausen

1201 Pennsylvania Ave. NW
Washington, DC 20004-2401

Tel: (202)662-6000
Fax: (202)662-6291
Registered: LDA

EMail: cely@cov.com
Law Clerk to Judge Richard T. Rives, U.S. Court of Appeals, Fifth Circuit, 1972-73.

Employers
Covington & Burling (Partner)

Clients Represented
On Behalf of Covington & Burling
Nat'l Food Processors Ass'n

EMANUEL, Adam

One Massachusetts Ave. NW
Suite 330
Washington, DC 20001

Tel: (703)448-3060
Fax: (703)448-3060
Registered: LDA

Employers
Adam Emanuel and Associates (President)
Law Office of Zel E. Lipsen

Clients Represented
On Behalf of Adam Emanuel and Associates
Ancore Corp.
EFW Corp.
Israel Aircraft Industries, Ltd.
On Behalf of Law Office of Zel E. Lipsen
Ancore Corp.
British Ministry of Defence
EFW Corp.
Northrop Grumman Corp.

EMERICK, Kelli

601 13th St. NW
Suite 410 South
Washington, DC 20005

Tel: (202)737-0100
Fax: (202)628-3965

Employers
R. Duffy Wall and Associates (V. President)

EMERLING, Stanley J.

2713 Berryland Dr.
Oakton, VA 22124-1404

Tel: (703)620-6036
Fax: (703)620-5989

Former Member, National Advisory Committee for Meat and Poultry Inspection, Department of Agriculture.

Employers
Self-employed as an independent consultant.

Clients Represented
As an independent consultant
North American Meat Processors Ass'n

EMERY, Jack M.

1101 Vermont Ave. NW
12th Floor
Washington, DC 20005-3583

Tel: (202)789-7414
Fax: (202)789-7581
Registered: LDA

Employers
American Medical Ass'n (Assistant Director, Federal Affairs)

EMERY, Rodney

601 13th St. NW
Suite 410 South
Washington, DC 20005

Tel: (202)737-0100
Fax: (202)628-3965
Registered: LDA

Employers
R. Duffy Wall and Associates (V. President)

Clients Represented
On Behalf of R. Duffy Wall and Associates
Florence, South Carolina, City of
Gardena, California, City of

EMLING, Gretchen

1627 I St. NW
Suite 900
Washington, DC 20006

Tel: (202)833-8994
Fax: (202)835-0707
Registered: LDA

Employers
The Williams Companies (Manager, Government Affairs)

EMLING, John

1201 F St. NW
Suite 200
Washington, DC 20004

Tel: (202)554-9000
Fax: (202)484-1566
Registered: LDA

Employers
Nat'l Federation of Independent Business (Manager, Legislative Affairs/House)

EMMER, Matthew D.

1400 16th St. NW
Suite 600
Washington, DC 20036

Tel: (202)939-7900
Fax: (202)745-0916

Employers
Fleischman and Walsh, L.L.P. (Partner)

EMMETT, Edward M.

1700 N. Moore St.
Suite 1900
Arlington, VA 22209-1904
EMail: emmett@nitl.org

Tel: (703)524-5011
Fax: (703)524-5017
Registered: LDA

Employers
Nat'l Industrial Transportation League (President and Chief Operating Officer)

EMMONS, Rachel A.

418 C St. NE
Washington, DC 20002
EMail: rachele@mail.greystone-group.com

Tel: (202)547-8530
Fax: (202)547-8532

Employers
Sara Garland (and Associates) (Exec. Associate)

Clients Represented
On Behalf of Sara Garland (and Associates)
American Indian Higher Education Consortium
Minot State University
Sesame Workshop
Swope Parkway Health Center

EMORD, Jonathan W.

1050 17th St. NW
Suite 600
Washington, DC 20036

Tel: (202)466-6937
Fax: (202)466-6938
Registered: LDA

Employers
Emord & Associates, P.C. (President)

Clients Represented
On Behalf of Emord & Associates, P.C.
American Preventive Medical Ass'n
The JAG Group, Inc.
Meditrend, Inc.
Pure Encapsulations, Inc.
Rx Vitamins, Inc.
UroStar, Inc.
Weider Nutritional Group
XCEL Medical Pharmacy, Ltd.

ENCE, Ronald K.

One Thomas Circle NW
Suite 400
Washington, DC 20005

Tel: (202)659-8111
Fax: (202)659-9216
Registered: LDA

Employers
Independent Community Bankers of America (Director, Legislative Affairs)

ENDEAN, Erin M.

1200 19th St. NW
Suite 201
Washington, DC 20036-2065

Tel: (202)822-4700
Fax: (202)822-4710

Former Director, Japanese Affairs, Office of U.S. Trade Representative. Former Senior Economic Analyst on China, Central Intelligence Agency.

Employers
Hills & Company, International Consultants (Managing Director)

ENDEAN, Jr., Howard John

1730 K St. NW
Suite 1200
Washington, DC 20006

Tel: (202)822-9300
Fax: (202)467-4070
Registered: LDA

Employers
American Business Conference (V. President, Policy)

ENDRES, Jr., Arthur P. "Skip"

1001 G St. NW
Suite 1210-W
Washington, DC 20001-4545
EMail: skip.endres@bnsf.com

Tel: (202)347-8662
Fax: (202)347-8675
Registered: LDA

Employers
Burlington Northern Santa Fe Railway (V. President, Government Affairs)

ENDRESON, Douglas B. L.

1250 I St. NW
Suite 1000
Washington, DC 20005

Tel: (202)682-0240
Fax: (202)682-0249

Employers
Sonosky, Chambers, Sachse & Endreson (Partner)

ENGEBRETSON, Gary D.

1200 G St. NW
Suite 510
Washington, DC 20005
EMail: gary@csa-dc.org

Tel: (202)347-0600
Fax: (202)347-0608
Registered: LDA

Employers
Contract Services Ass'n of America (President)

ENGEL, III, Charles J.

1299 Pennsylvania Ave. NW
Washington, DC 20004-2402
EMail: engelt@howrey.com

Tel: (202)783-0800
Fax: (202)383-6610

Employers
Howrey Simon Arnold & White (Partner)

Clients Represented
On Behalf of Howrey Simon Arnold & White
Marine Preservation Ass'n

ENGEL, Jeanne K.

1201 15th St. NW
Washington, DC 20005-2800
Tel: (202)822-0200
Fax: (202)822-0572

Employers

Nat'l Ass'n of Home Builders of the U.S. (V. President, Policy-Multi-Family Services Division)

ENGEL, John M.

750 17th St. NW
Suite 1100
Washington, DC 20006
Tel: (202)778-2300
Fax: (202)778-2330
Registered: LDA

Legislative Assistant and Professional Staff Member to Senator Steve Symms (R-ID), 1983-86.

Employers

FoxKiser

ENGLAND, M.D., Mary Jane

50 F St. NW
Suite 600
Washington, DC 20001
EMail: wbgh@wbgh.com
Tel: (202)628-9320
Fax: (202)628-9244

Employers

Washington Business Group on Health (President)

ENGLAND, Peggy P.

805 15th St. NW
Suite 430
Washington, DC 20005
EMail: peggy.england@wswa.org
Tel: (202)371-9792
Fax: (202)789-2405

Former Communications Director to Senator Mike DeWine (R-OH) and former Press Secretary to Rep. Barbara Vucanovich (R-NV).

Employers

Wine and Spirits Wholesalers of America (V. President, Public Affairs and Communications)

ENGLE, Craig

1050 Connecticut Ave. NW
Washington, DC 20036-5339
Tel: (202)857-6000
Fax: (202)857-6395

Former Executive Assistant to Commissioner Lee Ann Elliott, Federal Election Commission.

Employers

Arent Fox Kintner Plotkin & Kahn, PLLC (Counsel)

ENGLE, Kimberley A.

601 Pennsylvania Ave. NW
Suite 300
The North Bldg.
Washington, DC 20004
Tel: (202)628-3500
Fax: (202)628-0400
Registered: LDA

Employers

Waste Management, Inc. (Manager, Government Affairs)

ENGLERT, Greg

600 Pennsylvania Ave. SE
Suite 220
Washington, DC 20003
Tel: (202)544-8814
Fax: (202)544-8853

Employers

Highmark Blue Cross/ Blue Shield (Senior Government Affairs Representative)

ENGLISH, Jr., Charles M.

701 Pennsylvania Ave. NW
Suite 800
Washington, DC 20004
Tel: (202)508-4000
Fax: (202)508-4321
Registered: LDA

Employers

Thelen Reid & Priest LLP (Partner)

Clients Represented

On Behalf of Thelen Reid & Priest LLP

Anderson Erickson Dairy Co.
Horizon Organic Holding Co.
Tillamook County Creamery Ass'n
Upper Midwest Coalition

ENGLISH, Hon. Glenn

4301 Wilson Blvd.
Arlington, VA 22203-1860
Tel: (703)907-5540
Fax: (703)907-5511
Registered: LDA

Employers

Nat'l Rural Electric Cooperative Ass'n (Chief Exec. Officer)

ENGLISH, Marlene

1350 I St. NW
Suite 300
Washington, DC 20005
Tel: (202)639-5900
Fax: (202)639-5932

Employers

Nat'l Food Processors Ass'n (Director, Political Affairs)

ENGLISH, Pepper

1133 21st St. NW
Suite 900
Washington, DC 20036
EMail: pepper.english@bellsouth.com
Tel: (202)463-4100
Fax: (202)463-4633
Registered: LDA

Employers

BellSouth Corp. (V. President, Congressional Relations)

ENGLISH, Stephen M.

1100 17th St. NW
Seventh Floor
Washington, DC 20036
Tel: (202)223-8196
Fax: (202)872-1948
Registered: LDA

Employers

American Academy of Actuaries (Policy Analyst)

ENGLUND, Steven R.

555 12th St. NW
Washington, DC 20004-1206
EMail: Steven_Englund@aporter.com
Tel: (202)942-5000
Fax: (202)942-5999

Employers

Arnold & Porter (Partner)

ENGMAN, Patricia H.

1615 L St. NW
Suite 1100
Washington, DC 20036-5610
Tel: (202)872-1260
Fax: (202)466-3509
Registered: LDA

Employers

The Business Roundtable (Exec. Director)

ENGQUIST, Christopher P.

905 16th St. NW
Washington, DC 20006
Tel: (202)783-3545
Fax: (202)347-1721

Employers

Laborers-Employers Cooperation & Education Trust (Exec. Director)

ENNEKING, Patty

1300 Wilson Blvd.
Suite 800
Arlington, VA 22209
Tel: (703)253-0602
Fax: (703)253-0701

Employers

American Plastics Council (V. President, Non Durables)

ENNIS, Kate

6400 Goldsboro Rd.
Suite 500
Bethesda, MD 20817
EMail: kennis@epb.com
Tel: (301)263-2310
Fax: (301)263-2269

Employers

Earle Palmer Brown Public Relations (Account Director, EPB PR)

ENNS, Bill

11480 Commerce Park Dr.
Reston, VA 20191
Tel: (703)755-2000
Fax: (703)755-2623

Employers

Teleglobe Communications Corp. (V. President, Corporate Development and Regulatory Affairs)

ENRIGHT, Janice Ann

1300 Connecticut Ave. NW
Suite 600
Washington, DC 20036
EMail: jenright@griffinjohnson.com
Tel: (202)887-6726
Fax: (202)223-0358
Registered: LDA

Former Executive Assistant to the Deputy Chief of Staff, Executive Office of the President, The White House, during the Clinton Administration..

Employers

The Ickes & Enright Group (Partner)
Meyer, Suozzi, English & Klein, P.C. (Senior Advisor, Government Affairs)

Clients Represented

On Behalf of The Ickes & Enright Group

4C Foods Corp.
American Federation of Teachers
Brooklyn Public Library
Consortium for Worker Education
Deloitte Consulting
Farallon Capital Management
Greater New York Hospital Ass'n
HiSynergy Communications, Inc.
New York City, New York, Council of
The New York Historical Soc.
Service Employees Internat'l Union
United Airlines

ENSINGER, Robert

801 18th St. NW
Washington, DC 20006
Tel: (202)872-1300
Fax: (202)416-7641

Employers

Paralyzed Veterans of America (Director, Communications)

ENTIN, Stephen J.

1730 K St. NW
Suite 910
Washington, DC 20006
Tel: (202)463-1400
Fax: (202)463-6199

Employers

Institute for Research on the Economics of Taxation (IRET) (President and Exec. Director)

ENTMACHER, Joan M.

11 Dupont Circle NW
Suite 800
Washington, DC 20036
EMail: jentmacher@nwlc.org
Tel: (202)588-5180
Fax: (202)588-5185

Employers

Nat'l Women's Law Center (V. President, Family Economic Security Program)

ENVALL, Kirsten

316 Pennsylvania Ave. SE
Suite 300
Washington, DC 20003
Tel: (202)675-3362
Fax: (202)675-4230
Registered: LDA

Employers

United Parcel Service (Manager, Public Affairs)

ENZI, Michael Bradley

601 13th St. NW
Suite 410 South
Washington, DC 20005
Tel: (202)737-0100
Fax: (202)628-3965
Registered: LDA

Employers

R. Duffy Wall and Associates (V. President)

Clients Represented

On Behalf of R. Duffy Wall and Associates

NCR Corp.

EPPARD, Ann

211 N. Union St.
Suite 100
Alexandria, VA 22314
Tel: (703)739-2545
Fax: (703)739-2718
Registered: LDA

Former Chief of Staff to Rep. Bud Shuster (R-PA).

Employers

Ann Eppard Associates, Ltd. (President)

Clients Represented

On Behalf of Ann Eppard Associates, Ltd.

Air Transport Ass'n of America
Air-21 Coalition
Amadeus Global Travel Distribution SA
American Beverage Institute
American Maritime Officers Service
Anthony Timberlands, Inc.
Boucher & James
Calspan University of Buffalo Research Center
COMARCO Wireless Technology
Dade County Board of Commissioners
Daniel, Mann, Johnson & Mendenhall
Day & Zimmermann, Inc.
Delta Development Group, Inc.
FedEx Corp.
George Zamias Developers
Harlingen Area Chamber of Commerce
Indiana County Development Corp.
Jefferson Government Relations, L.L.C.
Outdoor Advertising Ass'n of America
Pennsylvania Pyrotechnics Ass'n
Pennsylvania Turnpike Commission
Pine Bluff Sand and Gravel Co.
Thelen Reid & Priest LLP
Traffic.com
Union Pacific
United Airlines

EPSTEIN, Anita K.

2300 N St. NW
Washington, DC 20037-1128
Tel: (202)663-8000
Fax: (202)663-8007
Registered: LDA, FARA
EMail: anita.epstein@shawpittman.com

Employers
Shaw Pittman (Government Relations Advisor)

Clients Represented

On Behalf of Shaw Pittman

Memphis, Tennessee, City of
Mexico, Secretaria de Comercio y Fomento Industrial (SECOFI)
Southern Ass'n of Forestry Economics

EPSTEIN, Christopher

1701 Pennsylvania Ave. NW
Suite 500
Washington, DC 20006
Tel: (202)861-0660
Fax: (202)861-0437

Employers
Mitsui and Co. (U.S.A.), Inc. (Export Controls Manager)

EPSTEIN, Gary M.

555 11th St. NW
Suite 1000
Washington, DC 20004
Tel: (202)637-2200
Fax: (202)637-2201
Registered: LDA
Chief, Common Carrier Bureau, Federal Communications Commission, 1981-83.

Employers
Latham & Watkins (Partner)

EPSTEIN, Gordon

2001 Pennsylvania Ave. NW
Suite 700
Washington, DC 20006
Tel: (202)331-7301
Fax: (202)331-7277
EMail: gordon_epstein@micusa.com

Employers
Mitsubishi Internat'l Corp. (Manager)

EPSTEIN, Jason

1640 Rhode Island Ave. NW
Washington, DC 20036-3278
Tel: (202)857-6613
Fax: (202)857-6689
Registered: LDA
EMail: jepstein@bnaibrith.org

Employers
B'nai B'rith Internat'l (Director, Legislative Affairs)

EPSTEIN, Joshua M.

1775 Massachusetts Ave. NW
Washington, DC 20036-2188
Tel: (202)797-6000
Fax: (202)797-6004
Former International Affairs Fellow, Council on Foreign Relations, Department of State and Senate Armed Services Committee.

Employers
The Brookings Institution (Senior Fellow, Economic Studies)

EPSTEIN, Louise

1500 Pennsylvania Ave. NW
MS: 1006
Washington, DC 20220
Tel: (202)622-1778

Employers
Department of Treasury - Tax Policy (Associate Tax Legislative Counsel)

EPSTEIN, Mark

4350 East West Hwy.
Suite 401
Bethesda, MD 20814-4411
Tel: (301)718-6537
Fax: (301)656-0989

Employers
PAI Management Corp. (Senior Account Executive)

Clients Represented

On Behalf of PAI Management Corp.

Internat'l Soc. for Pharmacoepidemiology

EPSTEIN, Michael

325 Seventh St. NW
Suite 1100
Washington, DC 20004-2802
Tel: (202)783-7971
Fax: (202)737-2849

Employers
Nat'l Retail Federation (Manager, Communications)

EPSTEIN, M.Ed.,CTRS, Rikki S.

22377 Belmont Ridge Rd.
Ashburn, VA 20148-4501
Tel: (703)858-2151
Fax: (703)858-0794
EMail: NTRSNRPA@aol.com

Employers
Nat'l Therapeutic Recreation Soc. (Exec. Director)

EPSTEIN, Tom

1320 Braddock Pl.
Alexandria, VA 22314
Tel: (703)739-5000
Fax: (703)739-0775

Employers
Public Broadcasting Service (V. President, Communications and Public Relations, National Press Relations)

EPSTIEN, Jay A.

1200 19th St. NW
Washington, DC 20036-2430
Tel: (202)861-3850
Fax: (202)223-2085
EMail: jay.epstien@piperrudnick.com

Employers
Piper Marbury Rudnick & Wolfe LLP (Co-Managing Partner)

EQUALE, Paul A.

412 First St. SE
Suite 300
Washington, DC 20003
Tel: (202)863-7000
Fax: (202)863-7015
Registered: LDA

Employers
Independent Insurance Agents of America, Inc. (Chief Exec. Officer, Capitol Hill Office)

EQUIHUA, Xavier

717 D St. NW
Suite 310
Washington, DC 20004
Tel: (202)626-0560
Fax: (202)393-5728
Registered: LDA, FARA
EMail: xfe@fedstrategies.com

Employers
Federal Strategies Group (V. President)

Clients Represented

On Behalf of Federal Strategies Group

AFINOA
Argentine Citrus Ass'n

ERAMIAN, Dan

1625 K St. NW
Suite 1100
Washington, DC 20006-1604
Tel: (202)857-0244
Fax: (202)857-0237
EMail: deramian@bio.org

Employers
Biotechnology Industry Organization (V. President, Communications)

ERAT, Donna

1120 19th St. NW
Eighth Floor
Washington, DC 20036
Tel: (202)467-6900
Fax: (202)467-6910
Registered: LDA

Employers
Womble Carlyle Sandridge & Rice, P.C.

Clients Represented

On Behalf of Womble Carlyle Sandridge & Rice, P.C.

North Carolina Electric Membership Corp.
North Carolina Global TransPark Authority
North Carolina, Hurricane Floyd Redevelopment Center of State of

ERB TULLY, Valerie

228 Seventh St. SE
Washington, DC 20003
Tel: (202)543-4357
Fax: (202)547-9312

Employers
Speak Out! USA (Managing Director, Public Relations)

ERBACH, Donald C.

445 12th St. NW
Room 8-C457
Washington, DC 20554
Tel: (202)418-1900
Fax: (202)418-2806

Employers
Federal Communications Commission (Senior Advisor, Legislative and Intergovernmental Affairs)

ERD, Steven J.

225 Reinekers Lane
Suite 300
Alexandria, VA 22314
Tel: (703)548-8600
Fax: (703)684-1581
Registered: LDA
EMail: serd@caionline.org

Employers
Community Ass'ns Institute (CAI) (Director, Government and Public Affairs)

ERDENGIZ, Ahmet

1667 K St. NW
Suite 690
Washington, DC 20006
Tel: (202)887-6198
Fax: (202)467-0685
Registered: FARA

Employers
Turkish Republic of Northern Cyprus, Embassy of (Representative)

ERDHEIM, Eric

1300 N. 17th St.
Suite 1847
Rosslyn, VA 22209
Tel: (703)841-3249
Fax: (703)841-3349
Registered: LDA
EMail: ric_erdheim@nema.org

Employers
Nat'l Electrical Manufacturers Ass'n (Senior Manager, Environmental Health and Safety)

ERDMANN, Richard L.

1800 N. Kent St.
Suite 1120
Arlington, VA 22209
Tel: (703)525-6300
Fax: (703)525-4610

Employers
The Conservation Fund (Sr. V. President and General Counsel)

ERDREICH, Hon. Ben L.

801 Pennsylvania Ave. NW
Suite 230
Washington, DC 20004
Tel: (202)393-7150
Fax: (202)347-1684
Registered: LDA
EMail: berdreich@bradleyarant.com
Chairman, Merit Systems Protection Board, 1993-2000. Member, U.S. House of Representatives (D-AL), 1982-92. First Lieutenant, U.S. Army, 1963-65.

Employers
Bradley Arant Rose & White LLP (Partner)

ERGER, Nurit

810 Vermont Ave. NW
Room 506
Washington, DC 20420
Tel: (202)273-5628
Fax: (202)273-6791

Employers
Department of Veterans Affairs (Director, Congressional Relations)

ERICKSEN, Jack

1310 G St. NW
12th Floor
Washington, DC 20005

Tel: (202)626-4780
Fax: (202)626-4833
Registered: LDA

Employers
Blue Cross Blue Shield Ass'n (Exec. Director, Congressional Relations)

ERICKSON, Audrae

600 Maryland Ave. SW
Suite 800
Washington, DC 20024

Tel: (202)484-3600
Fax: (202)484-3604
Registered: LDA

Employers
American Farm Bureau Federation (Director, International Trade, Policy, and Negotiations)

ERICKSON, Markham C.

400 N. Capitol St. NW
Suite 585
Washington, DC 20001
EMail: markham0010@att.net

Tel: (202)783-5300
Fax: (202)393-5218
Registered: LDA

Employers
McGuiness & Holch (Associate)

Clients Represented
On Behalf of McGuiness & Holch
Arch Mineral Corp.
Barr Laboratories
Council for Responsible Nutrition
Major League Baseball Players Ass'n
NetCoalition.Com
Oneida Indian Nation of New York
Project to Promote Competition and Innovation in the Digital Age
Wine and Spirits Wholesalers of America

ERICKSON, R. Brent

1625 K St. NW
Suite 1100
Washington, DC 20006-1604

Tel: (202)857-0244
Fax: (202)857-0237

Employers
Biotechnology Industry Organization (Director, Industrial and Environmental Section)

ERICKSON, Steve

2000 L St. NW
Suite 300
Washington, DC 20036-0646

Tel: (202)835-8800
Fax: (202)835-8879

Employers
Ketchum (Sr. V. President, Healthcare)

ERIKSON, Donald

21 Dupont Circle NW
Suite 700
Washington, DC 20036
EMail: dre@opastco.org

Tel: (202)659-5990
Fax: (202)659-4619
Registered: LDA

Employers
Organization for the Promotion and Advancement of Small Telecommunications Cos. (Director, Legislative Relations)

ERIKSON, R. Brent

1220 L St. NW
Washington, DC 20005

Tel: (202)682-8420
Fax: (202)682-8294
Registered: LDA

Employers
American Petroleum Institute (Washington Representative)

ERLENBORN, Hon. John N.

233 Pennsylvania Ave. SE
Suite 200
Washington, DC 20003-1107
EMail: usafmc1@mindspring.com

Tel: (202)543-8676
Fax: (202)543-7145

Member, U.S. House of Representatives (R-IL), 1965-85.

Employers
U.S. Ass'n of Former Members of Congress (President)

ERLING, Christina

1920 L St. NW
Washington, DC 20036
EMail: cerling@kamber.com

Tel: (202)223-8700
Fax: (202)659-5559

Employers
The Kamber Group (Exec. Assistant to the President)

Clients Represented
On Behalf of The Kamber Group
Nat'l Energy Management Institute

ERNST, Don

1703 N. Beauregard St.
Alexandria, VA 22311-1714
EMail: dernst@ascd.org

Tel: (703)575-5611
Fax: (703)575-5400

Employers
Ass'n for Supervision and Curriculum Development (Government Relations Director)

ERNST, Julia

1146 19th St. NW
Washington, DC 20036

Tel: (202)530-2975
Fax: (202)530-2976

Employers
Center for Reproductive Law and Policy (International Legislative Counsel)

ERNST, Martin C.

3000 K St. NW
Suite 300
Washington, DC 20007

Tel: (202)424-7500
Fax: (202)424-7643

Employers
Swidler Berlin Shereff Friedman, LLP

Clients Represented
On Behalf of Swidler Berlin Shereff Friedman, LLP
Entertainment Made Convenient

ERSKINE, Lt. Cdr. James M.

Rayburn House Office Bldg.
Room B324
Washington, DC 20515
EMail: erskine.james@hq.navy.mil

Tel: (202)225-1398

Employers
Department of Navy (Director, Management Division, Office of Legislative Affairs)

ERSTLING, Mark D.

1350 Connecticut Ave. NW
Suite 200
Washington, DC 20036
EMail: mark@apts.org

Tel: (202)887-1700
Fax: (202)293-2422

Employers
Ass'n of America's Public Television Stations (Senior V. President)

ERVIN, James L.

106 North Carolina Ave. SE
Washington, DC 20003
EMail: JimETA@aol.com

Tel: (202)863-0001
Fax: (202)863-0096
Registered: LDA

Director, House Affairs Office of the Secretary, Department of Defense, 1987. Former Lobbyist, Office of Legislative Liaison, Department of the Air Force.

Employers
Ervin Technical Associates, Inc. (ETA) (President)

Clients Represented
On Behalf of Ervin Technical Associates, Inc. (ETA)
ACS Defense, Inc.
Chamberlain Manufacturing Corp.
Computer Coalition for Responsible Exports
General Dynamics Corp.
Ingalls Shipbuilding
Kaiser-Hill Co., L.L.C.
Kaman Diversified Technologies Corp.
Lister Bolt & Chain Co.
Lockheed Martin Corp.
Martins Point Health Care
Northrop Grumman Corp.
Sarnoff Corp.
Science Applications Internat'l Corp. (SAIC)
SKF USA, Inc.
United Defense, L.P.
Video Network Communications

ERVIN, Susan C.

1775 I St. NW
Washington, DC 20006
EMail: susan.ervin@dechert.com

Tel: (202)261-3300
Fax: (202)261-3333

Employers
Dechert (Partner)*

ESBECK, Carl H.

4208 Evergreen Ln.
Suite 222
Annandale, VA 22003
EMail: cesbeck@clsnet.org

Tel: (703)642-1070
Fax: (703)642-1075
Registered: LDA

Employers
Christian Legal Soc. (Director, Center for Law and Religious Freedom)

ESBER, Brett M.

600 New Hampshire Ave. NW
11th Floor
Washington, DC 20037
EMail: bme@dejlaw.com

Tel: (202)944-3000
Fax: (202)944-3068
Registered: LDA, FARA

Employers
Dyer Ellis & Joseph, P.C. (Partner)

Clients Represented
On Behalf of Dyer Ellis & Joseph, P.C.
China Shipping (Group) Co.
DaimlerChrysler Corp.
Fruit Shippers Ltd.

ESBIN, Barbara

1200 New Hampshire Ave. NW
Suite 800
Washington, DC 20036-6802
EMail: besbin@dlalaw.com

Tel: (202)776-2000
Fax: (202)776-2222

Employers
Dow, Lohnes & Albertson, PLLC (Member)

ESCOBEDO, Esperanza

655 National Press Bldg.
Washington, DC 20045

Tel: (202)737-8400
Fax: (202)737-8406

Employers
John Adams Associates Inc.

Clients Represented
On Behalf of John Adams Associates Inc.
GlobalNet Holdings Corp.

ESDERS, Ingolf G.

1101 17th St. NW
Suite 400
Washington, DC 20036

Tel: (202)955-6304
Fax: (202)955-6048

Employers
Internat'l Longshoremen's Ass'n (Legislative Representative)

ESHELMAN, Jeffrey

1150 17th St. NW
Suite 701
Washington, DC 20036
EMail: jeffreye@dittus.com

Tel: (202)775-1401
Fax: (202)775-1404

Employers
Dittus Communications (Senior Director)

Clients Represented
On Behalf of Dittus Communications
Digital Focus
Hess
Statoil Energy
Surviving Selma
TCS

ESHERICK, Mark

701 Pennsylvania Ave. NW
Suite 720
Washington, DC 20004

Tel: (202)434-4800
Fax: (202)347-4015

Employers
Siemens Corp.

ESHMAN, Carrie

1299 Pennsylvania Ave. NW
Suite 800 West
Washington, DC 20004
Tel: (202)785-0500
Fax: (202)785-5277

Employers
The Carmen Group

ESKIN, Andrew D.

901 15th St. NW
Suite 700
Washington, DC 20005-2301
Tel: (202)371-6000
Fax: (202)371-6279
Registered: LDA
EMail: adeskin@verner.com
Legislative Director to Senator Richard Bryan (D-NV), 1989-90. Attorney, Bureau of Competition, Federal Trade Commission, 1985-86. Legislative Aide to Rep. James Santini (D-NV), 1977-78.

Employers
Verner, Liipfert, Bernhard, McPherson and Hand, Chartered (Member of Firm)

Clients Represented

On Behalf of Verner, Liipfert, Bernhard, McPherson and Hand, Chartered
Alere Medical Inc.
American Share Insurance
Citigroup
Federal Home Loan Bank of Indianapolis
Lehman Brothers
Mars, Inc.
Merrill Lynch & Co., Inc.
Rite Aid Corp.
VISA U.S.A., Inc.
Winstar Petroleum

ESPERNE, Jeanine

1001 19th St. North
Suite 800
Arlington, VA 22209-3901
Tel: (703)276-5100
Fax: (703)276-5057
Registered: LDA
EMail: jeanine.esperne@trw.com

Employers
TRW Inc. (Director, Government Relations-Defense and Nat'l Security Programs)

ESPINOSA, William H.

1133 Connecticut Ave. NW
Suite 1200
Washington, DC 20036
Tel: (202)775-9800
Fax: (202)833-8491

Employers
Winthrop, Stimson, Putnam & Roberts (Associate)

Clients Represented

On Behalf of Winthrop, Stimson, Putnam & Roberts
Sargeant Marine, Inc.

ESPOSITO, Sante J.

1909 K St. NW
Suite 820
Washington, DC 20006
Tel: (202)777-7700
Fax: (202)777-7763
Registered: LDA
EMail: sesposito@lmm-law.com
Democratic Chief Counsel, House Committee on Transportation and Infrastructure, 1981-98. Counsel, House Committee on the Budget, 1978-81. Counsel, Congressional Budget Office, 1975-78.

Employers
Lawler, Metzger & Milkman, LLC (Partner)

Clients Represented

On Behalf of Lawler, Metzger & Milkman, LLC
Advocates for Highway and Auto Safety
Assumption College
Brotherhood of Maintenance of Way Employees
Canadian Nat'l Railroad/Illinois Central Railroad
Canadian Nat'l Railway Co.
Currie Technologies, Inc.
Electric Transportation Co.
EVA Corp.
Fairfield University
Great Projects Film Co., Inc.
Highway 53 Longrange Improvement Citizens' Task Force
ORBITZ
Portals Development Associates L.P.
Provideo Productions
Rutgers University
ZapWorld.com
Zuckert, Scoutt and Rasenberger, L.L.P.

ESQUIBEL, Amanda R.

901 E St. NW
Suite 600
Washington, DC 20004
Tel: (202)783-4444
Fax: (202)783-4085
Executive Assistant to Senator Jeff Bingaman (D-NM), 1988-91.

Employers
Nat'l Treasury Employees Union (Director, TEPAC)

ESSER, Peter J. C.

1627 I St. NW
Suite 550
Washington, DC 20006
Tel: (202)659-4777
Fax: (202)659-4779
Registered: LDA, FARA

Employers
Representative of German Industry and Trade (Government Affairs Counsel)

Clients Represented

On Behalf of Representative of German Industry and Trade
Ass'n of German Chambers of Industry & Commerce (DIHT)
Federation of German Industries (BDI)

ESTELL, Anita R.

1420 New York Ave. NW
Suite 1050
Washington, DC 20005
Tel: (202)638-1950
Fax: (202)638-1928
Registered: LDA
EMail: aestell@vsadc.com
Former advisor to Secretary of Education Richard Riley; Associate Staff for Congressman Louis Stokes (D-OH), House Appropriations Committee.

Employers
Van Scoyoc Associates, Inc. (V. President)

Clients Represented

On Behalf of Van Scoyoc Associates, Inc.
Baltimore, Maryland, City of
Bristol-Myers Squibb Co.
Chicago State University
Jackson State University
Nat'l Ass'n for Equal Opportunity in Higher Education
Nat'l Commission on Correctional Health Care
Sickle Cell Disease Ass'n of America
Spelman College

ESTEREICHER, Christine

1401 H St. NW
Suite 700
Washington, DC 20005
Tel: (202)414-6713
Fax: (202)414-6745
Registered: LDA

Employers
DaimlerChrysler Corp. (Representative, External Affairs)

ESTES, Charles D.

1600 Wilson Blvd.
Suite 900
Arlington, VA 22209-2505
Tel: (703)526-7850
Fax: (703)526-7805
Registered: LDA
EMail: cestes@gri.org
Staff Director, Interior Subcommittee, Committee on Appropriations, U.S. Senate, 1979-92. Served in various staff positions, Department of Energy, 1971-79.

Employers
Charles D. Estes & Associates (President)

Clients Represented

On Behalf of Charles D. Estes & Associates
American Gas Ass'n
Appalachian-Pacific Coal Mine Methane Power Co., LLC
Gas Research Institute

ESTES, Deborah M.

400 N. Capitol St. NW
Washington, DC 20001
Tel: (202)824-7208
Fax: (202)824-7090
Registered: LDA
EMail: destes@aga.org

Employers
American Gas Ass'n (Managing Director, Government Relations)

ESTES, III, John N.

1440 New York Ave. NW
Washington, DC 20005
Tel: (202)371-7000
Fax: (202)393-5760

Employers
Skadden, Arps, Slate, Meagher & Flom LLP (Partner)

ESTES, John T.

1300 Pennsylvania Ave. NW
Suite 600
Washington, DC 20004
Tel: (202)220-9798
Fax: (202)289-7675
Registered: LDA
EMail: burntree@mindspring.com
Former Attorney, National Labor Relations Board.

Employers
Estes Associates (Exec. Director)

Clients Represented

On Behalf of Estes Associates
Coalition for Competitive Rail Transportation
Main Street Coalition for Postal Fairness

ESTEVEZ, Mareza I.

701 Pennsylvania Ave. NW
Suite 800
Washington, DC 20004
Tel: (202)508-4000
Fax: (202)508-4321
Registered: LDA

Employers
Thelen Reid & Priest LLP

Clients Represented

On Behalf of Thelen Reid & Priest LLP
Washington Soccer Partners

ESTRADA, Lisa

1050 Connecticut Ave. NW
Washington, DC 20036-5339
Tel: (202)857-6000
Fax: (202)857-6395

Employers
Arent Fox Kintner Plotkin & Kahn, PLLC (Associate)

Clients Represented

On Behalf of Arent Fox Kintner Plotkin & Kahn, PLLC
Mercy Hospital of Des Moines, Iowa

ESTY, Sandi

1160 Air Force Pentagon
Room 5D912
Washington, DC 20330-1160
Tel: (703)697-1500
Fax: (703)697-2001

Employers
Department of Air Force (Chief, Air Operations Officer, Legislative Liaison)

ETHERTON, Jonathan

1250 I St. NW
Suite 1200
Washington, DC 20005-3924
Tel: (202)371-8533
Fax: (202)371-8470
Registered: LDA

Employers
Aerospace Industries Ass'n of America (Assistant V. President, Legislative Affairs)

ETKA, Steven D.

4502 Highland Green Ct.
Alexandria, VA 22312
Tel: (703)354-3303
Fax: (703)354-3336
Registered: LDA
Legislative Assistant/Deputy Legislative Director to Senator Herbert Kohl (D-WI), 1992-97.

Employers
Etka Consulting (Principal)

Clients Represented

On Behalf of Etka Consulting
American Farmland Trust
Rural Advancement Foundation Internat'l - USA
Upper Midwest Dairy Coalition

ETTLINGER, Michael P.

1320 19th St. NW
Suite M-1
Washington, DC 20036
Tel: (202)293-0222
Fax: (202)293-0202

Employers
Public Campaign (Deputy Director)

EULE, Margo Grimm

1667 K St. NW
Suite 1210
Washington, DC 20006
Tel: (202)296-5550
Registered: LDA

Employers
Hyundai Motor Co.

EUSTICE, Mary Jo

8400 W. Park Dr.
McLean, VA 22102
Tel: (202)547-5500
Fax: (202)479-0168

Employers
Nat'l Automobile Dealers Ass'n (Senior Legislative Representative)

EVANS, Barbara

1120 20th St. NW
Suite 1000
Washington, DC 20036
Registered: LDA

Employers
Concert USA

EVANS, Billy Lee

210 Seventh St. SE
Washington, DC 20003
Tel: (202)547-6808
Fax: (202)546-5425
Registered: LDA

Member, U.S. House of Representatives (D-GA), 1977-83.

Employers
Kessler & Associates Business Services, Inc.

Clients Represented

On Behalf of Kessler & Associates Business Services, Inc.

Burlington Northern Santa Fe Railway
Dunn-Edwards Corp.
Exelon Corp.
Nat'l Ass'n of Securities Dealers, Inc. (NASD)
Pharmacia Corp.
Philip Morris Management Corp.
Planet Electric

EVANS, Catherine A.

499 S. Capitol St. SW
Suite 502A
Washington, DC 20003
Tel: (202)554-3060
Fax: (202)554-3160
Registered: LDA
EMail: cevans@motor-freight.com

Aide to Rep. Jack Brooks (D-TX); House Public Works Committee.

Employers
Motor Freight Carriers Ass'n (V. President, Government Affairs)

EVANS, Christy Carson

700 13th St. NW
Suite 400
Washington, DC 20005
Tel: (202)347-0773
Fax: (202)347-0785
Registered: LDA
EMail: cevans@cassidy.com

Policy and Planning Coordinator, House Republican Conference, 1994-98. Special Assistant to Rep. John Boehner (R-OH), 1992-94. Strategy Whip Assistant 1990-92, Legislative Assistant 1989-90 to Rep. Newt Gingrich, (R-GA). Staff Assistant to Deputy Assistant Secretary for Congressional and Legislative Affairs, Department of Commerce, 1988-89.

Employers
Cassidy & Associates, Inc. (V. President)

Clients Represented

On Behalf of Cassidy & Associates, Inc.

Abtech Industries
Air Products and Chemicals, Inc.
CNF Transportation, Inc.
eCharge Corp.
Edward Health Services
Internat'l Snowmobile Manufacturers Ass'n
Memorial Hermann Health Care System
Ocean Spray Cranberries
Ohio State University
Orange, California, County of
Sacramento Area Flood Control Agency
Subaru of America
Tiffany & Co.
VoiceStream Wireless Corp.
Widener University

EVANS, Hon. Dave

406 Third St. SE
Washington, DC 20003
Tel: (202)546-9634
Registered: LDA

Member, U.S. House of Representatives (D-IN), 1975-83.

Employers
Dave Evans Associates (President)

Clients Represented

On Behalf of Dave Evans Associates

Dunn-Edwards Corp.
Harmon-Motive
Internat'l Game Technology
Manufactured Housing Ass'n for Regulatory Reform
United California Savings Bank

EVANS, David C.

1301 K St. NW
Suite 1100-East Tower
Washington, DC 20005
Tel: (202)414-9200
Fax: (202)414-9299
Registered: LDA

Employers
Reed, Smith, LLP (Partner)

Clients Represented

On Behalf of Reed, Smith, LLP

Brick Industry Ass'n
Golf Course Superintendents Ass'n of America
Nat'l Ass'n of Dental Laboratories
Owens-Illinois, Inc.

EVANS, David V.

3549 S. Utah St.
Arlington, VA 22206-1815
Tel: (703)998-0894
Registered: LDA

Former Staff Director, U.S. Senate Subcommittee on Education, Arts and Humanities.

Employers
Self-employed as an independent consultant.

EVANS, Eddie D.

801 Pennsylvania Ave. NW
Suite 725
Washington, DC 20004
Tel: (202)628-0500
Fax: (202)682-0538
Registered: LDA
EMail: eddie.evants@aventis.com

Health Affairs Congressional Liaison, Office of the Assistant Secretary of Defense, 1992-93; Chief, Congressional Actions Branch, Office of the Army Surgeon General, 1992-88; Senior Program Analyst, Office of the Army Surgeon General, 1987-88.

Employers
Aventis Pharmaceuticals, Inc. (V. President, Federal Government Relations)

EVANS, Eric

1250 Connecticut Ave. NW
Suite 610
Washington, DC 20036
Tel: (202)955-3005
Fax: (202)955-1087
EMail: eevans@welfaretowork.org

Employers
Welfare to Work Partnership (V. President, Communications)

EVANS, Gail

1901 L St. NW
Suite 500
Washington, DC 20036
Tel: (202)862-7200
Fax: (202)862-7230

Employers
Nat'l Railway Labor Conference (Exec. Administrator)

EVANS, Gordon R.

1300 I St. NW
Suite 400 West
Washington, DC 20005
Tel: (202)515-2527
Fax: (202)336-7922

Employers
Verizon Communications (V. President, Federal Regulatory)

EVANS, Holly

2500 Wilson Blvd.
Arlington, VA 22201-3834
Tel: (703)907-7576
Fax: (703)907-7501
Registered: LDA
EMail: hevans@eia.org

Employers
Electronic Industries Alliance (Director, Environmental Affairs)

EVANS, Jr., K. Stewart

600 14th St. NW
Suite 500
Washington, DC 20005
Tel: (202)220-1200
Fax: (202)220-1665

Employers
Pepper Hamilton LLP (Partner)

EVANS, Lawrence H.

5201 Auth Way
Fifth Floor
Camp Springs, MD 20746
Tel: (301)423-3335
Fax: (301)423-0634

Employers
Transportation Institute (Director, Domestic Marine Affairs)

EVANS, Linda C.

1301 K St. NW
Suite 1200-West Tower
Washington, DC 20005-3307
Tel: (202)515-5526
Fax: (202)515-5078
Registered: LDA
EMail: levans@us.ibm.com

Employers
Internat'l Business Machines Corp. (Program Director, Taxes and Finance)

EVANS, M. Stanton

800 Maryland Ave. NE
Washington, DC 20002
Tel: (202)546-1710
Fax: (202)546-3489

Employers
Education and Research Institute (Chairman)

EVANS, Mica

Ten G St. NE
Suite 700
Washington, DC 20002
Tel: (202)216-5900
Fax: (202)216-0875

Employers
Interstate Natural Gas Ass'n of America (PAC Administrator)

EVANS, Rae Forker

1615 L St. NW
Suite 1220
Washington, DC 20036-5610
Tel: (202)659-0946
Fax: (202)659-4972
Registered: LDA
EMail: rfevans@winstarmail.com

Employers
Evans & Black, Inc. (President)

Clients Represented

On Behalf of Evans & Black, Inc.

American Business Media
Brinker Internat'l
Girl Scouts of the U.S.A. - Washington Office
Hallmark Cards, Inc.
Komen Breast Cancer Foundation, The Susan G.
Nat'l Osteoporosis Foundation
Newspaper Ass'n of America

EVANS, Robert D.

740 15th St. NW
Ninth Floor
Washington, DC 20005
Tel: (202)662-1765
Fax: (202)662-1762
Registered: LDA

Employers
American Bar Ass'n (Associate Exec. Director)

EVANS, William C.

901 15th St. NW
Suite 700
Washington, DC 20005-2301
Tel: (202)371-6000
Fax: (202)371-6279
Registered: LDA

Employers
Verner, Liipfert, Bernhard, McPherson and Hand, Chartered (Member of Firm)

EVANS, JR., Hon. Thomas B.

700 13th St. NW
Suite 950
Washington, DC 20005
Tel: (202)333-8777
Fax: (202)333-8722
Registered: LDA, FARA

Member, U.S. House of Representatives (R-DE), 1977-83.

Employers
The Evans Group, Ltd. (Chairman)

Clients Represented

On Behalf of The Evans Group, Ltd.

Cyprus, Government of the Republic of
Kazakhstan 21st Century Foundation
Naigai, Inc.
PetrolRem, Inc.
Unideal Navitankers
WorldWide Minerals Ltd.

EVE, Eric

1300 I St. NW
Suite 400 West
Washington, DC 20005
Tel: (202)515-2559
Fax: (202)336-7921
Registered: LDA

Employers

Verizon Communications (Assistant V. President, Federal Government Relations)

EVENS, Mark F.

701 Pennsylvania Ave. NW
Suite 800
Washington, DC 20004
Tel: (202)508-4053
Fax: (202)508-4321
EMail: mevens@thelenreid.com

Employers

Thelen Reid & Priest LLP (Partner)

EVERED, Stephen A.

One Massachusetts Ave. NW
Suite 880
Washington, DC 20001
Tel: (202)371-0782
Fax: (202)371-1178
Registered: LDA
EMail: severed841@aol.com

Employers

Robison Internat'l, Inc. (V. President)

Clients Represented

On Behalf of Robison Internat'l, Inc.

Honeywell Internat'l, Inc.
Simula, Inc.

EVERETT, Ralph B.

1299 Pennsylvania Ave. NW
Tenth Floor
Washington, DC 20004-2400
Tel: (202)508-9500
Fax: (202)508-9700
Registered: LDA
EMail: ralpheverett@paulhastings.com
Chief Counsel and Staff Director (1987-89) and Minority Chief Counsel and Staff Director (1983-87), Senate Committee on Commerce, Science and Transportation. Legislative Assistant (1979-82) and Minority Special Assistant (1977-78) to Senator Ernest Hollings (D-SC), 1977-78.

Employers

Paul, Hastings, Janofsky & Walker LLP (Partner)

Clients Represented

On Behalf of Paul, Hastings, Janofsky & Walker LLP

American Trucking Ass'ns
CFSBdirect Inc.
Chamber of Shipping of America
Cumulus Media, Inc.
INTELSAT - Internat'l Telecommunications Satellite Organization
Mead Johnson Nutritional Group
Norfolk Southern Corp.
Personal Communications Industry Ass'n (PCIA)
SBC Communications Inc.
SCC Communications Corp.
U.S. Figure Skating Ass'n
Union Pacific

EVERETT, Susan

636 I St. NW
Washington, DC 20001
Tel: (202)216-9034
Fax: (202)292-1185
EMail: severett@asla.org

Employers

Landscape Architecture Foundation (Exec. Director)

EVERSOLE, Kellye A.

3208 Park View Rd.
Chevy Chase, MD 20815
Tel: (301)951-3345
Fax: (301)951-1846
Registered: LDA
Legislative Assistant to Senator David Boren (D-OK), 1979-88; Professional Staff Member, Senate Committee on Agriculture, Nutrition and Forestry, 1988-89; Executive Director, Commission for Improvement of Federal Crop Insurance, 1989-90.

Employers

Eversole Associates (President)

Clients Represented

On Behalf of Eversole Associates

American Seed Trade Ass'n
Nat'l Corn Growers Ass'n

EWALT, Jim

1724 Massachusetts Ave. NW
Washington, DC 20036-1969
Tel: (202)775-3550
Fax: (202)775-1055

Employers

Nat'l Cable Television Ass'n (V. President, Public Affairs)

EWART, Andrea

2099 Pennsylvania Ave. NW
Suite 100
Washington, DC 20006
Tel: (202)955-3000
Fax: (202)955-5564
EMail: aewart@hklaw.com

Employers

Holland & Knight LLP (Associate)

EWART, Gary

1726 M St. NW
Suite 902
Washington, DC 20036
Tel: (202)785-3355
Fax: (202)452-1805
Registered: LDA

Employers

American Thoracic Soc. (Legislative Representative)

EWING, Kevin

2000 K St. NW
Suite 500
Washington, DC 20006-1872
Tel: (202)828-5800
Fax: (202)223-1225

Employers

Bracewell & Patterson, L.L.P.

Clients Represented

On Behalf of Bracewell & Patterson, L.L.P.

Council of Industrial Boiler Owners (CIBO)

EWING, Richard S.

555 12th St. NW
Washington, DC 20004-1206
Tel: (202)942-5000
Fax: (202)942-5999
EMail: Richard_Ewing@aporter.com

Employers

Arnold & Porter (Partner)

EWING, Hon. Thomas

1455 Pennsylvania Ave. NW
Suite 1200
Washington, DC 20004
Tel: (202)347-2230
Fax: (202)393-3310
Member, U.S. House of Representatives (R-IL), 1991-2001.

Employers

Davis & Harman LLP

EXLEY, Robbie

1016 16th St. NW
Suite 300
Washington, DC 20036
Tel: (202)862-4400
Fax: (202)862-4432

Employers

Nat'l Federation of Federal Employees (Specialist, Labor Relations)

EYMAN, Barbara D. A.

1001 Pennsylvania Ave. NW
Suite 600
Washington, DC 20004
Tel: (202)347-0066
Fax: (202)624-7222
Registered: LDA
EMail: beyman@pgfm.com
Legislative Assistant to Rep. Leon Panetta (D-CA), 1985-86.

Employers

Powell, Goldstein, Frazer & Murphy LLP (Counsel)

Clients Represented

On Behalf of Powell, Goldstein, Frazer & Murphy LLP

Nat'l Ass'n of Public Hospitals and Health Systems

EZZELL, William

555 12th St. NW
Suite 500
Washington, DC 20004-1207
Tel: (202)879-5385
Fax: (202)879-5309
Registered: LDA
EMail: wezzel@dttus.com

Employers

Deloitte & Touche LLP Nat'l Office - Washington (Partner in Charge, Government Affairs)

FABERMAN, Edward P.

1500 K St. NW
Suite 250
Washington, DC 20005-1714
Tel: (202)639-7501
Fax: (202)639-7505
Registered: LDA
EMail: epfaberman@uhlaw.com
Deputy Chief Counsel (1980-88) and Assistant Chief Counsel for Regulation and Enforcement (1970-80), Federal Aviation Administration.

Employers

Air Carrier Ass'n of America (Exec. Director)
Ungaretti & Harris (Partner)

Clients Represented

On Behalf of Ungaretti & Harris

Air Carrier Ass'n of America
Air Tran Airways
Akron-Canton Airport
Colgan Air, Inc.
Frontier Airlines
Lincoln Airport
Radius, The Global Travel Co.

FABIANI, James P.

700 13th St. NW
Suite 400
Washington, DC 20005
Tel: (202)347-0773
Fax: (202)347-0785
Registered: LDA, FARA
EMail: jfabiani@cassidy.com
Senior Minority Staff Member, Subcommittee on Labor, Health and Human Services, and Education, House Committee on Appropriations, 1979-82.

Employers

Cassidy & Associates, Inc. (Chairman and Chief Exec. Officer)

Clients Represented

On Behalf of Cassidy & Associates, Inc.

Boston College

FABRY, Ph.D., David

8300 Greensboro Dr.
Suite 750
McLean, VA 22102
Tel: (703)790-8466
Fax: (703)790-8631

Employers

American Academy of Audiology (President)

FAENZA, Michael M.

1021 Prince St.
Alexandria, VA 22314-2971
Tel: (703)684-7722
Fax: (703)684-5968
Registered: LDA

Employers

Nat'l Mental Health Ass'n (President and CEO)

FAGA, Betsy

600 Maryland Ave. SW
Suite 305 West
Washington, DC 20024
Tel: (202)484-2200
Ext: 104
Fax: (202)488-7416
EMail: betsyfaga@aol.com

Employers

North American Millers' Ass'n (President)

FAGAN, Janet

The Pentagon
Room 2C631
Washington, DC 20310-1600
Tel: (703)697-2583
Fax: (703)697-0690

Employers

Department of Army (Acting Chief, Congressional Inquiry Division, Legislative Liaison)

FAGAN, Patrick F.

214 Massachusetts Ave. NE
Washington, DC 20002
Tel: (202)546-4400
Fax: (202)546-8328

Employers

Heritage Foundation (William H.G. FitzGerald Senior Fellow in Family and Cultural Issues)

FAGER, Dan L.
1401 I St. NW
Suite 1200
Washington, DC 20005-2225
EMail: dfag@chevron.com
Tel: (202)408-5857
Fax: (202)408-5845
Registered: LDA

Employers
The Chevron Companies (Federal Relations Manager)
Chevron, U.S.A.

FAGIN, Darryl H.
1625 K St. NW
Suite 210
Washington, DC 20006
EMail: dfaigin@adaction.com
Tel: (202)785-5980
Fax: (202)785-5969
Registered: LDA

Employers
Americans for Democratic Action (Legislative Director)

FAGNANI, Lynn P.
1301 Pennsylvania Ave. NW
Suite 950
Washington, DC 20004
EMail: lfagnani@naph.org
Tel: (202)585-0100
Fax: (202)585-0101
Registered: LDA

Employers
Nat'l Ass'n of Public Hospitals and Health Systems (V. President, Finance and Reimbursement)

FAGRE, Danielle
1666 K St. NW
Suite 500
Washington, DC 20006-2803
Tel: (202)887-1400
Fax: (202)466-2198
Registered: LDA

Employers
O'Connor & Hannan, L.L.P. (Associate)

Clients Represented
On Behalf of O'Connor & Hannan, L.L.P.
American Free Trade Ass'n
Bear, Stearns and Co.
California Tax Credit Allocation Committee
Coalition for Tax Equity
The Metris Companies, Inc.
State Street Bank and Trust Co.
Tyson's Governmental Sales, LLC
UBS Warburg
VISA U.S.A., Inc.

FAHA, Joseph D.
5600 Fishers Ln.
Room 12C-15
Rockville, MD 20857
EMail: jfaha@samhsa.gov
Tel: (301)443-4640
Fax: (301)443-1450

Employers
Department of Health and Human Services - Substance Abuse and Mental Health Services Administration (Director, Division of Legislative and External Affairs)

FAHERTY, Robert L.
1775 Massachusetts Ave. NW
Washington, DC 20036-2188
Tel: (202)797-6250
Fax: (202)797-6004

Employers
The Brookings Institution (Director, Brookings Institution Press)

FAHEY, John
1145 17th St. NW
Washington, DC 20036
Tel: (202)857-7000
Fax: (202)775-6141

Employers
Nat'l Geographic Soc. (President and Chief Exec. Officer)

FAHEY, Mary L.
1200 G St. NW
Suite 300
Washington, DC 20005
EMail: mfahey@tei.org
Tel: (202)638-5601
Fax: (202)638-5607

Employers
Tax Executives Institute, Inc. (Tax Counsel)

FAHRENKOPF, Jr., Frank J.
555 13th St. NW
Suite 1010 East
Washington, DC 20004
Tel: (202)637-6500
Fax: (202)637-6507
Registered: LDA

Employers
American Gaming Ass'n (President and Chief Exec. Officer)

FAHY, Thomas E.
4000 Cathedral Ave. NW
Suite 705 B
Washington, DC 20016-5261
EMail: tfahycapitol@hotmail.com
Tel: (202)337-6954
Fax: (202)337-6959
Registered: LDA

Employers
Capitol Campaign Consultants (President)

Clients Represented
On Behalf of Capitol Campaign Consultants
Broadcast Compliance Services
Maryland, DC, Delaware Broadcasters Ass'n
Mid-Atlantic Broadcast Partners

FAIRBANKS, John
1334 G St. NW
Suite 300
Washington, DC 20005-3169
Tel: (202)628-3030
Fax: (202)347-2417

Employers
Families U.S.A. Foundation (Media Director)

FAIRBARNS, Jacqueline
4600 Duke St.
Suite 430
P.O. Box 22397
Alexandria, VA 22304
Tel: (703)823-9690
Fax: (703)823-9695

Employers
Ass'n for Education and Rehabilitation of the Blind & Visually Impaired (Assistant Exec. Director)

FAIRCHILD, MacLellan
P.O. Box 3008
Alexandria, VA 22302-0008
Tel: (703)931-4107
Fax: (703)931-3127
Registered: LDA

Employers
The Conaway Group LLC (Consultant)

Clients Represented
On Behalf of The Conaway Group LLC
Lockheed Martin Corp.

FAIRCHILD, Roger C.
14500 Avion Pkwy.
Suite 300
Chantilly, VA 20151
Tel: (703)818-1320
Fax: (703)818-8813
Registered: LDA

Employers
Shutler and Low

Clients Represented
On Behalf of Shutler and Low
Japan Automobile Standards Internat'l Center
Nissan North America Inc.
Toyota Motor Manufacturing North America
Toyota Technical Center U.S.A. Inc.

FAIRWEATHER, Allison
5211 Auth Rd.
Suitland, MD 20746
Tel: (301)899-3500
Fax: (301)899-8136

Employers
Air Force Sergeants Ass'n (Manager, Legislative Affairs)

FAITH, Brian
1825 Connecticut Ave. NW
Fifth Floor
Washington, DC 20009
EMail: brian.faith@widmeyer.com
Tel: (202)667-0901
Fax: (202)667-0902

Employers
Widmeyer Communications, Inc. (V. President)

FALB, Robert J.
1275 K St. NW
Suite 1212
Washington, DC 20005
Tel: (703)787-0000
Fax: (202)312-5005
Registered: LDA

Employers
Healthcare Distribution Management Ass'n (Director, Congressional Affairs)

FALCO, Mathea
1575 I St. NW
Suite 210
Washington, DC 20005
Tel: (202)663-6090
Fax: (202)414-6199

Employers
Drug Strategies (President)

FALCOFF, Mark
1150 17th St. NW
Washington, DC 20036
EMail: mfalcoff@aei.org
Tel: (202)862-5800
Fax: (202)862-7177

Employers
American Enterprise Institute for Public Policy Research (Resident Scholar)

FALCON, M.P.P., Adolph P.
1501 16th St. NW
Washington, DC 20036-1401
Tel: (202)387-5000
Fax: (202)797-4353

Employers
Nat'l Alliance for Hispanic Health (V. President for Science and Policy)

FALEY, Kevin O.
1620 L St. NW
Suite 600
Washington, DC 20036
EMail: kfaley@owdlaw.com
Tel: (202)312-8000
Fax: (202)312-8100
Registered: LDA

Chief Counsel and Exec. Director (1978-80) and General Counsel (1977-78), Subcommittee on the Constitution and Counsel (1974-77), Subcommittee on Juvenile Delinquency, Judiciary Committee, U.S. Senate.

Employers
Oppenheimer Wolff & Donnelly LLP (Partner)

Clients Represented
On Behalf of Oppenheimer Wolff & Donnelly LLP
CBI Industries
ComEd
Cook Group
Crown Butte Mines, Inc.
ICN Pharmaceuticals, Inc.
Illinois Tool Works
Nat'l Basketball Ass'n
NISH - Creating Employment Opportunities for People with Severe Disabilities
Real Estate Capital Resources Ass'n

FALK, Donald M.
1909 K St. NW
Washington, DC 20006
Tel: (202)263-3000
Fax: (202)263-3300
Registered: LDA

Employers
Mayer, Brown & Platt (Partner)

Clients Represented
On Behalf of Mayer, Brown & Platt
Oracle Corp.

FALK, Sr., James H.
One Westin Center
2445 M St. NW
Suite 260
Washington, DC 20037
Tel: (202)833-8700
Fax: (202)872-1725
Registered: LDA

Employers
Falk Law Firm, plc (President)

FALK, John M.
2445 M St. NW
Suite 260
Washington, DC 20037
Tel: (202)342-0204
Fax: (202)337-0034
Registered: LDA

Employers
Kyros & Cummins Associates (V. President)
The Willard Group

Clients Represented
On Behalf of Kyros & Cummins Associates
Allsup Inc.
Ass'n of Administrative Law Judges
Board of Veterans Appeals Professional Ass'n
Cooperative of American Physicians
Defense Administrative Judges Professional Ass'n
Joint Steering Committee for Public Policy
Merit Systems Protection Board

On Behalf of The Willard Group
Kyros & Cummins Associates
J. T. Rutherford & Associates

FALLETTA, Patricia

1755 Massachusetts Ave. NW
Suite 418
Washington, DC 20036
Tel: (202)232-5020
Fax: (202)797-8947
Registered: LDA
EMail: patriciaf@erols.com

Employers
American Soc. for the Prevention of Cruelty to Animals National Legislative Office (Coordinator, Fed. Govt. Affairs, Nat'l Legislative Office)

FALLON, Paul

1201 15th St. NW
Washington, DC 20005-2800
Tel: (202)822-0470
Fax: (202)822-0572

Employers
Nat'l Ass'n of Home Builders of the U.S. (Director, Public Opinion Research)

FALLON, Willard G.

1200 Wilson Blvd.
Arlington, VA 22209-1989
Tel: (703)465-3677
Fax: (703)465-3004
Registered: LDA

Employers
The Boeing Co. (Legislative Affairs, Army Programs/V-22)

FALVEY, Cheryl

1333 New Hampshire Ave. NW
Suite 400
Washington, DC 20036
Tel: (202)887-4000
Fax: (202)887-4288

Employers
Akin, Gump, Strauss, Hauer & Feld, L.L.P. (Partner)

FAMIGLIETTI, Kimberly M.

555 12th St. NW
Suite 740
Washington, DC 20004
Tel: (202)638-3752
Fax: (202)638-3833
Registered: LDA
EMail: kimberly.famiglietti@schwab.com

Employers
Charles Schwab & Co., Inc., (V. President, Government Affairs)

FANCHER, Marilyn

1615 L St. NW
Suite 900
Washington, DC 20036
Tel: (202)778-1000
Fax: (202)466-6002
EMail: mfancher@apcoworldwide.com

Employers
APCO Worldwide (V. President and Creative Director)

FANFALONE, Michael D.

1150 17th St. NW
Suite 702
Washington, DC 20036
Tel: (202)293-7277
Fax: (202)293-7727
Registered: LDA

Employers
Professional Airways Systems Specialists (AFL-CIO) (National President)

FANG, William

701 Pennsylvania Ave. NW
Washington, DC 20004-2696
Tel: (202)508-5617
Fax: (202)508-5673
Registered: LDA

Employers
Edison Electric Institute (Associate General Counsel, Industry Affairs)

FANNON, Peter F.

1620 L St. NW
Suite 1150
Washington, DC 20036
Tel: (202)223-2575
Fax: (202)223-2614
Registered: LDA

Employers
Matsushita Electric Corp. of America (V. President, Technology Policy and Regulatory Affairs)

FAQIRI, Seena

8400 Westpark Dr.
McLean, VA 22102
Tel: (703)827-7411

Employers
Automotive Consumer Action Program

FARAG, Kathleen N.

122 S. Royal St.
Alexandria, VA 22314-3328
Tel: (703)838-0373
Fax: (703)838-1698

Employers
Cordia Cos. (Assistant)

FARAH, Robert

P.O. 57263
Washington, DC 20037
Tel: (202)255-3106
Fax: (703)751-5327
Registered: FARA
EMail: lirc@erols.com

Employers
Lebanese Information and Research Center (Exec. Director)

FARAH, William J.

1333 New Hampshire Ave. NW
Suite 400
Washington, DC 20036
Tel: (202)887-4000
Fax: (202)887-4288
Registered: LDA

Employers
Akin, Gump, Strauss, Hauer & Feld, L.L.P. (Senior Counsel)

Clients Represented
On Behalf of Akin, Gump, Strauss, Hauer & Feld, L.L.P.
Barrick Goldstrike Mines, Inc.
Brunswick Corp.
Motion Picture Ass'n of America
Westar Group, Inc.

FARB, Anita B.

814 Thayer Ave.
Suite 250
Silver Spring, MD 20910
Tel: (301)587-1788
Fax: (301)587-1791

Employers
Nat'l Ass'n of the Deaf (Associate Exec. Director, Administration)

FARB, Warren

1666 K St. NW
Suite 800
Washington, DC 20006
Tel: (202)481-7000
Fax: (202)862-7098
Registered: LDA

Employers
Arthur Andersen LLP (Manager)

Clients Represented
On Behalf of Arthur Andersen LLP
Eagle-Picher Personal Injury Settlement Trust

FARBER, David J.

2550 M St. NW
Washington, DC 20037-1350
Tel: (202)457-6000
Fax: (202)457-6315
Registered: LDA
EMail: dfarber@pattonboggs.com

Employers
Patton Boggs, LLP (Partner)

Clients Represented
On Behalf of Patton Boggs, LLP
Brink's Inc.
James Hardie Building Products Inc.
Rock of Ages Corp.

FARBER, Judith

1526 Pennsylvania Ave. SE
Washington, DC 20003
Tel: (202)544-5300
Fax: (202)544-6600

Employers
JHP, Inc. (Jobs Have Priority) (Exec. Director)

FARBER, Ted B.

6101 Montrose Rd.
Rockville, MD 20852
Tel: (301)230-7200
Fax: (301)230-7265

Employers
Jewish Federation of Greater Washington (Exec. V. President)

FARBERMAN, Rhea K.

750 First St. NE
Washington, DC 20002-4242
Tel: (202)336-5709
Fax: (202)336-5708

Employers
American Psychological Ass'n (Exec. Director, Public Communications)

FARBMAN, Andrea H.

8455 Colesville Rd.
Suite 1000
Silver Spring, MD 20910-3392
Tel: (301)589-3300
Fax: (301)589-5175
EMail: farbman@musictherapy.org

Employers
American Music Therapy Ass'n (Exec. Director)

FARBSTEIN, Marcus

808 17th St. NW
Suite 250
Washington, DC 20006
Tel: (202)296-7272
Fax: (202)296-7290

Employers
Genentech, Inc. (Federal Government Liaison)

FARFONE, Frank

1776 I St. NW
Suite 1050
Washington, DC 20006
Tel: (202)429-3466
Fax: (202)429-3467
Registered: LDA

Employers
The Dow Chemical Co. (V. President, International Affairs)

FARHAT, Ann C.

1901 L St. NW
Suite 250
Washington, DC 20036
Tel: (202)833-4190
Fax: (202)833-3084

Employers
Bechtel & Cole (Managing Principal)

FARIA, Wendell M.

1299 Pennsylvania Ave. NW
Tenth Floor
Washington, DC 20004-2400
Tel: (202)508-9500
Fax: (202)508-9700
EMail: wendellfaria@paulhastings.com
Former Deputy Chief, Division of Investment Management, Securities and Exchange Commission.

Employers
Paul, Hastings, Janofsky & Walker LLP (Of Counsel)

FARIS, Jack

1201 F St. NW
Suite 200
Washington, DC 20004
Tel: (202)554-9000
Fax: (202)554-0496
Registered: LDA

Employers
Nat'l Federation of Independent Business (President and Chief Exec. Officer)

FARKAN, Pani

1079 Papermill Ct. NW
Washington, DC 20007
Tel: (202)337-6008
Fax: (202)337-6193
Registered: LDA
EMail: pFarkhan@aol.com

Employers
Richard W. Bliss (Director, Legislative Affairs)

Clients Represented
On Behalf of Richard W. Bliss
Nat'l Paint and Coatings Ass'n
Nat'l Spa and Pool Institute
Niki Trading Co.

FARMER, Anthony

1413 K St. NW
Seventh Floor
Washington, DC 20005-3442
Tel: (202)898-0414
Fax: (202)898-0435
Registered: LDA
EMail: tfarmer@napwa.org

Employers
Nat'l Ass'n of People with AIDS, Inc. (Deputy Exec. Director)

FARMER, David M.

1211 Connecticut Ave. NW
Suite 400
Washington, DC 20036
EMail: dfarmer@allianceai.org
Tel: (202)822-8811
Fax: (202)872-1885
Registered: LDA

Employers
Alliance of American Insurers (Senior V. President, Federal Affairs)

FARMER, Greg

801 Pennsylvania Ave. NW
Suite 700
Washington, DC 20004
EMail: gfarmer@nortelnetworks.com
Tel: (202)347-4610
Fax: (202)508-3612
Registered: LDA

Employers
Nortel Networks (V. President, Government Relations - International Trade)

FARMER, Thomas L.

2121 K St. NW
Suite 701
Washington, DC 20037
EMail: tom@baft.org
Tel: (202)452-0952
Fax: (202)452-0959
Registered: LDA

Employers
Bankers' Ass'n for Finance and Trade (General Counsel)

FARNHAM, Peter

9650 Rockville Pike
Bethesda, MD 20814
EMail: pfarnham@asbmb.faseb.org
Tel: (301)530-7145
Fax: (301)571-1824
Registered: LDA

Employers
American Soc. for Biochemistry and Molecular Biology (Public Affairs Officer)

FARNSWORTH, Eric

1501 M St. NW
Suite 700
Washington, DC 20005-1702
EMail: efarnsworth@manatt.com
Tel: (202)463-4300
Fax: (202)463-4394
Registered: LDA, FARA

Policy Director, Office of the Counselor to the President and Special Envoy to the Americas, The White House, 1995. Staff Member, Bureau of Western Hemishpere Affairs, Department of State, 1990-95.

Employers
Manatt, Phelps & Phillips, LLP (Senior Advisor)

Clients Represented
On Behalf of Manatt, Phelps & Phillips, LLP
Asociacion Columbiana de Exportadores de Flores (ASOCOLFLORES)
BellSouth Corp.
Bolivia, Embassy of
Congo, Republic of
Land Grant Development
Mexico, Embassy of
Mitsubishi Motors America, Inc.
SWIPCO, U.S.

FARQUHAR, Douglas B.

700 13th St. NW
Suite 1200
Washington, DC 20005
EMail: dbf@hpm.com
Tel: (202)737-9624
Fax: (202)737-9329
Registered: LDA

Assistant U.S. Attorney for the District of Maryland, Department of Justice, 1990-97.

Employers
Hyman, Phelps & McNamara, P.C. (Partner)

Clients Represented
On Behalf of Hyman, Phelps & McNamara, P.C.
Medeva Pharmaceuticals

FARQUHAR, Michele

555 13th St. NW
Washington, DC 20004-1109
Tel: (202)637-5600
Fax: (202)637-5910

Employers
Hogan & Hartson L.L.P.

Clients Represented
On Behalf of Hogan & Hartson L.L.P.
Western Wireless Internat'l

FARR, Dagmar T.

655 15th St. NW
Washington, DC 20005-5701
EMail: dfarr@fmi.org
Tel: (202)220-0619
Fax: (202)220-0873
Registered: LDA

Employers
Food Marketing Institute (Group V. President, Legislative and Consumer Affairs)

FARR, Stephen

1615 L St. NW
Suite 900
Washington, DC 20036
EMail: sfarr@apcoworldwide.com
Tel: (202)778-1000
Fax: (202)466-6002

Employers
APCO Worldwide (V. President, Corporate Community Strategies)

FARRAR, Jay C.

1800 K St. NW
Washington, DC 20005
Tel: (202)887-0200
Fax: (202)775-3199

Former Deputy Assistant Secretary of Legislative Affairs, Department of Defense and former Director of Legislative Affairs, National Security Council, Executive Office of the President, The White House. Also served as Legislative Assistant to the Chairman, Joint Chiefs of Staff, Department of Defense. Served over 22 years in the U.S. Marine Corps.

Employers
Center for Strategic and Internat'l Studies (V. President, External Relations)

FARRELL, Chris

606 N. Washington St.
Alexandria, VA 22314
Tel: (703)838-7760
Fax: (703)838-7782
Registered: LDA

Employers
Nat'l Ass'n of Retired Federal Employees (Legislative Representative)

FARRELL, Dianne

P.O. Box 2999
Reston, VA 20191
EMail: dfarrell@rvia.org
Tel: (703)620-6003
Ext: 315
Fax: (703)620-5071

Employers
Recreation Vehicle Industry Ass'n (V. President, Government Affairs)

FARRELL, Edward J.

900 17th St. NW
Suite 1000
Washington, DC 20006
Tel: (202)530-7437
Fax: (202)463-6915

Employers
Blank Rome Comisky & McCauley, LLP (Partner)

Clients Represented
On Behalf of Blank Rome Comisky & McCauley, LLP
Canadian Cattlemen's Ass'n
Meat New Zealand
New Zealand Dairy Board

FARRELL, Pamela

1299 Pennsylvania Ave. NW
Suite 1100 West
Washington, DC 20004-2407
Tel: (202)637-4000
Fax: (202)637-4612

Employers
General Electric Co. (Technology, Research and Development)

FARRELL, Richard

805 15th St. NW
Suite 500
Washington, DC 20005
Tel: (202)371-9770
Fax: (202)371-6601

Employers
Chambers Associates Inc. (Senior V. President)
Council of Infrastructure Financing Authorities (Exec. Director)

FARREN, J. Michael

1401 H St. NW
Suite 200
Washington, DC 20005
Tel: (202)414-1285
Fax: (202)414-1217
Registered: LDA

Employers
Xerox Corp. (Corporate V. President, External Affairs)

FARRIS, Elaine

1701 Pennsylvania Ave. NW
Suite 300
Washington, DC 20006
Tel: (202)662-2700
Fax: (202)662-2739

Employers
Andrews and Kurth, L.L.P.

FARROW, Frank

1575 I St. NW
Suite 500
Washington, DC 20006
Tel: (202)371-1565
Fax: (202)371-1472

Employers
Center for the Study of Social Policy (Director, Washington Office)

FARTHING, Penelope S.

2550 M St. NW
Washington, DC 20037-1350
EMail: pfarthing@pattonboggs.com
Tel: (202)457-6000
Fax: (202)457-6315
Registered: LDA

Special Assistant to the Administrator, Food Safety and Quality Service, Department of Agriculture, 1977-78. Congressional Liaison, Federal Trade Commission, 1974-77. Staff Attorney, Federal Communications Commission, 1970-72.

Employers
Patton Boggs, LLP (Partner)

Clients Represented
On Behalf of Patton Boggs, LLP
American Advertising Federation
American Ass'n of Advertising Agencies
Ass'n of Nat'l Advertisers
AutoNation, Inc.
Commco, L.L.C.
Crane Co.
The Limited Inc.
Magazine Publishers of America
MCI WorldCom Corp.
Nat'l Stroke Ass'n
Outdoor Advertising Ass'n of America
Point of Purchase Advertising Institute
US Airways
WQED Pittsburgh

FASCIONE, Nina

1101 14th St. NW
Suite 1400
Washington, DC 20005
EMail: nfascione@defenders.org
Tel: (202)682-9400
Fax: (202)682-1331

Employers
Defenders of Wildlife (Director, Carnivore Conservation)

FASS, Heather

1850 M St. NW
Suite 550
Washington, DC 20036
Tel: (202)289-5900
Fax: (202)289-4141
Registered: LDA

Employers
Chlopak, Leonard, Schechter and Associates

FATH, Marie

1120 Connecticut Ave. NW
Suite 1060
Washington, DC 20036
Tel: (202)833-6395
Fax: (202)833-0018

Employers
Textile Rental Services Ass'n of America (Director, Government Affairs)

FAUCETTE, Douglas P.

5101 Wisconsin Ave. NW
Washington, DC 20016
Tel: (202)362-0840
Fax: (202)966-9409

Senior Associate General Counsel for Securities and Business Transactions (1980-81) and Associate General Counsel and Director, Securities Division (1977-80), Federal Home Loan Bank Board.

Employers
Muldoon, Murphy & Faucette, LLP (Partner)

FAULK, Page

1500 K St. NW
Suite 250
Washington, DC 20005-1714
Tel: (202)639-7519
Fax: (202)639-7505
EMail: pfaulk@uhlaw.com

Legislative Assistant to Senator Ben Nighthorse Campbell (R-CO), 1999-2001. Legislative Aide to Senator Rick Santorum (R-PA), 1996-98. Law Intern, Senate Judiciary Commitee, 1996.

Employers
Ungaretti & Harris (Associate)

Clients Represented
On Behalf of Ungaretti & Harris
Air Carrier Ass'n of America
Air Tran Airways
Cardinal Health Inc.
Frontier Airlines
United Defense, L.P.

FAULKNER, Tamara

2201 C St. NW
Room 7251
Washington, DC 20520-7261
Tel: (202)647-8722
Fax: (202)647-2762

Employers
Department of State - Bureau of Legislative Affairs (International Crime, Counter Narcotics & Legal Affairs Legislative Management Officer)

FAULS, Brian J.

1575 I St. NW
Suite 400
Washington, DC 20005
Tel: (202)289-1818
Fax: (202)289-6578
Registered: LDA

Employers
American Ass'n of Museums (Senior Legislative Assistant)

FAUSS, Gloria

4245 N. Fairfax Dr.
Suite 100
Arlington, VA 20003-1606
Tel: (703)841-3754
Fax: (703)841-7400
Registered: LDA

Employers
The Nature Conservancy (Director, State Government Relations)

FAUST, Marcus G.

332 Constitution Ave. NE
Washington, DC 20002
Tel: (202)547-5400
Fax: (202)543-5740
Registered: LDA
EMail: marcusfaust@msn.com

Employers
Marcus G. Faust, P.C. (President)

Clients Represented
On Behalf of Marcus G. Faust, P.C.
Central Utah Water Conservancy District
Clark County Department of Aviation
Clark County, Nevada, Office of the County Manager
Clark County-McCarran Internat'l Airport
Colorado River Commission of Nevada
Contra Costa Water District
Las Vegas Valley Water District
Public Service Co. of New Mexico
Regional Transportation Commission
Sierra Pacific Resources

FAUST, Michelle M.

1500 K St. NW
Suite 250
Washington, DC 20005-1714
Tel: (202)639-7503
Fax: (202)639-7505
Registered: LDA
EMail: mmfaust@uhlaw.com

Former Legislative Research Assistant to Rep. Sonny Bono (R-CA).

Employers
Ungaretti & Harris (Associate)

Clients Represented
On Behalf of Ungaretti & Harris
Air Carrier Ass'n of America
Air Tran Airways
Allegiance Healthcare Corp.
Frontier Airlines
Radius, The Global Travel Co.
Stepan Co.

FAUST, Thomas N.

1450 Duke St.
Alexandria, VA 22314-3490
Tel: (703)836-7827
Fax: (703)683-6541

Employers
Nat'l Sheriffs' Ass'n (Exec. Director)

FAUSTI, John J.

4301 Connecticut Ave. NW
Suite 453
Washington, DC 20008
Tel: (202)237-0505
Fax: (202)237-7566
Registered: LDA

Employers
John J. Fausti & Associates, LLC (Owner/Attorney)

Clients Represented
On Behalf of John J. Fausti & Associates, LLC
Nat'l Ass'n of Aircraft and Communication Suppliers

FAUTH, III, Gerald W.

116 S. Royal St.
Alexandria, VA 22314
Tel: (703)549-6161
Fax: (703)549-6162
Registered: LDA
EMail: gfauth@aol.com

Employers
G.W. Fauth & Associates Inc. (President)

Clients Represented
On Behalf of G.W. Fauth & Associates Inc.
U.S. Clay Producers Traffic Ass'n

FAUX, Jeff

1660 L St. NW
Suite 1200
Washington, DC 20036
Tel: (202)775-8810
Fax: (202)775-0819
EMail: epi@epinet.org

Employers
Economic Policy Institute (President)

FAWCETT, W. H. "Buzz"

607 14th St. NW
Suite 700
Washington, DC 20005-2011
Tel: (202)434-1636
Fax: (202)434-1690
Registered: LDA
EMail: fawcw@perkinscoie.com

Former Legislative Director to Senator Dirk Kempthorne (R-ID).

Employers
Perkins Coie LLP (Partner)

Clients Represented
On Behalf of Perkins Coie LLP
AuctionWatch.com
Avenue A, Inc.
Intermountain Forest Industry Ass'n
Ocean Futures Soc., Inc.
Spokane, Washington, City of

FAWCETT-HOOVER, Jane

801 Pennsylvania Ave. NW
Suite 720
Washington, DC 20004-2604
Tel: (202)393-3408
Fax: (202)393-4606
Registered: LDA
EMail: hoover.jf@pg.com

Employers
The Procter & Gamble Company (V. President, National Government Relations)

FAY, Dan

2033 K St. NW
Suite 850
Washington, DC 20006
Tel: (202)872-4688
Fax: (202)872-4689

Employers
Valent U.S.A. Corp. (Manager, Federal Registration and Regulatory Affairs)

FAY, Kevin J.

2111 Wilson Blvd.
Eighth Floor
Arlington, VA 22201-3058
Tel: (703)841-0626
Fax: (703)243-2874
Registered: LDA
EMail: fay@alcalde-fay.com

Employers
Alcalde & Fay (President)
Internat'l Climate Change Partnership (Exec. Director)

Clients Represented
On Behalf of Alcalde & Fay
Alliance for Responsible Atmospheric Policy
Earthshell Container Corp.
Fairfax County Water Authority
Intel Corp.
Internat'l Climate Change Partnership
NEDA

FAY, Msgr. William

3211 Fourth St. NE
Washington, DC 20017
Tel: (202)541-3100
Fax: (202)541-3322

Employers
United States Catholic Conference (General Secretary)

FAY, William D.

1776 Massachusetts Ave. NW
Suite 500
Washington, DC 20036
Tel: (202)857-1200
Fax: (202)857-1220
Registered: LDA

Employers
American Highway Users Alliance (President and Chief Exec. Officer)

FAZIO, Jr., Hon. Vic H.

1775 I St. NW
Suite 700
Washington, DC 20006
Tel: (202)261-4000
Fax: (202)261-4001
Registered: LDA

Member, U.S. House of Representatives (D-CA), 1979-98.

Employers
Clark & Weinstock, Inc. (Partner)

Clients Represented
On Behalf of Clark & Weinstock, Inc.
American Ass'n of Homes and Services for the Aging
AT&T
Rabbi Milton Balkany
Calpine Corp.
Cargill, Inc.
Delta Wetlands Project
The Ferguson Group
Foundation Health Federal Services, Inc.
Hefner, Stark & Marois LLP
Infrastructure Defense Inc.
Lockheed Martin Corp.
Microsoft Corp.
Nat'l Prostate Cancer Coalition Co.
Pharmaceutical Research and Manufacturers of America
Remy, Thomas & Moose, LLP
Rubber Manufacturers Ass'n
Sacramento, California, City of
Schering-Plough Corp.
Sodexho Marriott Services, Inc.
Vivendi Universal

FEAGLES, Prentiss

555 13th St. NW
Washington, DC 20004-1109
Tel: (202)637-5781
Fax: (202)637-5910
Registered: LDA
EMail: pefeagles@hhlaw.com

Assistant to the General Counsel, Office of the Secretary, U.S. Army, 1976-80.

Employers
Hogan & Hartson L.L.P. (Partner)

Clients Represented
On Behalf of Hogan & Hartson L.L.P.
HMSHost Corp.

FEDDIS, Nessa E.

1120 Connecticut Ave. NW
Washington, DC 20036
Tel: (202)663-5000
Fax: (202)828-5052
Registered: LDA

Employers
American Bankers Ass'n (Senior Federal Counsel)

FEDER, Gerald

1350 Connecticut Ave. NW
Suite 600
Washington, DC 20036
Tel: (202)955-8305
Fax: (202)955-8311

Member, ERISA Advisory Council, Department of Labor, 1978-85. Chairman, Minimum Wage Study Commission, 1978-79. Chief Counsel, Subcommittee on Labor, Senate Committee on Labor and Human Resources, 1969-74.

Employers
Feder, Semo, Clarke & Bard (Senior Partner)

FEDERICI, Tara

1200 G St. NW
Suite 400
Washington, DC 20005
Tel: (202)783-8700
Fax: (202)783-8750
Registered: LDA

Employers
AdvaMed (Associate V. President, Government Affairs)

FEDEWA, Kirsten A.

310 First St. SE
Washington, DC 20003
Tel: (202)863-8587
Ext: 7

Employers
Republican Governors Ass'n (Director, Communications)

FEDOR, John D.

1911 Fort Myer Dr.
Suite 600
Arlington, VA 22209
Tel: (703)741-0546
Fax: (703)741-0529
Registered: LDA

Employers
Alliant Techsystems, Inc. (Director, Congressional Relations)

FEDORCHAK, Jeff

3927 Old Lee Hwy.
Suite 102
Fairfax, VA 22030
Tel: (703)503-4000
Registered: LDA
EMail: jeff.fedorchak@impact-strategies.com
Chief of Staff to Rep. Bob Inglis (R-SC), 1993-96 and Chief of Staff to Rep. Frank Riggs (R-CA), 1991-92.

Employers
Impact Strategies (President)

Clients Represented
On Behalf of Impact Strategies
R. R. Donnelley & Sons
Environmental Commonsense Coalition
Placer County Water Agency
The Tekamah Corp.
The Timken Co.

FEENEY, Susan

Hamilton Square
600 14th St. NW, Fifth Floor
Washington, DC 20005
Tel: (202)783-1980
Fax: (202)783-1918

Employers
Valente Lopatin & Schulze

Clients Represented
On Behalf of Valente Lopatin & Schulze
Keating Technologies Inc.
System & Computer Technology Corp.

FEHRENBACH, John

1400 L St. NW
Washington, DC 20005-3502
Tel: (202)371-5925
Fax: (202)371-5950
EMail: jfehrenbach@winston.com
Trial Attorney, Environmental Enforcement Section, Department of Justice, 1987-89. Senior Trial Attorney, Office of the Solicitor, Department of Energy, 1982-87. Senior Attorney, Office of Air, Noise and Radiation Enforcement (1980-82), Attorney, Pesticides and Toxic Substances Enforcement Division (1979-80), and Attorney, Mobile Source Enforcement Division (1978-79), all at the Environmental Protection Agency.

Employers
Winston & Strawn (Partner, Environmental Practice)

Clients Represented
On Behalf of Winston & Strawn
Becker-Underwood, Inc.

FEIBUSCH, Morris D.

1500 K St. NW
Suite 875
Washington, DC 20005
Tel: (202)783-3195
Fax: (202)783-4862

Employers
Bituminous Coal Operators Ass'n (V. President, Public Affairs)

FEIDLER, Linda

1385 Piccard Dr.
Rockville, MD 20850-4340
Tel: (301)869-5800
Fax: (301)990-9690
EMail: lfeidler@mcaa.org

Employers
Mechanical Contractors Ass'n of America (Director, Executive & Administrative Services)

FEIGHAN, Alison

1250 I St. NW
Suite 902
Washington, DC 20005
Tel: (202)393-5225
Fax: (202)393-3034
Registered: LDA
EMail: Alison@Rapoza.org

Employers
Robert A. Rapoza Associates (V. President)

Clients Represented
On Behalf of Robert A. Rapoza Associates
Community Development Venture Capital Ass'n
Community Transportation Ass'n of America
Nat'l Ass'n of SBA Microloan Intermediaries
Nat'l Rural Development & Finance Corp.
Nat'l Rural Housing Coalition
Woman's Opportunities Resource Center

FEIN, Bruce

6515 Sunny Hill Court
McLean, VA 22101
Tel: (703)448-1279
Fax: (703)448-5765
Registered: FARA

Employers
Self-employed as an independent consultant.

Clients Represented
As an independent consultant
Togo, Embassy of the Republic of

FEIN, Richard

1010 N. Fairfax St.
Alexandria, VA 22314-1574
Tel: (703)549-6400
Fax: (703)549-2984
EMail: rfein@nsaccl.org

Employers
Nat'l Soc. of Accountants (Director, Federal Affairs and Taxation)

FEINBERG, Peter H.

1200 New Hampshire Ave. NW
Suite 800
Washington, DC 20036-6802
Tel: (202)776-2000
Fax: (202)776-2222
EMail: pfeinberg@dlalaw.com

Employers
Dow, Lohnes & Albertson, PLLC (Member)

FEINMAN, Dori

700 13th St. NW
Suite 400
Washington, DC 20005
Tel: (202)347-0773
Fax: (202)347-0785
EMail: dfeinman@cassidy.com

Employers
Cassidy & Associates, Inc. (Account Executive)

FEINSTEIN, Margaret

2101 L St. NW
Washington, DC 20037-1526
Tel: (202)785-9700
Fax: (202)887-0689
Registered: LDA

Employers
Dickstein Shapiro Morin & Oshinsky LLP

Clients Represented
On Behalf of Dickstein Shapiro Morin & Oshinsky LLP
American Greyhound Track Operators Ass'n

FEISTRITZER, C. Emily

4401A Connecticut Ave. NW
PMB 212
Washington, DC 20008-2322
Tel: (202)362-3444
Fax: (202)362-3493

Employers
Nat'l Center for Education Information (Director)

FEITH, Douglas J.

1300 19th St. NW
Suite 400
Washington, DC 20036
Tel: (202)293-1600
Fax: (202)293-8965
Deputy Assistant Secretary for Negotiations Policy (1984-86) and Special Counsel to the Assistant Secretary for International Security Affairs (1982-84), Department of Defense. Member, National Security Council Staff, The White House, 1981-82.

Employers
Feith & Zell, P.C. (Partner)

Clients Represented
On Behalf of Feith & Zell, P.C.
Loral Space and Communications, Ltd.
Mas-Hamilton Group

FELDBAUM, Carl B.

1625 K St. NW
Suite 1100
Washington, DC 20006-1604
Tel: (202)857-0244
Fax: (202)857-0237
Registered: LDA
EMail: cfeldbaum@bio.org
Former Chief of Staff, Senator Arlen Spector (R-PA). Inspector General, Defense Intelligence, Department of Defense, 1976-79. Assistant to the Secretary, Department of Energy, 1979-80.

Employers
Biotechnology Industry Organization (President)

FELDESMAN, James L.

2001 L St. NW
Second Floor
Washington, DC 20036
Tel: (202)466-8960
Fax: (202)293-8103
General Counsel, President's Council on Youth Opportunity, 1969-70. Staff Attorney, Office of the Solicitor, Department of Labor, 1965-68.

Employers
Feldesman, Tucker, Leifer, Fidell & Bank (Partner)

Clients Represented
On Behalf of Feldesman, Tucker, Leifer, Fidell & Bank
Nat'l Ass'n of Community Health Centers
Nat'l Family Planning and Reproductive Health Ass'n

FELDGARDEN, Robert

600 13th St. NW
Washington, DC 20005-3096
Tel: (202)756-8304
Fax: (202)756-8087
EMail: rfeldgarden@mwe.com
Attorney-Advisor, Office of Tax Legislative Counsel, Treasury Department, 1968-72; Attorney, Office of Chief Counsel, Internal Revenue Service, 1965-68.

Employers
McDermott, Will and Emery (Partner)

FELDMAN, Howard J.

1050 Thomas Jefferson St. NW
Seventh Floor
Washington, DC 20007
Tel: (202)298-1800
Fax: (202)338-2416
Registered: LDA, FARA
EMail: hjf@vnf.com
Chief Counsel, Permanent Subcommittee on Investigations, Senate Committee on Government Operations, 1973-77. Attorney, Appellate Section, Tax Division, Department of Justice, 1964-1968.

Employers
Van Ness Feldman, P.C. (Member)

Clients Represented
On Behalf of Van Ness Feldman, P.C.
Arctic Slope Regional Corp.
Geothermal Resources Ass'n
Large Public Power Council
Mack Trucks, Inc.
McKesson Corp.
Petro Star, Inc.
Princess Tours
Sealaska Corp.
Toyota Motor North America, U.S.A., Inc.

FELDMAN, Jay

701 E St. SE
Suite 200
Washington, DC 20003
Tel: (202)543-5450
Fax: (202)543-4791
EMail: ncamp@igc.apc.org

Employers
Nat'l Coalition Against the Misuse of Pesticides (Exec. Director)

FELDMAN, Laura S.

401 Wythe St.
Alexandria, VA 22314
Tel: (703)684-1355
Fax: (703)684-1589
Registered: LDA
EMail: lfeldman@nachri.org

Employers
Nat'l Ass'n of Children's Hospitals Inc. (Director, Grants Project and Policy)

FELDMAN, Mark B.

1300 19th St. NW
Suite 400
Washington, DC 20036
Tel: (202)293-1600
Fax: (202)293-8965
Registered: LDA
Acting Legal Advisor (1981) and Deputy Legal Advisor (1974-80), Department of State.

Employers
Feith & Zell, P.C. (Partner)

Clients Represented
On Behalf of Feith & Zell, P.C.
Corporacion de Exportaciones Mexicanas, S.A. de C.V. and Marvin Roy Feldman
Loral Space and Communications, Ltd.

FELDMAN, Sandra

555 New Jersey Ave. NW
Washington, DC 20001
Tel: (202)879-4440
Fax: (202)879-4545

Employers
American Federation of Teachers (President)

FELDMAN, Steven

700 13th St. NW
Suite 1000
Washington, DC 20005
Tel: (202)347-6633
Fax: (202)347-8713
Registered: LDA
Former Aide to Senator Donald W. Riegle, Jr. (D-MI).

Employers
Powell Tate (V. President)

FELDMAN, Timothy

1300 N. 17th St.
Suite 1847
Rosslyn, VA 22209
Tel: (703)841-3251
Fax: (703)841-3351
Registered: LDA
EMail: tim_feldman@nema.org

Employers
Nat'l Electrical Manufacturers Ass'n (V. President, Government Affairs)

FELDMAN, Warren

11 Dupont Circle NW
Suite 700
Washington, DC 20036
Tel: (202)293-5886
Fax: (202)939-6969
Registered: LDA

Employers
Multinat'l Government Services, Inc.

Clients Represented
On Behalf of Multinat'l Government Services, Inc.
CIGNA Corp.

FELLER, Mimi A.

1100 Wilson Blvd.
Arlington, VA 22234
Tel: (703)284-6046
Registered: LDA

Employers
Gannett Co., Inc. (Senior V. President, Public Affairs and Gov't Relations)

FELLER, Peter Buck

1900 K St. NW
Washington, DC 20006
Tel: (202)496-7500
Fax: (202)496-7756
EMail: peter_feller@mckennacuneo.com
Attorney/Advisor, Office of Tax International Counsel (1969-71) and Attorney/Advisor, Office of General Counsel (1964-68), Department of the Treasury.

Employers
McKenna & Cuneo, L.L.P. (Partner)

Clients Represented
On Behalf of McKenna & Cuneo, L.L.P.
American Pipe Fittings Ass'n
Cast Iron Pipefittings Committee
U.S. Fittings Group

FELLMAN, Steven John

1054 31st St. NW
Suite 200
Canal Square
Washington, DC 20007
Tel: (202)342-5200
Fax: (202)342-5219
EMail: sfellman@gkmg.com
Trial Attorney, Federal Trade Commission, 1962-64.

Employers
Galland, Kharasch, Greenberg, Fellman & Swirsky, P.C. (Managing Partner)

Clients Represented
On Behalf of Galland, Kharasch, Greenberg, Fellman & Swirsky, P.C.
Nat'l Ass'n of Theatre Owners

FELLNER, Baruch A.

1050 Connecticut Ave. NW
Washington, DC 20036-5306
Tel: (202)955-8500
Fax: (202)467-0539
EMail: bfellner@gdclaw.com
Associate General Counsel, Pension Benefit Guaranty Corporation, 1980-86. Counsel for Appellate and Regional Litigation, Office of the Solicitor, Occupational Safety and Health Administration, Department of Labor, 1972-80.

Employers
Gibson, Dunn & Crutcher LLP (Partner)

FELLS, Robert M.

1895 Preston White Dr.
Reston, VA 22091-5434
Tel: (703)391-8400
Fax: (703)391-8416

Employers
Internat'l Cemetery and Funeral Ass'n (Chief Operating Officer, External Affairs)

FELRICE, Barry

1401 H St. NW
Suite 700
Washington, DC 20005
Tel: (202)414-6730
Fax: (202)414-6738
Registered: LDA

Employers
DaimlerChrysler Corp. (Senior Manager, Regulatory Affairs)

FELS, Nicholas W.

1201 Pennsylvania Ave. NW
Washington, DC 20004-2401
Tel: (202)662-5900
Fax: (202)662-6291
EMail: nfels@cov.com
Law Clerk to Judge John Minor Wisdom, U.S. Court of Appeals, Fifth Circuit, 1968-69.

Employers
Covington & Burling (Partner)

FELT, Emily

1707 L St. NW
Suite 950
Washington, DC 20036
Tel: (202)296-2588
Fax: (202)331-7792
Registered: LDA
EMail: ncjwdc@aol.com

Employers
Nat'l Council of Jewish Women (Legislative Associate)

FELTMAN, Kenneth E.

927 15th St. NW
Suite 1000
Washington, DC 20005
Tel: (202)659-4300
Registered: LDA
EMail: infoecfc@ecfc.org

Employers
Employers Council on Flexible Compensation (Exec. Director)

FELTON, Reginald

1680 Duke St.
Alexandria, VA 22314-3407
Tel: (703)838-6722
Fax: (703)683-7590

Employers
Nat'l School Boards Ass'n (Director, Federal Relations)

FENDLEY, Stan G.

1350 I St. NW
Suite 500
Washington, DC 20005-3305
Tel: (202)682-3200
Fax: (202)682-3130
Tax Counsel, Senate Committee on Finance, 1998-2000. Legislative Assistant to Senator Dale Bumpers (D-AR), 1997-98. Tax Counsel, Senate Committee on Small Business, 1993-97.

Employers
Corning Inc. (Director, Legislative and Regulatory Policy)

FENIG, David

1801 K St. NW
Suite 901-L
Washington, DC 20006
Tel: (202)530-0500
Fax: (202)530-4800
Registered: LDA, FARA
EMail: David_Fenig@bm.com
Former Legislative Director for Senator Spark Matsunaga (D-HI).

Employers
BKSH & Associates (Director)

Clients Represented
On Behalf of BKSH & Associates
M-Unit

FENNAR, Miya

801 Pennsylvania Ave. NW
Suite 245
Washington, DC 20004-2604
Tel: (202)624-1500
Fax: (202)737-6462
EMail: miya@americashospitals.com

Employers
Federation of American Hospitals (Office Manager and PAC Contact)

FENNELL, Karen S.

818 Connecticut Ave. NW
Suite 900
Washington, DC 20006
Tel: (202)728-9860
Fax: (202)728-9897
Registered: LDA
EMail: kfennell@acnm.org

Employers
American College of Nurse-Midwives (Senior Policy Analyst)

FENNELL, Rosalyn

1615 M St. NW
Washington, DC 20036
Tel: (202)833-2300
Fax: (202)429-3945
Registered: LDA
EMail: rose_fennell@tws.org

Employers
The Wilderness Soc. (Director, Nat'l Parks)

FENNIE, Bruce

305 E. Capitol St. SE
Washington, DC 20003
Tel: (202)543-2143

Employers
Bruce Fennie & Associates

Clients Represented
On Behalf of Bruce Fennie & Associates
BAE SYSTEMS North America

FENNINGER, Randolph B.

1101 17th St. NW
Suite 803
Washington, DC 20036
Tel: (202)833-0007
Fax: (202)833-0086
Registered: LDA

Employers
MARC Associates, Inc. (Exec. V. President)

Clients Represented
On Behalf of MARC Associates, Inc.
American Ass'n of Clinical Urologists, Inc.
American Soc. for Gastrointestinal Endoscopy
American Soc. of Nuclear Cardiology
American Urological Ass'n
Sunstone Behavioral Health

FENSTERHEIM, G. David

1250 Connecticut Ave. NW
Suite 700
Washington, DC 20005
Tel: (202)637-6667
Fax: (202)842-2869

Employers
Fensterheim & Bean, P.C. (Partner)
RECRA (Exec. Director)

Clients Represented
On Behalf of Fensterheim & Bean, P.C.
RECRA

FENTON, Anne

1730 Rhode Island Ave. NW
Suite 717
Washington, DC 20036
EMail: media@hoffmangroup.com

Tel: (202)728-0800
Fax: (202)728-0802
Registered: LDA

Employers
The Hoffman Group (Senior Account Executive)

FENTON, Dawn D.H.

555 12th St. NW
Suite 350
N. Tower
Washington, DC 20004

Tel: (202)639-4064
Fax: (202)737-1311
Registered: LDA

Employers
ABB, Inc. (Manager, Government Affairs)

FENTON, Frank

801 Pennsylvania Ave. NW
Suite 1117
Washington, DC 20004

Tel: (202)628-1117
Fax: (202)783-6309
Registered: LDA

Employers
Self-employed as an independent consultant.

Clients Represented

As an independent consultant
Bethlehem Steel Corp.
USX Corp.

FENTON, Jr., G. F. "Ric"

1130 17th St. NW
Washington, DC 20036-4677
EMail: rfenton@nma.org

Tel: (202)463-3241
Fax: (202)833-1965
Registered: LDA

Employers
Nat'l Mining Ass'n (V. President, Congressional Affairs)

FENTON, Rick

200 Independence Ave. SW
Room 337D
Washington, DC 20201
EMail: rfenton@hcfa.gov

Tel: (202)690-8501

Employers
Department of Health and Human Services - Center for Medicaid and State Operations (Acting Director, Intergovernmental and Tribal Affairs Group)

FEORE, Jr., John R.

1200 New Hampshire Ave. NW
Suite 800
Washington, DC 20036-6802
EMail: jfeore@dlalaw.com

Tel: (202)776-2000
Fax: (202)776-2222
Registered: LDA

Employers
Dow, Lohnes & Albertson, PLLC (Member)

Clients Represented

On Behalf of Dow, Lohnes & Albertson, PLLC
BET Holdings II, Inc.

FERENBACH, Gregory

1320 Braddock Pl.
Alexandria, VA 22314

Tel: (703)739-5063
Fax: (703)739-5358

Employers
Public Broadcasting Service (Senior V. President and General Counsel)

FERENC, Sue

1010 Wisconsin Ave. NW
Ninth Floor
Washington, DC 20007
EMail: sferenc@gmabrands.com

Tel: (202)337-9400
Fax: (202)337-4508

Employers
Grocery Manufacturers of America (V. President, Science and Regulatory Affairs)

FERGUSON, Charles H.

1775 Massachusetts Ave. NW
Washington, DC 20036-2188

Tel: (202)797-6000
Fax: (202)797-6004

Employers
The Brookings Institution (Senior Fellow, Economic Studies)

FERGUSON, Denise G.

801 Pennsylvania Ave.
Suite 650
Washington, DC 20004
EMail: denise.ferguson@aexp.com

Tel: (202)624-0761
Fax: (202)624-0775
Registered: LDA

Employers
American Express Co. (V. President, Government Affairs)

FERGUSON, Edward E.

440 First St. NW
Eighth Floor
Washington, DC 20001
EMail: efurguso@naco.org

Tel: (202)942-4214
Fax: (202)737-0480

Employers
Nat'l Ass'n of Counties (Director, County Services)
Nat'l Ass'n of County Administrators (Director, County Services)
Nat'l Ass'n of County Recorders, Election Officials and Clerks (Contact)

FERGUSON, Edward L.

1299 Pennsylvania Ave. NW
Washington, DC 20004-2402

Tel: (202)783-0800
Fax: (202)383-6610
Registered: LDA

Employers
Howrey Simon Arnold & White

Clients Represented

On Behalf of Howrey Simon Arnold & White
Battery Council Internat'l
Nat'l Ass'n for Plastic Container Recovery

FERGUSON, Jack

203 Maryland Ave. NE
Washington, DC 20002
EMail: jackferguson@mindspring.com

Tel: (202)544-6655
Fax: (202)544-5763
Registered: LDA

Administrative Aide to Assistant Minority Leader, Senator Ted Stevens (R-AK), 1976-78. Administrative Aide to Rep. Don Young (R-AK), 1973-76. Legislative Aide to Rep. Floyd Hicks (D-WA), 1970-73.

Employers
Jack Ferguson Associates, Inc. (President)

Clients Represented

On Behalf of Jack Ferguson Associates, Inc.
The 13th Regional Corp.
Alaska Airlines
Arctic Power
AT&T
Dillingham Construction, Inc.
Edison Electric Institute
Fantasma Networks, Inc.
Global Marine, Inc.
Icicle Seafoods, Inc.
Kennecott/Borax
Maersk Inc.
Mortgage Insurance Companies of America
Nat'l Ski Area Ass'n
Northern Air Cargo
Northland Holdings, Inc.
PanAmSat Corp.
Sea Containers America, Inc.
U.S. Borax, Inc.
United Airlines
University of Oklahoma

FERGUSON, Sydney

1211 Connecticut Ave. NW
Suite 608
Washington, DC 20036
EMail: sferguson@qorvis.com

Tel: (202)496-1000
Fax: (202)496-1300

Employers
Qorvis Communications (Managing Director)

FERGUSON, Jr., William

1130 Connecticut Ave. NW
Suite 300
Washington, DC 20036

Tel: (202)331-8500
Fax: (202)331-1598
Registered: LDA

Employers
The Ferguson Group, LLC (Chief Exec. Officer)
McConnell/Ferguson Group

Clients Represented

On Behalf of The Ferguson Group, LLC
Alabama A & M University
Arcadia, California, City of
Brea, California, City of
Broward, Florida, County of
California State University Fullerton
Central Valley Project Water Ass'n
Fairfield, California, City of
Imperial Irrigation District
Inglewood, California, City of
Interstate 5 Consortium
The Irvine Co.
Lennar Partners
Logan, Utah, City of (Transit District)
Long Beach Transit
Mecklenburg, North Carolina, County of
Modesto/Turlock Irrigation District
Norwalk, California, City of
Novato, California, City of
Oakland, California, City of
Oceanside, California, City of
Pico Rivera, California, City of
San Diego, California, City of
Santa Ana, California, City of
Sierra Madre, California, City of
Stop It Now!
Transportation Corridor Agencies
Yuma, Arizona, City of

On Behalf of McConnell/Ferguson Group
Transportation Corridor Agencies

FERGUSON LOVE, Georgane

1776 D St. NW
Washington, DC 20006-5303

Tel: (202)628-1776
Fax: (202)879-3252

Employers
Daughters of the American Revolution (Immediate Past President General)

FERMAN, John H.

444 N. Capitol St. NW
Suite 821
Washington, DC 20001

Tel: (202)737-3390
Fax: (202)628-3607
Registered: LDA

Employers
Health Policy Alternatives, Inc. (Principal)

FERRAND, Louis G.

1211 Connecticut Ave. NW
Suite 202
Washington, DC 20036

Tel: (202)466-5944
Fax: (202)466-5946

Employers
Inter-American Bar Ass'n (Secretary General)

FERRANDINO, Dr. Vincent

1615 Duke St.
Alexandria, VA 22314-3483

Tel: (703)684-3345
Fax: (703)548-6021

Employers
Nat'l Ass'n of Elementary School Principals (Exec. Director)

FERREE, Kandy

1400 I St. NW
Suite 1220
Washington, DC 20005

Tel: (202)408-4848
Fax: (202)408-1818

Employers
Nat'l AIDS Fund (President)

FERREIRA, Joseph L.

219 N. Washington St.
Alexandria, VA 22314
EMail: joe.ferreira@pal-aerospace.com

Tel: (703)836-7990
Fax: (703)836-9739
Registered: LDA

Employers
Peduzzi Associates, Ltd. (Associate)

Clients Represented

On Behalf of Peduzzi Associates, Ltd.
DRS - EOSG
Integrated Medical Systems
Lord Corp.
Marconi Flight Systems, Inc.
Skyhook Technologies, Inc.

FERRELL, DeDe

1501 M St. NW
Suite 1100
Washington, DC 20005
Tel: (202)785-7300
Fax: (202)785-6360
Registered: LDA

Employers
Viacom Inc. (V. President, Government Affairs)

FERRELL, Kirk

122 C St. NW
Suite 875
Washington, DC 20001
Tel: (202)347-3600
Fax: (202)347-5265
Registered: LDA

Employers
Nat'l Pork Producers Council (V. President, Public Policy)

FERRELL, Michael J.

1201 New York Ave. NW
Suite 1000
Washington, DC 20005
Tel: (202)962-4800
Fax: (202)962-8300

Employers
Venable

FERRELL, Michael L.

1234 Massachusetts Ave. NW
Washington, DC 20005
Tel: (202)347-8870
Fax: (202)347-7279
EMail: mferrell@dccfh.org

Employers
Coalition for the Homeless (Exec. Director)

FERRIGNO, Edward

601 13th St. NW
Suite 600 South
Washington, DC 20005-3807
Tel: (202)626-3634
Fax: (202)638-6635
Registered: LDA
EMail: ferrigno@psca.org

Employers
Profit Sharing/401 (k) Council of America (V. President, Washington Affairs)

FERRIN, Richard P.

607 14th St. NW
Washington, DC 20005
Tel: (202)434-0700
Fax: (202)912-6000
Registered: FARA

Employers
Rogers & Wells (Associate)

Clients Represented

On Behalf of Rogers & Wells
Dofasco, Inc.

FERRIS, Charles D.

701 Pennsylvania Ave. NW
Suite 900
Washington, DC 20004-2608
Tel: (202)434-7300
Fax: (202)434-7400
Registered: LDA, FARA
EMail: cferris@mintz.com
Chairman, Federal Communications Commission, 1977-81. Chief Counsel to Speaker of the House, Rep. Carl B. Albert (D-OK), 1976-77. General Counsel to Senate Majority Leader, Senator Michael J. Mansfield (D-MT) and General Counsel and Staff Director, Senate Democratic Policy Committee, 1964-76. Trial Attorney, Department of Justice, 1961-63.

Employers
Mintz, Levin, Cohn, Ferris, Glovsky and Popeo, P.C. (Chairman)

Clients Represented

On Behalf of Mintz, Levin, Cohn, Ferris, Glovsky and Popeo, P.C.
Cablevision Systems Corp.

FERRIS, Frank

901 E St. NW
Suite 600
Washington, DC 20004
Tel: (202)783-4444
Fax: (202)783-4085

Employers
Nat'l Treasury Employees Union (National Exec. V. President)

FERRIS, Robert M.

1101 14th St. NW
Suite 1400
Washington, DC 20005
Tel: (202)682-9400
Fax: (202)682-1331
EMail: rferris@defenders.org

Employers
Defenders of Wildlife (V. President, Species Conservation)

FERRUGIARO, John E.

700 11th St. NW
Washington, DC 20001-4507
Tel: (202)383-1077
Fax: (202)383-7584
EMail: jferrugiaro@realtors.org

Employers
Nat'l Ass'n of Realtors (Political Representative)

FERTEL, Marvin

1776 I St. NW
Suite 400
Washington, DC 20006-3708
Tel: (202)739-8000
Fax: (202)785-4019
Registered: LDA

Employers
Nuclear Energy Institute (Senior V. President, Business Operations)

FESH, Anne C.

1155 15th St. NW
Suite 1004
Washington, DC 20005
Tel: (202)467-5081
Fax: (202)467-5085
EMail: afesh@acb.org

Employers
American Council of the Blind (Administrative Coordinator)

FETGATTER, James A.

700 13th St. NW
Suite 950
Washington, DC 20005
Tel: (202)434-4510
Fax: (202)434-4509
EMail: jaf@afire.org

Employers
Ass'n of Foreign Investors in U.S. Real Estate (Chief Executive)

FEUER, Marvin

440 First St. NW
Suite 600
Washington, DC 20001
Tel: (202)639-5200
Registered: LDA

Employers
American Israel Public Affairs Committee (Defense and Strategic Issues Director)

FEULNER, Jr., Edwin J.

214 Massachusetts Ave. NE
Washington, DC 20002
Tel: (202)546-4400
Fax: (202)546-8328

Employers
Heritage Foundation (President and Chief Exec. Officer)

FICHTHORN, Norman W.

1900 K St. NW
Washington, DC 20006-1109
Tel: (202)955-1500
Fax: (202)778-2201
Registered: LDA

Employers
Hunton & Williams (Partner)

Clients Represented

On Behalf of Hunton & Williams
American Road and Transportation Builders Ass'n (ARTBA)
Clean Air Regulatory Information Group

FICHTNER, Shelley

1050 Thomas Jefferson St. NW
Seventh Floor
Washington, DC 20007
Tel: (202)298-1800
Fax: (202)338-2416

Employers
Van Ness Feldman, P.C. (Associate Director, Gov't Issues)

FIDLER, Shelley N.

1050 Thomas Jefferson St. NW
Seventh Floor
Washington, DC 20007
Tel: (202)298-1800
Fax: (202)338-2416
Registered: LDA

Employers
Van Ness Feldman, P.C. (Principal)

FIELDING, F. C.

1725 Jefferson Davis Hwy.
Suite 706
Arlington, VA 22202
Tel: (703)413-6200
Fax: (703)413-6384

Employers
Oshkosh Truck Corp. (V. President, Government Operations)

FIELDING, Fred F.

1776 K St. NW
Washington, DC 20006
Tel: (202)719-7000
Fax: (202)719-7049
Counsel (1981-86), Deputy Counsel (1972-74) and Assistant Counsel (1970-72) to the President, The White House.

Employers
Wiley, Rein & Fielding (Partner)

Clients Represented

On Behalf of Wiley, Rein & Fielding
U.S. Banknote Corp.
United Parcel Service

FIELDING, John

444 N. Capitol St. NW
Suite 701
Washington, DC 20001
Tel: (202)624-7790
Fax: (202)624-8579
EMail: JFielding@naic.org

Employers
Nat'l Ass'n of Insurance Commissioners (Senior Counsel, Financial Services)

FIELDS, Cheryl

1307 New York Ave. NW
Suite 400
Washington, DC 20005-4722
Tel: (202)478-6040
Fax: (202)478-6046

Employers
Nat'l Ass'n of State Universities and Land-Grant Colleges (Director, Public Affairs)

FIELDS, Craig

8001 Forbes Pl.
Suite 102
Springfield, VA 22151
Tel: (703)321-8585
Fax: (703)321-8408
Registered: LDA

Employers
Gun Owners of America (Director, Electronic Communications)

FIELDS, Drew

1020 19th St. NW
Washington, DC 20036
Tel: (202)429-0303
Fax: (202)293-0561
Registered: LDA

Employers
Qwest Communications (Exec. Director, Congressional Affairs)

FIELDS, Jr., Hon. Jack M.

434 New Jersey Ave. SE
Washington, DC 20003
Tel: (202)488-2800
Fax: (202)488-3150
Registered: LDA
EMail: twenty-firstcenturygroup@worldnet.att.net
Member, U.S. House of Representatives (R-TX), 1981-97. Served as Chairman, Subcommittee on Telecommunications and Finance, House Commerce Committee and Ranking Member, House Committee on Merchant Marine and Fisheries.

Employers
Twenty-First Century Group (Chief Exec. Officer)

Clients Represented

On Behalf of Twenty-First Century Group
Electronic Industries Alliance
Longhorn Pipeline
Personal Communications Industry Ass'n (PCIA)
SBC Communications Inc.
Taxpayers Against Fraud, The False Claims Legal Center
Telecommunications Industry Ass'n
Verizon Communications

FIER, Steven I.

4301 N. Fairfax Dr.
Suite 550
Arlington, VA 22203-1627
Tel: (703)527-8655
Fax: (703)527-2649
Registered: LDA
EMail: sfier@elamail.com

Employers
Equipment Leasing Ass'n of America (Director, Federal Government Relations)

FIERCE, Donald L.

600 New Hampshire Ave. NW
Tenth Floor
Washington, DC 20037
Tel: (202)333-8667
Fax: (202)298-9109
Registered: LDA
Former Aide to Rep. James Broyhill (R-NC). Professional Staff Member, Office of Congressional Affairs at the General Services Administration, 1973-75.

Employers
Fierce and Isakowitz (President)

Clients Represented

On Behalf of Fierce and Isakowitz
American Ass'n of Nurse Anesthetists
American Gaming Ass'n
Credit Union Nat'l Ass'n, Inc.
DuPont
Federation of American Hospitals
Generic Pharmaceutical Ass'n
Health Insurance Ass'n of America
Liberty Maritime Co.
MCI WorldCom Corp.
Pegasus Communications
Rubber Manufacturers Ass'n
Tricon Global Restaurants Inc.

FIGEL, Brad G.

507 Second St. NE
Washington, DC 20002
Tel: (202)543-6453
Fax: (202)544-6453
Registered: LDA
EMail: brad.figel@nike.com

Employers
Nike, Inc. (Director, Governmental Affairs and International Trade Counsel)

FIGUA, Emily

1627 K St. NW 12th Floor
Washington, DC 20006
Tel: (202)293-3114
Fax: (202)293-1990
Registered: LDA

Employers
Nat'l Family Planning and Reproductive Health Ass'n (Senior Public Policy Analyst)

FIGUEROA, Darryl Lynette

1201 16th St. NW
Washington, DC 20036
Tel: (202)833-4000

Employers
Nat'l Education Ass'n of the U.S. (Senior Professional Associate, Media Relations Staff)

FIKE, Robert

1920 L St. NW
Suite 200
Washington, DC 20036
Tel: (202)785-0266
Fax: (202)785-0261
Registered: LDA
EMail: rfike@atr.dc.org

Employers
Americans for Tax Reform (Manager, Federal Affairs)
Anti-Value Added Tax Coalition (Director)

FILES, Amory

600 13th St. NW
Washington, DC 20005-3096
Tel: (202)756-8686
Fax: (202)756-8087
Registered: LDA
EMail: afiles@mwe.com

Employers
McDermott, Will and Emery (Law Clerk)

Clients Represented

On Behalf of McDermott, Will and Emery
Internat'l Ass'n of Professional Numismatists

FILIPOVIC, Mark

9000 Machinists Pl.
Upper Marlboro, MD 20772-2687
Tel: (301)967-4500
Fax: (301)967-4591

Employers
Internat'l Ass'n of Machinists and Aerospace Workers (Railroad Coordinator)

FILIPPONE, Desiree

555 12th St. NW
Suite 650
Washington, DC 20004-1205
Tel: (202)393-7950
Fax: (202)393-7960

Employers
Eli Lilly and Co. (Manager, International and Public Government Relations)

FILLER, Marshall S.

117 N. Henry St.
Alexandria, VA 22314
Tel: (703)299-0784
Fax: (703)299-0254
Registered: LDA
EMail: msf@fillerweller.com

Employers
Filler & Weller, P.C. (President)

FILLICHIO, Carl A.

1301 K St. NW
Suite 450 West
Washington, DC 20005
Tel: (202)728-0418
Fax: (202)728-0422
Deputy Assistant Secretary for Public Affairs, Department of Labor, 19995-2001.

Employers
Council for Excellence in Government (Director, Public Affairs)

FILLIP, Christine

410 First St. SE
Third Floor
Washington, DC 20003
EMail: cfillip@dcsgroup.com
Tel: (202)484-2776
Fax: (202)484-7016

Employers
The DCS Group (Senior V. President)

FINDARO, Joseph T.

201 Maryland Ave. NE
Washington, DC 20002
Tel: (202)543-7200
Fax: (202)543-0616
Registered: LDA
EMail: joe@mgninc.com
Deputy Assistant Secretary, Department of Interior, 1985-87.

Employers
McClure, Gerard & Neuenschwander, Inc. (Principal)

Clients Represented

On Behalf of McClure, Gerard & Neuenschwander, Inc.
American Gaming Ass'n
Barrick Goldstrike Mines, Inc.
Boise State University
Brush Wellman, Inc.
Coachella Valley Water District
Echo Bay Mining
Family Farm Alliance (Project Transfer Council)
Harquehala Irrigation District
Hecla Mining Co.
Helli USA Airways
Henderson, Nevada, City of
Howard Hughes Corp.
Idaho Power Co.
Independence Mining Co., Inc.
Internat'l Bottled Water Ass'n
Nat'l Endangered Species Act Reform Coalition
Native American Mohegans Inc.
Nevada Test Site Development Corp.
Newmont Mining Corp.
Pershing Co. Water Conservation District of Nevada
Placer Dome U.S. Inc.
Private Fuels Storage, L.L.C.
Quest Nevada, Inc.
Space Imaging, Inc.
Stirling Energy Systems
Verizon Wireless
Wellton-Mohawk Irrigation and Drainage District
Westlands Water District
The Williams Companies

FINDER, Jodi

800 Connecticut Ave. NW
Suite 500
Washington, DC 20006
Tel: (202)331-3100
Fax: (202)331-3101
Registered: LDA

Employers
Greenberg Traurig, LLP

Clients Represented

On Behalf of Greenberg Traurig, LLP
Nat'l Center for Genome Research

FINDLAY, Linda D.

1420 New York Ave. NW
Suite 210
Washington, DC 20005
Tel: (202)789-1745
Fax: (202)371-1731
Registered: LDA

Employers
Phelps Dodge Corp. (V. President, Government Relations)

FINDLEY, Hon. Paul

1250 Fourth St. SW
Suite WG-1
Washington, DC 20024
EMail: count@igc.apc.org
Tel: (202)863-2951
Fax: (202)863-2952
Member, U.S. House of Representatives (R-IL), 1961-83.

Employers
Council for the Nat'l Interest (Founding Chairman)

FINE, David

1401 I St. NW
Suite 1100
Washington, DC 20005
Tel: (202)326-8870
Fax: (202)408-4803
Registered: LDA

Employers
SBC Communications Inc. (Assistant V. President, Government and International Relations)

FINE, Hyman

8605 Cameron St.
Suite M5
Silver Spring, MD 20910
Tel: (301)562-3141
Fax: (301)562-3141

Employers
Hyman Fine Associates

FINE, Michael E.

1001 Pennsylvania Ave. NW
Suite 600
Washington, DC 20004
Tel: (202)347-0066
Fax: (202)624-7222
Registered: LDA
EMail: mfine@pgfm.com
Law Clerk, U.S. Court of Appeals, District of Columbia Circuit, 1982-83.

Employers
Powell, Goldstein, Frazer & Murphy LLP (Partner)

Clients Represented

On Behalf of Powell, Goldstein, Frazer & Murphy LLP
American Committee for the Weizmann Institute of Science
Hong Kong Trade Development Council
Joint Stock Company Severstal
Koyo Seiko Co., Ltd.
Nissan North America Inc.
Organization for Internat'l Investment
Rollerblade, Inc.

FINE, Sharon R.

1776 K St. NW
Washington, DC 20006
Tel: (202)719-7000
Fax: (202)719-7049
Registered: LDA

Employers
Wiley, Rein & Fielding

Clients Represented

On Behalf of Wiley, Rein & Fielding
Birmingham Steel Corp.
Co-Steel Raritan
Connecticut Steel Corp.
Keystone Consolidated Industries, Inc.
Northwestern Steel and Wire Co.
Verizon Wireless
Washington Citizens for World Trade

FINEGAN, P. Cole

1615 L St. NW
Suite 450
Washington, DC 20036
Tel: (202)296-7353
Fax: (202)296-7009
Registered: LDA

Employers
Brownstein Hyatt & Farber, P.C.

Clients Represented
On Behalf of Brownstein Hyatt & Farber, P.C.
Discount Refrigerants Inc.

FINERFROCK, William A.

426 C St. NE
Washington, DC 20002
Tel: (202)544-1880
Fax: (202)543-2565
Registered: LDA
EMail: bf@capitolassociates.com
Legislative Assistant, U.S. Senate, 1977-84.

Employers
Capitol Associates, Inc. (V. President, Health Policy)

Clients Represented
On Behalf of Capitol Associates, Inc.
American Ass'n for Marriage and Family Therapy
American Soc. of Radiologic Technologists
Ass'n of Surgical Technologists
DeBrunner and Associates, Inc.
Health Quest
Healthcare Billing and Management Ass'n
MedReview, Inc.
Nat'l Ass'n of Medical Equipment Suppliers (NAMES)
Nat'l Ass'n of Rural Health Clinics
Urban Health Care Coalition of Pennsylvania

FINGER, Larry E.

6110 Executive Blvd.
Suite 800
Rockville, MD 20852-3927
Tel: (301)984-9400
Fax: (301)984-9610
EMail: lfinger@washreit.com

Employers
Washington Real Estate Investment Trust (Senior V. President and Chief Financial Officer)

FINK, Marc J.

1850 M St. NW
Suite 900
Washington, DC 20036
Tel: (202)463-2500
Fax: (202)463-4950
Registered: LDA, FARA
EMail: mfink@shebla.com
Trial Attorney, Civil Division, Department of Justice, 1974-77. Law Clerk, Trial Division, U.S. Court of Claims, 1973-74.

Employers
Sher & Blackwell (Partner)

Clients Represented
On Behalf of Sher & Blackwell
Apex Marine Ship Management Co. LLC
Carriers Against Harbor Tax
Council of European and Japanese Nat'l Shipowners' Ass'ns
Internat'l Brotherhood of Teamsters
Maersk Inc.
Ocean Carriers Working Group
Transpacific Stabilization Agreement

FINK, Matthew P.

1401 H St. NW
12th Floor
Washington, DC 20005-2148
Tel: (202)326-5801
Fax: (202)326-5806

Employers
Investment Co. Institute (President)

FINK, Patricia M.

1385 Piccard Dr.
Rockville, MD 20850-4340
Tel: (301)869-5800
Fax: (301)990-9690
EMail: pfink@mcaa.org

Employers
Mechanical Contractors Ass'n of America (Director, Affiliate Support Services)

FINK, Paula

P.O. Box 1804
Department 599
Washington, DC 20013
Tel: (301)341-4398
Fax: (301)618-4968

Employers
Giant Food Inc. (Communications Manager)

FINK, Richard H.

655 15th St. NW
Suite 445
Washington, DC 20005
Tel: (202)737-1977

Employers
Koch Industries, Inc. (Exec. V. President)

FINK, Seth D.

1385 Piccard Dr.
Rockville, MD 20850-4340
Tel: (301)869-5800
Fax: (301)990-9690
EMail: sfink@mcaa.org

Employers
Mechanical Contractors Ass'n of America (Exec. Director, Finance and Business Operations)

FINKE, Rupert

1615 H St. NW
Washington, DC 20062-2000
Tel: (202)659-6000
Fax: (202)463-5836

Employers
Chamber of Commerce of the U.S.A. (Associate Director, Eurasia, International Division)

FINKEL, E. Jay

1919 Pennsylvania Ave. NW
Suite 500
Washington, DC 20006-3434
Tel: (202)778-3000
Fax: (202)778-3063
EMail: jfinkel@porterwright.com

Employers
Porter, Wright, Morris & Arthur, LLP (Partner)

Clients Represented
On Behalf of Porter, Wright, Morris & Arthur, LLP
Atanor, S.A.
Harza Engineering Co.
Huntington Bancshares

FINKELNBURG, Marjorie C.

325 Seventh St. NW
Suite 1200
Washington, DC 20004-1007
Tel: (202)783-7070
Fax: (202)347-2044

Employers
Pfizer, Inc. (Assistant Director, Government Relations)

FINKELSTEIN, Ben

1350 New York Ave. NW
Suite 1100
Washington, DC 20005-4798
Tel: (202)879-4000
Fax: (202)393-2866
Registered: LDA
EMail: finkelsb@spiegelmcd.com

Employers
Spiegel & McDiarmid (Partner)

Clients Represented
On Behalf of Spiegel & McDiarmid
Holyoke Department of Gas and Electricity

FINKENBINDER, David O.

1130 17th St. NW
Washington, DC 20036-4677
Tel: (202)463-2636
Fax: (202)463-3257
Registered: LDA
EMail: dfinkenbinder@nma.org

Employers
Nat'l Mining Ass'n (V. President, Lands Policy)

FINKLE, Jeffrey A.

1730 K St. NW
Suite 700
Washington, DC 20006
Tel: (202)223-4735
Fax: (202)223-4745
EMail: jfinkle@urbandevelopment.com

Employers
Council for Urban Economic Development (President, Chief Exec. Officer)
Nat'l Ass'n of Installation Developers (Exec. Director)

FINLAY-DICK, Brian

1755 Massachusetts Ave. NW
Suite 400
Washington, DC 20036
Tel: (202)387-0400
Fax: (202)483-9430
EMail: finlay@tcf.org

Employers
The Century Foundation (Program Officer)

FINLAYSON, Joseph

2131 K St. NW
Suite 710
Washington, DC 20037-1810
Tel: (202)347-6787
Fax: (202)737-4727
Registered: LDA

Employers
The Roth Group (Exec. Director)

Clients Represented
On Behalf of The Roth Group
Johnson Controls, Inc.
Nat'l Cash Register

FINLEY, Catherine

444 N. Capitol St. NW
Suite 200
Washington, DC 20001
Tel: (202)624-5897
Fax: (202)624-7797
EMail: sga@sso.org

Employers
Southern Governors Ass'n (Policy Analyst)

FINLEY, Elise K.

2400 Clarendon Blvd.
Suite 616
Arlington, VA 22201

Employers
Conscience of a Conservative PAC (Contact)
Southern Co. (Manager, Federal Legislative Affairs)

FINNEGAN, David B.

1909 K St. NW
Washington, DC 20006
Tel: (202)263-3000
Fax: (202)263-3300
Registered: LDA
Counsel, Committee on Energy and Commerce, U.S. House of Representatives, 1976-94. Counsel, Committee on Science and Technology, U.S. House of Representatives, 1974-76. Counsel, Committee on Government Operations, U.S. House of Representatives, 1969-74. Assistant Legislative Counsel (1967-69), Attorney, Office of Legislative Counsel (1963-67), and Attorney, Office of the Solicitor (1960-63), Department of the Interior.

Employers
Mayer, Brown & Platt (Senior Counsel)

Clients Represented
On Behalf of Mayer, Brown & Platt
Cable & Wireless, Inc.
Edison Electric Institute
Ford Motor Co.

FINNEGAN, Dr. Niall B.

1101 Vermont Ave. NW
Suite 710
Washington, DC 20005-3521
Tel: (202)789-0007
Fax: (202)842-4360
Registered: LDA

Employers
American Veterinary Medical Ass'n (Director, Governmental Relations Division)

FINNIGAN, Thomas D.

801 Pennsylvania Ave. NW
Suite 230
Washington, DC 20004
Tel: (202)393-0962
Fax: (202)347-1684
Registered: LDA
EMail: Tom_Finnigan@Praxair.com
Served on Staff to Rep. Glenn Davis (R-WI), 1970-71.

Employers
Praxair, Inc. (Director, Government Relations)

FINSTOM, Susan

1100 15th St. NW
Suite 900
Washington, DC 20005
Tel: (202)835-3400
Fax: (202)835-3414
Registered: LDA

Employers
Pharmaceutical Research and Manufacturers of America (Assistant V. President, International)

FINUCANE, Alexandra K.

4351 Garden City Dr.
Landover, MD 20785
Tel: (301)459-3700
Fax: (301)459-0340
EMail: afinucane@efa.org

Employers
Epilepsy Foundation of America (V. President, Legal and Government Affairs)

FINZEL, Ben

1615 L St. NW
Suite 1000
Washington, DC 20036
Tel: (202)659-0330
Fax: (202)296-6119

Employers
Fleishman-Hillard, Inc (V. President)

FIORDELLISI, Maria

815 16th St. NW
Washington, DC 20006
Tel: (202)637-5000
Fax: (202)637-5058
Registered: LDA

Employers
AFL-CIO (American Federation of Labor and Congress of Industrial Organizations) (Legislative Representative)

FIORE, Maria

815 15th St. NW
Suite 538
Washington, DC 20005
EMail: mfiore@nhc.org
Tel: (202)393-5772
Fax: (202)393-5656

Employers
Nat'l Housing Conference (Policy Manager)

FIRE, Ed

1275 K St. NW
Suite 600
Washington, DC 20005
Tel: (202)513-6300

Employers
Internat'l Union of Electronic, Electrical, Salaried, Machine, and Furniture Workers-Communications Workers of America (President)

FIRESTONE, Jean Ann

1000 Thomas Jefferson St. NW
Suite 515
Washington, DC 20007
Tel: (202)342-8086
Fax: (202)342-9063

Employers
Leather Industries of America (Communications Coordinator)

FIRMAN, Ed.D., James P.

409 Third St. SW
Second Floor
Washington, DC 20024
Tel: (202)479-1200
Fax: (202)479-0735

Employers
Nat'l Council on the Aging (President and Chief Exec. Officer)
Nat'l Institute on Financial Issues and Services for Elders

FIRTH, Adrianne

332 Constitution Ave. NE
Washington, DC 20002
EMail: mgfpc@msn.com
Tel: (202)547-5400
Fax: (202)543-5740
Registered: LDA

Employers
Marcus G. Faust, P.C. (Legislative Consultant)

Clients Represented

On Behalf of Marcus G. Faust, P.C.
Central Utah Water Conservancy District
Clark County Department of Aviation
Clark County, Nevada, Office of the County Manager
Contra Costa Water District
Public Service Co. of New Mexico
Regional Transportation Commission
Sierra Pacific Resources

FIRVIDA, Cristina Begona

11 Dupont Circle NW
Suite 800
Washington, DC 20036
EMail: cfirvida@nwlc.org
Tel: (202)588-5180
Fax: (202)588-5185

Employers
Nat'l Women's Law Center (Senior Counsel)

FISCHBECK, Kyra

1001 Pennsylvania Ave. NW
Suite 600
Washington, DC 20004
Tel: (202)347-0066
Fax: (202)624-7222
Registered: LDA

Employers
Powell, Goldstein, Frazer & Murphy LLP (Associate)

Clients Represented

On Behalf of Powell, Goldstein, Frazer & Murphy LLP
Bayer Corp. / Agriculture Division

FISCHER, Alison

1413 K St. NW
Tenth Floor
Washington, DC 20005
Tel: (202)347-8772
Fax: (202)393-5886

Employers
United States Student Ass'n (President)

FISCHER, Danna S.

8200 Jones Branch Dr.
McLean, VA 22102
Tel: (703)903-2000
Fax: (703)903-2447
Registered: LDA

Employers
Federal Home Loan Mortgage Corp. (Freddie Mac) (Director, Government and Industry Relations)

FISCHER, L. Richard

2000 Pennsylvania Ave. NW
Suite 5500
Washington, DC 20006
EMail: lfischer@mofo.com
Tel: (202)887-1500
Fax: (202)887-0763
Registered: LDA

Employers
Morrison & Foerster LLP (Partner)

Clients Represented

On Behalf of Morrison & Foerster LLP
VISA U.S.A., Inc.

FISCHIONE, Deborah A.

Ten G St. NE
Suite 710
Washington, DC 20002
EMail: daf@nasaa.org
Tel: (202)737-0900
Fax: (202)783-3571
Registered: LDA

Employers
North American Securities Administrators Ass'n (NASAA) (Director of Policy)

FISCHMAN, Brent

1025 Connecticut Ave. NW
Suite 501
Washington, DC 20036
Tel: (202)828-6853
Fax: (202)828-6849

Employers
GenCorp (Director, International Marketing and Sales)

FISE, Mary Ellen

1424 16th St. NW
Suite 604
Washington, DC 20036
EMail: merf@home.com
Tel: (202)387-6121
Fax: (202)265-7989
Registered: LDA

Employers
Consumer Federation of America (General Counsel)

FISE, Thomas F.

4900-B S. 31st St.
Arlington, VA 22206
Tel: (703)820-7400
Fax: (703)931-4520

Employers
American College of Gastroenterology (Exec. Director)
Ass'n and Government Relations Management, Inc. (Principal)

Clients Represented

On Behalf of Ass'n and Government Relations Management, Inc.
American College of Gastroenterology
American Dental Trade Ass'n

FISH, Andrew C.

750 17th St. NW
Suite 1100
Washington, DC 20006
Tel: (202)778-2300
Fax: (202)778-2330

Employers
FoxKiser

FISH, John H.

1201 F St. NW
Suite 1000
Washington, DC 20004-1077
Tel: (202)626-7210
Fax: (202)626-7208
Registered: LDA

Employers
R. J. Reynolds Tobacco Co. (V. President, Federal Government Affairs)

FISHBEIN, Ellen

1101 Connecticut Ave. NW
Suite 400
Washington, DC 20036-4303
Tel: (202)530-7878
Fax: (202)530-7879
Registered: LDA

Employers
AOL Time Warner (Assistant General Counsel)

FISHBEIN, Julie W.

9901 Avenel Farm Dr.
Potomac, MD 20854
Tel: (301)767-1690
Fax: (301)767-1692
Registered: LDA

Employers
Fishbein Associates, Inc. (Chairman)

FISHBEIN, Rand H.

9901 Avenel Farm Dr.
Potomac, MD 20854
Tel: (301)767-1690
Fax: (301)767-1692
Registered: LDA

Former Special Assistant for National Security Affairs to Senator Daniel K. Inouye (D-HI). Also served as Professional Staff Member, Subcommittee on Defense and Subcommittee on Foreign Operations, Senate Committee on Appropriations.

Employers
Fishbein Associates, Inc. (Partner)

FISHBURNE, Jonathan

2450 N St. NW
Washington, DC 20037-1126
Tel: (202)828-0525
Fax: (202)862-6218
Registered: LDA

Employers
Ass'n of American Medical Colleges (Senior Legislative Analyst)

FISHEL, Alan

1050 Connecticut Ave. NW
Washington, DC 20036-5339
Tel: (202)857-6000
Fax: (202)857-6395

Employers
Arent Fox Kintner Plotkin & Kahn, PLLC (Member)

Clients Represented

On Behalf of Arent Fox Kintner Plotkin & Kahn, PLLC
France Telecom America do Sul Ltda.

FISHER, Bart S.

1919 Pennsylvania Ave. NW
Suite 500
Washington, DC 20006-3434
EMail: bfisher@porterwright.com
Tel: (202)778-3000
Fax: (202)778-3063
Registered: LDA

Employers
Porter, Wright, Morris & Arthur, LLP (Of Counsel)

Clients Represented

On Behalf of Porter, Wright, Morris & Arthur, LLP
Huffy Bicycles
Huffy Sports
Nature's Farm Products

FISHER, Colleen M.

121 N. Washington St.
Suite 301
Alexandria, VA 22314
Tel: (703)837-9001
Fax: (703)837-8467

Formely employed at Resolution Trust Corp. (1993-95) and U.S. Senate (1976-83).

Employers
Council for Affordable and Rural Housing (Exec. Director)

FISHER, CAE, Dr. Donald W.

1422 Duke St.
Alexandria, VA 22314
Tel: (703)838-0033 Ext: 331
Fax: (703)548-1890
Registered: LDA

Employers

American Medical Group Ass'n (President and Chief Exec. Officer)

FISHER, Donna J.

1120 Connecticut Ave. NW
Washington, DC 20036
Tel: (202)663-5000
Fax: (202)828-4548
Registered: LDA

Employers

American Bankers Ass'n (Director, Tax and Accounting)

FISHER, J. Paris

1700 K St. NW
Suite 800
Washington, DC 20006
Tel: (202)862-9705
Fax: (202)862-9710
Registered: LDA
EMail: parisfisher@aol.com

Employers

Martin, Fisher & Associates, Inc. (Senior V. President)

Clients Represented

On Behalf of Martin, Fisher & Associates, Inc.

AAI Corp.
Nat'l Soft Drink Ass'n
United Defense, L.P.

FISHER, John R.

2300 Wilson Blvd.
Arlington, VA 22201
Tel: (703)528-1775
Fax: (703)528-2333
EMail: jfisher@navyleague.org

Employers

Navy League of the United States (Nat'l President)

FISHER, Linda L.

905 16th St. NW
Washington, DC 20006
Tel: (202)737-8320
Fax: (202)737-2754

Employers

Laborers' Internat'l Union of North America (Director, Public Affairs)

FISHER, Lynn

1140 19th St. NW
Suite 600
Washington, DC 20036
Tel: (202)822-8200
Fax: (202)822-8205

Employers

Violence Policy Center (Communications Assistant)

FISHER, Robert

1200 19th St. NW
Suite 201
Washington, DC 20036-2065
Tel: (202)822-4700
Fax: (202)822-4710
Former Director, Mexican Affairs, Office of U.S. Trade Representative.

Employers

Hills & Company, International Consultants (Managing Director)

Clients Represented

On Behalf of Hills & Company, International Consultants

The Procter & Gamble Company

FISHER, Steven A.

P.O. Box 76228
Washington, DC 20013-6228
Tel: (202)625-2102
Fax: (202)625-2104
Registered: LDA

Employers

Fisher Consulting (Washington Representative)

Clients Represented

On Behalf of Fisher Consulting

American Great Lakes Ports
Ball State University
Build Indiana Council
Chicago Southshore and South Bend Railroad

FISHER, Tim

1909 K Street NW
Suite 810
Washington, DC 20006
Tel: (202)872-0127
Fax: (202)872-0736
Registered: LDA

Employers

ACE INA (Assistant V. President, Global Government Affairs)

FISHER, William E.

12251 Tech Rd.
Silver Spring, MD 20904
Tel: (301)622-1900
Fax: (301)236-9320
Registered: LDA

Employers

Internat'l Fabricare Institute (Chief Exec. Officer)

FISHER, William P.

1201 New York Ave. NW
Suite 600
Washington, DC 20005-3931
Tel: (202)289-3100
Fax: (202)289-3199
EMail: bfisher@ahma.com

Employers

American Hotel and Lodging Ass'n (President and Chief Exec. Officer)

FISKE, Edward

1825 Connecticut Ave. NW
Fifth Floor
Washington, DC 20009
Tel: (202)667-0901
Fax: (202)667-0902

Employers

Widmeyer Communications, Inc. (Senior Counsel)

FISKUM, David

1275 K St. NW
Suite 810
Washington, DC 20005
Tel: (202)408-2100
Fax: (202)408-2115
Registered: LDA

Employers

Conkling, Fiskum & McCormick (Partner)

Clients Represented

On Behalf of Conkling, Fiskum & McCormick

New Edge Networks

FITCH, Jr., John H.

400 C St. NE
Washington, DC 20002
Tel: (202)547-0441
Fax: (202)547-0726
Registered: LDA
EMail: jfitch@nfda.org

Employers

Nat'l Funeral Directors Ass'n (Director, Government Relations)

FITCH, Robert J.

1215 Jefferson Davis Hwy.
Suite 1500
Arlington, VA 22202
Tel: (703)416-7800
Fax: (703)415-1459
Registered: LDA
EMail: robert.fitch@baesystems.com

Employers

BAE SYSTEMS North America (V. President, Government Relations)

FITHIAN, John F.

2550 M St. NW
Washington, DC 20037-1350
Tel: (202)457-6000
Fax: (202)457-6315
Registered: LDA
EMail: jfithian@pattonboggs.com

Employers

Patton Boggs, LLP (Partner)

Clients Represented

On Behalf of Patton Boggs, LLP

American Ass'n of Advertising Agencies
Ass'n of Nat'l Advertisers
Commco, L.L.C.
Major League Baseball Players Ass'n
Mars, Inc.
MCI WorldCom Corp.
Nat'l Ass'n of Theatre Owners
Outdoor Advertising Ass'n of America
Point of Purchase Advertising Institute
Supra Telecom & Information Systems, Inc.
Wayne, Michigan, County of

FITZGERALD, Brian W.

3000 K St. NW
Suite 300
Washington, DC 20007
Tel: (202)424-7500
Fax: (202)424-7643
Registered: LDA
Law Clerk, Senate Judiciary Subcommittee on the Constitution, 1979-80.

Employers

Swidler Berlin Shereff Friedman, LLP (Partner)

Clients Represented

On Behalf of Swidler Berlin Shereff Friedman, LLP

Aventis Pharmaceuticals, Inc.
Dairy.com
Florida Power and Light Co.
Merrill Lynch & Co., Inc.
Microsoft Corp.
Newman & Associates
Niagara Mohawk Power Corp.
Reusable Industrial Packaging Ass'n
RSR Corp.
Schering Corp.
Suiza Foods Corp.
Transkaryotic Therapies Inc.

FITZGERALD, David A.

901 15th St. NW
Suite 700
Washington, DC 20005-2301
Tel: (202)371-6000
Fax: (202)371-6279
Registered: LDA
EMail: dafitzgerald@verner.com

Employers

Verner, Liipfert, Bernhard, McPherson and Hand, Chartered (Associate)

Clients Represented

On Behalf of Verner, Liipfert, Bernhard, McPherson and Hand, Chartered

MBIA Insurance Corp.
Oglethorpe Power Corp.
Southeastern Federal Power Customers, Inc.

FITZGERALD, Eileen

1990 M St. NW
Suite 340
Washington, DC 20036
Tel: (202)223-6222
Fax: (202)785-0687
Registered: LDA

Employers

Kent & O'Connor, Inc. (Consultant)

Clients Represented

On Behalf of Kent & O'Connor, Inc.

American Supply Ass'n
Internat'l Academy of Compounding Pharmacists

FITZGERALD, Jayne T.

1150 17th St. NW
Suite 601
Washington, DC 20036
Tel: (202)293-7474
Fax: (202)293-8811
Registered: LDA
Tax Counsel, House Ways and Means Committee, 19992-93 and 1980-85.

Employers

Washington Council Ernst & Young (Partner)

Clients Represented

On Behalf of Washington Council Ernst & Young

Aetna Inc.
Aetna Life & Casualty Co.
Allegiance Healthcare Corp.
Allen & Co.
American Express Co.
American Insurance Ass'n
American Staffing Ass'n
Anheuser-Busch Cos., Inc.
Antitrust Coalition for Consumer Choice in Health Care
Apartment Investment and Management Co.
Ass'n of American Railroads
Ass'n of Home Appliance Manufacturers
AT&T
AT&T Capital Corp.
Avco Financial Services
Aventis Pharmaceuticals, Inc.
Baxter Healthcare Corp.
BHC Communications, Inc.
Bulmer Holding PLC, H. P.
Cash Balance Coalition
Chamber of Shipping of America
Citigroup
Coalition for Fairness in Defense Exports
Coalition to Preserve Tracking Stock
ComEd
The Connell Co.
Deferral Group
Directors Guild of America
Doris Duke Charitable Foundation
Eaton Vance Management Co.
Eden Financial Corp.
The Enterprise Foundation
Fannie Mae
FedEx Corp.
Ford Motor Co.
GE Capital Assurance
General Electric Co.
General Motors Corp.
Global Competitiveness Coalition
Grasslands Water District
Group Health, Inc.
Haz-X Support Services Corp.
HEREIU
Gilbert P. Hyatt, Inventor
Investment Co. Institute
Large Public Power Council
Local Initiatives Support Corp.
Lockheed Martin Corp.
MacAndrews & Forbes Holdings, Inc.
Marsh & McLennan Cos.
MCG Northwest, Inc.
McLane Co.
Merrill Lynch & Co., Inc.
Metropolitan Banking Group
Microsoft Corp.
Nat'l Ass'n for State Farm Agents
Nat'l Ass'n of Professional Employer Organizations
Nat'l Ass'n of Real Estate Investment Trusts
Nat'l Ass'n of State Farm Agents
Nat'l Cable Television Ass'n
Nat'l Defined Contribution Council
Nat'l Foreign Trade Council, Inc.
Nat'l Multi-Housing Council
PaineWebber Group, Inc.
Pfizer, Inc.
R&D Tax Credit Coalition
R&D Tax Regulation Group
Recording Industry Ass'n of America
Reed-Elsevier Inc.
R. J. Reynolds Tobacco Co.
Charles Schwab & Co., Inc.,
Securities Industry Ass'n
Sierra Pacific Industries
Skadden, Arps, Slate, Meagher & Flom LLP
Straddle Rules Tax Group
Tax Fairness Coalition
Tax/Shelter Coalition
TransOceanic Shipping
TU Services
TXU Business Services
U.S. Oncology
USA Biomass Power Producers Alliance
Viaticus, Inc.
Wilkie Farr & Gallagher
Ziff Investors Partnership

FITZGERALD, John

13826 Castle Cliff Way
Silver Spring, MD 20904-5464
Tel: (301)384-6629
Registered: LDA

Employers
Self-employed as an independent consultant.

FITZGERALD, Kevin C.

401 Ninth St. NW
Suite 1000
Washington, DC 20004
Tel: (202)274-2955
Fax: (202)274-2994
Registered: LDA

Employers
Troutman Sanders LLP (Managing Partner)

Clients Represented

On Behalf of Troutman Sanders LLP

Minnesota Power
Otter Tail Power Co.
Southern Co.

FITZGERALD, Mary Clare

401 Ninth St. NW
Suite 1000
Washington, DC 20004
Tel: (202)274-2950
Fax: (202)274-2994
Registered: LDA

Employers
Troutman Sanders LLP

Clients Represented

On Behalf of Troutman Sanders LLP

American Institute of Certified Public Accountants
Electronic Commerce Forum
ezgov.com
Federal Home Loan Bank of Des Moines

FITZGERALD, Thomas F.

1701 Pennsylvania Ave. NW
Suite 1200
Washington, DC 20006
EMail: tff@groom.com
Tel: (202)857-0620
Fax: (202)659-4503
Registered: LDA

Employers
Groom Law Group, Chartered (Member)

Clients Represented

On Behalf of Groom Law Group, Chartered

Blue Cross Blue Shield Ass'n

FITZGIBBONS, Dennis B.

1401 H St. NW
Suite 700
Washington, DC 20005
Tel: (202)414-6764
Fax: (202)414-6741
Registered: LDA

Employers
DaimlerChrysler Corp. (Director, Public Policy)

FITZGIBBONS, Ellen B.

1850 K St. NW
Suite 850
Washington, DC 20006
Tel: (202)331-1760
Fax: (202)822-9376
Registered: LDA

Former Press Secretary to Rep. Mickey Leland (D-TX). Former Assistant Press Secretary to Speaker of the House, Rep. Thomas P. O'Neill (D-MA).

Employers
Timmons and Co., Inc. (V. President)

Clients Represented

On Behalf of Timmons and Co., Inc.

American Council of Life Insurers
American Petroleum Institute
American Soc. of Anesthesiologists
Anheuser-Busch Cos., Inc.
Asbestos Working Group
AT&T
Bay Harbor Management, L.C.
Bristol-Myers Squibb Co.
Cox Enterprises Inc.
DaimlerChrysler Corp.
Farallon Capital Management
Federal Home Loan Mortgage Corp. (Freddie Mac)
Micron Technology, Inc.
Napster, Inc.
Nat'l Rifle Ass'n of America
New York Life Insurance Co.
Northrop Grumman Corp.
TruePosition Inc.
Union Pacific
University of Utah
UNOCAL Corp.
VISA U.S.A., Inc.

FITZHUGH, Estrellita Jones

1250 24th St. NW
Washington, DC 20037
Tel: (202)293-4800
Fax: (202)293-9211
Registered: LDA

Employers
World Wildlife Fund

FITZMAURICE, Sena

1317 F St. NW
Suite 600
Washington, DC 20004
Tel: (202)638-2121
Fax: (202)638-7045
Registered: LDA
EMail: fitzmaurice@wexlergroup.com

Employers
The Wexler Group (Principal)

Clients Represented

On Behalf of The Wexler Group

Comcast Corp.

FITZPATRICK, Eileen B.

8200 Jones Branch Dr.
McLean, VA 22102
Tel: (703)903-2446
Fax: (703)903-2447
EMail: eileen_fitzpatrick@freddiemac.com

Employers
Federal Home Loan Mortgage Corp. (Freddie Mac) (Media Relations Specialist)

FITZPATRICK, James F.

555 12th St. NW
Washington, DC 20004-1206
Tel: (202)942-5878
Fax: (202)942-5999
Registered: LDA
EMail: James_Fitzpatrick@aporter.com

Law Clerk to Chief Judge John S. Hastings, U.S. Court of Appeals, Seventh Circuit, 1959-61.

Employers
Arnold & Porter (Partner)

Clients Represented

On Behalf of Arnold & Porter

Bruce Vladek
Health Services of Kansas and Mid Missouri
Nat'l Ass'n of Dealers in Ancient, Oriental and Primitive Art
State Farm Insurance Cos.

FITZPATRICK, Joan

600 Pennsylvania Ave. SE
Suite 400
Washington, DC 20003
Tel: (202)546-0007
Fax: (202)544-5002

Employers
Democratic Leadership Council (Controller)

FITZPATRICK, John F.

818 Connecticut Ave. NW
Second Floor
Washington, DC 20006
Tel: (202)289-2001
Fax: (202)289-1327
EMail: jfitzpatrick@stratacomm.net

Former Deputy Public Affairs Director, Federal Railroad Administration, Department of Transportation. Former Communications Director, White House Conference on Travel and Tourism.

Employers
Strat@Comm (Strategic Communications Counselors) (Senior Counselor)

FITZPATRICK, Kellyanne

1220 Connecticut Ave. NW
Second Floor
Washington, DC 20036
Tel: (202)667-6557
Fax: (202)467-6551
Registered: LDA
EMail: Kellyanne@pollingcompany.com

Employers
The Polling Company (President)

Clients Represented

On Behalf of The Polling Company

Export Control Coalition

FITZPATRICK, Maggie

1615 L St. NW
Suite 900
Washington, DC 20036
Tel: (202)778-1000
Fax: (202)466-6002
EMail: mfitzpat@apcoworldwide.com

Employers
APCO Worldwide (V. President and Director, Internet Positioning)

FITZSIMMONS, Ron

206 King St.
Second Floor
Alexandria, VA 22314
EMail: ronncap@aol.com

Tel: (703)684-0055
Fax: (703)684-5051
Registered: LDA

Employers
Nat'l Coalition of Abortion Providers (Exec. Director)

FITZSIMON, Leo R.

1101 Connecticut Ave. NW
Suite 910
Washington, DC 20036

Tel: (202)887-1798
Fax: (202)887-0432
Registered: LDA

Employers
NOKIA

FIX, Donald J.

2100 Pennsylvania Ave. NW
Suite 560
Washington, DC 20037
EMail: dfix@hyjekfix.com

Tel: (202)223-4800
Fax: (202)223-2011
Registered: LDA, FARA

Office of Congressional Liaison, Department of the Army, 1981-86.

Employers
Hyjek & Fix, Inc. (Partner)

Clients Represented
On Behalf of Hyjek & Fix, Inc.
BAE SYSTEMS North America
Bombardier Aerospace
Gelco Government Services
IT Group, Inc.
Mobile Climate Control
The Oneida County Edge
Shelby, Tennessee, County of
U.S. Display Consortium

FIX, Michael E.

2100 M St. NW
Washington, DC 20037

Tel: (202)833-7200
Fax: (202)429-0687

Employers
The Urban Institute (Director, Immigrant Policy Research)

FIX, Michael W.

2100 Pennsylvania Ave. NW
Suite 560
Washington, DC 20037
EMail: mfix@hyjekfix.com

Tel: (202)223-4800
Fax: (202)223-2011

Employers
Hyjek & Fix, Inc. (Financial Director)

FLACK, Susan Garber

1200 19th St. NW
Seventh Floor
Washington, DC 20006
EMail: sgflack@aol.com

Tel: (202)822-6288
Fax: (202)659-2609
Registered: LDA

Employers
Flack Associates (Principal)

Clients Represented
On Behalf of Flack Associates
Spiegel Inc.
Target Corp.

FLAGG, Robert B.

1300 Wilson Blvd.
Arlington, VA 22209

Tel: (703)741-5903
Fax: (703)741-6097
Registered: LDA

EMail: robert_flagg@americanchemistry.com

Employers
American Chemistry Council (Senior Director, Federal Relations)

FLAHERTY, Linda Doorfee

601 13th St. NW
Suite 900 South
Washington, DC 20005
EMail: flaherty@bracywilliams.com

Tel: (202)783-5588
Fax: (202)783-5595
Registered: LDA

Employers
Bracy Williams & Co. (Associate)

Clients Represented
On Behalf of Bracy Williams & Co.
American Institute for Foreign Studies
College Parents of America
Council on Internat'l Educational Exchange
Girl Scouts of the U.S.A. - Washington Office
MedStar Health
Nassif & Associates
Nat'l Ass'n for Girls and Women in Sport
Women's Sports Foundation
YWCA of the USA

FLAHERTY, Richard

2101 L St. NW
Suite 202
Washington, DC 20037
EMail: rflaherty@aacc.org

Tel: (202)857-0717
Fax: (202)887-5093

Employers
American Ass'n for Clinical Chemistry, Inc. (Exec. V. President)

FLAHERTY, Stephen

1250 H St. NW
Suite 700
Washington, DC 20005-3908
EMail: sflaherty@cse.org

Tel: (202)783-3870
Fax: (202)783-4687

Employers
Citizens for a Sound Economy (Director, Grassroots)

FLAHIVE, Lynn

10801 Rockville Pike
Rockville, MD 20852

Tel: (301)897-5700
Fax: (301)897-7350

Employers
Nat'l Student Speech Language Hearing Ass'n (Exec. Director)

FLAJSER, Steven H.

1755 Jefferson Davis Hwy.
Suite 1007
Arlington, VA 22202-4159

Tel: (703)414-1042
Fax: (703)414-1071
Registered: LDA

Employers
Loral Space and Communications, Ltd. (V. President, Legislative Relations)

FLAMBERG, Gemma

9000 Rockville Pike
Bldg. One, Room 244
Bethesda, MD 20892
EMail: flamberg@od.nih.gov

Tel: (301)496-3471
Fax: (301)496-0840

Employers
Department of Health and Human Services - Nat'l Institutes of Health (Legislative Analyst)

FLANAGAN, Brendan

1200 17th St. NW
Washington, DC 20036-3097
EMail: bflanagan@dineout.org

Tel: (202)331-5900
Fax: (202)973-5373

Employers
Nat'l Restaurant Ass'n (Legislative Representative)

FLANAGAN, Hon. Michael Patrick

1317 F St. NW
Suite 600
Washington, DC 20004

Tel: (202)638-2121
Fax: (202)638-7045
Registered: LDA

Member, U.S. House of Representatives (R-IL), 1995-96.

Employers
The Wexler Group (Principal/Senior Director)

Clients Represented
On Behalf of The Wexler Group
Alliance of Automobile Manufacturers, Inc.
Burger King Corp.
General Motors Corp.

FLANAGAN, Newman

99 Canal Center Plaza
Suite 510
Alexandria, VA 22314
EMail: newman.flanagan@ndaa-apri.org

Tel: (703)549-9222
Fax: (703)836-3195

Employers
Nat'l District Attorneys Ass'n (Exec. Director)

FLANAGAN, Richard W.

4647 Forbes Blvd.
Lanham, MD 20706-4380

Tel: (301)459-9600
Fax: (301)459-7924

Employers
AMVETS (American Veterans of World War II, Korea and Vietnam) (National Public Relations Director)

FLANAGAN, Sarah A.

1025 Connecticut Ave. NW
Suite 700
Washington, DC 20036

Tel: (202)785-8866
Fax: (202)835-0003
Registered: LDA

Former Staff Director to the Subcommittee on Children, Family, Drugs and Alcoholism, U.S Senate. Former Staff Member to Senator Christopher Dodd (D-CT). Former Staff Member of the Subcommittee on Education, Arts, and Humanities, U.S. Senate.

Employers
Nat'l Ass'n of Independent Colleges and Universities (V. President, Government Relations)

FLANAGAN, Susan J.P.

1120 19th St. NW
Suite 310
Washington, DC 20036-3605
EMail: sjflanagan@ime.org

Tel: (202)429-9280
Fax: (202)293-2420

Employers
Institute of Makers of Explosives (Counsel, Environmental Affairs)

FLANAGAN, Troy

1010 Wisconsin Ave. NW
Ninth Floor
Washington, DC 20007
EMail: tflanagan@gmabrands.com

Tel: (202)337-9400
Fax: (202)337-4508
Registered: LDA

Employers
Grocery Manufacturers of America (Manager, State Affairs)

FLANIGAN, Matthew J.

2500 Wilson Blvd.
Suite 300
Arlington, VA 22201
EMail: mflaniga@tia.eia.org

Tel: (703)907-7700
Fax: (703)907-7727
Registered: LDA

Employers
Telecommunications Industry Ass'n (President)

FLANNERY, Ellen J.

1201 Pennsylvania Ave. NW
Washington, DC 20004-2401

Tel: (202)662-6000
Fax: (202)662-6291
Registered: LDA

EMail: eflannery@cov.com
Court Law Clerk and Law Clerk to Judge David Bazelon, U.S. Court of Appeals for the District of Columbia, 1978-79.

Employers
Covington & Burling (Partner)

Clients Represented
On Behalf of Covington & Burling
Schering-Plough Corp.

FLANNERY, Kellen

1440 N St. NW
Suite 1016
Washington, DC 20005

Tel: (202)462-5911
Fax: (202)588-8094

Employers
Federal Management Strategies, Inc. (President)

Clients Represented
On Behalf of Federal Management Strategies, Inc.
Federal Advocacy for California Education

FLANNIGAN, Michael

1325 Pennsylvania Ave. NW
Seventh Floor
Washington, DC 20004

Tel: (202)393-0266
Fax: (202)393-0232
Registered: LDA

Employers
Kennecott/Borax (Director, Federal Government Affairs)

FLATER, M. E. Rhett

217 N. Washington St.
Alexandria, VA 22314
Tel: (703)684-6777
Fax: (703)739-9279
EMail: rflater@vtol.org

Employers
American Helicopter Soc. Internat'l (Exec. Director)
Vertical Flight Foundation

FLATLEY, John

One Thomas Circle NW
Tenth Floor
Washington, DC 20005
Tel: (202)530-5910
Fax: (202)530-0659
Registered: LDA

Employers
Navista, Inc. (V. President)

Clients Represented
On Behalf of Navista, Inc.
American Ceramics Soc.
Corporate Environmental Enforcement Council (CEEC)

FLAVIN, Christopher

1776 Massachusetts Ave. NW
Washington, DC 20036
Tel: (202)452-1999
Fax: (202)296-7365
EMail: cflavin@worldwatch.org

Employers
Worldwatch Institute (President)

FLAVIN, Deborah C.

888 16th St. NW
Suite 305
Washington, DC 20006
Tel: (202)833-1880
Fax: (202)833-2338
EMail: flavin@bipac.org

Employers
Business-Industry Political Action Committee (V. President, Development and Marketing)

FLAVIN, Lisa

1220 L St. NW
Washington, DC 20005
Tel: (202)682-8000
Fax: (202)682-8232
Registered: LDA

Employers
American Petroleum Institute

FLAX, Samuel A.

555 12th St. NW
Washington, DC 20004-1206
Tel: (202)942-5000
Fax: (202)942-5999
EMail: Samuel_Flax@aporter.com
Law Clerk to Judge H. Emory Widener, Jr., U.S. Court of Appeals, Fourth Circuit, 1981-82.

Employers
Arnold & Porter (Partner)

FLEEK, Susan

1200 18th St. NW
Suite 800
Washington, DC 20036
Tel: (202)331-7300
Fax: (202)659-8339

Employers
American Farmland Trust (Director, Government Relations)

FLEENOR, Camille

1015 15th St. NW
Suite 802
Washington, DC 20005
Tel: (202)347-7474
Fax: (202)898-0068
Registered: LDA
EMail: cfleemor@acec.org

Employers
American Consulting Engineers Council (Director, Procurement Programs and Federal Markets)

FLEENOR, Patrick

1250 H St. NW
Suite 750
Washington, DC 20005
Tel: (202)783-2760
Fax: (202)783-6868
EMail: pfleenor@taxfoundation.org

Employers
Tax Foundation, Inc. (Chief Economist)

FLEGEL, Laura

1407 S St. NW
Washington, DC 20009
Tel: (202)797-3500
Fax: (202)797-3504

Employers
Whitman-Walker Clinic (Legal Director)

FLEISCHAKER, Marc L.

1050 Connecticut Ave. NW
Washington, DC 20036-5339
Tel: (202)857-6000
Fax: (202)857-6395
Registered: LDA

Employers
Arent Fox Kintner Plotkin & Kahn, PLLC (Member)

Clients Represented
On Behalf of Arent Fox Kintner Plotkin & Kahn, PLLC
American Plywood Ass'n
Motor and Equipment Manufacturers Ass'n
Nat'l Ass'n of College Stores
Nat'l Grain and Feed Ass'n

FLEISCHER, Ruth Frances

5459 Nebraska Ave. NW
Washington, DC 20015
Tel: (202)966-9179
Registered: LDA

Employers
Self-employed as an independent consultant.

Clients Represented
As an independent consultant
Scenic Hudson

FLEISCHMAN, Aaron I.

1400 16th St. NW
Suite 600
Washington, DC 20036
Tel: (202)939-7900
Fax: (202)745-0916

Employers
Fleischman and Walsh, L.L.P. (Partner)

FLEISCHMAN, Janet

1630 Connecticut Ave. NW
Suite 500
Washington, DC 20009
Tel: (202)612-4321
Fax: (202)612-4333

Employers
Human Rights Watch (Washington Director, Human Rights Watch - Africa Division)

FLEISHMAN, Robert W.

1330 Connecticut Ave. NW
Washington, DC 20036-1795
Tel: (202)429-3000
Fax: (202)429-3902
Registered: FARA
EMail: rfleishman@steptoe.com
Attorney/Advisor to the Commissioner, Federal Trade Commission, 1974-75. Trial Attorney, Bureau of Competition, Federal Trade Commission, 1973-74.

Employers
Steptoe & Johnson LLP (Partner)

FLEMING, Britt S.

1050 Thomas Jefferson St. NW
Seventh Floor
Washington, DC 20007
Tel: (202)298-1800
Fax: (202)338-2416
Registered: LDA
EMail: BSF@vnf.com

Employers
Van Ness Feldman, P.C. (Associate)

Clients Represented
On Behalf of Van Ness Feldman, P.C.
The Electric Vehicle Ass'n of the Americas (EVAA)

FLEMING, Col. Dan G.

The Pentagon
4C678
Washington, DC 20350
Tel: (703)697-5395

Employers
Department of Navy - United States Marine Corps (Deputy to the Legislative Director, Office of the Legislative Assistant to the Commandant)

FLEMING, Daniel E.

1755 Jefferson Davis Hwy.
Suite 1107
Arlington, VA 22202
Tel: (703)415-0344
Fax: (703)415-0182
Registered: LDA

Employers
The PMA Group (Associate)

Clients Represented
On Behalf of The PMA Group
AAI Corp.
Cartwright Electronics
CRYPTEK Secure Communications, LLC
Dynamics Research Corp.
Electro-Radiation Inc.
Fidelity Technologies Corp.
Guild Associates
Kollsman, Inc.
L-3 Communications Corp.
Laguna Industries, Inc.
Laguna, New Mexico, City of
Lockheed Martin Corp.
MIC Industries, Inc.
SIGCOM, Inc.
Textron Inc.

FLEMING, Daniel J.

1733 King St.
Alexandria, VA 22314
Tel: (703)549-7464
Fax: (703)549-6980

Employers
Legislative Solutions (Partner)

Clients Represented
On Behalf of Legislative Solutions
Intermodal Ass'n of North America
Truck Renting and Leasing Ass'n

FLEMING, Elizabeth W.

1735 New York Ave. NW
Suite 500
Washington, DC 20006-4759
Tel: (202)628-1700
Fax: (202)331-1024

Employers
Preston Gates Ellis & Rouvelas Meeds LLP (Of Counsel)

FLEMING, Julie

1130 Connecticut Ave. NW
Suite 1200
Washington, DC 20036-3954
Tel: (202)862-0500
Fax: (202)862-0537
Registered: LDA

Employers
American Textile Manufacturers Institute (Assistant Director, Government Relations)

FLEMING, Michael J.

4301 N. Fairfax Dr.
Suite 550
Arlington, VA 22203-1627
Tel: (703)527-8655
Fax: (703)527-2649
Registered: LDA
EMail: mfleming@elamail.com

Employers
Equipment Leasing Ass'n of America (President)

FLEMING, Roger T.

1020 19th St. NW
Washington, DC 20036
Tel: (202)429-0303
Fax: (202)293-0561

Employers
Qwest Communications (Exec. Director, Congressional Affairs)

FLEMING, Scott S.

Healy Hall
Third Floor
Box 571243
37th & O Sts. NW
Washington, DC 20057
Tel: (202)687-3455
Fax: (202)687-1656
Assistant Secretary for Legislation and Congressional Affairs, Department of Education. Former Chief of Staff to Rep. Nita M. Lowey (D-NY). Legislative Assistant, Legislative Staff Director and Administrative Assistant to Rep. Dan Glickman (D-KS), 1977-88. Policy Analyst, Forest Service, Department of Agriculture, 1976. Staff Assistant to Senator Stuart Symington (D-MO), 1972-75. Also serves as Acting Director, Legislation Staff for the Department of Education.

Employers
Georgetown University (Assistant to the President for Federal Relations)

FLEMING, Sean

1101 30th St. NW
Suite 500
Washington, DC 20007
Tel: (202)625-4890
Fax: (202)625-4363

Employers
Law Offices of Pamela L. Meredith (Associate)

FLEMING, Tony

420 Seventh St. SE
Washington, DC 20003
Tel: (202)546-3950
Fax: (202)546-3749

Employers
World Federalist Ass'n (Director, Media Relations)

FLEPS, Christina W.

1666 K St. NW
Suite 500
Washington, DC 20006-2803
EMail: cwf@oh-mail.com
Tel: (202)887-1400
Fax: (202)466-2198
Registered: LDA

Employers
O'Connor & Hannan, L.L.P. (Partner)

Clients Represented

On Behalf of O'Connor & Hannan, L.L.P.
California Debt Limit Allocation Committee
Healthcare Financing Study Group
Kendall-Jackson Winery
New England Mobile X-Ray

FLETCHER, Amy

700 11th St. NW
Washington, DC 20001-4507
EMail: afletcher@realtors.org
Tel: (202)383-1234
Fax: (202)383-7540
Registered: LDA

Employers
Nat'l Ass'n of Realtors (Legislative Representative)

FLETCHER, Bill

815 16th St. NW
Washington, DC 20006
Tel: (202)637-5000
Fax: (202)637-5058

Employers
AFL-CIO (American Federation of Labor and Congress of Industrial Organizations) (Assistant to the President)

FLETCHER, Clinton

1156 15th St. NW
Suite 1100
Washington, DC 20005
Tel: (202)293-8830
Fax: (202)872-8543

Employers
Nat'l Small Business United (Government Affairs Coordinator)

FLETCHER, Francis

1301 K St. NW
Suite 900
East Tower
Washington, DC 20005
Tel: (202)408-7100
Fax: (202)289-1504

Employers
Gardner, Carton and Douglas

Clients Represented

On Behalf of Gardner, Carton and Douglas
Andrew Corp.

FLETCHER, Jeff

1301 Pennsylvania Ave. NW
Suite 550
Washington, DC 20004-1701
EMail: fletcher@nlc.org
Tel: (202)626-3120
Fax: (202)626-3043

Employers
Nat'l League of Cities (Director, Center for Public Affairs)

FLETCHER, Nancy J.

1850 M St. NW
Suite 1040
Washington, DC 20036
Tel: (202)833-5566
Fax: (202)833-1522

Employers
Outdoor Advertising Ass'n of America (President and CEO)

FLICKER, Scott M.

1299 Pennsylvania Ave. NW
Tenth Floor
Washington, DC 20004-2400
EMail: scottflicker@paulhastings.com
Tel: (202)508-9500
Fax: (202)508-9700
Registered: LDA, FARA

Employers
Paul, Hastings, Janofsky & Walker LLP (Partner)

Clients Represented

On Behalf of Paul, Hastings, Janofsky & Walker LLP
Kawasaki Motors Corp., USA
The Marine and Fire Insurance Ass'n of Japan, Inc.

FLIEGER, Neal

1875 I St. NW
Suite 900
Washington, DC 20005
Tel: (202)371-0200
Fax: (202)371-2858
Registered: LDA, FARA

Employers
Edelman Public Relations Worldwide (General Manger)

Clients Represented

On Behalf of Edelman Public Relations Worldwide
Speedway Motorsports
Verizon Communications

FLINT, Alex

The Willard Office Bldg.
1455 Pennsylvania Ave. NW, Suite 200
Washington, DC 20004
Tel: (202)737-0683
Fax: (202)737-0693
Registered: LDA

Former Clerk, Subcommittee on Energy and Water Development, Senate Committee on Appropriations. Former Staff Member to Senator Pete V. Domenici (R-NM).

Employers
Johnston & Associates, LLC (Partner)

Clients Represented

On Behalf of Johnston & Associates, LLC
EG&G
Morgan, Lewis & Bockius LLP
Riverdeep Inc.
USEC, Inc.
Westinghouse Government Services Group
Xcel Energy, Inc.

FLINT, Myles

1722 I St. NW
Washington, DC 20006
Tel: (202)736-8000
Fax: (202)736-8711
Registered: LDA

Employers
Sidley & Austin

Clients Represented

On Behalf of Sidley & Austin
Appleton Papers, Inc.

FLIPPO, Hon. Ronnie G.

1101 30th St. NW
Suite 500
Washington, DC 20007
Tel: (202)289-5490
Fax: (202)289-5495
Registered: LDA

Member, U.S. House of Representatives (D-AL), 1977-91.

Employers
R. G. Flippo and Associates, Inc. (President)

Clients Represented

On Behalf of R. G. Flippo and Associates, Inc.
Alabama Nursing Homes Ass'n
Huntsville, Alabama, City of
Huntsville-Madison County Airport
Spectrum Astro, Inc.
Tensor Technologies, Inc.
Troy State University - Montgomery

FLOCKEN, Jeff

1400 16th St. NW
Suite 501
Washington, DC 20036-2266
EMail: flocken@nwf.org
Tel: (202)797-6800
Fax: (202)797-6646

Employers
Nat'l Wildlife Federation - Office of Federal and Internat'l Affairs (National Endangered Species Grassroots Coordinator)

FLORES, Anna

801 Pennsylvania Ave.
Suite 650
Washington, DC 20004
EMail: anna.flores@aexp.com
Tel: (202)624-0761
Fax: (202)624-0775

Employers
American Express Co. (Manager, Government Affairs)

FLORES, Jolynne

4245 N. Fairfax Dr.
Suite 750
Arlington, VA 22203
Tel: (703)516-9300
Fax: (703)516-9308

Employers
American Soc. of Pension Actuaries (Manager, Government Affairs)

FLORINI, Karen

1875 Connecticut Ave. NW
Suite 1016
Washington, DC 20009
Tel: (202)387-3500
Fax: (202)319-8590
Registered: LDA

Employers
Environmental Defense Fund (Senior Staff Attorney, Toxics Program)

FLORIO, Dale

1200 G St. NW
Suite 800
Washington, DC 20005
Tel: (202)434-8768
Fax: (202)434-8707

Employers
Winning Strategies Washington, D.C., LLC

FLORY, David L.

1022 29th St. NW
Washington, DC 20007
EMail: dflory@wincapitol.com
Tel: (202)333-3232
Fax: (202)333-5001
Registered: LDA

Employers
WinCapitol, Inc. (Chairman and Chief Exec. Officer)

Clients Represented

On Behalf of WinCapitol, Inc.
AFL-CIO (Union Label and Service Trades Department)
American Green Network
Danaher Corp.

FLORY, Mark

Ariel Rios Federal Bldg.
(1301-MC)
1200 Pennsylvania Ave. NW
3rd Floor
Washington, DC 20460
EMail: flory.mark@epa.gov
Tel: (202)564-7803
Fax: (202)501-1540

Employers
Environmental Protection Agency (State/Local Team Leader, Office of Congressional and Intergovernmental Affairs)

FLOWER, Ruth L.

1012 14th St. NW
Suite 500
Washington, DC 20005
EMail: rflower@aaup.org
Tel: (202)737-5900
Fax: (202)737-5526
Registered: LDA

Employers
American Ass'n of University Professors (Director, Government Relations)

FLOYD, Craig W.

605 E St. NW
Washington, DC 20004
EMail: nleomcwf@erols.com
Tel: (202)737-3400
Fax: (202)737-3405

Employers
Nat'l Law Enforcement Officers Memorial Fund (Chairman)

FLOYD, Jr., Donald T.

7100 Connecticut Ave.
Chevy Chase, MD 20815
EMail: floyd@fourhcouncil.edu
Tel: (301)961-2800
Fax: (301)961-2894

Employers
Nat'l 4-H Council (President and Chief Exec. Officer)

FLOYD, Veronica McCann

5906 Ashby Manor Place
Alexandria, VA 22310-2267
Tel: (703)960-2223
Fax: (703)960-2696
Registered: LDA

Employers
Floyd Associates

Clients Represented

On Behalf of Floyd Associates
Brunswick Corp.

FLUG, James F.

1615 M St. NW
Suite 800
Washington, DC 20036-3203
Tel: (202)467-6370
Fax: (202)467-6379
EMail: jff@dwgp.com

Chief Counsel, Administrative Practice and Procedure Subcommittee, Judiciary Committee, U.S. Senate, 1969-73. Legislative Assistant to Senator Edward Kennedy (D-MA), 1967-69. Confidential Assistant to the Attorney General (1965-67) and Legal Assistant to Assistant Attorney General, Tax Division (1964-65), Department of Justice.

Employers
Duncan, Weinberg, Genzer & Pembroke, P.C. (Of Counsel)

Clients Represented

On Behalf of Duncan, Weinberg, Genzer & Pembroke, P.C.
Connecticut, Office of the Attorney General of the State of
Georgia, Office of the Attorney General of the State of
Idaho, Office of the Attorney General of the State of
Indiana, Office of the Attorney General of the State of
Maryland, Office of the Attorney General of the State of
Michigan, Office of the Attorney General of the State of
Nevada, Office of the Attorney General
Ohio, Office of the Attorney General of the State of
South Dakota, Office of the Attorney General of the State of
West Virginia, Office of the Attorney General of the State of
Wisconsin, Office of the Attorney General of the State of
Wyoming, Office of the Attorney General of the State of

FLUHARTY, J. John

1800 K St. NW
Suite 1122
Washington, DC 20006
Tel: (202)463-9677
Fax: (202)463-9680
Registered: LDA

Employers
Chesapeake Enterprises, Inc. (V. President)

Clients Represented

On Behalf of Chesapeake Enterprises, Inc.
Diamond Games
Internat'l Raw Materials
Ketchum
Paucatuck Eastern Pequot Tribal Nation
Shakopee Mdewakanton Sioux Tribe
Tiger Fund

FLYNN, Brian

1440 New York Ave. NW
Washington, DC 20005
Tel: (202)371-7000
Fax: (202)393-5760
Registered: LDA

Employers
Skadden, Arps, Slate, Meagher & Flom LLP (Legislative Consultant)

Clients Represented

On Behalf of Skadden, Arps, Slate, Meagher & Flom LLP
The Stanley Works

FLYNN, Dan

4455 Connecticut Ave. NW
Suite 330
Washington, DC 20008
Tel: (202)364-3085
Fax: (202)364-4098
EMail: cr@aim.org

Employers
Accuracy in Academia (Exec. Director)

FLYNN, Jack

1090 Vermont Ave. NW
Third Floor
Washington, DC 20005
Tel: (202)842-5000
Fax: (202)789-4293

Employers
Millian Byers Associates, LLC (Senior Labor Advisor)

FLYNN, James C.

1660 L St. NW
Fourth Floor
Washington, DC 20036
Tel: (202)775-5092
Registered: LDA

Employers
General Motors Corp. (Washington Representative - Locomotive Group)

FLYNN, Janet F.

1300 Wilson Blvd.
Arlington, VA 22209
Tel: (703)741-5827
Fax: (703)741-6827
EMail: janet_flynn@cmahq.com

Employers
Chlorine Chemistry Council (Director, Public Affairs)

FLYNN, John

815 15th St. NW
Washington, DC 20005
Tel: (202)783-3788
Fax: (202)393-0219

Employers
Internat'l Union of Bricklayers and Allied Craftsworkers (President)

FLYNN, Kevin W.

1050 Thomas Jefferson St. NW
Seventh Floor
Washington, DC 20007
Tel: (202)298-1800
Fax: (202)338-2416
EMail: kwf@vnf.com

Legal Intern, Office of Administrative Litigation, Federal Energy Regulatory Commission, 2000. Legislative Staff Assistant, Senate Committee on Judiciary, 1997. Legislative Staff Assistant, Senate Committee on Agriculture, Nutrition and Forestry, 1995-96. Staff Assistant to Senator Patrick Leahy (D-VT), 1993-95.

Employers
Van Ness Feldman, P.C. (Associate)

FLYNN, Mike

910 17th St. NW
Fifth Floor
Washington, DC 20006
Tel: (202)466-3800
Fax: (202)466-3801

Employers
American Legislative Exchange Council (Director, Legislation and Policy)

FLYNN, Paul M.

1200 G St. NW
Suite 600
Washington, DC 20005-3802
Tel: (202)393-1200
Fax: (202)393-1240
EMail: flynn@wrightlaw.com

Employers
Wright & Talisman, P.C.

FLYNN, Ray

448 New Jersey Ave. SE
Washington, DC 20003
Tel: (202)544-9600
Fax: (202)318-0789

Employers
Catholic Alliance (President)

FOER, Esther

1199 N. Fairfax St.
Suite 1000
Alexandria, VA 22314
Tel: (703)299-4499
Fax: (703)299-4488
Registered: LDA
EMail: efoer@hawthorngroup.com

Employers
The Hawthorn Group, L.C. (Vice Chairman)

Clients Represented

On Behalf of The Hawthorn Group, L.C.
AT&T Wireless Services, Inc.
Electronic Industries Ass'n of Japan
Honda North America, Inc.

FOGARASI, Andre P.

1666 K St. NW
Suite 800
Washington, DC 20006
Tel: (202)481-7000
Fax: (202)862-7098

Employers
Arthur Andersen LLP (Managing Director, Office of Federal Tax Services)

FOGARTY, Sarah

1010 Wisconsin Ave. NW
Ninth Floor
Washington, DC 20007
Tel: (202)337-9400
Fax: (202)337-4508
Registered: LDA
EMail: sfogarty@gmabrands.com

Employers
Grocery Manufacturers of America (Director, International Trade)

FOGARTY, Sean

1755 Jefferson Davis Hwy.
Suite 1107
Arlington, VA 22202
Tel: (703)415-0344
Fax: (703)415-0182
Registered: LDA

Employers
The PMA Group (Associate)

Clients Represented

On Behalf of The PMA Group
AAI Corp.
Advanced Acoustic Concepts, Inc.
AEPTEC
ARC Global Technologies
Concurrent Technologies Corp.
Coronado, California, City of
CRYPTEK Secure Communications, LLC
Dynamics Research Corp.
B. F. Goodrich Co.
Lockheed Martin Federal Systems
Marconi Communications Federal
Planning Systems, Inc.
Titan Corp.

FOGEL, Robert

440 First St. NW
Eighth Floor
Washington, DC 20001
Tel: (202)942-4217
Fax: (202)942-4281
EMail: rfogel@naco.org

Employers
Nat'l Ass'n of Counties (Associate Legislative Director, Transportation)
Nat'l Ass'n of County Engineers (Contact)
Nat'l Democratic County Officials Organization (Contact)

FOGELMAN-BEYER, Alisa

600 New Hampshire Ave. NW
Suite 601
Washington, DC 20037
Tel: (202)333-7400
Fax: (202)333-1638

Employers
Hill and Knowlton, Inc. (Sr. Managing Director, Director of Technology Practice)

FOIS, Sonia P.

555 12th St. NW
Washington, DC 20004-1206
Tel: (202)942-5000
Fax: (202)942-5999
Registered: LDA, FARA
EMail: Sonia_Fois@aporter.com

Employers
Arnold & Porter (Partner)

FOLEY, Beth

1110 N. Glebe Rd.
Arlington, VA 22201-5704
Tel: (703)620-3660
Ext: 409
Fax: (703)620-4334
Registered: LDA
EMail: bethf@cec.sped.org

Employers
Council for Exceptional Children (Policy Specialist, Government Relations)

FOLEY, Cathy

1111 19th St. NW
Suite 800
Washington, DC 20036
Tel: (202)463-2700
Fax: (202)463-2785

Employers
American Paperboard Packaging Environment Council (Exec. Director, Bleached Paperboard)

FOLEY, Donald J.

700 13th St. NW
Suite 1000
Washington, DC 20005
Tel: (202)347-6633
Fax: (202)347-8713

Employers
Powell Tate (Managing Director and Chief Operating Officer)

FOLEY, Joseph P.

P.O. Box 61303
Potomac, MD 20859
Tel: (301)294-0937
Registered: LDA
EMail: info@FoleyCoInc.com

Legislative Affairs Officer, Selective Service System and Federal Emergency Management Agency, 1981-86. Congressional Liaison, Executive Office of the President, The White House, 1980. House Floor Assistant to the Chairman, Appropriations Subcommittee, 1974-80.

Employers
Foley Government and Public Affairs, Inc. (President)

Clients Represented

On Behalf of Foley Government and Public Affairs, Inc.
Megaseal Corp.
Nat'l Federation of Croatian Americans
Pyrocap International Corp., Inc.
Technology Resource Centers
Thompson Lighting Protection Inc.
Unified Industries, Inc.
Upland, California, City of
Zone Therapeutics, Inc.

FOLEY, III, Leander J.

810 First St. NE
Suite 530
Washington, DC 20002
Tel: (202)842-4721
Fax: (202)842-0551
Registered: LDA

Employers
Moss McGee Bradley & Foley (Partner)

Clients Represented

On Behalf of Moss McGee Bradley & Foley
Center for Employment Training
Committee for Farmworker Programs
Community Development Financial Institutions (CDFI)
Green Thumb, Inc.
Greenpoint Manufacturing and Design Center (GMDC)
Indian Hills Community College
Internat'l Ass'n of Personnel in Employment Security
The Learning Disabilities Ass'n
Nat'l Center for Appropriate Technology
Nat'l Community Action Foundation
TELACU
Telacu Carpenter
Three Affiliated Tribes of Fort Berthold Reservation
USA WORKS!
Western Alliance of Farmworker Advocates, Inc. (WAFA)

FOLEY, Leigh

430 S. Capitol St. SE
Washington, DC 20003
Tel: (202)863-8000
Fax: (202)863-8174

Employers
Democratic Nat'l Committee (Director, Specialty Media)

FOLEY, Martin E.

2200 Mill Rd.
Alexandria, VA 22314
Tel: (703)838-1818
Fax: (703)683-1094

Employers
Nat'l Motor Freight Traffic Ass'n (Exec. Director)

FOLEY, Walter J. "Chip"

1667 K St. NW
Suite 460
Washington, DC 20006
Tel: (202)496-9686
Registered: LDA
EMail: wjfoley@worldnet.att.net

Employers
Steel Recycling Institute (Director, Government Relations - Recycling)

FOLGER, Ph.D., Peter

2000 Florida Ave. NW
Washington, DC 20009
Tel: (202)777-7509
Fax: (202)328-0566
Registered: LDA
EMail: pfolger@agu.org

Employers
American Geophysical Union (Manager, Public Affairs)

FOLK, Cassie

1630 Duke St.
Alexandria, VA 22314
Tel: (703)684-5545
Fax: (703)548-8735
Registered: LDA

Employers
Nat'l Rural Letter Carriers' Ass'n (Assistant Director, Government Affairs)

FOLK, Nicole

513 Capitol Ct. NE
Suite 300
Washington, DC 20002
Tel: (202)546-0100
Fax: (202)547-0936

Employers
Congressional Management Foundation (IT Writer/Analyst)

FOLKERTS, Brian

1341 G St. NW
Suite 900
Washington, DC 20005
Tel: (202)637-1598
Fax: (202)637-1517
Registered: LDA

Employers
Philip Morris Management Corp. (Director, Government Affairs, Food)

FOLSOM, R. D.

1317 F St. NW
Suite 600
Washington, DC 20004
Tel: (202)638-2121
Fax: (202)638-7045
Registered: LDA
EMail: folsom@wexlergroup.com

Employers
The Wexler Group (Principal/Senior Director)

Clients Represented

On Behalf of The Wexler Group
Comcast Corp.
Electronic Industries Alliance
Guardian Industries Corp.
Hong Kong Economic and Trade Office

FOLTIN, Richard T.

1156 15th St. NW
Suite 1201
Washington, DC 20005
Tel: (202)785-4200
Fax: (202)785-4115
Registered: LDA

Employers
American Jewish Committee (Director, Legislative Affairs and Counsel)

FONES, Linda L.

601 Pennsylvania Ave. NW
Suite 540
North Bldg.
Washington, DC 20004
Tel: (202)223-8290
Fax: (202)293-2913

Employers
Ashland Inc. (Administrative Coordinator)

FONTAINE, Monita W.

1819 L St. NW
Suite 700
Washington, DC 20036
Tel: (202)721-1621
Fax: (202)861-1181
Registered: LDA

Employers
Personal Watercraft Industry Ass'n (Exec. Director)

FONTES, Brian F.

1818 N St. NW
Eighth Floor
Washington, DC 20036
Tel: (202)293-1707
Registered: LDA

Employers
Cingular Wireless

FONTHEIM, Claude G. B.

601 13th St. NW
Suite 1100
Washington, DC 20005
Tel: (202)429-2217
Fax: (202)296-8727
Registered: LDA

Employers
Fontheim Internat'l, LLC (Managing Director)
Fontheim Partners, PC (Partner)

Clients Represented

On Behalf of Fontheim Internat'l, LLC
Microsoft Corp.
Vivendi Universal

On Behalf of Fontheim Partners, PC
American Internat'l Group, Inc.
Citizen's Educational Foundation
The Limited Inc.

FOOSANER, Robert

2001 Edmund Halley Dr.
Reston, VA 20191
Tel: (703)433-4000

Employers
Nextel Communications, Inc.

FOOSHE, Alexis

600 Army-Navy Dr.
Arlington, VA 22202
Tel: (202)307-9220
Fax: (202)307-5228

Employers
Department of Justice - United States Marshals Service (Legislative Affairs Specialist)

FOOTE, David

1090 Vermont Ave. NW
Suite 1225
Washington, DC 20005
Tel: (202)842-2818
Fax: (202)682-0168

Employers
American Transit Services Council (Managing Director)

FOOTE, George M.

1775 I St. NW
Suite 600
Washington, DC 20006-2401
Tel: (202)721-4600
Fax: (202)721-4646

Employers
Bracewell & Patterson, L.L.P.
Hughes Hubbard & Reed LLP (Partner)

FOOTE, Melvin P.

2400 N St. NW
Suite 510
Washington, DC 20037
Tel: (202)371-0588
Fax: (202)371-9017
EMail: mfoote@cfanet.org

Employers
Constituency for Africa (President and Chief Exec. Officer)

FORBURGER, Melissa T.

1255 23rd St. NW
Suite 200
Washington, DC 20037-1174
Tel: (202)452-8100
Fax: (202)833-3636
EMail: mforburger@hauck.com

Employers
Electromagnetic Energy Ass'n (Exec. Director)
Hauck and Associates (Account Exec.)
Nat'l Ass'n of Healthcare Consultants (Exec. Director)

Clients Represented

On Behalf of Hauck and Associates
American Academy of Wound Management
Electromagnetic Energy Ass'n
Nat'l Ass'n of Healthcare Consultants

FORD, Anne J.

1707 L St. NW
Suite 800
Washington, DC 20036
Tel: (202)296-5469
Fax: (202)296-5427
Registered: LDA

Employers
Nat'l Center for Tobacco-Free Kids (Manager, Federal Relations)

FORD, Anne K.

1050 Connecticut Ave. NW
Suite 1100
Washington, DC 20036-5304
Tel: (202)861-1500
Fax: (202)861-1790
EMail: Aford@baker-hostetler.com

Employers
Baker & Hostetler LLP (Partner)

FORD, Gary M.

1701 Pennsylvania Ave. NW
Suite 1200
Washington, DC 20006
EMail: gmf@groom.com
Tel: (202)857-0620
Fax: (202)659-4503
Registered: LDA

Employers
Groom Law Group, Chartered (Managing Principal)

Clients Represented
On Behalf of Groom Law Group, Chartered
Buffalo Carpenters Pension Fund
Montgomery Ward & Co., Inc.
Production Service & Sales District Council Pension Fund

FORD, Martha

1730 K St. NW
Washington, DC 20006
EMail: ford@thearc.org
Tel: (202)785-3388
Fax: (202)467-4179
Registered: LDA

Employers
The Arc (Director of Legal Advocacy)

FORD, Mr. Pat

1801 K St. NW
Suite 1000L
Washington, DC 20006
EMail: pat_ford@washbm.com
Tel: (202)530-0400
Fax: (202)530-4500

Employers
Burson-Marsteller (Managing Director, Public Affairs Practice)

FORD, Patricia

1313 L St. NW
Washington, DC 20005
Tel: (202)898-3200
Fax: (202)898-3304
Registered: LDA

Employers
Service Employees Internat'l Union (Exec. V. President)

FORD, Tim

1730 K St. NW
Suite 700
Washington, DC 20006
EMail: tford@urbandevelopment.com
Tel: (202)822-5256
Fax: (202)822-8819

Employers
Nat'l Ass'n of Installation Developers (Deputy Exec. Director)

FORD, Hon. Wendell H.

2101 L St. NW
Washington, DC 20037-1526
EMail: fordw@dsmo.com
Tel: (202)785-9700
Fax: (202)887-0689
Registered: LDA
Member, U.S. Senate (D-KY), 1974-98.

Employers
Dickstein Shapiro Morin & Oshinsky LLP (Senior Counsel)

Clients Represented
On Behalf of Dickstein Shapiro Morin & Oshinsky LLP
Cigar Ass'n of America
Delta Air Lines
Electric Power Supply Ass'n
Hydro-Quebec
Kerr-McGee Corp.
Lorillard Tobacco Co.
PG&E Generating Co.
Pipe Tobacco Council, Inc.
Smokeless Tobacco Council

FORD-ROEGNER, Pat

888 17th St. NW
Suite 800
Washington, DC 20006
EMail: pfroegner@heimag.com
Tel: (202)822-8060
Fax: (202)822-9088

Employers
Heidepriem & Mager, Inc. (Senior Policy Analyst)

Clients Represented
On Behalf of Heidepriem & Mager, Inc.
Nat'l Asian Women's Health Organization
Nat'l Council of Juvenile and Family Court Judges
Pharmacia Corp.

FORDING, Jr., Edmund H.

1850 M St. NW
Suite 700
Washington, DC 20036
EMail: ed.fording@socma.com
Tel: (202)721-4100
Fax: (202)296-8120

Employers
Synthetic Organic Chemical Manufacturers Ass'n (President)

FOREHAND, Lon

300 E St. SW
Room 9M32
Washington, DC 20546
Tel: (202)358-1948
Fax: (202)358-4340

Employers
Nat'l Aeronautics and Space Administration (Legislative Affairs Specialist)

FOREMAN, Christopher

1775 Massachusetts Ave. NW
Washington, DC 20036-2188
Tel: (202)797-6000
Fax: (202)797-6004

Employers
The Brookings Institution (Senior Fellow, Governmental Studies)

FOREMAN, Donald D.

1201 F St. NW
Suite 1000
Washington, DC 20004-1077
Tel: (202)626-7230
Fax: (202)626-7208
Registered: LDA

Employers
R. J. Reynolds Tobacco Co. (Director, Federal Government Affairs)

FORKENBROCK, John

444 N. Capitol St. NW
Suite 419
Washington, DC 20001
EMail: nafis@sso.org
Tel: (202)624-5455
Fax: (202)624-5468
Registered: LDA

Employers
Nat'l Ass'n of Federally Impacted Schools (Exec. Director)

FORLENZA, Paul P.

1301 K St. NW
Suite 1200-West Tower
Washington, DC 20005-3307
Tel: (202)515-5019
Fax: (202)515-5078
Registered: LDA

Employers
Internat'l Business Machines Corp. (Government Relations Director, Latin America)

FORMAN, Ira N.

777 N. Capitol St. NE
Suite 305
Washington, DC 20002
Tel: (202)216-9060
Fax: (202)216-9061

Employers
Nat'l Jewish Democratic Council (Exec. Director)

FORMICA, Michael

1020 19th St. NW
Suite 400
Washington, DC 20036
EMail: mformica@aol.com
Tel: (202)331-9100
Fax: (202)331-9060
Registered: LDA

Employers
Baise + Miller, P.C. (Associate)

Clients Represented
On Behalf of Baise + Miller, P.C.
Martinizing Environmental Group

FORNOS, Werner

107 Second St. NE
Washington, DC 20002
EMail: wfornos@populationinstitute.org
Tel: (202)544-3300
Fax: (202)544-0068

Employers
Population Institute (President)

FORRER, Graydon G.

750 17th St. NW
Suite 1100
Washington, DC 20006
Tel: (202)778-2300
Fax: (202)778-2330

Employers
FoxKiser

FORSCEY, Michael A.

818 Connecticut Ave. NW
Suite 1004
Washington, DC 20006
EMail: main@forstin.com
Tel: (202)530-7185
Fax: (202)530-7189
Registered: LDA
Chief Minority Counsel, Senate Committee on Labor and Human Resources, 1981-85. Special Assistant to Rep. John Brademas (D-IN), 1980-81. Counsel, Subcommittee on Labor, Senate Committee on Labor and Human Resources, 1977-80.

Employers
Forscey & Stinson, PLLC (Managing Partner)
The National Group, LLP (Partner)

Clients Represented
On Behalf of Forscey & Stinson, PLLC
Adventist Health System/Sunbelt, Inc.
Law Offices of Peter Angelos
Ass'n of Trial Lawyers of America
Barr Laboratories
Bituminous Coal Operators Ass'n
Westhill Partners

FORSGREN, D. Lee

409 Ninth St. NW
Suite 610 South
Washington, DC 20004
EMail: forsgrend@arlaw.com
Tel: (202)737-3234
Fax: (202)737-0264
Registered: LDA
Counsel, House Water Resources Committee, 1995-99.

Employers
Adams and Reese LLP (Special Counsel)

Clients Represented
On Behalf of Adams and Reese LLP
AHL Shipping Co.
Baton Rouge, Louisiana, City of
Bollinger Shipyards
First American Aircraft Title
First American Title Aircraft
GE Capital Corp.
Lehtinen O'Donnell
Miccosukee Indians
Project ACTA

FORSHT, Ralph

909 N. Washington St.
Suite 400
Alexandria, VA 22314
Tel: (703)535-3825

Employers
America's Promise (V. President, Government Relations)

FORSTER, Johann R.

827 25th St. South
Arlington, VA 22202
Tel: (703)548-1360
Fax: (703)836-2608
Former Chief U.S. Navy Foreign Liaison and Head U.S. Navy Foreign Military Sales, PACOM.

Employers
Forster & Associates (President)

Clients Represented
On Behalf of Forster & Associates
Bruker Meerestechnik GmbH
Fentek Internat'l Pty. Ltd.
Friede, Goldman, & Halter, Inc.
In-Pipe Technology
PMSC-Irby Steel

FORSTER, Theresa M.

228 Seventh St. SE
Washington, DC 20003-4306
EMail: tmf@nahc.org
Tel: (202)547-7424
Fax: (202)547-9559
Registered: LDA

Employers
Nat'l Ass'n for Home Care (V. President, Policy)

FORTE, Patrick A.

888 17th St. NW
Suite 312
Washington, DC 20006
EMail: afshc@ibm.net
Tel: (202)223-6575
Fax: (202)331-3836
Registered: LDA

Employers
Ass'n of Financial Services Holding Companies (President)

FORTENBERRY, Amy

700 13th St. NW
Suite 800
Washington, DC 20005
Tel: (202)508-5800
Fax: (202)508-5858

Employers
Kilpatrick Stockton LLP

FORTH, Patrick

903 Russell Ave.
Suite 400
Gaithersburg, MD 20879

Employers
Mid-Atlantic Regional Joint Board UNITE PAC (PAC Administrator)

FORTIER, Alison

1725 Jefferson Davis Hwy.
Crystal Square 2, Suite 300
Arlington, VA 22202
Tel: (703)413-5979
Fax: (703)413-5908
Registered: LDA

Employers
Lockheed Martin Corp. (V. President, Space and Strategic Missile Legislative Affairs)

FORTIER, Michael P.

601 Pennsylvania Ave. NW
Suite 900
South Bldg.
Washington, DC 20004
EMail: mfortie@erols.com
Tel: (202)338-1829
Fax: (202)338-1879
Registered: LDA

Employers
The Fortier Group, LLC (Principal)

Clients Represented
On Behalf of The Fortier Group, LLC
Caretenders Health Corp.
ClaimTraq, Inc.
CNA Insurance Cos.

FORTNAM, Anthony

1850 K St. NW
Suite 300
Washington, DC 20006
Tel: (202)331-9068
Fax: (202)466-3745
Registered: LDA, FARA

Employers
British Airways Plc (V. President, Government and Industry Affairs)

FORTNEY, Mary Martha

1655 N. Fort Myer Dr.
Suite 300
Arlington, VA 22209
Tel: (703)528-8351
Fax: (703)528-3248
Registered: LDA

Employers
Nat'l Ass'n of State Credit Union Supervisors (V. President, Public Affairs and Accreditation)

FORTSON, Tracy

818 Connecticut Ave. NW
Suite 200
Washington, DC 20006
EMail: tfortson@nabr.org
Tel: (202)857-0540
Fax: (202)659-1902
Registered: LDA

Employers
Nat'l Ass'n for Biomedical Research (V. President)

FORTUNATO, Edward

1800 Diagonal Rd.
Suite 606
Alexandria, VA 22314
Tel: (703)684-3132
Fax: (703)549-6245

Employers
Crowley Maritime Corp. (Washington Representative)

FORTUNE, Terence J.

1615 L St. NW
Suite 1300
Washington, DC 20036
EMail: tfortune@paulweiss.com
Tel: (202)223-7300
Fax: (202)223-7420
Registered: LDA, FARA
Assistant Legal Advisor, Department of State, 1977-83.

Employers
Paul, Weiss, Rifkind, Wharton & Garrison (Partner)

Clients Represented
On Behalf of Paul, Weiss, Rifkind, Wharton & Garrison
American Agip MTBE Sales Division
Le Groupe de Soleil

FORTUNO, Victor M.

750 First St. NE
Suite 1000
Washington, DC 20002-4250
EMail: vfortuno@lsc.gov
Tel: (202)336-8800
Fax: (202)336-8954

Employers
Legal Services Corp. (V. President and General Counsel)

FOSCARINIS, Maria

1411 K St. NW
Suite 1400
Washington, DC 20005
Tel: (202)638-2535
Fax: (202)628-2737

Employers
Nat'l Law Center on Homelessness and Poverty (Exec. Director)

FOSS, Murray F.

1150 17th St. NW
Washington, DC 20036
EMail: mfoss@aei.org
Tel: (202)862-5800
Fax: (202)862-7177

Employers
American Enterprise Institute for Public Policy Research (Visiting Scholar)

FOSS, Richard A.

5225 Wisconsin Ave. NW
Suite 600
Washington, DC 20015-2014
EMail: dfoss@nasbp.org
Tel: (202)686-3700
Fax: (202)686-3656

Employers
Nat'l Ass'n of Surety Bond Producers (Exec. V. President)

FOSSEDAL, Gregory

1611 N. Kent St.
Suite 901
Arlington, VA 22209
Tel: (703)351-4969
Fax: (703)351-0090

Employers
Alexis de Tocqueville Institution (Chairman)

FOSTER, F. David

1150 18th St. NW
Ninth Floor
Washington, DC 20036
EMail: dfoster@ablondifoster.com
Tel: (202)296-3355
Fax: (202)296-3922
Registered: FARA
Trade Counsel, Senate Committee on Finance, 1977-81. Assistant to the Chairman (1975-77) and Attorney/Advisor, Office of the General Counsel (1973-75), International Trade Commission.

Employers
Ablondi, Foster, Sobin & Davidow, P.C. (Partner)

Clients Represented
On Behalf of Ablondi, Foster, Sobin & Davidow, P.C.
United States Beet Sugar Ass'n

FOSTER, Hope S.

701 Pennsylvania Ave. NW
Suite 900
Washington, DC 20004-2608
EMail: hfoster@mintz.com
Tel: (202)661-8758
Fax: (202)434-7400
Registered: LDA

Employers
Mintz, Levin, Cohn, Ferris, Glovsky and Popeo, P.C. (Partner)

FOSTER, J. William

499 S. Capitol St. SW
Suite 504
Washington, DC 20003
Tel: (202)554-3626
Fax: (202)554-1961

Employers
R. V. Davis and Associates (Principal)

Clients Represented
On Behalf of R. V. Davis and Associates
Ball Aerospace & Technology Corp.
Insyte Corp.
Spectrum Astro, Inc.
United Space Alliance
Zenware Solutions, Inc.

FOSTER, Lisa

888 17th St. NW
Suite 800
Washington, DC 20006
EMail: lfoster@heimag.com
Tel: (202)822-8060
Fax: (202)822-9088
Registered: LDA

Employers
Heidepriem & Mager, Inc. (Associate)

Clients Represented
On Behalf of Heidepriem & Mager, Inc.
CIGNA Corp.
The Dow Chemical Co.

FOSTER, Maurice

4609 Pinecrest Office Park Dr.
Suite F
Second Floor
Alexandria, VA 22312
Tel: (703)658-1529
Fax: (703)658-9479

Employers
Nat'l Organization of Black Law Enforcement Executives (Chief Exec. Officer)

FOSTER, Nancy E.

1156 15th St. NW
Suite 400
Washington, DC 20005
Tel: (202)296-1585
Fax: (202)463-0474
Registered: LDA

Employers
American Crop Protection Ass'n (V. President, Legislative Affairs)

FOSTER, Robert B.

1800 Diagonal Rd.
Suite 600
Alexandria, VA 22314
Tel: (703)684-4446
Fax: (703)836-2450
Registered: LDA
Former Staff Director, House Appropriations Subcommittee on Agriculture, Rural Development, FDA and Related Agencies.

Employers
Bob Foster and Associates (President)

Clients Represented
On Behalf of Bob Foster and Associates
American Indian Higher Education Consortium
American Sugar Alliance

FOSTER, Ron

316 Pennsylvania Ave. SE
Suite 300
Washington, DC 20003
Tel: (202)675-4235
Fax: (202)675-4230
Registered: LDA

Employers
United Parcel Service (V. President, Public Affairs)

FOSTER, Stephenie

2000 M St. NW
Suite 400
Washington, DC 20036
Tel: (202)467-4999
Fax: (202)293-2672

Employers
People for the American Way (Director, Public Policy)

FOTI, Anthony

1333 New Hampshire Ave. NW
Suite 400
Washington, DC 20036
Tel: (202)887-4000
Fax: (202)887-4288
Registered: LDA

Employers
Akin, Gump, Strauss, Hauer & Feld, L.L.P.

Clients Represented
On Behalf of Akin, Gump, Strauss, Hauer & Feld, L.L.P.
Americans for Affordable Electricity
Howland Hook Container Terminal Inc.
Nehemiah Progressive Housing Development Corp.
New York Bus Service
Niagara Frontier Transportation Authority
St. Barnabas Healthcare System

FOTI, Suzanne

1030 15th St. NW
Suite 800
Washington, DC 20005
EMail: sfoti@uscib-dc.org
Tel: (202)371-1316
Fax: (202)371-8249

Employers
United States Council for Internat'l Business (Manager, Biotechnology and Agriculture)

FOTIS, James J.

7700 Leesburg Pike
Suite 421
Falls Church, VA 22043
Tel: (703)847-2677
Fax: (703)556-6485

Employers
Law Enforcement Alliance of America (Exec. Director)

FOTIS, Stephen C.

1050 Thomas Jefferson St. NW
Seventh Floor
Washington, DC 20007
EMail: scf@vnf.com
Tel: (202)298-1800
Fax: (202)338-2416
Registered: LDA

Employers
Van Ness Feldman, P.C. (Member)

Clients Represented
On Behalf of Van Ness Feldman, P.C.
American Electric Power Co.
Large Public Power Council

FOUBERG, Robert J.

1120 Connecticut Ave. NW
Washington, DC 20036
Tel: (202)663-5000
Fax: (202)828-4548
Registered: LDA

Employers
American Bankers Ass'n (Senior Counsel)

FOULKES, Tom

1000 Vermont Ave. NW
Suite 700
Washington, DC 20005
Tel: (202)408-0808
Fax: (202)408-0876
Former Deputy Press Secretary to Senator Richard Bryan (D-NV)

Employers
Susan Davis Internat'l (Senior Account Executive)

FOURNIER, Susan

One Thomas Circle NW
Suite 400
Washington, DC 20005
Tel: (202)659-8111
Fax: (202)659-9216

Employers
Independent Community Bankers of America (Director, Information Center)

FOUSHEE, Ph.D., Clay

901 15th St. NW
Suite 310
DCA 1150
Washington, DC 20005
Tel: (202)842-3193
Fax: (202)289-6834
Registered: LDA

Employers
Northwest Airlines, Inc. (V. President, International and Regulatory Affairs)

FOWLER, Marianne W.

1100 17th St. NW
Tenth Floor
Washington, DC 20036
Tel: (202)331-9696
Registered: LDA

Employers
Rails to Trails Conservancy (Senior V. President, Programs)

FOWLER, Mary Litton

2111 Wilson Blvd.
Eighth Floor
Arlington, VA 22201-3058
Tel: (703)841-0626
Fax: (703)243-2874

Employers
Alcalde & Fay (Associate)

Clients Represented
On Behalf of Alcalde & Fay
Fairfax County Water Authority
Palm Springs, California, City of
Virginia Beach, Virginia, City of

FOWLER, Hon. Tillie K.

2099 Pennsylvania Ave. NW
Suite 100
Washington, DC 20006
EMail: tfowler@hklaw.com
Tel: (202)955-3000
Fax: (202)955-5564
Member, U.S. House of Representatives (R-FL), 1993-2001 (Deputy Majority Whip, 1995-2001). Deputy General Counsel and General Counsel, Office of Consumer Affairs, The White House, 1970-71. Legislative Assistant to Rep. Robert Stephens, Jr. (D-GA), 1967-70.

Employers
Holland & Knight LLP (Partner)

FOX, Alissa

1310 G St. NW
12th Floor
Washington, DC 20005
Tel: (202)626-4780
Fax: (202)626-4833
Registered: LDA

Employers
Blue Cross Blue Shield Ass'n (Exec. Director, Policy)

FOX, Allan M.

750 17th St. NW
Suite 1100
Washington, DC 20006
Tel: (202)778-2326
Fax: (202)778-2330
Registered: LDA
Chief of Staff and Chief Legislative Assistant to Senator Jacob K. Javits (D-NY), 1977-79. General Counsel, Subcommittee on Health and Scientific Research, Senate Committee on Labor and Public Welfare, 1975-77.

Employers
FoxKiser

Clients Represented
On Behalf of FoxKiser
Bristol-Myers Squibb Co.
NitroMed, Inc.

FOX, Amy

1150 17th St. NW
Suite 701
Washington, DC 20036
EMail: amy.fox@dittus.com
Tel: (202)775-1401
Fax: (202)775-1404

Employers
Dittus Communications (Associate Director)

Clients Represented
On Behalf of Dittus Communications
Magazine Publishers of America

FOX, Barbara

1101 Pennsylvania Ave. NW
Suite 950
Washington, DC 20004
Tel: (202)434-8600
Fax: (202)434-8626
Registered: LDA

Employers
Federal Home Loan Mortgage Corp. (Freddie Mac) (Director, Government Relations (Senate))

FOX, Cheryl

1200 G St. NW
Suite 800
Washington, DC 20005
EMail: cherylf@tcbinc.org
Tel: (202)661-6101
Fax: (202)628-2040
Registered: LDA

Employers
The Community Builders, Inc. (Director of Policy)

FOX, David

525 School St. SW
Suite 500
Washington, DC 20024
Tel: (202)484-0103
Fax: (202)488-7595

Employers
WAVE, Inc. (Chairman)

FOX, David E.

1325 18th St. NW
Suite 103
Washington, DC 20036
Tel: (202)887-0725
Fax: (202)872-0200

Employers
David E. Fox and Associates (Principal)

FOX, Eric R.

1700 Pennsylvania Ave. NW
Suite 600
Washington, DC 20006
Tel: (202)393-7600
Fax: (202)393-7601
Registered: LDA

Employers
Ivins, Phillips & Barker (Partner)

Clients Represented
On Behalf of Ivins, Phillips & Barker
Bass Hotels and Resorts, Inc.

FOX, Howard I.

1625 Massachusetts Ave. NW
Suite 702
Washington, DC 20036
Tel: (202)667-4500
Fax: (202)667-2356

Employers
Earthjustice Legal Defense Fund (Managing Attorney)

FOX, Jamie

1200 G St. NW
Suite 800
Washington, DC 20005
Tel: (202)434-8768
Fax: (202)434-8707

Employers
Winning Strategies Washington, D.C., LLC

FOX, Sr., Joseph L.

801 18th St. NW
Washington, DC 20006
Tel: (202)872-1300
Fax: (202)785-4452

Employers
Paralyzed Veterans of America (National President)

FOX, Leann

1101 Vermont Ave. NW
Suite 700
Washington, DC 20005
EMail: lfox@aaodc.org
Tel: (202)737-6662
Fax: (202)737-7061

Employers
American Academy of Ophthamology - Office of Federal Affairs (Political Affairs Coordinator)

FOX, Russell H.

701 Pennsylvania Ave. NW
Suite 900
Washington, DC 20004-2608
EMail: rfox@mintz.com
Tel: (202)434-7300
Fax: (202)434-7400
Registered: LDA

Employers
Mintz, Levin, Cohn, Ferris, Glovsky and Popeo, P.C. (Partner)

FOX, Steve

One Massachusetts Ave. NW
Suite 333
Washington, DC 20001
EMail: sfox@cnponline.org
Tel: (202)682-1800
Fax: (202)682-1818

Employers
Center for Nat'l Policy (Deputy Director, External Relations)

FOX, Susan

1150 17th St. NW
Suite 400
Washington, DC 20036
Tel: (202)222-4700
Fax: (202)222-4799
Former Deputy Chief, Mass Media Bureau and former Senior Legal Advisor to Chairman William Kennard, Federal Communications Commission.

Employers
The Walt Disney Co. (V. President, Government Relations)

FOX, Thomas A.

1990 M St. NW
Suite 500
Washington, DC 20036
Tel: (202)776-0700
Fax: (202)776-0720
Registered: LDA

Employers
Schwartz & Ballen (Associate)

Clients Represented

On Behalf of Schwartz & Ballen

American Council of Life Insurers
American Insurance Ass'n

FOX, Wayne

526 King St.
Suite 511
Alexandria, VA 22314
Tel: (703)683-8630
Fax: (703)683-8634
Registered: LDA
EMail: wayne.fox@nahma.org

Employers

Nat'l Affordable Housing Management Ass'n (President Elect)

FRAAS, Charlotte

555 New Jersey Ave. NW
Tenth Floor
Washington, DC 20001
Tel: (202)879-4728
Fax: (202)879-4402
Registered: LDA

Employers

Federation of Nurses and Health Professionals/AFT (Director, Federal Legislation)

FRAAS, Phillip L.

1025 Thomas Jefferson St. NW
Suite 407 West
Washington, DC 20007
Tel: (202)342-1300
Fax: (202)342-5880
Registered: LDA, FARA

Chief Counsel, House Committee on Agriculture, 1985-89.

Employers

Tuttle, Taylor & Heron (Of Counsel)

Clients Represented

On Behalf of Tuttle, Taylor & Heron

Bell Equipment Ltd.
Cheese Importers Ass'n of America
Darigold, Inc.
DEIP (Dairy Export Incentive Program) Coalition
Philip Morris Management Corp.
South African Sugar Ass'n
Western United Dairymen

FRADKIN, Hillel

1150 17th St. NW
Washington, DC 20036
Tel: (202)862-5800
Fax: (202)862-7177
EMail: hfradkin@aei.org

Employers

American Enterprise Institute for Public Policy Research (Resident Scholar)

FRAIOLI, Michael J.

80 F St. NW
Suite 804
Washington, DC 20001
Tel: (202)347-3042
Fax: (202)347-3046

Employers

Fraioli/Siggins (President)

FRAKER, Mary E.

700 13th St. NW
Suite 1000
Washington, DC 20005
Tel: (202)347-6633
Fax: (202)347-8713

Employers

Powell Tate (V. President)

FRANASIAK, David E.

1155 21st St. NW
Suite 300
Washington, DC 20036
Tel: (202)659-8201
Fax: (202)659-5249
Registered: LDA, FARA
EMail: defranasiak@wms-jen.com

Staff Director, Subcommittee on Tax Oversight, House Small Business Committee, 1979-81. Aide to Rep. Henry J. Nowak (D-NY), 1979-81.

Employers

Williams & Jensen, P.C. (Partner)

Clients Represented

On Behalf of Williams & Jensen, P.C.

Aegon USA
Alexander's Inc.
American Home Products Corp.
Asahi Glass Co.
Chandis Securities Co.
Chicago Deferred Exchange Corp.
The Church Alliance
CIGNA Corp.
Colonial Pipeline Co.
Credit Suisse First Boston Corp.
Fannie Mae
First Union Corp.
Gateway, Inc.
Genentech, Inc.
Keystone, Inc.
Knight Trading Group
J. P. Morgan Chase & Co.
J. P. Morgan Securities
Oklahoma Gas and Electric Co.
Perdue Farms Inc.
Reinsurance Ass'n of America
Securities Traders Ass'n
Texaco Group Inc.

FRANC, Michael G.

214 Massachusetts Ave. NE
Washington, DC 20002
Tel: (202)546-4400
Fax: (202)546-8328

Employers

Heritage Foundation (V. President, Government Relations)

FRANCHOT, Peter

700 13th St. NW
Suite 400
Washington, DC 20005
Tel: (202)347-0773
Fax: (202)347-0785

Employers

Cassidy & Associates, Inc. (Consultant)

FRANCIS, Barbara L.

700 13th St. NW
Suite 1000
Washington, DC 20005
Tel: (202)347-6633
Fax: (202)347-8713
Registered: LDA, FARA

Employers

Powell Tate

Clients Represented

On Behalf of Powell Tate

Taiwan Studies Institute

FRANCIS, Fran

1350 New York Ave. NW
Suite 1100
Washington, DC 20005-4798
Tel: (202)879-4000
Fax: (202)393-2866
Registered: LDA
EMail: francisf@spiegelmcd.com

Attorney (1969-70) and Assistant to the Commissioner (1965-68), Federal Power Commission.

Employers

Spiegel & McDiarmid (Partner)

Clients Represented

On Behalf of Spiegel & McDiarmid

Holyoke Department of Gas and Electricity
Northern California Power Agency

FRANCIS, Frann G.

1050 17th St. NW
Suite 300
Washington, DC 20036
Tel: (202)296-3390
Fax: (202)296-3399
Registered: LDA

Employers

Apartment and Office Building Ass'n of Metropolitan Washington (General Counsel)

FRANCIS, Les

1800 K St. NW
Suite 900
Washington, DC 20006
Tel: (202)659-0616
Fax: (202)659-8075

Employers

Educational Testing Service (V. President, Communications and Public Affairs)

FRANCIS, Michael A.

1615 M St. NW
Washington, DC 20036
Tel: (202)833-2300
Fax: (202)429-3945
Registered: LDA
EMail: Michael_Francis@tws.org

Employers

The Wilderness Soc. (Director, National Forests Program)

FRANCIS, Patricia A.

1200 New Hampshire Ave. NW
Suite 800
Washington, DC 20036-6802
Tel: (202)776-2000
Fax: (202)776-2222
EMail: pfrancis@dlalaw.com

Employers

Dow, Lohnes & Albertson, PLLC (Member)

FRANCIS, Shari L.

2010 Massachusetts Ave. NW
Suite 500
Washington, DC 20036-1023
Tel: (202)466-7496
Fax: (202)296-6620
EMail: shari@ncate.org

Employers

Nat'l Council for Accreditation of Teacher Education (V. President, State Relations)

FRANCISCO, Stephen R.

1150 17th St. NW
Suite 300
Washington, DC 20036
Tel: (202)778-4384
Fax: (202)293-5308
Registered: LDA
EMail: sfrancisco@uswa.org

Employers

United Steelworkers of America (Legislative Representative)

FRANCO, Patricia A.

1300 I St. NW
Suite 1070 East
Washington, DC 20005
Tel: (202)962-8550
Fax: (202)962-8560
Registered: LDA

Employers

Philips Electronics North America Corp. (Legislative and Regulatory Counsel)

FRANK, Abe L.

1101 Pennsylvania Ave. NW
Suite 1000
Washington, DC 20004
Tel: (202)879-6881
Fax: (202)783-4460
EMail: frank@citi.com

Employers

Citigroup (State Government Relations Deputy Director)

FRANK, David

1825 Connecticut Ave. NW
Fifth Floor
Washington, DC 20009
Tel: (202)667-0901
Fax: (202)667-0902
EMail: david.frank@widmeyer.com

Former Communications Director and Public Affairs Officer, Department of Education and former speechwriter for Secretary of State Warren Christopher.

Employers

Widmeyer Communications, Inc. (Senior V. President and Group Director)

FRANK, Dr. Martin

9650 Rockville Pike
Bethesda, MD 20814-3991
Tel: (301)530-7118
Fax: (301)571-8305

Employers

American Physiological Soc. (Exec. Director)

FRANK, Matthew

1200 Wilson Blvd.
Arlington, VA 22209-1989
Tel: (703)465-3500
Fax: (703)465-3001

Employers

The Boeing Co. (Director, Federal Health, Safety, and Environment)

FRANK, Peter M.

1667 K St. NW
Suite 250
Washington, DC 20006
Tel: (202)728-9600
Fax: (202)728-9587
Registered: LDA

Employers
Kerr-McGee Corp. (V. President, Public Affairs)

FRANK, Richard L.

1400 16th St. NW
Suite 400
Washington, DC 20036-2220
Tel: (202)518-6363
Fax: (202)234-3550
Registered: LDA
EMail: rfrank@ofwlaw.com

Employers
Olsson, Frank and Weeda, P.C. (Managing Partner)

Clients Represented
On Behalf of Olsson, Frank and Weeda, P.C.
Adheris, Inc.
Beef Products, Inc.
Chocolate Manufacturers Ass'n of the U.S.A.
Food Distributors Internat'l (NAWGA-IFDA)
Health Resource Publishing Co.
Nat'l Confectioners Ass'n
Nat'l Frozen Pizza Institute
The Pillsbury Co.
San Tomo Group

FRANK, Susan

Six Montgomery Village Ave.
Suite 403
Gaithersburg, MD 20879-3557
Tel: (240)632-9716
Fax: (240)632-1321

Employers
American Congress on Surveying and Mapping (PAC Contact)

FRANK, Theodore

555 12th St. NW
Washington, DC 20004-1206
Tel: (202)942-5000
Fax: (202)942-5999
EMail: Theodore_Frank@aporter.com

Employers
Arnold & Porter (Partner)

FRANKEL, Matthew

600 Pennsylvania Ave. SE
Suite 400
Washington, DC 20003
Tel: (202)546-0007
Fax: (202)546-0628
EMail: mfrankel@dlcppi.org

Employers
Democratic Leadership Council (Press Secretary)

FRANKEN, Mark

3211 Fourth St. NE
Washington, DC 20017
Tel: (202)541-3352
Fax: (202)541-3322

Employers
United States Catholic Conference (Exec. Director, Migration and Refugee Services)

FRANKFORT, Faye B.

9312 Old Georgetown Rd.
Bethesda, MD 20814-1621
Tel: (301)581-9232
Fax: (301)530-2752
Registered: LDA
EMail: fbfrankfort@apma.org

Employers
American Podiatric Medical Ass'n (Director, Legislative Advocacy)

FRANKLAND, Jr., Walter L.

1730 M St. NW
Suite 911
Washington, DC 20036-4505
Tel: (202)785-3066
Fax: (202)659-5760
Served in U.S. Army (1946-66); retired as Lt. Colonel.

Employers
Compass Internat'l Inc. (Secretary-Treasurer)
Silver Users Ass'n (Exec. V. President)

FRANKLIN, Bobby

601 Pennsylvania Ave. NW
Suite 720
Washington, DC 20004
Tel: (202)783-3978
Fax: (202)783-3982
Registered: LDA

Employers
Alltel Corporation (V. President, Federal Legislative Affairs)

FRANKLIN, C. Anson

1101 Connecticut Ave. NW
Suite 1200
Washington, DC 20036
Tel: (202)298-8107
Fax: (202)298-8108
Registered: LDA
EMail: frabur@aol.com
Assistant Press Secretary, The White House, 1983-85. Director, Communications (1985-87), Principal Deputy Assistant Secretary (1987-88), and Assistant Secretary for Congressional, Intergovernmental and Public Affairs (1988-89), all for the Department of Energy. Assistant Administrator, External Affairs, Agency for Internat'l Development, 1990.

Employers
Franklin & Burling (Partner)

FRANKLIN, Desiree

1156 15th St. NW
Suite 1019
Washington, DC 20005
Tel: (202)296-4820

Employers
United States Beet Sugar Ass'n (PAC Contact)

FRANKLIN, Jr., Joe T.

1500 King St.
Suite 201
Alexandria, VA 22314
Tel: (703)838-0050
Fax: (703)684-0242
EMail: franklin@agma.org

Employers
American Gear Manufacturers Ass'n (President)

FRANKLIN, Kathleen

1900 M St. NW
Suite 800
Washington, DC 20036-3508
Tel: (202)295-6650
Fax: (202)296-7585
EMail: kfranklin@comptel.org

Employers
Competitive Telecommunications Ass'n (COMPTEL) (Director, Communications)

FRANKLIN, Laura M.

6110 Executive Blvd.
Suite 800
Rockville, MD 20852-3927
Tel: (301)984-9400
Fax: (301)984-9610
EMail: lfranklin@washreit.com

Employers
Washington Real Estate Investment Trust (V. President and Chief Accounting Officer)

FRANKLIN, Pat

1911 Fort Myer Dr.
Suite 702
Arlington, VA 22209-1603
Tel: (703)276-9800
Fax: (703)276-9587
EMail: cri@container-recycling.org

Employers
Container Recycling Institute (Director)

FRANKLIN, Reed

10801 Rockville Pike
Rockville, MD 20852
Tel: (301)897-5700
Fax: (301)571-0457

Employers
American Speech, Language, and Hearing Ass'n (Director, Congressional Constituent Relations)

FRANKLIN, Shai

1640 Rhode Island Ave. NW
Suite 501
Washington, DC 20036
Tel: (202)898-2500
Fax: (202)898-0822
EMail: ncsj@ncsj.org

Employers
NCSJ: Advocates on Behalf of Jews in Russia, Ukraine, the Baltic States and Eurasia (Director, Government Relations)

FRANKLIN, Thomas M.

5410 Grosvenor Ln.
Bethesda, MD 20814
Tel: (301)897-9770
Fax: (301)530-2471
EMail: tws@wildlife.org

Employers
The Wildlife Soc. (Director, Wildlife Policy)

FRANKO, Sara

1300 I St. NW
Suite 520 West
Washington, DC 20005-3314
Tel: (202)408-0090
Fax: (202)408-1750
Registered: LDA

Employers
Hoffmann-La Roche Inc. (Director, Federal Government Affairs)

FRANKOVICH, Kevin

733 15th St. NW
Suite 912
Washington, DC 20005
Tel: (202)393-0683
Fax: (202)393-0922
Registered: LDA

Employers
CGR Associates, Inc. (Principal)

Clients Represented
On Behalf of CGR Associates, Inc.
Ass'n of Air Medical Services
Fringe Benefit Group, Inc

FRANTZ, David J.

1818 N St. NW
Suite 700
Washington, DC 20036
Tel: (202)331-7050
Fax: (202)331-9306

Employers
Conlon, Frantz, Phelan & Pires (Partner)

Clients Represented
On Behalf of Conlon, Frantz, Phelan & Pires
American Anthropological Ass'n
Paper Machine Clothing Council

FRANZ, Jerry

1701 N. Beauregard St.
Alexandria, VA 22311
Tel: (703)549-1500
Ext: 2054
Fax: (703)549-6249
EMail: jfranz@diabetes.org

Employers
American Diabetes Ass'n (V. President, Communications)

FRANZ, Keira E.

122 C St. NW
Suite 510
Washington, DC 20001
Tel: (202)628-7001
Fax: (202)628-1933
Registered: LDA
EMail: franz@dc.ncga.com

Employers
Nat'l Corn Growers Ass'n (Director, Public Policy)

FRANZ, Liesyl

1331 Pennsylvania Ave. NW
Suite 1300 North
Washington, DC 20004
Tel: (202)637-6722
Fax: (202)637-6759
EMail: liesyl.franz@eds.com

Employers
EDS Corp. (Director, Financial Industry Policy)

FRANZ, Marian C.

2121 Decatur Pl. NW
Washington, DC 20008
Tel: (202)483-3751
Fax: (202)986-0667
Registered: LDA
EMail: info@peacetax.com

Employers
Nat'l Campaign for a Peace Tax Fund (Exec. Director)

FRANZ, Mark A.

1901 Pennsylvania Ave. NW
Suite 700
Washington, DC 20006
Tel: (202)955-9091
Fax: (202)955-9039

Employers
University of Texas Office of Federal Relations (V. Chancellor for Federal Relations)

FRANZ, Ph.D., Wanda

419 Seventh St. NW
Suite 500
Washington, DC 20004
Tel: (202)626-8800
Fax: (202)737-9189

Employers
Nat'l Right to Life Committee (President)

FRANZEL, Brent S.

1747 Pennsylvania Ave. NW
Suite 300
Washington, DC 20006

Tel: (202)293-0398
Fax: (202)393-0363
Registered: LDA

Employers
Tighe, Patton, Tabackman & Babbin

Clients Represented
On Behalf of Tighe, Patton, Tabackman & Babbin
The Boeing Co.
Citigroup
SPACEHAB, Inc.

FRANZEN, IV, Nicholas J.

444 N. Capitol St. NW
Suite 840
Washington, DC 20001

Employers
Citizens for a Conservative Majority (PAC Administrator)

FRASCELLA, Albert

3501 Newark St. NW
Washington, DC 20016

Tel: (202)966-7840
Fax: (202)966-2061

Employers
Nat'l Council for the Social Studies (Director, Communications and Government Relations)

FRASER, Bryna Shore

1825 Connecticut Ave. NW
Seventh Floor
Washington, DC 20009
EMail: bfraser@aed.org

Tel: (202)884-8186
Fax: (202)884-8422

Employers
Academy for Educational Development - Nat'l Institute for Work and Learning (Deputy Director)

FRASER, Edie

1146 19th St. NW
Third Floor
Washington, DC 20036
Government service, 1965-73.

Tel: (202)466-8209
Fax: (202)466-6572

Employers
Public Affairs Group, Inc. (President and Chief Exec. Officer)

FRASER, Heather

625 Slaters Ln.
Suite 200
Alexandria, VA 22314-1171

Tel: (703)836-6263
Fax: (703)836-6730

Employers
American Ass'n for Homecare (PAC Contact)

FRASER, USN, Cdr. James

1300 Defense Pentagon
Room 3D919
Washington, DC 20301-1300

Tel: (703)695-7104

Employers
Department of Defense (Director, Senate Affairs, Office of Legislative Affairs)

FRASER, Kimberley M.

601 13th St. NW
Suite 1150 South
Washington, DC 20005

Tel: (202)393-7790
Fax: (202)628-0225

Employers
Manatos & Manatos, Inc. (V. President)

Clients Represented
On Behalf of Manatos & Manatos, Inc.
American University
Committee for Citizen Awareness

FRATARANGELO, USMC (Ret.), Maj. Gen. Paul

11 Canal Center Plaza
Suite 103
Alexandria, VA 22314

Tel: (703)683-4222
Fax: (703)683-0645
Registered: LDA

Employers
The Spectrum Group

Clients Represented
On Behalf of The Spectrum Group
ADSI Inc.
Raydon Corp.
Tetra Tech

FRATKIN, Susan

2322 20th St. NW
Washington, DC 20009

Tel: (202)265-5410
Fax: (202)332-8538
Registered: LDA

EMail: sue@internet2.edu

Employers
Fratkin Associates (Principal)

Clients Represented
On Behalf of Fratkin Associates
Coalition of Academic Scientific Computation (CASC)

FRAZEE, Elizabeth

1101 Connecticut Ave. NW
Suite 400
Washington, DC 20036-4303

Tel: (202)530-7878
Fax: (202)530-7879

Employers
AOL Time Warner (Law and Public Affairs Group)

FRAZER, John C.

11250 Waples Mill Rd.
Fairfax, VA 22030-7400

Tel: (202)651-2568
Fax: (202)651-2577
Registered: LDA

Employers
Nat'l Rifle Ass'n of America (Federal Liaison)

FRAZER, Paul

2300 Clarendon Blvd.
Suite 610
Arlington, VA 22201-3367
EMail: pfrazer@golinharris.com

Tel: (703)351-5666
Fax: (703)351-5667

Employers
Golin/Harris Internat'l (Exec. V. President)

FRAZIER, Adrienne

1010 Wisconsin Ave. NW
Ninth Floor
Washington, DC 20007
EMail: afrazier@gmabrands.com

Tel: (202)337-9400
Fax: (202)337-4508

Employers
Grocery Manufacturers of America (Representative, Government Affairs)

FRAZIER, Harry

1615 L St. NW
Suite 1000
Washington, DC 20036
EMail: frazierh@fleishman.com
Former Deputy Press Secretary to Senator John W. Warner (R-VA).

Tel: (202)659-0330
Fax: (202)467-4382

Employers
Fleishman-Hillard, Inc (Senior V. President)

FRAZIER, Lauren

1401 Wilson Blvd.
Suite 1100
Arlington, VA 22209

Tel: (703)284-5358
Fax: (703)525-2279
Registered: LDA

EMail: lfrazier@itaa.org

Employers
Information Technology Ass'n of America (ITAA) (Exec. Assistant, Government Affairs)

FRAZIER, Lita

1299 Pennsylvania Ave. NW
Suite 1175
Washington, DC 20004

Tel: (202)638-3838
Fax: (202)638-5799
Registered: LDA

EMail: lita1213@erols.com

Employers
Chicago Mercantile Exchange (Director, Government Relations)

FRAZIER, Mike

400 Seventh St. SW
MS: 10100
Washington, DC 20590

Tel: (202)366-4687
Fax: (202)366-7153

Employers
Department of Transportation (Assistant Secretary for Governmental Affairs)

FREBERG, II, Douglas

400 N. Capitol St. NW
Washington, DC 20001

Tel: (202)824-7214
Fax: (202)824-7090
Registered: LDA

EMail: dfreberg@aga.org

Employers
American Gas Ass'n (Director, Government Relations)

FREDERICK, Jeannie P.

1100 New York Ave. NW
12th Floor
Washington, DC 20527
EMail: jfred@opic.gov

Tel: (202)336-8648
Fax: (202)336-7949

Employers
Overseas Private Investment Corp. (Congressional Assistant)

FREDERICK, Robert M.

1616 H St. NW
Washington, DC 20006

Tel: (202)628-3507
Fax: (202)347-1091

EMail: rfrederick@nationalgrange.org

Employers
Nat'l Grange (Director, Administrative Services)

FREDRICKSON, Debi

1350 I St. NW
Suite 1030
Washington, DC 20005-3305

Tel: (202)682-1280
Fax: (202)682-1412
Registered: LDA

EMail: fredrickson.debi@principal.com

Employers
Principal Financial Group (Compliance Analyst, Fed. Gov't Relations)

FREE, Brant

One Massachusetts Ave. NW
Suite 350
Washington, DC 20001

Tel: (202)408-8123
Fax: (202)296-7683
Registered: LDA

EMail: bfree@chubb.com

Employers
The Chubb Corp. (Senior V. President and Director, Internat'l External Affairs)

FREE, James C.

1401 K St. NW
12th Floor
Washington, DC 20005

Tel: (202)393-4760
Fax: (202)393-3516
Registered: LDA

EMail: jfree@smithfree.com
Former Special Assistant to the President for Congressional Liaison, The White House during the Carter Administration.

Employers
The Smith-Free Group (President and Chief Exec. Officer)

Clients Represented
On Behalf of The Smith-Free Group
AT&T
Broadcast Music Inc. (BMI)
CSX Corp.
HCA Healthcare Corp.
Kennecott/Borax
MasterCard Internat'l
MBNA America Bank NA
Nuclear Energy Institute
Paucatuck Eastern Pequot Tribal Nation
Sandia Pueblo
Sony Music Entertainment Inc.
Sony Pictures Entertainment Inc.
Southern Co.
U.S. Wireless Data, Inc.
VISA U.S.A., Inc.
Washington Group Internat'l
Washington Mutual Bank
Westinghouse Government Services Group
Xcel Energy, Inc.

FREEBURG, Kara E.

4200 Evergreen Ln.
Suite 315
Annandale, VA 22003
EMail: karancor@radix.net

Tel: (703)642-6614
Fax: (703)642-0497
Registered: LDA

Employers
American Network of Community Options and Resources (ANCOR) (Analyst, Public Policy)

FREED, Bruce F.

426 C St. NE
Washington, DC 20002
EMail: BFFreed@att.net

Tel: (202)544-1880
Fax: (202)543-2565

Chief Investigator, Senate Banking Committee 1978-81; Staff Director, House Small Business Oversight Subcommittee, 1981-83; Special Assistant to Rep. Mary Rose Oakar (D-OH), 1983-85. Special Assistant to Rep. Bill Alexander (D-AR), 1985-86.

Employers
Integrated Strategies/Strategic Communications (Principal)

FREEDENBERG, Paul H.

7901 Westpark Dr.
McLean, VA 22102-4206
EMail: phf@mfgtech.org

Tel: (703)827-5282
Fax: (703)749-2742
Registered: LDA

Employers
The Ass'n For Manufacturing Technology (AMT) (Government Relations Director)

FREEDENBERG, Sam

666 11th St. NW
Suite 750
Washington, DC 20001
EMail: sfreeden@nasbic.org

Tel: (202)628-5055
Fax: (202)628-5080

Employers
Nat'l Ass'n of Small Business Investment Companies (Director, Communications)

FREEDMAN, Anthony S.

601 13th St. NW
Suite 800 North
Washington, DC 20005

Tel: (202)682-1480
Fax: (202)682-1497

Deputy Assistant Secretary, Housing Policy and Budget, Department of Housing and Urban Development, 1979-81. Deputy Director, Legislation, Environmental Protection Agency, 1977-78. Staff, Budget Committee, U.S. House of Representatives, 1976-77.

Employers
Hawkins, Delafield & Wood (Partner)

FREEDMAN, Dara

1875 I St. NW
Suite 600
Washington, DC 20006
EMail: dfreedman@nareit.com

Tel: (202)739-9400
Fax: (202)739-9401
Registered: LDA

Employers
Nat'l Ass'n of Real Estate Investment Trusts (Counsel)

FREEMAN, Ali

1001 Connecticut Ave. NW
Suite 1250
Washington, DC 20036

Tel: (202)331-1010
Fax: (202)331-0640

Employers
Competitive Enterprise Institute (Environmental Policy Analyst)

FREEMAN, Anthony G.

1828 L St. NW
Suite 600
Washington, DC 20036

Tel: (202)653-7652
Fax: (202)653-7687

Employers
Internat'l Labor Office (Director)

FREEMAN, Jr., Chas W.

1730 M St. NW
Suite 512
Washington, DC 20036
EMail: info@mepc.org

Tel: (202)296-6767
Fax: (202)296-5791

Employers
Middle East Policy Council (President)

FREEMAN, Jr., David F.

555 12th St. NW
Washington, DC 20004-1206
EMail: David_Freeman@aporter.com

Tel: (202)942-5000
Fax: (202)942-5999
Registered: LDA

Employers
Arnold & Porter (Partner)

Clients Represented

On Behalf of Arnold & Porter
Metropolitan Mortgage and Securities, Inc.

FREEMAN, Jeffrey B.

11250 Waples Mill Rd.
Fairfax, VA 22030-7400

Tel: (202)651-2565
Fax: (202)651-2577
Registered: LDA

Employers
Nat'l Rifle Ass'n of America (Federal Liaison)

FREEMAN, III, Joseph E.

444 N. Capitol St. NW
Suite 214
Washington, DC 20001
EMail: jfreeman@gov.state.va.us

Tel: (202)783-1769
Fax: (202)783-7687

Employers
Virginia Liaison Office (Director, Virginia Liaison Office)

FREEMAN, Jr., Lewis R.

1801 K St. NW
Suite 600K
Washington, DC 20006

Tel: (202)371-5220
Fax: (202)296-7218
Registered: LDA

Employers
Soc. of the Plastics Industry (Chief Lobbyist and Senior Gov't Affairs Fellow)

FREEMAN, Michael

900 17th St. NW
Suite 600
Washington, DC 20006

Tel: (202)452-8700
Fax: (202)296-9561
Registered: LDA

Employers
Healthcare Leadership Council (V. President, Communications)

FREEMAN, Rosemary B.

901 15th St. NW
Suite 700
Washington, DC 20005-2301

Tel: (202)371-6000
Fax: (202)371-6279
Registered: LDA, FARA

Employers
Verner, Liipfert, Bernhard, McPherson and Hand, Chartered (Director, Public Affairs)

Clients Represented

On Behalf of Verner, Liipfert, Bernhard, McPherson and Hand, Chartered
Alere Medical Inc.
Alliance Pipeline, L.P.
Biovail Corp. Internat'l
Chlorine Chemistry Council
Federal Home Loan Bank of Indianapolis
General Motors Corp.
Genesee County Drain Commissioner
"I Have a Dream" Foundation
Kasten Chase Applied Research Limited
Kellogg Co.
Kelly Services, Inc.
Kmart Corp.
Merrill Lynch & Co., Inc.
Northwest Airlines, Inc.
Olympic Aid
Rite Aid Corp.
University of Michigan Medical Center

FREEMAN, Sharon K.

450 Fifth St. NW
Room 6100
Washington, DC 20549

Tel: (202)942-0010
Fax: (202)942-9650

Employers
Securities and Exchange Commission (Legislative Assistant)

FREEMAN, Terri Lee

1112 16th St. NW
Suite 340
Washington, DC 20036
EMail: cfncrtfreeman@erols.com

Tel: (202)955-5890
Fax: (202)955-8084

Employers
The Community Foundation for the Nat'l Capital Region (President)

FREEMAN, Yvonne

555 New Jersey Ave. NW
Washington, DC 20001

Tel: (202)879-4400
Fax: (202)638-2589

Employers
American Federation of Teachers (Treasurer, Staff Union)

FREEMAN-SIMMONS, Shayla

1849 C St. NW
Room 6255
Washington, DC 20240
EMail: shayla_simmons@ios.doi.gov

Tel: (202)208-7693
Fax: (202)208-7619

Employers
Department of Interior (Acting Director, Office of Congressional and Legislative Affairs)

FREEMYER, Windsor

1301 Pennsylvania Ave. NW
Suite 401
Washington, DC 20004
EMail: windsor.freemyer@sugarcaneleague.org

Tel: (202)785-4020
Fax: (202)659-8581
Registered: LDA

Legislative Staff Member to Representatives; Christopher Cannon (R-UT), 1998-2001, John Ensign (R-NV), 1995-98, Scott McInnis (R-CO), 1994-95.

Employers
Florida Sugar Cane League, Inc. (Director, Government Relations)
Gay & Robinson, Inc. (Washington Representative)
Hawaiian Commercial and Sugar Company (Washington Representative)
Rio Grande Valley Sugar Growers (Washington Representative)

FREER, David W.

1001 G St. NW
Sixth Floor East
Washington, DC 20001-4545
EMail: dfreer@sempra.com

Tel: (202)662-1704
Fax: (202)293-2887
Registered: LDA

Employers
Sempra Energy (Regional V. President, Federal Government Affairs)

FREER, Paula D.

1101 Pennsylvania Ave. NW
Suite 510
Washington, DC 20004

Tel: (202)783-6333
Fax: (202)783-6309
Registered: LDA

Employers
USX Corp. (Manager, Governmental Affairs)

FREER, Jr., Robert E.

1020 19th St. NW
Suite 400
Washington, DC 20036

Tel: (202)331-9100
Fax: (202)331-9060
Registered: LDA

Executive Assistant to the General Counsel, Department of Transportation, 1971-74. Attorney-Advisor to the Chairman and Assistant to the General Counsel (1970-71) and Trial Attorney (1966-69), Federal Trade Commission.

Employers
Lawyers for the Republic (Principal Activist)

FREILICH, Harold I.

901 15th St. NW
Suite 700
Washington, DC 20005-2301

Tel: (202)371-6000
Fax: (202)371-6279
Registered: LDA

Employers
Verner, Liipfert, Bernhard, McPherson and Hand, Chartered (Member of Firm)

FREITAG, Douglas Ward

21150 New Hampshire Ave.
Brookeville, MD 20833

Tel: (301)570-3821
Registered: LDA

Employers
Self-employed as an independent consultant.

Clients Represented

As an independent consultant

Inter-Associates, Inc.

FREITAS, Joseph

100 Daingerfield Rd.
Alexandria, VA 22314-2888
Tel: (703)684-9606
Fax: (703)684-9675

Employers

IBFI - The Internat'l Ass'n for Document and Information Management Solutions (President)

FRELICK, Bill

1717 Massachusetts Ave. NW
Suite 200
Washington, DC 20036
Tel: (202)347-3507
Fax: (202)347-3418
Registered: LDA
EMail: bill.frelick@irsa-uscr.org

Employers

United States Committee for Refugees (Director, Policy)

FRENCH, Claudia

1906 Sunderland Pl. NW
Washington, DC 20036
Tel: (202)530-8030
Fax: (202)530-8031

Employers

AIDS Action Council (Exec. Director)

FRENCH, David

201 Park Washington Ct.
Falls Church, VA 22046-4621
Tel: (703)532-9400
Fax: (703)538-4673
Registered: LDA
EMail: dfrench@fdi.org

Employers

ENS Resources, Inc.
Food Distributors Internat'l (NAWGA-IFDA) (Director, Government Relations)

FRENCH, David

701 Pennsylvania Ave. NW
Suite 725
Washington, DC 20004
Tel: (202)638-7429
Fax: (202)628-4763

Employers

Novartis Corp. (Director, Communications and Public Affairs)

FRENCH, Michael P.

555 12th St. NW
Suite 620 North
Washington, DC 20004
Tel: (202)955-9312
Fax: (202)833-1630
Registered: LDA
EMail: mike.french@fluor.com

Employers

Fluor Corp. (Senior Director, Government Relations)

FRENCH, Verrick O.

601 13th St. NW
Suite 370 South
Washington, DC 20005
Tel: (202)783-7272
Fax: (202)783-4345
Registered: LDA

Employers

French & Company (President)

Clients Represented

On Behalf of French & Company

Bendich, Stobaugh & Strong
Encapco Technologies, LLC
Information Spectrum Inc.
Internat'l Biometric Industry Ass'n
Internat'l Electronics Manufacturers and Consumers of America
Levine-Fricke Restoration Corp.
Montgomery Ward & Co., Inc.
Nossaman, Gunther, Knox & Elliott

FRENKEL, Orit

1299 Pennsylvania Ave. NW
Suite 1100 West
Washington, DC 20004-2407
Tel: (202)637-4000
Fax: (202)637-4300
Registered: LDA

Employers

General Electric Co. (Senior Manager, International Law and Policy)

FRENZEL, Hon. Bill

501 Capitol Ct. NE
Suite 300
Washington, DC 20002
Tel: (202)546-1292
Fax: (202)547-6560
Member, U.S. House of Representatives (R-MN), 1971-91.

Employers

Ripon Society (President)

FRERICHS, Stephen

One Massachusetts Ave. NW
Suite 800
Washington, DC 20001-1431
Tel: (202)842-2345
Fax: (202)408-7763

Employers

McLeod, Watkinson & Miller (Economist/Budget Analyst)

Clients Represented

On Behalf of McLeod, Watkinson & Miller

American Ass'n of Crop Insurers

FRESE, Elizabeth Norris

1501 M St. NW
Suite 1100
Washington, DC 20005
Tel: (202)785-7300
Fax: (202)785-6360

Employers

Viacom Inc. (Office Manager, Government Affairs)

FRESHMAN, John D.

1050 Thomas Jefferson St. NW
Sixth Floor
Washington, DC 20007
Tel: (202)298-1895
Fax: (202)298-1699
Registered: LDA

Employers

John Freshman Associates, Inc. (President)

Clients Represented

On Behalf of John Freshman Associates, Inc.

#10 Enterprises LLC
Anheuser-Busch Cos., Inc.
Gulf Coast Waste Disposal Authority
Lewis and Clark Rural Water System, Inc.
Los Angeles County Sanitation District
Metropolitan St. Louis Sewer District
Mid Dakota Rural Water System
Monterey County Water Resources Agency
Nat'l Audubon Soc.
Oregon Water Trust
Pharmacia Corp.
Sacramento, California, Department of Utilities of

FRESHOUR, Paul

555 12th St. NW
Washington, DC 20004-1206
Tel: (202)942-5000
Fax: (202)942-5999
EMail: Paul_Freshour@aporter.com

Employers

Arnold & Porter (Partner)

FREUND, Jeffrey R.

1000 Connecticut Ave. NW
Suite 1300
Washington, DC 20036
Tel: (202)842-2600
Fax: (202)842-1888
Legal Assistant, Federal Communications, 1971-72. Law Clerk to Judge Alfonso Zirpoli, U.S. District Court for the Northern District of California, 1970-71.

Employers

Bredhoff & Kaiser (Partner)

Clients Represented

On Behalf of Bredhoff & Kaiser

Bakery, Confectionery and Tobacco Workers Internat'l Union

FREY, Scott

Ten G St. NE
Suite 600
Washington, DC 20002-4215
Tel: (202)216-0420
Fax: (202)216-0446
Registered: LDA
EMail: freys@ncpssm.org

Employers

Nat'l Committee to Preserve Social Security and Medicare (Senior Legislative Representative)

FRICK, G. William

1220 L St. NW
Washington, DC 20005
Tel: (202)682-8240
Fax: (202)682-8232
Registered: LDA

Employers

American Petroleum Institute (V. President, General Counsel and Secretary)

FRIDAY SCOTT, Lisa

700 11th St. NW
Washington, DC 20001-4507
Tel: (202)383-1270
Fax: (202)383-7580
Registered: LDA

Employers

Nat'l Ass'n of Realtors (Political Programs Representative)

FRIEBERG, Ronna

1001 Pennsylvania Ave. NW
Suite 760 North
Washington, DC 20004
Tel: (202)661-7060
Fax: (202)661-7066
Former Director, Legislative Affairs, Office of the V. President (during the Clinton Adminstration) and Legislative Affairs Staff (during the Carter Adminsitration), Executive Office of the President, The White House.

Employers

The Legislative Strategies Group, LLC

FRIED, Bruce

2300 N St. NW
Washington, DC 20037-1128
Tel: (202)663-8006
Fax: (202)663-8007
Registered: LDA
EMail: bruce.fried@shawpittman.com
Director, Center for Health Plans and Providers, Department of Health and Human Services, 1997-98. Office of Managed Care, Department of Health and Human Services, 1995-97.

Employers

Shaw Pittman (Partner)

Clients Represented

On Behalf of Shaw Pittman

American Ass'n for Homecare
Detroit Medical Center
Liberty Medical Supply
Medicare Cost Contractors Alliance
Nat'l IPA Coalition

FRIEDBACHER, Todd

1001 Pennsylvania Ave. NW
Suite 600
Washington, DC 20004
Tel: (202)347-0066
Fax: (202)624-7222
EMail: tfriedba@pgfm.com

Employers

Powell, Goldstein, Frazer & Murphy LLP (Associate)

FRIEDLAND, David M.

1350 I St. NW
Suite 700
Washington, DC 20005
Tel: (202)789-6000
Fax: (202)789-6190

Employers

Beveridge & Diamond, P.C. (Partner)

FRIEDLANDER, Lisa L.

1735 New York Ave. NW
Suite 500
Washington, DC 20006-4759
Tel: (202)628-1700
Fax: (202)331-1024

Employers

Preston Gates Ellis & Rouvelas Meeds LLP (Associate)

Clients Represented

On Behalf of Preston Gates Ellis & Rouvelas Meeds LLP

Northpoint Technology, Ltd.
Prime Time 24

FRIEDMAN, Barry A.

1920 N St. NW
Washington, DC 20036
Tel: (202)331-8800
Fax: (202)331-8330
EMail: bfriedman@thf.com

Employers

Thompson, Hine and Flory LLP (Partner)

FRIEDMAN, David

1100 Connecticut Ave. NW
Suite 1020
Washington, DC 20036
Tel: (202)452-8320
Fax: (202)296-2371

Employers
Anti-Defamation League (Director, Washington, DC, Maryland, Northern Virginia Region)

FRIEDMAN, Dorian

1250 Connecticut Ave. NW
Suite 610
Washington, DC 20036
EMail: dfriedman@welfaretowork.org
Tel: (202)955-3005
Fax: (202)955-1087

Employers
Welfare to Work Partnership (V. President, Policy and Planning)

FRIEDMAN, Jim

600 New Hampshire Ave. NW
Suite 601
Washington, DC 20037
EMail: JFriedman@hillandknowlton.com
Tel: (202)333-7400
Fax: (202)333-1638

Employers
Hill and Knowlton, Inc. (Senior Managing Director, Director of Health Care)

Clients Represented
On Behalf of Hill and Knowlton, Inc.
GlaxoSmithKline

FRIEDMAN, Laura

1815 H St. NW
Suite 920
Washington, DC 20006
EMail: lfriedman@peacenow.org
Tel: (202)728-1893
Fax: (202)728-1895

Employers
Americans for Peace Now (Legislative Director)

FRIEDMAN, Margery Sinder

1800 M St. NW
Washington, DC 20036
Tel: (202)467-7000
Fax: (202)467-7176
Registered: LDA
EMail: mfriedman@morganlewis.com

Employers
Morgan, Lewis & Bockius LLP

Clients Represented
On Behalf of Morgan, Lewis & Bockius LLP
Bituminous Coal Operators Ass'n

FRIEDMAN, Miles

12884 Harbor Dr.
Woodside, VA 20192
EMail: mfriedman@nasda.com
Tel: (703)490-6777
Fax: (703)492-4404

Employers
Nat'l Ass'n of State Development Agencies (President and CEO)

FRIEDMAN, Paul H.

1775 I St. NW
Washington, DC 20006
Tel: (202)261-3398
Fax: (202)261-3333

Employers
Dechert (Partner)

FRIEDMAN, Philip S.

888 16th St. NW
Suite 400
Washington, DC 20006
Tel: (202)835-7466
Fax: (202)296-8791

Employers
Friedman Law Offices, P.L.L.C. (Partner)

Clients Represented
On Behalf of Friedman Law Offices, P.L.L.C.
American Israel Public Affairs Committee

FRIEDMAN, Robert

777 N. Capitol St. NE
Suite 410
Washington, DC 20002
EMail: friedman@cfeb.org
Tel: (202)408-9788
Fax: (202)408-9793
Registered: LDA

Employers
Corporation for Enterprise Development (Chair and Founder)

FRIEDMAN, Susan

1090 Vermont Ave. NW
Suite 510
Washington, DC 20005
Tel: (202)414-0140
Fax: (202)544-3525
Registered: LDA

Employers
American Osteopathic Ass'n (Deputy Director, Government Relations)

FRIEDMANN, Gay H.

Ten G St. NE
Suite 700
Washington, DC 20002
Tel: (202)216-5900
Fax: (202)216-0875
Registered: LDA

Employers
Interstate Natural Gas Ass'n of America (Senior V. President, Legislative Affairs and Secretary)

FRIEDMANN, Peter

1275 Pennsylvania Ave. NW
Ninth Floor
Washington, DC 20004
Tel: (202)467-8383
Fax: (202)467-8381
Registered: LDA

Employers
Lindsay Hart Neil & Weigler (Of Counsel)

Clients Represented
On Behalf of Lindsay Hart Neil & Weigler
Agriculture Ocean Transportation Coalition
Coalition of New England Companies for Trade
Maritime Fire and Safety Ass'n
Oregon Economic Development Department
Pacific Coast Council of Customs Brokers and Freight Forwarders Ass'n
Redwood City, California, Port of
Reebok Internat'l

FRIEND, Patricia

1275 K St. NW
Fifth Floor
Washington, DC 20005
EMail: pfriend@afanet.org
Tel: (202)712-9799

Employers
Ass'n of Flight Attendants (President)

FRIESS, Katherine

1801 K St. NW
Suite 901-L
Washington, DC 20006
Tel: (202)530-0500
Fax: (202)530-4800
Registered: LDA
EMail: Katherine_Friess@bm.com
Former Tax and Trade Counsel to U.S. Senators Larry Pressler (R-SD) and Dave Durenberger (R-MN). Former Aide to Rep. Bill Frenzel, (R-MN).

Employers
BKSH & Associates (Director)

Clients Represented
On Behalf of BKSH & Associates
UST Public Affairs, Inc.

FRIGIOLA, Jim

3602 Tristan Ct.
Annandale, VA 22003
Tel: (703)641-9455
Fax: (703)641-8831
Registered: LDA

Employers
Self-employed as an independent consultant.

Clients Represented
As an independent consultant
Fifty Caliber Shooters Policy Institute, Inc.

FRISA, Hon. Dan

499 S. Capitol St. SW
Suite 420
Washington, DC 20003
Tel: (202)302-0465
Member, House of Representatives (R-NY), 1995-96.

Employers
Monfort & Wolfe (Senior Political Advisor)

FRISBY, Bradford V.

1130 17th St. NW
Washington, DC 20036-4677
EMail: bfrisby@nma.org
Tel: (202)463-2643
Fax: (202)463-3257
Registered: LDA

Employers
Nat'l Mining Ass'n (Assistant General Counsel)

FRISBY, Jr., H. Russell

1900 M St. NW
Suite 800
Washington, DC 20036-3508
EMail: rfrisby@comptel.org
Tel: (202)296-6650
Fax: (202)296-7585
Registered: LDA

Employers
Competitive Telecommunications Ass'n (COMPTEL) (President)

FRISBY, Michael

1909 K St. NW
Fourth Floor
Washington, DC 20006
Tel: (202)973-5800
Fax: (202)973-5858

Employers
Porter/Novelli (Senior V. President, Public Affairs)

Clients Represented
On Behalf of Porter/Novelli
American Fidelity Life Insurance Co.

FRISBY, R. Larson

740 15th St. NW
Ninth Floor
Washington, DC 20005
Tel: (202)662-1098
Fax: (202)662-1762
Registered: LDA

Employers
American Bar Ass'n (Legislative Counsel)

FRISHBERG, Ivan

218 D St. SE
Second Floor
Washington, DC 20003
Tel: (202)546-9707
Fax: (202)546-2461
Registered: LDA

Employers
U.S. Public Interest Research Group (Higher Education Project Director)

FRITTS, Charles H.

400 N. Capitol St. NW
Washington, DC 20001
EMail: cfritts@aga.org
Tel: (202)824-7220
Fax: (202)824-7090
Registered: LDA

Employers
American Gas Ass'n (V. President, Government Relations)

FRITTS, Edward O.

1771 N St. NW
Washington, DC 20036-2891
Tel: (202)429-5444
Fax: (202)429-5410
Registered: LDA

Employers
Nat'l Ass'n of Broadcasters (President and Chief Exec. Officer)

FRITTS, Kimberley

1001 G St. NW
Suite 900 E
Washington, DC 20001-4545
EMail: fritts@podesta.com
Tel: (202)393-1010
Fax: (202)393-5510
Registered: LDA
Former Legislative aide to Senator Connie Mack III (R-FL).

Employers
Podesta/Mattoon (Principal)

Clients Represented
On Behalf of Podesta/Mattoon
American Psychological Ass'n
AOL Time Warner
Celera Genomics
Motion Picture Ass'n of America
Nat'l Ass'n of Broadcasters
News America Inc.
Northpoint Technology, Ltd.
Recording Industry Ass'n of America
SITV
Teligent, Inc.
Vivendi Universal

FRITTS, Linda A.

1200 New Hampshire Ave. NW
Suite 800
Washington, DC 20036-6802
EMail: lfritts@dlawlaw.com
Tel: (202)776-2000
Fax: (202)776-2222

Employers
Dow, Lohnes & Albertson, PLLC (Member)

FRITZ, Alison

2300 M St. NW
Suite 900
Washington, DC 20037
EMail: alison@publicforuminstitute.com
Tel: (202)467-2770
Fax: (202)293-5717

Employers
Public Forum Institute (Vice President)

FRITZEL, Charles H.

444 N. Capitol St. NW
Suite 801
Washington, DC 20001
Tel: (202)639-0490
Fax: (202)639-0494
Registered: LDA

Employers
Nat'l Ass'n of Independent Insurers (Assistant V. President, Government Relations)

FROELICH, M.D., F. Edwin

2011 Pennsylvania Ave. NW
Suite 301
Washington, DC 20006
Tel: (202)296-2810
Fax: (202)331-7479
Registered: LDA
Physician Advisor to Republicans, Senate Committee on Labor and Human Resources, 1985-89.

Employers
Nat'l Ass'n of Waterfront Employers (Assistant General Counsel)
Wilcox, Carroll & Froelich, PLLC (Partner)

Clients Represented
On Behalf of Wilcox, Carroll & Froelich, PLLC
Nat'l Ass'n of Waterfront Employers
Nat'l Maritime Safety Ass'n
Shell Oil Co.

FROELICH, Sara L.

1422 Duke St.
Alexandria, VA 22314
Tel: (703)838-0033
Fax: (703)548-1890
Registered: LDA

Employers
American Medical Group Ass'n (V. President, Public Policy and Political Affairs)

FROGUE, James

214 Massachusetts Ave. NE
Washington, DC 20002
Tel: (202)546-4400
Fax: (202)546-8328

Employers
Heritage Foundation (Health Care Policy Analyst)

FROH, Richard B.

1700 K St. NW
Suite 601
Washington, DC 20006
Tel: (202)296-1314
Fax: (202)296-4067
Registered: LDA

Employers
Kaiser Permanente (V. President, Government Relations)

FROHMAN, Charles

1828 L St. NW
Suite 705
Washington, DC 20036
Tel: (202)296-3671
Fax: (202)223-5843
Registered: LDA

Employers
American Land Title Ass'n (Director, Grassroots)

FROM, Alvin

600 Pennsylvania Ave. SE
Suite 400
Washington, DC 20003
Tel: (202)546-0007
Fax: (202)544-5002

Employers
Democratic Leadership Council (Founder and C.E.O.)

FROMM, Chuck

11 Dupont Circle NW
Suite 700
Washington, DC 20036
Tel: (202)293-5886
Fax: (202)939-6969
Registered: LDA

Employers
Multinat'l Government Services, Inc.

Clients Represented
On Behalf of Multinat'l Government Services, Inc.
Rhone-Polenc Inc.

FROMYER, Mary O.

818 Connecticut Ave. NW
Suite 1200
Washington, DC 20006
EMail: mfromyer@ibgc.com
Tel: (202)872-8181
Fax: (202)872-8696

Employers
Internat'l Business-Government Counsellors, Inc. (V. President)

FRONING, Denise

214 Massachusetts Ave. NE
Washington, DC 20002
Tel: (202)546-4400
Fax: (202)546-8328

Employers
Heritage Foundation (Policy Analyst, Trade and Internat'l Economics)

FRONT, Alan

666 Pennsylvania Ave. SE
Suite 401
Washington, DC 20003
Tel: (202)543-7552
Fax: (202)544-4723
Registered: LDA

Employers
Trust for Public Land (Senior V. President)

FROST, Ellen L.

11 Dupont Circle NW
Suite 620
Washington, DC 20036
EMail: elfrost@iie.com
Tel: (202)328-9000
Fax: (202)328-5432

Employers
Institute for Internat'l Economics (Visiting Fellow)

FROYD, Erica

2450 N St. NW
Washington, DC 20037-1126
Tel: (202)828-0525
Fax: (202)862-6218
Registered: LDA

Employers
Ass'n of American Medical Colleges (Legislative Analyst)

FRUCHTERMAN, III, Richard L.

1133 19th St. NW
Washington, DC 20036
Tel: (202)887-3844
Fax: (202)736-6880
Registered: LDA
EMail: richard.fruchterman@wcom.com

Employers
MCI WorldCom Corp. (Director, Government Relations)

FRULLA, David E.

923 15th St. NW
Washington, DC 20005
Tel: (202)662-9700
Fax: (202)737-7565
Registered: LDA
EMail: dfrulla@brand-frulla.com

Employers
Brand & Frulla, P.C. (Partner)

Clients Represented
On Behalf of Brand & Frulla, P.C.
United Airlines

FRUMKIN, Lara

750 First St. NE
Washington, DC 20002-4242
Tel: (202)336-5500
Fax: (202)336-6069
Registered: LDA

Employers
American Psychological Ass'n

FRY, Edmund M.

7500 Old Georgetown Rd.
Suite 620
Bethesda, MD 20814
EMail: fry@pda.org
Tel: (301)986-0293
Fax: (301)986-0296

Employers
PDA (President)

FRY, Richard

100 N. Pitt
Suite 400
Alexandria, VA 22314
Tel: (703)683-8416
Fax: (703)683-8417

Employers
Academy of Managed Care Pharmacy (Senior Director, Pharmacy Affairs)

FRY, Tom

1120 G St. NW
Suite 900
Washington, DC 20005-3801
EMail: tomf@noia.org
Tel: (202)347-6900
Fax: (202)347-8650

Employers
Nat'l Ocean Industries Ass'n (President)

FRYDENLUND, John

1301 Connecticut Ave. NW
Fourth Floor
Washington, DC 20036
Tel: (202)467-5300
Fax: (202)467-4253
Served in the Department of Agriculture during the Reagan and Bush I Administrations.

Employers
Citizens Against Government Waste (Fellow, Food and Agriculture Policy)

FRYE, Cary

1250 H St. NW
Suite 900
Washington, DC 20005
EMail: cfrye@idfa.org
Tel: (202)737-4332
Fax: (202)331-7820

Employers
Internat'l Dairy Foods Ass'n (V. President, Regulatory and Scientific Affairs)

FRYE, Jocelyn C.

1875 Connecticut Ave. NW
Suite 710
Washington, DC 20009
Tel: (202)986-2600
Fax: (202)986-2539

Employers
Nat'l Partnership for Women and Families (Director, Legal and Public Policy)

FUENTES, Rodolfo

2300 N St. NW
Washington, DC 20037-1128
Tel: (202)663-8240
Fax: (202)663-8007
Registered: LDA
EMail: rudy.fuentes@shawpittman.com
Senior Advisor to the Director, Minority Business Development Agency, Department of Commerce, 1995-98

Employers
Shaw Pittman (Associate)

Clients Represented
On Behalf of Shaw Pittman
Memphis, Tennessee, City of
Nat'l Coalition for Minority Business
Texaco Group Inc.

FUGERE, Patricia M.

1800 Massachusetts Ave. NW
Washington, DC 20036
Tel: (202)872-1494
Fax: (202)872-1932

Employers
Washington Legal Clinic for the Homeless (Director)

FUJII, Noboru

196 Van Buren St.
Suite 450
Herndon, VA 20170
Tel: (703)456-2563
Fax: (703)456-2551

Employers
Nissan North America Inc. (Director, Technical Affairs)

FUJITO, Wayne T.

1330 Connecticut Ave. NW
Suite 210
Washington, DC 20036-1704
EMail: wfujito@itta.com
Tel: (202)828-2614
Fax: (202)828-2617

Employers
Internat'l Technology & Trade Associates, Inc. (ITTA, Inc.) (President and C.O.O.)

FULCHER, Juley

1532 16th St. NW
Washington, DC 20036
Tel: (202)745-1211
Fax: (202)745-0088

Employers
Nat'l Coalition Against Domestic Violence (Director, Public Policy)

FULLER, Carolyn

1420 New York Ave. NW
Suite 1050
Washington, DC 20005
EMail: cfuller@vsadc.com
Tel: (202)638-1950
Fax: (202)638-7714
Registered: LDA

Former Staff Director, Subcommittee on Military Construction, Senate Appropriations Committee. Counsel to Senator Bob Kerrey (D-NE).

Employers
Van Scoyoc Associates, Inc. (V. President)

Clients Represented

On Behalf of Van Scoyoc Associates, Inc.
Coalition of EPSCoR States
Federation of State Humanities Councils
Great Cities' Universities
Montana State University
The Nat'l Space Grant Alliance
Space Grant Coalition
University of Idaho
University of Nebraska
University of New Orleans Foundation
University of North Carolina at Chapel Hill

FULLER, Craig L.

P.O. Box 1417-D49
Alexandria, VA 22313-1417
Tel: (703)549-3001
Fax: (703)836-4869

Employers
Nat'l Ass'n of Chain Drug Stores (President and C.E.O.)

FULLER, Daniel

1680 Duke St.
Alexandria, VA 22314-3407
Tel: (703)838-6722
Fax: (703)683-7590

Employers
Nat'l School Boards Ass'n (Director, Federal Programs)

FULLER, David R.

600 13th St. NW
Washington, DC 20005-3096
EMail: dfuller@mwe.com
Tel: (202)756-8302
Fax: (202)756-8087

Former Assistant Branch Chief in Employee Benefits and Exempt Organizations Division, Internal Revenue Service.

Employers
McDermott, Will and Emery (Partner)

Clients Represented

On Behalf of McDermott, Will and Emery
Nat'l Ass'n of Professional Employer Organizations

FULLER, Douglas

1112 16th St. NW
Suite 240
Washington, DC 20036
Tel: (202)835-0952
Fax: (202)835-0155

Employers
Klein & Saks, Inc.

Clients Represented

On Behalf of Klein & Saks, Inc.
The Gold and Silver Institute

FULLER, Elizabeth A.

800 Connecticut Ave. NW
Suite 1100
Washington, DC 20006
EMail: elizabeth_fuller@baxter.com
Tel: (202)223-4016
Fax: (202)296-7177

Employers
Baxter Healthcare Corp. (PAC and Grassroots Associate)

FULLER, Jon

1025 Connecticut Ave. NW
Suite 700
Washington, DC 20036
Tel: (202)785-8866
Fax: (202)835-0003
Registered: LDA

Former Special Assistant to the Assistant Secretary of Education, Department of Health, Education, and Welfare. Former Special Assistant to the Commissioner of Education, Department of Health, Education, and Welfare.

Employers
Nat'l Ass'n of Independent Colleges and Universities (Senior Fellow)

FULLER, Kathryn S.

1250 24th St. NW
Washington, DC 20037
Tel: (202)293-4800
Fax: (202)293-9211

Employers
World Wildlife Fund (President)

FULLER, Lee O.

1201 15th St. NW
Third Floor
Washington, DC 20005
EMail: lfuller@ipaa.org
Tel: (202)857-4722
Fax: (202)857-4799
Registered: LDA

Employers
Independent Petroleum Ass'n of America (V. President, Government Relations)

FULLER, Richard B.

801 18th St. NW
Washington, DC 20006
Tel: (202)872-1300
Fax: (202)785-4452
Registered: LDA

Employers
Paralyzed Veterans of America (National Legislation Director)

FULLER, Rick

1200 Wilson Blvd.
Arlington, VA 22209-1989
Tel: (703)465-3500
Fax: (703)465-3001

Employers
The Boeing Co. (Director, Communications)

FULLER, Thomas D.

1666 K St. NW
Suite 800
Washington, DC 20006
Tel: (202)481-7000
Fax: (202)862-7098
Registered: LDA

Employers
Arthur Andersen LLP (Principal)

Clients Represented

On Behalf of Arthur Andersen LLP
Hybrid Branch Coalition

FULLER, Tim M.

733 15th St. NW
Suite 437
Washington, DC 20005
EMail: tfuller@graypanthers.org
Tel: (202)737-6637
Fax: (202)737-1160

Employers
Gray Panthers Nat'l Office in Washington (Exec. Director)

FULLERTON, Lawrence R.

1001 Pennsylvania Ave. NW
Suite 600
Washington, DC 20004
Tel: (202)347-0066
Fax: (202)624-7222
Registered: LDA

Deputy Assistant Attorney General, Antitrust Division, Department of Justice, 1995-98.

Employers
Powell, Goldstein, Frazer & Murphy LLP (Partner)

FULLUM, Karen

1771 N St. NW
Washington, DC 20036-2891
Tel: (202)429-5430
Fax: (202)775-3526
Registered: LDA

Employers
Nat'l Ass'n of Broadcasters (V. President, Regulatory Affairs)

FULTON, C. Michael

2300 Clarendon Blvd.
Suite 610
Arlington, VA 22201-3367
EMail: mfulton@golinharris.com
Tel: (703)351-5666
Fax: (703)351-5667
Registered: LDA

Associate Counsel, House Appropriations Committee, and Aide to Reps. Alan and Robert Mollohan (D-WV), 1979-1988.

Employers
Golin/Harris Internat'l (Exec. V. President)

Clients Represented

On Behalf of Golin/Harris Internat'l
Alliance Community Hospital
Brown General Hospital
Flexsys America
Go-Mart, Inc.
Grenada Lake Medical Center
John Harland Co.
Kent State University
Our Lady of the Lake Regional Medical Center
Joel Pomerene Hospital
Sacred Heart University
Southeast Missouri State University
University Health Associates, Inc.

FULTON, Kathryn

1299 Pennsylvania Ave. NW
Suite 1100 West
Washington, DC 20004-2407
Tel: (202)637-4000
Fax: (202)637-4066
Registered: LDA

Director, Office of Legislative Affairs, Securities and Exchange Commission, 1991-95.

Employers
GE Capital Corp. (Manager, Government Relations (GE Capital))
General Electric Co. (Manager, Federal Government Relations, GE Capital)

FULTON, Kenneth R.

2101 Constitution Ave. NW
Washington, DC 20418
Tel: (202)334-2000
Fax: (202)334-1684

Employers
Nat'l Academy of Sciences (Exec. Director)

FULTON, Ralph Thomas

4020 Ellicott St.
Alexandria, VA 22304-1012
Tel: (703)845-0487
Registered: LDA

Employers
Big Sky Consulting, Inc. (President)

Clients Represented

On Behalf of Big Sky Consulting, Inc.
Nat'l Fastener Distributors Ass'n

FUMENTO, Michael

1015 18th St. NW
Suite 300
Washington, DC 20036
Tel: (202)223-7770
Fax: (202)223-8537

Employers
Hudson Institute (Senior Fellow)

FUNDERBURK, Hon. David

1735 New York Ave. NW
Suite 500
Washington, DC 20006-4759
EMail: david@prestongates.com
Tel: (202)628-1700
Fax: (202)331-1024
Registered: LDA

Member, U.S. House of Representatives (R-NC), 1995-97. U.S. Ambassador to Romania, Department of State, 1981-85

Employers
Preston Gates Ellis & Rouvelas Meeds LLP (Government Affairs Counselor)

Clients Represented

On Behalf of Preston Gates Ellis & Rouvelas Meeds LLP
Americans for Computer Privacy
Chitimacha Tribe of Louisiana
eLottery, Inc.
Future of Puerto Rico Inc.
Magazine Publishers of America
Nat'l Center for Economic Freedom, Inc.
Nat'l Produce Production Inc.
VoiceStream Wireless Corp.
Voor Huisen Project Mgmt. Serv. Bedryt B.V., Ltd.

FUNDERBURK, Tripp

1401 K St. NW
Suite 400
Washington, DC 20005
Tel: (202)789-2111
Fax: (202)789-4883
Registered: LDA
EMail: trippf@thewashingtongroup.com

Employers
The Washington Group (Director, Policy)

Clients Represented
On Behalf of The Washington Group
American Hospital Ass'n
AT&T
BD
IVAX Corp.
Korea Information & Communication, Ltd.
Microsoft Corp.
News Corporation Ltd.
SAMPCO Companies
Texas Municipal Power Agency

FUNK, Karen J.

2120 L St. NW
Suite 700
Washington, DC 20037
Tel: (202)822-8282
Fax: (202)296-8834
Registered: LDA
EMail: kfunk@hsdwdc.com

Employers
Hobbs, Straus, Dean and Walker, LLP (Legislative Affairs Specialist)

Clients Represented
On Behalf of Hobbs, Straus, Dean and Walker, LLP
Alamo Navajo School Board
Alaska Native Health Board
Black Mesa Community School Board
Bristol Bay Area Health Corp.
Choctaw Indians, Mississippi Band of
Maniilaq Ass'n
Menominee Indian Tribe
Metlakatla Indian Community
Miccosukee Tribe of Indians of Florida
Nat'l Indian Child Welfare Ass'n
Pinon Community School Board
Rock Point Community School
Rough Rock Community School
Seldovia Native Ass'n, Inc.
Seminole Tribe of Indians of Florida
Shiprock Alternative Schools, Inc.
Shoalwater Bay Indian Tribe
St. Regis Mohawk Tribe
Susanville Indian Rancheria
Three Affiliated Tribes of Fort Berthold Reservation
United Tribes Technical College

FUNK, Robert E.

1775 K St. NW
Washington, DC 20006
Tel: (202)223-3111
Fax: (202)466-1562

Employers
United Food and Commercial Workers Internat'l Union (General Counsel)

FURA, Shannon

1300 Pennsylvania Ave. NW
Suite 400
Ronald Reagan Bldg.
Washington, DC 20004
Tel: (202)638-2230
Fax: (202)638-2236
Registered: LDA
Former Assistant to the Director of Consular Affairs, Department of State.

Employers
Sandler, Travis & Rosenberg, P.A. (Trade Advisor)

Clients Represented
On Behalf of Sandler, Travis & Rosenberg, P.A.
Babcock & Wilcox
Commercial Services Internat'l

FURCHTGOTT-ROTH, Diana

1150 17th St. NW
Washington, DC 20036
Tel: (202)862-5800
Fax: (202)862-7177
EMail: afr@aei.org

Employers
American Enterprise Institute for Public Policy Research (Resident Fellow)

FURMAN, II, Harold W.

1401 K St. NW
Suite 450
Washington, DC 20005
Tel: (202)737-0700
Fax: (202)737-0455
EMail: hwfurman@furmangroup.com
Former Deputy Assistant Secretary of Interior for Water and Science.

Employers
The Furman Group (Chief Exec. Officer/President)

FURMAN, Pamela J.

1400 16th St. NW
Suite 400
Washington, DC 20036-2220
Tel: (202)518-6367
Fax: (202)234-0399
Registered: LDA
EMail: pfurman@ofwlaw.com

Employers
Olsson, Frank and Weeda, P.C. (Principal)

Clients Represented
On Behalf of Olsson, Frank and Weeda, P.C.
American Academy of Audiology
Ass'n of Medical Device Reprocessors
Nat'l Ass'n of Pharmaceutical Manufacturers

FURUYA, Toshihiko

1901 L St. NW
Suite 720
Washington, DC 20036
Tel: (202)457-0790
Fax: (202)457-0810

Employers
The Tokyo Electric Power Company, Inc. (General Manager and Director)

FUSILIER, VeTalle

1211 Connecticut Ave. NW
Suite 608
Washington, DC 20036
Tel: (202)496-1000
Fax: (202)496-1300
EMail: vfusilier@qorvis.com

Employers
Qorvis Communications (Managing Director)

FUSS, Wendy Smith

12500 Fair Lakes Circle
Suite 375
Fairfax, VA 22033
Tel: (703)502-1550
Fax: (703)502-7852
Registered: LDA

Employers
American Soc. for Therapeutic Radiology and Oncology (Director, Healthcare Policy)

FUTRELL, J. William

1616 P St. NW
Suite 200
Washington, DC 20036
Tel: (202)939-3800
Fax: (202)939-3868

Employers
Environmental Law Institute (President)

FYFFE, Kathleen

1201 F St. NW
Suite 500
Washington, DC 20004
Tel: (202)824-1600
Fax: (202)824-1651
Registered: LDA

Employers
Health Insurance Ass'n of America (Federal Regulatory Director)

GABA, Michael M.

2099 Pennsylvania Ave. NW
Suite 100
Washington, DC 20006
Tel: (202)955-3000
Fax: (202)955-5564
Registered: LDA
EMail: mgaba@hklaw.com

Employers
Holland & Knight LLP (Partner)

GABAUER, Peter

1130 17th St. NW
Washington, DC 20036-4677
Tel: (202)463-2615
Fax: (202)463-3257
Registered: LDA
EMail: pgabauer@nma.org

Employers
Nat'l Mining Ass'n (Deputy General Counsel)

GABELNICK, Tamar

307 Massachusetts Ave. NE
Washington, DC 20002
Tel: (202)546-3300
Fax: (202)675-1010
Registered: LDA

Employers
Federation of American Scientists (Editor, Arms Sales Monitor)

GABLE, Melinda D.

303 Pennsylvania Ave. SE
Washington, DC 20003
Tel: (202)543-6850
Fax: (202)543-6853

Employers
Congressional Sportsmen's Foundation (Exec. Director)

GABLE, Wayne E.

655 15th St. NW
Suite 445
Washington, DC 20005
Tel: (202)737-1977

Employers
Koch Industries, Inc. (Managing Director, Federal Affairs)

GABRIEL, Anthony

1300 L St. NW
Suite 825
Washington, DC 20005
Tel: (202)289-8335
Fax: (202)842-4439

Employers
Nat'l Ass'n of Urban Bankers, Inc. (Acting Exec. Director)

GABRIEL, USAF (Ret.), Gen. Charles A.

10640 Main St.
Suite 200
Fairfax, VA 22030
Tel: (703)352-3400
Fax: (703)385-6470

Employers
JGW Internat'l Ltd.

GACKENBACH, Julie Leigh

444 N. Capitol St. NW
Suite 801
Washington, DC 20001
Tel: (202)639-0490
Fax: (202)639-0494
Registered: LDA

Employers
Nat'l Ass'n of Independent Insurers (Director, Government Relations)

GADBAW, R. Michael

1299 Pennsylvania Ave. NW
Suite 1100 West
Washington, DC 20004-2407
Tel: (202)637-4000
Fax: (202)637-4300
Registered: LDA

Employers
General Electric Co. (V. President and Senior Counsel, International Law and Policy)

GADDY, Clifford

1775 Massachusetts Ave. NW
Washington, DC 20036-2188
Tel: (202)797-6000
Fax: (202)797-6004

Employers
The Brookings Institution (Fellow, Foreign Policy Studies)

GADSBY, William

1120 G St. NW
Suite 850
Washington, DC 20005
Tel: (202)347-3190
Fax: (202)393-0993
EMail: wgadsby@napawash.org

Employers
Nat'l Academy of Public Administration (Director, Management Studies)

GAFF, Jerry

1818 R St. NW
Washington, DC 20009
Tel: (202)387-3760
Fax: (202)265-9532

Employers
Ass'n of American Colleges and Universities (V. President, Education and Institutional Renewal)

GAFFNEY, Jr., Frank J.

1920 L St. NW
Suite 210
Washington, DC 20036
Tel: (202)835-9077
Fax: (202)835-9066
EMail: info@security-policy.org

Employers
Center for Security Policy (President and C.E.O.)

GAFFNEY-CAMPANELLA, Susan

1750 K St. NW
Suite 350
Washington, DC 20006
Tel: (202)429-2750
Fax: (202)429-2755
EMail: sgaffney-campanella@gfoa.org

Employers
Government Finance Officers Ass'n, Federal Liaison Center (Director, Federal Liaison Center)

GAGE, Alexander P.

1199 N. Fairfax St.
Suite 400
Alexandria, VA 22314
Tel: (703)535-8505
Fax: (703)535-8517

Employers
Market Strategies Inc. (President)

GAGE, Kit

3321 12th St. NE
Third Floor
Washington, DC 20017
Tel: (202)529-4225
Fax: (202)526-4611

Employers
Nat'l Committee Against Repressive Legislation (Washington Representative)

GAGE, Larry S.

1001 Pennsylvania Ave. NW
Suite 600
Washington, DC 20004
Tel: (202)347-0066
Fax: (202)624-7222

Employers
Powell, Goldstein, Frazer & Murphy LLP (Partner)

GAGER, William C.

4401 Fair Lakes Ct.
Suite 210
Fairfax, VA 22033-3848
Tel: (703)968-2772
Fax: (703)968-2878
Registered: LDA
EMail: gager@BuyReman.com

Employers
Automotive Parts Rebuilders Ass'n (President)

GAGLIARDI, Tiffany

1850 M St. NW
Suite 550
Washington, DC 20036
Tel: (202)289-5900
Fax: (202)289-4141
Registered: LDA

Employers
Chlopak, Leonard, Schechter and Associates

Clients Represented

On Behalf of Chlopak, Leonard, Schechter and Associates
Hyundai Electronics Industries Co., LTD
Wilkie Farr & Gallagher

GAIBLER, Floyd D.

1156 15th St. NW
Suite 302
Washington, DC 20005
Tel: (202)457-0825
Fax: (202)457-0864
Registered: LDA

Employers
Agricultural Retailers Ass'n (V. President, Government Affairs)
North American Equipment Dealers Ass'n (Legislative Director)

GAINE, John G.

2025 M St. NW
Suite 800
Washington, DC 20036
Tel: (202)367-2100
Fax: (202)367-1200
Registered: LDA
EMail: john_gaine@dc.sba.com

Employers
Smith, Bucklin and Associates, Inc.

Clients Represented

On Behalf of Smith, Bucklin and Associates, Inc.
Managed Funds Ass'n

GAINER, Ronald L.

1920 N St. NW
Suite 250
Washington, DC 20036
Tel: (202)408-8000
Fax: (202)408-0888
Director, Penal Law Reform Project (1989); Deputy Associate Attorney General (1986-88, 1983-85); Associate Deputy Attorney General (1985-86); Deputy Assistant Attorney General, Office of Legal Policy (1981-83); Deputy Assistant Attorney General, Office for Improvements in the Administration of Justice (1977-81); Director (1976-77) and Deputy Director (1975-76), Office of Policy and Planning; Chief (1974-75) and Deputy Chief (1969-73), Legislation and Special Projects Section, Criminal Division; and Appellate Attorney, Criminal Division (1963-69), Department of Justice.

Employers
Gainer & Rient (Partner)

GAINES, Kristi

740 15th St. NW
Ninth Floor
Washington, DC 20005
Tel: (202)662-1763
Fax: (202)662-1762
Registered: LDA

Employers
American Bar Ass'n (Legislative Counsel)

GAINES, Robert A.

1000 Connecticut Ave. NW
Suite 302
Washington, DC 20036
Tel: (202)835-0740
Fax: (202)775-8526
Registered: LDA, FARA
EMail: bobg@sda-inc.com

Employers
Smith Dawson & Andrews, Inc.

Clients Represented

On Behalf of Smith Dawson & Andrews, Inc.
Fontana, California, City of
Upland, California, City of

GALANO, Mike

2099 Pennsylvania Ave. NW
Suite 100
Washington, DC 20006
Tel: (202)955-3000
Fax: (202)955-5564
Registered: LDA
EMail: mgalano@hklaw.com

Employers
Holland & Knight LLP (Legislative Assistant)

Clients Represented

On Behalf of Holland & Knight LLP
American Chemistry Council
DuPont
FMC Corp.
S.C. Johnson and Son, Inc.
Mille Lacs Band of Ojibwe Indians
Murphy Oil U.S.A.
Nassau County Health Care Corp.
Nat'l Paint and Coatings Ass'n
Placer, California, County of
Rockdale, Georgia, County of, Board of Commissioners of
Somerville Housing Group
Water Systems Council

GALBRAITH, J. Alan

725 12th St. NW
Washington, DC 20005
Tel: (202)434-5000
Fax: (202)434-5029

Employers
Williams & Connolly (Partner)

Clients Represented

On Behalf of Williams & Connolly
Internat'l Truck and Engine Corp.

GALBRAITH, Suellen

4200 Evergreen Ln.
Suite 315
Annandale, VA 22003
Tel: (703)642-6614
Fax: (703)642-0497
Registered: LDA
EMail: suellenancor@radix.net

Employers
American Network of Community Options and Resources (ANCOR) (Director, Public Policy)

GALE, Michael R.

801 Pennsylvania Ave. NW
Suite 640
Washington, DC 20004
Tel: (202)737-3800
Fax: (202)393-1004
Acting Assistant Secretary of Commerce for Legislative and Intergovernmental Affairs, and Deputy Assistant for Legal Affairs, 1989-82.

Employers
Warnaco, Inc. (V. President, International Trade and Government Relations)

GALE, William

1775 Massachusetts Ave. NW
Washington, DC 20036-2188
Tel: (202)797-6000
Fax: (202)797-6004
Former Senior Staff Economist, President's Council of Economic Advisers, 1991-92.

Employers
The Brookings Institution (Senior Fellow, Economic Studies)

GALEN, Christopher

2101 Wilson Blvd.
Suite 400
Arlington, VA 22201
Tel: (703)243-6111
Fax: (703)841-9328
EMail: cgalen@nmpf.org

Employers
Nat'l Milk Producers Federation (V. President, Communications)

GALEY, Shannon

700 13th St. NW
Suite 400
Washington, DC 20005
Tel: (202)347-0773
Fax: (202)347-0785
EMail: sgaley@cassidy.com

Employers
Cassidy & Associates, Inc. (Account Executive)

GALIHER-OTT, Kathleen

1001 19th St. North
Suite 800
Arlington, VA 22209-3901
Tel: (703)276-5016
Fax: (703)276-5057
Registered: LDA
EMail: kathy.ott@trw.com

Employers
TRW Inc. (Director, Government Relations)

GALLAGHER, Christopher R.

1640 Wisconsin Ave. NW
Washington, DC 20007
Tel: (202)337-2701
Fax: (202)337-4271
Registered: LDA
EMail: cgallagher@facs.org

Employers
American College of Surgeons (Senior Government Affairs Associate)

GALLAGHER, Cristy

400 N. Capitol St. NW
Suite 376
Washington, DC 20001
Tel: (202)624-7720
Fax: (202)624-5855
EMail: cgallagher@sso.org

Employers
Missouri, Washington Office of the State of (Director, Washington Office)

GALLAGHER, Edward G.

1101 Connecticut Ave. NW
Suite 800
Washington, DC 20036
Tel: (202)463-0600
Fax: (202)463-0606

Employers
Surety Ass'n of America (General Counsel)

GALLAGHER, Henry

517 Second St. NE
Washington, DC 20002
Tel: (202)543-3744
Fax: (202)543-3509
Registered: LDA

Employers
David Turch & Associates (Associate)

Clients Represented

On Behalf of David Turch & Associates
Rialto, California, City of
San Bernardino, California, County of

GALLAGHER, James L.

1133 Connecticut Ave. NW
Suite 1200
Washington, DC 20036
Tel: (202)775-9800
Fax: (202)833-8491

Employers
Winthrop, Stimson, Putnam & Roberts (Associate)

GALLAGHER, James P.

1800 N. Kent St.
Suite 907
Arlington, VA 22209
Tel: (703)527-1135
Fax: (703)524-1005
Registered: LDA

Administrative Assistant (1994-95) and Legislative Director (1993-94) to Senator Judd Gregg (R-NH). Director of Congressional Affairs, Defense Base Closure and Realignment Commission, 1991-93.

Employers
The Gallagher Group, LLC

Clients Represented
On Behalf of The Gallagher Group, LLC
American Automar
Commonwealth Consulting Corp.
General Dynamics Corp.
NoFire Technologies, Inc.

GALLAGHER, John

2120 Washington Blvd.
Suite 200
Arlington, VA 22204
Tel: (703)920-7070
Fax: (703)920-7177

Employers
Designers & Planners, Inc. (President)

GALLAGHER, Linda Parke

715 E. Capitol St. SE
Washington, DC 20003
Tel: (202)544-9489
Fax: (202)544-9490

Employers
Linda Parke Gallagher & Assoc. (President)

Clients Represented
On Behalf of Linda Parke Gallagher & Assoc.
Affordable Housing Preservation Center
Multi-Family Housing Institute
Nat'l Corp. for Housing Partnerships, Inc. (NCHP)

GALLAGHER, Lynn M.

3000 K St. NW
Suite 300
Washington, DC 20007
Tel: (202)424-7500
Fax: (202)424-7643

Employers
Swidler Berlin Shereff Friedman, LLP (Counsel)

GALLAGHER, Mark J.

3211 Fourth St. NE
Washington, DC 20017
Tel: (202)541-3142
Fax: (202)541-3313

Employers
United States Catholic Conference (Associate Director, Government Liaison)

GALLAGHER, Steve

2201 Cooperative Way
Third Floor
Herndon, VA 22071
Tel: (703)904-7100
Fax: (703)904-7942
Registered: LDA

Employers
Nat'l Ass'n of Industrial and Office Properties (Assistant V. President, State and Local Affairs)

GALLAGHER, Steven G.

601 Pennsylvania Ave. NW
Suite 700
Washington, DC 20004-2676
EMail: gallaghers@adr.org
Tel: (202)737-1460
Fax: (202)737-2418

Employers
American Arbitration Ass'n (Senior V. President)

GALLANT, Gary

3000 K St. NW
Suite 300
Washington, DC 20007
Tel: (202)424-7500
Fax: (202)424-7643
Registered: LDA

Chief of Staff (1997-98), Press Secretary (1995-98) and District Representative (1989-95) to Rep. Jim Saxton (R-NJ). Senior Counsel, Joint Economic Committee, U.S. Congress, 1995-97.

Employers
Swidler Berlin Shereff Friedman, LLP (Associate)

Clients Represented
On Behalf of Swidler Berlin Shereff Friedman, LLP
Ry Cooder
Florida Power and Light Co.
Merrill Lynch & Co., Inc.
Newman & Associates
Niagara Mohawk Power Corp.
Schering Corp.
Transkaryotic Therapies Inc.

GALLANT, Karl

9506 Gauge Dr.
Fairfax Station, VA 22039
Tel: (703)690-4450
Fax: (703)690-4451

Employers
Gallant Co. (President)

Clients Represented
On Behalf of Gallant Co.
Alexander Strategy Group
Salem Communications Corp.

GALLANT, Louis E.

808 17th St. NW
Suite 410
Washington, DC 20006
Tel: (202)293-0090
Fax: (202)293-1250

Employers
Nat'l Ass'n of State Alcohol and Drug Abuse Directors (NASADAD) (Exec. Director)

GALLAS, Philip

1300 Pennsylvania Ave. NW
Suite 400
Ronald Reagan Bldg.
Washington, DC 20004
Tel: (202)638-2230
Fax: (202)638-2236
Registered: LDA

Former Attorney, Office of Antidumping Compliance, International Trade Administration, Department of Commerce. Former Attorney, Office of Regulations and Rulings, U.S. Customs Service, Department of the Treasury.

Employers
Sandler, Travis & Rosenberg, P.A. (Member)

Clients Represented
On Behalf of Sandler, Travis & Rosenberg, P.A.
Tailored Clothing Ass'n

GALLEGOS, Gilbert G.

309 Massachusetts Ave. NE
Washington, DC 20002
EMail: natlfop@wizard.net
Tel: (202)547-8189
Fax: (202)547-8190
Registered: LDA

Employers
Fraternal Order of Police (National President)

GALLUBO, Gary

2200 Claredon Blvd.
Suite 1401
Arlington, VA 22201
Tel: (703)465-2700

Employers
Nat'l Board for Professional Teaching Standards (NBPTS) (V. President)

GALLUP, David

1012 14th St. NW
Suite 1106
Washington, DC 20005
Tel: (202)638-2662
Fax: (202)638-0638

Employers
World Government of World Citizens (President, Administration)
World Service Authority (President)

GALPER, Harvey

2001 M St. NW
Fourth Floor
Washington, DC 20036
Tel: (202)533-5660
Fax: (202)533-8580

Former Director, Office of Tax Analysis, Department of the Treasury.

Employers
Barents Group LLC (Managing Director)

GALSTER, Geoff

1250 I St. NW
Suite 500
Washington, DC 20005
EMail: ggalster@anla.org
Tel: (202)789-2900
Ext: 3015
Fax: (202)789-1893

Employers
American Nursery and Landscape Ass'n (Director, Regulatory Affairs)
Wholesale Nursery Growers of America (Administrator)

GALVAN, Gail

2001 M St. NW
Washington, DC 20036
Tel: (202)467-3000
Fax: (202)533-8500
Registered: LDA

Employers
KPMG, LLP

Clients Represented
On Behalf of KPMG, LLP
The KPMG FSC Coalition
Sara Lee Corp.

GALVIN, E. William

1830 Connecticut Ave. NW
Washington, DC 20009
Tel: (202)483-2220
Fax: (202)483-1246
Registered: LDA

Employers
Center on Conscience and War/NISBCO

GALVIN, Jane

1310 G St. NW
12th Floor
Washington, DC 20005
Tel: (202)626-4780
Fax: (202)626-4833

Employers
Blue Cross Blue Shield Ass'n (Senior Regulatory Consultant)

GALVIN, Roger

2111 Eisenhower Ave.
Alexandria, VA 22314-4698
EMail: rgalvin.nspi.org
Tel: (703)838-0083
Fax: (703)549-0493

Employers
Nat'l Spa and Pool Institute (Chief Exec. Officer)

GAMACHE, Nicole B.

700 N. Fairfax St.
Suite 601
Alexandria, VA 22314
EMail: gamache@rpi.org
Tel: (703)836-2332
Fax: (703)548-0058
Registered: LDA

Employers
Railway Progress Institute (Assistant V. President)

GAMBRELL, Brooke

1300 Pennsylvania Ave. NW
Suite 700
Washington, DC 20004
Registered: LDA

Employers
U.S. Family Network

GAMPEL, Gwen

444 N. Capitol St. NW
Suite 532
Washington, DC 20001
EMail: ccgampel@erols.com
Tel: (202)544-6264
Fax: (202)544-3610
Registered: LDA

Former Professional Staff Member, Subcommittee on Health, House Committee on Ways and Means, 1984-89.

Employers
Congressional Consultants (President)

Clients Represented
On Behalf of Congressional Consultants
Aksys, Ltd.
Alliance Medical Corp.
Dialysis Clinic, Inc.
Nat'l Renal Administrators Ass'n
Renal Leadership Council
Schein Pharmaceutical, Inc.
SterilMed, Inc.
Vanguard Medical Concepts, Inc.

GANDY, Henry M.

2100 Pennsylvania Ave. NW
Suite 500
Washington, DC 20037
Tel: (202)728-1100
Fax: (202)728-1123
Registered: LDA

Former White House liaison officer under President Ronald Reagan; Aide to Rep. Tom Loeffler (R-TX); and Aide to House Minority Whip Trent Lott (R-MS).

Employers
The Duberstein Group, Inc. (V. President)

Clients Represented

On Behalf of The Duberstein Group, Inc.
Amerada Hess Corp.
American Apparel & Footwear Ass'n
American Ass'n of Health Plans (AAHP)
American Council of Life Insurers
American Gaming Ass'n
The American Water Works Co.
AOL Time Warner
The Business Roundtable
Comcast Corp.
Conoco Inc.
CSX Corp.
Direct Marketing Ass'n, Inc.
Dow Corning Corp.
Fannie Mae
General Motors Corp.
Goldman, Sachs and Co.
Marathon Oil Co.
Nat'l Cable Television Ass'n
Pharmacia Corp.
Project to Promote Competition and Innovation in the Digital Age
Sara Lee Corp.
Transportation Institute
United Airlines
USX Corp.

GANDY, Kim A.

733 15th St. NW 2nd Floor
Washington, DC 20005
Tel: (202)628-8669
Fax: (202)785-8576

Employers
Nat'l Organization for Women (Exec. V. President)

GANGLOFF, Deborah

910 17th St. NW
Suite 600
Washington, DC 20006
Tel: (202)955-4500
Fax: (202)955-4588

Employers
American Forests (Exec. Director)

GANGONE, Ed.D., Lynn M.

1325 18th St. NW
Suite 210
Washington, DC 20036
EMail: lgangone@nawe.org
Tel: (202)659-9330
Fax: (202)457-0946

Employers
NAWE: Advancing Women in Higher Education (Exec. Director)

GANNETT, Craig

1500 K St. NW
Suite 450
Washington, DC 20005
Tel: (202)508-6600
Fax: (202)508-6699

Employers
Davis Wright Tremaine LLP

Clients Represented

On Behalf of Davis Wright Tremaine LLP
Ass'n of Oil Pipelines

GANNON, Cheryl

Ten G St. NE
Suite 600
Washington, DC 20002-4215
EMail: gannonc@ncpssm.org
Tel: (202)216-0420
Fax: (202)216-0446
Registered: LDA

Employers
Nat'l Committee to Preserve Social Security and Medicare (Director, Government Relations and Policy)

GANNON, Leo J.

905 16th St. NW
Washington, DC 20006
Tel: (202)783-3545
Fax: (202)347-1721
Registered: LDA

Employers
Laborers-Employers Cooperation & Education Trust (Legislative Director)

GANNON, Richard

1200 G St. NW
Suite 800
Washington, DC 20005
Tel: (202)434-8768
Fax: (202)434-8707
Registered: LDA

Employers
Winning Strategies Washington, D.C., LLC

GANS, Curtis B.

421 New Jersey Ave. SE
Washington, DC 20003
EMail: csnag@erols.com
Tel: (202)546-3221
Fax: (202)546-3571

Employers
Committee for the Study of the American Electorate (Director)

GANS, John A.

2215 Constitution Ave. NW
Washington, DC 20037-2985
Tel: (202)628-4410
Fax: (202)783-2351

Employers
American Pharmaceutical Ass'n (Exec. V. President and Chief Exec. Officer)

GANTER, Mark

3114 Circle Hill Rd.
Alexandria, VA 22305-1606
EMail: info@itctrade.com
Tel: (703)548-1234
Fax: (703)548-6216

Employers
Internat'l Trade Council (Director, Economic Research)

GANZGLASS, Evelyn

444 N. Capitol St. NW
Suite 267
Washington, DC 20001-1512
EMail: eganzglass@nga.org
Tel: (202)624-5394
Fax: (202)624-5313

Employers
Nat'l Governors' Ass'n (Policy Studies Director of Employment and Social Services)

GANZGLASS, Martin

1300 L St. NW
Suite 1200
Washington, DC 20005-4178
Tel: (202)898-1707
Fax: (202)682-9276

Employers
O'Donnell, Schwartz & Anderson, P.C.

GARA, Nicole

950 N. Washington St.
Alexandria, VA 22314-1552
Tel: (703)836-2272
Fax: (703)684-1924

Employers
American Academy of Physician Assistants (V. President, Government and Professional Affairs)

GARAGIOLA, Rob

800 Connecticut Ave. NW
Suite 500
Washington, DC 20006
EMail: garagiolar@gtlaw.com
Tel: (202)331-3110
Fax: (202)261-0110
Registered: LDA

Employers
Greenberg Traurig, LLP (Assistant Director, Government Affairs)

Clients Represented

On Behalf of Greenberg Traurig, LLP
American Health Care Ass'n
American Speech, Language, and Hearing Ass'n
Community Health Systems, Inc.
Fresenius Medical Care North America
LifePoint Hospitals, Inc.
Nat'l Ass'n for the Support of Long Term Care
Nat'l Ass'n of Community Health Centers
Province Healthcare, Inc.

GARAY, Mark

555 12th St. NW
Suite 500
Washington, DC 20004-1207
Tel: (202)879-5600
Fax: (202)879-5309
Registered: LDA

Employers
Deloitte & Touche LLP Nat'l Office - Washington (Manager)

Clients Represented

On Behalf of Deloitte & Touche LLP Nat'l Office - Washington
Liz Robbins Associates

GARBER, Jr., William E.

2600 Virginia Ave. NW
Suite 123
Washington, DC 20037
EMail: bgarber@appraisalinstitute.org
Tel: (202)298-6449
Fax: (202)298-5547
Registered: LDA

Employers
Appraisal Institute (Director, Government Affairs)

GARBINI, Robert A.

900 Spring St.
Silver Spring, MD 20910
Tel: (301)587-1400
Fax: (301)585-4219

Employers
Concrete Plant Manufacturers Bureau (Exec. Secretary)
Nat'l Ready Mixed Concrete Ass'n (President)
Truck Mixer Manufacturers Bureau (Exec. Secretary)

GARBOUSHIAN, Ralph

1401 K St. NW
Suite 700
Washington, DC 20005
Tel: (202)842-5430
Fax: (202)842-5051
Registered: LDA

Employers
Barbara T. McCall Associates (Legislative Assistant)

Clients Represented

On Behalf of Barbara T. McCall Associates
Austin, Texas, City of
Columbia, South Carolina, City of
Dallas, Texas, City of
Denton, Texas, City of
Henderson, Nevada, City of
Huntsville, Alabama, City of
Lubbock, Texas, City of
Plano, Texas, City of

GARCIA, Greg

1201 Pennsylvania Ave. NW
Suite 300
Washington, DC 20004
Tel: (202)661-4608
Fax: (202)661-4618

Employers
3Com Corp. (Director, Global Government Relations)

GARCIA, Isabelle

1201 16th St. NW
Washington, DC 20036
Tel: (202)833-4000
Registered: LDA

Employers
Nat'l Education Ass'n of the U.S. (Senior Professional Associate, Government Relations)

GARCIA, CAE, Lou

801 N. Fairfax St.
Suite 404
Alexandria, VA 22314-1757
Tel: (703)519-3700
Fax: (703)549-4886

Employers
Soc. of Consumer Affairs Professionals in Business (Exec. Director)

GARCIA, Nelson

1211 Connecticut Ave. NW
Suite 400
Washington, DC 20036
Tel: (202)822-8811
Fax: (202)872-1885
Registered: LDA

Employers
Alliance of American Insurers

GARCIA, Hon. Robert

1666 K St. NW
Suite 500
Washington, DC 20006
EMail: garciaasoc@aol.com
Tel: (202)778-2149
Fax: (202)296-6907
Registered: LDA

Member, U.S. House of Representatives (D-NY), 1978-90.

Employers
Robert Garcia and Associates, Inc (Washington Representative)

Clients Represented

On Behalf of Robert Garcia and Associates, Inc

Verizon Communications

GARDEPE, William M,

3190 Fairview Park Dr.
Falls Church, VA 22042
Tel: (703)271-7525
Fax: (703)271-7401
Registered: LDA

Employers

General Dynamics Corp. (Director, Legislative Affairs)

GARDNER, C. Randal

901 Massachusetts Ave. NW
Washington, DC 20001
Tel: (202)628-5823
Fax: (202)628-5024

Employers

United Ass'n of Journeymen and Apprentices of the Plumbing and Pipe Fitting Industry of the U.S. and Canada (Assistant General President)

GARDNER, Courtney C.

1575 I St. NW
Washington, DC 20005-1103
EMail: cgardner@asaenet.org
Tel: (202)626-2734
Fax: (202)371-1673

Employers

American Soc. of Ass'n Executives (Director, Public Relations)

GARDNER, Lori B.

5400 Grosvenor Ln.
Bethesda, MD 20814-2198
EMail: gardnerl@safnat.org
Tel: (301)897-8720
Fax: (301)897-3690

Employers

Soc. of American Foresters (Director, Communications and Member Services)

GARDNER, Marilyn

17904 Georgia Ave.
Suite 215
Olney, MD 20832-2277
Tel: (301)570-2111
Fax: (301)570-2212

Employers

Ass'n for Childhood Education Internat'l (Director, Membership and Marketing)

GARDNER, Mark

1101 Connecticut Ave. NW
Suite 500
Washington, DC 20036
Tel: (202)833-9095
Fax: (202)833-0008

Employers

Nat'l Postal Mail Handlers Union (National Secretary-Treasurer)

GARDNER, Matthew

1311 L St. NW
Fourth Floor
Washington, DC 20005
EMail: mattg@ctj.org
Tel: (202)626-3780
Fax: (202)638-3486

Employers

Citizens for Tax Justice (Analyst)

GARDNER, Michael R.

1150 Connecticut Ave. NW
Suite 710
Washington, DC 20036
EMail: MRGPC@aol.com
Tel: (202)785-2828
Fax: (202)785-1504
Registered: LDA

Employers

Law Offices of Michael R. Gardner, P.C.

Clients Represented

On Behalf of Law Offices of Michael R. Gardner, P.C.

Universal Wireless Communications Consortium

GARDNER, Robert W.

7901 Westpark Dr.
McLean, VA 22102-4206
EMail: rwg@mfgtech.org
Tel: (703)827-5275
Fax: (703)893-1151

Employers

The Ass'n For Manufacturing Technology (AMT) (V. President, Communications)

GARDNER-OUTLAW, Tom

1300 19th St. NW
Second Floor
Washington, DC 20036
Tel: (202)557-3400
Fax: (202)728-4177
Registered: LDA

Employers

Population Action Internat'l (Policy Analyst)

GARFIELD, Robert L.

2000 Corporate Ridge
Suite 1000
McLean, VA 22102
EMail: rgarfield@affi.com
Tel: (703)821-0770
Fax: (703)821-1350
Registered: LDA

Employers

American Frozen Food Institute (Senior V. President, Regulatory and Technical Affairs)
Nat'l Frozen Pizza Institute (Exec. Director)
Nat'l Yogurt Ass'n (V. President, Regulatory and Technical Affairs)

GARFINKEL, Andrew

1299 Pennsylvania Ave. NW
Suite 800 West
Washington, DC 20004
Tel: (202)785-0500
Fax: (202)785-5277
Registered: LDA

Employers

The Carmen Group (Associate)

Clients Represented

On Behalf of The Carmen Group

GELCO Information Network GSD, Inc.

GARFINKEL, Jennifer

1150 17th St. NW
Suite 701
Washington, DC 20036
EMail: jennifer.garfinkel@dittus.com
Tel: (202)775-1401
Fax: (202)775-1404

Employers

Dittus Communications (Director)

Clients Represented

On Behalf of Dittus Communications

American Ass'n of Preferred Provider Organizations
Andrx Pharmaceutical Corp.
Exolve
R - Tech Veno
Uniformed Services Family Health Plan

GARIKES, Margaret

1101 Vermont Ave. NW
12th Floor
Washington, DC 20005-3583
Tel: (202)789-7409
Fax: (202)789-7581
Registered: LDA

Employers

American Medical Ass'n (Director, Federal Affairs)

GARLAND, Kristine

50 S. Picket St.
Suite 110
Alexandria, VA 22304-7206
Tel: (703)823-7234
Fax: (703)823-7237

Employers

Composite Can and Tube Institute (Exec. V. President)

GARLAND, Nancy

1111 N. Fairfax St.
Alexandria, VA 22314
Tel: (703)684-2782
Fax: (703)684-7343
Registered: LDA

Employers

American Physical Therapy Ass'n (Director, Government Affairs)

GARLAND, Sara G.

418 C St. NE
Washington, DC 20002
Tel: (202)547-8530
Fax: (202)547-8532
Registered: LDA
EMail: sarag@mail.greystone-group.com

Former aide to Senator Quentin Burdick (D-ND), and Chief of Staff to Senator Kent Conrad (D-ND).

Employers

Sara Garland (and Associates) (Principal)

Clients Represented

On Behalf of Sara Garland (and Associates)

Ad Hoc Public Television Group
American Indian Higher Education Consortium
Fort Abraham Lincoln Foundation
Minot State University
Oglala Lakota College
Red River Trade Council
Sesame Workshop
Swope Parkway Health Center
Turtle Mountain Community College
University of North Dakota

GARLIKOV, Andrew J.

5810 Kingstowne Center Dr.
Suite 120-740
Alexandria, VA 22315
Tel: (703)921-5070
Fax: (703)921-9217
Registered: FARA

Employers

Pro Advance Inc. (President)

Clients Represented

On Behalf of Pro Advance Inc.

Tai Ji Men Qigong Academy

GARMAN, Cathleen

1200 G St. NW
Suite 510
Washington, DC 20005
EMail: cathleen@csa-dc.org
Tel: (202)347-0600
Fax: (202)347-0608
Registered: LDA

Employers

Contract Services Ass'n of America (V. President, Public Policy)

GARMAN, Susan

1801 K St. NW
Suite 1000L
Washington, DC 20006
EMail: susan_garman@washbm.com
Tel: (202)530-0400
Fax: (202)530-4500

Employers

Burson-Marsteller (Managing Director, Public Affairs Practice)

GARMENT, Suzanne

1150 17th St. NW
Washington, DC 20036
EMail: sgarment@aei.org
Tel: (202)862-5800
Fax: (202)862-7177

Employers

American Enterprise Institute for Public Policy Research (Resident Scholar)

GARNER, Bob

1755 Jefferson Davis Highway
Suite 1101
Arlington, VA 22202
Tel: (703)416-6666
Fax: (703)416-1517
Registered: LDA

Employers

FLIR Systems, Inc.

GAROFALO, Gary B.

1201 Connecticut Ave. NW
Suite 700
Washington, DC 20036
EMail: ggarofalo@bgairlaw.com
Tel: (202)822-9070
Fax: (202)822-9075
Registered: FARA

Staff Attorney, Federal Aviation Administration, 1965-68.

Employers

Boros & Garofalo (Partner)

Clients Represented

On Behalf of Boros & Garofalo

Great Britain, Government of

GARON, Richard J.

901 15th St. NW
Suite 700
Washington, DC 20005-2301
Tel: (202)371-6000
Fax: (202)371-6279

Chief of Staff, House Committee on International Relations, 1995-2001. Republican Chief of Staff, House Committee on Foreign Affairs, 1993-95. Republican Deputy Staff Director, House Committee on Post Office and Civil Service, 1989-92. Administrative Assistant to Rep. Benjamin A. Gilman (R-NY), Minority Staff Consultant, House Committee on Foreign Affairs, 1983-85. Republican Staff Assistant, House Committee on Post Office and Civil Service, 1979-83. Legislative Assistant to Rep. Gilman, 1977-79.

Employers
Verner, Liipfert, Bernhard, McPherson and Hand, Chartered (Senior Advisor, International Relations)

GARRETT, Anthony

1701 K St. NW
Suite 750
Washington, DC 20006
Tel: (202)833-5740
Ext: 102
Fax: (202)833-5745
Registered: LDA

Employers
Self-employed as an independent consultant.

Clients Represented

As an independent consultant
Internews

GARRETT, Debbie

1133 Connecticut Ave. NW
Fifth Floor
Washington, DC 20036
Tel: (202)457-1110
Fax: (202)457-1130

Employers
Quinn Gillespie & Associates (Public Relations Associate)

Clients Represented

On Behalf of Quinn Gillespie & Associates
Coalition to Repeal the Tax on Talking

GARRETT, Harley

1215 Jefferson Davis Hwy.
Suite 307
Arlington, VA 22202
Tel: (703)416-2211
Fax: (703)416-2213

Employers
SCI Systems, Inc. (Manager, Northeast Region)

GARRETT, John C.

2550 M St. NW
Washington, DC 20037-1350
Tel: (202)457-6000
Fax: (202)457-6315
Registered: LDA

Employers
Patton Boggs, LLP (Defense Systems Consultant)

Clients Represented

On Behalf of Patton Boggs, LLP
Syntroleum Corp.

GARRETT, Judith Simon

320 First St. NW
Washington, DC 20534
Tel: (202)514-9663
Fax: (202)514-5935

Employers
Department of Justice - Federal Bureau of Prisons (Chief, Office of Congressional Affairs)

GARRETT, Peter

1825 Connecticut Ave. NW
Suite 650
Washington, DC 20009
EMail: pgarrett@gyhllc.com
Tel: (202)745-5100
Fax: (202)234-6159

Employers
Garrett Yu Hussein LLC (Senior Partner)

GARRETT, Robert A.

555 12th St. NW
Washington, DC 20004-1206
Tel: (202)942-5000
Fax: (202)942-5999
EMail: Robert_Garrett@aporter.com

Counsel, Special Commission on the U.S. Military Academy (Borman Commission), 1976-77. Assistant to the General Counsel, Department of the Army, 1975-76. Law Clerk to Judge John Paul Stevens, U.S. Court of Appeals, Seventh Circuit, 1974.

Employers
Arnold & Porter (Partner)

GARRETT, Steven

909 N. Washington St.
Suite 301
Alexandria, VA 22314
Tel: (703)684-1981
Fax: (703)548-4876

Employers
The Retired Enlisted Ass'n (Legislative Assistant)

GARRETT, Theodore L.

1201 Pennsylvania Ave. NW
Washington, DC 20004-2401
Tel: (202)662-6000
Fax: (202)662-6291
EMail: tgarrett@cov.com

Law Clerk to Chief Justice Warren E. Burger, U.S. Supreme Court, 1970-71 and to Judge J. Joseph Smith, U.S. Court of Appeals, Second Circuit, 1968-69. Special Assistant to Assistant Attorney General, Office of Legal Counsel, Department of Justice, 1969-70.

Employers
Covington & Burling (Partner)

GARRETT-NELSON, LaBrenda

1150 17th St. NW
Suite 601
Washington, DC 20036
Tel: (202)293-7474
Fax: (202)293-8811
Registered: LDA

Senior Legislation Attorney, Joint Committee on Taxation, 1982-87.

Employers
Washington Council Ernst & Young (Partner)

Clients Represented

On Behalf of Washington Council Ernst & Young
Aetna Inc.
Aetna Life & Casualty Co.
Allegiance Healthcare Corp.
Allen & Co.
American Express Co.
American Insurance Ass'n
American Staffing Ass'n
Anheuser-Busch Cos., Inc.
Antitrust Coalition for Consumer Choice in Health Care
Apartment Investment and Management Co.
Ass'n of American Railroads
Ass'n of Home Appliance Manufacturers
AT&T
AT&T Capital Corp.
Avco Financial Services
Aventis Pharmaceuticals, Inc.
Baxter Healthcare Corp.
BHC Communications, Inc.
Bulmer Holding PLC, H. P.
Cash Balance Coalition
Chamber of Shipping of America
Citigroup
Coalition for Fairness in Defense Exports
Coalition to Preserve Tracking Stock
ComEd
The Connell Co.
Deferral Group
Directors Guild of America
Doris Duke Charitable Foundation
Eaton Vance Management Co.
Eden Financial Corp.
The Enterprise Foundation
Fannie Mae
FedEx Corp.
Ford Motor Co.
GE Capital Assurance
General Electric Co.
General Motors Corp.
Global Competitiveness Coalition
Grasslands Water District
Group Health, Inc.
Haz-X Support Services Corp.
HEREIU
Gilbert P. Hyatt, Inventor
Investment Co. Institute
Large Public Power Council
Local Initiatives Support Corp.
Lockheed Martin Corp.
MacAndrews & Forbes Holdings, Inc.
Marsh & McLennan Cos.
MCG Northwest, Inc.
McLane Co.
Merrill Lynch & Co., Inc.
Metropolitan Banking Group
Microsoft Corp.
Nat'l Ass'n for State Farm Agents
Nat'l Ass'n of Professional Employer Organizations
Nat'l Ass'n of Real Estate Investment Trusts
Nat'l Ass'n of State Farm Agents
Nat'l Cable Television Ass'n
Nat'l Defined Contribution Council
Nat'l Foreign Trade Council, Inc.
Nat'l Multi-Housing Council
PaineWebber Group, Inc.
Pfizer, Inc.
R&D Tax Credit Coalition
R&D Tax Regulation Group
Recording Industry Ass'n of America
Reed-Elsevier Inc.
R. J. Reynolds Tobacco Co.
Charles Schwab & Co., Inc.,
Securities Industry Ass'n
Sierra Pacific Industries
Skadden, Arps, Slate, Meagher & Flom LLP
Straddle Rules Tax Group
Tax Fairness Coalition
Tax/Shelter Coalition
TransOceanic Shipping
TU Services
TXU Business Services
U.S. Oncology
USA Biomass Power Producers Alliance
Viaticus, Inc.
Wilkie Farr & Gallagher
Ziff Investors Partnership

GARRIGAN, Lee

1816 Jefferson Place NW
Washington, DC 20036
Tel: (202)833-2672
Fax: (202)833-4657
Registered: LDA
EMail: lgarrigan@amsa-cleanwater.org

Employers
Ass'n of Metropolitan Sewerage Agencies (Manager, Government Affairs)

GARRISON, Charles

1531 T St. NW
Washington, DC 20009
Tel: (202)234-6888
Fax: (202)234-6887
Registered: LDA

Employers
The Garrison Group (Consultant)

Clients Represented

On Behalf of The Garrison Group
Southeast Dairy Farmer Ass'n

GARRISON, David F.

1120 G St. NW
Suite 850
Washington, DC 20005
EMail: dgarrison@napawash.org
Tel: (202)347-3190
Fax: (202)393-0993

Employers
Nat'l Academy of Public Administration (V. President)

GARRISON, Ph.D., Ellen G.

750 First St. NE
Washington, DC 20002-4242
Tel: (202)336-5500
Fax: (202)336-6069
Registered: LDA

Employers
American Psychological Ass'n (Director, Public Interest Policy)

GARRISON, Dr. Howard

9650 Rockville Pike
Bethesda, MD 20814-3998
Tel: (301)571-0657
Fax: (301)571-0686

Employers
Federation of American Societies for Experimental Biology (Director, Office of Public Affairs)

GARRITSON, Dean

1331 Pennsylvania Ave. NW
Sixth Floor
Washington, DC 20004-1790
Tel: (202)637-3050
Fax: (202)637-3182

Employers

Nat'l Ass'n of Manufacturers (V. President, Small and Medium Manufacturers)

GARRO, Dianne B.

500 E St. SW
Eighth Floor
Room 869
Washington, DC 20254-0001
EMail: diane.b.garro@ssa.gov

Tel: (202)358-6086
Fax: (202)358-6074

Employers

Social Security Administration-Office of Legislation and Congressional Affairs (Assistant Deputy Commissioner for Legislative and Congressional Affairs)

GARTLAND, John C.

214 Massachusetts Ave. NE
Suite 210
Washington, DC 20002

Tel: (202)547-5005
Fax: (202)547-3483
Registered: LDA

EMail: John_Gartland@alticor.com

Employers

Alticor, Inc. (Director, Government Affairs)

GARTMAN, Heather

6400 Goldsboro Rd.
Suite 500
Bethesda, MD 20817
EMail: hgartman@epb.com

Tel: (301)263-2309
Fax: (301)263-2269

Employers

Earle Palmer Brown Public Relations (Director, Client Services/Group Director, EPB PR)

GARVIE, Pamela J.

1735 New York Ave. NW
Suite 500
Washington, DC 20006-4759

Tel: (202)628-1700
Fax: (202)331-1024
Registered: LDA, FARA

Chief Counsel, Subcommittees on Aviation, Surface Transportation and Business, Trade and Tourism (1986-87) and Counsel (1981-86), Senate Commerce Committee. Assistant Legislative Counsel, Interstate Commerce Commission, 1978-80. Counsel to Rep. Robert Duncan (D-OR), 1976-78.

Employers

Preston Gates Ellis & Rouvelas Meeds LLP (Partner)

Clients Represented

On Behalf of Preston Gates Ellis & Rouvelas Meeds LLP

Amgen
Brown-Forman Corp.
Burlington Northern Santa Fe Railway
Maryland Department of Transportation
PPL
Prime Time 24
Pulse Medical Instruments
United States Maritime Coalition
VoiceStream Wireless Corp.

GARVIN, June

444 N. Capitol St. NW
Suite 546
Washington, DC 20001

Tel: (202)624-5844
Fax: (202)624-5847

Employers

Ohio, Washington Office of the State of (Director)

GARVIN, Lana

601 Pennsylvania Ave. NW
Suite 1200
North Bldg.
Washington, DC 20036

Tel: (202)638-4170
Fax: (202)638-3670

Employers

Merck & Co. (PAC Administrator)

GARWOOD, Suzanne

3138 N. Tenth St.
Arlington, VA 22201

Tel: (703)522-4770
Fax: (703)522-0594

Employers

Nat'l Ass'n of Federal Credit Unions (Director, Regulatory Affairs)

GARY, W. Bradford

1030 15th St. NW
Suite 1028-A
Washington, DC 20005

Tel: (202)289-6772
Fax: (202)289-7129
Registered: LDA

EMail: gary_brad@allergan.com

Employers

Allergan, Inc. (V. President, Government Affairs)

GARY, Sr., William H.

9815 Godwin Dr.
Manassas, VA 22111

Tel: (703)361-0884
Fax: (703)330-8967

EMail: whgary@aol.com

Employers

NAVCOM Systems, Inc. (V. President, Business Development/Operations)

GARZA, Chris

600 Maryland Ave. SW
Suite 800
Washington, DC 20024

Tel: (202)484-3600
Fax: (202)484-3604

Employers

American Farm Bureau Federation (Assistant Director, Regulatory Affairs)

GASAWAY, Robert R.

655 15th St. NW
Suite 1200
Washington, DC 20005

Tel: (202)879-5000
Fax: (202)879-5200
Registered: LDA

Employers

Kirkland & Ellis (Associate)

Clients Represented

On Behalf of Kirkland & Ellis

Chamber of Commerce of the U.S.A.

General Motors Corp.

GASCON, Sharon

1725 K St. NW
Suite 1212
Washington, DC 20006

Tel: (202)833-8383
Fax: (202)331-7442
Registered: LDA

Employers

Nat'l Ass'n of Water Companies (Deputy Exec. Director)

GASKIN, Lillian B.

740 15th St. NW
Ninth Floor
Washington, DC 20005

Tel: (202)662-1768
Fax: (202)662-1762
Registered: LDA

Employers

American Bar Ass'n (Senior Legislative Counsel)

GASPER, Gary J.

1150 17th St. NW
Suite 601
Washington, DC 20036

Tel: (202)293-7474
Fax: (202)293-8811
Registered: LDA

Senior Tax Advisor (1991-93) and Assistant to the Commissioner, Internal Revenue Service (1989-91), Department of the Treaury. Attorney/Advisor, U.S. Tax Court, 1983-84.

Employers

Washington Council Ernst & Young (Partner)

Clients Represented

On Behalf of Washington Council Ernst & Young

Aetna Inc.
Aetna Life & Casualty Co.
Allegiance Healthcare Corp.
Allen & Co.
American Express Co.
American Insurance Ass'n
American Staffing Ass'n
Anheuser-Busch Cos., Inc.
Antitrust Coalition for Consumer Choice in Health Care
Apartment Investment and Management Co.
Ass'n of American Railroads
Ass'n of Home Appliance Manufacturers
AT&T
AT&T Capital Corp.
Avco Financial Services
Aventis Pharmaceuticals, Inc.
Baxter Healthcare Corp.
BHC Communications, Inc.
Bulmer Holding PLC, H. P.
Cash Balance Coalition
Chamber of Shipping of America
Citigroup
Coalition for Fairness in Defense Exports
Coalition to Preserve Tracking Stock
ComEd
The Connell Co.
Deferral Group
Directors Guild of America
Doris Duke Charitable Foundation
Eaton Vance Management Co.
Eden Financial Corp.
The Enterprise Foundation
Fannie Mae
FedEx Corp.
Ford Motor Co.
GE Capital Assurance
General Electric Co.
General Motors Corp.
Global Competitiveness Coalition
Grasslands Water District
Group Health, Inc.
Haz-X Support Services Corp.
HEREIU
Gilbert P. Hyatt, Inventor
Investment Co. Institute
Large Public Power Council
Local Initiatives Support Corp.
Lockheed Martin Corp.
MacAndrews & Forbes Holdings, Inc.
Marsh & McLennan Cos.
MCG Northwest, Inc.
McLane Co.
Merrill Lynch & Co., Inc.
Metropolitan Banking Group
Microsoft Corp.
Nat'l Ass'n for State Farm Agents
Nat'l Ass'n of Professional Employer Organizations
Nat'l Ass'n of Real Estate Investment Trusts
Nat'l Ass'n of State Farm Agents
Nat'l Cable Television Ass'n
Nat'l Defined Contribution Council
Nat'l Foreign Trade Council, Inc.
Nat'l Multi-Housing Council
PaineWebber Group, Inc.
Pfizer, Inc.
R&D Tax Credit Coalition
R&D Tax Regulation Group
Recording Industry Ass'n of America
Reed-Elsevier Inc.
R. J. Reynolds Tobacco Co.
Charles Schwab & Co., Inc.,
Securities Industry Ass'n
Sierra Pacific Industries
Skadden, Arps, Slate, Meagher & Flom LLP
Straddle Rules Tax Group
Tax Fairness Coalition
Tax/Shelter Coalition
TransOceanic Shipping
TU Services
TXU Business Services
U.S. Oncology
USA Biomass Power Producers Alliance
Viaticus, Inc.
Wilkie Farr & Gallagher
Ziff Investors Partnership

GASQUE, Henry

535 Herndon Pkwy.
Herndon, VA 22070-4370

Tel: (703)481-4456
Fax: (703)689-4370

Employers

Air Line Pilots Ass'n Internat'l (Manager, Communications)

GASSTER, Elizabeth

1120 20th St. NW
Suite 1000
Washington, DC 20036

Tel: (202)457-2081
Fax: (202)457-2267
Registered: LDA

EMail: egasster@att.com

Employers
AT&T (Director, Federal Government Affairs)

GAST, Lisa S.

1615 M St. NW
Suite 800
Washington, DC 20036-3203
EMail: lsg@dwgp.com
Tel: (202)467-6370
Fax: (202)467-6379

Employers
Duncan, Weinberg, Genzer & Pembroke, P.C. (Associate)

GASTON, Beth

1400 Independence Ave. SW
Room 1180-S
Washington, DC 20250
Tel: (202)720-9113
Fax: (202)720-5704

Employers
Department of Agriculture - Food Safety and Inspection Service (Chief Press Officer, Congressional and Public Affairs Staff)

GASTON, Carole

1101 17th St. NW
Eighth Floor
Washington, DC 20036
Tel: (202)463-8880
Fax: (202)833-3584
Communications Committee for the Republican National Committee, 1984-94; Finance Committee for the 50th Presidential Inaugural.

Employers
Bonner & Associates (V. President)

GASTON, Patrick G.

1300 I St. NW
Suite 400 West
Washington, DC 20005
Tel: (202)515-2520
Fax: (202)336-7925

Employers
Verizon Communications (Exec. Director, Strategic Alliances)

GASTWIRTH, DPM, Glenn B.

9312 Old Georgetown Rd.
Bethesda, MD 20814-1621
EMail: gbgastwirth@apma.org
Tel: (301)571-9200
Fax: (301)530-2752

Employers
American Podiatric Medical Ass'n (Exec. Director)

GATES, Bruce A.

1150 17th St. NW
Suite 601
Washington, DC 20036
Tel: (202)293-7474
Fax: (202)293-8811
Registered: LDA
Former Legislative Assistant to Rep. Carroll A. Campbell, Jr. (R-SC).

Employers
Health Benefits Coalition (Exec. Director)
Washington Council Ernst & Young (Partner)

Clients Represented
On Behalf of Washington Council Ernst & Young
Aetna Inc.
Aetna Life & Casualty Co.
Allegiance Healthcare Corp.
Allen & Co.
American Express Co.
American Insurance Ass'n
American Staffing Ass'n
Anheuser-Busch Cos., Inc.
Antitrust Coalition for Consumer Choice in Health Care
Apartment Investment and Management Co.
Ass'n of American Railroads
Ass'n of Home Appliance Manufacturers
AT&T
AT&T Capital Corp.
Avco Financial Services
Aventis Pharmaceuticals, Inc.
Baxter Healthcare Corp.
BHC Communications, Inc.
Bulmer Holding PLC, H. P.
Cash Balance Coalition
Chamber of Shipping of America
Citigroup
Coalition for Fairness in Defense Exports
Coalition to Preserve Tracking Stock
ComEd
The Connell Co.
Deferral Group
Directors Guild of America
Doris Duke Charitable Foundation
Eaton Vance Management Co.
Eden Financial Corp.
The Enterprise Foundation
Fannie Mae
FedEx Corp.
Ford Motor Co.
GE Capital Assurance
General Electric Co.
General Motors Corp.
Global Competitiveness Coalition
Grasslands Water District
Group Health, Inc.
Haz-X Support Services Corp.
Health Benefits Coalition
Gilbert P. Hyatt, Inventor
Investment Co. Institute
Large Public Power Council
Local Initiatives Support Corp.
Lockheed Martin Corp.
MacAndrews & Forbes Holdings, Inc.
Marsh & McLennan Cos.
MCG Northwest, Inc.
McLane Co.
Merrill Lynch & Co., Inc.
Metropolitan Banking Group
Microsoft Corp.
Nat'l Ass'n for State Farm Agents
Nat'l Ass'n of Professional Employer Organizations
Nat'l Ass'n of Real Estate Investment Trusts
Nat'l Ass'n of State Farm Agents
Nat'l Cable Television Ass'n
Nat'l Defined Contribution Council
Nat'l Foreign Trade Council, Inc.
Nat'l Multi-Housing Council
PaineWebber Group, Inc.
Pfizer, Inc.
R&D Tax Credit Coalition
R&D Tax Regulation Group
Recording Industry Ass'n of America
Reed-Elsevier Inc.
R. J. Reynolds Tobacco Co.
Charles Schwab & Co., Inc.,
Securities Industry Ass'n
Sierra Pacific Industries
Skadden, Arps, Slate, Meagher & Flom LLP
Straddle Rules Tax Group
Tax Fairness Coalition
Tax/Shelter Coalition
TransOceanic Shipping
TU Services
TXU Business Services
U.S. Oncology
USA Biomass Power Producers Alliance
Viaticus, Inc.
Wilkie Farr & Gallagher
Ziff Investors Partnership

GATI, Toby T.

1333 New Hampshire Ave. NW
Suite 400
Washington, DC 20036
Tel: (202)887-4000
Fax: (202)887-4288
Registered: LDA

Employers
Akin, Gump, Strauss, Hauer & Feld, L.L.P.

Clients Represented
On Behalf of Akin, Gump, Strauss, Hauer & Feld, L.L.P.
Tyumen Oil Company

GATTI, Michael

325 Seventh St. NW
Suite 1100
Washington, DC 20004-2802
Tel: (202)783-7971
Fax: (202)737-2849

Employers
Nat'l Retail Federation (V. President, Marketing and Public Relations)

GATTI, Peter

1700 N. Moore St.
Suite 1900
Arlington, VA 22209-1904
EMail: gatti@nitl.org
Tel: (703)524-5011
Fax: (703)524-5017
Registered: LDA

Employers
Nat'l Industrial Transportation League (Director of Policy)

GATTUSO, James

1001 Connecticut Ave. NW
Suite 1250
Washington, DC 20036
Tel: (202)331-1010
Fax: (202)331-0640

Employers
Competitive Enterprise Institute (V. President for Policy and Management)

GAUCLETTE, Eugene

1300 Pennsylvania Ave. NW
Suite 700
Washington, DC 20004
Registered: LDA

Employers
Curson Koopersmith Partners, Inc. (Principal)

Clients Represented
On Behalf of Curson Koopersmith Partners, Inc.
Internet Action PAC

GAUDETTE, Sylvia

1140 Connecticut Ave. NW
Suite 1050
Washington, DC 20036
Tel: (202)331-5790
Fax: (202)331-9334

Employers
American Health Quality Ass'n (Director, Government Relations)

GAUDINO, Dr. James L.

1765 N St. NW
Washington, DC 20036
EMail: jgaudino@scassn.org
Tel: (202)464-4622
Fax: (202)464-4600

Employers
Nat'l Communication Ass'n (Exec. Director)

GAUGLER, Tiki

888 17th St. NW
Suite 900
Washington, DC 20006
Tel: (202)969-2587
Fax: (202)969-2581

Employers
Ass'n for Local Telecommunications Services (Senior Attorney)

GAUJACQ, Catherine

1730 Rhode Island Ave. NW
Suite 509
Washington, DC 20036
EMail: cgaujacq@edfina.com
Tel: (202)429-2527
Fax: (202)429-2532

Employers
Electricite de France Internat'l North America, Inc. (President)

GAULT, Polly L.

555 Twelfth St. NW
Suite 640
Washington, DC 20004
Tel: (202)393-3075
Fax: (202)393-1497
Registered: LDA

Employers
Edison Internat'l (V. President, Washington Region)

GAUVIN, Charles F.

1500 Wilson Blvd.
Suite 310
Arlington, VA 22209
Tel: (703)522-0200
Fax: (703)284-9400

Employers
Trout Unlimited (President and Chief Exec. Officer)

GAVILAN, Horacio

8201 Greensboro Dr.
Suite 300
McLean, VA 22102
Tel: (703)610-9000
Fax: (703)610-9005

Employers
Ass'n Management Group

Clients Represented
On Behalf of Ass'n Management Group
Ass'n of Hispanic Advertising Agencies

GAVIN, Anne

444 N. Capitol St. NW
Suite 400
Washington, DC 20001
Tel: (202)624-7713
Fax: (202)624-7714

Employers
Massachusetts, Commonwealth of (Director, Office of Federal-State Relations)

GAVIN, III, Joseph G.

1030 15th St. NW
Suite 800
Washington, DC 20005
EMail: jgavin@uscib-dc.org
Tel: (202)371-1316
Fax: (202)371-8249

Employers
United States Council for Internat'l Business (V. President, Trade Policy)

GAVIN, Stephen Diaz

2550 M St. NW
Washington, DC 20037-1350
EMail: sgavin@pattonboggs.com
Tel: (202)457-6000
Fax: (202)457-6315
Registered: LDA

Employers
Patton Boggs, LLP (Partner)

Clients Represented
On Behalf of Patton Boggs, LLP
BET Holdings II, Inc.
Commco, L.L.C.
IVIDCO, LLC
Nassau Broadcasting Inc.

GAVORA, Carrie J.

1001 Pennsylvania Ave. NW
Suite 760 North
Washington, DC 20004
Tel: (202)661-7060
Fax: (202)661-7066
Republican Staff Member, House Committee on Commerce, 1999-2001. Former Aide to Senator Frank Murkowski (R-AK) and Staff Member, Senate Committee on Veterans' Affairs.

Employers
The Legislative Strategies Group, LLC (Health Policy Analyst)

GAWELL, Karl

209 Pennsylvania Ave. SE
Washington, DC 20003
EMail: karl@geo-energy.org
Tel: (202)454-5261
Fax: (202)454-5265

Employers
Geothermal Energy Ass'n (Exec. Director)

GAY, Barbara L.

2519 Connecticut Ave. NW
Washington, DC 20008-1520
Tel: (202)783-2242
Fax: (202)783-2255
Registered: LDA

Employers
American Ass'n of Homes and Services for the Aging (Director, Information)

GAY, John F.

1201 New York Ave. NW
Suite 600
Washington, DC 20005-3931
EMail: jgay@ahma.com
Tel: (202)289-3123
Fax: (202)289-3185
Registered: LDA

Employers
American Hotel and Lodging Ass'n (V. President, Government Affairs)

GAY, Tim

410 First St. SE
Third Floor
Washington, DC 20003
EMail: tgay@dcsgroup.com
Tel: (202)484-2776
Fax: (202)484-7016

Employers
The DCS Group (Senior V. President)

GAYAT, Francois

99 Canal Center Plaza
Suite 450
Alexandria, VA 22314
Tel: (703)838-9685
Fax: (703)838-1688

Employers
Thales (Chairman and Chief Exec. Officer)

GAYNER, Lewis

214 Massachusetts Ave. NE
Washington, DC 20002
Tel: (202)546-4400
Fax: (202)546-8328

Employers
Heritage Foundation (V. President, Administration and Chief Financial Officer)

GAZIANO, Todd

214 Massachusetts Ave. NE
Washington, DC 20002
Tel: (202)546-4400
Fax: (202)546-8328

Employers
Heritage Foundation (Director, Center for Legal and Judicial Studies)

GEANACOPOULOS, David

1333 New Hampshire Ave. NW
Suite 400
Washington, DC 20036
Tel: (202)887-4000
Fax: (202)887-4288
Registered: LDA, FARA
Legislative Assistant to U.S. Rep. Edward P. Boland, 1979-83.

Employers
Akin, Gump, Strauss, Hauer & Feld, L.L.P. (Partner)

Clients Represented
On Behalf of Akin, Gump, Strauss, Hauer & Feld, L.L.P.
APKINDO
Bolivia, Government of the Republic of
Bombardier, Inc.
Bridgestone/Firestone, Inc.
British Columbia, Canada, Government of the Province of
Colombia, Government of the Republic of
Exxon Mobil Corp.
The Robert Mondavi Winery
OMNIPLEX World Services Corp.
Stamps.com
Uniden Corp.
Volkswagen, AG
Woodmont Corporation

GEBHARDTSBAUER, Ronald

1100 17th St. NW
Seventh Floor
Washington, DC 20036
Tel: (202)223-8196
Fax: (202)872-1948
Registered: LDA

Employers
American Academy of Actuaries (Senior Pension Fellow)

GEDDINGS, Kristine Phillips

1655 N. Fort Myer Dr.
Suite 700
Arlington, VA 22209
EMail: kris@geddings.com
Tel: (202)965-6680
Registered: LDA
Communications Director, U.S. Senate Special Committee on Aging, 1989-91.

Employers
Geddings Communications LLC (Co-Owner)

Clients Represented
On Behalf of Geddings Communications LLC
Nat'l Committee to Preserve Social Security and Medicare

GEDMIN, Jeffrey

1150 17th St. NW
Washington, DC 20036
EMail: jgedmin@aei.org
Tel: (202)862-5800
Fax: (202)862-7177

Employers
American Enterprise Institute for Public Policy Research (Research Fellow)

GEGG, Joseph C.

805 15th St. NW
Suite 430
Washington, DC 20005
EMail: joseph.gegg@wswa.org
Tel: (202)371-9792
Fax: (202)789-2405

Employers
Wine and Spirits Wholesalers of America (Senior V. President)

GEHLHAART, Donna

1101 Pennsylvania Ave. NW
Suite 200
Washington, DC 20004
EMail: donna.gehlhaart@ipaper.com
Tel: (202)628-1223
Fax: (202)628-1368
Registered: LDA

Employers
Internat'l Paper (Washington Representative)

GEHLMANN, Gregory

1501 M St. NW
Suite 700
Washington, DC 20005-1702
Tel: (202)463-4300
Fax: (202)463-4394

Employers
Manatt, Phelps & Phillips, LLP (Partner)

GEHMAN, Julian

1909 K St. NW
Washington, DC 20006
Tel: (202)263-3000
Fax: (202)263-3300
Registered: LDA

Employers
Mayer, Brown & Platt (Counsel)

Clients Represented
On Behalf of Mayer, Brown & Platt
Bertelsmann AG

GEHRING, Jennifer

324 Fourth St. NE
Washington, DC 20002
Tel: (202)546-7584
Fax: (202)546-9289

Employers
Nat'l Roofing Contractors Ass'n (Director, Federal Affairs)

GEHRISCH, Michael

2225 M St. NW
Suite 500
Washington, DC 20036
Tel: (202)296-7888
Fax: (202)296-7889

Employers
Internat'l Ass'n of Convention and Visitor Bureaus (President and Chief Exec. Officer)

GEIB, Ruthann

1156 15th St. NW
Suite 1101
Washington, DC 20005
EMail: asga@aol.com
Tel: (202)833-2398
Fax: (202)833-2962
Registered: LDA

Employers
American Sugarbeet Growers Ass'n (V. President)

GEIGER, Lisa M.

2215 Constitution Ave. NW
Washington, DC 20037-2985
Tel: (202)628-4410
Fax: (202)783-2351
Registered: LDA

Employers
American Pharmaceutical Ass'n (Director, State and Federal Policy)

GEIGER, Susan B.

1735 New York Ave. NW
Suite 500
Washington, DC 20006-4759
Tel: (202)628-1700
Fax: (202)331-1024
Registered: LDA
Senior Staff Member, Office of Management and Budget, 1970-80.

Employers
Preston Gates Ellis & Rouvelas Meeds LLP (Partner)

Clients Represented
On Behalf of Preston Gates Ellis & Rouvelas Meeds LLP
Air Nauru
American Soc. for Therapeutic Radiology and Oncology
Chicago Title & Trust Co.
Chicago Title Insurance
Interlake Holding Corp.
Island Express Boat Lines Ltd.
Lake Carriers Ass'n
Marine Transport Corp.
Nat'l Council on Compensation Insurance
Southeast Alaska Regional Health Corp. (SEARHC)
Transportation Institute
United States Maritime Coalition

GEISSER, John E.

100 N. Pitt
Suite 400
Alexandria, VA 22314
Tel: (703)683-8416
Fax: (703)683-8417
Registered: LDA

Employers
Academy of Managed Care Pharmacy (Director, Government Affairs)

GEIST, Brenda S.

The Pentagon
MS: 5E677
Washington, DC 20350-1300
EMail: geist.brenda@hq.navy.mil
Tel: (703)693-5764
Fax: (703)614-6060

Employers
Department of Navy (Director, Congressional Travel Division, Office of Legislative Affairs)

GELAK, Deanna R.

7505 Inzer St.
Springfield, VA 22151
Tel: (703)256-0829
Registered: LDA

Employers
Family and Medical Leave Act Technical Corrections Coalition (Exec. Director)
Working for the Future, LLC

Clients Represented

On Behalf of Working for the Future, LLC
Family and Medical Leave Act Technical Corrections Coalition
Soc. for Human Resource Management

GELB, Michael

700 13th St. NW
Suite 1000
Washington, DC 20005
Tel: (202)347-6633
Fax: (202)347-8713
Registered: FARA

Employers
Powell Tate (Senior V. President and Director, Editorial Services and Media Relations)

Clients Represented

On Behalf of Powell Tate
Saudi Arabia, Royal Embassy of

GELBAND, Stephen L.

1000 Potomac St. NW
Suite 300
Washington, DC 20007
Tel: (202)337-6200
Fax: (202)333-0871
Trial Attorney, Bureau of Economic Regulation, Civil Aeronautics Board, 1957-60. Attorney, Office of the U.S. Attorney for the Southern District of New York, Department of Justice, 1955.

Employers
Hewes, Gelband, Lambert & Dann, P.C. (Partner)

Clients Represented

On Behalf of Hewes, Gelband, Lambert & Dann, P.C.
Conquest Tours Ltd.
Orion Air
Tower Air, Inc.

GELETA, Abiyu

1810 Ninth St. NW
Washington, DC 20001
Tel: (202)462-5477
Fax: (202)332-7011
Registered: FARA

Employers
Oromo Liberation Front (OLF Representative)

GELLER, Howard S.

1001 Connecticut Ave. NW
Suite 801
Washington, DC 20036
Tel: (202)429-8873
Fax: (202)429-2248
Registered: LDA

Employers
American Council for an Energy-Efficient Economy (Exec. Director)

GELLER, Kenneth

1909 K St. NW
Washington, DC 20006
Tel: (202)263-3000
Fax: (202)263-3300

Employers
Mayer, Brown & Platt

Clients Represented

On Behalf of Mayer, Brown & Platt
Chamber of Commerce of the U.S.A.

GELMAN, Matthew

1001 G St. NW
Suite 900 E
Washington, DC 20001-4545
EMail: gelman@podesta.com
Tel: (202)393-1010
Fax: (202)393-5510
Registered: LDA
Former Floor Assistant to House Minority Whip, Rep. David Bonior (D-MI) and former Legislative aide to House Minority Leader, Rep. Richard A. Gephardt (D-MO).

Employers
Podesta/Mattoon (Principal)

Clients Represented

On Behalf of Podesta/Mattoon
American Council of Life Insurers
AOL Time Warner
Chiquita Brands Internat'l, Inc.
Genentech, Inc.
Interactive Gaming Council
MCI WorldCom Corp.
Motion Picture Ass'n of America
Mount Sinai/NYU Health
Nat'l Ass'n of Broadcasters
Recording Industry Ass'n of America
SiTV
Trans World Airlines, Inc.
Vivendi Universal

GELNOVATCH, Valerie

1130 Connecticut Ave. NW
Suite 300
Washington, DC 20036
EMail: vgelnovatch@tfgnet.com
Tel: (202)331-8500
Fax: (202)331-1598
Registered: LDA

Employers
The Ferguson Group, LLC (Senior Associate)

GELTMAN, Edward A.

1201 Pennsylvania Ave. NW
P.O. Box 407
Washington, DC 20044-0407
EMail: egeltman@ssd.com
Tel: (202)626-6600
Fax: (202)626-6780
Registered: FARA
Trial Attorney, Federal Trade Commission, 1971-73.

Employers
Squire, Sanders & Dempsey L.L.P. (Partner)

Clients Represented

On Behalf of Squire, Sanders & Dempsey L.L.P.
United Technologies Carrier

GELULA, Richard

1522 K St. NW
Suite 500
Washington, DC 20005
Tel: (202)347-3471
Fax: (202)347-3472

Employers
Nat'l Sleep Foundation (Exec. Director)

GEMEINHARDT, Elise A.

1225 New York Ave. NW
Suite 475
Washington, DC 20005
Tel: (202)371-1303
Fax: (202)371-5569
Registered: LDA
Former Legislative Assistant to Senator Alan K. Simpson (R-WY). Former Professional Staff Member, Subcommittee on Health, House Ways and Means Committee.

Employers
United Health Group (V. President, Federal Affairs)

GEMMA, Jr., Peter B.

56 McPherson Circle
Potomac Falls, VA 20165
EMail: peterjo@ix.netcom.com
Tel: (703)444-4445
Fax: (703)444-7887

Employers
Gemma & Associates (President)

GEMMA, Suzanne

1120 Connecticut Ave. NW
Suite 1100
Washington, DC 20036
Tel: (202)861-5899
Fax: (202)861-5795
Registered: LDA

Employers
GPC Internat'l

Clients Represented

On Behalf of GPC Internat'l
The Providence Plan
Providence Redevelopment Agency

GEMMELL, Michael K.

1101 15th St. NW
Suite 910
Washington, DC 20005
EMail: mkg@asph.org
Tel: (202)296-1099
Ext: 126
Fax: (202)296-1252

Employers
Ass'n of Schools of Public Health (Exec. Director)

GEMSKI, Liz

426 C St. NE
Washington, DC 20002
EMail: lg@capitolassociates.com
Tel: (202)544-1880
Fax: (202)543-2565
Registered: LDA

Employers
Capitol Associates, Inc. (Associate)

Clients Represented

On Behalf of Capitol Associates, Inc.
American Psychological Ass'n
Bastyr University
Health Physics Soc.
Lymphoma Research Foundation of America, Inc.
Nat'l Ass'n of Community Health Centers
Nat'l Coalition for Cancer Research
Nat'l Nutritional Foods Ass'n
Parkinson's Action Network
Rotary Foundation

GENDERSON, Bruce R.

725 12th St. NW
Washington, DC 20005
Tel: (202)434-5000
Fax: (202)434-5029
Law Clerk to Judge Irving L. Goldberg, U.S. Court of Appeals, Fifth Circuit, 1977-78.

Employers
Williams & Connolly (Partner)

Clients Represented

On Behalf of Williams & Connolly
McKechnie Brothers (South Africa) Ltd.

GENESON, David F.

1900 K St. NW
Washington, DC 20006-1109
EMail: dgeneson@hunton.com
Tel: (202)955-1500
Fax: (202)778-2201

Employers
Hunton & Williams (Partner)

GENNARO, Mary M.

1234 Massachusetts Ave. NW
Suite 103
Washington, DC 20005
EMail: naddc@naddc.org
Tel: (202)347-1234
Fax: (202)347-4023

Employers
Nat'l Ass'n of Developmental Disabilities Councils (Director, Governmental Affairs)

GENO, Sharon

1250 I St. NW
Suite 900
Washington, DC 20005
Tel: (202)783-2800
Fax: (202)783-0550
Registered: LDA

Employers
Reno & Cavanaugh, PLLC (Associate)

Clients Represented

On Behalf of Reno & Cavanaugh, PLLC
Council of Large Public Housing Authorities

GENOVESI, Jacqueline

801 Pennsylvania Ave. NW
Suite 720
Washington, DC 20004-2604
Tel: (202)393-3400
Fax: (202)393-4606
Registered: LDA

Employers
The Procter & Gamble Company (Legislative Assistant)

GENTILLE, John R.

1385 Piccard Dr.
Rockville, MD 20850-4340
EMail: jgentille@mcaa.org
Tel: (301)869-5800
Fax: (301)990-9690
Registered: LDA

Employers
Mechanical Contractors Ass'n of America (Exec. V. President & Chief Exec. Officer)

GENTRY, Margaret

1501 M St. NW
Suite 700
Washington, DC 20005-1702
EMail: mgentry@manatt.com
Tel: (202)463-4300
Fax: (202)463-4394
Registered: LDA, FARA

Employers
Manatt, Phelps & Phillips, LLP (Legislative Advisor)

Clients Represented

On Behalf of Manatt, Phelps & Phillips, LLP
Congo, Republic of
DAG Petroleum

GENTZER, Rick

409 Third St. SW
Second Floor
Washington, DC 20024-6682
Tel: (202)479-6689
Fax: (202)479-0735

Employers
Nat'l Interfaith Coalition on Aging (Chairman)

GENZER, Jeffrey C.

1615 M St. NW
Suite 800
Washington, DC 20036-3203
EMail: jcg@dwgp.com
Tel: (202)467-6370
Fax: (202)467-6379
Registered: LDA

Employers
Duncan, Weinberg, Genzer & Pembroke, P.C. (Principal)
Nat'l Ass'n of Energy Service Companies

Clients Represented

On Behalf of Duncan, Weinberg, Genzer & Pembroke, P.C.
Bergen, New York, Village of
Boonville, New York, Village of
Center for Clean Air Policy
Churchville, New York, Village of
Colorado Energy Assistance Foundation
Eclipse Energy Systems, Inc./Insyte, Inc.
Energy House Capital Corp.
Energy Programs Consortium
Export Council for Energy Efficiency
Freeport, New York, Electric Department of the Village of
Geothermal Energy Ass'n
Hawaii, Department of Business and Economic Development of the State of
Internat'l Energy Consultants
Jamestown, New York, Board of Public Utilities
Massena, New York, Town of
Mid-West Electric Consumers Ass'n
Municipal Electric Utilities Ass'n of New York State
Nat'l Ass'n of Energy Service Companies
Nat'l Ass'n of State Energy Officials
Nat'l Energy Assistance Directors' Ass'n
New York Municipal Power Agency
Penn Yan, New York, Village of
Plattsburgh, New York, City of
Renewable Energy Policy Project
Rockville Centre, New York, Village of
Salamanca, New York, City Board of Public Utilities of
Sherburne, New York, Village of
City of Sherrill, New York
Solar Electric Light Co.
Solar Energy Industries Ass'n (SEIA)
Solar Energy Research and Education Foundation
Solvay, New York, Village of
Trinity Public Utilities District

GEOGHEGAN, William A.

1301 K St. NW
Suite 1100-East Tower
Washington, DC 20005
Tel: (202)414-9200
Fax: (202)414-9299
Registered: LDA
Former Assistant Deputy Attorney General, Department of Justice, 1961-65.

Employers
Reed, Smith, LLP (Counsel)

GEORGE, Keith E.

600 13th St. NW
Washington, DC 20005-3096
EMail: kgeorge@mwe.com
Tel: (202)756-8603
Fax: (202)756-8087
Patent Examiner, Patent and Trademark Office, 1978-90.

Employers
McDermott, Will and Emery (Partner)

GEORGE, Larry

1725 Jefferson Davis Hwy.
Crystal Square 2, Suite 300
Arlington, VA 22202
Tel: (703)413-5611
Fax: (703)413-5617
Registered: LDA

Employers
Lockheed Martin Corp. (V. President, Classified Programs)

GEORGE, Melinda

1730 M St. NW
Suite 700
Washington, DC 20036-4510
EMail: mgeorge@siia.net
Tel: (202)452-1600
Fax: (202)223-8756
Registered: LDA

Employers
Software & Information Industry Ass'n (SIIA) (Director, Education Policy)

GEORGE, W. Peyton

1200 G St. NW
Suite 800
Washington, DC 20005
Tel: (202)833-1420
Fax: (202)434-8992
Registered: LDA
Washington, DC Legislative Liaison Officer, Office of the Secretary and Executive Assistant to the General Counsel, Department of Agriculture, 1969-73. Special Agent, Federal Bureau of Investigation, Department of Justice, 1962-69.

Employers
Lathrop & Gage, L.C. (Member)

Clients Represented

On Behalf of Lathrop & Gage, L.C.
Wendy's Internat'l, Inc.

GEORGIA, Paul J.

1001 Connecticut Ave. NW
Suite 1250
Washington, DC 20036
Tel: (202)331-1010
Fax: (202)331-0640

Employers
Competitive Enterprise Institute (Environmental Policy Analyst)

GEORGINE, Robert A.

111 Massachusetts Ave. NW
Washington, DC 20001
Tel: (202)682-0900
Fax: (202)682-6784
Registered: LDA

Employers
The Union Labor Life Insurance Co. (President, Chairman, and Chief Exec. Officer)

GERARD, Jack N.

1130 17th St. NW
Washington, DC 20036-4677
Tel: (202)463-2601
Fax: (202)463-3258
Registered: LDA
Legislative Director to Senator James McClure (R-ID), 1985-90. Legislative Assistant to Rep. George Hansen (R-ID), 1981-84.

Employers
Nat'l Mining Ass'n (President and Chief Exec. Officer)

GERARD, Leo

1150 17th St. NW
Suite 300
Washington, DC 20036
Tel: (202)778-4384
Fax: (202)293-5308

Employers
United Steelworkers of America (President)

GERASSIMEDES, Pam

444 N. Capitol St. NW
Suite 142
Washington, DC 20001
Tel: (202)431-8020
Fax: (202)434-8033

Employers
Nat'l Ass'n of State Workforce Agencies (Marketing and Outreach Coordinator)

GERBER, Louis M.

501 Third St. NW
Washington, DC 20001-2797
Tel: (202)434-1315
Fax: (202)434-1318
Registered: LDA

Employers
Communications Workers of America (Administrative Assistant to Secretary-Treasurer/Chief Lobbyist)

GERDANO, Samuel J.

44 Canal Center Plaza
Suite 404
Alexandria, VA 22314
EMail: sgerdano@abiworld.org
Tel: (703)739-0800
Fax: (703)739-1060

Employers
American Bankruptcy Institute (Exec. Director)

GERDES, Ronald W.

1300 Pennsylvania Ave. NW
Suite 400
Ronald Reagan Bldg.
Washington, DC 20004
EMail: rgerdes@strtrade.com
Tel: (202)638-2230
Fax: (202)638-2236
Registered: LDA, FARA
Assistant Chief Counsel, Administration and Legislation (1980-85) and Senior Attorney, Office of Regulation and Rulings (1973-1980), U.S. Customs Service, Department of the Treasury.

Employers
Sandler, Travis & Rosenberg, P.A. (Senior Member)

Clients Represented

On Behalf of Sandler, Travis & Rosenberg, P.A.
U.S. Apparel Industry Council

GEREN, Natalia W.

600 New Hampshire Ave. NW
11th Floor
Washington, DC 20037
Tel: (202)944-3000
Fax: (202)944-3068
Registered: LDA

Employers
Dyer Ellis & Joseph, P.C. (Associate)

Clients Represented

On Behalf of Dyer Ellis & Joseph, P.C.
Heerema Marine Contractors Nederland B.V.

GERKE, Scott A.

955 L'Enfant Plaza SW
Suite 5300
Washington, DC 20024
Tel: (202)554-1650
Fax: (202)488-3542
Registered: LDA

Employers
Honda North America, Inc. (Specialist, Government Relations)

GERKEN, David A.

300 Third St. NE
Suite 204
Washington, DC 20002
Tel: (202)544-0003
Fax: (202)544-6635
Registered: LDA
Former Legislative Advisor to Rep. Tony Coelho (D-CA).

Employers
Alvarado & Gerken (Partner)

Clients Represented

On Behalf of Alvarado & Gerken
Mas-Hamilton Group
MCI WorldCom Corp.
Puerto Rico Senate
TransNat'l Business Development Corp.

GERKIN, Daniel R.

1130 17th St. NW
Washington, DC 20036-4677
EMail: dgerkin@nma.org
Tel: (202)463-2659
Fax: (202)857-0135

Employers
Nat'l Mining Ass'n (Senior V. President Public and Constituent Relations)

GERMAN, Brad

8200 Jones Branch Dr.
McLean, VA 22102
EMail: brad_german@freddiemac.com
Tel: (703)903-2437
Fax: (703)903-2447

Employers
Federal Home Loan Mortgage Corp. (Freddie Mac) (Manager, Public Relations)

GERMOND, Alice Travis

1156 15th St. NW
Suite 700
Washington, DC 20005
Tel: (202)973-3000
Fax: (202)973-3096

Employers
Nat'l Abortion and Reproductive Rights Action League (Exec. V. President)

GERMROTH, David S.

300 N. Lee St.
Suite 500
Alexandria, VA 22314
Tel: (703)518-8600
Fax: (703)518-8611
Registered: LDA

Employers
R. J. Hudson Associates (Senior Lobbyist of Senior V. President)
PACE-CAPSTONE (Partner)

Clients Represented
On Behalf of R. J. Hudson Associates
Nat'l Licensed Beverage Ass'n
On Behalf of PACE-CAPSTONE
Guam AFGE
Guam Internat'l Airport Authority
Guam, Washington Office of the Governor
Honolulu Shipyard
Internat'l Facilities Management Ass'n

GERSH, Mark H.

122 C St. NW
Suite 650
Washington, DC 20001
Tel: (202)639-8300
Fax: (202)639-5038

Employers
Nat'l Committee for an Effective Congress (Washington Director)

GERSHMAN, Carl S.

1101 15th St. NW
Suite 700
Washington, DC 20005
Tel: (202)293-9072
Fax: (202)223-6042

Employers
Nat'l Endowment for Democracy (President)

GERSON, David

1150 17th St. NW
Washington, DC 20036
Tel: (202)862-5800
Fax: (202)862-7177
EMail: david@aei.org

Employers
American Enterprise Institute for Public Policy Research (Exec. V. President)

GERSON, Matthew T.

1401 I St. NW
Suite 1220
Washington, DC 20005
Tel: (202)898-6400
Fax: (202)898-6454
Registered: LDA

Employers
Vivendi Universal (V. President, Entertainment Public Policy)

GERST, Leesa

1201 New York Ave. NW
Suite 725
Washington, DC 20005
Tel: (202)216-2740
Fax: (202)289-7618
EMail: lmgerst@aol.com

Employers
Nat'l Coalition for Advanced Manufacturing (Director, Communications)

GERUM, Laura M.

1155 16th St. NW
Washington, DC 20036
Tel: (202)872-4600
Fax: (202)872-4615
Registered: LDA

Employers
American Chemical Soc.

GERVASIO, Jr., Ralph J.

P.O. Box 61303
Potomac, MD 20859
Tel: (301)294-0937
Registered: LDA
EMail: info@FoleyCoInc.com
Legislative Aide to Rep. David Bonior (D-MI), 1974-80.

Employers
Foley Government and Public Affairs, Inc. (Legislative Assistant)

Clients Represented
On Behalf of Foley Government and Public Affairs, Inc.
Pyrocap International Corp., Inc.
Technology Resource Centers

GERWIN, Jr., Edward F.

1400 L St. NW
Washington, DC 20005-3502
Tel: (202)371-5740
Fax: (202)371-5950
Registered: LDA, FARA
EMail: egerwin@winston.com

Employers
Winston & Strawn (Partner, Corporate Practice)

Clients Represented
On Behalf of Winston & Strawn
Benrus Watch Co.
CAMECO Corp.
Gildan Activewear
Virgin Islands Watch and Jewelry Manufacturers Ass'n

GESSEMAN, Donald

819 Seventh St. NW
Washington, DC 20001
Tel: (202)833-8940
Fax: (202)833-8943
Registered: LDA

Employers
EOP Group, Inc.

Clients Represented
On Behalf of EOP Group, Inc.
American Petroleum Institute
The Boeing Co.
The Business Roundtable
Nuclear Energy Institute

GEST, Kathryn Waters

700 13th St. NW
Suite 1000
Washington, DC 20005
Tel: (202)347-6633
Fax: (202)347-8713
Registered: LDA, FARA
Press Secretary to Senator William S. Cohen (R-ME), 1987-96.

Employers
Powell Tate (Senior V. President and Director, International Issues Group)

Clients Represented
On Behalf of Powell Tate
Gabonese Republic, Government of the
Saudi Arabia, Royal Embassy of
Taiwan Studies Institute

GETTER, Pat

1156 15th St. NW
Suite 400
Washington, DC 20005
Tel: (202)296-1585
Fax: (202)463-0474

Employers
American Crop Protection Ass'n (V. President, Communications)

GETTINGS, Robert M.

113 Oronoco St.
Alexandria, VA 22314
Tel: (703)683-4202
Fax: (703)684-1395

Employers
Nat'l Ass'n of State Directors of Developmental Disabilities Services, Inc. (Exec. Director)

GETTLEMAN, Marna

1025 Thomas Jefferson St. NW
Suite 400 East
Washington, DC 20007-0805
Tel: (202)965-8116
Fax: (202)965-6403
Registered: LDA

Employers
Jorden Burt LLP (Assistant Director, Grant Services)

Clients Represented
On Behalf of Jorden Burt LLP
American Museum of Natural History
Assurant Group
Atlantic Health Systems
The Colonial Williamsburg Foundation
Florida State University System
Gainesville Regional Utilities
Gainesville, Florida, City of
Lovelace Respiratory Research Institute
Miami Beach, Florida, City of
New York University
Newark, New Jersey, City of
University of Medicine and Dentistry of New Jersey
University of Miami
University of Tulsa
University of Virginia

GHANNAM, Jeff

5400 Grosvenor Ln.
Bethesda, MD 20814-2198
Tel: (301)897-8720
Fax: (301)897-3690
EMail: ghannamm@safnet.org

Employers
Soc. of American Foresters (Director, Media Relations)

GHAZAL, Maria M.

1212 New York Ave. NW
Suite 1250
Washington, DC 20005-3987
Tel: (202)289-6700
Fax: (202)289-4582
Registered: LDA

Employers
American Benefits Council (Director, Health Policy)

GHORBANI, Daniel D.

1331 Pennsylvania Ave. NW
Suite 508
Washington, DC 20004
Tel: (202)783-4087
Fax: (202)783-4075
EMail: mharrdg@aol.com

Employers
Manufactured Housing Ass'n for Regulatory Reform (President)

GIAIMO, USAF (Ret.), Col. Christopher J.

201 N. Washington St.
Alexandria, VA 22314
Tel: (800)245-8762
Fax: (703)838-8173
Registered: LDA
EMail: chrisg@troa.org

Employers
The Retired Officers Ass'n (TROA) (Director, Chapter Affairs)

GIANBERARDINO, Marco

1201 New York Ave. NW
Suite 300
Washington, DC 20005
Tel: (202)326-6365
Fax: (202)371-0181
EMail: mgianberardino@boma.org

Employers
Building Owners and Managers Ass'n Internat'l (Assistant Exec. Director, Government and Industry Affairs)

GIANCOLA, Anthony R.

440 First St. NW
Washington, DC 20001
Tel: (202)393-5041
Fax: (202)393-2630

Employers
Nat'l Ass'n of County Engineers (Exec. Director)

GIANELLI, William R.

1225 I St. NW
Suite 500
Washington, DC 20005
Tel: (202)312-2005
Fax: (202)289-8683
EMail: dawsonassociates@worldnet.att.net
Former Assistant Secretary of the Army for Civil Works, U.S. Army Corps of Engineers, Department of the Army. Former Chairman of the Board of Directors, Panama Canal Commission.

Employers
Dawson & Associates, Inc. (Senior Advisor)

GIANINY, James

1029 N. Royal St.
Suite 400
Alexandria, VA 22314
Tel: (703)684-1245
Fax: (703)684-1249
EMail: JGianiny@directimpact.com

Employers
The Direct Impact Co. (Senior V. President)

GIBBENS, Wayne

801 Pennsylvania Ave. NW
Suite 840
Washington, DC 20004-2615
Tel: (202)638-4400
Fax: (202)638-5967
Registered: LDA

Employers
U.S. Oil and Gas Ass'n (President)

GIBBIN, Holly

810 Vermont Ave. NW
Washington, DC 20420
Tel: (202)273-9419
Fax: (202)273-9988

Employers
Department of Veterans Affairs (Legislative Analyst)

GIBBONS, Clifford S.

The Willard Office Bldg.
1455 Pennsylvania Ave. NW
Washington, DC 20004
Tel: (202)783-6000
Fax: (202)783-4171
Registered: LDA, FARA
EMail: gibbons@gibbonsco.com
Special Assistant, U.S. Trade Representative, Executive Office of the President, The White House, 1979-81.

Employers
Gibbons & Company, Inc. (President and Chief Exec. Officer)

Clients Represented
On Behalf of Gibbons & Company, Inc.
Aso Corp.
Elettronica Veneta & IN.EL.
ETREMA Products, Inc./Edge Technologies
Kellogg Co.
Lloyd's of London
Moffit Cancer Research Hospital
MONY Life Insurance Co.
Playtex Products, Inc.

GIBBONS, Hon. Sam M.

The Willard Office Bldg.
1455 Pennsylvania Ave. NW
Washington, DC 20004
Tel: (202)783-6000
Fax: (202)783-4171
Registered: LDA
Member, U.S. House of Representatives (D-FL), 1962-1997. (Served as Chairman, House Committee on Ways and Means.)

Employers
Gibbons & Company, Inc. (Chairman of the Board)

Clients Represented
On Behalf of Gibbons & Company, Inc.
Aso Corp.
ETREMA Products, Inc./Edge Technologies
Moffit Cancer Research Hospital
MONY Life Insurance Co.
Playtex Products, Inc.

GIBBS, Jeffrey L.

1000 Connecticut Ave. NW
Suite 1300
Washington, DC 20036
Tel: (202)842-2600
Fax: (202)842-1888

Employers
Bredhoff & Kaiser (Partner)

GIBBS, Jeffrey N.

700 13th St. NW
Suite 1200
Washington, DC 20005
Tel: (202)737-5600
Fax: (202)737-9329

Employers
Hyman, Phelps & McNamara, P.C. (Partner)

GIBBS, Lawrence B.

655 15th St. NW
Suite 900
Washington, DC 20005-5701
Tel: (202)626-5800
Fax: (202)628-0858
Registered: LDA
EMail: lgibbs@milchev.com
Commissioner of Internal Revenue (1986-89), Assistant Commissioner - Technical (1973-76), Acting Chief Counsel (1973), and Deputy Chief Counsel (1972-73), Internal Revenue Service.

Employers
Miller & Chevalier, Chartered (Member)

Clients Represented
On Behalf of Miller & Chevalier, Chartered
Ernest & Julio Gallo Winery
Keidanren
U.S. Chamber Task Force on Punitive Damages

GIBBS, Lois Marie

150 S. Washington St.
Suite 300
P.O. Box 6806
Falls Church, VA 22046-6806
Tel: (703)237-2249
Fax: (703)237-8389

Employers
Center for Health, Environment and Justice (Exec. Director)

GIBERGA, Elena

2550 M St. NW
Washington, DC 20037-1350
Tel: (202)457-6000
Fax: (202)457-6315
Registered: LDA
EMail: egiberga@pattonboggs.com

Employers
Patton Boggs, LLP (Legislative Specialist)

Clients Represented
On Behalf of Patton Boggs, LLP
African Coalition for Trade, Inc.
American Advertising Federation
American Ass'n of Advertising Agencies
AOL Time Warner
Ass'n of Nat'l Advertisers
DFS Group Ltd.
EchoStar Communications Corp.
Major League Baseball Players Ass'n
MCI WorldCom Corp.
Nat'l Ass'n of Theatre Owners
Nat'l Oilheat Research Alliance (NORA)
Outdoor Advertising Ass'n of America
Point of Purchase Advertising Institute
Ventura County Citizens Against Radar Emissions (VCCARE)
Wheeling Pittsburgh Steel Corp.

GIBLIN, Christopher M.

801 Pennsylvania Ave. NW
Suite 620
Washington, DC 20004-2604
Tel: (202)783-7220
Fax: (202)783-8127
Registered: LDA
EMail: chris_giblin@reliantenergy.com

Employers
Reliant Energy, Inc. (Manager, Federal Relations)

GIBSON, Barbara

1133 19th St. NW
Washington, DC 20036
Tel: (202)887-2757
Fax: (202)887-2023

Employers
MCI WorldCom Corp. (Senior Manager, Coporate Communications)

GIBSON, Churchill J.

1518 K St. NW
Suite 206
Washington, DC 20005
Tel: (202)638-1526
Fax: (202)638-4664

Employers
Nat'l Alliance to End Homelessness (Exec. Director)

GIBSON, James O.

2100 M St. NW
Washington, DC 20037
Tel: (202)833-7200
Fax: (202)429-0687

Employers
The Urban Institute (Consultant)

GIBSON, Jennifer

122 C St. NW
Suite 540
Washington, DC 20001
Tel: (202)628-1558
Fax: (202)628-1601
Registered: LDA
EMail: jcromwell@namic.org

Employers
Nat'l Ass'n of Mutual Insurance Companies (Director, Federal Affairs)

GIBSON, Mary Jo

601 E St. NW
Washington, DC 20049
Tel: (202)434-3896
Fax: (202)434-6480
EMail: mjgibson@aarp.org

Employers
AARP (American Ass'n of Retired Persons) (Associate Director, Public Policy Institute)

GIBSON, Michael

1029 N. Royal St.
Suite 400
Alexandria, VA 22314
Tel: (703)684-1245
Fax: (703)684-1249
EMail: mgibson@directimpact.com

Employers
The Direct Impact Co. (V. President)

GIBSON, Nan

1660 L St. NW
Suite 1200
Washington, DC 20036
Tel: (202)775-8810
Fax: (202)775-0819
EMail: epi@epinet.org

Employers
Economic Policy Institute (Communications Director)

GIBSON, Shannon M.

2550 M St. NW
Washington, DC 20037-1350
Tel: (202)457-6000
Fax: (202)457-6315
Registered: LDA
EMail: sgibson@pattonboggs.com

Employers
Patton Boggs, LLP (Legislative Affairs Specialist)

Clients Represented
On Behalf of Patton Boggs, LLP
Baltimore Symphony Orchestra
Cincinnati, Ohio, City of
Houston, Texas, City of
Illinois Department of Human Services
Sierra Military Health Services, Inc.

GIBSON, Thomas C.

1595 Spring Hill Rd.
Suite 330
Vienna, VA 22182
Tel: (703)506-3260
Fax: (703)506-3266

Employers
Ass'n Management Bureau (President/Chief Exec. Officer)

Clients Represented
On Behalf of Ass'n Management Bureau
Emergency Department Practice Management Ass'n (EDPMA)

GIDDINGS, L. Val

1625 K St. NW
Suite 1100
Washington, DC 20006-1604
Tel: (202)857-0244
Fax: (202)857-0237
Registered: LDA
EMail: lvg@bio.org

Employers
Biotechnology Industry Organization (V. President, Food and Agriculture)

GIERE, John

1634 I St. NW
Suite 600
Washington, DC 20006-4083
Tel: (202)783-2200
Fax: (202)783-2206
Registered: LDA

Employers
Ericsson Inc. (V. President, Marketing and Public Affairs)

GIESE, Robert B.

1101 Connecticut Ave. NW
Suite 900
Washington, DC 20036
Tel: (202)828-2300
Fax: (202)828-2322

Employers
Chris-Craft Broadcasting, Inc. (V. President and Counsel)

GIESECKE, Anne

1350 I St. NW
Suite 1290
Washington, DC 20005
Tel: (202)789-0300
Fax: (202)898-1164
Registered: LDA

Employers
American Bakers Ass'n (V. President, Environmental Activities)

GIESECKE, Stephanie

1025 Connecticut Ave. NW
Suite 700
Washington, DC 20036
Tel: (202)785-8866
Fax: (202)835-0003
Former Legislative Assistant to Rep. William V. Alexander (D-AR).

Employers
Nat'l Ass'n of Independent Colleges and Universities (Director, Budget and Appropriations)

GIGLIO, Christopher F.

1401 K St. NW
Suite 700
Washington, DC 20005
EMail: giglio@capitaledge.com
Tel: (202)842-4930
Fax: (202)842-5051
Registered: LDA

Employers
Carolyn C. Chaney & Associates (V. President)

Clients Represented
On Behalf of Carolyn C. Chaney & Associates
Beaumont, Texas, City of
Farmers Branch, Texas, City of
Lincoln, Nebraska, City of
Pasadena, California, City of
Reno, Nevada, City of
Santa Cruz County Regional Transportation Commission
Santa Cruz Metropolitan Transit District
Santa Cruz Redevelopment Agency
Santa Cruz, California, County of
Scottsdale, Arizona, City of

GIGLIO, Mary

One Massachusetts Ave. NW
Suite 820
Washington, DC 20001
EMail: mgiglio@ethandrfa.org
Tel: (202)289-3835
Fax: (202)289-7519

Employers
Renewable Fuels Ass'n (Director, Congressional and Public Affairs)

GIGUERE, Michelle E.

1455 F St. NW
Suite 225
Washington, DC 20005
EMail: mgiguere@bjllp.com
Tel: (202)638-3307
Fax: (202)783-6947
Registered: LDA
Legislative Director for Rep. Les AuCoin (D-OR), 1979-88.

Employers
Ball Janik, LLP (Government Relations Specialist)

Clients Represented
On Behalf of Ball Janik, LLP
Cascade General, Inc.
Clackamas, Oregon, County of
Clatsop Community College
Concentrex
Grants Pass Irrigation District
Guardian Marine Internat'l LLC
Highline School District Educational Resources
Hood River, Oregon, Port of
Oregon Department of Transportation
Schnitzer Steel Industries, Inc.
Tukwila, Washington, City of

GILBERG, Anders K.

1717 Pennsylvania Ave. NW
Suite 600
Washington, DC 20006
Tel: (202)293-3450
Fax: (202)293-2787
Registered: LDA

Employers
Medical Group Management Ass'n (Field Representative)

GILBERT, David

1301 Pennsylvania Ave. NW
Suite 1050
Washington, DC 20004
Tel: (202)942-9840
Fax: (202)942-9847
Registered: LDA

Employers
Constellation Energy Group (Federal Relations Representative)

GILBERT, Donald M.

325 Seventh St. NW
Suite 1100
Washington, DC 20004-2802
Tel: (202)783-7971
Fax: (202)737-2849
Registered: LDA

Employers
Nat'l Retail Federation (Senior V. President, Information Technology)

GILBERT, Gerald

555 13th St. NW
Washington, DC 20004-1109
Tel: (202)637-5600
Fax: (202)637-5910

Employers
Hogan & Hartson L.L.P.

GILBERT, Jr., John A.

700 13th St. NW
Suite 1200
Washington, DC 20005
Tel: (202)737-4293
Fax: (202)737-9329
Registered: LDA
Attorney/Advisor, Office of the Chief Counsel (1993-95) and Law Clerk, Office of Administrative Judges (1992-93), Drug Enforcement Administration, Department of Justice.

Employers
Hyman, Phelps & McNamara, P.C. (Partner)

Clients Represented
On Behalf of Hyman, Phelps & McNamara, P.C.
Hoffmann-La Roche Inc.
Medeva Pharmaceuticals

GILBERT, Robert A.

1300 L St. NW
Suite 1020
Washington, DC 20005
EMail: bghsmai@aol.com
Tel: (202)789-0089
Fax: (202)789-1725

Employers
Hospitality Sales and Marketing Ass'n Internat'l (President and Chief Exec. Officer)

GILBERT, Robin H.

3050 K St. NW
Washington, DC 20007
Tel: (202)342-8400
Fax: (202)342-8451
Registered: LDA
EMail: rgilbert@colliershannon.com

Employers
Collier Shannon Scott, PLLC (Member)

Clients Represented
On Behalf of Collier Shannon Scott, PLLC
Municipal Castings Fair Trade Council

GILBERT, Sandra A.

One Massachusetts Ave. NW
Suite 880
Washington, DC 20001
EMail: sgilb94810@aol.com
Tel: (202)371-0945
Fax: (202)371-1178
Registered: LDA

Employers
Robison Internat'l, Inc. (Director, Government Relations)

Clients Represented
On Behalf of Robison Internat'l, Inc.
Alliant Techsystems, Inc.
The Boeing Co.
General Electric Co.
Honeywell Internat'l, Inc.
Lockheed Martin Tactical Systems
United Defense, L.P.

GILBERTI, Eric

440 First St. NW
Eighth Floor
Washington, DC 20001
Tel: (202)942-4207
Fax: (202)393-2630

Employers
Nat'l Ass'n of Counties (Assistant Legislative Director, Rural Action Caucus)

GILBERTSON, Lisa

1700 N. Moore St.
Suite 2250
Arlington, VA 22209
Tel: (703)841-2300
Fax: (703)841-1183

Employers
Internat'l Mass Retailers Ass'n (Director of Tax and Financial Issues)

GILBERTSON, Richard

119 N. Henry St.
Third Floor
Alexandria, VA 22314-2903
Tel: (703)921-9111
Fax: (703)836-8009
Registered: LDA

Employers
CAREY/NEALON & Associates, L.L.C. (Senior Associate)

GILBERTSON, Ronald

1615 L St. NW
Suite 1200
Washington, DC 20036
Tel: (202)466-6300
Fax: (202)463-0678

Employers
Bell, Boyd & Lloyd

GILCHREST, Donald

440 First St. NW
Suite 430
Washington, DC 20001
Tel: (202)737-7523
Fax: (202)737-6788
Registered: LDA

Employers
Honberger and Walters, Inc. (Associate)

Clients Represented
On Behalf of Honberger and Walters, Inc.
Calleguas Municipal Water District, California
Monterey Salinas Transit
North San Diego County Transit Development Board
Pechanga Band of Luiseno Mission Indians
Riverside, California, County of
San Diego Metropolitan Transit Development Board
San Diego, California, County of
San Joaquin, California, County of
Sweetwater Authority
Ventura, California, County of

GILDER, Josh

1030 15th St. NW
Suite 1100
Washington, DC 20005
Tel: (202)783-4600
Fax: (202)783-4601
Chief Speechwriter to the V. President and Senior Speechwriter to the President, during the Reagan Administration.

Employers
White House Writers Group (Senior Director)

GILES, Lance

444 N. Capitol St. NW
Suite 201
Washington, DC 20001
Tel: (202)638-0631
Fax: (202)638-2296

Employers
New Jersey, Washington Office of the State of (Associate Director)

GILFOYLE, Nathalie

750 First St. NE
Washington, DC 20002-4242
Tel: (202)336-6186
Fax: (202)336-6069

Employers
American Psychological Ass'n (Deputy General Counsel)

GILIBERTI, Mary

1101 15th St. NW
Suite 1212
Washington, DC 20005
EMail: maryg@bazelon.org
Tel: (202)467-5730
Ext: 15
Fax: (202)223-0409

Employers
Bazelon Center for Mental Health Law, Judge David L. (Staff Attorney, Children's Issues)

GILL, Bates

1775 Massachusetts Ave. NW
Washington, DC 20036-2188
Tel: (202)797-6000
Fax: (202)797-6004

Employers
The Brookings Institution (Senior Fellow, Foreign Policy Studies/Director, Northeast Asian Policy Studies)

GILL, Jr., Edward J.

700 14th St. NW
Suite 900
Washington, DC 20005
Tel: (202)508-1000
Fax: (202)508-1010
Registered: LDA
Office of the Chief Counsel, Urban Mass Transportation Administration, 1978-89. Office of the Chief Counsel, Division of Regulations and Administrative Law, U.S. Coast Guard, 1973-78.

Employers
Thompson Coburn LLP (Partner)

Clients Represented
On Behalf of Thompson Coburn LLP
Taxicab, Limousine and Paratransit Ass'n

GILL, Gregory M.

700 13th St. NW
Suite 400
Washington, DC 20005
EMail: ggill@cassidy.com
Tel: (202)347-0773
Fax: (202)347-0785
Registered: LDA, FARA
Former Associate Staff Member and Legislative Director, House Appropriations Committee. Former Legislative Director to Rep. Steny Hoyer (D-MD). Former Legislative Assistant to Senator Donald Riegle (D-MI).

Employers
Cassidy & Associates, Inc. (Senior V. President, General Counsel)

Clients Represented

On Behalf of Cassidy & Associates, Inc.
American Chamber of Commerce in Egypt
Crane & Co.
Dimensions Healthcare System
Draft Worldwide
Gabon, Nat'l Assembly of
Gabonese Republic, Office of the President of the
Hampton University
Hawaii, State of
Hospital for Special Surgery
Lifebridge Health
Miami-Dade Community College
Monroe Community College
Montefiore Medical Center
New Jersey Institute of Technology
Pierce College
Tiffany & Co.
Tougaloo College

GILL, John J.

1120 Connecticut Ave. NW
Washington, DC 20036
Tel: (202)663-5000
Fax: (202)828-4548

Employers
American Bankers Ass'n (General Counsel)

GILL, Michael

2000 Corporate Ridge
Suite 1000
McLean, VA 22102
Tel: (703)821-0770
Fax: (703)821-1350

Employers
American Frozen Food Institute (V. President, Legislative Affairs)
Frozen Potato Products Institute

GILL, Rick

1156 15th St. NW
Suite 502
Washington, DC 20005-1799
Tel: (202)862-4811
Fax: (202)862-4829
Registered: LDA
EMail: rrgill@jcpenney.com

Employers
J. C. Penney Co., Inc. (V. President and Director, Government Relations)

GILLAN, Jacqueline S.

750 First St. NE
Suite 901
Washington, DC 20002
Tel: (202)408-1711
Fax: (202)408-1699
Registered: LDA
EMail: jgillan@saferoads.org

Employers
Advocates for Highway and Auto Safety (V. President)

GILLCASH, Robert S.

4114 Legato Rd.
Fairfax, VA 22033
Tel: (703)267-8000
Fax: (703)227-5507
Registered: LDA
Former Senior Legislative Assistant to Senator Christopher J. Dodd (D-CT).

Employers
American Management Systems (Director, Government Affairs)

GILLEECE, Mary Ann

1501 M St. NW
Suite 700
Washington, DC 20005-1702
Tel: (202)463-4300
Fax: (202)463-4394
Registered: LDA
EMail: mgilleece@manatt.com
Deputy Under Secretary for Research and Engineering (Acquisition Management), Department of Defense, 1983-85. Counsel, Committee on Armed Services, U.S. House of Representatives, 1972-77.

Employers
Manatt, Phelps & Phillips, LLP (Attorney)

Clients Represented

On Behalf of Manatt, Phelps & Phillips, LLP
R. R. Donnelley & Sons
Eaton Corp., Cutler Hammer
Honeywell Internat'l, Inc.
Inflatable Survival Systems, Inc.
Jacobs Engineering Group Inc.
Miami Valley Economic Coalition
Racal Communications Inc.
Sabreliner Corp.
Stewart & Stevenson Services, Inc.

GILLEN, Neal P.

1725 K St. NW
Suite 1404
Washington, DC 20006
Tel: (202)296-7116
Fax: (202)659-5322
Registered: LDA
EMail: Gillen@aol.com

Employers
American Cotton Shippers Ass'n (Exec. V. President and General Counsel)
Washington Discussion Group (Secretary-Treasurer)

GILLERMAN, Gordon

1850 M St. NW
Suite 1000
Washington, DC 20036
Tel: (202)296-7840
Fax: (202)872-1576

Employers
Underwriters Laboratories Inc. (Manager, Governmental Affairs)

GILLESPIE, Cathy

P.O. Box 6136
Alexandria, VA 22306
Tel: (703)360-8386
Fax: (703)619-1122
EMail: cathy_gillespie@msn.com
Chief of Staff, 1988-98, Special Assistant, 1985-88, to Rep Joe Barton (R-TX)

Employers
Texas Freedom Fund (Exec. Director)

GILLESPIE, Charles A.

900 17th St. NW
Suite 500
Washington, DC 20006
Tel: (202)296-9312
Fax: (202)296-9395
EMail: Gillespie@scowfront.com
Former Ambassador to Colombia, Chile and Grenada; retired Foreign Service Officer; and Staff member, Nat'l Security Council during the Bush I administration.

Employers
The Scowcroft Group (Senior Associate)

GILLESPIE, Edward A.

1301 K St. NW
Suite 1200-West Tower
Washington, DC 20005-3307
Tel: (202)515-5187
Fax: (202)525-4943
EMail: eag@us.ibm.com

Employers
Internat'l Business Machines Corp. (Senior Program Manager, Environmental Issues)

GILLESPIE, Edward W.

1133 Connecticut Ave. NW
Fifth Floor
Washington, DC 20036
Tel: (202)457-1110
Fax: (202)457-1130
Registered: LDA
Former Aide to House Majority Leader, Rep. Dick Armey (R-TX).

Employers
Quinn Gillespie & Associates (Principal)

Clients Represented

On Behalf of Quinn Gillespie & Associates
American Hospital Ass'n
American Insurance Ass'n
British Columbia Lumber Trade Council
Instinet
LVMH Moet Hennessy Louis Vuitton S.A.
Recording Industry Ass'n of America
SBC Communications Inc.
Technology Network
USEC, Inc.

GILLETTE, David

440 First St. NW
Suite 600
Washington, DC 20001
Tel: (202)639-5200
Registered: LDA

Employers
American Israel Public Affairs Committee (Senior Legislative Liaison)

GILLIAM, Arleen

815 16th St. NW
Washington, DC 20006
Tel: (202)637-5235
Fax: (202)637-5058

Employers
AFL-CIO (American Federation of Labor and Congress of Industrial Organizations) (Assistant to the President)

GILLIAM, Loralei

1001 Connecticut Ave. NW
Suite 1250
Washington, DC 20036
Tel: (202)331-1010
Fax: (202)331-0640

Employers
Competitive Enterprise Institute (Director of Marketing for Development)

GILLIAM, Jr., Reginald E.

600 New Hampshire Ave. NW
Suite 601
Washington, DC 20037
Tel: (202)333-7400
Fax: (202)333-1638
Registered: LDA, FARA
EMail: rgilliam@hillandknowlton.com

Employers
Hill and Knowlton, Inc. (Senior Managing Director, Public Affairs)

Clients Represented

On Behalf of Hill and Knowlton, Inc.
Cleveland, Ohio, City of
Great Lakes Science Center
Kohler Corp.

GILLICK, John E.

1133 Connecticut Ave. NW
Suite 1200
Washington, DC 20036
Tel: (202)775-9800
Fax: (202)833-8491
Registered: LDA

Employers
Winthrop, Stimson, Putnam & Roberts (Partner)

Clients Represented

On Behalf of Winthrop, Stimson, Putnam & Roberts
Air Transat
El Al Israel Airlines, Ltd.
LOT Polish Airlines

GILLIGAN, Charles W.

4748 Wisconsin Ave. NW
Washington, DC 20016
Tel: (202)362-0041

Employers
O'Donoghue & O'Donoghue

GILLIGAN, Thomas J.

3513 McKinley St. NW
Washington, DC 20015-2513
Tel: (202)244-6450
Fax: (202)244-6570
Registered: LDA

Employers
Self-employed as an independent consultant.

Clients Represented

As an independent consultant
Ass'n for Electronic Healthcare Transaction
MBNA America Bank NA

GILLILAND, C. Michael

555 13th St. NW
Washington, DC 20004-1109
Tel: (202)637-5619
Fax: (202)637-5910
Registered: LDA
EMail: cmgilliland@hhlaw.com
Staff Attorney, Subcommittee on Courts, Senate Judiciary Committee, 1980-81. Legislative Director for Senator Howell Heflin (D-AL), 1981-86.

Employers
Hogan & Hartson L.L.P. (Partner)

Clients Represented

On Behalf of Hogan & Hartson L.L.P.

AAA MidAtlantic
American Registry of Pathology
Andalex Resources, Inc.
Brandeis University
CUNA Mutual Group
Danaher Corp.
The Danny Foundation,
Grocery Manufacturers of America
Health and Hospital Corp. of Marion County
HMSHost Corp.
Irvine, California, City of
Kongsberg Simrad
Laguna Woods, California, City of
Lee County Port Authority
The McConnell Foundation
Michelin North America
Michigan Consolidated Gas Co.
Nat'l Chicken Council
Nat'l College Access Network
Nestle USA, Inc.
Olney Boys and Girls Club
Plasma Protein Therapeutics Ass'n
S1 Corp.
Southern Methodist University
The St. Joe Co.
Vulcan Materials Co.
WebMD

GILLILAND, David W.

2099 Pennsylvania Ave. NW
Suite 100
Washington, DC 20006
EMail: dwgillil@hklaw.com
Tel: (202)955-3000
Fax: (202)955-5564

Employers

Holland & Knight LLP (Senior Public Affairs Advisor)

GILLILAND, John

499 S. Capitol St. SW
Suite 600
Washington, DC 20003
EMail: dwawashdc@aol.com
Tel: (202)554-1222
Fax: (202)554-1230
Registered: LDA

Employers

Don Wallace Associates, Inc.

Clients Represented

On Behalf of Don Wallace Associates, Inc.

American Sugar Cane League of the U.S.A.
Cotton Warehouse Ass'n of America
Service Corp. Internat'l

GILLIS, Jack

1424 16th St. NW
Suite 604
Washington, DC 20036
EMail: jgillis@essential.org
Tel: (202)737-0766
Fax: (202)737-2214

Employers

Consumer Federation of America (Public Affairs Director)

GILLIS, Michael

2099 Pennsylvania Ave. NW
Suite 100
Washington, DC 20006
EMail: mgillis@hklaw.com
Tel: (202)955-3000
Fax: (202)955-5564
Registered: LDA

Employers

Holland & Knight LLP (Legislative Assistant)

Clients Represented

On Behalf of Holland & Knight LLP

Capitol Broadcasting Co.
S.C. Johnson and Son, Inc.
Somerville Housing Group
Spirit Airlines
Wyeth-Ayerst Pharmaceuticals

GILLON, Peter M.

800 Connecticut Ave. NW
Suite 500
Washington, DC 20006
EMail: gillonp@gtlaw.com
Tel: (202)331-3145
Fax: (202)331-3101
Registered: LDA

Employers

Greenberg Traurig, LLP (Shareholder)

Clients Represented

On Behalf of Greenberg Traurig, LLP

Environmental Redevelopers Ass'n
Health Partners
Uniroyal Technology Corp.

GILMAN, Bradley D.

2300 Clarendon Blvd.
Suite 1010
Arlington, VA 22201
Tel: (703)527-4414
Fax: (703)527-0421
Registered: LDA

Employers

Robertson, Monagle & Eastaugh (Director)

Clients Represented

On Behalf of Robertson, Monagle & Eastaugh

Alaska Groundfish Data Bank
Aleutians East Borough
American Steamship Co.
CSX Corp.
CSX Lines LLC
Friede, Goldman, & Halter, Inc.
The Glacier Bay Group
Kodiak Island, Alaska, Borough of
Kodiak, Alaska, City of
Lunds Fisheries, Inc.
Maersk Inc.
Ocean Shipholding, Inc.
Ounalashka Corp.
Pacific States Marine Fisheries Commission
Petersburg, Alaska, City of
Seafreeze
Seward, Alaska, City of
Transportation Institute
Trident Seafood Corp.
U.S. Marine Corp.
Unalaska, Alaska, City of
Verner, Liipfert, Bernhard, McPherson and Hand, Chartered
Wrangell, Alaska, City of

GILMAN, Maureen

901 E St. NW
Suite 600
Washington, DC 20004
Tel: (202)508-3708
Fax: (202)783-4085
Registered: LDA

Employers

Nat'l Treasury Employees Union (Director of Legislation)

GILMAN, Nicholas

600 Pennsylvania Ave. SE
Washington, DC 20003
Tel: (202)547-9080
Fax: (202)547-8944

Aviation Trial Attorney (1976-79) and Assistant U.S. Attorney for the District of Columbia (1972-76), Department of Justice. Law Clerk to Judge John Biggs, Jr., U.S. Court of Appeals, Third Circuit, 1971-72.

Employers

Gilman & Associates

GILMARTIN, William J.

1615 L St. NW
Suite 650
Washington, DC 20036
EMail: bgilmartin@jeffersongr.com
Tel: (202)626-8535
Fax: (202)626-8593
Registered: LDA

Former Legislative Director to former Rep. Bob Traxler (D-MI), 1986-93. Assistant Secretary of Housing and Urban Development for Congressional and Intergovernmental Relations, 1993-95.

Employers

Jefferson Government Relations, L.L.C. (V. President)

Clients Represented

On Behalf of Jefferson Government Relations, L.L.C.

AFL-CIO Housing Investment Trust
Bethune-Cookman College
Carlsberg Management Co.
Daytona Beach, City of
Edison Welding Institute
NAHB Research Center
Nat'l Ass'n of Home Builders Research Center, Inc.

GILROY, Daniel T.

601 13th St. NW
Suite 600 South
Washington, DC 20005
Tel: (202)626-3600
Fax: (202)639-9355

Employers

White & Case LLP (Legislative Affairs Specialist)

GILROY, Edwin J.

430 First St. SE
Washington, DC 20003
Tel: (202)544-6245
Fax: (202)544-6568
Registered: LDA

Employers

American Trucking Ass'ns (Director, Legislative Affairs)

GILSON, Marla

5100 Wisconsin Ave. NW
Washington, DC 20016
EMail: mgilson@hadassah.org
Tel: (202)363-4600
Fax: (202)363-4651
Registered: LDA

Employers

Hadassah, The Women's Zionist Organization of America (Director)

GILSON, Susan E.

1299 Pennsylvania Ave. NW
Suite 800 West
Washington, DC 20004
Tel: (202)785-0500
Fax: (202)785-5277
Registered: LDA

Employers

The Carmen Group
Council of Development Finance Agencies (Director, Communications)
LMRC, Inc. (Senior Associate)
Nat'l Ass'n of Flood and Stormwater Management Agencies (Director of Legislative and Regulatory Affairs)

Clients Represented

On Behalf of The Carmen Group

Interstate Council on Water Policy
Nat'l Ass'n of Flood and Stormwater Management Agencies

GILSTAD, USAFR (Ret.), Col. Claire

One Constitution Ave. NE
Washington, DC 20002
Tel: (202)479-2200
Fax: (202)479-0416
Registered: LDA

Employers

Reserve Officers Ass'n of the U.S. (Director, Air Force Affairs)

GIMBEL, Tod I.

1341 G St. NW
Suite 900
Washington, DC 20005
Tel: (202)637-1558
Fax: (202)637-1537

Employers

Philip Morris Management Corp. (District Director, East)

GINGLES, Andre J.

11785 Beltsville Dr.
Tenth Floor
Calverton, MD 20705
Tel: (301)572-7900
Fax: (301)572-6655
Registered: LDA

Employers

O'Malley, Miles, Nylen & Gilmore, P.A. (Senior Partner)

Clients Represented

On Behalf of O'Malley, Miles, Nylen & Gilmore, P.A.

Peterson Cos., Inc.

GINGRICH, Candace

919 18th St. NW
Suite 800
Washington, DC 20006
Tel: (202)628-4160
Fax: (202)347-5323

Employers

Human Rights Campaign Fund (NCOP Associate Manager)

GINGRICH, Claud

5400 Albia Rd.
Bethesda, MD 20816
Tel: (301)320-4125
Fax: (301)320-0762
Registered: LDA

Employers

GCS Inc. (President)

Clients Represented

On Behalf of GCS Inc.

Anheuser-Busch Cos., Inc.

GINGRICH, Hon. Newt

1150 17th St. NW
Washington, DC 20036
EMail: ngingrich@aei.org
Tel: (202)862-5800
Fax: (202)862-7177

Employers
American Enterprise Institute for Public Policy Research (Senior Fellow)

GINSBERG, Benjamin L.

2550 M St. NW
Washington, DC 20037-1350
Tel: (202)457-6000
Fax: (202)457-6315
Registered: LDA
EMail: bginsberg@pattonboggs.com

Employers
Patton Boggs, LLP (Partner)

Clients Represented
On Behalf of Patton Boggs, LLP
Air Force Memorial Foundation
American Insurance Ass'n
Commco, L.L.C.
Jacksonville, Florida, City of
Save Barton Creek
Security Capital Group

GINSBERG, Dr. Mark

1509 16th St. NW
Washington, DC 20036-1426
Tel: (202)232-8777
Fax: (202)328-1846

Employers
Nat'l Ass'n for the Education of Young Children (Exec. Director)

GINSBERG, Richard W.

601 Pennsylvania Ave. NW
South Bldg., Suite 900
Washington, DC 20004
Tel: (202)434-8163
Fax: (202)639-8238

Employers
Lockridge Grindal & Nauen, P.L.L.P.

GINSBURG, David

1001 Pennsylvania Ave. NW
Suite 600
Washington, DC 20004
EMail: dginsbur@pgfm.com
Tel: (202)347-0066
Fax: (202)624-7222
Administrative Assistant to Senator M. M. Neely (D-WV), 1950. General Counsel, Office of Price Administration, 1940-42. Law Clerk, U.S. Supreme Court, 1939. Attorney, Securities and Exchange Commission, 1935-39.

Employers
Powell, Goldstein, Frazer & Murphy LLP (Senior Counsel)

GINSBURG, Jack

2011 Pennsylvania Ave. NW
Suite 800
Washington, DC 20006-1808
Tel: (202)261-4542
Fax: (202)835-0443
Registered: LDA
EMail: jginsburg@mail.acponline.org

Employers
American College of Physicians-American Soc. of Internal Medicine (ACP-ASIM) (Director, Health Policy Analysis and Research)

GINSBURG, Mindy

2000 Pennsylvania Ave. NW
Suite 500
Washington, DC 20006
Tel: (202)887-1574
Registered: LDA

Employers
Viatel, Inc. (V. President, Regulatory Affairs)

GIOFFRE, Michele

700 13th St. NW
Suite 400
Washington, DC 20005
EMail: mgioffre@cassidy.com
Tel: (202)347-0773
Fax: (202)347-0785
Former Staff Member to Senator Joseph R. Biden, Jr. (D-DE).

Employers
Cassidy & Associates, Inc. (Associates)

Clients Represented
On Behalf of Cassidy & Associates, Inc.
Draft Worldwide
Major League Baseball
Rush Presbyterian-St. Luke's Medical Center

GIORDANO, Nick

1150 17th St. NW
Suite 601
Washington, DC 20036
Tel: (202)293-7474
Fax: (202)293-8811
Registered: LDA
Chief Minority Tax Counsel, Senate Committee on Finance, 1997-99. Legislative Director and Tax Counsel to Senator Max Baucus (D-SD), 1993-95.

Employers
Washington Council Ernst & Young (Partner)

Clients Represented
On Behalf of Washington Council Ernst & Young
Aetna Inc.
Aetna Life & Casualty Co.
Allen & Co.
American Express Co.
American Insurance Ass'n
American Staffing Ass'n
Anheuser-Busch Cos., Inc.
Antitrust Coalition for Consumer Choice in Health Care
Apartment Investment and Management Co.
Ass'n of American Railroads
Ass'n of Home Appliance Manufacturers
AT&T
AT&T Capital Corp.
Aventis Pharmaceuticals, Inc.
Baxter Healthcare Corp.
BHC Communications, Inc.
Bulmer Holding PLC, H. P.
Cash Balance Coalition
Citigroup
Coalition for Fairness in Defense Exports
Coalition to Preserve Tracking Stock
ComEd
The Connell Co.
Deferral Group
Directors Guild of America
Doris Duke Charitable Foundation
Eaton Vance Management Co.
Eden Financial Corp.
The Enterprise Foundation
Fannie Mae
FedEx Corp.
Ford Motor Co.
GE Capital Assurance
General Electric Co.
General Motors Corp.
Global Competitiveness Coalition
Grasslands Water District
Group Health, Inc.
Haz-X Support Services Corp.
HEREIU
Hewlett-Packard Co.
Gilbert P. Hyatt, Inventor
Investment Co. Institute
Large Public Power Council
Local Initiatives Support Corp.
Lockheed Martin Corp.
MacAndrews & Forbes Holdings, Inc.
Marsh & McLennan Cos.
MCG Northwest, Inc.
McLane Co.
Merrill Lynch & Co., Inc.
Metropolitan Banking Group
Microsoft Corp.
Mutual of Omaha Insurance Companies
Nat'l Ass'n for State Farm Agents
Nat'l Ass'n of Professional Employer Organizations
Nat'l Ass'n of Real Estate Investment Trusts
Nat'l Ass'n of State Farm Agents
Nat'l Cable Television Ass'n
Nat'l Defined Contribution Council
Nat'l Foreign Trade Council, Inc.
Nat'l Multi-Housing Council
PaineWebber Group, Inc.
Pfizer, Inc.
R&D Tax Credit Coalition
R&D Tax Regulation Group
Recording Industry Ass'n of America
Reed-Elsevier Inc.
R. J. Reynolds Tobacco Co.
Charles Schwab & Co., Inc.,
Securities Industry Ass'n
Sierra Pacific Industries
Skadden, Arps, Slate, Meagher & Flom LLP
Straddle Rules Tax Group
Tax Fairness Coalition
Tax/Shelter Coalition
TransOceanic Shipping
TU Services
TXU Business Services
U.S. Oncology
USA Biomass Power Producers Alliance
Viaticus, Inc.
Wilkie Farr & Gallagher
Ziff Investors Partnership

GIORDANO, Nick D.

122 C St. NW
Suite 875
Washington, DC 20001
Tel: (202)347-3600
Fax: (202)347-5265
Registered: LDA

Employers
Nat'l Pork Producers Council (International Trade Counsel)

GIORGIO, Cynthia

1150 17th St. NW
Suite 701
Washington, DC 20036
EMail: cynthiag@dittus.com
Tel: (202)775-1401
Fax: (202)775-1404

Employers
Dittus Communications (Assistant V. President)

Clients Represented
On Behalf of Dittus Communications
Business Software Alliance
eLink
Internat'l Limousine
Microsoft Corp.
SurfControl
Surviving Selma

GIOVANIELLO, Gerard

700 11th St. NW
Washington, DC 20001-4507
Tel: (202)383-1115
Fax: (202)383-7540
Registered: LDA

Employers
Nat'l Ass'n of Realtors (V. President, Government Affairs)

GIPP, Dr. Gerald

121 Oronoco St.
Alexandria, VA 22314
EMail: ggipp@aihec.org
Tel: (703)838-0400
Fax: (703)838-0388

Employers
American Indian Higher Education Consortium (Exec. Director)

GIRARDOT, Dean

9000 Machinists Pl.
Upper Marlboro, MD 20772-2687
Tel: (301)967-4500
Fax: (301)967-4515

Employers
Internat'l Ass'n of Machinists and Aerospace Workers (Exec. Assistant)

GIROUX, Angela

1320 19th St. NW
Suite 300
Washington, DC 20036
Tel: (202)887-1970
Fax: (202)887-0950
Registered: LDA

Employers
Ass'n of Local Television Stations (Director, Congressional Relations)

GIROUX, Terrence J.

99 Canal Center Plaza
Suite 320
Alexandria, VA 22314
Tel: (703)684-9444
Fax: (703)684-9445

Employers
Horatio Alger Ass'n of Distinguished Americans (Exec. Director)

GIRTON-MITCHELL, Brenda

110 Maryland Ave. NE
Washington, DC 20002
EMail: bgirtonm@ncccusa.org
Tel: (202)544-2350
Fax: (202)543-1297

Employers
Nat'l Council of the Churches of Christ in the USA (Director, Washington Office)

GIST, John

601 E St. NW
Washington, DC 20049
EMail: jgist@aarp.org
Tel: (202)434-3870
Fax: (202)434-6402

Employers
AARP (American Ass'n of Retired Persons) (Associate Director, Public Policy Institute)

GITENSTEIN, Mark H.

1909 K St. NW
Washington, DC 20006
Tel: (202)263-3000
Fax: (202)263-3300
Registered: LDA
EMail: mgitenstein@mayerbrown.com
Chief Counsel, Senate Judiciary Committee, 1987-89. Minority Chief Counsel, Senate Judiciary Committee, 1981-87. Chief Counsel, Senate Subcommittee on Criminal Justice of the Judiciary Committee, 1978-81. Counsel, Senate Intelligence Committee, 1976-78.

Employers
Mayer, Brown & Platt (Partner)

Clients Represented
On Behalf of Mayer, Brown & Platt
Accenture
ACE INA
Ace Ltd.
Ameritech
Ass'n of Publicly Traded Companies
Burlington Northern Santa Fe Railway
Cable & Wireless, Inc.
Chicago Stock Exchange, Inc.
Ernst & Young LLP
General Dynamics Corp.
KPMG, LLP
Lockheed Martin Corp.
Oracle Corp.
PriceWaterhouseCoopers
Technology Network
United Defense, L.P.
United Technologies Corp.

GITTELMAN, Lynn

119 Oronoco St.
Alexandria, VA 22314-2015
Tel: (703)683-5400
Fax: (703)548-5728
EMail: lynngittelman@presidentialclassroom

Employers
A Presidential Classroom for Young Americans, Inc. (Director of Marketing)

GIUGNI, Henry K.

700 13th St. NW
Suite 400
Washington, DC 20005
Tel: (202)347-0773
Fax: (202)347-0785
Registered: LDA, FARA
EMail: hgiugni@cassidy.com
Sergeant at Arms, U.S. Senate, 1986-90. Administrative Assistant to Senator Daniel Inouye (D-HI), 1963-86.

Employers
Cassidy & Associates, Inc. (V. Chairman)

Clients Represented
On Behalf of Cassidy & Associates, Inc.
Bishop Museum
The Boeing Co.
Boston University
Chicago Mercantile Exchange
Henry Ford Health System
Hawaii, State of
Kuakini Hospital
The Nature Conservancy

GIVENS, Veronica I.

Theodore Roosevelt Federal Bldg.
1900 E St. NW
MS: 5H30
Washington, DC 20415
Tel: (202)606-1300
Fax: (202)606-1344

Employers
Office of Personnel Management (Legislative Analyst)

GIVHAN, Lt. Col. Walter

1160 Air Force Pentagon
Room 5D928
Washington, DC 20330-1160
Tel: (703)695-1292
Fax: (703)697-2001

Employers
Department of Air Force (Chief, Congressional Action Division, Legislative Liaison)

GLAKAS, Nicholas

Ten G St. NE
Suite 750
Washington, DC 20002-4213
Tel: (202)336-6700
Fax: (202)336-6828
EMail: NickG@career.org

Employers
Career College Ass'n (President)

GLASER, Howard B.

1919 Pennsylvania Ave. NW
Seventh Floor
Washington, DC 20006-3488
Tel: (202)557-2700
Registered: LDA
Formerly Deputy General Counsel, Department of Housing and Urban Development.

Employers
Mortgage Bankers Ass'n of America (Senior Staff V. President and General Counsel)

GLASGOW, James A.

1800 M St. NW
Washington, DC 20036
Tel: (202)467-7000
Fax: (202)467-7176
Registered: LDA
EMail: jglasgow@morganlewis.com

Employers
Morgan, Lewis & Bockius LLP

Clients Represented
On Behalf of Morgan, Lewis & Bockius LLP
Credit Suisse First Boston Corp.

GLASHEEN, Megan

1250 I St. NW
Suite 900
Washington, DC 20005
Tel: (202)783-2800
Fax: (202)783-0550
Registered: LDA
EMail: Mglasheen@renocavanaugh.com

Employers
Reno & Cavanaugh, PLLC (Member)

GLASS, Jonathan

1200 New Hampshire Ave. NW
Suite 800
Washington, DC 20036-6802
Tel: (202)776-2000
Fax: (202)776-2222
Registered: LDA
EMail: jglass@dlalaw.com

Employers
Dow, Lohnes & Albertson, PLLC (Member)

Clients Represented
On Behalf of Dow, Lohnes & Albertson, PLLC
Middlesex Community-Technical College
St. Matthew's University School of Medicine

GLAUB, Richard

1150 Connecticut Ave. NW
Suite 201
Washington, DC 20036
Tel: (202)955-6200
Fax: (202)955-6215
EMail: rglaub@gcwdc.com

Employers
Goddard Claussen (Senior V. President)

GLAVES, Dennis

1300 I St. NW
Suite 400 West
Washington, DC 20005
Tel: (202)515-2565
Fax: (202)336-7925

Employers
Verizon Communications (V. President, Federal Government Relations)

GLAZA, Gordon

1120 Connecticut Ave. NW
Washington, DC 20036
Tel: (202)663-5000
Fax: (202)828-5052
Registered: LDA

Employers
American Bankers Ass'n (Regulatory Counsel)

GLAZE, James E.

1250 I St. NW
Suite 1000
Washington, DC 20005
Tel: (202)682-0240
Fax: (202)682-0249

Employers
Sonosky, Chambers, Sachse & Endreson (Associate)

GLAZE, Steve

801 Pennsylvania Ave. NW
Suite 730
Washington, DC 20004
Tel: (202)756-2416
Fax: (202)756-2417
Registered: LDA
EMail: Glaze@howdc.com
Tax Counsel to Senator David Pryor, 1990-96. Chairman, Subcommittee on Taxation and IRS Oversight, Senate Committee on Finance, 1990-96.

Employers
Hooper Owen & Winburn (Principal)

Clients Represented
On Behalf of Hooper Owen & Winburn
AFL-CIO (American Federation of Labor and Congress of Industrial Organizations)
American Soc. of Pension Actuaries
Apple Computer, Inc.
Bessemer Securities Corp.
Cox Enterprises Inc.
The Hartford
KPMG, LLP
Metropolitan Life Insurance Co.
Parsons Corp.
Stephens Group, Inc.
Waste Management, Inc.
Wine and Spirits Wholesalers of America

GLAZER, Melinda

1300 N. 17th St.
Eighth Floor
Rosslyn, VA 22209-3801
Tel: (703)812-2000
Fax: (703)820-2
EMail: glazer@abc.org

Employers
Associated Builders and Contractors (Legislative Assistant)

GLAZIER, Jonathan H.

4301 Wilson Blvd.
Arlington, VA 22203-1860
Tel: (703)907-5798
Fax: (703)907-5517
Registered: LDA
EMail: jonathan.glazier@nreca.org

Employers
Nat'l Rural Electric Cooperative Ass'n (Association Counsel)

GLAZIER, Mitch

1330 Connecticut Ave. NW
Suite 300
Washington, DC 20036
Tel: (202)775-0101
Fax: (202)775-7253
Former Chief Counsel, Subcommittee on Courts and Intellectual Property, House Committee on the Judiciary.

Employers
Recording Industry Ass'n of America (Senior V. President, Government Relations and Legislative Counsel)

GLEASON, Barbara

1703 N. Beauregard St.
Alexandria, VA 22311-1714
Tel: (703)575-5610
Fax: (703)575-5400
EMail: bgleason@ascd.org

Employers
Ass'n for Supervision and Curriculum Development (Director, Public Information)

GLEASON, Carolyn B.

600 13th St. NW
Washington, DC 20005-3096
Tel: (202)756-8215
Fax: (202)756-8087
Registered: LDA
EMail: cgleason@mwe.com

Employers
McDermott, Will and Emery (Partner)

Clients Represented
On Behalf of McDermott, Will and Emery
Alaska Seafood Marketing Institute
Blue Anchor, Inc.
California Canning Peach Ass'n
California Cling Peach Growers Advisory Board
Chase Nat'l Kiwi Farms
Chiquita Brands Internat'l, Inc.
Florida Fruit and Vegetable Ass'n
U.S. Mink Export Development Council
Welch's Foods, Inc.

GLEASON, Donna

1200 Wilson Blvd.
Arlington, VA 22209
Tel: (703)465-3263
Fax: (703)465-3004
Registered: LDA

Employers
The Boeing Co. (Director, Corporate Legislation)

GLEASON, Kathryn L.

1800 M St. NW
Washington, DC 20036
Tel: (202)467-7000
Fax: (202)467-7176
Registered: LDA
EMail: kgleason@morganlewis.com

Employers
Morgan, Lewis & Bockius LLP (Partner)

Clients Represented
On Behalf of Morgan, Lewis & Bockius LLP
Cord Blood Registry, Inc.

GLEASON, Robert E.

1101 17th St. NW
Suite 400
Washington, DC 20036
Tel: (202)955-6304
Fax: (202)955-6048

Employers
Internat'l Longshoremen's Ass'n (Secretary/Treasurer)

GLEASON, Stefan H.

8001 Braddock Rd.
Springfield, VA 22160
Tel: (703)321-8510
Fax: (703)321-9319

Employers
Nat'l Right to Work Legal Defense Foundation (V. President)

GLEASON, Teresa A.

815 Connecticut Ave. NW
Suite 900
Washington, DC 20006-4078
Tel: (202)452-7000
Fax: (202)452-7073
Registered: LDA

Employers
Baker & McKenzie (Partner)

Clients Represented
On Behalf of Baker & McKenzie
R. G. Barry
ChemFirst Inc.
Storck U.S.A.
Wm. Wrigley Jr. Co.

GLEDHILL, Jonathan

819 Seventh St. NW
Washington, DC 20001
Tel: (202)833-8940
Fax: (202)833-8943
Registered: LDA

Employers
EOP Group, Inc.

Clients Represented
On Behalf of EOP Group, Inc.
American Petroleum Institute
Dow AgroSciences
The Dow Chemical Co.
Edison Electric Institute
FMC Corp.
Fort Howard Corp.
Internat'l Food Additives Council
Monsanto Co.
Novartis Crop Protection
Price Costco

GLEIBER, John

P.O. Box 3719
Georgetown Station
Washington, DC 20007
Tel: (202)337-2334
Fax: (202)338-9478

Employers
Soc. for Animal Protective Legislation (Exec. Secretary)

GLENN, Robert E.

4041 Powder Mill Rd.
Suite 402
Calverton, MD 20705
Tel: (301)595-5550
Fax: (301)595-3303

Employers
Nat'l Industrial Sand Ass'n (President)

GLENNON, Margie Fleming

1616 H St. NW
Third Floor
Washington, DC 20006
Tel: (202)737-3700
Fax: (202)737-0530

Employers
Internat'l Center for Journalists (Director, Communications)

GLENNON, Jr., Robert E.

1155 21st St. NW
Suite 300
Washington, DC 20036
Tel: (202)659-8201
Fax: (202)659-5249
Registered: LDA, FARA
EMail: reglennon@wms-jen.com

Employers
Williams & Jensen, P.C. (Partner)

Clients Represented
On Behalf of Williams & Jensen, P.C.
ACE INA
Aegon USA
Alexander's Inc.
American Home Products Corp.
AOL Time Warner
Bass Enterprises Production Co.
Chandis Securities Co.
CIGNA Corp.
The Coca-Cola Company
Credit Suisse First Boston Corp.
Estee Lauder, Inc.
Fannie Mae
First Union Corp.
Keystone, Inc.
La Quinta Inns, Inc.
MeriStar Hospitality Corp.
J. P. Morgan Chase & Co.
J. P. Morgan Securities
Norfolk Southern Corp.
Owens-Illinois, Inc.
Perdue Farms Inc.
Pier 1 Imports
Pilgrim's Pride
Reinsurance Ass'n of America
Texaco Group Inc.
Texas Pacific Group
USAA - United Services Automobile Ass'n
Vornado Inc.

GLESKE, Elmer G.

1201 Pennsylvania Ave. NW
Suite 300
Washington, DC 20004-2401
Tel: (202)661-4700
Fax: (202)661-4799
EMail: gleskea@fsi001.flightsafety.com

Employers
FlightSafety Internat'l (V. President, Governmental Affairs)

GLEW, Jr., William B.

3000 K St. NW
Suite 300
Washington, DC 20007
Tel: (202)424-7500
Fax: (202)424-7643
Registered: LDA

Employers
Swidler Berlin Shereff Friedman, LLP (Counsel)

Clients Represented
On Behalf of Swidler Berlin Shereff Friedman, LLP
Newman & Associates
Niagara Mohawk Power Corp.

GLICK, Helene L.

1800 M St. NW
Washington, DC 20036
Tel: (202)467-7000
Fax: (202)467-7176
Registered: LDA
EMail: hglick@morganlewis.com

Employers
Morgan, Lewis & Bockius LLP (Associate)

Clients Represented
On Behalf of Morgan, Lewis & Bockius LLP
The Church Alliance
Coalition of Supporters of the Shipping Act

GLICK, Leslie Alan

1919 Pennsylvania Ave. NW
Suite 500
Washington, DC 20006-3434
Tel: (202)778-3000
Fax: (202)778-3063
Registered: FARA
EMail: lglick@porterwright.com
Counsel, Subcommittee on International Trade, House Select Committee on Small Business, 1973-74.

Employers
Porter, Wright, Morris & Arthur, LLP (Partner)

Clients Represented
On Behalf of Porter, Wright, Morris & Arthur, LLP
ACS Industries, Inc.
Asociacion Nacional de la Industria Quimica (ANIQ), A.C
Ass'n of Brazilian Ceramic Tile Producers
Ass'n of Brazilian Tire Producers
Industrial Minera Mexicana
Kemet Electronics Co.
TEKSID/Fiat U.S.A.
Vishay Intertechnologies, Inc.

GLICK, Nancy L.

600 New Hampshire Ave. NW
Suite 601
Washington, DC 20037
Tel: (202)333-7400
Fax: (202)333-1638
EMail: nglick@hillandknowlton.com
Formerly served with the Food and Drug Administration press office.

Employers
Hill and Knowlton, Inc. (Sr. Managing Director, Sr. Counselor for Health, Nutrition and Consumer Issues)

GLICK, Warren W.

1828 L St. NW
Eleventh Floor
Washington, DC 20036-5109
Tel: (202)467-8807
Fax: (202)467-8900
EMail: glickwa@vssp.com
V. President and Senior V. President for Financing, 1969-73; Acting Exec. V. President, 1973-75; and General Counsel, 1975-84, Export-Import Bank of the United States.

Employers
Vorys, Sater, Seymour and Pease, LLP (Counsel)

Clients Represented
On Behalf of Vorys, Sater, Seymour and Pease, LLP
Arab American Bank
Australia and New Zealand Banking Group
Banco Portugues do Atlantico, S.A.
Camac Holdings, Inc.
Chadwick Internat'l, Inc.
M&W Pump Corp.
J. P. Redd Inc.
Texuna Internat'l USA Ltd.

GLICKMAN, Hon. Daniel R.

1333 New Hampshire Ave. NW
Suite 400
Washington, DC 20036
Tel: (202)887-4000
Fax: (202)887-4288
Secretary, Department of Agriculture, 1995-2001. Member, U.S. House of Representatives (D-KS), 1977-75. Attorney, Securities and Exchange Commission, 1969-70.

Employers
Akin, Gump, Strauss, Hauer & Feld, L.L.P. (Partner)

GLISSON, JoAnne

1250 H St. NW
Suite 880
Washington, DC 20005
Tel: (202)637-9466
Fax: (202)637-2050
Registered: LDA
EMail: glisson@clinical-labs.org

Employers
American Clinical Laboratory Ass'n (V. President, Government Relations)

GLISSON, Laine

412 First St. SE
Suite 100
Washington, DC 20003
Tel: (202)484-4884
Fax: (202)484-0109
Registered: LDA
Former Press Secretary to Senator John Breaux (D-LA).

Employers
The Dutko Group, Inc.

GLITZENSTEIN, Eric

1601 Connecticut Ave. NW
Suite 700
Washington, DC 20009-1056
Tel: (202)588-5206
Fax: (202)588-5049

Employers
Meyer & Glitzenstein (Partner)

GLOTFELTY, Rick

801 18th St. NW
Washington, DC 20006
Tel: (202)872-1300
Fax: (202)785-4452

Employers
Paralyzed Veterans of America (Associate Exec. Director, Veterans Benefits)

GLOVER, Gregory J.

1301 K St. NW
Suite 800 East
Washington, DC 20005
EMail: gglover@ropesgray.com
Tel: (202)626-3926
Fax: (202)626-3961

Employers
Ropes & Gray (Partner)

GLOVER, Rebecca

8725 John J. Kingman Rd.
Suite 2533
Ft. Belvoir, VA 22060-6221
Tel: (703)767-5292
Fax: (703)767-6312

Employers
Department of Defense - Defense Logistics Agency (Congressional Affairs Specialist)

GLOVER, Ph.D., Robert W.

66 Canal Center Plaza
Suite 302
Alexandria, VA 22314
Tel: (703)739-9333
Fax: (703)548-9517

Employers
Nat'l Ass'n of State Mental Health Program Directors (Exec. Director)

GLOWAKY, Ph.D., Raymond

7900 Westpark Dr.
Suite A-320
McLean, VA 22102
Tel: (703)790-5011
Fax: (703)790-5752

Employers
American Cocoa Research Institute (Senior V. President, Scientific and Regulatory Affairs)

GLOZER, Ken

11 Dupont Circle NW
Suite 700
Washington, DC 20036
Tel: (202)293-5886
Fax: (202)939-6969
Registered: LDA

Employers
Multinat'l Government Services, Inc.

Clients Represented

On Behalf of Multinat'l Government Services, Inc.
Edison Electric Institute

GLUCK, Adam

25 E St. NW
Washington, DC 20001
Tel: (202)628-8787
Fax: (202)662-3550
Registered: LDA
EMail: agluck@childrensdefense.org

Employers
Children's Defense Fund (Senior House Associate)

GLUCK, Richard D.

1000 Potomac St. NW
Suite 500
Washington, DC 20007
Tel: (202)965-7880
Fax: (202)965-1729
Registered: LDA
EMail: rgluck@gsblaw.com

Employers
Garvey, Schubert & Barer (Partner)

Clients Represented

On Behalf of Garvey, Schubert & Barer
American Internat'l Freight Ass'n
China Ocean Shipping Co.

GLUCKSMAN, Daniel I.

1901 N. Moore St.
Suite 808
Arlington, VA 22209
Tel: (703)525-1695
Fax: (703)528-2148
Registered: LDA
EMail: dglucksman@safetyequipment.org

Employers
Internat'l Safety Equipment Ass'n (ISEA) (Director, Public Affairs)

GLUECK, Kenneth

1667 K St. NW
Suite 640
Washington, DC 20006-1605
Tel: (202)721-4815
Fax: (202)467-4250
Registered: LDA
EMail: kenneth.glueck@oracle.com
Former Aide to Senator Joseph Lieberman (D-CT).

Employers
Oracle Corp. (V. President, Government Affairs)

GLUNZ, Kathleen

1301 Pennsylvania Ave. NW
Suite 404
Washington, DC 20004-1727
Tel: (202)783-0911
Fax: (202)783-3524

Employers
Chicago, Illinois, Washington Office of the City of (Deputy Director)

GOCH, David P.

1747 Pennsylvania Ave. NW
Suite 1000
Washington, DC 20006
Tel: (202)785-9500
Fax: (202)835-0243
Registered: LDA, FARA

Employers
Webster, Chamberlain & Bean (Partner)

Clients Represented

On Behalf of Webster, Chamberlain & Bean
American Soc. of Radiologic Technologists
Commercial Law League of America

GODDARD, Montrice D.

1015 18th St. NW
Suite 1100
Washington, DC 20036-5725
EMail: mgodard@csbsdc.org
Tel: (202)296-2840
Fax: (202)296-1928

Employers
Conference of State Bank Supervisors (Senior V. President, Regulation)

GODFREY, Jr., Carl Franklin

700 13th St. NW
Suite 400
Washington, DC 20005
Tel: (202)347-0773
Fax: (202)347-0785
Registered: LDA, FARA
EMail: fgodfrey@cassidy.com
Former Executive Assistant, Senior Legislative Assistant, and Legislative Assistant to Rep. Thomas P. O'Neill Jr. (D-MA). Staff Member of Subcommittee on Consumer Protection and Finance, House Committee on Energy and Commerce.

Employers
Cassidy & Associates, Inc. (Exec. V. President)

Clients Represented

On Behalf of Cassidy & Associates, Inc.
The Auxiliary Service Corporations
Boston University
Columbia University
Condell Medical Center
DRAKA USA Corp.
Fairfield University
Gabonese Republic, Office of the President of the
Hampton University
Internat'l Snowmobile Manufacturers Ass'n
Maersk Inc.
Ocean Spray Cranberries
Philadelphia College of Textiles and Science
San Diego, University of
Texas Tech University System
Tufts University School of Veterinary Medicine
University of Dubuque
University of Puerto Rico
University of the Sciences
Westminster College
Wheelchairs for the World Foundation

GODFREY, David F.

P.O. Box 6394
Alexandria, VA 22306
Tel: (703)780-2462
Fax: (703)780-6123
Registered: LDA

Employers
Self-employed as an independent consultant.

Clients Represented

As an independent consultant
Dal Mac Investment Corp.
Indian Pueblos Federal Development Corp.
Keating Development Corp.
W. G. Yates & Sons Construction Co.

GODFREY, John

1250 I St. NW
Suite 200
Washington, DC 20005
Tel: (202)737-8888
Fax: (202)638-4922
Registered: LDA

Employers
Information Technology Industry Council (Director, Technology Policy)

GODLES, Joseph A.

1229 19th St. NW
Washington, DC 20036
Tel: (202)429-4900
Fax: (202)429-4912
Registered: LDA
EMail: general@g2w2.com

Employers
Goldberg, Godles, Wiener & Wright (Partner)

GODLEY, Gene E.

2000 K St. NW
Suite 500
Washington, DC 20006-1872
Tel: (202)828-5870
Fax: (202)223-1225
Registered: LDA
EMail: ggodley@bracepatt.com
Assistant Secretary for Legislative Affairs, Department of Treasury, 1977-80. General Counsel, Senate District Committee, 1970-71. General Counsel, Senate Labor and Public Welfare Committee, 1969-70. Administrative Assistant to Senator Ralph Yarborough (D-TX), 1967-69.

Employers
Bracewell & Patterson, L.L.P. (Partner)

Clients Represented

On Behalf of Bracewell & Patterson, L.L.P.
Africa Resources Trust USA
Air Conditioning Contractors of America
Alltel Corporation
American Registry for Internet Numbers (ARIN)
Baldwin Piano and Organ Co.
Cement Kiln Recycling Coalition
Continental Cement Co., Inc.
Council of Industrial Boiler Owners (CIBO)
Enron Corp.
Envirocare of Utah, Inc.
FBI Agents Ass'n
Gary-Williams Energy Corp.
Gas Processors Ass'n
Houston, Texas, Port Authority of the City of
Huntsman Corp.
Independent Oil and Gas Ass'n of Pennsylvania
Lyondell Chemical Co.
Nat'l Cable Television Ass'n
Oxygenated Fuels Ass'n
Physician Insurers Ass'n of America
Placid Refining Co.
Solex Environmental Systems, Inc.
Southdown, Inc.
Sterling Chemical Co.
Texas Petrochemicals Corp.
Texas Windstorm Insurance Ass'n
Valero Energy Corp.
Welcon, Inc.

GODLEY, Patricia Fry

1050 Thomas Jefferson St. NW
Seventh Floor
Washington, DC 20007
Tel: (202)298-1800
Fax: (202)338-2416
Registered: LDA
EMail: PFG@vnf.com
Assistant Secretary for Fossil Energy (1994-98), and Special Assistant to the Deputy Secretary (1993-94), Department of Energy.

Employers
Van Ness Feldman, P.C. (Member)

Clients Represented

On Behalf of Van Ness Feldman, P.C.
Alaska North Slope LNG Project

GODLOWSKI, Matt

1401 I St. NW
Suite 1220
Washington, DC 20005
Tel: (202)898-6400
Fax: (202)898-6454

Employers
Vivendi Universal (Manager, Public Policy)

GODSON, Dr. Roy

1730 Rhode Island Ave. NW
Suite 500
Washington, DC 20036
EMail: nsic@ix.netcom.com
Tel: (202)429-0129
Fax: (202)659-5429

Employers
Nat'l Strategy Information Center (President)

GODWIN, Jean C.

1010 Duke St.
Alexandria, VA 22314-3589
Tel: (703)684-5700
Fax: (703)684-6321
Registered: LDA

Employers
American Ass'n of Port Authorities (Exec. V. President and General Counsel)

GODWIN, Mike

1634 I St. NW
Suite 1100
Washington, DC 20006-4003
Tel: (202)637-9800
Fax: (202)637-0968

Employers
Center for Democracy and Technology (Senior Fellow)

GOEAS, Carole

503 Second St. NE
Washington, DC 20002
EMail: cgoeas@patrickmurphy.com
Tel: (202)544-8490
Fax: (202)543-7804

Employers
Patrick M. Murphy & Associates (Associate)

GOEDHARD, Bart

3927 Old Lee Hwy.
Suite 101A
Fairfax, VA 22030
Tel: (703)691-2777
Fax: (703)691-4173

Employers
The Propeller Club of the United States (Exec. V. President)

GOEHLER, David J.

515 Prince St.
Alexandria, VA 22314-3115
EMail: dave.goehler@jeppesen.com
Tel: (703)519-5295
Fax: (703)519-5296

Employers
Jeppesen Sanderson, Inc. (Director, Washington Office)

GOEL, Ankur J.

600 13th St. NW
Washington, DC 20005-3096
EMail: agoel@mwe.com
Tel: (202)756-8234
Fax: (202)756-8087
Former Attorney, Department of Justice.

Employers
McDermott, Will and Emery (Partner)

GOELDNER, Dean

1101 Vermont Ave. NW
Suite 710
Washington, DC 20005-3521
Tel: (202)789-0007
Fax: (202)842-4360

Employers
American Veterinary Medical Ass'n (Assistant Director, Government Relations)

GOELZ, Peter

1615 L St. NW
Suite 900
Washington, DC 20036
Tel: (202)778-1000
Fax: (202)466-6002
Registered: LDA
Former Managing Director, National Transportation Safety Board,

Employers
APCO Worldwide

Clients Represented
On Behalf of APCO Worldwide
Alaska Airlines

GOERGEN, Michael

5400 Grosvenor Ln.
Bethesda, MD 20814-2198
EMail: goergenm@safnet.org
Tel: (301)897-8720
Fax: (301)897-3690

Employers
Soc. of American Foresters (Director, Forest Policy)

GOETEL, Katie

1225 I St. NW
Suite 1000
Washington, DC 20005-3914
Tel: (202)842-7400
Fax: (202)842-0022

Employers
Institute for a Drug-Free Workplace (Assistant Counsel)

GOETZE, Richard

4701 Sangamore Rd.
Suite N100
Bethesda, MD 20816-2508
Tel: (301)229-5800
Fax: (301)229-5045
Registered: LDA

Employers
Burdeshaw Associates, Ltd. (Associate)

GOFF, Donald G.

1200 Wilson Blvd.
Arlington, VA 22209-1989
Tel: (703)465-3218
Fax: (703)465-3004
Registered: LDA

Employers
The Boeing Co. (Director, Legislative Affairs)

GOFF, Jackie

2215 M St. NW
Washington, DC 20037
Tel: (202)785-1614
Fax: (202)785-1568

Employers
Federal Bar Ass'n (President)

GOGAL, Laura S.

801 Pennsylvania Ave. NW
Suite 245
Washington, DC 20004-2604
EMail: lgogal@americashospitals.com
Tel: (202)624-1526
Fax: (202)737-6462
Registered: LDA

Employers
Federation of American Hospitals (V. President and Chief Counsel)

GOGOL, David U.

805 15th St. NW
Suite 700
Washington, DC 20005
EMail: dugogol@bakerd.com
Tel: (202)312-7400
Fax: (202)312-7441
Registered: LDA
Legislative Director to Senator Richard Lugar (R-IN), 1983-85. Assistant to the Chairman, Senate Subcommittee on Housing and Urban Affairs, 1981-83. Legislative Assistant to Senator Lugar, 1978-81.

Employers
Sagamore Associates, Inc. (President)

Clients Represented
On Behalf of Sagamore Associates, Inc.
2001 World Police and Fire Games
Allegheny County, Pennsylvania, Housing Authority
Cinergy PSI
Fort Wayne, Indiana, City of
Historic Landmarks Foundation of Indiana
Marion, Indiana, City of
Medford, Oregon, City of
Polk, Iowa, County of
Recreation Vehicle Industry Ass'n
Shake-A-Leg
Spring Hill Camps
U.S. Olympic Committee
Walsh Enterprises Internat'l
Ways to Work

GOHEEN, John

One Massachusetts Ave. NW
Washington, DC 20001
Tel: (202)789-0031
Fax: (202)682-9358

Employers
Nat'l Guard Ass'n of the U.S. (Director, Communications)

GOLAB, Thomas

1001 Connecticut Ave. NW
Suite 1250
Washington, DC 20036
Tel: (202)331-1010
Fax: (202)331-0640

Employers
Competitive Enterprise Institute (V. President for Development)

GOLD, Jonathan E.

1700 N. Moore St.
Suite 2250
Arlington, VA 22209
EMail: jongold@imra.org
Tel: (703)841-2300
Fax: (703)841-1184
Registered: LDA

Employers
Internat'l Mass Retailers Ass'n (Legislative Representative)

GOLD, Josh

112 Elden St.
Unit J
Herndon, VA 20170
Tel: (703)709-8299
Fax: (703)709-1036

Employers
Barrack Ass'n Management (Account Executive)
Nat'l Ass'n of Metal Finishers (Deputy Director)
Washington Technical Professional Forum (WTPF) (Deputy Director)

GOLD, Laurence

1000 Connecticut Ave. NW
Suite 1300
Washington, DC 20036
Tel: (202)842-2600
Fax: (202)842-1888
Attorney, Office of the General Counsel, Supreme Court Branch, National Labor Relations Board, 1963-65. Law Clerk to Judge Joe Ingraham, U.S. District Court for Houston, Texas, 1962-63.

Employers
Bredhoff & Kaiser (Of Counsel)

GOLD, Martin B.

1001 Pennsylvania Ave. NW
Suite 760 North
Washington, DC 20004
Tel: (202)661-7060
Fax: (202)661-7066
Registered: LDA
Former Counsel to Senate Majority Leader Howard Baker, Jr. (R-TN); Minority Staff Director and Counsel, Senate Rules Committee; Professional Staff, Select Senate Committee on Intelligence; and Legal Assistant to Senator Mark Hatfield (R-OR).

Employers
The Legislative Strategies Group, LLC (Chairman)

Clients Represented
On Behalf of The Legislative Strategies Group, LLC
Allscripts Inc.
American Academy of Dermatology
American College of Cardiology
American Hospital Ass'n
Citizens Flag Alliance
Eye Bank Ass'n of America
Federal Home Loan Bank of San Francisco
Harcourt General
Hopi Indian Tribe
Joint Commission on the Accreditation of Health Care Organizations
MedPartners, Inc.
Nat'l Football League
Nat'l Orthotics Manufacturers Ass'n

GOLD, Richard M.

2099 Pennsylvania Ave. NW
Suite 100
Washington, DC 20006
EMail: rgold@hklaw.com
Tel: (202)457-7143
Fax: (202)955-5564
Registered: LDA
Special Assistant to the Administrator, Environmental Protection Agency, 1993-94. Special Assistant to Senator Lloyd Bentsen (D-TX), 1991-92.

Employers
Holland & Knight LLP (Partner)

Clients Represented
On Behalf of Holland & Knight LLP
American Chemistry Council
Benova, Inc.
Consortium for Plant Biotechnology Research
Consortium Plant Biotech Research
DuPont
FirstEnergy Co.
Florida Gas Utility
FMC Corp.
S.C. Johnson and Son, Inc.
Mille Lacs Band of Ojibwe Indians
Murphy Oil U.S.A.
Nassau County Health Care Corp.
Nat'l Paint and Coatings Ass'n
Placer, California, County of
Rockdale, Georgia, County of, Board of Commissioners of
Sarasota, Florida, City of
Sarasota, Florida, County of
Somerville Housing Group
Southern Coalition for Advanced Transportation
United Airlines
Water Systems Council
West Palm Beach, Florida, City of
Wyeth-Ayerst Pharmaceuticals

GOLD, Stephen

1331 Pennsylvania Ave. NW
Sixth Floor
Washington, DC 20004-1790
Tel: (202)637-3104
Fax: (202)637-3182

Employers
Nat'l Ass'n of Manufacturers (Exec. Director, Associations Council)

GOLDBERG, Adam

1666 Connecticut Ave. NW
Suite 310
Washington, DC 20009
EMail: goldad@consumer.org
Tel: (202)462-6262
Fax: (202)265-9548
Registered: LDA

Employers
Consumers Union of the United States (Policy Analyst)

GOLDBERG, Avrum M.

1333 New Hampshire Ave. NW
Suite 400
Washington, DC 20036
Tel: (202)887-4000
Fax: (202)887-4288
Attorney, Division of Litigation, Office of the General Counsel, National Labor Relations Board, 1969-73.

Employers
Akin, Gump, Strauss, Hauer & Feld, L.L.P. (Partner)

GOLDBERG, Dara

1320 Braddock Pl.
Alexandria, VA 22314
Tel: (703)739-5000
Fax: (703)739-0775

Employers
Public Broadcasting Service (Director, Corporate Communications)

GOLDBERG, Deborah

1000 Wisconsin Ave. NW
Washington, DC 20007
EMail: goldbergd@commchange.com
Tel: (202)342-0567
Fax: (202)333-5462

Employers
Center for Community Change (Co-Director, Neighborhood Revitalization Project)

GOLDBERG, Jr., Fred T.

1440 New York Ave. NW
Washington, DC 20005
Tel: (202)371-7000
Fax: (202)393-5760
Registered: LDA
Commissioner, Internat'l Revenue Service, 1989-92; Assistant Secretary for Tax Policy, Department of the Treasury, 1992.

Employers
Skadden, Arps, Slate, Meagher & Flom LLP (Partner)

Clients Represented
On Behalf of Skadden, Arps, Slate, Meagher & Flom LLP
Clark/Bardes, Inc.
Fidelity Charitable Gift Fund
Fort Howard Corp.
MCI WorldCom Corp.
Pharmaceutical Research and Manufacturers of America
Tax Fairness Coalition

GOLDBERG, Henry

1229 19th St. NW
Washington, DC 20036
EMail: general@g2w2.com
Tel: (202)429-4900
Fax: (202)429-4912
Registered: LDA

Employers
Goldberg, Godles, Wiener & Wright (Partner)

Clients Represented
On Behalf of Goldberg, Godles, Wiener & Wright
PanAmSat Corp.

GOLDBERG, James M.

888 16th St. NW
Suite 700
Washington, DC 20006-4103
EMail: jimcounsel@aol.com
Tel: (202)835-8282
Fax: (202)835-8293
Registered: LDA

Employers
Goldberg & Associates, PLLC (Partner)

Clients Represented
On Behalf of Goldberg & Associates, PLLC
American Peanut Council
American School Counselor Ass'n
Michigan Retailers Ass'n
Nat'l Alcohol Beverage Control Ass'n
Nat'l Ass'n of School Music Dealers
North American Retail Dealers Ass'n

GOLDBERG, Joan R.

2025 M St. NW
Suite 800
Washington, DC 20036
EMail: joan_goldberg@dc.sba.com
Tel: (202)367-2100
Fax: (202)367-1200

Employers
Smith, Bucklin and Associates, Inc.

Clients Represented
On Behalf of Smith, Bucklin and Associates, Inc.
American Soc. for Bone and Mineral Research

GOLDBERG, Kevin M.

1920 N St. NW
Suite 300
Washington, DC 20036-1622
EMail: kmg@cohnmarks.com
Tel: (202)293-3860
Fax: (202)293-4827
Registered: LDA

Employers
Cohn and Marks (Associate)

Clients Represented
On Behalf of Cohn and Marks
American Soc. of Newspaper Editors

GOLDBERG, Michael I.

1752 N St. NW
Washington, DC 20036
Tel: (202)737-3600
Fax: (202)942-9333

Employers
American Soc. for Microbiology (Exec. Director)

GOLDBERG, Neal M.

1724 Massachusetts Ave. NW
Washington, DC 20036-1969
Tel: (202)775-3550
Fax: (202)775-3603
Registered: LDA

Employers
Nat'l Cable Television Ass'n (General Counsel)

GOLDBERG, Robert

1700 K St. NW
Suite 1150
Washington, DC 20006
EMail: robert.goldberg@ujc.org
Tel: (202)736-5881
Fax: (202)785-4937

Employers
United Jewish Communities, Inc. (Senior Legislative Associate)

GOLDBERG, Sherwood D.

1155 15th St. NW
Suite 800
Washington, DC 20005
Tel: (202)429-9788
Fax: (202)833-5296
Former Chief of Staff to the Secretary, Department of State. Retired Officer, Department of the Army, Department of Defense.

Employers
Worldwide Associates, Inc (Managing Director)

GOLDBERG, Thomas R.

1020 19th St. NW
Suite 520
Washington, DC 20036
EMail: t.r.goldberg@att.net
Tel: (202)429-9714
Fax: (202)467-5469
Registered: LDA

Employers
GHL Inc. (President)

Clients Represented
On Behalf of GHL Inc.
3Tex
Brewer Science Inc.
Foster-Miller, Inc.
Seemann Composites LLC
Sensor Research and Development Corp.
Wilson Composites Group

GOLDBLATT, Howard I.

1012 14th St. NW
Suite 200
Washington, DC 20005
Tel: (202)393-7330
Fax: (202)393-7329

Employers
Coalition Against Insurance Fraud (Director, Government Affairs)

GOLDEN, Jennifer

444 N. Capitol St.
Suite 841
Washington, DC 20001
Tel: (202)638-5333
Fax: (202)638-5335
Registered: LDA
Legislative Counsel to Rep. Cliff Stearns (R-FL), 1997-99.

Employers
Davis O'Connell, Inc. (Counsel)

Clients Represented
On Behalf of Davis O'Connell, Inc.
Contra Costa Community College District
Florida Department of Education
LifeLink Foundation

GOLDEN, CAE, Mark J.

8224 Old Courthouse Rd.
Vienna, VA 22182-3808
EMail: mgolden@ncrahq.org
Tel: (703)556-6272
Fax: (703)556-6291

Employers
Nat'l Court Reporters Ass'n (Exec. Director)

GOLDEN, Myron

440 R St. NW
Washington, DC 20001
Tel: (202)462-3614
Fax: (202)387-1034

Employers
Africare (Director, Francophone West Africa Region)

GOLDFIELD, Harold P.

3000 K St. NW
Suite 300
Washington, DC 20007
Tel: (202)424-7500
Fax: (202)424-7643
Registered: LDA, FARA
Assistant Secretary, Department of Commerce, 1984-87. Associate Counsel to the President (1982-83) and Assistant Counsel (1981-82), the White House. Member, National Advisory on Juvenile Justice and Delinquency Prevention, 1976-80.

Employers
Swidler Berlin Shereff Friedman, LLP (Senior Partner)

Clients Represented
On Behalf of Swidler Berlin Shereff Friedman, LLP
Artichoke Enterprises, Inc.
Aventis Pharmaceuticals, Inc.
BroadSpan Communications, Inc.
Conoco Inc.
Ry Cooder
Florida Power and Light Co.
Hyundai Semiconductor America, Inc.
Matsushita Electric Corp. of America
Merrill Lynch & Co., Inc.
Microsoft Corp.
Napster, Inc.
Nat'l Ass'n of Chain Drug Stores
Nat'l Sediments Coalition
Newman & Associates
Niagara Mohawk Power Corp.
Suiza Foods Corp.
Transkaryotic Therapies Inc.

GOLDGEIER, James M.

1775 Massachusetts Ave. NW
Washington, DC 20036-2188
Tel: (202)797-6000
Fax: (202)797-6004
Former Council on Foreign Relations International Affairs Fellow at State Department and National Security Staff.

Employers
The Brookings Institution (Non-Resident Senior Fellow, Foreign Policy Studies)

GOLDMAN, Janlori

2233 Wisconsin Ave. NW
Suite 525
Georgetown University
Washington, DC 20007
Tel: (202)687-0880
Fax: (202)687-3110

Employers
Institute for Health Care Research and Policy (Director, Health Privacy Project)

GOLDMAN, Leslie J.

1440 New York Ave. NW
Washington, DC 20005
Tel: (202)371-7000
Fax: (202)393-5760

Former Assistant Secretary for International Affairs, Department of Energy; former Deputy Assistant Secretary for Policy, Department of Energy; former General Counsel to the Senate Commerce Committee's Subcommittee on Oil and Natural Gas Production.

Employers
Skadden, Arps, Slate, Meagher & Flom LLP (Partner)

GOLDMAN, Michael

1101 30th St. NW
Suite 120
Washington, DC 20007
Tel: (202)944-3301
Fax: (202)944-3306
Registered: LDA

Employers
Silverberg, Goldman & Bikoff, LLP (Partner)

Clients Represented
On Behalf of Silverberg, Goldman & Bikoff, LLP
Societe Air France

GOLDMAN, Patricia R.

325 Seventh St. NW
Washington, DC 20004
Tel: (202)638-1100
Fax: (202)626-4638
Registered: LDA

Employers
American Hospital Ass'n (Senior Associate Director, Legislative Affairs)

GOLDMAN, Stanley I.

1700 K St. NW
Suite 301
Washington, DC 20006
Tel: (202)833-8884
Fax: (202)833-8886

Attorney-Advisor, Office of Proceedings, Interstate Commerce Commission, 1965-67.

Employers
Denning & Wohlstetter (Partner)

Clients Represented
On Behalf of Denning & Wohlstetter
Household Goods Forwarders Tariff Bureau

GOLDMAN, William L.

600 13th St. NW
Washington, DC 20005-3096
Tel: (202)756-8305
Fax: (202)756-8087
EMail: wgoldman@mwe.com

Attorney in Appellate Section, Tax Division, Department of Justice, 1968-72.

Employers
McDermott, Will and Emery (Partner)

GOLDMEIER GREEN, Karen E.

1333 New Hampshire Ave. NW
Suite 400
Washington, DC 20036
Tel: (202)887-4000
Fax: (202)887-4288
Registered: LDA
EMail: kgoldmeier@akingump.com

Health Counsel to Rep. Robert T. Matsui (D-CA), 1995-98.

Employers
Akin, Gump, Strauss, Hauer & Feld, L.L.P. (Associate)

Clients Represented
On Behalf of Akin, Gump, Strauss, Hauer & Feld, L.L.P.
Alliance for Quality Nursing Home Care
Avax Technologies, Inc.
Base Ten Systems, Inc.
Granite Broadcasting Co.
Heard Goggan Blair & Williams
Knoll Pharmaceutical Co.
Susan G. Komen Breast Cancer Foundation
New York State Health Facilities Ass'n
Serono Laboratories, Inc.

GOLDSCHMIDT, Kathy

513 Capitol Ct. NE
Suite 300
Washington, DC 20002
Tel: (202)546-0100
Fax: (202)547-0936

Employers
Congressional Management Foundation (Director, IT Services)

GOLDSMITH, Jerry

2101 L St. NW
Suite 202
Washington, DC 20037
EMail: jgoldsmith@aacc.org
Tel: (202)857-0717
Fax: (202)887-5093

Employers
American Ass'n for Clinical Chemistry, Inc. (V. President, Marketing Programs)

GOLDSMITH, Kenneth

740 15th St. NW
Ninth Floor
Washington, DC 20005
Tel: (202)662-1780
Fax: (202)662-1762

Employers
American Bar Ass'n (Staff Director, State Legislation)

GOLDSMITH, Marta

1025 Thomas Jefferson St. NW
Suite 500 W
Washington, DC 20007-5201
EMail: mgoldsmith@uli.org
Tel: (202)624-7000
Fax: (202)624-7140

Employers
Urban Land Institute (V. President, Policy and Practice)

GOLDSON, Christopher

1220 19th St. NW
Washington, DC 20036
Tel: (202)775-0436
Registered: LDA

Employers
Ass'n of Maternal and Child Health Programs (AMCHP)

GOLDSPIEL, Eileen

New Hampshire Ave. & F St. NW
Washington, DC 20566
Tel: (202)416-8000
Fax: (202)416-8205

Employers
Kennedy Center for the Performing Arts, John F. (Associate Managing Director, Government Liaison)

GOLDSTEIN, Ellen

1299 Pennsylvania Ave. NW
Suite 1100 West
Washington, DC 20004-2407
Tel: (202)637-4000
Fax: (202)637-4066
Registered: LDA
EMail: ellen.goldstein@corporate.ge.com

Employers
General Electric Co. (Manager, Federal Government Relations (GE Medical Systems))

GOLDSTEIN, James

1350 I St. NW
Suite 400
Washington, DC 20005-3306
Tel: (202)371-6900
Fax: (202)842-3578
Registered: LDA

Employers
Motorola, Inc. (Director, U.S. Government Relations, CGISS)

GOLDSTEIN, Jennifer

2550 M St. NW
Washington, DC 20037-1350
Tel: (202)457-6000
Fax: (202)457-6315
Registered: LDA

Employers
Patton Boggs, LLP (Associate)

Clients Represented
On Behalf of Patton Boggs, LLP
Salton, Inc.

GOLDSTEIN, Michael B.

1200 New Hampshire Ave. NW
Suite 800
Washington, DC 20036-6802
Tel: (202)776-2000
Fax: (202)776-2222
Registered: LDA
EMail: mgoldstein@dlalaw.com

Employers
Dow, Lohnes & Albertson, PLLC (Member)

Clients Represented
On Behalf of Dow, Lohnes & Albertson, PLLC
St. Matthew's University School of Medicine

GOLDSTEIN, Morris

11 Dupont Circle NW
Suite 620
Washington, DC 20036
EMail: mgldstne@iie.com
Tel: (202)328-9000
Fax: (202)328-5432

Employers
Institute for Internat'l Economics (Senior Fellow)

GOLDSTEIN, Nick

1050 Thomas Jefferson St. NW
Seventh Floor
Washington, DC 20007
EMail: nxg@vnf.com
Tel: (202)298-1800
Fax: (202)338-2416

Intern, American Indian Environmental Office, Environmental Protection Agency, 1995.

Employers
Van Ness Feldman, P.C. (Associate)

GOLDSTEIN, Richard S.

401 Ninth St. NW
Suite 900
Washington, DC 20004
Tel: (202)585-8060
Fax: (202)585-8080
Registered: LDA
EMail: rgoldstein@nixonpeabody.com

Employers
Nixon Peabody LLP (Partner)

Clients Represented
On Behalf of Nixon Peabody LLP
Affordable Housing Tax Credit Coalition
Cornerstone Florida Corp., Ltd.

GOLDSTEIN, Ricky

1630 Connecticut Ave. NW
Suite 500
Washington, DC 20009
Tel: (202)612-4321
Fax: (202)612-4333

Employers
Human Rights Watch (Acting Director, Human Rights Watch - Middle East Division)

GOLDWATER, James

345 S. Patrick St.
Alexandria, VA 22314
Tel: (703)836-3654
Fax: (703)836-6086
Registered: LDA

Employers
Bob Lawrence & Associates (V. President)

Clients Represented
On Behalf of Bob Lawrence & Associates
Brandegee, Inc.
Irrigation Ass'n
Nat'l Ass'n of Tower Erectors

GOLDWIN, Robert A.

1150 17th St. NW
Washington, DC 20036
EMail: rgoldwin@aei.org
Tel: (202)862-5800
Fax: (202)862-7177

Employers
American Enterprise Institute for Public Policy Research (Resident Scholar)

GOLEC, Janice

One GEICO Plaza
Washington, DC 20076-0001
Tel: (301)986-3000

Employers
GEICO Corp. (Director, Business and Government Relations)

GOLLNICK, Donna M.

2010 Massachusetts Ave. NW
Suite 500
Washington, DC 20036-1023
EMail: donna@ncate.org
Tel: (202)466-7496
Fax: (202)296-6620

Employers
Nat'l Council for Accreditation of Teacher Education (Senior V. President)

GOLODNER, Linda F.

1701 K St. NW
Suite 1200
Washington, DC 20006
Tel: (202)835-3323
Fax: (202)835-0747

Employers
Nat'l Consumers League (President)

GOLTZMAN, Michael

800 Connecticut Ave. NW
Suite 711
Washington, DC 20006
Tel: (202)973-2657
Fax: (202)296-0047

Employers
The Coca-Cola Company (International Relations)

GOLUB, Judith E.

918 F St. NW
Washington, DC 20004-1400
Tel: (202)216-2400
Fax: (202)371-9449
Registered: LDA
EMail: jgolub@aila.org

Employers
American Immigration Lawyers Ass'n (Director, Advocacy and Public Affairs)

GOLUB, PhD, Sidney

9650 Rockville Pike
Bethesda, MD 20814-3998
Tel: (301)530-7000
Fax: (301)530-7001

Employers
Federation of American Societies for Experimental Biology (Exec. Director)

GOLUBOCK, Carol

1313 L St. NW
Washington, DC 20005
Tel: (202)898-3200
Fax: (202)898-3304
Registered: LDA

Employers
Service Employees Internat'l Union (Attorney)

GOMBAR, Robert C.

600 13th St. NW
Washington, DC 20005-3096
Tel: (202)756-8242
Fax: (202)756-8087
EMail: rgombar@mwe.com
Former Attorney, General Counsel and Chief Legal Office, Occupational Safety and Health Review Commission.

Employers
McDermott, Will and Emery (Partner)

GOMEZ, Diego A.

401 Ninth St. NW
Suite 1000
Washington, DC 20004
Tel: (202)274-2870
Fax: (202)654-5644
Attorney-Advisor, Office of the General Counsel, Federal Energy Regulatory Commission.

Employers
Troutman Sanders LLP (Associate)

GOMEZ, Esperanza

801 Pennsylvania Ave. NW
Suite 730
Washington, DC 20004
Tel: (202)756-2408
Fax: (202)756-2409
Registered: LDA, FARA
EMail: Gomez@howdc.com

Employers
Hooper Owen & Winburn (Senior Legislative Specialist)

Clients Represented
On Behalf of Hooper Owen & Winburn
Azerbaijan, Embassy of the Republic of
Pakistan, Government of the Islamic Republic of

GOMEZ, Humberto

1201 F St. NW
Suite 1000
Washington, DC 20004-1077
Tel: (202)626-7225
Fax: (202)626-7208
Registered: LDA

Employers
R. J. Reynolds Tobacco Co. (Manager, Federal Government Affairs)

GOMPF, Soledad

1101 14th St. NW
11th Floor
Washington, DC 20005-5601
Tel: (202)682-1510
Fax: (202)682-1535
EMail: sgompf@villagebanking.org

Employers
FINCA Internat'l Inc., The Foundation for Internat'l Community Assistance (Director, Development)

GONDLES, Jr., CAE, James A.

4380 Forbes Blvd.
Lanham, MD 20706-4322
Tel: (301)918-1800
Fax: (301)918-1900

Employers
American Correctional Ass'n (Exec. Director)

GONELLA, Geoff

700 13th St. NW
Suite 400
Washington, DC 20005
Tel: (202)347-0773
Fax: (202)347-0785
EMail: ggonella@cassidy.com

Employers
Cassidy & Associates, Inc. (Senior V. President, New Business Development)

GONYEA, Dr. Meredith A.

3223 Quesada St. NW
Washington, DC 20015
Tel: (202)244-5383
Fax: (202)364-1926

Employers
Center for Studies in Health Policy (President)

GONZALES, Bridget

919 18th St. NW
Tenth Floor
Washington, DC 20006
Tel: (202)263-2900
Fax: (202)263-2960

Employers
Issue Dynamics Inc. (Senior Consultant)

GONZALES, Walter

1501 M St. NW
Suite 700
Washington, DC 20005-1702
Tel: (202)463-4300
Fax: (202)463-4394
Registered: LDA
Former Senior Legislative Assistant to Rep. Gene Green (D-TX).

Employers
Manatt, Phelps & Phillips, LLP (Legislative Assistant)

Clients Represented
On Behalf of Manatt, Phelps & Phillips, LLP
Campbell Foundry Co.
Computer and Communications Industry Ass'n (CCIA)

GONZALEZ, Emilio

1710 N St. NW
Washington, DC 20036
Registered: LDA

Employers
Strategy Group Internat'l (V. President)

Clients Represented
On Behalf of Strategy Group Internat'l
Secure Wrap, Inc.

GONZALEZ, USAF, Lt. Col. Fernando

1300 Defense Pentagon
Room 3D918
Washington, DC 20301-1300
Tel: (703)697-4491

Employers
Department of Defense (Special Assistant for Personnel Policy, Office of Legislative Liaison)

GONZALEZ, Henry P.

1710 Rhode Island Ave. NW
Tenth Floor
Washington, DC 20036
Tel: (202)293-3300
Fax: (202)293-3307
Registered: LDA
EMail: gonzalez@rofgw.com

Employers
Rodriguez O'Donnell Fuerst Gonzalez & Williams (Partner)

GONZALEZ, John A.

Commonwealth Towers
1300 Wilson Blvd., Suite 200
Arlington, VA 22209-2307
Tel: (703)516-8228
Fax: (703)516-8295
Registered: LDA
EMail: jagonzal@collins.rockwell.com

Employers
Rockwell Collins (Director, Congressional Relations - Government Programs)

GONZALEZ, Laura L.

1300 I St. NW
11th Floor East
Washington, DC 20005-3314
Tel: (202)216-4200
Fax: (202)775-8741
Registered: LDA

Employers
Schnader Harrison Segal & Lewis LLP

Clients Represented
On Behalf of Schnader Harrison Segal & Lewis LLP
Internat'l Air Transport Ass'n

GONZALEZ, USA (Ret.), Lt. Col. Roberto

908 Pennsylvania Ave. SE
Washington, DC 20003
Tel: (202)544-5666
Fax: (202)544-4647
EMail: rgonzalez@advantage-dc.com
Former Military Advisor to the Assistant Secretary for Health Affairs, Department of Defense. Lieutenant Colonel, U.S. Army.

Employers
Advantage Associates, Inc. (Professional Staff)

GONZALEZ, Rose

600 Maryland Ave. SW
Suite 100 West
Washington, DC 20024-2571
Tel: (202)651-7000
Fax: (202)651-7001
Registered: LDA

Employers
American Nurses Ass'n (Associate Director, Federal Government Relations)

GONZALEZ-NOGUERA, Maria Christina

1850 M St. NW
Suite 550
Washington, DC 20036
Tel: (202)289-5900
Fax: (202)289-4141
Registered: LDA

Employers
Chlopak, Leonard, Schechter and Associates (Senior Associate)

Clients Represented
On Behalf of Chlopak, Leonard, Schechter and Associates
Hyundai Electronics Industries Co., LTD
Wilkie Farr & Gallagher

GOOD, Larry

1432 Fenwick Ln.
Suite 200
Silver Spring, MD 20910
Tel: (301)608-1141

Employers
Electronic Commerce Ass'n (Senior V. President)
Good & Associates (President)

GOODE, Bernard N.

1225 I St. NW
Suite 500
Washington, DC 20005
Tel: (202)312-2005
Fax: (202)289-8683
Registered: LDA
EMail: dawsonassociates@worldnet.att.net
Former Chief, National Regulatory Program, U.S. Army Corps of Engineers, Department of the Army.

Employers
Dawson & Associates, Inc. (Senior Advisor)

GOODELL, Jeffrey

1101 17th St. NW
Suite 602
Washington, DC 20036
Tel: (202)467-8202
Fax: (202)467-8204
EMail: jeffrey.goodell@sabre.com

Employers
Sabre Inc. (V. President, Government Affairs)
Travelocity.com (V. President, Government Affairs)

GOODFELLOW, William C.

1755 Massachusetts Ave. NW
Suite 550
Washington, DC 20036
Tel: (202)232-3317
Fax: (202)232-3440
EMail: wcg@ciponline.org

Employers
Center for Internat'l Policy (Director)

GOODIN, Mark W.

8617 Cross Chase Ct.
Fairfax Station, VA 22039
Tel: (703)690-3590
Registered: LDA

Employers
Self-employed as an independent consultant.

Clients Represented
As an independent consultant
American Ass'n of Health Plans (AAHP)
Former Governors of Puerto Rico
The PGA Tour, Inc.
Puerto Rico, Commonwealth of
Southern Auto Sales, Inc.

GOODKIND, Arthur

2099 Pennsylvania Ave. NW
Suite 100
Washington, DC 20006
EMail: agoodkin@hklaw.com
Tel: (202)955-3000
Fax: (202)955-5564

Employers
Holland & Knight LLP (Partner)

GOODMAN, Alan

1615 L St. NW
Suite 1000
Washington, DC 20036
Tel: (202)659-0330
Fax: (202)296-6119

Employers
Fleishman-Hillard, Inc (V. President)

GOODMAN, Alice C.

550 17th St. NW
MS: 6076
Washington, DC 20429-9990
Tel: (202)898-8730
Fax: (202)898-3745

Employers
Federal Deposit Insurance Corp. (Director, Office of Legislative Affairs)

GOODMAN, Amy

1050 Connecticut Ave. NW
Washington, DC 20036-5306
EMail: agoodman@gdclaw.com
Tel: (202)955-8500
Fax: (202)467-0539

Former Associate Director (EDGAR); Deputy Associate Director; Assistant Chief, Office of Disclosure Policy; and Chief, Task Force on Corporate Accountability; Securities and Exchange Commission. Also served as Legal Assistant and Special Counsel to Chairman Harold Williams and as Staff Attorney, Division of Investment Management; Securities and Exchange Commission.

Employers
Gibson, Dunn & Crutcher LLP (Of Counsel)

Clients Represented
On Behalf of Gibson, Dunn & Crutcher LLP
The Business Roundtable

GOODMAN, Collette C.

1800 Massachusetts Ave. NW
Washington, DC 20036
Tel: (202)828-2000
Fax: (202)828-2195

Employers
Shea & Gardner

Clients Represented
On Behalf of Shea & Gardner
Iraqi Nat'l Congress

GOODMAN, Edward

1200 New Hampshire Ave. NW
Suite 410
Washington, DC 20036
EMail: egoodman@vha.com
Tel: (202)721-8100
Fax: (202)721-8105
Registered: LDA

Employers
VHA Inc. (V. President, Public Policy)

GOODMAN, G. Thomas

440 First St. NW
Eighth Floor
Washington, DC 20001
EMail: tgoodman@naco.org
Tel: (202)942-4222
Fax: (202)393-2630

Employers
Nat'l Ass'n of Counties (Director, Public Affairs)
Nat'l Ass'n of County Information Officers

GOODMAN, Jack N.

1771 N St. NW
Washington, DC 20036-2891
Tel: (202)429-5430
Fax: (202)775-3526
Registered: LDA

Employers
Nat'l Ass'n of Broadcasters (Senior V. President, Policy Counsel)

GOODMAN, John

1300 I St. NW
Suite 400 West
Washington, DC 20005
Tel: (202)515-2563
Fax: (202)336-7925

Employers
Verizon Communications (Assistant General Counsel)

GOODMAN, Joni

1620 I St. NW
Suite 300
Washington, DC 20006
EMail: misrael@primanet.com
Tel: (202)429-0160
Fax: (202)293-3109

Employers
Mark S. Israel (Legislative Analyst)

GOODMAN, Mark

1815 N. Fort Myer Dr.
Suite 900
Arlington, VA 22209-1817
Tel: (703)807-1904
Fax: (703)807-2109

Employers
Student Press Law Center (Exec. Director)

GOODMAN, Ruthanne

1730 N. Lynn St.
Suite 504
Arlington, VA 22209
Tel: (703)276-1412
Fax: (703)276-1415
Registered: LDA

Employers
Balzano Associates (Account Executive)

Clients Represented
On Behalf of Balzano Associates
Boeing Defense and Space Group
The Business Roundtable
Lockheed Martin Corp.
Nat'l Institute for Aerospace Studies and Services Inc.

GOODMAN, Stephen L.

555 12th St. NW
Suite 950 North
Washington, DC 20004
Tel: (202)371-9100
Fax: (202)371-1497

Served as Deputy Chief, Industry Analysis Division, Federal Communications Commission, 1983-88.

Employers
Halprin, Temple, Goodman & Maher (Partner)

GOODRICH, Kristina

1142 Walker Rd.
Suite E
Great Falls, VA 22066
Tel: (703)759-0100
Fax: (703)759-7679

Employers
Industrial Designers Soc. of America (Exec. Director)

GOODRICH, Jr., William W.

1050 Connecticut Ave. NW
Washington, DC 20036-5339
Tel: (202)857-6000
Fax: (202)857-6395

Law Clerk to Judge Marion T. Bennett, U.S. Court of Appeals for the Federal Circuit, 1975-76.

Employers
Arent Fox Kintner Plotkin & Kahn, PLLC (Member)

GOODSTEIN, Richard F.

1130 Connecticut Ave. NW
Suite 710
Washington, DC 20036
Tel: (202)659-1324
Fax: (202)659-1328
Registered: LDA

Legislative Assistant to Senator Abraham Ribicoff (D-CT), 1974-78.

Employers
Air Products and Chemicals, Inc. (Washington Representative)
Goodstein & Associates (President)

Clients Represented
On Behalf of Goodstein & Associates
Air Products and Chemicals, Inc.
Bennett Environmental Inc.
Lexmark Internat'l
Micell Technologies, Inc.
U.S. Postal Service

GOODWEATHER, Melvin

499 S. Capitol St. SW
Suite 600
Washington, DC 20003
Tel: (202)289-9881
Fax: (202)289-9877
Registered: LDA

Employers
The Livingston Group, LLC (Associate)

Clients Represented
On Behalf of The Livingston Group, LLC
American Ass'n of Nurse Anesthetists
Broward, Florida, County of
Committee of Unsecured Creditors
General Category Tuna Ass'n
Gray Morrison
Great Western Cellular Partnership
Link Plus Co.
Marine Desalination Systems LLC
Mesa, Arizona, City of
New Orleans, Louisiana, Port of
Schering-Plough Corp.
Stewart Enterprises, Inc.

GOODWIN, Lee M.

701 Pennsylvania Ave. NW
Suite 800
Washington, DC 20004
EMail: lgoodwin@thelenreid.com
Tel: (202)508-4346
Fax: (202)508-4321

Employers
Thelen Reid & Priest LLP (Partner)

GOODWIN, Robert K.

1400 I St. NW
Suite 800
Washington, DC 20005
EMail: rgoodwin@pointsoflight.org
Tel: (202)729-8000
Fax: (202)729-8100

Employers
The Points of Light Foundation (President and Chief Exec. Officer)

GOODWIN, Thomas

1199 N. Fairfax St.
Suite 1000
Alexandria, VA 22314
EMail: tgoodwin@hawthorngroup.com
Tel: (703)299-4499
Fax: (703)299-4488

Employers
The Hawthorn Group, L.C. (Senior Counselor)

GOOF, Dale

Eight Herbert St.
Alexandria, VA 22305-2600
Tel: (703)683-9027
Fax: (703)683-6820

Employers
Nat'l Ass'n of Postmasters of the U.S. (Secretary-Treasurer)

GOOLD, Linda

700 11th St. NW
Washington, DC 20001-4507
EMail: lgoold@realtors.org
Tel: (202)383-1083
Fax: (202)383-7540
Registered: LDA

Employers
Nat'l Ass'n of Realtors (Director, Federal Taxation)

GOON, Julie

1129 20th St. NW
Suite 600
Washington, DC 20036-3421
EMail: jgoon@aahp.org
Tel: (202)778-3200
Fax: (202)778-8479
Registered: LDA

Employers
American Ass'n of Health Plans (AAHP) (V. President, Government Affairs)

GOOSE, Stephen D.

1630 Connecticut Ave. NW
Suite 500
Washington, DC 20009
Tel: (202)612-4321
Fax: (202)612-4333

Employers
Human Rights Watch (Program Director, Arms Project)

GORDEN, Mark

2011 Pennsylvania Ave. NW
Suite 800
Washington, DC 20006-1808
EMail: mgorden@mail.acponline.org
Tel: (202)264-4544
Fax: (202)835-0443

Employers
American College of Physicians-American Soc. of Internal Medicine (ACP-ASIM) (Senior Associate, Managed Care and Regulatory Affairs)

GORDLEY, John

600 Pennsylvania Ave. SE
Suite 320
Washington, DC 20003
EMail: jgordley@gordley.com
Tel: (202)969-8900
Fax: (202)331-7036
Registered: LDA

Employers
Gordley Associates (President)

Clients Represented

On Behalf of Gordley Associates
American Soybean Ass'n
Iowa Pork Producers Ass'n
Nat'l Barley Growers Ass'n
Nat'l Sunflower Ass'n
Nebraska Wheat Board
U.S. Canola Ass'n
Wild Bird Feeding Institute

GORDON, Al

700 13th St. NW
Suite 400
Washington, DC 20005
EMail: agordon@cassidy.com
Tel: (202)347-0773
Fax: (202)347-0785

Employers
Cassidy & Associates, Inc. (Director, New Business Development Consulting)

GORDON, Anthony

818 Connecticut Ave. NW
Suite 801
Washington, DC 20006
EMail: Anthony_Gordon@seaboardcorp.com
Tel: (202)955-6111
Fax: (202)955-6118
Registered: LDA

Employers
Seaboard Corp. (Government Affairs Assistant)

GORDON, Bonny Kanter

One GEICO Plaza
Washington, DC 20076-0001
Tel: (301)986-3000

Employers
GEICO Corp. (Senior Counsel)

GORDON, Bradley

440 First St. NW
Suite 600
Washington, DC 20001
Tel: (202)639-5200
Registered: LDA

Employers
American Israel Public Affairs Committee (Legislative Director/Lobbyist)

GORDON, Harold

8009 Carita Ct.
Bethesda, MD 20817
Tel: (301)770-2540
Fax: (301)770-2183

Employers
Internat'l Healthcare Safety Professional Certification Board (Exec. Director)

GORDON, Lincoln

1775 Massachusetts Ave. NW
Washington, DC 20036-2188
Tel: (202)797-6000
Fax: (202)797-6004

Assistant Secretary of State for Inter-American Affairs, 1966-68; Ambassador to Brazil, 1961-66; Director of the Marshall Plan Mission and Minister for Economic Affairs, U.S. Embassy, London, 1952-55.

Employers
The Brookings Institution (Guest Scholar, Foreign Policy Studies)

GORDON, Mary F.

c/o Nat'l League of Cities
1301 Pennsylvania Ave. NW, Suite 550
Washington, DC 20004
EMail: gordon@nlc.org
Tel: (202)626-3169
Fax: (202)626-3043

Employers
Nat'l Black Caucus of Local Elected Officials (Manager, Constituency Groups)

GORDON, Mary S.

801 Pennsylvania Ave. NW
Suite 700
Washington, DC 20004
EMail: mgordon@nortelnetworks.com
Tel: (202)347-4610
Fax: (202)508-3612
Registered: LDA

Employers
Nortel Networks (V. President, Government Relations - Congressional Affairs)

GORDON, Megan

701 Pennsylvania Ave. NW
Suite 650
Washington, DC 20004
EMail: mgordon@cancer.org
Tel: (202)661-5716
Fax: (202)661-5750
Registered: LDA

Employers
American Cancer Soc. (Manager, Federal Government Relations)

GORDON, Philip H.

1775 Massachusetts Ave. NW
Washington, DC 20036-2188
Tel: (202)797-6000
Fax: (202)797-6004

Former Director for European Affairs, National Security Council.

Employers
The Brookings Institution (Senior Fellow, Foreign Policy Studies/Director, Center on the U.S. and France)

GORDON, Randall C.

1250 I St. NW
Suite 1003
Washington, DC 20005-3917
EMail: rgordon@ngfa.org
Tel: (202)289-0873
Fax: (202)289-5388
Registered: LDA

Employers
Nat'l Grain and Feed Ass'n (V. President, Communications and Government Relations)

GORDON, Richard A.

1666 K St. NW
Suite 800
Washington, DC 20006
Tel: (202)481-7000
Fax: (202)862-7098
Registered: LDA

Former Deputy Chief of Staff, Joint Congressional Committee on Taxation.

Employers
Arthur Andersen LLP (Partner)

Clients Represented

On Behalf of Arthur Andersen LLP
Coalition on Royalties Taxation
Hybrid Branch Coalition
Microsoft Corp.
Oracle Corp.
UtiliCorp United, Inc.

GORDON, Jr., Robert E.

P.O. Box 25766
Washington, DC 20007
Tel: (703)836-7404
Fax: (703)836-7405

Employers
Nat'l Wilderness Institute (Director)

GORDON, Stephen

475 L'Enfant Plaza SW
MS: 10801
Washington, DC 20260
Tel: (202)268-3751
Fax: (202)268-4977

Employers
United States Postal Service (Public Policy Planning and Analysis)

GORDON, Stuart J.

10005 Sorrel Ave.
Potomac, MD 20854
Tel: (301)299-8844
Fax: (301)983-8865
Registered: LDA

Served as Administrative Assistant to Senator Daniel Patrick Moynihan (D-NY).

Employers
Self-employed as an independent consultant.

Clients Represented

As an independent consultant
Major League Baseball

GORE, Elizabeth

Eisenhower Exec. Office Bldg.
725 17th St. NW
Washington, DC 20503
Tel: (202)395-4790
Fax: (202)395-3888

Employers
Executive Office of the President - Office of Management and Budget (Special Assistant for Policy and Legislation)

GORE, Jennifer

805 15th St. NW
Suite 300
Washington, DC 20005-2207
Tel: (202)682-4200
Fax: (202)682-9054
Registered: LDA

Employers
Credit Union Nat'l Ass'n, Inc. (Manager, Public and Congressional Affairs)

GORE, Laura

2121 K Street NW
Suite 325
Washington, DC 20037
EMail: lgore@acep.org
Tel: (202)728-0610
Fax: (202)728-0617

Employers
American College of Emergency Physicians (Director, Public Relations)

GORELICK, Jamie S.

3900 Wisconsin Ave. NW
Washington, DC 20016
Tel: (202)752-7000
Fax: (202)752-6099

Employers
Fannie Mae (V. Chair)

GORENFLO, Richard W.

Four Taft Ct.
Rockville, MD 20850
Tel: (800)331-2102
Fax: (301)762-5728

Employers
Mid-Atlantic Medical Services, Inc. (V. President, Regulatory Affairs)

GOREZYCA, Dolores A.

8630 Fenton St.
Suite 400
Silver Spring, MD 20910-3803
Tel: (301)565-9016
Fax: (301)565-0018
Registered: LDA

Employers
Internat'l Federation of Professional and Technical Engineers (Secretary-Treasurer)

GORIN, David

113 Park Ave.
Falls Church, VA 22046
EMail: dgarvc@aol.com
Tel: (703)241-8801
Fax: (703)241-1004

Employers
Nat'l Ass'n of RV Parks and Campgrounds (President and Chief Exec. Officer)

GORIN, Susan

4340 East-West Hwy.
Suite 402
Bethesda, MD 20814
EMail: sgorin@naspweb.org
Tel: (301)657-0270
Ext: 221
Fax: (301)657-0275

Employers
Nat'l Ass'n of School Psychologists (Exec. Director)

GORLIN, Jacques

2300 M St. NW
Suite 800
Washington, DC 20037
Tel: (202)973-2870
Fax: (202)296-8407
Registered: LDA
EMail: jgorlin@erols.com

Employers
The Gorlin Group (President)

Clients Represented
On Behalf of The Gorlin Group
Bristol-Myers Squibb Co.
Intellectual Property Committee
Pfizer, Inc.
Pharmaceutical Research and Manufacturers of America

GORMAN, Bridget

1733 King St.
Alexandria, VA 22314
Tel: (703)739-9500
Fax: (703)739-0124
EMail: gormanb@cmaa.org

Employers
Club Managers Ass'n of America (Manager, Public Affairs)

GORMAN, Carolyn

1730 Rhode Island Ave.
Suite 710
Washington, DC 20036
Tel: (202)833-1580
Fax: (202)223-5779

Employers
Insurance Information Institute (V. President, Washington Office)

GORMAN, David W.

807 Maine Ave. SW
Washington, DC 20024
Tel: (202)554-3501
Fax: (202)554-3581
Registered: LDA

Employers
Disabled American Veterans (Exec. Director, Washington Headquarters)

GORMAN, John K.

1350 I St. NW
Suite 870
Washington, DC 20005
Tel: (202)638-0550
Fax: (202)737-1947
EMail: gorman@capalliance.com
Staff Director (1993) and Senior Legislative Assistant (1991-92) to Rep. John Conyers, Jr. (D-MI). Deputy Press Secretary, House Committee on Government Operations, 1990-91. Formerly served in the Health Care Financing Administration.

Employers
Managed Care Compliance Solutions, Inc. (President)

GORMAN, John S.

1015 18th St. NW
Suite 1100
Washington, DC 20036-5725
Tel: (202)728-5726
Fax: (202)296-1928
Registered: LDA
EMail: jgorman@csbsdc.org

Employers
Conference of State Bank Supervisors (General Counsel)

GORMAN, Mark S.

1250 I St. NW
Suite 400
Washington, DC 20005-3998
Tel: (202)628-3544
Fax: (202)682-8888
Registered: LDA
EMail: mgorman@discus.org

Employers
Distilled Spirits Council of the United States, Inc. (Senior V. President, Office of Government Relations)

GORMAN, Teresa

3000 K St. NW
Suite 300
Washington, DC 20007
Tel: (202)295-8787
Fax: (202)295-8799
Registered: LDA
Former Special Assistant to the President for Energy, the Environment, and Natural Resources, The White House, during the George H. W. Bush Administration. Former Professional Committee Staff Member, House Committee on Commerce.

Employers
The Harbour Group (Advisor)
LPI Consulting, Inc. (Advisor)

Clients Represented
On Behalf of LPI Consulting, Inc.
Albright & Wilson Americas
General Electric Co.
Koch Industries, Inc.
Swidler Berlin Shereff Friedman, LLP

GORMAN, Tori

1129 20th St. NW
Suite 600
Washington, DC 20036-3421
Tel: (202)778-3200
Fax: (202)778-8479
Senior Legislative Assistant to Rep. Jim Kolbe (R-AZ), 1997-2000. Former Social Security Policy Advisor to Senator Rick Santorum (R-PA).

Employers
American Ass'n of Health Plans (AAHP) (Director, Policy and Research)

GORMAN-GRAUL, Faye

1133 Connecticut Ave. NW
Suite 200
Washington, DC 20036-4305
Tel: (202)785-5536
Fax: (202)785-0421
Registered: LDA

Employers
Dow Corning Corp. (Director, Government Relations/Washington Office)

GORRELL, J. Warren

555 13th St. NW
Washington, DC 20004-1109
Tel: (202)637-5600
Fax: (202)637-5910

Employers
Hogan & Hartson L.L.P. (Chairman)

Clients Represented
On Behalf of Hogan & Hartson L.L.P.
Foodmaker Internat'l Franchising Inc.
HMSHost Corp.

GORTENBURG, Gary

440 First St. NW
Washington, DC 20001
Tel: (202)393-6226
Fax: (202)942-4281

Employers
Nat'l Ass'n of County Training and Employment Professionals (Director, Employment and Training)

GOSE, Richard

805 15th St. NW
Suite 300
Washington, DC 20005-2207
Tel: (202)682-4200
Fax: (202)682-9054

Employers
Credit Union Nat'l Ass'n, Inc. (V. President, Political Action and Grassroots)

GOSIER, Ann M.

1310 G St. NW
Suite 770
Washington, DC 20005
Tel: (202)508-0800
Fax: (202)508-0818
Registered: LDA

Employers
Guidant Corp. (V. President, Government Affairs)

GOSLIN, Dr. David A.

3333 K St. NW
Suite 300
Washington, DC 20007
Tel: (202)342-5000
Fax: (202)342-5033

Employers
American Institutes for Research (President and Chief Exec. Officer)

GOSS, (Ret.), Col. Bill

One Massachusetts Ave. NW
Washington, DC 20001
Tel: (202)789-0031
Fax: (202)682-9358

Employers
Nat'l Guard Ass'n of the U.S. (Director, Legislative Affairs)

GOSS, Elizabeth

1900 K St. NW
Suite 750
Washington, DC 20006
Tel: (202)833-4500
Fax: (202)833-2859
Registered: LDA

Employers
Bennett Turner & Coleman, LLP (Partner)

Clients Represented
On Behalf of Bennett Turner & Coleman, LLP
American Soc. of Clinical Oncology
Bristol-Myers Squibb Co.
Cancer Leadership Council
The Children's Cause Inc.
Cure for Lymphoma Foundation
Cystic Fibrosis Foundation
Leukemia & Lymphoma Soc.
Nat'l Coalition for Cancer Survivorship
Nat'l Patient Advocate Foundation
North American Brain Tumor Coalition

GOSS, Kenneth A.

1501 Lee Hwy.
Arlington, VA 22209-1198
Tel: (703)247-5804
Fax: (703)247-5853
EMail: kgoss@afa.org

Employers
Air Force Ass'n (Director, Government Relations)

GOSSENS, Myra Peabody

808 17th St. NW
Suite 600
Washington, DC 20006
Tel: (202)466-7800
Fax: (202)887-0905

Employers
Ruder Finn Washington (President, Public Relations, Washington)

GOTTEHRER, Barry

115 S. Union St.
P310
Alexandria, VA 22314
Tel: (703)549-8280
Fax: (703)549-8271
Registered: LDA
EMail: gottehrerandco@aol.com

Employers
Gottehrer and Co. (President)

Clients Represented
On Behalf of Gottehrer and Co.
Bay State Health Systems
Take The Field, Inc.
UST Public Affairs, Inc.
Wright, Lindsey & Jennings

GOTTEMOELLER, Rose E.

1779 Massachusetts Ave. NW
Washington, DC 20036
Tel: (202)483-7600
Fax: (202)483-1840
Acting Deputy Administrator for Defense Nuclear Nonproliferation, Department of Energy, 2000.

Employers
Carnegie Endowment for Internat'l Peace (Senior Associate)

GOTTLIEB, Brian

1300 Wilson Blvd.
Arlington, VA 22209
Tel: (703)741-5948
Fax: (703)741-6097
Registered: LDA
EMail: brian_gottlieb@americanchemistry.com

Employers
American Chemistry Council (Manager)

GOTWALS, Amy E.

666 11th St. NW
Suite 700
Washington, DC 20001
Tel: (202)783-6686
Fax: (202)638-2356
Registered: LDA

Employers
Older Women's League (Director, Public Policy)

GOULD, Lt. Cdr. Austin

400 Seventh St. SW
Suite 10402
Washington, DC 20590
Tel: (202)366-4280
Fax: (202)366-7124
EMail: agould@comdit.uscg.mil

Employers
Department of Transportation - United States Coast Guard (Government Liaison, Congressional Affairs Staff, Office of Governmental and Congressional Affairs)

GOULD, Christopher

888 17th St. NW
Suite 800
Washington, DC 20006
Tel: (202)822-8060
Fax: (202)822-9088
Registered: LDA
EMail: cgould@heimag.com
Legislative Assistant to Rep. Chester G. Atkins (D-MA), 1990-93 and Democratic Study Group, U.S. House of Representatives.

Employers
Heidepriem & Mager, Inc. (Associate)

Clients Represented
On Behalf of Heidepriem & Mager, Inc.
EXACT Laboratories
Pharmacia Corp.
Serono Laboratories, Inc.
United Airlines

GOULD, Geoffrey C.

1300 I St. NW
Suite 400 West
Washington, DC 20005
Registered: LDA

Employers
Verizon Communications (Senior V. President, State Government Relations)

GOULD, George B.

100 Indiana Ave. NW
Washington, DC 20001
Tel: (202)393-4695
Fax: (202)756-7400
Registered: LDA

Employers
Nat'l Ass'n of Letter Carriers of the United States of America (Assistant to the President for Legislative and Political Affairs)

GOULD, Patrick

1615 H St. NW
Washington, DC 20062-2000
Tel: (202)659-6000
Fax: (202)463-5836

Employers
Chamber of Commerce of the U.S.A. (Associate Director, Congressional and Public Affairs)

GOULD, Rebecca M. J.

1225 I St. NW
Suite 920
Washington, DC 20005
Tel: (202)408-5538
Fax: (202)408-7664
Minority Counsel, House Energy and Commerce Committee, 1984-88.

Employers
Alliance to Promote Software Innovations (Manager, Public Policy)
Dell Computer Corp. (Director, Public Policy)

GOULD, Rob

1909 K St. NW
Fourth Floor
Washington, DC 20006
Tel: (202)973-5800
Fax: (202)973-5858

Employers
Porter/Novelli (Partner, Washington Health Care Practice)

GOULDEN, Jody

One GEICO Plaza
Washington, DC 20076-0001
Tel: (301)986-3000

Employers
GEICO Corp. (Director, Public Relations)

GOURLAY, Diana

1523 New Hampshire Ave. NW
Washington, DC 20036
Tel: (202)588-0002
Fax: (202)785-2669
Registered: LDA
EMail: diana.gourlay@ucop.edu
Staff Member, U.S. Senate, 1986-93.

Employers
University of California, Office of Federal Government Relations (Legislative Director)

GOURLEY, Jacquelyn

One Dupont Circle NW
Suite 520
Washington, DC 20036-1171
Tel: (202)263-0282
Fax: (202)872-8857
EMail: gourleyj@aacrao.org

Employers
American Ass'n of Collegiate Registrars and Admissions Officers (Assistant Director, Government Relations and Communications)

GOVAN, Michael J.

1713 Birch Rd.
McLean, VA 22101
Tel: (703)917-0942
Fax: (703)917-0947
Registered: LDA

Employers
The Legacy Group (President)

Clients Represented
On Behalf of The Legacy Group
Puerto Rico House of Representatives

GOVER, Kevin

1330 Connecticut Ave. NW
Washington, DC 20036-1795
Tel: (202)429-3000
Fax: (202)429-3902
EMail: kgover@steptoe.com
Assistant Secretary for Indian Affairs, Department of the Interior, 1997-2001.

Employers
Steptoe & Johnson LLP (Partner)

GOYETTE, Diane P.

1275 K St. NW
Suite 1212
Washington, DC 20005
Tel: (703)787-0000
Fax: (202)312-5005

Employers
Healthcare Distribution Management Ass'n (Director, Regulatory Affairs)

GOZONSKY, Moses

409 Third St. SW
Second Floor
Washington, DC 20024-6682
Tel: (202)479-6693

Employers
Nat'l Institute of Senior Housing

GRAB, Glenn

1350 I St. NW
Suite 400
Washington, DC 20005-3306
Tel: (202)371-6900
Fax: (202)842-3578
Registered: LDA

Employers
Motorola, Inc. (Director, U.S. Government Relations)

GRABER, Edmund C.

2302 N. Jackson St.
Arlington, VA 22201
Tel: (703)469-3066
Fax: (703)469-3064
Registered: LDA

Employers
Self-employed as an independent consultant.

Clients Represented
As an independent consultant
American Concrete Pavement Ass'n (ACPA)
American Road and Transportation Builders Ass'n (ARTBA)
Crown American Realty Trust
Design-Build Institute of America
Dredging Contractors of America
Frederick Area Committee on Transportation (FACT)
Illinois Public Transit Ass'n (IPTA)
Nat'l Utility Contractors Ass'n (NUCA)
Safety Warning System, L.C.

GRABOWSKI, Gene

1010 Wisconsin Ave. NW
Ninth Floor
Washington, DC 20007
Tel: (202)337-9400
Fax: (202)337-4508
EMail: ggrabowski@gmabrands.com

Employers
Grocery Manufacturers of America (V. President, Communications)

GRACE, David R.

1201 Pennsylvania Ave. NW
Washington, DC 20004-2401
Tel: (202)662-6000
Fax: (202)662-6291
Registered: LDA
EMail: dgrace@cov.com
Office of the Chief Counsel, U.S. Army Corps of Engineers, 1981-84.

Employers
Covington & Burling (Of Counsel)

Clients Represented
On Behalf of Covington & Burling
American Watch Ass'n
Canon USA, Inc.
Canon, Inc.
Christie's Inc.
Internat'l Jelly and Preserve Ass'n
Sotheby's Holdings Inc.

GRACE, Jennifer L.

600 New Hampshire Ave. NW
Suite 601
Washington, DC 20037
Tel: (202)333-7400
Fax: (202)333-1638

Employers
Hill and Knowlton, Inc. (Sr. Managing Director, Technology Practice)

GRACE, Sharon

2500 Wilson Blvd.
Suite 300
Arlington, VA 22201
Tel: (703)907-7713
Fax: (703)907-7727
EMail: sgrace@tia.eia.org

Employers
Telecommunications Industry Ass'n (Director, Marketing Communications Services)

GRADISON, Hon. Willis "Bill" D.

2550 M St. NW
Washington, DC 20037-1350
Tel: (202)457-6184
Fax: (202)457-6315
Registered: LDA
EMail: wgradison@pattonboggs.com
Member, U.S. House of Representatives (R-OH), 1975-93. Assistant to the Secretary, Department of Health, Education, and Welfare, 1955-57. Assistant to the Undersecretary, Department of the Treasury, 1953-55.

Employers
Patton Boggs, LLP (Senior Public Policy Counselor)

Clients Represented
On Behalf of Patton Boggs, LLP
Alliance of Catholic Health Care Systems
Bristol-Myers Squibb Co.
Cincinnati, Ohio, City of
Illinois Department of Human Services
Nat'l Stroke Ass'n
Schering-Plough Corp.
Valley Children's Hospital

GRADY, Cmdr. Chris

The Pentagon
MS: 5C760
Washington, DC 20350-1300
Tel: (703)697-7146
Fax: (703)614-7089
EMail: grady.chris@hq.navy.mil

Employers
Department of Navy (Exec. Assistant, Office of Legislative Affairs)

GRADY, Gregory

1200 G St. NW
Suite 600
Washington, DC 20005-3802
Tel: (202)393-1200
Fax: (202)393-1240
EMail: grady@wrightlaw.com
Attorney, Federal Power Commission, 1973-74.

Employers
Wright & Talisman, P.C. (V. President and Secretary)

Clients Represented
On Behalf of Wright & Talisman, P.C.
GPM Gas Corp.
Transcontinental Gas Pipeline Corp.
Williams Pipelines Central, Inc.

GRADY, John

2425 Wilson Blvd.
Arlington, VA 22201-3385
Tel: (703)841-4300
Ext: 213
Fax: (703)525-9039
EMail: jgrady@ausa.org

Employers
Ass'n of the United States Army (Director, Communications)

GRAEFE, Erin

430 S. Capitol St. SE
Second Floor
Washington, DC 20003
Tel: (202)863-1500
Fax: (202)485-3427

Employers
Democratic Congressional Campaign Committee (Director, Washington Fundraising)

GRAEFE, Frederick H.

1050 Connecticut Ave. NW
Suite 1100
Washington, DC 20036-5304
Tel: (202)861-1500
Fax: (202)861-1790
Registered: LDA, FARA
EMail: Fgraefe@baker-hostetler.com
Law Clerk to Judge Howard F. Corcoran, U.S. District Court for the District of Columbia, 1973-75.

Employers
Baker & Hostetler LLP (Partner)

Clients Represented
On Behalf of Baker & Hostetler LLP
American Concrete Pavement Ass'n (ACPA)
American Electric Power Co.
American Fidelity Life Insurance Co.
American Resort Development Ass'n
Capitol American Financial Corp.
Central Reserve Life
Children's Mercy Hospital
The Chubb Corp.
The Council of Insurance Agents & Brokers
D. H. Blair Investment Banking Corp.
Eagle-Picher Personal Injury Settlement Trust
Edison Electric Institute
Federation of American Hospitals
Flexi-Van Leasing
Florida Residential and Casualty Joint Underwriting Ass'n
Florida Windstorm Underwriting Ass'n
Froedtert Memorial Lutheran Hospital
Icelandship Steamship Co. Ltd.
Invacare Corp.
Kettering Medical Center
Medical Mutual of Ohio
Nat'l Ass'n of Optometrics and Opticians
Nat'l Ass'n of Real Estate Investment Trusts
RMS Disease Management Inc.
Schering Berlin Inc.
Trans World Assurance Co.
Transportation Institute
Verizon Communications
Washington Regional Transplant Consortium
The Wireless Communications Council

GRAF, II, James E.

601 Pennsylvania Ave. NW
Suite 625
North Bldg.
Washington, DC 20004
Tel: (202)639-8222
Fax: (202)434-8867
Registered: LDA
EMail: james.graf@btna.com

Employers
BT North America Inc. (President, BT North America, Inc.)

GRAF, Ronald P.

1130 Connecticut Ave. NW
Suite 710
Washington, DC 20036
Tel: (202)833-5724
Fax: (202)833-5728
Registered: LDA

Employers
Hershey Foods Corp. (Federal Government Relations Manager)

GRAFF, Brian H.

4245 N. Fairfax Dr.
Suite 750
Arlington, VA 22203
Tel: (703)516-9300
Fax: (703)516-9308
Registered: LDA

Employers
American Soc. of Pension Actuaries (Exec. Director)

GRAFF, Gretchen

805 15th St. NW
Suite 300
Washington, DC 20005-2207
Tel: (202)682-4200
Fax: (202)682-9054
Registered: LDA

Employers
Credit Union Nat'l Ass'n, Inc. (Grassroots Manager)

GRAFF, John R.

1448 Duke St.
Alexandria, VA 22314
Tel: (703)836-4800
Fax: (703)836-4801
Registered: LDA
EMail: jgraff@iaapa.org

Employers
Internat'l Ass'n of Amusement Parks and Attractions (President, Chief Exec. Officer and Counsel)

GRAFMEYER, Richard

1666 K St. NW
Suite 800
Washington, DC 20006
Tel: (202)481-7000
Fax: (202)862-7098
Deputy Chief of Staff, Joint Committee on Taxation, 1998-2000. Former Tax Counsel, Senate Committee on Finance.

Employers
Arthur Andersen LLP (Partner)

GRAHAM, Carol

1775 Massachusetts Ave. NW
Washington, DC 20036-2188
Tel: (202)797-6000
Fax: (202)797-6004

Employers
The Brookings Institution (Sr. Fellow, Foreign Policy Studies/Co-Dir., Center on Social & Economic Dynamics)

GRAHAM, IV, John H.

1701 N. Beauregard St.
Alexandria, VA 22311
Tel: (703)549-1500
Ext: 2001
Fax: (703)836-7439
EMail: jgraham@diabetes.org

Employers
American Diabetes Ass'n (Chief Exec. Officer)

GRAHAM, Katherine

325 Seventh St. NW
Suite 1100
Washington, DC 20004-2802
Tel: (202)783-7971
Fax: (202)737-2849
Registered: LDA

Employers
Nat'l Retail Federation (Senior Director)

GRAHAM, Lawrence T.

8320 Old Courthouse Rd.
Suite 300
Vienna, VA 22182
Tel: (703)790-5011
Fax: (703)790-5752
Registered: LDA

Employers
American Cocoa Research Institute (President)
Chocolate Manufacturers Ass'n of the U.S.A. (President)
Nat'l Confectioners Ass'n (President)

GRAHAM, Michael A.

1111 14th St. NW
Suite 1200
Washington, DC 20005-5603
Tel: (202)789-5167
Fax: (202)898-2437
Registered: LDA
EMail: grahamm@ada.org

Employers
American Dental Ass'n (Senior Congressional Lobbyist)

GRAHAM, Neil E.

P.O. Box 1096
McLean, VA 22101-1096
Tel: (703)821-8700
Fax: (703)827-7761
Registered: LDA

Employers
Stephens Law Firm (Senior Attorney)

Clients Represented
On Behalf of Stephens Law Firm
American Rental Ass'n

GRAHAM, Thomas

1730 Pennsylvania Ave. NW
Suite 1200
Washington, DC 20006-4706
Tel: (202)737-0500
Fax: (202)626-3737
Deputy General Counsel, Office of the United States Trade Representative, Executive Office of the President, The White House, 1974-79.

Employers
King & Spalding (Partner)

GRAHAM, Jr., Thomas

1901 Pennsylvania Ave. NW
Suite 201
Washington, DC 20006
Tel: (202)745-2450
Fax: (202)667-0444

Employers
Lawyers Alliance for World Security (President and Ambassador)

GRAIG, Ian C.

1101 16th St. NW
Washington, DC 20036
Tel: (202)496-1550
Fax: (202)496-1552
Registered: FARA

Employers
Global Policy Group, Inc. (Chief Exec.)

GRAMLEY, Lyle E.

1919 Pennsylvania Ave. NW
Seventh Floor
Washington, DC 20006-3488
Tel: (202)557-2700

Employers
Mortgage Bankers Ass'n of America (Consulting Economist)

GRANBERG, Chris

309 Massachusetts Ave. NE
Washington, DC 20002
Tel: (202)547-8189
Fax: (202)547-8190
Registered: LDA
EMail: clgranberg@aol.com

Employers
Fraternal Order of Police (Legislative Assistant)

GRANDISON, W. George

1330 Connecticut Ave. NW
Washington, DC 20036-1795
Tel: (202)429-3000
Fax: (202)429-3902
Registered: LDA
EMail: wgrandis@steptoe.com
Captain, Office of the Judge Advocate General, International Affairs Division, U.S. Army, 1972-76.

Employers
Steptoe & Johnson LLP (Partner)

Clients Represented
On Behalf of Steptoe & Johnson LLP
B.C. Softwood Lumber Trade Council
British Columbia Softwood Lumber Trade Council
Canadian Wheat Board

GRANDY, Ph.D., John W.

2100 L St. NW
Washington, DC 20037
Tel: (202)452-1100
Fax: (202)778-6132
Registered: LDA

Employers
Humane Soc. of the United States (V. President, Wildlife and Habitat Protection)

GRANESE, Nancy

555 13th St. NW
Washington, DC 20004-1109
Tel: (202)637-5697
Fax: (202)637-5910
Registered: LDA
EMail: nlgranese@hhlaw.com

Employers
Hogan & Hartson L.L.P. (Government Affairs Advisor)

Clients Represented
On Behalf of Hogan & Hartson L.L.P.
Blount Parrish & Co., Inc.
CELOTEX
DIAGEO
eBay Inc.
Grocery Manufacturers of America
Guardian Industries Corp.
HMSHost Corp.
Institute for Civil Soc.
Kinder-Care Learning Centers, Inc.
MedPro, Inc.
Mennonite Mutual Aid Ass'n
Michelin North America
Nat'l Board for Professional Teaching Standards (NBPTS)
Nat'l Structured Settlements Trade Ass'n
Nestle USA, Inc.
Parker Jewish Geriatric Institute
Polyisocyanurate Insulation Manufacturers Ass'n
Staff Builders, Inc.
UPMC Presbyterian

GRANGER, Jim

1363 Beverly Rd.
McLean, VA 22101
Tel: (703)556-0001
Fax: (703)893-3811

Employers
Wirthlin Worldwide (Chief Exec. Officer and President)

GRANNIS, Mark

1200 18th St. NW
Suite 1200
Washington, DC 20036
Tel: (202)730-1300
Fax: (202)730-1301
Former Senior Legal Advisor, International Bureau, Federal Communications Commission.

Employers
Harris, Wiltshire & Grannis LLP (Partner)

GRANRUD, USA (Ret.), Lt. Gen. Jerome H.

11 Canal Center Plaza
Suite 103
Alexandria, VA 22314
Tel: (703)683-4222
Fax: (703)683-0645
Registered: LDA
Former Commanding General, Japan and IX Corps, U.S. Army.

Employers
The Spectrum Group

Clients Represented
On Behalf of The Spectrum Group
Tri-City Regional Port District

GRANT, Andrea J.

901 15th St. NW
Suite 700
Washington, DC 20005-2301
Tel: (202)371-6000
Fax: (202)371-6279
Registered: LDA
Attorney on the Oil Import Appeals Board, 1974-76.

Employers
Verner, Liipfert, Bernhard, McPherson and Hand, Chartered (Member of Firm)

Clients Represented
On Behalf of Verner, Liipfert, Bernhard, McPherson and Hand, Chartered
Independent Fuel Terminal Operators Ass'n
The Limited Inc.
Lubrizol
New England Fuel Institute
Petroport, Inc.

GRANT, Dr. Carl N.

1615 H St. NW
Washington, DC 20062-2000
Tel: (202)463-5425
Fax: (202)463-5593
Registered: LDA
EMail: cgrant@uschamber.com

Employers
Chamber of Commerce of the U.S.A. (Senior V. President, Communications)

GRANT, H. Morton

2100 M St. NW
Washington, DC 20037
Tel: (202)833-7200
Fax: (202)429-0687

Employers
The Urban Institute (V. President, Controller and Treasurer)

GRANT, Hon. James William "Bill"

908 Pennsylvania Ave. SE
Washington, DC 20003
Tel: (202)544-5666
Fax: (202)544-4647
Registered: LDA
EMail: bgrant@advantage-dc.com
Member, U.S. House of Representatives (D-FL), 1987-89 and (R-FL), 1989-91.

Employers
Advantage Associates, Inc. (Partner)

GRANT, Jason D.

5225 Wisconsin Ave. NW
Suite 600
Washington, DC 20015-2014
Tel: (202)686-7463
Fax: (202)686-3656
EMail: jgrant@sio.org

Employers
Surety Information Office (Manager, Communications Programs)

GRANT, Jay B.

801 Pennsylvania Ave. NW
Suite 245
Washington, DC 20005
Tel: (202)624-1512
Fax: (202)318-0338
Registered: LDA
EMail: jay@healthupdate.com

Employers
Jay Grant & Associates (Counsel)

Clients Represented
On Behalf of Jay Grant & Associates
Arkansas, Office of the Governor of the State of
Fort Smith Regional Airport
Nat'l Ass'n of Insurance Commissioners
Protective Life Insurance Co.
Travelocity.com

GRANT, Jill E.

816 Connecticut Ave. NW
Suite 300
Washington, DC 20006
Tel: (202)530-1270
Fax: (202)530-1920
Registered: LDA

Employers
Nordhaus Haltom Taylor Taradash & Bladh LLP (Partner)

Clients Represented
On Behalf of Nordhaus Haltom Taylor Taradash & Bladh LLP
Navajo Nation Oil and Gas Co., Inc.
Santa Ana Pueblo

GRANT, Patrick J.

555 12th St. NW
Washington, DC 20004-1206
Tel: (202)942-5000
Fax: (202)942-5999
EMail: Patrick_Grant@aporter.com

Employers
Arnold & Porter (Partner)

GRANT, Susan

1701 K St. NW
Suite 1200
Washington, DC 20006
Tel: (202)835-3323
Fax: (202)835-0747

Employers
Nat'l Consumers League (V. President, Public Policy)

GRANWELL, Alan

1700 Pennsylvania Ave. NW
Suite 600
Washington, DC 20006
Tel: (202)393-7600
Fax: (202)393-7601
Registered: LDA

Employers
Ivins, Phillips & Barker (Partner)

Clients Represented
On Behalf of Ivins, Phillips & Barker
Bass Hotels and Resorts, Inc.

GRASSER, John L. C.

1130 17th St. NW
Washington, DC 20036-4677
Tel: (202)463-2622
Fax: (202)857-0135
EMail: jgrasser@nma.org

Employers
Nat'l Mining Ass'n (V. President, External Communications)

GRASSO, Jeanne Marie

600 New Hampshire Ave. NW
11th Floor
Washington, DC 20037
Tel: (202)944-3000
Fax: (202)944-3068
Registered: LDA
EMail: jmg@dejlaw.com
Formerly served on the staff of the House Committee on Merchant Marine and Fisheries, 1985-86; and formerly served in the Nat'l Oceanic and Atmospheric Ass'n, 1986-91.

Employers
Dyer Ellis & Joseph, P.C. (Partner)

Clients Represented
On Behalf of Dyer Ellis & Joseph, P.C.
American Coke and Coal Chemicals Institute
Bender Shipbuilding & Repair Co., Inc.
Fruit Shippers Ltd.
Glass Packaging Institute
Heerema Marine Contractors Nederland B.V.
Hornblower Marine Services, Inc.
Hvide Marine Inc.
Kvaerner Philadelphia Shipyard Inc.
Marine Spill Response Corporation
The Trump Organization

GRAU, John

Three Bethesda Metro Center
Suite 1100
Bethesda, MD 20814
Tel: (301)657-3110
Fax: (301)215-4500

Employers
Associated Specialty Contractors (President)
Nat'l Electrical Contractors Ass'n (Exec. V. President and Chief Exec. Officer)

GRAUL, Michael R.

9200 Rockville Pike
Bethesda, MD 20814-3896
Tel: (301)530-6500
Fax: (301)530-1516
Registered: LDA
EMail: mgraul@goodwill.org

Employers
Goodwill Industries Internat'l, Inc. (Director, Governmental Affairs)

GRAUSE, Marie Beatrice

1747 Pennsylvania Ave. NW
Suite 1200
Washington, DC 20006
Tel: (202)223-1200
Fax: (202)785-6687
Registered: LDA
EMail: bgrause@fhe.com

Employers
Foley, Hoag & Eliot LLP (Counsel)

Clients Represented
On Behalf of Foley, Hoag & Eliot LLP
Massachusetts Hospital Ass'n
Massachusetts Water Resources Authority
THA: An Ass'n of Hospitals and Health Systems

GRAVELINE, Denise T.

1155 16th St. NW
Washington, DC 20036
Tel: (202)872-4600
Fax: (202)872-4615
EMail: d_graveline@acs.org

Employers
American Chemical Soc. (Director, Communications)

GRAVELY, Clay

11350 Random Hills Rd.
Suite 800
Fairfax, VA 22030
Tel: (703)620-4914
Fax: (703)620-4709
Registered: LDA
EMail: cgravely@cpiva.com

Employers
Capital Partnerships (VA) Inc. (Associate)

Clients Represented
On Behalf of Capital Partnerships (VA) Inc.
Anoka County Regional Railroad Authority
Denver, Colorado, City and County of
Douglas, Colorado, County of
Friedlob, Sanderson, Raskin, Paulson, Toutillott
North Metro Mayors Coalition
Policy Advantage
Southeast Business Partnership
Taxicab, Limousine and Paratransit Ass'n

GRAVES, Charles H.

1660 L St. NW
Suite 1050
Washington, DC 20036
Tel: (202)659-2229
Fax: (202)659-5234
Registered: LDA
EMail: chg@foxislands.net
Former Senior Executive, Federal Transit Administration.

Employers
Charles H. Graves & Associates (President)

Clients Represented

On Behalf of Charles H. Graves & Associates
Bridgeport, Connecticut, City of
Central Ohio Regional Transit Authority
Corpus Christi Regional Transportation Authority
Utah Transit Authority
Washoe County Regional Transportation Commission

GRAVES, David

50 F St. NW
Suite 900
Washington, DC 20001
Tel: (202)626-8700
Fax: (202)626-8722
Registered: LDA
EMail: dgraves@ncfc.org

Employers
Nat'l Council of Farmer Cooperatives (President)

GRAVES, Donet D.

1615 L St. NW
Suite 1100
Washington, DC 20036-5610
Tel: (202)872-1260
Fax: (202)466-3509

Employers
The Business Roundtable (Exec. Director, BusinessLINC)

GRAVES, Edwin C.

1401 K St. NW
Suite 450
Washington, DC 20005
Tel: (202)737-0700
Fax: (202)737-0455
Registered: LDA, FARA
Press Secretary and Administrative Assistant to Senator Walter Huddleston (D-KY), 1973-84.

Employers
Edwin C. Graves & Associates (President)

Clients Represented

On Behalf of Edwin C. Graves & Associates
Azerbaijan, Embassy of the Republic of
CBI Sugar Group

GRAVES, Shannon

2300 Wilson Blvd.
Arlington, VA 22201
Tel: (703)528-1775
Fax: (703)528-2333
Registered: LDA
EMail: sgraves@navyleague.org

Employers
Navy League of the United States (Director of Legislative Affairs)

GRAVES, Thomas J.

1500 Rhode Island Ave. NW
Washington, DC 20005-5597
Tel: (202)462-6272
Fax: (202)462-8549

Employers
Nat'l Paint and Coatings Ass'n (General Counsel)

GRAVES-MOORE, Pamela

1455 F St. NW
Suite 450
Washington, DC 20004
Tel: (202)393-6040
Fax: (202)393-6050
Registered: LDA

Employers
Pharmacia Corp. (Manager, Federal Government Affairs)

GRAY, Alan G.

218 N. Lee St.
Alexandria, VA 22314
Tel: (703)329-1670
Fax: (703)329-1670
EMail: aggray@worldnet.att.net

Employers
The Lonington Group (Managing Director)

Clients Represented

On Behalf of The Lonington Group
Harborlink, LLC
Metromarine Holdings, Inc.

GRAY, Albert C.

601 Wythe St.
Alexandria, VA 22314-1994
Tel: (703)684-2400
Fax: (703)684-2492
EMail: agray@wef.org

Employers
Water Environment Federation (Deputy Exec. Director - Technical)

GRAY, C. Boyden

2445 M St. NW
Washington, DC 20037-1420
Tel: (202)663-6000
Fax: (202)663-6363
Registered: LDA
EMail: bgray@wilmer.com
Counsel to the President (1989-93) and Counsel to the V. President (1981-89), The White House, 1981-89. Clerk to Justice Earl Warren, U.S. Supreme Court, 1968.

Employers
Wilmer, Cutler & Pickering (Partner)

Clients Represented

On Behalf of Wilmer, Cutler & Pickering
Amgen
Clean Air Action Corp.
Deutsche Telekom, Inc.
Genzyme Corp.
Loral Space and Communications, Ltd.
Tiger Management Corp.

GRAY, Carolyn Doppelt

1227 25th St. NW
Suite 700
Washington, DC 20037
Tel: (202)861-0900
Fax: (202)296-2882

Employers
Epstein Becker & Green, P.C. (Partner)

Clients Represented

On Behalf of Epstein Becker & Green, P.C.
Coalition on Accessibility

GRAY, Charles D.

1101 Vermont Ave. NW
Suite 200
Washington, DC 20005
Tel: (202)898-2208
Fax: (202)898-2213
EMail: cgray@naruc.org

Employers
Nat'l Ass'n of Regulatory Utility Commissioners (Exec. Director)

GRAY, Chris

1155 15th St. NW
Suite 1004
Washington, DC 20005
Tel: (202)467-5081
Fax: (202)467-5085

Employers
Braille Revival League (President)

GRAY, Davon

1747 Pennsylvania Ave. NW
Suite 1150
Washington, DC 20006
Tel: (202)557-2971
Fax: (202)296-4507

Employers
The MWW Group (Legislative Associate)

Clients Represented

On Behalf of The MWW Group
Little Havana Activities and Nutrition Centers
Michigan Bulb
Ross University School of Medicine in Dominica
United States Education Finance Corp.

GRAY, Delna

1201 15th St. NW
Washington, DC 20005-2800
Tel: (202)822-0470
Fax: (202)822-0572

Employers
Nat'l Ass'n of Home Builders of the U.S. (Legislative Director, Tax Policy)

GRAY, Don

122 C St. NW
Suite 700
Washington, DC 20001
Tel: (202)628-1400
Ext: 1882
Fax: (202)628-1825
EMail: dgray@eesi.org

Employers
Environmental and Energy Study Institute (Director, Water and Sustainable Communities Program)

GRAY, Edward C.

1525 Wilson Blvd.
Suite 600
Arlington, VA 22209
Tel: (703)527-1670
Fax: (703)527-5477
Registered: LDA

Employers
Jellinek, Schwartz & Connolly

Clients Represented

On Behalf of Jellinek, Schwartz & Connolly
FQPA Implementation Working Group

GRAY, Geoffrey P.

888 17th St. NW
Suite 312
Washington, DC 20006
Tel: (202)223-6575
Fax: (202)331-3836
Registered: LDA
EMail: afshc@ibm.net

Employers
Ass'n of Financial Services Holding Companies (Director, Government Relations)

GRAY, Gerald

910 17th St. NW
Suite 600
Washington, DC 20006
Tel: (202)955-4500
Fax: (202)955-4588

Employers
American Forests (V. President, Resource Policy)

GRAY, John M.

201 Park Washington Ct.
Falls Church, VA 22046-4621
Tel: (703)532-9400
Fax: (703)538-4673
Registered: LDA
EMail: johngray@fdi.org

Employers
Food Distributors Internat'l (NAWGA-IFDA) (President, IFDA and Exec. V. President, General Counsel, FDI)

GRAY, Neil A.

2120 L St. NW
Suite 305
Washington, DC 20037
Tel: (202)659-4620
Fax: (202)659-0500
Registered: LDA
EMail: ngray@ibtta.org

Employers
Internat'l Bridge, Tunnel and Turnpike Ass'n (Director, Government Relations)

GRAY, Odyssey E.

4301 Connecticut Ave. NW
Suite 453
Washington, DC 20008
Tel: (202)237-0505
Fax: (202)237-7566
Registered: LDA

Employers
John J. Fausti & Associates, LLC (Law Clerk)

Clients Represented

On Behalf of John J. Fausti & Associates, LLC
Nat'l Ass'n of Aircraft and Communication Suppliers

GRAY, Robert J.

205 S. Whiting St.
Suite 308
Alexandria, VA 22304
Tel: (703)751-8022
Fax: (703)751-5735
Registered: LDA
EMail: BGray15452@aol.com

Employers
The GrayWell Group, Inc.
Resource Management Consultants, Inc. (President)

Clients Represented

On Behalf of The GrayWell Group, Inc.
Horizon Organic Dairy, Inc.
Nat'l Cooperative Business Ass'n

On Behalf of Resource Management Consultants, Inc.
Council of Northeast Farmer Cooperatives
Nat'l Center for Appropriate Technology
Organic Trade Ass'n
Southeast Dairy Farmer Ass'n
Waves States Ratification Committee

GRAY, Robert Reed

1133 Connecticut Ave. NW
Suite 1200
Washington, DC 20036
Tel: (202)775-9800
Fax: (202)833-8491
Registered: LDA
Assistant Chief, International and Rules Division (1953-55) and Staff of General Counsel (1951-52), Civil Aeronautics Board.

Employers
Winthrop, Stimson, Putnam & Roberts (Of Counsel)

Clients Represented

On Behalf of Winthrop, Stimson, Putnam & Roberts

Transportes Aereos Mercantiles Panamericanos

GRAY, Roz

9000 Rockville Pike
Bldg. One, Room 244
Bethesda, MD 20892
EMail: grayr@od.nih.gov
Tel: (301)496-3471
Fax: (301)496-0840

Employers

Department of Health and Human Services - Nat'l Institutes of Health (Deputy Director, Office of Legislative Policy and Analysis)

GRAY, Todd D.

1200 New Hampshire Ave. NW
Suite 800
Washington, DC 20036-6802
EMail: tgray@dlalaw.com
Tel: (202)776-2000
Fax: (202)776-2222
Registered: LDA

Employers

Dow, Lohnes & Albertson, PLLC (Member)

Clients Represented

On Behalf of Dow, Lohnes & Albertson, PLLC

Nat'l ITFS Ass'n
St. Louis Regional Education and Public Television Commission
University of Puerto Rico

GRAY, Tom

333 N. Fairfax St.
Suite 302
Alexandria, VA 22314
Tel: (703)548-5868
Fax: (703)548-5869
Registered: LDA

Former Chief Economist, U.S. Small Business Administration. Former Deputy Assistant Director, Policy Planning, Budget and Evaluation, ACTION. Former Deputy Director, Peace Corps.

Employers

The Argus Group, L.L.C. (Of Counsel)

GRAYKAUSKI, John

600 New Hampshire Ave. NW
11th Floor
Washington, DC 20037
Tel: (202)944-3000
Fax: (202)944-3068

Employers

Dyer Ellis & Joseph, P.C.

Clients Represented

On Behalf of Dyer Ellis & Joseph, P.C.

FastShip, Inc.
Friede Goldman Halter
Kvaerner Philadelphia Shipyard Inc.

GRAYSON, Cherry

1500 Pennsylvania Ave. NW
Room 3025MT
Washington, DC 20220
Tel: (202)622-0555
Fax: (202)622-0534

Employers

Department of Treasury (Legislative Assistant)

GRAYSON, Helen

P.O. Box 916
Alexandria, VA 22313
Tel: (703)893-4631

Employers

American Restaurant China Council (Exec. Director)

GRAYSON, Mark

1100 15th St. NW
Suite 900
Washington, DC 20005
Tel: (202)835-3400
Fax: (202)835-3414

Employers

Pharmaceutical Research and Manufacturers of America (Senior Director, Communications)

GRAZ, John

12501 Old Columbia Pike
Silver Spring, MD 20904
EMail: 74532,240@compuserve.com
Tel: (301)680-6680
Fax: (301)680-6695

Employers

General Conference of Seventh-day Adventists (Director, Public Affairs and Religious Liberty)
Internat'l Religious Liberty Ass'n (Secretary-General)

GREALY, Mary R.

900 17th St. NW
Suite 600
Washington, DC 20006
Tel: (202)452-8700
Fax: (202)296-9561
Registered: LDA

Employers

Healthcare Leadership Council (President)

GREALY, Robert F.

1090 Vermont Ave. NW
Third Floor
Washington, DC 20005
Tel: (202)842-5000
Fax: (202)789-4293

40 years in U.S. Foreign Service , primarily in Asia.

Employers

Millian Byers Associates, LLC (Senior International Advisor)

Clients Represented

On Behalf of Millian Byers Associates, LLC

Siemens Corp.

GREBE, Michael W.

3000 K St. NW
Suite 500
Washington, DC 20007-5109
EMail: mgrebe@foleylaw.com
Tel: (202)672-5465
Fax: (202)672-5399

Employers

Foley & Lardner (Chairman and Chief Exec. Officer)

GRECO, Dawn R.

277 S. Washington St.
Suite 200
Alexandria, VA 22314
EMail: dgreco@staffingtoday.net
Tel: (703)253-2037
Fax: (703)253-2053
Registered: LDA

Employers

American Staffing Ass'n (Assistant Counsel)

GRECZYN, Mary Anne

198 Van Buren St.
Herndon, VA 20170
Tel: (703)834-3400
Fax: (703)834-3593

Employers

Airbus Industrie of North America, Inc. (Communications Manager)

GREELEY, Christopher J.

1001 Pennsylvania Ave. NW
Suite 450 North
Washington, DC 20004
Tel: (202)789-4040
Fax: (202)789-4242
Registered: LDA

Employers

Commonwealth Group, Ltd.

Clients Represented

On Behalf of Commonwealth Group, Ltd.

Nexia Biotechnologies, Inc.
OraVax, Inc.

GREELEY, Donald R.

2801 Beechwood Circle
Arlington, VA 22207

Executive Assistant to Senator Ernest Gruening (D-AK), 1966-68. Administrative Assistant to Rep. Ralph J. Rivers (D-AK), 1959-66.

Employers

Self-employed as an independent consultant.

Clients Represented

As an independent consultant

American Fiber Manufacturers Ass'n

GREEN, Carl J.

1900 K St. NW
Suite 800
Washington, DC 20006
Tel: (202)828-9272
Fax: (202)828-9277

Employers

Hitachi, Ltd. (Deputy Senior Representative)

GREEN, Carol Lynn

7315 Wisconsin Ave.
Suite 800W
Bethesda, MD 20814
Tel: (301)941-8038
Fax: (301)961-8648

Employers

Law Offices of Carol Green (Attorney)

Clients Represented

On Behalf of Law Offices of Carol Green

Nat'l Funeral Directors Ass'n

GREEN, Douglas H.

1200 19th St. NW
Washington, DC 20036-2430
EMail: douglas.green@piperrudnick.com
Tel: (202)861-3847
Fax: (202)223-2085
Registered: LDA

Employers

Piper Marbury Rudnick & Wolfe LLP (Partner)

GREEN, Edward M.

1001 Pennsylvania Ave. NW
Suite 1100
Washington, DC 20004-2595
EMail: egreen@cromor.com
Tel: (202)624-2500
Fax: (202)628-5116
Registered: LDA

Special Assistant to the Administrator, Mining Enforcement and Safety Administration (1975-77); Counsel to the Secretary for Surface Mining and Reclamation (1973-74); and Attorney-Advisor, Office of the Solicitor, Division of Mine Health and Safety (1970-73), Department of Interior.

Employers

Crowell & Moring LLP (Of Counsel)

Clients Represented

On Behalf of Crowell & Moring LLP

Cyprus Amex Minerals Co.
Franco-Nevada Mining Corp., Inc.
Homestake Mining
Independence Mining Co., Inc.
Placer Dome U.S. Inc.

GREEN, George R.

655 15th St. NW
Washington, DC 20005-5701
EMail: ggreen@fmi.org
Tel: (202)220-0613
Fax: (202)220-0873
Registered: LDA

Employers

Food Marketing Institute (V. President and General Counsel)

GREEN, James F.

227 Massachusetts Ave. NE
Suite One
Washington, DC 20002
EMail: green@tongoursimpson.com
Tel: (202)544-7600
Fax: (202)544-6770
Registered: LDA

Special Detailer to Senator Byron Dorgan (D-ND) and Senator Thomas A. Daschle (D-SD), 1999-2000. Special Counsel, Wireless Telecommunications Bureau (1998-99), and Deputy and Interim Director, Office of Legislative and Intergovernmental Affairs (1997-98), Federal Communications Commission.

Employers

Tongour Simpson Holsclaw Green (Partner)

Clients Represented

On Behalf of Tongour Simpson Holsclaw Green

Corning Inc.
SBC Communications Inc.

GREEN, John M.

1212 New York Ave. NW
Suite 350
Washington, DC 20005
EMail: johngreen@erols.com
Tel: (202)842-5077
Fax: (202)842-5010
Registered: LDA, FARA

Deputy Chief of Staff (1995-96) and Legislative Aide (1993-95) to Senator Trent Lott (R-MS).

Employers

Hall, Green, Rupli, LLC (Partner)

Clients Represented

On Behalf of Hall, Green, Rupli, LLC

American Ass'n of Nurse Anesthetists
BellSouth Corp.
BellSouth Telecommunications, Inc.
Birmingham Airport Authority
Colsa Corp.
Community Financial Services Ass'n
DaimlerChrysler Corp.
FedEx Corp.
Huntsville Madison Chamber of Commerce
MemberWorks, Inc.
Nat'l Ass'n of Business Political Action Committees
Nat'l Rifle Ass'n of America
Pernod Ricard
Philip Morris Management Corp.
Southern Research Institute
U.S. Space & Rocket Center
United States Telecom Ass'n
University of Alabama - Huntsville
University of South Alabama
UST Public Affairs, Inc.

GREEN, Kaylene

1755 Jefferson Davis Hwy.
Suite 1107
Arlington, VA 22202
Tel: (703)415-0344
Fax: (703)415-0182
Registered: LDA

Employers

American Accreditation Healthcare Commission/URAC (Chair)
The PMA Group (Director)

Clients Represented

On Behalf of The PMA Group

AAI Corp.
ADSIL
Advanced Acoustic Concepts, Inc.
Advanced Programming Concepts
AEPTEC
Ag/Bio Con
Alliance
American Academy of Audiology
Applied Marine Technologies, Inc.
ARC Global Technologies
AsclepiusNet
Ass'n of Medical Device Reprocessors
Autometric Inc.
Battelle
Biocontrol Technology, Inc.
Cartwright Electronics
Caterpillar Inc.
Chamberlain Manufacturing Corp.
Cheese of Choice Coalition
Chicago Mercantile Exchange
CHIM
CoBank, ACB
Concurrent Technologies Corp.
Condor Systems
Coronado, California, City of
CPU Technology
CRYPTEK Secure Communications, LLC
Diamond Antenna & Microwave Corp.
Dynacom Industries
Dynamics Research Corp.
Electro-Radiation Inc.
Electronic Warfare Associates, Inc.
Environmental Technology Unlimited
Fidelity Technologies Corp.
FLIR Systems, Inc.
Florida Sugar Cane League, Inc.
Foundation Health Federal Services, Inc.
General Atomics
Generic Pharmaceutical Ass'n
Gentex Corp.
B. F. Goodrich Co.
Guild Associates
IIT Research Institute
IMSSCO Inc.
Innovative Productivity, Inc.
Joint Healthcare Information Technology Alliance
Kollsman, Inc.
L-3 Communications Corp.
Laguna Industries, Inc.
Laguna, New Mexico, City of
Life Cell
Lockheed Martin Corp.
Lockheed Martin Federal Systems
Lockheed Martin MS/Gaithersburg
Lucent Technologies
Marconi Communications Federal
McLean Hospital
MIC Industries, Inc.
Microvision, Inc.
J. E. Morgan Knitting Mills
MTS Systems Inc.
Nat'l Ass'n of RC&D Councils
Nat'l Ass'n of Resource Conservation
Nat'l Cattleman's Beef Ass'n
Nat'l Cooperative Bank
Nat'l Pork Producers Ass'n
New Mexico Tech
Northrop Marine
Omega Air
Opportunity Medical, Inc.
Orange Shipbuilding Co., Inc.
Oxley
Pathfinder Technology Inc.
Planning Systems, Inc.
Prologic
Sabreliner Corp.
SACO Defense
SatoTravel
Schweizer Aircraft Corp.
Science Applications Internat'l Corp. (SAIC)
Spatial Integrated Systems
Stanly County Airport Authority
SVS, Inc.
Teledyne Controls, Inc.
TeleFlex Canada, Ltd.
Textron Inc.
Titan Corp.
Trex Enterprises
Triosyn Corp.
U.S. Rice Producers Ass'n
University Emergency Medicine Foundation
Weidlinger Associates, Inc.

GREEN, Kimberly A.

444 N. Capitol St. NW
Suite 830
Washington, DC 20001
Tel: (202)737-0303
Fax: (202)737-1106
Registered: LDA

Employers

Nat'l Ass'n of State Directors of Vocational Technical Education Consortium (Exec. Director)

GREEN, Lori Valencia

750 First St. NE
Washington, DC 20002-4242
Tel: (202)336-5931
Fax: (202)336-6063
Registered: LDA

Employers

American Psychological Ass'n (Senior Legislative/Federal Affairs Representative)

GREEN, Merritt J.

1497 Chain Bridge Rd.
Suite 300
McLean, VA 22101
EMail: mgreen@ilalaw.com
Tel: (703)893-7071
Fax: (703)893-8020
Registered: LDA

Employers

Institutional Labor Advisors (Associate)

Clients Represented

On Behalf of Institutional Labor Advisors

Coal Act Fairness Alliance
Freeman United Coal Mining Co.
Retiree Benefits Alliance

GREEN, Micah S.

1399 New York Ave. NW
Eighth Floor
Washington, DC 20005-4711
EMail: mgreen@bondmarkets.com
Tel: (202)434-8400
Fax: (202)434-8456
Registered: LDA

Staff, House Committee on Post Office and Civil Service, 1983-85. Former Legislative Assistant to Rep. Don Albosta (D-MI). Served as Legislative Assistant to Rep. Ronald Sarasin (R-CT).

Employers

The Bond Market Ass'n (President)

GREEN, Paul

1401 H St. NW
Suite 600
Washington, DC 20005-2136
Tel: (202)326-7300
Fax: (202)326-7333

Employers

United States Telecom Ass'n (V. President, Development and Marketing)

GREEN, Peter M.

1819 H St. NW
Suite 1250
Washington, DC 20006-3690
EMail: pgreenbadc@aol.com
Tel: (202)223-6600
Fax: (202)293-3388

Employers

Bar Ass'n of the District of Columbia (Exec. Director)

GREEN, Randy

One Massachusetts Ave. NW
Suite 800
Washington, DC 20001-1431
EMail: rgreen@mwmlaw.com
Tel: (202)842-2345
Fax: (202)408-7763
Registered: LDA

Employers

McLeod, Watkinson & Miller (Senior Government Relations Consultant)

Clients Represented

On Behalf of McLeod, Watkinson & Miller

Coalition for Sugar Reform

GREEN, Richard

1111 14th St. NW
Suite 1200
Washington, DC 20005-5603
EMail: greenr@ada.org
Tel: (202)789-5170
Fax: (202)898-2437

Employers

American Dental Ass'n (Director, Washington Communications)

GREEN, Rob J.

1200 17th St. NW
Washington, DC 20036-3097
Tel: (202)331-5900
Fax: (202)973-5373

Former Work Force Policy Coordinator, House Committee on Education and the Workforce, 1996-2001. Former Legislative Director to Rep. Harris W. Fawell (R-IL) and Chief of Staff to Rep. William F. Goodling (R-PA).

Employers

Nat'l Restaurant Ass'n (Director, Work Force Policy)

GREEN, Robert R.

One Massachusetts Ave. NW
Suite 800
Washington, DC 20001-1431
Tel: (202)842-2345
Fax: (202)408-7763
Registered: LDA

Employers

McLeod, Watkinson & Miller

Clients Represented

On Behalf of McLeod, Watkinson & Miller

United Egg Ass'n
United Egg Producers

GREEN, Roy

601 E St. NW
Washington, DC 20049
Tel: (202)434-3800
Fax: (202)434-6477
Registered: LDA

Employers

AARP (American Ass'n of Retired Persons) (Legislative Representative)

GREEN, Sally

919 18th St. NW
Suite 800
Washington, DC 20006
Tel: (202)628-4160
Fax: (202)347-5323

Employers

Human Rights Campaign Fund (Northern Field Organizer)

GREEN, Scott H.

8150 Leesburg Pike
Suite 900
Vienna, VA 22182
Tel: (703)760-1550
Fax: (703)760-8870
Registered: LDA

Employers
Lafayette Group, Inc. (Partner)

Clients Represented

On Behalf of Lafayette Group, Inc.
Boys and Girls Clubs of America
D.A.R.E. America

GREEN, Seth

One Thomas Circle NW
Suite 1100
Washington, DC 20005
Tel: (202)862-7859
Fax: (202)429-3301
Registered: LDA
EMail: smg@capdale.com
Associate Tax Legislative Counsel (1997-98) and Attorney-Advisor (1994-97), Office of Tax Policy, Department of Treasury.

Employers
Caplin & Drysdale, Chartered (Member)

Clients Represented

On Behalf of Caplin & Drysdale, Chartered
The Chubb Corp.
The Hartford

GREEN, Steven K.

518 C St. NE
Washington, DC 20002
Tel: (202)466-3234
Fax: (202)466-2587
Registered: LDA

Employers
Americans United for Separation of Church and State (Legal Director)

GREEN, William J.

1455 Pennsylvania Ave. NW
Suite 300
Washington, DC 20004
Tel: (202)628-2600
Fax: (202)638-2072
Registered: LDA

Employers
MacAndrews & Forbes Holdings, Inc. (V. President, Government Affairs)

GREENAN, Barbara

9111 Old Georgetown Rd.
Bethesda, MD 20814
Tel: (301)897-2692
Fax: (301)897-8757
Registered: LDA
EMail: bgreenan@acc.org

Employers
American College of Cardiology (Director, Legislative Affairs)

GREENAWAY, Douglas A.

2001 S St. NW
Suite 580
Washington, DC 20009
Tel: (202)232-5492
Fax: (202)387-5281
EMail: nawdexdir@aol.com

Employers
Nat'l Ass'n of WIC Directors (Exec. Director)

GREENBERG, Eldon V. C.

1000 Potomac St. NW
Suite 500
Washington, DC 20007
Tel: (202)965-7880
Fax: (202)965-1729
Registered: LDA
EMail: egreenberg@gsblaw.com
General Counsel, National Oceanic and Atmospheric Administration, Department of Commerce, 1978-81. Deputy General Counsel, Agency for International Development, 1977. Law Clerk to Judge Edward C. McLean, U.S. District Court for the Southern District of New York, 1969-70.

Employers
Garvey, Schubert & Barer (Partner)

Clients Represented

On Behalf of Garvey, Schubert & Barer
Bolsa Chica Land Trust
East Coast Tuna Ass'n
Nat'l Fisheries Institute

GREENBERG, Frankee

1700 K St. NW
Suite 1150
Washington, DC 20006
Tel: (202)736-5866
Fax: (202)785-4937
EMail: frankee.greenberg@ujc.org

Employers
United Jewish Communities, Inc. (Deputy Director, Human Services and Social Policy Pillar)

GREENBERG, Kenneth

810 Vermont Ave. NW
Room 505
Washington, DC 20420
Tel: (202)273-5628
Fax: (202)273-6792

Employers
Department of Veterans Affairs (Director, Congressional Reports and Correspondence)

GREENBERG, Mark H.

1616 P St. NW
Suite 150
Washington, DC 20036
Tel: (202)328-5132
Fax: (202)328-5195
EMail: mhgreen@clasp.org

Employers
Center for Law and Social Policy (Senior Staff Attorney)

GREENBERG, Mark S.

1615 L St. NW
Suite 650
Washington, DC 20036
Tel: (202)626-8511
Fax: (202)626-8593
Registered: LDA
EMail: mark_greenberg@jeffersongr.com
Former Special Assistant to the President for Legislative Affairs, The White House, during the Reagan Administration. Former Administrative Assistant and Legislative Director to Senator Paul Trible (R-VA).

Employers
Jefferson Government Relations, L.L.C. (V. President)

Clients Represented

On Behalf of Jefferson Government Relations, L.L.C.
An Achievable Dream, Inc.
Aurora, Colorado, City of
Christopher Newport University

GREENBERG, Pamela

700 13th St. NW
Suite 950
Washington, DC 20005
Tel: (202)434-4565
Fax: (202)434-4564

Employers
American Managed Behavioral Healthcare Ass'n (Exec. Director)

GREENBERG, Robert B.

7910 Woodmont Ave.
Suite 700
Bethesda, MD 20814
Tel: (301)654-2055
Fax: (301)654-5920

Employers
American Gastroenterological Ass'n (Exec. V. President)

GREENBERG, Sally

1666 Connecticut Ave. NW
Suite 310
Washington, DC 20009
Tel: (202)462-6262
Fax: (202)265-9548
Registered: LDA
EMail: greesa@consumer.org

Employers
Consumers Union of the United States (Senior Product Safety Counsel)

GREENBERGER, Leonard

2025 M St. NW
Suite 350
Washington, DC 20036
Tel: (202)466-7391
Fax: (202)463-1338
Registered: LDA

Employers
Potomac Communications Group

GREENBERGER, Marcia D.

11 Dupont Circle NW
Suite 800
Washington, DC 20036
Tel: (202)588-5180
Fax: (202)588-5185

Employers
Nat'l Women's Law Center (Co-President)

GREENBERGER, M.S.W., Phyllis M.

1828 L St. NW
Suite 625
Washington, DC 20036
Tel: (202)223-8224
Fax: (202)833-3472
EMail: phyllis@womens-health.org

Employers
Soc. for Women's Health Research (President and Chief Exec. Officer)

GREENBURG, Jerry

1615 M St. NW
Washington, DC 20036
Tel: (202)833-2300
Fax: (202)429-8443
EMail: jerry_greenburg@tws.org

Employers
The Wilderness Soc. (V. President, Communications)

GREENE, Elizabeth

1518 K St. NW
Suite 503
Washington, DC 20005
Tel: (202)737-0202
Fax: (202)638-4833

Employers
Sufka & Associates

GREENE, USA (Ret.), Col. Fred W.

400 N. Capitol St. NW
Suite 363
Washington, DC 20001
Tel: (202)783-0280
Fax: (202)737-4518
Registered: LDA
Former Chief of Staff, U.S. Army Armor Center, Fort Knox, Kentucky.

Employers
Denny Miller McBee Associates (Consultant)

Clients Represented

On Behalf of Denny Miller McBee Associates
Asbestos Recycling Inc.

GREENE, H. Thomas

8400 W. Park Dr.
McLean, VA 22102
Tel: (202)547-5500
Fax: (202)479-0168
Registered: LDA

Employers
Nat'l Automobile Dealers Ass'n (Chief Operating Officer, Legislative Affairs)

GREENE, Joe L.

1729 21st St. NW
Washington, DC 20009-1101
Tel: (202)986-4209
Fax: (202)986-4211

Employers
American Federation of School Administrators (President)

GREENE, John C.

2000 N. 14th St.
Suite 450
Arlington, VA 22201
Tel: (703)276-0220
Fax: (703)841-7797
Registered: LDA
EMail: jgreene@nahu.org

Employers
Nat'l Ass'n of Health Underwriters (Manager, Federal Regulatory Affairs)

GREENE, Ronald J.

2445 M St. NW
Washington, DC 20037-1420
Tel: (202)663-6000
Fax: (202)663-6363
Registered: LDA
EMail: rgreene@wilmer.com
Law Clerk to Justice Thurgood Marshall, U.S. Supreme Court, 1968.

Employers
Wilmer, Cutler & Pickering (Partner)

Clients Represented

On Behalf of Wilmer, Cutler & Pickering
AdvaMed
Lederle Laboratories
Trans Ocean Leasing Corp.

GREENE, Sarah

1651 Prince St.
Alexandria, VA 22314
Tel: (703)739-0875
Fax: (703)739-0878
EMail: sgreene@nhsa

Employers
Nat'l Head Start Ass'n (Chief Exec. Officer)

GREENER, Charles V.

1909 K St. NW
Fourth Floor
Washington, DC 20006
Tel: (202)973-5800
Fax: (202)973-5858

Former Administrative Assistant to Rep. Bob McEwen (R-OH). Special Assistant, Legislative Affairs Office, The White House, during the Reagan Administration.

Employers
Porter/Novelli (Senior Partner and General Manager)

GREENER, III, William I.

1875 I St. NW
Suite 540
Washington, DC 20006
Tel: (202)822-0655
Fax: (202)822-2022
EMail: wgreener@greenerandhook.com

Director, Public Affairs, Department of Energy, 1981. Staff Member, Office of Communications, The White House, 1976. Staff Member, Media Relations, Department of Treasury, 1976.

Employers
Greener and Hook, LLC (Partner)

GREENFIELD, Jr., Arthur W.

1815 N. Fort Myer Dr.
Suite 500
Arlington, VA 22209-1805
Tel: (703)527-0226
Fax: (703)527-0229

Employers
Nat'l Aeronautic Ass'n of the U.S.A. (Secretary, Contest and Records Board)

GREENHALGH, Ronald K.

4301 Wilson Blvd.
Arlington, VA 22203-1860
Tel: (703)907-5831
Fax: (703)907-5517
Registered: LDA
EMail: ron.greenhalgh@nreca.org

Employers
Nat'l Rural Electric Cooperative Ass'n (Chief Engineer)

GREENHOUSE, Robin L.

600 13th St. NW
Washington, DC 20005-3096
Tel: (202)756-8204
Fax: (202)756-8087
EMail: rgreenhouse@mwe.com

Trial Attorney, Tax Division, Department of Justice, 1984-88.

Employers
McDermott, Will and Emery (Partner)

GREENSTEIN, Robert

820 First St. NE
Suite 510
Washington, DC 20002
Tel: (202)408-1080
Fax: (202)408-1056
Registered: LDA

Administrator, Food and Nutrition Service, Department of Agriculture, 1979-80.

Employers
Center on Budget and Policy Priorities (Exec. Director)

GREENSTEIN, Seth D.

600 13th St. NW
Washington, DC 20005-3096
Tel: (202)756-8088
Fax: (202)756-8087
Registered: LDA
EMail: sgreenstein@mwe.com

Employers
McDermott, Will and Emery (Partner)

Clients Represented
On Behalf of McDermott, Will and Emery
Digital Media Ass'n
Electronic Industries Ass'n of Japan

GREENWALD, John D.

2445 M St. NW
Washington, DC 20037-1420
Tel: (202)663-6000
Fax: (202)663-6363
Registered: LDA
EMail: jgreenwald@wilmer.com

Deputy Assistant Secretary for Import Administration, Department of Commerce, 1980-81. Deputy General Counsel, Office of U.S. Trade Representative, Executive Office of the President, The White House, 1978-79.

Employers
Wilmer, Cutler & Pickering (Partner)

Clients Represented
On Behalf of Wilmer, Cutler & Pickering
DuPont
Milliken and Co.
RMI Titanium Co.

GREENWALT, Pamela

1920 L St. NW
Washington, DC 20036
Tel: (202)223-8700
Fax: (202)659-5559
EMail: pgreenwalt@kamber.com

Employers
The Kamber Group (Senior V. President and Director, Media Production)

Clients Represented
On Behalf of The Kamber Group
Amalgamated Transit Union
Internat'l Longshoremen's Ass'n
Laborers' Internat'l Union of North America

GREENWOOD, Jr., Allen Beau

Three LaFayette Centre
1155 21st St. NW
Room 9002
Washington, DC 20581
Tel: (202)418-5075
Fax: (202)418-5542
EMail: bgreenwood@cftc.gov

Employers
Commodity Futures Trading Commission (Director, Office of Legislative and Intergovernmental Affairs)

GREENWOOD, Mark A.

1301 K St. NW
Suite 800 East
Washington, DC 20005
Tel: (202)626-3900
Fax: (202)626-3961
Registered: LDA
EMail: mgreenwo@ropesgray.com

Director, Office of Pollution, Prevention and Toxics, Environmental Protection Agency (1990-94), Associate General Counsel, Office of Pesticides and Toxics (1988-90), and Assistant General Counsel, Resource Conservation and Recovery Act and Superfund (1983-88), Environmental Protection Agency.

Employers
Ropes & Gray (Partner)

Clients Represented
On Behalf of Ropes & Gray
Coalition for Effective Environmental Information

GREENWOOD, Maureen

600 Pennsylvania Ave. SE
Fifth Floor
Washington, DC 20003
Tel: (202)544-0200
Fax: (202)546-7142
Registered: LDA

Employers
Amnesty Internat'l U.S.A. (Advocacy Director for Europe)

GREENWOOD, Sheila M.

400 N. Washington St.
Alexandria, VA 22314-9980
Tel: (703)836-9340
Fax: (703)836-1279
Registered: LDA
EMail: sheilamc@pianet.org

Employers
Nat'l Ass'n of Professional Insurance Agents (Assistant V. President, Government Affairs)

GREER, Ann

1250 New York Ave. NW
Washington, DC 20005
Tel: (202)783-5000
Fax: (202)393-3235

Employers
Nat'l Museum of Women in the Arts (Director, Public Relations)

GREER, Frank

1010 Wisconsin Ave. NW
Suite 800
Washington, DC 20007
Tel: (202)338-8700
Fax: (202)338-2334

Employers
Greer, Margolis, Mitchell, Burns & Associates (Partner)

Clients Represented
On Behalf of Greer, Margolis, Mitchell, Burns & Associates
Campaign for the Northwest

GREER, Linda

1200 New York Ave. NW
Suite 400
Washington, DC 20005
Tel: (202)289-6868
Fax: (202)289-1060

Employers
Natural Resources Defense Council (Senior Scientist)

GREER, Stanley

8001 Braddock Rd.
Springfield, VA 22160
Tel: (703)321-9820
Fax: (703)321-7342

Employers
Nat'l Right to Work Committee (Director, News and Information)

GREESON, Jennifer

1341 G St. NW
Suite 1100
Washington, DC 20005
Tel: (202)393-2260
Fax: (202)393-0712
Registered: LDA

Former Communications Director for Senator Blanche Lambert Lincoln (D-AR).

Employers
Computer Coalition for Responsible Exports (Manager, Communications Outreach)
Computer Systems Policy Project (Manager, Communications Outreach)
Infotech Strategies, Inc. (Director, Communications)

Clients Represented
On Behalf of Infotech Strategies, Inc.
Computer Coalition for Responsible Exports
Computer Systems Policy Project

GREFRATH, Bruce

1217 E St. NE
Washington, DC 20002
Tel: (202)544-6156
Fax: (202)547-7513

Employers
American Land Rights Ass'n (Washington Representative)
League of Private Property Voters

GREGG, Donna C.

1776 K St. NW
Washington, DC 20006
Tel: (202)719-7000
Fax: (202)719-7049

Attorney, Federal Communications Commission, 1974-75.

Employers
Wiley, Rein & Fielding (Partner)

Clients Represented
On Behalf of Wiley, Rein & Fielding
Blade Communications

GREGG, John P.

1140 19th St. NW
Suite 700
Washington, DC 20036
Tel: (202)296-2960
Fax: (202)296-0166

Employers
Miller, Balis and O'Neil, P.C. (Managing Partner)

Clients Represented
On Behalf of Miller, Balis and O'Neil, P.C.
American Public Gas Ass'n

GREGG, Sarah Massengale

800 Connecticut Ave. NW
Suite 1100
Washington, DC 20006
Tel: (202)223-4016
Fax: (202)296-7177
Registered: LDA
EMail: sarah_gregg@baxter.com

Employers
Baxter Healthcare Corp. (V. President, Federal Legislative Affairs and Payment Planning)

GREGOR, Janet R.

1020 N. Fairfax St.
Fourth Floor
Alexandria, VA 22314
Tel: (703)684-5236
Fax: (703)684-3417
Registered: LDA
EMail: jgregor@pass1.com

Employers
Vienna, Gregor & Associates (V. President)

Clients Represented

On Behalf of Vienna, Gregor & Associates

California Board of Equalization
California Franchise Tax Board
California Public Employees' Retirement System
California State Senate
The Pacific Stock Exchange, Inc.

GREGORY, Ginger

1600 Pennsylvania Ave. NW
2nd Fl, W. Wing
Washington, DC 20500
Tel: (202)456-2230
Fax: (202)456-1806

Employers

Executive Office of the President - The White House (Exec. Assistant to the Director of Legislative Affairs)

GREGORY, Hayden W.

740 15th St. NW
Ninth Floor
Washington, DC 20005
Tel: (202)662-1772
Fax: (202)662-1762
Registered: LDA

Employers

American Bar Ass'n (Consultant)

GREGORY, Jack

601 13th St. NW
Suite 410 South
Washington, DC 20005
Tel: (202)737-0100
Fax: (202)628-3965
Registered: LDA, FARA

Employers

R. Duffy Wall and Associates (V. President)

GREGORY, Jamie

700 11th St. NW
Washington, DC 20001-4507
Tel: (202)383-1027
Fax: (202)383-7540
Registered: LDA
EMail: jgregory@realtors.org

Employers

Nat'l Ass'n of Realtors (Legislative Representative)

GREGORY, Janice M.

1400 L St. NW
Suite 350
Washington, DC 20005
Tel: (202)789-1400
Fax: (202)789-1120
Registered: LDA

Employers

The ERISA Industry Committee (ERIC) (V. President)

GREGORY, Kay

8101 Glenbrook Rd.
Bethesda, MD 20814-2749
Tel: (301)907-6977
Fax: (301)907-6895

Employers

American Ass'n of Blood Banks (Director, Regulatory Affairs)

GREGORY, Neal

One Massachusetts Ave. NW
Suite 840
Washington, DC 20001
Tel: (202)371-0440
Fax: (202)371-0411
Registered: LDA
Staff Director, Information and Policy, Committee on House Administration, 1976-81.

Employers

The Gregory Co. (President)

Clients Represented

On Behalf of The Gregory Co.

Benevolent and Protective Order of Elks (BPOE)
Lake Preservation Coalition

GREISSING, Jr., Edward F.

1455 F St. NW
Suite 450
Washington, DC 20004
Tel: (202)393-6040
Fax: (202)393-6050
Registered: LDA

Employers

Pharmacia Corp. (V. President, Government Affairs)

GRENIER, Jr., Edward J.

1275 Pennsylvania Ave. NW
Washington, DC 20004-2415
Tel: (202)383-0100
Fax: (202)637-3593
Law Clerk to Chief Judge E. Barrett Prettyman, U.S. Court of Appeals, District of Columbia Circuit, 1959-60.

Employers

Sutherland Asbill & Brennan LLP (Partner)

Clients Represented

On Behalf of Sutherland Asbill & Brennan LLP

Armco Inc.

GRESHAM, Julie

1350 I St. NW
Suite 1255
Washington, DC 20005
Tel: (202)626-0089
Fax: (202)626-0088

Employers

Law Offices of Mark Barnes (Attorney at Law)

GREY, Jerry

1801 Alexander Bell Dr.
Suite 500
Reston, VA 20191
Tel: (703)264-7500
Fax: (703)264-7551

Employers

American Institute of Aeronautics and Astronautics (Consultant)

GRIBBIN, D. J.

655 15th St. NW
Suite 445
Washington, DC 20005
Tel: (202)737-1977

Employers

Koch Industries, Inc. (Director, Government Affairs)

GRIBBON, Daniel M.

1201 Pennsylvania Ave. NW
Washington, DC 20004-2401
Tel: (202)662-6000
Fax: (202)662-6291
EMail: dgribbon@cov.com
Former Law Clerk to Judge Learned Hand, U.S. Court of Appeals, Second Circuit.

Employers

Covington & Burling (Senior Counsel)

GRIEBOSKI, Joseph K.

1101 15th St. NW
Suite 115
Washington, DC 20005
Tel: (202)835-8760
Fax: (202)318-4017
EMail: grieboski@religionandpolicy.org

Employers

Institute on Religion and Public Policy (President)

GRIESING, Dennis

1500 K St. NW
Suite 300
Washington, DC 20005
Tel: (202)347-2900
Fax: (202)347-4110
Registered: LDA
EMail: dgriesing@sdahq.org

Employers

Soap and Detergent Ass'n (V. President, Government Affairs)

GRIFF, Marvin T.

1133 Connecticut Ave. NW
Suite 1200
Washington, DC 20036
Tel: (202)775-9800
Fax: (202)833-8491
Senior Trial Attorney, Office of General Counsel, Gas and Oil Litigation Section, Federal Energy Regulatory Commission, 1987-89.

Employers

Winthrop, Stimson, Putnam & Roberts (Counsel)

GRIFFIN, Charles

1120 20th St. NW
Suite 1000
Washington, DC 20036
Tel: (202)457-3926
Fax: (202)457-3110
Registered: LDA
EMail: cgrif@att.com

Employers

AT&T (Director, Federal Government Affairs)

GRIFFIN, Janice B.

1825 I St. NW
Suite 400
Washington, DC 20006
Tel: (202)857-5210
Fax: (202)429-6834
Registered: LDA

Employers

Griffin & Associates (President)

Clients Represented

On Behalf of Griffin & Associates

Prudential Insurance Co. of America

GRIFFIN, III, L. George

700 11th St. NW
Washington, DC 20001-4507
Tel: (202)383-1102
Fax: (202)383-7540
Registered: LDA
EMail: ggriffin@realtors.org

Employers

Nat'l Ass'n of Realtors (Real Estate Finance Policy Representative)

GRIFFIN, Luanne

196 Van Buren St.
Suite 450
Herndon, VA 20170
Tel: (703)456-2564
Fax: (703)456-2551

Employers

Nissan North America Inc. (Manager, Government Affairs)

GRIFFIN, Mark E.

1455 Pennsylvania Ave. NW
Suite 1200
Washington, DC 20004
Tel: (202)347-2230
Fax: (202)393-3310
Registered: LDA

Employers

Davis & Harman LLP (Partner)

GRIFFIN, Melanie

408 C St. NE
Washington, DC 20002
Tel: (202)547-1141
Fax: (202)547-6009
Registered: LDA

Employers

Sierra Club (Director, Land Protection Program)

GRIFFIN, Molly

2001 Jefferson Davis Hwy.
Suite 209
Arlington, VA 22202
Tel: (703)413-0090
Fax: (703)413-4467
Registered: LDA
EMail: mgriffin@mehlgriffinbartek.com
Legislative Assistant to Rep. Martin Lancaster (D-NC), 1988-93. Staff Member, Office of the Chief of Legislative Liaison, U.S. Army, 1981-83.

Employers

Mehl, Griffin & Bartek Ltd. (President)

Clients Represented

On Behalf of Mehl, Griffin & Bartek Ltd.

AMI Aircraft Seating Systems
Battelle Memorial Institute
Chandler Evans Control Systems
D3 Internat'l Energy, LLC
El Camino Resources, Ltd.
Exide Corp.
Galaxy Aerospace Co., LP
General Atomics
Irvine Sensors Corp.
LSP Technologies
Motorola Space and Systems Technology Group
Nat'l Veterans Foundation
Pacific Northwest Nat'l Laboratory
Turbine Controls, Inc.

GRIFFIN, Patrick J.

1300 Connecticut Ave. NW
Suite 600
Washington, DC 20036
Tel: (202)775-8116
Fax: (202)223-0358
Registered: LDA
Former Assistant to the President and Director, Legislative Affairs, The White House, during the Clinton Administration.

Employers

Griffin, Johnson, Dover & Stewart (President)

Clients Represented

On Behalf of Griffin, Johnson, Dover & Stewart

American Agrisurance
American Fish Spotters Ass'n
American Petroleum Institute
American Soc. of Anesthesiologists
Arthur Andersen LLP
Avue Technologies
Dell Computer Corp.
Deloitte Consulting
Deutsche Telekom, Inc.
Directors Guild of America
Fannie Mae
The Justice Project, Inc.
Monsanto Co.
Nat'l Music Publishers' Ass'n
United Technologies Corp.
Vietnam Veterans of America Foundation
Wilmer, Cutler & Pickering
Wine and Spirits Wholesalers of America

GRIFFIN, Jr., Richard B.

2200 Foxhall Rd. NW
Washington, DC 20007
Tel: (202)337-1870
Fax: (202)337-0165
Registered: LDA

Employers

RBG Associates (Managing Director)

Clients Represented

On Behalf of RBG Associates

Ultratech Stepper Inc.
Wabtec Corp.

GRIFFIN, Royce

Ten G St. NE
Suite 710
Washington, DC 20002
Tel: (202)737-0900
Fax: (202)783-3571

Employers

North American Securities Administrators Ass'n (NASAA) (General Counsel)

GRIFFIN, Susan

3501 Newark St. NW
Washington, DC 20016
Tel: (202)966-7840
Fax: (202)966-2061

Employers

Nat'l Council for the Social Studies (Exec. Director)

GRIFFITH, Benjamin G.

1341 G St. NW
Suite 200
Washington, DC 20005
Tel: (202)737-3655
Fax: (202)347-5941
Registered: LDA
Staff Assistant to Senator Nancy Kassebaum (R-KS), 1995-97.

Employers

Sacramento-Potomac Consulting, Inc. (Senior Associate)

Clients Represented

On Behalf of Sacramento-Potomac Consulting, Inc.

Abide Internat'l, Inc.
California State University Fresno
Community Hospitals of Central California

GRIFFITH, David

277 S. Washington St.
Alexandria, VA 22314
Tel: (703)684-4000
Fax: (703)836-2313

Employers

Nat'l Ass'n of State Boards of Education (Director, Governmental Affairs)

GRIFFITH, Jr., G. O. Lanny

1275 Pennsylvania Ave. NW
Tenth Floor
Washington, DC 20004
Tel: (202)333-4936
Fax: (202)833-9392
Registered: LDA, FARA
Special Assistant to President for Intergovernmental Affairs, The White House, 1989-91. Assistant Secretary for Intergovernmental and Interagency Affairs, Department of Education, during the Bush I administration.

Employers

Barbour Griffith & Rogers, Inc. (Chief Operating Officer)

Clients Represented

On Behalf of Barbour Griffith & Rogers, Inc.

Air Transport Ass'n of America
Alliance for Quality Nursing Home Care
American Maritime Congress
American Trucking Ass'ns
Amgen
Artists Coalition
Avioimpex
Bay Harbor Management, L.C.
BellSouth Telecommunications, Inc.
Better World Campaign
Bristol-Myers Squibb Co.
Broadcast Music Inc. (BMI)
Brown and Williamson Tobacco Corp.
Canadian Nat'l Railway Co.
Citizens for Jobs and the Economy
DaimlerChrysler Corp.
Delta Air Lines
Education Networks of America
FM Watch
GlaxoSmithKline
Illinois State Board of Education
INTELSAT - Internat'l Telecommunications Satellite Organization
Lyondell Chemical Co.
Makedonski Telekomunikacii
Microsoft Corp.
Oxygenated Fuels Ass'n
Professional Benefit Trust
Qwest Communications
RJR Co.
Southern Co.
State Street Bank and Trust Co.
Tulane University
United Health Group
University of Mississippi
University of Mississippi Medical Center
University of Southern Mississippi
The Winterthur Group
Yazoo County, Mississippi Port Commission

GRIFFITH, Gary W.

1300 Wilson Blvd.
Arlington, VA 22209
Tel: (703)741-5914
Fax: (703)741-6097
Registered: LDA
EMail: gary_griffith@americanchemistry.com

Employers

American Chemistry Council (Director)

GRIFFITH, Laura

7700 Leesburg Pike
Suite 421
Falls Church, VA 22043
Tel: (703)847-2677
Fax: (703)556-6485

Employers

Law Enforcement Alliance of America (Director, Federal Legislative)

GRIFFITH, Patricia

1312 18th St. NW
Suite 300
Washington, DC 20036
Tel: (202)296-4563
Fax: (202)887-9178

Employers

Agribusiness Council (Secretary-Treasurer)

GRIFFITH, Spencer S.

1333 New Hampshire Ave. NW
Suite 400
Washington, DC 20036
Tel: (202)887-4000
Fax: (202)887-4288
Registered: FARA

Employers

Akin, Gump, Strauss, Hauer & Feld, L.L.P. (Partner)

Clients Represented

On Behalf of Akin, Gump, Strauss, Hauer & Feld, L.L.P.

British Columbia, Canada, Government of the Province of

GRIFFITHS, Ann Mills

1001 Connecticut Ave. NW
Suite 919
Washington, DC 20036
Tel: (202)223-6846
Fax: (202)785-9410
EMail: info@pow-miafamilies.org

Employers

Nat'l League of Families of American Prisoners and Missing in Southeast Asia (Exec. Director)

GRIFFITHS, William D.

1420 Spring Hill Rd.
Suite 490
McLean, VA 22102
Tel: (703)821-1550
Fax: (703)821-0920
EMail: bgriffiths@eberle1.com

Employers

Bruce W. Eberle & Assoc., Inc. (Chief Financial Officer)

GRIGG, Kenneth A.

2550 M St. NW
Washington, DC 20037-1350
Tel: (202)457-6000
Fax: (202)457-6315
Registered: LDA
EMail: kgrigg@pattonboggs.com

Employers

Patton Boggs, LLP (Partner)

Clients Represented

On Behalf of Patton Boggs, LLP

Mars, Inc.

GRIGG, Steven A.

1280 Maryland Ave. SW
Suite 280
Washington, DC 20024
Tel: (202)863-0300
Fax: (202)863-4049

Employers

Republic Properties Corp. (President)

GRIGSBY, McGee

555 11th St. NW
Suite 1000
Washington, DC 20004
Tel: (202)637-2200
Fax: (202)637-2201
Law Clerk to Judge Theodore Tannenwald, U.S. Tax Court, 1970-71.

Employers

Latham & Watkins (Partner)

GRILES, J. Steven

2600 Virginia Ave. NW
Suite 600
Washington, DC 20037
Tel: (202)333-2524
Fax: (202)338-5950
Registered: LDA

Employers

J. Steven Griles & Associates (President)
Nat'l Environmental Strategies (Principal)
NES, Inc.

Clients Represented

On Behalf of J. Steven Griles & Associates

Advanced Power Technologies, Inc.
APTI
Caithness Energy, LLC
Devon Energy Corp.
RAPOCA Energy Co.
Redstone

GRILL, Philip M.

1735 New York Ave. NW
Suite 500
Washington, DC 20006
Tel: (202)662-8455
Fax: (202)331-1024
Registered: LDA

Employers

Matson Navigation Co. (V. President, Government Relations)

GRIMALDI, Alan M.

1299 Pennsylvania Ave. NW
Washington, DC 20004-2402
Tel: (202)783-0800
Fax: (202)383-6610
EMail: grimaldia@howrey.com
Law Clerk to Judge Barrington D. Parker, U.S. District Court for the District of Columbia, 1971-72.

Employers

Howrey Simon Arnold & White (Partner)

Clients Represented

On Behalf of Howrey Simon Arnold & White

Air & Water Technologies
Huffy Corp.

GRIMM, Jr., Norman E.

12600 Fair Lakes Circle
Fairfax, VA 22033-4904
Tel: (703)222-4100
Fax: (703)802-8621

Employers

AAA MidAtlantic (Director, Traffic Safety)

GRIMM, Paul

1420 New York Ave. NW
Suite 1050
Washington, DC 20005
Tel: (202)638-1950
Fax: (202)638-1928
Registered: LDA
EMail: pgrimm@vsadc.com
Former Acting Assistant Secretary for Environmental Management, Department of Energy.

Employers
Van Scoyoc Associates, Inc. (V. President)

Clients Represented
On Behalf of Van Scoyoc Associates, Inc.
Alcoa Inc.
Archimedes Technology Group
Burns and Roe Enterprises, Inc.
Clemson University
Communications Training Analysis Corp. (C-TAC)
Duke Solutions
Johnson Controls, Inc.
Lockheed Martin Hanford
Virginia Polytechnic Institute and State University
Wackenhut Services, Inc.

GRIMM, CPPO, CPPB, Rick

151 Spring St.
Suite 300
Herndon, VA 20170
Tel: (703)736-8900
Ext: 235
Fax: (703)736-9644
EMail: rgrimm@nigp.org

Employers
Nat'l Institute of Governmental Purchasing (Exec. V. President)

GRINCEWICH, Katherine C.

3211 Fourth St. NE
Washington, DC 20017
Tel: (202)541-3000

Employers
U.S. Catholic Conference (Assistant General Counsel)

GRINDAL, H. Theodore

601 Pennsylvania Ave. NW
South Bldg., Suite 900
Washington, DC 20004
Tel: (202)434-8163
Fax: (202)639-8238

Employers
Lockridge Grindal & Nauen, P.L.L.P. (Partner)

GRINER, Allison

430 S. Capitol St. SE
Washington, DC 20003
Tel: (202)224-2447
Fax: (202)485-3120

Employers
Democratic Senatorial Campaign Committee (Director, DSCC Roundtable)

GRINER, G Christopher

The McPherson Bldg.
901 15th St. NW, Suite 1100
Washington, DC 20005
Tel: (202)682-3500
Fax: (202)682-3580

Employers
Kaye Scholer LLP (Managing Partner)

Clients Represented
On Behalf of Kaye Scholer LLP
BNFL, Inc.

GRINSTEAD, Darrel J.

555 13th St. NW
Washington, DC 20004-1109
Tel: (202)637-5600
Fax: (202)637-5910
Registered: LDA
EMail: djgrinstead@hhlaw.com
Chief Counsel, Health Care Financing Administration (1988-97), Assistant General Counsel, Business and Administrative Law Division (1979-88) and Attorney, Office of General Counsel (1969-79), Department of Health and Human Services.

Employers
Hogan & Hartson L.L.P. (Partner)

Clients Represented
On Behalf of Hogan & Hartson L.L.P.
American Ambulance Ass'n
Federation of American Hospitals

GRISOLD, Ray

481 N. Frederick Ave.
Suite 405
Gaithersburg, MD 20877
Tel: (301)417-0047
Fax: (301)417-0746

Employers
AECL Technologies (Treasurer and Acting President)

GRISSO, Cynthia Powers

1201 15th St. NW
Third Floor
Washington, DC 20005
Tel: (202)857-4722
Fax: (202)857-4799
Registered: LDA
EMail: cgrisso@ipaa.org

Employers
Independent Petroleum Ass'n of America (V. President, Administration)

GRISSO, Michael E.

P.O. Box 230010
Centreville, VA 20120
Tel: (703)802-1682
Fax: (703)802-0289
Registered: LDA
EMail: mgrisso@grissoconsulting.com
Former Legislative Assistant to the Speaker, U.S. House of Representatives.

Employers
Grisso Consulting (President)
R. Duffy Wall and Associates (V. President)

Clients Represented
On Behalf of Grisso Consulting
Commercial Service Co., Ltd.
Health Policy Strategies
Hees Interests, Ltd.
Medical Records Internat'l, Inc.
Nat'l Ass'n of Children's Hospitals Inc.
TriWest Healthcare Alliance, Inc.

GRIZZLE, Charles L.

1400 16th St. NW
Suite 400
Washington, DC 20036
Tel: (202)234-2101
Fax: (202)234-1614
Registered: LDA
Assistant Administrator, Administration and Resource Management, Environmental Protection Agency, 1988-91. Former Deputy Assistant Secretary for Administration, Department of Agriculture, 1983-87.

Employers
The Grizzle Company (Chairman)

Clients Represented
On Behalf of The Grizzle Company
al group Lonza
Ashland Inc.
ENTEK Corp.
GSE Systems, Inc.
Internat'l Council of Shopping Centers
ManTech Internat'l
Mas-Hamilton Group
NTS Mortgage Income Fund
Regional Airport Authority of Louisville & Jefferson Co.
University of Louisville
WPC Brands, Inc.

GRKAVAC, Olga

1401 Wilson Blvd.
Suite 1100
Arlington, VA 22209
Tel: (703)522-5055
Fax: (703)525-2279
Registered: LDA
EMail: ogrkavac@itaa.org

Employers
Information Technology Ass'n of America (ITAA) (Exec. V. President, Enterprise Systems Division)

GROCHALA, Ann M.

One Thomas Circle NW
Suite 400
Washington, DC 20005
Tel: (202)659-8111
Fax: (202)659-9216
Registered: LDA

Employers
Independent Community Bankers of America (Director of Bank Operations)

GROGAN, James

1776 Massachusetts Ave. NW
Suite 301
Washington, DC 20036
Tel: (202)785-2388
Fax: (202)429-0568

Employers
Internat'l Ass'n of Heat and Frost Insulators and Asbestos Workers (General Secretary-Treasurer)

GRONOND, Gail

3138 N. Tenth St.
Arlington, VA 22201
Tel: (703)522-4770
Fax: (703)522-0594

Employers
Nat'l Ass'n of Federal Credit Unions (Editor Manager, Member Services)

GROOBERT, David

600 New Hampshire Ave. NW
Suite 601
Washington, DC 20037
Tel: (202)333-7400
Fax: (202)333-1638
EMail: dgroober@hillandknowlton.com

Employers
Hill and Knowlton, Inc. (Senior Managing Director, Director of Marketing Communications)

GROOBERT, Edward A.

1300 I St. NW
Suite 300 West
Washington, DC 20005
Tel: (202)522-8600
Fax: (202)522-8669
Registered: LDA
Attorney, Appellate Section, Civil Division, Department of Justice, 1961-63.

Employers
Dykema Gossett PLLC (Member)

GROOM, Theodore R.

1701 Pennsylvania Ave. NW
Suite 1200
Washington, DC 20006
Tel: (202)857-0620
Fax: (202)659-4503
Registered: LDA
EMail: trg@groom.com

Employers
Groom Law Group, Chartered (Partner)

Clients Represented
On Behalf of Groom Law Group, Chartered
Mutual Tax Committee
Prudential Insurance Co. of America

GROS, Simon

210 Seventh St. SE
Washington, DC 20003
Tel: (202)547-6808
Fax: (202)546-5425
Registered: LDA

Employers
Kessler & Associates Business Services, Inc.

Clients Represented
On Behalf of Kessler & Associates Business Services, Inc.
Grocery Manufacturers of America
Henry H. Kessler Foundation
Pharmacia Corp.

GROSBERG, Joel R.

600 13th St. NW
Washington, DC 20005-3096
Tel: (202)756-8207
Fax: (202)756-8087
EMail: jgrosberg@mwe.com
Former Attorney, Bureau of Competition, Federal Trade Commission.

Employers
McDermott, Will and Emery (Associate)

GROSS, Anne

2501 M St. NW
Suite 400
Washington, DC 20037
Tel: (202)861-2500
Fax: (202)861-2583

Employers
Nat'l Ass'n of College and University Business Officers (Director, Policy Research and Analysis)

GROSS, Dr. Debbie

1250 I St. NW
Suite 901A
Washington, DC 20005
Tel: (202)638-1300
Fax: (202)638-2364
EMail: dgross@cipha.org

Employers
Council of Large Public Housing Authorities (Research Director)

GROSS, Kenneth A.

1440 New York Ave. NW
Washington, DC 20005
Tel: (202)371-7000
Fax: (202)371-7956
Former Associate General Counsel, Chief of Enforcement, Federal Election Commission, 1980-86.

Employers
Skadden, Arps, Slate, Meagher & Flom LLP (Partner)

Clients Represented
On Behalf of Skadden, Arps, Slate, Meagher & Flom LLP
Century 21 Real Estate Corp.

GROSS, Lauren

9650 Rockville Pike
Bethesda, MD 20814-3994
Tel: (301)530-7178
Fax: (301)571-1816

Employers
American Ass'n of Immunologists (Director, Public Policy and Government Affairs)

GROSS, Leslie Sacks

1001 Connecticut Ave. NW
Suite 507
Washington, DC 20036
Tel: (202)466-0001
Fax: (202)466-0002
Registered: LDA

Employers
Craig Associates (Legislative Analyst)

Clients Represented
On Behalf of Craig Associates
County Welfare Directors Ass'n of California
Dakota, Minnesota, County of
San Bernardino County Social Services Department

GROSS, Mark C.

901 N. Stuart St.
Suite 900
Arlington, VA 22203
Tel: (703)527-7600
Fax: (703)527-8811
Registered: LDA

Employers
Nat'l Accrediting Commission of Cosmetology Arts & Sciences, Inc. (Chief Executive Officer)

GROSS, Tarneisha

1811 R St. NW
Washington, DC 20009-1659
Tel: (202)265-6280
Fax: (202)234-5662
EMail: jwv@erols.com

Employers
Jewish War Veterans of the U.S.A. (National Director, Public Relations)

GROSSI, Jr., Peter T.

555 12th St. NW
Washington, DC 20004-1206
Tel: (202)942-5000
Fax: (202)942-5999
EMail: Peter_Grossi@aporter.com
Law Clerk to Judge J. Joseph Smith, U.S. Court of Appeals, Second Circuit, 1973-74.

Employers
Arnold & Porter (Partner)

GROSSI, Ralph E.

1200 18th St. NW
Suite 800
Washington, DC 20036
Tel: (202)331-7300
Fax: (202)659-8339

Employers
American Farmland Trust (President)

GROSSMAN, MPH, Donna Brown

1100 17th St. NW
Second Floor
Washington, DC 20036
Tel: (202)783-5550
Fax: (202)783-1583

Employers
Nat'l Ass'n of County and City Health Officials (Director, Public Health Advocacy)

GROSSMAN, Jerome

110 Maryland Ave. NE
Suite 409
Washington, DC 20002
Tel: (202)543-4100
Fax: (202)543-6297
Registered: LDA
EMail: jdi@clw.org

Employers
Council for a Livable World (Chairman)

GROSSMAN, Lawrence C.

700 13th St. NW
Suite 400
Washington, DC 20005
Tel: (202)347-0773
Fax: (202)347-0785
Registered: LDA, FARA
EMail: lgrossman@cassidy.com
Former Staff Member, House Armed Services Committee. Speechwriter for Rep. Les Aspin (D-WI).

Employers
Cassidy & Associates, Inc. (Senior V. President)

Clients Represented
On Behalf of Cassidy & Associates, Inc.
Agassi Enterprises, Inc.
Air Products and Chemicals, Inc.
American Superconductor Corp.
The Boeing Co.
Boston College
Boston University
CMS Defense Systems, Inc.
Council on Superconductivity for American Competitiveness
Electro Energy, Inc.
General Dynamics Corp.
IBP Aerospace, Inc.
Idaho State University
Lockheed Martin Corp.
Saudi Arabia, Royal Embassy of
United Service Organization
University Medical Center of Southern Nevada
University of Nevada - Las Vegas
VoiceStream Wireless Corp.

GROSSMAN, Marla P.

901 15th St. NW
Suite 700
Washington, DC 20005-2301
Tel: (202)371-6000
Fax: (202)371-6279
Registered: LDA
EMail: mgrossman@verner.com
Democratic Counsel, Senate Judiciary Committee, 1997-99.

Employers
Verner, Liipfert, Bernhard, McPherson and Hand, Chartered (Member of Firm)

Clients Represented
On Behalf of Verner, Liipfert, Bernhard, McPherson and Hand, Chartered
EqualFooting.com
Firstdoor.com
getpress.com
Interactive Digital Software Ass'n
Magna Entertainment Corp.

GROSVENOR, Gilbert M.

1145 17th St. NW
Washington, DC 20036
Tel: (202)857-7000
Fax: (202)775-6141

Employers
Nat'l Geographic Soc. (Chairman of the Board)

GROUNDWATER, John

1600 Wilson Blvd.
Suite 1000-A
Arlington, VA 22209
Tel: (703)807-0100
Fax: (703)807-0103

Employers
Passenger Vessel Ass'n (Exec. Director)

GROVE, Donald H.

816 Connecticut Ave. NW
Suite 300
Washington, DC 20006
Tel: (202)530-1270
Fax: (202)530-1920
Registered: LDA

Employers
Nordhaus Haltom Taylor Taradash & Bladh LLP (Associate)

GROVER, Steve

1200 17th St. NW
Washington, DC 20036-3097
Tel: (202)331-5900
Fax: (202)973-5373

Employers
Nat'l Restaurant Ass'n (V. President, Regulatory Affairs)

GRUBB, Debbie

1155 15th St. NW
Suite 1004
Washington, DC 20005
Tel: (202)467-5081
Fax: (202)467-5085

Employers
Guide Dog Users, Inc. (President)

GRUBOR, Justina

420 Seventh St. SE
Washington, DC 20003
Tel: (202)546-3950
Fax: (202)546-3749

Employers
World Federalist Ass'n (Director, Partners Program)

GRUENBURG, Drew

1601 Duke St.
Alexandria, VA 22314-3406
Tel: (703)836-8700
Fax: (703)836-8705
EMail: dgruenbu@safnow.org

Employers
Soc. of American Florists (Senior V. President, Government Relations)

GRUENEBAUM, Jane

1875 Connecticut Ave. NW
Suite 710
Washington, DC 20009
Tel: (202)387-6030
Fax: (202)986-2539

Employers
Center for Policy Alternatives (Chief Operating Officer)

GRUPE, Michael

1875 I St. NW
Suite 600
Washington, DC 20006
Tel: (202)739-9400
Fax: (202)739-9401
EMail: mgrupe@nareit.com

Employers
Nat'l Ass'n of Real Estate Investment Trusts (Senior V. President, Research)

GRYCE, David

1050 Connecticut Ave. NW
Washington, DC 20036-5339
Tel: (202)857-6000
Fax: (202)857-6395

Employers
Arent Fox Kintner Plotkin & Kahn, PLLC (Member)

GRYMES, Susan P.

1400 16th St. NW
Suite 400
Washington, DC 20036-2220
Tel: (202)518-6324
Fax: (202)234-1560
Registered: LDA
EMail: sgrymes@ofwlaw.com

Employers
Olsson, Frank and Weeda, P.C. (Associate)

Clients Represented
On Behalf of Olsson, Frank and Weeda, P.C.
Adheris, Inc.
American Academy of Audiology
American Commodity Distribution Ass'n
American School Food Service Ass'n
Ass'n of Medical Device Reprocessors
Aventis Pasteur
Beef Products, Inc.
California Canning Peach Ass'n
Chocolate Manufacturers Ass'n of the U.S.A.
Duramed Pharmaceuticals, Inc.
Food Distributors Internat'l (NAWGA-IFDA)
General Mills
Gentrac Inc.
Health Resource Publishing Co.
Institute of Food Technologists
Kraft Foods, Inc.
Lower Brule Sioux Tribe
Mead Johnson Nutritional Group
Nat'l Ass'n of Margarine Manufacturers
Nat'l Ass'n of Pharmaceutical Manufacturers
Nat'l Coalition of Food Importers Ass'n
Nat'l Confectioners Ass'n
Nat'l Food Processors Ass'n
Nat'l Meat Ass'n
PennField Oil Co.
The Pillsbury Co.
San Tomo Group
Schwan's Sales Enterprises
SteriGenics Internat'l
Titan Scan
Transhumance Holding Co., Inc.
United Fresh Fruit and Vegetable Ass'n
Urner Barry Publications, Inc.

GRZEBIEN, John C.

1105 N. Pitt St.
Suite 3C
Alexandria, VA 22314
Tel: (703)836-7615
Registered: LDA

Professional Staff Member for the Majority, Senate Environment and Public Works Committee, 1989-96. Legislative Assistant to Senator John H. Chafee (R-RI), 1987-89.

Employers
Self-employed as an independent consultant.

Clients Represented
As an independent consultant
Dredging Contractors of America
Edison Community College
Heritage Harbor Museum
Professional Facilities Management
Providence City Arts for Youth, Inc.
Providence Performing Arts Center
SafeWorks, LLC
Save the Bay
Shea's Performing Arts Center
Tampa Bay Performing Arts Center

GUAIS, Jean Claude

7401 Wisconsin Ave.
Suite 500
Bethesda, MD 20814
Tel: (301)986-8585
Fax: (301)652-5690
Registered: FARA

Employers
COGEMA, Inc. (V. President, Strategic Development)

GUARISCO, Annette J.

1001 Pennsylvania Ave. NW
Suite 700 South
Washington, DC 20004
Tel: (202)662-2644
Fax: (202)662-2674
Registered: LDA

Employers
Honeywell Internat'l, Inc. (Corporate Director, Public Policy and Government Relations)

GUARRIELLO, Joseph L.

Four Taft Ct.
Rockville, MD 20850
Tel: (800)331-2102
Fax: (301)762-5728

Employers
Mid-Atlantic Medical Services, Inc. (Exec. V. President, General Counsel and Secretary)

GUAY, Richard F.

1900 M St. NW
Suite 500
Washington, DC 20036
Tel: (202)785-2635
Fax: (202)785-4037
Registered: LDA

Employers
BNFL, Inc. (V. President, Government Relations)

GUCCIONE, Andrew

1111 N. Fairfax St.
Alexandria, VA 22314
Tel: (703)684-2782
Fax: (703)684-7343

Employers
American Physical Therapy Ass'n (Senior V. President, Practice and Research)

GUCLU, Damla

1667 K St. NW
Suite 690
Washington, DC 20006
Tel: (202)887-6198
Fax: (202)467-0685
Registered: FARA

Employers
Turkish Republic of Northern Cyprus, Embassy of (First Secretary)

GUDE, Kalbak

1133 Connecticut Ave. NW
Suite 675
Washington, DC 20036
EMail: kgude@panamsat.com
Tel: (202)223-3511
Fax: (202)861-4368

Employers
PanAmSat Corp. (V. President, Government and Regulatory Affairs and Associate General Counsel)

GUELI, Charles A.

1101 Vermont Ave. NW
Suite 1001
Washington, DC 20005
Tel: (202)429-4649
Fax: (202)659-6126

Employers
Italian-American Democratic Leadership Council (Treasurer)

GUENTHER, Kenneth A.

One Thomas Circle NW
Suite 400
Washington, DC 20005
Tel: (202)659-8111
Fax: (202)659-9216
Registered: LDA

Employers
Independent Community Bankers of America (Exec. V. President)

GUENTHER, Kurt

1010 Wisconsin Ave. NW
Suite 800
Washington, DC 20007
Tel: (202)338-8700
Fax: (202)338-2334

Employers
Greer, Margolis, Mitchell, Burns & Associates (Partner)

GUENTHER, Robert L.

727 N. Washington St.
Alexandria, VA 22314
EMail: rguenther@uffva.org
Tel: (703)836-3410
Fax: (703)836-2049

Employers
United Fresh Fruit and Vegetable Ass'n (V. President, Government Public Affairs)

GUENTHER-PETERSON, Nance

1055 N. Fairfax St.
Suite 201
Alexandria, VA 22314-3563
EMail: nguent@aol.com
Tel: (703)739-7999
Fax: (703)739-7995
Registered: LDA

Employers
U.S. Strategies Corp. (Senior V. President, Intergovernmental Relations)

Clients Represented
On Behalf of U.S. Strategies Corp.
AdvoServe
Harrah's Entertainment, Inc.
Healthsouth Corp.
Home Access Health
Integrated Health Services, Inc.

GUERNEY, Janis

601 13th St. NW
Suite 400 North
Washington, DC 20005
EMail: jguerney@aap.org
Tel: (202)347-8600
Fax: (202)393-6137
Registered: LDA

Employers
American Academy of Pediatrics (Assistant Director)

GUERRY, Jr., William M.

3050 K St. NW
Washington, DC 20007
EMail: wguerry@colliershannon.com
Tel: (202)342-8400
Fax: (202)342-8451
Registered: LDA

Employers
Collier Shannon Scott, PLLC (Member)

Clients Represented
On Behalf of Collier Shannon Scott, PLLC
Metals Industry Recycling Coalition
Outdoor Power Equipment Institute

GUERTIN, Dr. Donald L.

910 17th St. NW
Tenth Floor
Washington, DC 20006
EMail: dlguertin@erols.com
Tel: (202)778-4963
Fax: (202)463-7241

Employers
Atlantic Council of the United States (Director, Economics, Energy and Environment Program)

GUEST, Michael

2201 C St. NW
Room 7261
Washington, DC 20520-7261
Tel: (202)647-1050
Fax: (202)647-2762

Employers
Department of State - Bureau of Legislative Affairs (Deputy Assistant Secretary - Regional Political Affairs)

GUFFAIN, Pamela D.

501 Second St. NE
Washington, DC 20002
EMail: pguffain@tfi.org
Tel: (202)675-8250
Fax: (202)544-8123
Registered: LDA

Employers
The Fertilizer Institute (Director, Government Relations)

GUGGOLZ, Richard A.

11250 Roger Bacon Dr.
Suite Eight
Reston, VA 20190
Tel: (703)437-4377
Fax: (703)435-4390

Employers
Drohan Management Group (V. President)
Nat'l Ass'n of Rehabilitation Agencies (Exec. Director)

Clients Represented
On Behalf of Drohan Management Group
Sports Lawyers Ass'n

GUHL, Jennifer

601 Pennsylvania Ave. NW
Suite 600
North Bldg.
Washington, DC 20004
EMail: jennifer.guhl@aeanet.org
Tel: (202)682-9110
Fax: (202)682-9111
Registered: LDA

Employers
American Electronics Ass'n (Manager, International Trade Policy)

GUIDO, George

1801 K St. NW
Suite 1000L
Washington, DC 20006
EMail: george_guido@washbm.com
Tel: (202)530-0400
Fax: (202)530-4500

Employers
Burson-Marsteller (Director, Public Affairs Practice)

GUIDOS, Robert J.

99 Canal Center Plaza
Suite 210
Alexandria, VA 22314
EMail: rguidos@idsociety.org
Tel: (703)299-0200
Fax: (703)299-0204
Registered: LDA

Legislative Analyst (1999-2000) and Regulatory Counsel/Legislative Analyst, Food and Drug Administration (1993-99), Department of Health and Human Services.

Employers
Infectious Diseases Soc. of America, Inc. (Director, Public Policy)

GUIDRY, Jerene B.

50 F St. NW
Suite 1050
Washington, DC 20001
EMail: jerene_guidry@fmi.com
Tel: (202)737-1400
Fax: (202)737-1568
Registered: LDA

Employers
Freeport-McMoRan Copper & Gold Inc. (Legislative Assistant)

GUILLORY, L. Marie

4121 Wilson Blvd.
Tenth Floor
Arlington, VA 22203
Tel: (703)351-2000
Registered: LDA

Employers
Nat'l Telephone Cooperative Ass'n (V. President, Legal and Industry)

GUIRARD, Jr., James E.

600 Water St. SW
Suite B 14
Washington, DC 20024
Tel: (202)488-2722
Fax: (202)488-2729
Registered: LDA

An attorney and government relations consultant. Administrative Assistant to Senator Russell Long (D-LA), 1972-80; to Senator Allen Ellender (D-LA), 1968-72; and to Rep. Edwin E. Willis (D-LA), 1964-68.

Employers
Self-employed as an independent consultant.

Clients Represented

As an independent consultant

Analytical Systems, Inc.
Newpark Resources/SOLOCO
SIGCOM, Inc.

GUITERMAN, Susan L.

P.O. Box 1417-D49
Alexandria, VA 22313-1417
Tel: (703)549-3001
Fax: (703)836-4869

Employers

Nat'l Ass'n of Chain Drug Stores (Senior V. President, Communications and External Affairs)

GULDI, Virginia

1201 Connecticut Ave. NW
Suite 600
Washington, DC 20036
Tel: (202)778-1800
Fax: (202)822-8106
Registered: LDA

Employers

Zuckerman Spaeder L.L.P.

Clients Represented

On Behalf of Zuckerman Spaeder L.L.P.

The Bureau of Nat'l Affairs, Inc.

GULICK, Karen

1200 18th St. NW
Suite 1200
Washington, DC 20036
Tel: (202)730-1300
Fax: (202)730-1301
Registered: LDA

Held positions at the Federal Communications Commission, 1995-99.

Employers

Harris, Wiltshire & Grannis LLP (Partner)

Clients Represented

On Behalf of Harris, Wiltshire & Grannis LLP

VoiceStream Wireless Corp.

GULLEDGE, Lisa

600 New Hampshire Ave. NW
Suite 601
Washington, DC 20037
Tel: (202)333-7400
Fax: (202)333-1638

Employers

Hill and Knowlton, Inc. (Managing Director)

Clients Represented

On Behalf of Hill and Knowlton, Inc.

GlaxoSmithKline

GUMP, David

4350 N. Fairfax Dr.
Suite 900
Arlington, VA 22203
Tel: (703)207-4500
Registered: LDA

Employers

LunaCorp, Inc. (President)

Clients Represented

On Behalf of LunaCorp, Inc.

Rotary Rocket Co.

GUMPER, Frank J.

1300 I St. NW
Suite 400 West
Washington, DC 20005
Tel: (202)515-2538
Fax: (202)336-7922

Employers

Verizon Communications (V. President, Public Policy Development)

GUNDERSON, Hon. Steve

1000 Wilson Blvd.
Suite 2710
Arlington, VA 22209
Tel: (703)243-8242
Fax: (703)243-8377
EMail: gundersonsc@greystonegp.com

Member, U.S. House of Representatives (R-WI), 1981-96.

Employers

The Greystone Group (VA) (Managing Director)

Clients Represented

On Behalf of The Greystone Group (VA)

Republican Main Street Partnership

GUNDLING, Rick

1301 Connecticut Ave. NW
Suite 300
Washington, DC 20036
Tel: (202)296-2920
Fax: (202)223-9771
Registered: LDA
EMail: rgundling@hfma.org

Employers

Healthcare Financial Management Ass'n (Technical Director)

GUNN, Susan H.

1615 M St. NW
Washington, DC 20036
Tel: (202)833-2300
Fax: (202)429-3945
Registered: LDA
EMail: sue_gunn@tws.org

Employers

The Wilderness Soc. (Director, Budget and Appropriations)

GUNNING, Anne C.

1030 15th St. NW
Suite 820
Washington, DC 20005-1503
Tel: (202)535-7800
Fax: (202)535-7801
EMail: agunning@kearnswest.com

Employers

Kearns & West, Inc. (V. President)

GUNNULFSEN, Jeffrey

1850 M St. NW
Suite 700
Washington, DC 20036
Tel: (202)721-4198
Fax: (202)296-8548
Registered: LDA
EMail: jeff.gunnulfsen@socma.com

Employers

Synthetic Organic Chemical Manufacturers Ass'n (Manager, Government Affairs)

GUNTER, Linda

1717 Massachusetts Ave. NW
Suite 106
Washington, DC 20036
Tel: (202)483-8491 Ext: 13
Fax: (202)234-9194
EMail: lcpentz@erols.com

Employers

Safe Energy Communication Council (Communications Director)

GUNTER, Paul

1424 16th St. NW
Suite 404
Washington, DC 20036
Tel: (202)328-0002
Fax: (202)462-2183

Employers

Nuclear Information and Resource Service (Director, Reactor Watchdog Project)

GUNTHER, Jr., James J.

1909 K St. NW
Suite 800
Washington, DC 20006
Tel: (202)715-3707
Fax: (202)715-3715
Registered: LDA

Employers

Alcatel USA (Senior Manager, Regulatory Affairs)

GUNZBURG, Dr. Frank

9525 Georgia Ave.
Suite 203
Silver Spring, MD 20910-1439
Tel: (301)588-5800
Fax: (301)588-5870
EMail: dr-efg@resourcebuilder.com

Employers

Center for Health Care Practice in the Public Interest (Exec. Director)

GUPTA, Geeta Rao

1717 Massachusetts Ave. NW
Suite 302
Washington, DC 20036
Tel: (202)797-0007
Fax: (202)797-0020

Employers

Internat'l Center for Research on Women (President)

GURLAND, Christine Slowikowski

400 Seventh St. SW
7206 F
Washington, DC 20590
Tel: (202)366-1707
Fax: (202)366-3890

Employers

Department of Transportation - Maritime Administration (Director, Office of Congressional and Public Affairs)

GURLEY, John

1050 Connecticut Ave. NW
Washington, DC 20036-5339
Tel: (202)857-6000
Fax: (202)857-6395

Employers

Arent Fox Kintner Plotkin & Kahn, PLLC (Member)

GUSKY, David

1401 K St. NW
Suite 600
Washington, DC 20005
Tel: (202)835-9898
Fax: (202)853-9893
Registered: LDA

Employers

ASCENT (Ass'n of Community Enterprises) (Exec. V. President)

GUSLER, Dorothy

1111 19th St. NW
Suite 800
Washington, DC 20036
Tel: (202)463-2700
Fax: (202)463-2785
Registered: LDA

Employers

American Forest & Paper Ass'n (Director, International Trade)

GUSS, Phyllis A.

1200 K St. NW
Suite 1200
Washington, DC 20005
Tel: (202)414-3500
Registered: LDA

Employers

Lockheed Martin IMS (V. President, Legislative Affairs and Marketing)

GUSTAFSON, Erick

1250 H St. NW
Suite 700
Washington, DC 20005-3908
Tel: (202)783-3870
Fax: (202)783-4687
Registered: LDA
EMail: egustafson@cse.org

Employers

Citizens for a Sound Economy (Director, Technology and Communications Policy)

GUSTAFSON, Julia

1155 Connecticut Ave. NW
Suite 1200
Washington, DC 20036
Tel: (202)659-5800
Fax: (202)659-1027
Registered: LDA

Employers

Birch, Horton, Bittner & Cherot

Clients Represented

On Behalf of Birch, Horton, Bittner & Cherot

America Outdoors
Bibb, Georgia, Board of Commissioners of the County of
Internat'l Snowmobile Manufacturers Ass'n
Wildlife Legislative Fund of America

GUSTAFSON, Robert C.

1175 Reston Ave.
Herndon, VA 20170
Tel: (703)450-9066
Registered: LDA
EMail: rcg@gustafsonassoc.com

Chief of Staff (1993-95), Legislative Director (1990-93) and Legislative Assistant (1987-90) to Rep. John E. Porter (R-IL).

Employers

Gustafson Associates (President)

Clients Represented

On Behalf of Gustafson Associates

Center for Aging Policy
EarthVoice
Internat'l Campaign for Tibet
Internat'l Trust Fund for Demining and Mine Victims Assistance in Bosnia-Herzigovina
Interns for Peace Internat'l
Nat'l Spiritual Assembly of the Baha'is of the United States

GUSTAVSON, Dr. E. Brandt

7839 Ashton Ave.
Manassas, VA 20109
Tel: (703)330-7000
Fax: (703)330-7100

Employers
Nat'l Religious Broadcasters (President)

GUSTINI, Raymond J.

401 Ninth St. NW
Suite 900
Washington, DC 20004
Tel: (202)585-8000
Fax: (202)585-8080
Registered: LDA
EMail: rgustini@nixonpeabody.com

Employers
Nixon Peabody LLP (Partner)

GUTHRIE, Anne

227 Massachusetts Ave. NE
Suite 200
Washington, DC 20002
Tel: (202)543-1147
Fax: (202)543-4466

Employers
Alliance to End Childhood Lead Poisoning (Director, Health Policy)

GUTHRIE, Kathy

245 Second St. NE
Washington, DC 20002
Tel: (202)547-6000
Fax: (202)547-6019
Registered: LDA

Employers
Friends Committee on Nat'l Legislation (Field Program Coordinator)

GUTHRIE, Susan

1201 15th St. NW
Washington, DC 20005-2800
Tel: (202)822-0200
Fax: (202)822-0572

Employers
Nat'l Ass'n of Home Builders of the U.S. (Acting Senior Staff V. President, Staff V. President, Operations and Communications (Multi-Family Services))

GUTMAN, Harry L.

2001 M St. NW
Washington, DC 20036
Tel: (202)467-3044
Fax: (202)533-8500
Registered: LDA
EMail: hgutman@kpmg.com
Chief of Staff, Joint Committee on Taxation, 1991-93. Deputy Tax Legislative Counsel (1978-80) and Attorney-Advisor (1977-78), Department of the Treasury.

Employers
The KPMG FSC Coalition
KPMG, LLP (Partner)

Clients Represented

On Behalf of KPMG, LLP
Air Transport Ass'n of America
Apple Computer, Inc.
The INDOPCO Coalition
The KPMG FSC Coalition
Nat'l Council of Farmer Cooperatives
Sara Lee Corp.

GUTMAN, Howard W.

725 12th St. NW
Washington, DC 20005
Tel: (202)434-5000
Fax: (202)434-5029
Special Assistant to the Director, Federal Bureau of Investigation, Department of Justice, 1985-86. Law Clerk to Justice Potter Stewart, U.S. Supreme Court, 1981-82, and to Judge Irving L. Goldberg, U.S. Court of Appeals, Fifth Circuit, 1980-81.

Employers
Williams & Connolly (Partner)

GUTTER, Sam

1722 I St. NW
Washington, DC 20006
Tel: (202)736-8000
Fax: (202)736-8711

Employers
Sidley & Austin (Partner)

Clients Represented

On Behalf of Sidley & Austin
American Petroleum Institute

GUTTING, Jr., Richard

1901 N. Fort Myer Dr.
Suite 700
Arlington, VA 22209
Tel: (703)524-8884
Fax: (703)524-4619
Registered: LDA
EMail: rgutting@nfi.org

Employers
Nat'l Fisheries Institute (Exec. V. President)

GUTTMAN, Daniel

1135 15th St. NW
Suite 410
Washington, DC 20006
Tel: (202)638-6050
Fax: (202)637-2977
Registered: LDA
Former Commissioner, Occupational Safety and Health Review Commission.

Employers
Self-employed as an independent consultant.

GUTTMAN, Robert M.

219 Ninth St. SE
Washington, DC 20003
Tel: (202)547-1840
Fax: (202)547-7668

Employers
Self-employed as an independent consultant.

Clients Represented

As an independent consultant
Nat'l Council for Adoption

GUTTMANN, Jr., John S.

1350 I St. NW
Suite 700
Washington, DC 20005
Tel: (202)789-6000
Fax: (202)789-6190
Law Clerk to Judge Aubrey E. Robinson, Jr., U.S. District Court for the District of Columbia, 1978-80.

Employers
Beveridge & Diamond, P.C. (Partner)

GUTTUSO, Joseph

1401 Constitution Ave. NW
Room 4898
Washington, DC 20230
Tel: (202)482-1551
Fax: (202)482-1635

Employers
Department of Commerce - Nat'l Telecommunications and Information Administration (Acting Director, Office of Congressional Affairs)

GUY, IV, John H.

1625 K St. NW
Suite 600
Washington, DC 20006
Tel: (202)393-6100
Fax: (202)331-8539
EMail: jguy@npc.org

Employers
Nat'l Petroleum Council (Deputy Exec. Director)

GUZIK, John

1133 21st St. NW
Suite 700
Washington, DC 20036
Tel: (202)887-6900
Fax: (202)887-6970
Former Chief of Staff to Rep. David Camp (R-MI).

Employers
Janus-Merritt Strategies, L.L.C.

Clients Represented

On Behalf of Janus-Merritt Strategies, L.L.C.
Fannie Mae
Napster, Inc.

GUZZETTI, Arthur L.

1666 K St. NW
Washington, DC 20006
Tel: (202)296-4700
Fax: (202)496-4324
Registered: LDA
EMail: aguzzetti@apta.com

Employers
American Public Transportation Ass'n (Director, Policy Development and Member Mobilization)

GWADZ, Joyce T.

1200 New Hampshire Ave. NW
Suite 800
Washington, DC 20036-6802
Tel: (202)776-2000
Fax: (202)776-2222
EMail: jgwadz@dlalaw.com

Employers
Dow, Lohnes & Albertson, PLLC (Member)

GWALTNEY, W. David

1755 Jefferson Davis Hwy.
Suite 1107
Arlington, VA 22202
Tel: (703)415-0344
Fax: (703)415-0182
Former Professional Staff Member, Subcommittee on Energy and Water Development, Senate Committee on Appropriations. Served in the U.S. Air Force, 1967-72.

Employers
The PMA Group

GWINN, W. Roger

1130 Connecticut Ave. NW
Suite 300
Washington, DC 20036
Tel: (202)331-8500
Fax: (202)331-1598
Registered: LDA
Legislative Director (1987-93), Legislative Assistant (1985-87), and Press Secretary (1979-85) to Rep. Vic Fazio (D-CA). Legislative and Press Assistant (1978-79) and Intern (1977) to Rep. Richardson Preyer (D-NC), 1977.

Employers
The Ferguson Group, LLC (President)

Clients Represented

On Behalf of The Ferguson Group, LLC
Alcalde & Fay
Arcadia, California, City of
Camp Dresser and McKee, Inc.
Central Valley Project Water Ass'n
Colusa Basin Drainage District
Fairfield, California, City of
Family Farm Alliance (Project Transfer Council)
Folsom, California, City of
Glenn-Colusa Irrigation District
Gridley, California, City of/Northern California Power Agency
Huntington Beach, California, City of
Imperial Irrigation District
The Irvine Co.
Kaweah Delta Water Conservation District
Mecklenburg, North Carolina, County of
Modesto/Turlock Irrigation District
Natomas
Northern California Power Agency
Norwalk, California, City of
Oceanside, California, City of
Sacramento, California, Public Works Agency of the County of
San Luis Obispo, California, County of
Santa Monica, California, City of
Somach, Simmons & Dunn
Southeast Water Coalition
Sutter, California, County of
Transportation Corridor Agencies
Wake, North Carolina, County of
Washoe County
West Valley City, Utah

GWYN, Brigitte S.

1615 L St. NW
Suite 1100
Washington, DC 20036-5610
Tel: (202)872-1260
Fax: (202)466-3509
Legislative Assistant to Rep. Jim Kolbe (R-AZ), 1995-98.

Employers
The Business Roundtable (Legislative Director)

GWYNN, Peter

One Dupont Circle NW
Suite 615
Washington, DC 20036-1168
Tel: (202)659-3130
Fax: (202)785-0374

Employers
University Continuing Education Ass'n (Director, Government Relations and Program Development)

HAAKE, Timothy M.

1301 K St. NW
Suite 900, East Tower
Washington, DC 20005
Tel: (202)408-8701
Fax: (202)408-8704
Registered: LDA
EMail: thaake@haake-dc.com

Employers
Haake and Associates (Counsel)

Clients Represented

On Behalf of Haake and Associates

American Ass'n of Orthodontists
American Orthotic and Prosthetic Ass'n
EMC Corp.
Free Trade Lumber Council
Jewelers of America
The Lansdale Company
North American Insulation Manufacturers Ass'n
Ortho Concepts
The Pillsbury Co.
Saint-Gobain Corp.
Science Applications Internat'l Corp. (SAIC)
Seal Beach, California, City of
Tanimura & Antle, Inc.
Titan Corp.

HAAKER, Ryan

1025 Thomas Jefferson St. NW
Suite 400 East
Washington, DC 20007-0805
Tel: (202)965-8100
Fax: (202)965-6403

Employers

Jorden Burt LLP (Director of Administration and Special Projects)

HAAS, Joseph

700 S. Washington St.
Suite 300
Alexandria, VA 22314
Tel: (703)739-3900
Fax: (703)739-3915

Employers

American School Food Service Ass'n (Government Affairs/Media Relations Specialist)

HAAS, Richard T.

1300 N. 17th St.
Eighth Floor
Rosslyn, VA 22209-3801
EMail: haas@abc.org
Tel: (703)812-2000
Fax: (703)812-8203

Employers

Associated Builders and Contractors (V. President, Public Affairs)

HAAS, Rosemary T.

1710 Rhode Island Ave. NW
Suite 300
Washington, DC 20036
Tel: (202)659-8524
Fax: (202)466-8386
Registered: LDA

Employers

Abbott Laboratories (Regional Director, Government Affairs)

HAASS, Richard N.

1775 Massachusetts Ave. NW
Washington, DC 20036-2188
Tel: (202)797-6000
Fax: (202)797-6004

Employers

The Brookings Institution (V. President and Director, Foreign Policy Studies)

HABEEB, W. Mark

888 16th St. NW
Washington, DC 20006
Tel: (202)835-8177
Fax: (202)835-8161
Registered: LDA, FARA

Foreign Policy Assistant for Senator Gary Hart.

Employers

Bannerman and Associates, Inc.

Clients Represented

On Behalf of Bannerman and Associates, Inc.

Palestinian Authority

HABER, Jon

1615 L St. NW
Suite 1000
Washington, DC 20036
EMail: haberj@fleishman.com
Tel: (202)659-0330
Fax: (202)296-6119

Chief of Staff to Senator Dianne Feinstein (D-CA), 1993. Counsel and Communications Director, Senate Committee on Agriculture, 1989-93.

Employers

Fleishman-Hillard, Inc (Senior V. President)

HABER, Sherry J.

1275 K St. NW
Suite 1212
Washington, DC 20005
Tel: (703)787-0000
Fax: (202)312-5005
Registered: LDA

Employers

Healthcare Distribution Management Ass'n (V. President, Government and Professional Affairs)

HABERMAN-GOMEZ, Amy

1800 R St. NW
Suite C-4
Washington, DC 20009
EMail: chair@winonline.org
Tel: (202)347-2827
Fax: (202)347-1418

Employers

Women's Information Network (Chairperson)

HABIB, Amy

1015 15th St. NW
Suite 1200
Washington, DC 20005
Tel: (202)789-8600
Fax: (202)789-1708

Employers

McGuiness Norris & Williams, LLP (Associate)

Clients Represented

On Behalf of McGuiness Norris & Williams, LLP

Labor Policy Ass'n (LPA)

HACAJ, Sylvia

2120 L St. NW
Suite 400
Washington, DC 20037
Tel: (202)223-9541
Fax: (202)223-9579
Registered: LDA

Employers

M & R Strategic Services (Director, Government Relations)

Clients Represented

On Behalf of M & R Strategic Services

Greater New York Automobile Dealers Ass'n
Lesbian & Gay Community Center Hetrick-Martin Institute

HACK, Ted

3190 Fairview Park Dr.
Falls Church, VA 22042
Tel: (703)876-3000
Fax: (703)876-3600
Registered: LDA

Employers

General Dynamics Corp. (Director, Government Relations - Submarine Programs)

HACKER, George A.

1875 Connecticut Ave. NW
Suite 300
Washington, DC 20009
Tel: (202)332-9110
Fax: (202)265-4954
Registered: LDA

Employers

Center for Science in the Public Interest (Director of Alchohol Policies Project)
Coalition for the Prevention of Alcohol Problems (Chairman)

HACKETT, David L.

1320 Fenwick Lane
Suite 506
Silver Spring, MD 20910
Tel: (301)585-0580
Fax: (301)585-0584

Employers

Youth Policy Institute (Exec. Director)

HACKETT, Susan J.

1025 Connecticut Ave. NW
Suite 200
Washington, DC 20036
EMail: hackett@acca.com
Tel: (202)293-4103
Fax: (202)293-4701

Employers

American Corporate Counsel Ass'n (Senior V. President and General Counsel)

HACKMAN, Charles H.

1725 I St. NW
Suite 600
Washington, DC 20006
EMail: chackman@ncb.com
Tel: (202)336-7657
Fax: (202)336-7801
Registered: LDA

Employers

Nat'l Cooperative Bank (Managing Director)

HACKMAN, Timothy B.

1301 K St. NW
Suite 1200-West Tower
Washington, DC 20005-3307
EMail: thackman@us.ibm.com
Tel: (202)515-5115
Fax: (202)515-4943
Registered: LDA

Employers

Internat'l Business Machines Corp. (Director, Public Affairs, Science and Technology)

HACKNEY, Richard

1750 New York Ave. NW
Washington, DC 20006
Tel: (202)637-0700
Fax: (202)637-0771
Registered: LDA

Employers

Internat'l Union of Painters and Allied Trades

HADDOW, C. McClain

2921 Mother Well Ct.
Herndon, VA 20171
Tel: (703)471-5210
Fax: (703)481-3682
Registered: LDA

Employers

C. McClain Haddow & Associates (Director)

Clients Represented

On Behalf of C. McClain Haddow & Associates

Somerset Pharmaceuticals

HADDOW, John M.

233 Constitution Ave. NE
Washington, DC 20002
Tel: (202)547-4000
Fax: (202)543-5044
Registered: LDA

EMail: j.haddow@att.net

Former Aide to Senator Orrin G. Hatch (R-UT).

Employers

Parry, Romani, DeConcini & Symms (V. President)

Clients Represented

On Behalf of Parry, Romani, DeConcini & Symms

AIDS Healthcare Foundation
Andrx Pharmaceutical Corp.
Armstrong World Industries, Inc.
Asphalt Systems, Inc.
Aventis Pharmaceutical Products
Avondale, Arizona, City of
Bank of New York
Bristol-Myers Squibb Co.
Coalition Against Database Piracy
Composites Fabricators Ass'n
Ferraro, USA
Formosan Ass'n for Public Affairs
GlaxoSmithKline
Herbalife Internat'l, Inc.
Hoechst Marion Roussel Deutschland GmbH
Inter-Cal Corp.
Katten Muchin & Zavis
Motion Picture Ass'n of America
Nat'l Air Cargo, Inc.
Nat'l Nutritional Foods Ass'n
Nat'l Retail Federation
Nogales, Arizona, City of
Nu Skin Internat'l Inc.
Owens Corning
Peoria, Arizona, City of
Pfizer, Inc.
Pharmacia Corp.
Policy Development Group, Inc.
Project to Promote Competition and Innovation in the Digital Age
Research & Development Laboratories
Research Corp. Technology
Rexall Sundown
SBC Communications Inc.
SOL Source Technologies, Inc.
Styrene Information and Research Center
Taxpayers Against Fraud, The False Claims Legal Center
TCOM, L.P.
Unilever United States, Inc.
Utah Natural Products Alliance

HADFIELD, Victoria

1401 K St. NW
Suite 601
Washington, DC 20005
EMail: vhadfield@semi.org
Tel: (202)289-0440
Fax: (202)289-0441
Registered: LDA

Employers
Semiconductor Equipment and Materials Internat'l (V. President, Public Policy)

HADIDIAN, John

2100 L St. NW
Washington, DC 20037
Tel: (202)452-1100
Fax: (202)778-6132

Employers
Humane Soc. of the United States (Director, Suburban Wildlife Protection)

HADLEY, Jr., Joseph E.

1815 H St. NW
Suite 500
Washington, DC 20006-3604
Tel: (202)296-6300
Fax: (202)775-5929

Employers
Hadley & McKenna

Clients Represented

On Behalf of Hadley & McKenna
Aniline Ass'n, Inc.
Ethylene Oxide Sterilization Ass'n, Inc.
Nitrobenzene Ass'n
Tetrahydrofuran Task Force

HAEFELI, Jennifer A.

1850 M St. NW
Suite 550
Washington, DC 20036
Tel: (202)289-5900
Fax: (202)289-4141

Employers
Chlopak, Leonard, Schechter and Associates (Senior Associate)

HAFT, William S.

555 13th St. NW
Washington, DC 20004-1109
Tel: (202)637-5600
Fax: (202)637-5910
Registered: LDA

Employers
Hogan & Hartson L.L.P.

Clients Represented

On Behalf of Hogan & Hartson L.L.P.
S1 Corp.
WebMD

HAGAN, James G.

1776 I St. NW
Suite 400
Washington, DC 20006-3708
Tel: (202)739-8000
Fax: (202)785-4019
Registered: LDA

Employers
Nuclear Energy Institute (Director, Legislative Programs)

HAGAN, Paul E.

1350 I St. NW
Suite 700
Washington, DC 20005
Tel: (202)789-6000
Fax: (202)789-6190
Registered: LDA

Employers
Beveridge & Diamond, P.C. (Partner)

HAGEL, Lawrence

801 18th St. NW
Washington, DC 20006
Tel: (202)872-1300
Fax: (202)785-4452

Employers
Paralyzed Veterans of America (General Counsel)

HAGER, Susan

1090 Vermont Ave. NW
Third Floor
Washington, DC 20005
EMail: shager@hagersharp.com
Tel: (202)842-3600
Fax: (202)842-4032

Employers
Hager Sharp Inc. (Chair and Chief Exec. Officer)

HAGERUP, Stefan A.

1333 New Hampshire Ave. NW
Suite 400
Washington, DC 20036
Tel: (202)887-4000
Fax: (202)887-4288
Registered: FARA
Law Clerk to Judge John L. Coffey, U.S. Court of Appeals, Seventh Circuit, 1990-92.

Employers
Akin, Gump, Strauss, Hauer & Feld, L.L.P. (Associate)

HAGGART, Veronica

1350 I St. NW
Suite 400
Washington, DC 20005-3306
Tel: (202)371-6900
Fax: (202)842-3578

Employers
Motorola, Inc. (Corporate V. President and Director, One Motorola Ventures, Eastern Region)

HAGGINS, Marrietta

Ariel Rios Federal Bldg.
(1301-MC)
1200 Pennsylvania Ave. NW
Third Floor
Washington, DC 20460
EMail: haggins.marrietta@epa.gov
Tel: (202)564-5200
Fax: (202)501-1519

Employers
Environmental Protection Agency (Staff Assistant, Congressional and Intergovernmental Affairs)

HAGMANN, Patrice

701 Pennsylvania Ave. NW
Washington, DC 20004-2696
Tel: (202)508-5000
Fax: (202)508-5759

Employers
Edison Electric Institute (Media Relations Representative)

HAGOOD, Susan

2100 L St. NW
Washington, DC 20037
Tel: (202)452-1100
Fax: (202)778-6132
Registered: LDA

Employers
Humane Soc. of the United States (Wildlife Issues Specialist)

HAHN, Adriennne M.

1666 Connecticut Ave. NW
Suite 310
Washington, DC 20009
EMail: Hhnadr@consumer.org
Tel: (202)462-6262
Fax: (202)265-9548
Registered: LDA

Employers
Consumers Union of the United States (Sr. Legislative Counsel)

HAHN, Beth D.

6776 Little Falls Rd.
Arlington, VA 22213
EMail: Amerhome@aol.com
Tel: (703)536-7776
Fax: (703)536-0003

Employers
American Homeowners Grassroots Alliance (Exec. V. President)

HAHN, Bruce N.

6776 Little Falls Rd.
Arlington, VA 22213
EMail: bhahn@compTIA.org
Tel: (703)536-0002
Fax: (703)536-0003
Registered: LDA

Employers
Computing Technology Industry Ass'n (Director, Public Policy)

HAHN, Colleen

808 17th St. NW
Suite 600
Washington, DC 20006
Tel: (202)466-7800
Fax: (202)887-0905

Employers
Ruder Finn Washington (Senior V. President, Technology Practice)

HAHN, Dr. Lorna

1629 K St. NW
Suite 802
Washington, DC 20006
Tel: (202)331-8455
Fax: (202)775-7465

Employers
Ass'n on Third World Affairs (Exec. Director)

HAHN, Mary

1401 H St. NW
Suite 600
Washington, DC 20005-2136
Tel: (202)326-7300
Fax: (202)326-7333

Employers
United States Telecom Ass'n (V. President, Administration)

HAHN, Robert A.

1400 16th St. NW
Suite 400
Washington, DC 20036-2220
EMail: rhahn@ofwlaw.com
Tel: (202)518-6388
Fax: (202)234-3583

Employers
Olsson, Frank and Weeda, P.C. (Associate)

HAHN, Robert W.

1150 17th St. NW
Washington, DC 20036
EMail: rhahn@crosslink.net
Tel: (202)862-5800
Fax: (202)862-7177

Employers
American Enterprise Institute for Public Policy Research (Resident Scholar)

HAIFLEY, Gregg

25 E St. NW
Washington, DC 20001
EMail: ghaifley@childrensdefense.org
Tel: (202)628-8787
Fax: (202)662-3560
Registered: LDA

Employers
Children's Defense Fund (Senior Health Associate)

HAIG, Jr., Alexander M.

1155 15th St. NW
Suite 800
Washington, DC 20005
Secretary of State, 1981-82.
Tel: (202)429-9788
Fax: (202)833-5296

Employers
Worldwide Associates, Inc (Chairman and President)

HAILEY, Gary D.

1201 New York Ave. NW
Suite 1000
Washington, DC 20005
EMail: gdhailey@venable.com
Tel: (202)962-4997
Fax: (202)962-8300
Attorney/Advisor to Commissioner Mary L. Azcuenaga, Federal Trade Commission, 1985-91. Staff Attorney and Program Advisor, Bureau of Consumer Protection, Federal Trade Commission, 1977-85.

Employers
Venable (Of Counsel)

HAILPERN, Nancy

1700 K St. NW
Suite 1150
Washington, DC 20006
EMail: nancy.hailpern@ujc.org
Tel: (202)736-5878
Fax: (202)785-4937

Employers
United Jewish Communities, Inc. (Director, Washington Mission Programs)

HAINES, Robert W.

2001 Pennsylvania Ave. NW
Suite 300
Washington, DC 20006
Tel: (202)862-0245
Fax: (202)862-0269
Registered: LDA

Employers
Exxon Mobil Corp. (Manager, International Relations)

HAJJAR, Anton G.

1300 L St. NW
Suite 1200
Washington, DC 20005-4178
Tel: (202)898-1707
Fax: (202)682-9276
Attorney, Office of the General Counsel, Division of Enforcement Litigation, Appellate Court Branch and Contempt Litigation Section (1979-81) and Field Attorney, Region 15 (1975-79), National Labor Relations Board. Law Clerk to Judge John Minor Wisdom, U.S. Court of Appeals, Fifth Circuit, 1975-75.

Employers
O'Donnell, Schwartz & Anderson, P.C. (Principal)

Clients Represented

On Behalf of O'Donnell, Schwartz & Anderson, P.C.

American Postal Workers Union

HAJOST, Scott A.

1630 Connecticut Ave. NW
Third Floor
Washington, DC 20009
EMail: postmaster@iucnus.org
Tel: (202)387-4826
Fax: (202)387-4823

Employers

IUCN - The World Conservation Union (US) (Exec. Director)

HAKIM, Peter

1211 Connecticut Ave. NW
Suite 510
Washington, DC 20036
Tel: (202)822-9002
Fax: (202)822-9553

Employers

Inter-American Dialogue (President)

HALAMANDARIS, Val

228 Seventh St. SE
Washington, DC 20003-4306
Tel: (202)547-7424
Fax: (202)547-3540

Employers

Caring Institute (Exec. Director)
Nat'l Ass'n for Home Care (President)

HALE, Elizabeth

1001 Connecticut Ave. NW
Suite 310
Washington, DC 20036
Tel: (202)822-8405
Fax: (202)872-4050

Employers

Institute for Educational Leadership (V. President)

HALE, Malia

1400 16th St. NW
Suite 501
Washington, DC 20036-2266
Tel: (202)797-6800
Fax: (202)797-6646
Registered: LDA

Employers

Nat'l Wildlife Federation - Office of Federal and Internat'l Affairs

HALE, M.D., Ralph

409 12th St. SW
P.O. Box 96920
Washington, DC 20090-6920
Tel: (202)863-2525
Fax: (202)863-1643

Employers

American College of Obstetricians and Gynecologists (Exec. V. President)

HALEDJIAN, Gregory

10302 Eaton Pl.
Suite 340
Fairfax, VA 22030
Tel: (703)385-5300
Fax: (703)385-5301

Employers

American Public Communications Council (Government Relations Manager)

HALES, Shirley I.

1001 19th St. North
Suite 800
Arlington, VA 22209-3901
EMail: shirley.hales@trw.com
Tel: (703)276-5043
Fax: (703)276-5024
Registered: LDA

Employers

TRW Inc. (Director, Government Relations)

HALES, Stuart

2101 Wilson Blvd.
Suite 500
Arlington, VA 22201-3062
EMail: commdir@eap-association.org
Tel: (703)387-1000
Fax: (703)522-4585

Employers

Employee Assistance Professionals Ass'n (Director, Communications)

HALEY, Daniel D.

412 First St. SE
Suite One
Washington, DC 20003
Tel: (202)484-2773
Fax: (202)484-0770
Registered: LDA

Former Administrator, Agricultural Marketing Services, Department of Agriculture.

Employers

Haley and Associates (President)
Meyers & Associates (General Counsel)

Clients Represented

On Behalf of Haley and Associates

CalCot
California Prune Board
California Strawberry Commission
California Walnut Commission
Ingersoll-Rand Co.
Sun Diamond Growers, Inc.
SunSweet Growers, Inc.
Valley Fig Growers

HALEY, John

1717 H St. NW
Washington, DC 20006

Employers

The Watson Wyatt Worldwide Co. (Chief Exec. Officer)

HALEY, Roberta

750 First St. NE
Suite 1010
Washington, DC 20002
EMail: r.savage@asiwpca.org
Tel: (202)898-0905
Fax: (202)898-0929

Employers

Ass'n of State and Interstate Water Pollution Control Administrators (Exec. Director)

HALICKI, Tom

444 N. Capital St. NW
Suite 208
Washington, DC 20001
EMail: thalicki@sso.org
Tel: (202)624-3553
Fax: (202)624-3554

Employers

Nat'l Ass'n of Towns and Townships (Exec. Director)

HALKIAS, Rebecca

444 N. Capitol St. NW
Suite 700
Washington, DC 20001
Tel: (202)624-7828
Fax: (202)624-7831

Employers

Pennsylvania, Washington Office of the Commonwealth of (Deputy Chief of Staff for Federal Affairs)

HALL, Ph.D., Clarence

440 R St. NW
Washington, DC 20001
Tel: (202)462-3614
Fax: (202)387-1034

Employers

Africare (Director, HIV/AIDS Programs)

HALL, Cynthia A.

409 12th St. SW
Suite 310
Washington, DC 20024
EMail: cindy@womenspolicy.org
Tel: (202)554-2323
Fax: (202)554-2346

Legislative Director to Rep. Constance Morella (R-MD), 1987-98.

Employers

Women's Policy, Inc. (President)

HALL, Darcy

1090 Vermont Ave. NW
Third Floor
Washington, DC 20005
Tel: (202)842-3600
Fax: (202)842-4032

Employers

Hager Sharp Inc. (Account Assistant)

HALL, Debra J.

1301 Pennsylvania Ave. NW
Suite 900
Washington, DC 20004
Tel: (202)638-3690
Fax: (202)638-0936

Employers

Reinsurance Ass'n of America (V. President and General Counsel)

HALL, Fletcher R.

2200 Mill Rd.
Alexandria, VA 22314
EMail: fhall@trucking.org
Tel: (703)838-1897
Fax: (703)519-1866

Employers

Agricultural Transporters Conference (Exec. Director)

HALL, G. Stewart

1212 New York Ave. NW
Suite 350
Washington, DC 20005
EMail: stewarthall@erols.com
Tel: (202)842-5077
Fax: (202)842-5010
Registered: LDA, FARA

Legislative Director for Senator Richard C. Shelby (R-AL), 1992-96.

Employers

Hall, Green, Rupli, LLC (President and Partner)

Clients Represented

On Behalf of Hall, Green, Rupli, LLC

American Ass'n of Nurse Anesthetists
Bay Area Rapid Transit District
BellSouth Corp.
BellSouth Telecommunications, Inc.
Birmingham Airport Authority
Colsa Corp.
Community Financial Services Ass'n
DaimlerChrysler Corp.
FedEx Corp.
Flight Safety Technologies, Inc.
Huntsville Madison Chamber of Commerce
MemberWorks, Inc.
Nat'l Ass'n of Business Political Action Committees
Nat'l Rifle Ass'n of America
Pernod Ricard
Philip Morris Management Corp.
Southern Research Institute
U.S. Space & Rocket Center
United States Telecom Ass'n
University of Alabama - Huntsville
University of South Alabama

HALL, Gerri L.

1420 King St.
Suite 401
Alexandria, VA 22314
EMail: ghall@oli.org
Tel: (703)739-0308
Fax: (703)519-8267

Employers

Operation Lifesaver Inc. (President)

HALL, J. Michael

1875 I St. NW
12th Floor
Washington, DC 20006
Tel: (202)466-6550
Fax: (202)785-1756

Clerk, Subcommittee on Labor, Health and Human Services and Education, Committee on Appropriations, U.S. Senate, 1987-93. Staff Director, Subcommittee on District of Columbia and Subcommittee on Treasury and General Government, Subcommittee on Transportation, Committee on Appropriations, U.S. Senate, 1976-87. Staff, Office of Management and Budget, 1971-75. Volunteer, Peace Corps, 1967-69.

Employers

Powers Pyles Sutter & Verville, PC (Director, Government Relations)

Clients Represented

On Behalf of Powers Pyles Sutter & Verville, PC

American Ass'n of Colleges of Nursing
American Foundation for the Blind - Governmental Relations Group
American Liver Foundation
American Psychological Ass'n
California School of Professional Psychology
Nat'l Mental Health Ass'n
Southeastern Universities Research Ass'n
University of Florida Health Science Center

HALL, James E.

1101 Pennsylvania Ave. NW
Sixth Floor
Washington, DC 20004
Tel: (202)312-0600
Fax: (202)312-0606

Chairman (1994-2001) and Member (1993-1994), National Transportation Safety Board. Chief of Staff to Senator Harlan Matthews (D-TN), 1993. Advance Man for the President and Vice President of the United States, 1976-80. General Counsel, Subcommittee on Intergovernmental Relations, Senate Committee on Government Operations, 1972-75. Special Assistant to Senator Albert J. Gore, Sr. (D-TN), 1970.

Employers

Dillon, Hall & Lungershausen (Partner)

Clients Represented

On Behalf of Dillon, Hall & Lungershausen

DaimlerChrysler Corp.

HALL, Jason Y.

1575 I St. NW
Suite 400
Washington, DC 20005
Tel: (202)289-9125
Fax: (202)289-6578
Registered: LDA

Employers

American Ass'n of Museums (Director, Government and Public Affairs)

HALL, John

1201 Pennsylvania Ave. NW
Washington, DC 20004-2401
Tel: (202)662-6000
Fax: (202)662-6291
EMail: jhall@cov.com

Assistant U.S. Attorney for the Eastern District of Missouri, Department of Justice, 1989-91. Legislative Counsel to Senator John C. Danforth (R-MO), 1985-86. Law Clerk to Judge Eugene F. Lynch, U.S. District Court for the Northern District of California, 1984-85.

Employers

Covington & Burling (Of Counsel)

HALL, Jr., USAF (Ret.), Lt. Gen. John B "Skip"

11 Canal Center Plaza
Suite 103
Alexandria, VA 22314
Tel: (703)683-4222
Fax: (703)683-0645
Registered: LDA

Employers

The Spectrum Group

Clients Represented

On Behalf of The Spectrum Group

ADSI Inc.
Simula, Inc.

HALL, Joseph C.

1615 M St. NW
Suite 800
Washington, DC 20036-3203
Tel: (202)467-6370
Fax: (202)467-6379
EMail: jch@dwgp.com

Employers

Duncan, Weinberg, Genzer & Pembroke, P.C. (Associate)

HALL, Joseph M.

1201 E. Abingdon Dr.
Suite 300
Alexandria, VA 22314
Tel: (703)739-1927
Fax: (703)739-2775
Registered: LDA
EMail: jhall04@harris.com

Employers

Harris Corp. (Director, Congressional Relations)

HALL, Lauren

1730 M St. NW
Suite 700
Washington, DC 20036-4510
Tel: (202)452-1600
Fax: (202)223-8756
Registered: LDA
EMail: lhall@siia.net

Employers

Software & Information Industry Ass'n (SIIA) (Exec. V. President)

HALL, Louise

9300 Livingston Rd.
Fort Washington, MD 20744
Tel: (301)248-6200
Fax: (301)248-7104
EMail: louise@ntma.org

Employers

Nat'l Tooling and Machining Ass'n (PAC Administrator)

HALL, Mardel

409 Third St. SW
Suite 7900
Washington, DC 20416
Tel: (202)205-6700
Fax: (202)205-7374
EMail: mardel.hall@sba.gov

Employers

Small Business Administration (Staff Assistant, Legislative Affairs)

HALL, Martin L.

311 Maryland Ave. NE
Suite One
Washington, DC 20002
Tel: (202)544-4256
Fax: (202)544-4207
Registered: LDA

Employers

Self-employed as an independent consultant.

Clients Represented

As an independent consultant

Gulfstream TLC, Inc.

HALL, Jr., Ridgway M.

1001 Pennsylvania Ave. NW
Suite 1100
Washington, DC 20004-2595
Tel: (202)624-2500
Fax: (202)628-5116

Associate General Counsel, Environmental Protection Agency, 1976-77.

Employers

Crowell & Moring LLP (Partner)

HALL, III, Robert P.

655 15th St. NW
Suite 445
Washington, DC 20005
Tel: (202)737-1977
Registered: LDA

Employers

Koch Industries, Inc. (Director, Government Affairs)

HALL, III, Robert T.

701 Pennsylvania Ave. NW
Suite 800
Washington, DC 20004
Tel: (202)508-4160
Fax: (202)508-4321
EMail: rhall@thelenreid.com

Employers

Thelen Reid & Priest LLP (Partner)

HALL, Stephanie

1850 M St. NW
Suite 550
Washington, DC 20036
Tel: (202)289-5900
Fax: (202)289-4141

Employers

Chlopak, Leonard, Schechter and Associates (Managing Associate)

HALL, Terre McFillen

1350 Beverly Rd.
Suite 108
McLean, VA 22101
Tel: (703)748-0400
Fax: (703)748-0402
Registered: LDA
EMail: terrehall@patientadvocacy.org

Employers

Center for Patient Advocacy (President)

HALL, USN (Ret.), Rear Adm. Thomas F.

1619 King St.
Alexandria, VA 22314-2793
Tel: (703)548-5800
Fax: (703)683-3647

Employers

Naval Reserve Ass'n (Exec. Director)

HALL, William N.

1400 L St. NW
Washington, DC 20005-3502
Tel: (202)371-5928
Fax: (202)371-5950
EMail: whall@winston.com

Employers

Winston & Strawn (Partner, Environmental Practice)

Clients Represented

On Behalf of Winston & Strawn

Nat'l Paint and Coatings Ass'n

HALLAGAN, John B.

1620 I St. NW
Suite 925
Washington, DC 20006
Tel: (202)293-5800
Fax: (202)463-8998

Employers

The Roberts Group

Clients Represented

On Behalf of The Roberts Group

American Spice and Trade Ass'n
Flavor and Extract Manufacturers Ass'n
Fragrance Materials Ass'n
Internat'l Ass'n of Color Manufacturers

HALLER, G. Keith

8120 Woodmont Ave.
Suite 650
Bethesda, MD 20814
Tel: (301)656-7900
Fax: (301)656-7903

Employers

Potomac Incorporated (President)

HALLER, Susan C.

1150 Connecticut Ave. NW
Suite 700
Washington, DC 20036
Tel: (202)296-8000
Fax: (202)296-8803
Registered: LDA

Employers

Mullenholz, Brimsek & Belair

Clients Represented

On Behalf of Mullenholz, Brimsek & Belair

Center for Civic Education
ChoicePoint
The Coalition on Motor Vehicle Privacy
Constitutional Rights Foundation
Equifax Inc.
First Data Corp./Telecheck
SEARCH Group, Inc.
Street Law Inc.

HALLER, Tracy

701 Pennsylvania Ave. NW
Suite 725
Washington, DC 20004
Tel: (202)638-7429
Fax: (202)628-4763
Registered: LDA

Employers

Novartis Corp. (Director, Federal Government Relations)
Novartis Services, Inc.

HALLETT, Carol B.

1301 Pennsylvania Ave. NW
Suite 1100
Washington, DC 20004-1707
Tel: (202)626-4000
Fax: (202)626-4166
Registered: LDA

Employers

Air Transport Ass'n of America (President and Chief Exec. Officer)

HALLISAY, Paul L.

1625 Massachusetts Ave. NW
Washington, DC 20036
Tel: (202)797-4033
Fax: (202)797-4030
Registered: LDA

Employers

Air Line Pilots Ass'n Internat'l (Director, Government Affairs)

HALLMAN, Kristina

1899 L St. NW
Suite 200
Washington, DC 20036
Tel: (202)833-8121
Fax: (202)833-8155

Employers

Devillier Communications (V. President)

Clients Represented

On Behalf of Devillier Communications

Capital Concerts

HALLMAN, Paul W.

515 King St.
Suite 300
Alexandria, VA 22314
Tel: (703)684-1110
Fax: (703)684-7912
EMail: phallman@multistate.com

Deputy Director, Compliance, Bureau of Product Safety, Food and Drug Administration, 1971-73; Ass't General Counsel, U.S. Consumer Product Safety Commission, 1973-74.

Employers

MultiState Associates (Principal)

HALLORAN, Deirdre

3211 Fourth St. NE
Washington, DC 20017
Tel: (202)541-3300
Fax: (202)541-3337

Employers
United States Catholic Conference (Associate General Counsel)

HALLORAN, James

818 Connecticut Ave. NW
Suite 600
Washington, DC 20006-2702
Tel: (202)466-0671
Fax: (202)466-0684

Employers
Caterpillar Inc. (Washington Manager, Governmental Affairs)

HALLOWAY, Lorraine B.

1001 Pennsylvania Ave. NW
Suite 1100
Washington, DC 20004-2595
Tel: (202)624-2500
Fax: (202)628-5116
Registered: LDA

Trial Attorney, Civil Division, Department of Justice, 1979-80.

Employers
Crowell & Moring LLP (Partner)

Clients Represented

On Behalf of Crowell & Moring LLP
Helicopter Ass'n Internat'l

HALPERIN, Samuel

1836 Jefferson Place NW
Washington, DC 20036
Tel: (202)775-9731
Fax: (202)775-9733

Employers
American Youth Policy Forum (Senior Fellow)

HALPERN, Ilisa

1050 Connecticut Ave. NW
Washington, DC 20036-5339
Tel: (202)857-6000
Fax: (202)857-6395

Served as Aide to Senator Dianne Feinstein (D-CA).

Employers
Arent Fox Kintner Plotkin & Kahn, PLLC (Government Relations Director)

HALPERN, Naomi J. L.

1400 16th St. NW
Suite 400
Washington, DC 20036-2220
EMail: nhalpern@ofwlaw.com
Tel: (202)518-6325
Fax: (202)234-3550

Employers
Olsson, Frank and Weeda, P.C. (Associate)

HALPERT, James J.

1200 19th St. NW
Washington, DC 20036-2430
Tel: (202)861-3938
Fax: (202)223-2085
Registered: LDA

EMail: jim.halpert@piperrudnick.com

Employers
Piper Marbury Rudnick & Wolfe LLP (Partner)

Clients Represented

On Behalf of Piper Marbury Rudnick & Wolfe LLP
AOL Time Warner
Commercial Internet Exchange Ass'n
Direct Marketing Ass'n, Inc.
Individual Reference Services Group
Internat'l Telecommunications, Inc.
Lexis-Nexis
NetCoalition.Com
Omnipoint Corp.
PrimeTEC Internat'l, Inc.
PSINet Inc.
USP&C

HALPIN, Katherine L.

507 C St. NE
Washington, DC 20002-5809
Tel: (202)544-7944
Fax: (202)544-7975
Registered: LDA

EMail: khalpin@beacon-group.net

Employers
Beacon Consulting Group, Inc. (Senior Legislative Assistant)

Clients Represented

On Behalf of Beacon Consulting Group, Inc.
Boston Symphony Orchestra
Carnegie Hall Corp.
Mystic Seaport Museum
Ohio Wesleyan University
Old Sturbridge Village

HALPIN, Peter G.

1120 Connecticut Ave. NW
Suite 1100
Washington, DC 20036
Tel: (202)861-5899
Fax: (202)861-5795
Registered: LDA

EMail: phalpin@gpcusa.com

Managing Director, Congressional and Intergovernmental Affairs, Overseas Private Investment Corp., 1997-2000. Director, Congressional Affairs, Department of Transportation, 1995-97.

Employers
GPC Internat'l (V. President and Managing Director, Federal Relations)

Clients Represented

On Behalf of GPC Internat'l
Alcan Aluminum Corp.
Harbor Philadelphia Center City Office, Ltd.
Puerto Rico, Commonwealth of
YouBet.com

HALPRIN, Albert

555 12th St. NW
Suite 950 North
Washington, DC 20004
Tel: (202)371-9100
Fax: (202)371-1497
Registered: LDA

Served as Director, Common Carrier Bureau, Federal Communications Commission, 1984-87.

Employers
Halprin, Temple, Goodman & Maher (Partner)

Clients Represented

On Behalf of Halprin, Temple, Goodman & Maher
Yellow Pages Publishers Ass'n

HALPRIN, Lawrence P.

1001 G St. NW
Suite 500 West
Washington, DC 20001
EMail: halprin@khlaw.com
Tel: (202)434-4100
Fax: (202)434-4646

Law Clerk to Judge Charles R. Johnston, U.S. Tax Court, 1977-78.

Employers
Keller and Heckman LLP (Partner)

HALSEY, Steven C.

2111 Wilson Blvd.
Suite 600
Arlington, VA 22201
Tel: (703)351-5077
Fax: (703)351-5827
Registered: LDA

EMail: steven@halseyrains.com

Technical Information Specialist, Library and Research Center, The White House, 1985-86.

Employers
Halsey, Rains & Associates, LLC (Managing Member)

Clients Represented

On Behalf of Halsey, Rains & Associates, LLC
American Board of Medical Specialties in Podiatry
American Medical Technologists
American Soc. of Military Comptrollers
Ass'n of Government Accountants
Board for Orthotists/Prosthetist Certification
Cardiovascular Credentialing Internat'l
The Chauncey Group Internat'l
Coalition for Professional Certification
Computer Adaptive Technologies
Internat'l Board of Lactation Consultant Examiners
Internat'l Electrical Testing Ass'n
Nat'l Ass'n of Portable X-Ray Providers
Nat'l Commission for the Certification of Crane Operators
Nat'l Council on Family Relations
Nat'l Institute for Certification in Engineering Technologies
Oklahoma Ass'n Serving Impacted Schools

HALTEMAN, Marsha

1717 K St. NW
Suite 800
Washington, DC 20006
EMail: info@jinsa.org
Tel: (202)833-0020
Fax: (202)296-6452

Employers
Jewish Institute for Nat'l Security Affairs (Director, Corporate and Community Relations)

HALTMEYER, Kris

1310 G St. NW
12th Floor
Washington, DC 20005
Tel: (202)626-4780
Fax: (202)626-4833
Registered: LDA

Employers
Blue Cross Blue Shield Ass'n (Senior Policy Consultant)

HALVERSON, James

1330 Connecticut Ave. NW
Washington, DC 20036-1795
Tel: (202)429-3000
Fax: (202)429-3902
Registered: FARA

EMail: jhalvers@steptoe.com

Director, Bureau of Competition, Federal Trade Commission, 1972-75. Acting General Counsel, Federal Trade Commission, 1972.

Employers
Steptoe & Johnson LLP (Partner)

HALVORSEN, Jerald V.

Ten G St. NE
Suite 700
Washington, DC 20002
Tel: (202)216-5900
Fax: (202)216-0870

Employers
Interstate Natural Gas Ass'n of America (President)

HAM, Douglas B.

P.O. Box 50037
Arlington, VA 22205
Tel: (703)536-2956
Fax: (703)241-0539
Registered: LDA

EMail: dham@dbhcon.com

Acting Administrator (1992-93) and Deputy Administrator (1989-93), Research and Special Programs Administration, Department of Transportation. Professional Staff Member, Senate and House of Representatives, 1977-86.

Employers
DBH Consulting

Clients Represented

On Behalf of DBH Consulting
Alcalde & Fay

HAM, Shane

600 Pennsylvania Ave. SE
Suite 400
Washington, DC 20003
EMail: sham@dlcppi.org
Tel: (202)547-0001
Fax: (202)544-5014

Employers
Progressive Policy Institute (Technology Policy Analyst)

HAMAD, Said

1717 K St. NW
Suite 407
Washington, DC 20036
Tel: (202)785-8394
Fax: (202)887-5337
Registered: LDA

EMail: shamad9950@aol.com

Employers
PLO Mission (Deputy Chief of Mission)

HAMANN, Jennifer

441-E Carlisle Dr.
Herndon, VA 20170-4802
Tel: (703)709-2293
Fax: (703)709-2296

Employers
Safari Club Internat'l (Legislative Assistant)

HAMBEL, John

159 D St. SE
Washington, DC 20003
Tel: (202)547-7566
Fax: (202)546-8630
Registered: LDA

Employers
Kehoe & Hambel

Clients Represented

On Behalf of Kehoe & Hambel
Niche Plan Sponsors, Inc.

HAMBERGER, Edward R.

50 F St. NW
12th Floor
Washington, DC 20001
Tel: (202)639-2525
Fax: (202)639-2526
Registered: LDA

Assistant Secretary for Government Affairs, Department of Transportation, 1988-89. Counsel and Executive Director, House Republican Policy Committee, 1979-80. Staff Aide to Senator Hugh Scott (R-PA), 1970-76.

Employers
Ass'n of American Railroads (President and Chief Exec. Officer)

HAMBERGER, Martin G.

227 Massachusetts Ave. NE
Suite One
Washington, DC 20002
Tel: (202)548-8470
Fax: (202)548-8472
Registered: LDA
EMail: mghamberger@fortessa.com

Former Chief of Staff to Senator Hugh Scott, Jr. (R-PA).

Employers
Martin G. Hamberger & Associates (President)

Clients Represented

On Behalf of Martin G. Hamberger & Associates
American Public Transportation Ass'n
Michael Baker Corp.
Eschenbach USA, Inc.
Fortessa, Inc.
GATCO of VA, Inc.
Northrop Grumman Corp.
Westinghouse Government Services Group

HAMBLEY, Winthrop D.

20th and C Sts. NW
MS: 2125
Washington, DC 20551
Tel: (202)452-3352
Fax: (202)452-2611

Employers
Federal Reserve System (Deputy Congressional Liaison)

HAMBRICK, Edith

1050 Connecticut Ave. NW
Washington, DC 20036-5339
Tel: (202)857-6000
Fax: (202)857-6395

Employers
Arent Fox Kintner Plotkin & Kahn, PLLC (Associate)

Clients Represented

On Behalf of Arent Fox Kintner Plotkin & Kahn, PLLC
American Ass'n of Physician Specialists

HAMBURG, Richard S.

1150 Connecticut Ave. NW
Suite 810
Washington, DC 20036
Tel: (202)785-7900
Fax: (202)785-7950
Registered: LDA
EMail: rhamburg@heart.org

Employers
American Heart Ass'n (Director, Government Relations)

HAMBURGER, Margaret

1747 Pennsylvania Ave. NW
7th Floor
Washington, DC 20006
Tel: (202)296-4810
Fax: (202)296-4811

Former Assistant Secretary for Planning and Evaluation, Department of Health and Human Services.

Employers
Nuclear Threat Initiative (V. President for Biological Programs)

HAMBURGER, Paul

600 13th St. NW
Washington, DC 20005-3096
Tel: (202)756-8306
Fax: (202)756-8087
Registered: LDA
EMail: phamburger@mwe.com

Employers
McDermott, Will and Emery (Partner)

Clients Represented

On Behalf of McDermott, Will and Emery
Applied Benefits Research Corp.

HAMBY, Martha R.

1101 Connecticut Ave. NW
Suite 800
Washington, DC 20036
Tel: (202)463-0600
Fax: (202)463-0606
Registered: LDA
EMail: mhamby@surety.org

Employers
Surety Ass'n of America (V. President)

HAMBY, Zhi Marie

9200 Centerway Rd.
Gaithersburg, MD 20879
Tel: (301)840-6642
Fax: (301)840-8502
EMail: zhi@nmia.org

Employers
Nat'l Military Intelligence Ass'n (Exec. Director)
Operations Security Professionals Soc. (Exec. Director)
Real Trends (President)

Clients Represented

On Behalf of Real Trends
CyberWynd Publications
Nat'l Military Intelligence Ass'n
Operations Security Professionals Soc.

HAMELBURG, Mark

1255 23rd St. NW
Suite 250
Washington, DC 20037
Tel: (202)263-3900
Fax: (202)296-0909
Registered: LDA

Employers
William M. Mercer, Inc. (Attorney)

Clients Represented

On Behalf of William M. Mercer, Inc.
Nat'l Ass'n of Manufacturers

HAMER, Glenn

1616 H St. NW
Suite 800
Washington, DC 20006-4999
Tel: (202)628-7979
Fax: (202)628-7779

Employers
Solar Energy Industries Ass'n (SEIA) (Exec. Director)

HAMILTON, Charles A.

5025 Overlook Rd. NW
Washington, DC 20016-1911
Tel: (202)237-8142
Fax: (202)237-8146
Registered: LDA
EMail: cahallc@worldnet.att.net

Deputy Director, Strategic Trade, Office of the Secretary, Department of Defense, 1982-90. Executive Assistant, Office of the Chairman, U.S. International Trade Commission, 1971-81. Assistant to the Secretary for Congressional Liaison, Department of Interior, 1970-71.

Employers
Charles A. Hamilton Associates LLC (President)

Clients Represented

On Behalf of Charles A. Hamilton Associates LLC
Airbus Industrie of North America, Inc.

HAMILTON, David

1200 18th St. NW
Suite 900
Washington, DC 20036
Tel: (202)857-0666
Fax: (202)331-9588
Registered: LDA

Employers
Alliance to Save Energy (Director, State and Federal Policy)

HAMILTON, Heather

1200 19th St. NW
Washington, DC 20036-2430
Tel: (202)861-3900
Fax: (202)223-2085

Employers
Piper Marbury Rudnick & Wolfe LLP
World Federalist Ass'n (ICC Project Director)

Clients Represented

On Behalf of Piper Marbury Rudnick & Wolfe LLP
NetCoalition.Com

HAMILTON, James

3000 K St. NW
Suite 300
Washington, DC 20007
Tel: (202)424-7500
Fax: (202)424-7643
Registered: LDA

Member, Investigative Task Force, General Accounting Office, 1985. Special Counsel, Subcommittee on Human Resources, House Committee on the Post Office and Civil Service, 1983-84. Assistant Chief Counsel, Senate Select Committee on Presidential Campaign Activities, 1973-74.

Employers
Swidler Berlin Shereff Friedman, LLP (Partner)

Clients Represented

On Behalf of Swidler Berlin Shereff Friedman, LLP
American Bakers Ass'n
Artichoke Enterprises, Inc.
Nat'l Housing and Rehabilitation Ass'n
Shakopee Mdewakanton Sioux Tribe
WRD Venture/NWD Venture

HAMILTON, John

1523 New Hampshire Ave. NW
Washington, DC 20036
Tel: (202)588-0002
Fax: (202)785-2669
Registered: LDA
EMail: john.hamilton@ucop.edu

Legislative Assistant to Rep. Jerome B. "Bob" Traxler (D-MI), 1990-92.

Employers
University of California, Office of Federal Government Relations (Legislative Director)

HAMILTON, Katherine

3225 N. Pershing Dr.
Arlington, VA 22201
Tel: (703)516-4444
Fax: (703)516-4444
Registered: LDA

Employers
Katherine Hamilton

Clients Represented

On Behalf of Katherine Hamilton
American Bioenergy Ass'n
Bob Lawrence & Associates
Midwest Research Institute

HAMILTON, Larry

1000 Wilson Blvd.
Suite 2300
Arlington, VA 22209
Tel: (703)875-8400
Fax: (703)243-3190

Employers
Northrop Grumman Corp. (Director, Washington Public Affairs)

HAMILTON, Parker

600 Pennsylvania Ave. SE
Suite 301
Washington, DC 20003
Tel: (202)608-1411
Fax: (202)608-1429

Employers
College Republican Nat'l Committee (Exec. Director)

HAMILTON, Philip W.

1828 L St. NW
Suite 906
Washington, DC 20036
Tel: (202)785-3756
Fax: (202)429-9417
EMail: hamiltonp@asme.org

Employers
American Soc. of Mechanical Engineers (Managing Director, Public Affairs)

HAMILTON, Rae M.

1300 N. 17th St.
Suite 1847
Rosslyn, VA 22209
Tel: (703)841-3256
Fax: (703)841-3356
EMail: rae_hamilton@nema.org

Employers
Nat'l Electrical Manufacturers Ass'n (V. President, Communications and Publications)

HAMILTON, Stephen W.

1440 New York Ave. NW
Washington, DC 20005
Tel: (202)371-7000
Fax: (202)393-5760

Employers
Skadden, Arps, Slate, Meagher & Flom LLP (Partner)

HAMLIN, Charles E.

1735 New York Ave. NW
Washington, DC 20006
Tel: (202)626-7300
Fax: (202)626-7365
EMail: chamlin@aia.org

Employers
The American Institute of Architects (Managing Director, Communications)

HAMM, Peter

1199 N. Fairfax St.
Suite 1000
Alexandria, VA 22314
Tel: (703)299-4499
Fax: (703)299-4488
EMail: phamm@hawthorngroup.com
Formerly at Department of Labor.

Employers
The Hawthorn Group, L.C. (V. President)

HAMM, Ron

1130 Connecticut Ave. NW
Suite 300
Washington, DC 20036
Tel: (202)331-8500
Fax: (202)331-1598
Registered: LDA
EMail: rhamm@tfgnet.com

Employers
The Ferguson Group, LLC (Senior Associate)

Clients Represented
On Behalf of The Ferguson Group, LLC
Alabama A & M University
Stop It Now!

HAMMELMAN, Suzanne

1199 N. Fairfax St.
Suite 1000
Alexandria, VA 22314
Tel: (703)299-4499
Fax: (703)299-4488
EMail: shammelman@hawthorngroup.com

Employers
The Hawthorn Group, L.C. (V. President)

Clients Represented
On Behalf of The Hawthorn Group, L.C.
Georgia-Pacific Corp.

HAMMER, Amy R.

2001 Pennsylvania Ave. NW
Suite 300
Washington, DC 20006
Tel: (202)862-0216
Fax: (202)862-0267

Employers
Exxon Mobil Corp. (Washington Representative, U.S. Senate)

HAMMER, John H.

21 Dupont Circle NW
Suite 604
Washington, DC 20036
Tel: (202)296-4994
Fax: (202)872-0884
Registered: LDA
EMail: jhammer@cni.org

Employers
Nat'l Humanities Alliance (Director)

HAMMER, Nancy

699 Prince St.
Alexandria, VA 22314-3175
Tel: (703)235-3900
Fax: (703)274-2222

Employers
Nat'l Center for Missing and Exploited Children (General Counsel)

HAMMER, Thomas A.

3231 Valley Lane
Falls Church, VA 22044
Tel: (703)532-9360
Fax: (703)532-9361

Employers
Hammer & Co. (President)
Sweetener Users Ass'n (President)

Clients Represented
On Behalf of Hammer & Co.
Sweetener Users Ass'n

HAMMON, Wayne L.

415 Second St. NE
Suite 300
Washington, DC 20002-4993
Tel: (202)547-7800
Fax: (202)546-2638
Registered: LDA

Employers
Nat'l Ass'n of Wheat Growers (Director, Government Relations)

HAMMOND, David C.

1001 Pennsylvania Ave. NW
Suite 600
Washington, DC 20004
Tel: (202)347-0066
Fax: (202)624-7222
EMail: dhammond@pgfm.com

Employers
Powell, Goldstein, Frazer & Murphy LLP (Partner)

HAMMOND, Keith

122 C St. NW
Suite 240
Washington, DC 20001
Tel: (202)546-2215
Fax: (202)544-5197
Registered: LDA

Employers
Southern Utah Wilderness Alliance

HAMMOND, Mike

8001 Forbes Pl.
Suite 102
Springfield, VA 22151
Tel: (703)321-8585
Fax: (703)321-8408
Registered: LDA

Employers
Gun Owners of America (Counsel)

HAMMOND, Ross

1707 L St. NW
Suite 800
Washington, DC 20036
Tel: (202)296-5469
Fax: (202)296-5427

Employers
Campaign for Tobacco-Free Kids (Latin American Specialist)

HAMMOND-CHAMBERS, Rupert

1700 N. Moore St.
Suite 1703
Arlington, VA 22209
Tel: (703)465-2930
Fax: (703)465-2937

Employers
US-ROC (Taiwan) Business Council (President)

HAMMONDS, Timothy M.

655 15th St. NW
Washington, DC 20005-5701
Tel: (202)452-8444
Fax: (202)429-4519
Registered: LDA
EMail: thammonds@fmi.org

Employers
Food Marketing Institute (President and Chief Exec. Officer)

HAMOR, Kathy V.

1300 Pennsylvania Ave. NW
Suite 700
Washington, DC 20024
Tel: (202)204-3004
Fax: (202)204-3026
Registered: LDA
EMail: khamor@savingscoalition.org

Employers
Savings Coalition of America (Exec. Director)

HAMPARIAN, Aram

888 17th St. NW
Suite 904
Washington, DC 20006
Tel: (202)775-1918
Fax: (202)775-1918

Employers
Armenian Nat'l Committee of America (Exec. Director)

HAMPE, Carl W.

1615 L St. NW
Suite 1300
Washington, DC 20036
Tel: (202)223-7426
Fax: (202)223-7420
Registered: LDA
EMail: champe@paulweiss.com
Deputy Assistant Attorney General , Office of Legislative Affairs, Department of Justice, 1992-93. Minority Counsel, Subcommittee on Immigration and Refugee Affairs, Senate Judiciary Committee, 1983-92.

Employers
Paul, Weiss, Rifkind, Wharton & Garrison (Of Counsel)

Clients Represented
On Behalf of Paul, Weiss, Rifkind, Wharton & Garrison
Alliance of Motion Picture & Television Producers
Bouchard Transportation Co.
Commission on Graduates of Foreign Nursing Schools
The Devereux Foundation
Federation of Korean Industries
General Atlantic Service Corp.
IBP, Inc.
INTELSAT - Internat'l Telecommunications Satellite Organization
Nat'l Music Publishers' Ass'n
SpaceData Internat'l

HAMPTON, Frank R.

1399 New York Ave. NW
Eighth Floor
Washington, DC 20005-4711
Tel: (202)434-8400
Fax: (202)434-8456
Registered: LDA
EMail: fhampton@bondmarkets.com
Former Legislative Director and Legislative Assistant to Rep. Bill Archer (R-TX).

Employers
The Bond Market Ass'n (V. President, Legislative Affairs)

HAMPTON, Maura

805 15th St. NW
Suite 300
Washington, DC 20005-2207
Tel: (202)682-4200
Fax: (202)682-9054
Registered: LDA

Employers
Credit Union Nat'l Ass'n, Inc. (Manager, House Legislative Affairs)

HAMPTON, Ronald E.

3251 Mount Pleasant St. NW
Washington, DC 20010
Tel: (202)986-2070
Fax: (202)986-0410

Employers
Nat'l Black Police Ass'n (Exec. Director)

HAMRE, Dr. John J.

1800 K St. NW
Washington, DC 20005
Tel: (202)775-3227
Fax: (202)775-3199
EMail: jhamre@csis.org
Deputy Secretary (1997-99) and Undersecretary (1993-97) of Defense. Professional Staff Member, Senate Committee on Armed Services, 1984-93. Deputy Assistant Director for National Affairs, Congressional Budget Office, 1978-84.

Employers
Center for Strategic and Internat'l Studies (President and Chief Exec. Officer)

HAMRICK, David

444 N. Capitol St. NW
Suite 230
Washington, DC 20001
Tel: (202)624-7724
Fax: (202)624-5495

Employers
Delaware, Washington Office of the State of (Director, Washington Office)

HAMRICK, Mary Moore

1001 Pennsylvania Ave. NW
Suite 580 North
Washington, DC 20004-2505
Tel: (202)783-1354
Fax: (202)393-2769
Registered: LDA

Employers
New York Life Insurance Co. (V. President, Government Relations)

HAN, Joanna S.

2099 Pennsylvania Ave. NW
Suite 100
Washington, DC 20006
Tel: (202)955-3000
Fax: (202)955-5564
Registered: LDA
EMail: jshan@hklaw.com

Employers
Holland & Knight LLP (Associate)

Clients Represented
On Behalf of Holland & Knight LLP
Nat'l Coalition of Minority Businesses
Texaco Group Inc.

HANADA, Yuko

196 Van Buren St.
Suite 450
Herndon, VA 20170
Tel: (703)456-2562
Fax: (703)456-2551

Employers
Nissan North America Inc. (Analyst, Government Affairs)

HANAGAN, Mary Dreape

112 S. West St.
Suite 310
Alexandria, VA 22314
Tel: (703)684-8880
Fax: (703)836-5256

Employers
Americans for Free Internat'l Trade (AFIT PAC) (Exec. Director)

HANCE, Kenneth G.

401 Ninth St. NW
Suite 900
Washington, DC 20004
Tel: (202)585-8000
Fax: (202)585-8080
Registered: LDA
EMail: khance@nixonpeabody.com

Employers
Nixon Peabody LLP (Partner)

HANCE, Hon. Kent R.

1150 17th St. NW
Suite 601
Washington, DC 20036
Tel: (202)296-2638
Fax: (202)296-9266
Registered: LDA
Member, U.S. House of Representatives, 1979-85.

Employers
Hance, Scarborough & Wright (Partner)

Clients Represented
On Behalf of Hance, Scarborough & Wright
American Soc. of Ass'n Executives

HANCOCK, Charles C.

9650 Rockville Pike
Bethesda, MD 20814
Tel: (301)530-7145
Fax: (301)571-1824

Employers
American Soc. for Biochemistry and Molecular Biology (Exec. Officer)

HANCOCK, J. B.

2111 Wilson Blvd.
Eighth Floor
Arlington, VA 22201-3058
Tel: (703)841-0626
Fax: (703)243-2874
EMail: hancock@alcalde-fay.com

Employers
Alcalde & Fay (Partner)

Clients Represented
On Behalf of Alcalde & Fay
CORFAC, Internat'l
E.ssociation
Office of Naval Research

HAND, Lloyd N.

901 15th St. NW
Suite 700
Washington, DC 20005-2301
Tel: (202)371-6000
Fax: (202)371-6279
Registered: LDA
Chief of Protocol, Department of State, 1965-66. Assistant to Senate Majority Leader and V. President Lyndon B. Johnson, 1957-61.

Employers
Verner, Liipfert, Bernhard, McPherson and Hand, Chartered (Member of Firm)

Clients Represented
On Behalf of Verner, Liipfert, Bernhard, McPherson and Hand, Chartered
GenCorp
Lockheed Martin Tactical Systems
MBIA Insurance Corp.
Merrill Lynch & Co., Inc.
Newport News Shipbuilding Inc.
Northwest Airlines, Inc.
Oerlikon Aerospace, Inc.
Peterson Cos., Inc.
Sarnoff Corp.
Stewart & Stevenson Services, Inc.
Virginia Commonwealth Trading Co.

HANDLESMAN, Jacob

1111 19th St. NW
Suite 800
Washington, DC 20036
Tel: (202)463-2700
Fax: (202)463-2785
Registered: LDA
EMail: jacob_handlesman@afandpa.org

Employers
American Forest & Paper Ass'n (Director, International Research)

HANDLOS, Brian

1101 Connecticut Ave. NW
Suite 1000
Washington, DC 20036
Tel: (202)828-2400
Fax: (202)828-2488
Registered: LDA

Employers
Kutak Rock LLP

Clients Represented
On Behalf of Kutak Rock LLP
First Nat'l of Nebraska

HANEN, Laura

444 N. Capitol St. NW
Suite 339
Washington, DC 20001
Tel: (202)434-8091
Fax: (202)434-8092

Employers
Nat'l Alliance of State and Territorial AIDS Directors (Director, Government Relations)

HANEY, Hance

1020 19th St. NW
Washington, DC 20036
Tel: (202)429-0303
Fax: (202)293-0561
Registered: LDA

Employers
Qwest Communications (Exec. Director, Regulatory Affairs)

HANEY, Mark

1317 F St. NW
Third Floor
Washington, DC 20004
Tel: (202)955-6155
Fax: (202)955-5786

Employers
Internat'l Business and Economic Research Corp. (President)

HANEY, Peggy

801 Pennsylvania Ave.
Suite 650
Washington, DC 20004
Tel: (202)624-0761
Fax: (202)624-0775
Registered: LDA
EMail: peggy.haney@aexp.com

Employers
American Express Co. (V. President, Public Responsibility)

HANKA, William W.

1130 Connecticut Ave. NW
Suite 300
Washington, DC 20036
Tel: (202)331-8500
Fax: (202)331-1598
Registered: LDA
Investigative Counsel, House Government Reform Committee, 1997-98. Legislative Director to Rep. George Nethercutt (R-WA), 1995-97. Deputy Director of Legislative Affairs, Office of the V. President, Executive Office of the President, The White House, 1989-93. Assistant to the Minority Counsel, Senate Labor Subcommittee, 1987-89.

Employers
The Ferguson Group, LLC (Principal)
McConnell/Ferguson Group

HANKIN, Christopher G.

1300 I St. NW
Suite 420 East
Washington, DC 20005
Tel: (202)326-7520
Fax: (202)326-7525

Employers
Sun Microsystems (Director, Federal Affairs)

HANKS, Sara

607 14th St. NW
Washington, DC 20005
Tel: (202)434-0700
Fax: (202)912-6000
Former Chief of Internat'l Corporate Finance, Securities and Exchange Commission.

Employers
Rogers & Wells (Partner, Latin American Division)

HANLEY, John

One Thomas Circle NW
Suite 400
Washington, DC 20005
Tel: (202)659-8111
Fax: (202)659-9216
Registered: LDA

Employers
Independent Community Bankers of America (Legislative Counsel)

HANLON, Blake

1730 K St. NW
Suite 1106
Washington, DC 20006
Tel: (202)466-3561
Fax: (202)466-3583

Employers
Household Financial Group, Ltd. (Federal Director)

HANLON, Patrick M.

1800 Massachusetts Ave. NW
Washington, DC 20036
Tel: (202)828-2000
Fax: (202)828-2195
Registered: LDA
Law Clerk to Chief Judge Irving R. Kaufman, U.S. Court of Appeals, Second Circuit, 1976-77.

Employers
Shea & Gardner (Partner)

Clients Represented
On Behalf of Shea & Gardner
Center for Claims Resolution
Internat'l Federation of Inspection Agencies, North American Committee
SGS Government Programs, Inc.
SGS North America, Inc.
Societe Generale de Surveillance Holding S.A.

HANLON, William R.

1800 Massachusetts Ave. NW
Washington, DC 20036
Tel: (202)828-2000
Fax: (202)828-2195
Law Clerk to Judge Arlin M. Adams, U.S. Court of Appeals, Third Circuit, 1979-80.

Employers
Shea & Gardner (Partner)

Clients Represented
On Behalf of Shea & Gardner
Center for Claims Resolution

HANNAFORD, Peter D.

1299 Pennsylvania Ave. NW
Suite 800 West
Washington, DC 20004
Tel: (202)785-0500
Fax: (202)785-5277

Employers
The Carmen Group (Public Relations Counsel)

HANNAPEL, Jeff

1120 Connecticut Ave. NW
Suite 490
Washington, DC 20036
Tel: (202)457-0670
Fax: (202)457-0638

Employers
The Policy Group (V. President)

HANNAWAY, Jane

2100 M St. NW
Washington, DC 20037
Tel: (202)833-7200
Fax: (202)429-0687

Employers
The Urban Institute (Director, Education Policy Center)

HANNEGAN, Timothy

1317 F St. NW
Suite 600
Washington, DC 20004
Tel: (202)638-2121
Fax: (202)638-7045
Registered: LDA
EMail: hannegan@wexlergroup.com

Employers
The Wexler Group (Principal/Senior Director)

Clients Represented

On Behalf of The Wexler Group

Air Transport Ass'n of America
American Airlines
British Airways Plc
Chattanooga Metropolitan Airport Authority
Mammoth Mountain
Midwest Express Airlines
ORBITZ

HANNEMAN, Richard L.

700 N. Fairfax St. Tel: (703)549-4648
Suite 600 Fax: (703)548-2194
Alexandria, VA 22314-2040
EMail: Hanneman_Dick@salthinstitute.org

Employers

Salt Institute (President)

HANNES, Steven P.

600 13th St. NW Tel: (202)756-8218
Washington, DC 20005-3096 Fax: (202)756-8087
EMail: shannes@mwe.com
Associate International Tax Counsel, Office of Assistant Secretary for Tax Policy, Department of the Treasury, 1976-82; Attorney, Internal Revenue Service, 1971-76.

Employers

McDermott, Will and Emery (Partner)

HANNETT, Frederick J.

1350 I St. NW Tel: (202)638-6012
Suite 870 Fax: (202)737-1947
Washington, DC 20005 Registered: LDA

Employers

The Capitol Alliance (Managing Principal)
Hannett & Associates (President)
Managed Care Compliance Solutions, Inc. (Principal)

Clients Represented

On Behalf of Hannett & Associates

Amerigroup Corp.
Anthem Alliance
Healtheon/Web MD
Kaiser Permanente

HANNON, Sandra

1615 L St. NW Tel: (202)659-0330
Suite 1000 Fax: (202)296-6119
Washington, DC 20036

Employers

Fleishman-Hillard, Inc (V. President)

HANRAHAN, Kathleen

4733 Bethesda Ave. Tel: (301)656-0003
Suite 750 Fax: (301)907-0878
Bethesda, MD 20814

Employers

Nat'l Foundation for Infectious Diseases (Director, Special Projects)

HANRAHAN, Hon. Robert P.

7268 Evans Mill Rd. Tel: (703)448-0931
McLean, VA 22101-3423 Fax: (703)448-1141
Registered: LDA
Deputy Assistant Secretary, Department of Education, 1975-77. Member, U.S. House of Representatives (R-IL), 1973-75.

Employers

Advantage Associates, Inc. (Partner)
RPH & Associates, L.L.C. (President)

Clients Represented

On Behalf of Advantage Associates, Inc.

Esat, Inc.
Professional Services Council

On Behalf of RPH & Associates, L.L.C.

Advantage Associates, Inc.
Fon Digital Network Clearpoint Communications, Inc.
Hello Arabia Corp.

HANSBERGER, Patricia B.

9000 Rockville Pike Tel: (301)496-3471
Bldg. One, Room 244 Fax: (301)496-0840
Bethesda, MD 20892
EMail: brandtp@od.nih.gov

Employers

Department of Health and Human Services - Nat'l Institutes of Health (Legislative Analyst)

HANSELL, Herbert J.

51 Louisiana Ave. NW Tel: (202)879-3939
Washington, DC 20001 Fax: (202)626-1700
EMail: hjhansell@jonesday.com
Legal Advisor, Department of State, 1977-79.

Employers

Jones, Day, Reavis & Pogue (Senior Counsel)

Clients Represented

On Behalf of Jones, Day, Reavis & Pogue

China, Embassy of the People's Republic of

HANSELL, Jr., William H.

777 N. Capitol St. NE Tel: (202)289-4262
Suite 500 Fax: (202)962-3500
Washington, DC 20002-4201

Employers

Internat'l City/County Management Ass'n (Exec. Director)

HANSEN, Charles M.

2600 Virginia Ave. NW Tel: (202)333-2524
Suite 600 Fax: (202)338-5950
Washington, DC 20037 Registered: LDA
Former Director of Congressional Liaison, International Trade Commission and former Legislative Aide to Senator Lloyd Bentsen (D-TX).

Employers

Nat'l Environmental Strategies

HANSEN, Christopher W.

1200 Wilson Blvd. Tel: (703)465-3602
Arlington, VA 22209-1989 Fax: (703)465-3044
Registered: LDA

Employers

The Boeing Co. (Senior V. President, Government Relations)

HANSEN, Gregory L.

1755 Jefferson Davis Hwy. Tel: (703)415-0344
Suite 1107 Fax: (703)415-0182
Arlington, VA 22202 Registered: LDA

Employers

The PMA Group (Associate)

Clients Represented

On Behalf of The PMA Group

ADSIL
Advanced Acoustic Concepts, Inc.
AEPTEC
ARC Global Technologies
Caterpillar Inc.
Coronado, California, City of
CPU Technology
FLIR Systems, Inc.
B. F. Goodrich Co.
Innovative Productivity, Inc.
L-3 Communications Corp.
Lockheed Martin Federal Systems
MTS Systems Inc.
Northrop Marine
Orange Shipbuilding Co., Inc.
Titan Corp.

HANSEN, Jake

444 N. Capitol St. NW Tel: (202)393-6599
Suite 722 Fax: (202)638-3386
Washington, DC 20001-0000 Registered: LDA

Employers

Barr Laboratories (V. President, Government Affairs)

HANSEN, Jay

5100 Forbes Blvd. Tel: (301)731-4748
Suite 200 Fax: (301)731-4621
Lanham, MD 20706

Employers

Nat'l Asphalt Pavement Ass'n (V. President, Government Affairs)

HANSEN, Joseph T.

1775 K St. NW Tel: (202)223-3111
Washington, DC 20006 Fax: (202)466-1562

Employers

United Food and Commercial Workers Internat'l Union (International Secretary and Treasurer)

HANSEN, Kenneth

1200 New Hampshire Ave. NW Tel: (202)974-5600
Washington, DC 20036 Fax: (202)974-5602
EMail: kenneth.hansen@chadbourne.com

Employers

Chadbourne and Parke LLP (Partner)

HANSEN, Kip L.

1215 Jefferson Davis Hwy. Tel: (703)416-8000
Suite 1004 Fax: (703)416-8010
Arlington, VA 22202 Registered: LDA

Employers

DRS Technologies, Inc. (V. President, Government Relations)

HANSEN, Linda

1341 G St. NW Tel: (202)347-5990
Suite 200 Fax: (202)347-5941
Washington, DC 20005 Registered: LDA
EMail: lihansen@clj.com

Employers

Copeland, Lowery & Jacquez (Assistant)

HANSEN, Paul W.

707 Conservation Ln. Tel: (301)548-0150
Gaithersburg, MD 20878 Fax: (301)548-0149
EMail: phansen@iwla.org

Employers

Izaak Walton League of America (Exec. Director)

HANSEN, Suzanne

401 Wythe St. Tel: (703)684-1355
Alexandria, VA 22314 Fax: (703)684-1589
EMail: shansen@nachri.org

Employers

Nat'l Ass'n of Children's Hospitals Inc. (Director, Medicaid and State Policy)

HANSEN, William D.

1155 15th St. NW Tel: (202)466-8621
Suite 801 Fax: (202)466-8643
Washington, DC 20005 Registered: LDA
Former Assistant Secretary of Education.

Employers

Education Finance Council (Exec. Director)

HANSEN-KUHN, Karen

927 15th St. NW Tel: (202)898-1566
Fourth Floor Fax: (202)898-1612
Washington, DC 20005

Employers

Development Group for Alternative Policies (Latin American Coordinator)

HANSON, Eric R.

1055 N. Fairfax St. Tel: (703)739-7999
Suite 201 Fax: (703)739-7995
Alexandria, VA 22314-3563

Employers

U.S. Strategies Corp. (Chief Exec. Officer)

HANSON, Heidi

1055 N. Fairfax St. Tel: (703)739-7999
Suite 201 Fax: (703)739-7995
Alexandria, VA 22314-3563 Registered: LDA
EMail: heidih@usstrategies.com

Employers

U.S. Strategies Corp. (Senior V. President, Public Affairs)

Clients Represented

On Behalf of U.S. Strategies Corp.

AdvoServe
Harrah's Entertainment, Inc.
Healthsouth Corp.
Home Access Health
Integrated Health Services, Inc.
JRL Enterprises
Nat'l Ass'n of Community Health Centers
Palm Beach, Florida, County of

HANSON, Jennifer

729 15th St. NW
Third Floor
Washington, DC 20005
EMail: jhanson@bonnergrp.com
Tel: (202)737-5877
Fax: (202)737-6061

Employers
Bonner Group, Inc. (Political Director)

HANSON, Jodi L.

888 Sixteenth St. NW
Seventh Floor
Washington, DC 20006-4103
Tel: (202)835-8225
Fax: (202)835-8136
Registered: LDA
Former Legislative Assistant, House of Representatives.

Employers
Foley & Lardner (Lobbyist)

Clients Represented

On Behalf of Foley & Lardner

AAAE-ACI
Canadian Nat'l Railway Co.
ComEd
Bruce Givner, Attorney
Grand Trunk Corp.
Illinois Housing Development Authority
Illinois Institute of Technology
Kerr-McGee Corp.
Nat'l Realty Committee
Northwestern Memorial Hospital
PG&E Nat'l Energy Group
USAA - United Services Automobile Ass'n
YouBet.com

HANSON, John N.

1350 I St. NW
Suite 700
Washington, DC 20005
Tel: (202)789-6000
Fax: (202)789-6190
Assistant Chief, Enforcement, Civil Division (1978-79) and Trial Attorney (1972-77), Department of Justice.

Employers
Beveridge & Diamond, P.C. (Partner)

HANSON, Marshall A.

1619 King St.
Alexandria, VA 22314-2793
Tel: (703)548-5800
Fax: (703)683-3647
Registered: LDA
EMail: info@navy-reserve.org

Employers
Naval Reserve Ass'n (Legislative Director)

HANSON, Robert

1500 Pennsylvania Ave. NW
MS: 1322
Washington, DC 20220
Tel: (202)622-1776

Employers
Department of Treasury - Tax Policy (Deputy Tax Legislative Counsel for Regulatory Affairs)

HAQUE, Bradley O.

1676 International Dr.
McLean, VA 22102
Tel: (703)891-7500
Fax: (703)891-7501
Registered: LDA

Employers
Akin, Gump, Strauss, Hauer & Feld, L.L.P. (Associate)

HARACZNAK, Stephen R.

1255 23rd St. NW
Suite 200
Washington, DC 20037-1174
EMail: stevenh@hauck.com
Tel: (202)452-8100
Fax: (202)833-3636

Employers
American Ambulance Ass'n (Exec. V. President)
Hauck and Associates (Account Exec.)

HARADA, Daisaku

1001 Connecticut Ave. NW
Suite 425
Washington, DC 20036
Tel: (202)955-5663
Fax: (202)955-6125

Employers
Japan Productivity Center for Socio-Economic Development (Senior Advisor)

HARAHAN, Samuel F.

1717 K St. NW
Suite 510
Washington, DC 20036
EMail: harahan@courtexcellence.org
Tel: (202)785-5917
Fax: (202)785-5922

Employers
Council for Court Excellence (Exec. Director)

HARBISON, Stacy

1050 Connecticut Ave. NW
Washington, DC 20036-5339
Tel: (202)857-6000
Fax: (202)857-6395
Registered: LDA
Former Legislative Aide to Senator Bill Frist (R-TN).

Employers
Arent Fox Kintner Plotkin & Kahn, PLLC (Government Relations Director)

Clients Represented

On Behalf of Arent Fox Kintner Plotkin & Kahn, PLLC

American Ass'n of Bioanalysts
American College of Nurse Practitioners
American Hospital Ass'n
Amputee Coalition
Arthritis Foundation
Ass'n of Pain Management Anesthesiologist
Datahr Rehabilitation Institute
Epilepsy Foundation of America
Exeter Architectural Products
Lakeland Regional Medical Center
Landmine Survivors
Medix Pharmaceuticals
Middlesex Hospital Home Care
Nat'l Ass'n of Pediatric Nurse Associates and Practitioners
Nat'l Ass'n of School Nurses
Prevent Blindness America
Priority Care
Sabolich Research & Development
Soc. for Vascular Surgery
Soc. of Diagnostic Medical Sonographers
Soc. of Vascular Technology
State University of New York (SUNY)

HARCAR, Mary

1111 19th St. NW
Suite 800
Washington, DC 20036
Tel: (202)463-2700
Fax: (202)463-2785
Registered: LDA

Employers
American Forest & Paper Ass'n (Director, Tax Policy)

HARDEN, Krysta

600 Pennsylvania Ave. SE
Suite 320
Washington, DC 20003
EMail: kharden@gordley.com
Tel: (202)969-8900
Fax: (202)331-7036
Registered: LDA
Former Staff Director, House Agriculture Peanuts and Tobacco Subcommittee.

Employers
Gordley Associates (Associate)

Clients Represented

On Behalf of Gordley Associates

American Soybean Ass'n
Iowa Pork Producers Ass'n
Nat'l Barley Growers Ass'n
Nat'l Sunflower Ass'n

HARDIMAN, Michael

508 First St. SE
Washington, DC 20003

Employers
Constitution PAC

HARDIN, Charles G.

3124 N. Tenth St.
Arlington, VA 22201
Tel: (703)243-7400
Fax: (703)243-7403
Registered: LDA
EMail: chardin@govreform.org
Former Assistant Secretary of Governmental Affairs, U.S. Department of Transportation. Former Staff Director of the Appropriations Subcommittee on Transportation, U.S. Senate. Former Professional Staff Member to the Appropriations Committee, U.S. House of Representatives.

Employers
Council for Government Reform (President and Chief Exec. Officer)

HARDING, Robert B.

600 13th St. NW
Washington, DC 20005-3096
Tel: (202)756-8205
Fax: (202)756-8087
Registered: LDA
EMail: rharding@mwe.com
Former Attorney, Securities and Exchange Commission; Legislative Assistant, House of Representatives; Special Assistant to Secretary for Congressional Affairs, Department of Health, Education and Welfare.

Employers
McDermott, Will and Emery (Partner)

Clients Represented

On Behalf of McDermott, Will and Emery

The Chevron Companies
H. B. Fuller Co.
Eli Lilly and Co.
Maxus Energy Corp.
Murphy Oil U.S.A.
Prudential Insurance Co. of America

HARDING, Sandra

950 N. Washington St.
Alexandria, VA 22314-1552
Tel: (703)836-2272
Fax: (703)684-1924
Registered: LDA

Employers
American Academy of Physician Assistants (Director, Federal Affairs)

HARDISON, Ann

1615 L St. NW
Suite 1000
Washington, DC 20036
Tel: (202)659-0330
Fax: (202)296-6119

Employers
Fleishman-Hillard, Inc (V. President)

HARDISTY, John

1090 Vermont Ave. NW
Suite 800
Washington, DC 20005
Tel: (202)408-7023
Fax: (202)289-2639

Employers
Ameron Internat'l Corp. (Washington Representative)

HARDMAN, Kenneth E.

1828 L St. NW
Suite 901
Washington, DC 20036
Tel: (202)223-3772
Fax: (202)833-2416
Registered: LDA

Employers
Moir & Hardman (Principal)

HARDOCK, Randolf H.

1455 Pennsylvania Ave. NW
Suite 1200
Washington, DC 20004
Tel: (202)347-2230
Fax: (202)393-3310
Registered: LDA
Benefits Tax Counsel, Office of Tax Policy, Department of the Treasury, 1993-95. Tax Counsel, Senate Finance Committee, 1986-93.

Employers
Davis & Harman LLP (Partner)

Clients Represented

On Behalf of Davis & Harman LLP

Administaff
American Benefits Council
Citigroup
Committee of Annuity Insurers
Coors Brewing Company
Financial Executives International
Greyhound Lines
Health Insurance Ass'n of America
Lincoln Nat'l Corp.
Merrill Lynch & Co., Inc.
Mutual of Omaha Insurance Companies
Nat'l Ass'n of Professional Employer Organizations
Paul, Hastings, Janofsky & Walker LLP

HARDY, Jr., George

1275 K St. NW
Suite 800
Washington, DC 20005
Tel: (202)371-9090
Fax: (202)371-9797

Employers

Ass'n of State and Territorial Health Officials (Exec. Director)

HARDY, John D.

2000 Massachusetts Ave. NW
Washington, DC 20036
Tel: (202)785-1712
Fax: (202)785-1807
Registered: LDA

Employers

Self-employed as an independent consultant.

Clients Represented

As an independent consultant

Marine Engineers Beneficial Ass'n (District No. 1 - PCD)

HARDY, Margaret

5550 Friendship Blvd.
Suite 300
Chevy Chase, MD 20815-7201
Tel: (301)968-2642
Fax: (301)968-4195
Registered: LDA

Employers

American Osteopathic Healthcare Ass'n (Director, Government Relations)
Ass'n of Osteopathic Directors and Medical Educators (V. President, Federal Relations & Policy)

HARDY, Jr., Ralph W.

1200 New Hampshire Ave. NW
Suite 800
Washington, DC 20036-6802
EMail: rhardy@dlalaw.com
Tel: (202)776-2000
Fax: (202)776-2222

Employers

Dow, Lohnes & Albertson, PLLC (Member)

HARDY HAVENS, Debra M.

426 C St. NE
Washington, DC 20002
Tel: (202)544-1880
Fax: (202)543-2565
Registered: LDA

Former Health Legislative Assistant to Rep. George M. O'Brien (R-IL).

Employers

Capitol Associates, Inc. (Chief Exec. Officer)

Clients Represented

On Behalf of Capitol Associates, Inc.

Academic Health Center Coalition
American Ass'n for Marriage and Family Therapy
Aunt Martha's Youth Service Center
California Ass'n of Marriage and Family Therapists
DeBrunner and Associates, Inc.
Health Quest
Healthcare Billing and Management Ass'n
Fred Hutchinson Cancer Research Center
Illinois Collaboration on Youth
Joint Council of Allergy, Asthma and Immunology
MedReview, Inc.
Nat'l Ass'n of Children's Hospitals Inc.
Nat'l Ass'n of Medical Equipment Suppliers (NAMES)
Nat'l Ass'n of Pediatric Nurse Associates and Practitioners
New York University Medical Center
Northwestern Memorial Hospital
Urban Health Care Coalition of Pennsylvania

HARE, Neil

1615 H St. NW
Washington, DC 20062
Tel: (202)463-5500
Fax: (202)463-3129

Employers

Nat'l Chamber Foundation (Director, Programs)

HARFF, James W.

901 15th St. NW
Suite 370
Washington, DC 20005
Tel: (202)371-9600
Fax: (202)371-0808
Registered: LDA, FARA

Former Chief of Staff to Rep. Robert Kasten (R-WI).

Employers

Global Communicators (Chairman and Chief Exec. Officer)

Clients Represented

On Behalf of Global Communicators

Jordan Tourism Board
Switzerland, Economic Development, State of Vaud

HARGETT, Jack

1968 Crescent Park Dr.
Reston, VA 20190
EMail: wjackhargett@msn.com
Tel: (703)707-9793
Registered: LDA

Employers

Hargett Consulting (Principal)

Clients Represented

On Behalf of Hargett Consulting

AAI Corp.
Information Handling Services
The Williamson Group

HARGETT, Michael

120 S. Payne St.
Alexandria, VA 22314
EMail: mhargett@bahrinc.com
Tel: (703)684-7300
Fax: (703)684-7302
Registered: LDA

Served in the Army, 1970-95.

Employers

Bentley, Adams, Hargett, Riley and Co., Inc. (Treasurer)

Clients Represented

On Behalf of Bentley, Adams, Hargett, Riley and Co., Inc.

InWork Technologies
Munitions Industrial Base Task Force
Sister Cities Internat'l

HARGIS, Lynn

1200 New Hampshire Ave. NW
Washington, DC 20036
EMail: lynn.hargis@chadbourne.com
Tel: (202)974-5600
Fax: (202)974-5602
Registered: LDA

Assistant General Counsel for Electric Rates, Federal Energy Regulatory Commission, 1979-85. Assistant to Senator Ralph Yarborough (D-TX), 1964-66.

Employers

Chadbourne and Parke LLP (Counsel)

Clients Represented

On Behalf of Chadbourne and Parke LLP

American Forest & Paper Ass'n

HARGRAVES, Dirck

919 18th St. NW
Tenth Floor
Washington, DC 20006
Tel: (202)263-2900
Fax: (202)263-2960

Employers

Issue Dynamics Inc. (Senior Consultant)

HARITON, David P.

1701 Pennsylvania Ave. NW
Suite 800
Washington, DC 20006
Tel: (202)956-7500
Fax: (202)293-6330
Registered: LDA

Employers

Sullivan & Cromwell (Partner)

Clients Represented

On Behalf of Sullivan & Cromwell

Securities Industry Ass'n

HARJO, Suzan Shown

611 Pennsylvania Ave. SE
Washington, DC 20003
Tel: (202)547-5531
Fax: (202)546-6724

Employers

Morning Star Institute, The (President and Exec. Director)

HARJU, Lori

501 Capitol Ct. NE
Suite 300
Washington, DC 20002
EMail: lharju@riponsoc.org
Tel: (202)546-1292
Fax: (202)547-6560

Employers

Ripon Society (Exec. Director)

HARKER, Drew A.

555 12th St. NW
Washington, DC 20004-1206
EMail: Drew_Harker@aporter.com
Tel: (202)942-5000
Fax: (202)942-5999

Professional Staff Member, Senate Committee on Armed Services, 1981-86.

Employers

Arnold & Porter (Partner)

HARKIN, Ruth R.

1401 I St. NW
Suite 600
Washington, DC 20005
Tel: (202)336-7400
Fax: (202)336-7479

Employers

United Technologies Corp. (Senior V. President, International Affairs and Government Relations)

HARKINS, Elizabeth M.

277 S. Washington St.
Suite 200
Alexandria, VA 22314
EMail: eharkins@staffingtoday.net
Tel: (703)253-2039
Fax: (703)253-2053
Registered: LDA

Employers

American Staffing Ass'n (Director, Government Affairs)

HARKINS, Malcolm J.

1233 20th St. NW
Suite 800
Washington, DC 20036-2396
EMail: MHarkins@prskauer.com
Tel: (202)416-6800
Fax: (202)416-6899

Employers

Proskauer Rose LLP (Partner)

HARKRADER, Mary

440 First St. NW
Washington, DC 20001
Tel: (202)393-6226
Fax: (202)737-0480

Employers

Nat'l Ass'n of County Recorders, Election Officials and Clerks (President)

HARLES, Charles

P.O. Box 15318
Washington, DC 20003
Tel: (202)546-2847
Fax: (202)546-2854
Registered: LDA

Employers

Harles & Associates (Director)

Clients Represented

On Behalf of Harles & Associates

Internat'l Ass'n of Business, Industry and Rehabilitation
Rehabilitation Engineering and Assistive Technology Soc. of North America

---

HARLEY, William

341 S. Patrick St.
Alexandria, VA 22314
Tel: (703)549-7600
Fax: (703)549-7604

Employers

Outdoor Power Equipment Institute (President and Chief Exec. Officer)

HARLOW, Bryce L. "Larry"

1850 K St. NW
Suite 850
Washington, DC 20006
Tel: (202)331-1760
Fax: (202)822-9376
Registered: LDA

Deputy Undersecretary for Legislative Affairs, Department of the Treasury, 1989-90. Special Assistant to the President for Legislative Affairs (1985-89) and Associate Director for Legislative Affairs, Office of Management and Budget (1985-86), Executive Office of the President, The White House. Chief Lobbyist, Federal Trade Commission, 1981-85. Legislative

Specialist, Environmental Protection Agency, 1972-76. Staff Assistant to Senator Howard Baker (R-TN), 1969-71.

Employers
Timmons and Co., Inc. (President and Managing Partner)

Clients Represented

On Behalf of Timmons and Co., Inc.
American Council of Life Insurers
American Petroleum Institute
American Soc. of Anesthesiologists
Anheuser-Busch Cos., Inc.
Asbestos Working Group
AT&T
Bay Harbor Management, L.C.
Bristol-Myers Squibb Co.
Cox Enterprises Inc.
DaimlerChrysler Corp.
Farallon Capital Management
Federal Home Loan Mortgage Corp. (Freddie Mac)
Micron Technology, Inc.
Napster, Inc.
Nat'l Rifle Ass'n of America
New York Life Insurance Co.
Northrop Grumman Corp.
TruePosition Inc.
Union Pacific
University of Utah
UNOCAL Corp.
VISA U.S.A., Inc.

HARMALA, Robert

1666 K St. NW
Suite 500
Washington, DC 20006-2803
Tel: (202)887-1400
Fax: (202)466-2198
Registered: LDA

Employers
O'Connor & Hannan, L.L.P.

Clients Represented

On Behalf of O'Connor & Hannan, L.L.P.
California Debt Limit Allocation Committee
Celera Genomics

HARMAN, John R.

1301 K St. NW
Washington, DC 20005-3333
Tel: (202)414-1000
Fax: (202)414-1301
Registered: LDA
EMail: john.r.harman@us.pwcglobal.com
Former Assistant Secretary for Legislative Affairs, Department of Treasury and Assistant Minority Tax Counsel, Committee on Ways and Means, U.S. House of Representatives.

Employers
PriceWaterhouseCoopers (Senior Manager, Tax Policy)

HARMAN, Jr., William B.

1455 Pennsylvania Ave. NW
Suite 1200
Washington, DC 20004
Tel: (202)347-2230
Fax: (202)393-3310
Registered: LDA
EMail: wbharman@davis-harman.com
Attorney, Office of Tax Legislative Counsel, Department of Treasury, 1959-61. Attorney, Legislation and Regulations Division, Office of the Chief Counsel, Internal Revenue Service, Department of Treasury, 1958-59.

Employers
Davis & Harman LLP (Partner)

Clients Represented

On Behalf of Davis & Harman LLP
Allstate Insurance Co.
Committee of Annuity Insurers
Stock Co. Information Group

HARMON, Herbert

1010 Vermont Ave. NW
Suite 810
Washington, DC 20005
Tel: (202)783-9100
Fax: (202)783-9103

Employers
Harmon & Wilmot, L.L.P. (Partner)

HARMON, Linda

2025 M St. NW
Suite 800
Washington, DC 20036
EMail: linda_harmon@dc.sba.com
Tel: (202)367-2100
Fax: (202)367-1200

Employers
Smith, Bucklin and Associates, Inc.

Clients Represented

On Behalf of Smith, Bucklin and Associates, Inc.
Lamaze Internat'l

HARNAGE, Sr., Bobby L.

80 F St. NW
Washington, DC 20001
Tel: (202)639-6435
Fax: (202)639-6490

Employers
American Federation of Government Employees (AFL-CIO) (National President)

HARNED, Karen Reis

1400 16th St. NW
Suite 400
Washington, DC 20036-2220
EMail: kharned@ofwlaw.com
Tel: (202)518-6346
Fax: (202)234-2686
Registered: LDA

Employers
Olsson, Frank and Weeda, P.C. (Associate)

Clients Represented

On Behalf of Olsson, Frank and Weeda, P.C.
Adheris, Inc.
American Commodity Distribution Ass'n
American School Food Service Ass'n
Ass'n of Medical Device Reprocessors
Aventis Pasteur
Beef Products, Inc.
California Canning Peach Ass'n
Chocolate Manufacturers Ass'n of the U.S.A.
Duramed Pharmaceuticals, Inc.
Food Distributors Internat'l (NAWGA-IFDA)
Gentrac Inc.
Health Resource Publishing Co.
Institute of Food Technologists
Kraft Foods, Inc.
Lower Brule Sioux Tribe
Mead Johnson Nutritional Group
Nat'l Ass'n of Margarine Manufacturers
Nat'l Ass'n of Pharmaceutical Manufacturers
Nat'l Coalition of Food Importers Ass'n
Nat'l Confectioners Ass'n
Nat'l Food Processors Ass'n
Nat'l Meat Ass'n
PennField Oil Co.
The Pillsbury Co.
San Tomo Group
Schwan's Sales Enterprises
SteriGenics Internat'l
Titan Scan
Transhumance Holding Co., Inc.
United Fresh Fruit and Vegetable Ass'n
Urner Barry Publications, Inc.

HARNED, Ph.D., Patricia J.

1747 Pennsylvania Ave. NW
Suite 400
Washington, DC 20006
EMail: pat@ethics.org
Tel: (202)737-2258
Fax: (202)737-2227
Registered: LDA

Employers
Ethics Resource Center Inc. (Director of Character Development)

HAROLD-FOSTER, Toni

1775 K St. NW
Washington, DC 20006
Tel: (202)223-3111
Fax: (202)466-1562
Registered: LDA

Employers
United Food and Commercial Workers Internat'l Union (Lobbyist)

HAROOTYAN, Linda K.

1030 15th St. NW
Suite 250
Washington, DC 20005-1503
EMail: geron@geron.org
Tel: (202)842-1275
Fax: (202)842-1150

Employers
Gerontological Soc. of America (Deputy Director)

HARPEL, Richard

1307 New York Ave. NW
Suite 400
Washington, DC 20005-4722
Tel: (202)478-6040
Fax: (202)478-6046

Employers
Nat'l Ass'n of State Universities and Land-Grant Colleges (Director, Federal Relations-Higher Education)

HARPER, Dal

1299 Pennsylvania Ave. NW
Suite 800 West
Washington, DC 20004
Tel: (202)785-0500
Fax: (202)785-5277

Employers
The Carmen Group (Operations Manager)
LMRC, Inc. (Operations Manager)

HARPER, Diane

1000 Wilson Blvd.
Suite 2300
Arlington, VA 22209
Tel: (703)875-8400
Fax: (703)276-0711
Registered: LDA

Employers
Northrop Grumman Corp. (Manager, Legislative Affairs)

HARPER, James W.

P.O. Box 77476
Washington, DC 20013
EMail: jimharper@policycounsel.com
Tel: (202)486-0824
Counsel, Subcommittee on Commercial and Administrative Law, House Committee on the Judiciary, 1997-2000. Counsel, Senate Committee on Government Affairs, 1996-97. Legal Fellow, Senate Committee on the Judiciary, 1996.

Employers
PolicyCounsel.com (Founder and Principal)

HARPER, Stephen F.

1634 I St. NW
Suite 300
Washington, DC 20006
Tel: (202)626-4399
Fax: (202)628-2525
Registered: LDA

Employers
Intel Corp. (Manager, Environmental Health and Safety)

HARPLE, Charles E.

25 Louisiana Ave. NW
Washington, DC 20001-2198
Tel: (202)624-6800
Fax: (202)624-8973
Registered: LDA

Employers
Internat'l Brotherhood of Teamsters (Legislative Representative)

HARPS, Gina

818 Connecticut Ave. NW
Suite 900
Washington, DC 20006
EMail: gharps@acnm.org
Tel: (202)728-9860
Fax: (202)728-9897

Employers
American College of Nurse-Midwives (Manager, Marketing/Public Relations)

HARRELL, Adele

2100 M St. NW
Washington, DC 20037
Tel: (202)833-7200
Fax: (202)429-0687

Employers
The Urban Institute (Director, Program on Law and Behavior)

HARRINGTON, Alex J.

225 N. Washington St.
Alexandria, VA 22314
EMail: aharring@ncoausa.org
Tel: (703)549-0311
Fax: (703)549-0245

Employers
Non Commissioned Officers Ass'n of the U.S.A. (Director, Legislative Affairs)

HARRINGTON, Clifford M.

2300 N St. NW
Washington, DC 20037-1128
Tel: (202)663-8000
Fax: (202)663-8007
Registered: LDA
EMail: clifford.harrington@shawpittman.com
Task Force on Adjudicatory Reregulation (1974-75) and Office of Opinions and Review (1972-74), Federal Communications Commission.

Employers
Shaw Pittman (Partner)

Clients Represented

On Behalf of Shaw Pittman
Christian Broadcasting Network

HARRINGTON, Eugene

8100 Oak St.
Dunn Loring, VA 22027
Tel: (703)573-8330
Fax: (703)573-4116
EMail: gharrington@pestworld.org

Employers
Nat'l Pest Control Ass'n (Manager, Government Affairs)

HARRINGTON, Gerald T.

601 Pennsylvania Ave. NW
Suite 900 South Bldg.
Washington, DC 20004
Tel: (202)434-8211
Fax: (202)638-7124
Registered: LDA

Employers
Capitol City Group

Clients Represented

On Behalf of Capitol City Group
American Biophysics Corp.
Cranston, Rhode Island, City of
CVS, Inc.
Greater Providence Chamber of Commerce
Landmark Medical Center
Rhode Island Resource Recovery Center

HARRINGTON, Kathleen

1201 F St. NW
Suite 500
Washington, DC 20004
Tel: (202)824-1600
Fax: (202)824-1651
Registered: LDA

Employers
Health Insurance Ass'n of America (Senior V. President, Federal Affairs)

HARRINGTON, Toni

955 L'Enfant Plaza SW
Suite 5300
Washington, DC 20024
Tel: (202)554-1650
Fax: (202)488-3542
Registered: LDA

Employers
Honda North America, Inc. (Assistant V. President, Government and Industry Relations)

HARRINGTON, W. Brendan

1101 15th St. NW
Suite 1000
Washington, DC 20005
Tel: (202)530-8160
Fax: (202)530-8180
Registered: LDA
EMail: brendan_harrington@cargill.com

Employers
Cargill, Inc. (Assistant V. President)

HARRIS, II, A. J.

1155 21st St. NW
Suite 300
Washington, DC 20036
Tel: (202)659-8201
Fax: (202)659-5249
Registered: LDA

Employers
Williams & Jensen, P.C. (Partner)

HARRIS, Barry Lambert

2121 Crystal Dr.
Suite 706
Arlington, VA 22202
Tel: (703)746-0670
Fax: (703)746-0671
Registered: LDA

Employers
Galaxy Aerospace Co., LP

HARRIS, C. Coleman

1410 King St.
Suite 400
Alexandria, VA 22314
Tel: (703)838-5889
Fax: (703)838-5888
EMail: coleman_harris@ffa.org

Employers
Nat'l FFA Organization (National Exec. Secretary)

HARRIS, Collette

2000 L St. NW
Suite 805
Washington, DC 20036
Tel: (202)872-9222
Fax: (202)293-2697

Employers
Electric Power Research Institute (Washington Representative)

HARRIS, David A.

777 N. Capitol St. NE
Suite 305
Washington, DC 20002
Tel: (202)216-9060
Fax: (202)216-9061

Employers
Nat'l Jewish Democratic Council (Deputy Exec. Director)

HARRIS, FAIA, David A.

1090 Vermont Ave. NW
Suite 700
Washington, DC 20005-4905
Tel: (202)289-7800
Fax: (202)289-1092
EMail: dharris@nibs.org

Employers
Nat'l Institute of Building Sciences (President)

HARRIS, Ellen

1101 15th St. NW
Suite 1212
Washington, DC 20005
Tel: (202)467-5730 Ext: 32
Fax: (202)223-0409
EMail: ellenh@bazelon.org

Employers
Bazelon Center for Mental Health Law, Judge David L. (Staff Attorney, Committee on Mental Health Issues)

HARRIS, George

801 Pennsylvania Ave. NW
Suite 230
Washington, DC 20004
Tel: (202)393-7150
Fax: (202)347-1684
Registered: LDA
EMail: gbharris@bradleyarant.com

Employers
Bradley Arant Rose & White LLP (Partner)

HARRIS, II, Hon. Herbert E.

The Watergate
Suite 1113
2600 Virginia Ave. NW
Washington, DC 20037-1905
Tel: (202)337-8338
Fax: (202)337-6685
Registered: LDA
Member, U.S. House of Representatives (D-VA), 1975-81.

Employers
Harris Ellsworth & Levin (Partner)

Clients Represented

On Behalf of Harris Ellsworth & Levin
American Railway Car Institute
Ass'n of Food Industries, Inc.
Cheese Importers Ass'n of America
Committee of Domestic Steel Wire Rope and Specialty Cable Manufacturers
Wood Corp.

HARRIS, James "Jay"

1850 M St. NW
Suite 540
Washington, DC 20036
Tel: (202)974-2300
Fax: (202)775-0112
Registered: LDA

Employers
Nat'l Multi-Housing Council (V. President, Property Management)

HARRIS, Jean A.

1640 Wisconsin Ave. NW
Washington, DC 20007
Tel: (202)337-2701
Fax: (202)337-4271
EMail: jharris@facs.org

Employers
American College of Surgeons (Regulatory and Coding Specialist)

HARRIS, Jeffrey

1155 Connecticut Ave.
Sixth Floor
Washington, DC 20036
Tel: (202)861-0870
Fax: (202)429-0657
Deputy Associate Attorney General (1981-83) and Executive Director, Attorney General's Task Force on Violent Crime (1981), Department of Justice. Deputy Chief Counsel, House Committee on Standards of Official Conduct, 1977-79. Chief Attorney General's Investigation Review Unit (1976-77) and Assistant U.S. Attorney, Southern District of New York (1972-76), Department of Justice.

Employers
Rubin, Winston, Diercks, Harris & Cooke (Partner)

HARRIS, Judith L.

1301 K St. NW
Suite 1100-East Tower
Washington, DC 20005
Tel: (202)414-9200
Fax: (202)414-9299
Registered: LDA
Former Director, Office of Legislative and Intergovernmental Affairs, Federal Communications Commission.

Employers
Reed, Smith, LLP (Counsel)

Clients Represented

On Behalf of Reed, Smith, LLP
Washington, Department of Information of the State of

HARRIS, Leslie A.

2120 L St. NW
Suite 400
Washington, DC 20037
Tel: (202)478-6301
Fax: (202)478-6171
Registered: LDA

Employers
Leslie Harris & Associates (President)

Clients Represented

On Behalf of Leslie Harris & Associates
American Library Ass'n
AOL Time Warner
Consortium for School Networking
EdLinc
Internat'l Soc. for Technology in Education
Leadership Conference on Civil Rights
Media Access Project
Nat'l School Boards Ass'n
Verizon Communications

HARRIS, Ph.D., Marilyn A.

1101 Pennsylvania Ave. NW
Suite 510
Washington, DC 20004
Tel: (202)783-6315
Fax: (202)783-6309
Registered: LDA

Employers
USX Corp. (General Manager, Federal Government Affairs)

HARRIS, Marshall F.

901 15th St. NW
Suite 700
Washington, DC 20005-2301
Tel: (202)371-6000
Fax: (202)371-6279
Registered: LDA

Employers
Verner, Liipfert, Bernhard, McPherson and Hand, Chartered

Clients Represented

On Behalf of Verner, Liipfert, Bernhard, McPherson and Hand, Chartered
Washington Group Internat'l

HARRIS, Martin

440 First St. NW
Eighth Floor
Washington, DC 20001
Tel: (202)661-8805
Fax: (202)393-2630
EMail: mharris@naco.org

Employers
Nat'l Ass'n of Counties (Co-Director, Joint Center for Sustainable Development)

HARRIS, USAF (Ret.), Col. Marvin J.

201 N. Washington St.
Alexandria, VA 22314
Tel: (800)245-8762
Fax: (703)838-8173
EMail: marvh@troa.org

Employers
The Retired Officers Ass'n (TROA) (Director, Public Relations)

HARRIS, Renee

810 Vermont Ave. NW
Washington, DC 20420
Tel: (202)273-9419
Fax: (202)273-9988

Employers
Department of Veterans Affairs (Legislative Analyst)

HARRIS, IV, Robert A.

8300 Greensboro Dr.
Suite 1080
McLean, VA 22102
Tel: (703)883-0102
Fax: (703)883-0108

Employers
Sack & Harris, P.C. (V. President)

HARRIS, Robert L.

1455 Pennsylvania Ave. NW
Suite 225
Washington, DC 20004
Tel: (202)289-7400
Fax: (202)289-7414
Registered: LDA

Served as Aide to Senator Jennings Randolph (D-WV) and on the staff of the Senate Committee on Labor and Public Welfare and the Nat'l Commission on Water Quality. Served on the staff of the Appalachian Regional Commission.

Employers
Nutter & Harris, Inc. (Exec. V. President)

Clients Represented

On Behalf of Nutter & Harris, Inc.
The Aluminum Ass'n
Lead Industries Ass'n
Plum Creek Timber Co.

HARRIS, Scott Blake

1200 18th St. NW
Suite 1200
Washington, DC 20036
Tel: (202)730-1300
Fax: (202)730-1301
Registered: LDA

Chief, Internat'l Bureau, Federal Communications Commission, 1994-96. Former Chief Counsel, Export Administration, Department of Commerce.

Employers
Harris, Wiltshire & Grannis LLP (Managing Partner)

Clients Represented

On Behalf of Harris, Wiltshire & Grannis LLP
3Com Corp.
Apple Computer, Inc.
Cisco Systems Inc.
North American GSM Alliance, LLC
Time Domain Corp.
VoiceStream Wireless Corp.
Winstar Communications, Inc.

HARRIS, Stuart H.

1299 Pennsylvania Ave. NW
Washington, DC 20004-2402
EMail: harriss@howrey.com
Tel: (202)783-0800
Fax: (202)383-6610

Employers
Howrey Simon Arnold & White (Partner)

Clients Represented

On Behalf of Howrey Simon Arnold & White
General Signal Corp.
Timex Corp.

HARRIS, William D.

818 Connecticut Ave. NW
Suite 1100
Washington, DC 20006
EMail: wharris@oldaker-harris.com
Tel: (202)728-1010
Fax: (202)728-4044
Registered: LDA

Employers
Great Northwest Classic Committee (PAC Treasurer)
Oldaker and Harris, LLP (Partner)

Clients Represented

On Behalf of Oldaker and Harris, LLP
Fajardo, Puerto Rico, Municipality of
Guaynabo, Puerto Rico, City of
Mayaguez, Puerto Rico, Municipality of
Telecorp PCS Inc.

HARRIS, Ph.D., William G.

1201 Pennsylvania Ave. NW
Suite 300
Washington, DC 20004
Tel: (202)857-8444

Employers
Ass'n of Test Publishers (Exec. Director)

HARRIS BERRY, Gail

1500 Pennsylvania Ave. NW
Room 2205MT
Washington, DC 20220
Tel: (202)622-4401
Fax: (202)622-0534

Employers
Department of Treasury (Legislative Research Assistant)

HARRIS-AIKENS, Donna

1101 Vermont Ave. NW
Suite 400
Washington, DC 20005
EMail: aikens@dbmlaw.com
Tel: (202)289-3900
Fax: (202)371-0197
Registered: LDA

Employers
Dean Blakey & Moskowitz (Associate Attorney)

HARRISON, Alisa

1301 Pennsylvania Ave. NW
Suite 300
Washington, DC 20004
Tel: (202)347-0228
Fax: (202)638-0607

Employers
Nat'l Cattleman's Beef Ass'n (Director, Public Affairs)

HARRISON, Donald

1050 Connecticut Ave. NW
Washington, DC 20036-5306
EMail: dharrison@gdclaw.com
Tel: (202)955-8500
Fax: (202)467-0539

Law Clerk to Judge Francis L. Van Dusen, U.S. Court of Appeals, Third Circuit, 1971-72.

Employers
Gibson, Dunn & Crutcher LLP (Partner)

HARRISON, Gail

700 13th St. NW
Suite 1000
Washington, DC 20005
Tel: (202)347-6633
Fax: (202)347-8713

Employers
Powell Tate (Principal)

HARRISON, Joseph M.

1611 Duke St.
Alexandria, VA 22314
Tel: (703)683-7410
Fax: (703)683-7527
Registered: LDA

Employers
American Moving and Storage Ass'n (President)

HARRISON, Kim

1444 I St. NW
Suite 700
Washington, DC 20005-2210
EMail: kharrison@bostromdc.com
Tel: (202)216-9623
Fax: (202)216-9646

Employers
Automotive Maintenance and Repair Ass'n (Director of Accreditation)
Bostrom Corp. (Director, Administration)

HARRISON, Michael

1111 19th St. NW
Suite 800
Washington, DC 20036
Tel: (202)463-2700
Fax: (202)463-2785

Employers
American Forest & Paper Ass'n (Coordinator, Congressional Affairs)

HARRISON, Nancy F.

1849 C St. NW
Room 6246
Washington, DC 20240
EMail: nancy_harrison@ois.doi.gov
Tel: (202)208-6797
Fax: (202)208-7619

Employers
Department of Interior (Chief, Legislative Service Branch, Office of Legislative Counsel)

HARRISON, Sabrina

1801 L St. NW
MS: 9311
Washington, DC 20507
Tel: (202)663-4900
Fax: (202)663-4912

Employers
Equal Employment Opportunity Commission (Congressional Liaison Assistant)

HARRISON, Selig

1755 Massachusetts Ave. NW
Suite 400
Washington, DC 20036
EMail: hart@tcf.org
Tel: (202)387-0400
Fax: (202)483-9430

Employers
The Century Foundation (Writer, Foreign Policy Background and Korean Issues)

HARRISON, Tandy

1301 Pennsylvania Ave. NW
Suite 300
Washington, DC 20004
Tel: (202)347-0228
Fax: (202)638-0607

Employers
Nat'l Cattleman's Beef Ass'n (Associate, PACS and PES)

HARRISON-CLARK, Anne

2100 M St. NW
Fifth Floor
Washington, DC 20037
Tel: (301)565-6710
Fax: (301)565-7850

Employers
Population Ass'n of America (Public Affairs Consultant)

HARSANYI, Dr. Fruzsina M.

555 12th St. NW
Suite 350
N. Tower
Washington, DC 20004
Tel: (202)639-4060
Fax: (202)737-1311
Registered: LDA

Employers
ABB, Inc. (V. President, Public Affairs and Corporate Communications)

HARSHA, Barbara

750 First St. NE
Suite 720
Washington, DC 20002
EMail: bharsha@naghsr.org
Tel: (202)789-0942
Fax: (202)789-0946

Employers
Nat'l Ass'n of Governors' Highway Safety Representatives (Exec. Director)

HARSHBARGER, Scott

1250 Connecticut Ave. NW
Washington, DC 20036
Tel: (202)833-1200
Fax: (202)659-3716

Employers
Common Cause (President)

HART, Bill

700 13th St. NW
Suite 1000
Washington, DC 20005
Tel: (202)347-6633
Fax: (202)347-8713

Employers
Powell Tate (Senior V. President)

HART, Jr., Clyde J.

1100 New York Ave. NW
Suite 1050
Washington, DC 20005
EMail: chart@buses.org
Tel: (202)842-1645
Fax: (202)842-0850

Employers
American Bus Ass'n (V. President, Government Affairs)

HART, Dennis M.

1301 Pennsylvania Ave. NW
Suite 500
Washington, DC 20004
EMail: dhart@butera-andrews.com
Tel: (202)347-6875
Fax: (202)347-6876

Employers
Butera & Andrews (Partner)

Clients Represented

On Behalf of Butera & Andrews
British Nuclear Fuels plc

HART, J. Steven

1155 21st St. NW
Suite 300
Washington, DC 20036
Tel: (202)659-8201
Fax: (202)659-5249
Registered: LDA, FARA

Special Assistant to the Assistant Attorney General for Legal Policy, Department of Justice, 1981-82. Assistant to the Chair, President's Task Force on ERISA Reorganization, Office of Management and Budget, Executive Office of the President, The White House, 1978-79.

Employers
Arena PAC (Director)
Tailored Clothing Ass'n (PAC Director)
Williams & Jensen, P.C. (Chairman and Chief Exec. Officer)

Clients Represented

On Behalf of Williams & Jensen, P.C.
Ad Hoc Coalition of Commercial and Investment Banks
Aegon USA
American Home Products Corp.
American Share Insurance
The Anschutz Co.
AOL Time Warner
Applera Corp.
Arena PAC
Asahi Glass Co.
The Church Alliance
CIGNA Corp.
The Coca-Cola Company
Colonial Pipeline Co.
Continental Airlines Inc.
Credit Suisse First Boston Corp.
Fannie Mae
First Union Corp.
Gateway, Inc.
Genentech, Inc.
HP Global Workplaces, Inc.
Internat'l Ass'n of Amusement Parks and Attractions
Keystone, Inc.
Knight Trading Group
KSL Development Corp.
Nat'l Audubon Soc.
Nat'l Cable Television Ass'n
Nat'l Underground Railroad Freedom Center
Owens-Illinois, Inc.
Perdue Farms Inc.
Pharmaceutical Research and Manufacturers of America
The Pittston Co.
Qwest Communications
Recording Industry Ass'n of America
Reuters America Inc.
Securities Traders Ass'n
Smithfield Foods Inc.
Tailored Clothing Ass'n
Tejon Ranch Co.
Texaco Group Inc.

HART, Joe

430 First St. SE
Washington, DC 20003
Tel: (202)544-6245
Fax: (202)675-6568
Registered: LDA

Employers
American Trucking Ass'ns (V. President, Legislative and Government Affairs)

HART, Jonathan D.

1200 New Hampshire Ave. NW
Suite 800
Washington, DC 20036-6802
EMail: jhart@dlalaw.com
Tel: (202)776-2000
Fax: (202)776-2222

Employers
Dow, Lohnes & Albertson, PLLC (Member)

HART, Norma Alexander

1513 P St. NW
Washington, DC 20005-1909
Tel: (202)588-5432
Fax: (202)588-5443

Employers
Nat'l Bankers Ass'n (President)

HART, Thomas H.

110 Maryland Ave. NE
Suite 309
Washington, DC 20002
EMail: tom.hart@dfms.org
Tel: (202)547-7300
Fax: (202)547-4457

Employers
Episcopal Church, Office of Government Relations (Director, Government Relations)

HART, Vicki E.

901 15th St. NW
Suite 700
Washington, DC 20005-2301
EMail: vhart@verner.com
Tel: (202)371-6000
Fax: (202)371-6279
Registered: LDA, FARA
Former Special Assistant to Majority Leader Senator Trent Lott (R-MS) and to Majority Leader Senator Robert Dole (R-KS).

Employers
Bob Dole Enterprises
Verner, Liipfert, Bernhard, McPherson and Hand, Chartered (Director, Legislation and Federal Affairs)

Clients Represented

On Behalf of Bob Dole Enterprises
Johnson & Johnson, Inc.

On Behalf of Verner, Liipfert, Bernhard, McPherson and Hand, Chartered
Alere Medical Inc.
American Ass'n of Blood Banks
American Soc. of Anesthesiologists
Amgen
Austin, Texas, City of
Continuum Healthcare Systems
Envirocare of Texas, Inc.
Genentech, Inc.
Healthcare Leadership Council
Lehman Brothers
Lockheed Martin Corp.
Merrill Lynch & Co., Inc.
Mexico, Government of
Muscular Dystrophy Ass'n
Petroport, Inc.
Pharmaceutical Research and Manufacturers of America
Polycistic Kidney Disease Foundation
Public Broadcasting Entities
Rite Aid Corp.
RJR Nabisco Holdings Co.
Staples, Inc.
Starwood Lodging/Starwood Capital Group, L.P.
Thomson Consumer Electronics, Inc.
University of Michigan Medical Center
Vanderbilt University Medical Center
VISA U.S.A., Inc.
Vitas Healthcare Corp.

HARTEL, Ph.D., Christine R.

750 First St. NE
Washington, DC 20002-4242
Tel: (202)336-6000
Fax: (202)336-5953

Employers
American Psychological Ass'n (Associate Exec. Director, Science)

HARTENBERGER, Werner K.

1200 New Hampshire Ave. NW
Suite 800
Washington, DC 20036-6802
EMail: whartenber@dlalaw.com
Tel: (202)776-2000
Fax: (202)776-2222
Registered: LDA
Attorney, Federal Communications Commission, 1970-77.

Employers
Dow, Lohnes & Albertson, PLLC (Of Counsel)

HARTER, Kiran

1615 H St. NW
Washington, DC 20062
Tel: (202)463-5500
Fax: (202)463-3129

Employers
Nat'l Chamber Foundation (Program Coordinator)

HARTING, Erin

1219 Prince St.
Alexandria, VA 22314
EMail: eangus@eangus.org
Tel: (703)519-3846
Fax: (703)519-3849
Registered: LDA

Employers
Enlisted Ass'n of the Nat'l Guard of the United States (Legislative Analyst)

HARTKE, Vance

7637 Leesburg Pike
Falls Church, VA 22043
Tel: (703)734-2810
Registered: LDA

Employers
Hartke & Hartke

Clients Represented

On Behalf of Hartke & Hartke
Vortec Corp.

HARTKE, Wayne

7637 Leesburg Pike
Falls Church, VA 22043
Tel: (703)734-2810
Registered: LDA

Employers
Hartke & Hartke

Clients Represented

On Behalf of Hartke & Hartke
Vortec Corp.

HARTL, Gabriel A.

2300 Clarendon Blvd.
Suite 711
Arlington, VA 22201
EMail: atca@worldnet.att.net
Tel: (703)522-5717
Fax: (703)527-7251

Employers
Air Traffic Control Ass'n (President)

HARTLE, Allyson J.

601 Pennsylvania Ave. NW
South Bldg., Suite 900
Washington, DC 20004
Tel: (202)434-8163
Fax: (202)639-8238

Employers
Lockridge Grindal & Nauen, P.L.L.P.

HARTLE, Terry W.

One Dupont Circle NW
Suite 835
Washington, DC 20036-1193
EMail: t_w_hartle@ace.nche.edu
Tel: (202)939-9300
Fax: (202)833-4762
Registered: LDA

Employers
American Council on Education (Senior V. President, Government and Public Affairs)

HARTMAN, Arthur A.

1615 L St. NW
Suite 900
Washington, DC 20036
Tel: (202)778-1000
Fax: (202)466-6002
Former U.S. Ambassador to the Soviet Union and to France.

Employers
APCO Worldwide (Senior Consultant)

HARTMAN, Chester

3000 Connecticut Ave. NW
Suite 200
Washington, DC 20008
EMail: chartman@prrac.org
Tel: (202)387-9887
Fax: (202)387-0764

Employers
Poverty and Race Research Action Council (President and Exec. Director)

HARTMAN, Edward E.

807 Maine Ave. SW
Washington, DC 20024
Tel: (202)554-3501
Fax: (202)554-3581

Employers
Disabled American Veterans (Assistant National Director, Volunteer Services)

HARTMANN, David

560 Herndon Pkwy.
Suite 340
Herndon, VA 20170
Tel: (703)471-5370
Fax: (703)471-9895

Employers
Fellowship Square Foundation, Inc. (President)

HARTNESS, Norman

819 Seventh St. NW
Washington, DC 20001
Tel: (202)833-8940
Fax: (202)833-8943
Registered: LDA

Employers
EOP Group, Inc.

Clients Represented

On Behalf of EOP Group, Inc.
The Business Roundtable
FMC Corp.

HARTNETT, Barbara A.

1215 Jefferson Davis Hwy.
Suite 1500
Arlington, VA 22202
EMail: barbara.hartnett@baesystems.com
Tel: (703)236-6247
Fax: (703)236-6205

Employers
BAE SYSTEMS North America (Public Affairs Specialist)

HARTQUIST, David A.

3050 K St. NW
Washington, DC 20007
Tel: (202)342-8450
Fax: (202)342-8451
Registered: LDA, FARA
EMail: dhartqui@colliershannon.com
General Counsel, Council on International Economic Policy, The White House, 1974-76. Assistant to the President, Overseas Private Investment Corp., 1973-74. Legislative Assistant to Senator Richard S. Schweiker, 1970-1973.

Employers
Collier Shannon Scott, PLLC (Member)

Clients Represented

On Behalf of Collier Shannon Scott, PLLC
Allegheny Technologies, Inc.
Bicycle Manufacturers Ass'n of America
Coalition for Safe Ceramicware
Copper and Brass Fabricators Council
Damascus Tubular Products
Internat'l Crystal Federation
Miller Co.
Pfaltzgraff
Specialty Steel Industry of North America
Specialty Tubing Group
Valve Manufacturers Ass'n of America

HARTSOE, Joseph R.

1775 I St. NW
Suite 800
Washington, DC 20006
Tel: (202)466-9150
Fax: (202)828-3372

Employers
Enron Corp. (V. President and Federal Regulatory Counsel)

HARTWELL, Keith O.

122 C St. NW
Suite 850
Washington, DC 20001
Tel: (202)638-7790
Fax: (202)638-1045
Registered: LDA
EMail: keith.hartwell@cchinc.com
Former Administrative Assistant to Rep. Marvin Esch (R-MI), 1971-76.

Employers
Chambers, Conlon & Hartwell (President)

Clients Represented

On Behalf of Chambers, Conlon & Hartwell
American Short Line and Regional Railroad Ass'n
Canadian Nat'l Railway Co.
Nat'l Railroad and Construction Maintenance Ass'n
Norfolk Southern Corp.
Rail Supply and Service Coalition

HARTZ, Michelle

700 13th St. NW
Suite 1000
Washington, DC 20005
Tel: (202)347-6633
Fax: (202)347-8713
Registered: FARA

Employers
Powell Tate (Consultant)

HARVEY, Linda

1101 17th St. NW
Suite 300
Washington, DC 20036
Tel: (202)331-1770
Fax: (202)331-1969

Employers
Cosmetic, Toiletry and Fragrance Ass'n (Director, Publications and Communications)

HARVEY, Pharis J.

733 15th St. NW
Suite 920
Washington, DC 20005
EMail: laborrights@igc.org
Tel: (202)347-4100
Fax: (202)347-4885

Employers
Internat'l Labor Rights Fund (Exec. Director)

HARVIE, Christopher J.

701 Pennsylvania Ave. NW
Suite 900
Washington, DC 20004-2608
Tel: (202)434-7300
Fax: (202)434-7400
Registered: LDA
EMail: charvie@mintz.com
Counsel, Subcommittee on Antitrust, Monopolies and Business Rights, Senate Committee on Judiciary, 1988-93.

Employers
Mintz, Levin, Cohn, Ferris, Glovsky and Popeo, P.C. (Partner)

HARVISON, Clifford J.

2200 Mill Rd.
Suite 620
Alexandria, VA 22314
EMail: nttc@juno.com
Tel: (703)838-1960
Fax: (703)684-5753

Employers
Nat'l Tank Truck Carriers (President)

HARWOOD, Jr., John H.

2445 M St. NW
Washington, DC 20037-1420
Tel: (202)663-6000
Fax: (202)663-6363
Registered: LDA
EMail: jharwood@wilmer.com

Employers
Wilmer, Cutler & Pickering (Partner)

Clients Represented

On Behalf of Wilmer, Cutler & Pickering
Deutsche Telekom, Inc.

HASELTINE, Ph.D., William

133 H. St. NW
Suite 600
Washington, DC 20005
Tel: (202)737-2670
Fax: (202)347-4285

Employers
Nat'l Health Museum (Chairman)

HASKINS, Ronald T.

1775 Massachusetts Ave. NW
Washington, DC 20036-2188
Tel: (202)797-6000
Fax: (202)797-6004
Staff Director, Subcommittee on Human Resources (1994-2000) and Welfare Counsel (1986-94), House Committee on Ways and Means. Congressional Science Fellow for Senator Paul Simon (D-IL), 1985-86.

Employers
The Brookings Institution (Senior Fellow, Economic Studies Program)

HASSELL, John

1299 Pennsylvania Ave. NW
Suite 800 West
Washington, DC 20004
Tel: (202)785-0500
Fax: (202)785-5277
Registered: LDA

Employers
The Carmen Group

Clients Represented

On Behalf of The Carmen Group
Maryland Department of Transportation
Missouri Highway and Transportation Department
Montgomery County, Maryland, Division of Transportation
Stafford, Virginia, County of

HASSELMO, Nils

1200 New York Ave. NW
Suite 550
Washington, DC 20005
Tel: (202)408-7500
Fax: (202)408-8184

Employers
Ass'n of American Universities (President)

HASSETT, Jace

1717 Pennsylvania Ave. NW
Suite 400
Washington, DC 20006
Tel: (202)857-3000
Fax: (202)857-3030
Registered: LDA

Employers
Occidental Internat'l Corporation (Director, Legislative and Regulatory Affairs)

HASSETT, Kevin

1150 17th St. NW
Washington, DC 20036
Tel: (202)862-5800
Fax: (202)862-7177
EMail: khassett@aei.org

Employers
American Enterprise Institute for Public Policy Research (Resident Scholar)

HASSOUNA, Dr. Hussein

1100 17th St. NW
Suite 602
Washington, DC 20036
Tel: (202)265-3210
Fax: (202)331-1525
Registered: FARA

Employers
League of Arab States/Arab Information Center (Chief Representative)

HASTAD, Anne-Marye

2301 M St. NW
Washington, DC 20037-1484
Tel: (202)467-2950
Fax: (202)467-2910
EMail: ahastad@APPAnet.org

Employers
American Public Power Ass'n (Legislative Research Assistant)

HASTY, Claudia

909 N. Washington St.
Alexandria, VA 22314
Tel: (703)549-4455
Fax: (703)706-5961

Employers
Armed Forces Benefit Ass'n (Exec. Officer)

HATCH, Paul D.

700 13th St. NW
Suite 400
Washington, DC 20005
Tel: (202)347-0773
Fax: (202)347-0785
Registered: LDA

Employers
Cassidy & Associates, Inc. (Senior Consultant)
Ed XL PAC (PAC Administrator)

HATCH, Scott D.

233 Constitution Ave. NE
Washington, DC 20002
Tel: (202)547-4000
Fax: (202)543-5044
Registered: LDA
EMail: sd35@erols.com

Employers
Parry, Romani, DeConcini & Symms (Research Director)

Clients Represented

On Behalf of Parry, Romani, DeConcini & Symms
AIDS Healthcare Foundation
Andrx Pharmaceutical Corp.
Armstrong World Industries, Inc.
Asphalt Systems, Inc.
Aventis Pharmaceutical Products
Avondale, Arizona, City of
Bank of New York
Bristol-Myers Squibb Co.
Coalition Against Database Piracy
Composites Fabricators Ass'n
Ferraro, USA
Formosan Ass'n for Public Affairs
GlaxoSmithKline
Herbalife Internat'l, Inc.
Hoechst Marion Roussel Deutschland GmbH
Inter-Cal Corp.
Katten Muchin & Zavis
Motion Picture Ass'n of America
Nat'l Air Cargo, Inc.
Nat'l Nutritional Foods Ass'n
Nat'l Retail Federation
Nogales, Arizona, City of
Nu Skin Internat'l Inc.
Owens Corning
Peoria, Arizona, City of
Pfizer, Inc.
Pharmacia Corp.
Policy Development Group, Inc.
Project to Promote Competition and Innovation in the Digital Age
Research & Development Laboratories
Research Corp. Technology
Rexall Sundown
SBC Communications Inc.
SOL Source Technologies, Inc.
Styrene Information and Research Center
Taxpayers Against Fraud, The False Claims Legal Center
TCOM, L.P.
Unilever United States, Inc.
Utah Natural Products Alliance

HATCHER, Jennifer L.

655 15th St. NW
Washington, DC 20005-5701
Tel: (202)220-0734
Fax: (202)220-0873
Registered: LDA
EMail: jhatcher@fmi.org

Employers
Food Marketing Institute (Director, Government Relations)

HATCHER, Michael R.

2099 Pennsylvania Ave. NW
Suite 100
Washington, DC 20006
Tel: (202)955-3000
Fax: (202)955-5564
Registered: LDA
EMail: mhatcher@hklaw.com

Employers
Holland & Knight LLP (Partner)

Clients Represented
On Behalf of Holland & Knight LLP
Nat'l Coalition of Minority Businesses
Texaco Group Inc.

HATFIELD, Dr. Thomas A.

1916 Association Dr.
Reston, VA 20191-1590
Tel: (703)860-8000
Fax: (703)860-2960
EMail: naea@dgs.dgsys.com

Employers
Nat'l Art Education Ass'n (Exec. Director)

HATHAWAY, Julia

1849 C St. NW
Washington, DC 20240
Tel: (202)208-5403
Fax: (202)208-7059

Employers
Department of Interior - Fish and Wildlife Service (Legislative Specialist)

HATHAWAY, Kris

2111 Wilson Blvd.
Eighth Floor
Arlington, VA 22201-3058
Tel: (703)841-0626
Fax: (703)243-2874
EMail: hathaway@alcalde-fay.com

Employers
Alcalde & Fay (Associate)

Clients Represented
On Behalf of Alcalde & Fay
Earthshell Container Corp.
Internat'l Climate Change Partnership

HATRY, Harry P.

2100 M St. NW
Washington, DC 20037
Tel: (202)833-7200
Fax: (202)429-0687

Employers
The Urban Institute (Director, State and Local Government Research)

HATTON, Bruce N.

1820 N. Fort Myer Dr.
Suite 804
Arlington, VA 22209
Tel: (703)351-6301
Fax: (703)351-6417
Registered: LDA

Employers
McDermott Internat'l, Inc./Babcock & Wilcox (V. President and General Manager, Washington Operations)

HATTON, Melinda Reid "Mindy"

325 Seventh St. NW
Washington, DC 20004
Tel: (202)638-1100
Fax: (202)626-2254
Antitrust Counsel, Subcommittee on Antitrust, Monopolies and Business Rights, Senate Judiciary Committee, 1990-95.

Employers
American Hospital Ass'n (V. President and Chief Washington Counsel)

HATZER, Dawn

444 N. Capitol St. NW
Suite 345
Washington, DC 20001
Tel: (202)434-4850
Fax: (202)434-4851

Employers
Academy for State and Local Government (Coordinator)

HATZIKONSTANTINOU, Maria E.

2111 Wilson Blvd.
Suite 1200
Arlington, VA 22201
Tel: (703)522-1845
Fax: (703)351-6634
EMail: mhatzikonstantinou@columbuspublicaffairs.com

Employers
Columbus Public Affairs (Associate)

HAUCK, Graham S.

1255 23rd St. NW
Suite 200
Washington, DC 20037-1174
Tel: (202)452-8100
Fax: (202)833-3636
EMail: gsh@hauck.com

Employers
American Ambulance Ass'n (Director of Meetings and Member Services)
Ass'n of Meeting Professionals (Exec. Director)
Hauck and Associates (Account Exec.)

HAUCK, Jay

1255 23rd St. NW
Suite 200
Washington, DC 20037-1174
Tel: (202)452-8100
Fax: (202)833-3636
EMail: jhauck@hauck.com

Employers
Hauck and Associates (Account Exec.)

Clients Represented
On Behalf of Hauck and Associates
DFK Internat'l/USA, Inc.

HAUCK, Sheldon J.

1255 23rd St. NW
Suite 200
Washington, DC 20037-1174
Tel: (202)452-8100
Fax: (202)833-3636
EMail: shauck@hauck.com

Employers
Hauck and Associates (President)

Clients Represented
On Behalf of Hauck and Associates
Nat'l Oilseed Processors Ass'n
Soy Protein Council

HAUPT, Chris

1875 I St. NW
Suite 900
Washington, DC 20005
Tel: (202)371-0200
Fax: (202)371-2858

Employers
Edelman Public Relations Worldwide (V. President)

HAUPTLI, Todd J.

601 Madison
Suite 400
Alexandria, VA 22314
Tel: (703)824-0500
Fax: (703)820-1395
Registered: LDA
EMail: todd.hauptli@airportnet.org
Congressional Relations Officer for Aviation Affairs, Department of Transportation, 1989-91.

Employers
AAAE-ACI (Senior V. President, Federal Affairs)
Airports Council Internat'l - North America (Senior V. President, Federal Affairs)
American Ass'n of Airport Executives (Senior V. President, Legislative Affairs)

HAUSER, Debra

1025 Vermont Ave. NW
Suite 200
Washington, DC 20005
Tel: (202)347-5700
Fax: (202)347-2263
Registered: LDA

Employers
Advocates for Youth (V. President)

HAUSER, Eric W.

1782 Columbia Rd. NW
Washington, DC 20009
Tel: (202)518-8047
Fax: (202)518-8048
EMail: Eric@thgweb.com
Director of Communications to Senator Bill Bradley (D-NJ), 1991-94. Director of Communications to Rep. Charles E. Schumer (D-NY), 1989-91. Press Secretary to Rep. Glenn English (D-OK), 1987-89. Press Secretary to Del. Fofo I. F. Sunia (D-American Samoa), 1985-87.

Employers
Hauser Group (President)

HAUSER, Katheryn

1250 I St. NW
Suite 200
Washington, DC 20005
Tel: (202)737-8888
Fax: (202)638-4922

Employers
Information Technology Industry Council (Director, Internat'l Trade)

HAUSER, Richard H.

1050 Connecticut Ave. NW
Suite 1100
Washington, DC 20036-5304
Tel: (202)861-1500
Fax: (202)861-1790
Registered: LDA
EMail: rhauser@baker-hostetler.com
Deputy Counsel to the President, The White House, 1981-86. Assistant Director, Office of Policy and Planning, Department of Justice, 1974-75. Associate Counsel to the President, The White House, 1973-74. Attorney-Advisor, Office of the Deputy Attorney General, Department of Justice, 1971-73. Assistant U.S. Attorney, Southern District of Florida, 1970-71. Law Clerk to Judge Charles B. Fulton, U.S. District Court for Southern District of Florida, 1968-70.

Employers
Baker & Hostetler LLP (Partner)

Clients Represented
On Behalf of Baker & Hostetler LLP
Eagle-Picher Personal Injury Settlement Trust
Medical Mutual of Ohio
Nat'l Ass'n of Optometrics and Opticians
Pardee Construction Co.
Verizon Communications

HAUSMAN, Shawn

1001 Pennsylvania Ave. NW
Washington, DC 20004-2599
Tel: (202)624-2000
Fax: (202)624-2319

Employers
American Council of Life Insurers (Deputy Vice President, Public Affairs)

HAUSRATH, Jan E.

1615 L St. NW
Suite 900
Washington, DC 20036
Tel: (202)778-1000
Fax: (202)466-6002
Registered: FARA
EMail: jhausrat@apcoworldwide.com

Employers
APCO Worldwide (Senior V. President and Director, Strategic Communications)

HAUTER, Wenonah

215 Pennsylvania Ave. SE
Washington, DC 20003
Tel: (202)546-4996

Employers
Public Citizen, Inc. (Director, Critical Mass Energy Project)

HAVENS, Arnie I.

1331 Pennsylvania Ave. NW
Suite 560
Washington, DC 20004
Tel: (202)783-8124
Fax: (202)783-5929
Registered: LDA

Employers
CSX Corp. (Corporate V. President, Federal Affairs)

HAVENS, III, Charles W.

1875 Connecticut Ave. NW
Suite 1200
Washington, DC 20009-5728
Tel: (202)986-8000
Fax: (202)986-8102

Employers
LeBoeuf, Lamb, Greene & MacRae L.L.P. (Of Counsel)

HAWKINS, III, Charles E.

2101 Wilson Blvd.
Suite 100
Arlington, VA 22201
Tel: (703)525-8788

Employers
Nat'l Stone, Sand, and Gravel Ass'n (V. President and Chief Exec. Officer)

HAWKINS, Jr., Daniel R.

1330 New Hampshire Ave. NW
Suite 122
Washington, DC 20036
Tel: (202)296-0131
Fax: (202)296-3526
Registered: LDA
Assistant Secretary for Planning and Evaluation, Department of Health and Human Services, 1977-81.

Employers
Nat'l Ass'n of Community Health Centers (V. President, Federal and State Affairs)

HAWKINS, David A.

1631 Prince St.
Alexandria, VA 22314-2818
Tel: (703)836-2222
Fax: (703)836-8015
Registered: LDA

Employers
Nat'l Ass'n for College Admission Counseling (Director, Government Relations)

HAWKINS, David G.

1200 New York Ave. NW
Suite 400
Washington, DC 20005
Tel: (202)289-6868
Fax: (202)289-1060
Registered: LDA

Employers
Natural Resources Defense Council (Senior Attorney)

HAWKINS, James W.

1101 16th St. NW
Suite 500
Washington, DC 20036
Tel: (202)659-9111
Fax: (202)659-6387
Registered: LDA
Former Aide to Senator James M. Jeffords (R-VT). Former Professional Staff Member, Senate Health, Education, Labor and Pensions Committee.

Employers
Bergner Bockorny Castagnetti and Hawkins (Principal)

Clients Represented
On Behalf of Bergner Bockorny Castagnetti and Hawkins
AdvaMed
Agilent Technologies
Amgen
Biogen, Inc.
Bristol-Myers Squibb Co.
Cerner Corp.
Chicago Board Options Exchange
Dell Computer Corp.
Everglades Defense Council
First Health Group Corp.
Genzyme Corp.
Medtronic, Inc.
Nat'l Ass'n of Real Estate Investment Trusts
Ovations/United Health Group
Premium Standard Farms
Qwest Communications
UDV North America, Inc.

HAWKINS, III, John R.

1801 K St. NW
Suite 601 L
Washington, DC 20006
Tel: (202)756-7100
Fax: (202)756-7200

Employers
Cohn & Wolfe (Exec. V. President)

HAWKINS, Steven

1436 U St. NW
Suite 104
Washington, DC 20009
EMail: shawkins@ncadp.org
Tel: (202)387-3890
Fax: (202)387-5590

Employers
Nat'l Coalition to Abolish the Death Penalty (Exec. Director)

HAWKINSON, Brian P.

2033 K St. NW
Suite 700
Washington, DC 20006
Tel: (202)872-1790
Fax: (202)835-8343

Employers
Public Affairs Council (Director, Center for Public Affairs Management)

HAWKS, John K.

7500 Old Georgetown Rd.
Suite 1300
Bethesda, MD 20814-6161
EMail: jhawks@usgen.com
Tel: (301)718-6805
Fax: (301)718-6659

Employers
PG&E Generating Co. (V. President, Public Affairs and Government Relations)

HAWLEY, Buzz

1420 New York Ave. NW
Suite 1050
Washington, DC 20005
Tel: (202)638-1950
Fax: (202)638-1928
Registered: LDA
Senior Legislative Assistant to Rep. Frank Wolf (R-VA), 1991-97.

Employers
Van Scoyoc Associates, Inc. (Legislative Counsel)

Clients Represented
On Behalf of Van Scoyoc Associates, Inc.
Alcoa Inc.
Archimedes Technology Group
British Trade and Commerce Bank
Burns and Roe Enterprises, Inc.
Communications Training Analysis Corp. (C-TAC)
Greater New Orleans Expressway Commission
Johnson Controls, Inc.
Krebs, LaSalle, LeMieux Consultants, Inc.
Lockheed Martin Hanford
University of New Orleans Foundation
Virginia Polytechnic Institute and State University
Wackenhut Services, Inc.
Washington Consulting Group

HAWLEY, Noelle M.

901 15th St. NW
Suite 700
Washington, DC 20005-2301
EMail: nmhawley@verner.com
Tel: (202)371-6000
Fax: (202)371-6279
Registered: LDA

Employers
Verner, Liipfert, Bernhard, McPherson and Hand, Chartered (Associate)

Clients Represented
On Behalf of Verner, Liipfert, Bernhard, McPherson and Hand, Chartered
Goldman, Sachs and Co.
Staples, Inc.
Virginia Commonwealth Trading Co.

HAY, John C.

1200 Wilson Blvd.
Arlington, VA 22209-1989
Tel: (703)465-3264
Fax: (703)465-3004
Registered: LDA

Employers
The Boeing Co. (Director, Legislative Affairs)

HAY, Matt

1235 Jefferson Davis Hwy.
Suite 305
Arlington, VA 22202
EMail: mhay.escowdc@seistl.com
Tel: (703)416-7600
Fax: (703)416-7606
Registered: LDA

Employers
Engineered Support System, Inc. (ESSI) (V. President, Washington Operations)

HAYDEN, Cheryl A.

1350 I St. NW
Suite 880
Washington, DC 20005
EMail: chayden@aad.org
Tel: (202)842-3555
Fax: (202)842-4355
Registered: LDA

Employers
American Academy of Dermatology (Assistant Director, Federal Affairs)

HAYDEN, J. Michael

1033 N. Fairfax St.
Suite 200
Alexandria, VA 22314
EMail: asasishing@aol.com
Tel: (703)519-9691
Fax: (703)519-1872

Employers
American Sportfishing Ass'n (President)

HAYDEN, Lou

1201 15th St. NW
Washington, DC 20005-2800
Tel: (202)822-0470
Fax: (202)822-0572
Registered: LDA

Employers
Nat'l Ass'n of Home Builders of the U.S. (Legislative Director, Energy, Environment and Trade)

HAYDEN, Jr., Ludwig

1401 I St. NW
Suite 1200
Washington, DC 20005-2225
EMail: lhay@chevron.com
Tel: (202)408-5861
Fax: (202)408-5845
Registered: LDA

Employers
The Chevron Companies (Federal Relations Manager)
Chevron, U.S.A.

HAYDEN, Martin

1625 Massachusetts Ave. NW
Suite 702
Washington, DC 20036
Tel: (202)667-4500
Fax: (202)667-2356
Registered: LDA

Employers
Earthjustice Legal Defense Fund (Legislative Director)

HAYES, Carla

1155 15th St. NW
Suite 1004
Washington, DC 20005
Tel: (202)467-5081
Fax: (202)467-5085

Employers
Independent Visually Impaired Enterprisers (President)

HAYES, Carnie

One Massachusetts Ave. NW
Suite 700
Washington, DC 20001-1431
Tel: (202)408-5505
Fax: (202)408-8072
Registered: LDA

Employers
Council of Chief State School Officers (Director, Federal-State Relations)

HAYES, David J.

555 11th St. NW
Suite 1000
Washington, DC 20004
Tel: (202)637-2200
Fax: (202)637-2201
Former Deputy Secretary, Department of the Interior, during the Clinton Administration.

Employers
Latham & Watkins (Partner)

HAYES, Dennis

1822 Jefferson Place NW
Washington, DC 20036
Tel: (202)530-1894
Fax: (202)530-2444

Employers
Cuban American Nat'l Foundation/Cuban American Foundation (Exec. V. President)

HAYES, Hon. James A. "Jimmy"

409 Ninth St. NW
Suite 610 South
Washington, DC 20004
EMail: hayesja@arlaw.com
Tel: (202)737-3234
Fax: (202)737-0264
Registered: LDA
Member, U.S. House of Representatives (D-LA), 1987-97.

Employers
Adams and Reese LLP (Special Counsel)

Clients Represented
On Behalf of Adams and Reese LLP
AHL Shipping Co.
Baton Rouge, Louisiana, City of
Bollinger Shipyards
Coastal Impact Assistance & Reinvestment
First American Aircraft Title
First American Title Aircraft
Lafayette Airport Commission
Lehtinen O'Donnell
Louisiana Credit Union Ass'n
Louisiana State University
Miccosukee Indians
New Orleans, Louisiana, Regional Transit Authority of
NiSource Inc.
South Louisiana, Port of
Swiftships
Technology Integration Group
Textron Marine and Land
Z-Tel Communications Inc.
Zachery Taylor Parkway Commission

HAYES, Richard

1707 H St. NW
Suite 600
Washington, DC 20006-3919
Tel: (202)223-6133
Fax: (202)223-6162

Employers
Union of Concerned Scientists (Media Director)

HAYES, Robert G.

1455 F St. NW
Suite 225
Washington, DC 20005
Tel: (202)638-3307
Fax: (202)783-6947
Registered: LDA

Deputy Director, Office of Industry Services (1980-84) and Deputy Assistant General Counsel for Fisheries (1979-80), National Marine Fisheries Service and Southeast Regional Counsel, National Oceanic and Atmospheric Administration (1978-79), Department of Commerce.

Employers
Ball Janik, LLP (Partner)

Clients Represented

On Behalf of Ball Janik, LLP

Alcoa Inc.
American Dehydrated Onion and Garlic Ass'n
American Sportfishing Ass'n
ATOFINA
Billfish Foundation
Coastal Conservation Ass'n
Columbia Falls Aluminum Co.
Goldendale Aluminum
Hager Hinge Co.
Kaiser Aluminum & Chemical Corp.
Northwest Aluminum Co.
Restore America's Estuaries

HAYES, Stephen

1100 17th St.
Suite 1100
Washington, DC 20036
EMail: shayes@africacncl.org
Tel: (202)835-1115
Fax: (202)835-1117

Employers
Corporate Council on Africa (President)

HAYES, Tammi

444 N. Capitol St. NW
Suite 841
Washington, DC 20001
Tel: (202)393-6412
Fax: (202)638-4584
Registered: LDA
EMail: tammi.hayes@capitalstrategiesgroup.com

Former Assistant to Senator Edward Kennedy (D-MA).

Employers
Capital Strategies Group, Inc. (President/Chief Exec. Officer)

Clients Represented

On Behalf of Capital Strategies Group, Inc.

3gi, Inc.
allacrossamerica.com
Allthane Technologies Internat'l
The Capital Hill Group, Inc.
The Castano Group
China.com
Corel Corp.
Internat'l Public Relations Co.
Millenium 2100
Toyota Motor Corp.
Visitalk.com

HAYLER, Susan

2500 Wilson Blvd.
Suite 300
Arlington, VA 22201
EMail: shayler@tia.eia.org
Tel: (703)907-7704
Fax: (703)907-7727

Employers
Telecommunications Industry Ass'n (Director, Standards Development & Promotion)

HAYNES, Mark

2001 Pennsylvania Ave. NW
Suite 650
Washington, DC 20006
Tel: (202)496-8200
Fax: (202)659-1110
Registered: LDA
EMail: haynes@ga.radix.net

Employers
General Atomics (V. President, Washington Operations)

HAYNES, Mildred

1101 15th St. NW
Suite 1100
Washington, DC 20005
Tel: (202)331-2812
Fax: (202)331-2805
Registered: LDA
EMail: mwhaynes@mmm.com

Employers
Minnesota Mining and Manufacturing Co. (3M Co.) (Manager, Government Relations)

HAYS, F. Wallace

1250 I St. NW
Suite 1105
Washington, DC 20005
Tel: (202)682-5151
Fax: (202)682-2185
Registered: LDA

Publications Assistant to Rep. Lee H. Hamilton (D-IN), 1987-94.

Employers
Andreae, Vick & Associates, L.L.C. (Senior Associate)

HAYS, John J.

50 F St. NW
Suite 900
Washington, DC 20001
EMail: hays@fccouncil.com
Tel: (202)879-0853
Fax: (202)626-8718

Employers
Farm Credit Council (V. President)

HAYS, Michael D.

1200 New Hampshire Ave. NW
Suite 800
Washington, DC 20036-6802
Tel: (202)776-2000
Fax: (202)776-2222
Registered: LDA
EMail: mhays@dlalaw.com

Employers
Dow, Lohnes & Albertson, PLLC (Member)

Clients Represented

On Behalf of Dow, Lohnes & Albertson, PLLC

Questcom
Stoll Stoll Berne Lokting & Shlachter, P.C.

HAYWARD, Barbara

1350 Connecticut Ave. NW
Suite 605
Washington, DC 20036
Tel: (202)862-3952
Fax: (202)862-3956
Registered: FARA

Director of Public Liaison and Conference Management, Conference for a Drug Free America (1987-88) Associate Director, Political Office (1985-87), Executive Assistant to the Chief of Staff (1983-85) and Personal Assistant to the V. President (1980-83), The White House.

Employers
Hayward Internat'l (President)

Clients Represented

On Behalf of Hayward Internat'l

Chad, Government of the Republic of

HAYWOOD, Alyson M.

1875 I St. NW
12th Floor
Washington, DC 20006
Tel: (202)466-6550
Fax: (202)785-1756
Registered: LDA

Employers
Powers Pyles Sutter & Verville, PC (Legislative Director)

Clients Represented

On Behalf of Powers Pyles Sutter & Verville, PC

American Foundation for the Blind - Governmental Relations Group
American Liver Foundation
California School of Professional Psychology
Nat'l Mental Health Ass'n
University of Florida Health Science Center

HAYWOOD, Elizabeth B.

2101 L St. NW
Washington, DC 20037-1526
Tel: (202)785-9700
Fax: (202)887-0689
Registered: LDA
EMail: haywoode@dsmo.com

Former Legislative Assistant to Rep. Richard Burr (R-NC) and Rep. Mark Sanford (R-SC).

Employers
Dickstein Shapiro Morin & Oshinsky LLP (Associate)

Clients Represented

On Behalf of Dickstein Shapiro Morin & Oshinsky LLP

American Greyhound Track Operators Ass'n
American Public Communications Council
Cigar Ass'n of America
Electric Power Supply Ass'n
Harbour Group Industries, Inc.
Hydro-Quebec
Incentive Federation Sweepstakes Trust Fund
Internat'l Brotherhood of Teamsters
Lorillard Tobacco Co.
PG&E Generating Co.
Pipe Tobacco Council, Inc.
The Reader's Digest Ass'n
Smokeless Tobacco Council

HAYWOOD, Michael S.

401 Ninth St. NW
Suite 1100
Washington, DC 20004
Tel: (202)331-8090
Fax: (202)331-1181

Legislative Assistant to Senator Jim Bunning (R-KY), 1995-2001. Staff Assistant and Legislative Assistant to Rep. David Camp (R-MI), 1992-95

Employers
Duke Energy (Director, Federal Governmental Affairs)

HAZARD, Holly Elisabeth

227 Massachusetts Ave. NE
Suite 100
Washington, DC 20002
EMail: info@ddal.org
Tel: (202)546-1761
Fax: (202)546-2193

Employers
Doris Day Animal League (Exec. Director)

HAZARD, Jr., John W.

1747 Pennsylvania Ave. NW
Suite 1000
Washington, DC 20006
Tel: (202)785-9500
Fax: (202)835-0243

Employers
Webster, Chamberlain & Bean (Partner)

HAZEN, Paul

1401 New York Ave. NW
Suite 1100
Washington, DC 20005
Tel: (202)638-6222
Fax: (202)628-6726

Employers
Nat'l Cooperative Business Ass'n (President and Chief Exec. Officer)

HAZLE, Jeffery

1899 L St. NW
Suite 1000
Washington, DC 20036
EMail: jeff_hazle@npradc.org
Tel: (202)457-0480
Fax: (202)457-0486

Employers
Nat'l Petrochemical Refiners Ass'n (Director, Lubricants, Waxes, and Maintenance)

HAZLETT, Thomas W.

1150 17th St. NW
Washington, DC 20036
EMail: thazlett@aei.org
Tel: (202)862-5800
Fax: (202)862-7177

Employers
American Enterprise Institute for Public Policy Research (Resident Scholar)

HAZLEWOOD, Catherine

600 Pennsylvania Ave. SE
Suite 340
Washington, DC 20003
EMail: clhazlewood@coastalliance.org
Tel: (202)546-9554
Fax: (202)546-9609

Employers
Coast Alliance (Counsel, Pollution Program)

HEAD, Bill

1455 Pennsylvania Ave. NW
Suite 575
Washington, DC 20004
Tel: (202)638-4076
Fax: (202)638-1096

Employers
WellPoint Health Networks/Blue Cross of California/UNICARE (Manager, Legislative Affairs)

HEAD, Terry

2320 Mill Rd.
Suite 102
Alexandria, VA 22314
Tel: (703)684-3780
Fax: (703)684-3784
EMail: hhgfaa@aol.com

Employers

Household Goods Forwarders Ass'n of America, Inc. (President)

HEADINGTON, Edward

1156 15th St. NW
Suite 1100
Washington, DC 20005
Tel: (202)293-8830
Fax: (202)872-8543
EMail: eheadington@nsbu.org

Employers

Nat'l Small Business United (Manager, Media Affairs)

HEALEY, James C.

1801 K St. NW
Suite 901-L
Washington, DC 20006
Tel: (202)530-0500
Fax: (202)530-4800
Registered: LDA, FARA
EMail: Jim_Healey@bm.com
Former Senior Advisor to Rep. Dan Rostenkowski (D-IL), House Ways and Means Committee.

Employers

BKSH & Associates (Managing Director)

Clients Represented

On Behalf of BKSH & Associates

M-Unit
UST Public Affairs, Inc.

HEALEY, Maureen

1801 K St. NW
Suite 600K
Washington, DC 20006
Tel: (202)974-5219
Fax: (202)296-7218
Registered: LDA

Employers

Soc. of the Plastics Industry (Chief State and Regulatory Affairs Officer)

HEALY, Jr., Robert L.

1666 K St. NW
Washington, DC 20006
Tel: (202)296-4700
Fax: (202)496-4324
Registered: LDA
EMail: rhealy@apta.com

Employers

American Public Transportation Ass'n (Director, Government Relations)
The Wexler Group (Principal/Senior Director)

Clients Represented

On Behalf of The Wexler Group

Alaska, Washington Office of the State of
Asea Brown Boveri, Inc.
BP Amoco Corp.

HEALY, Thomas R.

1211 Connecticut Ave. NW
Suite 608
Washington, DC 20036
Tel: (703)299-9800
Fax: (703)299-9803
EMail: thealy@webermerritt.com

Employers

Qorvis Communications (Director, Business Development)

HEARD, Keith

1300 Connecticut Ave. NW
Suite 600
Washington, DC 20036
Tel: (202)775-8116
Fax: (202)223-0358
Registered: LDA
Legislative Aide to Senator Thad Cochran (R-MS), 1978-85.

Employers

Griffin, Johnson, Dover & Stewart (Lobbyist)

Clients Represented

On Behalf of Griffin, Johnson, Dover & Stewart

Alliance for Reasonable Regulation of Insecticides
American Agrisurance
American Fish Spotters Ass'n
American Home Products Corp.
Avue Technologies
Coalition of Commercial and Investment Banks
Dell Computer Corp.
Deloitte Consulting
Fannie Mae
The Justice Project, Inc.
Local Initiatives Support Corp.
United Technologies Corp.
Wilmer, Cutler & Pickering
Wine and Spirits Wholesalers of America

HEARNEY, Richard D.

1717 Pennsylvania Ave. NW
Suite 350
Washington, DC 20006
Tel: (202)296-2125
Fax: (202)296-2490
EMail: rhearney@bens.org

Employers

Business Executives for Nat'l Security (President and Chief Exec. Officer)

HEATON, Erin R.

3190 Fairview Park Dr.
Falls Church, VA 22042
Tel: (703)876-3000
Fax: (703)876-3600
Registered: LDA

Employers

General Dynamics Corp. (Director, Legislative Affairs)

HEBERLEE, Brent

1401 I St. NW
Suite 1100
Washington, DC 20005
Tel: (202)326-8892
Fax: (202)408-8717

Employers

SBC Communications Inc. (Exec. Director, Federal Relations)

HEBERT, David E.

412 First St. SE
Suite 12
Washington, DC 20003
Tel: (202)484-8400
Fax: (202)484-8408
Registered: LDA
Legislative Director to Rep. Jack Buechner (R-MO), 1987-88.

Employers

American Ass'n of Nurse Anesthetists (Director, Federal Government Affairs)

HEBERT, Marc C.

2000 K St. NW
Suite 500
Washington, DC 20006-1872
Tel: (202)828-5838
Fax: (202)223-1225
Registered: LDA
EMail: mhebert@bracepatt.com
Former Majority Staff Member, Subcommittee on National Economic Growth, Natural Resources and Regulatory Affairs, House Government Reform and Oversight Committee.

Employers

Bracewell & Patterson, L.L.P. (Associate)

Clients Represented

On Behalf of Bracewell & Patterson, L.L.P.

Africa Resources Trust USA
Air Conditioning Contractors of America
Alltel Corporation
American Registry for Internet Numbers (ARIN)
Baldwin Piano and Organ Co.
Cement Kiln Recycling Coalition
Continental Cement Co., Inc.
Council of Industrial Boiler Owners (CIBO)
Enron Corp.
Envirocare of Utah, Inc.
FBI Agents Ass'n
Gary-Williams Energy Corp.
Houston, Texas, Port Authority of the City of
Huntsman Corp.
Lyondell Chemical Co.
Nat'l Cable Television Ass'n
Oxygenated Fuels Ass'n
Physician Insurers Ass'n of America
Placid Refining Co.
Solex Environmental Systems, Inc.
Southdown, Inc.
Sterling Chemical Co.
Texas Petrochemicals Corp.
Texas Windstorm Insurance Ass'n
Valero Energy Corp.
Welcon, Inc.

HEBERT, Thomas R.

1156 15th St. NW
Suite 400
Washington, DC 20005
Tel: (202)872-3865
Fax: (202)296-0833
Registered: LDA
EMail: thebert@capitolink.com
Deputy Undersecretary, National Resources Conservation Service, Department of Agriculture, 1994-98.

Employers

Capitolink, LLC (Senior Associate)

Clients Represented

On Behalf of Capitolink, LLC

American Crop Protection Ass'n
Nat'l Ass'n of Conservation Districts
SePRO Corp.
Vantage Point Network, LLC

HECHT, Jim

1440 New York Ave. NW
Washington, DC 20005
Tel: (202)371-7000
Fax: (202)393-5760
Chief Counsel to Senate Majority Leader, Senator Trent Lott (R-MS), 1998-2001.

Employers

Skadden, Arps, Slate, Meagher & Flom LLP (Partner)

HECHT, Timothy P.

499 S. Capitol St. SW
Suite 507
Washington, DC 20003
Tel: (202)554-2881
Registered: LDA

Employers

Hecht, Spencer & Associates (V. President)

Clients Represented

On Behalf of Hecht, Spencer & Associates

Boy Scouts of America
Brown and Williamson Tobacco Corp.
Minnesota Mining and Manufacturing Co. (3M Co.)
Norfolk Southern Corp.
J. C. Penney Co., Inc.
The Charles E. Smith Companies
TECO Energy, Inc.
Tulalip Tribes

HECHT, William H.

499 S. Capitol St. SW
Suite 507
Washington, DC 20003
Tel: (202)554-2881
Registered: LDA

Employers

Hecht, Spencer & Associates (President)

Clients Represented

On Behalf of Hecht, Spencer & Associates

Boy Scouts of America
Brown and Williamson Tobacco Corp.
Minnesota Mining and Manufacturing Co. (3M Co.)
Norfolk Southern Corp.
Patton Boggs, LLP
J. C. Penney Co., Inc.
The Charles E. Smith Companies
TECO Energy, Inc.
Tulalip Tribes

HECK, Patrick G.

1225 Connecticut Ave. NW
Washington, DC 20036
Tel: (202)327-8774
Fax: (202)327-6719
Registered: LDA
EMail: patrick.heck@ey.com
Assistant Counsel, Subcommittee on Oversight, House Ways and Means Committee, 1988-94. Trial Attorney, Office of Chief Counsel, Tax Litigation Division (1985-88) and Employee Plans and Exempt Organizations (1983-85), Internal Revenue Service, Department of Treasury. Staff Assistant to Rep. Thomas L. Ashley (D-OH), 1976-81.

Employers

Ernst & Young LLP (Senior Manager)

Clients Represented

On Behalf of Ernst & Young LLP

E-Commerce Coalition
Edison Electric Institute
General Ore Internat'l Corp. Ltd.
INCOL 2000
Interest Netting Coalition
Koch Industries, Inc.
MassMutual Financial Group
Nordstrom, Inc.
Repeal the Tax on Talking Coalition
Tax Policy Coalition

HECK, Wade

1275 Pennsylvania Ave. NW
Tenth Floor
Washington, DC 20004
Tel: (202)347-6000
Fax: (202)347-6001
Registered: LDA

Employers
Balch & Bingham LLP (Director, Federal Affairs)

Clients Represented
On Behalf of Balch & Bingham LLP
Alabama Space Science Exhibits Commission
Coleman Research Corp.
Computer Systems Technologies, Inc.
Elmco, Inc.
Emerging Technology Partners, LLC
Madison Research Corp.
Mas-Hamilton Group

HECKER, James

1717 Massachusetts Ave. NW
Suite 800
Washington, DC 20036
EMail: jhecker@tlpj.org
Tel: (202)797-8600
Fax: (202)232-7203

Employers
Trial Lawyers for Public Justice, P.C. (Environmental Attorney)

HECKER, CAE, Larry

1444 I St. NW
Suite 700
Washington, DC 20005-2210
EMail: lhecker@bostromdc.com
Tel: (202)216-9623
Fax: (202)216-9646

Employers
Automotive Maintenance and Repair Ass'n (President)
Bostrom Corp. (V. President)

Clients Represented
On Behalf of Bostrom Corp.
Automotive Maintenance and Repair Ass'n

HECKLER, Hon. Margaret

805 15th St. NW
Suite 500
Washington, DC 20005
Tel: (202)371-9770
Fax: (202)371-6601
Secretary, Department of Health and Human Services, 1983-85. Member, U.S. House of Representatives (R-MA), 1967-83. Former Ambassador to Ireland, Department of State.

Employers
Chambers Associates Inc. (Senior Advisor)

HECKMAN, Julie L.

4808 Moorland Ln.
Suite 109
Bethesda, MD 20814
Tel: (301)907-8181
Registered: LDA

Employers
American Pyrotechnics Ass'n (Exec. Director)
Americans Supporting the Pyrotechnics Industry

HEDLUND, James B.

1320 19th St. NW
Suite 300
Washington, DC 20036
Tel: (202)887-1970
Fax: (202)887-0950

Employers
Ass'n of Local Television Stations (President)

HEENAN, Michael T.

1110 Vermont Ave. NW
Suite 400
Washington, DC 20005
EMail: mheenan@harlaw.com
Tel: (202)887-0800
Fax: (202)775-8518
Trial Attorney, Division of Mine Health and Safety, Office of the Solicitor, Department of the Interior, 1973-74.

Employers
Heenan, Althen & Roles (Partner)

Clients Represented
On Behalf of Heenan, Althen & Roles
General Portland Inc.
Hulcher Quarry, Inc.
Lone Star Florida, Inc.
Lone Star Industries
Nemacolin Mines Corp.
Peter White Coal Mining Co.
Youngstown Mines Corp.

HEESEN, Mark G.

1655 N. Fort Myer Dr.
Suite 850
Arlington, VA 22209
Tel: (703)524-2549
Fax: (703)524-3940
Registered: LDA

Employers
Nat'l Venture Capital Ass'n (President)

HEETER, Charles P.

1666 K St. NW
Suite 800
Washington, DC 20006
Tel: (202)481-7000
Fax: (202)862-7098
Registered: LDA

Employers
Arthur Andersen LLP (Partner, Officer of Government Affairs)

HEFFERNAN, Barbara D.

1776 I St. NW
Suite 200
Republic Place
Washington, DC 20006
Tel: (202)293-9494
Fax: (202)223-9594

Employers
Anheuser-Busch Cos., Inc. (Director, National Affairs)

HEFFERNAN, Claire M.

1225 New York Ave. NW
Suite 300
Washington, DC 20005
Tel: (202)393-6362
Fax: (202)737-3742
Registered: LDA
Former Senior Legislative Assistant to Senator Christopher S. "Kit" Bond (R-MO).

Employers
Motor and Equipment Manufacturers Ass'n (V. President, Government Relations)

HEFFERNAN, Elizabeth B.

555 13th St. NW
Washington, DC 20004-1109
EMail: ebheffernan@hhlaw.com
Tel: (202)637-8676
Fax: (202)637-5910
Registered: LDA

Employers
Hogan & Hartson L.L.P. (Partner)

Clients Represented
On Behalf of Hogan & Hartson L.L.P.
Nat'l College Access Network

HEFTI, M. L. "Buzz"

1001 Pennsylvania Ave. NW
Suite 700 South
Washington, DC 20004
Tel: (202)662-2683
Fax: (202)662-2624
Registered: LDA

Employers
Honeywell Internat'l, Inc. (Staff V. President, Government Relations)

HEGG, Richard Y

816 Connecticut Ave. NW
Tenth Floor
Washington, DC 20006
EMail: rick@ptomac.com
Tel: (202)783-3460
Fax: (202)783-2432
Registered: LDA

Employers
Potomac Group (Legislative Consultant)

Clients Represented
On Behalf of Potomac Group
American Psychological Ass'n
Ass'n of American Railroads
Maersk Inc.
Rapid Mat LLC
R. J. Reynolds Tobacco Co.
Seafarers Internat'l Union of North America
Seafarers Mobilization Action Research Team
Transportation Institute
Union Pacific
Walgreen Co.
Watson Energy

HEGYI, Gwynn Geiger

1101 17th St. NW
Eighth Floor
Washington, DC 20036
EMail: ghegyi@bonnerandassociates.com
Tel: (202)463-8880
Fax: (202)833-3584

Employers
Bonner & Associates (Partner)

HEIBERG, Lt. Gen. Vald

1225 I St. NW
Suite 500
Washington, DC 20005
Tel: (202)312-2005
Fax: (202)289-8683
Registered: LDA
EMail: dawsonassociates@worldnet.att.net
Former Chief of Engineers, Director of Civil Works, and Deputy Chief of Engineers; U.S. Army Corps of Engineers; Department of the Army.

Employers
Dawson & Associates, Inc. (Senior Advisor)

Clients Represented
On Behalf of Dawson & Associates, Inc.
Chemical Land Holdings, Inc.
Florida Citrus Mutual
Florida Farm Bureau
Florida Sugar Cane League, Inc.
Sugar Cane Growers Cooperative of Florida

HEIDEMAN, Richard D.

1640 Rhode Island Ave. NW
Washington, DC 20036-3278
EMail: rdheideman@bnabrith.org
Tel: (202)857-6500
Fax: (202)296-0638

Employers
B'nai B'rith Internat'l (President)

HEIDEPRIEM, Nikki

888 17th St. NW
Suite 800
Washington, DC 20006
Tel: (202)822-8060
Fax: (202)822-9088
Registered: LDA
EMail: nheidepriem@heimag.com
Special Assistant to the Secretary, Department of Health, Education and Welfare, 1978-79.

Employers
Heidepriem & Mager, Inc. (President)

Clients Represented
On Behalf of Heidepriem & Mager, Inc.
American Home Products Corp.
CIGNA Corp.
Citigroup
The Dow Chemical Co.
EXACT Laboratories
Nat'l Council of Juvenile and Family Court Judges
Pharmacia Corp.
R2 Technology, Inc.
Serono Laboratories, Inc.
United Airlines

HEIDER, Claret M.

1090 Vermont Ave. NW
Suite 700
Washington, DC 20005-4905
Tel: (202)289-7800
Fax: (202)289-1092

Employers
Nat'l Institute of Building Sciences (V. President, BSC/MMC)

HEIGHT, Dr. Dorothy I.

1629 K St. NW
Suite 1010
Washington, DC 20006
Tel: (202)466-3311
Fax: (202)466-3435

Employers
Leadership Conference on Civil Rights (Chairperson)
Nat'l Council of Negro Women (Chair and Chief Exec. Officer)

HEILIG, Paul T.

1200 Wilson Blvd.
Arlington, VA 22209-1989
Tel: (703)465-3666
Fax: (703)465-3004
Registered: LDA

Employers
The Boeing Co. (Legislative Affairs, Navy/USMC/Joint Programs)

HEIMAN, Bruce J.

1735 New York Ave. NW
Suite 500
Washington, DC 20006-4759
Tel: (202)628-1700
Fax: (202)331-1024
Registered: LDA, FARA
EMail: bruceh@prestongates.com
Legislative Director and Trade Counsel to Senator Daniel P. Moynihan (D-NY), 1984-87.

Employers
Preston Gates Ellis & Rouvelas Meeds LLP (Partner)

Clients Represented

On Behalf of Preston Gates Ellis & Rouvelas Meeds LLP

American Classic Voyages Co.
Americans for Computer Privacy
Business Software Alliance
Dredging Contractors of America
Great Lakes Dredge & Dock
Magazine Publishers of America
Microsoft Corp.
Nat'l Produce Production Inc.
Pitney Bowes, Inc.
Prime Time 24
RSA Security Inc.
Tate and Lyle North American Sugars Inc.
Transportation Institute
United States Maritime Coalition

HEIMBACH, Jay

1001 G St. NW
Suite 700 E
Washington, DC 20001-4545
Tel: (202)879-9321
Fax: (202)879-9340
Former Director of Legislative Affairs, Federal Communications Commission, 1999-2001.

Employers
Ricchetti Inc. (V. President)

HEIMBERG, Gary A.

1333 New Hampshire Ave. NW
Suite 400
Washington, DC 20036
Tel: (202)887-4000
Fax: (202)887-4288
Registered: LDA
Attorney-Advisor to the Chief Administrative Judge, Board of Contract Appeals, Department of Transportation, 1985-87.

Employers
Akin, Gump, Strauss, Hauer & Feld, L.L.P. (Counsel)

Clients Represented

On Behalf of Akin, Gump, Strauss, Hauer & Feld, L.L.P.

Alliance Capital Management LP
Citizen's Educational Foundation
Collagen Corp.
Educational Foundation for Citizenship and Statehood Project
Johnson & Johnson, Inc.
Serono Laboratories, Inc.
St. Barnabas Healthcare System
Sunscreen Coalition
Wartsila Diesel, Inc.

HEIN, Dr. Warren

One Physics Ellipse
College Park, MD 20740-3845
Tel: (301)209-3300
Fax: (301)209-0845
EMail: whein@aapt.org

Employers
American Ass'n of Physics Teachers (Associate Exec. Officer)

HEINE, Kristine E.

901 15th St. NW
Suite 370
Washington, DC 20005
Tel: (202)371-9600
Fax: (202)371-0808
Registered: LDA, FARA
EMail: kheine@globalcommunicators.com
Director of Public Liaison, Agency for Independent Development, 1990-93. Press Secretary to Rep. Charles Grassley (R-IA), 1976-77.

Employers
Global Communicators (Exec. V. President)

Clients Represented

On Behalf of Global Communicators

Switzerland, Economic Development, State of Vaud

HEINE, Robert M.

601 Pennsylvania Ave. NW
Suite 325, North Bldg.
Washington, DC 20004
Tel: (202)728-3661
Fax: (202)728-3649
Registered: LDA

Employers
DuPont (Director, International Trade and Investment)

HEINZE, Ph.D., John E.

655 National Press Bldg.
Washington, DC 20045
Tel: (202)737-8400
Fax: (202)737-8406
EMail: jheinze@johnadams.com

Employers
John Adams Associates Inc. (Senior V. President and Senior Science Advisor)

HEINZE, Mary Kayne

1001 Connecticut Ave. NW
Suite 204
Washington, DC 20036
Tel: (202)822-9000
Fax: (202)822-5077

Employers
Center for Education Reform (Director, Media Relations)

HEISSENBUTTEL, John

1111 19th St. NW
Suite 800
Washington, DC 20036
Tel: (202)463-2700
Fax: (202)463-2785
Registered: LDA
EMail: john_heissenbuttel@afandpa.org

Employers
American Forest & Paper Ass'n (V. President, Forestry and Wood Products)

HEKIMIAN, Christopher M.

888 17th St. NW
Suite 904
Washington, DC 20006
Tel: (202)775-1918
Fax: (202)775-1918

Employers
Armenian Nat'l Committee of America (Director, Government Relations)

HELIN, Willy

2300 M St. NW
Third Floor
Washington, DC 20037-1434
Tel: (202)862-9500
Fax: (202)429-1766

Employers
European Commission Delegation (Director, Office of Press and Public Affairs)

HELLEM, Steven B.

One Thomas Circle NW
Tenth Floor
Washington, DC 20005
Tel: (202)530-5910
Fax: (202)530-0659
Registered: LDA

Employers
Navista, Inc. (President)

Clients Represented

On Behalf of Navista, Inc.

Corporate Environmental Enforcement Council (CEEC)

HELLER, Jack I.

1101 15th St. NW
Suite 205
Washington, DC 20005-1714
Tel: (202)466-4700
Fax: (202)223-4826
EMail: 2133282@mcimail.com
Director of Programs, Latin America (1972-74), Director of Operations, Brazil (1967-68), and Member, Office of the Legal Advisor, Latin America Bureau (1963-67), Agency for International Development, Department of State.

Employers
Heller & Rosenblatt (Partner)

HELLER, Lauren M.

1001 19th St. North
Suite 800
Arlington, VA 22209-3901
Tel: (703)276-5086
Fax: (703)276-5057
EMail: lauren.heller@trw.com

Employers
TRW Inc. (Manager, Government Relations)

HELLER, Mark

1455 Pennsylvania Ave. NW
Suite 1000
Washington, DC 20004
Tel: (202)942-8400
Fax: (202)942-8484
EMail: mark.heller@haledorr.com
Former Associate Chief Counsel of Medical Devices, Food and Drug Administration.

Employers
Hale and Dorr LLP (Senior Partner)

Clients Represented

On Behalf of Hale and Dorr LLP

AdvaMed
Cook Inc.
Hearing Industries Ass'n
Hillenbrand Industries, Inc.
Molecular BioSystems, Inc.

HELLER, Stephen

1401 I St. NW
Suite 1220
Washington, DC 20005
Tel: (202)898-6400
Fax: (202)898-6454
Registered: LDA

Employers
Vivendi Universal (Associate, Government Affairs)

HELLERT, William E.

811 Vermont Ave. NW
Room 1261
Washington, DC 20571
Tel: (202)565-3233
Fax: (202)565-3236
EMail: william.hellert@exim.gov

Employers
Export-Import Bank (Deputy Vice President, Congressional and External Affairs)

HELLINGER, Douglas

927 15th St. NW
Fourth Floor
Washington, DC 20005
Tel: (202)898-1566
Fax: (202)898-1612
EMail: dgap@igc.org

Employers
Development Group for Alternative Policies (Exec. Director)

HELLINGER, Stephen

927 15th St. NW
Fourth Floor
Washington, DC 20005
Tel: (202)898-1566
Fax: (202)898-1612
EMail: shellinger@igc.org

Employers
Development Group for Alternative Policies (President)

HELLMAN, Chris

1779 Massachusetts Ave. NW
Suite 615
Washington, DC 20036
Tel: (202)332-0600
Fax: (202)462-4559

Employers
Center for Defense Information (Senior Analyst)

HELLMAN, Richard A.

2013 Q St. NW
Washington, DC 20009-1009
Tel: (202)234-3600
Fax: (202)332-3221
Registered: LDA
EMail: rahmercl@tidalwave.net

Employers
Christians' Israel Public Action Campaign, Inc. (President and Exec. Director)

HELLMANN, Donald J.

18th and C Sts. NW
Room 3210
Washington, DC 20240
Tel: (202)208-5656
Fax: (202)208-5683
EMail: don_hellmann@nps.gov

Employers
Department of Interior - Nat'l Park Service (Acting Assistant Director, Legislative and Congressional Affairs)

HELM, Brig. Gen. Lewis M.

7000 Millwood Rd.
Bethesda, MD 20817
Tel: (301)229-1550
Fax: (301)229-4905

Employers
Senior Army Reserve Commanders Ass'n (Executive Director)

HELM, Robert W.

1000 Wilson Blvd.
Suite 2300
Arlington, VA 22209
Tel: (703)875-8400
Fax: (703)276-0711
Registered: LDA

Employers
Northrop Grumman Corp. (Corporate V. President, Government Relations)

HELM, Suzanne

1775 Massachusetts Ave. NW
Washington, DC 20036-2188
Tel: (202)797-6000
Fax: (202)797-6004

Employers
The Brookings Institution (Director, Development - External Affairs)

HELM-KHANI, Julie

1350 I St. NW
Suite 1000
Washington, DC 20005
Tel: (202)962-5365
Fax: (202)336-7228
Registered: LDA
EMail: jkhani@ford.com

Employers
Ford Motor Co. (Legislative Manager, Healthcare and Labor)

HELMANIS, Ansis M.

1225 I St. NW
Suite 1150
Washington, DC 20005
Tel: (202)457-0300
Fax: (202)331-8746

Employers
Barnes, Richardson and Colburn (Special Counsel)

Clients Represented

On Behalf of Barnes, Richardson and Colburn
Wyeth-Ayerst Laboratories

HELME, Edward A. "Ned"

750 First St. NE
Suite 940
Washington, DC 20002
Tel: (202)408-9260
Fax: (202)408-8896

Employers
Center for Clean Air Policy (Exec. Director)

HELMES, Dr. C. Tucker

1850 M St. NW
Suite 700
Washington, DC 20036
Tel: (202)721-4154
Fax: (202)296-8120

Employers
Ecological and Toxicological Ass'n of Dyes and Organic Pigments Manufacturers (Exec. Director)

HELMS, David

1801 K St. NW
Suite 701-L
Washington, DC 20006
Tel: (202)292-6700
Fax: (202)292-6800

Employers
Alpha Center for Health Planning (President)
Coalition for Health Services Research (Chief Exec. Officer/President)

HELMS, Robert

1150 17th St. NW
Washington, DC 20036
Tel: (202)862-5800
Fax: (202)862-7177
EMail: rhelms@aei.org

Employers
American Enterprise Institute for Public Policy Research (Resident Scholar and Director, Health Policy Studies)

HELMSLEY, E. Molly

529 14th St. NW
Suite 440
Washington, DC 20045-1402
Tel: (202)783-4697
Fax: (202)783-4699
Registered: LDA
EMail: leahm@naa.org

Employers
Newspaper Ass'n of America (Director, Government Affairs and Legislative Counsel)

HELSING, Craig R.

1101 Pennsylvania Ave. NW
Washington, DC 20004
Tel: (202)872-3822
Fax: (202)756-7444

Employers
BMW (U.S.) Holding Corp. (V. President)

HELTZER, Harold J.

1001 Pennsylvania Ave. NW
Suite 1100
Washington, DC 20004-2595
Tel: (202)624-2500
Fax: (202)628-5116
Registered: LDA
Attorney-Advisor, Office of Tax Legislative Counsel, Department of the Treasury, 1972-74. Attorney, Civil and Tax Divisions, Department of Justice, 1966-72.

Employers
Crowell & Moring LLP (Partner)

Clients Represented

On Behalf of Crowell & Moring LLP
Avon Products, Inc.
Eagle-Picher Industries
ICF Consulting
United Cities Gas Co.
The Wyatt Co.

HELWIG, H. Kurt

950 Herndon Pkwy.
Suite 390
Herndon, VA 20170
Tel: (703)435-9800
Fax: (703)435-7157
EMail: kurthelwig@aol.com

Employers
Electronic Funds Transfer Ass'n (Exec. Director)

HEMENWAY, Russell D.

122 C St. NW
Suite 650
Washington, DC 20001
Tel: (202)639-8300
Fax: (202)639-5038

Employers
Nat'l Committee for an Effective Congress (National Director)

HEMMENDINGER, Henry

30 Ivy St. SE
Washington, DC 20003
Tel: (202)543-2035
Fax: (202)479-4273
EMail: hhdemo@aol.com

Employers
Nat'l Democratic Club (General Manager)

HEMPHILL, Holly K.

600 13th St. NW
Washington, DC 20005-3096
Tel: (202)756-8211
Fax: (202)756-8087
EMail: hhemphill@mwe.com
Former Director, Office of Employment Policy and Grievance Review, Department of Army; Chair, Defense Advisory Committee on Women in the Services.

Employers
McDermott, Will and Emery (Partner)

HEMPHILL, John

1655 N. Fort Myer Dr.
Suite 700
Arlington, VA 22209
Tel: (703)351-5252
Fax: (703)351-5261

Employers
North American Soc. for Trenchless Technology (Deputy, Operations)

HEMPHILL, Melissa M.

1920 N St. NW
Suite 800
Washington, DC 20036
Tel: (202)216-9270
Fax: (202)216-9662
EMail: melissa@railcompetition.org

Employers
Alliance for Rail Competition (Manager, Operations and Development)

HENCHY, Geraldine

1875 Connecticut Ave. NW
Suite 540
Washington, DC 20009
Tel: (202)986-2200
Ext: 3019
Fax: (202)986-2525
EMail: ghenchy@frac.org

Employers
Food Research and Action Center (Senior Policy Analyst)

HENDEL, Patricia J.

8630 Fenton St.
Suite 934
Silver Spring, MD 20910-3803
Tel: (301)585-8101
Fax: (301)585-3445

Employers
Nat'l Ass'n of Commissions for Women (President)

HENDERSON, Basil W.

1775 Pennsylvania Ave. NW
Suite 200
Washington, DC 20006
Tel: (202)862-1000
Fax: (202)862-1093
Registered: LDA

Employers
Dewey Ballantine LLP (Specialist)

Clients Represented

On Behalf of Dewey Ballantine LLP
Automatic Data Processing, Inc
Northwestern Memorial Hospital
Railroad Retirement Tax Working Group

HENDERSON, Debra

1025 Vermont Ave. NW
Suite 900
Washington, DC 20005
Tel: (202)347-7430
Fax: (202)347-0786
Registered: LDA

Employers
Council for Opportunity in Education (Director, Public Policy)

HENDERSON, James E.

1750 K St. NW
12th Floor East
Washington, DC 20006
Tel: (202)857-2330
Fax: (202)835-0643
EMail: jhender@clin.org

Employers
Community Learning and Information Network, Inc. (V. President, Operations)

HENDERSON, Sr., James M.

1650 Diagonal Rd.
Fifth Floor
Alexandria, VA 22314
Tel: (703)740-1450
Fax: (703)837-8510
EMail: jmhaclj@aol.com

Employers
American Center for Law and Justice (Senior Counsel)

HENDERSON, John

600 New Hampshire Ave. NW
11th Floor
Washington, DC 20037
Tel: (202)944-3000
Fax: (202)944-3068

Employers
Dyer Ellis & Joseph, P.C.

Clients Represented

On Behalf of Dyer Ellis & Joseph, P.C.
Kvaerner Shipholding, Inc.

HENDERSON, K.

900 S. Washington St.
Suite G-13
Falls Church, VA 22046
Tel: (703)237-8616
Fax: (703)533-1153

Employers
Nat'l Ass'n of Dental Assistants (Membership Director)

HENDERSON, Shannon Davis

233 Constitution Ave. NE
Washington, DC 20002
Tel: (202)547-4000
Fax: (202)543-5044
Registered: LDA
EMail: SDHenderson@erols.com
Legislative Assistant (1992-94) and Office Manager (1991-92) to Rep. Sam Johnson (R-TX).

Employers
Parry, Romani, DeConcini & Symms (Director, Congressional Affairs)

Clients Represented

On Behalf of Parry, Romani, DeConcini & Symms

AIDS Healthcare Foundation
Andrx Pharmaceutical Corp.
Armstrong World Industries, Inc.
Asphalt Systems, Inc.
Aventis Pharmaceutical Products
Avondale, Arizona, City of
Bank of New York
Bristol-Myers Squibb Co.
Coalition Against Database Piracy
Composites Fabricators Ass'n
Ferraro, USA
Formosan Ass'n for Public Affairs
GAF Corp.
GlaxoSmithKline
Herbalife Internat'l, Inc.
Hoechst Marion Roussel Deutschland GmbH
Inter-Cal Corp.
Katten Muchin & Zavis
Motion Picture Ass'n of America
Nat'l Air Cargo, Inc.
Nat'l Nutritional Foods Ass'n
Nat'l Retail Federation
Nogales, Arizona, City of
Nu Skin Internat'l Inc.
Owens Corning
Peoria, Arizona, City of
Pfizer, Inc.
Pharmacia Corp.
Pharmanex
Policy Development Group, Inc.
Project to Promote Competition and Innovation in the Digital Age
Research & Development Laboratories
Research Corp. Technology
Rexall Sundown
SBC Communications Inc.
SOL Source Technologies, Inc.
Styrene Information and Research Center
Taxpayers Against Fraud, The False Claims Legal Center
TCOM, L.P.
Unilever United States, Inc.
Utah Natural Products Alliance

HENDERSON, Jr., Thomas H.

1050 31st St. NW
Washington, DC 20007
Tel: (202)965-3500
Fax: (202)342-5484

Employers
Ass'n of Trial Lawyers of America (Chief Exec. Officer)

HENDERSON, Thomas J.

1401 New York Ave. NW
Suite 400
Washington, DC 20005
EMail: thenders@lawyerscomm.org
Tel: (202)662-8330
Fax: (202)783-5113

Employers
Lawyers' Committee for Civil Rights Under Law (Deputy Director for Litigation)

HENDERSON, Wade J.

1629 K St. NW
Suite 1010
Washington, DC 20006
EMail: henderson@civilrights.org
Tel: (202)466-3311
Fax: (202)466-3435
Registered: LDA

Employers
Leadership Conference on Civil Rights (Exec. Director)

HENDERSON, Wallace J.

1401 I St. NW
Suite 220
Washington, DC 20005
Tel: (202)216-8910
Fax: (202)216-8901
Registered: LDA

Chief Counsel (1997-99) and Chief of Staff (1980-83) to Rep. Wilbert J. Tauzin (R-LA). Chief of Staff to Senator John B. Breaux (D-LA), 1987-93. Staff Director, Subcommittee on Panama Canal/Outer Continental Shelf, House Committee on Merchant Marine and Fisheries, 1986-87.

Employers
Public Strategies, Inc.

Clients Represented

On Behalf of Public Strategies, Inc.

Bridgestone/Firestone, Inc.
Cellular Telecommunications and Internet Ass'n
Fantasma Networks, Inc.
ITRON, Inc.
United States Telecom Ass'n

HENDRICK, Scott

1875 Connecticut Ave. NW
Suite 540
Washington, DC 20009
Tel: (202)986-2200 Ext: 3017
Fax: (202)986-2525

Employers
Food Research and Action Center (Legislative Associate)

HENDRICKS, Karen

601 13th St. NW
Suite 400 North
Washington, DC 20005
EMail: khendricks@aap.org
Tel: (202)347-8600
Fax: (202)393-6137
Registered: LDA

Employers
American Academy of Pediatrics (Assistant Director)

HENDRICKSON, Dr. Connie

515 King St.
Suite 420
Alexandria, VA 22314
Tel: (703)836-2090
Fax: (703)684-6048

Employers
American Institute of Chemists (President)

HENDRICKSON, Florence

445 12th St. NW
Room 8-C432
Washington, DC 20554
Tel: (202)418-1900
Fax: (202)418-2806

Employers
Federal Communications Commission (Staff Assistant, Legislative and Intergovermental Affairs)

HENDRICKSON, Gail

701 Pennsylvania Ave. NW
Third Floor
Washington, DC 20004
Tel: (202)508-5995
Fax: (202)508-5924
Registered: LDA

Employers
The Electric Vehicle Ass'n of the Americas (EVAA) (Associate Director)

HENDRICKSON, Ron

1110 N. Glebe Rd.
Suite 1000
Arlington, VA 22201
EMail: chiro@erols.com
Tel: (703)528-5000
Fax: (703)528-5023

Employers
Foundation for the Advancement of Chiropractic Tenets and Science (Exec. Director)
Internat'l Chiropractors Ass'n (Exec. Director)

HENDRIX, R. Brian

2550 M St. NW
Washington, DC 20037-1350
EMail: bhendrix@pattonboggs.com
Tel: (202)457-6000
Fax: (202)457-6315
Registered: LDA

Employers
Patton Boggs, LLP (Associate)

Clients Represented

On Behalf of Patton Boggs, LLP

Chesapeake Bay Foundation

HENIGAN, Dennis

1225 I St. NW
Suite 1100
Washington, DC 20005
Tel: (202)898-0792
Fax: (202)371-9615

Employers
Handgun Control, Inc. (General Counsel and Director, Legal Action Project)

HENINGER, Lynn W.

1735 Jefferson Davis Hwy.
Suite 1001
Arlington, VA 22202-3461
Tel: (703)413-6300
Fax: (703)413-6316
Registered: LDA

Employers
Thiokol Propulsion (Director, Legislative Liaison (Space))

HENLEY, Tracey G.

801 Pennsylvania Ave. NW
Suite 350
Washington, DC 20004
EMail: thenley@nnsdc.com
Tel: (202)783-2262
Fax: (202)783-1746

Employers
Newport News Shipbuilding Inc. (Manager, PAC)

HENNEBERGER, Lawrence F.

1050 Connecticut Ave. NW
Washington, DC 20036-5339
Tel: (202)857-6000
Fax: (202)857-6395
Registered: LDA

Employers
Arent Fox Kintner Plotkin & Kahn, PLLC (Member)

Clients Represented

On Behalf of Arent Fox Kintner Plotkin & Kahn, PLLC

Motor and Equipment Manufacturers Ass'n
Parker Hannifin Corp.

HENNEBERRY, Brian

555 11th St. NW
Suite 750
Washington, DC 20005
Tel: (202)637-3506
Fax: (202)637-3504

Legislative Aide, Sen. Sam Brownback (R-KA), 1996-2000; Inspector, Bureau of Alcohol, Tobacco and Firearms (BATF), 1994-95; Public Affairs Specialist, BATF, 1993-94.

Employers
El Paso Corporation (Federal Government Affairs Representative)

HENNEBERRY, Joan

444 N. Capitol St. NW
Suite 267
Washington, DC 20001-1512
EMail: jhenneberry@nga.org
Tel: (202)624-3644
Fax: (202)624-5313

Employers
Nat'l Governors' Ass'n (Policy Studies Director for Health)

HENNEBERRY, Margaretha M.

1000 Connecticut Ave. NW
Suite 202
Washington, DC 20036
Tel: (202)466-5428
Fax: (202)452-8540

Employers
World Jurist Ass'n of the World Peace Through Law Center (Exec. V. President)

HENNESSEY, Mary C.

1301 K St. NW
Suite 800 East
Washington, DC 20005
EMail: mhenness@ropesgray.com
Tel: (202)626-3900
Fax: (202)626-3961

Employers
Ropes & Gray (Associate)

HENNESSY, Tom

444 N. Capitol St. NW
Suite 601B
Washington, DC 20001
EMail: info@futuretrends.org
Tel: (202)347-9001
Fax: (202)347-9004

Employers
Congressional Institute for the Future (Exec. Director)

HENNEY, Cmdr. Fred

The Pentagon
MS: 5C768
Washington, DC 20350-1300
EMail: fred.henney@hq.navy.mil
Tel: (703)695-0395
Fax: (703)614-7089

Employers
Department of Navy (Director, Public Affairs and Contract Notifications Division, Legislative Affairs)

HENNING, C. Randall

11 Dupont Circle NW
Suite 620
Washington, DC 20036
EMail: henning@iie.com
Tel: (202)328-9000
Fax: (202)328-5432

Employers
Institute for Internat'l Economics (Visiting Fellow)

HENNING, Stephanie

555 13th St. NW
Washington, DC 20004-1109
Tel: (202)637-5600
Fax: (202)637-5910

Employers
Hogan & Hartson L.L.P.

Clients Represented
On Behalf of Hogan & Hartson L.L.P.
Payless Shoe Source

HENRI, Erica

734 15th St. NW
Suite 500
Washington, DC 20005
Tel: (202)393-8164
Fax: (202)393-0649

Employers
Women's Campaign Fund (Political Director)

HENRICH, Carolyn

1090 Vermont Ave. NW
Suite 1200
Washington, DC 20005
Tel: (202)289-6790
Fax: (202)289-6791
Registered: LDA

Employers
Nat'l Congress of Parents and Teachers (Government Relations Specialist)

HENRICKS, Jayd

2131 K St. NW
Suite 710
Washington, DC 20037-1810
Tel: (202)347-6787
Fax: (202)737-4727

Employers
The Roth Group (Legislative Director)

Clients Represented
On Behalf of The Roth Group
Ass'n of Retail Travel Agents
Johnson Controls, Inc.

HENRIKSEN, Melissa

1655 N. Fort Meyer Dr.
Suite 510
Arlington, VA 22209
Tel: (703)525-0511
Fax: (703)525-0743

Employers
Composites Fabricators Ass'n (Exec. Director)

HENRY, Darrell

400 N. Capitol St. NW
Washington, DC 20001
Tel: (202)824-7000
Fax: (202)824-7115
Registered: LDA

Employers
American Gas Ass'n (Director, Public Affairs)

HENRY, Denise M.

1001 Pennsylvania Ave. NW
Suite 760 North
Washington, DC 20004
Tel: (202)661-7060
Fax: (202)661-7066
Registered: LDA
Former Staff Member, Select Committee on Aging, U.S. Senate.

Employers
The Legislative Strategies Group, LLC (Lobbyist)

Clients Represented
On Behalf of The Legislative Strategies Group, LLC
Allscripts Inc.
American Academy of Dermatology
American College of Cardiology
American Hospital Ass'n
Amgen
Eye Bank Ass'n of America
Hoffmann-La Roche Inc.
Joint Commission on the Accreditation of Health Care Organizations
Eli Lilly and Co.
MedPartners, Inc.
Nat'l Orthotics Manufacturers Ass'n

HENRY, Fred

425 Second St. NW
Washington, DC 20001
Tel: (202)393-4409
Fax: (202)783-3254

Employers
Community for Creative Non-Violence (V. President and Co-Spokesperson)

HENRY, James L.

5201 Auth Way
Fifth Floor
Camp Springs, MD 20746
Tel: (301)423-3335
Fax: (301)423-0634
Registered: LDA

Employers
Transportation Institute (Chairman and President)

HENRY, Jeffrey W.

507 C St. NE
Washington, DC 20002-5809
Tel: (202)544-7944
Fax: (202)544-7975
Registered: LDA
EMail: jhenry@beacon-group.net

Employers
Beacon Consulting Group, Inc. (Legislative Director)

Clients Represented
On Behalf of Beacon Consulting Group, Inc.
American Trauma Soc.
Cummins-Allison Corp.
Museum of Science and Industry
Nat'l Crime Prevention Council
Oregon Health Sciences University
Public/Private Ventures

HENRY, Ronald K.

The McPherson Bldg.
901 15th St. NW, Suite 1100
Washington, DC 20005
Tel: (202)682-3500
Fax: (202)682-3580
Registered: LDA

Employers
Kaye Scholer LLP (Partner)

HENRY, Wayne O.

401 Ninth St. NW
Suite 1100
Washington, DC 20004
EMail: whenry@duke-energy.com
Tel: (202)331-8090
Fax: (202)331-1181

Employers
Duke Energy (Director, Federal Government Affairs)

HENSING, David J.

400 Virginia Ave. SW
Suite 800
Washington, DC 20024-2370
Tel: (202)484-4847
Fax: (202)484-3483

Employers
Intelligent Transportation Soc. of America (President)

HENSLER, David J.

555 13th St. NW
Washington, DC 20004-1109
Tel: (202)637-5600
Fax: (202)637-5910
Registered: LDA

Employers
Hogan & Hartson L.L.P.

Clients Represented
On Behalf of Hogan & Hartson L.L.P.
Michigan Consolidated Gas Co.
Warland Investment Co.

HENSLEY, William L.

1667 K St. NW
Suite 1230
Washington, DC 20006
Tel: (202)466-3866
Fax: (202)466-3886
Registered: LDA
EMail: Hensleywl@alyeska-pipeline.com

Employers
Alyeska Pipeline Service Co. (Manager, Federal Government Relations)

HENTELEFF, Thomas O.

1140 19th St. NW
Suite 900
Washington, DC 20036
EMail: toh@kkblaw.com
Tel: (202)223-5120
Fax: (202)223-5619
Law Clerk for Judge David T. Lewis, U.S. Court of Appeals, Tenth Circuit, 1968-69.

Employers
Kleinfeld, Kaplan and Becker (Partner)

Clients Represented
On Behalf of Kleinfeld, Kaplan and Becker
Contact Lens Institute

HEPBURN, Michael A.

1200 New Hampshire Ave. NW
Suite 800
Washington, DC 20036-6802
EMail: mhepburn@dlalaw.com
Tel: (202)776-2000
Fax: (202)776-2222

Employers
Dow, Lohnes & Albertson, PLLC (Member)

HERBERT, Allen

2291 Wood Oak Dr.
Herndon, VA 20171
Tel: (703)709-4621
Registered: LDA

Employers
Self-employed as an independent consultant.

Clients Represented
As an independent consultant
Computer Associates Internat'l, Inc.

HERBOLSHEIMER, Robert T.

733 15th St. NW
Suite 1120
Washington, DC 20005
Tel: (202)628-9200
Fax: (202)628-9201
Registered: LDA

Employers
Law Offices of Robert T. Herbolsheimer (Partner)

Clients Represented
On Behalf of Law Offices of Robert T. Herbolsheimer
Bowling Proprietors' Ass'n of America

HERLIHY, Thomas W.

400 Seventh St. SW
MS: 10100
Washington, DC 20590
Tel: (202)366-4687
Fax: (202)366-7153

Employers
Department of Transportation (Assistant General Counsel, Office of Legislation)

HERMAN, Andrew D.

923 15th St. NW
Washington, DC 20005
Tel: (202)662-9700
Fax: (202)737-7565
Registered: LDA
EMail: aherman@brand-frulla.com

Employers
Brand & Frulla, P.C. (Associate)

Clients Represented
On Behalf of Brand & Frulla, P.C.
United Airlines

HERMAN, Angela D.

1130 Connecticut Ave. NW
Suite 1000
Washington, DC 20036
Tel: (202)828-7100
Fax: (202)293-1219
Registered: LDA
EMail: aherman@aiadc.org

Employers
American Insurance Ass'n (Director, Federal Affairs)

HERMAN, Betsy M.

9312 Old Georgetown Rd.
Bethesda, MD 20814
Tel: (301)493-9667
Fax: (301)530-2752

Employers
American Podiatric Medical Students Ass'n (Exec. Director)

HERMAN, Doug

1875 Connecticut Ave. NW
Suite 414
Washington, DC 20009
Tel: (202)745-4900
Fax: (202)745-0215

Employers
The Rendon Group, Inc.

HERMANDORFER, Wayne

1725 Jefferson Davis Hwy.
Crystal Square 2, Suite 300
Arlington, VA 22202
Tel: (703)413-5600
Fax: (703)413-5617
Registered: LDA

Employers
Lockheed Martin Corp. (Director, Legislative Affairs)

HERMANN, Ronda

1201 New York Ave. NW
Suite 600
Washington, DC 20005-3931
Tel: (202)289-3100
Fax: (202)289-3199

Employers
American Hotel and Lodging Ass'n (Manager, Legislative Communications)

HERMES, James

One Dupont Circle NW
Suite 410
Washington, DC 20036
Tel: (202)728-0200
Fax: (202)833-2467

Employers
American Ass'n of Community Colleges (Legislative Associate)

HERNANDEZ, Mary

409 Third St. SW
Suite 7900
Washington, DC 20416
EMail: mary.hernandez@sba.gov
Tel: (202)205-6700
Fax: (202)205-7374

Employers
Small Business Administration (Congressional Relations Specialist)

HEROLD, Arthur

1747 Pennsylvania Ave. NW
Suite 1000
Washington, DC 20006
Tel: (202)785-9500
Fax: (202)835-0243

Employers
Webster, Chamberlain & Bean (Partner)

Clients Represented

On Behalf of Webster, Chamberlain & Bean
American Soc. of Radiologic Technologists
American Staffing Ass'n
Ass'n of School Business Officials Internat'l
Internat'l Safety Equipment Ass'n (ISEA)
Taxicab, Limousine and Paratransit Ass'n

HEROLD, Eve

15825 Shady Grove Rd.
Suite 140
Rockville, MD 20850
EMail: eherold@ahaf.org
Tel: (301)948-3244
Fax: (301)258-9454

Employers
American Health Assistance Foundation (Public Education Manager)

HERON, Jr., Julian B.

1025 Thomas Jefferson St. NW
Suite 407 West
Washington, DC 20007
Tel: (202)342-1300
Fax: (202)342-5880
Registered: LDA

Employers
Tuttle, Taylor & Heron (Senior Partner)

Clients Represented

On Behalf of Tuttle, Taylor & Heron
Blue Diamond Growers
Crop Growers Insurance Co.
Sunkist Growers, Inc.

HERR, Wendy W.

Ten Pidgeon Hill Dr.
Suite 150
Sterling, VA 20165
EMail: wendy@debrunnerandassociates.com
Tel: (703)444-4091
Fax: (703)444-3029
Registered: LDA

Employers
DeBrunner and Associates, Inc. (Associate)

Clients Represented

On Behalf of DeBrunner and Associates, Inc.
Catholic Healthcare West
Health Quest
Nat'l Ass'n of Urban Hospitals
Susquehanna Health System

HERRARA-DAVILA, Nina V.W.

901 15th St. NW
Suite 370
Washington, DC 20005
Tel: (202)371-9600
Fax: (202)371-0808

Employers
Global Communicators

Clients Represented

On Behalf of Global Communicators
Jordan Tourism Board

HERRERA, George

2175 K St. NW
Suite 100
Washington, DC 20036
Tel: (202)842-1212
Fax: (202)842-3221

Employers
U.S. Hispanic Chamber of Commerce (President and Chief Exec. Officer)

HERRERA, Juan J.

504 C St. NE
Washington, DC 20002
Tel: (202)543-1771
Fax: (202)546-2143

Employers
Congressional Hispanic Caucus Institute (CHCI) (Communications Director)

HERRIN, Carl A.

1776 Massachusetts Ave. NW
Suite 700
Washington, DC 20036
EMail: herrin@actr.org
Tel: (202)833-7522
Fax: (202)872-9178
Registered: LDA

Employers
American Councils for Internat'l Education: ACTR/ACCELS (Director, Government Relations)

HERRING, Lee

1015 15th St. NW
Suite 802
Washington, DC 20005
EMail: lherring@acec.org
Tel: (202)347-7474
Fax: (202)898-0068

Employers
American Consulting Engineers Council (Director, Public Affairs)

HERRITY, John F.

10335 Democracy Ln.
Fairfax, VA 22030
Tel: (703)352-0225
Fax: (703)352-8894
Registered: LDA

Employers
Solutions Group (President)

Clients Represented

On Behalf of Solutions Group
Wheelabrator-Cleanwater Systems-BioGro Division

HERRITY, Thomas M.

1029 N. Royal St.
Suite 400
Alexandria, VA 22314
EMail: THerrity@directimpact.com
Tel: (703)684-1245
Fax: (703)684-1249

Employers
The Direct Impact Co. (President)

HERRNSTADT, Owen

9000 Machinists Pl.
Upper Marlboro, MD 20772-2687
Tel: (301)967-4500
Fax: (301)967-4588

Employers
Internat'l Ass'n of Machinists and Aerospace Workers (Director, International Affairs)

HERSH, Alexis

1223 Potomac St. NW
Washington, DC 20007-0231
EMail: alexishersh@mindspring.com
Tel: (202)333-8190
Fax: (202)337-3809
Registered: LDA

Employers
Robert N. Pyle & Associates (Senior V. President)

Clients Represented

On Behalf of Robert N. Pyle & Associates
Bulgarian-American Business Center
Elkem Metals Co.
Independent Bakers Ass'n
Internat'l Dairy-Deli-Bakery Ass'n
McKee Foods Corp.
Orbex Resources
Strategic Minerals Corp.
Welch's Foods, Inc.

HERSHAFT, Alex

P.O. Box 30654
Bethesda, MD 20824
EMail: farm@farmusa.org
Tel: (301)530-1737
Fax: (301)530-5747

Employers
Farm Animal Reform Movement (FARM) (President)

HERSHMAN, Esther

901 N. Pitt St.
Suite 320
Alexandria, VA 22314
Tel: (703)836-4880
Fax: (703)836-6941

Employers
Nat'l Ass'n of Partners in Education (Symposium Coordinator)

HERSHOW, Sheila

1130 Connecticut Ave. NW
Suite 600
Washington, DC 20036
Tel: (202)296-0263
Fax: (202)452-9371

Employers
Nichols-Dezenhall Communication Management Group, Ltd. (V. President)

HERSON, Michael

1800 K St. NW
Suite 1010
Washington, DC 20006
EMail: mhersonadi@aol.com
Tel: (202)296-5030
Fax: (202)296-4750
Registered: LDA, FARA

Special Assistant, Office of the Secretary, Department of Defense, 1990-93.

Employers
American Defense Internat'l, Inc. (President)

Clients Represented

On Behalf of American Defense Internat'l, Inc.
Barber Colman Co.
Beretta U.S.A. Corp.
Bofors Defence AB
Dialogic Communications Corp.
Drexel University
East/West Industries
Ensign-Bickford Co.
EWA Land Information Group, Inc.
Fibernet LLC
Friction Free Technologies Inc.
Ganaden Biotech Inc.
GEO Centers, Inc.
GIAT Industries
Hagglunds Moelv AS
InformaTech, Inc.
InvenCom LLC
Koable Co., Ltd.
Large Scale Biology
Le Meilleur Co., Ltd.
Longworth Industries Inc.
Marine Desalination Systems LLC
MEGAXESS, Inc.
Ordnance Development and Engineering Co. of Singapore
Pacific Consolidated Industries
PDI Ground Support Systems, Inc.
Raytheon Missile Systems
Saab AB
Sarnoff Corp.
SINTEF Telecom and Informatics
Smiths Industries Aerospace and Defense Systems
Stidd Systems, Inc.
Stratus Systems Inc.
Syntroleum Corp.
Time Domain Corp.
University Hospital of Tromso
Virtual Drug Development
Virtual Impact Productions
VISICU
ViTel Net
Xeta Internat'l Corp.
Youyang

HERT, James

1815 N. Fort Myer Dr.
Suite 1020
Arlington, VA 22209
Tel: (703)528-7701
Fax: (703)528-7966

Employers
Public Risk Management Ass'n (Interim Exec. Director)

HERTEL, Hon. Dennis M.

1100 Connecticut Ave. NW
Suite 1000
Washington, DC 20036
Tel: (202)321-1800
Fax: (703)759-6231
Registered: LDA
Former Member, U.S. House of Representative (D-MI), 1981-93.

Employers
Dennis M. Hertel & Associates (President)

Clients Represented
On Behalf of Dennis M. Hertel & Associates
Boysville
Detroit Metropolitan Airport
Henry Ford Museum in Greenfield Village
Northwood Inc.
Sault Ste. Marie Tribe of Chippewa Indians

HERTZBERG, Michael A.

1299 Pennsylvania Ave. NW
Washington, DC 20004-2402
Tel: (202)783-0800
Fax: (202)383-6610
EMail: hertzbergm@howrey.com

Employers
Howrey Simon Arnold & White (Partner)

Clients Represented
On Behalf of Howrey Simon Arnold & White
Kyocera Corp.
LEP Scientific Ltd.
USA/Scientific Plastics Inc.

HERTZOG, Linda

40 Ivy St. SE
Washington, DC 20003
Tel: (202)547-2230
Fax: (202)547-7640
EMail: linda@dealer.org

Employers
Nat'l Lumber and Building Material Dealers Ass'n (Director, Member Services)

HERWITT, Allison

1156 15th St. NW
Suite 700
Washington, DC 20005
Tel: (202)973-3000
Fax: (202)973-3096
Registered: LDA
EMail: aherwitt@naral.org

Employers
Nat'l Abortion and Reproductive Rights Action League (Director, Government Relations)

HERZFELD, Shannon S. S.

1100 15th St. NW
Suite 900
Washington, DC 20005
Tel: (202)835-3400
Fax: (202)835-3414
Registered: LDA

Employers
Pharmaceutical Research and Manufacturers of America (Senior V. President, International)

HERZOG, John

2800 Shirlington Rd.
Suite 300
Arlington, VA 22206
Tel: (703)824-8842
Fax: (703)575-4449
Registered: LDA

Employers
Air Conditioning Contractors of America (Staff V. President, Public Policy)

HESCHELES, Heather

2200 Clarendon Blvd.
Suite 1202
Arlington, VA 22201
Tel: (703)284-5400
Fax: (703)284-5449

Employers
Ball Aerospace & Technologies Corp. (Manager, Lesgislative Affairs)

HESS, Catherine

1220 19th St. NW
Washington, DC 20036
Tel: (202)775-0436
Registered: LDA

Employers
Ass'n of Maternal and Child Health Programs (AMCHP)

HESS, Doug

1875 Connecticut Ave. NW
Suite 540
Washington, DC 20009
Tel: (202)986-2200
Ext: 3004
Fax: (202)986-2525

Employers
Food Research and Action Center (Policy Analyst/Researcher)

HESS, Stephen

1775 Massachusetts Ave. NW
Washington, DC 20036-2188
Tel: (202)797-6000
Fax: (202)797-6004
U.S. Representative to United Nations General Assembly, 1976; Editor-in-Chief of Republican Party Platform, 1976; Chairman, White House Committee on Children and Youth, 1970-71; Presidential Advisor for Urban Affairs, 1969; Presidential Speechwriter, 1959-61.

Employers
The Brookings Institution (Senior Fellow, Governmental Studies)

HESSBURG, Laura

409 12th St. SW
P.O. Box 96920
Washington, DC 20090-6920
Tel: (202)863-2534
Fax: (202)488-3985
Registered: LDA
EMail: lhessburg@acog.org

Employers
American College of Obstetricians and Gynecologists (Senior Federal Government Relations Representative)

HESSE, Christine

1333 New Hampshire Ave. NW
Suite 400
Washington, DC 20036
Tel: (202)887-4000
Fax: (202)887-4288

Employers
Akin, Gump, Strauss, Hauer & Feld, L.L.P.

Clients Represented
On Behalf of Akin, Gump, Strauss, Hauer & Feld, L.L.P.
EMC Corp.
Mortgage Insurance Companies of America

HESSE, III, John

1275 Pennsylvania Ave. NW
Suite 800
Washington, DC 20004
Tel: (202)293-5760
Fax: (202)463-4569
Registered: LDA

Employers
Direct Selling Ass'n (Senior Attorney and Director, Government Relations)

HESSE, Richard J.

1060 Leigh Mill Rd.
Great Falls, VA 22066
Tel: (703)759-6746
Fax: (703)438-0743

Employers
Harza Engineering Co. (Manager, Washington Office and Senior Consultant)

HESSEL, Arthur R.

1050 17th St. NW
Suite 900
Washington, DC 20036
Tel: (202)466-5300
Fax: (202)466-5508
Special Assistant to the Assistant Secretary, Department of Housing and Urban Development, 1969-72.

Employers
Hessel and Aluise, P.C. (Principal)

HESSLER, Clare

1325 G St. NW
Suite 1000
Washington, DC 20005-3104
Tel: (202)737-1770
Fax: (202)626-0900
Registered: LDA

Employers
Institute of Scrap Recycling Industries, Inc. (Director, Federal and State Policy)

HESTER, Theodore M.

1730 Pennsylvania Ave. NW
Suite 1200
Washington, DC 20006-4706
Tel: (202)737-0500
Fax: (202)626-3737
Registered: LDA

Employers
King & Spalding (Partner)

Clients Represented
On Behalf of King & Spalding
Blue Cross Blue Shield Ass'n
Bridgestone/Firestone, Inc.
Georgia Electric Membership Corp.
Lockheed Martin Corp.
Minnesota Mining and Manufacturing (3M Pharmaceuticals)
Salt Lake City Olympic Organizing Committee
Southern Tier Cement Committee
Teledyne-Commodore, LLC

HETTINGER, Michael

2550 M St. NW
Washington, DC 20037-1350
Tel: (202)457-6000
Fax: (202)457-6315
Registered: LDA
Former Chief of Staff to Rep. Thomas Davis (R-VA).

Employers
Patton Boggs, LLP (Public Policy Counselor)

Clients Represented
On Behalf of Patton Boggs, LLP
Internet Safety Ass'n

HEUNEMAN, Donna Z.

1234 Massachusetts Ave. NW
Suite 103
Washington, DC 20005
Tel: (202)347-1234
Fax: (202)347-4023
EMail: naddc@naddc.org

Employers
Nat'l Ass'n of Developmental Disabilities Councils (Exec. Director)

HEWES, Jr., C. Alexander

1000 Potomac St. NW
Suite 300
Washington, DC 20007
Tel: (202)337-6200
Fax: (202)333-0871
Assistant Counsel, Senate Committee on Banking, Housing and Urban Affairs, 1970-73.

Employers
Hewes, Gelband, Lambert & Dann, P.C. (Managing Partner)

HEWITT, Charles C.

225 Reinekers Ln.
Suite 600
Alexandria, VA 22314
Tel: (703)549-6990
Fax: (703)549-7640
Registered: LDA

Employers
Satellite Broadcasting and Communications Ass'n (President)

HEWITT, Mary E.

1332 Independence Ave. SE
Washington, DC 20003-2365
Tel: (202)543-4600

Employers
Morgan Casner Associates, Inc. (V. President)

HEYDON, Douglas A.

601 13th St. NW
Suite 710 North
Washington, DC 20005
Tel: (202)628-3936
Fax: (202)628-3949
EMail: dh@arianespace-inc.com

Employers
ArianeSpace, Inc. (Chairman)

HEYL, Michael S.

1850 M St. NW
Suite 700
Washington, DC 20036
Tel: (202)721-4100
Fax: (202)296-8120
Registered: LDA
EMail: mike.heyl@socma.com

Employers
Synthetic Organic Chemical Manufacturers Ass'n (Manager, Government Relations)

HEYWOOD, Christopher A.

1120 20th St. NW
Suite 700 North
Washington, DC 20036-3406
Tel: (202)973-1200
Fax: (202)973-1212

Employers
Hall, Estill, Hardwick, Gable, Golden & Nelson (Associate)

HEZIR, Joseph

819 Seventh St. NW
Washington, DC 20001
Tel: (202)833-8940
Fax: (202)833-8943
Registered: LDA

Employers
EOP Group, Inc.

Clients Represented

On Behalf of EOP Group, Inc.
American Petroleum Institute
The Boeing Co.
The Business Roundtable
Central Illinois Public Service Co.
Chlorine Chemistry Council
Continental Grain Co.
Edison Electric Institute
FMC Corp.
Gas Research Institute
Internat'l Food Additives Council
Monsanto Co.
Nuclear Energy Institute
Uranium Producers of America
Zirconia Sales America

HIATT, Jonathan

815 16th St. NW
Washington, DC 20006
Tel: (202)637-5000
Fax: (202)637-5058

Employers
AFL-CIO (American Federation of Labor and Congress of Industrial Organizations) (General Counsel)

HIBBERT, Robert G.

600 13th St. NW
Washington, DC 20005-3096
Tel: (202)756-8216
Fax: (202)756-8087
EMail: rhibbert@mwe.com
Former Trial Attorney, Department of Agriculture.

Employers
McDermott, Will and Emery (Partner)

Clients Represented

On Behalf of McDermott, Will and Emery
Campbell Soup Co.

HICKEY, Christopher

1001 Pennsylvania Ave. NW
Suite 700 South
Washington, DC 20004
Tel: (202)662-2650
Fax: (202)662-2674
Registered: LDA

Employers
Honeywell Internat'l, Inc. (Director, Aerospace Government Relations)

HICKEY, Daniel

1301 Pennsylvania Ave. NW
Suite 1100
Washington, DC 20004-1707
Tel: (202)626-4000
Fax: (202)626-4208
Registered: LDA

Employers
Air Transport Ass'n of America (Director, Government Affairs)

HICKEY, James J.

1100 Wilson Blvd.
Suite 1500
Arlington, VA 22209
Tel: (703)841-5725
Fax: (703)841-5792
Registered: LDA
EMail: james_j_hickey@raytheon.com

Employers
Raytheon Co. (Director, Congressional Relations, Army Programs)

HICKEY, Jr., James J.

1700 K St. NW
Suite 300
Washington, DC 20006
Tel: (202)296-4031
Fax: (202)296-1970
Registered: LDA
EMail: ahc@horsecouncil.org

Employers
American Horse Council, Inc. (President)

HICKEY, John A.

1050 Thomas Jefferson St. NW
Seventh Floor
Washington, DC 20007
Tel: (202)298-1800
Fax: (202)338-2416
EMail: JAH@vnf.com

Employers
Van Ness Feldman, P.C. (Associate)

HICKIE, Jane

901 15th St. NW
Suite 700
Washington, DC 20005-2301
Tel: (202)371-6000
Fax: (202)371-6279
Registered: LDA
EMail: vjhickie@verner.com

Employers
Verner, Liipfert, Bernhard, McPherson and Hand, Chartered (Member of Firm)

Clients Represented

On Behalf of Verner, Liipfert, Bernhard, McPherson and Hand, Chartered
Austin, Texas, City of
Baca Land and Cattle Co.
Capital Metropolitan Transportation Authority
Envirocare of Texas, Inc.
Ferrocarril Mexicano, S.A. de C.V.
Lockheed Martin Tactical Systems
Mills Corporation
Nat'l Broadcasting Co.
RJR Nabisco Holdings Co.
SBC Communications Inc.
Texas Manufactured Housing Ass'n

HICKMAN, USN (Ret.), RAdm. Donald "Smoke"

11 Canal Center Plaza
Suite 103
Alexandria, VA 22314
Tel: (703)683-4222
Fax: (703)683-0645
Registered: LDA

Employers
The Spectrum Group

HICKMAN, Peter

200 Independence Ave. SW
Room 341H
Washington, DC 20201
Tel: (202)690-5950
Fax: (202)690-8168

Employers
Department of Health and Human Services - Health Care Financing Administration (Director, Medicare Part B Analysis Group)

HICKMOTT, Robert

1401 K St. NW
12th Floor
Washington, DC 20005
Tel: (202)393-4760
Fax: (202)393-3516
Registered: LDA

Employers
The Smith-Free Group (Senior V. President)

Clients Represented

On Behalf of The Smith-Free Group
Paucatuck Eastern Pequot Tribal Nation
U.S. Wireless Data, Inc.
Washington Group Internat'l
Westinghouse Government Services Group
Xcel Energy, Inc.

HICKOX, Amy

606 E. Capitol St. NE
Washington, DC 20003
Tel: (202)546-1493
Fax: (202)546-7807
EMail: amyhickox@hotmail.com
Principal Director for Strategy, Plans and Analysis (1997-98), Acting Principal Deputy Assistant Secretary (1996-97), Director, Civil- Military Programs (1993-96), and Special Assistant to the Secretary (1993), Department of Defense. Research Assistant, House Armed Services Committee, 1991-93. Staff Assistant to Rep. Tom McMillen (D-MD).

Employers
Broad-Band Solutions (Principal)

Clients Represented

On Behalf of Broad-Band Solutions
Register.com

HICKS, Carol A.

P.O. Box 2115
Springfield, VA 22152
Tel: (703)866-4290
Fax: (703)866-4928

Employers
Hicks-Richardson Associates (Managing Partner)

Clients Represented

On Behalf of Hicks-Richardson Associates
East Valley Water District
Tarrant Regional Water District

HICKS, Fred B.

1401 New York Ave. NW
Suite 640
Washington, DC 20005
Tel: (202)628-8303
Fax: (202)628-2846
Registered: LDA

Employers
American Water Works Ass'n (Washington Representative, American Water Works Foundation)
Hicks-Richardson Associates (Partner)

Clients Represented

On Behalf of Hicks-Richardson Associates
East Valley Water District
San Gabriel Valley Water Ass'n
Tarrant Regional Water District

HICKS, Louis

1150 17th St. NW
Washington, DC 20036
Tel: (202)862-5800
Fax: (202)862-7177
EMail: lhicks@aei.org

Employers
American Enterprise Institute for Public Policy Research (Research Fellow)

HICKS, Nancy

600 New Hampshire Ave. NW
Suite 601
Washington, DC 20037
Tel: (202)333-7400
Fax: (202)333-1638

Employers
Hill and Knowlton, Inc. (Sr. Managing Director, Sr. Counselor Health)

Clients Represented

On Behalf of Hill and Knowlton, Inc.
American Red Cross

HIDEN, Barbara L.

1101 16th St. NW
Washington, DC 20036-4877
Tel: (202)463-6740
Fax: (202)659-5349
Registered: LDA

Employers
Nat'l Soft Drink Ass'n (Director, Federal Affairs)

HIEBERT, Peter N.

1400 L St. NW
Washington, DC 20005-3502
Tel: (202)371-5716
Fax: (202)371-5950
Registered: LDA
EMail: phiebert@winston.com

Employers
Winston & Strawn (Partner, Legislative and Regulatory Practice)

Clients Represented

On Behalf of Winston & Strawn
Benrus Watch Co.
Columbia Ventures, LLC
DHL Airways, Inc.
Puerto Rico, Commonwealth of
University of California at Los Angeles
Virgin Islands Watch and Jewelry Manufacturers Ass'n
Virgin Islands, Government of the

HIEMSTRA, Hal D.

1455 F St. NW
Suite 225
Washington, DC 20005
Tel: (202)638-3307
Fax: (202)783-6947
Registered: LDA
EMail: hhiemstra@bjllp.com

Employers
Ball Janik, LLP (Government Relations Consultant)

Clients Represented

On Behalf of Ball Janik, LLP

Clackamas, Oregon, County of
Greenbrier Companies
Highline School District Educational Resources
Oregon Department of Transportation
Restore America's Estuaries
Tukwila, Washington, City of

HIESTAND, Mike

1815 N. Fort Myer Dr.
Suite 900
Arlington, VA 22209-1817
Tel: (703)807-1904
Fax: (703)807-2109

Employers

Student Press Law Center (Staff Attorney)

HIGGINBOTHAM, J. Thomas

1455 Pennsylvania Ave. NW
Suite 400
Washington, DC 20004-1081
Tel: (202)737-6600
Fax: (202)638-4512
Registered: LDA
EMail: Internet: thigginbotham@aicpa.org

Employers

American Institute of Certified Public Accountants (V. President, Congressional and Political Affairs)

HIGGINS, Kathryn

1785 Massachusetts Ave. NW
Washington, DC 20036
Tel: (202)588-6000
Fax: (202)588-6059
Registered: LDA

Employers

Nat'l Trust for Historic Preservation (V. President, Public Policy)

HIGGINS, Lauren

9000 Rockville Pike
Bldg. One, Room 244
Bethesda, MD 20892
Tel: (301)496-3471
Fax: (301)496-0840
EMail: higginsl@od.nih.gov

Employers

Department of Health and Human Services - Nat'l Institutes of Health (Legislative Analyst)

HIGGINS, Lawrence

1620 L St. NW
Suite 1210
Washington, DC 20036
Tel: (202)955-6062
Fax: (202)955-6070
Registered: LDA

Employers

Higgins, McGovern & Smith, LLC (Partner)

Clients Represented

On Behalf of Higgins, McGovern & Smith, LLC

Metropolitan Life Insurance Co.
Northwestern Mutual Life Insurance Co.

HIGGINS, Terrence S.

1899 L St. NW
Suite 1000
Washington, DC 20036
Tel: (202)457-0480
Fax: (202)457-0486
Registered: LDA
EMail: terry_higgins@npradc.org

Employers

Nat'l Petrochemical Refiners Ass'n (Ass't Treasurer & Technical Director)

HIGHT, Martin

1015 15th St. NW
Suite 600
Washington, DC 20005
Tel: (202)789-2200
Fax: (202)289-6797
Registered: LDA
EMail: mhight@dc.asce.org

Employers

American Soc. of Civil Engineers (Senior Manager, Government Relations)

HIGLEY, Charlie

215 Pennsylvania Ave. SE
Washington, DC 20003
Tel: (202)546-4996

Employers

Public Citizen, Inc. (Senior Energy Policy Analyst)

HILBERT, II, John W.

900 Second St. NE
Suite 201
Washington, DC 20002
Tel: (202)842-0219
Fax: (202)842-0439
Registered: LDA
EMail: jhilbert@kinghornassociates.com

Employers

Kinghorn & Associates, L.L.C. (V. President, Legislative and Regulatory Affairs)

Clients Represented

On Behalf of Kinghorn & Associates, L.L.C.

Ferroalloys Ass'n
Non-Ferrous Founders' Soc.
South Carolina Research Authority
Tri-County Alliance

HILDEBRAND, Bruce

600 New Hampshire Ave. NW
Suite 601
Washington, DC 20037
Tel: (202)333-7400
Fax: (202)333-1638
Registered: LDA

Employers

Hill and Knowlton, Inc. (Senior Managing Director, Media Relations)

Clients Represented

On Behalf of Hill and Knowlton, Inc.

Ass'n of American Publishers
Cadmus/Energy Star
Fresenius Medical Care North America

HILDEBRAND, Daniel

1909 K St. NW
Washington, DC 20006
Tel: (202)263-3000
Fax: (202)263-3300

Employers

Mayer, Brown & Platt

Clients Represented

On Behalf of Mayer, Brown & Platt

Illinois, State of

HILDEBRAND, Jerry

200 Constitution Ave. NW
Washington, DC 20210
Tel: (202)693-3038
Fax: (202)693-3229
EMail: ghildebrand@doleta.gov

Employers

Department of Labor - Office of Workforce Security (Chief, Division of Legislation)

HILDEBRAND, Sarah M.

1111 19th St. NW
Suite 800
Washington, DC 20036
Tel: (202)463-2746
Fax: (202)463-2424
Registered: LDA
EMail: sarah_hildebrand@afandpa.org

Employers

American Forest & Paper Ass'n (V. President, Congressional Affairs)

HILDEBRANDT, David A.

601 13th St. NW
Suite 600 South
Washington, DC 20005
Tel: (202)626-3600
Fax: (202)639-9355

Employers

White & Case LLP

Clients Represented

On Behalf of White & Case LLP

Profit Sharing/401 (k) Council of America

HILDEBRANDT, Susan

2021 Massachusetts Ave. NW
Washington, DC 20036
Tel: (202)232-9033
Fax: (202)232-9044
Registered: LDA
EMail: shildebrandt@aafp.org

Employers

American Academy of Family Physicians (Assistant Director, Washington Office)

HILDEBRANT, Jeffrey P.

2099 Pennsylvania Ave. NW
Suite 100
Washington, DC 20006
Tel: (202)955-3000
Fax: (202)955-5564
Registered: LDA
EMail: jphildebe@hklaw.com

Employers

Holland & Knight LLP (Senior Counsel)

Clients Represented

On Behalf of Holland & Knight LLP

Nat'l Coalition of Minority Businesses
Texaco Group Inc.

HILDWINE, Regina

1350 I St. NW
Suite 300
Washington, DC 20005
Tel: (202)639-5900
Fax: (202)639-5932
Registered: LDA

Employers

Nat'l Food Processors Ass'n (Director, Technical Regulatory Affairs-FDA)

HILER, Bruce A.

555 13th St. NW
Suite 500 West
Washington, DC 20004
Tel: (202)383-5300
Fax: (202)383-5414
EMail: bhiler@omm.com

Associate Director (1990-94), Assistant Director (1985-90), Branch Chief (1981-85), Special Counsel (1981), and Staff Attorney (1978-80), all at the Securities and Exchange Commission.

Employers

O'Melveny and Myers LLP (Partner)

HILL, A. Karen

400 N. Capitol St. NW
Washington, DC 20001
Tel: (202)824-7225
Fax: (202)824-7115
EMail: khill@aga.org

Employers

American Gas Ass'n (V. President, Regulatory Affairs)

HILL, Alyce

1625 Massachusetts Ave. NW
Suite 400
Washington, DC 20036
Tel: (202)667-5636
Fax: (202)265-6332
EMail: ahill@aaionline.org

Employers

The Africa-America Institute (V. President)

HILL, Ann

601 Madison St.
Suite 300
Alexandria, VA 22314-1756
Tel: (703)739-6700
Fax: (703)739-6708

Employers

Flight Safety Foundation (Director, Membership and Development)

HILL, Carlisa

8200 Jones Branch Dr.
McLean, VA 22102
Tel: (703)903-3814
Fax: (703)903-3585

Employers

Federal Home Loan Mortgage Corp. (Freddie Mac) (Grants Manager, Freddie Mac Foundation)

HILL, Carolyn C.

601 Pennsylvania Ave. NW
Suite 720
Washington, DC 20004
Tel: (202)783-3974
Fax: (202)783-3982
Registered: LDA

Employers

Alltel Corporation (V. President, Federal Government Affairs)

HILL, Edward J.

730 15th St. NW
Fifth Floor
Washington, DC 20005
Tel: (202)624-4185
Fax: (202)383-3475
Registered: LDA
EMail: edward.j.hill@bankofamerica.com

Employers

Bank of America (V. President, Government Relations)

HILL, Eleanor

1730 Pennsylvania Ave. NW
Suite 1200
Washington, DC 20006-4706
Tel: (202)737-0500
Fax: (202)626-3737
Registered: LDA

Employers
King & Spalding

Clients Represented

On Behalf of King & Spalding
Blue Cross Blue Shield Ass'n
Bridgestone/Firestone, Inc.

HILL, Fiona

1775 Massachusetts Ave. NW
Washington, DC 20036-2188
Tel: (202)797-6000
Fax: (202)797-6004

Employers
The Brookings Institution (Fellow, Foreign Policy Studies)

HILL, Frank H.

P.O. Box 1807
Alexandria, VA 22313
Tel: (703)876-0920
Registered: LDA
EMail: headhill@evestamail.com
Chief of Staff to Rep. Alex McMillan (R-NC), 1985-94.

Employers
McMillan, Hill & Associates

HILL, Jerry C.

600 13th St. NW
Washington, DC 20005-3096
Tel: (202)756-8217
Fax: (202)756-8087
Registered: LDA
EMail: jhill@mwe.com
Deputy Assistant Secretary for Marketing and Transportation, Department of Agriculture, 1977-81. Legislative Counsel to Senator (1971-77) and Rep. (1965-71) John V. Tunney (D-CA), 1965-76.

Employers
McDermott, Will and Emery (Partner)

Clients Represented

On Behalf of McDermott, Will and Emery
American Spice and Trade Ass'n
California Avocado Commission
California Cling Peach Growers Advisory Board
California Kiwi Fruit Commission
Chiquita Brands Internat'l, Inc.
Crop Protection Coalition
Florida Fruit and Vegetable Ass'n
The Good Sam Club
Guatemalan Development Foundation (FUNDESA)
Minor Crop Farmer Alliance
Nat'l Potato Council
Nat'l Potato Promotion Board
Stroh Brewing Co.
U.S. Mink Export Development Council

HILL, Jerry W.

1776 I St. NW
Suite 1000
Washington, DC 20006
Tel: (202)785-4888
Fax: (202)457-6597
Registered: LDA

Employers
BP Amoco Corp. (Director, Federal Government Affairs)

HILL, Jim

1400 Spring St.
Suite 260
Silver Spring, MD 20910
Tel: (301)587-8570
Fax: (301)587-8573

Employers
Internat'l Soc. for Performance Improvement (President)

HILL, John S.

2100 Pennsylvania Ave. NW
Suite 500
Washington, DC 20037
Tel: (202)728-1100
Fax: (202)728-1123
Former Legislative Assistant to Rep. Jim Davis (D-FL) and Rep. Pete Peterson (D-FL).

Employers
The Duberstein Group, Inc. (Director, Legislative Affairs)

HILL, Jonathan B.

1200 New Hampshire Ave. NW
Suite 800
Washington, DC 20036-6802
EMail: jhill@dlalaw.com
Tel: (202)776-2000
Fax: (202)776-2222
Attorney, Federal Aviation Administration, Department of Transportation, 1969-72.

Employers
Dow, Lohnes & Albertson, PLLC (Member)

Clients Represented

On Behalf of Dow, Lohnes & Albertson, PLLC
Hawaiian Airlines

HILL, Joseph M.

1275 K St. NW
Suite 1212
Washington, DC 20005
Tel: (703)787-0000
Fax: (202)312-5005

Employers
Healthcare Distribution Management Ass'n (Associate Director, State Legislative Affairs)

HILL, Julie S.

1401 K St. NW
Suite 600
Washington, DC 20005
Tel: (202)835-9898
Fax: (202)853-9893

Employers
ASCENT (Ass'n of Community Enterprises) (Director, Marketing)

HILL, Karen K.

122 S. Royal St.
Alexandria, VA 22314-3328
Tel: (703)838-0373
Fax: (703)838-1698

Employers
Cordia Cos. (Assistant)

HILL, Micheal

3211 Fourth St. NE
Washington, DC 20017
Tel: (202)541-3161
Fax: (202)541-3313

Employers
United States Catholic Conference (Associate Director, Government Liaison)

HILL, Nick

One Marriott Dr.
Department 977.01
Washington, DC 20058
Tel: (202)380-3000

Employers
Marriott Internat'l, Inc. (Director, Corporate Information)

HILL, Norman

1444 I St. NW
Suite 300
Washington, DC 20005
EMail: nhill@aprihq.org
Tel: (202)289-2774
Fax: (202)289-5289

Employers
A. Philip Randolph Educational Fund (President)
A. Philip Randolph Institute (President)

HILL, Patricia K.

1120 G St. NW
Suite 1050
Washington, DC 20005
Tel: (202)347-4446

Employers
Georgia-Pacific Corp. (Manager, Federal Regulatory Affairs)

HILL, Richard B.

8720 Georgia Ave.
Suite 501
Silver Spring, MD 20910-3602
EMail: rhill@asis.org
Tel: (301)495-0900
Fax: (301)495-0810

Employers
American Soc. for Information Science (Exec. Director)

HILL, Richard E.

1615 L St. NW
Suite 1200
Washington, DC 20036
Tel: (202)466-6300
Fax: (202)463-0678

Employers
Bell, Boyd & Lloyd (Of Counsel)

HILL, Richard G.

224 Second St. SE
Washington, DC 20003
Tel: (202)546-7711
Fax: (202)546-1755

Employers
Nat'l Indian Gaming Ass'n (Chairman)

HILL, Robert L.

927 15th St. NW
Suite 200
Washington, DC 20005
EMail: aabe@erols.com
Tel: (202)371-9530
Fax: (202)371-9218

Employers
American Ass'n of Blacks in Energy (Exec. Director)

HILL, Terry

1350 New York Ave. NW
Suite 900
Washington, DC 20005
Tel: (202)628-8000
Fax: (202)628-0812

Employers
Internat'l Franchise Ass'n (V. President, Communications)

HILL, Thomas M.

700 11th St. NW
Suite 250
Washington, DC 20001
Tel: (202)638-3502
Fax: (202)638-3522
Registered: LDA
EMail: thomas.hill@pge-corp.com

Employers
PG&E Corp. (Manager, Federal Governmental Relations)

HILL, Yvette

1615 M St. NW
Washington, DC 20036
Tel: (202)833-2300
Fax: (202)429-3945
Registered: LDA
EMail: yvette_hill@tws.org

Employers
The Wilderness Soc. (Policy Associate)

HILL-ARDOIN, Priscilla

1401 I St. NW
Suite 1100
Washington, DC 20005
Tel: (202)326-8836
Fax: (202)289-3699

Employers
SBC Communications Inc. (Senior V. President-FCC)

HILLA, Elizabeth B.

66 Canal Center Plaza
Suite 520
Alexandria, VA 22314-1591
EMail: hilla@hida.org
Tel: (703)549-4432
Fax: (703)549-6495

Employers
Health Industry Distributors Ass'n (Exec. Director, HIDA Educational Foundation)

HILLER, Michelle A.

Ariel Rios Federal Bldg.
(1301-MC)
1200 Pennsylvania Ave. NW
3rd Floor
Washington, DC 20460
EMail: hiller.michelle@epa.gov
Tel: (202)564-3702
Fax: (202)501-1545

Employers
Environmental Protection Agency (Acting Deputy Associate Administrator for State/Local Relations)

HILLIER, Troy

819 Seventh St. NW
Washington, DC 20001
Tel: (202)833-8940
Fax: (202)833-8945
Registered: LDA

Employers
EOP Group, Inc.

Clients Represented

On Behalf of EOP Group, Inc.
Edison Electric Institute
FMC Corp.
Novartis Crop Protection

HILLINGS, E. Joseph

1775 I St. NW
Suite 800
Washington, DC 20006
Tel: (202)466-9145
Fax: (202)828-3372
Registered: LDA

Employers
Enron Corp. (V. President and General Manager, Federal Government Affairs)

HILLMAN, A. William

4301 N. Fairfax Dr.
Suite 360
Arlington, VA 22203-1627
Tel: (703)358-9300
Fax: (703)358-9307
Registered: LDA

Employers
Clean Water Council
Nat'l Utility Contractors Ass'n (NUCA) (Exec. V. President)

HILLS, Carla A.

1200 19th St. NW
Suite 201
Washington, DC 20036-2065
Tel: (202)822-4700
Fax: (202)822-4710
Assistant Attorney General, Civil Division, Department of Justice, 1974-75. Secretary, Department of Housing and Urban Development, 1975-77. U.S. Trade Representative, 1989-93.

Employers
Hills & Company, International Consultants (Chairman and Chief Exec. Officer)

Clients Represented
On Behalf of Hills & Company, International Consultants
The Procter & Gamble Company

HILSEN, Louise

1101 Pennsylvania Ave. NW
Suite 600
Washington, DC 20004
Tel: (202)756-2299
Fax: (202)756-7556

Employers
Nestle USA, Inc. (Director, Government Relations)

HILTON, Cynthia

1120 19th St. NW
Suite 310
Washington, DC 20036-3605
Tel: (202)429-9280
Fax: (202)293-2420

Employers
Institute of Makers of Explosives (Exec. V. President)

HILTON, Steven M.

1001 Pennsylvania Ave. NW
Suite 760 North
Washington, DC 20004
Tel: (202)661-7060
Fax: (202)661-7066
Deputy Assistant to the President and Deputy Director, Office of Public Liaison, The White House, 1993-95. Minority Chief Counsel and Staff Director, Subcommittee on the Constitution, Senate Judiciary Committee, 1987-89.

Employers
The Legislative Strategies Group, LLC (Lobbyist)

Clients Represented
On Behalf of The Legislative Strategies Group, LLC
Allscripts Inc.
Citizens Flag Alliance
Federal Home Loan Bank of San Francisco
Hopi Indian Tribe
Nat'l Football League
Nat'l Orthotics Manufacturers Ass'n

HILTSCHER, Brad L.

1015 18th St. NW
Suite 600
Washington, DC 20036
Tel: (202)296-3551
Fax: (202)296-6741
Registered: LDA
EMail: bradhiltscher@mwd.dst.ca.us

Employers
The Metropolitan Water District of Southern California (Principal Legislative Representative)

HILTY, Christine

80 F St. NW
Suite 804
Washington, DC 20001
Tel: (202)347-3042
Fax: (202)347-3046

Employers
Fraioli/Siggins

HIMELFARB, Phyllis R.

P.O. Box 2000
Merrifield, VA 22116-2000
Tel: (703)359-2830
Fax: (703)359-2834

Employers
Optical Laboratories Ass'n (Manager, Membership and Communications)

HIMMELBERG, John M.

1666 K St. NW
Suite 500
Washington, DC 20006-2803
Tel: (202)887-1400
Fax: (202)466-2198
Registered: LDA
Deputy Director, Hearings and Appeals, Commodity Futures Trading Commission, 1975-76.

Employers
O'Connor & Hannan, L.L.P. (Partner)

Clients Represented
On Behalf of O'Connor & Hannan, L.L.P.
Brooks Tropicals, Inc.
Florida Citrus Alliance
Florida Department of Citrus
Florida Tomato Exchange
Indian River Citrus League
Kanowitz Fruit & Produce Co.
Kendall-Jackson Winery
Nat'l Peach Council

HIMMELMAN, Harold

1350 I St. NW
Suite 700
Washington, DC 20005
Tel: (202)789-6000
Fax: (202)789-6190
Attorney, Civil Rights Division, Department of Justice, 1967-69.

Employers
Beveridge & Diamond, P.C. (Partner)

HIMMELSTEIN, Marc I.

2600 Virginia Ave. NW
Suite 600
Washington, DC 20037
Tel: (202)333-2524
Fax: (202)338-5950
Registered: LDA
EMail: Marchimmel@aol.com

Employers
Nat'l Environmental Strategies (President)
NES, Inc.

Clients Represented
On Behalf of Nat'l Environmental Strategies
American Chemistry Council
American Gas Ass'n
American Petroleum Institute
Bristol-Myers Squibb Co.
Coors Brewing Company
Edison Electric Institute
Ethyl Petroleum Additives, Inc.
Nat'l Mining Ass'n
OXY USA Inc.
Oxygenated Fuels Ass'n
Reilly Industries
Sunoco, Inc.

On Behalf of NES, Inc.
The Dow Chemical Co.

HIMPLER, Bill

1275 Pennsylvania Ave. NW
Tenth Floor
Washington, DC 20004
Tel: (202)333-4936
Fax: (202)833-9392
Registered: LDA
Former Tax Counsel and Legislative Director, Tax, Trade and Pensions to Rep. Gerald C. Weller (R-IL) and Senior Legislative Assistant to Rep. Charles T. Canady (R-FL).

Employers
Barbour Griffith & Rogers, Inc. (Director, Legislative Affairs)

Clients Represented
On Behalf of Barbour Griffith & Rogers, Inc.
Alliance for Quality Nursing Home Care
American Maritime Congress
FM Watch
GCG Partners
Illinois State Board of Education
INTELSAT - Internat'l Telecommunications Satellite Organization
Lyondell Chemical Co.
Oxygenated Fuels Ass'n
Professional Benefit Trust
Southern Co.

HINAMAN, Randy

601 Madison St.
Suite 200
Alexandria, VA 22314
Tel: (703)684-9188
Registered: LDA

Employers
Smith, Hinaman & Associates

Clients Represented
On Behalf of Smith, Hinaman & Associates
Ibex
US Acqua Sonics Corp.

HINCHMAN, Grace L.

1615 L St. NW
Suite 1320
Washington, DC 20036
Tel: (202)457-6203
Fax: (202)857-0230
Registered: LDA
EMail: ghinchman@feidc.org

Employers
Financial Executives International (Senior V. President, Public Affairs)

HIND, Edwin A.

1330 Connecticut Ave. NW
Suite 210
Washington, DC 20036-1704
Tel: (202)828-2614
Fax: (202)828-2617
EMail: ehind@itta.com

Employers
Internat'l Technology & Trade Associates, Inc. (ITTA, Inc.) (Exec. V. President)

HIND, Richard

702 H. Street NW
Suite 300
Washington, DC 20001
Tel: (202)462-1177
Fax: (202)462-4507

Employers
Greenpeace, U.S.A. (Legislative Director, Toxics Campaign)

HINDS, Richard deC.

2000 Pennsylvania Ave. NW
Washington, DC 20006
Tel: (202)974-1500
Fax: (202)974-1999
Registered: FARA
Special Assistant to Assistant Secretary for Tariff and Trade Affairs, Department of Treasury, 1971-73. Law Clerk to Judge Leonard P. Moore, U.S. Court of Appeals, Second Circuit, 1967-68.

Employers
Cleary, Gottlieb, Steen and Hamilton (Partner)

HINES, J. Michael

1200 New Hampshire Ave. NW
Suite 800
Washington, DC 20036-6802
Tel: (202)776-2000
Fax: (202)776-2222
Registered: LDA
EMail: mhines@dlalaw.com
Served in the Judge Advocate General's Office, U.S. Air Force, 1971-74.

Employers
Dow, Lohnes & Albertson, PLLC (Member)

Clients Represented
On Behalf of Dow, Lohnes & Albertson, PLLC
R. R. Donnelley & Sons

HINES, John

3900 Wisconsin Ave. NW
Washington, DC 20016
Tel: (202)752-6585
Fax: (202)752-6099
Registered: LDA

Employers
Fannie Mae (Manager, Government Relations)

HINES, Richard T.

809 Princess St.
Alexandria, VA 22314
Tel: (703)519-6165
Fax: (703)519-9669
Registered: FARA

Employers
Richard T. Hines Consulting, Inc.

Clients Represented
On Behalf of Richard T. Hines Consulting, Inc.
Cambodian People's Party

HINES, Terri

196 Van Buren St.
Suite 450
Herndon, VA 20170

Tel: (703)456-2552
Fax: (703)456-2551

Employers
Nissan North America Inc. (Manager, Corporate Communications)

HINES, Verna B.

Administration Bldg.
Room A1109
Quince Orchard & Clopper Rds.
Gaithersburg, MD 20899-1002
EMail: verna.hines@nist.gov

Tel: (301)975-3080
Fax: (301)926-2569

Employers
Department of Commerce - Nat'l Institute of Standards and Technology (Director, Congressional and Legislative Affairs)

HINGELEY, Anne

888 16th St. NW
Washington, DC 20006

Tel: (202)835-8177
Fax: (202)835-8161
Registered: LDA, FARA

Employers
Bannerman and Associates, Inc.

Clients Represented

On Behalf of Bannerman and Associates, Inc.
Assurance Technology Corp.
Egypt, Government of the Arab Republic of
El Salvador, Embassy of the Republic of
Internat'l College
Lebanese American University
Palestinian Authority

HINKLE, USN (Ret.), RAdm. James B.

11 Canal Center Plaza
Suite 103
Alexandria, VA 22314

Tel: (703)683-4222
Fax: (703)683-0645
Registered: LDA

Former Deputy Chief of Personnel, Department of the Navy.

Employers
The Spectrum Group

Clients Represented

On Behalf of The Spectrum Group
KPMG, LLP
Tetra Tech
TRW Inc.

HINTON, Pamela J.

700 11th St. NW
Suite 510
Washington, DC 20001-4511

Tel: (202)737-1150
Fax: (202)737-8796

Employers
Soc. of Industrial and Office Realtors (Exec. V. President)

HINTON, Steve

1300 N. 17th St.
Eighth Floor
Rosslyn, VA 22209-3801
EMail: hinton@abc.org

Tel: (703)812-2000
Fax: (703)812-8202
Registered: LDA

Employers
Associated Builders and Contractors (PAC Coordinator)

HIPP, Duke

801 Pennsylvania Ave. NW
Suite 245
Washington, DC 20004-2604
EMail: dhipp@americashospitals.com

Tel: (202)624-1509
Fax: (202)737-6462

Employers
Federation of American Hospitals (Director, Communications)

HIPP, Kelly

1505 Prince St.
Suite 300
Alexandria, VA 22314

Tel: (703)739-9200
Fax: (703)739-9497
Registered: LDA

Employers
American Optometric Ass'n (Assistant Director, Government Relations)

HIPP, Jr., Van D.

1800 K St. NW
Suite 1010
Washington, DC 20006
EMail: vanhippadi@aol.com

Tel: (202)296-5030
Fax: (202)296-4750
Registered: LDA, FARA

Deputy Assistant Secretary, Department of the Army, 1990-92. Principal Deputy General Counsel, Department of the Navy, 1992-93.

Employers
American Defense Internat'l, Inc. (Chairman)

Clients Represented

On Behalf of American Defense Internat'l, Inc.
3D Metrics Inc.
ANSAR Inc.
Barber Colman Co.
Beretta U.S.A. Corp.
Bofors Defence AB
Dialogic Communications Corp.
Drexel University
East/West Industries
Eickhorn-Solingen
Ensign-Bickford Co.
EWA Land Information Group, Inc.
Fibernet LLC
Friction Free Technologies Inc.
Ganaden Biotech Inc.
Gentex Corp.
GEO Centers, Inc.
GIAT Industries
Hagglunds Moelv AS
InformaTech, Inc.
Internat'l Trade Resources Group
InvenCom LLC
Koable Co., Ltd.
Large Scale Biology
Le Meilleur Co., Ltd.
Longworth Industries Inc.
Marine Desalination Systems LLC
MEGAXESS, Inc.
Ordnance Development and Engineering Co. of Singapore
Pacific Consolidated Industries
PDI Ground Support Systems, Inc.
Raytheon Missile Systems
Saab AB
Sarnoff Corp.
SINTEF Telecom and Informatics
Smiths Industries Aerospace and Defense Systems
Stidd Systems, Inc.
Stratus Systems Inc.
Swiss Munition Enterprise
Syntroleum Corp.
Time Domain Corp.
University Hospital of Tromso
Virtual Drug Development
Virtual Impact Productions
VISICU
ViTel Net
Xeta Internat'l Corp.
Youyang

HIRD, David B.

1615 L St. NW
Suite 700
Washington, DC 20036-5610
EMail: david.hird@weil.com

Tel: (202)682-7000
Fax: (202)857-0939
Registered: LDA

Employers
Weil, Gotshal & Manges, LLP (Partner)

Clients Represented

On Behalf of Weil, Gotshal & Manges, LLP
Real Estate Roundtable

HIRSCH, David

1025 Vermont Ave. NW
Third Floor
Washington, DC 20005

Tel: (202)783-7400
Ext: 215
Fax: (202)783-0444
Registered: LDA

Employers
Friends of the Earth (Transportation Policy Coordinator)

HIRSCH, Paul J.

444 N. Capitol St.
Suite 545
Washington, DC 20001

Tel: (202)347-1223
Fax: (202)347-1225
Registered: LDA

Employers
Madison Government Affairs (President)

Clients Represented

On Behalf of Madison Government Affairs
Clean Air Now
DCH Technology Inc.
Fairfield, California, City of
Food Bank of the Virginia Peninsula
NASA Aeronautics Support Team
Nat'l Community Reinvestment Coalition
Newport News, Virginia, Industrial Development Authority of the City of
Nottoway, Virginia, County of
Pensacola Chamber of Commerce
REM Engineering
SM&A
Systems Simulation Solutions Inc.
Team Santa Rosa Economic Development Council
University of West Florida
USS Wisconsin Foundation
Virginia Living Museum
Roy F. Weston, Inc.

HIRSCH, Robert

2200 Mill Rd.
Third Floor
Alexandria, VA 22314

Tel: (703)838-1950
Fax: (703)836-6610

Employers
Truckload Carriers Ass'n (President)

HIRSCHE, Evan

1901 Pennsylvania Ave. NW
Suite 1100
Washington, DC 20006

Tel: (202)861-2242
Fax: (202)861-4290
Registered: LDA

Employers
Nat'l Audubon Soc. (Director, Foundation)

HIRSCHHORN, Eric L.

1400 L St. NW
Washington, DC 20005-3502
EMail: ehirschh@winston.com

Tel: (202)371-5706
Fax: (202)371-5950
Registered: LDA

Deputy Assistant Secretary for Export Administration, Department of Commerce, 1980-81. Deputy Associate Director for International Affairs and Trade, Office of Management and Budget, The White House, 1977-80. Chief Counsel, Subcommittee on Government Information and Individual Rights, House Committee on Government Operations, 1975-77. Legislative Assistant to Rep. Bella S. Abzug (D-NY), 1971-73.

Employers
Winston & Strawn (Partner, Corporate Practice)

Clients Represented

On Behalf of Winston & Strawn
Barr Laboratories
DHL Airways, Inc.

HIRSCHMANN, David

1615 H St. NW
Washington, DC 20062

Tel: (202)463-5500
Fax: (202)463-3129
Registered: LDA

Employers
Chamber of Commerce of the U.S.A. (Exec. V. President, National Chamber Foundation)
Nat'l Chamber Foundation (Exec. V. President)

HIRSHBERG, Jennefer A.

2111 Wilson Blvd.
Eighth Floor
Arlington, VA 22201-3058

Tel: (703)841-0626
Fax: (703)243-2874

Employers
Alcalde & Fay (Partner)

Clients Represented

On Behalf of Alcalde & Fay
Grand Valley State University
Metromedia Co.
Nat'l Peace Foundation

HIRST, Peter G.

1225 19th St. NW
Suite 800
Washington, DC 20036

Tel: (202)955-6067
Fax: (202)293-0307

Employers
Berliner, Candon & Jimison (Associate)

HISHTA, John

320 First St. SE
Washington, DC 20003
Tel: (202)479-7000
Fax: (202)863-0693

Employers
Nat'l Republican Congressional Committee (Exec. Director)

HITCHCOCK, Cornish F.

1100 17th St. NW
Tenth Floor
Washington, DC 20036-4601
Tel: (202)974-5111
Registered: LDA

Employers
Self-employed as an independent consultant.

Clients Represented
As an independent consultant
Tax Analysis

HITCHCOCK, Donald

919 18th St. NW
Suite 800
Washington, DC 20006
Tel: (202)628-4160
Fax: (202)347-5323

Employers
Human Rights Campaign Fund (Southern Field Organizer)

HITOV, Steve

1101 14th St. NW
Suite 405
Washington, DC 20005
Tel: (202)289-7661
Fax: (202)289-7724

Employers
Nat'l Health Law Program (Staff Attorney)

HIU, Patrick

1755 Jefferson Davis Hwy.
Suite 1107
Arlington, VA 22202
Tel: (703)415-0344
Fax: (703)415-0182
Registered: LDA

Employers
The PMA Group (Associate)

Clients Represented
On Behalf of The PMA Group
AsclepiusNet
Autometric Inc.
Biocontrol Technology, Inc.
Concurrent Technologies Corp.
CRYPTEK Secure Communications, LLC
Foundation Health Federal Services, Inc.
Gentex Corp.
IIT Research Institute
L-3 Communications Corp.
Life Cell
McLean Hospital
Microvision, Inc.
MTS Systems Inc.
Nat'l Cooperative Bank
Opportunity Medical, Inc.
Planning Systems, Inc.
Spatial Integrated Systems
Trex Enterprises
Triosyn Corp.
University Emergency Medicine Foundation

HIVLEY, Dawn

444 N. Capitol St. NW
Suite 214
Washington, DC 20001
EMail: dhivley@gov.state.va.us
Tel: (202)783-1769
Fax: (202)783-7687

Employers
Virginia Liaison Office (Special Assistant, State/Federal Relations)

HIXSON, Sheila E.

500 K St. NW
Suite 350
Washington, DC 20005-1209
Tel: (202)393-0159
Fax: (202)638-2780
Registered: LDA

Employers
Cook and Associates (President)

Clients Represented
On Behalf of Cook and Associates
Agr Foods
Duffy Internat'l
J. R. Gray & Co.
Seamans-Rome

HOAGLAND, Dr. K. Elaine

734 15th St. NW
Suite 550
Washington, DC 20005
EMail: cur@cur.org
Tel: (202)783-4810
Fax: (202)783-4811

Employers
Council on Undergraduate Research (National Exec. Officer)

HOAGLAND, Hon. Peter J.

1331 F St. NW
Suite 800
Washington, DC 20004
EMail: hoagland@csandh.com
Tel: (202)347-8000
Fax: (202)347-8920
Member, U.S. House of Representatives (D-NE), 1989-95. Law Clerk to Judge Oliver Gasch, U.S. District Court for the District of Columbia, 1969-70.

Employers
Colling Swift & Hynes (Principal)

Clients Represented
On Behalf of Colling Swift & Hynes
Molina Healthcare

HOBBIE, Kenneth

1400 K St. NW
Suite 1200
Washington, DC 20005
Tel: (202)789-0789
Fax: (202)898-0522

Employers
U.S. Grains Council (President)

HOBBIE, Ph.D., Richard

444 N. Capitol St. NW
Suite 142
Washington, DC 20001
Tel: (202)431-8020
Fax: (202)434-8033

Employers
Nat'l Ass'n of State Workforce Agencies (Unemployment Insurance Director)

HOBBS, III, Caswell O.

1800 M St. NW
Washington, DC 20036
EMail: chobbs@morganlewis.com
Tel: (202)467-7200
Fax: (202)467-7176
Director, Office of Policy Planning (1972-73), Assistant to the Chairman (1970-72) and Attorney (1967-70), Federal Trade Commission.

Employers
Morgan, Lewis & Bockius LLP (Partner, Washington Office)

HOBBS, David W.

1600 Pennsylvania Ave. NW
112 E. Wing
Washington, DC 20500
Tel: (202)456-6620
Fax: (202)456-2604
Former Aide to House Majority Leader, Rep. Dick Armey (R-TX).

Employers
Executive Office of the President - The White House (Deputy Assistant to the President for Legislative Affairs/House Liaison)

HOBBS, Douglas

1849 C St. NW
Washington, DC 20240
Tel: (202)208-5403
Fax: (202)208-6965

Employers
Department of Interior - Fish and Wildlife Service (Legislative Specialist)

HOBBS, Monica

1146 19th St. NW
Washington, DC 20036
Tel: (202)530-2975

Employers
Center for Reproductive Law and Policy (Federal Legislative Counsel)

HOBERMAN, Mary

1120 20th St. NW
Suite 1000
Washington, DC 20036
Registered: LDA

Employers
Concert USA

HOBGOOD, James L.

P.O. Box 3008
Alexandria, VA 22302-0008
Tel: (703)931-4107
Fax: (703)931-3127
Registered: LDA

Employers
The Conaway Group LLC (Consultant)

Clients Represented
On Behalf of The Conaway Group LLC
Accenture
AGS Defense, Inc.
Comtel Secure Fiber Telecommunications, Inc.
EDS Corp.
Essential Technologies, Inc.
Mountain Top Technologies, Inc.

HOBSON, David F.

1300 N. 17th St.
Suite 750
Arlington, VA 22209
EMail: hobson@utsa.com
Tel: (703)247-2600
Fax: (703)841-4750

Employers
Uniform and Textile Service Ass'n (President and Chief Exec. Officer)

HOBSON, Joseph W.

4041 Powder Mill Rd.
Suite 404
Calverton, MD 20705-3106
Tel: (301)348-2002
Fax: (301)348-2020

Employers
Asphalt Roofing Manufacturers Ass'n (Director, Communications/Public Affairs)

HOBSON, Jr., Julius W.

1101 Vermont Ave. NW
12th Floor
Washington, DC 20005-3583
Tel: (202)789-7456
Fax: (202)789-7485
Registered: LDA

Employers
American Medical Ass'n (Director, Congressional Affairs)

HOCHBERG, Philip R.

901 15th St. NW
Suite 700
Washington, DC 20005-2301
Tel: (202)371-6000
Fax: (202)371-6279
Registered: LDA
Special Counsel, Subcommittee on Communications, House Committee on Commerce, Science and Transportation, 1977.

Employers
Verner, Liipfert, Bernhard, McPherson and Hand, Chartered (Of Counsel)

Clients Represented
On Behalf of Verner, Liipfert, Bernhard, McPherson and Hand, Chartered
Nat'l Basketball Ass'n
Nat'l Football League
Nat'l Hockey League
Rite Aid Corp.
Thomson Consumer Electronics, Inc.

HOCHBERG, Sheldon E.

1330 Connecticut Ave. NW
Washington, DC 20036-1795
Tel: (202)429-3000
Fax: (202)429-3902
Registered: LDA
EMail: shochberg@steptoe.com
Attorney, Office of the Legal Advisor, Economic Affairs, Department of State, 1967-69.

Employers
Steptoe & Johnson LLP (Partner)

Clients Represented
On Behalf of Steptoe & Johnson LLP
Sterling Internat'l Consultants, Inc.

HOCHSTEIN, Amos

700 13th St. NW
Suite 400
Washington, DC 20005
Tel: (202)347-0773
Fax: (202)347-0785
Registered: LDA, FARA
EMail: ahochstein@cassidy.com
Former Senior Policy Advisor to Rep. Sam Gejdenson (D-CT), House Committee on International Relations. Staff member of House Subcommittee on International Economic Policy and Trade.

Employers
Cassidy & Associates, Inc. (Sr. V. President)

Clients Represented

On Behalf of Cassidy & Associates, Inc.

The Boeing Co.
Polytechnic University
Smartforce
Taiwan Studies Institute
Wheelchairs for the World Foundation

HOCHSTETLER, Paula P.

908 King St.
Suite 100
Alexandria, VA 22314
EMail: paula.bline@ACConline.org
Tel: (703)683-5900
Fax: (703)683-2564

Employers

Airport Consultants Council (Exec. Director)

HOCKER, Jean

1331 H St. NW
Suite 400
Washington, DC 20005-4711
Tel: (202)638-4725
Fax: (202)638-4730

Employers

Land Trust Alliance (President)

HOCKER, Stephen A.

300 I St. NE
Suite 102
Washington, DC 20002
Tel: (202)544-7770
Fax: (202)546-8249

Employers

District of Columbia Special Olympics (Exec. Director)

HODGDON, Harry E.

5410 Grosvenor Ln.
Bethesda, MD 20814
EMail: tws@wildlife.org
Tel: (301)897-9770
Fax: (301)530-2471

Employers

The Wildlife Soc. (Exec. Director)

HODGDON, S. A.

300 N. Lee St.
Suite 500
Alexandria, VA 2214

Employers

Take Back the House (PAC Administrator)

HODGE, Debbie A.

Unit 50
USDA Riverside
4700 River Rd.
Riverdale, MD 20737
EMail: debbie.a.hodge@usda.gov
Tel: (301)734-5386
Fax: (301)734-8405

Employers

Department of Agriculture - Animal and Plant Health Inspection Service (Management Analyst, Legislative and Public Affairs)

HODGE, Scott A.

1250 H St. NW
Suite 750
Washington, DC 20005
Tel: (202)783-2760
Fax: (202)783-6868
Registered: LDA

Employers

Tax Foundation, Inc. (Exec. Director)

HODGES, James H.

1700 N. Moore St.
Suite 1600
Arlington, VA 22209
Tel: (703)841-2400
Fax: (703)527-0938
Registered: LDA

Employers

American Meat Institute (Senior V. President, Regulatory Affairs)

HODGES, John A.

1776 K St. NW
Washington, DC 20006
Tel: (202)719-7000
Fax: (202)719-7049
Registered: FARA

Employers

Wiley, Rein & Fielding (Partner)

Clients Represented

On Behalf of Wiley, Rein & Fielding

Marine Mammal Coalition

HODGES, Paulette J.

451 Seventh St. SW
Room 10148
Washington, DC 20410
EMail: paulette_j._hodges@hud.gov
Tel: (202)708-0380
Fax: (202)708-1350

Employers

Department of Housing and Urban Development (Assistant to the Deputy Assistant Secretary, Office of Congressional Relations)

HODGKINSON, Harold L.

1001 Connecticut Ave. NW
Suite 310
Washington, DC 20036
Tel: (202)822-8405
Fax: (202)872-4050

Employers

Institute for Educational Leadership (Director, Center for Demographic Policy)

HODGSON, Barry

750 First St. NE
9th Floor
Washington, DC 20002
Tel: (202)745-2900
Fax: (202)745-2901

Employers

Capital Consultants Corp. (Senior Consultant)

Clients Represented

On Behalf of Capital Consultants Corp.

Chehalis Reservation, Confederated Tribes of the Omaha Tribe of Nebraska

HOE, E. Sanderson

1900 K St. NW
Washington, DC 20006
Tel: (202)496-7500
Fax: (202)496-7756
Registered: FARA
EMail: sandy_hoe@mckennacuneo.com

Employers

McKenna & Cuneo, L.L.P. (Partner)

HOECK, Kenneth J.

6617 Jill Ct.
Suite 100
McLean, VA 22101
Tel: (703)728-9500
Fax: (703)442-0749

Employers

Gilbert A. Robinson, Inc. (Exec. V. President)

Clients Represented

On Behalf of Gilbert A. Robinson, Inc.

Chemcrete Technologies Russia (RIS/NIS), Inc.
Internat'l Marketing for Russia and NIS

HOEL, John

1341 G St. NW
Suite 900
Washington, DC 20005
Tel: (202)637-1524
Fax: (202)637-1537
Registered: LDA
Former Counsel to Rep. Bart Gordon (D-TN).

Employers

Philip Morris Management Corp. (District Director, South)

HOELTER, Herbert J.

3125 Mount Vernon Ave.
Alexandria, VA 22305
EMail: ncia@igc.apc.org
Tel: (703)684-0373
Fax: (703)684-6037

Employers

Nat'l Center on Institutions and Alternatives (Director)

HOENICKE, Jeanne E.

1001 Pennsylvania Ave. NW
Washington, DC 20004-2599
Tel: (202)624-2000
Fax: (202)624-2319
Registered: LDA

Employers

American Council of Life Insurers (V. President and Deputy General Counsel)

HOEWING, C. Lincoln "Link"

1300 I St. NW
Suite 400 West
Washington, DC 20005
Tel: (202)515-2420
Fax: (202)336-7866

Employers

Verizon Communications (Assistant V. President, Internet)

HOFER, Lydia

151 D St. SE
Washington, DC 20003
Tel: (202)546-7255
Fax: (202)543-9289
Registered: LDA

Employers

Lydia Hofer & Associates (Director, Washington Office)
Manuel Lujan Associates (Associate)

Clients Represented

On Behalf of Lydia Hofer & Associates

Piliero Mazza & Pargament

On Behalf of Manuel Lujan Associates

Legix Co.
Pojoaque Pueblo

HOFF, Paul S.

1000 Potomac St. NW
Suite 500
Washington, DC 20007
EMail: phoff@gsblaw.com
Tel: (202)965-7880
Fax: (202)965-1729
Registered: LDA, FARA
Associate Chief Counsel, Senate Governmental Affairs Committee, 1975-81.

Employers

Garvey, Schubert & Barer (Partner)

Clients Represented

On Behalf of Garvey, Schubert & Barer

Coalition on the Implementation of the AFA
Japan Fisheries Ass'n
Japan Wood-Products Information and Research Center

HOFFA, James P.

25 Louisiana Ave. NW
Washington, DC 20001-2198
Tel: (202)624-6800
Fax: (202)624-8973

Employers

Internat'l Brotherhood of Teamsters (President)

HOFFER, Larry

105 N. Alfred St.
Alexandria, VA 22314
EMail: lhoffer@biausa.org
Tel: (703)236-6000
Fax: (703)236-6001

Employers

Brain Injury Ass'n (Director, Communications)

HOFFMAN, Adonis E.

1899 L St. NW
Suite 700
Washington, DC 20036
EMail: ahoffman@aaaadc.org
Tel: (202)331-7345
Fax: (202)857-3675
Registered: LDA

Employers

American Ass'n of Advertising Agencies (Senior V. President and Counsel)

HOFFMAN, Ann F.

888 16th St. NW
Suite 303
Washington, DC 20006
EMail: ahoffman@unitedunion.org
Tel: (202)347-7417
Fax: (202)347-0708
Registered: LDA

Employers

Union of Needletrades, Industrial, and Textile Employees (UNITE) (Associate Legislative Director)

HOFFMAN, Beverly R.

1555 Connecticut Ave. NW
Suite 200
Washington, DC 20036-1126
Tel: (202)462-0992
Fax: (202)462-9043

Employers

Friends of the Nat'l Institute of Dental and Craniofacial Research (Exec. Director)
Friends of the Nat'l Library of Medicine (Exec. Director)

HOFFMAN, Bruce

1200 S. Hayes St.
Arlington, VA 22202-5050
Tel: (703)413-1100
Fax: (703)413-8111

Employers

RAND Corp. (Director)

HOFFMAN, Carrie

1255 23rd St. NW
Suite 200
Washington, DC 20037-1174
Tel: (202)452-8100
Fax: (202)833-3636

Employers
Hauck and Associates
Nat'l Ass'n of Healthcare Consultants (Director of Meetings)

Clients Represented
On Behalf of Hauck and Associates
Nat'l Ass'n of Healthcare Consultants

HOFFMAN, Eric

1875 I St. NW
Suite 900
Washington, DC 20005
Tel: (202)371-0200
Fax: (202)371-2858

Employers
Edelman Public Relations Worldwide (V. President)

Clients Represented
On Behalf of Edelman Public Relations Worldwide
Americans for Sensible Estate Tax Solutions (ASSETS)
Ass'n for Advanced Life Underwriting
Rhythms NetConnections

HOFFMAN, Gail H.

1730 Rhode Island Ave. NW
Suite 717
Washington, DC 20036
Tel: (202)728-0800
Fax: (202)728-0802
Registered: LDA
EMail: hoffman@hoffmangroup.com
Director of Public Liaison and Intergovernmental Affairs, Department of Justice, 1993-95. Special Assistant to the Attorney General for Legislative Affairs, Department of Justice, 1993. Former Staff member, Office of the Deputy Chief of Staff and Counsel's Office, The White House, during the Clinton administration.

Employers
The Hoffman Group (President)

Clients Represented
On Behalf of The Hoffman Group
Saf T Hammer

HOFFMAN, Jody A.

1317 F St. NW
Suite 600
Washington, DC 20004
Tel: (202)638-2121
Fax: (202)638-7045
Registered: LDA
EMail: hoffman@wexlergroup.com

Employers
The Wexler Group (Principal/Senior Director)

Clients Represented
On Behalf of The Wexler Group
American Dental Ass'n
Blue Cross and Blue Shield of California
Immunex Corp.
IMS Health Inc.
PacifiCare Health Systems
VISA U.S.A., Inc.
Wyeth-Ayerst Laboratories

HOFFMAN, Joel E.

1275 Pennsylvania Ave. NW
Washington, DC 20004-2415
Tel: (202)383-0100
Fax: (202)637-3593
Registered: LDA
Trial Attorney, Appellate Section, Antitrust Division, Department of Justice, 1960-63.

Employers
Sutherland Asbill & Brennan LLP (Of Counsel)

HOFFMAN, Laurence J.

1333 New Hampshire Ave. NW
Suite 400
Washington, DC 20036
Tel: (202)887-4000
Fax: (202)887-4288
Attorney, National Labor Relations Board, 1967-68.

Employers
Akin, Gump, Strauss, Hauer & Feld, L.L.P. (Partner)

HOFFMAN, Marshall

5683 Columbia Pike
Suite 200
Falls Church, VA 22041
Tel: (703)820-2244
Fax: (703)820-2271
Registered: FARA

Employers
Hoffman & Hoffman Public Relations (President)

Clients Represented
On Behalf of Hoffman & Hoffman Public Relations
Central Bank of Turkey

HOFFMAN, Scott

420 Seventh St. SE
Washington, DC 20003
Tel: (202)546-3950
Fax: (202)546-3749

Employers
World Federalist Ass'n (Field Director)

HOFFMAN, Scott P.

1133 21st St. NW
Suite 700
Washington, DC 20036
Tel: (202)887-6900
Fax: (202)887-6970
Registered: LDA
EMail: shoffman@janus-merritt.com

Employers
Janus-Merritt Strategies, L.L.C. (Principal)

Clients Represented
On Behalf of Janus-Merritt Strategies, L.L.C.
AFIN Securities
American Business for Legal Immigration
Banorte Casa de Bolsa
Camara Nacional de la Industria Pesquera
Camara Nacional de las Industrias Azucarera y Alcoholera
CDM Fantasy Sports
CEMEX Central, S.A. de C.V.
COVAD Communications Co.
DSL Access Telecommunications Ass'n (DATA)
EchoStar Communications Corp.
Fannie Mae
First Amendment Coalition for Expression
Fraternal Order of Police (U.S. Park Police Labor Committee)
Free ANWAR Campaign
Grupo Financiero Banorte
HarvardNet, Inc.
Interactive Gaming Council
Interactive Services Ass'n
Napster, Inc.
Nat'l Indian Gaming Ass'n
Rhythms NetConnections
Scribe Communications, Inc.
Secured Access Portals, Inc.
Viejas Band of Kumeyaay Indians
Vivendi Universal

HOFFMAN, III, William H.

1033 N. Fairfax St.
Suite 404
Alexandria, VA 22314
Tel: (703)549-7404
Fax: (703)549-8712
Registered: LDA
EMail: whoffman@icsc.org

Employers
Internat'l Council of Shopping Centers (Manager, Environmental Issues)

HOFFMAN, William L.

516 First St. SE
Washington, DC 20003
Tel: (202)546-5639
Fax: (202)544-0473
Registered: LDA
EMail: whoffman@worldnet.att.net
Former Chief of Staff to Senator Mike Gravel (D-AK).

Employers
Gryphon Internat'l

Clients Represented
On Behalf of Gryphon Internat'l
American University of Beirut
Richardson Lawrie Associates

HOFFMANN, Justin

1775 Pennsylvania Ave. NW
Suite 1250
Washington, DC 20006
Tel: (202)347-1041
Fax: (202)628-0669
Registered: LDA

Employers
The Trade Partnership (Trade Policy Analyst)

HOFFMEIER, Donna L.

1717 Pennsylvania Ave. NW
Suite 1300
Washington, DC 20006
Tel: (202)452-6925
Fax: (202)452-6190
Registered: LDA

Employers
Astra Solutions, LLC

Clients Represented
On Behalf of Astra Solutions, LLC
Spectrum Health Care Resources, Inc.
United Concordia Companies, Inc.

HOFGARD, Jefferson F.

1200 Wilson Blvd.
Arlington, VA 22209-1989
Tel: (703)465-3500
Fax: (703)465-3001

Employers
The Boeing Co. (Director, International Policy)

HOGAN, Gerald F.

1401 I St. NW
Suite 1100
Washington, DC 20005
Tel: (202)326-8815
Fax: (202)408-4797
Registered: LDA

Employers
SBC Communications Inc. (Exec. Director, Federal Relations)

HOGAN, J. Michael

1201 L St. NW
Washington, DC 20005-4014
Tel: (202)842-4444
Fax: (202)842-3860
Registered: LDA

Employers
American Health Care Ass'n (Senior Director, Legislative Affairs)

HOGAN, John J.

601 Pennsylvania Ave. NW
Suite 900 South Bldg.
Washington, DC 20004
Tel: (202)434-8211
Fax: (202)638-7124
Registered: LDA

Employers
Capitol City Group

Clients Represented
On Behalf of Capitol City Group
American Biophysics Corp.
Cranston, Rhode Island, City of
CVS, Inc.
Greater Providence Chamber of Commerce
Landmark Medical Center
Rhode Island Resource Recovery Center

HOGAN, Liz

1133 19th St. NW
Washington, DC 20036
Tel: (202)887-2934
Fax: (202)887-3123
Registered: LDA
EMail: liz.hogan@wcom.com

Employers
MCI WorldCom Corp. (Senior Policy Advisor, Government Relations)

HOGAN, Mark B.

2302 Horse Pen Rd.
Herndon, VA 20171-3499
Tel: (703)713-1900
Fax: (703)713-1910
EMail: mhogan@ncma.org

Employers
Nat'l Concrete Masonry Ass'n (President)

HOGAN, Matt

303 Pennsylvania Ave. SE
Washington, DC 20003
Tel: (202)543-6850
Fax: (202)543-6853

Employers
Congressional Sportsmen's Foundation (Director, Conservation Policy)

HOGAN, Maureen Flatley

1025 Connecticut Ave. NW
Suite 1012
Washington, DC 20036
EMail: dcgmh@usa.net

Employers
Adopt America (Exec. Director)
Dublin Castle Group (President)

Clients Represented

On Behalf of Dublin Castle Group

Adopt America
Bicopas, Ltd.
Catholic Alliance
Family Advocacy Services
Foster America, Inc.
Janus Solutions, Inc.
Link Romania, Inc.
Nat'l Adoption Foundation
Nat'l Ass'n of Foster Care Review Boards
Romanian Orphans Connection, Inc.
Small Property Owners Ass'n of America

HOGAN, Thomas P.

601 Pennsylvania Ave. NW
Suite 900 South Bldg.
Washington, DC 20004
EMail: thoganccg@aol.com
Tel: (202)434-8211
Fax: (202)638-7124
Registered: LDA

Employers

Capitol City Group (Managing Director)

Clients Represented

On Behalf of Capitol City Group

American Biophysics Corp.
Cranston, Rhode Island, City of
CVS, Inc.
Greater Providence Chamber of Commerce
Landmark Medical Center
Rhode Island Resource Recovery Center

HOGAN, Tim

1899 L St. NW
Suite 1000
Washington, DC 20036
EMail: tim_hogan@npradc.org
Tel: (202)457-0480
Fax: (202)457-0486

Employers

Nat'l Petrochemical Refiners Ass'n (Technical Analyst)

HOGEN, Phillip N.

2099 Pennsylvania Ave. NW
Suite 100
Washington, DC 20006
EMail: phogen@hklaw.com
Tel: (202)955-3000
Fax: (202)955-5564
Registered: LDA

Employers

Holland & Knight LLP (Of Counsel)

HOGGARD, Jack

1820 N. Fort Myer Dr.
Suite 804
Arlington, VA 22209
EMail: jhhoggard@mcdermott.com
Tel: (703)351-6301
Fax: (703)351-6417
Registered: LDA

Employers

McDermott Internat'l, Inc./Babcock & Wilcox (Manager, Legislative Affairs)

HOGGARTH, Robert

500 Montgomery St.
Suite 700
Alexandria, VA 22314-1561
Tel: (703)739-0300
Fax: (703)836-1608
Registered: LDA

Employers

Personal Communications Industry Ass'n (PCIA) (Senior V. President, Paging and Narrowband)

HOGUE, Bonnie

1319 F St. NW
Suite 710
Washington, DC 20004
Tel: (202)393-7737
Fax: (202)393-2109
Registered: LDA

Senior Health Policy Advisor, Senate Democratic Policy Committee, 1999-2000. Legislative Assistant to Rep. John Francis "Jack" Reed (D-RI), 1997-98. Professional Staff, Senate Committee on Aging, 1989-96.

Employers

Alzheimer's Ass'n (Director, Federal and State Policy)

HOHENTHANER, Thomas

1200 New Hampshire Ave. NW
Washington, DC 20036
EMail: thomas.hohenthaneer@chadbourne.com
Tel: (202)974-5600
Fax: (202)974-5602

Chief Counsel and Deputy Staff Director, Senate Commerce Committee, 1994-96. Chief Counsel, Senate Small Business Committee, 1993-94. Legislative Director to Senator Larry Pressler (R-SD), 1990-93.

Employers

Chadbourne and Parke LLP (Associate)

HOHLT, Richard F.

1100 New York Ave. NW
Suite 700 East
Washington, DC 20005
EMail: rick@hohlt.com
Tel: (202)833-8999
Fax: (202)833-1587
Registered: LDA

Board of Directors, Student Loan Marketing Ass'n, 1990-94. Board of Directors, Overseas Private Investment Corporation, 1983-85. Board of Advisors, U.S. Peace Corps, 1982-83. Exec. Assistant to Senator Richard Lugar (R-IN), 1977-81.

Employers

Hohlt & Associates

Clients Represented

On Behalf of Hohlt & Associates

BMW Financial Services of North America, Inc.
Bristol-Myers Squibb Co.
Clark/Bardes, Inc.
Dime Savings Bank of New York
FISERV, Inc.
Guaranty Bank, SSB
Kelly and Associates, Inc.
J. P. Morgan Chase & Co.
Nuclear Energy Institute
Sallie Mae, Inc.
Washington Mutual Bank
Wilmington Savings Fund Society

HOKE, Robert J.

Theodore Roosevelt Federal Bldg.
1900 E St. NW
MS: 5H30
Washington, DC 20415
Tel: (202)606-1300
Fax: (202)606-1344

Employers

Office of Personnel Management (Deputy Director, Office of Congressional Relations)

HOLAHAN, John F.

2100 M St. NW
Washington, DC 20037
Tel: (202)833-7200
Fax: (202)429-0687

Employers

The Urban Institute (Director, Health Policy Center)

HOLBEIN, James R.

2100 M St. NW
Suite 200
Washington, DC 20037
EMail: jholbein@stewartlaw.com
Tel: (202)785-4185
Fax: (202)466-1286

Former Director, North American Free Trade Agreement Secretariat, Office of Deputy Assistant Secretary for Agreements Compliance, Office of Assistant Secretary for Market Access and Compliance, Department of Commerce.

Employers

Stewart and Stewart (Of Counsel)

HOLCH, Niels C.

400 N. Capitol St. NW
Suite 585
Washington, DC 20001
Tel: (202)783-5300
Fax: (202)393-5218
Registered: LDA

Former Chief of Staff to Senator Mitch McConnell (R-KY).

Employers

McGuiness & Holch (Partner)

Clients Represented

On Behalf of McGuiness & Holch

Nat'l Horse Show Commission
Oneida Indian Nation of New York

HOLCOMBE, Kathleen "Kay"

818 Connecticut Ave. NW
Suite 325
Washington, DC 20006
EMail: kholcombe@poldir.com
Tel: (202)776-0071
Fax: (202)776-0083
Registered: LDA

Professional Staff member, Committee on Commerce, U.S. House of Representatives, 1993-97.

Employers

Policy Directions, Inc. (Exec. V. President)

Clients Represented

On Behalf of Policy Directions, Inc.

Amgen
Aventis Behring
Aventis Pharmaceuticals, Inc.
Baxter Healthcare Corp.
Baylor College of Medicine
Cosmetic, Toiletry and Fragrance Ass'n
CP Pharmaceuticals, Ltd.
Genelabs Technologies, Inc.
Grocery Manufacturers of America
Kraft Foods, Inc.
Merck & Co.
Nat'l Ass'n for Biomedical Research
Orphan Medical, Inc.
Pharmaceutical Research and Manufacturers of America
Philip Morris Management Corp.
Reckitt & Colman Pharmaceuticals Inc.
Soc. of the Plastics Industry
Transkaryotic Therapies Inc.
Transkaryotic Therapies Inc.
U.S. Oncology
Visible Genetics
Visx, Inc.

HOLDER, Debra

150 Elden St.
Suite 270
Herndon, VA 20170
Tel: (703)736-9666
Fax: (703)736-9668

Employers

Associated Landscape Contractors of America (Exec. Director)

HOLDSWORTH, Eric

1275 K St. NW
Suite 890
Washington, DC 20005
Tel: (202)682-9161
Fax: (202)638-1043

Employers

Global Climate Coalition (Deputy Director)

HOLDSWORTH, Thomas W.

P.O. Box 3000
Leesburg, VA 20177
EMail: twh@skillsusa.org
Tel: (703)777-8810 Ext: 607
Fax: (703)777-8999

Employers

Skills USA-VICA (Director, Communications and Public Affairs)

HOLGATE, Laura

1747 Pennsylvania Ave. NW
7th Floor
Washington, DC 20006
Tel: (202)296-4810
Fax: (202)296-4811

Formerly served in the Departments of Energy and Defense.

Employers

Nuclear Threat Initiative (V. President for Russia)

HOLLAND, Judith

601 F St. NW
Washington, DC 20004
Tel: (202)661-5000
Fax: (202)661-5108

Employers

Washington Sports & Entertainment, L.P. (V. President, Community Relations)

HOLLAND, Lisa

1100 17th St. NW
Suite 500
Washington, DC 20036
Tel: (202)265-7546
Fax: (202)265-8850

Employers

Nat'l Ass'n of Community Action Agencies (Coordinator, Marketing and Public Relations)

HOLLAND, M. Elaine

601 13th St. NW
Suite 400 North
Washington, DC 20005
EMail: eholland@aap.org
Tel: (202)347-8600
Fax: (202)393-6137
Registered: LDA

Employers

American Academy of Pediatrics (Assistant Director, Government Liaison)

HOLLEMAN, Deirdre Park

909 N. Washington St. Tel: (703)684-1981
Suite 301 Fax: (703)548-4876
Alexandria, VA 22314

Employers
The Retired Enlisted Ass'n (Deputy Legislative Director)

HOLLESTELLE, Kay

725 15th St. NW Tel: (202)347-3300
Suite 505 Fax: (202)347-3382
Washington, DC 20005
EMail: cfwashdc@aol.com

Employers
Children's Foundation (Exec. Director)

HOLLEYMAN, II, Robert W.

1150 18th St. NW Tel: (202)872-5500
Suite 700 Fax: (202)872-5501
Washington, DC 20036 Registered: LDA

Employers
Business Software Alliance (President and C.E.O.)

HOLLINGSWORTH, Jr., E. Boyd

1600 Wilson Blvd. Tel: (703)841-9300
Suite 1000 Fax: (703)841-0389
Arlington, VA 22209 Registered: LDA
EMail: bhollingsworth@vesselalliance.com
Former Deputy Assistant to the President for Legislative Affairs - Senate, Executive Office of the President, The White House, during the first Bush administration.

Employers
American Waterways Operators (V. President, Legislative Affairs)

HOLLINGSWORTH, Joe G.

1350 I St. NW Tel: (202)898-5800
Ninth Floor Fax: (202)682-1639
Washington, DC 20005-3304

Employers
Spriggs & Hollingsworth (Senior Partner)

HOLLIS, Nicholas E.

1312 18th St. NW Tel: (202)296-4563
Suite 300 Fax: (202)887-9178
Washington, DC 20036

Employers
Agribusiness Council (President)

HOLLMAN, Holly

200 Maryland Ave. NE Tel: (202)544-4226
Suite 303 Fax: (202)544-2094
Washington, DC 20002

Employers
Baptist Joint Committee on Public Affairs (General Counsel)

HOLLON, Michael

900 Second St. NE Tel: (202)898-1444
Suite 109 Fax: (202)898-0188
Washington, DC 20002 Registered: LDA

Employers
Waterman & Associates

Clients Represented
On Behalf of Waterman & Associates
California State Ass'n of Counties

HOLLOWAY, Anne

2750 Prosperity Ave. Tel: (703)204-0500
Suite 550 Fax: (703)204-4610
Fairfax, VA 22031-4312 Registered: LDA

Employers
American Wood Preservers Institute (Manager, Legislative Affairs)

HOLLRAH, Russell A.

1225 I St. NW Tel: (202)842-3400
Suite 1000 Fax: (202)842-0011
Washington, DC 20005 Registered: LDA

Employers
Independent Contractor Ass'n of America, Inc.
Littler Mendelson, P.C. (Shareholder)

Clients Represented
On Behalf of Littler Mendelson, P.C.
Independent Contractor Ass'n of America, Inc.
Private Care Ass'n, Inc.

HOLLY, William F.

1101 Connecticut Ave. NW Tel: (202)785-3575
Suite 950 Fax: (202)785-3023
Washington, DC 20036

Employers
Fireman's Fund Insurance Cos. (Assistant V. President, Government and Industry Affairs)

HOLMAN, Barry R.

3125 Mount Vernon Ave. Tel: (703)684-0373
Alexandria, VA 22305 Fax: (703)684-6037
EMail: bholman@ncianet.org

Employers
Coalition for Federal Sentencing Reform (Project Coordinator)

HOLMAN, Jr., Francis W.

1525 Wilson Blvd. Tel: (703)841-9000
Suite 900 Fax: (703)841-9514
Arlington, VA 22209
EMail: fholman@mapi.net

Employers
Manufacturers Alliance/MAPI Inc. (V. President and Secretary)

HOLMAN, Linda P.

1133 19th St. NW Tel: (202)887-3830
Washington, DC 20036 Fax: (202)736-6880
EMail: linda.holman@wcom.com

Employers
MCI WorldCom Corp. (Manager, Tax Legislative Affairs)

HOLMAN, Mark

900 17th St. NW Tel: (202)530-7400
Suite 1000 Fax: (202)530-7476
Washington, DC 20006 Registered: LDA
Chief of Staff and Administrative Assistant to Rep. Tom Ridge (R-PA), 1983-91. Staff Assistant to Senator Henry John Heinz III (R-PA), 1980-82.

Employers
Blank Rome Comisky & McCauley, LLP (Principal, Government Relations)

HOLMER, Alan F.

1100 15th St. NW Tel: (202)835-3420
Suite 900 Fax: (202)835-3414
Washington, DC 20005 Registered: LDA

Employers
Pharmaceutical Research and Manufacturers of America (President and Chief Exec. Officer)

HOLMES, Anne

1100 15th St. NW Tel: (202)835-3400
Suite 900 Fax: (202)835-3414
Washington, DC 20005

Employers
Pharmaceutical Research and Manufacturers of America (PAC Contact and Federal Affairs Coordinator)

HOLMES, Bucky

1500 K St. NW Tel: (202)682-4292
Suite 850 Fax: (202)682-5150
Washington, DC 20005
EMail: bholmes@compete.org

Employers
Council on Competitiveness (Director, Administration)

HOLMES, Constance D.

1130 17th St. NW Tel: (202)463-2654
Washington, DC 20036-4677 Fax: (202)833-9636
Registered: LDA
EMail: cholmes@nma.org

Employers
Nat'l Mining Ass'n (Senior V. President, Policy Analysis)

HOLMES, Diana

1775 Pennsylvania Ave. NW Tel: (202)862-1000
Suite 200 Fax: (202)862-1093
Washington, DC 20006

Employers
Dewey Ballantine LLP (Associate)

HOLMES, Diane

555 12th St. NW Tel: (202)955-9300
Suite 620 North Fax: (202)833-1630
Washington, DC 20004 Registered: LDA
EMail: diane.holmes@fluor.com

Employers
Fluor Corp. (Senior Washington Representative)

HOLMES, Dr. Kim R.

214 Massachusetts Ave. NE Tel: (202)546-4400
Washington, DC 20002 Fax: (202)546-8328

Employers
Heritage Foundation (V. President, Foreign Policy and Defense Studies)

HOLMES, Marty

1910 Association Dr. Tel: (703)758-1900
Reston, VA 20191-1547 Fax: (703)758-8001

Employers
North American Meat Processors Ass'n (Exec. V. President)

HOLMES, Peter E.

600 13th St. NW Tel: (202)756-8213
Washington, DC 20005 Fax: (202)756-8087
Registered: LDA

Employers
Puerto Rico U.S.A. Foundation (Consultant)

HOLMES, Richard

1023 15th St. NW Tel: (202)289-5920
Washington, DC 20005 Fax: (202)289-5938

Employers
Nat'l U.S.-Arab Chamber of Commerce (President)

HOLMES, Robert

499 S. Capitol St. SW Tel: (202)488-8001
Suite 600 Fax: (202)488-8003
Washington, DC 20003
EMail: bholmes@lmcinc.org
Aide to Rep. J.D. Hayworth (R-AZ), 1994-2000.

Employers
Landry, Creedon & Associates, Inc. (V. President/Managing Director)

HOLMES, Tommy

1401 New York Ave. NW Tel: (202)628-8303
Suite 640 Fax: (202)628-2846
Washington, DC 20005 Registered: LDA

Employers
American Water Works Ass'n (Legislative Programs Manager)

HOLMSTEAD, Jeff

555 11th St. NW Tel: (202)637-2200
Suite 1000 Fax: (202)637-2201
Washington, DC 20004

Employers
Latham & Watkins (Partner)

HOLOVIAK, Judy

2000 Florida Ave. NW Tel: (202)777-7520
Washington, DC 20009 Fax: (202)328-0566

Employers
American Geophysical Union (Director, Publications)

HOLRAN, Peter T.

1317 F St. NW
Suite 600
Washington, DC 20004
Tel: (202)638-2121
Fax: (202)638-7045
Registered: LDA
EMail: holran@wexlergroup.com

Employers
The Wexler Group (Principal/Deputy General Manager)

Clients Represented
On Behalf of The Wexler Group
AstroVision Inc.
Burst Networks Inc.
DCH Technology Inc.
Dreamtime, Inc.
EarthWatch, Inc.
Lockheed Martin Corp.
MENC: The Nat'l Ass'n for Music Education
Nat'l Ass'n of Music Merchants
Rocket Development Co.
Rosenbaum Trust
Sechan Electronics

HOLSCLAW, John Bradley "Brad"

227 Massachusetts Ave. NE
Suite One
Washington, DC 20002
Tel: (202)544-7600
Fax: (202)544-6770
Registered: LDA
EMail: holsclaw@tongoursimpson.com
Staff member, Republican Leader Floor Operations, U.S. Senate, 1987-98.

Employers
Tongour Simpson Holsclaw Green (Partner)

Clients Represented
On Behalf of Tongour Simpson Holsclaw Green
American Ass'n of Nurse Anesthetists
Aventis Pharmaceuticals, Inc.
Communities in Schools, Inc.
Corning Inc.
CSX Corp.
Pharmaceutical Research and Manufacturers of America
SCANA Corp.
TXU Business Services

HOLSTEIN, Howard

555 13th St. NW
Washington, DC 20004-1109
Tel: (202)637-5600
Fax: (202)637-5910

Employers
Hogan & Hartson L.L.P.

Clients Represented
On Behalf of Hogan & Hartson L.L.P.
Kensey Nash Corp.

HOLT, M.D., G. Richard

One Prince St.
Alexandria, VA 22314-3357
Tel: (703)836-4444
Fax: (703)683-5100
EMail: grholt@entnet.org

Employers
American Academy of Otolaryngology-Head and Neck Surgery (Exec. V. President)

HOLT, James S.

1015 15th St. NW
Suite 1200
Washington, DC 20005
Tel: (202)789-8600
Fax: (202)789-1708
Registered: LDA

Employers
McGuiness Norris & Williams, LLP (Consultant)

Clients Represented
On Behalf of McGuiness Norris & Williams, LLP
American Kennel Club
American Nursery and Landscape Ass'n
Nat'l Council of Agricultural Employers
Western Range Ass'n

HOLT, Timothy

8300 Colesville Rd.
Suite 250
Silver Spring, MD 20910
Tel: (301)495-0240
Fax: (301)495-3330
EMail: nssea@aol.com

Employers
Nat'l School Supply and Equipment Ass'n (C.E.O.)

HOLTZ, Patrick J.

1225 I St. NW
Suite 500
Washington, DC 20005
Tel: (202)682-4759
Fax: (202)789-0406
Registered: LDA

Employers
American Motorcyclist Ass'n

HOLTZ, William E.

750 17th St. NW
Suite 1100
Washington, DC 20006
Tel: (202)778-2300
Fax: (202)778-2330

Employers
FoxKiser

HOLTZMAN, Jill K.

1719 Dogwood Dr.
Alexandria, VA 22302

Employers
PACAmerica Inc.

HOLWILL, Richard N.

214 Massachusetts Ave. NE
Suite 210
Washington, DC 20002
Tel: (202)547-0300
Fax: (202)547-5008
EMail: Richard_Holwill@alticor.com

Employers
Alticor, Inc. (Director, International Affairs)

HOLY, Lori

1771 N St. NW
Washington, DC 20036-2891
Tel: (202)429-5466
Fax: (202)775-2157
Registered: LDA

Employers
Nat'l Ass'n of Broadcasters (Legislative Counsel)

HOLZ, Hans

555 12th St. NW
Suite 350
N. Tower
Washington, DC 20004
Tel: (202)639-4067
Fax: (202)737-6286

Employers
ABB, Inc. (Director, Multilateral Project Finance)

HOLZWORTH, David A.

1225 19th St. NW
Suite 600
Washington, DC 20036
Tel: (202)857-0242
Fax: (202)857-0189
EMail: dah@lmwh.com

Employers
Lepon McCarthy White & Holzworth, PLLC (Partner)

Clients Represented
On Behalf of Lepon McCarthy White & Holzworth, PLLC
Chilean Exporters Ass'n

HOMAN, Bill

2659 S. Shirlington Rd.
Arlington, VA 22206
Tel: (703)979-9400
Fax: (703)979-8632

Employers
Design Cuisine (President)

HOMER, Peter

4004 David Lane
Alexandria, VA 22311
Tel: (703)998-8177
Registered: LDA

Employers
Self-employed as an independent consultant.

Clients Represented
As an independent consultant
Colorado River Indian Tribes

HOMMES, Caryn D.

1111 19th St. NW
Suite 900
Washington, DC 20036
Tel: (202)296-3920
Fax: (202)296-3948
EMail: chommes@cnfa.org

Employers
Citizens Network for Foreign Affairs (CNFA) (Director, Operations and Compliance)

HONBERG, Ron

Colonial Place Three
2107 Wilson Blvd., Suite 300
Arlington, VA 22201-3042
Tel: (703)524-7600
Fax: (703)524-9094
Registered: LDA

Employers
Nat'l Alliance for the Mentally Ill (Deputy Exec. Director, Legal Affairs)

HONBERGER, Roger F.

440 First St. NW
Suite 430
Washington, DC 20001
Tel: (202)737-7523
Fax: (202)737-6788
Registered: LDA

Employers
Honberger and Walters, Inc. (Partner)

Clients Represented
On Behalf of Honberger and Walters, Inc.
Pechanga Band of Luiseno Mission Indians

HONEY, Martha

733 15th St. NW
Suite 1020
Washington, DC 20005
Tel: (202)234-9382
Fax: (202)387-7915

Employers
Institute for Policy Studies (Fellow)

HONEYCUTT, Michael

2800 Shirlington Rd.
Suite 300
Arlington, VA 22206
Tel: (703)824-8850
Fax: (703)575-9082
EMail: michael@ms.acca.org

Employers
Air Conditioning Contractors of America (Senior Staff V. President)

HONEYGOSKY, Paulette

1200 G St. NW
Suite 800
Washington, DC 20005
Tel: (202)434-8977
Fax: (202)775-8427
Registered: LDA
EMail: paulette_honeygosky@apl.com

Employers
APL Limited (Government Affairs Specialist)

HONG, Jocelyn

1225 I St. NW
Suite 600
Washington, DC 20005
Tel: (202)661-6180
Fax: (202)661-6182
Registered: LDA
EMail: jocelynhong@morganmeguire.com

Employers
Morgan Meguire, LLC (Principal)

Clients Represented
On Behalf of Morgan Meguire, LLC
Burke Venture Capital
Longhorn Pipeline
Manatee, Florida, County of

HONG, Peter

900 19th St. NW
Suite 400
Washington, DC 20006
Tel: (202)857-3100
Fax: (202)296-8716

Employers
America's Community Bankers (Government Relations)

HONIGMAN, Steven S.

701 Pennsylvania Ave. NW
Suite 800
Washington, DC 20004
Tel: (202)508-4006
Fax: (202)508-4321
EMail: shonigman@thelenreid.com
General Counsel, Department of the Navy, 1993-98. Lieutenant, Judge Advocate General's Corps, Department of the Navy, 1973-77. Law Clerk to Judge Jacob Mishler, U.S. District Court for the the Eastern District of New York, 1972-73.

Employers
Thelen Reid & Priest LLP (Partner)

Clients Represented

On Behalf of Thelen Reid & Priest LLP

Metro Machine Corp. of Virginia

HONOR, USA (Ret.), Lt. Gen. Edward

50 S. Pickett St. Tel: (703)751-5011
Suite 220 Fax: (703)823-8761
Alexandria, VA 22304
EMail: ndta@ndtahq.com

Employers

Nat'l Defense Transportation Ass'n (President)

HONTZ, Karen

409 Third St. SW Tel: (202)205-6700
Suite 7900 Fax: (202)205-7374
Washington, DC 20416
EMail: Karen.hontz@sba.gov

Employers

Small Business Administration (Legislative Affairs Specialist)

HONTZ, Lloyd

1350 I St. NW Tel: (202)639-5900
Suite 300 Fax: (202)639-5932
Washington, DC 20005 Registered: LDA

Employers

Nat'l Food Processors Ass'n (Director, Technical Regulatory Affairs-USDA)

HOOD, Elouise

Ronald Reagan Bldg. Tel: (202)712-4063
1300 Pennsylvania Ave. NW Fax: (202)216-3237
MS: 6.10-060
Washington, DC 20523
EMail: ehood@usaid.gov

Employers

Agency for Internat'l Development (Congressional Correspondence/Documents Legislation Program Specialist)

HOOD, Cpt. George

615 Slaters Ln. Tel: (703)684-5526
Alexandria, VA 22313 Fax: (703)684-5538

Employers

Salvation Army (Director of Public Affairs)

HOODYE, Tanya R.

1919 M St. NW Tel: (202)912-1000
Suite 200 Fax: (202)912-1030
Washington, DC 20036
EMail: thoodye@conservation.org

Employers

Conservation Internat'l Foundation (Operations Coordinator)

HOOG, Michael

2550 M St. NW Tel: (202)457-6000
Washington, DC 20037-1350 Fax: (202)457-6315
Registered: LDA
EMail: mhoog@pattonboggs.com

Employers

Patton Boggs, LLP (Associate)

Clients Represented

On Behalf of Patton Boggs, LLP

Greenwood Village, Colorado, City of

HOOK, Michael J.

1875 I St. NW Tel: (202)822-0655
Suite 540 Fax: (202)822-2022
Washington, DC 20006
EMail: mhook@greenerandhook.com
District Director (1989-92) and Chief of Staff (1993-96) to Rep. L. William Paxon (R-NY).

Employers

Greener and Hook, LLC (Partner)

HOOPER, Candice Shy

3733 N. Tazewell St. Tel: (703)241-4007
Arlington, VA 22207-4572 Registered: LDA
Legislative Assistant to Rep. Charles Wilson (D-TX), 1973-78.

Employers

Contango LLC (Principal)

Clients Represented

On behalf of Contango LLC

Barrick Goldstrike Mines, Inc.
Sherritt Internat'l

HOOPER, Heidi

1401 Wilson Blvd. Tel: (703)522-5055
Suite 1100 Fax: (703)525-2279
Arlington, VA 22209 Registered: LDA

Employers

Information Technology Ass'n of America (ITAA)

HOOPER, Helen

4245 N. Fairfax Dr. Tel: (703)841-7426
Suite 100 Fax: (703)841-7400
Arlington, VA 20003-1606 Registered: LDA

Employers

The Nature Conservancy (Director, Congressional Affairs)

HOOPER, Lindsay D.

801 Pennsylvania Ave. NW Tel: (202)756-2400
Suite 730 Fax: (202)756-2401
Washington, DC 20004 Registered: LDA
EMail: Hooper@howdc.com
Tax Counsel and Legislative Director to Senator Malcolm Wallop (R-WY), 1980-84.

Employers

Hooper Owen & Winburn (Principal)

Clients Represented

On Behalf of Hooper Owen & Winburn

AFL-CIO (American Federation of Labor and Congress of Industrial Organizations)
Apple Computer, Inc.
Barrick Goldstrike Mines, Inc.
Borden Chemicals & Plastics, Inc.
Gary-Williams Energy Corp.
Hallmark Cards, Inc.
The Hillman Co.
Hubbell, Inc.
Kansas City Southern Industries
KPMG, LLP
Morgan Stanley Dean Witter & Co.
Parsons Corp.
Philip Morris Management Corp.
Stilwell Financial Inc.
TECO Energy, Inc.
TerraPoint
Trizec Hahn Corp.
Wine and Spirits Wholesalers of America

HOOPER, Theresa

1101 15th St. NW Tel: (202)331-6949
Suite 1100 Fax: (202)331-2805
Washington, DC 20005 Registered: LDA
EMail: tdhooper@mmm.com

Employers

Minnesota Mining and Manufacturing Co. (3M Co.) (Manager, Government Relations)

HOOPER, Thomas A.

2111 Wilson Blvd. Tel: (703)351-5058
Suite 700 Fax: (703)351-6239
Arlington, VA 22201 Registered: LDA
Colonel, U.S. Army, 1967-98.

Employers

Collins & Company, Inc. (Federal Privatization Programs)

Clients Represented

On Behalf of Collins & Company, Inc.

Citizens Network for Foreign Affairs (CNFA)
EarthData Holdings
Hawaii Economic Development Alliance, State of
Internat'l Agriculture and Rural Development Group
Internat'l Fund for Agricultural Development
Loral Space and Communications, Ltd.
Marquette University
Nat'l Telephone Cooperative Ass'n
NewMarket Global Consulting Group
Northrop Grumman Corp.
Pacific Marine
PADCO, Inc.
Population Action Internat'l
Textron Systems Division
Trex Enterprises

HOOPES, Jr., Robert B.

700 13th St. NW Tel: (202)347-6633
Suite 1000 Fax: (202)347-8713
Washington, DC 20005

Employers

Powell Tate (Group V. President)

HOOVER, Karen

490 L'Enfant Plaza East SW Tel: (202)479-1133
Suite 7204 Fax: (202)479-1136
Washington, DC 20024 Registered: LDA

Employers

American Maritime Officers Service (Assistant Legislative Director)

HOOVER, Kimberly

888 16th St. NW Tel: (202)363-6426
Suite 300 Fax: (202)296-7302
Washington, DC 20006 Registered: LDA
EMail: kim@hooperpartners.com

Employers

Hoover Partners (Founder)

Clients Represented

On Behalf of Hoover Partners

Ass'n of Bank Couriers
Financial Technology Industry Council
UMonitor.com

HOOVER, Lesa N.

1050 17th St. NW Tel: (202)296-3390
Suite 300 Fax: (202)296-3399
Washington, DC 20036 Registered: LDA

Employers

Apartment and Office Building Ass'n of Metropolitan Washington (V. President, Governmental Affairs-MD)

HOPE, Doreen C.

1100 H St. NW Tel: (202)624-6033
Washington, DC 20080 Fax: (202)624-6221
Registered: LDA
EMail: dhope@washgas.com

Employers

Washington Gas (Director, Federal Affairs)

HOPE, Judith Richards

1299 Pennsylvania Ave. NW Tel: (202)508-9500
Tenth Floor Fax: (202)508-9700
Washington, DC 20004-2400
EMail: judithrichardshope@paulhastings.com
V. Chairman, President's Commission on Organized Crime, 1983-86. Member, National Highway Traffic Safety Commission, 1977-78. Associate Director, The Domestic Council, The White House, 1975-77.

Employers

Paul, Hastings, Janofsky & Walker LLP (Senior Counsel)

Clients Represented

On Behalf of Paul, Hastings, Janofsky & Walker LLP

General Aviation Manufacturers Ass'n

HOPE, Patrick

701 Pennsylvania Ave. NW Tel: (202)434-7300
Suite 900 Fax: (202)434-7400
Washington, DC 20004-2608 Registered: LDA
EMail: phope@mintz.com

Employers

Mintz, Levin, Cohn, Ferris, Glovsky and Popeo, P.C. (Associate)

Clients Represented

On Behalf of Mintz, Levin, Cohn, Ferris, Glovsky and Popeo, P.C.

CVS, Inc.

HOPE, Samuel

11250 Roger Bacon Dr.
Suite 21
Reston, VA 20190-5202
Tel: (703)437-0700
Fax: (703)437-6312

Employers

Nat'l Ass'n of Schools of Art and Design (Exec. Director)

Nat'l Ass'n of Schools of Dance (Exec. Director)

Nat'l Ass'n of Schools of Music (Exec. Director)

Nat'l Ass'n of Schools of Theatre (Exec. Director)

HOPKINS, Ed

408 C St. NE
Washington, DC 20002
Tel: (202)547-1141
Fax: (202)547-6009
Registered: LDA

Employers

Sierra Club (Director, Environmental Quality Program)

HOPKINS, Marian E.

1615 L St. NW
Suite 1100
Washington, DC 20036-5610
Tel: (202)872-1260
Fax: (202)466-3509
Registered: LDA

Employers

The Business Roundtable (Director, Legislation)

HOPKINS, Mark D.

1200 18th St. NW
Suite 900
Washington, DC 20036
Tel: (202)857-0666
Fax: (202)331-9588

Employers

Alliance to Save Energy (V. President)

HOPKINS, Mark D.

1401 I St. NW
Suite 1200
Washington, DC 20005-2225
Tel: (202)408-5813
Fax: (202)408-5845
Registered: LDA
EMail: mhop@chevron.com

Employers

The Chevron Companies (Federal Relations Manager)

Chevron, U.S.A.

HOPP, R. Richard

4748 Wisconsin Ave. NW
Washington, DC 20016
Tel: (202)362-0041

Employers

O'Donoghue & O'Donoghue

HOPPE, Rodney

1133 Connecticut Ave. NW
Suite 300
Washington, DC 20036
Tel: (202)293-1177
Fax: (202)293-3411
Registered: LDA

Former Deputy Press Secretary, House Commerce Committee.

Employers

Ryan, Phillips, Utrecht & MacKinnon (Legislative Associate)

Clients Represented

On Behalf of Ryan, Phillips, Utrecht & MacKinnon

Air Transport Ass'n of America
Ass'n of American Railroads
Coeur d'Alene Mines Corp.
Cook Inlet Region Inc.
R. R. Donnelley & Sons
Edison Electric Institute
Florida Power and Light Co.
General Communications, Inc.
Investment Co. Institute
Kerr-McGee Corp.
Lockheed Martin Corp.
MultiDimensional Imaging, Inc.
Nat'l Cable Television Ass'n
New York Stock Exchange
Pfizer, Inc.
Philip Morris Management Corp.
Progress Energy
Sault Ste. Marie Tribe of Chippewa Indians
Southern Co.
TXU Business Services
U.S. Interactive
United Pan-Europe Communications, NV
VoiceStream Wireless Corp.

HOPPER, Gary B.

1755 Jefferson Davis Highway
Suite 1101
Arlington, VA 22202
EMail: gary.hopper@flir.com
Tel: (703)416-6666
Fax: (703)416-1517
Registered: LDA

Employers
FLIR Systems, Inc.

HOPPERT, Don

800 I St. NW
Washington, DC 20001
Tel: (202)777-2510
Fax: (202)777-2534
Registered: LDA

Employers
American Public Health Ass'n (Federal Affairs Associate)

HORAN, John G.

600 13th St. NW
Washington, DC 20005-3096
EMail: jhoran@mwe.com
Tel: (202)756-8298
Fax: (202)756-8087

Former Assistant U.S. Attorney, U.S. Attorney's Office, District of Columbia.

Employers
McDermott, Will and Emery (Partner)

HORANBURG, Richard C.

1100 New York Ave. NW
12th Floor
Washington, DC 20527
EMail: rhora@opic.gov
Tel: (202)336-8417
Fax: (202)336-7949

Employers
Overseas Private Investment Corp. (Director, Congressional Affairs)

HORBLITT, Steve

5301 Wisconsin Ave. NW
Suite 700
Washington, DC 20015
EMail: steve@caii-dc.com
Tel: (202)966-5804
Fax: (202)363-4771
Registered: LDA

Legislative Director to Rep. Walter E. Fauntroy (D-DC), 1976-90.

Employers
Creative Associates Internat'l (Director, External Relations)

HORD, Ben F.

11 Canal Center Plaza
Suite 103
Alexandria, VA 22314
Tel: (703)683-4222
Fax: (703)683-0645
Registered: LDA

Employers
The Spectrum Group

Clients Represented

On Behalf of The Spectrum Group

AAI Corp.

HORDELL, Michael A.

700 13th St. NW
Suite 800
Washington, DC 20005
Tel: (202)508-5800
Fax: (202)508-5858

Employers
Kilpatrick Stockton LLP

HORDES, Jess N.

1100 Connecticut Ave. NW
Suite 1020
Washington, DC 20036
Tel: (202)452-8320
Fax: (202)296-2371
Registered: LDA

Employers
Anti-Defamation League (Director, Government and National Affairs Office)

HORINKO, Marianne Lamont

1701 Pennsylvania Ave. NW
Suite 1200
Washington, DC 20006
EMail: info@clayassociates.com
Tel: (202)861-0160
Fax: (202)861-3101

Former Special Assistant to the Assistant Administrator for Solid Waste and Emergency Response, Environmental Protection Agency.

Employers
Clay Associates, Inc. (President)

HORLICK, Gary N.

555 13th St. NW
Suite 500 West
Washington, DC 20004
EMail: ghorlick@omm.com
Tel: (202)383-5300
Fax: (202)383-5414
Registered: LDA

Deputy Assistant Secretary for Import Administration, Department of Commerce, 1981-83. Staff, Senate Committee on Finance, 1981.

Employers
O'Melveny and Myers LLP (Partner)

Clients Represented

On Behalf of O'Melveny and Myers LLP

American Consumers for Affordable Homes
Canada, Government of
Cargill, Inc.
Chile, Government of the Republic of
CIGNA Corp.
Coalition for Truth in Environmental Marketing Information, Inc.

HORN, Colleen

2121 K Street NW
Suite 325
Washington, DC 20037
Tel: (202)728-0610
Fax: (202)728-0617

Employers
American College of Emergency Physicians (Manager, Public Relations)

HORN, Joseph

611 Cameron St.
Alexandria, VA 22314
Tel: (703)683-1077
Fax: (703)683-1272

Employers
Foundation Endowment (President)

HORN, Robert J.

601 Pennsylvania Ave. NW
Suite 350
North Bldg.
Washington, DC 20004
EMail: hornr@dteenergy.com
Tel: (202)347-8420
Fax: (202)347-8423
Registered: LDA

Employers
Detroit Edison Co. (Assistant V. President and Manager, Federal Affairs)

HORN, Ryan

1920 L St. NW
Suite 200
Washington, DC 20036
Tel: (202)785-0266
Fax: (202)785-0261
Registered: LDA

Employers
Americans for Tax Reform (Manager, Federal Affairs)

HORN, William P.

1155 Connecticut Ave. NW
Suite 1200
Washington, DC 20036
EMail: whorn@dc.bhb.com
Tel: (202)659-5800
Fax: (202)659-1027
Registered: LDA

Staff Member, House Committee on Interior and Insular Affairs, 1977-81. Deputy Under Secretary, Department of Interior, 1981-85. Assistant Secretary, Fish, Wildlife and Parks, Department of Interior, 1985-88.

Employers
Birch, Horton, Bittner & Cherot (Shareholder)
Wildlife Legislative Fund of America (Washington Counsel)

Clients Represented

On Behalf of Birch, Horton, Bittner & Cherot
Alaska Legislature
Alaska Professional Hunters Ass'n
Alaska State Snowmobile Ass'n
America Outdoors
Anchorage, Alaska, Municipality of
Bibb, Georgia, Board of Commissioners of the County of
Blue Ribbon Coalition
Clearwater Environmental, Inc.
CSX Corp.
DuPont
Fairbanks, Alaska, North Star Borough of
Feld Entertainment Inc.
Florida Power and Light Co.
ICRC Energy, Inc.
Internat'l Snowmobile Manufacturers Ass'n
ITRI, Ltd.
Kent Gamebore
Quinnat Landing Hotel
Salt River Pima Maricopa Indian Community
Sportsmen's Legal Defense Fund
Tanadgusix Corp.
Turlock Irrigation District
University of Alaska
Wildlife Legislative Fund of America
Yukon Pacific

HORNBACK, Chris

1816 Jefferson Place NW
Washington, DC 20036
Tel: (202)833-2672
Fax: (202)833-4657
Registered: LDA
EMail: chornback@amsa-cleanwater.org

Employers
Ass'n of Metropolitan Sewerage Agencies (Director, Government Affairs)

HORNE, Jennifer

515 N. Washington St.
Alexandria, VA 22314
Tel: (703)836-6767
Fax: (703)836-4543

Employers
Internat'l Ass'n of Chiefs of Police (Legislative Assistant)

HORNE, Katherine M.

1401 H St. NW
Suite 900
Washington, DC 20005
Tel: (202)326-5525
Fax: (202)326-5595
Registered: LDA

Employers
Alliance of Automobile Manufacturers, Inc. (Manager, Government Affairs)

HORNE, Michael S.

1201 Pennsylvania Ave. NW
Washington, DC 20004-2401
Tel: (202)662-6000
Fax: (202)662-6291
EMail: mhorne@cov.com

Employers
Covington & Burling (Partner)

HORNE, Scott J.

1325 G St. NW
Suite 1000
Washington, DC 20005-3104
Tel: (202)737-1770
Fax: (202)626-0900
Registered: LDA

Employers
Institute of Scrap Recycling Industries, Inc. (Manager, Government Relations and Counsel)

HORNER, Charles

1015 18th St. NW
Suite 300
Washington, DC 20036
Tel: (202)223-7770
Fax: (202)223-8537

Employers
Hudson Institute (Senior Fellow)

HORNER, Christopher C.

1001 Connecticut Ave. NW
Suite 1250
Washington, DC 20036
Tel: (202)331-1010
Fax: (202)331-0640
EMail: chorner@cei.org

Employers
Self-employed as an independent consultant.

Clients Represented

As an independent consultant
Competitive Enterprise Institute
Cooler Heads Coalition

HORNER, Constance J.

1775 Massachusetts Ave. NW
Washington, DC 20036-2188
Tel: (202)797-6000
Fax: (202)797-6004
White House Director of Presidential Personnel and Deputy Secretary, Department of Health and Human Services in Bush I Administration. Head, U.S. Office of Personnel Management; Associate Director for Economics and Government, Office of Management and Budget; and Director of VISTA all in Reagan Administration

Employers
The Brookings Institution (Guest Scholar, Governmental Studies)

HORNER, Michael J.

1725 K St. NW
Suite 1212
Washington, DC 20006
Tel: (202)833-8383
Fax: (202)331-7442

Employers
Nat'l Ass'n of Water Companies (Director, Administration and Membership)

HORNING, Mark F.

1330 Connecticut Ave. NW
Washington, DC 20036-1795
Tel: (202)429-3000
Fax: (202)429-3902
EMail: mhorning@steptoe.com

Employers
Steptoe & Johnson LLP (Partner)

HORNING, Robert S.

600 13th St. NW
Washington, DC 20005-3096
Tel: (202)756-8338
Fax: (202)756-8087
EMail: rhorning@mwe.com
Attorney, Department of Labor.

Employers
McDermott, Will and Emery (Partner)

HOROWITZ, Michael J.

1015 18th St. NW
Suite 300
Washington, DC 20036
Tel: (202)223-7770
Fax: (202)223-8537

Employers
Hudson Institute (Senior Fellow)

HORSLEY, John

444 N. Capitol St. NW
Suite 249
Washington, DC 20001
Tel: (202)624-5800
Fax: (202)624-5806

Employers
American Ass'n of State Highway and Transportation Officials (Exec. Director)

HORSTMAN, Douglass C.

1310 G St. NW
Suite 720
Washington, DC 20005
Tel: (202)639-9420
Fax: (202)639-9421
Registered: LDA
EMail: dhorst@maytag.com

Employers
Maytag Corp. (V. President, Government Affairs)

HORTON, Hon. Frank J.

1201 New York Ave. NW
Suite 1000
Washington, DC 20005
Tel: (202)962-4956
Fax: (202)962-8300
Registered: LDA
EMail: fjhorton@venable.com
Member, U.S. House of Representatives (R-NY), 1963-93.

Employers
Venable (Of Counsel)

Clients Represented

On Behalf of Venable
Connaught Laboratories Inc.
Nat'l Council of Juvenile and Family Court Judges

HORTON, Katie

1001 Pennsylvania Ave. NW
Suite 600
Washington, DC 20004
Tel: (202)347-0066
Fax: (202)624-7222
Registered: FARA

Employers
Powell, Goldstein, Frazer & Murphy LLP (Senior Policy Advisor)

HORTON, Jr., Oliver James

1132 Valley Dr.
Alexandria, VA 22302
Tel: (703)671-1408
Fax: (202)429-4342
Registered: LDA

Employers
Self-employed as an independent consultant.

Clients Represented

As an independent consultant
Agri Business Council of Arizona
Arizona Power Authority
Giant Industries, Inc.

HORWITZ, Jamie

555 New Jersey Ave. NW
Washington, DC 20001
Tel: (202)879-4447
Fax: (202)879-4556

Employers
American Federation of Teachers (Assistant Director, Public Affairs)

HORWITZ, Joshua M.

1023 15th St. NW
Suite 600
Washington, DC 20005
Tel: (202)408-7560
Ext: 101
Fax: (202)408-0062

Employers
Educational Fund to Stop Gun Violence (Exec. Director)

HORWITZ, Reid B.

1775 I St. NW
Washington, DC 20006
Tel: (202)261-3365
Fax: (202)261-3333
EMail: reid.horwitz@dechert.com
Antitrust Division, Department of Justice, 1993-2000; Assistant Chief, Merger Task Force, 1995-2000; Bureau of Competition (1988-93) and Bureau of Consumer Protection (1982-88), Federal Trade Commission.

Employers
Dechert (Partner)

HOSKING, James H.

6301 Stevenson Ave.
Suite One
Alexandria, VA 22304
Tel: (703)823-1732
Fax: (703)823-5064

Employers
Strother & Hosking, Inc. (Assistant Exec. V. President)

HOSKINS, David

1725 DeSales St. NW
Suite 600
Washington, DC 20036
Tel: (202)429-5609
Fax: (202)872-0619

Employers
Center for Marine Conservation (V. President of Govt. Affairs and General Counsel)

HOSKINS, Jim

1363 Beverly Rd.
McLean, VA 22101
Tel: (703)556-0001
Fax: (703)893-3811

Employers
Wirthlin Worldwide (Senior V. President)

HOSKINS, Kathy

11250 Roger Bacon Dr.
Suite Eight
Reston, VA 20190
Tel: (703)437-4377
Fax: (703)435-4390

Employers
Drohan Management Group (Account Executive)
Internat'l Biometric Ass'n (Eastern North American Region) (Exec. Director)
Nat'l Renal Administrators Ass'n (Deputy Director)

Clients Represented

On Behalf of Drohan Management Group

Internat'l Biometric Ass'n (Eastern North American Region)

HOSKINSON, Samuel M.

1401 K St. NW
Tenth Floor
Washington, DC 20005
Tel: (202)216-2200
Fax: (202)216-2999
Registered: LDA, FARA

Former Deputy Under Secretary for Economic Policy, Department of State during the Bush I administration. Former senior member of the National Security Council staff, The White House. Former Vice Chairman, National Intelligence Council.

Employers

Jefferson-Waterman Internat'l, LLC (Exec. V. President)

Clients Represented

On Behalf of Jefferson-Waterman Internat'l, LLC

Bulgaria, Ministry of Foreign Affairs of the Republic of
Chevron Chemical Co., LLC

HOSTETLER, James S.

655 15th St. NW
Suite 1200
Washington, DC 20005
Tel: (202)879-5000
Fax: (202)879-5200

Employers

Kirkland & Ellis (Partner)

Clients Represented

On Behalf of Kirkland & Ellis

Professional Services Council

HOTINE, Susan J.

1875 I St. NW
Suite 1050
Washington, DC 20006-5409
Tel: (202)331-8585
Fax: (202)331-2032
Registered: LDA

Legislative Staff Attorney, Joint Committee on Taxation, 1981-85. Attorney and Assistant Branch Chief, Interpretive Division, Chief Counsel's Office, Internal Revenue Service, Department of the Treasury, 1973-81.

Employers

Scribner, Hall & Thompson, LLP (Partner)

Clients Represented

On Behalf of Scribner, Hall & Thompson, LLP

CNA Financial Corp.
Pacific Life Insurance Co.
Transamerica Corp.

HOTKA, M. Cathy

325 Seventh St. NW
Suite 1100
Washington, DC 20004-2802
Tel: (202)783-7971
Fax: (202)737-2849
Registered: LDA

Employers

Nat'l Retail Federation (V. President, Information Technology)

HOTRA, Michael

1850 M St. NW
Suite 1095
Washington, DC 20036
EMail: mhotra@atra.org
Tel: (202)682-1163
Fax: (202)682-1022

Employers

American Tort Reform Ass'n (Director, Public Education)

HOUCK, Caryn

1735 New York Ave. NW
Suite 500
Washington, DC 20006-4759
Tel: (202)628-1700
Fax: (202)331-1024

Employers

Preston Gates Ellis & Rouvelas Meeds LLP (Associate)

HOUGENS, Lori

419 Seventh St. NW
Suite 500
Washington, DC 20004
Tel: (202)626-8800
Fax: (202)737-9189
Registered: LDA

Employers

Nat'l Right to Life Committee (Senior Congressional Liaison, Department of Medical Ethics)

HOUGH, Clayton L.

2550 M St. NW
Washington, DC 20037-1350
Tel: (202)457-6000
Fax: (202)457-6315
Registered: LDA
EMail: chough@pattonboggs.com

Legislative Director to Rep. Elton Gallegly (R-CA), 1987 and to Rep. Bobbi Fiedler (R-CA), 1984-86.

Employers

Patton Boggs, LLP (Partner)

Clients Represented

On Behalf of Patton Boggs, LLP

American Feed Industry Ass'n
Beauty and Barber Supply Industries, Inc.
Crane Co.
Dictaphone Corp.
EchoStar Communications Corp.
Mars, Inc.
Pechanga Band of California Luiseno Indians
Tip Tax Coalition
Tribune Co.
Ventura County Citizens Against Radar Emissions (VCCARE)
WQED Pittsburgh

HOUGH, Henry A.

1655 N. Fort Myer Dr.
Suite 355
Arlington, VA 22209
Tel: (703)807-2070
Fax: (703)807-2073
Registered: LDA
EMail: hhough_60plus@yahoo.com

Employers

The 60/Plus Ass'n, Inc. (Exec. V. President)

HOUGH, Jessica A.

1440 New York Ave. NW
Washington, DC 20005
Tel: (202)371-7000
Fax: (202)393-5760
Registered: LDA

Employers

Skadden, Arps, Slate, Meagher & Flom LLP

Clients Represented

On Behalf of Skadden, Arps, Slate, Meagher & Flom LLP

Fidelity Charitable Gift Fund

HOULE, Alison

1200 New Hampshire Ave NW
Suite 430
Washington, DC 20036
Tel: (202)955-3030
Fax: (202)955-1147
Registered: LDA

Employers

Murray, Scheer, Montgomery, Tapia & O'Donnell

Clients Represented

On Behalf of Murray, Scheer, Montgomery, Tapia & O'Donnell

Jasper, Alabama, City of
Marshall, Alabama, County of

HOULE, Ronald G.

431 18th St. NW
Washington, DC 20006
Tel: (202)639-3125
Fax: (202)639-6116
EMail: houler@usa.redcross.org

Employers

American Red Cross (Director, Legislative Affairs)

HOULIHAN, David P.

601 13th St. NW
Suite 600 South
Washington, DC 20005
EMail: houlida@washdc.whitecase.com
Tel: (202)626-3600
Fax: (202)639-9355

Employers

White & Case LLP (Partner)

Clients Represented

On Behalf of White & Case LLP

Dalmine
Siderar S.A.I.C.
Siderca Corp.
Siderurgica del Orinoco (Sidor), C.A.
TAMSA
Toshiba Corp.

HOULIHAN, Peggy A.

11654 Plaza America Dr.
Suite 200
Reston, VA 20190
Tel: (703)713-9410
Fax: (703)713-0263
Registered: LDA
EMail: pah@houlihanconsulting.com

Employers

Houlihan Consulting L.L.C. (President and Chief Exec. Officer)

HOUSE, Doug

1655 N. Fort Meyer Dr.
Suite 800
Arlington, VA 22209
Tel: (703)312-6004
Fax: (703)527-4586

Employers

Washington Researchers (President)

HOUSE, Michael P.

The McPherson Bldg.
901 15th St. NW, Suite 1100
Washington, DC 20005
Tel: (202)682-3543
Fax: (202)682-3580
Registered: LDA
EMail: mhouse@kayscholer.com

Employers

Kaye Scholer LLP (Partner)

Clients Represented

On Behalf of Kaye Scholer LLP

Korean Semiconductor Industry Ass'n

HOUSE, William Michael

555 13th St. NW
Washington, DC 20004-1109
Tel: (202)637-5636
Fax: (202)637-5910
Registered: LDA
EMail: wmhouse@hhlaw.com

Chief of Staff to Senator Howell Heflin (D-AL), 1979-86. Legislative Assistant to Rep. James M. Collins (R-TX), 1971-72.

Employers

FM Watch (Exec. Director)
Hogan & Hartson L.L.P. (Partner)

Clients Represented

On Behalf of Hogan & Hartson L.L.P.

AAA MidAtlantic
Air Transport Ass'n of America
American Express Co.
Andalex Resources, Inc.
Blount Parrish & Co., Inc.
Brother Internat'l Co.
CELOTEX
Cendant Corp.
Chlorine Chemistry Council
CUNA Mutual Group
Dana Corp.
DIAGEO
Milton S. Eisenhower Foundation
Executive Jet
Financial Planning Ass'n
FM Watch
Grocery Manufacturers of America
HMSHost Corp.
Intergraph Corp.
Kinder-Care Learning Centers, Inc.
Lee County Port Authority
Michelin North America
Mortgage Insurance Companies of America
Nat'l Board for Professional Teaching Standards (NBPTS)
Nestle USA, Inc.
Nissan North America Inc.
NTT America
Polyisocyanurate Insulation Manufacturers Ass'n
Public Service Co. of Colorado
Qwest Communications
SI Corp.
Southern Methodist University
The St. Joe Co.
Toyota Motor North America, U.S.A., Inc.
Vulcan Materials Co.

HOUSEMAN, Alan W.

1616 P St. NW
Suite 150
Washington, DC 20036
EMail: ahouse@clasp.org
Tel: (202)328-5141
Fax: (202)328-5195

Employers

Center for Law and Social Policy (Exec. Director)

HOUSER, Anne

9000 Rockville Pike
Bldg. One, Room 244
Bethesda, MD 20892
EMail: housera@od.nih.gov
Tel: (301)496-3471
Fax: (301)496-0840

Employers
Department of Health and Human Services - Nat'l Institutes of Health (Legislative Analyst)

HOUSER, Susan

811 Vermont Ave. NW
Room 1261
Washington, DC 20571
EMail: susan.houser@exim.gov
Tel: (202)565-3232
Fax: (202)565-3236

Employers
Export-Import Bank (Senior Congressional Analyst)

HOUSMAN, Robert F.

2000 K St. NW
Suite 500
Washington, DC 20006-1872
Tel: (202)828-7637
Fax: (202)223-1225
Registered: LDA
EMail: rhousman@bracepatt.com
Assistant Director for Strategic Planning, Office of National Drug Control Policy, Executive Office of the President, The White House, 1997-2000.

Employers
Bracewell & Patterson, L.L.P. (Associate)

HOUSTLE, Peter M.

14239 Park Center Dr.
Laurel, MD 20707
Tel: (301)725-2149
Fax: (301)725-2187

Employers
Retailers Bakery Ass'n (Exec. V. President)

HOUSTON, Ian

1717 Massachusetts Ave. NW
Suite 701
Washington, DC 20036
EMail: ihouston@interaction.org
Tel: (202)667-8227
Fax: (202)667-8236

Employers
InterAction (Director, Public Policy)

HOUSTON, Paul

1801 N. Moore St.
Arlington, VA 22209
EMail: phouston@aasa.org
Tel: (703)528-0700
Fax: (703)528-2146

Employers
American Ass'n of School Administrators (Exec. Director)

HOUSTON, Russell

1099 14th St. NW
Suite 300 West
Washington, DC 20005-3438
Tel: (202)289-0222
Fax: (202)289-7722

Employers
Institute of Transportation Engineers (Government Relations Associate)

HOUSTON, III, William H.

1300 Pennsylvania Ave. NW
Suite 400
Ronald Reagan Bldg.
Washington, DC 20004
Tel: (202)638-2230
Fax: (202)638-2236
Registered: LDA

Employers
Sandler, Travis & Rosenberg, P.A. (Trade Advisor)

Clients Represented

On Behalf of Sandler, Travis & Rosenberg, P.A.
Confederation of Garment Exporters of the Philippines
Sri Lanka Apparel Exporters Ass'n

HOUTON, Dan

201 Massachusetts Ave. NE
Suite C-8
Washington, DC 20002
EMail: dhouton@celi.org
Tel: (202)546-5007
Fax: (202)546-7037

Employers
Congressional Economic Leadership Institute (Program Manager)

HOUTON, Jamie

21 Dupont Circle NW
Fifth Floor
Washington, DC 20036
Tel: (202)263-5900
Fax: (202)263-5901
Registered: LDA

Employers
Microsoft Corp. (Manager, Federal Government Affairs)

HOUTON, Robert

1201 New York Ave. NW
Suite 300
Washington, DC 20005
EMail: rhouton@boma.org
Tel: (202)326-6365
Fax: (202)371-0181

Employers
Building Owners and Managers Ass'n Internat'l (Manager, State and Local Affairs)

HOVERMALE, David J.

1255 23rd St. NW
Suite 200
Washington, DC 20037-1174
EMail: dhovermale@hauck.com
Tel: (202)452-8100
Fax: (202)833-3636
Registered: LDA

Employers
Hauck and Associates (Director, Government Relations)
Nat'l Oilseed Processors Ass'n (Director, Government and Public Relations)

HOWARD, Angelina S.

1776 I St. NW
Suite 400
Washington, DC 20006-3708
Tel: (202)739-8000
Fax: (202)785-4019

Employers
Nuclear Energy Institute (Exec. V. President, Policy, Planning and External Affairs)

HOWARD, Ann B.

1320 Fenwick Ln.
Suite 100
Silver Spring, MD 20910
Tel: (301)588-1454
Fax: (301)588-4732
Registered: LDA

Employers
American Federation of Home Care Providers (Exec. Director)

HOWARD, Bill

1010 Wayne Ave.
Suite 920
Silver Spring, MD 20910
Tel: (301)588-8994
Fax: (301)588-4629

Employers
Wildlife Habitat Council (President)

HOWARD, Edward F.

1900 L St. NW
Suite 512
Washington, DC 20036
Tel: (202)466-5626
Fax: (202)466-6525

Employers
Alliance for Health Reform (Exec. V. President)

HOWARD, Elizabeth Johns

1001 Pennsylvania Ave. NW
Suite 600
Washington, DC 20004
Tel: (202)347-0066
Fax: (202)624-7222
Registered: LDA
EMail: ejhoward@pgfm.com
International Trade Specialist, Office of Japan (1991-94) and Export Administration Specialist, Bureau of Export Administration (1989-91), Department of Commerce.

Employers
Powell, Goldstein, Frazer & Murphy LLP (Trade Policy Analyst)

Clients Represented

On Behalf of Powell, Goldstein, Frazer & Murphy LLP
American Committee for the Weizmann Institute of Science

HOWARD, Eve

555 13th St. NW
Washington, DC 20004-1109
Tel: (202)637-5600
Fax: (202)637-5910

Employers
Hogan & Hartson L.L.P. (Partner)

HOWARD, Gerald M.

1201 15th St. NW
Washington, DC 20005-2800
Tel: (202)822-0200
Fax: (202)822-0374
Registered: LDA

Employers
Nat'l Ass'n of Home Builders of the U.S. (Exec. V. President and Chief Exec. Officer)

HOWARD, Jack

1600 Pennsylvania Ave. NW
2nd Fl, W. Wing
Washington, DC 20500
Tel: (202)456-2230
Fax: (202)456-1806

Employers
Executive Office of the President - The White House (Deputy Assistant to the President and Deputy Director for Legislative Affairs)

HOWARD, Jane A.

1015 15th St. NW
Suite 700
Washington, DC 20005-2605
Tel: (202)828-5200
Fax: (202)785-2645
Registered: LDA

Employers
Bechtel Group, Inc. (Senior International Trade Representative (BCorp))

HOWARD, Janet

800 Connecticut Ave. NW
Suite 711
Washington, DC 20006
Tel: (202)973-2650
Fax: (202)296-0047

Employers
The Coca-Cola Company (V. President, International Relations)

HOWARD, John E.

1615 H St. NW
Washington, DC 20062-2000
Tel: (202)463-5460
Fax: (202)463-3114
Registered: LDA

Employers
Chamber of Commerce of the U.S.A. (Director, Policy and Programs International)

HOWARD, Lauren R.

3050 K St. NW
Washington, DC 20007
Tel: (202)342-8505
Fax: (202)342-8451
Registered: LDA
EMail: lhoward@colliershannon.com

Employers
Collier Shannon Scott, PLLC (Member)

Clients Represented

On Behalf of Collier Shannon Scott, PLLC
American Textile Machinery Ass'n
Berry Amendment Glove Coalition
Coalition Against Australian Leather Subsidies
Federal Glove Contractors Coalition
Leather Industries of America
Maui Pineapple Co.
Military Footwear Coalition
Military Glove Coalition
Nat'l Cosmetology Ass'n
Specialty Steel Industry of North America
Tanners Countervailing Duty Coalition

HOWARD, Marcia

444 N. Capitol St. NW
Suite 642
Washington, DC 20001
EMail: mhoward@sso.org
Tel: (202)624-5382
Fax: (202)624-7745

Employers
Federal Funds Information for States (Director)

HOWARD, Thomas L.

801 Pennsylvania Ave. NW
Suite 800
Washington, DC 20004
EMail: thoward@bdbc.com
Tel: (202)508-3400
Fax: (202)508-3402
Attorney, Office of the Chief Counsel, Internal Revenue Service, 1971-75.

Employers
Baker, Donelson, Bearman & Caldwell, P.C. (Shareholder)

HOWARTH, Thomas J.

1001 G St. NW
Suite 400 East
Washington, DC 20001
Tel: (202)638-3730
Fax: (202)638-3516
Registered: LDA
EMail: thowarth@peyser.com
Former Legislative Assistant to Senator Frank Lautenberg (D-NJ).

Employers
Peyser Associates, Inc. (V. President, Client Relations)

Clients Represented
On Behalf of Peyser Associates, Inc.
Federal Home Loan Bank of Seattle
Mothers Against Drunk Driving (MADD)
Philadelphia, Pennsylvania, City of
Seattle, Washington, City of
Sound Transit
Southeastern Pennsylvania Transit Authority

HOWE, Allynn

1050 17th St. NW
Suite 510
Washington, DC 20036
Tel: (202)775-0079
Fax: (202)785-0477
Registered: LDA
EMail: AllynnH@aol.com

Employers
Government Relations, Inc. (Consultant)

Clients Represented
On Behalf of Government Relations, Inc.
The Home Depot

HOWE, Jr., Jerald S.

1200 S. Hay St.
Suite 1100
Arlington, VA 22202
Tel: (703)575-3100
Fax: (703)575-3200

Employers
Veridian Corp. (Senior V. President and General Counsel)

HOWE, Louise

1455 Pennsylvania Ave. NW
Suite 1000
Washington, DC 20004
EMail: louise.howe@haledorr.com
Tel: (202)942-8400
Fax: (202)942-8484

Employers
Hale and Dorr LLP (Senior Partner)

Clients Represented
On Behalf of Hale and Dorr LLP
Cook Inc.
Hillenbrand Industries, Inc.

HOWE, Shippen

1050 Thomas Jefferson St. NW
Seventh Floor
Washington, DC 20007
EMail: sxh@vnf.com
Tel: (202)298-1800
Fax: (202)338-2416

Employers
Van Ness Feldman, P.C. (Of Counsel)

HOWE, Todd

1919 Pennsylvania Ave. NW
Seventh Floor
Washington, DC 20006-3488
Tel: (202)557-2700
Registered: LDA
Formerly Deputy Chief of Staff, U.S. Department of Housing and Urban Development.

Employers
Mortgage Bankers Ass'n of America

HOWE, William H.

1747 Pennsylvania Ave. NW
Suite 1050
Washington, DC 20006
EMail: hhowe@haspc.com
Tel: (202)296-5680
Fax: (202)331-8049

Employers
Howe, Anderson & Steyer, P.C. (Partner)

Clients Represented
On Behalf of Howe, Anderson & Steyer, P.C.
Ass'n of Bituminous Contractors

HOWELL, Andrew

1615 H St. NW
Washington, DC 20062
Tel: (202)463-5500
Fax: (202)463-3129

Employers
Nat'l Chamber Foundation (V. President)

HOWELL, Barbara

50 F St. NW
Suite 500
Washington, DC 20001
Tel: (301)608-2400
Fax: (301)608-2401
Registered: LDA
EMail: bhowell@bread.org

Employers
Bread for the World (Director, Government Relations)

HOWELL, Chandler

919 18th St. NW
Tenth Floor
Washington, DC 20006
Tel: (202)263-2900
Fax: (202)263-2960

Employers
Issue Dynamics Inc. (Assistant V. President)

HOWELL, James P.

50 F St. NW
Suite 900
Washington, DC 20001
Tel: (202)626-8700
Fax: (202)626-8722
Registered: LDA
EMail: jhowell@ncfc.org

Employers
Nat'l Council of Farmer Cooperatives (V. President, Congressional and Regulatory Affairs)

HOWELL, Jane

1015 15th St. NW
Suite 600
Washington, DC 20005
EMail: jhowell@dc.asce.org
Tel: (202)789-2200
Fax: (202)289-6797

Employers
American Soc. of Civil Engineers (Director, Communications)

HOWELL, Marcela E.

1025 Vermont Ave. NW
Suite 200
Washington, DC 20005
Tel: (202)347-5700
Fax: (202)347-2263
Registered: LDA
EMail: marcela@advocatesforyouth.org

Employers
Advocates for Youth (Director, Public Affairs)

HOWELL, Mary L.

1101 Pennsylvania Ave. NW
Suite 400
Washington, DC 20004-2504
Tel: (202)637-3800
Fax: (202)637-3860
Registered: LDA

Employers
Textron Inc. (Exec. V. President, Government, Internat'l Investor Relations & Corp. Commun.)

HOWELL, Steve

4245 N. Fairfax Dr.
Suite 100
Arlington, VA 20003-1606
Tel: (703)841-5316
Fax: (703)841-8796

Employers
The Nature Conservancy (Acting V. President and Chief Operating Officer)

HOWELL, Thomas R.

1775 Pennsylvania Ave. NW
Suite 200
Washington, DC 20006
Tel: (202)429-2354
Fax: (202)862-1093
Registered: LDA

Employers
Dewey Ballantine LLP (Partner)

Clients Represented
On Behalf of Dewey Ballantine LLP
American Natural Soda Ash Corp.

HOWES, Joanne M.

1818 N St. NW
Suite 450
Washington, DC 20036
Tel: (202)530-2900
Fax: (202)530-2901
Registered: LDA
EMail: jhowes@basshowes.com
Legislative Director for Rep. Barbara Mikulski (D-MD), 1977-79.

Employers
Bass and Howes, Inc. (Principal)

Clients Represented
On Behalf of Bass and Howes, Inc.
Family Violence Prevention Fund
Genentech, Inc.
Nat'l Breast Cancer Coalition
Nat'l Partnership for Women and Families

HOWES, John A.

700 13th St. NW
Suite 950
Washington, DC 20005
EMail: jahowes@aol.com
Tel: (202)434-8918
Fax: (202)638-5129

Employers
Redland Energy Group

Clients Represented
On Behalf of Redland Energy Group
TVA Watch

HOWIE, Irene E.

7321 Masonville Dr.
Annadale, VA 22003
Tel: (703)573-0635
Fax: (703)573-0066
Registered: LDA
Former Senior Staff Member, Federal Aviation Administration, Department of Transportation.

Employers
Law Offices of Irene E. Howie (Principal)

Clients Represented
On Behalf of Law Offices of Irene E. Howie
Air Methods/Mercy Air

HOWLETT, Jr., C. T. "Kip"

1300 Wilson Blvd.
Arlington, VA 22209
Tel: (703)741-5850
Fax: (703)741-6850
Registered: LDA
EMail: kip_howlett@cmahq.com

Employers
American Chemistry Council (V. President, Chlorine Chemistry Council)
Chlorine Chemistry Council (V. President and Exec. Director)

HOWLEY, John

1313 L St. NW
Washington, DC 20005
Tel: (202)898-3200
Fax: (202)898-3304
Registered: LDA

Employers
Service Employees Internat'l Union (Director, Public Policy)

HOXIE, Lance

350 John Carlyle St.
Suite 200
Alexandria, VA 22314
Tel: (703)836-7114
Ext: 3012
Fax: (703)836-0838
EMail: lhoxie@opoffice.org

Employers
American Board for Certification in Orthotics and Prosthetics, Inc. (ABC) (Exec. Director)

HOYDYSH, Dan

1901 Pennsylvania Ave. NW
Suite 302
Washington, DC 20006
Tel: (202)293-7720
Fax: (202)293-7757
Registered: LDA

Employers
Unisys Corp. (Director, Washington Office)

HOYLE, Peggy A.

1875 Connecticut Ave. NW
Suite 1200
Washington, DC 20009-5728
Tel: (202)986-8000
Fax: (202)986-8102
Registered: LDA

Employers
LeBoeuf, Lamb, Greene & MacRae L.L.P.

Clients Represented

On Behalf of LeBoeuf, Lamb, Greene & MacRae L.L.P.
Candle Corp.

HOYLER, Maureen

1025 Vermont Ave. NW
Suite 900
Washington, DC 20005
Tel: (202)347-7430
Fax: (202)347-0786
Registered: LDA

Employers
Council for Opportunity in Education (Exec. V. President)

HOYT, Robert F.

2445 M St. NW
Washington, DC 20037-1420
Tel: (202)663-6000
Fax: (202)663-6363
EMail: rhoyt@wilmer.com

Employers
Wilmer, Cutler & Pickering (Associate)

HRVATIN, Claudia

2300 N St. NW
Washington, DC 20037-1128
Tel: (202)663-8245
Fax: (202)663-8007
Registered: LDA
EMail: claudia.hrvatin@shawpittman.com
Legislative Director to Representative Chris Cannon (R-UT), 1997-99. Senior Legislative Assistant to Representative John T. Doolittle (R-CA), 1994-97.

Employers
Shaw Pittman (Government Relations Advisor)

Clients Represented

On Behalf of Shaw Pittman
The Boeing Co.
Mexico, Secretaria de Comercio y Fomento Industrial (SECOFI)
Southern Ass'n of Forestry Economics

HSU, Fiona

1311 L St. NW
Fourth Floor
Washington, DC 20005
EMail: fiona@ctj.org
Tel: (202)626-3780
Fax: (202)638-3486

Employers
Citizens for Tax Justice (Tax Analyst)

HUBAND, Dr. Frank L.

1818 N St. NW
Suite 600
Washington, DC 20036
EMail: f.huband@asee.org
Tel: (202)331-3545
Fax: (202)265-8504

Employers
American Soc. for Engineering Education (Exec. Director)

HUBBARD, Alan

2101 L St. NW
Washington, DC 20037-1526
Tel: (202)785-9700
Fax: (202)887-0689
Registered: LDA
EMail: hubbarda@dsmo.com

Employers
Dickstein Shapiro Morin & Oshinsky LLP (Counsel)

Clients Represented

On Behalf of Dickstein Shapiro Morin & Oshinsky LLP
American Public Communications Council

HUBBARD, David S.

1225 I St. NW
Suite 300
Washington, DC 20005
Tel: (202)408-9494
Fax: (202)408-0877
Registered: LDA

Employers
American Portland Cement Alliance (Director, Legislative Affairs)

HUBBARD, Gary L.

1150 17th St. NW
Suite 300
Washington, DC 20036
EMail: ghubbard@uswa.org
Tel: (202)778-4384
Fax: (202)293-5308

Employers
United Steelworkers of America (Director, Public Affairs)

HUBBARD, Henry W.

1615 L St. NW
Suite 1000
Washington, DC 20036
EMail: hubbardh@fleishman.com
Tel: (202)659-0330
Fax: (202)239-8105

Employers
Fleishman-Hillard, Inc (Senior V. President and Partner)

HUBBARD, James

2111 Wilson Blvd.
Suite 600
Arlington, VA 22201
Tel: (703)351-5077
Fax: (703)351-5827
Registered: LDA
EMail: jim@halseyrains.com

Employers
Halsey, Rains & Associates, LLC (Member)

Clients Represented

On Behalf of Halsey, Rains & Associates, LLC
American Board of Medical Specialties in Podiatry
American Medical Technologists
American Soc. of Military Comptrollers
Ass'n of Government Accountants
Board for Orthotists/Prosthetist Certification
Cardiovascular Credentialing Internat'l
The Chauncey Group Internat'l
Coalition for Professional Certification
Computer Adaptive Technologies
Internat'l Board of Lactation Consultant Examiners
Internat'l Electrical Testing Ass'n
Nat'l Ass'n of Portable X-Ray Providers
Nat'l Commission for the Certification of Crane Operators
Nat'l Council on Family Relations
Nat'l Institute for Certification in Engineering Technologies

HUBBARD, R. Glenn

1150 17th St. NW
Washington, DC 20036
Tel: (202)862-5800
Fax: (202)862-7177
EMail: rgh1@columbia.edu

Employers
American Enterprise Institute for Public Policy Research (Visiting Scholar)

HUBBARD, Richard L.

555 12th St. NW
Washington, DC 20004-1206
Tel: (202)942-5000
Fax: (202)942-5999
EMail: Richard_Hubbard@aporter.com
Law Clerk to Judge Arnold Raum, U.S. Tax Court, 1967-69.

Employers
Arnold & Porter (Partner)

HUBBARD, Sherry L.

1225 19th St. NW
Suite 450
Washington, DC 20036
Tel: (202)296-4933
Fax: (202)296-4951
Registered: LDA

Employers
Cox Enterprises Inc. (Director of Operations)

HUBER, Robert T.

1776 Massachusetts Ave. NW
Suite 700
Washington, DC 20036
Registered: LDA

Employers
American Councils for Internat'l Education: ACTR/ACCELS (Consultant)

HUBERTY, Robert M.

1513 16th St. NW
Washington, DC 20036
Tel: (202)483-6900
Fax: (202)483-6990
EMail: rhuberty@capitalresearch.org

Employers
Capital Research Center (V. President and Director, Research)

HUCKABY, Stan

425 Second St. NE
Washington, DC 20002
Tel: (202)675-6000
Fax: (202)675-6058

Employers
Nat'l Republican Senatorial Committee (Treasurer)

HUDAK, Stephen P.

1777 F St. NW
Room 426
Washington, DC 20006
EMail: hudaks@fhfb.gov
Tel: (202)408-2998
Fax: (202)408-2947

Employers
Federal Housing Finance Board (Acting Director, Office of Congressional Affairs)

HUDDLESON, III, Edwin E.

1230 31st St. NW
Second Floor
Washington, DC 20007
Tel: (202)333-1360
Fax: (202)298-6699
Registered: LDA
EMail: huddleson@aol.com
Attorney, Civil Division, Department of Justice, 1971-77, Law Clerk to Judge Charles M. Merrill, U.S. Court of Appeals, Ninth Circuit, 1970-71.

Employers
Self-employed as an independent consultant.

Clients Represented

As an independent consultant
Equipment Leasing Ass'n of America

HUDDLESTON, Andrew

919 18th St. NW
Suite 800
Washington, DC 20006
Tel: (202)628-4160
Fax: (202)347-5323

Employers
Human Rights Campaign Fund (Political Assistant)

HUDDLESTON, Hon. Walter D.

499 S. Capitol St. SW
Suite 507
Washington, DC 20003
Tel: (202)554-2881
Registered: LDA, FARA
Member, U.S. Senate (D-KY), 1973-85.

Employers
Hecht, Spencer & Associates (Consultant)

HUDGENS, Capt. Tom

502 H St. SW
Washington, DC 20024-2726
Tel: (202)544-5150
Fax: (202)544-3742
EMail: atunite@aol.com

Employers
Ass'n to Unite the Democracies (President and Chief Exec. Officer)

HUDGINS, Edward L.

1000 Massachusetts Ave. NW
Washington, DC 20001
Tel: (202)842-0200
Fax: (202)842-3490

Employers
Cato Institute (Director, Regulatory Studies)

HUDSON, Betty

1145 17th St. NW
Washington, DC 20036
Tel: (202)857-7000
Fax: (202)775-6141

Employers
Nat'l Geographic Soc. (Senior V. President, Communications)

HUDSON, Cynthia

1801 K St. NW
Suite 1000L
Washington, DC 20006
EMail: cynthia_hudson@washbm.com
Tel: (202)530-0400
Fax: (202)530-4500

Employers
Burson-Marsteller (Managing Director, Public Affairs Practice)

HUDSON, Dana W.

1700 Pennsylvania Ave. NW
Suite 950
Washington, DC 20006
Tel: (202)393-5055
Fax: (202)393-0120
Registered: LDA
EMail: danahudson@starpower.net

Employers
Trade Ass'n Liaison Council (Coordinator)
Valis Associates (Account Exec.)

Clients Represented

On Behalf of Valis Associates
Citizens for Civil Justice Reform
Coalition for Open Markets and Expanded Trade
The Doctors' Co.
Exxon Mobil Corp.
New Majority Soc.
Trade Ass'n Liaison Council

HUDSON, J. Michael

1919 Pennsylvania Ave. NW
Suite 600
Washington, DC 20006
Tel: (202)326-1530
Fax: (202)547-1105
Registered: LDA
Deputy Administrator, Health Care Financing Administration, Department of Health and Human Services, during the Bush I administration.

Employers
Health Policy Group (Senior Partner)

Clients Represented

On Behalf of Health Policy Group
Ass'n of Organ Procurement Organizations
Ralin Medical
Teletech Teleservices, Inc.
University of Texas Health Systems
Vector Research, Inc.

HUDSON, J. William

7315 Wisconsin Ave.
Suite 1200N
Bethesda, MD 20814
Tel: (301)652-5674
Fax: (301)652-7269
EMail: bhudson@iarw.org

Employers
Internat'l Ass'n of Refrigerated Warehouses (President and C.E.O.)

HUDSON, James H.

1212 New York Ave. NW
Suite 525
Washington, DC 20005
Tel: (202)898-1661
Fax: (202)371-9744
Registered: LDA

Employers
Nat'l Fair Housing Alliance (Director of Public Policy)

HUDSON, Laura C.

1150 Connecticut Ave. NW
Suite 1025
Washington, DC 20036
Tel: (202)367-2775
Fax: (202)367-2790
Registered: LDA

Employers
UNOCAL Corp. (Federal and International Affairs)

HUDSON, Peggy Renken

1225 I St. NW
Suite 300
Washington, DC 20005
Tel: (202)408-9494
Fax: (202)408-0877
Registered: LDA

Employers
American Portland Cement Alliance (V. President, Legislative Affairs)

HUDSON, Rebecca J.

P.O Box 20652
Alexandria, VA 22320-1652
Tel: (703)660-9246
Fax: (703)660-9240
Registered: LDA

Employers
R. J. Hudson Associates (President)

Clients Represented

On Behalf of R. J. Hudson Associates
Coalition of Hawaii Movers
DeWitt Cos. of Guam and Saipan

HUDSON, Thomas H.

1615 L St. NW
Suite 450
Washington, DC 20036
Tel: (202)296-7353
Fax: (202)296-7009
Registered: LDA
EMail: tomhudson@erols.com
Former Chief of Staff to Sen. John Breaux (D-LA).

Employers
Brownstein Hyatt & Farber, P.C.

Clients Represented

On Behalf of Brownstein Hyatt & Farber, P.C.
AT&T Broadband & Internet Service
Delta Petroleum Corp.
Express One Internat'l Inc.
Global Crossing North America, Inc.
Mariner Post Acute Network
Nat'l Cable Television Ass'n
Oracle Corp.
Pacific Capital Group, Inc.
Shaw Group
Teletech Teleservices, Inc.

HUERTA, Michael P.

5225 Wisconsin Ave. NW
Suite 409
Washington, DC 20015
Tel: (202)466-5542
Fax: (202)466-5548
Registered: LDA

Employers
Cambridge Systematics, Inc (Principal)

Clients Represented

On Behalf of Cambridge Systematics, Inc
Salt Lake City Olympic Organizing Committee

HUETER, Ernest B.

1000 16th St. NW
Suite 500
Washington, DC 20036
Tel: (202)296-1683
Fax: (202)293-2118
EMail: info@nlcpi.org

Employers
Nat'l Legal Center for the Public Interest (President)

HUEY, Erik V.

1501 M St. NW
Suite 700
Washington, DC 20005-1702
Tel: (202)463-4300
Fax: (202)463-4394
Registered: LDA
EMail: ehuey@manatt.com

Employers
Manatt, Phelps & Phillips, LLP (Associate)

Clients Represented

On Behalf of Manatt, Phelps & Phillips, LLP
BellSouth Corp.
Congo, Republic of
Kean Tracers, Inc.
Verizon Communications

HUEY, Robert H.

1050 Connecticut Ave. NW
Washington, DC 20036-5339
Tel: (202)857-6000
Fax: (202)857-6395

Employers
Arent Fox Kintner Plotkin & Kahn, PLLC (Member)

HUFFMAN, Robert K.

655 15th St. NW
Suite 900
Washington, DC 20005-5701
Tel: (202)626-5800
Fax: (202)628-0858
EMail: rhuffman@milchev.com

Employers
Miller & Chevalier, Chartered (Member)

HUG, Jim

1225 Otis St. NE
Washington, DC 20017
Tel: (202)635-2757
Fax: (202)832-9494
EMail: jhug@coc.org

Employers
Center of Concern (President)

HUGE, Harry

1001 Pennsylvania Ave. NW
Suite 600
Washington, DC 20004
Tel: (202)347-0066
Fax: (202)624-7222
EMail: hhuge@pgfm.com
Special Master, U.S. District Court for the District of Columbia, 1983-85. Member, President's General Advisory Committee on Arms Control and Disarmament, The White House, 1977-81.

Employers
Powell, Goldstein, Frazer & Murphy LLP (Partner)

HUGEL, Max

1299 Pennsylvania Ave. NW
Suite 800 West
Washington, DC 20004
Tel: (202)682-3901
Fax: (202)842-0621
Deputy Director, Central Intelligence Agency.

Employers
LMRC, Inc. (Vice Chairman)

HUGGINS, James B.

601 Pennsylvania Ave. NW
Suite 900
Washington, DC 20004
Tel: (202)547-3566
Fax: (202)639-8238
Registered: LDA
Professional Staff member, Senate Appropriations Committee, 1991. State Director to Sen. Robert C. Byrd (D-WV), 1973-91.

Employers
Cottone and Huggins Group (President and Chief Exec. Officer)

Clients Represented

On Behalf of Cottone and Huggins Group
Center for Sino-American Trade
CESD/WVU
Civil Air Patrol
CTC Corp.
Dulles Networking Associates
EER Systems
Galaxy Global Corp.
Hardy County Industrial Ass'n
HARSCO Corp.
Marshall Research Corp.
MICAH Software Systems
OAO Corp.
Science Applications Internat'l Corp. (SAIC)
Spectrum Astro, Inc.
Strictly Business Software System
TMC Technologies
University of Tennessee

HUGHES, Della

1319 F St. NW
Suite 401
Washington, DC 20004
Tel: (202)783-7949
Fax: (202)783-7955

Employers
Nat'l Network for Youth (Exec. Director)

HUGHES, Gary E.

1001 Pennsylvania Ave. NW
Washington, DC 20004-2599
Tel: (202)624-2000
Fax: (202)624-2319
Registered: LDA

Employers
American Council of Life Insurers (Senior V. President and General Counsel)

HUGHES, J. Vance

700 13th St. NW
Suite 800
Washington, DC 20005
Tel: (202)508-5800
Fax: (202)508-5858
Formerly with the Environmental Protection Agency and the Department of Justice.

Employers
Kilpatrick Stockton LLP (Partner)

Clients Represented

On Behalf of Kilpatrick Stockton LLP
Atlanta, Georgia, City of
Georgia Ports Authority
Zirconium Environmental Committee (ZEC)

HUGHES, Jennifer P.

1730 Rhode Island Ave. NW
Suite 209
Washington, DC 20036-3120
Tel: (202)331-8690
Fax: (202)331-8738
Registered: LDA

Employers
Morriset, Schlosser, Ayer & Jozwiak (Attorney)

Clients Represented

On Behalf of Morriset, Schlosser, Ayer & Jozwiak
Alaska Eskimo Whaling Commission
Kake, Alaska, Organized Village of
Paucatuck Eastern Pequot Tribal Nation
Quechan Indian Tribe
Saginaw Chippewa Indian Tribe of Michigan

HUGHES, John P.

1333 H St. NW
West Tower
Eighth Floor
Washington, DC 20005
EMail: elcon@elcon.org
Tel: (202)682-1390
Fax: (202)289-6370
Registered: LDA

Employers
Electricity Consumers Resource Council (ELCON) (Director, Technical Affairs)

HUGHES, Kristin

900 17th St. NW
Suite 1100
Washington, DC 20006
EMail: kristin_hughes@hp.com
Tel: (202)884-7035
Fax: (202)884-7070
Registered: LDA

Employers
Hewlett-Packard Co. (Manager, Federal Public Policy)

HUGHES, Mary Rose

607 14th St. NW
Suite 700
Washington, DC 20005-2011
Tel: (202)628-6600
Fax: (202)434-1690
Deputy Assistant Secretary for Environment, Health and Natural Resources, Department of State, 1982-84. Chief Legislative Assistant to Rep. Jack Kemp (R-NY), 1973-77.

Employers
Perkins Coie LLP (Partner)

HUGHES, Meredith

1100 New York Ave. NW
Suite 450
Washington, DC 20005
Tel: (202)408-8422
Fax: (202)408-1255

Employers
Travel Industry Ass'n of America (Manager, Legislative Affairs)

HUGHES, Nancy

950 N. Washington St.
Alexandria, VA 22314-1552
Tel: (703)836-2272
Fax: (703)684-1924

Employers
American Academy of Physician Assistants (V. President, Communication and Information Services)

HUGHES, Phyllis E.

1050 Connecticut Ave. NW
Washington, DC 20036-5366
EMail: phughes@flks.com
Tel: (202)672-5300
Fax: (202)672-5399
Registered: LDA

Employers
Freedman, Levy, Kroll & Simonds (Legislative Specialist)
Women in Government Relations, Inc. (President)

HUGHES, Robert

1225 I St. NW
Suite 500
Washington, DC 20005
Tel: (202)466-2100
Fax: (202)466-2123

Employers
Nat'l Ass'n for the Self-Employed (President)

HUGHES, Robert

P.O. Box 4062
Merrifield, VA 22116

Employers
Nat'l Pro-Life Alliance PAC (PAC Administrator)

HUGHES, Scott

1875 I St. NW
Suite 540
Washington, DC 20006
EMail: shughes@greenerandhook.com
Tel: (202)822-0655
Fax: (202)822-2022
Confidential Assistant, Department of Education, 1990-93.

Employers
Greener and Hook, LLC (Senior Associate)

HUGHES, Sharon M.

1112 16th St. NW
Suite 920
Washington, DC 20036
EMail: agemployers@aol.com
Tel: (202)728-0300
Fax: (202)728-0303
Registered: LDA

Employers
Nat'l Council of Agricultural Employers (Exec. V. President)

HUGHES, Timothy

1500 K St.
Suite 1100
Washington, DC 20005
Tel: (202)842-8800
Fax: (202)842-8465
Registered: LDA

Employers
Drinker Biddle & Reath LLP

Clients Represented

On Behalf of Drinker Biddle & Reath LLP
Nat'l Community Capital Ass'n

HUGHES, William G.

1101 Vermont Ave. NW
Suite 710
Washington, DC 20005-6308
Tel: (202)289-6334
Fax: (202)842-4360

Employers
Nat'l Ass'n of Federal Veterinarians (General Counsel)

HUGO, Timothy D.

1129 20th St. NW
Suite 200
Washington, DC 20036
EMail: timhugo@bot.org
Tel: (202)857-5936
Fax: (202)223-2648
Chief of Staff to Rep. Bud Shuster (R-PA), 1996-99. Legislative Staff, House Administration Committee, 1994-95. Legislative Director to Rep. Jennifer Dunn (R-WA), 1993-95. Intelligence Action Officer, Legislative Affairs, Department of Defense, 1992.

Employers
Greater Washington Board of Trade (Director, CapNet and Federal Affairs)

HUIZENGA, Walter E.

99 Canal Center Plaza
Suite 500
Alexandria, VA 22314-1538
EMail: goaiada@aiada.org
Tel: (703)519-7800
Fax: (703)519-7810
Registered: LDA

Employers
American Internat'l Automobile Dealers Ass'n (President)

HUIZINGA, James A.

1722 I St. NW
Washington, DC 20006
EMail: jhuizinga@sidley.com
Tel: (202)736-8000
Fax: (202)736-8711

Employers
Sidley & Austin (Partner)

HULL, Bob

919 18th St. NW
Tenth Floor
Washington, DC 20006
Tel: (202)263-2900
Fax: (202)263-2960

Employers
Issue Dynamics Inc. (Assistant V. President)

HULL, Brenda J.

1001 19th St. North
Suite 800
Arlington, VA 22209-3901
EMail: brenda.hull@trw.com
Tel: (703)276-5124
Fax: (703)276-5119
Registered: LDA

Employers
TRW Inc. (Director, Government Relations, Defense and National Security Programs)

HULL, Jeanine

1350 New York Ave. NW
11th Floor
Washington, DC 20005
Tel: (202)628-3123
Fax: (202)628-3339
Registered: LDA

Employers
Strategic Energy Advisors (Principal)

HULSHART, Mark

3009 Federal Hill Dr.
Falls Church, VA 22044
Tel: (703)241-5501
Exec. Assistant and Regional District Director to Sen. John Heinz (R-PA), 1982-84.

Employers
Hulshart & Associates (Principal)

HULSMAN, John

214 Massachusetts Ave. NE
Washington, DC 20002
Tel: (202)546-4400
Fax: (202)546-8328

Employers
Heritage Foundation (Research Fellow, NATO and Europe)

HUME, Greg

1775 Pennsylvania Ave. NW
Suite 200
Washington, DC 20006
Tel: (202)862-1000
Fax: (202)862-1093
Registered: LDA

Employers
Dewey Ballantine LLP (Economist)

HUME, Hamish

1500 K St. NW
Suite 200
Washington, DC 20005
Tel: (202)220-9600
Fax: (202)220-9601
Registered: LDA

Employers
Cooper, Carvin & Rosenthal

Clients Represented

On Behalf of Cooper, Carvin & Rosenthal
Real Access Alliance

HUME, John P.

607 14th St. NW
Suite 700
Washington, DC 20005-2011
Tel: (202)628-6600
Fax: (202)434-1690
Principal Assistant U.S. Attorney (1983-85), Director, District Court Operations (1981-83), Chief, Felony Trial Division (1975-79), and Assistant U.S. Attorney (1970-75), District of Columbia, Department of Justice. Lieutenant, U.S. Navy, 1965-70.

Employers
Perkins Coie LLP (Partner)

HUME, Virginia

1133 Connecticut Ave. NW
Fifth Floor
Washington, DC 20036
Tel: (202)457-1110
Fax: (202)457-1130

Employers
Quinn Gillespie & Associates (Public Relations Associate)

HUMES, Traci D.

1747 Pennsylvania Ave. NW
Suite 1200
Washington, DC 20006
EMail: thumes@fhe.com
Tel: (202)223-1200
Fax: (202)785-6687
Registered: LDA, FARA

Employers
Foley, Hoag & Eliot LLP (Of Counsel)

Clients Represented

On Behalf of Foley, Hoag & Eliot LLP
Uganda, Embassy of the Republic of
Uganda, Government of the Republic of

HUMMERS, Jr., Edward

2099 Pennsylvania Ave. NW
Suite 100
Washington, DC 20006
EMail: ehummers@hklaw.com
Tel: (202)955-3000
Fax: (202)828-1868

Employers
Holland & Knight LLP (Partner)

HUMPHREY, Cliff

4301 Wilson Blvd.
Arlington, VA 22203-1860
Tel: (703)907-5806
Fax: (703)907-5516
Registered: LDA
EMail: cliff.humphrey@nreca.org

Employers
Nat'l Rural Electric Cooperative Ass'n (Legislative Representative)

HUMPHREY, Margot Smiley

2099 Pennsylvania Ave. NW
Suite 100
Washington, DC 20006
EMail: mhumphre@hklaw.com
Tel: (202)955-3000
Fax: (202)955-5564

Employers
Holland & Knight LLP (Partner)

HUMPHREYS, David J.

P.O. Box 2999
Reston, VA 20191
Tel: (703)620-6003
Ext: 335
Fax: (703)620-5071

Employers
Recreation Vehicle Industry Ass'n (President)

HUMPHREYS, Fred

1090 Vermont Ave. NW
Suite 600
Washington, DC 20005
Tel: (202)371-0600
Fax: (202)898-7777

Employers
Home Builders Institute (President and Chief Exec. Officer)

HUMPHREYS, Robert R.

4319 Reno Rd. NW
Washington, DC 20008
Tel: (202)363-2200
Fax: (202)363-7464
Registered: LDA

Employers
Self-employed as an independent consultant.

Clients Represented
As an independent consultant
Helen Keller Nat'l Center for Deaf Blind Youths and Adults

HUMPHRIES, Derrick

1025 Vermont Ave. NW
Suite 910
Washington, DC 20005
Tel: (202)347-7000
Fax: (202)347-2424

Employers
Self-employed as an independent consultant.

Clients Represented
As an independent consultant
Internat'l Ass'n of Black Professional Fire Fighters

HUMPHRIES, Heather

1424 16th St. NW
Suite 300
Washington, DC 20036-2211
EMail: info@ncne.com
Tel: (202)518-6500
Fax: (202)588-0314

Employers
Nat'l Center for Neighborhood Enterprise (Public Relations Director)

HUMPHRIES, John M.

1401 I St. NW
Suite 600
Washington, DC 20005
Tel: (202)336-7400
Fax: (202)336-7529
Registered: LDA

Employers
United Technologies Corp. (Congressional Relations Representative)

HUMPHRYS, Deborah

1818 R St. NW
Washington, DC 20009
Tel: (202)387-3760
Fax: (202)265-9532

Employers
Ass'n of American Colleges and Universities (V. President, Communications and Public Relations)

HUNNICUTT, Charles A.

1801 K St. NW
Washington, DC 20006
Tel: (202)775-0725
Fax: (202)223-8604
Registered: LDA

Assistant Secretary of Transportation for Aviation and International Affairs, Department of Transportation, 1996-99. Legal Advisor to the Chairwoman, International Trade Commission, 1980-87. Executive Assistant to the UnderSecretary of Commerce for International Trade, Department of Commerce, 1979-80. Assistant to the Deputy Assistant Secretary of Commerce, Department of Commerce, 1977-79.

Employers
Robins, Kaplan, Miller & Ciresi L.L.P. (Partner)

Clients Represented
On Behalf of Robins, Kaplan, Miller & Ciresi L.L.P.
North Dakota Wheat Commission
Northwest Airlines, Inc.
Pacific Maritime Ass'n
R.M.S. Titanic, Inc.

HUNNICUTT, John E.

1455 Pennsylvania Ave. NW
Suite 400
Washington, DC 20004-1081
Tel: (202)737-6600
Fax: (202)638-4512
Registered: LDA
EMail: Internet: JHunnicutt@aicpa.org

Employers
American Institute of Certified Public Accountants (Senior V. President, Public Affairs)

HUNNICUTT, Patrick A.

1301 K St. NW
Suite 1200-West Tower
Washington, DC 20005-3307
EMail: path@us.ibm.com
Tel: (202)515-5184
Fax: (202)515-4943

Employers
Internat'l Business Machines Corp. (Regional Manager, Government Relations)

HUNT, David W.

601 13th St. NW
Suite 600 South
Washington, DC 20005
EMail: huntdav@washdc.whitecase.com
Tel: (202)626-3600
Fax: (202)639-9355

Employers
White & Case LLP (Partner)

Clients Represented
On Behalf of White & Case LLP
CalEnergy Co., Inc.

HUNT, Jr., Frederick D.

Two Wisconsin Circle
Suite 670
Chevy Chase, MD 20815-7003
Tel: (301)718-7722
Fax: (301)718-9440

Employers
Hunt Management Systems (President)
Soc. of Professional Benefit Administrators (President)

Clients Represented
On Behalf of Hunt Management Systems
Soc. of Professional Benefit Administrators

HUNT, Margaret

701 Pennsylvania Ave. NW
Washington, DC 20004-2696
Tel: (202)508-5634
Fax: (202)508-5403
Registered: LDA

Employers
Edison Electric Institute (Director, Government Relations)

HUNT, Scott

4350 East-West Hwy.
Suite 500
Bethesda, MD 20814-4110
Tel: (301)941-0205
Fax: (301)941-0259

Employers
Endocrine Soc. (Exec. Director)

HUNT, Tim

1111 19th St. NW
Suite 800
Washington, DC 20036
Tel: (202)463-2700
Fax: (202)463-2785
Registered: LDA

Employers
American Forest & Paper Ass'n (Director, Air Quality Program)

HUNTER, Angie

112 S. West St.
Fourth Floor
Alexandria, VA 22314
Tel: (703)836-6200
Fax: (703)836-6550
Registered: LDA
EMail: anghunter@cahi.org

Employers
Council for Affordable Health Insurance (Director, Federal Affairs)

HUNTER, Bruce

1801 N. Moore St.
Arlington, VA 22209
Tel: (703)528-0700
Fax: (703)528-2146
Registered: LDA
EMail: bhunter@aasa.org

Employers
American Ass'n of School Administrators (Senior Associate Exec. Director)

HUNTER, Caroline

1299 Pennsylvania Ave. NW
Suite 800 West
Washington, DC 20004
Tel: (202)785-0500
Fax: (202)785-5277

Employers
The Carmen Group (Associate)

HUNTER, David

1825 K St. NW
Suite 1100
Washingon, DC 20006
Tel: (202)785-2908
Fax: (202)835-8931
Registered: LDA

Employers
Local Initiatives Support Corp.

HUNTER, Edward L.

6525 Belcrest Rd.
Room 1120
Hyattsville, MD 20782
Tel: (301)458-4100
Fax: (301)458-4021

Employers
Department of Health and Human Services - Nat'l Center for Health Statistics (Associate Director for Planning, Budget, and Legislation)

HUNTER, J. Robert

2202 N. 24th St.
Arlington, VA 22207
Tel: (703)528-0062
Fax: (703)528-0062
Registered: LDA

Federal Insurance Administrator, Department of Housing and Urban Development, 1974-78.

Employers
Consumer Federation of America (Director, Insurance)
Consumer Federation of America's Insurance Group (Director)

HUNTER, Justin

1875 I St. NW
12th Floor
Washington, DC 20006
Tel: (202)466-6550
Fax: (202)785-1756
Registered: LDA
EMail: jhunter@ppsv.com

Employers
Powers Pyles Sutter & Verville, PC (Legislative Director)

HUNTER, Kenneth

4200 Wilson Blvd.
Suite 800
Arlington, VA 22203-1838
EMail: khunter@cbbb.bbb.org
Tel: (703)276-0100
Fax: (703)525-8277

Employers
Council of Better Business Bureaus (President and Chief Exec. Officer)

HUNTER, Richard C.

1021 Prince St.
Alexandria, VA 22314
Tel: (703)838-7543
Fax: (703)519-7648

Employers
World Federation for Mental Health (Deputy Secretary General)

HUNTINGTON, Erin B.

555 12th St. NW
Suite 650
Washington, DC 20004-1205
Tel: (202)393-7950
Fax: (202)393-7960
Registered: LDA

Employers
Eli Lilly and Co. (Manager, International and Public Government Relations)

HURD, Frank

1300 Wilson Blvd.
Arlington, VA 22209
Tel: (703)741-5852
Fax: (703)741-6852
Registered: LDA
EMail: frank_hurd@cmahq.com

Employers
Chlorine Chemistry Council (Managing Director, Operations and Finance and Director, Government Relations)

HUREWITZ, Barry J.

1455 Pennsylvania Ave. NW
Suite 1000
Washington, DC 20004
Tel: (202)942-8400
Fax: (202)942-8484
Registered: LDA
EMail: barry.hurewitz@haledorr.com

Employers
Hale and Dorr LLP (Junior Partner)

Clients Represented

On Behalf of Hale and Dorr LLP
Diamond Antenna & Microwave Corp.
Ostex Internat'l Inc.

HUREWITZ, Lane S.

2100 M St. NW
Suite 200
Washington, DC 20037
Tel: (202)785-4185
Fax: (202)466-1286
EMail: lhurewitz@stewartlaw.com

Employers
Stewart and Stewart (Of Counsel)

HURLBURT, Carol J.

1899 Preston White Dr.
Reston, VA 20191-4367
Tel: (703)264-7200
Fax: (703)620-0994
EMail: churlbur@npes.org

Employers
NPES, The Ass'n for Suppliers of Printing, Publishing, and Converting Technologies (Director, Communications and Marketing)

HURLEY, Charles A.

1025 Connecticut Ave. NW
Suite 1200
Washington, DC 20036
Tel: (202)293-2270
Fax: (202)293-0032
EMail: hurleyc@nsc.org

Employers
Nat'l Safety Council (Exec. Director, Public Affairs)

HURLEY, Gerald

4041 Powder Mill Rd.
Suite 402
Calverton, MD 20705
Tel: (301)595-5550
Fax: (301)595-3303

Employers
Nat'l Industrial Sand Ass'n (V. President)

HURLEY, Judith

555 12th St. NW
Washington, DC 20004-1206
Tel: (202)942-5000
Fax: (202)942-5999
EMail: Judith_Hurley@aporter.com

Employers
Arnold & Porter (Exec. Dir. and Chief Financial Officer)

HURLEY, Michael W.

1899 Preston White Dr.
Reston, VA 20191-4367
Tel: (703)264-7200
Fax: (703)620-0994
EMail: mhurley@npes.org

Employers
NPES, The Ass'n for Suppliers of Printing, Publishing, and Converting Technologies (Director, International Trade)

HURLEY, Robert F.

1225 I St. NW
Suite 810
Washington, DC 20005
Tel: (202)289-9800
Fax: (202)289-3588
Registered: LDA
EMail: rhurley@theaccordgroup.com
Former Chief of Staff to Senator John H. Chafee (R-RI). Republican Staff Director, Senate Committee on the Environmental and Public Works, 1980-90.

Employers
The Accord Group (Principal)

Clients Represented

On Behalf of The Accord Group
American Forest & Paper Ass'n
Ass'n of American Railroads
Ciba Specialty Chemicals Corp.
DuPont
Novartis Corp.
Water Infrastructure Network

HURLEY GRAVES, Caroline

601 Pennsylvania Ave. NW
Suite 600
North Bldg.
Washington, DC 20004
Tel: (202)682-9110
Fax: (202)682-9111
Registered: LDA

Employers
American Electronics Ass'n (Tax Counsel and Director, Tax Policy)

HURSON, John

2000 L St. NW
Suite 300
Washington, DC 20036-0646
Tel: (202)835-8800
Fax: (202)835-8879
Registered: LDA

Employers
Ketchum (Consultant)

HURST, Lisa

1025 Connecticut Ave. NW
Suite 1012
Washington, DC 20036
Tel: (202)258-2301
Registered: LDA
EMail: lhurst@smithallinglane.com

Employers
Smith Alling Lane, P.S.

Clients Represented

On Behalf of Smith Alling Lane, P.S.
PE Biosystems
Sagem Morpho
Washington Ass'n of Sheriffs and Police Chiefs

HURST, Paul R.

1330 Connecticut Ave. NW
Washington, DC 20036-1795
Tel: (202)429-3000
Fax: (202)429-3902
Registered: LDA
EMail: phurst@steptoe.com

Employers
Steptoe & Johnson LLP (Associate)

Clients Represented

On Behalf of Steptoe & Johnson LLP
Motorola, Inc.
Netscape Communications Corp.

HURSTON, Pat

7500 Old Georgetown Rd.
Suite 1300
Bethesda, MD 20814-6161
Tel: (301)280-6800
Fax: (301)280-6900

Employers
PG&E Generating Co. (Corporate Communications Specialist)

HURT, Frank

10401 Connecticut Ave.
Kensington, MD 20895
Tel: (301)933-8600
Fax: (301)946-8452

Employers
Bakery, Confectionery and Tobacco Workers Internat'l Union (President)

HURT, Robert H.

505 Capitol Ct. NE
Suite 200
Washington, DC 20002
Tel: (202)543-9398
Fax: (202)543-7844
Registered: LDA
EMail: bobhurt@hurtnorton.com
Administrative Assistant to Senator Sam Nunn (D-GA), 1992-96. Administrative Assistant to Rep. Lindsay Thomas (D-GA), 1983-92. Administrative Assistant and Press Aide (1977-82) and Senior Legislative Assistant and Press Aide (1973-77) to Rep. Bo Ginn (D-GA). Served in the U.S. Army, 1966-68.

Employers
Hurt, Norton & Associates (Partner)

Clients Represented

On Behalf of Hurt, Norton & Associates
21st Century Partnership
Air Tran Airways
Auburn University
Caswell Internat'l Corp.
The Coca-Cola Company
Georgia Ports Authority
Intergraph Corp. Federal Systems Division
Lockheed Martin Aeronautical Systems Co.
Mercer Engineering Research Center
Mercer University
Pemco Aviation Group, Inc.
Phoenix Air Group, Inc.
Quad City Development Group
Savannah Airport Commission
Scientific Research Corp.
Sierra Military Health Services, Inc.
Visiting Nurses Health System
Westinghouse Electric Co.

HURWITZ, Geoffrey B.

1300 Wilson Blvd.
Suite 1220
Arlington, VA 22209
Tel: (703)741-5881
Fax: (703)741-5884
Registered: LDA

Employers
Rohm and Haas Co. (Director, Federal and State Government Relations)

HUSSEY, Michael F.

1220 L St. NW
Suite 500
Washington, DC 20005
Tel: (202)371-6700
Fax: (202)289-8544
Registered: LDA
EMail: mhussey@arda.org

Employers
American Resort Development Ass'n (Senior V. President, Public Affairs)

HUT, Stephen

2445 M St. NW
Washington, DC 20037-1420
Tel: (202)663-6000
Fax: (202)663-6363

Employers
Wilmer, Cutler & Pickering

HUTA, Leda

P.O. Box 19367
Washington, DC 20036
Tel: (202)387-8030
Fax: (202)234-5176

Employers
Government Purchasing Project (Director)

HUTCHERSON, Carolyn

1050 Connecticut Ave. NW
Washington, DC 20036-5339
Tel: (202)857-6000
Fax: (202)857-6395

Employers
Arent Fox Kintner Plotkin & Kahn, PLLC (Healthcare Specialist)

HUTCHESON, John

119 C St. SE
Washington, DC 20003
Tel: (202)548-2563
Registered: LDA

Employers
People Advancing Christian Education (PACE)

HUTCHINGS, Suzanne

1730 Rhode Island Ave. NW
Suite 1000
Washington, DC 20036
Tel: (202)721-0960
Fax: (202)296-8953
Registered: LDA

Employers
Teledesic Corp. (Regulatory Counsel)

HUTCHINS, Julia

218 D St. SE
Second Floor
Washington, DC 20003
Tel: (202)546-9707
Fax: (202)546-2461
Registered: LDA

Employers
U.S. Public Interest Research Group (Democracy Advocate)

HUTCHINS, Dr. Michael

8403 Colesville Rd.
Suite 710
Silver Spring, MD 20910
Tel: (301)562-0777
Fax: (301)562-0888
Registered: LDA

Employers
American Zoo and Aquarium Ass'n (Dir., American Zoo and Aquarium Ass'n Conservation & Science)

HUTCHINSON, Suzanne C.

727 15th St. NW
12th Floor
Washington, DC 20005
Tel: (202)393-5566
Fax: (202)393-5557

Employers
Mortgage Insurance Companies of America (Exec. V. President)

HUTCHISON, Fred H.

1620 I Street NW
Suite 900
Washington, DC 20006
EMail: fred_hutchison@plexusconsulting.com
Tel: (202)785-8940
Fax: (202)785-8949

Employers
The Plexus Consulting Group (Senior Partner)

Clients Represented

On Behalf of The Plexus Consulting Group
Iceland, Ministry of Fisheries, Government of
Institute of Internal Auditors
Space Station Associates
Wallcovering Ass'n

HUTCHISON, Karen B.

4330 East West Hwy.
Suite 310
Bethesda, MD 20814
EMail: ppema1@msn.com
Tel: (301)652-0774
Fax: (301)654-6138
Registered: LDA

Employers
Portable Power Equipment Manufacturers Ass'n (V. President)

HUTHER, Christopher S.

1735 New York Ave. NW
Suite 500
Washington, DC 20006-4759
Tel: (202)628-1700
Fax: (202)331-1024

Employers
Preston Gates Ellis & Rouvelas Meeds LLP (Partner)

HUTMAN, Ken

601 13th St. NW
Suite 1100
Washington, DC 20005
Tel: (202)429-2217
Fax: (202)296-8727
Registered: LDA

Employers
Fontheim Partners, PC (Director, International Trade and Finance)

Clients Represented

On Behalf of Fontheim Partners, PC
Citizen's Educational Foundation

HUTSON, Harrison D.

1735 New York Ave. NW
Suite 500
Washington, DC 20006-4759
Tel: (202)628-1700
Fax: (202)331-1024

Employers
Preston Gates Ellis & Rouvelas Meeds LLP (Of Counsel)

HUTT, Peter Barton

1201 Pennsylvania Ave. NW
Washington, DC 20004-2401
Tel: (202)662-6000
Fax: (202)662-6291
Registered: LDA
EMail: phutt@cov.com
Chief Counsel, Food and Drug Administration, 1971-1975.

Employers
Covington & Burling (Partner)

Clients Represented

On Behalf of Covington & Burling
Consumer Healthcare Products Ass'n
Cosmetic, Toiletry and Fragrance Ass'n
Council for Responsible Nutrition
Grocery Manufacturers of America
Pharmaceutical Research and Manufacturers of America
Pizza Hut, Inc.

HUTTER, Lindsay

1605 King St.
Alexandria, VA 22314-2792
Tel: (703)684-3600
Fax: (703)836-4564

Employers
Nat'l Ass'n of Convenience Stores (V. President, Industry Relations and Communications)

HUYNH, Phuong

1600 I St. NW
Washington, DC 20006
Tel: (202)293-1966
Fax: (202)296-7410

Employers
Motion Picture Ass'n of America (Director, Public Relations)

HWA, Nancy

1225 I St. NW
Suite 1100
Washington, DC 20005
Tel: (202)289-7319
Fax: (202)408-1851

Employers
The Center to Prevent Handgun Violence (Assistant Director, Communications)

HYATT, David

8400 W. Park Dr.
McLean, VA 22102
Tel: (703)821-7000

Employers
Nat'l Automobile Dealers Ass'n (Group Exec. Director, Public Affairs)

HYATT, Thomas K.

1401 H St. NW
Suite 500
Washington, DC 20005-3324
Tel: (202)408-8400
Fax: (202)408-0640

Employers
Ober, Kaler, Grimes & Shriver (Shareholder)

Clients Represented

On Behalf of Ober, Kaler, Grimes & Shriver
Health Industry Initiative

HYDE, Margaret

2300 Clarendon Blvd.
Suite 610
Arlington, VA 22201-3367
EMail: mhyde@golinharris.com
Tel: (703)351-5666
Fax: (703)351-5667
Confidential Staff Assistant to the Deputy Assistant Secretary for Public Affairs, Department of Health and Human Services, 1999-2001.

Employers
Golin/Harris Internat'l (Account Exec.)

HYDE, Myra

1301 Pennsylvania Ave. NW
Suite 300
Washington, DC 20004
EMail: mbh@ncanet.org
Tel: (202)347-0228
Fax: (202)638-0607
Registered: LDA

Employers
Nat'l Cattleman's Beef Ass'n (Director, Private Lands)

HYDE, Sharon

1849 C St. NW
Room 6254
Washington, DC 20240
EMail: sharon_hyde@ios.doi.gov
Tel: (202)208-7693
Fax: (202)208-7619

Employers
Department of Interior (Assistant to the Director, Office of Congressional and Legislative Affairs)

HYDE, Terrill A.

2445 M St. NW
Washington, DC 20037-1420
Tel: (202)663-6000
Fax: (202)663-6363
Registered: FARA
EMail: thyde@wilmer.com
Tax Legislative Counsel (1991-92) and Deputy Tax Legislative Counsel for Regulatory Affairs (1989-91), Department of the Treasury.

Employers
Wilmer, Cutler & Pickering (Partner)

Clients Represented

On Behalf of Wilmer, Cutler & Pickering
AutoNation, Inc.
Republic Industries, Inc.

HYJEK, Steven M.

2100 Pennsylvania Ave. NW
Suite 560
Washington, DC 20037
Tel: (202)223-4800
Fax: (202)223-2011
Registered: LDA, FARA
EMail: shyjek@hyjekfix.com
Former Staff Aide to Senator Robert Stafford (R-VT). Staff Member, Office of the Sergeant-at-Arms, U.S. Senate.

Employers
Hyjek & Fix, Inc. (Partner)

Clients Represented

On Behalf of Hyjek & Fix, Inc.
BAE SYSTEMS North America
Bombardier Aerospace
Gelco Government Services
Intermec Corp.
IT Group, Inc.
Mobile Climate Control
Niagara Area Chamber of Commerce
The Oneida County Edge
Pilkington Thorn
Shelby, Tennessee, County of
Shorts Missile Systems
U.S. Display Consortium

HYLAND, Gigi

805 15th St. NW
Suite 300
Washington, DC 20005-2207
Tel: (202)682-4200
Fax: (202)682-9054
Registered: LDA

Employers
Credit Union Nat'l Ass'n, Inc. (Regulatory Staff Attorney)

HYLAND, Thomas R.

1050 17th St. NW
Suite 300
Washington, DC 20036
Tel: (202)296-3390
Fax: (202)296-3399
Registered: LDA

Employers
Apartment and Office Building Ass'n of Metropolitan Washington (V. President, Governmental Affairs-VA)

HYMAN, Elizabeth

1333 New Hampshire Ave. NW
Suite 400
Washington, DC 20036
Tel: (202)887-4000
Fax: (202)887-4288
Registered: LDA
Former Attorney, Office of the U.S. Trade Representative, Executive Office of the President, The White House.

Employers
Akin, Gump, Strauss, Hauer & Feld, L.L.P. (Associate)

Clients Represented

On Behalf of Akin, Gump, Strauss, Hauer & Feld, L.L.P.
American Home Products Corp.
Frederic R. Harris, Inc.
Mitsubishi Corp.
Pegasus Capital Advisors, L.P.
Quad Dimension
Tyumen Oil Company

HYMAN, Lester S.

3000 K St. NW
Suite 300
Washington, DC 20007
Tel: (202)424-7500
Fax: (202)424-7643
Registered: LDA, FARA
Attorney, Securities and Exchange Commission, 1955-56.

Employers
Swidler Berlin Shereff Friedman, LLP (Senior Counsel)

Clients Represented

On Behalf of Swidler Berlin Shereff Friedman, LLP

Artichoke Enterprises, Inc.
Aventis Pharmaceuticals, Inc.
British Virgin Islands, Government of the
Florida Power and Light Co.
Hyundai Semiconductor America, Inc.
Matsushita Electric Corp. of America
Merrill Lynch & Co., Inc.
Newman & Associates
Schering Corp.

HYMEL, Gary G.

600 New Hampshire Ave. NW
Suite 601
Washington, DC 20037
Tel: (202)333-7400
Fax: (202)333-1638
Registered: LDA, FARA
EMail: ghymel@hillandknowlton.com
Former Administrative Assistant to Speaker of the House, Rep. Thomas P. O'Neill (D-MA).

Employers

Hill and Knowlton, Inc. (Chief Lobbyist and V. Chairman, Sr. Counselor Government Relations)

Clients Represented

On Behalf of Hill and Knowlton, Inc.

Ariba
Blue Cross and Blue Shield of Florida
Eurapair International, Inc.
Internat'l Olympic Committee
Kohler Corp.
Mazda Motor Corp.
Orange, California, County of
Petro-Canada
Royal Netherlands, Embassy of the
Woods Hole Oceanographic Institution

HYNES, Jr., Robert J.

1101 Pennsylvania Ave. NW
Suite 810
The Evening Star Building
Washington, DC 20004
Tel: (202)638-1101
Fax: (202)638-1102
Registered: LDA
Minority Counsel to the House Rules Committee, 1964-71, and former Legislative Counsel to Rep. Gerald R. Ford (R-MI).

Employers

Colling Swift & Hynes (Principal)
Davidson & Company, Inc. (Of Counsel)

Clients Represented

On Behalf of Colling Swift & Hynes

Frank Beam and Co.
Caraustar
Chuck & Rock Adventure Productions, Inc.
Garden State Paper Co., Inc.
Greenman Technologies Inc.
Media General, Inc.
The Newark Group
NewsHunter.net, LLC
Opportunity Internat'l
Paper Recycling Coalition
PrediWave
Quest Diagnostics Inc.
Rock-Tenn Co.
Smurfit Stone Container Corp.
Talgo
White Pigeon Paper Co.

HYNES, Scott

1133 Connecticut Ave. NW
Fifth Floor
Washington, DC 20036
Tel: (202)457-1110
Fax: (202)457-1130
Registered: LDA
Former Assistant to the Chief of Staff, Executive Office of the President, The White House.

Employers

Quinn Gillespie & Associates (Associate)

HYPS, Brian M.

15501 Monona Dr.
Rockville, MD 20855
Tel: (301)251-0560
Fax: (301)279-2996
Registered: LDA
EMail: bhyps@aspp.org
Former counsel to House Veterans Affairs Subcommittee on Hospitals and Health Care.

Employers

American Soc. of Plant Physiologists (Director, Public Affairs)

HYSELL, Donald R.

601 13th St. NW
Suite 200 North
Washington, DC 20005
Tel: (202)682-9462
Registered: LDA

Employers

BASF Corporation (Director, Government Relations)

IADAROLA, Elizabeth A.

1747 Pennsylvania Ave. NW
Suite 1150
Washington, DC 20006
Tel: (202)557-2961
Fax: (202)296-4507
Registered: LDA
EMail: eklein@mww.com
Public Relations Coordinator to Senator John Ashcroft (R-MO).

Employers

The MWW Group (Deputy Director, Federal Affairs)

Clients Represented

On Behalf of The MWW Group

Bacardi-Martini, USA, Inc.
Cuban American Nat'l Foundation/Cuban American Foundation
GAF Corp.
Hadassah Medical Relief Fund
Kmart Corp.
Michigan Bulb
Nat'l Ass'n of Jai-Alai Frontons, Inc.
Puerto Ricans for Civic Action

IANDOLI, Matthew

201 Maryland Ave. NE
Washington, DC 20002
Tel: (202)543-7200
Fax: (202)543-0616
Registered: LDA
EMail: matt@mgninc.com

Employers

McClure, Gerard & Neuenschwander, Inc.

Clients Represented

On Behalf of McClure, Gerard & Neuenschwander, Inc.

American Gaming Ass'n
Barrick Goldstrike Mines, Inc.
Boise State University
Brush Wellman, Inc.
Coachella Valley Water District
Echo Bay Mining
Family Farm Alliance (Project Transfer Council)
Harquehala Irrigation District
Hecla Mining Co.
Helli USA Airways
Henderson, Nevada, City of
Howard Hughes Corp.
Idaho Power Co.
Independence Mining Co., Inc.
Internat'l Bottled Water Ass'n
Nat'l Endangered Species Act Reform Coalition
Native American Mohegans Inc.
Nevada Test Site Development Corp.
Newmont Mining Corp.
Pershing Co. Water Conservation District of Nevada
Placer Dome U.S. Inc.
Private Fuels Storage, L.L.C.
Quest Nevada, Inc.
Space Imaging, Inc.
Stirling Energy Systems
Verizon Wireless
Wellton-Mohawk Irrigation and Drainage District
Westlands Water District
The Williams Companies

IARROBINO, Paul

1420 New York Ave. NW
Suite 1050
Washington, DC 20005
Tel: (202)638-1950
Fax: (202)638-7714
Registered: LDA

Employers

Van Scoyoc Associates, Inc.

Clients Represented

On Behalf of Van Scoyoc Associates, Inc.

Archimedes Technology Group
Greater New Orleans Expressway Commission
Virginia Polytechnic Institute and State University

IBRAHIM, Tod

2501 M St. NW
Suite 550
Washington, DC 20037-1308
Tel: (202)861-7700
Fax: (202)861-9731
Registered: LDA
EMail: Ibrahim@im.org

Employers

Ass'n of Professors of Medicine (Exec. Director)

IBSON, Ralph

1021 Prince St.
Alexandria, VA 22314-2971
Tel: (703)684-7722
Fax: (703)684-5968
Registered: LDA
EMail: ribson@nmha.org
Former Staff Director and Counsel, Subcommittee on Health, House Committee on Veterans Affairs.

Employers

Nat'l Mental Health Ass'n (V. President, Government Affairs)

ICHORD, J. William

1150 Connecticut Ave. NW
Suite 1025
Washington, DC 20036
Tel: (202)367-2773
Fax: (202)367-2790
Registered: LDA

Employers

UNOCAL Corp. (General Manager and V. President, Washington Office)

ICHTER, Ralph

1150 18th St. NW
Suite 275
Washington, DC 20036
Tel: (202)466-6330
Fax: (202)466-6334

Employers

Euroconsultants, Inc. (Partner/President)

ICIEK, James E.

8401 Corporate Dr.
Suite 605
Landover, MD 20785
Tel: (301)577-4828
Fax: (301)577-3880

Employers

Nat'l Academy of Opticianry (Exec. Director)

ICKES, Harold M.

1300 Connecticut Ave. NW
Suite 600
Washington, DC 20036
Tel: (202)887-6726
Fax: (202)223-0358
Registered: LDA
EMail: hickes@griffinjohnson.com
Former Deputy Chief of Staff, Executive Office of the President, The White House, during the Clinton Administration.

Employers

The Ickes & Enright Group (Partner)
Meyer, Suozzi, English & Klein, P.C. (Partner)

Clients Represented

On Behalf of The Ickes & Enright Group

4C Foods Corp.
American Federation of Teachers
Brooklyn Public Library
Consortium for Worker Education
Deloitte Consulting
Farallon Capital Management
Greater New York Hospital Ass'n
HiSynergy Communications, Inc.
New York City, New York, Council of
The New York Historical Soc.
Service Employees Internat'l Union
United Airlines

IDRISS, Shamil

1601 Connecticut Ave. NW
Suite 200
Washington, DC 20009
Tel: (202)265-4300
Fax: (202)232-6718
EMail: sidriss@sfgc.org

Employers

Search for Common Ground (C.O.O.)

IGNAGNI, Karen M.

1129 20th St. NW
Suite 600
Washington, DC 20036-3421
Tel: (202)778-3200
Fax: (202)778-8479
Registered: LDA
EMail: kignagni@aahp.org
Former Professional Staff Member, Senate Committee on Labor and Human Resources.

Employers

American Ass'n of Health Plans (AAHP) (President and Chief Exec. Officer)

IGO, Shirley

1090 Vermont Ave. NW
Suite 1200
Washington, DC 20005
Tel: (202)289-6790
Fax: (202)289-6791

Employers
Nat'l Congress of Parents and Teachers (President-Elect)

IKENBERRY, Stanley O.

One Dupont Circle NW
Suite 835
Washington, DC 20036-1193
Tel: (202)939-9300
Fax: (202)659-2212

Employers
American Council on Education (President)

IKENSON, Frederick L.

1621 New Hampshire Ave. NW
Washington, DC 20009
Tel: (202)483-8900
Fax: (202)483-9368
An attorney. Assistant Chief (1971-73) and Trial Attorney (1968-71) Customs Section, Civil Division, Department of Justice.

Employers
Self-employed as an independent consultant.

Clients Represented
As an independent consultant
Cooper Tire and Rubber Co.
GE Lighting Group
General Electric Co.
Hand Tools Institute
Zenith Electronics Corp.

IKETA, Yukio

1825 K St. NW
Suite 1203
Washington, DC 20006
Tel: (202)466-3585
Fax: (202)466-3586

Employers
Japan Federation of Construction Contractors, Inc. (Representative)

ILEM, Joy J.

807 Maine Ave. SW
Washington, DC 20024
Tel: (202)554-3501
Fax: (202)554-3581

Employers
Disabled American Veterans (Assistant National Legislative Director)

IMBERGAMO, Bill

444 N. Capitol St. NW
Suite 540
Washington, DC 20001
Tel: (202)624-5415
Fax: (202)624-5407

Employers
Nat'l Ass'n of State Foresters (Exec. Director)

IMIG, David G.

1307 New York Ave. NW
Suite 300
Washington, DC 20005-4701
Tel: (202)293-2450
Fax: (202)457-8095

Employers
American Ass'n of Colleges for Teacher Education (President)

IMUS, Scot E.

499 S. Capitol St. SW
Suite 502
Washington, DC 20003
EMail: seimus@natso.com
Tel: (202)554-2510
Fax: (202)554-2520
Registered: LDA

Employers
NATSO, Inc. (V. President, Government Affairs)

ING, Charles E.

1850 M St. NW
Suite 600
Washington, DC 20036
Tel: (202)775-1700
Fax: (202)822-0928
Registered: LDA

Employers
Toyota Motor North America, U.S.A., Inc. (Director, Government Affairs)

ING, Edwin T. C.

2121 K St. NW
Suite 800
Washington, DC 20037
Tel: (202)457-6630
Fax: (202)293-0027
Registered: LDA
Legislative Counsel to Senator Spark Matsunaga (D-HI), 1977-83. Tax Law Specialist, Internal Revenue Service, 1975-77.

Employers
Self-employed as an independent consultant.

Clients Represented
As an independent consultant
Hawaiian Electric Co.
Kamehameha Schools
United States Windpower, Inc.

INGEBRETSON, Charles L.

2000 K St. NW
Suite 500
Washington, DC 20006-1872
EMail: cingebretson@bracepatt.com
Tel: (202)828-5800
Fax: (202)223-1225
Registered: LDA
General Counsel, House Committee on Commerce, 1995-98. Counsel, House Committee on Energy and Commerce, 1990-94. Legislative Director, Rep. Dan Coats (R-IN), 1981-84.

Employers
Bracewell & Patterson, L.L.P. (Associate)

Clients Represented
On Behalf of Bracewell & Patterson, L.L.P.
Air Conditioning Contractors of America
Alltel Corporation
Council of Industrial Boiler Owners (CIBO)
Envirocare of Utah, Inc.
FBI Agents Ass'n
Gary-Williams Energy Corp.
Houston, Texas, Port Authority of the City of
Huntsman Corp.
Lyondell Chemical Co.
Oxygenated Fuels Ass'n
Placid Refining Co.
Solex Environmental Systems, Inc.
Texas Petrochemicals Corp.
Texas Windstorm Insurance Ass'n
UST Public Affairs, Inc.
Welcon, Inc.

INGIS, Stuart P.

1200 19th St. NW
Washington, DC 20036-2430
EMail: stuart.ingis@piperrudnick.com
Tel: (202)861-6468
Fax: (202)223-2085
Registered: LDA

Employers
Piper Marbury Rudnick & Wolfe LLP (Associate)

Clients Represented
On Behalf of Piper Marbury Rudnick & Wolfe LLP
Acxiom Corp.
AOL Time Warner
Commercial Internet Exchange Ass'n
Direct Marketing Ass'n, Inc.
Individual Reference Services Group
Lexis-Nexis
NetCoalition.Com
PSINet Inc.

INGLE, Cynthia

1825 Connecticut Ave. NW
Fifth Floor
Washington, DC 20009
Tel: (202)667-0901
Fax: (202)667-0902

Employers
Widmeyer Communications, Inc. (Assistant V. President)

INGLEE, William

1725 Jefferson Davis Hwy.
Crystal Square 2, Suite 300
Arlington, VA 22202
Tel: (703)413-5600
Fax: (703)413-5613

Employers
Lockheed Martin Corp. (V. President, Legislative Affairs)

INGRAHAM, Margaret B.

1414 Prince St.
Suite 302
Alexandria, VA 22314
Tel: (703)548-3692
Fax: (703)548-8024
Registered: LDA
Special Assistant to the Deputy Assistant Secretary for Legislation, 1987-88, and Deputy Assistant Secretary for Legislation, 1988-89, Department of Health and Human Services.

Employers
The Borden Group, Inc. (Exec. V. President)

Clients Represented
On Behalf of The Borden Group, Inc.
Meals on Wheels Ass'n of America

INGRAM, Charles W.

1156 15th St. NW
Suite 1020
Washington, DC 20005
EMail: charlie@nasda-hq.org
Tel: (202)296-9680
Fax: (202)296-9686

Employers
Nat'l Ass'n of State Departments of Agriculture (Manager, Legislative and Regulatory Affairs)

INGRAM, Chris

1000 Wilson Blvd.
Suite 950
Arlington, VA 22209
Tel: (703)358-0080
Fax: (703)358-0089

Employers
Luntz Research Cos. (Senior V. President)

INGRAM, Marc

2500 Wilson Blvd.
Suite 300
Arlington, VA 22201
EMail: marc@getcommstuff.com
Tel: (703)907-7725
Fax: (703)907-7727

Employers
Telecommunications Industry Ass'n (Director, GetCommStuff.com)

INGRAM, Richard T.

One Dupont Circle NW
Suite 400
Washington, DC 20036
EMail: tomi@agb.org
Tel: (202)296-8400
Fax: (202)223-7053

Employers
Ass'n of Governing Boards of Universities and Colleges (President)

INGRAO, Mike

888 16th Street NW
Suite 650
Washington, DC 20006
Tel: (202)628-9262
Fax: (202)628-0391

Employers
AFL-CIO - Transportation Trades Department (Chief of Staff)

INGRASSIA, Jill

1440 New York Ave. NW
Suite 200
Washington, DC 20005
Tel: (202)942-2050
Fax: (202)783-4798
Registered: LDA

Employers
American Automobile Ass'n (Manager, Congressional Relations)

INGRASSIA, Phil

3930 University Dr.
Fairfax, VA 22030-2515
Tel: (703)591-7130
Fax: (703)591-0734

Employers
Recreation Vehicle Dealers Ass'n of North America (Director, Communications)

INMAN, Julie

21 Dupont Circle NW
Fifth Floor
Washington, DC 20036
Tel: (202)263-5900
Fax: (202)263-5901
Registered: LDA

Employers
Microsoft Corp. (Legislative Assistant)

INNES, Andrea L.

1130 17th St. NW
Washington, DC 20036-4677
EMail: ainnes@nma.org
Tel: (202)463-2645
Fax: (202)833-1965

Employers
Nat'l Mining Ass'n (V. President, Political Affairs)

INNES, Richard

1101 14th St. NW
Suite 420
Washington, DC 20005
Tel: (301)774-3568
Registered: LDA
Former Staff Member, Senate Committee on Environment and Public Works, 1987-93. Senior Program Analyst, Environmental Protection Agency, 1984-87.

Employers
Conservation Strategies, LLC (Principal)

Clients Represented
On Behalf of Conservation Strategies, LLC
Nat'l Wildlife Federation - Office of Federal and Internat'l Affairs

IOVINO, Peter

1350 I St. NW
Suite 1000
Washington, DC 20005
Tel: (202)962-5376
Fax: (202)336-7223
Registered: LDA
EMail: piovino@ford.com

Employers
Ford Motor Co. (Legislative Manager, International Trade and Tax)

IPPOLITO, Frank

Office of Govermental Affairs
3101 Park Center Dr.
Room 910
Alexandria, VA 22302
Tel: (703)305-2010
Fax: (703)305-2312
EMail: frank.ippolito@fns.usda.gov

Employers
Department of Agriculture - Food and Nutrition Service (Director, Governmental Affairs Staff)

IPSEN, Jeanine

1023 15th St. NW
Suite 1000
Washington, DC 20005
Tel: (202)289-3933
Fax: (202)289-3962
EMail: jipsen@transport.bombardier.com

Employers
Bombardier Transportation/Bombardier Transit Corporation (Government Relations Manager)

IRACE, Mary

1625 K St. NW
Suite 1090
Washington, DC 20006-1604
Tel: (202)887-0278
Fax: (202)452-8160
Registered: LDA

Employers
Nat'l Foreign Trade Council, Inc. (V. President, Trade and Export Finance)

IRBY, Richard

819 Seventh St. NW
Washington, DC 20001
Tel: (202)833-8940
Fax: (202)833-8945
Registered: LDA

Employers
EOP Group, Inc.

Clients Represented
On Behalf of EOP Group, Inc.
Gas Research Institute
Uranium Producers of America

IRELAND, Hon. Andy

499 S. Capitol St.
Suite 600
Washington, DC 20003
Tel: (202)554-0473
Fax: (202)554-0393
Registered: LDA
EMail: AIreland@zeliffireland.com
Member, U.S. House of Representatives (D-FL), 1977-84, and (R-FL), 1984-93.

Employers
Zeliff, Ireland, and Associates

Clients Represented
On Behalf of Zeliff, Ireland, and Associates
Boys Town USA
Feld Entertainment Inc.
Schering-Plough Corp.

IRELAND, Kathleen

700 13th St. NW
Suite 350
Washington, DC 20005
Tel: (202)637-0040
Fax: (202)637-0041
Registered: LDA
Former Legislative Assistant to Rep. Michael G. Oxley (R-OH), Vice Chairman of the House Telecommunications Subcommittee.

Employers
Rhoads Group (V. President)

Clients Represented
On Behalf of Rhoads Group
AAAE-ACI
Airports Council Internat'l - North America
American Management Systems
Dick Corp.
The Justice Project, Inc.
PNC Bank, N.A.
SWATH Ocean Systems, Inc.
Taiwan Studies Institute
United States Enrichment Corp.

IRELAND, Patricia

733 15th St. NW 2nd Floor
Washington, DC 20005
Tel: (202)628-8669
Fax: (202)785-8576

Employers
Nat'l Organization for Women (President)

IRION, Mark S.

412 First St. SE
Suite 100
Washington, DC 20003
Tel: (202)484-4884
Fax: (202)484-0109
Registered: LDA
EMail: mirion@dutkogroup.com
Legislative Assistant to Senator Alan Dixon (D-IL), 1987-90.

Employers
The Dutko Group, Inc. (President)

Clients Represented
On Behalf of The Dutko Group, Inc.
Alcatel USA
American Herbal Products Ass'n
Ass'n for Competitive Technology
Biotech Research and Development Center
Carpet and Rug Institute
CITGO Petroleum Corp.
Level 3 Communications LLC
Longhorn Pipeline
Oregon Garden Foundation
Recovermat Technologies LLC
SEFBO Pipeline Bridge, Inc.

IRONFIELD, Susan B.

727 15th St. NW
12th Floor
Washington, DC 20005
Tel: (202)393-5566
Fax: (202)393-5557

Employers
Mortgage Insurance Companies of America (Director, Legislative and Regulatory Relations)

IRVIN, Nicole

1755 Massachusetts Ave. NW
Suite 600
Washington, DC 20036
Tel: (202)667-5881
Fax: (202)667-5890
EMail: naf@prochoice.org

Employers
Nat'l Abortion Federation (Director, Government Relations)

IRVINE, Reed J.

4455 Connecticut Ave. NW
Suite 330
Washington, DC 20008
Tel: (202)364-4401
Fax: (202)364-4098
EMail: ar1@aim.org
Economist, Federal Reserve Board, 1952-77.

Employers
Accuracy in Media (Chairman of the Board)

IRVING, John

655 15th St. NW
Suite 1200
Washington, DC 20005
Tel: (202)879-5000
Fax: (202)879-5200

Employers
Kirkland & Ellis (Partner)

Clients Represented
On Behalf of Kirkland & Ellis
American Staffing Ass'n

IRVING, Paul D.

950 H St. NW
Room 8350
Washington, DC 20001
Tel: (202)406-5676
Fax: (202)406-5740
EMail: pirving@usss.treas.gov

Employers
Department of Treasury - United States Secret Service (Deputy Assistant Director, Congressional Affairs)

IRWIN, Paul G.

2100 L St. NW
Washington, DC 20037
Tel: (202)452-1100
Fax: (202)778-6132

Employers
Humane Soc. of the United States (President)

IRWIN, William

1401 I St. NW
Suite 1200
Washington, DC 20005-2225
Tel: (202)408-5854
Fax: (202)408-5842
Registered: LDA
EMail: wmir@chevron.com

Employers
The Chevron Companies (International Relations Manager)

ISAAC, William M.

7799 Leesburg Pike
Suite 800 North
Falls Church, VA 22043
Tel: (703)749-0823
Fax: (703)749-1688
Chairman, Federal Deposit Insurance Corp., 1981-85.

Employers
The Secura Group (Chairman and Managing Director)

ISAACS, Amy

1625 K St. NW
Suite 210
Washington, DC 20006
Tel: (202)785-5980
Fax: (202)785-5969
Registered: LDA
EMail: adaction@ix.netcom.com

Employers
Americans for Democratic Action (National Director)

ISAACS, David

900 17th St. NW
Suite 1100
Washington, DC 20006
Tel: (202)884-7033
Fax: (202)884-7070
Registered: LDA
EMail: david_isaacs@hp.com

Employers
Hewlett-Packard Co. (Manager, Government Policy)

ISAACS, John D.

110 Maryland Ave. NE
Suite 409
Washington, DC 20002
Tel: (202)543-4100
Fax: (202)543-6297
Registered: LDA
EMail: jdi@clw.org

Employers
Council for a Livable World (President and Lobbyist)
Council for a Livable World Education Fund (Senior Director)

ISAACS, Joseph C.

P.O. Box 31220
4720 Montgomery Ln.
Bethesda, MD 20824-1220
Tel: (301)652-2682
Fax: (301)652-7711

Employers
American Occupational Therapy Ass'n, Inc. (Exec. Director)

ISAACSON, Ben

1301 Connecticut Ave. NW
Fifth Floor
Washington, DC 20036
Tel: (202)408-0008
Fax: (202)408-0111

Employers
Ass'n for Interactive Media (Exec. Director)

ISAACSON, Jason F.

1156 15th St. NW
Suite 1201
Washington, DC 20005
Tel: (202)785-4200
Fax: (202)785-4115

Employers
American Jewish Committee (Director, Government and International Affairs)

ISAKOWER, Kyle

1220 L St. NW
Washington, DC 20005

Tel: (202)682-8000
Fax: (202)682-8232
Registered: LDA

Employers
American Petroleum Institute

ISAKOWITZ, Mark W.

600 New Hampshire Ave. NW
Tenth Floor
Washington, DC 20037

Tel: (202)333-8667
Fax: (202)298-9109
Registered: LDA

EMail: misakowitz@erols.com
Former Press Secretary to Rep. Paul E. Gillmor (R-OH).

Employers
Fierce and Isakowitz (Partner)

Clients Represented
On Behalf of Fierce and Isakowitz
American Ass'n of Nurse Anesthetists
American Ass'n of Preferred Provider Organizations
American Gaming Ass'n
Credit Union Nat'l Ass'n, Inc.
DuPont
Edison Electric Institute
Federation of American Hospitals
Generic Pharmaceutical Ass'n
Health Insurance Ass'n of America
Liberty Maritime Co.
MCI WorldCom Corp.
Pegasus Communications
Tricon Global Restaurants Inc.

ISBERG, Joan

One Massachusetts Ave. NW
Washington, DC 20001

Tel: (202)789-0031
Fax: (202)682-9358

Employers
Nat'l Guard Ass'n of the U.S. (Deputy Director, Army Activities)

ISEMAN, Vicki L.

2111 Wilson Blvd.
Eighth Floor
Arlington, VA 22201-3058

Tel: (703)841-0626
Fax: (703)243-2874
Registered: LDA

EMail: iseman@alcalde-fay.com

Employers
Alcalde & Fay (Partner)

Clients Represented
On Behalf of Alcalde & Fay
American Maglev Technology Inc.
AMFM, Inc.
Carnival Foundation
Christian Network, Inc.
Computer Sciences Corp.
Glencairn, Ltd.
Hispanic Broadcasting Inc.
Jovan Broadcasting
Paxson Communications Corp.
Telemundo

ISHII, Tsutomu

1900 K St. NW
Suite 800
Washington, DC 20006

Tel: (202)828-9272
Fax: (202)828-9277
Registered: LDA

Employers
Hitachi, Ltd. (Senior Representative and Director)

ISLER, Micaela

1730 K St. NW
Suite 1106
Washington, DC 20006

Tel: (202)466-3561
Fax: (202)466-3583

Employers
Household Internat'l, Inc. (PAC Director)

ISRAEL, Benjamin L.

401 Ninth St. NW
Suite 1000
Washington, DC 20004

Tel: (202)274-2964
Fax: (202)274-2994

Employers
Troutman Sanders LLP (Partner)

ISRAEL, Kenneth

4701 Sangamore Rd.
Suite N100
Bethesda, MD 20816-2508

Tel: (301)229-5800
Fax: (301)229-5045
Registered: LDA

EMail: kisrael@burdeshaw.com

Employers
Burdeshaw Associates, Ltd. (Senior V. President, Air Force Programs)

Clients Represented
On Behalf of Burdeshaw Associates, Ltd.
Martin-Baker Aircraft Co., Ltd.

ISRAEL, Mark S.

1620 I St. NW
Suite 300
Washington, DC 20006

Tel: (202)429-0160
Fax: (202)293-3109

Employers
Mark S. Israel

ISRAEL, Sheryl R.

2300 N St. NW
Washington, DC 20037-1128

Tel: (202)663-8000
Fax: (202)663-8007
Registered: LDA

EMail: sheryl.israel@shawpittman.com

Employers
Shaw Pittman (Counsel)

Clients Represented
On Behalf of Shaw Pittman
Air Foyle, Ltd.
Big Sky Airlines
Chromalloy Gas Turbine Corp.
Midway Airlines Corp.
Vanguard Airlines, Inc.

ITLE, Carissa

2101 Wilson Blvd.
Suite 400
Arlington, VA 22201
EMail: citle@nmpf.org

Tel: (703)243-6111
Fax: (703)841-9328

Employers
Nat'l Milk Producers Federation (Director, Environmental Progams)

ITRRALDE, Rodrigo

701 Pennsylvania Ave. NW
Suite 500
Washington, DC 20004

Tel: (202)508-5017
Fax: (202)508-5080

Employers
Internat'l Utility Efficiency Partnerships (IUEP) (Project Manager)

ITURREGUI, Carlos E.

1120 Connecticut Ave. NW
Suite 1100
Washington, DC 20036

Tel: (202)861-5899
Fax: (202)861-5795
Registered: LDA

EMail: citurregui@gpcusa.com
Administrative Judge, District of Columbia, 1992-93.

Employers
GPC Internat'l (Senior Director)

Clients Represented
On Behalf of GPC Internat'l
Puerto Rico, Commonwealth of

ITURREGUI, Juan Carlos

800 Connecticut Ave. NW
Suite 500
Washington, DC 20006

Tel: (202)331-3103
Fax: (202)331-3101
Registered: LDA

Legislative Assistant to Resident Commissioner Carlos Romero-Barcelo (D-PR), 1993-95.

Employers
Greenberg Traurig, LLP (Shareholder)

ITZKOFF, Donald M.

888 Sixteenth St. NW
7th Floor
Washington, DC 20006-4103

Tel: (202)835-8182
Fax: (202)835-8136
Registered: LDA

Deputy Administrator, Federal Railroad Administration, Department of Transportation, 1994-99. Staff Counsel and Senior Counsel, Subcommittee on Surface Transportation, Committee on Commerce, 1991-94.

Employers
Foley & Lardner (Partner)

Clients Represented
On Behalf of Foley & Lardner
Siemens Transportation Systems, Inc.

ITZKOFF, Mark L.

1400 16th St. NW
Suite 400
Washington, DC 20036-2220
EMail: mitzkoff@ofwlaw.com

Tel: (202)518-6327
Fax: (202)234-2686

Employers
Olsson, Frank and Weeda, P.C. (Of Counsel)

IUCULANO, Russel

1620 L St. NW
Suite 800
Washington, DC 20036-5617

Tel: (202)659-3575
Fax: (202)659-1026
Registered: LDA

Employers
Metropolitan Life Insurance Co. (V. President, Government and Industry Relations)

IVANCIE, Thomas

1513 16th St. NW
Washington, DC 20036

Tel: (202)483-6900
Fax: (202)483-6902

EMail: tivancie@capitalresearch.org

Employers
Capital Research Center (Director, Development)

IVENSON, Christine

200 Constitution Ave. NW
Room S-1325
Washington, DC 20210

Tel: (202)693-4600
Fax: (202)693-4642

Employers
Department of Labor (Assistant Secretary, Office of Congressional and Intergovernmental Affairs)

IVERSON, William D.

1201 Pennsylvania Ave. NW
Washington, DC 20004-2401

Tel: (202)662-6000
Fax: (202)662-6291

EMail: wiverson@cov.com
Law Clerk to Judge David L. Bazelon, U.S. Court of Appeals for the District of Columbia Circuit, 1968-69.

Employers
Covington & Burling (Partner)

IVEY, Glenn

1735 New York Ave. NW
Suite 500
Washington, DC 20006-4759

Tel: (202)628-1700
Fax: (202)331-1024

Former Chief Counsel to Senator Tom Daschle (D-SD).

Employers
Preston Gates Ellis & Rouvelas Meeds LLP (Partner)

IVEY, Mary E.

6120 Oregon Ave. NW
Washington, DC 20015

Tel: (202)686-1216
Fax: (202)686-0598

Employers
Nat'l Ass'n of Minority Political Families, USA, Inc. (President and Chief Exec. Officer)

IVINS, II, Benjamin F. P.

1771 N St. NW
Washington, DC 20036-2891

Tel: (202)429-5430
Fax: (202)775-3526
Registered: LDA

Employers
Nat'l Ass'n of Broadcasters (Senior Associate, General Counsel)

IVORY, Elenora G.

110 Maryland Ave. NE
Suite 104
Washington, DC 20002

Tel: (202)543-1126
Fax: (202)543-7755

Employers
Presbyterian Church (U.S.A.) (Director, Washington Office)

IVORY, Glo

1806 New Hampshire Ave. NW
Washington, DC 20009
Tel: (202)483-4206
Fax: (202)462-7253

Employers
Nat'l Ass'n of Negro Business & Professional Women's Clubs, Inc. (Exec. Director)

IVORY, Megan

1200 G St. NW
Suite 400
Washington, DC 20005
Tel: (202)783-8700
Fax: (202)783-8750
Former Legislative Assistant to Rep. Jim Ramstad (R-MN).

Employers
AdvaMed (Director, Federal Government Relations)

IWANCIW, Eugene M.

P.O. Box 5748
Arlington, VA 22205-5748
Tel: (703)536-0725
Fax: (703)536-0738
Registered: LDA
EMail: emiwanciw@aol.com

Employers
EMI Associates, Ltd. (President)

Clients Represented

On Behalf of EMI Associates, Ltd.
Battelle Memorial Institute
Citizens Network for Foreign Affairs (CNFA)
ERIM
Loyola College
Romyr Associates
Scientech Corp.
Ukrainian Nat'l Ass'n, Inc.

JABLON, Robert A.

1350 New York Ave. NW
Suite 1100
Washington, DC 20005-4798
Tel: (202)879-4000
Fax: (202)393-2866
EMail: jablonr@spiegelmcd.com
Trial Attorney and Supervisory Trial Attorney, Federal Power Commission, 1962-70.

Employers
Spiegel & McDiarmid (Partner)

Clients Represented

On Behalf of Spiegel & McDiarmid
Michigan Municipal/Cooperative Group

JABLOW, Judy W.

722 Jackson Place NW
Washington, DC 20503-0002
Tel: (202)395-5750
Fax: (202)456-6546

Employers
Executive Office of the President - Council on Environmental Quality (Associate Director for Congressional Relations)

JACKMAN, Jennifer

1600 Wilson Blvd.
Suite 801
Arlington, VA 22209
Tel: (703)522-2214
Fax: (703)522-2219

Employers
Feminist Majority (Director, Policy and Research)

JACKMAN, Ph.D., William Jay

1410 King St.
Suite 400
Alexandria, VA 22314
Tel: (703)838-5885
Fax: (703)838-5888
EMail: jjackman@teamaged.org

Employers
Nat'l Ass'n of Agricultural Educators (NAAE) (Exec. Director)

JACKSON, Aletia

444 N. Capitol St. NW
Suite 701
Washington, DC 20001
Tel: (202)624-7790
Fax: (202)624-8579
EMail: AJackson@naic.org

Employers
Nat'l Ass'n of Insurance Commissioners (Assistant Counsel, Health Policy)

JACKSON, Alex

600 Maryland Ave. SW
Suite 800
Washington, DC 20024
Tel: (202)484-3600
Fax: (202)484-3604

Employers
American Farm Bureau Federation (Director, Trade Relations and Development)

JACKSON, Alvin B.

1101 16th St. NW
Suite 500
Washington, DC 20036
Tel: (202)659-9111
Fax: (202)659-6387
Registered: LDA

Employers
Bergner Bockorny Castagnetti and Hawkins

Clients Represented

On Behalf of Bergner Bockorny Castagnetti and Hawkins
The Boeing Co.
Chicago Board Options Exchange

JACKSON, Benjamin R.

14500 Avion Pkwy.
Suite 300
Chantilly, VA 20151
Tel: (703)818-1320
Fax: (703)818-8813
Registered: LDA
Former Deputy Assistant Administrator, Environmental Protection Agency.

Employers
Shutler and Low (Partner)

JACKSON, Bobby J.

1130 17th St. NW
Washington, DC 20036-4677
Tel: (202)463-2610
Fax: (202)833-1965
Registered: LDA
EMail: bjackson@nma.org

Employers
Nat'l Mining Ass'n (V. President, Human Resources)

JACKSON, Brian

1800 F St. NW
MS: 6107
Washington, DC 20405
Tel: (202)501-0563
Fax: (202)219-5742

Employers
General Services Administration (Special Assistant, Congressional and Intergovernmental Affairs)

JACKSON, Chris

1520 18th St. NW
Washington, DC 20036
Tel: (202)331-8947
Fax: (202)331-8958

Employers
Hong Kong Economic and Trade Office (Director General)

JACKSON, Elizabeth

910 17th St. NW
Suite 210
Washington, DC 20006-2603
Tel: (202)293-4505
Fax: (202)293-4509
EMail: bjackson@ida-downtown.org

Employers
Internat'l Downtown Ass'n (President)

JACKSON, Glenn F.

1627 I St. NW
Suite 900
Washington, DC 20006
Tel: (202)833-8994
Fax: (202)835-0707
Registered: LDA

Employers
The Williams Companies (Director, Government Affairs)

JACKSON, Jr., Jack C.

1301 Connecticut Ave. NW
Suite 200
Washington, DC 20036
Tel: (202)466-7767
Fax: (202)466-7797
EMail: jackjacksonjr@erols.com

Employers
Nat'l Congress of American Indians (Director, Government Affairs)

JACKSON, Janice

927 15th St. NW
Sixth Floor
Washington, DC 20036
Tel: (202)296-8130
Fax: (202)296-8134
EMail: jjackson@n4a.org

Employers
Nat'l Ass'n of Area Agencies on Aging (Exec. Director)

JACKSON, Sr., Rev. Jesse L.

1002 Wisconsin Ave. NW
Washington, DC 20007
Tel: (202)333-5270
Fax: (202)728-1192

Employers
Rainbow/Push Coalition (National Bureau) (President and Founder)

JACKSON, Kristie

1735 New York Ave. NW
Suite 500
Washington, DC 20006-4759
Tel: (202)628-1700
Fax: (202)331-1024

Employers
Preston Gates Ellis & Rouvelas Meeds LLP (Associate)

JACKSON, Leslie

P.O. Box 31220
4720 Montgomery Ln.
Bethesda, MD 20824-1220
Tel: (301)652-2682
Fax: (301)652-7711

Employers
American Occupational Therapy Ass'n, Inc. (Representative, Federal Affairs)

JACKSON, Lorie D.

2001 Pennsylvania Ave. NW
Suite 300
Washington, DC 20006
Tel: (202)862-0255
Fax: (202)862-0269

Employers
Exxon Mobil Corp. (Washington Representative, International Issues)

JACKSON, Ph.D., Marcia

9111 Old Georgetown Rd.
Bethesda, MD 20814
Tel: (301)897-5400
Fax: (301)897-9745
EMail: mjackson@acc.org

Employers
American College of Cardiology (Senior Associate Exec. V. President, Education)

JACKSON, Michael D.

1015 18th St. NW
Suite 600
Washington, DC 20036
Tel: (202)429-4344
Fax: (202)429-4342
Deputy Staff Director and Professional Staff Director (1999-2000), Professional Staff Member (1997-98), Special Assistant to the Chairman (1995-96), and Special Assistant to the Vice Chairman (1991-94), all with the Senate Committee on Indian Affairs. Consultant on Water and Power (1985-91), Consultant on Indian Affairs and Public Lands (1977-78) and Consultant on Indian Affairs (1974-85), House Committee on Interior and Insular Affairs. Staff Assistant to Rep. Craig Hosmer (R-CA), 1973-74. Research Analyst, Department of Justice, 1971-73. Corporal, U.S. Marine Corps, 1967-68.

Employers
Will and Carlson, Inc. (Senior Associate)

JACKSON, Nancy Izzo

1150 17th St. NW
Suite 406
Washington, DC 20036
Tel: (202)261-2840
Fax: (202)861-6490
Registered: FARA
EMail: njackson@crinternational.com

Employers
C/R Internat'l, L.L.C (V. President)

JACKSON, Neal

635 Massachusetts Ave. NW
Washington, DC 20001
Tel: (202)414-2000

Employers
Nat'l Public Radio (General Counsel)

JACKSON, Pamela Patrice

426 C St. NE
Washington, DC 20002
Tel: (202)544-1880
Fax: (202)543-6539
Registered: LDA
EMail: pj@capitolassociates.com

Assistant to Speaker Thomas P. (Tip) O'Neill (D-MA), U.S House of Representatives, 1974-87.

Employers
Capitol Associates, Inc. (V. President, Public Affairs)

Clients Represented
On Behalf of Capitol Associates, Inc.
FDA-NIH Council
Friends of CDC
Nat'l Coalition for Cancer Research

JACKSON, Patricia

1701 Clarendon Blvd.
Arlington, VA 22209
Tel: (703)276-8800
Fax: (703)243-2593

Employers
American Chiropractic Ass'n (V. President, Professional Development and Research)

JACKSON, Raynard

P.O. Box 2404
Washington, DC 20013
Tel: (202)543-7778
Fax: (202)543-7384

Employers
Americans for a Brighter Future (Chairman)

JACKSON, Ronald G.

P.O. Box 29260
Washington, DC 20017
Tel: (301)853-4500
Fax: (301)853-7671
Registered: LDA
EMail: jacksonr@adw.org

Employers
D.C. Catholic Conference - Archdiocese of Washington (Exec. Director)

JACKSON, Selina

316 Pennsylvania Ave. SE
Suite 300
Washington, DC 20003
Tel: (202)675-4220
Fax: (202)675-4230

Employers
United Parcel Service (Manager, Public Affairs)

JACKSON, Tami S.

601 Pennsylvania Ave. NW
Suite 325, North Bldg.
Washington, DC 20004
Tel: (202)728-3661
Fax: (202)728-3649

Employers
DuPont (Manager, State Government and Public Affairs)

JACKSON, Thomas C.

1200 19th St. NW
Suite 500
Washington, DC 20036
EMail: tjackson@kelleydrye.com
Tel: (202)955-9600
Fax: (202)955-9792

Employers
Kelley, Drye & Warren LLP (Partner)

JACKSON, William D.

1625 Massachusetts Ave. NW
Suite 400
Washington, DC 20036
EMail: wjackson@aaionline.org
Tel: (202)667-5636
Fax: (202)265-6332

Congressional Fellow, office of Senator James M. Jeffords (R-VT), 1996-97

Employers
The Africa-America Institute (Director, Government Relations and Policy)

JACKSON BELLINGER, Julia

1800 Duke St.
Alexandria, VA 22314
Tel: (703)548-3440
Fax: (703)836-0367

Employers
Soc. for Human Resource Management (Manager, Tax Benefits Regulation and Legislation)

JACOB, Amy

601 13th St. NW
Suite 410 South
Washington, DC 20005
Tel: (202)737-0100
Fax: (202)628-3965
Registered: LDA

Employers
R. Duffy Wall and Associates (V. President)

JACOB, Anne Marie L.

1130 17th St. NW
Washington, DC 20036-4677
Tel: (202)463-2649
Fax: (202)833-1965
Registered: LDA
EMail: ajacob@nma.org

Employers
Nat'l Mining Ass'n (Manager, Congressional Affairs)

JACOB, Paul

10 G St. NE
Suite 410
Washington, DC 20002
EMail: pjlimits@concentric.net
Tel: (202)379-3000
Fax: (202)379-3010

Employers
U.S. Term Limits (National Director)

JACOB, Thomas R.

601 Pennsylvania Ave. NW
Suite 325, North Bldg.
Washington, DC 20004
Tel: (202)728-3661
Fax: (202)728-3649
Registered: LDA

Employers
DuPont (Manager, International and Industry Affairs)

JACOBS, Barry

1156 15th St. NW
Suite 1201
Washington, DC 20005
Tel: (202)785-4200
Fax: (202)785-4115

Employers
American Jewish Committee (Director, Strategic Studies)

JACOBS, Brenda A.

1001 Pennsylvania Ave. NW
Suite 600
Washington, DC 20004
Tel: (202)347-0066
Fax: (202)624-7222
Registered: LDA, FARA
EMail: bjacobs@pgfm.com

Senior Counsel, Textiles and Trade Agreements, Office of the General Counsel, Department of Commerce, 1985-89. Attorney/Advisor, Office of the General Counsel, International Trade Commission, 1983-85.

Employers
Powell, Goldstein, Frazer & Murphy LLP (Partner)

Clients Represented
On Behalf of Powell, Goldstein, Frazer & Murphy LLP
Carpet Export Promotion Council
China, Embassy of the People's Republic of
DCS Group
Footwear Distributors and Retailers of America
Hong Kong Economic and Trade Office
PROEXPORT
U.S. Ass'n of Importers of Textiles and Apparel

JACOBS, Jerald A.

1575 I St. NW
Washington, DC 20005-1103
Tel: (202)626-2723
Fax: (202)371-1673

Employers
American Soc. of Ass'n Executives (General Counsel)

JACOBS, Lynn S.

2001 Pennsylvania Ave. NW
Suite 350
Washington, DC 20006-1825
Tel: (202)775-2681
Fax: (202)296-2521
Registered: LDA
EMail: lynn.jacobs@cigna.com

Employers
CIGNA Corp. (V. President, Government Affairs)

JACOBS, Stephen I.

666 11th St. NW
Suite 600
Washington, DC 20001
Tel: (202)783-0070
Fax: (202)783-0534
Registered: LDA
EMail: sjacobs@ccianet.org

Employers
Computer and Communications Industry Ass'n (CCIA) (V. President and Chief Counsel)

JACOBSEN, Jennifer

1101 Connecticut Ave. NW
Suite 400
Washington, DC 20036-4303
Tel: (202)530-7878
Fax: (202)530-7879
Registered: LDA

Employers
AOL Time Warner (Director, Domestic Public Policy)

JACOBSEN, Mary Jeanne

1145 17th St. NW
Washington, DC 20036
Tel: (202)857-7000
Fax: (202)775-6141

Employers
Nat'l Geographic Soc. (V. President, Communications)

JACOBSEN, Jr., Raymond A.

600 13th St. NW
Washington, DC 20005-3096
Tel: (202)756-8028
Fax: (202)756-8087

Employers
McDermott, Will and Emery (Partner)

Clients Represented
On Behalf of McDermott, Will and Emery
Lockheed Martin Corp.

JACOBSOHN, Alice P.

4301 Connecticut Ave. NW
Suite 300
Washington, DC 20008
Tel: (202)244-4700
Fax: (202)966-4818

Employers
Environmental Industry Ass'ns (Acting Director, Industry Research and Communications)

JACOBSOHN, David B.

901 15th St. NW
Suite 700
Washington, DC 20005-2301
Tel: (202)371-6000
Fax: (202)371-6279
Registered: LDA
EMail: dbjacobsohn@verner.com

Special Assistant to the Director, Federal Deposit Insurance Corporation, 1978-79. Director, Securities Disclosure Division, Comptroller of the Currency, Department of the Treasury, 1972-78. Attorney, Securities and Exchange Commission, 1969-72.

Employers
Verner, Liipfert, Bernhard, McPherson and Hand, Chartered (Of Counsel)

Clients Represented
On Behalf of Verner, Liipfert, Bernhard, McPherson and Hand, Chartered
Citigroup
Merrill Lynch & Co., Inc.
Nat'l Ass'n of Government Guaranteed Lenders
New York Stock Exchange

JACOBSON, Carolyn

10401 Connecticut Ave.
Kensington, MD 20895
Tel: (301)933-8600
Fax: (301)946-8452

Employers
Bakery, Confectionery and Tobacco Workers Internat'l Union (Director, Publications)

JACOBSON, Craig A.

2120 L St. NW
Suite 700
Washington, DC 20037
Tel: (202)822-8282
Fax: (202)296-8834
Registered: LDA

Employers
Hobbs, Straus, Dean and Walker, LLP

Clients Represented
On Behalf of Hobbs, Straus, Dean and Walker, LLP
Shoalwater Bay Indian Tribe

JACOBSON, David E.

701 Pennsylvania Ave. NW
Suite 800
Washington, DC 20004
Tel: (202)508-4300
Fax: (202)508-4321
EMail: djacobson@thelenreid.com

Tax Counsel, Senate Committee on Finance, 1979-81. Attorney/Advisor, Office of the Chief Counsel, Internal Revenue Service, 1974-79.

Employers

Thelen Reid & Priest LLP (Partner)

Clients Represented

On Behalf of Thelen Reid & Priest LLP

Progress Energy

JACOBSON, Jack

1225 I St. NW
Suite 600
Washington, DC 20005
Tel: (202)661-6180
Fax: (202)661-6182
Registered: LDA
EMail: jackjacobson@morganmeguire.com

Employers

Morgan Meguire, LLC (Legislative Assistant)

Clients Represented

On Behalf of Morgan Meguire, LLC

Burke Venture Capital
Longhorn Pipeline
Manatee, Florida, County of

JACOBSON, Judith M.

700 13th St. NW
Suite 400
Washington, DC 20005
Tel: (202)347-0773
Fax: (202)347-0785
Registered: LDA
EMail: jjacobson@cassidy.com

Employers

Cassidy & Associates, Inc. (Consultant)

Clients Represented

On Behalf of Cassidy & Associates, Inc.

Hampton University
Rochester Institute of Technology

JACOBSON, Dr. Michael F.

1875 Connecticut Ave. NW
Suite 300
Washington, DC 20009
Tel: (202)332-9110
Fax: (202)265-4954

Employers

Center for Science in the Public Interest (Exec. Director)

JACOBSON, Myron M.

444 N. Capitol St.
Suite 545
Washington, DC 20001
Tel: (202)347-1223
Fax: (202)347-1225
Registered: LDA
EMail: mmjmga@aol.com

Former Legislative Assistant to Rep. James E. Rogan (R-CA).

Employers

Madison Government Affairs (Director, Legislative Affairs)

Clients Represented

On Behalf of Madison Government Affairs

DCH Technology Inc.
Nat'l Community Reinvestment Coalition
Nottoway, Virginia, County of
REM Engineering
SM&A
University of West Florida
USS Wisconsin Foundation
Virginia Living Museum
Roy F. Weston, Inc.

JACOBY, Irene

1000 16th St. NW
Suite 500
Washington, DC 20036
Tel: (202)296-1683
Fax: (202)293-2118
EMail: info@nlcpi.org

Employers

Nat'l Legal Center for the Public Interest (Senior V. President, Administration)

JACOBY, Peter G.

1120 20th St. NW
Suite 1000
Washington, DC 20036
Tel: (202)457-2050
Fax: (202)457-2267
EMail: pgjacoby@att.com

Former Special Assistant to the President for House Legislative Affairs, Executive Office of the President, The White House, during the Clinton administration. Former Legislative Aide to Rep. Mike Synar (D-OK).

Employers

AT&T (V. President, Congressional Affairs)

JACQUEZ, Lynnette C.

1341 G St. NW
Suite 200
Washington, DC 20005
Tel: (202)347-5990
Fax: (202)347-5941
Registered: LDA
EMail: ljacquez@clj.com

Counsel, House Committee on the Judiciary, 1984-87. Assistant Counsel, Subcommittee on Immigration, Refugees, and International Law, House Committee on the Judiciary, 1984-87.

Employers

Copeland, Lowery & Jacquez (Partner)

Clients Represented

On Behalf of Copeland, Lowery & Jacquez

CALSTART
Hollister Ranch Owners' Ass'n
March Joint Powers Authority
Merced, California, County of
Riverside, California, City of
Santa Barbara Electric Transit Institute
Santa Barbara Metropolitan Transit District
Ventura County Community-Navy Action Partnership

JADCZAK, Jeremy

1201 15th St. NW
Washington, DC 20005-2800
Tel: (202)822-0470
Fax: (202)822-0572

Employers

Nat'l Ass'n of Home Builders of the U.S. (Congressional Representative and Grassroots Regional Director)

JAEGER, Arthur R.

1424 16th St. NW
Suite 604
Washington, DC 20036
Tel: (202)387-6121
Fax: (202)265-7989

Employers

Consumer Federation of America (Assistant Director)

JAFARI, Beth

1730 Pennsylvania Ave. NW
Suite 1200
Washington, DC 20006-4706
Tel: (202)737-0500
Fax: (202)626-3737
Registered: LDA

Former Legislative Director to Rep. Joe Barton (R-TX).

Employers

King & Spalding

Clients Represented

On Behalf of King & Spalding

Bridgestone/Firestone, Inc.

JAFFE, Daniel L.

1120 20th St. NW
Suite 520 South
Washington, DC 20036
Tel: (202)296-1883
Fax: (202)296-1430
Registered: LDA

Employers

Ass'n of Nat'l Advertisers (Exec. V. President, Director of Washington Office)

JAFFE, Jim

820 First St. NE
Suite 510
Washington, DC 20002
Tel: (202)408-1080
Fax: (202)408-1056
EMail: jaffe@cbpp.org

Employers

Center on Budget and Policy Priorities (Director, Communications)

JAFFE, Kenneth G.

3000 K St. NW
Suite 300
Washington, DC 20007
Tel: (202)424-7500
Fax: (202)424-7643
Registered: LDA

Employers

Swidler Berlin Shereff Friedman, LLP (Partner)

Clients Represented

On Behalf of Swidler Berlin Shereff Friedman, LLP

California Independent System Operator

JAFFE, Michael Evan

1050 Connecticut Ave. NW
Washington, DC 20036-5339
Tel: (202)857-6000
Fax: (202)857-6395
Registered: LDA

Employers

Arent Fox Kintner Plotkin & Kahn, PLLC (Member)

JAGTIANI, Patricia Wilson

805 15th St. NW
Suite 510
Washington, DC 20005
Tel: (202)326-9300
Fax: (202)326-9330
EMail: pjagtiani@ngsa.org

Employers

Natural Gas Supply Ass'n (Director, Regulatory Affairs)

JAKUBEK, Wolfgang

1020 19th St. NW
Suite 850
Washington, DC 20036
Tel: (202)452-9100
Fax: (202)452-9555

Employers

Deutsche Telekom, Inc. (Managing Director)

JAMES, A. Everette

1875 Connecticut Ave. NW
Suite 1200
Washington, DC 20009-5728
Tel: (202)986-8120
Fax: (202)986-8102
EMail: aejames@llgm.com

Former Deputy Assistant Secretary for Industries and Finance, Department of Commerce

Employers

LeBoeuf, Lamb, Greene & MacRae L.L.P. (Partner)

Clients Represented

On Behalf of LeBoeuf, Lamb, Greene & MacRae L.L.P.

Candle Corp.
Lloyd's of London
Nationwide Global

JAMES, Allen

1156 15th St. NW
Suite 400
Washington, DC 20005
Tel: (202)872-3860
Fax: (202)463-0474
Registered: LDA

Employers

RISE (Responsible Industry for a Sound Environment) (President)

JAMES, April

1255 23rd St. NW
Suite 200
Washington, DC 20037-1174
Tel: (202)452-8100
Fax: (202)833-3636
EMail: ajames@hauck.com

Employers

Hauck and Associates (Senior Associate)

JAMES, Claudia

1001 G St. NW
Suite 900 E
Washington, DC 20001-4545
Tel: (202)393-1010
Fax: (202)393-5510
Registered: LDA, FARA
EMail: james@podesta.com

Former Senior Legislative Assistant to Rep. Peter Peyser (D-NY) and Legislative Assistant, Judiciary to Rep. Christopher J. Dodd (D-CT).

Employers

Podesta/Mattoon (President)

Clients Represented

On Behalf of Podesta/Mattoon

AOL Time Warner
Ass'n for Local Telecommunications Services
Ass'n of Directory Publishers
eBay Inc.
MCI WorldCom Corp.
Motion Picture Ass'n of America
Nat'l Ass'n of Broadcasters
Newspaper Ass'n of America
North American GSM Alliance, LLC
Northpoint Technology, Ltd.
Recording Industry Ass'n of America
SiTV
Teligent, Inc.
Vivendi Universal

JAMES, Dan

1455 F St. NW
Suite 225
Washington, DC 20005
Tel: (202)638-3307
Fax: (202)783-6947
Registered: LDA
EMail: djames@bjllp.com

Employers

Ball Janik, LLP (Government Relations Consultant)

Clients Represented

On Behalf of Ball Janik, LLP

Grants Pass Irrigation District

JAMES, Diane

1575 I St. NW
Washington, DC 20005-1103
Tel: (202)626-2723
Fax: (202)371-1673

Employers

American Soc. of Ass'n Executives (Director, Allied Partners)

JAMES, Edgar N.

1146 19th St. NW
Suite 600
Washington, DC 20036
Tel: (202)496-0500
Fax: (202)496-0555
Registered: LDA

Employers

James & Hoffman, P.C. (Partner)

JAMES, Harriet

1133 Connecticut Ave. NW
Fifth Floor
Washington, DC 20036
Tel: (202)457-1110
Fax: (202)457-1130
Registered: LDA

Employers

Quinn Gillespie & Associates (Associate)

Clients Represented

On Behalf of Quinn Gillespie & Associates

British Columbia Lumber Trade Council
LVMH Moet Hennessy Louis Vuitton S.A.

JAMES, Marie

700 13th St. NW
Suite 400
Washington, DC 20005
Tel: (202)347-0773
Fax: (202)347-0785
Registered: LDA
EMail: mjames@cassidy.com

Employers

Cassidy & Associates, Inc. (Senior Associate)

Clients Represented

On Behalf of Cassidy & Associates, Inc.

The BOSE Corp.
Carondelet Health System
Community General Hospital of Sullivan County
Community Health Partners of Ohio
FedEx Corp.
Hospital for Special Surgery
Santa Rosa Memorial Hospital
University of Massachusetts Memorial Health System

JAMES, Philip J.

8200 Greensboro Dr.
Suite 302
McLean, VA 22102-3881
Tel: (703)442-4890
Fax: (703)442-0630
Registered: LDA
EMail: nga@glass.org

Employers

Nat'l Glass Ass'n (President and Chief Exec. Officer)

JAMES, Raymond K.

1100 Connecticut Ave. NW
Suite 1000
Washington, DC 20036
Tel: (202)728-1070
Fax: (202)293-2448
Registered: LDA

Chief Counsel, Federal Railroad Administration, Department of Transportation, 1977-81. Chief Counsel, Subcommittee on Housing and Community Development, House Committee on Banking, Finance and Urban Affairs, 1973-77. Assistant General Counsel for Legislation (1971-73) and Legislative Attorney (1967-71), Department of Housing and Urban Development. Counsel, House Judiciary Committee, 1963-66.

Employers

Coan & Lyons (Partner)

Clients Represented

On Behalf of Coan & Lyons

Akron Tower Housing Partnership
Coalition for Affordable Housing Preservation
Council for Affordable and Rural Housing
Hempstead, New York, Village of
Presidential Towers, Ltd.
Public Housing Authorities Directors Ass'n
State Street Development Co. of Boston
Weinberg Investments, Inc.

JAMES, Thomas M.

1401 K St. NW
Suite 450
Washington, DC 20005
Tel: (202)737-0700
Fax: (202)737-0455
Registered: LDA
EMail: tmjames@furmangroup.com

Employers

The Furman Group (Senior V. President)

Clients Represented

On Behalf of The Furman Group

California Water Service Co.
Central Basin Municipal Water District
Imperial Beach, California, City of
Leucadia County Water District
Mesquite Resort Ass'n
Mesquite, Nevada, City of
Olivenhain Municipal Water District
Paradise Canyon Resort
San Elijo Joint Powers Authority
San Gabriel Basin Water Quality Authority
Tooele, Utah, City of
Upper San Gabriel Municipal Water District
Virgin Valley Water District
Watsonville, California, City of
West Basin Municipal Water District
West Hills Community College District

JAMES, Timothy P.

1125 17th St. NW
Washington, DC 20036
Tel: (202)429-9100
Fax: (202)778-2680
Registered: LDA

Employers

Internat'l Union of Operating Engineers (Director, Department of Politics, Corporate and Government Affairs)

JAMESON, Booth S.

1331 Pennsylvania Ave. NW
Suite 1300 North
Washington, DC 20004
Tel: (202)637-6741
Fax: (202)637-6759

Legislative Director (1996-2000) and Senior Legislative Assistant (1993-96) to Rep. Michael N. Castle (R-DE). Legislative Assistant for Foreign Affairs to Del. Ben Blaz (R-GU), 1991-92. Legislative Correspondent and Legislative Assistant to Senator Conrad Burns (R-MT), 1989-91.

Employers

EDS Corp. (Director, Global Government Affairs)

JAMESON, Paul W.

1455 Pennsylvania Ave. NW
Suite 1000
Washington, DC 20004
Tel: (202)942-8400
Fax: (202)942-8484
Registered: LDA
EMail: paul.jameson@haledorr.com

Employers

Hale and Dorr LLP (Of Counsel)

JAMIESON, Paul W.

1200 19th St. NW
Washington, DC 20036-2430
Tel: (202)861-6817
Fax: (202)223-2085
Registered: LDA
EMail: paul.jamieson@piperrudnick.com

Employers

Piper Marbury Rudnick & Wolfe LLP (Associate)

Clients Represented

On Behalf of Piper Marbury Rudnick & Wolfe LLP

Individual Reference Services Group
PSINet Inc.

JAMISON, Delos Cy

306 Constitution Ave. NE
Washington, DC 20002
Tel: (202)546-9060
Fax: (202)546-9160
Registered: LDA, FARA

Director, Bureau of Land Management, Department of the Interior, 1989-93.

Employers

Jamison and Sullivan, Inc. (Chairman)

Clients Represented

On Behalf of Jamison and Sullivan, Inc.

Ass'n of O & C Counties
Ass'n of Oregon Counties
Counterpart Internat'l
Douglas, Oregon, County of
The Fanning Corp.
Flight Landata, Inc.
Greystar Resources, Ltd.
Internat'l Utility Efficiency Partnerships (IUEP)
D. R. Johnson Lumber
Malheur Timber Operators
Prairie Wood Products
Umatilla Water Users
Upper Klamath Water Users

JANETOS, Anthony

Ten G St. NE
Suite 800
Washington, DC 20002
Tel: (202)729-7600
Fax: (202)729-7610

Employers

World Resources Institute (Senior V. President, Programs)

JANGER, Lee J.

2111 Wilson Blvd.
Suite 1200
Arlington, VA 22201
Tel: (703)522-1845
Fax: (703)351-6634
EMail: LJanger@columbuspublicaffairs.com

Contrator, Civic Division (Frauds), Department of Justice.

Employers

Columbus Public Affairs (Senior Associate)

JANGER, Stephen A.

44 Canal Center Plaza
Alexandria, VA 22314
Tel: (703)706-3328
Fax: (703)706-3684
Registered: LDA
EMail: jangers@closeup.org

Employers

Close Up Foundation (President and Chief Exec. Officer)

JANKO, Julie A.

2025 M St. NW
Suite 800
Washington, DC 20036
Tel: (202)367-2100
Fax: (202)367-1200
EMail: julie_janko@dc.sba.com

Employers

Smith, Bucklin and Associates, Inc.

JANKOWSKY, Joel

1333 New Hampshire Ave. NW
Suite 400
Washington, DC 20036
Tel: (202)887-4000
Fax: (202)887-4288
Registered: LDA

Legislative Assistant to the Speaker of the House, Rep. Carl B. Albert (D-OK), 1972-76.

Employers

Akin, Gump, Strauss, Hauer & Feld, L.L.P. (Partner)

Clients Represented

On Behalf of Akin, Gump, Strauss, Hauer & Feld, L.L.P.

Alliance for Quality Nursing Home Care
American Express Co.
American Family Enterprises
American Legion
AOL Time Warner
Asbury Automotive Group
AT&T
Bankers Trust Co.
Bear, Stearns and Co.
Competitive Consumer Lending Coalition
Fontana Union Water Co.
Granite Broadcasting Co.
Manufactured Housing Institute
Mortgage Insurance Companies of America
Motion Picture Ass'n of America
PG&E Corp.
PG&E Gas Transmission Northwest
The Project Leadership Committee, Lincoln Center for the Performing Arts
Texas Manufactured Housing Ass'n
Transamerica Financial Services Co.

JANOSKO, A.J.

2500 Wilson Blvd.
Suite 300
Arlington, VA 22201
EMail: ajanosko@tia.eia.org
Tel: (703)907-7499
Fax: (703)907-7727

Employers

Telecommunications Industry Ass'n (Director, Trade Show Operations)

JANOW, Joshua

1615 L St. NW
Suite 700
Washington, DC 20036-5610
EMail: joshua.janow@weil.com
Tel: (202)682-7000
Fax: (202)857-0939
Registered: LDA

Employers

Weil, Gotshal & Manges, LLP (Legislative Specialist)

Clients Represented

On Behalf of Weil, Gotshal & Manges, LLP

Nomura Internat'l plc

JANS, Megan C.

1200 Wilson Blvd.
Arlington, VA 22209-1989
Tel: (703)465-3687
Fax: (703)465-3004

Employers

The Boeing Co. (Legislative Affairs, Army Programs)

JARAMILLO, Felipe

1701 Pennsylvania Ave. NW
Suite 560
Washington, DC 20006
Tel: (202)887-9000
Fax: (202)223-0526

Employers

Colombian Government Trade Bureau (Director)

JARBOE, Kenan Patrick

711 Tenth St. SE
Washington, DC 20003
Tel: (202)547-7064
Registered: LDA

Employers

Jarboe & Associates

Clients Represented

On Behalf of Jarboe & Associates

Fontheim Internat'l

JARBOE, Mark

1001 Pennsylvania Ave. NW
Suite 300S
Washington, DC 20004
Tel: (202)824-8800
Fax: (202)824-8990
Registered: LDA

Employers

Dorsey & Whitney LLP

Clients Represented

On Behalf of Dorsey & Whitney LLP

Central Council of Tlingit and Haida Indian Tribes of Alaska
Cow Creek Umpqua Tribe of Oregon
Hoopa Valley Tribal Council
Little River Band of Ottawa Indians
Red Lake Band of Chippewa Indians
Shakopee Mdewakanton Sioux Tribe

JARDOT, Leo C.

1667 K St. NW
Suite 1270
Washington, DC 20006
Tel: (202)659-8320
Fax: (202)496-2448
Registered: LDA

Employers

American Home Products Corp. (V. President, Government Relations)

JARMAN, Daniel

1275 K St. NW
Suite 810
Washington, DC 20005
EMail: danj@cfmdc.com
Tel: (202)408-2100
Fax: (202)408-2115
Registered: LDA

Employers

Conkling, Fiskum & McCormick (V. President, Federal Affairs)

Clients Represented

On Behalf of Conkling, Fiskum & McCormick

Electric Lightwave, Inc.
Electro Scientific Industries, Inc.
Industrial Customers of Northwest Utilities
Mentor Graphics Corp.
New Edge Networks
Oregon Graduate Institute of Science and Technology
Sisters of Providence Health Systems

JARMAN, Richard B.

1250 H St. NW
Suite 800
Washington, DC 20005
Tel: (202)857-3400
Fax: (202)857-3401
Registered: LDA

Employers

Eastman Kodak Co. (Director, Advanced Manufacturing Affairs)

JARMAN, Rick

1350 I St. NW
Suite 300
Washington, DC 20005
Tel: (202)639-5900
Fax: (202)639-5932
Registered: LDA

Employers

Nat'l Food Processors Ass'n (Senior Director, Technical Regulatory Affairs-EPA)

JARMIN, Gary L.

208 N. Patrick St.
Alexandria, VA 22314
EMail: jarmoninc@aol.com
Tel: (703)548-4904
Fax: (703)548-1424
Registered: LDA

Employers

Jar-Mon Consultants, Inc. (President)

JARMIN, Gina

208 N. Patrick St.
Alexandria, VA 22314
EMail: jm2consult@aol.com
Tel: (703)548-4904
Fax: (703)548-1424
Registered: LDA

Employers

Jar-Mon Consultants, Inc. (Senior V. President)

Clients Represented

On Behalf of Jar-Mon Consultants, Inc.

American Federation of Senior Citizens

JARREAU, Bert

440 First St. NW
Eighth Floor
Washington, DC 20001
EMail: bjarreau@naco.org
Tel: (202)942-4248
Fax: (202)393-2630

Employers

Nat'l Ass'n of Counties (Chief Technology Officer)

JARRELL, Kent

1615 L St. NW
Suite 900
Washington, DC 20036
Tel: (202)778-1000
Fax: (202)466-6002

Employers

APCO Worldwide (Senior V. President, PA Practice)

JARRELL, William P.

2300 Clarendon Blvd.
Suite 401
Arlington, VA 22201
EMail: williamj@washingtonstrategies.com
Tel: (703)516-4787
Fax: (703)522-2628
Registered: LDA

Former Deputy Chief of Staff and Administrative Assistant to House Majority Whip, Rep. Tom DeLay (R-TX). Former Chief of Staff to Rep. James Saxton (R-NJ) and Rep. Donald Lukens (R-Ohio). Former Communications Director to Senator Steve Symms (R-ID). Former Press Aide to Rep. Mickey Edwards (R-OK). Former Deputy Director of Communications, Department of the Interior.

Employers

Washington Strategies, L.L.C.

Clients Represented

On Behalf of Washington Strategies, L.L.C.

Ballard, Spahr, Andrews & Ingersoll LLP
Corning Inc.
Internat'l Longevity Center
Maersk Inc.
New York Institute of Technology
Personal Watercraft Industry Ass'n
Recreational Fishing Alliance
University Technology Park
West Chester University
Widener University

JARVIS, Charles W.

3900 Jermantown Rd.
Suite 450
Fairfax, VA 22030
Tel: (703)359-6500
Fax: (703)359-6510

Employers

United Seniors Ass'n (President)

JARVIS, John T.

1901 L St. NW
Suite 300
Washington, DC 20036
Tel: (202)452-9515
Fax: (202)466-8016
Registered: LDA

Employers

Forest Products Industry Nat'l Labor-Management Committee (Exec. Director)
McGlotten & Jarvis

Clients Represented

On Behalf of McGlotten & Jarvis

Chlorine Chemistry Council
Computer Sciences Corp.
CSX Corp.
Edison Electric Institute
Forest Products Industry Nat'l Labor-Management Committee
Internat'l Dairy Foods Ass'n
Internat'l Franchise Ass'n
Investment Co. Institute
United Mine Workers of America

JARVIS, Steve

600 Jefferson Plaza
Suite 350
Rockville, MD 20852
EMail: sjarvis@forestresources.org
Tel: (301)838-9385
Fax: (301)838-9481

Employers

Forest Resources Ass'n (Director, Forestry Programs)

JASINOWSKI, Isabel H.

1420 New York Ave. NW
Suite 200
Washington, DC 20005
EMail: ihjasinowski@goodyear.com
Tel: (202)682-9250
Fax: (202)682-1533
Registered: LDA

Employers

Goodyear Tire and Rubber Co. (V. President, Governmental Relations)

JASINOWSKI, Jerry J.

1331 Pennsylvania Ave. NW
Sixth Floor
Washington, DC 20004-1790
Tel: (202)637-3106
Fax: (202)637-3182
Registered: LDA

Employers

Nat'l Ass'n of Manufacturers (President)

JASKOT, John J.

499 S. Capitol St. SW
Suite 600
Washington, DC 20003
Tel: (202)828-8363
Fax: (202)828-6907
Registered: LDA
EMail: jjaskot@joneswalker.com
U.S. Coast Guard Liaison, U.S. Senate, 1993-96. Fellow, Subcommittee on Transportation, Senate Appropriations Committee.

Employers
Jones, Walker, Waechter, Poitevent, Carrere & Denegre, L.L.P. (Of Counsel)

Clients Represented
On Behalf of Jones, Walker, Waechter, Poitevent, Carrere & Denegre, L.L.P.
ACS Government Solutions Group
American Ass'n of Nurse Anesthetists
The Audubon Institute
Avondale Industries, Inc.
Bailey Link
Baton Rouge, Louisiana, City of
Boys Town USA
Broward, Florida, County of
Burk-Kleinpeter, Inc.
Canal Barge Co., Inc.
Columbus General, L.L.C.
Committee of Unsecured Creditors
General Category Tuna Ass'n
General Electric Co.
Imedia.IT, Inc.
Ingram Barge Company
Internat'l Shipholding Corp.
Internat'l Technology Resources, Inc.
Jacobus Tenbroek Memorial Fund
JRL Enterprises
LA Center for the Blind
Lockheed Martin Global Telecommunications
Louisiana Superdome
Martinez and Curtis
Mechanical Equipment Co., Inc.
Mesa, Arizona, City of
The MetroVision Chamber
New Orleans, Louisiana, Port of
Oracle Corp.
Peoplesoft USA, Inc.
Petroleum Helicopters
Raytheon Co.
Science & Engineering Associates, Inc.
Sewerage and Water Board of New Orleans
St. Gabriel, Louisiana, Town of
Stewart Enterprises, Inc.
TransOceanic Shipping
Tulane University
United Special Transport Air Resources, LLC (USTAR)
University of New Orleans Foundation

JASNY, Henry

750 First St. NE
Suite 901
Washington, DC 20002
EMail: hjasney@saferoads.org
Tel: (202)408-1711
Fax: (202)408-1699

Employers
Advocates for Highway and Auto Safety (Legal Counsel)

JAWETZ, Steven M.

1350 I St. NW
Suite 700
Washington, DC 20005
Tel: (202)789-6000
Fax: (202)789-6190
Registered: LDA

Employers
Beveridge & Diamond, P.C.

JAY, Dennis

1012 14th St. NW
Suite 200
Washington, DC 20005
Tel: (202)393-7330
Fax: (202)393-7329

Employers
Coalition Against Insurance Fraud (Exec. Director)

JAYNE, Jr., Edwin S.

1625 L St. NW
Washington, DC 20036-5687
Tel: (202)429-1188
Fax: (202)223-3413
Registered: LDA
EMail: ejayne@afscme.org

Employers
American Federation of State, County and Municipal Employees (Associate Director, Legislation)

JEALOUS, Benjamin

3200 13th St. NW
Washington, DC 20010-2410
Tel: (202)588-8764
Fax: (202)588-5029

Employers
Nat'l Newspaper Publishers Ass'n (Exec. Director)

JEANNERET, Matthew

1010 Massachusetts Ave. NW
Washington, DC 20001
Tel: (202)289-4434
Fax: (202)289-4435

Employers
American Road and Transportation Builders Ass'n (ARTBA) (V. President, Communications)

JEANSONNE, Angela

1090 Vermont Ave. NW
Suite 510
Washington, DC 20005
Tel: (202)414-0140
Fax: (202)544-3525
Registered: LDA

Employers
American Osteopathic Ass'n (Assistant Director, Federal Education Issues)

JEFFCOAT, Scott

1600 Pennsylvania Ave. NW
102 E. Wing
Washington, DC 20500
Tel: (202)456-6493
Fax: (202)456-2604

Employers
Executive Office of the President - The White House (Legislative Assistant, House Liaison Office)

JEFFERS, Margaret O.

1050 17th St. NW
Suite 300
Washington, DC 20036
Tel: (202)296-3390
Fax: (202)296-3399
Registered: LDA

Employers
Apartment and Office Building Ass'n of Metropolitan Washington (Exec. V. President)

JEFFERSON, John

1608 K St. NW
Washington, DC 20006
Tel: (202)861-2700
Fax: (202)861-2786
Registered: LDA

Employers
American Legion (Assistant Legislative Director)

JEFFERSON, Sally

1615 H St. NW
Washington, DC 20062-2000
Tel: (202)463-5533
Fax: (202)887-3445

Employers
Chamber of Commerce of the U.S.A. (Director, Congressional and Public Affairs)

JELLINEK, Steven D.

1525 Wilson Blvd.
Suite 600
Arlington, VA 22209
EMail: SteveJ@jscinc.com
Tel: (703)527-1670
Fax: (703)547-5477
Former Assistant Administrator of Pesticides and Toxic Substances, Environmental Protection Agency and former Staff Director, Council on Environmental Quality.

Employers
Jellinek, Schwartz & Connolly (Chairman)

JEMMOTT, Diane

1299 Pennsylvania Ave. NW
Suite 800 West
Washington, DC 20004
Tel: (202)785-0500
Fax: (202)785-5277
Registered: LDA
EMail: jemmottd@carmengroup.com

Employers
The Carmen Group (V. President)

Clients Represented
On Behalf of The Carmen Group
Major Medicaid Hospital Coalition
Metropolitan Washington Airports Authority
Missouri Highway and Transportation Department
Pembroke Real Estate, Inc.
Stafford, Virginia, County of
Sunrise Assisted Living
Washington Sports & Entertainment, L.P.
Western Development

JENCKES, Linda

210 Seventh St. SE
Washington, DC 20003
Tel: (202)547-6808
Fax: (202)546-5425
Registered: LDA

Employers
Linda Jenckes & Associates (President)
Kessler & Associates Business Services, Inc.

Clients Represented
On Behalf of Linda Jenckes & Associates
Henry H. Kessler Foundation
On Behalf of Kessler & Associates Business Services, Inc.
Mercy Health System of Northwest Arkasas

JENDRZEJCZYK, Mike

1630 Connecticut Ave. NW
Suite 500
Washington, DC 20009
Tel: (202)612-4321
Fax: (202)612-4333

Employers
Human Rights Watch (Washington Director, Human Rights Watch - Asia Division)

JENKINS, Dana

Ronald Reagan Bldg.
1300 Pennsylvania Ave. NW
MS: 6.10-015
Washington, DC 20523
Tel: (202)712-0071
Fax: (202)216-3237

Employers
Agency for Internat'l Development (Administrative Officer, Bureau for Legislative and Public Affairs)

JENKINS, II, David M.

8000 Towers Crescent Dr.
Suite 1350
Tysons Corner, VA 22182
Tel: (703)760-7888
Fax: (703)821-8694
Registered: LDA
EMail: dmj2wash@aol.com
Congressional Liaison, Department of the Interior, 1971-72. Administrative Assistant to Rep. Tom Railsback (R-IL), 1969-71.

Employers
Washington Liaison Group, LLC (V. President and General Counsel)

Clients Represented
On Behalf of Washington Liaison Group, LLC
Reckitt & Colman Pharmaceuticals Inc.
Serono Laboratories, Inc.

JENKINS, Ellen D.

1610 Dewitt Avenue
Alexandria, VA 22301
Tel: (703)262-6434
Fax: (703)860-3187

Employers
Pediatrix Medical Group, Inc. (Director, Federal Affairs)

JENKINS, Jr., Harry

1650 Tysons Blvd.
Suite 1700
McLean, VA 22201
Tel: (703)790-6300
Fax: (703)790-6365

Employers
ITT Industries (Director, Congressional Liaison and Business Development)

JENKINS, Jennifer

2011 Pennsylvania Ave. NW
Suite 800
Washington, DC 20006-1808
EMail: jjenkins@mail.acponline.org
Tel: (202)261-4536
Fax: (202)835-0443

Employers
American College of Physicians-American Soc. of Internal Medicine (ACP-ASIM) (Associate, Grassroots Advocacy)

JENKINS, John S.

555 13th St. NW
Washington, DC 20004-1109
Tel: (202)637-5600
Fax: (202)637-5910
Registered: LDA

Employers
Hogan & Hartson L.L.P.

Clients Represented

On Behalf of Hogan & Hartson L.L.P.

Warland Investment Co.

JENKINS, Judy P.

1300 I St. NW
Suite 300 West
Washington, DC 20005
Tel: (202)522-8600
Fax: (202)522-8669
Registered: LDA

Former aide to Senator Carl Levin (D-MI), 1979-86.

Employers

Dykema Gossett PLLC (Associate)

JENKINS, Kimberly

601 N. Pennsylvania Ave. NW
Suite 250
Washington, DC 20004
Tel: (202)628-3900
Fax: (202)628-3922

Employers

Internet Policy Institute (President)

JENKINS, Linda M.

499 S. Capitol St. SW
Suite 502
Washington, DC 20003
Tel: (202)554-2510
Fax: (202)554-2520
Registered: LDA
EMail: ljenkins@natso.com

Former Legislative Correspondent for Senator Judd Gregg (R-NH).

Employers

NATSO, Inc. (Director, Government Affairs)

JENKINS, Pam

1901 L St. NW
Suite 300
Washington, DC 20036
Tel: (202)466-7590
Fax: (202)466-7598
EMail: pam.jenkins@dc.ogilvypr.com

Employers

Ogilvy Public Relations Worldwide (Senior V. President, Group Head, Health and Medical)

JENKINS, Timothy W.

1666 K St. NW
Suite 500
Washington, DC 20006-2803
Tel: (202)887-1400
Fax: (202)466-2198
Registered: LDA, FARA

Investigator, Subcommittee on Investigations and General Oversight, Senate Labor Committee, 1980-82.

Employers

O'Connor & Hannan, L.L.P. (Partner)

Clients Represented

On Behalf of O'Connor & Hannan, L.L.P.

Amgen
Associated Credit Bureaus, Inc.
Bear, Stearns and Co.
Capital One Financial Corp.
Celera Genomics
Coalition for Tax Equity
Lockheed Martin Corp.
The Metris Companies, Inc.
Santa Fe, New Mexico, County of
State Government Affairs Council
State Street Bank and Trust Co.
UBS Warburg
VISA U.S.A., Inc.
Nidal Z. Zayed and Associates

JENNER, Gregory F.

1301 K St. NW
Washington, DC 20005-3333
Tel: (202)414-1000
Fax: (202)414-1301
Registered: LDA
EMail: gregory.f.jenner@us.pwcglobal.com

Employers

PriceWaterhouseCoopers (Partner)

JENNING, Steven

1100 New York Ave. NW
Suite 200M
Washington, DC 20005
Tel: (202)367-0440
Fax: (202)367-0470
Registered: LDA
EMail: steven@caphg.com

Chief of Staff to Senator Ron Wyden (D-OR), 1996-97. Staff Director, Subcommittee on Regulation, Business Opportunities and Technology, Committee on Small Business, U.S. House of Representatives, 1987-95. Policy Director to Rep. Wyden, 1986-87.

Employers

Capitol Health Group, LLC (Principal)

Clients Represented

On Behalf of Capitol Health Group, LLC

Abbott Laboratories
Beverly Enterprises
Bristol-Myers Squibb Co.
Express Scripts Inc.
Greater New York Hospital Ass'n
Healthcare Leadership Council
Humana Inc.
Johnson & Johnson, Inc.
Medassets.com
Nat'l Ass'n of Psychiatric Health Systems
Northwestern Memorial Hospital
Pfizer, Inc.
Soc. of Thoracic Surgeons

JENNINGS, Allison

1776 I St. NW
Suite 1030
Washington, DC 20006
Tel: (202)822-1690
Fax: (202)822-1693
Registered: LDA

Employers

Solutia Inc. (Government Affairs Specialist)

JENNINGS, Ph.D., R.N, Carole P.

P.O. Box 40130
Washington, DC 20016
Tel: (202)966-6414
Fax: (202)966-2856
Registered: LDA

Employers

American Academy of Nurse Practitioners (Washington Representative)

JENNINGS, Deborah E.

1200 19th St. NW
Washington, DC 20036-2430
Tel: (202)861-3842
Fax: (202)223-2085
Registered: LDA
EMail: deborah.jennings@piperrudnick.com

Employers

Piper Marbury Rudnick & Wolfe LLP (Partner)

Clients Represented

On Behalf of Piper Marbury Rudnick & Wolfe LLP

Alliant Energy

JENNINGS, III, Horace

44 Canal Center Plaza
Alexandria, VA 22314
Tel: (703)706-3567
Fax: (703)706-3356
Registered: LDA
EMail: jenningsh@closeup.org

Employers

Close Up Foundation (Director, Government Relations)

JENNINGS, Jim

600 New Hampshire Ave. NW
Suite 601
Washington, DC 20037
Tel: (202)333-7400
Fax: (202)333-1638
Registered: LDA
EMail: JJennings@hillandknowlton.com

Employers

Hill and Knowlton, Inc. (Exec. Managing Director, Co-Director, U.S. Healthcare Practice)

JENNINGS, Patricia

1611 Duke St.
Alexandria, VA 22314
Tel: (703)683-7410
Fax: (703)683-7527

Employers

American Moving and Storage Ass'n (V. President, Programs and Services)
Nat'l Institute of Certified Moving Consultants (V. President, Programs and Services)

JENNY, Louis J.

1725 K St. NW
Suite 1212
Washington, DC 20006
Tel: (202)833-8383
Fax: (202)331-7442
Registered: LDA

Employers

Nat'l Ass'n of Water Companies (Director, Congressional Relations)

JENSEN, Alexa

810 Vermont Ave. NW
Room 510
Washington, DC 20420
Tel: (202)273-5615
Fax: (202)273-6791

Employers

Department of Veterans Affairs (Congressional Relations Officer)

JENSEN, Amy

1201 F St. NW
Suite 200
Washington, DC 20004
Tel: (202)554-9000
Fax: (202)554-0496

Aide to Speaker of the House and Chief Deputy Whip, Rep. J. Dennis Hastert (R-IL), 1995-2001.

Employers

Nat'l Federation of Independent Business (Director, Public Policy/House)

JENSEN, James E.

2101 Constitution Ave. NW
Washington, DC 20418
Tel: (202)334-2000
Fax: (202)334-1684

Employers

Nat'l Academy of Sciences (Director, Congressional and Government Affairs)

JENSEN, John E.

2300 N St. NW
Washington, DC 20037-1128
Tel: (202)663-8000
Fax: (202)663-8007
Registered: LDA
EMail: john.jensen@shawpittman.com

Attorney/Advisor, Office of General Counsel, Environmental Protection Agency, 1987-90.

Employers

Shaw Pittman (Partner)

Clients Represented

On Behalf of Shaw Pittman

Nat'l Coalition for Minority Business
Universal Systems and Technology Inc.

JENSEN, Paul H.

700 13th St. NW
Suite 1000
Washington, DC 20005
Tel: (202)347-6633
Fax: (202)347-8713
Registered: FARA

Former Executive Assistant and Counselor to the U.S. Secretary of Labor.

Employers

Powell Tate (Consultant)

JENSEN, Thomas C.

401 Ninth St. NW
Suite 1000
Washington, DC 20004
Tel: (202)274-2945
Fax: (202)274-2994
Registered: LDA

Associate Director, Natural Resources, Council on Environmental Quality, The White House, 1992-97.Counsel, Senate Committee on Energy and Natural Resources, 1989-92.

Employers

Troutman Sanders LLP (Partner)

Clients Represented

On Behalf of Troutman Sanders LLP

Cinergy Corp.
Longhorn Pipeline
PG&E Corp.
Trigen Energy Corp.
Wisconsin Energy Corp.

JEPSON, Frank

1133 15th St. NW
Suite 640
Washington, DC 20005
Tel: (202)466-2520
Fax: (202)296-4419
EMail: frank@ala-national.org

Employers

American Logistics Ass'n (V. President, Exchange and MWR Affairs)

JERNIGAN, Bryan

1101 15th St. NW
Suite 600
Washington, DC 20005
Tel: (202)785-1122
Ext: 20
Fax: (202)785-5019

Employers

Sugar Ass'n, Inc. (Director, Communications)

JESIEN, George

8630 Fenton St.
Suite 410
Silver Spring, MD 20910
Tel: (301)588-8252
Fax: (301)588-2842

Employers
American Ass'n of University Affiliated Programs for Persons with Developmental Disabilities (Exec. Director)

JETTON, Jr., C. Loring

2445 M St. NW
Washington, DC 20037-1420
Tel: (202)663-6000
Fax: (202)663-6363
Registered: LDA, FARA

Employers
Wilmer, Cutler & Pickering (Partner)

JEWELL-KELLY, Starla

3929 Old Lee Hwy.
Suite 91-A
Fairfax, VA 22030-2401
EMail: starla@ncea.com
Tel: (703)359-8973
Fax: (703)359-0972

Employers
Nat'l Community Education Ass'n (Exec. Director)

JIMENEZ, Michael C.

444 N. Capitol St. NW
Suite 840
Washington, DC 20001
Tel: (202)434-8013
Fax: (202)434-8018
Registered: LDA

Associate Staff Member to Rep. Jim Kolbe (R-AZ) and the House Appropriations Committee, 1995-98. Professional Staff Member, Senate Committee on Governmental Affairs, 1994. Special Assistant to the Deputy Assistant Secretary for Congressional Affairs and Acting Director for Congressional Affairs, Department of Veterans Affairs, 1989-93. Aide to Senator John S. McCain, III (R-AZ), 1984-89. Served in the U.S. Air Force, 1972-76.

Employers
Strategic Impact, Inc. (Principal)

Clients Represented

On Behalf of Strategic Impact, Inc.
Central Arizona Irrigation and Drainage District
Commercial Weather Services Ass'n (CWSA)
Hispanic Ass'n of Colleges and Universities
Internat'l Arid Lands Consortium
Maricopa-Stanfield Irrigation and Drainage District
Pascua Yaqui Tribe of Arizona
Santa Cruz Water and Power Districts Ass'n
Southwest Border Technology Project

JIMISON, John W.

1225 19th St. NW
Suite 800
Washington, DC 20036
Tel: (202)955-6067
Fax: (202)293-0307
Registered: LDA, FARA

Counsel, Subcommittee on Fossil and Synthetic Fuels, House Committee on Energy and Commerce, 1981. Head of Energy Section, Congressional Research Service, Library of Congress, 1976-80. Professional Staff Member, Senate Commerce Committee, 1974-75. Energy Policy Analyst, Congressional Research Service, Library of Congress, 1972-74.

Employers
Berliner, Candon & Jimison (Partner)

Clients Represented

On Behalf of Berliner, Candon & Jimison
Wireless Location Industry Ass'n

JINDAL, Gorav

1775 I St. NW
Washington, DC 20006
Tel: (202)261-3482
Fax: (202)261-3333

Former Staff Attorney, Bureau of Competition, Federal Trade Commission.

Employers
Dechert (Associate)

JIPPING, Thomas L.

717 Second St. NE
Washington, DC 20002
EMail: tjipping@freecongress.org
Tel: (202)546-3000
Fax: (202)543-5605

Employers
Free Congress Research and Education Foundation (V. President, Policy)

JOCHUM, Jim

800 Connecticut Ave. NW
Washington, DC 20006
Tel: (202)533-1100
Fax: (202)533-1134

Employers
Accenture (Senior Manager, Government Affairs)

JODREY, Darrel Cox

1350 I St. NW
Suite 1210
M/S 1006
Washington, DC 20005-3305
Tel: (202)589-1006
Fax: (202)589-1001
Registered: LDA

Employers
Johnson & Johnson, Inc. (Director, Federal Affairs)

JOFFE, Bruce

10015 Main St.
Fairfax, VA 22031-3489
EMail: sgia@sgia.org
Tel: (703)385-1335
Fax: (703)273-0456

Employers
Screenprinting & Graphic Imaging Ass'n Internat'l (Director, Communication)

JOFFE, Mark S.

1800 K St. NW
Suite 720
Washington, DC 20006
Tel: (202)457-6633
Fax: (202)457-6636

Employers
Law Offices of Mark S. Joffe

JOFFE, Paul L.

1400 16th St. NW
Suite 501
Washington, DC 20036-2266
Tel: (202)797-6800
Fax: (202)797-6646

Employers
Nat'l Wildlife Federation - Office of Federal and Internat'l Affairs (Associate Director, Advocacy)

JOGE, Carmen

504 C St. NE
Washington, DC 20002
Tel: (202)543-1771
Fax: (202)546-2143

Employers
Congressional Hispanic Caucus Institute (CHCI) (Programs Director)

JOHANNES, Mary P.

1350 I St. NW
Suite 1060
Washington, DC 20005
Tel: (202)962-5384
Fax: (202)336-7223
Registered: LDA

Employers
Ford Motor Co. (Legislative Manager Financial Services)
Self-employed as an independent consultant.

Clients Represented

As an independent consultant
Ford Motor Credit Co. (Legal Department)

JOHANSEN, Lawrence A.

1100 17th St. NW
Seventh Floor
Washington, DC 20036
Tel: (202)223-8196
Fax: (202)872-1948

Employers
American Academy of Actuaries (President)

JOHANSEN, Marc

6352 Rolling Mill Pl.
Suite 102
Springfield, VA 22152-2354
Tel: (703)866-0020
Fax: (703)866-3526

Employers
American Astronautical Soc. (V. President, Public Policy)

JOHANSON, David S.

2100 M St. NW
Suite 200
Washington, DC 20037
EMail: djohanson@stewartlaw.com
Tel: (202)785-4185
Fax: (202)466-1286
Registered: LDA

Employers
Stewart and Stewart (Associate)

Clients Represented

On Behalf of Stewart and Stewart
Floral Trade Council
The Gates Rubber Co.
Libbey, Inc.
PPG Industries
Ranchers-Cattlemen Legal Action Fund
The Timken Co.
Torrington Co.

JOHN, David

214 Massachusetts Ave. NE
Washington, DC 20002
Tel: (202)546-4400
Fax: (202)546-8328

Employers
Heritage Foundation (Senior Policy Analyst, Social Security)

JOHNS, Karin L.

1025 Connecticut Ave. NW
Suite 700
Washington, DC 20036
Tel: (202)785-8866
Fax: (202)835-0003
Registered: LDA

Former Legislative Director to Rep. Phil English (R-PA). Former Legislative Assistant to Rep. Fred Grandy (R-IA).

Employers
Nat'l Ass'n of Independent Colleges and Universities (Director, Tax Policy)

JOHNS, Marie C.

1710 H St. NW
11th Floor
Washington, DC 20006
EMail: marie.c.johns@verizon.com
Tel: (202)392-3700
Fax: (202)887-9195

Employers
Verizon Washington, DC, Inc. (President and Chief Exec. Officer)

JOHNS, Robert S.

3517 16th St. NW
Washington, DC 20010
Tel: (202)588-1697
Fax: (202)588-1244

Employers
Nat'l Dental Ass'n (Exec. Director)

JOHNSEN, R. Christian

499 S. Capitol St. SW
Suite 600
Washington, DC 20003
EMail: cjohnsen@joneswalker.com
Tel: (202)828-8363
Fax: (202)828-6907
Registered: LDA

Employers
Jones, Walker, Waechter, Poitevent, Carrere & Denegre, L.L.P. (Managing Partner)

Clients Represented

On Behalf of Jones, Walker, Waechter, Poitevent, Carrere & Denegre, L.L.P.
ACS Government Solutions Group
American Ass'n of Nurse Anesthetists
The Audubon Institute
Avondale Industries, Inc.
Bailey Link
Baton Rouge, Louisiana, City of
Boys Town USA
Broward, Florida, County of
Burk-Kleinpeter, Inc.
Canal Barge Co., Inc.
Columbus General, L.L.C.
Committee of Unsecured Creditors
General Category Tuna Ass'n
General Electric Co.
Imedia.IT, Inc.
Ingram Barge Company
Internat'l Shipholding Corp.

Internat'l Technology Resources, Inc.
Jacobus Tenbroek Memorial Fund
JRL Enterprises
LA Center for the Blind
Lockheed Martin Global Telecommunications
Louisiana Superdome
Martinez and Curtis
Mechanical Equipment Co., Inc.
Mesa, Arizona, City of
The MetroVision Chamber
New Orleans, Louisiana, Port of
Oracle Corp.
Peoplesoft USA, Inc.
Petroleum Helicopters
Raytheon Co.
Science & Engineering Associates, Inc.
Sewerage and Water Board of New Orleans
St. Gabriel, Louisiana, Town of
Stewart Enterprises, Inc.
TransOceanic Shipping
Tulane University
United Special Transport Air Resources, LLC (USTAR)
University of New Orleans Foundation

JOHNSEN, Wayne D.

1776 K St. NW
Washington, DC 20006
Tel: (202)719-7000
Fax: (202)719-7049

Employers
Wiley, Rein & Fielding (Partner)

JOHNSON, Adam

One Dupont Circle NW
Suite 340
Washington, DC 20036-1170
EMail: johnsona@act.org
Tel: (202)223-2318
Fax: (202)293-2223

Employers
ACT, Inc. (Government Relations Assistant)

JOHNSON, Aleck

2120 L St. NW
Suite 400
Washington, DC 20037
Tel: (202)478-6301
Fax: (202)478-6171

Employers
Leslie Harris & Associates (Senior Policy Analyst)

Clients Represented

On Behalf of Leslie Harris & Associates
AOL Time Warner
EdLinc
Leadership Conference on Civil Rights

JOHNSON, Dr. Alice

1225 New York Ave. NW
Suite 400
Washington, DC 20005
Tel: (202)898-0100
Fax: (202)898-0203
Registered: LDA

Employers
Nat'l Turkey Federation (V. President, Scienctific and Regulatory Affairs)

JOHNSON, Allen F.

1255 23rd St. NW
Suite 200
Washington, DC 20037-1174
EMail: ajohnson@hauck.com
Tel: (202)452-8100
Fax: (202)833-3636

Employers
Hauck and Associates (Exec. V. President)
Nat'l Oilseed Processors Ass'n (President)

Clients Represented

On Behalf of Hauck and Associates
Nat'l Oilseed Processors Ass'n

JOHNSON, Amy

601 Pennsylvania Ave. NW
South Bldg., Suite 900
Washington, DC 20004
EMail: amjohnson@locklaw.com
Tel: (202)434-8163
Fax: (202)639-8238
Registered: LDA

Employers
Lockridge Grindal & Nauen, P.L.L.P. (Senior Federal Relations Specialist)

Clients Represented

On Behalf of Lockridge Grindal & Nauen, P.L.L.P.
Joint Powers Board
St. Louis/Lake Counties Regional Rail Authority

JOHNSON, Angela

1300 Pennsylvania Ave. NW
Suite 700
Washington, DC 20004
EMail: aljnaic@aol.com
Tel: (202)289-4336
Fax: (202)289-4329

Employers
Nat'l Ass'n of Investment Companies (Chief Administrator)

JOHNSON, Betsy

1001 Connecticut Ave. NW
Suite 925
Washington, DC 20036
Tel: (202)457-0540
Fax: (202)457-0549

Employers
Washington Council of Agencies (Exec. Director)

JOHNSON, Broderick D.

1120 20th St. NW
Suite 1000
Washington, DC 20036
Tel: (202)457-3810
Fax: (202)457-2244
Deputy Assistant to the President for Legislative Affairs, Executive Office of the President, The White House, 1998-2000. Chief Minority Counsel, House Committee on Education and the Workforce, 1995-98.

Employers
AT&T (V. President of Congressional Relations)

JOHNSON, Hon. C. Donald "Don"

2550 M St. NW
Washington, DC 20037-1350
Tel: (202)457-6000
Fax: (202)457-6315
Member, U.S. House of Representatives, 1993-95 (D-GA); Chief Textile Negotiator, U.S. Trade Representative.

Employers
Patton Boggs, LLP (Partner)

JOHNSON, Calvin P.

600 13th St. NW
Washington, DC 20005-3096
Tel: (202)756-8348
Fax: (202)756-8087
Registered: LDA
EMail: cjohnson@mwe.com
Senior Legislative Assistant to Senator Richard S. Schweiker (R-PA), 1975-76.

Employers
McDermott, Will and Emery (Legislative Director)

Clients Represented

On Behalf of McDermott, Will and Emery
American College of Gastroenterology
American Import Shippers Ass'n
Applied Benefits Research Corp.
Coalition for Employment Opportunities
Coalition for Reasonable and Fair Taxation (CRAFT)
Fashion Accessories Shippers Ass'n
Georgia-Pacific Corp.
Government Development Bank of Puerto Rico
Internat'l Hearing Soc.
Mariner Health Group, Inc.
McGlotten & Jarvis
RJR Nabisco Holdings Co.
Rural Referral Centers Coalition
Telecorp PCS Inc.
TJTC Recovery Project Coalition
VIVRA
WOTC Project

JOHNSON, Candice

501 Third St. NW
Washington, DC 20001-2797
Tel: (202)434-1100
Fax: (202)434-1377

Employers
Communications Workers of America (Associate Director, Communications)

JOHNSON, Carl T.

1725 Jefferson Davis Hwy.
Suite 1004
Arlington, VA 22202-4102
EMail: cjohnson@cganet.com
Tel: (703)412-0900
Fax: (703)412-0128
Registered: LDA

Employers
Compressed Gas Ass'n (President)

JOHNSON, Cass

1130 Connecticut Ave. NW
Suite 1200
Washington, DC 20036-3954
Tel: (202)862-0500
Fax: (202)862-0570

Employers
American Textile Manufacturers Institute (Assistant Director, International Trade Division)

JOHNSON, IV, Charles W.

1333 New Hampshire Ave. NW
Suite 400
Washington, DC 20036
Tel: (202)887-4000
Fax: (202)887-4288
Registered: LDA

Employers
Akin, Gump, Strauss, Hauer & Feld, L.L.P. (Counsel)

Clients Represented

On Behalf of Akin, Gump, Strauss, Hauer & Feld, L.L.P.
American Legion
Banro American Resources Inc.
Bombardier, Inc.
Bridgestone/Firestone, Inc.
Capital Gaming Internat'l, Inc.
Granite Broadcasting Co.
OMNIPLEX World Services Corp.
Pfizer, Inc.
Wartsila Diesel, Inc.
Woodmont Corporation

JOHNSON, Ph.D., Craig

8300 Greensboro Dr.
Suite 750
McLean, VA 22102
Tel: (703)790-8466
Fax: (703)790-8631

Employers
American Academy of Audiology (Chair, Government Affairs Committee)

JOHNSON, Cynthia K.

1455 Pennsylvania Ave. NW
Suite 375
M/S 4072
Washington, DC 20004
EMail: ckjohnson@ti.com
Tel: (202)628-3133
Fax: (202)628-2980
Registered: LDA

Employers
Texas Instruments (Director, Government Relations-International Trade)

JOHNSON, D. Lynn

1300 Wilson Blvd.
Suite 900
Arlington, VA 22209
EMail: dlynn@eastman.com
Tel: (703)524-7660
Fax: (703)524-7707
Registered: LDA

Employers
Eastman Chemical Co. (V. President, Government Relations)

JOHNSON, Darwin G.

2001 M St. NW
Fourth Floor
Washington, DC 20036
Tel: (202)533-5660
Fax: (202)533-8580
Former Chief, Fiscal Analysis Branch, Office of Management and Budget, Executive Office of the President, The White House.

Employers
Barents Group LLC (Chairman)

JOHNSON, David

1010 Wisconsin Ave. NW
Ninth Floor
Washington, DC 20007
EMail: djohnson@gmabrands.com
Tel: (202)337-9400
Fax: (202)337-4508

Employers
Grocery Manufacturers of America (Representative, Government Affairs)

JOHNSON, David E.

1300 Connecticut Ave. NW
Suite 600
Washington, DC 20036
Tel: (202)775-8116
Fax: (202)223-0358
Registered: LDA, FARA
Former Executive Director, Democratic Senatorial Campaign Committee, 1985-86; Administrative Assistant to Senator George Mitchell (D-ME); Deputy Assistant Secretary, Department of Health and Human Services; Counsel, U.S. Governmental Affairs Committee, U.S. Senate.

Employers
Griffin, Johnson, Dover & Stewart (V. President)

Clients Represented

On Behalf of Griffin, Johnson, Dover & Stewart

Air Transport Ass'n of America
American Agrisurance
American Fish Spotters Ass'n
American Petroleum Institute
American Soc. of Anesthesiologists
Arthur Andersen LLP
Avue Technologies
Computer Coalition for Responsible Exports
Council of Smaller Enterprises
Dell Computer Corp.
Deloitte Consulting
Delta Dental Plans Ass'n
Fannie Mae
Hong Kong Economic and Trade Office
The Justice Project, Inc.
Nat'l Music Publishers' Ass'n
United Technologies Corp.
Wilmer, Cutler & Pickering
Wine and Spirits Wholesalers of America

JOHNSON, David T.

1779 Massachusetts Ave. NW
Suite 615
Washington, DC 20036
Tel: (202)332-0600
Fax: (202)462-4559

Employers

Center for Defense Information (Research Director)

JOHNSON, Dennis R.

1400 16th St. NW
Suite 400
Washington, DC 20036-2220
Tel: (202)518-6311
Fax: (202)234-3550
Registered: LDA
EMail: djohnson@ofwlaw.com

Employers

Olsson, Frank and Weeda, P.C. (Principal)

Clients Represented

On Behalf of Olsson, Frank and Weeda, P.C.

Schwan's Sales Enterprises

JOHNSON, Denny

1776 Massachusetts Ave. NW
Suite 400
Washington, DC 20036
Tel: (202)872-0611
Fax: (202)872-0643
EMail: djohnson@planning.org

Employers

American Planning Ass'n (Information Coordinator)

JOHNSON, Don

200 Independence Ave. SW
Room 341H
Washington, DC 20201
Tel: (202)690-5500
Fax: (202)690-8168

Employers

Department of Health and Human Services - Health Care Financing Administration (Deputy Director, Office of Legislation)

JOHNSON, Douglas D.

419 Seventh St. NW
Suite 500
Washington, DC 20004
Tel: (202)626-8820
Fax: (202)347-3668
Registered: LDA

Employers

Nat'l Right to Life Committee (Legislative Director)

JOHNSON, Douglas K.

2500 Wilson Blvd.
Arlington, VA 22201-3834
Tel: (703)907-7686
Fax: (703)907-7693
Registered: LDA
EMail: djohnson@ce.org

Employers

Consumer Electronics Ass'n (Director, Technology Policy)

JOHNSON, Frances Brigham

1312 18th St. NW
Suite 300
Washington, DC 20036
Tel: (202)296-4563
Fax: (202)887-9178

Employers

Agribusiness Council (Director, Enterprise Policy and Development)

JOHNSON, Haley

515 King St.
Suite 420
Alexandria, VA 22314-3103
Tel: (703)684-5570
Fax: (703)684-6048
EMail: hjohnson@clarionmr.com

Employers

CLARION Management Resources, Inc. (Account Executive)
Internat'l Soc. of Hospitality Consultants (Administrative Director)

Clients Represented

On Behalf of CLARION Management Resources, Inc.

Ass'n of Women in the Metal Industries
Internat'l Soc. of Hospitality Consultants

JOHNSON, Hugh N. "Rusty"

600 Pennsylvania Ave. SE
Suite 304
Washington, DC 20003
Tel: (202)544-9614
Fax: (202)544-9618
Registered: LDA

Employers

Brown and Company, Inc.

Clients Represented

On Behalf of Brown and Company, Inc.

American Defense Internat'l, Inc.
American Shipbuilding Ass'n
Bird-Johnson Co.
Merant PVCS
Sperry Marine Inc.

JOHNSON, James H.

1275 Pennsylvania Ave. NW
Tenth Floor
Washington, DC 20004
Tel: (202)347-1434
Fax: (202)833-9392
Registered: LDA
Former aide to Senator Trent Lott (R-MS).

Employers

Barbour Griffith & Rogers, Inc. (Of Counsel)
Johnson Co. (Principal)

Clients Represented

On Behalf of Barbour Griffith & Rogers, Inc.

Delta Air Lines
Lockheed Martin Corp.
University of Southern Mississippi

On Behalf of Johnson Co.

Coffee Reserve
DATRON, Inc.
Hattiesburg, Mississippi, City of
Kongsberg Defense & Aerospace

JOHNSON, Jr., James L.

1120 20th St. NW
Suite 1000
Washington, DC 20036
Tel: (202)457-2255
Fax: (202)457-2746
EMail: jljohnson@att.com

Employers

AT&T (V. President, Congressional Affairs)

JOHNSON, Jr., James W. M.

1156 15th St. NW
Suite 1019
Washington, DC 20005
Tel: (202)296-4820

Employers

United States Beet Sugar Ass'n (President)

JOHNSON, Jay S.

1455 F St. NW
Suite 225
Washington, DC 20005
Tel: (202)638-3307
Fax: (202)783-6947
Registered: LDA
EMail: jjohnson@bjllp.com
Deputy General Counsel (1988-2000), Assistant General Counsel for Fisheries (1979-88), and Assistant General Counsel for Administration (1976-79), all at the National Oceanic and Atmospheric Administration, Department of Commerce.

Employers

Ball Janik, LLP (Of Counsel)

Clients Represented

On Behalf of Ball Janik, LLP

Icicle Seafoods, Inc.

JOHNSON, Joel

3000 K St. NW
Suite 300
Washington, DC 20007
Tel: (202)295-8787
Fax: (202)295-8799
Former Senior Advisor to the President for Policy and Communications, The White House, during the Clinton administration. Former Aide to Senator Tom Daschle (D-SD).

Employers

The Harbour Group (Managing Director)

JOHNSON, Joel L.

1250 I St. NW
Suite 1200
Washington, DC 20005-3924
Tel: (202)371-8420
Fax: (202)371-8471

Employers

Aerospace Industries Ass'n of America (V. President, International Affairs)

JOHNSON, Jr., John Griffith

1299 Pennsylvania Ave. NW
Tenth Floor
Washington, DC 20004-2400
Tel: (202)508-9578
Fax: (202)508-8578
EMail: johngriffithjohnson@paulhastings.com

Employers

Paul, Hastings, Janofsky & Walker LLP (Partner)

Clients Represented

On Behalf of Paul, Hastings, Janofsky & Walker LLP

Pappas Telecasting Cos.

JOHNSON, Joyce L.

440 First St. NW
Third Floor
Washington, DC 20001-2085
Tel: (202)638-2952
Fax: (202)638-4004

Employers

Child Welfare League of America (Press Secretary)

JOHNSON, Karen

733 15th St. NW 2nd Floor
Washington, DC 20005
Tel: (202)628-8669
Fax: (202)785-8576

Employers

Nat'l Organization for Women (V. President, Membership)

JOHNSON, Kay N.

1501 Wilson Blvd.
Suite 1100
Arlington, VA 22209
Tel: (703)524-0810
Fax: (703)524-1921
EMail: aif@aif.org

Employers

Animal Industry Foundation (V. President)

JOHNSON, Kimberly

1420 New York Ave. NW
Suite 1050
Washington, DC 20005
Tel: (202)638-1950
Fax: (202)638-7714
Registered: LDA
Former Legislative Assistant, Project Director to Rep. Carolyn Kilpatrick (D-MI).

Employers

Van Scoyoc Associates, Inc. (Legislative Counsel)

Clients Represented

On Behalf of Van Scoyoc Associates, Inc.

Baltimore, Maryland, City of
Bristol-Myers Squibb Co.
Chicago State University
Jackson State University
Sickle Cell Disease Ass'n of America

JOHNSON, Kirt C.

1301 K St. NW
Washington, DC 20005-3333
Tel: (202)414-1616
Fax: (202)414-1301
Registered: LDA
EMail: kirt.c.johnson@us.pwcglobal.com
Former Chief of Staff/Tax Counsel to Rep. Philip M. Crane (R-IL).

Employers

PriceWaterhouseCoopers (Director)

Clients Represented

On Behalf of PriceWaterhouseCoopers

Alliance Capital Management LP
American Ass'n of Nurse Anesthetists
Plum Creek Timber Co.
Steam Generator Coalition

JOHNSON, Kristin A.

700 13th St. NW
Suite 350
Washington, DC 20005
Tel: (202)637-0040
Fax: (202)637-0041

Employers

Rhoads Group (Exec. Assistant)

JOHNSON, L. Oakley

1399 New York Ave. NW
Suite 900
Washington, DC 20005
Tel: (202)585-5804
Fax: (202)585-5820
Registered: LDA

Employers

American Internat'l Group, Inc. (Senior V. President, Corporate and International Affairs)

JOHNSON, Laurindo

1776 K St.
Washington, DC 20006
Tel: (202)452-7941
Fax: (202)452-7989

Employers

Buchanan Ingersoll, P.C.

JOHNSON, Leah

1101 Pennsylvania Ave. NW
Suite 1000
Washington, DC 20004
Tel: (202)879-6800
Fax: (202)783-1873
Registered: LDA

Employers

Citigroup (Director, Public Affairs)

JOHNSON, Lionel C.

1101 Pennsylvania Ave. NW
Suite 1000
Washington, DC 20004
Tel: (202)879-6855
Fax: (202)783-4460
Registered: LDA
EMail: johnsonli@citi.com

Employers

Citigroup (V. President, International Government Relations)

JOHNSON, Lori A.

122 S. Royal St.
Alexandria, VA 22314-3328
Tel: (703)838-0373
Fax: (703)838-1698
EMail: lori@cordia.com

Employers

Cordia Cos. (Exec. Assistant)

JOHNSON, Mark R.

1101 17th St. NW
Suite 610
Washington, DC 20036
Tel: (202)887-6770
Fax: (202)887-5014
Registered: LDA

Employers

Maersk Inc. (V. President, Government Affairs)

JOHNSON, Marlene M.

1307 New York Ave. NW
Eighth Floor
Washington, DC 20009-5728
Tel: (202)737-3699
Fax: (202)737-3657
EMail: marlenej@nafsa.org

Employers

NAFSA: Ass'n of Internat'l Educators (Exec. Director and Chief Exec. Officer)

JOHNSON, Marvin

122 Maryland Ave. NE
Washington, DC 20002
Tel: (202)544-1681
Fax: (202)546-0738
Registered: LDA

Employers

American Civil Liberties Union (Legislative Counsel, Free Speech)

JOHNSON, Michele I.

2021 Massachusetts Ave. NW
Washington, DC 20036
Tel: (202)232-9033
Fax: (202)232-9044
EMail: mjohnson@aafp.org

Employers

American Academy of Family Physicians (Government Relations Representative)

JOHNSON, Mike

805 15th St. NW
Suite 430
Washington, DC 20005
Tel: (202)371-9792
Fax: (202)789-2405
EMail: mike.johnson@wswa.org

Employers

Wine and Spirits Wholesalers of America (Director, Government Relations)

JOHNSON, Nancie S.

601 Pennsylvania Ave. NW
Suite 325, North Bldg.
Washington, DC 20004
Tel: (202)728-3661
Fax: (202)728-3649

Employers

DuPont (V. President, Government Affairs)

JOHNSON, Nils W.

201 Maryland Ave. NE
Washington, DC 20002
Tel: (202)543-7200
Fax: (202)543-0616
Registered: LDA
EMail: nils@mgninc.com

Director of Energy, Environment and Natural Resources to Senator Larry E. Craig (R-ID), 1991-2000. Senior Legislative Assistant to Rep. Larry E. Craig (R-ID), 1987-90. Professional Staff, House Committee on Interior and Insular Affairs, 1987-90. Staff, Forest Service, Department of Agriculture, 1970-87.

Employers

McClure, Gerard & Neuenschwander, Inc. (Principal)

Clients Represented

On Behalf of McClure, Gerard & Neuenschwander, Inc.

American Gaming Ass'n
Barrick Goldstrike Mines, Inc.
Boise State University
Brush Wellman, Inc.
Coachella Valley Water District
Echo Bay Mining
Family Farm Alliance (Project Transfer Council)
Harquehala Irrigation District
Hecla Mining Co.
Helli USA Airways
Henderson, Nevada, City of
Howard Hughes Corp.
Idaho Power Co.
Independence Mining Co., Inc.
Internat'l Bottled Water Ass'n
Nat'l Endangered Species Act Reform Coalition
Native American Mohegans Inc.
Nevada Test Site Development Corp.
Newmont Mining Corp.
Pershing Co. Water Conservation District of Nevada
Placer Dome U.S. Inc.
Private Fuels Storage, L.L.C.
Quest Nevada, Inc.
Space Imaging, Inc.
Stirling Energy Systems
Verizon Wireless
Wellton-Mohawk Irrigation and Drainage District
Westlands Water District
The Williams Companies

JOHNSON, Jr., O. Thomas

1201 Pennsylvania Ave. NW
Washington, DC 20004-2401
Tel: (202)662-6000
Fax: (202)662-6291
EMail: ojohnson@cov.com

Employers

Covington & Burling (Partner)

Clients Represented

On Behalf of Covington & Burling

AT&T

JOHNSON, Owen M.

1333 New Hampshire Ave. NW
Suite 400
Washington, DC 20036
Tel: (202)887-4000
Fax: (202)887-4288

Employers

Akin, Gump, Strauss, Hauer & Feld, L.L.P. (Partner)

JOHNSON, Paul W.

1615 L St. NW
Suite 1000
Washington, DC 20036
Tel: (202)659-0330
Fax: (202)467-4382
Registered: LDA, FARA
EMail: johnsonp@fleishman.com

Former Chief of Staff to Rep. Eugene A. Chappie (R-CA).

Employers

Fleishman-Hillard, Inc (Exec. V. President, Senior Partner and General Manager)

Clients Represented

On Behalf of Fleishman-Hillard, Inc

Jacobs Engineering Group Inc.
Knoll Pharmaceutical Co.
SBC Communications Inc.

JOHNSON, Randel K.

1615 H St. NW
Washington, DC 20062-2000
Tel: (202)463-5448
Fax: (202)463-3445

Employers

Chamber of Commerce of the U.S.A. (V. President, Labor Policy)

JOHNSON, Randy

1350 I St. NW
Suite 400
Washington, DC 20005-3306
Tel: (202)371-6900
Fax: (202)842-3578

Employers

Motorola, Inc. (Director, U.S. Human Resource Legislative Affairs)

JOHNSON, Richard A.

555 12th St. NW
Washington, DC 20004-1206
Tel: (202)942-5000
Fax: (202)942-5999
Registered: FARA
EMail: Richard_Johnson@aporter.com

Law Clerk to Judge Eugene A. Wright, U.S. Court of Appeals, Ninth Circuit, Seattle, Washington, 1976-77. Associate General Counsel for International Trade, Department of Commerce, 1980-81.

Employers

Arnold & Porter (Partner)

JOHNSON, Robert L.

One BET Plaza
1900 W Pl. NE
Washington, DC 20018
Tel: (202)608-2000
Fax: (202)608-2595

Employers

BET Holdings II, Inc. (Chief Exec. Officer/Chairman)

JOHNSON, II, Robert W.

Watergate Office Bldg.
Suite 508
2600 Virginia Ave. NW
Washington, DC 20037
Tel: (202)337-6817
Fax: (202)337-3462
Registered: LDA, FARA

Member, Commodity Policy Advisory Committee, Office of the U.S. Trade Representative, 1984-86. Senior Staff Assistant to the Chairman, Committee on Appropriations, U.S. House of Representatives, 1978-79. Attorney, Office of the General Counsel, Department of Agriculture, 1976-77. Colonel, U.S. Marine Corps Reserves, 1968-71.

Employers

Johnson, Rogers & Clifton, L.L.P.

JOHNSON, Sheldon

119 Oronoco St.
Suite 300
Alexandria, VA 22314-2015
Tel: (703)519-7555
Fax: (703)519-7747
EMail: sheldon@careauto.org

Employers

Coalition for Auto Repair Equality (CARE) (Operations Director)

JOHNSON, Stephen

214 Massachusetts Ave. NE
Washington, DC 20002
Tel: (202)546-4400
Fax: (202)546-8328

Employers

Heritage Foundation (Latin America Policy Analyst)

JOHNSON, Stephen R.

901 15th St. NW
Suite 700
Washington, DC 20005-2301
Tel: (202)371-6000
Fax: (202)371-6279
Registered: LDA, FARA

Employers

Verner, Liipfert, Bernhard, McPherson and Hand, Chartered (Associate)

JOHNSON, Steven A.

1920 L St. NW
Washington, DC 20036
EMail: sjohnson@kamber.com
Tel: (202)223-8700
Fax: (202)659-5559

Employers

The Kamber Group (V. President)

Clients Represented

On Behalf of The Kamber Group

Sheet Metal Workers' Internat'l Ass'n

JOHNSON, Susan E.

1090 Vermont Ave NW
Eighth Floor
Washington, DC 20005
EMail: respro@erols.com
Tel: (202)408-7038
Fax: (202)408-0948
Registered: LDA

Employers

Sue E. Johnson Associates (Exec. Director)

Clients Represented

On Behalf of Sue E. Johnson Associates

Council of Urban and Economic Development
First Nationwide Bank
Real Estate Services Providers Council

JOHNSON, Victor

1307 New York Ave. NW
Eighth Floor
Washington, DC 20009-5728
Tel: (202)737-3699
Fax: (202)737-3657

Employers

NAFSA: Ass'n of Internat'l Educators (Director, Government Relations)

JOHNSON, W. Stanfield

1001 Pennsylvania Ave. NW
Suite 1100
Washington, DC 20004-2595
Tel: (202)624-2500
Fax: (202)628-5116

Employers

Crowell & Moring LLP (Partner)

Clients Represented

On Behalf of Crowell & Moring LLP

United Technologies Corp.

JOHNSTON, Ann Thomas G.

601 13th St. NW
Suite 410 South
Washington, DC 20005
Tel: (202)737-0100
Fax: (202)628-3965
Registered: LDA

Employers

R. Duffy Wall and Associates (V. President)

Clients Represented

On Behalf of R. Duffy Wall and Associates

American Gas Ass'n
CIGNA Corp.
Entergy Services, Inc.
Novartis Corp.

JOHNSTON, Jr., Charles R.

801 Pennsylvania Ave. NW
Suite 800
Washington, DC 20004
EMail: crj@bdbc.com
Tel: (202)508-3423
Fax: (202)508-3402
Registered: FARA

Counsel, Subcommittee on Trade, Senate Finance Committee, 1978-80. Attorney-Advisor, International Trade Commission, 1976-78.

Employers

Baker, Donelson, Bearman & Caldwell, P.C. (Shareholder)

Clients Represented

On Behalf of Baker, Donelson, Bearman & Caldwell, P.C.

American Friends of Turkey
American-Turkish Council
Azerbaijan, Embassy of the Republic of
Dillingham Construction, Inc.
E-Tech
Gibson Guitar Corp.
Howard Energy Internat'l
Pakistani-American Business Ass'n
U.S.-Azerbaijan Council, Inc.

JOHNSTON, David A.

1010 Massachusetts Ave. NW
Suite 350
Washington, DC 20001
EMail: djohnston@dbia.org
Tel: (202)682-0110
Fax: (202)682-5877

Employers

Design-Build Institute of America (Director, Technical Programs and PAC)

JOHNSTON, Hon. J. Bennett

The Willard Office Bldg.
1455 Pennsylvania Ave. NW, Suite 200
Washington, DC 20004
Tel: (202)737-0683
Fax: (202)737-0693
Registered: LDA

Member, U.S. Senate (D-LA), 1972-97.

Employers

Johnston & Associates, LLC (Partner)

Clients Represented

On Behalf of Johnston & Associates, LLC

The AES Corp.
Aiken and Edgenfield Counties, South Carolina, Economic Development Partnership of
Alliance for Competitive Electricity
American Animal Husbandry Coalition PAC
Avondale Industries, Inc.
Battelle Memorial Institute
Burns and Roe Enterprises, Inc.
California, State of
COGEMA, Inc.
Coushatta Tribe of Louisiana
Drexel University
Edison Internat'l
EG&G
Enron Corp.
Hearthstone
The Ickes & Enright Group
Jefferson Parish Council
Lockheed Martin Corp.
Louisiana State University Medical Center Foundation
Morgan, Lewis & Bockius LLP
MTS Systems Inc.
New Orleans Internat'l Airport
New Orleans, Louisiana, Regional Transit Authority of
Northrop Grumman Corp.
Nuclear Energy Institute
Oregon, State of
Regional Transit Authority
Riverdeep Inc.
Tulane University
Tunica Biloxi Indians of Louisiana
United Gamefowl Breeders Ass'n, Inc.
University of New Orleans
University of Southwestern Louisiana
USEC, Inc.
Washington, State of
Xcel Energy, Inc.

JOHNSTON, James

1150 17th St. NW
Washington, DC 20036
EMail: jjohnston@aei.org
Tel: (202)862-5800
Fax: (202)862-7177

Employers

American Enterprise Institute for Public Policy Research (Resident Fellow)

JOHNSTON, Kelly D.

1350 I St. NW
Suite 300
Washington, DC 20005
Tel: (202)639-5900
Fax: (202)639-5932
Registered: LDA

Employers

Nat'l Food Processors Ass'n (Exec. V. President, Government Affairs and Communications)

JOHNSTON, Matthew

1201 F St. NW
Suite 500
Washington, DC 20004
Tel: (202)824-1600
Fax: (202)824-1651
Registered: LDA

Employers

Health Insurance Ass'n of America (Assistant Federal Legislative Director/Political Affairs Director)

JOHNSTON, Megan

1600 Pennsylvania Ave. NW
107 E. Wing
Washington, DC 20500
Tel: (202)456-2230
Fax: (202)456-1806

Employers

Executive Office of the President - The White House (Exec. Assistant to the Deputy Director for Legislation)

JOHNSTON, N. Hunter

The Willard Office Bldg.
1455 Pennsylvania Ave. NW, Suite 200
Washington, DC 20004
Tel: (202)737-0683
Fax: (202)737-0693
Registered: LDA

Employers

Johnston & Associates, LLC (Partner)

Clients Represented

On Behalf of Johnston & Associates, LLC

Aiken and Edgenfield Counties, South Carolina, Economic Development Partnership of
Alliance for Competitive Electricity
Avondale Industries, Inc.
COGEMA, Inc.
Coushatta Tribe of Louisiana
Edison Internat'l
The Ickes & Enright Group
Jefferson Parish Council
Lockheed Martin Corp.
Louisiana State University Medical Center Foundation
New Orleans Internat'l Airport
New Orleans, Louisiana, Regional Transit Authority of
Northrop Grumman Corp.
Nuclear Energy Institute
Regional Planning Commission
Regional Transit Authority
Riverdeep Inc.
Sewerage and Water Board of New Orleans
Tulane University
Tunica Biloxi Indians of Louisiana
University of New Orleans
University of Southwestern Louisiana

JOHNSTON, Philip W.

1330 New Hampshire Ave. NW
Suite 122
Washington, DC 20036
Tel: (202)659-8008
Fax: (202)659-8519
Registered: LDA

Employers

Philip W. Johnston Associates (President)

Clients Represented

On Behalf of Philip W. Johnston Associates

Bio-Vascular, Inc.
Dimock Community Health Center
East Boston Neighborhood Health Center
Holyoke Hospital
Massachusetts Extended Care Federation
Nat'l Ass'n of Community Health Centers
Springfield, Massachusetts, City of

JOLLIE, Susan

913 E. Taylor Run Pkwy.
Suite 303
Alexandria, VA 22302
Tel: (703)548-3676
Fax: (703)548-0926
Registered: LDA

Employers

Cash, Smith & Wages

Clients Represented

On Behalf of Cash, Smith & Wages

Nat'l Women's History Museum

JOLLY, Ernest

1010 Wisconsin Ave. NW
Suite 520
Washington, DC 20007
Tel: (202)298-8226
Fax: (202)298-8074

Employers

Executive Leadership Council and Foundation (Interim Exec. Director)

JOLLY, Thomas R.

818 Connecticut Ave. NW
Tenth Floor
Washington, DC 20006
Tel: (202)293-3330
Fax: (202)293-3515
Registered: LDA
EMail: tjolly@jollyrissler.com
Legislative Assistant (1970-73) and Legislative Counsel (1973-78) to Rep. William Ford (D-MI). Counsel and Staff Director, Subcommittee on Agricultural Labor (1973-77) and Subcommittee on Postsecondary Education (1977-78), House Committee on Education and Labor.

Employers
Jolly/Rissler, Inc. (Chairman)

Clients Represented

On Behalf of Jolly/Rissler, Inc.
AFLAC, Inc.
CNA Insurance Cos.
Internat'l Union of Police Ass'ns
Sallie Mae, Inc.

JONAS, John F.

2550 M St. NW
Washington, DC 20037-1350
Tel: (202)457-6000
Fax: (202)457-6315
Registered: LDA
EMail: jjonas@pattonboggs.com
Tax Counsel, House Committee on Ways and Means, 1981-86. Legislative Director to Rep. Bob Shamansky (D-OH), 1980-81. Legislative Counsel to Rep. Elizabeth Holtzman (D-NY), 1978-80. Office of the General Counsel, Department of Health, Education and Welfare, 1976-78.

Employers
Patton Boggs, LLP (Partner)

Clients Represented

On Behalf of Patton Boggs, LLP
American College of Gastroenterology
American Family Mutual Insurance Co.
American Medical Rehabilitation Providers Ass'n
Ass'n for Advanced Life Underwriting
Bristol-Myers Squibb Co.
Business Insurance Coalition
Forethought Group/Forethought Life Insurance Co.
HCR-Manor Care, Inc.
Hoffmann-La Roche Inc.
Illinois Department of Human Services
Mars, Inc.
MassMutual Financial Group
Minimed, Inc.
Mutual Legislative Committee
New York Life Insurance Co.
New York State Ass'n of Health Care Providers
Newport Group
Newspaper Ass'n of America
Northwestern Mutual Life Insurance Co.
Patient Access to Transplantation (PAT) Coalition
Preneed Insurers Government Programs Coalition
Schoenke & Associates
University Medical Associates

JONAS, III, W. James

1801 K St. NW
Washington, DC 20006
Tel: (202)775-7100
Fax: (202)857-0172
EMail: jjonas@arterhadden.com

Employers
Arter & Hadden (Partner)

Clients Represented

On Behalf of Arter & Hadden
South West Florida Enterprises, Inc.
Tesoro Petroleum Corp.

JONES, Anne

1317 F St. NW
Suite 600
Washington, DC 20004
Tel: (202)638-2121
Fax: (202)638-7045
Registered: LDA
EMail: jones@wexlergroup.com

Employers
The Wexler Group (Principal/Director)

Clients Represented

On Behalf of The Wexler Group
Burst Networks Inc.
DCH Technology Inc.
EarthWatch, Inc.
Lockheed Martin Corp.

JONES, Arnita

400 A St. SE
Washington, DC 20003
Tel: (202)544-2422
Fax: (202)544-8307
EMail: ajones@theaha.org

Employers
American Historical Ass'n (Exec. Director)

JONES, Barbara

1150 18th St. NW
Suite 200
Washington, DC 20036
Tel: (202)223-0820
Fax: (202)223-2385
Registered: LDA
EMail: barbara.jones1@halliburton.com

Employers
Halliburton/Brown & Root (Director, Government Affairs)

JONES, Belva W.

1101 15th St. NW
Suite 202
Washington, DC 20005
Tel: (202)785-3232
Fax: (202)223-9741
EMail: bjones@assnhq.com

Employers
The Kellen Company (Account Executive)

JONES, Beverly E.

409 Ninth St. NW
Suite 610 South
Washington, DC 20004
Tel: (202)737-3234
Fax: (202)737-0264
EMail: jonesbe@arlaw.com
Worked for Securities and Exchange Commission.

Employers
Adams and Reese LLP (Special Counsel)

Clients Represented

On Behalf of Adams and Reese LLP
Dominion Resources, Inc.
Technology Integration Group

JONES, C. Todd

1718 Connecticut Ave. NW
Suite 700
Washington, DC 20009
Tel: (202)518-0847
Fax: (202)785-3849

Employers
Nat'l Education Knowledge Industry Ass'n (NEKIA) (President)

JONES, Carolyn

1200 G St. NW
Suite 400
Washington, DC 20005
Tel: (202)783-8700
Fax: (202)783-8750
Registered: LDA

Employers
AdvaMed (Associate V. President, Technology and Regulatory Affairs)

JONES, Cathy L.

8001 Braddock Rd.
Springfield, VA 22160
Tel: (703)321-8519
Fax: (703)321-7342
EMail: clj@nrtw.org

Employers
Concerned Educators Against Forced Unionism (Coordinator)

JONES, Clara

Ariel Rios Federal Bldg.
(1301-MC)
1200 Pennsylvania Ave. NW
3rd Floor
Washington, DC 20460
Tel: (202)564-3701
Fax: (202)501-1545
EMail: jones.clara@epa.gov

Employers
Environmental Protection Agency (Staff Assistant, Congressional and Intergovernmental Relations)

JONES, Diane R.

1250 H St. NW
Suite 800
Washington, DC 20005
Tel: (202)857-3462
Fax: (202)857-3401
Registered: LDA
EMail: diane.r.jones@kodak.com

Employers
Eastman Kodak Co. (Director, Health Imaging Affairs)

JONES, E. Dale

19564 Club House Rd.
Mont. Village, MD 20886
Tel: (301)670-6733
Fax: (301)670-6735
EMail: atllp@aol.com

Employers
Ass'n for Transportation, Law, Logistics and Policy (Exec. Director)

JONES, Elizabeth F.

1717 K St. NW
Suite 200
Washington, DC 20006
Tel: (202)452-9545
Fax: (202)452-9328
EMail: info@aic-faic.org

Employers
American Institute for Conservation of Historic and Artistic Works (Exec. Director)

JONES, Erika Z.

1909 K St. NW
Washington, DC 20006
Tel: (202)263-3000
Fax: (202)263-3300
Registered: LDA

Employers
Mayer, Brown & Platt (Partner)

Clients Represented

On Behalf of Mayer, Brown & Platt
Alliance of Automobile Manufacturers, Inc.
Cable & Wireless, Inc.

JONES, Jake

1401 H St. NW
Suite 700
Washington, DC 20005
Tel: (202)414-6746
Fax: (202)414-6743
Registered: LDA

Employers
DaimlerChrysler Corp. (Sr. Manager, Legislative Affairs)

JONES, James

1310 G St. NW
Suite 690
Washington, DC 20005-3000
Tel: (202)639-0724
Fax: (202)639-0794

Employers
Mexico-U.S. Business Committee, U.S. Council (Chairman)

JONES, James D. E.

1001 Connecticut Ave. NW
Suite 610
Washington, DC 20036
Tel: (202)887-5240
Fax: (202)887-0282
EMail: jjones@panynj.gov
Former Aviation Bilateral Negotiator, Department of Transportation, 1974-80.

Employers
Port Authority of New York and New Jersey (Deputy Washington Representative)

JONES, James R.

1501 M St. NW
Suite 700
Washington, DC 20005-1702
Tel: (202)463-4300
Fax: (202)463-4394
Registered: LDA, FARA
EMail: jjones@manatt.com
Ambassador to Mexico, 1993-97. Member, U.S. House of Representatives (D-OK), 1973-87. Appointments Secretary to the President, White House, 1965-69. Legislative Assistant to Congressman Ed Edmondson (D-OK), 1961-64.

Employers
Manatt, Phelps & Phillips, LLP (Senior Counsel)

Clients Represented

On Behalf of Manatt, Phelps & Phillips, LLP
BellSouth Corp.
Bolivia, Embassy of
CEMEX Central, S.A. de C.V.
Congo, Republic of
DAG Petroleum
Land Grant Development
Pelican Butte Corp.
Poseidon Resources Corp.
Verizon Communications

JONES, Janet L.

1500 Pennsylvania Ave. NW
Room 3025MT
Washington, DC 20220
Tel: (202)622-0581
Fax: (202)622-0534

Employers
Department of Treasury (Scheduling Coordinator to the Assistant Secretary, Office of Legislative Affairs)

JONES, Jeffrey

1701 Pennsylvania Ave. NW
Suite 520
Washington, DC 20006
Tel: (202)739-9180
Fax: (202)659-5920

Employers
U.S.-Russia Business Council (Program Manager)

JONES, Jerry D.

8315 Lee Hwy.
Fairfax, VA 22031
Tel: (703)208-7200
Fax: (703)208-7132

Employers
United Mine Workers of America (V. President)

JONES, Jerry H.

2121 K St. NW
Suite 650
Washington, DC 20037
EMail: Jerry@GlobalUSAinc.com
Tel: (202)296-2400
Fax: (202)296-2409

Staff Assistant to the President; Special Assistant to the President; and Staff Secretary to the President, The White House, 1971-72.

Employers
Global USA, Inc. (Advisor)

JONES, Kevin Darrow

1120 19th St. NW
Eighth Floor
Washington, DC 20036
Tel: (202)467-6900
Fax: (202)467-6910
Registered: LDA

Legislative Assistant to Senator Lloyd Bentsen (D-TX), 1991-93. Legislative Assistant to Senator Bob Krueger (D-TX), 1993.

Employers
Womble Carlyle Sandridge & Rice, P.C.

Clients Represented

On Behalf of Womble Carlyle Sandridge & Rice, P.C.
Alameda Corridor-East Construction Authority
North Carolina Global TransPark Authority

JONES, Leroy D.

Ten G St. NE
Suite 480
Washington, DC 20002
Tel: (202)347-7936
Fax: (202)347-5237
Registered: LDA

Employers
Brotherhood of Locomotive Engineers (V. President and National Legislative Representative)

JONES, Lora Lynn

2760 Eisenhower Ave.
Suite 250
Alexandria, VA 22314
Tel: (703)329-1982
Fax: (703)329-2411

Employers
The Stone Group, Inc. (Senior V. President)

JONES, Michael

1849 C St. NW
Room 6253
Washington, DC 20240
EMail: michael_j_jones@ios.doi.gov
Tel: (202)208-7693
Fax: (202)208-7619

Employers
Department of Interior (Special Assistant to the Director, Office of Congressional and Legislative Affairs)

JONES, Michael J.

3328 S. Second St.
Arlington, VA 22204
Tel: (703)521-8844
Fax: (703)521-8866
Registered: LDA

Employers
Capitol Capital Group

Clients Represented

On Behalf of Capitol Capital Group
Washington Consulting Group

JONES, Murray W.

1201 F St. NW
Suite 1000
Washington, DC 20004-1077
Tel: (202)626-7235
Fax: (202)626-7208
Registered: LDA

Employers
R. J. Reynolds Tobacco Co. (Director, Federal Government Affairs)

JONES, Nolan

444 N. Capitol St. NW
Suite 267
Washington, DC 20001-1512
EMail: njones@nga.org
Tel: (202)624-5360
Fax: (202)624-5313

Employers
Nat'l Governors' Ass'n (Director, Human Resources Group)

JONES, Randall T.

50 F St. NW
Suite 900
Washington, DC 20001
EMail: rjones@ncfc.org
Tel: (202)626-8700
Fax: (202)626-8722
Registered: LDA

Employers
Nat'l Council of Farmer Cooperatives (Senior V. President, Government and Public Affairs)

JONES, Richard

4647 Forbes Blvd.
Lanham, MD 20706-4380
Tel: (301)459-9600
Fax: (301)459-7924

Employers
AMVETS (American Veterans of World War II, Korea and Vietnam) (National Legislative Director)

JONES, Richard M.

One Physics Ellipse
College Park, MD 20740-3843
Tel: (301)209-3100
Fax: (301)209-0846

Employers
American Institute of Physics (Senior Liaison, Government and Institutional Relations)

JONES, Robert C.

2550 M St. NW
Washington, DC 20037-1350
EMail: rjones@pattonboggs.com
Tel: (202)457-6000
Fax: (202)457-6315
Registered: LDA, FARA

Legislative Assistant to Senator Barbara Mikulski (D-MD), 1989-90. Counsel (1987-89) and Professional Staff Member (1986-87), Senate Appropriations Committee.

Employers
Patton Boggs, LLP (Partner)

Clients Represented

On Behalf of Patton Boggs, LLP
500 C Street Associates, L.P.
Baltimore Symphony Orchestra
Barat College
Cambridge Technologies
Cellular Telecommunications and Internet Ass'n
General Aviation Manufacturers Ass'n
Genome Dynamics, Inc.
Kansas City Southern Industries
Massachusetts Maritime Academy
MCI WorldCom Corp.
Nat'l Aquarium
Sebesta, Blomberg and Associates, Inc.
Sheriff Jefferson Parrish, Louisiana
Union Pacific Railroad Co.

JONES, Robert J.

555 12th St. NW
Washington, DC 20004-1206
EMail: Robert_Jones@aporter.com
Tel: (202)942-5000
Fax: (202)942-5999

Employers
Arnold & Porter (Partner)

JONES, Roberts T.

1201 New York Ave. NW
Suite 700
Washington, DC 20005
Tel: (202)289-2888
Fax: (202)289-1303

Employers
Nat'l Alliance of Business (President and Chief Exec. Officer)

JONES, Jr., Roy S.

1155 Connecticut Ave. NW
Suite 1200
Washington, DC 20036
EMail: rjones@dc.bhb.com
Tel: (202)659-5800
Fax: (202)659-1027
Registered: LDA

Employers
Birch, Horton, Bittner & Cherot (Shareholder)

Clients Represented

On Behalf of Birch, Horton, Bittner & Cherot
Cordova, Alaska, City of
Elim Native Corp.
Emmonak Corp.
The Eyak Corp.
Feld Entertainment Inc.
Leisnoi
Old Harbor Native Corp.
Prince William Sound Regional Citizen's Advisory Council
Salt River Pima Maricopa Indian Community

JONES, Shelton

1150 17th St. NW
Suite 701
Washington, DC 20036
EMail: sheltonj@dittus.com
Tel: (202)775-1401
Fax: (202)775-1404

Employers
Dittus Communications (Senior Director)

Clients Represented

On Behalf of Dittus Communications
CapNet
Citigroup
Council for Affordable Reliable Energy (CARE)
Dell Computer Corp.
FM Watch
Intel Corp.
Pernod Ricard
VeriSign/Network Solutions, Inc.

JONES, Stephen A.

1730 Pennsylvania Ave. NW
Suite 1200
Washington, DC 20006-4706
Tel: (202)737-0500
Fax: (202)626-3737

Employers
King & Spalding (Partner)

JONES, Susan Henshaw

401 F St. NW
Washington, DC 20001
Tel: (202)272-2448
Fax: (202)272-2564

Employers
Nat'l Building Museum (President)

JONES, Terry

1001 G St. NW
Suite 500 West
Washington, DC 20001
Tel: (202)434-4100
Fax: (202)434-4646

Employers
Keller and Heckman LLP

Clients Represented

On Behalf of Keller and Heckman LLP
Food Distributors Internat'l (NAWGA-IFDA)

JONES, Thomas

1111 19th St. NW
Suite 403
Washington, DC 20036
EMail: tjones@aaes.org
Tel: (202)296-2237
Fax: (202)296-1151

Employers
American Ass'n of Engineering Societies (Director, Public Policy)

JONES, Lt. Col. Tom

615 Slaters Ln.
Alexandria, VA 22313
Tel: (703)684-5500
Fax: (703)684-3478

Employers
Salvation Army (National Community Relations and Development Secretary)

JONES, Vera M.

14th and Constitution Ave. NW
Room 7814A
Washington, DC 20230
Tel: (202)482-2309
Fax: (202)501-4828

Employers
Department of Commerce - Economic Development Administration (Communications and Congressional Liaison Assistant)

JONES, W. Proctor

The Willard Office Bldg.
1455 Pennsylvania Ave. NW,
Suite 200
Washington, DC 20004
Tel: (202)737-0683
Fax: (202)737-0693
Registered: LDA

Staff Member, Senate Committee on Appropriations, 1970-97. Staff Director, Subcommittee on Energy and Water Development, Senate Committee on Appropriations, 1972-80 and 1986-92.

Employers
Johnston & Associates, LLC (Partner)

Clients Represented
On Behalf of Johnston & Associates, LLC
Aiken and Edgenfield Counties, South Carolina, Economic Development Partnership of
Battelle Memorial Institute
Burns and Roe Enterprises, Inc.
COGEMA, Inc.
Coushatta Tribe of Louisiana
Drexel University
EG&G
The Ickes & Enright Group
Jefferson Parish Council
Lockheed Martin Corp.
Louisiana State University Medical Center Foundation
Minnesota Valley Alfalfa Producers
Morgan, Lewis & Bockius LLP
MTS Systems Inc.
New Orleans Internat'l Airport
Northrop Grumman Corp.
Nuclear Energy Institute
Regional Planning Commission
Riverdeep Inc.
Sewerage and Water Board of New Orleans
Tulane University
Tunica Biloxi Indians of Louisiana
University of New Orleans
USEC, Inc.
Westinghouse Government Services Group
Xcel Energy, Inc.

JONES, Wiley N.

1747 Pennsylvania Ave. NW
Suite 850
Washington, DC 20006
Tel: (202)393-0100
Fax: (202)393-0102
Registered: LDA
EMail: wiley.jones@qwestisp.net

Employers
The Anschutz Co. (V. President and Washington Counsel)

JONKERS, Roy K.

6723 Whittier Ave.
Suite 303A
McLean, VA 22101
Tel: (703)790-0320
Fax: (703)790-0264

Employers
Ass'n of Former Intelligence Officers (Exec. Director)

JORAY, Millie

4301 Wilson Blvd.
Arlington, VA 22203-1860
Tel: (703)907-5808
Fax: (703)907-5516
EMail: millie.joray@nreca.org

Employers
Nat'l Rural Electric Cooperative Ass'n (Manager, Advocacy Tools Division)

JORDAN, Daryle

2300 N St. NW
Washington, DC 20037-1128
Tel: (202)663-8000
Fax: (202)663-8007
Registered: LDA
EMail: daryle.jordan@shawpittman.com

Employers
Shaw Pittman (Associate)

JORDAN, G. Harris

1030 15th St. NW
Suite 1028
Washington, DC 20005
Tel: (202)216-9116
Fax: (202)216-0363
Registered: LDA
EMail: prg@his.com

Served as Legislative Director for Rep. Phil Crane (R-IL), a member of the House Committee on Ways and Means, 1978-88.

Employers
The Potomac Research Group LLC (Managing Partner)

Clients Represented
On Behalf of The Potomac Research Group LLC
Bayer Corp.
Biotechnology Industry Organization
Safety Reasearch Center, Inc.
Spatial Technologies Industry Ass'n
United States Cane Sugar Refiners' Ass'n

JORDAN, Josie

1555 Connecticut Ave.
Suite 200
Washington, DC 20036
Tel: (202)483-1057
Fax: (202)462-9043
EMail: josie@fnider.org

Employers
Friends of the Nat'l Institute of Dental and Craniofacial Research (Deputy Exec. Director)

JORDAN, Lloyd J.

2099 Pennsylvania Ave. NW
Suite 100
Washington, DC 20006
Tel: (202)955-3000
Fax: (202)955-5564
EMail: ljjordan@hklaw.com

Employers
Holland & Knight LLP (Senior Counsel)

JORDAN, Patricia

1401 K St. NW
Suite 700
Washington, DC 20005
Tel: (202)842-5030
Fax: (202)842-5048
Registered: LDA
EMail: pjordan757@aol.com

Legislative aide to Rep. Glenn Anderson (D-CA), 1981-82. Legislative aide to Rep. Olympia Snowe (R-ME), 1983-86.

Employers
Jordan & Associates, Inc. (President)

Clients Represented
On Behalf of Jordan & Associates, Inc.
Imperial Beach, California, City of
Livermore Amador Valley Transit Ass'n
Livermore, California, City of
Provo, Utah, City of
South Salt Lake, Utah, City of

JORDAN, Robert

1330 Connecticut Ave. NW
Washington, DC 20036-1795
Tel: (202)429-3000
Fax: (202)429-3902
Registered: LDA
EMail: rjordan@steptoe.com

General Counsel and Special Assistant to the Secretary for Civil Functions (1967-71), Deputy General Counsel (1967), Department of the Army. Executive Assistant for Enforcement, Office of the Secretary, Department of the Treasury, 1965-67. Assistant U.S. Attorney, Department of Justice, 1964-65. Special Assistant for Civil Rights, Office of the Secretary, Department of Defense, 1963-64.

Employers
Steptoe & Johnson LLP (Partner)

Clients Represented
On Behalf of Steptoe & Johnson LLP
TAPS Renewal Task Force

JORDAN, Stephen

1615 H St. NW
Washington, DC 20062-2000
Tel: (202)659-6000
Fax: (202)463-5836
Registered: LDA
EMail: sjordan@uschamber.com

Employers
Chamber of Commerce of the U.S.A. (Director, Trade Policy Latin America)

JORDAN, Wendy

321 D St. NE
Washington, DC 20002
Tel: (202)548-8322
Fax: (202)548-8326
Registered: LDA
EMail: wjordan@siscorpdc.com

Special Assistant for International Security Affairs (1999-2001), and Office of NATO Policy (1998-1999), Department of Defense.

Employers
SISCORP

Clients Represented
On Behalf of SISCORP
Science Applications Internat'l Corp. (SAIC)
Textron Inc.
ThermoTrex Corp.

JORDAN, Whit

1133 21st St. NW
Suite 900
Washington, DC 20036
Tel: (202)463-4100
Fax: (202)463-4198
EMail: whit.jordan@bellsouth.com

Employers
BellSouth Corp. (V. President, Federal Regulatory)

JORDAN, William

1200 G St. NW
Suite 900
Washington, DC 20005-3802
Tel: (202)383-3700
Fax: (202)383-3718
Registered: LDA

Employers
McGraw-Hill Cos., The (Director, Government Affairs and Communications)

JORGE, M. Fabiana

1300 Connecticut Ave. NW
Suite 600
Washington, DC 20036
Tel: (202)223-7017
Fax: (202)223-7013
Registered: LDA
EMail: mfjorge@aol.com

Employers
MFJ Internat'l (Principal)

JORPELAND, Marshall S.

8224 Old Courthouse Rd.
Vienna, VA 22182-3808
Tel: (703)556-6272
Fax: (703)556-6291
EMail: mjorpeland@ncrahq.org

Employers
Nat'l Court Reporters Ass'n (Director, Communications)

JORY, David C.

601 13th St. NW
Suite 410 South
Washington, DC 20005
Tel: (202)737-0100
Fax: (202)628-3965
Registered: LDA

Legislative Counsel to Senator Robert Packwood (R-OR), 1983-85. Legislative Counsel to Rep. James Weaver (D-OR), 1981-83.

Employers
R. Duffy Wall and Associates (Senior V. President)

Clients Represented
On Behalf of R. Duffy Wall and Associates
BHP (USA) Inc.
Entergy Services, Inc.
Metropolitan Mortgage and Securities, Inc.
Oracle Corp.
Software Finance and Tax Executives Council
Verizon Communications
Waddell & Reed Financial, Inc.

JOSEFIAK, Thomas

310 First St. SE
Washington, DC 20003
Tel: (202)863-8500
Fax: (202)863-8820

Employers
Republican Nat'l Committee (Chief Counsel)

JOSEPH, Bruce G.

1776 K St. NW
Washington, DC 20006
Tel: (202)719-7000
Fax: (202)719-7049
Registered: LDA

Employers
Wiley, Rein & Fielding (Partner)

Clients Represented
On Behalf of Wiley, Rein & Fielding
Prodigy

JOSEPH, Jeff

2500 Wilson Blvd.
Arlington, VA 22201-3834
Tel: (703)907-7664
Fax: (703)907-7690
EMail: jjoseph@ce.org

Employers
Consumer Electronics Ass'n (V. President, CEA Communications and Strategic Relationships)

JOSEPH, Joel

317 Massachusetts Ave. NE
Suite 300
Washington, DC 20002
Tel: (202)789-3960
Fax: (202)789-1813

Employers
The Cuneo Law Group, P.C. (Of Counsel)

JOSEPH, Kevin

1225 I St. NW
Washington, DC 20005
Tel: (202)289-0425

Employers
Allegiance Telecom, Inc. (V. President, Government Affairs)

JOSEPH, Michael

600 New Hampshire Ave. NW
11th Floor
Washington, DC 20037
EMail: mj@dejlaw.com
Tel: (202)944-3000
Fax: (202)944-3068
Registered: LDA

Employers
Dyer Ellis & Joseph, P.C. (Partner)

Clients Represented

On Behalf of Dyer Ellis & Joseph, P.C.
Avondale Industries, Inc.

JOSEPH, Rachel

518 C St. NE
Washington, DC 20002
Tel: (202)466-3234
Fax: (202)466-2587
Registered: LDA

Employers
Americans United for Separation of Church and State (Legislative Associate)

JOSEPH, III, Thomas L.

440 First St. NW
Suite 440
Washington, DC 20001
EMail: tjoseph@naco.org
Tel: (202)393-2404
Fax: (202)393-2666

Employers
Los Angeles, California, County of (Deputy Chief Legislative Representative)

JOSEPHSON, Marvin

600 Pennsylvania Ave. SE
Washington, DC 20003
Tel: (202)879-7710
Fax: (202)879-7728

Employers
The Nat'l PAC (Treasurer)

JOSHI, Sangeeta

816 Connecticut Ave. NW
Suite 300
Washington, DC 20006
Tel: (202)530-1270
Fax: (202)530-1920
Registered: LDA

Employers
Nordhaus Haltom Taylor Taradash & Bladh LLP (Paralegal)

JOSI, Christian

1007 Cameron St.
Alexandria, VA 22314
Tel: (703)836-8602
Fax: (703)836-8606

Employers
American Conservative Union (Exec. Director)

JOST, John C.

1200 New Hampshire Ave. NW
Suite 800
Washington, DC 20036-6802
EMail: jjost@dlalaw.com
Tel: (202)776-2000
Fax: (202)776-2222

Employers
Dow, Lohnes & Albertson, PLLC (Member)

JOSTEN, R. Bruce

1615 H St. NW
Washington, DC 20062-2000
EMail: bjosten@uschamber.com
Tel: (202)463-5310
Fax: (202)887-3403
Registered: LDA

Employers
Chamber of Commerce of the U.S.A. (Exec. V. President)

JOURNEY, Drexel D.

1101 Connecticut Ave. NW
Suite 600
Washington, DC 20036
Tel: (202)778-6400
Fax: (202)778-6460
Legal Staff Member (1952-74) and General Counsel (1974-77), Federal Power Commission.

Employers
Schiff Hardin & Waite (Partner)

JOWYK, Xenia

1420 New York Ave. NW
Suite 1100
Washington, DC 20005
EMail: xjowyk@rer.org
Tel: (202)639-8400
Fax: (202)639-8442

Employers
Real Estate Roundtable (Director, Publications)

JOY, Michele F.

1101 Vermont Ave. NW
Suite 604
Washington, DC 20005-3521
EMail: mjoy@aopl.org
Tel: (202)408-7970
Fax: (202)408-7983
Registered: LDA

Employers
Ass'n of Oil Pipelines (General Counsel and Secretary)

JOYCE, Chris

8219 Leesburg Pike
Vienna, VA 22182-2625
Tel: (703)790-5300
Fax: (703)442-8819

Employers
Cable & Wireless, Inc. (V. President, Chief Financial Officer and Treasurer)

JOYCE, Cynthia

Hubert H. Humphrey Bldg.
200 Independence Ave. SW
Room 406G
Washington, DC 20201
EMail: cjoyce@os.dhhs.gov
Tel: (202)690-6786
Fax: (202)690-7380

Employers
Department of Health and Human Services (Correspondence Specialist, Congressional Liaison)

JOYCE, Frederick

601 Pennsylvania Ave. NW
11th Floor, North Bldg.
Washington, DC 20004-2601
Tel: (202)756-3300
Fax: (202)756-3333

Employers
Alston & Bird LLP (Partner)

JOYCE, Jonathan R.

1333 New Hampshire Ave. NW
Suite 400
Washington, DC 20036
Tel: (202)887-4000
Fax: (202)887-4288
Registered: LDA

Employers
Akin, Gump, Strauss, Hauer & Feld, L.L.P.

Clients Represented

On Behalf of Akin, Gump, Strauss, Hauer & Feld, L.L.P.
Bombardier, Inc.

JOYCE, Sherman

1850 M St. NW
Suite 1095
Washington, DC 20036
EMail: SJoyce@ATRA.org
Tel: (202)682-1163
Fax: (202)682-1022
Registered: LDA

Employers
American Tort Reform Ass'n (President)

JOYNER, Nelson T.

11800 Sunrise Valley Drive
Suite 210
Reston, VA 20191
EMail: njoyner@fita.org
Tel: (703)620-1588
Fax: (703)620-4922

Employers
Federation of Internat'l Trade Ass'ns (FITA) (Chairman)

JUARBE, Jr., Frederico

200 Maryland Ave. NE
Washington, DC 20002
EMail: fjuarbe@vfwdc.org
Tel: (202)543-2239
Fax: (202)547-3196
Registered: LDA

Employers
Veterans of Foreign Wars of the U.S. (Director, National Veterans Service)

JUBERT, Drew Ann

910 17th St. NW
Tenth Floor
Washington, DC 20006
EMail: dajubert@acus.org
Tel: (202)778-4953
Fax: (202)463-7241

Employers
Atlantic Council of the United States (Director, Finance and Administration)

JUDD, Terry W.

1615 L St. NW
Suite 900
Washington, DC 20036
EMail: tjudd@apcoworldwide.com
Tel: (202)778-1000
Fax: (202)466-6002
Registered: FARA

Employers
APCO Worldwide (V. President)

JUDGE, Clark S.

1030 15th St. NW
Suite 1100
Washington, DC 20005
Tel: (202)783-4600
Fax: (202)783-4601
Speechwriter and Special Assistant to V. President, George Bush (1984-86) and President Ronald Reagan (1986-89).

Employers
White House Writers Group (Managing Director)

JUDGE, Dolly A.

325 Seventh St. NW
Suite 1200
Washington, DC 20004-1007
Tel: (202)783-7070
Fax: (202)347-2044

Employers
Pfizer, Inc. (Senior Director, Federal Relations)

JUDGE, J. Steven

1401 I St. NW
Suite 1000
Washington, DC 20005
EMail: sjudge@sia.com
Tel: (202)296-9410
Fax: (202)408-1913
Registered: LDA

Employers
Securities Industry Ass'n (Senior V. President, Government Affairs)

JULA, Tom

18928 Premiere Ct.
Gaithersburg, MD 20879
Tel: (301)670-0604
Fax: (301)840-1252

Employers
Composite Panel Ass'n (President)

JULIANO, Robert E.

2555 M St. NW
Suite 327
Washington, DC 20037
Tel: (202)223-3352
Registered: LDA

Employers
J/T Group (Co-Chairman)
Robert E. Juliano Associates (Chairman)

Clients Represented

On Behalf of J/T Group
AFL-CIO - Building and Construction Trades Department
Coalition for Group Legal Services
Internat'l Speedway Corp.
University Village Ass'n/Near West Side Conservation Community Council

JULIHN, Lawrence

1133 21st St. NW
Suite 710
Washington, DC 20036
Tel: (202)223-7683
Fax: (202)223-7687
Registered: FARA
EMail: ljulihn@samuelsinternational.com
Country Director (Europe) and Director, Bosnia Task Force, U.S. Navy, Office of the Secretary, Department of Defense, 1990-93. U.S. Navy, 1967-93.

Employers
Samuels Internat'l Associates, Inc. (Senior V. President)

Clients Represented
On Behalf of Samuels Internat'l Associates, Inc.
Angola, Government of the Republic of

JUNEMANN, Gregory J.

8630 Fenton St.
Suite 400
Silver Spring, MD 20910-3803
Tel: (301)565-9016
Fax: (301)565-0018
Registered: LDA
EMail: gjjunemann@worldnet.att.net

Employers
Internat'l Federation of Professional and Technical Engineers (International President)

JURKOVICH, Celesta S.

1455 Pennsylvania Ave. NW
Suite 1225
Washington, DC 20004
Tel: (202)783-1190
Fax: (202)347-5835
Registered: LDA

Employers
Chicago Board of Trade (Senior V. President, Government Relations)

JURKOVICH, Tom

21 Dupont Circle NW
Fifth Floor
Washington, DC 20036
Tel: (202)263-5900
Fax: (202)263-5901
Registered: LDA

Employers
Microsoft Corp. (Manager, Federal Government Affairs)

JURVELIN, Linda E.

Rayburn House Office Bldg.
Room B328
Washington, DC 20515
Tel: (202)225-2280
Fax: (292)453-5225

Employers
Department of Veterans Affairs (Assistant Director, Congressional Liaison Services)

KABEL, Robert J.

1501 M St. NW
Suite 700
Washington, DC 20005-1702
Tel: (202)463-4300
Fax: (202)463-4394
Registered: LDA
EMail: rkabel@manatt.com
Special Assistant to the President, The White House, 1982-84. Legislative Director for Senator Richard Lugar (R-IN), 1977-82. Former Legislative Assistant to Senator Paul Fannin (R-AZ).

Employers
The Bank Private Equity Coalition (Legislative Counsel)
Manatt, Phelps & Phillips, LLP (Partner)

Clients Represented
On Behalf of Manatt, Phelps & Phillips, LLP
AIS, Inc.
Alameda Corridor Transportation Authority
Asociacion Columbiana de Exportadores de Flores (ASOCOLFLORES)
The Bank Private Equity Coalition
Bolivia, Embassy of
CEMEX Central, S.A. de C.V.
Coalition for Global Perspectives
Downey Financial Corp.
Kean Tracers, Inc.
Land Grant Development
SESAC, Inc.
SWIPCO, U.S.
US Airways

KABOUS, Julie

400 N. Capitol St. NW
Washington, DC 20001
Tel: (202)824-7000
Fax: (202)824-7115
Registered: LDA

Employers
American Gas Ass'n (Manager, Government Relations)

KADEN, Alan S.

1001 Pennsylvania Ave. NW
Suite 800
Washington, DC 20004-2505
Tel: (202)639-7000
Fax: (202)639-7008
EMail: alan_kaden@ffhsj.com

Employers
Fried, Frank, Harris, Shriver & Jacobson (Partner)

KADRICH, Lee

4600 East-West HWy.
Suite 300
Bethesda, MD 20814
Tel: (301)654-6664
Fax: (301)654-3299
Registered: LDA

Employers
Automotive Aftermarket Industry Ass'n
Automotive Parts and Service Alliance (V. President, Government Affairs and International Trade)

KADROFSKE, Alan

1401 New York Ave. NW
Tenth Floor
Washington, DC 20005-2102
Tel: (202)737-1900
Fax: (202)659-3458
Registered: LDA
EMail: akadrofske@connerton-ray.com

Employers
Connerton & Ray (Legislative Assistant)

Clients Represented
On Behalf of Connerton & Ray
Internat'l Brotherhood of Teamsters
Laborers Health & Safety Fund
Laborers Institute for Training and Education
Laborers' Internat'l Union of North America
Laborers-AGC Education and Training Fund
Nat'l Environmental Education and Training Center

KADZIK, Peter J.

2101 L St. NW
Washington, DC 20037-1526
Tel: (202)785-9700
Fax: (202)887-0689
Registered: LDA, FARA
EMail: kadzikp@dsmo.com
Member, Justice Cluster, Presidential Transition Team, 1992. Assistant U.S. Attorney for the District of Columbia, Department of Justice, 1978-80. Law Clerk to Judge Thomas A. Flannery, U.S. District Court for the District of Columbia Circuit, 1977-78.

Employers
Dickstein Shapiro Morin & Oshinsky LLP (Partner)

Clients Represented
On Behalf of Dickstein Shapiro Morin & Oshinsky LLP
CaseNewHolland Inc.
Harbour Group Industries, Inc.
Internat'l Brotherhood of Teamsters
Malaysian Palm Oil Promotion Council
Nat'l Ass'n of Chain Drug Stores

KAEHLER, Norma H.

900 19th St. NW
Suite 350
Washington, DC 20006
Tel: (202)457-4762
Fax: (202)457-4767
Registered: LDA

Employers
Trans World Airlines, Inc. (V. President, Government Affairs)

KAFER, Krista

214 Massachusetts Ave. NE
Washington, DC 20002
Tel: (202)546-4400
Fax: (202)546-8328
Former Legislative Director to Rep. David McIntosh (R-IN).

Employers
Heritage Foundation (Education Policy Analyst)

KAFFKA, Jerry L.

2000 N. 14th St.
Suite 250
Arlington, VA 22201
Tel: (703)522-9500
Fax: (703)522-6847
Registered: LDA
EMail: rgijerry@aol.com

Employers
Rooney Group Internat'l, Inc. (Associate)

Clients Represented
On Behalf of Rooney Group Internat'l, Inc.
Deere Co. Worldwide Commercial & Consumer Equipment Division
DuPont Agricultural Products
General Atomics
Noesis Inc.

KAGANOWICH, Gar

1200 S. Hayes St.
Arlington, VA 22202-5050
Tel: (703)413-1100
Ext: 5632
Fax: (703)413-8111
Registered: LDA
EMail: gar_kaganowich@rand.org

Employers
RAND Corp. (Director, Washington External Affairs)

KAGDIS, J. A.

1401 I St. NW
Suite 600
Washington, DC 20005
Tel: (202)336-7400
Fax: (202)336-7527

Employers
United Technologies Corp. (Comanche Market Director)

KAGEN, Lynn

1509 16th St. NW
Washington, DC 20036-1426
Tel: (202)232-8777
Fax: (202)328-1846

Employers
Nat'l Ass'n for the Education of Young Children (President)

KAHANOVITZ, M.D., Neil

1350 Beverly Rd.
Suite 108
McLean, VA 22101
Tel: (703)748-0400
Fax: (703)748-0402
Registered: LDA
EMail: neilkahanovitz@patientadvocacy.org

Employers
Center for Patient Advocacy (Founder)

KAHLENBERG, Richard

1755 Massachusetts Ave. NW
Suite 400
Washington, DC 20036
Tel: (202)387-0400
Fax: (202)483-9430
EMail: kahlenberg@tcf.org

Employers
The Century Foundation (Senior Fellow)

KAHN, III, Charles N. "Chip"

1201 F St. NW
Suite 500
Washington, DC 20004
Tel: (202)824-1858
Fax: (202)824-1651
Registered: LDA
Staff Director, Subcommittee on Health (1995-98) and Republican Health Counsel (1986-93), House Committee on Ways and Means. Senior Health Policy Advisor to Senator David Durenburger (R-MN), 1984-86. Legislative Assistant for Health Policy to Senator Danforth Quayle (R-IN), 1983-84.

Employers
Health Insurance Ass'n of America (President)

KAHN, Melissa Jan

1620 L St. NW
Suite 800
Washington, DC 20036-5617
Tel: (202)659-3575
Fax: (202)659-1026
Registered: LDA

Employers
Metropolitan Life Insurance Co. (V. President)

KAHN, Peter J.

725 12th St. NW
Washington, DC 20005
Tel: (202)434-5000
Fax: (202)434-5029

Employers
Williams & Connolly (Partner)

KAHN, Sarah E.

555 12th St. NW
Washington, DC 20004-1206
Tel: (202)942-5000
Fax: (202)942-5999
EMail: Sarah_Kahn@aporter.com

Employers
Arnold & Porter (Partner)

KAIL, Michael

1330 Connecticut Ave. NW
Washington, DC 20036-1795
Tel: (202)429-3000
Fax: (202)429-3902
Registered: LDA
EMail: mkail@steptoe.com

Employers
Steptoe & Johnson LLP (Partner)

KAISER, Michael David

750 First St. NE
9th Floor
Washington, DC 20002
Tel: (202)745-2900
Fax: (202)745-2901
Registered: FARA
EMail: mkaiser@capitalconsultantscorp.com

Employers
Capital Consultants Corp. (President)

Clients Represented

On Behalf of Capital Consultants Corp.
American Indian Ass'n
Brookhill Redevelopment
Chehalis Reservation, Confederated Tribes of the
Cherokee Investment Partners, LLC
Development Corporation of Nevada
Dolce Internat'l
Emory University, Department of Internat'l Health-PAMM, USAID
Energy Conservation Program, Inc.
Guaynabo, Puerto Rico, City of
Hercules Development Corp.
Moscow State University
Omaha Tribe of Nebraska
Sister Cities Internat'l
South African Government/World Bank
Sports Corp., Ltd.
Trinity Partners, Inc.

KAISER, Timothy G.

511 Capitol Ct. NE
Suite 200
Washington, DC 20002-4937
Tel: (202)546-5445
Fax: (202)546-2280
Registered: LDA

Employers
Public Housing Authorities Directors Ass'n (Exec. Director)

KAJIKAWA, Makoto

1901 L St. NW
Suite 600
Washington, DC 20036
Tel: (202)466-6781
Fax: (202)466-6758
Registered: LDA
EMail: kajikawa@denjiren.com

Employers
Federation of Electric Power Cos. of Japan (Chief Representative)

KAKESAKO, Susan

2201 C St. NW
Room 7251
Washington, DC 20520-7261
Tel: (202)647-8722
Fax: (202)647-2762

Employers
Department of State - Bureau of Legislative Affairs (Legislative Management Officer)

KALAVRITINOS, Jack

1015 15th St. NW
Suite 802
Washington, DC 20005
Tel: (202)347-7474
Fax: (202)898-0068
Registered: LDA
EMail: jkalavritinos@acec.org

Employers
American Consulting Engineers Council (Director, Government Affairs and General Counsel)

KALEN, Pam

1299 Pennsylvania Ave. NW
Suite 800 West
Washington, DC 20004
Tel: (202)785-0500
Fax: (202)785-5277
Registered: LDA

Employers
The Carmen Group (V. President)
LMRC, Inc. (Senior Associate)
Managed Health Care Ass'n (Exec. Director)

Clients Represented

On Behalf of LMRC, Inc.
Managed Health Care Ass'n

KALEN, Sam

1050 Thomas Jefferson St. NW
Seventh Floor
Washington, DC 20007
Tel: (202)298-1800
Fax: (202)338-2416
EMail: smk@vnf.com
Special Assistant to Associate Solicitor, Office of the Solicitor, Department of the Interior, 1994-96.

Employers
Van Ness Feldman, P.C. (Of Counsel)

KALER, Robert G.

14500 Avion Pkwy.
Suite 300
Chantilly, VA 20151
Tel: (703)818-1320
Fax: (703)818-8813
Registered: LDA

Employers
Shutler and Low

Clients Represented

On Behalf of Shutler and Low
Japan Automobile Standards Internat'l Center
Nissan North America Inc.
Toyota Technical Center U.S.A. Inc.

KALIK, Robert G.

5247 Wisconsin Ave. NW
Suite Five
Washington, DC 20015
Tel: (202)537-2290
Fax: (202)537-2291
Registered: LDA

Employers
Kalik Lewin (Partner)

Clients Represented

On Behalf of Kalik Lewin
American Vintners Ass'n
American Wine Heritage Alliance
Citrosuco North America, Inc.

KALISH, Susan

4405 East-West Hwy.
Suite 405
Bethesda, MD 20814-9139
Tel: (301)913-9517
Fax: (301)913-9520
EMail: run@americanrunning.org

Employers
American Running and Fitness Ass'n (Exec. Director)

KALOI, Laura W.

418 C St. NE
Washington, DC 20002
Tel: (202)546-2663
Fax: (202)546-0057

Employers
Nat'l Center for Learning Disabilities (NCLD) (Director, Public Policy)

KALOMIRIS, Paul

1730 K St. NW
Suite 700
Washington, DC 20006
Tel: (202)223-4735
Fax: (202)223-4745
EMail: pkalomiris@urbandevelopment.com

Employers
Council for Urban Economic Development (Legislative Director)

KAMASAKI, Charles K.

1111 19th St. NW
Suite 1000
Washington, DC 20036
Tel: (202)785-1670
Fax: (202)776-1792
Registered: LDA

Employers
Nat'l Council of La Raza (Senior V. President, Office of Research, Advocacy and Legislation)

KAMBER, Victor S.

1920 L St. NW
Washington, DC 20036
Tel: (202)223-8700
Fax: (202)659-5559
Registered: LDA

Employers
The Kamber Group (President, Chief Exec. Officer and Chairman of the Board)

Clients Represented

On Behalf of The Kamber Group
Amalgamated Transit Union
Internat'l Union of Painters and Allied Trades
Laborers' Internat'l Union of North America
North American Communications Corp.
Sheet Metal Workers' Internat'l Ass'n

KAMBROD, Mathew R.

1800 N. Kent St.
Suite 907
Arlington, VA 22209
Tel: (703)416-1401
Fax: (703)418-3649
Registered: LDA

Employers
Kambrod Associates Ltd. (President)

Clients Represented

On Behalf of Kambrod Associates Ltd.
Microvision, Inc.

KAMEN, Hershel

1350 I St. NW
Suite 1250
Washington, DC 20005
Tel: (202)289-6060
Fax: (202)289-1546
Registered: LDA

Employers
Continental Airlines Inc.

KAMEN, Laurel

801 Pennsylvania Ave.
Suite 650
Washington, DC 20004
Tel: (202)624-0761
Fax: (202)624-0775
Registered: LDA
EMail: laurel.kamen@aexp.com

Employers
American Express Co. (V. President, Government Affairs)

KAMENAR, Paul D.

2009 Massachusetts Ave. NW
Washington, DC 20036
Tel: (202)588-0302
Fax: (202)588-0386

Employers
Washington Legal Foundation (Senior Exec. Counsel)

KAMESAKI, Mutsuya

800 Connecticut Ave. NW
Suite 1000
Washington, DC 20006
Tel: (202)785-9210
Fax: (202)861-0690

Employers
Sumitomo Corp. of America (Director, Business Development)

KAMIN, Deborah

1900 Duke St.
Suite 200
Alexandria, VA 22314
Tel: (703)299-1050
Fax: (703)299-1044
Registered: LDA
EMail: kamind@asco.org

Employers
American Soc. of Clinical Oncology (Senior Director, Public Policy)

KAMINOW, Ira P.

1700 K St. NW
Suite 1200
Washington, DC 20006
Tel: (202)857-0001
Fax: (202)857-0209
EMail: ikaminow@cig1.com

Employers
Capital Insights Group (President and Chief Exec. Officer)

KAMINSKI, Jim

1050 Connecticut Ave. NW
Washington, DC 20036-5339
Tel: (202)857-6000
Fax: (202)857-6395
Worked for Federal Trade Commission.

Employers
Arent Fox Kintner Plotkin & Kahn, PLLC (Associate)

KAMMER, SJ, Father Fred

1731 King St.
Suite 200
Alexandria, VA 22314
Tel: (703)549-1390
Fax: (703)549-1656
EMail: fkammer@catholiccharitiesusa.org

Employers
Catholic Charities USA (President)

KAMP, John

1776 K St. NW
Washington, DC 20006
Tel: (202)719-7000
Fax: (202)719-7049
Registered: LDA

Employers
Wiley, Rein & Fielding

Clients Represented
On Behalf of Wiley, Rein & Fielding
Internet Advertising Bureau

KAMPINSKY, Lois

440 First St. NW
Eighth Floor
Washington, DC 20001
EMail: lkampkins@naco.org
Tel: (202)942-4267
Fax: (202)737-0480

Employers
Nat'l Ass'n of Counties (Director, Telecommunications and Training)

KAMPMAN, Rosalba

9650 Rockville Pike
Bethesda, MD 20814-3998
Tel: (301)530-7114
Fax: (301)530-7133
EMail: rkampman@biophysics.faseb.org

Employers
Biophysical Soc. (Exec. Director)

KANDER, Mark

10801 Rockville Pike
Rockville, MD 20852
Tel: (301)897-5700
Ext: 4139
Fax: (301)571-0457
Registered: LDA
EMail: mkander@asha.org

Employers
American Speech, Language, and Hearing Ass'n (Director, Medicare and Medicaid Branch)

KANDO-PINEDA, Carol A.

600 Pennsylvania Ave. NW
MS: 402
Washington, DC 20580
EMail: ckando@ftc.gov
Tel: (202)326-3152
Fax: (202)326-3585

Employers
Federal Trade Commission (Legislative Counsel, Office of Congressional Relations)

KANE, Annette P.

1275 K St. NW
Suite 975
Washington, DC 20005
Tel: (202)682-0334
Fax: (202)682-0338

Employers
Nat'l Council of Catholic Women (Exec. Director)

KANE, Betty Ann

1155 Connecticut Ave. NW
Suite 1000
Washington, DC 20036-4306
Tel: (202)785-0600
Fax: (202)785-1234
Registered: LDA

Employers
Betty Ann Kane & Co. (President)
Miller & Van Eaton, P.L.L.C. (Federal Relations Advisor)

Clients Represented
On Behalf of Betty Ann Kane & Co.
DC Land Title Ass'n
Laredo, Texas, City of
NCRIC, Inc.
Sprint Corp.
Tort Reform Institute
On Behalf of Miller & Van Eaton, P.L.L.C.
Laredo, Texas, City of
Northern Mariana Islands, Commonwealth of the

KANE, Jr., James L.

1315 Vincent Place
McLean, VA 22101
Tel: (703)790-5287
Registered: LDA

Employers
Law Offices of James L. Kane (Attorney)

Clients Represented
On Behalf of Law Offices of James L. Kane
The Smith, Korach, Hayet, Haynie Partnership

KANE, John E.

1776 I St. NW
Suite 400
Washington, DC 20006-3708
Tel: (202)739-8000
Fax: (202)785-4019

Employers
Nuclear Energy Institute (V. President, Governmental Affairs)

KANE, Kevin

1801 F St. NW
Washington, DC 20006
EMail: kkane@usnzcouncil.org
Tel: (202)842-0772
Fax: (202)842-0749

Employers
The United States-New Zealand Council (Exec. Director)

KANE, Lesley

666 Pennsylvania Ave. SE
Suite 401
Washington, DC 20003
Tel: (202)543-7552
Fax: (202)544-4723
Registered: LDA

Employers
Trust for Public Land (V. President, Legislative Affairs)

KANE, Stacey

801 Pennsylvania Ave. NW
North Bldg., Suite 252
Washington, DC 20004-2604
Tel: (202)737-4444
Fax: (202)737-0951

Employers
Coors Brewing Company (Manager, Federal Government Affairs)

KANEGIS, Aura

2120 L St. NW
Suite 700
Washington, DC 20037
Tel: (202)822-8282
Fax: (202)296-8834

Employers
Hobbs, Straus, Dean and Walker, LLP

Clients Represented
On Behalf of Hobbs, Straus, Dean and Walker, LLP
Black Mesa Community School Board
Bristol Bay Area Health Corp.
Pinon Community School Board
Pueblo de Conchiti
Rock Point Community School
Rough Rock Community School
Seminole Tribe of Indians of Florida
Shoalwater Bay Indian Tribe

KANIA, John

1400 I St. NW
Suite 540
Washington, DC 20005-2208
EMail: jkania@sayer.com
Tel: (202)638-4434
Fax: (202)296-1074
Registered: LDA

Employers
R. Wayne Sayer & Associates (Director, Legislative Affairs)

Clients Represented
On Behalf of R. Wayne Sayer & Associates
Applied Materials
Candescent Technologies
IPC Washington Office
Schott Corp.
Silicon Valley Group

KANIEWSKI, Donald

905 16th St. NW
Washington, DC 20006
Tel: (202)737-8320
Fax: (202)737-2754
Registered: LDA

Employers
Laborers' Internat'l Union of North America (Legislative and Political Director)

KANNER, Martin B.

122 C St. NW
Suite 500
Washington, DC 20001
EMail: mkanner@kannerandassoc.com
Tel: (202)347-6625
Fax: (202)347-6605
Registered: LDA

Employers
Kanner & Associates (President)

Clients Represented
On Behalf of Kanner & Associates
Eugene Water and Electric Board
Idaho Energy Authority, Inc.
Missouri River Energy Services
Northern California Power Agency
Ohio Municipal Electric Ass'n
Oregon Utility Resource Coordination Ass'n (OURCA)
Public Power Council

KANSTEINER, Walter H.

900 17th St. NW
Suite 500
Washington, DC 20006
EMail: Kansteiner@scowcroft.com
Tel: (202)296-9312
Fax: (202)296-9395
Served on the staff of the National Security Council under President George Bush.

Employers
Forum for Internat'l Policy (Senior Associate)
The Scowcroft Group (Principal)

KANTER, Arnold

900 17th St. NW
Suite 500
Washington, DC 20006
Tel: (202)296-9312
Fax: (202)296-9395
Former Undersecretary, Political Affairs, Department of State and Special Assistant to the President and Senior Director, Arms Control and Defense Policy, National Security Council, The White House during the Bush I administration.

Employers
Forum for Internat'l Policy (Senior Associate)
The Scowcroft Group (Principal)

KANTER, Beth

1630 Connecticut Ave. NW
Suite 201
Washington, DC 20009
Tel: (202)785-1100
Fax: (202)785-3605

Employers
Nat'l Women's Political Caucus (Political Director)

KANTOR, Doug

3050 K St. NW
Washington, DC 20007
EMail: dkantor@colliershannon.com
Tel: (202)342-8400
Fax: (202)342-8451
Former Deputy Chief of Staff for Programs, Department of Housing and Urban Development.

Employers
Collier Shannon Scott, PLLC (Associate)

Clients Represented
On Behalf of Collier Shannon Scott, PLLC
Fannie Mae

KANTOR, Mickey

1909 K St. NW
Washington, DC 20006
Tel: (202)263-3000
Fax: (202)263-3300
Former U.S. Trade Representative.

Employers
Mayer, Brown & Platt (Partner)

KAPEN, Karen

1919 Pennsylvania Ave. NW
Seventh Floor
Washington, DC 20006-3488
Tel: (202)557-2700
Registered: LDA

Employers
Mortgage Bankers Ass'n of America (Associate Director/Counsel)

KAPLAN, Alan H.

1140 19th St. NW
Suite 900
Washington, DC 20036
EMail: akaplan@kkblaw.com
Tel: (202)223-5120
Fax: (202)223-5619
Trial Attorney, Food and Drug Division, Office of General Counsel, Department of Health, Education and Welfare, 1957-60.

Employers
Kleinfeld, Kaplan and Becker (Partner)

Clients Represented

On Behalf of Kleinfeld, Kaplan and Becker

Adria Laboratories, Inc.
Carter-Wallace, Inc.
Cord Laboratories
Mead Johnson and Co.
Par Pharmaceutical, Inc.
Quad Pharmaceutical Inc.
Vitarine Pharmaceuticals Inc.

KAPLAN, Donald A.

1735 New York Ave. NW
Suite 500
Washington, DC 20006-4759
Tel: (202)628-1700
Fax: (202)331-1024

Special Litigation Counsel (1981-90), Chief, Energy Section (1978-81), Assistant Chief, Energy Section (1977-78), and Trial Attorney, Foreign Commerce Section (1975-77), all in the Antitrust Division, Department of Justice. Law Clerk to Judge John Dooling, U.S. District Court for the Eastern District of New York, 1970-71.

Employers

Preston Gates Ellis & Rouvelas Meeds LLP (Partner)

KAPLAN, Gilbert B.

1455 Pennsylvania Ave. NW
Suite 1000
Washington, DC 20004
Tel: (202)942-8400
Fax: (202)942-8484
Registered: LDA
EMail: gilbert.kaplan@haledorr.com

Acting Assistant Secretary (1987-88) and Deputy Assistant Secretary (1985-88), Import Administration and Director, Office of Investigations (1983-85), Department of Commerce.

Employers

Hale and Dorr LLP (Senior Partner)

Clients Represented

On Behalf of Hale and Dorr LLP

Bethlehem Steel Corp.
Committee to Support U.S. Trade Laws
Micron Technology, Inc.
Neiman Marcus Group
Pixtech, Inc.

KAPLAN, Jim

1701 Clarendon Blvd.
Arlington, VA 22209
Tel: (703)276-8800
Fax: (703)243-2593

Employers

American Chiropractic Ass'n (Director, Political Action Committee)

KAPLAN, Karen

1620 Eye St. NW Suite 202
Washington, DC 20006
Tel: (202)296-8071
Fax: (202)296-8352
EMail: pfc@partnershipforcaring.org

Employers

Partnership for Caring (President)

KAPLAN, Lionel

440 First St. NW
Suite 600
Washington, DC 20001
Tel: (202)639-5200

Employers

American Israel Public Affairs Committee (President)

KAPLAN, Melissa

1828 L St. NW
Suite 625
Washington, DC 20036
Tel: (202)496-5014
Fax: (202)833-3472
EMail: melissa@womens-health.org

Employers

Soc. for Women's Health Research (Government Relations Assistant)

KAPLAN, Philip S.

2550 M St. NW
Washington, DC 20037-1350
Tel: (202)457-6000
Fax: (202)457-6315
Registered: FARA
EMail: pkaplan@pattonboggs.com

Ambassador, U.S. Embassy (Vienna Disarmament Conference - 1989-91), Minister/Charge d'affaires, U.S. Embassy (Manila, Philippines - 1985-87), Deputy Assistant Secretary for Planning (1981-85), Foreign Service Officer (Washington, DC - 1975-80; Vienna, Austria - 1974-75; Bonn, Germany - 1970-74; Brussels, Belgium - 1968-70), Department of State.

Employers

Patton Boggs, LLP (Partner)

Clients Represented

On Behalf of Patton Boggs, LLP

Philippines, Department of Trade and Industry of the Republic of

KAPLAN, Steven L.

555 12th St. NW
Washington, DC 20004-1206
Tel: (202)942-5000
Fax: (202)942-5999
Registered: FARA
EMail: Steven_Kaplan@aporter.com

Employers

Arnold & Porter (Partner)

KAPLAR, Richard T.

1000 Potomac St. NW
Suite 301
Washington, DC 20007
Tel: (202)298-7512
Fax: (202)337-7092

Employers

Media Institute (V. President)

KAPP, Robert A.

1818 N St. NW
Suite 200
Washington, DC 20036
Tel: (202)429-0340
Fax: (202)775-2476

Employers

U.S.-China Business Council (President)

KAPP, Robert H.

555 13th St. NW
Washington, DC 20004-1109
Tel: (202)637-5600
Fax: (202)637-5910

Employers

Hogan & Hartson L.L.P.

Clients Represented

On Behalf of Hogan & Hartson L.L.P.

American Gaming Ass'n

KAPPEL, Brett G.

1001 Pennsylvania Ave. NW
Suite 600
Washington, DC 20004
Tel: (202)624-7330
Fax: (202)624-7222
Registered: LDA
EMail: bkappel@pgfm.com

Employers

Powell, Goldstein, Frazer & Murphy LLP (Partner)

Clients Represented

On Behalf of Powell, Goldstein, Frazer & Murphy LLP

Bayer Corp. / Agriculture Division
EUTELSAT
Kinetic Biosystems Inc.
Qualcomm Inc.
Walker Digital Corp.

KAPPELER, Joyce

1919 Pennsylvania Ave. NW
Seventh Floor
Washington, DC 20006-3488
Tel: (202)557-2700

Employers

Mortgage Bankers Ass'n of America (Senior Staff V. Prsident, Education)

KARALEKAS, S. Steven

1211 Connecticut Ave. NW
Suite 302
Washington, DC 20036
Tel: (202)466-7330
Fax: (202)955-5879
Registered: LDA, FARA

Chief Assistant to Rep. Paul W. Cronin (R-MA), 1973-74. Staff Assistant to the President, The White House, 1971-73.

Employers

Karalekas & Noone (Partner)

Clients Represented

On Behalf of Karalekas & Noone

American Retirees Ass'n
Johns Hopkins University-Applied Physics Lab

KARAS, William

1330 Connecticut Ave. NW
Washington, DC 20036-1795
Tel: (202)429-3000
Fax: (202)429-3902
Registered: LDA
EMail: wkaras@steptoe.com

Employers

Steptoe & Johnson LLP (Partner)

KARCHER, David A.

4000 Legato Rd.
Suite 850
Fairfax, VA 22033
Tel: (703)591-2220
Fax: (703)591-0614

Employers

American Soc. of Cataract and Refractive Surgery (Exec. Director)

KARDELL, Lisa R.

601 Pennsylvania Ave. NW
Suite 300
The North Bldg.
Washington, DC 20004
Tel: (202)628-3500
Fax: (202)628-0400
Registered: LDA
EMail: lkardell@wm.com

Employers

Waste Management, Inc. (Manager, Government Affairs)

KARDY, Walter M.

P.O. Box 42558
Northwest Station
Washington, DC 20015-0558
Tel: (301)933-7430

Employers

Instrument Technicians Labor-Management Cooperation Fund (Fund Administrator)
Masonry Industry Ventures, Inc. (President)
Specialty Contractors Management, Inc. (President)

Clients Represented

On Behalf of Specialty Contractors Management, Inc.

Instrument Technicians Labor-Management Cooperation Fund
Internat'l Council of Employers of Bricklayers and Allied Craftsmen
Masonry Industry Ventures, Inc.

KARG, Kathlene

1211 Connecticut Ave. NW
Suite 600
Washington, DC 20036
Tel: (202)833-4372
Fax: (202)833-4431
Registered: LDA

Employers

Interactive Digital Software Ass'n (Director, Intellectual Property and Public Policy)

KARIM, Talib I.

1140 Connecticut Ave. NW
Suite 1142
Washington, DC 20036
Tel: (202)862-4383
Fax: (202)331-5562
Registered: LDA

Legal Honors Program and the International Bureau, Federal Communications Commission. Former Aide to Rep. Mervyn Dymally (D-CA). Former Aide, Subcommittee on Africa, House Committee on International Relations.

Employers

Technology, Entertainment and Communications (TEC) Law Group

Clients Represented

On Behalf of Technology, Entertainment and Communications (TEC) Law Group

WorldSpace Corp.

KARIS, Katherine

1620 L St. NW
Suite 1150
Washington, DC 20036
Tel: (202)223-2575
Ext: 117
Fax: (202)223-2614

Employers

Matsushita Electric Industrial Co., Ltd. (International Research Coordinator)

KARL, Edward

1455 Pennsylvania Ave. NW
Suite 400
Washington, DC 20004-1081
Tel: (202)737-6600
Fax: (202)638-4512
Registered: LDA
EMail: ekarl@aicpa.org

Employers
American Institute of Certified Public Accountants (Director, Taxation)

KARLSON, Ph.D., David

2501 M St. NW
Suite 575
Washington, DC 20037
Tel: (202)887-5150
Fax: (202)887-5405

Employers
Soc. of General Internal Medicine (Exec. Director)

KARMOL, David L.

2111 Eisenhower Ave.
Alexandria, VA 22314-4698
Tel: (703)838-0083
Fax: (703)549-0493
Registered: LDA
EMail: dkarmol@nspi.org

Employers
Nat'l Spa and Pool Institute (General Counsel and Director, Government Relations)

KARNES, Dave

1101 Connecticut Ave. NW
Suite 1000
Washington, DC 20036
Tel: (202)828-2400
Fax: (202)828-2488
Registered: LDA

Employers
Kutak Rock LLP

Clients Represented
On Behalf of Kutak Rock LLP
First Nat'l of Nebraska

KARNS, Christopher

1001 Pennsylvania Ave. NW
Suite 300S
Washington, DC 20004
Tel: (202)824-8800
Fax: (202)824-8990
Registered: LDA
EMail: karns.christopher@dorseylaw.com

Employers
Dorsey & Whitney LLP (Partner)

Clients Represented
On Behalf of Dorsey & Whitney LLP
Central Council of Tlingit and Haida Indian Tribes of Alaska
Cow Creek Umpqua Tribe of Oregon
Grand Traverse Band of Chippewa and Ottawa Indians
Hoopa Valley Tribal Council
Red Lake Band of Chippewa Indians
Saginaw Chippewa Indian Tribe of Michigan
St. George Island Traditional Council

KAROL, Kathryn Dickey

555 12th St. NW
Suite 650
Washington, DC 20004-1205
Tel: (202)393-7950
Fax: (202)393-7960
Registered: LDA

Employers
Eli Lilly and Co. (Director, International and Public Government Relations)

KARPINSKI, Gene

218 D St. SE
Second Floor
Washington, DC 20003
Tel: (202)546-9707
Fax: (202)546-2461
Registered: LDA

Employers
U.S. Public Interest Research Group (Exec. Director)

KARR, Susan

10801 Rockville Pike
Rockville, MD 20852
Tel: (301)897-5700
Fax: (301)571-0457
Registered: LDA

Employers
American Speech, Language, and Hearing Ass'n (Director, School Services)

KARSTING, Philip C.

816 Connecticut Ave. NW
Tenth Floor
Washington, DC 20006
Tel: (202)783-3460
Fax: (202)783-2432
Registered: LDA
EMail: phil@ptomac.com
Senior Budget Analyst for Commerce, Housing, Telecommunications, Agriculture and Regional Development, Minority Staff, Senate Committee on the Budget, 1995-98. Legislative Assistant for Natural Resources to Senator J. James Exon (D-NE), 1985-95.

Employers
Potomac Group (Director, Federal Affairs)

Clients Represented
On Behalf of Potomac Group
American Psychological Ass'n
Ass'n of American Railroads
Maersk Inc.
Rapid Mat LLC
R. J. Reynolds Tobacco Co.
Seafarers Internat'l Union of North America
Seafarers Mobilization Action Research Team
Transportation Institute
Union Pacific
Walgreen Co.
Watson Energy

KASHDAN, Alan

1775 I St. NW
Suite 600
Washington, DC 20006-2401
Tel: (202)721-4600
Fax: (202)721-4646

Employers
Hughes Hubbard & Reed LLP (Of Counsel)

KASINITZ, Barry

1750 New York Ave. NW
Washington, DC 20006
Tel: (202)737-8484
Fax: (202)737-8418
Registered: LDA

Employers
Internat'l Ass'n of Fire Fighters (Legislative Director)

KASLOW, Amy

1500 K St. NW
Suite 850
Washington, DC 20005
Tel: (202)682-4292
Fax: (202)682-5150

Employers
Council on Competitiveness (Senior Fellow)

KASSIR, Allison

1730 Pennsylvania Ave. NW
Suite 1200
Washington, DC 20006-4706
Tel: (202)737-0500
Fax: (202)626-3737
Registered: LDA
Legislative Assistant to Rep. Paul McHale (D-PA), 1993-95. Staff Assistant, Office of the Secretary, Department of Defense, 1993. Staff Assistant, House Armed Services Committee, 1990-93.

Employers
King & Spalding (Government Affairs Representative)

Clients Represented
On Behalf of King & Spalding
Bridgestone/Firestone, Inc.
ESR Children's Health Care System
Healthcare Recoveries Inc.
Salt Lake City Olympic Organizing Committee

KAST, Lawrence P.

1050 Thomas Jefferson St. NW
Sixth Floor
Washington, DC 20007
Tel: (202)298-1895
Fax: (202)298-1699
Registered: LDA

Employers
John Freshman Associates, Inc. (Director)

Clients Represented
On Behalf of John Freshman Associates, Inc.
#10 Enterprises LLC
Anheuser-Busch Cos., Inc.
Gulf Coast Waste Disposal Authority
Lewis and Clark Rural Water System, Inc.
Los Angeles County Sanitation District
Metropolitan St. Louis Sewer District
Mid Dakota Rural Water System
Monterey County Water Resources Agency
Nat'l Audubon Soc.
Oregon Water Trust
Pharmacia Corp.
Sacramento, California, Department of Utilities of

KASTEN, Jr., Robert W.

888 16th St. NW
Suite 700
Washington, DC 20006
Tel: (202)223-9151
Fax: (202)223-9814
Registered: LDA

Employers
Kasten & Co. (President)

Clients Represented
On Behalf of Kasten & Co.
Information Practices Coalition of Washington, D.C.
Newsbank, Inc.

KASTNER, Kenneth M.

700 13th St. NW
Suite 700
Washington, DC 20005-3960
Tel: (202)508-6000
Fax: (202)508-6200
EMail: kmkastner@bryancave.com

Employers
Bryan Cave LLP (Partner)

KASTNER, Michael E.

1300 19th St. NW
Fifth Floor
Washington, DC 20036
Tel: (202)628-2010
Fax: (202)628-2011
Registered: LDA
EMail: mkastner@ntea.com

Employers
Nat'l Truck Equipment Ass'n (Director, Government Relations)

KASUNICH, Cheryl

950 N. Washington St.
Alexandria, VA 22314-1552
Tel: (703)836-2272
Fax: (703)684-1924

Employers
American Academy of Physician Assistants (V. President and Chief Operating Officer)

KASWELL, Stuart J.

1401 I St. NW
Suite 1000
Washington, DC 20005
Tel: (202)296-9410
Fax: (202)326-5358
Registered: LDA
EMail: skaswell@sia.com

Employers
Securities Industry Ass'n (Senior V. President and General Counsel)

KATIC, Lisa

1010 Wisconsin Ave. NW
Ninth Floor
Washington, DC 20007
Tel: (202)337-9400
Fax: (202)337-4508
EMail: lkatic@gmabrands.com

Employers
Grocery Manufacturers of America (Director, Scientific and Nutrition Policy)

KATOH, Masanobu

1776 I St. NW
Suite 880
Washington, DC 20006
Tel: (202)331-8750
Fax: (202)331-8797
EMail: mkatoh@wdc.fujitsu.com

Employers
Fujitsu Limited (General Manager)

KATRICHIS, Harry

1050 Connecticut Ave. NW
Washington, DC 20036-5339
Tel: (202)857-6000
Fax: (202)857-6395
Former Majority Chief Counsel and Minority Chief Counsel, House Committee on Small Business. Former Assistant to the Attorney General, Department of Justice. Former Associate Chief Counsel, Office of Advocacy, Small Business Administration. Former Special Counsel, Office of the General Counsel, Department of Commerce.

Employers
Arent Fox Kintner Plotkin & Kahn, PLLC (Counsel)

KATSURINIS, Stephen A.

1050 Connecticut Ave. NW
Suite 1200
Washington, DC 20036
Tel: (202)857-2912
Fax: (202)857-1737
Registered: LDA, FARA
EMail: skatsurinis@mwcllc.com
Counsel to Rep Dana Rohrabacher (R-CA), 1991-94.

Employers
McGuireWoods L.L.P. (V. President, McGuire Woods Consulting)

Clients Represented

On Behalf of McGuireWoods L.L.P.

Alexandria, Virginia, Sanitation Authority of the City of
Allegiance Healthcare Corp.
Center for Governmental Studies of the University of Virginia
CSO Partnership
CSX Corp.
Eastman Chemical Co.
Families of Anthoniessen, Bekaert, Eyskens, Van den Heede, and Vermander
Fibrowatt, Inc.
Financial Services Council
GE Financial Assurance
Georgia-Pacific Corp.
Huntington Sanitary Board
Lynchburg, Virginia, City of
Prince William County Service Authority
Richmond, Virginia, City of
Smithfield Foods Inc.
Trigon Healthcare Inc.
University of Miami
Verizon Communications
Virginia Power Co.
Wheeling, West Virginia, City of

KATZ, Bruce J.

1775 Massachusetts Ave. NW
Washington, DC 20036-2188
Tel: (202)797-6000
Fax: (202)797-6004

Chief of Staff, Department of Housing and Urban Development, 1993-96; Staff Director, Senate Subcommittee on Housing and Urban Affairs, 1987-92.

Employers

The Brookings Institution (Senior Fellow, Econ. Studies & Director, Center on Urban & Metropolitan Policy)

KATZ, Daniel E.

518 C St. NE
Washington, DC 20002
Tel: (202)466-3234
Fax: (202)466-2587

Employers

Americans United for Separation of Church and State (Director, Legislative Affairs)

KATZ, Daniel F.

725 12th St. NW
Washington, DC 20005
Tel: (202)434-5000
Fax: (202)434-5029

Employers

Williams & Connolly (Partner)

KATZ, Irv

1319 F St. NW
Suite 601
Washington, DC 20004
Tel: (202)347-2080
Fax: (202)393-4517

Employers

Nat'l Assembly of Health and Human Service Organizations (President and Chief Exec. Officer)
Nat'l Collaboration for Youth (Contact)

KATZ, Jennifer

1707 L St. NW
Suite 1060
Washington, DC 20036
Tel: (202)296-7477
Fax: (202)265-6854
Registered: LDA
EMail: jkatz@natlbcc.org

Legislative Assistant to Rep. Sherrod Brown (D-OH), 1996-98.

Employers

Nat'l Breast Cancer Coalition (Deputy Director, Government Relations)

KATZ, John W.

444 N. Capitol St. NW
Suite 336
Washington, DC 20001
Tel: (202)624-5858
Fax: (202)624-5857

Employers

Alaska, Washington Office of the State of (Director of State/Federal Relations)

KATZ, Jonathan

1029 Vermont Ave. NW
Second Floor
Washington, DC 20005
Tel: (202)347-6352
Fax: (202)737-0526

Employers

Nat'l Assembly of State Arts Agencies (Chief Exec. Officer)

KATZ, Marc N.

1605 King St.
Alexandria, VA 22314-2792
Tel: (703)684-3600
Fax: (703)836-4564
Registered: LDA

Employers

Nat'l Ass'n of Convenience Stores (V. President, Government Relations)

KATZ, Philip

1001 Pennsylvania Ave. NW
Suite 1100
Washington, DC 20004-2595
Tel: (202)624-2500
Fax: (202)628-5116

Employers

Crowell & Moring LLP (Partner)

KAUFFMAN, Amy

1015 18th St. NW
Suite 300
Washington, DC 20036
Tel: (202)223-7770
Fax: (202)223-8537

Employers

Hudson Institute (Research Fellow)

KAUFFMAN, Frank

1615 L St. NW
Suite 1000
Washington, DC 20036
Tel: (202)659-0330
Fax: (202)293-8105
Registered: FARA
EMail: kauffmaf@fleishman.com

Employers

Fleishman-Hillard, Inc (Senior V. President)

Clients Represented

On Behalf of Fleishman-Hillard, Inc

SBC Communications Inc.

KAUFFMAN, Vanessa C.

1010 Wayne Ave.
Suite 920
Silver Spring, MD 20910
Tel: (301)588-8994
Fax: (301)588-4629

Employers

Wildlife Habitat Council (Director of Marketing and Communications)

KAUFMAN, Alison

444 N. Capitol St. NW
Suite 317
Washington, DC 20001
Tel: (202)347-4535
Fax: (202)347-7151

Employers

Connecticut, Washington Office of the Governor of the State of (Director, Washington Office)

KAUFMAN, Beth

1500 Pennsylvania Ave. NW
MS: 1014
Washington, DC 20220
Tel: (202)622-1766

Employers

Department of Treasury - Tax Policy (Associate Tax Legislative Counsel)

KAUFMAN, Kenneth S.

1200 G St. NW
Suite 600
Washington, DC 20005-3802
Tel: (202)393-1200
Fax: (202)393-1240
EMail: kaufman@wrightlaw.com

Employers

Wright & Talisman, P.C.

KAUFMAN, Ronald C.

412 First St. SE
Suite 100
Washington, DC 20003
Tel: (202)484-4884
Fax: (202)484-0109
Registered: LDA
EMail: rkaufman@dutkogroup.com

Political Director and Deputy Assistant to the President, The White House, 1991-92; Deputy Assistant to the President for Personnel, The White House, 1989-90; Senior Counselor to the Secretary and Executive Officer, U.S. Department of Health and Human Services, 1983.

Employers

The Dutko Group, Inc. (Senior Managing Partner)

Clients Represented

On Behalf of The Dutko Group, Inc.

Eastern Pequot Indians
JM Family Enterprises
Longhorn Pipeline
Mills Corporation
Nat'l Aviary in Pittsburgh
Orange, Florida, County of

KAUFMAN, IV, W. Campbell

700 13th St. NW
Suite 400
Washington, DC 20005
Tel: (202)347-0773
Fax: (202)347-0785
Registered: LDA

Former Communications Director to Rep. John Cooksey (R-LA) and former Press Secretary to Rep. Jim McCrery (R-LA).

Employers

Cassidy & Associates, Inc. (V. President)

Clients Represented

On Behalf of Cassidy & Associates, Inc.

Abtech Industries
AdMeTech
Community Hospital Telehealth Consortium
Dimensions Healthcare System
eCharge Corp.
Idaho State University
Internat'l Snowmobile Manufacturers Ass'n
Lake Charles Memorial Hospital
Liberty Science Center
Memorial Hermann Health Care System
North American Datacom
Research Foundation of the City University of New York
Smartforce
Trinity Health
Valley Hospital Foundation
VoiceStream Wireless Corp.
Vollmer Public Relations

KAULBACK, Laura

740 15th St. NW
Ninth Floor
Washington, DC 20005
Tel: (202)662-1000
Fax: (202)662-1032

Employers

American Bar Ass'n (Legislative Assistant)

KAVANAGH, Anthony P.

801 Pennsylvania Ave. NW
Suite 214
Washington, DC 20004
Tel: (202)628-1645
Fax: (202)628-4276
Registered: LDA

Employers

American Electric Power Co. (V. President, Governmental Affairs)

KAVANAUGH, E. Edward

1101 17th St. NW
Suite 300
Washington, DC 20036
Tel: (202)331-1770
Fax: (202)331-1969
Registered: LDA

Employers

Cosmetic, Toiletry and Fragrance Ass'n (President)

KAVJIAN, Edward M.

1660 L St. NW
Fourth Floor
Washington, DC 20036
Tel: (202)775-5086
Fax: (202)775-5045
Registered: LDA

Employers

General Motors Corp. (Senior Washington Representative)

KAWASHITA, Haruhisa

1101 17th St. NW
Suite 1001
Washington, DC 20036
Tel: (202)331-8696
Fax: (202)293-3932

Employers

Development Bank of Japan (Chief Representative)

KAY, Kenneth R.

1341 G St. NW
Suite 1100
Washington, DC 20005
Tel: (202)393-2260
Fax: (202)393-0712
Registered: LDA

Legislative Director to Senator Max Baucus (D-MT), 1982-84. Counsel, Senate Judiciary Committee, 1979-82. Legislative Assistant, Rep. Ed Koch (D-NY), 1976-77.

Employers
Computer Coalition for Responsible Exports (Exec. Director)
Computer Systems Policy Project (Exec. Director)
Infotech Strategies, Inc. (Chairman)

Clients Represented

On Behalf of Infotech Strategies, Inc.
CEO Forum on Education and Technology
Computer Coalition for Responsible Exports
Computer Systems Policy Project

KAYE, Bronwen A.

1667 K St. NW
Suite 1270
Washington, DC 20006
Tel: (202)659-8320
Fax: (202)496-2448
Registered: LDA

Employers
American Home Products Corp. (Director, Government Relations)

KAYE, D. Michael

1333 New Hampshire Ave. NW
Suite 400
Washington, DC 20036
Tel: (202)887-4000
Fax: (202)887-4288
Registered: LDA
International Trade Attorney, Office of General Counsel, Department of Commerce, 1990-92.

Employers
Akin, Gump, Strauss, Hauer & Feld, L.L.P. (Partner)

KAYE, Stephen S.

700 13th St. NW
Suite 700
Washington, DC 20005-3960
EMail: sskaye@bryancave.com
Tel: (202)508-6000
Fax: (202)508-6200

Employers
Bryan Cave LLP (Partner)

KAYMAK, Alev

2101 L St. NW
Washington, DC 20037-1526
Tel: (202)785-9700
Fax: (202)887-0689
Registered: LDA
EMail: kaymaka@dsmo.com

Employers
Dickstein Shapiro Morin & Oshinsky LLP (International Trade Consultant)

Clients Represented

On Behalf of Dickstein Shapiro Morin & Oshinsky LLP
Colakoglu Group
Habas Group

KAYSER, Susan

1050 Connecticut Ave. NW
Washington, DC 20036-5339
Tel: (202)857-6000
Fax: (202)857-6395
Registered: LDA

Employers
Arent Fox Kintner Plotkin & Kahn, PLLC (Member)

Clients Represented

On Behalf of Arent Fox Kintner Plotkin & Kahn, PLLC
Assisted Living Federation of America

KAZEMZADEH, Dr. Firuz

1320 19th St. NW
Suite 701
Washington, DC 20036
Tel: (202)833-8990
Fax: (202)833-8988

Employers
Nat'l Spiritual Assembly of the Baha'is of the United States (Secretary, Office of External Affairs)

KAZMAN, Sam

1001 Connecticut Ave. NW
Suite 1250
Washington, DC 20036
Tel: (202)331-1010
Fax: (202)331-0640

Employers
Competitive Enterprise Institute (General Counsel)

KAZON, Peter M.

701 Pennsylvania Ave. NW
Suite 900
Washington, DC 20004-2608
Tel: (202)661-8739
Fax: (202)434-7400
Registered: LDA
EMail: pkazon@mintz.com
Attorney, Bureau of Competition, Federal Trade Commission, 1979-84.

Employers
Mintz, Levin, Cohn, Ferris, Glovsky and Popeo, P.C. (Partner)

Clients Represented

On Behalf of Mintz, Levin, Cohn, Ferris, Glovsky and Popeo, P.C.
American Clinical Laboratory Ass'n
Ass'n of American Blood Banks

KEALY, Edward R.

122 C St. NW
Suite 280
Washington, DC 20001
Tel: (202)383-0083
Fax: (202)383-0097
Registered: LDA
EMail: ekealy@cef.org

Employers
Committee for Education Funding (Exec. Director)

KEAN, Eileen

919 Prince St.
Alexandria, VA 22314
Tel: (703)684-6098
Fax: (703)684-7138
Registered: LDA

Employers
Bond & Company, Inc. (Senior V. President)

Clients Represented

On Behalf of Bond & Company, Inc.
Hackensack University Medical Center Foundation
openNET Coalition
Service Employees Internat'l Union
United Brotherhood of Carpenters and Joiners of America

KEANE, William K.

1801 K St. NW
Washington, DC 20006
Tel: (202)775-7100
Fax: (202)857-0172

Employers
Arter & Hadden (Partner)

Clients Represented

On Behalf of Arter & Hadden
Manufacturers Radio Frequency Advisory Committee, Inc.
Taxicab, Limousine and Paratransit Ass'n

KEANEY, David

655 15th St. NW
Suite 300
Washington, DC 20005
Tel: (202)783-0900
Fax: (202)783-2308
Registered: LDA
EMail: dave.keaney@bms.com

Employers
Bristol-Myers Squibb Co. (Director, Federal Government Affairs)

KEARNS, Ph.D., Kenneth D.

1030 15th St. NW
Suite 820
Washington, DC 20005-1503
EMail: kkearns@kearnswest.com
Tel: (202)535-7800
Fax: (202)535-7801

Employers
Kearns & West, Inc. (Principal)

KEARNS, Kevin L.

910 16th St. NW
Suite 300
Washington, DC 20006
Tel: (202)728-1980
Fax: (202)728-1981
Registered: LDA
EMail: council@usbusiness.org

Employers
United States Business and Industry Council (President)

KEAST, Robert

1250 Connecticut Ave. NW
Suite 610
Washington, DC 20036
Tel: (202)955-3005
Fax: (202)955-1087

Employers
Welfare to Work Partnership (Director, Policy)

KEATING, Daniel L.

1150 18th St. NW
Suite 400
Washington, DC 20036
Tel: (202)223-9347
Fax: (202)872-0347

Employers
Municipal Securities Rulemaking Board (Chairman)

KEATING, David

1776 K St. NW
Suite 300
Washington, DC 20006
Tel: (202)955-5500
Fax: (202)955-9466
EMail: dkeating@clubforgrowth.org

Employers
Club for Growth (Exec. Director)

KEATING, David L.

1100 New York Ave. NW
Suite 750
West Tower
Washington, DC 20005
Tel: (202)223-2555
Registered: LDA

Employers
Citizen Strategies (President)
Club for Growth

Clients Represented

On Behalf of Citizen Strategies
Nat'l Taxpayers Union

KEATING, Raymond I.

1920 L St. NW
Suite 200
Washington, DC 20036
Tel: (202)785-0238
Fax: (202)822-8118

Employers
Small Business Survival Committee (Chief Economist)

KEATING, Richard F.

1776 I St. NW
Suite 200
Republic Place
Washington, DC 20006
Tel: (202)293-9494
Fax: (202)223-9594
Registered: LDA

Employers
Anheuser-Busch Cos., Inc. (V. President and Sr. Government Affairs Officer)

KEATING, Ted

1727 King St.
Suite 400
Alexandria, VA 22314-2753
Tel: (703)836-9660
Fax: (703)836-9665

Employers
Nat'l Ass'n of Postal Supervisors (Exec. V. President)

KEATING, Thomas

1350 I St. NW
Suite 690
Washington, DC 20005
Tel: (202)898-4746
Fax: (202)898-4756
Registered: LDA
EMail: tkeating@ob-cgroup.com
Served as Director of Police Services and House Sergeant, Arms Control Bureau, Department of Defense.

Employers
The OB-C Group, LLC (Principal)

Clients Represented

On Behalf of The OB-C Group, LLC

American Airlines
Anheuser-Busch Cos., Inc.
AT&T
Biotechnology Industry Organization
Blue Cross Blue Shield Ass'n
Fannie Mae
Goodyear Tire and Rubber Co.
Healthcare Distribution Management Ass'n
Investment Co. Institute
Merrill Lynch & Co., Inc.
Motorola, Inc.
Nat'l Thoroughbred Racing Ass'n, Inc.
Newport News Shipbuilding Inc.
The Rouse Company
Sears, Roebuck and Co.
Securities Industry Ass'n
TIAA-CREF
United Parcel Service
WellPoint Health Networks/Blue Cross of California/UNICARE
Wilmer, Cutler & Pickering

KEATING, Timothy J.

1850 K St. NW
Suite 850
Washington, DC 20006
Tel: (202)331-1760
Fax: (202)822-9376
Registered: LDA

Former Special Assistant to the President and Staff Director, Legislative Affairs, Executive Office of the President, The White House, during the Clinton administration and Assistant Floor Manager for Democratic Leadership and Special Assistant to Doorkeeper, U.S. House of Representatives.

Employers

Timmons and Co., Inc. (Chairman and Managing Partner)

Clients Represented

On Behalf of Timmons and Co., Inc.

American Council of Life Insurers
American Petroleum Institute
American Soc. of Anesthesiologists
Anheuser-Busch Cos., Inc.
Asbestos Working Group
AT&T
Bay Harbor Management, L.C.
Bristol-Myers Squibb Co.
Cox Enterprises Inc.
DaimlerChrysler Corp.
Farallon Capital Management
Federal Home Loan Mortgage Corp. (Freddie Mac)
Micron Technology, Inc.
Napster, Inc.
Nat'l Rifle Ass'n of America
New York Life Insurance Co.
Northrop Grumman Corp.
TruePosition Inc.
Union Pacific
University of Utah
UNOCAL Corp.
VISA U.S.A., Inc.

KECK, Christine

2500 Wilson Blvd.
Suite 300
Arlington, VA 22201
EMail: ckeck@tia.eia.org
Tel: (703)907-7011
Fax: (703)907-7727

Employers

Telecommunications Industry Ass'n (Director, Global Services Provider Relations)

KEDZIOR, Dennis M.

700 13th St. NW
Suite 400
Washington, DC 20005
Tel: (202)347-0773
Fax: (202)347-0785
Registered: LDA

Senior Staff Assistant, U.S. House Committee on Appropriations, 1980-98. Assistant to the Secretary, Department of Transportation, 1978-80. Chief of Budget Operations, House Committee on the Budget, 1974-77.

Employers

Cassidy & Associates, Inc. (Senior V. President)

Clients Represented

On Behalf of Cassidy & Associates, Inc.

ADI Ltd.
AdMeTech
Alenia Aerospazig
American Superconductor Corp.
Arnold & Porter
Boston University
Columbia University
Crane & Co.
Dakota Wesleyan University
Fairview Hospital and Healthcare Services
Institute for Student Achievement
Lifebridge Health
Matthews Media Group, Inc.
Northern Essex Community College Foundation
Ohio State University
Rochester Institute of Technology
Saint Coletta of Greater Washington, Inc.
Texas Tech University System
United Service Organization
University of Puerto Rico
Valley Hospital Foundation

KEE, Esther G.

232 E. Capitol St. NE
Washington, DC 20003
Tel: (202)544-3181
Fax: (202)543-1748

Employers

US-Asia Institute (Secretary/Treasurer)

KEEBLER, Barbara

1077 30th St. NW
Suite 100
Washington, DC 20007
Tel: (202)337-6232
Fax: (202)333-6706

Employers

Nat'l Catholic Educational Ass'n (Director, Public Relations)

KEEFE, Kenneth

1450 G St. NW
Suite 500
Washington, DC 20005
Registered: LDA

Employers

Auyua Inc.

KEEFE, Marilyn J.

1627 K St. NW 12th Floor
Washington, DC 20006
EMail: marilynkeefe@nfprha.org
Tel: (202)293-3114
Fax: (202)293-1990
Registered: LDA

Employers

Nat'l Family Planning and Reproductive Health Ass'n (Director of Public Policy and Service Delivery)

KEEFE, Patrick

3138 N. Tenth St.
Arlington, VA 22201
Tel: (703)522-4770
Fax: (703)522-0594

Employers

Nat'l Ass'n of Federal Credit Unions (V. President, Communications and Technology)

KEEFE, Robert J.

1775 Pennsylvania Ave. NW
Suite 1050
Washington, DC 20006
Tel: (202)638-7030
Fax: (202)318-0491
Registered: LDA, FARA

Employers

TKC Internat'l, Inc. (Chairman and Chief Exec. Officer)

KEEFE, Tom

1201 S. Eads St.
Suite Two
Arlington, VA 22202
EMail: tkeefe@wheatgr.com
Tel: (703)271-8775
Fax: (703)271-9594
Registered: LDA

Executive Assistant, Department of Veterans Affairs, 2000-2001. Deputy Assistant Secretary (1998-2000) and Special Assistant/Chief of Staff, Veterans Employment and Training Services (1994-98), Department of Labor.

Employers

Wheat & Associates, Inc. (Senior V. President)

Clients Represented

On Behalf of Wheat & Associates, Inc.

Global Encasement, Inc.

KEEFFE, Mary Ann

1350 Connecticut Ave. NW
Suite 1102
Washington, DC 20036
EMail: maryannk@ccicorporate.com
Tel: (202)223-4747
Ext: 14
Fax: (202)223-4245

Deputy Administrator, Foreign Agricultural Services (1997-2000) and Deputy Undersecretary, Food, Nutrition, and Consumer Services (1993-97), Department of Agriculture.

Employers

The Clinton Group (V. President, Grassroots Services)

KEEGAN, Michael G.

1200 New Hampshire Ave NW
Suite 430
Washington, DC 20036
EMail: nrwainfo@nrwa.com
Tel: (202)955-4555
Fax: (202)955-1147
Registered: LDA

Employers

Murray, Scheer, Montgomery, Tapia & O'Donnell (Policy Analyst)

Clients Represented

On Behalf of Murray, Scheer, Montgomery, Tapia & O'Donnell

Ground Water Protection Council
Nat'l Rural Water Ass'n

KEEHAN, Timothy E.

1909 K St. NW
Washington, DC 20006
Tel: (202)263-3000
Fax: (202)263-3300
Registered: LDA

Employers

Mayer, Brown & Platt (Partner)

Clients Represented

On Behalf of Mayer, Brown & Platt

New Life Corp. of America

KEELEN, Matthew B.

P.O. Box 2776
Arlington, VA 22202
EMail: keelencommunications@erols.com
Tel: (703)548-0092
Fax: (703)548-9821

Employers

Keelen Communications (President)

Clients Represented

On Behalf of Keelen Communications

Nat'l Ass'n of Convenience Stores

KEELER, Jeffrey

1775 I St. NW
Suite 800
Washington, DC 20006
EMail: jkeeler@enron.com
Tel: (202)466-9157
Fax: (202)828-3372
Registered: LDA

Employers

Enron Corp. (Director, Federal Government Affairs)

KEELER, Tim

1500 Pennsylvania Ave. NW
Room 3202
Washington, DC 20220
Tel: (202)622-0585
Fax: (202)622-0534

Employers

Department of Treasury (Deputy to the Assistant Secretary (International))

KEELING, J. Michael

1726 M St. NW
Suite 501
Washington, DC 20036
EMail: michael@esopassociation.org
Tel: (202)293-2971
Fax: (202)293-7568
Registered: LDA

Employers

The ESOP (Employee Stock Ownership Plan) Ass'n (President)

KEELING, John R.

1325 G St. NW
Suite 700
Washington, DC 20005
EMail: jkeeling@ahi.org
Tel: (202)637-2440
Fax: (202)393-1667
Registered: LDA

Employers

Animal Health Institute (V. President, Legislative Affairs)

KEELOR, Dr. Richard

1101 15th St. NW
Suite 600
Washington, DC 20005
Tel: (202)785-1122
Ext: 14
Fax: (202)785-5019

Employers
Sugar Ass'n, Inc. (President and Chief Exec. Officer)

KEELTY, Lana

4301 Wilson Blvd.
Arlington, VA 22203-1860
Tel: (703)907-6028
Fax: (703)907-5508
Registered: LDA

Employers
Nat'l Rural Electric Cooperative Ass'n (Legislative Representative)

KEENAN, Laurie E.

1700 Pennsylvania Ave. NW
Suite 600
Washington, DC 20006
Tel: (202)393-7600
Fax: (202)393-7601
Registered: LDA

Employers
Ivins, Phillips & Barker (Partner)

KEENAN, Theresa Anne

601 E St. NW
Washington, DC 20049
Tel: (202)434-3772
Fax: (202)434-6477
Registered: LDA

Employers
AARP (American Ass'n of Retired Persons) (Senior Research Advisor)

KEENE, David A.

1299 Pennsylvania Ave. NW
Suite 800 West
Washington, DC 20004
Tel: (202)785-0500
Fax: (202)785-5277
Registered: LDA

Employers
American Conservative Union
The Carmen Group (Managing Associate)
Conservative Political Action Conference (Chairman)
LMRC, Inc. (Managing Associate)

Clients Represented
On Behalf of The Carmen Group
Air Transport Ass'n of America
Illinois Department of Transportation
Northeast Illinois Regional Commuter Railroad Corp.
United Seniors Ass'n
US Bancorp
Wisconsin Public Service Corp.
World Wrestling Federation Entertainment Inc.

KEENE, Kerry

1299 Pennsylvania Ave. NW
Suite 800 West
Washington, DC 20004
Tel: (202)785-0500
Fax: (202)785-5277
Registered: LDA

Employers
The Carmen Group (Project Manager)

KEENER, Melvin E.

1133 Connecticut Ave. NW
Suite 1023
Washington, DC 20036
Tel: (202)775-9869
Fax: (202)833-8491
Registered: LDA

Employers
Coalition for Responsible Waste Incineration (Exec. Director)

KEENEY, Andrea

1015 15th St. NW
Suite 802
Washington, DC 20005
EMail: akeeney@acec.org
Tel: (202)347-7474
Fax: (202)898-0068

Employers
American Consulting Engineers Council (Webmaster)

KEENEY, Regina M.

1909 K St. NW
Suite 820
Washington, DC 20006
Tel: (202)777-7700
Fax: (202)777-7763
Registered: LDA
EMail: gkeeney@lmm-law.com
Chief, International Bureau (1997-99); Chief, Common Carrier Bureau (1995-97); and Chief, Wireless Telecommunications Bureau (1994-95), all with the Federal Communications Commission. Senior Counsel for Communications, Senate Committee on Commerce, Science and Transportation, 1985-94. Attorney-Advisor, Tariff Division, Common Carrier Bureau, Federal Communications Commission, 1983-85.

Employers
Lawler, Metzger & Milkman, LLC (Partner)

Clients Represented
On Behalf of Lawler, Metzger & Milkman, LLC
Allegiance Telecom, Inc.
MCI WorldCom Corp.

KEENUM, Rhonda

1875 I St. NW
Suite 900
Washington, DC 20005
Tel: (202)371-0200
Fax: (202)371-2858

Employers
Edelman Public Relations Worldwide (Senior V. President)

KEENY, Jr., Spurgeon M.

1726 M St. NW
Suite 201
Washington, DC 20036
EMail: aca@armscontrol.org
Tel: (202)463-8270
Fax: (202)463-8273

Employers
Arms Control Ass'n (President and Exec. Director)

KEESE, III, James P.

2111 Wilson Blvd.
Suite 1200
Arlington, VA 22201
Tel: (703)522-1845
Fax: (703)351-6634
Registered: LDA
EMail: jkeese@columbuspublicaffairs.com
Special Assistant to Senator John Heinz (R-PA).

Employers
Columbus Public Affairs (V. President)

Clients Represented
On Behalf of Columbus Public Affairs
CIGNA Corp.

KEETON, Pamela

700 13th St. NW
Suite 1000
Washington, DC 20005
Tel: (202)347-6633
Fax: (202)347-8713

Employers
Powell Tate (Director, Defense Group)

KEFAUVER, Jenny

122 S. Patrick St.
Alexandria, VA 22314
Tel: (703)739-5920
Fax: (703)739-5924

Employers
Craig Shirley & Associates

Clients Represented
On Behalf of Craig Shirley & Associates
Southeastern Legal Foundation

KEHL, David

801 Pennsylvania Ave. NW
Suite 245
Washington, DC 20005
Tel: (202)624-1511
Fax: (202)318-0338
Registered: LDA
EMail: dkehl@healthupdate.com
Served as Legislative Director to Rep. Robert Michel (R-IL) for 22 years.

Employers
Jay Grant & Associates (Counsel)

Clients Represented
On Behalf of Jay Grant & Associates
Arkansas, Office of the Governor of the State of

KEHOE, Brien E.

1615 New Hampshire Ave. NW
Suite 200
Washington, DC 20009
Tel: (202)319-0800
Fax: (202)319-0804
Executive Assistant to the Maritime Administrator (1982-83) and Marine Legal Consultant (1981-82), Department of Transportation. General Counsel, Federal Maritime Commission, 1979-81.

Employers
Hill, Betts & Nash L.L.P. (Counsel)

Clients Represented
On Behalf of Hill, Betts & Nash L.L.P.
Orient Overseas Container Line
Resources Trucking Inc.

KEHOE, Danea M.

159 D St. SE
Washington, DC 20003
Tel: (202)547-7566
Fax: (202)546-8630
Registered: LDA

Employers
Kehoe & Hambel

Clients Represented
On Behalf of Kehoe & Hambel
American Soc. of Pension Actuaries
Nat'l Ass'n of Insurance and Financial Advisors
Niche Plan Sponsors, Inc.

KEHOE, Kerry

444 N. Capitol St. NW
Suite 322
Washington, DC 20001
Tel: (202)508-3860
Fax: (202)508-3843

Employers
Coastal States Organization (Legislative Counsel)

KEHOE, Stephen

1501 M St. NW
Suite 600
Washington, DC 20005-1710
Tel: (202)739-0200
Fax: (202)659-8287

Employers
BSMG Worldwide (Managing Director)

KEIGHTLEY, John

1731 King St.
Suite 200
Alexandria, VA 22314
EMail: jkeightley@catholiccharitiesusa.org
Tel: (703)549-1390
Fax: (703)549-1656

Employers
Catholic Charities USA (Director of Development)

KEINER, Jr., R. Bruce

1001 Pennsylvania Ave. NW
Suite 1100
Washington, DC 20004-2595
EMail: rbkeiner@cromor.com
Tel: (202)624-2500
Fax: (202)628-5116

Employers
Crowell & Moring LLP (Partner)

Clients Represented
On Behalf of Crowell & Moring LLP
Aer Lingus

KEINER, Suellen Terrill

1120 G St. NW
Suite 850
Washington, DC 20005
EMail: skeiner@napawash.org
Tel: (202)347-3190
Fax: (202)393-0993

Employers
Nat'l Academy of Public Administration (Director, Center for the Economy and Environment)

KEITH, Kendell W.

1250 I St. NW
Suite 1003
Washington, DC 20005-3917
EMail: kkeith@ngfa.org
Tel: (202)289-0873
Fax: (202)289-5388
Registered: LDA

Employers
Nat'l Grain and Feed Ass'n (President)

KEITH, Kenton W.

1630 Crescent Pl. NW
Washington, DC 20009-4099
Tel: (202)667-6800
Fax: (202)667-1475

Employers
Meridian Internat'l Center (Senior V. President)

KEITH, Stephen T.

1619 King St.
Alexandria, VA 22314-2793
EMail: info@navy-reserve.org
Tel: (703)548-5800
Fax: (703)683-3647

Employers
Naval Reserve Ass'n (Deputy Exec. Director)

KEITH, Susan

122 C St. NW
Suite 510
Washington, DC 20001
EMail: keith@dc.ncga.com
Tel: (202)628-7001
Fax: (202)628-1933
Registered: LDA

Employers
Nat'l Corn Growers Ass'n (Senior Director, Public Policy)

KEITHLEY, Carter E.

1601 N. Kent St.
Suite 1001
Arlington, VA 22209
EMail: keithley@hearthassociation.org
Tel: (703)522-0086
Fax: (703)522-0548

Employers
Hearth Products Ass'n (President and Chief Exec. Officer)

KEITHLEY, Jay

401 Ninth St. NW
Suite 400
Washington, DC 20004
Tel: (202)585-1920
Fax: (202)585-1896

Employers
Sprint Corp. (V. President, Federal Regulatory-LTD)

KELER, Marianne M.

11600 Sallie Mae Dr.
Reston, VA 20193
Tel: (703)810-5208
Fax: (703)810-7695

Employers
Sallie Mae, Inc. (Senior V. President and General Counsel)

KELLER, Elizabeth

777 N. Capitol St. NE
Suite 500
Washington, DC 20002-4201
Tel: (202)289-4262
Fax: (202)962-3500

Employers
Internat'l City/County Management Ass'n (Deputy Director)

KELLER, L. Charles

2300 N St. NW
Suite 700
Washington, DC 20037-1128
EMail: ckeller@wbklaw.com
Tel: (202)783-4141
Fax: (202)783-5851

Employers
Wilkinson, Barker and Knauer, LLP (Partner)

KELLER, Matthew

1250 Connecticut Ave. NW
Washington, DC 20036
Tel: (202)833-1200
Fax: (202)639-3716
Registered: LDA

Employers
Common Cause (Legislative Director)

KELLER, Jr., Roger A.

1400 L St. NW
Washington, DC 20005-3502
EMail: rkeller@winston.com
Tel: (202)371-5873
Fax: (202)371-5950
Registered: LDA

Counsel, House Committee on Small Business, 1999-2000.

Employers
Winston & Strawn (Associate, Environmental)

Clients Represented

On Behalf of Winston & Strawn
American Airlines
Columbia Ventures, LLC
Nat'l Paint and Coatings Ass'n
South Carolina Department of Transportation

KELLER, Thomas C.

1420 New York Ave. NW
Suite 550
Washington, DC 20005
Tel: (202)783-4805
Fax: (202)783-4804
Registered: LDA

Former Director of Projects for Senator Dan Coats (R-IN).

Employers
Russ Reid Co. (Account Supervisor)

Clients Represented

On Behalf of Russ Reid Co.
Alfalit Internat'l
Boys Town Nat'l Research Hospital
Corporation for Business, Work and Learning
Detroit Rescue Mission Ministries
Earth University, Inc.
Fuller Theological Seminary
Gospel Rescue Ministries of Washington
Light of Life Ministries
New College
Touro College
Vanguard University
Village of Kiryas Joel
William Tyndale College

KELLER, Thomas J.

901 15th St. NW
Suite 700
Washington, DC 20005-2301
EMail: tjkeller@verner.com
Tel: (202)371-6000
Fax: (202)371-6279
Registered: LDA

Employers
Verner, Liipfert, Bernhard, McPherson and Hand, Chartered (Member of Firm)

Clients Represented

On Behalf of Verner, Liipfert, Bernhard, McPherson and Hand, Chartered
Lockheed Martin Corp.

KELLEY, Angela

220 I St. NE
Suite 220
Washington, DC 20002
Tel: (202)544-0004
Fax: (202)544-1905
Registered: LDA

Employers
Nat'l Immigration Forum (Deputy Exec. Director)

KELLEY, Colleen M.

901 E St. NW
Suite 600
Washington, DC 20004
Tel: (202)783-4444
Fax: (202)628-3930

Employers
Nat'l Treasury Employees Union (National President)

KELLEY, J. Tyrone

655 15th St. NW
Washington, DC 20005-5701
EMail: tkelley@fmi.org
Tel: (202)220-0629
Fax: (202)220-0873
Registered: LDA

Employers
Food Marketing Institute (Director, Government Relations)

KELLEY, Joseph B.

555 12th St. NW
Suite 650
Washington, DC 20004-1205
Tel: (202)393-7950
Fax: (202)393-7960

Employers
Eli Lilly and Co. (Director, State Government Affairs)

KELLEY, Michael T.

7800 Foxhound Rd.
McLean, VA 22102
Tel: (703)821-3179
Fax: (703)448-3515
Registered: LDA

Deputy Assistant Secretary for Trade and Basic Industries, Department of Commerce, 1983-89. Deputy Assistant Secretary for Congressional Affairs, Department of Energy, 1981-83. Legislative Assistant to Rep. Silvio Conte (R-MA), 1966-67.

Employers
Berkshire Inc. (President)

Clients Represented

On Behalf of Berkshire Inc.
Advanced Refractory Technologies, Inc.
Hydrocarbon Technologies Inc.
IIT Research Institute
Synzyme Technologies, Inc.

KELLEY, USMC (Ret.), General Paul X.

700 13th St. NW
Suite 400
Washington, DC 20005
EMail: pkelley@cassidy.com
Tel: (202)347-0773
Fax: (202)347-0785

Commander, President's Rapid Deployment Task Force, 1980. Commandant of the U.S. Marine Corps, 1983-87. Member Joint Chiefs of Staff, Department of Defense, 1983-87.

Employers
Cassidy & Associates, Inc. (V. Chairman Emeritus)

KELLEY, Robert K.

321 D. St. NE
Washington, DC 20002
Tel: (301)654-3734
Registered: FARA

Employers
Robert K. Kelley Law Offices

Clients Represented

On Behalf of Robert K. Kelley Law Offices
Japan Automobile Manufacturers Ass'n

KELLEY, Ronald L.

499 S. Capitol St. SW
Suite 420
Washington, DC 20003
EMail: RonKelley@aol.com
Tel: (202)256-5211
Fax: (703)827-7766
Registered: LDA

Employers
Strategic Partners Inc. (President)

Clients Represented

On Behalf of Strategic Partners Inc.
Materials Research Soc.

KELLEY, Timothy J.

1200 New Hampshire Ave. NW
Suite 800
Washington, DC 20036-6802
EMail: tkelley@dlalaw.com
Tel: (202)776-2000
Fax: (202)776-2222

Employers
Dow, Lohnes & Albertson, PLLC (Member)

KELLEY, W. Curtis

1901 L St. NW
Suite 200
Washington, DC 20036
Tel: (202)659-1800
Fax: (202)296-2964
Registered: LDA

Employers
March of Dimes Birth Defects Foundation (Deputy Director, Federal Affairs)

KELLEY, William E.

2025 M St. NW
Suite 800
Washington, DC 20036
EMail: bill_kelley@dc.sba.com
Tel: (202)367-2100
Fax: (202)367-1200

Employers
Smith, Bucklin and Associates, Inc.

Clients Represented

On Behalf of Smith, Bucklin and Associates, Inc.
Community Financial Services Ass'n
Viatical Ass'n of America

KELLEY-RIESETT, Kathleen

21 Dupont Circle NW
Suite 700
Washington, DC 20036
EMail: kkr@opastco.org
Tel: (202)659-5990
Fax: (202)659-4619

Employers
Organization for the Promotion and Advancement of Small Telecommunications Cos. (Director, Education)

KELLIHER, Joseph T.

1875 Connecticut Ave. NW
Suite 1200
Washington, DC 20009-5728
Tel: (202)986-8000
Fax: (202)986-8102
Majority Counsel, House Commerce Commitee, 1995-2000. Former Legislative Assistant to Rep. Joseph Barton (R-TX).

Employers
LeBoeuf, Lamb, Greene & MacRae L.L.P. (Senior Counsel)

Clients Represented
On Behalf of LeBoeuf, Lamb, Greene & MacRae L.L.P.
Candle Corp.

KELLNER, Stephen S.

1913 I St. NW
Washington, DC 20006
Tel: (202)872-8110
Fax: (202)872-8114
Registered: LDA
EMail: skeller@csma.org

Employers
Consumer Specialties Products Ass'n (Senior Vice President, Legal Affairs)

KELLY, Anne Marie

1730 Massachusetts Ave. NW
Washington, DC 20036-1903
Tel: (202)371-0101
Fax: (202)728-9614

Employers
IEEE Computer Society (Acting Exec. Director)

KELLY, Biruta P.

1875 I St. NW
Suite 1050
Washington, DC 20006-5409
Tel: (202)331-8585
Fax: (202)331-2032

Employers
Scribner, Hall & Thompson, LLP (Partner)

KELLY, Bradley L.

701 Pennsylvania Ave. NW
Suite 900
Washington, DC 20004-2608
Tel: (202)434-7300
Fax: (202)434-7400
Registered: LDA
EMail: bkelly@mintz.com
Assistant U.S. Attorney, U.S. Attorney's Office for the District of Columbia (1984-89) and Attorney/Advisor, Office of Legal Policy (1983-84), Department of Justice.

Employers
Mintz, Levin, Cohn, Ferris, Glovsky and Popeo, P.C. (Partner)

KELLY, Brian

1150 17th St. NW
Suite 400
Washington, DC 20036
Tel: (202)222-4700
Fax: (202)222-4799

Employers
The Walt Disney Co. (Director, Government Relations)

KELLY, Brian

2500 Wilson Blvd.
Arlington, VA 22201-3834
Tel: (703)907-7525
Fax: (703)907-7501
Registered: LDA
EMail: bkelly@eia.org

Employers
Electronic Industries Alliance (Sr. V. President, Government Relations and Communications)

KELLY, Carol

1200 G St. NW
Suite 400
Washington, DC 20005
Tel: (202)783-8700
Fax: (202)783-8750

Employers
AdvaMed (Exec. V. President, Health Systems and Federal Legislative Policy)

KELLY, Charles J.

701 Pennsylvania Ave. NW
Washington, DC 20004-2696
Tel: (202)508-5155
Fax: (202)508-5186
Registered: LDA

Employers
Edison Electric Institute (Manager, Human Resource, Regulatory and Legislative Issues)

KELLY, Claire

1215 Jefferson Davis Hwy.
Suite 1500
Arlington, VA 22202
Tel: (703)236-4531
Fax: (703)415-1459
Registered: LDA
EMail: claire.kelly@baesystems.com

Employers
BAE SYSTEMS North America (Director, Legislative Initiatives)

KELLY, Clare M.

401 Wythe St.
Alexandria, VA 22314
Tel: (703)684-1355
Fax: (703)684-1589
Registered: LDA
EMail: ckelly@nachri.org

Employers
Nat'l Ass'n of Children's Hospitals Inc. (Associate, Public Policy)

KELLY, Colleen

805 15th St. NW
Suite 300
Washington, DC 20005-2207
Tel: (202)682-4200
Fax: (202)682-9054

Employers
Credit Union Nat'l Ass'n, Inc. (V. President, State Governmental Affairs)

KELLY, Donald E.

2600 Virginia Ave. NW
Suite 123
Washington, DC 20037
Tel: (202)298-5583
Fax: (202)298-5547
Registered: LDA
EMail: dkelly@appraisalinstitute.org

Employers
Appraisal Institute (V. President, Public Affairs)

KELLY, Doug

430 S. Capitol St. SE
Washington, DC 20003
Tel: (202)863-8000
Fax: (202)863-8174

Employers
Democratic Nat'l Committee (Director, Research)

KELLY, III, Ernest B.

1401 K St. NW
Suite 600
Washington, DC 20005
Tel: (202)835-9898
Fax: (202)853-9893
Registered: LDA

Employers
ASCENT (Ass'n of Community Enterprises) (President)

KELLY, Frank

555 12th St. NW
Suite 740
Washington, DC 20004
Tel: (202)638-3752
Fax: (202)638-3823
Registered: LDA
EMail: frank.kelly@schwab.com

Employers
Charles Schwab & Co., Inc., (Senior V. President and Head of Government Affairs)

KELLY, Frank X.

1023 15th St. NW
Suite 900
Washington, DC 20005-2602
Tel: (202)289-7200
Fax: (202)289-7698
EMail: fkelly@gbmdc.com
Office of the General Counsel, Federal Power Commission, 1972-74.

Employers
Gallagher, Boland and Meiburger (Partner)

Clients Represented
On Behalf of Gallagher, Boland and Meiburger
Enron Corp.

KELLY, Glenn

1275 K St. NW
Suite 890
Washington, DC 20005
Tel: (202)682-9161
Fax: (202)638-1043
Registered: LDA

Employers
Global Climate Coalition (Exec. Director)

KELLY, Harry J.

401 Ninth St. NW
Suite 900
Washington, DC 20004
Tel: (202)585-8000
Fax: (202)585-8080
Registered: LDA
EMail: nkelly@nixonpeabody.com

Employers
Nixon Peabody LLP (Partner)

KELLY, Ph.D., Heather O'Beirne

750 First St. NE
Washington, DC 20002-4242
Tel: (202)336-5500
Fax: (202)336-6069
Registered: LDA

Employers
American Psychological Ass'n (Legislative and Federal Affairs Officer)

KELLY, Henry C.

307 Massachusetts Ave. NE
Washington, DC 20002
Tel: (202)546-3300
Fax: (202)675-1010
EMail: fas@fas.org

Employers
Federation of American Scientists (President/Editor, FAS Public Interest Report)

KELLY, James

1825 Connecticut Ave. NW
Fifth Floor
Washington, DC 20009
Tel: (202)667-0901
Fax: (202)667-0902
EMail: james.kelly@widmeyer.com

Employers
Widmeyer Communications, Inc.

KELLY, Jennifer A.

1600 Wilson Blvd.
Suite 1000
Arlington, VA 22209
Tel: (703)841-9300
Fax: (703)841-0389
Registered: LDA

Employers
American Waterways Operators (Senior V. President, Government Affairs and Policy Analysis)

KELLY, Jennine

1401 New York Ave. NW
Suite 1100
Washington, DC 20005
Tel: (202)638-6222
Fax: (202)628-6726
EMail: jkenney@ncba.org

Employers
Nat'l Cooperative Business Ass'n (Director of Communications and Public Policy)

KELLY, John A.

925 15th St. NW
5th Floor
Washington, DC 20005
Tel: (202)342-9610
Fax: (202)342-0650
Registered: LDA
EMail: jkelly@kellylobbyshop.com
Deputy Executive Director, 1989 Presidential Inaugural Committee. Member, Presidential Transition Team, 1980. Legislative Assistant to Rep. Charles Rangel (D-NY), 1974-78. Major, U.S. Army Reserve, 1972-99.

Employers
Kelly and Associates, Inc. (Chief Exec. Officer)

Clients Represented
On Behalf of Kelly and Associates, Inc.
Academic Medicine Development Corp.
AMDeC Policy Group, Inc.
BMW (U.S.) Holding Corp.
BMW Financial Services of North America, Inc.
BMW Manufacturing Corp.
BMW of North America, Inc.
Internat'l Narcotic Enforcement Officers Ass'n
Morse Diesel Internat'l Inc.
Peachtree Settlement Funding
Perdue Farms Inc.
Qwest Communications
Showell Farms Inc.
Singer Assett Finance, Inc.

KELLY, John F.

1455 Pennsylvania Ave. NW
Suite 950
Washington, DC 20004-1087
Tel: (202)661-7100
Fax: (202)661-7110
Registered: LDA

Employers
Merrill Lynch & Co., Inc. (V. President, Government Relations)

KELLY, Kenneth

1701 K St. NW
Suite 600
Washington, DC 20006-1503
Tel: (202)833-5900
Fax: (202)833-0075

Employers
Global Health Council (Grassroots Officer)

KELLY, Kerry

1300 Wilson Blvd.
Arlington, VA 22209
Tel: (703)741-5163
Fax: (703)741-6092
Registered: LDA
EMail: kerry_kelly@americanchemistry.com

Employers
American Chemistry Council (Director)

KELLY, Kevin F.

1420 New York Ave. NW
Suite 1050
Washington, DC 20005
Tel: (202)638-1950
Fax: (202)638-1928
Registered: LDA
EMail: kkelly@vsadc.com
Former Floor Assistant to the Secretary, Senate Democratic Conference; former Majority Staff Director, Subcommittee on Veterans Affairs, Housing and Urban Development and Independent Agencies, Senate Committee on Appropriations. Legislative Assistant for Appropriations to Senator Barbara Mikulski (D-MD), 1987-88. Professional Staff Member, Subcommittee on Oceanography, House Committee on Merchant Marine and Fisheries, 1985-86.

Employers
Van Scoyoc Associates, Inc. (V. President)

Clients Represented

On Behalf of Van Scoyoc Associates, Inc.
APG Army Alliance
Arista Knowledge Systems, Inc.
Ass'n of Schools of Public Health
Ass'n of Universities for Research in Astronomy, Inc.
Baltimore, Maryland, City of
Bethesda Academy for the Performing Arts
Board on Human Sciences
Chesapeake Bay Foundation
Computer Data Systems, Inc.
Computer Sciences Corp.
Federal Home Loan Bank of San Francisco
Johns Hopkins School of Hygiene and Public Health
Johns Hopkins University-Applied Physics Lab
Lehigh University
Lockheed Martin Venture Star
Morgan State University
Mount Sinai School of Medicine
NASA Aeronautics Support Team
Nat'l Ass'n for Equal Opportunity in Higher Education
Orasure Technologies
Reno & Cavanaugh, PLLC
Space Explorers Inc.
University of Arizona
University of Connecticut
University of Missouri
University of New Orleans Foundation
UNOCAL Corp.
Washington Consulting Group

KELLY, Kevin S.

1030 15th St. NW
Suite 325
Washington, DC 20005
Tel: (202)289-9020
Fax: (202)289-7051

Employers
Nat'l Congress for Community Economic Development (Assistant V. President, Programs)

KELLY, Kimberly A.

One BET Plaza
1900 W Pl. NE
Washington, DC 20018
Tel: (202)608-2000
Fax: (202)608-2595
EMail: Kimberly.Kelly@bet.net

Employers
BET Holdings II, Inc. (Counsel, Government Affairs and Affiliate Regulations)

KELLY, Maureen

600 Pennsylvania Ave. SE
Suite 320
Washington, DC 20003
Tel: (202)969-8900
Fax: (202)969-7036
Registered: LDA
EMail: mkelly@gordley.com

Employers
Gordley Associates (Associate)

Clients Represented

On Behalf of Gordley Associates
Nat'l Barley Growers Ass'n

KELLY, Peter

4041 Powder Mill Rd.
Suite 404
Calverton, MD 20705-3106
Tel: (301)348-2002
Fax: (301)348-2020

Employers
Asphalt Roofing Manufacturers Ass'n (General Manager)

KELLY, Ross

1401 K St. NW
Suite 900
Washington, DC 20005
Tel: (202)626-8550
Fax: (202)626-8578

Employers
Jefferson Consulting Group (V. President)

KELLY, Rusty

625 Slaters Ln.
Suite 200
Alexandria, VA 22314-1171
Tel: (703)836-6263
Fax: (703)836-6730
EMail: rustyk@aahomecare.org

Employers
American Ass'n for Homecare (Director of Communications)

KELLY, Jr., William C.

555 11th St. NW
Suite 1000
Washington, DC 20004
Tel: (202)637-2200
Fax: (202)637-2201
Registered: LDA
Executive Assistant to the Secretary, Department of Housing and Urban Development, 1975-77. Assistant to Special Counsel, Office of the Secretary, Department of the Navy, 1973-75. Law Clerk to Justice Lewis F. Powell, Jr., U.S. Supreme Court, 1972-73, and to Judge Frank M. Coffin, U.S. Court of Appeals, First Circuit, 1971-72.

Employers
Latham & Watkins (Partner)

Clients Represented

On Behalf of Latham & Watkins
ElderCare Companies

KELLY, William G.

11 Dupont Circle NW
Suite 700
Washington, DC 20036
Tel: (202)293-5886
Fax: (202)939-6969
Registered: LDA

Employers
Multinat'l Government Services, Inc.

Clients Represented

On Behalf of Multinat'l Government Services, Inc.
Rhone-Polenc Inc.

KELLY-JOHNSON, Mary Kate

700 13th St. NW
Suite 400
Washington, DC 20005
Tel: (202)347-0773
Fax: (202)347-0785
EMail: mjohnson@cassidy.com
Finance Director for 2001 Presidential Inaugural Committee and Deputy Finance Director of Bush-Cheney 2000.

Employers
Cassidy & Associates, Inc. (V. President)

Clients Represented

On Behalf of Cassidy & Associates, Inc.
Barry University
Ocean Spray Cranberries
Sherwin Williams Co.
University of Massachusetts Memorial Health System
VoiceStream Wireless Corp.

KELVIE, William C.

3900 Wisconsin Ave. NW
Washington, DC 20016
Tel: (202)752-8640

Employers
Fannie Mae (Exec. V. President, Chief Information Officer)

KEMMER, Mark L.

1660 L St. NW
Fourth Floor
Washington, DC 20036
Tel: (202)775-5066
Fax: (202)775-5097
Registered: LDA

Employers
General Motors Corp. (Senior Washington Representative)

KEMP, Geoffrey

1615 L St. NW
Suite 1250
Washington, DC 20036
Tel: (202)887-1000
Fax: (202)887-5222

Employers
Nixon Center, The (Director, Regional Strategic Programs)

KEMP, John D.

1300 Connecticut Ave. NW
Suite 700
Washington, DC 20036
Tel: (202)628-2800
Fax: (202)737-0725

Employers
Very Special Arts (President and Chief Exec. Officer)

KEMP, Steven C.

2025 M St. NW
Suite 800
Washington, DC 20036
Tel: (202)367-2100
Fax: (202)367-1200
EMail: kemp_steven@dc.sba.com

Employers
Smith, Bucklin and Associates, Inc.

Clients Represented

On Behalf of Smith, Bucklin and Associates, Inc.
American Urogynecologic Soc.
Nat'l Ass'n of Healthcare Access Management

KEMP, Tonya

2501 M St. NW
Suite 350
Washington, DC 20037
Tel: (202)659-3729
Fax: (202)887-5159

Employers
Manufactured Imports Promotion Organization (MIPRO) (Research Analyst)

KEMPER, III, Jackson

444 N. Capitol St.
Suite 545
Washington, DC 20001
Tel: (202)347-1223
Fax: (202)347-1225
Registered: LDA
EMail: jk3mga@aol.com

Employers
Madison Government Affairs (V. President, Business Development)

Clients Represented

On Behalf of Madison Government Affairs
Nat'l Community Reinvestment Coalition
Newport News, Virginia, Industrial Development Authority of the City of
Pensacola Chamber of Commerce
REM Engineering
SM&A
Systems Simulation Solutions Inc.
Team Santa Rosa Economic Development Council
University of West Florida
USS Wisconsin Foundation

KEMPER, Jr., Jackson

2600 Virginia Ave. NW
Suite 210
Washington, DC 20037
Tel: (202)337-5019
Fax: (202)337-5310
Registered: LDA

Employers
The Kemper Co. (President and Chief Exec. Officer)

Clients Represented

On Behalf of The Kemper Co.
Circuit Services, Inc.
CRYPTEK Secure Communications, LLC
Flight Safety Technologies, Inc.
Kildare Corp.
Progeny Systems
Qualtec, Inc.
Science Applications Internat'l Corp. (SAIC)
Scientific Fishery Systems, Inc.
Sonetech Corp.
Technology Systems, Inc.

KEMPF, Kyle W.

40 Ivy St. SE
Washington, DC 20003
Tel: (202)547-2230
Fax: (202)547-7640
Registered: LDA
EMail: kyle@dealer.org

Employers
Nat'l Lumber and Building Material Dealers Ass'n (Legislative Assistant)

KEMPNER, Jonathan L.

1919 Pennsylvania Ave. NW
Seventh Floor
Washington, DC 20006-3488
Tel: (202)557-2700
Former Staff Assistant to Senator Abraham Ribicoff (D-CT). Former Staff Assistant to the Subcommittee on Representation of Citizen Interests, Senate Committee on the Judiciary.

Employers
Mortgage Bankers Ass'n of America (Chief Operating Officer)

KEMPNER, Michael W.

1747 Pennsylvania Ave. NW
Suite 1150
Washington, DC 20006
Tel: (202)296-6222
Fax: (202)296-4507
Registered: LDA
EMail: mkempner@mww.com
Legislative Director to Rep. Bob Torricelli (D-NJ), 1983-85.

Employers
The MWW Group (President and Chief Exec. Officer)

Clients Represented
On Behalf of The MWW Group
GAF Corp.

KEMPS, David

1401 H St. NW
12th Floor
Washington, DC 20005-2148
Tel: (202)371-5406
Fax: (202)326-8313
Registered: LDA

Employers
Investment Co. Institute (Legislative Representative - Pension)

KENDALL, David E.

725 12th St. NW
Washington, DC 20005
Tel: (202)434-5000
Fax: (202)434-5029
Law Clerk to Justice Byron R. White, U.S. Supreme Court, 1971-72.

Employers
Williams & Connolly (Partner)

Clients Represented
On Behalf of Williams & Connolly
MCA Inc.

KENDALL, Deborah A.

475 L'Enfant Plaza SW
MS: 10907
Washington, DC 20260
Tel: (202)268-3420
Fax: (202)268-3775

Employers
United States Postal Service (Manager, Policy/Strategy)

KENDALL, William T.

50 E St. SE
Washington, DC 20003
Tel: (202)546-2600
Fax: (202)484-1979
Registered: LDA

Employers
Kendall and Associates (Chairman)

Clients Represented
On Behalf of Kendall and Associates
Toyota Motor North America, U.S.A., Inc.

KENDARDINE, Melanie

1600 Wilson Blvd.
Suite 900
Arlington, VA 22209
Tel: (703)526-7800
Fax: (703)526-7805

Employers
Gas Research Institute (V. President, Government Relations)

KENDRICK, Ethel

1801 L St. NW
MS: 9315
Washington, DC 20507
Tel: (202)663-4900
Fax: (202)663-4912

Employers
Equal Employment Opportunity Commission (Congressional Liaison Specialist)

KENDRICK, Glenda

810 Seventh St. NW
MS: 6328
Washington, DC 20531
Tel: (202)307-0703
Fax: (202)514-5958

Employers
Department of Justice - Office of Justice Programs (Associate Deputy Director, Office of Congressional and Public Affairs)

KENDRICK, Martha M.

2550 M St. NW
Washington, DC 20037-1350
Tel: (202)457-6520
Fax: (202)457-6315
Registered: LDA
EMail: mkendrick@pattonboggs.com
Professional Staff Member, Department of Health and Human Services, 1973-85.

Employers
Patton Boggs, LLP (Partner)

Clients Represented
On Behalf of Patton Boggs, LLP
America's Blood Centers
American College of Gastroenterology
American Medical Rehabilitation Providers Ass'n
American Medical Security
Forethought Group/Forethought Life Insurance Co.
HCR-Manor Care, Inc.
Hoffmann-La Roche Inc.
Illinois Department of Human Services
Intercultural Cancer Council
Mars, Inc.
Nat'l Marrow Donor Program
New York State Ass'n of Health Care Providers
Patient Access to Transplantation (PAT) Coalition
Preneed Insurers Government Programs Coalition
University Medical Associates
Valley Children's Hospital
Wayne, Michigan, County of

KENIRY, Daniel J.

1600 Pennsylvania Ave. NW
112 E. Wing
Washington, DC 20500
Tel: (202)456-6620
Fax: (202)456-2604

Employers
Executive Office of the President - The White House (Special Assistant to the President for Legislative Affairs, House Liaison Office)

KENKEL, Mary

701 Pennsylvania Ave. NW
Washington, DC 20004-2696
Tel: (202)508-5662
Fax: (202)508-5403

Employers
Edison Electric Institute (Director, Public Policy and Issue Management)

KENNEBECK, Joseph W.

1300 Pennsylvania Ave. NW
Suite 860
Washington, DC 20004
Tel: (202)842-5800
Fax: (202)842-8612
Registered: LDA

Employers
Volkswagen of America, Inc. (Director, Government Affairs)

KENNEDY, Brian

1801 K St. NW
Suite 601 L
Washington, DC 20006
Tel: (202)756-7100
Fax: (202)756-7200
EMail: brian_kennedy@was.cohnwolfe.com

Employers
Cohn & Wolfe (Senior Account Executive)

KENNEDY, Caroline

1101 14th St. NW
Suite 1400
Washington, DC 20005
Tel: (202)682-9400
Fax: (202)682-1331
EMail: CKennedy@defenders.org

Employers
Defenders of Wildlife (Program Associate)

KENNEDY, Charlene Dziak

1275 K St. NW
Suite 1200
Washington, DC 20005
Tel: (202)216-0700
Fax: (202)216-0824
Registered: LDA

Employers
Delta Air Lines (Manager, Government Affairs)

KENNEDY, Craig

1330 New Hampshire Ave. NW
Suite 122
Washington, DC 20036
Tel: (202)296-3073
Fax: (202)296-3526
Registered: LDA
EMail: ckennedy@nachc.com
Legislative Director to Rep. Doc Hastings (R-WA). Senior Legislative Assistant to Rep. Jim Bunn (R-OR). Legislative Correspondent, Senate Committee on Finance, 1992-95.

Employers
Nat'l Ass'n of Community Health Centers (Federal Affairs Representative)

KENNEDY, Craig R.

11 Dupont Circle NW
Suite 750
Washington, DC 20036
Tel: (202)745-3950
Fax: (202)265-1662

Employers
German Marshall Fund of the United States (President)

KENNEDY, Daniel E.

1015 15th St. NW
Suite 700
Washington, DC 20005-2605
Tel: (202)828-5200
Fax: (202)785-2645
Registered: LDA

Employers
Bechtel Group, Inc. (V. President and Manager, Government Affairs (BNI))

KENNEDY, J. Keith

801 Pennsylvania Ave. NW
Suite 800
Washington, DC 20004
Tel: (202)508-3438
Fax: (202)508-3402
Registered: LDA, FARA
EMail: kkennedy@bdbc.com
Majority Staff Director, Senate Committee on Appropriations, 1980-96.

Employers
Baker, Donelson, Bearman & Caldwell, P.C. (Senior Public Policy Advisor)

Clients Represented
On Behalf of Baker, Donelson, Bearman & Caldwell, P.C.
American Trucking Ass'ns
Amgen
Deutsche Telekom, Inc.
FLIR Systems, Inc.
Leap Wireless Internat'l
Newspaper Ass'n of America
Nextwave Telecom
PacifiCorp
Ventura Port District
VoiceStream Wireless Corp.
The Washington Post Co.

KENNEDY, Jerry W.

313 South Carolina Ave. SE
Washington, DC 20003-4213
Tel: (202)547-0971
Fax: (202)547-2672
Registered: LDA

Employers
Kennedy Government Relations (Attorney)

Clients Represented
On Behalf of Kennedy Government Relations
El Dorado Irrigation District
General Atomics

KENNEDY, Judith A.

2121 K St. NW
Suite 700
Washington, DC 20037
Tel: (202)293-9850
Fax: (202)293-9852
Registered: LDA

Employers
Nat'l Ass'n of Affordable Housing Lenders (President)

KENNEDY, Kara

444 North Capitol St. NW
Suite 535
Washington, DC 20001
Tel: (202)478-6859
EMail: kara@petrizzogroup.com

Chief of Staff (1999-2001), Communications Director (1999), and Press Secretary (1998-99) to Rep. Jennifer Dunn (R-WA). Former Aide to Speaker of the House, Rep. Newt Gingrich (R-GA).

Employers
The Petrizzo Group, Inc. (V. President)

Clients Represented
On Behalf of The Petrizzo Group, Inc.
Airborne Express
Central Puget Sound Regional Transit Authority (Sound Transit)
Coalition for American Financial Security
Eddie Bauer Co.
Electronic Industries Alliance
Group Health Cooperative
Renton, Washington, City of
Frank Russell Co.
Vulcan Northwest Inc.

KENNEDY, Michael D.

1350 I St. NW
Suite 400
Washington, DC 20005-3306
Tel: (202)371-6900
Fax: (202)842-3578
Registered: LDA

Employers
Motorola, Inc. (Corporate V. President and Director, Global Government Relations)

KENNEDY, Patricia C.

3220 Juniper Ln.
Falls Church, VA 22044
Tel: (703)533-2035
Registered: LDA

Employers
Self-employed as an independent consultant.

Clients Represented
As an independent consultant
DaimlerChrysler Corp.
PEI Electronics

KENNEDY, Thomas

444 N. Capitol St. NW
Suite 315
Washington, DC 20001
Tel: (202)624-5828
Fax: (202)624-7875

Employers
Ass'n of State and Territorial Solid Waste Management Officials (Exec. Director)

KENNELLY, Hon. Barbara Bailey

1050 Connecticut Ave. NW
Suite 1100
Washington, DC 20036-5304
Tel: (202)861-1529
Fax: (202)861-1790

Associate Commissioner for Retirement Policy, Social Security Administration, 1999-2000. Member, U.S. House of Representatives (D-CT), 1982-99

Employers
Baker & Hostetler LLP

KENNETT, Earle

1090 Vermont Ave. NW
Suite 700
Washington, DC 20005-4905
Tel: (202)289-7800
Fax: (202)289-1092
EMail: ekennett@nibs.org

Employers
Nat'l Institute of Building Sciences (V. President)

KENNEY, Joan M.

655 15th St. NW
Suite 300
Washington, DC 20005
Tel: (202)783-0900
Fax: (202)783-2308
EMail: joan.kenney@bms.com

Employers
Bristol-Myers Squibb Co. (Director, Regulatory Relations and Policy)

KENNGOTT, Chris

430 S. Capitol St. SE
Washington, DC 20003
Tel: (202)863-8000
Fax: (202)863-8174

Employers
Democratic Nat'l Committee (Director, State Party Fundraising)

KENNY, Brendan M.

1625 Massachusetts Ave. NW
Washington, DC 20036
Tel: (202)797-4033
Fax: (202)797-4030
Registered: LDA

Employers
Air Line Pilots Ass'n Internat'l (Legislative Representative)

KENNY, G. Michael

1015 Duke St.
Alexandria, VA 22314-3551
Tel: (703)549-8444
Fax: (703)549-6526
EMail: g.michael.kenny@us-mongolia.org

Employers
U.S.-Mongolia Business Council, Inc. (Exec. Director)

KENNY, John

1341 G St. NW
Suite 1100
Washington, DC 20005
Tel: (202)585-0202
Fax: (202)393-0712
Registered: LDA

Employers
Infotech Strategies, Inc. (President)

KENNY, Lynn

1030 15th St. NW
Suite 870
Washington, DC 20005
Tel: (202)393-1780
Fax: (202)393-0336
EMail: lkenny@kellenco.com

Employers
American College of Construction Lawyers (Exec. Director)
American College of Tax Counsel (Administrator)
American Tax Policy Institute (Administrator)
The Kellen Company (Account Executive)

Clients Represented
On Behalf of The Kellen Company
American College of Construction Lawyers
American College of Tax Counsel
American Tax Policy Institute

KENT, Jonathan H.

1990 M St. NW
Suite 340
Washington, DC 20036
Tel: (202)223-6222
Fax: (202)785-0687
Registered: LDA

Employers
Kent & O'Connor, Inc. (Chairman)

Clients Represented
On Behalf of Kent & O'Connor, Inc.
American Soc. of Plastic and Reconstructive Surgeons
American Supply Ass'n
Condea Vista Chemical Co.
Internat'l Academy of Compounding Pharmacists
Internat'l Ass'n of Airport Duty Free Stores
Internat'l Trademark Ass'n
Liz Claiborne Internat'l
Nat'l Customs Brokers and Forwarders Ass'n of America

KENT, Judy

1001 Connecticut Ave. NW
Suite 1250
Washington, DC 20036
Tel: (202)331-1010
Fax: (202)331-0640

Employers
Competitive Enterprise Institute (Media Contact, Center for Private Conservation)

KENT, Linda

1401 H St. NW
Suite 600
Washington, DC 20005-2136
Tel: (202)326-7300
Fax: (202)326-7333
EMail: Lkent@usta.org

Employers
United States Telecom Ass'n (Associate General Counsel)

KENT, Norma G.

One Dupont Circle NW
Suite 410
Washington, DC 20036
Tel: (202)728-0200
Ext: 209
Fax: (202)833-2467
EMail: nkent@aacc.nche.edu

Employers
American Ass'n of Community Colleges (Director, Communications)

KENTOFF, David R.

555 12th St. NW
Washington, DC 20004-1206
Tel: (202)942-5000
Fax: (202)942-5999
EMail: David_Kentoff@aporter.com

Employers
Arnold & Porter (Partner)

KENTZ, Andrew W.

1775 Pennsylvania Ave. NW
Suite 200
Washington, DC 20006
Tel: (202)862-1086
Fax: (202)862-1093
Registered: LDA

Chief of Staff and Counsel to Senator Byron L. Dorgan (D-ND), 1986-1989.

Employers
Dewey Ballantine LLP (Partner)

Clients Represented
On Behalf of Dewey Ballantine LLP
American Natural Soda Ash Corp.
Automatic Data Processing, Inc
Coalition for Fair Lumber Imports
Railroad Retirement Tax Working Group
Scull Law Firm, David L.
Thompson Publishing, Inc.
Tribune Co.
Union Pacific

KENWORTHY, William D.

11803 Wayland St.
Oakton, VA 22124-2229
Tel: (703)716-4846
Fax: (703)716-0043
Registered: LDA

Employers
Governmental Strategies, Inc. (V. President)

Clients Represented
On Behalf of Governmental Strategies, Inc.
El Paso Electric Co.

KENYON, Allyson

1021 Prince St.
Alexandria, VA 22314-2971
Tel: (703)684-7722
Fax: (703)684-5968
EMail: akenyon@nmha.org

Employers
Nat'l Mental Health Ass'n (Government Affairs Associate)

KERAMIDAS, Sherry

11300 Rockville Pike
Suite 1000
Rockville, MD 20852-3048
Tel: (301)770-2920
Fax: (301)770-2924

Employers
Regulatory Affairs Professionals Soc. (Exec. Director)

KERCHNER, George

1299 Pennsylvania Ave. NW
Washington, DC 20004-2402
Tel: (202)783-0800
Fax: (202)383-6610
Registered: LDA

Employers
Howrey Simon Arnold & White

Clients Represented
On Behalf of Howrey Simon Arnold & White
Portable Rechargeable Battery Ass'n

KERKHOVEN, Paul

1100 Wilson Blvd.
Suite 850
Arlington, VA 22209
Tel: (703)527-3022
Fax: (703)527-3025
Registered: LDA
EMail: pkerkhoven@ngvc.org

Employers
Natural Gas Vehicle Coalition (Director, Government Relations)

KERMAN, Candace

1255 23rd St. NW
Suite 800
Washington, DC 20037
Tel: (202)973-7739
Fax: (202)973-7750

Employers
Affordable Housing Tax Credit Coalition (Director)

KERMAN, Leslie

818 Connecticut Ave. NW
#1007
Washington, DC 20006

Employers
Campaign Accountability Project (Contact, Political Action Committee)

KERN, Thomas E.

1015 15th St. NW
Suite 802
Washington, DC 20005
Tel: (202)347-7474
Fax: (202)898-0068
Registered: LDA
EMail: tkern@acec.org

Employers
American Consulting Engineers Council (Deputy Exec. V. President, Operations)

KERR, Eleanor

701 Pennsylvania Ave. NW
Suite 720
Washington, DC 20004
Tel: (202)434-4800
Fax: (202)347-4015
Registered: LDA
Formerly worked in the Department of Health and Human Services, during the Bush I Administration.

Employers
Siemens Corp.

KERR, Gordon

1785 Massachusetts Ave. NW
Washington, DC 20036
Tel: (202)588-6000
Fax: (202)588-6059
Registered: LDA

Employers
Nat'l Trust for Historic Preservation (Director, Congressional Relations)

KERR, Stuart

1615 New Hampshire Ave. NW
Washington, DC 20009
Tel: (202)483-3036
Fax: (202)483-3029

Employers
Internat'l Law Institute (Exec. Director)

KERR, Suzanne S.

110 Maryland Ave. NE
Suite 409
Washington, DC 20002
Tel: (202)543-4100
Fax: (202)543-6297
Registered: LDA
EMail: skerr@clw.org

Employers
Council for a Livable World (Legislative Director)
Council for a Livable World Education Fund

KERRIGAN, Karen

1920 L St. NW
Suite 200
Washington, DC 20036
Tel: (202)785-0238
Fax: (202)822-8118
Registered: LDA

Employers
Small Business Survival Committee (Chairman)

KERRIGAN, Kathleen M.

1050 Connecticut Ave. NW
Suite 1100
Washington, DC 20036-5304
Tel: (202)861-1500
Fax: (202)861-1790
Registered: LDA

Employers
Baker & Hostetler LLP

Clients Represented

On Behalf of Baker & Hostetler LLP
Citigroup
The Council of Insurance Agents & Brokers
Federation of American Hospitals
Froedtert Memorial Lutheran Hospital
Invacare Corp.
Nat'l Ass'n of Real Estate Investment Trusts
RMS Disease Management Inc.
Schering Berlin Inc.

KERRIGAN, Michael J.

1104 Dapple Grey Court
Great Falls, VA 22066
Tel: (703)757-2829
Fax: (703)757-2884
Registered: LDA
EMail: kerrigan@tagnet.com

Employers
Kerrigan & Associates, Inc. (President)

Clients Represented

On Behalf of Kerrigan & Associates, Inc.
L. P. Conwood Co.
GCI-Wisconsin
Maptech
New York Institute for Special Education
Science Applications Internat'l Corp. (SAIC)

KERSHOW, Michael R.

3050 K St. NW
Washington, DC 20007
Tel: (202)342-8580
Fax: (202)342-8451
Registered: LDA, FARA
EMail: mkershow@colliershannon.com

Employers
Collier Shannon Scott, PLLC (Of Counsel)

Clients Represented

On Behalf of Collier Shannon Scott, PLLC
American Sheep Industry Ass'n
Bicycle Manufacturers Ass'n of America
Coalition for Safe Ceramicware
Gerico
Internat'l Crystal Federation
Pfaltzgraff

KERTTULA, Ph.D, Anna M.

444 N. Capitol St. NW
Suite 336
Washington, DC 20001
Tel: (202)624-5858
Fax: (202)624-5857

Employers
Alaska, Washington Office of the State of (Associate Director)

KERWIN, Mary D.

300 E St. SW
Room 9L33
Washington, DC 20546
Tel: (202)358-1827
Fax: (202)358-4340
EMail: mkerwin@hq.nasa.gov

Employers
Nat'l Aeronautics and Space Administration (Acting Associate Administrator, Legislative Affairs)

KESS, Linda E.

200 Independence Ave. SW
Room 341H
Washington, DC 20201
Tel: (202)690-5413
Fax: (202)690-8168

Employers
Department of Health and Human Services - Health Care Financing Administration (Exec. Officer, Office of Legislation)

KESSER, Sheri

1615 L St. NW
Suite 900
Washington, DC 20036
Tel: (202)778-1000
Fax: (202)466-6002
EMail: skesser@apcoworldwide.com

Employers
APCO Worldwide (V. President, Global Services)

KESSLER, J. Christian

2201 C St. NW
Washington, DC 20520
Tel: (202)736-4242
Fax: (202)736-4250

Employers
Department of State - Non-Proliferation Bureau (Director, Office of Congressional and Public Affairs)

KESSLER, Judd L.

1919 Pennsylvania Ave. NW
Suite 500
Washington, DC 20006-3434
Tel: (202)778-3000
Fax: (202)778-3063
Registered: FARA
EMail: jkessler@porterwright.com
Chief Counsel for Near East Programs (1980-82), Chief Counsel for Latin American and Caribbean Affairs (1976-80), Chief Counsel for Legislative Affairs (1975-76), and Assistant General Counsel (1975-82), all at the U.S. Agency for International Development, U.S. International Development Cooperation Agency.

Employers
Porter, Wright, Morris & Arthur, LLP (Partner)

Clients Represented

On Behalf of Porter, Wright, Morris & Arthur, LLP
Harza Engineering Co.

KESSLER, Lee

100 N. Pitt St.
Suite 202
Alexandria, VA 22314
Tel: (703)519-7778
Fax: (703)519-7557

Employers
Pride Africa (Director)

KESSLER, Liza

2120 L St. NW
Suite 400
Washington, DC 20037
Tel: (202)478-6301
Fax: (202)478-6171
EMail: lkessler@lharris.com

Employers
Leslie Harris & Associates (Senior Policy Counsel)

Clients Represented

On Behalf of Leslie Harris & Associates
American Library Ass'n
Leadership Conference on Civil Rights

KESSLER, Lorence L.

1015 15th St. NW
Suite 1200
Washington, DC 20005
Tel: (202)789-8600
Fax: (202)789-1708

Employers
McGuiness Norris & Williams, LLP (Of Counsel)

KESSLER, Richard S.

210 Seventh St. SE
Washington, DC 20003
Tel: (202)547-6808
Fax: (202)546-5425
Registered: LDA

Employers
Kessler & Associates Business Services, Inc. (President)

Clients Represented

On Behalf of Kessler & Associates Business Services, Inc.
Amgen
Burlington Northern Santa Fe Railway
Dunn-Edwards Corp.
Exelon Corp.
Grocery Manufacturers of America
Henry H. Kessler Foundation
Mercy Health System of Northwest Arkasas
Nat'l Ass'n of Securities Dealers, Inc. (NASD)
Novartis Corp.
Pfizer, Inc.
Pharmacia Corp.
Philip Morris Management Corp.
Planet Electric
Ripon Society
Sallie Mae, Inc.

KEST, Steven

739 Eighth St. SE
Washington, DC 20003
Tel: (202)547-2500
Fax: (202)546-2483

Employers
ACORN (Ass'n of Community Organizations for Reform Now) (Exec. Director)

KESTENBAUM, Leon M.

401 Ninth St. NW
Suite 400
Washington, DC 20004
Tel: (202)585-1913
Fax: (202)585-1897

Employers
Sprint Corp. (V. President, Federal Regulatory - LDD)

KESTER, John G.

725 12th St. NW
Washington, DC 20005
Tel: (202)434-5000
Fax: (202)434-5029
Special Assistant to the Secretary and Deputy Secretary, Department of Defense, 1977-78. Deputy Assistant Secretary, Department of the Army, 1969-72. Captain, Judge Advocate General Corps, U.S. Army, 1965-68. Law Clerk to Justice Hugo L. Black, U.S. Supreme Court, 1963-65.

Employers
Williams & Connolly (Partner)

KESTON, Joan

P.O. Box 75248
Washington, DC 20013-5248
Tel: (202)927-4926
Fax: (202)927-4920

Employers
Public Employees Roundtable (Chair)

KETCH, Todd

1120 Connecticut Ave. NW
Suite 480
Washington, DC 20036-3989
EMail: tketch@eatright.com
Tel: (202)775-8277
Fax: (202)775-8284
Registered: LDA

Employers
American Dietetic Ass'n (Director, Government Affairs)

KETTER, Joni

555 New Jersey Ave. NW
Tenth Floor
Washington, DC 20001
EMail: fnhpaft@aft.org
Tel: (202)879-4491
Fax: (202)879-4597

Employers
Federation of Nurses and Health Professionals/AFT (Senior Associate)

KEULEMAN, Christopher

1201 15th St. NW
Washington, DC 20005-2800
Tel: (202)822-0470
Fax: (202)822-0572
Registered: LDA

Employers
Nat'l Ass'n of Home Builders of the U.S. (Director, Political Affairs/Democrat)

KEUP, Wayne A.

600 New Hampshire Ave. NW
11th Floor
Washington, DC 20037
EMail: wak@dejlaw.com
Tel: (202)944-3000
Fax: (202)944-3068
Registered: LDA

Employers
Dyer Ellis & Joseph, P.C. (Partner)

Clients Represented

On Behalf of Dyer Ellis & Joseph, P.C.
John Crane-LIPS, Inc.
DaimlerChrysler Corp.
Electronic Design Inc.
TI Group Inc.

KEVICH, Fran

1300 19th St. NW
Suite 300
Washington, DC 20036
Tel: (202)223-6722
Fax: (202)659-0650

Employers
Nat'l Parks Conservation Ass'n

KEVILL, Paige

1055 Thomas Jefferson St. NW
Suite 500
Washington, DC 20007
Tel: (202)625-2111
Fax: (202)424-7900

Employers
RTC Direct (Management Supervisor)

KEYES, Jr., J.D., Joseph A.

2450 N St. NW
Washington, DC 20037-1126
Tel: (202)828-0555
Fax: (202)828-1125

Employers
Ass'n of American Medical Colleges (General Counsel, Senior V. President)

KEYES, IV, William A.

1706 New Hampshire Ave. NW
Washington, DC 20009
EMail: wkeyes@tfas.org
Tel: (202)986-0384
Fax: (202)986-0390

Employers
Fund for American Studies (Exec. Director, Institute on Political Journalism)

KEYS, III, G. Chandler

1301 Pennsylvania Ave. NW
Suite 300
Washington, DC 20004
EMail: qck@ncanet.org
Tel: (202)347-0228
Fax: (202)638-0607
Registered: LDA

Employers
Nat'l Cattleman's Beef Ass'n (V. President, Public Policy)

KEYSERLING, Jonathan

1700 Diagonal Rd.
Suite 300
Alexandria, VA 22314
EMail: jkeyserling@nhpco.org
Tel: (703)837-3153
Fax: (703)525-5762

Employers
Nat'l Hospice & Palliative Care Organization (V. President, Legislative and Regulatory Affairs)

KEYWORK, II, Ph.D., George A. "Jay"

1301 K St. NW
Suite 550E
Washington, DC 20005
Tel: (202)289-8928
Fax: (202)289-6079

Employers
The Progress Freedom Foundation (Chairman, Senior Fellow and Co-Founder)

KHACHIGIAN, Kristy

1706 New Hampshire Ave. NW
Washington, DC 20009
EMail: kkhachig@tfas.org
Tel: (202)986-0384
Fax: (202)986-0390

Employers
Fund for American Studies (Director, Engalitcheff Institute and Bryce Harlow Institute)

KHAN, Ayesha

518 C St. NE
Washington, DC 20002
Tel: (202)466-3234
Fax: (202)466-2587

Employers
Americans United for Separation of Church and State (Litigator)

KHAN, Mohamed

1500 K St. NW
Suite 850
Washington, DC 20005
EMail: mkhan@compete.org
Tel: (202)682-4292
Fax: (202)682-5150

Employers
Council on Competitiveness (Director, Information Technology)

KHARE, Joe

2800 Shirlington Rd.
Suite 401
Arlington, VA 22206
EMail: joekhare@asic-dc.com
Tel: (703)824-0300
Fax: (703)824-0320
Registered: LDA

Employers
American Systems Internat'l Corp. (Consultant)

Clients Represented

On Behalf of American Systems Internat'l Corp.
Elbet Forth Worth
SRA Corp.

KHARFEN, Michael

1250 Connecticut Ave. NW
Suite 610
Washington, DC 20036
Director, Administration for Children, Youth and Families, Department of Health and Human Services, 1994-2001.
Tel: (202)955-3005
Fax: (202)955-1087

Employers
Welfare to Work Partnership (Chief Operating Officer)

KHLOPIN, Derek

1300 Pennsylvania Ave. NW
Suite 350
Washington, DC 20044
EMail: dkhlopin@tia.eia.org
Tel: (202)383-1486
Fax: (202)383-1495

Employers
Telecommunications Industry Ass'n (Director, Law and Public Policy)

KHOURY, Dr. Bernard V.

One Physics Ellipse
College Park, MD 20740-3845
EMail: bkhoury@aapt.org
Tel: (301)209-3300
Fax: (301)209-0845

Employers
American Ass'n of Physics Teachers (Exec. Officer)

KIBBE, Mark

1220 L St. NW
Washington, DC 20005
Tel: (202)682-8425
Fax: (202)682-8232
Registered: LDA

Employers
American Petroleum Institute (Legislative Analyst)

KIBBE, Matt

1250 H St. NW
Suite 700
Washington, DC 20005-3908
EMail: mkibbe@cse.org
Tel: (202)783-3870
Fax: (202)783-4687

Employers
Citizens for a Sound Economy (Exec. V. President, Public Policy)

KIDDOO, Jean L.

3000 K St. NW
Suite 300
Washington, DC 20007
Tel: (202)424-7500
Fax: (202)424-7643

Employers
Swidler Berlin Shereff Friedman, LLP (Partner)

Clients Represented

On Behalf of Swidler Berlin Shereff Friedman, LLP
CAIS Internet

KIEFER, Catherine B.

1050 Thomas Jefferson St. NW
Sixth Floor
Washington, DC 20007
Tel: (202)298-1895
Fax: (202)298-1699
Registered: LDA

Employers
John Freshman Associates, Inc.

Clients Represented

On Behalf of John Freshman Associates, Inc.
#10 Enterprises LLC
Anheuser-Busch Cos., Inc.
Gulf Coast Waste Disposal Authority
Lewis and Clark Rural Water System, Inc.
Los Angeles County Sanitation District
Metropolitan St. Louis Sewer District
Mid Dakota Rural Water System
Monterey County Water Resources Agency
Nat'l Audubon Soc.
Oregon Water Trust
Pharmacia Corp.
Sacramento, California, Department of Utilities of

KIEFFER, Charles

Eisenhower Exec. Office Bldg.
725 17th St. NW
Washington, DC 20503
Tel: (202)395-4790
Fax: (202)395-3729

Employers
Executive Office of the President - Office of Management and Budget (Acting Associate Director, Legislative Affairs)

KIEFFER, Dr. Jarold A.

9019 Hamilton Dr.
Fairfax, VA 22031
Tel: (703)591-8328
Fax: (703)359-4244

Employers
Advanced Transit Ass'n (Former Chairman)

KIEFFER, Margaret

300 E St. SW
Room 9L33
Washington, DC 20546
EMail: mkieffer@hq.nasa.gov
Tel: (202)358-1055
Fax: (202)358-4340

Employers
Nat'l Aeronautics and Space Administration (Legislative Affairs Specialist)

KIEHL, Kristina

1010 Wisconsin Ave. NW
Suite 410
Washington, DC 20007
Tel: (202)944-5080
Fax: (202)944-5081

Employers
Voters For Choice (Democratic Chair)

KIEL, Fred

5683 Columbia Pike
Suite 200
Falls Church, VA 22041
Tel: (703)820-2244
Fax: (703)820-2271
Registered: FARA

Employers
Hoffman & Hoffman Public Relations (V. President)

KIELY, Bruce F.

1299 Pennsylvania Ave. NW
Suite 1300 West
Washington, DC 20004-2400
Tel: (202)639-7700
Fax: (202)639-7890

Member, Office of General Counsel, Federal Power Commission, 1972-73. Office of General Counsel, U.S. Army Selective Service System, 1971-72.

Employers
Baker Botts, L.L.P. (Partner)

KIELY, Elise P. W.

1625 Massachusetts Ave. NW
Suite 300
Washington, DC 20036
Tel: (202)955-6300
Fax: (202)955-6460
Registered: LDA
EMail: elise@technologylaw.com

Employers
Blumenfeld & Cohen (Associate)

KIENITZ, Roy

1100 17th St. NW
Suite Ten
Washington, DC 20036
Tel: (202)466-2636
Fax: (202)466-2247

Employers
Surface Transportation Policy Project (Exec. Director)

KIERIG, Chris

1341 G St. NW
Suite 200
Washington, DC 20005
Tel: (202)347-5990
Fax: (202)347-5941
EMail: ckierig@clj.com

Employers
Copeland, Lowery & Jacquez (Legislative Associate)

KIERN, Lawrence I.

1400 L St. NW
Washington, DC 20005-3502
Tel: (202)371-5811
Fax: (202)371-5950
Registered: LDA

Employers
Winston & Strawn (Of Counsel, Health Care Practice)

Clients Represented

On Behalf of Winston & Strawn
First American Bulk Carriers Corp.
Kirby Corp./Dixie Carriers
Liberty Maritime Co.
Marinette Marine Corp.
Maximum Information Technology Inc.
Northland Holdings, Inc.

KIERNAN, Peter S.

450 Fifth St. NW
Room 6104
Washington, DC 20549
Tel: (202)942-0015
Fax: (202)942-9650

Employers
Securities and Exchange Commission (Legislative Counsel)

KIERNAN, Thomas C.

1300 19th St. NW
Suite 300
Washington, DC 20036
Tel: (202)223-6722
Fax: (202)659-0650

Employers
Nat'l Parks Conservation Ass'n (President)

KIES, Kathleen Clark

3050 K St. NW
Washington, DC 20007
Tel: (202)342-8528
Fax: (202)342-8451
Registered: LDA, FARA
EMail: kkies@colliershannon.com

Former Legislative Assistant to Rep. Don Pease (D-OH).

Employers
Collier Shannon Scott, PLLC (Assistant Director, Government Relations)

Clients Represented

On Behalf of Collier Shannon Scott, PLLC
American Flange Producers Marking Coalition
American Sheep Industry Ass'n
Bicycle Manufacturers Ass'n of America
Fannie Mae
Fresh Garlic Producer Ass'n
GATX Corp.
Nat'l Ass'n of Convenience Stores
Nat'l Juice Products Ass'n
Soc. of Independent Gasoline Marketers of America
Symbol Technologies, Inc.
Toolex USA, Inc.
Vitol, S.A., Inc.
Wickland Oil Co.

KIES, Kenneth J.

1301 K St. NW
Washington, DC 20005-3333
Tel: (202)414-1616
Fax: (202)414-1301
Registered: LDA
EMail: kenneth.j.kies@us.pwcglobal.com

Chief of Staff, Joint Committee on Taxation, U.S. Congress, 1995-98. Chief Minority Tax Counsel, Committee on Ways and Means, 1982-86.

Employers
PriceWaterhouseCoopers (Managing Partner, Washington National Tax Service)

Clients Represented

On Behalf of PriceWaterhouseCoopers
Alliance Capital Management LP
American Ass'n of Nurse Anesthetists
American Council of Life Insurers
Automobile Manufacturers R&D Coalition
Bank of America
Blue Cross Blue Shield Ass'n
Cigar Ass'n of America
Clark/Bardes, Inc.
Coalition for Fair Tax Credits
Coalition of Corporate Taxpayers
Conoco Inc.
Contract Manufacturing Coalition
Council for Energy Independence
Edison Electric Institute
General Motors Corp.
Goldman, Sachs and Co.
Household Internat'l, Inc.
Interest Allocation Coalition
Latona Associates, Inc.
Owens Corning
Placid Refining Co.
Plum Creek Timber Co.
PwC Contract Manufacturing Coalition
PwC Leasing Coalition
Ralston Purina Co.
Tupperware Corp.
United Parcel Service

KIKUCHI, Hiroshi "Andy"

1620 L St. NW
Suite 1150
Washington, DC 20036
Tel: (202)223-2575
Ext: 107
Fax: (202)223-2614
Registered: LDA

Employers
Matsushita Electric Industrial Co., Ltd. (Director)

KILBERG, William J.

1050 Connecticut Ave. NW
Washington, DC 20036-5306
Tel: (202)955-8500
Fax: (202)467-0539
Registered: LDA
EMail: wkilberg@gdclaw.com

Deputy Team Leader, Reagan-Bush Transition Team (1980-81), Solicitor (1973-77) and Associate Solicitor (1971-73), all at the Department of Labor. General Counsel, Federal Mediation and Conciliation Service, 1970-71. White House Fellow, Special Assistant to the Secretary, Department of Labor, 1969-70.

Employers
Gibson, Dunn & Crutcher LLP (Partner)

KILBOURN, Seth

919 18th St. NW
Suite 800
Washington, DC 20006
Tel: (202)628-4160
Fax: (202)347-5323
Registered: LDA

Employers
Human Rights Campaign Fund (National Field Director)

KILBOURNE, Brett

1140 Connecticut Ave. NW
Suite 1140
Washington, DC 20036
Tel: (202)872-0030
Fax: (202)872-1331
Registered: LDA
EMail: bkilbour@utc.org

Employers
United Telecom Council (Associate Counsel)

KILCULLEN, Peter

1615 L St. NW
Suite 1200
Washington, DC 20036
Tel: (202)466-6300
Fax: (202)463-0678

Employers
Bell, Boyd & Lloyd

KILEY, Edward J.

1730 M St. NW
Suite 400
Washington, DC 20036
Tel: (202)296-2900
Fax: (202)296-1370

Employers
Grove, Jaskiewicz, and Cobert (Partner)

KILEY, Roger J.

1909 K St. NW
Washington, DC 20006
Tel: (202)263-3000
Fax: (202)263-3300
Registered: LDA

Employers
Mayer, Brown & Platt (Partner)

KILGANNON, Thomas P.

22570 Market Court
Suite 240
Dulles, VA 20166
Tel: (703)444-7940
Fax: (703)444-9893
EMail: tom.kilgannon@freedomalliance.org

Employers
The Freedom Alliance (Exec. Director)

KILGORE, Ed

600 Pennsylvania Ave. SE
Suite 400
Washington, DC 20003
Tel: (202)546-0007
Fax: (202)544-5002

Employers
Democratic Leadership Council (Policy Director)

KILGORE, Gregory

401 Ninth St. NW
Suite 400
Washington, DC 20004
Tel: (202)585-1900
Fax: (202)585-1899
Registered: LDA

Employers
Sprint Corp. (Director, Government Affairs)

KILGORE, Peter

1200 17th St. NW
Washington, DC 20036-3097
Tel: (202)331-5900
Fax: (202)973-5373
EMail: pkilgore@dineout.org

Employers
Nat'l Restaurant Ass'n (Senior V. President and General Counsel)

KILLEEN, John J.

2020 K St. NW
Suite 400
Washington, DC 20006
Tel: (202)530-8905
Fax: (202)530-5641
Registered: LDA

Employers
Science Applications Internat'l Corp. (SAIC) (Senior V. President, Government Affairs)

KILLION, Frederick J.

1400 L St. NW
Washington, DC 20005-3502
Tel: (202)371-5700
Fax: (202)371-5950

Employers
Winston & Strawn

Clients Represented
On Behalf of Winston & Strawn
Barr Laboratories

KILLMER, William P.

1201 15th St. NW
Washington, DC 20005-2800
Tel: (202)822-0470
Fax: (202)822-0572

Employers
Nat'l Ass'n of Home Builders of the U.S. (Senior Staff V. President, Government Affairs Division)

KILLORIDE, Patrick

1310 G St. NW
Suite 690
Washington, DC 20005-3000
EMail: pkilloride@as-coa.org
Tel: (202)639-0724
Fax: (202)639-0794

Employers
Council of the Americas (Director, Governmental Affairs)

KILMER, Debbie

401 Ninth St.
Second Floor
Washington, DC 20004-2037
Tel: (202)879-9600
Fax: (202)879-9700

Employers
Corporation for Public Broadcasting (V. President, Government Relations)

KILMER, Paul F.

2099 Pennsylvania Ave. NW
Suite 100
Washington, DC 20006
EMail: pkilmer@hklaw.com
Tel: (202)955-3000
Fax: (202)955-5564

Employers
Holland & Knight LLP (Partner)

KIM, Anne

600 Pennsylvania Ave. SE
Suite 400
Washington, DC 20003
Tel: (202)547-0001
Fax: (202)544-5014

Employers
Progressive Policy Institute (Director, Working Families Project)

KIM, Baker

1401 Wilson Blvd.
Suite 1100
Arlington, VA 22209
Tel: (703)522-5055
Fax: (703)525-2279
Registered: LDA

Employers
Information Technology Ass'n of America (ITAA)

KIM, Christina

2500 Wilson Blvd.
Suite 300
Arlington, VA 22201
EMail: ckim@tia.eia.org
Tel: (703)907-7729
Fax: (703)907-7727

Employers
Telecommunications Industry Ass'n (Controller)

KIM, David S.

444 N. Capitol St. NW
Suite 134
Washington, DC 20001
Tel: (202)624-5270
Fax: (202)624-5280

Employers
California, Washington Office of the State of (Deputy Director)

KIM, Hank

1750 New York Ave. NW
Washington, DC 20006
Tel: (202)737-8484
Fax: (202)737-8418
Registered: LDA

Employers
Internat'l Ass'n of Fire Fighters

KIM, Harold

2550 M St. NW
Washington, DC 20037-1350
EMail: hkim@pattonboggs.com
Tel: (202)457-6000
Fax: (202)457-6315
Registered: LDA

Employers
Patton Boggs, LLP (Associate)

Clients Represented
On Behalf of Patton Boggs, LLP
Swan Creek River Confederated Ojibbwa Tribes of Michigan

KIM, Hwan

555 13th St. NW
Suite 500 West
Washington, DC 20004
EMail: hwankim@omm.com
Tel: (202)383-5300
Fax: (202)383-5414
Registered: LDA

Employers
O'Melveny and Myers LLP

Clients Represented
On Behalf of O'Melveny and Myers LLP
Samsung Heavy Industries Co., Ltd.

KIM, Richard Y.

600 13th St. NW
Washington, DC 20005-3096
EMail: rkim@mwe.com
Former Attorney, Patent and Trademark Office.
Tel: (202)756-8295
Fax: (202)756-8087

Employers
McDermott, Will and Emery (Associate)

KIM, Sukhan

1333 New Hampshire Ave. NW
Suite 400
Washington, DC 20036
Tel: (202)887-4000
Fax: (202)887-4288

Employers
Akin, Gump, Strauss, Hauer & Feld, L.L.P. (Partner)

KIMBALL, Amy B.

1730 M St. NW
Suite 200
Washington, DC 20036-4530
EMail: akimball@selleryinc.com
Tel: (202)296-3522
Fax: (202)296-7713
Registered: LDA

Employers
Sellery Associates, Inc. (V. President)

Clients Represented
On Behalf of Sellery Associates, Inc.
American Soc. for Quality
Coalition for Uniform Product Liability Law
The Mead Corp.

KIMBALL, Daryl

110 Maryland Ave. NE
Suite 201
Washington, DC 20002
EMail: kimball@clw.org
Tel: (202)546-0795
Fax: (202)546-5142
Registered: LDA

Employers
Council for a Livable World Education Fund (Director, Coalition to Reduce Nuclear Dangers)

KIMBALL, Florence

245 Second St. NE
Washington, DC 20002
Tel: (202)547-6000
Fax: (202)547-6019
Registered: LDA

Employers
Friends Committee on Nat'l Legislation (Legislative Education Secretary)

KIMBALL, Kevin

Administration Bldg.
Room A1109
Quince Orchard & Clopper Rds.
Gaithersburg, MD 20899-1002
EMail: kevin.kimball@nist.gov
Tel: (301)975-5675
Fax: (301)926-2569

Employers
Department of Commerce - Nat'l Institute of Standards and Technology (Senior Legislative Analyst)

KIMBALL, Mark

2021 K St. NW
Suite 305
Washington, DC 20006-1003
Tel: (202)293-2856
Fax: (202)785-8574

Employers
Alliance for Aging Research (Director, Finance and Administration)

KIMBELL, Jeffrey J.

3504 Whitehaven Pkwy. NW
Washington, DC 20007
Tel: (202)338-6066
Fax: (202)338-6446
Registered: LDA
Former Aide to Senator Howard H. Baker (R-TN). Former Aide to Lawrence S. Eagleburger, Secretary of State, during the Bush I administration.

Employers
Jeffrey J. Kimbell & Associates (Chief Exec. Officer)

Clients Represented
On Behalf of Jeffrey J. Kimbell & Associates
HemaSure, Inc.
Sepracor, Inc.

KIMBERLY, Richard H.

901 15th St. NW
Suite 440
Washington, DC 20005
EMail: kimberlyconsulting@att.net
Tel: (202)312-3026
Fax: (202)312-3027
Registered: LDA

Employers
Kimberly Consulting, LLC (President)

Clients Represented
On Behalf of Kimberly Consulting, LLC
The Asheville School
Chesapeake Bay Maritime Museum
Easton Airport
Georgetown University-McDonough School of Business
Georgetown University-School of Nursing
Kimberly-Clark Corp.
Pinkering Corp.
Tricap Management Corp.
Wayland Academy
Zamorano

KIMMEL, Adele

1717 Massachusetts Ave. NW
Suite 800
Washington, DC 20036
EMail: akimmel@tlpj.org
Tel: (202)797-8600
Fax: (202)232-7203

Employers
Trial Lawyers for Public Justice, P.C. (Staff Attorney)

KIMMELL, Thomas H.

6540 Arlington Blvd.
Falls Church, VA 22042
EMail: tom@irrigation.org
Tel: (703)536-7080
Fax: (703)536-7019

Employers
Irrigation Ass'n (Exec. Director)

KIMMELMAN, Gene

1666 Connecticut Ave. NW
Suite 310
Washington, DC 20009
EMail: kimmge@consumer.org
Tel: (202)462-6262
Fax: (202)265-9548
Registered: LDA

Employers
Consumers Union of the United States (Co-Director, Washington Office)

KIMMITT, Joseph S.

1730 M St. NW
Suite 911
Washington, DC 20036
Tel: (202)293-4762
Fax: (202)659-5760
Registered: LDA

Employers
Self-employed as an independent consultant.
Kimmitt, Coates & McCarthy (Chairman)

Clients Represented
As an independent consultant
The Boeing Co.

KIN, Moo Han

1800 K St. NW
Suite 700
Washington, DC 20006
Tel: (202)828-4400
Fax: (202)828-4404

Employers

Korea Internat'l Trade Ass'n (V. President)

KINCAIDE, Gail G.

2000 L St. NW
Suite 740
Washington, DC 20036
EMail: gailk@awhonn.org
Tel: (202)261-2400
Fax: (202)728-0575

Employers

Ass'n of Women's Health, Obstetric and Neonatal Nurses (Exec. Director)

KINCHELOE, James Jeffrey

228 Seventh St. SE
Washington, DC 20003-4306
Tel: (202)547-7424
Fax: (202)547-9559
Registered: LDA

Employers

Nat'l Ass'n for Home Care (Deputy Director, Government Affairs)

KING, Aubrey C.

1156 15th St. NW
Suite 505
Washington, DC 20005
EMail: aubking@aol.com
Tel: (202)659-2979
Fax: (202)659-3020
Registered: LDA

Employers

Albertine Enterprises, Inc. (Principal)

Clients Represented

On Behalf of Albertine Enterprises, Inc.

American Ass'n of Entrepreneurs
Carlson Cos.
Energy Absorption Systems, Inc.
Internat'l Snowmobile Manufacturers Ass'n
Nat'l Ass'n of RV Parks and Campgrounds
Western States Tourism Policy Council

KING, Charles W.

1220 L St. NW
Suite 410
Washington, DC 20005
Tel: (202)371-9156
Fax: (202)842-4966

Employers

Snavely, King, Majoros, O'Connor and Lee, Inc. (President)

Clients Represented

On Behalf of Snavely, King, Majoros, O'Connor and Lee, Inc.

Dow Jones & Co., Inc.
Wall Street Journal

KING, Craig S.

1050 Connecticut Ave. NW
Washington, DC 20036-5339
Tel: (202)857-6000
Fax: (202)857-6395
Registered: LDA

Former Chief Counsel, U.S. Navy.

Employers

Arent Fox Kintner Plotkin & Kahn, PLLC (Member)

Clients Represented

On Behalf of Arent Fox Kintner Plotkin & Kahn, PLLC

Avondale Industries, Inc.
Raytheon Co.

KING, D. Brady

444 N. Capitol St. NW
Suite 419
Washington, DC 20001
Tel: (202)624-5455
Fax: (202)624-5468
Registered: LDA

Employers

Nat'l Ass'n of Federally Impacted Schools (Director, Government Relations)

KING, Dan G.

The Mercury Bldg.
1925 K St. NW
Washington, DC 20423-0001
EMail: kingd@stb.dot.gov
Tel: (202)565-1592
Fax: (202)565-9016

Director, Office of Public Services, Surface Transportation Board, 1995-97. Director, Office of Public Assistance (1991-95), Acting Director (1990-91), Deputy Director (1986-90), Director, Small Business Assistance Office (1981-86), Legal Counsel to the Commissioner (1980-81), Legislative Counsel's Office, Motor Carrier Act of 1980 (1979), Legal Counsel to the Commissioner (1974-79), and Staff Attorney, Section of Finance (1971-74) all at the Interstate Commerce Commission.

Employers

Department of Transportation - Surface Transportation Board (Director, Congressional and Public Services)

KING, USA, Lt. Col. Greg

1300 Defense Pentagon
Room 3D918
Washington, DC 20301-1300
Tel: (703)614-6150

Employers

Department of Defense (Special Assistant for Guard & Reserve Affairs, Logistics, Readiness, Office of Legislative Liaison)

KING, Gregory

555 New Jersey Ave. NW
Washington, DC 20001
Tel: (202)393-6387
Fax: (202)434-4699

Employers

American Federation of Teachers (Press Secretary)

KING, Jennifer

1120 Connecticut Ave. NW
Suite 1100
Washington, DC 20036
Tel: (202)861-5899
Fax: (202)861-5795
Registered: LDA

Former Research Assistant to Senator Kay Bailey Hutchison (R-TX).

Employers

GPC Internat'l

Clients Represented

On Behalf of GPC Internat'l

Applied Terravision Systems

KING, Kathleen

50 F St. NW
Suite 600
Washington, DC 20001
Tel: (202)628-9320
Fax: (202)628-9244

Employers

Washington Business Group on Health (V. President)

KING, Lynn

409 Third St. SW
Suite 210
Washington, DC 20024
Tel: (202)205-3850
Fax: (202)205-6825

Employers

Nat'l Women's Business Council (Deputy Director)

KING, Mitch

475 L'Enfant Plaza SW
MS: 10846
Washington, DC 20260
Tel: (202)268-3740

Employers

United States Postal Service (Government Relations Manager)

KING, Neil J.

2445 M St. NW
Washington, DC 20037-1420
EMail: nking@wilmwer.com
Tel: (202)663-6000
Fax: (202)663-6363
Registered: LDA

Member, Advisory Committee on Trade and the Environment, Environmental Protection Agency, 1992-93. Former Law Clerk to Judge Henry J. Friendly, U.S. Court of Appeals, Second Circuit.

Employers

Wilmer, Cutler & Pickering (Partner)

Clients Represented

On Behalf of Wilmer, Cutler & Pickering

Internat'l Metals Reclamation Co.

KING, Peter

1401 K St. NW
11th Floor
Washington, DC 20005
Tel: (202)408-9541
Fax: (202)408-9542

Employers

American Public Works Ass'n (Exec. Director)

KING, Rachel C.

122 Maryland Ave. NE
Washington, DC 20002
Tel: (202)544-1681
Fax: (202)546-0738
Registered: LDA

Employers

American Civil Liberties Union (Legislative Counsel, Criminal Justice)

KING, Rachel K.

701 Pennsylvania Ave. NW
Suite 725
Washington, DC 20004
Tel: (202)662-4364
Fax: (202)628-4764
Registered: LDA

Employers

Novartis Corp. (Senior V. President, Corporate Government Relations)
Novartis Services, Inc.

KING, Robin

900 19th St. NW
Suite 300
Washington, DC 20006
EMail: rking@aluminum.com
Tel: (202)862-5100
Fax: (202)862-5164

Employers

The Aluminum Ass'n (V. President, Public Affairs)

KING, Roland H.

1025 Connecticut Ave. NW
Suite 700
Washington, DC 20036
Tel: (202)785-8866
Fax: (202)835-0003

Employers

Nat'l Ass'n of Independent Colleges and Universities (V. President, Public Affairs)

KING, W. Russell

50 F St. NW
Suite 1050
Washington, DC 20001
EMail: russell_king@fmi.com
Tel: (202)737-1400
Fax: (202)737-1568
Registered: LDA

Former Legislative Director to Sen. Herman E. Talmadge (D-GA).

Employers

Freeport-McMoRan Copper & Gold Inc. (Senior V. President, International Relations and Federal Affairs)

KING, William K.

1350 I St. NW
Suite 1000
Washington, DC 20005
EMail: bking2@ford.com
Tel: (202)962-5379
Fax: (202)336-7228
Registered: LDA

Employers

Ford Motor Co. (Regulatory Manager, Safety and Energy)

KING-HOLMES, Alexis

2300 Clarendon Blvd.
Suite 610
Arlington, VA 22201-3367
EMail: akholmes@golinharris.com
Tel: (703)351-5666
Fax: (703)351-5667

Associate Director, Senate Democratic Steering and Coordination Committee, 1998-2000. Policy Team Member for Senator John D. Rockefeller IV (D-WV), 1996-98.

Employers

Golin/Harris Internat'l (Senior Account Exec.)

KINGHORN, Jr., Edward J.

900 Second St. NE
Suite 201
Washington, DC 20002
EMail: tkinghorn@kinghornassociates.com
Tel: (202)842-2767
Fax: (202)842-0439
Registered: LDA

Executive Assistant to Senator Strom Thurmond (R-SC).

Employers

Kinghorn & Associates, L.L.C. (President)

Clients Represented

On Behalf of Kinghorn & Associates, L.L.C.

Advanced Technology Institute
American Metalcasting Consortium
Ferroalloys Ass'n
Remediation Financial, Inc.
South Carolina Research Authority
South Carolina Technology Alliance
Tri-County Alliance

KINGSBURY, Cathryn J.

801 Pennsylvania Ave. NW
Suite 750
Washington, DC 20004
Tel: (202)628-3750
Fax: (202)624-0659
EMail: CathrynKingsbury@solomongroup.com

Employers

The Solomon Group, LLC (Director, Research/Legislative Analyst)

KINGSCOTT, Kathleen N.

1301 K St. NW
Suite 1200-West Tower
Washington, DC 20005-3307
Tel: (202)515-5193
Fax: (202)515-4943
Registered: LDA
EMail: tking@us.ibm.com

Employers

Internat'l Business Machines Corp. (Director, Public Policy Programs)

KINGSLEY, Daniel T.

1030 15th St. NW
Suite 1028
Washington, DC 20005
Tel: (202)216-9116
Fax: (202)216-0363
Former Special Assistant to the President and Director of Presidential Personnel, Nixon administration. Former Commissioner, General Services Administration. Former Administrator for Operations, Small Business Administration.

Employers

The Potomac Research Group LLC (Senior Partner)

KINGSLEY, G. Thomas

2100 M St. NW
Washington, DC 20037
Tel: (202)833-7200
Fax: (202)429-0687

Employers

The Urban Institute (Senior Fellow)

KINGSLEY, Ph.D., Roger P.

12609 Pentenville Rd.
Silver Spring, MD 20904-3526
Tel: (301)622-0433
Fax: (301)625-8711
Registered: LDA
EMail: rpkingsley@aol.com

Employers

Polity Consulting (Principal)

Clients Represented

On Behalf of Polity Consulting

Brain Injury Ass'n
Internat'l Code Council
Internat'l Dyslexia Ass'n, The
Nat'l Ass'n of Developmental Disabilities Councils

KINGSLEY, Steven

845 Ninovan Rd. SE
Vienna, VA 22180-2017
Tel: (703)284-5818
Fax: (703)284-5819

Employers

Self-employed as an independent consultant.

Clients Represented

As an independent consultant

Citizens' Scholarship Foundation of America
Nat'l Computer Systems

KINNAIRD, Jula J.

1300 L St. NW
Suite 925
Washington, DC 20005
Tel: (202)842-0400
Fax: (202)789-7223

Employers

Nat'l Grain Trade Council (President)

KINNEY, Charles L.

1400 L St. NW
Washington, DC 20005-3502
Tel: (202)371-5765
Fax: (202)371-5950
Registered: LDA
EMail: ckinney@winston.com
Former Chief Floor Counsel to Senate Majority Leader, Senator George Mitchell (D-ME), 1989-93, and Floor Counsel and Judiciary Counsel to Senate Democratic Leader, Senator Robert C. Byrd (D-WV), 1974-88.

Employers

Winston & Strawn (Partner, Legislative and Regulatory Practice)

Clients Represented

On Behalf of Winston & Strawn

American Airlines
American General Financial Group
American Healthways, Inc.
Barr Laboratories
DMJM + Harris
The ESOP (Employee Stock Ownership Plan) Ass'n
EyeTicket Corp.
Federal Judges Ass'n
Federal Magistrate Judges Ass'n
Gildan Activewear
Heller Financial Inc.
Internat'l Council of Shopping Centers
Leukemia and Lymphoma Soc. of America
Liberty Maritime Co.
Lockheed Martin Corp.
Marinette Marine Corp.
Motor Coach Industries, Inc.
Nat'l Geographic Soc.
Nat'l Organization of Social Security Claimants' Representatives
Norfolk Southern Corp.
Panda Energy Internat'l
Puerto Rico, Commonwealth of
Research Planning, Inc.
Virgin Islands, Government of the
Yellow Corp.

KINNEY, Janie Ann

1500 K St. NW
Suite 650
Washington, DC 20005
Tel: (202)715-1000
Fax: (202)715-1001
Registered: LDA

Employers

GlaxoSmithKline (V. President, Federal Government Relations and Public Policy)

KINSELLA, Michael T.

925 15th St. NW
Fifth Floor
Washington, DC 20006
Tel: (202)296-0784
Fax: (202)293-2768
Former Chief of Staff to Senator Alfonse D'Amato (R-NY).

Employers

Royer & Babyak (Partner)

Clients Represented

On Behalf of Royer & Babyak

New York, State of

KINSMAN, John

701 Pennsylvania Ave. NW
Washington, DC 20004-2696
Tel: (202)508-5711
Fax: (202)508-5150
Registered: LDA

Employers

Edison Electric Institute (Manager, Atmospheric Science)

KINTER, Marcia

10015 Main St.
Fairfax, VA 22031-3489
Tel: (703)385-1335
Fax: (703)273-0456
EMail: sgia@sgia.org

Employers

Screenprinting & Graphic Imaging Ass'n Internat'l (V. President, Government Affairs)

KINZLER, Peter

7310 Stafford Rd.
Alexandria, VA 22307
Tel: (703)660-0799
Fax: (703)660-0799
Registered: LDA
Staff Director, Subcommittee on Financial Institutions, House Banking Committee, 1993-95. Counsel (1992-93), Staff Director, Subcommittee on Consumer Affairs (1987-89), and Minority Counsel, Subcommittee on Financial Institutions (1981-86), all with the Senate Committee on Banking, Housing and Urban Affairs. Legislative Director to Senator Christopher Dodd (D-CT), 1989-92. Counsel, Subcommittee on Oversight and Investigations, House Committee on Energy and Commerce, 1979-81. Counsel, Subcommittee on Consumer Protection and Finance, House Committee on Interstate and Foreign Commerce, 1975-79. Attorney, Federal Trade Commission, 1974-75. Legislative Assistant to Rep. Thomas Ashley (D-OH), 1969-74.

Employers

Coalition for Auto-Insurance Reform
Self-employed as an independent consultant.

Clients Represented

As an independent consultant

Coalition for Auto-Insurance Reform
Massachusetts Mutual Life Insurance Co.
Prudential Insurance Co. of America

KIPREOS, Thanos

1300 Pennsylvania Ave. NW
Suite 350
Washington, DC 20044
Tel: (202)383-1484
Fax: (202)383-1495
Registered: LDA
EMail: tkipreos@tia.eia.org

Employers

Telecommunications Industry Ass'n (Senior Director, Global Standards and Technology)

KIRBY, Craig A.

P.O. Box 2999
Reston, VA 20191
Tel: (703)620-6003
Ext: 312
Fax: (703)620-5071
EMail: ckirby@rvia.org

Employers

Recreation Vehicle Industry Ass'n (V. President and General Counsel)

KIRBY, John B.

5413-B Backlick Rd.
Springfield, VA 22151
Tel: (703)642-5360
Fax: (703)642-2054
EMail: info@purpleheart.org

Employers

Military Order of the Purple Heart of the U.S.A. (Adjutant General)

KIRBY, Kathleen A.

1776 K St. NW
Washington, DC 20006
Tel: (202)719-7000
Fax: (202)719-7049

Employers

Wiley, Rein & Fielding (Counsel)

Clients Represented

On Behalf of Wiley, Rein & Fielding

Radio-Television News Directors Ass'n

KIRBY, Michael

1100 Pennsylvania Ave. NW
Room 524
Washington, DC 20506
Tel: (202)682-5434
Fax: (202)682-5638
EMail: kirbym@arts.endow.gov

Employers

Nat'l Endowment for the Arts (Deputy Director, Congressional and White House Liaison)

KIRBY, Sheila

1200 S. Hayes St.
Arlington, VA 22202-5050
Tel: (703)413-1100
Fax: (703)413-8111

Employers

RAND Corp. (Associate Director)

KIRBY, Thomas W.

1776 K St. NW
Washington, DC 20006
Tel: (202)719-7000
Fax: (202)719-7049
Law Clerk to Judge Myron Bright, U.S. Court of Appeals, Eighth Circuit, 1975-76.

Employers

Wiley, Rein & Fielding (Partner)

KIRCHHOFF, Richard W.

1156 15th St. NW
Suite 1020
Washington, DC 20005
Tel: (202)296-9680
Fax: (202)296-9686
EMail: nasda@patriot.net

Employers

Nat'l Ass'n of State Departments of Agriculture (Exec. V. President and C.E.O.)

KIRK, Keith A.

2000 L St. NW
Suite 300
Washington, DC 20036-0646
Tel: (202)835-8800
Fax: (202)835-8879
Registered: LDA

Employers

Ketchum (V. President for Grassroots)

KIRK, Ken

1816 Jefferson Place NW
Washington, DC 20036
Tel: (202)833-2672
Fax: (202)833-4657
Registered: LDA

EMail: kkirk@amsa-cleanwater.org

Employers

Ass'n of Metropolitan Sewerage Agencies (Exec. Director)

KIRK, Michael K.

2001 Jefferson Davis Hwy.
Suite 203
Arlington, VA 22202
Tel: (703)415-0780
Fax: (703)415-0786
Registered: LDA

EMail: mkirk@aipla.org

Employers

American Intellectual Property Law Ass'n (Exec. Director)

KIRK, Michael W.

1500 K St. NW
Suite 200
Washington, DC 20005
Tel: (202)220-9600
Fax: (202)220-9601

Employers

Cooper, Carvin & Rosenthal (Partner)

KIRK, Jr., Paul G.

1025 Connecticut Ave. NW
Suite 1000
Washington, DC 20036
Tel: (202)775-8190
Fax: (202)293-2275
Registered: LDA

Employers

Sullivan & Worcester LLP (Of Counsel)

Clients Represented

On Behalf of Sullivan & Worcester LLP

Hoechst Marion Roussel Deutschland GmbH

KIRK, Sharon

1899 L St. NW
Suite 1000
Washington, DC 20036
Tel: (202)457-0480
Fax: (202)457-0486
Registered: LDA

EMail: sharon_kirk@npradc.org

Employers

Nat'l Petrochemical Refiners Ass'n (Director, Congressional Affairs)

KIRK, Jr., William A.

701 Pennsylvania Ave. NW
Suite 800
Washington, DC 20004
Tel: (202)508-4353
Fax: (202)508-4321
Registered: LDA

EMail: wkirk@thelenreid.com

Professional Staff, House Committee on Ways and Means, 1980-85. Legislative Aide to Rep. John Conyers (D-MI), 1975-80.

Employers

Thelen Reid & Priest LLP (Partner)

Clients Represented

On Behalf of Thelen Reid & Priest LLP

Airport Minority Advisory Council
Airports Council Internat'l - North America
Capital Dimensions Venture Fund Inc.
Capital Region Airport Commission
Corpus Christi Port Authority
Denver Internat'l Airport
Denver, Colorado, City of
Fulcrum Venture Capital Corp.
J & B Management Co.
The Jewelers' Security Alliance
LM Capital Corp.
MCA Inc.
Medallion Funding Corp.
Metro Machine Corp. of Virginia
Metro Machine of Pennsylvania, Inc.
Metroplex Corp.
MMG Ventures LP
Myriad Capital Inc.
Nat'l Ass'n of Investment Companies
Opportunity Capital Corp.
Pacific 17
Parsons Brinckerhoff Inc.
Recording Industry Ass'n of America
Suiza Foods Corp.
TSG Ventures Inc.

KIRKLAND, J. R.

1620 L St. NW
Suite 875
Washington, DC 20036
Tel: (202)833-5881
Fax: (202)833-5924
Registered: LDA

EMail: fba@clark.net

Form staff member, The White House during the Carter administration.

Employers

F.B.A. (President)

Clients Represented

On Behalf of F.B.A.

Medco Containment Services, Inc.
Ohio Supercomputing Center
Old Dominion University
RGK Foundation
Science Applications Internat'l Corp. (SAIC)
Stetson University
Sun Microsystems
University of Akron
University of Alaska
University of Nevada - Las Vegas
University of Vermont
Westinghouse Electric Co.

KIRKLAND, James A.

701 Pennsylvania Ave. NW
Suite 900
Washington, DC 20004-2608
Tel: (202)434-7300
Fax: (202)434-7400
Registered: LDA

EMail: jkirkland@mintz.com

Employers

Mintz, Levin, Cohn, Ferris, Glovsky and Popeo, P.C. (Partner)

Clients Represented

On Behalf of Mintz, Levin, Cohn, Ferris, Glovsky and Popeo, P.C.

AOL Time Warner

KIRKLAND, Katherine H.

1010 Vermont Ave. NW
Suite 513
Washington, DC 20005
EMail: aoec@aoec.org
Tel: (202)347-4976
Fax: (202)347-4950

Employers

Ass'n of Occupational and Environmental Clinics (Exec. Director)

KIRKMAN, Larry

950 18th St. NW
Washington, DC 20006
Tel: (202)638-5770
Fax: (202)638-5771

Employers

Benton Foundation/Communications Policy Project (President)

KIRKPATRICK, C. Kris

801 Pennsylvania Ave. NW
Suite 750
Washington, DC 20004
Tel: (202)737-9212
Fax: (202)624-0659
Registered: LDA

EMail: longlawfirm@aol.com

Employers

Long Law Firm (Partner)

Clients Represented

On Behalf of Long Law Firm

Bristol-Myers Squibb Co.
Employee Stock Ownership Assn
Louisiana Tobacco Group
United Companies Financial Corp.

KIRKPATRICK, James R.

6352 Rolling Mill Pl.
Suite 102
Springfield, VA 22152-2354
Tel: (703)866-0020
Fax: (703)866-3526

Employers

American Astronautical Soc. (Exec. Director)

KIRKPATRICK, Jeane J.

1150 17th St. NW
Washington, DC 20036
EMail: jkirkpatrick@aei.org
Tel: (202)862-5800
Fax: (202)862-7177

Employers

American Enterprise Institute for Public Policy Research (Senior Fellow and Director, Foreign Policy and Defense Studies)

KIRSCH, Jeff

1334 G St. NW
Suite 300
Washington, DC 20005-3169
Tel: (202)628-3030
Fax: (202)347-2417

Employers

Families U.S.A. Foundation (Field Director)

KIRSHENBERG, Seth

1101 Connecticut Ave. NW
Suite 1000
Washington, DC 20036
Tel: (202)828-2400
Fax: (202)828-2488
Registered: LDA

Employers

Kutak Rock LLP (Partner)

Clients Represented

On Behalf of Kutak Rock LLP

Alameda, California, City of
Energy Communities Alliance, Inc.
Farm Progress Cos.
Highland Park, Illinois, City of Highwood Local Redevelopment Authority and the City of
Los Alamos, New Mexico, County of
New London Development Corp.
Oak Ridge, Tennessee, City of
Orlando, Florida, City of
San Francisco, City of
Seaside, California, City of
Team Stratford
Tustin, California, City of

KIRSHNER, Robert

1111 19th St. NW
Suite 800
Washington, DC 20036
EMail: robert_kirshner@afandpa.org
Tel: (202)463-2700
Fax: (202)463-2785

Employers

American Forest & Paper Ass'n (V. President and General Counsel)

KIRST, Michael E.

1900 M St. NW
Suite 500
Washington, DC 20036
Tel: (202)945-6400
Fax: (202)945-6404
Registered: LDA

Employers

Westinghouse Electric Co. (Director, Government and International Affairs)

KIRSTEIN, David M.

1050 Connecticut Ave. NW
Suite 1100
Washington, DC 20036-5304
Tel: (202)861-1500
Fax: (202)861-1790
Registered: LDA, FARA

EMail: Dkirstein@baker-hostetler.com

Majority Counsel, Aviation Subcommittee, Senate Committee on Commerce, Science and Transportation, 1982.

Employers

Baker & Hostetler LLP (Partner)

KIRTLAND, John C.

1400 L St. NW
Washington, DC 20005-3502
Tel: (202)371-5700
Fax: (202)371-5950
Registered: LDA

Counsel, Senate Committee on Commerce, Science and Transportation, 1971-77.

Employers
Winston & Strawn (Partner, Legislative and Regulatory Practice)

Clients Represented
On Behalf of Winston & Strawn
Cooper Tire and Rubber Co.
Corning Inc.
Jackson County, Mississippi Board of Supervisors
Jackson Municipal Airport Authority
Jackson, Mississippi, City of
Liberty Maritime Co.
Maximum Information Technology Inc.
Puerto Rico, Commonwealth of
Virgin Islands, Government of the
Waggoner Engineering, Inc.

KIRTMAN, Deanna M.

1725 Jefferson Davis Hwy.
Crystal Square 2, Suite 300
Arlington, VA 22202
Tel: (703)413-5600
Fax: (703)413-5613

Employers
Lockheed Martin Corp. (Director, Legislative Affairs, Navy Programs)

KISER, Cherie R.

701 Pennsylvania Ave. NW
Suite 900
Washington, DC 20004-2608
Tel: (202)434-7300
Fax: (202)434-7400
Registered: LDA
EMail: ckiser@mintz.com

Employers
Mintz, Levin, Cohn, Ferris, Glovsky and Popeo, P.C. (Partner)

KISER, John Daniel

750 17th St. NW
Suite 1100
Washington, DC 20006
Tel: (202)778-2326
Fax: (202)778-2330
Registered: LDA

Special Assistant to the Deputy General Counsel (1983-85), Senior Attorney/Litigation, Public Health Division (1980-83), and Assistant Regional Attorney (1976-80), Department of Health and Human Services.

Employers
FoxKiser

Clients Represented
On Behalf of FoxKiser
Bristol-Myers Squibb Co.
NitroMed, Inc.

KISH, Carla

1225 19th St. NW
Suite 800
Washington, DC 20036
Tel: (202)955-6067
Fax: (202)293-0307
Registered: LDA

Legislative Assistant to Senator Carl Levin (D-MI), 1981-84. Staff member, Subcommittee on Energy and the Environment, House Interior Committee, 1976-80.

Employers
Berliner, Candon & Jimison (Director, Federal Legislative Affairs)

Clients Represented
On Behalf of Berliner, Candon & Jimison
California Primary Care Ass'n
Cedars-Sinai Medical Center
Los Angeles, California, County of
Tarzana Treatment Center
Wireless Location Industry Ass'n

KISSEL, Peter C.

1500 K St. NW
Suite 330
Washington, DC 20005
Tel: (202)408-5400
Fax: (202)408-5406
Registered: LDA
EMail: pckissel@grkse-law.com

Trial Attorney, Office of the General Counsel, Federal Power Commission, 1972-77.

Employers
GKRSE (Partner)

Clients Represented
On Behalf of GKRSE
Kootenai Electric Cooperative, Inc.

KISSICK, Ralph L.

888 17th St. NW
Suite 600
Washington, DC 20006-3959
Tel: (202)298-8660
Fax: (202)342-0683
EMail: rlkissick@zsrlaw.com

Law Clerk to the Commissioners, U.S. Court of Claims, 1969-70.

Employers
Zuckert, Scoutt and Rasenberger, L.L.P. (Partner)

KISSLING, Frances

1436 U St. NW
Suite 301
Washington, DC 20009
Tel: (202)986-6093
Fax: (202)332-7995

Employers
Catholics for a Free Choice (President)

KITCHEN, Charles A.

1200 N. Nash St.
Suite 1150
Arlington, VA 22209
Tel: (703)527-2099
Fax: (703)527-2092
Registered: LDA
EMail: charles.kitchen@atofina.com

Employers
ATOFINA Chemicals, Inc. (Director, Government Relations)

KITCHEN, Jr., Emmett B. "Jay"

500 Montgomery St.
Suite 700
Alexandria, VA 22314-1561
Tel: (703)739-0300
Fax: (703)836-1608

Employers
Personal Communications Industry Ass'n (PCIA) (President)

KITTLEMAN, Trent

One Marriott Dr.
Department 977.01
Washington, DC 20058
Tel: (202)380-3000
Registered: LDA

Employers
Marriott Internat'l, Inc.

KITTO, Joseph L.

2099 Pennsylvania Ave. NW
Suite 100
Washington, DC 20006
Tel: (202)955-3000
Fax: (202)955-5564
Registered: LDA
EMail: jlkitto@hklaw.com

Employers
Holland & Knight LLP (Associate)

Clients Represented
On Behalf of Holland & Knight LLP
Hualapai Nation

KITTRIE, Nicholas N.

2023 Q St. NW
Washington, DC 20009-1009
Tel: (202)387-3624
Fax: (202)387-3629

Employers
Independents Committee for Future America (Treasurer)

KIYOSHI, Michael J.

2121 R St. NW
Washington, DC 20008-1908
Tel: (202)673-5869
Fax: (202)673-5873

Employers
Northern Mariana Islands, Commonwealth of the (Federal Programs Coordinator)

KIZER BALL, Julie L.

600 Pennsylvania Ave. SE
Suite 400
Washington, DC 20003
Tel: (202)546-0007
Fax: (202)544-5002
EMail: jkizerball@dlcppi.org

Employers
Democratic Leadership Council (Administrative Director)

KJAER, Lars

1015 15th St. NW
Suite 450
Washington, DC 20005
Tel: (202)589-1234
Fax: (202)589-1231
Registered: LDA
EMail: lkjaer@worldshipping.org

Employers
World Shipping Council (V. President)

KJELLBERG, Sandra D.

1775 K St. NW
Suite 200
Washington, DC 20006
Tel: (202)463-6505
Fax: (202)223-9093
Registered: LDA

Employers
Maritime Institute for Research and Industrial Development (Government Relations)

KLAHR, Pamela

4232 King St.
Alexandria, VA 22302
Tel: (703)998-0072
Fax: (703)931-5624
EMail: pklahr@acce.org

Employers
American Chamber of Commerce Executives (V. President, Marketing)

KLAIN, Ronald A.

555 13th St. NW
Suite 500 West
Washington, DC 20004
Tel: (202)383-5300
Fax: (202)383-5414
Registered: LDA
EMail: rklain@omm.com

Assistant to the President and Chief of Staff to the Vice President, The White House, 1995-99. Staff Director, Senate Democratic Leadership Committee, 1995. Chief of Staff to the Attorney General, Department of Justice, 1994-95. Associate Counsel to the President, The White House, 1993-94. Chief Counsel, Senate Committee on the Judiciary, 1989-92. Law Clerk to Justice Byron White, U.S. Supreme Court, 1989-92.

Employers
O'Melveny and Myers LLP (Partner)

Clients Represented
On Behalf of O'Melveny and Myers LLP
Coalition for Asbestos Resolution
US Airways

KLASS, USAF (Ret.), Col. Richard L.

1401 K St. NW
Tenth Floor
Washington, DC 20005
Tel: (202)216-2200
Fax: (202)216-2999

Employers
Jefferson-Waterman Internat'l, LLC (Senior V. President)

Clients Represented
On Behalf of Jefferson-Waterman Internat'l, LLC
Alenia Marconi Systems
Vietnam Veterans of America Foundation

KLATT, III, Victor F.

1420 New York Ave. NW
Suite 1050
Washington, DC 20005
Tel: (202)638-1950
Fax: (202)638-7714
Registered: LDA

Former Education Coordinator, House Former Staffer, House Committee on Education and the Workforce. Also worked in the Congressional Affairs Office, The White House, during the Bush I administration.

Employers
Van Scoyoc Associates, Inc.

Clients Represented
On Behalf of Van Scoyoc Associates, Inc.
Abrams & Co. Publishers Inc.
Charter Schools Development Corp.
Education Leaders Council
New American School
Teach for America
University of Phoenix

KLAUSNER, Joseph A.

2550 M St. NW
Washington, DC 20037-1350
Tel: (202)457-6000
Fax: (202)457-6315
Registered: LDA
EMail: jklausner@pattonboggs.com

Employers
Patton Boggs, LLP (Of Counsel)

KLAYMAN, Larry

501 School St. SW
Suite 725
Washington, DC 20024
Tel: (202)646-5172
Fax: (202)646-5199

Employers
Judicial Watch, Inc. (Chief Exec. Officer and General Counsel)

KLEIN, Allen J.

2300 N St. NW
Washington, DC 20037-1128
Tel: (202)663-8000
Fax: (202)663-8007
Registered: LDA
EMail: allen.klein@shawpittman.com
Legislation Attorney, U.S. Congress Joint Committee on Taxation, 1984-85.

Employers
Shaw Pittman (Partner)

KLEIN, Andrew M.

1101 Connecticut Ave. NW
Suite 600
Washington, DC 20036
Tel: (202)778-6400
Fax: (202)778-6460
Special Counsel (1973-74), Assistant Director (1974-75), Associate Director (1975-77), and Director (1977-79), Division of Market Regulation, Securities and Exchange Commission.

Employers
Schiff Hardin & Waite (Partner)

KLEIN, Benjamin

1150 Connecticut Ave. NW
Suite 810
Washington, DC 20036
Tel: (202)785-7900
Fax: (202)785-7950
EMail: benk@heart.org

Employers
American Heart Ass'n (Government Relations Representative)

KLEIN, Carol Doran

1666 K St. NW
Suite 800
Washington, DC 20006
Tel: (202)481-7000
Fax: (202)862-7098
Registered: LDA

Employers
Arthur Andersen LLP (Partner)

Clients Represented

On Behalf of Arthur Andersen LLP
UtiliCorp United, Inc.

KLEIN, Christian A.

121 N. Henry St.
Alexandria, VA 22314
Tel: (703)739-9485
Fax: (703)739-9488
Registered: LDA

Employers
Associated Equipment Distributors (PAC Contact)
Obadal and MacLeod, p.c. (Senior Associate)

Clients Represented

On Behalf of Obadal and MacLeod, p.c.
Alsatian American Chamber of Commerce
Associated Equipment Distributors

KLEIN, Dennis

1775 I St. NW
Suite 600
Washington, DC 20006-2401
Tel: (202)721-4600
Fax: (202)721-4646

Employers
Hughes Hubbard & Reed LLP (Managing Partner)

KLEIN, Gary J.

901 15th St. NW
Suite 700
Washington, DC 20005-2301
Tel: (202)371-6000
Fax: (202)371-6279
Registered: LDA
EMail: gjklein@verner.com
Legislative Assistant to Senator Jacob Javits (R-NY), 1973-75. Minority Counsel, Energy Subcommittee, Senate Government Affairs Committee, 1975-77. Heads the Energy Consumer Tax Coalition.

Employers
Verner, Liipfert, Bernhard, McPherson and Hand, Chartered (Member of Firm)

Clients Represented

On Behalf of Verner, Liipfert, Bernhard, McPherson and Hand, Chartered
Alliance Pipeline, L.P.
Amgen
Bacardi-Martini, USA, Inc.
Biovail Corp. Internat'l
Caribe Waste Technologies
Flow Internat'l Corp.
Goldman, Sachs and Co.
Independent Fuel Terminal Operators Ass'n
Lehman Brothers
Petroleum Heat and Power Co., Inc.

KLEIN, Gary S.

2500 Wilson Blvd.
Arlington, VA 22201-3834
Tel: (703)907-7677
Fax: (703)907-7693
Registered: LDA
EMail: gklein@ce.org

Employers
Consumer Electronics Ass'n (V. President, Government and Legal Affairs)

KLEIN, James A.

1212 New York Ave. NW
Suite 1250
Washington, DC 20005-3987
Tel: (202)289-6700
Fax: (202)289-4582
Registered: LDA

Employers
American Benefits Council (President)

KLEIN, Kenneth H.

1401 H St. NW
Suite 200
Washington, DC 20005
Tel: (202)414-1287
Fax: (202)414-1217
Registered: LDA

Employers
Xerox Corp. (Director, International External Affairs)

KLEIN, D.V.M., Patrice

2100 L St. NW
Washington, DC 20037
Tel: (202)452-1100
Fax: 202)778-6132
Registered: LDA

Employers
Humane Soc. of the United States (Wildlife Veterinarian)

KLEIN, Philip

1913 I St. NW
Washington, DC 20006
Tel: (202)872-8110
Fax: (202)872-8114
Registered: LDA
EMail: pklein@csma.org

Employers
Consumer Specialties Products Ass'n (Senior V. President, Federal and State Legislative Affairs)

KLEIN, Scott

1001 19th St. North
Suite 800
Arlington, VA 22209-3901
Tel: (703)276-5042
Fax: (703)276-5029
Registered: LDA
EMail: scott.klein@trw.com

Employers
TRW Inc. (Manager, Government Relations)

KLEIN, William

1200 G St. NW
Suite 500
Washington, DC 20005
Tel: (202)434-8821
Fax: (202)393-5453
EMail: bklein@atis.org

Employers
Alliance for Telecommunications Industry Solutions (V. President, Finance and Operations)

KLEINE, Douglas M.

1401 New York Ave. NW
Suite 1100
Washington, DC 20005
Tel: (202)737-0797
Fax: (202)783-7869

Employers
Nat'l Ass'n of Housing Cooperatives (Exec. Director)

KLEINE, Thomas C.

1660 Internat'l Dr.
Suite 600
McLean, VA 22102
Tel: (703)734-4334
Fax: (703)734-4340
Registered: LDA

Employers
Troutman Sanders Mays & Valentine L.L.P. (Associate)

KLEINMAN, Ronald W.

800 Connecticut Ave. NW
Suite 500
Washington, DC 20006
Tel: (202)331-3146
Fax: (202)331-3101
Registered: LDA
EMail: kleinmar@gtlaw.com
Office of the Legal Advisor, Department of State, 1982-89. Law Clerk to Senior Judge Luther W. Youngdahl, U.S. District Court for the District of Columbia, 1976-78.

Employers
Greenberg Traurig, LLP (Shareholder)

Clients Represented

On Behalf of Greenberg Traurig, LLP
Armando Alejandre, Estate of
Costa, Carlos Alberto, Estate of
Mario M. de la Pena, Estate of
Uniroyal Technology Corp.

KLEMOW, Marvin G.

1700 N. Moore St.
Suite 1210
Arlington, VA 22209
Tel: (703)875-3723
Fax: (703)875-3740
Registered: FARA
EMail: klemow.iaii@psinet.com

Employers
Self-employed as an independent consultant.

Clients Represented

As an independent consultant
Israel Aircraft Industries, Ltd.

KLEPNER, Jerry

1801 K St. NW
Suite 901-L
Washington, DC 20006
Tel: (202)530-0500
Fax: (202)530-4800
Registered: LDA
EMail: Jerry_Klepner@bm.com
Former Assistant Secretary for Legislation, Department of Health and Human Services during the Clinton administration.

Employers
BKSH & Associates (Managing Director)

Clients Represented

On Behalf of BKSH & Associates
Safety-Kleen Corp.

KLETTER, Joni

11 Dupont Circle NW
Second Floor
Washington, DC 20036
Tel: (202)822-6070
Fax: (202)822-6068

Employers
Alliance for Justice (Law Fellow)

KLINE, Stephan

1700 K St. NW
Suite 1150
Washington, DC 20006
Tel: (202)736-5864
Fax: (202)785-4937
Registered: LDA
EMail: stephan.kline@ujc.org

Employers
United Jewish Communities, Inc. (Director, Legislative Affairs)

KLINE, Steven L.

700 11th St. NW
Suite 250
Washington, DC 20001
Tel: (202)638-3518
Fax: (202)638-3522
Registered: LDA

Employers
PG&E Corp. (V. President, Federal Governmental and Regulatory Relations)

KLINEFELTER, William J.

1150 17th St. NW
Suite 300
Washington, DC 20036
Tel: (202)778-4384
Fax: (202)293-5308
Registered: LDA
EMail: wklinefelter@uswa.org

Employers
United Steelworkers of America (Legislative and Political Director)

KLINGELHOFER, Philip T.

333 John Carlyle St.
Suite 530
Alexandria, VA 22314
EMail: pklingelhofer@ceednet.org
Tel: (703)684-6292
Fax: (703)684-6297

Employers
Center for Energy and Economic Development (V. President, Finance and Administration)

KLINK, Hon. Ron

2600 Virginia Ave. NW
Suite 600
Washington, DC 20037
EMail: ronpklink@aol.com
Tel: (202)338-6550
Fax: (202)338-5950
Member, U.S. House of Representatives (D-PA), 1993-2001

Employers
O'Brien, Klink & Associates (Partner)

KLINKE, Diane G.

1150 18th St. NW
Suite 400
Washington, DC 20036
EMail: dklinke@msrb.org
Tel: (202)223-9347
Fax: (202)872-0347

Employers
Municipal Securities Rulemaking Board (General Counsel)

KLIPPER, Michael R.

923 15th St. NW
Washington, DC 20005
Tel: (202)637-0850
Fax: (202)637-0851
Registered: LDA
EMail: klipper@erols.com
Chief Counsel, Subcommittee on Criminal Law (1981-82) and Counsel (1975-80), Senate Judiciary Committee.

Employers
Meyer & Klipper, PLLC

Clients Represented

On Behalf of Meyer & Klipper, PLLC
Coalition Against Database Piracy
Magazine Publishers of America
Property Owners Remedy Alliance

KLISMET, Kurt J.

1101 15th St. NW
Suite 115
Washington, DC 20005
EMail: klismet@religionandpolicy.org
Tel: (202)835-8760
Fax: (202)318-4017

Employers
Institute on Religion and Public Policy (Director of Research)

KLITZMAN, Stephen H.

445 12th St. NW
Room 8-C468
Washington, DC 20554
Tel: (202)418-1900
Fax: (202)418-2806

Employers
Federal Communications Commission (Associate Director, Legislative and Intergovernmental Affairs)

KLONOSKI, Grace

2010 Massachusetts Ave. NW
Washington, DC 20036
Tel: (202)416-1422
Fax: (202)416-1440

Employers
Optical Soc. of America (Strategic Marketing and Membership)

KLOSE, Christopher

655 National Press Bldg.
Washington, DC 20045
Tel: (202)737-8400
Fax: (202)737-8406

Employers
John Adams Associates Inc. (Principal and Senior Partner)

KLOSE, Eliza K.

1601 Connecticut Ave. NW
Suite 301
Washington, DC 20009
EMail: eliza@isar.org
Tel: (202)387-3034
Fax: (202)667-3291

Employers
ISAR, Initiative for Social Action and Renewal in Eurasia (Exec. Director)

KLOSE, Kevin

635 Massachusetts Ave. NW
Washington, DC 20001
Tel: (202)414-2000
Registered: LDA

Employers
Nat'l Public Radio (President and Chief Exec. Officer)

KLUCSARTIS, Ann

214 Massachusetts Ave. NE
Washington, DC 20002
Tel: (202)546-4400
Fax: (202)546-8328

Employers
Heritage Foundation (Director, Development Programs)

KLUGH, Gloria J.

Ten Pidgeon Hill Dr.
Suite 150
Sterling, VA 20165
Tel: (703)444-4091
Fax: (703)444-3029
Registered: LDA

Employers
DeBrunner and Associates, Inc. (Associate)

Clients Represented

On Behalf of DeBrunner and Associates, Inc.
Nat'l Ass'n of Urban Hospitals

KLUNDT, Scott

1301 Pennsylvania Ave. NW
Suite 300
Washington, DC 20004
Tel: (202)347-5355
Fax: (202)737-4086

Employers
Public Lands Council (Associate Director)

KNAB, Karen

2300 N St. NW
Washington, DC 20037-1128
EMail: karen.knab@shawpittman.com
Tel: (202)663-8000
Fax: (202)663-8007

Employers
Shaw Pittman (Exec. Director)

KNAB, Sarah T.

1233 20th St. NW
Suite 200
Washington, DC 20036
Tel: (202)833-0009
Fax: (202)833-0113

Employers
Partnership for Prevention (Projects Manager)

KNAPP, David C.

8403 Arlington Blvd.
Suite 100
Fairfax, VA 22031
EMail: dknapp@interfacinc.com
Tel: (703)876-6800
Fax: (703)876-0515

Employers
Interface Inc. (President)

Clients Represented

On Behalf of Interface Inc.
Bacharach
Church and Dwight ArmaKleen
Foamex
Hunter Ceiling Fans
Pressure Island
Safety-Kleen Corp.
USF Surface Preparation

KNAPP, John

1310 19th St. NW
Washington, DC 20036
Tel: (202)466-6555
Fax: (202)466-6596
Registered: LDA

Employers
O'Neill, Athy & Casey, P.C.

Clients Represented

On Behalf of O'Neill, Athy & Casey, P.C.
Temple University Health System

KNAPP, John J.

1001 Pennsylvania Ave. NW
Suite 600
Washington, DC 20004
EMail: jknapp@pgfm.com
Tel: (202)347-0066
Fax: (202)624-7222
Registered: LDA
General Counsel, Department of Housing and Urban Development, 1981-86.

Employers
Powell, Goldstein, Frazer & Murphy LLP (Partner)

Clients Represented

On Behalf of Powell, Goldstein, Frazer & Murphy LLP
Starrett City Associates

KNAPP, Michael

2020 K St. NW
Suite 400
Washington, DC 20006
EMail: mknapp@telcordia.com
Tel: (202)776-5454
Fax: (202)776-5424

Employers
Telcordia Technologies, Inc. (Exec. Director, Federal and State Regulatory Relations)

KNAPP, Ph.D., Richard M.

2450 N St. NW
Washington, DC 20037-1126
Tel: (202)828-0410
Fax: (202)862-6218
Registered: LDA

Employers
Ass'n of American Medical Colleges (Exec. V. President)

KNAPPEN, Theodore C.

1001 G St. NW
Suite 400 East
Washington, DC 20001
Tel: (202)638-3490
Fax: (202)638-3516
Registered: LDA

Employers
Self-employed as an independent consultant.

Clients Represented

As an independent consultant
Greyhound Lines
Martz Group
Mid-Atlantic Medical Services, Inc.

KNAUER, Leon T.

2300 N St. NW
Suite 700
Washington, DC 20037-1128
Tel: (202)783-4141
Fax: (202)783-5851
Registered: FARA
Law Clerk to Judge Charles F. McLaughlin, U.S. District Court for the District of Columbia, 1961-62.

Employers
Wilkinson, Barker and Knauer, LLP (Partner)

Clients Represented

On Behalf of Wilkinson, Barker and Knauer, LLP
Panama, Public Service Regulatory Entity of the Government of the Republic of

KNAUSS, Charles H.

3000 K St. NW
Suite 300
Washington, DC 20007
Tel: (202)424-7500
Fax: (202)424-7643
Registered: LDA
Minority Counsel, House Energy and Commerce Committee, 1987-90.

Employers
Swidler Berlin Shereff Friedman, LLP (Partner)

Clients Represented

On Behalf of Swidler Berlin Shereff Friedman, LLP
Exxon Chemical Co.
General Electric Co.
Nat'l Sediments Coalition

KNEBEL, John A.

1771 N St. NW
Washington, DC 20036-2891
Tel: (202)429-5386
Fax: (202)429-5410

Employers
Nat'l Ass'n of Broadcasters (Exec. V. President, Operations and Business Development)

KNEISS, Sharon H.

1111 19th St. NW
Suite 800
Washington, DC 20036
Tel: (202)463-2700
Fax: (202)463-2785
Registered: LDA

Employers
American Forest & Paper Ass'n (V. President, Regulatory Affairs)

KNETTEL, Anthony J.

1400 L St. NW
Suite 350
Washington, DC 20005
Tel: (202)789-1400
Fax: (202)789-1120
Registered: LDA

Employers
The ERISA Industry Committee (ERIC) (V. President, Health Policy)

KNEUER, John M. R.

901 15th St. NW
Suite 700
Washington, DC 20005-2301
Tel: (202)371-6000
Fax: (202)371-6279
Registered: LDA
EMail: jmrkneuer@verner.com

Employers
Verner, Liipfert, Bernhard, McPherson and Hand, Chartered

Clients Represented
On Behalf of Verner, Liipfert, Bernhard, McPherson and Hand, Chartered
NOKIA
Thomson Consumer Electronics, Inc.

KNIGHT, Aaron

420 Seventh St. SE
Washington, DC 20003
Tel: (202)546-3950
Fax: (202)546-3749

Employers
World Federalist Ass'n (Chief of Staff)

KNIGHT, Bruce I.

122 C St. NW
Suite 510
Washington, DC 20001
Tel: (202)628-7001
Fax: (202)628-1933
Registered: LDA
EMail: knight@dc.ncga.com

Employers
Nat'l Corn Growers Ass'n (V. President, Public Policy)

KNIGHT, Delos

1199 N. Fairfax St.
Suite 1000
Alexandria, VA 22314
Tel: (703)299-4499
Fax: (703)299-4488
EMail: delosk@aol.com

Employers
The Hawthorn Group, L.C. (Senior Counselor)

KNIGHT, Guyon H.

1150 15th St. NW
Washington, DC 20071
Tel: (202)334-6000
Fax: (202)334-4536
EMail: knightc@washpost.com

Employers
The Washington Post Co. (V. President, Corporate Communications)

KNIGHT, James

Ten G St. NE
Suite 460
Washington, DC 20002
Tel: (202)638-2135
Fax: (202)737-3085
Registered: LDA

Employers
Brotherhood of Maintenance of Way Employees (Director, Government Affairs)

KNIGHT, Laurie

1100 S. Washington St.
First Floor
Alexandria, VA 22314-4494
Tel: (703)683-4300
Fax: (703)683-8965
Registered: LDA
EMail: lknight@nbwa.org

Employers
Nat'l Beer Wholesalers Ass'n (Washington Representative)

KNIGHT, Mark A.

2301 Mount Vernon Ave.
Suite 100
Alexandria, VA 22301
Tel: (703)836-2274
Fax: (703)836-0083
EMail: markaabh@aabh.org

Employers
Ass'n for Ambulatory Behavioral Healthcare (Exec. Director)

KNIGHT, Robert

1201 New York Ave. NW
Suite 350
Washington, DC 20005
Tel: (202)289-2950
Fax: (202)289-2846

Employers
Nat'l Ass'n of Private Industry Councils (President)

KNIGHT, Yvonne

4400 Massachusetts Ave. NW
Washington, DC 20016
Tel: (202)885-2166

Employers
American University (Director, Government Relations Office)

KNIGHTS, Josh

1615 H St. NW
Washington, DC 20062-2000
Tel: (202)659-6000
Fax: (202)463-5836

Employers
Chamber of Commerce of the U.S.A. (Director, Asia Trade Policy, International Division)

KNIPPERS, Diane L.

1110 Vermont Ave. NW
Suite 1180
Washington, DC 20005-3544
Tel: (202)969-8430
Fax: (202)969-8429
EMail: mail@ird-renew.org

Employers
Institute on Religion and Democracy (President)

KNISELY, Evan

1420 New York Ave. NW
Suite 1050
Washington, DC 20005
Tel: (202)638-1950
Fax: (202)638-7714
Registered: LDA
Former Staff Assistant to Rep. John Bryant (D-TX), 1992-93. Former Clerk, Budget Services, Department of Education.

Employers
Van Scoyoc Associates, Inc. (Legislative Assistant)

Clients Represented
On Behalf of Van Scoyoc Associates, Inc.
American Psychological Ass'n
Ass'n of Schools of Public Health
DGME Fairness Initiative
Fargo-Cass County Development Corp.
Johns Hopkins University-Applied Physics Lab
Nat'l Ass'n of Foster Grandparent Program Directors
Patient Access to Transplantation (PAT) Coalition
University of Nebraska

KNISELY, Robert L.

1420 New York Ave. NW
Suite 1050
Washington, DC 20005
Tel: (202)638-1950
Fax: (202)638-7714
Registered: LDA
Professional Staff member, Subcommittee on Labor, HHS, Education and Related Services, House Committee on Appropriations, 1972-1999. Budget Analyst, Department of Housing and Urban Development, 1970-72.

Employers
Van Scoyoc Associates, Inc.

Clients Represented
On Behalf of Van Scoyoc Associates, Inc.
American Library Ass'n
American Psychological Ass'n
Nat'l Ass'n of Foster Grandparent Program Directors
New American School
Recording for the Blind and Dyslexic, Inc.
Regents College
Science Applications Internat'l Corp. (SAIC)
Teach for America
University of Phoenix

KNOBLOCH, Karen

325 Seventh St. NW
Suite 1100
Washington, DC 20004-2802
Tel: (202)783-7971
Fax: (202)737-2849

Employers
Nat'l Retail Federation (Senior V. President, Membership)

KNOLL, Albert B.

1130 Connecticut Ave. NW
Suite 710
Washington, DC 20036
Tel: (202)628-1010
Fax: (202)628-1041
Registered: LDA
EMail: albert_b_knoll@sunoil.com

Employers
Sunoco, Inc. (Senior Legislative Representative)

KNOLL, E. Joseph

1850 M St. NW
Suite 400
Washington, DC 20036
Tel: (202)293-8200
Fax: (202)872-0145
Registered: LDA
Attorney, Federal Housing Administration, 1964-68.

Employers
Krooth & Altman (Partner)

Clients Represented
On Behalf of Krooth & Altman
Healthcare Financing Study Group

KNOPMAN, Debra

600 Pennsylvania Ave. SE
Suite 400
Washington, DC 20003
Tel: (202)546-4482
Fax: (202)544-5014
EMail: dknopman@pf.org

Employers
Center for Innovation and the Environment, Progressive Foundation (Director)

KNOPP, Greg

700 11th St. NW
Washington, DC 20001-4507
Tel: (202)383-1207
Fax: (202)383-7540
Registered: LDA
EMail: gknopp@realtors.org

Employers
Nat'l Ass'n of Realtors (Senior RPAC Representative)

KNOTT, Bob

1875 I St. NW
Suite 900
Washington, DC 20005
Tel: (202)371-0200
Fax: (202)371-2858

Employers
Edelman Public Relations Worldwide (V. President)

Clients Represented
On Behalf of Edelman Public Relations Worldwide
Capital Confirmation
U.S. Senate Federal Credit Union
Windsor Group

KNOTT, Kerry

21 Dupont Circle NW
Fifth Floor
Washington, DC 20036
Tel: (202)263-5900
Fax: (202)263-5901
Registered: LDA

Employers
Microsoft Corp. (Senior Manager, Federal Affairs)

KNOWLES, Gearold L.

1101 Connecticut Ave. NW
Suite 600
Washington, DC 20036
Tel: (202)778-6400
Fax: (202)778-6460
Registered: FARA
Attorney, Division of Corporate Regulation, Securites and Exchange Commission, 1973-76.

Employers
Schiff Hardin & Waite (Partner)

Clients Represented
On Behalf of Schiff Hardin & Waite
China, Directorate General of Telecommunications, Ministry of Communications of the Republic of

KNOWLES, Jeffrey D.

1201 New York Ave. NW
Suite 1000
Washington, DC 20005
Tel: (202)962-4860
Fax: (202)962-8300

EMail: jdknowles@venable.com

Employers

Venable (Partner)

Clients Represented

On Behalf of Venable

Electronic Retailing Ass'n

KNOWLTON, William A.

1301 K St. NW
Suite 800 East
Washington, DC 20005
Tel: (202)626-3900
Fax: (202)626-3961

EMail: wknowlton@ropesgray.com

Employers

Ropes & Gray (Partner)

KNUTSON, Kent

21 Dupont Circle NW
Fifth Floor
Washington, DC 20036
Tel: (202)263-5900
Fax: (202)263-5901
Registered: LDA

Employers

Microsoft Corp. (Manager, Federal Government Affairs)

KNUTSON, Marcia

1350 Connecticut Ave. NW
Suite 200
Washington, DC 20036
Tel: (202)887-1700
Fax: (202)293-2422
Registered: LDA

EMail: marcia@apts.org

Employers

Ass'n of America's Public Television Stations (Congressional Representative)

KOBLENZ, Andrew

8400 W. Park Dr.
McLean, VA 22102
Tel: (703)821-7000

Employers

Nat'l Automobile Dealers Ass'n (Exec. Director, Industry Affairs)

KOBOR, Patricia C.

750 First St. NE
Washington, DC 20002-4242
Tel: (202)336-5933
Fax: (202)336-6063
Registered: LDA

EMail: pck.apa@email.apa.org

Employers

American Psychological Ass'n (Senior, Science Policy)

KOCH, Cathy

1150 17th St. NW
Suite 601
Washington, DC 20036
Tel: (202)293-7474
Fax: (202)293-8811
Registered: LDA

Employers

Washington Council Ernst & Young (Senior Manager)

Clients Represented

On Behalf of Washington Council Ernst & Young

Aetna Life & Casualty Co.
American Insurance Ass'n
American Staffing Ass'n
Antitrust Coalition for Consumer Choice in Health Care
Apartment Investment and Management Co.
Ass'n of American Railroads
AT&T
Aventis Pharmaceuticals, Inc.
Baxter Healthcare Corp.
BHC Communications, Inc.
Bulmer Holding PLC, H. P.
Citigroup
ComEd
The Connell Co.
Directors Guild of America
Doris Duke Charitable Foundation
Eaton Vance Management Co.
The Enterprise Foundation
Fannie Mae
FedEx Corp.
General Electric Co.
Global Competitiveness Coalition
Grasslands Water District
Gilbert P. Hyatt, Inventor
Large Public Power Council
Local Initiatives Support Corp.
MacAndrews & Forbes Holdings, Inc.
Marsh & McLennan Cos.
MCG Northwest, Inc.
McLane Co.
Merrill Lynch & Co., Inc.
Nat'l Ass'n for State Farm Agents
Nat'l Ass'n of Professional Employer Organizations
Nat'l Ass'n of Real Estate Investment Trusts
Nat'l Defined Contribution Council
Nat'l Foreign Trade Council, Inc.
Nat'l Multi-Housing Council
Pfizer, Inc.
R&D Tax Credit Coalition
Recording Industry Ass'n of America
Reed-Elsevier Inc.
R. J. Reynolds Tobacco Co.
Charles Schwab & Co., Inc.,
Securities Industry Ass'n
Tax Fairness Coalition
TXU Business Services
U.S. Oncology
USA Biomass Power Producers Alliance
Viaticus, Inc.
Wilkie Farr & Gallagher
Ziff Investors Partnership

KOCH, Christopher L.

1015 15th St. NW
Suite 450
Washington, DC 20005
Tel: (202)589-1230
Fax: (202)589-1231
Registered: LDA
EMail: ckoch@worldshipping.org

Chairman, Federal Maritime Commission, 1990-93. Chief of Staff to Senator John McCain (R-AZ), 1987-90. Chief of Staff to Senator Slade Gorton (R-WA), 1983-87. General Counsel to the Committee on Commerce, Science and Transportation, U.S. Senate, 1977-81.

Employers

World Shipping Council (President and Chief Exec. Officer)

KOCH, F. James

1112 16th St. NW
Suite 300
Washington, DC 20036
Tel: (202)296-4336
Fax: (202)331-8523

Employers

Nat'l Parking Ass'n (Legislative Director)

KOCH, Gary

900 19th St. NW
Suite 700
Washington, DC 20006
Tel: (202)530-7000
Fax: (202)530-7042
Registered: LDA

Employers

Lucent Technologies (Director, Global Public Affairs)

KOCH, George W.

1800 Massachusetts Ave. NW
Second Floor
Washington, DC 20036-1800
Tel: (202)778-9110
Fax: (202)778-9100
Registered: LDA

Employers

Kirkpatrick & Lockhart LLP (Legislative Consultant)

Clients Represented

On Behalf of Kirkpatrick & Lockhart LLP

American Financial Group
Grocery Manufacturers of America
Independent Grocers' Alliance
Nat'l Court Reporters Ass'n

KOCH, Patrick C.

1620 L St. NW
Suite 1210
Washington, DC 20036
Tel: (202)955-6062
Fax: (202)955-6070
Registered: LDA

Employers

Higgins, McGovern & Smith, LLC
Self-employed as an independent consultant.

Clients Represented

On Behalf of Higgins, McGovern & Smith, LLC

AT&T
New Skies Satellites N.V.

As an independent consultant

Mercy Health Corp.

KOCH, Robert P.

601 13th St. NW
Suite 580 South
Washington, DC 20005
Tel: (202)408-0870
Fax: (202)371-0061
Registered: LDA

Employers

Wine Institute (Senior V. President)

KOCHEISEN, Carol

1301 Pennsylvania Ave. NW
Suite 550
Washington, DC 20004-1701
Tel: (202)626-3020
Fax: (202)626-3043
EMail: kocheisen@nlc.org

Employers

Nat'l League of Cities (Senior Legislative Counsel)

KOCHENDERFER, Karil L.

1010 Wisconsin Ave. NW
Ninth Floor
Washington, DC 20007
Tel: (202)337-9400
Fax: (202)337-4508
Registered: LDA
EMail: kkochenderfer@gmabrands.com

Employers

Coalition for Truth in Environmental Marketing Information, Inc. (Contact)
Grocery Manufacturers of America (Director, International Trade and Environmental Affairs)

KOCHES, Paul A.

1050 Connecticut Ave. NW
Washington, DC 20036-5339
Tel: (202)857-6000
Fax: (202)857-6395

Employers

Arent Fox Kintner Plotkin & Kahn, PLLC (Member)

KOCOL, John M.

101 North Carolina St. SE
Suite 401
Washington, DC 20003
Tel: (202)543-8331
Fax: (202)543-4225
EMail: john@swimwiththesharks.com

Employers

SwimWithTheSharks.com (Chief Exec. Officer)

KOCOT, S. Lawrence

P.O. Box 1417-D49
Alexandria, VA 22313-1417
Tel: (703)549-3001
Fax: (703)549-0772

Employers

Nat'l Ass'n of Chain Drug Stores (Senior V. President, Government Affairs and General Counsel)

KODIS, Martin

1849 C St. NW
Washington, DC 20240
Tel: (202)208-5403
Fax: (202)208-6965

Employers

Department of Interior - Fish and Wildlife Service (Legislative Specialist)

KOEHL, Dexter

1100 New York Ave. NW
Suite 450
Washington, DC 20005
Tel: (202)408-2137
Fax: (202)408-1255

Employers
Travel Industry Ass'n of America (V. President, Public Relations and Communications)

KOEHLER, Robert H.

2550 M St. NW
Washington, DC 20037-1350
Tel: (202)457-6000
Fax: (202)457-6315
EMail: rkoehler@pattonboggs.com
Trial Attorney, Contract Appeals Division, Office of the Judge Advocate General, 1971-73. Legal Advisor, U.S. Army Procurement Agency (Vietnam), 1970-71.

Employers
Patton Boggs, LLP (Partner)

Clients Represented
On Behalf of Patton Boggs, LLP
Sierra Military Health Services, Inc.

KOENIG, Eric

21 Dupont Circle NW
Fifth Floor
Washington, DC 20036
Tel: (202)263-5900
Fax: (202)263-5901
Registered: LDA

Employers
Microsoft Corp. (Senior Manager, Federal Government Affairs)

KOENIG, Col. Lyle

U.S. Senate Russell Bldg.
Room 182
Washington, DC 20510
Tel: (202)685-2573
Fax: (202)685-2575

Employers
Department of Air Force (Senate Liaison, Legislative Liaison)

KOENIG, Peter J.

1150 18th St. NW
Ninth Floor
Washington, DC 20036
Tel: (202)296-3355
Fax: (202)296-3922
EMail: pkoenig@ablondifoster.com
Office of Policy, Federal Trade Commission, 1983.

Employers
Ablondi, Foster, Sobin & Davidow, P.C. (Partner)

KOENIGS, Craig A.

1666 K St. NW
Suite 500
Washington, DC 20006-2803
Tel: (202)887-1400
Fax: (202)466-2198
Registered: LDA

Employers
O'Connor & Hannan, L.L.P. (Associate)

KOEPPER, Ken

1300 N. 17th St.
Suite 750
Arlington, VA 22209
Tel: (703)247-2600
Fax: (703)841-4750
EMail: koepper@utsa.com

Employers
Uniform and Textile Service Ass'n (Director, Communications)

KOFF, Alexander

1001 Pennsylvania Ave. NW
Suite 600
Washington, DC 20004
Tel: (202)347-0066
Fax: (202)624-7222

Employers
Powell, Goldstein, Frazer & Murphy LLP (Associate)

Clients Represented
On Behalf of Powell, Goldstein, Frazer & Murphy LLP
DCS Group

KOGAN, Richard

820 First St. NE
Suite 510
Washington, DC 20002
Tel: (202)408-1080
Fax: (202)408-1056
Former Staff Member, House Committee on the Budget.

Employers
Center on Budget and Policy Priorities (Senior Fellow for Budge Policy)

KOGEL, Ross

11921 Freedom Dr.
Suite 550
Reston, VA 20190
Tel: (703)736-8082
Fax: (703)904-4339
EMail: rkogel@gte.net

Employers
Tire Ass'n of North America (Exec. V. President)

KOGOVSEK, Hon. Raymond P.

1001 Pennsylvania Ave. NW
Suite 760 North
Washington, DC 20004
Tel: (202)661-7060
Fax: (202)661-7066
Registered: LDA, FARA
Member, U.S. House of Representatives (D-CO), 1979-85.

Employers
Kogovsek & Associates (President)
The Legislative Strategies Group, LLC

Clients Represented
On Behalf of Kogovsek & Associates
The Legislative Strategies Group, LLC
Rio Grande Water Conservation District
Signal Behavioral Health Network
Southern Ute Indian Tribe
Southwestern Water Conservation District
Ute Mountain Ute Indian Tribe
Wolf Springs Ranches, Inc.

KOHL, Kay J.

One Dupont Circle NW
Suite 615
Washington, DC 20036-1168
Tel: (202)659-3130
Fax: (202)785-0374

Employers
University Continuing Education Ass'n (Exec. Director)

KOHLMOOS, James W.

1420 New York Ave. NW
Suite 1050
Washington, DC 20005
Tel: (202)638-1950
Fax: (202)638-7714
Registered: LDA
Assistant Secretary for Elementary and Secondary Education, Department of Education, during the Clinton Administration.

Employers
Van Scoyoc Associates, Inc. (V. President)

Clients Represented
On Behalf of Van Scoyoc Associates, Inc.
Abrams & Co. Publishers Inc.
American Library Ass'n
Recording for the Blind and Dyslexic, Inc.
Regents College
Teach for America
ZapMe! Corp.

KOHN, Gary J.

805 15th St. NW
Suite 300
Washington, DC 20005-2207
Tel: (202)682-4200
Fax: (202)682-9054
Registered: LDA

Employers
Credit Union Nat'l Ass'n, Inc. (V. President and Senior Legislative Counsel)

KOHR, Howard

440 First St. NW
Suite 600
Washington, DC 20001
Tel: (202)639-5200
Registered: LDA

Employers
American Israel Public Affairs Committee (Exec. Director)

KOHUT, Carleen C.

325 Seventh St. NW
Suite 1100
Washington, DC 20004-2802
Tel: (202)783-7971
Fax: (202)737-2849

Employers
Nat'l Retail Federation (Senior V. President)

KOLAR, Alexander Peter

2121 Crystal Dr.
Suite 706
Arlington, VA 22202
Tel: (703)746-0670
Registered: LDA

Employers
Galaxy Aerospace Co., LP

KOLAR, Joseph M.

1717 Pennsylvania Ave. NW
Washington, DC 20006
Tel: (202)974-1000
Fax: (202)331-9330
Registered: LDA

Employers
Goodwin, Procter & Hoar LLP (Partner)

Clients Represented
On Behalf of Goodwin, Procter & Hoar LLP
Consumer Mortgage Coalition

KOLAR, CAE, Mary Jane

526 King St.
Alexandria, VA 22314
Tel: (703)706-9580
Fax: (703)706-9583

Employers
The Alexandria Group (President and Chief Exec. Officer)

KOLARAS, Demo

1909 Q St. NW
Suite 500
Washington, DC 20009-1007
Tel: (202)232-6300
Fax: (202)232-2140

Employers
American Hellenic Educational Progressive Ass'n (AHEPA) (Exec. Director)

KOLASKY, Jr., William J.

2445 M St. NW
Washington, DC 20037-1420
Tel: (202)663-6000
Fax: (202)663-6363
EMail: wkolasky@wilmer.com
Former Law Clerk to Judge Bailey Aldrich, U.S. Court of Appeals, First Circuit.

Employers
Wilmer, Cutler & Pickering (Partner)

KOLB, Charles

2000 L St. NW
Suite 700
Washington, DC 20036
Tel: (202)296-5860
Fax: (202)223-0776
EMail: kolb@ced.org

Employers
Committee for Economic Development (President)

KOLBE, Diane

918 F St. NW
Washington, DC 20004-1400
Tel: (202)216-2400
Fax: (202)371-9449

Employers
American Immigration Lawyers Ass'n (Associate Director, Membership)

KOLBE, Jr., Stanley E.

305 Fourth St. NE
Washington, DC 20002
Tel: (202)547-8202
Fax: (202)547-8810
Registered: LDA
EMail: SKolbe@smacna.org

Employers
Sheet Metal and Air Conditioning Contractors' Nat'l Ass'n (Director, Legislation)

KOLEDA, Michael S.

1110 N. Glebe Rd.
Suite 610
Arlington, VA 22201
Tel: (703)276-0600
Fax: (703)276-7662
EMail: mkoleda@hcikh.com

Employers
Koleda Childress & Co. (Principal)

KOLESNIK, Kris

3238 P St. NW
Washington, DC 20007
Tel: (202)342-1902
Fax: (202)342-1904
EMail: kjk@whistleblowers.org

Employers
Nat'l Whistleblower Center (Exec. Director)

KOLKER, Ann

910 17th St. NW
Suite 413
Washington, DC 20006
Tel: (202)331-1332
Registered: LDA

Employers
Ovarian Cancer Nat'l Alliance (Exec. Director)

KOLODZIEJ, Richard

1100 Wilson Blvd.
Suite 850
Arlington, VA 22209
Tel: (703)527-3022
Fax: (703)527-3025

Employers
Natural Gas Vehicle Coalition (President)

KOLSTAD, Katherine C.

700 13th St. NW
Suite 1000
Washington, DC 20005
Tel: (202)347-6633
Fax: (202)347-8713
Registered: LDA, FARA

Employers
Powell Tate (Account Executive)

Clients Represented

On Behalf of Powell Tate
Saudi Arabia, Royal Embassy of
Taiwan Studies Institute

KOLSTAND, James L.

1560 Wilson Blvd.
Suite 1250
Arlington, VA 22209
Tel: (703)527-6223
Fax: (703)527-7747

Employers
Nat'l Ass'n of Chemical Distributors (President and Chief Operating Officer)

KOLTON, Adam

122 C Street NW
Suite 240
Washington, DC 20001
Tel: (202)544-5205
Fax: (202)544-5197
Registered: LDA

Employers
Alaska Wilderness League

KOLTON, Eleanor A.

1050 17th St. NW
Suite 600
Washington, DC 20036
Tel: (202)466-6937
Fax: (202)466-6938
Registered: LDA

Employers
Emord & Associates, P.C. (Senior Associate)

Clients Represented

On Behalf of Emord & Associates, P.C.
American Preventive Medical Ass'n
The JAG Group, Inc.
Meditrend, Inc.
Pure Encapsulations, Inc.
Rx Vitamins, Inc.
UroStar, Inc.
Weider Nutritional Group
XCEL Medical Pharmacy, Ltd.

KOMAR, Brian

1629 K St. NW
Suite 1010
Washington, DC 20006
Tel: (202)466-3311
Fax: (202)466-3435
Registered: LDA
EMail: komar@civilrights.org

Employers
Leadership Conference on Civil Rights (Legislative Analyst)

KOMAROW, Jeffrey D.

1200 G St. NW
Suite 600
Washington, DC 20005-3802
Tel: (202)393-1200
Fax: (202)393-1240
EMail: komarow@wrightlaw.com
Law Clerk to Judge Edward Allen Tamm, U.S. Court of Appeals, District of Columbia Circuit, 1974-75.

Employers
Wright & Talisman, P.C.

Clients Represented

On Behalf of Wright & Talisman, P.C.
Alabama Gas Corp.

KOMIFAR, Harriet

2233 Wisconsin Ave. NW
Suite 525
Georgetown University
Washington, DC 20007
Tel: (202)687-0880
Fax: (202)687-3110

Employers
Institute for Health Care Research and Policy (Co-Director)

KOMINUS, Nicholas

1730 Rhode Island Ave. NW
Suite 608
Washington, DC 20036
Tel: (202)331-1458
Fax: (202)785-5110
Registered: LDA

Employers
United States Cane Sugar Refiners' Ass'n (President)

KOMOROSKE, John H.

1735 K St. NW
Washington, DC 20006-1506
Tel: (202)728-8475
Fax: (202)728-8419
Registered: LDA
EMail: john.komoroske@nasd.com

Employers
Nat'l Ass'n of Securities Dealers, Inc. (NASD) (Director, Governmental Relations)

KONDOH, Yasushi

2001 Pennsylvania Ave. NW
Suite 750
Washington, DC 20006
Tel: (202)785-2424
Fax: (202)785-2426
EMail: ykondoh@mriusa.com

Employers
Mitsubishi Research Institute (Chief Representative)

KONDRATAS, Anna

2100 M St. NW
Washington, DC 20037
Tel: (202)833-7200
Fax: (202)429-0687

Employers
The Urban Institute (Deputy Director, Assessing the New Federalism Project)

KONIGSBERG, Chuck

1500 K St. NW
Suite 250
Washington, DC 20005-1714
Tel: (202)639-7507
Fax: (202)639-7505
EMail: ckonigsberg@uhlaw.com
Minority Chief Health Counsel and General Counsel (1999-2000), Assistant Director for Legislative Affairs, Office of Management and Budget (1995-99), and General Counsel (1993-94), Senate Finance Committee. Minority Chief Counsel, Counsel, Deputy Counsel, Senate Rules Committee, 1987-92. Staff Attorney, Senate Budget Committee, 1983-86.

Employers
Ungaretti & Harris (Partner)

Clients Represented

On Behalf of Ungaretti & Harris
Cardinal Health Inc.
United Defense, L.P.

KONNOR, PharmMS, Delbert D.

2300 Ninth St. South
Suite 210
Arlington, VA 22204
Tel: (703)920-8480
Fax: (703)920-8491
EMail: ddkonnor@pcmanet.org

Employers
American Managed Care Pharmacy Ass'n (President and Chief Exec. Officer)
Pharmaceutical Care Management Ass'n (President and Chief Exec. Officer)

KONO, Makato

1776 I St. NW
Suite 880
Washington, DC 20006
Tel: (202)331-8750
Fax: (202)331-8797
EMail: mkono@wdc.fujitsu.com

Employers
Fujitsu Limited (Liaison Representative)

KONOSHIMA, Joji

232 E. Capitol St. NE
Washington, DC 20003
Tel: (202)544-3181
Fax: (202)543-1748

Employers
US-Asia Institute (President and Trustee)

KONTIO, Peter

601 Pennsylvania Ave. NW
11th Floor, North Bldg.
Washington, DC 20004-2601
Tel: (202)756-3300
Fax: (202)756-3333

Employers
Alston & Bird LLP

Clients Represented

On Behalf of Alston & Bird LLP
GTE Mobilnet

KOON, Danielle M.

919 18th St. NW
Suite 300
Washington, DC 20006
Tel: (202)296-5544
Fax: (202)223-0321
Registered: LDA

Employers
American Financial Services Ass'n (Director, Federal Government Affairs)

KOONCE, Norman L.

1735 New York Ave. NW
Washington, DC 20006
Tel: (202)626-7300
Fax: (202)626-7420

Employers
The American Institute of Architects (Exec. V. President/C.E.O.)

KOONTZ, John R.

1385 Piccard Dr.
Rockville, MD 20850-4340
Tel: (301)869-5800
Fax: (301)990-9690
EMail: jkoontz@mcaa.org

Employers
Mechanical Contractors Ass'n of America (National Director, Project Management and Supervisory Education)

KOOP, M.D., Sc.D, C. Everett

133 H. St. NW
Suite 600
Washington, DC 20005
Tel: (202)737-2670
Fax: (202)347-4285

Employers
Nat'l Health Museum (Chairman Emeritus)

KOOPERSMITH, Jeffrey M.

1300 Pennsylvania Ave. NW
Suite 700
Washington, DC 20004
Registered: LDA

Employers
Curson Koopersmith Partners, Inc. (Managing Partner)

Clients Represented

On Behalf of Curson Koopersmith Partners, Inc.
Internet Action PAC
Underwriters Digital Research, Inc.

KOOPERSMITH, Theodore B.

1300 Pennsylvania Ave. NW
Suite 700
Washington, DC 20004
Registered: LDA

Employers
Curson Koopersmith Partners, Inc. (Principal)

Clients Represented

On Behalf of Curson Koopersmith Partners, Inc.
Internet Action PAC
Underwriters Digital Research, Inc.

KOPECKY, Sr., John

1401 I St. NW
Suite 600
Washington, DC 20005
Tel: (202)336-7400
Fax: (202)336-7515
Registered: LDA

Employers
United Technologies Corp. (Director, Space and Aero Propulsion Programs)

KOPETSKI, Michael J.

517 Colecroft Ct.
Alexandria, VA 22314
Registered: LDA

Employers
Self-employed as an independent consultant.

Clients Represented
As an independent consultant
The Boeing Co.
The Business Roundtable
Downey McGrath Group, Inc.

KOPP, George S.
2121 K St. NW
Suite 650
Washington, DC 20037
Tel: (202)296-2400
Fax: (202)296-2409
Registered: LDA, FARA
EMail: George@GlobalUSAinc.com
Staff Director and Chief Counsel, House Subcommittee on Natural Resources and Environment, 1980-88. Counsel, Committee on Energy and Commerce, 1978-80.

Employers
Global USA, Inc. (Senior V. President and General Counsel)

Clients Represented
On Behalf of Global USA, Inc.
All Nippon Airways Co.
Artel, Inc.
Dade, Florida, County of
DRC, Inc.
Hyundai Motor Co.
K-Mortgage Corp.
Psychemedics Corp.
SBC Communications Inc.
Taipei Economic and Cultural Representative Office in the United States
Takata Corp.

KOPP, Harry
1101 Connecticut Ave. NW
Suite 1200
Washington, DC 20036
Tel: (202)739-0129
Registered: LDA

Employers
Harry Kopp LLC (President)

Clients Represented
On Behalf of Harry Kopp LLC
Philippine Sugar Alliance

KOPPEL, Robert
1133 19th St. NW
Washington, DC 20036
Tel: (202)887-2248
Fax: (202)736-6434
EMail: robert.koppel@wcom.com

Employers
MCI WorldCom Corp. (V. President, Regulatory)

KOPPEN, Christopher
1330 New Hampshire Ave. NW
Suite 122
Washington, DC 20036
Tel: (202)296-2175
Fax: (202)296-3526
Registered: LDA
EMail: ckoppen@nachc.com
Former Legislative Assistant to Rep. Charlie Norwood (R-GA).

Employers
Nat'l Ass'n of Community Health Centers (Associate Director, Federal Affairs)

KOPPERUD, Steve
818 Connecticut Ave. NW
Suite 325
Washington, DC 20006
Tel: (202)776-0071
Fax: (202)776-0083
Registered: LDA
EMail: skopperund@poldir.com

Employers
American Feed Industry Ass'n (PAC Contact)
Policy Directions, Inc. (Senior V. President)

Clients Represented
On Behalf of Policy Directions, Inc.
American Feed Industry Ass'n
Grocery Manufacturers of America
Kraft Foods, Inc.
Nestle USA, Inc.

KOPPI, Susan
4350 East-West Hwy.
Suite 500
Bethesda, MD 20814-4110
Tel: (301)941-0252
Fax: (301)941-0259
Registered: LDA

Employers
Endocrine Soc. (Director, Public Affairs)

KORANDA, Donald J.
1815 N. Fort Myer Dr.
Suite 500
Arlington, VA 22209-1805
Tel: (703)527-0226
Fax: (703)527-0229

Employers
Nat'l Aeronautic Ass'n of the U.S.A. (President)

KORB, Thomas
1922 F St. NW
Fourth Floor
Washington, DC 20006
Tel: (202)331-6081
Fax: (202)331-2164

Employers
Ass'n for Advanced Life Underwriting (Director, Government Affairs)

KORDOSKI, Ph.D, Edward W.
1850 M St. NW
Suite 700
Washington, DC 20036
Tel: (202)721-4145
Fax: (202)296-8120

Employers
Chlorobenzene Producers Ass'n (Exec. Director)
Institute for Polyacrylate Absorbents, Inc. (Exec. Director)
Tetrahydrofuran Task Force (Exec. Director)

KORENS, Michael E.
2201 Wisconsin Ave. NW
Suite 105
Washington, DC 20007
Tel: (202)965-9810
Fax: (202)965-9812
Registered: LDA
EMail: mkorens@mindspring.com
Former Counsel, Subcommittee on Aviation, Senate Committee on Commerce, Science and Transportation.

Employers
Self-employed as an independent consultant.

Clients Represented
As an independent consultant
NAV Canada
Northwest Airlines, Inc.
United Airlines

KORKUCH, Marylou
One Massachusetts Ave. NW
Suite 350
Washington, DC 20001
Tel: (202)408-8123
Fax: (202)296-7683
EMail: mkorvuch@chubb.com

Employers
The Chubb Corp. (Assistant V. President)

KORMAN, Paul I.
1050 Thomas Jefferson St. NW
Seventh Floor
Washington, DC 20007
Tel: (202)298-1800
Fax: (202)338-2416
EMail: PIK@vnf.com
Assistant Secretary to Commissioner George Hall (1977-79), Special Assistant (1975-77), Federal Energy Regulatory Commission, Department of Energy.

Employers
Van Ness Feldman, P.C. (Member)

KORNEGAY, Amanda
1771 N St. NW
Washington, DC 20036-2891
Tel: (202)495-5427
Fax: (202)775-2157

Employers
Nat'l Ass'n of Broadcasters (TARPAC Manager)

KORNS, John H.
1620 L St. NW
Suite 600
Washington, DC 20036
Tel: (202)312-8000
Fax: (202)312-8100
Registered: LDA, FARA
EMail: jkorns@owdlaw.com
Assistant U.S. Attorney for the District of Columbia, Department of Justice, 1976-80. Law Clerk to Chief Justice Warren E. Burger, U.S. Supreme Court, 1971-72, and Judge John Minor Wisdom, U.S. Court of Appeals, Fifth Circuit, 1970-71.

Employers
Oppenheimer Wolff & Donnelly LLP (Partner)

Clients Represented
On Behalf of Oppenheimer Wolff & Donnelly LLP
Association des Constructeurs Europeens de Motocycles
NYK Bulkship, Inc.

KOROLISHLIN, Jennifer
1451 Dolley Madison Blvd.
McLean, VA 22101-3850
Tel: (703)761-2600
Fax: (703)761-4334
EMail: info@iafis.org

Employers
Internat'l Ass'n of Food Industry Suppliers (Director, Communications)

KOROLOGOS, Tom C.
1850 K St. NW
Suite 850
Washington, DC 20006
Tel: (202)331-1760
Fax: (202)822-9376
Registered: LDA
Deputy Assistant to the President for Legislative Affairs, The White House, 1970-74. Former Assistant to Senator Wallace F. Bennett (R-UT).

Employers
Timmons and Co., Inc. (Chairman, Exec. Committee)

Clients Represented
On Behalf of Timmons and Co., Inc.
American Council of Life Insurers
American Petroleum Institute
American Soc. of Anesthesiologists
Anheuser-Busch Cos., Inc.
Asbestos Working Group
AT&T
Bay Harbor Management, L.C.
Bristol-Myers Squibb Co.
Cox Enterprises Inc.
DaimlerChrysler Corp.
Farallon Capital Management
Federal Home Loan Mortgage Corp. (Freddie Mac)
Micron Technology, Inc.
Napster, Inc.
Nat'l Rifle Ass'n of America
New York Life Insurance Co.
Northrop Grumman Corp.
TruePosition Inc.
Union Pacific
University of Utah
UNOCAL Corp.
VISA U.S.A., Inc.

KORSMO, Chris
1780 Massachusetts Ave. NW
Washington, DC 20036
Tel: (202)785-3351
Fax: (202)293-4349
Registered: LDA

Employers
Planned Parenthood Federation of America (Director, Government Relations)

KORTH, Fritz-Alan
1700 K St. NW
Suite 501
Washington, DC 20006
Tel: (202)223-3630
Fax: (202)223-1878

Employers
Korth & Korth (Principal)

Clients Represented
On Behalf of Korth & Korth
Del Norte Technology

KOSAR, David A.
1275 K St. NW
Suite 1212
Washington, DC 20005
Tel: (703)787-0000
Fax: (202)312-5005

Employers
Healthcare Distribution Management Ass'n (Director, State Legislative Affairs)

KOSH, Ronald W.
12600 Fair Lakes Circle
Fairfax, VA 22033-4904
Tel: (703)222-4100
Fax: (703)222-4915

Employers
AAA MidAtlantic (V. President)

KOSIAK, Steven
1730 Rhode Island Ave.
Suite 912
Washington, DC 20036
Tel: (202)331-7990
Fax: (202)331-8019

Employers
Center for Strategic and Budgetary Assessments (Senior Budget Analyst)

KOSTERS, Marvin H.

1150 17th St. NW
Washington, DC 20036
EMail: mkosters@aei.org

Tel: (202)862-5800
Fax: (202)862-7177

Employers
American Enterprise Institute for Public Policy Research (Resident Scholar and Director, Economic Policy)

KOSTIW, Michael V.

1050 17th St. NW
Suite 500
Washington, DC 20036

Tel: (202)331-1427
Fax: (202)785-4702
Registered: LDA

Employers
Texaco Group Inc. (General Manager, International Relations)

KOSTUK, Barbara M.

1301 Pennsylvania Ave. NW
Suite 1100
Washington, DC 20004-1707

Tel: (202)626-4000
Fax: (202)626-4208
Registered: LDA

Employers
Air Transport Ass'n of America (Director, Government Affairs)

KOSTYACK, John F.

1400 16th St. NW
Suite 501
Washington, DC 20036-2266
EMail: kostyack@nwf.org

Tel: (202)797-6800
Fax: (202)797-6646
Registered: LDA

Employers
Nat'l Wildlife Federation - Office of Federal and Internat'l Affairs (Counsel, Endangered Habitats)

KOTEEN, Bernard

2099 Pennsylvania Ave. NW
Suite 100
Washington, DC 20006
EMail: bkoteen@hklaw.com

Tel: (202)955-3000
Fax: (202)955-5564

Employers
Holland & Knight LLP (Partner)

KOTIF, Linda

1225 19th St. NW
Suite 710
Washington, DC 20036

Tel: (202)296-4426
Fax: (202)296-4319

Employers
Nat'l Institute for Health Care Management (Senior Director, Policy and Program Development)

KOTLER, Sarah B.

555 12th St. NW
Washington, DC 20004-1206
EMail: sarah_kotler@aporter.com

Tel: (202)942-5994
Fax: (202)942-5999
Registered: LDA

Employers
Arnold & Porter (Associate)

KOTLOVE, Douglas

8555 16th St.
Suite 500
Silver Spring, MD 20910

Tel: (301)589-8100

Employers
USLaw.com (Director, Public Relations)

KOURY, Joseph S.

1200 G St. NW
Suite 600
Washington, DC 20005-3802
EMail: koury@wrightlaw.com

Tel: (202)393-1200
Fax: (202)393-1240

Attorney, Pipeline Rates and Valuation Section (1983-84) and Attorney, Electric Rates and Corporate Regulation Section (1980-83), Federal Energy Regulatory Commission.

Employers
Wright & Talisman, P.C.

KOURY, Kate

1015 15th St. NW
Suite 802
Washington, DC 20005
EMail: kkoury@acec.org

Tel: (202)347-7474
Fax: (202)898-0068
Registered: LDA

Employers
American Consulting Engineers Council (Director, Liability and Regulatory Affairs)

KOUTSOUMPAS, J. Thomas

555 13th St. NW
Suite Three East
Washington, DC 20004
EMail: tom@vitas.com

Tel: (202)637-7228
Fax: (202)637-8715

Employers
Vitas Healthcare Corp. (V. President, Public Affairs)

KOVACS, William L.

1615 H St. NW
Washington, DC 20062-2000

Tel: (202)659-6000
Fax: (202)463-5836

Employers
Chamber of Commerce of the U.S.A. (V. President for Environment and Regulatory Affairs)

KOVAKA, Michael G.

1200 New Hampshire Ave. NW
Suite 800
Washington, DC 20036-6802
EMail: mkovaka@dlalaw.com

Tel: (202)776-2000
Fax: (202)776-2222

Employers
Dow, Lohnes & Albertson, PLLC (Member)

KOVAR, Carrie

1101 Vermont Ave. NW
Suite 700
Washington, DC 20005
EMail: ckovar@aaodc.org

Tel: (202)737-6662
Fax: (202)737-7061
Registered: LDA

Employers
American Academy of Ophthamology - Office of Federal Affairs (Manager of Public Health Manpower Policy)

KOVEY, Mark H.

1875 I St. NW
Suite 1050
Washington, DC 20006-5409

Tel: (202)331-8585
Fax: (202)331-2032

Employers
Scribner, Hall & Thompson, LLP (Partner)

KOWALCZUK, Paula

1300 Connecticut Ave. NW
Suite 600
Washington, DC 20036

Tel: (202)293-0231
Fax: (202)223-0358

Employers
American Strategies, Inc. (President)

KOYANAGI, Christine

1101 15th St. NW
Suite 1212
Washington, DC 20005

Tel: (202)467-5730
Ext: 18
Fax: (202)223-0409
Registered: LDA

Employers
Bazelon Center for Mental Health Law, Judge David L. (Policy Director)

KOZAK, Jerome J.

2101 Wilson Blvd.
Suite 400
Arlington, VA 22201
EMail: jkozak@nmpf.org

Tel: (703)243-6111
Fax: (703)841-9328

Employers
American Butter Institute (Exec. Director)
Nat'l Milk Producers Federation (Chief Exec. Officer)

KOZICHAROW, Eugene

1101 Pennsylvania Ave. NW
Suite 400
Washington, DC 20004-2504

Tel: (202)637-3800
Fax: (202)637-3860

Employers
Textron Inc. (Exec. Director, Public Affairs)

KOZLOW, Bess

1120 Connecticut Ave. NW
Washington, DC 20036

Tel: (202)663-5000
Fax: (202)828-5212
Registered: LDA

Employers
American Bankers Ass'n (Assistant Director, Grassroots)

KOZLOWSKI, Richard G.

1050 Thomas Jefferson St. NW
Seventh Floor
Washington, DC 20007
EMail: rgk@vnf.com

Tel: (202)298-1800
Fax: (202)338-2416

Employers
Van Ness Feldman, P.C. (Of Counsel)

Clients Represented

On Behalf of Van Ness Feldman, P.C.
Newport News, Virginia, City of

KOZUCH, Randy J.

11250 Waples Mill Rd.
Fairfax, VA 22030-7400

Tel: (703)267-1000
Fax: (703)267-3976

Employers
Nat'l Rifle Ass'n Institute for Legislative Action (Director, State and Local Affairs)

KRACOV, Daniel A.

2550 M St. NW
Washington, DC 20037-1350
EMail: dkracov@pattonboggs.com

Tel: (202)457-6000
Fax: (202)457-6315
Registered: LDA, FARA

Employers
Patton Boggs, LLP (Partner)

Clients Represented

On Behalf of Patton Boggs, LLP
drugstore.com
Hoffmann-La Roche Inc.
Pharmanex
Salton, Inc.

KRAEMER, Jay R.

1001 Pennsylvania Ave. NW
Suite 800
Washington, DC 20004-2505
EMail: jay_kraemer@ffhsj.com

Tel: (202)639-7000
Fax: (202)639-7008
Registered: LDA

Law Clerk to Judge James R. Miller, Jr., U.S. District Court for the District of Maryland, 1973-74.

Employers
Fried, Frank, Harris, Shriver & Jacobson (Partner)

Clients Represented

On Behalf of Fried, Frank, Harris, Shriver & Jacobson
GE Nuclear Energy

KRAGIE, Scott T.

1201 Pennsylvania Ave. NW
P.O. Box 407
Washington, DC 20044-0407
EMail: skragie@ssd.com

Tel: (202)626-6600
Fax: (202)626-6780

Assistant U.S. Attorney, Office of the U.S. Attorney for the District of Columbia, Department of Justice, 1979-86.

Employers
Squire, Sanders & Dempsey L.L.P. (Partner)

Clients Represented

On Behalf of Squire, Sanders & Dempsey L.L.P.
American Soc. of Anesthesiologists

KRAHN, Joe

900 Second St. NE
Suite 109
Washington, DC 20002

Tel: (202)898-1444
Fax: (202)898-0188
Registered: LDA

Employers
Waterman & Associates (Associate)

Clients Represented

On Behalf of Waterman & Associates
California State Ass'n of Counties
Milwaukee, Wisconsin, County of

KRAM, Sally W.

One Dupont Circle NW
Suite 200
Washington, DC 20036-1131
EMail: kram@consortium.org
Tel: (202)331-8080
Fax: (202)331-7925

Employers
Consortium of Universities of the Washington Metropolitan Area (Director, Government and Community Relations)

KRAMER, Albert H.

2101 L St. NW
Washington, DC 20037-1526
EMail: kramera@dsmo.com
Tel: (202)785-9700
Fax: (202)887-0689
Director, Bureau of Consumer Protection, Federal Trade Commission, 1977-81.

Employers
Dickstein Shapiro Morin & Oshinsky LLP (Partner)

Clients Represented
On Behalf of Dickstein Shapiro Morin & Oshinsky LLP
American Public Communications Council

KRAMER, Charlene K.

3900 Wisconsin Ave. NW
Washington, DC 20016
Tel: (202)752-7128

Employers
Fannie Mae (V. President, Corporate Communications)

KRAMER, Craig

1350 I St. NW
Suite 1210
Washington, DC 20005-3305
Tel: (202)589-1012
Fax: (202)589-1001
Registered: LDA

Employers
Johnson & Johnson, Inc. (Director, Federal Affairs)

KRAMER, Donald J.

700 13th St. NW
Suite 200
Washington, DC 20005
EMail: dkramer@opa.easter-seals.org
Tel: (202)347-3066
Fax: (202)737-7914
Registered: LDA

Employers
Easter Seals (Senior Information Specialist)

KRAMER, Elizabeth

1615 L St. NW
Suite 1000
Washington, DC 20036
Tel: (202)659-0330
Fax: (202)296-6119

Employers
Fleishman-Hillard, Inc (V. President)

KRAMER, George R.

1401 I St. NW
Suite 1000
Washington, DC 20005
EMail: gkramer@sia.com
Tel: (202)296-9410
Fax: (202)296-9775
Registered: LDA

Employers
Securities Industry Ass'n (V. President and Associate General Counsel)

KRAMER, Harri J.

810 Seventh St. NW
MS: 6338
Washington, DC 20531
Tel: (202)307-0703
Fax: (202)514-5958

Employers
Department of Justice - Office of Justice Programs (Director, Office of Congressional and Public Affairs)

KRAMER, Jeff A.

601 E St. NW
Washington, DC 20049
Tel: (202)434-3800
Fax: (202)434-6477
Registered: LDA

Employers
AARP (American Ass'n of Retired Persons) (Legislative Representative)

KRAMER, John E.

1717 Pennsylvania Ave. NW
Suite 200
Washington, DC 20006
EMail: jkramer@ij.org
Tel: (202)955-1300
Fax: (202)955-1329

Employers
Institute for Justice (V. President, Communications)

KRAMER, Steve

600 New Hampshire Ave. NW
Suite 601
Washington, DC 20037
Tel: (202)333-7400
Fax: (202)333-1638

Employers
Hill and Knowlton, Inc. (Sr. Managing Director, Marketing Communications)

Clients Represented
On Behalf of Hill and Knowlton, Inc.
U.S. Mint

KRAMER, William D.

901 15th St. NW
Suite 700
Washington, DC 20005-2301
EMail: wdkramer@verner.com
Tel: (202)371-6000
Fax: (202)371-6279

Employers
Verner, Liipfert, Bernhard, McPherson and Hand, Chartered (Member of Firm)

KRANOWITZ, Alan M.

1725 K St. NW
Suite 300
Washington, DC 20006
Tel: (202)872-0885
Fax: (202)296-5940
Registered: LDA
Deputy Assistant to the President for Legislative Affairs - House, Executive Office of the President, The White House, during the Reagan administration. Floor Assistant to the House Minority Whip, Rep. Richard Cheney (R-WY), 1989.

Employers
Nat'l Ass'n of Wholesaler-Distributors (Senior V. President, Government Relations)

KRANZ, Sally

1734 N St. NW
Washington, DC 20036-2990
EMail: gfwc@gfwc.org
Tel: (202)347-3168
Fax: (202)835-0246

Employers
General Federation of Women's Clubs (Director, Public Relations)

KRANZFELDER, Kathy

One Information Way
Bethesda, MD 20892-3560
Tel: (301)654-3327
Fax: (301)907-8906

Employers
Nat'l Diabetes Information Clearinghouse (Project Director)
Nat'l Digestive Diseases Information Clearinghouse (Director)
Nat'l Kidney and Urologic Diseases Information Clearinghouse (Project Officer)

KRASH, Abe

555 12th St. NW
Washington, DC 20004-1206
EMail: Abe_Krash@aporter.com
Tel: (202)942-5000
Fax: (202)942-5999
Member, President's Commission on Crime in the District of Columbia, 1965-66.

Employers
Arnold & Porter (Partner)

KRASNER, Wendy L.

600 13th St. NW
Washington, DC 20005-3096
EMail: wkrasner@mwe.com
Tel: (202)756-8064
Fax: (202)756-8087
Registered: LDA
Office of General Counsel, Department of Health and Human Services, 1978-80.

Employers
McDermott, Will and Emery (Partner)

Clients Represented
On Behalf of McDermott, Will and Emery
American Dental Hygienists' Ass'n
Comprehensive Health Services
Council of Women's and Infant's Specialty Hospitals
Hutzel Medical Center
Inova Fairfax Hospital
Magee Women's Health Foundation
Nat'l Perinatal Ass'n
Northside Hospital
Northside Savings Bank
PHP Healthcare Corp.
Rural Health Network Coalition
Rural Referral Centers Coalition
St. Peter's Medical Center
Women and Infants' Hospital
Women's Hospital
Women's Hospital of Greensboro

KRASOW, Cristina L.

1300 Connecticut Ave. NW
Suite 600
Washington, DC 20036
Tel: (202)775-8116
Fax: (202)223-0358
Registered: LDA
Senior Cloakroom Assistant, Senate Democrat Cloakroom, 1994-98.

Employers
Griffin, Johnson, Dover & Stewart

KRATTENMAKER, Thomas G.

701 Pennsylvania Ave. NW
Suite 900
Washington, DC 20004-2608
EMail: tkrattenmaker@mintz.com
Tel: (202)661-8738
Fax: (202)434-7400
Former Director of Research, Office of Plans and Policy, Federal Communications Commission.

Employers
Mintz, Levin, Cohn, Ferris, Glovsky and Popeo, P.C. (Partner)

KRAULAND, Edward J.

1330 Connecticut Ave. NW
Washington, DC 20036-1795
EMail: ekrauland@steptoe.com
Tel: (202)429-3000
Fax: (202)429-3902
Office of the Legal Advisor, Department of State, 1979. Nonproliferation Analyst, Nuclear Regulatory Commission, 1976-77.

Employers
Steptoe & Johnson LLP (Partner)

Clients Represented
On Behalf of Steptoe & Johnson LLP
Canadian Wheat Board
FIAMM S.p.A.
FIAMM Technologies, Inc.
Sterling Internat'l Consultants, Inc.

KRAUS, Angela

601 13th St. NW
Suite 410 South
Washington, DC 20005
Tel: (202)737-0100
Fax: (202)628-3965

Employers
R. Duffy Wall and Associates (Assistant V. President)

KRAUS, Don

420 Seventh St. SE
Suite C
Washington, DC 20003-0270
EMail: dkraus@cunr.org
Tel: (202)546-3956
Fax: (202)546-8703
Registered: LDA

Employers
Campaign for United Nations Reform (Exec. Director)

KRAUS, Margery

1615 L St. NW
Suite 900
Washington, DC 20036
EMail: info@apcoworldwide.com
Tel: (202)778-1000
Fax: (202)466-6002
Registered: LDA, FARA

Employers
APCO Worldwide (President and Chief Exec. Officer)

KRAUSE, Charles

1615 L St. NW
Suite 900
Washington, DC 20036
Tel: (202)778-1000
Fax: (202)466-6002

Employers
APCO Worldwide (Senior V. President, Global Services)

KRAUSE, Paul D.

1341 G St. NW
Fifth Floor
Washington, DC 20005
Tel: (202)626-7660
Fax: (202)628-3606

Employers
Wilson, Elser, Moskowitz, Edelman & Dicker LLP (Managing Partner)

KRAUSER, Katherine M.

1615 L St. NW
Suite 650
Washington, DC 20036
Tel: (202)626-8589
Fax: (202)626-8593
Registered: LDA
EMail: kkrauser@jeffersongr.com
Former Legislative Assistant to Rep. Mel Hancock (R-MO).

Employers
Jefferson Government Relations, L.L.C. (Director)

Clients Represented

On Behalf of Jefferson Government Relations, L.L.C.
Bass Hotels and Resorts, Inc.
Edison Welding Institute
Westmoreland Coal Co.

KRAUSHAAR, Kevin J.

1150 Connecticut Ave. NW
12th Floor
Washington, DC 20036
Tel: (202)429-9260
Fax: (202)223-6835
Registered: LDA

Employers
Consumer Healthcare Products Ass'n (V. President and Director, Government Relations)

KRAUSS, Julia

500 E. Street SW
Suite 920
Washington, DC 20024
Tel: (202)479-4050
Fax: (202)484-1312
Registered: LDA
EMail: julia.krauss@aopa.org

Employers
Aircraft Owners and Pilots Ass'n (Director, Legislative Affairs)

KRAUTHAMER, Judith

1828 L St. NW
Suite 906
Washington, DC 20036-5104
Tel: (202)775-5966
Fax: (202)429-9417

Employers
Marine Technology Soc. (Exec. Director)

KRAVETZ, Lauri

1700 K St. NW
Suite 1150
Washington, DC 20006
EMail: lauri.kravetz@ujc.org
Tel: (202)736-5860
Fax: (202)785-4937

Employers
United Jewish Communities, Inc. (Legislative Assistant)

KRAVITZ, Cheryl

1815 H St. NW
Suite 1050
Washington, DC 20006
Tel: (202)822-6110
Fax: (202)822-6114

Employers
Nat'l Conference of Christians and Jews (Exec. Director)

KRAVITZ, Peter

1455 Pennsylvania Ave. NW
Suite 400
Washington, DC 20004-1081
EMail: Internet:Pkravitz@aicpa.org
Tel: (202)737-6600
Fax: (202)638-4512

Employers
American Institute of Certified Public Accountants (Director Congressional and Political Affairs)

KRAWITZ, David

700 13th St. NW
Suite 1000
Washington, DC 20005
Tel: (202)347-6633
Fax: (202)347-8713

Employers
Powell Tate (President)

KREBS, Frederick J.

1025 Connecticut Ave. NW
Suite 200
Washington, DC 20036
EMail: krebs@acca.com
Tel: (202)293-4103
Fax: (202)293-4701

Employers
American Corporate Counsel Ass'n (President and Chief Operating Officer)

KRECHTING, John

600 Pennsylvania Ave. NW
Suite 200
North Bldg.
Washington, DC 20004
Tel: (202)628-2748
Fax: (202)628-1007
Registered: LDA

Employers
TXU Business Services (Manager, Federal Regulatory Affairs)

KREIG, Andrew T.

1140 Connecticut Ave. NW
Suite 810
Washington, DC 20036
EMail: president@wcai.com
Tel: (202)452-7823
Fax: (202)452-0041

Employers
Wireless Communications Ass'n (President)

KREMSNER, Sarah

1700 K St. NW
Suite 1150
Washington, DC 20006
EMail: sarah.kremsner@ujc.org
Tel: (202)736-5871
Fax: (202)785-4937

Employers
United Jewish Communities, Inc. (Legislative Assistant)

KRENIK, Edward

Ariel Rios Federal Bldg.
(1301-MC)
1200 Pennsylvania Ave. NW
3rd. Floor
Washington, DC 20460
EMail: krenik.ed@epa.gov
Tel: (202)564-5200
Fax: (202)501-1519

Employers
Environmental Protection Agency (Associate Administrator for Congressional and Intergovernmental Relations)

KREPINEVICH, Andrew

1730 Rhode Island Ave.
Suite 912
Washington, DC 20036
Tel: (202)331-7990
Fax: (202)331-8019

Employers
Center for Strategic and Budgetary Assessments (Exec. Director)

KREY, James M.

1875 Connecticut Ave. NW
Suite 1200
Washington, DC 20009-5728
Tel: (202)986-8000
Fax: (202)986-8102
Registered: LDA

Employers
LeBoeuf, Lamb, Greene & MacRae L.L.P. (Legislative Assistant)

Clients Represented

On Behalf of LeBoeuf, Lamb, Greene & MacRae L.L.P.
Internat'l Underwriting Ass'n of London
Lloyd's of London

KRHOUINK, Kimberly

2201 C St. NW
Room 7261
Washington, DC 20520-7261
Tel: (202)647-4204
Fax: (202)647-2762

Employers
Department of State - Bureau of Legislative Affairs (Special Assistant, Congressional Affairs)

KRICHTEN, Leo

441 N. Lee St.
Alexandria, VA 22314
Tel: (703)549-3622
Fax: (703)684-5196

Employers
Catholic War Veterans of the U.S.A. (Exec. Director)

KRIEGER, Kathy L.

1146 19th St. NW
Suite 600
Washington, DC 20036
Tel: (202)496-0500
Fax: (202)496-0555

Employers
James & Hoffman, P.C. (Partner)

KRIESBERG, Simeon M.

1909 K St. NW
Washington, DC 20006
Tel: (202)263-3000
Fax: (202)263-3300
Registered: LDA
EMail: skreisberg@mayerbrown.com

Employers
Mayer, Brown & Platt (Partner)

KRIKORIAN, Mark

1522 K St. NW
Suite 820
Washington, DC 20005
EMail: center@cis.org
Tel: (202)466-8185
Fax: (202)466-8076

Employers
Center for Immigration Studies (Exec. Director)

KRINKIE, Mary Ramsey

601 Pennsylvania Ave. NW
South Bldg., Suite 900
Washington, DC 20004
Tel: (202)434-8163
Fax: (202)639-8238

Employers
Lockridge Grindal & Nauen, P.L.L.P.

KRIPKE, Gawain

1025 Vermont Ave. NW
Third Floor
Washington, DC 20005
Tel: (202)783-7400
Ext: 212
Fax: (202)783-0444
Registered: LDA
EMail: gkripke@foe.org

Employers
Friends of the Earth (Director, Appropriations Project)

KRIPOWICZ, Mary Jo

1016 16th St. NW
Fifth Floor
Washington, DC 20036
Tel: (202)293-5794
Fax: (202)223-6178
Registered: LDA

Employers
Consumers Energy Co. (Director, Federal Affairs)

KRISHNAMOORTI, Mala

1201 15th St. NW
Washington, DC 20005-2800
Tel: (202)822-0470
Fax: (202)822-0572

Employers
Nat'l Ass'n of Home Builders of the U.S. (Legislative Director, Labor, Small Business, and Health Care)

KRISTIANSEN, Lars B.

16410 Heritage Blvd.
Mitchellville, MD 20716
Tel: (301)352-4409
Fax: (301)352-5454

Employers
Nationwide Mutual Insurance Co. (Representative, Legislative Affairs)

KRISTOF, Dawn C.

P.O. Box 17402 Dulles Internat'l Airport
Washington, DC 20041
EMail: wwema@erols.com
Tel: (703)444-1777
Fax: (703)444-1779

Employers
Water and Wastewater Equipment Manufacturers Ass'n (President)

KRISTOFF, Sandra J.

1001 Pennsylvania Ave. NW
Suite 580 North
Washington, DC 20004-2505
Tel: (202)783-9070
Fax: (202)393-2769
Registered: LDA

Employers
New York Life Insurance Co. (Senior V. President)

KRISTOL, Irving

1150 17th St. NW
Washington, DC 20036
Tel: (202)862-5800
Fax: (202)862-7177

Employers
American Enterprise Institute for Public Policy Research (John M. Olin Distinguished Fellow)

KRIVIT, Daniel H.

1120 G St. NW
Suite 200
Washington, DC 20005
Tel: (202)544-1112
Fax: (202)737-4933
EMail: krivlaw@iamdigex.net
Counsel, House Subcommittee on Manpower, Compensation, Health and Safety (1974-76), House Select Subcommittee on Labor (1969-74), and House Select Committee on Education (1967-69).

Employers
Krivit & Krivit, P.C. (President)

Clients Represented
On Behalf of Krivit & Krivit, P.C.
Bayonne Housing Authority
Bayonne, New Jersey, City of
East Chicago Public Housing Authority

KROEMER, Kurt

431 18th St. NW
Washington, DC 20006
Tel: (202)639-3125
Fax: (202)639-6116
EMail: kroemerk@usa.redcross.org

Employers
American Red Cross (Director, Regulatory Affairs)

KROLOFF, George

9158 Rothbury Dr.
Suite 168
Gaithersburg, MD 20886
Tel: (301)977-5008
Fax: (301)258-0016
Senior Professional Staff member, Senate Foreign Relations Committee, 1974-78; Special Assistant to Postmaster General and Director, Special Projects, United States Postal Service. Public Affairs Consultant, U.S. Agency for International Development.

Employers
George Kroloff & Associates (Senior Principal)

Clients Represented
On Behalf of George Kroloff & Associates
America's Charities
Commission on Presidential Debates

KROMER, John P.

1717 Pennsylvania Ave. NW
Washington, DC 20006
Tel: (202)974-1000
Fax: (202)331-9330

Employers
Goodwin, Procter & Hoar LLP

KROMER, Kathi J.

1111 19th St. NW
Suite 402
Washington, DC 20036
Tel: (202)434-7484
Fax: (202)434-7400
Registered: LDA

Employers
Ass'n of Home Appliance Manufacturers (Manager, Gov't Relations)

KROMKOWSKI, John A.

P.O. Box 20
Cardinal Station
Washington, DC 20064
Tel: (202)232-3600
Fax: (202)319-6289
EMail: kromkowki@lua.edu

Employers
Nat'l Center for Urban Ethnic Affairs (President)

KRONMILLER, Theodore George

601 Pennsylvania Ave. NW
Suite 900
South Bldg.
Washington, DC 20004
Tel: (202)434-8208
Fax: (202)639-8238
Registered: LDA, FARA
Former Counsel, House Subcommittees on Oceanography and Fisheries and Wildlife Conservation and the Environment; Counsel for International Law, National Oceanic and Atmospheric Administation, Department of Commerce; Deputy Assistant Secretary (Ambassador) for Ocean and Fisheries Affairs, Department of State; and Lieutenant, Office of The Judge Advocate General, Department of the Navy.

Employers
Self-employed as an independent consultant.

Clients Represented
As an independent consultant
Iceland, Government of the Republic of
Marshall Islands, Republic of the

KRUEGER, Keith

1555 Connecticut Ave. NW
Suite 200
Washington, DC 20036
Tel: (202)462-9600
Fax: (202)462-9043

Employers
Consortium for School Networking (Exec. Director)
Non-Profit Management Associates, Inc. (President)

Clients Represented
On Behalf of Non-Profit Management Associates, Inc.
Consortium for School Networking
Friends of the Nat'l Library of Medicine

KRUG, Peter

1776 K St. NW
Washington, DC 20006
Tel: (202)719-7000
Fax: (202)719-7049
Registered: LDA

Employers
Wiley, Rein & Fielding

Clients Represented
On Behalf of Wiley, Rein & Fielding
Verizon Wireless

KRUGER, Robert M.

1150 18th St. NW
Suite 700
Washington, DC 20036
Tel: (202)872-5500
Fax: (202)872-5501

Employers
Business Software Alliance (V. President, Enforcement)

KRULISCH, Lee

7833 Walker Dr.
Suite 410
Greenbelt, MD 20770
Tel: (301)345-3500
Fax: (301)345-3503
EMail: info@scaw.com

Employers
Scientists Center for Animal Welfare (Exec. Director)

KRULWICH, Andrew S.

1776 K St. NW
Washington, DC 20006
Tel: (202)719-7000
Fax: (202)719-7049
General Counsel, Consumer Product Safety Commission, 1979-81.

Employers
Wiley, Rein & Fielding (Partner)

KRUMHOLTZ, Jack

21 Dupont Circle NW
Fifth Floor
Washington, DC 20036
Tel: (202)263-5900
Fax: (202)263-5901
Registered: LDA

Employers
Microsoft Corp. (Associate General Counsel/Federal Affairs)

KRUMHOLZ, Sheila

1101 14th St. NW
Suite 1030
Washington, DC 20005-5635
Tel: (202)857-0044
Fax: (202)857-7809

Employers
Center for Responsive Politics (Research Director)

KRUPNICK, Allen

1616 P St. NW
Washington, DC 20036
Tel: (202)328-5000

Employers
Resources for the Future (Director, Quality of the Environment Division)

KRUPP, Aaron

1717 Pennsylvania Ave. NW
Suite 600
Washington, DC 20006
Tel: (202)293-3450
Fax: (202)293-2787

Employers
Medical Group Management Ass'n (Government Affairs Representative)

KRUSE, USN (Ret.), Capt. Dennis

1452 Duke St.
Alexandria, VA 22314-3458
Tel: (703)836-6727
Fax: (703)836-7491
EMail: dkruse@navalengineers.org

Employers
American Soc. of Naval Engineers (Exec. Director)

KRUSE, Earl J.

1660 L St. NW
Suite 800
Washington, DC 20036
Tel: (202)463-7663
Fax: (202)463-6906

Employers
United Union of Roofers, Waterproofers and Allied Workers (International President)

KRYS, Susan

2500 Wilson Blvd.
Suite 300
Arlington, VA 22201
Tel: (703)907-7981
Fax: (703)907-7727
EMail: skrys@tia.eia.org

Employers
Telecommunications Industry Ass'n (Director, Trade Show Exhibitor Sales & Marketing)

KRZYMINSKI, James S.

50 F St. NW
Suite 900
Washington, DC 20001
Tel: (202)626-8700
Fax: (202)626-8722

Employers
Nat'l Council of Farmer Cooperatives (Senior V. President, Corporate Services, General Counsel and Secretary)

KU, Charlotte

2223 Massachusetts Ave. NW
Washington, DC 20008-2864
Tel: (202)939-6000
Fax: (202)797-7133
EMail: cku@asil.org

Employers
American Soc. of Internat'l Law (Exec. Director)

KUBIAK, Greg

444 N. Capitol St. NW
Suite 200
Washington, DC 20001
Tel: (202)624-5897
Fax: (202)624-7797
EMail: sga@sso.org

Employers
Southern Governors Ass'n (Senior Policy and Program Manager)

KUBIK, Rob

1350 I St. NW
Suite 400
Washington, DC 20005-3306
Tel: (202)371-6900
Fax: (202)842-3578

Employers
Motorola, Inc. (Manager, Spectrum and Regulatory Policy)

KUCHNICKI, Richard P.

5203 Leesburg Pike
Suite 600
Falls Church, VA 22041
Tel: (703)931-4533
Fax: (703)379-1546

Employers
Internat'l Code Council (Exec. V. President)

KUE, Chia

611 Pennsylvania Ave. SE
Suite 340
Washington, DC 20003
Tel: (202)543-1444
Fax: (202)318-0652
Registered: LDA

Employers
Philip S. Smith & Associates, Inc.

Clients Represented

On Behalf of Philip S. Smith & Associates, Inc.
Lao Progressive Institute
Lao Veterans of America, Inc.

KUE, Lisa

611 Pennsylvania Ave. SE
Suite 340
Washington, DC 20003
Tel: (202)543-1444
Fax: (202)318-0652
Registered: LDA

Employers
Philip S. Smith & Associates, Inc.

Clients Represented

On Behalf of Philip S. Smith & Associates, Inc.
Lao Progressive Institute
Lao Veterans of America, Inc.

KUFFNER, Mary

1101 Vermont Ave. NW
12th Floor
Washington, DC 20005-3583
Tel: (202)789-8510
Fax: (202)789-7401
Registered: LDA

Employers
American Medical Ass'n (Washington Counsel)

KUGLER, Ellen J.

Ten Pidgeon Hill Dr.
Suite 150
Sterling, VA 20165
Tel: (703)444-4091
Fax: (703)444-3029
Registered: LDA
EMail: ellen@debrunnerandassociates.com

Employers
DeBrunner and Associates, Inc. (Director, Government Affairs)

Clients Represented

On Behalf of DeBrunner and Associates, Inc.
Albert Einstein Medical Center
Catholic Healthcare West
Health Quest
Nat'l Ass'n of Urban Hospitals
Private Essential Access Community Hospitals (PEACH) Inc.
Southcoast Health System
Susquehanna Health System
Thomas Jefferson University Hospital

KUHLIK, Bruce N.

1201 Pennsylvania Ave. NW
Washington, DC 20004-2401
Tel: (202)662-6000
Fax: (202)662-6291
Registered: LDA
EMail: bkuhlik@cov.com
Assistant to the Solicitor General, Department of Justice, 1984-86. Law Clerk to Judge Levin H. Campbell, U.S. Court of Appeals, First Circuit, 1981-82.

Employers
Covington & Burling (Partner)

Clients Represented

On Behalf of Covington & Burling
Consumer Healthcare Products Ass'n
Merck & Co.
Pharmaceutical Research and Manufacturers of America

KUHN, James F.

2805 Washington Ave.
Chevy Chase, MD 20815
Tel: (301)588-8461
Fax: (301)495-6362
Registered: LDA

Employers
Tuvin Associates (Associate)

KUHN, Jennifer

1920 L St. NW
Suite 200
Washington, DC 20036
Tel: (202)785-0266
Fax: (202)785-0261
EMail: jkuhn@atr-dc.org

Employers
Americans for Tax Reform (V. President, Finance)

KUHN, Nancy R.

1800 M St. NW
Washington, DC 20036
Tel: (202)467-7000
Fax: (202)467-7176
Registered: FARA

Employers
Morgan, Lewis & Bockius LLP

KUHN, Thomas R.

701 Pennsylvania Ave. NW
Washington, DC 20004-2696
Tel: (202)508-5555
Fax: (202)508-5786
Registered: LDA
White House Liaison Officer to the Secretary, Department of the Navy, 1970-72.

Employers
Edison Electric Institute (President)

KUHNREICH, Jeff

1501 M St. NW
Suite 700
Washington, DC 20005-1702
Tel: (202)463-4300
Fax: (202)463-4394
Registered: LDA, FARA
EMail: jkuhnreich@manatt.com

Employers
Manatt, Phelps & Phillips, LLP (Legislative Advisor)

Clients Represented

On Behalf of Manatt, Phelps & Phillips, LLP
Bolivia, Embassy of
CEMEX Central, S.A. de C.V.
Eaton Corp., Cutler Hammer
Honeywell Internat'l, Inc.
Miami Valley Economic Coalition
Pelican Butte Corp.
Playa Vista
Racal Communications Inc.
Sabreliner Corp.
Stewart & Stevenson Services, Inc.
SWIPCO, U.S.
Yakima, Washington, City of

KUHNSMAN, David William

7900 Westpark Dr.
SuiteT-305
McLean, VA 22102
Tel: (703)506-8770
Registered: LDA

Employers
Self-employed as an independent consultant.

Clients Represented

As an independent consultant
Integrated Management Resources Group, Inc.

KULICK, Jeffery

625 Slaters Ln.
Suite 205
Alexandria, VA 22314
Tel: (703)684-3200
Fax: (703)684-3212

Employers
Nat'l School Transportation Ass'n (Exec. Director)

KULISH, Carol

1666 K St. NW
Suite 800
Washington, DC 20006
Tel: (202)481-7000
Fax: (202)862-7098
Registered: LDA
Tax Counsel, House Committee on Ways and Means, 1991-94.

Employers
Arthur Andersen LLP (Principal)

Clients Represented

On Behalf of Arthur Andersen LLP
Coalition for Job Growth and Internat'l Competitiveness Through AMT Reform
Coalition to Preserve Employee Ownership of S Corporation
Nat'l Ass'n of Investors Corporation (NAIC)

KUMAR, T.

600 Pennsylvania Ave. SE
Fifth Floor
Washington, DC 20003
Tel: (202)544-0200
Fax: (202)546-7142
Registered: LDA

Employers
Amnesty Internat'l U.S.A. (Advocacy Director for Asia)

KUMBALA-FRASER, Mondi

740 15th St. NW
Ninth Floor
Washington, DC 20005
Tel: (202)662-1789
Fax: (202)662-1762

Employers
American Bar Ass'n (Legislative Counsel)

KUNDE, Gerald "Chip"

1010 Wisconsin Ave. NW
Ninth Floor
Washington, DC 20007
Tel: (202)337-9400
Fax: (202)337-4508
Registered: LDA
EMail: ckunde@gmabrands.com

Employers
Grocery Manufacturers of America (V. President, State Affairs)

KUNDU, Jai

2200 Mill Rd.
Alexandria, VA 22314
Tel: (703)838-1852
Fax: (703)683-9752

Employers
American Trucking Ass'ns (V. President and Exec. Director, Safety Management Council)

KUNIN, Christy C.

1625 Massachusetts Ave. NW
Suite 300
Washington, DC 20036
Tel: (202)955-6300
Fax: (202)955-6460
Registered: LDA
EMail: christy@technologylaw.com

Employers
Blumenfeld & Cohen (Associate)

Clients Represented

On Behalf of Blumenfeld & Cohen
Rhythms NetConnections

KUNKA, Jane

1020 19th St. NW
Washington, DC 20036
Tel: (202)429-3121
Fax: (202)293-0561
Registered: LDA

Employers
Qwest Communications (Director, Public Policy, Regulatory and Legislative Affairs)

KUNKO, Damian

112 S. West St.
Alexandria, VA 22314
Tel: (703)683-9600
Fax: (703)836-5255
Registered: LDA

Employers
Strategic Management Associates (Policy Assistant)

KUNZ, David

1299 Pennsylvania Ave. NW
Suite 800 West
Washington, DC 20004
Tel: (202)785-0500
Fax: (202)785-5277

Employers
The Carmen Group (Associate)

KUO, Ellen

730 15th St. NW
Fifth Floor
Washington, DC 20005
Tel: (202)624-4295
Fax: (202)383-3475
Registered: LDA
EMail: ellen.kuo@bankofamerica.com

Employers
Bank of America (V. President, Government Relations)

KUPER, Susan

1400 K St. NW
Washington, DC 20005
Tel: (202)682-6000
Fax: (202)682-6850

Employers
American Psychiatric Ass'n (Director, Membership)

KUPFERMAN, Alon

1156 15th St. NW
Suite 1201
Washington, DC 20005
Tel: (202)785-4200
Fax: (202)785-4115

Employers
American Jewish Committee (Assistant Director, Legislative Affairs)

KUPFERSCHMID, Keith

1730 M St. NW
Suite 700
Washington, DC 20036-4510
Tel: (202)452-1600
Fax: (202)223-8756
Registered: LDA
EMail: kkupfer@siia.net

Employers
Software & Information Industry Ass'n (SIIA) (Intellectual Property Counsel)

KURKUL, Douglas R.

1331 Pennsylvania Ave. NW
Sixth Floor
Washington, DC 20004-1790
Tel: (202)637-3085
Fax: (202)637-3182
Registered: LDA
EMail: dkurkul@nam.org

Employers
Nat'l Ass'n of Manufacturers (Assistant V. President, Member Communications)

KURLAND, Pamela S.

1101 Vermont Ave. NW
12th Floor
Washington, DC 20005-3583
Tel: (202)789-7481
Fax: (202)789-7401
Registered: LDA

Employers
American Medical Ass'n (Washington Counsel)

KURLANDER, Stuart

555 11th St. NW
Suite 1000
Washington, DC 20004
Tel: (202)637-2200
Fax: (202)637-2201

Employers
Latham & Watkins (Partner)

Clients Represented

On Behalf of Latham & Watkins
Nat'l Orthotics Manufacturers Ass'n

KURMAN, Michael J.

1050 Connecticut Ave. NW
Washington, DC 20036-5339
Tel: (202)857-6000
Fax: (202)857-6395
Registered: LDA
Member, White House Domestic Policy Staff, 1979. Attorney, Solicitor's Honors Program and Division of Surface Mining, and Special Assistant to the Solicitor, U.S. Department of Interior, 1977-81.

Employers
Arent Fox Kintner Plotkin & Kahn, PLLC (Member)

Clients Represented

On Behalf of Arent Fox Kintner Plotkin & Kahn, PLLC
Navajo Nation

KURNICK, Robert D.

1125 15th St. NW
Suite 801
Washington, DC 20005
Tel: (202)785-9300
Fax: (202)775-1950

Employers
Sherman, Dunn, Cohen, Leifer & Yellig, P.C.

KURRLE, Jonathan

7901 Westpark Dr.
McLean, VA 22102-4206
Tel: (703)827-5227
Fax: (703)749-2742
Registered: LDA
EMail: jkurrle@mfgtech.org
Former Legislative Assistant to Rep. J. Dennis Hastert (R-IL).

Employers
The Ass'n For Manufacturing Technology (AMT) (Legislative Director)

KURTZMAN, Andrew

2500 Wilson Blvd.
Suite 300
Arlington, VA 22201
Tel: (703)907-7413
Fax: (703)907-7727
EMail: akurtzman@getcommstuff.com

Employers
Telecommunications Industry Ass'n (Managing Director, GetCommStuff.com)

KURUCZA, Robert M.

2000 Pennsylvania Ave. NW
Suite 5500
Washington, DC 20006
Tel: (202)887-1500
Fax: (202)887-0763
EMail: rkurucza@mofo.com
Securities and Exchange Commission, 1978-80. Office of the Comptroller of the Currency, 1980-82.

Employers
Morrison & Foerster LLP (Partner)

KURZ, Ester

440 First St. NW
Suite 600
Washington, DC 20001
Tel: (202)639-5200
Registered: LDA

Employers
American Israel Public Affairs Committee (Director, Legislative Strategy and Policy)

KURZWEIL, Jeffrey

1212 New York Ave. NW
Suite 350
Washington, DC 20005
Tel: (202)842-7663
Fax: (202)842-5010
Registered: LDA
EMail: jkurz@bellatlantic.net
Special Assistant to the General Counsel, Department of Commerce, 1978-79.

Employers
Kurzweil & Associates (Principal)

Clients Represented

On Behalf of Kurzweil & Associates
Cabazon Band of Mission Indians
Hilton Hotels Corp.
HMSHost Corp.
Marriott Internat'l, Inc.
Nordstrom, Inc.
Sodexho Marriott Services, Inc.

KUSHAN, Jeff

1001 Pennsylvania Ave. NW
Suite 600
Washington, DC 20004
Tel: (202)347-0066
Fax: (202)624-7222
Registered: LDA
EMail: jkushan@pgfm.com
Attorney-Advisor, Office of Legislative and International Affairs (1997-98 and 1991-95) and Biotech Patent Examiner (1987-91), U.S. Patent and Trademark Office, Department of Commerce. Attache for Intellecutal Propery Affairs, United States Mission to the World Trade Organization, Office of the U.S. Trade Representative, 1995-97.

Employers
Powell, Goldstein, Frazer & Murphy LLP (Partner)

Clients Represented

On Behalf of Powell, Goldstein, Frazer & Murphy LLP
Genentech, Inc.
Pharmaceutical Research and Manufacturers of America
Qualcomm Inc.

KUSHNER, David L.

5550 Friendship Blvd.
Suite 300
Chevy Chase, MD 20815-7201
Tel: (301)968-2642
Fax: (301)968-4195
EMail: dkushner@osteohdq.org

Employers
American College of Osteopathic Pediatricians (Exec. Director)
American Osteopathic Academy of Addiction Medicine (Exec. Director)
American Osteopathic Healthcare Ass'n (President and Chief Exec. Officer)
Ass'n of Osteopathic Directors and Medical Educators (President and Chief Exec. Officer)

KUSHNER, Gary Jay

555 13th St. NW
Washington, DC 20004-1109
Tel: (202)637-5856
Fax: (202)637-5910
Registered: LDA
EMail: gjkushner@hhlaw.com
Consultant on food labeling, Department of Health and Human Services (1989) and Office of Technology Assessment, U.S. Congress (1979).

Employers
Hogan & Hartson L.L.P. (Partner)

Clients Represented

On Behalf of Hogan & Hartson L.L.P.
American Frozen Food Institute
Grocery Manufacturers of America
Nat'l Chicken Council
Nat'l Pasta Ass'n
Protein Technologies Internat'l
Taylor Packing Co., Inc.

KUSIN, Susan

1150 17th St. NW
Suite 400
Washington, DC 20036
Tel: (202)222-4700
Fax: (202)222-4799

Employers
The Walt Disney Co. (Assistant)

KUSSKE, Kathryn A.

1909 K St. NW
Washington, DC 20006
Tel: (202)263-3000
Fax: (202)263-3300
Registered: LDA
EMail: kkusske@mayerbrown.com

Employers
Mayer, Brown & Platt (Partner)

KUTCHER, Joan L.

1201 Pennsylvania Ave. NW
Washington, DC 20004-2401
Tel: (202)662-6000
Fax: (202)662-6291
Registered: LDA
EMail: jkutcher@cov.com

Employers
Covington & Burling (Legislative Counsel)

Clients Represented

On Behalf of Covington & Burling
American Ass'n of Oral and Maxillofacial Surgeons
Ass'n of American Medical Colleges
Coalition of Boston Teaching Hospitals
Coalition on AFDC Quality Control Penalties
Coalition on EAF Funding
Coalition on Medicaid Reform
Missouri Department of Social Services
Public Broadcasting Service

KUTLER, Alison

1050 Connecticut Ave. NW
Washington, DC 20036-5339
Tel: (202)828-3421
Fax: (202)857-6395
Registered: LDA
EMail: kutlera@arentfox.com
Former Legislative Assistant to Congressman Peter Hoagland (D-NE).

Employers
Arent Fox Kintner Plotkin & Kahn, PLLC (Associate)

Clients Represented

On Behalf of Arent Fox Kintner Plotkin & Kahn, PLLC
Alaska Rainforest Campaign
American Amusement Machine Ass'n
Amusement and Music Operators Ass'n
Arthritis Foundation
Ass'n of Pain Management Anesthesiologist
Exeter Architectural Products
Global Associates
Guardian Angel Holdings, Inc.
S.C. Johnson and Son, Inc.
New Orleans, Louisiana, City of
Renewable Resources LLC
webwasher.com

KUTLER, Ed

1775 I St. NW
Suite 700
Washington, DC 20006
Tel: (202)261-4000
Fax: (202)261-4001
Registered: LDA
Assistant to House Speaker (1995-97) and House Republican Whip (1992-95), Rep. Newt Gingrich (R-GA).

Employers
Clark & Weinstock, Inc. (Managing Director)

Clients Represented

On Behalf of Clark & Weinstock, Inc.
American Ass'n of Health Plans (AAHP)
American Ass'n of Homes and Services for the Aging
AT&T
Rabbi Milton Balkany
CapCURE
Edison Electric Institute
The Ferguson Group
Guidant Corp.
Infrastructure Defense Inc.
The Island ECN
Lockheed Martin Corp.
Microsoft Corp.
Nat'l Center for Tobacco-Free Kids
Pharmaceutical Research and Manufacturers of America
Sallie Mae, Inc.
Schering-Plough Corp.

KUTNIK, Marc

1025 Thomas Jefferson St. NW
Suite 400 East
Washington, DC 20007-0805
Tel: (202)965-8100
Fax: (202)965-6403

Employers
Jorden Burt LLP (Grant Services Specialist)

KUTSKA, Helen M.

1899 L St. NW
Suite 1000
Washington, DC 20036
EMail: helen_kutska@npradc.org
Tel: (202)457-0480
Fax: (202)457-0486

Employers
Nat'l Petrochemical Refiners Ass'n (Director, Convention Services and Safety Programs)

KUWANA, Eric A.

2550 M St. NW
Washington, DC 20037-1350
Tel: (202)457-6000
Fax: (202)457-6315
Registered: LDA
EMail: ekuwana@pattonboggs.com
Department of Transportation, 1993-95. Office of Counsel to the President, The White House, 1992-93. Federal Highway Administration, Department of Transportation, 1991-92.

Employers
Patton Boggs, LLP (Partner)

Clients Represented
On Behalf of Patton Boggs, LLP
Eagle-Picher Industries
Minimed, Inc.

KUZAS, Kevin J.

1200 New Hampshire Ave. NW
Suite 800
Washington, DC 20036-6802
EMail: kkuzas@dlalaw.com
Tel: (202)776-2000
Fax: (202)776-2222

Employers
Dow, Lohnes & Albertson, PLLC (Member)

KUZE, Kazunori

900 17th St. NW
Suite 1220
Washington, DC 20006
EMail: kuze.kazunori@chuden.co.jp
Tel: (202)775-1960
Fax: (202)331-9256

Employers
Chubu Electric Power Co. (Chief Representative)

KWALWASSER, Marsha

1000 Wilson Blvd.
Suite 2300
Arlington, VA 22209
Tel: (310)201-3398
Registered: LDA

Employers
Northrop Grumman Corp.

KWIATKOWSKI, Holly E.

1100 17th St. NW
Seventh Floor
Washington, DC 20036
Tel: (202)223-8196
Fax: (202)872-1948
Registered: LDA

Employers
American Academy of Actuaries (Policy Analyst)

KWITOWSKI, Jeff

1701 Pennsylvania Ave. NW
Suite 900
Washington, DC 20006-5805
Tel: (202)452-8200
Fax: (202)833-0388

Employers
Empower America (Spokesperson)

KYNOCH, Brent

4915 Auburn Ave.
Suite 204
Bethesda, MD 20814
EMail: bkynock@eia-usa.org
Tel: (301)961-4999
Fax: (301)961-3094

Employers
Environmental Information Ass'n (Managing Director)

KYROS, Hon. Peter N.

2445 M St. NW
Suite 260
Washington, DC 20037
Tel: (202)342-0204
Fax: (202)337-0034
Registered: LDA
Member, U.S. House of Representatives (D-ME), 1967-75.

Employers
Kyros & Cummins Associates (President)

Clients Represented
On Behalf of Kyros & Cummins Associates
Allsup Inc.
American Soc. for Biochemistry and Molecular Biology
American Soc. for Cell Biology
Ass'n of Administrative Law Judges
Board of Veterans Appeals Professional Ass'n
Cooperative of American Physicians
Defense Administrative Judges Professional Ass'n
Joint Steering Committee for Public Policy
Merit Systems Protection Board

KYTE, John

1801 K St. NW
Suite 901-L
Washington, DC 20006
EMail: john_kyte@bm.com
Tel: (202)530-0500
Fax: (202)530-4800
Registered: LDA

Employers
BKSH & Associates (Managing Director)

Clients Represented
On Behalf of BKSH & Associates
Nat'l Power
Safety-Kleen Corp.
Tripoli Rocketry Ass'n

LA NAVE, Anna

1301 Pennsylvania Ave. NW
Suite 1100
Washington, DC 20004-1707
Tel: (202)626-4000
Fax: (202)626-0707

Employers
Air Transport Ass'n of America (Director, State Government Affairs)

LA ROCQUE, USN (Ret), Rear Adm. Gene R.

1779 Massachusetts Ave. NW
Suite 615
Washington, DC 20036
Tel: (202)332-0600
Fax: (202)462-4559

Employers
Center for Defense Information (Founder)

LA SALA, Jim

5025 Wisconsin Ave. NW
Washington, DC 20016
Tel: (202)537-1645
Fax: (202)244-7824

Employers
Amalgamated Transit Union (Internat'l President)

LABOMBARD, Susan

701 Pennsylvania Ave. NW
Suite 300
Washington, DC 20004
Tel: (202)508-5044
Registered: LDA

Employers
Ameren Services (Federal Affairs Representative)

LABONTE, Christopher

919 18th St. NW
Suite 800
Washington, DC 20006
Tel: (202)628-4160
Fax: (202)347-5323

Employers
Human Rights Campaign Fund (Senior Policy Advocate)

LABOSCHIN, Debra

2550 M St. NW
Washington, DC 20037-1350
Tel: (202)457-6000
Fax: (202)457-6315
Registered: LDA

Employers
Patton Boggs, LLP (Associate)

Clients Represented
On Behalf of Patton Boggs, LLP
Illinois Department of Human Services

LABUDA, Laurie

1615 L St. NW
Suite 900
Washington, DC 20036
Tel: (202)778-1000
Fax: (202)466-6002

Employers
APCO Worldwide (V. President, Public Affairs)

LACEY, Jamie P.

701 Pennsylvania Ave. NW
Suite 725
Washington, DC 20004
EMail: jamie.lacey@group.novartis.com
Tel: (202)638-7429
Fax: (202)628-4763

Employers
Novartis Corp. (Director, Communications and Public Affairs)

LACEY, Pamela A.

400 N. Capitol St. NW
Washington, DC 20001
Tel: (202)824-7340
Fax: (202)824-7082
Registered: LDA
EMail: placey@aga.org

Employers
American Gas Ass'n (Senior Manging Counsel)

LACEY, Stephen L.

1400 16th St. NW
Suite 400
Washington, DC 20036-2220
Tel: (202)518-6330
Fax: (202)234-3550
Registered: LDA
EMail: slacey@ofwlaw.com
Former Assistant, Senate Committee on Agriculture, Nutrition and Forestry.

Employers
Olsson, Frank and Weeda, P.C. (Associate)

Clients Represented
On Behalf of Olsson, Frank and Weeda, P.C.
Adheris, Inc.
American Academy of Audiology
American Commodity Distribution Ass'n
American School Food Service Ass'n
Ass'n of Medical Device Reprocessors
Aventis Pasteur
Beef Products, Inc.
Black Hills Forest Resource Ass'n
California Canning Peach Ass'n
Chocolate Manufacturers Ass'n of the U.S.A.
Clement Pappas & Co., Inc.
Cliffstar Corp.
Duramed Pharmaceuticals, Inc.
Food Distributors Internat'l (NAWGA-IFDA)
General Mills
Gentrac Inc.
Health Resource Publishing Co.
Institute of Food Technologists
Kraft Foods, Inc.
Lower Brule Sioux Tribe
Mead Johnson Nutritional Group
Nat'l Ass'n of Margarine Manufacturers
Nat'l Ass'n of Pharmaceutical Manufacturers
Nat'l Coalition of Food Importers Ass'n
Nat'l Confectioners Ass'n
Nat'l Food Processors Ass'n
Nat'l Meat Ass'n
PennField Oil Co.
The Pillsbury Co.
San Tomo Group
Schwan's Sales Enterprises
SteriGenics Internat'l
Titan Scan
Transhumance Holding Co., Inc.
United Fresh Fruit and Vegetable Ass'n
Urner Barry Publications, Inc.

LACHICA, Eric

2500 Massachusetts Ave. NW
Washington, DC 20008
Tel: (202)246-1998
Fax: (301)963-1720
Registered: LDA
EMail: ericlachica@msn.com
Worked for the Bureau of the Census, Department of Commerce, 1989.

Employers
American Coalition for Filipino Veterans (Exec. Director)

LACIVITA, Chris

425 Second St. NE
Washington, DC 20002
Tel: (202)675-6000
Fax: (202)675-6058

Employers
Nat'l Republican Senatorial Committee (Political Director)

LACKMAN, Carey A.

1101 30th St. NW
Suite 220
Washington, DC 20007
Tel: (202)337-3137
Fax: (202)337-6660
Registered: LDA

Employers
Lackman & Associates, L.L.C. (Manager)

Clients Represented

On Behalf of Lackman & Associates, L.L.C.
Please Touch Museum, The Children's Museum of Philadelphia

LACKRITZ, Marc E.

1401 I St. NW
Suite 1000
Washington, DC 20005
EMail: mlackritz@sia.com
Tel: (202)296-9410
Fax: (202)408-1918
Registered: LDA

Employers
Securities Industry Ass'n (President)

LACY, Peter

1616 P St. NW
Suite 100
Washington, DC 20036
EMail: ipcaft@rff.org
Tel: (202)328-5056
Fax: (202)328-5133

Employers
Internat'l Policy Council on Agriculture, Food and Trade (Exec. Director)

LADD, Richard B.

One Massachusetts Ave. NW
Suite 880
Washington, DC 20001
EMail: dickladd@aol.com
Tel: (202)371-1196
Fax: (202)371-1178
Registered: LDA, FARA

Employers
Robison Internat'l, Inc. (President)

Clients Represented

On Behalf of Robison Internat'l, Inc.
Armtec Defense Products
The Boeing Co.
The BOSE Corp.
General Electric Co.
Honeywell Internat'l, Inc.
L-3 Communications Corp.
Lockheed Martin Tactical Systems
Oshkosh Truck Corp.
United Defense, L.P.

LADD, Thomas E.

One Marriott Dr.
Department 977.01
Washington, DC 20058
Tel: (202)380-3000
Registered: LDA

Employers
Marriott Internat'l, Inc. (V. President, Government Affairs)

LADD, William D.

One Marriott Dr.
Department 977.01
Washington, DC 20058
Tel: (202)380-3000
Registered: LDA

Employers
Marriott Internat'l, Inc. (V. President, Legislative Affairs)

LADNER, Joyce A.

1775 Massachusetts Ave. NW
Washington, DC 20036-2188
Tel: (202)797-6000
Fax: (202)797-6004

Employers
The Brookings Institution (Senior Fellow, Governmental Studies)

LADSON, Damon

1200 18th St. NW
Suite 1200
Washington, DC 20036
Tel: (202)730-1300
Fax: (202)730-1301
Former Director, World Radio Conference, Federal Communications Commission.

Employers
Harris, Wiltshire & Grannis LLP (Technology Policy Advisor)

LAFEVRE, Sandra L.

1301 Pennsylvania Ave. NW
Suite 900
Washington, DC 20004
Tel: (202)638-3690
Fax: (202)638-0936

Employers
Reinsurance Ass'n of America (V. President and Assistant Secretary)

LAFFLY-MURPHY, Genevieve

1220 L St. NW
Washington, DC 20005
Tel: (202)682-8000
Fax: (202)682-8232

Employers
American Petroleum Institute (Washington Representative)

LAFIELD, Bill

1913 I St. NW
Washington, DC 20006
Tel: (202)872-8110
Fax: (202)872-8114

Employers
Consumer Specialties Products Ass'n (V. President, State Legislative Affairs)

LAFONTAINE, Paul

1920 L St. NW
Washington, DC 20036
EMail: plafontaine@kamber.com
Tel: (202)223-8700
Fax: (202)659-5559

Employers
The Kamber Group (Chief Financial Officer)

LAFORGE, William N.

1015 15th St. NW
Suite 1200
Washington, DC 20005
EMail: wlaforge@mnwlaw.net
Tel: (202)789-8600
Fax: (202)789-1708
Registered: LDA
Chief of Staff and Legislative Counsel to Senator Thad Cochran (R-MS), 1983-90. Chief Counsel and Staff Director, Subcommittee on Agriculture, Rural Development and Related Agencies, Senate Commitee on Appropriations, 1981-83. Congressional Liaison, The Peace Corps, 1979-81. Legislative Assistant to Rep. David Bowen (D-MS), 1976-79.

Employers
McGuiness Norris & Williams, LLP (Of Counsel)

Clients Represented

On Behalf of McGuiness Norris & Williams, LLP
American Kennel Club
American Nursery and Landscape Ass'n
Celanese Government Relations Office
Nat'l Council of Agricultural Employers
Nat'l Turfgrass Evaluation Program
Nisei Farmers League
PepsiCo, Inc.
San Joaquin Valley Wide Air Pollution Study Agency
Turfgrass Producers Internat'l
Western States Petroleum Ass'n
Wilke, Fleury, Hoffelt, Gould & Birney, LLP

LAGANA, Brian

16 Duke St.
Suite 220
Alexandria, VA 22314
EMail: brian.lagana@wpa.org
Tel: (703)519-1713
Fax: (703)519-1716

Employers
Conference of Private Operators for Response Towing (Exec. Director)

LAGASSE, Alfred

3849 Farragut Ave.
Kensington, MD 20895
EMail: alagasse@tlpa.org
Tel: (301)946-5701
Fax: (301)946-4641

Employers
Taxicab, Limousine and Paratransit Ass'n (Exec. V. President)

LAGOMARCINO, John

1299 Pennsylvania Ave. NW
Suite 800 West
Washington, DC 20004
Tel: (202)785-0500
Fax: (202)785-5277
Registered: LDA
Office of General Counsel, Department of Health, Education and Welfare, 1966-68.

Employers
The Carmen Group
LMRC, Inc. (Associate)

Clients Represented

On Behalf of The Carmen Group
New York Roadway Improvement Coalition
Northeast Illinois Regional Commuter Railroad Corp.
Omnitech Robotics Inc.
Riverside South Planning Corp.
Stafford, Virginia, County of

On Behalf of LMRC, Inc.
Colorado Ass'n of Transit Agencies
Colorado, Department of Transportation of the State of
Metra/Northeast Illinois Rail Corp.

LAGUARDA, Fernando R.

701 Pennsylvania Ave. NW
Suite 900
Washington, DC 20004-2608
EMail: flaguarda@mintz.com
Tel: (202)434-7300
Fax: (202)434-7400

Employers
Mintz, Levin, Cohn, Ferris, Glovsky and Popeo, P.C. (Associate)

Clients Represented

On Behalf of Mintz, Levin, Cohn, Ferris, Glovsky and Popeo, P.C.
Nat'l Network to End Domestic Violence

LAHAM, Carol

1776 K St. NW
Washington, DC 20006
Tel: (202)719-7000
Fax: (202)719-7049

Employers
Wiley, Rein & Fielding (Partner)

Clients Represented

On Behalf of Wiley, Rein & Fielding
Internat'l Paper

LAHAYE, Beverly

1015 15th St. NW
Suite 1100
Washington, DC 20005
Tel: (202)488-7000
Fax: (202)488-0806

Employers
Concerned Women for America (Founder and Chairman)

LAHEY, Michael

1101 14th St. NW
Suite 1400
Washington, DC 20005
Tel: (202)682-9400
Fax: (202)682-1331

Employers
Defenders of Wildlife (Counsel, Public Lands)

LAHEY, Shannon M.

2701 32nd St. NW
Washington, DC 20008
Tel: (202)333-6924
Registered: LDA

Employers
Shannon M. Lahey Associates (Principal)

Clients Represented

On Behalf of Shannon M. Lahey Associates
Ass'n for Los Angeles Deputy Sheriffs
California Correctional Peace Officers Ass'n
NYSCOPBA - New York State Correctional Officers & Police Benevolent Ass'n

LAHIFF, Christopher M.

600 13th St. NW
Washington, DC 20005-3096
Tel: (202)756-8000
Fax: (202)756-8087
Registered: LDA

Employers
McDermott, Will and Emery (Partner)

LAIBLE, Myron

1850 M St. NW
Suite 1040
Washington, DC 20036
EMail: mlaible@oaaa.org

Tel: (202)833-5566
Fax: (202)833-1522

Employers
American Property Rights Alliance (Contact)
Outdoor Advertising Ass'n of America (V. President, Regulatory Affairs and Operations)

LAJEUNESSE, Jr., Raymond J.

8001 Braddock Rd.
Springfield, VA 22160

Tel: (703)321-9820
Fax: (703)321-7342
Registered: LDA

Employers
Nat'l Right to Work Committee (Attorney)

LAKE, Jr., F. David

2445 M St. NW
Washington, DC 20037-1420

Tel: (202)663-6000
Fax: (202)663-6363
Registered: LDA

EMail: dlake@wilmer.com
Office of Tax Legislative Counsel and Special Assistant to the Assistant Secretary for Tax Policy, Department of the Treasury, 1969-71.

Employers
Wilmer, Cutler & Pickering (Partner)

Clients Represented
On Behalf of Wilmer, Cutler & Pickering
The Boeing Co.
IATA U.S. Frequent Flyer Tax Interest Group

LAKE, James

1275 Pennsylvania Ave. NW
Tenth Floor
Washington, DC 20004

Tel: (202)737-5339
Fax: (202)467-0810

Employers
Policy Impact Communications (President and Chief Exec. Officer)

LAKE, Monte B.

1015 15th St. NW
Suite 1200
Washington, DC 20005

Tel: (202)789-8600
Fax: (202)789-1708
Registered: LDA

Employers
McGuiness Norris & Williams, LLP (Partner)

Clients Represented
On Behalf of McGuiness Norris & Williams, LLP
American Nursery and Landscape Ass'n
Garden Centers of America
Nat'l Council of Agricultural Employers
Nat'l Turfgrass Evaluation Program
Nisei Farmers League
San Joaquin Valley Wide Air Pollution Study Agency
Turfgrass Producers Internat'l
Western States Petroleum Ass'n
Wholesale Nursery Growers of America

LAKE, William T.

2445 M St. NW
Washington, DC 20037-1420

Tel: (202)663-6000
Fax: (202)663-6363
Registered: LDA

EMail: wlake@wilmer.com
Deputy Legal Advisor, Department of State, 1980-81. Counsel, Council on Environmental Quality, Executive Office of the President, The White House, 1970-73. Law Clerk to Justice John M. Harlan, U.S. Supreme Court, 1968.

Employers
Wilmer, Cutler & Pickering (Partner)

Clients Represented
On Behalf of Wilmer, Cutler & Pickering
Deutsche Telekom, Inc.

LAKIN, David N.

1776 Massachusetts Ave. NW
Suite 500
Washington, DC 20036

Tel: (202)857-1200
Fax: (202)857-1220

Employers
American Highway Users Alliance (V. President, Public Liaison)

LALONDE, Gregory

3114 Circle Hill Rd.
Alexandria, VA 22305-1606
EMail: info@itctrade.com

Tel: (703)548-1234
Fax: (703)548-6216

Employers
Internat'l Trade Council (V. President and General Counsel)

LALUMONDIER, Richard

1300 N. 17th St.
Suite 1847
Rosslyn, VA 22209
EMail: ric_lalumondier@nema.org

Tel: (703)841-3237
Fax: (703)841-3337

Employers
Nat'l Electrical Manufacturers Ass'n (Scientist, Environment, Health and Safety)

LAMAR, Stephen E.

1601 N. Kent St.
Suite 120
Arlington, VA 22209

Tel: (703)524-1864
Fax: (703)522-6741
Registered: LDA

EMail: slamar@apperalandfootwear.org

Employers
American Apparel & Footwear Ass'n (Director, Government Relations)

LAMARCA, Louis

325 Seventh St. NW
Suite 1200
Washington, DC 20004-1007

Tel: (202)783-7070
Fax: (202)347-2044
Registered: LDA

Employers
Pfizer, Inc. (Director, Federal Relations)

LAMAUTE, Daniel

1400 East West Hwy.
Silver Spring, MD 20910

Employers
Caribbean American Leadership Council

LAMB, Deborah A.

1250 I St. NW
Suite 400
Washington, DC 20005-3998
EMail: dlamb@discus.org

Tel: (202)628-3544
Fax: (202)682-8888

Minority Chief Trade Counsel, Senate Committee on Finance, 1990-2000. Director for Korea and Taiwan, International Trade Administration (1982-88) and Economist, Bureau of East-West Trade (1978-82), Department of Commerce.

Employers
Distilled Spirits Council of the United States, Inc. (V. President, Internat'l Issues and Trade)

LAMB, Eugene

509 Capitol Ct. NE
Washington, DC 20002

Tel: (202)547-6223
Fax: (202)547-6450

EMail: eugene-lamb@nacdnet.org

Employers
Nat'l Ass'n of Conservation Districts (Director, Programs)

LAMB, Gerry F.

3190 Fairview Park Dr.
Falls Church, VA 22042

Tel: (703)876-3368
Fax: (703)876-3600
Registered: LDA

Employers
General Dynamics Corp. (Director, Government Relations - Naval Surface Warfare Programs)

LAMB, James C.

1133 Connecticut Ave. NW
Suite 300
Washington, DC 20036

Tel: (202)293-1177
Fax: (202)293-3411

Minority Counsel, Senate Governmental Affairs Committee, Special Investigation, 1997-98. District Field Representative to Rep. John Dingell (D-MI), 1991-92. Community and Economic Development Specialist to Senator Donald Riegle (D-MI), 1987-89.

Employers
Ryan, Phillips, Utrecht & MacKinnon (Associate)

Clients Represented
On Behalf of Ryan, Phillips, Utrecht & MacKinnon
Sault Ste. Marie Tribe of Chippewa Indians

LAMB, Kathy

1900 M St. NW
Suite 800
Washington, DC 20036-3508
EMail: klamb@comptel.org

Tel: (202)296-6650
Fax: (202)296-7585

Employers
Competitive Telecommunications Ass'n (COMPTEL) (Director, Member Services)

LAMB, Robert H.

1200 G St. NW
Suite 600
Washington, DC 20005-3802

Tel: (202)393-1200
Fax: (202)393-1240
Registered: LDA

EMail: lamb@wrightlaw.com
Professional Staff Member, House Committee on Energy and Commerce, 1976-81. Chief Legislative Assistant to Rep. David E. Satterfield, III (D-VA), 1974-76.

Employers
Wright & Talisman, P.C.

Clients Represented
On Behalf of Wright & Talisman, P.C.
Bristol Resource Recovery Facility Operating Committee
Columbia Natural Resources
Equitable Resources Energy Co.
Montgomery County, Ohio/Montgomery County Solid Waste District
PJM Interconnection, L.L.C.
Potlatch Corp.
Solid Waste Authority of Central Ohio
Sunoco, Inc.

LAMB, Shawn D.

1767 Business Center Dr.
Suite 302
Reston, VA 20190

Tel: (703)438-3101
Fax: (703)438-3113

Employers
Ass'n Innovation and Management, Inc. (President)

Clients Represented
On Behalf of Ass'n Innovation and Management, Inc.
Soc. of Toxicology

LAMB, Tony

1129 20th St. NW
Suite 600
Washington, DC 20036-3421
EMail: tlamb@aahp.org

Tel: (202)778-3200
Fax: (202)778-8479

Employers
American Ass'n of Health Plans (AAHP) (Director, Political Affairs)

LAMBERGMAN, Barry

1350 I St. NW
Suite 400
Washington, DC 20005-3306

Tel: (202)371-6900
Fax: (202)842-3578
Registered: LDA

Employers
Motorola, Inc. (Director, Satellite Regulatory Affairs)

LAMBERT, Chuck

1301 Pennsylvania Ave. NW
Suite 300
Washington, DC 20004

Tel: (202)347-0228
Fax: (202)638-0607
Registered: LDA

Employers
Nat'l Cattleman's Beef Ass'n (Chief Economist)

LAMBERT, III, David F.

P.O. Box 1417-D49
Alexandria, VA 22313-1417

Tel: (703)549-3001
Fax: (703)549-0772
Registered: LDA

Employers
Nat'l Ass'n of Chain Drug Stores (V. President, Government Affairs)

LAMBERT, Dennis

110 Maryland Ave. NE
Suite 304
Washington, DC 20002
Tel: (202)546-1299
Fax: (202)546-4025
EMail: faithpoll@aol.com

Employers
Faith & Politics Institute (Exec. Director)

LAMBERT, Eugene I.

1201 Pennsylvania Ave. NW
Washington, DC 20004-2401
Tel: (202)662-6000
Fax: (202)662-6291
Registered: LDA
EMail: elambert@cov.com
Motions Clerk, U.S. Court of Appeals for the District of Columbia, 1960.

Employers
Covington & Burling (Partner)

LAMBERT, Michael P.

1601 18th St. NW
Suite Two
Washington, DC 20009
Tel: (202)234-5100
Fax: (202)332-1386

Employers
Distance Education and Training Council (Exec. Director)

LAMBERT, Steven C.

888 Sixteenth St. NW
7th Floor
Washington, DC 20006-4103
Tel: (202)835-8052
Fax: (202)835-8136
Law Clerk to Chief Judge Wilson Cowen, U.S. Court of Claims, 1974-75.

Employers
Foley & Lardner (Partner)

LAMBRIX, Thomas

1199 N. Fairfax St.
Suite 1000
Alexandria, VA 22314
Tel: (703)299-4499
Fax: (703)299-4488
EMail: tlambrix@hawthorngroup.com

Employers
The Hawthorn Group, L.C. (Exec. V. President)

LAMM, Carolyn B.

601 13th St. NW
Suite 600 South
Washington, DC 20005
Tel: (202)626-3600
Fax: (202)639-9355
Registered: FARA
EMail: clamm@whitecase.com
Former Trial Attorney, Frauds Section, Civil Division and Assistant Director, Commercial Branch Civil Division, Department of Justice.

Employers
White & Case LLP (Partner)

Clients Represented

On Behalf of White & Case LLP
American-Uzbekistan Chamber of Commerce
Indonesia, Government of the Republic of
Techsnabexport, A.O.
Uzbekistan, Government of the Republic of

LAMM, William C.

809 Maryland Ave. NE
Washington, DC 20002

Employers
United Ass'n of Journeymen and Apprentices of the Plumbing and Pipe Fitting Industry of the U.S. and Canada ((Local 602))

LAMMI, Glenn G.

2009 Massachusetts Ave. NW
Washington, DC 20036
Tel: (202)588-0302
Fax: (202)588-0386

Employers
Washington Legal Foundation (Chief Counsel, Legal Studies Division)

LAMOND, Christopher

700 13th St. NW
Suite 400
Washington, DC 20005
Tel: (202)347-0773
Fax: (202)347-0785
Registered: LDA
EMail: clamond@cassidy.com
Systems Administrator for Senate Committee on Government Affairs, 1997-98. Legislative Correspondent to Senator Fred Thompson (R-TN), 1994-97.

Employers
Cassidy & Associates, Inc. (Associate)

Clients Represented

On Behalf of Cassidy & Associates, Inc.
Adelphi University
Agassi Enterprises, Inc.
Boston College
CNF Transportation, Inc.
Community Health Partners of Ohio
Council on Superconductivity for American Competitiveness
Crane & Co.
Edward Health Services
Hospital for Special Surgery
IBP Aerospace, Inc.
Jewish Family Service Ass'n of Cleveland
Major League Baseball
New Jersey Institute of Technology
North American Datacom
Northern Essex Community College Foundation
Philadelphia College of Osteopathic Medicine
Ramo Defense Systems, LLC
Research Foundation of the City University of New York
Rhode Island School of Design
University Medical Center of Southern Nevada
University of Nevada - Las Vegas

LAMORIELLO, Francine

801 Pennsylvania Ave. NW
Suite 800
Washington, DC 20004
Tel: (202)508-3400
Fax: (202)508-3402
Registered: LDA
EMail: flamoriello@bdbc.com
Senior Economist, European Community Division (1982-87) and Director, European Community Internal Market Office (1987-89), Department of Commerce.

Employers
Baker, Donelson, Bearman & Caldwell, P.C. (Senior Director, Internat'l Business Strategy)

Clients Represented

On Behalf of Baker, Donelson, Bearman & Caldwell, P.C.
American Standard Cos. Inc.
Buckeye Technologies
IMAX Corp.
Lincoln Nat'l Corp.
PacifiCorp
Phillips Petroleum Co.

LAMORUREUX, Nicole D.

1201 15th St. NW
Washington, DC 20005-2800
Tel: (202)822-0470
Fax: (202)822-0572

Employers
Nat'l Ass'n of Home Builders of the U.S. (Director of Operations, Government Affairs Division)

LAMOUREUX, Anne

7700 Wisconsin Ave.
Bethesda, MD 20814
Tel: (301)986-1999
Fax: (301)986-5998
Registered: LDA

Employers
Discovery Communications, Inc. (V. President, Government Relations)

LAMPHER, Michelle

1904 Association Dr.
Reston, VA 20191
Tel: (703)860-0200
Fax: (703)476-5432

Employers
Nat'l Ass'n of Secondary School Principals (Director, Communications)

LAMPI, Ruth

4455 Connecticut Ave. NW
Suite B500
Washington, DC 20008-2328
Tel: (202)537-5005
Fax: (202)537-3007

Employers
Lindesmith Center- Drug Policy Foundation (Director of Finance & Administration)

LAMPKIN, Marc

1133 Connecticut Ave. NW
Fifth Floor
Washington, DC 20036
Tel: (202)457-1110
Fax: (202)457-1130

Employers
Quinn Gillespie & Associates (Associate)

Clients Represented

On Behalf of Quinn Gillespie & Associates
American Insurance Ass'n

LAMPLEY, Virginia A.

900 17th St. NW
Suite 500
Washington, DC 20006
Tel: (202)296-9312
Fax: (202)296-9395
EMail: VLampley@scowcroft.com
Staff member, Nat'l Security Council during the Bush I administration.

Employers
Forum for Internat'l Policy (V. President)
The Scowcroft Group (Principal and Managing Director)

LAMPTEY, Peter

2101 Wilson Blvd.
Suite 700
Arlington, VA 22201
Tel: (703)516-9779
Fax: (703)516-9781

Employers
Family Health Internat'l (Project Director, Impact HIV/AIDS Prevention & Care Programs)

LAMSON, John

819 Seventh St. NW
Washington, DC 20001
Tel: (202)833-8940
Fax: (202)833-8943
Registered: LDA

Employers
EOP Group, Inc.

Clients Represented

On Behalf of EOP Group, Inc.
The Business Roundtable

LAMSON, Susan

11250 Waples Mill Rd.
Fairfax, VA 22030-7400
Tel: (703)267-1000
Fax: (703)267-1543
Registered: LDA

Employers
Nat'l Rifle Ass'n Institute for Legislative Action (Director, Conservation, Wildlife and Natural Resources Division)

LANAM, Linda L.

1001 Pennsylvania Ave. NW
Washington, DC 20004-2599
Tel: (202)624-2000
Fax: (202)624-2319

Employers
American Council of Life Insurers (V. President and Chief Counsel, State Relations)

LANCE, J.

1900 Association Dr.
Reston, VA 20191
Tel: (703)476-3437
Fax: (703)476-6638
EMail: jlance@aahperd.org

Employers
American Ass'n for Health Education (Coordinator, Government and Public Affairs)

LANCE, Linda

1615 M St. NW
Washington, DC 20036
Tel: (202)833-2300
Fax: (202)429-3945
Registered: LDA
EMail: linda_lance@tws.org
Former Associate Director, White House Council on Environmental Quality.Served as Senior Policy Analyst to the Vice President, The White House, during the Clinton administration. Also worked for the Departments of Justice and Health, Education, and Welfare and for the Senate Committee on Commerce, Science and Transportation.

Employers
The Wilderness Soc. (V. President, Public Policy)

LANCETTI, Luisa

401 Ninth St. NW
Suite 400
Washington, DC 20004
Tel: (202)585-1892

Employers
Sprint Corp. (V. President, Federal Regulatory - PCS)

LAND, Guy

1666 Connecticut Ave. NW
Suite 700
Washington, DC 20235-0001
EMail: guyland@arc.gov
Tel: (202)884-7674
Fax: (202)884-7693

Employers
Appalachian Regional Commission (Special Counsel and Director, Congressional Affairs)

LANDE, Jeffrey S.

1401 Wilson Blvd.
Suite 1100
Arlington, VA 22209
Tel: (703)522-5055
Fax: (703)525-2279
Registered: LDA

Legislative Assistant to Rep. Lane Evans (D-IL) and Professional Staff Member, Subcommittee on Oversight and Investigations, House Veterans' Affairs Committee, 1991-96. Special Legislative Assistant to Rep. Barbara Boxer (D-CA), 1991.

Employers
Information Technology Ass'n of America (ITAA) (V. President)

LANDE, Jim

2201 C St. NW
Room 7251
Washington, DC 20520-7261
Tel: (202)647-8728
Fax: (202)647-2762

Employers
Department of State - Bureau of Legislative Affairs (Legislative Management Officer)

LANDERS, David M.

1155 21st St. NW
Suite 300
Washington, DC 20036
Tel: (202)659-8201
Fax: (202)659-5249
Registered: LDA

Legislative Counsel to Senator Lauch Faircloth (R-NC), 1997-98. Legislative Counsel to Rep. Fred Heineman (R-NC), 1995-96. Legislative Assistant to Rep. Elton Gallegly (R-CA), 1993-94.

Employers
Williams & Jensen, P.C. (Associate)

Clients Represented

On Behalf of Williams & Jensen, P.C.
American Share Insurance
Credit Suisse First Boston Corp.
CT USA, Inc.
Fidelity Investments Co.
First Union Corp.
Reinsurance Ass'n of America
USAA - United Services Automobile Ass'n

LANDERS, Jay

P.O. Box 2999
Reston, VA 20191
Tel: (703)620-6003
Ext: 354
Fax: (703)620-5071
EMail: jlanders@rvia.org

Employers
Recreation Vehicle Industry Ass'n (Senior Director, Government Affairs)

LANDGRAF, L. Charles

1875 Connecticut Ave. NW
Suite 1200
Washington, DC 20009-5728
Tel: (202)986-8000
Fax: (202)986-8102
Registered: LDA, FARA

Legislative Director to Senator Robert Smith (R-NH), 1991-93.

Employers
LeBoeuf, Lamb, Greene & MacRae L.L.P. (Partner)

Clients Represented

On Behalf of LeBoeuf, Lamb, Greene & MacRae L.L.P.
Hydro-Quebec
Internat'l Underwriting Ass'n of London
Lloyd's of London
New York State Reliability Council

LANDRITH, III, George C.

1401 Wilson Blvd.
Suite 1007
Arlington, VA 22209
EMail: glandrith@ff.org
Tel: (703)527-8282
Fax: (703)527-8388

Employers
Frontiers of Freedom Institute (Exec. Director)

LANDRUM, J. Michael

300 N. Lee St.
Suite 500
Alexandria, VA 22314
Tel: (703)518-8600
Fax: (703)518-8611
Registered: LDA

Employers
PACE-CAPSTONE (Partner)

Clients Represented

On Behalf of PACE-CAPSTONE
Kern, California, County of
Nat'l Ass'n of Credit Management

LANDRY, Brock R.

1201 New York Ave. NW
Suite 1000
Washington, DC 20005
EMail: brlandry@venable.com
Tel: (202)962-4877
Fax: (202)962-8300

Employers
Venable (Partner)

Clients Represented

On Behalf of Venable
Amino and Phenolic Wood Adhesives Ass'n
Bicycle Council
Bicycle Product Suppliers Ass'n
Chlorine Chemistry Council
Composite Panel Ass'n
Cool Roof Rating Council
Hardwood Plywood and Veneer Ass'n
Internat'l Bicycle Ass'n
Metal Building Manufacturers Ass'n
Nat'l Bicycle Dealers Ass'n
North American Steel Framing Alliance
Recreation Vehicle Dealers Ass'n of North America
Roof Coatings Manufacturers Ass'n
Wood Products Indoor Air Consortium

LANDSIDLE, David W.

1710 Rhode Island Ave. NW
Suite 300
Washington, DC 20036
Tel: (202)659-8524
Fax: (202)466-8386
Registered: LDA

Employers
Abbott Laboratories (Divisional V. President, Federal Government Affairs)

LANE, Jan

431 18th St. NW
Washington, DC 20006
Tel: (202)639-3125
Fax: (202)639-6116
Registered: LDA
EMail: lanej@usa.redcross.org

Employers
American Red Cross (V. President, Government Relations)

LANE, Janet C.

601 E St. NW
Washington, DC 20049
Tel: (202)434-2277
Fax: (202)434-6477

Employers
AARP (American Ass'n of Retired Persons) (Director, Communications Operations)

LANE, Lee

1828 L St. NW
Suite 1000
Washington, DC 20036
Tel: (202)463-8453
Fax: (202)293-4598
Registered: LDA
EMail: leelane@aecs-inc.org

Employers
Self-employed as an independent consultant.

Clients Represented

As an independent consultant
Americans for Equitable Climate Solutions

LANE, Patrick J.

1615 H St. NW
Washington, DC 20062-2000
Tel: (202)659-6000
Fax: (202)463-5836

Employers
Chamber of Commerce of the U.S.A. (Director, Congressional and Public Affairs)

LANE, Scott H.

99 Canal Center Plaza
Suite 500
Alexandria, VA 22314-1538
EMail: scott@aiada.org
Tel: (703)519-7800
Fax: (703)519-7810
Registered: LDA

Employers
American Internat'l Automobile Dealers Ass'n (V. President, Government Relations)

LANE, William C.

818 Connecticut Ave. NW
Suite 600
Washington, DC 20006-2702
Tel: (202)466-0672
Fax: (202)466-0684
Registered: LDA

Employers
Caterpillar Inc. (Washington Director, Governmental Affairs)

LANG, Jeffrey M.

2445 M St. NW
Washington, DC 20037-1420
EMail: jlang@wilmer.com
Tel: (202)663-6000
Fax: (202)663-6363

Deputy U.S. Trade Representative, Office of the U.S. Trade Representative, Executive Office of the President, The White House, 1995-98. Chief International Trade Counsel (1986-90) and Professional Staff Member (1979-86), Senate Committee on Finance.Deputy General Counsel, International Trade Commission, 1975-79.

Employers
Wilmer, Cutler & Pickering (Partner)

LANG, Paul R.

1200 New Hampshire Ave. NW
Suite 800
Washington, DC 20036-6802
EMail: plang@dlalaw.com
Tel: (202)776-2000
Fax: (202)776-2222
Registered: LDA

Employers
Dow, Lohnes & Albertson, PLLC (Member)

Clients Represented

On Behalf of Dow, Lohnes & Albertson, PLLC
R. R. Donnelley & Sons

LANG, William G.

1426 Prince St.
Alexandria, VA 22314
EMail: wglang@aacp.org
Tel: (703)739-2330
Fax: (703)836-8982

Employers
American Ass'n of Colleges of Pharmacy (Director of Government Affairs)

LANGAN, Thomas P.

816 Connecticut Ave. NW
Seventh Floor
Washington, DC 20006-2705
EMail: tom.langan@unilever.com
Tel: (202)828-1010
Fax: (202)828-4550

Employers
Unilever United States, Inc. (Manager, Government Affairs)

LANGDON, Jr., James C.

1333 New Hampshire Ave. NW
Suite 400
Washington, DC 20036
Tel: (202)887-4000
Fax: (202)887-4288

Director, Office of Commercial Affairs, Department of the Treasury, 1974-75. Associate Administrator, Federal Energy Administration, 1973-74. Associate Administrator, Federal Energy Office, 1972-73.

Employers
Akin, Gump, Strauss, Hauer & Feld, L.L.P. (Partner)

LANGE, Gene C.

1660 L St. St. NW
Suite 506
Washington, DC 20036
Tel: (202)463-1260
Fax: (202)463-6328

Employers
Luman, Lange & Wheeler (Managing Partner)

Clients Represented

On Behalf of Luman, Lange & Wheeler
American Wholesale Marketers Ass'n
Ass'n of Schools of Public Health

LANGER, Andrew

1001 Connecticut Ave. NW
Suite 1250
Washington, DC 20036
Tel: (202)331-1010
Fax: (202)331-0640

Employers
Competitive Enterprise Institute (Associate Director for Development)

LANGER, Therese

1001 Connecticut Ave. NW
Suite 801
Washington, DC 20036
Tel: (202)429-8873
Fax: (202)429-2248

Employers
American Council for an Energy-Efficient Economy (Senior Associate)

LANGFELDT, Carl

1501 Lee Hwy.
Arlington, VA 22209-1198
EMail: clangfeldt@afa.org
Tel: (703)247-5800
Fax: (703)247-5853

Employers
Air Force Ass'n (Legislative Assistant)

LANGFORD, Carrie

1575 I St. NW
Washington, DC 20005-1103
EMail: clangford@asaenet.org
Tel: (202)626-2788
Fax: (202)371-1673
Registered: LDA

Employers
American Soc. of Ass'n Executives (Associate Manager, Public Policy)

LANGKNECHT, John M.

1725 Jefferson Davis Hwy.
Suite 601
Arlington, VA 22202
Tel: (703)418-0300
Fax: (703)413-0607

Employers
Ingalls Shipbuilding (Director, Government Relations)

LANGLEY, Ann

888 17th St. NW
Suite 800
Washington, DC 20006
Tel: (202)452-8290
Fax: (202)822-9088
Registered: LDA

Employers
Health Policy Strategies (President)

Clients Represented

On Behalf of Health Policy Strategies
Children's Hospital of Boston
La Rabida Children's Hospital Research Center
Nat'l Ass'n of Children's Hospitals Inc.

LANGLEY, Marty

1140 19th St. NW
Suite 600
Washington, DC 20036
Tel: (202)822-8200
Fax: (202)822-8205

Employers
Violence Policy Center (Policy Analyst)

LANGSTON, Ed

219 N. Washington St.
Alexandria, VA 22314
Tel: (703)836-7990
Fax: (703)836-9739

Employers
Peduzzi Associates, Ltd. (Associate)

LANIAK, Judy

1033 N. Fairfax St.
Suite 404
Alexandria, VA 22314
EMail: jlaniak@icsc.org
Tel: (703)549-7404
Fax: (703)549-8712

Employers
Internat'l Council of Shopping Centers (Government Relations Administrator)

LANIER, Robin W.

1620 I St. NW
Suite 615
Washington, DC 20006
Tel: (202)463-8493
Fax: (202)463-8497
Registered: LDA

Employers
Consumers for World Trade (President)
JBC Internat'l
Management Options, Inc.

Clients Represented

On Behalf of JBC Internat'l
Internat'l Mass Retailers Ass'n

LANKFORD, Thomas L.

1420 New York Ave. NW
Suite 1050
Washington, DC 20005
Tel: (202)638-1950
Fax: (202)638-1928
Registered: LDA

Senior Legislative Assistant to Senator Robert C. Smith (R-NH), 1990-97 and Legislative Assistant to Senator Gordon Humphrey (R-NH), 1988-90.

Employers
Van Scoyoc Associates, Inc. (V. President)

Clients Represented

On Behalf of Van Scoyoc Associates, Inc.
Alcoa Inc.
APG Army Alliance
Insight Technology, Inc.
Lockheed Martin Government Electronics Systems
Lockheed Martin Naval Electronics Surveillance Systems
Mentis Sciences Inc.
TRAUX Engineering
Universal Systems, Inc.
Xcellsis Corp.

LANNING, Karen

1100 Connecticut Ave. NW
12th Floor
Washington, DC 20036
EMail: klanning@nchelp.org
Tel: (202)822-2106
Fax: (202)822-2142

Employers
Nat'l Council of Higher Education Loan Programs (Communications Coordinator)

LANSING, Kathleen

1819 H St. NW
Suite 1200
Washington, DC 20006
EMail: ntlpeace@aol.com
Tel: (202)223-1770
Fax: (202)223-1718

Employers
Nat'l Peace Foundation (Deputy Director)

LANSING, Olga

1225 I St. NW
Suite 500
Washington, DC 20005
EMail: dawsonassociates@worldnet.att.net
Tel: (202)312-2005
Fax: (202)289-8683
Registered: LDA

Office of the Assistant Secretary of Defense for Environmental Security, Department of Defense, 1997-1998. U.S. Army Corps of Engineers, Department of the Army, 1956-97.

Employers
Dawson & Associates, Inc. (Senior Advisor)

Clients Represented

On Behalf of Dawson & Associates, Inc.
Great Lakes Dredge & Dock

LANVANHOVE, Scott

1150 18th St. NW
Suite 700
Washington, DC 20036
Tel: (202)872-5500
Fax: (202)872-5501

Employers
Business Software Alliance (V. President, Global Operations)

LANZA, Susanne

1201 F St. NW
Suite 500
Washington, DC 20004
Tel: (202)824-1600
Fax: (202)824-1651
Registered: LDA

Employers
Health Insurance Ass'n of America (Director, Managed Care Policy)

LAPAILLE, Gary J.

819 Seventh St. NW
Suite 200
Washington, DC 20001
EMail: gary.lapaille@mn.com
Tel: (202)296-5354
Ext: 223
Fax: (202)296-7248
Registered: LDA

Employers
Montgomery Watson (V. President, National and State Affairs)

LAPAS, Linda

1616 H St. NW
Eighth Floor
Washington, DC 20006-4999
Tel: (202)628-7979
Fax: (202)628-7779

Employers
Solar Energy Research and Education Foundation (Exec. Director)

LAPIDUS, Fern M.

8801 Montgomery Ave.
Chevy Chase, MD 20815
Tel: (301)986-5491
Fax: (301)986-1506
Registered: LDA

Employers
Self-employed as an independent consultant.

Clients Represented

As an independent consultant
Ass'n of Proprietary Colleges
Los Alamitos Unified School District
Nat'l Council for Impacted Schools
School of Visual Arts

LAPIERRE, Steven

1310 G St. NW
12th Floor
Washington, DC 20005
Tel: (202)626-4780
Fax: (202)626-4833
Registered: LDA

Employers
Blue Cross Blue Shield Ass'n (Exec. Washington Representative)

LAPIERRE, Jr., Wayne R.

11250 Waples Mill Rd.
Fairfax, VA 22030-7400
Tel: (703)267-1050
Fax: (703)267-3989
Registered: LDA

Employers
Nat'l Rifle Ass'n of America (Exec. V. President)

LAPKIN, Ted

1300 Wilson Blvd.
Arlington, VA 22209
Tel: (703)741-5850
Fax: (703)741-6084

Former Communications Director for Rep. Rick A. Lazio (R-NY).

Employers
Chlorine Chemistry Council (Senior Public Policy Analyst)

LAPLACA, Joseph

100 Indiana Ave. NW
Washington, DC 20001
Tel: (202)393-4695
Fax: (202)737-1540

Employers
Nat'l Ass'n of Letter Carriers of the United States of America (Director, Retired Members)

LAPLANTE, Clifford C.

1299 Pennsylvania Ave. NW
Suite 1100 West
Washington, DC 20004-2407
Tel: (202)637-4000
Fax: (202)637-4412
Registered: LDA

Employers
General Electric Co. (Manager, Congressional and Exec. Office Relations)

LAPORTE, Nicole

1403 King St.
Alexandria, VA 22314
Tel: (703)535-1093
Fax: (703)535-1094
Registered: LDA
EMail: nlaporte@ssci.org
Former Legislative Assistant to Rep. Don Young (R-AK).

Employers
Steel Service Center Institute (Manager, Governmental Affairs)

LAPORTE, Yolan

1901 L St. NW
Suite 300
Washington, DC 20036
Tel: (202)466-7590
Fax: (202)466-7598
EMail: yolan.laporte@dc.ogilvypr.com
Director, Joint Recruitment Advertising, Department of Defense, 1978-87.

Employers
Ogilvy Public Relations Worldwide (Senior V. President)

LAPPEN, Mark

707 N. Saint Asaph St.
Alexandria, VA 22314
Tel: (703)836-4012
Fax: (703)836-8353

Employers
Internat'l Sign Ass'n (President and Chief Exec. Officer)

LARCHER, Constance C.

2009 Massachusetts Ave. NW
Washington, DC 20036
Tel: (202)588-0302
Fax: (202)588-0371

Employers
Washington Legal Foundation (Exec. Director and President)

LARCOM, M. Kay

800 Connecticut Ave. NW
Suite 900
Washington, DC 20006
Tel: (202)467-1060
Fax: (202)467-1080
Registered: LDA

Employers
Conoco Inc.

LARDY, Nicholas R.

1775 Massachusetts Ave. NW
Washington, DC 20036-2188
Tel: (202)797-6000
Fax: (202)797-6004

Employers
The Brookings Institution (Senior Fellow and Interim Director of Foreign Policy Studies)

LARGER, Christine

2501 M St. NW
Suite 400
Washington, DC 20037
Tel: (202)861-2500
Fax: (202)861-2583

Employers
Nat'l Ass'n of College and University Business Officers (V. President, Public Policy and Government Relations)

LARIGAKIS, Nicholas

1220 16th St. NW
Washington, DC 20036
Tel: (202)659-4608
Fax: (202)785-5178
Registered: LDA

Employers
American Hellenic Institute Public Affairs Committee (Exec. Director)
American Hellenic Institute, Inc. (Exec. Director)

LARKIN, J. Stephen

900 19th St. NW
Suite 300
Washington, DC 20006
Tel: (202)862-5100
Fax: (202)862-5164
Registered: LDA
EMail: jlarkin@aluminum.org

Employers
The Aluminum Ass'n (President)

LARKIN, Jennifer

214 Massachusetts Ave. NE
Washington, DC 20002
Tel: (202)546-4400
Fax: (202)546-8328

Employers
Heritage Foundation (Director, Congressional Relations, U.S. House of Representatives)

LARKINS, J. McKinney

1341 Connecticut Ave. NW
Third Floor
Washington, DC 20036
Tel: (202)862-3900
Fax: (202)862-5500
Commissioned Officer, U.S. Army, retired. Former Program Manager, National Security Council, The White House, 1983-87.

Employers
Scribe Consulting & Communications (Senior Associate)

LAROCCA, Anthony J.

1330 Connecticut Ave. NW
Washington, DC 20036-1795
Tel: (202)429-3000
Fax: (202)429-3902
EMail: alarocca@steptoe.com

Employers
Steptoe & Johnson LLP (Partner)

LAROCCO, Christine B.

Six E St. SE
Washington, DC 20003
Tel: (202)547-6400
Fax: (202)547-8800
Registered: LDA
EMail: clarocco@aol.com

Employers
LaRocco & Associates (President)

Clients Represented
On Behalf of LaRocco & Associates
Education Assistance Foundation

LAROCCO, Hon. Lawrence P.

Six E St. SE
Washington, DC 20003
Tel: (202)547-6400
Fax: (202)547-8800
Registered: LDA, FARA
EMail: larrylarocco@aol.com
Member, U.S. House of Representatives (D-ID), 1991-95.

Employers
LaRocco & Associates (Chairman)
U.S. Ass'n of Former Members of Congress (V. President)

Clients Represented
On Behalf of LaRocco & Associates
American Bankers Ass'n
Education Assistance Foundation
Netivation.com
Spokane Area Chamber of Commerce

LAROCCO, Matthew

Six E St. SE
Washington, DC 20003
Tel: (202)547-6400
Fax: (202)547-8800
Registered: LDA
EMail: mllarocco@aol.com

Employers
LaRocco & Associates (Senior V. President)

Clients Represented
On Behalf of LaRocco & Associates
American Bankers Ass'n
Chase Electronic Investments
Education Assistance Foundation
Netivation.com
Spokane Area Chamber of Commerce

LAROCK, Joan W.

6728 Baron Rd.
McLean, VA 22101
Tel: (703)556-3324
Fax: (703)734-7763
Registered: LDA
United States Environmental Protection Agency, 1980-90, including Special Assistant to the Administrator, 1988. Congressional Fellow to Senator John Breaux (D-LA), 1989-90.

Employers
LaRock Associates, Inc. (President)

Clients Represented
On Behalf of LaRock Associates, Inc.
American Plastics Council

LARSEN, William L.

601 13th St. NW
Suite 800 South
Washington, DC 20005
Tel: (202)682-1498
Fax: (202)637-0217
Registered: LDA
EMail: wlarsen@nabl.org

Employers
Nat'l Ass'n of Bond Lawyers (Director, Governmental Affairs)

LARSON, Amy

800 N. Capitol St. NW
Room 1018
Washington, DC 20573
Tel: (202)523-5740
Fax: (202)523-5738
EMail: amyl@fmc.gov

Employers
Federal Maritime Commission (Legislative Counsel)

LARSON, Daniel M.

1455 Pennsylvania Ave. NW
Suite 375
M/S 4072
Washington, DC 20004
Tel: (202)628-3133
Fax: (202)628-2980
Registered: LDA
EMail: danlarson@ti.com

Employers
Texas Instruments (Director, Government and Media Relations)

LARSON, Dave

1050 Connecticut Ave. NW
Washington, DC 20036-5339
Tel: (202)857-6000
Fax: (202)857-6395
Former Health Policy Advisor to Senator Bill Frist (R-TN).

Employers
Arent Fox Kintner Plotkin & Kahn, PLLC (Government Relations Director)

LARSON, Jennifer

1101 17th St. NW
Suite 1102
Washington, DC 20036
Tel: (202)785-4500
Fax: (202)785-3539

Employers
Nat'l Park Foundation (Director, Public Relations)

LARSON, Lance

1341 G St. NW
Suite 200
Washington, DC 20005
Tel: (202)347-5990
Fax: (202)347-5941
EMail: llarson@clj.com

Employers
Copeland, Lowery & Jacquez (Assistant)

LARSON, Philip

555 13th St. NW
Washington, DC 20004-1109
Tel: (202)637-5738
Fax: (202)637-5910
Registered: LDA
EMail: pclarson@hhlaw.com
Formerly with the Veterans Administration Central Office, Department of Veterans Affairs, 1967-68.

Employers
Hogan & Hartson L.L.P. (Partner)

Clients Represented
On Behalf of Hogan & Hartson L.L.P.
United Parcel Service

LARSON, Reed E.

8001 Braddock Rd.
Springfield, VA 22160
Tel: (703)321-9820
Fax: (703)321-7342
Registered: LDA

Employers
Nat'l Right to Work Committee (President)
Nat'l Right to Work Legal Defense Foundation (President)

LARSON, Shane

1275 K St. NW
Fifth Floor
Washington, DC 20005
Tel: (202)712-9799
Registered: LDA

Employers
Ass'n of Flight Attendants

LARSON, Teresa J.

101 1/2 S. Union St.
Alexandria, VA 22314
Tel: (703)684-5100
Fax: (703)684-5424
EMail: tlarson@smithfairfield.com
Legislative Correspondent to Senator Bob Dole (R-KS), 1982-84.

Employers
Smith Fairfield, Inc. (Principal)

LASER, Rachel

1818 N St. NW
Suite 450
Washington, DC 20036
EMail: rlaser@basshowes.com
Tel: (202)530-2900
Fax: (202)530-2901
Registered: LDA

Employers
Bass and Howes, Inc. (Senior Program Associate)

Clients Represented
On Behalf of Bass and Howes, Inc.
Institute for Civil Soc.
Ross Abbott Laboratories

LASH, Jonathan

Ten G St. NE
Eighth Floor
Washington, DC 20002
Tel: (202)729-7600
Fax: (202)729-7759

Employers
Institutions and Governance Program (President)
World Resources Institute (President)

LASHER, Craig

1300 19th St. NW
Second Floor
Washington, DC 20036
Tel: (202)557-3400
Fax: (202)728-4177
Registered: LDA

Employers
Population Action Internat'l (Senior Policy Analyst)

LASHOF, Daniel A.

1200 New York Ave. NW
Suite 400
Washington, DC 20005
Tel: (202)289-6868
Fax: (202)289-1060
Registered: LDA

Employers
Natural Resources Defense Council (Senior Scientist)

LASKER, Helene C.

555 13th St. NW
Washington, DC 20004-1109
Tel: (202)637-5600
Fax: (202)637-5910
Registered: LDA

Employers
Hogan & Hartson L.L.P.

Clients Represented
On Behalf of Hogan & Hartson L.L.P.
Plasma Protein Therapeutics Ass'n

LASKO, Elizabeth W.

1806 Robert Fulton Dr.
Reston, VA 20191
EMail: elizabeth@menc.org
Tel: (703)860-4000
Fax: (703)860-1531

Employers
MENC: The Nat'l Ass'n for Music Education (Senior Manager, Public Relations, Marketing, and Media)

LASKY, Samantha

2000 L St. NW
Suite 300
Washington, DC 20036-0646
Tel: (202)835-8800
Fax: (202)835-8879
Registered: LDA

Employers
Ketchum (Account Executive)

Clients Represented
On Behalf of Ketchum
Regeneration Technologies Inc.

LASOFF, Laurence J.

3050 K St. NW
Washington, DC 20007
Tel: (202)342-8400
Fax: (202)342-8451
Registered: LDA
EMail: llasoff@colliershannon.com
Executive Assistant to the Assistant Secretary for International Trade (1977-79) and International Trade Specialist, Bureau of East-West Trade (1974-77), Department of Commerce.

Employers
Collier Shannon Scott, PLLC (Member)

Clients Represented
On Behalf of Collier Shannon Scott, PLLC
COMPACT
Internat'l Ass'n of Machinists and Aerospace Workers
Metro Internat'l Trade Services, Inc.
Oneida Ltd.
Outdoor Power Equipment Institute
Specialty Steel Industry of North America
Symbol Technologies, Inc.

LASS, Conrad

1130 Connecticut Ave. NW
Suite 830
Washington, DC 20036
Tel: (202)261-5000
Fax: (202)296-7937

Employers
Southern Co. (Manager, Federal Legislative Affairs)

LASSMAN, Malcolm

1333 New Hampshire Ave. NW
Suite 400
Washington, DC 20036
Tel: (202)887-4000
Fax: (202)887-4288

Employers
Akin, Gump, Strauss, Hauer & Feld, L.L.P. (Partner)
Policy Group (Treasurer)

Clients Represented
On Behalf of Akin, Gump, Strauss, Hauer & Feld, L.L.P.
Policy Group

LASSMAN, Prescott M.

1140 19th St. NW
Suite 900
Washington, DC 20036
EMail: plassman@kkblaw.com
Tel: (202)223-5120
Fax: (202)223-5619

Employers
Kleinfeld, Kaplan and Becker (Partner)

LASTOWKA, James A.

600 13th St. NW
Washington, DC 20005-3096
EMail: jlastowka@mwe.com
Tel: (202)756-8245
Fax: (202)756-8087
General Counsel (1981-84) and Commissioner (1984-90), Federal Mine Safety and Health Review Commission; Assistant General Counsel, Occupational Safety and Health Review Commission

Employers
McDermott, Will and Emery (Partner)

LASZAKOVITS, Greg

337 North Carolina Ave. SE
Washington, DC 20003
Tel: (202)546-3202
Fax: (202)544-5852

Employers
Church of the Brethren Washington Office (Coordinator)

LATE, Karen M.

444 N. Capitol St. NW
Suite 532
Washington, DC 20001
Tel: (202)544-6264
Fax: (202)544-3610
Registered: LDA

Employers
Congressional Consultants (Senior Associate)

Clients Represented
On Behalf of Congressional Consultants
Aksys, Ltd.
Alliance Medical Corp.
Nat'l Renal Administrators Ass'n
SterilMed, Inc.
Vanguard Medical Concepts, Inc.

LATHAM, Dawn

1575 I St. NW
Washington, DC 20005-1103
EMail: dlatham@asaenet.org
Tel: (202)626-2874
Fax: (202)371-1673
Registered: LDA

Employers
American Soc. of Ass'n Executives (Associate Director, Public Policy)

LATHAM, Weldon H.

2099 Pennsylvania Ave. NW
Suite 100
Washington, DC 20006
EMail: wlatham@hklaw.com
Tel: (202)955-3000
Fax: (202)955-5564
Registered: LDA
General Deputy Assistant Secretary, Department of Housing and Urban Development, 1979-81. Assistant General Counsel, Office of Management and Budget, Executive Office of the President, The White House, 1974-76. Office of the Secretary, General Counsel's Honors Program, Department of the Air Force, 1973-74.

Employers
Holland & Knight LLP (Partner)

Clients Represented
On Behalf of Holland & Knight LLP
Nat'l Coalition of Minority Businesses
Texaco Group Inc.

LATIMER, Helen

4701 Sangamore Rd.
Suite N100
Bethesda, MD 20816-2508
Tel: (301)229-5800
Fax: (301)229-5045
Registered: LDA

Employers
Burdeshaw Associates, Ltd. (Associate)

LATTANZIO, Ted

1341 G St. NW
Suite 900
Washington, DC 20005
Tel: (202)637-1500
Fax: (202)637-1505

Employers
Philip Morris Management Corp. (Director, Government Affairs Strategy and Development)

LATTIMORE, Neel

1501 M St. NW
Suite 600
Washington, DC 20005-1710
EMail: lattimore@bsmg.com
Tel: (202)739-0200
Fax: (202)659-8287
Registered: FARA

Employers
BSMG Worldwide (Senior Managing Director)

LATTIS, Richard

8403 Colesville Rd.
Suite 710
Silver Spring, MD 20910
Tel: (301)562-0777
Fax: (301)562-0888

Employers
American Zoo and Aquarium Ass'n (President/C.E.O. Zoo Atlanta)

LAUDERBAUGH, Richard

444 N. Capitol St. NW
Suite 821
Washington, DC 20001
Tel: (202)737-3390
Fax: (202)628-3607
Registered: LDA

Employers
Health Policy Alternatives, Inc. (Principal)

Clients Represented
On Behalf of Health Policy Alternatives, Inc.
American College of Emergency Physicians
American Hospital Ass'n
American Nurses Ass'n
Federation of American Hospitals

LAUDIEN, Lori E.

555 11th St. NW
Suite 750
Washington, DC 20005
Tel: (202)637-3506
Fax: (202)637-3504
Registered: LDA
Tax Counsel, Senate Committee on Finance, 1996-97. Tax Counsel to Senator William V. Roth, Jr. (R-DE), 1995-96.

Employers
El Paso Corporation (Director, Federal Government Affairs)

LAUGHLIN, Hon. Greg H.

2550 M St. NW
Washington, DC 20037-1350
Tel: (202)457-6000
Fax: (202)457-6315
Registered: LDA
EMail: glaughlin@pattonboggs.com
Member, U.S. House of Representatives (R-TX), (1995-96) and (D-TX), (1989-95).

Employers
Patton Boggs, LLP (Of Counsel)

Clients Represented
On Behalf of Patton Boggs, LLP
Crane Co.
Dole Food Co.
James Hardie Building Products Inc.
McKinsey & Co., Inc.
G. Murphy Trading
QSP Inc.
Union Pacific Railroad Co.
United Airlines

LAUGHLIN, Keith

1100 17th St. NW
Tenth Floor
Washington, DC 20036
Tel: (202)331-9696
Fax: (202)331-9680

Employers
Rails to Trails Conservancy (President)

LAV, Iris J.

820 First St. NE
Suite 510
Washington, DC 20002
EMail: lav@center.cbpp.org
Tel: (202)408-1080
Fax: (202)408-1056

Employers
Center on Budget and Policy Priorities (Deputy Director)

LAVALLEE, Adrienne C.

701 Pennsylvania Ave. NW
Suite 900
Washington, DC 20004-2608
EMail: alavallee@mintz.com
Tel: (202)434-7300
Fax: (202)434-7400

Employers
Mintz, Levin, Cohn, Ferris, Glovsky and Popeo, P.C. (Of Counsel)

LAVANTY, Deanna D.

46 S. Glebe Rd.
Suite 202
Arlington, VA 22204
Tel: (703)920-8001
Fax: (301)948-4463
Registered: LDA

Employers
J. T. Rutherford & Associates (Senior Associate, Government Relations)

Clients Represented
On Behalf of J. T. Rutherford & Associates
American College of Radiology
American Optometric Ass'n

LAVANTY, Donald F.

46 S. Glebe Rd.
Suite 202
Arlington, VA 22204
Tel: (703)920-8001
Fax: (301)948-4463
Registered: LDA

Employers
J. T. Rutherford & Associates (President)

Clients Represented
On Behalf of J. T. Rutherford & Associates
American College of Radiology
American Optometric Ass'n
American Soc. for Clinical Laboratory Science
Glossco Free Zone, N.V.

LAVERDY, Marina

409 Third St. SW
Suite 7900
Washington, DC 20416
EMail: marina.laverdy@sba.gov
Tel: (202)205-6700
Fax: (202)205-7374

Employers
Small Business Administration (Legislative Affairs Specialist)

LAVERY, Paul C.

P.O. Box 61303
Potomac, MD 20859
EMail: info@FoleyCoInc.com
Tel: (301)294-0937
Registered: LDA

Employers
Foley Government and Public Affairs, Inc. (Research Assistant)

Clients Represented
On Behalf of Foley Government and Public Affairs, Inc.
Thompson Lighting Protection Inc.

LAVERY, Susan

1616 H St. NW
Third Floor
Washington, DC 20006
Tel: (202)737-3700
Fax: (202)737-0530

Employers
Internat'l Center for Journalists (Senior Director, Programs)

LAVET, Lorraine

601 Pennsylvania Ave. NW
Suite 600
North Bldg.
Washington, DC 20004
Tel: (202)682-9110
Fax: (202)682-9111
Registered: LDA

Employers
American Electronics Ass'n (Exec. V. President and Chief Operating Officer)

LAVIE, Ann Ferrill

1825 K St. NW
Suite 703
Washington, DC 20006
Tel: (202)466-2800
Fax: (202)466-2090

Employers
Insurance Services Office, Inc. (Assistant V. President, Federal Affairs)

LAVIN, Laurence

1101 14th St. NW
Suite 405
Washington, DC 20005
EMail: lavin@healthlaw.org
Tel: (202)289-7661
Fax: (202)289-7724

Employers
Nat'l Health Law Program (Director)

LAVIOLETTE, Karry

655 15th St. NW
Washington, DC 20005-5701
EMail: klaviolette@fmi.org
Tel: (202)220-0627
Fax: (202)220-0872

Employers
Food Marketing Institute (Manager, Political Affairs)

LAVRAKAS, Susan C.

1000 Wilson Blvd.
Suite 2300
Arlington, VA 22209
Tel: (703)875-8400
Fax: (703)276-0711
Registered: LDA

Employers
Northrop Grumman Corp.

LAW, Steven

425 Second St. NE
Washington, DC 20002
Tel: (202)675-6000
Fax: (202)675-6058

Employers
Nat'l Republican Senatorial Committee (Exec. Director)

LAWLER, Gregory E.

1909 K St. NW
Suite 820
Washington, DC 20006
Tel: (202)777-7700
Fax: (202)777-7763
Registered: LDA
EMail: glawler@lmm-law.com
Senior Policy Advisor, Exec. Office of the President, The White House, 1993-94. Chief Counsel and Staff Director, Subcommittee on Commerce and Transportation, Committee on Energy and Commerce, U.S. House of Representatives, 1978-89.

Employers
Lawler, Metzger & Milkman, LLC (Managing Partner)

Clients Represented
On Behalf of Lawler, Metzger & Milkman, LLC
Brotherhood of Maintenance of Way Employees
Canadian Nat'l Railroad/Illinois Central Railroad
Canadian Nat'l Railway Co.
Currie Technologies, Inc.
Fairfield University
Great Projects Film Co., Inc.
Portals Development Associates L.P.
Provideo Productions
Rutgers University

LAWNICZAK, Jonathan

1801 K St. NW
Suite 700-L
Washington, DC 20006
Tel: (202)292-6700
Fax: (202)292-6800
Registered: LDA

Employers
Coalition for Health Services Research (Director, Government Relations)

LAWRENCE, Amanda

499 S. Capitol St. SW
Suite 417
Washington, DC 20003
Tel: (202)554-9494
Fax: (202)554-9454

Employers
Miccosukee Tribe of Indians of Florida (Legislative Assistant)

LAWRENCE, De'Arcy

3114 Circle Hill Rd.
Alexandria, VA 22305-1606
Tel: (703)548-1234
Fax: (703)548-6216

Employers
Internat'l Trade Council (Director, Administration)

LAWRENCE, Deborah B.

1627 I St. NW
Suite 900
Washington, DC 20006
Tel: (202)833-8994
Fax: (202)835-0707

Employers
The Williams Companies (V. President, Government Affairs)

LAWRENCE, Gregg

600 13th St. NW
Washington, DC 20005-3096
Tel: (202)756-8000
Fax: (202)756-8087

Employers
McDermott, Will and Emery (Partner)

LAWRENCE, H. Adam

1130 Connecticut Ave. NW
Suite 830
Washington, DC 20036
Tel: (202)261-5000
Fax: (202)296-7937
Registered: LDA

Employers
Southern Co. (Director, Federal Legislative Affairs)

LAWRENCE, Jeffrey

700 13th St. NW
Suite 400
Washington, DC 20005
Tel: (202)347-0773
Fax: (202)347-0785
Registered: LDA
EMail: jlawrence@cassidy.com
Associate Administrator for Legislative Affairs, National Aeronautics and Space Administration, 1993-97. Legislative Director to Rep. Bill Green (R-NY), 1983-93 and former Legislative Staff Member to Reps. Norman D'Amours (D-NH) and Daniel Akaka (D-HI).

Employers
Cassidy & Associates, Inc. (Senior V. President and Director, Aerospace and Technology Group)

Clients Represented
On Behalf of Cassidy & Associates, Inc.
Alcon Laboratories
Alenia Aerospazig
Arizona State University
Auspice, Inc.
Bishop Museum
The Boeing Co.
Boston University
California Museum Foundation
Chlorine Chemistry Council
Columbia University
Draft Worldwide
IBP Aerospace, Inc.
Liberty Science Center
Nat'l Rural Telecommunications Cooperative
Northern Essex Community College Foundation
Rhode Island School of Design
Rochester Institute of Technology
Summit Technology
Texas Tech University System
United Space Alliance
University of Hawaii

LAWRENCE, Jeffrey F.

1850 M St. NW
Suite 900
Washington, DC 20036
Tel: (202)463-2500
Fax: (202)463-4950
Registered: LDA, FARA

Legal Assistant to Commissioner (1978-79) and Staff Counsel (1977-78), Nuclear Regulatory Commission.

Employers
Sher & Blackwell (Partner)

Clients Represented

On Behalf of Sher & Blackwell
Massachusetts Heavy Industries
New York Waterways
Nippon Yusen Kaisha (NYK) Line
Rowan Companies, Inc.
Stuyvesant Dredging Co.

LAWRENCE, Jr., Dr. L. Robert

345 S. Patrick St.
Alexandria, VA 22314
Tel: (703)836-3654
Fax: (703)836-6086
Registered: LDA

Employers
Bob Lawrence & Associates (President)

Clients Represented

On Behalf of Bob Lawrence & Associates
Irrigation Ass'n
Minnesota Mining and Manufacturing Co. (3M Co.)

LAWRENCE, Lindsay

700 13th St. NW
Suite 400
Washington, DC 20005
Tel: (202)347-0773
Fax: (202)347-0785
Registered: LDA
EMail: llawrence@cassidy.com

Former aid to Rep. John Balducci (D-ME).

Employers
Cassidy & Associates, Inc. (Account Executive)

Clients Represented

On Behalf of Cassidy & Associates, Inc.
American Superconductor Corp.
Elmira College
Montefiore Medical Center
Tiffany & Co.

LAWRENCE, III, Thomas

1620 L St. NW
Suite 600
Washington, DC 20036
Tel: (202)312-8000
Fax: (202)312-8100

Employers
Oppenheimer Wolff & Donnelly LLP

LAWRENCE, Timothy W.

P.O. Box 3000
Leesburg, VA 20177
Tel: (703)777-8810
Fax: (703)777-8999

Employers
Skills USA-VICA (Exec. Director)

LAWS, Danielle

1913 I St. NW
Washington, DC 20006
Tel: (202)872-8110
Fax: (202)872-8114
Registered: LDA

Employers
Consumer Specialties Products Ass'n (Federal Legislative Specialist)

LAWSON, Elizabeth

1730 M St. NW
Suite 1000
Washington, DC 20036
Tel: (202)429-1965
Fax: (202)429-0854
Registered: LDA

Employers
League of Women Voters of the United States (Senior Lobbyist)

LAWSON, Eugene K.

1701 Pennsylvania Ave. NW
Suite 520
Washington, DC 20006
Tel: (202)739-9180
Fax: (202)659-5920

Employers
U.S.-Russia Business Council (President)

LAWSON, John M.

110 S. Union St.
Suite 250
Alexandria, VA 22314
Tel: (703)548-0010
Fax: (703)548-0726
Registered: LDA
EMail: jlawson@convg.com

Employers
Convergence Services, Inc. (President)

Clients Represented

On Behalf of Convergence Services, Inc.
Central Virginia Educational Telecommunications Corp.
CSRG Digital LLC
Detroit Public Television
Family Communications, Inc.
JASON Foundation for Education
KCTS
Lancit Media/Junior Net
Public Broadcasting Service
Tequity
WETA
WNVT/WNVC

LAWSON, Karen McGill

1629 K St. NW
Suite 1010
Washington, DC 20006
Tel: (202)466-3311
Fax: (202)466-3435
Registered: LDA
EMail: lawson@civilrights.org

Employers
Leadership Conference on Civil Rights (Policy Research Associate)

LAWSON, Keith

1401 H St. NW
12th Floor
Washington, DC 20005-2148
Tel: (202)326-5832
Fax: (202)326-5839
Registered: LDA

Employers
Investment Co. Institute (Senior Counsel)

LAWSON, Peter H.

1666 K St. NW
Suite 800
Washington, DC 20006
Tel: (202)481-7000
Fax: (202)862-7098

Legislative Assistant to Rep. James P. Moran (D-VA), 1998-2000.

Employers
Arthur Andersen LLP (Director, Government Affairs)

LAWSON, Quentin R.

310 Pennsylvania Ave. SE
Washington, DC 20003
Tel: (202)483-1549
Fax: (202)483-8323
EMail: nabse@naomoi.com

Employers
Nat'l Alliance of Black School Educators (Exec. Director)

LAWSON, Richard C.

1100 17th St. NW
Seventh Floor
Washington, DC 20036
Tel: (202)223-8196
Fax: (202)872-1948
Registered: LDA

Employers
American Academy of Actuaries (Exec. Director)

LAWSON, IV, W. David

800 Connecticut Ave. NW
9th Floor
Washington, DC 20006
Tel: (202)533-2100
Fax: (202)533-2124

Employers
J. P. Morgan Chase & Co. (Managing Director)

LAWTON, Jane

Department of Housing and Community Affairs
Division of Consumer Affairs
100 Maryland Ave., Suite 250
Rockville, MD 20850
Tel: (301)294-7760
Fax: (301)294-7697

Employers
Montgomery, Maryland, Cable Television Office of the County of (Cable Communications Administrator)

LAWTON, Stephen E.

1625 K St. NW
Suite 1100
Washington, DC 20006-1604
Tel: (202)857-0244
Fax: (202)857-0237

Chairman, Advisory Commission on Childhood Vaccines, Department of Health and Human Services, 1989-90. Chief Counsel, House Subcommittee on Health and the Environment, 1971-78.

Employers
Biotechnology Industry Organization (V. President, Regulatory Affairs and General Counsel)

LAXALT, Michelle D.

801 Pennsylvania Ave. NW
Suite 750
Washington, DC 20004
Tel: (202)393-0688
Fax: (202)393-7224
Registered: LDA

Aide to Senator Ted Stevens (R-AK), 1975-80. Director, Legislative Affairs, Agency for International Development, 1980-82. Congressional Affairs, Military and Security Assistance, Department of State, 1982-83.

Employers
The Laxalt Corp. (President)

Clients Represented

On Behalf of The Laxalt Corp.
Academy of Rail Labor Attorneys
Alliance for American Innovation, Inc.
BP Capital, LLC
Motion Picture Ass'n of America
Pickens Fuel Corp.
Unisite, Inc.

LAXALT, Hon. Paul D.

801 Pennsylvania Ave. NW
Suite 750
Washington, DC 20004
Tel: (202)624-0640
Fax: (202)624-0659
Registered: LDA

Member, U.S. Senate (R-NV), 1974-87.

Employers
The Paul Laxalt Group (President)

Clients Represented

On Behalf of The Paul Laxalt Group
AIG Environmental
The American Land Conservancy
American Soc. of Anesthesiologists
Apria Healthcare Group
CSX Corp.
IDT Corp.
Philip Morris Management Corp.
PolyMedica Corp.
Sierra Pacific Resources
Sirius Satellite Radio, Inc.
Yukon Pacific

LAXTON, Christopher E.

1275 K St. NW
Suite 1000
Washington, DC 20005
Tel: (202)789-1890
Fax: (202)789-1899
EMail: apicinfo@apic.org

Employers
Ass'n for Professionals in Infection Control and Epidemiology (Exec. Director)

LAY, Tillman L.

1900 K St. NW
Suite 1150
Washington, DC 20006
Tel: (202)429-5575
Fax: (202)331-1118
Registered: LDA
EMail: lay@millercanfield.com

Law Clerk for Hon. John C. Godbold, Chief Judge, U.S. Court of Appeals for the Fifth Circuit, 1980-81.

Employers
Miller, Canfield, Paddock & Stone, P.L.C. (Senior Counsel)

Clients Represented

On Behalf of Miller, Canfield, Paddock & Stone, P.L.C.
Nat'l League of Cities

LAYMAN, Heather

1133 Connecticut Ave. NW
Fifth Floor
Washington, DC 20036
Tel: (202)457-1110
Fax: (202)457-1130

Employers
Quinn Gillespie & Associates (Public Relations Associate)

LAYMAN, Thomas

2121 K St. NW
Suite 700
Washington, DC 20037

Tel: (202)296-9230
Fax: (202)862-5498
Registered: LDA

Employers
VISA U.S.A., Inc. (Senior V. President)

LAYTON, Elisabeth

555 13th St. NW
Suite 500 West
Washington, DC 20004
EMail: elayton@omm.com

Tel: (202)383-5300
Fax: (202)383-5414
Registered: LDA

Employers
O'Melveny and Myers LLP (Associate)

Clients Represented
On Behalf of O'Melveny and Myers LLP
CIGNA Corp.

LAYTON, Kevin

919 18th St. NW
Suite 800
Washington, DC 20006

Tel: (202)628-4160
Fax: (202)347-5323
Registered: LDA

Employers
Human Rights Campaign Fund (Senior Counsel)

LAZARO, Robin

2000 P St. NW
Suite 310
Washington, DC 20036
EMail: ccn@us.net

Tel: (202)296-4548
Fax: (202)296-4609
Registered: LDA

Employers
Carrying Capacity Network, Inc. (Network Coordinator)

LAZARUS, Maggi A.

801 Pennsylvania Ave. NW
Fifth Floor
Washington, DC 20004

Tel: (202)662-4720
Fax: (202)662-4748

Employers
John T. O'Rourke Law Offices (Associate)

LAZARUS, III, Simon

1001 Pennsylvania Ave. NW
Suite 600
Washington, DC 20004
EMail: slazarus@pgfm.com

Tel: (202)624-7242
Fax: (202)624-7222
Registered: LDA

Associate Director, Domestic Policy Staff, The White House, 1977-81. Legal Assistant to Commissioner Nicholas Johnson, Federal Communications Commission, 1967-68.

Employers
Powell, Goldstein, Frazer & Murphy LLP (Partner)

Clients Represented
On Behalf of Powell, Goldstein, Frazer & Murphy LLP
DuPont
The DuPont Pharmaceutical Co.
Nat'l Ass'n of Public Hospitals and Health Systems
Qualcomm Inc.
Walker Digital Corp.

LE BEAU, Josephine Aiello

655 15th St. NW
Suite 900
Washington, DC 20005-5701
EMail: jalebeau@milchev.com

Tel: (202)626-5800
Fax: (202)628-0858
Registered: FARA

Employers
Miller & Chevalier, Chartered (Associate)

LEACH, David

1775 Pennsylvania Ave. NW
Suite 200
Washington, DC 20006

Tel: (202)862-1000
Fax: (202)862-1093
Registered: LDA

Employers
Dewey Ballantine LLP (Communications Industry Advisor)

Clients Represented
On Behalf of Dewey Ballantine LLP
Nextwave Telecom
SBC Communications Inc.

LEACH, Debra A.

20 S. Quaker Ln.
Suite 230
Alexandria, VA 22314
EMail: dleach@nlba.org

Tel: (703)751-9730
Fax: (703)751-9748
Registered: LDA

Employers
Nat'l Licensed Beverage Ass'n (Exec. Director)

LEACH, Marianne

1625 K St. NW
Suite 500
Washington, DC 20006
EMail: leach@dc.care.org

Tel: (202)223-2277
Fax: (202)296-8695
Registered: LDA

Employers
CARE (Cooperative for Assistance and Relief Everywhere) (Exec. Director, Office of Public Policy and Govt. Relations)

LEADER, Martin R.

2300 N St. NW
Washington, DC 20037-1128
EMail: martin.leader@shawpittman.com

Tel: (202)663-8000
Fax: (202)663-8007
Registered: LDA

Office of Opinions and Review, Federal Communications Commission, 1965-67.

Employers
Shaw Pittman (Partner)

Clients Represented
On Behalf of Shaw Pittman
Glencairn, Ltd.
Sinclair Broadcast Group, Inc.

LEAHY, W. Christopher

1300 Pennsylvania Ave. NW
Suite 860
Washington, DC 20004

Tel: (202)842-5800
Fax: (202)842-8612
Registered: LDA

Employers
Volkswagen of America, Inc. (Manager, Government Relations)

LEAPE, James P.

1250 24th St. NW
Washington, DC 20037

Tel: (202)293-4800
Fax: (202)293-9211

Employers
World Wildlife Fund (V. President)

LEARY, James

1333 New Hampshire Ave. NW
Suite 400
Washington, DC 20036

Tel: (202)887-4000
Fax: (202)887-4288

Employers
Akin, Gump, Strauss, Hauer & Feld, L.L.P. (Exec. Director)

LEARY, Kristen

1001 G St. NW
Suite 900 E
Washington, DC 20001-4545

Tel: (202)393-1010
Fax: (202)393-5510
Registered: LDA

Employers
Podesta/Mattoon (Senior Associate)

Clients Represented
On Behalf of Podesta/Mattoon
Ass'n for Local Telecommunications Services
Chiquita Brands Internat'l, Inc.
MCI WorldCom Corp.
Motion Picture Ass'n of America
Nat'l Ass'n of Broadcasters
Northpoint Technology, Ltd.
Trans World Airlines, Inc.

LEARY, Mary Anne

409 12th St. SW
Suite 310
Washington, DC 20024
EMail: maryanne@womenspolicy.org

Tel: (202)554-2323
Fax: (202)554-2346

Press Secretary to Rep. Constance Morella (R-MD), 1989-98.

Employers
Women's Policy, Inc. (Exec. Director)

LEASON, Chris

1900 K St. NW
Washington, DC 20006

Tel: (202)496-7500
Fax: (202)496-7756

Employers
McKenna & Cuneo, L.L.P. (Partner)

Clients Represented
On Behalf of McKenna & Cuneo, L.L.P.
Nat'l Propane Gas Ass'n

LEASURE, Mark A.

99 Canal Center Plaza
Suite 210
Alexandria, VA 22314

Tel: (703)299-0200
Fax: (703)299-0204
Registered: LDA

Employers
Infectious Diseases Soc. of America, Inc. (Exec. Director)

LEASURE, Jr., William A.

1225 New York Ave. NW
Suite 300
Washington, DC 20005
EMail: tma_bill@ix.netcom.com

Tel: (202)638-7825
Fax: (202)737-3742

Director, Office of Crash Avoidance Research (1988-95) and Chief Heavy Vehicle Research Division (1978-88), National Highway Traffic Safety Administration, and Staff Member, Office of Noise Abatement, Office of the Secretary (1976-78), all at the Department of Transportation. Chief Applied Acoustics Section (1974-76) and Project Manager, Applied Acoustics Sectional (1970-74), both at National Bureau of Standards, Department of Commerce. Project Engineer, Advanced Technical Development Section, Goddard Space Flight Center, National Aeronautics and Space Administration, 1966-70.

Employers
Truck Manufacturers Ass'n (Exec. Director)

LEATH, Audrey T.

One Physics Ellipse
College Park, MD 20740-3843
EMail: atl@aip.org

Tel: (301)209-3094
Fax: (301)209-0843

Employers
American Institute of Physics (Liaison, Government and Institutional Relations)

LEATH, Hon. Marvin

2019 Mayfair McLean Ct.
Falls Church, VA 22043-1764

Tel: (703)536-5573
Fax: (703)536-8163
Registered: LDA

Member, U.S. House of Representatives (D-TX), 1979-90.

Employers
Marvin Leath Associates

Clients Represented
On Behalf of Marvin Leath Associates
Periodical Management Group, Inc.
Textron Inc.

LEATHERWOOD, Gloria Delgado

1401 I St. NW
Suite 1100
Washington, DC 20005

Tel: (202)326-8800
Fax: (202)408-4808
Registered: LDA

Employers
SBC Communications Inc. (Exec. Director, National Constituency Relations)

LEBEDEV, Gregori

1615 H St. NW
Washington, DC 20062-2000

Tel: (202)659-6000
Fax: (202)463-5836

Employers
Chamber of Commerce of the U.S.A. (Exec. V. President and Chief Operating Officer)

LEBLANC, Darian

1341 Connecticut Ave. NW
Third Floor
Washington, DC 20036

Tel: (202)862-3900
Fax: (202)862-5500

Employers
Scribe Consulting & Communications (Associate)

LEBLANC, James L.

601 Pennsylvania Ave. NW
Suite 900
South Bldg.
Washington, DC 20004
Tel: (202)638-6959
Fax: (703)799-2950

Employers
J. LeBlanc Internat'l, LLC (Managing Partner)

Clients Represented
On Behalf of J. LeBlanc Internat'l, LLC
APG Solutions and Technologies
Canada, Government of
CATA (Canadian Advanced Technology Ass'n)
Newbridge Networks
Veritas Communications

LEBLANC, Justin

1901 N. Fort Myer Dr.
Suite 700
Arlington, VA 22209
EMail: jleblanc@nfi.org
Tel: (703)524-8884
Fax: (703)524-4619
Registered: LDA

Employers
Nat'l Fisheries Institute (V. President, Government Relations)

LEBOEUF, Kerley

1605 King St.
Alexandria, VA 22314-2792
EMail: kerley@cstorecentral.com
Tel: (703)684-3600
Fax: (703)836-4564

Employers
Nat'l Ass'n of Convenience Stores (President)

LEBOURGEOIS, Ashton H.

2000 Pennsylvania Ave. NW
Washington, DC 20006
Tel: (202)974-1500
Fax: (202)974-1999
Registered: LDA

Employers
Cleary, Gottlieb, Steen and Hamilton (Legislative Analyst)

LEBOW, Edward M.

1919 Pennsylvania Ave. NW
Suite 610
Washington, DC 20006
Tel: (202)775-2400
Fax: (202)331-7538
Assistant General Counsel (1981) and Acting Chief, Unfair Import Investigations Division, Section 337 (1980), International Trade Commission.

Employers
Miller Thomson Wickens & Lebow LLP

LECHNER, Wendy

100 Daingerfield Rd.
Alexandria, VA 22314
EMail: wlechner@printing.org
Tel: (703)519-8100
Fax: (703)519-6481
Registered: LDA

Employers
Printing Industries of America (Legislative Director)

LECHTMAN, Vladimir

1333 New Hampshire Ave. NW
Suite 400
Washington, DC 20036
Tel: (202)887-4000
Fax: (202)887-4288

Employers
Akin, Gump, Strauss, Hauer & Feld, L.L.P.

Clients Represented
On Behalf of Akin, Gump, Strauss, Hauer & Feld, L.L.P.
Tyumen Oil Company

LECKAR, Stephen C.

1301 Pennsylvania Ave. NW
Suite 500
Washington, DC 20004
EMail: sleckar@butera-andrews.com
Tel: (202)347-6875
Fax: (202)347-6876
Trial Attorney, Commoditites Futures Trading Commission, 1976-78. Legislative Assistant to Senator Herman Talmadge (D-GA), 1974-75.

Employers
Butera & Andrews (Partner)

Clients Represented
On Behalf of Butera & Andrews
British Nuclear Fuels plc

LECKER, Barbara A.

5101 River Rd.
Suite 108
Bethesda, MD 20816
Tel: (301)656-1494
Fax: (301)656-7539
Registered: LDA

Employers
Nat'l Ass'n of Beverage Retailers (Manager, Government Affairs)

LECLAIR, Larry

1850 M St. NW
Suite 1095
Washington, DC 20036
Tel: (202)682-1163
Fax: (202)682-1022
Registered: LDA

Employers
American Tort Reform Ass'n (Director, Legislation)

LECOS, William D.

1129 20th St. NW
Suite 200
Washington, DC 20036
Tel: (202)857-5900
Fax: (202)223-2648

Employers
Greater Washington Board of Trade (Senior V. President, Advocacy Group)

LEDDY, Mark

2000 Pennsylvania Ave. NW
Washington, DC 20006
Tel: (202)974-1500
Fax: (202)974-1999
Registered: LDA
Deputy Assistant Attorney General (1984-86), Deputy Director of Operations (1979-84), Section Chief (1977-79), and Trial Attorney (1972-77), Department of Justice.

Employers
Cleary, Gottlieb, Steen and Hamilton (Partner)

Clients Represented
On Behalf of Cleary, Gottlieb, Steen and Hamilton
Asahi Glass Co.

LEDEEN, Michael A.

1150 17th St. NW
Washington, DC 20036
EMail: mledeen@aei.org
Tel: (202)862-5800
Fax: (202)862-7177

Employers
American Enterprise Institute for Public Policy Research (Resident Scholar)

LEDERER, Gerry

1201 New York Ave. NW
Suite 300
Washington, DC 20005
EMail: glederer@boma.org
Tel: (202)326-6350
Fax: (202)371-0181

Employers
Building Owners and Managers Ass'n Internat'l (Exec. Director, Government and Industry Affairs)

LEDERER, Jr., Robert F.

8100 Oak St.
Dunn Loring, VA 22027
EMail: lederer@pestworld.org
Tel: (703)573-8330
Fax: (703)573-4116

Employers
Nat'l Pest Control Ass'n (Exec. V. President)

LEDERMAN, Gordon N.

555 12th St. NW
Washington, DC 20004-1206
EMail: Gordon_Lederman@aporter.com
Tel: (202)942-5000
Fax: (202)942-5999
Registered: LDA

Employers
Arnold & Porter (Associate)

LEDFORD, Michael

1233 20th St. NW
Suite 610
Washington, DC 20036
Tel: (202)466-4111
Fax: (202)466-4123

Employers
Lewis-Burke Associates

Clients Represented
On Behalf of Lewis-Burke Associates
Associated Universities Inc.
Virginia Commonwealth University

LEDIG, Robert H.

1001 Pennsylvania Ave. NW
Suite 800
Washington, DC 20004-2505
EMail: robert_legig@ffhsj.com
Tel: (202)639-7000
Fax: (202)639-7008

Employers
Fried, Frank, Harris, Shriver & Jacobson (Partner)

LEDOUX, Marque I.

300 Maryland Ave. NE
Washington, DC 20002
Tel: (202)546-1631
Fax: (202)546-3309
Registered: LDA

Employers
FedEx Corp. (Senior Federal Affairs Representative)

LEDUC, David

1730 M St. NW
Suite 700
Washington, DC 20036-4510
EMail: dleduc@siia.net
Tel: (202)452-1600
Fax: (202)223-8756
Registered: LDA

Employers
Software & Information Industry Ass'n (SIIA) (Manager, Public Policy)

LEE, Anna

1201 L St. NW
Washington, DC 20005-4014
Tel: (202)842-4444
Fax: (202)842-3860

Employers
American Health Care Ass'n (PAC Administrator)

LEE, Beverlee A.

910 17th St. NW
Fifth Floor
Washington, DC 20006
Tel: (202)466-3800
Fax: (202)466-3801

Employers
American Legislative Exchange Council (Director, Finance and Administration)

LEE, David B.

1101 30th St. NW
Suite 200
Washington, DC 20007
Tel: (202)293-4584
Fax: (202)293-4588
Registered: LDA
Chief of Staff and Counsel to Rep. K. Gunn McKay (D-UT), 1976-81.

Employers
Lee & Smith P.C. (President)

Clients Represented
On Behalf of Lee & Smith P.C.
Environmental Land Technology Ltd.
North Dakota State University
Space Dynamics Laboratory
Utah State University

LEE, Eileen C.

1850 M St. NW
Suite 540
Washington, DC 20036
Tel: (202)974-2300
Fax: (202)775-0112
Registered: LDA
Former Staff Director for the Environmental Subcommittee of the Committee on Science, Space, and Technology, U.S. House of Representatives.

Employers
Nat'l Multi-Housing Council (V. President, Environment)

LEE, Eric

1301 K Street NW
Suite 325
Washington, DC 20005
EMail: lee@cix.org
Tel: (703)709-8200
Fax: (703)709-5249

Employers
Commercial Internet Exchange Ass'n (Director, Public Policy)

LEE, F. Gordon

1666 K St. NW
Suite 500
Washington, DC 20006-2803
Tel: (202)887-1400
Fax: (202)466-2198
Registered: LDA, FARA

Employers
O'Connor & Hannan, L.L.P. (Partner)

Clients Represented
On Behalf of O'Connor & Hannan, L.L.P.
University of Akron

LEE, Franklin M.

300 I St. NE
Suite 400
Washington, DC 20002
Tel: (202)289-1700
Fax: (202)289-1701

Employers
Minority Business Enterprise Legal Defense and Education Fund (Chief Counsel)

LEE, Gayle

1111 N. Fairfax St.
Alexandria, VA 22314
Tel: (703)684-2782
Fax: (703)684-7343
Registered: LDA

Employers
American Physical Therapy Ass'n (Assistant Director, Regulatory Affairs)

LEE, Jason

2111 Wilson Blvd.
Eighth Floor
Arlington, VA 22201-3058
Tel: (703)841-0626
Fax: (703)243-2874

Employers
Alcalde & Fay (Associate)

Clients Represented
On Behalf of Alcalde & Fay
Golden Gate Bridge Highway and Transportation District
Sonoma County Water Agency
Sonoma, California, County of

LEE, Jee Hang

2120 L St. NW
Suite 400
Washington, DC 20037
Tel: (202)478-6301
Fax: (202)478-6171

Employers
Leslie Harris & Associates (Senior Legislative Associate)

Clients Represented
On Behalf of Leslie Harris & Associates
Consortium for School Networking
EdLinc
Internat'l Soc. for Technology in Education

LEE, Jennifer

2021 Massachusetts Ave. NW
Washington, DC 20036
Tel: (202)232-9033
Fax: (202)232-9044

Employers
American Academy of Family Physicians (Government Relations Analyst)

LEE, Jonathan

1900 M St. NW
Suite 800
Washington, DC 20036-3508
Tel: (202)296-6650
Fax: (202)296-7585

Employers
Competitive Telecommunications Ass'n (COMPTEL) (V. President, Regulatory Affairs)

LEE, Judith A.

1050 Connecticut Ave. NW
Washington, DC 20036-5306
Tel: (202)955-8500
Fax: (202)467-0539
Registered: LDA
EMail: jalee@gdclaw.com

Employers
Gibson, Dunn & Crutcher LLP (Partner)

Clients Represented
On Behalf of Gibson, Dunn & Crutcher LLP
U.S. Business Alliance for Customs Modernization

LEE, Kenneth G.

1200 G St. NW
Suite 800
Washington, DC 20005
Tel: (202)434-8968
Fax: (202)737-5822
Registered: LDA

Employers
Stites & Harbison (Of Counsel)

Clients Represented
On Behalf of Stites & Harbison
Family Place
Montrose, Colorado, City of
Ogden, Utah, City of
Western Kentucky University

LEE, Ladonna Y.

900 Second St. NE
Suite 200
Washington, DC 20002
EMail: ladonna@temc.com
Tel: (202)842-4100
Fax: (202)842-4442

Employers
The Eddie Mahe Company (President)

Clients Represented
On Behalf of The Eddie Mahe Company
American Insurance Ass'n

LEE, III, Lansing B.

2550 M St. NW
Washington, DC 20037-1350
Tel: (202)457-6000
Fax: (202)457-6315
Registered: LDA
EMail: llee@pattonboggs.com

Employers
Patton Boggs, LLP (Of Counsel)

Clients Represented
On Behalf of Patton Boggs, LLP
African Coalition for Trade, Inc.
Augusta-Richmond, Georgia, County of
Discovery Place, Inc. (Charlotte Science Museum)
The Limited Inc.
Mars, Inc.
Ventura County Citizens Against Radar Emissions (VCCARE)

LEE, Richard

1220 L St. NW
Suite 410
Washington, DC 20005
Tel: (202)371-9151
Fax: (202)842-4966

Employers
Snavely, King, Majoros, O'Connor and Lee, Inc. (V. President)

LEE, Susan G.

555 12th St. NW
Washington, DC 20004-1206
EMail: Susan_Lee@aporter.com
Tel: (202)942-5000
Fax: (202)942-5999
Chief of Staff, Commodity Futures Trading Commission, 1996-99.

Employers
Arnold & Porter (Partner)

LEE, Thea

815 16th St. NW
Washington, DC 20006
Tel: (202)637-5000
Fax: (202)637-5058

Employers
AFL-CIO (American Federation of Labor and Congress of Industrial Organizations) (Assistant Director, Public Policy)

LEE, William J.

1100 Wilson Blvd.
Suite 1500
Arlington, VA 22209
EMail: william_j_lee@raytheon.com
Tel: (703)841-5730
Fax: (703)841-5792
Registered: LDA

Employers
Raytheon Co. (Director, Congressional Relations)

LEE, Yoon-Young

2445 M St. NW
Washington, DC 20037-1420
EMail: ylee@wilmer.com
Tel: (202)663-6000
Fax: (202)663-6363

Employers
Wilmer, Cutler & Pickering (Partner)

LEEPER, John E.

1627 K St. NW
Suite 700
Washington, DC 20006
Tel: (202)452-1252
Ext: 19
Fax: (202)452-0118
Registered: LDA

Employers
Smokeless Tobacco Council (Senior Director, Government Relations)

LEETH, Timothy B.

1101 Vermont Ave. NW
12th Floor
Washington, DC 20005-3583
Tel: (202)789-7411
Fax: (202)789-7485
Registered: LDA

Employers
American Medical Ass'n (Assistant Director, Congressional Affairs)

LEFEVRE, Jennifer

900 Spring St.
Silver Spring, MD 20910
Tel: (301)587-1400
Fax: (301)585-4219
Registered: LDA
EMail: jlefevre@nrmca.org

Employers
Nat'l Ready Mixed Concrete Ass'n (Manager, Government Relations)

LEFEVRE, Jessica S.

908 King St.
Suite 200
Alexandria, VA 22314
Tel: (703)836-3515
Fax: (703)548-3181
Registered: LDA

Employers
Self-employed as an independent consultant.

Clients Represented
As an independent consultant
Alaska Eskimo Whaling Commission

LEFKIN, Peter A.

1101 Connecticut Ave. NW
Suite 950
Washington, DC 20036
Tel: (202)785-3575
Ext: 14
Fax: (202)785-3023
Registered: LDA
EMail: plefkin@ffic.com

Employers
Fireman's Fund Insurance Cos. (Senior V. President, Government and Industry Affairs)

LEFRANCOIS, Ronald J.

1001 Pennsylvania Ave. NW
Suite 580 North
Washington, DC 20004-2505
Tel: (202)783-1366
Fax: (202)393-2769
Registered: LDA

Employers
New York Life Insurance Co. (V. President, Government Affairs)

LEFTWICH, Bruce

Ten G St. NE
Suite 750
Washington, DC 20002-4213
EMail: BruceL@career.org
Tel: (202)336-6700
Fax: (202)336-6828
Registered: LDA

Employers
Career College Ass'n (V. President, Government Relations)

LEFTWICH, Gail

1600 Wilson Blvd.
Suite 902
Arlington, VA 22209
Tel: (703)908-9700
Fax: (703)908-9706

Employers
Federation of State Humanities Councils (President)

LEGATO, Carmen D.

601 13th St. NW
Suite 600 South
Washington, DC 20005
EMail: legatca@washdc.whitecase.com
Tel: (202)626-3600
Fax: (202)639-9355

Employers
White & Case LLP (Partner)

LEGENDRE, Richard

499 S. Capitol St. SW
Suite 600
Washington, DC 20003
Tel: (202)289-9881
Fax: (202)289-9877

Employers
The Livingston Group, LLC (Principal)

Clients Represented

On Behalf of The Livingston Group, LLC
ACS Government Solutions Group
Baton Rouge, Louisiana, City of
Boys Town USA
Great Western Cellular Partnership
Illinois Department of Human Services
New Orleans, Louisiana, Port of
Stewart Enterprises, Inc.

LEGER, Elizabeth E.

412 First St. SE
Suite 300
Washington, DC 20003
Tel: (202)863-7000
Fax: (202)863-7015

Employers
Independent Insurance Agents of America, Inc. (Assistant V. President, Political Affairs)

LEGRANDE, David E.

501 Third St. NW
Washington, DC 20001-2797
Tel: (202)434-1100
Fax: (202)434-1318

Employers
Communications Workers of America (Director, Occupational Safety and Health)

LEGRO, Stanley W.

901 15th St. NW
Suite 700
Washington, DC 20005-2301
Tel: (202)371-6000
Fax: (202)371-6279
Registered: LDA
EMail: swlegro@verner.com
Assistant Administrator for Enforcement, Environmental Protection Agency, 1975-77. Served in the U.S. Marine Corps, 1959-63.

Employers
Verner, Liipfert, Bernhard, McPherson and Hand, Chartered (Of Counsel)

Clients Represented

On Behalf of Verner, Liipfert, Bernhard, McPherson and Hand, Chartered
Chlorine Chemistry Council

LEHMAN, Christopher M.

1800 N. Kent St.
Suite 907
Arlington, VA 22209
Tel: (703)524-0026
Fax: (703)524-1005
Registered: LDA
EMail: CLehman@commonwealthconsulting.com
Special Assistant to the President for National Security Affairs, The White House, 1983-85; Director of Strategic Nuclear Policy, Department of State, 1981-83; Staff, U.S. Senate, 1976-81.

Employers
Commonwealth Consulting Corp. (President)

Clients Represented

On Behalf of Commonwealth Consulting Corp.
Alpha Technologies Group Inc.
Atlantic Marine Holding Co.
Delex Systems, Inc.
IAI Internat'l
Lubbock, Texas, City of
Massa Products Corp.
Monroe, Florida, County of
Newport News Shipbuilding Inc.
NoFire Technologies, Inc.

LEHMAN, David E.

1212 New York Ave. NW
Suite 350
Washington, DC 20005
Tel: (202)842-5077
Fax: (202)842-5010
Chief of Staff (1998-2000) and Legislative Counsel (1997-98) to Rep. Bob Goodlatte (R-VA). Former Legislative Counsel to Rep. Lamar Smith (R-TX).

Employers
Hall, Green, Rupli, LLC (Associate)

LEHMAN, Dirksen

1600 Pennsylvania Ave. NW
107 E. Wing
Washington, DC 20500
Tel: (202)456-6493
Fax: (202)456-2604

Employers
Executive Office of the President - The White House (Special Assistant to the President for Legislative Affairs, Senate Liaison Office)

LEHMAN, Ph.D., Gregg

1015 18th St. NW
Suite 730
Washington, DC 20036
EMail: gl1nbch@aol.com
Tel: (202)775-9300
Fax: (202)775-1569

Employers
Nat'l Business Coalition on Health (President and Chief Exec. Officer)

LEHMAN, Hon. Richard H.

1341 G St. NW
Suite 200
Washington, DC 20005
Tel: (202)737-3655
Fax: (202)347-5941
Registered: LDA
Member, U.S. House of Representatives (D-CA), 1983-94.

Employers
Sacramento-Potomac Consulting, Inc. (President)

Clients Represented

On Behalf of Sacramento-Potomac Consulting, Inc.
Abide Internat'l, Inc.
California State University Fresno
Community Hospitals of Central California
Federal Home Loan Mortgage Corp. (Freddie Mac)
Mandolay Resort Group

LEHMAN, Sherri

1701 Pennsylvania Ave. NW
Suite 950
Washington, DC 20006
EMail: slehman@corn.org
Tel: (202)331-1634
Fax: (202)331-2054
Registered: LDA

Employers
Corn Refiners Ass'n, Inc. (Director, Congressional Affairs)

LEHMAN, Trent

1130 Connecticut Ave. NW
Suite 300
Washington, DC 20036
Tel: (202)331-8500
Fax: (202)331-1598

Employers
The Ferguson Group, LLC (Senior Associate)

Clients Represented

On Behalf of The Ferguson Group, LLC
Lake, Illinois, County of
Sierra Madre, California, City of

LEHN, Alfred M.

127 S. Fairfax St.
Suite 137
Alexandria, VA 22314
Tel: (703)495-0710
Fax: (703)495-9124
Registered: LDA, FARA
Former National Security Advisor to Senate Minority Leader, Senator Robert Dole (R-KS).

Employers
Symms, Lehn & Associates, Inc. (Principal)

Clients Represented

On Behalf of Symms, Lehn & Associates, Inc.
Ass'n of American Railroads

LEHNER, Thomas J.

919 18th St. NW
Suite 300
Washington, DC 20006
Tel: (202)296-5544
Fax: (202)223-0321
Registered: LDA
Former Chief of Staff to Senator Charles S. Robb (D-VA).

Employers
American Financial Services Ass'n (Exec. V. President, Government Affairs)

LEHNERD, Lori

8401 Colesville Rd.
Suite 505
Silver Spring, MD 20910
EMail: llehnerd@nasao.org
Tel: (301)588-0587
Fax: (301)585-1803

Employers
Nat'l Ass'n of State Aviation Officials (V. President)

LEHNHARD, Mary Nell

1310 G St. NW
12th Floor
Washington, DC 20005
Tel: (202)626-4780
Fax: (202)626-4833
Registered: LDA

Employers
Blue Cross Blue Shield Ass'n (Senior V. President, Office of Policy and Representation)

LEHRHOFF, Michael B.

1227 25th St. NW
Suite 700
Washington, DC 20037
Tel: (202)861-0900
Fax: (202)296-2882
Registered: LDA

Employers
Epstein Becker & Green, P.C.

Clients Represented

On Behalf of Epstein Becker & Green, P.C.
Coalition on Accessibility

LEHRMAN, Louis

412 First St. SE
Suite 100
Washington, DC 20003
Tel: (202)484-4884
Fax: (202)484-0109
Registered: LDA
EMail: llehrman@dutkogroup.com
Legislative Associate to Rep. J. Alex McMillan (R-NC), 1991-94.

Employers
The Dutko Group, Inc. (V. President)

Clients Represented

On Behalf of The Dutko Group, Inc.
Alcatel USA
ASCENT (Ass'n of Community Enterprises)
Ass'n for Competitive Technology
AT&T
AT&T Wireless Services, Inc.
Cable & Wireless, Inc.
Carolina PCS
EXCEL Communications Inc.
SkyBridge, LLC
SpaceData Internat'l
VeriSign/Network Solutions, Inc.
Winstar Communications, Inc.
XO Communications

LEHRMAN, Margie

1050 31st St. NW
Washington, DC 20007
Tel: (202)965-3500
Fax: (202)342-5484

Employers
Ass'n of Trial Lawyers of America (Senior Director, Legal Knowledge & Professional Development)

LEIBBRAND, Jane

2010 Massachusetts Ave. NW
Suite 500
Washington, DC 20036-1023
EMail: jane@ncate.org
Tel: (202)466-7496
Fax: (202)296-6620

Employers
Nat'l Council for Accreditation of Teacher Education (V. President, Communications)

LEIBENLUFT, Robert

555 13th St. NW
Washington, DC 20004-1109
Tel: (202)637-5789
Fax: (202)637-5910
Registered: LDA
EMail: rfleibenluft@hhlaw.com

Employers
Hogan & Hartson L.L.P. (Partner)

Clients Represented

On Behalf of Hogan & Hartson L.L.P.
Antitrust Coalition for Consumer Choice in Health Care

LEIBENSPERGER, Jr., Thomas

2000 L St. NW
Suite 300
Washington, DC 20036-0646
Tel: (202)835-8800
Fax: (202)835-8879
Registered: LDA

Employers
Ketchum (Account Supervisor)

LEIBIG, Michael

1025 Connecticut Ave. NW
Suite 712
Washington, DC 20036

Tel: (202)857-5000
Fax: (202)223-8417

Employers

Zwerdling, Paul, Leibig, Kahn, Thompson & Wolly, P.C. (General Counsel)

Clients Represented

On Behalf of Zwerdling, Paul, Leibig, Kahn, Thompson & Wolly, P.C.

Internat'l Union of Police Ass'ns

LEIBMAN, Sara F.

701 Pennsylvania Ave. NW
Suite 900
Washington, DC 20004-2608

Tel: (202)434-7300
Fax: (202)434-7400
Registered: LDA

EMail: sleibman@mintz.com

Former Special Counsel, Office of the General Counsel, Federal Communications Commission.

Employers

Mintz, Levin, Cohn, Ferris, Glovsky and Popeo, P.C. (Partner)

Clients Represented

On Behalf of Mintz, Levin, Cohn, Ferris, Glovsky and Popeo, P.C.

AT&T Wireless Services, Inc.

LEIBOLD, Peter M.

1025 Connecticut Ave. NW
Suite 600
Washington, DC 20036

Tel: (202)833-1100
Fax: (202)833-1105

Chief of Staff and Legislative Director to Sen. John C. Danforth (R-MO), 1993-94. Judicial Clerk to Judge Wilfred Feinberg, U.S. Court of Appeals, Second Circuit, 1988-89.

Employers

American Health Lawyers Ass'n (Exec. V. President)
Nat'l Health Lawyers Ass'n (Exec. V. President and Chief Exec. Officer)

LEIBOWITZ, Arnold H.

1875 I St. NW
12th Floor
Washington, DC 20006

Tel: (202)824-8183
Fax: (202)296-9246
Registered: LDA

Employers

Self-employed as an independent consultant.

Clients Represented

As an independent consultant

Hebrew Immigrant Aid Soc.

LEIBOWITZ, Lewis E.

555 13th St. NW
Washington, DC 20004-1109

Tel: (202)637-5638
Fax: (202)637-5910
Registered: LDA, FARA

EMail: leleibowitz@hhlaw.com

Law Clerk to Senior Judge Roszel C. Thomsen, U.S. District Court for the District of Maryland, 1975-76.

Employers

Hogan & Hartson L.L.P. (Partner)

Clients Represented

On Behalf of Hogan & Hartson L.L.P.

Brother Internat'l Co.
Michelin North America

LEIDL, Richard J.

701 Pennsylvania Ave. NW
Suite 800
Washington, DC 20004

Tel: (202)508-4130
Fax: (202)508-4321
Registered: LDA

EMail: rleidl@thelenreid.com

Employers

Thelen Reid & Priest LLP (Partner)

Clients Represented

On Behalf of Thelen Reid & Priest LLP

Abilene Industrial Foundation, Inc.
Airport Minority Advisory Council
Airports Council Internat'l - North America
Capital Region Airport Commission
Corpus Christi Port Authority
Denver Internat'l Airport
Denver, Colorado, City of
DRS Precision Echo Inc.
L.B. Foster Co.
The Jewelers' Security Alliance
Metro Machine Corp. of Virginia
Metro Machine of Pennsylvania, Inc.
Metroplex Corp.
Philadelphia Industrial Development Corp.
Philadelphia, Pennsylvania, City of
Power Paragon Inc.
SPD Technologies
Washington Soccer Partners

LEIFER, Elihu I.

1125 15th St. NW
Suite 801
Washington, DC 20005

Tel: (202)785-9300
Fax: (202)775-1950

Attorney, Civil Rights Division, Department of Justice, 1964-67.

Employers

Sherman, Dunn, Cohen, Leifer & Yellig, P.C. (Partner)

LEIFERT, Harvey

2000 Florida Ave. NW
Washington, DC 20009

Tel: (202)777-7507
Fax: (202)328-0566

EMail: hleifert@agu.org

Employers

American Geophysical Union (Public Information Manager)

LEIGHT, Elizabeth Ysla

Two Wisconsin Circle
Suite 670
Chevy Chase, MD 20815-7003

Tel: (301)718-7722
Fax: (301)718-9440

Serves as Director of Government Relations of the Soc. of Professional Benefit Administrators.

Employers

Hunt Management Systems (Director, Government Relations)
Soc. of Professional Benefit Administrators (Director, Government Relations)

Clients Represented

On Behalf of Hunt Management Systems

Soc. of Professional Benefit Administrators

LEIGHTON, Richard J.

1001 G St. NW
Suite 500 West
Washington, DC 20001

Tel: (202)434-4100
Fax: (202)434-4646

EMail: leighton@khlaw.com

Consultant, Subcommittee on Regulatory Reform, Senate Judiciary Committee, 1980.

Employers

Keller and Heckman LLP (Partner)

Clients Represented

On Behalf of Keller and Heckman LLP

Leprino Foods Co.

LEIKEN, Brian

1320 19th St. NW
Suite M-1
Washington, DC 20036

Tel: (202)293-0222
Fax: (202)293-0202

Employers

Public Campaign (Sr. Outreach and Legislative Associate)

LEIMAN, Karmi

5108 34th St. NW
Washington, DC 20008

Tel: (202)296-4790
Fax: (202)296-4791

EMail: DLTrade@aol.com

International Trade Analyst, US Department of Commerce, International Trade Administration, 1988-91.

Employers

Davis & Leiman, P.C. (Consultant, International Trade)

LEITCH, David G.

555 13th St. NW
Washington, DC 20004-1109

Tel: (202)637-5822
Fax: (202)637-5910

EMail: dgleitch@hhlaw.com

Deputy Assistant Attorney General (1992-93) and Senior Counsel (1990-92), Office of Legal Counsel, Department of Justice. Law Clerk to Chief Justice William Rehnquist, U.S. Supreme Court, 1986-87. Law Clerk to Judge J. Harvie Wilkinson, III, U.S. Court of Appeals, Fourth Circuit, 1985-86.

Employers

Hogan & Hartson L.L.P. (Partner)

LEITER, Jeffrey L.

3050 K St. NW
Washington, DC 20007

Tel: (202)342-8490
Fax: (202)342-8451
Registered: LDA

EMail: jleiter@colliershannon.com

Employers

Collier Shannon Scott, PLLC (Member)

Clients Represented

On Behalf of Collier Shannon Scott, PLLC

AAAE-ACI
Independent Lubricant Manufacturers Ass'n
Nat'l Ass'n of Convenience Stores
Soc. of Independent Gasoline Marketers of America

LEIVE, David M.

555 11th St. NW
Suite 1000
Washington, DC 20004

Tel: (202)637-2200
Fax: (202)637-2201

Employers

Latham & Watkins (Senior Communications Counsel)

LEMA, Joseph E.

1130 17th St. NW
Washington, DC 20036-4677

Tel: (202)463-2629
Fax: (202)463-9799
Registered: LDA

EMail: jlema@nma.org

Employers

Nat'l Mining Ass'n (V. President, Manufacturers and Services Division)

LEMASTER, Lynn

701 Pennsylvania Ave. NW
Washington, DC 20004-2696

Tel: (202)508-5475
Fax: (202)508-5786
Registered: LDA

Employers

Edison Electric Institute (Senior V. President, Policy, Issue Management and Internal Operations)

LEMIEUX, Jeff

600 Pennsylvania Ave. SE
Suite 400
Washington, DC 20003

Tel: (202)547-0001
Fax: (202)544-5014

Employers

Progressive Policy Institute (Director, Economic Studies)

LEMKE, Randal

11242 Waples Mill Rd.
Suite 200
Fairfax, VA 22030

Tel: (703)273-7200
Fax: (703)278-8082

Employers

Internat'l Communications Industries Ass'n (ICIA) (Exec. V. President)

LEMOINE, Barbara J.

820 First St. NE
Suite 400
Washington, DC 20002

Tel: (202)408-8169
Fax: (202)289-7880
Registered: LDA

EMail: blemoine@afb.net

Employers

American Foundation for the Blind - Governmental Relations Group (Legislative Assistant)

LEMON, Chrys D.

1155 15th St. NW
Suite 1101
Washington, DC 20005
Tel: (202)659-3900
Fax: (202)659-5763
Registered: LDA

Staff Officer, Office of the Assistant Secretary, Force Management and Personnel, Department of Defense, 1986-88.

Employers
McIntyre Law Firm, PLLC (Attorney)

Clients Represented

On Behalf of McIntyre Law Firm, PLLC
Ass'n of Banks in Insurance
Community Financial Services Ass'n
Internat'l Ass'n for Financial Planning
MemberWorks, Inc.
Risk and Insurance Management Soc., Inc. (RIMS)

LEMOV, Michael R.

1400 L St. NW
Washington, DC 20005-3502
Tel: (202)371-5749
Fax: (202)371-5950
Registered: LDA
EMail: mlemov@winston.com

Former Chairman, Federal Trade Commission Transition Team for the Clinton Administration. Chief Counsel, Subcommittee on Oversight and Investigations (1975-77) and Special Counsel, Subcommittee on Commerce and Finance (1971-75), House Committee on Commerce. Counsel, House Committee on Banking and Currency and Staff Director, Subcommittee on Foundations, House Committee on Small Business, 1970-71. General Counsel, National Commission on Product Safety, 1968-70. Trial Attorney, Department of Justice, 1966-68.

Employers
Winston & Strawn (Partner, Legislative and Regulatory Practice)

LEMUNYON, Glenn B.

233 Pennsylvania Ave. SE
Suite 300
Washington, DC 20003
Tel: (202)547-9050
Fax: (202)547-8991
Registered: LDA
EMail: glenn@tatelemunyon.com

Floor/Appropriations Aide to House Majority Whip, Rep. Tom DeLay (R-TX), 1985-96.

Employers
Tate-LeMunyon, LLC (Principal)

Clients Represented

On Behalf of Tate-LeMunyon, LLC
Alliance Air Services
Brownsville, Texas, Port of
Fannie Mae
Lockheed Martin Corp.
North American Superhighway Coalition
Orange, California, County of

LENARD, Thomas

1301 K St. NW
Suite 550E
Washington, DC 20005
Tel: (202)289-8928
Fax: (202)289-6079
EMail: tlenard@pff.org

Employers
The Progress Freedom Foundation (Senior Fellow and Director, Regulatory Studies)

LENDSEY, Jacquelyn L.

1900 N. Beauregard St.
Suite 103
Alexandria, VA 22311
Tel: (703)671-0500
Fax: (703)671-4489
EMail: jlendsey@wics.org

Employers
Women in Community Service (President/CEO)

LENEHAN, III, Daniel W.

1710 Rhode Island Ave. NW
Tenth Floor
Washington, DC 20036
Tel: (202)973-2990
Fax: (202)293-3307
EMail: ndirish@rofgw.com

Employers
Rodriguez O'Donnell Fuerst Gonzalez & Williams (Attorney-at-Law)

LENETT, Michael G.

317 Massachusetts Ave. NE
Suite 300
Washington, DC 20002
Tel: (202)789-3960
Fax: (202)789-1813
Registered: LDA

Democratic Counsel (1995-96) and Counsel, Subcommittee on Antitrust, Monopolies, and Business Rights (1993-95), Senate Judiciary Committee. Special Counsel (1993), Senior Counsel (1991-93), and Staff Attorney (1990-91), Office of the General Counsel, Securities and Exchange Commission.

Employers
The Cuneo Law Group, P.C.

Clients Represented

On Behalf of The Cuneo Law Group, P.C.
Nat'l Ass'n of Securities and Commercial Law Attorneys
Taxpayers Against Fraud, The False Claims Legal Center

LENFEST, Lauren

1667 K St. NW
Suite 640
Washington, DC 20006-1605
Tel: (202)721-4814
Fax: (202)467-4250
Registered: LDA
EMail: lauren.lenfest@oracle.com

Employers
Oracle Corp. (V. President, International Trade and Development)

LENHOFF, Donna R.

1875 Connecticut Ave. NW
Suite 710
Washington, DC 20009
Tel: (202)986-2600
Fax: (202)986-2539

Employers
Nat'l Partnership for Women and Families (V. President and General Counsel)

LENNAN, Anne C.

Two Wisconsin Circle
Suite 670
Chevy Chase, MD 20815-7003
Tel: (301)718-7722
Fax: (301)718-9440

Employers
Hunt Management Systems (V. President and Director of Federal Affairs)
Soc. of Professional Benefit Administrators (V. President and Director of Federal Affairs)

Clients Represented

On Behalf of Hunt Management Systems
Soc. of Professional Benefit Administrators

LENNOX, Jr., Maj. Gen. William J.

The Pentagon
Room 2C631
Washington, DC 20310-1600
Tel: (703)697-6767
Fax: (703)614-7599

Employers
Department of Army (Chief, Legislative Liaison)

LENNY, Peter L.

2600 Virginia Ave. NW
Suite 610
Washington, DC 20037
Tel: (202)337-6644
Fax: (202)337-2421
Registered: FARA

Employers
Louisiana Energy Services (President)
Urenco, Inc. (President/Chief Exec. Officer/Director)

LENOIR, Monique

1101 14th St. NW
11th Floor
Washington, DC 20005-5601
Tel: (202)682-1510
Fax: (202)682-1535
EMail: mlenoir@villagebanking.org

Employers
FINCA Internat'l Inc., The Foundation for Internat'l Community Assistance (Communications Coordinator)

LENT, III, Norman F.

915 15th St. NW
Suite 800
Washington, DC 20005
Tel: (202)347-3030
Fax: (202)347-3133
Registered: LDA
EMail: nlent3@lentdc.com

Former Legislative Assistant for Senator Connie Mack (R-FL).

Employers
Lent Scrivner & Roth LLC (Partner)

Clients Represented

On Behalf of Lent Scrivner & Roth LLC
American Soc. of Anesthesiologists
AOL Time Warner
Burlington Northern Santa Fe Railway
Cellular Telecommunications and Internet Ass'n
Chevron, U.S.A.
Futurewave General Partners, L.P.
Great Western Cellular Partnership
Iroquois Gas Transmission System
KeySpan Energy
Bernard L. Madoff Investment Securities
Monroe Telephone Services, L.P.
Nassau University Medical Center
Nat'l Center for Tobacco-Free Kids
New Skies Satellites N.V.
Pfizer, Inc.

LENT, Hon. Norman F.

915 15th St. NW
Suite 800
Washington, DC 20005
Tel: (202)347-3030
Fax: (202)347-3133
Registered: LDA
EMail: nlent@lentdc.com

Member, U.S. House of Representatives (R-NY), 1971-93.

Employers
Lent Scrivner & Roth LLC (Senior Partner)

Clients Represented

On Behalf of Lent Scrivner & Roth LLC
American Soc. of Anesthesiologists
AOL Time Warner
Burlington Northern Santa Fe Railway
Cellular Telecommunications and Internet Ass'n
Chevron, U.S.A.
Futurewave General Partners, L.P.
Great Western Cellular Partnership
Iroquois Gas Transmission System
KeySpan Energy
Bernard L. Madoff Investment Securities
Monroe Telephone Services, L.P.
Nassau University Medical Center
Nat'l Center for Tobacco-Free Kids
New Skies Satellites N.V.
Pfizer, Inc.

LENT, Susan H.

1333 New Hampshire Ave. NW
Suite 400
Washington, DC 20036
Tel: (202)887-4000
Fax: (202)887-4288
Registered: LDA

Counsel, Subcommittee on Surface Transportation, Committee on Transportation and Infrastructure, 1996-98.

Employers
Akin, Gump, Strauss, Hauer & Feld, L.L.P. (Senior Counsel)

Clients Represented

On Behalf of Akin, Gump, Strauss, Hauer & Feld, L.L.P.
Bridgestone/Firestone, Inc.
Gila River Indian Community
Harris, Beach & Wilcox
Frederic R. Harris, Inc.
Harris, Texas, Metropolitan Transit Authority of
Howland Hook Container Terminal Inc.
New York Bus Service
Niagara Frontier Transportation Authority
Pfizer, Inc.
San Gabriel Basin Water Quality Authority

LENZ, Edward A.

277 S. Washington St.
Suite 200
Alexandria, VA 22314
Tel: (703)253-2035
Fax: (703)253-2053
Registered: LDA
EMail: elenz@staffingtoday.net

Employers
American Staffing Ass'n (Senior V. President, Public Affairs and General Counsel)

LEON, Mary Reed

1201 F St. NW
Suite 200
Washington, DC 20004
Tel: (202)554-9000
Fax: (202)484-1566
Registered: LDA

Employers
Nat'l Federation of Independent Business (Manager, Legislative Affairs/House)

LEON, Miguelina

1931 13th St. NW
Washington, DC 20009
Tel: (202)483-6622 Ext: 324
Fax: (202)483-1135
EMail: mleon@nmac.org

Employers
Nat'l Minority AIDS Council (Director, Government Relations and Public Policy)

LEON, Paul

1650 Tysons Blvd.
Suite 1700
McLean, VA 22102
Tel: (703)790-6300
Fax: (703)790-6365

Employers
ITT Industries Defense (Director, Business Development, Technology, and Logistics)

LEONARD, Burleigh C. W.

3433 N. Albemarle St.
Arlington, VA 22207
Tel: (703)536-9118
Registered: LDA

Special Assistant to the President for Food and Agriculture, The White House, 1981-84. Professional Staff Member, Senate Committee on Agriculture, 1979-81. Legislative Assistant to Senator John Danforth (R-MO), 1977-79.

Employers
Leonard and Co. (President and Chief Exec. Officer)

Clients Represented

On Behalf of Leonard and Co.
Philip Morris Management Corp.

LEONARD, Charles G.

1850 M St. NW
Suite 550
Washington, DC 20036
Tel: (202)289-5900
Fax: (202)289-4141
Registered: LDA, FARA
EMail: cgl@clsdc.com

Former Nat'l Campaign Director, Nat'l Republican Congressional Committee.

Employers
Chlopak, Leonard, Schechter and Associates (Partner)

Clients Represented

On Behalf of Chlopak, Leonard, Schechter and Associates
GE Capital Mortgage Insurance Co. (GEMICO)
General Electric Appliances
General Electric Capital Mortgage Corp.
General Electric Co.
Hyundai Electronics Industries Co., LTD
Mexico, Office of the President of
Wilkie Farr & Gallagher

LEONARD, Jerris

888 Sixteenth St. NW
7th Floor
Washington, DC 20006-4103
Tel: (202)835-8032
Fax: (202)835-8136
Registered: LDA

Served in the U.S. Department of Justice, 1969-73.

Employers
Foley & Lardner (Partner)

Clients Represented

On Behalf of Foley & Lardner
AAAE-ACI
Canadian Nat'l Railway Co.
ComEd
Bruce Givner, Attorney
Kruger Internat'l (KI)
Save the Greenback Coalition
YouBet.com

LEONARD, Joe

1002 Wisconsin Ave. NW
Washington, DC 20007
Tel: (202)333-5270
Fax: (202)728-1192

Employers
Rainbow/Push Coalition (National Bureau) (Exec. Director)

LEONARD, Kathleen

888 Sixteenth St. NW
7th Floor
Washington, DC 20006-4103
Tel: (202)835-8124
Fax: (202)835-8136
Registered: LDA

Employers
Foley & Lardner (Lobbyist)

Clients Represented

On Behalf of Foley & Lardner
AAAE-ACI
Correctional Vendors Ass'n
Information Handling Services

LEONARD, Lloyd J.

1730 M St. NW
Suite 1000
Washington, DC 20036
Tel: (202)429-1965
Fax: (202)429-0854
Registered: LDA

Employers
League of Women Voters of the United States (Legislative Director)

LEONARD, Robert J.

1150 17th St. NW
Suite 601
Washington, DC 20036
Tel: (202)293-7474
Fax: (202)293-8811
Registered: LDA

Chief Counsel and Staff Director (1987-93), Chief Tax Counsel (1981-86) and Tax Counsel (1974-80), House Ways and Means Committee.

Employers
Washington Council Ernst & Young (Partner)

Clients Represented

On Behalf of Washington Council Ernst & Young
Aetna Inc.
Aetna Life & Casualty Co.
Allegiance Healthcare Corp.
Allen & Co.
American Express Co.
American Insurance Ass'n
American Staffing Ass'n
Anheuser-Busch Cos., Inc.
Antitrust Coalition for Consumer Choice in Health Care
Apartment Investment and Management Co.
Ass'n of American Railroads
Ass'n of Home Appliance Manufacturers
AT&T
AT&T Capital Corp.
Avco Financial Services
Aventis Pharmaceuticals, Inc.
Baxter Healthcare Corp.
BHC Communications, Inc.
Bulmer Holding PLC, H. P.
Cash Balance Coalition
Chamber of Shipping of America
Citigroup
Coalition for Fairness in Defense Exports
Coalition to Preserve Tracking Stock
ComEd
The Connell Co.
Deferral Group
Directors Guild of America
Doris Duke Charitable Foundation
Eaton Vance Management Co.
Eden Financial Corp.
The Enterprise Foundation
Fannie Mae
FedEx Corp.
Ford Motor Co.
GE Capital Assurance
General Electric Co.
General Motors Corp.
Global Competitiveness Coalition
Grasslands Water District
Group Health, Inc.
Haz-X Support Services Corp.
HEREIU
Gilbert P. Hyatt, Inventor
Investment Co. Institute
Large Public Power Council
Local Initiatives Support Corp.
Lockheed Martin Corp.
MacAndrews & Forbes Holdings, Inc.
Marsh & McLennan Cos.
MCG Northwest, Inc.
McLane Co.
Merrill Lynch & Co., Inc.
Metropolitan Banking Group
Microsoft Corp.
Nat'l Ass'n for State Farm Agents
Nat'l Ass'n of Professional Employer Organizations
Nat'l Ass'n of Real Estate Investment Trusts
Nat'l Ass'n of State Farm Agents
Nat'l Cable Television Ass'n
Nat'l Defined Contribution Council
Nat'l Foreign Trade Council, Inc.
Nat'l Multi-Housing Council
PaineWebber Group, Inc.
Pfizer, Inc.
R&D Tax Credit Coalition
R&D Tax Regulation Group
Recording Industry Ass'n of America
Reed-Elsevier Inc.
R. J. Reynolds Tobacco Co.
Charles Schwab & Co., Inc.,
Securities Industry Ass'n
Sierra Pacific Industries
Skadden, Arps, Slate, Meagher & Flom LLP
Straddle Rules Tax Group
Tax Fairness Coalition
Tax/Shelter Coalition
TransOceanic Shipping
TU Services
TXU Business Services
U.S. Oncology
USA Biomass Power Producers Alliance
Viaticus, Inc.
Wilkie Farr & Gallagher
Ziff Investors Partnership

LEONARD, Scott

900 Second St. NE
Suite 308
Washington, DC 20002-3557
Tel: (202)408-8362
Fax: (202)408-8287
Registered: LDA
EMail: narp@narprail.org

Employers
Nat'l Ass'n of Railroad Passengers (Assistant Director)

LEONARD, Tracy

1120 20th St. NW
Suite 750 South
Washington, DC 20036
Tel: (202)454-6400
Fax: (202)454-6401

Employers
Columbia Lighthouse for the Blind (Director, Communications)

LEONARD, Will E.

1150 18th St. NW
Ninth Floor
Washington, DC 20036
Tel: (202)296-3355
Fax: (202)296-3922
EMail: wleonard@ablondifoster.com

Chairman (1975-76) and Commissioner (1968-77), U.S. International Trade Commission. Professional Staff Member, Senate Committee on Finance, 1966-68. Legislative Assistant to Senator Russell B. Long (D-LA), 1960-66.

Employers
Ablondi, Foster, Sobin & Davidow, P.C. (Partner)

LEONHARDT, Jill L.

1701 Pennsylvania Ave. NW
Suite 1200
Washington, DC 20006
Tel: (202)857-0620
Fax: (202)659-4503
Registered: LDA
EMail: jll@groom.com

Employers
Groom Law Group, Chartered (Consultant)

Clients Represented

On Behalf of Groom Law Group, Chartered
Prudential Insurance Co. of America

LEPETIC, Alenna M.

1329 Connecticut Ave. NW
Washington, DC 20036-1825
Tel: (202)331-2830
Fax: (202)331-0050
EMail: nfcalepetic@aol.com

Employers
Nat'l Federation of Croatian Americans (National Coordinator)

LEPON, Jeffrey M.

1225 19th St. NW
Suite 600
Washington, DC 20036
EMail: jml@lmwh.com
Tel: (202)857-0242
Fax: (202)857-0189

Employers
Lepon McCarthy White & Holzworth, PLLC (Partner)

LERCH, Donald G.

1629 K St. NW
Suite 1100
Washington, DC 20006
Tel: (202)785-6705
Fax: (202)331-4212
Registered: FARA

Employers
Lerch & Co., Inc. (President)

Clients Represented
On Behalf of Lerch & Co., Inc.
Japan Internat'l Agricultural Council

LEREAH, David A.

1919 Pennsylvania Ave. NW
Seventh Floor
Washington, DC 20006-3488
Tel: (202)557-2700

Employers
Mortgage Bankers Ass'n of America (Senior Staff V. President and Chief Economist)

LERMAN, Robert

2100 M St. NW
Washington, DC 20037
Tel: (202)833-7200
Fax: (202)429-0687

Employers
The Urban Institute (Director, Human Resources Policy Center)

LERMAN, Steven

2000 K St. NW
Suite 600
Washington, DC 20006-1809
Tel: (202)429-8970
Fax: (202)293-7783

Employers
Leventhal, Senter & Lerman, P.L.L.C. (Managing Partner)

LERNER, Matthew D.

1330 Connecticut Ave. NW
Washington, DC 20036-1795
EMail: mlerner@steptoe.com
Tel: (202)429-3000
Fax: (202)429-3902

Employers
Steptoe & Johnson LLP (Partner)

LESCH, Peter C.

1023 15th St. NW
Suite 900
Washington, DC 20005-2602
EMail: plesch@gbmdc.com
Tel: (202)289-7200
Fax: (202)289-7698
Legal Advisor, Federal Energy Regulatory Commission, 1978-79. Staff Attorney, Federal Power Commission, 1973-77.

Employers
Gallagher, Boland and Meiburger (Partner)

Clients Represented
On Behalf of Gallagher, Boland and Meiburger
Cinergy Corp.
TECO Energy, Inc.

LESCOTT, Jaqueline

1300 N. 17th St.
Eighth Floor
Rosslyn, VA 22209-3801
EMail: lescott@abc.org
Tel: (703)812-2000
Fax: (703)812-8202

Employers
Associated Builders and Contractors (Regulatory Representative)

LESEUR, John H.

1224 17th St. NW
Washington, DC 20036
Tel: (202)347-7170
Fax: (202)347-3619
Registered: LDA

Employers
Slover & Loftus (Partner)

Clients Represented
On Behalf of Slover & Loftus
Western Coal Traffic League

LESHAN, Timothy E.

8120 Woodmont Ave.
Suite 750
Bethesda, MD 20814-2755
EMail: tleshan@ascb.org
Tel: (301)530-7153
Fax: (301)530-7139

Employers
American Soc. for Cell Biology (Director, Public Policy)
Joint Steering Committee for Public Policy (Director of Public Policy)

LESHER, William G.

1919 South Eads St.
Suite 103
Arlington, VA 22202-3028
Tel: (703)979-6900
Fax: (703)979-6906
Registered: LDA
Assistant Secretary for Economics, Department of Agriculture, 1981-85. Chief Economist, Senate Agricultural Committee, 1978-80.

Employers
Lesher & Russell, Inc. (President)

Clients Represented
On Behalf of Lesher & Russell, Inc.
Chicago Mercantile Exchange
Commerce Ventures
Federal Agricultural Mortgage Corp. (Farmer Mac)
Monsanto Co.
PepsiCo, Inc.
Philip Morris Management Corp.
USA Rice Federation

LESKOVSEK, Natasha

1900 K St. NW
Suite 750
Washington, DC 20006
Tel: (202)833-4500
Fax: (202)833-2859
Registered: LDA

Employers
Bennett Turner & Coleman, LLP (Associate)

Clients Represented
On Behalf of Bennett Turner & Coleman, LLP
Cure for Lymphoma Foundation
Cystic Fibrosis Foundation
Leukemia & Lymphoma Soc.
North American Brain Tumor Coalition

LESKY, Marcia

1400 16th St. NW
Suite 501
Washington, DC 20036-2266
Tel: (202)797-6800
Fax: (202)797-6646

Employers
Nat'l Wildlife Federation - Office of Federal and Internat'l Affairs (Population Policy Analyst)

LESLIE, Gregg

1815 N. Fort Myer Dr.
Suite 900
Arlington, VA 22209
Tel: (703)807-2100
Fax: (703)807-2109

Employers
Reporters Committee for Freedom of the Press (Director, Legal Defense)

LESLIE, J. Douglass

Three LaFayette Centre
1155 21st St. NW
Room 9156
Washington, DC 20581
Tel: (202)418-5075
Fax: (202)418-5542

Employers
Commodity Futures Trading Commission (Acting Senior Counsel, Office of Legislative and Intergovernmental Affairs)

LESSENCO, Gilbert B.

1920 N St. NW
Washington, DC 20036
EMail: glessenco@thf.com
Tel: (202)331-8800
Fax: (202)331-8330

Employers
Thompson, Hine and Flory LLP (Of Counsel)

Clients Represented
On Behalf of Thompson, Hine and Flory LLP
Home Baking Ass'n
The Toro Co.

LESSER, Jill A.

1101 Connecticut Ave. NW
Suite 400
Washington, DC 20036-4303
EMail: JillLess@aol.com
Tel: (202)530-7882
Fax: (202)530-7879
Registered: LDA

Employers
AOL Time Warner (V. President, Domestic Public Policy)

LESSER, William C.

200 Constitution Ave. NW
Washington, DC 20210
Tel: (202)219-8065
Ext: 107
Fax: (202)501-2583

Employers
Department of Labor - Solicitor (Legislative Communications Counsel)

LESSNER, Richard

801 G St. NW
Washington, DC 20001
Tel: (202)393-2100
Fax: (202)393-2134

Employers
American Renewal (Exec. Director)

LESSO, Maryann

2500 Wilson Blvd.
Suite 300
Arlington, VA 22201
EMail: mlesso@tia.eia.org
Tel: (703)907-7713
Fax: (703)907-7728

Employers
Telecommunications Industry Ass'n (Associate V. President, Member Relations)

LESTER, Patrick W.

1120 Connecticut Ave. NW
Suite 910
Washington, DC 20006
EMail: PWLESTER@chn.org
Tel: (202)223-2532
Fax: (202)223-2538

Employers
Coalition on Human Needs (Senior Legislative Associate)

LETOW, Jan

1385 Piccard Dr.
Rockville, MD 20850-4340
EMail: jletow@mcaa.org
Tel: (301)869-5800
Fax: (301)990-9690

Employers
Mechanical Contractors Ass'n of America (Director, Membership)

LETZLER, Kenneth A.

555 12th St. NW
Washington, DC 20004-1206
EMail: Kenneth_Letzler@aporter.com
Tel: (202)942-5000
Fax: (202)942-5999
Law Clerk, U.S. Court of Appeals, District of Columbia Circuit, 1968-69.

Employers
Arnold & Porter (Partner)

LEU, Jodi

1780 Massachusetts Ave. NW
Washington, DC 20036
Tel: (202)785-3351
Fax: (202)293-4349
Registered: LDA

Employers
Planned Parenthood Federation of America (Associate, Government Relations)

LEUCK, Jason

1300 Pennsylvania Ave. NW
Suite 350
Washington, DC 20044
EMail: jleuck@tia.eia.org
Tel: (202)383-1493
Fax: (202)383-1495

Employers
Telecommunications Industry Ass'n (Director, Latin America Programs)

LEVARIO, Andrea

9000 Rockville Pike
Bldg. One, Room 244
Bethesda, MD 20892
Tel: (301)496-3471
Fax: (301)496-0840

Employers
Department of Health and Human Services - Nat'l Institutes of Health (Legislative Analyst)

LEVENSON, Meredith

1350 I St. NW
Suite 830
Washington, DC 20005
EMail: mlev@pptaglobal.org
Tel: (202)789-3100
Fax: (202)789-4197

Employers
Plasma Protein Therapeutics Ass'n (Associate Director, Health Policy)

LEVENSON, Nancy R.

900 17th St. NW
Suite 402
Washington, DC 20006-5504
Tel: (202)331-1186
Fax: (202)659-2338
Registered: LDA

Employers
S.C. Johnson and Son, Inc. (Director, U.S. Federal Government Relations)

LEVENTHAL, Paul

1000 Connecticut Ave. NW
Suite 804
Washington, DC 20036
Tel: (202)822-8444
Fax: (202)452-0892
Registered: LDA

Employers
Nuclear Control Institute (President)

LEVER, Jack Q.

600 13th St. NW
Washington, DC 20005-3096
Tel: (202)756-8365
Fax: (202)756-8087
EMail: jlever@mwe.com
Deputy General Counsel for Patents (1980-81) and Patent Attorney (1975-80), Department of Energy; Patent Examiner, Patent and Trademark Office, 1970-75.

Employers
McDermott, Will and Emery (Partner)

LEVERICH, Bingham B.

1201 Pennsylvania Ave. NW
Washington, DC 20004-2401
Tel: (202)662-6000
Fax: (202)662-6291
EMail: bleverich@cov.com

Employers
Covington & Burling (Partner)

LEVEY, Jeffrey R.

1101 Pennsylvania Ave. NW
Suite 1000
Washington, DC 20004
Tel: (202)879-6818
Fax: (202)783-1873
Registered: LDA
EMail: jeffrey.levey@citicorp.com

Employers
Citigroup (V. President, Director, Tax Legislation)

LEVI, Gerron

905 16th St. NW
Washington, DC 20006
Tel: (202)737-8320
Fax: (202)737-2754
Registered: LDA

Employers
Laborers' Internat'l Union of North America (Legislative Representative)

LEVI, Robert

Eight Herbert St.
Alexandria, VA 22305-2600
Tel: (703)683-9027
Fax: (703)683-6820
Registered: LDA

Employers
Nat'l Ass'n of Postmasters of the U.S. (Director, Government Relations)

LEVIEN, Lawrence D.

1333 New Hampshire Ave. NW
Suite 400
Washington, DC 20036
Tel: (202)887-4000
Fax: (202)887-4288

Employers
Akin, Gump, Strauss, Hauer & Feld, L.L.P. (Partner)

LEVIN, Barbara

7200 Wisconsin Ave.
Suite 709
Bethesda, MD 20814
Tel: (301)656-7998
Fax: (301)656-5019

Employers
Forum For Investor Advice (Exec. Director)

LEVIN, David R.

700 13th St. NW
Suite 800
Washington, DC 20005
Tel: (202)508-5800
Fax: (202)508-5858
Special Counsel, Office of the General Counsel, Pension Benefit Guaranty Corp., 1978-83.

Employers
Kilpatrick Stockton LLP (Partner)

LEVIN, Jeffrey S.

The Watergate
Suite 1113
2600 Virginia Ave. NW
Washington, DC 20037-1905
Tel: (202)337-8338
Fax: (202)337-6685
Registered: LDA

Employers
Harris Ellsworth & Levin (Partner)

Clients Represented
On Behalf of Harris Ellsworth & Levin
Ass'n of Food Industries, Inc.
Committee of Domestic Steel Wire Rope and Specialty Cable Manufacturers
Wood Corp.

LEVIN, Mark B.

1640 Rhode Island Ave. NW
Suite 501
Washington, DC 20036
EMail: ncsj@ncsj.org
Tel: (202)898-2500
Fax: (202)898-0822

Employers
NCSJ: Advocates on Behalf of Jews in Russia, Ukraine, the Baltic States and Eurasia (Exec. Director, Washington Office)

LEVIN, Mark G.

11785 Beltsville Dr.
Tenth Floor
Calverton, MD 20705
Tel: (301)572-7900
Fax: (301)572-6655

Employers
O'Malley, Miles, Nylen & Gilmore, P.A. (Deputy Managing Partner)

LEVIN, Mark R.

445-B Carlisle Dr.
Herndon, VA 20170
Tel: (703)689-2370
Fax: (703)689-2373

Employers
Landmark Legal Foundation Center for Civil Rights (President)

LEVIN, Michael H.

1701 K St. NW
Suite 300
Washington, DC 20006
Tel: (202)223-2500
Fax: (202)223-2501
Registered: LDA
EMail: mhlevin@leonardhurt.com

Employers
Leonard Hurt Frost Lilly & Levin, PC

Clients Represented
On Behalf of Leonard Hurt Frost Lilly & Levin, PC
SBREFA Coalition

LEVIN, Sharon

11 Dupont Circle NW
Suite 800
Washington, DC 20036
EMail: slevin@nwlc.org
Tel: (202)588-5180
Fax: (202)588-5185

Employers
Nat'l Women's Law Center (Senior Counsel)

LEVIN-EPSTEIN, Jodie

1616 P St. NW
Suite 150
Washington, DC 20036
EMail: jodie@clasp.org
Tel: (202)328-5174
Fax: (202)328-5195

Employers
Center for Law and Social Policy (Senior State Policy Advocate)

LEVINAS, Randi

The McPherson Bldg.
901 15th St. NW, Suite 1100
Washington, DC 20005
Tel: (202)682-3500
Fax: (202)682-3580
Registered: LDA

Employers
Kaye Scholer LLP

Clients Represented
On Behalf of Kaye Scholer LLP
Korean Semiconductor Industry Ass'n

LEVINE, Arthur N.

555 12th St. NW
Washington, DC 20004-1206
Tel: (202)942-5000
Fax: (202)942-5999
EMail: Arthur_Levine@aporter.com
Deputy General Counsel, Litigation (1978-81) and Trial Attorney (1970-78), Food and Drug Administration.

Employers
Arnold & Porter (Partner)

LEVINE, David J.

600 13th St. NW
Washington, DC 20005-3096
Tel: (202)756-8153
Fax: (202)756-8087
EMail: dlevine@mwe.com
International Trade Analyst, Department of Commerce, 1985-87.

Employers
McDermott, Will and Emery (Partner)

LEVINE, Estee S.

450 Fifth St. NW
Room 6102
Washington, DC 20549
Tel: (202)942-0010
Fax: (202)942-9650

Employers
Securities and Exchange Commission (Director, Office of Congressional and Intergovernmental Affairs)

LEVINE, Ezra C.

1299 Pennsylvania Ave. NW
Washington, DC 20004-2402
Tel: (202)783-0800
Fax: (202)383-6610
Registered: LDA
EMail: levinee@howrey.com
Assistant General Counsel, Interpretations and Rulings (1977-78) and Deputy Assistant General Counsel, Compliance (1975-77), Federal Energy Administration, Department of Energy. Senior Litigation Attorney, Federal Energy Office, Executive Office of the President, The White House, 1974. Attorney, Office of Opinions and Review, Federal Communications Commission, 1968-69.

Employers
Howrey Simon Arnold & White (Partner)

Clients Represented
On Behalf of Howrey Simon Arnold & White
Non-Bank Funds Transmitters Group

LEVINE, Dr. Felice J.

1307 New York Ave. NW
Suite 700
Washington, DC 20005
EMail: executive.office@asanet.org
Tel: (202)383-9005
Fax: (202)638-0882

Employers
American Sociological Ass'n (Exec. Officer)

LEVINE, Ken

1225 I St. NW
Suite 350
Washington, DC 20005
Tel: (202)712-9134
Fax: (202)189-1110
Registered: LDA, FARA
EMail: klevinejd@aol.com
Director, Office of Congressional Consumer and Public Affairs, Federal Energy Regulatory Commission, Department of Energy, 1979-81. Deputy Assistant Secretary for Legislation, Department of Health Education and Welfare, 1977-79.

Administrative Assistant to Rep. Bob Eckhardt (D-TX) 1975-76.

Employers
Levine & Co. (Chairman)

Clients Represented
On Behalf of Levine & Co.
American Internat'l Group, Inc.
Bermuda, Government of
GAF Corp.
Kohlberg Kravis Roberts & Co.
Radiant Aviation Services, Inc.
Schering-Plough Corp.
Virgin Atlantic Airways

LEVINE, Leonard B.

4009 Mansion Dr. NW
Washington, DC 20007
Tel: (202)965-2788
Fax: (202)965-2672
Registered: LDA

Employers
Leonard B. Levine & Associates

Clients Represented
On Behalf of Leonard B. Levine & Associates
Express Pipeline Partnership and Platte Pipeline Co.

LEVINE, Lisa

805 15th St. NW
Suite 700
Washington, DC 20005
Tel: (202)312-7400
Fax: (202)312-7441
Registered: LDA
EMail: lalevine@bakerd.com

Employers
Sagamore Associates, Inc. (Assistant V. President)

Clients Represented
On Behalf of Sagamore Associates, Inc.
Allegheny County, Pennsylvania, Housing Authority
Arthritis Foundation

LEVINE, Hon. Meldon E.

1050 Connecticut Ave. NW
Washington, DC 20036-5306
Tel: (202)955-8500
Fax: (202)467-0539
Registered: LDA
EMail: mlevine@gdclaw.com
Member, U.S. House of Representatives (D-CA), 1983-93.

Employers
Gibson, Dunn & Crutcher LLP (Partner)

Clients Represented
On Behalf of Gibson, Dunn & Crutcher LLP
The Boeing Co.
Northrop Grumman Corp.

LEVINE, Peter J.

9608 Sotwood St.
Potomac, MD 20854
Tel: (301)983-1376
Registered: LDA

Employers
TransNat'l Business Development Corp. (President)

Clients Represented
On Behalf of TransNat'l Business Development Corp.
Trans-Ona S.A.M.C.I.F.

LEVINSON, Bruce

11 Dupont Circle NW
Suite 700
Washington, DC 20036
Tel: (202)293-5886
Fax: (202)939-6969
Registered: LDA

Employers
Multinat'l Government Services, Inc.

Clients Represented
On Behalf of Multinat'l Government Services, Inc.
TRW Inc.

LEVINSON, Ellen S.

1201 F St. NW
Suite 1100
Washington, DC 20004
Tel: (202)862-2256
Fax: (202)862-2400
Registered: LDA
EMail: ellen.levinson@cwt.com

Employers
Cadwalader, Wickersham & Taft (Government Relations Advisor)

Clients Represented
On Behalf of Cadwalader, Wickersham & Taft
New York Board of Trade

LEVINSON, Kenneth I.

601 13th St. NW
Suite 1100
Washington, DC 20005
Tel: (202)429-2217
Fax: (202)296-8727
Registered: LDA

Employers
Fontheim Internat'l, LLC (Director, International Trade and Finance)
Fontheim Partners, PC (Director, International Trade and Finance)

Clients Represented
On Behalf of Fontheim Internat'l, LLC
Enron Corp.
Microsoft Corp.
Vivendi Universal
On Behalf of Fontheim Partners, PC
American Internat'l Group, Inc.
The Limited Inc.
Susquehanna Investment Group

LEVINSON, Lawrence E.

901 15th St. NW
Suite 700
Washington, DC 20005-2301
Tel: (202)371-6000
Fax: (202)371-6279
Registered: LDA, FARA
EMail: lelevinson@verner.com
Deputy Special Counsel to the President, The White House, 1965-68. Judge Advocate Division, U.S. Army, 1955-57.

Employers
Verner, Liipfert, Bernhard, McPherson and Hand, Chartered (Member of Firm)

Clients Represented
On Behalf of Verner, Liipfert, Bernhard, McPherson and Hand, Chartered
Equal Justice Coalition
The Hamilton Group
Heritage Development
Kellogg Co.
Midroc Ethiopia
Montenegro, Government of
The Singer Group
Stanford Financial Group
Transportation Maritima Mexicana
Woodfin Suite Hotels

LEVINSON, Dr. Richard

800 I St. NW
Washington, DC 20001
Tel: (202)777-2510
Fax: (202)777-2534
Registered: LDA

Employers
American Public Health Ass'n (Associate Exec. Director, Programs and Policy)

LEVINSON, Riva

1801 K St. NW
Suite 901-L
Washington, DC 20006
Tel: (202)530-0500
Fax: (202)530-4800
Registered: LDA, FARA
EMail: Riva_Levinson@bm.com

Employers
BKSH & Associates (Managing Director)

Clients Represented
On Behalf of BKSH & Associates
Advertising Company ART-ERIA
Jigawa, Nigerian State of
Nat'l Power

LEVITAS, Hon. Elliott H.

700 13th St. NW
Suite 800
Washington, DC 20005
Tel: (202)508-5800
Fax: (202)508-5858
Registered: LDA
Member, U.S. House of Representatives (D-GA), 1975-85.

Employers
Kilpatrick Stockton LLP (Partner)

Clients Represented
On Behalf of Kilpatrick Stockton LLP
Blake Construction Co.
Hoffman Management, Inc.
Public Properties Policy Ass'n
Republic Properties Corp.

LEVITIN, Michael J.

1133 Connecticut Ave. NW
Suite 1200
Washington, DC 20036
Tel: (202)775-9800
Fax: (202)833-8491
Attorney/Advisor, Office of the General Counsel, Department of the Treasury, 1986-88.

Employers
Winthrop, Stimson, Putnam & Roberts (Associate)

LEVITT, Geoffrey M.

1201 New York Ave. NW
Suite 1000
Washington, DC 20005
Tel: (202)962-4923
Fax: (202)962-8300
EMail: dmlevitt@venable.com
Office of the Legal Advisor, Department of State, 1981-88.

Employers
Venable (Partner)

LEVITT, Ed.D., Nina Gail

750 First St. NE
Washington, DC 20002-4242
Tel: (202)336-6023
Fax: (202)336-6063
Registered: LDA

Employers
American Psychological Ass'n (Director, Education Policy)

LEVITT, Rachelle

1025 Thomas Jefferson St. NW
Suite 500 W
Washington, DC 20007-5201
Tel: (202)624-7000
Fax: (202)624-7140
EMail: rlevitt@uli.org

Employers
Urban Land Institute (Senior V. President, Policy and Practice)

LEVY, Charles S.

2445 M St. NW
Washington, DC 20037-1420
Tel: (202)663-6000
Fax: (202)663-6363
Registered: LDA
EMail: clevy@wilmer.com
Legal Advisor, International Trade Commission, 1979-80. Legislative Assistant to Senator Adlai E. Stevenson (D-IL), 1973-75. Counsel, Subcommittee on Foreign Economic Policy, House Committee on Foreign Affairs, 1971-73. Legislative Assistant to Rep. John C. Culver (D-IA), 1971.

Employers
Wilmer, Cutler & Pickering (Partner)

Clients Represented
On Behalf of Wilmer, Cutler & Pickering
AOL Time Warner
The Business Roundtable
Coalition of Service Industries
Computer Systems Policy Project
Deutsche Telekom, Inc.
Export Control Coalition
Hewlett-Packard Co.
Intellectual Property Committee

LEVY, David C.

500 17th St. NW
Washington, DC 20006-4804
Tel: (202)639-1700
Fax: (202)639-1779

Employers
The Corcoran Gallery of Art (President and Director)

LEVY, David L.

300 I St. NE
Suite 401
Washington, DC 20002
Tel: (202)547-6227
Fax: (202)546-4272
EMail: crcdc@erols.com

Employers
Children's Rights Council (President)

LEVY, David M.

1722 I St. NW
Washington, DC 20006
Tel: (202)736-8000
Fax: (202)736-8711
EMail: dlevy@sidley.com

Employers
Sidley & Austin (Partner)

Clients Represented
On Behalf of Sidley & Austin
Alliance of Nonprofit Mailers

LEVY, Frederic

1900 K St. NW
Washington, DC 20006
Tel: (202)496-7500
Fax: (202)496-7756

Employers
McKenna & Cuneo, L.L.P. (Managing Partner)

LEVY, Gregg H.

1201 Pennsylvania Ave. NW
Washington, DC 20004-2401
Tel: (202)662-6000
Fax: (202)662-6291
EMail: glevy@cov.com

Employers
Covington & Burling (Partner)

LEVY, Harold A.

3000 K St. NW
Suite 300
Washington, DC 20007
Tel: (202)424-7500
Fax: (202)424-7643
Registered: LDA
Chief Attorney (1990-92) and Attorney/Advisor (1979-90), Department of Housing and Urban Development.

Employers
Swidler Berlin Shereff Friedman, LLP (Of Counsel)

Clients Represented

On Behalf of Swidler Berlin Shereff Friedman, LLP
Associated Estates Co.
H & R Executive Towers
Manhattan Plaza Associates
Nat'l Housing and Rehabilitation Ass'n
Newman & Associates
Starrett Corp.

LEVY, Kathryn

750 First St. NE
Suite 700
Washington, DC 20002
Tel: (202)408-8600
Fax: (202)336-8311

Employers
Nat'l Ass'n of Social Workers (Political Affairs Associate)

LEVY, Lori C.

122 C St. NW
Suite 750
Washington, DC 20001-2109
Tel: (202)737-2337
Fax: (202)737-7004

Employers
Beer Institute (Director, Communications)

LEVY, Michael B.

1615 L St. NW
Suite 450
Washington, DC 20036
Tel: (202)296-7353
Fax: (202)296-7009
Registered: LDA
Senior Advisor to the Secretary (1995) and Assistant Secretary for Legislative Affairs (1993-95), Department of the Treasury, 1993-95; Administrative Assistant to Senator Lloyd Bentson (D-TX), 1987-93.

Employers
Brownstein Hyatt & Farber, P.C.

Clients Represented

On Behalf of Brownstein Hyatt & Farber, P.C.
American Salvage Pool Ass'n
Apollo Advisors
AT&T Broadband & Internet Service
Colorado Credit Union Systems
Delta Petroleum Corp.
Express One Internat'l Inc.
First Data Corp./Telecheck
Global Crossing North America, Inc.
Liggett Group, Inc.
Mariner Post Acute Network
Nat'l Cable Television Ass'n
NL Industries
Oracle Corp.
Pacific Capital Group, Inc.
Pfizer, Inc.
Rent-a-Center, Inc.
Rhythms NetConnections
Teletech Teleservices, Inc.
Timet-Titantium Metals Corp.
Vail Associates

LEVY, Michael R.

1201 Pennsylvania Ave. NW
Washington, DC 20004-2401
Tel: (202)662-6000
Fax: (202)662-6291
EMail: mlevy@cov.com
Law Clerk to Judge Arnold Raum, U.S. Tax Court, 1973-75.

Employers
Covington & Burling (Partner)

LEVY, Neil I.

700 13th St. NW
Suite 800
Washington, DC 20005
Tel: (202)508-5800
Fax: (202)508-5858

Employers
Kilpatrick Stockton LLP (Partner)

Clients Represented

On Behalf of Kilpatrick Stockton LLP
American Speech, Language, and Hearing Ass'n
Blake Construction Co.
Elcor Inc.
Hoffman Management, Inc.
Julien J. Studley, Inc.
Transrapid Internat'l

LEVY, Robin

1300 N. 17th St.
Eighth Floor
Rosslyn, VA 22209-3801
Tel: (703)812-2005
Fax: (703)812-8202
Registered: LDA
EMail: levy@abc.org

Employers
Associated Builders and Contractors (Government Affairs Assistant)

LEVY, Roger N.

1101 Pennsylvania Ave. NW
Suite 1000
Washington, DC 20004
Tel: (202)879-6823
Fax: (202)783-4461
Registered: LDA
EMail: levyr@citi.com

Employers
Citigroup (S. V. President and Director, Federal Government Relations)

LEWAN, Michael

1001 Pennsylvania Ave. NW
Suite 850N
Washington, DC 20004
Tel: (202)347-2222
Fax: (202)347-4242
Registered: LDA, FARA
EMail: michaellewanco@worldnet.att.net
Chief of Staff to Senator Joseph Lieberman (D-CT), 1989-93. Chief of Staff to Rep. Stephen Solarz (D-NY), 1975-89.

Employers
The Michael Lewan Co. (President)

Clients Represented

On Behalf of The Michael Lewan Co.
BellSouth Corp.
BSMG Worldwide
Capital City Economic Development Authority
Connecticut Resource Recovery Authority
McGraw-Hill Cos., The
Nat'l Center for Children in Poverty
NetCoalition.Com
Oracle Corp.
Phoenix Home Life Mutual Insurance Co.
Public Policy Partners

LEWANDOWSKI, William

1250 I St. NW
Suite 1200
Washington, DC 20005-3924
Tel: (202)371-8432
Fax: (202)371-8470

Employers
Aerospace Industries Ass'n of America (V. President, Supplier Management Council)

LEWIN, Martin J.

666 11th St. NW
Suite 315
Washington, DC 20001
Tel: (202)331-8045
Fax: (202)331-8191
Registered: LDA
EMail: MLewin@ix.netcom.com
Legal Advisor, U.S. International Trade Commission, 1978-79. Staff Member, House Committee on International Relations, 1977-78. Attorney/Advisor, Office of the General Counsel, General Accounting Office, 1974-77. Staff Attorney, Special Project Counsel, Interstate Commerce Commission, 1973-74.

Employers
Aitken, Irvin, Lewin, Berlin, Vrooman & Cohn (Partner)

Clients Represented

On Behalf of Aitken, Irvin, Lewin, Berlin, Vrooman & Cohn
American Import Shippers Ass'n
Colgate Palmolive

LEWIN, Nathan

701 Pennsylvania Ave. NW
Suite 900
Washington, DC 20004-2608
Tel: (202)434-7300
Fax: (202)434-7400
EMail: nlewin@minz.com
Deputy Assistant Attorney General, Civil Rights Division, Department of Justice, 1968-69. Deputy Administrator, Bureau of Security and Consular Affairs, Department of State, 1967-68. Assistant to the Solicitor General (1963-67) and Special Assistant to the Assistant Attorney General, Criminal Division (1962-63), Department of Justice. Law Clerk to Justice John M. Harlan, U.S. Supreme Court, 1961-62, and to Chief Judge J. Edward Lumbard, U.S. Court of Appeals, Second Circuit, 1960-61.

Employers
Mintz, Levin, Cohn, Ferris, Glovsky and Popeo, P.C. (Partner)

Clients Represented

On Behalf of Mintz, Levin, Cohn, Ferris, Glovsky and Popeo, P.C.
Internat'l Ass'n of Jewish Lawyers and Jurists

LEWIS, Catherine

1710 H St. NW
Ninth Floor
Washington, DC 20006
Tel: (202)392-1021
Fax: (202)392-1759
EMail: catherine.hogan.lewis@verizon.com

Employers
Verizon Washington, DC, Inc. (Senior Specialist, Media Relations)

LEWIS, Col. Dennis

The Pentagon
Room 2C638
Washington, DC 20310-0101
Tel: (703)697-9915
Fax: (703)693-7750

Employers
Department of Army (Chief, Programs Division, Legislative Liaison)

LEWIS, Elizabeth A.

1227 25th St. NW
Suite 700
Washington, DC 20037
Tel: (202)861-0900
Fax: (202)296-2882
Registered: LDA
EMail: llewis@ebglaw.com

Employers
Epstein Becker & Green, P.C. (Associate)

Clients Represented

On Behalf of Epstein Becker & Green, P.C.
Olsten Health Services

LEWIS, Flint H.

1155 16th St. NW
Washington, DC 20036
Tel: (202)872-4072
Fax: (202)872-6338
Registered: LDA
EMail: f_lewis@acs.org

Employers
American Chemical Soc. (Director, Government Relations and Assistant Secretary)

LEWIS, Fred

2111 Wilson Blvd.
Suite 400
Arlington, VA 22201
Tel: (703)522-1820
Fax: (703)243-1659

Employers
Nat'l Training Systems Ass'n (Exec. Director)

LEWIS, Gregory A.

635 Massachusetts Ave. NW
Washington, DC 20001
Tel: (202)414-2000
Registered: LDA

Employers
Nat'l Public Radio (Associate General Counsel)

LEWIS, James

818 Connecticut Ave. NW
Second Floor
Washington, DC 20006
EMail: jlewis@stratacomm.net
Tel: (202)289-2001
Fax: (202)289-1327

Employers
Strat@Comm (Strategic Communications Counselors) (Senior Counselor)

LEWIS, Jane

400 N. Capitol St. NW
Washington, DC 20001
Tel: (202)824-7226
Fax: (202)824-7115
Registered: LDA
EMail: jlewis@aga.org

Employers
American Gas Ass'n (Senior Managing Counsel and Director)

LEWIS, Jeffrey H.

1909 K St. NW
Washington, DC 20006
Tel: (202)263-3000
Fax: (202)263-3300
Registered: LDA
EMail: jhlewis@mayerbrown.com
Legislative Assistant to Senator John Breaux, 1995-99. Exec. Assistant to Congressman W.J. "Billy" Tauzin (D-LA), 1993-95.

Employers
Mayer, Brown & Platt (Associate)

Clients Represented
On Behalf of Mayer, Brown & Platt
Accenture
ED&F Man Inc.
Ernst & Young LLP
KPMG, LLP
Oracle Corp.
PriceWaterhouseCoopers
St. Paul Cos.
Technology Network

LEWIS, Joan H.

1250 I St. NW
Suite 700
Washington, DC 20005-3922
EMail: jlewis@dcha.org
Tel: (202)682-1581
Fax: (202)371-8151

Employers
District of Columbia Hospital Ass'n (Senior V. President)

LEWIS, Karen Judd

1155 21st St. NW
Suite 300
Washington, DC 20036
Tel: (202)659-8201
Fax: (202)659-5249
Registered: LDA
EMail: kjlewis@wms-jen.com
Former Aide to Senator Bob Packwood (R-OR).

Employers
Williams & Jensen, P.C. (Partner)

Clients Represented
On Behalf of Williams & Jensen, P.C.
American Home Products Corp.
CIGNA Corp.
Continental Airlines Inc.
Human Rights Campaign
Keystone, Inc.
Norfolk Southern Corp.
Owens-Illinois, Inc.
The Pittston Co.
Qwest Communications
Taxpayers Against Fraud, The False Claims Legal Center
TTX Co.
USAA - United Services Automobile Ass'n

LEWIS, Lauren

2101 Wilson Blvd.
Suite 610
Arlington, VA 22201
Tel: (703)558-0400
Fax: (703)558-0401

Employers
Manufactured Housing Institute (Director, Grassroots and PAC Activities)

LEWIS, Laurie D.

1001 Pennsylvania Ave. NW
Washington, DC 20004-2599
Tel: (202)624-2000
Fax: (202)624-2319
Registered: LDA

Employers
American Council of Life Insurers (Senior Counsel)

LEWIS, Linda R.

4301 Wilson Blvd.
Suite 400
Arlington, VA 22203-1861
EMail: llewis@aamva.org
Tel: (703)522-4200
Fax: (703)522-1553

Employers
American Ass'n of Motor Vehicle Administrators (President and Chief Exec. Officer)

LEWIS, Michael A.

1776 K St. NW
Washington, DC 20006
Tel: (202)719-7000
Fax: (202)719-7049

Employers
Wiley, Rein & Fielding (Consultant)

LEWIS, Michael J.

1801 Alexander Bell Dr.
Suite 500
Reston, VA 20191
Tel: (703)264-7500
Fax: (703)264-7551
Registered: LDA

Employers
American Institute of Aeronautics and Astronautics (Business Development Group)

LEWIS, Nicholas

316 Pennsylvania Ave. SE
Suite 300
Washington, DC 20003
Tel: (202)675-4222
Fax: (202)675-4230
Registered: LDA

Employers
United Parcel Service (Manager, Public Affairs)

LEWIS, Peggy

25 E St. NW
Washington, DC 20001
EMail: plewis@childrensdefense.org
Tel: (202)628-8787
Fax: (202)662-3530

Employers
Children's Defense Fund (Director, Communications)

LEWIS, Richard

600 Jefferson Plaza
Suite 350
Rockville, MD 20852
EMail: rlewis@forestresources.org
Tel: (301)838-9385
Fax: (301)838-9481

Employers
Forest Resources Ass'n (President)

LEWIS, Rita M.

1401 K St. NW
Suite 400
Washington, DC 20005
Tel: (202)789-2111
Fax: (202)789-4883
Registered: LDA, FARA
EMail: rlewis@thewashingtongroup.com
Former Aide to Senate Minority Leader, Senator Thomas Daschle (D-SD).

Employers
The Washington Group (Principal)

Clients Represented
On Behalf of The Washington Group
American Hospital Ass'n
American Resort Development Ass'n
AT&T
BD
The Boeing Co.
Bridgestone/Firestone, Inc.
Delta Air Lines
Global Waste Recycling, Inc.
IVAX Corp.
Korea Information & Communication, Ltd.
LCOR, Inc.
Microsoft Corp.
Nat'l Ass'n of Real Estate Investment Trusts
News Corporation Ltd.
Real Estate Roundtable
SAMPCO Companies
Texas Municipal Power Agency
Yankton Sioux Tribe

LEWIS, Robert J.

1725 K St. NW
Suite 1212
Washington, DC 20006
Tel: (202)833-8383
Fax: (202)331-7442
Registered: LDA

Employers
Nat'l Ass'n of Water Companies (Deputy Exec. Director, Federal Relations)

LEWIS-ENG, Claudia A.

1050 17th St. NW
Suite 600
Washington, DC 20036
Tel: (202)466-6937
Fax: (202)466-6938
Registered: LDA

Employers
Emord & Associates, P.C. (Senior Associate)

Clients Represented
On Behalf of Emord & Associates, P.C.
American Preventive Medical Ass'n
The JAG Group, Inc.
Meditrend, Inc.
Pure Encapsulations, Inc.
Rx Vitamins, Inc.
UroStar, Inc.
Weider Nutritional Group
XCEL Medical Pharmacy, Ltd.

LEYH, J. Robert

1000 16th St. NW
Suite 305
Washington, DC 20036
Tel: (202)659-3804
Fax: (202)296-1980
Registered: LDA

Employers
Waterman Steamship Co. (Senior V. President, Government Relations)

LEYLAND, Nora H.

1125 15th St. NW
Suite 801
Washington, DC 20005
Tel: (202)785-9300
Fax: (202)775-1950

Employers
Sherman, Dunn, Cohen, Leifer & Yellig, P.C.

LEZAMA, Michele

1454 Duke St.
Alexandria, VA 22314
Tel: (703)549-2207
Fax: (703)683-5312

Employers
Nat'l Soc. of Black Engineers (Exec. Director)

LEZY, Norm G.

1201 New York Ave. NW
Suite 200
Washington, DC 20005-3917
Tel: (202)962-4991
Fax: (202)962-4846

Employers
Wal-Mart Stores, Inc. (V. President, Federal and International Government Relations)

LIANZA, Cheryl

950 18th St. NW
Suite 220
Washington, DC 20006
Tel: (202)232-4300
Fax: (202)466-7656

Employers
Media Access Project (Deputy Director)

LIBBY, Sandra

1875 Connecticut Ave. NW
Suite 414
Washington, DC 20009
Tel: (202)745-4900
Fax: (202)745-0215

Employers
The Rendon Group, Inc. (Chief Financial Officer)

LIBERATORE, Robert G.

1401 H St. NW
Suite 700
Washington, DC 20005
Tel: (202)414-6747
Registered: LDA

Employers
DaimlerChrysler Corp. (Senior V. President, External Affairs and Public Policy)

LIBIN, Jerome B.

1275 Pennsylvania Ave. NW
Washington, DC 20004-2415
Tel: (202)383-0100
Fax: (202)637-3593
Registered: FARA
Law Clerk to Justice Charles E. Whittaker, U.S. Supreme Court, 1959-60.

Employers
Sutherland Asbill & Brennan LLP (Partner)

LIBONATI, John J.

1401 K St. NW
Suite 702
Washington, DC 20005
Tel: (202)216-1080
Fax: (202)216-1081
Registered: LDA
Former agent, U.S. Secret Service, Department of the Treasury.

Employers
Owens Corning (Director, Government and Public Affairs)

LIBOW, Daryl

1701 Pennsylvania Ave. NW
Suite 800
Washington, DC 20006
Tel: (202)956-7500
Fax: (202)293-6330

Employers
Sullivan & Cromwell (Partner)

Clients Represented
On Behalf of Sullivan & Cromwell
British Airways Plc

LIBRETTA, Donald F.

1850 M St. NW
Suite 400
Washington, DC 20036
Tel: (202)293-8200
Fax: (202)872-0145
Registered: LDA

Employers
Krooth & Altman (Partner)

Clients Represented
On Behalf of Krooth & Altman
Healthcare Financing Study Group

LIBRO, William J.

122 C St. NW
Suite 840
Washington, DC 20001
EMail: blibro@allete.com
Tel: (202)638-7707
Fax: (202)638-7710

Employers
Allete (Manager, Federal Affairs and Policy Development)

LIBSON, Nancy

1050 17th St. NW
Suite 900
Washington, DC 20036
Tel: (202)466-5300
Fax: (202)466-5508
Registered: LDA
Served with the Banking Committee, House of Representatives, 1990-97. Served with the Department of Housing and Urban Development, 1998-99.

Employers
Hessel and Aluise, P.C. (Director, Legislation and Public Policy)

Clients Represented
On Behalf of Hessel and Aluise, P.C.
Massachusetts Housing Finance Agency
Nat'l Cooperative Bank

LICHT, Eric

717 Second St. NE
Washington, DC 20002
Tel: (202)546-3003
Fax: (202)547-0392
Registered: LDA

Employers
Coalitions for America (President)

LICHTENBAUM, Greta L. H.

1455 Pennsylvania Ave. NW
Suite 700
Washington, DC 20004-1008
EMail: glichtenbaum@velaw.com
Tel: (202)639-6500
Fax: (202)639-6604
Registered: LDA

Employers
Vinson & Elkins L.L.P. (Of Counsel)

LICHTENBAUM, Peter

1330 Connecticut Ave. NW
Washington, DC 20036-1795
EMail: plichtenbaum@steptoe.com
Tel: (202)429-3000
Fax: (202)429-3902
Attorney/Advisor, Office of the General Counsel, Department of the Treasury, 1990-92.

Employers
Steptoe & Johnson LLP (Partner)

Clients Represented
On Behalf of Steptoe & Johnson LLP
Motorola, Inc.
Netscape Communications Corp.

LICHTENSTEIN, Jack D. P.

1625 Prince St.
Fifth Floor
Alexandria, VA 22314
EMail: jlichtenstein@erols.com
Tel: (703)518-1484
Fax: (703)518-1519
Registered: LDA
Former Executive Assistant to Senator Edward W. Brooke (R-MA); Director of Communications, President's Task Force on Management Reform, The White House; Acting Director, Public Affairs, Department of Commerce.

Employers
Leadership Counsel, LLC (Principal)
Self-employed as an independent consultant.

Clients Represented
On Behalf of Leadership Counsel, LLC
Aegis Research Corp.
American Soc. for Industrial Security
GenuOne
MindSim, Inc.
MPRI, Inc.
As an independent consultant
American Soc. for Industrial Security

LICHTER, S. Robert

2100 L St. NW
Washington, DC 20037
EMail: slichter@cmpa.com
Tel: (202)223-2942
Fax: (202)872-4014

Employers
Center for Media and Public Affairs (President)

LICHTMAN, Judith L.

1875 Connecticut Ave. NW
Suite 710
Washington, DC 20009
Tel: (202)986-2600
Fax: (202)986-2539

Employers
Nat'l Partnership for Women and Families (President)

LIDDLE, Jack W.

Crystal Gateway One
Suite 1102
1235 Jefferson Davis Hwy.
Arlington, VA 22202
Tel: (703)415-1600
Fax: (703)415-1608

Employers
Cubic Defense (V. President, Legislative Liaison)

LIDDLE, James

1200 18th St. NW
Washington, DC 20036
EMail: jliddle@environet.org
Tel: (202)887-8800
Fax: (202)887-8877
Registered: LDA

Employers
Nat'l Environmental Trust (Government Relations Associate)

LIEB, Bonnie

2000 L St. NW
Suite 300
Washington, DC 20036-0646
EMail: bonnie.lieb@ketchum.com
Tel: (202)835-8800
Fax: (202)835-8879

Employers
Ketchum (Sr. V. President, Technology)

Clients Represented
On Behalf of Ketchum
Capital One Financial Corp.

LIEBERMAN, Ben Charles

1001 Connecticut Ave. NW
Suite 1250
Washington, DC 20036
Tel: (202)331-1010
Fax: (202)331-0640

Employers
Competitive Enterprise Institute (Policy Analyst)

LIEBERMAN, Edward H.

1627 I St. NW
Suite 1200
Washington, DC 20006
Tel: (202)775-5100
Fax: (202)775-1168
Registered: FARA

Employers
Coudert Brothers (Partner)

Clients Represented
On Behalf of Coudert Brothers
The Khazakstan 21st Century Foundation

LIEBERMAN, Michael

1100 Connecticut Ave. NW
Suite 1020
Washington, DC 20036
Tel: (202)452-8320
Fax: (202)296-2371
Registered: LDA

Employers
Anti-Defamation League (Washington Counsel)

LIEBERMAN, Unice B.

701 Pennsylvania Ave. NW
Suite 650
Washington, DC 20004
EMail: unice.lieberman@cancer.org
Tel: (202)661-5711
Fax: (202)661-5750
Former Press Secretary to Senator Christopher J. Dodd (D-CT).

Employers
American Cancer Soc. (Director, Communications and Media Advocacy)

LIEBESMAN, Lawrence R.

1150 17th St. NW
Suite 302
Washington, DC 20036
Tel: (202)293-8510
Fax: (202)293-8513
Registered: LDA

Employers
Linowes and Blocher LLP (Partner)

Clients Represented
On Behalf of Linowes and Blocher LLP
Fire Island Ass'n

LIEBFRIED, Tom

12300 Twinbrook Pkwy.
Suite 320
Rockville, MD 20852
Tel: (301)984-6200

Employers
Nat'l Council for Community Behavioral Healthcare (Assistant V. President, Government Relations)

LIEBLER, Bernie

1200 G St. NW
Suite 400
Washington, DC 20005
Tel: (202)783-8700
Fax: (202)783-8750
Registered: LDA

Employers
AdvaMed (Director, Technology and Regulatory Affairs)

LIEBMAN, Bonnie F.

1875 Connecticut Ave. NW
Suite 300
Washington, DC 20009
Tel: (202)332-9110
Fax: (202)265-4954

Employers
Center for Science in the Public Interest (Director, Nutrition)

LIEBMAN, Diane S.

1331 Pennsylvania Ave. NW
Suite 560
Washington, DC 20004
Tel: (202)783-8124
Fax: (202)783-5929
Registered: LDA

Employers
CSX Corp. (V. President, Railroad Federal Affairs)

LIEBMAN, Murray

4413 Lowell St. NW
Washington, DC 20016
Tel: (202)966-5851
Registered: LDA

Employers
Liebman & Associates, Inc. (President)

Clients Represented
On Behalf of Liebman & Associates, Inc.
American Gas Ass'n
KeySpan Energy
Northern Indiana Public Service Co.

LIEBMAN, Ronald S.

2550 M St. NW
Washington, DC 20037-1350
Tel: (202)457-6000
Fax: (202)457-6315
Registered: FARA
EMail: rliebman@pattonboggs.com

Assistant U.S. Attorney for the District of Maryland, Department of Justice, 1972-78. Law Clerk to Chief Judge R. Dorsey Watkins, U.S. District Court for the District of Maryland, 1969-70.

Employers
Patton Boggs, LLP (Partner)

LIEF, Brett E.

1100 Connecticut Ave. NW
12th Floor
Washington, DC 20036
Tel: (202)822-2106
Fax: (202)822-2142
Registered: LDA
EMail: brettlief@aol.com

Employers
Nat'l Council of Higher Education Loan Programs (President)

LIEKWEG, John A.

3211 Fourth St. NE
Washington, DC 20017
Tel: (202)541-3300
Fax: (202)541-3337

Employers
United States Catholic Conference (Associate General Counsel)

LIESEMER, Ph.D., Ronald N.

1300 Wilson Blvd.
Suite 800
Arlington, VA 22209
Tel: (703)253-0700
Fax: (703)253-0701
EMail: rlieseme@ameriplas.org

Employers
American Plastics Council (V. President, Technology)

LIESS, Liz A.

1401 I St. NW
Suite 1000
Washington, DC 20005
Tel: (202)296-9410
Fax: (202)296-9775
EMail: lliess@sia.com

Employers
Securities Industry Ass'n (V. President and Director, Retirement Policy)

LIFSON, Arthur

2001 Pennsylvania Ave. NW
Suite 350
Washington, DC 20006-1825
Tel: (202)775-2680
Fax: (202)296-2521
Registered: LDA
EMail: arthur.lifson@cigna.com

Employers
CIGNA Corp. (V. President, Federal Affairs)

LIGGETT, Martha L.

1900 M St. NW
Suite 200
Washington, DC 20036-2422
Tel: (202)776-0544
Fax: (202)776-0545
Registered: LDA
EMail: mliggett@hematology.org

Employers
American Soc. of Hematology (Exec. Director)

LIGHT, Paul C.

1775 Massachusetts Ave. NW
Washington, DC 20036-2188
Tel: (202)797-6000
Fax: (202)797-6004

Former Senior Advisor, National Commission on the Public Service; former Senior Staff Member, Senate Governmental Affairs Committee.

Employers
The Brookings Institution (V. President and Director, Governmental Studies/Dir., Center for Public Service)

LIGHTFOOT, Jim R.

1 Massachusetts Ave. NW
Suite 310
Washington, DC 20001
Tel: (202)589-0440
Fax: (202)589-0861
Registered: LDA
EMail: jlightfoot@earthlink.net

Employers
Forensic Technology, Inc.

LIGHTHIZER, James

1331 H St. NW
Suite 1001
Washington, DC 20005
Tel: (202)367-1861
EMail: cwpt@civilwar.org

Employers
The Civil War Preservation Trust (President)

LIGHTHIZER, Robert E.

1440 New York Ave. NW
Washington, DC 20005
Tel: (202)371-7000
Fax: (202)393-5760
Registered: LDA

Chief Minority Counsel, Senate Committee on Finance, 1978-81. Chief Counsel and Staff Director, Senate Committee on Finance, 1981-83. Deputy United States Trade Representative, Ambassador, 1983-85.

Employers
Skadden, Arps, Slate, Meagher & Flom LLP (Partner)

Clients Represented

On Behalf of Skadden, Arps, Slate, Meagher & Flom LLP
Akzo America, Inc.
Amstel Hudson Management Corp.
Armco Inc.
Bethlehem Steel Corp.
Colgate Palmolive
Corning Inc.
Fruit of the Loom, Inc.
Inland Steel Industries, Inc.
Ispat Inland Steel Industries
LTV Steel Co.
MCI WorldCom Corp.
Milliken and Co.
Nat'l Steel Corp.
Pharmaceutical Research and Manufacturers of America
Sara Lee Corp.
US Steel Group

LIKEL, Charles

810 Vermont Ave. NW
Washington, DC 20420
Tel: (202)273-5615
Fax: (202)273-6791

Employers
Department of Veterans Affairs (Congressional Relations Officer)

LILLEY, James

1150 17th St. NW
Washington, DC 20036
Tel: (202)862-5800
Fax: (202)862-7177
EMail: jlilley@aei.org

Employers
American Enterprise Institute for Public Policy Research (Resident Fellow and Director of Asian Studies)

LILLEY, Justin W.

444 N. Capitol St. NW
Suite 740
Washington, DC 20001
Tel: (202)824-6500
Fax: (202)824-6510
Registered: LDA

Telecommunications Counsel, House Committee on Commerce, 1997-2000. Law Clerk to Judge Harold R. DeMoss, Jr., U.S. Court of Appeals, Fifth Circuit, 1993-95.

Employers
News Corporation Ltd. (V. President, Government Relations)

LILLO, Peter J.

536 First St. SE
Washington, DC 20003
Tel: (202)544-6259
Fax: (202)544-6141
Registered: LDA

Employers
New Jersey Hospital Ass'n (V. President, Government Relations)

LILYGREN, Sara J.

1700 N. Moore St.
Suite 1600
Arlington, VA 22209
Tel: (703)841-2400
Fax: (703)527-0938
Registered: LDA

Employers
American Meat Institute (Senior V. President, Legislative and Public Affairs)

LIMAURO, Nancy

1730 N. Lynn St.
Suite 504
Arlington, VA 22209
Tel: (703)276-1412
Fax: (703)276-1415
Registered: LDA

Employers
Balzano Associates (Account Executive)

Clients Represented

On Behalf of Balzano Associates
Nat'l Institute for Aerospace Studies and Services Inc.

LIMBACH, Bonnie M.

1801 K St. NW
Suite 600K
Washington, DC 20006
Tel: (202)974-5200
Fax: (202)296-7005

Employers
Soc. of the Plastics Industry (Chief Communications Officer)

LIMBACH, Dennis D.

1301 Pennsylvania Ave. NW
Suite 1030
Washington, DC 20004
Tel: (202)824-0404
Fax: (202)347-0132
EMail: dlimbac@alleghenyenergy.com

Employers
Allegheny Energy, Inc. (Manager, Federal Legislative Affairs)

LIMBACH, Mary "Mimi"

2025 M St. NW
Suite 350
Washington, DC 20036
Tel: (202)466-7391
Fax: (202)463-1338
Registered: LDA

Employers
Potomac Communications Group

LINCAMAOD, Melisa

801 N. Fairfax St.
Suite 400
Alexandria, VA 22314
Tel: (703)838-0500
Fax: (703)549-3864

Employers
American Medical Women's Ass'n (Deputy Exec. Director, Governmental Affairs and Communications)

LINCOLN, Edward J.

1775 Massachusetts Ave. NW
Washington, DC 20036-2188
Tel: (202)797-6000
Fax: (202)797-6004

Former Special Economic Advisor to Ambassador Walter Mondale in Tokyo, Japan, 1994-96.

Employers
The Brookings Institution (Senior Fellow, Foreign Policy Studies)

LINCOLN, Walter

102 Sheridan Ave.
Fort Myer, VA 22211-1110
Tel: (703)522-3060
Fax: (703)522-1336

Employers
Army & Air Force Mutual Aid Ass'n (President)

LIND, Keith D.

2099 Pennsylvania Ave. NW
Suite 100
Washington, DC 20006
Tel: (202)955-3000
Fax: (202)955-5564
Registered: LDA
EMail: klind@hklaw.com

Employers
Holland & Knight LLP (Senior Counsel)

Clients Represented

On Behalf of Holland & Knight LLP
Benova, Inc.
Nassau County Health Care Corp.
UroMedica Corp.

LIND, William S.

717 Second St. NE
Washington, DC 20002
Tel: (202)204-5312
Fax: (202)543-5605

Employers
Free Congress Research and Education Foundation (Director, Center for Cultural Conservatism)

LINDBERG, Brian

1101 Vermont Ave. NW
Suite 1001
Washington, DC 20005
Tel: (202)789-3606
Fax: (202)898-2389

Employers
Consumer Coalition for Quality Health Care (Exec. Director)

LINDBERG, Ernest T.

1301 K St. NW
Suite 900
East Tower
Washington, DC 20005
Tel: (202)408-8007
Fax: (202)408-8704
Former Attorney, Panama Canal Commission, Department of the Navy.

Employers
The Carter Group

LINDBERG, Gavin

507 Capitol Ct. NE
Suite 200
Washington, DC 20002
Tel: (202)544-7499
Fax: (202)546-7105
Registered: LDA

Employers
Health and Medicine Counsel of Washington (Legislative Director)

Clients Represented

On Behalf of Health and Medicine Counsel of Washington
Ass'n of Academic Health Sciences Library Directors
Ass'n of Minority Health Profession Schools
Crohn's and Colitis Foundation of America
Digestive Disease Nat'l Coalition
ESA, Inc.
Immune Deficiency Foundation, Inc.
Medical Library Ass'n/Ass'n of Academic Health Sciences Library Directors

LINDBERG, Roger

2300 M St. NW
Suite 900
Washington, DC 20037
Tel: (202)467-2761
Fax: (202)293-5717
EMail: roger@publicforuminstitute.com
Former Administrative Assistant to Rep. Robert T. Matsui (D-CA).

Employers
Public Forum Institute (Exec. Director)

LINDBLOM, Louise

2120 L St. NW
Suite 510
Washington, DC 20037
Tel: (202)986-1460
Fax: (202)986-1468

Employers
Nat'l Urban Coalition (Director, Media Relations)

LINDER, Diana

400 Maryland Ave. SW
Room 7E306
Washington, DC 20202-3100
Tel: (202)401-0023
Fax: (202)401-1438
EMail: diana_linder@ed.gov

Employers
Department of Education (Legislative Specialist)

LINDHOLM, Douglas

122 C St. NW
Suite 330
Washington, DC 20001
Tel: (202)484-5212
Fax: (202)484-5229

Employers
Committee On State Taxation (President and Exec. Director)

LINDNER, CAE, Randy

1444 I St. NW
Suite 700
Washington, DC 20005-2210
Tel: (202)216-9623
Fax: (202)216-9646
EMail: rlindner@bostromdc.com

Employers
Bostrom Corp. (Senior V. President and General Manager)

Clients Represented

On Behalf of Bostrom Corp.
Nat'l Ass'n of Boards of Examiners of Long Term Care Administrators

LINDSAY, David C.

1250 I St. NW
Suite 1003
Washington, DC 20005-3917
Tel: (202)289-0873
Fax: (202)289-5388
Registered: LDA
EMail: dlindsay@ngfa.org

Employers
Nat'l Grain and Feed Ass'n (Director, Legislative Affairs)

LINDSAY, J. Wade

2300 N St. NW
Suite 700
Washington, DC 20037-1128
Tel: (202)783-4141
Fax: (202)783-5851
EMail: jlindsay@wbklaw.com

Employers
Wilkinson, Barker and Knauer, LLP (Partner)

LINDSAY, James M.

1775 Massachusetts Ave. NW
Washington, DC 20036-2188
Tel: (202)797-6000
Fax: (202)797-6004
Director for Global Issues and Multilateral Affairs, National Security Council, 1996-97.

Employers
The Brookings Institution (Senior Fellow, Foreign Policy Studies)

LINDSAY, Linda P.

1420 King St.
Alexandria, VA 22314-2794
Tel: (703)684-2873
Fax: (703)836-4875
Registered: LDA
EMail: llindsay@nspe.org

Employers
Nat'l Soc. of Professional Engineers (Manager, Congressional and State Relations)

LINDSAY, Scott

1225 I St. NW
Suite 600
Washington, DC 20005
Tel: (202)661-6195
Fax: (202)661-6182
Registered: LDA
EMail: slindsay@morganmeguire.com
Former Legislative Assistant to Rep. Jennifer Dunn (R-WA).

Employers
Morgan Meguire, LLC (V. President)

Clients Represented

On Behalf of Morgan Meguire, LLC
Adroit Systems Inc.
Baker Electromotive, Inc.
BellSouth Corp.
Colorado River Energy Distributors Ass'n
Energy Northwest
Florida Municipal Power Agency
Goodman Manufacturing Co., L.P.
Longhorn Pipeline
Madison Gas & Electric Co.
Manatee, Florida, County of
Northern California Power Agency
Northwest Public Power Ass'n
Nuevo Energy
Redding, California, City of
Southern California Public Power Authority
Springfield, Missouri, City Utilities of
Tennessee Valley Public Power Ass'n
Transmission Access Policy Study Group
Washington Public Utility Districts Ass'n

LINDSEY, Elise

8201 Greensboro Dr.
Suite 300
McLean, VA 22102
Tel: (703)610-9000
Fax: (703)610-9005

Employers
Ass'n Management Group
Ass'n of Water Technologies (Exec. Director)

Clients Represented

On Behalf of Ass'n Management Group
Ass'n of Water Technologies

LINDSEY, Lawrence B.

1150 17th St. NW
Washington, DC 20036
Tel: (202)862-5800
Fax: (202)862-7177
EMail: llindsey@aei.org

Employers
American Enterprise Institute for Public Policy Research (Resident Scholar)

LINDSLEY, Thomas A.

1201 New York Ave. NW
Suite 700
Washington, DC 20005
Tel: (202)289-2932
Fax: (202)289-1303
EMail: lindsleyt@nab.com

Employers
Nat'l Alliance of Business (V. President, Policy and Government Relations)

LINDSTROM, Tom

1634 I St. NW
Suite 600
Washington, DC 20006-4083
Tel: (202)783-2200
Fax: (202)783-2206

Employers
Ericsson Inc. (Director, Regulatory Policy)

LINK, James E.

P.O. Box 1417-D49
Alexandria, VA 22313-1417
Tel: (703)549-3001
Fax: (703)836-4869
Deputy Director, Senate Republican Whip's Office and Legislative Assistant to Senator Alan K. Simpson (R-WY), 1992-94. Legislative Assistant to Rep. William L. Dickinson (R-AL), 1989-92. Also served as a Staff Assistant to Rep. Dick Cheney (R-WY).

Employers
Nat'l Ass'n of Chain Drug Stores (V. President, Federal Legislative Affairs)

LINK, Patric G.

1317 F St. NW
Suite 600
Washington, DC 20004
Tel: (202)638-2121
Fax: (202)638-7045
Registered: LDA

Employers
The Wexler Group (Principal/Senior Director)

Clients Represented

On Behalf of The Wexler Group
AstroVision Inc.
DCH Technology Inc.
EarthWatch, Inc.
ORBITZ
Virginia Center for Innovative Technology

LINN, Dane

444 N. Capitol St. NW
Suite 267
Washington, DC 20001-1512
Tel: (202)624-5300
Fax: (202)624-5313
EMail: dlinn@nga.org

Employers
Nat'l Governors' Ass'n (Policy Studies Director, Education)

LINNEY, Jr., Dr. Thomas J.

One Dupont Circle NW
Suite 430
Washington, DC 20036
Tel: (202)223-3791
Fax: (202)331-7157
Registered: LDA
EMail: tlinney@cgs.nche.edu

Employers
Council of Graduate Schools (V. President and Director, Government and Association Relations)

LINTHICUM, Kimberly

555 12th St. NW
Suite 650
Washington, DC 20004-1205
Tel: (202)393-7950
Fax: (202)393-7960

Employers
Eli Lilly and Co. (Sr. Associate, Federal Affairs)

LINTON, Ron M.

1299 Pennsylvania Ave. NW
Suite 800 West
Washington, DC 20004
Tel: (202)785-0500
Fax: (202)785-5277
Registered: LDA
Chairman, Task Force on Environmental Health, Department of Health, Education and Welfare, 1967-68. Staff Director, Public Works Committee, U.S. Senate, 1963-66. Director, Economic Utilization Policy, Department of Defense, 1961-63. Staff Member, Special Committee on Aging, U.S. Senate, 1961.

Employers
The Carmen Group
LMRC, Inc.

Clients Represented

On Behalf of The Carmen Group

ADVO, Inc.
Air Transport Ass'n of America

LIPMAN, Andrew D.

3000 K St. NW
Suite 300
Washington, DC 20007
Tel: (202)424-7500
Fax: (202)424-7643
Registered: LDA

Employers

Swidler Berlin Shereff Friedman, LLP (Partner)

Clients Represented

On Behalf of Swidler Berlin Shereff Friedman, LLP

Cable & Wireless, Inc.
German Competitive Carriers Ass'n

LIPMAN, Deborah Swartz

600 Fifth St. NW
Washington, DC 20001
Tel: (202)962-1003
Fax: (202)962-2466

Employers

Washington Metropolitan Area Transit Authority (Director, Government and Community Relations)

LIPNER, Robyn

1818 N St. NW
Suite 450
Washington, DC 20036
Tel: (202)530-2900
Fax: (202)530-2901
Registered: LDA
EMail: rlipner@basshowes.com

Former Staff Director, Subcommittee on Aging, Committee on Labor and Human Resources, U.S. Senate and Professional Staff for Senator Brock Adams (D-WA) and Rep. Patricia Schroeder (D-CO).

Employers

Bass and Howes, Inc. (Senior Program Manager)

Clients Represented

On Behalf of Bass and Howes, Inc.

Institute for Civil Soc.
Nat'l Breast Cancer Coalition
Nat'l Partnership for Women and Families
Ross Abbott Laboratories

LIPPINCOTT, Joan K.

21 Dupont Circle NW
Suite 800
Washington, DC 20036
Tel: (202)296-5098
Fax: (202)872-0884
EMail: joan@cni.org

Employers

Coalition for Networked Information (Associate Exec. Director)

LIPPMAN, Tom

1250 24th St. NW
Washington, DC 20037
Tel: (202)293-4800
Fax: (202)293-9211

Employers

World Wildlife Fund (V. President, Public Affairs)

LIPSCOMB, Renata

440 First St. NW
Eighth Floor
Washington, DC 20001
Tel: (202)942-4270
Fax: (202)393-2630
EMail: rlipscomb@naco.org

Employers

Nat'l Ass'n of Counties (Associate, Corporate Relations)

LIPSEN, Janice C.

1000 16th St. NW
Suite 400
Washington, DC 20036
Tel: (202)785-0550
Fax: (202)785-0210
Registered: LDA, FARA
EMail: cfmincdc@aol.com

Assistant to Speaker Carl Albert (D-OK), U.S. House of Representatives, 1970-75.

Employers

Counselors For Management, Inc. (President)

Clients Represented

On Behalf of Counselors For Management, Inc.

Alternative Systems, Inc.
American Samoa, Government of
Campbell Estate

LIPSEN, Linda A.

1050 31st St. NW
Washington, DC 20007
Tel: (202)965-3500
Fax: (202)342-5484
Registered: LDA

Employers

Ass'n of Trial Lawyers of America (Senior Director, Public and National Affairs)

LIPSEN, Zel E.

One Massachusetts Ave. NW
Suite 330
Washington, DC 20001
Tel: (703)448-3060
Fax: (703)448-3060
Registered: LDA

Legal Assistant, House Select Committee on Government Research and Development, 1964-65. Staff Assistant to Senator Clair Engle (D-CA), 1959-63.

Employers

Law Office of Zel E. Lipsen (Principal)

Clients Represented

On Behalf of Law Office of Zel E. Lipsen

British Ministry of Defence
Dames & Moore
Media Fusion L.L.C.
Northrop Grumman Corp.
PulseTech Products Corp.

LIPTAK, Elisabeth

1828 L St. NW
Suite 625
Washington, DC 20036
Tel: (202)496-5003
Fax: (202)833-3472
EMail: liz@womens-health.org

Employers

Soc. for Women's Health Research (Communications Director)

LIPTON, Karen Shoos

8101 Glenbrook Rd.
Bethesda, MD 20814-2749
Tel: (301)907-6977
Fax: (301)907-6895
Registered: LDA

Employers

American Ass'n of Blood Banks (Chief Exec. Officer)

LISACK, Jr., John

15501 Monona Dr.
Rockville, MD 20855
Tel: (301)251-0560
Fax: (301)279-2996
EMail: jlisack@aspp.org

Employers

American Soc. of Plant Physiologists (Exec. Director)

LISBOA-FARRON, Elizabeth

2175 K St. NW
Suite 100
Washington, DC 20036
Tel: (202)737-2622

Employers

U.S. Hispanic Chamber of Commerce (Chair)

LISEY, Diane

409 Third St. SW
Second Floor
Washington, DC 20024
Tel: (202)479-1200
Fax: (202)479-0735

Employers

Nat'l Council on the Aging (Public Policy Associate)

LISKER, Lisa R.

228 S. Washington St.
Suite 200
Alexandria, VA 22314

Employers

Impact America (Contact)

LISS, Cathy

P.O. Box 3719
Georgetown Station
Washington, DC 20007
Tel: (202)337-2334
Fax: (202)338-9478
Registered: LDA

Employers

Soc. for Animal Protective Legislation (Legislative Director)

LISS, Jeffrey F.

1200 19th St. NW
Washington, DC 20036-2430
Tel: (202)861-3940
Fax: (202)223-2085
Registered: LDA
EMail: jeffrey.liss@piperrudnick.com

Employers

Piper Marbury Rudnick & Wolfe LLP (Partner, Chief Operating Officer)

Clients Represented

On Behalf of Piper Marbury Rudnick & Wolfe LLP

Utility Solid Waste Activities Group

LISSAU, Jacqueline

1875 I St. NW
Suite 600
Washington, DC 20006
Tel: (202)739-9400
Fax: (202)739-9401
Registered: LDA
EMail: jlissau@nareit.com

Employers

Nat'l Ass'n of Real Estate Investment Trusts (Political Affairs Coordinator)

LISTER, James M.

1101 Vermont Ave. NW
Suite 401
Washington, DC 20005
Tel: (202)371-0690
Fax: (202)371-0692
Registered: FARA
EMail: jml@keia.org

Employers

Korea Economic Institute of America (V. President)

LISTER, V.D.M., Sarah

800 I St. NW
Washington, DC 20001
Tel: (202)777-2742
Fax: (202)777-2534

Employers

American Public Health Ass'n (Director, Congressional Affairs)

LITAN, Robert E.

Three Golden Crest Ct.
Rockville, MD 20854
Tel: (202)797-6120
Fax: (202)797-6181
Registered: LDA

Former Associate Director, General Government and Finance, Office of Management and Budget.

Employers

Robert E. Litan

Clients Represented

On Behalf of Robert E. Litan

Arnold & Porter

LITMAN, Gary V.

1615 H St. NW
Washington, DC 20062-2000
Tel: (202)463-5460
Fax: (202)463-3114
Registered: LDA
EMail: eurasia@uschamber.com

Employers

Chamber of Commerce of the U.S.A. (Director, Central Eastern Europe and Eurasia, International)

LITT, David

555 13th St. NW
Suite 500 West
Washington, DC 20004
Tel: (202)383-5300
Fax: (202)383-5414
Registered: LDA
EMail: dlitt@omm.com

Employers

O'Melveny and Myers LLP (Partner)

Clients Represented

On Behalf of O'Melveny and Myers LLP

CIGNA Corp.

LITTELL, Barbara

1775 Massachusetts Ave. NW
Washington, DC 20036-2188
Tel: (202)797-6000
Fax: (202)797-6004

Employers

The Brookings Institution (Senior Staff, Center for Public Policy Education)

LITTERST, Kristin

1150 17th St. NW
Suite 701
Washington, DC 20036
EMail: kristinl@dittus.com

Tel: (202)775-1401
Fax: (202)775-1404

Deputy Press Secretary for Sen. Malcom Wallop (R-WY), 1991-94. Legislative Correspondent for Sen. Alan Simpson (R-WY), 1989-91.

Employers
Dittus Communications (Assistant V. President)

Clients Represented
On Behalf of Dittus Communications
3Com Corp.
Americans for Computer Privacy
Business Software Alliance
CapNet
Comptel
COPA Commission
Intel Corp.
Nat'l Alliance Against Blacklisting
Pegasus Communications
Pernod Ricard
VeriSign/Network Solutions, Inc.

LITTERST, R. Nelson

1600 Pennsylvania Ave. NW
112 E. Wing
Washington, DC 20500

Tel: (202)456-6620
Fax: (202)456-2604

Former Aide to Rep. Gary Franks (R-CT). Former Aide to House Minority Leader, Rep. Bob Michel (R-IL).

Employers
Executive Office of the President - The White House (Special Assistant to the President for Legislative Affairs, House Liaison Office)

LITTIG, Melvin J.

1001 Pennsylvania Ave. NW
Suite 760 North
Washington, DC 20004

Tel: (202)661-7060
Fax: (202)661-7066
Registered: LDA

Former Military Specialist, Office of the Secretary, Department of the Army.

Employers
The Legislative Strategies Group, LLC

Clients Represented
On Behalf of The Legislative Strategies Group, LLC
American Systems Internat'l Corp.
ECC Internat'l Corp.
Institute for Human-Machine Cognition
Noesis Inc.

LITTLE, Barbara A.

1155 15th St. NW
Suite 611
Washington, DC 20005

Tel: (202)223-4411
Fax: (202)223-1849
Registered: LDA

Employers
Albemarle Corp. (V. President, Government Relations)
Ethyl Corp. (V. President, Government Relations)

LITTLE, C. Bryan

600 Maryland Ave. SW
Suite 800
Washington, DC 20024

Tel: (202)484-3600
Fax: (202)484-3604
Registered: LDA

Employers
American Farm Bureau Federation (Director, Agricultural Labor/Transportation/Regulatory Affairs)

LITTLE, Jeanne

1601 Duke St.
Alexandria, VA 22314-3406

Tel: (703)836-8700
Fax: (703)836-8705
Registered: LDA

EMail: jlittle@safnow.org

Employers
Soc. of American Florists (Director, Government Relations)

LITTLE, Linda A.

14th and Constitution Ave. NW
Room 7814A
Washington, DC 20230

Tel: (202)482-2309
Fax: (202)501-4828

Employers
Department of Commerce - Economic Development Administration (Communications and Congressional Liaison Specialist)

LITTLEFIELD, Amy

9420 Annapolis Rd.
Suite 307
Lanham, MD 20706

Tel: (301)577-4956
Ext: 102
Fax: (301)731-0039

Employers
Service Station Dealers of America and Allied Trades (Director, Federal Government Relations)

LITTLEFIELD, Cynthia A.

One Dupont Circle
Suite 405
Washington, DC 20036

Tel: (202)862-9893
Fax: (202)862-8523
Registered: LDA

EMail: cyndylit@aol.com

Employers
Ass'n of Jesuit Colleges and Universities (Director, Federal Relations)

LITTLEFIELD, Roy E.

9420 Annapolis Rd.
Suite 307
Lanham, MD 20706

Tel: (301)577-4956
Ext: 108
Fax: (301)731-0039

Employers
Service Station Dealers of America and Allied Trades (Exec. V. President)

LITTLEFIELD, Sean

8503 Pelham Rd.
Bethesda, MD 20817

Tel: (301)564-9708
Fax: (301)564-9706
Registered: LDA

Employers
Direct Impact, LLC

Clients Represented
On Behalf of Direct Impact, LLC
D.A.R.E. America

LITTLER, Charles N.

113 S. West St.
Fourth Floor
Alexandria, VA 22314

Tel: (703)838-2929
Fax: (703)838-2950

Employers
United Motorcoach Ass'n

LITTLETON, Joseph

1755 Jefferson Davis Hwy.
Suite 1107
Arlington, VA 22202

Tel: (703)415-0344
Fax: (703)415-0182
Registered: LDA

Employers
The PMA Group (Associate)

Clients Represented
On Behalf of The PMA Group
Condor Systems
CPU Technology
L-3 Communications Corp.
Lockheed Martin Federal Systems
Marconi Communications Federal
Microvision, Inc.
MTS Systems Inc.
Sabreliner Corp.
SVS, Inc.

LITTMAN, Andrew C.

1001 G St. NW
Suite 900 E
Washington, DC 20001-4545
EMail: littman@podesta.com

Tel: (202)393-1010
Fax: (202)393-5510

Former Policy Director to Senator Barbara Boxer (D-CA).

Employers
Podesta/Mattoon (Principal)

Clients Represented
On Behalf of Podesta/Mattoon
AOL Time Warner
Genentech, Inc.
Interactive Gaming Council
Mount Sinai/NYU Health
Nextel Communications, Inc.
Recording Industry Ass'n of America
SiTV
Vivendi Universal

LIVELY, Jr., H. R.

919 18th St. NW
Suite 300
Washington, DC 20006

Tel: (202)296-5544
Fax: (202)223-0321
Registered: LDA

Employers
American Financial Services Ass'n (President and Chief Exec. Officer)

LIVELY, P. Susan

1299 Pennsylvania Ave. NW
Tenth Floor
Washington, DC 20004-2400
EMail: susanlively@paulhastings.com

Tel: (202)508-9500
Fax: (202)508-9700

Trial Attorney, Environmental Enforcement Section, Environment and Natural Resources Division, Department of Justice, 1991-97. Clerk to Judge Jacques L. Weiner, Jr., U.S. Fifth Circuit for the Court of Appeals, 1990-91.

Employers
Paul, Hastings, Janofsky & Walker LLP (Associate)

Clients Represented
On Behalf of Paul, Hastings, Janofsky & Walker LLP
Chlorobenzene Producers Ass'n

LIVELY, Robert W.

1130 Connecticut Ave. NW
Suite 500
Washington, DC 20036

Tel: (202)463-7372
Fax: (202)463-8809
Registered: LDA

Employers
Schering-Plough Legislative Resources L.L.C. (Staff V. President, Congressional Relations)

LIVINGSTON, Burk

Eisenhower Exec. Office Bldg.
725 17th St. NW
Washington, DC 20503

Tel: (202)395-4790
Fax: (202)395-3888

Employers
Executive Office of the President - Office of Management and Budget (Legislative Assistant)

LIVINGSTON, Catherine E.

One Thomas Circle NW
Suite 1100
Washington, DC 20005
EMail: cel@capdale.com

Tel: (202)862-5089
Fax: (202)429-3301
Registered: LDA

Office of the Tax Legislative Counsel, Department of the Treasury, 1994-98

Employers
Caplin & Drysdale, Chartered (Member)

Clients Represented
On Behalf of Caplin & Drysdale, Chartered
Independent Sector

LIVINGSTON, Donald R.

1333 New Hampshire Ave. NW
Suite 400
Washington, DC 20036

Tel: (202)887-4000
Fax: (202)887-4288

General Counsel, Equal Employment Opportunity Commission, 1990-93.

Employers
Akin, Gump, Strauss, Hauer & Feld, L.L.P. (Partner)

LIVINGSTON, Jr., Hon. Robert L.

499 S. Capitol St. SW
Suite 600
Washington, DC 20003

Tel: (202)289-9881
Fax: (202)289-9877
Registered: LDA

Member, U.S. House of Representatives (R-LA), 1977-99.

Employers
The Livingston Group, LLC (Principal)

Clients Represented

On Behalf of The Livingston Group, LLC

ACS Government Solutions Group
American Ass'n of Nurse Anesthetists
Baton Rouge, Louisiana, City of
Boys Town USA
Broward, Florida, County of
Committee of Unsecured Creditors
Commonwealth Atlantic Properties
General Category Tuna Ass'n
General Electric Co.
Gray Morrison
Great Western Cellular Partnership
Illinois Department of Human Services
Internat'l Systems, Inc.
Jacobus Tenbroek Memorial Fund
Link Plus Co.
Marine Desalination Systems LLC
Mesa, Arizona, City of
MidAmerican Energy Holdings Co.
Nat'l Capitol Concerts
New Orleans, Louisiana, Port of
Raytheon Co.
Schering-Plough Corp.
Stewart Enterprises, Inc.
U.S. Oil and Gas Ass'n

LIVINGSTON, Jr., S. William

1201 Pennsylvania Ave. NW
Washington, DC 20004-2401
Tel: (202)662-6000
Fax: (202)662-6291
EMail: wlivington@cov.com

Former Law Clerk to Judge Charles M. Merrill, U.S. Court of Appeals, Ninth Circuit.

Employers

Covington & Burling (Partner)

LLOYD, David

1500 Rhode Island Ave. NW
Washington, DC 20005-5597
Tel: (202)462-6272
Fax: (202)462-8549

Employers

Nat'l Paint and Coatings Ass'n (V. President, Government Affairs)

LLOYD, Elizabeth J.

1400 Independence Ave. SW
Stop 3407, Room 1147, South Bldg.
Washington, DC 20250
Tel: (202)720-2511
Fax: (202)720-3982
EMail: elizabeth.j.lloyd@usda.gov

Employers

Department of Agriculture - Animal and Plant Health Inspection Service (Legislative Analyst)

LLOYD, Frank W.

701 Pennsylvania Ave. NW
Suite 900
Washington, DC 20004-2608
Tel: (202)434-7300
Fax: (202)434-7400
Registered: LDA
EMail: flloyd@mintz.com

Administrative Assistant to the Chairman, Federal Communications Commission, 1977-81. Office of Telecommunications Policy, Executive Office of the President, The White House, 1976-77.

Employers

Mintz, Levin, Cohn, Ferris, Glovsky and Popeo, P.C. (Partner)

Clients Represented

On Behalf of Mintz, Levin, Cohn, Ferris, Glovsky and Popeo, P.C.

California Cable Television Ass'n
New England Cable Television Ass'n
Television Ass'n of Programmers Latin America (TAP Latin America)

LLOYD, John G.

1090 Vermont Ave. NW
Suite 700
Washington, DC 20005-4905
Tel: (202)289-7800
Fax: (202)289-1092
EMail: jlloyd@nibs.org

Employers

Nat'l Institute of Building Sciences (V. President, Finance and Administration)

LOCHBAUM, David A.

1707 H St. NW
Suite 600
Washington, DC 20006-3919
Tel: (202)223-6133
Fax: (202)223-6162

Employers

Union of Concerned Scientists (Nuclear Safety Engineer)

LOCKE, W. Timothy

1401 K St. NW
12th Floor
Washington, DC 20005
Tel: (202)393-4760
Fax: (202)393-3516
Registered: LDA
EMail: tlock@smithfree.com

Former White House Assistant, U.S. Interior Department Official and Aide to Senator Howard Baker (R-TN).

Employers

The Smith-Free Group (Senior V. President)

Clients Represented

On Behalf of The Smith-Free Group

AT&T
Broadcast Music Inc. (BMI)
CSX Corp.
HCA Healthcare Corp.
MasterCard Internat'l
MBNA America Bank NA
Nuclear Energy Institute
Paucatuck Eastern Pequot Tribal Nation
Sandia Pueblo
Sony Music Entertainment Inc.
Sony Pictures Entertainment Inc.
Southern Co.
U.S. Wireless Data, Inc.
VISA U.S.A., Inc.
Washington Group Internat'l
Westinghouse Government Services Group

LOCKHART, Robert F.

1300 N. 17th St.
Suite 1850
Arlington, VA 22209
Tel: (703)841-7100
Fax: (703)841-7720
Registered: LDA

Employers

Oxygenated Fuels Ass'n (Director, Government Affairs)

LOCKWOOD, II, Charles H.

1001 19th St. North
Suite 1200
Arlington, VA 22209
Tel: (703)525-7788
Fax: (703)525-8817
EMail: clockwood@aiam.org

Employers

Ass'n of Internat'l Automobile Manufacturers (V. President and General Counsel)

LOCONTE, Joseph

214 Massachusetts Ave. NE
Washington, DC 20002
Tel: (202)546-4400
Fax: (202)546-8328

Employers

Heritage Foundation (William E. Simon Fellow in Religion and a Free Society)

LODGE, Stephen G.

8320 Old Courthouse Rd.
Suite 300
Vienna, VA 22182
Tel: (703)790-5011
Fax: (703)790-5752
Registered: LDA
EMail: steve.lodge@candyusa.org

Former Aide to Rep. Newt Steers (R-MD), Rep. John Paul Hammerschmidt (R-AR), Rep. Charles Dougherty (R-PA), and Rep. George Gekas (R-PA).

Employers

Chocolate Manufacturers Ass'n of the U.S.A. (V. President, Legislative Affairs)
Nat'l Confectioners Ass'n (V. President, Legislative Affairs)

LODGE, Terri

2201 C St. NW
Room 7251
Washington, DC 20520-7261
Tel: (202)647-8728
Fax: (202)647-2762

Employers

Department of State - Bureau of Legislative Affairs (Arms Control and Political-Military Issues Legislative Management Officer)

LOEB, Eric

1120 20th St. NW
Suite 1000
Washington, DC 20036
Registered: LDA

Employers

Concert USA

LOEB, G. Hamilton

1299 Pennsylvania Ave. NW
Tenth Floor
Washington, DC 20004-2400
Tel: (202)508-9500
Fax: (202)508-9700
Registered: LDA, FARA
EMail: hamiltonloeb@paulhastings.com

Law Clerk to Chief Judge James R. Browning, U.S. Court of Appeals, Ninth Circuit, 1978-79. Legislative Assistant to Rep. Robert H. Steele (R-CT), 1973-74.

Employers

Paul, Hastings, Janofsky & Walker LLP (Partner)

Clients Represented

On Behalf of Paul, Hastings, Janofsky & Walker LLP

Amdahl Corp.
Canada, Government of
The Marine and Fire Insurance Ass'n of Japan, Inc.
Tubos de Acero de Mexico, S.A.
U.S. Figure Skating Ass'n

LOEB, Laura E.

555 13th St. NW
Washington, DC 20004-1109
Tel: (202)637-5760
Fax: (202)637-5910
Registered: LDA
EMail: leloeb@hhlaw.com

Counsel, Congressional Caucus for Women's Issues, 1986-88.

Employers

Hogan & Hartson L.L.P. (Partner)

Clients Represented

On Behalf of Hogan & Hartson L.L.P.

American College of Osteopathic Surgeons
American Soc. of Orthopedic Physician Assistants

LOEFFLER, Robert H.

2000 Pennsylvania Ave. NW
Suite 5500
Washington, DC 20006
Tel: (202)887-1500
Fax: (202)887-0763
Registered: FARA
EMail: rloeffler@mofo.com

Employers

Morrison & Foerster LLP (Partner)

LOEFFLER, Stacey

1667 K St. NW
Suite 640
Washington, DC 20006-1605
Tel: (202)721-4807
Fax: (202)467-4250
EMail: stacey.loeffler@oracle.com

Employers

Oracle Corp. (Manager, Political Programs and Compliance)

LOEFFLER, Hon. Thomas G.

1801 K St. NW
Washington, DC 20006
Tel: (202)775-7100
Fax: (202)857-0172
Registered: LDA, FARA
EMail: tloeffler@arterhadden.com

Advisor to the President for Central American Legislative Affairs, Executive Office of the President, The White House, 1987. Member, U.S. House of Representatives (R-TX), 1978-86. Special Assistant to the President for Legislative Affairs, Executive Office of the President, The White House, 1975-77. Deputy for Congressional, Federal Energy Administration, 1974-75. Chief Legislative Counsel to Senator John Tower (R-TX), 1972-74. Legal Counsel, Department of Commerce, 1971-72.

Employers

Arter & Hadden (Partner)

Clients Represented

On Behalf of Arter & Hadden

Academy of Radiology Research
Americans for Fair Taxation
Billing Concepts, Inc.
BKK Corp.
Bristol-Myers Squibb Co.
Centerior Energy Corp.
Circus Circus Enterprises, Inc.
Citigroup
Fairchild Aircraft, Inc.
HCA Healthcare Corp.
Hicks, Muse, Tate & Furst
Houston, Texas, Port Authority of the City of
Metabolife
OnCare, Inc.
Pinpoint Communications
Sammons Enterprises, Inc.
San Antonio, Texas, City of
SBC Communications Inc.
South West Florida Enterprises, Inc.
Tesoro Petroleum Corp.
Tribal Alliance of Northern California
Whirlpool Corp.
H. B. Zachry

LOERA, Patricia

1220 L St. NW
Suite 605
Washington, DC 20005-4018
EMail: p_loera@nabe.org
Tel: (202)898-1829
Fax: (202)789-2866
Registered: LDA

Employers
Nat'l Ass'n for Bilingual Education (Legislative Director)

LOFTUS, C. Michael

1224 17th St. NW
Washington, DC 20036
Tel: (202)347-7170
Fax: (202)347-3619
Registered: LDA

Law Clerk to Judge Joseph H. Young, U.S. District Court for the District of Maryland, 1973-74.

Employers
Slover & Loftus (Partner)

LOFTUS, Robert E.

1775 Duke St.
Alexandria, VA 22314-3428
Tel: (703)518-6330
Fax: (703)518-6409

Employers
Nat'l Credit Union Administration (Director, Office of Public and Congressional Affairs)

LOGAN, Bryan J.

45 W. Watkins Mill Rd.
Gaithersburg, MD 20878
Tel: (301)948-8550
Fax: (301)963-2064

Employers
EarthData Holdings (Chief Exec. Officer)

LOGAN, Charles

1909 K St. NW
Suite 820
Washington, DC 20006
EMail: blogan@lmm-law.com
Tel: (202)777-7700
Fax: (202)777-7763
Registered: LDA

Chief (1998-99), Chief, Legal Branch (1996-98), and Staff Attorney, Legal Branch (1994-96), Policy and Rules Division, Mass Media Bureau, Federal Communications Commission.

Employers
Lawler, Metzger & Milkman, LLC (Partner)

Clients Represented

On Behalf of Lawler, Metzger & Milkman, LLC

MCI WorldCom Corp.

LOGAN, James A.

601 Madison St.
Suite 200
Alexandria, VA 22314
Tel: (703)549-9266
Fax: (703)549-9268

Employers
Allison Transmission Division, General Motors Corp. (Director, Washington Operations)

LOGAN, John E.

555 12th St. NW
Washington, DC 20004
Tel: (202)347-4964
Fax: (202)347-4961
Registered: LDA

Employers
Wallman Strategic Consulting, LLC

Clients Represented

On Behalf of Wallman Strategic Consulting, LLC

MediaOne Group
PanAmSat Corp.

LOGAN, John S.

1200 New Hampshire Ave. NW
Suite 800
Washington, DC 20036-6802
EMail: jlogan@dlalaw.com
Tel: (202)776-2000
Fax: (202)776-2222

Employers
Dow, Lohnes & Albertson, PLLC (Member)

LOGAN, Tammie

4121 Wilson Blvd.
Tenth Floor
Arlington, VA 22203
EMail: tlogan@ntca.org
Tel: (703)351-2000
Fax: (703)351-2001
Registered: LDA

Employers
Nat'l Telephone Cooperative Ass'n (Government Affairs Representative)

LOGE, Peter

50 F St. NW
Suite 1070
Washington, DC 20001
Tel: (202)638-5855
Fax: (202)638-6056
Registered: LDA

Former Chief of Staff and Communications Director for Rep. Brad Sherman (D-CA).

Employers
The Justice Project, Inc.
Vietnam Veterans of America Foundation

LOGOMASINI, Angela

1001 Connecticut Ave. NW
Suite 1250
Washington, DC 20036
Tel: (202)331-1010

Employers
Competitive Enterprise Institute (Director, Risk and Environmental Policy)

LOHMAN, Barbara

1899 L St. NW
Suite 200
Washington, DC 20036
Tel: (202)833-8121
Fax: (202)833-8155

Employers
Devillier Communications (V. President)

Clients Represented

On Behalf of Devillier Communications

Perkins School for the Blind

LOHMAN, Houda M.

555 12th St. NW
Suite 350
N. Tower
Washington, DC 20004
Tel: (202)639-4065
Fax: (202)737-1311
Registered: LDA

Employers
ABB, Inc. (Government Policy Analyst)

LOHNES, Robin C.

1000 29th St. NW
Suite T-100
Washington, DC 20007
Tel: (202)965-0500
Fax: (202)965-9621

Employers
American Horse Protection Ass'n (Exec. Director)

LOIELLO, John P.

1661 Crescent Place NW
Suite 608
Washington, DC 20009
EMail: gowran@erols.com
Tel: (202)387-1971
Fax: (202)387-1396
Registered: FARA

Former Associate Director of Educational and Cultural Affairs, United States Information Agency.

Employers
Gowran Internat'l Ltd. (President)

LOKOVIC, James

5211 Auth Rd.
Suitland, MD 20746
Tel: (301)899-3500
Fax: (301)899-8136
Registered: LDA

Employers
Air Force Sergeants Ass'n (Director, Military and Government Relations)

LOMBARD, Tanya

1341 G St. NW
Suite 900
Washington, DC 20005
Tel: (202)637-1577
Fax: (202)637-1549

Employers
Philip Morris Management Corp. (Director, Government Affairs)

LONDON, Sheldon I.

1156 15th St. NW
Suite 510
Washington, DC 20005
Tel: (202)639-8888
Fax: (202)296-5333

Employers
London and Satagaj, Attorneys-at-Law (Senior Partner)

Clients Represented

On Behalf of London and Satagaj, Attorneys-at-Law

American Hardware Manufacturers Ass'n
American Supply and Machinery Manufacturers' Ass'n
Manufacturing Jewelers and Suppliers of America
Photo Marketing Ass'n-Internat'l
Wood Machinery Manufacturers of America

LONG, Bernard J.

1200 New Hampshire Ave. NW
Suite 800
Washington, DC 20036-6802
EMail: blong@dlalaw.com
Tel: (202)776-2000
Fax: (202)776-2222

Employers
Dow, Lohnes & Albertson, PLLC (Member)

LONG, Christopher

1775 I St. NW
Suite 800
Washington, DC 20006
EMail: christopher.long@enron.com
Tel: (202)466-9158
Fax: (202)828-3372
Registered: LDA

Employers
Enron Corp. (Senior Director, Federal Government Affairs)

LONG, Christopher T.

8529 W. Oak Pl.
Vienna, VA 22182
Tel: (703)790-8093
Fax: (703)790-8257
Registered: LDA

Employers
Washington Resource Associates (President)

Clients Represented

On Behalf of Washington Resource Associates

Sabre Inc.
Sun Microsystems
United States Marine Repair

LONG, Dina

1101 King St.
Alexandria, VA 22314
Tel: (703)739-2782
Fax: (703)684-8319

Employers
American Soc. of Travel Agents (V. President, Communications)

LONG, Ph.D., Edward R.

426 C St. NE
Washington, DC 20002
Tel: (202)544-1880
Fax: (202)543-2565
Registered: LDA

Clerk, Subcommittee on Labor, Health and Human Services, and Education, Senate Committee on Appropriations, 1993-95. Legislative Director to Senator Tom Harkin (D-IA), 1991-93. Former Foreign Policy Legislative Assistant to Rep. Ted Weiss (D-NY). Former Aide to Rep. Tom Harkin (D-IA).

Employers
Capitol Associates, Inc. (V. President, Congressional Relations)

Clients Represented

On Behalf of Capitol Associates, Inc.

Academic Health Center Coalition
Albert Einstein Medical Center
American Psychological Ass'n
Bastyr University
Boys and Girls Clubs of America
Friends of CDC
Lymphoma Research Foundation of America, Inc.
Nat'l Ass'n of Community Health Centers
Nat'l Nutritional Foods Ass'n
Neurofibromatosis
New York Botanical Garden
New York University Medical Center
NF Inc. - Mass Bay Area
Northwest Regional Education Laboratory
Northwestern Memorial Hospital
Parkinson's Action Network
Pennsylvania Higher Education Assistance Agency
Rotary Foundation
Susquehanna Health System
Texas NF Foundation
Thomas Jefferson University Hospital
University of Pennsylvania/School of Dental Medicine
Western Michigan University

LONG, G. Thomas

1101 17th St. NW
Suite 500
Washington, DC 20036
Tel: (202)452-1102
Fax: (202)452-1885
Registered: LDA

Counsel and Health Policy Advisor to Senator Dan Coats (R-IN), 1989-91 and Chief of Staff to Rep. Coats, 1982-89. Legislative Director to Rep. David O'B. Martin (R-WY), 1981-82. Legislative Counsel to Rep. Robert C. McEwen (R-NY), 1974-81.

Employers

G. T. Long & Associates (President)

LONG, Matthew

1307 New York Ave. NW
Suite 1000
Washington, DC 20005
Tel: (202)328-5900
Fax: (202)387-4973

Employers

Council for Advancement and Support of Education (Government Relations Analyst)

LONG, Michael

Liberty Center
401 14th St. SW
MS: 556A
Washington, DC 20227
Tel: (202)874-6659
Fax: (202)874-7016
EMail: michael.long@fms.treas.gov

Employers

Department of Treasury - Financial Management Service (Legislative and Public Affairs Specialist)

LONG, Richard

P.O. Box 5320
Arlington, VA 22205
Tel: (703)536-2060
Fax: (703)536-8519

Employers

Internat'l Reading Ass'n (Director, Government Relations)
Richard Long & Associates

Clients Represented

On Behalf of Richard Long & Associates

Nat'l Council of Teachers of Mathematics

LONG, Robert S.

1130 17th St. NW
Washington, DC 20036-4677
Tel: (202)463-2663
Fax: (202)833-1965
Registered: LDA
EMail: rlong@nma.org

Employers

Nat'l Mining Ass'n (V. President, Government Affairs)

LONG, Hon. Russell B.

801 Pennsylvania Ave. NW
Suite 750
Washington, DC 20004
Tel: (202)737-9212
Fax: (202)624-0659

Member, U.S Senate (D-LA), 1948-86.

Employers

Long Law Firm (Partner)

LONGACRE, James B.

600 13th St. NW
Washington, DC 20005-3096
Tel: (202)756-8266
Fax: (202)756-8087
EMail: jlongacre@mwe.com

Former Economist, Department of Labor.

Employers

McDermott, Will and Emery (Associate)

LONGANO, Don R.

1301 K St. NW
Washington, DC 20005-3333
Tel: (202)414-1000
Fax: (202)414-1301
Registered: LDA
EMail: don.longano@us.pwcglobal.com

Chief Tax Counsel, Committee on Ways and Means, U.S. House of Representatives, 1985-94. Judicial Clerk, Commodity Futures Trading Commission, 1979-80.

Employers

PriceWaterhouseCoopers (Partner)

Clients Represented

On Behalf of PriceWaterhouseCoopers

Coalition of Corporate Taxpayers
Latona Associates, Inc.
Ralston Purina Co.

LONGMUIR, Shelley A.

1025 Connecticut Ave. NW
Suite 1210
Washington, DC 20036
Tel: (202)296-2337
Fax: (202)296-2873
Registered: LDA

Employers

United Airlines (Senior V. President, International, Regulatory, and Governmental Affairs)

LONGNECKER, Tom

Liberty Center
401 14th St. SW
MS: 556B
Washington, DC 20227
Tel: (202)874-4778
Fax: (202)874-7016
EMail: tom.longnecker@fms.treas.gov

Employers

Department of Treasury - Financial Management Service (Legislative Affairs Specialist)

LONGSTRETH, John L.

1735 New York Ave. NW
Suite 500
Washington, DC 20006-4759
Tel: (202)628-1700
Fax: (202)331-1024
Registered: LDA

Law Clerk to Judge Raymond J. Broderick of the U.S. District Court for the Eastern District of Pennsylvania, 1982-84.

Employers

Preston Gates Ellis & Rouvelas Meeds LLP (Partner)

Clients Represented

On Behalf of Preston Gates Ellis & Rouvelas Meeds LLP

Brown-Forman Corp.
Internat'l Council of Containership Operators
Mount Vernon Barge Service
Seattle, Washington, Port of
Sun Outdoor Advertising
Transpacific Stabilization Agreement
Transportation Institute
United States Maritime Coalition
Western Great Lakes Pilots Ass'n

LONIE, David M.

801 Pennsylvania Ave. NW
Suite 750
Washington, DC 20004
Tel: (202)628-3750
Fax: (202)624-0659
Registered: LDA, FARA
EMail: davelonie@solomongroup.com

Foreign Policy Advisor, House Rules Committee, 1989-95. Foreign Policy Aide to House Republicans, 1980-89.

Employers

The Solomon Group, LLC (Principal Partner)

Clients Represented

On Behalf of The Solomon Group, LLC

AAI Corp.
Alliance for American Innovation, Inc.
Ass'n of Small Business Development Centers
Clough, Harbour & Associates LLP
Espey Manufacturing and Electronics
General Electric Co.
Internat'l Medical Programs
JBA Consulting, Inc.
Morocco, Foreign Ministry of the Kingdom of
Safe Environment of America
Taipei Economic and Cultural Representative Office in the United States
Turkey, Government of the Republic of

LOOMIS, Laura

1300 19th St. NW
Suite 300
Washington, DC 20036
Tel: (202)223-6722
Fax: (202)659-0650

Employers

Nat'l Parks Conservation Ass'n (Visitor Experience)

LOOMIS, Ralph E.

633 Pennsylvania Ave. NW
Sixth Floor
Washington, DC 20004
Tel: (202)783-7959
Fax: (202)783-1489
Registered: LDA
EMail: ralph.loomis@us.ngrid.com

Employers

Nat'l Grid USA (V. President, Federal Affairs)

LOONEY, Jr. USMC (Ret.), Maj. Gen. Edmund P.

700 13th St. NW
Suite 400
Washington, DC 20005
Tel: (202)347-0773
Fax: (202)347-0785
Registered: LDA
EMail: elooney@cassidy.com

Employers

Cassidy & Associates, Inc. (Senior Consultant)

Clients Represented

On Behalf of Cassidy & Associates, Inc.

Maersk Inc.

LOONEY, Paul

1801 Alexander Bell Dr.
Suite 500
Reston, VA 20191
Tel: (703)264-7500
Fax: (703)264-7551
Registered: LDA

Employers

American Institute of Aeronautics and Astronautics (Government Relations Representative)

LOONEY, Robert J.

1745 Jefferson Davis Hwy.
Suite 404
Arlington, VA 22202
Tel: (703)413-9620
Fax: (703)413-9626
EMail: rlooney@cenexharveststates.com

Employers

CENEX, Inc. (Director, Federal Affairs)

LOPACH, Tom

227 Massachusetts Ave. NE
Suite 101
Washington, DC 20002
Tel: (202)544-4889
Fax: (202)546-2285

Employers

Committee for a Democratic Majority (Director)

LOPATIN, Alan G.

Hamilton Square
600 14th St. NW, Fifth Floor
Washington, DC 20005
Tel: (202)783-1980
Fax: (202)783-1918
Registered: LDA
EMail: VLLandS@aol.com

General Counsel, Committee on Education and Labor (1991-94); Deputy General Counsel, Committee on Post Office and Civil Service (1987-90); Deputy Chief Counsel (1986-87) and Counsel (1982-85), Committee on the Budget; and Counsel, Subcommittee on Civil Service, Committee on Post Office and Civil Service (1981-82), U.S. House of Representatives. Law Clerk, Federal Maritime Commission, 1980-81.

Employers

Ledge Counsel (Principal)
Valente Lopatin & Schulze (Principal)

Clients Represented

On Behalf of Valente Lopatin & Schulze

Alliance for Special Needs Children
American Collectors Ass'n
Columbus Educational Services
Columbus Medical Services
Dalton & Dalton P.C.
Kaplan Companies, Inc.
Nat'l and Community Service Coalition
Nat'l Ass'n of Retired and Senior Volunteer Program Directors
Nat'l Ass'n of Retired Federal Employees
Nat'l Ass'n of Senior Companion Project Directors
Nat'l Ass'n of Thrift Savings Plan Participants
Nat'l Center for Family Literacy
Nat'l Center for Learning Disabilities (NCLD)
Nat'l Education Ass'n of the U.S.
Nat'l Head Start Ass'n
Orkand Corp.
United Nations Development Programme
United Payors and United Providers

LOPES, Ana

1225 New York Ave. NW
Suite 300
Washington, DC 20005
Tel: (202)393-6362
Fax: (202)737-3742
Registered: LDA

Employers

Motor and Equipment Manufacturers Ass'n (Director, Public Relations)

LOPEZ, Anna M.

1193 Nat'l Press Building
Washington, DC 20045
EMail: alopez@nahj.org
Tel: (202)662-7145
Fax: (202)662-7144

Employers

Nat'l Ass'n of Hispanic Journalists (Exec. Director)

LOPEZ, Earl Francisco

1500 Farragut St. NW
Washington, DC 20011
EMail: eflopez@nild.org
Tel: (202)723-7241
Fax: (202)723-7246

Employers

Bert Corona Leadership Institute (President)

LOPEZ, John

444 N. Capitol St. NW
Suite 322
Washington, DC 20001
Tel: (202)508-3860
Fax: (202)508-3843

Employers

Coastal States Organization (Policy Analyst)

LOPEZ, John H.

20th and C Sts. NW
MS: 2125
Washington, DC 20551
Tel: (202)452-2533
Fax: (202)452-2611

Employers

Federal Reserve System (Congressional Liaison Assistant)

LOPEZ, Jr., Jorge J.

1333 New Hampshire Ave. NW
Suite 400
Washington, DC 20036
Tel: (202)887-4000
Fax: (202)887-4288
Registered: LDA

Employers

Akin, Gump, Strauss, Hauer & Feld, L.L.P. (Partner)

Clients Represented

On Behalf of Akin, Gump, Strauss, Hauer & Feld, L.L.P.

Johnson & Johnson, Inc.
Memorial Sloan-Kettering Cancer Center
St. Barnabas Healthcare System

LOPINA, Brian C.

2550 M St. NW
Washington, DC 20037-1350
Tel: (202)457-6000
Fax: (202)457-6315
Registered: LDA
EMail: blopina@pattonboggs.com

Administrative Aide to Rep. Ernest J. Istook, Jr. (R-OK), 1993-95. Legislative Liaison and Director, Interagency Affairs, Department of Education, 1987. Legislative Liaison, General Services Administration, 1982-84. Legislative Aide to Rep. Mark Siljander (R-MI), 1981. Also served as former Aide to Rep. John Porter (R-IL) and as a Professional Staff Member, Department of Transportation during the Reagan administration.

Employers

Patton Boggs, LLP (Of Counsel)

Clients Represented

On Behalf of Patton Boggs, LLP

Ass'n of Trial Lawyers of America
Clayton College of Natural Health
Coalition for Fair Competition in Rural Markets
Coalition to Preserve Mine Safety Standards
Ronald J. Cohen Investments
Direct Marketing Ass'n, Inc.
Farmland Industries, Inc.
H.A.H. of Wisconsin L.P.
Internet Safety Ass'n
Matsushita Electric Corp. of America
Mitsubishi Electronics America (Consumer Electronics Group)
Pioneer of North America
Professional Beauty Federation PAC
Salton, Inc.
Sanyo North American Corp.
Sharp Electronics Corp.
The Charles E. Smith Companies
Sony Electronics, Inc.
Tip Tax Coalition
Toshiba Consumer Products, Inc.
Weider Nutritional Group

LORANGER, Tom

801 Pennsylvania Ave. NW
Suite 750
Washington, DC 20004
EMail: TOLORANGER@aol.com
Tel: (202)624-0640
Fax: (202)624-0659
Registered: LDA

Press Secretary and Administrative Assistant to Senator Paul Laxalt (R-NV), 1982-86.

Employers

The Paul Laxalt Group (V. President)

Clients Represented

On Behalf of The Paul Laxalt Group

AIG Environmental
The American Land Conservancy
American Soc. of Anesthesiologists
Apria Healthcare Group
CSX Corp.
IDT Corp.
PolyMedica Corp.
Sierra Pacific Resources
Sirius Satellite Radio, Inc.
Yukon Pacific

LORBER, Leah

1001 Pennsylvania Ave. NW
Suite 1100
Washington, DC 20004-2595
Tel: (202)624-2500
Fax: (202)628-5116
Registered: LDA

Employers

Crowell & Moring LLP

Clients Represented

On Behalf of Crowell & Moring LLP

American Ass'n of Health Plans (AAHP)

LORD, USN (Ret.), Michael W.

8201 Corporate Dr.
Suite 560
Landover, MD 20785
EMail: mikecoa@aol.com
Tel: (301)731-9080
Fax: (301)731-9084
Registered: LDA

Employers

Commissioned Officers Ass'n of the U.S. Public Health Service (Exec. Director)

LORD, Susan B.

1225 I St. NW
Suite 500
Washington, DC 20005
EMail: Susan.Lord@Springs.com
Tel: (202)682-4711
Fax: (202)682-4591
Registered: LDA

Employers

Springs Industries, Inc. (V. President, Federal Government Relations)

LORE, Kenneth G.

3000 K St. NW
Suite 300
Washington, DC 20007
Tel: (202)424-7500
Fax: (202)424-7643
Registered: LDA

Employers

Swidler Berlin Shereff Friedman, LLP (Partner)

Clients Represented

On Behalf of Swidler Berlin Shereff Friedman, LLP

Associated Estates Co.
H & R Executive Towers
Manhattan Plaza Associates
Nat'l Housing and Rehabilitation Ass'n

LORENZ, Lance E.

1101 Connecticut Ave. NW
Suite 950
Washington, DC 20036
Tel: (202)785-3575
Fax: (202)785-3023

Employers

Fireman's Fund Insurance Cos. (Director, Government Affairs)

LORMAN, Alvin J.

701 Pennsylvania Ave. NW
Suite 900
Washington, DC 20004-2608
EMail: alorman@mintz.com
Tel: (202)434-7300
Fax: (202)434-7400
Registered: LDA

Professional Staff, House Select Committee on Crime, 1970-71; Professional Staff, Special Action Office for Drug Abuse Prevention, The White House, 1971-72; Member, Committee on State Food Labeling, Nat'l Academy of Sciences/Institute of Medicine, 1991-92.

Employers

Mintz, Levin, Cohn, Ferris, Glovsky and Popeo, P.C. (Partner)

Clients Represented

On Behalf of Mintz, Levin, Cohn, Ferris, Glovsky and Popeo, P.C.

Council for Advanced Agricultural Formulations, Inc.
Internat'l Specialty Products
N-Methylpyrrolidone Producers Group, Inc.
Soc. of Nuclear Medicine

LORSUNG, Thomas N.

3211 Fourth St. NE
Washington, DC 20017-1100
Tel: (202)541-3250
Fax: (202)541-3255

Employers

Catholic News Service (Director and Editor-in-Chief)

LOSEY, Frank W.

600 Pennsylvania Ave. SE
Suite 304
Washington, DC 20003
Tel: (202)544-9614
Fax: (202)544-9618
Registered: LDA

Employers

Brown and Company, Inc. (General Counsel)

Clients Represented

On Behalf of Brown and Company, Inc.

American Shipbuilding Ass'n
Bird-Johnson Co.
Sperry Marine Inc.

LOSEY, James A.

1440 New York Ave. NW
Washington, DC 20005
Tel: (202)371-7000
Fax: (202)393-5760
Registered: LDA

Employers

Skadden, Arps, Slate, Meagher & Flom LLP (Associate)

LOTSTEIN, Robert

5185 MacArthur Blvd. NW
Washington, DC 20016-3341
Tel: (202)237-6000
Ext: 110
Fax: (202)237-8900
Registered: LDA
EMail: lotstein@lotstienbuckman.com

Employers

Lotstein Buckman, Attorneys At Law (Attorney At Law)
Nat'l Ass'n of Mortgage Brokers (V. President, Government Affairs)

Clients Represented

On Behalf of Lotstein Buckman, Attorneys At Law

Nat'l Ass'n of Mortgage Brokers

LOTT, Brian H.

1801 K St. NW
Suite 1000L
Washington, DC 20006
Tel: (202)530-0400
Fax: (202)530-4500
Former Press Secretary and Chief of Staff to Rep. Jerry F. Costello (D-IL).

Employers
Burson-Marsteller (Director, Public Affairs)

Clients Represented
On Behalf of Burson-Marsteller
American Airlines
Monsanto Co.

LOTTERER, Steven A.

1050 Connecticut Ave. NW
Suite 1100
Washington, DC 20036-5304
Tel: (202)861-1500
Fax: (202)861-1790
Registered: LDA
EMail: slotterer@baker-hostetler.com

Employers
Baker & Hostetler LLP (Legislative Assistant)

Clients Represented
On Behalf of Baker & Hostetler LLP
Amwest Surety Insurance Co.
Blue Cross and Blue Shield of Ohio
Bristol-Myers Squibb Co.
Cafaro Co.
The Chubb Corp.
Citigroup
Coalition for Shareholder Fairness
The Council of Insurance Agents & Brokers
D. H. Blair Investment Banking Corp.
Eagle-Picher Personal Injury Settlement Trust
Edison Electric Institute
Emmis Broadcasting Corp.
Flexi-Van Leasing
Florida Residential and Casualty Joint Underwriting Ass'n
Florida Windstorm Underwriting Ass'n
Forest City Ratner Companies
Harvard University
I.O.T.A. Partners
Inman, Steinberg, Nye & Stone
KeyCorp, Inc.
Loeb & Loeb
Marsh & McLennan Cos.
Moose Internat'l Inc.
Motion Picture Ass'n of America
Nat'l Ass'n of Real Estate Investment Trusts
PSH Master L.P.I.
Rollins Hudig Hall
Sedgwick James, Inc.
Sutton & Sutton Solicitors
Transportation Institute

LOTZ, Denton

6733 Curran St.
McLean, VA 22101-6005
Tel: (703)790-8980
Fax: (703)893-5160
EMail: denton@bwanet.org

Employers
Baptist World Alliance (General Secretary)

LOUD, Ted

901 15th St. NW
Suite 700
Washington, DC 20005-2301
Tel: (202)371-6000
Fax: (202)371-6279
Registered: LDA

Employers
Verner, Liipfert, Bernhard, McPherson and Hand, Chartered (Public Relations Coordinator)

Clients Represented
On Behalf of Verner, Liipfert, Bernhard, McPherson and Hand, Chartered
Olympic Aid

LOUDA, Dale

1225 I St. NW
Suite 300
Washington, DC 20005
Tel: (202)408-9494
Fax: (202)408-0877
Registered: LDA

Employers
American Portland Cement Alliance (Director, Legislative Affairs)

LOUDY, Elizabeth A.

1255 23rd St. NW
Suite 200
Washington, DC 20037-1174
Tel: (202)728-0500
Fax: (202)833-3636

Employers
Hauck and Associates (V. President)
State Government Affairs Council (Exec. Director)

Clients Represented
On Behalf of Hauck and Associates
State Government Affairs Council

LOUGHERY, Richard M.

701 Pennsylvania Ave. NW
Washington, DC 20004-2696
Tel: (202)508-5647
Fax: (202)508-5150
Registered: LDA

Employers
Edison Electric Institute (Director, Environmental Programs)

LOUGHLIN, Peter J.

333 John Carlyle St.
Suite 200
Alexandria, VA 22314
Tel: (703)837-5366
Fax: (703)837-5407
Registered: LDA
EMail: loughlip@agc.org

Employers
Associated General Contractors of America (Director, Congressional Relations)

LOUGHLIN, Stephanie M.

1200 New Hampshire Ave. NW
Suite 800
Washington, DC 20036-6802
Tel: (202)776-2000
Fax: (202)776-2222
Registered: LDA
EMail: sloughlin@dlalaw.com

Employers
Dow, Lohnes & Albertson, PLLC (Member)

LOUIS, Claudia

1150 Connecticut Ave. NW
Suite 810
Washington, DC 20036
Tel: (202)785-7900
Fax: (202)785-7950
Registered: LDA
EMail: claudial@heart.org

Employers
American Heart Ass'n (Government Relations Manager)

LOUISON, Deborah L.

1615 L St. NW
Suite 900
Washington, DC 20036
Tel: (202)778-1000
Fax: (202)466-6002
EMail: dlouison@apcoworldwide.com
Deputy Assistant Secretary for Intergovernmental and Public Liaison, Department of Energy, 1989-93. Former Legislative Director to Rep. Barbara Vucanovich (R-NV).

Employers
APCO Worldwide (Senior V. President and Director, Global Services)

Clients Represented
On Behalf of APCO Worldwide
Ukraine, Government of

LOUSSEDES, Kelly

112 S. West St.
Fourth Floor
Alexandria, VA 22314
Tel: (703)836-6200
Fax: (703)836-6550
Registered: LDA
EMail: loussedes@cahi.org

Employers
Council for Affordable Health Insurance (Director, Public Affairs)

LOUTHIAN, III, Robert

600 13th St. NW
Washington, DC 20005-3096
Tel: (202)756-8172
Fax: (202)756-8087

Employers
McDermott, Will and Emery (Partner)

LOVAAS, Deron

408 C St. NE
Washington, DC 20002
Tel: (202)547-1141
Fax: (202)547-6009

Employers
Sierra Club (Associate Representative)

LOVAIN, Timothy B.

400 N. Capitol St. NW
Suite 363
Washington, DC 20001
Tel: (202)783-0280
Fax: (202)737-4518
Registered: LDA
Former Legislative Assistant to Senator Slade Gorton (R-WA) and Legislative Director to Rep. Helen Meyner (D-NJ).

Employers
Denny Miller McBee Associates (V. President and General Counsel)

LOVE, James P.

P.O. Box 19367
Washington, DC 20036
Tel: (202)387-8031
Fax: (202)234-5176

Employers
Consumer Project on Technology (Director)
Taxpayer Assets Project (Director)

LOVEJOY, Bret D.

1410 King St.
Alexandria, VA 22314
Tel: (703)683-3111
Fax: (703)683-7424
Registered: LDA

Employers
Ass'n for Career and Technical Education (Exec. Director)

LOVELESS, Charles M.

1625 L St. NW
Washington, DC 20036-5687
Tel: (202)429-1194
Fax: (202)223-3413
Registered: LDA
EMail: cloveless@afscme.org

Employers
American Federation of State, County and Municipal Employees (Director, Department of Legislation)

LOVELESS, Tom

1775 Massachusetts Ave. NW
Washington, DC 20036-2188
Tel: (202)797-6000
Fax: (202)797-6004

Employers
The Brookings Institution (Senior Fellow, Governmental Studies/Dir. Brown Center on Education Policy)

LOVENG, Jeff

801 Pennsylvania Ave. NW
Suite 310
Washington, DC 20004
Tel: (202)434-8140
Fax: (202)434-8156
Registered: LDA

Employers
GPU, Inc. (Manager, Federal Government Affairs)

LOVETT, A.E.

601 Pennsylvania Ave. NW
11th Floor, North Bldg.
Washington, DC 20004-2601
Tel: (202)756-3300
Fax: (202)756-3333

Employers
Alston & Bird LLP

Clients Represented
On Behalf of Alston & Bird LLP
Nat'l Coalition on E-Commerce and Privacy

LOVETT, David A.

317 Massachusetts Ave. NE
Suite 100
Washington, DC 20002
Tel: (202)546-4430
Fax: (202)546-5051
Registered: LDA

Employers
American Academy of Orthopaedic Surgeons (Director)

LOVETT, Steve

1111 19th St. NW
Suite 800
Washington, DC 20036
Tel: (202)463-2700
Fax: (202)463-2785
Registered: LDA
EMail: steve_lovett@afandpa.org

Employers
American Forest & Paper Ass'n (V. President, Fiber Resources and Products)

LOWE, Aaron M.

4600 East-West Hwy.
Suite 300
Bethesda, MD 20814-3415
Tel: (301)986-1500
Fax: (301)986-9633
Registered: LDA
EMail: aaron.lowe@aftermarket.org

Employers
Automotive Aftermarket Industry Ass'n
Automotive Parts and Service Alliance (V. President, Government Affairs)

LOWE, Florence Myeong-Hwa

1101 Vermont Ave. NW
Suite 401
Washington, DC 20005
Tel: (202)371-0690
Fax: (202)371-0692
Registered: FARA
EMail: fll@keia.org

Employers
Korea Economic Institute of America (Director, Financial Affairs, Publications)

LOWE, Jr., George H.

1211 Connecticut Ave. NW
Suite 805
Washington, DC 20036
Tel: (202)862-9835
Fax: (202)862-9838
Registered: LDA
EMail: lowedc@aol.com

Employers
Lowe & Associates, Ltd. (President)

Clients Represented
On Behalf of Lowe & Associates, Ltd.
Washington Parking Ass'n

LOWE, Roger

1909 K St. NW
Fourth Floor
Washington, DC 20006
Tel: (202)973-5800
Fax: (202)973-5858

Employers
Porter/Novelli (V. President, Public Affairs)

LOWE, Serena

805 15th St. NW
Suite 700
Washington, DC 20005
Tel: (202)312-7400
Fax: (202)312-7441
Registered: LDA
EMail: sdlowe@bakerd.com

Employers
Sagamore Associates, Inc. (Assistant V. President)

Clients Represented
On Behalf of Sagamore Associates, Inc.
Arthritis Foundation

LOWELL, Abbe David

1501 M St. NW
Suite 700
Washington, DC 20005-1702
Tel: (202)463-4300
Fax: (202)463-4394
Registered: LDA, FARA
Special Assistant U.S. Attorney (1981), Special Assistant to the Attorney General (1979-81) and Special Assistant to the Deputy Attorney General (1978-79), Department of Justice.

Employers
Manatt, Phelps & Phillips, LLP (Partner)

Clients Represented
On Behalf of Manatt, Phelps & Phillips, LLP
Mexico, Embassy of
Servicios Corporativos Cintra SA de CV

LOWENSTEIN, Douglas S.

1211 Connecticut Ave. NW
Suite 600
Washington, DC 20036
Tel: (202)833-4372
Fax: (202)833-4431

Employers
Interactive Digital Software Ass'n (President)

LOWER, Janice L.

1615 M St. NW
Suite 800
Washington, DC 20036-3203
EMail: jll@dwgp.com
Tel: (202)467-6370
Fax: (202)467-6379

Employers
Duncan, Weinberg, Genzer & Pembroke, P.C. (Principal)

Clients Represented
On Behalf of Duncan, Weinberg, Genzer & Pembroke, P.C.
Arab, Alabama, City of
Auburn, Avilla, Bluffton, Columbia City and Other Municipalities of Indiana
Braintree Electric Light Department
Central Montana Electric Power Cooperative, Inc.
Clayton, Dover, Lewes, Middletown, Milford, Newark, NewCastle, Seaford and Smyrna, Delaware, Municipalities of
Delaware Municipal Electric Corp. (DEMEC)
Front Royal, Virginia, Town of
Hagerstown, Maryland, Municipal Electric Light Plant of
Howard County, Maryland
Indiana and Michigan Municipal Distributors Ass'n
Mishawaka Utilities
Ocala, Florida, City of
Thurmont, Maryland, Town of
Williamsport, Maryland, Town of

LOWERY, Hon. William D.

1341 G St. NW
Suite 200
Washington, DC 20005
Tel: (202)347-5990
Fax: (202)347-5941
Registered: LDA
EMail: blowery@clj.com
Member, U.S. House of Representatives (R-CA), 1981-93.

Employers
Copeland, Lowery & Jacquez (Partner)

Clients Represented
On Behalf of Copeland, Lowery & Jacquez
ADCS, Inc.
The Boeing Co.
Children's Hospital and Health Center of San Diego
Children's Hospital Los Angeles
Digital System Resources, Inc.
El Toro Reuse Planning Authority
Hi-Desert Water District
Hollister Ranch Owners' Ass'n
Large Public Power Council
Loma Linda, California, City of
Orincon Corp.
Redlands, California, City of
Riverside Habitat Acquisition, County of
Salt Lake City Olympic Organizing Committee
San Diego Ass'n of Governments
San Diego State University Foundation
San Diego, California, City of
Science Applications Internat'l Corp. (SAIC)

LOWMAN, Rodney W.

1300 Wilson Blvd.
Suite 800
Arlington, VA 22209
Tel: (703)253-0700
Fax: (703)253-0701

Employers
American Plastics Council (Exec. V. President and Chief Staff Officer)

LOWTHER, Frederick M.

2101 L St. NW
Washington, DC 20037-1526
Tel: (202)785-9700
Fax: (202)887-0689
Registered: LDA
EMail: lowtherf@dsmo.com
Director, Office of Energy Programs, Department of Commerce, 1972-73. Special Assistant to General Counsel, Maritime Administration, 1971-72. Law Clerk to Judge Caleb M. Wright, U.S. District Court for the District of Delaware, 1968-69.

Employers
Dickstein Shapiro Morin & Oshinsky LLP (Partner)

Clients Represented
On Behalf of Dickstein Shapiro Morin & Oshinsky LLP
Poseidon Resources Corp.

LOWTHER, Kevin G.

440 R St. NW
Washington, DC 20001
Tel: (202)462-3614
Fax: (202)387-1034

Employers
Africare (Director, Southern Africa Region)

LOWY, Karen

1455 Pennsylvania Ave. NW
Suite 1000
Washington, DC 20004
EMail: karen.lowy@haledorr.com
Tel: (202)942-8400
Fax: (202)942-8484

Employers
Hale and Dorr LLP (Associate)

LOYLESS, Betsy

1920 L St. NW
Suite 800
Washington, DC 20036
Tel: (202)785-8683
Fax: (202)835-0491
Registered: LDA
EMail: lcv@lcv.org

Employers
League of Conservation Voters (Political Director)

LOZA, Moises

1025 Vermont Ave. NW
Suite 606
Washington, DC 20005
EMail: HAC@ruralhome.org
Tel: (202)842-8600
Fax: (202)347-3441

Employers
Housing Assistance Council (Exec. Director)

LUBAND, Charles

1001 Pennsylvania Ave. NW
Suite 600
Washington, DC 20004
Tel: (202)347-0066
Fax: (202)624-7222
Registered: LDA
EMail: clubinsk@pgfm.com

Employers
Powell, Goldstein, Frazer & Murphy LLP (Associate)

Clients Represented
On Behalf of Powell, Goldstein, Frazer & Murphy LLP
Nat'l Ass'n of Public Hospitals and Health Systems

LUBELL, Michael S.

529 14th St. NW
Suite 1050
Washington, DC 20045
Tel: (202)662-8700
Fax: (202)662-8711
Registered: LDA

Employers
American Physical Soc. (Director, Public Affairs)

LUBIN, J. E.

1120 20th St. NW
Suite 1000
M/S 5463C2
Washington, DC 20036
EMail: lubin@att.com
Tel: (202)457-3838
Fax: (202)457-3205

Employers
AT&T (Regulatory V. President)

LUBY, Arthur M.

1300 L St. NW
Suite 1200
Washington, DC 20005-4178
Tel: (202)898-1707
Fax: (202)682-9276
Registered: LDA

Employers
O'Donnell, Schwartz & Anderson, P.C. (Principal)

Clients Represented
On Behalf of O'Donnell, Schwartz & Anderson, P.C.
Transport Workers Union of America, AFL-CIO

LUCAS, Amy

900 Second St. NE
Suite 109
Washington, DC 20002
Tel: (202)898-1444
Fax: (202)898-0188
Registered: LDA

Employers
Waterman & Associates (Senior Associate)

Clients Represented
On Behalf of Waterman & Associates
American Foundrymen's Soc.
North American Die Casting Ass'n

LUCAS, C. Payne

440 R St. NW
Washington, DC 20001
Tel: (202)462-3614
Fax: (202)387-1034

Employers
Africare (President)

LUCAS, Jami

1990 M St. NW
Suite 680
Washington, DC 20036

Tel: (301)588-1800
Fax: (301)588-2454

Employers
American Academy of Otolaryngic Allergy (Exec. Director)

LUCAS, Jr., John A.

1079 Old Cedar Rd.
McLean, VA 22102

Tel: (703)827-5932
Fax: (703)448-6983
Registered: FARA

Employers
Institutional Development Associates (President)

Clients Represented
On Behalf of Institutional Development Associates
Saudi Arabia, Royal Embassy of

LUCAS, William L.

1100 15th St. NW
Suite 900
Washington, DC 20005

Tel: (202)835-3400
Fax: (202)835-3414
Registered: LDA

Employers
Pharmaceutical Research and Manufacturers of America (Associate V. President, State Government Affairs)

LUCCI, Mary Catherine

1133 19th St. NW
Washington, DC 20036

Tel: (202)872-1600
Fax: (202)887-3133

Employers
MCI WorldCom Corp. (Manager, Coporate Communications)

LUCEY, Anne C.

1501 M St. NW
Suite 1100
Washington, DC 20005

Tel: (202)785-7300
Fax: (202)785-6360
Registered: LDA

Employers
Viacom Inc. (V. President, Regulatory Affairs)

LUCKETT, Jill

1724 Massachusetts Ave. NW
Washington, DC 20036-1969

Tel: (202)775-3550
Fax: (202)775-1079

Employers
Nat'l Cable Television Ass'n (V. President, Program Network Policy)

LUCY, William

1625 L St. NW
Washington, DC 20036

Tel: (202)429-1200
Fax: (202)429-1102

Employers
American Federation of State, County and Municipal Employees (Internat'l Secretary-Treasurer)

LUDECKE, Kristen

One Massachusetts Ave. NW
Suite 710
Washington, DC 20001
EMail: kristen.ludecke@pseg.com

Tel: (202)408-0800
Fax: (202)408-0214
Registered: LDA

Employers
PSE&G (Manager, Governmental and Public Affairs)

LUDEMAN, Ruth L.

900 S. Washington St.
Suite G-13
Falls Church, VA 22046

Tel: (703)237-8616
Fax: (703)533-1153

Employers
Nat'l Ass'n of Executive Secretaries and Administrative Assistants (Exec. Director)

LUDOWAY, Natalie O.

1401 New York Ave.
Suite 600
Washington, DC 20005

Tel: (202)434-9100
Registered: LDA

Employers
Leftwich & Douglas

Clients Represented
On Behalf of Leftwich & Douglas
Verizon Washington, DC, Inc.

LUDWIG, Bob

2101 Constitution Ave. NW
Washington, DC 20418

Tel: (202)334-2000
Fax: (202)334-2158

Employers
Nat'l Academy of Engineering (Media Associate)

LUDWIG, Gabriele

517 C St. NE
Washington, DC 20002

Tel: (202)543-4455
Fax: (202)543-4586
Registered: LDA

Employers
Schramm, Williams & Associates, Inc.

Clients Represented
On Behalf of Schramm, Williams & Associates, Inc.
U.S. Citrus Science Council
Western Growers Ass'n

LUDWIG, Mark N.

700 13th St. NW
Suite 700
Washington, DC 20005-3960
EMail: mnludwig@bryancave.com

Tel: (202)508-6000
Fax: (202)508-6200
Registered: LDA

Employers
Bryan Cave LLP (Congressional Liaison)

Clients Represented
On Behalf of Bryan Cave LLP
Coin Acceptors, Inc.
Laclede Gas Co.

LUDWISZEWSKI, Raymond B.

1050 Connecticut Ave. NW
Washington, DC 20036-5306
EMail: rludwiszewski@gdclaw.com

Tel: (202)955-8500
Fax: (202)467-0539
Registered: LDA

General Counsel (1991-93) and Assistant Administrator for Enforcement (1990-91), Environmental Protection Agency. Associate Deputy Attorney General, Department of Justice, 1988-89. Special Counsel to the Assistant Attorney General for the Environment and Natural Resources, 1985-87. Law Clerk to Judge Henry J. Friendly, U.S. Court of Appeals, Second Circuit, 1984-85.

Employers
Gibson, Dunn & Crutcher LLP (Partner)

Clients Represented
On Behalf of Gibson, Dunn & Crutcher LLP
Lockheed Martin Corp.

LUERS, William H.

1779 Massachusetts Ave. NW
Suite 610
Washington, DC 20036

Tel: (202)462-3446
Registered: LDA

Employers
United Nations Ass'n of the U.S.A. (Chairman and President)

LUGAR, David

1133 Connecticut Ave. NW
Fifth Floor
Washington, DC 20036

Tel: (202)457-1110
Fax: (202)457-1130
Registered: LDA

Employers
Quinn Gillespie & Associates (Associate)

Clients Represented
On Behalf of Quinn Gillespie & Associates
British Columbia Lumber Trade Council
Instinet
Technology Network
USEC, Inc.

LUGGIERO, Carla

325 Seventh St. NW
Washington, DC 20004

Tel: (202)638-1100
Fax: (202)626-2254
Registered: LDA

Employers
American Hospital Ass'n (Senior Associate Director, Legislative Affairs)

LUGO, Ramon Luis

1000 Connecticut Ave. NW
Suite 302
Washington, DC 20036

Tel: (202)835-0740
Fax: (202)775-8526

Employers
Smith Dawson & Andrews, Inc.

Clients Represented
On Behalf of Smith Dawson & Andrews, Inc.
Caguas, Puerto Rico, City of
Carolina, Puerto Rico, City of
Ceiba, Puerto Rico, City of

LUHN, Kathy

1700 N. Moore St.
Suite 1900
Arlington, VA 22209-1904
EMail: luhn@nitl.org

Tel: (703)524-5011
Fax: (703)524-5017
Registered: LDA

Employers
Nat'l Industrial Transportation League (Director, Government Affairs)

LUKE, Anne Forristall

2000 L St. NW
Suite 300
Washington, DC 20036-0646
EMail: anne.forristall@ketchum.com

Tel: (202)835-8800
Fax: (202)835-8879
Registered: LDA

Former Senior Professional Committee Staff Member to Rep. Al Swift (D-WA); Legislative Director to Rep. Dennis Eckart (D-OH); and Legislative and Regulatory Policy Aid for the Land and Natural Resources Division, Deptartment of Justice.

Employers
Ketchum (Senior V. President, Public Affairs and Issues Management)

LUKE, Gina G.

1625 Massachusetts Ave. NW
Washington, DC 20036
EMail: lukeg@adea.org

Tel: (202)667-9433
Fax: (202)667-0642
Registered: LDA

Employers
American Dental Education Ass'n (Director, State Government Relations)

LUKE, Vern

1000 N. Payne St.
Alexandria, VA 22314

Tel: (703)549-1600
Fax: (703)549-2589

Employers
AOC (Exec. Director)

LUKEN, David D.

701 Pennsylvania Ave. NW
Washington, DC 20004-2696

Tel: (202)508-5480
Fax: (202)508-5403
Registered: LDA

Employers
Edison Electric Institute (Director, Government Relations)

LUKENS, David R.

333 John Carlyle St.
Suite 200
Alexandria, VA 22314
EMail: lukensl@agc.org

Tel: (703)548-3118
Registered: LDA

Employers
Associated General Contractors of America (Chief Operating Officer)

LUM, Christie

5999 Stevenson Ave.
Alexandria, VA 22304-3300

Tel: (703)823-9800
Ext: 354
Fax: (703)823-0252

Employers
American Counseling Ass'n (Administrative Assistant, Public Policy and Legislation)

LUMAN, Joseph C.

1660 L St. NW
Suite 506
Washington, DC 20036
EMail: jcluman@erols.com
Tel: (202)682-9191
Fax: (202)463-6328

Staff Director, Subcommittee on Manpower and Housing, House Government Operations Committee, 1966-82. Foreign Service Officer, Department of State, 1962-66.

Employers
J. C. Luman and Assoc. (President)
Luman, Lange & Wheeler (Of Counsel)

Clients Represented
On Behalf of J. C. Luman and Assoc.
Distance Education and Training Council
Nat'l Ass'n of Personnel Services

LUND, Lisa C.

Ariel Rios Federal Bldg.
(1301-MC)
1200 Pennsylvania Ave. NW
3rd Floor
Washington, DC 20460
EMail: lund.lisa@epa.gov
Tel: (202)564-3693
Fax: (202)501-1519

Employers
Environmental Protection Agency (Deputy Associate Administrator for Congressional and Intergovernmental Relations)

LUNDBERG, Rolf

One Marriott Dr.
Department 977.01
Washington, DC 20058
Tel: (202)380-3000

Employers
Marriott Internat'l, Inc. (V. President and Assistant General Counsel, Government and International Relations)

LUNNIE, Jr., Francis M.

2400 N St. NW
Fifth Floor
Washington, DC 20037
Tel: (202)728-1164
Fax: (202)728-2992
Registered: LDA

Employers
Ogletree Governmental Affairs, Inc. (Principal)

Clients Represented
On Behalf of Ogletree Governmental Affairs, Inc.
Coalition on Occupational Safety and Health
Electronic Industries Alliance
Nat'l Alliance Against Blacklisting

LUNNIE, Pete

c/o Nat'l Ass'n of Manufacturers
1331 Pennsylvania Ave. NW
Suite 600
Washington, DC 20004
Tel: (202)728-1164
Fax: (202)728-2992

Employers
Coalition on Occupational Safety and Health (Exec. Director)

LUNTZ, Frank I.

1000 Wilson Blvd.
Suite 950
Arlington, VA 22209
Tel: (703)358-0080
Fax: (703)358-0089

Employers
Luntz Research Cos. (President)

LUPO, Anthony V.

1050 Connecticut Ave. NW
Washington, DC 20036-5339
Tel: (202)857-6000
Fax: (202)857-6395

Employers
Arent Fox Kintner Plotkin & Kahn, PLLC (Member)

LUPO, Raphael V.

600 13th St. NW
Washington, DC 20005-3096
EMail: rlupo@mwe.com
Tel: (202)756-8366
Fax: (202)756-8087

Deputy Assistant General Counsel for Patents, Department of Energy, 1977-80; Associate Solicitor (1969-77) and Patent Examiner (1964-69), Patent and Trademark Office.

Employers
McDermott, Will and Emery (Partner)

LUSIS, Ingrid

1701 Clarendon Blvd.
Arlington, VA 22209
Tel: (703)276-8800
Fax: (703)243-2593
Registered: LDA

Employers
American Chiropractic Ass'n (Director, Government Relations)

LUSK, Cody

99 Canal Center Plaza
Suite 500
Alexandria, VA 22314-1538
EMail: cody@aiada.com
Tel: (703)519-7800
Fax: (703)519-7810
Registered: LDA

Employers
American Internat'l Automobile Dealers Ass'n (Director, Legislative Affairs)

LUSK, Michelle

1225 I St. NW
Suite 300
Washington, DC 20005
Tel: (202)789-1945
Fax: (202)408-9392
Registered: LDA

Employers
Cement Kiln Recycling Coalition (Director, Regulatory Affairs)

LUSKEY, Charlene E.

Rayburn House Office Bldg.
Room B332
Washington, DC 20515
Tel: (202)632-6296
Fax: (202)632-0832

Employers
Office of Personnel Management (Chief, Congressional Liaison)

LUSTIG, David Vernon

816 Connecticut Ave. NW
Seventh Floor
Washington, DC 20006-2705
EMail: david.lustig@unilever.com
Tel: (202)828-1010
Fax: (202)828-4550
Registered: LDA

Employers
Unilever United States, Inc. (Director, Government Relations)

LUSTIG, Ron

515 King St.
Suite 420
Alexandria, VA 22314-3103
Tel: (703)684-6681
Fax: (703)684-6048

Employers
Internat'l Soc. of Hospitality Consultants (Chairman)

LUTHER, Julie Renjilian

900 Spring St.
Silver Spring, MD 20910
EMail: jluther@nrmca.org
Tel: (301)587-1400
Fax: (301)585-4219
Registered: LDA

Employers
Nat'l Ready Mixed Concrete Ass'n (V. President, Government and Industry Relations)

LUTLEY, John H.

1112 16th St. NW
Suite 240
Washington, DC 20036
Tel: (202)835-0185
Fax: (202)835-0155

Employers
Klein & Saks, Inc. (Chairman)

LUTTER, Randall

1150 17th St. NW
Washington, DC 20036
EMail: rlutter@aei.org
Tel: (202)862-5800
Fax: (202)862-7177

Employers
American Enterprise Institute for Public Policy Research (Resident Scholar)

LUTZ, Martin T.

901 15th St. NW
Suite 700
Washington, DC 20005-2301
Tel: (202)371-6000
Fax: (202)371-6279

Employers
Verner, Liipfert, Bernhard, McPherson and Hand, Chartered (Member of Firm)

LUTZKER, Arnold P.

1000 Vermont Ave. NW
Suite 450
Washington, DC 20005
Tel: (202)408-7600
Fax: (202)408-7677
Registered: LDA

Employers
Lutzker & Lutzker LLP (Partner)

Clients Represented
On Behalf of Lutzker & Lutzker LLP
Directors Guild of America
Shared Legal Capability for Intellectual Property

LYDEN, Michael E.

2001 L St. NW
Suite 506
Washington, DC 20036-4919
Tel: (202)775-2790
Fax: (202)223-7225

Employers
Chlorine Institute (V. Pres., Storage and Transportation)

LYDER, Jane M.

1849 C St. NW
Room 6241
Washington, DC 20240
EMail: jane_lyder@ios.doi.gov
Tel: (202)208-6706
Fax: (202)208-7619

Employers
Department of Interior (Legislative Counsel)

LYDON, Tom

1629 K St. NW
Suite 301
Washington, DC 20006
Tel: (202)466-2929
Fax: (202)659-2184

Employers
Evergreen Internat'l Aviation (Director, Governmental Affairs)

LYMAN, Blair L.

666 11th St. NW
Suite 600
Washington, DC 20001
EMail: blyman@ccianet.org
Tel: (202)783-0070
Fax: (202)783-0534

Served as Senior Legislative Assistant to Rep. Karen McCarthy (D-MO) and Legislative Assistant to Rep. Matthew Martinez (R-CA).

Employers
Computer and Communications Industry Ass'n (CCIA) (Director, Public Policy)

LYMAN, Mary S.

805 15th St. NW
Suite 500
Washington, DC 20005
EMail: lyman@chambersinc.com
Tel: (202)371-9770
Fax: (202)371-6601
Registered: LDA

Former Tax Counsel to a member of the House Ways and Means Committee.

Employers
Chambers Associates Inc. (Project Manager, Tax Counsel)
Coalition of Publicly Traded Partnerships (Tax Counsel)

Clients Represented
On Behalf of Chambers Associates Inc.
Coalition of Publicly Traded Partnerships
Shea & Gardner

LYMN, Nadine

1707 H St. NW
Suite 400
Washington, DC 20006
EMail: nadine@esa.org
Tel: (202)833-8773
Fax: (202)833-8775

Employers
Ecological Soc. of America (Director, Public Affairs)

LYNAM, Clare

1501 M St. NW
Suite 600
Washington, DC 20005-1710
EMail: clynam@bsmg.com
Tel: (202)739-0200
Fax: (202)659-8287
Registered: FARA

Employers
BSMG Worldwide (Senior Managing Director)

LYNAM, Marshall L.

P.O. Box 76440
Washington, DC 20013-6440
Tel: (202)544-7996
Fax: (202)544-7996
Registered: LDA

Served as Administrative Assistant and Chief of Staff to House Speaker Jim Wright (D-TX).

Employers
Self-employed as an independent consultant.

Clients Represented

As an independent consultant
Dallas/Fort Worth Internat'l Airport Board
Radio Shack Corp.

LYNCH, II, Allen A.

401 Ninth St. NW
Suite 900
Washington, DC 20004
Tel: (202)585-8000
Fax: (202)585-8080
Registered: LDA
EMail: alynch@nixonpeabody.com

Employers
Nixon Peabody LLP

LYNCH, Ann-Marie

1100 15th St. NW
Suite 900
Washington, DC 20005
Tel: (202)835-3400
Fax: (202)835-3414

Staff Director, Subcommittee on Health (1998-2000) and Professional Staff (1997-98), House Committee on Ways and Means. Economist, Health Care Financing Administration, Department of Health and Human Services, 1990-95.

Employers
Pharmaceutical Research and Manufacturers of America (V. President, Policy)

LYNCH, Clifford A.

21 Dupont Circle NW
Suite 800
Washington, DC 20036
Tel: (202)296-5098
Fax: (202)872-0884
EMail: clifford@cni.org

Employers
Coalition for Networked Information (Exec. Director)

LYNCH, Connie

5225 Wisconsin Ave. NW
Suite 600
Washington, DC 20015-2014
Tel: (202)686-3700
Fax: (202)686-3656
Registered: LDA
EMail: clynch@nasbp.org

Employers
Nat'l Ass'n of Surety Bond Producers (Director, Government Relations)

LYNCH, David

600 Pennsylvania Ave. NW
Suite 200
North Bldg.
Washington, DC 20004
Tel: (202)628-1020
Fax: (202)628-1007
Registered: LDA

Employers
TXU Business Services (Governmental Affairs Manager)

LYNCH, Jessica

1201 15th St. NW
Washington, DC 20005-2800
Tel: (202)822-0470
Fax: (202)822-0572

Employers
Nat'l Ass'n of Home Builders of the U.S. (Staff V. President, Communication Operations Division)

LYNCH, Dr. John

1755 Jefferson Davis Hwy.
Suite 1107
Arlington, VA 22202
Tel: (703)415-0344
Fax: (703)415-0182
Registered: LDA

Former Associate Director, Office of Economic Adjustment, Department of Defense.

Employers
The PMA Group (Associate)
The Spectrum Group

Clients Represented

On Behalf of The PMA Group
ADSIL
Autometric Inc.
Concurrent Technologies Corp.
Coronado, California, City of
Diamond Antenna & Microwave Corp.
Dynamics Research Corp.
FLIR Systems, Inc.
Gentex Corp.
Kollsman, Inc.
Lockheed Martin Corp.
Lockheed Martin MS/Gaithersburg
Schweizer Aircraft Corp.
Teledyne Controls, Inc.

On Behalf of The Spectrum Group
Everett, Washington, Port of
Tri-City Regional Port District

LYNCH, John

1725 Duke St.
Suite 600
Alexandria, VA 22314-3457
Tel: (703)299-9120
Fax: (703)299-9115

Employers
Truck Renting and Leasing Ass'n (Manager, Government Affairs)

LYNCH, Karina

1155 21st St. NW
Suite 300
Washington, DC 20036
Tel: (202)659-8201
Fax: (202)659-5249
Registered: LDA
EMail: kvlynch@wms-jen.com

Counsel to Senate Permanent Subcommittee on Investigations, Committee on Government Affairs, 1999-2000; Investigative Counsel to Senate Special Committee on Aging, 1997-99.

Employers
Williams & Jensen, P.C. (Associate)

Clients Represented

On Behalf of Williams & Jensen, P.C.
Genentech, Inc.

LYNCH, Robert L.

1000 Vermont Ave. NW
12th Floor
Washington, DC 20005
Tel: (202)371-2830
Fax: (202)371-0424
Registered: LDA

Employers
Americans for the Arts (President/Chief Exec. Officer)

LYNCH, Scott

2025 M St. NW
Suite 800
Washington, DC 20036
Tel: (202)367-2100
Fax: (202)367-1200
EMail: scott_lynch@dc.sba.com

Employers
Smith, Bucklin and Associates, Inc.

Clients Represented

On Behalf of Smith, Bucklin and Associates, Inc.
American Bearing Manufacturers Ass'n

LYNCH, Timothy

1000 Massachusetts Ave. NW
Washington, DC 20001
Tel: (202)842-0200
Fax: (202)842-3490

Employers
Cato Institute (Assistant Director, Center for Constitutional Studies)

LYNCH, Timothy P.

499 S. Capitol St. SW
Suite 502A
Washington, DC 20003
Tel: (202)554-3060
Fax: (202)554-3160
Registered: LDA
EMail: tlynch@motor-freight.com

Senate Commerce Committee, 1978-82.

Employers
Motor Freight Carriers Ass'n (President and Chief Exec. Officer)

LYNN, Barry W.

518 C St. NE
Washington, DC 20002
Tel: (202)466-3234
Fax: (202)466-2587

Employers
Americans United for Separation of Church and State (Exec. Director)

LYNN, Jason M.

499 S. Capitol St. SW
Suite 502
Washington, DC 20003
Tel: (202)554-2510
Fax: (202)554-2520
Registered: LDA
EMail: jlynn@natso.com

Employers
NATSO, Inc. (Director, Government Affairs)

LYNN, John B.

1331 Pennsylvania Ave. NW
Suite 1300 North
Washington, DC 20004
Tel: (202)637-6757
Fax: (202)637-6759
Registered: LDA
EMail: john.lynn@eds.com

Employers
EDS Corp. (Director, Telecommunications Policy)

LYNN, John E.

800 Connecticut Ave. NW
Suite 620
Washington, DC 20006
Tel: (202)467-5050
Fax: (202)331-9055
Registered: LDA
EMail: jlynn@methanol.org

Employers
American Methanol Institute (President and Chief Exec. Officer)

LYON, III, Charles H.

6400 Arlington Blvd.
Suite 1100
Falls Church, VA 22042
Tel: (703)237-8061
Fax: (703)237-8085
EMail: clyon@rpihq.com

Employers
Research Planning, Inc. (Exec. V. President and V. President, Business Development)

LYON, Jill

1140 Connecticut Ave. NW
Suite 1140
Washington, DC 20036
Tel: (202)872-0030
Fax: (202)872-1331
Registered: LDA
EMail: jlyon@atc.org

Employers
United Telecom Council (V. President and General Counsel)

LYON, Sydelle

1215 Jefferson Davis Hwy.
Suite 1500
Arlington, VA 22202
Tel: (703)418-6208
Fax: (703)415-1459
EMail: sydelle.lyons@baesystems.com

Employers
BAE SYSTEMS North America (Legislative Coordinator, Government Relations)

LYONS, Clinton

1625 K St. NW
Suite 800
Washington, DC 20006
Tel: (202)452-0620
Fax: (202)872-1031

Employers
Nat'l Legal Aid and Defender Ass'n (Exec. Director)

LYONS, David Curtis

1350 I St. NW
Suite 1260
Washington, DC 20005-3305
Tel: (202)842-5114
Fax: (202)842-5099
Registered: LDA
EMail: lyonsd@ldcorp.com

Employers
Louis Dreyfus Corporation (V. President, Government Relations)

LYONS, Dennis G.

555 12th St. NW
Washington, DC 20004-1206
Tel: (202)942-5000
Fax: (202)942-5999
EMail: Dennis_Lyons@aporter.com

Law Clerk to Justice William Brennan, U.S. Supreme Court, 1958-60. Attorney, Office of the General Counsel, Department of the Air Force, 1955-58.

Employers
Arnold & Porter (Partner)

LYONS, James A.

1100 Connecticut Ave. NW
Suite 1000
Washington, DC 20036
Tel: (202)728-1070
Fax: (202)293-2448

Employers
Coan & Lyons (Of Counsel)

LYONS, John F.

1350 I St. NW
Suite 400
Washington, DC 20005-3306
Tel: (202)371-6900
Fax: (202)842-3578
Registered: LDA

Employers
Motorola, Inc. (Director, Telecommunications Strategy & Regulation)

LYONS, Kenneth T.

317 S. Patrick St.
Alexandria, VA 22314
Tel: (703)519-0300
Fax: (703)519-0311

Employers
Nat'l Ass'n of Government Employees (President)

LYONS, Lisbeth

1201 F St. NW
Suite 200
Washington, DC 20004
Tel: (202)554-9000
Fax: (202)554-0496

Employers
Nat'l Federation of Independent Business (Manager, Legislative and Grassroots Services)

LYONS, Matthew D.

1625 K St. NW
Suite 1100
Washington, DC 20006-1604
Tel: (202)857-0244
Fax: (202)857-0237
Former Legislative Director for Rep. Earl Hilliard (D-AL) and former Staff Member, House Committee on Commerce.

Employers
Biotechnology Industry Organization (Director, Government Relations, Food and Agriculture Section)

LYONS, William

1717 K St. NW
Suite 500
Washington, DC 20006
EMail: wtl@lyonsandco.com
Tel: (202)466-5636
Fax: (202)466-2331
Registered: LDA

Employers
Lyons & Co. (Owner)

Clients Represented
On Behalf of Lyons & Co.
Clariant Corp.
Holnam Inc.

LYONS-WYNNE, Lynn

605 E St. NW
Washington, DC 20004
EMail: nleomllw@erols.com
Tel: (202)737-3400
Fax: (202)737-3405

Employers
Nat'l Law Enforcement Officers Memorial Fund (Director, Public Liaison and Operations)

LYSTAD, Robert

1050 Connecticut Ave. NW
Suite 1100
Washington, DC 20036-5304
EMail: rlystad@baker-hostetler.com
Tel: (202)861-1500
Fax: (202)861-1790

Employers
Baker & Hostetler LLP (Associate)

Clients Represented
On Behalf of Baker & Hostetler LLP
Soc. of Professional Journalists

LYTLE, Gary R.

1401 H St. NW
Suite 600
Washington, DC 20005-2136
Tel: (202)326-7300
Fax: (202)326-7333
Registered: LDA

Employers
United States Telecom Ass'n (Interim President and Chief Exec. Officer)

LYTWAK, Ed

1101 14th St. NW
Suite 1400
Washington, DC 20005
EMail: elytwak@defenders.org
Tel: (202)682-9400
Fax: (202)682-1331

Employers
Defenders of Wildlife (Policy Coordinator)

MAATZ, Lisa

666 11th St. NW
Suite 700
Washington, DC 20001
Tel: (202)783-6686
Fax: (202)638-2356

Employers
Older Women's League (Deputy Director of Program Affairs)

MABEE, Ph.D., Marcia S.

11479 Waterview Cluster
Suite 200
Reston, VA 20190
EMail: mmabee@ix.netcom.com
Tel: (703)476-8060
Fax: (703)709-3003
Registered: LDA

Employers
Timothy Bell & Co. (President)

Clients Represented
On Behalf of Timothy Bell & Co.
Coalition for American Trauma Care
Coalition for Health Funding
Council of State and Territorial Epidemiologists

MABILE, Michael P.

1730 Pennsylvania Ave. NW
Suite 1200
Washington, DC 20006-4706
Tel: (202)737-0500
Fax: (202)626-3737
Registered: LDA
International Trade Counsel, Senate Committee on Finance, 1987-90. Assistant General Counsel for Litigation (1980-87) and Acting General Counsel (1984-85), International Trade Commission.

Employers
King & Spalding (Partner)

Clients Represented
On Behalf of King & Spalding
Southern Tier Cement Committee

MACALISTER, Rodney J.

800 Connecticut Ave. NW
Suite 900
Washington, DC 20006
EMail: rodney.j.macalister@usa.conoco.com
Tel: (202)467-1075
Fax: (202)467-1080
Registered: LDA

Employers
Conoco Inc. (Manager, Federal Affairs)

MACAULEY, Alastair

1201 15th St. NW
Washington, DC 20005-2800
Tel: (202)822-0470
Fax: (202)822-0572

Employers
Nat'l Ass'n of Home Builders of the U.S. (Senior Political Field Director)

MACBETH, Angus

1722 I St. NW
Washington, DC 20006
Tel: (202)736-8000
Fax: (202)736-8711

Employers
Sidley & Austin (Partner)

Clients Represented
On Behalf of Sidley & Austin
GE Lighting Group

MACCARTHY, Mark

2121 K St. NW
Suite 700
Washington, DC 20037
Tel: (202)296-9230
Fax: (202)862-5498

Employers
VISA U.S.A., Inc. (Senior V. President for Public Policy)

MACCARTHY, Timothy C.

1001 19th St. North
Suite 1200
Arlington, VA 22209
EMail: tmaccarthy@aiam.org
Tel: (703)525-7788
Fax: (703)525-8817
Registered: LDA

Employers
Ass'n of Internat'l Automobile Manufacturers (President and Chief Exec. Officer)

MACCONOMY, Scott D.

700 13th St. NW
Suite 400
Washington, DC 20005
EMail: smacconomy@cassidy.com
Tel: (202)347-0773
Fax: (202)347-0785
Legislative Assistant and Director to Senator Daniel Patrick Moynihan (D-NY), 1982-2000.

Employers
Cassidy & Associates, Inc. (Associate)

Clients Represented
On Behalf of Cassidy & Associates, Inc.
Alfred University
Arizona State University
Polytechnic University
Rochester Institute of Technology

MACDICKEN, Becky

11921 Freedom Dr.
Suite 550
Reston, VA 20190
EMail: becky.macdicken@gte.net
Tel: (703)736-8082
Fax: (703)904-4339
Registered: LDA

Employers
Tire Ass'n of North America (Director of Government Affairs)

MACDONALD, Catriona

1199 N. Fairfax St.
Suite 702
Alexandria, VA 22314
EMail: cmacdonalRG@aol.com
Tel: (703)548-8535
Fax: (703)548-8536
Registered: LDA
Legislative Director to Rep. Rosa DeLauro (D-CT), 1997-99. Senior Legislative Assistant to Rep. Steny Hoyer (D-MD), 1995-97.

Employers
Leonard Resource Group (V. President, Policy)

MACDONALD, Douglas

1747 Pennsylvania Ave. NW
Suite 1000
Washington, DC 20006
Tel: (202)785-9500
Fax: (202)835-0243

Employers
Webster, Chamberlain & Bean (Associate)

MACDONALD, Jennifer

50 F St. NW
12th Floor
Washington, DC 20001
Tel: (202)639-2525
Fax: (202)639-2526
Registered: LDA

Employers
Ass'n of American Railroads (Director, Government Affairs)

MACDONALD, Mary Lehman

555 New Jersey Ave. NW
Tenth Floor
Washington, DC 20001
EMail: fnhpaft@aft.org
Tel: (202)879-4491
Fax: (202)879-4597

Employers
Federation of Nurses and Health Professionals/AFT (Director)

MACDONALD, Sheila B.

2101 Wilson Blvd.
Suite 500
Arlington, VA 22201-3062
EMail: lppdir@eap-association.org
Tel: (703)387-1000
Ext: 309
Fax: (703)522-4585
Registered: LDA

Employers
Employee Assistance Professionals Ass'n (Director, Legislation and Public Policy)

MACDONALD, Tony

444 N. Capitol St. NW
Suite 322
Washington, DC 20001
Tel: (202)508-3860
Fax: (202)508-3843

Employers
Coastal States Organization (Exec. Director)

MACDOUGALL, Gordon P.

507 C St. NE
Washington, DC 20002-5809
Tel: (202)544-7944
Fax: (202)544-7975
Registered: LDA
EMail: gmacdougall@beacon-group.net
Former Administrative Assistant to Rep. John E. Porter (R-IL) and Associate Staff, House Appropriations Committee, 1984-87.

Employers
Beacon Consulting Group, Inc. (President)

Clients Represented
On Behalf of Beacon Consulting Group, Inc.
Access Community Health Network
Advance Paradigm
American Trauma Soc.
Big Brothers/Big Sisters of America
Boston Symphony Orchestra
Carnegie Hall Corp.
Center Point Inc.
Civic Ventures
Cummins-Allison Corp.
Haymarket Center
Metropolitan Family Services
Museum of Science and Industry
Mystic Seaport Museum
Nat'l Crime Prevention Council
Ohio Wesleyan University
Old Sturbridge Village
Oregon Health Sciences University
Public/Private Ventures
Safer Foundation
Westcare Foundation, Inc.

MACFARLANE, Cathy

1029 N. Royal St.
Suite 400
Alexandria, VA 22314
Tel: (703)684-1245
Fax: (703)684-1249
EMail: CMacFarlane@directimpact.com

Employers
The Direct Impact Co. (Exec. V. President)

MACGUINEAS, D. Biard

1300 I St. NW
Suite 300 West
Washington, DC 20005
Tel: (202)522-8600
Fax: (202)522-8669
Attorney, Office of the General Counsel, Federal Communications Commission, 1965-70.

Employers
Dykema Gossett PLLC (Member)

MACHAMER, Molly

1501 M St. NW
Suite 600
Washington, DC 20005-1710
Tel: (202)739-0200
Fax: (202)659-8287

Employers
BSMG Worldwide (Director, Public Affairs)

MACHIDA, Ado A.

1333 New Hampshire Ave. NW
Suite 400
Washington, DC 20036
Tel: (202)887-4000
Fax: (202)887-4288
Registered: LDA

Employers
Akin, Gump, Strauss, Hauer & Feld, L.L.P.

Clients Represented
On Behalf of Akin, Gump, Strauss, Hauer & Feld, L.L.P.
Gila River Indian Community
Howland Hook Container Terminal Inc.
Mitsubishi Corp.
Riggs Bank, N.A.

MACHOWSKY, Martin

1875 I St. NW
Suite 900
Washington, DC 20005
Tel: (202)371-0200
Fax: (202)371-2858
Registered: LDA

Employers
Edelman Public Relations Worldwide (Senior V. President)

MACK, III, Hon. Connie

2300 N St. NW
Washington, DC 20037-1128
Tel: (202)663-8000
Fax: (202)663-8007
Member, U.S. Senate (R-FL), 1989-2001. Member, U.S. House of Representatives (R-FL), 1983-89.

Employers
Shaw Pittman (Senior Policy Advisor)

MACK, David L.

1761 N St. NW
Washington, DC 20036-2882
Tel: (202)785-1141
Fax: (202)331-8861
EMail: vp@mideasti.org

Employers
Middle East Institute (V. President, General Programs)

MACK, James H.

7901 Westpark Dr.
McLean, VA 22102-4206
Tel: (703)827-5225
Fax: (703)749-2742
Registered: LDA
EMail: jhm@mfgtech.org

Employers
The Ass'n For Manufacturing Technology (AMT) (V. President, Government Relations)

MACK, John P.

1802 Fallbrook Rd.
Vienna, VA 22182
Tel: (202)295-9058
Fax: (202)295-9058
Registered: LDA
Executive Director, Democratic Steering and Policy Committee (1987-89), Executive Floor Assistant, Office of the Majority Leader (1979-86) and Assistant to Rep. Jim Wright (D-TX) (1975-78), U.S. House of Representatives, 1979-86.

Employers
Colex and Associates (Chief Exec. Officer)

Clients Represented
On Behalf of Colex and Associates
Bell, California, City of
DynCorp Aerospace Technology
The NARAS Foundation
Nat'l Rehabilitation Hospital
Palzcoe
St. Bernard Port, Harbor and Terminal District
Triad Design Group

MACK, Robert

1025 Connecticut Ave. NW
Suite 1012
Washington, DC 20036
Tel: (202)258-2301
Registered: LDA

Employers
Smith Alling Lane, P.S.

Clients Represented
On Behalf of Smith Alling Lane, P.S.
PE Biosystems
Sagem Morpho
Washington Ass'n of Sheriffs and Police Chiefs

MACKAY, David

600 New Hampshire Ave. NW
Suite 601
Washington, DC 20037
Tel: (202)333-7400
Fax: (202)333-1638
EMail: dmackay@hillandknowlton.com

Employers
Hill and Knowlton, Inc. (Sr. Managing Director; Sr. Counselor, Marketing Communications; and Director, U.S. Client Services)

Clients Represented
On Behalf of Hill and Knowlton, Inc.
The Aluminum Ass'n
U.S. Mint

MACKAY, Gordon D.

1011 Arlington Blvd.
Suite 304S
Arlington, VA 22209
Tel: (703)524-8293
Fax: (703)524-8398
Registered: LDA

Employers
GLOBEMAC Associates (Chairman)

Clients Represented
On Behalf of GLOBEMAC Associates
Massachusetts Software Council
Metropolitan Life Insurance Co.
New England Investment Co.
New England Life Insurance Co.

MACKAY, Ian

1455 Pennsylvania Ave. NW
Suite 400
Washington, DC 20004-1081
Tel: (202)737-6600
Fax: (202)638-4512
Registered: LDA
EMail: imackay@aicpa.org

Employers
American Institute of Certified Public Accountants (Director, Professional Standards and Services)

MACKELL, Jr., Thomas

1920 L St. NW
Washington, DC 20036
Tel: (202)223-8700
Fax: (202)659-5559
Former President, Advisory Council to the Secretary, Department of Labor.

Employers
The Kamber Group (Exec. V. President and Senior Counselor)

MACKENZIE, I. R.

P.O. Box 523225
Springfield, VA 22152
Tel: (703)913-7726
Fax: (703)913-7742
Registered: FARA

Employers
MacKenzie McCheyne, Inc. (Partner)

MACKEY, Connie

801 G St. NW
Washington, DC 20001
Tel: (202)393-2100
Fax: (202)393-2134
Registered: LDA

Employers
Family Research Council, Inc. (Director, Government Relations)

MACKIE, II, Robb S.

1350 I St. NW
Suite 1290
Washington, DC 20005
Tel: (202)789-0300
Fax: (202)898-1164
Registered: LDA

Employers
American Bakers Ass'n (V. President, Government Relations)

MACKIEWICZ, Edward R.

1330 Connecticut Ave. NW
Washington, DC 20036-1795
Tel: (202)429-3000
Fax: (202)429-3902
Registered: LDA
EMail: emackiewicz@steptoe.com
General Counsel, Pension Benefit Guaranty Corp., 1985-87. Counsel for Litigation, Civil Rights Division, Office of the Solicitor, Department of Labor, 1982-83.

Employers
Steptoe & Johnson LLP (Partner)

Clients Represented
On Behalf of Steptoe & Johnson LLP
The Hillman Co.

MACKINNON, Douglas M.

901 15th St. NW
Suite 700
Washington, DC 20005-2301
Tel: (202)371-6000
Fax: (202)371-6279
Registered: LDA
EMail: dmackinnon@verner.com

Employers
Verner, Liipfert, Bernhard, McPherson and Hand, Chartered (Director, Communications to the Office of Hon. Robert J. Dole)

Clients Represented
On Behalf of Verner, Liipfert, Bernhard, McPherson and Hand, Chartered
Washington Group Internat'l

MACKINNON, Gail G.
1501 M St. NW
Suite 1100
Washington, DC 20005
Tel: (202)785-7300
Fax: (202)785-6360
Registered: LDA

Employers
Viacom Inc. (V. President of Government Affairs)

MACKINNON, Jeff
P.O. Box 6136
Alexandria, VA 22306
Tel: (703)360-8386
Fax: (703)619-1122
Registered: LDA

Employers
Texas Freedom Fund (Treasurer)

MACKINNON, Jeffrey M.
1133 Connecticut Ave. NW
Suite 300
Washington, DC 20036
Tel: (202)293-1177
Fax: (202)293-3411
Registered: LDA
Legislative Director to Rep. Joe Barton (R-TX), 1985-93.

Employers
Ryan, Phillips, Utrecht & MacKinnon (Partner)

Clients Represented
On Behalf of Ryan, Phillips, Utrecht & MacKinnon
Air Transport Ass'n of America
Ass'n of American Railroads
Coeur d'Alene Mines Corp.
Cook Inlet Region Inc.
R. R. Donnelley & Sons
Edison Electric Institute
Florida Power and Light Co.
General Communications, Inc.
Investment Co. Institute
Kerr-McGee Corp.
Lockheed Martin Corp.
MultiDimensional Imaging, Inc.
Nat'l Cable Television Ass'n
New York Stock Exchange
Pfizer, Inc.
Philip Morris Management Corp.
Progress Energy
Southern Co.
TXU Business Services
U.S. Interactive
United Pan-Europe Communications, NV
VoiceStream Wireless Corp.

MACKINNON, Jessie
1300 Connecticut Ave. NW
Suite 700
Washington, DC 20036
Tel: (202)628-2800
Fax: (202)737-0725

Employers
Very Special Arts (V. President, Communications)

MACKINNON, Paul
1275 K St. NW
Fifth Floor
Washington, DC 20005
Tel: (202)712-9799

Employers
Ass'n of Flight Attendants (Secretary/Treasurer)

MACKINTOSH, Stuart
750 First St. NE
Suite 901
Washington, DC 20002
Tel: (202)408-1711
Fax: (202)408-1699

Employers
Advocates for Highway and Auto Safety (Director, Communications)

MACKLIN, Alice Y.
1120 20th St. NW
Suite 1000
Washington, DC 20036
Tel: (202)457-3820
Fax: (202)457-2571
Registered: LDA
EMail: amacklin@att.com

Employers
AT&T (Staff Manager, Federal Government Affairs)

MACKLLIN, Sheila
4201 Wilson Blvd.
Room 1245 S
Arlington, VA 22230
Tel: (703)292-8070
Fax: (703)292-9089
EMail: smacklin@nsf.gov

Employers
Nat'l Science Foundation

MACLEOD, Sarah
121 N. Henry St.
Alexandria, VA 22314
Tel: (703)739-9485
Fax: (703)739-9488

Employers
Obadal and MacLeod, p.c. (Managing Counsel)

Clients Represented
On Behalf of Obadal and MacLeod, p.c.
Aeronautical Repair Station Ass'n

MACLEOD, William C.
3050 K St. NW
Washington, DC 20007
Tel: (202)342-8400
Fax: (202)342-8451
EMail: wmacleod@colliershannon.com
Director, Bureau of Consumer Protection (1986-90) and Director, Chicago Regional Office (1983-86), Federal Trade Commission.

Employers
Collier Shannon Scott, PLLC (Member)

Clients Represented
On Behalf of Collier Shannon Scott, PLLC
Grocery Manufacturers of America

MACNEIL, C. Ellen
1666 K St. NW
Suite 800
Washington, DC 20006
Tel: (202)481-7000
Fax: (202)862-7098
Registered: LDA

Employers
Arthur Andersen LLP (Partner)

MACOMBER, Debbie
1120 20th St. NW
Suite 1000
Washington, DC 20036
Tel: (202)457-3810
Fax: (202)457-2571
EMail: dmacomber@att.com

Employers
AT&T (Staff Manager, Federal Govt. Affairs)

MACON, Charmayne
1130 Connecticut Ave. NW
Suite 300
Washington, DC 20036
Tel: (202)331-8500
Fax: (202)331-1598
Registered: LDA

Employers
The Ferguson Group, LLC (Principal)

Clients Represented
On Behalf of The Ferguson Group, LLC
Brea, California, City of
Fairfield, California, City of
Interstate 5 Consortium
Logan, Utah, City of (Transit District)
Long Beach Transit
Mooresville, North Carolina, Town of
Municipal Transit Operation Coalition
Norwalk, California, City of
Palo Alto, California, City of
Pico Rivera, California, City of

MACOY, Ian W.
13665 Dulles Technology Dr.
Suite 300
Herndon, VA 20171
Tel: (703)561-1100
Fax: (703)787-0996
EMail: imacoy@nacha.org

Employers
NACHA - The Electronic Payments Ass'n (Senior Director, Communications and Affiliate Services)

MACPHERSON, Jim
725 15th St. NW
Suite 700
Washington, DC 20005
Tel: (202)393-5725
Fax: (202)393-1282
Registered: LDA

Employers
America's Blood Centers (Chief Exec. Officer)

MADDALONI, Martin J.
901 Massachusetts Ave. NW
Washington, DC 20001
Tel: (202)628-5823
Fax: (202)628-5024
Registered: LDA

Employers
United Ass'n of Journeymen and Apprentices of the Plumbing and Pipe Fitting Industry of the U.S. and Canada (General President)

MADDEN, Andy
919 Prince St.
Alexandria, VA 22314
Tel: (703)684-6098
Fax: (703)684-7138
Registered: LDA

Employers
Bond & Company, Inc. (V. President)

Clients Represented
On Behalf of Bond & Company, Inc.
Service Employees Internat'l Union

MADDEN, Laura L.
601 13th St. NW
Suite 900 South
Washington, DC 20005
Tel: (202)783-5588
Fax: (202)783-5595
Registered: LDA
EMail: lmadden@bracywilliams.com

Employers
Bracy Williams & Co. (Associate)

Clients Represented
On Behalf of Bracy Williams & Co.
Atlanta, Georgia, City of
Bi-State Development Agency
Fort Worth Transportation Authority
Fort Worth, Texas, City of
St. Louis Airport Authority
St. Louis Metropolitan Sewer District
Tucson, Arizona, City of

MADDEN, Suzanne
1111 19th St. NW
Suite 800
Washington, DC 20036
Tel: (202)463-2700
Fax: (202)463-2785

Employers
American Forest & Paper Ass'n (Director, State Government Affairs)

MADDEN, Thomas J.
1201 New York Ave. NW
Suite 1000
Washington, DC 20005
Tel: (202)962-4803
Fax: (202)962-8300
Registered: LDA
EMail: tjmadden@venable.com
Advisor on Federal Assistance Programs, Office of Management and Budget, The White House, 1979-80. Director, National Advisory Commission on Criminal Justice Standards and Goals (1971-73) and General Counsel, Law Enforcement Assistance Administration (1972-79), Department of Justice.

Employers
Venable (Partner)

Clients Represented
On Behalf of Venable
Nat'l Council of Juvenile and Family Court Judges

MADDEN, Turner D.
1919 Pennsylvania Ave. NW
Suite 800
Washington, DC 20006
Tel: (202)434-8988
Fax: (202)861-1274
Registered: LDA

Employers
Internat'l Ass'n of Assembly Managers (General Counsel & Chief Lobbyist)
Self-employed as an independent consultant.

Clients Represented
As an independent consultant
Internat'l Ass'n of Assembly Managers

MADDOX, Lauren
1001 G St. NW
Suite 900 E
Washington, DC 20001-4545
Tel: (202)393-1010
Fax: (202)393-5510
Registered: LDA

Employers
Podesta/Mattoon (Principal)

Clients Represented
On Behalf of Podesta/Mattoon
Federation of American Hospitals
Mount Sinai/NYU Health

MADDY, Jim

1101 17th St. NW
Suite 1102
Washington, DC 20036
Tel: (202)785-4500
Fax: (202)785-3539

Employers

Nat'l Park Foundation (President)

MADEY, Stephen

1755 Jefferson Davis Hwy.
Suite 1107
Arlington, VA 22202
Tel: (703)415-0344
Fax: (703)415-0182
Registered: LDA

Employers

The PMA Group (Associate)

Clients Represented

On Behalf of The PMA Group

CPU Technology
Dynamics Research Corp.
Gentex Corp.
Microvision, Inc.
New Mexico Tech
Omega Air
SVS, Inc.
Weidlinger Associates, Inc.

MADIA, Michelle

2501 M St. NW
Suite 400
Washington, DC 20037
Tel: (202)861-2500
Fax: (202)861-2583

Employers

Nat'l Ass'n of College and University Business Officers (Information Manager)

MADIGAN, Michael J.

1333 New Hampshire Ave. NW
Suite 400
Washington, DC 20036
Tel: (202)887-4000
Fax: (202)887-4288

Chief Counsel, Senate Governmental Affairs Committee, 1997-98.

Employers

Akin, Gump, Strauss, Hauer & Feld, L.L.P. (Partner)

Clients Represented

On Behalf of Akin, Gump, Strauss, Hauer & Feld, L.L.P.

Corrections Corp. of America

MADIGAN, Peter T.

1300 Connecticut Ave. NW
Suite 600
Washington, DC 20036
Tel: (202)775-8116
Fax: (202)223-0358
Registered: LDA

Principal Deputy Assistant Secretary for Legislative Affairs, Department of State, 1988-90. Deputy Assistant Secretary of the Treasury, 1985-89. Special Assistant to the Assistant Secretary, Department of Health and Human Services. Legislative Assistant to Director of the Office of Management and Budget, The White House, 1983-85. Floor Assistant to the House Republican Chief Deputy Whip, 1981-83.

Employers

Griffin, Johnson, Dover & Stewart (Principal)

MADISON, Alan M.

410 First St. SE
Third Floor
Washington, DC 20003
Tel: (202)484-2776
Fax: (202)484-7016
EMail: amadison@dcsgroup.com

Employers

The DCS Group (Partner)

MADISON, Cliff

254A Maryland Ave. NE
Washington, DC 20002
Tel: (202)543-9395
Fax: (202)543-0684
Registered: LDA

Staff Member, House Public Works and Transportation Committee, 1974-78.

Employers

Cliff Madison Government Relations, Inc. (Partner)
MARC Associates, Inc.

Clients Represented

On Behalf of MARC Associates, Inc.

Los Angeles County Mass Transportation Authority
San Francisco, California, City and County of
University of California at Irvine Advanced Power and Energy Program

MADSEN, Grant

1201 15th St. NW
Washington, DC 20005-2800
Tel: (202)822-0200
Fax: (202)822-0572
Registered: LDA

Employers

Nat'l Ass'n of Home Builders of the U.S. (Legislative Director, Environment)

MADSEN, Marcia G.

655 15th St. NW
Suite 900
Washington, DC 20005-5701
EMail: mmadsen@milchev.com
Tel: (202)626-5800
Fax: (202)628-0858

Employers

Miller & Chevalier, Chartered (Member)

MADURO, Sr., Reynaldo P.

6400 Arlington Blvd.
Suite 1100
Falls Church, VA 22042
EMail: rmaduro@rpihq.com
Tel: (703)237-8061
Fax: (703)237-8085

Employers

Research Planning, Inc. (President)

MADUROS, Nicholas

1133 Connecticut Ave. NW
Fifth Floor
Washington, DC 20036
Tel: (202)457-1110
Fax: (202)457-1130
Registered: LDA

Employers

Quinn Gillespie & Associates (Associate)

Clients Represented

On Behalf of Quinn Gillespie & Associates

LVMH Moet Hennessy Louis Vuitton S.A.
Metropolitan Life Insurance Co.

MAEHARA, Paulette V.

1101 King St.
Suite 700
Alexandria, VA 22314
Tel: (703)684-0410
Fax: (703)684-0540

Employers

Ass'n of Fund Raising Professionals (President and Chief Exec. Officer)

MAESTRI, Bruno

1500 K St. NW
Suite 375
Washington, DC 20005
Tel: (202)383-4425
Fax: (202)383-4018

Employers

Norfolk Southern Corp. (V. President, Public Affairs)

MAGAN, Michael

1615 H St. NW
Washington, DC 20062
Tel: (202)463-5485
Fax: (202)463-3126
Registered: LDA

Employers

Ass'n of American Chambers of Commerce in Latin America (Exec. V. President)
Chamber of Commerce of the U.S.A. (Manager, Western Hemisphere)

MAGEE, Marybeth

1735 New York Ave. NW
Suite 500
Washington, DC 20006-4759
Tel: (202)628-1700
Fax: (202)331-1024

Employers

Preston Gates Ellis & Rouvelas Meeds LLP (Associate)

MAGER, Mimi

888 17th St. NW
Suite 800
Washington, DC 20006
EMail: mmager@heimag.com
Tel: (202)822-8060
Fax: (202)822-9088
Registered: LDA

Employers

Heidepriem & Mager, Inc. (Chief Exec. Officer)

Clients Represented

On Behalf of Heidepriem & Mager, Inc.

American Home Products Corp.
Cytyc Corp.
Nat'l Asian Women's Health Organization
Pharmacia Corp.
R2 Technology, Inc.
United Airlines
Wyeth-Ayerst Laboratories

MAGGI, Philip

1341 G St. NW
Suite 1100
Washington, DC 20005
Tel: (202)585-0238
Fax: (202)393-0712
Registered: LDA

Former Aide to Rep. Nancy Johnson (R-CT).

Employers

Computer Coalition for Responsible Exports (Coalition Policy Director)
Infotech Strategies, Inc. (Coalition Policy Director)

Clients Represented

On Behalf of Infotech Strategies, Inc.

Computer Coalition for Responsible Exports
Computer Systems Policy Project

MAGIELNICKI, Robert L.

1300 I St. NW
11th Floor East
Washington, DC 20005-3314
EMail: rmagielnicki@schnader.com
Tel: (202)216-4200
Fax: (202)775-8741
Registered: LDA

Employers

Schnader Harrison Segal & Lewis LLP

MAGLEBY, Curt N.

1350 I St. NW
Suite 1000
Washington, DC 20005
EMail: cmagleb1@ford.com
Tel: (202)962-5367
Fax: (202)336-7228

Employers

Ford Motor Co. (Legislative Manager, Clean Air and E-Commerce)

MAGLIOCCHETTI, Paul J.

1755 Jefferson Davis Hwy.
Suite 1107
Arlington, VA 22202
Tel: (703)415-0344
Fax: (703)415-0182
Registered: LDA

Former Professional Staff member, Subcommittee on Defense, House Committee on Appropriations. Former Professional Staff Member, General Accounting Office.

Employers

The PMA Group (President)

Clients Represented

On Behalf of The PMA Group

AAI Corp.
ADSIL
Advanced Acoustic Concepts, Inc.
Advanced Programming Concepts
AEPTEC
Ag/Bio Con
Alliance
American Academy of Audiology
Applied Marine Technologies, Inc.
ARC Global Technologies
AsclepiusNet
Ass'n of Medical Device Reprocessors
Autometric Inc.
Battelle
Biocontrol Technology, Inc.
Cartwright Electronics
Caterpillar Inc.
Chamberlain Manufacturing Corp.
Cheese of Choice Coalition
Chicago Mercantile Exchange
CHIM
CoBank, ACB
ConAgra Foods, Inc.
Concurrent Technologies Corp.
Condor Systems
Coronado, California, City of
CPU Technology
CRYPTEK Secure Communications, LLC
Diamond Antenna & Microwave Corp.
Dynacom Industries
Dynamics Research Corp.
Electro-Radiation Inc.
Electronic Warfare Associates, Inc.
Environmental Technology Unlimited
Fidelity Technologies Corp.
FLIR Systems, Inc.
Florida Sugar Cane League, Inc.
Foundation Health Federal Services, Inc.
General Atomics
General Mills
Generic Pharmaceutical Ass'n
Gentex Corp.
B. F. Goodrich Co.
Guild Associates
IIT Research Institute
IMSSCO Inc.
Innovative Productivity, Inc.
Joint Healthcare Information Technology Alliance
Kollsman, Inc.
L-3 Communications Corp.
Laguna Industries, Inc.
Laguna, New Mexico, City of
Life Cell
Lockheed Martin Corp.
Lockheed Martin Federal Systems
Lockheed Martin MS/Gaithersburg
Lucent Technologies
McLean Hospital
MIC Industries, Inc.
Microvision, Inc.
J. E. Morgan Knitting Mills
MTS Systems Inc.
Nat'l Ass'n of RC&D Councils
Nat'l Ass'n of Resource Conservation
Nat'l Cattleman's Beef Ass'n
Nat'l Cooperative Bank
Nat'l Pork Producers Ass'n
New Mexico Tech
Northrop Marine
Omega Air
Opportunity Medical, Inc.
Orange Shipbuilding Co., Inc.
Oxley
Pathfinder Technology Inc.
Planning Systems, Inc.
Prologic
Sabreliner Corp.
SACO Defense
SatoTravel
Schweizer Aircraft Corp.
Science Applications Internat'l Corp. (SAIC)
SIGCOM, Inc.
Spatial Integrated Systems
Stanly County Airport Authority
SVS, Inc.
Teledyne Controls, Inc.
TeleFlex Canada, Ltd.
Textron Inc.
Titan Corp.
Trex Enterprises
Triosyn Corp.
U.S. Rice Producers Ass'n
University Emergency Medicine Foundation
Weidlinger Associates, Inc.

MAGNO, Linda

325 Seventh St. NW
Washington, DC 20004
Tel: (202)638-1100
Fax: (202)626-4319
Registered: LDA

Employers

American Hospital Ass'n (Managing Director, Policy Development, Analysis, and Regulatory Affairs)

MAGNUS, John R.

1775 Pennsylvania Ave. NW
Suite 200
Washington, DC 20006
Tel: (202)862-1000
Fax: (202)862-1093
Registered: LDA

Employers

Dewey Ballantine LLP (Partner)

Clients Represented

On Behalf of Dewey Ballantine LLP

American Natural Soda Ash Corp.
Labor-Industry Coalition for Internat'l Trade

MAGNUSON, Norman G.

1090 Vermont Ave. NW
Suite 200
Washington, DC 20005-4905
Tel: (202)371-0910
Fax: (202)371-0134

Employers

Associated Credit Bureaus, Inc. (V. President, Public Affairs)

MAGRATH, C. Peter

1307 New York Ave. NW
Suite 400
Washington, DC 20005-4722
Tel: (202)478-6040
Fax: (202)478-6061

Employers

Nat'l Ass'n of State Universities and Land-Grant Colleges (President)

MAGRUDER, Coe

1300 I St. NW
Suite 1050-E
Washington, DC 20005
Tel: (202)336-5085

Employers

PaineWebber Group, Inc. (Senior V. President and District Manager, Washington)

MAGRUDER, Meghan

1455 Pennsylvania Ave. NW
Suite 1000
Washington, DC 20004
Tel: (202)942-8400
Fax: (202)942-8484

Employers

Hale and Dorr LLP (Senior Partner)

MAGUIRE, A. John

1521 New Hampshire Ave. NW
Washington, DC 20036
Tel: (202)745-7805
Fax: (202)483-4040
Registered: LDA
EMail: jmaguire@cotton.org

Employers

Nat'l Cotton Council of America (V. President, Washington Operations)

MAGUIRE, Margaret

7799 Leesburg Pike
Suite 800 North
Falls Church, VA 22043
Tel: (703)749-0823
Fax: (703)749-1688

Employers

The Secura Group (Managing Director)

MAGUIRE, Meg

801 Pennsylvania Ave. SE
Suite 300
Washington, DC 20003
Tel: (202)543-6200
Ext: 11
Fax: (202)543-9130
Registered: LDA
EMail: maguire@scenic.org

Senior Program Manager, Americorps; Deputy Director, Heritage Conservation and Recreation Service, Department of the Interior, 1977-81.

Employers

Scenic America (President)

MAGUIRE, II, Stephen J.

1615 L St. NW
Suite 1200
Washington, DC 20036
Tel: (202)466-6300
Fax: (202)463-0678
Registered: LDA

Employers

Bell, Boyd & Lloyd (Legislative Representative)

Clients Represented

On Behalf of Bell, Boyd & Lloyd

Computer Associates Internat'l

MAHE, Jr., Eddie

900 Second St. NE
Suite 200
Washington, DC 20002
EMail: eddie@temc.com
Tel: (202)842-4100
Fax: (202)842-4442

Employers

The Eddie Mahe Company (Chairman)

Clients Represented

On Behalf of The Eddie Mahe Company

American Insurance Ass'n

MAHEADY, Joseph

700 11th St. NW
Washington, DC 20001-4507
Tel: (202)383-1097
Fax: (202)383-7580
Registered: LDA
EMail: jmaheady@realtors.org

Employers

Nat'l Ass'n of Realtors (Environment Policy Representative)

MAHER, James R.

1828 L St. NW
Suite 705
Washington, DC 20036
EMail: jim_maher@alta.org
Tel: (202)296-3671
Fax: (202)223-5843

Employers

American Land Title Ass'n (Exec. V. President)

MAHER, Kevin L.

1201 New York Ave. NW
Suite 600
Washington, DC 20005-3931
Tel: (202)289-3147
Fax: (202)289-3185
Registered: LDA
EMail: kmaher@ahma.com

Employers

American Hotel and Lodging Ass'n (Director, Governmental Affairs)

MAHER, Nicole R.

900 Spring St.
Silver Spring, MD 20910
Tel: (301)587-1400
Fax: (301)587-1605

Employers

Truck Mixer Manufacturers Bureau (Bureau Administrator)

MAHER, William F.

630 I St. NW
Washington, DC 20001
Tel: (202)289-3400
Fax: (202)289-3401

Employers

Housing and Development Law Institute (Exec. Director and Counsel)

MAHER, Jr., William F.

555 12th St. NW
Suite 950 North
Washington, DC 20004
Tel: (202)371-9100
Fax: (202)371-1497

Employers

Halprin, Temple, Goodman & Maher (Partner)

MAHLE, Darlene

2500 Wilson Blvd.
Suite 300
Arlington, VA 22201
EMail: dmahle@tia.eia.org
Tel: (703)907-7716
Fax: (703)907-7727

Employers

Telecommunications Industry Ass'n (Director, Human Resources)

MAHLER, Jason M.

666 11th St. NW
Suite 600
Washington, DC 20001
Tel: (202)783-0070
Fax: (202)783-0534
Registered: LDA
EMail: jmahler@ccianet.org

Served as Legislative Assistant and Counsel to Rep. Zoe Lofgren (D-CA) and Legislative Assistant to Senator Frank R. Lautenberg (D-NJ).

Employers
Computer and Communications Industry Ass'n (CCIA) (V. President and General Counsel)

MAHLMANN, John J.

1806 Robert Fulton Dr.
Reston, VA 20191
Tel: (703)860-4000
Fax: (703)860-1531
EMail: cherylw@menc.org

Employers
MENC: The Nat'l Ass'n for Music Education (Exec. Director)

MAHON, William J.

1255 23rd St. NW
Suite 200
Washington, DC 20037-1174
Tel: (202)452-8100
Fax: (202)833-3636
EMail: wmahon@hauck.com

Employers
Hauck and Associates (Senior V. President)
Nat'l Health Care Anti-Fraud Ass'n (Exec. Director)

Clients Represented
On Behalf of Hauck and Associates
DFK Internat'l/USA, Inc.
Nat'l Health Care Anti-Fraud Ass'n

MAHONEY, Catherine

1101 Pennsylvania Ave. NW
Suite 1000
Washington, DC 20004
Tel: (202)879-6800
Fax: (202)783-4460

Employers
Citigroup (Assistant Director, PAC)

MAHONEY, Daniel

501 Third St. NW
Washington, DC 20001-2797
Tel: (202)434-1254
Fax: (202)434-1426
EMail: dmahoney@cwa-union.org

Employers
Nat'l Ass'n of Broadcast Employees and Technicians-Communications Workers of America, AFL-CIO (NABET-CWA) (Secretary-Treasurer)

MAHONEY, James E.

5103 Moorland Ln.
Bethesda, MD 20814
Tel: (301)657-2412
Fax: (301)426-2909
Registered: LDA

Employers
Results Cubed (President)

Clients Represented
On Behalf of Results Cubed
Matlack Systems, Inc.

MAHONEY, Mary

3900 Jermantown Rd.
Suite 450
Fairfax, VA 22030
Tel: (703)359-6500
Fax: (703)359-6510
Registered: LDA

Employers
United Seniors Ass'n (Director, Government Relations)

MAHONEY, Maureen E.

555 11th St. NW
Suite 1000
Washington, DC 20004
Tel: (202)637-2200
Fax: (202)637-2201

Deputy Solicitor General, Department of Justice, 1991-93. Law Clerk to Justice William H. Rehnquist, U.S. Supreme Court, 1979-80. Law Clerk to Judge Robert A. Sprecher, U.S. Court of Appeals, Seventh Circuit, 1978-79.

Employers
Latham & Watkins (Partner)

MAHONEY, William G.

1050 17th St. NW
Suite 590
Washington, DC 20036
Tel: (202)296-8500
Fax: (202)296-7143

Employers
Highsaw, Mahoney & Clarke (Partner)

Clients Represented
On Behalf of Highsaw, Mahoney & Clarke
Railway Labor Executives' Ass'n

MAHORMEY, William

1100 New York Ave. NW
Suite 1050
Washington, DC 20005
Tel: (202)842-1645
Fax: (202)842-0850

Employers
American Bus Ass'n (Director, Safety and Regulatory Programs)

MAHSETKY, Michael D.

5600 Fishers Ln.
Room 6-05
Rockville, MD 20857
Tel: (301)443-7261
Fax: (301)443-4794

Employers
Department of Health and Human Services - Indian Health Service (Director, Legislative Affairs)

MAI, Peter

3328 S. Second St.
Arlington, VA 22204
Tel: (703)521-8844
Fax: (703)521-8866
Registered: LDA

Employers
Capitol Capital Group

Clients Represented
On Behalf of Capitol Capital Group
Washington Consulting Group

MAIBACH, Michael C.

1634 I St. NW
Suite 300
Washington, DC 20006
Tel: (202)626-4383
Fax: (202)628-2525
Registered: LDA

Employers
Intel Corp. (V. President, Government Affairs)

MAILLAR, Townley

1651 Prince St.
Alexandria, VA 22314
Tel: (703)739-0875
Fax: (703)739-0878
EMail: thritz@nhsa.org

Employers
Nat'l Head Start Ass'n (Director, Government Affairs)

MAIMAN, Seth E.

1133 19th St. NW
Washington, DC 20036
Tel: (202)887-3830
Fax: (202)736-6880

Employers
MCI WorldCom Corp. (Government Affairs)

MAINE, Lucinda L.

2215 Constitution Ave. NW
Washington, DC 20037-2985
Tel: (202)628-4410
Fax: (202)783-2351

Employers
Academy of Pharmaceutical Research and Science (Senior V. President)
American Pharmaceutical Ass'n (Senior V. President, Professional and Public Affairs)

MAINES, Patrick D.

1000 Potomac St. NW
Suite 301
Washington, DC 20007
Tel: (202)298-7512
Fax: (202)337-7092

Employers
Media Institute (President)

MAIRENA, Mario D.

1913 I St. NW
Washington, DC 20006
Tel: (202)872-8110
Fax: (202)872-8114
Registered: LDA

Employers
Consumer Specialties Products Ass'n (Federal Legislative Representative)

MAISANO, Frank

2025 M St. NW
Suite 350
Washington, DC 20036
Tel: (202)466-7391
Fax: (202)463-1338
Registered: LDA
EMail: fmaisano@pcgpr.com

Employers
Potomac Communications Group (Director)

MAJOROS, Michael

1220 L St. NW
Suite 410
Washington, DC 20005
Tel: (202)371-9153
Fax: (202)842-4966

Employers
Snavely, King, Majoros, O'Connor and Lee, Inc. (V. President)

Clients Represented
On Behalf of Snavely, King, Majoros, O'Connor and Lee, Inc.
Puerto Rico Telephone Co.

MAKI, Reid

4350 N. Fairfax Dr.
Suite 410
Arlington, VA 22203
Tel: (703)528-4141
Ext: 140
Fax: (703)528-4145
EMail: maki@afop.org

Employers
Ass'n of Farmworker Opportunity Programs (Manager, Department of Labor Project)

MAKIN, John H.

1150 17th St. NW
Washington, DC 20036
Tel: (202)862-5800
Fax: (202)862-7177
EMail: jmakin@aei.org

Employers
American Enterprise Institute for Public Policy Research (Resident Scholar)

MAKINS, Christopher J.

910 17th St. NW
Tenth Floor
Washington, DC 20006
Tel: (202)778-4961
Fax: (202)463-7241
EMail: cmakins@acus.org

Employers
Atlantic Council of the United States (President)

MAKINSON, Larry

1101 14th St. NW
Suite 1030
Washington, DC 20005-5635
Tel: (202)857-0044
Fax: (202)857-7809

Employers
Center for Responsive Politics (Senior Fellow)

MAKOVSKY, David

1828 L St. NW
Suite 1050
Washington, DC 20036
Tel: (202)452-0650
Ext: 223
Fax: (202)223-5364
EMail: alanm@washingtoninstitute.org

Employers
Washington Institute for Near East Policy (Senior Fellow)

MAKRIS, Tony

201 N. Union St.
Suite 510
Alexandria, VA 22314
Tel: (703)299-9470
Fax: (703)299-9478
Registered: LDA

Employers
Mercury Group (President)

MAKSOUD, Ph.D., Hala

4201 Connecticut Ave. NW
Suite 300
Washington, DC 20008
Tel: (202)244-2990
Fax: (202)244-3196
EMail: adc@adc.org

Employers
American-Arab Anti-Discrimination Committee (ADC) (President)

MALAN, Todd M.

1901 Pennsylvania Ave. NW
Suite 807
Washington, DC 20006
EMail: toddmalan@aol.com
Tel: (202)659-1903
Fax: (202)659-2293
Registered: LDA

Employers
Organization for Internat'l Investment (Exec. Director)

MALARKEY, Faye A.

2025 M St. NW
Suite 800
Washington, DC 20036
EMail: faye_malarkey@dc.sba.com
Tel: (202)367-2100
Fax: (202)367-1200
Registered: LDA

Employers
Smith, Bucklin and Associates, Inc.

Clients Represented
On Behalf of Smith, Bucklin and Associates, Inc.
Regional Airline Ass'n

MALASKY, Alan R.

1919 Pennsylvania Ave. NW
Suite 600
Washington, DC 20006-3404
Tel: (202)326-1500
Fax: (202)326-1555

Employers
Jenkens & Gilchrist (Shareholder)

MALBIN, Irene L.

1101 17th St. NW
Suite 300
Washington, DC 20036
Tel: (202)331-1770
Fax: (202)331-1969

Employers
Cosmetic, Toiletry and Fragrance Ass'n (V. President, Public Affairs)

MALCOLM, Ellen R.

805 15th St. NW
Suite 400
Washington, DC 20005
Tel: (202)326-1400
Fax: (202)326-1415

Employers
EMILY'S List (President)

MALDONADO, Daniel C.

1101 17th St. NW
Suite 803
Washington, DC 20036
Tel: (202)833-0007
Fax: (202)833-0086
Registered: LDA

Employers
MARC Associates, Inc. (President)

Clients Represented
On Behalf of MARC Associates, Inc.
American Soc. of Anesthesiologists
Cerebral Palsy Council
Coalition for Health Services Research
Corporation for Supportive Housing
Fine Arts Museums of San Francisco
L.A. Care Health Plan
Los Angeles County Mass Transportation Authority
Los Angeles County Office of Education
Los Angeles, California, Community Development Commission of the County of
Los Angeles, California, County of
Nat'l Hemophilia Foundation
NI Industries
San Francisco, California, City and County of
TELACU
University of California at Irvine Advanced Power and Energy Program

MALES, Eric H.

200 N. Glebe Rd.
Suite 800
Arlington, VA 22203
EMail: natlime@lime.org
Tel: (703)243-5463
Fax: (703)243-5489
Registered: LDA

Employers
Nat'l Lime Ass'n (Director, Regulatory Issues and Special Projects)

MALIA, Gerald A.

1660 L St. NW
Suite 506
Washington, DC 20036
Tel: (202)639-8000
Fax: (202)463-6328
Registered: LDA

Employers
Self-employed as an independent consultant.

Clients Represented
As an independent consultant
American Bureau of Shipping

MALINA, Joel

1317 F St. NW
Suite 600
Washington, DC 20004
EMail: malina@wexlergroup.com
Tel: (202)638-2121
Fax: (202)638-7045
Registered: LDA

Employers
The Wexler Group (Principal/Senior Director)

Clients Represented
On Behalf of The Wexler Group
Alaska, Washington Office of the State of
Alliance for Understandable, Sensible and Accountable Government Regulations
BP Amoco Corp.
British Columbia Hydro and Power Authority
Burger King Corp.
Caterpillar Inc.
Hong Kong Economic and Trade Office
Hydroelectric Licensing Reform Task Force
MENC: The Nat'l Ass'n for Music Education
Nat'l Ass'n of Music Merchants

MALINA, Mary

1201 Connecticut Ave. NW
Suite 200
Washington, DC 20036-2636
EMail: mmalina@policefoundation.org
Tel: (202)833-1460
Fax: (202)659-9149

Employers
Police Foundation (Communications Director)

MALITO, Kenneth C.

444 N. Capitol St. NW
Washington, DC 20001
EMail: kmalito@aol.com
Tel: (202)347-1117
Fax: (202)638-4584
Registered: LDA

Employers
Davidoff & Malito, LLP (Assistant Director, Washington Office)

Clients Represented
On Behalf of Davidoff & Malito, LLP
American Museum of Natural History
Lou Levy & Sons Fashions, Inc.
Magellan Health Services
New City Development
New York Psychotherapy and Counseling Center
Project Return Foundation Inc.
Queens Borough Public Library
Soc. of Thoracic Surgeons
SOS Interpreting Ltd.
St. Vincent Catholic Medical Centers
Welch's Foods, Inc.

MALITO, Robert J.

444 N. Capitol St. NW
Washington, DC 20001
Tel: (202)347-1117
Fax: (202)638-4584
Registered: LDA

Employers
Davidoff & Malito, LLP (Partner)

Clients Represented
On Behalf of Davidoff & Malito, LLP
American Museum of Natural History
Lou Levy & Sons Fashions, Inc.
New City Development
New York Psychotherapy and Counseling Center
Soc. of Thoracic Surgeons
SOS Interpreting Ltd.
Trans World Airlines, Inc.
Welch's Foods, Inc.

MALLEN, Richard

1909 K St. NW
Suite 820
Washington, DC 20006
EMail: rmallen@lmm-law.com
Tel: (202)777-7700
Fax: (202)777-7763

Employers
Lawler, Metzger & Milkman, LLC (Associate)

MALLINO, Jr., David L.

1401 New York Ave. NW
Tenth Floor
Washington, DC 20005-2102
EMail: dlmjr@connerton-ray.com
Tel: (202)737-1900
Fax: (202)659-3458
Registered: LDA

Employers
Connerton & Ray (Legislative Representative)

Clients Represented
On Behalf of Connerton & Ray
Brotherhood of Locomotive Engineers
Coalition for Workers' Health Care Funds
Internat'l Brotherhood of Teamsters
Laborers Health & Safety Fund
Laborers-AGC Education and Training Fund
Laborers-Employers Cooperation & Education Trust

MALLINO, Sr., David L.

1615 L St. NW
Suite 650
Washington, DC 20036
Tel: (202)626-8517
Registered: LDA
Former Aide, Department of Labor. Former Aide, House Committee on Education and the Workforce.

Employers
Connerton & Ray (Director, Government Affairs)
Mallino Government Relations

Clients Represented
On Behalf of Connerton & Ray
Brotherhood of Locomotive Engineers
Coalition for Workers' Health Care Funds
Internat'l Brotherhood of Teamsters
Laborers Health & Safety Fund
Laborers Institute for Training and Education
Laborers' Internat'l Union of North America
Laborers-AGC Education and Training Fund
Laborers-Employers Cooperation & Education Trust
Nat'l Energy Management Institute
Nat'l Environmental Education and Training Center
On Behalf of Mallino Government Relations
Internat'l Brotherhood of Teamsters
Laborers Health & Safety Fund
Laborers' Internat'l Union of North America
Laborers-AGC Education and Training Fund
Laborers-Employers Cooperation & Education Trust
Nat'l Energy Management Institute

MALLON, Francis J.

1111 N. Fairfax St.
Alexandria, VA 22314
Tel: (703)684-2782
Ext: 3252
Fax: (703)706-8519

Employers
American Physical Therapy Ass'n (Chief Exec. Officer)

MALLORY, III, C. King

1900 K St. NW
Washington, DC 20006-1109
EMail: kmallory@hunton.com
Tel: (202)955-1500
Fax: (202)778-2201
Registered: LDA
Acting Assistant Secretary for Energy and Minerals (1974) and Deputy Assistant Secretary for Resources and Regulation (1973-74), Department of the Interior. Acting Executive Director, Securities and Exchange Commission, 1972-73. Lieutenant, U.S. Naval Reserve, 1961-64.

Employers
Hunton & Williams (Partner)

Clients Represented
On Behalf of Hunton & Williams
American Electric Power Co.
Edison Electric Institute

MALLORY, Michelle

21 Dupont Circle NW
Fifth Floor
Washington, DC 20036
Tel: (202)263-5900
Fax: (202)263-5901
Registered: LDA

Employers
Microsoft Corp. (Manager, Multi-State Government Affairs)

MALLOY, Claudia

1250 Connecticut Ave. NW
Washington, DC 20036
Tel: (202)833-1200
Fax: (202)659-3716
Registered: LDA

Employers
Common Cause (Secretary to the National Governing Board)

MALLOY, John Davis

815 15th St. NW
Suite 900
Washington, DC 20005
EMail: legalservices@thewala.org
Tel: (202)393-2826
Fax: (202)393-4444

Employers
Washington Area Lawyers for the Arts (Director of Legal Services)

MALLOY, Michelle

1101 Vermont Ave. NW
Suite 200
Washington, DC 20005
EMail: mmalloy@naruc.org
Tel: (202)898-2214
Fax: (202)898-2213

Employers
Nat'l Ass'n of Regulatory Utility Commissioners (Director, Meetings)

MALMGREN, Kurt

1100 15th St. NW
Suite 900
Washington, DC 20005
Tel: (202)835-3400
Fax: (202)835-3414

Employers
Pharmaceutical Research and Manufacturers of America (Senior V. President, Government Affairs)

MALONE, Harry

1725 Jefferson Davis Hwy.
Crystal Square 2, Suite 300
Arlington, VA 22202
Tel: (703)413-5600
Fax: (703)413-5613

Employers
Lockheed Martin Corp. (Director, Legislative Affairs, Army Programs)

MALONE, William

1155 Connecticut Ave. NW
Suite 1000
Washington, DC 20036-4306
EMail: wmalone@millervaneaton.com
Tel: (202)785-0600
Fax: (202)785-1234

Employers
Miller & Van Eaton, P.L.L.C. (Partner)

Clients Represented

On Behalf of Miller & Van Eaton, P.L.L.C.
Building Owners and Managers Ass'n Internat'l
Dayton, Ohio, Washington Office of the City of
Harvard Radio Broadcasting Co.
Kansas Electric Power Cooperative
Nat'l Apartment Ass'n
Nat'l Multi-Housing Council
Nebraska Public Power District
Northern Mariana Islands, Commonwealth of the
Real Estate Roundtable
Tucson, Arizona, City of

MALONEY, Barry C.

5225 Wisconsin Ave. NW
Suite 316
Washington, DC 20015-2014
EMail: BMaloney@maloneyknox.com
Tel: (202)293-1414
Fax: (202)293-1702
Senior Branch Attorney (1971) and Attorney/Advisor (1967-70), Division of Corporate Finance, Securities and Exchange Commission.

Employers
Maloney & Knox, LLP (Managing Partner)

Clients Represented

On Behalf of Maloney & Knox, LLP
Ass'n of Sales & Marketing Companies

MALONEY, Joseph

815 16th St. NW
Suite 600
Washington, DC 20006
Tel: (202)347-1461
Fax: (202)628-0724

Employers
AFL-CIO - Building and Construction Trades Department (Secretary-Treasurer)

MALONEY, Robert

3900 Wisconsin Ave. NW
Washington, DC 20016
Tel: (202)752-7958
Registered: LDA

Employers
Fannie Mae (V. President, Government Relations)

MALONEY, William A.

1101 King St.
Alexandria, VA 22314
Tel: (703)739-2782
Fax: (703)684-8319

Employers
American Soc. of Travel Agents (Exec V. President and Chief Operating Officer)

MALONI, Jason

410 First St. SE
Third Floor
Washington, DC 20003
EMail: jmaloni@dcsgroup.com
Tel: (202)484-2776
Fax: (202)484-7016

Employers
The DCS Group (Group Director)

MALONI, William Robert

3900 Wisconsin Ave. NW
Washington, DC 20016
Tel: (202)752-7120
Fax: (202)752-6099
Registered: LDA

Employers
Fannie Mae (Senior V. President, Government and Industrial Relations)

MALOUFF, Frank

12500 Fair Lakes Circle
Suite 375
Fairfax, VA 22033
Tel: (703)502-1550
Fax: (703)502-7852

Employers
American Soc. for Therapeutic Radiology and Oncology (Exec. Director)

MALOW, Jessica

1420 New York Ave. NW
Suite 1050
Washington, DC 20005
Tel: (202)638-1950
Fax: (202)638-7714

Employers
Van Scoyoc Associates, Inc. (Legislative Assistant)

Clients Represented

On Behalf of Van Scoyoc Associates, Inc.
Lockheed Martin Venture Star

MALSON, Robert A.

1250 I St. NW
Suite 700
Washington, DC 20005-3922
EMail: rmalson@dcha.org
Tel: (202)682-1581
Fax: (202)371-8151

Employers
District of Columbia Hospital Ass'n (President)

MAMET, Noah

P.O. Box 15187
Washington, DC 20003
Tel: (202)485-3437
Fax: (202)485-3427

Employers
Effective Government Committee (Treasurer)

MANAFORT, Paul J.

211 N. Union St.
Suite 250
Alexandria, VA 22314
EMail: pmanafort@dmfgroup.com
Tel: (703)299-9100
Fax: (703)299-9110
Registered: LDA

Employers
Davis Manafort, Inc. (Chief Exec. Officer)

MANASSE, Ph.D., Sc., Henri R.

7272 Wisconsin Ave.
Bethesda, MD 20814
Tel: (301)657-3000
Fax: (301)657-8278

Employers
American Soc. of Health System Pharmacists (Exec. V. President and Chief Exec. Officer)

MANATOS, Andrew E.

601 13th St. NW
Suite 1150 South
Washington, DC 20005
Tel: (202)393-7790
Fax: (202)628-0225
Registered: LDA
Legislative Assistant, U.S. Senate, 1969-1973; Associate Staff Director of full Senate Committee, 1973-1977; Assistant Secretary of Commerce for Legislation, Department of Commerce, 1977-1981.

Employers
Manatos & Manatos, Inc. (President)

Clients Represented

On Behalf of Manatos & Manatos, Inc.
American University
Pancyprian Ass'n of America
PSEKA, Internat'l Coordinating Committee, Justice for Cyprus
United Hellenic American Congress

MANATOS, Mike A.

601 13th St. NW
Suite 1150 South
Washington, DC 20005
Tel: (202)393-7790
Fax: (202)628-0225
Registered: LDA

Employers
Manatos & Manatos, Inc. (V. President)

Clients Represented

On Behalf of Manatos & Manatos, Inc.
Pancyprian Ass'n of America
PSEKA, Internat'l Coordinating Committee, Justice for Cyprus
United Hellenic American Congress

MANATT, Michelle A.

750 17th St. NW
Room 825
Washington, DC 20503
Tel: (202)395-6655
Fax: (202)395-6708
Senior Policy Advisor, Bureau of Western Hemisphere Affairs, Department of State, 1995-99.

Employers
Executive Office of the President - Office of Nat'l Drug Control Policy (Director, Office of Legislative Affairs)

MANCE, Katherine T.

325 Seventh St. NW
Suite 1100
Washington, DC 20004-2802
Tel: (202)783-7971
Fax: (202)737-2849

Employers
Nat'l Retail Federation (V. President, Research, Education and Community Affairs)

MANCINI, John

1100 Wayne Ave.
Suite 1100
Silver Spring, MD 20910
Tel: (301)587-8202
Fax: (301)587-2711

Employers
Ass'n for Information and Image Management Internat'l (President)

MANCUSI, Michael

7799 Leesburg Pike
Suite 800 North
Falls Church, VA 22043
Tel: (703)749-0823
Fax: (703)749-1688
Former Senior Deputy Comptroller of the Currency, Department of Treasury.

Employers
The Secura Group (Managing Director and Chief Exec. Officer)

MANDEL, Michael S.

1333 New Hampshire Ave. NW
Suite 400
Washington, DC 20036
Tel: (202)887-4000
Fax: (202)887-4288
Registered: LDA
Special Assistant to the Secretary, Department of Housing and Urban Development, 1979-81.

Employers
Akin, Gump, Strauss, Hauer & Feld, L.L.P. (Partner)

Clients Represented

On Behalf of Akin, Gump, Strauss, Hauer & Feld, L.L.P.

First Nationwide Bank
Texas Manufactured Housing Ass'n
Transamerica Financial Services Co.

MANDIGO, Michael

1615 L St. NW
Suite 1000
Washington, DC 20036
Tel: (202)659-0330
Fax: (202)223-8199
Registered: LDA
EMail: mandigom@fleishman.com
Former Legislative Counsel to Rep. Rick Boucher (D-VA) and Attorney-Advisor, International Policy Division, Common Carrier Bureau, Federal Communications Commission.

Employers
Fleishman-Hillard, Inc (V. President)

Clients Represented

On Behalf of Fleishman-Hillard, Inc

Enron Corp.
SBC Communications Inc.
Telefonos de Mexico

MANELLI, Daniel J.

2000 M St. NW
Suite 700
Washington, DC 20036
Tel: (202)261-1000
Fax: (202)887-0336
Registered: LDA

Employers
Contact Lens Manufacturers Ass'n (Treasurer)
Manelli Denison & Selter PLLC

Clients Represented

On Behalf of Manelli Denison & Selter PLLC

Contact Lens Manufacturers Ass'n

MANES, Julie

601 Pennsylvania Ave. NW
North Bldg., Suite 325
Washington, DC 20004
Tel: (202)728-3613

Employers
Pioneer Hi-Bred Internat'l, Inc. (Washington Representative)

MANESS, Alan D.

1710 Rhode Island Ave. NW
Suite 700
Washington, DC 20036-3007
Tel: (202)466-5208
Fax: (202)263-4435
Registered: LDA
Senior Minority Counsel, Senate Commerce Committee, 1986-94.

Employers
State Farm Insurance Cos. (Federal Affairs Director and Counsel)

MANESS, Katherine W.

600 13th St. NW
Suite 340
Washington, DC 20005
Tel: (202)662-0100
Fax: (202)662-0199
Registered: LDA

Employers
Union Pacific (Director, Washington Affairs - Political)

MANEY, Timothy J.

1615 H St. NW
Washington, DC 20062-2000
Tel: (202)659-6000
Fax: (202)463-5836

Employers
Chamber of Commerce of the U.S.A. (Director, Congressional and Public Affairs)

MANG, Jeff

555 13th St. NW
Washington, DC 20004-1109
Tel: (202)637-8703
Fax: (202)637-5910
Registered: LDA
EMail: jcmang@hhlaw.com

Employers
Hogan & Hartson L.L.P. (Legislative Services Manager)

Clients Represented

On Behalf of Hogan & Hartson L.L.P.

Brother Internat'l Co.

MANGAN, John J.

1440 New York Ave. NW
Washington, DC 20005
Tel: (202)371-7000
Fax: (202)393-5760
Registered: LDA

Employers
Skadden, Arps, Slate, Meagher & Flom LLP (Partner)

Clients Represented

On Behalf of Skadden, Arps, Slate, Meagher & Flom LLP

Nat'l Steel Corp.

MANGAS, Robert

2101 L St. NW
Washington, DC 20037-1526
Tel: (202)785-9700
Fax: (202)887-0689
Registered: LDA
EMail: mangasr@dsmo.com
Chief of Staff (1995-98) and Counsel (1987-94) to Senator Wendell Ford (D-KY).

Employers
Dickstein Shapiro Morin & Oshinsky LLP (Of Counsel)

Clients Represented

On Behalf of Dickstein Shapiro Morin & Oshinsky LLP

American Greyhound Track Operators Ass'n
American Public Communications Council
CaseNewHolland Inc.
Cigar Ass'n of America
Delta Air Lines
Electric Power Supply Ass'n
Hydro-Quebec
Internat'l Brotherhood of Teamsters
Kerr-McGee Corp.
Lorillard Tobacco Co.
Luiginos
Nat'l Ass'n of Water Companies
PG&E Generating Co.
Pipe Tobacco Council, Inc.
Ratcliff Strategies
The Reader's Digest Ass'n
Smokeless Tobacco Council

MANGIONE, Peter T.

1319 F St. NW
Suite 700
Washington, DC 20004
Tel: (202)737-5660
Fax: (202)638-2615
Registered: LDA

Employers
Footwear Distributors and Retailers of America (President)

MANHAN, Robert D.

200 Maryland Ave. NE
Washington, DC 20002
Tel: (202)543-2239
Fax: (202)543-0961
Registered: LDA
EMail: bmanhan@vfwdc.org

Employers
Veterans of Foreign Wars of the U.S. (Assistant Director, National Legislative Service)

MANHEIM, Bruce

1900 K St. NW
Suite 750
Washington, DC 20006
Tel: (202)833-4500
Fax: (202)833-2859

Employers
Bennett Turner & Coleman, LLP

Clients Represented

On Behalf of Bennett Turner & Coleman, LLP

Cystic Fibrosis Foundation
Serono Laboratories, Inc.

MANISCALCO, Msgr. Francis J.

3211 Fourth St. NE
Washington, DC 20017
Tel: (202)541-3200
Fax: (202)541-3129

Employers
United States Catholic Conference (Director, Communications)

MANISHIN, Glenn B.

1625 Massachusetts Ave. NW
Suite 300
Washington, DC 20036
Tel: (202)955-6300
Fax: (202)955-6460
Registered: LDA
EMail: gbm@clark.net
Trial Attorney, Antitrust Division, Department of Justice, 1982-85. Law Clerk to Judge Clifford Wallace, U.S. Court of Appeals, Ninth Circuit, 1981-82.

Employers
Blumenfeld & Cohen (Partner)

MANKIEWICZ, Frank

600 New Hampshire Ave. NW
Suite 601
Washington, DC 20037
Tel: (202)333-7400
Fax: (202)333-1638
Registered: LDA, FARA
Former Press Secretary to Senator Robert F. Kennedy (D-NY).

Employers
Hill and Knowlton, Inc. (V. Chairman)

Clients Represented

On Behalf of Hill and Knowlton, Inc.

Eurapair International, Inc.
Internat'l Olympic Committee
Woods Hole Oceanographic Institution

MANLEY, Jeffrey

2445 M St. NW
Washington, DC 20037-1420
Tel: (202)663-6000
Fax: (202)663-6363

Employers
Wilmer, Cutler & Pickering (Partner)

MANN, Curt

1101 Vermont Ave. NW
Suite 710
Washington, DC 20005
EMail: cjmann@aavmc.org
Tel: (202)371-9195
Fax: (202)842-0773

Employers
Ass'n of American Veterinary Medical Colleges (Exec. Director)

MANN, Mary M.

1101 Pennsylvania Ave. NW
Suite 200
Washington, DC 20004
Tel: (202)628-1223
Fax: (202)628-1368
Registered: LDA
EMail: mary.mann@ipaper.com

Employers
Internat'l Paper (Washington Representative)

MANN, Phillip L.

655 15th St. NW
Suite 900
Washington, DC 20005-5701
Tel: (202)626-5800
Fax: (202)628-0858
Registered: LDA
EMail: pmann@milchev.com
Tax Legislative Counsel (1974-75) and Deputy Tax Legislative Counsel (1973-74), Department of the Treasury.

Employers
Miller & Chevalier, Chartered (Member)

Clients Represented

On Behalf of Miller & Chevalier, Chartered

Mutual of America

MANN, Richard F.

1001 G St. NW
Suite 500 West
Washington, DC 20001
EMail: mann@khlaw.com
Tel: (202)434-4100
Fax: (202)434-4646

Employers
Keller and Heckman LLP (Partner)

Clients Represented

On Behalf of Keller and Heckman LLP

Leprino Foods Co.

MANN, Susan O.

1300 Connecticut Ave. NW
Suite 600
Washington, DC 20036
Tel: (202)775-8116
Fax: (202)223-0358
Registered: LDA, FARA
Former Counsel to the Office of Legislation and International Affairs, Patent and Trademark Office.

Employers
Griffin, Johnson, Dover & Stewart (Lobbyist)

Clients Represented

On Behalf of Griffin, Johnson, Dover & Stewart
American Agrisurance
American Fish Spotters Ass'n
American Petroleum Institute
Avue Technologies
Dell Computer Corp.
Deloitte Consulting
Fannie Mae
Hong Kong Economic and Trade Office
The Justice Project, Inc.
Nat'l Music Publishers' Ass'n
United Technologies Corp.
Wilmer, Cutler & Pickering
Wine and Spirits Wholesalers of America

MANN, Thomas E.

1775 Massachusetts Ave. NW Tel: (202)797-6000
Washington, DC 20036-2188 Fax: (202)797-6004

Employers
The Brookings Institution (Senior Fellow, Governmental Studies)

MANN, Wendy

66 Canal Center Plaza Tel: (703)549-4432
Suite 520 Fax: (703)549-6495
Alexandria, VA 22314-1591

Employers
Health Industry Distributors Ass'n (V. President, Communications and Editor-in-Chief)

MANNEN, Ted R.

805 15th St. NW Tel: (202)312-7440
Suite 700 Fax: (202)312-7460
Washington, DC 20005
EMail: trmannen@bakerd.com
Former Banking Committee Aide to Senator Adlai E. Stevenson III (D-IL). Former Attorney, Office of Legislative Counsel, U.S. House of Representatives.

Employers
Baker & Daniels (In-House Counsel)

MANNINA, Jr., George J.

1666 K St. NW Tel: (202)887-1400
Suite 500 Fax: (202)466-2198
Washington, DC 20006-2803 Registered: LDA, FARA
EMail: gmannina@oconnorhannan.com
Chief Minority Counsel (1982-85) and Counsel, Subcommittee on Fisheries, Wildlife, Conservation and the Environment (1975-83), House Committee on Merchant Marine and Fisheries. Legislative Assistant to Rep. Edwin B. Forsythe (R-NJ), 1973-75. Administrative Aide to Rep. Gilbert Gude (R-MD), 1971-73.

Employers
O'Connor & Hannan, L.L.P. (Partner)

Clients Represented

On Behalf of O'Connor & Hannan, L.L.P.
Alliance of Marine Mammal Parks and Aquariums
American Forest & Paper Ass'n
Ass'n of Chiropractic Colleges
ATOFINA Chemicals, Inc.
Exxon Mobil Corp.
Fishing Vessel Owners' Ass'n
FMC Corp.
General Electric Co.
Georgia-Pacific Corp.
P. H. Glatfelter
Lockheed Martin Corp.
Marine Mammal Coalition
Mirage Resorts, Inc.
Montrose Chemical Co.
Nat'l Paint and Coatings Ass'n
Pacific Seafood Processors Ass'n
Perry Institute for Marine Science
Plano Molding Co.
Solid Waste Agency of Northern Cook County
Southeast Alaska Seiners Ass'n
Trident Seafood Corp.
Wards Cove Packing Co.

MANNING, USN (Ret.), Capt. Lory

1750 New York Ave. NW Tel: (202)628-0444
Suite 350 Ext: 12
Washington, DC 20006 Fax: (202)628-0458

Employers
Women's Research and Education Institute (Director, Women in Military Project)

MANNING, Mary Jo

1776 K St. NW Tel: (202)719-7000
Washington, DC 20006 Fax: (202)719-7049
Registered: LDA

Employers
Wiley, Rein & Fielding (Counsel)

Clients Represented

On Behalf of Wiley, Rein & Fielding
Bell Atlantic Mobile
SnapTrack
Telephone Operators Caucus
Time Domain Corp.
Verizon Wireless

MANNING, Michael J.

801 Pennsylvania Ave. NW Tel: (202)662-4550
Washington, DC 20004-2604 Fax: (202)662-4643
EMail: mmanning@fulbright.com

Employers
Fulbright & Jaworski L.L.P. (Partner)

MANNION, Sean

Two Democracy Center Tel: (301)571-1940
6903 Rockledge Dr., Suite 1250 Fax: (301)571-8244
Bethesda, MD 20817-1831

Employers
Mutual of America (Senior V. President)

MANSKOPF, Dirk

408 C St. NE Tel: (202)547-1141
Washington, DC 20002 Fax: (202)547-6009

Employers
Sierra Club (Conservation Assistant, Environmental Quality)

MANSO, Angela

One Dupont Circle NW Tel: (202)728-0200
Suite 410 Ext: 249
Washington, DC 20036 Fax: (202)833-2467

Employers
American Ass'n of Community Colleges (Legislative Associate)

MANSON, III, Joseph L.

901 15th St. NW Tel: (202)371-6000
Suite 700 Fax: (202)371-6279
Washington, DC 20005-2301 Registered: LDA

Employers
Verner, Liipfert, Bernhard, McPherson and Hand, Chartered (Member of Firm)

MANTERIA, Bill

655 15th St. NW Tel: (202)220-0637
Washington, DC 20005-5701 Fax: (202)220-0873
EMail: bmanteria@fmi.org

Employers
Food Marketing Institute (V. President, State Government Relations)

MANTHEI, John R.

555 11th St. NW Tel: (202)637-2200
Suite 1000 Fax: (202)637-2201
Washington, DC 20004 Registered: LDA
Former Lead Staffer on U.S. House of Representatives Republican's Prescription Drug Task Force.

Employers
Latham & Watkins (Senior Associate)

Clients Represented

On Behalf of Latham & Watkins
Boston Scientific Corp.
Serono Laboratories, Inc.

MANTON, Hon. Thomas J.

1666 K St. NW Tel: (202)887-1400
Suite 500 Fax: (202)466-2198
Washington, DC 20006-2803
Member, U.S. House of Representatives (D-NY), 1985-98.

Employers
O'Connor & Hannan, L.L.P. (Of Counsel)

Clients Represented

On Behalf of O'Connor & Hannan, L.L.P.
CompTIA

MANTOOTH, Mark C.

1101 Vermont Ave. NW Tel: (202)789-7423
12th Floor Fax: (202)789-7401
Washington, DC 20005-3583 Registered: LDA

Employers
American Medical Ass'n (Senior Washington Counsel)

MANTZ, Jonathan

430 S. Capitol St. SE Tel: (202)863-1500
Second Floor Fax: (202)485-3427
Washington, DC 20003

Employers
Democratic Congressional Campaign Committee (National Finance Director)

MANUAL, Cleo A.

919 18th St. NW Tel: (202)263-2900
Tenth Floor Fax: (202)263-2960
Washington, DC 20006

Employers
Issue Dynamics Inc. (Senior Consultant)

MANUEL, Hilda

1330 Connecticut Ave. NW Tel: (202)429-3000
Washington, DC 20036-1795 Fax: (202)429-3902
Registered: LDA
EMail: hmanuel@steptoe.com
Former Deputy Commissioner, Bureau of Indian Affairs, Department of the Interior.

Employers
Steptoe & Johnson LLP (Special Counsel)

Clients Represented

On Behalf of Steptoe & Johnson LLP
Agua Caliente Band of Cahuilla Indians
Mashpee Wampanoag Indian Tribal Council, Inc.

MAPES, Jr., William R.

1667 K St. NW Tel: (202)776-7800
Suite 700 Fax: (202)776-7801
Washington, DC 20006
EMail: wrmapes@duanemorris.com

Employers
Duane, Morris & Heckscher LLP (Partner)

MAPLES, Robert Y.

1627 K St. NW Tel: (202)452-1252
Suite 700 Ext: 26
Washington, DC 20006 Fax: (202)452-0118
Registered: LDA

Employers
Smokeless Tobacco Council (President)

MARANEY, John V. "Skip"

324 E. Capitol St. NE Tel: (202)543-1661
Washington, DC 20003-3897 Fax: (202)543-8863
Registered: LDA

Employers
Nat'l Star Route Mail Contractors Ass'n (Exec. Director)

MARANGI, Karen L.

2550 M St. NW Tel: (202)457-6000
Washington, DC 20037-1350 Fax: (202)457-6315
Registered: LDA
Former Counsel to Rep. Patrick Leahy (D-VT).

Employers
Patton Boggs, LLP (Legislative Specialist)

Clients Represented

On Behalf of Patton Boggs, LLP

AOL Time Warner
Ass'n of Trial Lawyers of America
Dictaphone Corp.
Retractable Technologies, Inc.

MARANO, Alyson

409 12th St. SW
P.O. Box 96920
Washington, DC 20090-6920
EMail: amarano@acog.org
Tel: (202)863-2505
Fax: (202)488-3985

Employers

American College of Obstetricians and Gynecologists (Grassroots Representative)

MARCHAND, Lorraine H.

1909 K St. NW
Fourth Floor
Washington, DC 20006
Tel: (202)973-5800
Fax: (202)973-5858
Former Director, National Diabetes Outreach Program, National Institutes of Health.

Employers

Porter/Novelli (Sr. V. President, Healthcare Marketing and Patients First)

MARCHAND, Paul

1730 K St. NW
Washington, DC 20006
Tel: (202)785-3388
Fax: (202)467-4179
Registered: LDA
EMail: marchand@thearc.org

Employers

The Arc (Assistant Exec. Director for Policy and Advocacy)

MARCHANT, Byron

One BET Plaza
1900 W Pl. NE
Washington, DC 20018
Tel: (202)608-2037
Fax: (202)608-2509

Employers

BET Holdings II, Inc. (Exec. V. President and C.A.O.)

MARCHANT, Dawn D.

655 15th St. NW
Suite 1200
Washington, DC 20005
Tel: (202)879-5000
Fax: (202)879-5200
Registered: FARA
EMail: dawn_marchant@kirkland.com

Employers

Kirkland & Ellis (Associate)

MARCINIK, Dr. Ed

1800 K St. NW
Suite 1010
Washington, DC 20006
Tel: (202)296-5030
Fax: (202)296-4750
Registered: LDA

Employers

American Defense Internat'l, Inc.

Clients Represented

On Behalf of American Defense Internat'l, Inc.

Large Scale Biology

MARCOIS, Barton William

2600 Virginia Ave. NW
Suite 404
Washington, DC 20037
Tel: (202)338-0211
Fax: (202)965-3463
Registered: FARA

Employers

Self-employed as an independent consultant.

Clients Represented

As an independent consultant

Kuwait Information Office

MARCONE, Paul

1420 New York Ave. NW
Suite 550
Washington, DC 20005
Tel: (202)783-4805
Fax: (202)783-4804
Registered: LDA

Employers

Russ Reid Co.

Clients Represented

On Behalf of Russ Reid Co.

Corporation for Business, Work and Learning

MARCUS, Lindsey

701 Pennsylvania Ave. NW
Suite 600
Washington, DC 20004
EMail: lmarcus@lanlaw.com
Tel: (202)624-1200
Fax: (202)624-1298

Employers

Long, Aldridge & Norman, LLP (Government Affairs Consultant)

Clients Represented

On Behalf of Long, Aldridge & Norman, LLP

Biotechnology Industry Organization

MARCUS, Michael S.

1333 New Hampshire Ave. NW
Suite 400
Washington, DC 20036
Tel: (202)887-4000
Fax: (202)887-4288
Special Assistant to the Attorney General, Department of Justice, 1967-68.

Employers

Akin, Gump, Strauss, Hauer & Feld, L.L.P. (Partner)

MARCUS, Richard

3000 K St. NW
Suite 300
Washington, DC 20007
Tel: (202)295-8787
Fax: (202)295-8799

Employers

The Harbour Group (Managing Director)

MARCUSS, Stanley J.

700 13th St. NW
Suite 700
Washington, DC 20005-3960
EMail: sjmarcuss@bryancave.com
Tel: (202)508-6000
Fax: (202)508-6200
Acting Assistant Secretary for Industry and Trade (1979-80) and Senior Deputy Assistant Secretary for Industry and Trade (1977-79), Department of Commerce. Counsel, Subcommittee on International Finance, Senate Finance Committee, 1973-77.

Employers

Bryan Cave LLP (Partner)

Clients Represented

On Behalf of Bryan Cave LLP

Exxon Mobil Corp.
Fleishman-Hillard, Inc
Great Lakes Chemical Corp.
Nabisco, Inc.
Wells Fargo Bank, N.A.

MARDEN, Judith C.

200 N. Glebe Rd.
Suite 820
Arlington, VA 22203-3728
EMail: info@fwi.org
Tel: (703)807-2007
Fax: (703)807-0111

Employers

Financial Women Internat'l (Director, Public Affairs and Exec. Director, FWI Foundation)

MARES, Jan

819 Seventh St. NW
Washington, DC 20001
Tel: (202)833-8940
Fax: (202)833-8943
Registered: LDA

Employers

EOP Group, Inc.

Clients Represented

On Behalf of EOP Group, Inc.

American Petroleum Institute
Edison Electric Institute
FMC Corp.
Nuclear Energy Institute

MARESCA, Charles A.

1300 N. 17th St.
Eighth Floor
Rosslyn, VA 22209-3801
EMail: maresca@abc.org
Tel: (703)812-2000
Fax: (703)812-8202
Registered: LDA

Employers

Associated Builders and Contractors (Director, Legal and Regulatory Affairs)

MARGO, R.D. "Dee"

888 16th St. NW
Suite 305
Washington, DC 20006
Tel: (202)833-1880
Fax: (202)833-2338

Employers

Business-Industry Political Action Committee (Chairman)

MARGOLIN, Burt

1225 19th St. NW
Suite 800
Washington, DC 20036
Tel: (202)955-6067
Fax: (202)293-0307
Registered: LDA

Employers

Berliner, Candon & Jimison (Director, Public Policy)

Clients Represented

On Behalf of Berliner, Candon & Jimison

California Primary Care Ass'n
Cedars-Sinai Medical Center
Los Angeles, California, County of
Tarzana Treatment Center

MARGOLIS, Jim

1010 Wisconsin Ave. NW
Suite 800
Washington, DC 20007
Tel: (202)338-8700
Fax: (202)338-2334

Employers

Greer, Margolis, Mitchell, Burns & Associates (Partner)

Clients Represented

On Behalf of Greer, Margolis, Mitchell, Burns & Associates

Children's Action Network
Communications Workers of America

MARIANO, Joseph N.

1275 Pennsylvania Ave. NW
Suite 800
Washington, DC 20004
Tel: (202)293-5760
Fax: (202)463-4569
Registered: LDA

Employers

Direct Selling Ass'n (Senior V. President and Legal Counsel)

MARIASCHIN, Daniel S.

1640 Rhode Island Ave. NW
Washington, DC 20036-3278
Tel: (202)857-6500
Fax: (202)296-0638
Registered: LDA
EMail: dsm@bnaibrith.org

Employers

B'nai B'rith Internat'l (Exec. V. President)

MARIC, Zorica

1610 New Hampshire Ave. NW
Washington, DC 20009
Tel: (202)234-6108
Fax: (202)234-6109
Registered: FARA

Employers

Montenegro, Trade Mission to the U.S.A. of the Republic of (Acting Director)

MARICH, Mark

2300 M St. NW
Suite 900
Washington, DC 20037
EMail: mark@publicforuminstitute.com
Tel: (202)467-2776
Fax: (202)293-5717

Employers

Public Forum Institute (V. President)

MARIN, Mark

1233 20th St. NW
Suite 610
Washington, DC 20036
Tel: (202)466-4111
Fax: (202)466-4123
Registered: LDA
EMail: mark_marin@lewis-burke.org

Employers

Lewis-Burke Associates (Government Relations Assistant)

Clients Represented

On Behalf of Lewis-Burke Associates

Ass'n of Independent Research Institutes
Associated Universities Inc.
California Institute of Technology
Soc. for Industrial & Applied Mathematics
Universities Research Ass'n

MARIN, Monica M.

666 11th St. NW
Suite 600
Washington, DC 20001
EMail: mmarin@ccianet.org
Tel: (202)783-0070
Fax: (202)783-0534

Employers

Computer and Communications Industry Ass'n (CCIA) (Exec. Assistant)

MARINCOLA, Elizabeth

8120 Woodmont Ave.
Suite 750
Bethesda, MD 20814-2755
EMail: emarincola@ascb.org
Tel: (301)530-7153
Fax: (301)530-7139

Employers

American Soc. for Cell Biology (Exec. Director)
Joint Steering Committee for Public Policy (Exec. Director)

MARINELLI, Michelle

1627 I St. NW
Suite 950
Washington, DC 20006
Tel: (202)223-5115
Fax: (202)223-5118

Employers

ConAgra Foods, Inc. (Staff Assistant, Government Affairs)

MARIOTTE, Michael

1424 16th St. NW
Suite 404
Washington, DC 20036
Tel: (202)328-0002
Fax: (202)462-2183

Employers

Nuclear Information and Resource Service (Exec. Director)

MARISTCH, Rita

400 Seventh St. SW
Room 9316
Washington, DC 20590
Tel: (202)366-4011
Fax: (202)366-3809

Employers

Department of Transportation - Federal Transit Administration (Assistant Chief Counsel for Legislative and Regulatory Affairs)

MARK, Molly

1350 Connecticut Ave. NW
Suite 600
Washington, DC 20036
EMail: melmark@federlaw.com
Tel: (202)822-6432
Fax: (202)466-5109

Former Staff Assistant to Senator James Jeffords (R-VT).

Employers

Nat'l Employee Benefits Institute (Director, Government Affairs)

MARKARIAN, Michael

8121 Georgia Ave.
Suite 301
Silver Spring, MD 20910-4933
EMail: mmarkarian@fund.org
Tel: (301)585-2591
Fax: (301)585-2595

Employers

The Fund for Animals (Exec. V. President)

MARKETOS, James

1220 16th St. NW
Washington, DC 20036
Tel: (202)785-8430
Fax: (202)785-5178

Employers

American Hellenic Institute, Inc. (Chairman)

MARKEY, Barbara R.

1155 15th St. NW
Suite 1101
Washington, DC 20005
Tel: (202)822-9288
Fax: (202)822-0920
Registered: LDA

Employers

Markey and Associates (Legislative Consultant)

MARKEY, David J.

1133 21st St. NW
Suite 900
Washington, DC 20036
EMail: david.markey@bellsouth.com
Tel: (202)463-4103
Fax: (202)463-4141
Registered: LDA

Former Assistant Secretary and former Administrator, National Telecommunications and Information Adminstration, both with the Department of Commerce, during the Reagan administration. Former Special Advisor to the Chairman, Federal Communications Commission. Also served as Chief of Staff to Senators Frank Murkowski (R-AK) and J. Glenn Beall (R-MD).

Employers

BellSouth Corp. (V. President, Governmental Affairs)

MARKEY, Marybeth

1825 K St. NW
Suite 520
Washington, DC 20006
Tel: (202)785-1515
Fax: (202)785-4343
Registered: LDA

Employers

Internat'l Campaign for Tibet (Director, Government Relations)

MARKEY, Patricia E.

1155 15th St. NW
Suite 1101
Washington, DC 20005
Tel: (202)822-9288
Fax: (202)659-5763
Registered: LDA

Employers

Markey and Associates (Legislative Consultant)

Clients Represented

On Behalf of Markey and Associates

United Distribution Cos.

MARKHAM, Susan A.

236 Massachusetts Ave. NE
Suite 206
Washington, DC 20002
Tel: (202)543-5540
Fax: (202)543-5547

Employers

Participation 2000 Inc. (Exec. Director)

MARKIEWICZ, Stephanie J.

1120 20th St. NW
Suite 1000
Washington, DC 20036
EMail: smarkiewicz@att.com
Tel: (202)457-2130
Fax: (202)457-2571

Employers

AT&T (V. President, Congressional Affairs)

MARKOWITZ, Jennie

1700 K St. NW
Suite 1150
Washington, DC 20006
EMail: jennie.markowitz@ujc.org
Tel: (202)736-5871
Fax: (202)785-4937

Employers

United Jewish Communities, Inc. (Legislative Assistant)

MARKS, Deborah

666 Eleventh St. NW
Suite 202
Washington, DC 20001
Tel: (202)783-7030
Fax: (202)783-7040

Employers

Peace Links (Administrator)

MARKS, Herbert E.

1201 Pennsylvania Ave. NW
P.O. Box 407
Washington, DC 20044-0407
EMail: hmarks@ssd.com
Tel: (202)626-6600
Fax: (202)626-6780

Employers

Squire, Sanders & Dempsey L.L.P. (Partner)

Clients Represented

On Behalf of Squire, Sanders & Dempsey L.L.P.

Independent Data Communications Manufacturers Ass'n

MARKS, Jeffrey

1735 New York Ave. NW
Suite 500
Washington, DC 20006-4759
Tel: (202)628-1700
Fax: (202)331-1024

Employers

Preston Gates Ellis & Rouvelas Meeds LLP (Associate)

MARKS, Joel

3417 1/2 M St. NW
Washington, DC 20007
Tel: (202)337-0037

Employers

American Small Business Alliance (Exec. Director)

MARKS, John

1601 Connecticut Ave. NW
Suite 200
Washington, DC 20009
EMail: jmarks@sfcg.org
Tel: (202)265-4300
Fax: (202)232-6718

Served as Foreign Service Officer, 1966-70.

Employers

Search for Common Ground (President)

MARKS, Rick E.

2300 Clarendon Blvd.
Suite 1010
Arlington, VA 22201
Tel: (703)527-4414
Fax: (703)527-0421
Registered: LDA

Employers

Robertson, Monagle & Eastaugh

Clients Represented

On Behalf of Robertson, Monagle & Eastaugh

Alaska Groundfish Data Bank
Aleutians East Borough
CSX Corp.
CSX Lines LLC
Friede, Goldman, & Halter, Inc.
Garden State Seafood Ass'n
The Glacier Bay Group
Inter-Island Ferry Authority
Kenai Penninsula Borough
Kodiak Island, Alaska, Borough of
Kodiak, Alaska, City of
Lunds Fisheries, Inc.
Monroe County Commercial Fishermen, Inc.
Ocean Shipholding, Inc.
Ounalashka Corp.
Pacific States Marine Fisheries Commission
Petersburg, Alaska, City of
Seafreeze
Seward, Alaska, City of
Transportation Institute
Trident Seafood Corp.
U.S. Marine Corp.
Unalaska, Alaska, City of
Verner, Liipfert, Bernhard, McPherson and Hand, Chartered
Wrangell, Alaska, City of

MARKS, Steven M.

1330 Connecticut Ave. NW
Suite 300
Washington, DC 20036
Tel: (202)775-0101
Fax: (202)775-7253

Employers

Recording Industry Ass'n of America (Senior V. President, Business and Legal Affairs)

MARKS, Ph.D., Stuart

441-E Carlisle Dr.
Herndon, VA 20170-4802
Tel: (703)709-2293
Fax: (703)709-2296

Employers

Safari Club Internat'l (Senior Scientist)

MARKS, Susan Collin

1601 Connecticut Ave. NW
Suite 200
Washington, DC 20009
EMail: scmarks@sfcg.org
Tel: (202)265-4300
Fax: (202)232-6718

Employers

Search for Common Ground (Exec. V. President)

MARKSTEIN, Daniel

1730 Rhode Island Ave.
Suite 710
Washington, DC 20036
Tel: (202)833-1580
Fax: (202)223-5779

Employers

Insurance Information Institute (Public Affairs Specialist)

MARKWART, Luther A.

2111 Wilson Blvd.
Suite 700
Arlington, VA 22201
Tel: (703)351-5055
Fax: (703)351-6698
Registered: LDA

Employers
American Sugar Alliance (Chairman)
American Sugarbeet Growers Ass'n (Exec. V. President)

MARKWOOD, Sandy

440 First St. NW
Eighth Floor
Washington, DC 20001
EMail: smarkwoo@naco.org
Tel: (202)942-4235
Fax: (202)737-0480

Employers
Nat'l Ass'n of Counties (Deputy Director, County Services Department)
Nat'l Ass'n of County Aging Programs (Contact)
Nat'l Ass'n of County Planners (Contact)

MARKWOOD, Tricia K.

1300 I St. NW
Suite 300 West
Washington, DC 20005
Tel: (202)522-8600
Fax: (202)522-8669
Registered: LDA
Legislative Assistant to Rep. Howard Wolpe (D-MI), 1988-92.

Employers
Dykema Gossett PLLC (Legislative Associate)

Clients Represented
On Behalf of Dykema Gossett PLLC
Calhoun County Community Development
Citizen's Committee to Save the Federal Center
Detroit, Michigan, City of
ERIM
Ferris State University
Michigan Manufacturing Technology Center
The Modernization Forum

MARLAIS, Donald R.

1020 N. Fairfax St.
Fourth Floor
Alexandria, VA 22314
EMail: dmarlais@pass1.com
Tel: (703)684-5236
Fax: (703)684-3417

Employers
Vienna, Gregor & Associates (Senior Associate)

Clients Represented
On Behalf of Vienna, Gregor & Associates
California Board of Equalization
California Franchise Tax Board
California Public Employees' Retirement System
California State Senate
The Pacific Stock Exchange, Inc.

MARLENEE, Hon. Ron C.

10192B Ashbrooke Ct.
Oakton, VA 22124
Tel: (703)938-3797
Registered: LDA
Former Member of Congress (R-MT), 1977-93.

Employers
Self-employed as an independent consultant.

Clients Represented
As an independent consultant
Archery Manufactures & Merchants Organization
Everglades Coordinating Council
Flathead Joint Board of Control
Lower Yellowstone Irrigation Project
Safari Club Internat'l

MARLETTE, C. Alan

8400 Westpark Dr.
McLean, VA 22102
Tel: (703)821-7072
Fax: (703)556-8581

Employers
Automotive Trade Ass'n Executives (Exec. Director)

MARLIN, Ruth

1325 Massachusetts Ave. NW
Washington, DC 20005
Tel: (202)628-5451
Fax: (202)628-5767

Employers
Nat'l Air Traffic Controllers Ass'n (V. President)

MARLO, Stephen M.

900 19th St. NW
Suite 600
Washington, DC 20006-2105
Tel: (202)261-1900
Fax: (202)261-1949
Registered: LDA

Employers
Stone and Webster Engineering Corp. (Manager, Washington Operations)

MARLOWE, Howard

1667 K St. NW
Suite 480
Washington, DC 20006
Tel: (202)775-1796
Fax: (202)775-0214
Registered: LDA
EMail: Howard.Marlowe@mail.netlobby.com

Employers
Marlowe and Co. (President)

Clients Represented
On Behalf of Marlowe and Co.
American Coastal Coalition
Avalon, New Jersey, City of
Broward, Florida, Department of Natural Resource Protection of the County of
Encinitas, California, City of
Fire Island Ass'n
Galveston County, Texas
Jefferson Texas, County of
Lee County, Florida
Manatee, Florida, County of
MOTE Marine Lab
North Topsail Beach, North Carolina, Town of
Ocean Isle Beach, North Carolina, Town of
Ocean Village Property Owners Ass'n, Inc.
Port Aransas, Texas, City of
Sarasota, Florida, City of
Solana Beach, California, City of
St. Augustine Beach, Florida, City of
St. Lucie, Florida, County of
Venice, Florida, City of

MARMON, William F.

1133 19th St. NW
Washington, DC 20036
EMail: william.f.marmon@wcom.com
Tel: (202)872-1600

Employers
MCI WorldCom Corp. (V. President, Public Policy)

MARONE, Barbara

325 Seventh St. NW
Washington, DC 20004
Tel: (202)638-1100
Fax: (202)626-2254
Registered: LDA

Employers
American Hospital Ass'n (Associate Director, Public Policy Development, Analysis, and Regulatory Affairs)

MARONEY, Kevin

200 Constitution Ave. NW
Room S-1325
Washington, DC 20210
EMail: maroney-kevin@dol.gov
Tel: (202)693-4600
Fax: (202)693-4641

Employers
Department of Labor (Acting Assistant Secretary for Congressional and Intergovernmental Affairs)

MARONI, William

1501 M St. NW
Suite 600
Washington, DC 20005-1710
Tel: (202)739-0200
Fax: (202)659-8287
Registered: FARA
EMail: wmaroni@bsmg.com

Employers
BSMG Worldwide (Managing Director)

MAROULIS, Christine

1317 F St. NW
Suite 600
Washington, DC 20004
Tel: (202)638-2121
Fax: (202)638-7045
Registered: LDA
EMail: maroulis@wexlergroup.com

Employers
The Wexler Group (Senior Associate)

Clients Represented
On Behalf of The Wexler Group
Alliance for Understandable, Sensible and Accountable Government Regulations
Immunex Corp.
IMS Health Inc.
MENC: The Nat'l Ass'n for Music Education
Nat'l Ass'n of Music Merchants
PacifiCare Health Systems
Rosenbaum Trust
Wyeth-Ayerst Laboratories

MAROULIS-CRONMILLER, Alexandra

900 19th St. NW
Suite 400
Washington, DC 20006
Tel: (202)857-3100
Fax: (202)296-8716

Employers
America's Community Bankers (Director, Membership)

MARQUET, Megan

600 Pennsylvania Ave. SE
Suite 320
Washington, DC 20003
Tel: (202)969-8900
Fax: (202)331-7036
Registered: LDA
EMail: mmarquet@gordley.com

Employers
Gordley Associates (Assistant Director)

Clients Represented
On Behalf of Gordley Associates
American Soybean Ass'n
Iowa Pork Producers Ass'n
Nat'l Barley Growers Ass'n
Nat'l Sunflower Ass'n
U.S. Canola Ass'n

MARQUEZ, Jim J.

2099 Pennsylvania Ave. NW
Suite 100
Washington, DC 20006
EMail: jmarquez@hklaw.com
Tel: (202)457-7033
Fax: (202)955-5564
General Counsel, Department of Transportation, 1983-86. United States Attorney for Kansas, Department of Justice, 1981-83.

Employers
Holland & Knight LLP (Senior Counsel)

Clients Represented
On Behalf of Holland & Knight LLP
Greater Jamaica Development Corp.
Spirit Airlines

MARQUEZ, Joaquin A.

1500 K St.
Suite 1100
Washington, DC 20005
Tel: (202)842-8800
Fax: (202)842-8465
Registered: LDA
EMail: joaquin_marquez@dbr.com
Former Director, Puerto Rico Federal Affairs Administration in Washington.

Employers
Drinker Biddle & Reath LLP (Partner)

Clients Represented
On Behalf of Drinker Biddle & Reath LLP
Nat'l Community Capital Ass'n
Puerto Rico Bankers Ass'n
Puerto Rico Chamber of Commerce
Puerto Rico Manufacturers Ass'n

MARQUEZ, USAF (Ret.), Lt. Gen. Leo

11 Canal Center Plaza
Suite 103
Alexandria, VA 22314
Tel: (703)683-4222
Fax: (703)683-0645
Registered: LDA

Employers
The Spectrum Group

Clients Represented
On Behalf of The Spectrum Group
ADSI Inc.
Barksdale Foward

MARR, Brendan

1211 Connecticut Ave. NW
Suite 608
Washington, DC 20036
EMail: bmarr@qorvis.com
Tel: (703)299-9800
Fax: (703)299-9803

Employers
Qorvis Communications (Director)

MARRAPESE, Martha E.

1001 G St. NW
Suite 500 West
Washington, DC 20001
EMail: marrapese@khlaw.com
Tel: (202)434-4100
Fax: (202)434-4646

Employers
Keller and Heckman LLP (Partner)

Clients Represented
On Behalf of Keller and Heckman LLP
Tea Ass'n of the U.S.A., Inc.

MARRS, Danny D.

1501 Lee Hwy.
Arlington, VA 22209-1198
EMail: dmarrs@afa.org
Tel: (703)247-5840
Fax: (703)247-5853

Employers
Aerospace Education Foundation (Temporary Managing Director)
Air Force Ass'n (Assistant Exec. Director)

MARSAN, William P.

401 Ninth St. NW
Suite 1000
Washington, DC 20004
Tel: (202)274-2972
Fax: (202)654-5616
Registered: LDA
Legislative Director to Rep. Charles T. Canady (R-FL), 1995-96; Lieutenant, U.S. Navy Judge Advocate General's Corps, 1989-93.

Employers
Troutman Sanders LLP (Associate)

Clients Represented
On Behalf of Troutman Sanders LLP
Canadian Electricity Ass'n
ezgov.com
Minnesota Power
Otter Tail Power Co.
Paducah & Louisville Railroad
Southern Co.
Trigen Energy Corp.

MARSH, Joan

1120 20th St. NW
Suite 1000
Washington, DC 20036
EMail: joanmariemarsh@att.com
Tel: (202)457-3120
Fax: (202)457-2571
Registered: LDA

Employers
AT&T (Director, Federal Government Affairs)

MARSH, Robert H.

1660 L St. NW
Fourth Floor
Washington, DC 20036
Tel: (202)775-5092
Fax: (202)775-5024
Registered: LDA

Employers
General Motors Corp. (Deputy Director, Federal Affairs)

MARSH, William A.

2001 Jefferson Davis Hwy.
Suite 209
Arlington, VA 22202
EMail: wmarsh@mehlgriffinbartek.com
Tel: (703)413-0090
Fax: (703)413-4467
Registered: LDA
Military Legislative Assistant to Rep. Joel Hefley (R-CO), 1999-2000. Military Legislative Assistant to Rep. Van Hilleary (R-TN), 1997-99. Staff Assistant, House Armed Services Committee, 1995-1997.

Employers
Mehl, Griffin & Bartek Ltd. (Director, Government Affairs)

Clients Represented
On Behalf of Mehl, Griffin & Bartek Ltd.
AMI Aircraft Seating Systems
D3 Internat'l Energy, LLC
Exide Corp.
Galaxy Aerospace Co., LP
Irvine Sensors Corp.

MARSHALL, Beverly

401 Ninth St. NW
Suite 1100
Washington, DC 20004
EMail: bkmarshall@duke-energy.com
Tel: (202)331-8090
Fax: (202)331-1181
Registered: LDA

Employers
Duke Energy (V. President, Federal Government Affairs)

MARSHALL, C. Travis

1350 I St. NW
Suite 400
Washington, DC 20005-3306
Tel: (202)371-6900
Fax: (202)842-3578

Employers
Motorola, Inc. (Deputy, Motorola Chief Executive Office for Telecommunications Relations)

MARSHALL, Carmen

1738 Elton Rd.
Suite 314
Silver Spring, MD 20903
Tel: (301)445-2600
Fax: (301)445-1693

Employers
Nat'l Black Media Coalition (Exec. Director)

MARSHALL, David L.

1050 Connecticut Ave. NW
Suite 1100
Washington, DC 20036-5304
EMail: dmarshall@baker-hostetler.com
Tel: (202)861-1500
Fax: (202)861-1790
Registered: LDA

Employers
Baker & Hostetler LLP (Partner)

Clients Represented
On Behalf of Baker & Hostetler LLP
American Electric Power Co.
American Resort Development Ass'n
Cafaro Co.
The Chubb Corp.
Citigroup
The Council of Insurance Agents & Brokers
Eagle-Picher Personal Injury Settlement Trust
Florida Residential and Casualty Joint Underwriting Ass'n
Florida Windstorm Underwriting Ass'n
Forest City Ratner Companies
Marsh & McLennan Cos.
Nat'l Ass'n of Real Estate Investment Trusts
PSH Master L.P.I.
Transportation Institute

MARSHALL, Paul

1319 18th St. NW
Washington, DC 20036
Tel: (202)296-5101
Fax: (202)296-5078

Employers
The Center for Religious Freedom (Senior Fellow)

MARSHALL, Rolf

1735 New York Ave. NW
Suite 500
Washington, DC 20006-4759
Tel: (202)628-1700
Fax: (202)331-1024
Registered: LDA
Commander, U.S. Navy, 1964-91. Served on staff of the Chief of Naval Operations, 1986-91 and as Combat Systems Engineer for the Battleship Program at the Naval Sea Systems Command, Department of the Navy, 1984-86.

Employers
Preston Gates Ellis & Rouvelas Meeds LLP (Partner)

Clients Represented
On Behalf of Preston Gates Ellis & Rouvelas Meeds LLP
Dredging Contractors of America
Great Lakes Dredge & Dock
Ivarans Rederiasa
Mount Vernon Barge Service
Transportation Institute
United States Maritime Coalition

MARSHALL, Stephanie

1909 K St. NW
Fourth Floor
Washington, DC 20006
Tel: (202)973-5800
Fax: (202)973-5858

Employers
Porter/Novelli (V. President, Public Affairs)

MARSHALL, Terri R.

1627 I St. NW
Suite 950
Washington, DC 20006
Tel: (202)223-5115
Fax: (202)223-5118

Employers
ConAgra Foods, Inc. (Senior Representative, Government Affairs)

MARSHALL, Jr., Thurgood

3000 K St. NW
Suite 300
Washington, DC 20007
Tel: (202)424-7500
Fax: (202)424-7643
Registered: LDA
Assistant to the President and Cabinet Secretary (1997-2000) and Deputy Counsel and Director of Legislative Affairs, Office of the Vice President (1993-97), Executive Office of the President, The White House. Counsel, Subcommittee on Immigration and Refugee Affairs, Senate Committee on the Judiciary, 1988-92. Counsel, Subcommittee on Consumer, Senate Committee on Commerce, Science and Transportation, 1987. Governmental Affairs Committee Counsel to Senator Albert Gore, Jr. (D-TN), 1985-87. Law Clerk to Judge Barrington D. Parker, U.S. District Court for the District of Columbia, 1981-83.

Employers
Swidler Berlin Shereff Friedman, LLP (Partner)

MARSHALL, Will

600 Pennsylvania Ave. SE
Suite 400
Washington, DC 20003
Tel: (202)547-0001
Fax: (202)544-5014

Employers
Progressive Policy Institute (President)

MARSICO, Dale J.

1341 G St. NW
Tenth Floor
Washington, DC 20005
EMail: marsico@ctaa.org
Tel: (202)628-1480
Fax: (202)737-9197

Employers
Community Transportation Ass'n of America (Exec. Director)

MARTIN, Jr., Dr. A. Dallas

1129 20th St. NW
Suite 400
Washington, DC 20036-3489
Tel: (202)785-0453
Fax: (202)785-1487

Employers
Nat'l Ass'n of Student Financial Aid Administrators (President)

MARTIN, Bridget Powell

2722 Merrilee Dr.
Suite 360
Fairfax, VA 22031
Tel: (703)560-1493
Fax: (703)560-2584
Registered: LDA

Employers
Internat'l Brotherhood of Boilermakers, Iron Shipbuilders, Blacksmiths, Forgers and Helpers (Deputy Director, Legislation)

MARTIN, Catherine J.

14th and Constitution Ave. NW
Room 5717
Washington, DC 20230
Tel: (202)482-1684
Fax: (202)482-5924

Employers
Department of Commerce (Director, White House Liaison Office)

MARTIN, Chris

901 E St. NW
Fourth Floor
Washington, DC 20004
Tel: (202)969-8026
Fax: (202)969-8031

Employers
Sallie Mae, Inc. (Senior Government Relations Assistant)

MARTIN, Conrad

122 Maryland Ave. NE
Suite 300
Washington, DC 20002
Tel: (202)546-3799
Fax: (202)543-3156

Employers
Fund for Constitutional Government (Exec. Director)

MARTIN, Cynthia L.

1101 30th St. NW
Suite 500
Washington, DC 20007
Tel: (202)625-8380
Fax: (202)274-1967
Registered: LDA

Employers
E. E. & Company, L.L.C. (Managing Member)

MARTIN, D. Craig

808 17th St. NW
Suite 600
Washington, DC 20006
Tel: (202)466-7800
Fax: (202)887-0905
Registered: FARA

Former LBJ Intern with Senator John Heinz (R-PA) and Rep. Dick Schulz (R-PA).

Employers

Ruder Finn Washington (Managing Director)

Clients Represented

On Behalf of Ruder Finn Washington

Exportadora de Sal, S.A. de C.V.

MARTIN, David O'B.

1700 K St. NW
Suite 800
Washington, DC 20006
Tel: (202)862-9705
Fax: (202)862-9710
Registered: LDA
EMail: dobmartin@aol.com

Member, U.S. House of Representatives (R-NY), 1981-93.

Employers

Martin, Fisher & Associates, Inc. (President)

Clients Represented

On Behalf of Martin, Fisher & Associates, Inc.

AAI Corp.
Nat'l Soft Drink Ass'n
United Defense, L.P.

MARTIN, Gary C.

1300 L St. NW
Suite 900
Washington, DC 20005
Tel: (202)682-4030
Fax: (202)682-4033
Registered: LDA

Employers

North American Grain Export Ass'n, Inc. (President and Chief Exec. Officer)

MARTIN, Gregory

1660 L St. NW
Fourth Floor
Washington, DC 20036
Tel: (202)775-5095
Fax: (202)775-5045

Employers

General Motors Corp. (Manager, Media Relations)

MARTIN, Guy R.

607 14th St. NW
Suite 700
Washington, DC 20005-2011
Tel: (202)628-6600
Fax: (202)434-1690
Registered: LDA

Assistant Secretary for Land and Water Resources, Department of the Interior, 1977-81. Administrative Assistant to Rep. Nick Begich (D-AK), 1971-73.

Employers

Perkins Coie LLP (Partner)

Clients Represented

On Behalf of Perkins Coie LLP

Alaska Forest Ass'n
American Forest & Paper Ass'n
Bay Delta Urban Coalition
The Boeing Co.
Delta Wetlands Project
The Doe Run Co.
East Bay Municipal Utility District
Fort James Corp.
Kootznoowoo, Inc.
Ledyard, Connecticut, Town of
The Metropolitan Water District of Southern California
Nat'l Cattleman's Beef Ass'n
Western Urban Water Coalition
Weyerhaeuser Co.

MARTIN, J. Allen

499 S. Capitol St. SW
Suite 600
Washington, DC 20003
Tel: (202)289-9881
Fax: (202)289-9877
Registered: LDA

Former Chief of Staff to Rep. Bob Livingston (R-LA).

Employers

The Livingston Group, LLC (Principal)

Clients Represented

On Behalf of The Livingston Group, LLC

ACS Government Solutions Group
American Ass'n of Nurse Anesthetists
Baton Rouge, Louisiana, City of
Boys Town USA
Broward, Florida, County of
Committee of Unsecured Creditors
Commonwealth Atlantic Properties
General Category Tuna Ass'n
General Electric Co.
Gray Morrison
Great Western Cellular Partnership
Illinois Department of Human Services
Internat'l Systems, Inc.
Jacobus Tenbroek Memorial Fund
Link Plus Co.
Marine Desalination Systems LLC
Mesa, Arizona, City of
MidAmerican Energy Holdings Co.
Nat'l Capitol Concerts
Raytheon Co.
Schering-Plough Corp.
Stewart Enterprises, Inc.
U.S. Oil and Gas Ass'n

MARTIN, Jack W.

233 Constitution Ave. NE
Washington, DC 20002
Tel: (202)547-4000
Fax: (202)543-5044
Registered: LDA
EMail: prandd@aol.com

Employers

Parry, Romani, DeConcini & Symms (V. President, Government Relations)

Clients Represented

On Behalf of Parry, Romani, DeConcini & Symms

AIDS Healthcare Foundation
Andrx Pharmaceutical Corp.
Armstrong World Industries, Inc.
Asphalt Systems, Inc.
Aventis Pharmaceutical Products
Avondale, Arizona, City of
Bank of New York
Bristol-Myers Squibb Co.
Coalition Against Database Piracy
Composites Fabricators Ass'n
Ferraro, USA
Formosan Ass'n for Public Affairs
GAF Corp.
GlaxoSmithKline
Herbalife Internat'l, Inc.
Hoechst Marion Roussel Deutschland GmbH
Inter-Cal Corp.
Katten Muchin & Zavis
Motion Picture Ass'n of America
Nat'l Air Cargo, Inc.
Nat'l Nutritional Foods Ass'n
Nat'l Retail Federation
Nogales, Arizona, City of
Nu Skin Internat'l Inc.
Owens Corning
Peoria, Arizona, City of
Pfizer, Inc.
Pharmacia Corp.
Pharmanex
Policy Development Group, Inc.
Project to Promote Competition and Innovation in the Digital Age
Research & Development Laboratories
Research Corp. Technology
Rexall Sundown
SBC Communications Inc.
SOL Source Technologies, Inc.
Styrene Information and Research Center
Taxpayers Against Fraud, The False Claims Legal Center
TCOM, L.P.
Unilever United States, Inc.
Utah Natural Products Alliance

MARTIN, James L.

1655 N. Fort Myer Dr.
Suite 355
Arlington, VA 22209
Tel: (703)807-2070
Fax: (703)807-2073
Registered: LDA

Employers

The 60/Plus Ass'n, Inc. (President)

MARTIN, Jenifer

901 15th St. NW
Suite 700
Washington, DC 20005-2301
Tel: (202)371-6000
Fax: (202)371-6279
Registered: LDA

Employers

Verner, Liipfert, Bernhard, McPherson and Hand, Chartered (Associate)

Clients Represented

On Behalf of Verner, Liipfert, Bernhard, McPherson and Hand, Chartered

Alere Medical Inc.
Bombardier Transportation/Bombardier Transit Corporation
Citigroup
EqualFooting.com
Forest Soc. of Maine
Genesee County Drain Commissioner
Goldman, Sachs and Co.
G.E. Harris Harmon
Office of Hawaiian Affairs
Rite Aid Corp.
University of Michigan Medical Center
VISA U.S.A., Inc.

MARTIN, John C.

2550 M St. NW
Washington, DC 20037-1350
Tel: (202)457-6000
Fax: (202)457-6315
Registered: LDA
EMail: jmartin@pattonboggs.com

Trial Attorney, Land and Natural Resources Division, Environmental Enforcement Section, Department of Justice, 1982-85. Trial Attorney, Office of the Solicitor, Department of the Interior, 1981-82.

Employers

Patton Boggs, LLP (Partner)

Clients Represented

On Behalf of Patton Boggs, LLP

Homestake Mining
Save Barton Creek

MARTIN, Josephine C.

1201 F St. NW
Suite 500
Washington, DC 20004
Tel: (202)824-1600
Fax: (202)824-1651

Employers

Health Insurance Ass'n of America (Senior V. President for Public Affairs)

MARTIN, Kate

The George Washington University
Gelman Library, Suite 701
Washington, DC 20037
Tel: (202)994-7000
Fax: (202)994-7005

Employers

Nat'l Security Archive (General Counsel)

MARTIN, Keith

1200 New Hampshire Ave. NW
Washington, DC 20036
Tel: (202)974-5600
Fax: (202)974-5602
Registered: LDA, FARA
EMail: keith.martin@chadbourne.com

Legislative Counsel to Senator Daniel Patrick Moynihan (D-NY), 1979-82. Legislative Assistant to Senator Henry Jackson (D-WA), 1974-77.

Employers

Chadbourne and Parke LLP (Partner)

Clients Represented

On Behalf of Chadbourne and Parke LLP

The AES Corp.
Cogentrix, Inc.
Electric Power Supply Ass'n
Independent Power Tax Group
Magellan Carbon Fuels
Panda Energy Internat'l
The Purdue Frederick Co.
Ruan Leasing Co.
Sithe Energies

MARTIN, Krista

600 New Hampshire Ave. NW
Suite 601
Washington, DC 20037
Tel: (202)333-7400
Fax: (202)333-1638

Employers

Hill and Knowlton, Inc. (Sr. Account Supervisor)

MARTIN, Larry K.

1601 N. Kent St.
Suite 120
Arlington, VA 22209
Tel: (703)524-1864
Fax: (703)522-6741
Registered: LDA
EMail: lkmartin@apperalandfootwear.org

Employers
American Apparel & Footwear Ass'n (President and Chief Operating Officer)

MARTIN, R. Shawn

1090 Vermont Ave. NW
Suite 510
Washington, DC 20005
Tel: (202)414-0140
Fax: (202)544-3525
Registered: LDA

Employers
American Osteopathic Ass'n (Assistant Director, Congressional Affairs)

MARTIN, Wayne H.

One Massachusetts Ave. NW
Suite 700
Washington, DC 20001-1431
Tel: (202)408-5505
Fax: (202)408-8072

Employers
Council of Chief State School Officers (Director, State Education Assessment Center)

MARTIN, William F.

1025 Thomas Jefferson St. NW
Suite 411 West
Washington, DC 20007
Tel: (202)965-1161
Fax: (202)965-1177
Registered: LDA, FARA

Employers
Washington Policy & Analysis, Inc. (Chairman)

Clients Represented
On Behalf of Washington Policy & Analysis, Inc.
The Tokyo Electric Power Company, Inc.

MARTIN, William R.

1911 Fort Myer Dr.
Suite 600
Arlington, VA 22209
Tel: (703)741-0546
Fax: (703)741-0529
Registered: LDA

Employers
Alliant Techsystems, Inc. (V. President, Washington Operations)

MARTINDALE, III, Walter Reed

1200 G St. NW
Suite 800
Washington, DC 20005
Tel: (202)434-8779
Fax: (202)638-5127
Registered: LDA
EMail: Walter.Martindale@Gmills.com

Employers
Guilford Mills, Inc. (Washington Liaison, Governmental Affairs Director)

MARTINEZ, Jorge

1875 I St. NW
Suite 540
Washington, DC 20006
Tel: (202)822-0655
Fax: (202)822-2022
EMail: jmartinez@greenerandhook.com

Employers
Greener and Hook, LLC (Associate)

MARTINEZ, Lawrence

1900 L St. NW
Ninth Floor
Washington, DC 20036
Tel: (202)462-1400
Ext: 593
Fax: (202)721-0600
EMail: lmartinez@gciu.org

Employers
Graphic Communications Internat'l Union (V. President)

MARTINEZ, Michael L.

1920 N St. NW
Washington, DC 20036
Tel: (202)331-8800
Fax: (202)331-8330
EMail: mmartinez@thf.com
Assistant U.S. Attorney, 1983-93. Attorney Advisor, Urban Mass Transportation Administration, 1978-1983.

Employers
Thompson, Hine and Flory LLP

Clients Represented
On Behalf of Thompson, Hine and Flory LLP
Lyme Disease Foundation

MARTINEZ, Robert J.

1155 21st St. NW
Suite 300
Washington, DC 20036
Tel: (202)659-8201
Fax: (202)659-5249
Registered: LDA
EMail: rjmartinez@wms-jen.com

Employers
Williams & Jensen, P.C. (Partner)

Clients Represented
On Behalf of Williams & Jensen, P.C.
Dunn-Padre, Inc.
Nat'l Underground Railroad Freedom Center

MARTINEZ, Susanne M.

25 E St. NW
Washington, DC 20001
Tel: (202)628-8787
Fax: (202)662-3850
EMail: smartinez@childrensdefense.org

Employers
Children's Defense Fund (Director, Programs and Policy Department)

MARTINO, Laura

1660 L St. NW
Suite 216
Washington, DC 20036
Tel: (202)466-2823
Fax: (202)429-9602

Employers
Pure Food Campaign (Chief of Staff)

MARTINS, Jaqueline

122 C St. NW
Suite 510
Washington, DC 20001
Tel: (202)628-7001
Fax: (202)628-1933
Registered: LDA
EMail: martins@dc.ncga.com

Employers
Nat'l Corn Growers Ass'n (Director, Public Policy)

MARTONE, M.D., William J.

4733 Bethesda Ave.
Suite 750
Bethesda, MD 20814
Tel: (301)656-0003
Fax: (301)907-0878
EMail: wjmartone@aol.com

Employers
Nat'l Foundation for Infectious Diseases (Senior Exec. Director)

MARTS, Sherry

1828 L St. NW
Suite 625
Washington, DC 20036
Tel: (202)496-5019
Fax: (202)833-3472
EMail: sherry@womens-health.org

Employers
Soc. for Women's Health Research (Scientific Director)

MARTY, Elizabeth

810 Vermont Ave. NW
Room 515B
Washington, DC 20420
Tel: (202)224-9419
Fax: (202)273-9988

Employers
Department of Veterans Affairs (Legislative Affairs Officer)

MARUYAMA, Warren H.

555 13th St. NW
Washington, DC 20004-1109
Tel: (202)637-5709
Fax: (202)637-5910
Registered: LDA
EMail: whmaruyama@hhlaw.com
Associate Director, International Economic Policy (1992-93) and Deputy Associate Director (1989-92), Office of Policy Development, The White House. Associate General Counsel, Office of the U.S. Trade Representative, 1983-89. Attorney/Advisor, International Trade Commission, 1980-83.

Employers
Hogan & Hartson L.L.P. (Partner)

Clients Represented
On Behalf of Hogan & Hartson L.L.P.
Dana Corp.
Guardian Industries Corp.
Nat'l Foreign Trade Council, Inc.
Payless Shoe Source
Pharmaceutical Research and Manufacturers of America
Soap and Detergent Ass'n
Vulcan Materials Co.

MARVASO, Kathleen

1440 New York Ave. NW
Suite 200
Washington, DC 20005
Tel: (202)942-2050
Fax: (202)783-4798
Registered: LDA

Employers
American Automobile Ass'n (Managing Director)

MARVEL, Ph.D., Kevin B.

2000 Florida Ave. NW
Suite 400
Washington, DC 20009
Tel: (202)328-2010
Fax: (202)234-2560
Registered: LDA
EMail: marvel@aas.org

Employers
American Astronomical Soc. (Associate Officer, Public Policy)

MARVIN, Michael L.

1200 18th St. NW
Ninth Floor
Washington, DC 20036
Tel: (202)785-0507
Fax: (202)785-0514
Registered: LDA

Employers
Business Council for Sustainable Energy (President)

MARXUACH, Sergio

1400 L St. NW
Washington, DC 20005-3502
Tel: (202)371-5700
Fax: (202)371-5950

Employers
Winston & Strawn

MARZULLA, Nancie G.

1350 Connecticut Ave. NW
Suite 410
Washington, DC 20036
Tel: (202)822-6770
Fax: (202)822-6774

Employers
Defenders of Property Rights (President)

MASCH, Donald

1911 Fort Myer Dr.
Suite 600
Arlington, VA 22209
Tel: (703)741-0546
Fax: (703)741-0529

Employers
Alliant Techsystems, Inc. (Deputy Director, Government Relations)

MASLYN, Mark A.

600 Maryland Ave. SW
Suite 800
Washington, DC 20024
Tel: (202)484-3600
Fax: (202)484-3604
Registered: LDA

Employers
American Farm Bureau Federation (Deputy Exec. Director, Washington Office, Environment/Labor/Natural Resources)

MASON, Ann M.

1300 Wilson Blvd.
Arlington, VA 22209
Tel: (703)741-5204
Fax: (703)741-6204
EMail: ann_mason@cmahq.com

Employers
Chlorine Chemistry Council (Director, Science and Regulatory Policy)

MASON, Arthur D.

700 13th St. NW
Suite 400
Washington, DC 20005
Tel: (202)347-0773
Fax: (202)347-0785
Registered: LDA, FARA
EMail: amason@cassidy.com
Captain and First Lt., U.S. Army. Former Legal Staffer, Office of the Chief Counsel, Division of Trading and Markets Securities and Exchange Commission. Advisor, President's Committee on Review of National Policy Toward Gambling. U.S. Delegate, World Health Organization.

Employers
Cassidy & Associates, Inc. (Senior V. President)

Clients Represented

On Behalf of Cassidy & Associates, Inc.

Adelphi University
ADI Ltd.
Arnold & Porter
The Auxiliary Service Corporations
The Boeing Co.
Chlorine Chemistry Council
CNF Transportation, Inc.
D'Youville College
E Lottery
Elmira College
General Dynamics Corp.
Jewish Family Service Ass'n of Cleveland
Lewis and Clark College
Lockheed Martin IMS
Major League Baseball
Memorial Health System
Museum of Discovery and Science
North Shore Long Island Jewish Health System
Ocean Spray Cranberries
Ohio State University
Proctor Hospital
Saint Joseph's Health Center Foundation, Inc.
Saudi Arabia, Royal Embassy of
Sherwin Williams Co.
Subaru of America
United Service Organization
United Space Alliance
VoiceStream Wireless Corp.

MASON, G. David

1001 Pennsylvania Ave. NW
Suite 760 North
Washington, DC 20004
Tel: (202)661-7060
Fax: (202)661-7066
Registered: LDA

Employers

The Legislative Strategies Group, LLC

Clients Represented

On Behalf of The Legislative Strategies Group, LLC

Allscripts Inc.

MASON, Jana

1717 Massachusetts Ave. NW
Suite 200
Washington, DC 20036
Tel: (202)797-2105
Fax: (202)797-2363
Registered: LDA

Employers

Immigration and Refugee Service of America (Congressional Liaison)

MASON, Keith W.

701 Pennsylvania Ave. NW
Suite 600
Washington, DC 20004
Tel: (202)624-1200
Fax: (202)624-1298
Registered: LDA
EMail: kmason@lanlaw.com

Deputy Director to the President for Intergovernmental Affairs, Executive Office of the President, The White House, 1993-94.

Employers

Long, Aldridge & Norman, LLP (Partner)

Clients Represented

On Behalf of Long, Aldridge & Norman, LLP

AFLAC, Inc.
BellSouth Corp.

MASON, Kent A.

One Thomas Circle NW
Suite 1100
Washington, DC 20005
Tel: (202)862-7826
Fax: (202)429-3301
Registered: LDA
EMail: kam@capdale.com

Legislation Attorney, Joint Committee on Taxation, 1986-88. Attorney-Advisor, Office of the Tax Legislative Counsel, Department of Treasury, 1984-86. Law Clerk to Judge Phyllis A. Kravitch, U.S. Court of Appeals, Eleventh Circuit, 1980-81.

Employers

Caplin & Drysdale, Chartered (Member)

Clients Represented

On Behalf of Caplin & Drysdale, Chartered

American Benefits Council
Edward Jones Investments
Nat'l Rural Electric Cooperative Ass'n
Paul, Hastings, Janofsky & Walker LLP
Variable Annuity Life Insurance Co.

MASON, Michael D.

1300 I St. NW
Suite 250 West
Washington, DC 20005
Tel: (202)842-4900
Fax: (202)842-3492
Registered: LDA

Employers

American Maritime Congress (Director, Public Affairs)

MASON, Nancy H.

1020 19th St. NW
Washington, DC 20036
Tel: (202)429-3124
Fax: (202)293-0561
Registered: LDA

Employers

Qwest Communications (Exec. Director, Congressional Relations)

MASSA, III, Cliff

2550 M St. NW
Washington, DC 20037-1350
Tel: (202)457-6000
Fax: (202)457-6315
Registered: LDA
EMail: cmassa@pattonboggs.com

Employers

Patton Boggs, LLP (Partner)

Clients Represented

On Behalf of Patton Boggs, LLP

Direct Marketing Ass'n, Inc.
Mars, Inc.

MASSEY, Donald F.

321 D St. NE
Washington, DC 20002
Tel: (202)548-8322
Fax: (202)548-8326
Registered: LDA
EMail: dmassey@siscorpdc.com

Former Chief Counsel, Appropriations Committee; Counsel Rules and Administration Committee and Deputy Sergeant at Arms, U.S. Senate and Intelligence Analyst and Assistant Legislative Counsel, Central Intelligence Agency.

Employers

SISCORP

Clients Represented

On Behalf of SISCORP

Global Environment Facility
Harbor Branch Institute
Nintendo of America, Inc.
Providence St. Vincent Medical Center
PSI
SAT
Science Applications Internat'l Corp. (SAIC)

MASSEY, Eugene A.

1050 Connecticut Ave. NW
Washington, DC 20036-5339
Tel: (202)857-6000
Fax: (202)857-6395
Registered: LDA

Attorney, Office of the Legal Advisor, Department of State, 1967-72.

Employers

Arent Fox Kintner Plotkin & Kahn, PLLC (Member)

MASSEY, Paul

1501 M St. NW
Suite 600
Washington, DC 20005-1710
Tel: (202)739-0200
Fax: (202)659-8287

Employers

BSMG Worldwide (Senior Associate, Public Affairs Practice)

MASSIE, James D.

660 Pennsylvania Ave. SE
Suite 201
Washington, DC 20003
Tel: (202)547-1831
Fax: (202)547-4658
Registered: LDA
EMail: JMassie@alpinegroup.com

Employers

Alpine Group, Inc. (Partner)

Clients Represented

On Behalf of Alpine Group, Inc.

AgrEvo USA Co.
American Crop Protection Ass'n
BP Amoco Corp.
Bracco Diagnostics
Cinergy Corp.
Council on Radionuclides and Radiopharmaceuticals (CORAR)
Dow AgroSciences
El Paso Corporation
FMC Corp.
Jackson Nat'l Life Insurance
Medical Imaging Contrast Agent Ass'ns
Nat'l Ass'n of Insurance and Financial Advisors
Nat'l Corn Growers Ass'n
Pharmacia Corp.
Southwire, Inc.
U.S. Filter

MASSIMINO, Elisa

100 Maryland Ave. NE
Suite 500
Washington, DC 20002
Tel: (202)547-5692
Fax: (202)543-5999
EMail: wdc@lchr.org

Employers

Lawyers Committee for Human Rights (Director, Washington Office)

MASSON, Tonia

1767 Business Center Dr.
Suite 302
Reston, VA 20190
Tel: (703)438-3101
Fax: (703)438-3113
EMail: toniam@toxicology.org

Employers

Ass'n Innovation and Management, Inc. (Senior Account Executive)

Clients Represented

On Behalf of Ass'n Innovation and Management, Inc.

The Teratology Soc.

MASTEN, Mia

1010 Wisconsin Ave. NW
Ninth Floor
Washington, DC 20007
Tel: (202)337-9400
Fax: (202)337-4508
EMail: mmasten@gmabrands.com

Employers

Grocery Manufacturers of America (Manager, Federal Affairs)

MASTERSON, Ken

300 Maryland Ave. NE
Washington, DC 20002
Tel: (202)546-1631
Fax: (202)546-3309
Registered: LDA

Employers

FedEx Corp. (Executive V. President)

MASTRO, William

1150 17th St. NW
Suite 601
Washington, DC 20036
Tel: (202)293-7474
Fax: (202)293-8811
Registered: LDA

Employers

Washington Council Ernst & Young

Clients Represented

On Behalf of Washington Council Ernst & Young

BHC Communications, Inc.
Directors Guild of America

MASTROMARCO, Dan R.

333 N. Fairfax St.
Suite 302
Alexandria, VA 22314
Tel: (703)548-5868
Fax: (703)548-5869
Registered: LDA
EMail: drmargus@aol.com

Assistant Chief Counsel for Tax Policy, U.S. Small Business Administration, 1986-92. Special U.S. Trial Attorney, U.S. Department of Justice, 1983-85. Counsel, U.S. Senate Permanent Subcommittee on Investigations, Government Affairs, 1983-85.

Employers

The Argus Group, L.L.C. (Partner)

Clients Represented

On Behalf of The Argus Group, L.L.C.

America Outdoors
American Soc. of Travel Agents
Americans for Fair Taxation
Nat'l Park Hospitality Ass'n
Nat'l Tour Ass'n
Travel Council for Fair Competition
United Motorcoach Ass'n

MATELSKI, Wayne H.

1050 Connecticut Ave. NW
Washington, DC 20036-5339
Tel: (202)857-6000
Fax: (202)857-6395

Employers

Arent Fox Kintner Plotkin & Kahn, PLLC (Member)

MATHEIS, Cheryl

601 E St. NW
Washington, DC 20049
Tel: (202)434-3950
Fax: (202)434-3959
Registered: LDA

Employers

AARP (American Ass'n of Retired Persons) (Director, State Legislation)

MATHER, Judith A.

1200 New Hampshire Ave. NW
Suite 800
Washington, DC 20036-6802
Tel: (202)776-2000
Fax: (202)776-2222
EMail: jmather@dlalaw.com

Assistant General Counsel for Regulatory Litigation (1982-84) and Attorney-Advisor and Senior Trial Attorney (1978-82), Department of Energy. Law Clerk to Judge Herbert F. Murray, U.S. District Court for the District of Maryland, 1977-78.

Employers

Dow, Lohnes & Albertson, PLLC (Member)

MATHERLEE, Karen R.

2131 K St. NW
Suite 500
Washington, DC 20006
Tel: (202)872-1390
Fax: (202)862-9837

Employers

Nat'l Health Policy Forum (Co-Director)

MATHERS, Peter R.

1140 19th St. NW
Suite 900
Washington, DC 20036
Tel: (202)223-5120
Fax: (202)223-5619
EMail: pmathers@kkblaw.com

Employers

Kleinfeld, Kaplan and Becker (Partner)

Clients Represented

On Behalf of Kleinfeld, Kaplan and Becker

Contact Lens Institute
Inwood Laboratories, Inc.
Jones Medical Industries, Inc.

MATHEWS, Alexander S.

1325 G St. NW
Suite 700
Washington, DC 20005
Tel: (202)637-2440
Fax: (202)393-1667
Registered: LDA

Employers

Animal Health Institute (President and Chief Exec. Officer)

MATHEWS, Graham "Rusty"

2101 L St. NW
Washington, DC 20037-1526
Tel: (202)785-9700
Fax: (202)887-0689
Registered: LDA
EMail: mathewsg@dsmo.com

Former Minority Clerk, Subcommittee on Veterans Affairs, HUD & Independent Agencies, Senate Appropriations Committee, 1995-96. Assistant Majority Clerk, Subcommittee on Department of Interior and Related Agencies, Senate Committee on Appropriations, 1989-94.

Employers

Dickstein Shapiro Morin & Oshinsky LLP (Senior Legislative Advisor)

Clients Represented

On Behalf of Dickstein Shapiro Morin & Oshinsky LLP

American Greyhound Track Operators Ass'n
CaseNewHolland Inc.
Cigar Ass'n of America
DuPont
Electric Power Supply Ass'n
First USA Bank
Harbour Group Industries, Inc.
Homestake Mining
Hydro-Quebec
Incentive Federation Sweepstakes Trust Fund
Internat'l Brotherhood of Teamsters
Kerr-McGee Corp.
Lorillard Tobacco Co.
Luiginos
Nat'l Ass'n of Water Companies
PG&E Generating Co.
Pipe Tobacco Council, Inc.
The Reader's Digest Ass'n
Smokeless Tobacco Council

MATHEWS, James H.

1775 I St. NW
Suite 700
Washington, DC 20006
Tel: (202)261-4000
Fax: (202)261-4001
Registered: LDA

Chief of Staff to Rep. Thomas J. Manton (D-NY), 1997-99. Deputy Assistant Administrator, Environmental Protection Agency, 1995-97. Former staff member to Senators Harrison Williams (D-NJ) and Nicholas Brady (R-NJ).

Employers

Clark & Weinstock, Inc. (Director)

MATHEWS, Jessica

1779 Massachusetts Ave. NW
Washington, DC 20036
Tel: (202)483-7600
Fax: (202)483-1840
EMail: jmathews@ceip.org

Employers

Carnegie Endowment for Internat'l Peace (President)

MATHEWS, Lara Bernstein

600 New Hampshire Ave. NW
11th Floor
Washington, DC 20037
Tel: (202)944-3000
Fax: (202)944-3068
Registered: LDA
EMail: lbm@dejlaw.com

Law Clerk, White House Council on Environmental Quality, 1994-95.

Employers

Dyer Ellis & Joseph, P.C. (Associate)

Clients Represented

On Behalf of Dyer Ellis & Joseph, P.C.

American Coke and Coal Chemicals Institute
Cross Sound Ferry Services, Inc.
FastShip, Inc.
Gateway Clipper Fleet
Hvide Marine Inc.
Kvaerner Philadelphia Shipyard Inc.
Marine Spill Response Corporation
Put-in-Bay Boat Line Co.
The Trump Organization
Wendella Sightseeing Boats Inc.

MATHIAS, Charles

900 19th St. NW
Suite 700
Washington, DC 20006
Tel: (202)530-7000
Fax: (202)530-7042
Registered: LDA

Employers

Lucent Technologies (Director, EMEA Region)

MATHIAS, Edward J.

1001 Pennsylvania Ave. NW
Suite 220 South
Washington, DC 20004
Tel: (202)347-2626
Fax: (202)347-1818

Employers

The Carlyle Group (Managing Director)

MATHIAS, Richard D.

888 17th St. NW
Suite 600
Washington, DC 20006-3959
Tel: (202)298-8660
Fax: (202)342-0683
EMail: rdmathias@zsrlaw.com

Employers

Zuckert, Scoutt and Rasenberger, L.L.P. (Partner)

Clients Represented

On Behalf of Zuckert, Scoutt and Rasenberger, L.L.P.

Aerolineas Centrales de Colombia
Airtours Internat'l
Alitalia
JMC Airlines, Ltd.
Kenya Airways
Pakistan Internat'l Airlines

MATHIAS, Sarah Avellar

1523 New Hampshire Ave. NW
Washington, DC 20036
Tel: (202)588-0002
Fax: (202)785-2669
Registered: LDA
EMail: sarah.mathias@ucop.edu

Employers

University of California, Office of Federal Government Relations (Senior Consultant)

MATHIASCHECK, Susan

2550 M St. NW
Washington, DC 20037-1350
Tel: (202)457-6000
Fax: (202)457-6315
Registered: LDA
EMail: smathiascheck@pattonboggs.com

Employers

Patton Boggs, LLP (Partner)

Clients Represented

On Behalf of Patton Boggs, LLP

Wild Alabama

MATHIESEN, Sandra Windsor

400 N. Capitol St. NW
Suite 363
Washington, DC 20001
Tel: (202)783-0280
Fax: (202)737-4518
Registered: LDA

Legislative Assistant to Rep. Thomas Foley (D-WA), 1982-93.

Employers

Denny Miller McBee Associates (V. President)

MATHIS, Jennifer

1101 15th St. NW
Suite 1212
Washington, DC 20005
Tel: (202)467-5730
Ext: 22
Fax: (202)223-0409
EMail: jenniferm@bazelon.org

Employers

Bazelon Center for Mental Health Law, Judge David L. (Staff Attorney, ADA Issues)

MATHIS, Joshua

111 C St. SE
Lower Unit
Washington, DC 20003
Tel: (202)546-6335
Fax: (202)546-6401

Employers

The Freedom Project (Consultant)

MATHIS, Kevin S.

201 Massachusetts Ave. NE
Suite C-4
Washington, DC 20008
Tel: (202)547-5860
Registered: LDA

Employers

Campaign for Medical Research (Legislative Director)

MATHIS, Hon. M. Dawson

421 New Jersey Ave. SE
Washington, DC 20003
Tel: (202)547-2090
Fax: (202)547-2011
Registered: LDA

Member, U.S. House of Representatives (D-GA), 1971-81.

Employers

Dawson Mathis & Associates (President)

Clients Represented

On Behalf of Dawson Mathis & Associates

San Joaquin Regional Rail Commission
United Parcel Service

MATHIS, Mike

25 Louisiana Ave. NW
Washington, DC 20001-2198
Tel: (202)624-8741
Fax: (202)624-8973
Registered: LDA

Employers
Internat'l Brotherhood of Teamsters (Director, Government Affairs)

MATHISEN, William

1010 N. Fairfax St. Alexandria, VA 22314-1574 EMail: wrmathisen@nsacct.org
Tel: (703)549-6400 Fax: (703)549-2984

Employers
Nat'l Soc. of Accountants (Exec. V. President)

MATLACK, Jim

1822 R St. NW Washington, DC 20009
Tel: (202)483-3341 Fax: (202)232-3197

Employers
American Friends Service Committee (Director, Washington Office)

MATLACK, Michael

1111 N. Fairfax St. Alexandria, VA 22314
Tel: (703)706-3163 Fax: (703)838-8919

Employers
American Physical Therapy Ass'n (PAC Contact)

MATLICK, CAE, Susan J.

1738 Elton Rd. Suite 200 Silver Spring, MD 20903 EMail: smatlick@compuserve.com
Tel: (301)445-5400 Fax: (301)445-5499

Employers
Maryland Nat'l Capitol Building Ass'n (Exec. Director)

MATSON, Noah

1101 14th St. NW Suite 1400 Washington, DC 20005 EMail: nmatson@defenders.org
Tel: (202)682-9400 Fax: (202)682-1331

Employers
Defenders of Wildlife (Science Policy Analyst)

MATSUI, Doris O.

3050 K St. NW Washington, DC 20007 EMail: dmatsui@colliershannon.com
Tel: (202)342-8400 Fax: (202)342-8451
Deputy Assistant to the President and Deputy Director of Public Liaison, The White House, 1993-98.

Employers
Collier Shannon Scott, PLLC (Senior Advisor and Director, Government Relations and Public Policy)

Clients Represented

On Behalf of Collier Shannon Scott, PLLC
AdvaMed
American Flange Producers Marking Coalition
American Sheep Industry Ass'n
Fannie Mae
Verizon Communications

MATTAR, Philip

3501 M St. NW Washington, DC 20007-2624 EMail: pmattar@ipsjps.org
Tel: (202)342-3990 Fax: (202)342-3927

Employers
Institute for Palestine Studies (Exec. Director)

MATTHEWS, Carol L. B.

2099 Pennsylvania Ave. NW Suite 100 Washington, DC 20006 EMail: cmatthew@hklaw.com
Tel: (202)955-3000 Fax: (202)955-5564

Employers
Holland & Knight LLP (Partner)

MATTHEWS, Cassandra

440 First St. NW Eighth Floor Washington, DC 20001
Tel: (202)393-6226 Fax: (202)393-2630

Employers
Nat'l Ass'n of Counties (Associate Legislative Director, Community and Economic Development)

MATTHEWS, Sr., Darryl R.

7249-A Hanover Pkwy. Greenbelt, MD 20770 EMail: darrylmatthews@nabainc.org
Tel: (301)474-6222 Fax: (301)474-3114

Employers
Nat'l Ass'n of Black Accountants (Exec. Director)

MATTHEWS, III, David J.

1100 Wilson Blvd. Suite 1500 Arlington, VA 22209 EMail: david_j_matthews@raytheon.com
Tel: (703)841-5729 Fax: (703)841-5793 Registered: LDA

Employers
Raytheon Co. (Senior V. President, Congressional Relations)

MATTHEWS, Debbie

815 15th St. NW Washington, DC 20005
Tel: (202)783-3788 Fax: (202)393-0219 Registered: LDA

Employers
Internat'l Union of Bricklayers and Allied Craftsworkers (Program Assistant, Government Relations)

MATTHEWS, John E.

1800 M St. NW Washington, DC 20036
Tel: (202)467-7000 Fax: (202)467-7176 Registered: FARA

Employers
Morgan, Lewis & Bockius LLP

MATTHEWS, Marsha Dula

600 13th St. NW Washington, DC 20005-3096 EMail: mmatthews@mwe.com
Tel: (202)756-8042 Fax: (202)756-8335

Employers
McDermott, Will and Emery (Partner)

MATTHEWS, Nancy

1630 Crescent Pl. NW Washington, DC 20009-4099
Tel: (202)939-5518 Fax: (202)310-1306

Employers
Meridian Internat'l Center (V. President, Arts and Communication)

MATTHEWS, Odonna

P.O. Box 1804 Dept. 597 Washington, DC 20013
Tel: (301)341-4365 Fax: (301)618-4968

Employers
Giant Food Inc. (V. President, Consumer Affairs)

MATTHEWS, Robert A.

700 N. Fairfax St. Suite 601 Alexandria, VA 22314 EMail: matthews@rpi.org
Tel: (703)836-2332 Fax: (703)548-0058 Registered: LDA

Employers
Railway Progress Institute (President)

MATTHEWS, Stuart

601 Madison St. Suite 300 Alexandria, VA 22314-1756
Tel: (703)739-6700 Fax: (703)739-6708

Employers
Flight Safety Foundation (President, and Chief Exec. Officer)

MATTHEWS, Suzette

2300 Clarendon Blvd. Suite 711 Arlington, VA 22201 EMail: atca@worldnet.att.net
Tel: (703)522-5717 Fax: (703)527-7251

Employers
Air Traffic Control Ass'n (General Counsel)

MATTHEWS, William L.

1133 Connecticut Ave. NW Suite 1200 Washington, DC 20036
Tel: (202)775-9800 Fax: (202)833-8491 Registered: LDA, FARA

Employers
Winthrop, Stimson, Putnam & Roberts (Diretor, Non-Lawyer Trade Services)

Clients Represented

On Behalf of Winthrop, Stimson, Putnam & Roberts
SKW Chemicals, Inc.

MATTHYS, Allen

1350 I St. NW Suite 300 Washington, DC 20005
Tel: (202)639-5900 Fax: (202)639-5932 Registered: LDA

Employers
Nat'l Food Processors Ass'n (V. President, Regulatory Affairs)

MATTINGLEY, Jr., George M. "Matt"

1620 I St. NW Suite 615 Washington, DC 20006 EMail: matt@moinc.com
Tel: (202)463-8493 Fax: (202)463-8497 Registered: LDA

Employers
JBC Internat'l (V. President, Government Affairs)
Management Options, Inc.

Clients Represented

On Behalf of JBC Internat'l
Allen-Bradley
The BOSE Corp.
Meridian Worldwide
Uniroyal Chemical Co., Inc.
Wine Institute

On Behalf of Management Options, Inc.
American Teleservices Ass'n

MATTINGLY, C. Richard

6931 Arlington Rd. Suite 200 Bethesda, MD 20814
Tel: (301)951-4422 Fax: (301)951-6378

Employers
Cystic Fibrosis Foundation (Exec. V. President/Chief Operating Officer)

MATTINGLY, Joseph M.

2107 Wilson Blvd. Suite 600 Arlington, VA 22201
Tel: (703)525-7060 Fax: (703)525-6790 Registered: LDA

Employers
Gas Appliance Manufacturers Ass'n (V. President)

MATTISON, Allen

408 C St. NE Washington, DC 20002
Tel: (202)547-1141 Fax: (202)547-6009

Employers
Sierra Club (Director, Media Relations)

MATTISON, Lindsay

731 Eighth St. SE Washington, DC 20003 EMail: icnfp@erols.com
Tel: (202)547-3800 Ext: 104 Fax: (202)546-4784

Employers
Internat'l Center (Exec. Director)

MATTON, Michael N.

1200 Wilson Blvd. Arlington, VA 22209-1989
Tel: (703)465-3625 Fax: (703)465-3002 Registered: LDA

Employers
The Boeing Co. (V. President, Legislative Affairs)

MATTOON, Dan

1001 G St. NW Suite 900 E Washington, DC 20001-4545
Tel: (202)393-1010 Fax: (202)393-5510

Employers
Podesta/Mattoon (Partner)

MATTOS, Kate

1201 16th St. NW
Washington, DC 20036
Tel: (202)833-4000

Employers
Nat'l Education Ass'n of the U.S. (Director, Communications)

MATTOX, Barbara Groves

1455 Pennsylvania Ave. NW
Suite 1200
Washington, DC 20004
Tel: (202)347-2230
Fax: (202)393-3310
Registered: LDA

Tax Counsel, Senate Finance Committee, 1985-88. Law Clerk to Judge William M. Fay, U.S. Tax Court, 1980-82.

Employers
Davis & Harman LLP (Partner)

Clients Represented

On Behalf of Davis & Harman LLP

Aegon USA
Allstate Insurance Co.
Committee of Annuity Insurers
FMR Corp.
Lincoln Nat'l Corp.
Pharmaceutical Research and Manufacturers of America
Stock Co. Information Group

MATTOX, Richard B.

513 Capitol Court NE
Suite 100
Washington, DC 20002
Tel: (202)547-9505
Fax: (202)478-0279
Registered: LDA
EMail: richard@mattoxwoolfolk.com

Employers
Mattox Woolfolk, LLC (Partner)

Clients Represented

On Behalf of Mattox Woolfolk, LLC

Constituency for Africa
ICG Communications, Inc.
MCI WorldCom Corp.
Voices, Inc.

MATTOX, William C.

1700 Pennsylvania Ave. NW
Suite 500
Washington, DC 20006-4771
Tel: (202)393-6208
Fax: (202)639-8808
Registered: LDA
EMail: bill.mattox@mutualofomaha.com

Employers
Mutual of Omaha Insurance Companies (Exec. V. President, Federal Government Affairs)

MATTS, Dorothy Sharon

1762 Church St. NW
Washington, DC 20036
Tel: (202)939-8984
Fax: (202)939-8983
Registered: LDA

Employers
Burwell, Peters and Houston (Partner)

Clients Represented

On Behalf of Burwell, Peters and Houston

Barker Enterprises

MATZ, Marshall L.

1400 16th St. NW
Suite 400
Washington, DC 20036-2220
Tel: (202)789-1212
Fax: (202)234-3550
Registered: LDA
EMail: mmatz@ofwlaw.com

Special Counsel, Senate Committee on Agriculture, Nutrition and Forestry, 1978-80. Counsel and General Counsel, Senate Select Committee on Nutrition and Human Needs, 1973-77.

Employers
Olsson, Frank and Weeda, P.C. (Principal)

Clients Represented

On Behalf of Olsson, Frank and Weeda, P.C.

Adheris, Inc.
American Academy of Audiology
American Commodity Distribution Ass'n
American School Food Service Ass'n
Ass'n of Medical Device Reprocessors
Aventis Pasteur
Beef Products, Inc.
Black Hills Forest Resource Ass'n
California Canning Peach Ass'n
Chocolate Manufacturers Ass'n of the U.S.A.
Duramed Pharmaceuticals, Inc.
Food Distributors Internat'l (NAWGA-IFDA)
General Mills
Gentrac Inc.
Health Resource Publishing Co.
Institute of Food Technologists
Kraft Foods, Inc.
Lower Brule Sioux Tribe
Mead Johnson Nutritional Group
Nat'l Ass'n of Margarine Manufacturers
Nat'l Ass'n of Pharmaceutical Manufacturers
Nat'l Coalition of Food Importers Ass'n
Nat'l Confectioners Ass'n
Nat'l Food Processors Ass'n
Nat'l Frozen Pizza Institute
Nat'l Meat Ass'n
PennField Oil Co.
The Pillsbury Co.
San Tomo Group
Schwan's Sales Enterprises
SteriGenics Internat'l
Titan Scan
Transhumance Holding Co., Inc.
United Fresh Fruit and Vegetable Ass'n
Urner Barry Publications, Inc.

MATZ, Mike

122 C St. NW
Suite 240
Washington, DC 20001
Tel: (202)544-3691
Fax: (202)544-5197

Employers
Pew Wilderness Center (Exec. Director)

MATZ, Timothy B.

734 15th St. NW
12th Floor
Washington, DC 20005
Tel: (202)347-0300
Fax: (202)347-2172

Employers
Elias, Matz, Tiernan and Herrick (Managing Partner)

MAUCIERI, Mat

400 N. Capitol St. NW
Suite 357 South
Washington, DC 20001
Tel: (202)434-4760
Fax: (202)434-4763
Registered: LDA

Employers
Ass'n of California Water Agencies (Federal Relations Representative)

MAUER, Marc

514 10th St. NW
Suite 1000
Washington, DC 20005
EMail: mauer@sentencingproject.org
Tel: (202)628-0871
Fax: (202)628-1091

Employers
The Sentencing Project (Assistant Director)

MAUK, Alan R.

2121 Jamieson Ave.
Suite 1405
Alexandria, VA 22314
Tel: (703)567-2021
Registered: LDA

Employers
Alan Mauk Associates, Ltd. (President)

Clients Represented

On Behalf of Alan Mauk Associates, Ltd.

Ann Eppard Associates, Ltd.
Cambridge Management Inc.
Oklahoma Department of Transportation
Yukon City, Oklahoma, City of

MAURER, Eric J.

2033 K St. NW
Suite 850
Washington, DC 20006
EMail: eric.maurer@valent.com
Tel: (202)872-4688
Fax: (202)872-4689

Employers
Valent U.S.A. Corp. (Manager, Federal Registration)

MAURY, Samuel L.

1615 L St. NW
Suite 1100
Washington, DC 20036-5610
Tel: (202)872-1260
Fax: (202)466-3509
Registered: LDA

Employers
The Business Roundtable (President)

MAVES, M.D., Michael D.

1150 Connecticut Ave. NW
12th Floor
Washington, DC 20036
Tel: (202)429-9260
Fax: (202)223-6835

Employers
Consumer Healthcare Products Ass'n (President)

MAWBY, Michael

1701 N. Beauregard St.
Alexandria, VA 22311
Tel: (703)549-1500
Ext: 2059
Fax: (703)549-8748
Registered: LDA
EMail: mmawby@diabetes.org

Employers
American Diabetes Ass'n (V. President, Government Relations)

MAX, Derrick

1000 Massachusetts Ave. NW
Washington, DC 20001
Tel: (202)842-0200
Fax: (202)842-3490

Employers
Cato Institute (Director, Government Affairs)

MAXWELL, William A.

900 17th St. NW
Suite 1100
Washington, DC 20006
Tel: (202)884-7046
Fax: (202)884-7070
Registered: LDA
EMail: wmaxwell@hp.com

Employers
Hewlett-Packard Co. (Manager, International Trade Policy)

MAY, Clifford D.

1501 M St. NW
Suite 600
Washington, DC 20005-1710
Tel: (202)739-0200
Fax: (202)659-8287

Employers
BSMG Worldwide (Senior Managing Director)

MAY, James C.

1771 N St. NW
Washington, DC 20036-2891
Tel: (202)429-5302
Fax: (202)775-2157
Registered: LDA
EMail: jmay@nab.org

Employers
Nat'l Ass'n of Broadcasters (Exec. V. President, Government Relations)

MAY, John Paul

1101 Mercantile Ln.
Suite 100
Springdale, MD 20774
Tel: (301)925-1420
Fax: (301)925-1429
Registered: LDA

Employers
Ass'n Growth Enterprises (President and Chief Exec. Officer)

Clients Represented

On Behalf of Ass'n Growth Enterprises

American Military Soc.
Nat'l Ass'n for Uniformed Services

MAY, Richard E.

1101 Pennsylvania Ave. NW
Suite 810
The Evening Star Building
Washington, DC 20004
EMail: rem@davidsondc.com
Tel: (202)638-1101
Fax: (202)638-1102
Registered: LDA

Former Chief of Staff, House Budget Committee.

Employers
Davidson & Company, Inc. (Principal)

Clients Represented

On Behalf of Davidson & Company, Inc.
Advertising Tax Coalition
American Advertising Federation
American Ass'n for Homecare
American Ass'n of Advertising Agencies
AOL Time Warner
Apria Healthcare Group
Ass'n of Nat'l Advertisers
The Business Roundtable
Corporation for Enterprise Development
Direct Marketing Ass'n, Inc.
eBay Inc.
Ellicott Internat'l
Federal Home Loan Mortgage Corp. (Freddie Mac)
Grocery Manufacturers of America
The Hearst Corp.
Independent Contractor Coalition
Magazine Publishers of America
Nat'l Ass'n of Broadcasters
Newspaper Ass'n of America
The Reader's Digest Ass'n
Paul Scherer & Co., LLP
The Washington Post Co.
Yellow Pages Publishers Ass'n

MAY, Richard E.

1900 K St. NW
Washington, DC 20006-1109
Tel: (202)955-1500
Fax: (202)778-2201
Registered: LDA
EMail: rmay@hunton.com
Special Assistant to the Chief Counsel, Internal Revenue Service, Department of the Treasury, 1979-81. Lieutenant, U.S. Navy, 1968-71.

Employers
Hunton & Williams (Partner)

Clients Represented

On Behalf of Hunton & Williams
American Electric Power Co.

MAY, Stephen L.

1001 Pennsylvania Ave. NW
Suite 700 South
Washington, DC 20004
Tel: (202)662-2650
Fax: (202)662-2674
Registered: LDA

Employers
Honeywell Internat'l, Inc. (Director, Legislative and Regulatory Affairs)

MAY, Timothy J.

2550 M St. NW
Washington, DC 20037-1350
Tel: (202)457-6000
Fax: (202)457-6315
Registered: LDA
EMail: tmay@pattonboggs.com
General Counsel, U.S. Post Office Department, 1966-69. Managing Director, Federal Maritime Commission, 1963-66. Acting Chief Counsel, Senate Subcommittee on National Stockpile Investigation, 1962-63. Consultant, Executive Office of the President, The White House, 1961-62. Law Clerk to Judge John Danaher, U.S. Court of Appeals, District of Columbia Circuit, 1957-58.

Employers
Patton Boggs, LLP (Partner)

MAY, Vicki

1317 F St. NW
Suite 600
Washington, DC 20004
Tel: (202)638-2121
Fax: (202)638-7045
Registered: LDA
EMail: may@wexlergroup.com

Employers
The Wexler Group (Principal)

Clients Represented

On Behalf of The Wexler Group
Burst Networks Inc.
The Business Roundtable

MAYBERRY, Peter G.

252 N. Washington St.
Suite A
Falls Church, VA 22046
Tel: (703)538-8804
Fax: (703)538-6305
Registered: LDA
EMail: pgmayberry@aol.com

Employers
Mayberry & Associates LLC (President)

Clients Represented

On Behalf of Mayberry & Associates LLC
Ass'n of the Nonwoven Fabrics Industry - INDA
Healthcare Compliance Packaging Council

MAYCUMBER, Jill

1299 Pennsylvania Ave. NW
Suite 1175
Washington, DC 20004
Tel: (202)638-3838
Fax: (202)638-5799
Registered: LDA
EMail: jillmay@erols.com

Employers
Chicago Mercantile Exchange (Manager, Regulatory and Legislative Affairs)

MAYER, Joseph L.

1050 17th St. NW
Suite 440
Washington, DC 20036
Tel: (202)833-8575
Fax: (202)331-8267

Employers
Copper and Brass Fabricators Council (President)

MAYER, Marion R.

601 E St. NW
Washington, DC 20049
Tel: (202)434-3800
Fax: (202)434-3758
Registered: LDA

Employers
AARP (American Ass'n of Retired Persons) (Legislative Representative)

MAYER, Martin

1775 Massachusetts Ave. NW
Washington, DC 20036-2188
Tel: (202)797-6000
Fax: (202)797-6004
Member, President's Panel on Educational Research and Development in Kennedy and Johnson Administrations; Member, President's Commission on Housing, 1981-82.

Employers
The Brookings Institution (Guest Scholar, Economic Studies)

MAYER, Neal Michael

1000 Connecticut Ave. NW
Suite 400
Washington, DC 20036
EMail: hmcl@ix.netcom.com
Tel: (202)296-5460
Fax: (202)296-5463

Employers
Hoppel, Mayer and Coleman (Senior Partner)

Clients Represented

On Behalf of Hoppel, Mayer and Coleman
Tropical Shipping and Construction Co.

MAYER, Virginia M.

1660 L St. NW
Suite 1050
Washington, DC 20036
Tel: (202)496-9610
Fax: (202)659-5234
Registered: LDA

Employers
Boston, Massachusetts, City of (Director, Washington Office)
Self-employed as an independent consultant.

Clients Represented

As an independent consultant
Boston, Massachusetts, City of

MAYERS, Michael

1090 Vermont Ave. NW
Suite 510
Washington, DC 20005
Tel: (202)414-0140
Fax: (202)544-3525
Registered: LDA

Employers
American Osteopathic Ass'n (Assistant Director, Congressional Affairs)

MAYES, Paul

Park Center
107 E. Holly Ave., Suite 11
Sterling, VA 20164
Tel: (703)430-9668
Fax: (703)450-1745

Employers
Internat'l Soc. of Air Safety Investigators (V. President)

MAYHEW, Howard

P.O. Box 3008
Alexandria, VA 22302-0008
Tel: (703)931-4107
Fax: (703)931-3127
Registered: LDA

Employers
The Conaway Group LLC (Consultant)

MAYO, Philip R.

Rayburn House Office Bldg.
Room B328
Washington, DC 20515
Tel: (202)225-2280
Fax: (202)453-5225

Employers
Department of Veterans Affairs (Director, Congressional Liaison Services)

MAYRIDES, Maurice

1900 M St. NW
Suite 200
Washington, DC 20036-2422
Tel: (202)776-0544
Fax: (202)776-0545
Registered: LDA
EMail: mmayrides@hematology.org

Employers
American Soc. of Hematology (Government Affairs Director)

MAYS, Jeffrey G.

1505 Prince St.
Suite 300
Alexandria, VA 22314
Tel: (703)739-9200
Fax: (703)739-9497
Registered: LDA

Employers
American Optometric Ass'n (Deputy Exec. Director)

MAZAWEY, Louis T.

1701 Pennsylvania Ave. NW
Suite 1200
Washington, DC 20006
Tel: (202)857-0620
Fax: (202)659-4503
Registered: LDA

Employers
Groom Law Group, Chartered

Clients Represented

On Behalf of Groom Law Group, Chartered
Microsoft Corp.

MAZER, Michael E.

1850 M St. NW
Suite 400
Washington, DC 20036
Tel: (202)293-8200
Fax: (202)872-0145
Registered: LDA

Employers
Krooth & Altman (Managing Partner)

Clients Represented

On Behalf of Krooth & Altman
Healthcare Financing Study Group

MAZER, Robert A.

1455 Pennsylvania Ave. NW
Suite 700
Washington, DC 20004-1008
Tel: (202)639-6500
Fax: (202)639-6604
Registered: LDA
EMail: rmazer@velaw.com

Employers
Vinson & Elkins L.L.P. (Partner)

MAZER, Stacey

444 N. Capitol St. NW
Suite 642
Washington, DC 20001
Tel: (202)624-5382
Fax: (202)624-7745

Employers
Nat'l Ass'n of State Budget Officers (Senior Staff Associate)

MAZOR, John

535 Herndon Pkwy.
Herndon, VA 22070-4370
Tel: (703)481-4442
Fax: (703)689-4370

Employers
Air Line Pilots Ass'n Internat'l (Communications Specialist)

MAZURE, Kathleen L.

1615 M St. NW
Suite 800
Washington, DC 20036-3203
EMail: klm@dwgp.com
Tel: (202)467-6370
Fax: (202)467-6379

Attorney-Advisor, Federal Energy Regulatory Commission, Department of Energy 1986-88.

Employers

Duncan, Weinberg, Genzer & Pembroke, P.C. (Of Counsel)

Clients Represented

On Behalf of Duncan, Weinberg, Genzer & Pembroke, P.C.

Champlin Exploration, Inc.
Municipal Electric Utilities Ass'n of New York State
ONEOK Bushton Processing, LLC
ONEOK Energy Marketing & Trading Co.
ONEOK Field Services, Inc.
ONEOK Gas Transportation, LLC
ONEOK Midcontinent Market Center, Inc.
ONEOK Midstream Gas Supply, LLC
ONEOK OkTex Pipeline Co.

MAZZA, Pamela J.

888 17th St. NW
Suite 1100
Washington, DC 20006
Tel: (202)857-1000
Fax: (202)857-0200
Registered: LDA
EMail: pmazza@pmplawfirm.com

Employers

Piliero Mazza & Pargament (Senior Partner)

Clients Represented

On Behalf of Piliero Mazza & Pargament

Ysleta Del Sur Pueblo

MAZZARELLA, James A.

444 N. Capitol St. NW
Suite 301
Washington, DC 20001
Tel: (202)434-7100
Fax: (202)434-7110

Employers

New York State Office of Federal Affairs (Director)

MAZZELLA, Jeffrey

1667 K St. NW
Suite 480
Washington, DC 20006
Tel: (202)775-1796
Fax: (202)775-0214
Registered: LDA
EMail: jeff.mazzella@mail.netlobby.com

Employers

Marlowe and Co. (Legislative Representative)

Clients Represented

On Behalf of Marlowe and Co.

American Coastal Coalition
Avalon, New Jersey, City of
Broward, Florida, Department of Natural Resource Protection of the County of
Fire Island Ass'n
Galveston County, Texas
Jefferson Texas, County of
MOTE Marine Lab
North Topsail Beach, North Carolina, Town of
Ocean Isle Beach, North Carolina, Town of
Ocean Village Property Owners Ass'n, Inc.
Sarasota, Florida, City of
Solana Beach, California, City of
St. Augustine Beach, Florida, City of
St. Lucie, Florida, County of
Venice, Florida, City of

MCADAMS, Michael J.

1776 I St. NW
Suite 1000
Washington, DC 20006
Tel: (202)785-4888
Fax: (202)457-6597
Registered: LDA

Employers

BP Amoco Corp. (Director, Federal Government Affairs, Eastern U.S.)

MCALEENAN, Michael

1025 Connecticut Ave. NW
Suite 1012
Washington, DC 20036
Tel: (202)258-2301
Registered: LDA

Employers

Smith Alling Lane, P.S.

Clients Represented

On Behalf of Smith Alling Lane, P.S.

PE Biosystems
Sagem Morpho
Washington Ass'n of Sheriffs and Police Chiefs

MCALISTER-BUNN, Lynn

1331 Pennsylvania Ave. NW
Suite 1300 North
Washington, DC 20004
EMail: lynn.mcalister-bunn@eds.com
Tel: (202)637-6734
Fax: (202)637-6759

Employers

EDS Corp. (Director; Healthcare Policy)

MCALLISTER, John P.

1400 16th St. NW
Suite 600
Washington, DC 20036
Tel: (202)939-7900
Fax: (202)745-0916
Registered: LDA

Former Legislative Director to Rep. Bud Shuster (R-PA).

Employers

Fleischman and Walsh, L.L.P.

Clients Represented

On Behalf of Fleischman and Walsh, L.L.P.

ACTA Technology
American Airlines
Currenex
Forest Cities
Indigo
Katten Muchin & Zavis
Midway Airlines Corp.

MCALLISTER, Patricia H.

1800 K St. NW
Suite 900
Washington, DC 20006
EMail: pmcallister@ets.org
Tel: (202)659-0616
Fax: (202)659-8075

Employers

Educational Testing Service (Exec. Director, State and Federal Relations Office)

MCALPIN, K. C.

1666 Connecticut Ave. NW
Suite 400
Washington, DC 20009
Tel: (202)328-7004
Fax: (202)387-3447

Employers

Federation for American Immigration Reform (FAIR) (Deputy Director)

MCANDREWS, Lawrence A.

401 Wythe St.
Alexandria, VA 22314
EMail: lmcandrews@nachri.org
Tel: (703)684-1355
Fax: (703)684-1589

Employers

Nat'l Ass'n of Children's Hospitals Inc. (President and Chief Exec. Officer)

MCARVER, Jr., Robert D.

1615 L St. NW
Suite 650
Washington, DC 20036
Tel: (202)626-8514
Fax: (202)626-8774
Registered: LDA
EMail: rdm@jeffersongr.com

Employers

Jefferson Government Relations, L.L.C. (V. President)

Clients Represented

On Behalf of Jefferson Government Relations, L.L.C.

Ergodyne
Lafarge Corp.
Minnesota Mining and Manufacturing Co. (3M Co.)
Vinyl Institute

MCATEE, Daniel

1520 18th St. NW
Washington, DC 20036
Tel: (202)331-8947
Fax: (202)331-8958

Employers

Hong Kong Economic and Trade Office (Senior Information Officer)

MCAULEY, Sue S.

1400 Independence Ave. SW
Stop 3407, Room 1147, South Bldg.
Washington, DC 20250
EMail: susan.s.mcauley@usda.gov
Tel: (202)720-2511
Fax: (202)720-3982

Employers

Department of Agriculture - Animal and Plant Health Inspection Service (Assistant to the Director for Legislative Affairs)

MCAULIFFE, Mary E.

600 13th St. NW
Suite 340
Washington, DC 20005
Tel: (202)662-0100
Fax: (202)662-0199
Registered: LDA

Employers

Union Pacific (V. President, External Relations)

MCAULIFFE SMITH, Kate

1615 L St. NW
Suite 1300
Washington, DC 20036
Tel: (202)223-7300
Fax: (202)223-7420

Former Associate Counsel and Policy Advisor to Rep. Richard A. Gephardt (D-MO).

Employers

Paul, Weiss, Rifkind, Wharton & Garrison (Associate)

MCBARNETTE, Ellen

740 15th St. NW
Ninth Floor
Washington, DC 20005
Tel: (202)662-1767
Fax: (202)662-1762
Registered: LDA

Employers

American Bar Ass'n (Legislative Counsel)

MCBEE, Steve

400 N. Capitol St. NW
Suite 363
Washington, DC 20001
Tel: (202)783-0280
Fax: (202)737-4518
Registered: LDA
EMail: smcbee@millermcbee.com

Former National Security Assistant to Rep. Norm Dicks (D-WA) and Legislative Assistant to Rep. Al Swift (D-WA). Former Senior Policy Aide to Rep. Maria Cantwell (D-WA).

Employers

Denny Miller McBee Associates (Exec. V. President and Chief Operating Officer)

Clients Represented

On Behalf of Denny Miller McBee Associates

Asbestos Recycling Inc.

MCBETH, Danielle

2111 Wilson Blvd.
Eighth Floor
Arlington, VA 22201-3058
Tel: (703)841-0626
Fax: (703)243-2874
Registered: LDA
EMail: mcbeth@alcalde-fay.com

Employers

Alcalde & Fay (Partner)

Clients Represented

On Behalf of Alcalde & Fay

Clearwater, Florida, City of
Cruise Industry Charitable Foundation
Houston Independent School District
Miami-Dade County Public Schools
Miami-Dade, Florida, County of
North Miami Beach, Florida, City of
Riviera Beach, Florida, City of
Washington Workshops

MCBETH, Daryn

600 Pennsylvania Ave. SE
Suite 320
Washington, DC 20003
Tel: (202)969-8900
Fax: (202)331-7036
Registered: LDA
EMail: dmcbeth@gordley.com

Legislative Counsel to Rep. Earl Pomeroy (D-ND), 1997-98. Former Special Counsel, Natural Resources Conservation Service, Department of Agriculture.

Employers

Gordley Associates (Associate)

Clients Represented

On Behalf of Gordley Associates

Nat'l Barley Growers Ass'n
Nebraska Wheat Board
U.S. Canola Ass'n

MCBETH, Mark

1501 Farm Credit Dr.
MS: 4128
McLean, VA 22102-5090
Tel: (703)883-4056
Fax: (703)790-3260

Employers

Farm Credit Administration (Assistant Director for Congressional and Public Affairs)

MCBRIDE, Charlie

1101 17th St. NW
Suite 705
Washington, DC 20036
Tel: (202)466-4210
Fax: (202)466-4213
Registered: LDA

Former Exec. Director, Democratic Senatorial Campaign Committee.

Employers

Charlie McBride Associates, Inc. (President)

Clients Represented

On Behalf of Charlie McBride Associates, Inc.

Biomedical Research Foundation of Northwest Louisiana
Edison Chouest Offshore, Inc.
ExtrudeHone Corp.
Idaho Titanium Technologies, LLC
Louisiana Center for Manufacturing Sciences
North American Shipbuilding
Science and Engineering Associates, Inc.
Science Applications Internat'l Corp. (SAIC)
SRT Group
University Heights Science Park
Waterworks Internat'l, Inc.
Yukon Pacific

MCBRIDE, James W.

801 Pennsylvania Ave. NW
Suite 800
Washington, DC 20004
Tel: (202)508-3400
Fax: (202)508-3402

Employers

Baker, Donelson, Bearman & Caldwell, P.C. (Shareholder)

MCBRIDE, Lawrence G.

1050 Connecticut Ave. NW
Washington, DC 20036-5366
Tel: (202)672-5300
Fax: (202)672-5399
Registered: LDA
EMail: lmcbride@flks.com

Former Staff Member, Department of Justice, 1986-88. Assistant Section Chief, Land and Natural Resources Division, Department of the Interior, 1973-86. Former Assistant Solicitor, Office of the Solicitor.

Employers

Freedman, Levy, Kroll & Simonds (Partner)

Clients Represented

On Behalf of Freedman, Levy, Kroll & Simonds

Enron Corp.

MCBRIDE, Maurice H.

1899 L St. NW
Suite 1000
Washington, DC 20036
Tel: (202)457-0480
Fax: (202)457-0486
Registered: LDA
EMail: maurice_mcbride@npradc.org

Employers

Nat'l Petrochemical Refiners Ass'n (Corporate Secretary & Attorney)

MCBRIDE, Sharon

555 13th St. NW
Washington, DC 20004-1109
Tel: (202)637-5600
Fax: (202)637-5910

Employers

Hogan & Hartson L.L.P. (Legislative Specialist)

Clients Represented

On Behalf of Hogan & Hartson L.L.P.

FM Watch
Southern Methodist University

MCBRIDE, Timothy J.

1401 H St. NW
Suite 700
Washington, DC 20005
Tel: (202)414-6756
Fax: (202)414-6738
Registered: LDA

Employers

DaimlerChrysler Corp. (V. President, Washington Office)

MCBROOM, Marty

801 Pennsylvania Ave. NW
Suite 214
Washington, DC 20004
Tel: (202)628-1645
Fax: (202)628-4276
Registered: LDA

Employers

American Electric Power Co. (Director, Federal Environmental Affairs)

MCBURNEY, Shawn

1301 Connecticut Ave. NW
Fourth Floor
Washington, DC 20036
Tel: (202)467-5300
Fax: (202)467-4253
EMail: smcburney@cagw.org

Special Assistant to Rep. Edward R. Royce (R-CA), 1993-99.

Employers

Citizens Against Government Waste (Director, Government Relations)

MCCABE, Carrie

1010 Massachusetts Ave. NW
Washington, DC 20001
Tel: (202)289-4434
Fax: (202)289-4435

Employers

American Road and Transportation Builders Ass'n (ARTBA) (Editor, Transportation Builder)

MCCABE, Patrick

1825 Connecticut Ave. NW
Suite 650
Washington, DC 20009
Tel: (202)745-5100
Fax: (202)234-6159
EMail: pmccabe@gyhllc.com

Employers

Garrett Yu Hussein LLC (Partner)

MCCABE, Richard E.

1101 14th St. NW
Suite 801
Washington, DC 20005
Tel: (202)371-1808
Fax: (202)408-5059

Employers

Wildlife Management Institute (V. President)

MCCAIN, Mark

730 11th St. NW
Fourth Floor
Washington, DC 20001-4510
Tel: (202)638-1448
Ext: 117
Fax: (202)638-3429
EMail: mmcain@aupha.org

Employers

Ass'n of University Programs in Health Administration (Director, Marketing and Communications)

MCCALL, Barbara T.

1401 K St. NW
Suite 700
Washington, DC 20005
Tel: (202)842-5430
Fax: (202)842-5051
Registered: LDA
EMail: mccall@capitaledge.com

Employers

Barbara T. McCall Associates (President)

Clients Represented

On Behalf of Barbara T. McCall Associates

Austin, Texas, City of
Columbia, South Carolina, City of
Dallas, Texas, City of
Denton, Texas, City of
Henderson, Nevada, City of
Huntsville, Alabama, City of
Lubbock, Texas, City of
Plano, Texas, City of
Texas Cities Legislative Coalition (TCLC)

MCCALL, D. Mark

1701 Pennsylvania Ave. NW
Suite 800
Washington, DC 20006
Tel: (202)956-7500
Fax: (202)293-6330

Employers

Sullivan & Cromwell (Of Counsel)

Clients Represented

On Behalf of Sullivan & Cromwell

British Airways Plc

MCCALLION, Kerry

1775 Pennsylvania Ave. NW
Suite 200
Washington, DC 20006
Tel: (202)862-1000
Fax: (202)862-1093

Employers

Dewey Ballantine LLP (Legislative Assistant)

MCCALMON, Brian K.

1735 New York Ave. NW
Suite 500
Washington, DC 20006-4759
Tel: (202)628-1700
Fax: (202)331-1024

Employers

Preston Gates Ellis & Rouvelas Meeds LLP (Associate)

Clients Represented

On Behalf of Preston Gates Ellis & Rouvelas Meeds LLP

WABCO

MCCANN, Bart

444 N. Capitol St. NW
Suite 821
Washington, DC 20001
Tel: (202)737-3390
Fax: (202)628-3607

Employers

Health Policy Alternatives, Inc.

Clients Represented

On Behalf of Health Policy Alternatives, Inc.

AdvaMed
Johnson & Johnson, Inc.
Medtronic, Inc.

MCCANN, Nancey K.

4000 Legato Rd.
Suite 850
Fairfax, VA 22033
Tel: (703)591-2220
Fax: (703)591-0614
Registered: LDA
EMail: nmccann@ascrs.org

Employers

American Soc. of Cataract and Refractive Surgery (Director, Government Relations)

MCCANN, Patrick J.

1317 F St. NW
Suite 600
Washington, DC 20004
Tel: (202)638-2121
Fax: (202)638-7045
Registered: LDA
EMail: mccann@wexlergroup.com

Employers

The Wexler Group (Principal/Senior Director)

Clients Represented

On Behalf of The Wexler Group

AAAE-ACI
Air Transport Ass'n of America
American Airlines
ARINC, Inc.
Chamber of Commerce of the U.S.A.
Chicago Transit Authority
CSX Corp.
General Motors Corp.
InVision Technologies
Mammoth Mountain
Orange County Public Schools
ORBITZ
United Parcel Service
Wasatch Front Regional Council

MCCANN, Vonya B.

401 Ninth St. NW
Suite 400
Washington, DC 20004
Tel: (202)585-1902
Fax: (202)585-1899

Employers

Sprint Corp. (Senior V. President, Federal External Affairs)

MCCARLIE, Christine C.

1155 21st St. NW
Suite 300
Washington, DC 20036
Tel: (202)659-8201
Registered: LDA

Employers
Tailored Clothing Ass'n (Exec. Director)

MCCARRY, Michael

1776 Massachusetts Ave. NW
Suite 620
Washington, DC 20036
Tel: (202)293-6141
Fax: (202)293-6144
Registered: LDA
EMail: mmccarry@alliance-exchange.org

Employers
Alliance for Internat'l Educational and Cultural Exchange, The (Exec. Director)

MCCARTER, Katherine S.

1707 H St. NW
Suite 400
Washington, DC 20006
Tel: (202)833-8773
Fax: (202)833-8775
EMail: ksm@esa.org

Employers
Ecological Soc. of America (Exec. Director)

MCCARTER, Pender M.

1828 L St. NW
Suite 1202
Washington, DC 20036-5104
Tel: (202)785-0017
Fax: (202)785-0835
EMail: p.mccarter@ieee.org

Employers
Institute of Electrical and Electronics Engineers, Inc. (Director, Communications and Public Relations)

MCCARTHY, Amy

1401 K St. NW
Suite 600
Washington, DC 20005
Tel: (202)835-9898
Fax: (202)853-9893

Employers
ASCENT (Ass'n of Community Enterprises) (Director, Conference Services)

MCCARTHY, Andrea

7910 Science Application Court
Vienna, VA 22182
Tel: (703)676-1100
Fax: (703)903-1525
EMail: andrea.c.mccarthy@saic.com

Employers
Boeing Information Services (Director, Public Relations)

MCCARTHY, Bernie

6917 Arlington Rd.
Suite 210
Bethesda, MD 20814
Tel: (301)656-5824
Fax: (301)656-5825
EMail: bmccarthy@asphaltinstitute.org

Employers
Asphalt Institute (V. President)

MCCARTHY, Daniel

1600 Pennsylvania Ave. NW
112 E. Wing
Washington, DC 20500
Tel: (202)456-6493
Fax: (202)456-2604

Employers
Executive Office of the President - The White House (Staff Assistant for Correspondence, House Liaison Office)

MCCARTHY, Elizabeth

655 National Press Bldg.
Washington, DC 20045
Tel: (202)737-8400
Fax: (202)737-8406
EMail: emccarthy@johnadams.com

Employers
John Adams Associates Inc. (Senior V. President)

Clients Represented

On Behalf of John Adams Associates Inc.
Alliance for Chemical Awareness

MCCARTHY, Elizabeth S. "Bettie"

4845 Rock Spring Rd.
Arlington, VA 22207
Tel: (703)241-7977
Fax: (703)241-1035
Registered: LDA

Employers
Bettie McCarthy and Associates (President)

Clients Represented

On Behalf of Bettie McCarthy and Associates
Great Lakes Composites Consortium
Navy Joining Center
Proprietary Industries Ass'n

MCCARTHY, Francis

Federal Center Plaza
500 C St. SW
Room 820
Washington, DC 20472
Tel: (202)646-4500
Fax: (202)646-2531

Employers
Federal Emergency Management Agency (Acting Deputy Director, Office of Congressional and Legislative Affairs)

MCCARTHY, George D.

1730 M St. NW
Suite 911
Washington, DC 20036
Tel: (202)293-4762
Fax: (202)659-5760
Registered: LDA

Employers
Kimmitt, Coates & McCarthy (Secretary/Treasurer)

Clients Represented

On Behalf of Kimmitt, Coates & McCarthy
MSE, Inc.

MCCARTHY, James

801 Pennsylvania Ave. NW
Suite 720
Washington, DC 20004-2604
Tel: (202)393-3400
Fax: (202)393-4606
Registered: LDA

Employers
The Procter & Gamble Company (Director, National Government Relations)

MCCARTHY, James A.

1711 King St.
Suite One
Alexandria, VA 22314
Tel: (703)836-4500
Fax: (703)836-8262
Registered: LDA
EMail: jmccarthy@sfa.org

Employers
Snack Food Ass'n (President and Chief Exec. Officer)

MCCARTHY, Justin J.

325 Seventh St. NW
Suite 1200
Washington, DC 20004-1007
Tel: (202)783-7070
Fax: (202)347-2044
Registered: LDA

Employers
Pfizer, Inc. (Assistant Director, Government Relations)

MCCARTHY, Kevin

600 Pennsylvania Ave. SE
Suite 302
Washington, DC 20003
Tel: (202)608-1417
Fax: (202)608-1430

Employers
Young Republican Nat'l Federation, Inc. (Chairman)

MCCARTY, Kevin

1620 I St. NW
Suite 400
Washington, DC 20006
Tel: (202)293-7330
Fax: (202)293-2352

Employers
United States Conference of Mayors (Assistant Exec. Director)

MCCARTY, Michael N.

1025 Thomas Jefferson St. NW
Eighth Floor, West Tower
Washington, DC 20007
Tel: (202)342-0800
Fax: (202)342-0807
Registered: LDA
EMail: mmccarty@bbrslaw.com
Law Clerk to Judge Stanley S. Harris, U.S. Court of Appeals for the District of Columbia, 1979-80.

Employers
Brickfield, Burchette, Ritts & Stone (Partner)

Clients Represented

On Behalf of Brickfield, Burchette, Ritts & Stone
American Medical Technologists
Arizona Power Authority
Arvin-Edison Water Storage District
Colorado River Water Conservation District
Merced Irrigation District

MCCARTY, Philip A.

600 13th St. NW
Washington, DC 20005-3096
Tel: (202)756-8311
Fax: (202)756-8087
EMail: pmccarty@mwe.com
Former Associate Counsel, Office of Tax Policy, Department of the Treasury.

Employers
McDermott, Will and Emery (Partner)

MCCARTY, Ph.D., Richard

750 First St. NE
Washington, DC 20002-4242
Tel: (202)336-5500
Fax: (202)336-6069

Employers
American Psychological Ass'n (Exec. Director, Science Directorate)

MCCAUGHEY, Michelle

1201 15th St. NW
Third Floor
Washington, DC 20005
Tel: (202)857-4722
Fax: (202)857-4799
EMail: mmccaughey@ipaa.org

Employers
Independent Petroleum Ass'n of America (V. President, Communications)

MCCLANAHAN, Patricia

1401 I St. NW
Suite 1000
Washington, DC 20005
Tel: (202)296-9410
Fax: (202)296-9775
Registered: LDA
EMail: pmcclanahan@sia.com

Employers
Securities Industry Ass'n (V. President, Director of Tax Policy)

MCCLEAN, Scott D.

1301 K St. NW
Suite 900
East Tower
Washington, DC 20005
Tel: (202)408-8007
Fax: (202)408-8704
EMail: mcclean@thecartergroup-dc.com
Served as Major, Department of the Air Force Reserve, and Legislative Liaison, and Officer (1986-98), Department of the Air Force, Department of Defense.

Employers
The Carter Group
Lockheed Martin Corp. (Director, Aeronautics Legislative Affairs)

Clients Represented

On Behalf of The Carter Group
Airborne Tactical Advantage Co.
Military Order of the Purple Heart of the U.S.A.
Specialized Technical Services, Inc.
Vortex, Inc.

MCCLELLAN, Jr., Donald W.

707 D St. NW
Washington, DC 20004
Tel: (202)737-2000
Fax: (202)737-2688
Registered: LDA
EMail: donald.mcclellan@gateway.com

Employers
Gateway, Inc. (V. President, Government Relations)

MCCLELLAND, John

122 C St. NW
Suite 510
Washington, DC 20001
Tel: (202)628-7001
Fax: (202)628-1933
Registered: LDA
EMail: mcclelland@dc.ncga.com

Employers
Nat'l Corn Growers Ass'n (Director, Energy and Analysis)

MCCLENDON, Carol

409 Third St. SW
Second Floor
Washington, DC 20024

Tel: (202)479-1200
Fax: (202)479-0735

Employers

Health Promotion Institute
Nat'l Coalition on Rural Aging
Nat'l Council on the Aging (Staff Liaison)
Nat'l Institute on Community-Based Long-Term Care

MCCLENNY, Tricia

10201 Lee Hwy.
Suite 500
Fairfax, VA 22030

Tel: (703)691-1805
Fax: (703)691-1855

Employers

Soc. of Cardiovascular and Interventional Radiology (Assistant Exec. Director)

MCCLESKEY, James S.

444 N. Capitol St. NW
Suite 332
Washington, DC 20001
Staff, U.S. Senate, 1986-87.

Tel: (202)624-5830
Fax: (202)624-5836

Employers

North Carolina, Washington Office of the State of (Director, Washington Office)

MCCLINTOCK, Janis K.

1455 Pennsylvania Ave. NW
Suite 1200
Washington, DC 20004

Tel: (202)347-2230
Fax: (202)393-3310
Registered: LDA

Employers

Davis & Harman LLP (Legislative Coordinator)

Clients Represented

On Behalf of Davis & Harman LLP

Stock Co. Information Group

MCCLINTOCK, Luckie L.

901 Massachusetts Ave. NW
Washington, DC 20001

Tel: (202)628-5823
Fax: (202)628-5024
Registered: LDA

Employers

United Ass'n of Journeymen and Apprentices of the Plumbing and Pipe Fitting Industry of the U.S. and Canada (Director, Political and Legislative Affairs)

MCCLOSKEY, Amanda

1334 G St. NW
Suite 300
Washington, DC 20005-3169

Tel: (202)628-3030
Fax: (202)347-2417

Employers

Families U.S.A. Foundation (Director, Health Policy Analysis)

MCCLOSKEY, Colleen A.

1300 I St. NW
Suite 400 West
Washington, DC 20005

Tel: (202)515-2407
Fax: (202)336-7914

Employers

Verizon Communications (Senior V. President, Regulatory Planning)

MCCLOSKEY, Maureen A.

801 18th St. NW
Washington, DC 20006

Tel: (202)872-1300
Fax: (202)785-4452
Registered: LDA

Employers

Paralyzed Veterans of America (National Advocacy Director)

MCCLOSKEY, William J.

1133 21st St. NW
Suite 900
Washington, DC 20036
EMail: bill.mccloskey@bellsouth.com

Tel: (202)463-4100
Fax: (202)463-4612

Employers

BellSouth Corp. (Director, Media Relations)

MCCLOUD, David K.

1600 Wilson Blvd.
Suite 205
Arlington, VA 22209
Former Chief of Staff to Senator Charles Robb (D-VA).

Tel: (703)358-8600
Fax: (703)358-8885

Employers

The State Affairs Co. (Managing Partner)

MCCLOUD, Margaret M.

1225 I St. NW
Suite 350
Washington, DC 20005
EMail: mmcloud@dmggroup.com
Staff Assistant to Senator Byron Dorgan (D-ND), 1993; Staff Assistant to Rep. Thomas J. Downey (D-NY), 1991-92.

Tel: (202)789-1110
Fax: (202)789-1116
Registered: LDA

Employers

Downey McGrath Group, Inc. (Director)

Clients Represented

On Behalf of Downey McGrath Group, Inc.

Fuji Photo Film U.S.A., Inc.

MCCLOUD, Patrick

1600 Wilson Blvd.
Suite 205
Arlington, VA 22209

Tel: (703)358-8600
Fax: (703)358-8885

Employers

The State Affairs Co. (Associate)

MCCLOUD, Thomas H.

1301 Pennsylvania Ave. NW
Suite 800
Washington, DC 20004
EMail: mccloud@pti.nw.dc.us

Tel: (202)626-2400
Fax: (202)626-2498

Employers

Public Technology Inc. (Chief Operating Officer)

MCCLUER, Jess P.

1600 Wilson Blvd.
Suite 1000
Arlington, VA 22209
EMail: jmccluer@vesselalliance.com

Tel: (703)351-6734
Fax: (703)351-6736
Registered: LDA

Employers

Shipbuilders Council of America (Manager, Government and Administrative Affairs)

MCCLURE, Donovan

1920 L St. NW
Washington, DC 20036
EMail: dmcclure@kamber.com

Tel: (202)223-8700
Fax: (202)659-5559

Employers

The Kamber Group (Senior V. President)

Clients Represented

On Behalf of The Kamber Group

Communications Workers of America

MCCLURE, Frederick D.

1666 K St. NW
Suite 1200
Washington, DC 20005

Tel: (202)833-9200
Fax: (202)293-5939

Employers

Winstead, Sechrest & Minick, P.C. (Shareholder)

MCCLURE, Hon. James A.

201 Maryland Ave. NE
Washington, DC 20002
Member, U.S. Senate (R-ID), 1973-90. Member, U.S. House of Representatives (R-ID), 1967-72.

Tel: (202)543-7200
Fax: (202)543-0616
Registered: LDA

Employers

McClure, Gerard & Neuenschwander, Inc. (Principal)
Nat'l Endangered Species Act Reform Coalition (Chairman)

Clients Represented

On Behalf of McClure, Gerard & Neuenschwander, Inc.

American Gaming Ass'n
Barrick Goldstrike Mines, Inc.
Boise State University
Brush Wellman, Inc.
Coachella Valley Water District
Echo Bay Mining
Family Farm Alliance (Project Transfer Council)
Harquehala Irrigation District
Hecla Mining Co.
Helli USA Airways
Henderson, Nevada, City of
Howard Hughes Corp.
Idaho Power Co.
Independence Mining Co., Inc.
Internat'l Bottled Water Ass'n
Nat'l Endangered Species Act Reform Coalition
Native American Mohegans Inc.
Nevada Test Site Development Corp.
Newmont Mining Corp.
Pershing Co. Water Conservation District of Nevada
Placer Dome U.S. Inc.
Private Fuels Storage, L.L.C.
Quest Nevada, Inc.
Space Imaging, Inc.
Stirling Energy Systems
Verizon Wireless
Wellton-Mohawk Irrigation and Drainage District
Westlands Water District
The Williams Companies

MCCLURE, Kent D.

1325 G St. NW
Suite 700
Washington, DC 20005
EMail: kmcclure@ahi.org

Tel: (202)637-2440
Fax: (202)393-1667

Employers

Animal Health Institute (General Counsel)

MCCLURE, Sharon

1400 Independence Ave. SW
Room 5065 South
Washington, DC 20250

Tel: (202)720-6829
Fax: (202)720-8097

Employers

Department of Agriculture - Foreign Agricultural Service (Acting Director, Legislative Affairs Staff)

MCCLURE, William P.

601 13th St. NW
Suite 600 South
Washington, DC 20005
EMail: mccluwi@washdc.whitecase.com

Tel: (202)626-3600
Fax: (202)639-9355
Registered: LDA

Employers

White & Case LLP (Partner)

Clients Represented

On Behalf of White & Case LLP

The Coca-Cola Company
Koniag, Inc.
Motion Picture Ass'n of America
Perpetual Corp.

MCCLYMONT, Mary

1717 Massachusetts Ave. NW
Suite 701
Washington, DC 20036

Tel: (202)667-8227
Fax: (202)667-8236

Employers

InterAction (President and Chief Exec. Officer)

MCCOLL, William D.

4455 Connecticut Ave. NW
Suite B500
Washington, DC 20008-2328

Tel: (202)537-5005
Fax: (202)537-3007
Registered: LDA

Employers

Lindesmith Center- Drug Policy Foundation (Director, Legislative Affairs)

MCCOMBS, Julie

4301 N. Fairfax Dr.
Suite 425
Arlington, VA 22203

Tel: (703)524-8800
Fax: (703)528-3816

Employers

Air-Conditioning and Refrigeration Institute (Director, International Trade)

MCCONAGHY, Mark

1301 K St. NW
Washington, DC 20005-3333
Tel: (202)414-1000
Fax: (202)414-1301
Registered: LDA
EMail: mark.mcconaghy@us.pwcglobal.com
Former Chief of Staff, Joint Committee on Taxation, U.S. Congress.

Employers
PriceWaterhouseCoopers (Partner, Washington National Tax Service)

Clients Represented
On Behalf of PriceWaterhouseCoopers
Automobile Manufacturers R&D Coalition

MCCONAHY, Marc

915 15th St. NW
Suite 600
Washington, DC 20005-2302
Tel: (202)393-8444
Ext: 106
Fax: (202)393-8666
EMail: mmcconahy@dorfmanoneal.com
Served in the U.S. Navy, 1976-98. Former Deputy Director, Direct Delivery Fuels, Defense Energy Support Center and former Staff member to the Assistant Secretary of the Navy-Installations and Environment, U.S. Navy.

Employers
Dorfman & O'Neal, Inc. (V. President)

Clients Represented
On Behalf of Dorfman & O'Neal, Inc.
American Honda Motor Co., Inc.
FuelMaker Corp.

MCCONIHE, Michael H.

888 17th St. NW
Suite 1000
Washington, DC 20006
Tel: (202)298-6161
Fax: (202)293-1640
EMail: MMcConihe@aol.com
Assistant Director, Division of Enforcement, Securities and Exchange Commission, 1974-77.

Employers
O'Brien, Butler, McConihe & Schaefer (Senior Partner)

Clients Represented
On Behalf of O'Brien, Butler, McConihe & Schaefer
American Pharmaceutical Ass'n

MCCONKEY, Matthew J.

1050 Connecticut Ave. NW
Washington, DC 20036-5339
Tel: (202)857-6000
Fax: (202)857-6395

Employers
Arent Fox Kintner Plotkin & Kahn, PLLC (Associate)

Clients Represented
On Behalf of Arent Fox Kintner Plotkin & Kahn, PLLC
Motor and Equipment Manufacturers Ass'n

MCCONKEY PELTIER, Layna

1100 New York Ave. NW
Suite 200M
Washington, DC 20005
Tel: (202)367-0440
Fax: (202)367-0470
Registered: LDA
EMail: layna@caphg.com
Legislative Assistant to Rep. Jim Lightfoot (R-IA), 1991-95.

Employers
Capitol Health Group, LLC (Principal)

Clients Represented
On Behalf of Capitol Health Group, LLC
Abbott Laboratories
Beverly Enterprises
Bristol-Myers Squibb Co.
Express Scripts Inc.
Greater New York Hospital Ass'n
Healthcare Leadership Council
Humana Inc.
Johnson & Johnson, Inc.
Medassets.com
Nat'l Ass'n of Psychiatric Health Systems
Northwestern Memorial Hospital
Pfizer, Inc.
Soc. of Thoracic Surgeons

MCCONNAUGHEY, Robert S.

1001 Pennsylvania Ave. NW
Washington, DC 20004-2599
Tel: (202)624-2000
Fax: (202)624-2319

Employers
American Council of Life Insurers (Senior Counsel)

MCCONNELL, James F.

1130 Connecticut Ave. NW
Suite 300
Washington, DC 20036
Tel: (202)331-8500
Fax: (202)331-1598
Registered: LDA
EMail: jmcconnell@tfgnet.com

Employers
Self-employed as an independent consultant.
McConnell/Ferguson Group (Partner)

Clients Represented
As an independent consultant
Orange County Transportation Authority
Orange County Water District
Orange, California, County of
Santa Ana River Flood Protection Agency
On Behalf of McConnell/Ferguson Group
Transportation Corridor Agencies

MCCONNELL, Mark S.

555 13th St. NW
Washington, DC 20004-1109
Tel: (202)637-5796
Fax: (202)637-5910
Registered: LDA, FARA
EMail: msmcconnell@hhlaw.com
Presidential Transition Team, Office of the President Elect, 1980-81.

Employers
Hogan & Hartson L.L.P. (Partner)

Clients Represented
On Behalf of Hogan & Hartson L.L.P.
Algoma Steel, Inc.
Foodmaker Internat'l Franchising Inc.
General Motors Corp.
Nat'l Foreign Trade Council, Inc.
News Corporation Ltd.
Payless Shoe Source

MCCONNELL, Robert A.

1155 Connecticut Ave. NW
Suite 420
Washington, DC 20036
Tel: (202)467-8018
Fax: (202)467-2766
Registered: LDA
EMail: robert.mcconnell@hyi-usa.com
Assistant Attorney General, Office of Legislative and Intergovernmental Affairs, Department of Justice, 1981-84.

Employers
Law Office of Robert A. McConnell

Clients Represented
On Behalf of Law Office of Robert A. McConnell
Civil Justice Reform Group

MCCONNELL, Sally N.

1615 Duke St.
Alexandria, VA 22314-3483
Tel: (703)684-3345
Fax: (703)548-6021
Registered: LDA

Employers
Nat'l Ass'n of Elementary School Principals (Director, Government Relations)

MCCONNELL, Stephen R.

1319 F St. NW
Suite 710
Washington, DC 20004
Tel: (202)393-7737
Fax: (202)393-2109
Staff Director, Senate Special Committee on Aging, 1984-87.

Employers
Alzheimer's Ass'n (V. President, Public Policy)

MCCOOL, Jr., James M.

1130 Connecticut Ave. NW
Suite 830
Washington, DC 20036
Tel: (202)261-5000
Fax: (202)296-7937
Registered: LDA

Employers
Southern Co. (Director, Federal Legislative Affairs)

MCCORD, Rob

444 N. Capitol St. NW
Suite 601B
Washington, DC 20001
Tel: (202)347-9001
Fax: (202)347-9004

Employers
Congressional Institute for the Future (Senior Fellow)

MCCORMACK, Douglas

1050 Connecticut Ave. NW
Washington, DC 20036-5339
Tel: (202)857-6000
Fax: (202)857-6395
Registered: LDA

Employers
Arent Fox Kintner Plotkin & Kahn, PLLC (Associate)

Clients Represented
On Behalf of Arent Fox Kintner Plotkin & Kahn, PLLC
American Academy of Orthotists and Prosthetists
American Ass'n of Occupational Health Nurses
Amputee Coalition
Arthritis Foundation
Bassett Healthcare
Bergen Community College
Biomedical Research Institute
Dartmouth-Hitchcock Medical Center
Datahr Rehabilitation Institute
Diamond Manufacturing, Inc.
Education and Training Resources
Epilepsy Foundation of America
Exeter Architectural Products
Fresno Community Hospital and Medical Center
Fresno Metropolitan Museum
George Washington University Medical Center
Global Associates
Inoveon Corp.
Iowa Department of Public Health
Johns Hopkins University Hospital, School of Hygiene and Public Health
Lakeland Regional Medical Center
Landmine Survivors
Magnitude Information Systems
Medix Pharmaceuticals
Mercy Hospital of Des Moines, Iowa
Middlesex Hospital Home Care
Ovarian Cancer Nat'l Alliance
Phoenix Cardiovascular, Inc.
Prevent Blindness America
Priority Care
Christopher Reeve Paralysis Foundation
Research 2 Prevention
Sabolich Research & Development
State University of New York (SUNY)
TECHHEALTH.COM
University of Medicine and Dentistry of New Jersey - School of Health Related Professionals

MCCORMALLY, Timothy J.

1200 G St. NW
Suite 300
Washington, DC 20005
Tel: (202)638-5601
Fax: (202)638-5607
EMail: tmccormally@tei.org

Employers
Tax Executives Institute, Inc. (General Counsel and Director, Tax Affairs)

MCCORMICK, John L.

110 Maryland Ave. NE
Suite 408
Washington, DC 20002
Tel: (202)544-6210
Fax: (202)544-7164

Employers
Citizens Coal Council (Communications Coordinator)

MCCORMICK, Kelley

700 13th St. NW
Suite 1000
Washington, DC 20005
Tel: (202)347-6633
Fax: (202)347-8713

Employers
Powell Tate (Group V. President)

MCCORMICK, Matthew H.

2175 K St. NW
Suite 350
Washington, DC 20037-1845
Tel: (202)659-5700
Fax: (202)659-5711

Employers
Reddy, Begley, & McCormick, LLP (Partner)

Clients Represented
On Behalf of Reddy, Begley, & McCormick, LLP
Memphis Public Library and Information Center
Midwest Broadcasting Corp.

MCCORMICK, III, Patrick J.

1275 Pennsylvania Ave. NW
Tenth Floor
Washington, DC 20004
Tel: (202)347-6000
Fax: (202)347-6001
Registered: LDA

Former General Counsel to the Majority Whip, U.S. Senate; Chief Investigative Counsel, Committee on Government Reform and Oversight, U.S. House of Representatives; and Assistant U.S. Attorney for the District of Columbia, Department of Justice.

Employers
Balch & Bingham LLP (Partner)

Clients Represented
On Behalf of Balch & Bingham LLP
FirstEnergy Co.
informal coalition
Potomac Electric Power Co.
SCANA Corp.
Southern Co.
TVA Watch

MCCORMICK, Ruth

723 Upland Place
Alexandria, VA 22314
Tel: (703)549-1466
Fax: (703)549-1574
Registered: LDA

Employers
Self-employed as an independent consultant.

MCCORMICK, Steven J.

4245 N. Fairfax Dr.
Suite 100
Arlington, VA 20003-1606
Tel: (703)841-5300
Fax: (703)841-8796

Employers
The Nature Conservancy (President)

MCCORMICK, Thomas C.

2000 Pennsylvania Ave. NW
Suite 5500
Washington, DC 20006
EMail: tmccormick@mofo.com
Tel: (202)887-1500
Fax: (202)887-0763
Registered: LDA

Employers
Morrison & Foerster LLP (Associate)

Clients Represented
On Behalf of Morrison & Foerster LLP
VISA U.S.A., Inc.

MCCORMICK, Jr., Walter B.

2200 Mill Rd.
Alexandria, VA 22314
Tel: (703)838-1866
Fax: (703)838-5751
Registered: LDA

Employers
American Trucking Ass'ns (President and Chief Exec. Officer)

MCCOY, Garland T.

1301 K St. NW
Suite 550E
Washington, DC 20005
EMail: gmccoy@pff.org
Tel: (202)289-8928
Fax: (202)289-6079

Employers
The Progress Freedom Foundation (V. President, Development)

MCCOY, Michael

1767 Business Center Dr.
Suite 302
Reston, VA 20190
EMail: michael@toxicology.org
Tel: (703)438-3115
Fax: (703)438-3113

Employers
Ass'n Innovation and Management, Inc. (Director of Public Affairs)
Soc. of Toxicology (Director, Public Affairs)

MCCOY, USA (Ret.), Maj. Gen. Ray

11 Canal Center Plaza
Suite 103
Alexandria, VA 22314
Tel: (703)683-4222
Fax: (703)683-0645
Registered: LDA

Employers
The Spectrum Group

Clients Represented
On Behalf of The Spectrum Group
The Refinishing Touch

MCCOY, Tidal W.

1735 Jefferson Davis Hwy.
Suite 1001
Arlington, VA 22202-3461
Tel: (703)413-6300
Fax: (703)413-6316

Employers
Thiokol Propulsion (V. President, Government Relations)

MCCOY, Tim

1100 17th St.
Suite 1100
Washington, DC 20036
EMail: tmccou@africacncl.org
Tel: (202)835-1115
Fax: (202)835-1117

Employers
Corporate Council on Africa (Director, Communications)

MCCOY, Ty

2800 Shirlington Rd.
Suite 405
Arlington, VA 22206
Tel: (703)671-4116
Fax: (703)931-6432

Employers
Space Transportation Ass'n (Chairman)

MCCRACKEN, Todd

1156 15th St. NW
Suite 1100
Washington, DC 20005
EMail: tmccracken@nsbu.org
Tel: (202)293-8830
Fax: (202)872-8543
Registered: LDA

Employers
Nat'l Small Business United (President)

MCCRUDDEN, III, Charles J.

4301 N. Fairfax Dr.
Suite 360
Arlington, VA 22203-1627
Tel: (703)358-9300
Fax: (703)358-9307
Registered: LDA

Employers
Nat'l Utility Contractors Ass'n (NUCA) (Government Relations Representative)

MCCRUM, R. Timothy

1001 Pennsylvania Ave. NW
Suite 1100
Washington, DC 20004-2595
Tel: (202)624-2500
Fax: (202)628-5116
Registered: LDA

Attorney-Advisor, Office of the Solicitor, Department of the Interior, 1984-86.

Employers
Crowell & Moring LLP (Partner)

Clients Represented
On Behalf of Crowell & Moring LLP
Cyprus Amex Minerals Co.
Franco-Nevada Mining Corp., Inc.
Homestake Mining
Independence Mining Co., Inc.
Placer Dome U.S. Inc.

MCCULLOCH, Ned

1301 K St. NW
Suite 1200-West Tower
Washington, DC 20005-3307
EMail: nmcculloch@us.ibm.com
Tel: (202)515-4019

Employers
Internat'l Business Machines Corp. (Program Manager, Public Affairs)

MCCURDY, Dave

2500 Wilson Blvd.
Arlington, VA 22201-3834
EMail: dmccurdy@eia.org
Tel: (703)907-7508
Fax: (703)907-7501

Employers
Electronic Industries Alliance (President)

MCCURDY, Debra A.

1301 K St. NW
Suite 1100-East Tower
Washington, DC 20005
Tel: (202)414-9200
Fax: (202)414-9299

Former Legislative Assistant to Rep. Jim Courter (R-NJ); Deputy Legislative Director to Rep. Toby Roth (R-WI); and Minority Staff Director, Subcommittee on Housing and Consumer Interests, House Select Committee on Aging.

Employers
Reed, Smith, LLP (Health Policy Analyst)

MCCURDY, G. Lincoln

915 15th St. NW
7th Floor
Washington, DC 20005
Tel: (202)783-0483
Fax: (202)783-0511

Employers
American-Turkish Council (President)

MCCURRY, Mike

633 Pennsylvania Ave. NW
Fourth Floor
Washington, DC 20004
EMail: mmccurry@psw-inc.com
Tel: (202)783-2596
Fax: (202)628-5379

Former Press Secretary, Exec. Office of the President, The White House, during the Clinton Administration.

Employers
Grassroots Enterprise, Inc. (Chairman and Chief Exec. Officer)
Public Strategies Washington, Inc. (President)

MCCUTCHEN, Woodrow

8990 Burke Lake Rd.
Burke, VA 22015
EMail: woody@asbdc_us.org
Tel: (703)764-8950
Fax: (703)764-1234

Employers
Ass'n of Small Business Development Centers (President/Chief Exec. Officer)

MCDADE, Hon. Joseph M.

106 North Carolina Ave. SE
Washington, DC 20003
Tel: (202)863-0001
Fax: (202)863-0096
Registered: LDA

Member, U.S. House of Representatives (R-PA), 1962-98.

Employers
Ervin Technical Associates, Inc. (ETA)

Clients Represented
On Behalf of Ervin Technical Associates, Inc. (ETA)
Chamberlain Manufacturing Corp.
General Dynamics Corp.
Ingalls Shipbuilding
Lockheed Martin Corp.
Northrop Grumman Corp.
Science Applications Internat'l Corp. (SAIC)
ViaTronix
Winslow Press

MCDAID, Carol A.

1420 New York Ave. NW
Washington, DC 20005
Tel: (202)638-0326
Fax: (202)737-5154
Registered: LDA

Employers
VSAdc.com

Clients Represented
On Behalf of VSAdc.com
Caron Foundation
Betty Ford Center
Hazelden Foundation
Nat'l Council on Alcoholism and Drug Dependence
Partnership for Recovery Coalition
Texas Health Resources
Torchmark Corp.
Valley Hope Ass'n
Visiting Nurse Service of New York

MCDANIEL, Corey

819 Seventh St. NW
Washington, DC 20001
Tel: (202)833-8940
Fax: (202)833-8945
Registered: LDA

Employers
EOP Group, Inc.

Clients Represented
On Behalf of EOP Group, Inc.
American Petroleum Institute
Edison Electric Institute
FMC Corp.
Nuclear Energy Institute
Zirconia Sales America

MCDANIEL, USN (Ret.), Capt. Eugene B.

1055 N. Fairfax St.
Suite 200
Alexandria, VA 22314
Tel: (703)519-7000
Fax: (703)519-8627
EMail: ebm1@americandefins.org

Employers
American Defense Institute (President)

MCDAVID, Janet L.

555 13th St. NW
Washington, DC 20004-1109
Tel: (202)637-5600
Fax: (202)637-5910

Employers
Hogan & Hartson L.L.P.

Clients Represented
On Behalf of Hogan & Hartson L.L.P.
American Express Co.

MCDERMID, John F.

818 Connecticut Ave. NW
Suite 1200
Washington, DC 20006
Tel: (202)872-8181
Fax: (202)872-8696
Registered: LDA
EMail: jmcdermid@ibgc.com
Attorney, International Trade Commission, 1974-76. Attorney, Bureau of Competitions, Federal Trade Commission, 1976-78.

Employers
Internat'l Business-Government Counsellors, Inc. (President and Chief Operating Officer)

Clients Represented
On Behalf of Internat'l Business-Government Counsellors, Inc.
ANSAC
Campbell Soup Co.
ConAgra Foods, Inc.
Herbalife Internat'l, Inc.
PepsiCo, Inc.
Polaroid Corp.
The Procter & Gamble Company

MCDERMOTT, Ann

7361 Calhoun Place
Suite 300
Rockville, MD 20855
Tel: (240)453-8500

Employers
HCR-Manor Care, Inc. (V. President, Government Relations)

MCDERMOTT, Catherine

1100 Connecticut Ave. NW
Suite 545
Washington, DC 20036
Tel: (202)331-7535
Fax: (202)331-7532

Employers
Nat'l Committee for Quality Health Care (President)

MCDERMOTT, Daniel J.

1155 Connecticut Ave. NW
Suite 500
Washington, DC 20036
Tel: (202)429-6606
Fax: (202)785-4868
Registered: LDA

Employers
Providian Financial Corp. (V. President, Government Relations)

MCDERMOTT, Francis O.

888 Sixteenth St. NW
7th Floor
Washington, DC 20006-4103
Tel: (202)835-8094
Fax: (202)835-8136

Employers
Foley & Lardner (Of Counsel)

MCDERMOTT, Marianne

1030 15th St. NW
Suite 870
Washington, DC 20005
Tel: (202)393-1780
Fax: (202)393-0336
EMail: mmcdermott@kellenco.com

Employers
Greeting Card Ass'n (Exec. V. President)
Home Infusion Therapy Franchise Owners Ass'n (Exec. Director)
The Kellen Company (V. President)
Nat'l Candle Ass'n (Exec. V. President)

Clients Represented
On Behalf of The Kellen Company
Greeting Card Ass'n
Home Infusion Therapy Franchise Owners Ass'n
Nat'l Candle Ass'n

MCDERMOTT, Patrice

1742 Connecticut Ave. NW
Washington, DC 20009-1146
Tel: (202)234-8494
Fax: (202)234-8584
EMail: patrice@capacces.org

Employers
OMB Watch (Policy Analyst)

MCDERMOTT, Robert F.

51 Louisiana Ave. NW
Washington, DC 20001
Tel: (202)879-3939
Fax: (202)626-1700
EMail: rfmcdermott@jonesday.com
Assistant U.S. Attorney for the Eastern District of Virginia, U.S. Attorney's Office (1976-79), Associate Deputy Attorney General (1975), and Staff Assistant to the Deputy Attorney General (1974-75), all at Department of Justice. Staff Assistant to the President, The White House, 1971-72.

Employers
Jones, Day, Reavis & Pogue (Partner)

MCDERMOTT, Rose

2121 R St. NW
Washington, DC 20008-1908
Tel: (202)673-5869
Fax: (202)673-5873

Employers
Northern Mariana Islands, Commonwealth of the (Federal Programs Coordinator)

MCDIARMID, Robert C.

1350 New York Ave. NW
Suite 1100
Washington, DC 20005-4798
Tel: (202)879-4000
Fax: (202)393-2866
Registered: LDA
EMail: mcdiarmr@spiegelmcd.com
Assistant to the General Counsel, Federal Power Commission, 1968-70. Attorney, Civil Division, Appellate Section, Department of Justice, 1964-68.

Employers
Spiegel & McDiarmid (Partner)

Clients Represented
On Behalf of Spiegel & McDiarmid
Northern California Power Agency
Transmission Access Policy Study Group

MCDONALD, Dale

1077 30th St. NW
Suite 100
Washington, DC 20007
Tel: (202)337-6232
Fax: (202)333-6706

Employers
Nat'l Catholic Educational Ass'n (Public Policy Research Associate)

MCDONALD, Danny Lee

1612 K St. NW
Suite 300
Washington, DC 20006
Tel: (202)857-0999
Fax: (202)857-0027

Employers
American Council of Young Political Leaders (Chairman)

MCDONALD, Gavin

1920 L St. NW
Washington, DC 20036
Tel: (202)223-8700
Fax: (202)659-5559
Registered: LDA
EMail: gmcdonald@kamber.com

Employers
The Kamber Group (V. President)

Clients Represented
On Behalf of The Kamber Group
Internat'l Union of Painters and Allied Trades
North American Communications Corp.
Retail, Wholesale and Department Store Workers Union

MCDONALD, Gregory

800 Connecticut Ave. NW
Suite 500
Washington, DC 20006
Tel: (202)331-3100
Fax: (202)331-3101
Registered: LDA
EMail: mcdonaldg@gtlaw.com
Legislative Assistant to Rep. John Oliver (D-MA).

Employers
Greenberg Traurig, LLP (Legislative Analyst)

Clients Represented
On Behalf of Greenberg Traurig, LLP
Healtheon/Web MD
Smith Development, LLC

MCDONALD, Ingrid

1313 L St. NW
Washington, DC 20005
Tel: (202)898-3200
Fax: (202)898-3304
Registered: LDA

Employers
Service Employees Internat'l Union (Senior Policy Analyst)

MCDONALD, Hon. Jack H.

901 15th St. NW
Suite 700
Washington, DC 20005-2301
Tel: (202)371-6000
Fax: (202)371-6279
Registered: LDA, FARA
Member, U.S. House of Representatives (R-MI), 1967-73.

Employers
Self-employed as an independent consultant.
Verner, Liipfert, Bernhard, McPherson and Hand, Chartered (Consultant)

Clients Represented
As an independent consultant
India, Government of the Republic of
Mexico, Government of
Thera Matrix
Verner, Liipfert, Bernhard, McPherson and Hand, Chartered

MCDONALD, Jim

50 F St. NW
Suite 500
Washington, DC 20001
Tel: (301)608-2400
Fax: (301)608-2401
Registered: LDA
EMail: jmcdonald@bread.org

Employers
Bread for the World (International Analyst)

MCDONALD, Michael K.

Commonwealth Towers
1300 Wilson Blvd., Suite 200
Arlington, VA 22209-2307
Tel: (703)516-8230
Fax: (703)516-8298
Registered: LDA
EMail: mkmcdona@collins.rockwell.com

Employers
Rockwell Collins (V. President, Government Operations (Rockwell Collins))

MCDONALD, Michael P.

1233 20th St. NW
Suite 300
Washington, DC 20036
Tel: (202)833-8400 Ext: 102
Fax: (202)833-8410
EMail: cir@mail.wdn.com

Employers
Center for Individual Rights (President)

MCDONALD, Robert

700 13th St. NW
Suite 700
Washington, DC 20005-3960
Tel: (202)508-6303
Fax: (202)508-6305
Registered: LDA
Former Chief of Staff to Senator John C. Danforth (R-MO).

Employers
Emerson (V. President, Governmental Affairs)

MCDONALD, Stephen

1317 F St. NW
Suite 500
Washington, DC 20004
Tel: (202)783-6007
Fax: (202)783-6024
EMail: stevemac@sema.org

Employers
Specialty Equipment Market Ass'n (Director, Government and Technical Affairs)

MCDONALD, USN (Ret.), Adm. Wesley

1815 N. Fort Myer Dr.
Suite 500
Arlington, VA 22209-1805
Tel: (703)527-0226
Fax: (703)527-0229
Registered: LDA

Employers
Nat'l Aeronautic Ass'n of the U.S.A. (Chairman)
The Spectrum Group

Clients Represented

On Behalf of The Spectrum Group
Titanium Metals Corp.

MCDONNELL, James A.

1501 Lee Hwy.
Arlington, VA 22209-1198
Tel: (703)247-5810
Fax: (703)247-5853
EMail: jmcdonnell@afa.org

Employers
Air Force Ass'n (Chief, Military Relations)

MCDONNELL, Richard W.

1735 New York Ave. NW
Washington, DC 20006
Tel: (202)626-7300
Fax: (202)626-7365
EMail: rmcdonnell@aia.org

Employers
The American Institute of Architects (Program Manager, PAC/Grass Roots)

MCDONOUGH, John P.

11785 Beltsville Dr.
Tenth Floor
Calverton, MD 20705
Tel: (301)572-7900
Fax: (301)572-6655
Registered: LDA

Employers
O'Malley, Miles, Nylen & Gilmore, P.A. (Senior Partner)

Clients Represented

On Behalf of O'Malley, Miles, Nylen & Gilmore, P.A.
Peterson Cos., Inc.

MCDONOUGH, Peter

1200 G St. NW
Suite 800
Washington, DC 20005
Tel: (202)434-8768
Fax: (202)434-8707

Employers
Winning Strategies Washington, D.C., LLC

MCDONOUGH, Timothy J.

One Dupont Circle NW
Suite 835
Washington, DC 20036-1193
Tel: (202)939-9365
Fax: (202)833-4762
EMail: tim_mcdonough@ace.nche.edu

Employers
American Council on Education (Director, Public Affairs)

MCDOUGALL, Gay

1200 18th St. NW
Suite 602
Washington, DC 20036
Tel: (202)822-4600
Fax: (202)822-4606
EMail: humanrights@hrlawgroup.org

Employers
The Internat'l Human Rights Law Group (Exec. Director)

MCDOWELL, Ella

2001 S St. NW
Suite 580
Washington, DC 20009
Tel: (202)232-5492
Fax: (202)387-5281
EMail: nawdlegis@aol.com

Employers
Nat'l Ass'n of WIC Directors (Legislative Assistant)

MCDOWELL, G. Kendrick

2550 M St. NW
Washington, DC 20037-1350
Tel: (202)457-6000
Fax: (202)457-6315
Registered: LDA

Employers
Patton Boggs, LLP (Partner)

MCDOWELL, Heather L.

1201 New York Ave. NW
Suite 1000
Washington, DC 20005
Tel: (202)962-4897
Fax: (202)962-8300
EMail: hlmcdowell@venable.com

Employers
Venable (Partner)

MCDOWELL, Leila

1612 K St. NW
Suite 904
Washington, DC 20006
Tel: (202)833-9771
Fax: (202)833-9770

Employers
McKinney & McDowell Associates (V. President)

MCDOWELL, Marian E.

1401 I St. NW
Suite 1100
Washington, DC 20005
Tel: (202)326-8861
Fax: (202)408-8717
Registered: LDA

Employers
SBC Communications Inc. (Director, Federal Relations)

MCDOWELL, Robert

1900 M St. NW
Suite 800
Washington, DC 20036-3508
Tel: (202)296-6650
Fax: (202)296-7585
Registered: LDA
EMail: rmcdowell@comptel.org

Employers
Competitive Telecommunications Ass'n (COMPTEL) (V. President and Assistant General Counsel)

MCELLIGOTT, Tom

1120 Connecticut Ave. NW
Washington, DC 20036
Tel: (202)663-5000
Fax: (202)663-5212
Registered: LDA

Employers
American Bankers Ass'n (Program Manager, Washington Information)

MCELROY, Deborah C.

2025 M St. NW
Suite 800
Washington, DC 20036
Tel: (202)367-2100
Fax: (202)367-1200
Registered: LDA
EMail: deborah_mcelroy@dc.sba.com

Employers
Smith, Bucklin and Associates, Inc.

Clients Represented

On Behalf of Smith, Bucklin and Associates, Inc.
Regional Airline Ass'n

MCELROY, Edward

555 New Jersey Ave. NW
Washington, DC 20001
Tel: (202)879-4415
Fax: (202)393-7479

Employers
American Federation of Teachers (Secretary/Treasurer)

MCELROY, Sally

440 First St. NW
Eighth Floor
Washington, DC 20001
Tel: (202)942-4230
Fax: (202)393-2630
EMail: smcelroy@naco.org

Employers
Nat'l Ass'n of Counties (Associate Legislative Director, Health)

MCELVANEY, Jason

1156 15th St. NW
Suite 502
Washington, DC 20005-1799
Tel: (202)862-4818
Fax: (202)862-4829
Registered: LDA
EMail: jsmcelva@jcpenney.com

Employers
J. C. Penney Co., Inc. (Federal Government Relations Representative)

MCELWAIN, Mike

320 First St. SE
Washington, DC 20003
Tel: (202)479-7000
Fax: (202)863-0693

Employers
Nat'l Republican Congressional Committee (Political Director)

MCELWEE, George S.

919 18th St. NW
Suite 300
Washington, DC 20006
Tel: (202)296-5544
Fax: (202)223-0321

Employers
American Financial Services Ass'n (Manager, AFSAPAC & Gov't. Support)

MCENTEE, Christine

9111 Old Georgetown Rd.
Bethesda, MD 20814
Tel: (301)897-5400
Fax: (301)897-9745
EMail: cmcentee@acc.org

Employers
American College of Cardiology (Exec. V. President)

MCENTEE, Elliott C.

13665 Dulles Technology Dr.
Suite 300
Herndon, VA 20171
Tel: (703)561-1100
Fax: (703)787-0996

Employers
NACHA - The Electronic Payments Ass'n (President and Chief Exec. Officer)

MCENTEE, Gerald W.

1625 L St. NW
Washington, DC 20036
Tel: (202)429-1100
Fax: (202)429-1102

Employers
American Federation of State, County and Municipal Employees (Internat'l President)

MCENTEE, Joan M.

801 Pennsylvania Ave. NW
Suite 800
Washington, DC 20004
Tel: (202)508-3400
Fax: (202)508-3402
Registered: LDA
EMail: jmcentee@bdbc.com

Undersecretary for Export Administration (1989-93), Deputy Undersecretary for International Trade (1988-89), and Deputy Assistant Secretary for Trade Development (1986-88), all at the Department of Commerce. Deputy to the Chief of Staff to the Vice President, The White House, 1985-86. Staff Director and Chief Counsel, Senate Government Affairs Committee, 1981-85. Minority Staff Director, Subcommittee on Intergovernmental Relations, Senate Government Affairs Committee, 1978-81. Consultant, Consumer Product Safety Commission, 1977-78. Special Assistant to the Associate Director, Office of Management and Budget, The White House, 1975-77. Special Assistant to the Under Secretary (1974-75) and Assistant for Legislative Affairs (1971-73), both at the Department of Housing and Urban Development. Legislative Research Assistant to Senator Charles E. Goodell (R-NY), 1969-71.

Employers
Baker, Donelson, Bearman & Caldwell, P.C. (Shareholder)

Clients Represented

On Behalf of Baker, Donelson, Bearman & Caldwell, P.C.
American Standard Cos. Inc.
IMAX Corp.
Lincoln Nat'l Corp.
Motorola, Inc.
Phillips Petroleum Co.

MCEVOY, John T.

444 N. Capitol St. NW
Suite 438
Washington, DC 20001
Tel: (202)624-7710
Fax: (202)624-5899

Employers
Nat'l Council of State Housing Agencies (Exec. Director)

MCEWEN, Jr., Dr. Gerald N.

1101 17th St. NW
Suite 300
Washington, DC 20036
Tel: (202)331-1770
Fax: (202)331-1969

Employers
Cosmetic, Toiletry and Fragrance Ass'n (V. President, Science)

MCEWEN, Hon. Robert D.

1332 Independence Ave. SE
Washington, DC 20003-2365
Tel: (202)543-4600
Registered: LDA

Member, U.S. House of Representatives (R-OH), 1981-93.

Employers
Advantage Associates, Inc. (Partner)
Morgan Casner Associates, Inc. (Senior Associate)

Clients Represented
On Behalf of Advantage Associates, Inc.
Uniformed Services Dental Alliance

MCFADDEN, II, W. Clark

1775 Pennsylvania Ave. NW
Suite 200
Washington, DC 20006
Tel: (202)429-2533
Fax: (202)862-1093
Registered: LDA

President's Special Review Board (The Tower Commission), 1986-87. Special Counsel, Senate Committee on Foreign Relations, 1979. General Counsel, Senate Armed Services Committee, 1974-77.

Employers
Dewey Ballantine LLP (Partner)

Clients Represented
On Behalf of Dewey Ballantine LLP
CAMECO Corp.
SEMATECH, Inc.
Semiconductor Industry Ass'n

MCFARLAND, Jane J.

1730 M St. NW
Suite 300
Washington, DC 20036-4505
EMail: jmcfarland@osc.gov
Tel: (202)653-5163
Fax: (202)653-5161

Former Professional Staff Member, Senate Committee on Governmental Affairs and Senate Special Committee on Aging. Also served as an aide to Senator Robert C. Byrd (D-WV).

Employers
United States Office of Special Counsel (Director, Office of Legislative and Public Affairs)

MCFARLAND, Jeff

2025 M St. NW
Suite 800
Washington, DC 20036
EMail: jeff_mcfarland@dc.sba.com
Tel: (202)367-2100
Fax: (202)367-1200

Employers
Smith, Bucklin and Associates, Inc.

Clients Represented
On Behalf of Smith, Bucklin and Associates, Inc.
Soc. of Research Administrators

MCFARLANE, Carolyn Z.

250 E St. SW
MS: 9-18
Washington, DC 20219
Tel: (202)874-4840
Fax: (202)874-5305

Employers
Department of Treasury - Comptroller of the Currency (Director, Congressional Liaison)

MCGAHN, II, Donald F.

2550 M St. NW
Washington, DC 20037-1350
Tel: (202)457-6000
Fax: (202)457-6315
Registered: LDA
EMail: dmcgahn@pattonboggs.com

Employers
Patton Boggs, LLP (Associate)

Clients Represented
On Behalf of Patton Boggs, LLP
MCI WorldCom Corp.

MCGANN, James P.

1120 20th St. NW
Suite 1000
Washington, DC 20036
EMail: jpmcgann@att.com
Tel: (202)457-3942
Fax: (202)457-7490

Employers
AT&T (Director, Media Relations)

MCGARRY, III, J. Michael

1400 L St. NW
Washington, DC 20005-3502
EMail: jmcgarry@winston.com
Tel: (202)371-5733
Fax: (202)371-5950

Assistant U.S. Attorney, Department of Justice, 1970-73. Law Clerk to Judge Matthew F. McGuire, U.S. District Court for the District of Columbia, 1969-70.

Employers
Winston & Strawn (Managing Partner, Washington Office (Energy))

MCGEARY, Elizabeth A.

1200 New Hampshire Ave. NW
Suite 800
Washington, DC 20036-6802
EMail: emcgeary@dlalaw.com
Tel: (202)776-2000
Fax: (202)776-2222

Employers
Dow, Lohnes & Albertson, PLLC (Member)

MCGEE, Christi C.

1919 Pennsylvania Ave. NW
Seventh Floor
Washington, DC 20006-3488
Tel: (202)557-2700
Registered: LDA

Employers
Mortgage Bankers Ass'n of America

MCGEE, James

1628 11th St. NW
Washington, DC 20001
Tel: (202)939-6325
Fax: (202)939-6389

Employers
Nat'l Alliance of Postal and Federal Employees (President)

MCGEE, Kate

1667 K St. NW
Suite 640
Washington, DC 20006-1605
EMail: kate.mcgee@oracle.com
Tel: (202)721-4813
Fax: (202)467-4250
Registered: LDA

Employers
Oracle Corp. (V. President, Corporate Affairs)

MCGEE, Laura

801 G St. NW
Washington, DC 20001
Tel: (202)393-2100
Fax: (202)393-2134
Registered: LDA

Employers
Family Research Council, Inc.

MCGEE, Robert M.

1717 Pennsylvania Ave. NW
Suite 400
Washington, DC 20006
Tel: (202)857-3000
Fax: (202)857-3030
Registered: LDA

Employers
Occidental Internat'l Corporation (President and Chief Exec. Officer)
Occidental Petroleum Corporation (V. President)

MCGEHEE, Meredith

1250 Connecticut Ave. NW
Washington, DC 20036
Tel: (202)833-1200
Fax: (202)659-3716
Registered: LDA

Employers
Campaign Finance Reform Coalition (Contact)
Common Cause (Senior V. President)

MCGILLICUDDY, Hugh

9001 Braddock Rd.
Suite 390
Springfield, VA 22151
Tel: (703)239-1882
Fax: (703)239-1039

Employers
Hexcel Corp. (Contact, Hexel Corp. PAC)

MCGINLEY, Kathleen

1730 K St. NW
Washington, DC 20006
Tel: (202)785-3388
Fax: (202)467-4179
Registered: LDA
EMail: mcginley@thearc.org

Employers
The Arc (Director, Health and Housing Policy)

MCGINLY, Ph.D, CAE, Dr. William C.

313 Park Ave.
Suite 400
Falls Church, VA 22046
EMail: ahp@go-ahp.org
Tel: (703)532-6243
Fax: (703)532-7170

Employers
Ass'n for Healthcare Philanthropy (President and Chief Exec. Officer)

MCGINNIS, Patricia G.

1301 K St. NW
Suite 450 West
Washington, DC 20005
EMail: pmcginnis@excelgov.org
Tel: (202)728-0418
Fax: (202)728-0422

Employers
Council for Excellence in Government (President and Chief Exec. Officer)

MCGIVERN, Timothy

1401 I St. NW
Suite 1100
Washington, DC 20005
Tel: (202)326-8877
Fax: (202)408-4796

Employers
SBC Communications Inc. (Exec. Director, Federal Relations)

MCGLONE, William M.

655 15th St. NW
Suite 900
Washington, DC 20005-5701
Tel: (202)626-5800
Fax: (202)628-0858

Employers
Miller & Chevalier, Chartered

MCGLOTTEN, Robert M.

1901 L St. NW
Suite 300
Washington, DC 20036
Tel: (202)452-9515
Fax: (202)466-8016
Registered: LDA

Employers
McGlotten & Jarvis

Clients Represented
On Behalf of McGlotten & Jarvis
Computer Sciences Corp.
CSX Corp.
Edison Electric Institute
Internat'l Dairy Foods Ass'n
Internat'l Franchise Ass'n
Investment Co. Institute
Office and Professional Employees Internat'l Union
Philip Morris Management Corp.
Seafarers Internat'l Union of North America

MCGLOWAN, Angela

444 N. Capitol St. NW
Suite 740
Washington, DC 20001
Tel: (202)824-6500
Fax: (202)824-6510
Registered: LDA

Employers
News Corporation Ltd. (Director, Government Relations)

MCGOLDRICK, Jan

4245 N. Fairfax Dr.
Suite 100
Arlington, VA 20003-1606
Tel: (703)841-4229
Fax: (703)841-7400
Registered: LDA

Employers
The Nature Conservancy (Senior Policy Advisor, EPA)

MCGOVERN, Elissa M.

1750 Tysons Blvd.
12th Floor
McLean, VA 22102
EMail: mcgoverne@gtlaw.com
Tel: (703)749-1343
Fax: (703)749-1301

Employers
Greenberg Traurig, LLP (Of Counsel)

Clients Represented
On Behalf of Greenberg Traurig, LLP
BUNAC USA, Inc.

MCGOVERN, Jr., John J.

1620 L St. NW
Suite 1210
Washington, DC 20036
Tel: (202)955-6062
Fax: (202)955-6070
Registered: LDA

Employers
Higgins, McGovern & Smith, LLC (Partner)

Clients Represented

On Behalf of Higgins, McGovern & Smith, LLC
Mylan Laboratories, Inc.

MCGOVERN, Julie S.

1250 I St. NW
Suite 900
Washington, DC 20005
EMail: jmcgovern@renocavanaugh.com
Tel: (202)783-2800
Fax: (202)783-0550

Employers
Reno & Cavanaugh, PLLC (Associate)

MCGRADY, Michael

1651 Prince St.
Alexandria, VA 22314
EMail: mmcgrady@nhsa.org
Tel: (703)739-0875
Fax: (703)739-0878

Employers
Nat'l Head Start Ass'n (Deputy Director)

MCGRANE, Mary

1020 19th St. NW
Suite 550
Washington, DC 20036
EMail: mary.mcgrane@genzyme.com
Tel: (202)296-3280
Fax: (202)296-3411
Registered: LDA

Employers
Genzyme Corp. (V. President, Government Relations)

MCGRANN, Dennis

601 Pennsylvania Ave. NW
South Bldg., Suite 900
Washington, DC 20004
EMail: dmmcgrann@locklaw.com
Tel: (202)434-8163
Fax: (202)639-8238
Registered: LDA

Senior Consultant, U.S. Department of Energy, 1995; Staff Director, House Subcommittee on Civil Service, 1988-94; Staff Director, House Subcommittee on Human Resources, 1986-88; Chief of Staff, Rep. Gerry Sikorski (DFL-MN), 1983-86.

Employers
Lockridge Grindal & Nauen, P.L.L.P. (Director, Public Affairs)

Clients Represented

On Behalf of Lockridge Grindal & Nauen, P.L.L.P.
Ass'n of Minnesota Counties
Evangelical Lutheran Good Samaritan Soc.
Hennipin County Board of Commissioners
Jerome Foods
Joint Powers Board
Metropolitan Joint Powers Board
Minneapolis, Minnesota, City of
Minnesota Medical Group Management
Minnesota Transportation Alliance
Parent Centers FYI
Ramsey, Minnesota, Board of Commissioners of the County of
St. Louis, Minnesota, Board of Commissioners of the County
St. Louis/Lake Counties Regional Rail Authority
St. Paul, Minnesota, City of
Valley Pride Pack
Wakota Bridge Coalition
Washington, Minnesota, County of

MCGRARRITY, Gerard

430 S. Capitol St. SE
Second Floor
Washington, DC 20003
Tel: (202)863-1500
Fax: (202)485-3512

Employers
Democratic Congressional Campaign Committee (Director, Harriman Community Center)

MCGRATH, CAE, Charles

1444 I St. NW
Suite 700
Washington, DC 20005-2210
EMail: cmcgrath@bostromdc.com
Tel: (202)216-9623
Fax: (202)216-9646

Employers
Bostrom Corp. (V. President)

Clients Represented

On Behalf of Bostrom Corp.
Home Automation Ass'n
Interlocking Concrete Pavement Institute

MCGRATH, Dyan

1250 I St. NW
Suite 804
Washington, DC 20005
EMail: Dyan.McGrath@phwilm.zeneca.com
Tel: (202)289-2570
Fax: (202)289-2580

Employers
AstraZeneca Inc. (Senior Manager, Federal Government Affairs)

MCGRATH, Edward J.

901 15th St. NW
Suite 700
Washington, DC 20005-2301
EMail: ejmcgrath@verner.com
Tel: (202)371-6000
Fax: (202)371-6279
Registered: LDA

Employers
Verner, Liipfert, Bernhard, McPherson and Hand, Chartered (Member of Firm)

Clients Represented

On Behalf of Verner, Liipfert, Bernhard, McPherson and Hand, Chartered
Washington Group Internat'l

MCGRATH, K. Michael

701 Pennsylvania Ave. NW
Washington, DC 20004-2696
Tel: (202)508-5552
Fax: (202)508-5335
Registered: LDA

Employers
Edison Electric Institute (Group Director, Energy Supply)

MCGRATH, Matthew T.

1225 I St. NW
Suite 1150
Washington, DC 20005
EMail: mmcgrath@brc-dc.com
Tel: (202)457-0300
Fax: (202)331-8746
Registered: FARA

Employers
Barnes, Richardson and Colburn (Partner)

Clients Represented

On Behalf of Barnes, Richardson and Colburn
Agouron Pharmaceuticals, Inc.
Alcan Aluminum Corp.
American Ass'n of Exporters & Importers
American Ass'n of Fastener Importers
American Tourister, Inc.
Budd Co.
Consolidated Diesel Corp.
Durand Internat'l, J. G.
Florida Citrus Mutual
Florida Citrus Packers
Florida Citrus Processors Ass'n
Florida Farm Bureau Federation
Gulf Citrus Growers Ass'n
Indian River Citrus League
Italy-America Chamber of Commerce
Polaroid Corp.

MCGRATH, Hon. Raymond J.

1225 I St. NW
Suite 350
Washington, DC 20005
EMail: rmcgrath@dmggroup.com
Tel: (202)789-1110
Fax: (202)789-1116
Registered: LDA

Member, U.S. House of Representatives (R-NY), 1981-93.

Employers
Downey McGrath Group, Inc. (President)

Clients Represented

On Behalf of Downey McGrath Group, Inc.
American Soc. of Anesthesiologists
The Boeing Co.
Chevron, U.S.A.
Dental Recycling North America
Fantasma Networks, Inc.
Metropolitan Life Insurance Co.
Microsoft Corp.
The New York Structural Biology Center
SLM Holding Corp.
United Brotherhood of Carpenters and Joiners of America

MCGRAW, Chris

600 Pennsylvania Ave. SE
Fifth Floor
Washington, DC 20003
Tel: (202)544-0200
Fax: (202)546-7142
Registered: LDA

Employers
Amnesty Internat'l U.S.A. (Grassroots Advocacy Program Associate)

MCGRAW, Marvin A.

1200 G St. NW
Suite 822
Washington, DC 20009
Tel: (202)434-8738
Registered: LDA

Employers
Strategic Horizons Advisors, L.L.C.

Clients Represented

On Behalf of Strategic Horizons Advisors, L.L.C.
Guinea, Secretary General of the Presidency of the Republic of

MCGREEVY, Lisa

805 15th St. NW
Suite 600
Washington, DC 20005
Tel: (202)289-4322
Fax: (202)289-1903
Registered: LDA

Employers
The Financial Services Roundtable (Director, Government and Public Affairs)

MCGREGOR, Katy

1030 15th St. NW
Suite 1100
Washington, DC 20005
Tel: (202)783-4600
Fax: (202)783-4601

Communications Director, House Committee on Science, 1997-98. Congressional Affairs Officer, Office of the U.S. Trade Representative, Executive Office of the President, The White House, 1989-93. Legislative Assistant to Senator John McCain (R-AZ), 1987-89.

Employers
White House Writers Group (Senior Director)

MCGROARTY, Daniel

1030 15th St. NW
Suite 1100
Washington, DC 20005
Tel: (202)783-4600
Fax: (202)783-4601

Senior Speechwriter to Secretaries of Defense Frank C. Carlucci, III, and Caspar W. Weinberger. Special Assistant to the President for Communications, and Deputy Director of White House Speechwriting, 1989-93.

Employers
White House Writers Group (Senior Director)

MCGUINESS, Jeffrey C.

1015 15th St. NW
Suite 1200
Washington, DC 20005
Tel: (202)789-8600
Fax: (202)789-1708
Registered: LDA

Chairman, Civil Rights Reviewing Authority, Department of Health and Human Services, 1981-83. Special Counsel to Seantor Richard G. Lugar (R-IN), 1979.

Employers
Labor Policy Ass'n (LPA) (President)
McGuiness Norris & Williams, LLP (Partner)

Clients Represented

On Behalf of McGuiness Norris & Williams, LLP
Labor Policy Ass'n (LPA)

MCGUINESS, Kevin S.

400 N. Capitol St. NW
Suite 585
Washington, DC 20001
Tel: (202)783-5300
Fax: (202)393-5218
Registered: LDA

Former Chief of Staff to Senator Orrin G. Hatch (R-UT) and Republican Staff Director, Senate Committee on Labor and Human Resources.

Employers
McGuiness & Holch (Partner)

Clients Represented

On Behalf of McGuiness & Holch

Arch Mineral Corp.
Barr Laboratories
Council for Responsible Nutrition
Major League Baseball Players Ass'n
NetCoalition.Com
Project to Promote Competition and Innovation in the Digital Age
R. J. Reynolds Tobacco Co.
RJR Co.
Wine and Spirits Wholesalers of America

MCGUINESS, Martin

1150 17th St. NW
Suite 601
Washington, DC 20036
Tel: (202)293-7474
Fax: (202)293-8811
Registered: LDA

Employers

Washington Council Ernst & Young (Senior Manager)

MCGUIRE, Anne

1133 Connecticut Ave. NW
Fifth Floor
Washington, DC 20036
Tel: (202)457-1110
Fax: (202)457-1130
Registered: LDA

Employers

Quinn Gillespie & Associates (Associate)

Clients Represented

On Behalf of Quinn Gillespie & Associates

Instinet
LVMH Moet Hennessy Louis Vuitton S.A.

MCGUIRE, Mary Lee

444 N. Capitol St. NW
Suite 837
Washington, DC 20001
Tel: (202)637-9330
Fax: (202)544-5321
Registered: LDA

Employers

Self-employed as an independent consultant.

Clients Represented

As an independent consultant

Cook Inlet Region Inc.
The Metropolitan Water District of Southern California

MCGUIRE, Patricia

950 N. Washington St.
Alexandria, VA 22314-1552
Tel: (703)836-2272
Fax: (703)684-1924
Registered: LDA

Employers

American Academy of Physician Assistants (Administrator, Federal Affairs)

MCHALE, Alvina M.

Liberty Center
401 14th St. SW
MS: 555
Washington, DC 20227
EMail: alvina.mchale@fms.treas.gov
Tel: (202)874-6604
Fax: (202)874-7016

Employers

Department of Treasury - Financial Management Service (Director, Legislative and Public Affairs Office)

MCHALE, James M.

815 Connecticut Ave. NW
Suite 500
Washington, DC 20006-4004
Tel: (202)463-2400
Fax: (202)828-5393
Registered: FARA

Employers

Seyfarth, Shaw, Fairweather & Geraldson (Partner)

MCHALE, Jeanette

1615 H St. NW
Washington, DC 20062
Tel: (202)463-5500
Fax: (202)463-3129

Employers

Nat'l Chamber Foundation (Development Director)

MCHALE, Sharon

8200 Jones Branch Dr.
McLean, VA 22102
EMail: sharon_mchale@freddiemac.com
Tel: (703)903-2438
Fax: (703)903-3215

Employers

Federal Home Loan Mortgage Corp. (Freddie Mac) (Director, Public Relations)

MCHARG, Herb

122 C St. NW
Suite 240
Washington, DC 20001
Tel: (202)546-2215
Fax: (202)544-5197
Registered: LDA

Employers

Southern Utah Wilderness Alliance

MCHENRY, Paul T.

P.O. Box 206
Lothian, MD 20711
EMail: hquarter@sgaus.org
Tel: (301)261-9099
Fax: (301)261-9099

Employers

State Guard Ass'n of the U.S. (Exec. Director)

MCHUGH, Joe

60 Massachusetts Ave. NE
Washington, DC 20002
Tel: (202)906-3867
Fax: (202)906-3175

Employers

AMTRAK (Nat'l Rail Passenger Corp.) (Acting V. President, Government Affairs)

MCHUGH, Hon. Matthew F.

233 Pennsylvania Ave. SE
Suite 200
Washington, DC 20003-1107
EMail: usafmc1@mindspring.com
Tel: (202)543-8676
Fax: (202)543-7145

Member, U.S. House of Representatives (D-NY), 1975-93.

Employers

U.S. Ass'n of Former Members of Congress (Past President)

MCHUGH, Peter G.

1300 Wilson Blvd.
Suite 800
Arlington, VA 22209
Tel: (703)253-0694
Fax: (703)253-0701

Employers

American Plastics Council (Managing Counsel)

MCHUGH, Richard P.

1200 New Hampshire Ave. NW
Suite 800
Washington, DC 20036-6802
EMail: rmchugh@dlalaw.com
Tel: (202)776-2000
Fax: (202)776-2222

Employers

Dow, Lohnes & Albertson, PLLC (Member)

MCILRATH, Sharon

1101 Vermont Ave. NW
12th Floor
Washington, DC 20005-3583
Tel: (202)789-7417
Fax: (202)789-7581
Registered: LDA

Employers

American Medical Ass'n (Assistant Director, Federal Affairs)

MCILVAINE, Steve

2201 C St. NW
Room 7251
Washington, DC 20520-7261
Tel: (202)647-8722
Fax: (202)647-2762

Employers

Department of State - Bureau of Legislative Affairs (African Affairs Legislative Management Officer)

MCINESPIE, John

1301 Pennsylvania Ave. NW
Suite 500
Washington, DC 20004
EMail: jmcinespie@butera-andrews.com
Tel: (202)347-6875
Fax: (202)347-6876

Employers

Butera & Andrews (Partner)

Clients Represented

On Behalf of Butera & Andrews

British Nuclear Fuels plc

MCINTOSH, Joanna K.

1120 20th St. NW
Suite 1000
Washington, DC 20036
EMail: joannamcintosh@att.com
Tel: (202)457-3808
Fax: (202)457-2571

Employers

AT&T (V. President, International Affairs)

MCINTOSH, Lane

1776 K St. NW
Washington, DC 20006
Tel: (202)719-7000
Fax: (202)719-7049
Registered: LDA

Employers

Wiley, Rein & Fielding

Clients Represented

On Behalf of Wiley, Rein & Fielding

Verizon Wireless

MCINTOSH, Scott

555 13th St. NW
Washington, DC 20004-1109
EMail: samcintosh@hhlaw.com
Tel: (202)637-5588
Fax: (202)637-5910
Registered: LDA

Employers

Hogan & Hartson L.L.P. (Associate)

Clients Represented

On Behalf of Hogan & Hartson L.L.P.

Coste Enterprises Inc.

MCINTURFF, William D.

277 S. Washington St.
Suite 320
Alexandria, VA 22314
EMail: wdm@pos.org
Tel: (703)836-7655
Fax: (703)836-8117

Employers

Public Opinion Strategies (Managing Partner)

Clients Represented

On Behalf of Public Opinion Strategies

American Hospital Ass'n
Health Insurance Ass'n of America

MCINTYRE, Ann Marie

601 Pennsylvania Ave. NW
Suite 600
North Bldg.
Washington, DC 20004
Tel: (202)682-9110
Fax: (202)682-9111

Employers

American Electronics Ass'n (Director, Trade Regulation)

MCINTYRE, Gerald

1101 14th St. NW
Suite 400
Washington, DC 20005
Tel: (202)289-6976
Fax: (202)289-7224

Employers

Nat'l Senior Citizens Law Center (Acting Exec. Director)

MCINTYRE, James T.

1155 15th St. NW
Suite 1101
Washington, DC 20005
Tel: (202)659-3900
Fax: (202)659-5763
Registered: LDA

Director (1978-81) and Acting Director/Deputy Director (1977-78), Office of Management and Budget, The White House.

Employers

McIntyre Law Firm, PLLC (Managing Partner)

Clients Represented

On Behalf of McIntyre Law Firm, PLLC

Ass'n of Banks in Insurance
Community Financial Services Ass'n
Internat'l Ass'n for Financial Planning
MemberWorks, Inc.
Risk and Insurance Management Soc., Inc. (RIMS)

MCINTYRE, Jeff

750 First St. NE
Washington, DC 20002-4242
Tel: (202)336-6064
Fax: (202)336-6064
Registered: LDA

Employers
American Psychological Ass'n (Senior Legislative Assistant, Public Policy)

MCINTYRE, Maria

1090 Vermont Ave. NW
Suite 600
Washington, DC 20005
Tel: (202)371-0600
Fax: (202)898-7777

Employers
Home Builders Institute (Director, Job Development and Outreach)

MCINTYRE, Mark D.

1420 New York Ave. NW
Suite 550
Washington, DC 20005
Tel: (202)783-4805
Fax: (202)783-4804
Registered: LDA

Former Speechwriter for Vice President George Bush; former Press Secretary to Rep. Robert Livingtson (R-LA).

Employers
Russ Reid Co. (V. President and Director, Washington Office)

Clients Represented

On Behalf of Russ Reid Co.
Alfalit Internat'l
Boys Town Nat'l Research Hospital
Christian Herald Ass'n
Corporation for Business, Work and Learning
Detroit Rescue Mission Ministries
The Doe Fund
Dream Center/City Help
Earth University, Inc.
Fuller Theological Seminary
Gospel Rescue Ministries of Washington
Hebrew Academy for Special Children
Home Study Internat'l/Griggs University
Light of Life Ministries
New College
Touro College
Vanguard University
Village of Kiryas Joel
William Tyndale College

MCINTYRE, Marla

5225 Wisconsin Ave. NW
Suite 600
Washington, DC 20015-2014
EMail: mmcintyre@sio.org
Tel: (202)686-7463
Fax: (202)686-3656

Employers
Surety Information Office (Exec. Director)

MCINTYRE, Robert S.

1311 L St. NW
Fourth Floor
Washington, DC 20005
EMail: bmcintyr@ctj.org
Tel: (202)626-3780
Fax: (202)638-3486
Registered: LDA

Employers
Citizens for Tax Justice (Director)

MCKALIP, Douglas J.

12th and Independence Ave. SW
Room 5121, South Bldg.
Washington, DC 20250
Tel: (202)720-2771
Fax: (202)690-0854

Employers
Department of Agriculture - Natural Resources Conservation Service (Acting Director, Legislative Affairs)

MCKAY, Bruce C.

1200 18th St. NW
Suite 350
Washington, DC 20036
Tel: (202)833-3900
Fax: (202)833-3655
Registered: LDA

Employers
Dominion Resources, Inc. (Manager, Federal Policy)

MCKAY, Carol

1701 K St. NW
Suite 1200
Washington, DC 20006
Tel: (202)835-3323
Fax: (202)835-0747

Employers
Nat'l Consumers League (Assistant Director, Communications)

MCKAY, John

750 First St. NE
Suite 1000
Washington, DC 20002-4250
Tel: (202)336-8800
Fax: (202)336-8952

Employers
Legal Services Corp. (President)

MCKAY, Laurie

2101 L St. NW
Washington, DC 20037-1526
EMail: mckayl@dsmo.com
Tel: (202)785-9700
Fax: (202)887-0689
Registered: LDA

Employers
Dickstein Shapiro Morin & Oshinsky LLP (Legislative Assistant)

Clients Represented

On Behalf of Dickstein Shapiro Morin & Oshinsky LLP
Cigar Ass'n of America
Electric Power Supply Ass'n
Hydro-Quebec
Lorillard Tobacco Co.
PG&E Generating Co.
Pipe Tobacco Council, Inc.
Smokeless Tobacco Council

MCKAY, Michael

490 L'Enfant Plaza East SW
Suite 7204
Washington, DC 20024
Tel: (202)479-1133
Fax: (202)479-1136

Employers
American Maritime Officers Service (President)

MCKEAG, Jana

315 Queen St.
Alexandria, VA 22314
Tel: (703)684-1203
Fax: (703)684-1481
Registered: LDA

Employers
Self-employed as an independent consultant.

Clients Represented

As an independent consultant
Sodak Gaming Inc.
Venture Catalysts

MCKECHNIE, III, John J.

805 15th St. NW
Suite 300
Washington, DC 20005-2207
Tel: (202)682-4200
Fax: (202)682-9054
Registered: LDA

Employers
Credit Union Nat'l Ass'n, Inc. (V. President, Legislative Affairs)

MCKEEVER, III, Joseph F.

1455 Pennsylvania Ave. NW
Suite 1200
Washington, DC 20004
Tel: (202)347-2230
Fax: (202)393-3310
Registered: LDA

Law Clerk to Senior Judge Wilson Cowen, U.S. Court of Appeals for the Federal Circuit, 1979-80, and to Judge Harry Wood, U.S. Court of Federal Claims, 1978-79.

Employers
Davis & Harman LLP (Partner)

Clients Represented

On Behalf of Davis & Harman LLP
Committee of Annuity Insurers

MCKEEVER, Michele

Ariel Rios Federal Bldg.
(1301-MC)
1200 Pennsylvania Ave. NW
3rd Floor
Washington, DC 20460
EMail: mckeever.michele@epa.gov
Tel: (202)564-7101
Fax: (202)501-1540

Employers
Environmental Protection Agency (Waste and Superfund Team Leader, Office of Congressional and Intergovernmental Relations)

MCKENNA, Francis G.

206 N. Washington St.
Suite 330
Alexandria, VA 22304
EMail: francis_mckenna@hotmail.com
Tel: (703)683-4420
Fax: (703)683-4538
Registered: LDA

Office of the General Counsel, Federal Home Loan Bank Board, 1967-70. Hearing Division, Federal Communications Commission, 1966-68. Attorney, Antitrust Division, Department of Justice, 1962-66.

Employers
Anderson and Pendleton, C.A. (President)

Clients Represented

On Behalf of Anderson and Pendleton, C.A.
Tourist Railroad Ass'n, Inc.
West Virginia State Rail Authority

MCKENNA, Tiffany

2001 S St. NW
Suite 740
Washington, DC 20009
Tel: (202)483-9222

Employers
Vietnam Veterans of America Foundation (Director)

MCKENNEY, James

One Dupont Circle NW
Suite 410
Washington, DC 20036
EMail: jmckenney@aacc.nche.edu
Tel: (202)728-0200
Ext: 226
Fax: (202)833-2467

Employers
American Ass'n of Community Colleges (Director, Workforce Development)

MCKENZIE, Mary

800 Connecticut Ave. NW
Suite 200
Washington, DC 20006
EMail: mmckenzie@humana.com
Tel: (202)467-5821
Fax: (202)467-5825
Registered: LDA

Staff Director, House Committee on Small Business, 1996-99. Legislative Counsel/Director to Rep. James Talent (R-MO), 1993-96.

Employers
Humana Inc. (Director, Federal Relations and Treasurer)

MCKEON, Kit

1401 I St. NW
Suite 600
Washington, DC 20005
Tel: (202)336-7400
Fax: (202)336-7527

Employers
United Technologies Corp. (Director, OSD Requirements)

MCKERNAN, Kim F.

1350 I St. NW
Suite 690
Washington, DC 20005
EMail: kmckernan@ob-cgroup.com
Tel: (202)898-4746
Fax: (202)898-4756
Registered: LDA

Former Special Assistant to the President for Legislative Affairs (House of Representatives), The White House, during the Bush I administration. Former Special Advisor to Secretary Dick Cheney, Department of Defense.

Employers
The OB-C Group, LLC (Principal)

Clients Represented

On Behalf of The OB-C Group, LLC
American Airlines
Anheuser-Busch Cos., Inc.
AT&T
Biotechnology Industry Organization
Blue Cross Blue Shield Ass'n
Fannie Mae
Goodyear Tire and Rubber Co.
Healthcare Distribution Management Ass'n
Investment Co. Institute
Merrill Lynch & Co., Inc.
Motorola, Inc.
Nat'l Thoroughbred Racing Ass'n, Inc.
Newport News Shipbuilding Inc.
The Rouse Company
Sears, Roebuck and Co.
Securities Industry Ass'n
TIAA-CREF
United Parcel Service
WellPoint Health Networks/Blue Cross of California/UNICARE
Wilmer, Cutler & Pickering

MCKERNAN, Robert T.

99 Canal Center Plaza
Suite 200
Alexandria, VA 22314
Tel: (703)683-8512
Fax: (703)683-4622

Employers
Smith & Harroff, Inc. (Partner)

MCKEW, Robert E.

919 18th St. NW
Suite 300
Washington, DC 20006
Tel: (202)296-5544
Fax: (202)223-0321
Registered: LDA

Employers
American Financial Services Ass'n (V. President and General Counsel)

MCKINNEY, C.A. "Mack"

125 N. West St.
Alexandria, VA 22314-2754
Tel: (703)683-1400
Fax: (703)549-6610
Registered: LDA
Served in the U.S. Marine Corps, 1942-71.

Employers
Fleet Reserve Ass'n (Legislative Counsel)
The Military Coalition (Coordinator)

MCKINNEY, Dawn

409 12th St. SW
P.O. Box 96920
Washington, DC 20090-6920
EMail: dmckinney@acog.org
Tel: (202)863-2511
Fax: (202)488-3985

Employers
American College of Obstetricians and Gynecologists (Senior Legislative Assistant)

MCKINNEY, Gwen

1612 K St. NW
Suite 904
Washington, DC 20006
Tel: (202)833-9771
Fax: (202)833-9770

Employers
McKinney & McDowell Associates (President)

MCKINNEY, USN (Ret.), Rear Adm. Henry C.

701 Pennsylvania Ave. NW
Suite 123
Washington, DC 20004
Tel: (202)737-2300
Fax: (202)737-2308

Employers
United States Navy Memorial Foundation (President and Chief Exec. Officer)

MCKINNON, Jr., Daniel W.

2235 Cedar Ln.
Vienna, VA 22182
Tel: (703)560-6800
Fax: (703)849-8916

Employers
NISH - Creating Employment Opportunities for People with Severe Disabilities (President)

MCKINNON, Monette

927 15th St. NW
Sixth Floor
Washington, DC 20036
EMail: mmckinnon@n4a.org
Tel: (202)296-8130
Fax: (202)296-8134

Employers
Nat'l Ass'n of Area Agencies on Aging (Director, Field Communications)

MCKITTRICK, Beverly E.

1341 G St. NW
Suite 900
Washington, DC 20005
Tel: (202)637-1504
Fax: (202)637-1549
Registered: LDA
Former Assistant Chief, Policy and Rules Division, Mass Media Bureau, Federal Communications Commission and Counsel, Judiciary Committee, U.S. Senate.

Employers
Philip Morris Management Corp. (Director, Government Affairs, Tobacco)

MCKNIGHT, John

1819 L St. NW
Suite 700
Washington, DC 20036
Tel: (202)861-1180
Fax: (202)861-1181
Registered: LDA

Employers
Nat'l Marine Manufacturers Ass'n (Director, Environmental Relations)

MCKNIGHT, Steven G.

700 13th St. NW
Suite 350
Washington, DC 20005
Tel: (202)637-0040
Fax: (202)637-0041
Registered: LDA
Assistant U.S. Attorney (1989-94) and Trial Attorney (1987-89), Department of Justice.

Employers
Rhoads Group (Associate)

Clients Represented
On Behalf of Rhoads Group
AAAE-ACI
Airports Council Internat'l - North America
American Management Systems
Dick Corp.
The Justice Project, Inc.
Orange, California, County of
PNC Bank, N.A.
SWATH Ocean Systems, Inc.
Taiwan Studies Institute
United States Enrichment Corp.

MCKONE, Timothy P.

1401 I St. NW
Suite 1100
Washington, DC 20005
Tel: (202)326-8820
Fax: (202)408-4808

Employers
SBC Communications Inc. (V. President, Congressional Affairs)

MCLACHLAN, Jim

801 18th St. NW
Washington, DC 20006
Tel: (202)872-1300
Fax: (202)785-4452

Employers
Paralyzed Veterans of America (Associate Exec. Director, Development)

MCLAIN, Maydell E.

2615 Woodley Place NW
Washington, DC 20008
Tel: (202)462-2791

Employers
American War Mothers (National President)

MCLAIN, Patrick M.

1500 K St. NW
Suite 650
Washington, DC 20005
Tel: (202)715-1000
Fax: (202)715-1001
Registered: LDA

Employers
GlaxoSmithKline (Federal Government Relations)

MCLAUGHLIN, Christine

601 Pennsylvania Ave. NW
11th Floor, North Bldg.
Washington, DC 20004-2601
Tel: (202)756-3300
Fax: (202)756-3333

Employers
Alston & Bird LLP (Counsel)

MCLAUGHLIN, Francis X.

1111 14th St. NW
Suite 1200
Washington, DC 20005-5603
EMail: mclaughlinf@ada.org
Tel: (202)898-2424
Fax: (202)898-2437
Registered: LDA

Employers
American Dental Ass'n (Director, Political Affairs)

MCLAUGHLIN, P.E., Frank R.

1350 I St. NW
Suite 1240
Washington, DC 20005
Tel: (202)296-3840
Fax: (202)682-0146

Employers
Ashby and Associates (Associate)

MCLAUGHLIN, James D.

1120 Connecticut Ave. NW
Washington, DC 20036
Tel: (202)663-5000
Fax: (202)828-4548
Registered: LDA

Employers
American Bankers Ass'n (Director, Regulatory and Trust Affairs)

MCLAUGHLIN, Kathleen Tynan

1225 I St. NW
Suite 350
Washington, DC 20005
EMail: ktm@dmggroup.com
Tel: (202)789-1110
Fax: (202)789-1116
Chief of Staff (1988-92) and Staff Assistant (1980-88) to Rep. Thomas J. Downey (D-NY).

Employers
Downey McGrath Group, Inc. (Chief Operating Officer)

MCLAUGHLIN, Lindsay

1775 K St. NW
Suite 200
Washington, DC 20006
Tel: (202)463-6265
Fax: (202)467-4875
Registered: LDA

Employers
Internat'l Longshore and Warehouse Union (Washington Representative and Legislative Director)

MCLAUGHLIN, Michael J.

1400 L St. NW
Washington, DC 20005-3502
EMail: mjmclaug@winston.com
Tel: (202)371-5789
Fax: (202)371-5950
Former Republican Counsel, House Committee on Small Business.

Employers
Winston & Strawn (Associate, Federal and Regulatory Affairs Practice)

Clients Represented
On Behalf of Winston & Strawn
American Airlines
Puerto Rico, Commonwealth of
Yellow Corp.

MCLEAN, Catherine

1001 G St. NW
Suite 300 East
Washington, DC 20001
EMail: cmclean@deweysquare.com
Tel: (202)638-5616
Fax: (202)638-5612
Registered: LDA

Employers
Dewey Square Group (Partner)

MCLEAN, Chris

888 17th St. NW
12th Floor
Washington, DC 20006
Tel: (202)429-8744
Fax: (202)296-2962
Registered: LDA

Employers
Nat'l Strategies Inc. (V. President)

MCLEAN, Joseph

517 Second St. NE
Washington, DC 20002
Tel: (202)543-3744
Fax: (202)543-3509
Registered: LDA

Employers
David Turch & Associates (Associate)

MCLEAN, R. Bruce

1333 New Hampshire Ave. NW
Suite 400
Washington, DC 20036
Tel: (202)887-4000
Fax: (202)887-4288
Attorney, Appellate Court Branch, National Labor Relations Board, 1971-73.

Employers
Akin, Gump, Strauss, Hauer & Feld, L.L.P. (Chairman)

MCLEAN, Sandy

1120 Connecticut Ave. NW
Suite 1100
Washington, DC 20036
Tel: (202)861-5899
Fax: (202)861-5795

Employers
GPC Internat'l (V. President, Public Affairs)

MCLEARN, Donald

1615 L St. NW
Suite 1000
Washington, DC 20036
Tel: (202)659-0330
Fax: (202)833-3490
EMail: mclearnd@fleishman.com

Deputy Commissioner, Office of Public Affairs (1985-87), Press Officer, Publications Officer and Special Assistant to the Director, Center for Drugs and Biologics (1985-87), Staff Member, Office of Public Affairs (1980-85), Food and Drug Administration, Department of Health and Human Services. Staff Member, Office of Public Affairs, Department of Health, Education and Welfare, 1978-80. Office of the Assistant Secretary, Office of Public Affairs and the Office of Civil Rights, Department of Health, Education and Welfare, 1975-78. Journalist, U.S. Navy, 1966-70.

Employers
Fleishman-Hillard, Inc (Senior V. President)

MCLELLAN, Eileen

1015 18th St. NW
Suite 600
Washington, DC 20036
Tel: (202)429-4344
Fax: (202)429-4342

Employers
Will and Carlson, Inc.

MCLENNAN, Robert "Mac"

4301 Wilson Blvd.
Arlington, VA 22203-1860
Tel: (703)907-5809
Fax: (703)907-5516
EMail: mac.maclennan@nreca.org

Employers
Nat'l Rural Electric Cooperative Ass'n (Senior Representative, Legislative Affairs)

MCLEOD, Bruce

2300 Clarendon Blvd.
Suite 610
Arlington, VA 22201-3367
Tel: (703)351-5666
Fax: (703)351-5667
EMail: bmcleod@golinharris.com

Employers
Golin/Harris Internat'l (V. President)

MCLEOD, Jonathan

1111 14th St. NW
Suite 1200
Washington, DC 20005-5603
Tel: (202)898-2400
Fax: (202)789-2258
Registered: LDA

Employers
American Dental Ass'n (Manager, Legislative and Regulatory Policy)

MCLEOD, Michael R.

One Massachusetts Ave. NW
Suite 800
Washington, DC 20001-1431
Tel: (202)842-2345
Fax: (202)408-7763
Registered: LDA
EMail: MMcleod@mwmlaw.com

General Counsel and Staff Director (1974-78) and Counsel (1971-74), Senate Committee on Agriculture and Forestry. Legislative Assistant to Senator Herman E. Talmadge (D-GA), 1967-71.

Employers
American Ass'n of Crop Insurers (Exec. Director)
McLeod, Watkinson & Miller (Partner)

Clients Represented

On Behalf of McLeod, Watkinson & Miller
American Ass'n of Crop Insurers
American Mushroom Institute
American Peanut Product Manufacturers, Inc.
California Avocado Commission
Chicago Board of Trade
Coalition for Sugar Reform
Nat'l Frozen Food Ass'n
United Egg Ass'n
United Egg Producers

MCLERNON, Kevin

1300 I St. NW
Suite 400 West
Washington, DC 20005
Tel: (202)515-2442
Fax: (202)336-7920

Employers
Verizon Communications (Director, Federal Government Affairs)

MCLERNON, Nancy L.

1901 Pennsylvania Ave. NW
Suite 807
Washington, DC 20006
Tel: (202)659-1903
Fax: (202)659-2293
Registered: LDA
EMail: nancymcl@aol.com

Employers
Organization for Internat'l Investment (Director, Economic & Legislative Affairs)

MCLISH, Thomas

1333 New Hampshire Ave. NW
Suite 400
Washington, DC 20036
Tel: (202)887-4000
Fax: (202)887-4288

Employers
Akin, Gump, Strauss, Hauer & Feld, L.L.P. (Partner)

Clients Represented

On Behalf of Akin, Gump, Strauss, Hauer & Feld, L.L.P.
Food Lion, Inc.

MCLUCKIE, Jr., Frederick P.

25 Louisiana Ave. NW
Washington, DC 20001-2198
Tel: (202)624-8741
Fax: (202)624-8973
Registered: LDA

Employers
Internat'l Brotherhood of Teamsters (Legislative Representative)

MCMACKIN, Jr., John J.

1155 21st St. NW
Suite 300
Washington, DC 20036
Tel: (202)659-8201
Fax: (202)659-5249
Registered: LDA
EMail: jjmcmackin@wms-jen.com

Employers
Williams & Jensen, P.C. (Partner)

Clients Represented

On Behalf of Williams & Jensen, P.C.
Aegon USA
American Home Products Corp.
Fannie Mae
Nat'l Audubon Soc.
Norfolk Southern Corp.
Owens-Illinois, Inc.
Qwest Communications
Smith Barney Harris Upham & Co.
TTX Co.

MCMAHON, Anthony J.

6106 MacArthur Blvd.
Suite 110
Bethesda, MD 20816
Tel: (301)263-0585
Fax: (301)263-0587
Registered: LDA

Employers
Safety Reasearch Center, Inc. (President)

MCMAHON, Diane

1615 H St. NW
Washington, DC 20062-2000
Tel: (202)659-6000
Fax: (202)463-5836

Employers
Chamber of Commerce of the U.S.A. (Assistant Director, U.S.-India Business Council (USIBC))

MCMAHON, Joseph E.

1924 N St. NW
Washington, DC 20036
Tel: (202)293-6464
Fax: (202)293-6475
EMail: mcmahon@aol.com

Former Assistant to Senator Edward W. Brooke III (R-MA).

Employers
McMahon and Associates (President)

Clients Represented

On Behalf of McMahon and Associates
Covenant House
Rodale Press

MCMAHON, Kathryn M. T.

3050 K St. NW
Washington, DC 20007
Tel: (202)342-8400
Fax: (202)342-8451
Registered: LDA
EMail: kmcmahon@colliershannon.com

Employers
Collier Shannon Scott, PLLC (Member)

Clients Represented

On Behalf of Collier Shannon Scott, PLLC
Chrome Coalition

MCMAHON, Kevin P.

1001 19th St. North
Suite 800
Arlington, VA 22209-3901
Tel: (703)276-5035
Fax: (703)276-5024
Registered: LDA
EMail: kevin.mcmahon@trw.com

Employers
TRW Inc. (Director, Government Relations)

MCMAHON, Richard

701 Pennsylvania Ave. NW
Washington, DC 20004-2696
Tel: (202)508-5571
Fax: (202)508-5600
Registered: LDA

Employers
Edison Electric Institute (Group Director, Energy Supply)

MCMAHON, Shaine

1518 K St. NW
Suite 503
Washington, DC 20005
Tel: (202)737-0202
Fax: (202)638-4833

Employers
Sufka & Associates (Account Executive)

Clients Represented

On Behalf of Sufka & Associates
Nat'l Air Duct Cleaners Ass'n

MCMAHON, Steve

1029 N. Royal St.
Suite 350
Alexandria, VA 22314
Tel: (703)519-8600
Fax: (703)519-8604

Employers
Trippi, McMahon & Squier (Partner)

MCMAHON, Thomas E.

783 Station St.
Suite 1-D
Herndon, VA 20170
Tel: (703)435-1210
Fax: (703)435-6389

Employers
Nat'l Automatic Merchandising Ass'n (Senior V. President and Chief Counsel)

MCMANUS, James T.

1200 G St. NW
Suite 600
Washington, DC 20005-3802
Tel: (202)393-1200
Fax: (202)393-1240
EMail: mcmanus@wrightlaw.com

Attorney (1975-77) and Staff Witness and Engineer (1971-75), Federal Power Commission.

Employers
Wright & Talisman, P.C. (President)

Clients Represented

On Behalf of Wright & Talisman, P.C.
Bangor Hydro-Electric Co.
Iroquois Gas Transmission System
Maine Public Service Co.
Northwest Pipeline Corp
Williams Field Services

MCMANUS, Katherine D.

1299 Pennsylvania Ave. NW
Washington, DC 20004-2402
Tel: (202)783-0800
Fax: (202)383-6610
Registered: LDA
EMail: mcmanusk@howrey.com

Law Clerk to Judge Harold H. Greene, U.S. District Court for the District of Columbia, 1984-85. Foreign Affairs Officer, Arms Control and Disarmanent Agency, 1978-81.

Employers
Howrey Simon Arnold & White (Partner)

MCMANUS, Mary P.

900 19th St. NW
Suite 700
Washington, DC 20006
Tel: (202)530-7000
Fax: (202)530-7042
Registered: LDA

Employers
Lucent Technologies (V. President, Global Public Affairs)

MCMANUS, Paul E.

11 Canal Center Plaza
Suite 103
Alexandria, VA 22314
Tel: (703)683-4222
Fax: (703)683-0645
Registered: LDA

Employers
The Spectrum Group (Chief Exec. Officer)

Clients Represented

On Behalf of The Spectrum Group
AAI Corp.
ADSI Inc.
Barksdale Foward
PESystems, Inc.
PKC
The Refinishing Touch
Robertson Aviation
Simula, Inc.
Tetra Tech

MCMANUS, Fr. Sean

413 E. Capitol St. SE
Washington, DC 20003
Tel: (202)544-0568
Fax: (202)543-2491

Employers
Irish Nat'l Caucus (President)

MCMANUS, William A.

1101 16th St. NW
Washington, DC 20036-4877
Tel: (202)463-6740
Fax: (202)659-5346
Registered: LDA

Employers
Nat'l Soft Drink Ass'n (Manager, Federal Affairs)

MCMENAMIN, Peter

1101 Vermont Ave. NW
12th Floor
Washington, DC 20005-3583
Tel: (202)789-7437
Fax: (202)789-7485
Registered: LDA

Employers
American Medical Ass'n (Director, Health Policy Development)

MCMICKLE, John D.

1400 L St. NW
Washington, DC 20005-3502
Tel: (202)371-5833
Fax: (202)371-5950
EMail: jmcmickl@winston.com
Counsel, Subcommittee on Administrative Oversight and the Courts, Senate Committee on the Judiciary, 1995-2001.

Employers
Winston & Strawn (Associate, Federal and Regulatory Affairs Practice)

Clients Represented

On Behalf of Winston & Strawn
DMJM + Harris
Internat'l Council of Shopping Centers
Puerto Rico, Commonwealth of
Virgin Islands, Government of the
Yellow Corp.

MCMILLAN, Hon. J. Alex

P.O. Box 1807
Alexandria, VA 22313
Tel: (703)876-0920
Registered: LDA
Member, U.S. House of Representatives (R-NC), 1985-94.

Employers
McMillan, Hill & Associates

MCMILLAN, James G.

555 13th St. NW
Washington, DC 20004-1109
Tel: (202)637-5827
Fax: (202)637-5910
Registered: LDA
EMail: jgmcmillan@hhlaw.com
Counsel and Legislative Aide to Senate Minority Leader Robert J. Dole (R-KS), 1990-93.

Employers
Hogan & Hartson L.L.P. (Partner)

Clients Represented

On Behalf of Hogan & Hartson L.L.P.
Financial Planning Ass'n
Nat'l Ass'n of Personal Financial Advisors

MCMILLAN, Kurt

1200 G St. NW
Suite 510
Washington, DC 20005
Tel: (202)347-0600
Fax: (202)347-0608
Registered: LDA
EMail: kurt@csa-dc.org

Employers
Contract Services Ass'n of America (Director, Business Management)

MCMILLAN, Stephen

1250 I St. NW
Suite 804
Washington, DC 20005
Tel: (202)289-2570
Fax: (202)289-2580
Registered: LDA
EMail: Stephen.McMillan@phwilm.zeneca.com

Employers
AstraZeneca Inc. (Senior Manager, Pharmaceutical Federal Government Affairs)

MCMULLEN, Lynn

440 First St. NW
Suite 450
Washington, DC 20001
Tel: (202)783-7100
Fax: (202)783-2818
Registered: LDA
EMail: mcmullen@resultsusa.org

Employers
RESULTS (Exec. Director)

MCMURPHY, Michael A.

7401 Wisconsin Ave.
Suite 500
Bethesda, MD 20814
Tel: (301)986-8585
Fax: (301)652-5690
Registered: FARA

Employers
COGEMA, Inc. (President and Chief Exec. Officer)

MCMURTRY, Vanda B.

1501 M St. NW
Suite 400
Washington, DC 20005
Tel: (202)463-4022
Fax: (202)223-2821
Registered: LDA
EMail: mcmurtry.vanda@aetna.com

Employers
Aetna Inc. (Senior V. President, Federal Government Relations)

MCNALLY, Nancy Macan

1050 Thomas Jefferson St. NW
Seventh Floor
Washington, DC 20007
Tel: (202)298-1800
Fax: (202)338-2416
Registered: LDA
EMail: nmm@vnf.com

Employers
Van Ness Feldman, P.C. (Principal)

Clients Represented

On Behalf of Van Ness Feldman, P.C.
Consumers United for Rail Equity
Large Public Power Council
Mack Trucks, Inc.
McKesson Corp.
Nat'l Endangered Species Act Reform Coalition
Sonoma County Water Agency
Tecumseh Products Co.

MCNALLY, Susan V.

1330 New Hampshire Ave. NW
Suite 122
Washington, DC 20036
Tel: (202)296-0158
Fax: (202)296-3526
Registered: LDA
EMail: smcnally@nachc.com
Attorney/Advisor, Office of the Assistant Secretary for Legislative, Department of Health and Human Services, 1987-88. Assistant Counsel, Office of Legislative Counsel, U.S. Senate, 1977-87.

Employers
Nat'l Ass'n of Community Health Centers (Director Federal Affairs and Legislative Counsel)

MCNAMARA, Angela V.

1401 K St. NW
Suite 900
Washington, DC 20005
Tel: (202)626-8550
Fax: (202)626-8578
Registered: LDA

Employers
Jefferson Consulting Group (V. President)

Clients Represented

On Behalf of Jefferson Consulting Group
M.D. - I.P.A.

MCNAMARA, Chris

1150 17th St. NW
Suite 701
Washington, DC 20036
Tel: (202)775-1401
Fax: (202)775-1404
EMail: chris.mcnamara@dittus.com

Employers
Dittus Communications (V. President and Managing Director)

Clients Represented

On Behalf of Dittus Communications
American Ass'n of Preferred Provider Organizations
Andrx Pharmaceutical Corp.
Exolve
R - Tech Veno
Surviving Selma
Uniformed Services Family Health Plan

MCNAMARA, Daniel J.

700 13th St. NW
Suite 400
Washington, DC 20005
Tel: (202)347-0773
Fax: (202)347-0785
Registered: LDA
EMail: dmcnamara@cassidy.com
Assistant Legislative Director to Senator David Durenberger (R-MN), 1985-89. Former Professional Staff Member, Subcommittee on Intergovernmental Affairs, Senate Committee on Governmental Affairs. Former Staff Assistant to Senator Hubert H. Humphrey (D-MN). Former Staff Assistant to Senator Muriel B. Humphrey (D-MN).

Employers
Cassidy & Associates, Inc. (Senior V. President)

Clients Represented

On Behalf of Cassidy & Associates, Inc.
Alfred University
American Lung Ass'n of Minnesota
Central College
Chicago Board of Trade
Community Health Partners of Ohio
DRAKA USA Corp.
Forum Health
Internat'l Snowmobile Manufacturers Ass'n
Liberty Science Center
Lorain County Community College
Ocean Spray Cranberries
Palmdale, California, City of
Texas Tech University System
Villanova University

MCNAMARA, Michael T.

1050 Connecticut Ave. NW
Washington, DC 20036-5339
Tel: (202)857-6000
Fax: (202)857-6395
Registered: LDA
Worked for Department of Commerce.

Employers
Arent Fox Kintner Plotkin & Kahn, PLLC (Associate)

Clients Represented

On Behalf of Arent Fox Kintner Plotkin & Kahn, PLLC
Acxiom Corp.
Alaska Rainforest Campaign
American Airlines
American Amusement Machine Ass'n
American Plywood Ass'n
American Public Power Ass'n
Amusement and Music Operators Ass'n
Building Service Contractors Ass'n Internat'l
CIS Global
Engineering Animation, Inc.
Exeter Architectural Products
Fannie Mae
Guardian Angel Holdings, Inc.
Interactive Amusement and Tournament Video Game Coalition
S.C. Johnson and Son, Inc.
Kellogg Co.
Molina Medical Centers
Motor and Equipment Manufacturers Ass'n
Nat'l Ass'n of College Stores
Nat'l Ass'n of Retail Collection Attorneys
Nat'l Ass'n of School Nurses
New Orleans, Louisiana, City of
Parker Hannifin Corp.
Raytheon Co.
Renewable Resources LLC
Tyson Foods, Inc.
webwasher.com

MCNAMARA, Patrick H.

8201 Greensboro Dr.
Suite 1000
McLean, VA 22102
Tel: (703)394-8018
Fax: (703)394-8048
Registered: LDA
EMail: patrick_h_mcnamara@huntsman.com
Served in the United States Air Force.

Employers
Huntsman Corp. (Director, Government and Industry Relations)

MCNAMARA, Thomas J.

100 Daingerfield Rd.
Alexandria, VA 22314
Tel: (703)519-8197
Fax: (703)548-3227
Registered: LDA
Former Chief of Staff to Rep. Donald Sundquist (R-TN). Chief of Staff (1977-83) and Legislative Assistant (1975-77) to Rep. Robin Beard (R-TN).

Employers
McNamara & Associates (President)

Clients Represented

On Behalf of McNamara & Associates
Harrah's Entertainment, Inc.
The Nat'l Sports Center for the Disabled
Printing Industries of America
The Sharing Network

MCNEIL, J.E.

1830 Connecticut Ave. NW
Washington, DC 20009
Tel: (202)483-2220
Fax: (202)483-1246
Registered: LDA

Employers
Center on Conscience and War/NISBCO (Exec. Director)

MCNEIL, Sue

900 19th St. NW
Suite 700
Washington, DC 20006
Tel: (202)530-7000
Fax: (202)530-7042
Registered: LDA

Employers
Lucent Technologies (Director, Global Public Affairs)

MCNELIS, Marcie M.

515 King St.
Suite 300
Alexandria, VA 22314
Tel: (703)684-1110
Fax: (703)684-7912
EMail: mmcnelis@multistate.com

Employers
MultiState Associates (Principal)

MCNERNEY, John

1385 Piccard Dr.
Rockville, MD 20850-4340
Tel: (301)869-5800
Fax: (301)990-9690
Registered: LDA
EMail: jmcnerney@mcaa.org

Employers
Mechanical Contractors Ass'n of America (Director, Government/Labor Relations)

MCNEVIN, Anthony

1350 Piccard Dr.
Suite 322
Rockville, MD 20850
Tel: (301)990-7400
Fax: (301)990-2807
EMail: amcnevin@aacpm.org

Employers
American Ass'n of Colleges of Podiatric Medicine (President)

MCNICHOL, Elizabeth

820 First St. NE
Suite 510
Washington, DC 20002
Tel: (202)408-1080
Fax: (202)408-1056
EMail: mcnichol@center.cbpp.org

Employers
Center on Budget and Policy Priorities (Director, State Fiscal Project)

MCNICHOLAS, John P.

6701 Democracy Blvd.
Suite 300
Bethesda, MD 20817
Tel: (301)571-9404
Fax: (301)564-9619
Registered: LDA
EMail: J_McNicholas@juno.com
Chief, Information Policy, Office of Management and Budget, 1968-87. Program Analyst, Nat'l Aeronautics and Space Administration, 1961-68. United States Navy, 1961-68. United States Marine Corps, 1957-60.

Employers
Government Strategy Advisors (V. President)

MCNICKLE, Larry

2519 Connecticut Ave. NW
Washington, DC 20008-1520
Tel: (202)783-2242
Fax: (202)783-2255
Registered: LDA

Employers
American Ass'n of Homes and Services for the Aging (Director, Housing Policy)

MCNITT, Ben

1400 16th St. NW
Suite 501
Washington, DC 20036-2266
Tel: (202)797-6800
Fax: (202)797-6646
EMail: mcnitt@nwf.org

Employers
Nat'l Wildlife Federation - Office of Federal and Internat'l Affairs (Senior Communications Manager)

MCNITT, Townsend L.

1600 Pennsylvania Ave. NW
107 E. Wing
Washington, DC 20500
Tel: (202)456-6493
Fax: (202)456-2604

Employers
Executive Office of the President - The White House (Special Assistant to the President for Legislative Affairs, Senate Liaison Office)

MCNULTY, Robert H.

1429 21st St. NW
Second Floor
Washington, DC 20036
Tel: (202)887-5990
Fax: (202)466-4845

Employers
Partners for Livable Communities (President)

MCPHEE, Gerald T.

1717 Pennsylvania Ave. NW
Suite 400
Washington, DC 20006
Tel: (202)857-3000
Fax: (202)857-3030
Registered: LDA

Employers
Occidental Internat'l Corporation (V. President, Federal Relations)

MCPHEE, Jessica

1199 N. Fairfax St.
Suite 1000
Alexandria, VA 22314
Tel: (703)299-4499
Fax: (703)299-4488
EMail: jmcphee@hawthorngroup.com

Employers
The Hawthorn Group, L.C. (Sr. Account Coordinator)

MCPHEE, Shelley

1120 Connecticut Ave. NW
Suite 1100
Washington, DC 20036
Tel: (202)861-5899
Fax: (202)861-5795
Registered: LDA

Employers
GPC Internat'l

Clients Represented

On Behalf of GPC Internat'l
Mineral Technologies, Inc.

MCPHERSON, Harry C.

901 15th St. NW
Suite 700
Washington, DC 20005-2301
Tel: (202)371-6000
Fax: (202)371-6279
Registered: LDA
EMail: hcmcpherson@verner.com
Counsel and Special Counsel to the President, The White House, 1965-69. Assistant Secretary for Educational and Cultural Affairs, Department of State, 1964-65. Deputy Undersecretary for International Affairs, Department of the Army, 1963-64. General Counsel, Senate Democratic Policy Committee, 1956-63.

Employers
Verner, Liipfert, Bernhard, McPherson and Hand, Chartered (Member of Firm)

Clients Represented

On Behalf of Verner, Liipfert, Bernhard, McPherson and Hand, Chartered
Amgen
The Walt Disney Co.
Equal Justice Coalition
The Hamilton Group
Home Warranty Coalition
Lockheed Martin Tactical Systems
Midroc Ethiopia
Muscular Dystrophy Ass'n
Nat'l Broadcasting Co.
Northwest Airlines, Inc.
RJR Nabisco Holdings Co.
Stanford Financial Group
Washington Group Internat'l

MCPHERSON, Laura

700 11th St. NW
Washington, DC 20001-4507
Tel: (202)383-1131
Fax: (202)383-7540
Registered: LDA
EMail: lmcpherson@realtors.com

Employers
Nat'l Ass'n of Realtors (Legislative Representative)

MCPHERSON, Molly

2111 Wilson Blvd.
Eighth Floor
Arlington, VA 22201
Tel: (703)522-8463
Fax: (703)522-3811

Employers
Internat'l Council of Cruise Lines (Director, Communications)

MCQWEERY, James

1200 G St. NW
Suite 800
Washington, DC 20005
Tel: (202)434-8768
Fax: (202)434-8707
Registered: LDA

Employers
Winning Strategies Washington, D.C., LLC

MCREE, Diane B.

601 Pennsylvania Ave. NW
Suite 900
South Bldg.
Washington, DC 20004
Tel: (202)434-8205
Fax: (202)628-0565
Registered: LDA
Former aide to Rep. John Breaux (D-LA), 1972-86; Special Assistant to Senator John Breaux (D-LA), 1987-93.

Employers
Diane McRee Associates (President)

Clients Represented

On Behalf of Diane McRee Associates
3001, Inc.
GREX, Inc.
HUTCO, Inc.
Metamorphix, Inc.
Northrop Grumman Corp.
Port of Lake Charles
United States Tuna Foundation

MCRUNNEL, Karen

440 First St. NW
Eighth Floor
Washington, DC 20001
Tel: (202)942-4238
Fax: (202)393-2630
EMail: kmcrunnel@naco.org

Employers
Nat'l Ass'n of Counties (Executive Assistant and Board Liaison)

MCSHERRY, Carolyn

1001 Pennsylvania Ave. NW
Suite 600
Washington, DC 20004
Tel: (202)347-0066
Fax: (202)624-7222
Registered: LDA

Employers
Powell, Goldstein, Frazer & Murphy LLP (Analyst)

Clients Represented
On Behalf of Powell, Goldstein, Frazer & Murphy LLP
Cargill, Inc.

MCSHERRY, Michael T.

310 First St. SE
Washington, DC 20003
Tel: (202)863-8500
Fax: (202)863-8820

Employers
Republican Nat'l Committee (Director, Government Affairs)

MCSLARROW, Alison

6551 Kristina Ursula Court
Falls Church, VA 22044
Tel: (703)658-0138
Fax: (703)658-5040
Registered: LDA
Former Deputy Chief of Staff to Sen. Majority Leader Trent Lott (R-MS).

Employers
McSlarrow Consulting L.L.C. (Principal)

Clients Represented
On Behalf of McSlarrow Consulting L.L.C.
American Trucking Ass'ns
Fannie Mae
Microsoft Corp.
Qwest Communications
U.S. Oncology

MCSPADDEN, Gail

444 N. Capitol St. NW
Suite 419
Washington, DC 20001
Tel: (202)624-5455
Fax: (202)624-5468
Registered: LDA

Employers
Nat'l Ass'n of Federally Impacted Schools (Legislative Analyst)

MCSPADDEN, Steven

750 First St. NE
Suite 920
Washington, DC 20002-4241
Tel: (202)842-4420
Fax: (202)842-4396
Registered: LDA

Employers
Nat'l Ass'n of Police Organizations (General Counsel)

MCSTEEN, Martha A.

Ten G St. NE
Suite 600
Washington, DC 20002-4215
Tel: (202)216-0420
Fax: (202)216-0446
Registered: LDA

Employers
Nat'l Committee to Preserve Social Security and Medicare (President)

MCTAGGART, Brendan

1101 14th St. NW
Suite 405
Washington, DC 20005
EMail: brendan@healthlaw.org
Tel: (202)289-7661
Fax: (202)289-7724

Employers
Nat'l Health Law Program (Director, Communications)

MCTIGHE, Joe

13017 Wisteria Dr.
PMB 457
Germantown, MD 20874
Tel: (301)916-8460
Fax: (301)916-8485

Employers
Council for American Private Education (Exec. Director)

MCTIGHE MUSIL, Caryn

1818 R St. NW
Washington, DC 20009
Tel: (202)387-3760
Fax: (202)265-9532

Employers
Ass'n of American Colleges and Universities (V. President, Education and Diversity Initiatives)

MCVANEY, Jim

1300 Wilson Blvd.
Arlington, VA 22209
Tel: (703)741-5911
Fax: (703)741-6097
Registered: LDA
EMail: jim_mcvaney@americanchemistry.com

Employers
American Chemistry Council (Director)

MCVEY, Robert D.

2800 Shirlington Rd.
Suite 401
Arlington, VA 22206
EMail: bobmcvey@asic-dc.com
Tel: (703)824-0300
Fax: (703)824-0320
Registered: LDA

Employers
American Systems Internat'l Corp. (Chief Exec. Officer)

Clients Represented
On Behalf of American Systems Internat'l Corp.
Battelle Memorial Institute
Battelle Memorial Labs
Defence Evaluation and Research Agency
Elbet Forth Worth
FN Herstal, USA
Israel Aircraft Industries, Ltd.
Lockheed Martin Corp.
Logis-Tech, Inc.
Northrop Grumman Corp.
Pennsylvania Nat'l Guard Ass'n
Precision Lift
Production Technology, Inc.
Raytheon Co.
Safety Storage Inc.
SRA Corp.
Vision Systems Internat'l

MEAD, Sara

600 Pennsylvania Ave. SE
Suite 400
Washington, DC 20003
Tel: (202)547-0001
Fax: (202)544-5014
Confidential Assistant to the Senior Advisor to the Secretary, Department of Education, 2000.

Employers
Progressive Policy Institute (Policy Analyst, 21st Century Schools Project)

MEADE, David

750 17th St. NW
Suite 1100
Washington, DC 20006
Tel: (202)778-2300
Fax: (202)778-2330

Employers
FoxKiser

MEADE, Elizabeth

1635 Prince St.
Alexandria, VA 22314-3406
Tel: (703)683-4646
Fax: (703)683-4745

Employers
Helicopter Ass'n Internat'l (Exec. V. President, Administration)

MEADOWS, C. V.

219 N. Washington St.
Alexandria, VA 22314
Tel: (703)836-7990
Fax: (703)836-9739
Registered: LDA
EMail: jim.meadows@pal-aerospace.com

Employers
Peduzzi Associates, Ltd. (Associate)

Clients Represented
On Behalf of Peduzzi Associates, Ltd.
DRS - EOSG
Integrated Medical Systems
Lord Corp.
Marconi Flight Systems, Inc.
Skyhook Technologies, Inc.

MEADOWS, Johnette L.

1111 N. Fairfax St.
Alexandria, VA 22314
Tel: (703)684-2782
Fax: (703)684-7343

Employers
American Physical Therapy Ass'n (Director, Minority/International Affairs)

MEADOWS, Stephanie

1220 L St. NW
Washington, DC 20005
Tel: (202)682-8000
Fax: (202)682-8294
Registered: LDA

Employers
American Petroleum Institute (V. President, Head Assistant)

MEADOWS, III, William H.

1615 M St. NW
Washington, DC 20036
Tel: (202)833-2300
Fax: (202)429-3958
Registered: LDA
EMail: Bill_Meadows@tws.org

Employers
The Wilderness Soc. (President)

MEAKEM, John

1300 N. 17th St.
Suite 1847
Rosslyn, VA 22209
EMail: john_meakem@nema.org
Tel: (703)841-3243
Fax: (703)841-3343
Registered: LDA

Employers
Nat'l Electrical Manufacturers Ass'n (Manager, International Trade)

MEANS, James Gregory

660 Pennsylvania Ave. SE
Suite 201
Washington, DC 20003
EMail: GMeans@alpinegroup.com
Tel: (202)547-1831
Fax: (202)547-4658
Registered: LDA
Former Chief of Staff to Rep. Dennis Eckart (D-OH).

Employers
Alpine Group, Inc. (Partner)

Clients Represented
On Behalf of Alpine Group, Inc.
American Cable Ass'n
Arthur Andersen LLP
BP Amoco Corp.
FMC Corp.
Lafarge Corp.
Pharmacia Corp.
Swedish Match
TVA Watch
U.S. Filter

MEANS, Kathleen

2550 M St. NW
Washington, DC 20037-1350
Tel: (202)457-6000
Fax: (202)457-6315
Chief Health Care Analyst, Senate Committee on Finance, 1998-2001. Senior Health Insurance Policy Analyst, House Committee on Ways and Means, 1995-96. Director of Executive Operations, Health Care Financing Administration, Department of Health and Human Services, 1991-94. Senior Legislative Assistant to Senator Dave Durenberger (R-MN), 1989-91. Director of Health Financing Policy (1983-85) and Health Policy Analyst, Bureau of Health Insurance/Health Care Financing Administration (1969-82), Department of Health and Human Services

Employers
Patton Boggs, LLP (Senior Health Policy Advisor)

MEARS, Rachel

1750 New York Ave. NW
Suite 350
Washington, DC 20006
Tel: (202)628-0444
Ext: 11
Fax: (202)628-0458

Employers
Women's Research and Education Institute (Director, Women's Fellowship Program)

MEDAGLIA, III, Thomas J.

1776 I St. NW
Suite 1000
Washington, DC 20006
Tel: (202)785-4888
Fax: (202)457-6597
Registered: LDA

Employers
BP Amoco Corp. (Director, Government Affairs)

MEDALIE, Susan

734 15th St. NW
Suite 500
Washington, DC 20005
Tel: (202)393-8164
Fax: (202)393-0649

Employers
Women's Campaign Fund (Exec. Director)

MEDEROS, Carolina L.

2550 M St. NW
Washington, DC 20037-1350
Tel: (202)457-6000
Fax: (202)457-6315
Registered: LDA
EMail: cmederos@pattonboggs.com
Deputy Assistant Secretary for Policy and International Affairs (1988-90), Chair, Secretary's Safety Review Task Force

(1985-88), Director, Office of Programs and Evaluation (1981-88), Chief, Transportation Assistance Programs Division (1979-81), and Program Analyst (1976-79), all at the Department of Transportation.

Employers
Patton Boggs, LLP (Transportation Consultant)

Clients Represented
On Behalf of Patton Boggs, LLP
Hankin, Persson & Darnell
Houston, Texas, City of
I-69 Mid-Continent Highway Coalition
Mannesmann VDO
Pechanga Band of California Luiseno Indians
Save Barton Creek
Shreveport, Louisiana, City of
Wayne, Michigan, County of

MEDINE, David
555 13th St. NW
Washington, DC 20004-1109
Tel: (202)637-5600
Fax: (202)637-5910
Former Associate Director for Financial Practices, Bureau of Consumer Protection, Federal Trade Commission.

Employers
Hogan & Hartson L.L.P. (Partner)

MEDLEY, Joy
445 12th St. NW
Room 8-C721
Washington, DC 20554
Tel: (202)418-1900
Fax: (202)418-2806

Employers
Federal Communications Commission (Legislative Analyst)

MEDVED, Mary
1401 K St. NW
Suite 600
Washington, DC 20005
Tel: (202)835-9898
Fax: (202)853-9893

Employers
ASCENT (Ass'n of Community Enterprises) (Director of Administration)

MEECE, Ashley
1133 Connecticut Ave. NW
Fifth Floor
Washington, DC 20036
Tel: (202)457-1110
Fax: (202)457-1130

Employers
Quinn Gillespie & Associates (Associate)

MEEDS, Hon. Lloyd
1735 New York Ave. NW
Suite 500
Washington, DC 20006-4759
Tel: (202)628-1700
Fax: (202)331-1024
Registered: LDA, FARA
EMail: lloydm@prestongates.com
Member, U.S. House of Representatives (D-WA), 1965-79.

Employers
Preston Gates Ellis & Rouvelas Meeds LLP (Of Counsel)

Clients Represented
On Behalf of Preston Gates Ellis & Rouvelas Meeds LLP
Burlington Northern Santa Fe Railway
Future of Puerto Rico Inc.
Magazine Publishers of America
Nat'l Center for Economic Freedom, Inc.
Northpoint Technology, Ltd.
Pitney Bowes, Inc.
Prime Time 24
Southeast Alaska Regional Health Corp. (SEARHC)
United States Maritime Coalition
VoiceStream Wireless Corp.
Washington State Hospital Ass'n

MEEHAN, Bill
1750 New York Ave. NW
Washington, DC 20006
Tel: (202)637-0700
Fax: (202)637-0771

Employers
Internat'l Union of Painters and Allied Trades (Exec. General V. President)

MEENAHAN, Kathleen
8065 Leesburg Pike
Suite 400
Vienna, VA 22182
Tel: (703)762-5100
Fax: (703)762-5200

Employers
Teligent, Inc.

MEENAN, John M.
1301 Pennsylvania Ave. NW
Suite 1100
Washington, DC 20004-1707
Tel: (202)626-4000
Fax: (202)626-4166

Employers
Air Transport Ass'n of America (Senior V. President, Industry Policy)

MEESE, III, Edwin
214 Massachusetts Ave. NE
Washington, DC 20002
Tel: (202)546-4400
Fax: (202)546-8328

Employers
Heritage Foundation (Ronald Reagan Fellow in Public Policy)

MEGGESTO, James T.
1250 I St. NW
Suite 1000
Washington, DC 20005
Tel: (202)682-0240
Fax: (202)682-0249

Employers
Sonosky, Chambers, Sachse & Endreson (Associate)

MEGREGIAN, Scott S.
600 13th St. NW
Washington, DC 20005-3096
Tel: (202)756-8096
Fax: (202)756-8087
EMail: smegregian@mwe.com

Employers
McDermott, Will and Emery (Partner)

Clients Represented
On Behalf of McDermott, Will and Emery
Kvaerner US Inc.
Lockheed Martin Corp.

MEHALL, Nicole
51 Monroe St.
Suite 1402
Rockville, MD 20850
Tel: (301)610-5300
Fax: (301)610-5308

Employers
Interstitial Cystitis Ass'n (Administrative Manager)

MEHL, Theodore J.
2001 Jefferson Davis Hwy.
Suite 209
Arlington, VA 22202
Tel: (703)413-0090
Fax: (703)413-4467
Registered: LDA
EMail: tmehl@mehlgriffinbartek.com
Special Consultant to the Commissioner, U.S. Customs Service, Department of Treasury, 1986-87. Staff Director, Subcommittee on Government Information, Justice and Agriculture, House Committee on Government Operations, 1981-86. U.S. Army, 1959-81.

Employers
Mehl, Griffin & Bartek Ltd. (V. President)

Clients Represented
On Behalf of Mehl, Griffin & Bartek Ltd.
AMI Aircraft Seating Systems
Battelle Memorial Institute
Chandler Evans Control Systems
D3 Internat'l Energy, LLC
El Camino Resources, Ltd.
Exide Corp.
General Atomics
Irvine Sensors Corp.
Motorola Space and Systems Technology Group
Nat'l Veterans Foundation
Pacific Northwest Nat'l Laboratory
Turbine Controls, Inc.

MEHL, Wayne Edward
2725 Carter Farm Ct.
Alexandria, VA 22306
Tel: (703)780-1025
Fax: (703)799-9404
Registered: LDA
Legislative Assistant to Senator Vance Hartke (D-IN), 1976. Legislative Assistant to Senator John Melcher (D-MT), 1977-86. Legislative Director to Senator Harry Reid (D-NV), 1987-92.

Employers
Self-employed as an independent consultant.

Clients Represented
As an independent consultant
Nevada Resort Ass'n

MEHLMAN, Amy R.
509 C St. NE
Washington, DC 20002
Tel: (202)546-3800
Fax: (202)544-6771
Registered: LDA

Employers
Capitol Coalitions Inc. (Principal)

Clients Represented
On Behalf of Capitol Coalitions Inc.
Astro Vision Internat'l, Inc.
Big Sky Economic Development Authority
Corning Inc.
Houston, Texas, Department of Aviation of the City of
INTELSAT - Internat'l Telecommunications Satellite Organization
One Economy Corp.
Westinghouse Government Services Group

MEHLMAN, Bruce P.
601 Pennsylvania Ave. NW
Suite 520
North Bldg.
Washington, DC 20004
Tel: (202)661-4000
Fax: (202)661-4041
Registered: LDA
EMail: bmehlman@cisco.com
Former Policy Expert for Rep. J.C. Watts (R-OK).

Employers
Cisco Systems Inc. (Assistant Washington Representatives, Policy Counsel)

MEHLMAN, Wayne A.
1033 N. Fairfax St.
Suite 404
Alexandria, VA 22314
Tel: (703)549-7404
Fax: (703)549-8712
Registered: LDA
EMail: wmehlman@icsc.org

Employers
Internat'l Council of Shopping Centers (Director, Economic Issues)

MEHRA, Rekha
1717 Massachusetts Ave. NW
Suite 302
Washington, DC 20036
Tel: (202)797-0007
Fax: (202)797-0020

Employers
Internat'l Center for Research on Women (V. President)

MEIBURGER, George J.
1023 15th St. NW
Suite 900
Washington, DC 20005-2602
Tel: (202)289-7200
Fax: (202)289-7698

Employers
Gallagher, Boland and Meiburger (Senior Counsel)

MEIEHOEFER, Melissa G.
601 13th St. NW
Suite 300
Washington, DC 20005
Tel: (202)756-3670
Fax: (202)347-1420

Employers
Georgia Institute of Technology (Analyst, Federal Policy)

MEIGHAN, Katherine W.
607 14th St. NW
Washington, DC 20005
Tel: (202)434-0700
Fax: (202)912-6000
Registered: LDA
EMail: meighank@rw.com

Employers
Rogers & Wells (Associate)

Clients Represented
On Behalf of Rogers & Wells
Banque Paribas New York Branch

MEIGHER, Eugene J.
1050 Connecticut Ave. NW
Washington, DC 20036-5339
Tel: (202)857-6000
Fax: (202)857-6395
Registered: LDA
Attorney, Antitrust Division, Department of Justice, 1965-69.

Employers
Arent Fox Kintner Plotkin & Kahn, PLLC (Member)

MEIGS, Marilyn F.

1900 M St. NW
Suite 500
Washington, DC 20036
Tel: (202)785-2635
Fax: (202)785-4037
Registered: LDA

Employers
BNFL, Inc. (V. President, Fuel Cycle and Materials Processing)

MEIKLEJOHN, Nanine

1625 L St. NW
Washington, DC 20036-5687
Tel: (202)429-1199
Fax: (202)223-3413
Registered: LDA
EMail: n.meiklejohn@afscme.org

Employers
American Federation of State, County and Municipal Employees (Legislative Affairs Specialist)

MEINHOLD, Charles

7910 Woodmont Ave.
Suite 800
Bethesda, MD 20814
Tel: (301)657-2652
Fax: (301)907-8768
EMail: ncrp@ncrp.com

Employers
Nat'l Council on Radiation Protection and Measurement (President)

MEISINGER, Reese

1828 L St. NW
Suite 906
Washington, DC 20036
Tel: (202)785-3756
Fax: (202)429-9417

Employers
American Soc. of Mechanical Engineers (Director, Public Affairs)

MEISINGER, SPHR, Susan R.

1800 Duke St.
Alexandria, VA 22314
Tel: (703)548-3440
Fax: (703)836-0367
EMail: smeisinger@shrm.org

Employers
Soc. for Human Resource Management (Chief Operating Officer)

MEISSNER, Doris

1779 Massachusetts Ave. NW
Washington, DC 20036
Tel: (202)483-7600
Fax: (202)483-1840
Commissioner, Immigration and Naturalization Service, Department of Justice, 1993-2000.

Employers
Carnegie Endowment for Internat'l Peace (Senior Associate, Global Policy)

MEISSNER, Robert

321 D St. NE
Washington, DC 20002
Tel: (202)548-8322
Fax: (202)548-8326
Registered: LDA
EMail: bmeissner@siscorpdc.com
Senate Director, Legislative Affairs (1995) and House Director, Legislative Affairs (1989), Department of Defense. Legislative Fellow and Defense Legislative Assistant to Senator Phil Gramm (R-TX), 1988.

Employers
SISCORP

Clients Represented

On Behalf of SISCORP
Biostar Group, The
Dewey Electronics Corp.
Infusion Dynamics
Innovative Technical Solutions
Mercer Engineering Research Center
ThermoTrex Corp.
VLOC

MEISTER, Brenda G.

901 15th St. NW
Suite 700
Washington, DC 20005-2301
Tel: (202)371-6000
Fax: (202)371-6279
Registered: LDA
EMail: bgmeister@verner.com

Employers
Verner, Liipfert, Bernhard, McPherson and Hand, Chartered (Member of Firm)

Clients Represented

On Behalf of Verner, Liipfert, Bernhard, McPherson and Hand, Chartered
India, Government of the Republic of
Kelly Services, Inc.
Merrill Lynch & Co., Inc.
Starwood Lodging/Starwood Capital Group, L.P.
Stewart & Stevenson Services, Inc.

MEISTER, Norbert M.

1001 Pennsylvania Ave. NW
Suite 850N
Washington, DC 20004
Tel: (202)661-3593
Fax: (202)737-4242
Registered: LDA

Employers
Federal Health Strategies, Inc. (President)

Clients Represented

On Behalf of Federal Health Strategies, Inc.
USFHP Conference Group

MEITNER, Elizabeth M.

440 First St. NW
Third Floor
Washington, DC 20001-2085
Tel: (202)638-2952
Fax: (202)638-4004
Registered: LDA

Employers
Child Welfare League of America (Public Policy Director)

MEKELBURG, Andrew

1300 I St. NW
Suite 400 West
Washington, DC 20005
Tel: (202)515-2564
Fax: (202)336-7925

Employers
Verizon Communications (Assistant V. President, Federal Government Relations)

MELBERG, James K.

1317 F St. NW
Suite 600
Washington, DC 20004
Tel: (202)638-2121
Fax: (202)638-7045
Registered: LDA
EMail: melberg@wexlergroup.com

Employers
The Wexler Group (Principal)

Clients Represented

On Behalf of The Wexler Group
The Business Roundtable

MELBY, Eric D.K.

900 17th St. NW
Suite 500
Washington, DC 20006
Tel: (202)296-9312
Fax: (202)296-9395
EMail: Melby@scowcroft.com
Staff member, Nat'l Security Council during the Bush I administration.

Employers
Forum for Internat'l Policy (Senior Associate)
The Scowcroft Group (Principal)

MELCHER, Hon. John

230-B Maryland Ave. NE
Washington, DC 20002
Tel: (202)546-4084
Fax: (202)544-7609
Registered: LDA
Member U.S. Senate, 1977-88. Member U.S. House of Representatives, 1969-76.

Employers
Self-employed as an independent consultant.

Clients Represented

As an independent consultant
American Veterinary Medical Ass'n

MELE, Chris

1101 Vermont Ave. NW
Suite 200
Washington, DC 20005
Tel: (202)898-2200
Fax: (202)898-2213
EMail: cmele@naruc.org

Employers
Nat'l Ass'n of Regulatory Utility Commissioners (Legislative Director)

MELENDEZ, Sara E.

1200 18th St. NW
Second Floor
Washington, DC 20036
Tel: (202)467-6100
Fax: (202)467-6101

Employers
Independent Sector (President and Chief Executive Officer)

MELIA, Thomas O.

1717 Massachusetts Ave. NW
Suite 503
Washington, DC 20036
Tel: (202)328-3136
Fax: (202)939-3166

Employers
Nat'l Democratic Institute for Internat'l Affairs (V. President, Programs)

MELINCOFF, David R.

1666 K St. NW
Suite 500
Washington, DC 20006-2803
Tel: (202)887-1400
Fax: (202)466-2198
Registered: LDA, FARA
Member, Trial Section, Antitrust Division, Department of Justice, 1961-69.

Employers
O'Connor & Hannan, L.L.P. (Partner)

MELINSON, Gregg R.

1500 K St.
Suite 1100
Washington, DC 20005
Tel: (202)842-8800
Fax: (202)842-8465
Registered: LDA

Employers
Drinker Biddle & Reath LLP

Clients Represented

On Behalf of Drinker Biddle & Reath LLP
Nat'l Community Capital Ass'n

MELLNICK, Keith

1616 H St. NW
Washington, DC 20006
Tel: (202)628-8188
Fax: (202)628-8189

Employers
Internat'l Research and Exchanges Board (IREX) (Communications Officer)

MELLODY, Charles J.

1350 I St. NW
Suite 690
Washington, DC 20005
Tel: (202)898-4746
Fax: (202)898-4756
Registered: LDA
EMail: cmellody@ob-cgroup.com
Former aide to the Chairman, House Ways and Means Committee, 1984-94.

Employers
The OB-C Group, LLC (Principal)

Clients Represented

On Behalf of The OB-C Group, LLC
American Airlines
Anheuser-Busch Cos., Inc.
AT&T
Biotechnology Industry Organization
Blue Cross Blue Shield Ass'n
Fannie Mae
Goodyear Tire and Rubber Co.
Healthcare Distribution Management Ass'n
Investment Co. Institute
Merrill Lynch & Co., Inc.
Motorola, Inc.
Nat'l Thoroughbred Racing Ass'n, Inc.
Newport News Shipbuilding Inc.
The Rouse Company
Sears, Roebuck and Co.
Securities Industry Ass'n
TIAA-CREF
United Parcel Service
WellPoint Health Networks/Blue Cross of California/UNICARE
Wilmer, Cutler & Pickering

MELLON, Margaret

1707 H St. NW
Suite 600
Washington, DC 20006-3919
Tel: (202)223-6133
Fax: (202)223-6162
Registered: LDA

Employers
Union of Concerned Scientists (Director, Food and Environment)

MELLON, Regina M.

1725 DeSales St. NW
Suite 800
Washington, DC 20036
Tel: (202)659-6540
Fax: (202)659-5730
Registered: LDA

Employers
Whitten & Diamond (Government Affairs Representative)

Clients Represented

On Behalf of Whitten & Diamond
Gas Technology Institute
Philadelphia Internat'l Airport
Philadelphia, Pennsylvania, City of
Pioneer Hi-Bred Internat'l, Inc.
Temple University

MELLOR, William H.

1717 Pennsylvania Ave. NW
Suite 200
Washington, DC 20006
EMail: wmellor@ij.org
Tel: (202)955-1300
Fax: (202)955-1329

Employers
Institute for Justice (President and General Counsel)

MELMED, Matthew E.

734 15th St. NW
Suite 1000
Washington, DC 20005
Tel: (202)638-1144
Fax: (202)638-0851

Employers
ZERO TO THREE/Nat'l Center for Infants, Toddlers, and Families (Exec. Director)

MELNICK, Amy

2000 L St. NW
Suite 200
Washington, DC 20036
EMail: amelnick@naspe.org
Tel: (202)416-1871
Fax: (202)416-1841

Employers
North American Soc. of Pacing and Electrophysiology (Director, Government Relations)

MELNYKOVICH, George O.

200 Daingerfield Rd.
Alexandria, VA 22314
EMail: fpmsa@clark.net
Tel: (703)684-1080
Fax: (703)548-6563

Employers
Food Processing Machinery and Supplies Ass'n (President)

MELTON, Brenda

801 N. Fairfax St.
Suite 312
Alexandria, VA 22314
Tel: (703)683-2722
Fax: (703)683-1619

Employers
American School Counselor Ass'n (Chair, Public Relations)

MELTON, Carol

1501 M St. NW
Suite 1100
Washington, DC 20005
Tel: (202)785-7300
Fax: (202)785-6360
Registered: LDA

Employers
Viacom Inc. (Senior V. President, Government Affairs)

MELTSNER, Jim

1000 Wilson Blvd.
Suite 2300
Arlington, VA 22209
Tel: (703)875-8400
Fax: (703)276-0711
Registered: LDA

Employers
Northrop Grumman Corp. (Manager, Legislative Affairs)

MELTZER, Allan H.

1150 17th St. NW
Washington, DC 20036
EMail: am05@andrew.cmu.edu
Tel: (202)862-5800
Fax: (202)862-7177

Employers
American Enterprise Institute for Public Policy Research (Visiting Scholar)

MELTZER, David

3400 International Dr. NW
Washington, DC 20008-3090
Tel: (202)944-6873
Fax: (202)944-7898

Employers
INTELSAT - Internat'l Telecommunications Satellite Organization (V. President and General Counsel)

MELTZER, Donna Ledder

8630 Fenton St.
Suite 410
Silver Spring, MD 20910
Tel: (301)588-8252
Fax: (301)588-2842
Registered: LDA

Employers
American Ass'n of University Affiliated Programs for Persons with Developmental Disabilities (Director, Legislative Affairs)

MELTZER, Richard

1150 17th St. NW
Suite 601
Washington, DC 20036
Tel: (202)293-7474
Fax: (202)293-8811
Registered: LDA

Chief Minority Counsel, Select Subcommittee on Iranian Arms Transfers to Bosnia, 1996. Chief Counsel, House Committee on Natural Resources, 1991-94. Chief Legislative Assistant to Rep. Abner J. Mikva (D-IL), 1975-79.

Employers
Washington Council Ernst & Young (Partner)

Clients Represented

On Behalf of Washington Council Ernst & Young
Aetna Inc.
Aetna Life & Casualty Co.
Allegiance Healthcare Corp.
Allen & Co.
American Express Co.
American Insurance Ass'n
American Staffing Ass'n
Anheuser-Busch Cos., Inc.
Antitrust Coalition for Consumer Choice in Health Care
Apartment Investment and Management Co.
Ass'n of American Railroads
Ass'n of Home Appliance Manufacturers
AT&T
AT&T Capital Corp.
Avco Financial Services
Aventis Pharmaceuticals, Inc.
Baxter Healthcare Corp.
BHC Communications, Inc.
Bulmer Holding PLC, H. P.
Cash Balance Coalition
Chamber of Shipping of America
Citigroup
Coalition for Fairness in Defense Exports
Coalition to Preserve Tracking Stock
ComEd
The Connell Co.
Deferral Group
Directors Guild of America
Doris Duke Charitable Foundation
Eaton Vance Management Co.
Eden Financial Corp.
The Enterprise Foundation
Fannie Mae
FedEx Corp.
Ford Motor Co.
GE Capital Assurance
General Electric Co.
General Motors Corp.
Global Competitiveness Coalition
Grasslands Water District
Group Health, Inc.
Haz-X Support Services Corp.
Gilbert P. Hyatt, Inventor
Investment Co. Institute
Large Public Power Council
Local Initiatives Support Corp.
Lockheed Martin Corp.
Marsh & McLennan Cos.
MCG Northwest, Inc.
McLane Co.
Merrill Lynch & Co., Inc.
Metropolitan Banking Group
Microsoft Corp.
Nat'l Ass'n for State Farm Agents
Nat'l Ass'n of Professional Employer Organizations
Nat'l Ass'n of Real Estate Investment Trusts
Nat'l Ass'n of State Farm Agents
Nat'l Cable Television Ass'n
Nat'l Defined Contribution Council
Nat'l Foreign Trade Council, Inc.
Nat'l Multi-Housing Council
PaineWebber Group, Inc.
Pfizer, Inc.
R&D Tax Credit Coalition
R&D Tax Regulation Group
Recording Industry Ass'n of America
Reed-Elsevier Inc.
R. J. Reynolds Tobacco Co.
Charles Schwab & Co., Inc.
Securities Industry Ass'n
Sierra Pacific Industries
Skadden, Arps, Slate, Meagher & Flom LLP
Straddle Rules Tax Group
Tax Fairness Coalition
Tax/Shelter Coalition
TransOceanic Shipping
TU Services
TXU Business Services
U.S. Oncology
USA Biomass Power Producers Alliance
Viaticus, Inc.
Wilkie Farr & Gallagher
Ziff Investors Partnership

MELTZER, Ronald I.

2445 M St. NW
Washington, DC 20037-1420
EMail: rmeltzer@wilmer.com
Tel: (202)663-6000
Fax: (202)663-6363

Employers
Wilmer, Cutler & Pickering (Associate)

Clients Represented

On Behalf of Wilmer, Cutler & Pickering
Milliken and Co.

MELUGIN, Jessica

1001 Connecticut Ave. NW
Suite 1250
Washington, DC 20036
Tel: (202)331-1010
Fax: (202)331-0640

Employers
Competitive Enterprise Institute (Policy Analyst)

MEMBRINO, Joseph R.

1120 20th St. NW
Suite 700 North
Washington, DC 20036-3406
Tel: (202)973-1200
Fax: (202)973-1212
Registered: LDA

Employers
Hall, Estill, Hardwick, Gable, Golden & Nelson (Partner)

Clients Represented

On Behalf of Hall, Estill, Hardwick, Gable, Golden & Nelson
Hoopa Valley Tribal Council
Penobscot Indian Nation
San Pasqual Band of Mission Indians

MENARD, Barbara

919 18th St. NW
Suite 800
Washington, DC 20006
Tel: (202)628-4160
Fax: (202)347-5323

Employers
Human Rights Campaign Fund (Senior Policy Advocate)

MENARD, Marilee

418 N. Pitt St.
Alexandria, VA 22314
EMail: ammpa@aol.com
Tel: (703)549-0137
Fax: (703)549-0488

Employers
Alliance of Marine Mammal Parks and Aquariums (Exec. Director)

MENCHEY, Keith

1521 New Hampshire Ave. NW
Washington, DC 20036
Tel: (202)745-7805
Fax: (202)483-4040
EMail: kmenchey@cotton.org

Employers
Nat'l Cotton Council of America (Government Relations Representative)

MENDELSOHN, Bruce S.

1333 New Hampshire Ave. NW
Suite 400
Washington, DC 20036
Tel: (202)887-4000
Fax: (202)887-4288
Chief, Office of Regulatory Policy, Division of Investment Management (1982-83), Counsel to Commissioner (1980-82), Attorney and Special Counsel, Division of Corporation Finance (1977-80), Securities and Exchange Commission.

Employers
Akin, Gump, Strauss, Hauer & Feld, L.L.P. (Partner)

MENDELSOHN, Martin

901 15th St. NW
Suite 700
Washington, DC 20005-2301
Tel: (202)371-6000
Fax: (202)371-6279
Registered: LDA
Chief Counsel, Subcommittee on International Law, House Committee on the Judiciary. Deputy Director, Litigation, Office of Special Investigations (1979-80) and Chief, Special Litigation Unit, Immigration and Naturalization Service (1977-79), Department of Justice. Administrative Assistant, U.S. House of Representatives, 1976-77.

Employers
Verner, Liipfert, Bernhard, McPherson and Hand, Chartered (Member of Firm)

Clients Represented

On Behalf of Verner, Liipfert, Bernhard, McPherson and Hand, Chartered
Amgen
Citigroup
George Washington University, Office of Government Relations
Mars, Inc.
MBIA Insurance Corp.
Merrill Lynch & Co., Inc.
Platinum Guild Internat'l
Starwood Lodging/Starwood Capital Group, L.P.
Simon Weisenthal Center/Museum of Tolerance

MENDELSON, Ira

8300 Pennsylvania Ave.
Upper Marlboro, MD 20772
Tel: (301)420-6400
Fax: (301)967-4806

Employers
Murry's, Inc. (President and Chief Exec. Officer)

MENDENHALL, Greggory B.

1300 I St. NW
11th Floor East
Washington, DC 20005-3314
Tel: (202)216-4200
Fax: (202)775-8741
Registered: LDA
EMail: gmendenhall@schnader.com

Employers
Schnader Harrison Segal & Lewis LLP

Clients Represented

On Behalf of Schnader Harrison Segal & Lewis LLP
Internat'l Air Transport Ass'n
Marine Capital Management, LLC

MENDOZA, Julie C.

The McPherson Bldg.
901 15th St. NW, Suite 1100
Washington, DC 20005
Tel: (202)682-3500
Fax: (202)682-3580
Registered: LDA

Employers
Kaye Scholer LLP

Clients Represented

On Behalf of Kaye Scholer LLP
Korean Iron and Steel Ass'n

MENEZES, Mark W.

801 Pennsylvania Ave. NW
Suite 214
Washington, DC 20004
Tel: (202)628-1645
Fax: (202)628-4276
Registered: LDA

Employers
American Electric Power Co. (V. President and Associate General Counsel)
Repeal PUHCA Now Coalition (Director)

MENGEBIER, David G.

1016 16th St. NW
Fifth Floor
Washington, DC 20036
Tel: (202)293-5794
Fax: (202)223-6178
Registered: LDA

Employers
Consumers Energy Co. (V. President, Government and International Affairs)

MENGHETTI, Linda

1211 Connecticut Ave. NW
Suite 801
Washington, DC 20036
Tel: (202)659-5147
Fax: (202)659-1347
Former Chief Minority Trade Counsel, Senate Committee on Finance. Served as Trade and Foreign Affairs Aide to Senator Bill Bradley (D-NJ).

Employers
Emergency Committee for American Trade (V. President and Counsel)

MENICHELLI, Karen

950 18th St. NW
Washington, DC 20006
Tel: (202)638-5770
Fax: (202)638-5771

Employers
Benton Foundation/Communications Policy Project (V. President)

MENN, III, Henry W. ("Buddy")

1620 I St. NW
Suite 800
Washington, DC 20006
Tel: (202)833-9070
Fax: (202)833-9612
Registered: LDA

Employers
Generic Pharmaceutical Ass'n (V. President, Government Affairs)

MENOTTI, David E.

2300 N St. NW
Washington, DC 20037-1128
Tel: (202)663-8000
Fax: (202)663-8007
Registered: LDA
EMail: david.menotti@shawpittman.com
Associate General Counsel for Air, Noise and Radiation (1981-82), Associate General Counsel for Toxic Substances (1980), and Associate General Counsel for Pesticides (1978-80), all at the Environmental Protection Agency. Captain, Judge Advocate General Corps, U.S. Army, 1969-73.

Employers
Shaw Pittman (Partner)

Clients Represented

On Behalf of Shaw Pittman
American Coke and Coal Chemicals Institute
Nat'l Oilseed Processors Ass'n

MENTZ, J. Roger

601 13th St. NW
Suite 600 South
Washington, DC 20005
Tel: (202)626-3600
Fax: (202)639-9355
Registered: LDA
EMail: mentzro@washdc.whitecase.com
Assistant Secretary of Treasury for Tax Policy, 1985-87.

Employers
White & Case LLP (Partner)

Clients Represented

On Behalf of White & Case LLP
Alticor, Inc.
Koniag, Inc.
Liberty Check Printers
Mercedes-Benz of North America, Inc.
Methanex Inc.
The Williams Companies

MENTZER, Kenneth D.

44 Canal Center Plaza
Suite 310
Alexandria, VA 22314
Tel: (703)684-0084
Fax: (703)684-0427

Employers
North American Insulation Manufacturers Ass'n (President and Chief Exec. Officer)

MERBER, Selig S.

1299 Pennsylvania Ave. NW
Suite 1100 West
Washington, DC 20004-2407
Tel: (202)637-4000
Fax: (202)637-4300
Registered: LDA

Employers
General Electric Co. (Counsel, International Trade Regulation)

MERBETH, Russell

1615 L St. NW
Suite 1260
Washington, DC 20036
Tel: (202)367-7600
Fax: (202)659-1931

Employers
Winstar Communications, Inc. (V. President, State Regulatory Affairs)

MERCER, Lee W.

666 11th St. NW
Suite 750
Washington, DC 20001
Tel: (202)628-5055
Fax: (202)628-5080
Registered: LDA
EMail: lmercer@nasbic.org

Employers
Nat'l Ass'n of Small Business Investment Companies (President)

MERCER, William M.

1255 23rd St. NW
Suite 250
Washington, DC 20037
Tel: (202)263-3900
Fax: (202)296-0909

Employers
William M. Mercer, Inc.

Clients Represented

On Behalf of William M. Mercer, Inc.
The Business Roundtable
Nat'l Ass'n of Manufacturers

MEREDITH, John

9300 Livingston Rd.
Fort Washington, MD 20744
Tel: (301)248-6200
Fax: (301)248-7104
EMail: jmeredith@ntma.org

Employers
Nat'l Tooling and Machining Ass'n (Government Affairs Representative)

MEREDITH, M. Bruce

499 S. Capitol St. SW
Suite 520
Washington, DC 20003
Tel: (202)554-3714
Fax: (202)479-4657
Registered: LDA

Employers
The Van Fleet-Meredith Group (Managing Partner)

Clients Represented

On Behalf of The Van Fleet-Meredith Group
American Gas Ass'n
Donlee Technologies, Inc.
Lockheed Martin Corp.
Mantech Corp.
Miltope Corp.
PinPoint Systems Internat'l, LLC
United Defense, L.P.

MEREDITH, Pamela L.

1101 30th St. NW
Suite 500
Washington, DC 20007
Tel: (202)625-4890
Fax: (202)625-4363
Registered: LDA

Employers
Law Offices of Pamela L. Meredith (Attorney)

Clients Represented

On Behalf of Law Offices of Pamela L. Meredith
Spectrum Astro, Inc.

MEREDITH, Sandra K.

601 King St.
Alexandria, VA 22314
Tel: (202)364-8892
Fax: (202)364-8922
Registered: LDA, FARA

Employers
Meredith Concept Group, Inc. (President)

Clients Represented
On Behalf of Meredith Concept Group, Inc.
Messier-Dowty Internat'l
Societe Nationale d'Etude et Construction de Moteurs d'Aviation (SNECMA)

MERENDA, Daniel W.

901 N. Pitt St.
Suite 320
Alexandria, VA 22314
Tel: (703)836-4880
Fax: (703)836-6941

Employers
Nat'l Ass'n of Partners in Education (President and Chief Exec. Officer)

MERIDY, Mark

1640 Rhode Island Ave. NW
Washington, DC 20036-3278
EMail: mmeridy@bnaibrith.org
Tel: (202)857-6567
Fax: (202)857-6689

Employers
B'nai B'rith Internat'l (Deputy Director, B'nai B'rith Center for Public Policy)

MERIFIELD-TRIPOLDI, Cynthia E.

1600 I St. NW
Washington, DC 20006
Tel: (202)293-1966
Fax: (202)296-7410
Registered: LDA

Employers
Motion Picture Ass'n of America (V. President, Congressional Relations)

MERIN, Charles L.

1801 K St. NW
Suite 901-L
Washington, DC 20006
EMail: Charles_Merin@bm.com
Tel: (202)530-0500
Fax: (202)530-4800
Registered: LDA

Employers
BKSH & Associates (Managing Director)

MERISOTIS, Jamie P.

1320 19th St. NW
Suite 400
Washington, DC 20036
Tel: (202)861-8223
Fax: (202)861-9307

Employers
The Institute for Higher Education Policy (President)

MERKEL, Claire Sechler

1401 K St. NW
Tenth Floor
Washington, DC 20005
Tel: (202)216-2200
Fax: (202)216-2999
Registered: LDA, FARA
Former Legislative Assistant to Senator John McCain (R-AZ). Former Associate Director, Office of Cabinet Affairs, The White House, during the Bush I administration. Former Senior Intergovernmental Officer, Department of Labor.

Employers
Jefferson-Waterman Internat'l, LLC (European Consultant)

MERKOWITZ, David R.

426 C St. NE
Washington, DC 20002
EMail: drmerkowitz@compuserve.com
Tel: (202)544-1880
Fax: (202)543-2565

Employers
Integrated Strategies/Strategic Communications (Principal)

MERLIS, Edward A.

1301 Pennsylvania Ave. NW
Suite 1100
Washington, DC 20004-1707
Tel: (202)626-4000
Fax: (202)626-4208
Registered: LDA

Employers
Air Transport Ass'n of America (Senior V. President, Legislative and International Affairs)

MEROLA, Michael

700 13th St. NW
Suite 400
Washington, DC 20005
EMail: mmerola@cassidy.com
Tel: (202)347-0773
Fax: (202)347-0785
Registered: LDA
Former Deputy Chief of Staff to Senator Robert Torricelli (D-NJ).

Employers
Cassidy & Associates, Inc. (Senior Associate)

Clients Represented
On Behalf of Cassidy & Associates, Inc.
Alenia Aerospazig
American Lung Ass'n of Minnesota
Central College
Internat'l Snowmobile Manufacturers Ass'n
Liberty Science Center
Lifebridge Health
Maersk Inc.
Neumann College
New Jersey Institute of Technology
Northwestern University
Research Foundation of the City University of New York
Southeastern Pennsylvania Consortium for Higher Education
Subaru of America
University of Pittsburgh Medical Center (UPMC)
Valley Hospital Foundation
VoiceStream Wireless Corp.

MERONEY, Jane U.

555 New Jersey Ave. NW
Washington, DC 20001
Tel: (202)393-6308
Fax: (202)879-4402
Registered: LDA

Employers
American Federation of Teachers (Associate Director, Legislative Affairs)

MERRELL, Halley A.

1155 16th St. NW
Washington, DC 20036
EMail: h_merrell@acs.org
Tel: (202)872-4510
Fax: (202)872-4615

Employers
American Chemical Soc. (Assistant Exec. Director and Secretary)

MERRIGAN, John A.

901 15th St. NW
Suite 700
Washington, DC 20005-2301
EMail: jamerrigan@verner.com
Tel: (202)371-6000
Fax: (202)371-6279
Registered: LDA, FARA
Aide to Senator Russell Long (D-LA), 1971.

Employers
Verner, Liipfert, Bernhard, McPherson and Hand, Chartered (Member of Firm)

Clients Represented
On Behalf of Verner, Liipfert, Bernhard, McPherson and Hand, Chartered
Amgen
Bacardi-Martini, USA, Inc.
Citigroup
Federal Home Loan Mortgage Corp. (Freddie Mac)
Home Warranty Coalition
Investment Co. Institute
Lehman Brothers
Lockheed Martin Tactical Systems
Merrill Lynch & Co., Inc.
Nat'l Broadcasting Co.
Northwest Airlines, Inc.
Rite Aid Corp.
RJR Nabisco Holdings Co.
Starwood Lodging/Starwood Capital Group, L.P.
Transportation Maritima Mexicana
United Health Group
Vertical Net, Inc.
VISA U.S.A., Inc.

MERRILL, Greg

1300 Wilson Blvd.
Arlington, VA 22209
EMail: greg_merrill@cmahq.com
Tel: (703)741-5417
Fax: (703)741-6417

Employers
Chlorine Chemistry Council (Director, State Chlorine Issues)

MERRILL, Jo

1901 L St. NW
Suite 200
Washington, DC 20036
Tel: (202)659-1800
Fax: (202)296-2964
Registered: LDA

Employers
March of Dimes Birth Defects Foundation (Director, Government Affairs)

MERRILL, Peter R.

1301 K St. NW
Washington, DC 20005-3333
EMail: peter.merril@us.pwcglobal.com
Tel: (202)414-1000
Fax: (202)414-1301
Registered: LDA
Former aide, Joint Committee on Taxation, U.S. Congress.

Employers
PriceWaterhouseCoopers (Partner)

Clients Represented
On Behalf of PriceWaterhouseCoopers
Contract Manufacturing Coalition
Electronic Commerce Tax Study Group
Nat'l Foreign Trade Council, Inc.

MERRILL, Richard A.

1201 Pennsylvania Ave. NW
Washington, DC 20004-2401
EMail: rmerrill@cov.com
Tel: (202)662-6000
Fax: (202)662-6291
Registered: LDA
White House Office of Science and Technology, 1978-82. Chief Counsel, Food and Drug Administration, 1975-77. Law Clerk, District of Columbia Circuit, U.S. Court of Appeals, 1964-65.

Employers
Covington & Burling (Special Counsel)

MERRITT, Bernie

1211 Connecticut Ave. NW
Suite 608
Washington, DC 20036
EMail: bmerritt@qorvis.com
Tel: (202)496-1000
Fax: (202)496-1300

Employers
Qorvis Communications (Partner)

MERRITT, Gordon L.

8100 Crestridge Rd.
Fairfax Station, VA 22039
EMail: glmerritt@erols.com
Tel: (703)250-5224
Registered: LDA
Former Army-Congressional Liaison.

Employers
G.L. Merritt & Associates, Inc. (Principal)

Clients Represented
On Behalf of G.L. Merritt & Associates, Inc.
American Systems Internat'l Corp.
APTI
ASIC
Raytheon Missile Systems

MERRITT, Mark

1129 20th St. NW
Suite 600
Washington, DC 20036-3421
EMail: mmerritt@aahp.org
Tel: (202)778-3200
Fax: (202)778-8479

Employers
American Ass'n of Health Plans (AAHP) (V. President and Chief, Strategic Planning and Public Affairs)

MERSKI, Paul

One Thomas Circle NW
Suite 400
Washington, DC 20005
Tel: (202)659-8111
Fax: (202)659-9216
Registered: LDA

Employers
Independent Community Bankers of America (Tax Counsel)

MERSKI, Richard P.

1399 New York Ave. NW
Suite 900
Washington, DC 20005
Tel: (202)585-5807
Fax: (202)585-5820
Registered: LDA

Employers
American Internat'l Group, Inc. (V. President, Governmental Affairs)

MERSON, Gary N.

1212 New York Ave. NW
Eighth Floor
Washington, DC 20005
Tel: (202)223-5515
Registered: LDA

Employers
Fragomen, Del Rey, Bernsen & Loewy, PC (Government Affairs Counsel)

MERTZ, Alan B.

900 17th St. NW
Suite 600
Washington, DC 20006
Tel: (202)452-8700
Fax: (202)296-9561

Employers
Healthcare Leadership Council (Exec. V. President)

MERVES, Esther

1818 R St. NW
Washington, DC 20009
Tel: (202)387-3760
Fax: (202)265-9532

Employers
Ass'n of American Colleges and Universities (Director, Membership and External Affairs)

MESIROW, Harold E.

1801 K St. NW
Washington, DC 20006
Tel: (202)775-0725
Fax: (202)223-8604
Registered: LDA, FARA

Employers
Robins, Kaplan, Miller & Ciresi L.L.P. (Partner)

Clients Represented

On Behalf of Robins, Kaplan, Miller & Ciresi L.L.P.
The Boat Co.
Cal Dive Internat'l Inc.
Crystal Cruises
Internat'l Group of P&I Clubs
Pacific Maritime Ass'n
R.M.S. Titanic, Inc.

MESNIKOFF, Ann

408 C St. NE
Washington, DC 20002
Tel: (202)547-1141
Fax: (202)547-6009

Employers
Sierra Club (Associate Representative, Global Warming and Energy)

MESSICK, Neil

1299 Pennsylvania Ave. NW
Suite 1100 West
Washington, DC 20004-2407
Tel: (202)637-4000
Fax: (202)637-4400
Registered: LDA

Employers
General Electric Co. (Manager, Federal Government Relations)

MESSIH, Lillian

1701 K St. NW
Suite 200
Washington, DC 20006-1503
EMail: policy@alliance1.org
Tel: (202)223-3447
Fax: (202)331-7476

Employers
Alliance for Children and Families (Policy Analyst)

MESSINA, Raymond A.

1300 I St. NW
12th Floor
Washington, DC 20005
Tel: (202)326-3980
Fax: (202)326-3981
Registered: LDA

Employers
Morgan Stanley Dean Witter & Co. (Principal, Federal Government Affairs)

MESSINA-BOYER, Christine

2100 L St. NW
Washington, DC 20037
EMail: cboyer@cmpa.com
Tel: (202)223-2942
Fax: (202)872-4014

Employers
Center for Media and Public Affairs (Managing Director)

MESSING, Jr. USA (Ret.), Major F. Andy

1220 King St.
Suite 230
Alexandria, VA 22314
EMail: ndcf@erols.com
Tel: (703)836-3443
Fax: (703)836-5402

Employers
Nat'l Defense Council Foundation (Exec. Director)

MESTRICH, Keith

815 16th St. NW
Washington, DC 20006
Tel: (202)637-5000
Fax: (202)637-5058
Registered: LDA

Employers
AFL-CIO (American Federation of Labor and Congress of Industrial Organizations) (Press Secretary, Legislation Department)

MESZAROS, James A.

1501 M St. NW
Suite 600
Washington, DC 20005-1710
EMail: meszaros@bsmg.com
Tel: (202)739-0200
Fax: (202)659-8287
Registered: FARA

Employers
BSMG Worldwide (Principal)

METALITZ, Steven J.

1747 Pennsylvania Ave. NW
Suite 825
Washington, DC 20006-4604
EMail: metalitz@iipa.com
Tel: (202)833-4198
Fax: (202)872-0546
Registered: LDA

Former Special Counsel-Chief Nominations Counsel, Senate Judiciary Committee.

Employers
Internat'l Intellectual Property Alliance (V. President and General Counsel)
Smith & Metalitz, L.L.P. (Partner)

Clients Represented

On Behalf of Smith & Metalitz, L.L.P.
eBay Inc.
Internat'l Intellectual Property Alliance

METALLO, Michael C.

651 S. Washington St.
Alexandria, VA 22314
EMail: mmetallo@ilma.org
Tel: (703)684-5574
Fax: (703)836-8503

Employers
Independent Lubricant Manufacturers Ass'n (Exec. Director)

METCALF, Anne

321 S. Washington St.
Second Floor
Alexandria, VA 22314
Tel: (703)519-3983
Fax: (703)299-0857
Registered: LDA

Served on the Subcommittee Staff for Senator John Heinz (R-PA), 1987-89. Congressional Liason, Enivornmental Protection Agency, 1991-97.

Employers
Metcalf Federal Relations (Principal)

Clients Represented

On Behalf of Metcalf Federal Relations
Brain Research Foundation
Brookfield Zoo/Chicago Zoological Soc.
Chicago Botanic Garden
Columbia College Chicago
Green Door
Museum Campus Chicago
Natural History Museum of Los Angeles County
Philadelphia Zoo

METCALF, Kathy J.

1730 M St. NW
Suite 407
Washington, DC 20036
EMail: kmetcalf@knowships.org
Tel: (202)775-4399
Fax: (202)659-3795
Registered: LDA

Employers
Chamber of Shipping of America (Director, Maritime Affairs)

METELKO, Marta R.

600 Pennsylvania Ave. SE
Suite 300
Washington, DC 20003
Tel: (202)544-6700
Fax: (202)544-6869

Employers
Republican Nat'l Hispanic Assembly of the U.S. (Exec. Director)

METTIMANO, Joseph J.

1775 K St. NW
Suite 360
Washington, DC 20006
EMail: jmettimano@unicefusa.org
Tel: (202)296-4242
Fax: (202)296-4060
Registered: LDA

Employers
U.S. Fund for UNICEF (Assistant Director)

METZENBAUM, Hon. Howard M.

1424 16th St. NW
Suite 604
Washington, DC 20036
Tel: (202)387-6121
Fax: (202)265-7989
Registered: LDA

Member, U.S. Senate (D-OH), 1974; 1976-95.

Employers
Consumer Federation of America (Chairman)

METZGER, Jr., A. Richard

1909 K St. NW
Suite 820
Washington, DC 20006
EMail: rmetzger@lmm-law.com
Tel: (202)777-7700
Fax: (202)777-7763

Chief (1997-98) and Deputy Chief (1994-97), Common Carrier Bureau, Federal Communications Commission.

Employers
Lawler, Metzger & Milkman, LLC (Partner)

Clients Represented

On Behalf of Lawler, Metzger & Milkman, LLC
Allegiance Telecom, Inc.
Gemini Networks, Inc.
MCI WorldCom Corp.

METZGER, David P.

2099 Pennsylvania Ave. NW
Suite 100
Washington, DC 20006
EMail: dmetzger@hklaw.com
Tel: (202)955-3000
Fax: (202)955-5564
Registered: LDA

Employers
Holland & Knight LLP (Partner)

Clients Represented

On Behalf of Holland & Knight LLP
Consortium for Plant Biotechnology Research
Consortium Plant Biotech Research

METZLER, Christina A.

P.O. Box 31220
4720 Montgomery Ln.
Bethesda, MD 20824-1220
Tel: (301)652-2682
Fax: (301)652-7711
Registered: LDA

Employers
American Occupational Therapy Ass'n, Inc. (Director, Federal Affairs Department)

METZNER, David A.

2099 Pennsylvania Ave. NW
Suite 850
Washington, DC 20006
EMail: Metzner@acgrep.com
Tel: (202)419-2500
Fax: (202)419-2510
Registered: LDA

Employers
American Continental Group, Inc. (Managing Director)

Clients Represented

On Behalf of American Continental Group, Inc.
American Standard Cos. Inc.
Cisco Systems Inc.
Ernst & Young LLP
Fisher Imaging
Healthnow
OSI Systems, Inc.
Plasma-Therm, Inc.
Prudential Insurance Co. of America
Securify
Siemens Corp.
Stony Brook Foundation
Trifinery, Inc.
Vanguard Research, Inc.

MEYER, Aileen "Chuca"

1133 Connecticut Ave. NW
Suite 1200
Washington, DC 20036
Tel: (202)775-9800
Fax: (202)833-8491

Employers
Winthrop, Stimson, Putnam & Roberts (Counsel)

MEYER, Alden

1707 H St. NW
Suite 600
Washington, DC 20006-3919

Tel: (202)223-6133
Fax: (202)223-6162
Registered: LDA

Employers

Union of Concerned Scientists (Director, Government Relations)

MEYER, Brian M.

7272 Wisconsin Ave.
Bethesda, MD 20814

Tel: (301)657-3000
Fax: (301)657-1615
Registered: LDA

Employers

American Soc. of Health System Pharmacists (Director, Government Affairs Division)

MEYER, Daniel P.

2100 Pennsylvania Ave. NW
Suite 500
Washington, DC 20037

Tel: (202)728-1100
Fax: (202)728-1123
Registered: LDA

Chief of Staff to Rep. Newt Gingrich (R-GA), 1989-96. Administrative Assistant to Rep. Vin Weber (R-MN), 1986-89. Legislative Director (1982-86), Legislative Assistant (1980-82), and Projects Director (1979) to Senator Rudy Boschwitz (R-MN).

Employers

The Duberstein Group, Inc. (V. President)

Clients Represented

On Behalf of The Duberstein Group, Inc.

Amerada Hess Corp.
American Apparel & Footwear Ass'n
American Ass'n of Health Plans (AAHP)
American Council of Life Insurers
American Gaming Ass'n
The American Water Works Co.
AOL Time Warner
The Business Roundtable
Comcast Corp.
Conoco Inc.
CSX Corp.
Direct Marketing Ass'n, Inc.
Dow Corning Corp.
Fannie Mae
General Motors Corp.
Goldman, Sachs and Co.
Marathon Oil Co.
Nat'l Cable Television Ass'n
Pharmacia Corp.
Project to Promote Competition and Innovation in the Digital Age
Sara Lee Corp.
Transportation Institute
United Airlines
USX Corp.

MEYER, Don

600 New Hampshire Ave. NW
Suite 601
Washington, DC 20037

Tel: (202)333-7400
Fax: (202)333-1638
Registered: LDA

EMail: dmeyer@hillandknowlton.com

Employers

Hill and Knowlton, Inc. (Senoir Account Supervisor)

MEYER, Douglas

1275 K St. NW
Suite 600
Washington, DC 20005

Tel: (202)513-6300

Employers

Internat'l Union of Electronic, Electrical, Salaried, Machine, and Furniture Workers-Communications Workers of America (Director, Research and Public Policy)

MEYER, Jack A.

1015 18th St. NW
Suite 210
Washington, DC 20036

Tel: (202)833-8877
Fax: (202)833-8932

EMail: jmesrindp@aol.com

Employers

New Directions for Policy (President)

MEYER, Kathy

1601 Connecticut Ave. NW
Suite 700
Washington, DC 20009-1056

Tel: (202)588-5206
Fax: (202)588-5049

Employers

Meyer & Glitzenstein (Partner)

MEYER, Lindsay B.

1201 New York Ave. NW
Suite 1000
Washington, DC 20005

Tel: (202)962-4829
Fax: (202)962-8300

EMail: lbmeyer@venable.com

Employers

Venable (Partner)

MEYER, Lisa

2101 Wilson Blvd.
Suite 750
Arlington, VA 22201

Tel: (703)875-8059
Fax: (703)875-8922

EMail: meyer@pscouncil.org

Employers

Professional Services Council (V. President, Communications)

MEYERS, Bob

1211 Connecticut Ave. NW
Suite 310
Washington, DC 20026

Tel: (202)721-9100
Fax: (202)530-2855

Employers

Nat'l Press Foundation (President)

MEYERS, Craig A.

1317 F St. NW
Suite 200
Washington, DC 20004

Tel: (202)737-1800
Fax: (202)737-2485

Employers

Edington, Peel & Associates, Inc. (Associate)

Clients Represented

On Behalf of Edington, Peel & Associates, Inc.

Arrowhead Regional Medical Center
Kettering Medical Center
Pacific Union College
Paradise Valley Hospital

MEYERS, Edward R.

1311 L St. NW
Fourth Floor
Washington, DC 20005

Tel: (202)626-3780
Fax: (202)638-3486

EMail: edmeyers@ctj.org

Employers

Citizens for Tax Justice (Program Director)

MEYERS, Larry D.

412 First St. SE
Suite One
Washington, DC 20003

Tel: (202)484-2773
Fax: (202)484-0770
Registered: LDA

EMail: larrymeyers@meyersandassociates.com

Legislative Director to Senator Lloyd Bentsen (D-TX), 1972-76. Director, Congressional Affairs, Department of Agriculture, 1976-80.

Employers

Meyers & Associates (President)

Virginia-Carolina's Peanut Political Action Committee (Treasurer)

Clients Represented

On Behalf of Meyers & Associates

The Alliance for I-69 Texas
AMCOR Capital Corp.
American Beekeeping Federation
American Sheep Industry Ass'n
Canadian River Municipal Water Authority
Coalition for Maritime Education
Corpus Christi, City of
Council for Agricultural Science and Technology
Finnish American Corporate Team (F.A.C.T.)
Irrigation Projects Reauthorization Council
Las Cruces, New Mexico, City of
Minor Use, Minor Species Coalition
Nat'l Ass'n for Agricultural Stewardship
New Mexico State University
NOKIA
North Carolina Peanut Growers Ass'n
Rice Belt Warehouses
Rio Grande Valley Chamber of Commerce
Rio Grande Valley Irrigation
Southwest Peanut Growers
Southwest Peanut PAC
Space Access
Texas A&M Research Foundation
University of North Carolina at Greensboro
Virginia Peanut Growers Ass'n
Virginia-Carolina's Peanut Political Action Committee
Wool Fiber, Yarn Fabric Coalition

MEYERS, N. Marshall

1220 19th St. NW
Suite 400
Washington, DC 20036

Tel: (202)466-8270
Fax: (202)293-4377

Employers

Meyers & Alterman (Partner)
Pet Industry Joint Advisory Council (Exec. V. President and General Counsel)

Clients Represented

On Behalf of Meyers & Alterman

Pet Industry Joint Advisory Council

MEYERS, Nicholas

1400 K St. NW
Washington, DC 20005

Tel: (202)682-6164
Fax: (202)682-6850
Registered: LDA

Employers

American Psychiatric Ass'n (Deputy Director, Government Relations)

MEYERS, Richard L.

412 First St. SE
Suite One
Washington, DC 20003

Tel: (202)484-2773
Fax: (202)484-0770
Registered: LDA

EMail: rickmeyers@meyersandassociates.com

Employers

Meyers & Associates (Partner)

Clients Represented

On Behalf of Meyers & Associates

AMCOR Capital Corp.
American Beekeeping Federation
Corpus Christi, City of
Council for Agricultural Science and Technology
Finnish American Corporate Team (F.A.C.T.)
Geo-Seis Helicopters Inc.
Las Cruces, New Mexico, City of
Minor Use, Minor Species Coalition
Nat'l Ass'n for Agricultural Stewardship
New Mexico State Office of Research & Development
New Mexico State University
New Mexico State University, Department of Agriculture
New Mexico State University, Department of Engineering
NOKIA
North Carolina Peanut Growers Ass'n
Rice Belt Warehouses
Rio Grande Valley Chamber of Commerce
Southwest Peanut Growers
Space Access
University of North Carolina at Greensboro
Virginia Peanut Growers Ass'n
Wool Fiber, Yarn Fabric Coalition

MEYERSON, Adam

214 Massachusetts Ave. NE
Washington, DC 20002

Tel: (202)546-4400
Fax: (202)546-8328

Employers

Heritage Foundation (V. President, Educational Affairs)

MEZEY, Jennifer

11 Dupont Circle NW
Suite 800
Washington, DC 20036
EMail: jmezey@nwlc.org
Tel: (202)588-5180
Fax: (202)588-5185

Employers
Nat'l Women's Law Center (Fellow)

MEZINES, Basil J.

1100 Connecticut Ave. NW
Suite 1100
Washington, DC 20036
Tel: (202)737-7777
Fax: (202)296-8312
Executive Director (1971-73), Director, Bureau of Competition (1970), Executive Assistant to the Chairman (1970), Senior Trial Attorney (1961-70), Associate Executive Director (1960) and Attorney (1949-59), all with the Federal Trade Commission.

Employers
Stein, Mitchell & Mezines (Partner)

Clients Represented

On Behalf of Stein, Mitchell & Mezines
Automotive Warehouse Distributors Ass'n

MEZISTRANO, Scott

1225 I St. NW
Suite 500
Washington, DC 20005
Tel: (202)682-4786
Fax: (202)371-8892
Registered: LDA
EMail: scottmapa@aol.com

Employers
American Payroll Ass'n (Manager, Government Relations)

MIANO, Andrea

1775 Pennsylvania Ave. NW
Suite 200
Washington, DC 20006
Tel: (202)862-1000
Fax: (202)862-1093

Employers
Dewey Ballantine LLP (Associate)

MIANO, Anne

2550 M St. NW
Washington, DC 20037-1350
Tel: (202)457-6000
Fax: (202)457-6315
Registered: LDA
EMail: amiano@pattonboggs.com
Former Staff Director, Subcommittee on Transportation and Related Agencies, Senate Appropriations Committee and Aide to Senator Alfonse D'Amato (R-NY).

Employers
Patton Boggs, LLP (Counsel)

Clients Represented

On Behalf of Patton Boggs, LLP
Denver Regional Transportation District
New York State Department of Transportation
New York State Metropolitan Transportation Authority
New York State Thruway Authority
Save Barton Creek

MICA, Hon. Daniel A.

805 15th St. NW
Suite 300
Washington, DC 20005-2207
Tel: (202)682-4200
Fax: (202)682-9054
Registered: LDA
Member, U.S. House of Representatives (D-FL), 1979-89.

Employers
Credit Union Nat'l Ass'n, Inc. (President and Chief Exec. Officer)

MICALI, Mark A.

1111 19th St. NW
Suite 1100
Washington, DC 20036
Tel: (202)861-2422
Fax: (202)955-0085
Registered: LDA
EMail: markmicali@the-dma.org

Employers
Direct Marketing Ass'n, Inc. (V. President, Government Affairs)

MICHAEL, Laurie L.

601 Pennsylvania Ave. NW
Suite 1200
North Bldg.
Washington, DC 20036
Tel: (202)638-4170
Fax: (202)638-3670
Registered: LDA

Employers
Merck & Co. (Senior Director, Counsel, Federal Policy and Government Relations)

MICHAEL, Scott

1611 Duke St.
Alexandria, VA 22314
Tel: (703)683-7410
Fax: (703)683-7527
Registered: LDA

Employers
American Moving and Storage Ass'n (Assistant to the President)

MICHAEL, Stephen

818 Connecticut Ave. NW
Suite 325
Washington, DC 20006
Tel: (202)776-0071
Fax: (202)776-0083
Registered: LDA
EMail: smichael@poldir.com
Director of Legislative and Public Affairs, Rural Electrification Administration, 1992-93; Special Assistant, Legislative and Public Affairs, Farmers Home Administration, 1991-92; Legislative Director/Legislative Assistant to Rep. Bill Schuette (R-MI), 1985-89.

Employers
Policy Directions, Inc. (V. President)

Clients Represented

On Behalf of Policy Directions, Inc.
Anthra
Bausch & Lomb
Bayer Diagnostic
Baylor College of Medicine
Burger King Corp.
Cosmetic, Toiletry and Fragrance Ass'n
Nestle USA, Inc.
Orphan Medical, Inc.
Soc. for Neuroscience
State University of New York at Albany
U.S. Oncology
Visible Genetics
Visx, Inc.

MICHAELIS, Dan V.

1401 I St. NW
Suite 1000
Washington, DC 20005
EMail: dmichaelis@sia.com
Tel: (202)296-9410
Fax: (202)296-9775

Employers
Securities Industry Ass'n (Assistant V. President, Corporate Communications)

MICHAELS, Janet

15825 Shady Grove Rd.
Suite 140
Rockville, MD 20850
Tel: (301)948-3244
Fax: (301)258-9454

Employers
American Health Assistance Foundation (Exec. Director)

MICHAELSON, Leslie

6432 Quincy Pl.
Falls Church, VA 22042
EMail: smxus@aol.com
Tel: (703)237-8135
Fax: (703)533-9103

Employers
Shriner-Midland Co. (Manager, Association Research and Economics)

MICHAELSON, Martin

555 13th St. NW
Washington, DC 20004-1109
Tel: (202)637-5600
Fax: (202)637-5910
Registered: LDA

Employers
Hogan & Hartson L.L.P.

Clients Represented

On Behalf of Hogan & Hartson L.L.P.
Brandeis University

MICHAELSON, Michael G.

1201 Pennsylvania Ave. NW
Washington, DC 20004-2401
EMail: mmichaelson@cov.com
Tel: (202)662-6000
Fax: (202)662-6291
Law Clerk to Judge David L. Bazelon, U.S. Court of Appeals for the District of Columbia, 1984-85.

Employers
Covington & Burling (Special Counsel)

MICHALOPOULOS, Dino

1611 N. Kent St.
Suite 901
Arlington, VA 22209
Tel: (703)351-4969
Fax: (703)351-0090

Employers
Alexis de Tocqueville Institution (Visiting Fellow)

MICHALSKI, Richard P.

9000 Machinists Place
Upper Marlboro, MD 20772
Tel: (301)967-4575
Fax: (301)967-4595
Registered: LDA

Employers
Internat'l Ass'n of Machinists and Aerospace Workers (Director, Legislation and Political Action)

MICHAUD, Jay

1301 Pennsylvania Ave. NW
Suite 404
Washington, DC 20004-1727
Tel: (202)783-0911
Fax: (202)783-3524

Employers
Chicago, Illinois, Washington Office of the City of (Deputy Director)

MICHEL, Kyle G.

1225 I St. NW
Suite 600
Washington, DC 20005
Tel: (202)661-6191
Fax: (202)661-6182
Registered: LDA
EMail: kylemichel@morganmeguire.com
Special Assistant to the V. President, The White House, 1993. Legislative Assistant to Senator Al Gore, Jr. (D-TN), 1987-89.

Employers
Morgan Meguire, LLC (Senior V. President and General Counsel)

Clients Represented

On Behalf of Morgan Meguire, LLC
Adroit Systems Inc.
Air-Conditioning and Refrigeration Institute
Arctic Resources Co.
Baker Electromotive, Inc.
BellSouth Corp.
Burke Venture Capital
Colorado River Energy Distributors Ass'n
Energy Affairs Administration
Energy Northwest
Florida Municipal Power Agency
Goodman Manufacturing Co., L.P.
GovWorks.com
Just Valuations
Longhorn Pipeline
Madison Gas & Electric Co.
Manatee, Florida, County of
Northern California Power Agency
Northwest Public Power Ass'n
Nuevo Energy
Puerto Rico Electric Power Authority
Puerto Rico, Attorney General of
Redding, California, City of
Seven Seas Petroleum USA Inc.
Shell Oil Co.
Southern California Public Power Authority
Springfield, Missouri, City Utilities of
Tennessee Valley Public Power Ass'n
Transmission Access Policy Study Group
Truckee Donner Electric Power Utility District
Washington Public Utility Districts Ass'n

MICHEL, Hon. Robert H.

555 13th St. NW
Washington, DC 20004-1109
Tel: (202)637-5804
Fax: (202)637-5910
Registered: LDA
EMail: rhmichel@hhlaw.com
Member, U.S. House of Representatives (R-IL), 1957-95.

Employers
Hogan & Hartson L.L.P. (Senior Advisor, Corporate and Governmental Affairs)

Clients Represented

On Behalf of Hogan & Hartson L.L.P.

Air Transport Ass'n of America
American Registry of Pathology
Campaign for Medical Research
Discovery Science Center
eBay Inc.
Fujisawa Health Care Inc.
GE Capital Aviation Services
HMSHost Corp.
Nat'l Board for Professional Teaching Standards (NBPTS)
Nat'l Structured Settlements Trade Ass'n
News Corporation Ltd.
Public Service Co. of Colorado
Qwest Communications
United Special Transport Air Resources, LLC (USTAR)
UPMC Presbyterian

MICHELMAN, Kate

1156 15th St. NW
Suite 700
Washington, DC 20005
Tel: (202)973-3000
Fax: (202)973-3096

Employers

Nat'l Abortion and Reproductive Rights Action League (President)

MICHELS, Dina L.

1301 K St. NW
Suite 800 East
Washington, DC 20005
EMail: dmichels@ropesgray.com
Tel: (202)626-3900
Fax: (202)626-3961

Employers

Ropes & Gray (Partner)

MICHELS, Tom

1120 G St. NW
Suite 900
Washington, DC 20005-3801
EMail: tom@noia.org
Tel: (202)347-6900
Fax: (202)347-8650

Employers

Nat'l Ocean Industries Ass'n (Director, Public Affairs)

MICKEY, Anne E.

1850 M St. NW
Suite 900
Washington, DC 20036
Tel: (202)463-2500
Fax: (202)463-4950

General Counsel's Office, Federal Maritime Commission, 1977-80.

Employers

Sher & Blackwell (Partner)

MICKEY, Jr., Paul

2300 N St. NW
Washington, DC 20037-1128
EMail: paul.mickey@shawpittman.com
Tel: (202)663-8000
Fax: (202)663-8007

Employers

Shaw Pittman (Managing Partner)

MICOCCI, John

475 L'Enfant Plaza SW
MS: 10816
Washington, DC 20260
Tel: (202)268-3739
Fax: (202)268-4977

Employers

United States Postal Service (Public Policy Programs)

MIDMAN, Joy

1025 Connecticut Ave. NW
Suite 1012
Washington, DC 20036
EMail: naptcc@aol.com
Tel: (202)857-9735
Fax: (202)362-5145

Employers

Nat'l Ass'n of Psychiatric Treatment Centers for Children (Exec. Director)

MIERZWINSKI, Edmund

218 D St. SE
Second Floor
Washington, DC 20003
Tel: (202)546-9707
Fax: (202)546-2461
Registered: LDA

Employers

U.S. Public Interest Research Group (Consumer Program Director)

MIETUS, John R.

901 15th St. NW
Suite 700
Washington, DC 20005-2301
EMail: jrmietus@verner.com
Tel: (202)371-6000
Fax: (202)371-6279
Registered: LDA, FARA

Employers

Verner, Liipfert, Bernhard, McPherson and Hand, Chartered (Member of Firm)

Clients Represented

On Behalf of Verner, Liipfert, Bernhard, McPherson and Hand, Chartered

Bombardier Transportation/Bombardier Transit Corporation
Independent Fuel Terminal Operators Ass'n

MIGDAIL, Evan M.

901 15th St. NW
Suite 700
Washington, DC 20005-2301
EMail: emmigdail@verner.com
Tel: (202)371-6000
Fax: (202)371-6279
Registered: LDA

Employers

Verner, Liipfert, Bernhard, McPherson and Hand, Chartered (Member of Firm)

Clients Represented

On Behalf of Verner, Liipfert, Bernhard, McPherson and Hand, Chartered

American Financial Group
Management Insights, Inc.
The PGA Tour, Inc.

MIGNONI, Ellen

1615 L St. NW
Suite 900
Washington, DC 20036
EMail: emignoni@apcoworldwide.com
Tel: (202)778-1000
Fax: (202)466-6002

Employers

APCO Worldwide (Senior V. President and Director, Corporate Community Strategies)

MIHALSKI, Edmund J.

555 12th St. NW
Suite 650
Washington, DC 20004-1205
Tel: (202)393-7950
Fax: (202)393-7960
Registered: LDA

Employers

Eli Lilly and Co. (Director, Federal Affairs)

MIHAS, Tracy

1341 G St. NW
Suite 900
Washington, DC 20005
Tel: (202)637-1500
Fax: (202)637-1549

Employers

Philip Morris Management Corp. (Manager, Client Services - Pmmc/Issues Planning and Research)

MIKEL, John

701 Pennsylvania Ave. NW
Suite 720
Washington, DC 20004
Tel: (202)434-4800
Fax: (202)347-4015

Former Staff Member, House Committee on Appropriations.

Employers

Siemens Corp. (Director, Legislative Affairs)

MIKRUT, Joseph M.

1500 Pennsylvania Ave. NW
MS: 1308
Washington, DC 20220
Tel: (202)622-0180
Fax: (202)622-0646

Employers

Department of Treasury - Tax Policy (Tax Legislative Counsel)

MILANESE, Sylvia E.

Ballston Tower #3
4015 Wilson Blvd.
MS: 612
Arlington, VA 22203
EMail: smilanes@msha.gov
Tel: (703)235-1392
Fax: (703)235-4369

Employers

Department of Labor - Mine Safety and Health Administration (Congressional Liaison, Office of Congressional and Legislative Affairs)

MILANO, Madalene

1010 Wisconsin Ave. NW
Suite 800
Washington, DC 20007
Tel: (202)338-8700
Fax: (202)338-2334

Employers

Greer, Margolis, Mitchell, Burns & Associates (Partner)

Clients Represented

On Behalf of Greer, Margolis, Mitchell, Burns & Associates

Air Bag and Seat Belt Safety Campaign

MILBY, Helen Muir

600 Pennsylvania Ave. SE
Suite 400
Washington, DC 20003
EMail: hmilby@dlcppi.org
Tel: (202)546-0007
Fax: (202)544-5002

Employers

Democratic Leadership Council (Development Director)

MILES, David M.

1722 I St. NW
Washington, DC 20006
EMail: dmiles@sidley.com
Tel: (202)736-8000
Fax: (202)736-8711
Registered: LDA

Law Clerk to Judge George E. MacKinnon, U.S. Court of Appeals, District of Columbia Circuit, 1980-81, and to Chief Judge Edward S. Northrop, U.S. District Court for the District of Maryland, 1979-80.

Employers

Sidley & Austin (Partner)

Clients Represented

On Behalf of Sidley & Austin

Investment Co. Institute

MILES, Leslie K.

666 11th St. NW
Suite 600
Washington, DC 20001
EMail: lmiles@ccianet.org
Tel: (202)783-0070
Fax: (202)783-0534

Former Legislative Assistant to Barbara A. Mikulski (D-MD).

Employers

Computer and Communications Industry Ass'n (CCIA) (V. President, Communications and Industry Relations)

MILES, R. Jeffrey

14850 Conference Center Dr.
Suite 100
Chantilly, VA 20151-3831
EMail: r.jeffrey.miles@rollsroyce.com
Tel: (703)621-2850
Fax: (703)621-4989
Registered: LDA

Employers

Rolls-Royce North America Inc. (Director, Technology Programs)

MILEVA, Rali

2500 Wilson Blvd.
Suite 300
Arlington, VA 22201
EMail: rmileva@tia.eia.org
Tel: (703)907-7721
Fax: (703)907-7727

Employers

Telecommunications Industry Ass'n (Director, Public Relations)

MILGATE, Karen

1140 Connecticut Ave. NW
Suite 1050
Washington, DC 20036
Tel: (202)331-5790
Fax: (202)331-9334
Registered: LDA

Employers

American Health Quality Ass'n (Deputy Exec. V. President)

MILIUS, Pauline H.

Patrick Henry Bldg.
601 D St. NW, Room 8022
Washington, DC 20004
EMail: Pauline.Milius@usdoj.gov
Tel: (202)514-2586
Fax: (202)616-3362

Employers

Department of Justice - Environment and Natural Resources Division (Chief, Policy Legislation and Special Litigation Section)

MILK, Benjamin

7315 Wisconsin Ave.
Suite 1200N
Bethesda, MD 20814
Tel: (301)652-5674
Fax: (301)652-7269
EMail: bmilk@iarw.org

Executive Director, U.S. Securities and Exchange Commission, 1976-81.

Employers

Internat'l Ass'n of Refrigerated Warehouses (V. President and Secretary)

MILKEY, Dr. Robert

2000 Florida Ave. NW
Suite 400
Washington, DC 20009
Tel: (202)328-2010
Fax: (202)234-2560

Employers

American Astronomical Soc. (Exec. Officer)

MILKMAN, Ruth M.

1909 K St. NW
Suite 820
Washington, DC 20006
Tel: (202)777-7700
Fax: (202)777-7763
Registered: LDA
EMail: rmilkman@lmm-law.com

Deputy Chief (1997-87), Deputy Chief, Policy Division (1990-94), Attorney-Advisor, Office of General Counsel and Common Carrier Bureau (1986-90), Deputy Chief, International Bureau (1996-97), and Senior Legal Advisor to the Chairman (1994-96), Federal Communications Commission.

Employers

Lawler, Metzger & Milkman, LLC (Partner)

Clients Represented

On Behalf of Lawler, Metzger & Milkman, LLC

Allegiance Telecom, Inc.
INTELSAT - Internat'l Telecommunications Satellite Organization
MCI WorldCom Corp.
NorthPoint Communications, Inc.

MILLAN, William "Bill"

4245 N. Fairfax Dr.
Suite 100
Arlington, VA 20003-1606
Tel: (703)841-4228
Fax: (703)841-7400
Registered: LDA

Employers

The Nature Conservancy (Senior Policy Advisor, International)

MILLAR, Sheila A.

1001 G St. NW
Suite 500 West
Washington, DC 20001
Tel: (202)434-4100
Fax: (202)434-4646
EMail: millar@khlaw.com

Employers

Keller and Heckman LLP (Partner)

Clients Represented

On Behalf of Keller and Heckman LLP

Produce Marketing Ass'n

MILLAR, William W.

1666 K St. NW
Washington, DC 20006
Tel: (202)296-4700
Fax: (202)496-4324
Registered: LDA
EMail: wmillar@apta.com

Employers

American Public Transportation Ass'n (President)

MILLER, Alison

1299 Pennsylvania Ave. NW
Suite 800 West
Washington, DC 20004
Tel: (202)785-0500
Fax: (202)785-5277
Registered: LDA

Employers

The Carmen Group (Events Coordinator)

MILLER, Amy

4301 N. Fairfax Dr.
Suite 550
Arlington, VA 22203-1627
Tel: (703)527-8655
Fax: (703)527-2649

Employers

Equipment Leasing Ass'n of America (V. President, Communications)

MILLER, Andrew

600 Pennsylvania Ave. SE
Fifth Floor
Washington, DC 20003
Tel: (202)544-0200
Fax: (202)546-7142
Registered: LDA

Employers

Amnesty Internat'l U.S.A. (Advocacy Director for Latin America)

MILLER, Andrew Clark

700 13th St. NW
Suite 1000
Washington, DC 20005
Tel: (202)347-6633
Fax: (202)347-8713
Registered: FARA

Employers

Powell Tate (V. President)

Clients Represented

On Behalf of Powell Tate

Saudi Arabia, Royal Embassy of

MILLER, Andrew P.

2101 L St. NW
Washington, DC 20037-1526
Tel: (202)785-9700
Fax: (202)887-0689
Registered: LDA
EMail: millera@dsmo.com

Employers

Dickstein Shapiro Morin & Oshinsky LLP (Partner)

Clients Represented

On Behalf of Dickstein Shapiro Morin & Oshinsky LLP

The Reader's Digest Ass'n

MILLER, B. Jack

1755 Jefferson Davis Hwy.
Suite 1107
Arlington, VA 22202
Tel: (703)415-0146
Fax: (703)415-0147
Registered: LDA
EMail: BJackM@aol.com

Employers

Condor Electronic Systems (V. President, Washington Operations)

MILLER, B. Parker

1000 Wilson Blvd.
Suite 2300
Arlington, VA 22209
Tel: (703)875-8400
Fax: (703)276-0711
Registered: LDA

Employers

Northrop Grumman Corp. (Manager, Legislative Affairs)

MILLER, Bill

1615 H St. NW
Washington, DC 20062-2000
Tel: (202)659-6000
Fax: (202)463-5836

Employers

Chamber of Commerce of the U.S.A. (Political Director)

MILLER, Carol A.

1701 K St. NW
Suite 600
Washington, DC 20006-1503
Tel: (202)833-5900
Fax: (202)833-0075
Registered: LDA

Employers

Global Health Council (Director, Public Policy)

MILLER, Charles A.

1201 Pennsylvania Ave. NW
Washington, DC 20004-2401
Tel: (202)662-6000
Fax: (202)662-6291
Registered: LDA
EMail: cmiller@cov.com

Law Clerk, Supreme Court, 1958.

Employers

Covington & Burling (Partner)

Clients Represented

On Behalf of Covington & Burling

Coalition on Medicaid Reform

MILLER, Charles R.

1350 I St. NW
Suite 590
Washington, DC 20005
Tel: (202)354-7107
Fax: (202)354-7155
Registered: LDA
EMail: rmiller@cap.org

Employers

College of American Pathologists (Director, Political Programs and Grassroots Communication)

MILLER, Chaz

4301 Connecticut Ave. NW
Washington, DC 20008
Tel: (202)244-4700
Fax: (202)966-4818

Employers

Nat'l Solid Wastes Management Ass'n (Director, State Programs)

MILLER, USN, Cdr. Chip

1300 Defense Pentagon
Room 3D918
Washington, DC 20301-1300
Tel: (703)614-9115
Fax: (703)697-8299

Employers

Department of Defense (Special Assistant for Research, Testing & Evaluation, Office of Legislative Liaison)

MILLER, David H.

1710 Rhode Island Ave. NW
Fourth Floor
Washington, DC 20036
Tel: (202)467-0045
Fax: (202)467-0065
Registered: LDA

Legislative Assistant to Senator Edward Brooke (R-MA), 1975-77.

Employers

Federal Legislative Associates, Inc. (Principal)

Clients Represented

On Behalf of Federal Legislative Associates, Inc.

Commercial Finance Ass'n
FIRSTPLUS Financial Group Inc.
PenOp Inc.
Religious Technology Center
TV Radio Now Corp. (i Crave TV)

MILLER, Deborah E.

4301 N. Fairfax Dr.
Suite 425
Arlington, VA 22203
Tel: (703)524-8800
Fax: (703)528-3816
Registered: LDA
EMail: demiller@ari.org

Employers

Air-Conditioning and Refrigeration Institute (V. President, Government Affairs)

MILLER, Denny M.

400 N. Capitol St. NW
Suite 363
Washington, DC 20001
Tel: (202)783-0280
Fax: (202)737-4518
Registered: LDA
EMail: dmiller@millermcbee.com

Administrative Assistant to Senator Henry Jackson (D-WA), 1968-83. Former Professional Staff Member, Senate Committee on Energy and Natural Resources.

Employers

Denny Miller McBee Associates (President)

Clients Represented

On Behalf of Denny Miller McBee Associates

Asbestos Recycling Inc.

MILLER, Doug

700 11th St. NW
Washington, DC 20001-4507
Tel: (202)383-1117
Fax: (202)383-7540
Registered: LDA
EMail: dmiller@realtors.org

Employers

Nat'l Ass'n of Realtors (Representative, Commercial Finance Policy)

MILLER, Edward C.

700 11th St. NW
Washington, DC 20001-4507
Tel: (202)383-1171
Fax: (202)383-7540
Registered: LDA
EMail: emiller@realtors.org

Employers
Nat'l Ass'n of Realtors (Business Issues Policy Representative)

MILLER, Eleanor
4301 Wilson Blvd.
Arlington, VA 22203-1860
Tel: (703)907-5721
Fax: (703)907-5519
EMail: eleanor.miller@nreca.org

Employers
Nat'l Rural Electric Cooperative Ass'n (Manager, Media and Public Relations)

MILLER, Eric
666 11th St. NW
Suite 500
Washington, DC 20001
Tel: (202)347-1122
Fax: (202)347-1116

Employers
Project on Government Oversight, Inc. (Defense Specialist)

MILLER, Eugene P.
1735 New York Ave. NW
Suite 500
Washington, DC 20006-4759
Tel: (202)628-1700
Fax: (202)331-1024

Employers
Preston Gates Ellis & Rouvelas Meeds LLP (Partner)

MILLER, Garland
1010 Pennsylvania Ave. SE
Washington, DC 20003
Tel: (202)546-4995
Fax: (202)544-7926

Employers
Invest to Compete Alliance (Exec. Director)

MILLER, George E.
1111 19th St. NW
11th Floor
Washington, DC 20036
Tel: (703)528-7525
Fax: (703)807-0793

Employers
Direct Marketing Ass'n Nonprofit Federation (Postal Counsel)

MILLER, George W.
555 13th St. NW
Washington, DC 20004-1109
Tel: (202)637-6575
Fax: (202)637-5910
Registered: LDA
EMail: gwmiller@hhlaw.com
Office of the Assistant General Counsel (Logistics), Office of the General Counsel, Department of Defense, 1968-70. Active Duty, Judge Advocate General's Corps, U.S. Navy, 1967-70. Civil Law Division, Office of the Judge Advocate General, U.S. Navy, 1967-68.

Employers
Hogan & Hartson L.L.P. (Partner)

Clients Represented
On Behalf of Hogan & Hartson L.L.P.
Andalex Resources, Inc.

MILLER, Harris N.
1401 Wilson Blvd.
Suite 1100
Arlington, VA 22209
Tel: (703)522-5055
Fax: (703)525-2279
Registered: LDA
EMail: hmiller@itaa.org

Employers
Information Technology Ass'n of America (ITAA) (President)

MILLER, Hydi
P.O. Box 77235
National Capital Station
Washington, DC 20013
Tel: (202)874-1547
Fax: (202)874-1739
EMail: millerpma@aol.com

Employers
Professional Managers Ass'n (Legislative/Communications Director)

MILLER, III, James C.
1250 H St. NW
Suite 700
Washington, DC 20005-3908
Tel: (202)783-3870
Fax: (202)783-4687
EMail: jmiller@cse.org

Employers
Citizens for a Sound Economy (Counselor)

MILLER, James F.
800 Connecticut Ave. NW
Suite 500
Washington, DC 20006
Tel: (202)331-3166
Fax: (202)331-3101
Registered: LDA
EMail: millerj@gtlaw.com
Counsel, Office of Tax Policy, Department of Treasury, 1989-93. Counsel, Tax Division, Department of Justice, 1979-83.

Employers
Greenberg Traurig, LLP (Shareholder)

Clients Represented
On Behalf of Greenberg Traurig, LLP
Blue Cross and Blue Shield of California
Bowman Internat'l Corp.
Chicago Trust Co.
Englewood Hospital & Medical Center
Health Partners
Healtheon/Web MD
Starnet Communications Internat'l
Starwood Hotels & Resorts Worldwide, Inc.
United Healthcare
WellPoint Health Networks/Blue Cross of California/UNICARE

MILLER, Jeff
501 Third St. NW
Washington, DC 20001-2797
Tel: (202)434-1100
Fax: (202)434-1377

Employers
Communications Workers of America (Director, Communications)

MILLER, Ph.D., Jerome G.
3125 Mount Vernon Ave.
Alexandria, VA 22305
Tel: (703)684-0373
Fax: (703)684-6037
EMail: ncia@igc.apc.org

Employers
Nat'l Center on Institutions and Alternatives (President)

MILLER, Jim
400 N. Capitol St. NW
Suite 790
Washington, DC 20001
Tel: (202)554-1600
Fax: (202)554-1654
Registered: LDA

Employers
Nat'l Farmers Union (Farmers Educational & Co-operative Union of America) (Chief Economist)

MILLER, Joseph "Buzz"
1130 Connecticut Ave. NW
Suite 830
Washington, DC 20036
Tel: (202)261-5000
Fax: (202)296-7937

Employers
Southern Co. (V. President, Government Relations)

MILLER, Kimberly
444 N. Capitol St. NW
Suite 134
Washington, DC 20001
Tel: (202)624-5270
Fax: (202)624-5280

Employers
California, Washington Office of the State of (Deputy Director)

MILLER, Knute Michael
1909 K Street NW
Suite 810
Washington, DC 20006
Tel: (202)530-2706
Fax: (202)872-0736
Registered: LDA

Employers
ACE INA (V. President, Government and Industry Affairs)

MILLER, Kristine B.
1200 Wilson Blvd.
Arlington, VA 22209-1989
Tel: (703)465-3232
Fax: (703)465-3002
Registered: LDA

Employers
The Boeing Co. (PAC Manager)

MILLER, Lane F.
4200 Cathedral Ave. NW
Suite 715
Washington, DC 20016
EMail: lane_miller@hotmail.com

Employers
Transnat'l Development Consortium (Principal, International Investement/Trade and Strategic Alliances)

MILLER, Leonard A.
3000 K St. NW
Suite 300
Washington, DC 20007
Tel: (202)424-7500
Fax: (202)424-7643
Registered: LDA
Associate Deputy Assistant Administrator (1979-80), Permit Division Director (1976-79), Enforcement Division Director, Region X (1972-76), and Air Pollution Control Director (1970-72), all at the Environmental Protection Agency.

Employers
Swidler Berlin Shereff Friedman, LLP (Partner)

MILLER, Linda B.
818 18th St. NW
Suite 410
Washington, DC 20006
Tel: (202)659-0338
Fax: (202)659-0116
EMail: vt@sprintmail.com

Employers
Volunteer Trustees of Not-for-Profit Hospitals (President)

MILLER, Marc E.
One Massachusetts Ave. NW
Suite 800
Washington, DC 20001-1431
Tel: (202)842-2345
Fax: (202)408-7763
Registered: LDA
EMail: MMiller@mwmlaw.com
Administrative Assistant to Rep. Thomas J. Downey (D-NY), 1977, and to Rep. Lester L. Wolff (D-NY), 1972-75.

Employers
McLeod, Watkinson & Miller (Partner)

Clients Represented
On Behalf of McLeod, Watkinson & Miller
American Mushroom Institute

MILLER, Margaret L.
1200 New Hampshire Ave. NW
Suite 800
Washington, DC 20036-6802
Tel: (202)776-2000
Fax: (202)776-2222

Employers
Dow, Lohnes & Albertson, PLLC (Member)

MILLER, Marian
124 N. Alfred St.
Alexandria, VA 22314
Tel: (703)548-9688
Fax: (703)548-9836

Employers
Nat'l Federation of Republican Women (President)

MILLER, Marianne
1201 F St. NW
Suite 500
Washington, DC 20004
Tel: (202)824-1693
Fax: (202)824-1651
Registered: LDA

Employers
Health Insurance Ass'n of America (Director, Federal Regulatory Affairs Progra)

MILLER, Mark
700 13th St. NW
Suite 1000
Washington, DC 20005
Tel: (202)347-6633
Fax: (202)347-8713

Employers
Powell Tate (V. President, Writing)

MILLER, Mark H.
1050 17th St. NW
Suite 510
Washington, DC 20036
Tel: (202)775-0079
Fax: (202)785-0477
Registered: LDA

Employers
Government Relations, Inc. (Associate)

Clients Represented

On Behalf of Government Relations, Inc.

Aldaron Inc.
Ass'n for Commuter Transportation
Capital Area Transit Authority
Community Transit
Fairfax, Virginia, County of
Friends of ITS/ITS America
Gateway Cities
High Speed Ground Transportation Ass'n
Mass Transit Authority
Metropolitan Transportation Commission
Monroe, New York, County of
Oakland, Michigan, County of
Regional Public Tansportation Authority
Suburban Mobility Authority for Regional Transportation

MILLER, Mark L.

3222 M St. NW
Suite 501
Washington, DC 20007
Tel: (202)547-1700
Fax: (202)298-8787

Employers

Republican Leadership Council (Exec. Director)

MILLER, Marshall L.

1020 19th St. NW
Suite 400
Washington, DC 20036
EMail: envirlaw@aol.com
Tel: (202)331-9100
Fax: (202)331-9060
Registered: LDA

Acting Assistant Secretary for Occupational Safety and Health, Department of Labor, 1975-76. Associate Attorney General, Department of Justice, 1973-74. Special Assistant to Administrator, Chief EPA Judicial Officer, Environmental Protection Agency, 1971-73.

Employers

Baise + Miller, P.C. (Partner)

Clients Represented

On Behalf of Baise + Miller, P.C.

Citizens for Health
Ice Ban America, Inc.
Martinizing Environmental Group
Nat'l Calcium Council

MILLER, J.D., Michael J.

3330 Washington Blvd.
Suite 400
Arlington, VA 22201-4598
Tel: (703)525-4890
Fax: (703)276-0793

Employers

Ass'n for the Advancement of Medical Instrumentation (President)

MILLER, Mike

1130 Connecticut Ave. NW
Suite 300
Washington, DC 20036
Tel: (202)331-8500
Fax: (202)331-1598
Registered: LDA

Employers

The Ferguson Group, LLC (Principal)

Clients Represented

On Behalf of The Ferguson Group, LLC

Fairfield, California, City of
Folsom, California, City of
Roseville, California, City of
Sacramento Area Council of Governments
Transportation Corridor Agencies

MILLER, Mona

1199 N. Fairfax St.
Suite 1000
Alexandria, VA 22314
Tel: (703)299-4499
Fax: (703)299-4488

Former Director of Communications for Senator Barbara Mikulski (D-MD).

Employers

The Hawthorn Group, L.C. (V. President, Communications)

MILLER, Nancy L.

1020 N. Fairfax St.
Fourth Floor
Alexandria, VA 22314
EMail: nmiller@pass1.com
Tel: (703)684-5236
Fax: (703)684-3417
Registered: LDA

Employers

Vienna, Gregor & Associates (Senior Associate)

Clients Represented

On Behalf of Vienna, Gregor & Associates

California Board of Equalization
California Franchise Tax Board
California Public Employees' Retirement System
California State Senate
The Pacific Stock Exchange, Inc.

MILLER, Nicholas P.

1155 Connecticut Ave. NW
Suite 1000
Washington, DC 20036-4306
EMail: nmiller@millervaneaton.com
Tel: (202)785-0600
Fax: (202)785-1234
Registered: LDA

Employers

Miller & Van Eaton, P.L.L.C. (Managing Partner)

Clients Represented

On Behalf of Miller & Van Eaton, P.L.L.C.

Building Owners and Managers Ass'n Internat'l
Dearborn, Michigan, Department of Communication of
Dubuque, Iowa, Cable Television Division of
Kansas Electric Power Cooperative
Laredo, Texas, City of
Montgomery, Maryland, Cable Television Office of the County of
Nat'l Apartment Ass'n
Nat'l Multi-Housing Council
Prince George's, Maryland, County of
Real Estate Roundtable
San Francisco, California, City and County of
St. Louis Office of Cable Television

MILLER, Nina

1780 Massachusetts Ave. NW
Washington, DC 20036
Tel: (202)785-3351
Fax: (202)293-4349

Employers

Planned Parenthood Federation of America (Director, Planned Parenthood Action Fund, Inc. PAC)

MILLER, Paul A.

301 North Fairfax St.
Alexandria, VA 22314
EMail: pmiller@iopfda.org
Tel: (703)549-9040
Ext: 124
Fax: (703)683-7552
Registered: LDA

Employers

Independent Office Products and Furniture Dealers Ass'n (Director of Government Affairs)

MILLER, R. Scott

801 Pennsylvania Ave. NW
Suite 720
Washington, DC 20004-2604
EMail: miller.rs@pg.com
Tel: (202)393-3404
Fax: (202)393-4606
Registered: LDA

Employers

The Procter & Gamble Company (Director, National Government Relations)

MILLER, Richard W.

809 Princess St.
Alexandria, VA 22314
Tel: (703)683-1325
Fax: (703)519-9669
Registered: LDA

Employers

Miller & Co. (President)

Clients Represented

On Behalf of Miller & Co.

American Chiropractic Ass'n
Nat'l College
Tobacco Fairness Coalition

MILLER, Russell C.

701 S. Court House Rd.
Room 4320
Arlington, VA 22204-2199
Tel: (703)607-6700
Fax: (703)607-4081

Senior Executive Service since 1996. Chief of Plans, Command Control Communications System Management Support Office, Department of Defense, 1992-93. Chief of Plans, Office of Emergency Operations, White House Military Office, 1989-92. Research Assistant, Committee on Armed Services, U.S. Senate, 1984-87. Served with the U.S. Naval Reserve, 1982-85. Served with the U.S. Navy, 1977-82.

Employers

Department of Defense - Defense Information Systems Agency (Chief, Congressional Affairs)

MILLER, Sandra B.

400 N. Capitol St. NW
Suite 363
Washington, DC 20001
Tel: (202)783-0280
Fax: (202)737-4518
Registered: LDA

Employers

Denny Miller McBee Associates (Exec. V. President)

MILLER, Sarah

1120 Connecticut Ave. NW
Washington, DC 20036
Tel: (202)663-5000
Fax: (202)828-4548
Registered: LDA

Employers

American Bankers Ass'n (Director, Center for Securities, Trust and Investment)

MILLER, Scott A.

1310 G St. NW
Suite 690
Washington, DC 20005-3000
EMail: smiller@as-coa.org
Tel: (202)639-0724
Fax: (202)639-0794

Employers

Council of the Americas (Director, Public Affairs)
Mexico-U.S. Business Committee, U.S. Council (Exec. Director)

MILLER, Stephen L.

333 John Carlyle St.
Suite 530
Alexandria, VA 22314
EMail: smiller@ceednet.org
Tel: (703)684-6292
Fax: (703)684-6297

Employers

Center for Energy and Economic Development (President and Chief Exec. Officer)

MILLER, Steve

1101 Vermont Ave. NW
Suite 700
Washington, DC 20005
EMail: smiller@aaodc.org
Tel: (202)737-6662
Fax: (202)737-7061
Registered: LDA

Employers

American Academy of Ophthamology - Office of Federal Affairs (Director of OPHTPAC and Political Affairs)

MILLER, Susan M.

1200 G St. NW
Suite 500
Washington, DC 20005
EMail: smiller@atis.org
Tel: (202)434-8828
Fax: (202)393-5453

Employers

Alliance for Telecommunications Industry Solutions (President)

MILLER, Thomas H.

477 H St. NW
Washington, DC 20001-2694
EMail: bva@bva.org
Tel: (202)371-8880
Fax: (202)371-8258

Employers

Blinded Veterans Ass'n (Exec. Director)

MILLER, Thomas P.

1000 Massachusetts Ave. NW
Washington, DC 20001
Tel: (202)842-0200
Fax: (202)842-3490

Employers

Cato Institute (Director of Health Policy Studies)

MILLER, W. Kirk

1300 L St. NW
Suite 900
Washington, DC 20005
EMail: wkmiller@naega.org
Tel: (202)682-4030
Fax: (202)682-4033
Registered: LDA

Employers

North American Grain Export Ass'n, Inc. (Director, International Programs and Regulatory Affairs)

MILLER, Wayne

1025 Connecticut Ave. NW
Suite 600
Washington, DC 20036
Tel: (202)833-1100
Fax: (202)833-1105

Employers
Nat'l Health Lawyers Ass'n (Director, Finance and Administration)

MILLER, William T.

1140 19th St. NW
Suite 700
Washington, DC 20036
Tel: (202)296-2960
Fax: (202)296-0166
Law Clerk to Judge E. Barrett Prettyman, U.S. Court of Appeals, 1966-67.

Employers
Miller, Balis and O'Neil, P.C. (Principal)

Clients Represented
On Behalf of Miller, Balis and O'Neil, P.C.
American Public Gas Ass'n

MILLER, Yvette A.

1700 K St. NW
Suite 1150
Washington, DC 20006
EMail: yvette.miller@ujc.org
Tel: (202)736-5877
Fax: (202)785-4937

Employers
United Jewish Communities, Inc. (Director, Public and Community Affairs)

MILLIAN, John C.

1050 Connecticut Ave. NW
Washington, DC 20036-5306
Tel: (202)955-8500
Fax: (202)467-0539
Registered: FARA
EMail: jmillian@gdclaw.com
Law Clerk to Judge Gerhard A. Gesell, U.S. District Court for the District of Columbia, 1983-84.

Employers
Gibson, Dunn & Crutcher LLP (Partner)

MILLIAN, Kenneth Y.

1090 Vermont Ave. NW
Third Floor
Washington, DC 20005
EMail: kym@milbya.com
Tel: (202)842-5000
Fax: (202)789-4293
Held senior management positions in the U.S. Foreign Service in Asia and Latin America.

Employers
Millian Byers Associates, LLC (Chairman)

Clients Represented
On Behalf of Millian Byers Associates, LLC
American Chemistry Council
Chlorine Chemistry Council
Patton Boggs, LLP
Siemens Corp.

MILLIGAN, Susan M.

801 Pennsylvania Ave. NW
Suite 630
Washington, DC 20004-5878
Tel: (202)347-4300
Fax: (202)347-4370
Registered: LDA
EMail: smilligan@nysc.com

Employers
New York Stock Exchange (Counsel, Government Relations)

MILLING, Marcus E.

4220 King St.
Alexandria, VA 22302-1502
Tel: (703)379-2480
Fax: (703)379-7563

Employers
American Geological Institute (Exec. Director)

MILLMAN, Amy

409 Third St. SW
Suite 210
Washington, DC 20024
Tel: (202)205-3850
Fax: (202)205-6825

Employers
Nat'l Women's Business Council (Exec. Director)

MILLONIG, Marsha K.

1275 K St. NW
Suite 1212
Washington, DC 20005
Tel: (703)787-0000
Fax: (202)312-5005

Employers
Healthcare Distribution Management Ass'n (V. President, Research and Information)

MILLS, Christopher A.

1224 17th St. NW
Washington, DC 20036
Tel: (202)347-7170
Fax: (202)347-3619
Registered: LDA

Employers
Slover & Loftus

Clients Represented
On Behalf of Slover & Loftus
Western Coal Traffic League

MILLS, David E.

1200 New Hampshire Ave. NW
Suite 800
Washington, DC 20036-6802
EMail: dmills@dlalaw.com
Tel: (202)776-2000
Fax: (202)776-2222

Employers
Dow, Lohnes & Albertson, PLLC (Member)

MILLS, Penny

9111 Old Georgetown Rd.
Bethesda, MD 20814
EMail: pmills@acc.org
Tel: (301)897-5400
Fax: (301)897-9745

Employers
American College of Cardiology (Senior Associate Exec. V. President, Strategy, Finance, and Operations)

MILLS, Robert E.

1350 I St. NW
Suite 680
Washington, DC 20005-3305
Tel: (202)393-4841
Fax: (202)393-5596
Registered: LDA
EMail: bobby@advocacy.com
Legislative Assistant to Rep. Gillis Long (D-LA) 1974-75. Legislative Assistant to Senator William Proxmire (D-WI), 1974-75. Assistant Clerk, Senate Subcommittee on HUD, Space and Science, Senate Appropriations Committee, 1975-80. Staff Director, Subcommittee on Treasury, Postal Service and General Government, Senate Appropriations Committee, 1981-88.

Employers
The Advocacy Group

Clients Represented
On Behalf of The Advocacy Group
Ass'n of Chiropractic Colleges
Atlantic Corridor USA
BitWise Designs Inc.
Border Trade Alliance
Buffalo Economic Renaissance Corp.
Buffalo Sewer Authority
Buffalo, New York, City of
Daemen College
Detroit Internat'l Bridge Co./The Ambassador Bridge
Digital Descriptor Services, Inc.
Dowling College
Florida Atlantic University
Florida State University
Harbor Branch Institute
Logan College of Chiropractic
Palmer Chiropractic University
Sam Houston University
Siscorp
Southwest Texas State University
Texas Chiropractic College
University of Central Florida

MILLS, Robert G.

1300 Pennsylvania Ave. NW
Suite 700
Washington, DC 20004
Registered: LDA

Employers
U.S. Family Network (Exec. Director)

MILLS, Stephen

408 C St. NE
Washington, DC 20002
Tel: (202)547-1141
Fax: (202)547-6009

Employers
Sierra Club (Director, International Program)

MILLS, T. J.

607 14th St. NW
Suite 800
Washington, DC 20004

Employers
Tex-USA Fund (Contact)

MILLS, Thomas L.

1400 L St. NW
Washington, DC 20005-3502
Tel: (202)371-5714
Fax: (202)371-5950
Registered: LDA
EMail: tmills@winston.com
Lieutenant, U.S. Coast Guard, 1970-75.

Employers
Winston & Strawn (Partner, Health Care Practice)

Clients Represented
On Behalf of Winston & Strawn
American Healthways, Inc.
American Lithotripsy Soc.
First American Bulk Carriers Corp.
Kirby Corp./Dixie Carriers
Liberty Maritime Co.
Marinette Marine Corp.
Northland Holdings, Inc.
Van Ommeren Shipping (USA), Inc.

MILLS, Timothy B.

2550 M St. NW
Washington, DC 20037-1350
Tel: (202)457-6000
Fax: (202)457-6315
Registered: LDA
EMail: tmills@pattonboggs.com

Employers
Patton Boggs, LLP (Partner)

MILNE, John D.

1615 L St. NW
Suite 650
Washington, DC 20036
Tel: (202)626-8500
Fax: (202)626-8593
Registered: LDA

Employers
Jefferson Government Relations, L.L.C. (V. President)

MILNER, Claire

3105 South St. NW
Washington, DC 20007
Tel: (202)965-3652
Fax: (202)965-8913
Registered: LDA
EMail: cmilner@bruman.com

Employers
Brustein & Manasevit (Associate)

Clients Represented
On Behalf of Brustein & Manasevit
California Department of Education

MILNER, Neil

1015 18th St. NW
Suite 1100
Washington, DC 20036-5725
EMail: nmilner@csbsdc.org
Tel: (202)728-5702
Fax: (202)296-1928

Employers
Conference of State Bank Supervisors (President and Chief Exec. Officer)

MILO, Sara

426 C St. NE
Washington, DC 20002
Tel: (202)544-1880
Fax: (202)543-2565
Registered: LDA
EMail: sm@capitolassociates.com
Senior Legislative Staff, Rep. William J. Hughes (D-NJ), 1990-94.

Employers
Capitol Associates, Inc. (V. President)

Clients Represented
On Behalf of Capitol Associates, Inc.
American Soc. of Tropical Medicine and Hygiene
Nat'l Alliance for Eye and Vision Research
Research Soc. on Alcoholism
Soc. of Toxicology

MILT, Robert A.

600 Pennsylvania Ave. SE
Suite 400
Washington, DC 20003
Tel: (202)547-0001
Fax: (202)544-5014

Employers
Progressive Policy Institute (Project Assistant)

MINAMI, Kristine

1001 Connecticut Ave. NW
Suite 704
Washington, DC 20036
Tel: (202)223-1240
Fax: (202)296-8082

Employers
Japanese American Citizens League (Washington Representative)

MINARD, Richard "Dick"

600 New Hampshire Ave. NW
Suite 601
Washington, DC 20037
Tel: (202)333-7400
Fax: (202)333-1638
Registered: LDA

Former Chief of Staff to Rep. Robert F. Smith (R-OR). and Larry E. Craig (R-ID).

Employers
Hill and Knowlton, Inc. (Senior Managing Director and Deputy General Manager)

Clients Represented

On Behalf of Hill and Knowlton, Inc.
Motorola, Inc.

MINARDI-MOSER, Tara

1101 17th St. NW
Suite 1300
Washington, DC 20036-4700
Tel: (202)452-7198
Fax: (202)463-6573
Registered: LDA
EMail: tminardimoser@steel.org

Former Legislative Correspondent to Senator Daniel Patrick Moynihan (D-NY). Former Staff Assistant to Senator Herbert Kohl (D-WS)

Employers
American Iron and Steel Institute (Manager, Government Relations)

MINCBERG, Elliot M.

2000 M St. NW
Suite 400
Washington, DC 20036
Tel: (202)467-4999
Fax: (202)293-2672

Employers
People for the American Way (Exec. V. President and Director, Legal and General Counsel)

MINCHAK, Gregory N.

666 11th St. NW
Suite 600
Washington, DC 20001
Tel: (202)783-0070
Fax: (202)783-0534
EMail: gminchak@ccianet.org

Served as an intern to Rep. Harris W. Fawell (R-IL).

Employers
Computer and Communications Industry Ass'n (CCIA) (Senior Research Assistant)

MINER, Anuja

2101 Wilson Blvd.
Suite 400
Arlington, VA 22201
Tel: (703)243-6111
Fax: (703)841-9328
EMail: aminer@nmpf.org

Employers
American Butter Institute (Program Administrator)

MINER, William A.

888 16th St. NW
Washington, DC 20006
Tel: (202)835-8177
Fax: (202)835-8161
Registered: LDA, FARA

Retired Naval Officer. Former Military Planner, Joint Staff, and Policy Analyst for Iran, Iraq and Kuwait, OASD/ISA.

Employers
Bannerman and Associates, Inc.

Clients Represented

On Behalf of Bannerman and Associates, Inc.
Assurance Technology Corp.
Egypt, Government of the Arab Republic of
El Salvador, Embassy of the Republic of
Internat'l College
Lebanese American University
Palestinian Authority

MINES, Paul

444 N. Capitol St. NW
Suite 425
Washington, DC 20001
Tel: (202)624-8699
Fax: (202)624-8819
EMail: pmines@mtc.gov

Employers
Multistate Tax Commission (General Counsel)

MINGHETTI, Nancy

10801 Rockville Pike
Rockville, MD 20852
Tel: (301)897-5700
Fax: (301)571-0457

Employers
American Speech-Language-Hearing Foundation (Exec. Director)

MINGS, John

601 Pennsylvania Ave. NW
Suite 900
Washington, DC 20004
Tel: (202)547-3566
Fax: (202)639-8238

Employers
Cottone and Huggins Group (V. President, Proposal Development)

MINGS, Mike

919 18th St. NW
Suite 800
Washington, DC 20006
Tel: (202)628-4160
Fax: (202)347-5323

Employers
Human Rights Campaign Fund (Deputy Director, PAC)

MINIKES, Stephan M.

701 Pennsylvania Ave. NW
Suite 800
Washington, DC 20004
Tel: (202)508-4010
Fax: (202)508-4321
Registered: LDA
EMail: sminikes@thelenreid.com

Senior V. President, Export-Import Bank, 1974-77. Counsel to the Special Consultant for Energy to the President, The White House 1973. Counsel and Special Assistant to the Chief of Naval Operations, Department of Defense, 1972-74.

Employers
Thelen Reid & Priest LLP (Partner)

Clients Represented

On Behalf of Thelen Reid & Priest LLP
Abilene Industrial Foundation, Inc.
Airport Minority Advisory Council
Airports Council Internat'l - North America
Capital Region Airport Commission
Corpus Christi Port Authority
Denver Internat'l Airport
Denver, Colorado, City of
DRS Precision Echo Inc.
DRS Technologies, Inc.
L.B. Foster Co.
Horizon Organic Holding Co.
The Jewelers' Security Alliance
Metro Machine Corp. of Virginia
Metro Machine of Pennsylvania, Inc.
Metroplex Corp.
Parsons Brinckerhoff Inc.
Philadelphia Industrial Development Corp.
Philadelphia, Pennsylvania, City of
Power Paragon Inc.
SPD Technologies
Suiza Foods Corp.

MINJACK, Greg

805 15th St. NW
Suite 700
Washington, DC 20005
Tel: (202)312-7400
Fax: (202)312-7441
EMail: gaminjac@bakerd.com

Employers
Sagamore Associates, Inc. (V. President)

MINNIX, William L.

2519 Connecticut Ave. NW
Washington, DC 20008-1520
Tel: (202)783-2242
Fax: (202)783-2255

Employers
American Ass'n of Homes and Services for the Aging (President and Chief Exec.)

MINOR, William H.

901 15th St. NW
Suite 700
Washington, DC 20005-2301
Tel: (202)371-6000
Fax: (202)371-6279
Registered: LDA
EMail: whminor@verner.com

Legislative Assistant to Rep. Edward J. Markey (D-MA), 1989-92.

Employers
Verner, Liipfert, Bernhard, McPherson and Hand, Chartered (Associate)

Clients Represented

On Behalf of Verner, Liipfert, Bernhard, McPherson and Hand, Chartered
Accenture
Biovail Corp. Internat'l
Federal Home Loan Bank of Indianapolis
Federal Home Loan Mortgage Corp. (Freddie Mac)
Independent Fuel Terminal Operators Ass'n
Merle Hay Mall Limited Partners
Merrill Lynch & Co., Inc.
New Haven, Connecticut, City of

MINTER, William

110 Maryland Ave. NE
Suite 509
Washington, DC 20002
Tel: (202)546-7961
Fax: (202)546-1545

Employers
Africa Policy Information Center (Acting Director)

MINTZ, Alan L.

1050 Thomas Jefferson St. NW
Seventh Floor
Washington, DC 20007
Tel: (202)298-1800
Fax: (202)338-2416
Registered: LDA
EMail: alm@vnf.com

Senior Attorney, Office of Exceptions and Appeals, Federal Energy Administration, 1974-77.

Employers
Van Ness Feldman, P.C. (Member)

Clients Represented

On Behalf of Van Ness Feldman, P.C.
Alaska North Slope LNG Project
Arctic Slope Regional Corp.
Barron Collier Co.
Doyon, Ltd.
Koncor Forest Products Co.
North Slope Borough, Alaska
Petro Star, Inc.
Sealaska Corp.

MINTZ, Richard

1801 K St. NW
Suite 1000L
Washington, DC 20006
Tel: (202)530-0400
Fax: (202)530-4500
EMail: richard_mintz@washbm.com

Employers
Burson-Marsteller (Managing Director, Public Affairs Practice)

Clients Represented

On Behalf of Burson-Marsteller
American Airlines

MINTZ, Suzanne G.

10400 Connecticut Ave.
Suite 500
Kensington, MD 20895-3944
Tel: (800)896-3650
Fax: (301)942-2302
EMail: suzanne@nfcacares.org

Employers
Nat'l Family Caregivers Ass'n (President)

MIODUSKI, Mark

1755 Jefferson Davis Hwy.
Suite 1107
Arlington, VA 22202
Tel: (703)415-0344
Fax: (703)415-0182

Former Aide, Subcommittee on Labor, Health and Human Services, and Education, House Committee on Appropriations.

Employers
The PMA Group

MIRABAL, Manuel

1700 K St. NW
Suite 500
Washington, DC 20006
Tel: (202)223-3915
Fax: (202)429-2223
EMail: nprc@aol.com

Employers
Nat'l Puerto Rican Coalition (President)

MIRANDA, John Anthony

1775 K St. NW
Suite 320
Washington, DC 20006
EMail: jmiranda@iicwash.org
Tel: (202)458-3767
Fax: (202)458-6335

Assistant Deputy Administrator for International Cooperation and Development, Foreign Agricultural Service (1993-98); Acting Administrator (1992-93), Acting Associate Administrator (1991-92), and Assistant Administrator for Administration (1988-92), all at Department of Agriculture. Assistant to the Assistant Director General for Administration and Finance, Federal Accounting Office. Chief of the Financial Management Division, Office of Finance and Management, Department of Agriculture. Office of Budget and Management. Agriculture Subcommittee for Domestic Marketing, Consumer Relations, and Nutrition in House of Representatives.

Employers
Inter-American Institute for Cooperation on Agriculture (Director and U.S. Representative)

MIRANI, Viraj M.

927 15th St. NW
12th Floor
Washington, DC 20015
Tel: (202)833-4466
Fax: (202)833-2833
Registered: LDA

Employers
St. Maxens & Company

Clients Represented
On Behalf of St. Maxens & Company
Mattel, Inc.

MIRGA, Tomas F.

600 Pennsylvania Ave. SE
Suite 400
Washington, DC 20003
Tel: (202)546-0007
Fax: (202)544-5002

Employers
Democratic Leadership Council (Editor, Blueprint Magazine)

MIRICK, USAF(Ret.), Col. Steven C.

9320 Old Georgetown Rd.
Bethesda, MD 20814
EMail: stevem@amsus.org
Tel: (301)897-8800
Ext: 12
Fax: (301)530-5446

Employers
Ass'n of Military Surgeons of the U.S. (AMSUS) (Assistant Exec. Director)

MIRO, Carlos R. "Chuck"

1828 L St. NW
Suite 906
Washington, DC 20036-5104
EMail: cmiro@ashrae.org
Tel: (202)833-1830
Fax: (202)833-0118

Employers
American Soc. of Heating, Refrigerating and Air Conditioning Engineers (Director, Government Affairs)

MIROBALLI, Dana Lee

1101 Vermont Ave. NW
12th Floor
Washington, DC 20005-3583
Tel: (202)789-7424
Fax: (202)789-7401
Registered: LDA

Employers
American Medical Ass'n (Washington Counsel, Division of Legislative Counsel)

MIRON, George

1300 19th St. NW
Suite 400
Washington, DC 20036
Tel: (202)293-1600
Fax: (202)293-8965

Special Assistant to the Solicitor and Associate Solicitor for Reclamation and Power, Department of the Interior, 1965-68. Assistant Chief, General Litigation Section and Trial Attorney, Anti-trust Division, Department of Justice, 1959-1965.

Employers
Feith & Zell, P.C. (Partner)

MIRTCHEV, Alexander V.

2100 M St. NW
Suite 200
Washington, DC 20037
EMail: ibid@stewartlaw.com
Tel: (202)785-4185
Fax: (202)466-1286
Registered: FARA

Employers
Stewart and Stewart (Division Director)

MISHEL, Lawrence R.

1660 L St. NW
Suite 1200
Washington, DC 20036
EMail: epi@epinet.org
Tel: (202)775-8810
Fax: (202)775-0819

Employers
Economic Policy Institute (Research Director)

MISHKIN, David G.

901 15th St. NW
Suite 310
Washington, DC 20005
Tel: (202)842-3193
Fax: (202)289-6834
Registered: LDA

Employers
Northwest Airlines, Inc. (V. President, International and Regulatory Affairs)

MISKIEWICZ, Sophia

1612 K St.
Suite 410
Washington, DC 20006
Tel: (202)296-6955
Fax: (202)835-1565

Employers
Polish-American Congress (Exec. Director, Legislative and Public Affairs)

MISSOURI, Montre Aza

122 Maryland Ave. NE
Suite 300
Washington, DC 20002
Tel: (202)546-3799
Fax: (202)543-3156

Employers
Fund for Constitutional Government (Secretary)

MISTER, Steven M.

1150 Connecticut Ave. NW
12th Floor
Washington, DC 20036
Tel: (202)429-9260
Fax: (202)223-6835
Registered: LDA

Employers
Consumer Healthcare Products Ass'n (V. President)

MITCHEL, M. Lynn

526 King St.
Suite 423
Alexandria, VA 22314-3143
Tel: (703)518-4369
Fax: (703)706-9583

Employers
The Alexandria Group (Managing Partner)
Nat'l Ass'n of Government Communicators (Exec. Director)

MITCHELL, Carol C.

2300 Clarendon Blvd.
Suite 610
Arlington, VA 22201-3367
EMail: cmitchell@golinharris.com
Tel: (703)351-5666
Fax: (703)351-5667
Registered: LDA

Former Professional Staff Member, Senate Appropriations Committee and Legislative advisor to Senator Robert C. Byrd (D-WV).

Employers
Golin/Harris Internat'l (V. President)

Clients Represented
On Behalf of Golin/Harris Internat'l
Center for the Arts and Sciences
Concord College
John Harland Co.
Michigan Technological University
Nat'l Ass'n of City and County Health Officials
Ruby Memorial Hospital
St. Mary's Hospital
West Virginia University Hospitals, Inc.

MITCHELL, Cleta

1100 Connecticut Ave. NW
Suite 330
Washington, DC 20036
EMail: cmitchell@sullivanmitchell.com
Tel: (202)861-5900
Fax: (202)861-6065
Registered: LDA

Employers
Sullivan & Mitchell, P.L.L.C. (Attorney)

Clients Represented
On Behalf of Sullivan & Mitchell, P.L.L.C.
Americans Back in Charge Foundation

MITCHELL, Daniel J.

214 Massachusetts Ave. NE
Washington, DC 20002
Tel: (202)546-4400
Fax: (202)546-8328

Employers
Heritage Foundation (McKenna Senior Fellow in Political Economy)

MITCHELL, David E.

1010 Wisconsin Ave. NW
Suite 800
Washington, DC 20007
Tel: (202)338-8700
Fax: (202)338-2334

Employers
Greer, Margolis, Mitchell, Burns & Associates (Partner)

Clients Represented
On Behalf of Greer, Margolis, Mitchell, Burns & Associates
Air Bag and Seat Belt Safety Campaign
American Ass'n of Family Physicians
NHTSA
Ross/Nutrition Screening Initiative

MITCHELL, David F.

401 Ninth St. NW
Suite 1100
Washington, DC 20004
EMail: dmitchell@duke-energy.com
Tel: (202)331-8090
Fax: (202)331-1181

Employers
Duke Energy (Director, EHS Federal Government Affairs)

MITCHELL, Denise

815 16th St. NW
Washington, DC 20006
Tel: (202)637-5000
Fax: (202)637-5058

Employers
AFL-CIO (American Federation of Labor and Congress of Industrial Organizations) (Special Assistant to the President, Public Affairs)

MITCHELL, Erin

1150 17th St. NW
Suite 701
Washington, DC 20036
EMail: erin.mitchell@dittus.com
Tel: (202)775-1401
Fax: (202)775-1404

Employers
Dittus Communications (Associate Director)

Clients Represented
On Behalf of Dittus Communications
SurfControl

MITCHELL, Fran W.

927 15th St. NW
Suite 1000
Washington, DC 20005
Tel: (202)659-4300
Registered: LDA

Employers
Employers Council on Flexible Compensation (Exec. Assistant)

MITCHELL, Hon. George J.

901 15th St. NW
Suite 700
Washington, DC 20005-2301
Tel: (202)371-6000
Fax: (202)371-6279
Registered: LDA

Member, U.S. Senate (D-ME), 1980-94. Senate Majority Leader, 1989-94.

Employers
Verner, Liipfert, Bernhard, McPherson and Hand, Chartered (Special Counsel)

Clients Represented
On Behalf of Verner, Liipfert, Bernhard, McPherson and Hand, Chartered
The Limited Inc.
RJR Nabisco Holdings Co.

MITCHELL, Gina

2121 K St. NW
Suite 800
Washington, DC 20037
Tel: (202)261-6530

Employers
Stable Value Investments Ass'n (President)

MITCHELL, Gray

1130 Connecticut Ave. NW
Suite 1000
Washington, DC 20036
Tel: (202)828-7112
Fax: (202)293-1219

Employers
American Insurance Ass'n (Director, Political Programs)

MITCHELL, James K.

701 Pennsylvania Ave. NW
Suite 800
Washington, DC 20004
EMail: jmitchell@thelenreid.com
Tel: (202)508-4002
Fax: (202)508-4321

Employers
Thelen Reid & Priest LLP (Partner)

Clients Represented
On Behalf of Thelen Reid & Priest LLP
Green Mountain Power Corp.

MITCHELL, John T.

1919 Pennsylvania Ave. NW
Suite 600
Washington, DC 20006-3404
Tel: (202)326-1500
Fax: (202)326-1555
Registered: LDA

Employers
Jenkens & Gilchrist (Partner)

Clients Represented
On Behalf of Jenkens & Gilchrist
American Film Marketing Ass'n
Nat'l Ass'n of Recording Merchandisers

MITCHELL, Larry

1400 Independence Ave. SW
Room 3013 South
Washington, DC 20250
EMail: larry_mitchell@wdc.fsa.usda.gov
Tel: (202)720-3865
Fax: (202)720-9105

Employers
Department of Agriculture - Farm Service Agency (Deputy Administrator for Farm Programs)

MITCHELL, Maggie A.

600 13th St. NW
Washington, DC 20005-3096
Tel: (202)756-8005
Fax: (202)756-8087
Registered: LDA, FARA

Employers
McDermott, Will and Emery (Associate Legislative Director)

Clients Represented
On Behalf of McDermott, Will and Emery
American Dental Hygienists' Ass'n
California Cling Peach Growers Advisory Board
Council of Women's and Infant's Specialty Hospitals
Hutzel Medical Center
Inova Fairfax Hospital
Magee Women's Health Foundation
Northside Hospital
Public Employee Retirement Systems of Colorado
St. Peter's Medical Center
Stroh Brewing Co.
Women and Infants' Hospital
Women's Hospital
Women's Hospital of Greensboro

MITCHELL, Parren

300 I St. NE
Suite 400
Washington, DC 20002
Tel: (202)289-1700
Fax: (202)289-1701

Employers
Minority Business Enterprise Legal Defense and Education Fund (Founder and Chairman)

MITCHELL, Pat

1320 Braddock Pl.
Alexandria, VA 22314
Tel: (703)739-5000
Fax: (703)739-0775

Employers
Public Broadcasting Service (President)

MITCHELL, Patrick J.

444 N. Capitol St. NW
Suite 840
Washington, DC 20001
Tel: (202)434-8010
Fax: (202)434-8018
Registered: LDA

Chief of Staff to Representative Louise Slaughter (D-NY), 1988-89. Staff Assistant to Senator Dennis DeConcini (D-AZ), 1981-82.

Employers
Strategic Impact, Inc. (Principal)

Clients Represented
On Behalf of Strategic Impact, Inc.
Cantelme and Kaasa
ClaimTraq, Inc.
Commercial Weather Services Ass'n (CWSA)
Internat'l Arid Lands Consortium
Investment Co. Institute
Middle East Water and Energy Resource Institute
Pascua Yaqui Tribe of Arizona
Southwest Border Technology Project

MITCHELL, Peter

1275 K St. NW
Suite 600
Washington, DC 20005
Tel: (202)513-6300

Employers
Internat'l Union of Electronic, Electrical, Salaried, Machine, and Furniture Workers-Communications Workers of America (General Counsel)

MITCHELL, Samuel A.

1875 I St. NW
Suite 1050
Washington, DC 20006-5409
Tel: (202)331-8585
Fax: (202)331-2032

Employers
Scribner, Hall & Thompson, LLP (Associate)

MITCHEM, Dr. Arnold L.

1025 Vermont Ave. NW
Suite 900
Washington, DC 20005
EMail: katie@hqcoe.org
Tel: (202)347-7430
Fax: (202)347-0786

Employers
Council for Opportunity in Education (President)

MITOLA, Michele

1250 H St. NW
Suite 700
Washington, DC 20005-3908
EMail: mmitola@cse.org
Tel: (202)783-3870
Fax: (202)783-4687

Employers
Citizens for a Sound Economy (V. President, Public Policy)

MITROPOULOS, Nick

2141 Wisconsin Ave. NW
Suite H
Washington, DC 20007
Tel: (202)337-9600
Fax: (202)337-9620
Registered: LDA

Employers
Strategic Choices, Inc.

Clients Represented
On Behalf of Strategic Choices, Inc.
Colombian Coffee Federation

MITTERMEIER, Russell A.

1919 M St. NW
Suite 200
Washington, DC 20036
EMail: r.mittermeir@conservation.org
Tel: (202)912-1000
Fax: (202)912-1030

Employers
Conservation Internat'l Foundation (President)

MIX, Mark A.

8001 Braddock Rd.
Springfield, VA 22160
Tel: (703)321-9820
Fax: (703)321-7342
Registered: LDA

Employers
Nat'l Right to Work Committee (Senior V. President, Legislation)

MIX, Robert R.

225 N. Washington St.
Alexandria, VA 22314
Tel: (703)549-0311
Fax: (703)549-0245
Registered: LDA
EMail: rmix@ncoausa.org

Employers
Non Commissioned Officers Ass'n of the U.S.A.

MIYAZAWA, Mike K.

1776 I St. NW
Suite 725
Washington, DC 20006
Tel: (202)331-1167
Fax: (202)331-1319

Employers
Marubeni America Corp. (V. Preisdent and General Manager)

MIZEUR, Heather

1330 New Hampshire Ave. NW
Suite 122
Washington, DC 20036
Tel: (202)296-3410
Fax: (202)296-3526
Registered: LDA
EMail: hmizeur@nachc.com

Legislative Director to Rep. Joseph P. Kennedy (D-MA), 1995-98. Legislative Assistant to Reps. Sheila Jackson Lee (D-TX), 1995 and Marjorie Margolies-Mezvinsky (D-PA), 1993-94.

Employers
Nat'l Ass'n of Community Health Centers (Director, State Affairs)

MIZOGUCHI, Brian A.

901 15th St. NW
Suite 700
Washington, DC 20005-2301
Tel: (202)371-6000
Fax: (202)371-6279
Registered: LDA
EMail: bamizoguchi@verner.com

Trial Attorney, Civil Division, Commercial Litigation Branch, Department of Justice, 1987-90.

Employers
Verner, Liipfert, Bernhard, McPherson and Hand, Chartered (Member of Firm)

MLYNARCZYK, Matt

66 Canal Center Plaza
Suite 600
Alexandria, VA 22314
Tel: (703)683-1300
Ext: 215
Fax: (703)683-1217
Registered: LDA
EMail: mattm@nptc.org

Employers
Nat'l Private Truck Council (Director, Government Relations)

MLYNARCZYK, Tamara Tyrrell

1100 S. Washington St.
First Floor
Alexandria, VA 22314-4494
Tel: (703)683-4300
Fax: (703)683-8965
Registered: LDA
EMail: tamara@nbwa.org

Employers
Nat'l Beer Wholesalers Ass'n (Director, Public Affairs)

MOCHIZUKI, Mike

1775 Massachusetts Ave. NW
Washington, DC 20036-2188
Tel: (202)797-6000
Fax: (202)797-6004

Employers
The Brookings Institution (Non-Resident Senior Fellow, Foreign Policy Studies)

MOCK, Mary

1627 K St. NW
Suite 700
Washington, DC 20006
Tel: (202)452-1252
Ext: 25
Fax: (202)452-0118

Employers
Smokeless Tobacco Council (V. President, Secretary and Treasurer)

MOCKO, Madeline

370 L'Enfant Promenade SW
Fifth Floor
Washington, DC 20447
EMail: mmocko@acf.dhhs.gov
Tel: (202)401-9223
Fax: (202)401-4562

Employers
Department of Health and Human Services - Administration for Children and Families (Director, Office of Legislative Affairs and Budget)

MODE, Jr., Paul J.

2445 M St. NW
Washington, DC 20037-1420
Tel: (202)663-6000
Fax: (202)663-6363
Registered: FARA
Chief Counsel, Subcommittee on Constitutional Amendments, Senate Judiciary Committee, 1970-73.

Employers
Wilmer, Cutler & Pickering (Partner)

Clients Represented
On Behalf of Wilmer, Cutler & Pickering
UNOCAL Corp.

MODI, David T.

1120 G St. NW
Suite 1050
Washington, DC 20005
Tel: (202)347-4446
Registered: LDA

Employers
Georgia-Pacific Corp. (V. President, Government Affairs)

MODIANO, Albert L.

801 Pennsylvania Ave. NW
Suite 840
Washington, DC 20004-2615
Tel: (202)638-4400
Fax: (202)638-5967
Registered: LDA

Employers
U.S. Oil and Gas Ass'n (V. President)

MOE, Richard

1785 Massachusetts Ave. NW
Washington, DC 20036
Tel: (202)588-6000
Fax: (202)588-6059

Employers
Nat'l Trust for Historic Preservation (President)

MOEBIUS, Wanda

600 New Hampshire Ave. NW
Suite 601
Washington, DC 20037
Tel: (202)333-7400
Fax: (202)333-1638
EMail: wmoebius@hillandknowlton.com

Employers
Hill and Knowlton, Inc. (Senior Account Supervisor)

MOELLER, Jamie W.

1901 L St. NW
Suite 300
Washington, DC 20036
Tel: (202)466-7590
Fax: (202)466-7598
Registered: LDA
EMail: jamie.moeller@dc.ogilvypr.com

Employers
Ogilvy Public Relations Worldwide (Managing Director, Global Public Affairs Practice)

Clients Represented
On Behalf of Ogilvy Public Relations Worldwide
American Forest & Paper Ass'n
Edison Electric Institute
INTELSAT - Internat'l Telecommunications Satellite Organization

MOELLER, Julie Debolt

507 C St. NE
Washington, DC 20002-5809
Tel: (202)544-7944
Fax: (202)544-7975
Registered: LDA
EMail: jmoeller@beacon-group.net

Employers
Beacon Consulting Group, Inc. (Legislative Director)

Clients Represented
On Behalf of Beacon Consulting Group, Inc.
Access Community Health Network
Civic Ventures
Haymarket Center
Metropolitan Family Services
Safer Foundation

MOELLER, Karl

1150 Connecticut Ave. NW
Suite 810
Washington, DC 20036
Tel: (202)785-7900
Fax: (202)785-7950
Registered: LDA
EMail: karlm@heart.org

Employers
American Heart Ass'n (Manager, Government Relations)

MOERY, Diane

600 New Hampshire Ave. NW
Tenth Floor
Washington, DC 20037
Tel: (202)333-8667
Fax: (202)298-9109
Registered: LDA
Former Legislative Director to Senator Don Nickles (R-OK).

Employers
Fierce and Isakowitz

Clients Represented
On Behalf of Fierce and Isakowitz
American Ass'n of Nurse Anesthetists
Credit Union Nat'l Ass'n, Inc.
Edison Electric Institute
Edison Internat'l
Federation of American Hospitals
Generic Pharmaceutical Ass'n
Health Insurance Ass'n of America
MCI WorldCom Corp.
Pegasus Communications
Tricon Global Restaurants Inc.

MOETELL, Michael C.

2300 N St. NW
Washington, DC 20037-1128
Tel: (202)663-8000
Fax: (202)663-8007
Registered: LDA

Employers
Shaw Pittman

Clients Represented
On Behalf of Shaw Pittman
Ass'n of Banks of Israel

MOFFAT, Pamela

4341 Forest Ln. NW
Washington, DC 20007
Tel: (202)363-2192

Employers
Nat'l Council of Women of the U.S. (Washington Representative)

MOFFATT, J. Curtis

1050 Thomas Jefferson St. NW
Seventh Floor
Washington, DC 20007
Tel: (202)298-1800
Fax: (202)338-2416
Registered: LDA
EMail: jcm@vnf.com
Legal Assistant to the Chairman, Federal Energy Regulatory Commission, Department of Energy, 1977-79.

Employers
Van Ness Feldman, P.C. (Member)

Clients Represented
On Behalf of Van Ness Feldman, P.C.
Alaska North Slope LNG Project
Foothills Pipe Lines (Yukon), Ltd.

MOFFET, Barbara S.

1145 17th St. NW
Washington, DC 20036
Tel: (202)857-7000
Fax: (202)775-6141

Employers
Nat'l Geographic Soc. (Director, Plans and Programs)

MOFFETT-RIGOLI, Katy

1111 19th St. NW
Suite 800
Washington, DC 20036
Tel: (202)463-2700
Fax: (202)463-2785
Registered: LDA

Employers
American Forest & Paper Ass'n (Manager, Grassroots)

MOFFIT, Dr. Robert

214 Massachusetts Ave. NE
Washington, DC 20002
Tel: (202)546-4400
Fax: (202)546-8328

Employers
Heritage Foundation (Director, Domestic Policy Studies)

MOGIN, Paul

725 12th St. NW
Washington, DC 20005
Tel: (202)434-5000
Fax: (202)434-5029
Law Clerk to Justice Thurgood Marshall, U.S. Supreme Court, 1982-83, and to Judge Henry J. Friendly, U.S. Court of Appeals, Second Circuit, 1980-81.

Employers
Williams & Connolly (Partner)

Clients Represented
On Behalf of Williams & Connolly
Hatco Corp.

MOHACETTEZHPOUR, Shrine

1780 Massachusetts Ave. NW
Washington, DC 20036
Tel: (202)785-3351
Fax: (202)293-4349
Registered: LDA

Employers
Planned Parenthood Federation of America (Legislative Representative)

MOHIB, Mona

1001 G St. NW
Suite 400 East
Washington, DC 20001
Tel: (202)638-3730
Fax: (202)638-3516
Former Director, Intergovernmental Affairs, Department of Labor and former Staff Member, Office of Intergovernmental Affairs, The White House.

Employers
Peyser Associates, Inc.

MOHR, Christopher A.

923 15th St. NW
Washington, DC 20005
Tel: (202)637-0850
Fax: (202)637-0851
Registered: LDA
EMail: chrismohr@sprintmail.com

Employers
Meyer & Klipper, PLLC

Clients Represented
On Behalf of Meyer & Klipper, PLLC
Coalition Against Database Piracy
Magazine Publishers of America
Property Owners Remedy Alliance

MOHRMAN-GILLIS, Marilyn

1350 Connecticut Ave. NW
Suite 200
Washington, DC 20036
Tel: (202)887-1700
Fax: (202)293-2422

Employers
Ass'n of America's Public Television Stations (V. President, Policy and Legal Affairs)

MOHRMANN, George F.

1725 Jefferson Davis Hwy.
Crystal Square 2, Suite 300
Arlington, VA 22202
Tel: (703)413-5615
Fax: (703)413-5617
Registered: LDA

Employers
Lockheed Martin Corp. (V. President, Legislative Affairs, Navy Programs)

MOHUNLALL, Roop

910 17th St. NW
Fifth Floor
Washington, DC 20006
Tel: (202)466-3800
Fax: (202)466-3801

Employers
American Legislative Exchange Council (Director, Project Development)

MOIR, Brian R.

1828 L St. NW
Suite 901
Washington, DC 20036
Tel: (202)331-9852
Fax: (202)331-9854
Registered: LDA
EMail: BRMoir@worldnet.att.net
Senior Legal Counsel, House Energy and Commerce Committee, 1975-81. Staff Counsel, Federal Communications Commission, 1973-75.

Employers
Moir & Hardman (Principal)

MOIRE, Jennifer

1150 17th St. NW
Suite 701
Washington, DC 20036
EMail: jennifer.moire@dittus.com
Tel: (202)775-1401
Fax: (202)775-1404

Employers
Dittus Communications (Director)

Clients Represented

On Behalf of Dittus Communications
Business Software Alliance
Comptel
COPA Commission
Pegasus Communications
Pernod Ricard
SurfControl

MOLER, Elizabeth A.

400 Seventh St. NW
Fourth Floor
Washington, DC 20004
Tel: (202)347-7500
Fax: (202)347-7501

Employers
Exelon Corp. (Senior V. President, Government Affairs & Policy)

MOLINARI, Hon. Susan

4004 Sharp Place
Alexandria, VA 22304
Registered: LDA
Member, U.S. House of Representatives (R-NY), 1990-98.

Employers
Susan Molinari, L.L.P.

Clients Represented

On Behalf of Susan Molinari, L.L.P.
American Heart Ass'n
SBC Communications Inc.

MOLINARO, Peter A.

1776 I St. NW
Suite 1050
Washington, DC 20006
Tel: (202)429-3429
Registered: LDA

Employers
The Dow Chemical Co. (Director, Government Relations)

MOLINEAUX, Christopher

1100 15th St. NW
Suite 900
Washington, DC 20005
Tel: (202)835-3400
Fax: (202)835-3414

Employers
Pharmaceutical Research and Manufacturers of America (V. President, Public Affairs)

MOLINO, John

2425 Wilson Blvd.
Arlington, VA 22201-3385
Tel: (703)907-2637
Ext: 633
Fax: (703)525-9039
Registered: LDA
EMail: jmolino@ausa.org

Employers
Ass'n of the United States Army (Director, Government Affairs)

MOLINO, Mike

3930 University Dr.
Fairfax, VA 22030-2515
Tel: (703)591-7130
Fax: (703)591-0734

Employers
Recreation Vehicle Dealers Ass'n of North America (President)
Recreation Vehicle Rental Ass'n

MOLL, Gary

910 17th St. NW
Suite 600
Washington, DC 20006
Tel: (202)955-4500
Fax: (202)955-4588

Employers
American Forests (V. President, Urban Forestry)

MOLLINS, Stephanie

801 G St. NW
Washington, DC 20001
Tel: (202)393-2100
Fax: (202)393-2134
Registered: LDA

Employers
Family Research Council, Inc.

MOLLOY, James T.

9226 Ispahanloop
Laurel, MD 20708
Tel: (301)776-6128
Fax: (301)776-5070
Registered: LDA
Doorkeeper of the U.S. House of Representatives, 1969-70.

Employers
Self-employed as an independent consultant.

Clients Represented

As an independent consultant
Advanced Refractory Technologies, Inc.
Norfolk Southern Corp.
Philip Morris Management Corp.
Stanton & Associates
Union Pacific Railroad Co.

MOLLOY, Michelle

1730 Rhode Island Ave. NW
Suite 712
Washington, DC 20036
Tel: (202)331-1550
Fax: (202)331-1663

Employers
Robert M. Brandon and Associates

Clients Represented

On Behalf of Robert M. Brandon and Associates
A Greater Washington
Electric Consumers Alliance

MOLLURA, A. Dennis

901 15th St. NW
Suite 310
WAS 1186
Washington, DC 20005
Tel: (202)842-3193
Fax: (202)289-6834

Employers
Northwest Airlines, Inc. (Director, Corporate Communications)

MOLM, John R.

401 Ninth St. NW
Suite 1000
Washington, DC 20004
Tel: (202)274-2957
Fax: (202)274-2994
Registered: LDA

Employers
Troutman Sanders LLP (Partner)

MOLNAR, Yancy

1401 H St. NW
Suite 700
Washington, DC 20005
Tel: (202)414-6742
Fax: (202)414-6741
Registered: LDA

Employers
DaimlerChrysler Corp. (Analyst, International Trade)

MOLOFSKY, Robert A.

5025 Wisconsin Ave. NW
Washington, DC 20016
Tel: (202)537-1645
Fax: (202)244-7824
Registered: LDA

Employers
Amalgamated Transit Union (General Counsel)

MOLONEY, John M.

1275 K St. NW
Suite 1200
Washington, DC 20005
Tel: (202)216-0700
Fax: (202)216-0824
Registered: LDA

Employers
Delta Air Lines (General Manager, Government Affairs)

MOLOTSKY, Iris F.

1012 14th St. NW
Suite 500
Washington, DC 20005
Tel: (202)737-5900
Fax: (202)737-5526

Employers
American Ass'n of University Professors (Director, Public Relations)

MOLPUS, C. Manly

1010 Wisconsin Ave. NW
Ninth Floor
Washington, DC 20007
EMail: cmm@gmabrands.com
Tel: (202)337-9400
Fax: (202)337-4508
Registered: LDA

Employers
Grocery Manufacturers of America (President and Chief Exec. Officer)

MOLTZAN, Gunter W.

6701 Democracy Blvd.
Suite 300
Bethesda, MD 20817
Tel: (301)977-6104
Fax: (301)330-0790
Registered: FARA

Employers
Self-employed as an independent consultant.

Clients Represented

As an independent consultant
Baden-Wuerttemberg Agency for International Economic Cooperation

MONACO, Carol

1090 Vermont Ave. NW
Suite 510
Washington, DC 20005
Tel: (202)414-0140
Fax: (202)544-3525
Registered: LDA

Employers
American Osteopathic Ass'n (Assistant Director, Regulatory Affairs)

MONACO, Daniel J.

1000 Connecticut Ave. NW
Suite 202
Washington, DC 20036
EMail: wja@worldjurist.org
Tel: (202)466-5428
Fax: (202)452-8540

Employers
World Jurist Ass'n of the World Peace Through Law Center (President)

MONAHAN, Frank

3211 Fourth St. NE
Washington, DC 20017
Tel: (202)541-3140
Fax: (202)541-3313

Employers
Nat'l Conference of Catholic Bishops, Secretariat for Pro-Life Activities
United States Catholic Conference (Director, Office of Government Liaison)

MONDRES, Eric M.

900 19th St. NW
Suite 400
Washington, DC 20006
Tel: (202)857-3100
Fax: (202)296-8716
Registered: LDA

Employers
America's Community Bankers (Government Relations)

MONES, Seth

1200 G St. NW
Suite 800
Washington, DC 20005
Tel: (202)434-8768
Fax: (202)434-8707
Registered: LDA

Employers
Winning Strategies Washington, D.C., LLC

MONFORT, Charles A.

499 S. Capitol St. SW
Suite 420
Washington, DC 20003
Tel: (202)302-0465
Registered: LDA

Employers
Monfort & Wolfe (Associate)

Clients Represented

On Behalf of Monfort & Wolfe
Incorporated Research Institutions for Seismology
St. Elizabeth's Medical Center

MONGILLO, David

1350 I St. NW
Suite 590
Washington, DC 20005
EMail: dmongil@cap.org
Tel: (202)354-7110
Fax: (202)354-7155

Employers
College of American Pathologists (Director, Public Health and Scientific Affairs)

MONIHAN, Frank

3211 Fourth St. NE
Washington, DC 20017
Tel: (202)541-3000

Employers
U.S. Catholic Conference (Exec. Director, Office of Government Liason)

MONK, Carl C.

1201 Connecticut Ave. NW
Suite 800
Washington, DC 20036
EMail: cmonk@aals.org
Tel: (202)296-8851
Fax: (202)296-8869

Employers
Ass'n of American Law Schools (Exec. Director and Exec. V. President)

MONRO, Jr., Charles B.

1725 Jefferson Davis Hwy.
Crystal Square 2, Suite 300
Arlington, VA 22202
Tel: (703)413-5600
Fax: (703)413-5617
Registered: LDA

Employers
Lockheed Martin Corp. (Director, Airlift Programs, Aeronautics Sector, Washington Operations)

MONROE, Gary

1750 New York Ave. NW
Washington, DC 20006
Tel: (202)637-0798
Fax: (202)637-0771

Employers
Internat'l Union of Painters and Allied Trades (Administrator, Labor Management Cooperation Fund)

MONROE, Loren

1275 Pennsylvania Ave. NW
Tenth Floor
Washington, DC 20004
EMail: lomonroe@bgrdc.com
Tel: (202)333-4936
Fax: (202)833-9392
Registered: LDA, FARA

Former Legislative Aide to Senator Pete Domenici (R-NM).

Employers
Barbour Griffith & Rogers, Inc. (V. President and Director, Federal Affairs)

Clients Represented

On Behalf of Barbour Griffith & Rogers, Inc.
Air Transport Ass'n of America
Alliance for Quality Nursing Home Care
Amgen
Bay Harbor Management, L.C.
BellSouth Telecommunications, Inc.
Better World Campaign
Bristol-Myers Squibb Co.
Brown and Williamson Tobacco Corp.
Canadian Nat'l Railway Co.
Delta Air Lines
FM Watch
GlaxoSmithKline
INTELSAT - Internat'l Telecommunications Satellite Organization
LVMH Moet Hennessy Louis Vuitton S.A.
Lyondell Chemical Co.
MassMutual Financial Group
Microsoft Corp.
Oxygenated Fuels Ass'n
Professional Benefit Trust
Qwest Communications
RJR Co.
Southern Co.
Tulane University
United Health Group
University of Mississippi
University of Mississippi Medical Center
University of Southern Mississippi
The Winterthur Group

MONROE, Michael E.

1750 New York Ave. NW
Washington, DC 20006
Tel: (202)637-0700
Fax: (202)637-0771
Registered: LDA

Employers
Internat'l Union of Painters and Allied Trades (General President)

MONROE, Ned

1300 N. 17th St.
Eighth Floor
Rosslyn, VA 22209-3801
EMail: monroe@abc.org
Tel: (703)812-2000
Fax: (703)812-8202
Registered: LDA

Employers
Associated Builders and Contractors (Director, Political Development)

MONROE, Robert R.

1015 15th St. NW
Suite 700
Washington, DC 20005-2605
Tel: (202)828-5200
Fax: (202)785-2645

Employers
Bechtel Group, Inc. (V. President and Manager, Government Operations (BNI))

MONROE, Mr. Terry

1900 M St. NW
Suite 800
Washington, DC 20036-3508
EMail: tmonroe@comptel.org
Tel: (202)296-6650
Fax: (202)296-7585

Employers
Competitive Telecommunications Ass'n (COMPTEL) (V. President, Industry & Government Relations)

MONRONEY, Beth

801 Pennsylvania Ave. NW
Suite 750
Washington, DC 20004
Tel: (202)393-1132
Fax: (202)624-0659
Registered: LDA

Employers
Richard L. Spees, Inc.

MONTAGNA, Donald

7750 16th St. NW
Washington, DC 20012
Tel: (202)882-6650
Fax: (202)829-1354

Employers
Washington Ethical Soc. (Senior Leader)

MONTAGUE, R. Latane

555 13th St. NW
Washington, DC 20004-1109
Tel: (202)637-5600
Fax: (202)637-5910
Registered: LDA

Employers
Hogan & Hartson L.L.P.

Clients Represented

On Behalf of Hogan & Hartson L.L.P.
Nissan North America Inc.

MONTALBAN, Katrina

1560 Wilson Blvd.
Suite 1200
Arlington, VA 22209
EMail: ksolomon@mmsa.com
Tel: (703)525-4800
Fax: (703)525-6772

Employers
Mitsubishi Motors America, Inc. (Assistant Manager, Government Relations)

MONTANINO, Deborah

2000 M St. NW
Suite 400
Washington, DC 20036
Tel: (202)467-4999
Fax: (202)293-2672

Employers
People for the American Way (Director, Development)

MONTANO, William B.

1350 I St. NW
Suite 1240
Washington, DC 20005
Tel: (202)296-3840
Fax: (202)682-0146

Employers
Ashby and Associates (Associate)

Clients Represented

On Behalf of Ashby and Associates
American Security Resources, Inc.

MONTEILH, Richard

1213 K St. NW
Washington, DC 20005
Tel: (202)347-7201
Fax: (202)638-6764

Employers
District of Columbia Chamber of Commerce (President)

MONTESANO, Craig F.

1275 K St. NW
Suite 890
Washington, DC 20005
Tel: (202)682-9161
Fax: (202)638-1043
Registered: LDA

Employers
Global Climate Coalition (Manager, Government Relations and Public Affairs)

MONTGOMERY, Hon. G. V. "Sonny"

11 Canal Center Plaza
Suite 103
Alexandria, VA 22314
Tel: (703)683-4222
Fax: (703)683-0645
Registered: LDA

Member, U.S. House of Representatives (D-MS), 1967-96. Chairman, House Committee on Veterans' Affairs, 1981-94.

Employers
The Montgomery Group (President)
The Spectrum Group

Clients Represented

On Behalf of The Montgomery Group
American Ass'n of Community Colleges
Blue Cross Blue Shield of Mississippi
Lockheed Martin Corp.
Raytheon Co.

MONTGOMERY, George Cranwell

801 Pennsylvania Ave. NW
Suite 800
Washington, DC 20004
EMail: cmontgomery@bdbc.com
Tel: (202)508-3400
Fax: (202)508-3402
Registered: LDA, FARA

Ambassador to Oman, Department of State, 1985-89. Counsel to the Majority Leader, U.S. Senate, 1981-85. Legislative Aide to Senator Howard H. Baker, Jr. (R-TN), 1975-81.

Employers
Baker, Donelson, Bearman & Caldwell, P.C. (Shareholder)

Clients Represented

On Behalf of Baker, Donelson, Bearman & Caldwell, P.C.
American Standard Cos. Inc.
Azerbaijan, Embassy of the Republic of
Day & Zimmermann, Inc.
Loral Space and Communications, Ltd.
Phillips Petroleum Co.
Sikorsky Aircraft Corp.

MONTGOMERY, Gwen

14th and Constitution Ave. NW
Room 7814A
Washington, DC 20230
Tel: (202)482-2309
Fax: (202)501-4828

Employers
Department of Commerce - Economic Development Administration (Communications and Congressional Liaison Specialist)

MONTGOMERY, John H.

1200 New Hampshire Ave NW
Suite 430
Washington, DC 20036
Tel: (202)955-4555
Fax: (202)955-1147
Registered: LDA

Employers
Murray, Scheer, Montgomery, Tapia & O'Donnell (Partner)

Clients Represented

On Behalf of Murray, Scheer, Montgomery, Tapia & O'Donnell

Ass'n of Metropolitan Sewerage Agencies
Brownsville, Texas, City of
El Paso Water Utilities - Public Service Board
Ground Water Protection Council
Jasper, Alabama, City of
Long Beach, California, City of
Marshall, Alabama, County of
Nat'l Rural Water Ass'n
Native American Cultural & Educational Authority
Oklahoma City, Oklahoma, City of
Oklahoma State Medical Ass'n
Passaic Valley Sewerage Commissioners
San Jose, California, City of
Santa Clarita, California, City of
Southern California Ass'n of Governments
West Jordan, Utah, City of

MONTGOMERY, Ph.D., Kathryn

2120 L St. NW
Suite 200
Washington, DC 20037
Tel: (202)331-7833
Fax: (202)331-7841

Employers
Center for Media Education (President)

MONTGOMERY, Lynn

1900 Association Dr.
Suite ATE
Reston, VA 20191-1502
EMail: ate1@aol.com
Tel: (703)620-3110
Fax: (703)620-9530

Employers
Ass'n of Teacher Educators (Exec. Director)

MONTGOMERY, Margaret

14th and Constitution Ave. NW
Room 7814A
Washington, DC 20230
Tel: (202)482-2309
Fax: (202)501-4828

Employers
Department of Commerce - Economic Development Administration (Communications and Congressional Liaison Assistant)

MONTGOMERY, Jr., Robert E.

1615 L St. NW
Suite 1300
Washington, DC 20036
Tel: (202)223-7300
Fax: (202)223-7420
Registered: LDA, FARA
EMail: remontgomery@paulweiss.com
General Counsel, Federal Energy Administration, 1974-75. Assistant General Counsel, Federal Trade Commission, 1973. General Counsel, Office of Consumer Affairs, Executive Office of the President, The White House, 1971-72. Assistant to the General Counsel, Department of the Army, 1969-71. Infantry Captain, U.S. Army, 1960-66.

Employers
Paul, Weiss, Rifkind, Wharton & Garrison (Partner)

MONTGOMERY, Susan West

1350 Connecticut Ave. NW
Suite 401
Washington, DC 20036
Tel: (202)659-0915
Fax: (202)659-0189

Employers
Preservation Action (President)

MONTORFANO, Celina

1422 Fenwick Ln.
Silver Spring, MD 20910
Tel: (301)565-6704
Fax: (301)565-6714

Employers
American Hiking Soc. (Alliance Policy Coordinator)

MONTOYA, Ken

1325 Massachusetts Ave. NW
Washington, DC 20005
Tel: (202)628-5451
Ext: 437
Fax: (202)628-5767
Registered: LDA

Employers
Nat'l Air Traffic Controllers Ass'n (Legislative Director)

MONTWIELER, William J.

1750 K St. NW
Suite 460
Washington, DC 20006
Tel: (202)296-9880
Fax: (202)286-9884
Registered: LDA

Employers
Industrial Truck Ass'n (Exec. Director)

MOODIE, Michael

2111 Eisenhower Ave.
Suite 302
Alexandria, VA 22314
Tel: (703)739-1538
Fax: (703)739-1525

Employers
Chemical and Biological Arms Control Institute (President)

MOODY, Christopher

1250 I St. NW
Suite 902
Washington, DC 20005
Tel: (202)393-5225
Fax: (202)393-3034

Employers
Robert A. Rapoza Associates (Policy Associate)

MOODY, Randall

1201 16th St. NW
Washington, DC 20036
Tel: (202)833-4000
Registered: LDA

Employers
Nat'l Education Ass'n of the U.S. (Senior Professional Associate)

MOODY, Scott

1250 H St. NW
Suite 750
Washington, DC 20005
EMail: jsmoody@taxfoundation.org
Tel: (202)783-2760
Fax: (202)783-6868

Employers
Tax Foundation, Inc. (Economist)

MOON, Marilyn

2100 M St. NW
Washington, DC 20037
Tel: (202)833-7200
Fax: (202)429-0687

Employers
The Urban Institute (Senior Fellow)

MOONEY, Kathy

1526 New Hampshire Ave. NW
Washington, DC 20036
Tel: (202)232-7363
Fax: (202)986-2791

Employers
Woman's Nat'l Democratic Club (General Manager)

MOONEY, Robby A.

1615 L St. NW
Suite 1000
Washington, DC 20036
Tel: (202)659-0330
Fax: (202)223-8199
Registered: LDA
EMail: mooneyr@fleishman.com
Former Legislative Director to Rep. Joe Skubitz (R-KS); Legislative Director to Rep. Robert Whittaker (R-KS); and Republican Staff Director, Energy and Commerce Committee, U.S. House of Representatives.

Employers
Fleishman-Hillard, Inc (Senior V. President and Partner)

MOONEY, Saskia

1299 Pennsylvania Ave. NW
Washington, DC 20004-2402
Tel: (202)783-0800
Fax: (202)383-6610
Registered: LDA

Employers
Howrey Simon Arnold & White

Clients Represented

On Behalf of Howrey Simon Arnold & White

Nat'l Ass'n for Plastic Container Recovery
Portable Rechargeable Battery Ass'n

MOONIS, Anthony T.

122 C St. NW
Suite 505
Washington, DC 20001
Tel: (202)484-2282
Fax: (202)783-3306

Employers
GOPAC (Treasurer)

MOORE, Alan J.

9534 Clement Rd.
Silver Spring, MD 20910
Tel: (301)585-3838
Fax: (301)585-3838
Registered: LDA

Employers
Alan J. Moore, Washington Representative - Governmental Affairs (President)

Clients Represented

On Behalf of Alan J. Moore, Washington Representative - Governmental Affairs

Burlington Northern Santa Fe Railway

MOORE, Amy N.

1201 Pennsylvania Ave. NW
Washington, DC 20004-2401
Tel: (202)662-5900
Fax: (202)662-6291
Registered: LDA
EMail: anmoore@cov.com
Law Clerk to Judge Frank M. Coffin, U.S. Court of Appeals, First Circuit, 1983-84.

Employers
Covington & Burling (Partner)

MOORE, Andrew D.

1005 E St. SE
Washington, DC 20003
Tel: (202)546-5722
Fax: (202)546-5726
Registered: LDA
EMail: admoore@agaviation.org
Legislative Director, Former Rep. Andrea Seastrand (R-CA), 1995.

Employers
Nat'l Agricultural Aviation Ass'n (Director, Government Relations)

MOORE, Andrew E.

666 11th St. NW
Suite 1000
Washington, DC 20001-4542
EMail: amoore@nascc.org
Tel: (202)737-6272
Fax: (202)737-6277

Employers
Nat'l Ass'n of Service and Conservation Corps (V. President, Government Relations and Public Affairs)

MOORE, Carlos

1130 Connecticut Ave. NW
Suite 1200
Washington, DC 20036-3954
Tel: (202)862-0500
Fax: (202)862-0570
Registered: LDA

Employers
American Textile Manufacturers Institute (Exec. V. President)

MOORE, Christy

139 C St. SE
Washington, DC 20003
Tel: (202)547-8570
Fax: (202)546-6403

Employers
Traditional Values Coalition (Director, Communications)

MOORE, Cynthia L.

1911 North Fort Myer Dr.
Suite 702
Arlington, VA 22209
Tel: (703)243-1667
Fax: (703)243-1672
Registered: LDA
Former Legislative Staff to Representative Han Glickman (D-KS).

Employers
The Moore Law Firm, PLLC (President)

Clients Represented

On Behalf of The Moore Law Firm, PLLC

Nat'l Council on Teacher Retirement

MOORE, David B.

2450 N St. NW
Washington, DC 20037-1126
Tel: (202)828-0525
Fax: (202)862-6218
Registered: LDA

Employers
Ass'n of American Medical Colleges (Associate V. President, Governmental Relations)

MOORE, Evelyn K.

1101 15th St. NW
Suite 900
Washington, DC 20005
Tel: (202)833-2220
Fax: (202)833-8222

Employers
Nat'l Black Child Development Institute (President and Chief Exec. Officer)

MOORE, Frank M.

2025 M St. NW
Suite 800
Washington, DC 20036
Tel: (202)367-2100
Fax: (202)367-1200
Registered: LDA
EMail: frank_moore@dc.sba.com
Former Legislative Director to Rep. Robert Garcia (D-NY) and Counsel, Subcommittee on Policy Research and Insurance, Committee on Banking, Finance and Urban Affairs, U.S. House of Representatives.

Employers
Smith, Bucklin and Associates, Inc. (Director, Public Policy Practice Group, Government Relations)

Clients Represented
On Behalf of Smith, Bucklin and Associates, Inc.
Ass'n of Local Housing Finance Agencies
The Child Care Consortium
Internat'l Institute of Ammonia Refrigeration
Mobile Communications Holdings, Inc.
Nat'l Child Care Ass'n
Nat'l Organization for Competency Assurance

MOORE, Jerry

5100 Wisconsin Ave. NW
Suite 301
Washington, DC 20016
Tel: (202)966-8665
Fax: (202)966-3222

Employers
D.C. Building Industry Ass'n Political Action Committee (PAC Treasurer)

MOORE, Jesse W.

2200 Clarendon Blvd.
Suite 1202
Arlington, VA 22201
Tel: (703)284-5400
Fax: (703)284-5449

Employers
Ball Aerospace & Technologies Corp. (V. President, Washington Operations)

MOORE, Jon

1629 K St. NW
Suite 1100
Washington, DC 20006
Tel: (202)785-6710
Fax: (202)331-4212

Employers
Agri/Washington (Legislative Representative)

Clients Represented
On Behalf of Agri/Washington
American Ass'n of Grain Inspection and Weighing Agencies
American Grain Inspection Institute
Apple Processors Ass'n
Maryland Dairy Industry Ass'n

MOORE, Kathleen

1000 Wilson Blvd.
Suite 2500
Arlington, VA 22209-3908
Tel: (703)276-1750
Fax: (703)528-1290

Employers
Consumer Bankers Ass'n (Manager, Communications)

MOORE, Kirsten

1818 N St. NW
Suite 450
Washington, DC 20036
Tel: (202)530-2900
Fax: (202)530-2901
Registered: LDA
EMail: kmoore@basshowes.com

Employers
Bass and Howes, Inc. (Program Manager)

Clients Represented
On Behalf of Bass and Howes, Inc.
Physicians for Reproductive Choice and Health
Reproductive Health Technologies Project

MOORE, III, Lawrence

750 First St. NE
Suite 700
Washington, DC 20002
Tel: (202)408-8600
Fax: (202)336-8289
Registered: LDA

Employers
Nat'l Ass'n of Social Workers (Congressional Lobbyist)

MOORE, Lois

2111 Wilson Blvd.
Eighth Floor
Arlington, VA 22201-3058
Tel: (703)841-0626
Fax: (703)243-2874
Registered: LDA
EMail: moore@alcalde-fay.com

Employers
Alcalde & Fay (Partner)

Clients Represented
On Behalf of Alcalde & Fay
Cargill, Inc.
Clearwater, Florida, City of
Computer Sciences Corp.
Cruise Industry Charitable Foundation
Future Leaders of America
Hillsborough, Florida, County of
Houston Independent School District
Internat'l Council of Cruise Lines
Jacksonville Chamber of Commerce
Jacksonville, Florida, Port Authority of the City of
Miami-Dade County Public Schools
Miami-Dade, Florida, County of
Tampa Port Authority
Washington Workshops

MOORE, Lori

1750 New York Ave. NW
Washington, DC 20006
Tel: (202)737-8484
Fax: (202)737-8418
Registered: LDA

Employers
Internat'l Ass'n of Fire Fighters (Assistant to the General President, Membership Services, Technical Assistance, Information Resources)

MOORE, Margaret A.

1050 Thomas Jefferson St. NW
Seventh Floor
Washington, DC 20007
Tel: (202)298-1800
Fax: (202)338-2416
EMail: mam@vnf.com
Staff Attorney (1983-85), Office of General Counsel, Electric Rates and Corporate Reulation; and Attorney/Advisor (1982-83), Office of Administrative Law Judges, Federal Energy Regulatory Commission, Department of Energy.

Employers
Van Ness Feldman, P.C. (Member)

Clients Represented
On Behalf of Van Ness Feldman, P.C.
American Chemistry Council

MOORE, Michael D.

555 11th St. NW
Suite 750
Washington, DC 20005
Tel: (202)637-3506
Fax: (202)637-3504

Employers
El Paso Corporation (Director, Federal Agency Affairs)

MOORE, Michele

1015 15th St. NW
Suite 802
Washington, DC 20005
Tel: (202)347-7474
Fax: (202)898-0068
EMail: mmoore@acec.org

Employers
American Consulting Engineers Council (Assistant Director, International Affairs)

MOORE, Nuala

3615 Wisconsin Ave. NW
Washington, DC 20016
Tel: (202)966-7300
Fax: (202)966-1944
Registered: LDA

Employers
American Academy of Child and Adolescent Psychiatry (Assistant Director, Government Affairs)

MOORE, Powel A.

1300 Defense Pentagon
Room 3E966
Washington, DC 20301-1300
Tel: (703)697-6210
Fax: (703)693-5530

Employers
Department of Defense (Assistant Secretary for Legislative Affairs (Nominated))

MOORE, Stephen

1776 K St. NW
Suite 300
Washington, DC 20006
Tel: (202)955-5500
Fax: (202)955-4966

Employers
Club for Growth (President)

MOORE, Susan A.

1050 Thomas Jefferson St. NW
Seventh Floor
Washington, DC 20007
EMail: SAM@vnf.com
Tel: (202)298-1800
Fax: (202)338-2416

Employers
Van Ness Feldman, P.C. (Associate)

MOORE, Susan F.

1120 G St. NW
Suite 1050
Washington, DC 20005
Tel: (202)347-4446

Employers
Georgia-Pacific Corp. (V. President, Environmental Affairs)

MOORE, Susan P.

1300 Wilson Blvd.
Suite 800
Arlington, VA 22209
Tel: (703)253-0700
Fax: (703)253-0701

Employers
American Plastics Council (V. President, Communications)

MOORE, Thomas G.

214 Massachusetts Ave. NE
Washington, DC 20002
Tel: (202)546-4400
Fax: (202)546-8328

Employers
Heritage Foundation (Director, Kathryn & Shelby Collom Davis International Studies Center)

MOORE, Timothy X.

2900 M St. NW
Suite 300
Washington, DC 20007
Tel: (202)333-4318
Fax: (202)342-0418
Registered: LDA
EMail: timxavier@aol.com
Exec. Assistant to Rep. Timothy Wirth (D-CO), 1976-80. Legislative Assistant to Senator Richard Stone (D-FL), 1975-76.

Employers
Timothy X. Moore and Co. (President)

Clients Represented
On Behalf of Timothy X. Moore and Co.
Berkeley County Water & Sanitation Authority
Galena, Illinois, City of
Inventure Place
Santee Cooper (South Carolina Public Service Authority)
South Carolina Public Service Authority

MOORE, Hon. W. Henson

1111 19th St. NW
Suite 800
Washington, DC 20036
Tel: (202)463-2700
Fax: (202)463-2785
Registered: LDA
Member, U.S. House of Representatives (R-LA), 1975-87.

Employers
American Forest & Paper Ass'n (President and Chief Exec. Officer)

MOORE, W. John

1199 N. Fairfax St.
Suite 1000
Alexandria, VA 22314
Tel: (703)299-4499
Fax: (703)299-4488

Employers
The Hawthorn Group, L.C. (Senior V. President, Communications Services)

MOORE, Walter K.

808 17th St. NW
Suite 250
Washington, DC 20006
EMail: wmoore@gene.com
Tel: (202)296-7272
Fax: (202)296-7290
Registered: LDA

Employers
Genentech, Inc. (V. President, Government Affairs)

MOOREHEAD, Donald V.

2550 M St. NW
Washington, DC 20037-1350
Tel: (202)457-6000
Fax: (202)457-6315
Registered: LDA, FARA
EMail: dmoorehead@pattonboggs.com
Chief Minority Counsel, Senate Committee on Finance, 1975-76.

Employers
Patton Boggs, LLP (Partner)

Clients Represented
On Behalf of Patton Boggs, LLP
Aera Energy LLC
AutoNation, Inc.
FM Watch
Alan Hilburg & Associates
Internat'l Swaps and Derivatives Dealers Ass'n
Kaiser Aluminum & Chemical Corp.
Mars, Inc.
Security Capital Group
Shell Oil Co.
US Airways
Venetian Casino Resort, LLC
Walton Enterprises
Wegmans Food Markets, Inc.

MOORHEAD, Eileen M.

401 Ninth St. NW
Suite 1000
Washington, DC 20004
Tel: (202)274-2943
Fax: (202)274-2994

Employers
Troutman Sanders LLP (Associate)

Clients Represented
On Behalf of Troutman Sanders LLP
Longhorn Pipeline

MOORHEAD, Randall B.

1300 I St. NW
Suite 1070 East
Washington, DC 20005
Tel: (202)962-8550
Fax: (202)962-8560
Registered: LDA

Employers
Philips Electronics North America Corp. (V. President, Government Affairs)

MOORHEAD, Tracey

900 17th St. NW
Suite 600
Washington, DC 20006
EMail: tmoorehead@hlc.org
Tel: (202)452-1029
Fax: (202)296-9561
Registered: LDA

Employers
Alliance to Improve Medicare (Director)

MOORJANI, Neena

1150 17th St. NW
Suite 701
Washington, DC 20036
EMail: neena.moorjani@dittus.com
Tel: (202)775-1401
Fax: (202)775-1404

Employers
Dittus Communications (Associate Director)

Clients Represented
On Behalf of Dittus Communications
Magazine Publishers of America
Nat'l Cooperative Business Ass'n

MOORMAN, Jim

1220 19th St. NW
Suite 501
Washington, DC 20036
Tel: (202)296-4826
Fax: (202)296-4838

Employers
Taxpayers Against Fraud, The False Claims Legal Center (President/C.E.O.)

MORABITO, John S.

1615 L St. NW
Suite 450
Washington, DC 20036
EMail: john_morabito@globalcrossing.com
Tel: (202)872-0063
Registered: LDA

Employers
Global Crossing North America, Inc. (V. President, Federal Legislative & Regulatory Affairs)

MORAGO, Sheila

224 Second St. SE
Washington, DC 20003
EMail: SAMorago@indiangaming.org
Tel: (202)546-7711
Fax: (202)546-1755

Employers
Nat'l Indian Gaming Ass'n (Director, Public Relations)

MORAN, Anne E.

1330 Connecticut Ave. NW
Washington, DC 20036-1795
EMail: amoran@steptoe.com
Tel: (202)429-6449
Fax: (202)429-3902
Tax Counsel, Finance Committee, U.S. Senate, 1983-86.

Employers
Steptoe & Johnson LLP (Partner)

MORAN, Brian J.

119 N. Henry St.
Alexandria, VA 22314
Tel: (703)684-5755
Fax: (703)684-0472
Registered: LDA

Employers
Nealon & Moran, L.L.P.

Clients Represented
On Behalf of Nealon & Moran, L.L.P.
Washington Flyer Taxi Drivers Ass'n, Inc.

MORAN, Cynthia Root

1455 F St. NW
Suite 450
Washington, DC 20004
Tel: (202)393-6040
Fax: (202)393-6050
Registered: LDA

Employers
Pharmacia Corp. (Director, Government Affairs)

MORAN, Mark A.

1330 Connecticut Ave. NW
Washington, DC 20036-1795
Tel: (202)429-3000
Fax: (202)429-3902
Registered: LDA, FARA
EMail: mmoran@steptoe.com

Employers
Steptoe & Johnson LLP (Partner)

Clients Represented
On Behalf of Steptoe & Johnson LLP
B.C. Softwood Lumber Trade Council
British Columbia Softwood Lumber Trade Council
Canada, Embassy of
Trinidad and Tobago, Government of

MORAN, Mike

1350 I St. NW
Suite 1000
Washington, DC 20005
EMail: mmoran@ford.com
Tel: (202)962-5416
Fax: (202)962-5417

Employers
Ford Motor Co. (Director, Washington Regional Communications)

MORAN, Robert J.

1120 G St. NW
Suite 900
Washington, DC 20005-3801
Tel: (202)347-6900
Fax: (202)347-8650
Registered: LDA

Employers
Nat'l Ocean Industries Ass'n (Director, Government Affairs)

MORDHOFF, Keith

421 Aviation Way
Frederick, MD 21701
EMail: keith.mordhoff@aopa.org
Tel: (301)695-2000
Fax: (301)695-2375

Employers
Aircraft Owners and Pilots Ass'n (Senior V. President, Communications)

MORE, Jeffery T.

1225 I St. NW
Suite 810
Washington, DC 20005
EMail: jmore@theaccordgroup.com
Tel: (202)289-9800
Fax: (202)289-3588
Associate Counsel, House Water Resources and Environment Subcommittee, 1993-2000. Legislative Assistant, Rep. Sherwood Boehlert (R-NY), 1991-1993. Legislative Assistant, Rep. George Gekas (R-PA), 1989-91.

Employers
The Accord Group (Principal)
Science Leadership PAC (PAC Administrator)

Clients Represented
On Behalf of The Accord Group
The Clark Estates, Inc.
Ducks Unlimited Inc.
Water Infrastructure Network
Zurich Financial Services Group
Zurich U.S. Specialties

MORELAND, Edward W.

1225 I St. NW
Suite 500
Washington, DC 20005
EMail: edmoreland.ama@erols.com
Tel: (202)682-4750
Fax: (202)789-0406
Registered: LDA

Employers
American Motorcyclist Ass'n (Washington Representative)

MORELAND, Rick

601 F St. NW
Washington, DC 20004
Tel: (202)661-5000
Fax: (202)661-5108

Employers
Washington Sports & Entertainment, L.P. (V. President, Corporate Marketing)

MORELLI, Genevieve

1200 19th St. NW
Suite 500
Washington, DC 20036
Tel: (202)955-9600
Fax: (202)955-9792

Employers
Kelley, Drye & Warren LLP (Of Counsel)

MORENO, Lisa M.

1300 19th St. NW
Second Floor
Washington, DC 20036
Tel: (202)557-3400
Fax: (202)728-4177
Registered: LDA

Employers
Population Action Internat'l (Senior Legislative Policy Analyst)

MOREY, Richard S.

1140 19th St. NW
Suite 900
Washington, DC 20036
EMail: rmorey@kkblaw.com
Tel: (202)223-5120
Fax: (202)223-5619
Law Clerk for Judge Sterry R. Waterman, U.S. Court of Appeals, Second Circuit, 1966-67.

Employers
Kleinfeld, Kaplan and Becker (Partner)

Clients Represented
On Behalf of Kleinfeld, Kaplan and Becker
Cord Laboratories
Mead Johnson and Co.

MORGAN, Alan

1320 19th St. NW
Suite 350
Washington, DC 20036
EMail: dc@nrharural.org
Tel: (202)232-6200
Fax: (202)232-1133
Registered: LDA

Employers
Nat'l Rural Health Ass'n (V. President, Government Affairs and Policy)

MORGAN, Brian

1755 Jefferson Davis Hwy.
Suite 1107
Arlington, VA 22202
Tel: (703)415-0344
Fax: (703)415-0182

Employers
The PMA Group

MORGAN, Bruce

1350 I St. NW
Suite 400
Washington, DC 20005-3306
Tel: (202)371-6900
Fax: (202)842-3578

Employers
Motorola, Inc. (Manager, U.S. Government Relations)

MORGAN, Jr., Gerald D.

1133 Connecticut Ave. NW
Suite 1200
Washington, DC 20036
Tel: (202)775-9800
Fax: (202)833-8491

General Counsel, Agency for International Development (1976-77) and Vice President and General Counsel (1975-76), Deputy Vice President for Insurance (1974-75) and Attorney (1971-74), Overseas Private Investment Corporation, Executive Office of the President, The White House.

Employers
Winthrop, Stimson, Putnam & Roberts (Partner)

MORGAN, Herbert N.

1730 M St. NW
Suite 911
Washington, DC 20036-4505
Tel: (202)785-3066
Fax: (202)659-5760

Employers
Compass Internat'l Inc. (Chairman)

MORGAN, J. Railton

1350 I St. NW
Suite 1000
Washington, DC 20005
EMail: jmorgan9@ford.com
Tel: (202)962-5373
Fax: (202)336-7226
Registered: LDA

Employers
Ford Motor Co. (Legislative Manager, Environmental Quality)

MORGAN, Jack

1601 N. Kent St.
Suite 120
Arlington, VA 22209
EMail: jmorgan@apperalandfootwear.org
Tel: (703)524-1864
Fax: (703)522-6741

Employers
American Apparel & Footwear Ass'n (Director, Communications)

MORGAN, Jenna L.

40 Ivy St. SE
Washington, DC 20003
EMail: jenna@dealer.org
Tel: (202)547-2230
Fax: (202)547-7640
Registered: LDA

Employers
Nat'l Lumber and Building Material Dealers Ass'n (Director, Government Affairs)

MORGAN, Lance I.

1501 M St. NW
Suite 600
Washington, DC 20005-1710
EMail: lmorgan@bsmg.com
Tel: (202)739-0200
Fax: (202)659-8287
Registered: FARA

Employers
BSMG Worldwide (President and Partner)

Clients Represented
On Behalf of BSMG Worldwide
Grocery Manufacturers of America

MORGAN, Linda

4340 East-West Hwy.
Suite 402
Bethesda, MD 20814
EMail: lmorgan@naspweb.org
Tel: (301)657-0270
Fax: (301)657-0275

Employers
Nat'l Ass'n of School Psychologists (Director, Communications & Professional Projects)

MORGAN, Moya G.

1341 G St. NW
Suite 1100
Washington, DC 20005
Tel: (202)585-0215
Fax: (202)393-0712
Registered: LDA

Employers
Computer Systems Policy Project (Deputy Director)
Infotech Strategies, Inc. (Director, Coalition)

Clients Represented
On Behalf of Infotech Strategies, Inc.
Computer Systems Policy Project

MORGAN, Peter Denis

700 11th St. NW
Washington, DC 20001-4507
EMail: pmorgan@realtors.org
Tel: (202)383-1233
Fax: (202)383-7541
Registered: LDA

Employers
Nat'l Ass'n of Realtors (Senior Federal Regulations Representative)

MORGENWECK, Gail

1150 17th St. NW
Suite 400
Washington, DC 20036
Tel: (202)222-4700
Fax: (202)222-4799

Employers
The Walt Disney Co. (Manager)

MORIAK, Susan

P.O. Box 2999
Reston, VA 20191
EMail: smoriak@rvia.org
Tel: (703)620-6003
Ext: 318
Fax: (703)620-5071

Employers
Recreation Vehicle Industry Ass'n (Assistant Director, Government Affairs)

MORIARTY, Betty

700 13th St. NW
Suite 400
Washington, DC 20005
EMail: bmoriarty@cassidy.com
Tel: (202)347-0773
Fax: (202)347-0785

Department of Defense, 1971-88.

Employers
Cassidy & Associates, Inc. (V. President and Dir., New Business Development Research)

MORIARTY, Kevin

1775 K St. NW
Suite 360
Washington, DC 20006
EMail: kmoriarty@unicefusa.org
Tel: (202)296-4242
Fax: (202)296-4060
Registered: LDA

Employers
U.S. Fund for UNICEF (Legislative Coordinator and Program Manager)

MORIN, Cmdr. C. N.

The Pentagon
Washington, DC 20350-2000
Tel: (703)695-3480
Fax: (703)695-8993

Employers
Department of Navy - Chief of Naval Operations Office (Assistant for Legal and Legislative Matters)

MORIN, Jeanne L.

1615 L St. NW
Suite 650
Washington, DC 20036
EMail: jeanne_morin@jeffersongr.com
Tel: (202)626-8515
Fax: (202)626-8593
Registered: LDA

Minority Policy Director, House Committee on Small Business, 1990-92. Communications Director to Rep. Andy Ireland (R-FL), 1989-90.

Employers
Jefferson Government Relations, L.L.C. (Principal)

Clients Represented
On Behalf of Jefferson Government Relations, L.L.C.
Bass Hotels and Resorts, Inc.
Nat'l Industries for the Blind
Seminole Tribe of Indians of Florida

MORIN, William

1400 I St. NW
Suite 540
Washington, DC 20005-2208
EMail: wmorin@sayer.com
Tel: (202)638-4434
Fax: (202)296-1074
Registered: LDA

Employers
R. Wayne Sayer & Associates (V. President)

Clients Represented
On Behalf of R. Wayne Sayer & Associates
Applied Materials
Candescent Technologies
Coalition for Intelligent Manufacturing Systems (CIMS)
IPC Washington Office
Schott Corp.
Silicon Valley Group

MORISON, Karen A.

P.O. Box 7371
Fairfax Station, VA 22039-7371
Tel: (703)425-5347

Employers
Nat'l Ass'n to Protect Individual Rights (President)

MORITSUGU, Erika

1317 F St. NW
Suite 600
Washington, DC 20004
EMail: moritsugu@wexlergroup.com
Tel: (202)638-2121
Fax: (202)638-7045
Registered: LDA

Employers
The Wexler Group (Principal)

Clients Represented
On Behalf of The Wexler Group
The Business Roundtable
Immunex Corp.
Orange County Public Schools
Wyeth-Ayerst Laboratories

MORLEY, Jr., James E.

2501 M St. NW
Suite 400
Washington, DC 20037
Tel: (202)861-2500
Fax: (202)861-2583

Employers
Nat'l Ass'n of College and University Business Officers (President)

MORLEY, William J.

1615 H St. NW
Washington, DC 20062-2000
Tel: (202)659-6000
Fax: (202)463-5836

Special Counsel to Senator Arlen Specter (R-PA), 1995-97. Senior Republican Legislative Assistant, Subcommittee on the Constitution, Senate Committee on the Judiciary, 1987-88. Legislative Assistant to Senator Specter, 1986-88.

Employers
Chamber of Commerce of the U.S.A. (V. President, Congressional and Public Affairs)

MORNINGSTAR, Mary P.

1725 Jefferson Davis Hwy.
Crystal Square 2, Suite 300
Arlington, VA 22202
Tel: (703)413-5600
Fax: (703)413-5617
Registered: LDA

Employers
Lockheed Martin Corp. (Assistant General Counsel, Environmental Law)

MORNINGSTAR, Sara Eileen

Exec. Office Building
101 Monroe St.
Fourth Floor
Rockville, MD 20850
EMail: sara.morningstar@co.mo.md.us
Tel: (240)777-6553
Fax: (240)777-6551
Registered: LDA

Employers
Montgomery, Maryland, County of (Federal Relations Coordinator)

MORNINGSTAR, Warren

421 Aviation Way
Frederick, MD 21701
EMail: warren.morningstar@aopa.org
Tel: (301)695-2162
Fax: (301)695-2375

Employers
Aircraft Owners and Pilots Ass'n (V. President, Communications)

MORONEY, William

1140 Connecticut Ave. NW
Suite 1140
Washington, DC 20036
Tel: (202)872-0030
Fax: (202)872-1331
Registered: LDA

Employers
United Telecom Council (President/Chief Operating Exec.)

MORRA, Elizabeth

1001 G St. NW
Suite 900 E
Washington, DC 20001-4545
Tel: (202)393-1010
Fax: (202)393-5510
Communications Director, House Committee on Appropriations, 1995-2000, and former Press Secretary and Deputy Press Secretary to Senator Thad Cochran (R-MS).

Employers
Podesta/Mattoon (Principal)

MORRELL, Kay Allan

1101 30th St. NW
Suite 200
Washington, DC 20007
Tel: (202)342-2787
Fax: (202)342-2789
Registered: LDA
Former Counsel, Senate Committees on the Judiary and on Labor and Human Resources.

Employers
Self-employed as an independent consultant.

Clients Represented
As an independent consultant
Environmental Land Technology Ltd.
Scott J. Esparza & Co.
Space Dynamics Laboratory
Utah State University

MORRILL, James A.

1455 Pennsylvania Ave. NW
Suite 1260
Washington, DC 20004
Tel: (202)783-0350
Fax: (202)783-3332
Registered: LDA

Employers
Lincoln Nat'l Corp. (V. President and Director, Federal Relations)

MORRILL, Jennifer

50 F St. NW
Suite 900
Washington, DC 20001
EMail: morrill@fccouncil.com
Tel: (202)626-8710
Fax: (202)626-8718

Employers
Farm Credit Council (Director of Communications)

MORRIS, Carolyn Covey

1850 M St. NW
Suite 700
Washington, DC 20036
Tel: (202)721-4100
Fax: (202)296-8548
Registered: LDA
EMail: carolyn.coveymorris@socma.com

Employers
Synthetic Organic Chemical Manufacturers Ass'n (V. President, Public and Government Affairs)

MORRIS, Catherine

750 First St. NE
Suite 940
Washington, DC 20002
Tel: (202)408-9260
Ext: 209
Fax: (202)408-8896
EMail: cmorris@ccap.org

Employers
Center for Clean Air Policy (Deputy Director)

MORRIS, Dena S.

805 15th St. NW
Suite 700
Washington, DC 20005
Tel: (202)312-7400
Fax: (202)312-7441
Registered: LDA
EMail: dsmorris@bakerd.com

Employers
Sagamore Associates, Inc. (Senior V. President)

Clients Represented
On Behalf of Sagamore Associates, Inc.
Arthritis Foundation
Autism Soc. of America, Inc.
Historic Landmarks Foundation of Indiana
Indiana State University
Indianapolis Neighborhood Housing Partnership
Indianapolis Public Transportation Corp.
Marion, Indiana, City of
Nat'l Sleep Foundation
Northern Indiana Commuter Transportation District
South Bend, Indiana, City of
TRANSPO
U.S. Disabled Athletes Fund
U.S. Olympic Committee

MORRIS, Frederick E.

99 Canal Center Plaza
Suite 200
Alexandria, VA 22314
Tel: (703)683-8512
Fax: (703)683-4622
Registered: LDA

Employers
Smith & Harroff, Inc. (Partner)

MORRIS, Gerald

555 New Jersey Ave. NW
Washington, DC 20001
Tel: (202)879-4453
Fax: (202)879-4402
Registered: LDA

Employers
American Federation of Teachers (Director, Legislative Research)

MORRIS, Helen

1555 Connecticut Ave. NW
Suite 200
Washington, DC 20036
EMail: helen@cosn.org
Tel: (202)462-0992
Fax: (202)462-9043

Employers
Consortium for School Networking (Deputy Director)

MORRIS, Jon Paul

2550 M St. NW
Washington, DC 20037-1350
Tel: (202)457-6000
Fax: (202)457-6315
Registered: FARA
EMail: jpmorris@pattonboggs.com

Employers
Patton Boggs, LLP (Associate)

MORRIS, Kathy

Ronald Reagan Bldg.
1300 Pennsylvania Ave. NW
MS: 6.10-053
Washington, DC 20523
EMail: kmorris@usaid.gov
Tel: (202)712-4415
Fax: (202)216-3237

Employers
Agency for Internat'l Development (Congressional Notifications Legislative Program Specialist, Bureau of Legislative and Public Affairs)

MORRIS, Kristen

325 Seventh St. NW
Washington, DC 20004
Tel: (202)638-1100
Fax: (202)626-2254
Registered: LDA

Employers
American Hospital Ass'n (V. President, Legislative Affairs)

MORRIS, Rick

99 Canal Center Plaza
Suite 200
Alexandria, VA 22314
Tel: (703)683-8512
Fax: (703)683-4622
Registered: LDA

Employers
Alcan Aluminum Corp. (Washington Representative)
Consumer Aerosol Products Council

MORRIS, Sara W.

901 15th St. NW
Suite 700
Washington, DC 20005-2301
Tel: (202)371-6000
Fax: (202)371-6279
Registered: LDA
EMail: smorris@verner.com
Administrative Assistant, House Subcommittee on Telecommunications and Finance, 1987-94. Administrative Assistant, House Energy Conservation and Power, 1986-87.

Employers
Verner, Liipfert, Bernhard, McPherson and Hand, Chartered (Telecommunications Consultant)

Clients Represented
On Behalf of Verner, Liipfert, Bernhard, McPherson and Hand, Chartered
Lockheed Martin Corp.
Nat'l Broadcasting Co.
NxtWave Communications
Philips Electronics North America Corp.
Qwest Communications
Rite Aid Corp.
Thomson Consumer Electronics, Inc.

MORRIS, W. Patrick

444 N. Capitol St. NW
Suite 800
Washington, DC 20001
Tel: (202)638-5355
Fax: (202)638-5369
Registered: LDA

Employers
Marine Engineers Beneficial Ass'n (District No. 1 - PCD) (Director of Legislative and Legal Affairs)

MORRIS, William

1072 Thomas Jefferson St. NW
Washington, DC 20007
Tel: (202)965-7748
Fax: (202)965-7749
Registered: LDA
EMail: swmorris@erols.com
Former General Counsel, Senate Finance Committee; Trial Attorney, Internal Revenue Service, Department of Treasury; and Attorney-Advisor, U.S. Tax Court.

Employers
Moore & Bruce, LLP

Clients Represented
On Behalf of Moore & Bruce, LLP
Nat'l Automobile Dealers Ass'n

MORRISEY, Stephen J.

1025 Connecticut Ave. NW
Suite 1210
Washington, DC 20036
Tel: (202)296-2733
Fax: (202)296-2873
Registered: LDA

Employers
United Airlines (Director, Governmental Affairs)

MORRISON, Andrew F.

1455 Pennsylvania Ave. NW
Suite 575
Washington, DC 20004
Tel: (202)638-4076
Fax: (202)638-1096
Registered: LDA

Employers
WellPoint Health Networks/Blue Cross of California/UNICARE

MORRISON, Bruce A.

1120 Connecticut Ave. NW
Suite 1100
Washington, DC 20036
Tel: (202)861-5899
Fax: (202)861-5795
Registered: LDA

Employers
GPC Internat'l

Clients Represented
On Behalf of GPC Internat'l
Applied Terravision Systems
Educational Video Conferencing, Inc.
Harbor Philadelphia Center City Office, Ltd.
Mineral Technologies, Inc.
O'Grady Peyton Internat'l
Ultraprise.com

MORRISON, Ph.D., James W.

1012 Steeples Ct.
Falls Church, VA 22046
Tel: (703)536-1848
Fax: (703)536-1849
Registered: LDA
Former professional Staff Member, United States Senate. Former Consultant, U.S. House of Representatives.

Employers
The Morrison Group, Inc. (Chief Exec. Officer)

Clients Represented
On Behalf of The Morrison Group, Inc.
Nat'l Ass'n for the Self-Employed
Small Business Exporters Ass'n

MORRISON, Jill

11 Dupont Circle NW
Suite 800
Washington, DC 20036
EMail: jmorrison@nwlc.org
Tel: (202)588-5180
Fax: (202)588-5185

Employers
Nat'l Women's Law Center (Staff Counsel)

MORRISON, John W.

5535 Hempstead Way
Springfield, VA 22151
EMail: naus@ix.netcom.com
Tel: (703)750-1342
Fax: (703)354-4380
Registered: LDA

Employers
Nat'l Ass'n for Uniformed Services (Legislative Counsel)

MORRISON, Keith

1420 New York Ave. NW
Suite 1050
Washington, DC 20005
Tel: (202)638-1950
Fax: (202)638-7714
Legislative Officer, Department of State, 1999. Senior Advisor for Congressional Affairs, Arms Control and Disarmament Agency, 1997-99. Senior Advisor for Legislative Affairs, Office of the Secretary, Department of Commerce, 1995-97. Special Assistant for Policy, Economic Development Administration, Department of Commerce, 1994-95. Legislative Director to Rep. Thomas M. Foglietta (D-PA), 1988-93.

Employers
Van Scoyoc Associates, Inc. (Special Assistant to the President, Legislative Assistant)

Clients Represented
On Behalf of Van Scoyoc Associates, Inc.
University of North Carolina at Chapel Hill

MORRISON, Lynn

227 Massachusetts Ave. NE
Suite 300
Washington, DC 20002
EMail: healthadvocate@worldnet.att.net
Tel: (202)543-7460
Fax: (202)543-5327
Registered: LDA

Employers
Washington Health Advocates (President)

Clients Represented
On Behalf of Washington Health Advocates
American Federation for Medical Research
American Soc. for Clinical Pharmacology and Therapeutics
GCRC Program Directors Ass'n
Quintiles Transnational Corp.

MORRISON, Mark E.

1725 Jefferson Davis Hwy.
Crystal Square 2, Suite 300
Arlington, VA 22202
Tel: (703)413-5607
Fax: (703)413-5617
Registered: LDA

Employers
Lockheed Martin Corp. (Director, Space and Strategic Programs)

MORRISON, Richard

1001 Connecticut Ave. NW
Suite 1250
Washington, DC 20036
Tel: (202)331-1010
Fax: (202)331-0640

Employers
Competitive Enterprise Institute (Director of Media Relations)

MORRISON, William C.

1901 N. Fort Myer Dr.
Arlington, VA 22209
Tel: (703)522-1910

Employers
Meat Importers Council of America (Exec. Director)

MORRISSETTE, Peggy

1525 Wilson Blvd.
Suite 900
Arlington, VA 22209
EMail: pmorrissette@mapi.net
Tel: (703)841-9000
Fax: (703)841-9514
Legislative Affairs Staff, Department of Labor and U.S. General Services Administration.

Employers
Manufacturers Alliance/MAPI Inc. (Director, Public and Government Affairs)

MORRISSEY, Donald J.

1401 H St. NW
12th Floor
Washington, DC 20005-2148
Tel: (202)326-5895
Fax: (202)326-8313
Registered: LDA

Employers
Investment Co. Institute (V. President, Legislative Affairs)

MORRISSEY, Michael

1660 L St. NW
Fourth Floor
Washington, DC 20036
Tel: (202)775-5092
Fax: (202)775-5045

Employers
General Motors Corp. (Director, Communications)

MORRISSEY, Rafe

1615 L St. NW
Suite 1220
Washington, DC 20036-5610
EMail: rmorriss@winstarmail.com
Tel: (202)659-0946
Fax: (202)659-4972
Registered: LDA

Employers
Evans & Black, Inc. (Director, Operations and Strategic Planning)

Clients Represented
On Behalf of Evans & Black, Inc.
American Business Media
Brinker Internat'l
Hallmark Cards, Inc.
Internat'l Council of Shopping Centers
Newspaper Ass'n of America
Ticketmaster

MORROW, Hugh

P.O. Box 924
Great Falls, VA 22066-0924
EMail: icdamorrow@aol.com
Tel: (703)759-7400
Fax: (703)759-7003

Employers
Internat'l Cadmium Ass'n (President)

MORSE, M. Howard

1500 K St.
Suite 1100
Washington, DC 20005
EMail: howard_moore@dbr.com
Tel: (202)842-8800
Fax: (202)842-8465
Registered: LDA

Employers
Drinker Biddle & Reath LLP (Partner)

Clients Represented
On Behalf of Drinker Biddle & Reath LLP
RioPort, Inc.

MORTENSON, Lee E.

11600 Nebel St.
Suite 201
Rockville, MD 20852
Tel: (301)984-9496
Fax: (301)770-1949

Employers
Ass'n of Community Cancer Centers (Exec. Director)

MORTIMER, Edward L.

3601 Eisenhower Ave.
Suite 110
Alexandria, VA 22304-6439
EMail: mortimer@tianet.org
Tel: (703)329-1895
Fax: (703)329-1898
Registered: LDA

Employers
Transportation Intermediaries Ass'n (Director, Government Affairs)

MORTON, Andrew

555 11th St. NW
Suite 1000
Washington, DC 20004
Tel: (202)637-2200
Fax: (202)637-2201
Registered: LDA

Employers
Latham & Watkins

Clients Represented
On Behalf of Latham & Watkins
Nat'l Orthotics Manufacturers Ass'n

MORTON, Ann P.

2100 Pennsylvania Ave. NW
Suite 535
Washington, DC 20037
Tel: (202)822-1700
Fax: (202)822-1919
Registered: LDA
Former Legislative Counsel to Rep. Rick Boucher (D-VA).

Employers
Simon Strategies/Mindbeam (Senior V. President)

Clients Represented
On Behalf of Simon Strategies/Mindbeam
Catholic Television Network
Metricom, Inc.
Traffic.com

MORTON, Cynthia

1201 L St. NW
Washington, DC 20005-4014
Tel: (202)842-4444
Fax: (202)842-3860
Registered: LDA

Employers
American Health Care Ass'n (Director, Congressional Affairs)

MORTON, Evelyn

601 E St. NW
Washington, DC 20049
Tel: (202)434-3760
Fax: (202)434-3758
Registered: LDA

Employers
AARP (American Ass'n of Retired Persons) (Legislative Representative)

MORTON, Ted

600 Pennsylvania Ave. SE
Suite 210
Washington, DC 20003
EMail: tmorton@americanoceans.org
Tel: (202)544-3526
Fax: (202)544-5625

Employers
American Oceans Campaign (Director, Policy)

MOSEDALE, Susan

1448 Duke St.
Alexandria, VA 22314
EMail: smosedal@iaapa.org
Tel: (703)836-4800
Fax: (703)836-4801

Employers
Internat'l Ass'n of Amusement Parks and Attractions (V. President, Membership and Marketing)

MOSELEY, Phillip D.

1225 Connecticut Ave. NW
Washington, DC 20036
EMail: phil.moseley@ey.com
Tel: (202)327-6319
Fax: (202)327-6719
Registered: LDA
Chief of Staff (1995-96) and Republican Chief of Staff (1988-94), House Ways and Means Committee. Administrative Assistant and Chief of Staff to Rep. Bill Archer (R-TX), 1973-88.

Employers
Ernst & Young LLP (National Director, Legislative Services)
Washington Council Ernst & Young (Partner)

Clients Represented
On Behalf of Ernst & Young LLP
Cellular Depreciation Coalition
E-Commerce Coalition
Edison Electric Institute
General Ore Internat'l Corp. Ltd.
INCOL 2000
Interest Netting Coalition
Koch Industries, Inc.
MassMutual Financial Group
Nordstrom, Inc.
Repeal the Tax on Talking Coalition
Tax Policy Coalition

On Behalf of Washington Council Ernst & Young
Aetna Life & Casualty Co.
American Insurance Ass'n
American Staffing Ass'n
Anheuser-Busch Cos., Inc.
Antitrust Coalition for Consumer Choice in Health Care
Apartment Investment and Management Co.
Ass'n of American Railroads
Ass'n of Home Appliance Manufacturers
AT&T
Aventis Pharmaceuticals, Inc.
Baxter Healthcare Corp.
BHC Communications, Inc.
Bulmer Holding PLC, H. P.
Cash Balance Coalition
Citigroup
Coalition for Fairness in Defense Exports
Coalition to Preserve Tracking Stock
ComEd
The Connell Co.
Deferral Group
Directors Guild of America
Doris Duke Charitable Foundation
Eaton Vance Management Co.
Eden Financial Corp.
The Enterprise Foundation
Fannie Mae
FedEx Corp.
Ford Motor Co.
General Electric Co.
Global Competitiveness Coalition
Grasslands Water District
Group Health, Inc.
HEREIU
Gilbert P. Hyatt, Inventor
Investment Co. Institute
Large Public Power Council
Local Initiatives Support Corp.
MacAndrews & Forbes Holdings, Inc.
Marsh & McLennan Cos.
MCG Northwest, Inc.
McLane Co.
Merrill Lynch & Co., Inc.
Metropolitan Banking Group
Nat'l Ass'n for State Farm Agents
Nat'l Ass'n of Professional Employer Organizations
Nat'l Ass'n of Real Estate Investment Trusts
Nat'l Defined Contribution Council
Nat'l Foreign Trade Council, Inc.
Nat'l Multi-Housing Council
Pfizer, Inc.
R&D Tax Credit Coalition
R&D Tax Regulation Group
Recording Industry Ass'n of America
Reed-Elsevier Inc.
R. J. Reynolds Tobacco Co.
Charles Schwab & Co., Inc.,
Securities Industry Ass'n
Skadden, Arps, Slate, Meagher & Flom LLP
Straddle Rules Tax Group
Tax Fairness Coalition
TXU Business Services
U.S. Oncology
USA Biomass Power Producers Alliance
Viaticus, Inc.
Wilkie Farr & Gallagher
Ziff Investors Partnership

MOSELEY, Maj. Gen. T. Michael

1160 Air Force Pentagon
Room 4D927
Washington, DC 20330-1160
Tel: (703)697-8153
Fax: (703)697-2001

Employers
Department of Air Force (Director, Legislative Liaison)

MOSELY, Elizabeth

1730 Rhode Island Ave.
Suite 710
Washington, DC 20036
Tel: (202)833-1580
Fax: (202)223-5779

Employers
Insurance Information Institute (Communications Specialist)

MOSER, Charles E.

Eight Herbert St.
Alexandria, VA 22305-2600
Tel: (703)683-9027
Fax: (703)683-6820

Employers
Nat'l Ass'n of Postmasters of the U.S. (National President)

MOSER, Patricia

815 Connecticut Ave. NW
Suite 325
Washington, DC 20006
Tel: (202)728-1500
Fax: (202)728-0505

Employers
Asian Development Bank - North American Representative Office (Senior Liaison Officer)

MOSES, Indrani

1300 I St. NW
Suite 1070 East
Washington, DC 20005
Tel: (202)962-8550
Fax: (202)962-8560
EMail: indrani.moses@us.pna.philips.com

Employers
Philips Electronics North America Corp. (Government Affairs Representative)

MOSES, Dr. Yalonda

One Dupont Circle NW
Suite 360
Washington, DC 20036-1110
Tel: (202)293-6440
Fax: (202)293-0073

Employers
American Ass'n for Higher Education (President)

MOSHENBERG, Sammie

1707 L St. NW
Suite 950
Washington, DC 20036
Tel: (202)296-2588
Fax: (202)331-7792
Registered: LDA
EMail: ncjwdc@aol.com

Employers
Nat'l Council of Jewish Women (Director, Washington Operations)

MOSHER, Jeffrey

1717 K St. NW
Suite 801
Washington, DC 20036
Tel: (202)331-2820
Fax: (202)785-1845
Registered: LDA
EMail: jeff@amwa.net

Employers
Ass'n of Metropolitan Water Agencies (Director, Technical Services)

MOSHER, Jim

707 Conservation Ln.
Gaithersburg, MD 20878
Tel: (301)548-0150
Fax: (301)548-0149
EMail: jmosher@iwla.org

Employers
Izaak Walton League of America (Conservation Director)

MOSHER, Liese

700 13th St. NW
Suite 1000
Washington, DC 20005
Tel: (202)347-6633
Fax: (202)347-8713

Employers
Powell Tate (V. President)

MOSHER, Sol

1735 New York Ave. NW
Suite 500
Washington, DC 20006-4759
Tel: (202)628-1700
Fax: (202)331-1024
Registered: LDA, FARA
Assistant Trade Representative under Carla Hills and Clayton Yeutter, 1985-89. Assistant Secretary of Housing and Urban Development, 1973-76. Special Assistant to the Secretary of Commerce, 1969-72.

Employers
Preston Gates Ellis & Rouvelas Meeds LLP (Senior Advisor, Federal Affairs and International Trade)

Clients Represented

On Behalf of Preston Gates Ellis & Rouvelas Meeds LLP
Future of Puerto Rico Inc.
Nat'l Center for Economic Freedom, Inc.
Prime Time 24
Tate and Lyle North American Sugars Inc.
United States Maritime Coalition
VoiceStream Wireless Corp.

MOSKOWITZ, Laurie

430 S. Capitol St. SE
Washington, DC 20003
Tel: (202)863-8000
Fax: (202)863-8174

Employers
Democratic Nat'l Committee (PAC Administrator)

MOSKOWITZ, Saul L.

1101 Vermont Ave. NW
Suite 400
Washington, DC 20005
Tel: (202)289-3900
Fax: (202)371-0197
Registered: LDA
EMail: moskowitz@dbmlaw.com

Employers
Dean Blakey & Moskowitz (Partner)

Clients Represented

On Behalf of Dean Blakey & Moskowitz
Consumer Bankers Ass'n
Diversified Collection Services, Inc.
Fair Share Coalition
Financial Collection Agencies

MOSS, Bob

1150 Connecticut Ave. NW
Suite 201
Washington, DC 20036
Tel: (202)861-1282

Employers
Bob Moss Associates

Clients Represented

On Behalf of Bob Moss Associates
Advanced Vehicle Systems
American Chemistry Council
The Centech Group
Enron Corp.
General Motors Corp.
Oxygenated Fuels Ass'n

MOSS, Dorothy J.

1111 14th St. NW
Suite 1200
Washington, DC 20005-5603
Tel: (202)898-2400
Fax: (202)898-2437
Registered: LDA
EMail: mossd@ada.org

Employers
American Dental Ass'n (Director, Washington Office)

MOSS, Kate

1401 I St. NW
Suite 1100
Washington, DC 20005
Tel: (202)326-8908
Fax: (202)408-4797
Registered: LDA
Aide to Senator Charles Mathias (R-MD), 1968-70. Psychometrist, Central Intelligence Agency, 1966-68.

Employers
The Kate Moss Company (Principal)

Clients Represented

On Behalf of The Kate Moss Company
Bank of America
GE Capital Corp.
Morgan Stanley Dean Witter & Co.
SBC Communications Inc.
Trans Union Corp.

MOSS, Myla

1625 Massachusetts Ave. NW
Washington, DC 20036
Tel: (202)667-9433
Fax: (202)667-0642
Registered: LDA
EMail: mossm@adea.org

Employers
American Dental Education Ass'n (Director, Federal Relations)

MOSS, Ralph L.

818 Connecticut Ave. NW
Suite 801
Washington, DC 20006
Tel: (202)955-6111
Fax: (202)955-6118
Registered: LDA
EMail: seabrd@aol.com

Employers
Seaboard Corp. (Director, Government Affairs)

MOSSBERG, Christer L.

1275 Pennsylvania Ave. NW
Washington, DC 20004-2415
Tel: (202)383-0100
Fax: (202)637-3593

Employers
Sutherland Asbill & Brennan LLP (Counsel)

MOSSINGHOFF, Gerald J.

1530 Key Blvd.
Penthouse 28
Arlington, VA 22209
Tel: (703)276-8280
Fax: (703)276-1536
Registered: LDA

Employers
Self-employed as an independent consultant.

Clients Represented
As an independent consultant
Pharmaceutical Research and Manufacturers of America

MOSSLER, Diane L.

3190 Fairview Park Dr.
Falls Church, VA 22042
Tel: (703)876-3305
Fax: (703)876-3600

Employers
General Dynamics Corp. (Director, Government and Community Relations)

MOSTOFF, Allan S.

1775 I St. NW
Washington, DC 20006
Tel: (202)261-3300
Fax: (202)261-3333
Registered: FARA
EMail: allan.mostoff@dechert.com
Director, Division of Investment Management Regulation (1972-76), Associate Director, Division of Corporate Regulation (1968-72), and Staff Member (1962-68), Securities and Exchange Commission.

Employers
Dechert (Partner)

Clients Represented
On Behalf of Dechert
Japan Bank for Internat'l Cooperation
Japan, Embassy of

MOTEN, Beth

80 F St. NW
Washington, DC 20001
Tel: (202)639-6413
Fax: (202)639-6492
Registered: LDA

Employers
American Federation of Government Employees (AFL-CIO) (Legislative Director)

MOTLEY, III, John J.

655 15th St. NW
Washington, DC 20005-5701
Tel: (202)220-0610
Fax: (202)220-0872
Registered: LDA
EMail: jmotley@fmi.org

Employers
Food Marketing Institute (Senior V. President, Government and Public Affairs)

MOTLEY, Langhorne A.

1101 Connecticut Ave.
Suite 1200
Washington, DC 20036
Tel: (202)466-5529
Fax: (202)466-4144
Registered: LDA, FARA
Former U.S. Ambassador to Brazil. Former Assistant Secretary of State for Latin American Affairs.

Employers
L. A. Motley, L.L.C. (President and Chief Exec. Officer)

Clients Represented
On Behalf of L. A. Motley, L.L.C.
Anheuser-Busch Cos., Inc.
The Boeing Co.

MOTT, Andrew

1000 Wisconsin Ave. NW
Washington, DC 20007
Tel: (202)342-0519
Fax: (202)342-1132
EMail: andrewm@communitychange.org

Employers
Center for Community Change (Exec. Director)

MOTT, Jason N.

700 13th St. NW
Suite 350
Washington, DC 20005
Tel: (202)637-0040
Fax: (202)637-0041

Employers
Rhoads Group (Staff Assistant)

MOTT, Roger

1300 I St. NW
Suite 400 West
Washington, DC 20005
Tel: (202)515-2560
Fax: (202)336-7921
Registered: LDA

Employers
Verizon Communications (V. President, Federal Government Relations)

MOUNT, Michael

1200 17th St. NW
Washington, DC 20036-3097
Tel: (202)331-5900
Fax: (202)973-5373

Employers
Nat'l Restaurant Ass'n (Senior Manager, Media Relations)

MOW, Laura C.

1301 K St. NW
Suite 900
East Tower
Washington, DC 20005
EMail: lmow@dc.gcd.com
Tel: (202)408-7100
Fax: (202)289-1504

Employers
Gardner, Carton and Douglas (Partner)

MOWE, Jeanne C.

1350 Beverly Rd.
Suite 220A
McLean, VA 22101
EMail: mowej@aatb.org
Tel: (703)827-9582
Fax: (703)356-2198

Employers
American Ass'n of Tissue Banks (Exec. Director)

MOYE, Stacey

2025 M St. NW
Suite 800
Washington, DC 20036
Tel: (202)367-2100
Fax: (202)367-1200
Registered: LDA
EMail: stacey_moye@dc.sba.com

Employers
Smith, Bucklin and Associates, Inc. (Legislative Administrator, Government Relations)

Clients Represented
On Behalf of Smith, Bucklin and Associates, Inc.
The Child Care Consortium
Nat'l Child Care Ass'n
Nat'l Organization for Competency Assurance

MOYER, Bruce L.

2215 M St. NW
Washington, DC 20037
Tel: (202)785-1614
Fax: (202)785-1568
Registered: LDA

Employers
Federal Bar Ass'n (Government Relations Columnist)
The Moyer Group (President)

Clients Represented
On Behalf of The Moyer Group
Federal Bar Ass'n
Nat'l Ass'n of Postal Supervisors

MOYER, Carl

2100 M St. NW
Suite 200
Washington, DC 20037
Tel: (202)785-4185
Fax: (202)466-1286
Registered: LDA
EMail: cmoyer@stewartlaw.com

Employers
Stewart and Stewart (Trade Consultant)

Clients Represented
On Behalf of Stewart and Stewart
The Gates Rubber Co.
Ranchers-Cattlemen Legal Action Fund
The Timken Co.
Torrington Co.

MOYER, Jr., Homer E.

655 15th St. NW
Suite 900
Washington, DC 20005-5701
Tel: (202)626-5800
Fax: (202)628-0858
Registered: LDA, FARA
EMail: hmoyer@milchev.com
General Counsel (1980-81), Counsellor to the Secretary (1979), and Deputy General Counsel (1976-78), all at the Department of Commerce. Lieutenant-Commander, Judge Advocate General Corps, U.S. Navy, 1967-71.

Employers
Miller & Chevalier, Chartered (Member)

Clients Represented
On Behalf of Miller & Chevalier, Chartered
Canada, Government of
Exxon Mobil Corp.
Framatome, S.A.
Nat'l Foreign Trade Council, Inc.
SABIC Americas, Inc.

MOYER, Steven N.

1500 Wilson Blvd.
Suite 310
Arlington, VA 22209
Tel: (703)522-0200
Fax: (703)284-9400
Registered: LDA
EMail: smoyer@tu.org

Employers
Trout Unlimited (V. President, Conservation Program)

MOZINGO, Leslie Waters

1130 Connecticut Ave. NW
Suite 300
Washington, DC 20036
Tel: (202)331-8500
Fax: (202)331-1598
Registered: LDA
Former Legislative Assistant to Rep. E. Clay Shaw, Jr. (R-FL).

Employers
The Ferguson Group, LLC (Principal)

Clients Represented
On Behalf of The Ferguson Group, LLC
Fairfield, California, City of
Folsom, California, City of
Inglewood, California, City of
Interstate 5 Consortium
The Irvine Co.
Lake, Illinois, County of
Logan, Utah, City of (Transit District)
Long Beach Transit
Mecklenburg, North Carolina, County of
Metropolitan King County Council
Municipal Transit Operation Coalition
Norwalk, California, City of
Oceanside, California, City of
Santa Ana, California, City of
West Valley City, Utah

MUCKENFUSS, III, Cantwell Faulkner

1050 Connecticut Ave. NW
Washington, DC 20036-5306
Tel: (202)955-8500
Fax: (202)467-0539
Registered: LDA
EMail: cmuckenfuss@gdclaw.com
Senior Deputy Comptroller for Policy, Office of the Comptroller of the Treasury, Department of the Treasury, 1978-81. Counsel to the Chairman (1977-78) and Special Assistant to the Director (1974-77), Federal Deposit Insurance Corporation.

Employers
Gibson, Dunn & Crutcher LLP (Partner)

Clients Represented
On Behalf of Gibson, Dunn & Crutcher LLP
California Federal Bank
Dollar Bank
MacAndrews & Forbes Holdings, Inc.
New York Bankers Ass'n
Prudential Insurance Co. of America
Washington Mutual Bank

MUDRON, Maureen

325 Seventh St. NW
Washington, DC 20004
Tel: (202)638-1100
Fax: (202)626-4638

Employers
American Hospital Ass'n (Senior Counsel)

MUELLER, Gregory R.

1150 S. Washington St.
Third Floor
Alexandria, VA 22314
Tel: (703)683-5004
Fax: (703)683-1703

Employers
Creative Response Concepts (President)

MUELLER, Michael

1333 New Hampshire Ave. NW
Suite 400
Washington, DC 20036
Tel: (202)887-4000
Fax: (202)887-4288
Law Clerk to Judge Avern Cohn, U.S. District Court (Detroit), 1985-87.

Employers
Akin, Gump, Strauss, Hauer & Feld, L.L.P. (Partner)

Clients Represented
On Behalf of Akin, Gump, Strauss, Hauer & Feld, L.L.P.
Food Lion, Inc.

MUELLER, Ronald O.

1050 Connecticut Ave. NW
Washington, DC 20036-5306
Tel: (202)955-8500
Fax: (202)467-0539
Registered: LDA
EMail: rmueller@gdclaw.com
Legal Counsel to Commissioner Edward Fleischman, Securities and Exchange Commission, 1989-91.

Employers
Gibson, Dunn & Crutcher LLP (Partner)

MUELLER, Russell J.

800 Connecticut Ave. NW
Suite 500
Washington, DC 20006
Tel: (202)331-3100
Fax: (202)331-3101
Registered: LDA
EMail: muellerr@gtlaw.com

Employers
Greenberg Traurig, LLP (Director of Health and Retirement Policy)

Clients Represented
On Behalf of Greenberg Traurig, LLP
American Health Care Ass'n
American Speech, Language, and Hearing Ass'n
Amgen
The Business Roundtable
Community Health Systems, Inc.
Fresenius Medical Care North America
Genzyme Corp.
Humana Inc.
LifePoint Hospitals, Inc.
Miami-Dade, Florida, County of
Nat'l Ass'n for the Support of Long Term Care
Nat'l Ass'n of Community Health Centers
Province Healthcare, Inc.
Self-Insurance Institute of America, Inc.
Severance Trust Executive Program

MUFFETT, Carroll

1101 14th St. NW
Suite 1400
Washington, DC 20005
Tel: (202)682-9400
Fax: (202)682-1331
EMail: cmuffett@defenders.org

Employers
Defenders of Wildlife (International Counsel)

MUGG, Pamela

Rayburn House Office Bldg.
Room B328
Washington, DC 20515
Tel: (202)225-2280
Fax: (202)453-5225

Employers
Department of Veterans Affairs (House Liaison Representative)

MUHA, Denise B.

1818 N St. NW
Suite 405
Washington, DC 20036
Tel: (202)785-8888
Fax: (202)785-2008
Registered: LDA

Employers
Nat'l Leased Housing Ass'n (Exec. Director)

MUILENBURG, Terry L.

2000 L St. NW
Suite 402
Washington, DC 20036
Tel: (202)466-4306
Fax: (202)223-0145
Registered: LDA
EMail: tmuilenb@usafunds.org

Employers
USA Funds, Inc. (Senior V. President, Government and Industry Relations)

MUJICA, Mauro E.

1747 Pennsylvania Ave. NW
Suite 1100
Washington, DC 20006
Tel: (202)833-0100
Fax: (202)833-0108

Employers
U.S. English, Inc. (Chairman of the Board/Chief Exec. Officer)

MULCKHUYSE, Marlies

4232 King St.
Alexandria, VA 22302
Tel: (703)998-0072
Fax: (703)931-5624
EMail: mmulckhuyse@acce.org

Employers
American Chamber of Commerce Executives (V. President, Marketing and Association Development)

MULDER, Steven J.

1501 M St. NW
Suite 700
Washington, DC 20005-1702
Tel: (202)463-4300
Fax: (202)463-4394
Registered: LDA
EMail: smulder@manatt.com

Employers
The Bank Private Equity Coalition (Legislative Advisor)
Manatt, Phelps & Phillips, LLP (Legislative Advisor)
S-Corporation Ass'n (V. President and Legislative Director)

Clients Represented
On Behalf of Manatt, Phelps & Phillips, LLP
The Bank Private Equity Coalition
Bolivia, Embassy of
Coalition for Global Perspectives
Downey Financial Corp.
Employee-Owned S Corporations of America
Kean Tracers, Inc.
Mexico, Embassy of
Mitsubishi Motors America, Inc.
S-Corporation Ass'n

MULDOON, James

1500 K St. NW
Suite 350
Washington, DC 20005
Tel: (202)638-2788
Fax: (202)638-2780

Employers
Metcor, Ltd. (Chief Exec. Officer)

MULDOON, Sr., Joseph A.

5101 Wisconsin Ave. NW
Washington, DC 20016
Tel: (202)362-0840
Fax: (202)966-9409
Registered: LDA
Attorney, Federal Home Loan Bank Board, 1958-66.

Employers
Muldoon, Murphy & Faucette, LLP (Partner)

Clients Represented
On Behalf of Muldoon, Murphy & Faucette, LLP
GreenPoint Bank
Queens County Bancorp Inc.
Roslyn Bancorp Inc.

MULHERN, Jim

1615 L St. NW
Suite 1000
Washington, DC 20036
Tel: (202)659-0330
Fax: (202)223-8199
Registered: LDA
EMail: mulhernj@fleishman.com
Former Chief of Staff to Senator Herbert Kohl (D-WI) and Senior Campaign Advisor to Senator Russell D. Feingold (D-WI).

Employers
Fleishman-Hillard, Inc (Senior V. President)

Clients Represented
On Behalf of Fleishman-Hillard, Inc
Wheat Foods Council

MULLANEY, Kelley

1801 K St. NW
Suite 1000L
Washington, DC 20006
Tel: (202)530-0400
Fax: (202)530-4500
EMail: kelley_mullaney@washbm.com

Employers
Burson-Marsteller (Manager, Public Affairs Practice)

MULLENHOLZ, John J.

1150 Connecticut Ave. NW
Suite 700
Washington, DC 20036
Tel: (202)296-8000
Fax: (202)296-8803
Registered: LDA, FARA
Trial Attorney, Litigation Section, Tax Division, Department of Justice, 1968-73. Law Clerk to Judge Charles F. McLaughlin.

Employers
Mullenholz, Brimsek & Belair (Of Counsel)

MULLENS, Denise

500 17th St. NW
Washington, DC 20006-4804
Tel: (202)639-1700
Fax: (202)639-1779
EMail: dmullens@corcoran.org

Employers
The Corcoran Gallery of Art (Assoc. Dean, Corcoran School of Art)

MULLET, Mark S.

1300 I St. NW
Suite 400 West
Washington, DC 20005
Tel: (202)515-2553
Fax: (202)336-7921
Registered: LDA

Employers
Verizon Communications (V. President, Federal Government Relations)

MULLET, Melinda R.

1666 K St. NW
Suite 800
Washington, DC 20006
Tel: (202)481-7000
Fax: (202)862-7098
Registered: LDA

Employers
Arthur Andersen LLP (Congressional Specialist)

MULLETT, John A.

1525 Wilson Blvd.
Suite 700
Arlington, VA 22209
Tel: (703)312-6100
Fax: (703)312-6196
Registered: LDA
EMail: John_Mullet@udlp.com

Employers
United Defense, L.P. (V. President, Government Affairs)

MULLIGAN, Ann

518 C St. NE
Washington, DC 20002
Tel: (202)466-3234
Fax: (202)466-2587

Employers
Americans United for Separation of Church and State (State Legislative Coordinator)

MULLIGAN, Robert

One Massachusetts Ave. NW
Suite 350
Washington, DC 20001
Tel: (202)408-8123
Fax: (202)296-7683
Registered: LDA
EMail: rmulligan@chubb.com

Employers
The Chubb Corp. (Assistant V. President)

MULLIN, Tracy

325 Seventh St. NW
Suite 1100
Washington, DC 20004-2802
Tel: (202)783-7971
Fax: (202)737-2849
Registered: LDA

Employers
Nat'l Retail Federation (President and C.E.O.)

MULLINGS, Lisa J.

499 S. Capitol St. SW
Suite 502
Washington, DC 20003
Tel: (703)549-2100
Fax: (703)684-4525
Registered: LDA
EMail: lmullings@natso.com

Employers
NATSO, Inc. (V. President, Communications)

MULLINS, Geoff

1120 Connecticut Ave. NW
Washington, DC 20036
Tel: (202)663-5000
Fax: (202)663-5212
Registered: LDA

Employers
American Bankers Ass'n (Program Manager, Grassroots)

MULLINS, Karey E.

1225 I St. NW
Suite 920
Washington, DC 20005
Tel: (202)408-5538
Fax: (202)408-7664
Registered: LDA

Employers
Dell Computer Corp. (Policy Advisor)

MULLINS, Mike

1101 15th St. NW
Suite 1000
Washington, DC 20005
EMail: mike_mullins@cargill.com
Tel: (202)530-8160
Fax: (202)530-8180
Registered: LDA

Employers
Cargill, Inc. (Director, Public Policy)

MULLINS, William A.

401 Ninth St. NW
Suite 1000
Washington, DC 20004
Tel: (202)274-2953
Fax: (202)274-2994
Registered: LDA
Chief Counsel to Commissioners Andre, Emmett, and Walker, Interstate Commerce Commission, 1987-93.

Employers
Troutman Sanders LLP (Partner)

Clients Represented
On Behalf of Troutman Sanders LLP
Kansas City Southern Industries
Paducah & Louisville Railroad

MULLINS-GRISSOM, Janet

1350 I St. NW
Suite 1000
Washington, DC 20005
EMail: jgrissom@ford.com
Tel: (202)962-5400
Fax: (202)336-7226
Registered: LDA

Employers
Ford Motor Co. (V. President, Washington Affairs)

MULVEY, Kevin C. W.

1399 New York Ave. NW
Suite 900
Washington, DC 20005
Tel: (202)585-5811
Fax: (202)585-5820
Registered: LDA

Employers
American Internat'l Group, Inc. (Director, International Government Affairs)

MULVEY, William

1401 K St. NW
Suite 801
Washington, DC 20005
Tel: (202)682-1147
Fax: (202)682-1171

Employers
IT Group, Inc. (V. President, Communications)

MULVIHILL, David

1025 Thomas Jefferson St. NW
Suite 500 W
Washington, DC 20007-5201
EMail: dmulvihill@uli.org
Tel: (202)624-7000
Fax: (202)624-7140

Employers
Urban Land Institute (Director, Information Services)

MUMFORD, Ph.D., Geoffrey

750 First St. NE
Washington, DC 20002-4242
EMail: gkm.apa@email.apa.org
Tel: (202)336-6067
Fax: (202)336-6063
Registered: LDA

Employers
American Psychological Ass'n (Legislative/Federal Affairs Officer)

MUNDT, Michelle

701 Pennsylvania Ave. NW
Suite 900
Washington, DC 20004-2608
EMail: mmundt@mintz.com
Tel: (202)434-7300
Fax: (202)434-7400
Registered: LDA
Staff, House Committee on Energy and Commerce, 1988-94.

Employers
Mintz, Levin, Cohn, Ferris, Glovsky and Popeo, P.C. (Associate)

Clients Represented
On Behalf of Mintz, Levin, Cohn, Ferris, Glovsky and Popeo, P.C.
Cellular Telecommunications and Internet Ass'n

MUNK, Jeffrey W.

555 13th St. NW
Washington, DC 20004-1109
EMail: jwmunk@hhlaw.com
Tel: (202)637-6949
Fax: (202)637-5910
Registered: LDA, FARA
Legislative Counsel to Senator Kay Bailey Hutchison (R-TX), 1993-96.

Employers
Hogan & Hartson L.L.P. (Counsel)

Clients Represented
On Behalf of Hogan & Hartson L.L.P.
Air Transport Ass'n of America
Andalex Resources, Inc.
Brother Internat'l Co.
Cendant Corp.
Dana Corp.
Executive Jet
FM Watch
GE Capital Aviation Services
Grocery Manufacturers of America
Health and Hospital Corp. of Marion County
HMSHost Corp.
Institute for Civil Soc.
Koch Industries, Inc.
Mennonite Mutual Aid Ass'n
Michelin North America
Michigan Consolidated Gas Co.
Nissan North America Inc.
NTT America
Public Service Co. of Colorado
Qwest Communications
Southern Methodist University
Vulcan Materials Co.
Warland Investment Co.

MUNLEY, Evelyn Fieman

2519 Connecticut Ave. NW
Washington, DC 20008-1520
Tel: (202)783-2242
Fax: (202)783-2255

Employers
American Ass'n of Homes and Services for the Aging (Health Policy Analyst)

MUNOZ, Cecilia

1111 19th St. NW
Suite 1000
Washington, DC 20036
Tel: (202)785-1670
Fax: (202)776-1792
Registered: LDA

Employers
Nat'l Council of La Raza (V. President, Office of Research, Advocacy and Legislation)

MUNOZ, Kathy Jurado

2111 Wilson Blvd.
Eighth Floor
Arlington, VA 22201-3058
EMail: jurado@alcalde-com
Tel: (703)841-0626
Fax: (703)243-2874
Assistant Secretary, Public and Intergovernmental Affairs, Department of Veterans Affairs, 1993-98. Staff Assistant, House Committee on Post Office and Civil Service, 1983-84.

Employers
Alcalde & Fay (Partner)

Clients Represented
On Behalf of Alcalde & Fay
Earthshell Container Corp.
Houston Independent School District
Miami-Dade County Public Schools
Tampa, Florida, City of
Telemundo
University of Nevada - Las Vegas

MUNSAT, Susan Chertkof

1666 Connecticut Ave. NW
Suite 500
Washington, DC 20009
Tel: (202)328-1666
Fax: (202)328-9162

Employers
Lichtman, Trister, Singer & Ross (Attorney)

Clients Represented
On Behalf of Lichtman, Trister, Singer & Ross
Nat'l Writers Union/UAW Local 1981

MUNSON, Dick

218 D St. SE
Washington, DC 20003
EMail: dickmunson@nemw.org
Tel: (202)544-5200
Fax: (202)544-0043

Employers
Northeast-Midwest Institute (Exec. Director)

MUNUZ, K.C.

600 New Hampshire Ave. NW
Suite 601
Washington, DC 20037
Tel: (202)333-7400
Fax: (202)333-1638

Employers
Hill and Knowlton, Inc. (Managing Director)

MURAMATSU, Kazutoshi

1701 Pennsylvania Ave. NW
Suite 500
Washington, DC 20006
Tel: (202)861-0660
Fax: (202)861-0437

Employers
Mitsui and Co. (U.S.A.), Inc. (V. President and General Manager)

MURAVCHIK, Joshua

1150 17th St. NW
Washington, DC 20036
EMail: jmuravchik@aei.org
Tel: (202)862-5800
Fax: (202)862-7177

Employers
American Enterprise Institute for Public Policy Research (Resident Scholar)

MURCHIE, Gordon W.

P.O. Box 31342
Alexandria, VA 22310
EMail: thewinexchange@aol.com
Tel: (703)922-7049
Fax: (703)922-0617
Formerly served in the U.S. Information Agency and the Agency for International Development.

Employers
Vinifera Wine Growers Ass'n (President)
Virginia Wineries Ass'n (Exec. Director)

MURDOCK, III, J. E.

2300 N St. NW
Washington, DC 20037-1128
EMail: sandy.murdock@shawpittman.com
Tel: (202)663-8000
Fax: (202)663-8007
Registered: LDA
Chief Counsel, Federal Aviation Administration, 1981-85; Acting Deputy Administrator, Federal Aviation Administration, 1984.

Employers
Shaw Pittman (Partner)

Clients Represented
On Behalf of Shaw Pittman
Aviation Development Services
Chromalloy Gas Turbine Corp.
DHL Airways, Inc.
Embraer Aircraft Corp.
Greenville-Spartanburg Airport District
Hawaii, State of
Israel Aircraft Industries, Ltd.
Lucas Aerospace
The Nordam Group
North Carolina Global TransPark Authority
San Jose, California, City of

MURDOCK, Patricia C.

1201 16th St. NW
Washington, DC 20036
Tel: (202)833-4000

Employers
Nat'l Education Ass'n of the U.S. (Manager, Information Resources and Advocacy)

MUROYAMA, Paul

499 S. Capitol St. SW
Suite 506
Washington, DC 20003
EMail: paulmuroyama.washington@worldnet.att.net
Tel: (202)484-0785
Fax: (202)484-0788

Employers
Paul Muroyama & Assoc. (President and Chief Exec. Officer)

Clients Represented

On Behalf of Paul Muroyama & Assoc.

Dai-Ichi Life Insurance Co.
NTT America

MURPHY, Betty Southard

1050 Connecticut Ave. NW
Suite 1100
Washington, DC 20036-5304
Tel: (202)861-1500
Fax: (202)861-1790
EMail: Bmurphy@baker-hostetler.com

Chairman and Member, National Labor Relations Board, 1975-79. Administrator, Wage and Hour Division, Department of Labor, 1974-75.

Employers

Baker & Hostetler LLP (Partner)

MURPHY, Christopher M.

1255 23rd St. NW
Suite 200
Washington, DC 20037-1174
Tel: (202)452-8100
Fax: (202)833-3636
EMail: cmurphy@hauck.com

Employers

American Ass'n of Residential Mortgage Regulators (Exec. Director)
Ass'n of Meeting Professionals (Senior Director)
Hauck and Associates (V. President and Chief Operating Officer)
Internat'l Ass'n of Seed Crushers (V. President and Chief Operating Officer)
Internat'l Claim Ass'n (Director of Administration)

Clients Represented

On Behalf of Hauck and Associates

American Ass'n of Residential Mortgage Regulators
Internat'l Ass'n of Seed Crushers
Internat'l Claim Ass'n

MURPHY, Edward L.

1300 Wilson Blvd.
Arlington, VA 22209
Tel: (703)741-5936
Fax: (703)741-6097
Registered: LDA
EMail: ed_murphy@americanchemistry.com

Employers

American Chemistry Council (Senior Director, Grassroots and Political Activities)

MURPHY, Jack W.

1775 I St. NW
Washington, DC 20006
Tel: (202)261-3300
Fax: (202)261-3333
EMail: jack.murphy@dechert.com

Associate Director and Chief Counsel (1994-97); Staff Attorney and Special Counsel (1985-88), Division of Investment Management, Securities and Exchange Commission.

Employers

Dechert (Partner)

MURPHY, James J.

700 13th St. NW
Suite 700
Washington, DC 20005-3960
Tel: (202)508-6000
Fax: (202)508-6200
Registered: LDA
EMail: jjmurphy@bryancave.com

Legislative Assistant to Senator Thomas F. Eagleton (D-MO), 1969-76. Trial Attorney, Civil Rights Division, Department of Justice, 1965-68.

Employers

Bryan Cave LLP (Partner)

Clients Represented

On Behalf of Bryan Cave LLP

Laclede Gas Co.

MURPHY, Jeanne-Marie

730 15th St. NW
Fifth Floor
Washington, DC 20005
Tel: (202)624-4134
Fax: (202)383-3475
Registered: LDA
EMail: jeanne-marie.murphy@bankofamerica.com

Employers

Bank of America (Senior V. President and Director, Government Relations)

MURPHY, Jeremiah L.

One Dupont Circle NW
Suite 250
Washington, DC 20036
Tel: (202)939-9345
Fax: (202)833-4723
Registered: LDA

Employers

Business-Higher Education Forum (Exec. Director)

MURPHY, John

1615 H St. NW
Washington, DC 20062
Tel: (202)463-5485
Fax: (202)463-3126
Registered: LDA

Employers

Ass'n of American Chambers of Commerce in Latin America (Exec. Director)
Chamber of Commerce of the U.S.A.

MURPHY, Jr., John C.

2000 Pennsylvania Ave. NW
Washington, DC 20006
Tel: (202)974-1500
Fax: (202)974-1999
Registered: LDA, FARA

General Counsel, Federal Deposit Insurance Corporation, 1985-87. Chairman, Legal Advisory Group, Federal Financial Institutions Examination Council, 1984-85. Special Counsel, Office of the Bank Study, Securities and Exchange Commission, 1975-77.

Employers

Cleary, Gottlieb, Steen and Hamilton (Partner)

MURPHY, John C.

2025 M St. NW
Suite 800
Washington, DC 20036
Tel: (202)367-2100
Fax: (202)367-1200
Registered: LDA
EMail: john_murphy@dc.sba.com

Employers

Nat'l Ass'n of County Community and Economic Development (Exec. Director)
Smith, Bucklin and Associates, Inc.

Clients Represented

On Behalf of Smith, Bucklin and Associates, Inc.

Ass'n of Local Housing Finance Agencies
Nat'l Ass'n of County Community and Economic Development

MURPHY, Laura W.

122 Maryland Ave. NE
Washington, DC 20002
Tel: (202)675-2305
Fax: (202)547-2394
Registered: LDA

Employers

American Civil Liberties Union (Director, Washington National Office)

MURPHY, Lynda M.

499 S. Capitol St. SW
Suite 420
Washington, DC 20003
Tel: (202)302-0465

Employers

Monfort & Wolfe (Associate)

MURPHY, Meredith

1200 Wilson Blvd.
Arlington, VA 22209
Tel: (703)465-3621
Fax: (703)465-3014

Employers

The Boeing Co. (Director, Business Affairs and Acquisition Policy)

MURPHY, Michael J.

1125 17th St. NW
Washington, DC 20036
Tel: (202)429-9100
Fax: (202)778-2691

Employers

Internat'l Union of Operating Engineers (Treasurer, EPEC)

MURPHY, Michael J.

1200 G St. NW
Suite 300
Washington, DC 20005
Tel: (202)638-5601
Fax: (202)638-5607
EMail: mmurphy@tei.org

Employers

Tax Executives Institute, Inc. (Exec. Director)

MURPHY, Patricia

655 15th St. NW
Suite 300
Washington, DC 20005
Tel: (202)783-0900
Fax: (202)783-2308
Registered: LDA
EMail: patricia.murphy@bms.com

Employers

Bristol-Myers Squibb Co. (Administrator, Government Affairs, MIS Operations)

MURPHY, Patrick M.

503 Second St. NE
Washington, DC 20002
Tel: (202)544-8490
Fax: (202)543-7804
Registered: LDA
EMail: pmurphy@patrickmurphy.com

Employers

Patrick M. Murphy & Associates (President)

Clients Represented

On Behalf of Patrick M. Murphy & Associates

Education Networks of America
Santa Fe, New Mexico, County of
WebMD

MURPHY, Penny

409 12th St. SW
P.O. Box 96920
Washington, DC 20090-6920
Tel: (202)863-2827
Fax: (202)479-6826

Employers

American College of Obstetricians and Gynecologists (Director, Communications)

MURPHY, Pierre E.

2445 M St. NW
Suite 260
Washington, DC 20037
Tel: (202)872-1679
Fax: (202)872-1725
EMail: pmurphy@lopmurphy.com

Employers

Pierre E. Murphy Law Offices (Principal)

Clients Represented

On Behalf of Pierre E. Murphy Law Offices

APA Internat'l Air, S.A.
Apple Vacations, Inc.
Caraven Airlines (Carga Aerea Venezolana, S.A.)
Caribbean Airline Co. Ltd.
Faucett Airlines (Compania de Aviacion Faucett, S.A.)
Laker Airways (Bahamas) Ltd.
LAPA (Lineas Aereas Privadas, S.A.)
Southern Air Transport
Sun Jet Internat'l, Inc.
Worldwide Aviation Services, Ltd.

MURPHY, Rick

1010 Pennsylvania Ave. SE
Washington, DC 20003
Tel: (202)547-1005
Registered: LDA

Employers

R. B. Murphy & Associates (President)

Clients Represented

On Behalf of R. B. Murphy & Associates

Vern Clark & Associates
Internat'l Ass'n of Fire Fighters
Philip Morris Management Corp.

MURPHY, Robin

1919 M St. NW
Suite 200
Washington, DC 20036
Tel: (202)912-1000
Fax: (202)912-1030
EMail: r.murphy@conservation.org

Employers

Conservation Internat'l Foundation (V. President)

MURPHY, Sara Hope

401 Ninth St. NW
Suite 400
Washington, DC 20004
Tel: (202)585-1931
Fax: (202)585-1898
Registered: LDA

Employers

Sprint Corp. (Assistant V. President, Government Affairs)

MURRAY, Charles

1150 17th St. NW
Washington, DC 20036
Tel: (202)862-5800
Fax: (202)862-7177
EMail: chasmurray@earthlink.net

Employers
American Enterprise Institute for Public Policy Research (Bradley Fellow)

MURRAY, Chip

1111 19th St. NW
Suite 800
Washington, DC 20036
Tel: (202)463-2700
Fax: (202)463-2785
Registered: LDA
EMail: chip_murray@afandpa.org

Employers
American Forest & Paper Ass'n (Natural Resources Counsel)

MURRAY, D. Michael

1200 New Hampshire Ave NW
Suite 430
Washington, DC 20036
Tel: (202)955-3030
Fax: (202)955-1147
Registered: LDA, FARA
EMail: dmmo2a@aol.com
Executive Assistant to Chief of White House Congressional Office and Postmaster General, 1964-68.

Employers
Murray, Scheer, Montgomery, Tapia & O'Donnell (President)

Clients Represented

On Behalf of Murray, Scheer, Montgomery, Tapia & O'Donnell
Allmerica Financial
Ass'n of Industrialists and Businessmen of Tatarstan
California State Assembly - Committee on Rules
Cleveland Cliffs Iron Co.
Equitable Assurance Soc. of the United States
The Equitable Cos.
Iron Ore Ass'n
KQC Properties
Lafayette Consolidated Government
Metropolitan Life Insurance Co.
Mine Safety Appliances
MONY Life Insurance Co.
Nat'l Council of Coal Lessors
New England Financial
New England Life Insurance Co.
Pacific Life Insurance Co.
Passaic Valley Sewerage Commissioners
Penn Mutual Life Insurance Co.
PepsiCo, Inc.
Piedmont Environmental Council
PIMCO Advisors, L.P.
Porsche Cars North America, Inc.
Qualimetrics, Inc.
Science & Engineering Associates, Inc.
Sherwin Williams Co.
Shubert Organization Inc.
Southern California Ass'n of Governments
Swaziland Sugar Ass'n
Tatarstan, Republic of
Tricon Global Restaurants Inc.
United Biscuit
Wheeling & Lake Erie Railway Co.
Wisconsin Central Transportation Corp.

MURRAY, Daniel H.

2001 Cool Spring Dr.
Alexandria, VA 22308

Employers
Murray & Murray (Partner)

MURRAY, David P.

Three Lafayette Center
1155 21st St. NW
Washington, DC 20036-3384
Tel: (202)328-8000
Fax: (202)887-8979

Employers
Willkie Farr & Gallagher (Partner)

Clients Represented

On Behalf of Willkie Farr & Gallagher
Yamaha Motor Corp. U.S.A.

MURRAY, David T.

1615 L St. NW
Suite 1260
Washington, DC 20036
Tel: (202)367-7600
Fax: (202)659-1931
Registered: LDA

Employers
Winstar Communications, Inc. (Director, Government Affairs)

MURRAY, Donald

440 First St. NW
Eighth Floor
Washington, DC 20001
EMail: dmurray@naco.org
Tel: (202)942-4239
Fax: (202)942-4281

Employers
Nat'l Ass'n of Counties (Associate Legislative Director, Employment Justice and Public Safety)
Nat'l Ass'n of County Civil Attorneys (Contact)

MURRAY, Fred F.

1625 K St. NW
Suite 1090
Washington, DC 20006-1604
Tel: (202)887-0278
Fax: (202)452-8160
Registered: LDA

Employers
Nat'l Foreign Trade Council, Inc. (V. President, Tax Policy)

MURRAY, James V.

1776 I St. NW
Suite 1050
Washington, DC 20006
Tel: (202)429-3407
Registered: LDA

Employers
The Dow Chemical Co. (Director, Government Affairs)

MURRAY, Melissa R.

1111 19th St. NW
Suite 403
Washington, DC 20036
EMail: mmurray@aaes.org
Tel: (202)296-2237
Fax: (202)296-1151

Employers
American Ass'n of Engineering Societies (Public Policy Associate)

MURRAY, Nancy A.

2550 M St. NW
Washington, DC 20037-1350
Tel: (202)457-6000
Fax: (202)457-6315
Registered: LDA
EMail: nmurray@pattonboggs.com
Executive Assistant to the Undersecretary (1987-89), Executive Assistant to the Assistant Secretary for Housing, Federal Housing Commissioner (1986-87), and Executive Assistant to the Deputy Assistant Secretary, Multifamily Housing Programs (1985-86), all at the Department of Housing and Urban Development.

Employers
Patton Boggs, LLP (Of Counsel)

Clients Represented

On Behalf of Patton Boggs, LLP
The Limited Inc.

MURRAY, USAF (Ret.), Maj. Gen. Richard D.

5535 Hempstead Way
Springfield, VA 22151
Tel: (703)750-1342
Fax: (703)354-4380

Employers
Nat'l Ass'n for Uniformed Services (President)

MURRAY, Rosemary Griffin

Crystal Park Four
2345 Crystal Dr.
Arlington, VA 22227
Tel: (703)872-5140
Fax: (703)872-5109
Registered: LDA

Employers
US Airways (Director, Government Affairs)

MURRAY, Samuel H.

601 13th St. NW
Suite 600 South
Washington, DC 20005-3807
Tel: (202)626-3646
Fax: (202)638-6634
Registered: LDA
EMail: murray@psca.org

Employers
Profit Sharing/401 (k) Council of America (V. President, Government Affairs)

MURRAY, Ty

2001 Cool Spring Dr.
Alexandria, VA 22308

Employers
Murray & Murray (Partner)

MURRAY, Vanessa Allen

1111 Jefferson Davis Hwy.
Room 303
Arlington, VA 22202-4306
Tel: (703)604-6617
Fax: (703)604-6542

Employers
Department of Defense - Defense Security Cooperation Agency (Director, Legislation and Planning)

MUSANTE, Ramola

1225 I St. NW
Suite 600
Washington, DC 20005
Tel: (202)661-6180
Fax: (202)661-6182
Registered: LDA
EMail: rgmusante@morganmeguire.com

Employers
Morgan Meguire, LLC (V. President)

Clients Represented

On Behalf of Morgan Meguire, LLC
Air-Conditioning and Refrigeration Institute
Energy Affairs Administration
Texas A&M Engineering Experiment Station

MUSE, Donald N.

1775 I St. NW
Suite 520
Washington, DC 20006
EMail: dnmuse@muse-associates.com
Tel: (202)496-0200
Fax: (202)496-0201
Principal Analyst for Medicare and Medicaid, Congressional Budget Office, 1986-1990. Division Director, Office of Actuary, Health Care Financing Administration, Department of Health and Human Services, 1979-86. Professional Staff Member, Senate Committee on Finance, 1985-86.

Employers
Muse & Associates (President)

Clients Represented

On Behalf of Muse & Associates
Novartis Corp.
Pharmaceutical Research and Manufacturers of America
The Tri-Alliance of Rehabilitation Professionals

MUSE, Tonya W.

300 N. Washington St.
Suite 500
Alexandria, VA 22314-2530
Tel: (703)739-2200
Fax: (703)739-2209

Employers
Envelope Manufacturers Ass'n of America (V. President)

MUSHENO, Kim

1730 K St. NW
Washington, DC 20006
Tel: (202)785-3388
Fax: (202)467-4179
Registered: LDA
EMail: musheno@thearc.org

Employers
The Arc (Director of Governmental Affairs Communication)

MUSIL, Dr. Robert K.

1875 Connecticut Ave.
Suite 1012
Washington, DC 20029
Tel: (202)898-0150
Fax: (202)898-0172

Employers
Physicians for Social Responsibility (Exec. Director)

MUSKER, Joe

1310 G St. NW
12th Floor
Washington, DC 20005
Tel: (202)626-4780
Fax: (202)626-4833
Registered: LDA

Employers
Blue Cross Blue Shield Ass'n (Senior Legislative Policy Analyst)

MUSKETT, Margarete

2121 K St. NW
Suite 700
Washington, DC 20037
Tel: (202)296-9230
Fax: (202)862-5498
Registered: LDA

Employers
VISA U.S.A., Inc. (Exec. Assistant)

MUSKETT, Susan T.

499 S. Capitol St. SW
Suite 615
Washington, DC 20003
Tel: (202)479-6900
Fax: (202)479-4260
Registered: LDA

Employers
Christian Coalition of America (Government Relations Representative)

MUSSARA, Gerald

1725 Jefferson Davis Hwy.
Crystal Square 2, Suite 300
Arlington, VA 22202
Tel: (703)413-5812
Fax: (703)413-5617

Employers
Lockheed Martin Corp. (V. President, Trade and Regulatory Affairs)

MUSSER, Duane L.

517 C St. NE
Washington, DC 20002
Tel: (202)543-4455
Fax: (202)543-4586
Registered: LDA

Senior Legislative Assistant (1989-93) and Legislative Correspondent (1988-89) to Rep. Wally Herger (R-CA).

Employers
Schramm, Williams & Associates, Inc. (Associate)

Clients Represented

On Behalf of Schramm, Williams & Associates, Inc.
The Ass'n Healthcare Coalition
California Asparagus Commission
California Tomato Commission
Western Growers Ass'n
Western Growers Insurance Services
Western Pistachio Ass'n

MUSSER, James C.

210 Seventh St. SE
Washington, DC 20003
Tel: (202)547-6808
Fax: (202)546-5425
Registered: LDA

Former aide to Rep. Jim Bunning (R-KY).

Employers
Kessler & Associates Business Services, Inc. (Senior V. President, Tax Policy)

Clients Represented

On Behalf of Kessler & Associates Business Services, Inc.
Amgen
Burlington Northern Santa Fe Railway
Dunn-Edwards Corp.
Exelon Corp.
Grocery Manufacturers of America
Mercy Health System of Northwest Arkasas
Nat'l Ass'n of Securities Dealers, Inc. (NASD)
Pfizer, Inc.
Pharmacia Corp.
Philip Morris Management Corp.

MUSTAIN, Christopher

1301 K St. NW
Suite 1200-West Tower
Washington, DC 20005-3307
EMail: mustainc@us.ibm.com
Tel: (202)515-5062
Registered: LDA

Employers
Internat'l Business Machines Corp. (Program Manager, Public Affairs)

MYDLAND, Grant

6776 Little Falls Rd.
Arlington, VA 22213
Tel: (703)536-0002
Fax: (703)536-0003
Registered: LDA

Employers
Computing Technology Industry Ass'n (Manager, Government Affairs)

MYER, Lori

1680 Duke St.
Alexandria, VA 22314-3407
Tel: (703)838-6722
Fax: (703)683-7590

Employers
Nat'l School Boards Ass'n (Director, Federal Legislation)

MYERS, Charles

1000 Thomas Jefferson St. NW
Suite 515
Washington, DC 20007
Tel: (202)342-8086
Fax: (202)342-9063

Employers
Leather Industries of America (President)

MYERS, Chris

21700 Atlantic Blvd.
Dulles, VA 20166
Tel: (703)406-5000
Fax: (703)406-3502

Employers
Orbital Sciences Corp. (Manager, Government Relations)

MYERS, Dennis

1140 Connecticut Ave. NW
Suite 350
Washington, DC 20036
Tel: (202)872-7800
Fax: (202)872-7808
Registered: LDA

Employers
Elan Pharmaceutical Research Corp.

MYERS, Elissa Matulis

2101 Wilson Blvd.
Suite 1002
Arlington, VA 22201
EMail: lmyers@retailing.org
Tel: (703)841-1751
Fax: (703)841-1860

Employers
Electronic Retailing Ass'n (President and Chief Exec. Officer)

MYERS, Gary D.

501 Second St. NE
Washington, DC 20002
EMail: gmyers@tfi.org
Tel: (202)675-8250
Fax: (202)544-8123
Registered: LDA

Employers
The Fertilizer Institute (President)

MYERS, Jr., George C.

900 17th St. NW
Suite 1000
Washington, DC 20006
Tel: (202)530-7400
Fax: (202)463-6915

Employers
Blank Rome Comisky & McCauley, LLP (Partner)

Clients Represented

On Behalf of Blank Rome Comisky & McCauley, LLP
Southwire, Inc.

MYERS, James Pierce

1211 Connecticut Ave. NW
Suite 610
Washington, DC 20036
Tel: (202)296-3690
Fax: (202)296-0343
Registered: LDA

Special Counsel, Postal Rate Commission, 1995-97.

Employers
Self-employed as an independent consultant.
Parcel Shippers Ass'n (Exec. V. President)

Clients Represented

As an independent consultant
Preston Gates Ellis & Rouvelas Meeds LLP

MYERS, Jeff M.

1455 F St. NW
Suite 450
Washington, DC 20004
Tel: (202)393-6040
Fax: (202)393-6050
Registered: LDA

Employers
Pharmacia Corp. (Director, Government Affairs)

MYERS, Jeffrey A.

412 First St. SE
Suite 300
Washington, DC 20003
Tel: (202)863-7000
Fax: (202)863-7015

Employers
Independent Insurance Agents of America, Inc. (V. President, Public Affairs)

MYERS, Hon. John

1225 I St. NW
Suite 500
Washington, DC 20005
EMail: dawsonassociates@worldnet.att.net
Tel: (202)312-2005
Fax: (202)289-8683
Registered: LDA

Member, U.S. House of Representatives (R-IN), 1967-76. Also served in the U.S. Army.

Employers
Dawson & Associates, Inc. (Senior Advisor)

Clients Represented

On Behalf of Dawson & Associates, Inc.
AgriPartners
Anglogold Americas, Inc.
Chemical Land Holdings, Inc.
Florida Sugar Cane League, Inc.
Great Lakes Dredge & Dock
Sugar Cane Growers Cooperative of Florida

MYERS, Karen M.

1331 Pennsylvania Ave. NW
Suite 1300 North
Washington, DC 20004
EMail: karen.myers@eds.com
Tel: (202)637-6720
Fax: (202)637-6759
Registered: LDA

Employers
EDS Corp. (Director, Tax Policy)

MYERS, Matthew

1707 L St. NW
Suite 800
Washington, DC 20036
Tel: (202)296-5469
Fax: (202)296-5427
Registered: LDA

Employers
Nat'l Center for Tobacco-Free Kids (President)

MYERS, Molly M.

1655 N. Fort Myer Dr.
Suite 850
Arlington, VA 22209
Tel: (703)524-2549
Fax: (703)524-3940

Employers
Nat'l Venture Capital Ass'n (V. President, Administration and Program Development)

MYERS, Susan

1301 Connecticut Ave. NW
Suite 700
Washington, DC 20036
Tel: (202)462-4900
Fax: (202)462-2686
Registered: LDA

Employers
Better World Campaign (Legislative Director)

MYERS, Vickie R.

2111 Wilson Blvd.
Suite 700
Arlington, VA 22201
Tel: (703)351-5055
Fax: (703)351-6698
Registered: LDA

Employers
American Sugar Alliance (Exec. Director)

MYERS-NELSON, Mary

815 16th St. NW
Suite 5090
Washington, DC 20006
Tel: (202)637-5334
Fax: (202)508-6962

Employers
AFL-CIO - Broadcast Division (Contact)

MYHRE, William N.

1735 New York Ave. NW
Suite 500
Washington, DC 20006-4759
Tel: (202)628-1700
Fax: (202)331-1024
Registered: LDA, FARA

Employers
Preston Gates Ellis & Rouvelas Meeds LLP (Partner)

Clients Represented

On Behalf of Preston Gates Ellis & Rouvelas Meeds LLP

Alaska Ocean Seafoods L.P.
American Classic Voyages Co.
American Seafoods Inc.
Coalition for Stability in Marine Financing
Coastal Transportation Inc.
Dredging Contractors of America
Great Lakes Dredge & Dock
KB Holdings
Marine Resources Company Internat'l
Mount Vernon Barge Service
Seattle, Washington, Port of
Sunmar Shipping, Inc.
Transportation Institute
United States Maritime Coalition

MYRICK, Chris

1667 K St. NW
Suite 1270
Washington, DC 20006
Tel: (202)659-8320
Fax: (202)496-2448
Registered: LDA

Employers
American Home Products Corp. (Director, Government Relations)

MYRICK, Ronald

1255 23rd St. NW
Suite 200
Washington, DC 20037
Tel: (202)466-2396
Fax: (202)466-2893

Employers
Intellectual Property Owners Ass'n (President)

NAAKE, Larry E.

440 First St. NW
Eighth Floor
Washington, DC 20001
Tel: (202)942-4201
Fax: (202)942-4203

Employers
Nat'l Ass'n of Counties (Exec. Director)
Nat'l Ass'n of County Civil Attorneys (Contact)

NAAS, Penelope

14th and Constitution Ave. NW
Room 3434
Washington, DC 20230
Tel: (202)482-3015
Fax: (202)482-0900

Employers
Department of Commerce - Internat'l Trade Administration (Acting Director, Office of Legislative and Intergovernmental Affairs)

NAASZ, Kraig R.

6707 Old Dominion Dr.
Suite 320
McLean, VA 22101
Tel: (703)442-8850
Fax: (703)790-0845

Employers
U.S. Apple Ass'n (President and Chief Exec. Officer)

NABI FAI, Ghulam

733 15th St. NW
Suite 1100
Washington, DC 20005
EMail: kac@kashmiri.com
Tel: (202)628-6789
Fax: (202)393-0062

Employers
Kashmiri American Council (Exec. Director)

NADDAF, May

236 Massachusetts Ave. NE
Suite 400
Washington, DC 20002
Tel: (202)675-4511
Fax: (202)675-4512
Registered: LDA

Employers
AESOP Enterprises, Ltd. (V. President)

NADEL, Steve

1001 Connecticut Ave. NW
Suite 801
Washington, DC 20036
Tel: (202)429-8873
Fax: (202)429-2248
Registered: LDA

Employers
American Council for an Energy-Efficient Economy (Exec. Director)

NADER, Ralph

1600 20th St. NW
Washington, DC 20009
Tel: (202)588-1000
Fax: (202)588-7799

Employers
Center for the Study of Responsive Law (Managing Trustee)
Public Citizen, Inc. (Contact)

NADERI, Ms. Homa

611 Pennsylvania Ave. SE
Suite 340
Washington, DC 20003
Tel: (202)543-1444
Fax: (202)318-0652
Registered: LDA

Employers
Philip S. Smith & Associates, Inc.

NADHERNY, Steven T.

1001 G St. NW
Suite 100 East
Washington, DC 20001
Tel: (202)737-7575
Fax: (202)737-9090
Registered: LDA

Employers
CaseNewHolland Inc. (Manager, Government Affairs)

NADLER, Carl S.

601 13th St. NW
12th Floor
Washington, DC 20005
Tel: (202)639-6000
Fax: (202)639-6066
Law Clerk to Judge Alvin B. Rubin, U.S. Court of Appeals, Fifth Circuit, 1982-83.

Employers
Jenner & Block (Partner)

NADLER, Jonathan J.

1201 Pennsylvania Ave. NW
P.O. Box 407
Washington, DC 20044-0407
EMail: jnadler@ssd.com
Tel: (202)626-6600
Fax: (202)626-6780

Employers
Squire, Sanders & Dempsey L.L.P. (Partner)

Clients Represented

On Behalf of Squire, Sanders & Dempsey L.L.P.
Information Technology Ass'n of America (ITAA)

NAEGELE, Timothy D.

1201 Pennsylvania Ave. NW
Suite 300
Washington, DC 20004
EMail: naegelewdc@aol.com
Tel: (202)466-7500
Fax: (202)661-4699
Administrative Assistant to Senator Edward W. Brooke, III (R-MA), 1971-72. Assistant Counsel, Senate Committee on Banking, Housing and Urban Affairs, 1969-71.

Employers
Timothy D. Naegele & Associates (Principal)

Clients Represented

On Behalf of Timothy D. Naegele & Associates
Home Federal Savings and Loan Ass'n

NAEGLE, LaDawn

700 13th St. NW
Suite 700
Washington, DC 20005-3960
EMail: ldnaegle@bryancave.com
Tel: (202)508-6000
Fax: (202)508-6200

Employers
Bryan Cave LLP (Partner)

NAEVE, Clifford M.

1440 New York Ave. NW
Washington, DC 20005
Tel: (202)371-7000
Fax: (202)393-5760
Registered: LDA
Commissioner, Federal Energy Regulatory Commission, 1985-88. Legislative Director for Senator Lloyd Bentsen (D-TX), 1978-80.

Employers
Skadden, Arps, Slate, Meagher & Flom LLP (Partner)

Clients Represented

On Behalf of Skadden, Arps, Slate, Meagher & Flom LLP
Cinergy Corp.

NAFTALIN, Alan

2099 Pennsylvania Ave. NW
Suite 100
Washington, DC 20006
EMail: anaftali@hklaw.com
Tel: (202)955-3000
Fax: (202)955-5564

Employers
Holland & Knight LLP (Partner)

NAFTALIN, Charles

2099 Pennsylvania Ave. NW
Suite 100
Washington, DC 20006
EMail: cnaftali@hklaw.com
Tel: (202)955-3000
Fax: (202)955-5564

Employers
Holland & Knight LLP (Partner)

NAFTALIN, Micah

1819 H St. NW
Suite 230
Washington, DC 20006
Tel: (202)775-9770
Ext: 101
Fax: (202)775-9776
Acting Director, U.S. Holocaust Memorial Council, 1982-87.

Employers
Union of Councils for Soviet Jews (National Director)

NAFTZGER, J. Christopher

600 New Hampshire Ave. NW
11th Floor
Washington, DC 20037
EMail: jcn@dejlaw.com
Tel: (202)944-3000
Fax: (202)944-3068
Registered: LDA, FARA

Employers
Dyer Ellis & Joseph, P.C. (Associate)

Clients Represented

On Behalf of Dyer Ellis & Joseph, P.C.
FastShip, Inc.

NAGATA, Kenichiro

1560 Wilson Blvd.
Suite 1200
Arlington, VA 22209
Tel: (703)525-4800
Ext: 228
Fax: (703)525-6772

Employers
Mitsubishi Motors R&D of America, Inc. (V. President and General Manager)

NAGLE, Ann

Colonial Place Three
2107 Wilson Blvd., Suite 300
Arlington, VA 22201-3042
Tel: (703)524-7600
Fax: (703)524-9094

Employers
Nat'l Alliance for the Mentally Ill (Deputy Exec. Director, Operations)

NAGLE, B. Callan

700 13th St. NW
Suite 350
Washington, DC 20005
Tel: (202)637-0040
Fax: (202)637-0041
Registered: LDA
Staff Assistant to Sen. Mitch McConnell (R-KY), 1989.

Employers
Rhoads Group (V. President, Finance and Operations)

Clients Represented

On Behalf of Rhoads Group
American Management Systems
PNC Bank, N.A.

NAGLE, Kurt

1010 Duke St.
Alexandria, VA 22314-3589
Tel: (703)684-5700
Fax: (703)684-6321
Registered: LDA

Employers
American Ass'n of Port Authorities (President and Chief Exec. Officer)

NAGY, Edward C.

1029 Vermont Ave. NW
Suite 505
Washington, DC 20005
Tel: (202)347-5872
Fax: (202)347-5876
Registered: LDA

Employers
Academy of Radiology Research (Exec. Director)

NAH, Joseph

1850 M St. NW
Suite 900
Washington, DC 20036
Tel: (202)463-2500
Fax: (202)463-4950

Employers
Sher & Blackwell (Associate)

NAHRA, Kirk J.

1776 K St. NW
Washington, DC 20006
Tel: (202)719-7000
Fax: (202)719-7049

Employers
Wiley, Rein & Fielding (Partner)

NAIMON, Jeffrey P.

1717 Pennsylvania Ave. NW
Washington, DC 20006
Tel: (202)974-1000
Fax: (202)331-9330
Registered: LDA

Employers
Goodwin, Procter & Hoar LLP (Associate)

Clients Represented
On Behalf of Goodwin, Procter & Hoar LLP
Consumer Mortgage Coalition

NAISMITH, Martha

1350 I St. NW
Suite 1210
Washington, DC 20005-3305
Tel: (202)589-1015
Fax: (202)589-1001
Registered: LDA

Employers
Johnson & Johnson, Inc. (Director, Federal Affairs)

NAKAHATA, John T.

1200 18th St. NW
Suite 1200
Washington, DC 20036
Tel: (202)730-1300
Fax: (202)730-1301
Registered: LDA
Chief of Staff to the Chairman (1997-98), Chief of Competition Division (1997), Senior Legal Advisor (1996) and Legal Advisor (1995), all at the Federal Communications Commission. Aide to Senator Joseph Lieberman (D-CT), 1990-95.

Employers
Harris, Wiltshire & Grannis LLP (Partner)

Clients Represented
On Behalf of Harris, Wiltshire & Grannis LLP
Coalition for Affordable Local and Long Distance Services
VoiceStream Wireless Corp.

NAKAMURA, Kennon H.

2101 E St. NW
Washington, DC 20037
Tel: (202)338-4045
Fax: (202)338-6820
Registered: LDA
EMail: leg@asfa.org

Employers
American Foreign Service Ass'n (Director, Congressional Relations)

NAKANISHI, Hironori

2000 L St. NW
Suite 605
Washington, DC 20036
Tel: (202)822-9298
Fax: (202)822-9289

Employers
New Energy and Industrial Technology Development Organization (NEDO) (Chief Representative)

NALL, David A.

1201 Pennsylvania Ave. NW
P.O. Box 407
Washington, DC 20044-0407
Tel: (202)626-6600
Fax: (202)626-6780
EMail: dnall@ssd.com
Former Deputy Chief, Commercial Wireless Division, Federal Communications Division.

Employers
Squire, Sanders & Dempsey L.L.P. (Partner)

NALL, Mickey

1901 L St. NW
Suite 300
Washington, DC 20036
Tel: (202)466-7590
Fax: (202)466-7598
EMail: mickey.nall@dc.ogilvypr.com

Employers
Ogilvy Public Relations Worldwide (Senior V. President)

Clients Represented
On Behalf of Ogilvy Public Relations Worldwide
Internat'l Sleep Products Ass'n

NALLS, Charles H.

1725 K St. NW
Suite 402
Washington, DC 20006
Tel: (202)466-5258
Fax: (202)466-2360

Employers
Luxcore Public Affairs (Director, Government Affairs)

NANCE, D. Scott

601 13th St. NW
Suite 1100
Washington, DC 20005
Tel: (202)429-2217
Fax: (202)296-8727
Registered: LDA

Employers
Fontheim Partners, PC (Principal)

Clients Represented
On Behalf of Fontheim Partners, PC
The Limited Inc.

NANCE, Penny

P.O. Box 16069
Washington, DC 20041-6069
Tel: (703)904-7312
Fax: (703)478-9679
Registered: LDA

Employers
Justice Fellowship (Lobbyist)

NANNIS, Paul N.

Parklawn Bldg.
5600 Fishers Ln.
MS: 14-33
Rockville, MD 20857
Tel: (301)443-2460
Fax: (301)443-9270
EMail: pnannis@hrsa.gov

Employers
Department of Health and Human Services - Health Resources and Services Administration (Director, Office of Planning, Evaluation and Legislation)

NAPIER, David

1250 I St. NW
Suite 1200
Washington, DC 20005-3924
Tel: (202)371-8563
Fax: (202)371-8470

Employers
Aerospace Industries Ass'n of America (Director, Research)

NAPIER, Hon. John L.

1400 L St. NW
Washington, DC 20005-3502
Tel: (202)371-5982
Fax: (202)371-5950
Registered: LDA
EMail: jnapier@winston.com
Judge, U.S. Court of Federal Claims, 1986-89. Member, U.S. House of Representatives (R-SC), 1981-83. Chief Legislative Assistant to Senator Strom Thurmond (R-SC) and Minority Counsel, Subcommittee on Antitrust and Monopoly, Senate Committee on the Judiciary, 1976-78. Chief Counsel to the Minority, Senate Special Committee on Official Conduct, 1977. Professional Staff Member and Minority Counsel, Senate Veterans Affairs Committee, 1973-76. Legislative Assistant to Senator Strom Thurmond (R-SC) and Minority Counsel, Subcommittee on Administrative Practice and Procedure, Senate Committee on the Judiciary, 1972-73.

Employers
Winston & Strawn (Of Counsel, Legislative and Regulatory Practice)

Clients Represented
On Behalf of Winston & Strawn
Bank of America
Columbia Ventures, LLC
Cooper Tire and Rubber Co.
Eastern Band of Cherokee Indians
Federal Judges Ass'n
Federal Magistrate Judges Ass'n
Liberty Maritime Co.
Norfolk Southern Corp.
Panda Energy Internat'l
Research Planning, Inc.
South Carolina Department of Transportation

NAPPI, Doug

801 Pennsylvania Ave. NW
Suite 630
Washington, DC 20004-5878
Tel: (202)347-4300
Fax: (202)347-4370
Registered: LDA
EMail: dnappi@nyse.com

Employers
New York Stock Exchange (Vice President, Government Relations)

NAPPI, Sarah

1150 18th St. NW
Ninth Floor
Washington, DC 20036
Tel: (202)296-3355
Fax: (202)296-3922
Registered: FARA
EMail: snappi@ablondifoster.com

Employers
Ablondi, Foster, Sobin & Davidow, P.C. (Associate)

NARASAKI, Karen K.

1140 Connecticut Ave. NW
Suite 1200
Washington, DC 20036
Tel: (202)296-2300
Fax: (202)296-2318

Employers
Nat'l Asian Pacific American Legal Consortium (Exec. Director)

NARDOTTI, Michael J.

2550 M St. NW
Washington, DC 20037-1350
Tel: (202)457-6000
Fax: (202)457-6315
Registered: LDA

Employers
Patton Boggs, LLP (Partner)

Clients Represented
On Behalf of Patton Boggs, LLP
Crane Co.

NARVAIZ, Laura

1331 Pennsylvania Ave. NW
Sixth Floor
Washington, DC 20004-1790
Tel: (202)637-3087
Fax: (202)637-3182
EMail: lnarvaiz@nam.org

Employers
Nat'l Ass'n of Manufacturers (V. President, Communications)

NASER, Cristeena G.

1120 Connecticut Ave. NW
Washington, DC 20036
Tel: (202)663-5000
Fax: (202)828-4548
Registered: LDA

Employers
American Bankers Ass'n (Senior Counsel)

NASH, Bernard

2101 L St. NW
Washington, DC 20037-1526
Tel: (202)785-9700
Fax: (202)887-0689
Registered: LDA
EMail: nashb@dsmo.com
Counsel, Subcommittee on Antitrust and Monopolies, Senate Judiciary Committee, 1971-77. Special Counsel, Securities and Exchange Commission, 1966-71.

Employers
Dickstein Shapiro Morin & Oshinsky LLP (Partner)

Clients Represented
On Behalf of Dickstein Shapiro Morin & Oshinsky LLP
DuPont
Exxon Valdez Oil Spill Litigation Plaintiffs
First USA Bank
Home Box Office
Poseidon Resources Corp.

NASH, James A.

1090 Vermont Ave. NW
Third Floor
Washington, DC 20005
Tel: (202)842-5000
Fax: (202)789-4293

Employers
Millian Byers Associates, LLC (Advisor, Social and Ecological Ethics)

NASH, Jr., John F.

910 16th St. NW
Suite 402
Washington, DC 20006
Tel: (202)775-0084
Fax: (202)775-0784
Registered: LDA

Employers
Milliken and Co. (Washington Counsel)

NASH, Pamela A.

2101 L St. NW
Suite 202
Washington, DC 20037
Tel: (202)857-0717
Fax: (202)887-5093

Employers
American Ass'n for Clinical Chemistry, Inc. (V. President, Policy and Programming)

NASHASHIBI, Omar

1133 21st St. NW
Suite 700
Washington, DC 20036
EMail: onashashibi@janus-merritt.com
Tel: (202)887-6900
Fax: (202)887-6970

Employers
Janus-Merritt Strategies, L.L.C. (Director, Research)

Clients Represented
On Behalf of Janus-Merritt Strategies, L.L.C.
Free ANWAR Campaign
Viejas Band of Kumeyaay Indians

NASSAR, Josh

601 13th St. NW
Suite 900 South
Washington, DC 20005
EMail: jnassar@bracywilliams.com
Tel: (202)783-5588
Fax: (202)783-5595

Employers
Bracy Williams & Co. (Associate)

Clients Represented
On Behalf of Bracy Williams & Co.
Allied Pilots Ass'n
FedEx Pilots Ass'n

NASSEF, David

409 12th St. SW
Suite 701
Washington, DC 20024-2191
Tel: (703)566-2307
Fax: (703)566-2311

Employers
Pitney Bowes, Inc. (V. President, Federal Relations)

NASSIF, Thomas A.

2213 M St. NW
Third Floor
Washington, DC 20037
Tel: (202)223-9333
Fax: (202)223-1399

Employers
American Task Force for Lebanon (Chairman)

NASSIRIAN, Barmak

One Dupont Circle NW
Suite 520
Washington, DC 20036-1171
EMail: nassirianb@aacrao.org
Tel: (202)293-9161
Fax: (202)872-8857
Former member, Panel on Alternative Student Loan Indices, Department of Education, 1999. Steering Committee, Project EASI, 1995.

Employers
American Ass'n of Collegiate Registrars and Admissions Officers (Associate Exec. Director)

NATALE, Patrick

1420 King St.
Alexandria, VA 22314-2794
EMail: pnatale@nspe.org
Tel: (703)684-2820
Fax: (703)836-4875

Employers
Nat'l Soc. of Professional Engineers (Exec. Director)

NATALIE, Ronald B.

901 15th St. NW
Suite 700
Washington, DC 20005-2301
EMail: rbnatalie@verner.com
Tel: (202)371-6000
Fax: (202)371-6279
Registered: LDA

Employers
Verner, Liipfert, Bernhard, McPherson and Hand, Chartered (Member of Firm)

NATHAN, Irvin B.

555 12th St. NW
Washington, DC 20004-1206
EMail: Irvin_Nathan@aporter.com
Tel: (202)942-5000
Fax: (202)942-5999
Special Minority Counsel, Senate Select Committee on Intelligence, 1981. Deputy Assistant Attorney General for Criminal Enforcement, Department of Justice, 1979-81. Law Clerk to Judge Simon Sobeloff, U.S. Court of Appeals, Fourth Circuit, 1967-68.

Employers
Arnold & Porter (Partner)

NATHANSON, Paul

2000 L St. NW
Suite 835
Washington, DC 20006
EMail: paul.nathanson@pbnco.com
Tel: (202)466-6210
Fax: (202)466-6205
Registered: FARA

Employers
PBN Company (V. President and Managing Director)

Clients Represented
On Behalf of PBN Company
Srpska, Government of the Republic of

NATIVIDAD, Amarie C.

419 Seventh St. NW
Suite 500
Washington, DC 20004
Tel: (202)626-8800
Fax: (202)737-9189

Employers
Nat'l Right to Life Committee (Controller)

NATSUME, Takeo

2501 M St. NW
Suite 350
Washington, DC 20037
Tel: (202)659-3729
Fax: (202)887-5159

Employers
Manufactured Imports Promotion Organization (MIPRO) (Director)

NAUSBAUM, Howard

1220 L St. NW
Suite 500
Washington, DC 20005
Tel: (202)371-6700
Fax: (202)289-8544

Employers
American Resort Development Ass'n (President)

NAVALON, Jose

1401 K St. NW
Suite 900
Washington, DC 20005
Tel: (202)626-8550
Fax: (202)626-8578

Employers
Jefferson Consulting Group (V. President)

NAVARRETE, Lisa

1111 19th St. NW
Suite 1000
Washington, DC 20036
Tel: (202)785-1670
Fax: (202)776-1792

Employers
Nat'l Council of La Raza (Deputy V. President, Public Information)

NAVARRO, Bruce C.

1742 N St. NW
Washington, DC 20036
Tel: (202)955-6006
Fax: (202)785-2210
Registered: LDA
Special Assistant (Legal) to V. Chair, Consumer Product Safety Commission, 1992-95. Deputy Assistant Attorney General, Office of Legislative Affairs, Department of Justice, 1990-91. Director, Office of Congressional Relations, Office of Personnel Management, 1986-89. Acting Deputy Under Secretary, Office of Legislative Affairs, Department of Labor, 1984-85.

Employers
Navarro Legislative & Regulatory Affairs (Principal)

Clients Represented
On Behalf of Navarro Legislative & Regulatory Affairs
Ass'n for Healthcare Philanthropy
Health Risk Management Group, Inc.

NAVARRO-BOWMAN, Chandri

1300 Pennsylvania Ave. NW
Suite 400
Ronald Reagan Bldg.
Washington, DC 20004
EMail: cnb@strtrade.com
Tel: (202)638-2230
Fax: (202)638-2236
Registered: LDA, FARA

Employers
Sandler, Travis & Rosenberg, P.A. (Member)

Clients Represented
On Behalf of Sandler, Travis & Rosenberg, P.A.
American Apparel & Footwear Ass'n
Consejo Nacional de Zonas Frarcas de Exportacion
Intradeco
Skipps Cutting
Tailored Clothing Ass'n
U.S. Apparel Industry Council

NAVIN, Allison

1775 I St. NW
Suite 800
Washington, DC 20006
EMail: allison.navin@enron.com
Tel: (202)466-9141
Fax: (202)828-3372

Employers
Enron Corp. (Manager, Federal Government Affairs)

NAY, Mary Alice

1600 21st St. NW
Washington, DC 20009-1090
Tel: (202)387-2151
Fax: (202)387-2436

Employers
The Phillips Collection (Director, Corporate Membership)

NAYBACK, Kyle T.

1441 L St. NW
Ninth Floor
Washington, DC 20005
Tel: (202)632-7003
Fax: (202)632-7006

Employers
Nat'l Indian Gaming Commission (Director, Congressional and Public Affairs)

NAYLOR, Michael W.

1808 I St. NW
Eighth Floor
Washington, DC 20006
Tel: (202)223-4817
Fax: (202)296-0011
Registered: LDA

Employers
Deere & Co. (V. President, Washington Affairs)

NEAL, Laura A.

700 13th St. NW
Suite 400
Washington, DC 20005
EMail: lneal@cassidy.com
Tel: (202)347-0773
Fax: (202)347-0785
Registered: LDA
Former Special Projects Staff Assistant to Senator Frank R. Lautenberg (D-NJ) and Rep. Peter W. Rodino (D-NJ).

Employers
Cassidy & Associates, Inc. (V. President)

Clients Represented
On Behalf of Cassidy & Associates, Inc.
Alfred University
American Film Institute
Babyland Family Services, Inc.
California Hospital Medical Center Foundation
Central Piedmont Community College
Fairfield University
Idaho State University
Immaculata College
Lorain County Community College
Marietta College
Memorial Health System
Miami-Dade Community College
Museum of Discovery and Science
Nat'l Jewish Medical and Research Center
Proctor Hospital
Saint Joseph's Health Center Foundation, Inc.
Summit Technology
University of Dubuque
University of the Sciences

NEAL, Michael

P.O. Box 1222
Sterling, VA 20167
Tel: (703)379-9188

Employers
Council of Volunteer Americans (Director, Field Operations)

NEALER, Kevin G.

900 17th St. NW
Suite 500
Washington, DC 20006
Tel: (202)296-9312
Fax: (202)296-9395
EMail: Nealer@scowcroft.com
Staff member, Senate Democratic Policy Committee, 1982-87. Bureau for International Organization Affairs, Department of State, 1980-82.

Employers
The Scowcroft Group (Principal)

NEALON, Robert B.

119 N. Henry St.
Third Floor
Alexandria, VA 22314-2903
Tel: (703)921-9111
Fax: (703)836-8009
Registered: LDA
EMail: CareyNelon@aol.com

Employers
CAREY/NEALON & Associates, L.L.C. (Co-Chairman)

NEAS, Katy Beh

700 13th St. NW
Suite 200
Washington, DC 20005
Tel: (202)347-3066
Fax: (202)737-7914
Registered: LDA
EMail: kneas@opa.easter-seals.org

Employers
Easter Seals (Assistant V. President, Government Relations)

NEAS, Ralph G.

2000 M St. NW
Suite 400
Washington, DC 20036
Tel: (202)467-4999
Fax: (202)293-2672

Employers
People for the American Way (President)

NECAR SULMER, Peter

2000 L St. NW
Suite 835
Washington, DC 20006
Tel: (202)466-6210
Fax: (202)466-6205

Employers
PBN Company (Chairman and Chief Exec. Officer)

NEDD, Council

112 West St.
Suite 400
Alexandria, VA 22204
Tel: (703)837-1384
Fax: (703)836-6550
Registered: LDA
EMail: cnedd@sumlinassociates.com

Employers
Sumlin Associates (Principal)

Clients Represented
On behalf of Sumlin Associates
The 60/Plus Ass'n, Inc.
The Anderson Group
Anglican Catholic Church
Council for Affordable Health Insurance

NEDELCOVYCH, Mimi

1050 17th St. NW
Suite 600
Washington, DC 20036
Tel: (202)496-1285
Fax: (202)496-9620
Registered: LDA

Employers
Africa Global Partners (Partner)

Clients Represented
On Behalf of Africa Global Partners
Equatorial Guinea, Republic of
Swaziland, Kingdom of

NEDELL, Jackie R.

1909 K St. NW
Fourth Floor
Washington, DC 20006
Tel: (202)973-5800
Fax: (202)973-5858
Former Communications Director to the Secretary, Department of Health and Human Services.

Employers
Porter/Novelli (V. President, MessageMark Media Services)

NEE, Amy B.

2099 Pennsylvania Ave. NW
Suite 100
Washington, DC 20006
Tel: (202)955-3000
Fax: (202)955-5564
Registered: LDA
EMail: abnee@hklaw.com

Employers
Holland & Knight LLP (Public Affairs Advisor)

Clients Represented
On Behalf of Holland & Knight LLP
Nat'l Coalition of Minority Businesses

NEE, Patrick

1120 Connecticut Ave. NW
Suite 1100
Washington, DC 20036
Tel: (202)861-5899
Fax: (202)861-5795
Registered: LDA
EMail: pnee@gpcusa.com
Staff Assistant to Senator Edward M. Kennedy (D-MA), 1993-97.

Employers
GPC Internat'l (Account Executive/Office Manager)

Clients Represented
On Behalf of GPC Internat'l
Country Hen
Hanover Capital Partners Ltd.

NEEDELS, Christopher

1440 Duke St.
Alexandria, VA 22314
Tel: (703)836-3495
Fax: (703)836-2843
EMail: cneedels@uspa.org

Employers
United States Parachute Ass'n (Exec. Director)

NEEL, Anne

2300 M St. NW
Suite 900
Washington, DC 20037
Tel: (202)467-2774
Fax: (202)293-5717
EMail: anne@publicforuminstitute.com

Employers
Public Forum Institute (Director)

NEELY, Susan

2450 N St. NW
Washington, DC 20037-1126
Tel: (202)828-0400
Fax: (202)828-1125

Employers
Ass'n of American Medical Colleges (Sr. V. President, Communications)

NEFF, Julie

1015 15th St. NW
Suite 1100
Washington, DC 20005
Tel: (202)488-7000
Fax: (202)488-0806
Registered: LDA
EMail: jneff@cwfa.org

Employers
Concerned Women for America (Legislative Coordinator)

NEGRONI, Andrea Lee

1717 Pennsylvania Ave. NW
Washington, DC 20006
Tel: (202)974-1000
Fax: (202)331-9330

Employers
Goodwin, Procter & Hoar LLP

NEHRA, DeAnne

P.O. Box 96920
Washington, DC 20090-6920
Tel: (202)638-5577
Fax: (202)863-4994

Employers
Council on Resident Education in Obstetrics and Gynecology (Associate Director)

NEHRING, Ron

1920 L St. NW
Suite 200
Washington, DC 20036
Tel: (202)785-0266
Fax: (202)785-0261
Registered: LDA
EMail: rnehring@atr-dc.org

Employers
Americans for Tax Reform (Senior Consultant)

NEIHARDT, Jonas

2000 K St. NW
Suite 375
Washington, DC 20036
Tel: (202)263-0000
Fax: (202)263-0010
Registered: LDA

Employers
Qualcomm Inc. (V. President, Government Affairs)

NEILSON, Mikol S.

901 15th St. NW
Suite 700
Washington, DC 20005-2301
Tel: (202)371-6000
Fax: (202)371-6279
Registered: LDA

Employers
Verner, Liipfert, Bernhard, McPherson and Hand, Chartered (Of Counsel)

Clients Represented
On Behalf of Verner, Liipfert, Bernhard, McPherson and Hand, Chartered
Lehman Brothers
RJR Nabisco Holdings Co.

NELLIGAN, William D.

9111 Old Georgetown Rd.
Bethesda, MD 20814-1699
Tel: (301)493-2360
Fax: (301)493-2376

Employers
American Soc. of Nuclear Cardiology (Exec. Director)

NELSEN, Dr. Peter T.

3114 Circle Hill Rd.
Alexandria, VA 22305-1606
Tel: (703)548-1234
Fax: (703)548-6216
EMail: nelsen@itctrade.com

Employers
Internat'l Trade Council (President)

NELSON, C. Richard

910 17th St. NW
Tenth Floor
Washington, DC 20006
Tel: (202)778-4969
Fax: (202)463-7241
EMail: CRnelson@acus.org

Employers
Atlantic Council of the United States (Director, International Security)

NELSON, Carl A.

1101 17th St. NW
Suite 600
Washington, DC 20036
Tel: (202)857-4246
Fax: (202)496-5660
Registered: LDA
EMail: carl.nelson@aa.com

Employers
American Airlines (Associate General Counsel)

NELSON, Cathy

919 18th St. NW
Suite 800
Washington, DC 20006
Tel: (202)628-4160
Fax: (202)347-5323

Employers
Human Rights Campaign Fund (Development Director)

NELSON, Charles A.

1101 15th St. NW
Suite 503
Washington, DC 20005
Tel: (202)785-3885
Fax: (202)785-3887
EMail: CNelson@Bunge.com

Employers
Bunge Corp. (V. President and Washington Representative)

NELSON, David

119 N. Henry St.
Third Floor
Alexandria, VA 22314-2903
EMail: careynelon@aol.com
Tel: (703)921-9111
Fax: (703)836-8009
Registered: LDA

Employers
CAREY/NEALON & Associates, L.L.C. (Senior Associate)

NELSON, David E.

750 First St. NE
Washington, DC 20002-4242
Tel: (202)336-5500
Fax: (202)336-6069

Employers
American Psychological Ass'n (Director, Federal Advocacy, Practice Directorate)

NELSON, David W.

400 N. Capitol St. NW
Suite 585
Washington, DC 20001
Tel: (202)237-8848
Fax: (202)393-5218
Registered: LDA

Employers
David Nelson & Associates (President)

Clients Represented
On Behalf of David Nelson & Associates
Barr Laboratories
Pfizer, Inc.

NELSON, Jr., Donald M.

1341 G St. NW
Suite 900
Washington, DC 20005
Tel: (202)637-1588
Fax: (202)637-1506

Employers
Philip Morris Management Corp. (V. President, International Trade Relations)

NELSON, E. Colette

1004 Duke St.
Alexandria, VA 22314-3588
Tel: (703)684-3450
Ext: 310
Fax: (703)836-3482
EMail: cnelson@asa-hq.com

Employers
American Subcontractors Ass'n, Inc. (Executive V. President)

NELSON, Edward I.

8180 Greensboro Dr.
Suite 1070
McLean, VA 22102
EMail: ednelson@usbc.org
Tel: (703)356-6568
Registered: LDA

Employers
U.S. Border Control (President)

NELSON, Eric

2500 Wilson Blvd.
Suite 300
Arlington, VA 22201
EMail: enelson@tia.eia.org
Tel: (703)907-7719
Fax: (703)907-7727
Registered: LDA

Employers
Telecommunications Industry Ass'n (V. President, Global Network Marketing)

NELSON, Greg

733 15th St. NW
Suite 700
Washington, DC 20005
EMail: greg@ctsg.com
Tel: (202)347-5280
Fax: (202)347-5283

Employers
Carol/Trevelyan Strategy Group (Director, DC Office)

NELSON, Joseph B.

1050 Thomas Jefferson St. NW
Seventh Floor
Washington, DC 20007
EMail: jbn@vnf.com
Tel: (202)298-1800
Fax: (202)338-2416
Registered: LDA

Employers
Van Ness Feldman, P.C. (Associate)

Clients Represented
On Behalf of Van Ness Feldman, P.C.
Delta Wetlands Project
Nat'l Endangered Species Act Reform Coalition

NELSON, Justin

1101 Vermont Ave. NW
Suite 700
Washington, DC 20005
EMail: jnelson@aaodc.org
Tel: (202)737-6662
Fax: (202)737-7061

Employers
American Academy of Ophthamology - Office of Federal Affairs (Washington Representative)

NELSON, Kathleen

1250 H St. NW
Suite 900
Washington, DC 20005
Tel: (202)737-4332
Fax: (202)331-7820
Registered: LDA

Employers
Internat'l Dairy Foods Ass'n (Director, Legislative Affairs)

NELSON, Lisa

1101 Connecticut Ave. NW
Suite 400
Washington, DC 20036-4303
Tel: (202)530-7878
Fax: (202)530-7879
Registered: LDA

Employers
AOL Time Warner (Director, Domestic Public Policy)

NELSON, Marian Barell

1350 I St. NW
Suite 400
Washington, DC 20005-3306
Tel: (202)371-6900
Fax: (202)842-3578
Registered: LDA

Employers
Motorola, Inc. (V. President and Director, Global Trade Policy)

NELSON, Mark D.

1300 Wilson Blvd.
Arlington, VA 22209
Tel: (703)741-5900
Fax: (703)741-6097
Registered: LDA
EMail: mark_nelson@americanchemistry.com

Employers
American Chemistry Council (V. President, Federal Relations)

NELSON, Maura

1201 New York Ave. NW
Suite 600
Washington, DC 20005-3931
EMail: mnelson@ahma.com
Tel: (202)289-3132
Fax: (202)289-3138

Employers
American Hotel and Lodging Ass'n (V. President, Communications and marketing)

NELSON, USAF (Ret), Lt. Gen. Michael A.

201 N. Washington St.
Alexandria, VA 22314
EMail: miken@troa.org
Tel: (800)245-8762
Fax: (703)838-8173
Registered: LDA

Employers
The Retired Officers Ass'n (TROA) (President)

NELSON, Patricia A.

1350 I St. NW
Suite 690
Washington, DC 20005
EMail: pnelson@ob-cgroup.com
Tel: (202)898-4746
Fax: (202)898-4756
Registered: LDA
Former Staff Member, House Ways and Means Committee.

Employers
The OB-C Group, LLC (Principal)

Clients Represented
On Behalf of The OB-C Group, LLC
American Airlines
Anheuser-Busch Cos., Inc.
AT&T
Biotechnology Industry Organization
Blue Cross Blue Shield Ass'n
Fannie Mae
Goodyear Tire and Rubber Co.
Healthcare Distribution Management Ass'n
Investment Co. Institute
Merrill Lynch & Co., Inc.
Motorola, Inc.
Nat'l Thoroughbred Racing Ass'n, Inc.
Newport News Shipbuilding Inc.
The Rouse Company
Sears, Roebuck and Co.
Securities Industry Ass'n
TIAA-CREF
United Parcel Service
WellPoint Health Networks/Blue Cross of California/UNICARE
Wilmer, Cutler & Pickering

NELSON, Paul

925 15th St. NW
Fifth Floor
Washington, DC 20006
Tel: (202)296-0784
Fax: (202)293-2768
Registered: LDA
EMail: pnelson@royerandbabyak.com
Former Staff Director, House Committee on Banking, Finance and Urban Affairs.

Employers
Royer & Babyak (Legislative Consultant)

Clients Represented
On Behalf of Royer & Babyak
Associated Credit Bureaus, Inc.
Tulane University

NELSON, Jr., Richard Y.

630 I St. NW
Washington, DC 20001-3736
Tel: (202)289-3500
Fax: (202)289-8181

Employers
Nat'l Ass'n of Housing and Redevelopment Officials (Exec. Director)

NELSON, Scott

420 C St. NE
Washington, DC 20002
Tel: (202)546-1086

Employers
Great Plains Leadership Fund

NELSON, Virginia

1010 N. Glebe Rd.
Suite 450
Arlington, VA 22201
Tel: (703)907-7900
Fax: (703)907-7901

Employers
Nat'l Newspaper Ass'n (Communications Director)

NELSON, William

1200 G St. NW
Suite 360
Washington, DC 20005
Tel: (202)783-2756
Ext: 123
Fax: (202)347-6341
Registered: LDA
EMail: bnelson@americanwineries.org

Employers
American Vintners Ass'n (V. President)

NELSON, William B.

13665 Dulles Technology Dr.
Suite 300
Herndon, VA 20171
EMail: bnelson@nacha.org
Tel: (703)561-1100
Fax: (703)787-0996

Employers
NACHA - The Electronic Payments Ass'n (Exec. V. President)

NEMEROFF, Michael A.

1722 I St. NW
Washington, DC 20006
Tel: (202)736-8000
Fax: (202)736-8711
EMail: mnemerof@sidley.com
Assistant Counsel, Subcommittee to Investigate Juvenile Delinquency, Senate Committee on the Judiciary, 1971-73.

Employers
Leadership for the Future (Treasurer)
Sidley & Austin (Partner)

Clients Represented

On Behalf of Sidley & Austin
American Medical Informatics Ass'n
Nat'l Community Pharmacists Ass'n
United States Cellular Corp.

NEMETZ, Miriam R.

1909 K St. NW
Washington, DC 20006
Tel: (202)263-3000
Fax: (202)263-3300
Registered: LDA

Former Associate Counsel to the President, The White House, during the Clinton administration.

Employers
Mayer, Brown & Platt (Partner)

Clients Represented

On Behalf of Mayer, Brown & Platt
Lockheed Martin Corp.
United Defense, L.P.
United Technologies Corp.

NEMTZOW, David M.

1200 18th St. NW
Suite 900
Washington, DC 20036
Tel: (202)857-0666
Fax: (202)331-9588
Registered: LDA

Employers
Alliance to Save Energy (President)

NESBITT, Elizabeth

919 18th St. NW
Suite 800
Washington, DC 20006
Tel: (202)628-4160
Fax: (202)347-5323

Employers
Human Rights Campaign Fund (Western Field Organizer)

NESLUND, Thomas R.

12501 Old Columbia Pike
Silver Spring, MD 20904-1600
EMail: 74617.2242@compuserve.com
Tel: (301)680-6719
Fax: (301)680-6090

Employers
Internat'l Commission for the Prevention of Alcoholism and Drug Dependency (Exec. Director)

NESS, Debra L.

1875 Connecticut Ave. NW
Suite 710
Washington, DC 20009
Tel: (202)986-2600
Fax: (202)986-2539

Employers
Nat'l Partnership for Women and Families (Exec. V. President)

NESSEL, Rudy R.

8403 Arlington Blvd.
Suite 100
Fairfax, VA 22031
EMail: rnessel@interfacinc.com
Tel: (703)876-6800
Fax: (703)876-0515

Employers
Interface Inc. (Chief Exec. Officer)

Clients Represented

On Behalf of Interface Inc.
Ecology and Environment
Reckitt Benckiser Professional

NESSEN, Ronald H.

1775 Massachusetts Ave. NW
Washington, DC 20036-2188
Tel: (202)797-6000
Fax: (202)797-6004

Employers
The Brookings Institution (V. President, Communications)

NESTEL, Daniel

One Dupont Circle NW
Suite 310
Washington, DC 20036
EMail: dnestel@ncaa.org
Tel: (202)293-3050
Fax: (202)293-3075
Registered: LDA

Employers
Nat'l Collegiate Athletic Ass'n (Sr. Assistant Director, Federal Relations)

NETCHVOLODOFF, Alexander V.

1225 19th St. NW
Suite 450
Washington, DC 20036
Tel: (202)296-4933
Fax: (202)296-4951
Registered: LDA

Employers
Cox Enterprises Inc. (V. President, Public Policy)

NEUBAUER, Julia

2320 S St. NW
Washington, DC 20008
Tel: (202)667-0441
Fax: (202)483-0994

Employers
The Textile Museum (Public Information Assistant)

NEUBERGER, Ed.D., J.D, Carmen G.

One Dupont Circle NW
Suite 300
Washington, DC 20036-1110
EMail: cgn@acpa.nche.edu
Tel: (202)835-2272
Fax: (202)296-3286

Employers
American College Personnel Ass'n (Exec. Director)

NEUENSCHWANDER, Tod O.

201 Maryland Ave. NE
Washington, DC 20002
Tel: (202)543-7200
Fax: (202)543-0616
Registered: LDA
EMail: tod@mgninc.com

Press Secretary (1975-84) and Chief of Staff (1984-90) to Senator James McClure (R-ID).

Employers
McClure, Gerard & Neuenschwander, Inc. (Principal)

Clients Represented

On Behalf of McClure, Gerard & Neuenschwander, Inc.
American Gaming Ass'n
Barrick Goldstrike Mines, Inc.
Boise State University
Brush Wellman, Inc.
Coachella Valley Water District
Echo Bay Mining
Family Farm Alliance (Project Transfer Council)
Harquehala Irrigation District
Hecla Mining Co.
Helli USA Airways
Henderson, Nevada, City of
Howard Hughes Corp.
Idaho Power Co.
Independence Mining Co., Inc.
Internat'l Bottled Water Ass'n
LC Technologies
Nat'l Endangered Species Act Reform Coalition
Native American Mohegans Inc.
Nevada Test Site Development Corp.
Newmont Mining Corp.
Pershing Co. Water Conservation District of Nevada
Placer Dome U.S. Inc.
Private Fuels Storage, L.L.C.
Quest Nevada, Inc.
Space Imaging, Inc.
Stirling Energy Systems
Verizon Wireless
Wellton-Mohawk Irrigation and Drainage District
Westlands Water District
The Williams Companies

NEUFVILLE, Mortimer H.

1307 New York Ave. NW
Suite 400
Washington, DC 20005-4722
Tel: (202)478-6040
Fax: (202)478-6046

Employers
Nat'l Ass'n of State Universities and Land-Grant Colleges (Exec. V. President)

NEUMAN, Robert A.

1317 F St. NW
Suite 900
Washington, DC 20004
EMail: neumanco@aol.com
Tel: (202)628-2075
Fax: (202)628-2077
Registered: LDA

Former Press Secretary, Campaign Advisor and Chief of Staff to Rep. Morris Udall (D-AZ).

Employers
Neuman and Co. (President)

Clients Represented

On Behalf of Neuman and Co.
Amgen
Center for Deliberative Polling
The Economist Newspaper Group
Episcopal Diocese of Washington
The Frontier Press
Johns Hopkins Center for Gun Policy and Research
Joyce Foundation
Kids Voting USA
Nat'l Center on Addiction and Substance Abuse
Pew Center for Civic Journalism
White Mountain Apache Tribe

NEUMANN, E. John

701 Pennsylvania Ave. NW
Washington, DC 20004-2696
Tel: (202)508-5446
Fax: (202)508-5403
Registered: LDA

Former Staffer, Republican Policy Committee. Former Minority Staffer, House Appropriations Committee.

Employers
Edison Electric Institute (V. President, Government Affairs)

NEUMANN, Joanne Snow

400 N. Capitol St. NW
Suite 388
Washington, DC 20001
Tel: (202)624-7704
Fax: (202)624-7707

Employers
Utah, State of (Director, Washington Office)

NEUMANN, Thomas

1717 K St. NW
Suite 800
Washington, DC 20006
EMail: info@jinsa.org
Tel: (202)833-0020
Fax: (202)296-6452

Employers
Jewish Institute for Nat'l Security Affairs (Exec. Director)

NEVE, Maria F.

915 15th St. NW
Suite 600
Washington, DC 20005-2302
EMail: mneve@dorfmanoneal.com
Tel: (202)393-8444
Ext: 108
Fax: (202)393-8666

Employers
Dorfman & O'Neal, Inc. (Program Manager)

Clients Represented

On Behalf of Dorfman & O'Neal, Inc.
American Honda Motor Co., Inc.
FuelMaker Corp.

NEVINS, Louis H.

1301 Pennsylvania Ave. NW
Suite 500
Washington, DC 20004
EMail: nevinslh@aol.com
Tel: (202)737-5113
Fax: (202)737-6017
Registered: LDA

Employers
Western League of Savings Institutions (President)

NEVINS, Patrick

555 13th St. NW
Washington, DC 20004-1109
EMail: jpnevins@hhlaw.com
Tel: (202)637-6441
Fax: (202)637-5910
Registered: LDA

Employers
Hogan & Hartson L.L.P. (Associate)

Clients Represented

On Behalf of Hogan & Hartson L.L.P.
Public Service Co. of Colorado

NEW, Barry

14850 Conference Center Dr.
Suite 100
Chantilly, VA 20151-3831
EMail: barry.new@rollsroyce.com
Tel: (703)621-2850
Fax: (703)621-4989
Registered: LDA

Employers
Rolls-Royce North America Inc. (Senior V. President, Government Relations)

NEWBERGER, Stuart

1001 Pennsylvania Ave. NW
Suite 1100
Washington, DC 20004-2595
Tel: (202)624-2500
Fax: (202)628-5116
Registered: LDA

Employers
Crowell & Moring LLP

Clients Represented
On Behalf of Crowell & Moring LLP
Kenya Bombing Families

NEWBERRY, Edward J.

2550 M St. NW
Washington, DC 20037-1350
Tel: (202)457-6000
Fax: (202)457-6315
Registered: LDA
EMail: enewberry@pattonboggs.com
Appropriations Staff and Press Secretary to Rep. Frank Wolf (R-VA), 1984-91.

Employers
Patton Boggs, LLP (Partner)

Clients Represented
On Behalf of Patton Boggs, LLP
Coalition for Electronic Commerce
Coalition for Fair Competition in Rural Markets
Denver Regional Transportation District
DFS Group Ltd.
Dimensions Internat'l
Federal Communications Bar Ass'n
George Mason University Foundation
Illinois Department of Human Services
Internat'l Swaps and Derivatives Dealers Ass'n
Jacksonville, Florida, City of
Laquidara & Edwards, P.A.
Mannesmann VDO
Nat'l Center for Manufacturing Sciences
Nat'l Oilheat Research Alliance (NORA)
Shreveport, Louisiana, City of
The Charles E. Smith Companies
Travel Industry Ass'n of America
Valley Children's Hospital
Ventura County Citizens Against Radar Emissions (VCCARE)

NEWBORN, Steven A.

607 14th St. NW
Washington, DC 20005
Tel: (202)434-0700
Fax: (202)912-6000
EMail: newborns@rw.com
Director of Litigation (1991-94) and Assistant Director for Litigation (1988-91), Bureau of Competition, Federal Trade Commission. Special Assistant U.S. Attorney, Criminal Division, Eastern District of Virginia, U.S. Attorney's Office, Department of Justice, 1982-84.

Employers
Rogers & Wells (Partner, Anti-Trust Division)

NEWBOULD, E. Jack

206 Vassar Pl.
Alexandria, VA 22314
Tel: (703)370-5750

Employers
Nat'l Clay Pipe Institute (Corporate Counsel)

NEWBOULD, Peter E.

750 First St. NE
Washington, DC 20002-4242
Tel: (202)336-5800
Fax: (202)336-5797
Registered: LDA

Employers
American Psychological Ass'n (Director, Congressional Affairs)

NEWBURG, Janice

1360 Beverly Rd.
Suite 201
McLean, VA 22101
Tel: (703)448-1000
Fax: (703)790-3460

Employers
DeHart and Darr Associates, Inc.

NEWCOMBE, Anne

1385 Piccard Dr.
Rockville, MD 20850-4340
Tel: (301)869-5800
Fax: (301)990-9690
EMail: anewcombe@mcaa.org

Employers
Mechanical Contractors Ass'n of America (Director, Communications)

NEWCOMER WILLIAMS, Mary

1201 Pennsylvania Ave. NW
Washington, DC 20004-2401
Tel: (202)662-6000
Fax: (202)662-6291
Registered: LDA
EMail: mwilliams@cov.com

Employers
Covington & Burling (Associate)

NEWHOUSE, Neil S.

277 S. Washington St.
Suite 320
Alexandria, VA 22314
Tel: (703)836-7655
Fax: (703)836-8117
EMail: newhouse@pos.org

Employers
Public Opinion Strategies (Partner)

Clients Represented
On Behalf of Public Opinion Strategies
Cellular Telecommunications and Internet Ass'n

NEWLAND, Dee E. "Ned"

1301 K St. NW
Washington, DC 20005-3333
Tel: (202)414-1000
Fax: (202)414-1301
Registered: LDA
Former Economist, Congressional Committee on Taxation, U.S. Congress.

Employers
PriceWaterhouseCoopers (Manager, Tax Policy Economics)

NEWMAN, Colleen

1025 Thomas Jefferson St. NW
Eighth Floor, West Tower
Washington, DC 20007
Tel: (202)342-0800
Fax: (202)342-0807
EMail: cnewman@bbrslaw.com

Employers
Brickfield, Burchette, Ritts & Stone (Government Relations Advisor)

Clients Represented
On Behalf of Brickfield, Burchette, Ritts & Stone
American Medical Technologists
Arizona Power Authority
Arvin-Edison Water Storage District
Colorado River Water Conservation District
East Texas Electric Cooperative
Merced Irrigation District
Northeast Texas Electric Cooperative
Sam Rayburn G&T Electric Cooperative, Inc.
Tex-La Electric Cooperative of Texas

NEWMAN, Helen L.

1000 Wilson Blvd.
Suite 2701
Arlington, VA 22209
Tel: (703)276-9500
Fax: (703)276-9504

Employers
Gulfstream Aerospace Corp. (Senior V. President, Government Operations)

NEWMAN, Karol Lyn

555 13th St. NW
Washington, DC 20004-1109
Tel: (202)637-5786
Fax: (202)637-5910
Registered: LDA
EMail: klnewman@hhlaw.com

Employers
Hogan & Hartson L.L.P. (Partner)

Clients Represented
On Behalf of Hogan & Hartson L.L.P.
Public Service Co. of Colorado

NEWMAN, Melissa

1020 19th St. NW
Washington, DC 20036
Tel: (202)429-3121
Fax: (202)293-0561

Employers
Qwest Communications (V. President, Regulatory Affairs)

NEWMAN, Michael

408 C St. NE
Washington, DC 20002
Tel: (202)547-1141
Fax: (202)547-6009

Employers
Sierra Club (National Political Representative)

NEWMAN, William A.

8400 W. Park Dr.
McLean, VA 22102
Tel: (703)821-7000
Fax: (703)821-7030

Employers
Nat'l Automobile Dealers Ass'n (Chief Legal Counsel)

NEWMAN, Jr., William B.

1000 Connecticut Ave. NW
Suite 302
McLean, VA 20036
Tel: (202)835-0740
Registered: LDA
Professional Staff Member, House Committee on Energy and Commerce, 1978-81.

Employers
Self-employed as an independent consultant.

Clients Represented
As an independent consultant
Americans for Equitable Climate Solutions

NEWMASTER, Carol

2300 Clarendon Blvd.
Suite 711
Arlington, VA 22201
Tel: (703)522-5717
Fax: (703)527-7251
EMail: atca@worldnet.att.net

Employers
Air Traffic Control Ass'n (Senior V. President)

NEWPHER, Richard W.

600 Maryland Ave. SW
Suite 800
Washington, DC 20024
Tel: (202)484-3600
Fax: (202)484-3604
Registered: LDA

Employers
American Farm Bureau Federation (Exec. Director, Washington Office)

NEWSOME, Robert "Bo"

1025 Connecticut Ave. NW
Suite 700
Washington, DC 20036
Tel: (202)785-8866
Fax: (202)835-0003

Employers
Nat'l Ass'n of Independent Colleges and Universities (Outreach Coordinator)

NEWSON, Graham H.

601 13th St. NW
Suite 400 North
Washington, DC 20005
Tel: (202)347-8600
Fax: (202)393-6137
Registered: LDA
EMail: gnewson@aap.org

Employers
American Academy of Pediatrics (Director, Government Liaison)

NEWTON, Elisabeth G.

8370 Greensboro Dr.
Suite 4-814
McLean, VA 22102
Tel: (703)827-9597
Fax: (703)893-9557
EMail: e.g.newton@worldnet.att
Served in the Department of Interior as fossil fuel program manager and policy advisor, 1980-87.

Employers
Self-employed as an independent consultant.

Clients Represented
As an independent consultant
Morgan Stanley Dean Witter & Co.

NEWTON, Hugh C.

214 Massachusetts Ave. NE
Suite 520
Washington, DC 20002
Tel: (202)608-6150
Fax: (202)544-6979

Employers
Hugh C. Newton & Assoc. (President)

Clients Represented
On Behalf of Hugh C. Newton & Assoc.
Heritage Foundation

NEWTON, Susan

805 15th St. NW
Suite 300
Washington, DC 20005-2207
Tel: (202)682-4200
Fax: (202)682-9054

Employers
Credit Union Nat'l Ass'n, Inc. (Senior V. President, League Services)

NEWTON, Vanessa

1850 M St. NW
Suite 700
Washington, DC 20036
Tel: (202)721-4100
Fax: (202)296-8548

Employers
Synthetic Organic Chemical Manufacturers Ass'n (Manager, Communications)

NEZER, Melanie R.

1717 Massachusetts Ave. NW
Suite 200
Washington, DC 20036
Tel: (202)797-2105
Fax: (202)797-2363
Registered: LDA
EMail: mnezer@irsa-uscr.org

Employers
Immigration and Refugee Service of America (Attorney)

NGUYEN, H. T.

1201 16th St. NW
Washington, DC 20036
Tel: (202)822-7850
Fax: (202)822-7867

Employers
Federal Education Ass'n (Exec. Director and General Counsel)

NGUYEN, Mark D.

601 13th St. NW
Suite 600 South
Washington, DC 20005
Tel: (202)626-3600
Fax: (202)639-9355
EMail: nuyema@washdc.whitecase.com

Employers
White & Case LLP (Director, Multilateral Trade Service)

NGUYEN, Natalie D.

1130 Connecticut Ave. NW
Suite 1000
Washington, DC 20036
Tel: (202)828-7100
Fax: (202)293-1219

Employers
American Insurance Ass'n (Assistant V. President, Federal Affairs)

NI, Ph.D., Chuanliu

601 Pennsylvania Ave. NW
Suite 900
Washington, DC 20004
Tel: (202)547-3566
Fax: (202)639-8238

Employers
Cottone and Huggins Group (Senior V. President, Economics and International Finance)

NIBLETT, Robin

1800 K St. NW
Washington, DC 20005
Tel: (202)775-3226
Fax: (202)775-3199
EMail: rniblett@csis.org

Employers
Center for Strategic and Internat'l Studies (V. President, Strategic Planning and Senior Fellow, Europe Program)

NICELY, Matthew

Three Lafayette Center
1155 21st St. NW
Washington, DC 20036-3384
Tel: (202)328-8000
Fax: (202)887-8979

Employers
Willkie Farr & Gallagher (Associate Attorney)

Clients Represented
On Behalf of Willkie Farr & Gallagher
Meat and Livestock Australia

NICHOLAS, Michael

1399 New York Ave. NW
Eighth Floor
Washington, DC 20005-4711
Tel: (202)434-8400
Fax: (202)434-8456
EMail: mnicholas@bondmarkets.com
District Field Representative to Rep. Don Sundquist (R-TN), 1991-93.

Employers
The Bond Market Ass'n (Director, Issues Relations and Grassroots Programs)

NICHOLAS, Robert B.

600 13th St. NW
Washington, DC 20005-3096
Tel: (202)756-8170
Fax: (202)756-8087
Registered: LDA
EMail: rnicholas@mwe.com
Chief Counsel and Staff Director, Subcommittee on Investigations and Oversight, House Committee on Science and Technology, 1982-85. Senior Staff Member for Toxic Substances and Environmental Health, President's Council on Environmental Quality, The White House, 1977-81.

Employers
McDermott, Will and Emery (Partner)

Clients Represented
On Behalf of McDermott, Will and Emery
Bayer Corp. / Agriculture Division
Respiratory Medication Providers Coalition

NICHOLS, David

805 15th St. NW
Suite 700
Washington, DC 20005
Tel: (202)312-7400
Fax: (202)312-7441
Registered: LDA
EMail: dcnichol@bakerd.com

Employers
Sagamore Associates, Inc. (V. President)

Clients Represented
On Behalf of Sagamore Associates, Inc.
American Nuclear Soc.
Arthritis Foundation
Autism Soc. of America, Inc.
Hill-Rom Co., Inc.
Indiana State University
Indianapolis Public Transportation Corp.
Nat'l Sleep Foundation
Northern Indiana Commuter Transportation District
Nuclear Energy Institute
TRANSPO
Union Hospital

NICHOLS, David A.

1130 Connecticut Ave. NW
Suite 600
Washington, DC 20036
Tel: (202)296-0263
Fax: (202)452-9370
Registered: FARA

Employers
Nichols-Dezenhall Communication Management Group, Ltd. (Chairman)

Clients Represented
On Behalf of Nichols-Dezenhall Communication Management Group, Ltd.
Meat Industry Council

NICHOLS, Frederic A.

1331 Pennsylvania Ave. NW
Sixth Floor
Washington, DC 20004-1790
Tel: (202)637-3039
Fax: (202)637-3182
Registered: LDA
EMail: fnichols@nam.org

Employers
Nat'l Ass'n of Manufacturers (V. President, Public Affairs and Political Director)

NICHOLS, Holly B.

801 Pennsylvania Ave. NW
Suite 620
Washington, DC 20004-2604
Tel: (202)783-7220
Fax: (202)783-8127
EMail: holly_b_nichols@reliantenergy.com

Employers
Reliant Energy, Inc. (Manager, Federal Relations)

NICHOLS, Johnnie

2101 Wilson Blvd.
Suite 400
Arlington, VA 22201
Tel: (703)243-6111
Fax: (703)841-9328
EMail: jnichols@nmpf.org

Employers
Nat'l Milk Producers Federation (Director, Technical Services)

NICHOLS, Julie L.

1101 17th St. NW
Suite 600
Washington, DC 20036
Tel: (202)496-5649
Fax: (202)496-5660
Registered: LDA
EMail: julie.nichols@aa.com

Employers
American Airlines (Managing Director, Government Affairs)

NICHOLS, Len

2100 M St. NW
Washington, DC 20037
Tel: (202)833-7200
Fax: (202)429-0687

Employers
The Urban Institute (Principal Research Associate, Health Policy Center)

NICHOLS, Marshall W.

1625 K St. NW
Suite 600
Washington, DC 20006
Tel: (202)393-6100
Fax: (202)331-8539
EMail: mnichols@npc.org

Employers
Nat'l Petroleum Council (Exec. Director)

NICHOLS, W. John

1100 Wilson Blvd.
Suite 1500
Arlington, VA 22209
Tel: (703)841-5723
Fax: (703)841-5792
Registered: LDA
EMail: w_john_nichols@raytheon.com

Employers
Raytheon Co. (V. President, Defense Programs and Congressional Relations)

NICHOLSON, Anne

1801 K St. NW
Suite 601 L
Washington, DC 20006
Tel: (202)756-7100
Fax: (202)756-7200
EMail: anne_nicholson@was.cohnwolfe.com

Employers
Cohn & Wolfe (V. President)

NICHOLSON, E. Bruce

740 15th St. NW
Ninth Floor
Washington, DC 20005
Tel: (202)662-1769
Fax: (202)662-1762
Registered: LDA

Employers
American Bar Ass'n (Legislative Counsel)

NICHOLSON, Richard S.

1200 New York Ave. NW
Washington, DC 20005
Tel: (202)326-6400
Fax: (202)371-9526

Employers
American Ass'n for the Advancement of Science (Exec. Officer)

NICKEL, Henry V.

1900 K St. NW
Washington, DC 20006-1109
Tel: (202)955-1500
Fax: (202)778-2201
Registered: LDA
EMail: hnickel@hunton.com

Employers
Hunton & Williams (Partner)

Clients Represented
On Behalf of Hunton & Williams
Clean Air Regulatory Information Group
Edison Electric Institute
Utility Air Regulatory Group

NICKEL, Leslie A.

555 12th St. NW
Washington, DC 20004-1206
Tel: (202)942-5000
Fax: (202)942-5999
Registered: LDA
EMail: Leslie_Nickel@aporter.com

Employers
Arnold & Porter (Associate)

NICKELSON, Daniel E.

2000 L St. NW
Suite 200
Washington, DC 20036
Tel: (202)861-0955
Fax: (202)872-0834
Registered: LDA
EMail: nickeld@ccf.org

Employers
Cleveland Clinic Foundation (Director, Government Affairs)
North American Soc. of Pacing and Electrophysiology (Government Relations Liaison)

NICKENS, Jacqueline

1399 New York Ave. NW
Suite 900
Washington, DC 20005
Tel: (202)585-5800
Fax: (202)585-5820
Registered: LDA

Employers
American Internat'l Group, Inc. (Receptionist, Government Affairs)

NICKERSON, William

1666 K St. NW
Suite 500
Washington, DC 20006-2803
Tel: (202)887-1400
Fax: (202)466-2198
Registered: LDA

Employers
O'Connor & Hannan, L.L.P.

Clients Represented
On Behalf of O'Connor & Hannan, L.L.P.
UBS Warburg

NICKLAS, Bob

80 F St. NW
Washington, DC 20001
Tel: (202)639-6457
Fax: (202)639-6490

Employers
American Federation of Government Employees (AFL-CIO) (PAC Director)

NICKLES, Peter J.

1201 Pennsylvania Ave. NW
Washington, DC 20004-2401
EMail: pnickles@cov.com
Tel: (202)662-6000
Fax: (202)662-6291

Employers
Covington & Burling (Partner)

Clients Represented
On Behalf of Covington & Burling
Bazelon Center for Mental Health Law, Judge David L.

NICKLES, Thomas P.

325 Seventh St. NW
Washington, DC 20004
Tel: (202)638-1100
Fax: (202)626-2254
Registered: LDA

Employers
American Hospital Ass'n (Senior V. President, Federal Relations)

NICKSON, Ronald G.

1850 M St. NW
Suite 540
Washington, DC 20036
Tel: (202)974-2300
Fax: (202)775-0112

Employers
Nat'l Multi-Housing Council (V. President, Building Codes)

NICOLAS, Suzanne

601 13th St. NW
Suite 570 South
Washington, DC 20005-3807
EMail: snicolas@amseed.org
Tel: (202)638-3128
Fax: (202)638-3171

Employers
American Seed Research Foundation (Secretary)
American Seed Trade Ass'n (Director, Programs and Services)
Nat'l Council of Commercial Plant Breeders (Secretary)

NICOLL, David L.

1724 Massachusetts Ave. NW
Washington, DC 20036-1969
Tel: (202)775-3550
Fax: (202)775-3603
Registered: LDA

Employers
Nat'l Cable Television Ass'n (Associate General Counsel)

NICOLL, Eric

655 15th St. NW
Washington, DC 20005-5701
EMail: enicoll@fmi.org
Tel: (202)220-0626
Fax: (202)220-0873
Registered: LDA

Employers
Food Marketing Institute (Director, Government Relations)

NICOLL, Jill D.

1101 17th St. NW
Suite 1102
Washington, DC 20036
Tel: (202)785-4500
Fax: (202)785-3539

Employers
Nat'l Park Foundation (Exec. V. President)

NIDER, Steven

600 Pennsylvania Ave. SE
Suite 400
Washington, DC 20003
Tel: (202)547-0001
Fax: (202)544-5014

Employers
Progressive Policy Institute (Director, Foreign Policy and Defense Working Groups)

NIEDRINGHAUS, Stephanie

801 Pennsylvania Ave. SE
Suite 460
Washington, DC 20003
EMail: network@networklobby.org
Tel: (202)547-5556
Fax: (202)547-5510

Employers
NETWORK, A Nat'l Catholic Social Justice Lobby (Communications Coordinator)

NIEHOFF, Jodi

400 N. Capitol St. NW
Suite 790
Washington, DC 20001
Tel: (202)554-1600
Fax: (202)554-1654
Registered: LDA

Employers
Nat'l Farmers Union (Farmers Educational & Co-operative Union of America) (Government Relations Representative)

NIELDS, Jr., John

1299 Pennsylvania Ave. NW
Washington, DC 20004-2402
Tel: (202)783-0800
Fax: (202)383-6610

Employers
Howrey Simon Arnold & White (Partner)

NIELSEN, Catherine R.

1001 G St. NW
Suite 500 West
Washington, DC 20001
EMail: nielsen@khlaw.com
Tel: (202)434-4100
Fax: (202)434-4646
Registered: FARA

Employers
Keller and Heckman LLP (Partner)

NIELSEN, Louisa A.

1771 N St. NW
Washington, DC 20036
EMail: lnielsen@nab.org
Tel: (202)429-5354
Fax: (202)775-2981

Employers
Broadcast Education Ass'n (Exec. Director)

NIELSON, Scott K.

One Massachusetts Ave. NW
Suite 300
Washington, DC 20001
EMail: sknielson@tva.gov
Tel: (202)898-2999
Fax: (202)898-2998

Employers
Tennessee Valley Authority - Washington Office (Representative)

NIERO, Christine

8201 Greensboro Dr.
Suite 300
McLean, VA 22102
EMail: cniero@amg-inc.com
Tel: (703)610-9000
Fax: (703)610-9005

Employers
Ass'n Management Group

Clients Represented
On Behalf of Ass'n Management Group
Nat'l Certification Board for Therapeutic Massage and Bodywork

NIKPOURFAND, Dariush "Nick"

1385 Piccard Dr.
Rockville, MD 20850-4340
EMail: nnikpourfand@mcaa.org
Tel: (301)869-5800
Fax: (301)990-9690

Employers
Mechanical Contractors Ass'n of America (Exec. Director, NCPWB)
Nat'l Certified Pipe Welding Bureau (Exec. Director)

NILLES, Kathleen M.

1301 K St. NW
Suite 900
East Tower
Washington, DC 20005
EMail: knilles@dc.gcd.com
Tel: (202)408-7100
Fax: (202)289-1504
Registered: LDA
Tax Counsel, House Ways and Means Committee, 1990-95.

Employers
Gardner, Carton and Douglas (Partner)

Clients Represented
On Behalf of Gardner, Carton and Douglas
American Council on Education
The Council of Insurance Agents & Brokers
Nat'l Indian Gaming Ass'n
Partnership Defense Fund Trust
VHA Inc.

NILSEN, Michael

1101 King St.
Suite 700
Alexandria, VA 22314
EMail: mnilsen@afpnet.org
Tel: (703)684-0410
Fax: (703)684-0540
Registered: LDA

Employers
Ass'n of Fund Raising Professionals (Manager, Public Affairs)

NIOUS, Lionel

1101 14th St. NW
Suite 405
Washington, DC 20005
Tel: (202)289-7661
Fax: (202)289-7724

Employers
Nat'l Health Law Program (Administrative Assistant)

NIPP, Terry

236 Massachusetts Ave. NE
Suite 400
Washington, DC 20002
Tel: (202)675-4511
Fax: (202)675-4512
Registered: LDA

Employers
AESOP Enterprises, Ltd. (President)

Clients Represented
On Behalf of AESOP Enterprises, Ltd.
Internat'l Committee on Organization & Policy

NIPPER, James J.

2301 M St. NW
Washington, DC 20037-1484
EMail: jnipper@APPAnet.org
Tel: (202)467-2931
Fax: (202)467-2910
Registered: LDA

Employers
American Public Power Ass'n (Senior V. President, Government Relations)

NIRENBERG, Darryl D.

2550 M St. NW
Washington, DC 20037-1350
EMail: dnirenberg@pattonboggs.com
Tel: (202)457-6000
Fax: (202)457-6315
Registered: LDA
Chief of Staff to Senator Jesse Helms (R-NC), 1991-95. Deputy Staff Director (1990-91), Associate Minority Counsel (1989-90), and Professional Staff Member (1987-88), Foreign Relations Committee, U.S. Senate. Professional Staff Member, Committee on Agriculture, Nutrition and Forestry, U.S. Senate, 1983-87. Legislative Assistant to Senator S. I. Hayakawa (R-NC), 1981-82.

Employers
Patton Boggs, LLP (Partner)

Clients Represented

On Behalf of Patton Boggs, LLP

American Management
Ass'n of Trial Lawyers of America
Barringer Technologies
Condor-Pacific Industries
L. P. Conwood Co.
Discovery Place, Inc. (Charlotte Science Museum)
Electro Design Manufacturing, Inc.
Gilbarco, Inc.
Information Technology Ass'n of America (ITAA)
Mars, Inc.
G. Murphy Trading
Nat'l Ass'n of Consumer Bankruptcy Attorneys
Nat'l Soft Drink Ass'n
Point of Purchase Advertising Institute
QSP Inc.
Security Capital Group

NIRENBERG, Lori H.

1100 Wilson Blvd.
Suite 1500
Arlington, VA 22209
EMail: lori_h_nirenberg@raytheon.com
Tel: (703)841-5731
Fax: (703)841-5792
Registered: LDA

Employers

Raytheon Co. (Director, Congressional Relations, Tax and Trade Issues)

NISBET, Miriam M.

1301 Pennsylvania Ave. NW
Suite 403
Washington, DC 20004
EMail: mmn@alawash.org
Tel: (202)628-8410
Fax: (202)628-8419
Registered: LDA

Employers

American Library Ass'n (Legislative Counsel)

NISKANEN, William A.

1000 Massachusetts Ave. NW
Washington, DC 20001
Tel: (202)842-0200
Fax: (202)842-3490

Employers

Cato Institute (Chairman)

NISSALKE, Alan

1133 15th St. NW
Suite 640
Washington, DC 20005
Tel: (202)466-2520
Fax: (202)296-4419

Employers

American Logistics Ass'n (V. President, Government Relations and Commissary Affairs)

NISSENBAUM, Beverly

One Prince St.
Alexandria, VA 22314-3357
EMail: bnissen@entnet.org
Tel: (703)836-4444
Fax: (703)683-5100
Registered: LDA

Employers

American Academy of Otolaryngology-Head and Neck Surgery (Director, Department of Health Policy and Government Affairs)

NISSENBAUM, Ellen

820 First St. NE
Suite 510
Washington, DC 20002
EMail: nissenbaum@center.cbpp.org
Tel: (202)408-1080
Fax: (202)408-1056
Registered: LDA

Employers

Center on Budget and Policy Priorities (Legislative Director)

NIVOLA, Pietro S.

1775 Massachusetts Ave. NW
Washington, DC 20036-2188
Tel: (202)797-6000
Fax: (202)797-6004

Employers

The Brookings Institution (Senior Fellow, Governmental Studies)

NIX, Clayton J.

1227 25th St. NW
Suite 700
Washington, DC 20037
EMail: cnix@ebglaw.com
Tel: (202)861-0900
Fax: (202)296-2882
Registered: LDA

Employers

Epstein Becker & Green, P.C. (Associate)

NIX, Michael E.

1545 18th St. NW
Suite 711
Washington, DC 20036
Tel: (202)234-1086
Fax: (202)234-1088
Registered: LDA

Employers

Michael E. Nix Consulting (President)

Clients Represented

On Behalf of Michael E. Nix Consulting

Distributed Power Coalition of America

NIXON, Duncan A.

1707 L St. NW
Suite 725
Washington, DC 20036
EMail: customs@sharretts-paley
Tel: (202)223-4433
Fax: (202)659-3904
Registered: LDA

Employers

Sharretts, Paley, Carter and Blauvelt

Clients Represented

On Behalf of Sharretts, Paley, Carter and Blauvelt

Toy Manufacturers of America

NIXON, William

1620 I St. NW
Suite 800
Washington, DC 20006
Tel: (202)833-9070
Fax: (202)833-9612

Employers

Generic Pharmaceutical Ass'n (President and C.E.O.)

NIZANKIEWICZ, Mike

8201 Greensboro Dr.
Suite 300
McLean, VA 22102
Tel: (703)610-9000
Fax: (703)610-9005

Employers

Ass'n Management Group

Clients Represented

On Behalf of Ass'n Management Group

Nat'l Ass'n of Mortgage Brokers

NOACK, William H.

1660 L St. NW
Fourth Floor
Washington, DC 20036
Tel: (202)775-5008
Fax: (202)775-5095
Registered: LDA

Employers

General Motors Corp. (Director, Regional Offices, Corporate Communications)

NOBLE, Bethany

1133 21st St. NW
Suite 700
Washington, DC 20036
EMail: bnoble@janus-merritt.com
Tel: (202)887-6900
Fax: (202)887-6970
Registered: LDA

Employers

Janus-Merritt Strategies, L.L.C. (Principal, Campaign Finance Director)

Clients Represented

On Behalf of Janus-Merritt Strategies, L.L.C.

AFIN Securities
American Business for Legal Immigration
CEMEX Central, S.A. de C.V.
EchoStar Communications Corp.
First Amendment Coalition for Expression
Interactive Gaming Council
Interactive Services Ass'n
Nat'l Indian Gaming Ass'n
Scribe Communications, Inc.
Secured Access Portals, Inc.
Szlavik, Hogan & Miller
Viejas Band of Kumeyaay Indians
Vivendi Universal

NOBLE, Lawrence M.

1101 14th St. NW
Suite 1030
Washington, DC 20005-5635
Tel: (202)857-0044
Fax: (202)857-7809

General Counsel (1987-2000); Deputy General Counsel (1983-87); Assistant General Counsel (1979-83); and Litigation Attorney (1977-79), all with the Federal Election Commission.

Employers

Center for Responsive Politics (Exec. Director and General Counsel)

NOCERA, Barbara

1025 Connecticut Ave. NW
Suite 910
Washington, DC 20036
Tel: (202)467-5088
Registered: LDA

Employers

Mazda North America Operations (Director, Government and Industry Affairs)

NOE, A. Allan

1156 15th St. NW
Suite 400
Washington, DC 20005
Tel: (202)296-1585
Fax: (202)463-0474
Registered: LDA

Employers

American Crop Protection Ass'n (V. President, State Affairs, Biotechnology and Water Programs)

NOE, Jeff

8200 Jones Branch Dr.
McLean, VA 22102
EMail: jeff_noe@freddiemac.com
Tel: (703)903-2408
Fax: (703)903-5324

Employers

Federal Home Loan Mortgage Corp. (Freddie Mac) (Manager)

NOEL, Elizabeth A.

1133 15th St. NW
Suite 500
Washington, DC 20005-2710
EMail: ccceo@opc-dc.gov
Tel: (202)727-3071
Fax: (202)727-1014

Employers

Office of the People's Counsel for the District of Columbia (People's Counsel)

NOGUEIRA, Ricardo

1050 Thomas Jefferson St. NW
Seventh Floor
Washington, DC 20007
EMail: rpn@vnf.com
Tel: (202)298-1800
Fax: (202)338-2416

Employers

Van Ness Feldman, P.C. (Associate)

NOJEIM, Gregory T.

122 Maryland Ave. NE
Washington, DC 20002
Tel: (202)675-2326
Fax: (202)546-0738
Registered: LDA

Employers

American Civil Liberties Union (Associate Director and Chief Legislative Counsel)

NOLAN, Ellin J.

1101 Vermont Ave. NW
Suite 400
Washington, DC 20005
EMail: enolan@dbmlaw.com
Tel: (202)289-3900
Fax: (202)371-0197
Registered: LDA

Employers

Dean Blakey & Moskowitz (Director, Government Relations)

Clients Represented

On Behalf of Dean Blakey & Moskowitz

American Psychological Ass'n
Ass'n of Technology Act Projects
Coalition of Higher Education Assistance Organizations
Economics America
Internat'l Technology Education Ass'n
Management Concepts, Inc.
Nat'l Alliance of Sexual Assault Coalitions
Nat'l Collegiate Athletic Ass'n
Nat'l Council of Teachers of Mathematics
Nat'l Science Teachers Ass'n
Nat'l Writing Project
University of Vermont
Very Special Arts

NOLAN, Janne

1755 Massachusetts Ave. NW
Suite 400
Washington, DC 20036
EMail: nolan@tcf.org
Tel: (202)387-0400
Fax: (202)483-9430

Employers
The Century Foundation (Director, International Programs)

NOLAN, Jean

1625 L St. NW
Washington, DC 20036-5687
Tel: (202)429-1133
Fax: (202)429-1084

Employers
American Federation of State, County and Municipal Employees (Director, Public Affairs)

NOLAN, Jennifer

419 Seventh St. NW
Suite 500
Washington, DC 20004
Tel: (202)626-8800
Fax: (202)737-9189
Registered: LDA

Employers
Nat'l Right to Life Committee (Legislative Aide, Department of Medical Ethics)

NOLAN, Martha

1620 L St. NW
Suite 800
Washington, DC 20036-5617
Tel: (202)659-3575
Fax: (202)659-1026
Registered: LDA

Employers
Metropolitan Life Insurance Co. (Assistant V. President)

NOLAN, Michael J.

2301 M St. NW
Washington, DC 20037-1484
Tel: (202)467-2930
Fax: (202)467-2910
Registered: LDA
EMail: mnolan@APPAnet.org

Employers
American Public Power Ass'n (Government Relations Representative)

NOLAN, Pat

P.O. Box 16069
Washington, DC 20041-6069
Tel: (703)904-7312
Fax: (703)478-9679
Registered: LDA

Employers
Justice Fellowship (President)

NOLAN, Walker F.

818 Connecticut Ave. NW
Suite 1100
Washington, DC 20006
Tel: (202)728-1010
Fax: (202)728-4044
Registered: LDA
EMail: wnolan@oldaker-harris.com
Congressional Liaison, The White House, 1980-81. Counsel on several Senate panels during the 1970's.

Employers
Self-employed as an independent consultant.
Oldaker and Harris, LLP (Special Counsel)

Clients Represented

As an independent consultant
Edison Electric Institute
NSTAR
Reliant Energy, Inc.
TXU Business Services

On Behalf of Oldaker and Harris, LLP
Edison Electric Institute

NOLAND, Marcus

11 Dupont Circle NW
Suite 620
Washington, DC 20036
EMail: mnoland@iie.com
Tel: (202)328-9000
Fax: (202)328-5432

Employers
Institute for Internat'l Economics (Senior Fellow)

NOLEN, Leslie

4600 East-West Highway
Suite 300
Bethesda, MD 20814
Registered: LDA

Employers
Automotive Aftermarket Industry Ass'n

NOLLA, Teresita

600 13th St. NW
Washington, DC 20005-3096
Tel: (202)756-8000
Fax: (202)756-8087
Registered: LDA

Employers
McDermott, Will and Emery (Associate Legislative Director)

Clients Represented

On Behalf of McDermott, Will and Emery
Northwest Airlines, Inc.

NOLT, Kristin

1200 17th St. NW
Washington, DC 20036-3097
Tel: (202)331-5900
Fax: (202)973-5373

Employers
Nat'l Restaurant Ass'n (V. President, Media Relations)

NOONE, Amy E.

1655 N. Fort Myer Dr.
Suite 355
Arlington, VA 22209
Tel: (703)807-2070
Fax: (703)807-2073
Registered: LDA

Employers
The 60/Plus Ass'n, Inc. (Assistant to the President)

NOONE, James A.

1211 Connecticut Ave. NW
Suite 302
Washington, DC 20036
Tel: (202)466-7330
Fax: (202)955-5879
Registered: LDA
Writer/Editor, U.S. Information Agency, 1979-81 and 1974-77. Served in the U.S. Navy, 1967-69.

Employers
Karalekas & Noone (Partner)

Clients Represented

On Behalf of Karalekas & Noone
American Retirees Ass'n
Johns Hopkins University & Hospital
Johns Hopkins University-Applied Physics Lab

NOORIGIAN, Nicole

1146 19th St. NW
Washington, DC 20036
Tel: (202)530-2975
Fax: (202)530-2976

Employers
Center for Reproductive Law and Policy (Fellowship Attorney, Federal Legislative Program)

NORBERG, Tracey

1400 K St. NW
Suite 900
Washington, DC 20005
EMail: tracey@rma.org
Tel: (202)682-4800
Fax: (202)682-4854

Employers
Rubber Manufacturers Ass'n (Director, Environmental Affairs)

NORCROSS, David A.

900 17th St. NW
Suite 1000
Washington, DC 20006
Tel: (202)530-7400
Fax: (202)463-6915
Registered: LDA
EMail: norcross@blankrome.com
Former General Counsel, Republican National Committee.

Employers
Blank Rome Comisky & McCauley, LLP (Partner)

Clients Represented

On Behalf of Blank Rome Comisky & McCauley, LLP
Aetna/U.S. Healthcare, Inc.
American Insurance Ass'n
CIGNA Corp.
D.C. Wiring
Delaware River and Bay Authority
Delaware River Port Authority
Home Health Assembly of New Jersey, Inc.
LDW, Inc.
Maritime Exchange for the Delaware River and Bay
North American Securities Administrators Ass'n (NASAA)
On-Line Investment Services
Pilots' Ass'n of the Bay and River Delaware
U.S. Healthcare

NORD, Nancy A.

1250 H St. NW
Suite 800
Washington, DC 20005
Tel: (202)857-3400
Fax: (202)857-3401
Registered: LDA

Employers
Eastman Kodak Co. (Director, Federal Government Affairs)

NORDBERG, Jr., Carl A.

600 13th St. NW
Washington, DC 20005-3096
Tel: (202)756-8231
Fax: (202)756-8087
EMail: cnordberg@mwe.com
Former International Counsel, Congressional Joint Committee on Taxation; Attorney, Office of Chief Counsel, Internal Revenue Service.

Employers
McDermott, Will and Emery (Counsel)

NORDEN, Don

122 C St. NW
Suite 850
Washington, DC 20001
Tel: (202)638-7790
Fax: (202)638-1045
Registered: LDA
EMail: don.norden@cchinc.com
Legislative Counsel to Senator James Exon (D-NE), 1987-92.

Employers
Chambers, Conlon & Hartwell (Partner and Counsel)

Clients Represented

On Behalf of Chambers, Conlon & Hartwell
Alaska Railroad
American Short Line and Regional Railroad Ass'n
The False Claims Act Legal Center
Florida East Coast Industries Inc.
Investment Counsel Ass'n of America
Michigan State Department of Transportation
Nat'l Railroad and Construction Maintenance Ass'n
New York Metropolitan Transportation Authority
Norfolk Southern Corp.
Rail Supply and Service Coalition

NORDHAUS, Robert

1050 Thomas Jefferson St. NW
Seventh Floor
Washington, DC 20007
Tel: (202)298-1910
Fax: (202)338-2416
Registered: LDA
EMail: rrn@vnf.com
General Counsel (1993-97) and General Counsel (1977-80) and Assistant Administrator (1977), Federal Energy Regulatory Commission, all at the Department of Energy. Counsel, House Committee on Interstate and Foreign Commerce, 1975-76. Assistant Counsel, House Office of Legislative Counsel, 1963-74.

Employers
Van Ness Feldman, P.C. (Member)

Clients Represented

On Behalf of Van Ness Feldman, P.C.
Chelan County Public Utility District
Large Public Power Council
Public Generating Pool

NORDHEIMER, Jennifer

919 18th St. NW
Tenth Floor
Washington, DC 20006
Tel: (202)263-2900
Fax: (202)263-2960

Employers
Issue Dynamics Inc. (Senior Consultant)

NORDSTROM, Adam

122 C St. NW
Suite 850
Washington, DC 20001
Tel: (202)638-7790
Fax: (202)638-1045
Registered: LDA
EMail: adam.nordstrom@cchinc.com

Employers
Chambers, Conlon & Hartwell (Legislative Assistant)

Clients Represented

On Behalf of Chambers, Conlon & Hartwell
American Short Line and Regional Railroad Ass'n

NORDSTROM, Jane

1300 L St. NW
Suite 1020
Washington, DC 20005
Tel: (202)789-0089
Fax: (202)789-1725

Employers
Hospitality Sales and Marketing Ass'n Internat'l (Director, Education)

NORDSTROM, Paul E.

901 15th St. NW
Suite 700
Washington, DC 20005-2301
Tel: (202)371-6000
Fax: (202)371-6279
Registered: LDA
EMail: penordstrom@verner.com

Employers
Verner, Liipfert, Bernhard, McPherson and Hand, Chartered (Member of Firm)

Clients Represented

On Behalf of Verner, Liipfert, Bernhard, McPherson and Hand, Chartered
New Orleans, Louisiana, City of

NORMAN, Marcia

2201 C St. NW
Room 7260
Washington, DC 20520-7261
Tel: (202)647-1714
Fax: (202)647-2762

Employers
Department of State - Bureau of Legislative Affairs (Director, Office of Legislative Operations)

NORMAN, III, W. Caffey

2550 M St. NW
Washington, DC 20037-1350
Tel: (202)457-6000
Fax: (202)457-6315
Registered: LDA
EMail: cnorman@pattonboggs.com
Senior Counsel for Banking, Department of the Treasury, 1986-87. Law Clerk to Judge Walter P. Gewin, U.S. Court of Appeals, Fifth Circuit, 1977-78.

Employers
Patton Boggs, LLP (Partner)

Clients Represented

On Behalf of Patton Boggs, LLP
Halogenated Solvents Industry Alliance

NORMAN, William S.

1100 New York Ave. NW
Suite 450
Washington, DC 20005
Tel: (202)408-2137
Fax: (202)408-1255
Registered: LDA

Employers
Travel Industry Ass'n of America (President and Chief Exec. Officer)

NORMANDY, Joseph

8201 Greensboro Dr.
Suite 300
McLean, VA 22102
Tel: (703)610-9000
Fax: (703)610-9005

Employers
Ass'n Management Group
Nat'l Ass'n of Independent Life Brokerage Agency (Exec. Director)

Clients Represented

On Behalf of Ass'n Management Group
Nat'l Ass'n of Independent Life Brokerage Agency

NORQUIST, Grover G.

1920 L St. NW
Suite 200
Washington, DC 20036
Tel: (202)785-0266
Fax: (202)785-0261
Registered: LDA

Employers
Americans for Tax Reform (President)
Anti-Value Added Tax Coalition (Principal)
Citizens Against a Nat'l Sales Tax/Value-Added Tax (Principal)

NORRELL, Julia J.

601 Pennsylvania Ave. NW
Suite 900, S. Bldg.
Washington, DC 20004
Tel: (202)434-8192
Fax: (202)783-6304
Registered: LDA
EMail: jnorrell@erols.com

Employers
Julia J. Norrell & Associates (President)

Clients Represented

On Behalf of Julia J. Norrell & Associates
The Chubb Corp.
Metropolitan Life Insurance Co.
Minnesota Mining and Manufacturing Co. (3M Co.)
UNUM/Provident Corp.

NORRIS, Frances M.

1341 G St. NW
Suite 900
Washington, DC 20005
Tel: (202)637-1554
Fax: (202)637-1505

Employers
Kraft Foods, Inc. (V. President, Federal Government Affairs/Food)
Philip Morris Management Corp. (V. President, Government Affairs, Food)

NORRIS, Jeffrey A.

1015 15th St. NW
Suite 1200
Washington, DC 20005
Tel: (202)789-8600
Fax: (202)789-1708
Chief Counsel to Board Member Peter Walther, National Labor Relations Board, 1976-77.

Employers
McGuiness Norris & Williams, LLP (Partner)

NORRIS, Robert S.

1200 New York Ave. NW
Suite 400
Washington, DC 20005
Tel: (202)289-6868
Fax: (202)289-1060

Employers
Natural Resources Defense Council (Senior Research Analyst)

NORRIS, Uley

1350 I St. NW
Suite 1255
Washington, DC 20005
Tel: (202)626-0089
Fax: (202)626-0088

Employers
Law Offices of Mark Barnes (Attorney at Law)

NORTH, Nan F.

1350 I St. NW
Suite 870
Washington, DC 20005
Tel: (202)638-0551
Fax: (202)737-1947
Registered: LDA
EMail: north@capalliance.com

Employers
Health Policy Analysts (Associate)

Clients Represented

On Behalf of Health Policy Analysts
Corporate Health Care Coalition
Employer Health Care Innovation Project

NORTH, Tristan M.

1255 23rd St. NW
Suite 200
Washington, DC 20037-1174
Tel: (202)452-8100
Fax: (202)833-3636
Registered: LDA
Professional Staff Member, House Committee on Banking and Financial Services, 1992-95.

Employers
American Ambulance Ass'n (Director, Government Affairs)
Hauck and Associates (Director, Government Affairs)

Clients Represented

On Behalf of Hauck and Associates
American Ambulance Ass'n

NORTHCOTT, Hao

2010-A Eisenhower Ave.
Alexandria, VA 22314
Tel: (703)549-7351
Fax: (703)549-7448

Employers
Independent Electrical Contractors, Inc. (V. President, Government Affairs)

NORTHINGTON, John

2600 Virginia Ave. NW
Suite 600
Washington, DC 20037
Tel: (202)333-2524
Fax: (202)338-5950
Registered: LDA

Employers
J. Steven Griles & Associates
Nat'l Environmental Strategies (V. President)

Clients Represented

On Behalf of J. Steven Griles & Associates
Redstone

NORTHROP, Carl W.

1299 Pennsylvania Ave. NW
Tenth Floor
Washington, DC 20004-2400
Tel: (202)508-9500
Fax: (202)508-9700
Registered: LDA
EMail: carlnorthrop@paulhastings.com

Employers
Paul, Hastings, Janofsky & Walker LLP (Partner)

NORTHRUP, Steve

1900 K St. NW
Suite 100
Washington, DC 20006
Tel: (202)496-7150
Fax: (202)496-7756
Registered: LDA
EMail: snorthrup@medicaldevices.org

Employers
Medical Device Manufacturers Ass'n (Exec. Director)

NORTHUP, Clifford R.

700 13th St. NW
Suite 350
Washington, DC 20005
Tel: (202)637-0040
Fax: (202)637-0041
Registered: LDA
Legislative Assistant to Senator William L. Armstrong (R-CO), 1985-88. Deputy Assistant Secretary, Legislative Affairs, Department of Treasury, 1991-93.

Employers
Rhoads Group (V. President)

Clients Represented

On Behalf of Rhoads Group
AAAE-ACI
Airports Council Internat'l - North America
American Management Systems
Dick Corp.
The Justice Project, Inc.
PNC Bank, N.A.
SWATH Ocean Systems, Inc.
Taiwan Studies Institute
United States Enrichment Corp.

NORTHUP, Katherine

1711 King St.
Suite One
Alexandria, VA 22314
Tel: (703)836-4500
Fax: (703)836-8262
Registered: LDA

Employers
Snack Food Ass'n (Government Relations Representative)

NORTON, Frank

505 Capitol Ct. NE
Suite 200
Washington, DC 20002
Tel: (202)543-9398
Fax: (202)543-7844
Registered: LDA
EMail: fn@hurtnorton.com
Former staff member, Senate Armed Services Committee and as Secretary's Principal Liaison to the Senate and Military Liaison to the House, Department of the Army.

Employers
Hurt, Norton & Associates (Partner)

Clients Represented

On Behalf of Hurt, Norton & Associates
21st Century Partnership
Air Tran Airways
Auburn University
Caswell Internat'l Corp.
The Coca-Cola Company
Georgia Ports Authority
Intergraph Corp. Federal Systems Division
Lockheed Martin Aeronautical Systems Co.
Mercer Engineering Research Center
Mercer University
Pemco Aviation Group, Inc.
Phoenix Air Group, Inc.
Quad City Development Group
Savannah Airport Commission
Scientific Research Corp.
Sierra Military Health Services, Inc.
Visiting Nurses Health System
Westinghouse Electric Co.

NORTON, Lisa K.

1730 Pennsylvania Ave. NW
Suite 1200
Washington, DC 20006-4706
Tel: (202)737-0500
Fax: (202)626-3737
Legislative Assistant to Senator Robert F. Bennett (R-UT), 1995-98.

Employers
King & Spalding (Associate)

Clients Represented
On Behalf of King & Spalding
Agrium Inc.
Internet Security Systems, Inc.
Salt Lake City Olympic Organizing Committee

NORTON, Marlee

4121 Wilson Blvd.
Tenth Floor
Arlington, VA 22203
EMail: mnorton@ntca.org
Tel: (703)351-2007
Fax: (703)351-2001

Employers
Nat'l Telephone Cooperative Ass'n (Director, International Development)

NORTON, Rita E.

1300 I St. NW
Suite 470 East
Washington, DC 20005
Tel: (202)354-6100
Fax: (202)289-7448
Registered: LDA

Employers
Amgen (V. President, Government Relations)

NORTON, Thomas C.

1020 19th St. NW
Suite 800
Washington, DC 20036-6110
EMail: tcn@spectrumscience.com
Tel: (202)955-6222
Ext: 18
Fax: (202)955-0044

Employers
SPECTRUM Science Public Relations, Inc. (Senior V. President)

Clients Represented
On Behalf of SPECTRUM Science Public Relations, Inc.
Biotechnology Industry Organization

NOTMAN, Liz

1111 20th St. NW
Washington, DC 20526
Tel: (202)692-2244
Fax: (202)692-2101

Employers
Peace Corps (Deputy Director, Congressional Relations)

NOTO, Anne D.

1250 I St. NW
Suite 1000
Washington, DC 20005
Tel: (202)682-0240
Fax: (202)682-0249

Employers
Sonosky, Chambers, Sachse & Endreson (Partner)

NOTTINGHAM, Ellis T.

1001 Pennsylvania Ave. NW
Suite 700 South
Washington, DC 20004
Tel: (202)662-2650
Fax: (202)662-2674
Registered: LDA

Employers
Honeywell Internat'l, Inc. (Director, Aerospace Government Affairs)

NOVAK, John

701 Pennsylvania Ave. NW
Washington, DC 20004-2696
Tel: (202)508-5655
Fax: (202)508-5150
Registered: LDA

Employers
Edison Electric Institute (Director, Environmental Programs)

NOVAK, Michael

1150 17th St. NW
Washington, DC 20036
EMail: mnovak@aei.org
Tel: (202)862-5800
Fax: (202)862-7177

Employers
American Enterprise Institute for Public Policy Research (Director, Social and Political Studies and G. F. Jewett Scholar)

NOVELLI, William D.

601 E St. NW
Washington, DC 20049
Tel: (202)434-2510
Fax: (202)434-2525

Employers
AARP (American Ass'n of Retired Persons) (Associate Exec. Director)

NOVICK, Amy R.

918 F St. NW
Washington, DC 20004-1400
Tel: (202)216-2400
Fax: (202)371-9449

Employers
American Immigration Lawyers Ass'n (Deputy Director for Programs)

NOVICK, Len

4733 Bethesda Ave.
Suite 750
Bethesda, MD 20814
EMail: lennovick@aol.com
Tel: (301)656-0003
Fax: (301)907-0878

Employers
Nat'l Foundation for Infectious Diseases (Exec. Director)

NOVOTNY, Louise

501 Third St. NW
Washington, DC 20001-2797
Tel: (202)434-1100
Fax: (202)434-1318

Employers
Communications Workers of America (Research Economist (Health Policy Analyst))

NOYES, Elizabeth J.

601 13th St. NW
Suite 400 North
Washington, DC 20005
EMail: jnoyes@aap.org
Tel: (202)347-8600
Fax: (202)393-6137
Registered: LDA

Employers
American Academy of Pediatrics (Associate Exec.)
Pediatricians for Children Inc. (Treasurer)

NUBERN, Chris

2101 Wilson Blvd.
Suite 400
Arlington, VA 22201
Tel: (703)243-6111
Fax: (703)841-9328

Employers
Nat'l Milk Producers Federation (Director, Economic Research)

NUCKOLLS, C. Randall

701 Pennsylvania Ave. NW
Suite 600
Washington, DC 20004
EMail: cnuckolls@lanlaw.com
Tel: (202)624-1200
Fax: (202)624-1298
Registered: LDA
Chief Counsel and Legislative Director to Senator Sam Nunn (D-GA), 1980-86. Legislative Counsel to Senator Herman Talmadge (D-GA), 1977-80.

Employers
Long, Aldridge & Norman, LLP (Partner)

Clients Represented
On Behalf of Long, Aldridge & Norman, LLP
Consortium on Government Relations for Student Affairs
DeChiaro Properties
Florida Internat'l University
Nat'l Ass'n of Professional Forestry Schools and Colleges
Nat'l Franchisee Ass'n
Santa Fe Natural Tobacco Co.
University of Georgia
Weather Channel

NUEBIG, Tom S.

1225 Connecticut Ave. NW
Washington, DC 20036
Tel: (202)327-6000
Fax: (202)327-6200
Registered: LDA

Employers
Ernst & Young LLP

Clients Represented
On Behalf of Ernst & Young LLP
Bankruptcy Issues Council
Cellular Depreciation Coalition
Groom Law Group, Chartered
Thelen Reid & Priest LLP

NUGENT, Jr., John M.

1350 I St. NW
Suite 680
Washington, DC 20005-3305
EMail: Jack@advocacy.com
Tel: (202)393-4841
Fax: (202)393-5596
Registered: LDA
Special Assistant, Congressional Affairs, Federal Energy Administration, 1975-76. Director, Energy and Natural Resources Task Force, 1972-75.

Employers
The Advocacy Group

Clients Represented
On Behalf of The Advocacy Group
Fuels Management Inc.
Nuclear Energy Institute
Rineco Chemical Industries
TRW Inc.
Westinghouse Government Services Group

NUGENT, Patrick J.

1133 19th St. NW
Washington, DC 20036
EMail: patrick.nugent@wcom.com
Tel: (202)887-3830
Fax: (202)736-6880

Employers
MCI WorldCom Corp. (Director, Tax Legislation and Regulation)

NUNN, Hon. Sam

1730 Pennsylvania Ave. NW
Suite 1200
Washington, DC 20006-4706
Tel: (202)737-0500
Fax: (202)626-3737
Member, U.S. Senate (D-GA), 1972-97. Served as Chairman, Senate Armed Services Committee.

Employers
King & Spalding (Partner)

NURICK, Lester

2445 M St. NW
Washington, DC 20037-1420
EMail: lnurick@wilmer.com
Tel: (202)663-6000
Fax: (202)663-6363

Employers
Wilmer, Cutler & Pickering (Counsel)

NURNBERGER, Ralph D.

1735 New York Ave. NW
Suite 500
Washington, DC 20006-4759
EMail: ralphn@prestongates.com
Tel: (202)628-1700
Fax: (202)331-1024
Registered: LDA
Former Director, Congressional Affairs, Bureau of Export Administration, Department of Commerce. Former Professional Staff Member, Subcommittee on Foreign Economic Policy, Senate Committee on Foreign Relations. Former Legislative Assistant for Foreign Policy and Defense to Senator James Pearson (R-KS). Former Special Assistant to the Administrator, General Services Administration.

Employers
Nurnberger and Associates
Preston Gates Ellis & Rouvelas Meeds LLP (Government Affairs Counselor)

Clients Represented
On Behalf of Nurnberger and Associates
McDonald's Corp.
On Behalf of Preston Gates Ellis & Rouvelas Meeds LLP
Akzo Nobel Chemicals, Inc.
Magazine Publishers of America
Nat'l Center for Economic Freedom, Inc.
Nat'l Produce Production Inc.
Orange, California, County of
Pulse Medical Instruments
Silverline Technologies, Inc.
Tan Holdings Corp.
VoiceStream Wireless Corp.

NUSCHLER, Robin M.

1333 New Hampshire Ave. NW
Suite 400
Washington, DC 20036
Tel: (202)887-4000
Fax: (202)887-4288
Registered: LDA

Employers
Akin, Gump, Strauss, Hauer & Feld, L.L.P. (Partner)

Clients Represented

On Behalf of Akin, Gump, Strauss, Hauer & Feld, L.L.P.
PG&E Corp.

NUSGART, Marcia

5225 Pooks Hill Rd.
Suite 1626 North
Bethesda, MD 20814
Tel: (301)530-7846
Fax: (301)530-7946
Registered: LDA

Employers
Nusgart Consulting, LLC (President)

Clients Represented

On Behalf of Nusgart Consulting, LLC
Augustine Medical
BD
Cascade Designs
Coloplast Corp.
Contemporary Products Inc.
ConvaTec
Crown Therapeutics, Inc.
Dumex Medical
Essex Medical Systems Plus
Freedom Designs
Hill-Rom Co., Inc.
Hollister Inc.
Hyperion Medical
Kendall Healthcare Products Co.
Medline Industries Inc.
Pegasus Airwave
Precision Medical
ReGin Manufacturing Inc.
Respironics
ROHO, Inc.
Smith & Nephew, Inc.
Sunrise Medical
Tempur-Medical Inc.

NUSSBAUM, Jonathan

2201 C St. NW
Room 7251
Washington, DC 20520-7261
Tel: (202)647-8728
Fax: (202)647-2762

Employers
Department of State - Bureau of Legislative Affairs (Consular, Population & Refugees Affairs Legislative Management Officer)

NUSSBAUM, Karen

815 16th St. NW
Washington, DC 20006
Tel: (202)637-5000
Fax: (202)637-5058

Employers
AFL-CIO (American Federation of Labor and Congress of Industrial Organizations) (Director, Working Women's Department)

NUSSDORF, Melanie Franco

1330 Connecticut Ave. NW
Washington, DC 20036-1795
Tel: (202)429-3000
Fax: (202)429-3902
Registered: LDA
EMail: mnussdor@steptoe.com
Executive Assistant to the Solicitor, Department of Labor, 1977-78.

Employers
Steptoe & Johnson LLP (Partner)

NUSSMAN, J. Michael

1033 N. Fairfax St.
Suite 200
Alexandria, VA 22314
Tel: (703)519-9691
Fax: (703)519-1872
Registered: LDA
EMail: mnussman@asafishing.org
Former Staff Director for the National Ocean Policy Study, of the Commerce, Science and Transportation Committee, U.S. Senate.

Employers
American Sportfishing Ass'n (V. President for Government Affairs)

NUTT, Fred

8400 W. Park Dr.
McLean, VA 22102
Tel: (703)547-5500
Registered: LDA

Employers
Nat'l Automobile Dealers Ass'n (Legislative Representative)

NUTTER, Franklin W.

1301 Pennsylvania Ave. NW
Suite 900
Washington, DC 20004
Tel: (202)638-3690
Fax: (202)638-0936

Employers
Reinsurance Ass'n of America (President)

NUTTER, Jack O.

1455 Pennsylvania Ave. NW
Suite 225
Washington, DC 20004
Tel: (202)289-7400
Fax: (202)289-7414
Minority Tax Counsel, Senate Finance Committee under Senator Robert Dole (R-KS).

Employers
Nutter & Harris, Inc. (President)

Clients Represented

On Behalf of Nutter & Harris, Inc.
Fisher Scientific Worldwide
Reheis, Inc.

NUZUM, Janet

1250 H St. NW
Suite 900
Washington, DC 20005
Tel: (202)737-4332
Fax: (202)331-7820
Registered: LDA

Employers
Internat'l Dairy Foods Ass'n (V. President and General Counsel)

NUZZACO, Mark J.

1899 Preston White Dr.
Reston, VA 20191-4367
Tel: (703)264-7200
Fax: (703)620-0994
EMail: mnuzzaco@npes.org

Employers
NPES, The Ass'n for Suppliers of Printing, Publishing, and Converting Technologies (Director, Government Affairs)

NYHART, Nick

1320 19th St. NW
Suite M-1
Washington, DC 20036
Tel: (202)293-0222
Fax: (202)293-0202

Employers
Public Campaign (Exec. Director)

NYKWEST, Beverly C.

1700 K St. NW
13th Floor
Washington, DC 20006-0011
Tel: (202)457-0710
Ext: 20
Fax: (202)269-9352
EMail: nykwest@narc.org

Employers
Nat'l Ass'n of Regional Councils (Director of Policy)

NYQUIST, Christina

1310 G St. NW
12th Floor
Washington, DC 20005
Tel: (202)626-4780
Fax: (202)626-4833
Registered: LDA

Employers
Blue Cross Blue Shield Ass'n (Director, Policy)

O'BANNON, H. K. "Obie"

50 F St. NW
Suite 12500
Washington, DC 20001
Tel: (202)639-2537
Fax: (202)639-2526
Registered: LDA

Employers
Ass'n of American Railroads (V. President, Government Affairs)

O'BANNON, Michael

819 Seventh St. NW
Washington, DC 20001
Tel: (202)833-8940
Fax: (202)833-8943
Registered: LDA

Employers
EOP Group, Inc.

Clients Represented

On Behalf of EOP Group, Inc.
American Petroleum Institute
The Business Roundtable
Central Illinois Public Service Co.
Chlorine Chemistry Council
Continental Grain Co.
Dow AgroSciences
The Dow Chemical Co.
Edison Electric Institute
FMC Corp.
Fort Howard Corp.
Internat'l Food Additives Council
Monsanto Co.
Novartis Crop Protection
Price Costco
Trident Seafood Corp.
Zirconia Sales America

O'BRIEN, Colleen T.

1320 19th St. NW
Suite 400
Washington, DC 20036
Tel: (202)861-8223
Fax: (202)861-9307

Employers
The Institute for Higher Education Policy (V. President)

O'BRIEN, David D.

2600 Virginia Ave. NW
Suite 600
Washington, DC 20037
Tel: (202)338-6650
Fax: (202)338-5950
Registered: LDA, FARA
EMail: dobrien1@aol.com

Employers
Wayne Arny & Assoc. (Partner)
David O'Brien and Associates (President)
O'Brien, Klink & Associates (President)

Clients Represented

On Behalf of Wayne Arny & Assoc.
John Crane-LIPS, Inc.
Cruising America Coalition
DRS Technologies, Inc.
Jered Industries, Inc.
The Kinetics Group
MacGregor
Robbins-Gioia, Inc.
San Francisco Wholesale Produce Ass'n

On Behalf of David O'Brien and Associates
John Crane-LIPS, Inc.
Cruising America Coalition
DRS
MacGregor
Robbins-Gioia, Inc.
Wi-LAN, Inc.

On Behalf of O'Brien, Klink & Associates
The Kinetics Group
PetrolRem, Inc.
Zinc Corp. of America

O'BRIEN, Edward L.

1600 K St. NW
Suite 602
Washington, DC 20006-2801
Tel: (202)293-0088
Ext: 235
Fax: (202)293-0089
EMail: eobrien@streetlaw.org

Employers
Street Law Inc. (Exec. Director)

O'BRIEN, Elizabeth

1111 N. Fairfax St.
Alexandria, VA 22314
Tel: (703)684-2782
Fax: (703)684-7343

Employers
American Physical Therapy Ass'n (Assistant Director, Federal Regulatory Affairs)

O'BRIEN, Kevin M.

815 Connecticut Ave. NW
Suite 900
Washington, DC 20006-4078
Tel: (202)452-7000
Fax: (202)452-7073
Registered: LDA

Employers
Baker & McKenzie (Partner)

Clients Represented

On Behalf of Baker & McKenzie
Drives Inc.
Storck U.S.A.
Wm. Wrigley Jr. Co.

O'BRIEN, Kevin P.

1700 Pennsylvania Ave. NW
Suite 600
Washington, DC 20006

Tel: (202)393-7600
Fax: (202)393-7601
Registered: LDA

Employers
Ivins, Phillips & Barker (Partner)

O'BRIEN, III, Lawrence F.

1350 I St. NW
Suite 690
Washington, DC 20005
EMail: lobrien@ob-cgroup.com

Tel: (202)898-4746
Fax: (202)898-4756
Registered: LDA

Deputy for Tax Legislation to the Assistant Secretary for Legislative Affairs, Department of Treasury, 1977-79.

Employers
The OB-C Group, LLC

Clients Represented

On Behalf of The OB-C Group, LLC
American Airlines
Anheuser-Busch Cos., Inc.
AT&T
Biotechnology Industry Organization
Blue Cross Blue Shield Ass'n
Fannie Mae
Goodyear Tire and Rubber Co.
Healthcare Distribution Management Ass'n
Investment Co. Institute
Merrill Lynch & Co., Inc.
Motorola, Inc.
Nat'l Thoroughbred Racing Ass'n, Inc.
Newport News Shipbuilding Inc.
The Rouse Company
Sears, Roebuck and Co.
Securities Industry Ass'n
TIAA-CREF
United Parcel Service
WellPoint Health Networks/Blue Cross of California/UNICARE
Wilmer, Cutler & Pickering

O'BRIEN, Michael E.

901 15th St. NW
Suite 700
Washington, DC 20005-2301
EMail: mobrien@verner.com

Tel: (202)371-6000
Fax: (202)371-6279
Registered: LDA

Former Legislative Assistant to Senator Dan Coats (R-IN).

Employers
Verner, Liipfert, Bernhard, McPherson and Hand, Chartered (Legislative Consultant)

Clients Represented

On Behalf of Verner, Liipfert, Bernhard, McPherson and Hand, Chartered
Pharmaceutical Research and Manufacturers of America
United Defense, L.P.
Washington Group Internat'l

O'BRIEN, Nancy

1410 King St.
Alexandria, VA 22314

Tel: (703)683-3111
Fax: (703)683-7424
Registered: LDA

Employers
Ass'n for Career and Technical Education (Assistant Exec. Director, Government Relations)

O'BRIEN, Patrick J.

325 Pennsylvannia Ave. SE
Washington, DC 20003

Tel: (202)546-8527
Fax: (202)546-8528
Registered: LDA

Employers
Nat'l Forest Recreation Ass'n (Exec. Director)

O'BRIEN, Richard

1899 L St. NW
Suite 700
Washington, DC 20036
EMail: dobrien@aaaadc.org

Tel: (202)331-7345
Fax: (202)857-3675

Employers
American Ass'n of Advertising Agencies (Exec. V. President and Director, Government Relations)

O'BRIEN, Rosemary L.

1401 I St. NW
Suite 340
Washington, DC 20005
EMail: robrien@cfindustries.com

Tel: (202)371-9279
Fax: (202)371-9169
Registered: LDA

Employers
C F Industries, Inc. (V. President, Public Affairs)

O'BRIEN, Shaun

815 16th St. NW
Washington, DC 20006

Tel: (202)637-5000
Fax: (202)637-5058
Registered: LDA

Employers
AFL-CIO (American Federation of Labor and Congress of Industrial Organizations) (Senior Policy Analyst)

O'BRIEN, Tom

444 N. Capitol St. NW
Suite 134
Washington, DC 20001

Tel: (202)624-5270
Fax: (202)624-5280

Employers
California, Washington Office of the State of (Deputy Director)

O'BRYON, David S.

4424 Montgomery Ave.
Suite 102
Bethesda, MD 20814
EMail: obryonco@aol.com

Tel: (301)652-5066
Fax: (301)913-9146

Served on the Congressional staffs of Rep. Newton Steers (R-MD), 1977-79 and Rep. Gilbert Gude (R-MD), 1972-77.

Employers
O'Bryon & Co. (President)
Retirement Industry Trust Ass'n (Exec. Director)

Clients Represented

On Behalf of O'Bryon & Co.
American Ass'n of Limited Partners
Ass'n of Chiropractic Colleges
Retirement Industry Trust Ass'n

O'CONNELL, Ed

1010 Duke St.
Alexandria, VA 22314-3589

Tel: (703)684-5700
Fax: (703)684-6321
Registered: LDA

Employers
American Ass'n of Port Authorities (Director, Membership Services)

O'CONNELL, Edward J.

1200 New Hampshire Ave. NW
Suite 800
Washington, DC 20036-6802
EMail: eoconnell@dlalaw.com

Tel: (202)776-2000
Fax: (202)776-2222

Employers
Dow, Lohnes & Albertson, PLLC (Member)

O'CONNELL, Elizabeth

1860 19th St. NW
Washington, DC 20009
EMail: elizabet@niaf.org

Tel: (202)387-0600
Fax: (202)387-0800

Employers
Nat'l Italian American Foundation (Director, Public Policy and Ethnic Affairs)

O'CONNELL, James J.

1300 I St. NW
Suite 420 East
Washington, DC 20005

Tel: (202)789-6525
Fax: (202)789-6593
Registered: LDA

Employers
Ceridian Corp. (V. President, Government Relations)

O'CONNELL, Kelly

1600 I St. NW
Washington, DC 20006

Tel: (202)293-1966
Fax: (202)296-7410

Employers
Motion Picture Ass'n of America (PAC Contact)

O'CONNELL, Lynn

950 N. Washington St.
Alexandria, VA 22314-1552

Tel: (703)836-2272
Fax: (703)684-1924

Employers
American Academy of Physician Assistants (Foundation Director)

O'CONNELL, Maureen A.

444 N. Capitol St. NW
Suite 740
Washington, DC 20001
EMail: moconnell@newscorp.com

Tel: (202)824-6503
Fax: (202)824-6510
Registered: LDA

Employers
News Corporation Ltd. (V. President, Regulatory and Government Relations)

O'CONNELL, Mia

1299 Pennsylvania Ave. NW
Suite 800 West
Washington, DC 20004

Tel: (202)785-0500
Fax: (202)785-5277
Registered: LDA

Legislative Assistant to Rep. John Fary (D-IL), 1980-83; Legislative Assistant to Rep. Jim McNulty (D-AZ), 1984-86.

Employers
The Carmen Group
LMRC, Inc. (Senior Associate)

Clients Represented

On Behalf of The Carmen Group
Maryland Department of Transportation
Metropolitan Water Reclamation District of Greater Chicago
Napa County, California, Flood and Water Conservation District
Northwest Municipal Conference
Riverside County, California, Flood Control and Water Conservation District
Santa Clara Valley Water District

On Behalf of LMRC, Inc.
Chicago, Illinois, Department of the Environment of the City of
Chicago, Illinois, Washington Office of the City of

O'CONNELL, Pete

1776 K St. NW
Washington, DC 20006

Tel: (202)719-7000
Fax: (202)719-7049

Employers
Wiley, Rein & Fielding (Of Counsel)

Clients Represented

On Behalf of Wiley, Rein & Fielding
Gannett Co., Inc.

O'CONNELL, Sheila

805 15th St. NW
Suite 400
Washington, DC 20005

Tel: (202)326-1400
Fax: (202)326-1415

Employers
EMILY'S List (Political Director)

O'CONNELL, Terrence M.

444 N. Capitol St.
Suite 841
Washington, DC 20001
EMail: toconnell@davisoconnell.com

Tel: (202)638-5333
Fax: (202)638-5335
Registered: LDA

Employers
Davis O'Connell, Inc. (Chief Operating Officer)

Clients Represented

On Behalf of Davis O'Connell, Inc.
Constellation Technology Corp.
Contra Costa Community College District
Illinois Community College Board
Lockheed Martin Corp.
Raydon Corp.
Science Applications Internat'l Corp. (SAIC)
St. Petersburg Community College
Washington and Jefferson College

O'CONNOR, Charles P.

1800 M St. NW
Washington, DC 20036
EMail: coconnor@morganlewis.com

Tel: (202)467-7000
Fax: (202)467-7176

Attorney, National Labor Relations Board, 1967-68.

Employers
Morgan, Lewis & Bockius LLP (Managing Partner)

O'CONNOR, Christine A.

700 13th St. NW
Suite 400
Washington, DC 20005
Tel: (202)347-0773
Fax: (202)347-0785
Legislative Director to Rep. William F. Goodling (R-PA), 1993-2000.

Employers
Cassidy & Associates, Inc. (Associate)

Clients Represented
On Behalf of Cassidy & Associates, Inc.
Boston College
Dominican College of Blauvelt
Lorain County Community College
North Shore Long Island Jewish Health System
Philadelphia University
Phoenix, Arizona, City of

O'CONNOR, Edward C.

1800 N. Beauregard St.
Suite 150
Alexandria, VA 22311
Tel: (703)250-0916
Fax: (703)239-0122
Registered: LDA

Employers
GMA Internat'l

Clients Represented
On Behalf of GMA Internat'l
Singapore Technologies Automotive

O'CONNOR, James E.

900 19th St. NW
Suite 400
Washington, DC 20006
Tel: (202)857-3100
Fax: (202)296-8716
Registered: LDA

Employers
America's Community Bankers (Government Relations)

O'CONNOR, Jerry J.

1125 15th St. NW
Washington, DC 20005
Tel: (202)833-7000
Fax: (202)467-6316

Employers
Internat'l Brotherhood of Electrical Workers (International Secretary-Treasurer)

O'CONNOR, III, John J.

700 13th St. NW
Suite 700
Washington, DC 20005-3960
EMail: jjoconnor@bryancave.com
Tel: (202)508-6000
Fax: (202)508-6200

Employers
Bryan Cave LLP (Partner)

O'CONNOR, Judith

1828 L St. NW
Suite 900
Washington, DC 20036-5104
Tel: (202)452-6262
Fax: (202)452-6299

Employers
Nat'l Center for Nonprofit Boards (President and Chief Exec. Officer)

O'CONNOR, Kelly A.

1850 M St. NW
Suite 900
Washington, DC 20036
Tel: (202)463-2500
Fax: (202)463-4950

Employers
Sher & Blackwell (Associate)

O'CONNOR, Kevin

1750 New York Ave. NW
Washington, DC 20006
Tel: (202)737-8484
Fax: (202)737-8418

Employers
Internat'l Ass'n of Fire Fighters (Assistant to the General President, Govenmental and Public Affairs)

O'CONNOR, Kevin M.

1775 Pennsylvania Ave. NW
Suite 200
Washington, DC 20006
Tel: (202)862-1000
Fax: (202)862-1093
Registered: LDA

Employers
Dewey Ballantine LLP (Legislative Assistant)

Clients Represented
On Behalf of Dewey Ballantine LLP
Labor-Industry Coalition for Internat'l Trade

O'CONNOR, Michael J.

600 New Hampshire Ave. NW
Suite 1000
Washington, DC 20037
Tel: (202)333-4141
Fax: (202)298-9109
Registered: LDA

Employers
O'Connor & Fierce Associates (President)

Clients Represented
On Behalf of O'Connor & Fierce Associates
Powerware
Thorn Microwave Devices

O'CONNOR, Patrick C.

1990 M St. NW
Suite 340
Washington, DC 20036
Tel: (202)223-6222
Fax: (202)785-0687
Registered: LDA

Employers
Kent & O'Connor, Inc. (President)

Clients Represented
On Behalf of Kent & O'Connor, Inc.
American College of Occupational and Environmental Medicine
American Supply Ass'n
FedEx Corp.
Internat'l Warehouse Logistics Ass'n
Mont Blanc, Inc.
Nat'l Ass'n of Fleet Administrators
Richemont Internat'l Ltd.

O'CONNOR, Patrick J.

1666 K St. NW
Suite 500
Washington, DC 20006-2803
Tel: (202)887-1400
Fax: (202)466-2198
Registered: LDA, FARA

Employers
O'Connor & Hannan, L.L.P. (Senior Partner)

Clients Represented
On Behalf of O'Connor & Hannan, L.L.P.
Southeast Alaska Seiners Ass'n
St. Croix Chippewa Indians of Wisconsin
Nidal Z. Zayed and Associates

O'CONNOR, Teresa

1350 I St. NW
Suite 400
Washington, DC 20005-3306
Tel: (202)371-6900
Fax: (202)842-3578
Registered: LDA

Employers
Motorola, Inc. (Director, Global Regulatory Relations)

O'CONNOR, Thomas

3501 Newark St. NW
Washington, DC 20016
Tel: (202)966-6800
Fax: (202)895-1104

Employers
Youth For Understanding Internat'l Exchange (V. President, Public Affairs, Develpoment and Planning)

O'CONNOR, Tom

1220 L St. NW
Suite 410
Washington, DC 20005
EMail: skmoltom1@aol.com
Tel: (202)371-9149
Fax: (202)842-4966
Economist, Interstate Commerce Commission, 1973-75. Manager, Local Rail Planning, United States Railroad Administration, 1975-77.

Employers
Snavely, King, Majoros, O'Connor and Lee, Inc. (V. President)

Clients Represented
On Behalf of Snavely, King, Majoros, O'Connor and Lee, Inc.
Canadian Pacific
Kansas City Southern Industries
Montana, State of
Occidental Chemical Corporation
Washington Construction Co.

O'DAY, Paul T.

1150 17th St. NW
Suite 310
Washington, DC 20036
Tel: (202)296-6508
Fax: (202)296-3052

Employers
American Fiber Manufacturers Ass'n (President)

O'DELL, Barbara

1112 16th St. NW
Suite 300
Washington, DC 20036
Tel: (202)296-4336
Fax: (202)331-8523

Employers
Nat'l Parking Ass'n (Exec. Director)

O'DONNELL, James

500 E St. SW
Eighth Floor
Room 803
Washington, DC 20254-0001
Tel: (202)358-6028
Fax: (202)358-6074

Employers
Social Security Administration-Office of Legislation and Congressional Affairs (Social Insurance Program Advisor, Office of Legislative and Congressional Affairs)

O'DONNELL, John A.

801 Pennsylvania Ave. NW
Suite 212
Washington, DC 20004
Tel: (202)783-5505
Fax: (202)783-6873
Registered: LDA

Employers
Xcel Energy, Inc. (Director, Federal Public Affairs)

O'DONNELL, John R.

1200 New Hampshire Ave NW
Suite 430
Washington, DC 20036
Tel: (202)955-4555
Fax: (202)955-1147
Registered: LDA

Employers
Murray, Scheer, Montgomery, Tapia & O'Donnell (Partner)

Clients Represented
On Behalf of Murray, Scheer, Montgomery, Tapia & O'Donnell
Albuquerque, New Mexico, City of
Bernalillo, New Mexico, County of
Brownsville Public Utilities Board
Brownsville, Texas, City of
El Paso Water Utilities - Public Service Board
Freeport, New York, Village of
Hempstead, New York, Village of
Humboldt Harbor Recreation
Jasper, Alabama, City of
Long Beach, California, City of
Marshall, Alabama, County of
Monterey, California, County of
Oxnard Harbor District
Oxnard, California, City of
Passaic Valley Sewerage Commissioners
Phoenix, Arizona, City of
Salinas, California, City of
Santa Clarita, California, City of
Southern California Ass'n of Governments
Water Replenishment District of Southern California
West Jordan, Utah, City of

O'DONNELL, Katie

1500 Pennsylvania Ave. NW
Room 3204MT
Washington, DC 20220
Tel: (202)622-9014
Fax: (202)622-0534

Employers
Department of Treasury (Special Assistant to the Assistant Secretary, Office of Legislative Affairs)

O'DONNELL, Kelly

112 S. West St.
Fourth Floor
Alexandria, VA 22314
EMail: ktodonnell@cahi.org
Tel: (703)836-6200
Fax: (703)836-6550

Employers
Council for Affordable Health Insurance (Director, Operations)

O'DONNELL, Patrick E.

1666 K St. NW
Suite 500
Washington, DC 20006-2803
Tel: (202)887-1400
Fax: (202)466-2198
Registered: LDA, FARA
EMail: podonnell@oconnorhannon.com

Special Assistant to the President for Legislative Affairs, The White House, 1974-76, 1973-74, 1970-73. Deputy Assistant Attorney General for Legislative Affairs, Department of Justice, 1973-74. Legal Assistant to the Chairman, Federal Communications Commission, 1970-72.

Employers

O'Connor & Hannan, L.L.P. (Partner)

Clients Represented

On Behalf of O'Connor & Hannan, L.L.P.

Allergan, Inc.
American Forest & Paper Ass'n
American Free Trade Ass'n
ATOFINA Chemicals, Inc.
Bear, Stearns and Co.
California Debt Limit Allocation Committee
Celera Genomics
Education Finance Council
Exxon Mobil Corp.
FMC Corp.
General Electric Co.
Georgia-Pacific Corp.
P. H. Glatfelter
Kendall-Jackson Winery
Lockheed Martin Corp.
Montrose Chemical Co.
Mortgage Bankers Ass'n of America
Nat'l Paint and Coatings Ass'n
Netherlands Antilles, Government of
Portland Cellular Partnership
Student Loan Funding Corp.
Taipei Economic and Cultural Representative Office in the United States
Tyson's Governmental Sales, LLC
University of Akron
VISA U.S.A., Inc.
Nidal Z. Zayed and Associates

O'DONNELL, Thomas P.

2550 M St. NW
Washington, DC 20037-1350
Tel: (202)457-6000
Fax: (202)457-6315
Registered: LDA, FARA
EMail: todonnell@pattonboggs.com

Special Assistant to the President and Chief of Staff, Nat'l Economic Council, The White House, 1995-97. Chief of Staff and General Counsel, Council of Economic Advisors, 1993-95.

Employers

Patton Boggs, LLP (Of Counsel)

Clients Represented

On Behalf of Patton Boggs, LLP

American Advertising Federation
Clayton College of Natural Health
McKinsey & Co., Inc.
Outdoor Advertising Ass'n of America
Point of Purchase Advertising Institute
Roizman & Cos.
United States Enrichment Corp.

O'DRISCOLL, Gerald

214 Massachusetts Ave. NE
Washington, DC 20002
Tel: (202)546-4400
Fax: (202)546-8328

Employers

Heritage Foundation (Director, Center for International Trade and Economics)

O'DUDEN, Gregory J.

901 E St. NW
Suite 600
Washington, DC 20004
Tel: (202)783-4444
Fax: (202)783-4085

Employers

Nat'l Treasury Employees Union (General Counsel)

O'FLAHERTY, J. Daniel

1625 K St. NW
Suite 1090
Washington, DC 20006-1604
Tel: (202)887-0278
Fax: (202)452-8160
Registered: LDA

Employers

Nat'l Foreign Trade Council, Inc. (V. President and Exec. Director, U.S.-South Africa Business Council)

O'FLAHERTY, Michael J.

1400 16th St. NW
Suite 400
Washington, DC 20036-2220
Tel: (202)518-6320
Fax: (202)234-2686
EMail: moflaherty@ofwlaw.com

Employers

Olsson, Frank and Weeda, P.C. (Principal)

Clients Represented

On Behalf of Olsson, Frank and Weeda, P.C.

Mead Johnson Nutritional Group
United Fresh Fruit and Vegetable Ass'n

O'FLAHERTY, Neil F.

1400 16th St. NW
Suite 400
Washington, DC 20036-2220
Tel: (202)789-1212
Fax: (202)234-3550
EMail: noflaherty@ofwlaw.com

Employers

Olsson, Frank and Weeda, P.C. (Principal)

O'GARA, James F. X.

1150 17th St. NW
Suite 503
Washington, DC 20036
Tel: (202)822-8333
Fax: (202)822-8325

Employers

The Philanthropy Roundtable (Exec. Director)

O'GRADY, Richard

1444 I St. NW
Suite 200
Washington, DC 20005
Tel: (202)628-1500
Ext: 258
Fax: (202)628-1509
EMail: rogrady@aibs.org

Employers

American Institute of Biological Sciences (Exec. Director)

O'HAGAN, Malcolm

1300 N. 17th St.
Suite 1847
Rosslyn, VA 22209
Tel: (703)841-3200
Fax: (703)841-3300
EMail: mal_ohagan@nema.org

Employers

Nat'l Electrical Manufacturers Ass'n (President)

O'HANLON, G. John

1401 K St. NW
Suite 400
Washington, DC 20005
Tel: (202)789-2111
Fax: (202)789-4883
Registered: LDA, FARA
EMail: johno@thewashingtongroup.com

Former Aide to House Minority Leader, Rep. Richard Gephardt (D-MO).

Employers

The Washington Group (Principal)

Clients Represented

On Behalf of The Washington Group

American Hospital Ass'n
American Resort Development Ass'n
AT&T
BD
Bridgestone/Firestone, Inc.
Delta Air Lines
Everglades Trust
Global Waste Recycling, Inc.
IVAX Corp.
Korea Information & Communication, Ltd.
LCOR, Inc.
Microsoft Corp.
Nat'l Ass'n of Real Estate Investment Trusts
News Corporation Ltd.
Real Estate Roundtable
SAMPCO Companies
Texas Municipal Power Agency
WinStar Internat'l
Yankton Sioux Tribe

O'HANLON, Michael E.

1775 Massachusetts Ave. NW
Washington, DC 20036-2188
Tel: (202)797-6000
Fax: (202)797-6004

Defense and Foreign Policy Budget Analyst, National Security Division, Congressional Budget Office, 1989-94.

Employers

The Brookings Institution (Senior Fellow, Foreign Policy Studies)

O'HARA, Barbara E.

1101 King St.
Alexandria, VA 22314
Tel: (703)739-2782
Fax: (703)684-8319
Registered: LDA
EMail: barbo@astahq.com

Employers

American Soc. of Travel Agents (V. President, Government Affairs)

O'HARA, Bartley M.

1825 I St. NW
Suite 400
Washington, DC 20006
Tel: (202)429-2019
Fax: (202)775-4187
Registered: LDA

Employers

Self-employed as an independent consultant.

Clients Represented

As an independent consultant

Arctic Power
Internat'l Union of Bricklayers and Allied Craftsworkers
Norfolk Southern Corp.
San Bernardino Valley Municipal Water District
United Parcel Service

O'HARA, James T.

51 Louisiana Ave. NW
Washington, DC 20001
Tel: (202)879-3939
Fax: (202)626-1700
EMail: jtohara@jonesday.com

Section Chief, Reorganization Branch, Internal Revenue Service, 1967-69.

Employers

Jones, Day, Reavis & Pogue (Partner)

O'HARA, Marie "Mimi"

2550 M St. NW
Washington, DC 20037-1350
Tel: (202)457-6000
Fax: (202)457-6315

Assistant to Speaker of the House, Rep. Thomas Foley (D-WA), 1989-94. Executive Floor Assistant (1987-89) and Director of Research (1981-87) to Rep. Foley. Legislative Assistant to Rep. John Brademas (D-IN), 1977-80. Former Deputy Director, House Democratic Steering Policy Committee.

Employers

Patton Boggs, LLP (Legislative Affairs Specialist)

O'HARA, Mark A.

444 N. Capitol St. NW
Suite 618
Washington, DC 20001
Tel: (202)624-1440
Fax: (202)508-3859

Employers

Nat'l Criminal Justice Ass'n (Government Affairs Counsel)

O'HARA, Thomas G.

Suite 510
1140 Connecticut Ave. NW
Washington, DC 20036
Tel: (202)293-1676
Registered: LDA

Employers

Prudential Insurance Co. of America (V. President, Government Relations)

O'HARA-MATHERS, Kathleen

501 Second St. NE
Washington, DC 20002
Tel: (202)675-8250
Fax: (202)544-8123
EMail: kmathers@tfi.org

Employers

The Fertilizer Institute (V. President, Public Affairs)

O'HARE, Andrew

1225 I St. NW
Suite 300
Washington, DC 20005
Tel: (202)408-9494
Fax: (202)408-0877
Registered: LDA

Employers

American Portland Cement Alliance (V. President, Environmental Affairs)

O'HARE, Don

1015 15th St. NW
Suite 450
Washington, DC 20005
Tel: (202)589-1230
Fax: (202)589-1231
Registered: LDA
EMail: dohare@worldshipping.org

Employers
World Shipping Council (V. President)

O'HARE, Kerry

444 N. Capitol St. NW
Suite 301
Washington, DC 20001
Tel: (202)434-7100
Fax: (202)434-7110

Employers
New York State Office of Federal Affairs (Deputy Director)

O'HARE, Patricia

400 N. Capitol St. NW
Suite 585
Washington, DC 20001
Tel: (202)737-1960
Fax: (202)737-5585
Registered: LDA

Employers
Wise & Associates

O'HOLLAREN, Hilary

1120 20th St. NW
Suite 1000
Washington, DC 20036
Tel: (202)457-2089
Fax: (202)457-2571
Registered: LDA
EMail: hohollaren@att.com

Employers
AT&T (Director, Federal Government Affairs)

O'KEEFE, Patricia

600 13th St. NW
Washington, DC 20005-3096
Tel: (202)756-8123
Fax: (202)756-8087

Employers
McDermott, Will and Emery (Associate Legislative Director)

O'KEEFE, Rush

300 Maryland Ave. NE
Washington, DC 20002
Tel: (202)546-1631
Fax: (202)546-3309
Registered: LDA

Employers
FedEx Corp. (V. President, Regulatory)

O'KEEFE, Stephanie

1825 K St. NW
Suite 1100
Washington, DC 20006
Tel: (202)785-2908
Fax: (202)835-8931
Registered: LDA

Employers
Local Initiatives Support Corp.

O'KEEFE, William

1461 Carrington Ridge Ln.
Vienna, VA 22182
Tel: (703)893-1814
Registered: LDA
EMail: okeefew@worldnet.att.net

Employers
Marshall Institute, George C. (Managing Director)
Self-employed as an independent consultant.

O'KELLY, James S.

1225 I St. NW
Suite 1150
Washington, DC 20005
Tel: (202)457-0300
Fax: (202)331-8746
Trial Attorney, Customs Section, Civil Division, Department of Justice, 1964-66.

Employers
Barnes, Richardson and Colburn (Partner)

O'LEARY, Joseph E.

1400 L St. NW
Washington, DC 20005-3502
Tel: (202)371-5804
Fax: (202)371-5950
Registered: LDA
EMail: joleary@winston.com
Held several Congressional staff positions, 1969-75. Former Colonel, U.S. Army.

Employers
Winston & Strawn (Consultant, Legislative and Regulatory Practice)

Clients Represented
On Behalf of Winston & Strawn
Barr Laboratories
Corning Inc.
DMJM + Harris
Motor Coach Industries, Inc.
Norfolk Southern Corp.
Northland Holdings, Inc.
Robinson Terminal
Yellow Corp.

O'LEARY, Kathleen

1200 17th St. NW
Washington, DC 20036-3097
Tel: (202)331-5900
Fax: (202)973-5373
Registered: LDA
EMail: koleary@dineout.org
Former Legislative Aide on Capitol Hill, 1987-97.

Employers
Nat'l Restaurant Ass'n (Director, Tax Policy)

O'LEARY, Maureen

4330 East-West Hwy.
Room 720
Bethesda, MD 20207
Tel: (301)504-0515
Fax: (301)504-0016
EMail: moleary@cpsc.gov

Employers
Consumer Product Safety Commission (Director, Office of Congressional Relations)

O'LEARY, Stella

3744 Oliver St. NW
Washington, DC 20015
Tel: (202)362-9064
Fax: (202)237-5141
EMail: irldems@erols.com

Employers
Irish American Democrats (President/Treasurer)

O'MALIA, Scott

901 F St. NW
Suite 800
Washington, DC 20004
Tel: (202)585-3800
Fax: (202)585-3806
Former Aide to Senator Mitch McConnell (R-KY).

Employers
Mirant (Director, Federal Legislative Affairs)

O'MALLEY, Cindy

1735 New York Ave. NW
Suite 500
Washington, DC 20006-4759
Tel: (202)628-1700
Fax: (202)331-1024
Registered: LDA
EMail: cindyo@prestongates.com
Former Deputy Project Manager for Systematic Management Services, Department of Energy. Former Legislative Director to Rep. Robert W. Davis (R-MI). Former Professional Staff Member, Subcommittee on Research and Development, House Armed Services Committee.

Employers
Preston Gates Ellis & Rouvelas Meeds LLP (Government Affairs Analyst)

Clients Represented
On Behalf of Preston Gates Ellis & Rouvelas Meeds LLP
Battelle Memorial Institute
BWXT, Inc.
Envirocare of Utah, Inc.
Foster Wheeler Environmental Corp.
Magazine Publishers of America
Northern Michigan University
Pitney Bowes, Inc.
Stone and Webster Engineering Corp.
USFHP Conference Group

O'MALLEY, E. Michael

2300 N St. NW
Washington, DC 20037-1128
Tel: (202)663-8000
Fax: (202)663-8007
Registered: FARA
EMail: michael.omalley@shawpittman.com

Employers
Shaw Pittman (Government Relations Advisor)

Clients Represented
On Behalf of Shaw Pittman
Mexico, Secretaria de Comercio y Fomento Industrial (SECOFI)

O'NEAL, John F.

One Massachusetts Ave. NW
Suite 800
Washington, DC 20001
Tel: (202)628-0210
Fax: (202)628-2482
Registered: LDA

Employers
John F. O'Neal Law Offices (President)

Clients Represented
On Behalf of John F. O'Neal Law Offices
Nat'l Rural Telecom Ass'n

O'NEALL, Nancy

633 Pennsylvania Ave. NW
Fourth Floor
Washington, DC 20004
Tel: (202)783-2596
Fax: (202)628-5379
Registered: LDA
EMail: noneall@psw-inc.com

Employers
Public Strategies Washington, Inc.

Clients Represented
On Behalf of Public Strategies Washington, Inc.
AngloGold North America
Edison Electric Institute

O'NEIL, John M.

10640 Main St.
Suite 200
Fairfax, VA 22030
Tel: (703)352-3400
Fax: (703)385-6470
Registered: LDA

Employers
JGW Internat'l Ltd. (V. President)

Clients Represented
On Behalf of JGW Internat'l Ltd.
Graseby Plc

O'NEIL, Michael J.

1735 New York Ave. NW
Suite 500
Washington, DC 20006-4759
Tel: (202)628-1700
Fax: (202)331-1024
Registered: LDA
Former General Counsel to the Central Intelligence Agency; Counselor to the Department of Defense; and Counsel to Rep. Thomas S. Foley (D-WA).

Employers
Preston Gates Ellis & Rouvelas Meeds LLP (Partner)

Clients Represented
On Behalf of Preston Gates Ellis & Rouvelas Meeds LLP
Brown-Forman Corp.
Burlington Northern Santa Fe Railway
eLottery, Inc.
Microsoft Corp.
VoiceStream Wireless Corp.

O'NEIL, III, Thomas F.

1133 19th St. NW
Washington, DC 20036
Tel: (202)736-6412
Fax: (202)735-6710
Former U.S. Attorney for the District of Maryland and former Clerk to Judge Alexander Harvey, II, U.S. District Court for the District of Maryland.

Employers
MCI WorldCom Corp. (General Counsel, MCI Division)

O'NEILL, Alison

1223 Potomac St. NW
Washington, DC 20007-0231
Tel: (202)333-8190
Fax: (202)337-3809
EMail: aoneill@mindspring.com

Employers
Robert N. Pyle & Associates (V. President)

Clients Represented
On Behalf of Robert N. Pyle & Associates
Bulgarian-American Business Center
Elkem Metals Co.
Independent Bakers Ass'n
Internat'l Dairy-Deli-Bakery Ass'n
McKee Foods Corp.
Orbex Resources
Strategic Minerals Corp.
Welch's Foods, Inc.

O'NEILL, Brian

1005 N. Glebe Rd.
Suite 800
Arlington, VA 22201
EMail: boneill@iihs.org

Tel: (703)247-1500
Fax: (703)247-1678

Employers

Insurance Institute for Highway Safety (President)

O'NEILL, Christopher R.

1310 19th St. NW
Washington, DC 20036

Tel: (202)466-6555
Fax: (202)466-6596
Registered: LDA, FARA

Counsel to U.S. Senate Committee on Commerce, Science and Transportation, 1976-77.

Employers

Democratic Candidate Fund (Treasurer)
O'Neill, Athy & Casey, P.C. (Partner)

Clients Represented

On Behalf of O'Neill, Athy & Casey, P.C.

American Hospital Ass'n
AT&T
Beth Israel/Deaconess Medical Center
Boston Museum of Science
Coalition of Boston Teaching Hospitals
Des Moines University, Osteopathic Medical Center
Glass Packaging Institute
JM Family Enterprises
Lehman Brothers
Marathon Oil Co.
Massachusetts General/Brigham and Women's Hospital
New England Medical Center
Northeastern University
Partners Healthcare System, Inc.
TXU Business Services
USX Corp.
Viacom Inc.

O'NEILL, Daniel J.

1401 K St. NW
Tenth Floor
Washington, DC 20005

Tel: (202)216-2200
Fax: (202)216-2999
Registered: LDA, FARA

Former Legislative Assistant to Senator Brock Adams (D-WA) and Peace Corps Volunteer to Ghana.

Employers

Jefferson-Waterman Internat'l, LLC (Senior V. President)

Clients Represented

On Behalf of Jefferson-Waterman Internat'l, LLC

Japan External Trade Organization (JETRO)
Matsushita Electric Industrial Co., Ltd.
Sumitomo Corp. of America

O'NEILL, Eileen

601 Wythe St.
Alexandria, VA 22314-1994
EMail: eoneill@wef.org

Tel: (703)684-2400
Fax: (703)684-2492

Employers

Water Environment Federation (Director, Technical and Educational Services)

O'NEILL, J. Vincent

1828 L St. NW
Suite 1202
Washington, DC 20036-5104
EMail: v.oneill@ieee.org

Tel: (202)785-0017
Fax: (202)785-0835
Registered: LDA

Employers

Institute of Electrical and Electronics Engineers, Inc. (Senior Legislative Representative, Career Activities)

O'NEILL, Joseph P.

633 Pennsylvania Ave. NW
Fourth Floor
Washington, DC 20004
EMail: joneill@psw-inc.com

Tel: (202)783-2596
Fax: (202)628-5379
Registered: LDA, FARA

Administrative Assistant to Senator Lloyd Bentsen (D-TX), 1978-84.

Employers

Public Strategies Washington, Inc. (President)

Clients Represented

On Behalf of Public Strategies Washington, Inc.

Affiliated Computer Services
American Methanol Institute
AngloGold North America
Anheuser-Busch Cos., Inc.
Bristol-Myers Squibb Co.
Chamber of Commerce of the U.S.A.
Edison Electric Institute
Greater El Paso Chamber of Commerce
Honda North America, Inc.
Hutchison Whampo, LTD
Lockheed Martin IMS
Mexico, Secretaria de Comercio y Fomento Industrial (SECOFI)
Reuters America Inc.
Southwest Airlines

O'NEILL, Robert

127 Park St. NE
Vienna, VA 22180-4602
EMail: info@mss-hq.com

Tel: (703)281-6613
Fax: (703)281-6671

Employers

Manufacturers Standardization Soc. of the Valve and Fitting Industry, Inc. (Exec. Director)

O'NEILL, Robert J.

1120 G St. NW
Suite 850
Washington, DC 20005
EMail: roneill@napawash.org

Tel: (202)347-3190
Fax: (202)393-0993

Employers

Nat'l Academy of Public Administration (President)

O'NEILL, Sean

1750 New York Ave. NW
Washington, DC 20006

Tel: (202)737-8484
Fax: (202)737-8418

Former Legislative Assistant to Rep. Jack Quinn (R-NY).

Employers

Internat'l Ass'n of Fire Fighters (Governmental Affairs Representative)

O'NEILL, William S.

401 Ninth St. NW
Suite 400
Washington, DC 20004

Tel: (202)585-1933
Fax: (202)585-1899
Registered: LDA

Employers

Sprint Corp. (Director, Government Affairs)

O'QUINN, Beth

2750 Prosperity Ave.
Suite 620
Fairfax, VA 22031-4312

Tel: (703)698-0291
Fax: (703)698-0297

Employers

Specialized Carriers and Rigging Ass'n (V. President)

O'REGAN, Charles R.

1717 K St. NW
Suite 500
Washington, DC 20006

Tel: (202)466-9000
Fax: (202)466-9009
Registered: LDA

Former Chief of Staff to Rep. Dante Fascell (D-FL).

Employers

Palumbo & Cerrell, Inc. (V. President, Government Affairs)

Clients Represented

On Behalf of Palumbo & Cerrell, Inc.

American Soc. of Composers, Authors and Publishers
American Trans Air
HT Medical
K Capital Partners
Music Educators Nat'l Conference

O'REILLY, Mary

701 Pennsylvania Ave. NW
Suite 725
Washington, DC 20004
EMail: mary.oreilly@group.novartis.com

Tel: (202)638-7429
Fax: (202)628-4763
Registered: LDA

Employers

Novartis Corp. (Manager, Legislative Affairs)

O'ROURKE, John T.

801 Pennsylvania Ave. NW
Fifth Floor
Washington, DC 20004

Tel: (202)662-4720
Fax: (202)662-4748
Registered: LDA

Minority Staff Member, House Banking Committee, 1982-84. Legislative Assistant to Rep. Edwin R. Bethune, Jr. (R-AR), 1981-82. Economist, Department of Labor, 1974-77.

Employers

John T. O'Rourke Law Offices (Principal)

Clients Represented

On Behalf of John T. O'Rourke Law Offices

Alliance Data Systems
First American
Goldman, Sachs and Co.
Herzog, Heine, Geduld, Inc.
Internat'l Game Technology
The Limited Inc.
Securities Industry Ass'n

O'ROURKE, Peter

1319 F St. NW
Suite 301
Washington, DC 20004

Tel: (202)393-3240
Fax: (202)393-4385
Registered: LDA

Employers

Sparber and Associates (V. President)

Clients Represented

On Behalf of Sparber and Associates

Great Lakes Chemical Corp.
Marathon Ashland Petroleum, LLC
U.S. Steel

O'ROURKE, Thomas J.

1100 Connecticut Ave. NW
Suite 900
Washington, DC 20036-4101

Tel: (202)463-8400
Fax: (202)833-8082

Senior Trial Attorney, District Counsel for Washington, DC (1978-80), Staff Assistant to the Regional Counsel for the Midwest Region (1975-78), and Attorney, Office of Chief Counsel (1974-83), Internal Revenue Service, Department of the Treasury.

Employers

Shaw, Bransford, Veilleux & Roth (Of Counsel)

O'ROURKE, Timothy J.

1200 New Hampshire Ave. NW
Suite 800
Washington, DC 20036-6802
EMail: torourke@dlalaw.com

Tel: (202)776-2000
Fax: (202)776-2222

Deputy Assistant Attorney General and Counselor to the Assistant Attorney General for Civil Division of Department of Justice, 1992-93.

Employers

Dow, Lohnes & Albertson, PLLC (Member)

O'SHAUGHNESSY, John J.

112 S. West St.
Alexandria, VA 22314

Tel: (703)683-9600
Fax: (703)836-5255
Registered: LDA

Assistant Secretary for Management and Budget, Department of Health and Human Services, 1983-86. Republican Staff Director, House Budget Committee, 1980-83.

Employers

Strategic Management Associates (President)

O'SHEA, Sean

700 13th St. NW
Suite 400
Washington, DC 20005
EMail: soshea@cassidy.com

Tel: (202)347-0773
Fax: (202)347-0785
Registered: LDA

Former Senior Advisor to Cabinet Secretary at White House Office of Cabinet Affairs. Executive Assistant to Office of Secretary at Department of Agriculture.

Employers

Cassidy & Associates, Inc. (Account Executive)

Clients Represented

On Behalf of Cassidy & Associates, Inc.

Air Products and Chemicals, Inc.
Fairview Hospital and Healthcare Services
Nat'l Jewish Medical and Research Center
Northwestern University
Ocean Spray Cranberries
University of Massachusetts Memorial Health System

O'STEEN, Ph.D., David N.

419 Seventh St. NW
Suite 500
Washington, DC 20004
Tel: (202)626-8820
Fax: (202)737-9189
Registered: LDA

Employers
Nat'l Right to Life Committee (Exec. Director)

O'SULLIVAN, Lynda Troutman

655 15th St. NW
Suite 900
Washington, DC 20005-5701
EMail: losullivan@milchev.com
Tel: (202)626-5800
Fax: (202)628-0858
Registered: LDA

Employers
Miller & Chevalier, Chartered (Member)

O'SULLIVAN, Terence M.

905 16th St. NW
Washington, DC 20006
Tel: (202)737-8320
Fax: (202)737-2754

Employers
Laborers' Internat'l Union of North America (Staff Assistant to the General President)

O'TOOLE, Diane

1000 Wilson Blvd.
Suite 2300
Arlington, VA 22209
Tel: (703)875-8400
Fax: (703)276-0711
Registered: LDA

Employers
Northrop Grumman Corp. (Manager, Legislative Affairs)

O'TOOLE, Eve

1101 17th St. NW
Suite 803
Washington, DC 20036
Tel: (202)833-0007
Fax: (202)833-0086
Registered: LDA

Employers
MARC Associates, Inc. (Legislative Associate)

Clients Represented
On Behalf of MARC Associates, Inc.
Corporation for Supportive Housing
Fine Arts Museums of San Francisco
League of California Cities
Los Angeles to Pasadena Metro Blue Line Construction Authority
Los Angeles, California, Community Development Commission of the County of
Los Angeles, California, County of
San Francisco, California, City and County of
TELACU
University of California at Irvine Advanced Power and Energy Program

O'TOOLE, J. Denis

1730 K St. NW
Suite 1106
Washington, DC 20006
Tel: (202)466-3561
Fax: (202)466-3583
Registered: LDA

Employers
Household Financial Group, Ltd. (V. President, Federal Governmental Relations)

O'TOOLE, Patrice

750 First St. NE
Suite 5007
Washington, DC 20002-4242
EMail: potoole@apa.org
Tel: (202)336-5920
Fax: (202)336-5953

Employers
Federation of Behavioral, Psychological and Cognitive Sciences (Acting Director)

O'TOOLE, Robert M.

1919 Pennsylvania Ave. NW
Seventh Floor
Washington, DC 20006-3488
Tel: (202)557-2700

Employers
Mortgage Bankers Ass'n of America (Senior Staff V. President, Residential Finance/Government Agency Relations)

O'TOOLE, Stephen E.

1660 L St. NW
Fourth Floor
Washington, DC 20036
Tel: (202)775-5056
Fax: (202)775-5045
Registered: LDA

Employers
General Motors Corp. (Senior Washington Representative)

O'TOOLE, Thomas

700 13th St. NW
Suite 1000
Washington, DC 20005
Tel: (202)347-6633
Fax: (202)347-8713

Employers
O'Toole Consulting (President)
Powell Tate (Consultant)

Clients Represented
On Behalf of O'Toole Consulting
Discovery Communications, Inc.

OAKERSON, Bill

880 S. Pickett St.
Alexandria, VA 22304
EMail: boakerson@boatus.com
Tel: (703)461-2864
Fax: (703)461-2845

Employers
Boat Owners Ass'n of The United States (BOAT/U.S.) (President)

OAKES, Maribeth

1090 Vermont Ave. NW
Suite 1200
Washington, DC 20005
Tel: (202)289-6790
Fax: (202)289-6791
Registered: LDA

Employers
Nat'l Congress of Parents and Teachers (Director, Legislation)

OAKLEY, Diane

555 12th St. NW
Suite 700 South
Washington, DC 20004
Tel: (202)637-8915
Fax: (202)637-8950

Employers
TIAA-CREF (V. President, Government Relations)

OAKLEY, Janet

444 N. Capitol St. NW
Suite 249
Washington, DC 20001
Tel: (202)624-5800
Fax: (202)624-5806

Employers
American Ass'n of State Highway and Transportation Officials (Director, Government Relations)

OAKLEY, Robert L.

E.B. Williams Law Library
Georgetown University Law Center
111 G St. NW
Washington, DC 20001-1417
EMail: oakley@law.georgetown.edu
Tel: (202)662-9160
Fax: (202)662-9168
Registered: LDA

Employers
American Ass'n of Law Libraries (Washington Affairs Representative)

OBADAL, Anthony J.

121 N. Henry St.
Alexandria, VA 22314
Tel: (703)739-9485
Fax: (703)739-9488
Registered: LDA

Employers
Obadal and MacLeod, p.c. (Partner)

Clients Represented
On Behalf of Obadal and MacLeod, p.c.
American Concrete Pipe Ass'n
Associated Equipment Distributors

OBER, Ann

110 Maryland Ave. NE
Suite 205
Washington, DC 20002
Tel: (202)543-8505
Fax: (202)675-6469

Employers
Women's Action for New Directions (WAND)/Women Legislators' Lobby (WILL) (WILL Washington Director)

OBERBROECKLING, Laura J.

701 Pennsylvania Ave. NW
Suite 900
Washington, DC 20004-2608
EMail: loberbroeckling@mintz.com
Tel: (202)434-7300
Fax: (202)434-7400
Registered: LDA

Employers
Mintz, Levin, Cohn, Ferris, Glovsky and Popeo, P.C. (Partner)

OBERDORFER, John L.

2550 M St. NW
Washington, DC 20037-1350
Tel: (202)457-6000
Fax: (202)457-6315
Registered: LDA
EMail: joberdorfer@pattonboggs.com
Member, Clinton-Gore Transition Team, 1992. Attorney, Office of the General Counsel, Department of Transportation, 1971-74.

Employers
Patton Boggs, LLP (Partner)

OBIECUNAS, Robert J.

666 11th St. NW
Suite 600
Washington, DC 20001
EMail: bobiecun@ccianet.org
Tel: (202)783-0070
Fax: (202)783-0534

Employers
Computer and Communications Industry Ass'n (CCIA) (Controller)

OBRINSKY, Mark H.

1850 M St. NW
Suite 540
Washington, DC 20036
Tel: (202)974-2300
Fax: (202)775-0112

Employers
Nat'l Multi-Housing Council (V. President, Research and Chief Economist)

OBUCHOWSKI, Janice

555 12th St. NW
Suite 950N
Washington, DC 20004
Tel: (202)371-2220
Fax: (202)371-1497
Former Assistant Secretary, Department of Commerce, Nat'l Telecommunications Information Administration.

Employers
Freedom Technologies, Inc. (President)

OCCHIONERO, Anthony

400 N. Capitol St. NW
Washington, DC 20001
EMail: tocchionero@agcc.org
Tel: (202)824-7140
Fax: (202)824-7093

Employers
American Gas Cooling Center (Exec. Director)

OCHOA, Mario

12501 Old Columbia Pike
Silver Spring, MD 20904
Tel: (301)680-6380
Fax: (301)680-6370

Employers
Adventist Development and Relief Agency Internat'l (Exec. V. President)

ODAY, Larry A.

1455 Pennsylvania Ave. NW
Suite 700
Washington, DC 20004-1008
EMail: loday@velaw.com
Tel: (202)639-6792
Fax: (202)639-6604
Registered: LDA

Employers
Vinson & Elkins L.L.P. (Partner)

Clients Represented
On Behalf of Vinson & Elkins L.L.P.
Aon Corp.
Foundation for Hematopoietic Cell Therapy Accreditation
Ohio Hospital Ass'n
Scott & White Hospital

ODEEN, Phil

1001 19th St. North
Suite 800
Arlington, VA 22209-3901
EMail: phil.odeen@trw.com
Tel: (703)276-5050
Fax: (703)276-5057
Registered: LDA

Employers
TRW Inc. (Exec. V. President, Washington Operations)

ODENTHAL, Nancy A.

1850 M St. NW
Suite 1040
Washington, DC 20036
EMail: nodenthal@oaaa.org
Tel: (202)833-5566
Fax: (202)833-1522

Employers
Outdoor Advertising Ass'n of America (Manager, Legislative Services)

ODETTE, Ken

1655 N. Fort Meyer Dr.
Suite 510
Arlington, VA 22209
Tel: (703)525-0511
Fax: (703)525-0743

Employers
Composites Fabricators Ass'n (Director, Government Affairs)

ODLAND, Gerald C.

17904 Georgia Ave.
Suite 215
Olney, MD 20832-2277
EMail: aceihq@aol.com
Tel: (301)570-2111
Fax: (301)570-2212

Employers
Ass'n for Childhood Education Internat'l (Exec. Director)

ODLE, Bob Glen

555 13th St. NW
Washington, DC 20004-1109
Tel: (202)637-5600
Fax: (202)637-5910

Employers
Hogan & Hartson L.L.P. (Partner)

ODLE, Jr., Robert C.

1615 L St. NW
Suite 700
Washington, DC 20036-5610
Tel: (202)682-7180
Fax: (202)857-0939
Registered: LDA
Assistant Secretary, Department of Energy, 1981-85. Deputy Assistant Secretary, Department of Housing and Urban Development, 1973-76. Staff Assistant to the President, The White House, 1969-71.

Employers
Weil, Gotshal & Manges, LLP (Partner)

Clients Represented

On Behalf of Weil, Gotshal & Manges, LLP
Empire Blue Cross and Blue Shield
GAF Corp.
General Motors Corp.
Nat'l Football League Players Ass'n
Nomura Internat'l plc

ODOM, Jr., James C. "Cal"

701 Pennsylvania Ave. NW
Washington, DC 20004-2696
Tel: (202)508-5774
Fax: (202)508-5403
Registered: LDA
Former Aide to Rep. Clyde Holloway (R-LA).

Employers
Edison Electric Institute (Senior Legislative Representative)

ODOM, USA (Ret), Lt. Gen. William E.

1015 18th St. NW
Suite 300
Washington, DC 20036
Tel: (202)223-7770
Fax: (202)223-8537

Employers
Hudson Institute (Director, National Security Studies)

ODUM, Mark

1010 Wayne Ave.
Suite 800
Silver Spring, MD 20910
Tel: (301)562-2400
Fax: (301)562-2401

Employers
Nat'l Rehabilitation Information Center (Project Director)

OFFEN, Neil H.

1275 Pennsylvania Ave. NW
Suite 800
Washington, DC 20004
Tel: (202)293-5760
Fax: (202)463-4569
Registered: LDA

Employers
Direct Selling Ass'n (President)

OFORI, Kofi Asiedu

1140 Connecticut Ave. NW
Suite 1142
Washington, DC 20036
Tel: (202)862-4383
Fax: (202)331-5562

Employers
Technology, Entertainment and Communications (TEC) Law Group

OGILVIE, Donald G.

1120 Connecticut Ave. NW
Washington, DC 20036
Tel: (202)663-5000
Fax: (202)663-7533
Registered: LDA

Employers
American Bankers Ass'n (Exec. V. President)

OGRODZINSKI, Henry M.

8401 Colesville Rd.
Suite 505
Silver Spring, MD 20910
EMail: henryo@nasao.org
Tel: (301)588-0587
Fax: (301)585-1803

Employers
Nat'l Ass'n of State Aviation Officials (President and Chief Exec. Officer)

OGSBURY, James

499 S. Capitol St. SW
Suite 600
Washington, DC 20003
EMail: jogsbury@joneswalker.com
Tel: (202)828-8363
Fax: (202)828-6907
Registered: LDA
Former Staff Director, Subcommittee on Energy and Water Development, House Committee on Appropriations.

Employers
Jones, Walker, Waechter, Poitevent, Carrere & Denegre, L.L.P. (Special Counsel)

Clients Represented

On Behalf of Jones, Walker, Waechter, Poitevent, Carrere & Denegre, L.L.P.
ACS Government Solutions Group
Baton Rouge, Louisiana, City of
Boys Town USA
Broward, Florida, County of
Committee of Unsecured Creditors
General Category Tuna Ass'n
General Electric Co.
Jacobus Tenbroek Memorial Fund
Martinez and Curtis
Mesa, Arizona, City of
Raytheon Co.
Stewart Enterprises, Inc.

OHLSEN, John W.

9271 Old Keene Mill Rd.
Suite 200
Burke, VA 22015-4202
Tel: (703)451-1200
Fax: (703)451-1201

Employers
Defense Orientation Conference Ass'n (Exec. Vice President)

OHLSON, Barry

1615 L St. NW
Suite 1260
Washington, DC 20036
Tel: (202)367-7600
Fax: (202)659-1931

Employers
Winstar Communications, Inc. (Counsel)

OHMANS, Karen

2000 P St. NW
Suite 300
Washington, DC 20036
Tel: (202)828-5170
Fax: (202)785-3862

Employers
American Labor Education Center (Director)

OILMAN, Betsy

1501 M St. NW
Suite 600
Washington, DC 20005-1710
Tel: (202)739-0200
Fax: (202)659-8287

Employers
BSMG Worldwide (Senior Associate)

OJAKLI, Ziad S.

1600 Pennsylvania Ave. NW
107 E. Wing
Washington, DC 20500
Tel: (202)456-6493
Fax: (202)456-2604
Former Aide to Senator Paul Coverdell (R-GA).

Employers
Executive Office of the President - The White House (Deputy Assistant to the President for Legislative Affairs, Senate Liaison Office)

OKA, Mr. Takashi

2555 Pennsylvania Ave. NW
Suite 503
Washington, DC 20037
Tel: (202)463-9279
Fax: (202)463-9283
Registered: FARA

Employers
Self-employed as an independent consultant.

Clients Represented

As an independent consultant
Liberal Party of Japan

OKONSKI, Kendra

1001 Connecticut Ave. NW
Suite 1250
Washington, DC 20036
Tel: (202)331-1010
Fax: (202)331-0640

Employers
Competitive Enterprise Institute (Research Assistant)

OKUN, B. Robert

1299 Pennsylvania Ave. NW
Suite 1100 West
Washington, DC 20004-2407
Tel: (202)637-4000
Fax: (202)637-4006
Registered: LDA

Employers
General Electric Co. (V. President, NBC Washington)
Nat'l Broadcasting Co. (V. President, NBC Washington Office)

OKUN, Steven R.

316 Pennsylvania Ave. SE
Suite 300
Washington, DC 20003
Tel: (202)675-4220
Fax: (202)675-4230

Employers
United Parcel Service (Manager, Public Affairs)

OLADEINDE, Fred

1900 L St. NW
Suite 414
Washington, DC 20036
Tel: (202)331-1333
Fax: (202)331-8547

Employers
Foundation for Democracy in Africa (President)

OLANOFF, Mark

909 N. Washington St.
Suite 301
Alexandria, VA 22314
Tel: (703)684-1981
Fax: (703)548-4876
Registered: LDA

Employers
The Retired Enlisted Ass'n (Legislative Director)

OLCOTT, John W.

1200 18th St. NW
Suite 400
Washington, DC 20036-2506
Tel: (202)783-9000
Fax: (202)331-8364

Employers
Nat'l Business Aviation Ass'n (President)

OLDAKER, William C.

818 Connecticut Ave. NW
Suite 1100
Washington, DC 20006
EMail: weo@oldaker-harris.com
Tel: (202)728-1010
Fax: (202)728-4044
Registered: LDA
General Counsel, Federal Election Commission, 1976-79. Special Assistant to the Chairman, Equal Employment Opportunity Commission, 1969-73. Attorney, Federal Communications Commission, 1968-69.

Employers
Committee for a Democratic Majority (Treasurer)
Future Fund (PAC Administrator)
Glacier PAC
The National Group, LLP (Partner)
Oldaker and Harris, LLP (Partner)

Clients Represented

On Behalf of The National Group, LLP

Biotechnology Industry Organization

On Behalf of Oldaker and Harris, LLP

Committee for a Democratic Majority
Edison Electric Institute
Fajardo, Puerto Rico, Municipality of
Guaynabo, Puerto Rico, City of
Mayaguez, Puerto Rico, Municipality of
Monsanto Co.
Puerto Rico Senate
Searchlight Victory Fund
Tohono O'Odham Nation

OLDHAM, Judith L.

3050 K St. NW
Washington, DC 20007
Tel: (202)342-8400
Fax: (202)342-8451
EMail: joldham@colliershannon.com

Employers

Collier Shannon Scott, PLLC (Member)

Clients Represented

On Behalf of Collier Shannon Scott, PLLC

Outdoor Power Equipment Institute

OLESON, Peter C.

P.O. Box 383
Galesville, MD 20765-0383
Tel: (301)261-9990
Registered: LDA

Employers

Potomac Strategies & Analysis, Inc. (President)

Clients Represented

On Behalf of Potomac Strategies & Analysis, Inc.

Autometric Inc.
Sarnoff Corp.

OLEYNIK, Ronald A.

2099 Pennsylvania Ave. NW
Suite 100
Washington, DC 20006
Tel: (202)457-7183
Fax: (202)828-1868
Registered: LDA, FARA
EMail: roleynik@hklaw.com

Employers

Holland & Knight LLP (Partner)

Clients Represented

On Behalf of Holland & Knight LLP

ESPN, Inc.

OLINGER, John Peter

1225 I St. NW
Suite 350
Washington, DC 20005
Tel: (202)789-1110
Fax: (202)789-1116
Registered: LDA
EMail: jolinger@dmggroup.com
Staff Director, Subcommittee on Human Services, House Select Committee on Aging, 1989-93. Chief of Staff (1985-88) and Staff Assistant (1984) to Rep. Thomas J. Downey (D-NY).

Employers

Downey McGrath Group, Inc. (V. President)

Clients Represented

On Behalf of Downey McGrath Group, Inc.

American Foundation for AIDS Research
American Soc. of Anesthesiologists
AOL Time Warner
DuPont
Energy Efficiency Systems, Inc.
Fannie Mae
Fuji Photo Film U.S.A., Inc.
Healthcare Ass'n of New York State
Kalkines, Arky, Zall and Bernstein
The Limited Inc.
Metropolitan Life Insurance Co.
The New York Structural Biology Center
Philipp Brothers Chemicals, Inc.

OLIPHANT, III, C. Frederick

655 15th St. NW
Suite 900
Washington, DC 20005-5701
Tel: (202)626-5800
Fax: (202)628-0858
Registered: LDA
EMail: foliphant@milchev.com

Employers

Miller & Chevalier, Chartered (Member)

Clients Represented

On Behalf of Miller & Chevalier, Chartered

American Staffing Ass'n

OLIVE, David A.

1776 I St. NW
Suite 880
Washington, DC 20006
Tel: (202)331-8750
Fax: (202)331-8797
EMail: dolive@wdc.fujitsu.com

Employers

Fujitsu Limited (Deputy General Manager)

OLIVE, David M.

801 Pennsylvania Ave. NW
Suite 245
Washington, DC 20005
Tel: (202)624-1512
Fax: (202)318-0338
Registered: LDA
EMail: dolive@jaygrant.com
Former Chief of Staff to Asa Hutchinson (R-AR).

Employers

Jay Grant & Associates (Federal Counsel)

Clients Represented

On Behalf of Jay Grant & Associates

Arkansas, Office of the Governor of the State of
Fort Smith Regional Airport
Travelocity.com
Vision Technologies, Inc.

OLIVE, Jr., John T.

515 King St.
Suite 420
Alexandria, VA 22314-3103
Tel: (703)684-5570
Fax: (703)684-6048
EMail: jolive@clarionmr.com

Employers

Better Hearing Institute (Exec. Director)
CLARION Management Resources, Inc. (Account Executive)

Clients Represented

On Behalf of CLARION Management Resources, Inc.

Better Hearing Institute

OLIVER, Janice

25 Louisiana Ave. NW
Washington, DC 20001-2198
Tel: (202)624-8741
Fax: (202)624-8973
Registered: LDA

Employers

Internat'l Brotherhood of Teamsters (Legislative Representative)

OLIVER, Linda L.

555 13th St. NW
Washington, DC 20004-1109
Tel: (202)637-6527
Fax: (202)637-5910
Registered: LDA
EMail: lloliver@hhlaw.com
Legal Advisor to Commissioner Ervin S. Duggan (1990-94), Trial Attorney, Litigation Division, Office of General Counsel (1982-90), Attorney, Administrative Law Division, Office of the General Counsel (1980-82), and Law Student Intern, Office of the Chairman (1979), all at the Federal Communications Commission.

Employers

Hogan & Hartson L.L.P. (Partner)

Clients Represented

On Behalf of Hogan & Hartson L.L.P.

ASCENT (Ass'n of Community Enterprises)

OLIVER, R. Teel

601 Pennsylvania Ave. NW
Suite 1200
North Bldg.
Washington, DC 20036
Tel: (202)638-4170
Fax: (202)638-3670
Registered: LDA

Employers

Merck & Co. (V. President, Federal Policy and Government Relations)

OLIVERI, Ann

1025 Thomas Jefferson St. NW
Suite 500 W
Washington, DC 20007-5201
Tel: (202)624-7000
Fax: (202)624-7140
EMail: aoliveri@uli.org

Employers

Urban Land Institute (Senior V. President, Leadership and Outreach)

OLMER, Lionel H.

1615 L St. NW
Suite 1300
Washington, DC 20036
Tel: (202)223-7300
Fax: (202)223-7420
EMail: lolmer@paulweiss.com
Undersecretary for International Trade and head of the International Trade Administration, Department of Commerce, 1981-85. Executive Staff, President's Foreign Intelligence Advisory Board, 1973-77.

Employers

Paul, Weiss, Rifkind, Wharton & Garrison (Partner)

Clients Represented

On Behalf of Paul, Weiss, Rifkind, Wharton & Garrison

Federation of Korean Industries

OLSEN, Christie

1022 29th St. NW
Washington, DC 20007
Tel: (202)333-3232
Fax: (202)333-5001
Registered: LDA
EMail: colsen@wincapitol.com

Employers

WinCapitol, Inc. (Principal)

Clients Represented

On Behalf of WinCapitol, Inc.

AFL-CIO (Union Label and Service Trades Department)
American Green Network
Danaher Corp.

OLSEN, Darcy

1000 Massachusetts Ave. NW
Washington, DC 20001
Tel: (202)842-0200
Fax: (202)842-3490

Employers

Cato Institute (Director, Education and Child Policy)

OLSEN, George G.

1155 21st St. NW
Suite 300
Washington, DC 20036
Tel: (202)659-8201
Fax: (202)659-5249
Registered: LDA
EMail: ggolsen@wms-jen.com

Employers

Williams & Jensen, P.C. (Partner)

Clients Represented

On Behalf of Williams & Jensen, P.C.

Abbott Laboratories
Aegon USA
American Home Products Corp.
Applera Corp.
AstraZeneca Inc.
Bayer Corp.
The Church Alliance
CIGNA Corp.
Credit Suisse First Boston Corp.
The DuPont Pharmaceutical Co.
Genentech, Inc.
Girling Health Care
Keystone, Inc.
J. P. Morgan Chase & Co.
J. P. Morgan Securities
Nat'l Ass'n of Rehabilitation Agencies
Novartis Corp.
Oklahoma Gas and Electric Co.
Pharmaceutical Research and Manufacturers of America
Private Practice Section of the American Physical Therapy Ass'n
Texas Pacific Group

OLSEN, Nathan M.

1301 K St. NW
Suite 900, East Tower
Washington, DC 20005
Tel: (202)408-8700
Fax: (202)408-8704
Registered: LDA
EMail: nolsen@haake-dc.com

Employers

Haake and Associates (Counsel)

Clients Represented

On Behalf of Haake and Associates

American Ass'n of Orthodontists
American Orthotic and Prosthetic Ass'n
EMC Corp.
Free Trade Lumber Council
Jewelers of America
The Lansdale Company
North American Insulation Manufacturers Ass'n
Ortho Concepts
Saint-Gobain Corp.
Science Applications Internat'l Corp. (SAIC)
Seal Beach, California, City of
Tanimura & Antle, Inc.
Titan Corp.

OLSHAN, Mark

1640 Rhode Island Ave. NW
Washington, DC 20036-3278
Tel: (202)857-6535
Fax: (202)857-0980
Registered: LDA
EMail: molshan@bnaibrith.org

Employers

B'nai B'rith Internat'l (Director, Senior Housing and Services)

OLSON, Barbara K.

1275 Pennsylvania Ave. NW
Tenth Floor
Washington, DC 20004
Tel: (202)347-6000
Fax: (202)347-6001

Employers

Balch & Bingham LLP (Partner)

Clients Represented

On Behalf of Balch & Bingham LLP

Bay Harbor Management, L.C.
informal coalition
Interstate Wine Coalition

OLSON, Beth

1111 19th St. NW
Suite 800
Washington, DC 20036
Tel: (202)463-2700
Fax: (202)463-2785

Employers

American Forest & Paper Ass'n (Director, Regulatory Affairs)

OLSON, Erik D.

1200 New York Ave. NW
Suite 400
Washington, DC 20005
Tel: (202)289-6868
Fax: (202)289-1060

Employers

Natural Resources Defense Council (Senior Attorney)

OLSON, James W.

1299 Pennsylvania Ave. NW
Washington, DC 20004-2402
Tel: (202)783-0800
Fax: (202)383-6610
Former Chief, Competition Division, Federal Communications Commission.

Employers

Howrey Simon Arnold & White

OLSON, Jeffrey H.

1615 L St. NW
Suite 1300
Washington, DC 20036
Tel: (202)223-7300
Fax: (202)223-7420
EMail: jolson@paulweiss.com

Employers

Paul, Weiss, Rifkind, Wharton & Garrison (Associate)

Clients Represented

On Behalf of Paul, Weiss, Rifkind, Wharton & Garrison

SkyBridge, LLC

OLSON, John F.

1050 Connecticut Ave. NW
Washington, DC 20036-5306
Tel: (202)955-8500
Fax: (202)467-0539
Registered: LDA
EMail: jolson@gdclaw.com

Employers

Gibson, Dunn & Crutcher LLP (Partner)

Clients Represented

On Behalf of Gibson, Dunn & Crutcher LLP

The Business Roundtable

OLSON, Mattie

4301 Wilson Blvd.
Arlington, VA 22203-1860
Tel: (703)907-5544
Fax: (703)907-5511
EMail: mattie.olson@nreca.org

Employers

Nat'l Rural Electric Cooperative Ass'n (Director, Education and Training)

OLSON, CAE, Michael S.

1575 I St. NW
Washington, DC 20005-1103
Tel: (202)626-2741
Fax: (202)371-1673
Registered: LDA
EMail: molson@asaenet.org

Employers

American Soc. of Ass'n Executives (President and Chief Exec. Officer)

OLSON, Raelynn

1010 Wisconsin Ave. NW
Suite 800
Washington, DC 20007
Tel: (202)338-8700
Fax: (202)338-2334

Employers

Greer, Margolis, Mitchell, Burns & Associates (Partner)

OLSON, Sydney

1090 Vermont Ave. NW
Suite 510
Washington, DC 20005
Tel: (202)414-0140
Fax: (202)544-3525
Registered: LDA

Employers

American Osteopathic Ass'n (Director, Government Relations)

OLSON, Theodore B.

1050 Connecticut Ave. NW
Washington, DC 20036-5306
Tel: (202)955-8500
Fax: (202)467-0539
Registered: LDA
EMail: tolson@gdclaw.com
Assistant Attorney General, Office of Legal Counsel, Department of Justice, 1981-84.

Employers

Gibson, Dunn & Crutcher LLP (Partner)

OLSON, Thomas P.

2445 M St. NW
Washington, DC 20037-1420
Tel: (202)663-6000
Fax: (202)663-6363
EMail: tolson@wilmer.com
Staff Counsel, Subcommittee on Patents, Copyrights and Trademarks, Senate Judiciary Committee, 1983-84.

Employers

Wilmer, Cutler & Pickering (Partner)

OLSSON, Philip C.

1400 16th St. NW
Suite 400
Washington, DC 20036-2220
Tel: (202)518-6366
Fax: (202)234-3550
Registered: LDA, FARA
EMail: polsson@ofwlaw.com
Deputy Assistant Secretary for Marketing and Consumer Services (1971-73) and Assistant to the Assistant Secretary for Marketing and Consumer Services (1969-71), Department of Agriculture. Legislative Assistant to Rep. Bob Mathias (R-CA), 1967-69, and to Rep. Hastings Keith (R-MA), 1967.

Employers

Olsson, Frank and Weeda, P.C. (Principal)

Clients Represented

On Behalf of Olsson, Frank and Weeda, P.C.

Nat'l Ass'n of Margarine Manufacturers
Nat'l Meat Ass'n
Transhumance Holding Co., Inc.
Urner Barry Publications, Inc.

OMAN, Ralph

1775 I St. NW
Washington, DC 20006
Tel: (202)261-3339
Fax: (202)261-3333
Registered: LDA
EMail: ralph.oman@dechert.com
U.S. Register of Copyrights, 1985-93. Chief Counsel, Subcommittee on Patents, Copyrights and Trademarks (1983-85) and Staff Director and Chief Counsel, Subcommittee on Criminal Law (1981-83), Senate Judiciary Committee. Legislative Counsel to Senator Charles McC. Mathias (R-MD), 1977-81. Legislative Assistant to Senator Hugh Scott (R-PA), 1975-77. Attorney, Antitrust Division, Department of Justice, 1974-75. Foreign Service Officer, Department of State, 1962-64. Law Clerk to Judge C. Stanley Blair, U.S. District Court for the District of Maryland.

Employers

Dechert (Counsel)

Clients Represented

On Behalf of Dechert

Broadcast Music Inc. (BMI)

OMOREGIE, Zuwa

1401 I St. NW
Suite 1200
Washington, DC 20005-2225
Tel: (202)408-5800
Fax: (202)408-5842
Registered: LDA
EMail: zsom@chevron.com

Employers

The Chevron Companies (Director, International Relations)

ONAGHISE, Tryphene

413 New York Ave. SE
Washington, DC 20003
Tel: (202)543-3486
Fax: (202)543-1680
Registered: LDA

Employers

Jacobs Engineering Group Inc. (Exec. Assistant)

ONDECK, Christopher

1919 Pennsylvania Ave. NW
Suite 600
Washington, DC 20006-3404
Tel: (202)326-1500
Fax: (202)326-1555

Employers

Jenkens & Gilchrist (Associate, Federal Practice)

ONES, Leyla

2121 K St. NW
Suite 650
Washington, DC 20037
Tel: (202)296-2400
Fax: (202)296-2409
Registered: LDA
EMail: Leyla@GlobalUSAinc.com

Employers

Global USA, Inc. (Senior Associate)

Clients Represented

On Behalf of Global USA, Inc.

All Japan Postal Labor Union
Takata Corp.

ONG, George

1001 Connecticut Ave. NW
Suite 601
Washington, DC 20036
Tel: (202)223-5500
Fax: (202)296-0540

Employers

Organization of Chinese Americans, Inc. (National President)

ONIEAL, Marie Eileen

325 Pennsylvania Ave. SE
Washington, DC 20003
Tel: (202)675-6350

Employers

Nat'l Alliance of Nurse Practitioners (Chair)

ONOFF, Tim

700 13th St. NW
Suite 400
Washington, DC 20005
Tel: (202)347-0773
Fax: (202)347-0785
EMail: tonoff@cassidy.com
Deputy Upstate New York Coordinator, 1992 Clinton Gore Campaign.

Employers

Cassidy & Associates, Inc. (Director, Consultant Network)

OOMS, Van Doorn

2000 L St. NW
Suite 700
Washington, DC 20036
Tel: (202)296-5860
Fax: (202)223-0776
EMail: ooms@ced.org

Employers
Committee for Economic Development (Senior V. President, Director of Research)

OOSTERHUIS, Paul W.

1440 New York Ave. NW
Washington, DC 20005
Tel: (202)371-7000
Fax: (202)393-5760
Registered: LDA

Legislation Attorney, Joint Committee on Taxation, U.S. Congress, 1973-76 and 1977-78.

Employers
Skadden, Arps, Slate, Meagher & Flom LLP (Partner)

Clients Represented
On Behalf of Skadden, Arps, Slate, Meagher & Flom LLP
MCI WorldCom Corp.
Pharmaceutical Research and Manufacturers of America

OPINSKY, Howard S.

1501 M St. NW
Suite 600
Washington, DC 20005-1710
Tel: (202)739-0200
Fax: (202)659-8287

Employers
BSMG Worldwide (Managing Director)

ORASIN, Charles

1101 14th St. NW
Suite 1400
Washington, DC 20005
EMail: corasin@defenders.org
Tel: (202)682-9400
Fax: (202)682-1331

Employers
Defenders of Wildlife (V. President, Operations)

OREM, Bayly

818 Connecticut Ave. NW
Suite 600
Washington, DC 20006-2702
Tel: (202)466-0672
Fax: (202)466-0684

Employers
Caterpillar Inc. (Washington Manager, Government Marketing)

ORLANDO, John S.

1771 N St. NW
Washington, DC 20036-2891
Tel: (202)429-5308
Fax: (202)775-2157

Employers
Nat'l Ass'n of Broadcasters (Senior V. President, External Relations)

ORLANDO, Ron

1724 Massachusetts Ave. NW
Washington, DC 20036-1969
Tel: (202)775-3550
Fax: (202)775-3696

Employers
Nat'l Cable Television Ass'n (Director, Industry Grassroots Development)

ORLOFF, Jonathan M.

601 Pennsylvania Ave. NW
Suite 900 South
Washington, DC 20004
Tel: (202)220-3181
Registered: LDA

Legislative Assistant to Senator Edward Kennedy, (D-MA), 1977-86

Employers
Capitol Partners (Principal)

Clients Represented
On Behalf of Capitol Partners
American Chiropractic Ass'n
Biochemics
Biogen, Inc.
Biomatrix
Cambridge Redevelopment Authority
Concord Family and Adolescent Services
Emmanuel College
FLIR Systems, Inc.
Kessler Medical Rehabilitation Research & Education Corp.
Smith & Wesson

ORNDORFF, Charles

450 Maple Ave. East
Suite 309
Vienna, VA 22180
Tel: (703)281-6782
Fax: (703)281-4108

Employers
Conservative Caucus Research, Analysis and Education Foundation (Administrative V. President)
The Conservative Caucus (Administrative V. Chairman)

ORNST, Patty

1775 K St. NW
Suite 500
Washington, DC 20006
Tel: (202)293-8500
Fax: (202)887-5365

Employers
AAAE-ACI (Manager, Legislative Affairs)

ORNSTEIN, Norman J.

1150 17th St. NW
Washington, DC 20036
EMail: nornstein@aei.org
Tel: (202)862-5800
Fax: (202)862-7177

Employers
American Enterprise Institute for Public Policy Research (Resident Scholar and Political Analyst)

ORR, Beverly

P.O. Box 19367
Washington, DC 20036
EMail: beverly@essential.org
Tel: (202)387-8030
Fax: (202)234-5176

Employers
Center for the Study of Responsive Law (Business Manager)

ORR, Mark

1225 I St. NW
Suite 500
Washington, DC 20005
Tel: (202)218-3525
Registered: LDA

Employers
Pernod Ricard (V. President, North American Affairs)

ORR, Paul Welles

1030 15th St. NW
Suite 1028
Washington, DC 20005
EMail: prg@his.com
Tel: (202)216-9116
Fax: (202)216-0363
Registered: LDA

Former Assistant U. S. Trade Representative for Congressional Affairs in the Bush I administration, 1989-93; and Special Assistant to the Assistant Secretary of State, Bureau of Near Eastern/South Asian Affairs, Department of State, 1988-89.

Employers
The Potomac Research Group LLC (Partner)

Clients Represented
On Behalf of The Potomac Research Group LLC
Bayer Corp.
Biotechnology Industry Organization
Safety Reasearch Center, Inc.
Spatial Technologies Industry Ass'n
United States Cane Sugar Refiners' Ass'n

ORRICO, Kate O.

725 15th St. NW
Suite 800
Washington, DC 20005
EMail: korrico@neursurgery.org
Tel: (202)628-2072
Fax: (202)628-5264
Registered: LDA

Employers
American Ass'n of Neurological Surgeons/Congress of Neurological Surgeons (Director, Washington Office)

ORSECK, Gary A.

1909 K St. NW
Washington, DC 20006
Tel: (202)263-3000
Fax: (202)263-3300
Registered: LDA

Employers
Mayer, Brown & Platt (Partner)

ORTMAN, Glen J.

901 15th St. NW
Suite 700
Washington, DC 20005-2301
EMail: gjortman@verner.com
Tel: (202)371-6000
Fax: (202)371-6279
Registered: LDA

Employers
Verner, Liipfert, Bernhard, McPherson and Hand, Chartered (Member of Firm)

Clients Represented
On Behalf of Verner, Liipfert, Bernhard, McPherson and Hand, Chartered
New Orleans, Louisiana, City of

ORTMANS, Jonathan F.

2300 M St. NW
Suite 900
Washington, DC 20037
EMail: jonathan@publicforuminstitute.com
Tel: (202)467-2777
Fax: (202)293-5717

Employers
Public Forum Institute (President)

ORTNER, Blake C.

801 18th St. NW
Washington, DC 20006
Tel: (202)872-1300
Fax: (202)785-4452
Registered: LDA

Employers
Paralyzed Veterans of America (Associate Legislative Director)

ORTON, Hon. Bill

908 Pennsylvania Ave. SE
Washington, DC 20003
Tel: (202)544-5666
Fax: (202)544-4647
Registered: LDA

Member, U.S. House of Representatives (D-UT), 1991-96.

Employers
Advantage Associates, Inc. (Partner)

ORZA, Tony

1225 I St. NW
Suite 1100
Washington, DC 20005
Tel: (202)898-0792
Fax: (202)371-9615

Employers
Handgun Control, Inc. (Director, Government Relations and Legislative Counsel)

OSANN, Edward R.

1001 Connecticut Ave. NW
Washington, DC 20036
Tel: (202)429-8873
Ext: 711
Registered: LDA

Employers
Potomac Resources, Inc. (President)

Clients Represented
On Behalf of Potomac Resources, Inc.
American Council for an Energy-Efficient Economy
California Urban Water Conservation Council
Toto USA, Inc.

OSBORNE, Arison

733 15th St. NW
Suite 640
Washington, DC 20005
Tel: (202)478-6546
Fax: (202)347-5868

Employers
Share Our Strength (Director, Public Relations)

OSBORNE, Beth

444 N. Capitol St. NW
Suite 200
Washington, DC 20001
EMail: bosborne@sso.org
Tel: (202)624-5897
Fax: (202)624-7797

Employers
Southern Governors Ass'n (Policy Analyst)

OSBORNE, Jason M.

11250 Waples Mill Rd.
Fairfax, VA 22030-7400
Tel: (202)651-2563
Fax: (202)651-2577
Registered: LDA

Employers
Nat'l Rifle Ass'n of America (Federal Liaison)

OSBORNE, Valerie Rogers

700 13th St. NW
Suite 400
Washington, DC 20005
EMail: vosborne@cassidy.com
Tel: (202)347-0773
Fax: (202)347-0785
Registered: LDA

Former Senior Legislative Assistant to Rep. Frank Riggs (R-CA), 1994-96; Staff Person, House Subcommittee on Labor, Health and Human Services and Education, and Staff Person,

House Economic and Educational Opportunities Committee. Legislative Assistant to Rep. Peter Torkildsen (R-MA), 1993-95. Constituent Services Representative and Special Events Coordinator, Rep. Frank Riggs (R-CA), 1990-92.

Employers
Cassidy & Associates, Inc. (V. President)

Clients Represented

On Behalf of Cassidy & Associates, Inc.
American Film Institute
California Hospital Medical Center Foundation
California Museum Foundation
Columbia University
Condell Medical Center
The Core Center
Draft Worldwide
El Segundo, California, City of
Marymount University
Montefiore Medical Center
Nat'l Jewish Medical and Research Center
Nat'l SAFE KIDS Campaign
San Diego, University of
Santa Rosa Memorial Hospital
Texas Tech University System
University of Pittsburgh Medical Center (UPMC)
University of San Diego

OSBOURN, Stephanie

440 First St. NW
Eighth Floor
Washington, DC 20001
EMail: sosbourn@naco.org
Tel: (202)393-4269
Fax: (202)393-2630

Employers
Nat'l Ass'n of Counties (Associate Legislative Director, Environment/Energy/Land Use)

OSCEOLA-BRANCH, Marie

2120 L St. NW
Suite 700
Washington, DC 20037
EMail: mosceola-branch@hsdwdc.com
Tel: (202)822-8282
Fax: (202)296-8834
Registered: LDA

Employers
Hobbs, Straus, Dean and Walker, LLP (Legislative Affairs Specialist)

Clients Represented

On Behalf of Hobbs, Straus, Dean and Walker, LLP
Black Mesa Community School Board
Bristol Bay Area Health Corp.
Choctaw Indians, Mississippi Band of
Menominee Indian Tribe
Metlakatla Indian Community
Miccosukee Tribe of Indians of Florida
Norton Sound Health Corp.
Seldovia Native Ass'n, Inc.
Seminole Tribe of Indians of Florida
Shoalwater Bay Indian Tribe
Susanville Indian Rancheria

OSOLINIK, Carolyn P.

1909 K St. NW
Washington, DC 20006
EMail: cosolinik@mayerbrown.com
Tel: (202)263-3000
Fax: (202)263-3300
Registered: LDA

Chief Counsel to Senator Edward Kennedy, Senate Judiciary Committee, 1984-92. Counsel to Senator Edward Kennedy (D-MA), 1981-84. Land and Natural Resources Division, Department of Justice, 1979-81. Solicitor's Office, Department of Interior, 1977-79.

Employers
Mayer, Brown & Platt (Partner)

Clients Represented

On Behalf of Mayer, Brown & Platt
ED&F Man Inc.
Ernst & Young LLP
First Church of Christ, Scientist
General Dynamics Corp.
General Electric Co.
Lockheed Martin Corp.
St. Paul Cos.
United Defense, L.P.
United Technologies Corp.

OSSI, Gregory J.

1497 Chain Bridge Rd.
Suite 300
McLean, VA 22101
EMail: gossi@ilalaw.com
Tel: (703)893-7071
Fax: (703)893-8020
Registered: LDA

Employers
Institutional Labor Advisors (Associate)

Clients Represented

On Behalf of Institutional Labor Advisors
Coal Act Fairness Alliance
Freeman United Coal Mining Co.
Retiree Benefits Alliance

OSTEN, Neal

444 N. Capitol St. NW
Suite 515
Washington, DC 20001
Tel: (202)624-5400
Fax: (202)737-1069

Employers
Nat'l Conference of State Legislatures (Director of Commerce and Communications)

OSTERWEIS, Ph.D., Marian

1400 16th St. NW
Suite 720
Washington, DC 20036
Tel: (202)265-9600

Employers
Ass'n of Academic Health Centers (Exec. V. President)

OSTRONIC, Judith M.

99 Canal Center Plaza
Suite 500
Alexandria, VA 22314-1538
Tel: (703)519-7800
Fax: (703)519-7810

Employers
American Internat'l Automobile Dealers Ass'n (Grassroots Program Manager)

OTERO, Juan

1301 Pennsylvania Ave. NW
Suite 550
Washington, DC 20004-1701
EMail: otero@nlc.org
Tel: (202)626-3020
Fax: (202)626-3043

Employers
Nat'l League of Cities (Legislative Counsel)

OTERO, Wilfred J.

1101 17th St. NW
Suite 1004
Washington, DC 20036
EMail: wotero@dc.npga.org
Tel: (202)466-7200
Fax: (202)466-7205

Employers
Nat'l Propane Gas Ass'n (Political Affairs Coordinator)

OTT, Jim

2011 Pennsylvania Ave. NW
Suite 800
Washington, DC 20006-1808
Tel: (202)261-4500
Fax: (202)835-0443

Employers
American College of Physicians-American Soc. of Internal Medicine (ACP-ASIM) (Director, Operations)

OTT, Robert B.

555 12th St. NW
Washington, DC 20004-1206
EMail: Robert_Ott@aporter.com
Tel: (202)942-5000
Fax: (202)942-5999

Employers
Arnold & Porter (Partner)

OTTAVIANO, Deanne M.

1050 Connecticut Ave. NW
Washington, DC 20036-5339
Tel: (202)857-6000
Fax: (202)857-6395

Worked for the Department of Agriculture and the House Committee on Agriculture.

Employers
Arent Fox Kintner Plotkin & Kahn, PLLC (Member)

Clients Represented

On Behalf of Arent Fox Kintner Plotkin & Kahn, PLLC
Motor and Equipment Manufacturers Ass'n
Nat'l Ass'n of Retail Collection Attorneys

OTTEN, Norbert

1401 H St. NW
Suite 700
Washington, DC 20005
Tel: (202)414-6744
Fax: (202)414-6741

Employers
DaimlerChrysler Corp. (Director, International Affairs)

OTTER, Jean

8101 Glenbrook Rd.
Bethesda, MD 20814-2749
Tel: (301)907-6977
Fax: (301)907-6895

Employers
American Ass'n of Blood Banks (Division Director, Educational Programs)

OTTINGER, Larry

2000 M St. NW
Suite 400
Washington, DC 20036
Tel: (202)467-4999
Fax: (202)293-2672

Employers
People for the American Way (Senior Staff Attorney)

OTTMAN, Kathryn Jo

1101 15th St. NW
Suite 200
Washington, DC 20005-5002
EMail: kjottman@ysa.org
Tel: (202)296-2992
Ext: 20
Fax: (202)296-4030

Employers
Youth Service America (V. President of Development)

OTTO, Dale

1120 20th St. NW
Suite 750 South
Washington, DC 20036
EMail: info@clb.org
Tel: (202)454-6400
Fax: (202)454-6401

Employers
Columbia Lighthouse for the Blind (President and Chief Exec. Officer)

OTTO, Joyce M.

7023 Little River Tnpk.
Suite 207
Annandale, VA 22003
Tel: (703)916-8856
Fax: (703)916-7966

Employers
Opticians Ass'n of America (Exec. Director)

OTTOSEN, Karl J.

6916 Wolf Run Shoals
Fairfax Station, VA 22039
Tel: (703)978-8037
Fax: (703)978-8039
Registered: LDA

Employers
NL Industries (PAC Contact)
Ottosen and Associates (Partner)

Clients Represented

On Behalf of Ottosen and Associates
Contran Corp.
EWI-Re Ltd.
Kronos, Inc.
NL Industries
U.S. Federation of Small Businesses, Inc.
Valhi, Inc.

OTZENBURGER, Stephen J.

1233 20th St. NW
Suite 301
Washington, DC 20036-1250
Tel: (202)429-0311
Fax: (202)429-0149

Employers
College and University Professional Ass'n for Human Resources (Exec. Director)

OURSLER, Leonard

1111 Constitution Ave. NW
Room 3230
Washington, DC 20224
EMail: Lenny.Oursler@irs.gov
Tel: (202)622-3740
Fax: (202)622-4739

Former Senate aide, 1979-95.

Employers
Department of Treasury - Internal Revenue Service (Branch Chief, Congressional Affairs)

OUTMAN, II, William D.

815 Connecticut Ave. NW
Suite 900
Washington, DC 20006-4078
Tel: (202)452-7000
Fax: (202)452-7073
Registered: LDA

Employers
Baker & McKenzie (Partner)

OVENDEN, Thomas D.

1300 I St. NW
Suite 1000 West
Washington, DC 20005
Tel: (202)962-8531
Fax: (202)962-8542
Registered: LDA
EMail: tovenden@rcra.com
U.S Environmental Protection Agency, 1989-91.

Employers
The Technical Group LLC (Partner)

Clients Represented
On Behalf of The Technical Group LLC
Nat'l Environmental Development Ass'n, Inc.
RSR Corp.

OVERBEY, Dr. Mary Margaret

4350 N. Fairfax Dr.
Suite 640
Arlington, VA 22203-1620
Tel: (703)528-1902
Fax: (703)528-3546
EMail: poverbey@aaanet.org

Employers
American Anthropological Ass'n (Director, Government Relations)

OVERSTREET, Jack C.

1725 Jefferson Davis Hwy.
Crystal Square 2, Suite 300
Arlington, VA 22202
Tel: (703)413-5600
Fax: (703)413-5617
Registered: LDA

Employers
Lockheed Martin Corp. (V. President, Legislative Affairs - Aircraft Programs)

OVERTON, Alica A.

1101 15th St. NW
Suite 600
Washington, DC 20005
Tel: (202)785-1122
Ext: 13
Fax: (202)785-5019

Employers
Sugar Ass'n, Inc. (V. President and Treasurer)

OVIEDO, Nina

444 N. Capitol St. NW
Suite 349
Washington, DC 20001
Tel: (202)624-5885
Fax: (202)624-5886

Employers
Florida, Washington Office of the State of (Director, Washington Office)

OWEN, Daryl H.

801 Pennsylvania Ave. NW
Suite 730
Washington, DC 20004
Tel: (202)756-2436
Fax: (202)756-2437
Registered: LDA
EMail: Owen@howdc.com
Energy Legislative Assistant and Administrative Assistant to Senator J. Bennett Johnston (D-LA), 1981-86; and Staff Director, Senate Committee on Energy and Natural Resources, 1986-90.

Employers
Hooper Owen & Winburn (Principal)

Clients Represented
On Behalf of Hooper Owen & Winburn
The Atlantic Co.
Borden Chemicals & Plastics, Inc.
Duke Energy
Entergy Corp.
Entergy Services, Inc.
Japan Nuclear Cycle Development Institute
TECO Energy, Inc.
United Pan-Europe Communications, NV
Waste Control Specialists, Inc.

OWEN, Holly

2011 Pennsylvania Ave. NW
Suite 800
Washington, DC 20006
Tel: (202)261-4554
Fax: (202)835-0442
EMail: hkoerber@mail.acponline.org

Employers
Medical Advocacy Services, Inc. (Government Affairs Representative)

Clients Represented
On Behalf of Medical Advocacy Services, Inc.
American College of Rheumatology
Renal Physicians Ass'n

OWEN, Rob

1771 N St. NW
Washington, DC 20036-2891
Tel: (202)429-5318
Fax: (202)775-2157

Employers
Nat'l Ass'n of Broadcasters (Director, Senate Congressional Liaison)

OWEN, Roberts B.

1201 Pennsylvania Ave. NW
Washington, DC 20004-2401
Tel: (202)662-6000
Fax: (202)662-6291
EMail: rowen@cov.com
Legal Advisor, Department of State, 1979-81.

Employers
Covington & Burling (Of Counsel)

OWEN, Jr., Stephen F.

5335 Wisconsin Ave. NW
Suite 920
Washington, DC 20015
Tel: (202)965-2650
Fax: (202)244-5167

Employers
Classroom Publishers Ass'n (General Counsel and Secretary)

OWENS, David K.

701 Pennsylvania Ave. NW
Washington, DC 20004-2696
Tel: (202)508-5527
Fax: (202)508-5786
Registered: LDA

Employers
Edison Electric Institute (Exec. V. President, Business Operations)

OWENS, Dedra

1920 L St. NW
Washington, DC 20036
Tel: (202)223-8700
Fax: (202)659-5559
Registered: LDA
EMail: dowens@kamber.com

Employers
The Kamber Group (Senior Account Executive)

OWENS, Joseph H.

P.O. Box 3776
Washington, DC 20007
Tel: (202)638-4634

Employers
Council of State Administrators of Vocational Rehabilitation (Exec. Director)

OWENS, Oscar

5025 Wisconsin Ave. NW
Washington, DC 20016
Tel: (202)537-1645
Fax: (202)244-7824

Employers
Amalgamated Transit Union (Internat'l Secretary-Treasurer)

OXENDINE, Tom

819 Seventh St. NW
Washington, DC 20001
Tel: (202)833-8940
Fax: (202)833-8943
Registered: LDA

Employers
EOP Group, Inc.

Clients Represented
On Behalf of EOP Group, Inc.
FMC Corp.
Fort Howard Corp.

OXFELD, Eric J.

1201 New York Ave. NW
Suite 750
Washington, DC 20005
Tel: (202)682-1515
Fax: (202)842-2556
Registered: LDA

Employers
UWC - Strategic Services on Unemployment and Workers' Compensation (President)

OXLEY, Merri

1899 L St. NW
Suite 200
Washington, DC 20036
Tel: (202)833-8121
Fax: (202)833-8155

Employers
Devillier Communications (V. President)

Clients Represented
On Behalf of Devillier Communications
All Kinds of Music
Lockheed Martin Corp.
Nat'l Ass'n of Health Underwriters

OYLER, Gregory K.

1875 I St. NW
Suite 1050
Washington, DC 20006-5409
Tel: (202)331-8585
Fax: (202)331-2032

Employers
Scribner, Hall & Thompson, LLP (Partner)

OZER, Kathy

110 Maryland Ave NE
Suite 307
Washington, DC 20002
Tel: (202)543-5675
Fax: (202)543-0978

Employers
Nat'l Family Farm Coalition (Exec. Director)

OZINGA, Bob

815 16th St. NW
Suite 600
Washington, DC 20006
Tel: (202)347-1461
Fax: (202)628-0724

Employers
AFL-CIO - Building and Construction Trades Department (Chief of Staff)

OZLU, Nina

1000 Vermont Ave. NW
12th Floor
Washington, DC 20005
Tel: (202)371-2830
Fax: (202)371-0424
Registered: LDA
EMail: nozlu@artsusa.org

Employers
Americans for the Arts (V. President, Government Affairs)

PAAL, Douglas H.

601 13th St. NW
Suite 1100 North
Washington, DC 20005
Tel: (202)223-7258
Fax: (202)223-7280

Employers
Asia Pacific Policy Center (President)

PABLO, Jeanette

One Massachusetts Ave. NW
Suite 300
Washington, DC 20001
Tel: (202)898-2999
Fax: (202)898-2998
EMail: jmpablo@tva.gov

Employers
Tennessee Valley Authority - Washington Office (Manager)

PACELLE, Wayne P.

2100 L St. NW
Washington, DC 20037
Tel: (202)452-1100
Fax: (202)778-6132
Registered: LDA
EMail: wpacelle@hsus.org

Employers
Humane Soc. of the United States (Senior V. President, Communications and Government Affairs)

PACHECO, Jack

1201 16th St. NW
Washington, DC 20036
Tel: (202)833-4000

Employers
Nat'l Education Ass'n of the U.S. (Manager, Political Affairs)

PACINO, Thomas L.

1101 Mercantile Ln.
Suite 100
Springdale, MD 20774
Tel: (301)925-1420
Fax: (301)925-1429
Registered: LDA

Employers
Ass'n Growth Enterprises (V. President)

Clients Represented
On Behalf of Ass'n Growth Enterprises
American Military Soc.
Nat'l Ass'n for Uniformed Services

PACKARD, Hon. Ron
1225 I St. NW
Suite 500
Washington, DC 20005
Tel: (202)312-2005
Fax: (202)289-8683
EMail: dawsonassociates@worldnet.att.net
Former Member of Congress (R-CA). Former Chairman, Subcommittees on Energy and Water Development, Military Construction, and the Legislative Branch, House Committee on Appropriations.

Employers
Dawson & Associates, Inc. (Senior Advisor)

PACKER, Joel
1201 16th St. NW
Washington, DC 20036
Tel: (202)833-4000
Registered: LDA

Employers
Nat'l Education Ass'n of the U.S. (Senior Professional Associate, Government Relations)

PACKWOOD, Hon. Bob
2201 Wisconsin Ave. NW
Suite 105
Washington, DC 20007
Tel: (202)965-9810
Fax: (202)965-9812
Registered: LDA
Member, U.S. Senate (R-OR), 1969-1995.

Employers
Sunrise Research Corp. (President)

Clients Represented
On Behalf of Sunrise Research Corp.
American Business Is Local Enterprise
American Public Power Ass'n
The Coal Coalition
GTE Service Corp.
Jones, Day, Reavis & Pogue
Marriott Internat'l, Inc.
Northwest Airlines, Inc.

PACOTTI, Linda
655 15th St. NW
Suite 300
Washington, DC 20005
Tel: (202)783-0900
Fax: (202)783-2308
Registered: LDA
EMail: linda.pacotti@bms.com

Employers
Bristol-Myers Squibb Co. (Associate Director, Government Affairs)

PACQUING, Juliet
P.O. Box 2484
Fairfax, VA 22031
Tel: (703)573-4380
Registered: LDA

Employers
Pacquing Consulting Inc. (President)

Clients Represented
On behalf of Pacquing Consulting Inc.
AAI Corp.
Armstrong Laser Technology
Law Office of Zel E. Lipsen
The Potomac Advocates
Production Technology, Inc.

PADDEN, Preston
1150 17th St. NW
Suite 400
Washington, DC 20036
Tel: (202)222-4700
Fax: (202)222-4799

Employers
The Walt Disney Co. (Exec. V. President, Government Relations)

PADILLA, Anthony
Three Research Place
Rockville, MD 20850
Tel: (301)948-4910
Fax: (301)330-7673
Registered: LDA

Employers
Transportation-Communications Internat'l Union (Assistant National Legislative Director)

PADILLA, Christopher A.
1250 H St. NW
Suite 800
Washington, DC 20005
Tel: (202)857-3400
Fax: (202)857-3401
Registered: LDA

Employers
Eastman Kodak Co. (Director, International Trade Relations)

PADWE, Gerry
1455 Pennsylvania Ave. NW
Suite 400
Washington, DC 20004-1081
Tel: (202)737-6600
Fax: (202)638-4512
Registered: LDA
EMail: GPadwe@aicpa.org

Employers
American Institute of Certified Public Accountants (V. President, Taxation)

PAEMEN, Hugo
555 13th St. NW
Washington, DC 20004-1109
Tel: (202)637-5600
Fax: (202)637-5910

Employers
Hogan & Hartson L.L.P. (Senior Advisor)

PAGANELLI, Virginia
1140 Connecticut Ave. NW
Suite 1050
Washington, DC 20036
Tel: (202)331-5790
Fax: (202)331-9334

Employers
American Health Quality Ass'n (Director, Scientific and Technical Affairs)

PAGE, C. Lee
801 18th St. NW
Washington, DC 20006
Tel: (202)872-1300
Fax: (202)785-4452
Registered: LDA

Employers
Paralyzed Veterans of America (Associate Advocacy Director)

PAGE, Holly
600 Pennsylvania Ave. SE
Suite 400
Washington, DC 20003
Tel: (202)546-0007
Fax: (202)544-5002
EMail: hpage@dlcppi.org

Employers
Democratic Leadership Council (V. President, Strategy and Innovation)

PAGE, Jennie
2000 Corporate Ridge
Suite 1000
McLean, VA 22102
Tel: (703)821-0770
Fax: (703)821-1350

Employers
American Frozen Food Institute (Manager, Regulatory and Technical Affairs)

PAGE, Jeremy
1300 Pennsylvania Ave. NW
Suite 400
Ronald Reagan Bldg.
Washington, DC 20004
Tel: (202)638-2230
Fax: (202)638-2236
Registered: LDA

Employers
Sandler, Travis & Rosenberg, P.A.

Clients Represented
On Behalf of Sandler, Travis & Rosenberg, P.A.
Babcock & Wilcox
Commercial Services Internat'l

PAGONIS, George G.
1620 I St. NW
Suite 202
Washington, DC 20006
Tel: (202)452-8811
Fax: (202)659-5427
Registered: LDA, FARA

Employers
Ibex Internat'l, Inc. (President)

Clients Represented
On Behalf of Ibex Internat'l, Inc.
Chase Manhattan Bank

PAHL, Tish E.
1400 16th St. NW
Suite 400
Washington, DC 20036-2220
Tel: (202)518-6317
Fax: (202)234-3583
EMail: tpahl@ofwlaw.com

Employers
Olsson, Frank and Weeda, P.C. (Associate)

PAIGE, Sean
1001 Connecticut Ave. NW
Suite 1250
Washington, DC 20036
Tel: (202)331-1010
Fax: (202)331-0640

Employers
Competitive Enterprise Institute (Warren Brookes Fellow in Environmental Journalism)

PAINTER, Dustin
3050 K St. NW
Washington, DC 20007
Tel: (202)342-8400
Fax: (202)342-8451

Employers
Collier Shannon Scott, PLLC (Government Relations Advisor)

PAINTER, Sally
1225 I St. NW
Suite 350
Washington, DC 20005
Tel: (202)789-1110
Fax: (202)789-1116
Deputy Director, Office of Business Liaison, Department of Commerce, 1993-95.

Employers
Downey McGrath Group, Inc. (Managing Director, International)

PALADINI, Vincent M.
1200 19th St. NW
Washington, DC 20036-2430
Tel: (202)861-3445
Fax: (202)223-2085
EMail: vincent.paldini@piperrudnick.com

Employers
Piper Marbury Rudnick & Wolfe LLP (Associate)

Clients Represented
On Behalf of Piper Marbury Rudnick & Wolfe LLP
Commercial Internet Exchange Ass'n

PALAFOUTAS, John P.
601 Pennsylvania Ave. NW
Suite 600
North Bldg.
Washington, DC 20004
Tel: (202)682-9110
Fax: (202)682-9111

Employers
American Electronics Ass'n (V. President, Domestic Policy and Congressional Relations)

PALASCHAK, Richard G.
1800 N. Kent St.
Suite 1050
Arlington, VA 22209
Tel: (703)276-1702
Fax: (703)276-1704

Employers
Munitions Industrial Base Task Force (Director, Operations)

PALATIELLO, John M.
1760 Reston Pkwy.
Suite 515
Reston, VA 20190
Tel: (703)787-6665
Fax: (703)787-7550
Registered: LDA
Former Legislative Assistant to Rep. Bill Hendon (R-NC) and Legislative Aide to Rep. John Myers (R-IN).

Employers
John M. Palatiello & Associates (Principal)

Clients Represented
On Behalf of John M. Palatiello & Associates
Council on Federal Procurement of Architectural and Engineering Services (COFPAES)
EarthData Holdings
Management Ass'n for Private Photogrammetric Surveyors
MAPPS PAC
Navigational Electronic Chart Systems Ass'n (NECSA)

PALCHICK, Mark G.

2099 Pennsylvania Ave. NW
Suite 100
Washington, DC 20006
EMail: mpalchic@hklaw.com
Tel: (202)955-3000
Fax: (202)955-5564

Employers
Holland & Knight LLP (Partner)

PALE MOON, Princess

6051 Arlington Blvd.
Falls Church, VA 22044
Tel: (703)538-1587
Fax: (703)532-1921

Employers
American Indian Heritage Foundation (President)

PALERMO, Lou

1733 King St.
Alexandria, VA 22314
EMail: palermo@cmaa.org
Tel: (703)739-9500
Fax: (703)739-0124

Employers
Club Managers Ass'n of America (Director, Education and Professional Development)

PALLADINO, Vincent

1727 King St.
Suite 400
Alexandria, VA 22314-2753
Tel: (703)836-9660
Fax: (703)836-9665

Employers
Nat'l Ass'n of Postal Supervisors (President)

PALLAS, Greg

1650 Tysons Blvd.
Suite 1700
McLean, VA 22102
Tel: (703)790-6300
Fax: (703)790-6365
Registered: LDA

Employers
ITT Industries Defense (Director, Congressional Liaison and Business Development)

PALLASCH, Brian T.

1015 15th St. NW
Suite 600
Washington, DC 20005
Tel: (202)789-2200
Fax: (202)289-6797
Registered: LDA

Employers
American Soc. of Civil Engineers (Director, Government Relations)
Ass'n of State Dam Safety Officials (Washington Representative)

PALMER, Brenda W.

1800 K St. NW
Washington, DC 20005
EMail: bpalmer@csis.org
Tel: (202)775-3275
Fax: (202)775-3199
Former Aide to the Inspector General, Department of Commerce.

Employers
Center for Strategic and Internat'l Studies (Senior V. President, Operations)

PALMER, Clifford A.

216 Justice Ct. NE
Suite A
Washington, DC 20002
Tel: (202)547-7721
Fax: (202)547-7835
Registered: LDA
Director of Projects and Legislative Assistant to Senator John Bennett Johnston, Jr. (D-LA), 1989-95.

Employers
The Palmer Group (Director)

Clients Represented
On Behalf of The Palmer Group
Ascension, Louisiana, Parish of
BOH Environmental, L.L.C.
Erin Engineering and Research, Inc.
Grand Isle Independent Levee District
Monroe, Louisiana, Chamber of Commerce of the City of
Monroe, Louisiana, City of
Orleans Levee District
Professional Engineering
West Jefferson Levee District

PALMER, Craig A.

1111 14th St. NW
Suite 1100
Washington, DC 20005-5603
Tel: (202)898-2400
Fax: (202)789-2258

Employers
American Dental Ass'n (Washington Editor, ADA News)

PALMER, David B.

1333 New Hampshire Ave. NW
Suite 400
Washington, DC 20036
Tel: (202)887-4000
Fax: (202)887-4288
Registered: LDA

Employers
Akin, Gump, Strauss, Hauer & Feld, L.L.P.

Clients Represented
On Behalf of Akin, Gump, Strauss, Hauer & Feld, L.L.P.
St. Barnabas Healthcare System

PALMER, Jeff

2121 Eisenhower Ave.
Suite 401
Alexandria, VA 22314
Tel: (703)684-1770
Fax: (703)684-1771

Employers
Powder Coating Institute (Director, Communications)

PALMER, Michael C.

1350 I St. NW
Suite 590
Washington, DC 20005
EMail: mpalmer@cap.org
Tel: (202)354-7100
Fax: (202)354-7155
Registered: LDA

Employers
College of American Pathologists (Director, Professional Affairs)

PALMER, Steven O.

1420 New York Ave. NW
Suite 1050
Washington, DC 20005
EMail: spalmer@vsadc.com
Tel: (202)638-1950
Fax: (202)638-7714
Registered: LDA
Assistant Secretary for Governmental Affairs, U.S. Department of Transportation 1993-98. Senior Professional Staff Member, Senate Committee on Commerce, Science and Transportation, 1983-93.

Employers
Van Scoyoc Associates, Inc. (V. President)

Clients Represented
On Behalf of Van Scoyoc Associates, Inc.
Alameda-Contra Costa Transit District
Ass'n of American Railroads
Calspan University of Buffalo Research Center
Clemson University
Hughes Space & Communications Co.
NASA Aeronautics Support Team
Nat'l Air Traffic Controllers Ass'n
Nat'l Asphalt Pavement Ass'n
Oldcastle Materials Group
Regional Airport Authority of Louisville & Jefferson Co.
Universal Systems, Inc.
Veridian Engineering
Xcellsis Corp.
Zuckert, Scoutt and Rasenberger, L.L.P.

PALMER, Susan

1818 N St. NW
Eighth Floor
Washington, DC 20036
Tel: (202)293-1707

Employers
Cingular Wireless (Regulatory Affairs)

PALMER, Tom G.

1000 Massachusetts Ave. NW
Washington, DC 20001
Tel: (202)842-0200
Fax: (202)842-3490

Employers
Cato Institute (Fellow in Social Thought)

PALMER-BARTON, Stacy

1620 I St. NW
Suite 600
Washington, DC 20006
EMail: sbarton@usmayors.org
Tel: (202)861-6778
Fax: (202)429-0422
Registered: LDA

Employers
The Barton Co. (President)
Dayton, Ohio, Washington Office of the City of (Associate Director)
Gary, Indiana, Washington Office of the City of (Associate Director)

Clients Represented
On Behalf of The Barton Co.
Dayton, Ohio, Washington Office of the City of
Gary Public Transportation Corp.
Gary Sanitary District
Gary, Indiana, Housing Authority of the City of
Gary, Indiana, Washington Office of the City of
Lynn, Massachusetts, City of

PALMIERI, Andrew

1000 Potomac St. NW
Suite 300
Washington, DC 20007
Tel: (202)337-6200
Fax: (202)333-0871

Employers
Hewes, Gelband, Lambert & Dann, P.C. (President)

PALMIERI, Suzanne

1111 20th St. NW
Washington, DC 20526
Tel: (202)692-2244
Fax: (202)692-2101

Employers
Peace Corps (Director, Congressional Relations)

PALOMBI, David R.

8200 Jones Branch Dr.
McLean, VA 22102
Tel: (703)903-2510
Fax: (703)903-2447

Employers
Federal Home Loan Mortgage Corp. (Freddie Mac) (V. President, Corporate Communications)

PALUMBO, Benjamin L.

1717 K St. NW
Suite 500
Washington, DC 20006
Tel: (202)466-9000
Fax: (202)466-9009
Registered: LDA
Administrative Assistant to Senator Harrison Williams (D-NJ), 1971-73. Staff Director, House Democratic Caucus, 1975-77. Staff Director, House Subcommittee on Government Activities, 1977-78.

Employers
Palumbo & Cerrell, Inc. (President)

Clients Represented
On Behalf of Palumbo & Cerrell, Inc.
American Soc. of Composers, Authors and Publishers
American Trans Air
HT Medical
K Capital Partners
Los Angeles, California, Metropolitan Transit Authority of
Music Educators Nat'l Conference

PAMPLIN, Ashby

1250 I St. NW
Suite 500
Washington, DC 20005
Tel: (202)789-2900
Fax: (202)789-1893

Employers
Horticultural Research Institute (Administrator and Director)

PANETTA, Michael J.

3509 Connecticut Ave. NW
Suite 175
Washington, DC 20008-2400
EMail: mpanetta@yahoo.com
Tel: (202)253-6534

Employers
X-PAC (Exec. Director)

PANGELINAN, Edward

2121 R St. NW
Washington, DC 20008-1908
EMail: pangel069@aol.com
Tel: (202)673-5869
Fax: (202)673-5873

Employers
Northern Mariana Islands, Commonwealth of the (Special Assistant, Washington Representative)

PANOPOULOS, Frank

601 13th St. NW
Suite 600 South
Washington, DC 20005
Tel: (202)626-3600
Fax: (202)639-9355
Registered: LDA

Employers
White & Case LLP

Clients Represented
On Behalf of White & Case LLP
Techsnabexport, A.O.

PANTAZIS, Cynthia

1640 King St.
P.O. Box 1443
Alexandria, VA 22313
EMail: cpantazis@astd.org
Tel: (703)683-8153
Fax: (703)548-2383
Registered: LDA

Employers
American Soc. for Training and Development (Director, Policy and Public Leadership)

PANTOS, George

1250 H St. NW
Suite 901
Washington, DC 20005
EMail: georgegjp@aol.com
Registered: LDA
Deputy Under Secretary of Commerce, Department of Commerce, 1973-74.

Employers
Kinder & Associates, Inc. (Washington Counsel)
Self-Insurance Institute of America, Inc. (Contact)

Clients Represented
On Behalf of Kinder & Associates, Inc.
Self-Insurance Institute of America, Inc.

PANTUSO, Peter J.

1100 New York Ave. NW
Suite 1050
Washington, DC 20005
Tel: (202)842-1645
Fax: (202)842-0850
Registered: LDA

Employers
American Bus Ass'n (President and Chief Exec. Officer)

PANVINI, Vincent A.

1750 New York Ave. NW
Sixth Floor
Washington, DC 20006
Tel: (202)783-5880
Fax: (202)662-0895
Registered: LDA

Employers
Italian-American Democratic Leadership Council (Chairman)
Sheet Metal Workers' Internat'l Ass'n (Director, Legislative Department)

PANZER, Carolyn

1301 K St. NW
Suite 1000 East
Washington, DC 20005
Tel: (202)715-1105
Fax: (202)715-1114
Registered: LDA

Employers
UDV North America, Inc. (Senior V. President, Public Policy)

PAPADOPOULOS, Daniel G.

1900 L St. NW
Suite 407
Washington, DC 20036
Tel: (202)293-3454
Fax: (202)393-3455
Registered: LDA
Correspondence Director (1992-96) and Assistant Correspondence Director (1990-91) to Senator Daniel P. Moynihan (D-NY).

Employers
Bristol Group, Inc. (V. President, Government Affairs)

Clients Represented
On Behalf of Bristol Group, Inc.
Boston Edison Co.
TAP/Air Portugal

PAPAVIZAS, Constantine G.

1400 L St. NW
Washington, DC 20005-3502
Tel: (202)371-5732
Fax: (202)371-5950
Registered: LDA

Employers
Winston & Strawn (Partner, Health Care Practice)

Clients Represented
On Behalf of Winston & Strawn
First American Bulk Carriers Corp.
Kirby Corp./Dixie Carriers
Liberty Maritime Co.
Marinette Marine Corp.
Northland Holdings, Inc.
Van Ommeren Shipping (USA), Inc.

PAPE, Stuart M.

2550 M St. NW
Washington, DC 20037-1350
EMail: spape@pattonboggs.com
Tel: (202)457-5240
Fax: (202)457-6315
Registered: LDA
Executive Assistant to the Commissioner (1978-79) and Associate Chief Counsel (1974-78), Food and Drug Administration.

Employers
Patton Boggs, LLP (Managing Partner)

Clients Represented
On Behalf of Patton Boggs, LLP
Bristol-Myers Squibb Co.
L. P. Conwood Co.
DFS Group Ltd.
drugstore.com
General Mills
Grocery Manufacturers of America
Hoffmann-La Roche Inc.
Mars, Inc.
Nat'l Soft Drink Ass'n
Nat'l Yogurt Ass'n
Pharmanex
Sierra Military Health Services, Inc.

PAPKIN, Robert D.

1201 Pennsylvania Ave. NW
P.O. Box 407
Washington, DC 20044-0407
EMail: rpapkin@ssd.com
Tel: (202)626-6600
Fax: (202)626-6780

Employers
Squire, Sanders & Dempsey L.L.P. (Partner)

Clients Represented
On Behalf of Squire, Sanders & Dempsey L.L.P.
Aerolineas Argentinas
Ansett Transport Industries
Avianca Airlines
Compania Mexicana de Aviacion
Lineas Aereas Costarricicenes (Lasca Airlines)
Polynesian Airlines
Servicios Aereos de Honduras (SAHSA)
VASP Airlines
VIASA

PAPP, Capt. Robert J.

400 Seventh St. SW
Suite 10402
Washington, DC 20590
EMail: rpapp@comdit.uscg.mil
Tel: (202)366-4280
Fax: (202)366-7124

Employers
Department of Transportation - United States Coast Guard (Chief, Congressional Affairs Staff, Office of Government and Public Affairs)

PAPP, Sharon

2101 E St. NW
Washington, DC 20037
EMail: papps@state.gov
Tel: (202)338-4045
Fax: (202)338-6820

Employers
American Foreign Service Ass'n (Legal Counsel)

PARCELL, John

1500 Pennsylvania Ave. NW
MS: 1010
Washington, DC 20220
Tel: (202)622-2578

Employers
Department of Treasury - Tax Policy (Acting Deputy Tax Legislative Counsel)

PARCELLS, Harriet

900 Second St. NE
Suite 109
Washington, DC 20002
Tel: (202)408-1808
Fax: (202)408-9565
Registered: LDA

Employers
American Passenger Rail Coalition (Exec. Director)

PARDE, David L.

119 Oronoco St.
Suite 300
Alexandria, VA 22314-2015
EMail: david@careauto.org
Tel: (703)519-7555
Fax: (703)519-7747
Registered: LDA

Employers
Coalition for Auto Repair Equality (CARE) (President)

PARDE, Duane A.

910 17th St. NW
Fifth Floor
Washington, DC 20006
Tel: (202)466-3800
Fax: (202)466-3801

Employers
American Legislative Exchange Council (Exec. Director)

PARET, Jonathan R.

1401 I St. NW
Suite 1000
Washington, DC 20005
EMail: jparet@sia.com
Tel: (202)296-9410
Fax: (202)296-9775
Registered: LDA

Employers
Securities Industry Ass'n (V. President and Legislative Counsel)

PARET, S. Pierre

601 Pennsylvania Ave. NW
Suite 700
Washington, DC 20004-2676
EMail: paretp@adr.org
Tel: (202)737-9191
Fax: (202)737-2418
Former Intergovernmental Relations Officer, Puerto Rico Federal Affairs Administration; Office of Governmental and Public Affairs, Tennessee Valley Authority.

Employers
American Arbitration Ass'n (Assistant V. President, Government Programs)

PARK, H.K.

600 13th St. NW
Suite 640
Washington, DC 20005-3096
EMail: hkp@cohengroup.net
Tel: (202)756-8500
Fax: (202)756-8510
Special Assistant to the Chief of Staff, Department of Defense, 1999-2001.

Employers
The Cohen Group (Senior Associate)

PARK, Hong

1735 New York Ave. NW
Suite 500
Washington, DC 20006-4759
Tel: (202)628-1700
Fax: (202)331-1024

Employers
Preston Gates Ellis & Rouvelas Meeds LLP (Associate)

PARK, Howard F.

1249 South Carolina Ave. SE
Washington, DC 20003
Tel: (202)544-6262
Fax: (202)544-6062
Former Special Assistant to Rep. William Clay (D-MO), 1980.

Employers
Self-employed as an independent consultant.

Clients Represented
As an independent consultant
American Watercraft Ass'n

PARK, Jaemin

1333 New Hampshire Ave. NW
Suite 400
Washington, DC 20036
EMail: jpark@akingump.com
Tel: (202)887-4000
Fax: (202)887-4288

Employers
Akin, Gump, Strauss, Hauer & Feld, L.L.P. (Partner)

PARK, Judith E.

606 N. Washington St.
Alexandria, VA 22314
Tel: (703)838-7760
Fax: (703)838-7782
Registered: LDA

Employers
Nat'l Ass'n of Retired Federal Employees (Director, Legislation)

PARK, Robert L.

529 14th St. NW
Suite 1050
Washington, DC 20045
EMail: opa@aps.org
Tel: (202)662-8700
Fax: (202)662-8711

Employers
American Physical Soc. (Director, Public Information)

PARK, Won-Kyung

1129 20th St. NW
Suite 410
Washington, DC 20036
EMail: dcktc5@bellatlantic.net
Tel: (202)857-7919
Fax: (202)857-7923

Employers
Korea Trade Center (Director General)

PARKER, Armetta

600 New Hampshire Ave. NW
Suite 601
Washington, DC 20037
Tel: (202)333-7400
Fax: (202)333-1638

Employers
Hill and Knowlton, Inc. (Managing Director)

PARKER, Bruce J.

4301 Connecticut Ave. NW
Suite 300
Washington, DC 20008
Tel: (202)244-4700
Fax: (202)966-4818
Registered: LDA

Employers
Environmental Industry Ass'ns (President and Chief Exec. Officer)
Nat'l Solid Wastes Management Ass'n (Exec. V. President)

PARKER, Craig W.

620 Michigan Ave. NE
Washington, DC 20064
EMail: parker@cua.edu
Tel: (202)319-5142
Fax: (202)319-5579

Employers
Catholic University of America (General Counsel)

PARKER, David N.

400 N. Capitol St. NW
Washington, DC 20001
EMail: dparker@aga.org
Tel: (202)824-7111
Fax: (202)824-7092

Employers
American Gas Ass'n (President and Chief Exec. Officer)

PARKER, Dionne

927 15th St. NW
Suite 200
Washington, DC 20005
EMail: dparker@aabe.org
Tel: (202)371-9530
Fax: (202)371-9218

Employers
American Ass'n of Blacks in Energy (Director, Member Services)

PARKER, Donald

12490 Sunrise Valley Dr.
Reston, VA 22096
Tel: (703)689-6000
Fax: (703)689-6715

Employers
Global One (Sr. V. President and General Counsel)

PARKER, Douglas L.

600 New Jersey Ave. NW
Suite 312
Washington, DC 20001
Tel: (202)662-9535
Fax: (202)662-9634

Employers
Institute for Public Representation (Director)

PARKER, Erich

2120 L St. NW
Suite 400
Washington, DC 20037
Tel: (202)478-6158
Fax: (202)223-9579

Employers
Aseptic Packaging Council (V. President, Communications)

PARKER, Larry

1611 N. Kent St.
Suite 901
Arlington, VA 22209
Tel: (703)351-4969
Fax: (703)351-0090

Employers
Alexis de Tocqueville Institution (Senior Reporter)

PARKER, Leonard

Ten G St. NE
Suite 440
Washington, DC 20002
Tel: (202)628-5935
Fax: (202)347-3548

Employers
Brotherhood of Railroad Signalmen (Legislative Representative)

PARKER, Lynn

1875 Connecticut Ave. NW
Suite 540
Washington, DC 20009
EMail: lparker@frac.org
Tel: (202)986-2200
Ext: 3012
Fax: (202)986-2525

Employers
Food Research and Action Center (Director, Child Nutrition Programs/Nutrition Policy)

PARKER, Mary Beth

818 Connecticut Ave. NW
Second Floor
Washington, DC 20006
EMail: mparker@stratcomm.net
Tel: (202)289-2001
Fax: (202)289-1327

Employers
Strat@Comm (Strategic Communications Counselors) (Account Executive)

PARKER, Richard B.

1761 N St. NW
Washington, DC 20036-2882
Tel: (202)785-1141
Fax: (202)331-8861

Employers
Middle East Institute (Resident Scholar Emeritus)

PARKER, Richard G.

555 13th St. NW
Suite 500 West
Washington, DC 20004
EMail: rparker@omm.com
Tel: (202)383-5300
Fax: (202)383-5414

Director, Bureau of Competition, Federal Trade Commission.

Employers
O'Melveny and Myers LLP (Partner)

PARKER, Rosalind

1140 Connecticut Ave. NW
Suite 1142
Washington, DC 20036
Tel: (202)862-4383
Fax: (202)331-5562
Registered: LDA

Majority Counsel, Senate Committee on Commerce, 1997-99.

Employers
Technology, Entertainment and Communications (TEC) Law Group

Clients Represented

On Behalf of Technology, Entertainment and Communications (TEC) Law Group
WorldSpace Corp.

PARKER, Wendy C.

801 Pennsylvania Ave. NW
Suite 245
Washington, DC 20004-2604
EMail: wparker@americashospitals.com
Tel: (202)624-1521
Fax: (202)737-6462
Registered: LDA

Employers
Federation of American Hospitals (Assistant V. President, Legislation)

PARKERSON, William

11250 Waples Mill Rd.
Fairfax, VA 22030-7400
Tel: (703)267-1000
Fax: (703)267-3980

Employers
Nat'l Rifle Ass'n Institute for Legislative Action (Director, Research and Information)

PARKINSON, Charles R.

801 Pennsylvania Ave. NW
Suite 800
Washington, DC 20004
EMail: cparkinson@bdbc.com
Tel: (202)508-3400
Fax: (202)508-3402
Registered: LDA

Professional Staff Member, House Committee on Appropriations, 1997-2001. Chief Republican Clerk, Subcommittee on Treasury, Postal Service and General Government, Senate Committee on Appropriations, 1992-97 and 1982-87. Associate Commission, U.S. Customs Service, Department of Treasury, 1987-92. Special Assistant to Senator James Abdnor (R-SD), 1981-82. Professional Staff, House Committee on Veterans Affairs, 1976-80.

Employers
Baker, Donelson, Bearman & Caldwell, P.C. (Senior Public Policy Advisor)

Clients Represented

On Behalf of Baker, Donelson, Bearman & Caldwell, P.C.
American Trucking Ass'ns
Amgen
Newspaper Ass'n of America
The Washington Post Co.

PARKS, Carl M.

805 15th St. NW
Suite 300
Washington, DC 20005-2207
Tel: (202)682-4200
Fax: (202)682-9054
Registered: LDA

Employers
Credit Union Nat'l Ass'n, Inc. (Senior V. President, Governmental Affairs)

PARKS, Prudence

1140 Connecticut Ave. NW
Suite 1140
Washington, DC 20036
EMail: pparks@erols.com
Tel: (202)872-0030
Fax: (202)872-1331
Registered: LDA

Employers
United Telecom Council

PARLIN, C. Christopher

1133 Connecticut Ave. NW
Suite 1200
Washington, DC 20036
Tel: (202)775-9800
Fax: (202)833-8491
Registered: LDA, FARA

Assistant U.S. Trade Representative for the Environment and Natural Resources (1995), Deputy Assistant U.S. Trade Representative for North American Affairs (1994), Deputy Assistant U.S. Trade Representative for Multilateral Trade Negotiations (1993-94), Legal Advisor to the U.S. Trade Representative Mission to the General Agreement on Tariffs and Trade (1987-93), and Associate General Counsel (1986-87), all in the Office of the U.S. Trade Representative, Executive Office of the President, The White House. Deputy for Policy to the Deputy Assistant Secretary for Import Administration (1984-86), Director, Office of Policy, Import Administration (1982-86), and Deputy Assistant Attorney General for Import Administration (1980-82), all at the Department of Commerce. Attorney-Advisor, Office of General Counsel, Department of the Treasury, 1977-79.

Employers
Winthrop, Stimson, Putnam & Roberts (Counsel)

Clients Represented

On Behalf of Winthrop, Stimson, Putnam & Roberts
Caribbean Banana Exporters Ass'n
Korean Semiconductor Industry Ass'n
SKW Chemicals, Inc.

PARMELEE, Ken

1630 Duke St.
Alexandria, VA 22314
Tel: (703)684-5545
Fax: (703)548-8735
Registered: LDA

Administrative Assistant to Rep. James J. Florio (D-NJ), 1977-80; Executive Assistant to Senator Vance Hartke (D-IN), 1975-76.

Employers
Nat'l Rural Letter Carriers' Ass'n (V. President, Governmental Affairs)

PAROBEK, Dennis A.

1015 15th St. NW
Suite 700
Washington, DC 20005-2605
Tel: (202)828-5200
Fax: (202)785-2645
Registered: LDA

Employers

Bechtel Group, Inc. (Manager, Government Affairs (BINFRA))

PARR, Michael

601 Pennsylvania Ave. NW
Suite 325, North Bldg.
Washington, DC 20004
Tel: (202)728-3661
Fax: (202)728-3649

Employers

DuPont (Manager, Government Affairs)

PARRA, Victor S.

113 S. West St.
Fourth Floor
Alexandria, VA 22314
Tel: (703)838-2929
Fax: (703)838-2950

Employers

United Motorcoach Ass'n

PARRIS, George E.

2750 Prosperity Ave.
Suite 550
Fairfax, VA 22031-4312
Tel: (703)204-0500
Fax: (703)204-4610

Employers

American Wood Preservers Institute (Director, Environmental and Regulatory Affairs)

PARRIS, Hon. Stanford E.

2101 L St. NW
Washington, DC 20037-1526
Tel: (202)785-9700
Fax: (202)887-0689
Registered: LDA

EMail: parriss@dsmo.com

Member, U.S. House of Representatives (R-VA), 1973-75 and 1981-91.

Employers

Dickstein Shapiro Morin & Oshinsky LLP (Of Counsel)

Clients Represented

On Behalf of Dickstein Shapiro Morin & Oshinsky LLP

Cigar Ass'n of America
Electric Power Supply Ass'n
Homestake Mining
Lorillard Tobacco Co.
PG&E Generating Co.
Pipe Tobacco Council, Inc.
Poseidon Resources Corp.
The Reader's Digest Ass'n
Smokeless Tobacco Council

PARRISH, Linda Jo

1828 L St. NW
Suite 625
Washington, DC 20036
Tel: (202)496-5008
Fax: (202)833-3472
EMail: lindajo@womens-health.org

Employers

Soc. for Women's Health Research (Development Director)

PARROTT, Katie

1225 I St. NW
Suite 600
Washington, DC 20005
Tel: (202)661-6193
Fax: (202)661-6182
Registered: LDA

EMail: kparrott@morganmeguire.com

Former Legislative Aide to Rep. Tom Coburn (R-OK).

Employers

Morgan Meguire, LLC (Associate)

Clients Represented

On Behalf of Morgan Meguire, LLC

Adroit Systems Inc.
Baker Electromotive, Inc.
BellSouth Corp.
Colorado River Energy Distributors Ass'n
Energy Northwest
Florida Municipal Power Agency
Goodman Manufacturing Co., L.P.
Longhorn Pipeline
Madison Gas & Electric Co.
Manatee, Florida, County of
Northern California Power Agency
Northwest Public Power Ass'n
Nuevo Energy
Redding, California, City of
Sacramento Municipal Utility District
Southern California Public Power Authority
Springfield, Missouri, City Utilities of
Tennessee Valley Public Power Ass'n
Transmission Access Policy Study Group
Washington Public Utility Districts Ass'n

PARSHALL, Janet

801 G St. NW
Washington, DC 20001
Tel: (202)393-2100
Fax: (202)393-2134

Employers

Family Research Council, Inc. (National Spokeswoman)

PARSLEY, Nancy L.

9312 Old Georgetown Rd.
Bethesda, MD 20814-1621
Tel: (301)581-9233
Fax: (301)530-2752
EMail: nlparsley@npma.org

Employers

American Podiatric Medical Ass'n (Director, Health Policy and Practice)

PARSONS, Oscar N.

601 Pennsylvania Ave. NW
11th Floor, North Bldg.
Washington, DC 20004-2601
Tel: (202)756-3300
Fax: (202)756-3333
Registered: LDA
EMail: opersons@alston.com

Employers

Alston & Bird LLP (Partner)

PARTEE, Glenda L.

1836 Jefferson Place NW
Washington, DC 20036
Tel: (202)775-9731
Fax: (202)775-9733

Employers

American Youth Policy Forum (Co-director)

PARTRIDGE, (Ret.), Col. Charles C.

5535 Hempstead Way
Springfield, VA 22151
Tel: (703)750-1342
Fax: (703)354-4380
Registered: LDA

EMail: naus@ix.netcom.com

Employers

Nat'l Ass'n for Uniformed Services (Legislative Director)

PARTRIDGE, Lee

810 First St. NE
Suite 500
Washington, DC 20002
Tel: (202)682-0100
Fax: (202)289-6555

Employers

Nat'l Ass'n of Medicaid Directors (Director, Health Policy)

PARVEN, Scott

1909 K St. NW
Washington, DC 20006
Tel: (202)263-3000
Fax: (202)263-3300
Registered: LDA

Employers

Mayer, Brown & Platt (Counsel)

Clients Represented

On Behalf of Mayer, Brown & Platt

AOL Time Warner
The Boeing Co.
Citigroup
New York Life Insurance Co.

PARVER, Alan K.

1001 Pennsylvania Ave. NW
Suite 600
Washington, DC 20004
Tel: (202)347-0066
Fax: (202)624-7222
Registered: LDA
EMail: aparver@pgfm.com

Employers

Powell, Goldstein, Frazer & Murphy LLP (Managing Partner)

Clients Represented

On Behalf of Powell, Goldstein, Frazer & Murphy LLP

Ass'n of Community Cancer Centers
Nat'l Alliance for Infusion Therapy

PARVIS, Cathy C.

4700 Silver Hill Rd. 0002
Room 2432
Washington, DC 20233-0002
Tel: (301)457-2495
Fax: (301)457-1782

Employers

Department of Commerce - Bureau of the Census (Administrative Contact)

PARZAKONIS, Joanna

The Willard Office Bldg.
1455 Pennsylvania Ave. NW
Washington, DC 20004
Tel: (202)783-6000
Fax: (202)783-4171
Registered: LDA

Employers

Gibbons & Company, Inc.

Clients Represented

On Behalf of Gibbons & Company, Inc.

Kellogg Co.

PASCHAL, Jeanette Diana

666 11th St. NW
Suite 750
Washington, DC 20001
Tel: (202)628-5055
Fax: (202)628-5080
EMail: jpaschal@nasbic.org

Employers

Nat'l Ass'n of Small Business Investment Companies (V. President)

PASCO, Jr., James O.

309 Massachusetts Ave. NE
Washington, DC 20002
Tel: (202)547-8189
Fax: (202)547-8190
Registered: LDA

Assistant Director for Congressional and Media Affairs, Bureau of Alcohol and Firearms, Department of the Treasury, 1982-94.

Employers

Fraternal Order of Police (Exec. Director)
Jim Pasco & Associates

Clients Represented

On Behalf of Jim Pasco & Associates

Computer Associates Internat'l
Miller Brewing Co.
Nat'l Air Cargo, Inc.
Philip Morris Management Corp.
Sony Music Entertainment Inc.

PASCO, Richard E.

One Massachusetts Ave. NW
Suite 800
Washington, DC 20001-1431
Tel: (202)842-2345
Fax: (202)408-7763
Registered: LDA
EMail: RPasco@mwmlaw.com

Legislative Assistant to Senator Edward Zorinsky (D-NE), 1985-87.

Employers

McLeod, Watkinson & Miller (Senior Associate)

Clients Represented

On Behalf of McLeod, Watkinson & Miller

American Peanut Product Manufacturers, Inc.
California Avocado Commission
Nat'l Frozen Food Ass'n

PASHKOFF, Lionel E.

1233 20th St. NW
Suite 800
Washington, DC 20036-2396
Tel: (202)416-6800
Fax: (202)416-6899
EMail: LPashkoff@proskauer.com

Employers
Proskauer Rose LLP (Senior Counsel)

PASSACANTANDO, John

702 H. Street NW
Suite 300
Washington, DC 20001
Tel: (202)462-1177
Fax: (202)462-4507

Employers
Greenpeace, U.S.A. (Exec. Director)

PASSEL, Jeffrey S.

2100 M St. NW
Washington, DC 20037
Tel: (202)833-7200
Fax: (202)429-0687

Employers
The Urban Institute (Director, Immigration Policy Research)

PASSIMENT, Elissa

7910 Woodmont Ave.
Suite 530
Bethesda, MD 20814
Tel: (301)657-2768
Fax: (301)657-2909
EMail: elissap@ascls.org

Employers
American Soc. for Clinical Laboratory Science (Exec. Director)

PASTER, Howard G.

600 New Hampshire Ave. NW
Suite 601
Washington, DC 20037
Tel: (202)333-7400
Fax: (202)333-1638
Registered: LDA
Assistant to the President, Director, Legislative Affairs, The White House, 1993.

Employers
Hill and Knowlton, Inc. (Chairman and Chief Exec. Officer)

PASTRICK, R. Scott

1801 K St. NW
Suite 901-L
Washington, DC 20006
Tel: (202)530-0500
Fax: (202)530-4800
Registered: LDA
EMail: Scott_Pastrick@BM.COM
Special Assistant, Office of Legislative Affairs, Department of the Treasury, 1978-80. Staff Director, Subcommittee on Census and Population, House Committee on Post Office and Civil Service, 1983.

Employers
BKSH & Associates (Managing Director)

PATANO, Paul

600 13th St. NW
Washington, DC 20005-3096
Tel: (202)756-8026
Fax: (202)756-8087
EMail: ppatano@mwe.com
Former Trial Attorney, Commodity Futures Trading Commission.

Employers
McDermott, Will and Emery (Partner)

PATASHNIK, Bernard

1101 17th St. NW
Suite 803
Washington, DC 20036
Tel: (202)833-0007
Fax: (202)833-0086
Registered: LDA

Employers
MARC Associates, Inc. (Senior Consultant)

Clients Represented

On Behalf of MARC Associates, Inc.
American Academy of Dermatology
American Academy of Otolaryngic Allergy
American Soc. of Anesthesiologists
American Soc. of Hematology
American Soc. of Nuclear Cardiology
American Speech, Language, and Hearing Ass'n
Urologix, Inc.

PATCH, Richard

2100 L St. NW
Washington, DC 20037
Tel: (202)452-1100
Fax: (202)778-6132
Registered: LDA

Employers
Humane Soc. of the United States (Legislative Specialist)

PATE, Michael L.

2000 K St. NW
Suite 500
Washington, DC 20006-1872
Tel: (202)828-5841
Fax: (202)223-1225
Registered: LDA
EMail: mpate@bracepatt.com
Former Legislative Director for Senator Lloyd Bentsen (D-TX), 1979-85.

Employers
Bracewell & Patterson, L.L.P. (Partner)

Clients Represented

On Behalf of Bracewell & Patterson, L.L.P.
Africa Resources Trust USA
Air Conditioning Contractors of America
Alltel Corporation
American Bus Ass'n
American Chemistry Council
American Registry for Internet Numbers (ARIN)
Baldwin Piano and Organ Co.
Cement Kiln Recycling Coalition
Centex Corp.
Continental Cement Co., Inc.
Council of Industrial Boiler Owners (CIBO)
Enron Corp.
Envirocare of Utah, Inc.
FBI Agents Ass'n
Gary-Williams Energy Corp.
Gas Processors Ass'n
Houston, Texas, Port Authority of the City of
Huntsman Corp.
Independent Oil and Gas Ass'n of Pennsylvania
Lyondell Chemical Co.
Nat'l Cable Television Ass'n
Oxygenated Fuels Ass'n
Placid Refining Co.
Solex Environmental Systems, Inc.
Southdown, Inc.
Sterling Chemical Co.
Texas Petrochemicals Corp.
Texas Windstorm Insurance Ass'n
UST Public Affairs, Inc.
Valero Energy Corp.
Welcon, Inc.

PATRICK, Amy

801 Pennsylvania Ave. NW
Suite 230
Washington, DC 20004
Tel: (202)393-7150
Fax: (202)347-1684
EMail: apatrick@bradleyarant.com

Employers
Bradley Arant Rose & White LLP (Coordinator, Washington Office)

PATRIZIA, Charles A.

1299 Pennsylvania Ave. NW
Tenth Floor
Washington, DC 20004-2400
Tel: (202)508-9500
Fax: (202)508-9700
Registered: LDA
EMail: charlespatrizia@paulhastings.com
Legal Advisor to the Special Mid-East Peace Negotiator and to Ambassador-at-Large, Department of State, 1982-85. Law Clerk to Senior Judge Caleb M. Wright, U.S. District Court for the District of Delaware, 1975-76.

Employers
Paul, Hastings, Janofsky & Walker LLP (Partner)

PATTEE, Suzanne R.

6931 Arlington Rd.
Suite 200
Bethesda, MD 20814
Tel: (301)951-4422
Fax: (301)951-6378
Registered: LDA

Employers
Cystic Fibrosis Foundation (V. President, Public Policy and Patient Affairs)

PATTERSON, Donna E.

555 12th St. NW
Washington, DC 20004-1206
Tel: (202)942-5000
Fax: (202)942-5999
Former Deputy Assistant Attorney General, Antitrust Division, Department of Justice.

Employers
Arnold & Porter (Partner)

PATTERSON, Eliza

1001 Connecticut Ave. NW
Suite 610
Washington, DC 20036
Tel: (202)887-5240
Fax: (202)887-0282
EMail: epatterson@panynj.gov
International Liaison (1988-92), Deputy Director, Office of the Executive (1988-92), Attorney Advisor, Office of the Chair (1987-88), and Attorney Advisor (1982-83), International Trade Commission. Attorney Advisor, Department of Agriculture, 1978-82.

Employers
Port Authority of New York and New Jersey (Legislative Representative)

PATTERSON, Hon. Jerry M.

908 Pennsylvania Ave. SE
Washington, DC 20003
Tel: (202)544-5666
Fax: (202)544-4647
Registered: LDA
EMail: jpatterson@advantage-dc.com
Member, U.S. House of Representatives (D-CA), 1975-85.

Employers
Advantage Associates, Inc. (Partner)

PATTERSON, Judy L.

555 13th St. NW
Suite 1010 East
Washington, DC 20004
Tel: (202)637-6500
Fax: (202)637-6507
Registered: LDA

Employers
American Gaming Ass'n (V. President and Exec. Director)

PATTERSON, Julie

2111 Wilson Blvd.
Eighth Floor
Arlington, VA 22201-3058
Tel: (703)841-0626
Fax: (703)243-2874
Registered: LDA
EMail: patterson@alcalde-fay.com

Employers
Alcalde & Fay (Associate)

Clients Represented

On Behalf of Alcalde & Fay
AMFM, Inc.
Christian Network, Inc.
Computer Sciences Corp.
Glencairn, Ltd.
Jovan Broadcasting
Las Vegas Convention and Visitors Authority
Paxson Communications Corp.

PATTERSON, Romaine

1700 Kalorama Dr. NW
#101
Washington, DC 20009
Tel: (202)986-0425
Fax: (202)986-0470

Employers
Gay and Lesbian Alliance Against Defamation (GLAAD) (Regional Media Manager)

PATTERSON, Walt

950 Herndon Pkwy.
Suite 390
Herndon, VA 20170
Tel: (703)435-9800
Fax: (703)435-7157

Employers
Electronic Funds Transfer Ass'n (Chairman)

PATTI, C. James

1775 K St. NW
Suite 200
Washington, DC 20006
Tel: (202)463-6505
Fax: (202)223-9093
Registered: LDA

Employers
Maritime Institute for Research and Industrial Development (President)

PATTI, Meredith L.

1775 K St. NW
Suite 200
Washington, DC 20006
Tel: (202)463-6505
Fax: (202)223-9093
Registered: LDA

Employers
Maritime Institute for Research and Industrial Development (Government Relations)

PATTON, Douglas J.

2099 Pennsylvania Ave. NW
Suite 100
Washington, DC 20006
Tel: (202)955-3000
Fax: (202)955-5564
Registered: LDA
EMail: dpatton@hklaw.com

Employers
Holland & Knight LLP (Senior Counsel)

Clients Represented

On Behalf of Holland & Knight LLP

Charter Schools Development Corp.
Somerville Housing Group
Thompson Publishing, Inc.

PATTON, Thomas B.

1300 I St. NW
Suite 1070 East
Washington, DC 20005
Tel: (202)962-8550
Fax: (202)962-8560
Registered: LDA

Employers

Philips Electronics North America Corp. (V. President, Government Relations)

PAUGH, Wayne

1255 23rd St. NW
Suite 200
Washington, DC 20037
Tel: (202)466-2396
Fax: (202)466-2893

Employers

Intellectual Property Owners Ass'n (Intellectual Property Counsel, Government Affairs)

PAUL, Andrew R.

225 Reinekers Ln.
Suite 600
Alexandria, VA 22314
Tel: (703)549-6990
Fax: (703)549-7640
Registered: LDA

Employers

Satellite Broadcasting and Communications Ass'n (Senior V. President)

PAUL, Doug

611 Second St. NE
Washington, DC 20002
Tel: (202)548-4001
Fax: (202)548-6115
EMail: dpaul@IMAPS.org

Employers

Internat'l Microelectronics and Packaging Soc. - IMAPS (Manager, Marketing and Membership)

PAUL, Heather

1301 Pennsylvania Ave. NW
Suite 1000
Washington, DC 20004
Tel: (202)662-0600
Fax: (202)393-2072
EMail: hpaul@safekids.org

Employers

Nat'l SAFE KIDS Campaign (Exec. Director)

PAUL, Raymond

1101 Vermont Ave. NW
Suite 604
Washington, DC 20005-3521
Tel: (202)408-7970
Fax: (202)408-7983
Registered: LDA
EMail: rpaul@aopl.org

Employers

Ass'n of Oil Pipelines (Director, Public Affairs)

PAUL, Robert D.

601 13th St. NW
Suite 600 South
Washington, DC 20005
Tel: (202)626-3600
Fax: (202)639-9355
EMail: paulrob@washdc.whitecase.com

General Counsel, Federal Trade Commission, 1986-88. Trial Attorney, Antitrust Division, Department of Justice, 1967-70.

Employers

White & Case LLP (Partner)

Clients Represented

On Behalf of White & Case LLP

Polyisocyanurate Insulation Manufacturers Ass'n

PAUL, USMC (Ret.), Brig. Gen. Terry

700 13th St. NW
Suite 400
Washington, DC 20005
Tel: (202)347-0773
Fax: (202)347-0785
Registered: LDA
EMail: tpaul@cassidy.com

Director of Legislative Affairs for Marine Corps, 1998-2000. Marine Corps liaison officer in Senate, 1988-98.

Employers

Cassidy & Associates, Inc. (Senior V. President and Director, Defense Group)

Clients Represented

On Behalf of Cassidy & Associates, Inc.

Abtech Industries
ADI Ltd.
American Superconductor Corp.
Arnold & Porter
The Boeing Co.
The Chauncey Group Internat'l
CMS Defense Systems, Inc.
Lockheed Martin Corp.
M2 Technologies Inc.
New Jersey Institute of Technology
Ramo Defense Systems, LLC
SWATH Ocean Systems, Inc.
Ultracard, Inc.
United Service Organization
United Space Alliance

PAUL, William M.

1201 Pennsylvania Ave. NW
Washington, DC 20004-2401
Tel: (202)662-6000
Fax: (202)662-6291
Registered: LDA
EMail: wpaul@cov.com

Deputy Tax Legislative Counsel, Department of Treasury, 1988-89. Law Clerk to Judge Thomas Gibbs Gee, U.S. Court of Appeals, Fifth Circuit, 1977-78.

Employers

Covington & Burling (Partner)

Clients Represented

On Behalf of Covington & Burling

Ad Hoc Coalition on Intermarket Coordination

PAULEY, Katharine A.

1200 19th St. NW
Washington, DC 20036-2430
Tel: (202)689-7124
Fax: (202)223-2085
Registered: LDA
EMail: kay.pauley@piperrudnick.com

Employers

Piper Marbury Rudnick & Wolfe LLP (Legal Assistant)

Clients Represented

On Behalf of Piper Marbury Rudnick & Wolfe LLP

AOL Time Warner
Direct Marketing Ass'n, Inc.
Lexis-Nexis
NetCoalition.Com
PSINet Inc.

PAULINO, Erin

1899 Preston White Dr.
Reston, VA 20191-4367
Tel: (703)264-7200
Fax: (703)620-0994
Registered: LDA
EMail: epaulino@npes.org

Employers

NPES, The Ass'n for Suppliers of Printing, Publishing, and Converting Technologies (Government Affairs Representative)

PAULSON, Kristin E.

1401 I St. NW
Suite 600
Washington, DC 20005
Tel: (202)336-7400
Fax: (202)336-7529
Registered: LDA

Employers

United Technologies Corp. (Manager, Congressional Affairs)

PAVEL, Mary J.

1250 I St. NW
Suite 1000
Washington, DC 20005
Tel: (202)682-0240
Fax: (202)682-0249
Registered: LDA

Employers

Sonosky, Chambers, Sachse & Endreson (Partner)

Clients Represented

On Behalf of Sonosky, Chambers, Sachse & Endreson

Assiniboine and Sioux Tribes (Fort Peck Reservation)
Ho-Chunk Nation
Puyallup Tribe of Indians
Standing Rock Sioux Tribe
Yukon-Kuskokwim Health Corp.

PAVEN, Andy

1120 Connecticut Ave. NW
Suite 1100
Washington, DC 20036
Tel: (202)861-5899
Fax: (202)861-5795
Registered: LDA
EMail: apaven@gpcusa.com

Employers

GPC Internat'l (V. President)

Clients Represented

On Behalf of GPC Internat'l

Bechtel/Parsons Brinkeroff Joint Venture
Boardman, Ohio, Township of
Fidelity Investments Co.
Puerto Rico, Commonwealth of

PAVIA, Francisco J.

1400 L St. NW
Washington, DC 20005-3502
Tel: (202)371-5700
Fax: (202)371-5950
Registered: LDA
EMail: fpavia@winston.com

Employers

Winston & Strawn (Of Counsel, Legislative and Regulatory Practice)

Clients Represented

On Behalf of Winston & Strawn

Puerto Rico, Commonwealth of

PAVLIK, Margaret C.

300 E St. SW
LP43
Washington, DC 20546
Tel: (202)358-1948
Fax: (202)358-4340

Employers

Nat'l Aeronautics and Space Administration (Congressional Correspondence Unit)

PAVLOVIC, Dejan

1667 K St. NW
Suite 640
Washington, DC 20006-1605
Tel: (202)721-4809
Fax: (202)467-4250
Registered: LDA
EMail: dejan.pavlovic@oracle.com

Employers

Oracle Corp. (Manager, Global Public Policy)

PAWELCZYK, Julie P.

426 C St. NE
Washington, DC 20002
Tel: (202)544-1880
Fax: (202)543-2565
Registered: LDA
EMail: jp@capitolassociates.com

Employers

Capitol Associates, Inc. (V. President)

Clients Represented

On Behalf of Capitol Associates, Inc.

Academic Health Center Coalition
Albert Einstein Medical Center
Nat'l Ass'n of Children's Hospitals Inc.
Nat'l Federation of State High School Ass'ns
Northwest Regional Education Laboratory
Pennsylvania Higher Education Assistance Agency
Susquehanna Health System
Thomas Jefferson University Hospital
Western Michigan University

PAWLOW, Jean A.

655 15th St. NW
Suite 900
Washington, DC 20005-5701
Tel: (202)626-5800
Fax: (202)628-0858
EMail: jpawlow@milchev.com

Employers

Miller & Chevalier, Chartered (Member)

PAWLSON, Greg

2000 L St. NW
Suite 500
Washington, DC 20036
Tel: (202)955-3500
Fax: (202)955-3599

Employers

Nat'l Committee for Quality Assurance (Exec. V. President)

PAXON, Hon. William L.

1333 New Hampshire Ave. NW
Suite 400
Washington, DC 20036
Tel: (202)887-4000
Fax: (202)887-4288
Registered: LDA

Member, U.S. House of Representatives (R-NY), 1989-98.

Employers
Akin, Gump, Strauss, Hauer & Feld, L.L.P. (Senior Advisor)
Americans for Affordable Electricity (Nat'l Chairman)

Clients Represented
On Behalf of Akin, Gump, Strauss, Hauer & Feld, L.L.P.
Americans for Affordable Electricity
Bridgestone/Firestone, Inc.
Competitive Broadband Coalition
Howland Hook Container Terminal Inc.
Niagara Frontier Transportation Authority
St. Barnabas Healthcare System

PAYETTE, Paul F.

499 S. Capitol St. SW
Suite 520
Washington, DC 20003
Tel: (202)554-3714
Fax: (202)479-4657
Registered: LDA

Employers
The Van Fleet-Meredith Group (Partner)

Clients Represented
On Behalf of The Van Fleet-Meredith Group
American Gas Ass'n
Donlee Technologies, Inc.
Lockheed Martin Corp.
Mantech Corp.
Miltope Corp.
PinPoint Systems Internat'l, LLC
United Defense, L.P.

PAYNE, Donna

919 18th St. NW
Suite 800
Washington, DC 20006
Tel: (202)628-4160
Fax: (202)347-5323

Employers
Human Rights Campaign Fund (Constituent Field Organizer)

PAYNE, J. Michael

1725 Duke St.
Suite 600
Alexandria, VA 22314-3457
EMail: jmpayne@trala.org
Tel: (703)299-9120
Fax: (703)299-9115

Employers
Truck Renting and Leasing Ass'n (President and Chief Exec. Officer)

PAYNE, Jeanne H.

888 16th St. NW
Suite 305
Washington, DC 20006
EMail: payne@bipac.org
Tel: (202)833-1880
Fax: (202)833-2338

Employers
Business-Industry Political Action Committee (Director, Member Services)

PAYNE, Jennifer Cover

1436 U St. NW
Suite 103
Washington, DC 20009-3997
Tel: (202)638-2406
Fax: (202)638-3388

Employers
Cultural Alliance of Greater Washington (Exec. Director)

PAYNE, Dr. Keith

3031 Javier Rd.
Suite 300
Fairfax, VA 22031
Tel: (703)698-0563
Fax: (703)698-0566

Employers
Nat'l Institute for Public Policy (President)

PAYNE, Jr., Hon. Lewis F.

1050 Connecticut Ave. NW
Suite 1200
Washington, DC 20036
Tel: (202)857-2903
Fax: (202)857-1737
Registered: LDA, FARA
EMail: lfpayne@mwcllc.com

Member, U.S. House of Representatives (D-VA), 1988-97. U.S. Army Reserve, 1971-73. U.S. Army, 1969-70.

Employers
McGuireWoods L.L.P. (President, McGuire Woods Consulting, LLC)

Clients Represented
On Behalf of McGuireWoods L.L.P.
Alexandria, Virginia, Sanitation Authority of the City of
Allegiance Healthcare Corp.
Center for Governmental Studies of the University of Virginia
CSX Corp.
Families of Anthoniessen, Bekaert, Eyskens, Van den Heede, and Vermander
Fibrowatt, Inc.
GE Financial Assurance
Georgia-Pacific Corp.
Lynchburg, Virginia, City of
Richmond, Virginia, City of
Smithfield Foods Inc.
Trigon Healthcare Inc.
Wheeling, West Virginia, City of

PAYNE, Michael L.

2025 M St. NW
Suite 800
Washington, DC 20036
EMail: michael_payne@dc.sba.com
Tel: (202)367-2100
Fax: (202)367-1200

Employers
Smith, Bucklin and Associates, Inc. (Exec. V. President)

Clients Represented
On Behalf of Smith, Bucklin and Associates, Inc.
Internat'l Ass'n of Airport Duty Free Stores

PAYNE, Dr. N. Joyce

1307 New York Ave. NW
Suite 400
Washington, DC 20005
EMail: paynej@nasulgc.org
Tel: (202)478-6049
Fax: (202)478-6046

Employers
Office for the Advancement of Public Black Colleges (Director)

PAYNE, Nell

1000 Jefferson Dr. SW
Suite T360
Washington, DC 20560
Tel: (202)357-2962
Fax: (202)786-2274

Special Assistant to the President for Legislative Affairs, Executive Office of the President, The White House, 1989-91. Chief Counsel (1984-87) and Staff Attorney and Counsel (1982-84), Senate Committee on the Budget.

Employers
Smithsonian Institution (Director, Government Relations)

PAYNE, Phillis

1401 New York Ave. NW
Tenth Floor
Washington, DC 20005-2102
Tel: (202)737-1900
Fax: (202)659-3458
Registered: LDA
EMail: ppayne@connerton-ray.com

Employers
Connerton & Ray (Partner)

Clients Represented
On Behalf of Connerton & Ray
Laborers' Internat'l Union of North America
Laborers-Employers Cooperation & Education Trust

PAYTON, John

2445 M St. NW
Washington, DC 20037-1420
Tel: (202)663-6000
Fax: (202)663-6363

Employers
Wilmer, Cutler & Pickering (Partner)

PAZ-SOLDAN, C. Mateo

2600 Virginia Ave. NW
Suite 1000
Washington, DC 20037-1905
Tel: (202)333-8800
Fax: (202)337-6065
Registered: LDA

Employers
Schmeltzer, Aptaker & Shepard, P.C.

Clients Represented
On Behalf of Schmeltzer, Aptaker & Shepard, P.C.
Ass'n of Maquiladores
Honduras, Embassy of
St. Paul, Alaska, City of

PEACE, Chris

1401 I St. NW
Suite 600
Washington, DC 20005
Tel: (202)336-7400
Fax: (202)336-7529

Former Appropriations Committee Associate for Rep. Dave Hobson (R-OH).

Employers
United Technologies Corp. (Congressional Relations Representative)

PEACE, Jr., J. Leon

1120 Connecticut Ave. NW
Washington, DC 20036
Tel: (202)663-5000
Fax: (202)828-4548
Registered: LDA

Employers
American Bankers Ass'n (Senior Counsel, Tax Legislation)

PEAKE, Suzanne

1849 C St. NW
Washington, DC 20240
EMail: sue_peake@ios.doi.gov
Tel: (202)208-7693
Fax: (202)208-7619

Employers
Department of Interior (Staff Assistant to the Director, Office of Congressional and Legislative Affairs)

PEARCE, Christopher P.

1120 Connecticut Ave. NW
Suite 1080
Washington, DC 20036
Tel: (202)466-7362
Fax: (202)429-4915
Registered: LDA

Employers
American Furniture Manufacturers Ass'n (Director, Congressional and Regulatory Affairs)

PEARCE, Karen H.

4201 Wilson Blvd.
Room 1245 S
Arlington, VA 22230
EMail: kpearce@nsf.gov
Tel: (703)292-8070
Fax: (703)292-9089

Employers
Nat'l Science Foundation (Legislative Policy Analyst)

PEARL, Marc A.

2300 N St. NW
Washington, DC 20037-1128
EMail: marc.pearl@shawpittman.com
Tel: (202)663-8000
Fax: (202)663-8007

Employers
Shaw Pittman (Partner)

Clients Represented
On Behalf of Shaw Pittman
American Insurance Ass'n

PEARLMAN, Donald H.

2550 M St. NW
Washington, DC 20037-1350
Tel: (202)457-6000
Fax: (202)457-6315
Registered: LDA
EMail: dpearlman@pattonboggs.com

Executive Assistant to the Secretary, Department of the Interior, 1985-89. Executive Assistant to the Secretary, Department of Energy, 1982-85. Law Clerk to Chief Judge John R. Ross, U.S. District Court for Nevada, 1960-61.

Employers
Patton Boggs, LLP (Partner)

Clients Represented
On Behalf of Patton Boggs, LLP
The Climate Council,

PEARLMAN, Ronald A.

1201 Pennsylvania Ave. NW
Washington, DC 20004-2401
Tel: (202)662-6000
Fax: (202)662-6291
Registered: LDA
EMail: rpearlman@cov.com

Chief of Staff, Joint Committee on Taxation, 1988-90. Assistant Secretary (1984-85) and Deputy Assistant Secretary (1983-84) for Tax Policy, Department of the Treasury. Office of the Chief Counsel, Internal Revenue Service, 1965-69.

Employers
Covington & Burling (Partner)

Clients Represented

On Behalf of Covington & Burling

The Business Roundtable
Zeigler Coal Holding Co.

PEARSON, Cindy

514 Tenth St. NW
Suite 400
Washington, DC 20004
Tel: (202)347-1140
Fax: (202)347-1168

Employers

Nat'l Women's Health Network (Exec. Director)

PEARSON, Harriet P.

1301 K St. NW
Suite 1200-West Tower
Washington, DC 20005-3307
Tel: (202)515-5023
Fax: (202)515-5055
Registered: LDA
EMail: hpearson@us.ibm.ocm

Employers

Internat'l Business Machines Corp. (Chief Privacy Officer)

PEARSON, Mr. Kerry S.

1225 19th St. NW
Suite 825
Washington, DC 20036
Tel: (202)331-7080
Fax: (202)331-7082
Registered: LDA

Employers

The Kerry S. Pearson LLC (Chairman and Chief Exec. Officer)

Clients Represented

On Behalf of The Kerry S. Pearson LLC

Doctors Community Healthcare Corp.

PEARSON, Mary Frances

1225 Connecticut Ave. NW
Washington, DC 20036
Tel: (202)327-8395
Fax: (202)327-6738
Registered: LDA
EMail: maryfrances.pearson@ey.com
Former Majority Tax Counsel, Committee on Finance, U.S. Senate and Attorney, Office of Chief Counsel, Internal Revenue Service, Department of Treasury.

Employers

Ernst & Young LLP (Director, Federal Relations)

PEARSON, Ronald W.

104 North Carolina Ave. SE
Washington, DC 20003
Tel: (202)547-7177
Registered: LDA, FARA
Former Chief of Staff to Rep. John Ashbrook (R-OH).

Employers

Pearson & Pipkin, Inc. (President)

Clients Represented

On Behalf of Pearson & Pipkin, Inc.

The 60/Plus Ass'n, Inc.
Christian Action Network
Conservative Victory Fund
Young America's Foundation

PEASE, Kendall

3190 Fairview Park Dr.
Falls Church, VA 22042
Tel: (703)876-3000
Fax: (703)876-3600

Employers

General Dynamics Corp. (V. President, Communications)

PECK, Carol

1731 King St.
Suite 200
Alexandria, VA 22314
Tel: (703)549-1390
Fax: (703)549-1656
EMail: cpeck@catholiccharitiesusa.org

Employers

Catholic Charities USA (Program Dir. for Family Support)

PECK, Jeffrey J.

1666 K St. NW
Suite 800
Washington, DC 20006
Tel: (202)481-7000
Fax: (202)862-7098
Registered: LDA
Former Senate Judiciary Committee Aide to Senator Joseph R. Biden, Jr. (D-DE).

Employers

Arthur Andersen LLP (Managing Partner, Office of Government Affairs)

PECK, Jonathan

100 N. Pitt St.
Suite 235
Alexandria, VA 22314-3134
Tel: (703)684-5880
Fax: (703)684-0640
EMail: jpeck@altfutures.com

Employers

Institute for Alternative Futures (V. President)

PECK, Robert

1050 31st St. NW
Washington, DC 20007
Tel: (202)965-3500
Fax: (202)342-5484

Employers

Ass'n of Trial Lawyers of America (Director, Legal Affairs)

PECKARSKY, Lee

11408 Stonewood Ln.
Rockville, MD 20852
Tel: (301)468-6965
Registered: LDA
Counsel and Staff Director, House Banking Committee.

Employers

Self-employed as an independent consultant.

Clients Represented

As an independent consultant

HomeStreet Bank

PECKHAM, Gardner

1801 K St. NW
Suite 901-L
Washington, DC 20006
Tel: (202)530-0500
Fax: (202)530-4800
Registered: LDA
EMail: gardner_peckham@bm.com
Former Senior Policy Analyst to Speaker of the House, Rep. Newt Gingrich (R-GA). Deputy Chief of Staff and Senior Staff Consultant, and Staff Consultant, Subcommittee on Africa, all at the House Committee on Foreign Affairs.Former Director of Legislative Affairs to the National Security Advisor, Executive Office of the President, The White House.

Employers

BKSH & Associates (Managing Director)

Clients Represented

On Behalf of BKSH & Associates

Citizens for Liberty in Cuba (Cuba Libertad)
General Development Corp.

PECKINPAUGH, Tim L.

1735 New York Ave. NW
Suite 500
Washington, DC 20006-4759
Tel: (202)628-1700
Fax: (202)331-1024
Registered: LDA
EMail: timp@prestongates.com
Technical Consultant, House Committee on Science and Technology, 1985. Legislative Assistant to Rep. Sid Morrison (R-WA), 1982-84. Research Associate, House Republican Study Committee, 1981-82.

Employers

Preston Gates Ellis & Rouvelas Meeds LLP (Partner)

Clients Represented

On Behalf of Preston Gates Ellis & Rouvelas Meeds LLP

Acme Software
Adobe
American Nuclear Insurers
Amgen
Battelle Memorial Institute
Blaine, Washington, City of
BWXT, Inc.
East Tennessee Economic Council
Envirocare of Utah, Inc.
Environmental Business Action Coalition
Foster Wheeler Environmental Corp.
Future of Puerto Rico Inc.
Grant County P.U.D., Washington
MG Financial Group
Money Garden Corp.
Nat'l Center for Economic Freedom, Inc.
Northern Michigan University
Pac Med Clinics
Port Angeles, Washington, City of
PPL
Schlumberger Technology Corp.
Seattle Housing Authority
Seattle, Washington, Port of
Stone and Webster Engineering Corp.
Tri-City Industrial Development Council
United States Maritime Coalition
USFHP Conference Group
H. D. Vest Financial Service
VoiceStream Wireless Corp.

PECQUEX, Francis X.

815 16th St. NW
Sixth Floor
Washington, DC 20006
Tel: (202)628-6300
Fax: (202)637-3989
Registered: LDA

Employers

AFL-CIO - Maritime Trades Department (Exec. Secretary-Treasurer)

PEDDICORD, Ph.D., Douglas

227 Massachusetts Ave. NE
Suite 300
Washington, DC 20002
Tel: (202)543-7460
Fax: (202)543-5327
Registered: LDA
EMail: healthadvocate@worldnet.att.net

Employers

Washington Health Advocates (V. President)

Clients Represented

On Behalf of Washington Health Advocates

American Health Information Management Ass'n
American Medical Informatics Ass'n
American Soc. for Clinical Pharmacology and Therapeutics
Center for Healthcare Information Management
GCRC Program Directors Ass'n
Jewish Guild for the Blind
Quintiles Transnational Corp.

PEDERSEN, Wes

2033 K St. NW
Suite 700
Washington, DC 20006
Tel: (202)872-1790
Fax: (202)835-8343

Employers

Public Affairs Council (Director, Communications and Public Relations)

PEDERSEN, Jr., William F.

2300 N St. NW
Washington, DC 20037-1128
Tel: (202)663-8000
Fax: (202)663-8007
EMail: bill.pedersen@shawpittman.com
Served in the Environmental Protection Agency from 1972-85 as Staff Attorney, Deputy General Counsel and Associate General Counsel for Air and Radiation. Also served as Staff Counsel to the Senate Committee on Government Operations.

Employers

Shaw Pittman (Partner)

PEDROSO, Margo

1100 Pennsylvania Ave. NW
Room 510
Washington, DC 20506
Tel: (202)606-8339
Fax: (202)606-8591
EMail: mpedroso@imls.gov

Employers

Institute for Museum and Library Services (Congressional Affairs Specialist)

PEDULLA, Diane

750 First St. NE
Washington, DC 20002-4242
Tel: (202)336-5500
Fax: (202)336-6069
Registered: LDA

Employers

American Psychological Ass'n

PEDUZZI, Lawrence P.

219 N. Washington St.
Alexandria, VA 22314
Tel: (703)836-7990
Fax: (703)836-9739
Registered: LDA
EMail: pal@pal-aerospace.com

Employers

Peduzzi Associates, Ltd. (President)

Clients Represented

On Behalf of Peduzzi Associates, Ltd.

DRS - EOSG
Integrated Medical Systems
Lord Corp.
Marconi Flight Systems, Inc.
Skyhook Technologies, Inc.

PEEL, Terry R.

1317 F St. NW
Suite 200
Washington, DC 20004
Tel: (202)737-1800
Fax: (202)737-2485
Registered: LDA

Former Minority Staff Director, Subcommittee on Foreign Operations, Export Financing and Related Programs, House Appropriations Committee.

Employers
Edington, Peel & Associates, Inc. (Principal)

Clients Represented

On Behalf of Edington, Peel & Associates, Inc.
Florida State University
Helen Keller Worldwide
Kettering Medical Center
Kiwanis Internat'l
Nat'l Council for Eurasian and East European Research
Pacific Union College
Pan American Health Organization
U.S. Fund for UNICEF

PEELE, III, B. Thomas

815 Connecticut Ave. NW
Suite 900
Washington, DC 20006-4078
Tel: (202)452-7000
Fax: (202)452-7073
Registered: LDA, FARA

Employers
Baker & McKenzie (Partner)

Clients Represented

On Behalf of Baker & McKenzie
British Columbia Softwood Lumber Trade Council

PEELE, Jo Anne

700 13th St. NW
Suite 700
Washington, DC 20005-3960
EMail: japeete@bryancave.com
Tel: (202)508-6000
Fax: (202)508-6200

Employers
Bryan Cave LLP (Partner)

PEELER, Alexandra

1731 King St.
Suite 200
Alexandria, VA 22314
EMail: apeeler@catholiccharitiesusa.org
Tel: (703)549-1390
Fax: (703)549-1656

Employers
Catholic Charities USA (Director of Communications)

PEEPLES, Lloyd

801 Pennsylvania Ave. NW
Suite 230
Washington, DC 20004
EMail: lpeeples@bradleyarant.com
Tel: (202)393-7150
Fax: (202)347-1684

Former Legislative Counsel to Senator Jeff Sessions (R-AL).

Employers
Bradley Arant Rose & White LLP (Associate)

PEGG, William D.

600 13th St. NW
Washington, DC 20005-3096
EMail: wpegg@mwe.com
Tel: (202)756-8395
Fax: (202)756-8087

Engineer/Inspector, Nuclear Regulatory Commission, 1990-95.

Employers
McDermott, Will and Emery (Associate)

PEHRSON, Judy

3007 Tilden St. NW
Suite 5L
Washington, DC 20008-3009
EMail: scholars@cies.iie.org
Tel: (202)686-4000
Fax: (202)362-3442

Employers
Council for Internat'l Exchange of Scholars (Director, External Relations)

PELAVIN, Mark

2027 Massachusetts Ave. NW
Washington, DC 20036
Tel: (202)387-2800
Fax: (202)667-9070

Employers
Religious Action Center of Reform Judaism (Associate Director)

PELAVIN, Sol H.

3333 K St. NW
Suite 300
Washington, DC 20007
Tel: (202)342-5000
Fax: (202)342-5033

Employers
American Institutes for Research (Exec. V. President)

PELIKAN, Thomas

801 Pennsylvania Ave. SE
Suite 300
Washington, DC 20003
EMail: pelikan@scenic.org
Tel: (202)543-6200
Fax: (202)543-9130
Registered: LDA

Employers
Scenic America (Director of Policy)

PELLERIN, Christine A.

1747 Pennsylvania Ave. NW
Suite 1150
Washington, DC 20006
EMail: cpellerin@mww.com
Tel: (202)557-2964
Fax: (202)296-4507
Registered: LDA

Former Associate Staff Member, Subcommittee on Labor, Health and Human Services, and Education, House Committee on Appropriations. Former Legislative Correspondent to Rep. Silvio O. Conte (R-MA). Former Legislative Assistant to Rep. Henry Bonilla (R-TX).

Employers
The MWW Group (V. President, Federal Affairs)

Clients Represented

On Behalf of The MWW Group
Bacardi-Martini, USA, Inc.
Century Financial Group
Delaware River Stevedores
Detroit Medical Center
GAF Corp.
Green County Health Care, Inc.
Kmart Corp.
Nat'l Ass'n of Community Health Centers
Puerto Ricans for Civic Action
United States Education Finance Corp.

PELLETIER, Eric

Eisenhower Exec. Office Bldg.
725 17th St. NW
Washington, DC 20503
Tel: (202)395-4790
Fax: (202)395-3888

Employers
Executive Office of the President - Office of Management and Budget (Associate Director, Legislative Affairs)

PELLETIER, Steve

1307 New York Ave. NW
Eighth Floor
Washington, DC 20009-5728
Tel: (202)737-3699
Fax: (202)737-3657

Employers
NAFSA: Ass'n of Internat'l Educators (Director, Publications)

PELTZ, Elin

1156 15th St. NW
Suite 400
Washington, DC 20005
Tel: (202)872-3844
Fax: (202)463-0474
Registered: LDA

Employers
American Crop Protection Ass'n (Senior Director, Federal Legislative Affairs)

PELTZ, Mara

600 Pennsylvania Ave. SE
Suite 320
Washington, DC 20003
EMail: mpeltz@themec.com
Tel: (202)969-8110
Fax: (202)969-7036
Registered: LDA

Employers
The Macon Edwards Co. (V. President)

Clients Represented

On Behalf of The Macon Edwards Co.
American Soc. of Farm Managers and Rural Appraisers
American Sugar Cane League of the U.S.A.
Capital Equipment Legislative Coalition
Coalition for Crop Insurance Improvement
First South Production Credit Ass'n
Gildan Activewear
Supima Ass'n of America

PEMBROKE, James D.

1615 M St. NW
Suite 800
Washington, DC 20036-3203
EMail: jdp@dwgp.com
Tel: (202)467-6370
Fax: (202)467-6379

Employers
Duncan, Weinberg, Genzer & Pembroke, P.C. (Secretary-Treasurer)

Clients Represented

On Behalf of Duncan, Weinberg, Genzer & Pembroke, P.C.
Auburn, Avilla, Bluffton, Columbia City and Other Municipalities of Indiana
Central Montana Electric Power Cooperative, Inc.
Indiana and Michigan Municipal Distributors Ass'n
M-S-R Public Power Agency
Mishawaka Utilities
Modesto/Turlock Irrigation District
Orlando Utilities Commission
Palo Alto, California, City of
Redding, California, Electric Department of the City of
Santa Clara, California, Electric Department of the City of
Southern California Public Power Authority
Transmission Agency of Northern California
Trinity Public Utilities District

PENA, Humberto R.

555 13th St. NW
Washington, DC 20004-1109
EMail: hrpena@hhlaw.com
Tel: (202)637-5938
Fax: (202)637-5910
Registered: LDA

Chief of Staff (1988-90) and Subcommittee Counsel (1977-80), House Committee on Agriculture.

Employers
Hogan & Hartson L.L.P. (Partner)

Clients Represented

On Behalf of Hogan & Hartson L.L.P.
Biogen, Inc.
BrokerTek Global, L.L.C.
Coalition for the American Agricultural Producer (CAAP)
Coste Enterprises Inc.
Discovery Science Center
Farm Credit Bank of Texas
Farmland Industries, Inc.
Golden Peanut Co.
InterAmerica's Group LLC
Meat New Zealand
New Zealand Dairy Board
Soap and Detergent Ass'n
Taco Bell Corp.
United Special Transport Air Resources, LLC (USTAR)
United States Sugar Corp.

PENAFIEL, Karen

1201 New York Ave. NW
Suite 300
Washington, DC 20005
EMail: kpenafiel@boma.org
Tel: (202)326-6323
Fax: (202)371-0181
Registered: LDA

Employers
Building Owners and Managers Ass'n Internat'l (Assistant Exec. Director, Government and Industry Affairs)

PENBERTHY, Shannon

1101 17th St. NW
Suite 803
Washington, DC 20036
Tel: (202)833-0007
Fax: (202)833-0086
Registered: LDA

Employers
MARC Associates, Inc. (Legislative Associate)

Clients Represented

On Behalf of MARC Associates, Inc.
American Soc. for Gastrointestinal Endoscopy
Cerebral Palsy Council
Coalition for Health Services Research
Corporation for Supportive Housing
Fine Arts Museums of San Francisco
Nat'l Hemophilia Foundation
TELACU

PENCAK, Lawrence

1700 N. Moore St.
Suite 1540
Arlington, VA 22209
Tel: (703)524-6686
Fax: (703)524-6630

Employers
RESNA (Exec. Director)

PENCE, Randall G.

P.O. Box 6594
Arlington, VA 22206
Tel: (703)593-3456
Fax: (703)534-7760
Registered: LDA

Legislative Director to Senator David Karnes (R-NE), 1987-88. Legislative Assistant to Senator Edward Zorinsky (D-NE), 1983-87.

Employers
Capitol Hill Advocates (President)

Clients Represented
On Behalf of Capitol Hill Advocates
American Soc. of Home Inspectors (ASHI)
American Wood Preservers Institute
Big Sky, Inc.
Nat'l Concrete Masonry Ass'n

PENDER, Jill

445 12th St. NW
Room 8-C478
Washington, DC 20554
Tel: (202)418-1900
Fax: (202)418-2806

Employers
Federal Communications Commission (Attorney/Advisor, Legislative and Intergovernmental Affairs)

PENDERGAST, Mary

1140 Connecticut Ave. NW
Suite 350
Washington, DC 20036
Tel: (202)872-7800
Fax: (202)872-7808
Registered: LDA

Employers
Elan Pharmaceutical Research Corp.

PENDLETON, Linda

Two Democracy Center
6903 Rockledge Dr., Suite 1250
Bethesda, MD 20817-1831
Tel: (301)571-1940
Fax: (301)571-8244

Employers
Mutual of America (Service Manager)

PENHILL, Laurel

1101 Vermont Ave. NW
Suite 500
Washington, DC 20005
Tel: (202)898-0089
Fax: (202)898-0159

Employers
American Advertising Federation (Senior V. President, Operations)

PENN, David

2301 M St. NW
Washington, DC 20037-1484
Tel: (202)467-2933
Fax: (202)467-2910
Registered: LDA
EMail: davepenn@APPAnet.org

Employers
American Public Power Ass'n (Exec. V. President)

PENN, Deane A.

4900-B South 31st. St.
Arlington, VA 22206
Tel: (703)820-7400
Fax: (703)931-4520

Employers
American College of Gastroenterology (PAC Contact)

PENN, Nicolas S.

1401 New York Ave.
Suite 600
Washington, DC 20005
Tel: (202)434-9100
Registered: LDA

Employers
Leftwich & Douglas

PENNA, Richard A.

1050 Thomas Jefferson St. NW
Seventh Floor
Washington, DC 20007
Tel: (202)298-1800
Fax: (202)338-2416
Registered: LDA
EMail: rap@vnf.com

Employers
Van Ness Feldman, P.C. (Member)

Clients Represented
On Behalf of Van Ness Feldman, P.C.
Mack Trucks, Inc.
Tecumseh Products Co.
Toyota Motor Manufacturing North America
Toyota Motor North America, U.S.A., Inc.

PENNA, Richard P.

1426 Prince St.
Alexandria, VA 22314
Tel: (703)739-2330
Fax: (703)836-8982

Employers
American Ass'n of Colleges of Pharmacy (Exec. V. President)

PENNE, R. Leo

444 N. Capitol St.
Suite 209
Washington, DC 20001
EMail: lpenne@sso.org
Tel: (202)624-5405
Fax: (202)624-8181

Employers
Nevada, Washington Office of the State of (Director, DC Office)

PENNER, Dr. Rudolph G.

2100 M St. NW
Washington, DC 20037
Tel: (202)833-7200
Fax: (202)429-0687

Employers
The Urban Institute (Senior Fellow)

PENNEY, Bradford A.

1201 North Pitt St.
Number 1B
Alexandria, VA 22314
Tel: (703)532-1427
Fax: (703)471-8688
Registered: LDA

Counsel to Senator Claiborne de Borda Pell (D-RI), 1978-87. Counsel, House Committee on Science, 1991-93.

Employers
Self-employed as an independent consultant.

Clients Represented
As an independent consultant
Classroom Publishers Ass'n

PENNING, Nicholas J.

1801 N. Moore St.
Arlington, VA 22209
EMail: npenning@aasa.org
Tel: (703)528-0700
Fax: (703)528-2146

Employers
American Ass'n of School Administrators (Senior Legislative Analyst)

PENNINGTON, Thomas W.

7401 Wisconsin Ave.
Suite 500
Bethesda, MD 20814
Tel: (301)986-8585
Fax: (301)652-5690
Registered: FARA

Employers
COGEMA, Inc. (V. President and General Counsel)

PENRY, Charles D.

4301 Wilson Blvd.
Arlington, VA 22203-1860
Tel: (703)907-5815
Fax: (703)907-5516
Registered: LDA
EMail: chuck.penry@nreca.org

Employers
Nat'l Rural Electric Cooperative Ass'n (Legislative Representative)

PENSABENE, Gregory M.

800 Connecticut Ave. NW
Suite 700
Washington, DC 20006
Tel: (202)861-8064
Fax: (202)861-8065
Registered: LDA

Employers
Anadarko Petroleum Corp. (V. President, Government Affairs and Corporate Communications)

PENSABENE, Judith K.

1301 Pennsylvania Ave. NW
Suite 1050
Washington, DC 20004
Tel: (202)942-9840
Fax: (202)942-9847
Registered: LDA

Former counsel, Senate Energy Committee.

Employers
Constellation Energy Group (Director, Federal Relations and Washington Counsel)

PEOPLES, Thomas E.

1025 Connecticut Ave. NW
Suite 501
Washington, DC 20036
EMail: tom.peoples@gencorp.com
Tel: (202)828-6800
Fax: (202)828-6858
Registered: LDA

Employers
GenCorp (Senior V. President, International and Washington Operations)

PEPER, Jennifer

1634 I St. NW
Suite 600
Washington, DC 20006-4083
Tel: (202)783-2200
Fax: (202)783-2206
Registered: LDA

Employers
Ericsson Inc. (Manager, Legislative Affairs)

PERA, Lonnie E.

888 17th St. NW
Suite 600
Washington, DC 20006-3959
EMail: lepera@zsrlaw.com
Tel: (202)298-8660
Fax: (202)342-0683

Employers
Zuckert, Scoutt and Rasenberger, L.L.P. (Partner)

Clients Represented
On Behalf of Zuckert, Scoutt and Rasenberger, L.L.P.
Empresa Consolidada Cubana de Aviacion
JMC Airlines, Ltd.

PERCY-JARRETT, Stephanie

1526 Pennsylvania Ave. SE
Washington, DC 20003
Tel: (202)544-5300
Fax: (202)628-5394

Employers
JHP, Inc. (Jobs Have Priority) (Deputy Director)

PERCY-MCDANIEL, Herma M.

122 C St. NW
Suite 240
Washington, DC 20001
EMail: herma@pewwildernesscenter.org
Tel: (202)544-3691
Fax: (202)544-5197

Employers
Pew Wilderness Center (Media Director)

PERES, Judith Rae

2519 Connecticut Ave. NW
Washington, DC 20008-1520
Tel: (202)783-2242
Fax: (202)783-2255

Employers
American Ass'n of Homes and Services for the Aging (Director, Health Policy)

PEREZ, Barbara Zientek

1120 G St. NW
Suite 200
Washington, DC 20005
EMail: barbzienteck@erols.com
Tel: (202)544-1112
Fax: (202)737-4933

Employers
Krivit & Krivit, P.C.

PEREZ, Esten F.

1025 Vermont Ave. NW
Third Floor
Washington, DC 20005
Tel: (202)783-7400
Fax: (202)783-0444

Employers
Friends of the Earth

PEREZ, Lauren

1300 Pennsylvania Ave. NW
Suite 400
Ronald Reagan Bldg.
Washington, DC 20004
EMail: lperez@strtrade.com
Tel: (202)638-2230
Fax: (202)638-2236
Registered: LDA

Employers
Sandler, Travis & Rosenberg, P.A. (IPR Trade Advisor)

Clients Represented

On Behalf of Sandler, Travis & Rosenberg, P.A.

American Free Trade Ass'n

PERITO, Paul L.

1299 Pennsylvania Ave. NW
Tenth Floor
Washington, DC 20004-2400
EMail: paulperito@paulhastings.com
Tel: (202)508-9500
Fax: (202)508-9700

Special Counsel to the Administrator, Drug Enforcement Administration, Department of Justice, 1974-75. General Counsel and Deputy Director, Special Action Office on Drug Abuse Prevention, Executive Office of the President, The White House, 1971-73. Chief Counsel and Staff Director, House Select Committee on Crime, 1970-71. Member, Special Prosecutions Unit and Assistant U.S. Attorney for the Southern District of New York, Department of Justice, 1966-70.

Employers

Paul, Hastings, Janofsky & Walker LLP (Senior Counsel)

Clients Represented

On Behalf of Paul, Hastings, Janofsky & Walker LLP

Star Tobacco & Pharmaceuticals Inc.

PERKINS, III, Charles S.

1500 K St. NW
Suite 875
Washington, DC 20005
Tel: (202)783-3195
Fax: (202)783-4862

Employers

Bituminous Coal Operators Ass'n (Secretary-Treasurer)

PERKINS, Nancy L.

555 12th St. NW
Washington, DC 20004-1206
EMail: Nancy_Perkins@aporter.com
Tel: (202)942-5000
Fax: (202)942-5999
Registered: LDA

Clerk to Judge Eugene H. Nickerson, U.S. District Court, Eastern District of New York, 1987-88.

Employers

Arnold & Porter (Partner)

Clients Represented

On Behalf of Arnold & Porter

State Farm Insurance Cos.
Vestal Group of Companies

PERKINS, Peter

1001 19th St. North
Suite 800
Arlington, VA 22209-3901
EMail: pete.perkins@trw.com
Tel: (703)276-5159
Fax: (703)276-5119

Employers

TRW Inc. (Director, Government Relations-Defense and Nat'l Security Programs)

PERKINS, Roy

1150 Connecticut Ave. NW
Suite 201
Washington, DC 20036
EMail: rperkins@gcwdc.org
Tel: (202)955-6200
Fax: (202)955-6215

Employers

Goddard Claussen (Senior V. President and Deputy Director)

PERLE, Linda

1616 P St. NW
Suite 150
Washington, DC 20036
EMail: lperle@clasp.org
Tel: (202)328-5146
Fax: (202)328-5195

Employers

Center for Law and Social Policy (Senior Staff Attorney)

PERLE, Richard N.

1150 17th St. NW
Washington, DC 20036
EMail: rperle@aei.org
Tel: (202)862-5800
Fax: (202)862-7177

Employers

American Enterprise Institute for Public Policy Research (Resident Fellow)

PERLMAN, Abigail

1341 G St. NW
Suite 900
Washington, DC 20005
Tel: (202)637-1519
Fax: (202)637-1549

Employers

Philip Morris Management Corp. (Director, Government Affairs)

PERLMAN, Jeffry L.

1101 Vermont Ave. NW
Suite 500
Washington, DC 20005
Tel: (202)898-0089
Fax: (202)898-0159
Registered: LDA

Employers

American Advertising Federation (Exec. V. President, Government Affairs and General Counsel)

PERLMAN, Spencer

1500 K St. NW
Suite 250
Washington, DC 20005-1714
EMail: soperlman@uhlaw.com
Tel: (202)639-7506
Fax: (202)639-7505

Director of Constituent Relations, Legislative Assistant, and Legislative Director for Rep. John Edward Porter (R-IL), 1997-2001.

Employers

Ungaretti & Harris (Legislative Affairs Manager)

Clients Represented

On Behalf of Ungaretti & Harris

Allegiance Healthcare Corp.
Cardinal Health Inc.
Medical Research Laboratories

PERLMUTTER, Deana

412 First St. SE
Suite 100
Washington, DC 20003
EMail: dperlmutter@dutkogroup.com
Tel: (202)484-4884
Fax: (202)484-0109
Registered: LDA

Employers

The Dutko Group, Inc. (Senior V. President)

Clients Represented

On Behalf of The Dutko Group, Inc.

Carpet and Rug Institute
Coalition to Advance Sustainable Technology
Level 3 Communications LLC

PERLSTEIN, William J.

2445 M St. NW
Washington, DC 20037-1420
EMail: wperlstein@wilmer.com
Tel: (202)663-6000
Fax: (202)663-6363

Employers

Wilmer, Cutler & Pickering (Partner)

PERMUT, Philip V.

1200 19th St. NW
Suite 500
Washington, DC 20036
EMail: ppermut@kelleydrye.com
Tel: (202)955-9600
Fax: (202)955-9792

Deputy Chief (1977-78); Chief, Policy and Rules Division (1976-77); Special Assistant to Bureau Chief (1974-76); and Trial Attorney, General Counsel's Office (1973-74), Common Carrier Bureau; and Appellate Litigator, Broadcast Bureau (1968-73); all at the Federal Communications Commission.

Employers

Kelley, Drye & Warren LLP (Partner)

PERNICK, Carol V.

818 Connecticut Ave. NW
Tenth Floor
Washington, DC 20006
Tel: (202)296-4662
Fax: (202)296-5547
Registered: LDA

Employers

CNA Financial Corp. (V. President, Congressional Relations)

PEROT, Ruth

440 First St. NW
Suite 430
Washington, DC 20001
EMail: rperot@shire-inc.org
Tel: (202)371-0277
Fax: (202)371-0460

Employers

Summit Health Institute for Research and Education (Exec. Director)

PERRELL, Beverly S.

11141 Georgia Ave.
Suite 412
Wheaton, MD 20902
EMail: aspesbo@aol.com
Tel: (301)929-8848
Fax: (301)929-0231

Employers

American Soc. of Professional Estimators (Director, Administration)

PERRIELLO, Mark

919 18th St. NW
Suite 800
Washington, DC 20006
Tel: (202)628-4160
Fax: (202)347-5323

Employers

Human Rights Campaign Fund (PAC Manager)

PERRIN, Cheryl D.

50 F St. NW
Suite 1198
Washington, DC 20001
EMail: cdperrin@aol.com
Tel: (202)628-0610
Fax: (202)628-0598
Registered: LDA

Employers

Campaign for America (Exec. Director)

PERRIN, Cidette S.

325 Seventh St. NW
Suite 625
Washington, DC 20004-2802
EMail: legis@naphs.org
Tel: (202)393-6700
Ext: 17
Fax: (202)783-6041
Registered: LDA

Employers

Nat'l Ass'n of Psychiatric Health Systems (Director, Legislative and Regulatory Affairs)

PERROS, Georgette

1455 F St. NW
Suite 420
Washington, DC 20004
Tel: (202)628-6442
Fax: (202)628-6537
Registered: LDA

Employers

USAA - United Services Automobile Ass'n (Federal Affairs Associate)

PERRY, Barbara F.

444 N. Capitol St. NW
Suite 418
Washington, DC 20001
EMail: bperry@u.washington.edu
Tel: (202)624-1420
Fax: (202)624-1429
Registered: LDA

Employers

University of Washington (Assistant V. President, University Relations/Director Federal Relations)

PERRY, Beverly

1900 Pennsylvania Ave. NW
Washington, DC 20068
Tel: (202)872-2000
Fax: (202)872-7967
Registered: LDA

Employers

Potomac Electric Power Co. (V. President, Government and Corporate Affairs)

PERRY, Daniel

2021 K St. NW
Suite 305
Washington, DC 20006-1003
EMail: dperry@agingresearch.org
Tel: (202)293-2856
Fax: (202)785-8574

Special Assistant to Senator Alan Cranston (D-CA), 1972-85. Press Secretary to the Senate Committee on Veterans Affairs, 1978-80.

Employers

Alliance for Aging Research (Exec. Director)

PERRY, Deborah L.

1050 N. Taylor St.
Suite 306
Arlington, VA 22201
Tel: (202)668-4447
Registered: LDA

Employers

Self-employed as an independent consultant.

Clients Represented

As an independent consultant

The Nat'l Foundation for Teaching Entrepreneurship

PERRY, Edmund F.

1301 K St. NW
Suite 1200-West Tower
Washington, DC 20005-3307
EMail: efp@us.ibm.com

Tel: (202)515-5039
Fax: (202)515-5906
Registered: LDA

Employers
Internat'l Business Machines Corp. (Director, Government Relations)

PERRY, George L.

1775 Massachusetts Ave. NW
Washington, DC 20036-2188

Tel: (202)797-6000
Fax: (202)797-6004

Senior Economist, President's Council of Economic Advisers, 1961-63.

Employers
The Brookings Institution (Senior Fellow, Economic Studies)

PERRY, Louie

700 13th St. NW
Suite 400
Washington, DC 20005
EMail: lperry@cassidy.com

Tel: (202)347-0773
Fax: (202)347-0785

Special Assistant and Projects Coordinator to Rep. Jerry Huckaby (D-LA), 1989-92.

Employers
Cassidy & Associates, Inc. (V. President)

Clients Represented

On Behalf of Cassidy & Associates, Inc.
Elmira College
Memorial Hermann Health Care System
Ocean Spray Cranberries

PERRY, Mark A.

1050 Connecticut Ave. NW
Washington, DC 20036-5306
EMail: mperry@gdclaw.com

Tel: (202)955-8500
Fax: (202)467-0539

Law Clerk to Justice Sandra Day O'Connor, Supreme Court, 1993-94. Attorney, Office of the Solicitor General of the United States, 1992-93. Law Clerk to Judge Alex Kozinski, U.S. Court of Appeals, Ninth Circuit, 1991-92.

Employers
Gibson, Dunn & Crutcher LLP (Partner)

Clients Represented

On Behalf of Gibson, Dunn & Crutcher LLP
Civil Justice Reform Group

PERRY, Steve

1451 Dolley Madison Blvd.
McLean, VA 22101-3850

Tel: (703)761-2600
Fax: (703)761-4334

Employers
Internat'l Ass'n of Food Industry Suppliers (Senior V. President)

PERRY, Steve

412 First St. SE
Suite 100
Washington, DC 20003
EMail: sperry@dutkogroup.com

Tel: (202)484-4884
Fax: (202)484-0109
Registered: LDA

Former Legislative Aide to Senator John Heinz (R-PA).

Employers
The Dutko Group, Inc. (Chief Exec. Officer)

Clients Represented

On Behalf of The Dutko Group, Inc.
Alcatel USA
ASCENT (Ass'n of Community Enterprises)
AT&T
AT&T Wireless Services, Inc.
Cable & Wireless, Inc.
Competitive Telecommunications Ass'n (COMPTEL)
European Telecommunications Standards Institute (ETSI)
EXCEL Communications Inc.
Satellite Broadcasting and Communications Ass'n
SkyBridge, LLC
SpaceData Internat'l
TV Guide, Inc.
VeriSign/Network Solutions, Inc.
Winstar Communications, Inc.
XO Communications

PERRY, Susan B.

141 12th St. NE
Washington, DC 20002

Tel: (202)547-4808
Fax: (202)547-1698
Registered: LDA

Employers
Self-employed as an independent consultant.

Clients Represented

As an independent consultant
American Public Transportation Ass'n

PERRY, William R.

1250 I St. NW
Suite 1000
Washington, DC 20005

Tel: (202)682-0240
Fax: (202)682-0249
Registered: LDA

Employers
Sonosky, Chambers, Sachse & Endreson (Partner)

Clients Represented

On Behalf of Sonosky, Chambers, Sachse & Endreson
American Ass'n of Acupuncture and Oriental Medicine
Assiniboine and Sioux Tribes (Fort Peck Reservation)
Bad River Band of Lake Superior Chippewa
Colville Business Council
Cook Inlet Regional Citizen Advisory Council
Fond du Lac Reservation, Washington Office of the
Ho-Chunk Nation
Jemez, New Mexico, Pueblo of
Mole Lake Band of the Sokaogon Chippewa Community
Sault Ste. Marie, Michigan, City of
Shoshone-Bannock Tribes of the Fort Hall Indian Reservation
St. Croix Chippewa Indians of Wisconsin
Standing Rock Sioux Tribe
Yukon-Kuskokwim Health Corp.

PERTSCHUK, Mark

1023 15th St. NW
Suite 600
Washington, DC 20005
EMail: csgv@csgv.org

Tel: (202)408-0061
Registered: LDA

Employers
Coalition to Stop Gun Violence (Director, Legislative Affairs)

PERTSCHUK, Michael

1629 K St. NW
Suite 200
Washington, DC 20006-1629
EMail: info@advocacy.org

Tel: (202)777-7575
Fax: (202)777-7577

Employers
The Advocacy Institute (Co-Director)

PESKE, Sherry E.

1667 K St. NW
Suite 650
Washington, DC 20006
EMail: sherry_peske@fwc.com

Tel: (202)296-9703
Fax: (202)296-7461
Registered: LDA

Employers
Foster Wheeler Corp. (V. President, Government Affairs)

PETER, Brendan M.

4301 Wilson Blvd.
Suite 400
Arlington, VA 22203-1861
EMail: bpeter@aamva.org

Tel: (703)522-4200
Fax: (703)908-5890

Employers
American Ass'n of Motor Vehicle Administrators (Director, Government Affairs)

PETER, John

1725 K St. NW
Suite 300
Washington, DC 20006

Tel: (202)872-0885
Fax: (202)785-0586

Employers
Nat'l Ass'n of Wholesaler-Distributors (V. President, Corporate Relations)

PETER, Phillips S.

1301 K St. NW
Suite 1100-East Tower
Washington, DC 20005

Tel: (202)414-9200
Fax: (202)414-9299
Registered: LDA

Employers
Reed, Smith, LLP (Counsel, Government Relations and Federal Group Head)

Clients Represented

On Behalf of Reed, Smith, LLP
Agilent Technologies
American Ass'n for Homecare
American Soc. of Consultant Pharmacists
Ass'n of Health Information Outsourcing Services
Boys and Girls Club of Brownsville, Inc.
Center for Research on Institutions and Social Policy
Dominion Resources, Inc.
Eclipse Surgical Technologies
Federated Investors, Inc.
General Electric Co.
Golf Course Superintendents Ass'n of America
Knoll Pharmaceutical Co.
Lason, Inc.
Mercy Medical
Omnicare, Inc.
Owens-Illinois, Inc.
PCS Health Systems, Inc.
Pure Energy Corp.
Respironics
Sunrise Medical
Techneglas, Inc.
USX Corp.
Washington, Department of Information of the State of
J. G. Wentworth

PETERS, Duane

1300 Piccard Dr.
Suite 200
Rockville, MD 20850
EMail: peters@lupus.org

Tel: (301)670-9292
Ext: 17
Fax: (301)670-9486
Registered: LDA

Employers
Lupus Foundation of America (V. President for Advocacy and Communications)

PETERS, Eugene

1401 New York Ave. NW
11th Floor
Washington, DC 20005
EMail: gpeters@epsa.org

Tel: (202)628-8200
Fax: (202)628-8260
Registered: LDA

Employers
Electric Power Supply Ass'n (V. President, Legislative Affairs)

PETERS, Eugene F.

1762 Church St. NW
Washington, DC 20036

Tel: (202)939-8984
Fax: (202)939-8983
Registered: LDA

Employers
Burwell, Peters and Houston (Partner)

Clients Represented

On Behalf of Burwell, Peters and Houston
Barker Enterprises

PETERS, Jeff

1050 Connecticut Ave. NW
Washington, DC 20036-5339

Tel: (202)857-6000
Fax: (202)857-6395
Registered: LDA

Employers
Arent Fox Kintner Plotkin & Kahn, PLLC (Associate)

Clients Represented

On Behalf of Arent Fox Kintner Plotkin & Kahn, PLLC
Ass'n of Pain Management Anesthesiologist
Internat'l Soc. of Refractive Surgery
Soc. for Excellence in Eyecare

PETERS, Rise J.

1350 New York Ave. NW
Suite 1100
Washington, DC 20005-4798
EMail: petersr@spiegelmcd.com

Tel: (202)879-4000
Fax: (202)393-2866

Employers
Spiegel & McDiarmid (Partner)

PETERS, Robert A.

1250 I St. NW
Suite 1200
Washington, DC 20005-3924
Tel: (202)371-8401
Fax: (202)371-8470

Employers
Aerospace Industries Ass'n of America (Director, Environmental Affairs and Occupational Safety and Health)

PETERS, Stephanie J.

2550 M St. NW
Washington, DC 20037-1350
Tel: (202)457-6000
Fax: (202)457-6315
Former Minority Counsel, House Committee on the Judiciary.

Employers
Patton Boggs, LLP (Associate)

PETERSEN, Bruce L.

1899 L St. NW
Suite 1000
Washington, DC 20036
Tel: (202)457-0480
Fax: (202)457-0486
Registered: LDA
EMail: bruce_petersen@npradc.org

Employers
Nat'l Petrochemical Refiners Ass'n (Petrochemical Director)

PETERSEN, LeeAnn M.

611 Pennsylvania Ave. SE
Suite 287
Washington, DC 20003
Tel: (202)544-3273
Fax: (202)544-3273

Employers
LegiServe (President)

PETERSEN, Robert R.

1300 L St. NW
Suite 925
Washington, DC 20005
Tel: (202)842-0400
Fax: (202)789-7223
Registered: LDA
EMail: bpetersen@ngtc.org

Employers
Nat'l Grain Trade Council (President)

PETERSON, Alan D.

1505 Prince St.
Suite 300
Alexandria, VA 22314
Tel: (703)739-9200
Fax: (703)739-9497
Registered: LDA

Employers
American Optometric Ass'n (Assistant Director, Government Relations)

PETERSON, Cathleen

2445 M St. NW
Washington, DC 20037-1420
Tel: (202)663-6000
Fax: (202)663-6363

Employers
Wilmer, Cutler & Pickering (Partner)

PETERSON, Charles H.

1800 M St. NW
Washington, DC 20036
Tel: (202)467-7000
Fax: (202)467-7176
Registered: LDA
EMail: cpeterson@morganlewis.com

Employers
Morgan, Lewis & Bockius LLP

Clients Represented

On Behalf of Morgan, Lewis & Bockius LLP
Credit Suisse First Boston Corp.

PETERSON, Erik R.

1800 K St. NW
Washington, DC 20005
Tel: (202)775-3258
Fax: (202)775-3199
EMail: epeterso@csis.org

Employers
Center for Strategic and Internat'l Studies (Senior V. President and Director of Studies; William A. Schreyer Chair in Global Analysis)

PETERSON, Geoffrey G.

801 Pennsylvania Ave. NW
Suite 725
Washington, DC 20004
Tel: (202)898-3192
Fax: (202)371-1107
Registered: LDA, FARA
EMail: jeff.peterson@aventis.com

Employers
Aventis Pasteur (Director, Federal Government Relations)

PETERSON, George E.

2100 M St. NW
Washington, DC 20037
Tel: (202)833-7200
Fax: (202)429-0687

Employers
The Urban Institute (Senior Fellow)

PETERSON, Grant C.

6400 Arlington Blvd.
Suite 1100
Falls Church, VA 22042
Tel: (703)237-8061
Fax: (703)237-8085
EMail: gpeterson@rpihq.com

Employers
Research Planning, Inc. (Senior V. President, Operations)

PETERSON, Helena Hutton

1101 15th St. NW
Washington, DC 20005
Tel: (202)331-6976
Fax: (202)331-2805
Registered: LDA
EMail: hpterson@mmm.com

Employers
Minnesota Mining and Manufacturing Co. (3M Co.) (Manager, Government Relations)

PETERSON, Mark

1666 K St. NW
Suite 800
Washington, DC 20006
Tel: (202)481-7000
Fax: (202)862-7098
Former Aide to Speaker of the House, Rep. Newt Gingrich (R-GA).

Employers
Arthur Andersen LLP

PETERSON, Matt

1523 New Hampshire Ave. NW
Washington, DC 20036
Tel: (202)588-0002
Fax: (202)785-2669

Employers
University of California, Office of Federal Government Relations (Senior Legislative Analyst)

PETERSON, Matthew D.

750 17th St. NW
Suite 1100
Washington, DC 20006
Tel: (202)778-2300
Fax: (202)778-2330

Employers
FoxKiser

PETERSON, Meg

1317 F St. NW
Suite 600
Washington, DC 20004
Tel: (202)638-2121
Fax: (202)638-7045
Registered: LDA
EMail: peterson@wexlergroup.com

Employers
The Wexler Group (Associate)

Clients Represented

On Behalf of The Wexler Group
The Business Roundtable

PETERSON, Patti McGill

3007 Tilden St. NW
Suite 5L
Washington, DC 20008-3009
Tel: (202)686-4000
Fax: (202)362-3442
EMail: scholars@cies.iie.org

Employers
Council for Internat'l Exchange of Scholars (Exec. Director)

PETERSON, R. Max

444 N. Capitol St. NW
Suite 544
Washington, DC 20001
Tel: (202)624-7890
Fax: (202)624-7891

Employers
Internat'l Ass'n of Fish and Wildlife Agencies (Exec. V. President)

PETERSON, Col. Tim

Russell Senate Office Bldg.
Suite 183
Washington, DC 20510
Tel: (703)224-2881
Fax: (703)685-2570

Employers
Department of Army (Chief, Senate Liaison Division, Legislative Liaison)

PETERSON, Vance

1307 New York Ave. NW
Suite 1000
Washington, DC 20005
Tel: (202)328-5900
Fax: (202)387-4973

Employers
Council for Advancement and Support of Education (President)

PETHERICK, Chris

300 Independence Ave. SE
Washington, DC 20003
Tel: (202)546-5611

Employers
Liberty Lobby (Editor)

PETITO, Margaret L.

6008 34th Place NW
Washington, DC 20015
Tel: (202)537-1327
Fax: (202)362-2414
Registered: LDA, FARA
EMail: petito@erols.com
VISTA Volunteer, ACTION, 1972-74.

Employers
Petito & Associates (Director/Principal)

Clients Represented

On Behalf of Petito & Associates
Cultural Partnership of the Americas

PETNIUNAS, Susan E.

3686 King St.
Suite 170
Alexandria, VA 22302
Tel: (703)379-6444
Fax: (703)379-9728
Registered: LDA
EMail: petnunas@bellatlantic.net

Employers
Public Affairs Resources, Inc. (Managing Principal)

Clients Represented

On Behalf of Public Affairs Resources, Inc.
Abitibi Consolidated Sales Corp.
American Consumers for Affordable Homes
Election Systems & Software
Free Trade Lumber Council

PETRICONE, Michael D.

2500 Wilson Blvd.
Arlington, VA 22201-3834
Tel: (703)907-7544
Fax: (703)907-7693
Registered: LDA
EMail: michaelp@ce.org

Employers
Consumer Electronics Ass'n (V. President, Technology Policy)

PETRIZZO, Thomas "T.J."

444 North Capitol St. NW
Suite 535
Washington, DC 20001
Tel: (202)478-6859
Registered: LDA
Chief of Staff and Legislative Director to Rep. Jennifer Dunn (R-WA), 1995-99. Former Legislative Aide to Rep. Rod Chandler (R-WA). Former Legislative Aide to Senator Olympia Snowe (R-ME).

Employers
The Petrizzo Group, Inc. (President)

Clients Represented

On Behalf of The Petrizzo Group, Inc.

Airborne Express
Central Puget Sound Regional Transit Authority (Sound Transit)
Coalition for American Financial Security
Eddie Bauer Co.
Electronic Industries Alliance
Group Health Cooperative
Renton, Washington, City of
Frank Russell Co.
Vulcan Northwest Inc.

PETRO, Michael J.

2000 L St. NW
Suite 700
Washington, DC 20036
EMail: petro@ced.org
Tel: (202)296-5860
Fax: (202)223-0776

Employers

Committee for Economic Development (Chief of Staff, V. President and Director, Business and Government Policy)

PETROVA, Irina

1200 17th St. NW
Washington, DC 20036-3097
Tel: (202)331-5900
Fax: (202)973-5373
EMail: ipetrova@dineout.org

Employers

Nat'l Restaurant Ass'n (Manager, Legislative Research Products)

PETRUZZELLO, Michael

1211 Connecticut Ave. NW
Suite 608
Washington, DC 20036
EMail: mjp@qorvis.com
Tel: (703)744-7800
Fax: (703)744-7840

Employers

Qorvis Communications (Managing Partner)

PETRY, Stephan

4301 Wilson Blvd.
Arlington, VA 22203-1860
Tel: (703)907-5816
Fax: (703)907-5516
Registered: LDA
EMail: stephan.petry@nreca.org

Employers

Nat'l Rural Electric Cooperative Ass'n (Legislative Director)

PETSONK, Annie

1875 Connecticut Ave. NW
Suite 1016
Washington, DC 20009
Tel: (202)387-3500
Fax: (202)319-8590
Registered: LDA

Employers

Environmental Defense Fund (Attorney)

PETTIT, John W.

1500 K St.
Suite 1100
Washington, DC 20005
Tel: (202)842-8800
Fax: (202)842-8465
Registered: LDA
EMail: john_pettit@dbr.com

General Counsel, Federal Communications Commission, 1972-74.

Employers

Drinker Biddle & Reath LLP (Partner)

Clients Represented

On Behalf of Drinker Biddle & Reath LLP

Radio Shack Corp.

PETTIT, Mitchell S.

1133 Connecticut Ave. NW
Suite 1000
Washington, DC 20036
Registered: LDA

Employers

MSP Strategic Communications, Inc. (Chief Exec. Officer)
Project to Promote Competition and Innovation in the Digital Age (Exec. Director)

Clients Represented

On Behalf of MSP Strategic Communications, Inc.

MasterCard Internat'l
Netscape Communications Corp.
Project to Promote Competition and Innovation in the Digital Age
Securify
Verizon Communications

PETTIT, Robert L.

1776 K St. NW
Washington, DC 20006
Tel: (202)719-7000
Fax: (202)719-7049
Registered: LDA

Former General Counsel, Federal Communications Commission, 1989-92; Associate Deputy Secretary of Transportation, 1988-89; Senior Legal Advisor to FCC Commissioner Mimi Dawson, 1982-86.

Employers

Wiley, Rein & Fielding (Partner)

Clients Represented

On Behalf of Wiley, Rein & Fielding

Hearst-Argyle Television, Inc.
Industrial Telecommunications Ass'n, Inc.
Verizon Wireless

PETTIT, Susan

2301 M St. NW
Washington, DC 20037-1484
Tel: (202)467-2900
Fax: (202)467-2910
Registered: LDA

Employers

American Public Power Ass'n (Government Relations Representative)

PETTY, Brian T.

1901 L St. NW
Suite 702
Washington, DC 20036
Tel: (202)293-0670
Registered: LDA

Employers

Internat'l Ass'n of Drilling Contractors (Senior V. President, Government Affairs)

PETTY, Gary F.

66 Canal Center Plaza
Suite 600
Alexandria, VA 22314
Tel: (703)683-1300
Fax: (703)683-1217

Employers

Nat'l Private Truck Council (President and Chief Exec. Officer)

PETTY, Michael D.

1900 K St. NW
Suite 750
Washington, DC 20006
Tel: (202)833-4500
Fax: (202)833-2859
Registered: LDA

Employers

Bennett Turner & Coleman, LLP (Partner)

Clients Represented

On Behalf of Bennett Turner & Coleman, LLP

Serono Laboratories, Inc.
SmithKline Beecham Consumer Healthcare, LLP

PETTY, Monica

445 12th St. NW
Room 8-C454
Washington, DC 20554
Tel: (202)418-1900
Fax: (202)418-2806

Employers

Federal Communications Commission (Special Assistant, Legislative and Intergovernmental Affairs)

PEYSER, Jr., Peter A.

1001 G St. NW
Suite 400 East
Washington, DC 20001
Tel: (202)638-3730
Fax: (202)638-3516
Registered: LDA
EMail: peter@peyser.com

Former Administrative Assistant to Rep. Geraldine Ferraro (D-NY); Former Legislative Assistant to Rep. James Delaney and Rep. Peter Kostmayer (D-PA).

Employers

Peyser Associates, Inc. (President)

Clients Represented

On Behalf of Peyser Associates, Inc.

Federal Home Loan Bank of Seattle
S.C. Johnson and Son, Inc.
Macon, City of
Monroe Center, LLC
Muncie, Indiana, City of (Delaware County)
Orange County Transportation Authority
Philadelphia, Pennsylvania, City of
Portland Tri-Met
Seattle, Washington, City of
Sound Transit
Southeastern Pennsylvania Transit Authority
TRI-MET Tri-County Metropolitan Transportation
Twentynine Palms Water District

PEYTON, Keiana

1002 Wisconsin Ave. NW
Washington, DC 20007
Tel: (202)333-5270
Fax: (202)728-1192

Employers

Rainbow/Push Coalition (National Bureau) (Press Secretary)

PEYTON, Ramona E.

409 Third St. SW
Suite 7900
Washington, DC 20416
EMail: ramona.peyton@sba.gov
Tel: (202)205-6700
Fax: (202)205-7374

Employers

Small Business Administration (Congressional Relations Specialist)

PFAFF, John

1801 N. Moore St.
Arlington, VA 22209
Tel: (703)875-0774
Fax: (703)807-1849

Employers

Nat'l Ass'n of Federal Education Program Administrators (President)

PFAUTCH, Roy

1050 Connecticut Ave. NW
Suite 870
Washington, DC 20036
Tel: (202)783-9150
Fax: (202)783-9150
Registered: LDA

Employers

Civic Service, Inc. (President)

Clients Represented

On Behalf of Civic Service, Inc.

American Ass'n of Clinical Endocrinologists
IPR Shandwick
Japan Federation of Construction Contractors, Inc.
Metcor, Ltd.
Nippon Telegraph and Telephone Corp.
The Sanwa Bank , Ltd.
Unisys Corp.

PFEIFER, Eugene M.

1730 Pennsylvania Ave. NW
Suite 1200
Washington, DC 20006-4706
Tel: (202)737-0500
Fax: (202)626-3737
Registered: LDA

Associate Chief Counsel for Enforcement (1975-79) and Trial Attorney (1968-73), Office of the General Counsel, Food and Drug Administration, Department of Health and Human Services. Attorney, Office of General Counsel, Federal Trade Commission, 1974.

Employers

King & Spalding (Partner)

PFEIFFER, Margaret K.

1701 Pennsylvania Ave. NW
Suite 800
Washington, DC 20006
Tel: (202)956-7500
Fax: (202)293-6330

Employers

Sullivan & Cromwell (Partner)

Clients Represented

On Behalf of Sullivan & Cromwell

N.V. Philips Gloeilampenfabrieken

PFIFFERLING, Sueanne

1525 Wilson Blvd.
Suite 600
Arlington, VA 22209
Tel: (703)527-1670
Fax: (703)547-5477
Registered: LDA, FARA
EMail: Sueanne@jscinc.com
Former Legislative Assistant to Senator Daniel P. Moynihan (D-NY).

Employers
Jellinek, Schwartz & Connolly (V. President)

PFISTER, Gail W.

3114 Circle Hill Rd.
Alexandria, VA 22305-1606
Tel: (703)548-1234
Fax: (703)548-6216
EMail: info@itctrade.com

Employers
Internat'l Trade Council (V. President, Research)

PFISTER, Steven J.

325 Seventh St. NW
Suite 1100
Washington, DC 20004-2802
Tel: (202)783-7971
Fax: (202)737-2849
Registered: LDA

Employers
Nat'l Retail Federation (Senior V. President, Government Relations)

PFOHL, Peter A.

1224 17th St. NW
Washington, DC 20036
Tel: (202)347-7170
Fax: (202)347-3619
Registered: LDA
Former Legislative Assistant to Rep. George J. Hochbruecker (D-NY).

Employers
Slover & Loftus (Associate)

Clients Represented

On Behalf of Slover & Loftus
Western Coal Traffic League

PFOTENHAUER, Nancy M.

P.O. Box 3058
Arlington, VA 22203-0058
Tel: (703)558-4991
Fax: (703)558-4994
EMail: info@iwf.org

Employers
Independent Women's Forum (President)

PFUNDER, Malcolm R.

1050 Connecticut Ave. NW
Washington, DC 20036-5306
Tel: (202)955-8500
Fax: (202)467-0539
EMail: mpfunder@gdclaw.com
Federal Trade Commission, 1977-81. Assistant Director for Evaluation, Bureau of Competition, Federal Trade Commission, 1978-81.

Employers
Gibson, Dunn & Crutcher LLP (Of Counsel)

PHAH, Quan

1025 Connecticut Ave. NW
Suite 200
Washington, DC 20036
Tel: (202)293-4103
Fax: (202)293-4701

Employers
American Corporate Counsel Ass'n (Contact)

PHARR, William Shaun

1050 17th St. NW
Suite 300
Washington, DC 20036
Tel: (202)296-3390
Fax: (202)296-3399
Registered: LDA

Employers
Apartment and Office Building Ass'n of Metropolitan Washington (V. President, Governmental Affairs-DC)

PHELAN, Dennis J.

1101 17th St. NW
Suite 609
Washington, DC 20036
Tel: (202)331-7736
Fax: (202)331-9686
Registered: LDA
EMail: djppspa@prodigy.net

Employers
Pacific Seafood Processors Ass'n (V. President)

PHELLEPS, Moya

1130 17th St. NW
Washington, DC 20036-4677
Tel: (202)463-2639
Fax: (202)833-9636
Registered: LDA
EMail: mphelleps@nma.org

Employers
Coal Exporters Ass'n of the U.S. (Exec. Director)
Nat'l Mining Ass'n (V. President, International Trade)

PHELPS, Francie

1150 Connecticut Ave. NW
Suite 1025
Washington, DC 20036
Tel: (202)367-2776
Fax: (202)367-2790
Registered: LDA

Employers
UNOCAL Corp. (Federal and International Affairs)

PHELPS, James R.

700 13th St. NW
Suite 1200
Washington, DC 20005
Tel: (202)737-4280
Fax: (202)737-9329
Registered: LDA
Former Trial Attorney, Office of the Chief Counsel, Food and Drug Administration, Department of Health and Human Services. Former Assistant U.S. Attorney for the District of Columbia, Department of Justice.

Employers
Hyman, Phelps & McNamara, P.C. (Partner)

Clients Represented

On Behalf of Hyman, Phelps & McNamara, P.C.
Medeva Pharmaceuticals

PHELPS, III, Kenneth D.

1725 Jefferson Davis Hwy.
Crystal Square 2, Suite 300
Arlington, VA 22202
Tel: (703)413-5947
Fax: (703)413-5847

Employers
Lockheed Martin Corp. (Treasurer, Lockheed Martin Employees Political Action Committee)

PHELPS, Laura L.

One Massachusetts Ave. NW
Suite 800
Washington, DC 20001-1431
Tel: (202)842-2345
Fax: (202)408-7763
Registered: LDA
EMail: LPhelps@mwmlaw.com

Employers
American Ass'n of Crop Insurers
McLeod, Watkinson & Miller (Government Relations Consultant)

Clients Represented

On Behalf of McLeod, Watkinson & Miller
American Ass'n of Crop Insurers
American Mushroom Institute
American Peanut Product Manufacturers, Inc.
United Egg Ass'n
United Egg Producers

PHIFER, Franklin C.

499 S. Capitol St. SW
Suite 507
Washington, DC 20003
Tel: (202)554-2881
Registered: LDA
Former Minority Counsel, Committee on Ways and Means, U.S. House of Representatives.

Employers
Hecht, Spencer & Associates (Senior V. President)

Clients Represented

On Behalf of Hecht, Spencer & Associates
Boy Scouts of America
Brown and Williamson Tobacco Corp.
Minnesota Mining and Manufacturing Co. (3M Co.)
Norfolk Southern Corp.
Patton Boggs, LLP
J. C. Penney Co., Inc.
The Charles E. Smith Companies
TECO Energy, Inc.
Tulalip Tribes

PHILBIN, Tamara

4232 King St.
Alexandria, VA 22302
Tel: (703)998-0072
Fax: (703)931-5624
EMail: tphilbin@acce.org

Employers
American Chamber of Commerce Executives (V. President, Management Information Services)

PHILLIPS, Barbara L.

1818 N St. NW
Eighth Floor
Washington, DC 20036
Tel: (202)293-1707

Employers
Cingular Wireless (Congressional Affairs)

PHILLIPS, Bernard

1010 N. Fairfax St.
Alexandria, VA 22314-1574
Tel: (703)549-6400
Fax: (703)549-2984
EMail: bphillips@nsacct.org

Employers
Nat'l Soc. of Accountants (Tax Manager)

PHILLIPS, Beth

1550 Wilson Blvd.
Suite 701
Arlington, VA 22209
Tel: (703)527-7505
Fax: (703)527-7512

Employers
Foodservice & Packaging Institute, Inc. (Director, Administrative and Member Services)

PHILLIPS, Charles M.

2550 M St. NW
Washington, DC 20037-1350
Tel: (202)457-6000
Fax: (202)457-6315
Former Counsel to Senator John Warner (R-VA).

Employers
Patton Boggs, LLP (Associate)

PHILLIPS, Christie

7100 Connecticut Ave.
Chevy Chase, MD 20815
Tel: (301)961-2800
Fax: (301)961-2894
EMail: phillips@fourhcouncil.edu

Employers
Nat'l 4-H Council (Director of Marketing)

PHILLIPS, Debra

499 S. Capitol St. SW
Suite 604
Washington, DC 20003
Tel: (202)484-9188
Fax: (202)484-9189
EMail: webmaster@nasstrac.org

Employers
Nat'l Small Shipments Traffic Conference - NASSTRAC (Exec. Director)

PHILLIPS, Douglas E.

1201 Pennsylvania Ave. NW
Washington, DC 20004-2401
Tel: (202)662-6000
Fax: (202)662-6291
Registered: LDA
EMail: dphillips@cov.com
Law Clerk, Ninth Circuit, U.S. Court of Appeals, 1980-81.

Employers
Covington & Burling (Of Counsel)

PHILLIPS, George

1800 K St. NW
Suite 1010
Washington, DC 20006
Tel: (202)296-5030
Fax: (202)296-4750
Registered: LDA

Employers
American Defense Internat'l, Inc.

Clients Represented

On Behalf of American Defense Internat'l, Inc.
Bofors Defence AB

PHILLIPS, Howard J.

450 Maple Ave. East
Suite 309
Vienna, VA 22180
Tel: (703)281-6782
Fax: (703)281-4108

Employers
Conservative Caucus Research, Analysis and Education Foundation (President)

PHILLIPS, James A.

214 Massachusetts Ave. NE
Washington, DC 20002
Tel: (202)546-4400
Fax: (202)546-8328

Employers
Heritage Foundation (Research Fellow, Middle East)

PHILLIPS, JoAnna

1020 19th St. NW
Lower Lobby-40
Washington, DC 20036
Tel: (202)833-2210
Fax: (202)833-2456

Employers
Japan-America Soc. of Washington (Exec. Director)

PHILLIPS, Karen Borlaug

601 Pennsylvania Ave. NW
Suite 500
Washington, DC 20004
Tel: (202)347-7196
Fax: (202)347-8237
Registered: LDA
EMail: karen.phillips@cn.ca

Commissioner and Vice Chairman, Interstate Commerce Commission, 1988-94; Chief Economist, Republican Staff, 1987-88; Tax Economist, Senate Finance Committee, 1985-87; Staff Member, Senate Commerce Committee, 1982-85; Economist, Department of Transportation, 1977-82.

Employers
Canadian Nat'l Railway Co. (V. President, U.S. Government Affairs)

PHILLIPS, Laura H.

1200 New Hampshire Ave. NW
Suite 800
Washington, DC 20036-6802
Tel: (202)776-2000
Fax: (202)776-2222
Registered: LDA
EMail: lphillips@dlalaw.com

Fomerly with Chief Counsel's Office of National Telecommunications and Information Administration.

Employers
Dow, Lohnes & Albertson, PLLC (Member)

PHILLIPS, Mark

316 Pennsylvania Ave. SE
Suite 401
Washington, DC 20003
Tel: (202)546-1516
Fax: (202)546-1543
Registered: LDA

Legislative Assistant to Rep. Wendell Wyatt, 1973-74. Special Assistant to the Assistant Secretary, Indian Affairs, Department of Interior, 1981.

Employers
Edwards Associates, Inc. (President)

Clients Represented

On Behalf of Edwards Associates, Inc.
Confederated Tribes of the Grand Ronde
Confederated Tribes of the Umatilla Reservation of Oregon
Confederated Tribes of Warm Springs Reservation
Coquille Indian Tribe
Intertribal Timber Council

PHILLIPS, Michael

1625 K St. NW
Suite 1100
Washington, DC 20006-1604
Tel: (202)857-0244
Fax: (202)857-0237

Employers
Biotechnology Industry Organization (Director, Food and Agriculture Section)

PHILLIPS, Paula

1156 15th St. NW
Suite 502
Washington, DC 20005-1799
Tel: (202)862-4823
Fax: (202)862-4829

Employers
J. C. Penney Co., Inc. (Government Relations Specialist)

PHILLIPS, Randall G.

201 14th St. SW
Fifth Floor SW
Washington, DC 20250
EMail: rphillips01@fs.fed.us
Tel: (202)205-1663
Fax: (202)205-0936

Employers
Department of Agriculture - Forest Service (Deputy Chief, Programs and Legislation)

PHILLIPS, Rosanne

1735 New York Ave. NW
Suite 500
Washington, DC 20006-4759
Tel: (202)628-1700
Fax: (202)331-1024

Employers
Preston Gates Ellis & Rouvelas Meeds LLP (Treasurer, Political Action Committee)

PHILLIPS, Steven R.

901 15th St. NW
Suite 700
Washington, DC 20005-2301
Tel: (202)371-6000
Fax: (202)371-6279
Registered: LDA
EMail: srphillips@verner.com

Former Legislative Director and Counsel to Senator Jesse Helms (R-NC)

Employers
Verner, Liipfert, Bernhard, McPherson and Hand, Chartered (Member of Firm)

Clients Represented

On Behalf of Verner, Liipfert, Bernhard, McPherson and Hand, Chartered
BellSouth Corp.
Biovail Corp. Internat'l
General Electric Co.
Home Warranty Coalition
Lockheed Martin Corp.
Lockheed Martin Tactical Systems
Merrill Lynch & Co., Inc.
Northwest Airlines, Inc.
Olympic Advocates Together Honorably (OATH)
Perry Tritech Inc.
Prowler Fisheries and Clipper Seafoods
Rite Aid Corp.
RJR Nabisco Holdings Co.
Stewart & Stevenson Services, Inc.
United Defense, L.P.
United Pan-Europe Communications, NV
Winstar Petroleum

PHILLIPS, Susan A.

801 Pennsylvania Ave. NW
Suite 700
Washington, DC 20004
Tel: (202)347-4610
Fax: (202)508-3612
Registered: LDA
EMail: aphillip@nortelnetworks.com

Employers
Nortel Networks (Director, Global Government Relations, eCommerce Policy)

PHILLIPS, Webster

500 E St. SW
Eighth Floor
Room 869
Washington, DC 20254-0001
Tel: (202)358-6027
Fax: (202)358-6074

Employers
Social Security Administration-Office of Legislation and Congressional Affairs (Associate Commissioner for Legislative and Congressional Affairs)

PHILLIPS, William D.

1133 Connecticut Ave. NW
Suite 300
Washington, DC 20036
Tel: (202)293-1177
Fax: (202)293-3411
Registered: LDA
EMail: wdp@rpum.com

Chief of Staff (1983-86) and Legislative Director and Legislative Assistant (1981-83) to Senator Ted Stevens (R-AK).

Employers
Ryan, Phillips, Utrecht & MacKinnon (Partner)

Clients Represented

On Behalf of Ryan, Phillips, Utrecht & MacKinnon
Air Transport Ass'n of America
Ass'n of American Railroads
Coeur d'Alene Mines Corp.
Cook Inlet Region Inc.
R. R. Donnelley & Sons
Edison Electric Institute
Florida Power and Light Co.
General Communications, Inc.
Investment Co. Institute
Kerr-McGee Corp.
Lockheed Martin Corp.
MultiDimensional Imaging, Inc.
Nat'l Cable Television Ass'n
Pfizer, Inc.
Progress Energy
Sault Ste. Marie Tribe of Chippewa Indians
Southern Co.
TXU Business Services
U.S. Interactive
United Pan-Europe Communications, NV
VoiceStream Wireless Corp.

PHIPPS, John G.

1776 I St. NW
Suite 725
Washington, DC 20006
Tel: (202)331-1167
Fax: (202)331-1319

Employers
Marubeni America Corp. (Manager, Internat'l Business Development and Strategic Planning)

PHIPPS, Dr. Ronald

1320 19th St. NW
Suite 400
Washington, DC 20036
Tel: (202)861-8223
Fax: (202)861-9307

Employers
The Institute for Higher Education Policy (Senior Associate)

PHYTHYON, Daniel

2445 M St. NW
Washington, DC 20037-1420
Tel: (202)663-6000
Fax: (202)663-6363
Registered: LDA

Employers
Wilmer, Cutler & Pickering

Clients Represented

On Behalf of Wilmer, Cutler & Pickering
Dell Computer Corp.
Deutsche Telekom, Inc.

PIANALTO, Antonella

1001 G St. NW
Suite 900 E
Washington, DC 20001-4545
Tel: (202)393-1010
Fax: (202)393-5510
Registered: LDA

Employers
Podesta/Mattoon

Clients Represented

On Behalf of Podesta/Mattoon
Trans World Airlines, Inc.

PICA, Erich

1025 Vermont Ave. NW
Third Floor
Washington, DC 20005
Tel: (202)783-7400
Ext: 229
Fax: (202)783-0444
Registered: LDA
EMail: epica@foe.org

Employers
Friends of the Earth (Policy Associate)

PICARD, B. Donovan

901 15th St. NW
Suite 700
Washington, DC 20005-2301
Tel: (202)371-6000
Fax: (202)371-6279

Employers
Verner, Liipfert, Bernhard, McPherson and Hand, Chartered (Shareholder)

Clients Represented

On Behalf of Verner, Liipfert, Bernhard, McPherson and Hand, Chartered
Yemen, Government of

PICCIANO, Lorette

1411 K St. NW
Suite 901
Washington, DC 20005
EMail: lpicciano@ruralco.org
Tel: (202)628-7160
Fax: (202)628-7165

Employers

Rural Coalition (Exec. Director)

PICCIGALLO, Ph.D., Philip R.

219 E St. NE
Washington, DC 20002
Tel: (202)547-2900
Fax: (202)546-8168

Employers

Order Sons of Italy in America/Sons of Italy Foundation (National Exec. Director and Chief Exec. Officer)

PICCIONE, Mary Elizabeth

1275 K St. NW
Suite 1200
Washington, DC 20005
Tel: (202)216-0700
Fax: (202)216-0824
Registered: LDA

Employers

Delta Air Lines (General Manager, Government Affairs)

PICCOLO, Joann

1350 I St. NW
Suite 400
Washington, DC 20005-3306
Tel: (202)371-6900
Fax: (202)842-3578
Registered: LDA

Employers

Motorola, Inc. (Corporate V. President and Director, North America Region Government Relations)

PICHE, Diane

2000 M St. NW
Suite 400
Washington, DC 20036
EMail: dpiche@cccr.com
Tel: (202)659-5565
Fax: (202)223-5302

Employers

Citizens' Commission on Civil Rights (Exec. Director)

PICHETTE, David A.

6930 Carroll Ave.
Suite 240
Takoma Park, MD 20912
Tel: (301)891-8777
Ext: 307
Fax: (301)891-8778

Employers

Mainstream, Inc. (Exec. Director)

PICKER, Colin

2445 M St. NW
Washington, DC 20037-1420
Tel: (202)663-6000
Fax: (202)663-6363
Registered: LDA

Employers

Wilmer, Cutler & Pickering (Associate)

PICKERING, John H.

2445 M St. NW
Washington, DC 20037-1420
EMail: jpickering@wilmer.com
Tel: (202)663-6000
Fax: (202)663-6363

Law Clerk to Justice Frank Murphy, U.S. Supreme Court, 1941-42.

Employers

Wilmer, Cutler & Pickering (Senior Counsel)

PICKUP, James A.

901 15th St. NW
Suite 700
Washington, DC 20005-2301
EMail: japickup@verner.com
Tel: (202)371-6000
Fax: (202)371-6279
Registered: LDA

Employers

Verner, Liipfert, Bernhard, McPherson and Hand, Chartered (Associate)

Clients Represented

On Behalf of Verner, Liipfert, Bernhard, McPherson and Hand, Chartered

Alere Medical Inc.
Biovail Corp. Internat'l
Forest Soc. of Maine
Home Warranty Coalition
RJR Nabisco Holdings Co.
Virginia Commonwealth Trading Co.
Washington Group Internat'l

PIDCOCK, Paulette C.

700 11th St. NW
Suite 250
Washington, DC 20001
EMail: paulette.pidcock@pge-corp.com
Tel: (202)638-3501
Fax: (202)638-3522
Registered: LDA

Employers

PG&E Corp. (Director, Federal Governmental Relations)

PIEPER, Michael

444 N. Capitol St.
Suite 209
Washington, DC 20001
EMail: mpieper@sso.org
Tel: (202)624-5405
Fax: (202)624-8181

Employers

Nevada, Washington Office of the State of (Director, DC Office)

PIERCE, Anthony

1333 New Hampshire Ave. NW
Suite 400
Washington, DC 20036
Tel: (202)887-4000
Fax: (202)887-4288

Employers

Akin, Gump, Strauss, Hauer & Feld, L.L.P. (Partner)

PIERCE, Bill

1310 G St. NW
12th Floor
Washington, DC 20005
Tel: (202)626-4780
Fax: (202)626-8654

Employers

Blue Cross Blue Shield Ass'n (Director, Public Affairs)

PIERCE, David C.

1724 Massachusetts Ave. NW
Washington, DC 20036-1969
Tel: (202)775-3550
Fax: (202)775-3675

Employers

Nat'l Cable Television Ass'n (Senior Director, Public Affairs)

PIERCE, Kenneth J.

Three Lafayette Center
1155 21st St. NW
Washington, DC 20036-3384
Tel: (202)328-8000
Fax: (202)887-8979

Legislative Assistant to Senator Patrick Leahy (D-VT), 1979-81.

Employers

Willkie Farr & Gallagher (Partner)

Clients Represented

On Behalf of Willkie Farr & Gallagher

Fuji Heavy Industries Ltd.
Subaru-Isuzu Automotive, Inc.

PIERCE, Melinda

408 C St. NE
Washington, DC 20002
Tel: (202)547-1141
Fax: (202)547-6009
Registered: LDA

Employers

Sierra Club (Washington Representative, Land Protection Program)

PIERCE, Sarah

1800 Duke St.
Alexandria, VA 22314
Tel: (703)548-3440
Fax: (703)836-0367

Employers

Soc. for Human Resource Management (Legislative Representative)

PIERCE, William F.

1750 K St. NW
12th Floor East
Washington, DC 20006
EMail: wpierce@clin.org
Tel: (202)857-2330
Fax: (202)835-0643
Registered: LDA

Employers

Community Learning and Information Network, Inc. (V. President, Education)

PIERCY, Clare

1900 M St. NW
Suite 500
Washington, DC 20036
Tel: (202)785-2635
Fax: (202)785-4037
Registered: LDA

Employers

BNFL, Inc. (Government and Media Relations Representative)

PIERCY, Craig

499 S. Capitol St. SW
Suite 508
Washington, DC 20003
Tel: (202)488-7267
Fax: (202)488-7269

Employers

Wayne State University (Assistant V. President, Federal Affairs)

PIETRANGELO, Renee L.

4200 Evergreen Ln.
Suite 315
Annandale, VA 22003
Tel: (703)642-6614
Fax: (703)642-0497
Registered: LDA

Employers

American Network of Community Options and Resources (ANCOR) (Chief Executive Officer)

PIETRANTON, Arlene

10801 Rockville Pike
Rockville, MD 20852
Tel: (301)897-5700
Ext: 4113
Fax: (301)571-0457
Registered: LDA

Employers

American Speech, Language, and Hearing Ass'n (Associate Director for Speech Language Pathology)

PIGG, B. J. "Bob"

1235 Jefferson Davis Hwy.
Suite 406
Arlington, VA 22202
Tel: (703)560-2980
Fax: (703)560-2985

Employers

Asbestos Information Ass'n/North America (President)

PIGG, Joseph

1120 Connecticut Ave. NW
Washington, DC 20036
Tel: (202)663-5000
Fax: (202)663-7541
Registered: LDA

Employers

American Bankers Ass'n (Senior Counsel)

PIKE, Jeffrey R.

1850 M St. NW
Suite 900
Washington, DC 20036
Tel: (202)463-2500
Fax: (202)463-4950
Registered: LDA

Served as Chief of Staff of the House Committee on Merchant Marine and Fisheries, 1993-94. Staff Director, Subcommittee on Fisherises and Wildlife Conservation and the Environment, House Committee on Merchant Marine and Fisheries, 1987-92. Regional Representative to Rep. Gerry E. Studds (D-MA), 1986.

Employers

Sher & Blackwell (Director, Government Relations)

Clients Represented

On Behalf of Sher & Blackwell

Apex Marine Ship Management Co. LLC
ASCENT (Ass'n of Community Enterprises)
AUPS/Mo Hussain
Carriers Against Harbor Tax
Dolphin Safe/Fair Trade Campaign
Focal Communications
General Category Tuna Ass'n
Humane Soc. of the United States
Icicle Seafoods, Inc.
Internat'l Fund for Animal Welfare
JS&A Environmental Services, Inc.
Level 3 Communications LLC
Martha's Vineyard Steamship Authority
Massachusetts Heavy Industries
Mindspring
Nat'l Marine Life Center
New York Waterways
Nippon Yusen Kaisha (NYK) Line
Nucentrix Broadband Networks
Ocean Carriers Working Group
PanAmSat Corp.
Performing Animal Welfare Soc.
Rowan Companies, Inc.
Sargeant Marine, Inc.
Separation Technologies
Stuyvesant Dredging Co.
United Catcher Boats
Winstar Communications, Inc.
Woods Hole Steamship Authority

PIKE, Walter

11303 Amherst Ave.
Suite Four
Wheaton, MD 20902
Tel: (301)933-6228
Fax: (301)933-3902

Employers

Nat'l Ass'n of Air Traffic Specialists (President)

PIKRALLIDAS, Susan G.

1440 New York Ave. NW
Suite 200
Washington, DC 20005
Tel: (202)942-2050
Fax: (202)783-4798
Registered: LDA

Employers

American Automobile Ass'n (V. President, Public and Government Relations)

PILAND, Julius L. "Bud"

1820 N. Fort Myer Dr.
Suite 804
Arlington, VA 22209
Tel: (703)351-6301
Fax: (703)351-6417
Registered: LDA
EMail: jlpiland@mcdermott.com

Employers

McDermott Internat'l, Inc./Babcock & Wilcox (Manager, Government Programs)

PILE, Elizabeth

888 16th Street NW
Suite 650
Washington, DC 20006
Tel: (202)628-9262
Fax: (202)628-0391

Employers

AFL-CIO - Transportation Trades Department (Manager, Legislative Affairs)

PILON, Roger

1000 Massachusetts Ave. NW
Washington, DC 20001
Tel: (202)842-0200
Fax: (202)842-3490

Employers

Cato Institute (Senior Fellow and Director, Center for Constitutional Studies)

PILOT, Larry R.

1900 K St. NW
Washington, DC 20006
Tel: (202)496-7500
Fax: (202)496-7756
EMail: larry_piolet@mckennacuneo.com

Director, Office of Compliance, Bureau of Medical Devices (1971-79), Associate Commissioner of Medical Affairs (1970-71), and Special Assistant to Commissioner (1969-70), all at the Food and Drug Administration. Special Assistant to the Assistant Secretary for Health and Scientific Affairs, Department of Health, Education and Welfare, 1969.

Employers

McKenna & Cuneo, L.L.P. (Partner)

PILZER, Arthur

1015 15th St. NW
Suite 700
Washington, DC 20005-2605
Tel: (202)828-5200
Fax: (202)785-2645

Employers

Bechtel Group, Inc. (V. President and Development and Finance Manager (Bechtel Enterprises))

PIMM, Harriet

6707 Old Dominion Dr.
Suite 320
McLean, VA 22101
Tel: (703)442-8850
Fax: (703)790-0845
EMail: hpimm@usapple.org

Employers

U.S. Apple Ass'n (Manager, Communications)

PINDER, Susan D.

1299 Pennsylvania Ave. NW
Suite 1100 West
Washington, DC 20004-2407
Tel: (202)637-4000
Fax: (202)637-4066

Employers

General Electric Co. (Manager, Government Relations)

PINE, Mel

2750 Prosperity Ave.
Suite 550
Fairfax, VA 22031-4312
Tel: (703)204-0500
Fax: (703)204-4610

Employers

American Wood Preservers Institute (Manager, Communication)

PINELO, Greg

1010 Wisconsin Ave. NW
Suite 800
Washington, DC 20007
Tel: (202)338-8700
Fax: (202)338-2334

Employers

Greer, Margolis, Mitchell, Burns & Associates (Partner)

Clients Represented

On Behalf of Greer, Margolis, Mitchell, Burns & Associates

Communications Workers of America

PINES, Wayne L.

1615 L St. NW
Suite 900
Washington, DC 20036
Tel: (202)778-1000
Fax: (202)466-6002
EMail: wpines@apcoworldwide.com

Former Chief, Consumer Education and Information; Chief, Press Relations; and Associate Commissioner for Public Affairs, Food and Drug Administration, 1978-82.

Employers

APCO Worldwide (President, Healthcare and Director, Crisis Communications)

PINKERTON, CSJ, Catherine

801 Pennsylvania Ave. SE
Suite 460
Washington, DC 20003
Tel: (202)547-5556
Fax: (202)547-5510
Registered: LDA
EMail: network@networklobby.org

Employers

NETWORK, A Nat'l Catholic Social Justice Lobby (Lobbyist)

PINKHAM, Douglas G.

2033 K St. NW
Suite 700
Washington, DC 20006
Tel: (202)872-1790
Fax: (202)835-8343

Employers

Public Affairs Council (President)

PINSON, Valerie

1724 Massachusetts Ave. NW
Washington, DC 20036-1969
Tel: (202)775-3550
Fax: (202)775-3671
Registered: LDA

Employers

Nat'l Cable Television Ass'n (Director, Government Relations)

PINSTRUP-ANDERSEN, Per

2033 K St. NW
Washington, DC 20006
Tel: (202)862-5600
Fax: (202)467-4439
EMail: ifpri@cgnet.com

Employers

Internat'l Food Policy Research Institute (Director General)

PINTO, Tiago

1900 L St. NW
Suite 407
Washington, DC 20036
Tel: (202)293-3454
Fax: (202)393-3455
Registered: LDA

Employers

Bristol Group, Inc. (Managing Director)

PINTO-RIDDICK, Blenda

700 13th St. NW
Suite 400
Washington, DC 20005
Tel: (202)347-0773
Fax: (202)347-0785
Registered: LDA
EMail: bpinto@cassidy.com

Former Chief Legislative Correspondent to Senator Frank Lautenberg (D-NJ).

Employers

Cassidy & Associates, Inc. (Sr. Account Executive)

Clients Represented

On Behalf of Cassidy & Associates, Inc.

Alcon Laboratories
American Superconductor Corp.
Babyland Family Services, Inc.
California Hospital Medical Center Foundation
California Institute for the Arts
The Chauncey Group Internat'l
Memorial Hermann Health Care System
New Jersey Institute of Technology
Philadelphia University
Rochester Institute of Technology
Sherwin Williams Co.
Texas Tech University System
Trinity Health
University of Puerto Rico
University of San Francisco
Villanova University

PIPER, W. Stephen

6121 Lincolnia Rd.
Suite 106
Alexandria, VA 22312-2707
Tel: (703)914-2680
Fax: (703)914-2610
EMail: PiperPacif@aol.com

Office of the Secretary, Department of Defense, 1984-87. Office of the U.S. Trade Representative (1978-84) and Council on International Economic Policy, Executive Office of the President (1974-77), The White House.

Employers

Piper Pacific Internat'l (Owner/President)

PIPESTEM, Wilson

1300 Pennsylvania Ave. NW
Suite 600
Washington, DC 20005
Tel: (202)898-0875

Employers

Ietan Consulting

Clients Represented

On Behalf of Ietan Consulting

Cabazon Band of Mission Indians
Mashantucket Pequot Tribal Nation
Oklahoma Indian Gaming Ass'n

PIRIUS, James C.

444 N. Capitol St. NW
Suite 841
Washington, DC 20001
Tel: (202)638-2000
Fax: (202)638-4584

Former Administrative Assistant to Rep. Bruce F. Vento (D-MN) and Director, Legislative Policy, Department of Education.

Employers

JCP Associates

Clients Represented

On Behalf of JCP Associates

Florida State University System
University of South Florida Research Foundation
Youth Guidance of Chicago

PISANO, Susan

1129 20th St. NW
Suite 600
Washington, DC 20036-3421
EMail: spisano@aahp.org
Tel: (202)778-3200
Fax: (202)778-8479

Employers
American Ass'n of Health Plans (AAHP) (V. President, Communications)

PISCITELLI, Julie

1156 15th St. NW
Suite 700
Washington, DC 20005
Tel: (202)973-3000
Fax: (202)973-3096

Employers
Nat'l Abortion and Reproductive Rights Action League (Director of Communications)

PITCHER, Robert C.

2200 Mill Rd.
Alexandria, VA 22314
Tel: (703)838-1879
Fax: (703)838-1992
Registered: LDA

Employers
American Trucking Ass'ns (Director, State Laws)

PITSOR, Kyle

1300 N. 17th St.
Suite 1847
Rosslyn, VA 22209
Tel: (301)587-9572
Fax: (301)589-2017

Employers
Nat'l Lighting Bureau (Exec. Director)

PITT, Harvey L.

1001 Pennsylvania Ave. NW
Suite 800
Washington, DC 20004-2505
EMail: harvey_pitt@ffhsj.com
Tel: (202)639-7000
Fax: (202)639-7008

General Counsel (1975-78), Executive Assistant to the Chairman (1973-75), Chief Counsel, Division of Market Regulation (1972-73) and Special Counsel, Office of the General Counsel (1971-72), Securities Exchange Commission.

Employers
Fried, Frank, Harris, Shriver & Jacobson (Managing Partner)

PITTMAN, C. Juliet

1111 14th St. NW
Suite 700
Washington, DC 20005
Tel: (202)628-1151
Fax: (202)638-4502
Registered: LDA

Employers
SENSE, INC. (President)

Clients Represented

On Behalf of SENSE, INC.
Choctaw Nation of Oklahoma
Hoopa Valley Tribal Council
Jamestown-S'Klallam Indian Tribe
Lummi Indian Nation
Noosack Indian Tribal council
Northwest Indian Fisheries Commission
Quinault Indian Nation
Sac & Fox Nation
Squaxin Island Indian Tribe
Swinomish Tribal Community
Sycuan Band of Mission Indians
Viejas Band of Kumeyaay Indians

PITTMAN, Edward L.

701 Pennsylvania Ave. NW
Suite 800
Washington, DC 20004
EMail: epittman@thelenreid.com
Tel: (202)508-4018
Fax: (202)508-4321
Registered: LDA

Former Assistant Chief Counsel and Counsel to Commissioner Roberts, Securities and Exchange Commission. Former Economics Assistant, Research Division, Commodity Futures Trading Commission

Employers
Thelen Reid & Priest LLP (Of Counsel)

Clients Represented

On Behalf of Thelen Reid & Priest LLP
Charles Schwab & Co. Inc.
Cincinnati Stock Exchange
The Island ECN
Charles Schwab & Co., Inc.,

PITTS, Alexandra

1849 C St. NW
Washington, DC 20240
Tel: (202)208-5403
Fax: (202)208-7059

Employers
Department of Interior - Fish and Wildlife Service (Chief, Division of Congressional and Legislative Affairs)

PITTS, James T.

1400 L St. NW
Washington, DC 20005-3502
EMail: jpitts@winston.com
Tel: (202)371-5793
Fax: (202)371-5950
Registered: LDA

Staff Member, Subcommittee on Commerce, Consumer and Monetary Affairs, House Committee on Government Operations, 1986. Assistant Director, Securities and Corporate Practices Division, Office of the Comptroller of the Currency, Department of Treasury, 1982-87.

Employers
Winston & Strawn (Partner, Federal Government Relations and Regulatory Affairs)

Clients Represented

On Behalf of Winston & Strawn
Certified Airline Passenger Services, LLC
Cooper Tire and Rubber Co.
Liberty Maritime Co.
Motor Coach Industries, Inc.
Northland Holdings, Inc.

PITTS, Tyrone S.

601 50th St. NE
Washington, DC 20019
Tel: (202)396-0558
Fax: (202)398-4998

Employers
Progressive Nat'l Baptist Convention (General Secretary)

PITTS, William R. "Billy"

6515 Haystack Rd.
Alexandria, VA 22310
Tel: (703)822-0575
Fax: (703)822-0576
Registered: LDA

Employers
mp3.com

PITZER, Jack

7801 Suffolk Court
Alexandria, VA 22315-4029
EMail: iwca@aol.com
Tel: (703)971-7771
Fax: (703)971-7772

Employers
Internat'l Window Cleaning Ass'n (Exec. Director)

PIVIK, Robert

1299 Pennsylvania Ave. NW
Washington, DC 20004-2402
Tel: (202)783-0800
Fax: (202)383-6610

Employers
Howrey Simon Arnold & White (Chief Operating Officer)

PIZANIAS, Helen

1225 I St. NW
Suite 1000
Washington, DC 20005-3914
EMail: pizanias@drugfreeworkplace.org
Tel: (202)842-7400
Fax: (202)842-0022

Employers
Institute for a Drug-Free Workplace (Fulfillment Manager)

PIZER, Charles L.

1530 Wilson Blvd.
Suite 900
Arlington, VA 22209
Tel: (703)312-4326
Fax: (703)312-4343
Registered: LDA

Employers
Self-employed as an independent consultant.

Clients Represented

As an independent consultant
Chicago School Reform Board of Trustees
City Colleges of Chicago

PIZZANO, Winifred A.

444 N. Capitol St. NW
Suite 240
Washington, DC 20001
EMail: winifred_pizzano@gov.state.il.us
Tel: (202)624-7760
Fax: (202)724-0689

Employers
Illinois, Washington Office of the State of (Senior Assistant to the Governor)

PLAINE, Daniel J.

1050 Connecticut Ave. NW
Washington, DC 20036-5306
EMail: dplaine@gdclaw.com
Tel: (202)955-8500
Fax: (202)467-0539

Employers
Gibson, Dunn & Crutcher LLP (Partner)

PLAISIER, Melinda K.

Parklawn Bldg. 15-57
5600 Fishers Ln.
Rockville, MD 20857
EMail: mplaisier@oc.fda.gov
Tel: (301)827-3793
Fax: (301)827-2567

Chief of Staff (1991-94), District Director (1986-90) and Staff Assistant (1985-86) to Rep. Frank McCloskey (D-IN).

Employers
Department of Health and Human Services - Food and Drug Administration (Associate Commissioner for Legislative Affairs)

PLANNING, Mark D.

1133 Connecticut Ave. NW
Suite 300
Washington, DC 20036
Tel: (202)293-1177
Fax: (202)293-3411
Registered: LDA

Staff Member, House Committee on Appropriations, 1988-89. Senior Legislative Assistant to Rep. Stan Parris (R-VA), 1983-86.

Employers
Ryan, Phillips, Utrecht & MacKinnon (Partner)

Clients Represented

On Behalf of Ryan, Phillips, Utrecht & MacKinnon
Air Transport Ass'n of America
Ass'n of American Railroads
Coeur d'Alene Mines Corp.
Cook Inlet Region Inc.
R. R. Donnelley & Sons
Edison Electric Institute
Florida Power and Light Co.
General Communications, Inc.
Investment Co. Institute
Kerr-McGee Corp.
Lockheed Martin Corp.
MultiDimensional Imaging, Inc.
Nat'l Cable Television Ass'n
Pfizer, Inc.
Philip Morris Management Corp.
Progress Energy
Sault Ste. Marie Tribe of Chippewa Indians
TXU Business Services
United Pan-Europe Communications, NV
VoiceStream Wireless Corp.

PLANT, Michelle Sutton

1101 15th St. NW
Suite 600
Washington, DC 20005
Tel: (202)785-1122
Ext: 116
Fax: (202)785-5019

Employers
Sugar Ass'n, Inc. (Director, Public Policy)

PLANTE, Robert P.

807 Maine Ave. SW
Washington, DC 20024
Tel: (202)554-3501
Fax: (202)554-3581

Employers
Disabled American Veterans (Assistant National Service Director)

PLANTY, Ambassador Donald J.

1818 N St. NW
Suite 500
Washington, DC 20036
Tel: (202)466-7464
Fax: (202)822-0075

Employers
Caribbean/Latin American Action (Exec. Director)

PLASTER, Amy S.

1250 H St. NW
Suite 800
Washington, DC 20005
EMail: amy.plaster@kodak.com
Tel: (202)857-3465
Fax: (202)857-3401
Registered: LDA

Employers
Eastman Kodak Co. (Director, Workforce Policy)

PLATNER, Michael L.

1220 L St. NW
Washington, DC 20005
Tel: (202)682-8418
Fax: (202)682-8294
Registered: LDA

Employers
American Petroleum Institute (Washington Representative)

PLATT, Alan A.

1050 Connecticut Ave. NW
Washington, DC 20036-5306
Tel: (202)955-8500
Fax: (202)467-0539
Registered: LDA
EMail: aplatt@gdclaw.com
Chief, Arms Transfer Division, Arms Control and Disarmament Agency. Principal Foreign Policy Advisor to Senator Edmund Muskie (D-ME).

Employers
Gibson, Dunn & Crutcher LLP (Principal)

Clients Represented
On Behalf of Gibson, Dunn & Crutcher LLP
The Boeing Co.
CNF Transportation, Inc.
Hughes Electronics Corp.
Loral Corp.
Monterey Institute
Northrop Grumman Corp.
Southern California Organ Procurement Consortium
Tensiodyne Scientific Corp.

PLATT, Alexander

1800 K St. NW
Suite 1018
Washington, DC 20006
Tel: (202)333-1277
Fax: (202)333-3128

Employers
Projects Internat'l (Exec. V. President and General Manager)

Clients Represented
On Behalf of Projects Internat'l
The Boeing Co.

PLATT, Roger

1420 New York Ave. NW
Suite 1100
Washington, DC 20005
Tel: (202)639-8400
Fax: (202)639-8442
Registered: LDA
EMail: rplatt@rer.org

Employers
Real Estate Roundtable (V. President and Counsel)

PLATT, Ronald L.

800 Connecticut Ave. NW
Suite 500
Washington, DC 20006
Tel: (202)331-3103
Fax: (202)261-0120
Registered: LDA
EMail: plattr@gtlaw.com
Former Aide to Senator Lloyd Bentsen (D-TX), Rep. Jack Brooks (D-TX) and Rep. Glenn English (D-OK).

Employers
Greenberg Traurig, LLP (Senior Director, Government Affairs)

Clients Represented
On Behalf of Greenberg Traurig, LLP
Applied Benefits Research Corp.
ARAMARK Corp.
Associated Financial Corp.
Bowman Internat'l Corp.
Campbell Soup Co.
E-Commerce Coalition
E-Commerce Payment Coalition
Fashion Accessories Shippers Ass'n
Healtheon/Web MD
Miller and Schroeder Financial, Inc.
Nat'l Ass'n of Computer Consultant Businesses
Nat'l Ass'n of State & Provincial Lotteries
Nat'l Center for Genome Research
Nat'l Housing Trust
NeuLevel
NICORE, Inc.
PHP Healthcare Corp.
Playboy Enterprises, Inc.
Rakisons, Ltd.
Singer Asset Management Co., L.L.C.
Smith Development, LLC
Starnet Communications Internat'l
TJTC Recovery Project Coalition
WOTC Project
Yankton Sioux Tribe

PLATT, Susan S.

10110 Walker Lake Dr.
Great Falls, VA 22066
Tel: (703)759-9622

Employers
Susan S. Platt Consulting

Clients Represented
On Behalf of Susan S. Platt Consulting
Philip Morris Management Corp.

PLATZER, Michaela

601 Pennsylvania Ave. NW
Suite 600
North Bldg.
Washington, DC 20004
Tel: (202)682-9110
Fax: (202)682-9111

Employers
American Electronics Ass'n (V. President, Research and Policy Analysis)

PLAUSHIN, Christopher

1440 New York Ave. NW
Suite 200
Washington, DC 20005
Tel: (202)942-2050
Fax: (202)783-4798
Registered: LDA

Employers
American Automobile Ass'n (Manager, Regulatory Affairs)

PLAUSHIN, Nina

1331 Pennsylvania Ave. NW
Suite 512
Washington, DC 20004
Tel: (202)662-8752
Fax: (202)662-8749
Registered: LDA

Employers
PPL (Manager, Federal Affairs)

PLEBANI, Jon W.

1801 K St. NW
Washington, DC 20006
Tel: (202)775-7100
Fax: (202)857-0172
Registered: LDA, FARA
EMail: jplebani@arterhadden.com
Former Chief of Staff to Majority Whip William H. Gray III (D-PA). Former Deputy Special Advisor to the President on Haiti during the Clinton administration.

Employers
Arter & Hadden (Principal)

Clients Represented
On Behalf of Arter & Hadden
Academy of Radiology Research
Americans for Fair Taxation
Ass'n for Responsible Thermal Treatment
Bristol-Myers Squibb Co.
Circus Circus Enterprises, Inc.
Citigroup
Fairchild Aircraft, Inc.
Financial Guaranty Insurance Corp.
HCA Healthcare Corp.
Hicks, Muse, Tate & Furst
Houston, Texas, Port Authority of the City of
Koyo Corp. of U.S.A.
Sammons Enterprises, Inc.
San Antonio, Texas, City of
SBC Communications Inc.
H. B. Zachry

PLESCH, Daniel T.

1012 14th St. NW
Suite 900
Washington, DC 20005
Tel: (202)347-8340
Fax: (202)347-4688
EMail: basicus@basicint.org

Employers
British American Security Information Council (Director)

PLESSER, Ronald L.

1200 19th St. NW
Washington, DC 20036-2430
Tel: (202)861-3969
Fax: (202)223-2085
Registered: LDA
EMail: ron.plesser@piperrudnick.com

Employers
Piper Marbury Rudnick & Wolfe LLP (Partner)

Clients Represented
On Behalf of Piper Marbury Rudnick & Wolfe LLP
Acxiom Corp.
AOL Time Warner
Commercial Internet Exchange Ass'n
Direct Marketing Ass'n, Inc.
Individual Reference Services Group
Lexis-Nexis
NetCoalition.Com
Omnipoint Corp.
PSINet Inc.

PLOCK, Mary

1200 G St. NW
Suite 400
Washington, DC 20005
Tel: (202)783-8700
Fax: (202)783-8750

Employers
AdvaMed (V. President, Public Affairs)

PLOTKIN, Mark

1201 Pennsylvania Ave. NW
Washington, DC 20004-2401
Tel: (202)662-6000
Fax: (202)662-6291
EMail: mplotkin@cov.com
Law Clerk, Office of the Legal Advisor, Department of State, 1986.

Employers
Covington & Burling (Partner)

PLOTKIN, Martha

1120 Connecticut Ave. NW
Suite 930
Washington, DC 20036
Tel: (202)466-7820
Fax: (202)466-7826

Employers
Police Executive Research Forum (Director, Communications and Legislative Affairs)

PLOTKIN, Robert

1299 Pennsylvania Ave. NW
Tenth Floor
Washington, DC 20004-2400
Tel: (202)508-9500
Fax: (202)508-9700
EMail: robertplotkin@paulhastings.com
Chief, Special Litigation Section, Civil Rights Division, Department of Justice, 1980-81.

Employers
Paul, Hastings, Janofsky & Walker LLP (Of Counsel)

PLOTT, Angela

2111 Wilson Blvd.
Eighth Floor
Arlington, VA 22201-3058
Tel: (703)841-0626
Fax: (703)243-2874
Registered: LDA
EMail: plott@alcalde-fay.com

Employers
Alcalde & Fay (Partner)

Clients Represented
On Behalf of Alcalde & Fay
Deerfield Beach, Florida, City of
Palm Beach, Florida, Port of
Virginia Beach, Virginia, City of

PLUMART, Perry

1901 Pennsylvania Ave. NW
Suite 1100
Washington, DC 20006
Tel: (202)861-2242
Fax: (202)861-4290

Employers
Nat'l Audubon Soc. (Director, Government Affairs)

PLUMER, Michael W.

909 N. Washington St.
Suite 300
Alexandria, VA 22314
Tel: (703)548-5568
Fax: (703)684-3258
Registered: LDA

Employers
TREA Senior Citizens League (TSCL) (Deputy Legislative Director)

PLUMMER, William B.

1101 Connecticut Ave. NW
Suite 910
Washington, DC 20036
Tel: (202)887-1798
Fax: (202)887-0432
Registered: LDA

Employers
NOKIA (V. President, Government and Industry Affairs)

PLUMP, Andrew R.

888 17th St. NW
Suite 600
Washington, DC 20006-3959
Tel: (202)298-8660
Fax: (202)342-0683

Employers
Zuckert, Scoutt and Rasenberger, L.L.P.

Clients Represented
On Behalf of Zuckert, Scoutt and Rasenberger, L.L.P.
All Nippon Airways Co.
Pakistan Internat'l Airlines

PLUNK, Daryl M.

2111 Wilson Blvd.
Suite 1200
Arlington, VA 22201
Tel: (703)522-1845
Fax: (703)351-6634
EMail: dplunk@columbuspublicaffairs.com
Former Legislative Assistant to Rep. Edwin Forsythe (R-NJ). Also served in the Peace Corps.

Employers
Columbus Public Affairs (Senior V. President for Asia Operations)

POAG, Mary "Molly" Woodson

1330 Connecticut Ave. NW
Washington, DC 20036-1795
Tel: (202)429-3000
Fax: (202)429-3902
Registered: LDA
EMail: mpoag@steptoe.com
Former Special Assistant to the Secretary, Department of the Interior.

Employers
Steptoe & Johnson LLP (Of Counsel)

PODESTA, Anthony T.

1001 G St. NW
Suite 900 E
Washington, DC 20001-4545
Tel: (202)393-1010
Fax: (202)393-5510
Registered: LDA, FARA
EMail: tpodesta@podesta.com
Former Counsel to Senator Edward M. Kennedy (D-MA). Former Assistant U.S. Attorney for the District of Columbia, Department of Justice.

Employers
Podesta/Mattoon (Chairman)

Clients Represented
On Behalf of Podesta/Mattoon
American Psychological Ass'n
AOL Time Warner
Ass'n of Directory Publishers
Aventis CropScience
Celera Genomics
Dow AgroSciences
Friends of Cancer Research
GE Power Systems
Genentech, Inc.
Horsehead Industries, Inc.
MCI WorldCom Corp.
Mount Sinai/NYU Health
Nat'l Environmental Strategies
Nat'l Food Processors Ass'n
News America Inc.
Nextel Communications, Inc.
Recording Industry Ass'n of America
Teligent, Inc.
Trans World Airlines, Inc.
Vivendi Universal

PODGORSKY, Arnold B.

1200 G St. NW
Suite 600
Washington, DC 20005-3802
Tel: (202)393-1200
Fax: (202)393-1240
EMail: podgorsky@wrightlaw.com
Attorney, Appellate Court Branch (1977-78) and Attorney, Advice Branch (1975-76), National Labor Relations Board.

Employers
Wright & Talisman, P.C.

Clients Represented
On Behalf of Wright & Talisman, P.C.
Marine Transport Lines, Inc.

PODOLSKE, Lewis R.

14th and Constitution Ave. NW
Room 7814A
Washington, DC 20230
Tel: (202)482-2309
Fax: (202)501-4828

Employers
Department of Commerce - Economic Development Administration (Acting Director, Office of Communications and Congressional Liaison)

POERIO, J. Mark

1299 Pennsylvania Ave. NW
Tenth Floor
Washington, DC 20004-2400
Tel: (202)508-9582
Fax: (202)508-9700
EMail: markpoerio@paulhastings.com

Employers
Paul, Hastings, Janofsky & Walker LLP (Of Counsel)

POINTON, Henry

1225 I St. NW
Suite 500
Washington, DC 20005
Tel: (202)312-2005
Fax: (202)289-8683
Registered: LDA
EMail: dawsonassociates@worldnet.att.net
Former Assistant Chief, Programs Division, Civil Works Directorate, Office of the Chief of Engineers, U.S. Army Corps of Engineers, Department of the Army. Also formerly served as Assistant Chief, Planning Programs, Management Branch and as former Chief, Engineering Branch, both at the Natural Resources Division, Inter-American Geodetic Survey (Fort Clayton, Canal Zone), Defense Mapping Agency, National Imagery and Mapping Agency, Department of the Army. Also served as an Advisor to the U.S. Agency for International Development.

Employers
Dawson & Associates, Inc. (Senior Advisor)

Clients Represented
On Behalf of Dawson & Associates, Inc.
Anglogold Americas, Inc.
Chemical Land Holdings, Inc.

POLANKO, Anna

815 16th St. NW
Suite 310
Washington, DC 20006
Tel: (202)347-4223
Fax: (202)347-5095

Employers
Labor Council for Latin American Advancement (LCLAA) (Assistant Director)

POLATNICK, Eden

2101 L St. NW
Washington, DC 20037-1526
Tel: (202)785-9700
Fax: (202)887-0689
EMail: polatnicke@dsmo.com

Employers
Dickstein Shapiro Morin & Oshinsky LLP (Associate)

POLEBAUM, Elliot E.

1001 Pennsylvania Ave. NW
Suite 800
Washington, DC 20004-2505
Tel: (202)639-7000
Fax: (202)639-7008
EMail: elliot_polebaum@ffhsj.com
Law Clerk to Justice William J. Brennan, Jr., U.S. Supreme Court, 1980-81 and to Judge James L. Oakes, U.S. Court of Appeals, Second Circuit, 1977-78.

Employers
Fried, Frank, Harris, Shriver & Jacobson (Partner)

POLESE, Donald J.

1225 I St. NW
Suite 500
Washington, DC 20005
Tel: (202)312-2005
Fax: (202)289-8683
Registered: LDA
EMail: dawsonassociates@worldnet.att.net
Former District Director for Chairman Ron Packard, Subcommittee on Energy and Water Development, House Committee on Appropriations.

Employers
Dawson & Associates, Inc. (Senior Advisor)

POLGAR, Thomas C.

122 C St. NW
Suite 520
Washington, DC 20001
Tel: (202)393-5100
Fax: (202)393-5110
Registered: LDA

Employers
Tyco Internat'l (US), Inc. (Senior V. President, Public Affairs)

POLIDORI, Jack

1201 16th St. NW
Washington, DC 20036
Tel: (202)833-4000

Employers
Nat'l Education Ass'n of the U.S. (Senior Professional Associate, Government Relations)

POLIKOFF, Stuart

21 Dupont Circle NW
Suite 700
Washington, DC 20036
Tel: (202)659-5990
Fax: (202)659-4619
Registered: LDA
EMail: sep@opastco.org

Employers
Organization for the Promotion and Advancement of Small Telecommunications Cos. (Director, Government Relations)

POLINER, Michael C.

1300 19th St. NW
Suite 400
Washington, DC 20036
Tel: (202)293-1600
Fax: (202)293-8965
Registered: LDA

Employers
Feith & Zell, P.C.

Clients Represented
On Behalf of Feith & Zell, P.C.
Loral Space and Communications, Ltd.

POLING, Michael

701 Pennsylvania Ave. NW
Suite 300
Washington, DC 20004
Tel: (202)508-5276
Fax: (202)508-5278

Employers
Kansas City Power & Light Co. (Manager, Federal Government Affairs)

POLK, Loretta P.

1724 Massachusetts Ave. NW
Washington, DC 20036-1969
Tel: (202)775-3550
Fax: (202)775-3603
Registered: LDA

Employers
Nat'l Cable Television Ass'n (Associate General Counsel)

POLLACK, Michael J.

1801 K St. NW
Washington, DC 20006
Tel: (202)775-7100
Fax: (202)857-0172
EMail: mpollack@arterhadden.com

Employers
Arter & Hadden (Partner)

POLLACK, Richard J.

325 Seventh St. NW
Washington, DC 20004
Tel: (202)638-1100
Fax: (202)626-2355
Registered: LDA

Employers
American Hospital Ass'n (Exec. V. President)

POLLACK, Ronald F.

1334 G St. NW
Suite 300
Washington, DC 20005-3169
Tel: (202)628-3030
Fax: (202)347-2417

Employers
Families U.S.A. Foundation (Exec. Director)

POLLAK, Michele

601 E St. NW
Washington, DC 20049
Tel: (202)434-3760
Fax: (202)434-3758
Registered: LDA

Employers
AARP (American Ass'n of Retired Persons) (Legislative Representative)

POLLARD, Jr., Albert W.

1401 I St. NW
Suite 600
Washington, DC 20005
Tel: (202)336-7400
Fax: (202)336-7527
Registered: LDA

Employers
United Technologies Corp. (Director, Internat'l Business Development)

POLLARD, Alfonso M.

501 Third St. NW
Tenth Floor
Washington, DC 20001
Tel: (202)628-5460
Fax: (202)628-5461
Registered: LDA
EMail: apollard@afm.org

Employers
American Federation of Musicians of the United States and Canada (National Legislative Director)

POLLEY, James

99 Canal Center Plaza
Suite 510
Alexandria, VA 22314
Tel: (703)549-9222
Fax: (703)836-3195
EMail: james.polley@ndaa-apri.org

Employers
Nat'l District Attorneys Ass'n (Director, Government Affairs)

POLLITZ, Karen

2233 Wisconsin Ave. NW
Suite 525
Georgetown University
Washington, DC 20007
Tel: (202)687-0880
Fax: (202)687-3110

Employers
Institute for Health Care Research and Policy (Co-Director)

POLLOCK, Hon. Howard

908 Pennsylvania Ave. SE
Washington, DC 20003
Tel: (202)544-5666
Fax: (202)544-4647
Registered: LDA
EMail: hpollock@advantage-dc.com
Member, U.S. House of Representatives (R-AK), 1966-71. Deputy Administrator, National Oceanic and Atmospheric Administration and Deputy Undersecretary, Department of Commerce.

Employers
Advantage Associates, Inc. (Partner)

POLLOCK, Richard

1000 Massachusetts Ave. NW
Washington, DC 20001
Tel: (202)842-0200
Fax: (202)842-3490

Employers
Cato Institute (V. President, Communications)

POLLY, Kris D.

3800 N. Fairfax Dr.
Suite 4
Arlington, VA 22203
Tel: (703)524-1544
Fax: (703)524-1548
Registered: LDA
EMail: kpolly@nwra.org

Employers
Nat'l Water Resources Ass'n (Director, Government Relations)

POLNIASZEK, Susan E.

2519 Connecticut Ave. NW
Washington, DC 20008-1520
Tel: (202)783-2242
Fax: (202)783-2255

Employers
American Ass'n of Homes and Services for the Aging (Reimbursement Policy Specialist)

POLO, Barbara Jeanne

600 Pennsylvania Ave. SE
Suite 210
Washington, DC 20003
Tel: (202)544-3526
Fax: (202)544-5625
EMail: bjpolo@americanoceans.org

Employers
American Oceans Campaign (Exec. Director)

POLYAK, Jeffrey V.

2111 Wilson Blvd.
Suite 1200
Arlington, VA 22201
Tel: (703)522-1845
Fax: (703)351-6634
EMail: jpolyak@columbuspublicaffairs.com
Former Assistant to the Chief Advisor to the Secretary, Department of Education.

Employers
Columbus Public Affairs (Associate)

POMERANCE, Jr., Ralph

2026 Allen Pl. NW
Washington, DC 20009
Tel: (202)232-6885
Fax: (202)298-8514
Registered: LDA
Former Deputy Ass't Secretary for Environment and Development, U.S. Department of State.

Employers
Self-employed as an independent consultant.

Clients Represented
As an independent consultant
Corporation for Enterprise Development

POMERANTZ, Mitch

1155 15th St. NW
Suite 1004
Washington, DC 20005
Tel: (202)467-5081
Fax: (202)467-5085

Employers
ACB Government Employees

POMERANTZ, Paul

10201 Lee Hwy.
Suite 500
Fairfax, VA 22030
Tel: (703)691-1805
Fax: (703)691-1855

Employers
Soc. of Cardiovascular and Interventional Radiology (Exec. Director)

POMERANZ, John

11 Dupont Circle NW
Second Floor
Washington, DC 20036
Tel: (202)822-6070
Fax: (202)822-6068
Registered: LDA

Employers
Alliance for Justice (Non-Profit Advocacy Counsel)

POMEROY, John H.

1200 New Hampshire Ave. NW
Suite 800
Washington, DC 20036-6802
Tel: (202)776-2000
Fax: (202)776-2222
EMail: jpomeroy@dlalaw.com

Employers
Dow, Lohnes & Albertson, PLLC (Member)

POMFRET, Jacqueline M.

1129 20th St. NW
Suite 600
Washington, DC 20036-3421
Tel: (202)778-3200
Fax: (202)778-8508
Registered: LDA

Employers
American Ass'n of Health Plans (AAHP) (Director, Legislative Affairs)

POMMER, Russell E.

901 15th St. NW
Suite 700
Washington, DC 20005-2301
Tel: (202)371-6000
Fax: (202)371-6279
Registered: LDA
EMail: repommer@verner.com

Employers
Verner, Liipfert, Bernhard, McPherson and Hand, Chartered (Member of Firm)

Clients Represented
On Behalf of Verner, Liipfert, Bernhard, McPherson and Hand, Chartered
Northwest Airlines, Inc.

PONDER, Dr. Henry

8701 Georgia Ave.
Suite 200
Silver Spring, MD 20910
Tel: (301)650-2440
Fax: (301)495-3306
Registered: LDA

Employers
Nat'l Ass'n for Equal Opportunity in Higher Education (President and Chief Exec. Officer)

PONEMAN, Daniel B.

555 13th St. NW
Washington, DC 20004-1109
Tel: (202)637-6904
Fax: (202)637-5910
Registered: LDA
EMail: dbponeman@hhlaw.com
Special Assistant to the President and Senior Director, Nonproliferation and Export Controls (1993-96) and Director, Defense Policy and Arms Control, National Security Council (1990-93), Executive Office of the President, The White House. Fellow, Department of Energy, 1989-90.

Employers
Hogan & Hartson L.L.P. (Partner)

Clients Represented
On Behalf of Hogan & Hartson L.L.P.
Brandeis University
Nat'l Foreign Trade Council, Inc.
News Corporation Ltd.
Payless Shoe Source

PONGRACE, Donald R.

1333 New Hampshire Ave. NW
Suite 400
Washington, DC 20036
Tel: (202)887-4000
Fax: (202)887-4288
Registered: LDA
Law Clerk to Judge H. E. Widener, Jr., U.S. Court of Appeals, Fourth Circuit, 1985-86.

Employers
Akin, Gump, Strauss, Hauer & Feld, L.L.P. (Partner)

Clients Represented
On Behalf of Akin, Gump, Strauss, Hauer & Feld, L.L.P.
Banro American Resources Inc.
Dow Jones & Co., Inc.
Gila River Indian Community
Poongsan Corporation
The Project Leadership Committee, Lincoln Center for the Performing Arts

PONTE, Joe

1200 18th St. NW
Suite 400
Washington, DC 20036-2506
Tel: (202)783-9452
Fax: (202)331-8364
EMail: jponte@nbaa.org

Employers
Nat'l Business Aviation Ass'n (V. President, Membership and Marketing)

POOLE, Hardy

1130 Connecticut Ave. NW
Suite 1200
Washington, DC 20036-3954
Tel: (202)862-0500
Fax: (202)862-0570

Employers
American Textile Manufacturers Institute (Director, Product Services Division)

POOLE, Mark N.

1612 K St. NW
Suite 300
Washington, DC 20006
Tel: (202)857-0999
Fax: (202)857-0027
EMail: mpoole@acypl.org

Employers
American Council of Young Political Leaders (Exec. Director)

POOLER-JOHNSON, Susanne J.

317 S. Patrick St.
Alexandria, VA 22314
Tel: (703)519-0300
Fax: (703)519-0311

Employers
Internat'l Brotherhood of Police Officers
Nat'l Ass'n of Government Employees (V. President)

POPEO, Daniel J.

2009 Massachusetts Ave. NW
Washington, DC 20036
Tel: (202)588-0302
Fax: (202)588-0371

Employers
Washington Legal Foundation (Chairman and General Counsel)

POPHAM, James

1320 19th St. NW
Suite 300
Washington, DC 20036
Tel: (202)887-1970
Fax: (202)887-0950
Registered: LDA

Employers
Ass'n of Local Television Stations (V. President, General Counsel)

POPKIN, Richard A.

3000 K St. NW
Suite 300
Washington, DC 20007
Tel: (202)424-7500
Fax: (202)424-7643
Registered: LDA, FARA

Confidential Assistant to the Under Secretary of Commerce for International Trade, 1984-85. Deputy Assistant Secretary of Commerce for Trade Administration, 1985-87.

Employers
Swidler Berlin Shereff Friedman, LLP (Partner)

Clients Represented
On Behalf of Swidler Berlin Shereff Friedman, LLP
Ry Cooder
Matsushita Electric Corp. of America

POPOVICH, Luke

99 Canal Center Plaza
Suite 200
Alexandria, VA 22314
Tel: (703)683-8512
Fax: (703)683-4622

Employers
Smith & Harroff, Inc. (Senior V. President)

Clients Represented
On Behalf of Smith & Harroff, Inc.
Sappi Fine Paper NA

PORDZIK, Wolfgang

4710 Bethesda Ave.
Suite 919
Bethesda, MD 20814
Registered: FARA

Employers
Self-employed as an independent consultant.

Clients Represented
As an independent consultant
Deutsche Post AG

PORRO, Jeff

2120 L St. NW
Suite 400
Washington, DC 20037
Tel: (202)223-9541
Fax: (202)223-9579

Employers
M & R Strategic Services (V. President)

PORTE, Phillip

5454 Wisconsin Ave.
Suite 1270
Chevy Chase, MD 20815
Tel: (301)718-0202
Fax: (301)718-2976
Registered: LDA
EMail: pporte@erols.com

Employers
GRQ, Inc. (Principal)

Clients Represented
On Behalf of GRQ, Inc.
American Ass'n of Cardiovascular and Pulmonary Rehabilitation
American College of Chest Physicians
HCR-Manor Care, Inc.
Mallinckrodt-Nellcor Puritan Bennett
Nat'l Ass'n for Medical Direction of Respiratory Care
Transtracheal Systems
Tri Path Inc.

PORTER, Daniel L.

Three Lafayette Center
1155 21st St. NW
Washington, DC 20036-3384
Tel: (202)328-8000
Fax: (202)887-8979
Registered: LDA

Employers
Willkie Farr & Gallagher (Partner)

Clients Represented
On Behalf of Willkie Farr & Gallagher
Fuji Photo Film U.S.A., Inc.
Hyundai Electronics Industries Co., LTD
Superior Metal Products

PORTER, David N.

1133 19th St. NW
Washington, DC 20036
Tel: (202)736-6808
Fax: (202)736-6815

Employers
MCI WorldCom Corp. (V. President, Government Affairs and Regulatory Economics)

PORTER, John D.

1225 Connecticut Ave. NW
Washington, DC 20036
Tel: (202)327-6410
Fax: (202)327-8836
Registered: LDA
EMail: john.porter@ey.com

Employers
Ernst & Young LLP (Senior Manager)
Washington Council Ernst & Young (Senior Manager)

Clients Represented
On Behalf of Ernst & Young LLP
General Ore Internat'l Corp. Ltd.
INCOL 2000
Koch Industries, Inc.
Repeal the Tax on Talking Coalition
On Behalf of Washington Council Ernst & Young
Aetna Life & Casualty Co.
American Insurance Ass'n
American Staffing Ass'n
Anheuser-Busch Cos., Inc.
Antitrust Coalition for Consumer Choice in Health Care
Apartment Investment and Management Co.
Ass'n of American Railroads
Ass'n of Home Appliance Manufacturers
AT&T
Aventis Pharmaceuticals, Inc.
Baxter Healthcare Corp.
BHC Communications, Inc.
Bulmer Holding PLC, H. P.
Cash Balance Coalition
Citigroup
Coalition for Fairness in Defense Exports
Coalition to Preserve Tracking Stock
ComEd
The Connell Co.
Deferral Group
Directors Guild of America
Doris Duke Charitable Foundation
Eaton Vance Management Co.
Eden Financial Corp.
The Enterprise Foundation
Fannie Mae
FedEx Corp.
Ford Motor Co.
General Electric Co.
Global Competitiveness Coalition
Grasslands Water District
Group Health, Inc.
HEREIU
Gilbert P. Hyatt, Inventor
Investment Co. Institute
Large Public Power Council
Local Initiatives Support Corp.
MacAndrews & Forbes Holdings, Inc.
Marsh & McLennan Cos.
MCG Northwest, Inc.
McLane Co.
Merrill Lynch & Co., Inc.
Metropolitan Banking Group
Nat'l Ass'n for State Farm Agents
Nat'l Ass'n of Professional Employer Organizations
Nat'l Ass'n of Real Estate Investment Trusts
Nat'l Defined Contribution Council
Nat'l Foreign Trade Council, Inc.
Nat'l Multi-Housing Council
Pfizer, Inc.
R&D Tax Credit Coalition
R&D Tax Regulation Group
Recording Industry Ass'n of America
Reed-Elsevier Inc.
R. J. Reynolds Tobacco Co.
Charles Schwab & Co., Inc.,
Securities Industry Ass'n
Skadden, Arps, Slate, Meagher & Flom LLP
Straddle Rules Tax Group
Tax Fairness Coalition
TXU Business Services
U.S. Oncology
USA Biomass Power Producers Alliance
Viaticus, Inc.
Wilkie Farr & Gallagher
Ziff Investors Partnership

PORTER, Hon. John Edward

555 13th St. NW
Washington, DC 20004-1109
Tel: (202)637-5600
Fax: (202)637-5910

Member, U.S. House of Representatives (R-IL), 1980-2001. Chairman House Appropriations Subcommittee on Labor, Health and Human Services, and Education, 1995-2001

Employers
Hogan & Hartson L.L.P. (Partner)

PORTER, Julia

1100 Connecticut Ave. NW
Suite 530
Washington, DC 20036
Tel: (202)293-7222
Fax: (202)293-2955
Registered: LDA
EMail: julia.porter@weyerhaeuser.com

Employers
Weyerhaeuser Co. (Manager, Government Affairs)

PORTER, Orson

507 Second St. NE
Washington, DC 20002
Tel: (202)543-6453
Fax: (202)544-6453
Registered: LDA
EMail: orson.porter@nike.com

Employers
Nike, Inc. (Deputy Director of Governmental Affairs)

PORTER, Robert W.

3050 K St. NW
Washington, DC 20007
Tel: (202)342-8646
Fax: (202)342-8451
Registered: LDA, FARA
EMail: rporter@colliershannon.com

Former Professional Staff, Senate Governmental Affairs Committee and Legislative Assistant to Senator William S. Cohen (R-ME).

Employers
Collier Shannon Scott, PLLC (Government Relations Advisor)

Clients Represented
On Behalf of Collier Shannon Scott, PLLC
AKT Developments
Allegheny Technologies, Inc.
American Iron and Steel Institute
Australian Dairy Corp.
Berry Amendment Glove Coalition
Coalition for Safe Ceramicware
Internat'l Crystal Federation
Maui Pineapple Co.
Metro Internat'l Trade Services, Inc.
Military Footwear Coalition
Military Glove Coalition
Nat'l Juice Products Ass'n
Oneida Ltd.
Planar Systems, Inc.
Specialty Steel Industry of North America
Specialty Tubing Group
Toolex USA, Inc.

PORTER, Tola

1199 N. Fairfax St.
Suite 1000
Alexandria, VA 22314
Tel: (703)299-4499
Fax: (703)299-4488
EMail: tporter@hawthorngroup.com

Employers
The Hawthorn Group, L.C. (Sr. Account Coordinator)

PORTER, Dr. Winston

1225 I St. NW
Suite 500
Washington, DC 20005
Tel: (202)312-2005
Fax: (202)289-8683
EMail: dawsonassociates@worldnet.att.net

Assistant Administrator for Solid Waste and Emergency Response, Environmental Protection Agency, 1985-89.

Employers
Dawson & Associates, Inc. (Senior Advisor)

PORTERFIELD, Lendell

1420 New York Ave. NW
Suite 1050
Washington, DC 20005
Tel: (202)638-1950
Fax: (202)638-7714

Former Staff Director, Subcommittee on Financial Institutions and Regulatory Relief (1995-97) and Financial Advisor (1997-2000), House Committee on Banking, Housing and Urban Affairs. Aide to Senator Richard C. Shelby (R-AL), 1994-95.

Employers
Van Scoyoc Associates, Inc. (Economist and Legislative Analyst)

PORTMAN, Robert M.

601 13th St. NW
12th Floor
Washington, DC 20005
Tel: (202)639-6000
Fax: (202)639-6066
Registered: LDA

Deputy Assistant Secretary, Office of the American Workplace (1993-94) and Special Assistant to the Secretary (1993),

Department of Labor. Law Clerk to Judge Mark Wolf, U.S. District Court for the District of Massachusetts, 1985-86.

Employers
Jenner & Block (Partner)

Clients Represented
On Behalf of Jenner & Block
American College of Emergency Physicians
American Soc. of Cataract and Refractive Surgery
Nat'l Coalition of Petroleum Dry Cleaners

PORTNER, MPA, Gregory A.

1775 I St. NW
Suite 520
Washington, DC 20006
Tel: (202)496-0200
Fax: (202)496-0201
EMail: gportner@muse-associates.com

Employers
Muse & Associates (Senior Research Manager)

Clients Represented
On Behalf of Muse & Associates
The Tri-Alliance of Rehabilitation Professionals

PORTNER, Linda E.

One White Flint North Bldg.
11555 Rockville Pike
MS: 16D6
Rockville, MD 20852
Tel: (301)415-1776
Fax: (301)415-8571
EMail: lep@nrc.gov

Employers
Nuclear Regulatory Commission (Associate Director/Assistant to the Chairman for Congressional Communications)

PORTNEY, Paul R.

1616 P St. NW
Washington, DC 20036
Tel: (202)328-5000
Fax: (202)939-3460

Employers
Resources for the Future (President)

PORTNOY, Elliott I.

1050 Connecticut Ave. NW
Washington, DC 20036-5339
Tel: (202)857-6000
Fax: (202)857-6395
Registered: LDA
Worked for the Senate Democratic Policy Committee.

Employers
Arent Fox Kintner Plotkin & Kahn, PLLC (Member)

Clients Represented
On Behalf of Arent Fox Kintner Plotkin & Kahn, PLLC
Alaska Rainforest Campaign
American Amusement Machine Ass'n
Amusement and Music Operators Ass'n
Building Service Contractors Ass'n Internat'l
Children and Adults with Attention Deficit Disorders (CHADD)
Earth Council Institute - Canada
Interactive Amusement and Tournament Video Game Coalition
Mercy Hospital of Des Moines, Iowa
Nat'l Ass'n of School Nurses
Navajo Nation
New Orleans, Louisiana, City of

PORTNOY, James S.

1201 Pennsylvania Ave. NW
Washington, DC 20004-2401
Tel: (202)662-6000
Fax: (202)662-6291
Registered: LDA
General Counsel to the Minority, House Committee on Oversight, 1996-97. Associate Special Counsel to the Minority, Senate Special Committee to Investigate the Whitewater Development Corp., 1995-96. Law Clerk to Judge Irving R. Kaufman, U.S. District Court of Appeals for the Second Circuit, District of New York, 1987-88.

Employers
Covington & Burling (Associate)

POSSNER, Karen B.

1133 21st St. NW
Suite 900
Washington, DC 20036
Tel: (202)463-4100
Fax: (202)463-4637
Registered: LDA
EMail: karen.possner@bellsouth.com

Employers
BellSouth Corp. (V. President, Strategic Policy)

POST, Dr. Diana

8940 Jones Mill Rd.
Chevy Chase, MD 20815
Tel: (301)652-1877
Fax: (301)587-3863
EMail: rccouncil@aol.com

Employers
Rachel Carson Council, Inc. (Exec. Director)

POST, Karen A.

1200 New Hampshire Ave. NW
Suite 800
Washington, DC 20036-6802
Tel: (202)776-2000
Fax: (202)776-2222
EMail: kpost@dlalaw.com

Employers
Dow, Lohnes & Albertson, PLLC (Senior Counsel)

POSTAR, Michael R.

1615 M St. NW
Suite 800
Washington, DC 20036-3203
Tel: (202)467-6370
Fax: (202)467-6379
EMail: mrp@dwgp.com
Federal Energy Regulatory Commission, 1981-92: Attorney-Advisor 1981-83; Assistant to the Chairman, 1983-86; Deputy Assistant General Counsel 1986-87; Trial Attorney, 1987-92; Supervisory Trial Attorney 1992.

Employers
Duncan, Weinberg, Genzer & Pembroke, P.C. (Principal)

Clients Represented
On Behalf of Duncan, Weinberg, Genzer & Pembroke, P.C.
Bergen, New York, Village of
Churchville, New York, Village of
College Station, Texas, City of
Corn Belt Energy Corp.
EnerStar Power Corp.
Knightstown, Indiana, Town of
The Metropolitan Water District of Southern California
Modesto/Turlock Irrigation District
Penn Yan, New York, Village of
Redding, California, Electric Department of the City of
Santa Clara, California, Electric Department of the City of
Southern California Public Power Authority
Southwestern Electric Cooperative, Inc.
Transmission Agency of Northern California
Yates County Cable TV Committee

POSTON, Ramsey

700 13th St. NW
Suite 1000
Washington, DC 20005
Tel: (202)347-6633
Fax: (202)347-8713

Employers
Powell Tate (V. President)

POTETZ, Lisa

1901 L St. NW
Suite 200
Washington, DC 20036
Tel: (202)659-1800
Fax: (202)296-2964

Employers
March of Dimes Birth Defects Foundation (Director, Public Policy Research)

POTHOLM, Eric

305 Cameron St.
Alexandria, VA 22314
Tel: (703)683-8326
Fax: (703)683-8826
EMail: epotholm@srcmedia.com

Employers
Stevens Reed Curcio & Co. (Partner)

POTTER, Edward E.

1015 15th St. NW
Suite 1200
Washington, DC 20005
Tel: (202)789-8600
Fax: (202)789-1708

Employers
Employment Policy Foundation (President)
McGuiness Norris & Williams, LLP (Partner)

Clients Represented
On Behalf of McGuiness Norris & Williams, LLP
United States Council for Internat'l Business

POTTER, J. Craig

1666 K St. NW
Suite 500
Washington, DC 20006-2803
Tel: (202)887-1400
Fax: (202)466-2198
Registered: LDA

Employers
O'Connor & Hannan, L.L.P. (Partner)

Clients Represented
On Behalf of O'Connor & Hannan, L.L.P.
Upper Sioux Indian Community

POTTER, James G.

10801 Rockville Pike
Rockville, MD 20852
Tel: (301)897-5700
Ext: 4125
Fax: (301)897-7356
Registered: LDA
EMail: jpotter@asha.org

Employers
American Speech, Language, and Hearing Ass'n (Director, Government Relations and Public Policy)

POTTER, Kathryn

1201 New York Ave. NW
Suite 600
Washington, DC 20005-3931
Tel: (202)289-3130
Fax: (202)289-3199
EMail: kpotter@ahma.com

Employers
American Hotel and Lodging Ass'n (Director, Communications)

POTTER, Philip H.

717 D St. NW
Suite 310
Washington, DC 20004
Tel: (202)626-0550
Fax: (202)393-5728
Registered: LDA
EMail: ppotter@fedstrategies.com

Employers
Federal Strategies Group (President)

POTTER, Robert A.

4000 Jones Bridge Rd.
Chevy Chase, MD 20815-6789
Tel: (301)215-8855
Fax: (301)215-8863

Employers
Howard Hughes Medical Institute (Director, Communications)

POTTER, Trevor

1776 K St. NW
Washington, DC 20006
Tel: (202)719-7000
Fax: (202)719-7049
Assistant General Counsel, Federal Communications Commission, 1983-85. Special Assistant, Office of Legal Policy, Department of Justice, 1982-83. Commissioner and Chairman, Federal Election Commission, 1981.

Employers
Wiley, Rein & Fielding (Partner)

POTTS, James S.

1900 Pennsylvania Ave. NW
Washington, DC 20068
Tel: (202)872-2000

Employers
Potomac Electric Power Co. (V. President, Environmental)

POTTS, Ramsay D.

2300 N St. NW
Washington, DC 20037-1128
Tel: (202)663-8000
Fax: (202)663-8007
EMail: ramsay.potts@shawpittman.com

Employers
Shaw Pittman (Senior Counsel)

POULAKIDAS, Jennifer

1523 New Hampshire Ave. NW
Washington, DC 20036
Tel: (202)588-0002
Fax: (202)785-2669

Employers
University of California, Office of Federal Government Relations (Legislative Director)

POULARD, Othello

1000 Wisconsin Ave. NW
Washington, DC 20007
Tel: (202)342-0519
Fax: (202)342-1132
EMail: poulardo@commchange.org

Employers
Center for Community Change (Director, Public Housing Initiative)

POULIN, Cmdr. Steven

400 Seventh St. SW
Suite 10402
Washington, DC 20590
EMail: spoulin@uscg.mil
Tel: (202)366-0009
Fax: (202)366-7124

Employers
Department of Transportation - United States Coast Guard (Chief, Legislative Liaison Staff)

POULOS, Anthi

1220 16th St. NW
Suite 400
Washington, DC 20036
Tel: (202)955-1052
Fax: (202)955-5562
Counsel to Sen. Judd Gregg (R-NH), 1997-98. Counsel to Sen. Hank Brown (R-CO), 1996-97. Legislative Director to Rep. Scott McInnis (R-CO), 1992-94. Assistant to the Director of Legislation to Sen. John Glenn (D-OH), 1975-81.

Employers
The Committee on the Parthenon (President)

POULOS, Bill N.

1331 Pennsylvania Ave. NW
Suite 1300 North
Washington, DC 20004
EMail: bill.poulos@eds.com
Tel: (202)637-6700
Fax: (202)637-6759
Registered: LDA

Employers
EDS Corp. (Director, Electronic Commerce Policy)

POVOLO, Cayetano

1211 Connecticut Ave. NW
Suite 202
Washington, DC 20036
Tel: (202)466-5944
Fax: (202)466-5946

Employers
Inter-American Bar Ass'n (President)

POWAR, Sherri

1000 Connecticut Ave. NW
Suite 302
Washington, DC 20036
EMail: sherrip@sda-inc.com
Tel: (202)835-0740
Fax: (202)775-8526
Registered: LDA

Employers
Smith Dawson & Andrews, Inc.

Clients Represented

On Behalf of Smith Dawson & Andrews, Inc.
Avecia, Inc.
Children's Hospital and Medical Center
Eugene, Oregon, City of
Georgia, State of
Haarmann & Reimer Corp.
Lane Transit District
Lane, Oregon, County of
Nat'l Ass'n of Foreign Trade Zones
NeoPharm, Inc.
Springfield, Oregon, City of
Springfield, Oregon, School District #19
Wound Ostomy Continence Nurses

POWELL, Anne

440 First St. NW
Eighth Floor
Washington, DC 20001
EMail: apowell@naco.org
Tel: (202)942-4245
Fax: (202)393-2630

Employers
Nat'l Ass'n of Counties (Database Manager)
Nat'l Ass'n of County Information Technology Administrators

POWELL, Aquila

1301 Pennsylvania Ave. NW
Suite 404
Washington, DC 20004-1727
Tel: (202)783-0911
Fax: (202)783-3524

Employers
Chicago, Illinois, Washington Office of the City of (Associate Director)

POWELL, Janet L.

801 Pennsylvania Ave. NW
Suite 800
Washington, DC 20004
EMail: jpowell@bdbc.com
Tel: (202)508-3400
Fax: (202)508-3402
Registered: LDA
Staff, Transportation Subcommittee, House Committee on Appropriations, 1991-95.

Employers
Baker, Donelson, Bearman & Caldwell, P.C. (Senior Public Policy Advisor)

Clients Represented

On Behalf of Baker, Donelson, Bearman & Caldwell, P.C.
Alameda Corridor-East Construction Authority
BAE Systems Controls
Bombardier, Inc.
Briartek, Inc.
Bridgestone/Firestone, Inc.
Foothill Transit
Indianapolis Rail Project
Pennsylvania Turnpike Commission
Prince William County, Virginia

POWELL, Jody

700 13th St. NW
Suite 1000
Washington, DC 20005
Tel: (202)347-6633
Fax: (202)347-8713
Registered: LDA, FARA
Former Press Secretary to President Jimmy Carter.

Employers
Powell Tate (Chairman and Chief Exec. Officer)

Clients Represented

On Behalf of Powell Tate
Delta Air Lines
Saudi Arabia, Royal Embassy of

POWELL, Lee

1444 I St. NW
Suite 700
Washington, DC 20005-2210
EMail: lpowell@bostromdc.com
Tel: (202)216-9623
Fax: (202)216-9646

Employers
Bostrom Corp. (Operations Manager)

POWELL, Linda L.

1500 Pennsylvania Ave. NW
Room 3028MT
Washington, DC 20220
Tel: (202)622-0535
Fax: (202)622-0534

Employers
Department of Treasury (Administrative Officer, Office of Legislative Affairs)

POWELL, Paul L.

1801 K St. NW
Suite 901-L
Washington, DC 20006
EMail: Paul_Powell@bm.com
Tel: (202)530-0500
Fax: (202)530-4800
Registered: LDA
Administrative Assistant to Rep. Jack Kingston (R-GA), 1993-94. Director, Congressional Affairs, International Trade Administration and Bureau of the Census, Department of Commerce, 1989-93. Senate Liaison, Office of the Secretary, Department of the Interior, 1981-85. Legislative Director to Rep. Tom Hagedorn (R-MN), 1979. Legislative Assistant to Rep. Bill Young (R-FL), 1978. Legislative Assistant to Rep. Bo Ginn (D-GA), 1973-75. Served in the U.S. Navy, 1969-72.

Employers
BKSH & Associates (Director)

POWELL, Richard

1133 Connecticut Ave. NW
Fifth Floor
Washington, DC 20036
Tel: (202)457-1110
Fax: (202)457-1130

Employers
Quinn Gillespie & Associates (Managing Director)

POWER, Ms. Bevin

815 16th St. NW
Suite 600
Washington, DC 20006
EMail: bevin@bctd.org
Tel: (202)347-1461
Fax: (202)756-4607
Registered: LDA

Employers
AFL-CIO - Building and Construction Trades Department (Legislative Representative)

POWER, John "Jay"

815 16th St. NW
Washington, DC 20006
Tel: (202)637-5084
Fax: (202)637-5058
Registered: LDA

Employers
AFL-CIO (American Federation of Labor and Congress of Industrial Organizations) (Legislative Representative)

POWER, Patricia A.

1615 L St. NW
Suite 650
Washington, DC 20036
EMail: patricia_power@jeffersongr.com
Tel: (202)626-8231
Fax: (202)626-8774
Registered: LDA
Former Legislative Assistant to Senator John Heinz (R-PA), 1987-89. Environmental Protection Agency, 1983-86.

Employers
Jefferson Government Relations, L.L.C. (V. President)

Clients Represented

On Behalf of Jefferson Government Relations, L.L.C.
Seminole Tribe of Indians of Florida
Vinyl Institute
Volusia, Florida, County of

POWER, Thomas W.

2300 Clarendon Blvd.
Suite 1107
Arlington, VA 22201
Tel: (703)841-1330
Fax: (703)841-1822

Employers
Power & Power (Partner)

POWER, Tracy

2300 Clarendon Blvd.
Suite 1107
Arlington, VA 22201
Tel: (703)841-1330
Fax: (703)841-1822

Employers
Power & Power (Partner)

POWERS, Bill

11250 Waples Mill Rd.
Fairfax, VA 22030-7400
Tel: (703)267-1000
Fax: (703)267-3907

Employers
Nat'l Rifle Ass'n Institute for Legislative Action (Director, Public Relations and Communications)

POWERS, Bob

815 16th St. NW
Suite 600
Washington, DC 20006
EMail: powers@bctd.org
Tel: (202)347-1461
Fax: (202)756-4607
Registered: LDA

Employers
AFL-CIO - Building and Construction Trades Department (Legislative and Political Director)

POWERS, Brian A.

4748 Wisconsin Ave. NW
Washington, DC 20016
Tel: (202)362-0041

Employers
O'Donoghue & O'Donoghue

POWERS, Charles H.

1909 K St. NW
Fourth Floor
Washington, DC 20006
Tel: (202)973-5800
Fax: (202)973-5858
Former Deputy Assistant Secretary, Department of Transportation. Former Republican Press Secretary, Senate Finance Committee. Former Deputy Assistant Secretary, Department of the Treasury.

Employers
Porter/Novelli (Senior V. President)

Clients Represented

On Behalf of Porter/Novelli
Federation of Electric Power Cos. of Japan
Japan Automobile Manufacturers Ass'n

POWERS, Craig

600 Pennsylvania Ave. SE
Fifth Floor
Washington, DC 20003
Tel: (202)544-0200
Fax: (202)546-7142

Employers
Amnesty Internat'l U.S.A. (Acting Grassroots Advocacy Director)

POWERS, Galen D.

1875 I St. NW
12th Floor
Washington, DC 20006
Tel: (202)466-6550
Fax: (202)785-1756
Assistant General Counsel for Health Care Financing, Department of Health, Education and Welfare, 1977-79.

Employers
Powers Pyles Sutter & Verville, PC (President)

POWERS, Michelle R.

200 Daingerfield Rd.
Suite 100
Alexandria, VA 22314
EMail: mpowers@tarnepowerspr.com
Tel: (703)684-8352
Fax: (703)684-5812

Employers
Tarne Powers & Associates (V. President)

Clients Represented
On Behalf of Tarne Powers & Associates
Da Vinci's Notebook
Physicians Ad hoc Coalition for Truth (PHACT)
Susan B. Anthony List

POWERS, Pamela

1300 I St. NW
Suite 400 West
Washington, DC 20005
Tel: (202)515-2440
Fax: (202)336-7920

Employers
Verizon Communications (Exec. Director, Political Operations)

POWERS, Tara

805 15th St. NW
Suite 500
Washington, DC 20005
EMail: cifa@chambersinc.com
Tel: (202)371-9770
Fax: (202)371-6601

Employers
Chambers Associates Inc. (Management Associate)

Clients Represented
On Behalf of Chambers Associates Inc.
Council of Infrastructure Financing Authorities

POWERS, Thomas G.

2008 Rockingham St.
McLean, VA 22101
Tel: (703)532-2163
Registered: LDA

Employers
Self-employed as an independent consultant.

Clients Represented
As an independent consultant
Ass'n of Small Business Development Centers
Nat'l Ass'n of Government Guaranteed Lenders

POWERS, Timothy

1001 G St. NW
Suite 900 E
Washington, DC 20001-4545
EMail: powers@podesta.com
Tel: (202)393-1010
Fax: (202)393-5510
Registered: LDA
Former Deputy Director for Legislative Affairs, Republican National Committee.

Employers
Podesta/Mattoon (Principal)

Clients Represented
On Behalf of Podesta/Mattoon
Ass'n for Local Telecommunications Services
California Poultry Industry Federation
E-LOAN, Inc.
Horsehead Industries, Inc.
Interactive Gaming Council
Mount Sinai/NYU Health
Nat'l Environmental Strategies
Pillowtex Corp.
Recording Industry Ass'n of America
Teligent, Inc.

PRAKASH, Ambari

701 Pennsylvania Ave. NW
Suite 800
Washington, DC 20004
EMail: aprakash@thelenreid.com
Tel: (202)508-4021
Fax: (202)508-4321
Registered: LDA

Employers
Thelen Reid & Priest LLP (Associate)

Clients Represented
On Behalf of Thelen Reid & Priest LLP
Cincinnati Stock Exchange

PRATS, Lisa

5301 Shawnee Rd.
Alexandria, VA 22312
Tel: (703)354-8851
Fax: (703)354-8106

Employers
APICS - The Educational Soc. for Resource Management (Director, Communications)

PRATT, Eric M.

8001 Forbes Pl.
Suite 102
Springfield, VA 22151
Tel: (703)321-8585
Fax: (703)321-8408
Registered: LDA

Employers
Gun Owners of America (Director, Communications)

PRATT, Lawrence D.

8001 Forbes Pl.
Suite 102
Springfield, VA 22151
Tel: (703)321-8585
Fax: (703)321-8408
Registered: LDA

Employers
Gun Owners of America (Exec. Director)

PRATT, Megan

1620 L St. NW
Suite 620
Washington, DC 20036
Tel: (202)429-3971
Fax: (202)429-3976

Employers
Council for Chemical Research, Inc. (Public Affairs Representative)

PRATT, Stuart K.

1090 Vermont Ave. NW
Suite 200
Washington, DC 20005-4905
Tel: (202)371-0910
Fax: (202)371-0134
Registered: LDA

Employers
Associated Credit Bureaus, Inc. (V. President, Government Relations)

PRAWDZIK, Chris

1611 N. Kent St.
Suite 901
Arlington, VA 22209
Tel: (703)351-4969
Fax: (703)351-0090

Employers
Alexis de Tocqueville Institution (V. President, Special Projects)

PREE, Curtis

2301 M St. NW
Washington, DC 20037-1484
EMail: cpree@APPAnet.org
Tel: (202)467-2928
Fax: (202)467-2910
Registered: LDA

Employers
American Public Power Ass'n (Government Relations Representative)

PREEDE, Kenneth M.

5100 Wisconsin Ave. NW
Suite 307
Washington, DC 20016
Tel: (202)237-0900
Registered: LDA

Employers
American Seniors Housing Ass'n (Director, Research and Policy)

PREISS, Jeremy

1401 I St. NW
Suite 600
Washington, DC 20005
Tel: (202)336-7400
Fax: (202)336-7515

Employers
United Technologies Corp. (Chief International Trade Counsel)

PRENDA, Brian J.

401 Ninth St. NW
Suite 1100
Washington, DC 20004
EMail: bjprenda@duke-energy.com
Tel: (202)331-8090
Fax: (202)331-1181

Employers
Duke Energy (Director, Federal Government Affairs)

PRENDERGAST, Jim

1331 Pennsylvania Ave. NW
Sixth Floor
Washington, DC 20004-1790
Tel: (202)637-3014
Fax: (202)637-3182

Employers
Nat'l Ass'n of Manufacturers (National Director, Field Division)

PRENTICE, William

1111 14th St. NW
Suite 1200
Washington, DC 20005-5603
EMail: prenticew@ada.org
Tel: (202)898-2400
Fax: (202)898-2437
Registered: LDA

Employers
American Dental Ass'n (Senior Congressional Lobbyist)

PRESCOTT, Heidi

8121 Georgia Ave.
Suite 301
Silver Spring, MD 20910-4933
EMail: hprescott@fund.org
Tel: (301)585-2591
Fax: (301)585-2595

Employers
The Fund for Animals (National Director)

PRESLEY, Gilda

409 Third St. SW
Suite 210
Washington, DC 20024
Tel: (202)205-3850
Fax: (202)205-6825

Employers
Nat'l Women's Business Council (Administrative Officer)

PRESS, Daniel S.

1050 Thomas Jefferson St. NW
Seventh Floor
Washington, DC 20007
EMail: dsp@vnf.com
Tel: (202)298-1800
Fax: (202)338-2416
Registered: LDA

Employers
Van Ness Feldman, P.C. (Member)

Clients Represented
On Behalf of Van Ness Feldman, P.C.
Blackfeet Tribe of Montana
Cheyenne River Sioux Tribe
Intertribal Monitoring Ass'n on Indian Trust Funds
Three Affiliated Tribes of Fort Berthold Reservation

PRESSLER, Hon. Larry

1666 K St. NW
Suite 500
Washington, DC 20006-2803
Tel: (202)887-1400
Fax: (202)466-2198
Registered: LDA
Member, U.S. Senate (R-SD), 1979-97. Member, U.S. House of Representatives, 1975-79. Staff member, Office of Legal Adviser to the Secretary, Department of State, 1971-74. Former Legislative Aide to Senator Francis Case (R-SD). U.S. Army, 1966-68.

Employers
O'Connor & Hannan, L.L.P. (Partner)

Clients Represented
On Behalf of O'Connor & Hannan, L.L.P.
Celera Genomics
Communication Service for the Deaf
CustomerLinx
Dakota Minnesota and Eastern Railroad
Futurewave General Partners, L.P.
Great Western Cellular Partnership
Lafarge Corp.
Morepen Laboratories, Ltd.
Nat'l Federation for the Blind
Stephens Group, Inc.
Verizon Communications

PRESSNELL, Sissy

1701 Pennsylvania Ave. NW
Suite 960
Washington, DC 20006
EMail: sissy_pressnell@bat.com
Tel: (202)463-6674
Fax: (202)463-7130
Registered: LDA

Employers
Brown and Williamson Tobacco Corp. (Manager, Government Affairs)

PREST, Albert H.

1301 Pennsylvania Ave. NW
Suite 1100
Washington, DC 20004-1707
Tel: (202)626-4000
Fax: (202)626-4149

Employers
Air Transport Ass'n of America (V. President, Operations)

PRESTI, Susan

6309 Beachway Dr.
Falls Church, VA 22044
Tel: (703)998-7121
Fax: (703)998-7123
Registered: LDA

Employers
Public Policy Resources (President)

Clients Represented
On Behalf of Public Policy Resources
Air Courier Conference of America
Nissan North America Inc.

PRESTON, Camille

750 First St. NE
Washington, DC 20002-4242
Tel: (202)336-5500
Fax: (202)336-6069

Employers
American Psychological Ass'n (Policy Fellow)

PRESTON, Tawana

630 I St. NW
Washington, DC 20001-3736
Tel: (202)289-3500
Fax: (202)289-8181

Employers
Nat'l Ass'n of Housing and Redevelopment Officials (Policy Analyst, Housing)

PRESTOWITZ, Jr., Clyde V.

1401 H St. NW
Suite 560
Washington, DC 20005
EMail: presto@econstrat.org
Tel: (202)289-1288
Fax: (202)289-1319

Employers
Economic Strategy Institute (President)

PREWITT, Elizabeth

2011 Pennsylvania Ave. NW
Suite 800
Washington, DC 20006-1808
Tel: (202)261-4540
Fax: (202)835-0443
Registered: LDA
EMail: eprewitt@mail.acponline.org

Employers
American College of Physicians-American Soc. of Internal Medicine (ACP-ASIM) (Director, Governmental Affairs and Public Policy)

PRIBBLE, Robert

2445 M St. NW
Washington, DC 20037-1420
Tel: (202)663-6000
Fax: (202)663-6363
Registered: FARA

Employers
Wilmer, Cutler & Pickering (Legislative Specialist)

PRICE, Alan H.

1776 K St. NW
Washington, DC 20006
Tel: (202)719-7000
Fax: (202)719-7049
Registered: LDA
Law Clerk to Senior Judge Louis Spector, U.S. Claims Court, 1983-84.

Employers
Wiley, Rein & Fielding (Partner)

PRICE, Anne

1220 L St. NW
Washington, DC 20005
Tel: (202)682-8000
Fax: (202)682-8232
Registered: LDA

Employers
American Petroleum Institute

PRICE, Daniel M.

1001 Pennsylvania Ave. NW
Suite 600
Washington, DC 20004
Tel: (202)347-0066
Fax: (202)624-7222
Registered: LDA
EMail: dprice@pgfm.com
Deputy General Counsel, Office of the U.S. Trade Representative, 1989-92. Deputy Agent of the U.S. to the Iran-U.S. Claims Tribunal, 1984-86. Office of the Legal Advisor, Department of State, 1982-84.

Employers
Powell, Goldstein, Frazer & Murphy LLP (Partner)

Clients Represented
On Behalf of Powell, Goldstein, Frazer & Murphy LLP
Austin, Nichols & Co., Inc.
Joint Stock Company Severstal
Nat'l Foreign Trade Council, Inc.
Organization for Internat'l Investment
Pernod Ricard
Shaklee Corp.

PRICE, Gary W.

4222 King St. West
Alexandria, VA 22302-1597
Tel: (703)379-7755
Fax: (703)931-9429

Employers
American Dental Trade Ass'n (President and Chief Exec. Officer)

PRICE, Joseph H.

1050 Connecticut Ave. NW
Washington, DC 20036-5306
Tel: (202)955-8500
Fax: (202)467-0539
EMail: jprice@gdclaw.com
Law Clerk to Justice Hugo L. Black, U.S. Supreme Court, 1967-68.

Employers
Gibson, Dunn & Crutcher LLP (Partner)

PRICE, Mary

1612 K St. NW
Suite 1400
Washington, DC 20006
Tel: (202)822-6700
Fax: (202)822-6704

Employers
Families Against Mandatory Minimums (General Counsel)

PRICE, CAE, Randall C.

11250 Roger Bacon Dr.
Suite Eight
Reston, VA 20190
Tel: (703)437-4377
Fax: (703)435-4390

Employers
Ass'n of Nurses in AIDS Care (Exec. Director)
Drohan Management Group (Account Executive)
Environmental Mutagen Soc. (Exec. Director)
HIV/AIDS Nursing Certification Board (Exec. Director)
Nat'l Organization for Associate Degree Nursing (Exec. Director)

Clients Represented
On Behalf of Drohan Management Group
Ass'n of Nurses in AIDS Care
Ass'n of Occupational Health Professionals in Healthcare
Environmental Mutagen Soc.
HIV/AIDS Nursing Certification Board
Nat'l Organization for Associate Degree Nursing

PRICE, Richard

2000 K St. NW
Suite 801
Washington, DC 20006
EMail: richard@akerpartners.com
Tel: (202)789-2424
Fax: (202)789-1818
Special Assistant to Rep. Charles Schumer, 1996-97.

Employers
The Aker Partners Inc. (Senior Associate)

PRICE, Richard M.

401 Ninth St. NW
Suite 900
Washington, DC 20004
Tel: (202)585-8000
Fax: (202)585-8080
Registered: LDA
EMail: rprice@nixonpeabody.com
Trial Attorney, Department of Housing and Urban Development, 1988-91.

Employers
Nixon Peabody LLP (Partner)

Clients Represented
On Behalf of Nixon Peabody LLP
Continental Wingate Co., Inc.
Highland Mortgage Co.
Mellon Mortgage Co.
MetroPlains Development, Inc.
Project Funding Corp. (PFC)
Reilly Mortgage Group Inc.
TRI Capital Corp.
WMF/Huntoon, Paige Associates Ltd.

PRICE, Thomas J.

1111 19th St. NW
Suite 403
Washington, DC 20036
EMail: tprice@aaes.org
Tel: (202)296-2237
Fax: (202)296-1151

Employers
American Ass'n of Engineering Societies (Exec. Director)

PRIDDY, Ronald N.

910 17th St. NW
Washington, DC 20006
Tel: (202)833-8200
Fax: (202)659-9479

Employers
Nat'l Air Carrier Ass'n (President)

PRIDE, Ann L.

1776 I St. NW
Suite 275
Washington, DC 20006
Tel: (202)530-7300
Fax: (202)530-7350
Registered: LDA
EMail: apride@entergy.com

Employers
Entergy Services, Inc. (Director, Public Affairs Policy and Strategy)

PRIESTAS, Lauren

2000 P St. NW
Suite 310
Washington, DC 20036
Tel: (202)296-4548
Fax: (202)296-4609
Registered: LDA
EMail: ccn@us.net

Employers
Carrying Capacity Network, Inc. (Associate Director)

PRIESTER, Joseph

900 19th St. NW
Suite 700
Washington, DC 20006
EMail: jpriester@lucent.com
Tel: (202)530-7015
Fax: (202)530-7007
Assistant to Sen. Lloyd Bentsen (D-TX), 1973-77.

Employers
Lucent Technologies (Exec. Assistant, Corporate V. President and PAC Treasurer)

PRILLAMAN, Hunter L.

200 N. Glebe Rd.
Suite 800
Arlington, VA 22203
Tel: (703)243-5463
Fax: (703)243-5489
Registered: LDA
EMail: natlime@lime.org

Employers
Nat'l Lime Ass'n (Director, Government Affairs)

PRIMOSCH, Robert

2300 N St. NW
Suite 700
Washington, DC 20037-1128
EMail: rprimosch@wbklaw.com
Tel: (202)783-4141
Fax: (202)783-5851

Employers
Wilkinson, Barker and Knauer, LLP (Partner)

Clients Represented
On Behalf of Wilkinson, Barker and Knauer, LLP
Wireless Communications Ass'n

PRIMUS, Wendell E.

820 First St. NE
Suite 510
Washington, DC 20002
EMail: primus@center.cbpp.org
Tel: (202)408-1080
Fax: (202)408-1056
Served as Deputy Assistant Secretary for Planning and Evaluation, Department of Health and Human Services, during the Clinton administration.

Employers
Center on Budget and Policy Priorities (Director, Income Security)

PRINCE, H. G.

1201 Connecticut Ave. NW
Suite 800
Washington, DC 20036
EMail: hgprince@aals.org
Tel: (202)296-8851
Fax: (202)296-8869

Employers
Ass'n of American Law Schools (Deputy Director)

PRINCIPATO, Gregory

1900 K St. NW
Washington, DC 20006-1109
Tel: (202)955-1663
Fax: (202)778-2201
Registered: LDA
EMail: gprincipato@hunton.com
Legislative Assistant to Sen. Joseph R. Biden, Jr. (D-DE) 1982-86. Legislative Staff Member, to former Sen. J. Bennett Johnston (D-LA), 1979-81.

Employers
Coalition for a Global Standard on Aviation Noise (Contact)
Hunton & Williams (Trade and Transportation Specialist)

Clients Represented
On Behalf of Hunton & Williams
Coalition for a Global Standard on Aviation Noise

PRINCIPI, Frank

444 N. Capitol St. NW
Suite 267
Washington, DC 20001-1512
Tel: (202)624-5300
Fax: (202)624-5313
Former Staff Member, House Committee on Energy and Commerce

Employers
Nat'l Governors' Ass'n (Legislative Associate)

PRIOLEAU, Florence W.

2550 M St. NW
Washington, DC 20037-1350
Tel: (202)457-6000
Fax: (202)457-6315
Registered: LDA
EMail: fprioleau@pattonboggs.com
Assistant Director, Domestic Policy Staff, Executive Office of the President, The White House, 1979-81. Professional Staff Member, House Committee on Ways and Means, 1976-79.

Employers
Patton Boggs, LLP (Partner)

Clients Represented
On Behalf of Patton Boggs, LLP
AutoNation, Inc.
Cincinnati, Ohio, City of
The Clorox Co.
drugstore.com
Houston, Texas, City of
Nat'l Stroke Ass'n
Sierra Military Health Services, Inc.

PRITCHETT, John M.

324 Fourth St. NE
Washington, DC 20002
Tel: (202)546-7584
Fax: (202)546-9289

Employers
Nat'l Roofing Contractors Ass'n (Manager, Public Affairs)

PROBST, Sydney

1832 Belmont Rd. NW
Washington, DC 20009
Tel: (202)986-6666
Fax: (202)986-6608
Registered: LDA
EMail: sydneyp446@aol.com

Employers
Self-employed as an independent consultant.

Clients Represented
As an independent consultant
Arkansas Blue Cross and Blue Shield
Kansas City Southern Industries
Stilwell Financial Inc.

PROCTOR, Jr., Stuart E.

1225 New York Ave. NW
Suite 400
Washington, DC 20005
Tel: (202)898-0100
Fax: (202)898-0203
Registered: LDA

Employers
Nat'l Turkey Federation (President and Chief Exec. Officer)

PROFIT, Michelle

805 15th St. NW
Suite 300
Washington, DC 20005-2207
Tel: (202)682-4200
Fax: (202)682-9054
Registered: LDA

Employers
Credit Union Nat'l Ass'n, Inc.

PROKOP, John A.

1444 I Street NW
Suite 400
Washington, DC 20005
EMail: jprokop@ilta.org
Tel: (202)659-2301
Fax: (202)466-4166

Employers
Independent Liquid Terminals Ass'n (President)

PROKOP, Susan

801 18th St. NW
Washington, DC 20006
Tel: (202)872-1300
Fax: (202)785-4452
Registered: LDA

Employers
Paralyzed Veterans of America (Associate Advocacy Director)

PROPP, Elizabeth

1301 Connecticut Ave. NW
Suite 300
Washington, DC 20036
EMail: epropp@hfma.org
Tel: (202)296-2920
Fax: (202)223-9771

Employers
Healthcare Financial Management Ass'n (V. President)

PROSSER, Norville

1033 N. Fairfax St.
Suite 200
Alexandria, VA 22314
EMail: npresser@asafishing.org
Tel: (703)519-9691
Fax: (703)519-1872

Employers
American Sportfishing Ass'n (V. President for Government Affairs)

PROTO, Neil T.

901 15th St. NW
Suite 700
Washington, DC 20005-2301
Tel: (202)371-6000
Fax: (202)371-6279
Registered: LDA
EMail: ntproto@verner.com
Special Assistant Attorney General for Environmental Matters, Connecticut (1988-89) and Attorney, Environment and Natural Resources Division (1972-79), Department of Justice.

Employers
Verner, Liipfert, Bernhard, McPherson and Hand, Chartered (Member of Firm)

Clients Represented
On Behalf of Verner, Liipfert, Bernhard, McPherson and Hand, Chartered
Bombardier Transportation/Bombardier Transit Corporation
Equal Justice Coalition
Heritage Development
Merle Hay Mall Limited Partners
New Haven, Connecticut, City of

PROUDFIT, Elizabeth M.

1666 K St. NW
Suite 800
Washington, DC 20006
Tel: (202)481-7000
Fax: (202)862-7098
Registered: LDA

Employers
Arthur Andersen LLP (Congressional Specialist)

PROUT, Gerald R.

1667 K St. NW
Suite 460
Washington, DC 20006
Tel: (202)956-5209
Fax: (202)956-5235
Registered: LDA
EMail: jerry_prout@fmc.com

Employers
FMC Corp. (V. President, Government Affairs)

PROWITT, Nancy Gibson

2111 Wilson Blvd.
Eighth Floor
Arlington, VA 22201-3058
Tel: (703)841-0626
Fax: (703)243-2874
Registered: LDA
EMail: prowitt@alcalde-fay.com
Former Legislative Assistant, House Appropriations Committee

Employers
Alcalde & Fay (Partner)

Clients Represented
On Behalf of Alcalde & Fay
Fairfax County Water Authority
Internat'l Council of Cruise Lines
Miami Heat
Palm Springs, California, City of
Virginia Beach, Virginia, City of

PROWITT, Peter D.

1299 Pennsylvania Ave. NW
Suite 1100 West
Washington, DC 20004-2407
Tel: (202)637-4000
Fax: (202)637-4400
Registered: LDA

Employers
General Electric Co. (Manager, Federal Government Relations)

PRUITT, James C.

1050 17th St. NW
Suite 500
Washington, DC 20036
Tel: (202)331-1427
Fax: (202)785-4702
Registered: LDA

Employers
Texaco Group Inc. (V. President, Government Relations)

PRUITT, Jana Lee

805 15th St. NW
Suite 700
Washington, DC 20005
EMail: jlpruitt@bakerd.com
Tel: (202)312-7440
Fax: (202)312-7460

Employers
Baker & Daniels (Partner)

PRUITT, Penny

1909 K Street NW
Suite 810
Washington, DC 20006
Tel: (202)466-5754
Fax: (202)872-0736
Registered: LDA

Employers
ACE INA (Federal Affairs Representative)

PRYCE, William T.

1310 G St. NW
Suite 690
Washington, DC 20005-3000
Tel: (202)639-0724
Fax: (202)639-0794
Registered: LDA
EMail: wpryce@as-coa.org

Employers
Council of the Americas (V. President, Washington Operations)
Mexico-U.S. Business Committee, U.S. Council (Exec. V. President)

PRYGA, Ellen A.

325 Seventh St. NW
Washington, DC 20004
Tel: (202)638-1100
Fax: (202)626-4626
Registered: LDA

Employers
American Hospital Ass'n (Director, Public Policy Development, Analysis, and Regulatory Affairs)

PRYOR, Jr., David

300 Maryland Ave. NE
Washington, DC 20002
Tel: (202)546-1631
Fax: (202)546-3309

Employers
FedEx Corp. (Senior Federal Affairs Representative)

PRYOR, Michael H.

701 Pennsylvania Ave. NW
Suite 900
Washington, DC 20004-2608
Tel: (202)434-7300
Fax: (202)434-7400
Former Deputy Chief of the Policy and Program Planning Division, Common Carrier Bureau, Federal Communications Commission.

Employers
Mintz, Levin, Cohn, Ferris, Glovsky and Popeo, P.C. (Partner)

PRYSOCK, Mark

3913 Old Lee Hwy.
Suite 33B
Fairfax, VA 22030
Tel: (703)359-0826
Fax: (703)359-2576
Registered: LDA
EMail: mprysock@pdca.org

Employers
Painting and Decorating Contractors of America (Director, Government Affairs; PAC Treasurer)

PUESCHEL, Jamie

1111 16th St. NW
Washington, DC 20036-4873
Tel: (202)785-7793
Fax: (202)466-7618
Registered: LDA
EMail: pueschelj@aauw.org

Employers
American Ass'n of University Women (Manager, Government Relations)

PUGH, Kristen

412 First St. SE
Suite 12
Washington, DC 20003
Tel: (202)484-8400
Fax: (202)484-8408
Registered: LDA

Employers
American Ass'n of Nurse Anesthetists (Director, Federal Government Affairs)

PUGH, Martha G.

600 13th St. NW
Washington, DC 20005-3096
Tel: (202)756-8391
Fax: (202)756-8087
Registered: LDA
EMail: mpugh@mwe.com

Employers
McDermott, Will and Emery (Partner)

PUGLIARESI, Lucian

3000 K St. NW
Suite 105
Washington, DC 20007-5116
Tel: (202)424-7820
Fax: (202)424-7763
EMail: lpiconsulting@mindspring.com
Nat'l Security Council in Reagan Administration, 1983-87; State Department Policy Planning Staff, 1979-83.

Employers
Moscow Internat'l Petroleum Club (Director, Washington Representative Office)

PUGLISI, Matthew L.

2010 Massachusetts Ave. NW
Washington, DC 20036
Tel: (202)416-1418
Fax: (202)416-6134
Registered: LDA

Employers
Optical Soc. of America (Government Relations Manager)

PULIZZI, Phil

819 Seventh St. NW
Washington, DC 20001
Tel: (202)833-8940
Fax: (202)833-8945
Registered: LDA

Employers
EOP Group, Inc.

Clients Represented

On Behalf of EOP Group, Inc.
Continental Grain Co.
FMC Corp.
Internat'l Food Additives Council

PULLEN, Rachel C.

3401 Columbia Pike
Suite 400
Arlington, VA 22204
Tel: (703)920-2720
Fax: (703)920-2889

Employers
Ass'n for Unmanned Vehicle Systems International (Manager, Marketing)

PULLIAM, Gary P.

1000 Wilson Blvd.
Suite 2600
Arlington, VA 22209-3988
Tel: (703)812-0612
Fax: (703)812-9415
EMail: gary.p.pulliam@aero.org

Employers
The Aerospace Corp. (General Manager, Corporate Business Division)

PUNKE, Michael W.

1909 K St. NW
Washington, DC 20006
Tel: (202)263-3000
Fax: (202)263-3300

Employers
Mayer, Brown & Platt (Partner)

Clients Represented

On Behalf of Mayer, Brown & Platt
Wheat Export Trade Education Committee

PUPKIN, Barry A.

1201 Pennsylvania Ave. NW
P.O. Box 407
Washington, DC 20044-0407
Tel: (202)626-6600
Fax: (202)626-6780
EMail: bpupkin@ssd.com
Trial Attorney, Federal Trade Commission, 1975-76.

Employers
Squire, Sanders & Dempsey L.L.P. (Partner)

PURCELL, F. Eugene

700 13th St. NW
Suite 400
Washington, DC 20005
Tel: (202)347-0773
Fax: (202)347-0785
Registered: LDA
EMail: epurcell@cassidy.com

Employers
Cassidy & Associates, Inc. (Senior Consultant)

PURCELL, Frank J.

412 First St. SE
Suite 12
Washington, DC 20003
Tel: (202)484-8400
Fax: (202)484-8408
Registered: LDA
Legislative Director to Rep. Randy Cunningham (R-CA), 1995-2000. Chief of Staff to Rep. Jim Ross Lightfoot (R-IA), 1994-95. Press Secretary to Rep. Randy Cunningham (R-CA), 1991-94. Press Secretary to Rep. Harold Rogers (R-KY), 1989-91. Press intern to Rep. Jack Buechner (R-MO), 1988.

Employers
American Ass'n of Nurse Anesthetists (Director, Federal Government Affairs)

PURCELL, Theresa

1000 Wilson Blvd.
Arlington, VA 22209
Tel: (703)351-8317
Fax: (703)351-8567
Registered: LDA

Employers
System Planning Corp.

Clients Represented

On Behalf of System Planning Corp.
Hebrew University of Jerusalem

PURSER, Craig

1100 S. Washington St.
First Floor
Alexandria, VA 22314-4494
Tel: (703)683-4300
Fax: (703)683-8965
Registered: LDA
EMail: cpurser@nbwa.org

Employers
Nat'l Beer Wholesalers Ass'n (V. President)

PURTILL, Patrick

1930 17th St. NW
Washington, DC 20009-6207
Tel: (202)328-1200
Fax: (202)332-0935

Employers
Nat'l Council for Adoption (President and Chief Exec. Officer)

PUSEY, Leigh Ann

1130 Connecticut Ave. NW
Suite 1000
Washington, DC 20036
Tel: (202)828-7100
Fax: (202)293-1219
Registered: LDA
EMail: Lpusey@aiadc.org

Employers
American Insurance Ass'n (Senior V. President, Federal Affairs)

PUTALA, Chris

1250 Connecticut Ave. NW
Suite 800
Washington, DC 20036
Tel: (202)785-0081
Fax: (202)776-0540
Registered: LDA

Employers
Cellular Telecommunications and Internet Ass'n (V. President, Congressional Affairs)

PUTNAM, Ronald A.

219 N. Washington St.
Alexandria, VA 22314
Tel: (703)836-7990
Fax: (703)836-9739
Registered: LDA

Employers
Peduzzi Associates, Ltd. (Associate)

Clients Represented

On Behalf of Peduzzi Associates, Ltd.
DRS - EOSG
Integrated Medical Systems
Lord Corp.
Marconi Flight Systems, Inc.
Skyhook Technologies, Inc.

PUVAK, Ken

1015 15th St. NW
Suite 802
Washington, DC 20005
Tel: (202)347-7474
Fax: (202)898-0068
EMail: kpuvak@acec.org

Employers
American Consulting Engineers Council (Director, International Department)

PUZO, Daniel

1875 I St. NW
Suite 900
Washington, DC 20005
Tel: (202)371-0200
Fax: (202)371-2858

Employers
Edelman Public Relations Worldwide (Senior V. President)

Clients Represented

On Behalf of Edelman Public Relations Worldwide
Foodbrands America, Inc.
Michel Richard's Citronell
Nat'l Nutritional Foods Ass'n

PYLAK, Artur

1010 Wisconsin Ave. NW
Ninth Floor
Washington, DC 20007
Tel: (202)337-9400
Fax: (202)337-4508
EMail: apylak@gmabrands.com

Employers
Grocery Manufacturers of America (Assistant, State Affairs and Internat'l Trade)

PYLE, Robert N.

1223 Potomac St. NW
Washington, DC 20007-0231
Tel: (202)333-8190
Fax: (202)337-3809
Registered: LDA
EMail: rpyle@independentbaker.org

Employers
Independent Bakers Ass'n (President)
Robert N. Pyle & Associates (Chairman)

Clients Represented

On Behalf of Robert N. Pyle & Associates
Bulgarian-American Business Center
Elkem Metals Co.
Independent Bakers Ass'n
Internat'l Dairy-Deli-Bakery Ass'n
McKee Foods Corp.
Orbex Resources
Ort's, Inc.
Stratcor
Strategic Minerals Corp.
Welch's Foods, Inc.

PYLES, James C.

1875 I St. NW
12th Floor
Washington, DC 20006
Tel: (202)466-6550
Fax: (202)785-1756
Registered: LDA

Litigation Attorney, Office of the General Counsel, Department of Health and Human Services, 1972-79.

Employers
Powers Pyles Sutter & Verville, PC (Principal)

Clients Represented
On Behalf of Powers Pyles Sutter & Verville, PC
American Ass'n for Homecare
American Psychoanalytic Ass'n
Coalition for Patient Rights

PYLPEC, Nestor N.

1301 Pennsylvania Ave. NW
Suite 1100
Washington, DC 20004-1707
Tel: (202)626-4000
Fax: (202)626-4264

Employers
Air Transport Ass'n of America (V. President, Industry Services)

QUACKENBUSH, Linda

3114 Circle Hill Rd.
Alexandria, VA 22305-1606
Tel: (703)548-1234
Fax: (703)548-6216

Employers
Internat'l Trade Council (V. President, Administration)

QUAINTON, Anthony C. E.

1424 16th St. NW
Suite 700
Washington, DC 20036
EMail: aquainton@npal.org
Tel: (202)265-7685
Fax: (202)797-5516

Employers
Nat'l Policy Ass'n (President and Chief Exec. Officer)

QUALE, John C.

1440 New York Ave. NW
Washington, DC 20005
Tel: (202)371-7000
Fax: (202)393-5760

Employers
Skadden, Arps, Slate, Meagher & Flom LLP (Partner)

Clients Represented
On Behalf of Skadden, Arps, Slate, Meagher & Flom LLP
Silver King Communications
TCI

QUALIANA, Mary K.

1200 New Hampshire Ave. NW
Suite 800
Washington, DC 20036-6802
EMail: mqualiana@dlalaw.com
Tel: (202)776-2000
Fax: (202)776-2222

Former Trial Attorney at Department of Transportation.

Employers
Dow, Lohnes & Albertson, PLLC (Member)

QUAM, David C.

1001 Pennsylvania Ave. NW
Suite 600
Washington, DC 20004
EMail: dquam@pgfm.com
Tel: (202)624-7228
Fax: (202)624-7222
Registered: LDA

Counsel, Subcommittee on the Constitution, Federalism and Property Rights, Senate Judiciary Committee, 1994-96.

Employers
Powell, Goldstein, Frazer & Murphy LLP (Associate)

Clients Represented
On Behalf of Powell, Goldstein, Frazer & Murphy LLP
Concurrent Technologies Corp.
EUTELSAT
Qualcomm Inc.
Walker Digital Corp.

QUARLES, Lynn T.

1400 Independence Ave. SW
Stop 3407, Room 1147, South Bldg.
Washington, DC 20250
EMail: lynn.t.quarles@usda.gov
Tel: (202)720-2511
Fax: (202)720-3982

Employers
Department of Agriculture - Animal and Plant Health Inspection Service (Deputy Director, Legislative and Public Affairs)

QUARLES, Steven P.

1001 Pennsylvania Ave. NW
Suite 1100
Washington, DC 20004-2595
EMail: squarles@cromor.com
Tel: (202)624-2665
Fax: (202)628-5116
Registered: LDA

Deputy Under Secretary (1979-81) and Director, Office of Coal Leasing, Planning and Coordination (1978-79), Department of the Interior. Counsel, Subcommittee on Public Lands and Resources, Senate Committee on Energy and Natural Resources, 1971-78.

Employers
Crowell & Moring LLP (Partner)

Clients Represented
On Behalf of Crowell & Moring LLP
Agricultural Air Group
American Forest & Paper Ass'n
The American Land Conservancy
Burlington Resources Oil & Gas Co.
Cook Inlet Region Inc.
Cyprus Amex Minerals Co.
Endangered Species Coordinating Council
Franco-Nevada Mining Corp., Inc.
Georgia-Pacific Corp.
Homestake Mining
Independence Mining Co., Inc.
Intermountain Forest Industry Ass'n
KATY-FM
Nat'l Park Foundation
Nat'l Pork Producers Council
North Miami, Florida, City of
Northwest Forestry Ass'n
Placer Dome U.S. Inc.
Rocking K Development
Del E. Webb Corp.

QUARLES, Susan D.

918 F St. NW
Washington, DC 20004-1400
Tel: (202)216-2400
Fax: (202)371-9449

Employers
American Immigration Lawyers Ass'n (Deputy Director for Finance and Administration)

QUARLES, W. Kam

50 F St. NW
Suite 1100
Washington, DC 20001
Tel: (202)879-0256
Fax: (202)628-8233

Employers
Sunkist Growers, Inc. (Assistant Director)

QUATRINI, Phillip A.

700 13th St. NW
Suite 700
Washington, DC 20005-3960
EMail: paquatrini@bryancave.com
Tel: (202)508-6000
Fax: (202)508-6200

Employers
Bryan Cave LLP (Associate)

QUATT, Charles W.

2233 Wisconsin Ave.
Suite 501
Washington, DC 20007
Tel: (202)363-7782
Fax: (202)338-1000

Employers
Charles W. Quatt Associates, Inc. (Principal)

QUEALY, Patricia A.

1133 21st St. NW
Suite 450
Washington, DC 20036
EMail: patquealy@firsthealth.com
Tel: (202)872-0556
Fax: (202)872-0908
Registered: LDA

Chief Counsel (1985-90) and Deputy Chief Counsel (1982-85), House Budget Committee.

Employers
First Health Group Corp. (V. President, Government Affairs)

QUEEN, Nathan R.

7917 Beechnut Rd.
Capitol Heights, MD 20743
Tel: (301)350-1990

Employers
Internat'l Ass'n of Black Professional Fire Fighters (Nat'l Legislative Liaison)

QUERAL, Alejandro

408 C St. NE
Washington, DC 20002
Tel: (202)547-1141
Fax: (202)547-6009

Employers
Sierra Club (Associate Representative)

QUEVLI, Elizabeth

1155 Connecticut Ave. NW
Suite 1200
Washington, DC 20036
EMail: equevli@dc.bhb.com
Tel: (202)659-5800
Fax: (202)659-1027
Registered: LDA

Employers
Birch, Horton, Bittner & Cherot (Legislative Assistant)

QUIGLEY, David

1333 New Hampshire Ave. NW
Suite 400
Washington, DC 20036
Tel: (202)887-4000
Fax: (202)887-4288
Registered: LDA

Employers
Akin, Gump, Strauss, Hauer & Feld, L.L.P.

Clients Represented
On Behalf of Akin, Gump, Strauss, Hauer & Feld, L.L.P.
Mitsubishi Corp.
San Gabriel Basin Water Quality Authority

QUIGLEY, Elizabeth

3417 Volta Pl. NW
Washington, DC 20007
Tel: (202)337-5220
Fax: (202)337-8314

Employers
Alexander Graham Bell Ass'n for the Deaf (Director, Marketing and Membership)

QUIGLEY, Jr., Joseph J.

1875 I St. NW
Suite 600
Washington, DC 20006
EMail: jquiqley@nareit.com
Tel: (202)739-9400
Fax: (202)739-9401
Registered: LDA

Employers
Nat'l Ass'n of Real Estate Investment Trusts (Director, Government Relations)

QUIGLEY, Thomas J.

1201 Pennsylvania Ave. NW
P.O. Box 407
Washington, DC 20044-0407
EMail: tquigley@ssd.com
Tel: (202)626-6600
Fax: (202)626-6780

Employers
Squire, Sanders & Dempsey L.L.P. (Counsel)

Clients Represented
On Behalf of Squire, Sanders & Dempsey L.L.P.
Belgium, Embassy of the Kingdom of

QUILL, Terry

1667 K St. NW
Suite 700
Washington, DC 20006
EMail: tfquill@duanemorries.com
Tel: (202)776-7800
Fax: (202)776-7801

Employers
Duane, Morris & Heckscher LLP (Partner)

QUILLAN, Mary

1341 G St. NW
Suite 1100
Washington, DC 20005
Tel: (202)393-2260
Fax: (202)393-0712

Employers
Infotech Strategies, Inc.

QUINLAN, Andrew F.

6023 Shaffer Dr.
Alexandria, VA 22310
Tel: (202)285-0244
Registered: LDA

Former Staff Member, Joint Economic Committee.

Employers
Center for Freedom and Prosperity (President and Chief Exec. Officer)
Self-employed as an independent consultant.

Clients Represented

As an independent consultant
Swiss Investors Protection Ass'n

QUINN, Christine D.

1501 Farm Credit Dr.
MS: 4126
McLean, VA 22102-5090
Tel: (703)883-4056
Fax: (703)790-3260

Employers
Farm Credit Administration (Assistant Director of Congressional and Public Affairs)

QUINN, Gail

3211 Fourth St. NE
Washington, DC 20017
Tel: (202)541-3070
Fax: (202)541-3054

Employers
Nat'l Conference of Catholic Bishops, Secretariat for Pro-Life Activities (Exec. Director, Secretariat for Pro-Life Activities)

QUINN, Gloria

555 Twelfth St. NW
Suite 640
Washington, DC 20004
Tel: (202)393-3075
Registered: LDA

Employers
Edison Internat'l

QUINN, Jr., Harold P.

1130 17th St. NW
Washington, DC 20036-4677
Tel: (202)463-2652
Fax: (202)463-3257
Registered: LDA
EMail: hquinn@nma.org

Employers
Nat'l Mining Ass'n (Senior V. President, Legal and Regulatory Affairs and General Counsel)

QUINN, John M. "Jack"

1133 Connecticut Ave. NW
Fifth Floor
Washington, DC 20036
Tel: (202)457-1110
Fax: (202)457-1130
Registered: LDA

Counsel to the President (1995-97) and Chief of Staff to the Vice President (1993-95), Executive Office of the President, The White House.

Employers
Quinn Gillespie & Associates (Principal)

Clients Represented

On Behalf of Quinn Gillespie & Associates
British Columbia Lumber Trade Council
The Chubb Corp.
Instinet
LVMH Moet Hennessy Louis Vuitton S.A.
Metropolitan Life Insurance Co.
Technology Network

QUINN, Katie

1500 Pennsylvania Ave. NW
Room 3021
Washington, DC 20220
Tel: (202)622-0725
Fax: (202)622-0534

Employers
Department of Treasury (Deputy Assistant Secretary (Enforcement))

QUINN, Kenneth P.

1133 Connecticut Ave. NW
Suite 1200
Washington, DC 20036
Tel: (202)775-9800
Fax: (202)833-8491
Registered: LDA

Chief Counsel, Federal Aviation Administration (1991-93) and Counselor to the Secretary (1989-91), Department of Transportation.

Employers
Winthrop, Stimson, Putnam & Roberts (Partner)

Clients Represented

On Behalf of Winthrop, Stimson, Putnam & Roberts
Chicago, Illinois, Department of Law, City of
Sabre Inc.

QUINN, Patrick H.

1225 I St. NW
Suite 810
Washington, DC 20005
Tel: (202)289-9800
Fax: (202)289-3588
Registered: LDA
EMail: pquinn@theaccordgroup.com

Chief of Staff to the Deputy Administrator and Associate Administrator for Congressional Affairs, Environmental Protection Agency, 1986-92.

Employers
The Accord Group (Principal)

Clients Represented

On Behalf of The Accord Group
Energy and Environment Coalition
Innovation Reform Group
Internat'l Paint Inc.
Natural Gas Vehicle Coalition

QUINN, Paul S.

1120 20th St. NW
Suite 800
Washington, DC 20036
Tel: (202)778-6150
Fax: (202)778-6155
Registered: LDA

Employers
Bingham Dana LLP

Clients Represented

On Behalf of Bingham Dana LLP
Fleet Financial Group, Inc.
FleetBoston Financial

QUINN, Richard

1300 Pennsylvania Ave. NW
Room 6.4A
Washington, DC 20229
Tel: (202)927-1760
Fax: (202)927-2152

Employers
Department of Treasury - United States Customs Service (Acting Assistant Commissioner, Congressional Affairs)

QUINN, Robert W.

1120 20th St. NW
Suite 1000
Washington, DC 20036
Tel: (202)457-3851
Fax: (202)457-2571
EMail: rquinn@att.com

Employers
AT&T (Director, Federal Government Affairs)

QUINN, Sara

701 Pennsylvania Ave. NW
Third Floor
Washington, DC 20004
Tel: (202)508-5500
Fax: (202)508-5222

Employers
Geothermal Heat Pump Consortium (Director, Marketing, Public and Governmental Affairs)

QUINN, Thomas H.

1666 K St. NW
Suite 500
Washington, DC 20006-2803
Tel: (202)887-1400
Fax: (202)466-2198
Registered: LDA, FARA

Attorney, Office of the Comptroller of the Currency, Department of the Treasury, 1963-1967.

Employers
O'Connor & Hannan, L.L.P. (Partner)

Clients Represented

On Behalf of O'Connor & Hannan, L.L.P.
Allergan, Inc.
Associated Credit Bureaus, Inc.
Bear, Stearns and Co.
California Debt Limit Allocation Committee
California Tax Credit Allocation Committee
Capital One Financial Corp.
Celera Genomics
Edison Electric Institute
Futurewave General Partners, L.P.
Great Western Cellular Partnership
Healthcare Financing Study Group
Lockheed Martin Corp.
Mortgage Bankers Ass'n of America
Muldoon, Murphy & Faucette, LLP
Nat'l Ass'n of Ticket Brokers
Portland Cellular Partnership
State Street Bank and Trust Co.
Student Loan Funding Corp.
Taipei Economic and Cultural Representative Office in the United States
U.S. Central Credit Union
UBS Warburg
UST Public Affairs, Inc.
VISA U.S.A., Inc.

QUINN, Warren

1250 I St. NW
Suite 500
Washington, DC 20005
Tel: (202)789-2900
Ext: 3009
Fax: (202)789-1893
EMail: wquinn@anla.org

Employers
American Nursery and Landscape Ass'n (Director, Operations)

QUINN, William H.

1101 Connecticut Ave. NW
Suite 500
Washington, DC 20036
Tel: (202)833-9095
Fax: (202)833-0008

Employers
Nat'l Postal Mail Handlers Union (President)

QUINONEZ, Jose

50 F St. NW
Suite 500
Washington, DC 20001
Tel: (301)608-2400
Fax: (301)608-2401
Registered: LDA
EMail: jquinonez@bread.org

Employers
Bread for the World (Policy Analyst)

QUINTER, Neil

600 13th St. NW
Washington, DC 20005-3096
Tel: (202)756-8027
Fax: (202)756-8087
Registered: LDA
EMail: nquinter@mwe.com

Employers
McDermott, Will and Emery (Partner)

Clients Represented

On Behalf of McDermott, Will and Emery
Digital Media Ass'n
Electronic Industries Ass'n of Japan
Hitachi Semiconductors of America
Huntington's Disease Soc. of America
Morgan Stanley Dean Witter & Co.
Nat'l Paint and Coatings Ass'n
Puerto Rico, Commonwealth of
Telecorp PCS Inc.
UBS Warburg

QUIRK, Daniel

1225 I St. NW
Suite 725
Washington, DC 20005
Tel: (202)898-2578
Fax: (202)898-2583
EMail: dquirkf@nasua.org

Employers
Nat'l Ass'n of State Units on Aging (Exec. Director)

QUIRK, Frank

11785 Beltsville Dr.
Calverton, MD 20705
Tel: (301)572-0200
Fax: (301)572-0999

Employers
Macro Internat'l (President)

QUIRK, Jr., Ronald

601 Pennsylvania Ave. NW
11th Floor, North Bldg.
Washington, DC 20004-2601
Tel: (202)756-3300
Fax: (202)756-3333

Employers
Alston & Bird LLP (Senior Associate)

QUIRK, Sherry A.

901 15th St. NW
Suite 700
Washington, DC 20005-2301
Tel: (202)371-6000
Fax: (202)371-6279
Registered: LDA

Attorney/Advisor, Office of Opinions and Review (1983-84) and Law Clerk to Administrative Law Judges (1982-83), Federal Energy Regulatory Commission.

Employers
Verner, Liipfert, Bernhard, McPherson and Hand, Chartered (Member of Firm)

Clients Represented

On Behalf of Verner, Liipfert, Bernhard, McPherson and Hand, Chartered
MBIA Insurance Corp.
New Orleans, Louisiana, City of
Oglethorpe Power Corp.
Southeastern Federal Power Customers, Inc.

QUIST, Earl C.

1850 M St. NW
Suite 600
Washington, DC 20036
Tel: (202)775-1700
Fax: (202)822-0928
Registered: LDA

Employers
Toyota Motor North America, U.S.A., Inc. (Director, Industry Affairs)

QUIWZOW, Yasmin

1620 I Street NW
Suite 900
Washington, DC 20006
Tel: (202)785-8940
Fax: (202)785-8949

Employers
The Plexus Consulting Group

Clients Represented

On Behalf of The Plexus Consulting Group
American Soc. for Bone and Mineral Research
Check Payment Systems Ass'n
Nat'l Cosmetology Ass'n
Nat'l Organization for Competency Assurance
Soc. of Thoracic Surgeons

RAABE, Mark J.

3300 Circle Hill Rd.
Alexandria, VA 22305
Tel: (202)638-4170
Fax: (202)638-3670
Registered: LDA

Former Counsel, House Committee on Energy and Commerce, and Staff Director, Chief Counsel and Counsel of its Subcommittee on Oversight. Attorney, Federal Trade Commission. Special Agent, Federal Bureau of Investigation, Department of Justice.

Employers
Self-employed as an independent consultant.

Clients Represented

As an independent consultant
Downey McGrath Group, Inc.
Merck & Co.

RABAUT, Thomas W.

1525 Wilson Blvd.
Suite 700
Arlington, VA 22209
Tel: (703)312-6100
Fax: (703)312-6196

Employers
United Defense, L.P. (President and Chief Exec. Offficer)

RABER, Dr. Roger W.

1828 L St. NW
Suite 801
Washington, DC 20036
Tel: (202)775-0509
Fax: (202)775-4857

Employers
Nat'l Ass'n of Corporate Directors (President and Chief Exec. Officer)

RABHAN, Jody

1707 L St. NW
Suite 950
Washington, DC 20036
Tel: (202)296-2588
Fax: (202)331-7792
Registered: LDA
EMail: ncjwdc@aol.com

Employers
Nat'l Council of Jewish Women (Associate Director)

RABIN, Glenn S.

601 Pennsylvania Ave. NW
Suite 720
Washington, DC 20004
Tel: (202)783-3976
Fax: (202)783-3982
Registered: LDA

Employers
Alltel Corporation (Assistant V. President-Federal Regulatory Affairs)

RABIN, Ken

808 17th St. NW
Suite 600
Washington, DC 20006
Tel: (202)466-7800
Fax: (202)887-0905

Employers
Ruder Finn Washington (Strategic Counselor)

RABIN, Philip

801 18th St. NW
Washington, DC 20006
Tel: (202)872-1300
Fax: (202)785-4452

Employers
Paralyzed Veterans of America (Director of Communication)

RABINOVITZ, Bruce

2445 M St. NW
Washington, DC 20037-1420
Tel: (202)663-6000
Fax: (202)663-6363

Employers
Wilmer, Cutler & Pickering (Partner)

RABINOWITZ, Julie M.

1667 K St. NW
Suite 1270
Washington, DC 20006
Tel: (202)659-8320
Fax: (202)496-2448
Registered: LDA

Employers
American Home Products Corp. (Director, Government Relations and Counsel)

RABON, Tom

900 19th St. NW
Suite 700
Washington, DC 20006
Tel: (202)530-7000
Fax: (202)530-7042
Registered: LDA

Employers
Lucent Technologies (V. President, Global Public Affairs)

RABOY, David G.

2550 M St. NW
Washington, DC 20037-1350
Tel: (202)457-6000
Fax: (202)457-6315
Registered: LDA
EMail: draboy@pattonboggs.com

Legislative Director for Senator William V. Roth, Jr. (R-DE), 1983-86.

Employers
Patton Boggs, LLP (Chief Economic Consultant)

Clients Represented

On Behalf of Patton Boggs, LLP
Dole Food Co.
Mars, Inc.

RABUN, John

699 Prince St.
Alexandria, VA 22314-3175
Tel: (703)235-3900
Fax: (703)274-2222

Employers
Nat'l Center for Missing and Exploited Children (V. President and Chief Operating Officer)

RACICOT, Marc

2000 K St. NW
Suite 500
Washington, DC 20006-1872
Tel: (202)828-5800
Fax: (202)223-1225

Employers
America's Promise (Chairman)
Bracewell & Patterson, L.L.P. (Partner)

RACOSKY, Rebecca M.

201 Massachusetts Ave. NE
Suite C-6
Washington, DC 20002
Tel: (202)544-9244
Fax: (202)544-9247

Employers
Nat'l Center for Manufacturing Sciences (V. President, Government Relations)

RADEMACHER, Richard

1820 N. Fort Myer Dr.
Suite 804
Arlington, VA 22209
Tel: (703)351-6301
Fax: (703)351-6417
Registered: LDA

Employers
McDermott Internat'l, Inc./Babcock & Wilcox (Manager, Government Programs (BWX Technologies))

RADEN, Lewis P.

650 Massachusetts Ave. NW
Room 8150
Washington, DC 20226
Tel: (202)927-8490
Fax: (202)927-8863

Employers
Department of Treasury - Bureau of Alcohol, Tobacco and Firearms (Executive Assistant, Legislative Affairs)

RADER, Frederick A.

601 Pennsylvania Ave. NW
Suite 900
Washington, DC 20004
Tel: (202)547-3566
Fax: (202)639-8238

Employers
Cottone and Huggins Group (V. President, Public Sector Relations and Training)

RADEWAGEN, Fred

P.O. Box 26142
Alexandria, VA 22313-6142
Tel: (703)519-7757
Fax: (703)548-0633
EMail: fredradewagen@mail.com

Staff Coordinator, Insular Affairs Office, Department of the Interior, 1969-75.

Employers
Pacific Islands Washington Office (President)

Clients Represented

On Behalf of Pacific Islands Washington Office
Forum for America's Island Republicans
Guam Legislature
Guam, Washington Office of the Governor
Marshall Islands Nuclear Claims Tribunal
The Micronesia Institute
Washington Pacific Publications, Inc.

RADZIEWICZ, Marianne

1755 Massachusetts Ave. NW
Suite 418
Washington, DC 20036
Tel: (202)232-5020
Fax: (202)797-8947
Registered: LDA
EMail: marianner@erols.com

Employers
American Soc. for the Prevention of Cruelty to Animals National Legislative Office (Associate Director, National Legislative Office)

RAEDER, Joseph L.

1130 Connecticut Ave. NW
Suite 300
Washington, DC 20036
Tel: (202)331-8500
Fax: (202)331-1598
Registered: LDA

Former Legislative Director to Rep. Calvin Dooley (D-CA) and former Legislative Assistant to House Majority Whip Tony Coelho (D-CA).

Employers
The Ferguson Group, LLC (Principal)

Clients Represented

On Behalf of The Ferguson Group, LLC

Central Valley Project Water Ass'n
Colusa Basin Drainage District
Family Farm Alliance (Project Transfer Council)
Folsom, California, City of
Glenn-Colusa Irrigation District
Imperial Irrigation District
The Irvine Co.
Kaweah Delta Water Conservation District
Kings River Interests
Modesto/Turlock Irrigation District

RAETHER, Carl

2201 C St. NW
Room 7261
Washington, DC 20520-7261
Tel: (202)647-2135
Fax: (202)647-2762

Employers

Department of State - Bureau of Legislative Affairs (Legislative Management Officer)

RAEZER, Joyce

6000 Stevenson Ave.
Suite 304
Alexandria, VA 22304-3526
Tel: (703)823-6632
Fax: (703)751-4857

Employers

Nat'l Military Family Ass'n (Associate Director, Government Affairs)

RAFFA, Connie A.

1050 Connecticut Ave. NW
Washington, DC 20036-5339
Tel: (202)857-6000
Fax: (202)857-6395
Registered: LDA

Worked for the Department of Health and Human Services.

Employers

Arent Fox Kintner Plotkin & Kahn, PLLC (Member)

Clients Represented

On Behalf of Arent Fox Kintner Plotkin & Kahn, PLLC

Datahr Rehabilitation Institute
Middlesex Hospital Home Care
Priority Care

RAFFAELLI, John D.

1401 K St. NW
Suite 400
Washington, DC 20005
Tel: (202)789-2111
Fax: (202)789-4883
Registered: LDA, FARA
EMail: jraffaelli@thewashingtongroup.com

Tax and Trade Counsel to Senator Lloyd Bentsen (D-TX), 1980-84.

Employers

The Washington Group (Principal)

Clients Represented

On Behalf of The Washington Group

American Hospital Ass'n
American Resort Development Ass'n
Ass'n of Progressive Rental Organizations
AT&T
BD
The Boeing Co.
Bridgestone/Firestone, Inc.
Delta Air Lines
Global Waste Recycling, Inc.
IVAX Corp.
Korea Information & Communication, Ltd.
LCOR, Inc.
Microsoft Corp.
Nat'l Ass'n of Real Estate Investment Trusts
News Corporation Ltd.
Real Estate Roundtable
SAMPCO Companies
SCAN Health Plan
Texas Municipal Power Agency
WinStar Internat'l
Yankton Sioux Tribe

RAFFAELLI, Reba A.

2201 Cooperative Way
Third Floor
Herndon, VA 22071
Tel: (703)904-7100
Fax: (703)904-7942

Employers

Nat'l Ass'n of Industrial and Office Properties (V. President, Government Affairs)

RAFFANIELLO, Pat

1301 K St. NW
Washington, DC 20005-3333
Tel: (202)414-1616
Fax: (202)414-1301
Registered: LDA
EMail: patrick.raffaneillo@us.pwcglobal.com

Employers

PriceWaterhouseCoopers (Managing Director)

Clients Represented

On Behalf of PriceWaterhouseCoopers

Alliance Capital Management LP
American Ass'n of Nurse Anesthetists
Cigar Ass'n of America
Clark/Bardes, Inc.
Coalition for Fair Tax Credits
Council for Energy Independence
Edison Electric Institute
Owens Corning
Plum Creek Timber Co.
Steam Generator Coalition
United Parcel Service

RAFFENSPERGER, Juliette M.

412 First St. SE
Suite 100
Washington, DC 20003
Tel: (202)484-4884
Fax: (202)484-0109
Registered: LDA
EMail: jraffensperger@dutkogroup.com

Former Professional Staff member, Senate Commerce Committee, 1984-87.

Employers

The Dutko Group, Inc. (V. President)

Clients Represented

On Behalf of The Dutko Group, Inc.

Accenture
Alcatel USA
ASCENT (Ass'n of Community Enterprises)
AT&T
AT&T Wireless Services, Inc.
Cable & Wireless, Inc.
Competitive Telecommunications Ass'n (COMPTEL)
European Telecommunications Standards Institute (ETSI)
EXCEL Communications Inc.
Satellite Broadcasting and Communications Ass'n
SkyBridge, LLC
SpaceData Internat'l
TV Guide, Inc.
VeriSign/Network Solutions, Inc.
Winstar Communications, Inc.
XO Communications

RAFFETTO, John K.

1341 G St. NW
Suite 1100
Washington, DC 20005
Tel: (202)393-0225
Fax: (202)393-0712

Former Communications Director, Senate Appropriations Committee.

Employers

Infotech Strategies, Inc. (Senior V. President, Public Relations)

RAFUSE, John L.

1150 Connecticut Ave. NW
Suite 1025
Washington, DC 20036
Tel: (202)367-2774
Fax: (202)367-2790
Registered: LDA

Employers

UNOCAL Corp. (Federal and International Affairs)

RAGAN, Lorri

1828 L St. NW
Suite 705
Washington, DC 20036
Tel: (202)296-3671
Fax: (202)223-5843

Employers

American Land Title Ass'n (V. President, Public Affairs)

RAGAN, Robert H.

1015 15th St. NW
Suite 700
Washington, DC 20005-2605
Tel: (202)828-5200
Fax: (202)785-2645
Registered: LDA

Employers

Bechtel Group, Inc. (Principal V. President and Manager (Bechtel Group, Inc.))

RAGOSTA, John A.

1775 Pennsylvania Ave. NW
Suite 200
Washington, DC 20006
Tel: (202)862-1025
Fax: (202)862-1093
Registered: LDA

Employers

Dewey Ballantine LLP (Partner)

Clients Represented

On Behalf of Dewey Ballantine LLP

American Forest & Paper Ass'n
Coalition for Fair Lumber Imports

RAHAL, Ed

425 Second St. NE
Washington, DC 20002
Tel: (202)675-6000
Fax: (202)675-6058

Employers

Nat'l Republican Senatorial Committee (Director, Corporate Affairs)

RAHEB, Walter

700 13th St. NW
Suite 400
Washington, DC 20005
Tel: (202)347-0773
Fax: (202)347-0785
Registered: LDA
EMail: wraheb@cassidy.com

Former advisor, U.S. Customs Service, Office of U.S. Trade Representatives, Department of Treasury and International Trade Commission. Former advisor to Rep. John Joseph Moakley (D-MA) and Rep. Richard Gebhardt (D-MO).

Employers

Cassidy & Associates, Inc. (Sr. V. President and Director of Global Trade Strategies)

Clients Represented

On Behalf of Cassidy & Associates, Inc.

The BOSE Corp.
FedEx Corp.

RAHER, Patrick M.

555 13th St. NW
Washington, DC 20004-1109
Tel: (202)637-5682
Fax: (202)637-5910
Registered: LDA
EMail: pmraher@hhlaw.com

Co-Chair, New Source Review Subcommittee (1996-98) and Member, Clean Air Act Advisory Committee (1995-98), Environmental Protection Agency. Law Clerk to Judge Roger Robb, U.S. Circuit Court for the District of Columbia Circuit, 1972-73.

Employers

Hogan & Hartson L.L.P. (Partner)

Clients Represented

On Behalf of Hogan & Hartson L.L.P.

InterAmerica's Group LLC
Mercedes-Benz of North America, Inc.
Michelin North America
Nissan North America Inc.

RAHMAN, Hasan Abdel

1717 K St. NW
Suite 407
Washington, DC 20036
Tel: (202)785-8394
Fax: (202)887-5337
Registered: FARA

Employers

PLO Mission (Director and Chief PLO Representative)

RAHN, Richard W.

1020 16th St. NW
Washington, DC 20036
Tel: (202)659-3200
Fax: (202)659-3215
EMail: novmgtco@aol.com

Employers

Novecon (President)

RAIBLE, Robert

1111 14th St. NW
Suite 1200
Washington, DC 20005-5603
Tel: (202)898-2400
Fax: (202)898-2437
EMail: raibler@ada.org

Employers

American Dental Ass'n (Coordinator, Washington Communications)

RAIDER, Ron

700 13th St. NW
Suite 800
Washington, DC 20005
Tel: (202)508-5800
Fax: (202)508-5858

Employers
Kilpatrick Stockton LLP (Partner)

Clients Represented

On Behalf of Kilpatrick Stockton LLP
Atlanta, Georgia, City of

RAILSBACK, Hon. Thomas F.

2099 Pennsylvania Ave. NW
Suite 100
Washington, DC 20006
EMail: trailsba@khlaw.com
Tel: (202)955-3000
Fax: (202)828-1868
Member, U.S. House of Representatives (R-IL), 1967-83.

Employers
Holland & Knight LLP (Of Counsel)

Clients Represented

On Behalf of Holland & Knight LLP
American Chemistry Council
Capitol Broadcasting Co.

RAIMONDO, Barbara

P.O. Box 466
Washington Grove, MD 20880

Employers
Self-employed as an independent consultant.

Clients Represented

As an independent consultant
American Soc. for Deaf Children
Conference of Educational Administrators of Schools and Programs for the Deaf

RAINES, Ghani

2120 L St. NW
Suite 400
Washington, DC 20037
EMail: graines@lharris.com
Tel: (202)478-6301
Fax: (202)478-6171

Employers
Leslie Harris & Associates (Legislative Associate)

Clients Represented

On Behalf of Leslie Harris & Associates
Consortium for School Networking
EdLinc
Internat'l Soc. for Technology in Education
Leadership Conference on Civil Rights

RAINES, Lisa J.

1020 19th St. NW
Suite 550
Washington, DC 20036
EMail: lraines@genzyme.com
Tel: (202)296-3280
Fax: (202)296-3411
Registered: LDA

Employers
Genzyme Corp. (Senior V. President, Government Relations)

RAINS, Alan T.

1910 Association Dr.
Reston, VA 20191
EMail: arains@fcclainc.org
Tel: (703)476-4900
Fax: (703)860-2713

Employers
Family, Career and Community Leaders of America (Exec. Director)

RAINS, Laurie D.

2111 Wilson Blvd.
Suite 600
Arlington, VA 22201
EMail: laurie@halseyrains.com
Tel: (703)351-5077
Fax: (703)351-5827
Registered: LDA
Former Legislative Director and Senior Policy Advisor to Senator James M. Inhofe (R-OK); Majority Staff Director, Government Programs Subcommittee, Committee on Small Business, U.S. House of Representatives; and Professional Staff, Committee on Small Business, U.S. House of Representatives.

Employers
Halsey, Rains & Associates, LLC (Member)

Clients Represented

On Behalf of Halsey, Rains & Associates, LLC
American Board of Medical Specialties in Podiatry
American Medical Technologists
American Soc. of Military Comptrollers
Ass'n of Government Accountants
Board for Orthotists/Prosthetist Certification
Cardiovascular Credentialing Internat'l
The Chauncey Group Internat'l
Coalition for Professional Certification
Computer Adaptive Technologies
Internat'l Board of Lactation Consultant Examiners
Internat'l Electrical Testing Ass'n
Nat'l Ass'n of Portable X-Ray Providers
Nat'l Commission for the Certification of Crane Operators
Nat'l Council on Family Relations
Nat'l Institute for Certification in Engineering Technologies
Oklahoma Ass'n Serving Impacted Schools

RAISLER, Kenneth M.

1701 Pennsylvania Ave. NW
Suite 800
Washington, DC 20006
Tel: (202)956-7500
Fax: (202)293-6330
Registered: LDA

Employers
Sullivan & Cromwell (Partner)

Clients Represented

On Behalf of Sullivan & Cromwell
The Foreign Exchange Committee
The Group of 20

RALLS, Dr. Stephen A.

839 Quince Orchard Blvd.
Suite J
Gaithersburg, MD 20878
EMail: seralls@facd.org
Tel: (301)977-3223
Fax: (301)977-3330

Employers
American College of Dentists (Exec. Director)

RALPH, Regan

1630 Connecticut Ave. NW
Suite 500
Washington, DC 20009
Tel: (202)612-4321
Fax: (202)612-4333

Employers
Human Rights Watch (Director, Women's Rights Division)

RALSTON, Jr., David

888 Sixteenth St. NW
7th Floor
Washington, DC 20006-4103
Tel: (202)835-8131
Fax: (202)835-8136
Registered: LDA

Employers
Foley & Lardner (Partner)

Clients Represented

On Behalf of Foley & Lardner
AAAE-ACI
Information Handling Services
Kruger Internat'l (KI)

RAMIREZ, Andres

1055 N. Fairfax St.
Suite 201
Alexandria, VA 22314-3563
Tel: (703)739-7999
Fax: (703)739-7995

Employers
U.S. Strategies Corp. (Legislative Assistant)

RAMIREZ, Jack

444 N. Capitol St. NW
Suite 801
Washington, DC 20001
Tel: (847)297-7800
Fax: (847)297-5064
Registered: LDA

Employers
Nat'l Ass'n of Independent Insurers (President and Chief Exec. Officer)

RAMIREZ, Lilia L.

1100 Wilson Blvd.
Suite 1500
Arlington, VA 22209
EMail: lilia_l_ramirez@raytheon.com
Tel: (703)841-5713
Fax: (703)841-5792
Registered: LDA

Employers
Raytheon Co. (Director, Congressional Relations, Navy Programs)

RAMMINGER, Scott

2750 Prosperity Ave.
Suite 550
Fairfax, VA 22031-4312
Tel: (703)204-0500
Fax: (703)204-4610

Employers
American Wood Preservers Institute (President)

RAMONAS, George A.

1350 I St. NW
Suite 680
Washington, DC 20005-3305
EMail: george@advocacy.com
Tel: (202)393-4841
Fax: (202)393-5596
Registered: LDA

Employers
The Advocacy Group

Clients Represented

On Behalf of The Advocacy Group
Arizona Science Center
Authentica Inc.
BitWise Designs Inc.
First American Real Estate Solutions LLC
Florida Atlantic University
Florida State University
Fluor Corp.
Greater Cleveland Regional Transit Authority
Internat'l Research and Exchanges Board (IREX)
Long Island University
Nuclear Energy Institute
Rineco Chemical Industries
Silicon Graphics/SGI
Tempe, Arizona, City of
TRW Inc.
University of Houston
University of Utah

RAMSAY, M.D., David J.

1400 16th St. NW
Suite 720
Washington, DC 20036
Tel: (202)265-9600
Fax: (202)265-7514

Employers
Ass'n of Academic Health Centers (Chair, Board of Directors)

RAMSAY, James Bradford

1101 Vermont Ave. NW
Suite 200
Washington, DC 20005
EMail: ramsay@naruc.org
Tel: (202)898-2207
Fax: (202)898-2213

Employers
Nat'l Ass'n of Regulatory Utility Commissioners (General Counsel)

RAMSEY, II, Forest

P.O. Box 3008
Alexandria, VA 22302-0008
Tel: (703)931-4107
Fax: (703)931-3127
Registered: LDA

Employers
The Conaway Group LLC (Consultant)

RAMSEY, Jr., Joe F.

4647 Forbes Blvd.
Lanham, MD 20706-4380
Tel: (301)459-9600
Fax: (301)459-7924

Employers
AMVETS (American Veterans of World War II, Korea and Vietnam) (Exec. Director, National Service Foundation)

RAMSEY, Kathleen

1771 N St. NW
Washington, DC 20036-2891
Tel: (202)429-5312
Fax: (202)775-2157

Employers
Nat'l Ass'n of Broadcasters (Senior V. President, Congressional Relations)

RAMSEY, Martha C.

601 E St. NW
Washington, DC 20049
Tel: (202)434-6850
Fax: (202)434-6883

Employers
AARP (American Ass'n of Retired Persons) (Director, Publications)

RAMSEY, William

810 Vermont Ave. NW
Room 8151
Washington, DC 20420
Tel: (202)273-5789
Fax: (202)273-6161

Employers

Department of Veterans Affairs - Veterans Health Administration (Director, Legislative Programs)

RAND, Kristen

1140 19th St. NW
Suite 600
Washington, DC 20036
Tel: (202)822-8200
Fax: (202)822-8205
Registered: LDA

Employers

Violence Policy Center (Legislative Director)

RANDALL, Albert B.

801 Pennsylvania Ave. NW
Suite 800
Washington, DC 20004
Tel: (202)508-3400
Fax: (202)508-3402
Registered: LDA
EMail: arandall@bdbc.com

Assistant Chief Counsel, Legislation, Federal Aviation Administration, Department of Transportation, 1977-97.

Employers

Baker, Donelson, Bearman & Caldwell, P.C. (Of Counsel)

Clients Represented

On Behalf of Baker, Donelson, Bearman & Caldwell, P.C.

AAAE-ACI
American Airlines
The Boeing Co.
Cleveland, City of/Cleveland Hopkins Internat'l Airport
L-3 Communications Corp.
Lockheed Martin Air Traffic Management
Northwest Airlines, Inc.

RANDALL, Deborah A.

1050 Connecticut Ave. NW
Washington, DC 20036-5339
Tel: (202)857-6000
Fax: (202)857-6395

Law Clerk to Judge Joseph H. Young, U.S. District Court for the District of Maryland, 1976-77. Attorney-Advisor, Federal Trade Commission, 1977-80. Attorney-Advisor, Department of Health and Human Services, 1980-82.

Employers

Arent Fox Kintner Plotkin & Kahn, PLLC (Member)

RANDEL, Amy

1010 Vermont Ave. NW
Suite 900
Washington, DC 20005
Tel: (202)628-9171
Ext: 114
Fax: (202)628-9169
EMail: arandel@hfhi.org

Employers

Habitat for Humanity Internat'l (Director, Government Relations)

RANDLE, Russell V.

2550 M St. NW
Washington, DC 20037-1350
Tel: (202)457-6000
Fax: (202)457-6315
Registered: LDA
EMail: rrandle@pattonboggs.com

Law Clerk to Judge John H. Pratt, U.S. District Court for the District of Columbia, 1980-81.

Employers

Patton Boggs, LLP (Partner)

Clients Represented

On Behalf of Patton Boggs, LLP

San Bernardino Valley Municipal Water District
San Bernardino, California, City of
United Technologies Corp.

RANDOL, III, A. G.

2001 Pennsylvania Ave. NW
Suite 300
Washington, DC 20006
Tel: (202)862-0220
Fax: (202)862-0267
Registered: LDA

Employers

Exxon Mobil Corp. (Senior Washington Representative, Environmental Issues)

RANDOLPH, Jr., Howard W.

Three Research Place
Rockville, MD 20850
Tel: (301)948-4910
Fax: (301)330-7673
Registered: LDA

Employers

Transportation-Communications Internat'l Union (International V. President and National Legislative Director)

RANGE, James D.

801 Pennsylvania Ave. NW
Suite 800
Washington, DC 20004
Tel: (202)508-3400
Fax: (202)508-3402
Registered: LDA

Minority Counsel, Senate Committee on Environment and Public Works, 1973-80. Chief Counsel for the Senate Majority Leader, 1980-84.

Employers

Baker, Donelson, Bearman & Caldwell, P.C. (Senior Advisor for Legislative, Regulatory and Environmental Affairs)

Clients Represented

On Behalf of Baker, Donelson, Bearman & Caldwell, P.C.

American Fly Fishing Trade Ass'n
Bridgestone/Firestone, Inc.
Fishable Waters Coalition
Internat'l Ass'n of Fish and Wildlife Agencies
Monsanto Co.
Montana Land Reliance
Nat'l Ecological Foundation
The Pacific Forest Trust
World Wildlife Fund

RANGE, Peter Ross

600 Pennsylvania Ave. SE
Suite 400
Washington, DC 20003
Tel: (202)546-0007
Fax: (202)544-5002

Employers

Democratic Leadership Council (Editor, Blueprint Magazine)

RANGER, William E.

400 N. Capitol St.
Suite 365
Washington, DC 20001
Tel: (202)624-5308
Fax: (202)624-5425

Employers

Minnesota, Washington Office of the State of (Director)

RANKIN, Al

1455 F St. NW
Suite 420
Washington, DC 20004
Tel: (202)628-6442
Fax: (202)628-6537

Employers

USAA - United Services Automobile Ass'n (Senior V. President and Chief Communications Officer)

RANKIN, Paul W.

8401 Corporate Dr.
Suite 450
Landover, MD 20785
Tel: (301)577-3786
Fax: (301)577-6476
Registered: LDA

Employers

Reusable Industrial Packaging Ass'n (President)

RANKIN, III, Samuel M.

1527 18th St. NW
Washington, DC 20036
Tel: (202)588-1100
Fax: (202)588-1853
EMail: smr@ams.org

Employers

American Mathematical Soc. (Associate Exec. Director)

RAPHAELSON, Ira R.

555 13th St. NW
Suite 500 West
Washington, DC 20004
Tel: (202)383-5300
Fax: (202)383-5414
EMail: iraphaelson@omm.com

Counselor to the Attorney General (1992-93); Special Counsel for Financial Institutions Crime (1991-93); U.S. Attorney (1990-91), First Assistant U.S. Attorney (1989-90), Chief, Special Prosecutions Division (1987-89), Chief, Criminal Litigation Division (1987), Deputy Chief, Special Prosecutions Division (1986-87) and Assistant U.S. Attorney (1980-86), U.S. Attorneys Office, Northern District of Illinois; Department of Justice.

Employers

O'Melveny and Myers LLP (Partner)

RAPOZA, Robert A.

1250 I St. NW
Suite 902
Washington, DC 20005
Tel: (202)393-5225
Fax: (202)393-3034
Registered: LDA
EMail: Bob@Rapoza.org

Employers

Nat'l Rural Housing Coalition (Legislative Director)
Robert A. Rapoza Associates (President)

Clients Represented

On Behalf of Robert A. Rapoza Associates

Alaska Village Initiatives
Arkansas Enterprise Group
Bedford Stuyvesant Restoration Corp.
Bethel New Life
Chicanos Por La Causa
Community Development Venture Capital Ass'n
Community Transportation Ass'n of America
Corporation for Supportive Housing
Delta Foundation
The Enterprise Foundation
Impact Services
Kentucky Highlands Investment Corp.
Local Initiatives Support Corp.
Massachusetts Housing Partnership Fund
Mercy Housing
Nat'l Ass'n of Housing Partnerships
Nat'l Ass'n of SBA Microloan Intermediaries
Nat'l Council of La Raza
Nat'l Migrant Head Start Ass'n
Nat'l Neighborhood Housing Network
Nat'l Rural Development & Finance Corp.
Nat'l Rural Housing Coalition
Northeast Entrepreneur Fund
Northeast Ventures Corp.
Northern Economic Initiatives Corp.
Rural Community Assistance Corp.
Shorebank Corp.
Suomi College
TELACU
Woman's Opportunities Resource Center
Youthbuild, USA

RAPPAPORT, Marvin S.

1200 New Hampshire Ave. NW
Suite 800
Washington, DC 20036
Tel: (202)776-2911
Fax: (202)776-2222
Registered: LDA

Former Chief of Staff to Rep. Matthew F. McHugh (D-NY).

Employers

Charter Communications, Inc. (V. President, Public Policy)
Self-employed as an independent consultant.

RAROG, Robert

1810 Plymouth St. NW
Washington, DC 20012
Tel: (202)882-0321
Fax: (202)882-1096
Registered: LDA
EMail: rrarog@aol.com

Computer Industry Analyst, Bureau of Export Administration, Department of Commerce, 1983-87. Legislative Fellow, Senate Banking Committee, 1986.

Employers

Self-employed as an independent consultant.

Clients Represented

As an independent consultant

Sun Microsystems

RARUS, Nancy B.

814 Thayer Ave.
Suite 250
Silver Spring, MD 20910
Tel: (301)587-1788
Fax: (301)587-1791

Employers

Nat'l Ass'n of the Deaf (Associate Exec. Director, Programs)

RASAVAGE, Roy

1635 Prince St.
Alexandria, VA 22314-3406
Tel: (703)683-4646
Fax: (703)683-4745

Employers

Helicopter Ass'n Internat'l (President)

RASCO, Carol H.

1233 20th St. NW
Washington, DC 20036-2304
Tel: (202)822-5900
Fax: (202)822-5920
Former Senior Advisor to the Secretary, Department of Education.

Employers
The College Board (Exec. Director for Government Relations)

RASELL, M. Edith

1660 L St. NW
Suite 1200
Washington, DC 20036
EMail: epi@epinet.org
Tel: (202)775-8810
Fax: (202)775-0819

Employers
Economic Policy Institute (Economist)

RASKIN, Marcus G.

733 15th St. NW
Suite 1020
Washington, DC 20005
Tel: (202)234-9382
Fax: (202)387-7915

Employers
Institute for Policy Studies (Distinguished Fellow)

RASMUS, John R.

1120 Connecticut Ave. NW
Washington, DC 20036
Tel: (202)663-5000
Fax: (202)828-4548
Registered: LDA

Employers
American Bankers Ass'n (Senior Federal Administrative Counsel)

RASMUSSEN, Erik

1615 L St. NW
Suite 650
Washington, DC 20036
EMail: erik.rasmussen@jeffersongr.com
Tel: (202)626-8500
Fax: (202)626-8593
Legislative Assistant to Rep. John Porter (R-IL), 1998-2000.

Employers
Jefferson Government Relations, L.L.C. (Director)

Clients Represented
On Behalf of Jefferson Government Relations, L.L.C.
Cummins-Allison Corp.
eHealth Insurance Services, Inc.

RASMUSSEN, Jeffery P.

1200 G St. NW
Suite 300
Washington, DC 20005
EMail: jrasmussen@tei.org
Tel: (202)638-5601
Fax: (202)638-5607

Employers
Tax Executives Institute, Inc. (Tax Counsel)

RASSAM, Dr. Gus

5410 Grosvenor Ln.
Suite 110
Bethesda, MD 20814-2199
EMail: grassam@fisheries.org
Tel: (301)897-8616
Ext: 209
Fax: (301)897-8096

Employers
American Fisheries Soc. (Exec. Director)

RASSMUSSEN, Garrett G.

2550 M St. NW
Washington, DC 20037-1350
EMail: grassmussen@pattonboggs.com
Tel: (202)457-6000
Fax: (202)457-6315

Employers
Patton Boggs, LLP (Partner)

Clients Represented
On Behalf of Patton Boggs, LLP
Clayton College of Natural Health
Crane Co.

RASTATTER, Edward

1700 N. Moore St.
Suite 1900
Arlington, VA 22209-1904
EMail: rastatter@nitl.org
Tel: (703)524-5011
Fax: (703)524-5017
Registered: LDA

Employers
Nat'l Industrial Transportation League (Director of Policy)

RATCHFORD, Hon. William R.

1615 L St. NW
Suite 650
Washington, DC 20036
Tel: (202)626-8500
Fax: (202)626-8593
Associate Administrator for Congressional Affairs, General Services Administration. Member, U.S. House of Representatives (D-CT), 1979-85.

Employers
Jefferson Government Relations, L.L.C.

RATHBUN, Dennis K.

One White Flint North Bldg.
11555 Rockville Pike
MS: 17A1
Rockville, MD 20852
EMail: dkr@nrc.gov
Tel: (301)415-1776
Fax: (301)415-8571

Employers
Nuclear Regulatory Commission (Director, Office of Congressional Affairs)

RATHBUN, Jill

2025 M St. NW
Suite 800
Washington, DC 20036
EMail: jill_rathbun@dc.sba.com
Tel: (202)367-2100
Fax: (202)367-1200
Registered: LDA

Employers
Smith, Bucklin and Associates, Inc. (Director, Health Care Practice Group)

Clients Represented
On Behalf of Smith, Bucklin and Associates, Inc.
Academy of Osseointegration
American Psychiatric Nurses Ass'n
American Soc. of Nephrology
American Urogynecologic Soc.
Nat'l Vision Rehabilitation Cooperative
Soc. of Gyneocologic Oncologists
Soc. of Maternal-Fetal Medicine
SonoSite

RATIGAN, John

1615 L St. NW
Suite 1300
Washington, DC 20036
Tel: (202)223-7300
Fax: (202)223-7420
Registered: LDA

Employers
Paul, Weiss, Rifkind, Wharton & Garrison

Clients Represented
On Behalf of Paul, Weiss, Rifkind, Wharton & Garrison
Commission on Graduates of Foreign Nursing Schools
Federation of Korean Industries

RATLIFF, Gerri L.

425 I St. NW
Room 7030
Washington, DC 20536
Tel: (202)514-5231
Fax: (202)514-1117

Employers
Department of Justice - Immigration and Naturalization Service (Acting Director, Office of Congressional Relations)

RATLIFF, J. O.

Eight E St. SE
Washington, DC 20003
Tel: (202)543-4172
Fax: (202)546-6294
Registered: LDA

Employers
Washington Public Affairs Group

RAUL, Alan C.

1722 I St. NW
Washington, DC 20006
Tel: (202)736-8000
Fax: (202)736-8711
Registered: LDA
Department of Agriculture, 1989-93. General Counsel, Office of Management and Budget (1988-89) and Associate Counsel to the President (1986-88), The White House.

Employers
Sidley & Austin (Partner)

Clients Represented
On Behalf of Sidley & Austin
IBP, Inc.
Medeva Pharmaceuticals
Nat'l Nutritional Foods Ass'n

RAULSTON, Carol

1341 G St. NW
Suite 200
Washington, DC 20005
Tel: (202)333-2533
Fax: (202)342-0763

Employers
Winner & Associates (Sr. V. President)

RAUSCH, James P.

441 G St. NW
Room 3F05
Washington, DC 20314-1000
EMail: james.p.rausch@hq02.usace.army.mil
Tel: (202)761-1059
Fax: (202)761-8843

Employers
Department of Army - U.S. Army Corps of Engineers (Chief, Office of Congressional Affairs)

RAVITZ, Georgia C.

1050 Connecticut Ave. NW
Washington, DC 20036-5339
Tel: (202)857-6000
Fax: (202)857-6395
Registered: LDA

Employers
Arent Fox Kintner Plotkin & Kahn, PLLC (Member)

Clients Represented
On Behalf of Arent Fox Kintner Plotkin & Kahn, PLLC
Salton, Inc.

RAVITZ SMITH, Ruth

701 Pennsylvania Ave. NW
Suite 300
Washington, DC 20004
EMail: smithrx@nu.com
Tel: (202)508-5301
Fax: (202)508-5304
Registered: LDA
Administrative Assistant (1987-89) and Legislative Assistant (1985-87) to Rep. John G. Rowland (R-CT).

Employers
Northeast Utilities (Director, Federal Governmental Affairs)

RAVIV, Sheila

1801 K St. NW
Suite 1000L
Washington, DC 20006
EMail: sheila_raviv@washbm.com
Tel: (202)530-0400
Fax: (202)530-4500

Employers
Burson-Marsteller (Managing Director, Constituency Relations Practice)

RAWLS, Lee

1625 K St. NW
Suite 1100
Washington, DC 20006-1604
Tel: (202)857-0244
Fax: (202)857-0237
Chief of Staff for Senator Bill Frist (R-TN), 1997-2000. Chief of Staff, Sen. Peter V. Domenici, (R-NM), 1982-85

Employers
Biotechnology Industry Organization (V. President, Government Relations)

RAWLS, Rodger

1215 Jefferson Davis Hwy.
Suite 1500
Arlington, VA 22202
EMail: rodger.rawls@baesystems.com
Tel: (703)416-7800
Fax: (703)415-1459
Registered: LDA

Employers
BAE SYSTEMS North America (V. President, Government Relations-Information Systems Sector)

RAWSON, Edward

420 Seventh St. SE
Suite C
Washington, DC 20003-0270
Tel: (202)546-3956
Fax: (202)546-8703

Employers
Campaign for United Nations Reform (Exec. V. President)

RAWSON, W. Randall

4001 North 9th St.
Suite 226
Arlington, VA 22203-1900
EMail: randy@abma.com
Tel: (703)522-7350
Fax: (703)522-2665
Legal Assistant to Rep. Mike McCormack (D-WA), 1971-78.

Employers
American Boiler Manufacturers Ass'n (V. President)

RAY, Ph.D., Bruce A.

636 A St. NE
Washington, DC 20002
Tel: (202)543-4935
Registered: LDA

Employers
Bruce Ray & Company (President)

Clients Represented
On Behalf of Bruce Ray & Company
Bayley Seton Hospital
Cumberland Packing Corp.
Fairview Hospital and Healthcare Services
Lutheran Medical Center

RAY, Charles G.

12300 Twinbrook Pkwy.
Suite 320
Rockville, MD 20852
Tel: (301)984-6200

Employers
Nat'l Council for Community Behavioral Healthcare (President and Chief Exec. Officer)

RAY, James S.

1401 New York Ave. NW
Tenth Floor
Washington, DC 20005-2102
Tel: (202)737-1900
Fax: (202)659-3458
Registered: LDA
EMail: jray@connerton-ray.com

Employers
Connerton & Ray (Partner)

RAY, John L.

1501 M St. NW
Suite 700
Washington, DC 20005-1702
Tel: (202)463-4300
Fax: (202)463-4394
Registered: LDA, FARA
EMail: jray@manatt.com

Employers
Manatt, Phelps & Phillips, LLP (Partner)

Clients Represented
On Behalf of Manatt, Phelps & Phillips, LLP
Congo, Republic of
Corrections Corp. of America
DAG Petroleum
Employee-Owned S Corporations of America
Verizon Communications

RAY, Melinda Mercer

2000 L St. NW
Suite 740
Washington, DC 20036
Tel: (202)261-2405
Fax: (202)728-0575
Registered: LDA
EMail: melindar@awhonn.org

Employers
Ass'n of Women's Health, Obstetric and Neonatal Nurses (Director, Health Policy and Advocacy)

RAY, Paula

1111 Constitution Ave. NW
Room 3238
Washington, DC 20224
EMail: paula.ray@irs.gov
Tel: (202)622-9590
Fax: (202)622-3772

Employers
Department of Treasury - Internal Revenue Service (Congressional Inquiries)

RAY, Thomas

1016 16th St. NW
Suite 300
Washington, DC 20036
Tel: (202)862-4400
Fax: (202)862-4432
Registered: LDA

Employers
Nat'l Federation of Federal Employees (Secretary-Treasurer)

RAY-STRUNK, Pamela

4805 N. 20th Place
Arlington, VA 22207
Tel: (703)522-8278
Fax: (703)526-0355
Registered: LDA

Employers
Pamela Ray-Strunk and Associates

Clients Represented
On Behalf of Pamela Ray-Strunk and Associates
Carr Public Affairs
Dallas Area Rapid Transit Authority
Suffolk, New York, County of
Touro Law Center

RAYBURN, Dorothy

Ronald Reagan Bldg.
1300 Pennsylvania Ave. NW
MS: 6.10A
Washington, DC 20523
EMail: drayburn@usaid.gov
Tel: (202)712-4300
Fax: (202)216-3036

Employers
Agency for Internat'l Development (Legislative Program Specialist, Congressional Liaison Division)

RAYDER, Scott

1755 Massachusetts Ave. NW
Suite 800
Washington, DC 20036
Tel: (202)332-0063
Fax: (202)232-8203
Former Staff Member, House Committee on Science

Employers
Consortium for Oceanographic Research and Education (CORE) (Director, Government Affairs)

RAYMAN, M.D., Russell B.

320 S. Henry St.
Alexandria, VA 22314
Tel: (703)739-2240
Fax: (703)739-9652
EMail: rrayman@asma.org

Employers
Aerospace Medical Ass'n (Exec. Director)

RAYMOND, Brian J.

1301 K St. NW
Suite 1200-West Tower
Washington, DC 20005-3307
Tel: (202)515-5434
Fax: (202)515-5906
Registered: LDA
EMail: braymond@us.ibm.com

Employers
Internat'l Business Machines Corp. (Program Manager, Grassroots and Political Programs)

RAYMOND, David A.

1015 15th St. NW
Suite 802
Washington, DC 20005
Tel: (202)347-7474
Fax: (202)898-0068

Employers
American Consulting Engineers Council (Exec. V. President, and C.E.O.)

RAYMOND, Sandra C.

1232 22nd St. NW
Washington, DC 20037
Tel: (202)223-2226
Fax: (202)223-2237

Employers
Nat'l Osteoporosis Foundation (Exec. Director)

RAYMOND, Sharon

1120 Connecticut Ave. NW
Washington, DC 20036
Tel: (202)663-5000
Fax: (202)663-5212
Registered: LDA

Employers
American Bankers Ass'n (Director, Grassroots Programs and Washington Information)

RAYNES, CAE, Jeffry W.

5301 Shawnee Rd.
Alexandria, VA 22312
Tel: (703)354-8851
Fax: (703)354-8106

Employers
APICS - The Educational Soc. for Resource Management (Exec. Director and Chief Operating Officer)

REA, Jr., Bryce

1707 L St. NW
Suite 570
Washington, DC 20006
Tel: (202)785-3700
Fax: (202)659-4934
Counsel, Transportation, Public Utilities and Fuels, Office of Price Stabilization, 1951-53.

Employers
Rea, Cross & Auchincloss (Partner)

Clients Represented
On Behalf of Rea, Cross & Auchincloss
Middle Atlantic Conference
New England Motor Rate Bureau

READ, Debbie

1200 18th St. NW
Washington, DC 20036
Tel: (202)887-8800
Fax: (202)887-8877
Registered: LDA
EMail: dread@environet.org

Employers
Nat'l Environmental Trust (Legislative Director)

READ, Douglas E.

2000 L St. NW
Suite 200
Washington, DC 20036
EMail: DouglasR@SAE.org
Tel: (202)416-1649
Fax: (202)416-1618

Employers
Soc. of Automotive Engineers (SAE Internat'l) (Manager, Washington Office)

READ, Marcia

444 N. Capitol St. NW
Suite 142
Washington, DC 20001
Tel: (202)431-8020
Fax: (202)434-8033

Employers
Nat'l Ass'n of State Workforce Agencies (Fiscal and Administrative Director)

READE, Claire E.

555 12th St. NW
Washington, DC 20004-1206
Tel: (202)942-5000
Fax: (202)942-5999
Registered: FARA
EMail: Claire_Reade@aporter.com

Employers
Arnold & Porter (Partner)

REAGAN, Deborah

1775 Pennsylvania Ave. NW
Suite 600
Washington, DC 20006
Tel: (202)862-4505
Fax: (202)862-1093
Registered: LDA

Employers
Coalition for Fair Lumber Imports (Manager, Legislative Affairs)

REAGAN, Joanna E.

815 15th St. NW
Washington, DC 20005
Tel: (202)783-3788
Fax: (202)393-0219
Registered: LDA

Employers
Internat'l Union of Bricklayers and Allied Craftsworkers (Director, Government Relations)

REAGAN, Kinsey S.

1140 19th St. NW
Suite 900
Washington, DC 20036
EMail: kreagan@kkblaw.com
Tel: (202)223-5120
Fax: (202)223-5619
Attorney, Department of Health and Human Services, 1975-80.

Employers
Kleinfeld, Kaplan and Becker (Partner)

Clients Represented
On Behalf of Kleinfeld, Kaplan and Becker
E. R. Squibb and Sons, Inc.

REAGAN, Margaret

444 N. Capitol St. NW
Suite 625
Washington, DC 20001
Tel: (202)393-0860
Fax: (202)393-0864
Registered: LDA

Employers
Premier, Inc. (Director, Federal Affairs)

REAGLE, George

10046 Cotton Mill Lane
Columbia, MD 21046
Tel: (301)596-0533
Fax: (301)596-0352
Registered: LDA

Employers
Self-employed as an independent consultant.

Clients Represented
As an independent consultant
Chamber of Commerce of the U.S.A.
Coalition for Vehicle Choice
Nat'l Safety Council

REAM, Kathleen A.

1620 L St. NW
Suite 620
Washington, DC 20036
Tel: (202)429-3971
Fax: (202)429-3976
Registered: LDA

Employers
Council for Chemical Research, Inc. (Public Affairs Representative)

REAM, Roger R.

1706 New Hampshire Ave. NW
Washington, DC 20009
EMail: rream@tfas.org
Tel: (202)986-0384
Fax: (202)986-0390

Employers
Fund for American Studies (President)

REAMY, Jeff

1776 I St. NW
Suite 700
Washington, DC 20006
Tel: (202)833-0922
Fax: (202)785-0639
Registered: LDA

Employers
Phillips Petroleum Co. (Environmental/Regulatory Affairs Coordinator)

REARDON, Susan

2101 E St. NW
Washington, DC 20037
EMail: exec@afsa.org
Tel: (202)338-4045
Fax: (202)338-6820

Employers
American Foreign Service Ass'n (Exec. Director)

RECFORD, Thomas J.

1090 Vermont Ave. NW
Third Floor
Washington, DC 20005
Tel: (202)842-5000
Fax: (202)789-4293
Former consultant to the Department of Commerce. Served in the Office of National Estimates, Central Intelligence Agency.

Employers
Millian Byers Associates, LLC (Senior International Advisor)

RECHT, Philip R.

1909 K St. NW
Washington, DC 20006
Tel: (202)263-3000
Fax: (202)263-3300
Registered: LDA

Employers
Mayer, Brown & Platt (Partner)

RECINOS, Maria

1459 Columbia Rd. NW
Washington, DC 20009
Tel: (202)332-1094
Fax: (202)667-7783

Employers
Casa del Pueblo Community Program (Exec. Director)

RECTOR, Clark E.

1101 Vermont Ave. NW
Suite 500
Washington, DC 20005
Tel: (202)898-0089
Fax: (202)898-0159
Registered: LDA

Employers
American Advertising Federation (V. President, State Government Affairs)

RECTOR, John M.

205 Daingerfield Rd.
Alexandria, VA 22314
Tel: (703)683-8200
Fax: (703)683-3619
Registered: LDA

Employers
Nat'l Community Pharmacists Ass'n (Senior V. President, Government Affairs and General Counsel)

RECTOR, Robert

214 Massachusetts Ave. NE
Washington, DC 20002
Tel: (202)546-4400
Fax: (202)546-8328

Employers
Heritage Foundation (Senior Research Fellow, Welfare and Family Issues)

REDDEN, K. La Verne

1275 K St. NW
Suite 975
Washington, DC 20005
EMail: nccw01@winstarmail.com
Tel: (202)682-0334
Fax: (202)682-0338

Employers
Nat'l Council of Catholic Women (President)

REDDING, J. Christopher

1200 New Hampshire Ave. NW
Suite 800
Washington, DC 20036-6802
EMail: credding@dlalaw.com
Tel: (202)776-2000
Fax: (202)776-2222

Employers
Dow, Lohnes & Albertson, PLLC (Member)

REDDING, Jr., Robert L.

313 Massachusetts Ave. NE
Washington, DC 20002
Tel: (202)543-7464
Fax: (202)543-4575
Registered: LDA

Employers
Automotive Service Ass'n
Self-employed as an independent consultant.

Clients Represented
As an independent consultant
Automotive Service Ass'n
CRT, Inc.
Georgia Commodity Commission for Peanuts
Georgia Cotton Commission
Nat'l Peanut Buying Point Ass'n
SICPA Industries of America, Inc.
Tobacco Quota Warehouse Alliance
University of Georgia - College of Agricultural and Environmental Sciences
Vidalia Onion Business Council

REDDING, Whitney

11200 Waples Mill Rd.
Suite 150
Fairfax, VA 22030-7407
Tel: (703)691-8100
Fax: (703)691-8106

Employers
Assisted Living Federation of America (Director, Media and Public Relations)

REDDY, Leo J.

1201 New York Ave. NW
Suite 725
Washington, DC 20005
EMail: leoreddy@aol.com
Tel: (202)216-2740
Fax: (202)289-7618

Employers
Nat'l Coalition for Advanced Manufacturing (President)

REDER, Nancy

1800 Diagonal Rd.
Suite 320
Alexandria, VA 22314
EMail: nreder@nasdse.org
Tel: (703)519-3800
Fax: (703)519-3808

Employers
Nat'l Ass'n of State Directors of Special Education (Deputy Exec. Director, Director of Government Relations)

REDFERN, Ed

P.O. Box 818
Great Falls, VA 22066-1824
Tel: (703)759-9388
Fax: (703)832-0516
Registered: LDA
Special Assistant to Senator Chuck Grassley (R-IA), 1983-89.

Employers
Arent Fox Kintner Plotkin & Kahn, PLLC (Government Relations Director)
Redfern Resources (Government Relations Director)

Clients Represented
On Behalf of Redfern Resources
Cedar Rapids, Iowa, City of
Iowa Public Transit Ass'n
Kansas City Area Transportation Authority
Kansas Public Transit Ass'n
Lennox Internat'l
Missouri Public Transit Ass'n
The Ruan Companies
Schering-Plough Corp.
Stine Seed Co.
Woodbury County, Iowa
World Food Prize

REDIFER, Paul

1301 K St. NW
Suite 1200-West Tower
Washington, DC 20005-3307
EMail: rediferp@us.ibm.com
Tel: (202)515-5000
Registered: LDA

Employers
Internat'l Business Machines Corp. (Regional Manager, Government Relations)

REDPATH, Tyson

1400 16th St. NW
Suite 400
Washington, DC 20036-2220
EMail: tredpath@ofwlaw.com
Tel: (202)789-1212
Fax: (202)234-3550

Employers
Olsson, Frank and Weeda, P.C. (Legislative Assistant)

Clients Represented
On Behalf of Olsson, Frank and Weeda, P.C.
Adheris, Inc.
American Academy of Audiology
American Commodity Distribution Ass'n
American School Food Service Ass'n
Ass'n of Medical Device Reprocessors
Aventis Pasteur
Beef Products, Inc.
California Canning Peach Ass'n
Chocolate Manufacturers Ass'n of the U.S.A.
Food Distributors Internat'l (NAWGA-IFDA)
Gentrac Inc.
Health Resource Publishing Co.
Institute of Food Technologists
Kraft Foods, Inc.
Lower Brule Sioux Tribe
McDonald's Corp.
Mead Johnson Nutritional Group
Nat'l Ass'n of Margarine Manufacturers
Nat'l Ass'n of Pharmaceutical Manufacturers
Nat'l Coalition of Food Importers Ass'n
Nat'l Confectioners Ass'n
Nat'l Food Processors Ass'n
Nat'l Frozen Pizza Institute
Nat'l Meat Ass'n
PennField Oil Co.
Philip Morris Management Corp.
The Pillsbury Co.
San Tomo Group
Schwan's Sales Enterprises
SteriGenics Internat'l
Titan Scan
Transhumance Holding Co., Inc.
United Fresh Fruit and Vegetable Ass'n

REED, Alan J.

701 Pennsylvania Ave. NW
Suite 800
Washington, DC 20004
EMail: ajreed@thelenreid.com
Tel: (202)508-4056
Fax: (202)508-4321
Registered: LDA
Special Counsel, Division of Market Regulation, Security and Exchange Commission, 1995-2000.

Employers
Thelen Reid & Priest LLP (Associate-Business & Finance)

Clients Represented
On Behalf of Thelen Reid & Priest LLP
Charles Schwab & Co. Inc.
Cincinnati Stock Exchange
Charles Schwab & Co., Inc.,

REED, Alyson

3420 Hamilton Street
Suite 200
Hyattsville, MD 20782
Tel: (301)277-1033
Fax: (301)277-4451
Registered: LDA
EMail: fairpay@aol.com

Employers
Nat'l Committee on Pay Equity (Exec. Director)

REED, Gerald R.

1820 11th St. NW
Washington, DC 20001-5015
Tel: (202)667-3280
Fax: (202)667-3705

Employers
Blacks in Government (National President)

REED, Jo

601 E St. NW
Washington, DC 20049
Tel: (202)434-3800
Fax: (202)434-6477
Registered: LDA

Employers
AARP (American Ass'n of Retired Persons) (Director, Federal Affairs, Consumer Issues)

REED, Kevin F.

1200 New Hampshire Ave. NW
Suite 800
Washington, DC 20036-6802
Tel: (202)776-2000
Fax: (202)776-2222
EMail: kreed@dlalaw.com

Employers
Dow, Lohnes & Albertson, PLLC (Member)

REED, Linda A.

233 Pennsylvania Ave. SE
Suite 200
Washington, DC 20003-1107
Tel: (202)543-8676
Fax: (202)543-7145
EMail: usafmc1@mindspring.com

Employers
U.S. Ass'n of Former Members of Congress (Exec. Director)

REED, Lydia

730 11th St. NW
Fourth Floor
Washington, DC 20001-4510
Tel: (202)638-1448
Ext: 131
Fax: (202)638-3429
EMail: lreed@aupha.org

Employers
Ass'n of University Programs in Health Administration (V. President and Chief Operating Officer)

REED, Michael L.

8000 Towers Crescent Dr.
Suite 1350
Tysons Corner, VA 22182
Tel: (703)760-7888
Fax: (703)836-7959
Registered: LDA
EMail: mikelreed@aol.com
Former Legislative Director to Speaker of the House Carl B. Albert (D-OK).

Employers
Washington Liaison Group, LLC (V. President and Secretary)

Clients Represented
On Behalf of Washington Liaison Group, LLC
Reckitt & Colman Pharmaceuticals Inc.
Serono Laboratories, Inc.

REED, III, Morgan W.

1666 K St. NW
Suite 500
Washington, DC 20006-2803
Tel: (202)887-1400
Fax: (202)466-2198
Registered: LDA, FARA

Employers
O'Connor & Hannan, L.L.P. (Legislative Consultant)

Clients Represented
On Behalf of O'Connor & Hannan, L.L.P.
Calhoun County, Alabama Commission
Telecorp PCS Inc.

REED, Pris I.

11600 Nebel St.
Suite 210
Rockville, MD 20852
Tel: (301)984-1336
Fax: (301)770-0580

Employers
American Leprosy Foundation (Administrative Director)

REED, Rex H.

8001 Braddock Rd.
Springfield, VA 22160
Tel: (703)321-8510
Fax: (703)321-9319

Employers
Nat'l Right to Work Legal Defense Foundation (Exec. V. President, Secretary and Legal Director)

REED, Rick

305 Cameron St.
Alexandria, VA 22314
Tel: (703)683-8326
Fax: (703)683-8826
EMail: rreed@srcmedia.com

Employers
Stevens Reed Curcio & Co. (Partner)

REED, Roxanne

2201 C St. NW
Room 5917
Washington, DC 20520-7261
Tel: (202)647-2163
Fax: (202)647-2762

Employers
Department of State - Bureau of Legislative Affairs (Congressional Inquiries Chief)

REED, Scott W.

1800 K St. NW
Suite 1122
Washington, DC 20006
Tel: (202)463-9677
Fax: (202)463-9680
Registered: LDA, FARA

Employers
Chesapeake Enterprises, Inc. (President)

Clients Represented
On Behalf of Chesapeake Enterprises, Inc.
GTECH Corp.
Ketchum
Nat'l Airline Passenger Coalition
Paucatuck Eastern Pequot Tribal Nation
Republican Leadership Coalition
SBC Communications Inc.
Shakopee Business Council
Sun Healthcare Group, Inc.

REED, Stephanie W.

600 Maryland Ave. SW
Suite 100 West
Washington, DC 20024-2571
Tel: (202)651-7088
Fax: (202)651-7001
Registered: LDA
Legislative Director to Rep. Dave McCurdy (D-OK), 1984-94. Staff, Sergeant-at-Arms, U.S. House of Representatives, 1969-71. Aide to Rep. Carl Albert (D-OK), 1967-68.

Employers
American Nurses Ass'n (Associate Director, Federal Government Relations)

REED, T. Dean

1155 15th St. NW
Suite 1003
Washington, DC 20005
Tel: (202)223-3532
Fax: (202)223-5609

Employers
T. Dean Reed Co. (President)

REED, Tamara C.

1401 H St. NW
12th Floor
Washington, DC 20005-2148
Tel: (202)326-5825
Fax: (202)326-5827
Registered: LDA

Employers
Investment Co. Institute (Associate Counsel)

REED, Tom

1341 G St. NW
Suite 900
Washington, DC 20005
Tel: (202)637-1557
Fax: (202)637-1537

Employers
Philip Morris Management Corp. (Director, Government Affairs, Network Operations)

REEDER, James A.

2550 M St. NW
Washington, DC 20037-1350
Tel: (202)457-6000
Fax: (202)457-6315
Registered: LDA
EMail: jareeder@pattonboggs.com
Special Projects Staff Member to Senator J. Bennett Johnson, Jr. (D-LA), 1972-90.

Employers
Patton Boggs, LLP (Partner)

Clients Represented
On Behalf of Patton Boggs, LLP
Aera Energy LLC
H.A.H. of Wisconsin L.P.
LA 1 Coalition
Midcoast Interstate Transmission, Inc.
Point of Purchase Advertising Institute
Save Barton Creek
United States Enrichment Corp.

REEDER, John E.

Ariel Rios Federal Bldg.
(1301-MC)
1200 Pennsylvania Ave. NW
3rd Floor
Washington, DC 20460
Tel: (202)564-3699
Fax: (202)501-1545
EMail: reeder.john@epa.gov

Employers
Environmental Protection Agency (Deputy Associate Administrator, Congressional Affairs)

REEDER, Joseph

800 Connecticut Ave. NW
Suite 500
Washington, DC 20006
Tel: (202)331-3100
Fax: (202)331-3101
Registered: LDA

Employers
Greenberg Traurig, LLP

Clients Represented
On Behalf of Greenberg Traurig, LLP
Singapore Technologies, Inc.

REEF, Grace

25 E St. NW
Washington, DC 20001
Tel: (202)628-8787
Fax: (202)662-3550
Registered: LDA
EMail: greef@childrensdefense.org

Employers
Children's Defense Fund (Director, Department of Intergovernmental Relations)

REES, Jr., Clifford H. "Ted"

4301 N. Fairfax Dr.
Suite 425
Arlington, VA 22203
Tel: (703)524-8800
Fax: (703)528-3816
Registered: LDA
EMail: trees@ari.org

Employers
Air-Conditioning and Refrigeration Institute (President)

REESE, Brenda Benjamin

1101 16th St. NW
Suite 500
Washington, DC 20036
Tel: (202)659-9111
Fax: (202)659-6387
Registered: LDA
Former Conference Coordinator, House Republican Conference.

Employers
Bergner Bockorny Castagnetti and Hawkins (Legislative Coordinator)

Clients Represented
On Behalf of Bergner Bockorny Castagnetti and Hawkins
Agilent Technologies
Biogen, Inc.
Chicago Board Options Exchange
Ovations/United Health Group
Premium Standard Farms

REESE, Evan

1050 Thomas Jefferson St. NW
Seventh Floor
Washington, DC 20007
Tel: (202)298-1800
Fax: (202)338-2416
EMail: ecr@vnf.com
Summer Law Clerk, Office of the Regional Counsel Region III, Environmental Protection Agency, 1998.

Employers
Van Ness Feldman, P.C. (Associate)

REESE, Melissa

2025 M St. NW
Suite 800
Washington, DC 20036
EMail: apna@dc.sba.com
Tel: (202)367-2100
Fax: (202)367-1200

Employers
Smith, Bucklin and Associates, Inc.

Clients Represented
On Behalf of Smith, Bucklin and Associates, Inc.
American Psychiatric Nurses Ass'n

REESE, Rebecca

1331 Pennsylvania Ave. NW
Suite 1300 North
Washington, DC 20004
EMail: rebecca.reese@eds.com
Tel: (202)637-6700
Fax: (202)637-6759

Employers
EDS Corp. (Director, International Economic Policy)

REESE, Jr., Robert S.

1341 G St. NW
Suite 900
Washington, DC 20005
Tel: (202)637-1526
Fax: (202)637-1531

Employers
Philip Morris Management Corp. (Director, Government Affairs, Tobacco)

REESE-HAWKINS, Angie

1112 16th St. NW
Suite 720
Washington, DC 20036
Tel: (202)232-6700
Fax: (202)797-4486

Employers
YMCA of Metropolitan Washington (President and Chief Exec. Officer)

REESMAN, Ann Elizabeth

1015 15th St. NW
Suite 1200
Washington, DC 20005
Tel: (202)789-8600
Fax: (202)789-1708

Employers
McGuiness Norris & Williams, LLP (Partner)

REEVES, David C.

401 Ninth St. NW
Suite 1000
Washington, DC 20004
Tel: (202)274-2932
Fax: (202)654-5624

Employers
Troutman Sanders LLP (Of Counsel)

Clients Represented
On Behalf of Troutman Sanders LLP
Kansas City Southern Industries
Paducah & Louisville Railroad

REEVES, Gregg

1820 11th St. NW
Washington, DC 20001-5015
Tel: (202)667-3280
Fax: (202)667-3705

Employers
Blacks in Government (Exec. V. President)

REEVES, J. Ronald

Crystal Park Four
2345 Crystal Dr.
Arlington, VA 22227
Tel: (703)872-5111
Fax: (703)872-5109
Registered: LDA

Employers
US Airways (V. President, Government Affairs)

REFFE, Paige E.

1801 K St. NW
Suite 1205L
Washington, DC 20006
Tel: (202)452-7330
Fax: (202)542-7333
Registered: LDA
Former Deputy Assistant to the President and Director of Advance, Executive Office of the President, The White House, during the Clinton administration.

Employers
Law Office of Paige E. Reffe (Attorney)

Clients Represented
On Behalf of Law Office of Paige E. Reffe
Ass'n of Bankruptcy Professionals, Inc.
Lithuania, Republic of
Slovakia, Government of
University of Colorado, Office of the President

REGALIA, Martin A.

1615 H St. NW
Washington, DC 20062-2000
Tel: (202)463-5620
Fax: (202)463-3174
Registered: LDA

Employers
Chamber of Commerce of the U.S.A. (V. President, Economic Policy and Chief Economist)

REGAN, Carol

1313 L St. NW
Washington, DC 20005
Tel: (202)898-3200
Fax: (202)898-3304
Registered: LDA

Employers
Service Employees Internat'l Union (Director, Health Policy)

REGAN, David

8400 W. Park Dr.
McLean, VA 22102
Tel: (202)547-5500
Fax: (202)479-0168

Employers
Nat'l Automobile Dealers Ass'n (Exec. Director, Legislative Affairs)

REGAN, James

818 Connecticut Ave. NW
Suite 1200
Washington, DC 20006
Tel: (202)872-8181
Fax: (202)872-8696

Employers
Internat'l Business-Government Counsellors, Inc. (Senior V. President)

REGAN, James J.

1001 Pennsylvania Ave. NW
Suite 1100
Washington, DC 20004-2595
Tel: (202)624-2500
Fax: (202)628-5116
Chief Counsel and Hearing Examiner, General Services Administration Board of Contract Appeals, 1982-86.

Employers
Crowell & Moring LLP (Partner)

REGAN, Michael

444 N. Capitol St. NW
Suite 740
Washington, DC 20001
Tel: (202)824-6500
Fax: (202)824-6510

Employers
News Corporation Ltd. (Senior V. President, Government Affairs)

REGAN, Jr., Michael

1101 Pennsylvania Ave. NW
Suite 805
Washington, DC 20004
Tel: (202)347-2771
Fax: (202)347-2822

Employers
Nextwave Telecom (Senior V. President, External Affairs)

REGAN, Timothy J.

1350 I St. NW
Suite 500
Washington, DC 20005-3305
EMail: regantj@corning.com
Tel: (202)682-3200
Fax: (202)682-3130
Registered: LDA

Employers
Corning Inc. (V. President and Director, Government Affairs)

REGELBRUGGE, Craig J.

1250 I St. NW
Suite 500
Washington, DC 20005
EMail: cregelbrugge@anla.org
Tel: (202)789-2900
Ext: 3013
Fax: (202)789-1893

Employers
American Nursery and Landscape Ass'n (Senior Director, Government Relations)
Nat'l Ass'n of Plant Patent Owners (Administrator)

REGNER, Col. M.

Russell Senate Office Bldg.
Room 152
Washington, DC 20510
Tel: (202)225-2832

Employers
Department of Navy - United States Marine Corps (House Liaison Officer)

REGNERY, Alfred S.

1001 G St. NW
Suite 500 West
Washington, DC 20001
EMail: regnery@khlaw.com
Tel: (202)434-4100
Fax: (202)434-4646
Administrator, Office of Juvenile Justice and Delinquency Prevention (1983-86) and Deputy Assistant Attorney General (1981-83), Department of Justice. Minority Counsel, Senate Committee on the Judiciary, 1978-81.

Employers
Keller and Heckman LLP (Counsel)

REHANZEL, Lenka

1710 Rhode Island Ave. NW
Fourth Floor
Washington, DC 20036
Tel: (202)467-0045
Fax: (202)467-0065
Registered: LDA

Employers
Federal Legislative Associates, Inc. (Legislative Coordinator)

REHG, Robert

1875 I St. NW
Suite 900
Washington, DC 20005
Tel: (202)371-0200
Fax: (202)371-2858
Registered: FARA
Former Chief of Staff for Rep. Bill Schuette (R-MI).

Employers
Edelman Public Relations Worldwide (General Manager)

Clients Represented
On Behalf of Edelman Public Relations Worldwide
American Worldwide
Church of Jesus Christ of Latter Day Saints
Fleet Capital
FleetBoston Financial
Portugal, Trade Commission of the Government of the Republic of

REHR, Ph.D., David K.

1100 S. Washington St.
First Floor
Alexandria, VA 22314-4494
Tel: (703)683-4300
Fax: (703)683-8965
Registered: LDA
Former Director, Government Relations, Nat'l Federation of Independent Business (NFIB). Also served on staff of the House Small Business Committee, and as aide to Rep. Vin Weber (R-MN).

Employers
Nat'l Beer Wholesalers Ass'n (President)

REICH, Alan A.

910 16th St. NW
Suite 600
Washington, DC 20006
Tel: (202)293-5960
Fax: (202)293-7999

Employers
Nat'l Organization on Disability (President)

REICH, Otto J.

5313 Lee Hwy.
Arlington, VA 22207
Tel: (703)536-8099
Fax: (703)536-8092
Registered: LDA
EMail: oreich@erols.com
Ambassador, U.S. Mission to Venezuela (1986-89), Special Advisor to the Secretary (1983-86), Department of State. Assistant Administrator, U.S. Agency for International Development, U.S. International Development Cooperation Agency, 1981-83.

Employers
RMA Internat'l, Inc. (President)

Clients Represented
On Behalf of RMA Internat'l, Inc.
Bacardi-Martini, USA, Inc.
Lockheed Martin Corp.
Marriott Internat'l, Inc.
Mobil Latin America & Caribbean, Inc.
Telegate, Inc.

REICH, Sheara
1920 L St. NW
Washington, DC 20036
EMail: sreich@kamber.com
Tel: (202)223-8700
Fax: (202)659-5559

Employers
The Kamber Group (Assistant Account Executive)

REICH, Thomas
2201 C St. NW
Room 7251
Washington, DC 20520-7261
Tel: (202)647-8351
Fax: (202)647-2762

Employers
Department of State - Bureau of Legislative Affairs (Balkans, Europe & NATO Affairs Legislative Management Officer)

REICHARDT, David L.
2000 Edmund Halley Dr.
Reston, VA 20191
Tel: (703)264-0330
Fax: (703)715-4450

Employers
DynCorp (Senior V. President and General Counsel)

REICHEL, Randi
1129 20th St. NW
Suite 600
Washington, DC 20036-3421
EMail: rreichel@aahp.org
Tel: (202)778-3200
Fax: (202)778-8479

Employers
American Ass'n of Health Plans (AAHP) (Exec. Director, State Affairs)

REICHENBERG, Neil E.
1617 Duke St.
Alexandria, VA 22314
EMail: nreichenberg@ipma-hr.org
Tel: (703)549-7100
Fax: (703)684-0948

Employers
Internat'l Personnel Management Ass'n (Exec. Director)

REICHERTS, Liz
1776 I St. NW
Suite 1000
Washington, DC 20006
Tel: (202)785-4888
Fax: (202)457-6597
Registered: LDA

Employers
BP Amoco Corp. (Associate Director, Government Affairs)

REICHLER, Paul S.
1747 Pennsylvania Ave. NW
Suite 1200
Washington, DC 20006
EMail: preichler@fhe.com
Tel: (202)223-1200
Fax: (202)785-6687
Registered: LDA, FARA

Employers
Foley, Hoag & Eliot LLP (Partner)

Clients Represented

On Behalf of Foley, Hoag & Eliot LLP
Guyana, Government of the Co-operative Republic of
Uganda, Embassy of the Republic of
Uganda, Government of the Republic of

REICHS, Kerry
1050 Connecticut Ave. NW
Washington, DC 20036-5339
Tel: (202)857-6000
Fax: (202)857-6395

Employers
Arent Fox Kintner Plotkin & Kahn, PLLC (Associate)

Clients Represented

On Behalf of Arent Fox Kintner Plotkin & Kahn, PLLC
Nat'l Ass'n of Retail Collection Attorneys

REID, Morris
1001 G St. NW
Suite 300 East
Washington, DC 20001
EMail: mreid@deweysquare.com
Tel: (202)638-5616
Fax: (202)638-5612
Registered: LDA

Employers
Dewey Square Group (V. President)

Clients Represented

On Behalf of Dewey Square Group
AT&T

REID, Myke
1300 L St. NW
Washington, DC 20005
EMail: mreid@apwu.org
Tel: (202)842-4211
Fax: (202)682-2528
Registered: LDA

Employers
American Postal Workers Union (Assistant Legislative Director)

REID, Nancy S.
1150 Connecticut Ave. NW
Suite 515
Washington, DC 20036
Tel: (202)296-2830
Fax: (202)294-4337

Employers
Armstrong World Industries, Inc. (Government Relations Specialist)

REID, Robert J.
815 15th St. NW
Suite 538
Washington, DC 20005
EMail: nhc@nhc.org
Tel: (202)393-5772
Fax: (202)393-5656

Employers
Nat'l Housing Conference (Exec. Director)

REIDER, Alan E.
1050 Connecticut Ave. NW
Washington, DC 20036-5339
Tel: (202)857-6000
Fax: (202)857-6395
Registered: LDA

Chief, Review Policy Branch, Office of Professional Standards Review Organizations, Health Care Financing Administration, Department of Health and Human Services, 1979-80. Analyst, Department of Health, Education and Welfare, 1975-79.

Employers
Arent Fox Kintner Plotkin & Kahn, PLLC (Member)

Clients Represented

On Behalf of Arent Fox Kintner Plotkin & Kahn, PLLC
Internat'l Soc. of Refractive Surgery
Soc. for Excellence in Eyecare

REIDY, Maura
1000 Jefferson Dr. SW
Suite T360
Washington, DC 20560
Tel: (202)357-2962
Fax: (202)786-2274

Employers
Smithsonian Institution (Senior Government Relations Specialist)

REIFF, Laura F.
1750 Tysons Blvd.
12th Floor
McLean, VA 22102
EMail: reiffl@gtlaw.com
Tel: (703)749-1372
Fax: (703)749-1301

Employers
Greenberg Traurig, LLP (Shareholder)

Clients Represented

On Behalf of Greenberg Traurig, LLP
Ingersoll-Rand Co.

REILLY, John R.
815 Connecticut Ave. NW
Suite 900
Washington, DC 20006-4078
Tel: (202)452-7000
Fax: (202)452-7073
Registered: LDA, FARA

Assistant to Deputy Attorney General, Chief of Executive Office for U.S. Attorney, 1961-64. Commissioner, Federal Trade Commission, 1964-67.

Employers
Baker & McKenzie (Of Counsel)

Clients Represented

On Behalf of Baker & McKenzie
British Columbia Softwood Lumber Trade Council

REILLY, Michael
1200 G St. NW
Suite 400
Washington, DC 20005
Tel: (202)783-8700
Fax: (202)783-8750

Employers
AdvaMed (Director, Government and Public Affairs)

REILLY, Shelia
1299 Pennsylvania Ave. NW
Suite 800 West
Washington, DC 20004
Tel: (202)785-0500
Fax: (202)785-5277
Registered: LDA

Employers
The Carmen Group (Events Director)

REILLY, William K.
1250 24th St. NW
Washington, DC 20037
Tel: (202)293-4800
Fax: (202)293-9211

Employers
World Wildlife Fund (Chairman of the Board)

REIMERS, Jean D.
801 Pennsylvania Ave. NW
Suite 725
Washington, DC 20004
EMail: jreimers@rp-agro.com
Tel: (202)628-0500
Fax: (202)628-6622
Registered: LDA

Employers
Aventis CropScience (Director, Government Affairs)

REIN, Bert W.
1776 K St. NW
Washington, DC 20006
Tel: (202)719-7000
Fax: (202)719-7049

Deputy Assistant Secretary for Economic and Business Affairs (1970-73) and Special Assistant to the Undersecretary (1969-70), Department of State. Law Clerk to Justice John M. Harlan, U.S. Supreme Court, 1966-67.

Employers
Wiley, Rein & Fielding (Partner)

Clients Represented

On Behalf of Wiley, Rein & Fielding
INTELSAT - Internat'l Telecommunications Satellite Organization

REINEMER, Michael
409 Third St. SW
Second Floor
Washington, DC 20024-6682
Tel: (202)479-1200
Fax: (202)479-0735

Employers
Nat'l Institute on Financial Issues and Services for Elders (Director, Marketing and Communications)

REINHARDT, Glenn
601 Wythe St.
Alexandria, VA 22314-1994
Tel: (703)684-2400
Fax: (703)684-2492

Employers
Water Environment Research Foundation (Exec. Director)

REINSCH, William A.
1625 K St. NW
Suite 1090
Washington, DC 20006-1604
Tel: (202)887-0278
Fax: (202)452-8160

Undersecretary for Export Administration, Department of Commerce, 1994-2001. Also served as a Congressional Aide.

Employers
Nat'l Foreign Trade Council, Inc. (President)

REINSDORF, Andrew
1771 N St. NW
Washington, DC 20036-2891
Tel: (202)429-5306
Fax: (202)775-2157
Registered: LDA

Employers
Nat'l Ass'n of Broadcasters (Director, House Congressional Liaison)

REIS, Sharon
1825 Connecticut Ave. NW
Suite 650
Washington, DC 20009
EMail: sreis@gyhllc.com
Tel: (202)745-5100
Fax: (202)234-6159

Employers
Garrett Yu Hussein LLC (Partner)

REISER, Marty

1250 H St. NW
Suite 700
Washington, DC 20005-3908
EMail: mreiser@csa.org
Tel: (202)783-3870
Fax: (202)783-4687

Employers
Citizens for a Sound Economy (V. President, Public Affairs)

REISER, Tom

2025 M St. NW
Suite 800
Washington, DC 20036
EMail: tom_reiser@dc.sba.com
Tel: (202)367-2100
Fax: (202)367-1200

Employers
Smith, Bucklin and Associates, Inc. (Account Executive)

Clients Represented

On Behalf of Smith, Bucklin and Associates, Inc.
Internat'l Bone and Mineral Soc.
Internat'l Soc. for Experimental Hematology

REITER, Jim

325 Seventh St. NW
Washington, DC 20004
Tel: (202)638-1100
Fax: (202)626-2287

Employers
American Hospital Ass'n (Director, Advocacy and Member Communications)

REITER, Mark

1325 G St. NW
Suite 1000
Washington, DC 20005-3104
Tel: (202)737-1770
Fax: (202)626-0900
Registered: LDA

Employers
Institute of Scrap Recycling Industries, Inc. (Director, Congressional and International Affairs)

RELIC, Becky

1725 DeSales St. NW
Suite 802
Washington, DC 20036
Tel: (202)887-8900
Fax: (202)887-8907
Registered: LDA

Employers
McDonald's Corp. (Staff Director, Federal Relations)

RELLER, Nancy

1951 Kidwell Dr.
Suite 205
Vienna, VA 22182
EMail: nreller@bballard.com
Tel: (703)827-8771
Fax: (703)827-0783

Employers
Barksdale Ballard & Co., Inc. (Senior V. President)

Clients Represented

On Behalf of Barksdale Ballard & Co., Inc.
Partnership for Caring
Robert Wood Johnson Foundation

REMES, David H.

1201 Pennsylvania Ave. NW
Washington, DC 20004-2401
EMail: dremes@cov.com
Tel: (202)662-6000
Fax: (202)662-6291
Registered: LDA

Employers
Covington & Burling (Partner)

Clients Represented

On Behalf of Covington & Burling
American Tobacco Co.
Loews Corp.

REMINGTON, Michael J.

1500 K St.
Suite 1100
Washington, DC 20005
EMail: michael_remington@dbr.com
Tel: (202)842-8800
Fax: (202)842-8465
Special Counsel (1991-92) and Chief Counsel (1983-91), Subcommittee on Courts, Intellectual Property, and the Administration of Justice, House Committee on the Judiciary. Deputy Legislative Affairs Officer, Administrative Office of U.S. Courts, 1981-83. Counsel, House Committee on the Judiciary, 1977-81. Attorney, Criminal Division, Department of Justice, 1975-77.

Employers
Drinker Biddle & Reath LLP (Partner)

Clients Represented

On Behalf of Drinker Biddle & Reath LLP
Broadcast Music Inc. (BMI)
Printing Industries of America
RioPort, Inc.

RENDALL, Shari

8224 Old Courthouse Rd.
Vienna, VA 22182-3808
EMail: srendall@ncrahq.org
Tel: (703)556-6272
Fax: (703)556-6291
Registered: LDA

Employers
Nat'l Court Reporters Ass'n (Assistant Manager, Government Relations)

RENDIN, Betty L.

1900 M St. NW
5th Floor
Washington, DC 20036
Tel: (202)638-6355
Fax: (202)638-1419

Employers
Washington Group Internat'l (Treasurer, Washington Group Internat'l PAC)

RENDON, Jr., John W.

1875 Connecticut Ave. NW
Suite 414
Washington, DC 20009
EMail: jrendon@rendon.com
Tel: (202)745-4900
Fax: (202)745-0215
Registered: FARA

Employers
The Rendon Group, Inc. (President)

Clients Represented

On Behalf of The Rendon Group, Inc.
Aruba, Government of

RENDON, Martin Stephen

1775 K St. NW
Suite 360
Washington, DC 20006
EMail: mrendon@unicefusa.org
Tel: (202)296-4242
Fax: (202)296-4060
Registered: LDA

Employers
U.S. Fund for UNICEF (V. President, Public Policy and Advocacy)

RENKES, Gregg D.

1330 Connecticut Ave. NW
Suite 200
Washington, DC 20036
Tel: (202)872-9380
Fax: (202)872-1377
Registered: LDA, FARA
Former Chief of Staff, Committee on Energy and Natural Resources, U.S. Senate.

Employers
The Renkes Group, Ltd. (President)

Clients Represented

On Behalf of The Renkes Group, Ltd.
AIG Environmental
Coeur d'Alene Mines Corp.
Cominco Alaska Inc.
Edison Electric Institute
FirstEnergy Co.
Florida Power and Light Co.
Fort Sumter Tours
Land Trust Alliance
Lockheed Martin Idaho Technologies Corp.
NAC Internat'l
Nuclear Energy Institute
Pinnacle West Capital Corp.
Princess Cruise Lines
Sealaska Corp.
Southern Co.
USA Biomass Power Producers Alliance

RENNA, Stephen M.

1420 New York Ave. NW
Suite 1100
Washington, DC 20005
EMail: srenna@rer.org
Tel: (202)639-8400
Fax: (202)639-8442
Registered: LDA

Employers
Real Estate Roundtable (V. President and Counsel)

RENO, Lee P.

1250 I St. NW
Suite 900
Washington, DC 20005
EMail: lreno@renocavanaugh.com
Tel: (202)783-2800
Fax: (202)783-0550

Employers
Reno & Cavanaugh, PLLC (Member)

Clients Represented

On Behalf of Reno & Cavanaugh, PLLC
Housing Assistance Council

RENTON, Susan

1300 Pennsylvania Ave. NW
Suite 400
Ronald Reagan Bldg.
Washington, DC 20004
EMail: srenton@strtrade.com
Tel: (202)638-2230
Fax: (202)638-2236
Registered: LDA
Attorney, Office of Regulations and Rulings, U.S. Customs Service, Department of the Treasury.

Employers
Sandler, Travis & Rosenberg, P.A. (Associate)

Clients Represented

On Behalf of Sandler, Travis & Rosenberg, P.A.
Tailored Clothing Ass'n

RENYI, Judith

1201 16th St. NW
Washington, DC 20036
Tel: (202)822-7840
Fax: (202)822-7779

Employers
Nat'l Foundation for the Improvement of Education (Exec. Director)

REPA, Ph.D., Edward A.

4301 Connecticut Ave. NW
Suite 300
Washington, DC 20008
Tel: (202)244-4700
Fax: (202)966-4818

Employers
Environmental Industry Ass'ns (Director, Environment Programs)
Nat'l Solid Wastes Management Ass'n (Director, Environmental Programs)

REPASS, David M.

1301 K St. NW
Washington, DC 20005-3333
Tel: (202)414-1000
Fax: (202)414-1301
Registered: LDA

Employers
PriceWaterhouseCoopers (Senior Manager)

RESCH, Rhone

805 15th St. NW
Suite 510
Washington, DC 20005
EMail: rresch@ngsa.org
Tel: (202)326-9300
Fax: (202)326-9330
Registered: LDA

Employers
Natural Gas Supply Ass'n (Director, Utility Regulation and Environmental Affairs)

RESKOVAC, J. R.

1420 New York Ave. NW
Washington, DC 20005
Tel: (202)638-0326
Fax: (202)737-5154
Registered: LDA

Employers
VSAdc.com

Clients Represented

On Behalf of VSAdc.com
59/Air Depot Road, Ltd.
Lawton/Fort Sill Chamber of Commerce & Industry
Midwest City Municipal Authority
Oklahoma, State of
Tulsa Airport Authority
Vance Development Authority

RESLER, Barclay T.

800 Connecticut Ave. NW
Suite 711
Washington, DC 20006
EMail: bresler@na.ko.com
Tel: (202)973-2660
Fax: (202)466-2262
Registered: LDA

Employers
The Coca-Cola Company (Assistant V. President, Governmental Relations)

RESNICK, Michael A.

1680 Duke St.
Alexandria, VA 22314-3407
Tel: (703)838-6722
Fax: (703)683-7590

Employers
Nat'l School Boards Ass'n (Assoc. Exec. Director, Advocacy and Issues Management)

RESNICK, Richard M.

1125 15th St. NW
Suite 801
Washington, DC 20005
Tel: (202)785-9300
Fax: (202)775-1950

Employers
Sherman, Dunn, Cohen, Leifer & Yellig, P.C.

RESNICK, Sarah Chamberlain

1350 I St. NW
Suite 560
Washington, DC 20003
EMail: sarahJQA@mindspring.com
Tel: (202)682-3143
Fax: (202)682-3943

Employers
Republican Main Street Partnership (Exec. Director)

REUBMAN, Elizabeth

1130 Connecticut Ave. NW
Suite 300
Washington, DC 20036
Tel: (202)331-8500
Fax: (202)331-1598
Registered: LDA

Employers
The Ferguson Group, LLC (Associate)

REUSING, Vincent P.

1620 L St. NW
Suite 800
Washington, DC 20036-5617
Tel: (202)659-3575
Fax: (202)659-1026
Registered: LDA

Employers
Metropolitan Life Insurance Co. (Senior V. President, Government and Industry Relations)

REUTHER, Alan V.

1350 I St. NW
Suite 510
Washington, DC 20005
Tel: (202)828-8500
Fax: (202)293-3457
Registered: LDA

Employers
United Automobile, Aerospace and Agricultural Implement Workers of America (UAW) (Legislative Director)

REUTHER, Mary Lacey

1900 K St. NW
Suite 100
Washington, DC 20006
Tel: (202)496-7150
Fax: (202)496-7756

Employers
Medical Device Manufacturers Ass'n (Deputy Exec. Director)

REVAZ, Cris R.

1455 Pennsylvania Ave. NW
Suite 1000
Washington, DC 20004
EMail: cris.revaz@haledorr.com
Tel: (202)942-8400
Fax: (202)942-8484
Registered: LDA

Employers
Hale and Dorr LLP (Of Counsel)

REYAZUDDIN, Mohammed

1030 15th St. NW
Suite 250
Washington, DC 20005-1503
EMail: geron@geron.org
Tel: (202)842-1275
Fax: (202)842-1150

Employers
Gerontological Soc. of America (Information Specialist)

REYES, Paul

2121 R St. NW
Washington, DC 20008-1908
EMail: jpaulreyes@aol.com
Tel: (202)673-5869
Fax: (202)673-5873

Employers
Northern Mariana Islands, Commonwealth of the (Assistant Fiscal Officer)

REYES, Victor

800 Connecticut Ave. NW
Suite 500
Washington, DC 20006
Tel: (202)331-3100
Fax: (202)331-3101

Employers
Greenberg Traurig, LLP (Shareholder)

REYNOLDS, Alan

1015 18th St. NW
Suite 300
Washington, DC 20036
Tel: (202)223-7770
Fax: (202)223-8537

Employers
Hudson Institute (Senior Fellow and Director, Economic Studies)

REYNOLDS, David L.

400 N. Capitol St. NW
Suite 357 South
Washington, DC 20001
Tel: (202)434-4760
Fax: (202)434-4763
Registered: LDA

Director of External Relations, Bureau of Reclamation, Department of Interior, 1989-93. Legislative Assistant to Rep. Nancy Johnson (R-CT), 1983-86.

Employers
Ass'n of California Water Agencies (Director, Federal Relations)

REYNOLDS, Dennis

4915 St. Elmo Ave.
Suite 401
Bethesda, MD 20814
Tel: (301)657-1291
Fax: (301)657-1296

Employers
American Medical Informatics Ass'n (Exec. Director)

REYNOLDS, E. Kenneth

1155 15th St. NW
Suite 1101
Washington, DC 20005
EMail: abi@erols.com
Tel: (202)833-7756
Fax: (202)833-1429
Registered: LDA

Employers
Ass'n of Banks in Insurance (Exec. Director)

REYNOLDS, Elizabeth

1213 K St. NW
Washington, DC 20005
Tel: (202)347-7201
Fax: (202)638-6764

Employers
District of Columbia Chamber of Commerce (Coordinator, Special Events/Administration)

REYNOLDS, III, John B.

1776 K St. NW
Washington, DC 20006
Tel: (202)719-7000
Fax: (202)719-7049
Registered: LDA

Attorney/Advisor, Office of the Legal Advisor, Department of State, 1982-88. Law Clerk to Judge Caleb M. Wright, U.S. District Court for the District of Delaware, 1981-82.

Employers
Wiley, Rein & Fielding (Partner)

REYNOLDS, John R.

1350 New York Ave. NW
Suite 900
Washington, DC 20005
Tel: (202)628-8000
Fax: (202)628-0812

Employers
Internat'l Franchise Ass'n (President, IFA Educational Foundation and Exec. V. President)

REYNOLDS, Nicholas S.

1400 L St. NW
Washington, DC 20005-3502
EMail: nreynold@winston.com
Tel: (202)371-5717
Fax: (202)371-5950

Attorney, Office of the General Counsel, Federal Trade Commission

Employers
Winston & Strawn (Partner, Energy Practice)

RHEINSTEIN, Valerie

2021 K St. NW
Suite 305
Washington, DC 20006-1003
EMail: press@agingresearch.org
Tel: (202)293-2856
Fax: (202)785-8574

Employers
Alliance for Aging Research (Director of Communications)

RHETT, Candace M.

8630 Fenton St.
Suite 400
Silver Spring, MD 20910-3803
EMail: c.rhett@worldnet.att.net
Tel: (301)565-9016
Fax: (301)565-0018
Registered: LDA

Employers
Internat'l Federation of Professional and Technical Engineers (Communications Director)

RHINELANDER, John B.

2300 N St. NW
Washington, DC 20037-1128
EMail: john.rhinelander@shawpittman.com
Tel: (202)663-8000
Fax: (202)663-8007

Undersecretary, Department of Housing and Urban Development, 1975-77. General Counsel, Department of Health, Education and Welfare, 1973-75. Legal Advisor to U.S. Soviet Arms Limitation Treaty (SALT) Delegation, Arms Control and Disarmament Agency, 1971-72. Deputy Legal Advisor, Department of State, 1969-71. Chief Counsel and Acting Deputy Director, Office of Foreign Direct Investments, Department of Commerce, 1968-69. Law Clerk to Justice John M. Harlan, U.S. Supreme Court, 1961-62.

Employers
Shaw Pittman (Senior Counsel)

RHOADS, Barry D.

700 13th St. NW
Suite 350
Washington, DC 20005
Tel: (202)637-0040
Fax: (202)637-0041
Registered: LDA

Deputy General Counsel, Base Realignment and Closure Commission, 1991. Trial Attorney, Tax Division, Department of Justice, 1986-89.

Employers
Rhoads Group (Senior V. President)

Clients Represented

On Behalf of Rhoads Group

AAAE-ACI
Airports Council Internat'l - North America
American Management Systems
Dick Corp.
The Justice Project, Inc.
Orange, California, County of
PNC Bank, N.A.
SWATH Ocean Systems, Inc.
Taiwan Studies Institute
United States Enrichment Corp.

RHODES, Frederick W.

1755 Jefferson Davis Hwy.
Suite 1007
Arlington, VA 22202-3051
EMail: frhodes@aol.com
Tel: (703)414-1041
Fax: (703)414-1071

Employers
Loral Space and Communications, Ltd. (V. President, Corporate Legislative Relations)

RHODES, III, Hon. John J.

c/o Hunton & Williams
1900 K St. NW
Washington, DC 20006-1109
Tel: (202)955-1523
Fax: (202)778-2201
Registered: LDA

Member, U.S. House of Representatives (R-AZ), 1987-93.

Employers
Self-employed as an independent consultant.

Clients Represented

As an independent consultant

Central Arizona Water Conservation District
Garrison Diversion Conservancy District
George Washington University, Office of Government Relations
Imperial Irrigation District
San Carlos Irrigation and Drainage District

RHODES, Jr., Robert L.

2099 Pennsylvania Ave. NW
Suite 100
Washington, DC 20006
Tel: (202)955-3000
Fax: (202)955-5564
Registered: LDA
EMail: rrhodes@hklaw.com
Served in the U.S. Air Force, 1972-76.

Employers
Holland & Knight LLP (Partner)

RHODES, Sage

606 E. Capitol St. NE
Washington, DC 20003
Tel: (202)546-1493
Fax: (202)546-7807
EMail: msage34404@aol.com

Employers
Broad-Band Solutions (Principal)

Clients Represented
On Behalf of Broad-Band Solutions
Register.com

RHOME, Anne M.

One Dupont Circle NW
Suite 530
Washington, DC 20036
Tel: (202)463-6930
Ext: 230
Fax: (202)785-8320
EMail: arhome@aacn.nche.edu

Employers
American Ass'n of Colleges of Nursing (Deputy Exec. Director)

RHONE, Adrienne G.

1301 K St. NW
Suite 1200-West Tower
Washington, DC 20005-3307
Tel: (202)515-5103
Fax: (202)515-5906
Registered: LDA
EMail: aag@us.ibm.com

Employers
Internat'l Business Machines Corp. (Manager, Government Relations)

RHOTEN, William C.

901 Massachusetts Ave. NW
Washington, DC 20001
Tel: (202)628-5823
Fax: (202)628-5024

Employers
United Ass'n of Journeymen and Apprentices of the Plumbing and Pipe Fitting Industry of the U.S. and Canada (Director, Department of Safety and Health)

RICCARDI, Jennifer

1775 Pennsylvania Ave. NW
Suite 200
Washington, DC 20006
Tel: (202)862-1000
Fax: (202)862-1093
Registered: LDA

Employers
Dewey Ballantine LLP (Associate)

Clients Represented
On Behalf of Dewey Ballantine LLP
Dutch Produce Ass'n

RICCELLI, Marcus M.

206 G St. NE
Washington, DC 20002
Tel: (202)543-3383
Fax: (202)544-7716
Registered: LDA

Employers
Evergreen Associates, Ltd.

Clients Represented
On Behalf of Evergreen Associates, Ltd.
Clover Park School District
Medical Lake School District
Washington State Impact Aid Ass'n

RICCHETTI, Jeff

1001 G St. NW
Suite 700 E
Washington, DC 20001-4545
Tel: (202)879-9321
Fax: (202)879-9340
Registered: LDA

Employers
Ricchetti Inc. (Principal)

Clients Represented
On Behalf of Ricchetti Inc.
American Gastroenterological Ass'n

RICCHETTI, Steve

1001 G St. NW
Suite 700 E
Washington, DC 20001-4545
Tel: (202)879-9321
Fax: (202)879-9340
Deputy Chief of Staff (1999-2001) and Deputy Assistant for Senate Legislative Affairs (1993-96), Executive Office of the President, The White House.

Employers
Ricchetti Inc. (Principal)

Clients Represented
On Behalf of Ricchetti Inc.
American Gastroenterological Ass'n
Fannie Mae

RICCI, Tiffany

440 First St. NW
Eighth Floor
Washington, DC 20001
Tel: (202)942-4220
Fax: (202)393-2630

Employers
Nat'l Ass'n of Counties

RICE, Edmund B.

1100 Connecticut Ave. NW
Suite 810
Washington, DC 20036
Tel: (202)296-6107
Fax: (202)296-9709
Registered: LDA
EMail: edmund.rice@usaexport.org

Employers
Coalition for Employment through Exports (President)

RICE, Lois Dickson

1775 Massachusetts Ave. NW
Washington, DC 20036-2188
Tel: (202)797-6000
Fax: (202)797-6004

Employers
The Brookings Institution (Guest Scholar, Economic Studies)

RICE, Paul Jackson

1050 Connecticut Ave. NW
Washington, DC 20036-5339
Tel: (202)857-6000
Fax: (202)857-6395
Registered: LDA
Chief Counsel, Nat'l Highway Traffic Safety Commission, Department of Transportation, 1990-91. Colonel, U.S. Army, 1962-90.

Employers
Arent Fox Kintner Plotkin & Kahn, PLLC (Member)

Clients Represented
On Behalf of Arent Fox Kintner Plotkin & Kahn, PLLC
Bombardier, Inc.
Engineering Animation, Inc.

RICH, Barbara A.

818 Connecticut Ave. NW
Suite 200
Washington, DC 20006
Tel: (202)857-0540
Fax: (202)659-1902
Registered: LDA
EMail: brich@nabr.org

Employers
Nat'l Ass'n for Biomedical Research (Exec. V. President)

RICH, Bruce

1875 Connecticut Ave. NW
Suite 1016
Washington, DC 20009
Tel: (202)387-3500
Fax: (202)319-8590

Employers
Environmental Defense Fund (Chairman, Internat'l Programs)

RICH, J. Curtis

1050 Thomas Jefferson St. NW
Seventh Floor
Washington, DC 20007
Tel: (202)298-1800
Fax: (202)338-2416
Registered: LDA
EMail: JCR@vnf.com
Natural Resource and Energy Policy Counsel to Senator Max Baucus (D-MT), 1992-96.

Employers
Van Ness Feldman, P.C. (Of Counsel)

Clients Represented
On Behalf of Van Ness Feldman, P.C.
Blackfeet Tribe of Montana
Nat'l Endangered Species Act Reform Coalition
Nat'l Rural Electric Cooperative Ass'n
Sisters of Charity of Leavenworth Health Services
Three Affiliated Tribes of Fort Berthold Reservation

RICH, Jr., James E.

1401 I St. NW
Suite 1030
Washington, DC 20005
Tel: (202)466-1425
Ext: 425
Fax: (202)466-1498
Registered: LDA

Employers
Shell Oil Co. (Washington Representative)

RICH, John Townsend

1800 Massachusetts Ave. NW
Washington, DC 20036
Tel: (202)828-2000
Fax: (202)828-2195
Law Clerk to Justice Harry A. Blackmun, U.S. Supreme Court, 1971-72, and to Chief Judge David L. Bazelon, U.S. Court of Appeals, District of Columbia Circuit, 1970-71.

Employers
Shea & Gardner (Partner)

RICH, Laurie M.

122 C St. NW
Suite 200
Washington, DC 20001
Tel: (202)638-3927
Fax: (202)628-1943

Employers
Texas, Office of State-Federal Relations of the State of (Exec. Director)

RICH, Peter D.

1333 H St. NW
Washington, DC 20005
Tel: (202)898-8300
Fax: (202)898-8383

Employers
Reuters America Inc. (V. President, Government Relations)

RICH, M.D., William L.

1101 Vermont Ave. NW
Suite 700
Washington, DC 20005
Tel: (202)737-6662
Fax: (202)737-7061
Registered: LDA
EMail: wrich@aaodc.org

Employers
American Academy of Ophthamology - Office of Federal Affairs (Secretary, Federal Affairs)

RICHARD, Eric

805 15th St. NW
Suite 300
Washington, DC 20005-2207
Tel: (202)682-4200
Fax: (202)682-9054
Registered: LDA

Employers
Credit Union Nat'l Ass'n, Inc. (General Counsel)

RICHARD, John

P.O. Box 19367
Washington, DC 20036
Tel: (202)387-8030
Fax: (202)234-5176
EMail: jrichard@essential.org

Employers
Center for the Study of Responsive Law (Exec. Director)
Essential Information Inc. (Secretary)

RICHARD, Michael T.

1776 I St. NW
Suite 400
Washington, DC 20006-3708
Tel: (202)739-8000
Fax: (202)785-4019

Employers
Nuclear Energy Institute (Director, Congressional Information Program)

RICHARD, Sue

1634 I St. NW
Suite 300
Washington, DC 20006
Tel: (202)628-1245
Fax: (202)628-2528
Deputy Associate Administrator (1989-90) and Associate Administrator for Public Affairs (1991-93), Nat'l Aeronautics and Space Administration. Special Assistant to the President and Director of Media Relations (1985-1987) and Deputy Director of Media Relations (1981-84), The White House.

Employers
Intel Corp. (Press Relations Manager)

RICHARDS, Ann W.

901 15th St. NW
Suite 700
Washington, DC 20005-2301
Tel: (202)371-6000
Fax: (202)371-6279
Registered: LDA

Employers
Verner, Liipfert, Bernhard, McPherson and Hand, Chartered (Senior Advisor)

Clients Represented

On Behalf of Verner, Liipfert, Bernhard, McPherson and Hand, Chartered
Austin, Texas, City of
Capital Metropolitan Transportation Authority
Ferrocarril Mexicano, S.A. de C.V.
Lockheed Martin Tactical Systems
Mills Corporation
Nat'l Broadcasting Co.
RJR Nabisco Holdings Co.
SBC Communications Inc.
Texas Manufactured Housing Ass'n

RICHARDS, Cory L.

1120 Connecticut Ave. NW
Suite 460
Washington, DC 20036
Tel: (202)296-4012
Fax: (202)223-5756
EMail: crichards@agi-usa.org

Employers
The Alan Guttmacher Institute (V. President, Public Policy)

RICHARDS, Jeff B.

1111 19th St. NW
Suite 1180
Washington, DC 20036
Tel: (202)955-8091
Fax: (202)955-8081
EMail: richards@internetalliance.org

Employers
Internet Alliance Inc. (Exec. Director)

RICHARDS, John B.

1001 G St. NW
Suite 500 West
Washington, DC 20001
Tel: (202)434-4100
Fax: (202)434-4653
EMail: richards@khlaw.com

Legal Assistant to Commissioner Mimi Weyforth Dawson (1984-86), Chief (1983-84), Deputy Chief (1981-82), Chief of Enforcement Branch (1978-80), and Trial Attorney (1976-78), Rules Branch, Land Mobile and Microwave Division, Private Radio Bureau; Federal Communications Commission.

Employers
Keller and Heckman LLP (Partner)

RICHARDS, Patricia M.

1101 Pennsylvania Ave. NW
Suite 510
Washington, DC 20004
Tel: (202)783-6333
Fax: (202)783-6309
Registered: LDA

Employers
USX Corp. (Manager, Governmental Affairs)

RICHARDS, Richard

1025 Thomas Jefferson St. NW
Suite 410E
Washington, DC 20007
Tel: (202)342-3830
Fax: (202)318-0065
Registered: FARA

Employers
Commerce Consultants Internat'l Ltd. (Chairman)

Clients Represented

On Behalf of Commerce Consultants Internat'l Ltd.
Sunrider Internat'l
Young Brothers Development (USA), Inc.

RICHARDS, Steve

1025 Thomas Jefferson St. NW
Suite 410E
Washington, DC 20007
Tel: (202)342-3830
Fax: (202)318-0065

Employers
Commerce Consultants Internat'l Ltd. (V. President)

Clients Represented

On Behalf of Commerce Consultants Internat'l Ltd.
Integrated Microcomputer Systems, Inc.
Thai Gypsum Products Co., Ltd.

RICHARDS, Timothy J.

1299 Pennsylvania Ave. NW
Suite 1100 West
Washington, DC 20004-2407
Tel: (202)637-4000
Fax: (202)637-4300
Registered: LDA

Employers
General Electric Co. (Senior Manager, International Trade and Investment)

RICHARDSON, Alan H.

2301 M St. NW
Washington, DC 20037-1484
Tel: (202)467-2901
Fax: (202)467-2910
Registered: LDA
EMail: arichardson@APPAnet.org

Employers
American Public Power Ass'n (President/Chief Exec. Officer)

RICHARDSON, Bill

702 H. Street NW
Suite 300
Washington, DC 20001
Tel: (202)462-1177
Fax: (202)462-4507

Employers
Greenpeace, U.S.A. (Manager, Office Facilities)

RICHARDSON, Bonnie

1600 I St. NW
Washington, DC 20006
Tel: (202)293-1966
Fax: (202)296-7410
Registered: LDA

Employers
Motion Picture Ass'n of America (V. President, Trade and Federal Affairs)

RICHARDSON, Charles T.

805 15th St. NW
Suite 700
Washington, DC 20005
Tel: (202)312-7440
Fax: (202)312-7460
EMail: ctrichar@bakerd.com

Employers
Baker & Daniels (Partner)

RICHARDSON, Craig

2300 Clarendon Blvd.
Suite 401
Arlington, VA 22201
Tel: (703)516-4787
Fax: (703)522-2628
Registered: LDA
EMail: craigr@washingtonstrategies.com

Employers
Washington Strategies, L.L.C.

RICHARDSON, Debi Q.

1801 K St. NW
Suite 600K
Washington, DC 20006
Tel: (202)974-5204
Fax: (202)296-7218
Registered: LDA

Employers
Soc. of the Plastics Industry (Assistant Director, Safety, Health and State Affairs)

RICHARDSON, Douglas C.

1400 L St. NW
Washington, DC 20005-3502
Tel: (202)371-5868
Fax: (202)371-5950
Registered: LDA
EMail: drichard@winston.com

Former Legislative Assistant to Rep. Lynn Martin (R-IL). Former Staff Assistant to Rep. Tom Tauke (R-IA).

Employers
Winston & Strawn (Legislative Advisor, Legislative and Regulatory Practice)

Clients Represented

On Behalf of Winston & Strawn
Barr Laboratories
Chicago, Regional Transportation Authority of
EyeTicket Corp.
Federal Judges Ass'n
Gildan Activewear
Heller Financial Inc.
Leukemia and Lymphoma Soc. of America
Liberty Maritime Co.
Motor Coach Industries, Inc.
Norfolk Southern Corp.
Northland Holdings, Inc.
Panda Energy Internat'l
Puerto Rico, Commonwealth of
Research Planning, Inc.
Rickenbacker Port Authority
Southern Illinois University
Yellow Corp.

RICHARDSON, Jeff

1920 L St. NW
Washington, DC 20036
Tel: (202)223-8700
Fax: (202)659-5559
EMail: jrichardson@kamber.com

Employers
The Kamber Group (Staff Assistant)

Clients Represented

On Behalf of The Kamber Group
Nat'l Energy Management Institute

RICHARDSON, Julie R.

1050 Thomas Jefferson St. NW
Seventh Floor
Washington, DC 20007
Tel: (202)298-1800
Fax: (202)338-2416
EMail: jrr@vnf.com

Staff member, Energy Policy and Planning Office, Executive Office of the President, The White House, 1977. Office of General Counsel, Litigation Division, Federal Energy Administration, 1975-76. Former Legislative Assistant to Rep. Philip Ruppe (R-MI).

Employers
Van Ness Feldman, P.C. (Member)

RICHARDSON, Kermit

1616 H St. NW
Washington, DC 20006
Tel: (202)628-3507
Fax: (202)347-1091
Registered: LDA
EMail: krichardson@usemail.com

Employers
Nat'l Grange (President)

RICHARDSON, Jr., Lawrence S.

4115 Wisconsin Ave. NW
Suite 211
Washington, DC 20016
Tel: (202)966-0440
Fax: (202)966-8336
EMail: larry@ngrc.com

Employers
Nat'l Grass Roots & Communications (President)

RICHARDSON, Rayna H.

1717 Pennsylvania Ave. NW
Suite 600
Washington, DC 20006
Tel: (202)293-3450
Fax: (202)293-2787
Registered: LDA

Employers
Medical Group Management Ass'n (Government Affairs Representative)

RICHARDSON, Sam

203 S. West St.
Alexandria, VA 22314-2826
Tel: (703)548-3055
Fax: (703)684-5191

Former Press Secretary to Senator Bob Dole (R-KS); Press Secretary, Senate Committee on Finance; Communications Director, National Congressional Campaign Committee; and Communications Director, Office of Tax Policy, Department of Treasury.

Employers
Self-employed as an independent consultant.

Clients Represented

As an independent consultant

Asset Management Consultants
Berwind Corp.
The Bortz Corp.
ESCO Corp.
Jones, Day, Reavis & Pogue
LTV Steel Co.
Moberly-Randolph County Economic Development
Mueller Industries, Inc.
NACCO Industries
Nat'l Federation of Pachyderm Clubs, Inc.
Ninth Congressional District Republican Committee
Palmer Coking & Coal Co.
Sheesley Construction Corp.

RICHARDSON, Steven

1050 Thomas Jefferson St. NW
Seventh Floor
Washington, DC 20007
Tel: (202)298-1800
Fax: (202)338-2416
Registered: LDA

Former Director of Policy and External Affairs, Commissioner's Office, Bureau of Reclamation, Department of the Interior. Served as Professional Staff Member, Subcommittee on Environment, Energy and Natural Resources, House Committee on Government Operations. Former Staff Director and Counsel, Subcommittee on Oversight and Investigations, House Committee on Interior and Insular Affairs. Served as Legislative Counsel to Rep. Edward J. Markey (D-MA). Former Counsel, Subcommittee on the Constitution, Senate Committee on the Judiciary.

Employers

Van Ness Feldman, P.C. (Member)

Clients Represented

On Behalf of Van Ness Feldman, P.C.

Blackfeet Tribe of Montana
Three Affiliated Tribes of Fort Berthold Reservation

RICHARDSON, Tim

6707 Old Stage Rd.
North Bethesda, MD 20852
Tel: (301)770-6496
Fax: (301)770-6497
Registered: LDA

Former Special Assistant to Senator Lloyd Bentsen (D-TX), 1988; Administrative Assistant to Rep. Greg Laughlin (D-TX), 1989-90.

Employers

Outdoor Media, Inc. (President)

Clients Represented

On Behalf of Outdoor Media, Inc.

Kodiak Brown Bear Trust
Theodore Roosevelt Conservation Alliance
Wildlife Forever

RICHARDSON, Timothy M.

309 Massachusetts Ave. NE
Washington, DC 20002
Tel: (202)547-8189
Fax: (202)547-8190
Registered: LDA

Employers

Fraternal Order of Police (Legislative Assistant)

RICHARDSON, Jr., William R.

2445 M St. NW
Washington, DC 20037-1420
Tel: (202)663-6000
Fax: (202)663-6363
EMail: wrichardson@wilmer.com

Former Law Clerk to Judge John C. Godbold, U.S. Court of Appeals, Fifth Circuit.

Employers

Wilmer, Cutler & Pickering (Partner)

Clients Represented

On Behalf of Wilmer, Cutler & Pickering

ValueVision Internat'l, Inc.

RICHARDSON, Yolonda

440 R St. NW
Washington, DC 20001
Tel: (202)462-3614
Fax: (202)387-1034

Employers

Africare (Senior V. President)

RICHBOURG, Donald E.

106 North Carolina Ave. SE
Washington, DC 20003
Tel: (202)863-0001
Fax: (202)863-0096
Registered: LDA

Former Staff, House Appropriations Committee; Chief Clerk, National Security Subcommittee; and Chief Clerk, Foreign Affairs Subcommittee.

Employers

Ervin Technical Associates, Inc. (ETA)

Clients Represented

On Behalf of Ervin Technical Associates, Inc. (ETA)

ACS Defense, Inc.
Computer Coalition for Responsible Exports
Ingalls Shipbuilding
Kaiser-Hill Co., L.L.C.
Kaman Diversified Technologies Corp.
Lister Bolt & Chain Co.
Lockheed Martin Corp.
Martins Point Health Care
Northrop Grumman Corp.
Science Applications Internat'l Corp. (SAIC)
United Defense, L.P.

RICHERSON, Lois

1724 Massachusetts Ave. NW
Washington, DC 20036-1969
Tel: (202)775-3550
Fax: (202)775-3671
Registered: LDA

Employers

Nat'l Cable Television Ass'n (Director, Government Relations)

RICHERT, Mark D.

820 First St. NE
Suite 400
Washington, DC 20002
EMail: mrichert@afb.net
Tel: (202)408-8170
Fax: (202)289-7880
Registered: LDA

Employers

American Foundation for the Blind - Governmental Relations Group (Governmental Relations Representative)

RICHESON, Darlene

1300 I St. NW
Suite 400 West
Washington, DC 20005
Tel: (202)515-2558
Fax: (202)336-7921

Employers

Verizon Communications (Assistant V. President, Federal Government Relations)

RICHEY, Cdr. Thomas

Russell Senate Office Bldg.
Room 183
Washington, DC 20510
EMail: trichey@comdit.uscg.mil
Tel: (202)224-2913
Fax: (202)755-1695

Employers

Department of Transportation - United States Coast Guard (Chief, Senate Liaison Staff, Congressional Relations Staff, Office of Government and Public Affairs)

RICHICHI, Thomas

1350 I St. NW
Suite 700
Washington, DC 20005
Tel: (202)789-6000
Fax: (202)789-6190

Law Clerk to Judge John J. Sirica, U.S. District Court for the District of Columbia, 1980-82.

Employers

Beveridge & Diamond, P.C. (Partner)

RICHIE, Robert

P.O. Box 60037
Washington, DC 20039
EMail: fairvote@compuserve.com
Tel: (301)270-4616
Fax: (301)270-4133

Employers

The Center for Voting and Democracy (Exec. Director)

RICHLAND, MPH, Jordan H.

1307 New York Ave. NW
Suite 200
Washington, DC 20005
EMail: jhr@acpm.org
Tel: (202)466-2044
Fax: (202)466-2662

Employers

American College of Preventive Medicine (Exec. Director)

RICHMAN, Dvorah A.

1730 Pennsylvania Ave. NW
Suite 1200
Washington, DC 20006-4706
Tel: (202)737-0500
Fax: (202)626-3737

Employers

King & Spalding (Partner)

RICHMAN, Jeffrey W.

555 12th St. NW
Washington, DC 20004-1206
Tel: (202)942-5098
Fax: (202)942-5999
Registered: LDA
EMail: Jeff_Richman@aporter.com

Employers

Arnold & Porter (Associate)

Clients Represented

On Behalf of Arnold & Porter

Health Services of Kansas and Mid Missouri
Johns Hopkins Center for Civilian Biodefense Studies

RICHMAN, Teri F.

1605 King St.
Alexandria, VA 22314-2792
Tel: (703)684-3600
Fax: (703)836-4564
EMail: trichman@cstorecentral.com

Employers

Nat'l Ass'n of Convenience Stores (Senior V. President, Research and Industry Affairs)

RICHMOND, Marilyn S.

750 First St. NE
Washington, DC 20002-4242
Tel: (202)336-5800
Fax: (202)336-5797
Registered: LDA

Employers

American Psychological Ass'n (Assistant Exec. Director, Government Relations)

RICHTER, Anna

3000 K St. NW
Suite 300
Washington, DC 20007
Tel: (202)295-8787
Fax: (202)295-8799

Former Assistant Director of Communications for Domestic Policy, Executive Office of the President during the Clinton administration.

Employers

The Harbour Group (Associate)

RICHTER, Christian

1120 Connecticut Ave. NW
Suite 490
Washington, DC 20036
Tel: (202)457-0670
Fax: (202)457-0638

Employers

The Policy Group (Principal)

Clients Represented

On Behalf of The Policy Group

Metal Finishing Suppliers Ass'n

RICHTMAN, Max

Ten G St. NE
Suite 600
Washington, DC 20002-4215
EMail: richtmanm@ncpssm.org
Tel: (202)216-0420
Fax: (202)216-0446
Registered: LDA

Employers

Nat'l Committee to Preserve Social Security and Medicare (Exec. V. President)

RICKARD, Lisa A.

1900 M St. NW
Suite 700
Washington, DC 20036
Tel: (202)463-7090
Fax: (202)463-1830
Registered: LDA

Employers

Ryder System, Inc. (Senior V. President, Government Relations)

RICKENBACH, Jessica J.

14th and Constitution Ave. NW
Room 7898C
Washington, DC 20230
EMail: jrickenb@doc.gov
Tel: (202)482-3052
Fax: (202)482-0567

Employers
Department of Commerce - Inspector General (Legislative and Intergovernmental Affairs Officer)

RICKER, Timothy

601 Wythe St.
Alexandria, VA 22314-1994
EMail: tricker@wef.org
Tel: (703)684-2400
Fax: (703)684-2492

Employers
Water Environment Federation (Deputy Exec. Director, Administration)

RICKMAN, Gregg

Wilbur G. Cohen Bldg.
330 Independence Ave. SW, Room 3360
Washington, DC 20547
Tel: (202)401-3736
Fax: (202)401-6605

Employers
Broadcasting Board of Governors (Congressional Outreach)

RIDDLE, Clarine Nardi

1850 M St. NW
Suite 540
Washington, DC 20036
Tel: (202)974-2300
Fax: (202)775-0112
Registered: LDA
Former Staff Assistant to U.S. Senator Joseph I. Lieberman (D-CT).

Employers
Nat'l Multi-Housing Council (Senior V. President)

RIDDLE, Gregory A.

1300 Wilson Blvd.
Suite 900
Arlington, VA 22209
Tel: (703)524-7647
Fax: (703)524-7707
Registered: LDA

Employers
Eastman Chemical Co. (Government Relations Associate)

RIDDLE, Mark

501 Capitol Ct. NE
Suite 200
Washington, DC 20002
EMail: mriddle@newdem.org
Tel: (202)544-9200
Fax: (202)547-2929

Employers
New Democrat Network (Political Secretary)

RIDDLE, R. Lucia

1350 I St. NW
Suite 1030
Washington, DC 20005-3305
EMail: riddle.lucia@principal.com
Tel: (202)682-1280
Fax: (202)682-1412
Registered: LDA

Employers
Principal Financial Group (V. President, Government Relations)

RIDENOUR, Amy Moritz

777 N. Capitol St. NE
Suite 803
Washington, DC 20002
EMail: aridenour@nationalcenter.org
Tel: (202)371-1400
Fax: (202)408-7773

Employers
Nat'l Center for Public Policy Research (President)

RIDENOUR, David A.

777 N. Capitol St. NE
Suite 803
Washington, DC 20002
EMail: dridenour@nationalcenter.org
Tel: (202)371-1400
Fax: (202)408-7773

Employers
Nat'l Center for Public Policy Research (V. President)

RIDINGS, Amy

236 Massachusetts Ave. NE
Suite 203
Washington, DC 20002-5702
Tel: (202)543-7780
Fax: (202)546-3266

Employers
American Humane Ass'n (Director, Legislative Affairs)

RIDINGS, Dorothy S.

1828 L St. NW
Suite 300
Washington, DC 20036
Tel: (202)466-6512
Fax: (202)785-3926

Employers
Council on Foundations (President)

RIDLEY, Sarah

1001 Pennsylvania Ave. NW
Suite 300S
Washington, DC 20004
EMail: ridley.sarah@dorseylaw.com
Tel: (202)824-8800
Fax: (202)824-8990
Registered: LDA

Employers
Dorsey & Whitney LLP (Legislative Assistant)

Clients Represented

On Behalf of Dorsey & Whitney LLP
Aleutian Pribilof Islands Community Development Ass'n
Bristol Bay Native Corp.
Gaming Management Internat'l II, Ltd.
Hoopa Valley Tribal Council
Little River Band of Ottawa Indians
Lower Elwaha S'Klallam Tribe
Nez Perce Tribal Executive Committee
Pascua Yaqui Tribe of Arizona
Quinault Indian Nation
Shakopee Mdewakanton Sioux Tribe
Spokane Tribe
Stockbridge-Munsee Community Band of Mohican Indians
Winnebago Tribe of Nebraska

RIDNOUER, Nathan

1401 Wilson Blvd.
Suite 1100
Arlington, VA 22209
EMail: nridenouer@itaa.org
Tel: (703)522-5055
Fax: (703)525-2279
Registered: LDA

Employers
Information Technology Ass'n of America (ITAA) (Sr. Program Manager, ASP Program)

RIEDEL, Bunnie

666 11th St. NW
Suite 740
Washington, DC 20001-4542
Tel: (202)393-2650
Fax: (202)393-2653

Employers
Alliance for Community Media (Exec. Director)

RIEDY, James A.

600 13th St. NW
Washington, DC 20005-3096
EMail: jriedy@mwe.com
Tel: (202)756-8314
Fax: (202)756-8087
Attorney, Tax Division, Department of Justice, 1977-81.

Employers
McDermott, Will and Emery (Partner)

RIEGLE, Jr., Hon. Donald W.

700 13th St. NW
Suite 1000
Washington, DC 20005
Tel: (202)347-6633
Fax: (202)347-8713
Member, U.S. Senate (D-MI), 1976-95. Member, U.S. House of Representatives (D-MI), 1967-76.

Employers
Powell Tate (Chairman)

RIEHL, Maureen

325 Seventh St. NW
Suite 1100
Washington, DC 20004-2802
Tel: (202)783-7971
Fax: (202)737-2849
Registered: LDA

Employers
Nat'l Retail Federation (V. President, State Industry Relations Counsel)

RIEHL, Scott

1350 I St. NW
Suite 300
Washington, DC 20005
Tel: (202)639-5900
Fax: (202)639-5932
Registered: LDA

Employers
Nat'l Food Processors Ass'n (Senior Director, State Government Affairs)

RIEL, Elizabeth

1010 Wisconsin Ave. NW
Suite 800
Washington, DC 20007
Tel: (202)338-8700
Fax: (202)338-2334

Employers
Greer, Margolis, Mitchell, Burns & Associates (Senior V. President)

Clients Represented

On Behalf of Greer, Margolis, Mitchell, Burns & Associates
Children's Action Network

RIEMAN, Garth B.

444 N. Capitol St. NW
Suite 438
Washington, DC 20001
Tel: (202)624-7710
Fax: (202)624-5899

Employers
Nat'l Council of State Housing Agencies (Director, Program Development)

RIENT, Peter F.

1920 N St. NW
Suite 250
Washington, DC 20036
Tel: (202)408-8000
Fax: (202)408-0888
Senior Counsel, Office of Legal Policy (1981-88); Deputy Assistant Attorney General (1979-81) and Senior Counsel (1975-79), Office for Improvements in the Administration of Justice; Legal Advisor, Office Policy and Planning (1975-76); Assistant Special Prosecutor, Watergate Special Prosecution Force (1973-75); Senior Counsel, Federal Criminal Code Reform Project, Criminal Division (1972-73); and Chief Appellate Attorney (1971-72) and Assistant U.S. Attorney (1969-72), U.S. Attorney's Office for the Southern District of New York, Department of Justice. Law Clerk to Judge Frederick van Pelt Bryan, U.S. District Court for the Southern District of New York.

Employers
Gainer & Rient (Partner)

RIFKA, Margaret Dillenburg

600 New Hampshire Ave. NW
11th Floor
Washington, DC 20037
EMail: mad@dejlaw.com
Tel: (202)944-3000
Fax: (202)944-3068
Registered: LDA
Attorney, Assistant General Counsel, General Services Administration, 1991-93.

Employers
Dyer Ellis & Joseph, P.C. (Counsel)

Clients Represented

On Behalf of Dyer Ellis & Joseph, P.C.
Bender Shipbuilding & Repair Co., Inc.
Electronic Design Inc.
TI Group Inc.

RIFKIN, Jeremy R.

1660 L St. NW
Suite 216
Washington, DC 20036
Tel: (202)466-2823
Fax: (202)429-9602

Employers
Foundation on Economic Trends (President)

RIGGIN, Philip

810 Vermont Ave. NW
Room 504
Washington, DC 20420
Tel: (202)273-5615
Fax: (202)273-6791

Employers
Department of Veterans Affairs (Deputy Assistant Secretary, Congressional Affairs)

RIGGS, Cathy A.

7203 Ludwood Ct.
Alexandria, VA 22306
Tel: (703)768-4484
Fax: (703)765-6739
Registered: LDA

Employers
Riggs Government Relations Consulting LLC

Clients Represented

On Behalf of Riggs Government Relations Consulting LLC

Charter Schools Development Corp.
Edupoint.com

RIGGS, David

1001 Connecticut Ave. NW
Suite 1250
Washington, DC 20036
Tel: (202)331-1010

Employers

Competitive Enterprise Institute (Director, Land and Natural Resource Policy)

RIGGS, Hon. Frank D.

7203 Ludwood Ct.
Alexandria, VA 22306
Tel: (703)768-4484
Fax: (703)765-6739
Registered: LDA

Former Member, U.S. House of Representatives (R-CA), 1995-99.

Employers

Riggs Government Relations Consulting LLC

Clients Represented

On Behalf of Riggs Government Relations Consulting LLC

Charter Schools Development Corp.
Edupoint.com

RIGGS, Russell

700 11th St. NW
Washington, DC 20001-4507
Tel: (202)383-1259
Fax: (202)434-9683
Registered: LDA
EMail: rriggs@realtors.org

Employers

Nat'l Ass'n of Realtors (Environmental Policy Representative)

RIGMAIDEN, Kenneth

1750 New York Ave. NW
Washington, DC 20006
Tel: (202)637-0700
Fax: (202)637-0771
Registered: LDA

Employers

Internat'l Union of Painters and Allied Trades (Assistant to the General President)

RIGNEY, P. Robert

1350 Beverly Rd.
Suite 220A
McLean, VA 22101
EMail: rigneyb@aatb.org
Tel: (703)827-9582
Fax: (703)356-2198

Employers

American Ass'n of Tissue Banks (Chief Exec. Officer)

RIGSBY, Deborah

1301 Pennsylvania Ave. NW
Suite 550
Washington, DC 20004-1701
EMail: rigsby@nlc.org
Tel: (202)626-3020
Fax: (202)626-3043

Employers

Nat'l League of Cities (Legislative Counsel)

RIITH, Michael

1130 Connecticut Ave. NW
Suite 830
Washington, DC 20036
Tel: (202)261-5000
Fax: (202)296-7937
Registered: LDA

Employers

Southern Co. (Manager, Federal Legislative Affairs)

RIKER, Derek

635 Slaters Lane
Suite 140
Alexandria, VA 22314
Tel: (703)684-7703
Fax: (703)684-7594
Registered: LDA
EMail: Derek.Riker@chwatco.com

Employers

Chwat and Company, Inc. (V. President, Government Relations)

Clients Represented

On Behalf of Chwat and Company, Inc.

AccuWeather
American Friends of the Czech Republic
American Radio Relay League
BCI, Inc.
Center for Regulatory Effectiveness
Federal Physicians Ass'n
Nat'l Ass'n of Assistant United States Attorneys
Newington-Cropsey Foundation
Security Industry Ass'n

RIKER, Ellen

1101 17th St. NW
Suite 803
Washington, DC 20036
Tel: (202)833-0007
Fax: (202)833-0086
Registered: LDA

Employers

MARC Associates, Inc. (Senior V. President)

Clients Represented

On Behalf of MARC Associates, Inc.

American Academy of Otolaryngic Allergy
American Clinical Neurophysiology Soc.
American Sleep Disorders Ass'n
American Soc. of Anesthesiologists
American Soc. of Hematology
Coalition for Health Services Research
Federation of State Medical Boards of the U.S.
Nat'l Ass'n of Epilepsy Centers
Nat'l Hemophilia Foundation
San Francisco, California, City and County of

RIKSEN, Michael R.

1201 E. Abingdon Dr.
Suite 300
Alexandria, VA 22314
EMail: mriksen@harris.com
Tel: (703)739-1946
Fax: (703)739-2775
Registered: LDA

Employers

Harris Corp. (Director, Government Relations)

RILEY, Carey J.

3190 Fairview Park Dr.
Falls Church, VA 22042
Tel: (703)876-3309
Fax: (703)876-3600
Registered: LDA

Employers

General Dynamics Corp. (Staff V. President, Government Relations)

RILEY, H. McGuire

120 S. Payne St.
Alexandria, VA 22314
Tel: (703)684-7300
Fax: (703)684-7302
Registered: LDA
EMail: mriley@bahrinc.com

Special Counsel, Department of the Air Force, 1991-92. Deputy Assistant Secretary of the Army, 1992-93.

Employers

Bentley, Adams, Hargett, Riley and Co., Inc. (V. President)

Clients Represented

On Behalf of Bentley, Adams, Hargett, Riley and Co., Inc.

InWork Technologies
Munitions Industrial Base Task Force
Sister Cities Internat'l

RILEY, Janet M.

1700 N. Moore St.
Suite 1600
Arlington, VA 22209
Tel: (703)841-2400
Fax: (703)527-0938

Employers

American Meat Institute (V. President, Public Affairs)

RILEY, Rev. Meg A.

2026 P St. NW
Suite Three
Washington, DC 20036-6944
EMail: mriley@uua.org
Tel: (202)296-4672
Fax: (202)296-4673

Employers

Unitarian Universalist Ass'n of Congregations (Director, Washington Office)

RILEY, Jr., Richard F.

888 Sixteenth St. NW
7th Floor
Washington, DC 20006-4103
Tel: (202)835-8057
Fax: (202)835-8136
Registered: LDA

Employers

Foley & Lardner (Partner)

Clients Represented

On Behalf of Foley & Lardner

ComEd
Bruce Givner, Attorney
USAA - United Services Automobile Ass'n

RILEY, Stephen F.

1150 17th St. NW
Suite 406
Washington, DC 20036
Tel: (202)261-2840
Fax: (202)861-6490
Registered: FARA

Employers

C/R Internat'l, L.L.C (Managing Member)

RILEY, Susan Mary

1000 Connecticut Ave. NW
Suite 302
Washington, DC 20036
EMail: susanr@sda-inc.com
Tel: (202)835-0740
Fax: (202)775-8526
Registered: LDA, FARA

Employers

Smith Dawson & Andrews, Inc.

Clients Represented

On Behalf of Smith Dawson & Andrews, Inc.

Council of Development Finance Agencies

RILL, James

1299 Pennsylvania Ave. NW
Washington, DC 20004-2402
Tel: (202)783-0800
Fax: (202)383-6610

Employers

Howrey Simon Arnold & White (Partner)

RIME, Monique

2500 Wilson Blvd.
Suite 300
Arlington, VA 22201
EMail: maime@tia.eia.org
Tel: (703)907-7471
Fax: (703)907-7727

Employers

Telecommunications Industry Ass'n (Director, Global Enterprise Market Development)

RIMES, Algis

400 Hurley Ave.
Rockville, MD 20850
Tel: (301)340-1954
Fax: (301)309-1406

Employers

Joint Baltic American Nat'l Committee, Inc. (Chairman)

RIMO, Tricia

2020 K St. NW
Suite 400
Washington, DC 20006
EMail: tricia.rimo@saic.com
Tel: (202)776-5466
Fax: (202)776-5424

Employers

Telcordia Technologies, Inc. (V. President, Government Affairs, SAIC)

RINALDO, Diane

700 13th St. NW
Suite 400
Washington, DC 20005
Tel: (202)347-0773
Fax: (202)347-0785
Registered: LDA
EMail: drinaldo@cassidy.com

Former Legislative Correspondent to Senator Olympia Snowe (R-ME).

Employers

Cassidy & Associates, Inc. (Account Exec.)

Clients Represented

On Behalf of Cassidy & Associates, Inc.

Alfred University
American Lung Ass'n of Minnesota
Arizona State University
Community Hospital Telehealth Consortium
Dominican College of Blauvelt
Internat'l Snowmobile Manufacturers Ass'n
Jewish Family Service Ass'n of Cleveland
Memorial Health System
North Shore Long Island Jewish Health System
Ohio State University
Proctor Hospital

RINALDO, Hon. Matthew J.

700 New Hampshire Ave. NW
Washington, DC 20037
Tel: (202)965-4282
Fax: (202)965-7628
Registered: LDA

Member, U.S. House of Representatives, 1973-93 (R-NJ).

Employers

Self-employed as an independent consultant.

RING, Elizabeth E.

2550 M St. NW
Washington, DC 20037-1350
Tel: (202)457-6000
Fax: (202)457-6315
Registered: LDA
EMail: ering@pattonboggs.com

Employers

Patton Boggs, LLP (Associate)

Clients Represented

On Behalf of Patton Boggs, LLP

American College of Gastroenterology
American Family Mutual Insurance Co.
American Medical Rehabilitation Providers Ass'n
Forethought Group/Forethought Life Insurance Co.
HCR-Manor Care, Inc.
Patient Access to Transplantation (PAT) Coalition
Preneed Insurers Government Programs Coalition
University Medical Associates

RING, John F.

1800 M St. NW
Washington, DC 20036
Tel: (202)467-7000
Fax: (202)467-7176
Registered: FARA

Employers

Morgan, Lewis & Bockius LLP

RING, Kevin

800 Connecticut Ave. NW
Suite 500
Washington, DC 20006
Tel: (202)331-3103
Fax: (202)331-3101
Registered: LDA

Former Counsel, Senate Judiciary Committee.

Employers

Greenberg Traurig, LLP (Associate)

RING, Russell C.

1700 Pennsylvania Ave. NW
Suite 500
Washington, DC 20006-4771
Tel: (202)393-6205
Fax: (202)639-8808
Registered: LDA
EMail: rusty.ring@mutualofomaha.com

Employers

Mutual of Omaha Insurance Companies (V. President and Deputy Head, Federal Government Affairs)

RINGO, D. W. "Skip"

1299 Pennsylvania Ave. NW
Suite 1100 West
Washington, DC 20004-2407
Tel: (202)637-4000
Fax: (202)637-4412
Registered: LDA

Employers

General Electric Co. (Manager, Aircraft Engine Programs)

RINGWOOD, Danielle

1615 L St. NW
Suite 900
Washington, DC 20036
Tel: (202)778-1000
Fax: (202)466-6002
Registered: LDA

Employers

APCO Worldwide (Junior Associate)

Clients Represented

On Behalf of APCO Worldwide

American Camping Ass'n

RINGWOOD, Irene

1455 F St. NW
Suite 225
Washington, DC 20005
Tel: (202)638-3307
Fax: (202)783-6947
Registered: LDA

Legislative Assistant to Rep. Thomas S. Foley (D-WA), 1986-89. Counsel, House Administration Committee, 1985-86.

Employers

Ball Janik, LLP (Partner)

Clients Represented

On Behalf of Ball Janik, LLP

Alcoa Inc.
American Dehydrated Onion and Garlic Ass'n
American Sportfishing Ass'n
ATOFINA
Basic American, Inc.
Coastal Conservation Ass'n
Columbia Falls Aluminum Co.
Goldendale Aluminum
Hager Hinge Co.
Kaiser Aluminum & Chemical Corp.
Northwest Aluminum Co.
Prio Corp.
U.S. Forest Capital

RINKER, Martha L.

9312 Old Georgetown Rd.
Bethesda, MD 20814-1621
Tel: (301)581-9230
Fax: (301)530-2752
Registered: LDA
EMail: mrinker@apma.org

Employers

American Podiatric Medical Ass'n (Director, Division of Policy, Practice and Advocacy)

RINKERMAN, Gary

600 14th St. NW
Suite 500
Washington, DC 20005
Tel: (202)220-1200
Fax: (202)220-1665

Employers

Pepper Hamilton LLP (Partner)

RINTYE, Peter

1201 15th St. NW
Washington, DC 20005-2800
Tel: (202)822-0470
Fax: (202)822-0572
Registered: LDA
EMail: printye@nahb.com

Employers

Nat'l Ass'n of Home Builders of the U.S. (Staff V. President, Political Affairs)

RIOPEL, Maj. Sue

The Pentagon
Room 2C631
Washington, DC 20310-1600
Tel: (703)695-3524
Fax: (703)697-3847

Employers

Department of Army (Assistant Exec. Officer, Legislative Liaison)

RIORDAN, Kelly J.

555 13th St. NW
Suite 500 West
Washington, DC 20004
Tel: (202)383-5300
Fax: (202)383-5414
Registered: LDA
EMail: kriordan@omm.com

Employers

O'Melveny and Myers LLP (Associate)

Clients Represented

On Behalf of O'Melveny and Myers LLP

Samsung Heavy Industries Co., Ltd.
US Airways

RIORDAN, Kevin J.

1299 Pennsylvania Ave. NW
Suite 1100 West
Washington, DC 20004-2407
Tel: (202)637-4000
Fax: (202)637-4006
Registered: LDA

Employers

General Electric Co. (Team Leader, Government Relations)

RIOS, Jennifer

6400 Goldsboro Rd.
Suite 500
Bethesda, MD 20817
Tel: (301)263-2305
Fax: (301)263-2269
EMail: jrios@epb.com

Worked for the Center for Food Safety and Applied Nutrition and served as Physical Science Assistant to the Food and Drug Administration, Department of Health and Human Services, 1990-93.

Employers

Earle Palmer Brown Public Relations (Account Service Manager, EPB PR)

RIPPERGER, Patricia

1667 K St. NW
Suite 460
Washington, DC 20006
Tel: (202)956-5204
Fax: (202)956-5235
EMail: patricia_ripperger@fmc.com

Employers

FMC Corp. (Government Affairs Analyst)

RIS, Jr., William K.

1101 17th St. NW
Suite 600
Washington, DC 20036
Tel: (202)496-5650
Fax: (202)496-5660
Registered: LDA
EMail: will.ris@aa.com

Employers

American Airlines (Senior V. President, Government Affairs)

RISHE, Melvin

1722 I St. NW
Washington, DC 20006
Tel: (202)736-8000
Fax: (202)736-8711
Registered: FARA
EMail: mrishe@sidley.com

Associate General Counsel, Claims and Litigation, Office of the General Counsel, Department of the Navy, 1967-74.

Employers

Sidley & Austin (Partner)

Clients Represented

On Behalf of Sidley & Austin

Israel, Goverment of the State of
Israel, Ministry of Defense of the State of

RISNER, Gary D.

1100 Connecticut Ave. NW
Suite 530
Washington, DC 20036
Tel: (202)293-7222
Fax: (202)293-2955
Registered: LDA
EMail: gary.risner@weyerhaeuser.com

Employers

Weyerhaeuser Co. (Manager, Federal Regulatory Affairs)

RISOTTO, Stephen P.

2001 L St. NW
Suite 506A
Washington, DC 20036-4919
Tel: (202)775-0232
Fax: (202)833-0381

Employers

Halogenated Solvents Industry Alliance (Exec. Director)

RISSEEUW, Hugh

1401 I St. NW
Suite 600
Washington, DC 20005
Tel: (202)336-7400
Fax: (202)336-7515
Registered: LDA

Employers

United Technologies Corp. (Director, Navy Programs)

RISSETTO, Christopher L.

1301 K St. NW
Suite 1100-East Tower
Washington, DC 20005
Tel: (202)414-9208
Fax: (202)414-9299
Registered: LDA

Attorney-Advisor, Office of the General Counsel, Environmental Protection Agency.

Employers

Reed, Smith, LLP (Partner)

Clients Represented

On Behalf of Reed, Smith, LLP

Baltimore, Maryland, City of
Calaveras County, California, Water District
Detroit, Michigan, City of
Eureka, California, City of
Flint, Michigan, City of
Humboldt Bay Municipal Water District
Landis, NJ Sewerage Authority
Ocean County, NJ Utilities Authority
Orlando, Florida, City of
Phoenix, Arizona, City of
Springettsbury, Pennsylvania, Township of

RISSING, Ed

1101 17th St. NW
Eighth Floor
Washington, DC 20036
Tel: (202)463-8880
Fax: (202)833-3584
Registered: LDA
EMail: erissing@bonnerandassociates.com

Employers

Bonner & Associates (V. President)

RISSLER, Jane

1707 H St. NW
Suite 600
Washington, DC 20006-3919
Tel: (202)223-6133
Fax: (202)223-6162

Employers

Union of Concerned Scientists (Senior Scientist, Food and Environment)

RISSLER, Patricia F.

818 Connecticut Ave. NW
Tenth Floor
Washington, DC 20006
Tel: (202)293-3330
Fax: (202)293-3515
Registered: LDA
EMail: prissler@jollyrissler.com

Staff Director, House Committee on Education and Labor, 1991-94. Staff Director (1989-91) and Deputy Staff Director (1981-89), House Committee on Post Office and Civil Service. Deputy Staff Director, Subcommittee on Postsecondary Education (1977-81) and Clerk, Subcommittee on Agricultural Labor (1973-77), House Committee on Education and Labor. Staff Assistant to Senator Philip A. Hart (D-MI), 1967-73. Staff Assistant to Senator Patrick McNamara (D-MI), 1965-67. Staff Assistant to Rep. Neil Staebler (D-MI), 1965-67.

Employers

Jolly/Rissler, Inc. (President)

Clients Represented

On Behalf of Jolly/Rissler, Inc.

AFLAC, Inc.
CNA Insurance Cos.
Internat'l Union of Police Ass'ns
Sallie Mae, Inc.

RITA, Pat

1111 19th St. NW
Suite 800
Washington, DC 20036
Tel: (202)463-2700
Fax: (202)463-2785
Registered: LDA

Employers

American Forest & Paper Ass'n (V. President, State Government Affairs)

RITCEY-DONOHUE, Joanna M.

601 13th St. NW
Suite 600 South
Washington, DC 20005
Tel: (202)626-3600
Fax: (202)639-9355
EMail: donohjo@washdc.whitecase.com

Employers

White & Case LLP (Director, International Trade Service)

RITTER, Curtis A.

1200 New Hampshire Ave. NW
Suite 800
Washington, DC 20036-6802
Tel: (202)776-2000
Fax: (202)776-2222
EMail: critter@dlalaw.com

Employers

Dow, Lohnes & Albertson, PLLC (Member)

RITTER, Daniel

1735 New York Ave. NW
Suite 500
Washington, DC 20006-4759
Tel: (202)628-1700
Fax: (202)331-1024
Registered: LDA

Employers

Preston Gates Ellis & Rouvelas Meeds LLP (Associate)

Clients Represented

On Behalf of Preston Gates Ellis & Rouvelas Meeds LLP

Akzo Nobel Chemicals, Inc.
Alaska Ocean Seafoods L.P.
American Seafoods Inc.
Chitimacha Tribe of Louisiana
Future of Puerto Rico Inc.
MG Financial Group
Nat'l Center for Economic Freedom, Inc.
Nat'l Produce Production Inc.
United States Maritime Coalition

RITTER, Hon. Don

1401 K Street NW
M 103
Washington, DC 20005
Tel: (202)857-4784
Fax: (202)833-5977
EMail: dritter@nep.org

Employers

Nat'l Environmental Policy Institute (Chairman)

RITTER, Lloyd

1707 H St. NW
Suite 600
Washington, DC 20006-3919
Tel: (202)223-6133
Fax: (202)223-6162
Registered: LDA

Employers

Union of Concerned Scientists (Policy Coordinator, Climate Change)

RITTLE, Marc

337 North Carolina Ave. SE
Washington, DC 20003
Tel: (202)546-3202
Fax: (202)544-5852

Employers

Church of the Brethren Washington Office (Legislative Associate)

RITTLER, Andy

1300 N. 17th St.
Eighth Floor
Rosslyn, VA 22209-3801
Tel: (703)812-2000
Fax: (703)812-8202
Registered: LDA
EMail: rittler@abc.org

Employers

Associated Builders and Contractors (Regional Field Representative)

RITTS, Frederick H.

1025 Thomas Jefferson St. NW
Eighth Floor, West Tower
Washington, DC 20007
Tel: (202)342-0800
Fax: (202)342-0807
EMail: fritts@bbrslaw.com

Employers

Brickfield, Burchette, Ritts & Stone (Partner)

RITTS, Leslie Sue

555 13th St. NW
Washington, DC 20004-1109
Tel: (202)637-6573
Fax: (202)637-5910
Registered: LDA
EMail: lsritts@hhlaw.com

Employers

Hogan & Hartson L.L.P. (Partner)

Clients Represented

On Behalf of Hogan & Hartson L.L.P.

Distilled Spirits Council of the United States, Inc.
Nat'l Environmental Development Ass'n, Inc.
Occidental Petroleum Corporation

RIVAS, Andrew

1731 King St.
Suite 200
Alexandria, VA 22314
Tel: (703)549-1390
Fax: (703)549-1656
EMail: arivas@catholiccharitiesusa.org

Employers

Catholic Charities USA (Legislative Liaison)

RIVAS, Jose S.

2000 M St. NW
Suite 740
Washington, DC 20036-3313
Tel: (202)463-6040
Fax: (202)785-5209
Registered: LDA

Employers

Barnett & Sivon, P.C. (Legislative Specialist)

Clients Represented

On Behalf of Barnett & Sivon, P.C.

Community Financial Services Ass'n
The Financial Services Roundtable

RIVERA, Cindy

1735 K St. NW
Washington, DC 20006-1506
Tel: (202)728-8921
Fax: (202)728-8419
EMail: cindy.rivera@nasd.com

Employers

Nat'l Ass'n of Securities Dealers, Inc. (NASD) (Administrative Assistant Governmental Affairs)

RIVERA, Ivette E.

8400 W. Park Dr.
McLean, VA 22102
Tel: (202)547-5500
Fax: (202)479-0168
Registered: LDA

Employers

Nat'l Automobile Dealers Ass'n (Director, Legislative Affairs)

RIVERA, Jose

600 Pennsylvania Ave. SE
Suite 300
Washington, DC 20003
Tel: (202)544-6700
Fax: (202)544-6869
EMail: rnha1@aol.com

Employers

Republican Nat'l Hispanic Assembly of the U.S. (Chairman)

RIVERA, Nelson

909 N. Washington St.
Suite 300
Alexandria, VA 22314
Tel: (703)548-5568
Fax: (703)684-3258

Employers

TREA Senior Citizens League (TSCL) (Administrative Director)

RIVERA, Wanda

701 Pennsylvania Ave. NW
Suite 500
Washington, DC 20004
Tel: (202)508-5507
Fax: (202)508-5080

Employers

Internat'l Utility Efficiency Partnerships (IUEP) (Exec. Assistant and Accounting Officer)

RIVERS, Phillip W.

1050 17th St. NW
Suite 500
Washington, DC 20036
Tel: (202)331-1427
Fax: (202)785-4702

Employers

Texaco Group Inc. (Senior Government Relations Representative)

RIVES, Elizabeth

1401 I St. NW
Suite 1000
Washington, DC 20005
Tel: (202)296-9410
Fax: (202)296-9775
Registered: LDA
EMail: erives@sia.com

Employers

Securities Industry Ass'n (V. President, Policy Analysis and Communications)

RIVKIN, Jr., David B.

1050 Connecticut Ave. NW
Suite 1100
Washington, DC 20036-5304
Tel: (202)861-1500
Fax: (202)861-1790

Associate General Counsel, Department of Energy, 1990-91. Deputy Director, Office of Policy Development, Department of Justice, 1988-90. Legal Advisor to the White House Counsel (1989-90) and Special Assistant to Counsel to the Vice President (1988-89), The White House.

Employers

Baker & Hostetler LLP

Clients Represented

On Behalf of Baker & Hostetler LLP

Croatia, Republic of

RIVLIN, Alice

441 Fourth St. NW
Room 570N
Washington, DC 20001
Tel: (202)504-3400
Fax: (202)504-3431
Vice Chair, Board of Governors, Federal Reserve System, 1996-99; Director (1994-96) and Deputy Director (1993-94), White House Office of Management and Budget; Founding Director, Congressional Budget Office, 1975-83; Assistant Secretary for Planning and Evaluation, Department of Health, Education, and Welfare, 1968-69.

Employers
The Brookings Institution (Senior Fellow, Economic Studies)
District of Columbia Financial Responsibility and Management Assistance Authority (Chair of the Board)

RIXON, Gregory

1000 Vermont Ave. NW
Suite 700
Washington, DC 20005
Tel: (202)408-0808
Fax: (202)408-0876
Registered: LDA

Employers
Susan Davis Internat'l (Senior V. President)

Clients Represented
On Behalf of Susan Davis Internat'l
Internet Council of Registrars

RIZNER, Glenn

1635 Prince St.
Alexandria, VA 22314-3406
Tel: (703)683-4646
Fax: (703)683-4745

Employers
Helicopter Ass'n Internat'l (V. President, Operations)

RIZZO, Eric

412 First St. SE
Suite 300
Washington, DC 20003
Tel: (202)863-7000
Fax: (202)863-7015

Employers
Independent Insurance Agents of America, Inc. (Manager, Grassroots Programs)

RIZZO, Sandra

1735 New York Ave. NW
Suite 500
Washington, DC 20006-4759
Tel: (202)628-1700
Fax: (202)331-1024
Registered: LDA

Employers
Preston Gates Ellis & Rouvelas Meeds LLP (Of Counsel)

Clients Represented
On Behalf of Preston Gates Ellis & Rouvelas Meeds LLP
American Soc. for Therapeutic Radiology and Oncology
Amgen

RIZZUTO, Chris

810 Seventh St. NW
MS: 6334
Washington, DC 20531
Tel: (202)307-0703
Fax: (202)514-5958

Employers
Department of Justice - Office of Justice Programs (Deputy Director, Office of Congressional and Public Affairs)

ROACH, Jr., Robert

9000 Machinists Pl.
Upper Marlboro, MD 20772-2687
Tel: (301)967-4500
Fax: (301)967-4588

Employers
Internat'l Ass'n of Machinists and Aerospace Workers (General V. President, Transportation)

ROACH, Dr. Virginia

277 S. Washington St.
Alexandria, VA 22314
Tel: (703)684-4000
Fax: (703)836-2313

Employers
Nat'l Ass'n of State Boards of Education (Deputy Exec. Director)

ROADY, Celia

1800 M St. NW
Washington, DC 20036
Tel: (202)467-7000
Fax: (202)467-7176
Registered: LDA
EMail: croady@morganlewis.com

Employers
Morgan, Lewis & Bockius LLP (Partner)

Clients Represented
On Behalf of Morgan, Lewis & Bockius LLP
Nat'l Geographic Soc.
Vanguard Charitable Endowment Program

ROBART, Andrew W.

701 Pennsylvania Ave. NW
Suite 720
Washington, DC 20004
Tel: (202)434-4818
Fax: (202)347-4015
Registered: LDA
EMail: andrew.robart@swpc.siemens.com

Employers
Siemens Westinghouse Power Corporation (Manager, Government Relations)

ROBBIN, Elizabeth

1800 Duke St.
Alexandria, VA 22314
Tel: (703)548-3440
Fax: (703)836-0367

Employers
Soc. for Human Resource Management (Employment Regulation and Legislation)

ROBBINS, Liz

441 New Jersey Ave. SE
Washington, DC 20003
Tel: (202)544-6093
Fax: (202)544-1465
Registered: LDA

Employers
Liz Robbins Associates (President)

Clients Represented
On Behalf of Liz Robbins Associates
EMI Music
H. J. Heinz Co.,
Illinois Hospital and Health Systems Ass'n
Lexis-Nexis
Parkinson's Disease Foundation
Reed-Elsevier Inc.
Scholastic, Inc.
Take The Field, Inc.
The Thomson Corp.
Warburg, Pincus & Co., Inc., E. M.

ROBBINS, Michelle E.

1725 Jefferson Davis Hwy.
Crystal Square 2, Suite 300
Arlington, VA 22202
Tel: (703)413-5612
Fax: (703)413-5617
Registered: LDA

Employers
Lockheed Martin Corp. (Director, NASA Programs)

ROBERSON, Alan

1401 New York Ave. NW
Suite 640
Washington, DC 20005
Tel: (202)628-8303
Fax: (202)628-2846

Employers
American Water Works Ass'n (Director, Regulatory Affairs)

ROBERT, III, Wade H.

1401 I St. NW
Suite 600
Washington, DC 20005
Tel: (202)336-7400
Fax: (202)336-7529
Registered: LDA

Employers
United Technologies Corp. (V. President, Government Relations)

ROBERTS, Adam M.

P.O. Box 3719
Georgetown Station
Washington, DC 20007
Tel: (202)337-2334
Fax: (202)338-9478
Registered: LDA

Employers
Soc. for Animal Protective Legislation (Legislative Assistant)

ROBERTS, Adrienne

1640 Wisconsin Ave. NW
Washington, DC 20007
Tel: (202)337-2701
Fax: (202)337-4271
EMail: aroberts@facs.org

Employers
American College of Surgeons (Government Affairs Associate)

ROBERTS, Alan

1101 Vermont Ave. NW
Suite 301
Washington, DC 20005-3521
Tel: (202)289-4550
Fax: (202)289-4074

Employers
Hazardous Materials Advisory Council (President)

ROBERTS, Anne B.

1015 15th St. NW
Suite 700
Washington, DC 20005-2605
Tel: (202)828-5200
Fax: (202)785-2645

Employers
Bechtel Group, Inc. (Senior Government Affairs Representative (BNI))

ROBERTS, Ashleigh

501 Capitol Ct. NE
Suite 300
Washington, DC 20002
Tel: (202)546-1292
Fax: (202)547-6560
EMail: roberts@riponsoc.org

Employers
Ripon Society (Director of Communications)

ROBERTS, Benson F.

1825 K St. NW
Suite 1100
Washington, DC 20006
Tel: (202)785-2908
Fax: (202)835-8931
Registered: LDA

Employers
Local Initiatives Support Corp. (V. President, Policy)

ROBERTS, Beth L.

555 13th St. NW
Washington, DC 20004-1109
Tel: (202)637-8626
Fax: (202)637-5910
Registered: LDA
EMail: blroberts@hhlaw.com

Employers
Hogan & Hartson L.L.P. (Associate)

Clients Represented
On Behalf of Hogan & Hartson L.L.P.
American Ass'n for Medical Transcription
American Soc. of Orthopedic Physician Assistants
Endocrine Soc.
Pharmaceutical Research and Manufacturers of America

ROBERTS, Brian

1255 23rd St. NW
Suite 200
Washington, DC 20037-1174
Tel: (202)452-8100
Fax: (202)833-3636

Employers
Hauck and Associates

Clients Represented
On Behalf of Hauck and Associates
Nat'l Corrugated Steel Pipe Ass'n

ROBERTS, Carole T.

1101 Pennsylvania Ave. NW
Suite 1000
Washington, DC 20004
Tel: (202)879-6826
Fax: (202)508-4511
Registered: LDA
EMail: robertsc@citi.com

Employers
Citigroup (V. President, Federal Government Affairs)

ROBERTS, Cecil E.

8315 Lee Hwy.
Fairfax, VA 22031
Tel: (703)208-7200
Fax: (703)208-7132

Employers
United Mine Workers of America (President)

ROBERTS, David

6515 Haystack Rd.
Alexandria, VA 22310
Tel: (703)822-0575
Fax: (703)822-0576
EMail: daver@mp3.com

Employers

mp3.com (Director, Government Relations)

ROBERTS, David G.

801 Pennsylvania Ave. NW
Suite 250
Washington, DC 20004
Tel: (202)783-5530
Fax: (202)783-5569
Registered: LDA

Employers

Progress Energy (Director, Public Affairs-Federal)

ROBERTS, George D.

1313 L St. NW
Washington, DC 20005
Tel: (202)898-3200
Fax: (202)898-3304
Registered: LDA

Employers

Service Employees Internat'l Union (Director, Legislative Department)

ROBERTS, Glenn

1620 I St. NW
Suite 925
Washington, DC 20006
Tel: (202)293-5800
Fax: (202)463-8998

Employers

The Roberts Group

Clients Represented

On Behalf of The Roberts Group

American Spice and Trade Ass'n
Flavor and Extract Manufacturers Ass'n
Fragrance Materials Ass'n
Internat'l Ass'n of Color Manufacturers

ROBERTS, James H.

1501 M St. NW
Suite 700
Washington, DC 20005-1702
EMail: jroberts@manatt.com
Tel: (202)463-4300
Fax: (202)463-4394

Chief of Government Contract Law, Internal Revenue Service, Department of Treasury, 1983-88. Attorney-Advisor, Procurement Law Division, Office of General Counsel, General Accounting Office, 1978-83. Legal Officer, Judge Advocate General Corps, U.S. Army, 1974-78.

Employers

Manatt, Phelps & Phillips, LLP (Partner)

Clients Represented

On Behalf of Manatt, Phelps & Phillips, LLP

Jacobs Engineering Group Inc.

ROBERTS, John W.

1100 Pennsylvania Ave. NW
Washington, DC 20506
Tel: (202)606-8373
Fax: (202)606-8588

Employers

Nat'l Endowment for the Humanities (Deputy Chairman)

ROBERTS, Karen

1129 20th St. NW
Suite 200
Washington, DC 20036
Tel: (202)857-5900
Fax: (202)223-2648

Employers

Greater Washington Board of Trade (Director, The Potomac Conference)

ROBERTS, Kim

1301 Pennsylvania Ave. NW
Suite 1100
Washington, DC 20004-1707
Tel: (202)626-4000
Fax: (202)626-4181

Employers

Air Transport Ass'n of America (Director, Communications)

ROBERTS, Mark B.

1800 Diagonal Rd.
Suite 520
Alexandria, VA 22314
Tel: (703)838-2050
Fax: (703)838-3610
Registered: LDA
EMail: roberts@naccb.org

Grants and Projects Coordinator, Office of Rep. Benjamin A. Gilman (R-NY), 1983-87.

Employers

Nat'l Ass'n of Computer Consultant Businesses (General Counsel)

ROBERTS, Michael G.

1909 K St. NW
Suite 600
Washington, DC 20006-1167
Tel: (202)585-6900
Fax: (202)585-6969
Registered: LDA

Employers

Thompson Coburn LLP (Partner)

Clients Represented

On Behalf of Thompson Coburn LLP

UniGroup, Inc.

ROBERTS, Michael J.

901 15th St. NW
Suite 700
Washington, DC 20005-2301
Tel: (202)371-6000
Fax: (202)371-6279

Aide to Rep. Carlton R. Sickles (D-MD), 1963-64.

Employers

Verner, Liipfert, Bernhard, McPherson and Hand, Chartered (Member of Firm)

ROBERTS, Michele

P.O. Box 55999
Washington, DC 20040-5999
Tel: (202)722-0808
Fax: (202)722-5941

Employers

Ass'n of Black Psychologists (National Administrator)

ROBERTS, Mike

7910 Woodmont Ave.
Suite 700
Bethesda, MD 20814
Tel: (301)654-2055
Fax: (301)654-5920
Registered: LDA

Employers

American Gastroenterological Ass'n (V. President, Public Policy and Government Relations)

ROBERTS, Paula

1616 P St. NW
Suite 150
Washington, DC 20036
EMail: proberts@clasp.org
Tel: (202)328-5142
Fax: (202)328-5195

Employers

Center for Law and Social Policy (Senior Staff Attorney)

ROBERTS, Peggy

1341 G St. NW
Suite 900
Washington, DC 20005
Tel: (202)637-1514
Fax: (202)637-1535

Employers

Philip Morris Management Corp. (Director, Corporate Communications)

ROBERTS, Richard L.

1330 Connecticut Ave. NW
Washington, DC 20036-1795
Tel: (202)429-3000
Fax: (202)429-3902
EMail: rroberts@steptoe.com

Employers

Steptoe & Johnson LLP (Partner)

ROBERTS, Richard Y.

701 Pennsylvania Ave. NW
Suite 800
Washington, DC 20004
Tel: (202)508-4148
Fax: (202)508-4321
Registered: LDA
EMail: rroberts@thelenreid.com

Commissioner, Securities and Exchange Commission, 1990-95. Administrative Assistant and Legislative Director to Senator Richard Shelby (D-AL), 1987-90. Administrative Assistant and Legislative Director to Rep. Shelby, 1979-83.

Employers

Thelen Reid & Priest LLP (Partner)

Clients Represented

On Behalf of Thelen Reid & Priest LLP

Airports Council Internat'l - North America
Capital Region Airport Commission
Charles Schwab & Co. Inc.
Cincinnati Stock Exchange
Denver, Colorado, City of
Dominion Resources, Inc.
E*TRADE Securities, Inc.
Electronic Traders Ass'n
The Island ECN
Opportunity Capital Corp.
Parsons Brinckerhoff Inc.
Charles Schwab & Co., Inc.,
SEC Roundtable Group
Standard & Poor's Corp.

ROBERTS, Roselee N.

1200 Wilson Blvd.
Arlington, VA 22209
Tel: (703)465-3681
Fax: (703)465-3003
Registered: LDA

Employers

The Boeing Co. (Director, Legislative Affairs - Space Legislation)

ROBERTS, Thomas C.

1050 Thomas Jefferson St. NW
Seventh Floor
Washington, DC 20007
Tel: (202)298-1930
Fax: (202)338-2416
Registered: LDA
EMail: tcr@vnf.com

Legislative Director, Environmental Protection Agency, 1990-95. Chief Counsel and Legislative Director, Sen. Frank Murkowski, (R-AK), 1985-90.

Employers

Van Ness Feldman, P.C. (Member)

Clients Represented

On Behalf of Van Ness Feldman, P.C.

Alaska North Slope LNG Project
American Chemistry Council
Council for Conservation and Reinvestment of OCS Revenue
Delta Wetlands Project
Foothills Pipe Lines (Yukon), Ltd.
Hawaiian Electric Co.
Methanex Inc.
Newport News, Virginia, City of
Petro Star, Inc.
Sealaska Corp.
Tacoma, Washington, City of

ROBERTS, William A.

1615 L St. NW
Suite 650
Washington, DC 20036
Tel: (202)626-8520
Fax: (202)626-8593
Registered: LDA
EMail: waroberts@jeffersongr.com

Former aide to V. President Hubert H. Humphrey, The White House, Chief Legislative Assistant to Rep. Claude Pepper (D-FL), 1964-67, and Senior Consultant, Congressional Commission on Administrative Reorganization.

Employers

Jefferson Government Relations, L.L.C. (Principal)

Clients Represented

On Behalf of Jefferson Government Relations, L.L.C.

ABB Daimler-Benz Transportation, N.A. (ADTRANZ)
ADTranz (Daimler Chrysler Rail Systems)
An Achievable Dream, Inc.
Aurora, Colorado, City of
Bethune-Cookman College
Carlsberg Management Co.
Christopher Newport University
Computer Intelligence 2
Dallas Area Rapid Transit Authority
Daytona Beach, City of
Embry-Riddle Aeronautical University
EV Rental Cars, LLC
Greater Orlando Aviation Authority
JDA Aviation Technology Systems
Seminole Tribe of Indians of Florida
University of Miami
Visalia, California, City of
Volusia, Florida, County of

ROBERTSON, Diane E.

750 17th St. NW
Suite 1100
Washington, DC 20006
Tel: (202)778-2300
Fax: (202)778-2330
Registered: LDA

Employers

FoxKiser

Clients Represented

On Behalf of FoxKiser

NitroMed, Inc.

ROBERTSON, Doug

1010 Wisconsin Ave. NW
Ninth Floor
Washington, DC 20007
Tel: (202)337-9400
Fax: (202)337-4508
EMail: drobertson@gmabrands.com

Employers

Grocery Manufacturers of America (Representative, State Affairs)

ROBERTSON, Linda L.

1775 I St. NW
Suite 800
Washington, DC 20006
Tel: (202)828-3360
Fax: (202)828-3372
EMail: linda.robertson@enron.com

Assistant Secretary for Legislative Affairs (1995-2000), and Deputy Assistant for Tax and Budget, Office of Legislative Affairs (1993-95), Department of the Treasury. Staff Member, Subcommittee on Social Security, House Committee on Ways and Means, 1985-87. Staff member to Rep. James R. Jones (D-OK), 1976-85.

Employers

Enron Corp. (V. President, Federal Government Affairs)

ROBERTSON, Mark J.

1133 21st St. NW
Suite 700
Washington, DC 20036
Tel: (202)887-6900
Fax: (202)887-6970
Registered: LDA
EMail: mrobertson@januspartners.com

Minority Staff Director, House Committee on the District of Columbia, 1986-90. Legislative Director to Rep. Stan Parris (R-VA), 1985-90. Aide to Senator John Warner (R-VA), 1979-85. Aide to Senator Paul Laxalt (R-NV), 1974-78.

Employers

Janus-Merritt Strategies, L.L.C. (Managing Partner)

Clients Represented

On Behalf of Janus-Merritt Strategies, L.L.C.

AFIN Securities
Banorte Casa de Bolsa
C.A. Vencemos
Camara Nacional de la Industria Pesquera
Camara Nacional de las Industrias Azucarera y Alcoholera
Cemento Bayano
Cementos Monterrey, S.A.
CEMEX Central, S.A. de C.V.
CEMEX USA
Corporacion Valenciana de Cementos Portland, S.A.
Corporacion Venezolana de Cementos, SACA
COVAD Communications Co.
DSL Access Telecommunications Ass'n (DATA)
EchoStar Communications Corp.
Fannie Mae
Fraternal Order of Police (U.S. Park Police Labor Committee)
Free ANWAR Campaign
Fundacion para la Preservacion de Flora y Fauna Marina
Grupo Carrousel (Mexico)
Grupo Empresarial Maya
Grupo Financiero Banorte
Grupo Maseca
Gulf Coast Portland Cement Co.
HarvardNet, Inc.
Houston Shell and Concrete
Interactive Gaming Council
Mexam Trade, Inc.
Mexican Crab Industry
Mexican Nat'l Spiny Lobster Industry
Napster, Inc.
Nat'l Indian Gaming Ass'n
Pacific Coast Cement
PINSA, S.A de CD
Pretium S.C (Mexico)
Rhythms NetConnections
Scribe Communications, Inc.
Secured Access Portals, Inc.
Sunbelt Cement
Tolmex
Viejas Band of Kumeyaay Indians
Vivendi Universal

ROBERTSON, Michael

10015 Main St.
Fairfax, VA 22031-3489
Tel: (703)385-1335
Fax: (703)273-0456
EMail: sgia@sgia.org

Employers

Screenprinting & Graphic Imaging Ass'n Internat'l (Exec. V. President)

ROBERTSON, Peter D.

2550 M St. NW
Washington, DC 20037-1350
Tel: (202)457-6000
Fax: (202)457-6315
Registered: LDA
EMail: probertson@pattonboggs.com

Chief of Staff and Acting Deputy Administrator, Environmental Protection Agency, 1995-99. Professional Staff Member, House Budget Committee, 1980-85. Legislative Assistant to Rep. James R. Jones, (D-OK), 1979-80.

Employers

Patton Boggs, LLP (Partner)

Clients Represented

On Behalf of Patton Boggs, LLP

W. R. Grace & Co.
Wild Alabama

ROBERTSON, Raymond J.

1750 New York Ave. NW
Suite 400
Washington, DC 20006
Tel: (202)383-4800
Fax: (202)638-4856

Employers

Internat'l Ass'n of Bridge, Structural, Ornamental and Reinforcing Iron Workers (General V. President)

ROBERTSON, Steve A.

1608 K St. NW
Washington, DC 20006
Tel: (202)861-2700
Fax: (202)861-2786
Registered: LDA

Employers

American Legion (Director, National Legislative Commission)

ROBESON, Jr., Robert E.

1250 I St. NW
Suite 1200
Washington, DC 20005-3924
Tel: (202)371-8415
Fax: (202)371-8471

Employers

Aerospace Industries Ass'n of America (V. President, Civil Aviation)

ROBEY, Michael

6506 Lois Dale Rd.
Suite 209
Springfield, VA 22150
Tel: (703)719-5800
Fax: (703)719-9144
EMail: mrobey@abo-ncle.org

Employers

American Board of Opticianry (Exec. Director)
Nat'l Contact Lens Examiners (Exec. Director)

ROBILLARD, Marda J.

1401 I Street NW Suite 520
Washington, DC 20005
Tel: (202)842-2003
Fax: (202)683-4008
Registered: LDA
EMail: marda.robillard@sunh.com

Chief of Staff to Rep. John D. Dingell (D-MI), 1993-2000. Chief of Staff to Rep. Howard Wolpe (D-MI), 1987-92. Michigan Liaison and Deputy Press Secretary (1980-87) and Deputy State Director (1978-80) to Senator Carl Levin (D-MI).

Employers

Sun Healthcare Group, Inc. (Senior V. President, Government Relations)

ROBINSON, Amy M.

1275 Pennsylvania Ave. NW
Suite 800
Washington, DC 20004
Tel: (202)293-5760
Fax: (202)463-4569
EMail: arobinson@dsa.org

Employers

Direct Selling Ass'n (Manager, Communications)

ROBINSON, Anthony W.

300 I St. NE
Suite 400
Washington, DC 20002
Tel: (202)289-1700
Fax: (202)289-1701

Employers

Minority Business Enterprise Legal Defense and Education Fund (President)

ROBINSON, Bernie

444 N. Capitol St. NW
Suite 240
Washington, DC 20001
Tel: (202)624-7760
Fax: (202)724-0689
EMail: bernie_robinson@gov.state.il.us

Employers

Illinois, Washington Office of the State of (Assistant to the Governor)

ROBINSON, British

1616 P St. NW
Suite 300
Washington, DC 20036
Tel: (202)462-0400
Fax: (202)328-9212

Employers

Jesuit Conference (Nat'l Director)

ROBINSON, Brooke

1700 K St. NW
Suite 300
Washington, DC 20006
Tel: (202)296-4031
Fax: (202)296-1970
Registered: LDA

Employers

American Horse Council, Inc. (Director, Legislative Affairs)

ROBINSON, Charles L.

2300 Wilson Blvd.
Arlington, VA 22201
Tel: (703)528-1775
Fax: (703)528-2333
Registered: LDA
EMail: crobinson@navyleague.org

Employers

Navy League of the United States (Nat'l Exec. Director)

ROBINSON, Clint

1133 19th St. NW
Washington, DC 20036
Tel: (202)887-2747
Fax: (202)887-3123

Employers

MCI WorldCom Corp. (Legislative Policy Advisor)

ROBINSON, Davis R.

1875 Connecticut Ave. NW
Suite 1200
Washington, DC 20009-5728
Tel: (202)986-8000
Fax: (202)986-8102

Legal Advisor (1981-85) and Foreign Service Officer (1961-69), Department of State.

Employers

LeBoeuf, Lamb, Greene & MacRae L.L.P. (Partner)

ROBINSON, Douglas

8200 Jones Branch Dr.
McLean, VA 22102
Tel: (703)903-2423
Fax: (703)903-2447
EMail: douglas_robinson@freddiemac.com

Employers

Federal Home Loan Mortgage Corp. (Freddie Mac) (Director, Public Relations)

ROBINSON, Gilbert A.

6617 Jill Ct.
Suite 100
McLean, VA 22101
Tel: (703)728-9500
Fax: (703)442-0749

Former Ambassador at Large, Department of State and Deputy Director, U.S. Information Agency.

Employers

Gilbert A. Robinson, Inc. (Chairman)

Clients Represented

On Behalf of Gilbert A. Robinson, Inc.

21st Century Space Foundation
Corporations to End World Hunger Foundation
Global Movies Corp.
Robert Schenk Internat'l Russia

ROBINSON, J. Lawrence

300 N. Washington St.
Suite 102
Alexandria, VA 22314
Tel: (703)684-4044
Fax: (703)684-1795
EMail: info@cpma.com

Employers

Color Pigments Manufacturers Ass'n, Inc. (President)

ROBINSON, Jeffrey D.

One Thomas Circle NW
Suite 200
Washington, DC 20005-5802
Tel: (202)833-8900
Fax: (202)466-5738
Registered: LDA

Employers
Baach Robinson & Lewis, PLLC (Partner)

ROBINSON, Kip

444 N. Capitol St. NW
Suite 545
Washington, DC 20001
Tel: (202)347-9710
Fax: (202)347-1225
Registered: LDA
Former Counsel to the Subcommittee on the Merchant Marine, U.S. House of Representatives. Served in the National Oceanic and Atmospheric Administration.

Employers
Self-employed as an independent consultant.

Clients Represented
As an independent consultant
Nat'l Weather Service Employees Organization

ROBINSON, Kristin

11 Dupont Circle NW
Suite 800
Washington, DC 20036
EMail: krobinson@nwlc.org
Tel: (202)588-5180
Fax: (202)588-5185

Employers
Nat'l Women's Law Center (V. President, Development)

ROBINSON, Michelle

1707 H St. NW
Suite 600
Washington, DC 20006-3919
Tel: (202)223-6133
Fax: (202)223-6162
Registered: LDA

Employers
Union of Concerned Scientists (Senior Advocate for Clean Vehicles)

ROBINSON, Peter

2000 L St. NW
Suite 300
Washington, DC 20036-0646
Tel: (202)835-8800
Fax: (202)835-8879
Registered: LDA, FARA
EMail: peter.robinson@ketchum.com
Former Counsel and Deputy Director, House Steering Committee and Assistant Parliamentarian, House of Representatives.

Employers
Ketchum (Sr. V. President and Counselor for Policy, Govt. Relations)

ROBINSON, Rachel

1401 I St. NW
Suite 1000
Washington, DC 20005
EMail: rrobinson@sia.com
Tel: (202)296-9410
Fax: (202)296-9775
Registered: LDA

Employers
Securities Industry Ass'n (V. President, Government Affairs)

ROBINSON, Randall

1744 R St. NW
Washington, DC 20009
Tel: (202)797-2301
Fax: (202)797-2382

Employers
TransAfrica Forum (President)

ROBINSON, Ron

110 Elden St.
Suite A
Herndon, VA 20170
Tel: (703)318-9608
Fax: (703)318-9122

Employers
Young America's Foundation (President)

ROBINSON, Roxanne

5301 Buckeystown Pike
Suite 350
Frederick, MD 21704-8307
Tel: (301)644-3208
Fax: (301)662-2974

Employers
American Ass'n for Laboratory Accreditation (V. President)

ROBINSON, Ms. Sullivan

1225 I St. NW
Suite 750
Washington, DC 20005-0908
Tel: (202)371-1091
Fax: (202)371-0908

Employers
Congress of Nat'l Black Churches (Exec. Director)

ROBSON, Kimberly

110 Maryland Ave. NE
Suite 205
Washington, DC 20002
Tel: (202)543-8505
Fax: (202)675-6469
Registered: LDA

Employers
Women's Action for New Directions (WAND)/Women Legislators' Lobby (WILL) (Director, Policy and Programs)

ROCHETTE, Peggy

1350 I St. NW
Suite 300
Washington, DC 20005
Tel: (202)639-5900
Fax: (202)639-5932

Employers
Nat'l Food Processors Ass'n

ROCHFORD, Susan P.

1001 Pennsylvania Ave. NW
Suite 700 South
Washington, DC 20004
Tel: (202)662-2650
Fax: (202)662-2674
Registered: LDA

Employers
Honeywell Internat'l, Inc. (Director, International Affairs)

ROCHMAN, Julie

1130 Connecticut Ave. NW
Suite 1000
Washington, DC 20036
Tel: (202)828-7100
Fax: (202)293-1219

Employers
American Insurance Ass'n (Senior V. President, Public Affairs)

ROCK, James W.

1150 17th St. NW
Suite 601
Washington, DC 20036
Tel: (202)296-2638
Fax: (202)296-9266
Registered: LDA
Legislative Assistant to Rep. Edgar Jenkins (D-GA) (1984-88) and Rep. Kent Hance (D-TX) (1980-84), Ways and Means Committee, U.S. House of Representatives.

Employers
Hance, Scarborough & Wright
Rock & Associates (President)

Clients Represented
On Behalf of Rock & Associates
American Soc. of Ass'n Executives
Coalition for Fair Taxation of Real Estate
eLottery, Inc.
Nat'l Ass'n of Industrial and Office Properties

ROCK, Michael A.

600 13th St. NW
Suite 340
Washington, DC 20005
Tel: (202)662-0100
Fax: (202)662-0199
Registered: LDA

Employers
Union Pacific (Assistant V. President, External Affairs)

ROCK, Mike J.

325 Seventh St. NW
Washington, DC 20004
Tel: (202)638-1100
Fax: (202)626-2254
Registered: LDA

Employers
American Hospital Ass'n (Senior Associate Director, Legislative Affairs)

ROCK, Patrick

1301 K St. NW
Suite 900
East Tower
Washington, DC 20005
EMail: prock@dc.gcd.com
Tel: (202)408-7100
Fax: (202)289-1504

Employers
Gardner, Carton and Douglas (Partner)

Clients Represented
On Behalf of Gardner, Carton and Douglas
Yukon Pacific

ROCKEFELLER, Edwin S.

1101 Connecticut Ave. NW
Suite 600
Washington, DC 20036
Tel: (202)778-6400
Fax: (202)778-6460
Executive Assistant to the Chairman (1960-61) and Assistant to General Counsel (1958-59), Federal Trade Commission.

Employers
Schiff Hardin & Waite (Partner)

ROCKEFELLER, Sharon

2775 S. Quincy St.
Arlington, VA 22206
Tel: (703)998-2600
Fax: (703)998-3401

Employers
Greater Washington Educational Telecommunications Ass'n (President and Chief Exec. Officer)

ROCKLER, Walter J.

555 12th St. NW
Washington, DC 20004-1206
EMail: Walter_Rockler@aporter.com
Tel: (202)942-5228
Fax: (202)942-5999
Director, Office of Special Investigations, Department of Justice, 1979-80. Former Prosecuter, Nuremburg War Crimes Trials, Office of the Chief Counsel for War Crimes, Department of War.

Employers
Arnold & Porter (Partner)

ROCKWOOD, John

102 Irving St. NW
Washington, DC 20010-2949
Tel: (202)877-1780
Fax: (202)829-5161

Employers
Nat'l Rehabilitation Hospital (Director, Development)

RODA, Anthony J.

1155 21st St. NW
Suite 300
Washington, DC 20036
EMail: ajroda@wms-jen.com
Tel: (202)659-8201
Fax: (202)659-5249
Registered: LDA, FARA
Director of Legislative Strategy to House Republican Whip, Rep. Newt Gingrich (R-GA), 1989-92. Legislative Director to Rep. Steve C. Gunderson (R-WI), 1987-88. Legislative Director (1985-86) and Legislative Assistant (1983-84) to Rep. Stewart B. McKinney (R-CT).

Employers
Williams & Jensen, P.C. (Partner)

Clients Represented
On Behalf of Williams & Jensen, P.C.
Aegon USA
Alexander's Inc.
American Home Products Corp.
AOL Time Warner
Applera Corp.
Asahi Glass Co.
Bass Enterprises Production Co.
Chandis Securities Co.
CIGNA Corp.
Credit Suisse First Boston Corp.
First Union Corp.
Gateway, Inc.
Genentech, Inc.
HP Global Workplaces, Inc.
Human Rights Campaign
Nat'l Cable Television Ass'n
Nat'l Underground Railroad Freedom Center
Owens-Illinois, Inc.
Perdue Farms Inc.
Pharmaceutical Research and Manufacturers of America
The Pittston Co.
Recording Industry Ass'n of America
Reuters America Inc.
Smithfield Foods Inc.
TTX Co.
The Vantage Group, Inc.
Western Coalition Political Action Committee

RODDY-BURNS, Lisa M.

10302 Eaton Pl.
Suite 340
Fairfax, VA 22030
Tel: (703)385-5300
Fax: (703)385-5301

Employers
American Public Communications Council (Exec. Director)

RODE, Daniel F.

1225 I St. NW
Suite 500
Washington, DC 20005
EMail: dan.rode@ahima.org
Tel: (202)218-3535
Fax: (202)682-0078

Employers
American Health Information Management Ass'n (V. President, Policy and Gov't Relations)

RODERER, David W.

1717 Pennsylvania Ave. NW
Washington, DC 20006
Tel: (202)974-1000
Fax: (202)331-9330
Registered: LDA

Employers
Goodwin, Procter & Hoar LLP (Counsel)

RODGERS, Jr., Clifton E.

1420 New York Ave. NW
Suite 1100
Washington, DC 20005
EMail: crodgers@rer.org
Tel: (202)639-8400
Fax: (202)639-8442
Registered: LDA

Employers
Real Estate Roundtable (V. President)

RODGERS, Mark W.

499 S. Capitol St. SW
Suite 502A
Washington, DC 20003
EMail: mrodgers@motor-freight.com
Tel: (202)554-3060
Fax: (202)554-3160

Employers
Motor Freight Carriers Ass'n (V. President, Industry Relations and Exec. Director TMI Division)

RODGERS, Peter H.

1275 Pennsylvania Ave. NW
Washington, DC 20004-2415
Tel: (202)383-0100
Fax: (202)637-3593

Employers
Sutherland Asbill & Brennan LLP (Partner)

RODGERS, Richard F.

300 Maryland Ave. NE
Washington, DC 20002
Tel: (202)546-1631
Fax: (202)546-3309
Registered: LDA

Employers
FedEx Corp. (Senior Federal Affairs Representative)

RODGERS, Richard L.

499 S. Capitol St. SW
Suite 600
Washington, DC 20003
Tel: (202)289-9881
Fax: (202)289-9877
Registered: LDA
Former Chief of Staff to Rep. Bob Livingston (R-LA).

Employers
The Livingston Group, LLC (Associate)

Clients Represented

On Behalf of The Livingston Group, LLC
ACS Government Solutions Group
American Ass'n of Nurse Anesthetists
Baton Rouge, Louisiana, City of
Boys Town USA
Broward, Florida, County of
Committee of Unsecured Creditors
General Category Tuna Ass'n
General Electric Co.
Gray Morrison
Illinois Department of Human Services
Internat'l Systems, Inc.
Jacobus Tenbroek Memorial Fund
Link Plus Co.
Marine Desalination Systems LLC
Mesa, Arizona, City of
MidAmerican Energy Holdings Co.
New Orleans, Louisiana, Port of
Raytheon Co.
Schering-Plough Corp.
Stewart Enterprises, Inc.

RODGERS, Ruth

1341 G St. NW
P.O. Box 14267
Washington, DC 20005
Tel: (202)628-9212
Fax: (202)628-9227

Employers
Digital Future Coalition (Contact)
Home Recording Rights Coalition (HRRC) (Exec. Director)

RODGERS, Thomas C.

3000 S. Randolph St.
Suite 517
Arlington, VA 22206
EMail: TCR666@worldnet.att.net
Tel: (703)837-8187
Registered: LDA

Employers
Carlyle Consulting (Owner/President)

Clients Represented

On Behalf of Carlyle Consulting
Levi Strauss and Co.
Nat'l Indian Gaming Ass'n
North of Ireland Free Trade Initiative
Tule River Tribal Council

RODI, `Katherine G.

1341 G St. NW
Suite 1100
Washington, DC 20005
Tel: (202)393-2260
Fax: (202)393-0712
Registered: LDA

Employers
Infotech Strategies, Inc. (Coalition Director)

RODMAN, Peter W.

1615 L St. NW
Suite 1250
Washington, DC 20036
Tel: (202)887-1000
Fax: (202)887-5222

Employers
Nixon Center, The (Director, National Security Programs)

RODMAN, Veronique

1150 17th St. NW
Washington, DC 20036
Tel: (202)862-5800
Fax: (202)862-7177

Employers
American Enterprise Institute for Public Policy Research (Director, Public Affairs)

RODRIGUEZ, Carlos

1710 Rhode Island Ave. NW
Tenth Floor
Washington, DC 20036
EMail: rodriguez@rofgw.com
Tel: (202)973-2999
Fax: (202)293-3307
Registered: LDA

Employers
Rodriguez O'Donnell Fuerst Gonzalez & Williams (Senior Partner)

Clients Represented

On Behalf of Rodriguez O'Donnell Fuerst Gonzalez & Williams
Bicycle Shippers Ass'n
Boston Consolidated Services, Inc.
Coalition for Fair Play in Ocean Shipping
Espee Trading Corp.
New York/New Jersey Foreign Freight Forwarders and Brokers Ass'n, Inc.
Summary Agency, Ltd.
Trailer Marine Transport Corp.
Votainer Consolidation Service

RODRIGUEZ, Eric

1111 19th St. NW
Suite 1000
Washington, DC 20036
Tel: (202)785-1670
Fax: (202)776-1792
Registered: LDA

Employers
Nat'l Council of La Raza (Poverty Policy Analyst)

RODRIGUEZ, Gladys

14th and Independence Ave. SW
Stop 2280
Washington, DC 20250-2280
Tel: (202)720-4465
Fax: (202)720-6882

Employers
Department of Agriculture - Research, Education, and Economics Mission Area (Director, Legislative Office)

RODRIGUEZ, M.D., Rene F.

1712 I St. NW
Suite 200
Washington, DC 20006
Tel: (202)467-4756
Fax: (202)467-4758

Employers
InterAmerican College of Physicians and Surgeons (President)

RODRIGUEZ, Virginia O.

1150 15th St. NW
Washington, DC 20071
Tel: (202)334-6000
Fax: (202)334-5609

Employers
The Washington Post Co. (Public Relations Director)

RODRIGUEZ-SOLIS, Jose

2101 Wilson Blvd.
Suite 400
Arlington, VA 22201
EMail: jrodriguez@nmpf.org
Tel: (703)243-6111
Fax: (703)841-9328

Employers
Nat'l Milk Producers Federation (Economics & Trade Analyst)

ROE, Christopher P.

1101 Connecticut Ave. NW
Suite 950
Washington, DC 20036
Tel: (202)785-3575
Fax: (202)785-3023

Employers
Fireman's Fund Insurance Cos. (Assistant V. President, Government and Industry Affairs)

ROE, Randall B.

1400 K St. NW
Suite 910
Washington, DC 20005
EMail: rbr1@worldnet.att.net
Tel: (202)898-1500
Fax: (202)898-1561
Registered: LDA

Employers
Burns and Roe Enterprises, Inc. (V. Chairman)

ROEGNER, Pat Ford

888 17th St. NW
Suite 800
Washington, DC 20006
Tel: (202)822-8060
Fax: (202)822-9088
Registered: LDA

Employers
Heidepriem & Mager, Inc.

Clients Represented

On Behalf of Heidepriem & Mager, Inc.
R2 Technology, Inc.

ROELS, Starla K.

2120 L St. NW
Suite 700
Washington, DC 20037
Tel: (202)822-8282
Fax: (202)296-8834
Registered: LDA

Employers
Hobbs, Straus, Dean and Walker, LLP

Clients Represented

On Behalf of Hobbs, Straus, Dean and Walker, LLP
Shoalwater Bay Indian Tribe

ROESCH, Shawana

Ariel Rios Federal Bldg.
(1301-MC)
1200 Pennsylvania Ave. NW
3rd Floor
Washington, DC 20460
EMail: roesch.shawana@epa.gov
Tel: (202)564-6991
Fax: (202)501-1549

Employers
Environmental Protection Agency (Water Team Leader, Office of Congressional and Intergovernmental Relations)

ROESING, William P.

1133 21st St. NW
Suite 700
Washington, DC 20036
Tel: (202)887-6900
Fax: (202)887-6970
Former Administrative Assistant to Senator John H. Chafee (R-RI).

Employers
Janus-Merritt Strategies, L.L.C. (Strategic Counsel)

ROGAN, Maura Walsh

733 15th St. NW
Suite 640
Washington, DC 20005
Tel: (202)478-6521
Fax: (202)347-5868

Employers
Share Our Strength (Deputy Director, Public Relations)

ROGERS, David

600 13th St. NW
Washington, DC 20005-3096
EMail: drogers@mwe.com
Tel: (202)756-8307
Fax: (202)756-8087

Employers
McDermott, Will and Emery (Partner)

Clients Represented
On Behalf of McDermott, Will and Emery
Nat'l Ass'n of Professional Employer Organizations

ROGERS, Jr., Edward M.

1275 Pennsylvania Ave. NW
Tenth Floor
Washington, DC 20004
Tel: (202)347-6000
Fax: (202)347-6001
Registered: LDA
Deputy Assistant to the President (1989-91). Senior Deputy Political Director (1987), The White House.

Employers
Balch & Bingham LLP (Of Counsel)
Barbour Griffith & Rogers, Inc. (V. Chairman)

Clients Represented
On Behalf of Barbour Griffith & Rogers, Inc.
Alliance for Quality Nursing Home Care
American Maritime Congress
American Trucking Ass'ns
Amgen
Bay Harbor Management, L.C.
BellSouth Telecommunications, Inc.
Better World Campaign
Bristol-Myers Squibb Co.
Brown and Williamson Tobacco Corp.
Delta Air Lines
FM Watch
GlaxoSmithKline
Lyondell Chemical Co.
Microsoft Corp.
Oxygenated Fuels Ass'n
Professional Benefit Trust
Qwest Communications
RJR Co.
Southern Co.
State Street Bank and Trust Co.
Yazoo County, Mississippi Port Commission

ROGERS, Joel W.

1150 18th St. NW
Ninth Floor
Washington, DC 20036
EMail: jrogers@ablondifoster.com
Tel: (202)296-3355
Fax: (202)296-3922
Registered: FARA

Employers
Ablondi, Foster, Sobin & Davidow, P.C. (Partner)

ROGERS, John C.

300 N. Lee St.
Suite 500
Alexandria, VA 22314
Tel: (703)518-8600
Fax: (703)518-8611
Registered: LDA

Employers
PACE-CAPSTONE (Partner)

ROGERS, Kathleen

P.O. Box 11191
Alexandria, VA 22312
Tel: (703)941-5844
Fax: (703)212-6951

Employers
Ex-Partners of Servicemembers for Equality (Director)

ROGERS, Kyle

400 N. Capitol St. NW
Washington, DC 20001
Tel: (202)824-7000
Fax: (202)824-7115
Registered: LDA

Employers
American Gas Ass'n (Director, Government Relations)

ROGERS, Margaret

1776 I St. NW
Suite 1050
Washington, DC 20006
Tel: (202)429-3403
Fax: (202)429-3467
Registered: LDA

Employers
The Dow Chemical Co. (Manager, Government Relations, Environmental Policy)

ROGERS, Millie D.

1650 Tysons Blvd.
Suite 1700
McLean, VA 22201
Tel: (703)790-6300
Fax: (703)790-6365

Employers
ITT Industries (Director, Communications)

ROGERS, Hon. Paul G.

555 13th St. NW
Washington, DC 20004-1109
Tel: (202)637-5753
Fax: (202)637-5910
Registered: LDA
EMail: pgrogers@hhlaw.com
Member, U.S. House of Representatives (D-FL), 1955-79.

Employers
Hogan & Hartson L.L.P. (Partner)

Clients Represented
On Behalf of Hogan & Hartson L.L.P.
American Registry of Pathology
Campaign for Medical Research

ROGERS, Richard H.

12850 Middlebrook Rd.
Suite 205
Germantown, MD 20874
Tel: (301)528-1960

Employers
Waste Policy Institute (Senior Manager, Communications)

ROGERS, Susan

1776 I St. NW
Suite 1000
Washington, DC 20006
Tel: (202)785-4888
Fax: (202)457-6597

Employers
BP Amoco Corp. (Senior Tax Advisor)

ROGERS, Thomas F.

2800 Shirlington Rd.
Suite 405
Arlington, VA 22206
Tel: (703)671-4116
Fax: (703)931-6432

Employers
Space Transportation Ass'n (Chief Scientist)

ROGERS, William C.

499 S. Capitol St. SW
Suite 502A
Washington, DC 20003
EMail: brogers@motor-freight.com
Tel: (202)554-3060
Fax: (202)554-3160

Employers
Motor Freight Carriers Ass'n (V. President, Safety Training and Technology)

ROGERS, William D.

555 12th St. NW
Washington, DC 20004-1206
Tel: (202)942-5000
Fax: (202)942-5999
Registered: FARA
EMail: William_Rogers@aporter.com
Co-Chairman, Bilateral Commission on Future of U.S.-Mexican Relations, 1982. Special Emissary to El Salvador (during the Carter administration), 1980. Undersecretary for Economic Affairs (1976-77) and Assistant Secretary for Inter-American Affairs, U.S. Coordinator, Alliance for Progress (1974-76), Department of State. Alternate U.S. Representative, Inter-American Eonomic and Social Council, 1964-65. Deputy U.S. Coordinator, Alliance for International Progress and Deputy Assistant Administrator, Agency for International Development, 1963-65. Special Counsel, U.S. Coordinator, Alliance for International Progress, 1962-63. Law Clerk to Justice Stanley Reed, U.S. Supreme Court, 1952-53. Law Clerk to Judge Charles E. Clark, U.S. Court of Appeals, Second Circuit, 1951-52.

Employers
Arnold & Porter (Partner)

ROGGENSACK, Margaret E.

555 13th St. NW
Washington, DC 20004-1109
Tel: (202)637-6524
Fax: (202)637-5910
Registered: LDA, FARA
EMail: meroggensack@hhlaw.com

Employers
Hogan & Hartson L.L.P. (Counsel)

ROGIN, Carole M.

515 King St.
Suite 420
Alexandria, VA 22314-3103
EMail: crogin@clarionmr.com
Tel: (703)684-5570
Fax: (703)684-6048

Employers
CLARION Management Resources, Inc. (President)

Clients Represented
On Behalf of CLARION Management Resources, Inc.
Alliance of Work/Life Professionals
Ass'n of Women in the Metal Industries
Hearing Industries Ass'n
Internat'l Soc. of Hospitality Consultants
Wireless Location Industry Ass'n

ROGSTAD, Barry K.

1730 K St. NW
Suite 1200
Washington, DC 20006
Tel: (202)822-9300
Fax: (202)467-4070
Registered: LDA

Employers
American Business Conference (President)

ROH, Jr., Charles E.

1615 L St. NW
Suite 700
Washington, DC 20036-5610
Tel: (202)682-7000
Fax: (202)857-0939
Registered: LDA
Assistant U.S. Trade Representative (1989-94) and Associate General Counsel (1983-89), Office of the U.S. Trade Representative. Staff Member, Senate Finance Committee, 1979-80. Member, Office of Legal Affairs, Department of State, 1973-79.

Employers
Weil, Gotshal & Manges, LLP (Partner)

Clients Represented
On Behalf of Weil, Gotshal & Manges, LLP
Copyright Clearance Center, Inc.
Nomura Internat'l plc

ROHDE, Barbara J.

1101 17th St. NW
Suite 500
Washington, DC 20036
Tel: (202)833-5575
Registered: LDA

Employers
Self-employed as an independent consultant.

Clients Represented
As an independent consultant
Fargo-Moorhead Metropolitan Council of Governments
Moorehead, Minnesota, City of

ROHDE, Clifford

1730 Rhode Island Ave. NW
Suite 712
Washington, DC 20036
Tel: (202)331-1550
Fax: (202)331-1663

Employers
Robert M. Brandon and Associates

Clients Represented
On Behalf of Robert M. Brandon and Associates
Localisation Industry Standards Ass'n
Nat'l Ass'n for Public Interest Law (NAPIL)

ROHDE, Wayne R.

1850 M St. NW
Suite 900
Washington, DC 20036
Tel: (202)463-2500
Fax: (202)463-4950

Employers
Sher & Blackwell (Associate)

ROHLFING, Joan

1747 Pennsylvania Ave. NW
7th Floor
Washington, DC 20006
Tel: (202)296-4810
Fax: (202)296-4811
Formerly served in the Departments of Energy and Defense.

Employers
Nuclear Threat Initiative (Senior V. President for Operations)

ROHLING, M. Guy

1911 N. Ft. Myer Dr.
Suite 707
Arlington, VA 22209
Tel: (703)358-9100
Fax: (703)358-9106
Registered: LDA
EMail: grohling@alberscom.com

Employers
Albers & Co. (Regional Manager - South)

Clients Represented
On Behalf of Albers & Co.
Infiltrator Systems, Inc.
Eli Lilly and Co.
May Department Stores Co.
Profit Recovery Group Internat'l

ROHN, David

2025 M St. NW
Suite 800
Washington, DC 20036
Tel: (202)367-2100
Fax: (202)367-1200
Registered: LDA

Employers
Smith, Bucklin and Associates, Inc.

Clients Represented
On Behalf of Smith, Bucklin and Associates, Inc.
American Bearing Manufacturers Ass'n

ROHOLT WESTDORP, Lara

801 Pennsylvania Ave. NW
Suite 750
Washington, DC 20004
Tel: (202)628-3750
Fax: (202)624-0659
Registered: LDA
EMail: lararoholt@yahoo.com
Professional Staff Member, House Armed Services Committee, 1997-98. Budget Analyst, Office of Management and Budget, Exec. Office of the President, 1992-97.

Employers
The Solomon Group, LLC (Associate)

Clients Represented
On Behalf of The Solomon Group, LLC
Internat'l Medical Programs
Safe Environment of America

ROISTACHER, Charles H.

1001 Pennsylvania Ave. NW
Suite 600
Washington, DC 20004
Tel: (202)347-0066
Fax: (202)624-7222
Registered: LDA
EMail: croistac@pgfm.com
Executive U.S. Attorney (1985-88) and Assistant U.S. Attorney (1969-89), District of Columbia, Department of Justice.

Employers
Powell, Goldstein, Frazer & Murphy LLP (Partner)

ROIT, Sheila

600 Maryland Ave. SW
Suite 100 West
Washington, DC 20024-2571
Tel: (202)651-7090
Fax: (202)651-7001
Registered: LDA

Employers
American Nurses Ass'n (Political Action Specialist)

ROJAS, Ernesto J.

409 12th St. SW
Suite 701
Washington, DC 20024-2191
Tel: (202)488-4464
Fax: (202)488-4396

Employers
Pitney Bowes, Inc. (Director, Regulatory Affairs)

ROKALA, Mark

1755 Jefferson Davis Hwy.
Suite 1107
Arlington, VA 22202
Tel: (703)415-0344
Fax: (703)415-0182
Former Agricultural Legislative Assistant, Rep. David Minge, (D-MN). Former Appropriations Staff Member, Sen. Herbert Kohl, (D-WI)

Employers
The PMA Group (Associate)

Clients Represented
On Behalf of The PMA Group
Ag/Bio Con
American Crop Protection Ass'n
Cheese of Choice Coalition
Generic Pharmaceutical Ass'n
Nat'l Ass'n of RC&D Councils
Nat'l Ass'n of Resource Conservation
Nat'l Cattleman's Beef Ass'n
Nat'l Pork Producers Ass'n
U.S. Rice Producers Ass'n

ROLAND, Catherine S.

1819 Pennsylvania Ave. NW
Suite 400
Washington, DC 20006-3603
Tel: (202)333-8845
Fax: (202)333-8898

Employers
Institute for Advanced Studies in Aging and Geriatric Medicine (Program Director)

ROLDAN, Richard R.

1101 17th St. NW
Suite 1004
Washington, DC 20036
Tel: (202)466-7200
Fax: (202)466-7205
Registered: LDA
EMail: rroldan@dc.npga.org

Employers
Nat'l Propane Gas Ass'n (V. President, Government Relations)

ROLFE, Katherine Elizabeth

900 17th St. NW
Suite 600
Washington, DC 20006
Tel: (202)452-8700
Fax: (202)296-9561
Former Legislative Assistant for Health to Senator Jeff Sessions (R-AL).

Employers
Healthcare Leadership Council (Policy Director)

ROLLIN, Mariam

1319 F St. NW
Suite 401
Washington, DC 20004
Tel: (202)783-7949
Fax: (202)783-7955

Employers
Nat'l Network for Youth (Public Policy Director)

ROLLINS, Billie

One Massachusetts Ave. NW
Suite 700
Washington, DC 20001-1431
Tel: (202)408-5505
Fax: (202)408-8072

Employers
Council of Chief State School Officers (Director, Strategic Planning and Communications)

ROLOFSON, George

1156 15th St. NW
Suite 400
Washington, DC 20005
Tel: (202)296-1585
Fax: (202)463-0474
Registered: LDA

Employers
American Crop Protection Ass'n (Senior V. President, Government Affairs)

ROMAN, Jeanette

8725 John J. Kingman Rd.
Suite 2533
Ft. Belvoir, VA 22060-6221
Tel: (703)767-6176
Fax: (703)767-6312

Employers
Department of Defense - Defense Logistics Agency (Congressional Affairs Specialist)

ROMAN, Nan

1518 K St. NW
Suite 206
Washington, DC 20005
Tel: (202)638-1526
Fax: (202)638-4664
EMail: nroman@naeh.org

Employers
Nat'l Alliance to End Homelessness (President)

ROMANI, Romano

233 Constitution Ave. NE
Washington, DC 20002
Tel: (202)547-4000
Fax: (202)543-5044
Registered: LDA
EMail: rr52@clark.net
Former Chief of Staff to Senator Dennis DeConcini (D-AZ) and former Legislative Director and Staff Director to Senator Vance Harke (D-IN).

Employers
Parry, Romani, DeConcini & Symms (President)

Clients Represented
On Behalf of Parry, Romani, DeConcini & Symms
AIDS Healthcare Foundation
Andrx Pharmaceutical Corp.
Armstrong World Industries, Inc.
Asphalt Systems, Inc.
Aventis Pharmaceutical Products
Avondale, Arizona, City of
Bank of New York
Bristol-Myers Squibb Co.
Coalition Against Database Piracy
Composites Fabricators Ass'n
Ferraro, USA
Formosan Ass'n for Public Affairs
GAF Corp.
GlaxoSmithKline
Herbalife Internat'l, Inc.
Hoechst Marion Roussel Deutschland GmbH
Inter-Cal Corp.
Katten Muchin & Zavis
Motion Picture Ass'n of America
Nat'l Air Cargo, Inc.
Nat'l Nutritional Foods Ass'n
Nat'l Retail Federation
Nogales, Arizona, City of
Nu Skin Internat'l Inc.
Owens Corning
Peoria, Arizona, City of
Pfizer, Inc.
Pharmacia Corp.
Pharmanex
Policy Development Group, Inc.
Project to Promote Competition and Innovation in the Digital Age
Research & Development Laboratories
Research Corp. Technology
Rexall Sundown
SBC Communications Inc.
SOL Source Technologies, Inc.
Styrene Information and Research Center
Taxpayers Against Fraud, The False Claims Legal Center
TCOM, L.P.
Unilever United States, Inc.
Utah Natural Products Alliance

ROMANO, John

444 N. Capitol St. NW
Suite 840
Washington, DC 20001-1512
Tel: (202)434-8016
Fax: (202)434-8018
Registered: LDA
Deputy Administrator, Rural Utilities Service, Department of Agriculture, 1995-2000. Legislative Assistant and Projects Director to Senator Patrick J. Leahy (D-VT), 1987-95.

Employers
Romano & Associates, LLC (Principal)

Clients Represented
On behalf of Romano & Associates, LLC
Housing Assistance Council
Nat'l Rural Development Ass'n
Sisseton-Wahpoton Sioux Indian Tribe

ROMANO, Salvatore

1919 Pennsylvania Ave. NW
Suite 600
Washington, DC 20006-3404
Tel: (202)326-1500
Fax: (202)326-1555

Employers
Jenkens & Gilchrist (Shareholder)

ROMANOW, Joshua I.

1133 Connecticut Ave. NW
Suite 1200
Washington, DC 20036
Tel: (202)775-9800
Fax: (202)833-8491
Registered: LDA

Employers
Winthrop, Stimson, Putnam & Roberts (Associate)

ROMANSKY, Michael A.

600 13th St. NW
Washington, DC 20005-3096
Tel: (202)756-8069
Fax: (202)756-8335
Registered: LDA
EMail: mromansky@mwe.com

Employers
McDermott, Will and Emery (Partner)

Clients Represented

On Behalf of McDermott, Will and Emery
Allergan, Inc.
American College of Gastroenterology
American Gastroenterological Ass'n
American Soc. of Ambulatory Surgery Centers
Arthroscopy Ass'n of North America
Ass'n of periOperative Registered Nurses
InterMountain Health Care Inc.
Outpatient Ophthalmic Surgery Soc.
Respiratory Medication Providers Coalition
VIVRA

ROMER, Joseph D.

700 13th St. NW
Suite 200
Washington, DC 20005
Tel: (202)347-3066
Fax: (202)737-7914
Registered: LDA
EMail: jromer@opa.easter-seals.org

Employers
Easter Seals (Exec. V. President, Public Affairs)

ROMERO, Jorge

1735 New York Ave. NW
Suite 500
Washington, DC 20006-4759
Tel: (202)628-1700
Fax: (202)331-1024

Employers
Preston Gates Ellis & Rouvelas Meeds LLP (Associate)

ROMNEY, Clyde

1225 I St. NW
Suite 500
Washington, DC 20005
Tel: (202)312-2005
Fax: (202)289-8683
Registered: LDA
EMail: dawsonassociates@worldnet.att.net
Former Chief of Staff to Chairman Ron Packard, Subcommittee on Energy and Water, House Committee on Appropriations.

Employers
Dawson & Associates, Inc. (Senior Advisor)

RONAN, Patrick

1201 F St. NW
Suite 500
Washington, DC 20004
Tel: (202)824-1600
Fax: (202)824-1651
Former Senior Legislative Assistant to Rep. John E. Peterson (R-PA) and aide to Rep. John Ensign (R-NV) and Rep. Jon Christensen (R-NE). Also served as an intern in the office of Rep. Barbara Vucanovich (R-NV).

Employers
Health Insurance Ass'n of America (Legislative Director, Federal Affairs)

RONAY, J. Christopher

1120 19th St. NW
Suite 310
Washington, DC 20036-3605
Tel: (202)429-9280
Fax: (202)293-2420
EMail: jcronay@ime.org

Employers
Institute of Makers of Explosives (President)

RONEY, John C. "Jack"

2111 Wilson Blvd.
Suite 700
Arlington, VA 22201
Tel: (703)351-5055
Fax: (703)351-6698
Registered: LDA

Employers
American Sugar Alliance (Director, Economics)

ROONEY, Curtis

325 Seventh St. NW
Washington, DC 20004
Tel: (202)638-1100
Fax: (202)626-2254
Registered: LDA

Employers
American Hospital Ass'n (Senior Associate Director)

ROONEY, Francis P.

8484 Georgia Ave.
Suite 700
Silver Spring, MD 20910
Tel: (301)608-1552
Fax: (301)608-1557

Employers
Biscuit and Cracker Manufacturers Ass'n (President)

ROONEY, Hon. Fred B.

700 13th St. NW
Suite 400
Washington, DC 20005
Tel: (202)347-0773
Fax: (202)347-0785
Registered: LDA
EMail: frooney@cassidy.com
Member, U.S. House of Representatives (D-PA), 1963-79.

Employers
Cassidy & Associates, Inc. (Senior Consultant)

Clients Represented

On Behalf of Cassidy & Associates, Inc.
Maersk Inc.
Philadelphia College of Textiles and Science
Southeastern Pennsylvania Consortium for Higher Education

ROONEY, James

11 Canal Center Plaza
Suite 103
Alexandria, VA 22314
Tel: (703)683-4222
Fax: (703)683-0645
Registered: LDA

Employers
The Spectrum Group

Clients Represented

On Behalf of The Spectrum Group
PESystems, Inc.
Simula, Inc.
TRW Inc.

ROONEY, James W.

2000 N. 14th St.
Suite 250
Arlington, VA 22201
Tel: (703)522-9500
Fax: (703)522-6847
Registered: LDA
EMail: rgirooney@ao.com

Employers
Rooney Group Internat'l, Inc. (Chief Exec. Officer)

Clients Represented

On Behalf of Rooney Group Internat'l, Inc.
Akers Laboratories, Inc.
Autometric Inc.
Celsius Tech Electronics
CHEMRING, Ltd.
Deere Co. Worldwide Commercial & Consumer Equipment Division
DuPont Agricultural Products
ECC Internat'l Corp.
Federal Procurement Consultants
General Atomics
Institute of Human and Machine Cognition
Intermarine USA
Lockheed Martin Fairchild Systems
Nammo Inc.
Noesis Inc.
Raufoss A/S, Defense Products Division
Scepter Manufacturing Co. LTD
Shelters, Inc.

ROONEY, Kathryn D.

Ten Pidgeon Hill Dr.
Suite 150
Sterling, VA 20165
Tel: (703)444-4091
Fax: (703)444-3029
Registered: LDA

Employers
DeBrunner and Associates, Inc. (Associate)

Clients Represented

On Behalf of DeBrunner and Associates, Inc.
Albert Einstein Medical Center
Catholic Healthcare West
Health Quest
Nat'l Ass'n of Urban Hospitals
Private Essential Access Community Hospitals (PEACH) Inc.
Southcoast Health System
Susquehanna Health System
Thomas Jefferson University Hospital

ROONEY, Peter

1500 K St. NW
Suite 850
Washington, DC 20005
Tel: (202)682-4292
Fax: (202)682-5150
EMail: rooney@compete.org

Employers
Council on Competitiveness (Exec. Director-Forum on Technology and Innovation)

ROOS, Judith A.

455 Spring Park Pl.
Suite 200
Herndon, VA 20170
Tel: (703)326-5600
Fax: (703)326-5660
EMail: jroos@msrc.org

Employers
Marine Spill Response Corporation (Manager, Marketing and Customer Service)

ROOSA, Christopher

505 Huntmar Park Dr.
Herndon, VA 20170
Tel: (703)742-0400

Employers
VeriSign/Network Solutions, Inc. (PAC Administrator)

ROOT, Laurie

2201 Cooperative Way
Third Floor
Herndon, VA 22071
Tel: (703)904-7100
Fax: (703)904-7942
EMail: root@naiop.org

Employers
Nat'l Ass'n of Industrial and Office Properties (V. President, Education)

ROOTS, John

122 C St. NW
Suite 850
Washington, DC 20001
Tel: (202)638-7790
Fax: (202)638-1045
Registered: LDA
EMail: john.roots@cchinc.com
Legislative Attorney for Senator Ted Stevens (R-AK) and Senate Appropraitons Committee, 1995-98. Colonel, U.S. Marine Corps Reserves, 1964-96.

Employers
Chambers, Conlon & Hartwell (Partner)

Clients Represented

On Behalf of Chambers, Conlon & Hartwell
Advanced Power Technologies, Inc.
The False Claims Act Legal Center
Florida East Coast Industries Inc.
Juneau, Alaska, City of

ROPER, Barbara L. N.

1424 16th St. NW
Suite 604
Washington, DC 20036
Tel: (202)387-6121
Fax: (202)265-7989
Registered: LDA
EMail: roper@rmi.net

Employers
Consumer Federation of America (Editor)

ROPER, Ray

100 Daingerfield Rd.
Alexandria, VA 22314
Tel: (703)519-8100
Fax: (703)548-3227
EMail: rroper@printing.org

Employers
Printing Industries of America (President and Chief Exec. Officer)

RORKE, Rebecca M.

1156 15th St. NW
Suite 820
Washington, DC 20005
Tel: (202)833-1717
Fax: (202)833-2686
EMail: rmrorke@danceusa.com

Employers
Dance/USA (Director, Government Affairs)

ROSADO, Edwin S.

440 First St. NW
Eighth Floor
Washington, DC 20001
Tel: (202)393-6226
Fax: (202)393-2630
EMail: erosado@naco.org

Employers
Nat'l Ass'n of Counties (Director, Legislative Affairs)

ROSAMOND, John

120 S. Payne St.
Alexandria, VA 22314
Tel: (703)684-7300
Fax: (703)684-7302
Registered: LDA
EMail: jrosamond@bahrinc.com
Deputy Assistant Secretary of Defense of Reserve Affairs, Materiel and Facilities, 1987-1997. Acting Director of the

Nat'l Committee for Employer Support of the Guard and Reserve, 1997. Served in the Army, 1959-87.

Employers
Bentley, Adams, Hargett, Riley and Co., Inc. (Director, Government Relations)

Clients Represented
On Behalf of Bentley, Adams, Hargett, Riley and Co., Inc.
InWork Technologies
Munitions Industrial Base Task Force
Sister Cities Internat'l

ROSAN, Richard
1025 Thomas Jefferson St. NW
Suite 500 W
Washington, DC 20007-5201
EMail: rrosan@uli.org
Tel: (202)624-7000
Fax: (202)624-7140

Employers
Urban Land Institute (President)

ROSAY, Debra L.
1201 E. Abingdon Dr.
Suite 300
Alexandria, VA 22314
EMail: drosay@harris.com
Tel: (703)739-1914
Fax: (703)739-2775
Registered: LDA

Employers
Harris Corp. (Manager, Congressional Relations)

ROSCOE, Dr. Wilma J.
8701 Georgia Ave.
Suite 200
Silver Spring, MD 20910
Tel: (301)650-2440
Fax: (301)495-3306
Registered: LDA

Employers
Nat'l Ass'n for Equal Opportunity in Higher Education (V. President)

ROSE, David
1634 I St. NW
Suite 300
Washington, DC 20006
Tel: (202)626-4390
Fax: (202)628-2525
Registered: LDA

Employers
Intel Corp. (Director, Export/Import Administration)

ROSE, George B.
100 Maryland Ave.
Suite 330
Rockville, MD 20850
Tel: (240)777-3636
Fax: (240)777-3768

Employers
Montgomery County, Maryland, Division of Consumer Affairs (Division Chief)

ROSE, Jason
2300 M St. NW
Suite 900
Washington, DC 20037
EMail: jason@publicforuminstitute.com
Tel: (202)467-2771
Fax: (202)293-5717

Employers
Public Forum Institute (Director, Corporate Affairs)

ROSE, John N.
21 Dupont Circle NW
Suite 700
Washington, DC 20036
EMail: jnr@opastco.org
Tel: (202)659-5990
Fax: (202)659-4619
Registered: LDA

Employers
Organization for the Promotion and Advancement of Small Telecommunications Cos. (President)

ROSE, Jonathan C.
51 Louisiana Ave. NW
Washington, DC 20001
Tel: (202)879-3939
Fax: (202)626-1700
Registered: LDA
EMail: jcrose@jonesday.com
Assistant Attorney General, Office of Legal Policy (1981-84), Deputy Assistant Attorney General, Antitrust Division (1975-77), Associate Deputy Attorney General and Director, Office of Justice Policy and Planning (1974-75), all at the Department of Justice. General Counsel, Council on International Economic Policy, 1972-74. Special Assistant to the President (1971-72) and Staff Assistant (1969-71), The White House.

Employers
Jones, Day, Reavis & Pogue (Partner)

Clients Represented
On Behalf of Jones, Day, Reavis & Pogue
The Coal Coalition

ROSE, Luke
1501 M St. NW
Suite 700
Washington, DC 20005-1702
Tel: (202)463-4300
Fax: (202)463-4394
Former Legislative Director, Rep. Heather Wilson, R-NM)

Employers
Manatt, Phelps & Phillips, LLP (Legislative Advisor)

Clients Represented
On Behalf of Manatt, Phelps & Phillips, LLP
Campbell Foundry Co.
Computer and Communications Industry Ass'n (CCIA)
Los Angeles Unified School District
Oracle Corp.

ROSE, Mitch F.
1150 17th St. NW
Suite 400
Washington, DC 20036
Tel: (202)222-4700
Fax: (202)222-4799
Chief of Staff and Principal Advisor on Aviation and Telecommunications (1997-2000) and Press Secretary and Legislative Aide (1991-96) to Senator Ted Stevens (R-AK). Legislative Aide to Rep. Don Young (R-AK), 1989-91.

Employers
The Walt Disney Co. (V. President, Government Relations)

ROSE, Ph.D., Naomi
2100 L St. NW
Washington, DC 20037
Tel: (202)452-1100
Fax: (202)778-6132

Employers
Humane Soc. of the United States (Marine Mammal Scientist)

ROSE, Peter J.
499 S. Capitol St. SW
Suite 520
Washington, DC 20003
Tel: (202)484-3537
Fax: (202)479-4657
Registered: LDA
Congressional Staff Member, 1986-96. Former Legislative Director to Rep. Michael R. McNulty (D-NY) Former Legislative Director to Rep. Peter Geren (D-TX).

Employers
Self-employed as an independent consultant.

Clients Represented
As an independent consultant
ARINC, Inc.
Day Care Ass'n of Tarrant County and Fort Worth Texas
HAECO, Inc.
La Sen, Inc.
Litton Life Support
Lockheed Martin Corp.
NAAS
NOW Solutions, Inc.
Osteopathic Health System of Texas
QTEAM
Rapid Reporting, Inc.
S-TEC Sentry

ROSE, Robert R.
1625 K St. NW
Suite 725
Washington, DC 20006
Tel: (202)785-8972
Fax: (202)785-4313
Registered: LDA

Employers
Rose Communications (President)

Clients Represented
On Behalf of Rose Communications
Fuel Cells for Transportation

ROSE, Stephen L.
4200 Wilson Blvd.
Suite 800
Arlington, VA 22203-1838
EMail: srose@cbbb.bbb.org
Tel: (703)276-0100
Fax: (703)525-8277

Employers
Council of Better Business Bureaus (V. President, Chief Information Officer)

ROSE, Dr. Wil
6051 Arlington Blvd.
Falls Church, VA 22044
Tel: (703)237-9490
Fax: (703)532-1921

Employers
American Indian Heritage Foundation (Chief Exec. Officer)

ROSEN, Burt E.
701 Pennsylvania Ave. NW
Suite 725
Washington, DC 20004
Tel: (202)638-7429
Fax: (202)628-4763
Registered: LDA

Employers
Novartis Corp. (V. President, Pharmaceutical Government Relations)

ROSEN, David L.
600 13th St. NW
Washington, DC 20005-3096
Tel: (202)756-8075
Fax: (202)756-8087
Registered: LDA
EMail: drosen@mwe.com
Formerly served in various supervisory positions, Food and Drug Administration.

Employers
McDermott, Will and Emery (Partner)

Clients Represented
On Behalf of McDermott, Will and Emery
Coalition for Reasonable and Fair Taxation (CRAFT)

ROSEN, Gerald R.
1700 K St. NW
Suite 1200
Washington, DC 20006
EMail: grosen@cig1.com
Tel: (202)857-0001
Fax: (202)857-0209

Employers
Capital Insights Group (Managing Director, International)

ROSEN, Hilary B.
1330 Connecticut Ave. NW
Suite 300
Washington, DC 20036
Tel: (202)775-0101
Fax: (202)775-7253
Registered: LDA

Employers
Recording Industry Ass'n of America (President and Chief Exec. Officer)

ROSEN, Mark
1615 L St. NW
Suite 1320
Washington, DC 20036
EMail: mrosen@feidc.org
Tel: (202)457-6204
Fax: (202)857-0230

Employers
Financial Executives International (Director, Govenment Relations)

ROSEN, Steve
440 First St. NW
Suite 600
Washington, DC 20001
Tel: (202)639-5200
Registered: LDA

Employers
American Israel Public Affairs Committee (Foreign Policy Issues Director)

ROSENBAUM, III, Albert B.
8403 Arlington Blvd.
Suite 100
Fairfax, VA 22031
EMail: arosenba@interfacinc.com
Tel: (703)876-6800
Fax: (703)876-0515

Employers
Interface Inc. (Government Representative)

Clients Represented
On Behalf of Interface Inc.
Diebold, Inc.
Douglas Battery
EO Tech
Heil Trucks
Lifeline
QuikWater
Weld-It Trucks

ROSENBAUM, Daniel B.

One Thomas Circle NW
Suite 1100
Washington, DC 20005
EMail: dbr@capdale.com
Tel: (202)862-5000
Fax: (202)429-3301
Registered: LDA

Attorney, Tax Division, Department of Justice, 1968-72.

Employers
Caplin & Drysdale, Chartered (Member)

Clients Represented
On Behalf of Caplin & Drysdale, Chartered
The Chubb Corp.
MedStar Health

ROSENBAUM, Robert D.

555 12th St. NW
Washington, DC 20004-1206
EMail: Robert_Rosenbaum@aporter.com
Tel: (202)942-5000
Fax: (202)942-5999
Registered: LDA

Employers
Arnold & Porter (Partner)

ROSENBAUM, Steven J.

1201 Pennsylvania Ave. NW
Washington, DC 20004-2401
EMail: srosenbaum@cov.com
Tel: (202)662-6000
Fax: (202)662-6291
Registered: LDA

Employers
Covington & Burling (Partner)

Clients Represented
On Behalf of Covington & Burling
Internat'l Dairy Foods Ass'n

ROSENBERG, Andrew M.

2550 M St. NW
Washington, DC 20037-1350
EMail: arosenberg@pattonboggs.com
Tel: (202)457-6323
Fax: (202)457-6315
Registered: LDA

Employers
Patton Boggs, LLP (Associate)

Clients Represented
On Behalf of Patton Boggs, LLP
Ass'n of Trial Lawyers of America
Illinois Department of Human Services
Medical Device Manufacturers Ass'n
Retractable Technologies, Inc.

ROSENBERG, Marvin

2099 Pennsylvania Ave. NW
Suite 100
Washington, DC 20006
EMail: mrosenb@hklaw.com
Tel: (202)955-3000
Fax: (202)828-1868
Registered: LDA, FARA

Employers
Holland & Knight LLP (Partner)

Clients Represented
On Behalf of Holland & Knight LLP
Capitol Broadcasting Co.
Cellular Telecommunications and Internet Ass'n

ROSENBERG, R. A.

1710 SAIC Dr.
McLean, VA 22102
Tel: (703)821-4300
Fax: (703)676-4305

Employers
Science Applications Internat'l Corp. (SAIC) (Exec. V. President, Washington Operations)

ROSENBERG, Robert

8100 Oak St.
Dunn Loring, VA 22027
EMail: bob_rosenberg@msn.com
Tel: (703)573-8330
Fax: (703)573-4116
Registered: LDA

Employers
Nat'l Pest Control Ass'n (Director, Government Affairs)

ROSENBERG, Simon

501 Capitol Ct. NE
Suite 200
Washington, DC 20002
Tel: (202)544-9200
Fax: (202)547-2929

Employers
New Democrat Network (Founder and President)

ROSENBLATT, Daniel

515 N. Washington St.
Alexandria, VA 22314
Tel: (703)836-6767
Fax: (703)836-4543

Employers
Internat'l Ass'n of Chiefs of Police (Exec. Director)

ROSENBLATT, Gerry

2500 Wilson Blvd.
Suite 300
Arlington, VA 22201
EMail: grosenbl@tia.eia.org
Tel: (703)907-7722
Fax: (703)907-7727

Employers
Telecommunications Industry Ass'n (Director, Technical and Regulatory Affairs)

ROSENBLATT, Peter R.

1101 15th St. NW
Suite 205
Washington, DC 20005-1714
EMail: ffddprosenblatt@erols.com
Tel: (202)466-4700
Fax: (202)223-4826
Registered: FARA

Personal Representative of the President to the Negotiations on the Future Political Status of Trust Territory of the Pacific Islands (rank of Ambassador), 1977-81. Judicial Office and Chairman of the Board of Contract Appeals, U.S. Post Office, 1968-69. Staff, The White House, 1966-68. Deputy Assistant General Counsel for Near East and South Asia, Agency for International Development, 1966.

Employers
Heller & Rosenblatt (Partner)

ROSENBLATT, Sherrie

1225 New York Ave. NW
Suite 400
Washington, DC 20005
Tel: (202)898-0100
Fax: (202)898-0203

Employers
Nat'l Turkey Federation (Director, Public Relations)

ROSENBLEETH, USA (Ret.), Col. Herb

1811 R St. NW
Washington, DC 20009-1659
EMail: jwv@erols.com
Tel: (202)265-6280
Fax: (202)234-5662
Registered: LDA

Employers
Jewish War Veterans of the U.S.A. (National Exec. Director)

ROSENBLOOM, H. David

One Thomas Circle NW
Suite 1100
Washington, DC 20005
EMail: hdr@capdale.com
Tel: (202)862-5037
Fax: (202)429-3301
Registered: LDA

International Tax Counsel, Office of International Tax Affairs (1978-81) and Special Assistant to the Deputy Assistant Secretary (1977), Department of Treasury. Law Clerk to Justice Abe Fortas, U.S. Supreme Court, 1967-68. Special Assistant to the U.S. Ambassador to United Nations, 1966-67.

Employers
Caplin & Drysdale, Chartered (Member)

Clients Represented
On Behalf of Caplin & Drysdale, Chartered
The Hartford

ROSENBLUM, Elyse

1818 N St. NW
Suite 450
Washington, DC 20036
EMail: erosenblum@basshowes.com
Tel: (202)530-2900
Fax: (202)530-2901

Employers
Bass and Howes, Inc. (Program Manager)

ROSENBLUM, Jay E.

1225 Connecticut Ave. NW
Washington, DC 20036
EMail: jay.rosenblum@ey.com
Tel: (202)327-6803
Fax: (202)327-6737
Registered: LDA

Former Special Assistant, Department of Labor.

Employers
Ernst & Young LLP (Director)

ROSENBLUM, Mark

1815 H St. NW
Suite 920
Washington, DC 20006
Tel: (202)728-1893
Fax: (202)728-1895
Registered: LDA

Employers
Americans for Peace Now (Founder, Political Director)

ROSENDAHL, Erik

1300 N. 17th St.
Eighth Floor
Rosslyn, VA 22209-3801
EMail: rosendahl@abc.org
Tel: (703)812-2000
Fax: (703)812-8202

Employers
Associated Builders and Contractors (Regional Field Representative)

ROSENKOETTER, Thomas J.

1155 21st St. NW
Suite 300
Washington, DC 20036
Tel: (202)659-8201
Fax: (202)659-5249
Registered: LDA

Legislative Assistant, Rep. Bill McCollum (R-FL), 1993-97.

Employers
Williams & Jensen, P.C.

ROSENMAN, Ph.D., Mark

1710 Rhode Island Ave. NW
Suite 1100
Washington, DC 20036
EMail: mrosenman@tui.edu
Tel: (202)496-1630
Fax: (202)496-1635

Employers
Union Institute - Office for Social Responsibility, The (V. President)

ROSENSTEIN, Peter D.

1707 L St. NW
Suite 550
Washington, DC 20036
EMail: pdr@nagc.org
Tel: (202)785-4268
Fax: (202)785-4248

Employers
Nat'l Ass'n for Gifted Children (Exec. Director)

ROSENTHAL, Bruce G.

1411 K St. NW
Suite 1350
Washington, DC 20005-3407
Tel: (202)638-3060
Fax: (202)638-3064

Employers
Nat'l Foundation for Women Business Owners (Manager, Public Relations)

ROSENTHAL, Donald L.

815 Connecticut Ave. NW
Suite 500
Washington, DC 20006-4004
Tel: (202)463-2400
Fax: (202)828-5393
Registered: LDA

Chief of Staff and Counselor (1981-82) and Deputy Solicitor (1981), Department of Labor. Assistant Minority Counsel, Senate Labor and Public Welfare Committee, 1975-76.

Employers
Seyfarth, Shaw, Fairweather & Geraldson (Partner)

Clients Represented
On Behalf of Seyfarth, Shaw, Fairweather & Geraldson
Agricultural Producers
Complete Business Solutions, Inc.
Hospitality Employers Ass'n
Information Technology Ass'n of America (ITAA)

ROSENTHAL, Douglas E.

1301 K St. NW
Suite 600E
Washington, DC 20005
Tel: (202)408-6400
Fax: (202)408-6399
Registered: LDA

Employers
Sonnenschein, Nath & Rosenthal

Clients Represented
On Behalf of Sonnenschein, Nath & Rosenthal
Quebec Lumber Manufacturers Ass'n

ROSENTHAL, Larry

1300 Pennsylvania Ave. NW
Suite 600
Washington, DC 20005
Tel: (202)898-0875
Former Commissioner, National Indian Gaming Commission. Former Chief of Staff, Rep. Dale Kildee, (D-MI)

Employers
Ietan Consulting

Clients Represented
On Behalf of Ietan Consulting
Cabazon Band of Mission Indians
Mashantucket Pequot Tribal Nation
Oklahoma Indian Gaming Ass'n

ROSENTHAL, Lynn

666 Pennsylvania Ave. SE
Suite 303
Washington, DC 20003
Tel: (202)543-5566
Fax: (202)543-5626
Registered: LDA

Employers
Nat'l Network to End Domestic Violence (Exec. Director)

ROSENTHAL, Paul C.

3050 K St. NW
Washington, DC 20007
Tel: (202)342-8400
Fax: (202)342-8451
Registered: LDA
EMail: prosenth@colliershannon.com
Counsel, Senate Committee on Governmental Affairs, 1975-81.

Employers
Collier Shannon Scott, PLLC (Member)

Clients Represented
On Behalf of Collier Shannon Scott, PLLC
AdvaMed
Allied Products Corp.
American Honey Producers Ass'n
American Sheep Industry Ass'n
Cast Iron Soil Pipe Institute
Idex Corp.
The Lykes Bros.
Municipal Castings Fair Trade Council
NACCO Industries
Nat'l Juice Products Ass'n
Nat'l Pork Producers Council
PC Strand Producers Coalition
Planar Systems, Inc.
Symbol Technologies, Inc.

ROSENTHAL, Roger C.

P.O. Box 53308
Washington, DC 20009
Tel: (202)462-7744

Employers
Migrant Legal Action Program (Exec. Director)

ROSENTHAL, Steve

815 16th St. NW
Washington, DC 20006
Tel: (202)637-5000
Fax: (202)637-5058

Employers
AFL-CIO (American Federation of Labor and Congress of Industrial Organizations) (Political Director)

ROSENTHAL, Steven M.

2001 M St. NW
Washington, DC 20036
Tel: (202)467-3000
Ext: 3813
Fax: (202)533-8500
Registered: LDA

Employers
KPMG, LLP (Partner, Washington National Tax)

ROSENTHAL, Steven S.

1500 K St. NW
Suite 200
Washington, DC 20005
Tel: (202)220-9600
Fax: (202)220-9601
Registered: LDA

Employers
Cooper, Carvin & Rosenthal (Partner)

Clients Represented
On Behalf of Cooper, Carvin & Rosenthal
Real Access Alliance

ROSENTHAL, Sylvia

919 18th St. NW
Tenth Floor
Washington, DC 20006
Tel: (202)263-2900
Fax: (202)263-2960

Employers
Issue Dynamics Inc. (V. President)

ROSICA, A. Joseph

119 Oronoco St.
Alexandria, VA 22314-2015
Tel: (703)683-5400
Fax: (703)548-5728
EMail: jrosica@presidentialclassroom.org

Employers
A Presidential Classroom for Young Americans, Inc. (Director, Communications)

ROSIER, Dr. Ronald

1529 18th St. NW
Washington, DC 20036
Tel: (202)293-1170
Fax: (202)265-2384
EMail: ronrosier@guvax.georgetown.edu

Employers
Conference Board of the Mathematical Sciences (Administrative Officer)

ROSKE, Monique M.

1100 Connecticut Ave. NW
Suite 810
Washington, DC 20036
Tel: (202)296-6107
Fax: (202)296-9709
Registered: LDA
EMail: moniquemr@usaexports.org

Employers
Coalition for Employment through Exports (Director, Government Relations)

ROSMAN, Michael

1233 20th St. NW
Suite 300
Washington, DC 20036
Tel: (202)833-8400
Ext: 104
Fax: (202)833-8410
EMail: cir@mail.wdn.com

Employers
Center for Individual Rights (General Counsel)

ROSS, Alan L.

1220 19th St. NW
Suite 400
Washington, DC 20036
Tel: (202)872-7300
Fax: (202)872-9030
Registered: LDA

Employers
A. L. Ross Associates, Inc. (President)

Clients Represented
On Behalf of A. L. Ross Associates, Inc.
EXPRO Chemical Products

ROSS, Carl

Four Library Ct. SE
Washington, DC 20003
Tel: (202)544-9219
Fax: (202)544-7462
Registered: LDA

Employers
Save America's Forests, Inc. (Director)

ROSS, Dennis B.

1828 L St. NW
Suite 1050
Washington, DC 20036
Tel: (202)452-0650
Fax: (202)223-5364
Former Director of Policy Planning, Department of State. Special Assistant and Senior Director for Near Eastern and South Asian Affairs, National Security Council, Executive Office of the President, The White House, during the Regan administration. Also served in the Department of Defense during the Carter administration.

Employers
Washington Institute for Near East Policy (Counselor and Distinguished Fellow)

ROSS, Donald K.

2120 L St. NW
Suite 400
Washington, DC 20037
Tel: (202)223-9541
Fax: (202)223-9579

Employers
M & R Strategic Services (Principal)

ROSS, Elisabeth H.

1155 Connecticut Ave. NW
Suite 1200
Washington, DC 20036
Tel: (202)659-5800
Fax: (202)659-1027
Registered: LDA
EMail: eross@dc.bhb.com

Employers
Birch, Horton, Bittner & Cherot (Shareholder)

Clients Represented
On Behalf of Birch, Horton, Bittner & Cherot
Missouri Public Service Co.
Pacific Telecom, Inc.

ROSS, Emily K.

1101 Vermont Ave. NW
Suite 1001
Washington, DC 20005
Tel: (202)789-0470
Fax: (202)682-3984
EMail: rossem@erols.com

Employers
Matz, Blancato & Associates, Inc. (Senior Associate)

ROSS, Frank K.

2001 M St. NW
Washington, DC 20036
Tel: (202)467-3009
Fax: (202)533-8500

Employers
KPMG, LLP (Managing Partner)

ROSS, Jeff

1666 K St. NW
Suite 250
Washington, DC 20006
Tel: (202)835-3016
Fax: (202)835-3008

Employers
Time Domain Corp. (V. President, Corporate Development and Strategy)

ROSS, Jeffrey

1055 Thomas Jefferson St. NW
Suite 500
Washington, DC 20007
Tel: (202)625-2111
Fax: (202)424-7900

Employers
RTC Direct (Senior V. President)

ROSS, Jerilyn

11900 Parklawn Dr.
Suite 100
Rockville, MD 20852-2624
Tel: (301)231-9350
Fax: (301)231-7392

Employers
Anxiety Disorders Ass'n of America (President, C.E.O.)

ROSS, Mr. Kelly

P.O. Box 77077
Washington, DC 20013-7077
Tel: (202)624-8136
Fax: (202)624-6901
Former Aide to Senator Paul Wellstone (D-MN) and to Rep. Norman Sisisky (D-VA).

Employers
Citizens Trade Campaign (Exec. Director)

ROSS, Lisa

1100 Connecticut Ave. NW
12th Floor
Washington, DC 20036
Tel: (202)822-2106
Fax: (202)822-2142
EMail: lisaross@nchelp.org

Employers
Nat'l Council of Higher Education Loan Programs (V. President, Government Relations and Deputy General Counsel)

ROSS, Lisa Osborne

1901 L St. NW
Suite 300
Washington, DC 20036
Tel: (202)466-7590
Fax: (202)466-7598
Former Communications Director, Office of American Workplace; Deputy Director, Federal Glass Ceiling Commission; and Director, Public Liaison, all at the Department of Labor. Also served as Deputy Director, Office for Women's Initiatives and Outreach, Executive Office of the President, The White House.

Employers
Ogilvy Public Relations Worldwide (Senior V. President, Public Affairs Practice)

ROSS, Lynne M.

750 First St. NE
Suite 1100
Washington, DC 20002
Tel: (202)326-6054
Fax: (202)408-6999

Employers
Nat'l Ass'n of Attorneys General (Exec. Director)

ROSS, Mary Starr

701 Pennsylvania Ave. NW
Suite 750
Washington, DC 20004
Tel: (202)783-4400
Fax: (202)783-4410

Employers
The Council of Insurance Agents & Brokers (PAC Contact)

ROSS, Michelle

1220 L St. NW
Washington, DC 20005
Tel: (202)682-8291
Fax: (202)682-8232
Registered: LDA

Employers
American Petroleum Institute (Public Liaison Projects Manager)

ROSS, Peter

1776 K St. NW
Washington, DC 20006
Tel: (202)719-7000
Fax: (202)719-7049

Employers
Wiley, Rein & Fielding (Partner)

Clients Represented
On Behalf of Wiley, Rein & Fielding
Engage Technologies

ROSS, Stanford G.

555 12th St. NW
Washington, DC 20004-1206
Tel: (202)942-5000
Fax: (202)942-5999
Registered: LDA
EMail: Stanford_Ross@aporter.com
Public Trustee, Social Security and Medicare Trust Funds, 1990-95. Consultant, President's Commission on Pension Policy, 1980-81. Commissioner of Social Security, 1978-79. Chairman, Advisory Council on Social Security, 1978. General Counsel, Department of Transportation, 1968-69. Executive Director, President's National Advisory Panel on Insurance in Riot-Affected Areas, National Advisory Commissionon Civil Disorders, 1967-68. Staff Assistant, The White House, 1967-68. Office of Tax Legislative Counsel, Department of the Treasury, 1961-63 (Assistant Tax Legislative Counsel, 1961-62).

Employers
Arnold & Porter (Partner)

Clients Represented
On Behalf of Arnold & Porter
State Farm Insurance Cos.

ROSS, Steve

888 16th St. NW
Suite 400
Washington, DC 20006-8791
Tel: (202)296-8600
Fax: (202)296-8791

Employers
Ross & Hardies (Hiring Attorney)

ROSS, Steven R.

1333 New Hampshire Ave. NW
Suite 400
Washington, DC 20036
Tel: (202)887-4000
Fax: (202)887-4288
Registered: LDA
General Counsel, U.S. House of Representatives, 1983-93.

Employers
Akin, Gump, Strauss, Hauer & Feld, L.L.P. (Partner)

Clients Represented
On Behalf of Akin, Gump, Strauss, Hauer & Feld, L.L.P.
American Legion
Citizen's Educational Foundation
Collagen Corp.
Corrections Corp. of America
Educational Foundation for Citizenship and Statehood Project
Sunscreen Coalition
Svenska Petroleum Exploration AB
Transamerica Financial Services Co.
Transamerica Occidental Life Insurance Co.

ROSS, Stuart

601 Pennsylvania Ave. NW
North Bldg.
Washington, DC 20004-2688
Tel: (202)662-2000
Fax: (202)662-2190

Employers
Ross, Dixon & Bell (Partner)

Clients Represented
On Behalf of Ross, Dixon & Bell
Motorcycle Industry Council

ROSS-ROBINSON, Hazel

1825 I St. NW
Suite 400
Washington, DC 20006
Tel: (202)408-7052
Fax: (202)682-3084
Registered: LDA, FARA
Foreign policy advisor, U.S. Congress, 1985-95.

Employers
Ross-Robinson & Associates (President)

Clients Represented
On Behalf of Ross-Robinson & Associates
Caribbean Banana Exporters Ass'n
Haiti, Office of the President of the Republic of

ROSSEN, Leslie E.

1099 14th St. NW
Suite 9120
Washington, DC 20570
Tel: (202)273-1749

Employers
Nat'l Labor Relations Board Professional Ass'n (President)

ROSSER, Ann W.

1891 Preston White Dr.
Reston, VA 20191-9312
Tel: (703)648-8900
Fax: (703)391-1757

Employers
American College of Radiology (Assistant Exec. Director)

ROSSIER, Richard T.

One Massachusetts Ave. NW
Suite 800
Washington, DC 20001-1431
Tel: (202)842-2345
Fax: (202)408-7763
Registered: LDA
EMail: RRossier@mwmlaw.com

Employers
McLeod, Watkinson & Miller (Partner)

ROSSIN, Bradley

800 Connecticut Ave. NW
Suite 1100
Washington, DC 20006
Tel: (202)416-4169
Fax: (202)296-7177
EMail: bradley_rossin@baxter.com

Employers
Baxter Healthcare Corp. (Legislative Manager)

ROSSITER, Caleb S.

5235 Sherier Place NW
Washington, DC 20016
Tel: (202)537-5104
Registered: LDA

Employers
Self-employed as an independent consultant.

Clients Represented
As an independent consultant
Jacksonville University, Davis College of Business

ROSSLER, Michael

701 Pennsylvania Ave. NW
Washington, DC 20004-2696
Tel: (202)508-5516
Fax: (202)508-5150
Registered: LDA

Employers
Edison Electric Institute (Manager, Environmental Programs)

ROSSO, Joseph L.

1620 L St. NW
Suite 1210
Washington, DC 20036
Tel: (202)955-6062
Fax: (202)955-6070
Registered: LDA

Employers
Higgins, McGovern & Smith, LLC (Principal)

Clients Represented
On Behalf of Higgins, McGovern & Smith, LLC
Chamber of Commerce of the U.S.A.
Freightliner Corp.

ROSSOTTI, Lynn

1600 21st St. NW
Washington, DC 20009-1090
Tel: (202)387-2151
Fax: (202)387-2436

Employers
The Phillips Collection (Director, Public Relations)

ROSTOW, Victoria P.

1050 Connecticut Ave. NW
Washington, DC 20036-5306
Tel: (202)955-8500
Fax: (202)467-0539
Registered: LDA
EMail: vrostow@gdclaw.com
Former Deputy Assistant Secretary for Legislation, Banking and Domestic Finance, Department of the Treasury. Former Law Clerk to Judge Stephen Reinhardt, U.S. Court of Appeals, Ninth Circuit.

Employers
Gibson, Dunn & Crutcher LLP (Of Counsel)

Clients Represented
On Behalf of Gibson, Dunn & Crutcher LLP
California Federal Bank
Dollar Bank
MacAndrews & Forbes Holdings, Inc.
New York Bankers Ass'n

ROTE, Kelly

1819 L St. NW
Suite 700
Washington, DC 20036
Tel: (202)861-1180
Fax: (202)861-1181
Registered: LDA

Employers
Nat'l Marine Manufacturers Ass'n (Director, Federal Government Relations)

ROTENBERG, Marc

1718 Connecticut Ave. NW
Suite 200
Washington, DC 20009
Tel: (202)483-1140
Fax: (202)483-1248

Employers
Electronic Privacy Information Center (Exec. Director)

ROTENBERGER, Lesli

1320 Braddock Pl.
Alexandria, VA 22314
Tel: (703)739-5000
Fax: (703)739-0775

Employers
Public Broadcasting Service (Senior V. President, Grand Management and Promotion Corporate Communication)

ROTH, Alan J.

915 15th St. NW
Suite 800
Washington, DC 20005
Tel: (202)347-3030
Fax: (202)347-3133
Registered: LDA
EMail: aroth@lentdc.com
Minority Staff Director and Chief Counsel, House Committee on Commerce, 1995-97. Majority Staff Director and Chief Counsel (1992-95) and Counsel (1985-92), House Committee on Energy and Commerce.

Employers
Lent Scrivner & Roth LLC (Partner)

Clients Represented
On Behalf of Lent Scrivner & Roth LLC
American Soc. of Anesthesiologists
AOL Time Warner
Burlington Northern Santa Fe Railway
Cellular Telecommunications and Internet Ass'n
Chevron, U.S.A.
Great Western Cellular Partnership
Iroquois Gas Transmission System
KeySpan Energy
Bernard L. Madoff Investment Securities
Monroe Telephone Services, L.P.
Nassau University Medical Center
Nat'l Center for Tobacco-Free Kids
New Skies Satellites N.V.
Pfizer, Inc.

ROTH, Debra L.

1100 Connecticut Ave. NW
Suite 900
Washington, DC 20036-4101
Tel: (202)463-8400
Fax: (202)833-8082

Employers
Shaw, Bransford, Veilleux & Roth (Partner)

ROTH, Lewis E.

1815 H St. NW
Suite 920
Washington, DC 20006
Tel: (202)728-1893
Fax: (202)728-1895

Employers
Americans for Peace Now (Director, Public Affairs)

ROTH, Mark D.

80 F St. NW
Washington, DC 20001
Tel: (202)639-6415
Fax: (202)639-6441

Employers
American Federation of Government Employees (AFL-CIO) (General Counsel)

ROTH, Robert L.

1001 Pennsylvania Ave. NW
Suite 1100
Washington, DC 20004-2595
Tel: (202)624-2500
Fax: (202)628-5116
Registered: LDA

Employers
Crowell & Moring LLP (Partner)

ROTH, Royal R.

430 First St. SE
Washington, DC 20003
EMail: rroth@trucking.org
Tel: (202)544-6245
Fax: (202)675-6568

Employers
American Trucking Ass'ns (V. President, Political Affairs)

ROTH, Sr., Hon. Toby

2131 K St. NW
Suite 710
Washington, DC 20037-1810
Tel: (202)347-6787
Fax: (202)737-4727
Registered: LDA
Member, U.S. House of Representatives (R-WI), 1979-97.

Employers
The Roth Group (President)

Clients Represented
On Behalf of The Roth Group
American Medical Security
Appleton Papers, Inc.
Ass'n of Retail Travel Agents
Hughes Electronics Corp.
Johnson Controls, Inc.
Nat'l Cash Register
Oracle Corp.
San Juan, Puerto Rico, City of

ROTHER, John C.

601 E St. NW
Washington, DC 20049
Tel: (202)434-3704
Fax: (202)434-3714
Registered: LDA

Employers
AARP (American Ass'n of Retired Persons) (Director, Legislation and Public Policy Division)

ROTHERHAM, Andrew

600 Pennsylvania Ave. SE
Suite 400
Washington, DC 20003
EMail: arotherham@dlcppi.org
Tel: (202)547-0001
Fax: (202)544-5014

Employers
Progressive Policy Institute (Director, 21st Century Schools Project)

ROTHFELD, Charles A.

1909 K St. NW
Washington, DC 20006
Tel: (202)263-3000
Fax: (202)263-3300
Registered: LDA

Employers
Mayer, Brown & Platt (Counsel)

Clients Represented
On Behalf of Mayer, Brown & Platt
Ernst & Young LLP
PriceWaterhouseCoopers
Technology Network

ROTHHOLZ, Mitchel C.

2215 Constitution Ave. NW
Washington, DC 20037-2985
Tel: (202)628-4410
Fax: (202)783-2351
Registered: LDA

Employers
American Pharmaceutical Ass'n (V. President, Professional Practice)

ROTHLEDER, Linda S.

1200 G St. NW
Suite 800
Washington, DC 20005
Tel: (202)434-8756
Fax: (202)737-2055
Registered: LDA

Employers
Rothleder Associates, Inc. (President)

ROTHMAN, Eric

1010 Massachusetts Ave. NW
Washington, DC 20001
Tel: (202)289-4434
Fax: (202)289-4435

Employers
American Road and Transportation Builders Ass'n (ARTBA) (Marketing Consultant)

ROTHMAN, Helen

300 E St. SW
Room 9040
Washington, DC 20546
EMail: hrothman@hq.nasa.gov
Tel: (202)358-1943
Fax: (202)358-4340

Employers
Nat'l Aeronautics and Space Administration (Director, Congressional Inquiries Division)

ROTHROCK, III, Aubrey A.

2550 M St. NW
Washington, DC 20037-1350
Tel: (202)457-6000
Fax: (202)457-6315
Registered: LDA
EMail: arothrock@pattonboggs.com

Employers
Patton Boggs, LLP (Partner)

Clients Represented
On Behalf of Patton Boggs, LLP
Barringer Technologies
Internat'l Swaps and Derivatives Dealers Ass'n
Major League Baseball Players Ass'n
Mars, Inc.
Minimed, Inc.
The Pacific Lumber Co.
Security Capital Group
Walton Enterprises
Wegmans Food Markets, Inc.

ROTHSCHILD, Edwin S.

1001 G St. NW
Suite 900 E
Washington, DC 20001-4545
Tel: (202)393-1010
Fax: (202)393-5510
Registered: LDA
EMail: rothschild@podesta.com

Employers
Podesta/Mattoon (Associate)

Clients Represented
On Behalf of Podesta/Mattoon
Alliance to Save Energy
E-LOAN, Inc.

ROTHSCHILD, Jan

500 17th St. NW
Washington, DC 20006-4804
EMail: jrothchild@corcoran.org
Tel: (202)639-1700
Fax: (202)639-1779

Employers
The Corcoran Gallery of Art (Chief Communications Officer)

ROTHSTEIN, Amy

1341 G St. NW
Suite 900
Washington, DC 20005
Tel: (202)637-1546
Fax: (202)637-1581

Employers
Philip Morris Management Corp. (Senior Counsel, Corporate Affairs)

ROTHSTEIN, Audrey R.

1233 20th St. NW
Suite 301
Washington, DC 20036-1250
Tel: (202)429-0311
Fax: (202)429-0149

Employers
College and University Professional Ass'n for Human Resources (Assistant Exec. Director, Planning and Operations)

ROTHSTEIN, Rachel

8219 Leesburg Pike
Vienna, VA 22182-2625
Tel: (703)790-5300
Fax: (703)442-8819
Registered: LDA

Employers
Cable & Wireless, Inc. (V. President, Regulatory and Government Affairs)

ROTHSTEIN, Robert G.

2200 Mill Rd.
Third Floor
Alexandria, VA 22314
Tel: (703)838-1950
Fax: (703)836-6610

Employers
Truckload Carriers Ass'n (General Counsel)

ROTONDARO, Fred

1860 19th St. NW
Washington, DC 20009
EMail: elizabet@niaf.org
Tel: (202)387-0600
Fax: (202)387-0800

Employers
Nat'l Italian American Foundation (Exec. Director)

ROUCH, Jeffrey D.

1090 Vermont Ave. NW
Suite 800
Washington, DC 20005
Tel: (202)326-5242
Fax: (202)408-0241

Employers
Nationwide Mutual Insurance Co. (Director, Federal Relations)

ROUGHEAD, Rear Adm Gary

The Pentagon
MS: 5C760
Washington, DC 20350-1300
EMail: roughead.gary@hq.navy.mil
Tel: (703)697-7146
Fax: (703)614-7089

Employers
Department of Navy (Chief, Office of Legislative Affairs)

ROULEAU, Mary

1350 I St. NW
Suite 510
Washington, DC 20005
Tel: (202)828-8500
Fax: (202)293-3457
Registered: LDA

Employers
United Automobile, Aerospace and Agricultural Implement Workers of America (UAW) (Deputy Legislative Director)

ROUNSAVILLE, Marcia Thomson

2300 M St. NW
Suite 800
Washington, DC 20037
Tel: (202)861-0981
Fax: (202)973-2881
Registered: LDA

Employers
Industrial Fabrics Ass'n Internat'l (Washington Representative)

ROUSE, James J.

2001 Pennsylvania Ave. NW
Suite 300
Washington, DC 20006
Tel: (202)862-0235
Fax: (202)862-0267
Registered: LDA

Employers
Exxon Mobil Corp. (V. President, Washington Office)

ROUSH, Corey

555 13th St. NW
Washington, DC 20004-1109
Tel: (202)637-5731
Fax: (202)637-5910
Registered: LDA
EMail: cwroush@hhlaw.com
Paralegal Specialist, General Counsel's Office, Nat'l Archives and Records Administration, 1995-97.

Employers
Hogan & Hartson L.L.P. (Associate)

Clients Represented
On Behalf of Hogan & Hartson L.L.P.
eBay Inc.

ROUSH, Michael

2400 N St. NW
Fifth Floor
Washington, DC 20037
Tel: (202)728-1164
Fax: (202)728-2992

Employers
Ogletree Governmental Affairs, Inc. (Principal)

Clients Represented
On Behalf of Ogletree Governmental Affairs, Inc.
American Academy of Adoption Attorneys
Nat'l Alliance Against Blacklisting

ROUSSEL, Jerry

1350 I St. NW
Suite 1000
Washington, DC 20005
Tel: (202)962-5386
Fax: (202)336-7226
Registered: LDA
EMail: groussel@ford.com

Employers
Ford Motor Co. (Regulatory Manager, Environment)

ROUTH, Steven S.

555 13th St. NW
Washington, DC 20004-1109
Tel: (202)637-5600
Fax: (202)637-5910

Employers
Hogan & Hartson L.L.P.

Clients Represented
On Behalf of Hogan & Hartson L.L.P.
Nat'l Board for Professional Teaching Standards (NBPTS)

ROUVELAS, Emanuel L.

1735 New York Ave. NW
Suite 500
Washington, DC 20006-4759
Tel: (202)628-1700
Fax: (202)331-1024
Registered: LDA
EMail: mannyr@prestongates.com
Member, Advisory Congressional Maritime Caucus, 1985-87. Member, Advisory Committees, Reagan-Bush Transition Team, 1980-81, and Carter-Mondale Transition Team, 1976. Chief Counsel, Subcommittees on Merchant Marine and Foreign Commerce and Tourism, Senate Commerce Committee, 1969-73.

Employers
Preston Gates Ellis & Rouvelas Meeds LLP (Chairman and Partner)

Clients Represented
On Behalf of Preston Gates Ellis & Rouvelas Meeds LLP
American Classic Voyages Co.
Brown-Forman Corp.
Burlington Northern Santa Fe Railway
Chicago Title & Trust Co.
Chicago Title Insurance
Chitimacha Tribe of Louisiana
Interlake Holding Corp.
Internat'l Council of Containership Operators
Magazine Publishers of America
Microsoft Corp.
Nat'l Produce Production Inc.
Pitney Bowes, Inc.
PPL
Prime Time 24
Seattle, Washington, Port of
Transportation Institute
United States Maritime Coalition
VoiceStream Wireless Corp.

ROUVELAS, Mary

701 Pennsylvania Ave. NW
Suite 650
Washington, DC 20004
Tel: (202)661-5709
Fax: (202)661-5750
Registered: LDA
EMail: mrouvelas@cancer.org

Employers
American Cancer Soc. (Legislative Counsel)

ROVERSI, Louis

1730 Rhode Island Ave. NW
Suite 509
Washington, DC 20036
Tel: (202)429-2527
Fax: (202)429-2532

Employers
Electricite de France Internat'l North America, Inc. (V. President)

ROWAN, James

700 13th St. NW
Suite 400
Washington, DC 20005
Tel: (202)347-0773
Fax: (202)347-0785
Registered: LDA, FARA
EMail: jrowan@cassidy.com

Employers
Cassidy & Associates, Inc. (Senior Consultant for Government Affairs)

Clients Represented
On Behalf of Cassidy & Associates, Inc.
Ocean Spray Cranberries
Taiwan Research Institute

ROWAN, Matt

66 Canal Center Plaza
Suite 520
Alexandria, VA 22314-1591
Tel: (703)549-4432
Fax: (703)549-6495

Employers
Health Industry Distributors Ass'n (President and C.E.O.)

ROWAN, Peter

1600 Pennsylvania Ave. NW
112 E. Wing
Washington, DC 20500
Tel: (202)456-6620
Fax: (202)456-2604

Employers
Executive Office of the President - The White House (Special Assistant to the President for Legislative Affairs, House Liaison Office)

ROWDEN, Marcus A.

1001 Pennsylvania Ave. NW
Suite 800
Washington, DC 20004-2505
Tel: (202)639-7000
Fax: (202)639-7008
EMail: marcus_rowden@ffhsj.com
Chairman and Commissioner, Nuclear Regulatory Commission, 1975-77. General Counsel, Atomic Energy Commission, 1973-75.

Employers
Fried, Frank, Harris, Shriver & Jacobson (Of Counsel)

ROWE, James H.

1850 M St. NW
Suite 550
Washington, DC 20036
Tel: (202)289-5900
Fax: (202)289-4141
Former Chief Counsel, Subcommittee on Crime and Criminal Justice, House Committee on the Judiciary and Investigator, Senate Special Committee on Watergate.

Employers
Chlopak, Leonard, Schechter and Associates (Partner and General Counsel)

ROWE, Esq., Kirsten S.

11250 Waples Mill Rd.
Fairfax, VA 22030-7400
Tel: (202)651-2581
Fax: (202)651-2577
Registered: LDA

Employers
Nat'l Rifle Ass'n of America (Federal Liaison)

ROWE, Richard H.

1233 20th St. NW
Suite 800
Washington, DC 20036-2396
Tel: (202)416-6800
Fax: (202)416-6899
EMail: RRowe@proskauer.com
Attorney, Securities and Exchange Commission, 1970-79, 1964-69.

Employers
Proskauer Rose LLP (Partner)

ROWE, Sylvia

1100 Connecticut Ave. NW
Suite 430
Washington, DC 20036
Tel: (202)296-6540
Fax: (202)296-6547
EMail: rowe@ific.org

Employers
Internat'l Food Information Council (President)

ROWLAND, Robert O.

1101 Pennsylvania Ave. NW
Suite 400
Washington, DC 20004-2504
Tel: (202)637-3800
Fax: (202)637-3862
Registered: LDA

Employers
Textron Inc. (Director, Congressional Relations)

ROWLISON, Jill

1150 17th St. NW
Suite 400
Washington, DC 20036
Tel: (202)222-4700
Fax: (202)222-4799

Employers
The Walt Disney Co. (PAC Administrator)

ROY, Michael L.

2120 L St. NW
Suite 700
Washington, DC 20037
Tel: (202)822-8282
Fax: (202)296-8834
Registered: LDA
EMail: mlroy@hsdwdc.com

Employers
Hobbs, Straus, Dean and Walker, LLP (Partner)

Clients Represented
On Behalf of Hobbs, Straus, Dean and Walker, LLP
Bristol Bay Area Health Corp.
Choctaw Indians, Mississippi Band of
Seminole Tribe of Indians of Florida
Susanville Indian Rancheria
Three Affiliated Tribes of Fort Berthold Reservation

ROY, Natalie

11 DuPont Circle NW
Suite 201
Washington, DC 20036
Tel: (202)466-7272
Fax: (202)466-7964

Employers
Nat'l Pollution Prevention Roundtable (Exec. Director)

ROYCE, Shannon

505 Second St. NE
Washington, DC 20002-4916
Tel: (202)547-8105
Fax: (202)547-8165

Employers
Ethics and Religious Liberty Commission of the Southern Baptist Convention (Director of Government Relations and Legislative Counsel)

ROYER, Robert Stewart

925 15th St. NW
Fifth Floor
Washington, DC 20006
Tel: (202)296-0784
Fax: (202)293-2768
Registered: LDA
EMail: rsroyer@royerandbabyak.com
Former Counsel, House Administration Committee; Counsel, Joint Committee on the Library of Congress; Special Counsel for Capital Markets, Subcommittee on International Development Institutions and Finance, House Banking Committee; and Special Counsel, Commission on Security and Cooperation in Europe.

Employers
Royer & Babyak (Partner)

Clients Represented
On Behalf of Royer & Babyak
American Collectors Ass'n
American Names Ass'n
Edison Properties L.L.C.
Federal Home Loan Bank of New York
Federal Home Loan Mortgage Corp. (Freddie Mac)
Internat'l Reciprocal Trade
MacAndrews & Forbes Holdings, Inc.
Michigan Trade Exchange
Rent-a-Center, Inc.
Trade Exchange of America

ROYKA, Sharon

Ten G St. NE
Suite 580
Washington, DC 20002
Tel: (202)216-9766
Fax: (202)216-9786

Employers
Columbia Gas Transmission Corp. (Regulatory Representative)

ROZELL, Denise M.

4600 Duke St.
Suite 430
P.O. Box 22397
Alexandria, VA 22304
EMail: drozell@aerbvi.org
Tel: (703)823-9690
Fax: (703)823-9695

Employers
Ass'n for Education and Rehabilitation of the Blind & Visually Impaired (Exec. Director)

ROZEN, Robert M.

1150 17th St. NW
Suite 601
Washington, DC 20036
Tel: (202)293-7474
Fax: (202)293-8811
Registered: LDA

Legislative Counsel (1989-94) and Legislative Assistant (1985-89) to Senator George J. Mitchell (D-ME). Legislative Assistant to Senator Wendell Ford (D-KY), 1980-85.

Employers
Washington Council Ernst & Young (Partner)

Clients Represented

On Behalf of Washington Council Ernst & Young

Aetna Inc.
Aetna Life & Casualty Co.
Allegiance Healthcare Corp.
Allen & Co.
American Express Co.
American Insurance Ass'n
American Staffing Ass'n
Anheuser-Busch Cos., Inc.
Antitrust Coalition for Consumer Choice in Health Care
Apartment Investment and Management Co.
Ass'n of American Railroads
Ass'n of Home Appliance Manufacturers
AT&T
AT&T Capital Corp.
Avco Financial Services
Aventis Pharmaceuticals, Inc.
Baxter Healthcare Corp.
BHC Communications, Inc.
Bulmer Holding PLC, H. P.
Cash Balance Coalition
Chamber of Shipping of America
Citigroup
Coalition for Fairness in Defense Exports
Coalition to Preserve Tracking Stock
ComEd
The Connell Co.
Deferral Group
Directors Guild of America
Doris Duke Charitable Foundation
Eaton Vance Management Co.
Eden Financial Corp.
The Enterprise Foundation
Fannie Mae
FedEx Corp.
Ford Motor Co.
GE Capital Assurance
General Electric Co.
General Motors Corp.
Global Competitiveness Coalition
Grasslands Water District
Group Health, Inc.
Haz-X Support Services Corp.
HEREIU
Gilbert P. Hyatt, Inventor
Investment Co. Institute
Large Public Power Council
Local Initiatives Support Corp.
Lockheed Martin Corp.
MacAndrews & Forbes Holdings, Inc.
Marsh & McLennan Cos.
MCG Northwest, Inc.
McLane Co.
Merrill Lynch & Co., Inc.
Metropolitan Banking Group
Microsoft Corp.
Nat'l Ass'n for State Farm Agents
Nat'l Ass'n of Professional Employer Organizations
Nat'l Ass'n of Real Estate Investment Trusts
Nat'l Cable Television Ass'n
Nat'l Defined Contribution Council
Nat'l Foreign Trade Council, Inc.
Nat'l Multi-Housing Council
PaineWebber Group, Inc.
Pfizer, Inc.
R&D Tax Credit Coalition
R&D Tax Regulation Group
Recording Industry Ass'n of America
Reed-Elsevier Inc.
R. J. Reynolds Tobacco Co.
Charles Schwab & Co., Inc.,
Securities Industry Ass'n
Sierra Pacific Industries
Skadden, Arps, Slate, Meagher & Flom LLP
Straddle Rules Tax Group
Tax Fairness Coalition
Tax/Shelter Coalition
TransOceanic Shipping
TU Services
TXU Business Services
U.S. Oncology
USA Biomass Power Producers Alliance
Viaticus, Inc.
Wilkie Farr & Gallagher
Ziff Investors Partnership

ROZENMAN, Eric

1640 Rhode Island Ave. NW
Washington, DC 20036-3278
Tel: (202)857-6646
Fax: (202)857-6689

Employers
B'nai B'rith Internat'l (Exec. Director, International Jewish Monthly Magazine, Associate Director, Communications of BBI)

ROZETT, Linda S.

1615 H St. NW
Washington, DC 20062-2000
Tel: (202)659-6000
Fax: (202)463-5836

Employers
Chamber of Commerce of the U.S.A. (V. President, Media Relations)

ROZSA, Gabor J.

700 13th St. NW
Suite 400
Washington, DC 20005
EMail: grozsa@cassidy.com
Tel: (202)347-0773
Fax: (202)347-0785
Registered: LDA

Minority Counsel, Subcommittee on Water Resources and Environment (1986-94) and Assistant Minority Counsel (1985-86), House Committee on Public Works and Transportation. Assistant Counsel (1980-85) and Attorney/Advisor, Real Estate (1975-80), U.S. Army Corps of Engineers.

Employers
Cassidy & Associates, Inc. (Senior V. President)

Clients Represented

On Behalf of Cassidy & Associates, Inc.

Abtech Industries
Central College
Maersk Inc.
Museum of Discovery and Science
New Jersey Institute of Technology
Ocean Spray Cranberries
Palmdale, California, City of
Phoenix, Arizona, City of
Sacramento Area Flood Control Agency

ROZYNSKI, Edward M.

1200 G St. NW
Suite 400
Washington, DC 20005
Tel: (202)783-8700
Fax: (202)783-8750
Registered: LDA

Employers
AdvaMed (Exec. V. President, Global Strategy and Analysis)

RUANE, Dr. T. Peter

1010 Massachusetts Ave. NW
Washington, DC 20001
Tel: (202)289-4434
Fax: (202)289-4435

Employers
American Road and Transportation Builders Ass'n (ARTBA) (President and Chief Exec. Officer)

RUBEL, Eric A.

555 12th St. NW
Washington, DC 20004-1206
EMail: Eric_Rubel@aporter.com
Tel: (202)942-5000
Fax: (202)942-5999

Former General Counsel, Consumer Product Safety Commission.

Employers
Arnold & Porter (Partner)

RUBENSTEIN, Bonnie

1311 L St. NW
Fourth Floor
Washington, DC 20005
EMail: bonnie@ctj.org
Tel: (202)626-3780
Fax: (202)638-3486

Employers
Citizens for Tax Justice (Development Director)

RUBENSTEIN, Michael

2033 K St. NW
Washington, DC 20006
Tel: (202)862-5600
Fax: (202)467-4439

Employers
Internat'l Food Policy Research Institute (Director of Information)

RUBIN, Blake D.

555 12th St. NW
Washington, DC 20004-1206
Tel: (202)942-5000
Fax: (202)942-5999

Attorney/Advisor, Office of Tax Legislative Counsel, Department of the Treasury, 1984-87.

Employers
Arnold & Porter (Partner)

RUBIN, Burt

1101 King St.
Alexandria, VA 22314
Tel: (703)739-2782
Fax: (703)684-8319

Employers
American Soc. of Travel Agents (General Counsel)

RUBIN, Cheryl

214 Massachusetts Ave. NE
Washington, DC 20002
Tel: (202)546-4400
Fax: (202)546-8328

Employers
Heritage Foundation (Director of Public Relations)

RUBIN, Eric M.

1155 Connecticut Ave.
Sixth Floor
Washington, DC 20036
Tel: (202)861-0870
Fax: (202)429-0657

Associate Director (1978), Assistant Director (1974-77) and Deputy Assistant Director (1974-77), all at the Federal Trade Commission. Staff Counsel, Council on Executive Reorganization, Executive Office of the President, The White House, 1969-70. Trial Attorney, Department of Justice, 1967-69.

Employers
Rubin, Winston, Diercks, Harris & Cooke (Partner)

Clients Represented

On Behalf of Rubin, Winston, Diercks, Harris & Cooke

Outdoor Advertising Ass'n of America

RUBIN, Gabriel N.

666 11th St. NW
Suite 600
Washington, DC 20001
EMail: grubin@ccianet.org
Tel: (202)783-0070
Fax: (202)783-0534

Served as Legislative Clerk, Subcommittee on National Economic Growth, Natural Resources, and Regulatory Affairs, House Committee on Government Reform and Legislative Intern to Rep. Tom Campbell (R-CA).

Employers
Computer and Communications Industry Ass'n (CCIA) (Senior Associate)

RUBIN, Harry

2300 N St. NW
Washington, DC 20037-1128
EMail: harry.rubin@shawpittman.com
Tel: (202)663-8000
Fax: (202)663-8007

Employers
Shaw Pittman (Partner)

RUBIN, James E.

1125 15th St. NW
Suite 801
Washington, DC 20005
Tel: (202)785-9300
Fax: (202)775-1950

Employers
Sherman, Dunn, Cohen, Leifer & Yellig, P.C.

RUBIN, Joshua

400 N. Capitol St. NW
Suite 585
Washington, DC 20001
Tel: (202)737-1960
Fax: (202)737-5585
Registered: LDA

Employers
Wise & Associates

Clients Represented

On Behalf of Wise & Associates
Cleveland Growth Ass'n
RPM, Inc.

RUBIN, Leonard J.

1001 Pennsylvania Ave. NW
Suite 600
Washington, DC 20004
Tel: (202)347-0066
Fax: (202)624-7222
Registered: FARA
Captain, Adjutant General, U.S. Army, 1967-69.

Employers
Powell, Goldstein, Frazer & Murphy LLP (Partner)

RUBIN, Michael

1401 H St. NW
Suite 600
Washington, DC 20005-2136
Tel: (202)326-7300
Fax: (202)326-7333
Registered: LDA

Employers
United States Telecom Ass'n (V. President, Government Relations)

RUBIN, Paul

2550 M St. NW
Washington, DC 20037-1350
Tel: (202)457-6000
Fax: (202)457-6315
Registered: LDA

Employers
Patton Boggs, LLP (Partner)

Clients Represented

On Behalf of Patton Boggs, LLP
Salton, Inc.

RUBIN, Richard

1676 International Dr.
McLean, VA 22102
Tel: (703)891-7500
Fax: (703)891-7501
Former Attorney-Advisor, Tariff Division, Common Carrier Bureau, Federal Communications Commission and former Legislative Counsel, Resident Commissioner of the Commonwealth of Puerto Rico, House of Representatives.

Employers
Akin, Gump, Strauss, Hauer & Feld, L.L.P. (Partner)

RUBINER, Laurie

1875 Connecticut Ave. NW
Suite 710
Washington, DC 20009
Tel: (202)986-2600
Fax: (202)986-2539

Employers
Nat'l Partnership for Women and Families (V. President, Program and Policy)

RUBINOFF, Edward L.

1333 New Hampshire Ave. NW
Suite 400
Washington, DC 20036
Tel: (202)887-4000
Fax: (202)887-4288
Registered: LDA

Employers
Akin, Gump, Strauss, Hauer & Feld, L.L.P. (Partner)

Clients Represented

On Behalf of Akin, Gump, Strauss, Hauer & Feld, L.L.P.
Poongsan Corporation
Svenska Petroleum Exploration AB

RUBINSON, Gail

1828 L St. NW
Suite 250
Washington, DC 20036
Tel: (202)857-1310
Fax: (202)857-1380

Employers
Jewish Women Internat'l (Exec. Director)

RUCH, Jeffrey

2001 S St. NW
Suite 570
Washington, DC 20009
EMail: jruch@peer.org
Tel: (202)265-7337
Fax: (202)265-4192

Employers
Public Employees for Environmental Responsibility (PEER) (Exec. Director)

RUCKELSHAUS, William D.

Ten G St. NE
Suite 800
Washington, DC 20002
Tel: (202)729-7600
Fax: (202)729-7610

Employers
World Resources Institute (Chairman, Board of Directors)

RUCKER, Pamela

325 Seventh St. NW
Suite 1100
Washington, DC 20004-2802
Tel: (202)783-7971
Fax: (202)737-2849

Employers
Nat'l Retail Federation (V. President, Public Relations)

RUCKERT, Edward M.

600 13th St. NW
Washington, DC 20005-3096
Tel: (202)756-8214
Fax: (202)756-8087
Registered: LDA, FARA
EMail: eruckert@mwe.com
Trial Attorney, Office of the General Counsel, Department of Agriculture, 1976-81.

Employers
McDermott, Will and Emery (Partner)

Clients Represented

On Behalf of McDermott, Will and Emery
American Spice and Trade Ass'n
California Avocado Commission
California Table Grape Commission
Crop Protection Coalition
Minor Crop Farmer Alliance
U.S. Apple Ass'n

RUDA, Richard

444 N. Capitol St. NW
Suite 345
Washington, DC 20001
Tel: (202)434-4850
Fax: (202)434-4851

Employers
Academy for State and Local Government (Chief Counsel)

RUDD, Dana

1776 I St. NW
Suite 700
Washington, DC 20006
Tel: (202)833-0914
Fax: (202)785-0639
Registered: LDA

Employers
Phillips Petroleum Co. (Federal Relations Representative)

RUDD, David

801 Pennsylvania Ave. NW
Suite 730
Washington, DC 20004
Tel: (202)756-2430
Fax: (202)756-2431
Registered: LDA
EMail: Rudd@howdc.com
Former Administrative Assistant to Senator Ernest Hollings (D-SC).

Employers
Hooper Owen & Winburn (Principal)

Clients Represented

On Behalf of Hooper Owen & Winburn
AT&T
BellSouth Corp.
Comcast Corp.
Fantasma Networks, Inc.
The Hartford
Hutchison Whampo, LTD
Microsoft Corp.
Nat'l Cable Television Ass'n
Norfolk Southern Railroad
PanAmSat Corp.
Pfizer, Inc.
United Airlines

RUDDER, Dr. Catherine E.

1527 New Hampshire Ave. NW
Washington, DC 20036
EMail: rudder@apsanet.org
Tel: (202)483-2512
Fax: (202)483-2657

Employers
American Political Science Ass'n (Exec. Director)

RUDDY, Robert E.

9106 Drumaldry Dr.
Bethesda, MD 20817
Tel: (301)530-1331
Fax: (301)530-9294
Registered: LDA
EMail: bob_ruddy@yahoo.com
Former Deputy Undersecretary, Department of Housing and Urban Development and Republican Staff Director, House Committee on Banking.

Employers
Ruddy & Associates (President)

Clients Represented

On Behalf of Ruddy & Associates
Mortgage Insurance Companies of America
Nat'l Ass'n of Housing Cooperatives

RUDEBUSCH, Thomas L.

1615 M St. NW
Suite 800
Washington, DC 20036-3203
EMail: tlr@dwgp.com
Tel: (202)467-6370
Fax: (202)467-6379
Attorney-Advisor, Office of Administrative Law Judges, Federal Energy Regulatory Commission, 1986-87.

Employers
Duncan, Weinberg, Genzer & Pembroke, P.C. (Principal)

Clients Represented

On Behalf of Duncan, Weinberg, Genzer & Pembroke, P.C.
Bergen, New York, Village of
Freeport, New York, Electric Department of the Village of
Greenport, New York, Village Electric Department of
Jamestown, New York, Board of Public Utilities
M-S-R Public Power Agency
Massena, New York, Town of
Municipal Electric Utilities Ass'n of New York State
New York Municipal Power Agency
Rockville Centre, New York, Village of

RUDEN, Paul M.

1101 King St.
Alexandria, VA 22314
Tel: (703)739-2782
Fax: (703)684-8319

Employers
American Soc. of Travel Agents (Senior V. President, Legal and Industry Affairs)

RUDMAN, Hon. Warren B.

1615 L St. NW
Suite 1300
Washington, DC 20036
Tel: (202)223-7300
Fax: (202)223-7420
Registered: LDA
EMail: wrudman@paulweiss.com
Member, U.S. Senate (R-NH), 1980-92.

Employers
Paul, Weiss, Rifkind, Wharton & Garrison (Partner)

RUDNICK, Amy G.

1050 Connecticut Ave. NW
Washington, DC 20036-5306
Tel: (202)955-8500
Fax: (202)467-0539
Registered: LDA
EMail: arudnick@gdclaw.com
Director, Office of Financial Enforcement, Department of Treasury, 1987-90. Trial Attorney, Criminal Division, Department of Justice, 1981-84. Law Clerk to Judge Ellen Bree Burns, U.S. District Court for the District of Connecticut, 1980-81.

Employers
Gibson, Dunn & Crutcher LLP (Partner)

RUDOLPH, Deborah K.

1828 L St. NW
Suite 1202
Washington, DC 20036-5104
Tel: (202)785-0017
Fax: (202)785-0835
Registered: LDA
EMail: d.rudolph@ieee.org

Employers
Institute of Electrical and Electronics Engineers, Inc. (Manager, Technology Policy Activities)

RUDOWITZ, Robin

200 Independence Ave. SW
Room 341H
Washington, DC 20201
Tel: (202)690-7762
Fax: (202)690-8168

Employers
Department of Health and Human Services - Health Care Financing Administration (Director, Medicare Analysis Group)

RUDY, Anthony C.

800 Connecticut Ave. NW
Suite 500
Washington, DC 20006
Tel: (202)533-2313
Fax: (202)331-3101
EMail: rudyt@gtlaw.com

Deputy Chief of Staff (1998-2000) and Press Secretary (1995-98) to House Majority Whip, Rep. Tom DeLay (R-TX). Law Clerk to Senator Lauch Faircloth (R-NC), 1995. Law Clerk, Organized Crime Division, Department of Justice, 1994. Press Secretary (1991-93) and Legislative Assistant (1989-91) to Rep. Dana Rohrabacher (R-CA). Assistant to the General Counsel, Senate Steering Committee, 1986-87.

Employers
Greenberg Traurig, LLP (Shareholder)

Clients Represented

On Behalf of Greenberg Traurig, LLP
Fannie Mae
SunCruz Casino

RUDY, Theresa Meeham

1612 K St. NW
Suite 510
Washington, DC 20006
Tel: (202)887-8255
Fax: (202)887-9699

Employers
HALT-An Organization of Americans for Legal Reform (Director of Programs)

RUEMPLER, Henry C.

1225 Connecticut Ave. NW
Washington, DC 20036
Tel: (202)327-8383
Fax: (202)327-6719
Registered: LDA
EMail: henry.ruempler@ey.com

Legislative Director for Senator Thad Cochran (R-MS), 1979-83. Staff Counsel, Government Operations Committee, U.S. House of Representatives, 1976-78.

Employers
Ernst & Young LLP (Partner)

Clients Represented

On Behalf of Ernst & Young LLP
E-Commerce Coalition
Edison Electric Institute
General Ore Internat'l Corp. Ltd.
INCOL 2000
Interest Netting Coalition
Koch Industries, Inc.
MassMutual Financial Group
Nordstrom, Inc.
Repeal the Tax on Talking Coalition
Tax Policy Coalition

RUFE, Roger

1725 DeSales St. NW
Suite 600
Washington, DC 20036
Tel: (202)429-5609
Fax: (202)872-0619

Employers
Center for Marine Conservation (President)

RUFFIN, Edmund

1625 K St. NW
Suite 1100
Washington, DC 20006-1604
Tel: (202)857-0244
Fax: (202)857-0237
Registered: LDA
EMail: mruffin@bio.org

Employers
Biotechnology Industry Organization (V. President, Business Development)

RUFFING, Sheryl McCluney

1001 Pennsylvania Ave. NW
Suite 700 South
Washington, DC 20004
Tel: (202)662-2640
Fax: (202)662-2624
Registered: LDA

Employers
Honeywell Internat'l, Inc. (Director, Aerospace Government Relations and Aviation Policy)

RUFFNER, Gary M.

815 16th St. NW
Washington, DC 20006
Tel: (202)347-8105
Fax: (202)347-4872
EMail: gruffner@aflcio.org

Employers
Utility Workers Union of America (National Secretary/Treasurer)

RUGE, Mark H.

1735 New York Ave. NW
Suite 500
Washington, DC 20006-4759
Tel: (202)628-1700
Fax: (202)331-1024
Registered: LDA

Deputy Minority Staff Director, House Merchant Marine and Fisheries Committee, 1990-92. Chief of Staff to Rep. Robert Davis (R-MI), 1988-90, 1993.

Employers
Preston Gates Ellis & Rouvelas Meeds LLP (Partner)

Clients Represented

On Behalf of Preston Gates Ellis & Rouvelas Meeds LLP
Akzo Nobel Chemicals, Inc.
American Soc. for Therapeutic Radiology and Oncology
Aventis Pharmaceutical Products
Dredging Contractors of America
Island Express Boat Lines Ltd.
Lake Carriers Ass'n
Mount Vernon Barge Service
Nat'l Marine Manufacturers Ass'n
Northern Michigan University
Northwestern Michigan College
Personal Watercraft Industry Ass'n
Prime Time 24
Rhodia, Inc.
St. Lawrence Seaway Pilots Ass'n
Tacoma, Washington, Port of
The Title XI Coalition
Transpacific Stabilization Agreement
Transportation Institute
United States Maritime Coalition
VoiceStream Wireless Corp.
Western Great Lakes Pilots Ass'n

RUGGIERI, Nicholas L.

1700 Rockville Pike
Suite 210
Rockville, MD 20852
Tel: (301)770-2597
Fax: (301)770-2589

Employers
Serono Laboratories, Inc. (V. President, Government Affairs)

RUGGIO, Michael

1919 Pennsylvania Ave. NW
Suite 600
Washington, DC 20006-3404
Tel: (202)326-1500
Fax: (202)326-1555

Employers
Jenkens & Gilchrist (Partner)

RUGH, Timothy R.

8201 Greensboro Dr.
Suite 300
McLean, VA 22102
Tel: (703)610-9000
Fax: (703)610-9005

Employers
Ass'n Management Group

Clients Represented

On Behalf of Ass'n Management Group
Internat'l Cast Polymer Ass'n

RUHE, Shirley L.

1420 New York Ave. NW
Suite 1050
Washington, DC 20005
Tel: (202)638-1950
Fax: (202)638-7714
Registered: LDA

Director, Budget and Economic Policy, House Committee on the Budget, 1975-94

Employers
SLR Budget and Legislative Consulting (President)
Van Scoyoc Associates, Inc. (Of Counsel)

RUHLEN, Stephen S.

Old Executive Office Bldg.
Room 276
Washington, DC 20501
Tel: (202)456-6774
Fax: (202)456-1606

Employers
Executive Office of the President - Office of the Vice President (Deputy Assistant to the V. President for Legislative Affairs (House))

RUIZ, Andrea

2445 M St. NW
Suite 260
Washington, DC 20037
Tel: (202)872-1679
Fax: (202)872-1725
EMail: aruiz@lopmurphy.com

Employers
Pierre E. Murphy Law Offices (Associate)

RUIZ, Art

1710 Rhode Island Ave. NW
Suite 700
Washington, DC 20036-3007
Tel: (202)466-5208
Fax: (202)263-4435

Employers
State Farm Insurance Cos. (Director, Federal Affairs)

RUIZ, Hiram A.

1717 Massachusetts Ave. NW
Suite 200
Washington, DC 20036
Tel: (202)347-3507
Fax: (202)347-3418
Registered: LDA
EMail: hiram.ruiz@irsa-uscr.org

Employers
United States Committee for Refugees (Senior Policy Analyst)

RUKAVINA, Steven

1329 Connecticut Ave. NW
Washington, DC 20036-1825
Tel: (202)331-2830
Fax: (202)331-0050

Employers
Nat'l Federation of Croatian Americans (Exec. V. President)

RULAND, Susan

1250 H St. NW
Suite 900
Washington, DC 20005
Tel: (202)737-4332
Fax: (202)331-7820

Employers
Internat'l Dairy Foods Ass'n (V. President, Communications and Meetings)

RULE, Charles F.

1001 Pennsylvania Ave. NW
Suite 800
Washington, DC 20004-2505
Tel: (202)639-7000
Fax: (202)639-7008

Assistant Attorney General (1986-89), Deputy Assistant Attorney General (1984-86), and Special Assistant to the Assistant Attorney General (1982-84), Antitrust Division, Department of Justice.

Employers
Fried, Frank, Harris, Shriver & Jacobson (Partner)

RUMBARGER, Charles D.

8201 Greensboro Dr.
Suite 300
McLean, VA 22102
Tel: (703)610-9000
Fax: (703)610-9005

Employers
Ass'n Management Group (Chairman)

RUMFELT, Chad

820 Gibbon St.
Suite 204
Alexandria, VA 22314
Tel: (703)838-2850
Fax: (703)838-0149
EMail: crumfelt@nboa.org

Employers
Nat'l Business Owners Ass'n (Director, Government Affairs)

RUNG, Anne

600 Pennsylvania Ave. SE
Suite 400
Washington, DC 20003
Tel: (202)546-0007
Fax: (202)544-5002

Employers
Democratic Leadership Council (Congressional Director)

RUNGE, Tom S.

1275 Pennsylvania Ave. NW
Ninth Floor
Washington, DC 20004
Tel: (202)662-6790
Fax: (202)624-0866
Registered: LDA

Employers
Stuntz, Davis & Staffier, P.C. (Of Counsel)

Clients Represented

On Behalf of Stuntz, Davis & Staffier, P.C.
Alliance for Competitive Electricity

RUNKEL, Deedie

666 Eleventh St. NW
Suite 202
Washington, DC 20001
EMail: ddrunkel@peacelinkusa.org
Tel: (202)783-7030
Fax: (202)783-7040

Employers
Peace Links (Director)

RUNYAN, John C.

1101 Pennsylvania Ave. NW
Suite 200
Washington, DC 20004
EMail: john.runyon@ipaper.com
Tel: (202)628-1223
Fax: (202)628-1368
Registered: LDA

Employers
Internat'l Paper (Washington Representative)

RUNYON, Rex A.

1501 Wilson Blvd.
Suite 1100
Arlington, VA 22209-3199
EMail: rrunyon@afia.org
Tel: (703)524-0810
Fax: (703)524-1921

Employers
American Feed Industry Ass'n (V. President, Public Relations)

RUOFF, Beth

1901 L St. NW
Suite 300
Washington, DC 20036
EMail: beth.ruoff@dc.ogilvypr.com
Tel: (202)466-7590
Fax: (202)466-7598

Employers
Ogilvy Public Relations Worldwide (Senior V. President)

RUPINSKI, Walter F.

1200 Wilson Blvd.
Arlington, VA 22209
Tel: (703)465-3648
Fax: (703)465-3031

Employers
The Boeing Co. (V. President, Export Management and Compliance)

RUPLI, Timothy R.

1212 New York Ave. NW
Suite 350
Washington, DC 20005
Tel: (202)842-5077
Fax: (202)842-5010
Registered: LDA
Formerly served in the Department of Health and Human Services, Department of the Interior and as Director, Exec. Secretariat of the Base Closure and Realignment Commission.

Employers
Hall, Green, Rupli, LLC (Partner)
Timothy R. Rupli and Associates, Inc.

Clients Represented

On Behalf of Hall, Green, Rupli, LLC
Community Financial Services Ass'n
MemberWorks, Inc.
Pernod Ricard

On Behalf of Timothy R. Rupli and Associates, Inc.
R. Duffy Wall and Associates
University of Texas

RUPP, John P.

1201 Pennsylvania Ave. NW
Washington, DC 20004-2401
EMail: jrupp@cov.com
Tel: (202)662-6000
Fax: (202)662-6291
Assistant to the Solicitor General, Department of Justice, 1974-77. Law Clerk, First Cicuit, U.S. Court of Appeals, 1974-77.

Employers
Covington & Burling (Partner)

RUPPERT, Carey D.

801 Pennsylvania Ave. NW
Suite 350
Washington, DC 20004
EMail: cruppert@nnsdc.com
Tel: (202)783-2370
Fax: (202)783-1746
Registered: LDA

Employers
Newport News Shipbuilding Inc. (Director, Government Relations)

RUSBULDT, Robert A.

412 First St. SE
Suite 300
Washington, DC 20003
Tel: (202)863-7000
Fax: (202)863-7015
Registered: LDA
Former Aide to Rep. Carroll Campbell (R-SC).

Employers
Independent Insurance Agents of America, Inc. (Exec. V. President)

RUSBY, P. Baman

1825 I St. NW
Suite 400
Washington, DC 20006
Tel: (202)429-2090
Fax: (202)429-9574
Registered: LDA

Employers
Millennium Intermarket Group, LLC

Clients Represented

On Behalf of Millennium Intermarket Group, LLC
Infilco Degremont, Inc.

RUSCIO, Domenic R.

317 Massachusetts Ave. NE
Suite 200
Washington, DC 20002
EMail: druscio@dc-crd.com
Tel: (202)546-4732
Fax: (202)546-1257
Registered: LDA
Deputy Assistant Secretary for Legislation, Department of Education, 1980-81. Deputy Assistant Secretary for Education, Department of Health Education and Welfare, 1978-80. Staff Member, Senate Committee on Appropriations, 1973-77. Budget Examiner, Department of Health, Education and Welfare, 1968-72.

Employers
Cavarocchi Ruscio Dennis Associates (Senior Partner)

Clients Represented

On Behalf of Cavarocchi Ruscio Dennis Associates
Alzheimer's Ass'n
American Indian Higher Education Consortium
American Soc. of General Surgeons
American Soc. of Pediatric Nephrology
Boys Town Nat'l Research Hospital
Delta Dental Plans Ass'n
Software Productivity Consortium

RUSHTON, Alexander A.

1200 18th St. NW
Suite 400
Washington, DC 20036-2506
EMail: arushton@nbaa.org
Tel: (202)783-9454
Fax: (202)331-8364

Employers
Nat'l Business Aviation Ass'n (Administrative Assistant, Government and Public Affairs)

RUSKIN, Gary

1611 Connecticut Ave. NW
Suite 3A
Washington, DC 20009
Tel: (202)296-2787
Fax: (202)833-2406

Employers
Congressional Accountability Project (Director)

RUSKIN, Glenn S.

1776 I St. NW
Suite 1030
Washington, DC 20006
Tel: (202)822-1690
Fax: (202)822-1693
Registered: LDA

Employers
Solutia Inc. (V. President, Public Affairs)

RUSS, Marnie

700 13th St. NW
Suite 400
Washington, DC 20005
EMail: mruss@cassidy.com
Tel: (202)347-0773
Fax: (202)347-0785
Registered: LDA
Former Professional Staff for the Senate Committee on Energy and Natural Resources.

Employers
Cassidy & Associates, Inc. (Sr. Account Executive)

Clients Represented

On Behalf of Cassidy & Associates, Inc.
Alenia Aerospazig
American Film Institute
The Auxiliary Service Corporations
The Boeing Co.
Central College
Central Piedmont Community College
Community Hospital Telehealth Consortium
Condell Medical Center
The Core Center
Idaho State University
United Space Alliance

RUSSELL, Barry

1201 15th St. NW
Third Floor
Washington, DC 20005
EMail: brussell@ipaa.org
Tel: (202)857-4722
Fax: (202)857-4799
Registered: LDA

Employers
Independent Petroleum Ass'n of America (President)

RUSSELL, Cheryl

1200 Wilson Blvd.
Rosslyn, VA 22209
Tel: (703)465-3613
Fax: (703)465-3034

Employers
The Boeing Co. (Director, Federal Affairs)

RUSSELL, Dianne J.

6930 Carroll Ave.
Suite 420
Takoma Park, MD 20912
Tel: (301)270-2900
Fax: (301)270-0610

Employers
Institute for Conservation Leadership (Exec. Director)

RUSSELL, Michael E.

1299 Pennsylvania Ave. NW
Suite 800 West
Washington, DC 20004
Tel: (202)785-0500
Fax: (202)785-5277

Employers
The Carmen Group (Chief Financial Officer)

Clients Represented

On Behalf of The Carmen Group
ADVO, Inc.

RUSSELL, Randall M.

1919 South Eads St.
Suite 103
Arlington, VA 22202-3028
Tel: (703)979-6900
Fax: (703)979-6906
Registered: LDA
Chief of Staff to the Secretary (1985), Deputy Assistant Secretary for Economics (1984), and Assistant to the Secretary (1981-82), all at the Department of Agriculture. Former Agriculture Legislative Assistant to Senator, Rudolf Eli Boschwitz (R-MN).

Employers
Lesher & Russell, Inc.

Clients Represented

On Behalf of Lesher & Russell, Inc.
Chicago Mercantile Exchange
Commerce Ventures
Federal Agricultural Mortgage Corp. (Farmer Mac)
Monsanto Co.
PepsiCo, Inc.
Philip Morris Management Corp.
USA Rice Federation

RUSSELL, Shannon M.

601 Pennsylvania Ave. NW
Suite 540
North Bldg.
Washington, DC 20004
EMail: smrussell@ashland.com

Tel: (202)223-8290
Fax: (202)293-2913
Registered: LDA

Employers
Ashland Inc. (Senior Washington Representative)

RUSSELL, William J.

1230 17th St. NW
Washington, DC 20036-3078

Tel: (202)223-9485
Fax: (202)775-1824

Employers
American Educational Research Ass'n (Exec. Director)
Nat'l Council on Measurement in Education (Exec. Officer)

RUSSELL-WILSON, Clarissa

1767 Business Center Dr.
Suite 302
Reston, VA 20190

Tel: (703)438-3101
Fax: (703)438-3113

Employers
Ass'n Innovation and Management, Inc. (Senior Account Executive)

RUSSO, Hon. Martin A.

700 13th St. NW
Suite 400
Washington, DC 20005
EMail: mrusso@cassidy.com
Member, U.S. House of Representatives (D-IL), 1975-93.

Tel: (202)347-0773
Fax: (202)347-0785
Registered: LDA, FARA

Employers
Cassidy & Associates, Inc. (Vice Chairman, President and Chief Operating Officer)

Clients Represented

On Behalf of Cassidy & Associates, Inc.
Adelphi University
Alenia Aerospazig
Boston College
Chicago Board of Trade
Chicago Mercantile Exchange
Columbia University
Community Health Partners of Ohio
The Core Center
Crane & Co.
Draft Worldwide
E Lottery
Fairfield University
Henry Ford Health System
General Dynamics Corp.
Institute for Student Achievement
Maersk Inc.
Major League Baseball
North Shore Long Island Jewish Health System
Northwestern University
Rush Presbyterian-St. Luke's Medical Center
Sacramento Area Flood Control Agency
Sherwin Williams Co.
Taiwan Research Institute
Taiwan Studies Institute
United Service Organization
United Space Alliance
University of Massachusetts Memorial Health System
VoiceStream Wireless Corp.

RUST-TIERNEY, Diann

122 Maryland Ave. NE
Washington, DC 20002

Tel: (202)675-2321
Fax: (202)546-0738
Registered: LDA

Employers
American Civil Liberties Union (Director, Death Penalty)

RUTH, Frederick A.

888 16th St. NW
Suite 700
Washington, DC 20006

Tel: (202)223-9151
Fax: (202)223-9814
Registered: LDA

Employers
Kasten & Co. (V. President)

Clients Represented

On Behalf of Kasten & Co.
Information Practices Coalition of Washington, D.C.
Newsbank, Inc.

RUTHERFORD, J. T.

46 S. Glebe Rd.
Suite 202
Arlington, VA 22204

Tel: (703)920-8005

Employers
J. T. Rutherford & Associates (Founder)

RUTT, James

505 Huntmar Park Dr.
Herndon, VA 20170

Tel: (703)742-0400

Employers
VeriSign/Network Solutions, Inc. (Chief Exec. Officer)

RUTTA, Randall L.

700 13th St. NW
Suite 200
Washington, DC 20005
EMail: rrutta@opa.easter-seals.org

Tel: (202)347-3066
Fax: (202)737-7914
Registered: LDA

Employers
Easter Seals (Senior V. President, Government Relations)

RUTTEN, Timothy M.

901 15th St. NW
Suite 700
Washington, DC 20005-2301
EMail: tmrutten@verner.com

Tel: (202)371-6000
Fax: (202)371-6279
Registered: LDA

Employers
Verner, Liipfert, Bernhard, McPherson and Hand, Chartered (Associate)

Clients Represented

On Behalf of Verner, Liipfert, Bernhard, McPherson and Hand, Chartered
Capital Metropolitan Transportation Authority
Commercial Information Systems, Inc.
Confederated Tribes of the Coos
Forest Soc. of Maine
Kansas City, Missouri, City of
Port of Tillamook Bay
Prowler Fisheries and Clipper Seafoods
Washington County, Oregon, Land Use and Transportation of

RUYAK, Robert

1299 Pennsylvania Ave. NW
Washington, DC 20004-2402

Tel: (202)783-0800
Fax: (202)383-6610

Employers
Howrey Simon Arnold & White (Chairman)

RYAN, Bruce D.

1299 Pennsylvania Ave. NW
Tenth Floor
Washington, DC 20004-2400
EMail: bruceryan@paulhastings.com
Former Law Clerk to Judge Gasch, U.S. District Court for the District of Columbia.

Tel: (202)508-9500
Fax: (202)508-9700
Registered: LDA

Employers
Paul, Hastings, Janofsky & Walker LLP (Partner)

Clients Represented

On Behalf of Paul, Hastings, Janofsky & Walker LLP
Cumulus Media, Inc.

RYAN, Cheryl Feik

1050 Thomas Jefferson St. NW
Seventh Floor
Washington, DC 20007
EMail: cfr@vnf.com

Tel: (202)298-1800
Fax: (202)338-2416

Employers
Van Ness Feldman, P.C. (Member)

RYAN, Chris

1522 K St. NW
Suite 836
Washington, DC 20005
EMail: ryanchrisf@aol.com

Tel: (202)842-3525
Fax: (202)842-2788
Registered: LDA

Employers
Consortium of Social Science Ass'ns (Associate Director, Public Affairs)

RYAN, Christine C.

1025 Thomas Jefferson St. NW
Eighth Floor, West Tower
Washington, DC 20007
EMail: cryan@bbrslaw.com
Law Clerk to Judge John L. Smith, U.S. District Court for the District of Columbia, 1982-83.

Tel: (202)342-0800
Fax: (202)342-0807
Registered: LDA

Employers
Brickfield, Burchette, Ritts & Stone (Partner)

Clients Represented

On Behalf of Brickfield, Burchette, Ritts & Stone
East Texas Electric Cooperative
Northeast Texas Electric Cooperative
Sam Rayburn G&T Electric Cooperative, Inc.
Tex-La Electric Cooperative of Texas

RYAN, Dan

1025 Connecticut Ave. NW
Suite 910
Washington, DC 20036

Tel: (202)467-5088

Employers
Mazda North America Operations (Manager, Government and Safety Affairs)

RYAN, Donald T.

227 Massachusetts Ave. NE
Suite 200
Washington, DC 20002

Tel: (202)543-1147
Fax: (202)543-4466

Employers
Alliance to End Childhood Lead Poisoning (Exec. Director)

RYAN, Elaine M.

810 First St. NE
Suite 500
Washington, DC 20002-4267

Tel: (202)682-0100
Fax: (202)289-6555

Employers
American Public Human Services Ass'n (Acting Exec. Director)

RYAN, Frank E.

1111 14th St. NW
Suite 1200
Washington, DC 20005-5603
EMail: ryanf@ada.org

Tel: (202)898-2424
Fax: (202)898-2437

Employers
American Dental Ass'n (Manager, Political Education)

RYAN, Jay T.

1050 Thomas Jefferson St. NW
Seventh Floor
Washington, DC 20007
EMail: jtr@vnf.com

Tel: (202)298-1800
Fax: (202)338-2416

Employers
Van Ness Feldman, P.C. (Associate)

RYAN, John

4301 Wilson Blvd.
Arlington, VA 22203-1860
EMail: john.ryan@nreca.org

Tel: (703)907-5822
Fax: (703)907-5516
Registered: LDA

Employers
Nat'l Rural Electric Cooperative Ass'n (Senior Principal, Legislative Affairs)

RYAN, John C.

1301 Pennsylvania Ave. NW
Suite 400
Washington, DC 20004
EMail: jryan@cla.ci.la.ca.us

Tel: (202)347-0915
Fax: (202)347-0919

Employers
Los Angeles, California, Washington Office of the City of (Legislative Representative)

RYAN, John G.

655 15th St. NW
Suite 300
Washington, DC 20005
EMail: john.ryan@bms.com

Tel: (202)783-0900
Fax: (202)783-2308
Registered: LDA

Employers
Bristol-Myers Squibb Co. (Senior Counsel and Director, Government Affairs)

RYAN, John L.

1015 18th St. NW
Suite 1100
Washington, DC 20036-5725
EMail: jryan@csbsdc.org
Tel: (202)728-5724
Fax: (202)296-1928
Registered: LDA

Employers
Conference of State Bank Supervisors (Senior V. President, Policy)

RYAN, John R.

1301 Pennsylvania Ave. NW
Suite 1100
Washington, DC 20004-1707
Tel: (202)626-4000
Fax: (202)626-4149

Employers
Air Transport Ass'n of America (V. President, Air Traffic Management)

RYAN, Joseph

One Marriott Dr.
Department 977.01
Washington, DC 20058
Tel: (202)380-3000

Employers
Marriott Internat'l, Inc. (Exec. V. President and General Counsel)

RYAN, Kevin

1701 Pennsylvania Ave. NW
Suite 300
Washington, DC 20006
Tel: (202)662-2700
Fax: (202)662-2739

Employers
Andrews and Kurth, L.L.P. (Associate)

RYAN, Lisa F.

2120 L St. NW
Suite 700
Washington, DC 20037
EMail: lryan@hsdwdc.com
Tel: (202)822-8282
Fax: (202)296-8834

Trial Attorney, Land and Natural Resources Division, Department of Justice, 1985-89.

Employers
Hobbs, Straus, Dean and Walker, LLP (Associate)

Clients Represented
On Behalf of Hobbs, Straus, Dean and Walker, LLP
Shiprock Alternative Schools, Inc.

RYAN, Mary Frances

1500 K St. NW
Suite 650
Washington, DC 20005
Tel: (202)715-1000
Fax: (202)715-1001

Employers
GlaxoSmithKline (Federal Government Relations)

RYAN, Maureen

300 D St. SW
Suite 814
Washington, DC 20024
Tel: (202)488-3500
Fax: (202)488-1300

Employers
SPACEHAB, Inc. (Director, Government Relations)

RYAN, Patricia

321 D St. NE
Washington, DC 20002
Tel: (202)547-4192
Fax: (202)547-4674

Former Professional Staff Member, House Committee on Appropriations.

Employers
The Potomac Advocates (Partner)

RYAN, Paul D.

1001 19th St. North
Suite 1200
Arlington, VA 22209
EMail: pryan@aiam.org
Tel: (703)525-7788
Fax: (703)525-3289

Employers
Ass'n of Internat'l Automobile Manufacturers (Director, Commercial Affairs)

RYAN, Russ

11480 Commerce Park Dr.
Reston, VA 20191
Tel: (703)755-2000
Fax: (703)755-2623

Employers
Teleglobe Communications Corp. (Manager, Marketing and Corporate Communications)

RYAN, Stephen M.

1501 M St. NW
Suite 700
Washington, DC 20005-1702
EMail: sryan@manatt.com
Tel: (202)463-4349
Fax: (202)463-4394
Registered: LDA

General Counsel, Senate Committee on Governmental Affairs, 1987-90. Assistant U.S. Attorney for the District of Columbia, Department of Justice, 1986. Deputy Counsel, President's Commission on Organized Crime, 1984-86. Law Clerk to Judge Robert A. Grant, Sr., U.S. District Court for Northern Indiana, 1979-81.

Employers
Manatt, Phelps & Phillips, LLP (Partner)

Clients Represented
On Behalf of Manatt, Phelps & Phillips, LLP
Agilent Technologies
Computer and Communications Industry Ass'n (CCIA)
Hewlett-Packard Co.
Intuit, Inc.
Oracle Corp.
Unisys Corp.

RYAN, Thomas M.

1133 Connecticut Ave. NW
Suite 300
Washington, DC 20036
Tel: (202)293-1177
Fax: (202)293-3411
Registered: LDA

Chief Counsel (1985-87) and Counsel (1977-84), House Committee on Energy and Commerce.

Employers
Ryan, Phillips, Utrecht & MacKinnon (Partner)

Clients Represented
On Behalf of Ryan, Phillips, Utrecht & MacKinnon
Air Transport Ass'n of America
Ass'n of American Railroads
Coeur d'Alene Mines Corp.
Cook Inlet Region Inc.
R. R. Donnelley & Sons
Edison Electric Institute
Florida Power and Light Co.
General Communications, Inc.
Investment Co. Institute
Kerr-McGee Corp.
Lockheed Martin Corp.
MultiDimensional Imaging, Inc.
Nat'l Cable Television Ass'n
New York Stock Exchange
Pfizer, Inc.
Philip Morris Management Corp.
Progress Energy
Sault Ste. Marie Tribe of Chippewa Indians
Southern Co.
TXU Business Services
U.S. Interactive
United Pan-Europe Communications, NV
VoiceStream Wireless Corp.

RYAN, Wendy

6733 Curran St.
McLean, VA 22101-6005
EMail: wendy@bwanet.org
Tel: (703)790-8980
Fax: (703)893-5160

Employers
Baptist World Alliance (Director, Division of Communications)

RYBECK, Walter

10615 Brunswick Ave.
Kensington, MD 20895
EMail: waltrybeck@aol.com
Tel: (301)933-0277

Employers
Center for Public Dialogue (Director)

RYBERG, Jr., Paul

1054 31st St. NW
Suite 300
Washington, DC 20007
EMail: pr@his.com
Tel: (202)333-4000
Fax: (202)965-3445
Registered: LDA

Employers
Ryberg and Smith LLP (Partner)

Clients Represented
On Behalf of Ryberg and Smith LLP
African Coalition for Trade, Inc.
Mauritius Sugar Syndicate
Mauritius, Chamber of Agriculture of
Mauritius-U.S. Business Ass'n Inc.

RYLAND, Barbara H.

1001 Pennsylvania Ave. NW
Suite 1100
Washington, DC 20004-2595
Tel: (202)624-2500
Fax: (202)628-5116
Registered: LDA

Employers
Crowell & Moring LLP (Of Counsel)

SAAS, Richard

1330 Connecticut Ave. NW
Washington, DC 20036-1795
EMail: rsaas@steptoe.com
Tel: (202)429-3000
Fax: (202)429-3902

Employers
Steptoe & Johnson LLP (Partner)

SABBATH, Lawrence E.

1730 M St. NW
Suite 200
Washington, DC 20036-4530
EMail: lsabbath@selleryinc.com
Tel: (202)296-3522
Fax: (202)296-7713
Registered: LDA

Staff Director, Subcommittee on Transportation, Tourism and Hazardous Materials, Committee on Energy and Commerce, U.S. House of Representatives, 1987-89. Staff Director, Subcommittee on Tax, Access to Equity Capital and Business Opportunities (1985-87) and Staff Director, Subcommittee on Antitrust and Restraint of Trade Activities Affecting Small Business (1982-85), Committee on Small Business, U.S. House of Representatives. Legislative Assistant (1979-82 and 1977-78), Acting Administrative Assistant (1978-79), and District Office Manager (1975-76) to Rep. James Santini (D-NV).

Employers
Sellery Associates, Inc. (V. President)

Clients Represented
On Behalf of Sellery Associates, Inc.
Financial Service Centers of America
Nat'l Armored Car Ass'n
Nat'l Burglar and Fire Alarm Ass'n
Nat'l Council of Investigative and Security Services Inc.
Security Companies Organized for Legislative Action

SABO, Douglas

1401 Wilson Blvd.
Suite 1100
Arlington, VA 22209
EMail: dsabe@itaa.org
Tel: (703)522-5055
Fax: (703)525-2279
Registered: LDA

Employers
Information Technology Ass'n of America (ITAA) (V. President, Information Security Programs)

SABO, Melanie

1735 New York Ave. NW
Suite 500
Washington, DC 20006-4759
Tel: (202)628-1700
Fax: (202)331-1024

Employers
Preston Gates Ellis & Rouvelas Meeds LLP (Partner)

SACCO, Michael

5201 Auth Way
Camp Springs, MD 20746
Tel: (301)899-0675
Fax: (301)899-7355

Employers
Seafarers Internat'l Union of North America (President)

SACHS, Lowell

1300 I St. NW
Suite 420 East
Washington, DC 20005
Tel: (202)326-7520
Fax: (202)326-7525
Registered: LDA

Employers
Sun Microsystems (Manager, Federal Affairs)

SACHS, Robert J.

1724 Massachusetts Ave. NW
Washington, DC 20036-1969
Tel: (202)775-3550
Fax: (202)775-3695
Registered: LDA

Employers
Nat'l Cable Television Ass'n (President and Chief Exec. Officer)

SACHSE, Harry R.

1250 I St. NW
Suite 1000
Washington, DC 20005
Tel: (202)682-0240
Fax: (202)682-0249

Assistant to the Solicitor General, Department of Justice, 1971-76. Assistant General Counsel, Agency for International Development, 1969-71.

Employers
Sonosky, Chambers, Sachse & Endreson (Partner)

Clients Represented

On Behalf of Sonosky, Chambers, Sachse & Endreson
Hopi Indian Tribe

SACILOTTO, Kara

607 14th St. NW
Suite 700
Washington, DC 20005-2011
Tel: (202)628-6600
Fax: (202)434-1690

Employers
Perkins Coie LLP (Partner)

SACK, James M.

8300 Greensboro Dr.
Suite 1080
McLean, VA 22102
Tel: (703)883-0102
Fax: (703)883-0108

Employers
Sack & Harris, P.C. (President)

SACKETT, III, Dean R.

1401 H St. NW
12th Floor
Washington, DC 20005-2148
Tel: (202)326-8319
Fax: (202)326-8313
Registered: LDA

Employers
Investment Co. Institute (Legislative Representative, Banking and Securitys)

SACKETT, Victoria A.

1825 Connecticut Ave. NW
Fifth Floor
Washington, DC 20009
Tel: (202)667-0901
Fax: (202)667-0902
EMail: victoria.sackett@widmeyer.com

Employers
Widmeyer Communications, Inc. (V. President)

SACKIN, Barry

700 S. Washington St.
Suite 300
Alexandria, VA 22314
Tel: (703)739-3900
Fax: (703)739-3915
Registered: LDA

Employers
American School Food Service Ass'n (Director, Government Affairs)

SACKNOFF, Scott

P.O. Box 5752
Bethesda, MD 20824-5752
Tel: (703)524-2766

Employers
Internat'l Space Business Council (President)

SACKS, Stephen M.

555 12th St. NW
Washington, DC 20004-1206
Tel: (202)942-5000
Fax: (202)942-5999
EMail: Stephen_Sacks@aporter.com

Assistant to the General Counsel, Department of the Army, 1967-1970.

Employers
Arnold & Porter (Partner)

SADLER, Linda C.

Commonwealth Towers
1300 Wilson Blvd., Suite 200
Arlington, VA 22209-2307
Tel: (703)516-8225
Fax: (703)516-8293
Registered: LDA
EMail: lcsadler@collins.rockwell.com

Employers
Rockwell Collins (Director, Governmental and Regulatory Affairs)

SADLIER, Lizanne

700 11th St. NW
Washington, DC 20001-4507
Tel: (202)383-1209
Fax: (202)383-7580
Registered: LDA
EMail: lsadlier@realtors.org

Employers
Nat'l Ass'n of Realtors (Political Representative)

SAFER, Nancy

1110 N. Glebe Rd.
Arlington, VA 22201-5704
Tel: (703)620-3660
Fax: (703)620-4334

Employers
Council for Exceptional Children (Exec. Director)

SAFFERT, Christopher

739 Eighth St. SE
Washington, DC 20003
Tel: (202)547-2500
Fax: (202)546-2483

Employers
ACORN (Ass'n of Community Organizations for Reform Now) (Legislative Director)

SAFFURI, Khalid

1920 L St. NW
Suite 200
Washington, DC 20036
Tel: (202)955-7174
Fax: (202)785-0261
Registered: LDA
EMail: kalforca@aol.com

Employers
Islamic Institute (Exec. Director)

SAFIR, Peter O.

1140 19th St. NW
Suite 900
Washington, DC 20036
Tel: (202)223-5120
Fax: (202)223-5619
EMail: psafir@kkblaw.com

Employers
Kleinfeld, Kaplan and Becker (Partner)

Clients Represented

On Behalf of Kleinfeld, Kaplan and Becker
Aventis CropScience
Carter-Wallace, Inc.
E. R. Squibb and Sons, Inc.

SAHR, David R.

2300 N St. NW
Washington, DC 20037-1128
Tel: (202)663-8000
Fax: (202)663-8007
Registered: LDA
EMail: david.sahr@shawpittman.com

Employers
Shaw Pittman (Partner)

Clients Represented

On Behalf of Shaw Pittman
Bank Hapoalim B.M.
Dresdner Bank AG
Federation of Japanese Bankers Ass'ns

SAILER, Brian

2103 O St. NW
Washington, DC 20037
Tel: (202)371-5600
Fax: (202)371-5608
Registered: LDA

Employers
Mark A. Siegel & Associates (Exec. V. President)

Clients Represented

On Behalf of Mark A. Siegel & Associates
Maldives, Government of the Republic of

SAILER, Francis J.

2101 L St. NW
Washington, DC 20037-1526
Tel: (202)785-9700
Fax: (202)887-0689
Registered: LDA
EMail: sailerf@dsmo.com

Employers
Dickstein Shapiro Morin & Oshinsky LLP (Partner)

Clients Represented

On Behalf of Dickstein Shapiro Morin & Oshinsky LLP
Habas Group

SAILER, Gill

421 New Jersey Ave. SE
Washington, DC 20003
Tel: (703)318-7169
Registered: LDA

Employers
Washington Consulting Alliance, Inc.

Clients Represented

On Behalf of Washington Consulting Alliance, Inc.
Metrocall Inc.

SAILER, Henry P.

1201 Pennsylvania Ave. NW
Washington, DC 20004-2401
Tel: (202)662-6000
Fax: (202)662-6291
EMail: hsailer@cov.com

Law Clerk to Judge John M. Harlan, U.S. Supreme Court, 1958-59.

Employers
Covington & Burling (Partner)

SAINT-LOUIS, Rudolph A.

The Mercury Bldg.
1925 K St. NW
Room 848
Washington, DC 20423-0001
Tel: (202)565-1592
Fax: (202)565-9016
EMail: saint-louisr@stb.dot.gov

Staff Attorney, Office of Public Assistance (1980-95) and Attorney/Advisor, Section of Rates (1977-80), Interstate Commerce Commission. Special Assistant to the U.S. Attorney, Office of the U.S. Attorney for the District of Columbia, Department of Justice, 1980.

Employers
Department of Transportation - Surface Transportation Board (Attorney/Advisor, Congressional and Public Services)

SAJKA, Janina

820 First St. NE
Suite 400
Washington, DC 20002
Tel: (202)408-8175
Fax: (202)289-7880
Registered: LDA
EMail: janina@afb.net

Employers
American Foundation for the Blind - Governmental Relations Group (Director, Technology Research and Development)

SAKOL, Jodi

3000 K St. NW
Suite 300
Washington, DC 20007
Tel: (202)295-8787
Fax: (202)295-8799

Former Deputy Communications Director, Office of V. President Al Gore, Executive Office of the President.

Employers
The Harbour Group (Senior Associate)

SALA, Joseph L.

1341 Connecticut Ave. NW
Third Floor
Washington, DC 20036
Tel: (202)862-3900
Fax: (202)862-5500

Employers
Scribe Consulting & Communications (Consultant)

SALAETS, Kenneth J.

1250 I St. NW
Suite 200
Washington, DC 20005
Tel: (202)737-8888
Fax: (202)638-4922
Registered: LDA

Employers
Information Technology Industry Council (Director of Domestic Policy Issues)

SALAS, Carlos

1033 N. Fairfax St.
Suite 404
Alexandria, VA 22314
Tel: (703)549-7404
Fax: (703)549-8712
EMail: csalas@icsc.org

Employers
Internat'l Council of Shopping Centers (Manager, State Relations)

SALAVANTIS, Peter J.

1560 Wilson Blvd.
Suite 1175
Arlington, VA 22209
Tel: (703)276-3519
Fax: (703)276-8168

Employers
Mitsubishi Electric & Electronics, USA (Director, Public Affairs)

SALEM, George R.

1333 New Hampshire Ave. NW
Suite 400
Washington, DC 20036
Tel: (202)887-4000
Fax: (202)887-4288
Registered: LDA

Employers
Akin, Gump, Strauss, Hauer & Feld, L.L.P. (Partner)

Clients Represented

On Behalf of Akin, Gump, Strauss, Hauer & Feld, L.L.P.
AOL Time Warner

SALEM, Steve

600 Jefferson Plaza
Suite 401
Rockville, MD 20852
EMail: ssalem@bgca.org
Tel: (301)251-6676
Fax: (301)294-3052

Employers
Boys and Girls Clubs of America (V. President, Government Relations)

SALEMME, R. Gerard

1730 Rhode Island Ave. NW
Suite 1000
Washington, DC 20036
Tel: (202)721-0999
Fax: (202)721-0995
Registered: LDA
Senior Telecommunications Policy Analyst, Subcommittee on Telecommunications and Finance, House Committee on Energy and Commerce. Chief of Staff to Rep. Edward J. Markey (D-MA).

Employers
Communications Consultants, Inc.

Clients Represented

On Behalf of Communications Consultants, Inc.
Eagle River, LLC

SALGADO, R. Anthony

600 New Hampshire Ave. NW
11th Floor
Washington, DC 20037
EMail: ras@dejlaw.com
Tel: (202)944-3000
Fax: (202)944-3068
Registered: LDA

Employers
Dyer Ellis & Joseph, P.C. (Partner)

Clients Represented

On Behalf of Dyer Ellis & Joseph, P.C.
Intermare Navigation SA
Kvaerner Philadelphia Shipyard Inc.

SALIBA, Khalil G. "Karl"

5802 Grosvenor Lane
Bethesda, MD 20814
Tel: (301)581-1140
Fax: (301)571-5367
Registered: LDA
Department of Energy, 1991-93.

Employers
Saliba Action Strategies, LLC (Principal)

Clients Represented

On Behalf of Saliba Action Strategies, LLC
Burger King Corp.
GOPMarketplace.com
New Media Strategies

SALINAS, Carlos

600 Pennsylvania Ave. SE
Fifth Floor
Washington, DC 20003
Tel: (202)544-0200
Fax: (202)546-7142
Registered: LDA

Employers
Amnesty Internat'l U.S.A. (Acting Director, Washington Office)

SALISBURY, Dallas L.

2121 K St. NW
Suite 600
Washington, DC 20037-2121
EMail: salisbury@ebri.org
Tel: (202)659-0670
Fax: (202)775-6312

Employers
Employee Benefit Research Institute (President and Chief Exec. Officer)

SALISBURY, Franklin C.

4600 East West Hwy.
Suite 525
Bethesda, MD 20814
Tel: (301)654-1250
Fax: (301)654-5824

Employers
Nat'l Foundation for Cancer Research (President)

SALISBURY, Keith

6903 Rockledge Dr.
Suite 730
Bethesda, MD 20817
EMail: salisbury_keith@emc.com
Tel: (301)272-2320
Fax: (301)272-2369
Registered: LDA

Employers
EMC Corp. (Manager, Government Affairs)

SALMON, John J.

1775 Pennsylvania Ave. NW
Suite 200
Washington, DC 20006
EMail: jsalmon@deweyballantine.com
Tel: (202)429-2309
Fax: (202)862-1093
Registered: LDA, FARA
Chief Counsel and Staff Director (1981-85) and Professional Staff Member (1975-81), House Ways and Means Committee.

Employers
Dewey Ballantine LLP (Partner)

Clients Represented

On Behalf of Dewey Ballantine LLP
Automatic Data Processing, Inc
Catholic Health Ass'n of the United States
Citigroup
Development Resources, Inc.
GE Investment Corp.
Railroad Retirement Tax Working Group
Thompson Publishing, Inc.
Union Pacific

SALMON, Scott

1101 Pennsylvania Ave. NW
Suite 510
Washington, DC 20004
Tel: (202)783-6333
Fax: (202)783-6309

Employers
USX Corp. (Manager, Government Affairs)

SALMON, Scott R.

1001 G St. NW
Suite 100 East
Washington, DC 20001
Tel: (202)737-7575
Fax: (202)737-9090
Registered: LDA

Employers
CaseNewHolland Inc. (Manager, Government Affairs)

SALMON, Shannon

1350 I St. NW
Suite 1210
Washington, DC 20005-3305
Tel: (202)589-1004
Fax: (202)589-1001
Registered: LDA

Employers
Johnson & Johnson, Inc. (V. President, Federal Affairs)

SALMON, Sheila C.

1100 Connecticut Ave. NW
Suite 1000
Washington, DC 20036
Tel: (202)728-1070
Fax: (202)293-2448
Registered: LDA

Employers
Coan & Lyons (Associate)

SALMON, Stephanie

900 Second St. NE
Suite 109
Washington, DC 20002
Tel: (202)898-1444
Fax: (202)898-0188

Employers
Waterman & Associates (Senior Associate)

SALMONSEN, David

600 Maryland Ave. SW
Suite 800
Washington, DC 20024
Tel: (202)484-3600
Fax: (202)484-3604
Registered: LDA

Employers
American Farm Bureau Federation (Director, Water Quality/Wetlands)

SALOMON, Kenneth D.

1200 New Hampshire Ave. NW
Suite 800
Washington, DC 20036-6802
EMail: ksalomon@dlalaw.com
Tel: (202)776-2000
Fax: (202)776-2222
Registered: LDA
Deputy Chief Counsel, National Telecommunications and Information Administration, Department of Commerce, 1978-80. Attorney, Federal Communications Commission, 1975-78 and 1970-72.

Employers
Dow, Lohnes & Albertson, PLLC (Member)

Clients Represented

On Behalf of Dow, Lohnes & Albertson, PLLC
Cox Enterprises Inc.
R. R. Donnelley & Sons
Iowa Telecommunications & Technology Commission
Nat'l ITFS Ass'n
St. Louis Regional Education and Public Television Commission
St. Matthew's University School of Medicine
Stelco Inc.
Stoll Stoll Berne Lokting & Shlachter, P.C.
University of Puerto Rico

SALONEN, Eric

2100 M St. NW
Suite 200
Washington, DC 20037
EMail: esalonen@stewartlaw.com
Tel: (202)785-4185
Fax: (202)466-1286
Registered: LDA

Employers
Stewart and Stewart (Of Counsel)

Clients Represented

On Behalf of Stewart and Stewart
Ranchers-Cattlemen Legal Action Fund

SALSBURY, Michael

1133 19th St. NW
Washington, DC 20036
Tel: (202)887-3373
Fax: (202)887-3353

Employers
MCI WorldCom Corp. (General Counsel)

SALTER, Howard

50 F St. NW
Suite 500
Washington, DC 20001
EMail: hsalter@bread.org
Tel: (202)639-9400
Ext: 261
Fax: (202)639-9401

Employers
Bread for the World (Director, Communications)

SALTZMAN, Joel

1220 L St. NW
Washington, DC 20005
Tel: (202)682-8406
Fax: (202)682-8232
Registered: LDA

Employers
American Petroleum Institute (Washington Representative)

SALTZMAN, Paul

1399 New York Ave. NW
Eighth Floor
Washington, DC 20005-4711
EMail: psaltzman@bondmarkets.com
Tel: (202)440-9459
Registered: LDA

Employers
The Bond Market Ass'n (Senior V. President and General Counsel)

SALVOSA, Donn

1401 New York Ave. NW
11th Floor
Washington, DC 20005
Tel: (202)628-8200
Fax: (202)628-8260

Employers
Electric Power Supply Ass'n (Manager, Government Affairs)

SALYER, Allison

400 C St. NE
Washington, DC 20002
Tel: (202)547-0887
Fax: (202)547-0726
EMail: asalyer@afda.org

Employers

Nat'l Funeral Directors Ass'n (Legislative Assistant)

SAMARA, Noah A.

2400 N St. NW
Washington, DC 20037
Tel: (202)969-6000
Fax: (202)969-6001
Registered: LDA

Employers

WorldSpace Corp. (Chief Exec. Officer)

SAMET, Andrew

1300 Pennsylvania Ave. NW
Suite 400
Ronald Reagan Bldg.
Washington, DC 20004
Tel: (202)638-2230
Fax: (202)638-2236

Former Deputy Undersecretary and Associate Deputy Undersecretary, Department of Labor, 1993-2001. Aide to Senator Daniel Patrick Moynihan (D-NY), 1987-93.

Employers

Sandler, Travis & Rosenberg, P.A.

SAMHAN, Helen Hatab

1600 K St. NW
Suite 601
Washington, DC 20006
Tel: (202)429-9210
Fax: (202)429-9214
EMail: hsamhan@aaiusa.org

Employers

Arab American Institute (Exec. V. President)

SAMMAN, Mazhar

1023 15th St. NW
Washington, DC 20005
Tel: (202)289-5920
Fax: (202)289-5938

Employers

Nat'l U.S.-Arab Chamber of Commerce (Exec. V. President)

SAMMIS, Elizabeth

Four Taft Ct.
Rockville, MD 20850
Tel: (800)331-2102
Fax: (301)762-5728
EMail: bsammis@mamsi.com

Employers

Mid-Atlantic Medical Services, Inc. (Senior Director, Communications)

SAMMIS, Jack C.

1110 N. Glebe Rd.
Suite 580
Arlington, VA 22201-4795
Tel: (703)908-0707
Fax: (703)908-0709

Employers

Foundation for Internat'l Meetings (President)

SAMOLIS, Frank R.

2550 M St. NW
Washington, DC 20037-1350
Tel: (202)457-5244
Fax: (202)457-6315
Registered: LDA, FARA
EMail: fsamolis@pattonboggs.com

Professional Staff, Committee on Ways and Means, Subcommittee on Trade, U.S. House of Representatives, 1977-80. Legislative Assistant to Rep. Charles A. Vanik (D-OH), 1976.

Employers

Patton Boggs, LLP (Partner)

Clients Represented

On Behalf of Patton Boggs, LLP

African Coalition for Trade, Inc.
AOL Time Warner
DFS Group Ltd.
Dole Food Co.
Gilbarco, Inc.
Mars, Inc.
Nat'l Ass'n of Theatre Owners
Nat'l Retail Federation
United States Enrichment Corp.
Wheeling Pittsburgh Steel Corp.

SAMORA, Jr., Joseph E.

1001 G St. NW
Suite 100 East
Washington, DC 20001
Tel: (202)737-7575
Fax: (202)737-9090
Registered: LDA

Employers

CaseNewHolland Inc. (V. President, Government Affairs)

SAMP, Richard A.

2009 Massachusetts Ave. NW
Washington, DC 20036
Tel: (202)588-0302
Fax: (202)588-0386

Employers

Washington Legal Foundation (Chief Counsel)

SAMPLE, Michael J.

455 Spring Park Pl.
Suite 200
Herndon, VA 20170
Tel: (703)326-5600
Fax: (703)326-5660

Employers

Marine Spill Response Corporation (V. President, General Counsel)

SAMPLES, John

1000 Massachusetts Ave. NW
Washington, DC 20001
Tel: (202)842-0200
Fax: (202)842-3490

Employers

Cato Institute (Director of the Center for Representative Government)

SAMPSON, John

21 Dupont Circle NW
Fifth Floor
Washington, DC 20036
Tel: (202)263-5900
Fax: (202)263-5901
Registered: LDA

Employers

Microsoft Corp. (Manager, Federal Government Affairs)

SAMPSON, Vincent T.

1201 New York Ave. NW
Suite 750
Washington, DC 20005
Tel: (202)682-1515
Fax: (202)842-2556
Registered: LDA

Employers

UWC - Strategic Services on Unemployment and Workers' Compensation (Associate Legislative Counsel)

SAMS, Larry L.

1776 I St. NW
Suite 1050
Washington, DC 20006
Tel: (202)429-3400
Fax: (202)429-3467

Employers

The Dow Chemical Co. (Director, Federal Technical/Business Development)

SAMUEL, Antoinette

2101 Wilson Blvd.
Suite 500
Arlington, VA 22201-3062
Tel: (703)387-1000
Fax: (703)522-4585
EMail: ceo@eap-association.org

Employers

Employee Assistance Professionals Ass'n (C.E.O.)

SAMUEL, William

815 16th St. NW
Washington, DC 20006
Tel: (202)637-5000
Fax: (202)637-5058

Employers

AFL-CIO (American Federation of Labor and Congress of Industrial Organizations) (Legislative Director)

SAMUELS, Charles A.

701 Pennsylvania Ave. NW
Suite 900
Washington, DC 20004-2608
Tel: (202)434-7300
Fax: (202)434-7400
Registered: LDA
EMail: csamuels@mintz.com

Special Assistant to the General Counsel of the Council on Wage and Price Stability, The White House, 1979-80.

Employers

Ass'n of Home Appliance Manufacturers (Government Relations Counsel)
Mintz, Levin, Cohn, Ferris, Glovsky and Popeo, P.C. (Partner)

Clients Represented

On Behalf of Mintz, Levin, Cohn, Ferris, Glovsky and Popeo, P.C.

Ass'n of American Blood Banks
Ass'n of Home Appliance Manufacturers
Biogen, Inc.
Nat'l Ass'n of Higher Educational Finance Authorities
Nat'l Council of Health Facilities Finance Authorities

SAMUELS, Michael

1133 21st St. NW
Suite 710
Washington, DC 20036
Tel: (202)223-7683
Fax: (202)223-7687
Registered: FARA
EMail: masamuels@samuelsinternational.com

U.S. Ambassador to the GATT and Deputy U.S. Trade Representative, 1986-89. U.S. Ambassador to Sierra Leone (1975-77) and Office of Legislative Affairs (1970-73), Department of State.

Employers

Samuels Internat'l Associates, Inc. (President)

Clients Represented

On Behalf of Samuels Internat'l Associates, Inc.

Angola, Government of the Republic of

SANCHEZ, Felix R.

1010 Wisconsin Ave. NW
Suite 210
Washington, DC 20007
Tel: (202)965-5151
Fax: (202)965-5252
Registered: LDA
EMail: fsanchez@terrastrategic.com

Legislative Aide to Senator Lloyd M. Bentsen, Jr. (D-TX), 1984-87.

Employers

TerraCom-Strategic Communications (Chief Exec. Officer)

Clients Represented

On Behalf of TerraCom-Strategic Communications

Dallas/Fort Worth Internat'l Airport Board
Euro-Fulton, S.A.
Sidem International Ltd.

SANCHEZ, Ignacio E.

901 15th St. NW
Suite 700
Washington, DC 20005-2301
Tel: (202)371-6000
Fax: (202)371-6279
EMail: iesanchez@verner.com

Employers

Verner, Liipfert, Bernhard, McPherson and Hand, Chartered

SANCHEZ, Oscar

815 16th St. NW
Suite 310
Washington, DC 20006
Tel: (202)347-4223
Fax: (202)347-5095
EMail: natlclaa@aol.com

Employers

Labor Council for Latin American Advancement (LCLAA) (Exec. Director)

SANDER, Raymond J.

1001 Pennsylvania Ave. NW
Suite 580 North
Washington, DC 20004-2505
Tel: (202)783-9070
Fax: (202)393-2769
Registered: LDA

Employers

New York Life Insurance Co. (V. President, N.Y. Life International)

SANDER, Stephen

1849 C St. NW
MS: 4319
Washington, DC 20240
Tel: (202)208-4754
Fax: (202)501-7759

Employers

Department of Interior - Office of Insular Affairs (Staff Assistant, Legislative Affairs)

SANDERS, Amy Ford

321 S. Washington St.
Second Floor
Alexandria, VA 22314
Tel: (703)519-3983
Fax: (703)299-0857

Employers

Metcalf Federal Relations

Clients Represented

On Behalf of Metcalf Federal Relations

Brain Research Foundation
Philadelphia Zoo

SANDERS, Celetta Lee

1350 I St. NW
Suite 1290
Washington, DC 20005
Tel: (202)789-0300
Fax: (202)898-1164
Registered: LDA

Employers

American Bakers Ass'n (V. President, Regulatory and Technical Services)

SANDERS, David P.

655 15th St. NW
Suite 1200
Washington, DC 20005
EMail: david_sanders@dc.kirkland.com
Tel: (202)879-5161
Fax: (202)879-5200

Employers

Kirkland & Ellis (Partner)

SANDERS, Michael

1001 Pennsylvania Ave. NW
Suite 600
Washington, DC 20004
EMail: msanders@pgfm.com
Tel: (202)347-0066
Fax: (202)624-7222

Employers

Powell, Goldstein, Frazer & Murphy LLP (Partner)

SANDERS, Rose Marie

1300 Wilson Blvd.
Arlington, VA 22209
Tel: (703)741-5905
Fax: (703)741-6097
Registered: LDA
EMail: rose_marie_sanders@americanchemistry.com

Employers

American Chemistry Council (Director)

SANDERS, Dr. S. King

505 Second St. NE
Washington, DC 20002-4916
Tel: (202)547-8105
Fax: (202)547-8165

Employers

Ethics and Religious Liberty Commission of the Southern Baptist Convention (Director of Constituent Relations)

SANDERS, Timothy K.

1755 Jefferson Davis Hwy.
Suite 1107
Arlington, VA 22202
Tel: (703)415-0344
Fax: (703)415-0182
Registered: LDA

Clerk (1996-98) and Staff Member (1983-95), Subcommittee on Agriculture, House Appropriations Committee.

Employers

The PMA Group (Associate)

Clients Represented

On Behalf of The PMA Group

American Academy of Audiology
American Crop Protection Ass'n
Ass'n of Medical Device Reprocessors
Cheese of Choice Coalition
Chicago Mercantile Exchange
CoBank, ACB
ConAgra Foods, Inc.
Concurrent Technologies Corp.
Florida Sugar Cane League, Inc.
General Atomics
General Mills
Generic Pharmaceutical Ass'n
Nat'l Ass'n of Resource Conservation
Nat'l Cattleman's Beef Ass'n
Nat'l Cooperative Bank
Nat'l Pork Producers Ass'n
Science Applications Internat'l Corp. (SAIC)
Titan Corp.

SANDERS, Wallace

1140 Connecticut Ave. NW
Suite 1210
Washington, DC 20036
Tel: (202)293-0801
Fax: (202)293-0903

Employers

Nat'l Council on U.S.-Arab Relations (Director, Programs)

SANDERS BECKNER, Helen

1030 15th St. NW
Suite 1100
Washington, DC 20005
Tel: (202)783-4600
Fax: (202)783-4601

Employers

White House Writers Group (Senior Director)

SANDERSON-AUSTIN, Julie

1422 Duke St.
Alexandria, VA 22314
Tel: (703)838-0033
Fax: (703)548-1890
Registered: LDA

Employers

American Medical Group Ass'n (V. President, Quality Management, Research and Operations)

SANDHERR, Stephen E.

333 John Carlyle St.
Suite 200
Alexandria, VA 22314
EMail: sandhers@agc.org
Tel: (703)837-5309
Registered: LDA

Employers

Associated General Contractors of America (Exec. V. President and Chief Operating Officer)

SANDIFER, Mike

2419 Chain Bridge Rd. NW
Washington, DC 20016
Tel: (202)244-8736
Fax: (202)244-8736
Registered: LDA

Staff member, Senate Agriculture Committee, 1985. Legislative Assistant to Senator Walter D. Huddleston (D-KY), 1981-84. Staff, Office of Legislative Information, U.S. House of Representatives.

Employers

Sandifer and Co. (President)

SANDLER, Charles E.

1220 L St. NW
Washington, DC 20005
Tel: (202)682-8400
Fax: (202)682-8294
Registered: LDA

Employers

American Petroleum Institute (V. President, Government Affairs)

SANDLER, Gilbert Lee

1300 Pennsylvania Ave. NW
Suite 400
Ronald Reagan Bldg.
Washington, DC 20004
EMail: lsandler@strtrade.com
Tel: (202)638-2230
Fax: (202)638-2236
Registered: LDA

Worked in the Department of Justice.

Employers

Sandler, Travis & Rosenberg, P.A. (Managing Director)

Clients Represented

On Behalf of Sandler, Travis & Rosenberg, P.A.

American Free Trade Ass'n

SANDLER, Marideth J.

444 N. Capitol St. NW
Suite 336
Washington, DC 20001
Tel: (202)624-5858
Fax: (202)624-5857

Employers

Alaska, Washington Office of the State of (Associate Director)

SANDLER, William

1050 17th St. NW
Suite 280
Washington, DC 20036
EMail: wsandler@vma.org
Tel: (202)331-8105
Ext: 306
Fax: (202)296-0378

Employers

Valve Manufacturers Ass'n of America (President)

SANDMAN, James

555 12th St. NW
Washington, DC 20004-1206
EMail: James_Sandman@aporter.com
Tel: (202)942-5000
Fax: (202)942-5999

Employers

Arnold & Porter (Managing Partner)

SANDMAN, Jeffrey M.

1100 Connecticut Ave. NW
12th Floor
Washington, DC 20036
Tel: (202)452-6500
Fax: (202)452-6502

Employers

IssueSphere (Managing Partner)

SANDRI, Jr., Joseph M.

1615 L St. NW
Suite 1260
Washington, DC 20036
Tel: (202)367-7612
Fax: (202)659-1931
Registered: LDA

Employers

Winstar Communications, Inc. (V. President and Regulatory Counsel)

SANDSTROM, Mark Roy

1920 N St. NW
Washington, DC 20036
EMail: msandstrom@thf.com
Tel: (202)331-8800
Fax: (202)331-8330

Employers

Thompson, Hine and Flory LLP (Partner)

Clients Represented

On Behalf of Thompson, Hine and Flory LLP

Yale Materials Handling Corp.

SANDUSKY, Vincent R.

10302 Eaton Pl.
Suite 340
Fairfax, VA 22030
Tel: (703)385-5300
Fax: (703)385-5301

Employers

American Public Communications Council (President)

SANER, II, Robert J.

1875 I St. NW
12th Floor
Washington, DC 20006
Tel: (202)466-6550
Fax: (202)785-1756
Registered: LDA

Assistant to the Administrator, Social and Rehabilitation Service, Department of Health, Education and Welfare, 1972-73.

Employers

Powers Pyles Sutter & Verville, PC (Principal)

Clients Represented

On Behalf of Powers Pyles Sutter & Verville, PC

Ass'n of Metropolitan Water Agencies
Medical Group Management Ass'n
Pain Care Coalition

SANERA, Ph.D., Michael

1001 Connecticut Ave. NW
Suite 1250
Washington, DC 20036
Tel: (202)331-1010
Fax: (202)331-0640

Employers

Competitive Enterprise Institute (Director of Center for Environmental Education Research)

SANFORD, Bruce W.

1050 Connecticut Ave. NW
Suite 1100
Washington, DC 20036-5304
EMail: Bsanford@baker-hostetler.com
Tel: (202)861-1500
Fax: (202)861-1790

Employers

Baker & Hostetler LLP (Partner)

Clients Represented

On Behalf of Baker & Hostetler LLP

Soc. of Professional Journalists

SANFORD, USN (Ret.), Rear Adm. Frederic G.

9320 Old Georgetown Rd.
Bethesda, MD 20814
EMail: freds@amsus.org
Tel: (301)897-8800
Fax: (301)530-5446

Employers

Ass'n of Military Surgeons of the U.S. (AMSUS) (Exec. Director)

SANFORD, Suzanne L.

2600 Virginia Ave. NW
Suite 1000
Washington, DC 20037-1905
Tel: (202)333-8800
Fax: (202)337-6065
Registered: LDA

Employers
Schmeltzer, Aptaker & Shepard, P.C. (Associate)

SANFUENTES, Vince

Ronald Reagan Bldg.
1300 Pennsylvania Ave. NW
MS: 6.10A
Washington, DC 20523
Tel: (202)712-4300
Fax: (202)216-3036

Employers
Agency for Internat'l Development (Legislative Program Specialist, Congressional Liaison Division)

SANKEY, C. Patrick

1010 Massachusetts Ave. NW
Suite 410
Washington, DC 20001
Tel: (202)371-5544
Fax: (202)371-5565

Employers
Internat'l Road Federation (Director General & Chief Exec. Officer)

SANSONI, Brian T.

1500 K St. NW
Suite 300
Washington, DC 20005
Tel: (202)347-2900
Fax: (202)347-4110

Employers
Soap and Detergent Ass'n (V. President, Communication and Education)

SANTA ANNA, Yvonne

228 Seventh St. SE
Washington, DC 20003-4306
Tel: (202)547-7424
Fax: (202)547-9559

Employers
Nat'l Ass'n for Home Care (Deputy Director, Gov't Affairs)

SANTANA, Susan I.

2099 Pennsylvania Ave. NW
Suite 100
Washington, DC 20006
EMail: sisantan@hklaw.com
Tel: (202)955-3000
Fax: (202)955-5564

Employers
Holland & Knight LLP (Associate)

SANTARELLI, Donald E.

1615 L St. NW
Suite 1200
Washington, DC 20036
Tel: (202)466-6300
Fax: (202)463-0678
Registered: LDA

Assistant U.S. Attorney, Department of Justice, 1966-67. Administrator, Law Enforcement Assistance Administration (1973-74) and Associate Deputy Attorney General (1969-73), Department of Justice. Special Counsel, Subcommittee on Constitutional Rights, Senate Judiciary Committee, 1968-69. Minority Counsel, House Judiciary Committee, 1967-68. Assistant U.S. Attorney, Department of Justice, 1966-67.

Employers
Bell, Boyd & Lloyd (Partner)

SANTINI, David L.

1444 I St. NW
Suite 700
Washington, DC 20005-2210
EMail: dsantini@bostromdc.com
Tel: (202)216-9623
Fax: (202)216-9646

Employers
Bostrom Corp. (Executive Director)

Clients Represented

On Behalf of Bostrom Corp.
Internat'l Biometric Ass'n (Eastern North American Region)
Internat'l Coach Federation

SANTINI, Hon. James D.

1101 King St.
Suite 350
Alexandria, VA 22314
Tel: (703)684-0755
Fax: (703)549-3682
Registered: LDA

Member, U.S. House of Representatives (D-NV), 1975-83.

Employers
Santini, Chartered

Clients Represented

On Behalf of Santini, Chartered
Grand Canyon Air Tour Council
Nat'l Park Hospitality Ass'n
Nat'l Tour Ass'n
United States Air Tour Ass'n

SANTONIELLO, Tom

6776 Little Falls Rd.
Arlington, VA 22213
Tel: (703)536-0002
Fax: (703)536-0003
Registered: LDA

Employers
Computing Technology Industry Ass'n (Manager, Public Policy)

SANTORA, Kathleen C.

One Dupont Circle NW
Suite 620
Washington, DC 20036
Tel: (202)833-8390
Fax: (202)296-8379

Employers
Nat'l Ass'n of College and University Attorneys (Chief Exec. Officer)

SANTORA, Ralph

1317 F St. NW
Suite 900
Washington, DC 20004-1105
Tel: (202)783-2900
Fax: (202)783-3477

Employers
Independent Action (Exec. Director)

SANTOS, Barbara J.

555 Twelfth St. NW
Suite 640
Washington, DC 20004
Tel: (202)393-3075
Fax: (202)393-1497

Employers
Edison Internat'l (Business Analyst)

SANTUCCI, Louis G.

1101 17th St. NW
Suite 300
Washington, DC 20036
Tel: (202)331-1770
Fax: (202)331-1969

Employers
Cosmetic, Toiletry and Fragrance Ass'n (V. President, International Affairs)

SANZ, Marilina

440 First St. NW
Eighth Floor
Washington, DC 20001
EMail: msanz@naco.org
Tel: (202)942-4260
Fax: (202)942-4281

Employers
Nat'l Ass'n of Counties (Associate Legislative Director, Human Services and Education)
Nat'l Ass'n of County Health Facility Administrators (Associate Legislative Director, Human Services)
Nat'l Ass'n of County Human Services Administrators (Associate Legislative Director, Human Services)
Nat'l Ass'n of Hispanic County Officials (Associate Legislative Director, Human Services)

SANZO, Kathleen M.

1800 M St. NW
Washington, DC 20036
Tel: (202)467-7209
Fax: (202)467-7176
Registered: LDA
EMail: ksanzo@morganlewis.com

Employers
Morgan, Lewis & Bockius LLP (Partner)

Clients Represented

On Behalf of Morgan, Lewis & Bockius LLP
Cord Blood Registry, Inc.

SAPERSTEIN, Rabbi David

2027 Massachusetts Ave. NW
Washington, DC 20036
Tel: (202)387-2800
Fax: (202)667-9070

Employers
Religious Action Center of Reform Judaism (Director)

SAPIRO, Miriam

505 Huntmar Park Dr.
Herndon, VA 20170
Tel: (703)742-0400

Special Assistant to the President and Counselor for Southeast European Stabilization (1999-2000) and former Director of European Affairs, National Security Council, Executive Office of the President, The White House. Also served as a Policy Planning Aide to the Secretary and a Legal Advisor, Department of State.

Employers
VeriSign/Network Solutions, Inc. (Director, International Policy)

SAPIRSTEIN, Eric

1747 Pennsylvania Ave. NW
Suite 420
Washington, DC 20006
Tel: (202)466-3755
Fax: (202)466-3787
Registered: LDA

Employers
ENS Resources, Inc. (President)

Clients Represented

On Behalf of ENS Resources, Inc.
California Ass'n of Sanitation Agencies
East Bay Municipal Utility District
Las Virgenes Municipal Water District
Orange County Sanitation Districts
Public Agencies for Audit Reform
Sacramento, California, Department of Utilities of
Sacramento, California, Public Works Agency of the County of
South Tahoe Public Utility District
Union Sanitary District
WateReuse Ass'n
Western Research Institute

SAPORTA, Vicki A.

1755 Massachusetts Ave. NW
Suite 600
Washington, DC 20036
EMail: naf@prochoice.org
Tel: (202)667-5881
Fax: (202)667-5890

Employers
Nat'l Abortion Federation (Exec. Director)

SAPPER, Arthur G.

600 13th St. NW
Washington, DC 20005-3096
EMail: asapper@mwe.com
Tel: (202)756-8246
Fax: (202)756-8087

Deputy General Counsel, Occupational Safety and Health Review Commission, 1974-78, 1980-87; Special Counsel and Assistant General Counsel, Federal Mine Safety and Health Review Commission, 1978-80.

Employers
McDermott, Will and Emery (Partner)

SARASIN, CAE, Leslie G.

2000 Corporate Ridge
Suite 1000
McLean, VA 22102
EMail: affi@pop.dn.net
Tel: (703)821-0770
Fax: (703)821-1350
Registered: LDA

Employers
American Frozen Food Institute (President and Chief Exec. Officer)
Internat'l Frozen Food Ass'n (Deputy Director General)
Nat'l Yogurt Ass'n (President)

SARCONE, Christine

1400 Independence Ave. SW
Room 3510 South Bldg.
Washington, DC 20250
EMail: chris.sarcone@usda.gov
Tel: (202)720-3203
Fax: (202)720-8477

Employers
Department of Agriculture - Agricultural Marketing Service (Legislative Staff Director)

SARFATI, CAE, Susan

1426 21st St. NW
Suite 200
Washington, DC 20036
Tel: (202)429-9370
Fax: (202)833-1129

Employers
Greater Washington Soc. of Ass'n Executives (President and Chief Exec. Officer)

SARGENT, Mary Jane

6429 Downing Ct.
Annandale, VA 22003

Employers
Federal Victory Fund (Contact, Political Action Committee)

SARJEANT, Larry

1401 H St. NW
Suite 600
Washington, DC 20005-2136
Tel: (202)326-7300
Fax: (202)326-7333

Employers
United States Telecom Ass'n (V. President, Legal and Regulatory Affairs)

SARMIENTO, Tony

8403 Colesville Rd.
Suite 1200
Silver Spring, MD 20910
Tel: (301)578-8422
Fax: (301)578-8847

Employers
Alliance for Retired Americans (Acting Exec. Director)

SARPALIUS, Hon. Bill

908 Pennsylvania Ave. SE
Washington, DC 20003
Tel: (202)544-5666
Fax: (202)544-4647
Registered: LDA
EMail: bsarpalius@advantage-dc.com
Member, U.S. House of Representatives (D-TX), 1989-96.

Employers
Advantage Associates, Inc. (President and Chief Exec. Officer)

Clients Represented
On Behalf of Advantage Associates, Inc.
Christus Health
Esat, Inc.
Professional Services Council
Sisters of Charity of the Incarnate Word
TCOM, L.P.
Uniformed Services Dental Alliance

SARRAILLE, William A.

1050 Connecticut Ave. NW
Washington, DC 20036-5339
Tel: (202)857-6000
Fax: (202)857-6395
Registered: LDA

Employers
Arent Fox Kintner Plotkin & Kahn, PLLC (Member)

Clients Represented
On Behalf of Arent Fox Kintner Plotkin & Kahn, PLLC
American Hospital Ass'n
Ass'n of Pain Management Anesthesiologist
Bergen Community College
Coalition for a Procompetitive Stark Law
Dartmouth-Hitchcock Medical Center
Fresno Community Hospital and Medical Center
George Washington University Medical Center
Molina Medical Centers
Phoenix Cardiovascular, Inc.
Soc. for Vascular Surgery
Soc. of Diagnostic Medical Sonographers
Soc. of Vascular Technology
University of Medicine and Dentistry of New Jersey - School of Health Related Professionals

SASSO, John A.

522 21st St. NW
Suite 120
Washington, DC 20006
EMail: ncda@ix.netcom.com
Tel: (202)293-7587
Fax: (202)887-5546

Employers
Nat'l Community Development Ass'n (Exec. Secretary)

SATAGAJ, John S.

1156 15th St. NW
Suite 510
Washington, DC 20005
Tel: (202)639-8888
Fax: (202)296-5333
Registered: LDA

Employers
London and Satagaj, Attorneys-at-Law (Managing Partner)

Clients Represented
On Behalf of London and Satagaj, Attorneys-at-Law
American Supply and Machinery Manufacturers' Ass'n
Hand Tools Institute
Nat'l Lumber and Building Material Dealers Ass'n
Photo Marketing Ass'n-Internat'l
Wood Machinery Manufacturers of America

SATLOFF, Robert

1828 L St. NW
Suite 1050
Washington, DC 20036
Tel: (202)452-0650
Ext: 301
Fax: (202)223-5364

Employers
Washington Institute for Near East Policy (Exec. Director)

SATO, Kazuo

1155 21st St. NW
Suite 600
Washington, DC 20036
Tel: (202)429-4766
Fax: (202)463-9032

Employers
Japan Iron and Steel Exporters Ass'n (General Manager)

SATTERFIELD, Gary T.

4301 Connecticut Ave. NW
Suite 300
Washington, DC 20008
Tel: (202)244-4700
Fax: (202)966-4818

Employers
Environmental Industry Ass'ns (Exec. V. President, Waste Equipement Technology Ass'n)

SATTERFIELD, L. Kendall

1055 Thomas Jefferson St. NW
Suite 601
Washington, DC 20007
Tel: (202)337-8000
Fax: (202)265-9363
Registered: FARA

Employers
Finkelstein, Thompson & Loughran (Partner)

Clients Represented
On Behalf of Finkelstein, Thompson & Loughran
Canadian Broadcasting Corp.

SATTERFIELD, Lee A.

1025 Connecticut Ave. NW
Suite 400
Washington, DC 20036
EMail: 2019267@mcimail.com
Tel: (202)659-6800
Fax: (202)331-0573
General Attorney, General Counsel's Office, Equal Employment Opportunity Commission, 1968. Trial Attorney, General Litigation Section, Tax Division, Department of Justice, 1964-67. Tax Law Specialist, Internal Revenue Service, Department of Treasury, 1962-64.

Employers
Whiteford, Taylor & Preston (Of Counsel)

SATTLER, Dwayne

400 N. Capitol St. NW
Suite 585
Washington, DC 20001
Tel: (202)737-1960
Fax: (202)393-5218
Registered: LDA

Employers
Wise & Associates

Clients Represented
On Behalf of Wise & Associates
Cleveland Growth Ass'n
Columbus State College
Greater Columbus Chamber
Ohio Bureau of Employment Services
Plaintiffs Committee for TWA 800 and Swissair Air III Crashes

SAUBER, Richard

1001 Pennsylvania Ave. NW
Suite 800
Washington, DC 20004-2505
EMail: richard_sauber@ffhsj.com
Tel: (202)639-7000
Fax: (202)639-7008
Chief, Defense Procurement Fraud Unit (1982-84) and Prosecutor, Criminal Fraud Section (1977-82), Department of Justice.

Employers
Fried, Frank, Harris, Shriver & Jacobson (Partner)

SAUER, Ann E.

1725 Jefferson Davis Hwy.
Crystal Square 2, Suite 300
Arlington, VA 22202
Tel: (703)413-5600
Fax: (703)413-5613

Employers
Lockheed Martin Corp. (Director, General Legislation and Budgetary Affairs)

SAUER, Edward W.

1201 Pennsylvania Ave. NW
P.O. Box 407
Washington, DC 20044-0407
EMail: esauer@ssd.com
Tel: (202)626-6600
Fax: (202)626-6780
Registered: FARA

Employers
Squire, Sanders & Dempsey L.L.P. (Partner)

Clients Represented
On Behalf of Squire, Sanders & Dempsey L.L.P.
Ansett Transport Industries
Lineas Aereas Costarricicenes (Lasca Airlines)
Polynesian Airlines
VASP Airlines
VIASA

SAUL, Jr., Richard

1100 15th St. NW
Suite 900
Washington, DC 20005
Tel: (202)835-3400
Fax: (202)835-3414
Registered: LDA

Employers
Pharmaceutical Research and Manufacturers of America (Deputy V. President, International)

SAULS, Michael L.

202 Jefferson St.
Alexandria, VA 22314
Tel: (202)543-2143
Registered: LDA

Employers
Self-employed as an independent consultant.

Clients Represented
As an independent consultant
Itera Internat'l Energy Consultants

SAULS, Stephen

701 Pennsylvania Ave. NW
Suite 600
Washington, DC 20004
EMail: saulss@fiu.edu
Tel: (305)348-3505
Fax: (202)624-1298

Employers
Florida Internat'l University (Vice Provost)

SAUNDERS, Albert C.

4806 Bentonbrook Dr.
Fairfax, VA 22030
Tel: (703)691-0898
Fax: (703)691-0898
Registered: LDA
Administrative Assistant to Senator Muriel Humphrey (D-MN), 1978. Director, Legislation to Senator Hubert H. Humphrey (D-MN), 1971-78.

Employers
Saunders Consulting (Principal)

Clients Represented
On Behalf of Saunders Consulting
Pharmaceutical Research and Manufacturers of America

SAUNDERS, Anne

1001 Pennsylvania Ave. NW
Suite 850N
Washington, DC 20004
Tel: (202)347-2222
Fax: (202)347-4242
Registered: LDA

Employers
The Michael Lewan Co. (Director, Legislative and Corporate Affairs)

Clients Represented
On Behalf of The Michael Lewan Co.
BSMG Worldwide
Capital City Economic Development Authority
Connecticut Resource Recovery Authority
Nat'l Center for Children in Poverty
NetCoalition.Com
Oracle Corp.
Phoenix Home Life Mutual Insurance Co.

SAUNDERS, David A.

1255 23rd St. NW
Suite 200
Washington, DC 20037-1174
EMail: dsaunders@hauck.com
Tel: (202)452-8100
Fax: (202)833-3636

Employers
American Coke and Coal Chemicals Institute (President)
Hauck and Associates (V. President)
Internat'l Oxygen Manufacturers Ass'n (Exec. Director)

Clients Represented

On Behalf of Hauck and Associates

American Coke and Coal Chemicals Institute
Internat'l Oxygen Manufacturers Ass'n
Nat'l Oilseed Processors Ass'n
Soy Protein Council

SAUNDERS, Donald M.

1625 K St. NW
Suite 800
Washington, DC 20006
Tel: (202)452-0620
Fax: (202)872-1031
EMail: civil@nlada.org

Employers

Nat'l Legal Aid and Defender Ass'n (Director, Civil Division)

SAUNDERS, Greg

1100 17th St.
Suite 1100
Washington, DC 20036
Tel: (202)835-1115
Fax: (202)835-1117
EMail: gsaunders@africacncl.org

Employers

Corporate Council on Africa (Director, Policy)

SAUNDERS, Harold H.

444 N. Capitol St. NW
Suite 434
Washington, DC 20001
Tel: (202)393-4478
Fax: (202)393-7644

Employers

Kettering Foundation (Director, Internat'l Affairs)

SAUNDERS, Jane L.

700 11th St. NW
Washington, DC 20001-4507
Tel: (202)383-1047
Fax: (202)434-9674
Registered: LDA
EMail: jsaunders@realtors.org

Employers

Nat'l Ass'n of Realtors (Political Representative)

SAUNDERS, Jane V.

1600 I St. NW
Washington, DC 20006
Tel: (202)293-1966
Fax: (202)296-7410

Employers

Motion Picture Ass'n of America (V. President, Commercial Affairs)

SAUNDERS, III, John E.

777 N. Capitol St. NE
Suite 807
Washington, DC 20002
Tel: (202)408-9300
Fax: (202)408-8558

Employers

Nat'l Forum for Black Public Administrators (Exec. Director)

SAUNDERS, Lee

1625 L St. NW
Washington, DC 20036-5687
Tel: (202)429-1103
Fax: (202)429-1102

Employers

American Federation of State, County and Municipal Employees (Assistant to the President)

SAUNDERS, Margot Freeman

1629 K St. NW
Suite 600
Washington, DC 20006
Tel: (202)986-6060
Ext: 104
Fax: (202)463-9462

Employers

Nat'l Consumer Law Center (Managing Attorney)

SAUNDERS, Paul

1615 L St. NW
Suite 1250
Washington, DC 20036
Tel: (202)887-1000
Fax: (202)887-5222

Employers

Nixon Center, The (Director)

SAUNDERS, Steven R.

1015 Duke St.
Alexandria, VA 22314-3551
Tel: (703)549-1555
Fax: (703)549-6526
Registered: FARA
EMail: saunderscompany@erols.com

Assistant U.S. Trade Representative, Executive Office of the President, The White House, 1981-82. Staff Director, Republican Conference of the Senate, 1979-81. Communications Director, Republican Senatorial Committee, 1977-79. Chief Legislative Assistant to Rep. Norman Lent (R-NY), 1975-77.

Employers

Saunders and Company (President)
U.S.-Mongolia Business Council, Inc. (President)

SAUNDERS, Tonya

1401 K St. NW
Suite 400
Washington, DC 20005
Tel: (202)789-2111
Fax: (202)789-4883
Registered: LDA, FARA
EMail: tsaunders@thewashingtongroup.com

Employers

The Washington Group (V. President)

Clients Represented

On Behalf of The Washington Group

American Hospital Ass'n
American Resort Development Ass'n
Ass'n of Progressive Rental Organizations
AT&T
The Boeing Co.
Delta Air Lines
Global Waste Recycling, Inc.
IVAX Corp.
Korea Information & Communication, Ltd.
Microsoft Corp.
Nat'l Ass'n of Real Estate Investment Trusts
News Corporation Ltd.
SCAN Health Plan
Texas Municipal Power Agency
Yankton Sioux Tribe

SAUNDRY, Ph.D., Peter D.

1725 K St. NW
Suite 212
Washington, DC 20006
Tel: (202)530-5810
Ext: 201
Fax: (202)628-4311
EMail: info@cnie.org

Employers

Nat'l Council for Science and the Environment (Exec. Director)

SAURES, Emeterio

2121 R St. NW
Washington, DC 20008-1908
Tel: (202)673-5869
Fax: (202)673-5873

Employers

Northern Mariana Islands, Commonwealth of the (Federal Programs Coordinator)

SAVAGE, CAE, Bruce A.

2101 Wilson Blvd.
Suite 610
Arlington, VA 22201
Tel: (703)558-0400
Fax: (703)558-0401

Employers

Manufactured Housing Institute (V. President, Public Affairs)

SAVAGE, Deirdre W.

331 Constitution Ave. NE
Washington, DC 20002
Tel: (202)547-0048
Fax: (202)547-9149

Employers

The New England Council, Inc. (V. President, Legislative Affairs)

SAVAGE, Shannon A.

1828 L St. NW
Suite 801
Washington, DC 20036
Tel: (202)775-0509
Fax: (202)775-4857
EMail: info@nacdonline.org

Employers

Nat'l Ass'n of Corporate Directors (Director, Marketing)

SAVARESE, James M.

700 13th St. NW
Suite 1000
Washington, DC 20005
Tel: (202)347-6633
Ext: 2709
Fax: (202)347-2672
Registered: FARA

Employers

Savarese & Associates

SAVARY TAYLOR, Mary Beth

325 Seventh St. NW
Washington, DC 20004
Tel: (202)638-1100
Fax: (202)626-2254
Registered: LDA

Employers

American Hospital Ass'n (Director, Exec. Branch Relations)

SAVERCOOL, John

1130 Connecticut Ave. NW
Suite 1000
Washington, DC 20036
Tel: (202)828-7100
Fax: (202)293-1219
Registered: LDA
EMail: jsavercool@aiadc.org

Employers

American Insurance Ass'n (V. President)

SAVICH, Beverly

1360 Beverly Rd.
Suite 201
McLean, VA 22101
Tel: (703)448-1000
Fax: (703)790-3460

Employers

DeHart and Darr Associates, Inc.

SAVIT, Mark N.

2550 M St. NW
Washington, DC 20037-1350
Tel: (202)457-6000
Fax: (202)457-6315
Registered: LDA
EMail: msavit@pattonboggs.com

Employers

Patton Boggs, LLP (Partner)

Clients Represented

On Behalf of Patton Boggs, LLP

AKZO Aramid Products Inc.
Homestake Mining
Martin Marietta Aggregates

SAVITT, Charles

1718 Connecticut Ave. NW
Suite 300
Washington, DC 20009
Tel: (202)232-7933
Fax: (202)234-1328

Employers

Center for Resource Economics (President)

SAVITZ, Jacqueline

600 Pennsylvania Ave. SE
Suite 340
Washington, DC 20003
Tel: (202)546-9554
Fax: (202)546-9609
EMail: jsavitz@coastalliance.org

Employers

Coast Alliance (Exec. Director)

SAVNER, David

3190 Fairview Park Dr.
Falls Church, VA 22042
Tel: (703)876-3000
Fax: (703)876-3600

Employers

General Dynamics Corp. (Senior V. President and General Counsel)

SAVNER, Steve

1616 P St. NW
Suite 150
Washington, DC 20036
Tel: (202)328-5118
Fax: (202)328-5195
EMail: ssavner@clasp.org

Employers

Center for Law and Social Policy (Senior Staff Attorney)

SAWAYA, Richard

714 21st St. NW
Third Floor
Washington, DC 20052
Tel: (202)994-9132
Fax: (202)994-1229
Registered: LDA

Employers

George Washington University, Office of Government Relations (Assistant V. President, Government Relations)

SAWHILL, Isabel V.

1775 Massachusetts Ave. NW
Washington, DC 20036-2188
Tel: (202)797-6000
Fax: (202)797-6004

Associate Director, Office of Management and Budget, 1993-95; former Director, National Commission for Employment Policy.

Employers

The Brookings Institution (Senior Fellow, Economic Studies)

SAWICKY, Max B.

1660 L St. NW
Suite 1200
Washington, DC 20036
EMail: epi@epinet.org
Tel: (202)775-8810
Fax: (202)775-0819

Employers

Economic Policy Institute (Economist)

SAWYER, Jeffrey

1629 K St. NW
Suite 1100
Washington, DC 20006
Tel: (202)785-6710
Fax: (202)331-4212

Employers

Agri/Washington

Clients Represented

On Behalf of Agri/Washington

Financial Executives International

SAXENIAN, James R.

1200 New Hampshire Ave. NW
Suite 800
Washington, DC 20036-6802
EMail: jsaxenian@dlalaw.com
Tel: (202)776-2000
Fax: (202)776-2222

Employers

Dow, Lohnes & Albertson, PLLC (Member)

SAYER, R. Wayne

1400 I St. NW
Suite 540
Washington, DC 20005-2208
EMail: rws@sayer.com
Tel: (202)638-4434
Fax: (202)296-1074
Registered: LDA

Employers

R. Wayne Sayer & Associates (President)

Clients Represented

On Behalf of R. Wayne Sayer & Associates

Applied Materials
Candescent Technologies
Coalition for Intelligent Manufacturing Systems (CIMS)
IPC Washington Office
MRS
Schott Corp.
Sheldahl, Inc.
Silicon Valley Group

SAYLE, Stephen Craig

412 First St. SE
Suite 100
Washington, DC 20003
EMail: ssayle@dutkogroup.com
Tel: (202)484-4884
Fax: (202)484-0109
Registered: LDA

Counsel, House Commerce Committee, 1995-98. Legislative Counsel to Rep. Joe Barton (R-TX), 1989-92.

Employers

The Dutko Group, Inc. (V. President)

Clients Represented

On Behalf of The Dutko Group, Inc.

Alcatel USA
ASCENT (Ass'n of Community Enterprises)
AT&T
AT&T Wireless Services, Inc.
Cable & Wireless, Inc.
Coalition for Auto Repair Equality (CARE)
Competitive Telecommunications Ass'n (COMPTEL)
European Telecommunications Standards Institute (ETSI)
EXCEL Communications Inc.
Satellite Broadcasting and Communications Ass'n
SkyBridge, LLC
SpaceData Internat'l
TV Guide, Inc.
VeriSign/Network Solutions, Inc.
Winstar Communications, Inc.
XO Communications

SAYLER, Allen

1250 H St. NW
Suite 900
Washington, DC 20005
EMail: asayler@idfa.org
Tel: (202)737-4332
Fax: (202)331-7820

Employers

Internat'l Dairy Foods Ass'n (Director, Regulatory Affairs and International Standards)

SAYLER, Robert N.

1201 Pennsylvania Ave. NW
Washington, DC 20004-2401
EMail: rsayler@cov.com
Tel: (202)662-6000
Fax: (202)662-6291

Member of Justice Working Group, Department of Justice, 1994-95.

Employers

Covington & Burling (Partner)

SAYLOR, Alice C.

1120 G St. NW
Suite 520
Washington, DC 20005-3889
Tel: (202)628-4500
Fax: (202)628-6430
Registered: LDA

Employers

American Short Line and Regional Railroad Ass'n (V. President and General Counsel)

SCALCO, Mary

12251 Tech Rd.
Silver Spring, MD 20904
Tel: (301)622-1900
Fax: (301)236-9320
Registered: LDA

Employers

Internat'l Fabricare Institute (Senior V. President)

SCALERA, Charles

321 D St. NE
Washington, DC 20002
Tel: (202)547-4192
Fax: (202)547-4674
Registered: LDA

Former Administrative Assistant to Rep. Peter W. Rodino, Jr. (D-NJ), Chairman of the House Committee on the Judiciary.

Employers

The Potomac Advocates (Partner)

Clients Represented

On Behalf of The Potomac Advocates

Adroit Systems Inc.
Argon Engineering Associates
Brashear Systems, L.L.P.
CUBRC
Eastman Kodak Co.
Eclipse
General Dynamics Corp.
B. F. Goodrich Co.
GTS
Northrop Grumman Corp.
SAFT America Inc.
SAFT R&D Center
Spot Image Corp.
SRI Internat'l
Veridian Corp.

SCANDLEN, Greg M.

655 15th St. NW Suite 375
Washington, DC 20005
Tel: (202)628-6671
Fax: (202)628-6474

Employers

Nat'l Center for Policy Analysis (Senior Fellow)

SCANLAN, Mark K.

One Thomas Circle NW
Suite 400
Washington, DC 20005
Tel: (202)659-8111
Fax: (202)659-9216
Registered: LDA

Employers

Independent Community Bankers of America (Agriculture-Rural America Representative)

SCANLAN, Susan

1750 New York Ave. NW
Suite 350
Washington, DC 20006
EMail: scanlan@wrei.org
Tel: (202)628-0444
Ext: 15
Fax: (202)628-0458

Employers

Women's Research and Education Institute (President)

SCANLON, Elizabeth K.

1111 19th St. NW
Suite 1100
Washington, DC 20036
EMail: elizabethscanlon@the-dma.org
Tel: (202)861-2422
Fax: (202)955-0085

Employers

Direct Marketing Ass'n, Inc. (Government Affairs)

SCANLON, Kerry

The McPherson Bldg.
901 15th St. NW, Suite 1100
Washington, DC 20005
Tel: (202)682-3500
Fax: (202)682-3580

Former Deputy Assistant Attorney General, Civil Rights Division, Department of Justice.

Employers

Kaye Scholer LLP (Partner)

SCANLON, Jr., Lawrence R.

1625 L St. NW
Washington, DC 20036-5687
Tel: (202)429-1185
Fax: (202)429-1197

Employers

American Federation of State, County and Municipal Employees (Director, Political Action)

SCANLON, Patrick M.

501 Third St. NW
Washington, DC 20001-2797
Tel: (202)434-1100
Fax: (202)434-1318

Employers

Communications Workers of America (General Counsel)

SCANLON, Terrence

1513 16th St. NW
Washington, DC 20036
EMail: tscanlon@capitalresearch.org
Tel: (202)483-6900
Fax: (202)483-6990

Member of Consumer Products Safety Commission during second Reagan Administration.

Employers

Capital Research Center (Chairman and President)

SCANLON, Thomas J.

3248 Prospect St. NW
Washington, DC 20007
Tel: (202)965-3983
Fax: (202)965-3987
Registered: LDA

Employers

Benchmarks, Inc. (President)

Clients Represented

On Behalf of Benchmarks, Inc.

Grupo Industrial Alfa, S.A.
Internat'l Health, Racquet and Sportsclub Ass'n

SCANNELL, Raymond F.

10401 Connecticut Ave.
Kensington, MD 20895
Tel: (301)933-8600
Fax: (301)946-8452

Employers

Bakery, Confectionery and Tobacco Workers Internat'l Union (Director of Research)

SCARABELLO, Judy

1120 20th St. NW
Suite 1000
Washington, DC 20036
EMail: jscarabell@att.com
Tel: (202)457-2205
Fax: (202)457-2571
Registered: LDA

Employers
AT&T (Director, Federal Government Affairs)

SCARAMASTRO, T. R.

5520 G Hempstead Way
Springfield, VA 22151
EMail: cgcpoa@aol.com
Tel: (703)941-0395
Fax: (703)941-0397

Employers
United States Coast Guard Chief Petty Officers Ass'n (Exec. Director)

SCARBOROUGH, Keith A.

1120 20th St. NW
Suite 520 South
Washington, DC 20036
Tel: (202)296-1883
Fax: (202)296-1430
Registered: LDA

Employers
Ass'n of Nat'l Advertisers (V. President, State Government Relations)

SCARCELLI, Pat

1775 K St. NW
Washington, DC 20006
Tel: (202)223-3111
Fax: (202)466-1562

Employers
United Food and Commercial Workers Internat'l Union (Director, Legislative and Political Affairs)

SCARDELLETTI, Robert A.

Three Research Place
Rockville, MD 20850
Tel: (301)948-4910
Fax: (301)948-1369

Employers
Transportation-Communications Internat'l Union (International President)

SCARMEAS, Christina

1700 N. Moore St.
Suite 1600
Arlington, VA 22209
Tel: (703)841-2400
Fax: (703)527-0938

Employers
American Meat Institute (Staff Assistant, Legislative and Public Affairs)

SCHACHTER, John

1615 L St. NW
Suite 1100
Washington, DC 20036-5610
Tel: (202)872-1260
Fax: (202)466-3509

Employers
The Business Roundtable (Deputy Director, Communications)

SCHAEFER, Brett

214 Massachusetts Ave. NE
Washington, DC 20002
Tel: (202)546-4400
Fax: (202)546-8328

Employers
Heritage Foundation (Jay Kingham Fellow in International Regulatory Affairs)

SCHAEFER, Hon. Dan

1700 Pennsylvania Ave. NW
Suite 950
Washington, DC 20006
EMail: dnschaefer@erols.com
Tel: (202)393-5055
Fax: (202)393-0120
Registered: LDA

Member, U.S. House of Representatives (R-CO), 1983-98.

Employers
Valis Associates (Senior Legislative Advisor)

Clients Represented
On Behalf of Valis Associates
Ass'n of American Railroads
CH2M Hill
Exxon Mobil Corp.
Grocery Manufacturers of America
Joint Southeast Public Improvement Council
Renewable Fuels Ass'n

SCHAEFER, Richard H.

8484 Georgia Ave.
Room 215
Silver Spring, MD 20910
Tel: (301)427-2014

Employers
Department of Commerce - Nat'l Marine Fisheries Service (Chief, Intergovernmental and Recreational Fisheries Staff)

SCHAEFFLER, John

1201 L St. NW
Washington, DC 20005-4014
Tel: (202)842-4444
Fax: (202)842-3860
Registered: LDA

Employers
American Health Care Ass'n (V. President, Legislative Affairs)

SCHAEFGEN, John R.

701 Pennsylvania Ave. NW
Suite 800
Washington, DC 20004
EMail: jschaefgen@thelenreid.com
Tel: (202)508-4040
Fax: (202)508-4321

Employers
Thelen Reid & Priest LLP (Partner)

Clients Represented
On Behalf of Thelen Reid & Priest LLP
Dayton Power and Light Co.

SCHAENGOLD, Michael J.

2550 M St. NW
Washington, DC 20037-1350
EMail: mschaengold@pattonboggs.com
Tel: (202)457-6000
Fax: (202)457-6315

Law Clerk to U.S. Court of Appeals for the Federal Circuit, 1987-88 and to Judge H. Robert Mayer, U.S. Claims Court, 1986-87.

Employers
Patton Boggs, LLP (Partner)

SCHAFER, Jennifer A.

499 S. Capitol St. SW
Suite 606
Washington, DC 20003
Tel: (202)554-5828
Fax: (202)554-2896
Registered: LDA

Employers
Cascade Associates (President)

Clients Represented
On Behalf of Cascade Associates
American Gas Cooling Center
Business Council for Sustainable Energy
Integrated Building and Construction Solutions
Nat'l Fenestration Rating Council
Robur Corp.
University of Oregon

SCHAFER, Larry

50 F St. NW
Suite 900
Washington, DC 20001
EMail: lschafer@ncfc.org
Tel: (202)626-8700
Fax: (202)626-8722
Registered: LDA

Employers
Nat'l Council of Farmer Cooperatives (V. President, Legal, Tax and Accounting Policy)

SCHAFF, Terry

1755 Massachusetts Ave. NW
Suite 800
Washington, DC 20036
Tel: (202)332-0063
Fax: (202)232-8203
Registered: LDA

Employers
Consortium for Oceanographic Research and Education (CORE) (Assistant to the President)

SCHAFFER, Amy E.

1111 19th St. NW
Suite 800
Washington, DC 20036
EMail: amy_schaffer@afandpa.org
Tel: (202)463-2700
Fax: (202)463-2785
Registered: LDA

Employers
American Forest & Paper Ass'n (Senior Director, Environmental Program Coordinator and Industrial Waste)

SCHAFFER, Judith

2000 M St. NW
Suite 400
Washington, DC 20036
Tel: (202)467-4999
Fax: (202)293-2672

Employers
People for the American Way (Deputy Director)

SCHAFFER, Robert P.

Ronald Reagan Bldg.
1300 Pennsylvania Ave. NW, Suite 400
Washington, DC 20004
Tel: (202)638-2230
Fax: (202)638-2236
Registered: LDA, FARA

Employers
Sandler & Travis Trade Advisory Services, Inc. (President)

Clients Represented
On Behalf of Sandler & Travis Trade Advisory Services, Inc.
Consejo Nacional de Zonas Francas de Exportacion
Haiti, Government of the Republic of

SCHAGRIN, Roger B.

1100 15th St. NW
Suite 700
Washington, DC 20005
EMail: schagrin@erols.com
Tel: (202)223-1700
Fax: (202)429-2522
Registered: LDA

Employers
Schagrin Associates (Partner and President)

Clients Represented
On Behalf of Schagrin Associates
Alliant Techsystems, Inc.
Allied Tube & Conduit Corp.
Bitrek Corp.
Century Tube Corp.
Committee on Pipe and Tube Imports
Geneva Steel Co.
Hannibal Industries
IPSCO Tubulars, Inc.
LTV Copperweld
Maverick Tube Corp.
Sharon Tube Co.
Vest Inc.
Weirton Steel Corp.
Western Tube & Conduit Co.
Wheatland Tube Co.

SCHAITBERGER, Harold A.

1750 New York Ave. NW
Washington, DC 20006
Tel: (202)737-8484
Fax: (202)737-8418
Registered: LDA

Employers
Internat'l Ass'n of Fire Fighters (General President)

SCHALL, John A.

601 Pennsylvania Ave. NW
11th Floor, North Bldg.
Washington, DC 20004-2601
Tel: (202)756-3300
Fax: (202)756-3333
Registered: LDA

Employers
Alston & Bird LLP

Clients Represented
On Behalf of Alston & Bird LLP
Nat'l Coalition on E-Commerce and Privacy

SCHALLER, Candy K.

1129 20th St. NW
Suite 600
Washington, DC 20036-3421
EMail: cschaller@aahp.org
Tel: (202)778-3200
Fax: (202)778-8479
Registered: LDA

Employers
American Ass'n of Health Plans (AAHP) (V. President, Regulatory Affairs)

SCHAMU, Nancy

444 N. Capitol St. NW
Suite 342
Washington, DC 20001
EMail: nmncshpo@sso.org
Tel: (202)624-5465
Fax: (202)624-5419

Employers
Nat'l Conference of State Historic Preservation Officers (Exec. Director)

SCHANER, Greg

1816 Jefferson Place NW
Washington, DC 20036
Tel: (202)833-2672
Fax: (202)833-4657
Registered: LDA
EMail: gschaner@amsa-cleanwater.org

Employers
Ass'n of Metropolitan Sewerage Agencies (Manager, Government Affairs)

SCHANER, Kenneth I.

3000 K St. NW
Suite 300
Washington, DC 20007
Tel: (202)424-7500
Fax: (202)424-7643
Attorney, Office of Chief Counsel, Legislation and Regulations Division, Internal Revenue Service, Department of the Treasury, 1966-70.

Employers
Swidler Berlin Shereff Friedman, LLP (Partner)

SCHANNON, Mark

2000 L St. NW
Suite 300
Washington, DC 20036-0646
Tel: (202)835-8800
Fax: (202)835-8879
EMail: mark.schannon@ketchum.com

Employers
Ketchum (Partner and Director)

SCHANTZ, Connie

Colonial Place Three
2107 Wilson Blvd., Suite 300
Arlington, VA 22201-3042
Tel: (703)524-7600
Fax: (703)524-9094

Employers
Nat'l Alliance for the Mentally Ill (Manager, Meetings and Exhibits)

SCHANTZ, Jeffery A.

10640 Main St.
Suite 200
Fairfax, VA 22030
Tel: (703)352-3400
Fax: (703)385-6470
Registered: LDA

Employers
JGW Internat'l Ltd. (Associate)

SCHAPIRO, Mary

1735 K St. NW
Washington, DC 20006
Tel: (202)728-8140
Fax: (202)728-8075

Employers
NASD Regulation (President)

SCHARDT, Arlie

1320 18th St. NW
Suite 500
Washington, DC 20036
Tel: (202)463-6670
Fax: (202)463-6671
EMail: ems@ems.org

Employers
Environmental Media Services (President)

SCHARFFENBERGER, George

1600 Wilson Blvd.
Suite 710
Arlington, VA 22209
Tel: (703)276-1800
Fax: (703)243-1865

Employers
Volunteers in Technical Assistance (President)

SCHATZ, Thomas A.

1301 Connecticut Ave. NW
Fourth Floor
Washington, DC 20036
Tel: (202)467-5300
Fax: (202)467-4253
EMail: tschatz@cagw.org
Legislative Director to Rep. Hamilton Fish Jr., (R-NY), 1980-86.

Employers
Citizens Against Government Waste (President)

SCHAUFFLER, Peter

1400 16th St. NW
Suite 715
Washington, DC 20036
Tel: (202)387-8787
Fax: (202)939-3458

Employers
Committee on the Constitutional System (Coordinator)

SCHAUMBERG, Tom M.

1200 17th St. NW
Fifth Floor
Washington, DC 20036
Tel: (202)467-6300
Fax: (202)466-2006
Registered: LDA
Attorney, Merger Division, Bureau of Restraint of Trade, Federal Trade Commission, 1964-67.

Employers
Adduci, Mastriani & Schaumberg, L.L.P. (Partner)

SCHECHTEL, Sharon

1250 I St. NW
Suite 500
Washington, DC 20005
Tel: (202)789-2900
Ext: 3004
Fax: (202)789-1893
EMail: sschechtel@anla.org

Employers
American Nursery and Landscape Ass'n (Director, Marketing and Retail Services)
Garden Centers of America (Administrator)

SCHECHTER, Karen

211 N. Union St.
Suite 100
Alexandria, VA 22314
Tel: (703)739-2545
Fax: (703)739-2718
Registered: LDA
Former Staff Assistant to Rep. Bud Shuster (R-PA).

Employers
Ann Eppard Associates, Ltd. (V. President)

Clients Represented

On Behalf of Ann Eppard Associates, Ltd.
Air-21 Coalition
Amadeus Global Travel Distribution SA
American Maritime Officers Service
Calspan University of Buffalo Research Center
Delta Development Group, Inc.
FedEx Corp.
Jefferson Government Relations, L.L.C.
Outdoor Advertising Ass'n of America
Union Pacific
United Airlines

SCHECHTER, Peter

1850 M St. NW
Suite 550
Washington, DC 20036
Tel: (202)289-5900
Fax: (202)289-4141
Registered: FARA
Former Senior Staff Assistant to the House Subcommittee on International Development Institutions and Finance.

Employers
Chlopak, Leonard, Schechter and Associates (Partner)

Clients Represented

On Behalf of Chlopak, Leonard, Schechter and Associates
Cruz Enverga & Raboca
Hoechst Marion Roussel Deutschland GmbH
Hyundai Electronics Industries Co., LTD
PromPeru
Wilkie Farr & Gallagher
World Health Organization

SCHECTER, Irene D.

2100 Pennsylvania Ave. NW
Suite 560
Washington, DC 20037
Tel: (202)223-4800
Fax: (202)223-2011
Registered: LDA
EMail: ischecter@hyjekfix.com
Legislative Director to Rep. W. G. "Bill" Hefner (D-NC), 1987-99. Associate Staff, Committee on the Budget, U.S. House of Representatives, 1983-87. Legislative Assistant to Rep. Hefner, 1981-83. Legislative Assistant to Rep. Richardson Preyer (D-NC), 1969-81.

Employers
Hyjek & Fix, Inc. (Senior Consultant)

Clients Represented

On Behalf of Hyjek & Fix, Inc.
BAE SYSTEMS North America
IT Group, Inc.
Niagara Area Chamber of Commerce
Shorts Missile Systems

SCHEIB, Lauren

1201 Pennsylvania Ave. NW
Suite 300
Washington, DC 20004
Tel: (202)857-8444

Employers
Ass'n of Test Publishers (Administrator)

SCHEIBEL, John

2000 Pennsylvania Ave NW
Washington, DC 20006
Tel: (202)887-6932
Registered: LDA
Former Staff Director, Subcommittee on International Economic Policy and Trade, House Committee on International Relations.

Employers
Yahoo!

SCHEINESON, Cathy Zeman

600 13th St. NW
Washington, DC 20005-3096
Tel: (202)756-8187
Fax: (202)756-8087
EMail: cscheineson@mwe.com

Employers
McDermott, Will and Emery (Partner)

SCHEINESON, Marc

1301 K St. NW
Suite 1100-East Tower
Washington, DC 20005
Tel: (202)414-9200
Fax: (202)414-9299
Registered: LDA
Associate Commissioner for Legislative Affairs, Food and Drug Administration, Department of Health and Human Services, 1991-92. Legislative Assistant to Rep. Bill Gradison (R-OH), 1981-82.

Employers
Reed, Smith, LLP (Partner)

Clients Represented

On Behalf of Reed, Smith, LLP
Ass'n of Health Information Outsourcing Services
Innovative Science Solutions
Internat'l Hearing Soc.
Oce-USA, Inc.
PCS Health Systems, Inc.
Pharmacia Corp.
Solus Research, Inc.

SCHELLBERG, Timothy

1025 Connecticut Ave. NW
Suite 1012
Washington, DC 20036
Tel: (202)258-2301
Registered: LDA
EMail: tims@smithallinglane.com

Employers
Smith Alling Lane, P.S.

Clients Represented

On Behalf of Smith Alling Lane, P.S.
PE Biosystems
Sagem Morpho
Washington Ass'n of Sheriffs and Police Chiefs

SCHELLER, Nora

2001 Pennsylvania Ave. NW
Suite 300
Washington, DC 20006
Tel: (202)862-0275
Fax: (202)862-0267
Registered: LDA

Employers
Exxon Mobil Corp. (Washington Representative, Government Agencies)

SCHENENDORF, Jack L.

1201 Pennsylvania Ave. NW
Washington, DC 20004-2401
Tel: (202)662-6000
Fax: (202)662-6291
Coordinator, Department of Transportation, for the Bush/Cheney Transition Team. Chief of Staff, House Committee on Transportation and Infrastructure, 1995-2001. Minority Chief Counsel (1983-95), Associate Minority Counsel (1980-83), and Assistant Minority Counsel for Surface Transportation (1976-80), all at the House Committee on Public Works and Transportation. Staff Counsel, National Commission on Water Quality, 1975-76. Served in the U.S. Navy, 1967-72.

Employers
Covington & Burling

SCHEPIS, Chris

400 N. Capitol St. NW
Suite 790
Washington, DC 20001
Tel: (202)554-1600
Fax: (202)554-1654
Registered: LDA

Employers
Nat'l Farmers Union (Farmers Educational & Co-operative Union of America) (Government Relations Representative)

SCHEPPACH, Raymond C.

444 N. Capitol St. NW
Suite 267
Washington, DC 20001-1512
Tel: (202)624-5300
Fax: (202)624-5313

Employers
Nat'l Governors' Ass'n (Exec. Director)

SCHER, Barry F.

P.O. Box 1804
Department 599
Washington, DC 20013
EMail: bscher@giantofmaryland.com
Tel: (301)341-4710
Fax: (301)618-4967

Employers
Giant Food Inc. (V. President, Public Affairs)

SCHER, Eddie

1200 New York Ave. NW
Suite 400
Washington, DC 20005
Tel: (202)289-2395
Fax: (202)289-1060

Employers
Clean Water Network (Director)

SCHER, Amb. Peter L.

1909 K St. NW
Washington, DC 20006
Tel: (202)263-3000
Fax: (202)263-3300
Registered: LDA

Special Trade Negotiator for Agriculture and Food Policy, Office of the U.S. Trade Representative, Executive Office of the President, The White House, 1998-2000. Chief of Staff, Department of Commerce, 1995-97. Chief of Staff to the U.S. Trade Representative, Executive Office of the President, The White House, 1993-95. Staff Director, Committee on Environment and Public Works, 1993-94. Chief of Staff to Senator Max Baucus (D-MT), 1991-93.

Employers
Mayer, Brown & Platt (Partner)

Clients Represented

On Behalf of Mayer, Brown & Platt
Ace Ltd.
CoBank, ACB
Elanco Animal Health
Monsanto Co.
News America Inc.
Pharmacia Corp.
United Airlines
United Parcel Service

SCHERDER, Daniel

1497 Chain Bridge Rd.
Suite 303
McLean, VA 22101
EMail: dscherder@willardgroup.com
Tel: (703)893-8409
Fax: (703)893-8020
Registered: LDA

Employers
The Willard Group (Managing Director)

Clients Represented

On Behalf of The Willard Group
AEI Resources
Bituminous Coal Operators Ass'n
Energy and Environment Coalition
EnviroPower
The Peabody Group

SCHERGENS, Becky

1899 L St. NW
Suite 200
Washington, DC 20036
Tel: (202)833-8121
Fax: (202)833-8155

Employers
Devillier Communications (V. President)

Clients Represented

On Behalf of Devillier Communications
Lockheed Martin Corp.

SCHERMAN, William S.

1440 New York Ave. NW
Washington, DC 20005
Tel: (202)371-7000
Fax: (202)393-5760
Registered: LDA

Former General Counsel, Federal Energy Regulatory Commission.

Employers
Skadden, Arps, Slate, Meagher & Flom LLP (Partner)

Clients Represented

On Behalf of Skadden, Arps, Slate, Meagher & Flom LLP
Entergy Services, Inc.

SCHERR, Marsha

888 17th St. NW
12th Floor
Washington, DC 20006
Tel: (202)429-8744
Fax: (202)296-2962

Employers
Nat'l Strategies Inc. (V. President)

Clients Represented

On Behalf of Nat'l Strategies Inc.
The Comcare Alliance
Shenandoah Valley

SCHERR, S. Jacob

1200 New York Ave. NW
Suite 400
Washington, DC 20005
Tel: (202)289-6868
Fax: (202)289-1060

Employers
Natural Resources Defense Council (Senior Staff Attorney)

SCHERS, Eric

503 Capitol Ct. NE
Suite 300
Washington, DC 20002
Tel: (202)546-4825
Fax: (202)546-4797

Employers
American College of Nurse Practitioners (Director)

SCHETTEWI, Jennifer B.

2550 M St. NW
Washington, DC 20037-1350
EMail: jschwettewi@pattonboggs.com
Tel: (202)457-5645
Fax: (202)457-6315

Employers
Patton Boggs, LLP (Associate)

SCHEUER, Sarah

325 Seventh St. NW
Suite 1100
Washington, DC 20004-2802
Tel: (202)783-7971
Fax: (202)737-2849

Employers
Nat'l Retail Federation (Manager, Media Relations)

SCHEUNEMAN, Byron L.

12501 Old Columbia Pike
Silver Spring, MD 20904
Tel: (301)680-6380
Fax: (301)680-6370

Employers
Adventist Development and Relief Agency Internat'l (Senior V. President)

SCHIAPPA, Cheryl

1101 17th St. NW
Suite 300
Washington, DC 20036
Tel: (202)331-1770
Fax: (202)331-1969

Employers
Cosmetic, Toiletry and Fragrance Ass'n (V. President, Administration)

SCHICK, Allen

1775 Massachusetts Ave. NW
Washington, DC 20036-2188
Tel: (202)797-6000
Fax: (202)797-6004

Employers
The Brookings Institution (Visiting Scholar, Governmental Studies)

SCHICK, Michael W.

1050 Connecticut Ave. NW
Suite 870
Washington, DC 20036
Tel: (202)783-9150
Fax: (202)783-9150
Registered: LDA

Former Deputy Press Secretary to Senator Strom Thurmond (R-SC).

Employers
Civic Service, Inc. (Senior Associate)

Clients Represented

On Behalf of Civic Service, Inc.
American Ass'n of Clinical Endocrinologists
IPR Shandwick
Japan Federation of Construction Contractors, Inc.
Nippon Telegraph and Telephone Corp.
The Sanwa Bank , Ltd.
Unisys Corp.

SCHIFF, Phil

8101 Glenbrook Rd.
Bethesda, MD 20814-2749
Tel: (301)907-6977
Fax: (301)907-6895

Employers
American Ass'n of Blood Banks (Administration and Business Development)

SCHILLING, III, Edward L.

8201 Corporate Dr.
Suite 850
Landover, MD 20785
EMail: cli@us.net
Tel: (301)459-1800
Fax: (301)459-1802

Employers
Contact Lens Institute (Exec. Director)

SCHIMMEL, Jo Ann P.

451 Seventh St. SW
Room 10234
Washington, DC 20410
Tel: (202)708-0030
Fax: (202)708-9981

Employers
Department of Housing and Urban Development (Intergovernmental Relations Information Management Specialist, Office of Intergovernmental Relations)

SCHIPANI, Meredith

2010 Massachusetts Ave. NW
Washington, DC 20036
Tel: (202)416-1421
Fax: (202)416-6130

Employers
Optical Soc. of America (Marketing Coordinator)

SCHLAGENHAUF, Jeffrey L.

1050 Connecticut Ave. NW
Suite 1200
Washington, DC 20036
EMail: jlschlag@mwcllc.com
Tel: (202)857-2906
Fax: (202)857-1737
Registered: LDA, FARA

Former Chief of Staff, Legislative Director and Speech Writer to Rep. Thomas J. Bliley, Jr. (R-VA).

Employers
McGuireWoods L.L.P. (Senior V. President, McGuire Woods Consulting, LLC)

Clients Represented

On Behalf of McGuireWoods L.L.P.
Alexandria, Virginia, Sanitation Authority of the City of
Financial Services Council
GE Financial Assurance
Huntington Sanitary Board
Lynchburg, Virginia, City of
Prince William County Service Authority
Richmond, Virginia, City of
Smithfield Foods Inc.
University of Miami
Verizon Communications
Virginia Power Co.
Wheeling, West Virginia, City of

SCHLAGER, Ivan A.

1440 New York Ave. NW
Washington, DC 20005
Tel: (202)371-7000
Fax: (202)393-5760
Registered: LDA

Former Staff Director and Democratic Chief Counsel, Sennate Committee on Commerce, Science, and Transportation.

Employers
Skadden, Arps, Slate, Meagher & Flom LLP

Clients Represented

On Behalf of Skadden, Arps, Slate, Meagher & Flom LLP
AOL Time Warner
Milliken and Co.
News Corporation Ltd.
SBC Communications Inc.
Union Pacific
US Airways

SCHLECHT, Eric V.

108 N. Alfred St.
Alexandria, VA 22314
Tel: (703)683-5700
Fax: (703)683-5722
Registered: LDA

Employers

Nat'l Taxpayers Union (Director, Congressional Relations)

SCHLEE, G. Michael

1608 K St. NW
Washington, DC 20006
Tel: (202)861-2730
Fax: (202)861-2786
Registered: LDA

Employers

American Legion (Director, National Security/Foreign Relations)

Military Ad Hoc Committee (Contact)

SCHLEFER, Mark

1901 Pennsylvania Ave. NW
Suite 201
Washington, DC 20006
Tel: (202)745-2450
Fax: (202)667-0444

Employers

Lawyers Alliance for World Security (Chairman)

SCHLEGEL, Nancy

1725 Jefferson Davis Hwy.
Crystal Square 2, Suite 300
Arlington, VA 22202
Tel: (703)413-5600
Fax: (703)413-5617
Registered: LDA

Employers

Lockheed Martin Corp. (Director, International Legislation)

SCHLEGEL, Paul

1100 Connecticut Ave. NW
Suite 530
Washington, DC 20036
Tel: (202)293-7222
Fax: (202)293-2955
Registered: LDA
EMail: paul.schlegel@weyerhaeuser.com

Employers

Weyerhaeuser Co. (Senior Federal Affairs Manager)

SCHLEIDT, Sabine

1615 L St. NW
Suite 900
Washington, DC 20036
Tel: (202)337-1022
Fax: (202)337-6678
EMail: imdimail@aol.com

Employers

Internat'l Management and Development Institute (Exec. V. President)

SCHLESINGER, Michael N.

1747 Pennsylvania Ave. NW
Suite 825
Washington, DC 20006-4604
Tel: (202)833-4198
Fax: (202)872-0546
Registered: LDA
EMail: schlesin@iipa.com

Employers

Internat'l Intellectual Property Alliance (Counsel)

Smith & Metalitz, L.L.P. (Associate)

Clients Represented

On Behalf of Smith & Metalitz, L.L.P.

Internat'l Intellectual Property Alliance

SCHLESINGER, Paul

2111 Wilson Blvd.
Eighth Floor
Arlington, VA 22201-3058
Tel: (703)841-0626
Fax: (703)243-2874
Registered: LDA
EMail: schlesinger@alcalde-fay.com

Employers

Alcalde & Fay (Partner)

Clients Represented

On Behalf of Alcalde & Fay

American Magline Group
CNF Transportation, Inc.
Dallas, Texas, City of
EC-MAC
Golden Gate Bridge Highway and Transportation District
Lake, California, County of
Marin, California, County of
Nat'l Ass'n of Gas Chlorinators
Sonoma County Water Agency
Sonoma, California, County of
Tulare, California, County of

SCHLESS, David S.

5100 Wisconsin Ave. NW
Suite 307
Washington, DC 20016
Tel: (202)237-0900
Fax: (202)237-1616
Registered: LDA
EMail: dschless@seniorshousing.org

Employers

American Seniors Housing Ass'n (President)

SCHLEY, Wayne

614 Massachusetts Ave. NE
Washington, DC 20002
Tel: (202)547-9476
Fax: (202)544-2454
Registered: LDA

Commissioner, Postal Rate Commission, 1992-95. Republican Staff Director, Senate Committee on Rules and Administration, 1987-92. Majority Staff Director (1981-86) and Minority Staff Director (1977-80), Subcommittee on Civil Service, Post Office and General Services, Senate Committee on Governmental Affairs. Special Assistant to Senator Ted Stevens (R-AK), 1971-77.

Employers

Self-employed as an independent consultant.

Clients Represented

As an independent consultant

United Parcel Service

SCHLICHT, James P.

1250 I St. NW
Suite 804
Washington, DC 20005
Tel: (202)289-2574
Fax: (202)289-2580
Registered: LDA
EMail: James.Schlicht@phwilm.zeneca.com

Employers

AstraZeneca Inc. (V. President, Government Affairs)

SCHLICKEISEN, Dr. Rodger O.

1101 14th St. NW
Suite 1400
Washington, DC 20005
Tel: (202)682-9400
Fax: (202)682-1331
EMail: rodger@defenders.org

Employers

Defenders of Wildlife (President and Chief Exec. Officer)

SCHLOESSER, Lynn L.

1300 Wilson Blvd.
Suite 900
Arlington, VA 22209
Tel: (703)524-7661
Fax: (703)524-7707
Registered: LDA

Employers

Eastman Chemical Co. (Director, Federal Affairs)

SCHLOMAN, Kenneth D.

1211 Connecticut Ave. NW
Suite 400
Washington, DC 20036
Tel: (202)822-8811
Fax: (202)872-1885
Registered: LDA

Employers

Alliance of American Insurers (Counsel, Federal Affairs)

SCHLOSSBERG, George R.

1101 Connecticut Ave. NW
Suite 1000
Washington, DC 20036
Tel: (202)828-2400
Fax: (202)828-2488
Registered: LDA

Senior Counsel, Office of the Secretary, Department of Defense, 1980-90.

Employers

Kutak Rock LLP (Partner)

Clients Represented

On Behalf of Kutak Rock LLP

Alameda, California, City of
Energy Communities Alliance, Inc.
Farm Progress Cos.
Highland Park, Illinois, City of Highwood Local Redevelopment Authority and the City of
New London Development Corp.
Orange, Florida, County of
Orlando, Florida, City of
San Francisco, City of
Seaside, California, City of
Team Stratford
Tustin, California, City of

SCHMALE, Lin

1601 Duke St.
Alexandria, VA 22314-3406
Tel: (703)836-8700
Fax: (703)836-8705
Registered: LDA
EMail: lschmale@safnow.org

Employers

Soc. of American Florists (Senior Director, Government Relations)

SCHMELTZER, Edward

2600 Virginia Ave. NW
Suite 1000
Washington, DC 20037-1905
Tel: (202)333-8800
Fax: (202)337-6065

Managing Director (1966-69) and Director, Bureau of Domestic Regulation (1961-66), Federal Maritime Board, and Trial Attorney (1955-60), Federal Maritime Commission. Served in the U.S. Air Force, 1943-46.

Employers

Schmeltzer, Aptaker & Shepard, P.C. (Partner)

SCHMELTZER, Kathryn R.

2300 N St. NW
Washington, DC 20037-1128
Tel: (202)663-8000
Fax: (202)663-8007
Registered: LDA
EMail: kathryn.schmeltzer@shawpittman.com

Former Attorney, Federal Communications Commission.

Employers

Shaw Pittman (Partner)

Clients Represented

On Behalf of Shaw Pittman

Cornerstone Television

SCHMERMUND, Robert P.

900 19th St. NW
Suite 400
Washington, DC 20006
Tel: (202)857-3100
Fax: (202)296-8716

Employers

America's Community Bankers (Director, Public Affairs)

SCHMID, Linda

805 15th St. NW
Suite 1110
Washington, DC 20005
Tel: (202)289-7460
Fax: (202)775-1726
Registered: LDA

Employers

Coalition of Service Industries (V. President and Director, Electronic Commerce)

SCHMIDT, David

1100 Connecticut Ave. NW
Suite 430
Washington, DC 20036
Tel: (202)296-6540
Fax: (202)296-6547
EMail: schmidt@ific.org

Employers

Internat'l Food Information Council (Senior V. President, Food Safety)

SCHMIDT, Eric

2323 Horsepen Rd.
Suite 600
Herndon, VA 20171
Tel: (703)713-3700
Fax: (703)713-3555
Registered: LDA

Employers

Novell, Inc.

SCHMIDT, Jeffrey

1211 Connecticut Ave. NW
Suite 608
Washington, DC 20036
Tel: (202)496-1000
Fax: (202)496-1300
EMail: jschmidt@qorvis.com

Employers
Qorvis Communications (Director)

SCHMIDT, John

1875 I St. NW
Suite 900
Washington, DC 20005
Tel: (202)371-0200
Fax: (202)371-2858
Registered: LDA, FARA

Employers
Edelman Public Relations Worldwide (Senior V. President)

Clients Represented
On Behalf of Edelman Public Relations Worldwide
American Health Care Ass'n

SCHMIDT, K. Peter

555 12th St. NW
Washington, DC 20004-1206
Tel: (202)942-5000
Fax: (202)942-5999
Registered: LDA

Employers
Arnold & Porter

SCHMIDT, Marsha K.

2120 L St. NW
Suite 700
Washington, DC 20037
Tel: (202)822-8282
Fax: (202)296-8834

Employers
Hobbs, Straus, Dean and Walker, LLP (Partner)

Clients Represented
On Behalf of Hobbs, Straus, Dean and Walker, LLP
Bristol Bay Area Health Corp.
Metlakatla Indian Community

SCHMIDT, Jr., Richard M.

1920 N St. NW
Suite 300
Washington, DC 20036-1622
Tel: (202)293-3860
Fax: (202)293-4827
Registered: LDA
EMail: rms@cohnmarks.com
General Counsel, U.S. Information Agency, 1965-68. Counsel, Senate Special Investigating Subcommittee, 1959-60.

Employers
Cohn and Marks (Of Counsel)

Clients Represented
On Behalf of Cohn and Marks
American Soc. of Newspaper Editors
Internat'l Sign Ass'n

SCHMIDT, Susan M.

1501 M St. NW
Suite 700
Washington, DC 20005-1702
Tel: (202)463-4300
Fax: (202)463-4394
Registered: LDA, FARA
EMail: sschmidt@manatt.com
Foreign Service Officer, Department of State, 1990-99.

Employers
Manatt, Phelps & Phillips, LLP (Of Counsel)

Clients Represented
On Behalf of Manatt, Phelps & Phillips, LLP
Asociacion Columbiana de Exportadores de Flores (ASOCOLFLORES)
AUGURA
BellSouth Corp.
Bolivia, Embassy of
Mexico, Embassy of
Secretaria de Agricultura, Granaderia y Desarrolo Rural (SAGAR)
SESAC, Inc.
SWIPCO, U.S.

SCHMIDT, William

1400 I St. NW
Suite 530
Washington, DC 20005
Tel: (202)371-0044
Fax: (202)371-2760
Registered: LDA

Employers
Juvenile Diabetes Foundation Internat'l (V. President, Public Affairs)

SCHMITT, Robert

P.O. Box 2999
Reston, VA 20191
Tel: (703)620-6003 Ext: 358
Fax: (703)620-5071
EMail: rschmitt@rvia.org

Employers
Recreation Vehicle Industry Ass'n (Assistant General Counsel)

SCHMITZ, John P.

1909 K St. NW
Washington, DC 20006
Tel: (202)263-3000
Fax: (202)263-3300
Registered: LDA
EMail: jschmitz@mayerbrown.com
Deputy White House Counsel in the Bush I administration.

Employers
Mayer, Brown & Platt (Partner)

Clients Represented
On Behalf of Mayer, Brown & Platt
Bertelsmann AG
Deutsche Lufthansa AG
Edison Mission Energy
Enron Corp.
General Electric Co.
Marathon Oil Co.

SCHMITZ, Joseph E.

2550 M St. NW
Washington, DC 20037-1350
Tel: (202)457-6000
Fax: (202)457-6315
Registered: LDA
EMail: jschmitz@pattonboggs.com
Special Assistant to the Attorney General, Department of Justice, 1987. Clerk to Judge James Buckley, U.S. Court of Appeals for the District of Columbia, 1986-87.

Employers
Patton Boggs, LLP (Partner)

Clients Represented
On Behalf of Patton Boggs, LLP
American Trans Air
Greenwood Village, Colorado, City of

SCHNABEL, Mark

1401 K St. NW
Suite 400
Washington, DC 20005
Tel: (202)789-2111
Fax: (202)789-4883
Registered: LDA
EMail: mschnabel@thewashingtongroup.com

Employers
The Washington Group (Principal)

Clients Represented
On Behalf of The Washington Group
American Hospital Ass'n
American Resort Development Ass'n
Ass'n of Progressive Rental Organizations
AT&T
BD
The Boeing Co.
Delta Air Lines
Everglades Trust
IVAX Corp.
Korea Information & Communication, Ltd.
Microsoft Corp.
Nat'l Ass'n of Real Estate Investment Trusts
News Corporation Ltd.
Real Estate Roundtable
SAMPCO Companies
SCAN Health Plan
Texas Municipal Power Agency

SCHNEEBAUM, Steven M.

2550 M St. NW
Washington, DC 20037-1350
Tel: (202)457-6000
Fax: (202)457-6315
Registered: LDA
EMail: sschneebaum@pattonboggs.com

Employers
Patton Boggs, LLP (Partner)

Clients Represented
On Behalf of Patton Boggs, LLP
Mars, Inc.

SCHNEIDAWIND, John

1133 21st St. NW
Suite 900
Washington, DC 20036
Tel: (202)463-4100
Fax: (202)463-4149
EMail: schneidawind.john@bsc.bls.com

Employers
BellSouth Corp. (Director, Media Relations)

SCHNEIDER, Andrew G.

1450 G St. NW
Suite 215
Washington, DC 20005
Tel: (202)393-6898
Fax: (202)393-6899
Registered: LDA

Employers
Medicaid Policy, L.L.C. (Principal)

Clients Represented
On Behalf of Medicaid Policy, L.L.C.
California Rural Indian Health Board, Inc.
Taxpayers Against Fraud, The False Claims Legal Center

SCHNEIDER, Anna-Maria

1560 Wilson Blvd.
Suite 1200
Arlington, VA 22209
Tel: (703)525-4800 Ext: 229
Fax: (703)525-6772
EMail: aschneider@mmsa.com

Employers
Mitsubishi Motors America, Inc. (Exec. Director, Government Relations, U.S. Operations)

SCHNEIDER, Carol

1818 R St. NW
Washington, DC 20009
Tel: (202)387-3760
Fax: (202)265-9532

Employers
Ass'n of American Colleges and Universities (President)

SCHNEIDER, Cornelia

444 N. Capitol St. NW
Suite 234
Washington, DC 20001
Tel: (202)624-5451
Fax: (202)624-5473

Employers
Nat'l Ass'n of State Auditors, Comptrollers and Treasurers (Director, Washington Office)

SCHNEIDER, E. Joseph

1801 N. Moore St.
Arlington, VA 22209
Tel: (703)528-0700
Fax: (703)528-2146
EMail: jschneider@aasa.org

Employers
American Ass'n of School Administrators (Deputy Exec. Director)

SCHNEIDER, Elizabeth G.

444 N. Capitol St. NW
Suite 200
Washington, DC 20001
Tel: (202)624-5897
Fax: (202)624-7797
EMail: sga@sso.org

Employers
Southern Governors Ass'n (Exec. Director)

SCHNEIDER, Gail

1101 17th St. NW
Eighth Floor
Washington, DC 20036
Tel: (202)463-8880
Fax: (202)833-3584
Registered: LDA
EMail: gailschneider@bonnerandassociates.com

Employers
Bonner & Associates (V. President)

SCHNEIDER, Jeffrey G.

555 13th St. NW
Washington, DC 20004-1109
Tel: (202)637-6516
Fax: (202)637-5910
Registered: LDA
EMail: jgschneider@hhlaw.com

Employers
Hogan & Hartson L.L.P. (Partner)

Clients Represented
On Behalf of Hogan & Hartson L.L.P.
Parker Jewish Geriatric Institute
Staff Builders, Inc.

SCHNEIDER, Johanna

1615 L St. NW
Suite 1100
Washington, DC 20036-5610
Tel: (202)872-1260
Fax: (202)466-3509

Employers
The Business Roundtable (Director, Communications)

SCHNEIDER, Kim

2100 Pennsylvania Ave. NW
Suite 535
Washington, DC 20037
Tel: (202)822-1700
Fax: (202)822-1919

Employers
Simon Strategies/Mindbeam (Policy Analyst)

SCHNEIDER, Lawrence A.

555 12th St. NW
Washington, DC 20004-1206
Tel: (202)942-5000
Fax: (202)942-5999
EMail: Lawrence_Schneider@aporter.com

Employers
Arnold & Porter (Partner)

SCHNEIDER, Mr. Leslie J.

1700 Pennsylvania Ave. NW
Suite 600
Washington, DC 20006
Tel: (202)393-7600
Fax: (202)393-7601
Registered: LDA
Special Assistant to the Assistant Secretary for Tax Policy (1973) and Office of the Legislative Counsel (1971-73), Department of the Treasury.

Employers
Ivins, Phillips & Barker (Partner)

Clients Represented

On Behalf of Ivins, Phillips & Barker
Allegheny Ludlum Corp.

SCHNEIDER, Matthew R.

1000 Potomac St. NW
Suite 500
Washington, DC 20007
Tel: (202)965-7880
Fax: (202)965-1729
Registered: LDA, FARA
EMail: mschneider@gsblaw.com
Chief of Staff to Senator Jeff Bingaman (D-NM), 1983-85. Senior Counsel, Division of Corporation Finance (1982) and Director, Office of Legislative Affairs (1979-81), Securities and Exchange Commission. Special Assistant to the Secretary, Department of Defense, 1977-79. Counsel, Senate Committee on Government Affairs, 1974-77. Staff Member, Senate Judiciary Subcommittee, 1973-74.

Employers
Garvey, Schubert & Barer (Managing Director)

Clients Represented

On Behalf of Garvey, Schubert & Barer
Changing Paradigms
Council of Appraisal and Property Professional Societies
GoTo.com Inc.
Nat'l Ass'n of Independent Fee Appraisers
Natural Technologies
Primavera Laboratories, Inc.
Harry Winston Research Foundation

SCHNEIDER, Richard C.

225 N. Washington St.
Alexandria, VA 22314
Tel: (703)549-0311
Fax: (703)549-0245
Registered: LDA
EMail: rschneid@ncoausa.org

Employers
Non Commissioned Officers Ass'n of the U.S.A. (Director, State and Veterans Affairs)

SCHNEIDER, Thomas J.

1666 K St. NW
Suite 500
Washington, DC 20006-2803
Tel: (202)887-1400
Fax: (202)466-2198

Employers
O'Connor & Hannan, L.L.P. (Of Counsel)

Clients Represented

On Behalf of O'Connor & Hannan, L.L.P.
Student Loan Funding Corp.

SCHNEIDER, William

1150 17th St. NW
Washington, DC 20036
Tel: (202)862-5800
Fax: (202)862-7177
EMail: wschneider@aei.org

Employers
American Enterprise Institute for Public Policy Research (Resident Fellow)

SCHNEIDERMAN, Mark

1730 M St. NW
Suite 700
Washington, DC 20036-4510
Tel: (202)452-1600
Fax: (202)223-8756
Registered: LDA

Employers
Software & Information Industry Ass'n (SIIA) (Manager, Federal Education Policy)

SCHNEIDERMAN, Michael

888 Sixteenth St. NW
7th Floor
Washington, DC 20006-4103
Tel: (202)835-8000
Fax: (202)835-8136

Employers
Foley & Lardner (Partner)

Clients Represented

On Behalf of Foley & Lardner
AAAE-ACI

SCHNEIER, Abraham L.

5765 F Burke Center Pkwy.
Suite 347
Burke, VA 22015
Tel: (202)822-0604
Fax: (202)452-9077
Registered: LDA
EMail: aschneier@earthserve.com
Formerly with the Internal Revenue Service, Manhattan District Office; past advisor to the Securities and Exchange Commission Forum on Small Business; Tax Resource to the 1980, 1986 and 1995 White House Conferences on Small Business.

Employers
Abraham Schneier and Associates (Principal)

Clients Represented

On Behalf of Abraham Schneier and Associates
Bureau of Wholesale Sales Representatives
Kelly Services, Inc.
Nat'l Federation of Independent Business

SCHODER, Paul

919 18th St. NW
Suite 900
Washington, DC 20006
Tel: (202)263-2970
Fax: (202)263-2960

Employers
Alliance for Public Technology (President)

SCHOELLHAMER, Paul E.

888 17th St. NW
Suite 600
Washington, DC 20006-3959
Tel: (202)973-7912
Fax: (202)342-0683
Registered: LDA
EMail: peschoellhamer@zsrlaw.com
Chief of Staff, House Transportation and Infrastructure Committee, 1993-95. Professional Staff, Subcommittee on Aviation, House Committee on Public Works and Transportation, 1981-85.

Employers
Zuckert, Scoutt and Rasenberger, L.L.P. (Partner and Director, Government Affairs)

Clients Represented

On Behalf of Zuckert, Scoutt and Rasenberger, L.L.P.
Air Transport Ass'n of America
Decatur Park District
Dunc LLC
Houston, Texas, Department of Aviation of the City of

SCHOENBRUN, Lois

6110 Executive Blvd.
Suite 506
Rockville, MD 20852
Tel: (301)984-1441
Ext: 3006
Fax: (301)984-4737

Employers
American Academy of Optometry (Exec. Director)

SCHOENEMAN, Frank

2550 M St. NW
Washington, DC 20037-1350
Tel: (703)527-7600
Fax: (703)527-8811

Employers
Professional Beauty Federation PAC (PAC Contact)

SCHOENFELD, Howard

1301 K St. NW
Washington, DC 20005-3333
Tel: (202)414-1000
Fax: (202)414-1301
Registered: LDA
EMail: howard.schoenfeld@us.pwcglobal.com

Employers
PriceWaterhouseCoopers (Director)

Clients Represented

On Behalf of PriceWaterhouseCoopers
Vanguard Charitable Endowment Program

SCHOENTHALER, Lisa W.

1724 Massachusetts Ave. NW
Washington, DC 20036-1969
Tel: (202)775-3550
Fax: (202)775-3696
Registered: LDA

Employers
Nat'l Cable Television Ass'n (Senior Director and Counsel, Office of Small System Operators)

SCHOETTLE, Peter D.

1775 Massachusetts Ave. NW
Washington, DC 20036-2188
Tel: (202)797-6000
Fax: (202)797-6004

Employers
The Brookings Institution (Senior Staff, Center for Public Policy Education)

SCHOLL, Wayne

750 First St. NE
9th Floor
Washington, DC 20002
Tel: (202)745-2900
Fax: (202)745-2901

Employers
Capital Consultants Corp. (V. President)

Clients Represented

On Behalf of Capital Consultants Corp.
Brookhill Redevelopment
Cherokee Investment Partners, LLC

SCHOLLENBERGER, Bard D.

1200 K St. NW
Suite 1200
Washington, DC 20005
Tel: (202)414-3500
Fax: (202)289-2695
Registered: LDA

Employers
Lockheed Martin IMS (Director, Government Relations, Children and Family Services)

SCHOMBURG, Paul

1620 L St. NW
Suite 1150
Washington, DC 20036
Tel: (202)223-2575
Ext: 114
Fax: (202)223-2614
Registered: LDA

Employers
Matsushita Electric Corp. of America (Manager, Government and Public Affairs)

SCHOMER, Christie

1523 New Hampshire Ave. NW
Washington, DC 20036
Tel: (202)588-0002
Fax: (202)785-2669

Employers
University of California, Office of Federal Government Relations (Legislative Analyst)

SCHOOLING, Robert

1615 L St. NW
Suite 900
Washington, DC 20036
Tel: (202)778-1000
Fax: (202)466-6002
EMail: rschooli@apcoworldwide.com

Employers
APCO Worldwide (Senior V. President and Director, Public Affairs)

SCHOONMAKER, Jan

1420 New York Ave. NW
Suite 1050
Washington, DC 20005
Tel: (202)638-1950
Fax: (202)638-7714
Registered: LDA
EMail: jans@vsadc.com
Former Legislative Director to Rep. Lindy Boggs (D-LA). Associate Staff, House Committee on Appropriations.

Employers
Van Scoyoc Associates, Inc. (V. President)

Clients Represented
On Behalf of Van Scoyoc Associates, Inc.
The Audubon Institute
Coalition of EPSCoR States
Nat'l Institute for Water Resources
Ochsner Medical Institutions
Tulane University
Virginia Tech Intellectual Properties, Inc.

SCHOTT, Anne

1730 Pennsylvania Ave. NW
Suite 1200
Washington, DC 20006-4706
Tel: (202)737-0500
Fax: (202)626-3737
Registered: LDA

Employers
King & Spalding (Associate)

SCHOTT, Jeffrey J.

11 Dupont Circle NW
Suite 620
Washington, DC 20036
EMail: jschott@iie.com
Tel: (202)328-9000
Fax: (202)328-5432

Employers
Institute for Internat'l Economics (Senior Fellow)

SCHOUMACHER, Stephanie

2000 M St. NW
Suite 400
Washington, DC 20036
Tel: (202)467-4999
Fax: (202)293-2672

Employers
People for the American Way (Senior V. President, Marketing Communications and Development)

SCHRAMM, Robert

517 C St. NE
Washington, DC 20002
Tel: (202)543-4455
Fax: (202)543-4586
Registered: LDA
Legislative Assistant to Senator Herman Talmadge, 1966-68.

Employers
Schramm, Williams & Associates, Inc.

Clients Represented
On Behalf of Schramm, Williams & Associates, Inc.
California Asparagus Commission
California Pistachio Commission
California Tomato Commission
Desert Grape Growers League
Dole Food Co.
Lana'i Co.
U.S. Citrus Science Council
Western Growers Ass'n
Western Growers Insurance Services
Western Pistachio Ass'n
Winegrape Growers of America

SCHRAYER, Elizabeth

1920 L St. NW
Seventh Floor
Washington, DC 20036
Tel: (202)955-1381
Fax: (202)861-0811
Registered: LDA

Employers
Schrayer and Associates, Inc. (President)

Clients Represented
On Behalf of Schrayer and Associates, Inc.
Campaign to Preserve U.S. Global Leadership
InterAction

SCHREPEL, Dawn

1225 I St. NW
Suite 600
Washington, DC 20005
Tel: (202)661-6180
Fax: (202)661-6182
Registered: LDA
EMail: dawnschrepel@morganmeguire.com

Employers
Morgan Meguire, LLC (Director, Project Development)

Clients Represented
On Behalf of Morgan Meguire, LLC
Texas A&M Engineering Experiment Station

SCHRIEFER, Shane

1250 I St. NW
Suite 400
Washington, DC 20005-3998
Tel: (202)682-8819
Fax: (202)682-8849
Registered: LDA
EMail: sschriefer@discus.org
Former Deputy Associate Director, Office of Cabinet Affairs, The White House, during the Bush I administration.

Employers
Distilled Spirits Council of the United States, Inc. (V. President, Office of Government Relations and Congressional Liaison)

SCHRIVER, Melinda L.

2011 Pennsylvania Ave. NW
Suite 800
Washington, DC 20006-1808
EMail: mschriver@mail.acponline.org
Tel: (202)261-4532
Fax: (202)835-0443

Employers
American College of Physicians-American Soc. of Internal Medicine (ACP-ASIM) (Associate, Public Policy)

SCHRODE, Kristi E.

1900 K St. NW
Suite 750
Washington, DC 20006
Tel: (202)833-4500
Fax: (202)833-2859
Registered: LDA

Employers
Bennett Turner & Coleman, LLP (Associate)

Clients Represented
On Behalf of Bennett Turner & Coleman, LLP
Cancer Leadership Council
The Children's Cause Inc.
Cure for Lymphoma Foundation
Leukemia & Lymphoma Soc.
Nat'l Coalition for Cancer Survivorship
North American Brain Tumor Coalition

SCHROEDER, Lee

2001 Jefferson Davis Hwy.
Suite 203
Arlington, VA 22202
Tel: (703)415-0780
Fax: (703)415-0786

Employers
American Intellectual Property Law Ass'n (Deputy Exec. Director)

SCHROEDER, Hon. Patricia

50 F St. NW
Fourth Floor
Washington, DC 20001-1564
Tel: (202)347-3375
Fax: (202)347-3690
Registered: LDA
Member, U.S. House of Representatives (D-CO), 1973-97.

Employers
Ass'n of American Publishers (President and Chief Exec. Officer)

SCHROEDER, Paul W.

820 First St. NE
Suite 400
Washington, DC 20002
Tel: (202)408-0200
Fax: (202)289-7880
Registered: LDA
EMail: ws@afb.net

Employers
American Foundation for the Blind - Governmental Relations Group (V. President, Government Relations)

SCHROEDER, Terri

122 Maryland Ave. NE
Washington, DC 20002
Tel: (202)675-2324
Fax: (202)546-0738
Registered: LDA

Employers
American Civil Liberties Union (Legislative Representative, Religious Freedom Issues)

SCHROETER, Lisa

c/o PricewaterhouseCoopers LLP
1900 K St. NW, Suite 900
Washington, DC 20009
Tel: (202)414-1293
Fax: (202)414-1217

Employers
The Transatlantic Business Dialogue (Exec. Director)

SCHROPP, Tyler

201 N. Union St.
Suite 510
Alexandria, VA 22314
Tel: (703)299-9470
Fax: (703)299-9478
Registered: LDA

Employers
Mercury Group (V. President)

SCHROTE, John E.

500 N. Washington St.
Alexandria, VA 22314
Tel: (703)551-2108
Fax: (703)551-2109
Director of Congressional Relations, Deputy Assistant Secretary for Policy, and Assistant Secretary for Policy, Office of Management and Budget (1989-92) and Deputy Director of Presidential Personnel (1982), The White House. Assistant Secretary, Department of Agriculture, 1981.

Employers
Blue Ridge Internat'l Group, L.L.C. (Agricultural and Natural Resources Advisor)

SCHUBERT, Lynn M.

1101 Connecticut Ave. NW
Suite 800
Washington, DC 20036
Tel: (202)463-0600
Fax: (202)463-0606

Employers
Surety Ass'n of America (President)

SCHUFREIDER, Jim

14th and Constitution Ave. NW
Room 5221
Washington, DC 20230
Tel: (202)482-4981
Fax: (202)482-4960

Employers
Department of Commerce - Nat'l Weather Service (Legislative Affairs Specialist)

SCHUKER, Jill A.

1920 L St. NW
Washington, DC 20036
EMail: jschuker@kamber.com
Tel: (202)223-8700
Fax: (202)659-5559

Employers
The Kamber Group (Managing Director, International Operations and Global Strategy Division)

Clients Represented
On Behalf of The Kamber Group
Bristol-Myers Squibb Co.

SCHULD, Kimberly

P.O. Box 3058
Arlington, VA 22203-0058
EMail: kschuld@iwf.org
Tel: (703)558-4991
Fax: (703)558-4994

Employers
Independent Women's Forum (Director of Policy)

SCHULER, Alexis

1906 Sunderland Pl. NW
Washington, DC 20036
Tel: (202)530-8030
Fax: (202)530-8031

Employers
AIDS Action Council (Director, Government Affairs)

SCHULKE, David G.

1140 Connecticut Ave. NW
Suite 1050
Washington, DC 20036
Tel: (202)331-5790
Fax: (202)331-9334
Registered: LDA
EMail: dschulke@ahqa.org
Chief Health Policy Advisor to the Hon. Ronald Wyden (D-OR), 1991-95. Chief of Oversight, 1989-91, Professional Staff, 1987-89, Investigator, 1983-87 for the Special Committee on Aging, U.S. Senate.

Employers
American Health Quality Ass'n (Exec. V. President)

SCHULKEN, Chad

1420 New York Ave. NW
Suite 1050
Washington, DC 20005
Tel: (202)638-1950
Fax: (202)638-7714
Registered: LDA
Former Aide, Senate Commerce, Science, and Transportation Committee to Senator Ernest F. Hollings (D-SC).

Employers
Van Scoyoc Associates, Inc. (Legislative Assistant)

Clients Represented

On Behalf of Van Scoyoc Associates, Inc.
Alameda-Contra Costa Transit District
Calspan University of Buffalo Research Center
Clemson University
FedEx Corp.
Glankler Brown, PLLC
Hughes Space & Communications Co.
Jefferson County Commission
Montgomery Airport Authority
NASA Aeronautics Support Team
Nat'l Air Traffic Controllers Ass'n
Nat'l Asphalt Pavement Ass'n
Regional Airport Authority of Louisville & Jefferson Co.
Veridian Engineering
Zuckert, Scoutt and Rasenberger, L.L.P.

SCHULMAN, Allison

1605 King St.
Alexandria, VA 22314-2792
Tel: (703)684-3600
Fax: (703)836-4564
Registered: LDA

Employers
Nat'l Ass'n of Convenience Stores (Legislative Representative)

SCHULMAN, Joseph R.

1500 K St. NW
Suite 250
Washington, DC 20005-1714
EMail: jrschulman@uhlaw.com
Tel: (202)639-7509
Fax: (202)639-7505

Employers
Ungaretti & Harris (Legislative Counsel)

Clients Represented

On Behalf of Ungaretti & Harris
Cardinal Health Inc.

SCHULMAN, Melissa

1101 16th St. NW
Suite 500
Washington, DC 20036
Tel: (202)659-9111
Fax: (202)659-6387
Registered: LDA

Policy Director to Rep. Steny Hoyer (D-MD), 1995-98. Floor Assistant and Exec. Director, House Democratic Caucus, 1990-94. Legislative Aide to Rep. Thomas Manton (D-NY), 1985. Staff Assistant to Rep. Geraldine Ferraro (D-NY), 1984.

Employers
Bergner Bockorny Castagnetti and Hawkins (V. President)

Clients Represented

On Behalf of Bergner Bockorny Castagnetti and Hawkins
AdvaMed
Agilent Technologies
American Bankers Ass'n
American Hospital Ass'n
Amgen
Biogen, Inc.
The Boeing Co.
Business Executives for Nat'l Security
Chicago Board Options Exchange
Computer Coalition for Responsible Exports
Dell Computer Corp.
Elanco Animal Health
First Health Group Corp.
GlaxoSmithKline
Lucent Technologies
Medtronic, Inc.
Monsanto Co.
Nat'l Ass'n of Real Estate Investment Trusts
Nat'l Soft Drink Ass'n
News Corporation Ltd.
Northwest Airlines, Inc.
Ovations/United Health Group
Petroleum Marketers Ass'n of America
Philip Morris Management Corp.
Premium Standard Farms
Qwest Communications
Taipei Economic and Cultural Representative Office in the United States

SCHULTE, Benena

1275 Pennsylvania Ave. NW
Tenth Floor
Washington, DC 20004
Tel: (202)737-5339
Fax: (202)467-0810
Registered: LDA

Employers
Policy Impact Communications

Clients Represented

On Behalf of Policy Impact Communications
Lake Worth Drainage District

SCHULTE, Linda

1350 I St. NW
Suite 830
Washington, DC 20005
EMail: lschulte@pptaglobal.org
Tel: (202)789-3100
Fax: (202)789-4197

Employers
Plasma Protein Therapeutics Ass'n (Director, Corporate Communications)

SCHULTE, Valerie

1771 N St. NW
Washington, DC 20036-2891
Tel: (202)429-5430
Fax: (202)775-3526
Registered: LDA

Employers
Nat'l Ass'n of Broadcasters (Senior Associate General Counsel)

SCHULTZ, Catherine

1133 19th St. NW
Washington, DC 20036
EMail: catherine.schultz@wcom.com
Tel: (202)887-3830
Fax: (202)736-6880

Employers
MCI WorldCom Corp. (Director, Tax Legislation and Regulations)

SCHULTZ, Jane

1426 21st St. NW
Suite 200
Washington, DC 20036
Tel: (202)429-9370
Fax: (202)833-1129

Employers
Greater Washington Soc. of Ass'n Executives (V. President, Communications)

SCHULTZ, Jim

1101 17th St. NW
Suite 1300
Washington, DC 20036-4700
EMail: jschultz@steel.org
Tel: (202)452-7100
Fax: (202)463-6573
Registered: LDA

Employers
American Iron and Steel Institute (V. President, Environment and Energy)

SCHULTZ, Cdr. Karl

Rayburn House Office Bldg.
Room B320
Washington, DC 20515
EMail: kschultz@uscg.mil
Tel: (202)225-4775
Fax: (202)426-6081

Employers
Department of Transportation - United States Coast Guard (House Liaison Staff, Congressional Affairs Staff, Office of Government and Public Affairs)

SCHULTZ, Mark

722 12th St. NW
Washington, DC 20005
Tel: (202)628-8382
Fax: (202)628-8392

Employers
Research Institute for Small & Emerging Business, Inc. (President and Chief Exec. Officer)

SCHULTZ, Max

1001 Connecticut Ave. NW
Suite 1250
Washington, DC 20036
Tel: (202)331-1010
Fax: (202)331-0640

Employers
Competitive Enterprise Institute (Editorial Director)

SCHULTZ, Tim

1747 Pennsylvania Ave. NW
Suite 1100
Washington, DC 20006
Tel: (202)833-0100
Fax: (202)833-0108

Employers
U.S. English, Inc. (Director, Communications)

SCHULTZ, Valerie A.

888 16th St. NW
Washington, DC 20006
Tel: (202)835-8177
Fax: (202)835-8161
Registered: LDA, FARA

Employers
Bannerman and Associates, Inc.

Clients Represented

On Behalf of Bannerman and Associates, Inc.
Assurance Technology Corp.
Egypt, Government of the Arab Republic of
El Salvador, Embassy of the Republic of
Internat'l College
Lebanese American University
Palestinian Authority

SCHULTZ, William B.

1201 Connecticut Ave. NW
Suite 600
Washington, DC 20036
Tel: (202)778-1800
Fax: (202)822-8106

Deputy Assistant Attorney General, Civil Division, Department of Justice, 1998-2000. Deputy Commissioner for Policy, Food and Drug Administration, Departmennt of Health and Human Services, 1994-98. Counsel, Subcommittee on Health and the Environment, House Committee on Commerce, 1989-94.

Employers
Zuckerman Spaeder L.L.P.

SCHULTZE, Charles L.

1775 Massachusetts Ave. NW
Washington, DC 20036-2188
Tel: (202)797-6000
Fax: (202)797-6004

Chairman, President's Council for Economic Advisors, 1977-80; Director, U.S. Bureau of the Budget, 1965-67.

Employers
The Brookings Institution (Senior Fellow Emeritus, Economic Studies)

SCHULZ, William

60 Massachusetts Ave. NE
Washington, DC 20002
Tel: (202)906-3860
Fax: (202)906-3306

Employers
AMTRAK (Nat'l Rail Passenger Corp.) (V. President, Corporate Communications)

SCHULZE, Nichole A.

1575 I St. NW
Suite 400
Washington, DC 20005
Tel: (202)218-7704
Fax: (202)289-6578
Registered: LDA

Employers
American Ass'n of Museums (Government and Public Affairs Specialist)

SCHULZE, Hon. Richard T.

1700 Pennsylvania Ave. NW
Suite 950
Washington, DC 20006
EMail: valis@erols.com
Tel: (202)393-5055
Fax: (202)393-0120
Registered: LDA

Member, U.S. House of Representatives (R-PA), 1975-93.

Employers
Advantage Associates, Inc. (Senior Legislative Director)
Valis Associates (Senior Legislative Director)

Clients Represented

On Behalf of Valis Associates
American Consulting Engineers Council
Ass'n for the Suppliers of Printing and Publishing Technology
Ass'n of American Railroads
CH2M Hill
Citizens for Civil Justice Reform
Coalition for Open Markets and Expanded Trade
Dairyland Power Cooperative
The Doctors' Co.
Environmental Action Group
Exxon Mobil Corp.
Grocery Manufacturers of America
New Majority Soc.
Norfolk Southern Corp.
NPES, The Ass'n for Suppliers of Printing, Publishing, and Converting Technologies
Renewable Fuels Ass'n
Tax Action Group
Telecommunications Industry Ass'n
Transportation Reform Alliance

SCHULZE, Jr., Richard T.

Hamilton Square
600 14th St. NW, Fifth Floor
Washington, DC 20005
Tel: (202)783-1980
Fax: (202)783-1918
Registered: LDA
EMail: VLLandS@aol.com

White House Liaison/Deputy Director, Office of Congressional Relations, Office of Personnel Management, 1986-93. Deputy Congressional Liaison Officer, Office of Congressional Affairs, Department of Labor, 1985-86. Research Assistant, House Committee on Agriculture, 1984.

Employers
RTS Consulting (Principal)
Valente Lopatin & Schulze (Principal)

Clients Represented

On Behalf of Valente Lopatin & Schulze
Alliance for Special Needs Children
Aventis Behring
Cohn & Wolfe
Columbus Educational Services
Columbus Medical Services
Dalton & Dalton P.C.
FBV Group
Internat'l Tax and Investment Center
Keating Technologies Inc.
The LTV Corp.
Mediware Information Systems, Inc.
Nat'l Ass'n of Thrift Savings Plan Participants
Orkand Corp.
OSHA Reform Coalition
Pepper Hamilton LLP
S-PAC
System & Computer Technology Corp.
United Nations Development Programme
United Payors and United Providers

SCHUMACHER, Barry J.

1615 L St. NW
Suite 900
Washington, DC 20036
Tel: (202)778-1000
Fax: (202)466-6002
Registered: LDA, FARA
EMail: bschumac@apcoworldwide.com

Employers
APCO Worldwide (Senior V. President and Director, International Policy)

Clients Represented

On Behalf of APCO Worldwide
COSCO Americas Inc.
Creme de la Creme, Inc.
Holy Land Trust
India, Government of the Republic of

SCHUMACHER, Edward

1100 15th St. NW
Suite 900
Washington, DC 20005
Tel: (202)835-3400
Fax: (202)835-3414
Registered: LDA

Employers
Pharmaceutical Research and Manufacturers of America (Senior Director, Policy)

SCHUMACHER, Randal P.

1615 L St. NW
Suite 650
Washington, DC 20036
Tel: (202)626-8523
Fax: (202)626-8774
Registered: LDA
EMail: rps@jeffersongr.com

Employers
Jefferson Government Relations, L.L.C. (Chairman and Principal)

Clients Represented

On Behalf of Jefferson Government Relations, L.L.C.
Bowling Transportation
Ergodyne
Lafarge Corp.
Minnesota Mining and Manufacturing Co. (3M Co.)
Vinyl Institute
Westmoreland Coal Co.

SCHUMAN, Michael

733 15th St. NW
Suite 1020
Washington, DC 20005
Tel: (202)234-9382
Fax: (202)387-7915

Employers
Institute for Policy Studies (Fellow)

SCHUST, Sunny Mays

444 N. Capitol St. NW
Suite 249
Washington, DC 20001
Tel: (202)624-5800
Fax: (202)624-5806

Employers
American Ass'n of State Highway and Transportation Officials (Director, Communications and Publications)

SCHUSTER, Ph.D., Darlene S.

1300 I St. NW
Suite 1090
East Tower
Washington, DC 20005-3314
Tel: (202)962-8690
Fax: (202)962-8699
Registered: LDA
EMail: darls@aiche.org

Employers
American Institute of Chemical Engineers (Director, Government Relations)

SCHUSTER, Neil D.

2120 L St. NW
Suite 305
Washington, DC 20037
Tel: (202)659-4620
Fax: (202)659-0500
Registered: LDA
EMail: schuster@ibtta.org

Employers
Internat'l Bridge, Tunnel and Turnpike Ass'n (Exec. Director)

SCHUTE, Diane J.

1430 Duke St.
Alexandria, VA 22314
Tel: (703)548-7700
Fax: (703)548-3149

Employers
Chemical Producers and Distributors Ass'n (Director, Legislative Affairs)

SCHUTE, Jr., William

601 13th St. NW
Suite 410 South
Washington, DC 20005
Tel: (202)737-0100
Fax: (202)628-3965

Employers
R. Duffy Wall and Associates (Senior V. President)

SCHUTT, David

1155 16th St. NW
Washington, DC 20036
Tel: (202)872-4477
Fax: (202)872-6206
Registered: LDA
EMail: d_schutt@acs.org

Employers
American Chemical Soc. (Assistant Director, Government Relations)

SCHUTZ, Carol A.

1030 15th St. NW
Suite 250
Washington, DC 20005-1503
Tel: (202)842-1275
Fax: (202)842-1150
EMail: geron@geron.org

Employers
Gerontological Soc. of America (Exec. Director)

SCHUTZER, George J.

2550 M St. NW
Washington, DC 20037-1350
Tel: (202)457-6000
Fax: (202)457-6315
Registered: LDA
EMail: gschutzer@pattonboggs.com

Employers
Patton Boggs, LLP (Partner)

Clients Represented

On Behalf of Patton Boggs, LLP
College Savings Bank
Tip Tax Coalition
Vulcan Materials Co.

SCHUYLER, Michael A.

1730 K St. NW
Suite 910
Washington, DC 20006
Tel: (202)463-1400
Fax: (202)463-6199

Employers
Institute for Research on the Economics of Taxation (IRET) (Senior Economist)

SCHUYLER, William J.

1500 K St. NW
Suite 650
Washington, DC 20005
Tel: (202)715-1000
Fax: (202)715-1001
Registered: LDA

Employers
GlaxoSmithKline (Federal Government Relations)

SCHWAB, Paul

8110 Gatehouse Rd.
Suite 101 West
Falls Church, VA 22042
Tel: (703)573-2676
Fax: (703)573-0578
EMail: pschwab@erols.ocm

Employers
Ass'n of Organ Procurement Organizations (Exec. Director)

SCHWAB, Richard F.

1200 Wilson Blvd.
Arlington, VA 22209-1989
Tel: (703)465-3686
Fax: (703)465-3002
Registered: LDA

Employers
The Boeing Co. (Legislative Affairs, Navy/USMC/Joint Programs)

SCHWALB, Kevin

1201 15th St. NW
Washington, DC 20005-2800
Tel: (202)822-0470
Fax: (202)822-0572
Registered: LDA

Employers
Nat'l Ass'n of Home Builders of the U.S. (Director, Political Affairs/Republican)

SCHWARTZ, Ari

1634 I St. NW
Suite 1100
Washington, DC 20006-4003
Tel: (202)637-9800
Fax: (202)637-0968
EMail: ari@cdt.org

Employers
Center for Democracy and Technology (Policy Analyst)

SCHWARTZ, Bryan Alan

2000 Pennsylvania Ave. NW
Suite 5500
Washington, DC 20006
Tel: (202)887-1500
Fax: (202)887-0763
EMail: bschwartz@mofo.com

Employers
Internat'l Trade Commission Trial Lawyers Ass'n (President)
Morrison & Foerster LLP (Of Counsel)

SCHWARTZ, Daniel C.

700 13th St. NW
Suite 700
Washington, DC 20005-3960
Tel: (202)508-6000
Fax: (202)508-6200
Registered: LDA
EMail: dcschwartz@bryancave.com

General Counsel, National Security Agency, 1979-81. Deputy Director (1977-79), Assistant Director for Evaluation (1975-77), and Assistant to the Director (1973-75), Bureau of Competition, Federal Trade Commission.

Employers
Bryan Cave LLP (Partner)

SCHWARTZ, Elinor

318 S. Abington St.
Arlington, VA 22204
Tel: (703)920-5389
Fax: (703)920-5402
Registered: LDA

Former Legislative Assistant and Appropriations Associate, House of Representatives.

Employers
Self-employed as an independent consultant.

Clients Represented

As an independent consultant
California State Lands Commission
New Mexico State Land Office
Western States Land Commissioners Ass'n

SCHWARTZ, Elizabeth Nash

1200 Wilson Blvd.
Arlington, VA 22209
Tel: (703)465-3668
Fax: (703)465-3003
Registered: LDA

Employers
The Boeing Co. (Director, Legislative Affairs - International Issues)

SCHWARTZ, Elliot

2000 L St. NW
Suite 700
Washington, DC 20036
Tel: (202)296-5860
Fax: (202)223-0776
EMail: elliot.schwartz@ced.org

Employers
Committee for Economic Development (V. President and Director, Economic Studies)

SCHWARTZ, Eric J.

1747 Pennsylvania Ave. NW
Suite 825
Washington, DC 20006-4604
Tel: (202)833-4198
Fax: (202)872-0546
Registered: LDA
EMail: schwartz@iipa.com

Employers
Internat'l Intellectual Property Alliance (Counsel)
Smith & Metalitz, L.L.P. (Partner)

Clients Represented

On Behalf of Smith & Metalitz, L.L.P.
Internat'l Intellectual Property Alliance

SCHWARTZ, Gilbert T.

1990 M St. NW
Suite 500
Washington, DC 20036
Tel: (202)776-0700
Fax: (202)776-0720
Registered: LDA
Associate General Counsel, Federal Reserve Board, 1974-85.

Employers
Schwartz & Ballen (Partner)

Clients Represented

On Behalf of Schwartz & Ballen
American Council of Life Insurers
American Insurance Ass'n
Financial Services Coordinating Council

SCHWARTZ, Gina

699 Prince St.
Alexandria, VA 22314-3175
Tel: (703)235-3900
Fax: (703)274-2222

Employers
Nat'l Center for Missing and Exploited Children (Media Director)

SCHWARTZ, Haidee

700 13th St. NW
Suite 1000
Washington, DC 20005
Tel: (202)347-6633
Fax: (202)347-8713
Registered: FARA

Employers
Powell Tate (V. President)

SCHWARTZ, Jeffrey H.

1525 Wilson Blvd.
Suite 600
Arlington, VA 22209
Tel: (703)527-1670
Fax: (703)547-5477
Registered: LDA
EMail: Jeff@jscinc.com
Counsel, Environmental Legislation, House Committee on Interstate and Foreign Commerce, 1973-79. Attorney, Office of General Counsel, Environmental Protection Agency, 1971-73. Attorney, Office of General Counsel, Department of Health, Education and Welfare.

Employers
Jellinek, Schwartz & Connolly (V. President)

SCHWARTZ, Jerry

1111 19th St. NW
Suite 800
Washington, DC 20036
Tel: (202)463-2700
Fax: (202)463-2785
Registered: LDA
EMail: jerry_schwartz@afandpa.org

Employers
American Forest & Paper Ass'n (Director, Water Quality Program)

SCHWARTZ, Michael

1015 15th St. NW
Suite 1100
Washington, DC 20005
Tel: (202)488-7000
Fax: (202)488-0806
Registered: LDA
EMail: mschwartz@ewfa.org
Administrative Director to Rep. Tom Coburn (R-OK), 1995-2000.

Employers
Concerned Women for America (President, Government Relations)

SCHWARTZ, Robert S.

600 13th St. NW
Washington, DC 20005-3096
Tel: (202)756-8081
Fax: (202)756-8087
Registered: LDA
EMail: rschwartz@mwe.com
Trial Attorney, Antitrust Division, Intellectual Property Section, Department of Justice, 1975-79. Law Clerk to Judge Caleb R. Layton, III, U.S. District Court for the District of Delaware, 1974-75.

Employers
McDermott, Will and Emery (Partner)

Clients Represented

On Behalf of McDermott, Will and Emery
Circuit City Stores, Inc.
Electronic Industries Ass'n of Japan

SCHWARTZ, Victor E.

1001 Pennsylvania Ave. NW
Suite 1100
Washington, DC 20004-2595
Tel: (202)624-2500
Fax: (202)628-5116
Registered: LDA, FARA
Exec. Director, Federal Interagency Council on Insurance, 1978-80. Chairman, Federal Interagency Task Force on Product Liability, 1976-80. Law Clerk to Judge Metzner, U.S. District Court for the Southern District of New York, 1965-66.

Employers
Crowell & Moring LLP (Partner)

Clients Represented

On Behalf of Crowell & Moring LLP
A.C.E. Insurance Co. (Bermuda) Ltd.
American Ass'n of Health Plans (AAHP)
American Tort Reform Ass'n
Bridgestone/Firestone, Inc.
CIGNA Corp.
Guidant Corp.
Eli Lilly and Co.
Nat'l Pork Producers Council
Product Liability Alliance, The
Product Liability Information Bureau
USAA - United Services Automobile Ass'n

SCHWARTZ, William

1158 15th St. NW
Washington, DC 20005
Tel: (202)463-9455
Fax: (202)463-9456

Employers
Nat'l Prostate Cancer Coalition Co. (President and Chief Exec. Officer)

SCHWARTZMAN, Andrew J.

950 18th St. NW
Suite 220
Washington, DC 20006
Tel: (202)232-4300
Fax: (202)466-7656

Employers
Media Access Project (President and Chief Exec. Officer)

SCHWARZ, Carl W.

600 13th St. NW
Washington, DC 20005-3096
Tel: (202)756-8065
Fax: (202)756-8087
EMail: cschwarz@mwe.com
Former Trial Attorney, Antitrust Division, Department of Justice; Member, Atomic Safety and Licensing Board, Atomic Energy Commission.

Employers
McDermott, Will and Emery (Partner)

SCHWARZ, Eli

1619 Duke St.
Alexandria, VA 22314-3406
Tel: (703)548-0066
Fax: (703)548-1883
EMail: research@iadr.com

Employers
American Ass'n for Dental Research (Exec. Director)
Internat'l Ass'n for Dental Research (Exec. Director)

SCHWARZ, Melbert E.

2001 M St. NW
Washington, DC 20036
Tel: (202)467-3000
Fax: (202)533-8500
Registered: LDA

Employers
KPMG, LLP

Clients Represented

On Behalf of KPMG, LLP
Apple Computer, Inc.
The INDOPCO Coalition
The KPMG FSC Coalition

SCHWARZ, Melvin

1775 I St. NW
Washington, DC 20006
Tel: (202)261-3305
Fax: (202)261-3333
EMail: melvin.schwarz@dechert.com
Special Counsel for Civil Enforcement, Senior Staff, Antitrust Division, Department of Justice, 1998-2000.

Employers
Dechert (Partner)

SCHWEIKER, Jane

1819 L St. NW
Sixth Floor
Washington, DC 20036
Tel: (202)293-8020
Fax: (202)293-9287
EMail: jschweik@ansi.org

Employers
American Nat'l Standards Institute (Director, Public Policy and Government Relations)

SCHWEITZER, James J.

317 Massachusetts Ave. NE
Suite 300
Washington, DC 20002
Tel: (202)789-3960
Fax: (202)789-1813
Registered: LDA
Counsel, House Judiciary Committee, 1981-89. Associate Staff Member, Select Committee to Investigate Covert Arms Transactions with Iran, 1987. Counsel, Subcommittee on Immigration, Refugees, and International Law, House Judiciary Committee, 1979-81. Legislative Director to Rep. Elizabeth Holtzman (D-NY), 1977-79. Attorney-Advisor, Federal Highway Administration, Department of Transportation, 1973-74.

Employers
The Cuneo Law Group, P.C.

Clients Represented

On Behalf of The Cuneo Law Group, P.C.
Nat'l Ass'n of Securities and Commercial Law Attorneys
Songwriters Guild of America
Taxpayers Against Fraud, The False Claims Legal Center

SCHWEITZER, Michele

1707 H St. NW
Suite 703
Washington, DC 20006
Tel: (202)478-5425
Registered: LDA

Employers
Washington Aviation Group

Clients Represented

On Behalf of Washington Aviation Group
Airline Suppliers Ass'n

SCHWEITZER, Richard P.

888 17th St. NW
Suite 600
Washington, DC 20006-3959
Tel: (202)298-8660
Fax: (202)342-0683
Registered: LDA
EMail: rpschweitzer@zsrlaw.com

Employers
Zuckert, Scoutt and Rasenberger, L.L.P. (Partner)

Clients Represented

On Behalf of Zuckert, Scoutt and Rasenberger, L.L.P.
American Bus Ass'n
Nat'l Private Truck Council
Nat'l Welding Supply Ass'n
Truck Renting and Leasing Ass'n

SCHWEITZER, William H.

1050 Connecticut Ave. NW
Suite 1100
Washington, DC 20036-5304
Tel: (202)861-1500
Fax: (202)861-1790
Registered: LDA
EMail: Wschweitzer@baker-hostetler.com
Assistant United States Attorney, Washington, DC 1970-73.

Employers
Baker & Hostetler LLP (Partner)

Clients Represented
On Behalf of Baker & Hostetler LLP
The Aluminum Ass'n
American Dental Ass'n
Emmis Broadcasting Corp.
Harvard University
Major League Baseball

SCHWEMER, Brett T.

1400 16th St. NW
Suite 400
Washington, DC 20036-2220
Tel: (202)518-6359
Fax: (202)234-2686
EMail: bschwemer@ofwlaw.com

Employers
Olsson, Frank and Weeda, P.C. (Associate)

SCHWENSEN, Carl

P.O. Box 17091
Alexandria, VA 22302
Tel: (703)683-3900
Fax: (703)549-8678

Employers
Schwensen and Associates

SCIAMANNA, John M.

440 First St. NW
Third Floor
Washington, DC 20001-2085
Tel: (202)638-2952
Fax: (202)638-4004
Registered: LDA

Employers
Child Welfare League of America (Senior Policy Analyst)

SCIARRINO, Dawn M.

2300 N St. NW
Washington, DC 20037-1128
Tel: (202)663-8000
Fax: (202)663-8007
Registered: LDA
EMail: dawn.sciarrino@shawpittman.com
Law Clerk and Intern, Fairness/Political Programming Branch, Enforcement Division, Mass Media Bureau, Federal Communications Commission, 1988.

Employers
Shaw Pittman (Counsel)

Clients Represented
On Behalf of Shaw Pittman
Pezold Management

SCITCHIK, Brian

1220 Connecticut Ave. NW
Second Floor
Washington, DC 20036
Tel: (202)667-6557
Fax: (202)467-6551
EMail: bscitchik@pollingcompany.com

Employers
The Polling Company (Research Analyst)

SCIULLA, Michael G.

880 S. Pickett St.
Alexandria, VA 22304
Tel: (703)461-2864
Fax: (703)461-2845
Registered: LDA
EMail: msciulla@boatus.com

Employers
Boat Owners Ass'n of The United States (BOAT/U.S.) (V. President and Lobbyist)

SCOBLIC, Peter

1726 M St. NW
Suite 201
Washington, DC 20036
Tel: (202)463-8270
Fax: (202)463-8273

Employers
Arms Control Ass'n (Editor, Arms Control Today Magazine)

SCOFIELD, Rupert

1101 14th St. NW
11th Floor
Washington, DC 20005-5601
Tel: (202)682-1510
Fax: (202)682-1535
EMail: rscofield@villagebanking.org

Employers
FINCA Internat'l Inc., The Foundation for Internat'l Community Assistance (Exec. Director)

SCOTT, Betty

490 East L'Enfant Plaza SW
Sixth Floor
Washington, DC 20594
Tel: (202)314-6121
Fax: (202)314-6122
EMail: scottb@ntsb.gov

Employers
Nat'l Transportation Safety Board (Deputy Director, Government Affairs, Office of Government, Public and Family Affairs)

SCOTT, Brett P.

509 C St. NE
Washington, DC 20002
Tel: (202)546-3800
Fax: (202)544-6771
Registered: LDA
EMail: scott@capitolcoalitions.com
Former Counsel, Subcommittee on Communications, Senate Committee on Commerce, Science and Transportation and General Counsel to Senator Conrad Burns (R-MT). Former Trial Attorney, Tax Division, Department of Justice.

Employers
Capitol Coalitions Inc. (President)

Clients Represented
On Behalf of Capitol Coalitions Inc.
Astro Vision Internat'l, Inc.
Big Sky Economic Development Authority
Corning Inc.
Deaconess Billings Clinic
EarthWatch, Inc.
Fanatasy Elections
Final Analysis, Inc.
Houston, Texas, Department of Aviation of the City of
INTELSAT - Internat'l Telecommunications Satellite Organization
One Economy Corp.
Pocket Science, Inc.
Trimble Navigation, Ltd.
VeriSign/Network Solutions, Inc.
Westinghouse Government Services Group

SCOTT, Charlie

4600 East-West Hwy.
Suite 300
Bethesda, MD 20814
Registered: LDA

Employers
Automotive Aftermarket Industry Ass'n

SCOTT, Doug

122 C St. NW
Suite 240
Washington, DC 20001
Tel: (202)544-3691
Fax: (202)544-5197

Employers
Pew Wilderness Center (Policy Director)

SCOTT, Edward M.

1440 Duke St.
Alexandria, VA 22314
Tel: (703)836-3495
Fax: (703)836-2843
Registered: LDA
EMail: EScott@uspa.org

Employers
United States Parachute Ass'n (Director, Government Affairs and Group Membership)

SCOTT, Edward P.

11 Canal Center Plaza
Suite 103
Alexandria, VA 20005
Tel: (703)683-6990
Fax: (703)683-0645
Registered: LDA

Employers
Brown & Associates

Clients Represented
On Behalf of Brown & Associates
GAF Corp.
Onehealthbank.com
Pharmaceutical Research and Manufacturers of America
Problem-Knowledge Coupler

SCOTT, Gregory M.

3050 K St. NW
Washington, DC 20007
Tel: (202)342-8400
Fax: (202)342-8451
Registered: LDA
EMail: gscott@colliershannon.com
Former Legislative Assistant to Rep. Tim Wirth (D-CO).

Employers
Collier Shannon Scott, PLLC (Associate)

Clients Represented
On Behalf of Collier Shannon Scott, PLLC
CARFAX, Inc.
Fannie Mae
Lion Oil Co.
Nat'l Ass'n of Convenience Stores
Soc. of Independent Gasoline Marketers of America
Vitol, S.A., Inc.

SCOTT, Gregory R.

1341 G St. NW
Suite 900
Washington, DC 20005
Tel: (202)637-1530
Fax: (202)637-1515

Employers
Philip Morris Management Corp. (Director, Government Affairs, Tobacco)

SCOTT, James L.

444 N. Capitol St. NW
Suite 625
Washington, DC 20001
Tel: (202)393-0860
Fax: (202)393-0864
Registered: LDA

Employers
Premier, Inc. (Senior V. President)

SCOTT, Jenny

1350 I St. NW
Suite 300
Washington, DC 20005
Tel: (202)639-5900
Fax: (202)639-5932
Registered: LDA

Employers
Nat'l Food Processors Ass'n (Senior Director, Food Safety Programs)

SCOTT, Jeremy

900 Second St. NE
Suite 201
Washington, DC 20002
Tel: (202)842-0219
Fax: (202)842-0439
Registered: LDA
EMail: jscott@kinghornassociates.com

Employers
Kinghorn & Associates, L.L.C. (Legislative Associates)

Clients Represented
On Behalf of Kinghorn & Associates, L.L.C.
Advanced Technology Institute
Ferroalloys Ass'n
Non-Ferrous Founders' Soc.
South Carolina Research Authority
South Carolina Technology Alliance
Tri-County Alliance

SCOTT, John C.

1212 New York Ave. NW
Suite 1250
Washington, DC 20005-3987
Tel: (202)289-6700
Fax: (202)289-4582
Registered: LDA

Employers
American Benefits Council (Director, Retirement Policy)

SCOTT, John H.

1300 I St. NW
Suite 400 West
Washington, DC 20005
Tel: (202)515-2400
Fax: (202)589-3780

Employers
Verizon Wireless

SCOTT, Judith

1146 19th St. NW
Suite 600
Washington, DC 20036
Tel: (202)496-0500
Fax: (202)496-0555

Employers
James & Hoffman, P.C. (Partner)

SCOTT, Julie

1111 14th St. NW
Suite 1200
Washington, DC 20005-5603
Tel: (202)898-2400
Fax: (202)789-2258
Registered: LDA
EMail: scottj@ada.org

Employers
American Dental Ass'n (Manager, Legislative and Regulatory Policy)

SCOTT, Leanne

1150 17th St. NW
Suite 701
Washington, DC 20036
EMail: leanne.scott@dittus.com

Tel: (202)775-1401
Fax: (202)775-1404

Employers

Dittus Communications (Account Executive)

Clients Represented

On Behalf of Dittus Communications

eLink

SCOTT, Michael

1101 Vermont Ave. NW
Suite 606
Washington, DC 20005
EMail: m.scott@asawash.org

Tel: (202)289-2222
Fax: (202)371-0384
Registered: LDA

Employers

American Soc. of Anesthesiologists (Director, Governmental and Legal Affairs)

SCOTT, Ray

Eight E St. SE
Washington, DC 20003

Tel: (202)543-4172
Fax: (202)546-6294
Registered: LDA

Former Administrative Assistant to Sen. David Pryor (D-AR).

Employers

Denison, Scott and Cohen (Partner)
Denison, Scott Associates (Partner)

Clients Represented

On Behalf of Denison, Scott and Cohen

The Friends of Democratic Congo

On Behalf of Denison, Scott Associates

Bristol-Myers Squibb Co.

SCOTT, Robert E.

1660 L St. NW
Suite 1200
Washington, DC 20036
EMail: epi@epinet.org

Tel: (202)775-8810
Fax: (202)775-0819

Employers

Economic Policy Institute (Economist)

SCOTT, Roxanne L.

1401 I St. NW
Suite 1100
Washington, DC 20005

Tel: (202)326-8873
Fax: (202)408-4796
Registered: LDA

Employers

SBC Communications Inc. (Manager, Federal Relations)

SCOTT, Shannon L.

2600 Virginia Ave. NW
Suite 600
Washington, DC 20037
EMail: ShannonLScott@aol.com

Tel: (202)338-6650
Fax: (202)338-5950
Registered: LDA

Employers

David O'Brien and Associates (Senior Associate)
O'Brien, Klink & Associates (Senior Associate)

Clients Represented

On Behalf of David O'Brien and Associates

Cruising America Coalition
Robbins-Gioia, Inc.
Wi-LAN, Inc.

On Behalf of O'Brien, Klink & Associates

The Kinetics Group
PetrolRem, Inc.
Zinc Corp. of America

SCOTT, Ted

2200 Mill Rd.
Alexandria, VA 22314

Tel: (703)838-1788
Fax: (703)838-1992

Employers

American Trucking Ass'ns (Director, Highway Policy)

SCOTT, William W.

3050 K St. NW
Washington, DC 20007

Tel: (202)342-8400
Fax: (202)342-8451
Registered: LDA, FARA

EMail: wscott@colliershannon.com
Law Clerk to Judge Charles F. McLaughlin, U.S. District Court for the District of Columbia, 1964-65.

Employers

Collier Shannon Scott, PLLC (Member)

Clients Represented

On Behalf of Collier Shannon Scott, PLLC

American Textile Machinery Ass'n
Nat'l Cosmetology Ass'n

SCOTT-MARTIN, Read

818 Connecticut Ave. NW
Suite 1006
Washington, DC 20006
EMail: rsmartin@raskydc.com

Tel: (202)530-7702
Fax: (202)530-7714

Former Communications Director to Senator Carol Moseley-Braun (D-IL).

Employers

The Rasky/Baerlein Group (V. President)

SCOWCROFT, USAF (Ret.), Lt. Gen. Brent

900 17th St. NW
Suite 500
Washington, DC 20006

Tel: (202)296-9312
Fax: (202)296-9395

Former Director, National Security Council during the Bush I administration.

Employers

Forum for Internat'l Policy (President)
The Scowcroft Group (President)

SCRIVNER, Kerrill K.

600 Pennsylvania Ave. NW
Suite 200
North Bldg.
Washington, DC 20004

Tel: (202)628-1020
Fax: (202)628-1007
Registered: LDA

Employers

TXU Business Services (V. President, Governmental Affairs)

SCRIVNER, Michael S.

915 15th St. NW
Suite 800
Washington, DC 20005
EMail: mscrivner@lentdc.com

Tel: (202)347-3030
Fax: (202)347-3133
Registered: LDA

Chief of Staff (1986-93) and Legislative Director (1981-86) to Rep. Norman Lent (R-NY). Legislative Assistant to Rep. John Duncan, Sr. (R-TN), 1978-81.

Employers

Lent Scrivner & Roth LLC (Partner)

Clients Represented

On Behalf of Lent Scrivner & Roth LLC

American Soc. of Anesthesiologists
AOL Time Warner
Burlington Northern Santa Fe Railway
Cellular Telecommunications and Internet Ass'n
Chevron, U.S.A.
Futurewave General Partners, L.P.
Great Western Cellular Partnership
Iroquois Gas Transmission System
KeySpan Energy
Bernard L. Madoff Investment Securities
Monroe Telephone Services, L.P.
Nassau University Medical Center
Nat'l Center for Tobacco-Free Kids
New Skies Satellites N.V.
Pfizer, Inc.

SCRIVNER, Peter C.

2111 Wilson Blvd.
Suite 400
Arlington, VA 22201-3061

Tel: (703)522-1820
Fax: (703)522-1885
Registered: LDA

Employers

Nat'l Defense Industrial Ass'n (Senior V. President, Government Policy)

SCRUGGS, John F.

1341 G St. NW
Suite 900
Washington, DC 20005

Tel: (202)637-1508
Fax: (202)637-1505

Former Assistant Secretary for Legislation, Department of Health and Human Services and Special Assistant to the President for Legislative Affairs, The White House, during the Reagan administration.

Employers

Philip Morris Management Corp. (V. President, Government Affairs)

SCUDERI, Roy

119 Oronoco St.
Alexandria, VA 22314-2015
EMail: rscuderi@presidentialclassroom.org

Tel: (703)683-5400
Fax: (703)548-5728

Employers

A Presidential Classroom for Young Americans, Inc. (Director, Finance and Administration)

SCULLY, Robert T.

750 First St. NE
Suite 920
Washington, DC 20002-4241

Tel: (202)842-4420
Fax: (202)842-4396
Registered: LDA

Employers

Nat'l Ass'n of Police Organizations (Exec. Director)

SCULLY, Thomas A.

801 Pennsylvania Ave. NW
Suite 245
Washington, DC 20004-2604
EMail: tscully@americashospitals.com

Tel: (202)624-1527
Fax: (202)737-6462
Registered: LDA

Deputy Assistant for Domestic Policy (1992-93) and Associate Director, Office of Management and Budget (1989-92), Executive Office of the President, The White House.

Employers

Federation of American Hospitals (President and Chief Exec. Officer)

SCULLY, Jr., Timothy H.

1341 G St. NW
Suite 900
Washington, DC 20005

Tel: (202)637-1551
Fax: (202)637-1549
Registered: LDA

Employers

Miller Brewing Co. (V. President, Government Affairs)
Philip Morris Management Corp. (V. President, Beer)

SCZUDLO, Rebecca

1801 K St. NW
Suite 901-L
Washington, DC 20006
EMail: Rebecca_Sczudlo@bm.com

Tel: (202)530-0500
Fax: (202)530-4800
Registered: LDA

Staff, Senate Committee on Energy and Natural Resources, 1981-89.

Employers

BKSH & Associates (Director)

Clients Represented

On Behalf of BKSH & Associates

Safety-Kleen Corp.

SCZUDLO, Walter

1101 King St.
Suite 700
Alexandria, VA 22314

Tel: (703)684-0410
Fax: (703)684-0540
Registered: LDA

Employers

Ass'n of Fund Raising Professionals (V. President, Public Affairs & General Counsel)

SEAGER, John

1400 16th St. NW
Suite 320
Washington, DC 20036

Tel: (202)332-2200
Fax: (202)332-2302

Employers

Zero Population Growth, Inc. (Exec. Director)

SEALANDER, Karen S.

600 13th St. NW
Washington, DC 20005-3096
EMail: ksealander@mwe.com

Tel: (202)756-8024
Fax: (202)756-8087
Registered: LDA

Employers

McDermott, Will and Emery (Legislative Counsel)

Clients Represented

On Behalf of McDermott, Will and Emery

American Dental Hygienists' Ass'n
Ass'n of periOperative Registered Nurses
Council of Women's and Infant's Specialty Hospitals
Hutzel Medical Center
Inova Fairfax Hospital
InterMountain Health Care Inc.
Internat'l Hearing Soc.
Magee Women's Health Foundation
Nat'l Perinatal Ass'n
Northside Hospital
Northside Savings Bank
Rural Referral Centers Coalition
St. Peter's Medical Center
Women and Infants' Hospital
Women's Hospital
Women's Hospital of Greensboro

SEALE, C. Stevens

1301 K St. NW
Suite 1100-East Tower
Washington, DC 20005
Tel: (202)414-9200
Fax: (202)414-9299
Registered: LDA

Former Chief Counsel to Senate Majority Leader, Senator Trent Lott (R-MS).

Employers

Reed, Smith, LLP (Partner)

Clients Represented

On Behalf of Reed, Smith, LLP

AKAL Security
Center for Research on Institutions and Social Policy
Dominion Resources, Inc.
Golf Course Superintendents Ass'n of America
Knoll Pharmaceutical Co.
Lason, Inc.
Owens-Illinois, Inc.
Professional Bail Agents of the United States
Ryder System, Inc.
USX Corp.

SEAMAN, Dr. Janet

1900 Association Dr.
Reston, VA 20191
Tel: (703)476-3430
Fax: (703)476-9527
EMail: jseaman@aahperd.org

Employers

American Ass'n for Active Lifestyles and Fitness (Exec. Director)

SEAMON, Harold P.

1680 Duke St.
Alexandria, VA 22314-3407
Tel: (703)838-6722
Fax: (703)683-7590

Employers

Nat'l School Boards Ass'n (Deputy Exec. Director)

SEAMON, Theodore I.

1000 Potomac St. NW
Suite 300
Washington, DC 20007
Tel: (202)337-6200
Fax: (202)333-0871

Employers

Hewes, Gelband, Lambert & Dann, P.C. (Of Counsel)

Clients Represented

On Behalf of Hewes, Gelband, Lambert & Dann, P.C.

Pilgrim Airlines
Wien Air Alaska

SEARS, Fred

1300 I St. NW
Suite 1000 West
Washington, DC 20005
Tel: (202)962-8531
Fax: (202)962-8542
EMail: esears@rcra.com

Employers

The Technical Group LLC (Senior Consultant)

SEARS, Patricia M.

1400 16th St. NW
Suite 100
Washington, DC 20036
Tel: (202)667-1142
Fax: (202)332-4496
EMail: pmsears@cedpa.org

Employers

Centre for Development and Population Activities (Senior Advisor, Special Projects)

SEARS, William P.

227 Massachusetts Ave. NE
Suite One
Washington, DC 20002
Tel: (202)548-8470
Fax: (202)548-8472
Registered: LDA

Employers

Martin G. Hámberger & Associates (Consultant)
The Peterson Group (President)

Clients Represented

On Behalf of The Peterson Group

Erie Internat'l Airport
Franklin Institute
Klett Rooney Lieber & Schorling
Seton Hill College

SEASE, Debbie

408 C St. NE
Washington, DC 20002
Tel: (202)547-1141
Fax: (202)547-6009
Registered: LDA

Employers

Sierra Club (Legislative Director)

SEATON, Liz

919 18th St. NW
Suite 800
Washington, DC 20006
Tel: (202)628-4160
Fax: (202)347-5323

Employers

Human Rights Campaign Fund (Field Deputy Director)

SEBRECHTS, Jadwiga S.

125 Michigan Ave. NE
Suite 340
Washington, DC 20017
Tel: (202)234-0443
Fax: (202)234-0445
EMail: jss@trinitydc.edu

Employers

Women's College Coalition (President)

SEBREE, John M.

700 11th St. NW
Washington, DC 20001-4507
Tel: (202)383-7580
Registered: LDA
EMail: jsebree@realtors.org

Employers

Nat'l Ass'n of Realtors (Legislative Representative)

SECHLER, Philip

725 12th St. NW
Washington, DC 20005
Tel: (202)434-5000
Fax: (202)434-5029
Registered: LDA

Employers

Williams & Connolly

Clients Represented

On Behalf of Williams & Connolly

R. J. Reynolds Tobacco Co.

SECHRIST, Amber

1140 Connecticut Ave.
Suite 502
Washington, DC 20036
Tel: (202)293-9101
Fax: (202)293-9111
Registered: LDA

Employers

Cartwright & Riley (Partner)

SECOR, Cathy

320 First St. SE
Washington, DC 20003
Tel: (202)479-7000
Fax: (202)863-0693

Employers

Nat'l Republican Congressional Committee (Director, Administration)

SECREST, III, Lawrence W.

1776 K St. NW
Washington, DC 20006
Tel: (202)719-7000
Fax: (202)719-7049
Registered: LDA

Employers

Wiley, Rein & Fielding (Partner)

Clients Represented

On Behalf of Wiley, Rein & Fielding

Nat'l Religious Broadcasters, Music License Committee

SEDDELMEYER, David

1099 14th St. NW
Suite 8824
Washington, DC 20570
Tel: (202)273-3771
Fax: (202)273-4283

Employers

Nat'l Labor Relations Board Professional Ass'n (Director, Legislative and Public Affairs)

SEDERHOLM, Pamela

1199 N. Fairfax St.
Suite 425
Alexandria, VA 22314
Tel: (703)548-8621
Fax: (703)236-1949

Employers

Leadership PAC 2002
SEDERHOLM Public Affairs, Inc. (President)

Clients Represented

On Behalf of SEDERHOLM Public Affairs, Inc.

American Automotive Leasing Ass'n
Internat'l Housewares Ass'n
Leadership PAC 2002
Wendy's Internat'l, Inc.

SEDKY, Julie

1700 K St. NW
Suite 1200
Washington, DC 20006
Tel: (202)857-0001
Fax: (202)857-0209
EMail: jsedky@cig1.com

Employers

Capital Insights Group (V. President)

SEDNEY, Diana

1401 I St. NW
Suite 1200
Washington, DC 20005-2225
Tel: (202)408-5829
Fax: (202)408-5842
Registered: LDA
EMail: dsed@chevron.com

Employers

The Chevron Companies (International Relations Manager)

SEE, Chad

1735 New York Ave. NW
Suite 500
Washington, DC 20006-4759
Tel: (202)628-1700
Fax: (202)331-1024
Registered: LDA

Former Staff Assistant to Senator Patty Murray (D-WA) and Senator Jay Rockefeller (D-WV).

Employers

Preston Gates Ellis & Rouvelas Meeds LLP

Clients Represented

On Behalf of Preston Gates Ellis & Rouvelas Meeds LLP

VoiceStream Wireless Corp.

SEEGER, Arline M.

200 N. Glebe Rd.
Suite 800
Arlington, VA 22203
Tel: (703)243-5463
Fax: (703)243-5489
Registered: LDA
EMail: natlime@lime.org

Employers

Nat'l Lime Ass'n (Exec. Director)

SEEGER, Christopher C.

1455 F St. NW
Suite 420
Washington, DC 20004
Tel: (202)628-6442
Fax: (202)628-6537
Registered: LDA

Employers

USAA - United Services Automobile Ass'n (V. President/Federal Legislative Affairs)

SEEGER, Kristin

1111 19th St. NW
Suite 800
Washington, DC 20036
Tel: (202)463-2700
Fax: (202)463-2785

Employers

American Forest & Paper Ass'n (V. President, Communications)

SEELEY, James F.

1301 Pennsylvania Ave. NW
Suite 400
Washington, DC 20004
EMail: jseeley@cla.ci.la.ca.us
Tel: (202)347-0915
Fax: (202)347-0919

Employers
Los Angeles, California, Washington Office of the City of (Chief Legislative Representative)

SEETIN, Mark

1331 Pennsylvania Ave. NW
Suite 550S
Washington, DC 20004
EMail: nymex2@unidial.com
Tel: (202)662-8770
Fax: (202)662-8765
Registered: LDA

Employers
New York Mercantile Exchange (V. President, Government Affairs)

SEGAL, Allen

100 Indiana Ave. NW
Washington, DC 20001
Tel: (202)393-4695
Fax: (202)756-7400
Registered: LDA

Employers
Nat'l Ass'n of Letter Carriers of the United States of America (Special Assistant, Legislation)

SEGAL, Ph.D., Jerome M.

8604 Second Ave.
PMB 317
Silver Spring, MD 20910
Tel: (301)589-8764
Fax: (301)589-2722

Employers
Jewish Peace Lobby (President)

SEGAL, Scott H.

2000 K St. NW
Suite 500
Washington, DC 20006-1872
EMail: ssegal@bracepatt.com
Tel: (202)828-5845
Fax: (202)223-1225
Registered: LDA, FARA

Employers
Bracewell & Patterson, L.L.P. (Partner)

Clients Represented

On Behalf of Bracewell & Patterson, L.L.P.
Africa Resources Trust USA
Air Conditioning Contractors of America
Alltel Corporation
Baldwin Piano and Organ Co.
Cement Kiln Recycling Coalition
Continental Cement Co., Inc.
Council of Industrial Boiler Owners (CIBO)
Enron Corp.
Envirocare of Utah, Inc.
FBI Agents Ass'n
Gary-Williams Energy Corp.
Gas Processors Ass'n
Houston, Texas, Port Authority of the City of
Huntsman Corp.
Independent Oil and Gas Ass'n of Pennsylvania
Lyondell Chemical Co.
Nat'l Cable Television Ass'n
Oxygenated Fuels Ass'n
Placid Refining Co.
Solex Environmental Systems, Inc.
Southdown, Inc.
Sterling Chemical Co.
Texas Petrochemicals Corp.
Texas Windstorm Insurance Ass'n
Valero Energy Corp.
Welcon, Inc.

SEGAL, Tad

316 Pennsylvania Ave. SE
Suite 300
Washington, DC 20003
Tel: (202)675-3381
Fax: (202)675-4230
Registered: LDA

Employers
United Parcel Service (Director, Public Relations)

SEGALL, Harold L.

1350 I St. NW
Suite 700
Washington, DC 20005
Tel: (202)789-6000
Fax: (202)789-6190

Employers
Beveridge & Diamond, P.C. (Partner)

SEGALL, Peter

1875 I St. NW
Suite 900
Washington, DC 20005
Tel: (202)371-0200
Fax: (202)371-2858

Employers
Edelman Public Relations Worldwide (Exec. V. President and Deputy General Manager)

Clients Represented

On Behalf of Edelman Public Relations Worldwide
American Health Care Ass'n
California Health Care Foundation
Nat'l Hospice & Palliative Care Organization
Nat'l Hospice Foundation
Ortho-McNeil Pharmaceutical Corp.
Schering-Plough Corp.

SEGERMARK, Howard

904 Massachusetts Ave. NE
Washington, DC 20002-6228
EMail: howard@segermark.com
Tel: (202)547-2222
Fax: (202)547-7417
Special Assistant to Senator Jesse Helms (R-NC), 1976-83. Legislative Assistant to Senator Harry Byrd (I-VA), 1974-76. Administrative Assistant to Rep. Steve Symms (R-ID), 1973-74. Legislative Assistant to Rep. Ancher Nelsen (R-MN), 1967-72.

Employers
The Segermark Associates, Inc. (President)

Clients Represented

On Behalf of The Segermark Associates, Inc.
Free Speech Coalition
Internat'l Prepaid Communications Ass'n

SEHER, Jake

1666 K St. NW
Fifth Floor
Washington, DC 20006
Tel: (202)887-1427
Fax: (202)466-3215
Registered: LDA

Employers
JFS Group, Ltd. (Principal)

Clients Represented

On Behalf of JFS Group, Ltd.
R. J. Reynolds Tobacco Co.

SEIDEL, Joseph L.

1401 I St. NW
Suite 910
Washington, DC 20005
Tel: (202)354-2800
Fax: (202)354-2808
General Counsel (1995), Minority General Counsel (1993-95), Deputy Minority General Counsel (1991-93), and Minority Counsel, Subcommittee on Consumer Affairs and Coinage (1987-91), House Committee on Banking and Financial Services. Legal Division, Federal Deposit Insurance Corporation, 1983-87.

Employers
Credit Suisse First Boston Corp.

SEIDEL, Mary

1301 Pennsylvania Ave. NW
Suite 900
Washington, DC 20004
Tel: (202)638-3690
Fax: (202)638-0936
Registered: LDA

Employers
Reinsurance Ass'n of America (Director, Federal Affairs)

SEIDLER, Phyllis

1200 S. Hay St.
Suite 1100
Arlington, VA 22202
EMail: pseidler@veridian.com
Tel: (703)575-3170
Fax: (703)575-3233

Employers
Veridian Corp. (Assistant Secretary)

SEIDMAN, David

1909 K St. NW
Suite 600
Washington, DC 20006-1167
Tel: (202)585-6900
Fax: (202)585-6969

Employers
Thompson Coburn LLP (Associate)

SEIFFERT, Grant E.

1300 Pennsylvania Ave. NW
Suite 350
Washington, DC 20044
EMail: gseiffer@tia.eia.org
Tel: (202)383-1483
Fax: (202)383-1495
Registered: LDA

Employers
Telecommunications Industry Ass'n (V. President, External Affairs and Global Policy)

SEIGEL, Charles

666 Pennsylvania Ave. SE
Suite 202
Washington, DC 20003
Tel: (202)546-5488
Fax: (202)546-5281
Registered: LDA

Employers
Apollo Group, Inc. (Senior V. President, National Affairs)

SEIGMANN, Peter A.

1919 M St. NW
Suite 200
Washington, DC 20036
Tel: (202)912-1000
Fax: (202)912-1030

Employers
Conservation Internat'l Foundation (Chief Exec. Officer/Charman)

SEILER, Elizabeth Avery

1711 King St.
Suite One
Alexandria, VA 22314
Tel: (703)836-4500
Fax: (703)836-8262
Registered: LDA

Employers
Snack Food Ass'n (Sr. V. President, Government and Public Affairs)

SEKLECKI, Mark

325 Seventh St. NW
Washington, DC 20004
Tel: (202)638-1100
Fax: (202)626-2332
Registered: LDA

Employers
American Hospital Ass'n (PAC Director)

SEKLEMIAN, Caroline

655 National Press Bldg.
Washington, DC 20045
EMail: cseklemian@johnadams.com
Tel: (202)737-8400
Fax: (202)737-8406

Employers
John Adams Associates Inc. (Senior V. President)

SEKULOW, Jay Alan

1650 Diagonal Rd.
Fifth Floor
Alexandria, VA 22314
Tel: (703)740-1450
Fax: (703)837-8510

Employers
American Center for Law and Justice (Chief Counsel)

SELBY, Beverly M.

236 Massachusetts Ave. NE
Suite 110
Washington, DC 20002
Tel: (202)546-8700
Fax: (202)546-7357
Registered: LDA

Employers
Alliance for American Innovation, Inc. (Exec. Director)

SELDEN, Jack W.

801 Pennsylvania Ave. NW
Suite 230
Washington, DC 20004
EMail: jselden@barw.com
Tel: (202)393-7150
Fax: (202)347-1684
Registered: LDA
U.S. Attorney, North District of Alabama, Department of Justice, 1992-93.

Employers
Bradley Arant Rose & White LLP (Partner)

SELDMAN, Neil N.

2425 18th St. NW
Washington, DC 20009-2096
Tel: (202)232-4108
Fax: (202)332-0463

Employers
Institute for Local Self-Reliance (President)

SELEY, Peter E.

1050 Connecticut Ave. NW
Washington, DC 20036-5306
Tel: (202)955-8500
Fax: (202)467-0539
Registered: LDA
EMail: pseley@gdclaw.com

Employers
Gibson, Dunn & Crutcher LLP (Associate)

Clients Represented
On Behalf of Gibson, Dunn & Crutcher LLP
Lockheed Martin Corp.

SELF, Laurie C.

1201 Pennsylvania Ave. NW
Washington, DC 20004-2401
Tel: (202)662-6000
Fax: (202)662-6291
Registered: LDA
EMail: lself@cov.com

Employers
Covington & Burling (Of Counsel)

Clients Represented
On Behalf of Covington & Burling
Council for Marketing and Opinion Research

SELF, Richard B.

1333 New Hampshire Ave. NW
Suite 400
Washington, DC 20036
Tel: (202)887-4000
Fax: (202)887-4288
Registered: FARA

Employers
Akin, Gump, Strauss, Hauer & Feld, L.L.P.

Clients Represented
On Behalf of Akin, Gump, Strauss, Hauer & Feld, L.L.P.
Saudi Arabia, Government of

SELFRIDGE, Greg

503 Second St. NE
Washington, DC 20002
Tel: (202)544-8490
Fax: (202)543-7804
EMail: gselfridge@patrickmurphy.com

Employers
Patrick M. Murphy & Associates (V. President)

SELIG, Wendy

701 Pennsylvania Ave. NW
Suite 650
Washington, DC 20004
Tel: (202)661-5704
Fax: (202)661-5750
EMail: wselig@cancer.org

Employers
American Cancer Soc. (Managing Director, Federal Government Relations)

SELIGMAN, Daniel

408 C St. NE
Washington, DC 20002
Tel: (202)547-1141
Fax: (202)547-6009
Registered: LDA

Employers
Sierra Club (Senior Trade Fellow, International Program)

SELIGMAN, Naomi

1140 19th St. NW
Suite 600
Washington, DC 20036
Tel: (202)822-8200
Fax: (202)822-8205

Employers
Violence Policy Center (Communications Director)

SELIGMAN, Scott D.

1401 I St. NW
Suite 600
Washington, DC 20005
Tel: (202)336-7400
Fax: (202)336-7530

Employers
United Technologies Corp. (Director, Public Relations)

SELL, Alisa M.

1301 Pennsylvania Ave. NW
Suite 401
Washington, DC 20004-1729
Tel: (202)785-4070
Fax: (202)659-8581
Registered: LDA
EMail: aselltexas@aol.com
Legislative Staff to Sen. Lloyd Bentsen (D-TX), 1988-90.

Employers
Florida Sugar Cane League, Inc. (Washington Representative)
Gay & Robinson, Inc. (Washington Representative)
Hawaiian Commercial and Sugar Company (Washington Representative)
Rio Grande Valley Sugar Growers (Washington Representative)

SELL, Jim

1500 Rhode Island Ave. NW
Washington, DC 20005-5597
Tel: (202)462-6272
Fax: (202)462-8549

Employers
Nat'l Paint and Coatings Ass'n (Senior Counsel)

SELLERS, Barney

8630 Fenton St.
Suite 412
Silver Spring, MD 20910
Tel: (301)587-6315
Fax: (301)587-2365
EMail: barneys@aspen.nutr.org

Employers
American Soc. for Parenteral and Enteral Nutrition (Exec. Director)

SELLERS, Richard

1501 Wilson Blvd.
Suite 1100
Arlington, VA 22209-3199
Tel: (703)524-0810
Fax: (703)524-1921
EMail: rsellers@afia.org

Employers
American Feed Industry Ass'n (V. President, Feed Control and Nutrition)

SELLERY, Jr., William C.

1730 M St. NW
Suite 200
Washington, DC 20036-4530
Tel: (202)296-3522
Fax: (202)296-7713
Registered: LDA
EMail: wsellery@selleryinc.com

Employers
Sellery Associates, Inc. (President)

Clients Represented
On Behalf of Sellery Associates, Inc.
American Soc. for Quality
Coalition for Uniform Product Liability Law
Financial Service Centers of America
Job Opportunities Business Symposium
The Mead Corp.
Nat'l Armored Car Ass'n
Nat'l Burglar and Fire Alarm Ass'n
Nat'l Council of Investigative and Security Services Inc.
Pilkington North America
Security Companies Organized for Legislative Action

SELLS, Bill

4301 Connecticut Ave. NW
Suite 300
Washington, DC 20008
Tel: (202)244-4700
Fax: (202)966-4818
Registered: LDA

Employers
Environmental Industry Ass'ns (Director, Federal Relations)

SELTZ, Judy

1801 N. Moore St.
Arlington, VA 22209
Tel: (703)528-0700
Fax: (703)528-2146
EMail: jseltz@aasa.org

Employers
American Ass'n of School Administrators (Director, Planning and Communications)

SELTZER, Tammy

1101 15th St. NW
Suite 1212
Washington, DC 20005
Tel: (202)467-5730
Ext: 16
Fax: (202)223-0409
Registered: LDA
EMail: tammy@bazelon.org

Employers
Bazelon Center for Mental Health Law, Judge David L. (Staff Attorney)

SELZ, Kathleen

666 11th St. NW
Suite 1000
Washington, DC 20001-4542
Tel: (202)737-6272
Fax: (202)737-6277
EMail: kselz@nascc.org

Employers
Nat'l Ass'n of Service and Conservation Corps (President)

SEMINARIO, Margaret M.

815 16th St. NW
Washington, DC 20006
Tel: (202)637-5000
Fax: (202)637-5058
Registered: LDA

Employers
AFL-CIO (American Federation of Labor and Congress of Industrial Organizations) (Director, Occupational Safety & Health Department)

SEMO, Joseph

1350 Connecticut Ave. NW
Suite 600
Washington, DC 20036
Tel: (202)822-6432
Fax: (202)466-5109

Employers
Nat'l Employee Benefits Institute (Exec. Director)

SEMPLE, Nathaniel M.

3604 Davis St. NW
Washington, DC 20007
Tel: (202)299-7118
Fax: (202)293-7119
Registered: LDA

Employers
The Observatory Group (President)

Clients Represented
On Behalf of The Observatory Group
Partnership for Organ Donation

SENATORE, Michael P.

1101 14th St. NW
Suite 1400
Washington, DC 20005
Tel: (202)682-9400
Fax: (202)682-1331
EMail: msenatore@defenders.org

Employers
Defenders of Wildlife (Director, Legal Department)

SENESE, Donald J.

1655 N. Fort Myer Dr.
Suite 355
Arlington, VA 22209
Tel: (703)807-2070
Fax: (703)807-2073
Registered: LDA

Employers
The 60/Plus Ass'n, Inc. (V. President, Research)

SENG, John J.

1020 19th St. NW
Suite 800
Washington, DC 20036-6110
Tel: (202)955-6222
Ext: 11
Fax: (202)955-0044
EMail: jjs@spectrumscience.com

Employers
SPECTRUM Science Public Relations, Inc. (President)

Clients Represented
On Behalf of SPECTRUM Science Public Relations, Inc.
Soc. for Women's Health Research

SENKEWICZ, Mary Beth

444 N. Capitol St. NW
Suite 701
Washington, DC 20001
Tel: (202)624-7790
Fax: (202)624-8579
EMail: MSenkewicz@naic.org

Employers
Nat'l Ass'n of Insurance Commissioners (Senior Counsel, Health Policy)

SENKOWSKI, R. Michael

1776 K St. NW
Washington, DC 20006
Tel: (202)719-7000
Fax: (202)719-7049
Administrative Assistant to the Chairman (1974-77) and Trial Attorney, Litigation Division (1971-74), Federal Communications Commission.

Employers
Wiley, Rein & Fielding (Partner)

SENN, W. Edward

1300 I St. NW
Suite 400 West
Washington, DC 20005
Tel: (202)515-2551
Fax: (202)336-7921
Registered: LDA

Employers
Verizon Communications (V. President, Federal Government Relations)

SENSIBA, Charles R.

1050 Thomas Jefferson St. NW
Seventh Floor
Washington, DC 20007
EMail: CRS@vnf.com
Tel: (202)298-1800
Fax: (202)338-2416

Employers
Van Ness Feldman, P.C. (Associate)

SENSIBAUGH, Cynthia B.

1710 Rhode Island Ave. NW
Suite 300
Washington, DC 20036
Tel: (202)659-8524
Fax: (202)466-8386
Registered: LDA

Employers
Abbott Laboratories (Director, Washington Affairs)

SENTER, Billy

1730 M St. NW
Suite 911
Washington, DC 20036
EMail: sentranda@aol.com
Tel: (202)331-4348
Fax: (202)463-0862
Registered: LDA

Employers
David Senter & Associates

Clients Represented

On Behalf of David Senter & Associates
American Corn Growers Ass'n

SENTER, David L.

1730 M St. NW
Suite 911
Washington, DC 20036
EMail: davidlsenter@aol.com
Tel: (202)331-4348
Fax: (202)463-0862
Registered: LDA

Employers
David Senter & Associates (Principal)

Clients Represented

On Behalf of David Senter & Associates
American Corn Growers Ass'n
Edison Electric Institute
Nat'l Ass'n of Farmer Elected Committees (NAFEC)

SEPP, Peter J.

108 N. Alfred St.
Alexandria, VA 22314
Tel: (703)683-5700
Fax: (703)683-5722
Registered: LDA

Employers
Nat'l Taxpayers Union (V. President, Communications)

SERAFIN, James J.

2500 Wilson Blvd.
Arlington, VA 22201-3834
EMail: jserafin@eia.org
Tel: (703)907-7585
Fax: (703)907-7501
Registered: LDA

Employers
Electronic Industries Alliance (Director, Marketing and Legislative Affairs)

SERIE, Terry L.

1111 19th St. NW
Suite 800
Washington, DC 20036
EMail: terry_serie@afandpa.org
Tel: (202)463-2700
Fax: (202)463-2785

Employers
American Forest & Paper Ass'n (V. President, Statistics)

SERKES, Kathryn A.

2111 Wisconsin Ave. NW
Suite 125
Washington, DC 20007
EMail: kdserkes@worldnet.att.net
Tel: (202)333-3855

Employers
Ass'n of American Physicians and Surgeons (Legislative Director)

SERRANTI, Tess

1875 Connecticut Ave. NW
Suite 1200
Washington, DC 20009-5728
Tel: (202)986-8000
Fax: (202)986-8102
Registered: LDA

Employers
LeBoeuf, Lamb, Greene & MacRae L.L.P. (Consultant)

SERUMGARD, John

1400 K St. NW
Suite 900
Washington, DC 20005
Tel: (202)682-4800
Fax: (202)682-4854
Registered: LDA

Employers
Rubber Manufacturers Ass'n (Exec. V. President)

SERVICE, Robert

1801 F St. NW
Washington, DC 20006
EMail: dacor@ix.netcom.com
Tel: (202)682-0500
Fax: (202)842-3295

Employers
Diplomatic and Consular Officers, Retired (Dacor) (Exec. Director)

SERVIDEA, Philip D.

1919 Pennsylvania Ave. NW
Suite 630
Washington, DC 20006-3411
EMail: phil.servidea@ncr.com
Tel: (202)312-1110
Fax: (202)312-1115
Registered: LDA

Employers
NCR Corp. (V. President, Government Affairs)

SESSION, Warner

1140 Connecticut Ave. NW
Suite 1142
Washington, DC 20036
Tel: (202)862-4383
Fax: (202)331-5562

Former Staff Director and Counsel, Subcommittee on Government Activities and Transportation, House Committee on Government Operations.

Employers
Technology, Entertainment and Communications (TEC) Law Group

SETH, Andy

1350 New York Ave. NW
Suite 1100
Washington, DC 20005-4798
EMail: setha@spiegelmcd.com
Tel: (202)879-4000
Fax: (202)393-2866
Registered: LDA

Employers
Spiegel & McDiarmid (Legislative Coordinator)

SEVCIK, Jesse J.

1350 I St. NW
Suite 1240
Washington, DC 20005
Tel: (202)783-5330
Fax: (202)783-4381
Registered: LDA

Employers
Farmland Industries, Inc. (Government Relations Specialist)

SEWELL, Richard A.

P.O. Box 4134
Merrifield, VA 22116
Tel: (703)573-8677

Employers
Friends of Free China (Exec. Director)

SEXTON, Alan

3000 K St. NW
Suite 300
Washington, DC 20007
Tel: (202)295-8787
Fax: (202)295-8799

Employers
The Harbour Group (Senior Associate)

SEXTON, Nicole

1776 K St. NW
Suite 300
Washington, DC 20006
EMail: nsexton@clubforgrowth.org
Tel: (202)955-5500
Fax: (202)955-9466

Employers
Club for Growth (Membership Director)

SEXTON, Robin M.

815 Connecticut Ave. NW
Suite 330
Washington, DC 20006
Tel: (202)263-6260

Employers
Quest Diagnostics Inc. (Politcal Action Coordinator)

SEYBOLD, Catherine

444 N. Capitol St. NW
Suite 267
Washington, DC 20001-1512
Tel: (202)624-5300
Fax: (202)624-5313

Employers
Nat'l Governors' Ass'n (Manager, Media Relations)

SEYMON-HIRSCH, Barbara N.

1455 Pennsylvania Ave. NW
Suite 1200
Washington, DC 20004
Tel: (202)347-2230
Fax: (202)393-3310
Registered: LDA

Reporting Program Advisory Committee, Internal Revenue Service, 1994-95.

Employers
Davis & Harman LLP (Partner)

SEYMOUR, Magda Lynn

80 F St. NW
Washington, DC 20001
Tel: (202)639-6419
Fax: (202)639-6441

Employers
American Federation of Government Employees (AFL-CIO) (Director, Communications)

SEYMOUR, Richard T.

1401 New York Ave. NW
Suite 400
Washington, DC 20005
EMail: rseymour@lawyerscomm.org
Tel: (202)662-8350
Fax: (202)783-5131

Employers
Lawyers' Committee for Civil Rights Under Law (Director, Employment Discrimination Project)

SGUEO, James M.

4216 King St. West
Alexandria, VA 22302-1507
Tel: (703)578-4200
Fax: (703)820-3551
Registered: LDA

Employers
Nat'l Alcohol Beverage Control Ass'n (Exec. Director)

SHACKELFORD, Lottie H.

2121 K St. NW
Suite 650
Washington, DC 20037
EMail: Lottie@GlobalUSAinc.com
Tel: (202)296-2400
Fax: (202)296-2409
Registered: LDA

Employers
Global USA, Inc. (Exec. V. President)

Clients Represented

On Behalf of Global USA, Inc.
Artel, Inc.
Dade, Florida, County of
FM Watch
Jacksonville Electric Authority
K-Mortgage Corp.
Psychemedics Corp.
SBC Communications Inc.

SHADE, Briggs

1755 Jefferson Davis Hwy.
Suite 1107
Arlington, VA 22202
Tel: (703)415-0344
Fax: (703)415-0182
Registered: LDA

Employers
The PMA Group (Associate)

Clients Represented

On Behalf of The PMA Group

AAI Corp.
CPU Technology
CRYPTEK Secure Communications, LLC
Dynamics Research Corp.
Fidelity Technologies Corp.
L-3 Communications Corp.
Lockheed Martin Corp.
Lockheed Martin Federal Systems
Omega Air
Pathfinder Technology Inc.
Planning Systems, Inc.
Textron Inc.

SHAFER, Raymond P.

1700 K St. NW
Suite 800
Washington, DC 20006
Tel: (202)862-9700
Fax: (202)862-9710
Registered: LDA

Employers

Dunaway & Cross (General Counsel)

Clients Represented

On Behalf of Dunaway & Cross

Industrial Truck Ass'n

SHAFFER, Erin E.

1101 Pennsylvania Ave. NW
Suite 200
Washington, DC 20004
Tel: (202)628-1223
Fax: (202)628-1368
Registered: LDA
EMail: erin.shaffer@ipaper.com

Employers

Internat'l Paper (Counsel, Federal Corporate Affairs)

SHAFFER, Mark

1101 14th St. NW
Suite 1400
Washington, DC 20005
Tel: (202)682-9400
Fax: (202)682-1331
EMail: mshaffer@defenders.org

Employers

Defenders of Wildlife (Senior V. President, Programs)

SHAILOR, Barbara

815 16th St. NW
Washington, DC 20006
Tel: (202)637-5000
Fax: (202)637-5058

Employers

AFL-CIO (American Federation of Labor and Congress of Industrial Organizations) (Director, Internat'l Affairs Department)

SHAINMAN, Larry

1801 K St. NW
Suite 1000L
Washington, DC 20006
Tel: (202)530-0400
Fax: (202)530-4500
EMail: larry_shainman@washbm.com

Employers

Burson-Marsteller (Manager, Public Affairs Practice)

SHAKIR, Adib A.

700 13th St. NW
Suite 400
Washington, DC 20005
Tel: (202)347-0773
Fax: (202)347-0785
EMail: ashakir@cassidy.com

Employers

Cassidy & Associates, Inc. (Consultant)

SHAKOW, Susannah W.

901 15th St. NW
Suite 700
Washington, DC 20005-2301
Tel: (202)371-6000
Fax: (202)371-6279
Registered: LDA
EMail: swshakow@verner.com

Employers

Verner, Liipfert, Bernhard, McPherson and Hand, Chartered (Associate)

Clients Represented

On Behalf of Verner, Liipfert, Bernhard, McPherson and Hand, Chartered

General Electric Co.

SHALGIAN, Christian

1640 Wisconsin Ave. NW
Washington, DC 20007
Tel: (202)337-2701
Fax: (202)337-4271
Registered: LDA
EMail: christian_shalgian@facs.org

Employers

American College of Surgeons (Senior Government Affairs Associate)

SHAMBON, Leonard M.

2445 M St. NW
Washington, DC 20037-1420
Tel: (202)663-6000
Fax: (202)663-6363
Registered: LDA
EMail: lshambon@wilmer.com

Director, Office of Compliance, Import Administration, Department of Commerce, 1980-86. Antitrust Counsel, House Judiciary Committee, 1975-79. Former Law Clerk to Judge Oscar H. Davis, U.S. Court of Claims.

Employers

Wilmer, Cutler & Pickering (Counsel)

Clients Represented

On Behalf of Wilmer, Cutler & Pickering

RMI Titanium Co.
United Defense, L.P.

SHANAHAN, James R.

1301 K St. NW
Washington, DC 20005-3333
Tel: (202)414-1000
Fax: (202)414-1301
Registered: LDA

Employers

PriceWaterhouseCoopers (Partner)

Clients Represented

On Behalf of PriceWaterhouseCoopers

Automobile Manufacturers R&D Coalition
Coalition for Fair Tax Credits
Electronic Commerce Tax Study Group

SHANAHAN, John

1130 17th St. NW
Washington, DC 20036-4677
Tel: (202)463-9793
Fax: (202)463-3257
Registered: LDA
EMail: jshanahan@nma.org

Employers

Nat'l Mining Ass'n (Director, Air Policy)

SHANBACKER, K. Edward

2175 K St. NW Suite 200
Washington, DC 20037
Tel: (202)466-1800
Ext: 101
Fax: (202)452-1542
EMail: shanbacker@msdc.org

Employers

Medical Soc. of the District of Columbia (Exec. Director)

SHANLEY, Claire

1444 I St. NW
Suite 700
Washington, DC 20005-2210
Tel: (202)216-9623
Fax: (202)216-9646
EMail: cshanley@bostromdc.com

Employers

Bostrom Corp. (Account Executive)

Clients Represented

On Behalf of Bostrom Corp.

American Soc. of Access Professionals
Greater Washington D.C. Chapter of CLU & ChFC

SHANNON, Deborah

1120 Connecticut Ave. NW
Washington, DC 20036
Tel: (202)663-5000
Fax: (202)828-4548
Registered: LDA

Employers

American Bankers Ass'n (Senior Federal Legislative Representative - House Manager)

SHANNON, Thomas F.

3050 K St. NW
Washington, DC 20007
Tel: (202)342-8400
Fax: (202)342-8451
Registered: LDA
EMail: tshannon@colliershannon.com

Chief Minority Counsel, Senate Appropriations Committee, 1957-58. Legislative Counsel to Senator Styles Bridges (R-NH), 1955-57.

Employers

Collier Shannon Scott, PLLC (Of Counsel)

SHAPIRO, Bernard M.

1301 K St. NW
Washington, DC 20005-3333
Tel: (202)414-1000
Fax: (202)414-1301
Registered: LDA
EMail: bob.shapiro@us.pwcglobal.com

Former Chief of Staff, Joint Committee on Taxation, U.S. Congress.

Employers

PriceWaterhouseCoopers (Managing Partner)

Clients Represented

On Behalf of PriceWaterhouseCoopers

Placid Refining Co.

SHAPIRO, Dina S.

1101 Pennsylvania Ave. NW
Suite 1000
Washington, DC 20004
Tel: (202)879-6822
Fax: (202)783-1873
Registered: LDA
EMail: dina.shapiro@citicorp.com

Employers

Citigroup (V. President, Deputy Director, Tax Legislation)

SHAPIRO, Gary

2500 Wilson Blvd.
Arlington, VA 22201-3834
Tel: (703)907-7610
Fax: (703)907-7608
EMail: gshapiro@ce.org

Employers

Consumer Electronics Ass'n (President and Chief Exec. Officer)

SHAPIRO, Hal S.

655 15th St. NW
Suite 900
Washington, DC 20005-5701
Tel: (202)626-5800
Fax: (202)628-0858
Registered: LDA

Former Senior Advisor for Economic Policy, The White House and former Associate General Counsel, Office of the U.S. Trade Representative.

Employers

Miller & Chevalier, Chartered (Partner)

Clients Represented

On Behalf of Miller & Chevalier, Chartered

Nat'l Foreign Trade Council, Inc.

SHAPIRO, Howard Eliot

1050 Thomas Jefferson St. NW
Seventh Floor
Washington, DC 20007
Tel: (202)298-1800
Fax: (202)338-2416
EMail: hes@vnf.com

Employers

Van Ness Feldman, P.C. (Member)

SHAPIRO, Ira S.

701 Pennsylvania Ave. NW
Suite 600
Washington, DC 20004
Tel: (202)624-1200
Fax: (202)624-1298

Former General Counsel and Chief Trade Negotiator for Japan and Canada, Office of the U.S. Trade Representative; Chief of Staff to Senator John D. Rockefeller IV (D-WV); Minority Staff Director and Chief Counsel, Senate Governmental Affairs Committee; and Legislative Counsel to Senator Gaylord Nelson (D-WI).

Employers

Long, Aldridge & Norman, LLP (Partner)

SHAPIRO, Joe

1920 L St. NW
Washington, DC 20036
Tel: (202)223-8700
Fax: (202)659-5559
EMail: jshapiro@kamber.com

Employers
The Kamber Group (Staff Assistant)

SHAPIRO, Judith A.

2120 L St. NW
Suite 700
Washington, DC 20037
Tel: (202)822-8282
Fax: (202)296-8834
Registered: LDA

Law Clerk to Judge Richard Owen, U.S. District Court for the Southern District of New York, 1983-85.

Employers
Hobbs, Straus, Dean and Walker, LLP (Partner)

Clients Represented

On Behalf of Hobbs, Straus, Dean and Walker, LLP
Menominee Indian Tribe
Seminole Tribe of Indians of Florida
Susanville Indian Rancheria

SHAPIRO, Lisa

1001 Pennsylvania Ave. NW
Suite 600
Washington, DC 20004
Tel: (202)347-0066
Fax: (202)624-7222
Registered: LDA

Employers
Powell, Goldstein, Frazer & Murphy LLP (Analyst)

Clients Represented

On Behalf of Powell, Goldstein, Frazer & Murphy LLP
Bayer Corp. / Agriculture Division

SHAPIRO, Richard H.

513 Capitol Ct. NE
Suite 300
Washington, DC 20002
Tel: (202)546-0100
Fax: (202)547-0936

Employers
Congressional Management Foundation (Exec. Director)

SHAPIRO, Robert A.

200 Constitution Ave. NW
Washington, DC 20210
Tel: (202)219-8201
Fax: (202)501-2583

Employers
Department of Labor - Solicitor (Associate Solicitor, Legislative and Legal Counsel)

SHAPIRO, Robert B.

1730 K St. NW
Washington, DC 20006
Tel: (202)452-8010
Fax: (202)296-2065

Senior Attorney, Securities and Exchange Commission, 1975-79.

Employers
Bernstein Law Firm, PLLC

Clients Represented

On Behalf of Bernstein Law Firm, PLLC
X.L. Insurance Co.

SHARARA, Norma N.

1776 K St.
Washington, DC 20006
Tel: (202)452-7945
Registered: LDA

Employers
Buchanan Ingersoll, P.C.

Clients Represented

On Behalf of Buchanan Ingersoll, P.C.
nPower Advisors, LLC

SHARK, Alan R.

1150 18th St. NW
Suite 250
Washington, DC 20036
EMail: ashark@amtausa.org
Tel: (202)331-7773
Fax: (202)331-9062

Employers
American Mobile Telecommunications Ass'n (President and Chief Exec. Officer)

SHARKEY, III, Andrew G.

1101 17th St. NW
Suite 1300
Washington, DC 20036
EMail: asharkey@steel.org
Tel: (202)452-7146
Fax: (202)463-6573

Member of Bush-Cheney Transition Advisory Team, 2001.

Employers
American Iron and Steel Institute (President and Chief Exec. Officer)
Trade Ass'n Liaison Council (Chairman)

SHARN, Christy

3930 University Dr.
Fairfax, VA 22030-2515
Tel: (703)591-7130
Fax: (703)591-0734

Employers
Recreation Vehicle Dealers Ass'n of North America (Manager, State Communications)

SHARON, Yehiam

7910 Woodmont Ave.
Suite 1410
Bethesda, MD 20814
EMail: yehiam@imiusa.com
Tel: (301)215-4817
Fax: (301)657-1446
Registered: LDA

Employers
IMI Services USA, Inc. (President)

SHARP, Adam

600 Maryland Ave. SW
Suite 800
Washington, DC 20024
Tel: (202)484-3600
Fax: (202)484-3604
Registered: LDA

Employers
American Farm Bureau Federation (Director, Ag Chemicals/Biotechnology/Air Quality)

SHARP, Gregory L.

11 Canal Center Plaza
Suite 103
Alexandria, VA 22314
Tel: (703)683-4222
Fax: (703)683-0645
Registered: LDA

Employers
The Spectrum Group (President)

Clients Represented

On Behalf of The Spectrum Group
AAI Corp.
ADSI Inc.
Nat'l Health Care Access Coalition
PKC
Raydon Corp.
The Refinishing Touch
Robertson Aviation
Simula, Inc.
SRI Internat'l
Student Loan Finance Corp.
Titanium Metals Corp.
Tri-City Regional Port District

SHARP, John Hunter

805 15th St. NW
Suite 510
Washington, DC 20005
EMail: jhsharp@ngsa.org
Tel: (202)326-9300
Fax: (202)326-9330
Registered: LDA

Employers
Natural Gas Supply Ass'n (V. President, Governmental Affairs and Counsel)

SHARP, Mark

1620 L St. NW
Suite 1150
Washington, DC 20036
Tel: (202)223-2575
Ext: 116
Fax: (202)223-2614
Registered: LDA

Employers
Matsushita Electric Corp. of America (General Manager, Corporate Environmental Department)

SHARP, Norman F.

1707 H St. NW
#800
Washington, DC 20006
Tel: (202)223-8207
Fax: (202)833-0379
Registered: LDA

Employers
Cigar Ass'n of America (President)
Pipe Tobacco Council, Inc. (President)

SHARPE, Angela L.

1522 K St. NW
Suite 836
Washington, DC 20005
EMail: alsharpe@aol.com
Tel: (202)842-3525
Fax: (202)842-2788
Registered: LDA

Employers
Consortium of Social Science Ass'ns (Associate Director, Government Affairs)

SHARPE, Clark D.

6600 Rockledge Dr.
Bethesda, MD 20817
Tel: (240)694-4100
Fax: (240)694-4623

Employers
HMSHost Corp. (V. President, Government Affairs)

SHARPE, Kieran

666 11th St. NW
Suite 315
Washington, DC 20001
Tel: (202)331-8045
Fax: (202)331-8191
Registered: LDA

Employers
Aitken, Irvin, Lewin, Berlin, Vrooman & Cohn (Associate)

Clients Represented

On Behalf of Aitken, Irvin, Lewin, Berlin, Vrooman & Cohn
Colgate Palmolive

SHARPSTENE, Elizabeth R.

700 13th St. NW
Suite 350
Washington, DC 20005
Tel: (202)637-0040
Fax: (202)637-0041
Registered: LDA

Exec. Assistant to Rep. Paul Kanjorski (D-PA), 1991-1995.

Employers
Rhoads Group (Associate)

Clients Represented

On Behalf of Rhoads Group
AAAE-ACI
Airports Council Internat'l - North America
The Justice Project, Inc.
SWATH Ocean Systems, Inc.
Taiwan Studies Institute
United States Enrichment Corp.

SHARRY, Frank P.

2201 St. NE
Suite 220
Washington, DC 20002
Tel: (202)544-0004
Fax: (202)544-1905
Registered: LDA

Employers
Nat'l Immigration Forum (Exec. Director)

SHATTUCK, Cathie A.

1227 25th St. NW
Suite 700
Washington, DC 20037
Tel: (202)861-0900
Fax: (202)296-2882
Registered: LDA

V. Chairman, Equal Employment Opportunity Commission, 1982-84.

Employers
Epstein Becker & Green, P.C. (Of Counsel)

Clients Represented

On Behalf of Epstein Becker & Green, P.C.
Coalition on Accessibility
The Home Depot

SHAUD, John A.

1501 Lee Hwy.
Arlington, VA 22209-1198
EMail: jshaud@afa.org
Tel: (703)247-5801
Fax: (703)247-5853

Employers
Air Force Ass'n (Exec. Director)

SHAUK, Amber

419 Seventh St. NW
Suite 500
Washington, DC 20004
Tel: (202)626-8800
Fax: (202)737-9189

Employers
Nat'l Right to Life Committee (Secretary, Department of Medical Ethics)

SHAVIN, Karen

128 M St. NW
First Floor
Washington, DC 20001
Tel: (202)842-9090
Fax: (202)842-9095

Employers
Bright Beginnings, Inc. (Exec. Director)

SHAW, Catherine H.

700 Army Navy Dr.
MS: 12228
Arlington, VA 22202
Tel: (202)307-7363
Fax: (202)307-4778
Chief of Congressional Affairs, Drug Enforcement Administration, Department of Justice, 1990-94. Special Assistant for Public Affairs, Bureau of International Narcotics Matters, Department of State, 1985-90. Professional Staff Member, House Select Committee on Narcotics, 1983-85. Press Secretary and Legislative Assistant to Rep. Benjamin Gilman (R-NY), 1976-83.

Employers
Department of Justice - Drug Enforcement Administration (Chief, Office of Congressional and Public Affairs)

SHAW, Daniel F.

c/o World Perspectives Inc.
1150 18th St. NW, Suite 275
Washington, DC 20036
Tel: (202)785-3345
Fax: (202)785-9227
Registered: LDA
EMail: danshaw@agrilink.com
Deputy Administrator, State and County Operations (1988-93) and Southwest Area Director (1986-88), Agricultural Stabilization Conservation Service, Department of Agriculture.

Employers
Daniel F. Shaw & Associates

Clients Represented

On Behalf of Daniel F. Shaw & Associates
MacKenzie Agricultural Research
Nat'l Grain Sorgum Producers

SHAW, Douglas B.

1101 15th St. NW
Suite 115
Washington, DC 20005
Tel: (202)835-8760
Fax: (202)318-4017
EMail: shaw@religionandpolicy.org

Employers
Institute on Religion and Public Policy (V. President, Programs and Policy)

SHAW, Edward W.

1000 Wilson Blvd.
Suite 2701
Arlington, VA 22209
Tel: (703)276-9500
Fax: (703)276-9504

Employers
Gulfstream Aerospace Corp. (Director, Washington Operations)

SHAW, Ellie A.

1776 I St. NW
Suite 400
Washington, DC 20006-3708
Tel: (202)739-8000
Fax: (202)785-4019
Registered: LDA

Employers
Nuclear Energy Institute (Governmental Affairs Coordinator)

SHAW, Jr., G. Jerry

P.O. Box 44808
Washington, DC 20026-4808
Tel: (202)927-7000
Fax: (202)927-5192
Registered: LDA
Attorney, Branch Chief and Director, General Legal Services Division, Office of the Chief Counsel, Internal Revenue Service, Department of the Treasury, 1975-81.

Employers
Senior Executives Ass'n (General Counsel)
Shaw, Bransford, Veilleux & Roth (Partner)

Clients Represented

On Behalf of Shaw, Bransford, Veilleux & Roth
Cendant Mobility Services
Federal Employees Education and Assistance Fund
Public Employees Roundtable
Senior Executives Ass'n

SHAW, John S.

2550 M St. NW
Washington, DC 20037-1350
Tel: (202)457-6058
Fax: (202)457-6315
Registered: LDA
EMail: jshaw@pattonboggs.com
Majority Counsel, Special Investigation, Senate Committee on Governmental Affairs, 1997. White House Intern, 1990

Employers
Patton Boggs, LLP (Associate)

Clients Represented

On Behalf of Patton Boggs, LLP
EchoStar Communications Corp.
Alan Hilburg & Associates
IVIDCO, LLC
Nassau Broadcasting Inc.

SHAW, Pam

1155 15th St. NW
Suite 1004
Washington, DC 20005
Tel: (202)467-5081
Fax: (202)467-5085

Employers
ACB Social Service Providers

SHAW, Rhod M.

660 Pennsylvania Ave. SE
Suite 201
Washington, DC 20003
Tel: (202)548-2312
Fax: (202)547-4658
Registered: LDA
EMail: Rshaw@alpinegroup.com
Former Chief of Staff and Legislative Director to Rep. Sherrod Brown (D-OH), 1993-95. Former Chief of Staff and Legislative Director to Rep. Jimmy Hayes (R-LA), 1987-93.

Employers
Alpine Group, Inc. (Partner)

Clients Represented

On Behalf of Alpine Group, Inc.
American Cable Ass'n
Arthur Andersen LLP
Business Software Alliance
Dynegy, Inc.
El Paso Corporation
Environmental Response Team of California
Environmental Response Team of Louisiana
FMC Corp.
Nat'l Ass'n of Insurance and Financial Advisors
Pharmacia Corp.
Recording Industry Ass'n of America
Seneca Resources Corporation
Toyota Motor North America, U.S.A., Inc.

SHAW, Susan

901 E St. NW
Suite 600
Washington, DC 20004
Tel: (202)783-4444
Fax: (202)783-4085
Registered: LDA

Employers
Nat'l Treasury Employees Union (Deputy Director of Legislation)

SHAW, William A.

15363 Worth Ct.
Centreville, VA 20120
Tel: (703)815-0954
Fax: (703)815-0970
Registered: LDA

Employers
F&T Network, Inc. (President)

Clients Represented

On Behalf of F&T Network, Inc.
KOSA

SHAW, Win

3190 Fairview Park Dr.
Falls Church, VA 22042
Tel: (703)876-3000
Fax: (703)876-3600
Registered: LDA

Employers
General Dynamics Corp. (Director, Aerospace Programs)

SHAY, Matthew R.

1350 New York Ave. NW
Suite 900
Washington, DC 20005
Tel: (202)628-8000
Fax: (202)628-0812
Registered: LDA

Employers
Internat'l Franchise Ass'n (V. President and Chief Counsel)

SHAY, Russell

1331 H St. NW
Suite 400
Washington, DC 20005-4711
Tel: (202)638-4725
Fax: (202)638-4730
EMail: rshay@lta.org
Legislative Aide to Senator Timothy E. Wirth (D-CO), 1988-92. Professional Staff Member, House Committee on Merchant Marine and Fisheries, 1987-88. Professional Staff Member, House Committee on Interior and Insular Affairs, 1985-87.

Employers
Land Trust Alliance (Director, Public Policy)

SHEA, Beverly

310 First St. SE
Washington, DC 20003
Tel: (202)863-8500
Fax: (202)863-8820

Employers
Republican Nat'l Committee (Finance Director)

SHEA, Dennis

1801 K St. NW
Suite 901-L
Washington, DC 20006
Tel: (202)530-0500
Fax: (202)530-4800
Registered: LDA
EMail: dennis_shea@bm.com
Former Counsel and Former Deputy Chief of Staff to Senate Majority Leader, Senator Robert J. Dole (R-KS).

Employers
BKSH & Associates (Director)

Clients Represented

On Behalf of BKSH & Associates
J. P. Morgan Chase & Co.

SHEA, Donald B.

1400 K St. NW
Suite 900
Washington, DC 20005
Tel: (202)682-4800
Fax: (202)682-4854

Employers
Rubber Manufacturers Ass'n (President and Chief Exec. Officer)

SHEA, Ernest C.

509 Capitol Ct. NE
Washington, DC 20002
Tel: (202)547-6223
Fax: (202)547-6450
EMail: ernie-shea@nacdnet.org

Employers
Nat'l Ass'n of Conservation Districts (Chief Exec. Officer)

SHEA, Gerald M.

815 16th St. NW
Washington, DC 20006
Tel: (202)637-5000
Fax: (202)637-5058
Registered: LDA

Employers
AFL-CIO (American Federation of Labor and Congress of Industrial Organizations) (Exec. Assistant to the President, Political and Government Affairs)

SHEA, Nina H.

1319 18th St. NW
Washington, DC 20036
Tel: (202)296-5101
Fax: (202)296-5078
EMail: religion@freedomhouse.org

Employers
The Center for Religious Freedom (Director)

SHEARER, Gail E.

1666 Connecticut Ave. NW
Suite 310
Washington, DC 20009
Tel: (202)462-6262
Fax: (202)265-9548
Registered: LDA
EMail: sheaga@consumer.org

Employers
Consumers Union of the United States (Director, Health Policy Analysis)

SHEARER, Scott

1350 I St. NW
Suite 1240
Washington, DC 20005
Tel: (202)783-5330
Fax: (202)783-4381
Registered: LDA
EMail: psshearer@farmland.com

Employers
Farmland Industries, Inc. (Director, National Relations)

SHEEHAN, Daniel J.

1615 L St. NW
Suite 650
Washington, DC 20036
Tel: (202)626-8229
Fax: (202)626-8593
Registered: LDA
EMail: bishop@jeffersongr.com

Former Legislative Assistant to Senator Charles Robb (D-VA) and Staff Member, Subcommittee on Exports, Tax Policy and Special Problems, House Small Business Committee. Former Legislative Assistant to Rep. Norman Sisisky (D-VA).

Employers
Jefferson Government Relations, L.L.C. (Director)

Clients Represented
On Behalf of Jefferson Government Relations, L.L.C.
Bass Hotels and Resorts, Inc.
Carlsberg Management Co.
Greater Orlando Aviation Authority
JDA Aviation Technology Systems
Visalia, California, City of
Volusia, Florida, County of
Westmoreland Coal Co.

SHEEHAN, Kathleen

808 17th St. NW
Suite 410
Washington, DC 20006
EMail: dcoffice@nasadad.org
Tel: (202)293-0090
Fax: (202)293-1250

Employers
Nat'l Ass'n of State Alcohol and Drug Abuse Directors (NASADAD) (Director, Public Policy)

SHEEHAN, Kenneth

600 14th St. NW
Suite 500
Washington, DC 20005
Tel: (202)220-1200
Fax: (202)220-1665

Employers
Pepper Hamilton LLP (Partner)

SHEEHAN, Maria

600 New Hampshire Ave. NW
Suite 601
Washington, DC 20037
EMail: msheehan@hillandknowlton.com
Tel: (202)333-7400
Fax: (202)333-1638

Employers
Hill and Knowlton, Inc. (Managing Director)

SHEEHAN, Shaun M.

1722 I St. NW
Suite 400
Washington, DC 20006
Tel: (202)775-7750
Fax: (202)223-3844
Registered: LDA
EMail: ssheenhan@tribune.com

Employers
Tribune Co. (V. President, Washington)

SHEEHY, Edward

11200 Waples Mill Rd.
Suite 150
Fairfax, VA 22030-7407
Tel: (703)691-8100
Fax: (703)691-8106

Employers
Assisted Living Federation of America (V. President, State Legislative and Regulatory Affairs)

SHEEHY, Terrence C.

1299 Pennsylvania Ave. NW
Washington, DC 20004-2402
Tel: (202)783-0800
Fax: (202)383-6610

Employers
Howrey Simon Arnold & White (Partner)

Clients Represented
On Behalf of Howrey Simon Arnold & White
Anheuser-Busch Cos., Inc.

SHEEHY, Timothy J.

1301 K St. NW
Suite 1200-West Tower
Washington, DC 20005-3307
Tel: (202)515-5077
Fax: (202)515-4943
Registered: LDA
EMail: sheehy@us.ibm.com

Employers
Internat'l Business Machines Corp. (Public Policy Program Director, Finance and Taxation)

SHEEKEY, Arthur

One Massachusetts Ave. NW
Suite 700
Washington, DC 20001-1431
Tel: (202)408-5505
Fax: (202)408-8072

Employers
Council of Chief State School Officers (Coordinator, Learning Technologies)

SHEEKEY, Kathleen D.

1629 K St. NW
Suite 200
Washington, DC 20006-1629
EMail: info@advocacy.org
Tel: (202)777-7575
Fax: (202)777-7577

Employers
The Advocacy Institute (Co-Director)

SHEETZ, Patty

513 Capitol Ct. NE
Suite 300
Washington, DC 20002
Tel: (202)546-0100
Fax: (202)547-0936

Employers
Congressional Management Foundation (Management Consultant)

SHEFFIELD, Victoria

7801 Norfolk Ave.
Bethesda, MD 20814
Tel: (301)986-1830
Fax: (301)986-1876

Employers
Internat'l Eye Foundation/Soc. of Eye Surgeons (Exec. Director)

SHEIRE, James B.

1333 H St. NW
Suite 630
Washington, DC 20004
Tel: (202)347-9292
Fax: (202)628-5498
Registered: LDA
EMail: jsheire@eabc.org

Legislative Assistant to Senator Ronald Wyden (D-OR), 1993-99.

Employers
European-American Business Council (Director, Government Affairs)

SHEKETOFF, Emily

1301 Pennsylvania Ave. NW
Suite 403
Washington, DC 20004
Tel: (202)628-8410
Fax: (202)628-8419
Registered: LDA
EMail: es@alawash.org

Employers
American Library Ass'n (Exec. Director, Washington Office)

SHELBY, Richard D.

400 N. Capitol St. NW
Washington, DC 20001
Tel: (202)824-7210
Fax: (202)824-7092
Registered: LDA
EMail: rshelby@aga.org

Employers
American Gas Ass'n (Exec. V. President, Public Affairs)

SHELBY, Sheryl W.

316 Pennsylvania Ave. SE
Suite 300
Washington, DC 20003
Tel: (202)675-4220
Fax: (202)675-4230
Registered: LDA

Employers
United Parcel Service (Manager, Public Affairs)

SHELDON, Rev. Louis P.

139 C St. SE
Washington, DC 20003
Tel: (202)547-8570
Fax: (202)546-6403
Registered: LDA

Employers
Traditional Values Coalition (Chairman)

SHELDON, Stuart A.

1200 New Hampshire Ave. NW
Suite 800
Washington, DC 20036-6802
EMail: ssheldon@dlalaw.com
Tel: (202)776-2000
Fax: (202)776-2222

Employers
Dow, Lohnes & Albertson, PLLC (Member)

SHELDON-LAFFERTY, Andrea A.

139 C St. SE
Washington, DC 20003
Tel: (202)547-8570
Fax: (202)546-6403
Registered: LDA

Employers
Traditional Values Coalition (Exec. Director, Government Relations)

SHELEF, Noam

1815 H St. NW
Suite 920
Washington, DC 20006
Tel: (202)728-1893
Fax: (202)728-1895
Registered: LDA

Employers
Americans for Peace Now (Grassroots Coordinator)

SHELIGA, Nancy A.

901 15th St. NW
Suite 700
Washington, DC 20005-2301
Tel: (202)371-6000
Fax: (202)371-6279
Registered: LDA

Employers
Verner, Liipfert, Bernhard, McPherson and Hand, Chartered (Legislative Assistant)

Clients Represented
On Behalf of Verner, Liipfert, Bernhard, McPherson and Hand, Chartered
Home Warranty Coalition
Mars, Inc.
New England Fuel Institute

SHELK, John E.

555 13th St. NW
Suite 1010 East
Washington, DC 20004
Tel: (202)637-6500
Fax: (202)637-6507
Registered: LDA

Employers
American Gaming Ass'n (V. President)

SHELK, Melissa Wolford

1130 Connecticut Ave. NW
Suite 1000
Washington, DC 20036
Tel: (202)828-7100
Fax: (202)293-1219
Registered: LDA
EMail: mshelk@aiadc.org

Employers
American Insurance Ass'n (V. President, Federal Affairs)

SHELTON, Hilary

1025 Vermont Ave. NW
Suite 1120
Washington, DC 20005
Tel: (202)638-2269
Fax: (202)638-5936
Registered: LDA

Employers
Nat'l Ass'n for the Advancement of Colored People, Washington Bureau (Director)

SHELTON, Todd

Ronald Reagan Bldg.
1300 Pennsylvania Ave. NW
MS: 6.10A
Washington, DC 20523
Tel: (202)712-4300
Fax: (202)216-3036

Employers
Agency for Internat'l Development (Legislative Program Specialist, Congressional Liaison Division)

SHEMDIN, Nijyar H.

10903 Amherst Ave.
Suite 231
Silver Spring, MD 20902
Tel: (301)946-1383
Fax: (301)946-1383
Registered: LDA, FARA

Employers
Self-employed as an independent consultant.

Clients Represented
As an independent consultant
Kurdistan Regional Government

SHEMTOV, Rabbi Abraham

2110 Leroy Pl. NW
Washington, DC 20008
Tel: (202)332-5600
Fax: (202)332-5642

Employers
American Friends of Lubavitch (National Director)

SHEMTOV, Rabbi Levi

2110 Leroy Pl. NW
Washington, DC 20008
Tel: (202)332-5600
Fax: (202)332-5642
EMail: leviwashdc@aol.com

Employers
American Friends of Lubavitch (Director, Washington Office)

SHEN, Andrew

1718 Connecticut Ave. NW
Suite 200
Washington, DC 20009
Tel: (202)483-1140
Fax: (202)483-1248

Employers
Electronic Privacy Information Center (Policy Analyst)

SHEPARD, Jennifer

412 First St. SE
Suite One
Washington, DC 20003
Tel: (202)484-2773
Fax: (202)484-0770
Registered: LDA

Employers
Meyers & Associates (Outside Associate)

Clients Represented

On Behalf of Meyers & Associates
The Alliance for I-69 Texas

SHEPARD, Linda

1130 17th St. NW
Suite 400
Washington, DC 20036
Tel: (202)463-2299
Fax: (202)463-9405

Employers
Nat'l Parent Network on Disabilities (Exec. Director)

SHEPARD, Stacey

1730 Rhode Island Ave.
Suite 912
Washington, DC 20036
Tel: (202)331-7990
Fax: (202)331-8019

Employers
Center for Strategic and Budgetary Assessments (Director, Public Affairs)

SHEPHERD, Rebecah Moore

2101 L St. NW
Washington, DC 20037-1526
Tel: (202)785-9700
Fax: (202)887-0689
Registered: LDA
EMail: shepherdr@dsmo.com
Former Aide to Rep. Richard Burr (R-NC).

Employers
Dickstein Shapiro Morin & Oshinsky LLP (Legislative Specialist)

Clients Represented

On Behalf of Dickstein Shapiro Morin & Oshinsky LLP
American Greyhound Track Operators Ass'n
American Public Communications Council
Cigar Ass'n of America
Electric Power Supply Ass'n
Home Box Office
Hydro-Quebec
Incentive Federation Sweepstakes Trust Fund
Internat'l Brotherhood of Teamsters
Lorillard Tobacco Co.
PG&E Generating Co.
Pipe Tobacco Council, Inc.
The Reader's Digest Ass'n
Smokeless Tobacco Council

SHEPLER, Bob

1615 L St. NW
Suite 1320
Washington, DC 20036
Tel: (202)659-3700
Fax: (202)857-0230
Registered: LDA
EMail: bshepler@feidc.org

Employers
Financial Executives International (Manager, Government Relations)

SHER, Jacky

1700 N. Moore St.
Suite 1600
Arlington, VA 22209
Tel: (703)841-3680
Fax: (703)527-0928

Employers
Nat'l Meat Canners Ass'n (Director, Administration)

SHER, Stanley O.

1850 M St. NW
Suite 900
Washington, DC 20036
Tel: (202)463-2500
Fax: (202)463-4950
Registered: LDA, FARA

Employers
Sher & Blackwell (Partner)

Clients Represented

On Behalf of Sher & Blackwell
Carriers Against Harbor Tax
Council of European and Japanese Nat'l Shipowners' Ass'ns
Nippon Yusen Kaisha (NYK) Line
Ocean Carriers Working Group
Transpacific Stabilization Agreement

SHERBURNE, Jane C.

2445 M St. NW
Washington, DC 20037-1420
Tel: (202)663-6000
Fax: (202)663-6363
EMail: jsherburne@wilmer.com
Special Counsel (1995-97) and Special Associate Counsel (1994) to the President, Executive Office of the President, The White House. Executive Assistant to the Commissioner, Social Security Administration, 1978-80. Legislative Assistant to Rep. Donal Fraser (D-MN), 1976-77.

Employers
Wilmer, Cutler & Pickering (Partner)

SHERIDAN, Anne

1001 G St. NW
Suite 300 East
Washington, DC 20001
Tel: (202)638-5616
Fax: (202)638-5612
EMail: asheridan@deweysquare.com

Employers
Dewey Square Group (Principal)

SHERIDAN, Richard

1201 New York Ave. NW
Suite 300
Washington, DC 20005
Tel: (202)326-6338
Fax: (202)371-0181
EMail: rsherida@boma.org

Employers
Building Owners and Managers Ass'n Internat'l (Assistant Exec. Director, Government and Industry Affairs)

SHERIDAN, Rosemary

1666 K St. NW
Washington, DC 20006
Tel: (202)296-4700
Fax: (202)496-4324
EMail: rsheridan@apta.com

Employers
American Public Transportation Ass'n (V. President, Communications and Marketing)

SHERIDAN, Thomas F.

1808 Swann St. NW
Washington, DC 20009
Tel: (202)462-7288
Fax: (202)483-1964
Registered: LDA

Employers
American AIDS Political Action Committee (President/Treasurer)
The Sheridan Group (President)

Clients Represented

On Behalf of The Sheridan Group
American AIDS Political Action Committee
American Cancer Soc.
Chronic Fatigue and Immune Dysfunction Syndrome Ass'n of America
Cities Advocating Emergency AIDS Relief (CAEAR)
Fenton Communications
Housing Works
Nat'l Ryan White Title III (b) Coalition
San Francisco AIDS Foundation

SHERK, Jon Arthur

1615 H St. NW
Washington, DC 20062-2000
Tel: (202)659-6000
Fax: (202)463-5836

Employers
Chamber of Commerce of the U.S.A. (Director, Technology Policy)

SHERMAN, Cary

1330 Connecticut Ave. NW
Suite 300
Washington, DC 20036
Tel: (202)775-0101
Fax: (202)775-7253
Registered: LDA

Employers
Recording Industry Ass'n of America (Senior Exec. V. President and General Counsel)

SHERMAN, Daniel

2001 M St. NW
Fourth Floor
Washington, DC 20036
Tel: (202)533-5660
Fax: (202)533-8580
Registered: LDA

Employers
Barents Group LLC (Healthcare)

SHERMAN, Gerald H.

1776 K St. NW
Suite 700
Washington, DC 20006
Tel: (202)452-7900
Fax: (202)452-7989
EMail: ghs@silvmul.com

Employers
Silverstein and Mullens, P.L.L.C. (Member)

Clients Represented

On Behalf of Silverstein and Mullens, P.L.L.C.
Ass'n for Advanced Life Underwriting

SHERMAN, Judith C.

1111 14th St. NW
Suite 1200
Washington, DC 20005-5603
Tel: (202)898-2400
Fax: (202)898-2437
Registered: LDA
EMail: shermanj@ada.org

Employers
American Dental Ass'n (Senior Congressional Lobbyist)

SHERMAN, Michael D.

3050 K St. NW
Washington, DC 20007
Tel: (202)342-8400
Fax: (202)342-8451
Registered: LDA, FARA
EMail: msherman@colliershannon.com

Employers
Collier Shannon Scott, PLLC (Member)

Clients Represented

On Behalf of Collier Shannon Scott, PLLC
GATX Corp.
Golden Gate Petroleum Internat'l, Ltd.
Vitol, S.A., Inc.
Wickland Oil Co.

SHERMAN, Patricia A.

701 Pennsylvania Ave. NW
Suite 720
Washington, DC 20004
Tel: (202)434-4800
Fax: (202)347-4015
Registered: LDA

Employers
Siemens Corp.

SHERMAN, Sandy L.

1101 Vermont Ave. NW
12th Floor
Washington, DC 20005-3583
Tel: (202)789-4585
Fax: (202)789-7581
Registered: LDA

Employers
American Medical Ass'n (Assistant Director, Federal Affairs)

SHERRY, Chris

1717 Massachusetts Ave. NW
Suite 106
Washington, DC 20036
Tel: (202)483-8491
Ext: 12
Fax: (202)234-9194
EMail: csherry@erols.com

Employers
Safe Energy Communication Council (Research Director)

SHERWOOD, Lori

750 First St. NE
Suite 901
Washington, DC 20002
Tel: (202)408-1711
Fax: (202)408-1699
EMail: lsherwood@saferoads.org

Employers
Advocates for Highway and Auto Safety (Manager, Legislative Affairs)

SHERZER, Harvey G.

1299 Pennsylvania Ave. NW
Washington, DC 20004-2402
Tel: (202)783-0800
Fax: (202)383-6610
EMail: sherzerh@howrey.com
Law Clerk to Chief Judge Wilson Cowen (1969-70) and to Trial Judges (1968-69), U.S. Court of Claims.

Employers
Howrey Simon Arnold & White (Partner)

Clients Represented
On Behalf of Howrey Simon Arnold & White
Allegheny Technologies, Inc.

SHEY, Brigid

4214 King St. West
Alexandria, VA 22302
Tel: (703)820-6696
Fax: (703)820-8550

Employers
IWPA - The Internat'l Wood Products Ass'n (Director, Government Affairs)

SHIELDS, Carolyn

700 13th St. NW
Suite 1000
Washington, DC 20005
Tel: (202)347-6633
Fax: (202)347-8713
Former Executive Assistant to the Press Secretary during the Carter Administration.

Employers
Powell Tate (Director, Special Events)

SHIELDS, Mary E.

700 13th St. NW
Suite 400
Washington, DC 20005
Tel: (202)347-0773
Fax: (202)347-0785
Registered: LDA
EMail: mshields@cassidy.com
Former Professional Staff Assistant to Senator William Roth (R-DE). Former Chairman Senate Committee on Government Affairs.

Employers
Cassidy & Associates, Inc. (Senior V. President)

Clients Represented
On Behalf of Cassidy & Associates, Inc.
Carondelet Health System
Dominican College of Blauvelt
Henry Ford Health System
Hospital for Special Surgery
Immaculata College
Institute for Student Achievement
Marymount University
Monroe Community College
Nat'l SAFE KIDS Campaign
Neumann College
Ohio State University
Saint Coletta of Greater Washington, Inc.
Southeastern Pennsylvania Consortium for Higher Education
University of San Francisco

SHIELDS, Peter D.

1776 K St. NW
Washington, DC 20006
Tel: (202)719-7000
Fax: (202)719-7049

Employers
Wiley, Rein & Fielding (Partner)

SHIELDS, Wayne C.

2401 Pennsylvania Ave. NW
Suite 350
Washington, DC 20037-1718
Tel: (202)466-3825
Fax: (202)466-3826
EMail: wshields@arhp.org

Employers
Ass'n of Reproductive Health Professionals (President and Chief Exec. Officer)

SHIFFMAN, Gary M.

800 Connecticut Ave. NW
Suite 500
Washington, DC 20006
Tel: (202)331-3100
Fax: (202)331-3101
Registered: LDA
Foreign Policy Advisor to Senator Connie Mack (R-FL), 1996-2000. Former Advisor to the Secretary of Defense and Chief of Naval Operations. Served in the U.S. Navy, 1988-96.

Employers
Greenberg Traurig, LLP (Director, Governmental Affairs)

Clients Represented
On Behalf of Greenberg Traurig, LLP
NeuLevel

SHIFLETT, Jr., Ronald C.

701 Pennsylvania Ave. NW
Suite 500
Washington, DC 20004
Tel: (202)508-5507
Fax: (202)508-5080
EMail: ronalsee@eei.org

Employers
Internat'l Utility Efficiency Partnerships (IUEP) (Exec. Director)

SHIFTER, Michael

1211 Connecticut Ave. NW
Suite 510
Washington, DC 20036
Tel: (202)822-9002
Fax: (202)822-9553

Employers
Inter-American Dialogue (V. President, Policy)

SHILTON, Mary Katherine

3903 Gresham Place
Alexandria, VA 22305
Tel: (703)836-0279
Fax: (703)836-0831
Registered: LDA

Employers
Self-employed as an independent consultant.

Clients Represented
As an independent consultant
Internat'l Community Corrections Ass'n

SHIMBERG, Steven J.

1400 16th St. NW
Suite 501
Washington, DC 20036-2266
Tel: (202)797-6800
Fax: (202)797-6646
Registered: LDA
EMail: shimberg@nwf.org

Employers
Nat'l Wildlife Federation - Office of Federal and Internat'l Affairs (V. President, Office of Federal and International Affairs)

SHIN, Hyun Kyu

1667 K St. NW
Suite 1210
Washington, DC 20006
Tel: (202)296-5550
Registered: LDA

Employers
Hyundai Motor Co.

SHINDELMAN, Bonnie

1800 K St. NW
Suite 1010
Washington, DC 20006
Tel: (202)296-5030
Fax: (202)296-4750
Registered: LDA

Employers
American Defense Internat'l, Inc.

Clients Represented
On Behalf of American Defense Internat'l, Inc.
East/West Industries
Friction Free Technologies Inc.
Stidd Systems, Inc.

SHINGLETON, A. Bradley

1020 19th St. NW
Suite 850
Washington, DC 20036
Tel: (202)452-9100
Fax: (202)452-9555
Registered: FARA
EMail: bradley.shingleton@usa.telekom.de

Employers
Deutsche Telekom, Inc. (Legal Counsel)

SHINHOLSTER, April

1155 15th St. NW
Suite 1004
Washington, DC 20005
Tel: (202)467-5081
Fax: (202)467-5085

Employers
Nat'l Alliance of Blind Students (President)

SHINODA, Hiroshi

1001 Connecticut Ave. NW
Suite 425
Washington, DC 20036
Tel: (202)955-5663
Fax: (202)955-6125

Employers
Japan Productivity Center for Socio-Economic Development (Director, U.S. Office)

SHIPLEY, Don

818 Connecticut Ave. NW
Second Floor
Washington, DC 20006
Tel: (202)289-2001
Fax: (202)289-1327
EMail: dshipley@stratacomm.net

Employers
Strat@Comm (Strategic Communications Counselors) (Senior Counselor)

SHIPP, Charlie

1120 20th St. NW
Suite 1000
Washington, DC 20036
Tel: (202)457-2101
Fax: (202)457-2571
Registered: LDA
EMail: cshipp@att.com

Employers
AT&T (V. President, Congressional Affairs)

SHIPP, Daniel K.

1901 N. Moore St.
Suite 808
Arlington, VA 22209
Tel: (703)525-1695
Fax: (703)528-2148
Registered: LDA
EMail: dshipp@safetyequipment.org

Employers
Internat'l Safety Equipment Ass'n (ISEA) (President)

SHIPP, William Jeffry

50 F St. NW
Suite 900
Washington, DC 20001
Tel: (202)879-0851
Fax: (202)626-8718
Registered: LDA
EMail: shipp@fccouncil.com

Employers
Farm Credit Council (Exec. V. President)

SHIRAS, Peter

1200 18th St. NW
Second Floor
Washington, DC 20036
Tel: (202)467-6100
Fax: (202)467-6101
Registered: LDA
EMail: peter@independentsector.org

Employers
Independent Sector (Senior V. President, Programs)

SHIRLEY, Craig P.

122 S. Patrick St.
Alexandria, VA 22314
Tel: (703)739-5920
Fax: (703)739-5924
Registered: LDA
EMail: craig@craigshirley.com

Employers
Craig Shirley & Associates (President)

Clients Represented
On Behalf of Craig Shirley & Associates
Citizens for State Power
Southeastern Legal Foundation

SHIRLEY, Graham E.

412 First St. SE
Suite One
Washington, DC 20003
Tel: (202)484-2773
Fax: (202)484-0770
Former Brigadier General, U.S. Air Force.

Employers
Meyers & Associates (Senior Associate)

SHLABACH, Rachelle

110 Maryland Ave. NE
Suite 502
Washington, DC 20002
EMail: Rachelle_Schlabach@mcc.org
Tel: (202)544-6564
Fax: (202)544-2820

Employers
Mennonite Central Committee Washington Office (Legislative Assistant)

SHOAF, Jeffrey D.

333 John Carlyle St.
Suite 200
Alexandria, VA 22314
EMail: shoafj@agc.org
Tel: (703)837-5362
Fax: (703)837-5407
Registered: LDA

Employers
Associated General Contractors of America (Exec. Director, Congressional Relations)

SHOAF, Mary L.

725 15th St. NW
Suite 800
Washington, DC 20005
EMail: lshoaf@neurosurgery@.org
Tel: (202)628-2072
Fax: (202)628-5264
Registered: LDA

Employers
American Ass'n of Neurological Surgeons/Congress of Neurological Surgeons (Senior Washington Associate)

SHOCKET, Phyllis G.

1120 G St. NW
Suite 850
Washington, DC 20005
EMail: pshocket@napawash.org
Tel: (202)347-3190
Fax: (202)393-0993

Employers
Nat'l Academy of Public Administration (Director, Academy Affairs)

SHOCKEY, Jeffrey S.

1341 G St. NW
Suite 200
Washington, DC 20005
EMail: jshockey@clj.com
Tel: (202)347-5990
Fax: (202)347-5941
Registered: LDA

Legislative Director (1995-99) and Legislative Assistant (1991-95) to Rep. Jerry Lewis (R-CA).

Employers
Copeland, Lowery & Jacquez (Partner)

Clients Represented

On Behalf of Copeland, Lowery & Jacquez
BeamHit America LLC
The Boeing Co.
California State University, San Bernardino Foundation
Cedars-Sinai Medical Center
Children's Hospital and Health Center of San Diego
Children's Hospital Los Angeles
Disaster Insurance Coalition/City of Hope Nat'l Medical Center
Environmental Systems Research Institute, Inc.
Hi-Desert Water District
Jacobs & Co. Public Affairs/Loma Linda University
Latham & Watkins
Loma Linda, California, City of
Murrieta, California, City of
Redlands, California, City of
Riverside Habitat Acquisition, County of
San Bernardino Valley Municipal Water District
San Joaquin Council of Governments
San Joaquin Regional Rail Commission
University of Redlands
City of Victorville Redevelopment Agency

SHOCKLEY, Ed

5211 Auth Rd.
Suitland, MD 20746
Tel: (301)899-3500
Fax: (301)899-8136

Employers
Air Force Sergeants Ass'n (Director, Member and Field Services)

SHOCKLEY, Larry G.

1133 15th St. NW
Suite 800
Washington, DC 20005
Fax: (202)775-6005

Employers
Parsons Corp. (V. President, Government Relations)

SHOEMAKER, Janet

1752 N St. NW
Washington, DC 20036
EMail: jshoemaker@asmusa.org
Tel: (202)737-3600
Fax: (202)942-9335
Registered: LDA

Employers
American Soc. for Microbiology (Director, Public Affairs)

SHOEMAKER, Priscilla

1201 L St. NW
Washington, DC 20005-4014
Tel: (202)842-4444
Fax: (202)842-3860

Employers
American Health Care Ass'n (Senior Director, Legal Services, Clinical & Facility Operations)

SHOGAN, Cindy

122 C Street NW
Suite 240
Washington, DC 20001
Tel: (202)544-5205
Fax: (202)544-5197

Employers
Alaska Wilderness League (Exec. Director)

SHONKWILER, Tatjana M.

1615 M St. NW
Suite 800
Washington, DC 20036-3203
EMail: tms@dwgp.com
Tel: (202)467-6370
Fax: (202)467-6379

Employers
Duncan, Weinberg, Genzer & Pembroke, P.C. (Principal)

Clients Represented

On Behalf of Duncan, Weinberg, Genzer & Pembroke, P.C.
Internat'l Energy Consultants
Jamestown, New York, Board of Public Utilities
Nat'l Ass'n of Energy Service Companies
Salamanca, New York, City Board of Public Utilities of
Solar Energy Research and Education Foundation

SHOOK, William A.

1735 New York Ave. NW
Suite 500
Washington, DC 20006-4759
Tel: (202)628-1700
Fax: (202)331-1024
Registered: LDA

Legislative Investigator, Senate Judiciary Committee, 1979-85, and Special Assistant on the House Oversight and Investigations Subcommittee of the Interstate and Foreign Commerce Committee, 1977-79.

Employers
Preston Gates Ellis & Rouvelas Meeds LLP (Partner)

Clients Represented

On Behalf of Preston Gates Ellis & Rouvelas Meeds LLP
Envirocare of Utah, Inc.

SHOR, Michael T.

555 12th St. NW
Washington, DC 20004-1206
EMail: Michael_Shor@aporter.com
Tel: (202)942-5000
Fax: (202)942-5999

Legal Assistant, U.S. Claims Tribunal, The Hague, Netherlands, 1984-86.

Employers
Arnold & Porter (Partner)

SHORE, Bill

733 15th St. NW
Suite 640
Washington, DC 20005
Tel: (202)393-2925
Fax: (202)347-5868

Employers
Share Our Strength (Exec. Director)

SHORE, Linda K.

1776 K St.
Washington, DC 20006
Tel: (202)452-7945
Registered: LDA

Employers
Buchanan Ingersoll, P.C.

Clients Represented

On Behalf of Buchanan Ingersoll, P.C.
nPower Advisors, LLC

SHORE, Steven M.

236 Massachusetts Ave. NE
Suite 110
Washington, DC 20002
Tel: (202)546-8700
Fax: (202)546-7357

Employers
Alliance for American Innovation, Inc. (President)

SHORT, Bradley W.

1891 Preston White Dr.
Reston, VA 20191-9312
Tel: (703)648-8900
Fax: (703)262-9319

Employers
American College of Radiology (Director, Member Development and Chapter Relations)

SHORT, Brenda A.

1800 F St. NW
MS: 6112
Washington, DC 20405
EMail: brenda.a.short@gsa.gov
Tel: (202)501-1250
Fax: (202)219-5742

Employers
General Services Administration (Congressional Liaison)

SHORT, Kelli

1755 Jefferson Davis Hwy.
Suite 1107
Arlington, VA 22202
Tel: (703)415-0344
Fax: (703)415-0182
Registered: LDA

Employers
The PMA Group (Associate)

Clients Represented

On Behalf of The PMA Group
Ag/Bio Con
Alliance
Applied Marine Technologies, Inc.
Autometric Inc.
Battelle
CHIM
CRYPTEK Secure Communications, LLC
Dynamics Research Corp.
Environmental Technology Unlimited
Joint Healthcare Information Technology Alliance
L-3 Communications Corp.
Lockheed Martin MS/Gaithersburg
Prologic
Schweizer Aircraft Corp.

SHORT, Larri A.

1050 Connecticut Ave. NW
Washington, DC 20036-5339
Tel: (202)857-6000
Fax: (202)857-6395
Registered: LDA

Employers
Arent Fox Kintner Plotkin & Kahn, PLLC (Associate)

Clients Represented

On Behalf of Arent Fox Kintner Plotkin & Kahn, PLLC
American Ass'n of Occupational Health Nurses

SHOTTES, Fran

321 D St. NE
Washington, DC 20002
Tel: (202)548-8322
Fax: (202)548-8326

Employers
SISCORP

Clients Represented

On Behalf of SISCORP
Biostar Group, The
Science Applications Internat'l Corp. (SAIC)
Textron Inc.
ThermoTrex Corp.

SHOTWELL, Lynn Frendt

1212 New York Ave. NW
Suite 425
Washington, DC 20005
EMail: lynn_shotwell@acip.com
Tel: (202)371-6789
Fax: (202)371-5524
Registered: LDA

Employers
American Council on Internat'l Personnel, Inc. (Legal Counsel and Director, Government Relations)

SHOTWELL, Scott

1775 Pennsylvania Ave. NW
Suite 600
Washington, DC 20006
EMail: fairlumber@cs.com
Tel: (202)862-4505
Fax: (202)862-1093
Registered: LDA

Employers
Coalition for Fair Lumber Imports (Exec. Director)

SHOWALTER, Charles

1891 Preston White Dr.
Reston, VA 20191-9312
Tel: (703)648-8900
Fax: (703)262-9312

Employers
American College of Radiology (Senior Director, Government Relations)

SHOWELL, Jill

1101 Pennsylvania Ave. NW
Suite 950
Washington, DC 20004
Tel: (202)434-8600
Fax: (202)434-8626
Registered: LDA

Employers
Federal Home Loan Mortgage Corp. (Freddie Mac) (Legislative Director)

SHOYER, Andrew

1001 Pennsylvania Ave. NW
Suite 600
Washington, DC 20004
EMail: ashoyer@pgfm.com
Tel: (202)347-0066
Fax: (202)624-7222
Registered: LDA

Legal Advisor, United States Mission to the World Trade Organization and Assistant General Counsel, Office of the U.S. Trade Representative, Executive Office of the President, The White House, 1990-97.

Employers
Powell, Goldstein, Frazer & Murphy LLP (Partner)

Clients Represented
On Behalf of Powell, Goldstein, Frazer & Murphy LLP
Qualcomm Inc.
Shaklee Corp.

SHRIBER, Maurice N.

11 Canal Center Plaza
Suite 103
Alexandria, VA 22314
Tel: (703)683-4222
Fax: (703)683-0645
Registered: LDA

Employers
The Spectrum Group

Clients Represented
On Behalf of The Spectrum Group
AAI Corp.

SHRINER, Robert D.

6432 Quincy Pl.
Falls Church, VA 22042
Tel: (703)237-8135
Fax: (703)533-9103

Employers
Shriner-Midland Co. (Managing Partner)

SHRINSKY, Jason

The McPherson Bldg.
901 15th St. NW, Suite 1100
Washington, DC 20005
Tel: (202)682-3500
Fax: (202)682-3580

Employers
Kaye Scholer LLP (Partner)

Clients Represented
On Behalf of Kaye Scholer LLP
Barnstable Broadcasting
Holt Communications Corp.
Katz Communications, Inc.
Keymarket Communications, Inc.
The Lincoln Group
Malrite Communications Group, Inc.
NewCity Communications, Inc.

SHRIVER, Rob

901 E St. NW
Suite 600
Washington, DC 20004
Tel: (202)783-4444
Fax: (202)783-4085

Employers
Nat'l Treasury Employees Union (Assistant Counsel)

SHRIVER, Ph.D., Timothy P.

1325 G St. NW
Suite 500
Washington, DC 20005
EMail: tshriverso@aol.com
Tel: (202)824-0242
Fax: (202)628-0067

Employers
Special Olympics, Inc. (President and Chief Exec. Officer)

SHROYER, Julie

426 C St. NE
Washington, DC 20002
EMail: js@capitolassociates.com
Tel: (202)544-1880
Fax: (202)543-2565
Registered: LDA

Employers
Capitol Associates, Inc. (V. President)

Clients Represented
On Behalf of Capitol Associates, Inc.
American Ass'n for Marriage and Family Therapy
California Ass'n of Marriage and Family Therapists
College on Problems of Drug Dependence
DeBrunner and Associates, Inc.
Healthcare Billing and Management Ass'n
Nat'l Ass'n of Pediatric Nurse Associates and Practitioners
Research Soc. on Alcoholism
Western Michigan University

SHRUM, Robert M.

2141 Wisconsin Ave. NW
Suite H
Washington, DC 20007
Tel: (202)337-9600
Fax: (202)337-9620
Registered: LDA

Employers
Strategic Choices, Inc.

Clients Represented
On Behalf of Strategic Choices, Inc.
Colombian Coffee Federation

SHU, Cindy

1200 G St. NW
Suite 510
Washington, DC 20005
EMail: cindy@csa-dc.org
Tel: (202)347-0600
Fax: (202)347-0608

Employers
Contract Services Ass'n of America (Legislative/Regulatory Manager)

SHUBIK, Philippe

1575 I St. NW
Suite 325
Washington, DC 20005
EMail: toxforum@clark.net
Tel: (202)659-0030
Fax: (202)789-0905

Employers
Toxicology Forum (President)

SHUFORD, Capt. Jacob

Russell Senate Office Bldg.
Room 182
Washington, DC 20510
EMail: shuford.jacob@hq.navy.mil
Tel: (202)685-6006
Fax: (202)685-6005

Employers
Department of Navy (Senate Liaison Principal Deputy, Office of Legislative Affairs)

SHULER, Liz

1125 15th St. NW
Washington, DC 20005
Tel: (202)833-7000
Fax: (202)728-6055
Registered: LDA

Employers
Internat'l Brotherhood of Electrical Workers (Political/Legislative Assistant Director)

SHULL, Darrell A.

888 16th St. NW
Suite 305
Washington, DC 20006
EMail: shull@bipac.org
Tel: (202)833-1880
Fax: (202)833-2338

Employers
Business-Industry Political Action Committee (V. President, Political Operations)

SHULMAN, Eric

5316 Edgewood Dr.
Alexandria, VA 22310
Tel: (703)971-7656
Registered: LDA

Employers
Eric Shulman & Associates (President)

Clients Represented
On Behalf of Eric Shulman & Associates
Local 511 Professional Employees, AFGE
Nat'l Border Patrol Council
Nat'l Immigration and Naturalization Services Council

SHULTZ, Kelly

1900 M St. NW
Suite 700
Washington, DC 20036
Tel: (202)463-7090
Fax: (202)463-1830

Employers
Ryder System, Inc. (PAC Administrator)

SHULTZ, Lexi

218 D St. SE
Second Floor
Washington, DC 20003
Tel: (202)546-9707
Fax: (202)546-2461

Employers
U.S. Public Interest Research Group (Staff Attorney)

SHUMSKI, Scot

1300 N. 17th St.
Eighth Floor
Rosslyn, VA 22209-3801
EMail: shumski@abc.org
Tel: (703)812-2000
Fax: (703)812-8202

Employers
Associated Builders and Contractors (Regional Field Representative)

SHUPACK, Martin

110 Maryland Ave. NE
Suite 502
Washington, DC 20002
EMail: Martin_Shupack@mcc.org
Tel: (202)544-6564
Fax: (202)544-2820

Employers
Mennonite Central Committee Washington Office (Legislative Associate, International Affairs)

SHUPING, CAE, Frances

2800 Shirlington Rd.
Suite 300
Arlington, VA 22206
Tel: (703)824-8846
Fax: (703)575-4449

Employers
Air Conditioning Contractors of America (Staff V. President, Communications and Technology)

SHUR, Stephen

1211 Connecticut Ave. NW
Suite 608
Washington, DC 20036
EMail: sshur@qorvis.com
Tel: (202)496-1000
Fax: (202)496-1300

Employers
Qorvis Communications (Principal)

SHUREN, Allison

1050 Connecticut Ave. NW
Washington, DC 20036-5339
Tel: (202)857-6000
Fax: (202)857-6395
Registered: LDA

Employers
Arent Fox Kintner Plotkin & Kahn, PLLC (Associate)

Clients Represented
On Behalf of Arent Fox Kintner Plotkin & Kahn, PLLC
American Ass'n of Occupational Health Nurses
American College of Nurse Practitioners
Ass'n of Pain Management Anesthesiologist
Coalition for a Procompetitive Stark Law
Mercy Hospital of Des Moines, Iowa
Nat'l Ass'n of Pediatric Nurse Associates and Practitioners
Nat'l Ass'n of School Nurses
Nat'l Council of State Boards of Nursing
Soc. for Excellence in Eyecare
Soc. for Vascular Surgery
Soc. of Diagnostic Medical Sonographers
Soc. of Vascular Technology

SHUST, Diane M.

1201 16th St. NW
Washington, DC 20036
Tel: (202)833-4000
Registered: LDA

Employers

Nat'l Education Ass'n of the U.S. (Senior Professional Associate, Government Relations)

SHYCOFF, Barbara

801 Pennsylvania Ave.
Suite 650
Washington, DC 20004
Tel: (202)624-0761
Fax: (202)624-0775
Registered: LDA
EMail: barbara.shycoff@aexp.com

Employers

American Express Co. (V. President, Government Affairs)

SICKLES, Mark D.

643 S. Washington St.
Alexandria, VA 22314
Tel: (703)518-8408
Fax: (703)518-8490
Registered: LDA

Employers

Dredging Contractors of America (Exec. Director)

SIDAK, J. Gregory

1150 17th St. NW
Washington, DC 20036
Tel: (202)862-5800
Fax: (202)862-7177
EMail: jgsidak@aei.org

Employers

American Enterprise Institute for Public Policy Research (Director, Telecommunications Deregulation Project/F.K. Weyerhauser Fellow)

SIDDALL, David R.

901 15th St. NW
Suite 700
Washington, DC 20005-2301
Tel: (202)371-6000
Fax: (202)371-6279
Registered: LDA

Employers

Verner, Liipfert, Bernhard, McPherson and Hand, Chartered (Member of Firm)

Clients Represented

On Behalf of Verner, Liipfert, Bernhard, McPherson and Hand, Chartered

BellSouth Corp.
Iridium, LLC
Lockheed Martin Corp.
NxtWave Communications
Philips Electronics North America Corp.
Thomson Consumer Electronics, Inc.

SIDDON, Arthur

7200 Wisconsin Ave.
Suite 709
Bethesda, MD 20814
Tel: (301)656-7998
Fax: (301)656-5019

Employers

Forum For Investor Advice (Director, Communications Services)

SIDES, Stephen R.

1500 Rhode Island Ave. NW
Washington, DC 20005-5597
Tel: (202)462-6272
Fax: (202)462-8549

Employers

Nat'l Paint and Coatings Ass'n (V. President, Health and Safety)

SIDMAN, Lawrence R.

901 15th St. NW
Suite 700
Washington, DC 20005-2301
Tel: (202)371-6000
Fax: (202)371-6279
Registered: LDA

Chief Counsel and Staff Director, Subcommittee on Telecommunications and Finance (1987-89) and Subcommittee on Energy Conservation and Power (1985-87), House Committee on Commerce.

Employers

Verner, Liipfert, Bernhard, McPherson and Hand, Chartered (Member of Firm)

Clients Represented

On Behalf of Verner, Liipfert, Bernhard, McPherson and Hand, Chartered

BET Holdings II, Inc.
CanWest
Harris Corp.
Lockheed Martin Corp.
Nat'l Broadcasting Co.
NOKIA
NxtWave Communications
Philips Electronics North America Corp.
Public Broadcasting Entities
Qwest Communications
Rite Aid Corp.
Sarnoff Corp.
Thomson Consumer Electronics, Inc.
Verizon Communications

SIEDLECKI, Kathleen

1615 L St. NW
Suite 1000
Washington, DC 20036
Tel: (202)659-0330
Fax: (202)223-8199
Registered: LDA
EMail: siedleck@fleishman.com

Staff member to Rep. Vic Fazio (D-CA).

Employers

Fleishman-Hillard, Inc (V. President)

Clients Represented

On Behalf of Fleishman-Hillard, Inc

Kahl Pownall Advocates
Knoll Pharmaceutical Co.

SIEGEL, Elisa

1150 Connecticut Ave. NW
Suite 201
Washington, DC 20036
Tel: (202)955-6200
Fax: (202)955-6215
EMail: esiegel@gcwdc.com

Employers

Goddard Claussen (Senior V. President)

SIEGEL, Mark A.

2103 O St. NW
Washington, DC 20037
Tel: (202)371-5600
Fax: (202)371-5608
Registered: LDA

Employers

Mark A. Siegel & Associates (President)

Clients Represented

On Behalf of Mark A. Siegel & Associates

Maldives, Government of the Republic of

SIEGEL, Richard D.

1400 16th St. NW
Suite 400
Washington, DC 20036-2220
Tel: (202)789-1212
Fax: (202)234-3583
Registered: LDA
EMail: rsiegel@ofwlaw.com

Former House and Senate Aide. Deputy Assistant Secretary for Natural Resources and Environment, Department of Agriculture, 1981-87.

Employers

Olsson, Frank and Weeda, P.C. (Senior Attorney)

Clients Represented

On Behalf of Olsson, Frank and Weeda, P.C.

Black Hills Forest Resource Ass'n

SIEGEL, Stan

1250 I St. NW
Suite 1200
Washington, DC 20005-3924
Tel: (202)371-8430
Fax: (202)371-8572

Employers

Aerospace Industries Ass'n of America (V. President, Technical Operations)
Nat'l Center for Advanced Technologies (President)

SIEGEL-VANN, Dina

1640 Rhode Island Ave. NW
Washington, DC 20036-3278
Tel: (202)857-6540
Fax: (202)857-6689

Employers

B'nai B'rith Internat'l (Director, Latin American Affairs)

SIEGL, Simon

1200 G St. NW
Suite 360
Washington, DC 20005
Tel: (202)783-2756
Fax: (202)347-6341
Registered: LDA
EMail: ssiegl@americanwineries.org

Employers

American Vintners Ass'n (President)

SIEGLER, Ellen

555 13th St. NW
Washington, DC 20004-1109
Tel: (202)637-5728
Fax: (202)637-5910
Registered: LDA
EMail: esiegler@hhlaw.com

Attorney, Environmental Protection Agency, 1978-86.
Attorney, Securities and Exchange Commission, 1974-78.

Employers

Hogan & Hartson L.L.P. (Counsel)

Clients Represented

On Behalf of Hogan & Hartson L.L.P.

American Frozen Food Institute
Nat'l Environmental Development Ass'n, Inc.

SIEGNER, Jr., A. Wes

700 13th St. NW
Suite 1200
Washington, DC 20005
Tel: (202)737-5600
Fax: (202)737-9329
Registered: LDA
EMail: aws@hpm.com

Employers

Hyman, Phelps & McNamara, P.C. (Partner)

Clients Represented

On Behalf of Hyman, Phelps & McNamara, P.C.

Dietary Supplement Safety and Science Coalition

SIEMIETKOWSKI, Susan M.

1301 K St. NW
Suite 1200-West Tower
Washington, DC 20005-3307
Tel: (202)515-5142
Fax: (202)515-5906
Registered: LDA

Employers

Internat'l Business Machines Corp. (Regional Manager, Government Relations)

SIENKO, Louise

2012 Massachusetts Ave. NW
Washington, DC 20036
Tel: (202)293-1100
Fax: (202)861-0298

Employers

Business and Professional Women/USA (Chair and PAC Contact)

SIEVERS, Sharon

3222 N St. NW
Suite 340
Washington, DC 20007
Tel: (202)965-3434
Fax: (202)965-1018

Employers

Washington Workshops (President)

SIFONTES, Marisa A.

1275 Pennsylvania Ave. NW
Ninth Floor
Washington, DC 20004
Tel: (202)662-6790
Fax: (202)624-0866
EMail: msifontes@sdsatty.com

Employers

Stuntz, Davis & Staffier, P.C. (Associate)

SIFRY, Micah

1320 19th St. NW
Suite M-1
Washington, DC 20036
Tel: (202)293-0222
Fax: (202)293-0202

Employers

Public Campaign (Senior Analyst)

SIGAL, Jill

P.O. Box 3037
Alexandria, VA 22302
Tel: (703)824-9013
Fax: (703)824-9014
Registered: LDA

Special Assistant, Office of the General Counsel, Department of Energy, 1985-89.

Employers
Jill Sigal Associates (President)

Clients Represented

On Behalf of Jill Sigal Associates
Nissan North America Inc.

SIGAL, Marcia

630 I St. NW
Washington, DC 20001-3736
Tel: (202)289-3500
Fax: (202)289-8181

Employers
Nat'l Ass'n of Housing and Redevelopment Officials (Policy Analyst, Community Development)

SIGALOF, George

1200 G St. NW
Suite 510
Washington, DC 20005
EMail: george@csa.dc.org
Tel: (202)347-0600
Fax: (202)347-0608

Employers
Contract Services Ass'n of America (Director, Public Relations)

SIGGINS, Robert G.

80 F St. NW
Suite 804
Washington, DC 20001
Tel: (202)347-3042
Fax: (202)347-3046

Employers
Fraioli/Siggins (V. President)

SIGNER, William A.

805 15th St. NW
Suite 500
Washington, DC 20005
Tel: (202)371-9770
Fax: (202)371-6601
Registered: LDA
EMail: signer@chambersinc.com
Professional Staff, Select Subcommittee on Revenue Measures (1985), Subcommittee on Oversight (1981-84), and Subcommittee on Health (1979-80), House Committee on Ways and Means. Health and Tax Counsel to Rep. Charles Rangel (D-NY), 1977-85. Senior Legislative Assistant to Rep. James H. Scheuer (D-NY), 1975-76.

Employers
Chambers Associates Inc. (Senior V. President)

Clients Represented

On Behalf of Chambers Associates Inc.
Alarm Industry Communications Committee
APG, Inc.
Greater New York Hospital Ass'n
Marriott Internat'l, Inc.
Micros, Inc.
Nat'l Ass'n of Convenience Stores
Nat'l Employment Opportunities Network
Nat'l Healthy Start Ass'n
New York Presbyterian Hospital - Cornell Medical Center
TMC, Inc.

SIGNORINO, Marc-Anthony

555 13th St. NW
Suite 300
Washington, DC 20004
Tel: (202)627-5984
Fax: (202)637-5940
Registered: LDA
EMail: msignori@ebay.com

Employers
eBay Inc. (Policy Analyst)

SIKORA, Clifford S.

401 Ninth St. NW
Suite 1000
Washington, DC 20004
Tel: (202)274-2966
Fax: (202)274-2994
Registered: LDA
Former Professional Minority Staff Member, Senate Energy and Natural Resources Committee and former employee of the Federal Energy Regulatory Commission.

Employers
Troutman Sanders LLP (Partner)

Clients Represented

On Behalf of Troutman Sanders LLP
Longhorn Pipeline
Minnesota Power
Otter Tail Power Co.
Southern Co.
Wisconsin Energy Corp.

SIKORSKI, Hon. Gerald E.

2099 Pennsylvania Ave. NW
Suite 100
Washington, DC 20006
Tel: (202)828-5007
Fax: (202)955-5564
Registered: LDA
EMail: gsikorsk@hklaw.com
Member, U.S. House of Representatives (D-MN), 1983-93.

Employers
Holland & Knight LLP (Partner)

Clients Represented

On Behalf of Holland & Knight LLP
Allina Health Systems
Bassford, Lockhart, Truesdell & Briggs, P.A.
Bridgestone/Firestone, Inc.
Capitol Broadcasting Co.
Cheyenne and Arapahoe Tribes of Oklahoma
General Mills
Hubbard Broadcasting, Inc.
Mille Lacs Band of Ojibwe Indians
Nassau County Health Care Corp.
Red Lake Band of Chippewa Indians
Save America's Forests, Inc.
Slim Fast Foods Co.
Spirit Airlines
Unisys Corp.
United Airlines
West Group

SILBERG, Jay E.

2300 N St. NW
Washington, DC 20037-1128
Tel: (202)663-8000
Fax: (202)663-8007
EMail: jay.silberg@shawpittman.com
Attorney, Office of The General Counsel, Atomic Energy Commission, 1966-69.

Employers
Shaw Pittman (Partner)

Clients Represented

On Behalf of Shaw Pittman
Centerior Energy Corp.
Toledo Edison Co.
Wolf Creek Nuclear Operating Corp.

SILBERGELD, Mark

1666 Connecticut Ave. NW
Suite 310
Washington, DC 20009
Tel: (202)462-6262
Fax: (202)265-9548
Registered: LDA
EMail: silbma@consumer.org

Employers
Consumers Union of the United States (Co-Director, Washington Office)

SILBERMAN, Karen

8201 Greensboro Dr.
Suite 300
McLean, VA 22102
EMail: ksilberman@amg-inc.com
Tel: (703)610-9000
Fax: (703)610-9005

Employers
Ass'n Management Group

Clients Represented

On Behalf of Ass'n Management Group
Consulting Engineers Council of Metropolitan Washington

SILBEY, Franklin R.

9430 Sunnyfield Ct.
Potomac, MD 20854
Tel: (202)639-4494
Fax: (202)639-4495
Registered: LDA

Employers
Self-employed as an independent consultant.

Clients Represented

As an independent consultant
Citigroup

SILCOX, Clark

1300 N. 17th St.
Suite 1847
Rosslyn, VA 22209
EMail: cla_silcox@nema.org
Tel: (703)841-3280
Fax: (703)841-3380

Employers
Nat'l Electrical Manufacturers Ass'n (Legal Counsel)

SILER, Duane A.

2550 M St. NW
Washington, DC 20037-1350
EMail: dsiler@pattonboggs.com
Tel: (202)457-6000
Fax: (202)457-6315

Employers
Patton Boggs, LLP (Partner)

SILER, Russell O.

122 C St. NW
Suite 125
Washington, DC 20001
EMail: russ.siler@ecunet.org
Tel: (202)783-7507
Fax: (202)783-7502

Employers
Lutheran Office for Governmental Affairs/Evangelical Lutheran Church in America (Director)

SILLS, Hilary

1700 K St. NW
Suite 1200
Washington, DC 20006
Tel: (202)857-0103
Fax: (202)857-0209
Registered: LDA

Employers
Sills Associates (President)

Clients Represented

On behalf of Sills Associates
Jacksonville Electric Authority
Municipal Electric Authority of Georgia
Psychemedics Corp.

SILVER, Bruce S.

1201 15th St. NW
Washington, DC 20005-2800
Tel: (202)822-0274
Fax: (202)861-2177

Employers
Nat'l Housing Endowment (President and Chief Exec. Officer)

SILVER, Howard J.

1522 K St. NW
Suite 836
Washington, DC 20005
Tel: (202)842-3525
Fax: (202)842-2788
Registered: LDA
EMail: silverhj@erols.com

Employers
Consortium of Social Science Ass'ns (Exec. Director)

SILVER, Jane

1828 L St. NW
Suite 802
Washington, DC 20036
Tel: (202)331-8600
Fax: (202)331-8606
Registered: LDA

Employers
American Foundation for AIDS Research (Director, Public Policy)

SILVER, Larry

818 Connecticut Ave. NW
Suite 900
Washington, DC 20006
Tel: (202)728-9860
Fax: (202)728-9897

Employers
American College of Nurse-Midwives (Policy Analyst)

SILVER, Martha K.

21 Dupont Circle NW
Suite 700
Washington, DC 20036
EMail: mks@opastco.org
Tel: (202)659-5990
Fax: (202)659-4619

Employers
Organization for the Promotion and Advancement of Small Telecommunications Cos. (Director, Public Relations)

SILVER, Steven W.

2300 Clarendon Blvd.
Suite 1010
Arlington, VA 22201
Tel: (703)527-4414
Fax: (703)527-0421
Registered: LDA

Employers
Robertson, Monagle & Eastaugh (Director)

Clients Represented

On Behalf of Robertson, Monagle & Eastaugh

Alaska Forest Ass'n
Alaska Pulp Corp.
Aleutians East Borough
Coalition Against Unfair U.S. Postal Service Competition
Continental Airlines Inc.
Craig, Alaska, City of
Echo Bay Mining
Federal Administrative Law Judges Conference
Fort James Corp.
Four Dam Pool
Greens Creek Mining Co.
Ketchikan Gateway Borough
Ketchikan Public Utilities
Kotzebue, Alaska, City of
MailBoxes Etc.
Northwest Airlines, Inc.
Ounalashka Corp.
Preston Gates Ellis & Rouvelas Meeds LLP
Seward, Alaska, City of
Southeast Conference
Temsco Helicopter, Inc.
Verner, Liipfert, Bernhard, McPherson and Hand, Chartered
Wasilla, Alaska, City of

SILVERBERG, Jason

777 N. Capitol St. NE
Suite 305
Washington, DC 20002
Tel: (202)216-9060
Fax: (202)216-9061

Employers

Nat'l Jewish Democratic Council (Political Director)

SILVERBERG, Kenneth H.

401 Ninth St. NW
Suite 900
Washington, DC 20004
Tel: (202)585-8000
Fax: (202)585-8080
Registered: LDA

Employers

Nixon Peabody LLP (Partner)

SILVERGLADE, Bruce A.

1875 Connecticut Ave. NW
Suite 300
Washington, DC 20009
Tel: (202)332-9110
Fax: (202)265-4954
Registered: LDA

Employers

Center for Science in the Public Interest (Director, Legal Affairs)

SILVERMAN, Arthur H.

412 First St. SE
Suite 100
Washington, DC 20003
Tel: (202)484-4884
Fax: (202)484-0109
Registered: LDA
EMail: asilverman@dutkogroup.com

Employers

The Dutko Group, Inc. (Senior Managing Partner and General Counsel)

Clients Represented

On Behalf of The Dutko Group, Inc.

Accenture
Biotech Research and Development Center
Distilled Spirits Council of the United States, Inc.
Michigan Biotechnology Institute
Nat'l Aviary in Pittsburgh
Sandy City, Utah, City of
Todhunter Internat'l, Inc.
UPMC Health System
The Washington Opera
Western Governors Ass'n
Western Governors University

SILVERMAN, Donald J.

1800 M St. NW
Washington, DC 20036
Tel: (202)467-7502
Fax: (202)467-7176

Employers

Morgan, Lewis & Bockius LLP (Partner)

SILVERMAN, Ed

1101 30th St. NW
Suite 500
Washington, DC 20007
Tel: (202)625-4880
Fax: (202)625-4881

Employers

Greenwich Capital Markets, Inc. (Senior V. President)

SILVERMAN, Marcia

1901 L St. NW
Suite 300
Washington, DC 20036
Tel: (202)466-7590
Fax: (202)775-8169
EMail: marcia.silverman@dc.ogilvypr.com

Employers

Ogilvy Public Relations Worldwide (President of the Americas)

SILVERMAN, Mark J.

1330 Connecticut Ave. NW
Washington, DC 20036-1795
Tel: (202)429-6450
Fax: (202)429-3902
Registered: LDA
EMail: msilverm@steptoe.com
Attorney/Advisor to Judge Samuel B. Sterrett, U.S. Tax Court, 1971-73.

Employers

Steptoe & Johnson LLP (Partner)

Clients Represented

On Behalf of Steptoe & Johnson LLP

The Hillman Co.
United Asset Management Corp.

SILVERMAN, Richard S.

555 13th St. NW
Washington, DC 20004-1109
Tel: (202)637-5881
Fax: (202)637-5910
Registered: LDA
EMail: rssilverman@hhlaw.com
Associate Chief Counsel for Enforcement, Food and Drug Administration, 1970-75.

Employers

Hogan & Hartson L.L.P. (Partner)

Clients Represented

On Behalf of Hogan & Hartson L.L.P.

Grocery Manufacturers of America
Nestle USA, Inc.

SILVERMAN, Stephanie E.

1501 M St. NW
Suite 700
Washington, DC 20005-1702
Tel: (202)463-4300
Fax: (202)463-4394
Registered: LDA
EMail: ssilverman@manatt.com

Employers

Manatt, Phelps & Phillips, LLP (Senior Advisor)
S-Corporation Ass'n (President and Chief Exec. Officer)

Clients Represented

On Behalf of Manatt, Phelps & Phillips, LLP

Asociacion Columbiana de Exportadores de Flores (ASOCOLFLORES)
BellSouth Corp.
CEMEX Central, S.A. de C.V.
Employee-Owned S Corporations of America
S-Corporation Ass'n

SILVERMAN, William

607 14th St. NW
Washington, DC 20005
Tel: (202)434-0700
Fax: (202)912-6000
EMail: silvermw@rw.com

Employers

Rogers & Wells (Partner)

Clients Represented

On Behalf of Rogers & Wells

Canadian Pulp and Paper Ass'n, Newsprint Section of
Dofasco, Inc.

SILVERS, Curt

888 16th St. NW
Washington, DC 20006
Tel: (202)835-8177
Fax: (202)835-8161
Registered: LDA, FARA
Served with the Office of Senator Thompson, Senate Governmental Affairs Committee, Senate Foreign Relations Committee.

Employers

Bannerman and Associates, Inc.

Clients Represented

On Behalf of Bannerman and Associates, Inc.

Egypt, Government of the Arab Republic of
El Salvador, Embassy of the Republic of
Internat'l College
Lebanese American University
Palestinian Authority

SILVERSTEIN, Leonard L.

1776 K St. NW
Suite 700
Washington, DC 20006
Tel: (202)452-7900
Fax: (202)452-7989
Registered: LDA
EMail: jll@silvmul.com
Special Tax Counsel, Small Business Administration, 1958-59. Member, Legal Advisory Staff (1952-54) and Attorney, Office of Chief Counsel, Internal Revenue Service (1951-52), Department of the Treasury.

Employers

Silverstein and Mullens, P.L.L.C. (Member)

SILVERTHORNE, Scott

2980 Fairview Park Dr.
Suite 1400
Falls Church, VA 22042
Tel: (703)289-7800
Fax: (703)205-1785
Registered: LDA

Employers

Capital One Financial Corp. (Director, Government Relations)

SIMERLING, Jeffrey

1301 Pennsylvania Ave. NW
Suite 702
Washington, DC 20004
Tel: (202)393-2427
Fax: (202)393-2400
Registered: LDA

Employers

Council of the Great City Schools (Director, Legislation)

SIMES, Dimitri K.

1615 L St. NW
Suite 1250
Washington, DC 20036
Tel: (202)887-1000
Fax: (202)887-5222

Employers

Nixon Center, The (President)

SIMI, Shelly Snyder

1400 K St. NW
Suite 801
Washington, DC 20005-2485
Tel: (202)393-1500
Fax: (202)842-4063

Employers

General Aviation Manufacturers Ass'n (V. President, Communications)

SIMMONS, Audrea

1450 G St. NW
Suite 210
Washington, DC 20005
Tel: (202)383-0090
Fax: (202)383-0093
Registered: LDA

Employers

Internat'l Capital Strategies (Government Relations)

SIMMONS, Charles

700 13th St. NW
Suite 800
Washington, DC 20005
Tel: (202)508-5800
Fax: (202)508-5858

Employers

Kilpatrick Stockton LLP (Partner)

Clients Represented

On Behalf of Kilpatrick Stockton LLP

Interface
Zirconium Environmental Committee (ZEC)

SIMMONS, M.D., Henry E.

1200 G St. NW
Suite 750
Washington, DC 20005
Tel: (202)638-7151
Fax: (202)638-7166

Employers

Nat'l Coalition on Health Care (President)

SIMMONS, Kyle

1133 Connecticut Ave. NW
Fifth Floor
Washington, DC 20036
Tel: (202)457-1110
Fax: (202)457-1130

Employers
Quinn Gillespie & Associates (Associate)

SIMMONS, Pope M.

12300 Twinbrook Pkwy.
Suite 320
Rockville, MD 20852
Tel: (301)984-6200
Registered: LDA

Employers
Nat'l Council for Community Behavioral Healthcare (V. President, Government Relations)

SIMMONS, Ralph A.

1001 G St. NW
Suite 500 West
Washington, DC 20001
EMail: simmons@khlaw.com
Tel: (202)434-4100
Fax: (202)434-4646

Employers
Keller and Heckman LLP (Partner)

Clients Represented
On Behalf of Keller and Heckman LLP
Produce Marketing Ass'n

SIMMONS, Rebecca J.

1701 Pennsylvania Ave. NW
Suite 800
Washington, DC 20006
Tel: (202)956-7500
Fax: (202)293-6330
Registered: LDA

Employers
Sullivan & Cromwell (Partner)

Clients Represented
On Behalf of Sullivan & Cromwell
The Group of 20

SIMMONS, Samuel J.

1424 K St. NW
Suite 500
Washington, DC 20005-2407
EMail: simmons@ncba-aged.org
Tel: (202)637-8400
Fax: (202)347-0895

Employers
Nat'l Caucus and Center on Black Aged (President)

SIMMONS, William

412 First St. SE
Suite 100
Washington, DC 20003
EMail: wsimmons@dutkogroup.com
Tel: (202)484-4884
Fax: (202)484-0109
Registered: LDA

Former Staff Director, Subcommittee on Forests and Forest Health, House Committee on Resources. Former Professional Staff Member, Subcommittee on National Parks, Forests and Lands, House Committee on Resources. Former Legislative Aide to Rep. Jim Hansen (R-UT).

Employers
The Dutko Group, Inc. (Senior V. President)

Clients Represented
On Behalf of The Dutko Group, Inc.
Accenture
Biotech Research and Development Center
Distilled Spirits Council of the United States, Inc.
Michigan Biotechnology Institute
Nat'l Aviary in Pittsburgh
Sandy City, Utah, City of
Todhunter Internat'l, Inc.
UPMC Health System
The Washington Opera
Western Governors Ass'n
Western Governors University

SIMMS, Kristine D.

1776 I St. NW
Suite 275
Washington, DC 20006
Tel: (202)530-7300
Fax: (202)530-7350
Registered: LDA

Employers
Entergy Services, Inc. (Director, Federal Government Affairs)

SIMMS, Margaret

1090 Vermont Ave. NW
Suite 1100
Washington, DC 20005-4961
Tel: (202)789-3500
Fax: (202)789-6390

Employers
Joint Center for Political and Economic Studies (V. President, Research)

SIMON, Barry S.

725 12th St. NW
Washington, DC 20005
Tel: (202)434-5000
Fax: (202)434-5029

Law Clerk to Justice Thurgood Marshall, U.S. Supreme Court, 1975-76, and to Judge Edward Weinfeld, U.S. District Court for the Southern District of New York, 1974-75.

Employers
Williams & Connolly (Partner)

Clients Represented
On Behalf of Williams & Connolly
Archer Daniels Midland Co.

SIMON, Carrie A.

607 14th St. NW
Washington, DC 20005
EMail: simonc@rw.com
Tel: (202)434-0700
Fax: (202)912-6000
Registered: LDA

Employers
Rogers & Wells (Counsel)

SIMON, David L.

1000 Connecticut Ave. NW
Suite 412
Washington, DC 20006
EMail: DLSimon@dlsimon.com
Tel: (202)481-9000
Fax: (202)481-9010

Employers
Law Offices of David L. Simon

Clients Represented
On Behalf of Law Offices of David L. Simon
Chang Mien Industry Co., Ltd.
Eregli Demir ve Celik Fab.
Habas Group
Industrie Alimentare Molisane
Pastavilla Makarnacilik A.S.
Pastificio Antonio Pallante
Pastificio Pagani
Turkey, Government of the Republic of
The Yucel Group

SIMON, Donald

1250 I St. NW
Suite 1000
Washington, DC 20005
Tel: (202)682-0240
Fax: (202)682-0249

Employers
Sonosky, Chambers, Sachse & Endreson (Partner)

Clients Represented
On Behalf of Sonosky, Chambers, Sachse & Endreson
Common Cause

SIMON, Ethan Z.

4330 East-West Hwy.
Suite 1100
Bethesda, MD 20814
Tel: (301)718-9500
Fax: (301)718-4290
Registered: LDA

Employers
Radius, The Global Travel Co. (V. President, Corporate Communications)

SIMON, Gregory C.

2100 Pennsylvania Ave. NW
Suite 535
Washington, DC 20037
Tel: (202)822-1700
Fax: (202)822-1919
Registered: LDA

Chief Domestic Policy Advisor to the Vice President, Office of the Vice President, The White House, 1993-96. Legislative Director to Senator Al Gore (D-TN), 1991-93. Staff Director and Counsel, Subcommittee on Investigations and Oversight, House Committee on Science, Space and Technology, 1985-92.

Employers
Simon Strategies/Mindbeam (Chief Exec. Officer)

Clients Represented
On Behalf of Simon Strategies/Mindbeam
AirCell, Inc.
Catholic Television Network
Metricom, Inc.
Motorola, Inc.
openNET Coalition
Time Domain Corp.
Traffic.com
USEC, Inc.

SIMON, Heather

700 13th St. NW
Suite 700
Washington, DC 20005-3960
Tel: (202)508-6304
Fax: (202)508-6305

Employers
Emerson (Legislative Assistant)

SIMON, Jonathon D.

1050 Thomas Jefferson St. NW
Seventh Floor
Washington, DC 20007
EMail: jds@vnf.com
Tel: (202)298-1800
Fax: (202)338-2416
Registered: LDA

Legal Intern, Office of the Solicitor, Division of Land and Water Resources, Department of the Interior, 1997. Summer Legal Intern, General Litigation Section, Environment and Natural Resources Division, Department of Justice, 1996. Special Project Assistant/Legislative Assistant (1995) Special Research Assistant (1994), Legislative Correspondent (1993-94) to Senator Frank R. Lautenberg (D-NJ).

Employers
Van Ness Feldman, P.C. (Associate)

Clients Represented
On Behalf of Van Ness Feldman, P.C.
Petro Star, Inc.

SIMON, Julie

1401 New York Ave. NW
11th Floor
Washington, DC 20005
EMail: jsimon@epsa.org
Tel: (202)628-8200
Fax: (202)628-8260
Registered: LDA

Employers
Electric Power Supply Ass'n (V. President, Policy)

SIMON, Kenneth M.

2101 L St. NW
Washington, DC 20037-1526
EMail: simonk@dsmo.com
Tel: (202)785-9700
Fax: (202)887-0689

Employers
Dickstein Shapiro Morin & Oshinsky LLP (Partner)

Clients Represented
On Behalf of Dickstein Shapiro Morin & Oshinsky LLP
PG&E Generating Co.

SIMON, Leonard S.

1660 L St. NW
Suite 1050
Washington, DC 20036
EMail: SimonCoDC@aol.com
Tel: (202)659-2229
Fax: (202)659-5234
Registered: LDA

Employers
Simon and Co., Inc. (President)

Clients Represented
On Behalf of Simon and Co., Inc.
AC Transit
Alameda Corridor Transportation Authority
American Water Works Ass'n
Carmel, Indiana, City of
Citrus Heights, California, City of
Easter Seals
Fresno, California, City of
Madison, Wisconsin, City of
Newark, California, City of
Oakley, California, City of
Pierce Transit
Portland, Oregon, City of
Sacramento Housing and Redeveloping Agency
Salt Lake City, Utah, City of
San Leandro, California, City of
Tacoma, Washington, City of
Tacoma, Washington, Public Utilities Department of

SIMON, Marsha

409 12th St. SW
P.O. Box 96920
Washington, DC 20090-6920
EMail: msimon@acog.org
Tel: (202)863-2511
Fax: (202)488-3985
Registered: LDA

Employers
American College of Obstetricians and Gynecologists (Director, Government Relations and Outreach)

SIMON, Neil A.

1341 G St. NW
Suite 1000
Washington, DC 20005

Tel: (202)626-8562
Fax: (202)626-8593
Registered: LDA

Employers
Nat'l Franchise Council (Exec. Director)

SIMON, Samuel A.

919 18th St. NW
Tenth Floor
Washington, DC 20006

Tel: (202)263-2900
Fax: (202)263-2960

Employers
Issue Dynamics Inc. (President)

SIMON, Susan C.

1700 K St. NW
Suite 1200
Washington, DC 20006
EMail: ssimon@cig1.com

Tel: (202)857-0001
Fax: (202)857-0209

Employers
Capital Insights Group (V. President)

SIMONE, Frank

1120 20th St. NW
Suite 1000
Washington, DC 20036
EMail: fsimone@att.com

Tel: (202)457-2321
Fax: (202)457-2571

Employers
AT&T (Director, Federal Government Affairs)

SIMONETTI, Arthur J.

1001 Pennsylvania Ave. NW
Suite 700 South
Washington, DC 20004

Tel: (202)662-2671
Fax: (202)662-2674
Registered: LDA

Employers
Honeywell Internat'l, Inc. (Manager, Trade Legislation and Regulation)

SIMONS, Dee

1200 G St. NW
Suite 400
Washington, DC 20005

Tel: (202)783-8700
Fax: (202)783-8750

Employers
AdvaMed (Associate V. President, Payment and Policy)

SIMONSON, Kristin

12500 Fair Lakes Circle
Suite 375
Fairfax, VA 22033

Tel: (703)502-1550
Fax: (703)502-7852
Registered: LDA

Employers
American Soc. for Therapeutic Radiology and Oncology (Coordinator, Government Relations)

SIMPKINS, Eric L.

1800 M St. NW
Suite 300
Washington, DC 20036
EMail: ercc@erols.com

Tel: (202)296-8790
Fax: (202)296-8681

Employers
Fuel Cell Energy, Inc. (V. President, Business Development)

SIMPKINS, Talmage E.

1150 17th St. NW
Suite 700
Washington, DC 20036

Tel: (202)955-5662
Fax: (202)872-0912
Registered: LDA

Employers
AFL-CIO Maritime Committee (Exec. Director)
Labor Management Maritime Committee, Inc. (Exec. V. President)

SIMPSON, Hon. Alan K.

227 Massachusetts Ave. NE
Suite One
Washington, DC 20002

Tel: (202)544-7600
Fax: (202)544-6770

Member, U.S. Senate (R-WY), 1979-97, Republican Whip, 1985-95.

Employers
Tongour Simpson Holsclaw Green (Partner)

Clients Represented
On Behalf of Tongour Simpson Holsclaw Green
Americans for Sensible Estate Tax Solutions (ASSETS)

SIMPSON, C. Kyle

1225 I St. NW
Suite 600
Washington, DC 20005
EMail: kylesimpson@morganmeguire.com

Tel: (202)661-6193
Fax: (202)661-6182
Registered: LDA

Senior Policy Advisor, (1997-98) and Assistant Deputy Secretary (1995-97), Department of Energy.

Employers
Morgan Meguire, LLC (President and Chief Exec. Officer)

Clients Represented
On Behalf of Morgan Meguire, LLC
Adroit Systems Inc.
Air-Conditioning and Refrigeration Institute
Arctic Resources Co.
Baker Electromotive, Inc.
BellSouth Corp.
Burke Venture Capital
Colorado River Energy Distributors Ass'n
Energy Affairs Administration
Energy Northwest
Florida Municipal Power Agency
Goodman Manufacturing Co., L.P.
GovWorks.com
Longhorn Pipeline
LVS Power Ltd.
Madison Gas & Electric Co.
Manatee, Florida, County of
Monsanto Co.
Northern California Power Agency
Northwest Public Power Ass'n
Nuevo Energy
Puerto Rico Electric Power Authority
Redding, California, City of
Sacramento Municipal Utility District
Seven Seas Petroleum USA Inc.
Shell Oil Co.
Southern California Public Power Authority
Springfield, Missouri, City Utilities of
Tennessee Valley Public Power Ass'n
Texas A&M Engineering Experiment Station
Transmission Access Policy Study Group
Truckee Donner Electric Power Utility District
Washington Public Utility Districts Ass'n

SIMPSON, Cal

325 Seventh St. NW
Washington, DC 20004

Tel: (202)638-1100
Fax: (202)626-2689
Registered: LDA

Employers
American Hospital Ass'n (Regional Exec.)

SIMPSON, Jr., Charles J.

888 17th St. NW
Suite 600
Washington, DC 20006-3959
EMail: cjsimpson@zsrlaw.com

Tel: (202)298-8660
Fax: (202)342-0683

Employers
Zuckert, Scoutt and Rasenberger, L.L.P. (Partner)

Clients Represented
On Behalf of Zuckert, Scoutt and Rasenberger, L.L.P.
All Nippon Airways Co.
LADECO
Lan Chile
Malaysian Airline System
Nippon Cargo Airlines
Royal Brunei Airways
Turkish Airlines

SIMPSON, MaryAnn

475 L'Enfant Plaza SW
MS: 10836
Washington, DC 20260

Tel: (202)268-3741

Employers
United States Postal Service (Government Relations Manager)

SIMPSON, Thomas D.

700 N. Fairfax St.
Suite 601
Alexandria, VA 22314
EMail: simpson@rpi.org

Tel: (703)836-2332
Fax: (703)548-0058
Registered: LDA

Employers
Railway Progress Institute (V. President)

SIMPSON, William G.

1156 15th St. NW
Suite 315
Washington, DC 20005
EMail: mcaden@erols.com

Tel: (202)452-1003
Fax: (202)452-1311
Registered: LDA

Former aide to Senator James Eastland (D-MS) and Deputy Assistant to the President, The White House, during the Carter administration.

Employers
Bill Simpson & Associates (President)

Clients Represented
On Behalf of Bill Simpson & Associates
ChemFirst Inc.
FedEx Corp.
Mississippi Chemical Corp.
Stephens Group, Inc.

SIMS, Edgar H.

701 Pennsylvania Ave. NW
Suite 600
Washington, DC 20004
EMail: esims@lanlaw.com

Tel: (202)624-1200
Fax: (202)624-1298
Registered: LDA

Employers
Long, Aldridge & Norman, LLP (Partner)

Clients Represented
On Behalf of Long, Aldridge & Norman, LLP
BellSouth Corp.
Monsanto Co.

SIMS, James T.

1022 29th St. NW
Washington, DC 20007
EMail: jsims@wincapitol.com

Tel: (202)333-3232
Fax: (202)333-5001
Registered: LDA

Employers
WinCapitol, Inc. (President)

Clients Represented
On Behalf of WinCapitol, Inc.
AFL-CIO (Union Label and Service Trades Department)
American Green Network
Danaher Corp.

SIMS, Joe

51 Louisiana Ave. NW
Washington, DC 20001
EMail: jsims@jonesday.com

Tel: (202)879-3939
Fax: (202)626-1700

Deputy Assistant Attorney General for Regulated Industries and Foreign Commerce (1977-78), Deputy Assistant Attorney General for Policy Planning and Legislation (1975-77), Special Assistant to the Assistant Attorney General (1973-75), and Trial Attorney (1970-73), Antitrust Division, Department of Justice.

Employers
Jones, Day, Reavis & Pogue (Partner)

Clients Represented
On Behalf of Jones, Day, Reavis & Pogue
AOL Time Warner

SIMS, Robert B.

1145 17th St. NW
Washington, DC 20036

Tel: (202)857-7000
Fax: (202)775-6141

Employers
Nat'l Geographic Soc. (Exec. V. President and President, Magazine Group)

SIMS, Roberta

1100 H St. NW
Washington, DC 20080

Tel: (202)624-6266
Fax: (202)624-6699

Employers
Washington Gas (V. President, Corporate Relations)

SIMS, Stephen F.

400 N. Capitol St. NW
Suite 585
Washington, DC 20001

Tel: (202)783-5300
Fax: (202)393-5218
Registered: LDA

Deputy Staff Director, Subcommittee on Oversight and Investigations, House Energy and Commerce Committee, 1976-92.

Employers
Stephen F. Sims and Associates

Clients Represented
On Behalf of Stephen F. Sims and Associates
Barr Laboratories
Beerman, Swerdlove, Woloshin, Barezky, Becken, Genin & London
Polytec Group
Victory Wholesale Grocers Inc.

SINCERE, Richard E.

1341 Connecticut Ave. NW
Third Floor
Washington, DC 20036
Tel: (202)862-3900
Fax: (202)862-5500

Employers
Scribe Consulting & Communications (Senior Consultant)

SINCLAIR, Van H.

1050 Connecticut Ave. NW
Washington, DC 20036-5339
Tel: (202)857-6000
Fax: (202)857-6395

Employers
Arent Fox Kintner Plotkin & Kahn, PLLC (Member)

SINCLAIR-SMITH, Susan

1825 K St. NW
Suite 1100
Washington, DC 20006
Tel: (202)785-2908
Fax: (202)835-8931
Registered: LDA

Employers
Local Initiatives Support Corp.

SINCLAIRE, William T.

1615 H St. NW
Washington, DC 20062-2000
Tel: (202)463-5620
Fax: (202)463-3174
Registered: LDA

Employers
Chamber of Commerce of the U.S.A. (Director, Tax Policy)

SINDER, Scott A.

3050 K St. NW
Washington, DC 20007
Tel: (202)342-8400
Fax: (202)342-8451
Registered: LDA
EMail: ssinder@colliershannon.com

Employers
Collier Shannon Scott, PLLC (Member)

Clients Represented
On Behalf of Collier Shannon Scott, PLLC
American Land Title Ass'n
The Council of Insurance Agents & Brokers
Fannie Mae
Independent Insurance Agents of America, Inc.
Nat'l Ass'n of Insurance and Financial Advisors
Nat'l Ass'n of Professional Insurance Agents
World Floor Covering Ass'n

SINDERBRAND, Paul J.

2300 N St. NW
Suite 700
Washington, DC 20037-1128
EMail: psinderbrand@wbklaw.com
Tel: (202)783-4141
Fax: (202)783-5851

Employers
Wilkinson, Barker and Knauer, LLP (Partner)

Clients Represented
On Behalf of Wilkinson, Barker and Knauer, LLP
Wireless Communications Ass'n

SINDT, Robert H.

1850 M St. NW
Suite 400
Washington, DC 20036
Tel: (202)466-4500
Fax: (202)775-5872
Registered: LDA

Employers
Self-employed as an independent consultant.

Clients Represented
As an independent consultant
Bethel Grain Co., LLC

SINEL, Norman M.

555 12th St. NW
Washington, DC 20004-1206
EMail: Norman_Sinel@aporter.com
Tel: (202)942-5000
Fax: (202)942-5999
Senior V. President, Corporate Management and General Counsel (1976-79), V. President and General Counsel (1973-76), and General Counsel (1971-73), Public Broadcasting Service. Law Clerk, U.S. District Court, Northern District of California, 1966-67.

Employers
Arnold & Porter (Partner)

Clients Represented
On Behalf of Arnold & Porter
New York City Board of Estimate

SINGER, Bonnie

923 15th St. NW
Washington, DC 20005
Tel: (202)628-0752
Fax: (202)737-7565
Registered: LDA

Employers
Washington Alliance Group, Inc. (President)

Clients Represented
On Behalf of Washington Alliance Group, Inc.
Central Michigan University
Coachella Valley Economic Partnership
College of the Desert
Columbia University/Institute for Learning Technologies
Institute of Simulation and Training
Mort Community College
New Orleans Environmental Systems Foundation
Palm Desert, California, City of
The Readnet Foundation
Riverside County Schools
TI Group Inc.
University of California at Riverside

SINGER, Carol S.

1612 K St. NW
Suite 1102
Washington, DC 20006
Tel: (202)986-6616
Fax: (202)530-4408

Employers
Nat'l Ass'n for Environmental Management (Exec. Director)

SINGER, Dale

4701 Randolph Rd.
Suite 102
Rockville, MD 20852
Tel: (301)468-3515
Fax: (301)468-3511

Employers
Renal Physicians Ass'n (Exec. Director)

SINGER, Linda R.

1666 Connecticut Ave. NW
Suite 500
Washington, DC 20009
Tel: (202)265-9572
Fax: (202)328-9162

Employers
Center for Dispute Settlement (President)

SINGER, Richard M.

1500 K St.
Suite 1100
Washington, DC 20005
EMail: richard_singer@dbr.com
Tel: (202)842-8800
Fax: (202)842-8465
Trial Attorney, Federal Communications Commission, 1971-74.

Employers
Drinker Biddle & Reath LLP (Partner)

SINGER, Ronald M.

1299 Pennsylvania Ave. NW
Suite 1100 West
Washington, DC 20004-2407
Tel: (202)637-4000
Fax: (202)637-4412

Employers
General Electric Co. (Manager, International Programs)

SINGER, Ms. Terry E.

1615 M St. NW
Suite 800
Washington, DC 20036-3203
EMail: tes@dwgp.com
Tel: (202)467-6370
Fax: (202)467-6379
Registered: LDA

Employers
Duncan, Weinberg, Genzer & Pembroke, P.C. (Of Counsel)
Nat'l Ass'n of Energy Service Companies (Exec. Director)

SINGER, William S.

655 15th St. NW
Suite 1200
Washington, DC 20005
Tel: (202)879-5000
Fax: (202)879-5200
Registered: LDA

Employers
Kirkland & Ellis (Partner)

Clients Represented
On Behalf of Kirkland & Ellis
Sara Lee Corp.

SINGERLING, Chris

111 C St. SE
Lower Unit
Washington, DC 20003
Tel: (202)546-6335
Fax: (202)546-6401

Employers
The Freedom Project (Manager)

SINGERLING, CCM, CEC, James B.

1733 King St.
Alexandria, VA 22314
EMail: jims@cmaa.org
Tel: (703)739-9500
Fax: (703)739-0124

Employers
Club Managers Ass'n of America (Exec. V. President and Chief Exec. Officer)

SINGERMAN, Fredric S.

815 Connecticut Ave. NW
Suite 500
Washington, DC 20006-4004
Tel: (202)463-2400
Fax: (202)828-5393

Employers
Seyfarth, Shaw, Fairweather & Geraldson (Partner)

Clients Represented
On Behalf of Seyfarth, Shaw, Fairweather & Geraldson
Information Technology Ass'n of America (ITAA)

SINGISER, Dana E.

1333 New Hampshire Ave. NW
Suite 400
Washington, DC 20036
EMail: dsingiser@akingump.com
Tel: (202)887-4000
Fax: (202)887-4288
Registered: LDA
Special Assistant, Office of Presidential Personnel, The White House, 1993-95. Former Law Clerk, Senate Committee on the Judiciary.

Employers
Akin, Gump, Strauss, Hauer & Feld, L.L.P.

Clients Represented
On Behalf of Akin, Gump, Strauss, Hauer & Feld, L.L.P.
Alliance for Quality Nursing Home Care

SINGLETON, Roni

1150 17th St. NW
Suite 701
Washington, DC 20036
EMail: roni.singleton@dittus.com
Tel: (202)775-1401
Fax: (202)775-1404

Employers
Dittus Communications (Director)

Clients Represented
On Behalf of Dittus Communications
Ronald Reagan Internat'l Center

SINGLETON, Solveig

1001 Connecticut Ave. NW
Suite 1250
Washington, DC 20036
Tel: (202)331-1010
Fax: (202)331-0640

Employers
Competitive Enterprise Institute (Senior Policy Analyst)

SINGLEY, Beth

11200 Waples Mill Rd.
Suite 150
Fairfax, VA 22030-7407
Tel: (703)691-8100
Fax: (703)691-8106

Employers
Assisted Living Federation of America (Director, Federal Relations)

SINICK, Marshall S.

1201 Pennsylvania Ave. NW
P.O. Box 407
Washington, DC 20044-0407
EMail: msinick@ssd.com
Tel: (202)626-6600
Fax: (202)626-6780
Trial Attorney, Bureau of Operating Rights, Civil Aeronautics Board, 1968-71.

Employers
Squire, Sanders & Dempsey L.L.P. (Partner)

Clients Represented

On Behalf of Squire, Sanders & Dempsey L.L.P.
Air India
Fast Air Carrier

SINICROPI, Pat

1250 I St. NW
Suite 902
Washington, DC 20005
Tel: (202)393-5225
Fax: (202)393-3034

Employers
Robert A. Rapoza Associates (Policy Associate)

SINKEZ, Stephen G.

1560 Wilson Blvd.
Suite 1200
Arlington, VA 22209
Tel: (703)525-4800
Ext: 230
Fax: (703)525-6772
Registered: LDA

Employers
Mitsubishi Motors R&D of America, Inc. (V. President, Regulatory Affairs)

SINOWAY, Linda

919 18th St. NW
Tenth Floor
Washington, DC 20006
Tel: (202)263-2900
Fax: (202)263-2960

Employers
Issue Dynamics Inc. (Senior Consultant)

SIRACUSE, Helen C.

505 Capitol Ct. NE
Suite 200
Washington, DC 20002
EMail: csiracuse@hurtnorton.com
Tel: (202)543-9398
Fax: (202)543-7844
Registered: LDA
Acting Deputy Assistant Secretary of Defense (House Affairs), Department of Defense, 1996-98. Director Congressional and Intergovernmental Affairs, Defense Base Closure and Realignment Commission, 1994-96. Legislative Assistant (Military Affairs) to Senator Sam Nunn (D-GA), 1991-94. Various duties with Senator Nunn, 1987-91.

Employers
Hurt, Norton & Associates (Senior Associate)

Clients Represented

On Behalf of Hurt, Norton & Associates
Pemco Aviation Group, Inc.
Sierra Military Health Services, Inc.

SISCO, John

1600 Pennsylvania Ave. NW
Washington, DC 20500
Tel: (202)456-5066
Fax: (202)456-2256

Employers
Executive Office of the President - The White House (Legislative Correspondent)

SISK, Marcus W.

Two Lafayette Center
1133 21st St. NW, Suite 500
Washington, DC 20036
Tel: (202)293-8815
Fax: (202)293-7994
Registered: LDA
Member, Trial Staff, Civil Rights Division, Department of Justice, 1964-65. Appellate Attorney, National Labor Relations Board, 1965-67. Assistant Attorney General and Legislative Counsel, American Samoa, 1967-69.

Employers
Bastianelli, Brown & Kelley (Consultant)

Clients Represented

On Behalf of Bastianelli, Brown & Kelley
Tosco Corp.

SISKA, Christine

630 I St. NW
Washington, DC 20001-3736
Tel: (202)289-3500
Fax: (202)289-8181

Employers
Nat'l Ass'n of Housing and Redevelopment Officials (Policy Analyst, Housing)

SISSON, Edward

555 12th St. NW
Washington, DC 20004-1206
EMail: Edward_Sisson@aporter.com
Tel: (202)942-5000
Fax: (202)942-5999

Employers
Arnold & Porter (Partner)

SITES, Tim

1150 17th St. NW
Suite 701
Washington, DC 20036
EMail: tim.sites@dittus.com
Tel: (202)775-1401
Fax: (202)775-1404

Employers
Dittus Communications (V. President and Managing Director)

Clients Represented

On Behalf of Dittus Communications
Business Software Alliance
Ronald Reagan Internat'l Center
SurfControl
Surviving Selma
TCS

SITTENFELD, Tiernan

218 D St. SE
Second Floor
Washington, DC 20003
Tel: (202)546-9707
Fax: (202)546-2461
Registered: LDA

Employers
U.S. Public Interest Research Group (Staff Attorney)

SITTNICK, Tammy

888 16th St. NW
Washington, DC 20006
Tel: (202)835-8177
Fax: (202)835-8161
Registered: LDA, FARA

Employers
Bannerman and Associates, Inc. (Staff Assistant)

Clients Represented

On Behalf of Bannerman and Associates, Inc.
Egypt, Government of the Arab Republic of
El Salvador, Embassy of the Republic of
Internat'l College
Lebanese American University

SIVON, James C.

2000 M St. NW
Suite 740
Washington, DC 20036-3313
Tel: (202)463-6040
Fax: (202)785-5209
Registered: LDA
Minority Staff Director (1980-83) and Professional Staff Member (1974-80), House Committee on Banking, Finance and Urban Affairs.

Employers
Barnett & Sivon, P.C. (Partner)

Clients Represented

On Behalf of Barnett & Sivon, P.C.
ABA Insurance Ass'n
Citigroup
Community Financial Services Ass'n
The Financial Services Roundtable

SIX, Robert

2300 Clarendon Blvd.
Suite 610
Arlington, VA 22201-3367
EMail: rsix@golinharris.com
Tel: (703)351-5666
Fax: (703)351-5667
Deputy Chief of Staff (1998-2000), Special Assistant (1997-98) and Junior Legislative Assistant (1995-97) to Senator John D. Rockefeller IV (D-WV).

Employers
Golin/Harris Internat'l (Account Director)

SKAGGS, Hon. David E.

555 13th St. NW
Washington, DC 20004-1109
Tel: (202)637-5600
Fax: (202)637-5910
Member, U.S. House of Representatives (D-CO), 1987-99.

Employers
Hogan & Hartson L.L.P.

SKANCKE, Nancy J.

1500 K St. NW
Suite 330
Washington, DC 20005
EMail: njskancke@grkse
Tel: (202)408-5400
Fax: (202)408-5406
Registered: LDA

Employers
GKRSE (Partner)

Clients Represented

On Behalf of GKRSE
Kootenai Electric Cooperative, Inc.

SKANDERSON, David M.

2001 M St. NW
Fourth Floor
Washington, DC 20036
Tel: (202)533-5660
Fax: (202)533-8580
Registered: LDA

Employers
Barents Group LLC (Manager)

Clients Represented

On Behalf of Barents Group LLC
John T. O'Rourke Law Offices
Verner, Liipfert, Bernhard, McPherson and Hand, Chartered

SKERNOLIS, Edmund J.

601 Pennsylvania Ave. NW
Suite 300
The North Bldg.
Washington, DC 20004
Tel: (202)628-3500
Fax: (202)628-0400
Registered: LDA

Employers
Waste Management, Inc. (Director, Regulatory Affairs)

SKIADOS, Don

535 Herndon Pkwy.
Herndon, VA 22070-4370
Tel: (703)481-4456
Fax: (703)689-4370

Employers
Air Line Pilots Ass'n Internat'l (Director, Communications)

SKIBBIE, USAF (Ret.), Lt. Gen. Lawrence

2111 Wilson Blvd.
Suite 400
Arlington, VA 22201-3061
Tel: (703)522-1820
Fax: (703)522-1885

Employers
Nat'l Defense Industrial Ass'n (President)

SKILLINGTON, G. Lee

1001 Pennsylvania Ave. NW
Suite 600
Washington, DC 20004
Tel: (202)347-0066
Fax: (202)624-7222
Former Attorney, Legislative and International Office, Patent and Trademark Office, Department of Commerce.

Employers
Powell, Goldstein, Frazer & Murphy LLP (Counsel)

SKINNER, Ph.D., John H.

1100 Wayne Ave.
Suite 700
Silver Spring, MD 20907-7219
EMail: jskinner@swana.org
Tel: (301)585-2898
Fax: (301)589-7068

Employers
Solid Waste Ass'n of North America (Exec. Director and Chief Exec. Officer)

SKIPPER, Jr., William H.

2800 Shirlington Rd.
Suite 401
Arlington, VA 22206
EMail: bskipper@asic-dc.com
Tel: (703)824-0300
Registered: LDA

Employers
American Systems Internat'l Corp. (President)

Clients Represented

On Behalf of American Systems Internat'l Corp.

Battelle Memorial Institute
Battelle Memorial Labs
Defence Evaluation and Research Agency
Education Options Inc.
Elbet Forth Worth
FN Herstal, USA
Israel Aircraft Industries, Ltd.
Lockheed Martin Corp.
Logis-Tech, Inc.
Northrop Grumman Corp.
Pennsylvania Nat'l Guard Ass'n
Precision Lift
Production Technology, Inc.
PulseTech Products Corp.
Raytheon Co.
Safety Storage Inc.
SRA Corp.
Vision Systems Internat'l

SKLADANY, Jr., Barney J.

1333 New Hampshire Ave. NW
Suite 400
Washington, DC 20036
Tel: (202)887-4000
Fax: (202)887-4288
Registered: LDA, FARA

Employers

Akin, Gump, Strauss, Hauer & Feld, L.L.P. (Partner)

Clients Represented

On Behalf of Akin, Gump, Strauss, Hauer & Feld, L.L.P.

Albertson's Inc.
American Airlines
American Consulting Engineers Council
American Express Co.
American Family Enterprises
AOL Time Warner
APKINDO
AT&T
Base Ten Systems, Inc.
The Boeing Co.
Bolivia, Government of the Republic of
Bombardier, Inc.
Bridgestone/Firestone, Inc.
Broadwave USA Inc.
CalEnergy Co., Inc.
Citizen's Educational Foundation
Collagen Corp.
Colombia, Government of the Republic of
Commerce Clause Coalition
Corrections Corp. of America
Educational Foundation for Citizenship and Statehood Project
EMC Corp.
Exxon Mobil Corp.
FirstEnergy Co.
Gila River Indian Community
Harris, Texas, Metropolitan Transit Authority of
Human Genome Sciences Inc.
Johnson & Johnson, Inc.
Joint Corporate Committee on Cuban Claims
Liberty Mutual Insurance Group
Memorial Sloan-Kettering Cancer Center
Mortgage Insurance Companies of America
Motion Picture Ass'n of America
Nat'l Ass'n of Chain Drug Stores
New York Public Library
New York State Health Facilities Ass'n
NiSource Inc.
Northpoint Technology, Ltd.
OMNIPLEX World Services Corp.
PerkinElmer Detection Systems
PG&E Corp.
Phillips Foods, Inc.
Quad Dimension
Ryder System, Inc.
Serono Laboratories, Inc.
St. Barnabas Healthcare System
Texas Manufactured Housing Ass'n
Tyumen Oil Company
Uniden Corp.
Wartsila Diesel, Inc.
Westar Group, Inc.

SKLADANY, Linda Arey

233 Constitution Ave. NE
Washington, DC 20002
Tel: (202)547-4000
Fax: (202)543-5044
Registered: LDA
EMail: PRDandS@aol.com

Acting Chairman (1989-91) and Commissioner (1989-91), Occupational Safety and Health Review Commission. Special Assistant to the President and Deputy Director, White House Office of Public Liaison, 1985-87. Special Assistant to the Deputy Secretary, Department of Transportation, 1983-84. Special Assistant to the Attorney General, Department of Justice, 1982-83. Special Assistant to the Executive Secretary, Department of Education, 1981-82.

Employers

Parry, Romani, DeConcini & Symms (V. President for Congressional Relations)

Clients Represented

On Behalf of Parry, Romani, DeConcini & Symms

AIDS Healthcare Foundation
Andrx Pharmaceutical Corp.
Armstrong World Industries, Inc.
Asphalt Systems, Inc.
Aventis Pharmaceutical Products
Avondale, Arizona, City of
Bank of New York
Bristol-Myers Squibb Co.
Coalition Against Database Piracy
Composites Fabricators Ass'n
Ferraro, USA
Formosan Ass'n for Public Affairs
GAF Corp.
GlaxoSmithKline
Herbalife Internat'l, Inc.
Hoechst Marion Roussel Deutschland GmbH
Inter-Cal Corp.
Katten Muchin & Zavis
Motion Picture Ass'n of America
Nat'l Air Cargo, Inc.
Nat'l Nutritional Foods Ass'n
Nat'l Retail Federation
Nogales, Arizona, City of
Nu Skin Internat'l Inc.
Owens Corning
Peoria, Arizona, City of
Pfizer, Inc.
Pharmacia Corp.
Pharmanex
Policy Development Group, Inc.
Project to Promote Competition and Innovation in the Digital Age
Research & Development Laboratories
Research Corp. Technology
Rexall Sundown
SBC Communications Inc.
SOL Source Technologies, Inc.
Styrene Information and Research Center
Taxpayers Against Fraud, The False Claims Legal Center
TCOM, L.P.
Unilever United States, Inc.
Utah Natural Products Alliance

SKLAR, Scott

706 N. Ivy St.
Arlington, VA 22201
Tel: (703)522-1195
Fax: (703)841-1634
EMail: solarsklar@aol.com

Former aide to Sen. Jacob K. Javits (R-NY).

Employers

The Stella Group, Ltd. (President)

SKLAR, Stella

706 N. Ivy St.
Arlington, VA 22201
Tel: (703)522-1195
Fax: (703)841-1634
Registered: LDA
EMail: stellasklar@aol.com

Stella, 5 1/2 years old, is registered to represent clients on behalf of her daddy, Scott Sklar.

Employers

The Stella Group, Ltd. (V. President)

Clients Represented

On Behalf of The Stella Group, Ltd.

Solar Energy Industries Ass'n (SEIA)

SKLAROW, Mark H.

3251 Old Lee Hwy
Suite 510
Fairfax, VA 22030-1504
Tel: (703)591-4850
Ext: 12
Fax: (703)591-4860
EMail: msklarow@iecaonline.com

Employers

Independent Educational Consultants Ass'n (Exec. Director)

SKOFF, Laura

1595 Spring Hill Rd.
Suite 330
Vienna, VA 22182
Tel: (703)506-3260
Fax: (703)506-3266

Employers

Ass'n Management Bureau (V. President)

Clients Represented

On Behalf of Ass'n Management Bureau

American Soc. of Women Accountants (ACC)
Soc. of Nat'l Ass'n Publications

SKOL, Michael M.

1133 Connecticut Ave. NW
Suite 650
Washington, DC 20036
Tel: (202)822-2077
Fax: (202)822-2078
Registered: LDA

Principal Deputy Assistant Secretary for Inter-American Affairs (1993-96) and Ambassador to Venezuela (1990-93), Department of State.

Employers

Skol & Associates, Inc. (President)

Clients Represented

On Behalf of Skol & Associates, Inc.

Colombian Banking and Financial Entities Ass'n (ASOBANCARIA)

SKOLFIELD, Melissa T.

2300 Clarendon Blvd.
Suite 610
Arlington, VA 22201-3367
Tel: (703)351-5666
Fax: (703)351-5667
EMail: mskolfield@golinharris.com

Assistant Secretary for Public Affairs (1995-2000) and Deputy Assistant Secretary for Public Affairs for Policy and Strategy (1993-95), Department of Health and Human Services. Press Secretary to Senator Dale L. Bumpers (D-AR), 1987-93. Press Secretary and Legislative Assistant to Rep. Michael A. Andrews (D-TX), 1985-87.

Employers

Golin/Harris Internat'l (V. President and Director, Health Care Practice Group)

SKOPEC, Monica

660 Pennsylvania Ave. SE
Suite 201
Washington, DC 20003
Tel: (202)547-1831
Fax: (202)547-4658
Registered: LDA

Employers

Alpine Group, Inc. (Associate)

Clients Represented

On Behalf of Alpine Group, Inc.

American Cable Ass'n
Medical Imaging Contrast Agent Ass'ns
Seneca Resources Corporation
Toyota Motor North America, U.S.A., Inc.

SKRABUT, Jr., Paul A.

1717 K St. NW
Suite 500
Washington, DC 20006
Tel: (202)466-9000
Fax: (202)466-9009
Registered: LDA

Former Crisis Management Specialist, Federal Emergency Management Agency and former Administrative Assistant and Legislative Director to Senator Harrison A. Williams (D-NJ).

Employers

Palumbo & Cerrell, Inc. (Senior V. President)

Clients Represented

On Behalf of Palumbo & Cerrell, Inc.

American Soc. of Composers, Authors and Publishers
American Trans Air
HT Medical
K Capital Partners
Los Angeles, California, Metropolitan Transit Authority of
Music Educators Nat'l Conference

SKUBEL, Marimichael O.

655 15th St. NW
Suite 1200
Washington, DC 20005
Tel: (202)879-5034
Fax: (202)879-5200
EMail: marimicheal_skubel@dc.kirkland.com

Former Senior Lawyer, Bureau of Competition, Federal Trade Commission.

Employers

Kirkland & Ellis (Partner)

SLABY, Patty

1155 15th St. NW
Suite 1004
Washington, DC 20005
Tel: (202)467-5081
Fax: (202)467-5085

Employers

Nat'l Ass'n of Blind Teachers (President)

SLACKMAN, Joel

1310 G St. NW
12th Floor
Washington, DC 20005
Tel: (202)626-4780
Fax: (202)626-4833
Registered: LDA

Employers
Blue Cross Blue Shield Ass'n (Director, Policy)

SLADE, David

818 Connecticut Ave. NW
Second Floor
Washington, DC 20006
Tel: (202)289-2001
Fax: (202)289-1327

Employers
Strat@Comm (Strategic Communications Counselors) (Senior Account Executive)

SLADE, Jonathan B.

1747 Pennsylvania Ave. NW
Suite 1150
Washington, DC 20006
Tel: (202)296-6222
Fax: (202)296-4507
Registered: LDA
EMail: jslade@mww.com
Legislative Assistant to Rep. Larry Smith (D-FL), 1983-86.

Employers
The MWW Group (Senior V. President)

Clients Represented

On Behalf of The MWW Group
Amerijet Internat'l Inc.
Bacardi-Martini, USA, Inc.
Century Financial Group
Cuban American Nat'l Foundation/Cuban American Foundation
Delaware River Stevedores
Detroit Medical Center
Domino's Pizza
GAF Corp.
Green County Health Care, Inc.
Hadassah Medical Relief Fund
Hadassah, The Women's Zionist Organization of America
Internat'l Distance Learning
Charles Klatskin and Co.
Kmart Corp.
Little Havana Activities and Nutrition Centers
Michigan Bulb
Nat'l Ass'n of Community Health Centers
Nat'l Ass'n of Jai-Alai Frontons, Inc.
New Sea Escape
Perry Tritech Inc.
Puerto Ricans for Civic Action
Puerto Rico Senate
Ross University School of Medicine in Dominica
Synapse
United States Education Finance Corp.

SLADE, Stephen J.

444 N. Capitol St. NW
Washington, DC 20001
Tel: (202)347-1117
Fax: (202)638-4584
Registered: LDA
EMail: sslade2475@aol.com

Employers
Davidoff & Malito, LLP (Director, Washington Office)

Clients Represented

On Behalf of Davidoff & Malito, LLP
American Museum of Natural History
Forest City Ratner Companies
Lou Levy & Sons Fashions, Inc.
Magellan Health Services
New City Development
New York Psychotherapy and Counseling Center
Orangeburg, New York, Town of
Project Return Foundation Inc.
Queens Borough Public Library
Soc. of Thoracic Surgeons
SOS Interpreting Ltd.
St. Vincent Catholic Medical Centers
Trans World Airlines, Inc.
Welch's Foods, Inc.

SLAFER, Anna

1200 18th St. NW
Suite 1100
Washington, DC 20036
Tel: (202)721-1545
Fax: (202)467-5780
EMail: renewamerica@counterpart.org

Employers
Renew America (Exec. Director)

SLAFKY, Aaryn

4121 Wilson Blvd.
Tenth Floor
Arlington, VA 22203
Tel: (703)351-2087
Fax: (703)351-2088
EMail: aslafky@ntca.org

Employers
Nat'l Telephone Cooperative Ass'n (Director, Communications)

SLAFSKY, Ted

1001 Pennsylvania Ave. NW
Suite 600
Washington, DC 20004
Tel: (202)347-0066
Fax: (202)624-7222
Registered: LDA
EMail: tslafsky@pgfm.com
Congressional Fellow, Senate Democratic Policy Committee, 1994.

Employers
Powell, Goldstein, Frazer & Murphy LLP (Coalition Manager)

Clients Represented

On Behalf of Powell, Goldstein, Frazer & Murphy LLP
Nat'l Ass'n of Public Hospitals and Health Systems
Public Hospital Pharmacy Coalition

SLAGLE, Jr., P. Roger

1200 N. Veitch St.
Suite 816
Arlington, VA 22201
Tel: (703)524-3495
Registered: LDA

Employers
Slagle & Associates (President)

Clients Represented

On Behalf of Slagle & Associates
Dallas Area Rapid Transit Authority
Denver, Regional Transportation District of

SLAIMAN, Gary D.

3000 K St. NW
Suite 300
Washington, DC 20007
Tel: (202)424-7500
Fax: (202)424-7643
Registered: LDA
Chief Counsel and Staff Director, Subcommittee on Labor and Human Resources, Senate Committee on Labor, 1992-93. Counsel, Subcommittee on Antitrust, Monopolies and Business Rights, Senate Committee on the Judiciary, 1989-92.

Employers
Swidler Berlin Shereff Friedman, LLP (Partner)

Clients Represented

On Behalf of Swidler Berlin Shereff Friedman, LLP
Aventis Pharmaceuticals, Inc.
BroadSpan Communications, Inc.
California Independent System Operator
Coalition to Ensure Responsible Billing
Florida Power and Light Co.
Frontier Communications Corp.
ICG Communications, Inc.
MCI WorldCom Corp.
McLeod USA, Inc.
Merrill Lynch & Co., Inc.
Napster, Inc.
Niagara Mohawk Power Corp.
Philip Morris Management Corp.
RCN Telecom Services Inc.
Renewable Fuels Ass'n
Schering Corp.
Suiza Foods Corp.
US Airways

SLAJER, Veronica A.

1667 K St. NW
Suite 1230
Washington, DC 20006
Tel: (202)466-3866
Fax: (202)466-3886
Registered: LDA
EMail: slajerva@alyeska-pipeline.com

Employers
Alyeska Pipeline Service Co. (Assistant Manager, Federal Government Relations)

SLAKEY, Francis

529 14th St. NW
Suite 1050
Washington, DC 20045
Tel: (202)662-8700
Fax: (202)662-8711
Registered: LDA

Employers
American Physical Soc. (Associate Director, Public Affairs)

SLAN, Allan G.

4330 East-West Hwy.
Suite 1100
Bethesda, MD 20814
Tel: (301)718-9500
Fax: (301)718-4290
Registered: LDA

Employers
Radius, The Global Travel Co. (Exec. V. President)

SLANEY, Joanna

3000 K St. NW
Suite 300
Washington, DC 20007
Tel: (202)295-8787
Fax: (202)295-8799
Special Assistant to the President for Legislative Affairs, Executive Office of the President during the Clinton administration. Former Press Secretary and Legislative Assistant to Senator Carol Moseley-Braun (D-IL).

Employers
The Harbour Group (Senior Associate)

SLATER, Alice

1150 17th St. NW
Suite 701
Washington, DC 20036
Tel: (202)298-9055
Fax: (202)298-8155
EMail: alice.slater@dittus.com

Employers
Dittus Communications (Associate Director)

Clients Represented

On Behalf of Dittus Communications
Community Financial Services Ass'n
Nat'l Alliance Against Blacklisting
Personal Watercraft Industry Ass'n

SLATER, Karen

1620 L St. NW
Room 401
Washington, DC 20036
Tel: (202)452-0358
Fax: (202)452-5287

Employers
Department of Interior - Bureau of Land Management (Intergovernmental Affairs Manager)

SLATER, Rodney

2550 M St. NW
Washington, DC 20037-1350
Tel: (202)457-5265
Fax: (202)457-6315
EMail: rslater@pattonboggs.com
Secretary of Transportation, 1997-2001; Administrator, Federal Highway Administration, 1993-97.

Employers
Patton Boggs, LLP (Partner)

SLATER, Valerie A.

1333 New Hampshire Ave. NW
Suite 400
Washington, DC 20036
Tel: (202)887-4000
Fax: (202)887-4288
Registered: LDA

Employers
Akin, Gump, Strauss, Hauer & Feld, L.L.P. (Partner)

Clients Represented

On Behalf of Akin, Gump, Strauss, Hauer & Feld, L.L.P.
Ad Hoc Nitrogen Committee
Brunswick Corp.
Cargill, Inc.
Committee for Fair Ammonium Nitrate Trade

SLATTERY, Hon. Jim

1776 K St. NW
Washington, DC 20006
Tel: (202)719-7000
Fax: (202)719-7049
Registered: LDA
Member, U.S. House of Representatives (D-KS), 1983-94.

Employers
U.S. Ass'n of Former Members of Congress (Secretary)
Wiley, Rein & Fielding (Partner)

Clients Represented

On Behalf of Wiley, Rein & Fielding
ARINC, Inc.
Birmingham Steel Corp.
Co-Steel Raritan
Columbia University
Connecticut Steel Corp.
Connecticut Student Loan Foundation
Earth, Energy & Environment
Kansas City Southern Industries
Kansas City Southern Railway Co.
Keystone Consolidated Industries, Inc.
Northwestern Steel and Wire Co.
Personal Communications Industry Ass'n (PCIA)
Washington Citizens for World Trade
Wheat Gluten Industry Council

SLAUGHTER, Kenneth S.

1201 New York Ave. NW
Suite 1000
Washington, DC 20005
Tel: (202)962-8385
Fax: (202)962-8300
EMail: ksslaughter@venable.com
Attorney/Advisor, Department of Treasury, 1976-79.

Employers
Venable (Partner)

SLAUGHTER, Robert

1899 L St. NW
Suite 1000
Washington, DC 20036
Tel: (202)457-0480
Fax: (202)429-7726
Registered: LDA
EMail: bob_slaughter@npradc.org

Employers
Nat'l Petrochemical Refiners Ass'n (Director, Public Policy)

SLAWTER, Shannon E.

2001 M St. NW
Fourth Floor
Washington, DC 20036
Tel: (202)533-5660
Fax: (202)533-8580
Registered: LDA

Employers
Barents Group LLC
KPMG, LLP

Clients Represented
On Behalf of Barents Group LLC
American Petroleum Institute
On Behalf of KPMG, LLP
Bracewell & Patterson, L.L.P.

SLEASE, III, Clyde H.

1620 L St. NW
Washington, DC 20036
Tel: (202)955-5080
Fax: (202)955-6070
Registered: LDA

Employers
Doepken Keevican & Weiss

Clients Represented
On Behalf of Doepken Keevican & Weiss
Nat'l Liberty Museum
Please Touch Museum, The Children's Museum of Philadelphia

SLESAR, Alex

1901 Pennsylvania Ave. NW
Suite 201
Washington, DC 20006
Tel: (202)745-2450
Fax: (202)667-0444

Employers
Lawyers Alliance for World Security (Director of Administration)

SLESINGER, Phyllis

1919 Pennsylvania Ave. NW
Seventh Floor
Washington, DC 20006-3488
Tel: (202)557-2700

Employers
Mortgage Bankers Ass'n of America (Staff V. President and General Counsel)

SLESINGER, Scott

734 15th St. NW
Suite 720
Washington, DC 20005
Tel: (202)783-0870
Ext: 13
Fax: (202)737-2038
Registered: LDA
EMail: sslesinger@etc.org
Minority Counsel for Energy and Environment, Senate Budget Committee, 1998. Legislative Assistant to Senator Frank Lautenberg (D-NJ), 1994-98. Associate Counsel, Subcommittee on Water Resources, House Committee on Public Works and Transportation, 1990-94. Attorney Advisor, Environmental Protection Agency, 1977-79.

Employers
Environmental Technology Council (V. President, Government Affairs)

SLIZ, Deborah R.

1225 I St. NW
Suite 600
Washington, DC 20005
Tel: (202)661-6192
Fax: (202)661-6182
Registered: LDA
EMail: dsliz@morganmeguire.com
Former Counsel, Subcommittee on Energy and Environment, Committee on Interior and Insular Affairs, U.S. House of Representatives and Legislative Aide to Rep. Morris K. Udall (D-AZ).

Employers
Morgan Meguire, LLC (Principal)

Clients Represented
On Behalf of Morgan Meguire, LLC
Adroit Systems Inc.
Baker Electromotive, Inc.
BellSouth Corp.
Colorado River Energy Distributors Ass'n
Energy Affairs Administration
Energy Northwest
Florida Municipal Power Agency
Goodman Manufacturing Co., L.P.
Longhorn Pipeline
Madison Gas & Electric Co.
Manatee, Florida, County of
Northern California Power Agency
Northwest Public Power Ass'n
Nuevo Energy
Puerto Rico Electric Power Authority
Redding, California, City of
Sacramento Municipal Utility District
Seven Seas Petroleum USA Inc.
Southern California Public Power Authority
Springfield, Missouri, City Utilities of
Tennessee Valley Public Power Ass'n
Transmission Access Policy Study Group
Truckee Donner Electric Power Utility District
Washington Public Utility Districts Ass'n

SLOAN, Judith A.

1800 K St. NW
Suite 1102
Washington, DC 20006
Tel: (202)833-2742
Fax: (202)833-0189

Employers
Asia Society (Director, Washington Center)

SLOAN, Kirsten A.

601 E St. NW
Washington, DC 20049
Tel: (202)434-3770
Fax: (202)434-3758
Registered: LDA

Employers
AARP (American Ass'n of Retired Persons) (Deputy Director, Federal Affairs, Health Issues)

SLOAN, Mary Margaret

1422 Fenwick Ln.
Silver Spring, MD 20910
Tel: (301)565-6704
Fax: (301)565-6714

Employers
American Hiking Soc. (President)

SLOAN, Virginia

50 F St. NW
Suite 110
Washington, DC 20001
Tel: (202)662-4240
Fax: (202)662-4241

Employers
Constitution Project (Exec. Director)

SLOANE, David

805 15th St. NW
Suite 430
Washington, DC 20005
Tel: (202)371-9792
Fax: (202)789-2405
Registered: LDA
EMail: david.sloane@wswa.org

Employers
Wine and Spirits Wholesalers of America (V. President, Federal Government Relations)

SLOBODOW, Arlen

641 Fifth St. NE
Washington, DC 20002
Tel: (202)544-6040
Fax: (202)548-6002
EMail: ajs@publicinterestvideo.com

Employers
Public Interest Video Network (Exec. Director)

SLOCUMB, Dennis

1421 Prince St.
Suite 400
Alexandria, VA 22314
Tel: (703)549-7473
Fax: (703)683-9048
Registered: LDA

Employers
Internat'l Union of Police Ass'ns (Exec. V. President)

SLOMINSKI, Jerry

1776 I St. NW
Suite 400
Washington, DC 20006-3708
Tel: (202)739-8000
Fax: (202)785-4019
Registered: LDA

Employers
Nuclear Energy Institute (Director, Legislative Programs)

SLOMOWITZ, Alan

800 Connecticut Ave. NW
Suite 500
Washington, DC 20006
Tel: (202)331-3103
Fax: (202)331-3101
Registered: LDA
Former Chief of Staff to Rep. Robert Borksi (D-PA). Former Professional Staff Member, Subcommittee on Oversight and Investigations, House Committee on Public Works and Transportation.

Employers
Greenberg Traurig, LLP

Clients Represented
On Behalf of Greenberg Traurig, LLP
ATOFINA Chemicals, Inc.

SLON, Deborah

444 N. Capitol St. NW
Suite 134
Washington, DC 20001
Tel: (202)624-5270
Fax: (202)624-5280

Employers
California, Washington Office of the State of (Legislative Affairs Liaison)

SLONE, Peter B.

1801 K St. NW
Suite 901-L
Washington, DC 20006
Tel: (202)530-0500
Fax: (202)530-4800
Registered: LDA
EMail: Peter_Slone@bm.com
Former Associate Staff Member, House Appropriations Committee and Legislative Assistant to Rep. William R. Ratchford (D-CT), 1978-83

Employers
BKSH & Associates (Managing Director)

SLOVAK, Dorothy C.

2099 Pennsylvania Ave. NW
Suite 100
Washington, DC 20006
Tel: (202)955-3000
Fax: (202)955-5564
EMail: dslovak@hklaw.com

Employers
Holland & Knight LLP (Associate)

SMALL, Michael E.

1200 G St. NW
Suite 600
Washington, DC 20005-3802
Tel: (202)393-1200
Fax: (202)393-1240
EMail: small@wrightlaw.com
Attorney, Office of the Solicitor (1984-85) and Special Assistant for Gas Pipeline and Electric Rates to the Deputy General Counsel for Litigation (1982-84), Federal Energy Regulatory Commission.

Employers
Wright & Talisman, P.C. (V. President and Assistant Secretary)

Clients Represented
On Behalf of Wright & Talisman, P.C.
Bangor Hydro-Electric Co.
Maine Public Service Co.
MidWest ISO Transmission Owners
Northwestern Public Service
Southwest Power Pool
Western Systems Coordinating Council
Western Systems Power Pool

SMALLEN, David

141 12th St. NE
Suite 18
Washington, DC 20002
Tel: (202)547-9494
Fax: (202)366-7270
Registered: LDA

Employers
Self-employed as an independent consultant.

SMARR, Lawrence E.

2275 Research Blvd.
Suite 250
Rockville, MD 20850
Tel: (301)947-9000
Fax: (301)947-9090
Registered: LDA

Employers
Physician Insurers Ass'n of America (President)

SMEAL, Eleanor

1600 Wilson Blvd.
Suite 801
Arlington, VA 22209
Tel: (703)522-2214
Fax: (703)522-2219

Employers
Feminist Majority (President)

SMEALLIE, Shawn H.

2099 Pennsylvania Ave. NW
Suite 850
Washington, DC 20006
Tel: (202)419-2500
Fax: (202)419-2510
Registered: LDA
EMail: Smeallie@acgrep.com
Special Assistant for Legislative Affairs (Senate), The White House, 1990-93. Special Assistant to Budget Director, Office of Management and Budget, 1989-90. Legislative Aide to Senator Alfonse D'Amato (R-NY), 1981-88.

Employers
American Continental Group, Inc. (Managing Director)

Clients Represented
On Behalf of American Continental Group, Inc.
American Standard Cos. Inc.
Ass'n of American Railroads
Campaign for Tobacco-Free Kids
Central European Media Enterprises
Coalition for Travel Industry Parity
Colorado Intermountain Fixed Guideway Authority
EEI
Ernst & Young LLP
Healthnow
Los Angeles County Metropolitan Transportation Authority
Northpoint Technology, Ltd.
OSI Systems, Inc.
Pennsylvania Higher Education Assistance Agency
PepsiCo, Inc.
Prudential Insurance Co. of America
Scholastic, Inc.
Siemens Corp.
Stony Brook Foundation
Tri-County Commuter Rail Authority
Trifinery, Inc.

SMEDBURG, Paul C.

1730 M St. NW
Suite 500
Washington, DC 20036
Tel: (202)785-3910
Fax: (202)785-5923

Employers
Nat'l Health Council (Director, Governmental Affairs)

SMERKO, Robert G.

2001 L St. NW
Suite 506
Washington, DC 20036-4919
Tel: (202)775-2790
Fax: (202)223-7225

Employers
Chlorine Institute (President)

SMERLING, Thomas

1030 15th St. NW
Suite 850
Washington, DC 20005
Tel: (202)842-1700
Fax: (202)842-1722

Employers
Israel Policy Forum (V. President, IDF Director, Washington Policy Center)

SMILACK, Stanley

1330 Connecticut Ave. NW
Washington, DC 20036-1795
Tel: (202)429-6464
Fax: (202)429-3902
Registered: LDA
EMail: ssmilack@steptoe.com

Employers
Steptoe & Johnson LLP (Of Counsel)

SMINK, Jeffrey

One Massachusetts Ave. NW
Suite 700
Washington, DC 20001-1431
Tel: (202)408-5505
Fax: (202)408-8072
Registered: LDA

Employers
Council of Chief State School Officers (Legislative Associate)

SMIROLDO, Diane

1150 18th St. NW
Suite 700
Washington, DC 20036
Tel: (202)872-5500
Fax: (202)872-5501

Employers
Business Software Alliance (V. President, Public Affairs)

SMITH, Ada-Saran E.

1819 Pennsylvania Ave. NW
Suite 400
Washington, DC 20006-3603
Tel: (202)333-8845
Fax: (202)333-8898

Employers
Institute for Advanced Studies in Aging and Geriatric Medicine (Program Director)

SMITH, Alicia W.

1401 K St. NW
12th Floor
Washington, DC 20005
Tel: (202)393-4760
Fax: (202)393-3516
Registered: LDA
EMail: asmith@smithfree.com
Former Assistant to the Political Director, The White House, during the Carter administration.

Employers
The Smith-Free Group (Senior V. President and Secretary)

Clients Represented
On Behalf of The Smith-Free Group
AT&T
Broadcast Music Inc. (BMI)
CSX Corp.
HCA Healthcare Corp.
Kennecott/Borax
Nuclear Energy Institute
Paucatuck Eastern Pequot Tribal Nation
Sandia Pueblo
Sony Music Entertainment Inc.
Sony Pictures Entertainment Inc.
Southern Co.
U.S. Wireless Data, Inc.

SMITH, Amy

1500 Pennsylvania Ave. NW
Room 2202
Washington, DC 20220
Tel: (202)622-6773
Fax: (202)622-0534

Employers
Department of Treasury (Deputy Assistant Secretary (Banking and Finance))

SMITH, Anne

620 Michigan Ave. NE
Washington, DC 20064
EMail: smith@cua.edu
Tel: (202)319-6977
Fax: (202)319-5579

Employers
Catholic University of America (Exec. Director, Public Affairs)

SMITH, Anne V.

1350 I St. NW
Suite 680
Washington, DC 20005-3305
Tel: (202)393-4841
Fax: (202)393-5596
Registered: LDA, FARA
Professional Staff Member and Deputy Director, European Subcommittee, Foreign Relations Committee, U.S. Senate, 1988-95.

Employers
The Advocacy Group
Self-employed as an independent consultant.

Clients Represented
On Behalf of The Advocacy Group
Internat'l Research and Exchanges Board (IREX)
As an independent consultant
Baltic American Freedom League
DeMil Internat'l
Internat'l Research and Exchanges Board (IREX)
Japan, Embassy of
Partido Accion Nacional (PAN)

SMITH, Anne W.

44965 Aviation Dr.
Suite 303
Dulles, VA 20166-7527
Tel: (703)260-3466
Fax: (703)260-3466
Registered: FARA

Employers
AWS Services (Bureau Coordinator)

Clients Represented
On Behalf of AWS Services
Ulster Unionist Party

SMITH, Bea Pace

8701 Georgia Ave.
Suite 200
Silver Spring, MD 20910
Tel: (301)650-2440
Fax: (301)495-3306
Registered: LDA

Employers
Nat'l Ass'n for Equal Opportunity in Higher Education (Director, Federal Relations)

SMITH, Becky J.

1900 Association Dr.
Reston, VA 20191
Tel: (703)476-3437
Fax: (703)476-6638
EMail: bsmith@aahe.org

Employers
American Ass'n for Health Education (Exec. Director and Coordinator, Government and Public Affairs)

SMITH, Ms. Bobbi

313 Park Ave.
Suite 400
Falls Church, VA 22046
EMail: ahp@go-ahp.org
Tel: (703)532-6243
Fax: (703)532-7170

Employers
Ass'n for Healthcare Philanthropy (Director, Foundation and Government Relations)

SMITH, Brian G.

655 15th St. NW
Washington, DC 20005-5701
EMail: bsmith@fmi.org
Tel: (202)220-0616
Fax: (202)220-0873

Employers
Food Marketing Institute (Director, Grassroots Advocacy)

SMITH, C. William

1101 30th St. NW
Suite 200
Washington, DC 20007
Tel: (202)293-4584
Fax: (202)293-4588
Registered: LDA
Former Staff Director, House Appropriations Subcommittee, 1974-95.

Employers
JBG Real Estate Associates
Lee & Smith P.C.

Clients Represented
On Behalf of Lee & Smith P.C.
Space Dynamics Laboratory
Utah State University

SMITH, Carl M.

1620 L St. NW
Suite 1210
Washington, DC 20036
Tel: (202)955-6062
Fax: (202)955-6070
Registered: LDA

Employers
Higgins, McGovern & Smith, LLC (Partner)

Clients Represented
On Behalf of Higgins, McGovern & Smith, LLC
APL Limited
Betac Corp.
Preston Gates Ellis & Rouvelas Meeds LLP
Trident Systems Inc.

SMITH, Carol

1600 Wilson Blvd.
Suite 205
Arlington, VA 22209
Tel: (703)358-8600
Fax: (703)358-8885

Employers
The State Affairs Co. (General Counsel)

Clients Represented

On Behalf of The State Affairs Co.

Sheep Ranch Rancheria

SMITH, Chad

1025 Vermont Ave.
Suite 720
Washington, DC 20005
EMail: amrivers@amrivers.org
Tel: (202)347-7550
Fax: (202)347-9240
Registered: LDA

Employers

American Rivers (Associate Director)

SMITH, Charles

1755 Jefferson Davis Hwy.
Suite 1107
Arlington, VA 22202
Tel: (703)415-0344
Fax: (703)415-0182
Registered: LDA

Employers

The PMA Group (Associate)

Clients Represented

On Behalf of The PMA Group

ARC Global Technologies
Autometric Inc.
Caterpillar Inc.
Chamberlain Manufacturing Corp.
Electro-Radiation Inc.
IIT Research Institute
Innovative Productivity, Inc.
L-3 Communications Corp.
Life Cell
Lockheed Martin Federal Systems
J. E. Morgan Knitting Mills
New Mexico Tech
Oxley
SACO Defense
TeleFlex Canada, Ltd.

SMITH, Christopher

1050 Connecticut Ave. NW
Washington, DC 20036-5339
Tel: (202)857-6000
Fax: (202)857-6395
Special Assistant to the Assistant Administrator for Enforcement and General Counsel, Environmental Protection Agency, 1973-74.

Employers

Arent Fox Kintner Plotkin & Kahn, PLLC (Member)

SMITH, Christopher H.

818 Connecticut Ave. NW
Suite 1007
Washington, DC 20006

Employers

Wildlife Conservation and Zoos PAC

SMITH, Clifton

1299 Pennsylvania Ave. NW
Suite 800 West
Washington, DC 20004
Tel: (202)785-0500
Fax: (202)785-5277
Registered: LDA

Employers

The Carmen Group (Managing Associate)
LMRC, Inc. (Managing Associate)

Clients Represented

On Behalf of The Carmen Group

Dillard University

SMITH, Constance

7910 Woodmont Ave.
Suite 530
Bethesda, MD 20814
Tel: (301)657-2768
Fax: (301)657-2909

Employers

American Soc. for Clinical Laboratory Science (PAC Contact)

SMITH, Conwell

1101 Vermont Ave. NW
12th Floor
Washington, DC 20005-3583
Tel: (202)789-7427
Fax: (202)789-7485
Registered: LDA

Employers

American Medical Ass'n (Assistant Director of Congressional Affairs)

SMITH, Col. Dan M.

1779 Massachusetts Ave. NW
Suite 615
Washington, DC 20036
Tel: (202)332-0600
Fax: (202)462-4559

Employers

Center for Defense Information (Chief of Research)

SMITH, Dan W.

1341 G St. NW
Suite 900
Washington, DC 20005
Tel: (202)637-1502
Fax: (202)637-1537

Employers

Philip Morris Management Corp. (Director, Government Affairs, Outreach)

SMITH, Daniel

1360 Beverly Rd.
Suite 201
McLean, VA 22101
Tel: (703)448-1000
Fax: (703)790-3460

Employers

DeHart and Darr Associates, Inc.

SMITH, Daniel C.

1815 H St. NW
Suite 1001
Washington, DC 20006
Tel: (202)822-5080
Fax: (202)822-5085
Attorney, Federal Trade Commission, 1966-69.

Employers

Canfield, Smith and Martin (Attorney)

Clients Represented

On Behalf of Canfield, Smith and Martin

Nat'l Field Selling Ass'n

SMITH, Daniel E.

701 Pennsylvania Ave. NW
Suite 650
Washington, DC 20004
EMail: dsmith@cancer.org
Tel: (202)661-5700
Fax: (202)661-5750

Employers

American Cancer Soc. (National V. President, Federal and State Government Relations)

SMITH, David

2500 Wilson Blvd.
Suite 300
Arlington, VA 22201
EMail: dsmith@tia.eia.org
Tel: (703)907-7738
Fax: (703)907-7727

Employers

Telecommunications Industry Ass'n (Webmaster & Director, Internet Development)

SMITH, David

1054 31st St. NW
Suite 300
Washington, DC 20007
EMail: dfbs@his.com
Tel: (202)333-4000
Fax: (202)965-3445

Employers

Ryberg and Smith LLP (Partner)

SMITH, David A.

1010 Wisconsin Ave. NW
Suite 800
Washington, DC 20007
Tel: (202)338-8700
Fax: (202)338-2334

Employers

Greer, Margolis, Mitchell, Burns & Associates (Partner)

Clients Represented

On Behalf of Greer, Margolis, Mitchell, Burns & Associates

Nutrition Screening Initiative, The
Ross/Nutrition Screening Initiative

SMITH, Jr., David C.

3050 K St. NW
Washington, DC 20007
Tel: (202)342-8400
Fax: (202)342-8451
Registered: LDA
EMail: dsmith@colliershannon.com
International Trade Analyst, International Trade Administration, Department of Commerce, 1990-92.

Employers

Collier Shannon Scott, PLLC (Of Counsel)

Clients Represented

On Behalf of Collier Shannon Scott, PLLC

American Honey Producers Ass'n

SMITH, David F.

1850 M St. NW
Suite 900
Washington, DC 20036
Tel: (202)463-2500
Fax: (202)463-4950
Registered: FARA

Employers

Sher & Blackwell (Partner)

SMITH, David M.

919 18th St. NW
Suite 800
Washington, DC 20006
Tel: (202)628-4160
Fax: (202)347-5323

Employers

Human Rights Campaign Fund (Director, Communications/Senior Strategist)

SMITH, David S.

1497 Chain Bridge Rd.
Suite 300
McLean, VA 22101
EMail: dsmith@ilalaw.com
Tel: (703)893-7071
Fax: (703)893-8020
Registered: LDA

Employers

Institutional Labor Advisors (Member of Firm)

Clients Represented

On Behalf of Institutional Labor Advisors

Coal Act Fairness Alliance
Freeman United Coal Mining Co.
Retiree Benefits Alliance

SMITH, Deya

513 Capitol Court NE
Suite 100
Washington, DC 20002
Tel: (202)547-9505
Fax: (202)478-0279
Registered: LDA

Employers

Mattox Woolfolk, LLC

Clients Represented

On Behalf of Mattox Woolfolk, LLC

Voices, Inc.

SMITH, Diane

601 Pennsylvania Ave. NW
Suite 720
Washington, DC 20004
Tel: (202)783-3973
Fax: (202)783-3982
Registered: LDA

Employers

Alltel Corporation (Senior V. President-Federal Government Affairs)

SMITH, Don

601 Madison St.
Suite 200
Alexandria, VA 22314
EMail: shagroup@bellatlantic.net
Tel: (703)684-9188
Registered: LDA

Employers

Smith, Hinaman & Associates (Principal)

Clients Represented

On Behalf of Smith, Hinaman & Associates

Burns and Roe Enterprises, Inc.
Gadsden State Community College
Ibex
US Acqua Sonics Corp.

SMITH, III, Duncan C.

600 New Hampshire Ave. NW
11th Floor
Washington, DC 20037
EMail: dcs@dejlaw.com
Tel: (202)944-3000
Fax: (202)944-3068
Registered: LDA, FARA
Chief Minority Counsel, House Merchant Marine and Fisheries Committee, 1980-90. Attorney, Office of the General Counsel, Department of the Treasury, 1978-80. Law Specialist, Office of Chief Counsel, U.S. Coast Guard, 1976-78.

Employers

Dyer Ellis & Joseph, P.C. (Partner and Treasurer)

Clients Represented

On Behalf of Dyer Ellis & Joseph, P.C.

Alaska Ship and Drydock, Inc.

American Coke and Coal Chemicals Institute

Avondale Industries, Inc.

Bender Shipbuilding & Repair Co., Inc.

BLNG, Inc.

Browning Transport Management

China Shipping (Group) Co.

John Crane-LIPS, Inc.

Cross Sound Ferry Services, Inc.

DaimlerChrysler Corp.

Electronic Design Inc.

FastShip, Inc.

Friede Goldman Halter

Fruit Shippers Ltd.

Gateway Clipper Fleet

Glass Packaging Institute

Heerema Marine Contractors Nederland B.V.

Hornblower Marine Services, Inc.

Hvide Marine Inc.

Intermare Navigation SA

Kvaerner Philadelphia Shipyard Inc.

Marine Spill Response Corporation

Nat'l Maritime Alliance

Nat'l Oilseed Processors Ass'n

Nat'l Steel and Shipbuilding Co.

Northrop Grumman Corp.

Offshore Rig Museum, Inc.

Put-in-Bay Boat Line Co.

Sea Ventures Inc.

TI Group Inc.

TransAtlantic Lines - Iceland ehf

The Trump Organization

Wendella Sightseeing Boats Inc.

SMITH, III, Dwight C.

601 Pennsylvania Ave. NW
11th Floor, North Bldg.
Washington, DC 20004-2601
Tel: (202)756-3300
Fax: (202)756-3333
Registered: LDA

EMail: dcsmith@alston.com

Deputy Chief Counsel, Business Transactions (1995-1999) and Deputy Chief Counsel, Legal Policy (1990-1994), Department of the Treasury.

Employers

Alston & Bird LLP (Counsel)

Clients Represented

On Behalf of Alston & Bird LLP

AFLAC, Inc.

The Assurant Group

Nat'l Coalition on E-Commerce and Privacy

SMITH, E. Del

1130 Connecticut Ave. NW
Suite 650
Washington, DC 20036
Tel: (202)822-8300
Fax: (202)832-8315
Registered: LDA

Employers

E. Del Smith and Co. (President)

Clients Represented

On Behalf of E. Del Smith and Co.

American Magline Group
Anaheim, California, City of
Anaheim, California, Public Utilities of the City of
Apple Valley, California, City of
Aquarium of the Pacific
Barstow, California, City of
BEMS W/L Associates
Bioelectromagnetics Soc.
California Independent Petroleum Ass'n
California-American Water Co.
Calleguas Creek Flood Prevention Committee
Chino Hills, California, City of
Contra Costa, California, Tenants of the County of
Corte Madera, California, Town of
Downey, California, Economic Development of the City of
Hesperia, California, City of
Hollis-Eden Pharmaceuticals, Inc.
InterMart Broadcasting
Laguna Beach, California, City of
Lake County Basin 2000
Long Beach Naval Shipyard Employees Ass'n
Long Beach Water Department
Long Beach, California, City of
Long Beach, California, Port of
Los Angeles, California, County of
Lynwood, California, City of
Morro Bay, California, City of
Nat'l Independent Private Schools Ass'n
Port Hueneme, California, City of
Rancho Palos Verdes, California, City of
Reusable Pallet and Container Coalition
Santa Barbara, California, City of (Waterfront)
Santa Barbara, California, Public Works Department
Santa Cruz, California, Port of
Seal Beach, California, City of
Stockton, California, Port of
Victorville, California, City of
Woods Hole Oceanographic Institution
Xybernaut

SMITH, Edward J.

317 S. Patrick St.
Alexandria, VA 22314
Tel: (703)519-0300
Fax: (703)519-0311

Employers

Internat'l Brotherhood of Police Officers
Nat'l Ass'n of Government Employees (Counsel)

SMITH, Eleanor H.

1201 Connecticut Ave. NW
Suite 600
Washington, DC 20036
Tel: (202)778-1800
Fax: (202)822-8106
Registered: LDA
EMail: esmith@zsgtk.com

Employers

Zuckerman Spaeder L.L.P. (Partner)

Clients Represented

On Behalf of Zuckerman Spaeder L.L.P.

The Bureau of Nat'l Affairs, Inc.

SMITH, Elise D.

1201 L St. NW
Washington, DC 20005-4014
Tel: (202)842-4444
Fax: (202)842-3860

Employers

American Health Care Ass'n (Senior Director, Finance and Managed Care)

SMITH, Elizabeth M.

555 New Jersey Ave. NW
Washington, DC 20001
Tel: (202)393-6375
Fax: (202)879-4402

Employers

American Federation of Teachers (Political Director)

SMITH, Eric H.

1747 Pennsylvania Ave. NW
Suite 825
Washington, DC 20006-4604
Tel: (202)833-4198
Fax: (202)872-0546
Registered: LDA
EMail: esmith@iipa.com

Employers

Internat'l Intellectual Property Alliance (President)
Smith & Metalitz, L.L.P. (Managing Partner)

Clients Represented

On Behalf of Smith & Metalitz, L.L.P.

Internat'l Intellectual Property Alliance

SMITH, Erik

430 S. Capitol St. SE
Second Floor
Washington, DC 20003
Tel: (202)863-1500
Fax: (202)485-3456

Employers

Democratic Congressional Campaign Committee (Director, Communications)

SMITH, Francis

441 Fourth St. NW
Room 570N
Washington, DC 20001
Tel: (202)504-3400
Fax: (202)504-3431

Employers

District of Columbia Financial Responsibility and Management Assistance Authority (Exec. Director)

SMITH, Jr., Fred L.

1001 Connecticut Ave. NW
Suite 1250
Washington, DC 20036
Tel: (202)331-1010
Fax: (202)331-0640

Employers

Competitive Enterprise Institute (President and Founder)

SMITH, G. Wayne

816 Connecticut Ave. NW
Tenth Floor
Washington, DC 20006
Tel: (202)783-3460
Fax: (202)783-2432
Registered: LDA
EMail: wayne@ptomac.com

Former Chief of Staff to Sen. John Breaux (D-LA). Former Professional Staff Member, Democratic Senatorial Campaign Committee.

Employers

Potomac Group (President and Chief Exec. Officer)

Clients Represented

On Behalf of Potomac Group

American Psychological Ass'n
Ass'n of American Railroads
Maersk Inc.
Rapid Mat LLC
R. J. Reynolds Tobacco Co.
Seafarers Internat'l Union of North America
Seafarers Mobilization Action Research Team
Transportation Institute
Union Pacific
Walgreen Co.
Watson Energy

SMITH, Gare A.

1747 Pennsylvania Ave. NW
Suite 1200
Washington, DC 20006
Tel: (202)223-1200
Fax: (202)785-6687
Registered: LDA, FARA
EMail: gsmith@fhe.com

Former Principal Deputy Assistant Secretary, Department of State.

Employers

Foley, Hoag & Eliot LLP (Counsel)

Clients Represented

On Behalf of Foley, Hoag & Eliot LLP

Guatemala, Government of the Republic of
Guyana, Government of the Co-operative Republic of
PET Coalition

SMITH, Ph.D., Gilbert E.

815 15th St. NW
Suite 508
Washington, DC 20005
Tel: (202)393-7140
Fax: (202)393-4059

Employers

Nat'l Registry in Clinical Chemistry (Exec. Director)

SMITH, Glenore

1015 15th St. NW
Suite 802
Washington, DC 20005
Tel: (202)347-7474
Fax: (202)898-0068
EMail: gsmith@acec.org

Employers

American Consulting Engineers Council (Director, International Department)

SMITH, Gordon

219 N. Washington St.
Alexandria, VA 22314
Tel: (703)836-7990
Fax: (703)836-9739

Employers
Peduzzi Associates, Ltd. (Associate)

SMITH, Gregory A.

1918 18th St. NW
Suite 24
Washington, DC 20009
Tel: (202)265-1551
Fax: (202)737-0693
Registered: LDA

Employers
Johnston & Associates, LLC (Partner)
Smith Law Firm (Attorney at Law)

Clients Represented
On Behalf of Smith Law Firm
Navajo Nation
Pueblo of Acoma

SMITH, Gregory K.

1400 L St. NW
Washington, DC 20005-3502
Tel: (202)371-5954
Fax: (202)371-5950
Registered: LDA
EMail: gsmith@winston.com

Employers
Winston & Strawn (Associate, Corporate Practice)

Clients Represented
On Behalf of Winston & Strawn
Nat'l Organization of Social Security Claimants' Representatives
Yellow Corp.

SMITH, Heather L.

1400 16th St. NW
Suite 320
Washington, DC 20036
Tel: (202)332-2200
Fax: (202)332-2302
Registered: LDA

Employers
Zero Population Growth, Inc. (Senior Legislative Associate)

SMITH, J. Anthony

2600 Virginia Ave. NW
Suite 1000
Washington, DC 20037-1905
Tel: (202)333-8800
Fax: (202)337-6065
Registered: LDA

Employers
Schmeltzer, Aptaker & Shepard, P.C. (Special Counsel)

Clients Represented
On Behalf of Schmeltzer, Aptaker & Shepard, P.C.
AfriSpace Corp.
Ass'n of Maquiladores
D.C. Historical Tourism Coalition
Honduras, Embassy of
Juneau, Alaska, City of
St. Paul, Alaska, City of

SMITH, J. Brian

99 Canal Center Plaza
Suite 200
Alexandria, VA 22314
Tel: (703)683-8512
Fax: (703)683-4622

Employers
Smith & Harroff, Inc. (President and Chief Exec. Officer)

SMITH, J. Sharpe

1110 N. Glebe Rd.
Suite 500
Arlington, VA 22201-5720
Tel: (703)797-5115
Fax: (703)524-1074

Employers
Industrial Telecommunications Ass'n, Inc. (Director, Industry and Public Affairs)

SMITH, James E.

1401 K St. NW
12th Floor
Washington, DC 20005
Tel: (202)393-4760
Fax: (202)393-3516
Registered: LDA
EMail: jsmith@smithfree.com
Former Deputy Undersecretary for Legislative Affairs and former Comptroller of the Currency, Department of the Treasury Department.

Employers
The Smith-Free Group (Chairman)

Clients Represented
On Behalf of The Smith-Free Group
Federal Home Loan Mortgage Corp. (Freddie Mac)
HCA Healthcare Corp.
MasterCard Internat'l
MBNA America Bank NA
Northwestern Mutual Life Insurance Co.
Star Systems
VISA U.S.A., Inc.
Washington Mutual Bank

SMITH, James P.

1000 Connecticut Ave. NW
Suite 302
Washington, DC 20036
Tel: (202)835-0740
Fax: (202)775-8526
Registered: LDA, FARA
EMail: jims@sda-inc.com

Employers
Smith Dawson & Andrews, Inc.

Clients Represented
On Behalf of Smith Dawson & Andrews, Inc.
Alston & Bird, LLP
American Federation of Television and Radio Artists
Avecia, Inc.
Bone Care Internat'l
Caguas, Puerto Rico, City of
Carolina, Puerto Rico, City of
Ceiba, Puerto Rico, City of
Certified Automotive Parts Ass'n
Children's Hospital and Medical Center
Council of Development Finance Agencies
Eugene, Oregon, City of
George Washington University, Office of Government Relations
Georgia Municipal Gas Ass'n
Georgia, State of
Haarmann & Reimer Corp.
Japan, Embassy of
Lane Transit District
Lane, Oregon, County of
Mothers Against Drunk Driving (MADD)
Nat'l Ass'n of Foreign Trade Zones
NeoPharm, Inc.
Sacramento, California, City of
Springfield, Oregon, City of
Springfield, Oregon, School District #19

SMITH, Jason

1825 Connecticut Ave. NW
Fifth Floor
Washington, DC 20009
Tel: (202)667-0901
Fax: (202)667-0902
EMail: jason.smith@widmeyer.com

Employers
Widmeyer Communications, Inc. (V. President)

SMITH, Jeffrey C.

1600 Duke St.
Suite 220
Alexandria, VA 22314
Tel: (703)519-1715
Fax: (703)519-1716
Registered: LDA
EMail: jcs@wpa.org

Employers
Washington Policy Associates, Inc. (President)

Clients Represented
On Behalf of Washington Policy Associates, Inc.
Commercial Weather Services Ass'n (CWSA)
The Maritime Consortium, Inc.
Nat'l Ass'n of Charterboat Operators (NACO)
Nat'l Ass'n of Collection Sites

SMITH, Jeffrey H.

555 12th St. NW
Washington, DC 20004-1206
Tel: (202)942-5115
Fax: (202)942-5999
Registered: LDA
EMail: jeffrey_Smith@aporter.com
General Counsel, Central Intelligence Agency, 1995-96. Member, Commission of Roles and Missions, Department of Defense, 1994-95. Chairman, Joint Security Commission, 1993. Chief, Clinton Transition Team, Department of Defense, 1992. General Counsel and Senior Counsel, Senate Armed Services Committee, 1984-88. Office of Legal Advisor, Department of State, 1975-84.

Employers
Arnold & Porter (Partner)

Clients Represented
On Behalf of Arnold & Porter
Johns Hopkins Center for Civilian Biodefense Studies

SMITH, Jeffrey T.

2550 M St. NW
Washington, DC 20037-1350
Tel: (202)457-6000
Fax: (202)457-6315
Registered: FARA
EMail: jsmith@pattonboggs.com

Employers
Patton Boggs, LLP (Partner)

Clients Represented
On Behalf of Patton Boggs, LLP
Syntroleum Corp.

SMITH, Jennifer K.

101 1/2 S. Union St.
Alexandria, VA 22314
Tel: (703)684-5100
Fax: (703)684-5424
Registered: LDA
EMail: jsmith@smithfairfield.com

Employers
Smith Fairfield, Inc. (President)

SMITH, Jennifer L.

1000 Connecticut Ave. NW
Suite 304
Washington, DC 20036
Tel: (202)296-4484
Fax: (202)293-3060
Registered: LDA

Employers
Masaoka & Associates, Inc. (Senior Associate)

Clients Represented
On Behalf of Masaoka & Associates, Inc.
Fresh Produce Ass'n of the Americas

SMITH, Jim

1200 G St. NW
Suite 400
Washington, DC 20005
Tel: (202)783-8700
Fax: (202)783-8750
Registered: LDA
Chief of Staff to Rep. Peter Deutsch (D-FL), 1993-97.

Employers
AdvaMed (V. President, Government Affairs)

SMITH, II, John T.

1201 Pennsylvania Ave. NW
Washington, DC 20004-2401
Tel: (202)662-6000
Fax: (202)662-6291
Registered: LDA
EMail: jsmith@cov.com
General Counsel, Department of Commerce, 1976-77.

Employers
Covington & Burling (Partner)

SMITH, Joseph

4301 N. Fairfax Dr.
Suite 360
Arlington, VA 22203-1627
Tel: (703)358-9300

Employers
Nat'l Utility Contractors Ass'n (NUCA) (Government Relations Assistant)

SMITH, Joyce E.

1631 Prince St.
Alexandria, VA 22314-2818
Tel: (703)836-2222
Fax: (703)836-8015

Employers
Nat'l Ass'n for College Admission Counseling (Exec. Director)

SMITH, Judy

1211 Connecticut Ave. NW
Suite 608
Washington, DC 20036
Tel: (202)496-1000
Fax: (202)496-1300
EMail: jsmith@qorvis.com

Employers
Qorvis Communications (Partner)

SMITH, Julia

927 15th St. NW
12th Floor
Washington, DC 20015
Tel: (202)833-4466
Fax: (202)833-2833
Registered: LDA

Employers
St. Maxens & Company

Clients Represented

On Behalf of St. Maxens & Company

Mattel, Inc.

SMITH, Kathleen A.

1155 15th St. NW
Suite 801
Washington, DC 20005
Tel: (202)466-8621
Fax: (202)466-8643

Employers

Education Finance Council (Director, Government Affairs)

SMITH, Kathleen T.

1875 I St. NW
Twelfth Floor
Washington, DC 20006
Tel: (202)296-8632
Fax: (202)296-8634
Registered: LDA

Employers

Fresenius Medical Care North America (V. President, Government Affairs)

SMITH, Keith H.

601 13th St. NW
Suite 370 South
Washington, DC 20005
Tel: (202)783-7272
Fax: (202)783-4345
Registered: LDA

Employers

French & Company (Exec. V. President)

Clients Represented

On Behalf of French & Company

Internat'l Electronics Manufacturers and Consumers of America

SMITH, Kelly L.

600 13th St. NW
Suite 1200
Washington, DC 20005
Tel: (202)756-8299
Fax: (202)756-8087
Registered: LDA

Employers

Circuit City Stores, Inc. (Washington Representative)

SMITH, Kristen

1150 18th St. NW
Ninth Floor
Washington, DC 20036
Tel: (202)296-3355
Fax: (202)296-3922

Employers

Ablondi, Foster, Sobin & Davidow, P.C. (Associate)

SMITH, Kristen R.

725 15th St. NW
Suite 700
Washington, DC 20005
Tel: (202)393-5725
Fax: (202)393-1282
Registered: LDA
EMail: krsmith@americasblood.org

Employers

America's Blood Centers (Director, Government Affairs)

SMITH, L. Bradley

1001 Pennsylvania Ave. NW
Washington, DC 20004-2599
Tel: (202)624-2000
Fax: (202)624-2319

Employers

American Council of Life Insurers (Managing Director, International Relations)

SMITH, Larry E.

1001 Pennsylvania Ave. NW
Suite 760 North
Washington, DC 20004
Tel: (202)661-7060
Fax: (202)661-7066
Registered: LDA

Sergeant at Arms (1983-85) and Deputy Sergeant at Arms (1981-83), United States Senate and Staff Director, Senate Rules Committee.

Employers

The Legislative Strategies Group, LLC (President)

Clients Represented

On Behalf of The Legislative Strategies Group, LLC

Americans for Responsible Recreational Areas
Cardinal Health Inc.
Harcourt General
Hong Kong Trade Development Council
Hopi Indian Tribe
Independent Telephone and Telecommunications Alliance
Nat'l Orthotics Manufacturers Ass'n

SMITH, Laura L.

1110 N. Glebe Rd.
Suite 500
Arlington, VA 22201-5720
Tel: (703)797-5114
Fax: (703)524-1074
Registered: LDA

Employers

Industrial Telecommunications Ass'n, Inc. (President and C.E.O.)

SMITH, Lavone

1101 Vermont Ave. NW
Suite 710
Washington, DC 20005-3521
Tel: (202)789-0007
Fax: (202)842-4360

Employers

American Veterinary Medical Ass'n (PAC Coordinator)

SMITH, USN (Ret.), Adm. Leighton W.

11 Canal Center Plaza
Suite 103
Alexandria, VA 22314
Tel: (703)683-4222
Fax: (703)683-0645
Registered: LDA

Former Commander, International Peacekeeping Forces in Bosnia-Herzegovina.

Employers

Self-employed as an independent consultant.
The Spectrum Group

Clients Represented

As an independent consultant

The Boeing Co.

SMITH, Linden C.

2001 M St. NW
Fourth Floor
Washington, DC 20036
Tel: (202)533-5660
Fax: (202)533-8580
Registered: LDA

Employers

Barents Group LLC (Managing Director)
KPMG, LLP

Clients Represented

On Behalf of Barents Group LLC

American Petroleum Institute
Gardere & Wayne, LLP
General Ore Internat'l Corp. Ltd.
John T. O'Rourke Law Offices
Verner, Liipfert, Bernhard, McPherson and Hand, Chartered

On Behalf of KPMG, LLP

Bracewell & Patterson, L.L.P.
Nextwave Telecom

SMITH, Liz

555 New Jersey Ave. NW
Tenth Floor
Washington, DC 20001
Tel: (202)879-4436
Fax: (202)393-6375

Employers

Federation of Nurses and Health Professionals/AFT (PAC Contact)

SMITH, Loren

1920 L St. NW
Suite 200
Washington, DC 20036
Tel: (202)785-0266
Fax: (202)785-0261

Employers

Americans for Tax Reform (Operations Director)

SMITH, Mark F.

1012 14th St. NW
Suite 500
Washington, DC 20005
Tel: (202)737-5900
Fax: (202)737-5526
Registered: LDA
EMail: marksmith@aaup.org

Employers

American Ass'n of University Professors (Associate Director, Government Relations)

SMITH, Mark H.

2300 N St. NW
Washington, DC 20037-1128
Tel: (202)663-8000
Fax: (202)663-8007
EMail: mark.smith@shawpittman.com

Legislative Assistant to Senator Connie Mack (R-FL), 1989-2001.

Employers

Shaw Pittman (Sr. Corporate Relations Advisor)

SMITH, Mark R.

20949 Lohengrin Court
Ashburn, VA 20147
Tel: (202)293-3144
Fax: (703)723-0916
Registered: LDA

Employers

The Da Vinci Group (Director, Government Relations)

Clients Represented

On Behalf of The Da Vinci Group

Alliance for American Innovation, Inc.
Atlantic Shores Healthcare, Inc.
Backweb Technologies, Inc.
Detroit/Wayne County Port Authority
N-Z Land Company
Peterson Cos., Inc.
Soave Enterprises
Wackenhut Corrections Corp.

SMITH, Mark T.

1615 H St. NW
Washington, DC 20062-2000
Tel: (202)659-6000
Fax: (202)463-5836

Employers

Chamber of Commerce of the U.S.A. (Associate Director, Latin American Affairs)

SMITH, Martha

1725 K St. NW
Suite 1404
Washington, DC 20006
Tel: (202)296-7116
Fax: (202)659-5322

Employers

American Cotton Shippers Ass'n (Director, Congressional Relations)

SMITH, Maureen H.

1111 19th St. NW
Suite 800
Washington, DC 20036
Tel: (202)463-2700
Fax: (202)463-2785
Registered: LDA
EMail: maureen_smith@afandpa.org

Employers

American Forest & Paper Ass'n (V. President, International Affairs)

SMITH, Megan S.

1117 Alden Rd.
Alexandria, VA 22308
Tel: (202)467-6540
Fax: (202)467-6541
Registered: LDA

Employers

MSS Consultants, LLC (President)

Clients Represented

On Behalf of MSS Consultants, LLC

Arkenol, Inc.
B.C. Internat'l Corp.
Battelle Memorial Institute
Cargill Dow

SMITH, Michael B.

2121 K St. NW
Suite 650
Washington, DC 20037
Tel: (202)296-2400
Fax: (202)296-2409
Registered: LDA
EMail: Mike@GlobalUSAinc.com

Former Ambassador to the General Agreement on Tariffs and Trade and Deputy U.S. Trade Representative.

Employers

Global USA, Inc. (V. Chairman)

Clients Represented

On Behalf of Global USA, Inc.

All Japan Postal Labor Union
Takata Corp.

SMITH, Jr., Myron

14501 Lee Jackson Memorial Hwy.
Suite A
Chantilly, VA 20151-1512
Tel: (703)817-1307
Fax: (703)817-1407
EMail: msmith@data-trans.org

Formerly with Civil Engineer Corps., U.S. Navy; Deputy Assistant Secretary, Department of Energy.

Employers

Dulles Area Transportation Ass'n (Exec. Director)

SMITH, Nick

601 Pennsylvania Ave. NW
Suite 900
Washington, DC 20004
Tel: (202)547-3566
Fax: (202)639-8238

Employers
Cottone and Huggins Group (V. President, Media Production)

SMITH, Patricia P.

601 E St. NW
Washington, DC 20049
Tel: (202)434-3770
Fax: (202)434-3758
Registered: LDA

Employers
AARP (American Ass'n of Retired Persons) (Director, Federal Affairs, Health Issues)

SMITH, Jr., Patrick F.

1717 Pennsylvania Ave. NW
Suite 600
Washington, DC 20006
Tel: (202)293-3450
Fax: (202)293-2787
Registered: LDA

Employers
Medical Group Management Ass'n (V. President, Government Affairs)

SMITH, Patrick J.

1700 Pennsylvania Ave. NW
Suite 600
Washington, DC 20006
Tel: (202)393-7600
Fax: (202)393-7601
Registered: LDA

Employers
Ivins, Phillips & Barker (Partner)

Clients Represented
On Behalf of Ivins, Phillips & Barker
Allegheny Ludlum Corp.

SMITH, Paul A.

1120 Connecticut Ave. NW
Washington, DC 20036
Tel: (202)663-5000
Fax: (202)828-4548
Registered: LDA

Employers
American Bankers Ass'n (Senior Federal Administrative Counsel)

SMITH, Paul C.

7500 Woodmont Ave.
Suite L08
Bethesda, MD 20814
Tel: (202)675-3380
Fax: (301)986-9346
Registered: LDA
Counsel and Republican Staff Director, Energy and Commerce Committee, U.S. House of Representatives, 1985-88. Assistant Legislative Counsel, Office of Legislative Counsel, U.S. House of Representatives, 1972-85.

Employers
Policy Consulting Services

Clients Represented
On Behalf of Policy Consulting Services
American Automotive Leasing Ass'n
IPALCO Enterprises, Inc./Indianapolis Power & Light Co.
United Parcel Service

SMITH, Peter F.

1200 New York Ave. NW
Suite 550
Washington, DC 20005
EMail: peter_smith@aau.edu
Tel: (202)408-7500
Fax: (202)408-8184

Employers
Ass'n of American Universities (Director, Public Affairs)

SMITH, Jr., Philip J.

611 Pennsylvania Ave. SE
Suite 340
Washington, DC 20003
Tel: (202)543-1444
Fax: (202)318-0652
Registered: LDA

Employers
Philip S. Smith & Associates, Inc.

Clients Represented
On Behalf of Philip S. Smith & Associates, Inc.
Lao Veterans of America, Inc.

SMITH, Philip S.

611 Pennsylvania Ave. SE
Suite 340
Washington, DC 20003
Tel: (202)543-1444
Fax: (202)318-0652
Registered: LDA
Asia Policy Advisor, House Republican Research Committee, 1993-95. Senior Legislative Assistant to Rep. Don Ritter (R-PA) 1988-93. Assistant, Subcommittee on Select Education, House Committee on Education and Labor, 1987-88.

Employers
Philip S. Smith & Associates, Inc. (President)

Clients Represented
On Behalf of Philip S. Smith & Associates, Inc.
Afghanistan Foundation
Lao Progressive Institute
Lao Veterans of America, Inc.
United Lao Congress for Democracy

SMITH, R.J.

1001 Connecticut Ave. NW
Suite 1250
Washington, DC 20036
Tel: (202)331-1010
Fax: (202)331-0640

Employers
Competitive Enterprise Institute (Sr. Environmental Scholar)

SMITH, Randy T.

2001 Pennsylvania Ave. NW
Suite 300
Washington, DC 20006
Tel: (202)862-0225
Fax: (202)862-0267
Registered: LDA

Employers
Exxon Mobil Corp. (Washington Representative, House of Representatives)

SMITH, Richard F.

1101 Pennsylvania Ave. NW
Suite 400
Washington, DC 20004-2504
Tel: (202)637-3800
Fax: (202)637-3860
Registered: LDA

Employers
Textron Inc. (V. President, Congressional Affairs)

SMITH, Rick

1129 20th St. NW
Suite 600
Washington, DC 20036-3421
EMail: rsmith@aahp.org
Tel: (202)778-3200
Fax: (202)778-8479

Employers
American Ass'n of Health Plans (AAHP) (V. President, Public Policy and Research)

SMITH, Robert

1300 I St. NW
Suite 420 East
Washington, DC 20005
Tel: (202)326-7520
Fax: (202)326-7525
Former Legislative Director for Rep. Wes Watkins (R-OK).

Employers
Sun Microsystems (Federal Affairs Representative)

SMITH, Robert E.

5903 Mount Eagle Dr.
Suite 1404
Alexandria, VA 22303
Tel: (703)329-9514
Fax: (703)329-1164
Registered: LDA

Employers
Self-employed as an independent consultant.

Clients Represented
As an independent consultant
Arch Chemical Inc.
Olin Corp.

SMITH, Robin

One Dupont Circle NW
Suite 430
Washington, DC 20036
Tel: (202)223-3791
Fax: (202)331-7157

Employers
Council of Graduate Schools (V. President)

SMITH, Rodney A.

1401 I St. NW
Suite 1100
Washington, DC 20005
Tel: (202)326-8818
Fax: (202)408-4796
Registered: LDA

Employers
SBC Communications Inc. (Exec. Director, Federal Relations)

SMITH, Russell L.

Three Lafayette Center
1155 21st St. NW
Washington, DC 20036-3384
Tel: (202)328-8000
Fax: (202)887-8979
Registered: LDA
Minority Counsel, House Committee on Energy and Commerce, 1984-88. Special Advisor, International Trade Administration, Department of Commerce, 1982-84. Attorney/Advisor, Department of Treasury, 1972-76.

Employers
Willkie Farr & Gallagher (Special Counsel)

Clients Represented
On Behalf of Willkie Farr & Gallagher
Ass'n of Directory Publishers
Bloomberg L.P.
Fuji Photo Film U.S.A., Inc.
Hamilton, Rabinovitz & Alschuler
Hyundai Electronics Industries Co., LTD
ICF Industries, Inc.
Japan Automobile Manufacturers Ass'n
Japan Iron and Steel Exporters Ass'n
Meat and Livestock Australia
J. P. Morgan Chase & Co.
Riverhead Community Development Agency
Sprint Corp.
Superior Metal Products
Yamaha Motor Corp. U.S.A.

SMITH, S. Marijke

1300 Pennsylvania Ave. NW
Suite 860
Washington, DC 20004
Tel: (202)842-5800
Fax: (202)842-8612

Employers
Volkswagen of America, Inc. (Government Relations Assistant)

SMITH, Shanna L.

1212 New York Ave. NW
Suite 525
Washington, DC 20005
EMail: nfha@erols.com
Tel: (202)898-1661
Fax: (202)371-9744

Employers
Nat'l Fair Housing Alliance (Exec. Director)

SMITH, Steven R.

1630 Duke St.
Alexandria, VA 22314
Tel: (703)684-5545
Fax: (703)548-8735

Employers
Nat'l Rural Letter Carriers' Ass'n (President)

SMITH, Susan Snyder

8320 Old Courthouse Rd.
Suite 300
Vienna, VA 22182
Tel: (703)790-5011
Fax: (703)790-5752
Registered: LDA
EMail: susan.smith@candyusa.org
Former aide to Sen. Roger Jepsen (R-IA) and Rep. Delbert Latta (R-OH).

Employers
Chocolate Manufacturers Ass'n of the U.S.A. (V. President, Public Affairs)
Nat'l Confectioners Ass'n (Senior V. President)

SMITH, Timothy E.

11803 Wayland St.
Oakton, VA 22124-2229
Tel: (703)716-4846
Fax: (703)716-0043
Registered: LDA

Employers
Governmental Strategies, Inc. (President)

Clients Represented
On Behalf of Governmental Strategies, Inc.
El Paso Electric Co.

SMITH, Todd

601 Madison St.
Suite 200
Alexandria, VA 22314
Tel: (703)684-9188
Registered: LDA

Employers
Smith, Hinaman & Associates

Clients Represented

On Behalf of Smith, Hinaman & Associates

Ibex

SMITH, Todd

1201 L St. NW
Washington, DC 20005-4014
Tel: (202)842-4444
Fax: (202)842-3860
Registered: LDA

Employers

American Health Care Ass'n (Director, Policy & Analysis)

SMITH, Tracy Heinzman

1299 Pennsylvania Ave. NW
Washington, DC 20004-2402
Tel: (202)783-0800
Fax: (202)383-6610
Registered: LDA

Employers

Howrey Simon Arnold & White (Partner)

Clients Represented

On Behalf of Howrey Simon Arnold & White

Portable Rechargeable Battery Ass'n

SMITH, Jr., Turner T.

1900 K St. NW
Washington, DC 20006-1109
Tel: (202)955-1500
Fax: (202)778-2201
Registered: LDA
EMail: tsmith@hunton.com

Employers

Hunton & Williams (Partner)

Clients Represented

On Behalf of Hunton & Williams

Edison Electric Institute

SMITH, Vaughan A.

11208 Waples Mill Rd.
Suite 109
Fairfax, VA 22030
Tel: (703)691-2242
Fax: (703)691-2247

Employers

American Ass'n of Healthcare Consultants (President)

SMITH, Victor H.

1201 Connecticut Ave. NW
Suite 700
Washington, DC 20036
Tel: (202)822-9070
Fax: (202)822-9075
Registered: FARA

Employers

Boros & Garofalo

SMITH, W. Lamar

2121 K St. NW
Suite 700
Washington, DC 20037
Tel: (202)296-9230
Fax: (202)862-5498
Registered: LDA

Employers

VISA U.S.A., Inc. (Senior V. President, Government Relations)

SMITH, Walter R.

One GEICO Plaza
Washington, DC 20076-0001
Tel: (301)986-3000

Employers

GEICO Corp. (Assistant V. President, Communications)

SMITH, Wayne

50 F St. NW
Suite 1070
Washington, DC 20001
Tel: (202)638-5855
Registered: LDA

Employers

The Justice Project, Inc. (Executive Director)

SMITH, Willa H.

Federal Relations Office
11 Dupont Circle NW, Suite 220
Washington, DC 20036
EMail: fron@erols.com
Tel: (202)863-9384
Fax: (202)863-9388

Employers

Tuskegee University, Office of (Director)

SMITH, William G.

200 Maryland Ave. NE
Washington, DC 20002
EMail: bsmith@vfwdc.org
Tel: (202)543-2239
Fax: (202)543-2746

Employers

Veterans of Foreign Wars of the U.S. (Director, Public Affairs)

SMITH NIGHTINGALE, Demetra

2100 M St. NW
Washington, DC 20037
Tel: (202)833-7200
Fax: (202)429-0687

Employers

The Urban Institute (Director, Welfare and Training Research)

SMITH-DEWAAL, Caroline

1875 Connecticut Ave. NW
Suite 300
Washington, DC 20009
Tel: (202)332-9110
Fax: (202)265-4954
Registered: LDA

Employers

Center for Science in the Public Interest (Director, Programs on Food Safety)

SMOLEN, Maggie

1101 Vermont Ave. NW
12th Floor
Washington, DC 20005-3583
Tel: (202)789-7432
Fax: (202)789-7485
Registered: LDA

Employers

American Medical Ass'n (Assistant Director, Congressional Affairs)

SMOLER, Barry

1350 New York Ave. NW
Suite 1100
Washington, DC 20005-4798
Tel: (202)879-4000
Fax: (202)393-2866

Former Deputy Assistant General Counsel for Hydroelectric Licensing; Assistant General Counsel for Rule Making and Environmental Law; and Deputy Assistant General counsel for Pipeline Certification, all at the Federal Energy Regulatory Commission, Department of Energy.

Employers

Spiegel & McDiarmid (Of Counsel)

SMOLONSKY, Marc

9000 Rockville Pike
Bldg. One, Room 244
Bethesda, MD 20892
EMail: smolonm@od.nih.gov
Tel: (301)496-3471
Fax: (301)496-0840

Employers

Department of Health and Human Services - Nat'l Institutes of Health (Associate Director, Office of Legislative Policy and Analysis)

SMOOT, Oliver R.

1250 I St. NW
Suite 200
Washington, DC 20005
Tel: (202)737-8888
Fax: (202)638-4922
Registered: LDA

Employers

Information Technology Industry Council (Exec. V. President and Treasurer)

SMOOTS, Carol A.

1900 K St. NW
Washington, DC 20006
EMail: carol_smoots@mckennacuneo.com
Tel: (202)496-7500
Fax: (202)496-7756

Employers

McKenna & Cuneo, L.L.P. (Partner)

SMUCKER, Bob

2040 S St. NW
Washington, DC 20009
Tel: (202)387-5048
Fax: (202)387-5149
Registered: LDA

Employers

Charity Lobbying in the Public Interest (Co-Director)

SMYTH, Matthew D.

900 19th St. NW
Suite 400
Washington, DC 20006
Tel: (202)857-3100
Fax: (202)296-8716

Employers

America's Community Bankers (Government Relations)

SMYTHE, USMC, Col. Ana

1300 Defense Pentagon
Room 3E966
Washington, DC 20301-1300
Tel: (703)697-6210
Fax: (703)693-5530

Employers

Department of Defense (Military Assistant, Office of Legislative Affairs)

SMYTHE, Leigh H.

3601 Eisenhower Ave.
Suite 110
Alexandria, VA 22304-6439
EMail: smythe@tianet.org
Tel: (703)329-0498
Fax: (703)329-1898

Employers

Transportation Intermediaries Ass'n (Manager, Communications)

SMYTHE, Marianne K.

2445 M St. NW
Washington, DC 20037-1420
Tel: (202)663-6000
Fax: (202)663-6363
Registered: LDA, FARA
EMail: msmythe@wilmer.com

Director, Division of Investment Management (1990-93), Executive Assistant to the Chairman (1990), and Associate Director, Division of Investment Management (1988-90), all at the Securities and Exchange Commission.

Employers

Wilmer, Cutler & Pickering (Partner)

Clients Represented

On Behalf of Wilmer, Cutler & Pickering

American Electric Power Co.
Citibank, N.A.
Fitch Investors Service, Inc.
Managed Funds Ass'n
Tiger Management Corp.

SMYTHE, Ph.D., Robert B.

4807 Wellington Dr.
Chevy Chase, MD 20815
Tel: (301)654-5661
Fax: (301)652-8710
EMail: rbsmytheprc@cs.com

Former Volunteer, Peace Corps, 1965-66. Professional Staff Member (1974-76) and Senior Staff Member for Natural Resources (1977-81) President's Council on Environmental Quality.

Employers

Potomac Resource Consultants (Owner/Principal)

SMYTHE, William K.

1899 Preston White Dr.
Reston, VA 20191-4367
Tel: (703)264-7200
Fax: (703)620-0994
EMail: ksmythe@npes.org

Employers

NPES, The Ass'n for Suppliers of Printing, Publishing, and Converting Technologies (V. President)

SMYTHERS, Mike

1331 Pennsylvania Ave. NW
Suite 560
Washington, DC 20004
Tel: (202)783-8124
Fax: (202)783-5929
Registered: LDA

Employers

CSX Corp. (Director, Federal Affairs)

SNAPE, Dale W.

1317 F St. NW
Suite 600
Washington, DC 20004
Tel: (202)638-2121
Fax: (202)638-7045
Registered: LDA
EMail: snape@wexlergroup.com

Employers

The Wexler Group (Principal/General Manager)

Clients Represented

On Behalf of The Wexler Group

American Airlines
American Forest & Paper Ass'n
Blue Cross and Blue Shield of California
Burst Networks Inc.
Caterpillar Inc.
Comcast Corp.
Hydroelectric Licensing Reform Task Force
Lockheed Martin Corp.
Orange County Public Schools
ORBITZ
PacifiCare Health Systems
Shivwitz Band of the Paiute Indian Tribe of Utah
Wyeth-Ayerst Laboratories

SNAPE, III, William

1101 14th St. NW
Suite 1400
Washington, DC 20005
Tel: (202)682-9400
Fax: (202)682-1331
Registered: LDA
EMail: wsnape@defenders.org

Employers

Defenders of Wildlife (V. President, Law and Litigation)

SNEED, James

600 13th St. NW
Washington, DC 20005-3096
Tel: (202)756-8006
Fax: (202)756-8087
EMail: jsneed@mwe.com
Former General Counsel, Director of Bureau of Consumer Protection and Assistant Director of Bureau of Competition, Federal Trade Commission.

Employers

McDermott, Will and Emery (Partner)

SNEED, Robert D.

2404-D S. Walter Reed Dr.
Arlington, VA 22203
Tel: (703)820-6372
Fax: (703)820-6373
Registered: LDA

Employers

Self-employed as an independent consultant.

Clients Represented

As an independent consultant

Advanced Power Technologies, Inc.
General Electric Co.
Hurt, Norton and Associates, Inc.
Kaman Diversified Technologies Corp.

SNEERINGER, Thomas M.

1101 17th St. NW
Suite 1300
Washington, DC 20036
Tel: (202)452-7183
Fax: (202)463-6573
Registered: LDA
EMail: tsneeringer@steel.org

Employers

American Iron and Steel Institute (Senior V. President, Public Policy and General Counsel)

SNIDER, Virginia L.

607 14th St. NW
Washington, DC 20005
Tel: (202)434-0700
Fax: (202)912-6000
EMail: sniderv@rw.com
Director of Special Projects, Supervising Merger Analyst and Senior Merger Analyst, Federal Trade Commission, 1973-94.

Employers

Rogers & Wells (Consultant, Anti-Trust Division)

SNIPES, James C.

1201 Pennsylvania Ave. NW
Washington, DC 20004-2401
Tel: (202)662-6000
Fax: (202)662-6291
EMail: jsnipes@cov.com
Law Clerk to Judge Caleb M. Wright, U.S. District Court for the District of Delaware, 1980-81.

Employers

Covington & Burling (Partner)

SNODGRASS, Randall

1250 24th St. NW
Washington, DC 20037
Tel: (202)293-4800
Fax: (202)293-9211
Registered: LDA

Employers

World Wildlife Fund (Director, Congressional Relations)

SNOOK, Sheldon

409 Third St. SW
Suite 7900
Washington, DC 20416
Tel: (202)205-6700
Fax: (202)205-7374
EMail: sheldon.snook@sba.gov

Employers

Small Business Administration (Legislative Affairs Specialist)

SNOW, Gerard C.

5201 Auth Way
Fifth Floor
Camp Springs, MD 20746
Tel: (301)423-3335
Fax: (301)423-0634
Registered: LDA

Employers

Transportation Institute (Director, Government Affairs)

SNOW, Howard

110 N. Royal St.
Suite 406
Alexandria, VA 22314
Tel: (703)548-7607
Fax: (703)519-8779

Employers

Marine Corps Reserve Officers Ass'n (Exec. Director)

SNOWDEN, Courtney

919 18th St. NW
Suite 800
Washington, DC 20006
Tel: (202)628-4160
Fax: (202)347-5323

Employers

Human Rights Campaign Fund (Policy Assistant)

SNOWLING, Randall

555 12th St. NW
Suite 500
Washington, DC 20004-1207
Tel: (202)879-5600
Fax: (202)879-5309
Registered: LDA

Employers

Deloitte & Touche LLP Nat'l Office - Washington (Partner)

SNYDER, Andrea

1156 15th St. NW
Suite 820
Washington, DC 20005
Tel: (202)833-1717
Fax: (202)833-2686
EMail: asnyder@danceusa.org

Employers

Dance/USA (Exec. Director)

SNYDER, Craig

1101 30th St. NW
Washington, DC 20006
Tel: (202)337-6600
Fax: (202)337-6660
Registered: LDA
Former Chief of Staff to Senator Arlen Specter (R-PA).

Employers

The Peterson Group
Schroth & Associates (Contract Lobbyist)
Craig Snyder & Associates (President)

Clients Represented

On Behalf of The Peterson Group

Erie Internat'l Airport
Franklin Institute

On Behalf of Schroth & Associates

Thomas Jefferson University

On Behalf of Craig Snyder & Associates

Tensiodyne Scientific Corp.

SNYDER, Dan

1909 K St. NW
Fourth Floor
Washington, DC 20006
Tel: (202)973-5800
Fax: (202)973-5858

Employers

Porter/Novelli (Partner, Food, Beverage and Nutrition)

SNYDER, Denise

P.O. Box 34125
Washington, DC 20043
Tel: (202)232-0789
Fax: (202)387-3812

Employers

D.C. Rape Crisis Center (Exec. Director)

SNYDER, John M.

1090 Vermont Ave. NW
Suite 800
Washington, DC 20005
Tel: (202)326-5259
Fax: (202)898-1939
Registered: LDA
EMail: gundean@aol.com

Employers

American Federation of Police & Concerned Citizens, Inc. (V. President, Public Relations)
Citizens Committee for the Right to Keep and Bear Arms (Director, Public Affairs)

SNYDER, Kenneth F.

1050 Connecticut Ave. NW
Suite 1100
Washington, DC 20036-5304
Tel: (202)861-1500
Fax: (202)861-1790
Registered: LDA
EMail: Ksnyder@baker-hostetler.com

Employers

Baker & Hostetler LLP (Partner)

Clients Represented

On Behalf of Baker & Hostetler LLP

American Resort Development Ass'n
KeyCorp, Inc.

SNYDER, Lynn S.

1227 25th St. NW
Suite 700
Washington, DC 20037
Tel: (202)861-0900
Fax: (202)296-2882
Registered: LDA
EMail: lsnyder@ebglaw.com

Employers

Epstein Becker & Green, P.C. (Member)

SNYDER, Patricia N.

1909 K St. NW
Suite 600
Washington, DC 20006-1167
Tel: (202)585-6900
Fax: (202)585-6969
Registered: LDA

Employers

Thompson Coburn LLP (Partner)

Clients Represented

On Behalf of Thompson Coburn LLP

Air Transport Ass'n of America

SNYDER, Paul M.

633 Pennsylvania Ave. NW
Fourth Floor
Washington, DC 20004
Tel: (202)783-2596
Fax: (202)628-5379
Registered: LDA, FARA
EMail: psnyder@psw-inc.com
Tax Counsel for Rep. Ed Jenkins (D-GA), 1989-92. Legislative Assistant to Speaker Thomas P. "Tip" O'Neill, Jr. (D-MA), U.S. House of Representatives, 1979-85.

Employers

Public Strategies Washington, Inc.

Clients Represented

On Behalf of Public Strategies Washington, Inc.

Advanced Micro Devices
American Methanol Institute
Anheuser-Busch Cos., Inc.
Bristol-Myers Squibb Co.
Edison Electric Institute
Mexico, Secretaria de Comercio y Fomento Industrial (SECOFI)
Southwest Airlines

SNYDER, Russell K.

4041 Powder Mill Rd.
Suite 104
Calverton, MD 20705
Tel: (301)348-2005
Fax: (301)348-2020
EMail: rsnyder@kellencompany.com

Employers

Asphalt Roofing Manufacturers Ass'n (Exec. V. President)
Builders Hardware Manufacturers Ass'n (Washington Representative)
Comic Magazine Ass'n of America (Washington Representative)
Home Fashion Products Ass'n (Exec. V. President)
The Kellen Company (Exec. V. President)
Roof Coatings Manufacturers Ass'n (Exec. V. President)
Window Covering Manufacturers Ass'n (Washington Representative)
Window Covering Safety Council (Washington Representative)

Clients Represented

On Behalf of The Kellen Company

Asphalt Roofing Manufacturers Ass'n
Builders Hardware Manufacturers Ass'n
Comic Magazine Ass'n of America
Home Fashion Products Ass'n
Roof Coatings Manufacturers Ass'n
Window Covering Manufacturers Ass'n
Window Covering Safety Council

SNYDER, Wallace S.

1101 Vermont Ave. NW
Suite 500
Washington, DC 20005
Tel: (202)898-0089
Fax: (202)898-0159
Registered: LDA

Employers

American Advertising Federation (President)

SOBEL, David

1718 Connecticut Ave. NW
Suite 200
Washington, DC 20009
Tel: (202)483-1140
Fax: (202)483-1248

Employers

Electronic Privacy Information Center (Legal Counsel)

SOBEL, Georgette J.

2023 Q St. NW
Washington, DC 20009-1009
Tel: (202)387-3624
Fax: (202)387-3629

Employers

Independents Committee for Future America (Secretary)

SOBEL, M.D., Ph.D, Mark E.

9650 Rockville Pike
Bethesda, MD 20814-3993
Tel: (301)530-7130
Fax: (301)571-1879

Employers

American Soc. for Investigative Pathology (Exec. Officer)

SOBER, Rynthia Manning

One GEICO Plaza
Washington, DC 20076-0001
Tel: (301)986-3000
Fax: (301)718-5234

Employers

GEICO Corp. (V. President, Public Affairs)

SOCCI, Laurence L.

2020 Pennsylvania Ave. NW
Suite 323
Washington, DC 20006-1846
Tel: (202)262-5843
Registered: LDA

Employers

The C.L.A. Group, LLC

Clients Represented

On Behalf of The C.L.A. Group, LLC

Colombian American Service Ass'n
Colombian American Trade Center

SOEBAGJO, Adryani

1015 18th St. NW
Suite 505
Washington, DC 20036
Tel: (202)887-4830
Fax: (202)887-4834
Registered: LDA
EMail: asoebagjo@mindspring.com

Employers

Japan Automobile Standards Internat'l Center (Research Assistant)

SOHN, Michael N.

555 12th St. NW
Washington, DC 20004-1206
Tel: (202)942-5000
Fax: (202)942-5999
EMail: Michael_Sohn@aporter.com
Member (1980-83) and Counsel (1978-80), Administrative Conference of the U.S. Member, Executive Committee, Regulatory Council of the U.S., 1978-80. General Counsel, Federal Trade Commission, 1977-80. Attorney and Supervising Attorney, General Counsel's Office, National Labor Relations Board, 1964-69.

Employers

Arnold & Porter (Partner)

SOJKA, Gary L.

321 D St. NE
Washington, DC 20002
Tel: (202)547-4192
Fax: (202)547-4674
Registered: LDA
Professional Staff Member, Senate Select Committee on Intelligence, 1994.

Employers

The Potomac Advocates (Partner)

Clients Represented

On Behalf of The Potomac Advocates

Adroit Systems Inc.
Argon Engineering Associates
Brashear Systems, L.L.P.
CUBRC
Eastman Kodak Co.
Eclipse
General Dynamics Corp.
B. F. Goodrich Co.
GTS
Northrop Grumman Corp.
Raytheon Co.
SAFT America Inc.
SAFT R&D Center
Spot Image Corp.
SRI Internat'l
Veridian Corp.

SOKLER, Bruce D.

701 Pennsylvania Ave. NW
Suite 900
Washington, DC 20004-2608
Tel: (202)434-7300
Fax: (202)434-7400
Registered: FARA
EMail: bsokler@mintz.com

Employers

Mintz, Levin, Cohn, Ferris, Glovsky and Popeo, P.C. (Partner)

Clients Represented

On Behalf of Mintz, Levin, Cohn, Ferris, Glovsky and Popeo, P.C.

AOL Time Warner

SOKOL, Eric W.

228 Seventh St. SE
Washington, DC 20003-4306
Tel: (202)547-7424
Fax: (202)547-9559
Registered: LDA
EMail: ews@nahc.org

Employers

Nat'l Ass'n for Home Care (Deputy Director, Government Affairs)

SOKUL, Stanley

1101 Pennsylvania Ave. NW
Suite 810
The Evening Star Building
Washington, DC 20004
Tel: (202)638-1101
Fax: (202)638-1102
EMail: ss@davidsondc.com
Former Chief of Staff to Senator Judd Gregg (R-NH).

Employers

Davidson & Company, Inc. (Principal)

Clients Represented

On Behalf of Davidson & Company, Inc.

Advertising Tax Coalition
American Advertising Federation
American Ass'n for Homecare
American Ass'n of Advertising Agencies
AOL Time Warner
Apria Healthcare Group
Ass'n of Nat'l Advertisers
The Business Roundtable
Corporation for Enterprise Development
Direct Marketing Ass'n, Inc.
eBay Inc.
Ellicott Internat'l
Federal Home Loan Mortgage Corp. (Freddie Mac)
Grocery Manufacturers of America
The Hearst Corp.
Independent Contractor Coalition
Magazine Publishers of America
Nat'l Ass'n of Broadcasters
Newspaper Ass'n of America
The Reader's Digest Ass'n
Paul Scherer & Co., LLP
The Washington Post Co.
Yellow Pages Publishers Ass'n

SOLARZ, Barry D.

1101 17th St. NW
Suite 1300
Washington, DC 20036-4700
Tel: (202)452-7139
Fax: (202)463-6573
Registered: LDA
EMail: bsolarz@steel.org

Employers

American Iron and Steel Institute (V. President, Tax and Trade)

SOLARZ, Hon. Stephen J.

1615 L St. NW
Suite 900
Washington, DC 20036
Tel: (202)778-1000
Fax: (202)466-6002
Registered: LDA, FARA
EMail: ssolarz@apcoworldwide.com
Member, U.S. House of Representatives (D-NY), 1975-93.

Employers

APCO Worldwide (Senior Counselor)

Clients Represented

On Behalf of APCO Worldwide

Creme de la Creme, Inc.
Formosan Ass'n for Public Affairs

SOLER, Lawrence A.

1400 I St. NW
Suite 530
Washington, DC 20005
Tel: (202)371-9746
Fax: (202)371-2760

Employers

Juvenile Diabetes Foundation Internat'l (Director, Government Relations)

SOLHEIM, Linda T.

2817-D S. Woodrow St.
Arlington, VA 22206
Tel: (703)671-4228
Fax: (703)671-4424
Registered: LDA
EMail: ltsolheim@earthlink.net
Director, Office of Legislative Affairs, Federal Communications Commission, 1989-93. Chief Counsel, National Telecommunications and Information Administration and Deputy General Counsel, Department of Commerce, 1985-89. Acting Chief of Staff and Deputy Chief of Staff, Department of Labor, 1983-85. Majority Counsel, Senate Committee on Government Affairs and Minority Counsel, Senate Committee on the Judiciary, 1979-83.

Employers

Townsend Solheim (Chief Exec.Officer)

Clients Represented

On Behalf of Townsend Solheim

Iridium, LLC
Personal Communications Industry Ass'n (PCIA)
VoiceStream Wireless Corp.
Wireless Technology Research, L.L.C.

SOLIS, Ali

415 Second St. NE
Second Floor
Washington, DC 20002
Tel: (202)543-4599
Fax: (202)543-8130
EMail: asolis@enterprisefoundation.org

Employers

The Enterprise Foundation (Deputy Director, Public Policy)

SOLIS, Lupe

666 11th St. NW
Suite 700
Washington, DC 20001
Tel: (202)783-6686
Fax: (202)638-2356

Employers

Older Women's League (President)

SOLLER, R. William

1150 Connecticut Ave. NW
12th Floor
Washington, DC 20036
Tel: (202)429-9260
Fax: (202)223-6835

Employers

Consumer Healthcare Products Ass'n (Director, Science and Technology and Senior V. President)

SOLMONESE, Joe

805 15th St. NW
Suite 400
Washington, DC 20005
Tel: (202)326-1400
Fax: (202)326-1415

Employers
EMILY'S List (Chief Operating Officer)

SOLOMON, Emily B.

1625 K St. NW
Suite 1090
Washington, DC 20006-1604
Tel: (202)887-0278
Fax: (202)452-8160
Registered: LDA

Employers
Nat'l Foreign Trade Council, Inc. (Managing Director, U.S.-South Africa Business Council)

SOLOMON, Hon. Gerald B. H.

801 Pennsylvania Ave. NW
Suite 750
Washington, DC 20004
Tel: (202)628-3750
Fax: (202)624-0659
Registered: LDA, FARA
EMail: gsolomon@solomongroup.com
Member, U.S. House of Representatives (R-NY), 1979-99. Served in the U.S. Marine Corps, 1951-58

Employers
The Solomon Group, LLC (President and Chief Exec. Officer)

Clients Represented

On Behalf of The Solomon Group, LLC
AAI Corp.
Alliance for American Innovation, Inc.
Apria Healthcare Group
Ass'n of Small Business Development Centers
Clough, Harbour & Associates LLP
Espey Manufacturing and Electronics
Finch-Pruyn Paper Co.
General Electric Co.
Institute for Entrepreneurship
Internat'l Medical Programs
JBA Consulting, Inc.
"K" Line America, Inc.
Morocco, Foreign Ministry of the Kingdom of
Nat'l Milk Producers Federation
Safe Environment of America
States Ratification Committee
SUNY Empire State College
Taipei Economic and Cultural Representative Office in the United States
Turkey, Embassy of the Republic of
Turkey, Government of the Republic of
The Vandervort Group, LLC

SOLOMON, Irica

1025 Connecticut Ave. NW
Suite 1210
Washington, DC 20036
Tel: (202)296-1967
Fax: (202)296-2873

Employers
United Airlines (Manager, Legislative Affairs)

SOLOMON, Karen

250 E St. SW
MS: 8-4
Washington, DC 20219
Tel: (202)874-5090
Fax: (202)874-5305

Employers
Department of Treasury - Comptroller of the Currency (Director, Legislative and Regulatory Activities, Office of Chief Counsel)

SOLOMON, Maura K.

805 15th St. NW
Suite 600
Washington, DC 20005
Tel: (202)289-4322
Fax: (202)289-1903
Registered: LDA
Congressional Affairs Specialist, Office of Thrift Supervision, Department of the Treasury, 1999-2000.

Employers
The Financial Services Roundtable (Director of Banking and Financial Services)

SOLOMON, Nicole

1350 I St. NW
Suite 1000
Washington, DC 20005
Tel: (202)962-5400
Fax: (202)336-7224
EMail: nsolomo3@ford.com

Employers
Ford Motor Co. (Director, Corporate Policy Communications)

SOLOMON, Peggy

1755 S. Jefferson Davis Hwy.
Suite 1200
Arlington, VA 22202
Tel: (703)413-8300
Fax: (703)413-8445

Employers
Mutual Broadcasting System (V. President, Operations)

SOLOWAY, Stan Z.

2101 Wilson Blvd.
Suite 750
Arlington, VA 22201
Tel: (703)875-8059
Fax: (703)875-8922

Employers
Professional Services Council (President)

SOMBROTTO, Vincent R.

100 Indiana Ave. NW
Washington, DC 20001
Tel: (202)393-4695
Fax: (202)756-7400

Employers
Fund for Assuring an Independent Retirement (Chairman)
Nat'l Ass'n of Letter Carriers of the United States of America (President)

SOMERS, Edward

1620 I St. NW
Suite 400
Washington, DC 20006
Tel: (202)293-7330
Fax: (202)293-2352

Employers
United States Conference of Mayors (Assistant Exec. Director)

SOMERS, Frederick P.

P.O. Box 31220
4720 Montgomery Ln.
Bethesda, MD 20824-1220
Tel: (301)652-2682
Fax: (301)652-7711
Registered: LDA

Employers
American Occupational Therapy Ass'n, Inc. (Associate Exec. Director for Professional Affairs)

SOMERVILLE, Nancy

636 I St. NW
Washington, DC 20001-3736
Tel: (202)898-2444
Fax: (202)898-1185

Employers
American Soc. of Landscape Architects (Exec. Director)

SOMMER, Jr., John F.

1608 K St. NW
Washington, DC 20006
Tel: (202)861-2700
Fax: (202)861-2786
Registered: LDA

Employers
American Legion (Exec. Director, Washington Office)

SOMMER, Judah C.

1101 Pennsylvania Ave. NW
Suite 900
Washington, DC 20004
Tel: (202)637-3700
Fax: (202)637-3773

Employers
Goldman, Sachs and Co. (Managing Director)

SOMMER, Peter R.

1200 Wilson Blvd.
Arlington, VA 22209-1989
Tel: (703)465-3555
Fax: (703)465-3042

Employers
The Boeing Co. (Director, International Defense Trade)

SOMMER, Robert G.

1747 Pennsylvania Ave. NW
Suite 1150
Washington, DC 20006
Tel: (202)296-6222
Fax: (202)296-4507
Registered: LDA
EMail: rsommer@mww.com
Staff Consultant, House Commerce Subcommittee, 1984-87. Presidential Management Assistant, Environmental Protection Agency, 1983.

Employers
The MWW Group (Exec. V. President)

Clients Represented

On Behalf of The MWW Group
GAF Corp.
Puerto Ricans for Civic Action
Puerto Rico Senate
Synapse

SOMMERS, Christina Hoff

1150 17th St. NW
Washington, DC 20036
Tel: (202)862-5800
Fax: (202)862-7177
EMail: csommers@aei.org

Employers
American Enterprise Institute for Public Policy Research (W. H. Brady Fellow)

SOMSON, Barbara

1350 I St. NW
Suite 510
Washington, DC 20005
Tel: (202)828-8500
Fax: (202)293-3457
Registered: LDA

Employers
United Automobile, Aerospace and Agricultural Implement Workers of America (UAW) (Deputy Legislative Director)

SONENSTEIN, Freya Lund

2100 M St. NW
Washington, DC 20037
Tel: (202)833-7200
Fax: (202)429-0687

Employers
The Urban Institute (Director, Population Studies Center)

SONKEN, Lori J.

1849 C St. NW
Room 7639
Washington, DC 20240
Tel: (202)513-0565
Fax: (202)513-0304
EMail: lsonken@usbr.gov
Former Professional Staff Member, House Committee on Natural Resources. Professional Staff Member, Subcommittee on Water and Power Resources, House Committee on Interior and Insular Affairs, 1985-88. Legislative Assistant to Senator S. I. Hayakawa (R-CA), 1980-82.

Employers
Department of Interior - Bureau of Reclamation (Chief, Congressional and Legislative Affairs Group)

SONNENFELDT, Helmut

1775 Massachusetts Ave. NW
Washington, DC 20036-2188
Tel: (202)797-6000
Fax: (202)797-6004
Counselor, Department of State, 1974-77; Senior Staff Member, National Security Council, 1969-74; Director, Office of Research on the Soviet Union and Eastern Europe, Department of State, 1952-69.

Employers
The Brookings Institution (Guest Scholar, Foreign Policy Studies)

SOOK LEE, Jin

815 16th St. NW
Washington, DC 20006
Tel: (202)842-1263
Fax: (202)842-1462

Employers
Asian Pacific American Labor Alliance, AFL-CIO (Exec. Director)

SOPHOS, Mary C.

1010 Wisconsin Ave. NW
Ninth Floor
Washington, DC 20007
Tel: (202)337-9400
Fax: (202)337-4508
Registered: LDA
EMail: msophos@gmabrands.com

Employers
Grocery Manufacturers of America (Senior V. President and Chief Government Affairs Officer)

SORENSEN, Sandra

110 Maryland Ave. NE
Suite 207
Washington, DC 20002
Tel: (202)543-1517
Fax: (202)543-5994
EMail: sorensens@ucc.org

Employers
United Church of Christ Justice and Witness Ministry (Associate, Communications & Media Advocacy)

SORGI, Donna

1133 19th St. NW
Washington, DC 20036
Tel: (202)887-3830
Fax: (202)736-6880
EMail: donna.sorgi@wcom.com

Employers
MCI WorldCom Corp. (V. President, Federal Advocacy)

SORINI, Ron

1300 Pennsylvania Ave. NW
Suite 400
Ronald Reagan Bldg.
Washington, DC 20004
EMail: rsorini@strtrade.com
Tel: (202)638-2230
Fax: (202)638-2236
Registered: LDA

Former Chief Textile Negotiator, Office of the U.S. Trade Representative, Executive Office of the President, The White House. Also worked in the Department of Commerce.

Employers
Sandler, Travis & Rosenberg, P.A. (President, Trade Negotiations and Legislative Affairs)

Clients Represented
On Behalf of Sandler, Travis & Rosenberg, P.A.
American Apparel & Footwear Ass'n
American Textile Co.
Babcock & Wilcox
Confederation of Garment Exporters of the Philippines
Elzay Ready Wear Manufacturing Co.
Grupo "J" S.A.
The Hosiery Ass'n
Intradeco
Skipps Cutting

SORKIN, Stuart

1000 Potomac St. NW
Suite 300
Washington, DC 20007
Tel: (202)337-6200
Fax: (202)333-0871

Employers
Hewes, Gelband, Lambert & Dann, P.C. (Of Counsel)

SORLEY, Dr. Lewis

9429 Garden Ct.
Potomac, MD 20854-3964
EMail: sorleydog@erols.com
Tel: (301)765-0695
Fax: (301)983-0583

Employers
Ass'n of Military Colleges and Schools of the U.S. (Exec. Director)

SOROSIAK, Camille

9111 Old Georgetown Rd.
Bethesda, MD 20814
EMail: csorosia@acc.org
Tel: (301)897-5400
Fax: (301)897-9745
Registered: LDA

Employers
American College of Cardiology (Associate Director, Legislative Affairs)

SORRELLS, John

1341 G St. NW
Suite 900
Washington, DC 20005
Tel: (202)637-1547
Fax: (202)637-1535

Employers
Philip Morris Management Corp. (Director, Media Relations)

SOTOMAYOR, Dr. Marta

2713 Ontario Rd. NW
Suite 200
Washington, DC 20009
Tel: (202)265-1288
Fax: (202)745-2522

Employers
Nat'l Hispanic Council on Aging (President)

SOTSKY, Rachel

700 13th St. NW
Suite 400
Washington, DC 20005
EMail: rsotsky@cassidy.com
Tel: (202)347-0773
Fax: (202)347-0785
Registered: LDA

Legislative Assistant and Speechwriter to Senator Warren Rudman (R-NH), 1985-92. Legislative Assistant to Senator Spark Matsunaga (D-HI), 1980-84. Legislative Correspondent to Senator Howard Metzenbaum (D-OH), 1979-80.

Employers
Cassidy & Associates, Inc. (Associate)

Clients Represented
On Behalf of Cassidy & Associates, Inc.
Northwestern University
Ohio State University
Saint Coletta of Greater Washington, Inc.

SOUCY, Philip E.

1215 Jefferson Davis Hwy.
Suite 1500
Arlington, VA 22202
EMail: phil.soucy@baesystems.com
Tel: (703)236-6246
Fax: (703)405-5010

Employers
BAE SYSTEMS North America (Director, Public Relations)

SOUDRIETTE, Richard W.

1101 15th St. NW
Third Floor
Washington, DC 20005
Tel: (202)828-8507
Fax: (202)452-0804

Employers
Internat'l Foundation for Election Systems (IFES) (President)

SOUK, Fred S.

1001 Pennsylvania Ave. NW
Suite 1100
Washington, DC 20004-2595
EMail: fsouk@cromor.com
Tel: (202)624-2500
Fax: (202)628-5116

Law Clerk to Chief Judge Northrop, U.S. District Court for the District of Maryland, 1975-76.

Employers
Crowell & Moring LLP (Partner)

SOULE, AICP, Jeffrey

1776 Massachusetts Ave. NW
Suite 400
Washington, DC 20036
EMail: jsoule@planning.org
Tel: (202)872-0611
Fax: (202)872-0643

Employers
American Planning Ass'n (Director, Policy)

SOUTH, Rebecca F.

900 17th St. NW
Suite 1000
Washington, DC 20006
Tel: (202)530-7400
Fax: (202)463-6915
Registered: LDA

Employers
Blank Rome Comisky & McCauley, LLP

Clients Represented
On Behalf of Blank Rome Comisky & McCauley, LLP
D.C. Wiring
LDW, Inc.
Valley Forge Flag Co.

SOUTHWICK, Jennifer M.

600 New Hampshire Ave. NW
11th Floor
Washington, DC 20037
EMail: jms@dejlaw.com
Tel: (202)944-3000
Fax: (202)944-3068
Registered: LDA, FARA

Staff Assistant, House Committee on Transportation and Infrastructure, 1995-98.

Employers
Dyer Ellis & Joseph, P.C. (Government Affairs Analyst)

Clients Represented
On Behalf of Dyer Ellis & Joseph, P.C.
American Coke and Coal Chemicals Institute
Bender Shipbuilding & Repair Co., Inc.
BLNG, Inc.
Browning Transport Management
China Shipping (Group) Co.
John Crane-LIPS, Inc.
Cross Sound Ferry Services, Inc.
DaimlerChrysler Corp.
Electronic Design Inc.
FastShip, Inc.
Friede Goldman Halter
Fruit Shippers Ltd.
Gateway Clipper Fleet
Glass Packaging Institute
Heerema Marine Contractors Nederland B.V.
Hornblower Marine Services, Inc.
Hvide Marine Inc.
Kvaerner Philadelphia Shipyard Inc.
Marine Spill Response Corporation
Nat'l Oilseed Processors Ass'n
Northrop Grumman Corp.
Offshore Rig Museum, Inc.
Put-in-Bay Boat Line Co.
Sea Ventures Inc.
The Trump Organization
Wendella Sightseeing Boats Inc.

SPAHR, Frederick T.

10801 Rockville Pike
Rockville, MD 20852
Tel: (301)897-5700
Ext: 4100
Fax: (301)571-0457
Registered: LDA

Employers
American Speech, Language, and Hearing Ass'n (Exec. Director)
The Tri-Alliance of Rehabilitation Professionals (Contact)

SPAK, Gregory J.

601 13th St. NW
Suite 600 South
Washington, DC 20005
EMail: spakgre@washdc.whitecase.com
Tel: (202)626-3600
Fax: (202)639-9355

Employers
White & Case LLP (Partner)

SPAK, Walter J.

601 13th St. NW
Suite 600 South
Washington, DC 20005
EMail: spakwal@washdc.whitecase.com
Tel: (202)626-3600
Fax: (202)639-9355

Employers
White & Case LLP (Partner)

Clients Represented
On Behalf of White & Case LLP
Malaysia Ministry of Trade
Minebea Thailand
Singapore, Embassy of the Republic of
Singapore, Government of the Republic of
Thailand, Department of Foreign Trade of

SPALDING, Dr. Matthew

214 Massachusetts Ave. NE
Washington, DC 20002
Tel: (202)546-4400
Fax: (202)546-8328

Employers
Heritage Foundation (Director, Lectures and Educational Programs)

SPANGLER, Barbara R.

415 Second St. NE
Suite 300
Washington, DC 20002
Tel: (202)547-2004
Fax: (202)546-2638

Employers
Wheat Export Trade Education Committee (Exec. Director)

SPANGLER, David C.

1150 Connecticut Ave. NW
12th Floor
Washington, DC 20036
Tel: (202)429-9260
Fax: (202)223-6835
Registered: LDA

Employers
Consumer Healthcare Products Ass'n (V. President-International and Assistant General Counsel)

SPANGLER, Jr., Thomas J.

1111 14th St. NW
Suite 1100
Washington, DC 20005-5603
EMail: spanglet@ada.org
Tel: (202)898-2400
Fax: (202)789-2258
Registered: LDA

Employers
American Dental Ass'n (Director, Legislative and Regulatory Policy; CGA)

SPANOGLE, Robert W.

1608 K St. NW
Washington, DC 20006
Tel: (202)861-2700
Fax: (202)861-2786
Registered: LDA

Employers
American Legion (National Adjutant)

SPAR, Edward J.

1429 Duke St.
Suite 402
Alexandria, VA 22314-3402
EMail: copars@aol.com
Tel: (703)836-0404
Fax: (703)684-2037

Employers
Council of Professional Ass'ns on Federal Statistics (Exec. Director)

SPARBER, Peter G.

1319 F St. NW
Suite 301
Washington, DC 20004
Tel: (202)393-3240
Fax: (202)393-4385
Registered: LDA

Employers
Sparber and Associates (President)

Clients Represented

On Behalf of Sparber and Associates
Great Lakes Chemical Corp.
Marathon Ashland Petroleum, LLC
Methyl Bromide Working Group
Sleep Products Safety Council
U.S. Steel

SPARKMAN, John S.

1331 Pennsylvania Ave. NW
Suite 512
Washington, DC 20004
Tel: (202)662-8755
Fax: (202)662-8749
Registered: LDA

Employers
PPL (Director, Federal Public Affairs)

SPARKS, Angela M.

801 Pennsylvania Ave. NW
N. Bldg., Suite 250
Washington, DC 20004
Tel: (202)783-5521
Fax: (202)783-5569
Registered: LDA

Employers
Energy East Management Corp. (V. President, Government Affairs)

SPARKS, John D.

910 17th St. NW
Suite 800
Washington, DC 20006
Tel: (212)262-5161
Fax: (212)262-5198
Registered: LDA
EMail: jsparks@symphony.org

Employers
American Symphony Orchestra League (V. President, Public and Government Affairs)

SPARLIN, Jr., D. Dean

1050 Connecticut Ave. NW
Washington, DC 20036-5306
Tel: (202)955-8500
Fax: (202)467-0539
Registered: LDA
EMail: dsparlin@gdclaw.com

Employers
Gibson, Dunn & Crutcher LLP (Associate)

SPARROWE, Rollin D.

1101 14th St. NW
Suite 801
Washington, DC 20005
Tel: (202)371-1808
Fax: (202)408-5059

Employers
Wildlife Management Institute (President)

SPATZ, Ian D.

601 Pennsylvania Ave. NW
Suite 1200
North Bldg.
Washington, DC 20036
Tel: (202)638-4170
Fax: (202)638-3670
Registered: LDA

Employers
Merck & Co. (Exec. Director, Federal Policy)

SPAULDING, Kimberly M.

412 First St. SE
Suite 100
Washington, DC 20003
Tel: (202)484-4884
Fax: (202)484-0109
Registered: LDA
EMail: kspaulding@dutkogroup.com
Staff Director and Professional Staff Member, Aging Subcommittee, Labor and Human Resources Committee, U.S. Senate, 1993-98. Special Assistant to Senator Warren B. Rodman (R-NH), 1991-92.

Employers
The Dutko Group, Inc. (V. President)

Clients Represented

On Behalf of The Dutko Group, Inc.
America's Community Bankers
American Herbal Products Ass'n
Distilled Spirits Council of the United States, Inc.
Eastern Pequot Indians
FedEx Corp.
Food Distributors Internat'l (NAWGA-IFDA)
Household Internat'l, Inc.
Oregon Garden Foundation
PacifiCare Health Systems
PlanetRx
Sprint Corp.
Union Pacific

SPAULDING, Romeo O.

8700 Central Ave.
Suite 306
Landover, MD 20785
Tel: (301)808-0804
Fax: (301)808-0807

Employers
Internat'l Ass'n of Black Professional Fire Fighters (Acting Exec. Director)

SPEAR, Jonathan B.

800 Connecticut Ave. NW
Suite 1100
Washington, DC 20006
Tel: (202)416-4164
Fax: (202)296-7177
Registered: LDA

Employers
Baxter Healthcare Corp. (V. President, Government Affairs and Public Policy)

SPEAR, Scott

1420 New York Ave. NW
Suite 1050
Washington, DC 20005
Tel: (202)638-1950
Fax: (202)638-7714
Registered: LDA

Employers
Van Scoyoc Associates, Inc.

Clients Represented

On Behalf of Van Scoyoc Associates, Inc.
DGME Fairness Initiative

SPEARS, Ph.D., John R.

601 Pennsylvania Ave. NW
Suite 900
Washington, DC 20004
Tel: (202)547-3566
Fax: (202)639-8238

Employers
Cottone and Huggins Group (Senior V. President, Research and Technology)

SPECTOR, Barry S.

1200 G St. NW
Suite 600
Washington, DC 20005-3802
EMail: spector@wrightlaw.com
Tel: (202)393-1200
Fax: (202)393-1240

Employers
Wright & Talisman, P.C. (V. President and Assistant Treasurer)

Clients Represented

On Behalf of Wright & Talisman, P.C.
PJM Interconnection, L.L.C.

SPECTOR, Jay R.

2201 Cooperative Way
Third Floor
Herndon, VA 22071
Tel: (703)904-7100
Fax: (703)904-7942

Employers
Nat'l Ass'n of Industrial and Office Properties (Director of Federal Affairs)

SPECTOR, Phillip L.

1615 L St. NW
Suite 1300
Washington, DC 20036
Tel: (202)223-7300
Fax: (202)223-7420
Registered: LDA

Employers
Paul, Weiss, Rifkind, Wharton & Garrison (Partner)

Clients Represented

On Behalf of Paul, Weiss, Rifkind, Wharton & Garrison
INTELSAT - Internat'l Telecommunications Satellite Organization
SkyBridge, LLC

SPEED-BOST, Regina

901 15th St. NW
Suite 700
Washington, DC 20005-2301
EMail: rspeed-bost@verner.com
Tel: (202)371-6000
Fax: (202)371-6279

Employers
Verner, Liipfert, Bernhard, McPherson and Hand, Chartered (Of Counsel)

Clients Represented

On Behalf of Verner, Liipfert, Bernhard, McPherson and Hand, Chartered
New Orleans, Louisiana, City of

SPEER, Dr. J. Alexander

1015 18th St. NW
Suite 601
Washington, DC 20036-5212
EMail: j_a_speer@minsocam.org
Tel: (202)775-4344
Fax: (202)775-0018

Employers
Mineralogical Soc. of America (Exec. Director)

SPEES, Richard L.

801 Pennsylvania Ave. NW
Suite 750
Washington, DC 20004
Tel: (202)393-1132
Fax: (202)624-0659
Registered: LDA

Employers
Richard L. Spees, Inc.

Clients Represented

On Behalf of Richard L. Spees, Inc.
American Psychological Ass'n
Chabot Space & Science Center
Consortium for Regional Climate Centers
Council of American Overseas Research Centers
Desert Research Institute
Internat'l Laboratory Technology Corp.
Miami Museum of Science & Space Transit Planetarium
Miami, Florida, City of
North American Interstate Weather Modification Council
Orange County Transportation Authority
Orange, Florida, County of
Pardee Construction Co.
Sensis Corp.
Tallahassee, Florida, City of
University of Nevada - Reno

SPEIL, Steven

801 Pennsylvania Ave. NW
Suite 245
Washington, DC 20004-2604
EMail: sspeil@americashospitals.com
Tel: (202)624-1529
Fax: (202)737-6462
Registered: LDA

Employers
Federation of American Hospitals (Senior V. President, Health Financing and Policy)

SPELLMAN, James D.

1401 I St. NW
Suite 1000
Washington, DC 20005
Tel: (202)296-9410
Fax: (202)296-9775
Registered: LDA
EMail: jspellman@sia.com

Employers
Securities Industry Ass'n (V. President and Director, Communication)

SPENCER, Anna

1050 Connecticut Ave. NW
Washington, DC 20036-5339
Tel: (202)857-6000
Fax: (202)857-6395

Employers
Arent Fox Kintner Plotkin & Kahn, PLLC (Associate)

SPENCER, Gordon

490 L'Enfant Plaza East SW
Suite 7204
Washington, DC 20024
Tel: (202)479-1133
Fax: (202)479-1136
Registered: LDA

Employers
American Maritime Officers Service (Legislative Director)

SPENCER, Jack

214 Massachusetts Ave. NE
Washington, DC 20002
Tel: (202)546-4400
Fax: (202)546-8328

Employers
Heritage Foundation (Policy Analyst, Defense and National Security)

SPENCER, Leon

212 E. Capitol St.
Washington, DC 20003
Tel: (202)547-7503
Fax: (202)547-7505
Registered: LDA
EMail: woa@igc.org

Employers
Washington Office on Africa (Exec. Director)

SPENCER, Linda M.

1317 F St. NW
Suite 500
Washington, DC 20004
EMail: lindas@sema.org
Tel: (202)783-6007
Fax: (202)783-6024

Employers
Specialty Equipment Market Ass'n (Director, International and Government Relations)

SPENCER, Richard

1400 16th St. NW
Suite 501
Washington, DC 20036-2266
Tel: (202)797-6800
Fax: (202)797-6646

Employers
Nat'l Wildlife Federation - Office of Federal and Internat'l Affairs (Grassroots Coordinator, Water Issues)

SPENCER, Stuart K.

499 S. Capitol St. SW
Suite 507
Washington, DC 20003
Tel: (202)554-2881
Registered: LDA

Employers
Hecht, Spencer & Associates (Chairman)

Clients Represented

On Behalf of Hecht, Spencer & Associates
Brown and Williamson Tobacco Corp.

SPENCER, William A.

1630 Connecticut Ave. NW
Washington, DC 20009
Tel: (202)797-2171
Fax: (202)797-2172

Employers
Washington Office on Latin American (Deputy Director)

SPENCER, William B.

1300 N. 17th St.
Eighth Floor
Rosslyn, VA 22209-3801
Tel: (703)812-2000
Fax: (703)812-8202
Registered: LDA
EMail: spencer@abc.org

Employers
Associated Builders and Contractors (V. President, Government Affairs)
Workplaces Against Salting Abuse (Contact)

SPERLING, Andrew

Colonial Place Three
2107 Wilson Blvd., Suite 300
Arlington, VA 22201-3042
Tel: (703)524-7600
Fax: (703)524-9094
Registered: LDA

Employers
Nat'l Alliance for the Mentally Ill (Deputy Exec. Director, Public Policy)

SPEY, Adam

919 18th St. NW
Suite 800
Washington, DC 20006
Tel: (202)628-4160
Fax: (202)347-5323

Employers
Human Rights Campaign Fund (PAC Coordinator)

SPIEGEL, Daniel L.

1333 New Hampshire Ave. NW
Suite 400
Washington, DC 20036
Tel: (202)887-4000
Fax: (202)887-4288
Registered: LDA
United States' Permanent Representative to the United Nations, Geneva, Switzerland, 1994-96.

Employers
Akin, Gump, Strauss, Hauer & Feld, L.L.P. (Partner)

Clients Represented

On Behalf of Akin, Gump, Strauss, Hauer & Feld, L.L.P.
Alliance Capital Management LP
American Home Products Corp.
AOL Time Warner
AT&T
Bridgestone/Firestone, Inc.
Brunswick Corp.
Human Genome Sciences Inc.
Lucent Technologies
Mitsubishi Corp.
Serono Laboratories, Inc.
Stamps.com
Tyumen Oil Company
Volkswagen, AG

SPIEGEL, Jayson L.

One Constitution Ave. NE
Washington, DC 20002
Tel: (202)479-2200
Fax: (202)479-0416
Registered: LDA

Employers
Reserve Officers Ass'n of the U.S. (Exec. Director)

SPIEGELMAN, James M.

One Dupont Circle NW Suite 700
Washington, DC 20036-1113
EMail: jim.spiegelman@aspeninstitute.org
Tel: (202)736-5800
Fax: (202)467-0790

Employers
Aspen Institute (Director, Public Affairs)

SPIELMAN, Andrew

1615 L St. NW
Suite 450
Washington, DC 20036
Tel: (202)296-7353
Fax: (202)296-7009
Registered: LDA

Employers
Brownstein Hyatt & Farber, P.C.

Clients Represented

On Behalf of Brownstein Hyatt & Farber, P.C.
Discount Refrigerants Inc.
Rhythms NetConnections

SPIELMANN, Solveig Bjorke

818 Connecticut Ave. NW
Suite 1200
Washington, DC 20006
EMail: sspielman@ibgc.com
Tel: (202)872-8181
Fax: (202)872-8696

Employers
Internat'l Business-Government Counsellors, Inc. (Chairman/Chief Exec. Officer)

SPILHAUS, Jr., Ph.D., A. F.

2000 Florida Ave. NW
Washington, DC 20009
Tel: (202)462-6900
Fax: (202)328-0566
Registered: LDA

Employers
American Geophysical Union (Exec. Director)

SPILIOTES, Nicholas J.

2000 Pennsylvania Ave. NW
Suite 5500
Washington, DC 20006
EMail: nspiliotes@mofo.com
Tel: (202)887-1500
Fax: (202)887-0763
Special Assistant, Office of the United States Representative, U.S. Mission to the United Nations, 1981. Junior Member, National Security Council, 1979-81.

Employers
Morrison & Foerster LLP (Partner)

SPILKER, Dr. Bert A.

1100 15th St. NW
Suite 900
Washington, DC 20005
Tel: (202)835-3400
Fax: (202)835-3414

Employers
Pharmaceutical Research and Manufacturers of America (Senior V. President, Scientific and Regulatory Affairs)

SPILLMAN-SIMONE, Hannah

701 Pennsylvania Ave. NW
Washington, DC 20004-2696
Tel: (202)508-5777
Fax: (202)508-5403

Employers
Edison Electric Institute (Manager, Political Programs)

SPINA, Sam

400 N. Capitol St. NW
Suite 363
Washington, DC 20001
Tel: (202)783-0280
Fax: (202)737-4518
Former Administrative Assistant, Senator Slade Gorton (R-WA); Legislative Director, Senator Brock Adams (D-WA); Legislative Director, Senator Daniel Evans (R-WA); Legislative Assistant, Senator Henry M. Jackson (D-WA); Legislative Assistant, Senator Warren Magnuson (D-WA).

Employers
Denny Miller McBee Associates (V. President and Special Counsel)

SPIRER, Julian H.

927 15th St. NW
Third Floor
Washington, DC 20005
Tel: (202)628-2900
Fax: (202)628-4608
Counsel to Rep. Benjamin S. Rosenthal (D-NY), 1975-78.

Employers
Spirer & Goldberg, P.C. (Managing Partner)

SPITLER, Eric J.

550 17th St. NW
MS: 6070
Washington, DC 20429-9990
Tel: (202)898-3837
Fax: (202)898-3745

Employers
Federal Deposit Insurance Corp. (Deputy Director, Office of Legislative Affairs)

SPITZER, Arthur

1400 20th St. NW
Suite 119
Washington, DC 20036
Tel: (202)457-0800

Employers
American Civil Liberties Union of the Nat'l Capital Area (Legal Director)

SPITZNAGEL, DeDe

900 17th St. NW
Suite 600
Washington, DC 20006
Tel: (202)452-8700
Fax: (202)296-9561
Registered: LDA

Employers
Healthcare Leadership Council (V. President, Policy)

SPOKES, Jennifer J.

2550 M St. NW
Washington, DC 20037-1350
EMail: jspokes@pattonboggs.com
Tel: (202)457-6472
Fax: (202)457-6315

Employers
Patton Boggs, LLP (Associate)

SPOLARICH, Audrey

1350 I St. NW
Suite 870
Washington, DC 20005
EMail: spolarich@capalliance.com
Tel: (202)638-0551
Fax: (202)737-1947
Registered: LDA
Formerly held staff positions at the Department of Health and Human Services and the Department of Labor.

Employers
Health Policy Analysts (Principal)

Clients Represented

On Behalf of Health Policy Analysts
Schering-Plough Legislative Resources L.L.C.

SPOONER, Gillian

2001 M St. NW
Washington, DC 20036
Tel: (202)467-3000
Fax: (202)533-8500
Registered: LDA
Former Professional Staff Member, Joint Committee on Taxation, U.S. Congress, 1982-85.

Employers
KPMG, LLP (Partner, Washington National Tax)

Clients Represented

On Behalf of KPMG, LLP
Air Transport Ass'n of America
Nat'l Council of Farmer Cooperatives

SPOONER, Nancy K.

3000 K St. NW
Suite 300
Washington, DC 20007
Tel: (202)424-7500
Fax: (202)424-7643
Registered: LDA

Employers
Swidler Berlin Shereff Friedman, LLP (Partner)

Clients Represented

On Behalf of Swidler Berlin Shereff Friedman, LLP
Intersil Corp.

SPOOR, Barbara

900 Second St. NE
Suite 211
Washington, DC 20002
Tel: (202)408-9514
Fax: (202)408-9520

Employers
Nat'l Ass'n of Protection and Advocacy Systems (NAPAS) (Deputy Director, Training and Technical Assistance)

SPORIDIS, Harry

210 Seventh St. SE
Washington, DC 20003
Tel: (202)547-6808
Fax: (202)546-5425
Registered: LDA
Former Senior Legislative Aide to Rep. James C. Greenwood (R-PA).

Employers
Kessler & Associates Business Services, Inc. (Legislative Associate)

Clients Represented

On Behalf of Kessler & Associates Business Services, Inc.
Dunn-Edwards Corp.
Exelon Corp.
Grocery Manufacturers of America
Henry H. Kessler Foundation
Novartis Corp.
Pharmacia Corp.
Tosco Corp.

SPRAGUE, Stephen G.

113 S. West St.
Fourth Floor
Alexandria, VA 22314
Tel: (703)838-2929
Fax: (703)838-2950

Employers
United Motorcoach Ass'n (Chief Operating Officer)

SPRANG, James

9000 Machinists Pl.
Upper Marlboro, MD 20772-2687
Tel: (301)967-4500
Fax: (301)967-4591

Employers
Internat'l Ass'n of Machinists and Aerospace Workers (Airline Coordinator)

SPRIGGS, William

1111 14th St. NW
Suite 1001
Washington, DC 20005
Tel: (202)898-1604
Fax: (202)408-1965

Employers
Nat'l Urban League (Director, Research and Public Policy)

SPRIGGS, William J.

1350 I St. NW
Ninth Floor
Washington, DC 20005-3304
Tel: (202)898-5800
Fax: (202)682-1639
Captain, U.S. Marine Corps, 1964-67.

Employers
Spriggs & Hollingsworth (Senior Partner)

SPRING, Andrea Leigh

c/o Internat'l Paper
1101 Pennsylvania Ave. NW, Suite 200
Washington, DC 20004
Tel: (202)347-6371
Registered: LDA

Employers
Americans for Affordable Electricity (Exec. Director)

SPRING, Heather M.

1850 M St. NW
Suite 900
Washington, DC 20036
Tel: (202)463-2500
Fax: (202)463-4950

Employers
Sher & Blackwell (Associate)

SPRING, Herbert Baker

214 Massachusetts Ave. NE
Washington, DC 20002
Tel: (202)546-4400
Fax: (202)546-8328

Employers
Heritage Foundation (Kirby Research Fellow in National Security Policy)

SPRINGER, David E.

1666 K St. NW
Suite 500
Washington, DC 20006-2803
Tel: (202)887-1400
Fax: (202)466-2198
Chief of Staff to Rep. Thomas J. Manton (D-NY), 1985-90. Legislative Director to Rep. Bill Richardson (D-NM), 1983-84. Legislative Assistant to Senator Howard Metzenbaum (D-OH), 1980-83.

Employers
O'Connor & Hannan, L.L.P. (Partner)

Clients Represented

On Behalf of O'Connor & Hannan, L.L.P.
Calhoun County, Alabama Commission
CompTIA
Telecorp PCS Inc.

SPRINGFIELD, Craig R.

1455 Pennsylvania Ave. NW
Suite 1200
Washington, DC 20004
Tel: (202)347-2230
Fax: (202)393-3310
Registered: LDA

Employers
Davis & Harman LLP (Partner)

Clients Represented

On Behalf of Davis & Harman LLP
Citigroup
Health Insurance Ass'n of America

SPULAK, Thomas J.

2300 N St. NW
Washington, DC 20037-1128
Tel: (202)663-8000
Fax: (202)663-8007
Registered: LDA, FARA
EMail: thomas.spulak@shawpittman.com
Former General Counsel, U.S. House of Representatives and General Counsel and Staff Director, House Rules Committee.

Employers
Shaw Pittman (Partner)

Clients Represented

On Behalf of Shaw Pittman
The Advocacy Group
BET Holdings II, Inc.
Chevy Chase Bank, F.S.B.
Detroit Medical Center
Dresdner Bank AG
Embraer Aircraft Corp.
Hawaii, State of
Institute of Internat'l Bankers
Medicare Cost Contractors Alliance
Mexico, Secretaria de Comercio y Fomento Industrial (SECOFI)
J. Milton & Associates
The MWW Group
Nat'l Marine Manufacturers Ass'n
Nortel Networks
R. J. Reynolds Tobacco Co.
Sibley Memorial Hospital
Southern Ass'n of Forestry Economics
Vulcan Chemicals

SPURGEON, Scott

8400 W. Park Dr.
McLean, VA 22102
Tel: (703)821-7000
Registered: LDA

Employers
Nat'l Automobile Dealers Ass'n (Legislative Representative)

SPURLOCK, James

1120 20th St. NW
Suite 1000
Washington, DC 20036
EMail: spurlock@att.com
Tel: (202)457-3878
Fax: (202)263-2571

Employers
AT&T (Director, Federal Government Affairs)

SQUAIR, Philip A.

1101 17th St. NW
Suite 1004
Washington, DC 20036
EMail: psquair@dc.npga.org
Tel: (202)466-7200
Fax: (202)466-7205
Registered: LDA

Employers
Nat'l Propane Gas Ass'n (Director, Regulatory Affairs)

SQUIER, Mark R.

1029 N. Royal St.
Suite 350
Alexandria, VA 22314
Tel: (703)519-8600
Fax: (703)519-8604

Employers
Trippi, McMahon & Squier (Partner)

SQUIRE, Daniel H.

2445 M St. NW
Washington, DC 20037-1420
EMail: dsquire@wilmer.com
Tel: (202)663-6000
Fax: (202)663-6363
Registered: LDA

Employers
Wilmer, Cutler & Pickering (Partner)

Clients Represented

On Behalf of Wilmer, Cutler & Pickering
Atlantic Gulf Communities

SRAMEK, Helen

1440 New York Ave. NW
Suite 200
Washington, DC 20005
Tel: (202)942-2050
Fax: (202)783-4798
Registered: LDA

Employers
American Automobile Ass'n (Director, Federal Relations)

SREMAC, Danielle

P.O. Box 32099
Washington, DC 20007
EMail: comments@balkanaffairs.org
Tel: (301)424-3220
Fax: (301)424-0192

Employers
Institute for Balkan Affairs (Director)

SRODES, Cecile

801 Pennsylvania Ave. NW
Suite 630
Washington, DC 20004-5878
EMail: csrodes@nyse.com
Tel: (202)347-4300
Fax: (202)347-4370
Registered: LDA

Employers
New York Stock Exchange (Counsel, Legislative Affairs)

SROUFE, Gerald E.

1230 17th St. NW
Washington, DC 20036-3078
Tel: (202)223-9485
Fax: (202)775-1824

Employers
American Educational Research Ass'n (Director, Government Relations)

ST. AMAND, Janet G.

1730 K St. NW
Suite 1106
Washington, DC 20006
Tel: (202)466-3561
Fax: (202)466-3583
Registered: LDA

Employers
Household Financial Group, Ltd. (Director/Counsel, Federal Government Relations)
Household Internat'l, Inc. (Federal Director/Counsel)

ST. LEDGER-ROTY, Judith

1200 19th St. NW
Suite 500
Washington, DC 20036
Tel: (202)955-9600
Fax: (202)955-9792

Employers
Kelley, Drye & Warren LLP (Partner)

ST. MARTIN, Darla

419 Seventh St. NW
Suite 500
Washington, DC 20004
Tel: (202)626-8800
Fax: (202)737-9189
Registered: LDA

Employers
Nat'l Right to Life Committee (Associate Exec. Director)

ST. MAXENS, II, Thomas F.

927 15th St. NW
12th Floor
Washington, DC 20015
Tel: (202)833-4466
Fax: (202)833-2833
Registered: LDA
Former Executive Director, Office of the United States Trade Representative.

Employers
St. Maxens & Company

Clients Represented

On Behalf of St. Maxens & Company
Binney & Smith Inc.
Hallmark Cards, Inc.
Mattel, Inc.
Thailand, Department of Foreign Trade of
US JVC Corp.

ST. PIERRE, Mary

228 Seventh St. SE
Washington, DC 20003-4306
Tel: (202)547-7424
Fax: (202)547-3540
EMail: mts@nahc.org

Employers
Nat'l Ass'n for Home Care (V. President, Regulatory Affairs)

ST. PIERRE, Tracey

919 18th St. NW
Suite 800
Washington, DC 20006
Tel: (202)628-4160
Fax: (202)347-5323
Registered: LDA

Employers
Human Rights Campaign Fund (Senior Policy Associate)

STABBE, Michael H.

1200 New Hampshire Ave. NW
Suite 800
Washington, DC 20036-6802
Tel: (202)776-2000
Fax: (202)776-2222
EMail: mstabbe@dlalaw.com

Employers
Dow, Lohnes & Albertson, PLLC (Member)

STABLES, Jr., Gordon W.

1627 K St. NW
Suite 900
Washington, DC 20006
Tel: (202)955-1450
Fax: (202)955-1457

Employers
Ingersoll-Rand Co. (Director, Government Affairs and Sales)

STACH, Deirdre

1775 I St. NW
Suite 700
Washington, DC 20006
Tel: (202)261-4000
Fax: (202)261-4001
Registered: LDA
Budget Analyst, House Science Committee, 1995-96. Legislative Director (1989-95), Legislative Assistant (1989), Legislative Correspondent (1988-89) and Junior Caseworker (1987-88) to Rep. Bob Walker (R-PA).

Employers
Clark & Weinstock, Inc. (Director)

Clients Represented

On Behalf of Clark & Weinstock, Inc.
American Ass'n of Health Plans (AAHP)
AT&T
Rabbi Milton Balkany
CapCURE
Cargill, Inc.
Edison Electric Institute
Lockheed Martin Corp.
Microsoft Corp.
Pharmaceutical Research and Manufacturers of America
Sallie Mae, Inc.
Schering-Plough Corp.

STACH, Kevin

1030 15th St. NW
Suite 1100
Washington, DC 20005
Tel: (202)783-4600
Fax: (202)783-4601
Special Assistant to the Secretary, Deputy Assistant for Public Policy, and Assistant to the Secretary for Communications, Department of Housing and Urban Development, 1989-92.

Employers
White House Writers Group (Senior Director)

STACHELBERG, Winnie

919 18th St. NW
Suite 800
Washington, DC 20006
Tel: (202)628-4160
Fax: (202)347-5323
Registered: LDA

Employers
Human Rights Campaign Fund (Political Director)

STACK, Mary Kay

810 Vermont Ave. NW
Room 512
Washington, DC 20420
Tel: (202)273-5628
Fax: (202)273-6791

Employers
Department of Veterans Affairs (Congressional Relations Officer)

STACK, Michael J.

1625 Prince St.
Alexandria, VA 22314
Tel: (703)519-6200
Fax: (703)519-6299

Employers
American Soc. for Industrial Security (Exec. Director)

STACY, Michael

4701 Sangamore Rd.
Suite N100
Bethesda, MD 20816-2508
Tel: (301)229-5800
Fax: (301)229-5045
Registered: LDA
EMail: jstacy@burdeshaw.com

Employers
Burdeshaw Associates, Ltd. (V. President, Business Development)

Clients Represented

On Behalf of Burdeshaw Associates, Ltd.
Martin-Baker Aircraft Co., Ltd.

STADULIS, Lawrence P.

1800 M St. NW
Washington, DC 20036
Tel: (202)467-7000
Fax: (202)467-7176
Registered: FARA

Employers
Morgan, Lewis & Bockius LLP

STAFFIER, John R.

1275 Pennsylvania Ave. NW
Ninth Floor
Washington, DC 20004
Tel: (202)662-6790
Fax: (202)624-0866
Registered: FARA
EMail: jstaffier@sdsatty.com

Employers
Stuntz, Davis & Staffier, P.C. (Principal)

Clients Represented

On Behalf of Stuntz, Davis & Staffier, P.C.
Pan-Alberta Gas Ltd.

STAHL, Rusty

1625 K St. NW
Suite 210
Washington, DC 20006
Tel: (202)785-5980
Fax: (202)785-5969

Employers
Leadership 2000 (V. Chairperson)

STAIGER, Roger

P.O. Box 136
Scotland, MD 20687
Tel: (202)737-1004
Fax: (301)872-9843
Registered: LDA
EMail: roger@staiger.com
Professional Staff member, Committee on Energy and Commerce, U.S. House of Representatives, 1979-91.

Employers
Staiger.com

STALKNECHT, Paul

2200 Mill Rd.
Alexandria, VA 22314
Tel: (703)838-1803
Fax: (703)836-2023

Employers
American Trucking Ass'ns (Senior V. President, Federation Relations)

STALLMER, Eric W.

2800 Shirlington Rd.
Suite 405
Arlington, VA 22206
Tel: (703)671-4116
Fax: (703)931-6432
EMail: stallmer@aol.com

Employers
Space Transportation Ass'n (President)

STALVEY, Allan

601 Pennsylvania Ave. NW
Suite 300
The North Bldg.
Washington, DC 20004
Tel: (202)628-3500
Fax: (202)628-0400
Registered: LDA
EMail: allan_stalvey@wastemanagement.com

Employers
Waste Management, Inc. (V. President, Government Affairs)

STANARD, Sylvia

1701 20th St. NW
Washington, DC 20009
Tel: (202)667-6404
Fax: (202)667-6314
EMail: osadc@aol.com

Employers
Church of Scientology Internat'l (Director)

STANBERRY, Thomas E.

1150 18th St. NW
Suite 400
Washington, DC 20036
Tel: (202)223-9347
Fax: (202)872-0347

Employers
Municipal Securities Rulemaking Board (Vice Chairman)

STANCEU, Timothy C.

555 13th St. NW
Washington, DC 20004-1109
Tel: (202)637-5844
Fax: (202)637-5910
Registered: LDA
EMail: tcstanceu@hhlaw.com
Department of the Treasury: Deputy Director, Office of Trade and Tariff Affairs (1985-89) and Special Assistant to the Assistant Secretary for Enforcement and Operations (1982-85).

Employers
Hogan & Hartson L.L.P. (Partner)

Clients Represented

On Behalf of Hogan & Hartson L.L.P.
American Frozen Food Institute
Kraft Foods, Inc.

STANDISH, James

12501 Old Columbia Pike
Silver Spring, MD 20904
Tel: (301)680-6000
Fax: (301)680-6090
EMail: jdstandish@compuserve.com

Employers
General Conference of Seventh-day Adventists (Assistant Director)

STANFILL, Allison

1819 L St. NW
Suite 700
Washington, DC 20036
Tel: (202)721-1621
Fax: (202)861-1181
Registered: LDA

Employers
Personal Watercraft Industry Ass'n (Legislative Assistant)

STANGES, Milly Crawford

555 12th St. NW
Suite 700 South
Washington, DC 20004
Tel: (202)637-0090
Fax: (202)637-8950
Registered: LDA
Former aide, House Committee on Education and Labor and House Committee on Ways and Means.

Employers
TIAA-CREF

STANLEY, Anne

1199 N. Fairfax St.
Suite 1000
Alexandria, VA 22314
EMail: astanley@hawthorngroup.com
Tel: (703)299-4499
Fax: (703)299-4488

Employers
The Hawthorn Group, L.C. (Senior V. President)

STANLEY, David M.

108 N. Alfred St.
Alexandria, VA 22314
Tel: (703)683-5700
Fax: (703)683-5722
Registered: LDA

Employers
Nat'l Taxpayers Union (Chairman)

STANLEY, David W.

317 Massachusetts Ave. NE
Suite 300
Washington, DC 20002
Tel: (202)789-3960
Fax: (202)789-1813
Law clerk to Hon. Gerard D. Reilly, Chief Judge, District of Columbia Court of Appeals, 1972-73. Assistant U.S. Attorney, U.S. Attorney's Office for the District of Columbia (Fraud Division), 1981-84. Assistant Chief Trial Attorney, Division of Enforcement, U.S. Securities and Exchange Commission, 1984-87.

Employers
The Cuneo Law Group, P.C. (Attorney)

STANLEY, Kathleen H.

801 Pennsylvania Ave. NW
Suite 725
Washington, DC 20004
Tel: (202)898-3189
Registered: LDA

Employers
Aventis Pharmaceutical Products

STANLEY, Margaret A.

1310 G St. NW
Suite 500
Washington, DC 20005-3004
EMail: stanleyola@aol.com
Tel: (202)272-7742
Fax: (202)272-7728

Employers
Railroad Retirement Board (Director, Office of Legislative Affairs)

STANSFIELD, Carol

Office of Govermental Affairs
3101 Park Center Dr.
Room 806
Alexandria, VA 22302
EMail: carol_stansfield@fns.usda.gov
Tel: (703)305-2010
Fax: (703)305-2312

Employers
Department of Agriculture - Food and Nutrition Service (Legislative Specialist)

STANTON, Hon. James V.

1747 Pennsylvania Ave. NW
Suite 105
Washington, DC 20006
Tel: (202)467-4333
Fax: (202)467-4353
Registered: LDA
Member, U.S. House of Representatives (D-OH), 1971-77.

Employers
Stanton & Associates (Principal)

Clients Represented

On Behalf of Stanton & Associates
Nat'l Ass'n of Bankruptcy Trustees

STANTON, John

1312 18th St. NW
Suite 300
Washington, DC 20036
Tel: (202)296-4563
Fax: (202)887-9178

Employers
Agribusiness Council (Director, Membership Services)

STANTON, John Maloney

1200 18th St. NW
Washington, DC 20036
EMail: jstanton@environet.org
Tel: (202)887-8800
Fax: (202)887-8877
Registered: LDA

Employers
Nat'l Environmental Trust (V. President)

STANTON, John S.

555 13th St. NW
Washington, DC 20004-1109
Tel: (202)637-5704
Fax: (202)637-5910
Registered: LDA, FARA
EMail: jsstanton@hhlaw.com
Law Clerk to Judge Robert J. Kelleher, U.S. District Court for the Central District of California, 1979-80. Professional Staff Member, House Banking Committee, 1974.

Employers
Hogan & Hartson L.L.P. (Partner)

Clients Represented

On Behalf of Hogan & Hartson L.L.P.
American Gaming Ass'n
California State Teachers' Retirement System
Medtronic, Inc.
Nat'l Structured Settlements Trade Ass'n

STANTON, Joseph M.

122 C St. NW
Suite 750
Washington, DC 20001-2109
Tel: (202)737-2337
Fax: (202)737-7004

Employers
Beer Institute (V. President, Federal Government Affairs)

STANTON, Matt

1250 I St. NW
Suite 400
Washington, DC 20005-3998
EMail: mstanton@discus.org
Tel: (202)682-8884
Fax: (202)682-8849

Employers
Distilled Spirits Council of the United States, Inc. (V. President, Office of Government Relations)

STANTON, Michael J.

1401 H St. NW
Suite 900
Washington, DC 20005
Tel: (202)326-5521
Fax: (202)326-5595
Registered: LDA

Employers
Alliance of Automobile Manufacturers, Inc. (V. President, Government Affairs)

STANTON, Richard P.

401 Ninth St. NW
Suite 900
Washington, DC 20004
Tel: (202)585-8000
Fax: (202)585-8080
Senior Counsel, Office of Independent Counsel, 1995-98. Counsel to U.S. House of Representatives, 1991-95. Attorney to Chief Judge Thomas D. Lambros, 1989-91. Legislative Assistant to House Banking Committee, 1989. Legislative Assistant to House Judiciary Committee, 1988-89.

Employers
Nixon Peabody LLP (Partner)

Clients Represented

On Behalf of Nixon Peabody LLP
iCall, Inc.
Ice Ban America, Inc.
Saf T Lok, Inc.
Welch's Foods, Inc.

STARCHVILLE, Amy

111 Park Place
Falls Church, VA 22046-4513
Tel: (703)533-0251
Fax: (703)241-5603

Employers
Ass'n and Soc. Management Internat'l Inc.

Clients Represented

On Behalf of Ass'n and Soc. Management Internat'l Inc.
Internat'l Ass'n of Emergency Managers

STARCK, Leslie E.

555 Twelfth St. NW
Suite 640
Washington, DC 20004
Tel: (202)393-3075
Fax: (202)393-1497
Registered: LDA

Employers
Edison Internat'l (Manager, Federal Regulatory Affairs, Southern California Edison)

STAREK, III, Roscoe Burton

1111 19th St. NW
Suite 1100
Washington, DC 20036
Tel: (202)955-5030
Fax: (202)955-0085

Employers
Direct Marketing Ass'n, Inc. (Senior V. President, Catalog Issues)

STARK, Krista

1400 16th St. NW
Suite 600
Washington, DC 20036
Tel: (202)939-7900
Fax: (202)745-0916

Employers
Fleischman and Walsh, L.L.P.

Clients Represented

On Behalf of Fleischman and Walsh, L.L.P.
ORBITZ
SBC Communications Inc.

STARK, USA, Col. Richard

1300 Defense Pentagon
Room 3D918
Washington, DC 20301-1300
Tel: (703)695-4131
Fax: (703)693-5530

Employers
Department of Defense (Special Assistant for Energy, Healthcare Policy, Legal Issues, Office of Legislative Liaison)

STARK, Rosalind

1000 Connecticut Ave. NW
Suite 615
Washington, DC 20036-5302
Tel: (202)659-6510
Fax: (202)223-4007

Employers
Radio-Television News Directors Ass'n (Exec. Director)

STARKS, Ora D.

1500 Pennsylvania Ave. NW
Room 2204MT
Washington, DC 20220
Tel: (202)622-0576
Fax: (202)622-0534

Employers
Department of Treasury (Congressional Inquiries Analyst, Office of Legislative Affairs)

STARKWEATHER, Kendall N.

1914 Association Dr.
Suite 201
Reston, VA 20191
Tel: (703)860-2100
Fax: (703)860-0353

Employers
Internat'l Technology Education Ass'n (Exec. Director)

STARLING, Kenneth G.

1200 19th St. NW
Washington, DC 20036-2430
Tel: (202)861-3830
Fax: (202)223-2085
EMail: kenneth.starling@piperrudnick.com
Deputy Assistant Attorney General, Antitrust Division, Department of Justice, 1987-89. Assistant Director, Bureau of Competition, Federal Trade Commission, 1979-85. Assistant U.S. Attorney, Department of Justice, 1977.

Employers
Piper Marbury Rudnick & Wolfe LLP (Partner)

STARR, David A.

1155 21st St. NW
Suite 300
Washington, DC 20036
Tel: (202)659-8201
Fax: (202)659-5249
Registered: LDA, FARA
EMail: dastarr@wms-jen.com
Legislative Director to Senator Howard Metzenbaum (D-OH), 1981-89.

Employers
Williams & Jensen, P.C. (Partner)

Clients Represented

On Behalf of Williams & Jensen, P.C.
American Home Products Corp.
The Church Alliance
The Pittston Co.
Securities Traders Ass'n
Tailored Clothing Ass'n

STARR, Michael

1050 31st St. NW
Washington, DC 20007
Tel: (202)965-3500
Fax: (202)342-5484

Employers

Ass'n of Trial Lawyers of America (General Counsel)

STARR, Sam

1301 K St. NW
Washington, DC 20005-3333
Tel: (202)414-1000
Fax: (202)414-1301
Registered: LDA

Employers

PriceWaterhouseCoopers (Partner)

STAS, Eric

11 Dupont Circle NW
Suite 700
Washington, DC 20036
Tel: (202)293-5886
Fax: (202)939-6969

Employers

Multinat'l Government Services, Inc.

Clients Represented

On Behalf of Multinat'l Government Services, Inc.

CIGNA Corp.
Rhone-Polenc Inc.

STATLER, Jean

1363 Beverly Rd.
McLean, VA 22101
Tel: (703)556-0001
Fax: (703)893-3811

Employers

Wirthlin Worldwide (Senior V. President)

STATLER, Stuart M.

1025 Connecticut Ave. NW
Suite 901
Washington, DC 20036
EMail: exec@nacdl.com
Tel: (202)872-8600
Fax: (202)872-8690

Employers

Nat'l Ass'n of Criminal Defense Lawyers (Exec. Director)

STATMAN, Alan J.

1200 G St. NW
Suite 600
Washington, DC 20005-3802
EMail: statman@wrightlaw.com
Tel: (202)393-1200
Fax: (202)393-1240

Law Clerk to Judges Eugene P. Spellman (1979-80) and C. Clyde Atkins (1978-79), U.S. District Court.

Employers

Wright & Talisman, P.C. (V. President and Treasurer)

Clients Represented

On Behalf of Wright & Talisman, P.C.

Southwestern Public Service Co.

STATON, Hon. David M.

831 S. King St.
Suite E
Leesburg, VA 20175
EMail: mick@caplink.com
Tel: (703)443-2311
Fax: (703)443-2315
Registered: LDA, FARA

Member, U.S. House of Representatives (R-WV), 1981-83.

Employers

Capitol Link, Inc. (President)

Clients Represented

On Behalf of Capitol Link, Inc.

Catamount Energy Corp.
Durham, North Carolina, City of
Madison County Commission
Micronesia, Embassy of the Federated States of
Mobile Area Water and Sewer System
Mobile, Alabama, City of

STATON, James D.

5211 Auth Rd.
Suitland, MD 20746
Tel: (301)899-3500
Fax: (301)899-8136
Registered: LDA

Employers

Air Force Sergeants Ass'n (Exec. Director)

STATON, Lynn S.

831 S. King St.
Suite E
Leesburg, VA 20175
EMail: lynn@caplink.com
Tel: (703)443-2311
Fax: (703)443-2315
Registered: LDA

Employers

Capitol Link, Inc. (Senior V. President)

STAUTZ, Shay D.

2111 Wilson Blvd.
Suite 700
Arlington, VA 22201
Tel: (703)351-5058
Fax: (703)522-1738
Registered: LDA

Employers

Collins & Company, Inc. (Programs and Legislation)

Clients Represented

On Behalf of Collins & Company, Inc.

The Boeing Co.
Citizens Network for Foreign Affairs (CNFA)
Derry Investment Initiatives
EarthData Holdings
Hawaii Economic Development Alliance, State of
Internat'l Agriculture and Rural Development Group
Internat'l Fund for Agricultural Development
Loral Space and Communications, Ltd.
Mari-Flite Ferries, Inc.
Marquette University
Nat'l Telephone Cooperative Ass'n
NewMarket Global Consulting Group
Northrop Grumman Corp.
Oracle Corp.
Pacific Marine
PADCO, Inc.
Population Action Internat'l
Science Applications Internat'l Corp. (SAIC)
Solipsys Corp.
Textron Systems Division
Trex Enterprises

STAYIN, Randolph J.

1401 I St. NW
Suite 500
Washington, DC 20005
EMail: rstayin@btlaw.com
Tel: (202)289-1313
Fax: (202)289-1330
Registered: LDA, FARA

Administrative Assistant and Director of Legislation to Senator Robert Taft, Jr. (R-OH), 1973-76.

Employers

Barnes & Thornburg (Partner)

Clients Represented

On Behalf of Barnes & Thornburg

Capital Goods Standards Coalition
Food Processing Machinery and Supplies Ass'n
Indiana Glass Co.
Kyocera Corp.
Nat'l Candle Ass'n
NATSO, Inc.
Process Equipment Manufacturers' Ass'n
Quebec Lumber Manufacturers Ass'n
Special Committee for Workplace Product Liability Reform
Water and Wastewater Equipment Manufacturers Ass'n
Wheat Gluten Industry Council

STEADMAN, Jr., Dr. Eugene

1530 Wilson Blvd.
Suite 210
Arlington, VA 22209
EMail: ESteadman@celanese.com
Tel: (703)358-2890
Fax: (703)358-9786
Registered: LDA

Employers

Celanese Government Relations Office (Director, Government Affairs)

STEARN, Mitchell A.

1919 Pennsylvania Ave. NW
Suite 500
Washington, DC 20006-3434
Tel: (202)778-3000
Fax: (202)778-3063

Employers

Porter, Wright, Morris & Arthur, LLP (Partner)

STEARNS, Joe

1300 Wilson Blvd.
Arlington, VA 22209
Tel: (703)741-5850
Fax: (703)741-6084

Employers

Chlorine Chemistry Council (Director, International Affairs)

STECKELBERG, Kathryn A.

701 Pennsylvania Ave. NW
Washington, DC 20004-2696
Tel: (202)508-5478
Fax: (202)508-5403
Registered: LDA

Former Legislative Director to Rep. Jack Kemp (R-NY).

Employers

Edison Electric Institute (Director, Government Relations)

STEED, Diane K.

818 Connecticut Ave. NW
Second Floor
Washington, DC 20006
EMail: dsteed@stratacomm.net
Tel: (202)289-2001
Fax: (202)289-1327
Registered: LDA

Former Administrator of the National Highway Traffic Safety Administration, Department of Transportation.

Employers

Strat@Comm (Strategic Communications Counselors) (Principal)

Clients Represented

On Behalf of Strat@Comm (Strategic Communications Counselors)

Continental Teves

STEEL, Aimee N.

1655 N. Fort Myer Dr.
Suite 355
Arlington, VA 22209
Tel: (703)807-2070
Fax: (703)807-2073

Employers

The 60/Plus Ass'n, Inc. (Communications Director)

STEEL, Laura N.

1341 G St. NW
Fifth Floor
Washington, DC 20005
Tel: (202)626-7660
Fax: (202)628-3606

Employers

Wilson, Elser, Moskowitz, Edelman & Dicker LLP (Partner)

STEELE-FLYNN, Donna

1225 Connecticut Ave. NW
Washington, DC 20036
EMail: donna.flynn@ey.com
Tel: (202)327-6664
Fax: (202)327-6719
Registered: LDA

Staff Director, Subcommittee on Oversight, House Committee on Ways and Means, 1994-98. Legislative Director to Rep. Bill Archer (R-TX), 1988-94.

Employers

Ernst & Young LLP (Senior Manager)
Washington Council Ernst & Young (Senior Manager)

Clients Represented

On Behalf of Ernst & Young LLP

E-Commerce Coalition
Edison Electric Institute
General Ore Internat'l Corp. Ltd.
INCOL 2000
Interest Netting Coalition
Koch Industries, Inc.
MassMutual Financial Group
Nordstrom, Inc.
Repeal the Tax on Talking Coalition
Tax Policy Coalition

On Behalf of Washington Council Ernst & Young
Aetna Life & Casualty Co.
American Insurance Ass'n
American Staffing Ass'n
Anheuser-Busch Cos., Inc.
Antitrust Coalition for Consumer Choice in Health Care
Apartment Investment and Management Co.
Ass'n of American Railroads
Ass'n of Home Appliance Manufacturers
AT&T
Aventis Pharmaceuticals, Inc.
Baxter Healthcare Corp.
BHC Communications, Inc.
Bulmer Holding PLC, H. P.
Cash Balance Coalition
Citigroup
Coalition for Fairness in Defense Exports
Coalition to Preserve Tracking Stock
ComEd
The Connell Co.
Deferral Group
Directors Guild of America
Doris Duke Charitable Foundation
Eaton Vance Management Co.
Eden Financial Corp.
The Enterprise Foundation
Fannie Mae
FedEx Corp.
Ford Motor Co.
General Electric Co.
Global Competitiveness Coalition
Grasslands Water District
Group Health, Inc.
HEREIU
Gilbert P. Hyatt, Inventor
Investment Co. Institute
Large Public Power Council
Local Initiatives Support Corp.
MacAndrews & Forbes Holdings, Inc.
Marsh & McLennan Cos.
MCG Northwest, Inc.
McLane Co.
Merrill Lynch & Co., Inc.
Metropolitan Banking Group
Nat'l Ass'n for State Farm Agents
Nat'l Ass'n of Professional Employer Organizations
Nat'l Ass'n of Real Estate Investment Trusts
Nat'l Defined Contribution Council
Nat'l Foreign Trade Council, Inc.
Nat'l Multi-Housing Council
Pfizer, Inc.
R&D Tax Credit Coalition
R&D Tax Regulation Group
Recording Industry Ass'n of America
Reed-Elsevier Inc.
R. J. Reynolds Tobacco Co.
Charles Schwab & Co., Inc.,
Securities Industry Ass'n
Skadden, Arps, Slate, Meagher & Flom LLP
Straddle Rules Tax Group
Tax Fairness Coalition
TXU Business Services
U.S. Oncology
USA Biomass Power Producers Alliance
Viaticus, Inc.
Wilkie Farr & Gallagher
Ziff Investors Partnership

STEELMAN, Deborah

555 12th St. NW
Suite 650
Washington, DC 20004-1205
Tel: (202)393-7950
Fax: (202)393-7960

Associate Director for Human Resources, Veterans and Labor, Office of Management and Budget (1986-87) and Deputy Assistant to the President and Director, Intergovernmental Affairs (1985), Executive Office of the President, The White House. Director, Office of Intergovernmental Liaison, Environmental Protection Agency, 1983-84. Legislative Director to Senator John Heinz (R-PA), 1982.

Employers
Eli Lilly and Co. (V. President, Corporate Affairs)

STEELMAN, Jerry

807 Maine Ave. SW
Washington, DC 20024
Tel: (202)554-3501
Fax: (202)554-3581

Employers
Disabled American Veterans (National Director, Voluntary Services)

STEEN, Daniel K.

1155 21st St. NW
Suite 310
Washington, DC 20036
EMail: danielsteen@owens-ill.com
Tel: (202)785-3559
Fax: (202)785-8534
Registered: LDA

Employers
Owens-Illinois, Inc. (Director, Government Affairs/Washington Office)

STEEN, Ellen

1001 Pennsylvania Ave. NW
Suite 1100
Washington, DC 20004-2595
Tel: (202)624-2500
Fax: (202)628-5116
Registered: LDA

Employers
Crowell & Moring LLP

Clients Represented
On Behalf of Crowell & Moring LLP
Nat'l Pork Producers Council

STEENSLAND, Ann M.

1010 Vermont Ave. NW
Suite 900
Washington, DC 20005
EMail: asteensland@hfhi.org
Tel: (202)628-9171
Ext: 106
Fax: (202)628-9169

Employers
Habitat for Humanity Internat'l (Director, External Relations)

STEEPER, Frederick T.

1199 N. Fairfax St.
Suite 400
Alexandria, VA 22314
Tel: (703)535-8505
Fax: (703)535-8517

Employers
Market Strategies Inc. (Principal)

STEFFLE, Jerry

1455 Pennsylvania Ave. NW
Suite 575
Washington, DC 20004
Tel: (202)638-4076
Fax: (202)638-1096
Registered: LDA

Employers
WellPoint Health Networks/Blue Cross of California/UNICARE

STEGEMANN, E. J.

6885 Elm St.
McLean, VA 22101
Tel: (703)821-4900
Fax: (703)448-9678

Employers
Mars, Inc. (V. President)

STEGENGA, Karl H.

2100 Pennsylvania Ave. NW
Suite 560
Washington, DC 20037
EMail: kstegenga@hyjekfix.com
Tel: (202)223-4800
Fax: (202)223-2011
Registered: LDA

Former Special Assistant for Installations and Logistics to the Assistant Secretary for Legislative Affairs, Department of Defense. Staff Member on defense issues to Senator Dan Quayle (R-IN), 1981-89.

Employers
Hyjek & Fix, Inc. (Director, Federal Marketing)

Clients Represented
On Behalf of Hyjek & Fix, Inc.
BAE SYSTEMS North America
Intermec Corp.
Niagara Area Chamber of Commerce
The Oneida County Edge
Pilkington Thorn
Shelby, Tennessee, County of
U.S. Display Consortium

STEHMER, Karl H.

300 E St. SW
Room 9017
Washington, DC 20546
EMail: kstehmer@hq.nasa.gov
Tel: (202)358-1948
Fax: (202)358-4340

Employers
Nat'l Aeronautics and Space Administration (Legislation)

STEIMER, Mark

6400 Goldsboro Rd.
Suite 500
Bethesda, MD 20817
EMail: msteimer@epb.com
Tel: (301)263-2347
Fax: (301)263-2269

Intern to Rep. Constance A. Morella (R-MD), 1991.

Employers
Earle Palmer Brown Public Relations (Account Director, EPB PR)

STEIN, Daniel A.

1666 Connecticut Ave. NW
Suite 400
Washington, DC 20009
Tel: (202)328-7004
Fax: (202)387-3447

Employers
Federation for American Immigration Reform (FAIR) (Exec. Director)

STEIN, Donald S.

1501 M St. NW
Suite 700
Washington, DC 20005-1702
EMail: dstein@manatt.com
Tel: (202)463-4300
Fax: (202)463-4394
Registered: LDA

Employers
Manatt, Phelps & Phillips, LLP (Partner)

Clients Represented
On Behalf of Manatt, Phelps & Phillips, LLP
Royal Wine Co.

STEIN, Ph.D., Gary C.

7272 Wisconsin Ave.
Bethesda, MD 20814
Tel: (301)657-3000
Fax: (301)657-1615
Registered: LDA

Employers
American Soc. of Health System Pharmacists (Director, Federal Regulatory Affairs)

STEIN, John Hollister

1757 Park Rd. NW
Washington, DC 20010
Tel: (202)232-6682
Fax: (202)462-2255

Employers
Nat'l Organization for Victim Assistance (Deputy Director)

STEIN, Kalman

3400 International Dr. NW
Suite 2K
Washington, DC 20008
Tel: (202)537-7100
Fax: (202)537-7101

Employers
Earth Share (President)

STEIN, Michael H.

1775 Pennsylvania Ave. NW
Suite 200
Washington, DC 20006
Tel: (202)429-2303
Fax: (202)862-1093
Registered: LDA

General Counsel, International Trade Commission, 1977-84. Trial Attorney, Appellate Section, Civil Division, Department of Justice, 1970-77.

Employers
Dewey Ballantine LLP (Partner)

STEIN, Sharon McCloe

1717 Massachusetts Ave. NW
Suite 101
Washington, DC 20009
Tel: (202)667-8950
Fax: (202)667-8953
Registered: LDA

Employers
Negative Population Growth, Inc. (NPG) (Exec. Director)

STEINBACH, Sheldon Elliott

One Dupont Circle NW
Suite 838
Washington, DC 20036-1193
EMail: sheldon_steinbach@ace.nce.edu
Tel: (202)939-9361
Fax: (202)833-4762
Registered: LDA

Employers
American Council on Education (V. President and General Counsel)

STEINBERG, Barry P.

1101 Connecticut Ave. NW
Suite 1000
Washington, DC 20036
Tel: (202)828-2400
Fax: (202)828-2488
Registered: LDA

Served in United States Army (1963-89), and while in the Army as Chief of the Environmental Law Division (1988-89) and Chief of the Litigation Division (1986-88).

Employers
Kutak Rock LLP (Partner)

Clients Represented

On Behalf of Kutak Rock LLP
Alameda, California, City of
Farm Progress Cos.
Highland Park, Illinois, City of Highwood Local Redevelopment Authority and the City of
New London Development Corp.
Orlando, Florida, City of
Pickett, Virginia, Local Redevelopment Authority
San Francisco, City of
Seaside, California, City of
Team Stratford

STEINBRUNER, John D.

1775 Massachusetts Ave. NW
Washington, DC 20036-2188
Tel: (202)797-6000
Fax: (202)797-6004

Employers
The Brookings Institution (Non-Resident Senior Fellow, Economic Policy Studies)

STEINBRUNER, Maureen S.

One Massachusetts Ave. NW
Suite 333
Washington, DC 20001
EMail: mstein@cnponline.org
Tel: (202)682-1800
Fax: (202)682-1818

Employers
Center for Nat'l Policy (President)

STEINDLER, Thomas

600 13th St. NW
Washington, DC 20005-3096
Tel: (202)756-8254
Fax: (202)756-8087
Registered: LDA
EMail: tsteindler@mwe.com

Employers
McDermott, Will and Emery (Partner)

Clients Represented

On Behalf of McDermott, Will and Emery
Electronic Industries Ass'n of Japan

STEINEM, Gloria

1010 Wisconsin Ave. NW
Suite 410
Washington, DC 20007
Tel: (202)944-5080
Fax: (202)944-5081

Employers
Voters For Choice (President)

STEINER, Arthur J.

600 13th St. NW
Washington, DC 20005-3096
Tel: (202)756-8605
Fax: (202)756-8087
EMail: asteiner@mwe.com
Administrative Patent Judge at Board of Patent Appeals and Interferences (1979-93), and Patent Examiner (1966-70, 1973-79), both at Patent and Trademark Office.

Employers
McDermott, Will and Emery (Partner)

STEINER, David P.

1310 G St. NW
Suite 720
Washington, DC 20005
EMail: dstein@maytag.com
Tel: (202)639-9420
Fax: (202)639-9421

Employers
Maytag Corp. (Director, Government Affairs)

STEINKULLER, William P.

3975 Fair Ridge Dr.
Suite 20-North
Fairfax, VA 22033-2906
EMail: steinkuller@autorecyc.org
Tel: (703)385-1001
Fax: (703)385-1494

Employers
Automotive Recyclers Ass'n (Exec. V. President)

STEINMAN, Susan

1050 31st St. NW
Washington, DC 20007
Tel: (202)965-3500
Fax: (202)342-5484
Registered: LDA

Employers
Ass'n of Trial Lawyers of America (Public Affairs Counsel)

STEINWAY, Daniel M.

1200 19th St. NW
Suite 500
Washington, DC 20036
EMail: dsteinway@kelleydrye.com
Tel: (202)955-9600
Fax: (202)955-9792
Minority Counsel, Subcommittees on National Resources, Agricultural Research and the Environment, and Energy Development and Applications, House Committee on Science and Technology, 1978-86. Attorney/Advisor, Office of Enforcement, Environmental Protection Agency, 1976-78.

Employers
Kelley, Drye & Warren LLP (Partner)

Clients Represented

On Behalf of Kelley, Drye & Warren LLP
Environmental Business Action Coalition

STEINWURTZEL, Robert N.

3000 K St. NW
Suite 300
Washington, DC 20007
Tel: (202)424-7500
Fax: (202)424-7643
Registered: LDA
Attorney, Office of Enforcement, Environmental Protection Agency, 1978-79. Special Assistant to the Assistant Secretary, Department of the Interior, 1975-77.

Employers
Swidler Berlin Shereff Friedman, LLP (Partner)

STELZER, Irwin

1015 18th St. NW
Suite 300
Washington, DC 20036
Tel: (202)223-7770
Fax: (202)223-8537

Employers
Hudson Institute (Senior Fellow and Director, Regulatory Studies)

STEMPSON, Brenda

8200 Greensboro Dr.
Suite 302
McLean, VA 22102-3881
Tel: (703)442-4890
Ext: 180
Fax: (703)442-0630

Employers
Nat'l Glass Ass'n (Exec. V. President)

STENRUD, Chris

2300 Clarendon Blvd.
Suite 610
Arlington, VA 22201-3367
EMail: cstenrud@golinharris.com
Tel: (703)351-5666
Fax: (703)351-5667
Special Assistant for Communications and Special Assistant for Policy and Strategy, Department of Health and Human Services, 1997-99.

Employers
Golin/Harris Internat'l (Account Group Supervisor)

STENSON, Jane

1731 King St.
Suite 200
Alexandria, VA 22314
EMail: jstenson@catholiccharitiesusa.org
Tel: (703)549-1390
Fax: (703)549-1656

Employers
Catholic Charities USA (Program Director for Community Services)

STENZEL, Aimee

1140 19th St. NW
Suite 600
Washington, DC 20036
Tel: (202)822-8200
Fax: (202)822-8205

Employers
Violence Policy Center (Publications Coordinator)

STENZEL, Thomas E.

727 N. Washington St.
Alexandria, VA 22314
Tel: (703)836-3410
Fax: (703)836-2049
Registered: LDA
EMail: tstenzel@uffva.org

Employers
Internat'l Banana Ass'n (President)
United Fresh Fruit and Vegetable Ass'n (President and C.E.O.)

STEPANCHUK, John

2201 C St. NW
Room 7251
Washington, DC 20520-7261
Tel: (202)647-8722
Fax: (202)647-2762

Employers
Department of State - Bureau of Legislative Affairs (European & Newly Independent States Affairs Legislative Management Officer)

STEPHEN, Christopher T.

1050 Connecticut Ave. NW
Suite 1100
Washington, DC 20036-5304
Tel: (202)861-1500
Fax: (202)861-1790
Registered: LDA

Employers
Baker & Hostetler LLP

Clients Represented

On Behalf of Baker & Hostetler LLP
American Fidelity Life Insurance Co.
Trans World Assurance Co.

STEPHENS, Jr., J. Gordon "Skip"

4700 N. 38th Pl.
Arlington, VA 22207-2915
Tel: (703)532-4900
Fax: (703)532-4986
Registered: LDA
Legislative Assistant to Speaker Carl Albert (D-OK), House of Representatives, 1973-77.

Employers
Stephens Law Offices (Principal)

Clients Represented

On Behalf of Stephens Law Offices
Degussa Corp.
Financial Advisory Services of Oklahoma, L.L.C.
Harnischfeger Industries, Inc.
Joy Mining Machinery
OBWEO
Roquette America

STEPHENS, Ronald

P.O. Box 57315
Washington, DC 20037
Tel: (202)679-6282
Fax: (202)872-1150
Special Assistant to Deputy Labor Secretary, Internat'l Labor, Department of Labor, 1988-89. Director, Business/Government Relations, Internat'l Trade Administration, Department of Commerce, 1982-85.

Employers
Stephens, Cross, Ihlenfeld & Boring, Inc. (Partner)

Clients Represented

On Behalf of Stephens, Cross, Ihlenfeld & Boring, Inc.
Alliance for American Innovation, Inc.
Austin Professional Systems, Inc.

STEPHENS, W. Dennis

1735 New York Ave. NW
Suite 500
Washington, DC 20006-4759
Tel: (202)628-1700
Fax: (202)331-1024
Registered: LDA, FARA
EMail: denniss@prestongates.com
Legislative Director to Rep. Roger Wicker (R-MS), 1995. Legislative Director to Rep. Joe Barton (R-TX), 1993-95. Legislative Director to Rep. Richard W. Pombo (R-CA), 1993. Legislative Assistant to Rep. Richard Armey (R-TX), 1989-93. Served in the Office of Presidential Personnel, The White House, during the Reagan administration.

Employers
Preston Gates Ellis & Rouvelas Meeds LLP (Government Affairs Analyst)

Clients Represented

On Behalf of Preston Gates Ellis & Rouvelas Meeds LLP
Brown-Forman Corp.
Burlington Northern Santa Fe Railway
Chitimacha Tribe of Louisiana
eLottery, Inc.
Envirocare of Utah, Inc.
Future of Puerto Rico Inc.
Magazine Publishers of America
Microsoft Corp.
Nat'l Center for Economic Freedom, Inc.
Pitney Bowes, Inc.
Prime Time 24
Stone and Webster Engineering Corp.
Tate and Lyle North American Sugars Inc.
United States Maritime Coalition
VoiceStream Wireless Corp.

STEPHENS, William L.

8200 Jones Branch Dr.
McLean, VA 22102
Tel: (703)903-2798
Fax: (703)903-2447

Employers
Federal Home Loan Mortgage Corp. (Freddie Mac) (V. President, Shareholder Relations)

STEPHENS, William T.

P.O. Box 1096
McLean, VA 22101-1096
Tel: (703)821-8700
Fax: (703)827-7761
Registered: LDA

Employers
Stephens Law Firm (Managing Attorney)

Clients Represented
On Behalf of Stephens Law Firm
American Rental Ass'n

STEPHENSON, Gregory

555 12th St. NW
Suite 500
Washington, DC 20004-1207
Tel: (202)879-5600
Fax: (202)879-5309
Registered: LDA

Employers
Deloitte & Touche LLP Nat'l Office - Washington (Partner)

Clients Represented
On Behalf of Deloitte & Touche LLP Nat'l Office - Washington
Torchmark Corp.

STEPHENSON, Mark

1707 L St. NW
Suite 650
Washington, DC 20036
Tel: (202)955-5777
Fax: (202)955-4549

Employers
The Steel Alliance (Exec. Director)

STEPHENSON, Richard E.

2000 Edmund Halley Dr.
Reston, VA 20191
Tel: (703)264-9314
Fax: (703)715-4450
Registered: LDA

Employers
DynCorp (V. President, Technology and Government Relations)

STEPHENSON KRIVIT, Sandra M.

1120 G St. NW
Suite 200
Washington, DC 20005
EMail: skrivit@erols.com
Tel: (202)544-1112
Fax: (202)737-4933

Employers
Krivit & Krivit, P.C.

STEPTOE, Mary Lou

1440 New York Ave. NW
Washington, DC 20005
Tel: (202)371-7000
Fax: (202)393-5760
Registered: LDA, FARA

Employers
Skadden, Arps, Slate, Meagher & Flom LLP (Partner)

STERLING, Charlotte

One Marriott Dr.
Department 977.01
Washington, DC 20058
Tel: (202)380-3000

Employers
Marriott Internat'l, Inc. (Senior V. President, Corporate Relations)

STERLING, Eric E.

1225 I St. NW
Suite 500
Washington, DC 20005
EMail: esterling@igc.org
Tel: (202)312-2015
Fax: (202)842-2620

Employers
The Criminal Justice Policy Foundation (President)

STERN, Andrew

1313 L St. NW
Washington, DC 20005
Tel: (202)898-3200
Fax: (202)898-3304
Registered: LDA

Employers
Service Employees Internat'l Union (President)

STERN, David

2120 L St. NW
Suite 450
Washington, DC 20037
EMail: dstern@napil.org
Tel: (202)466-3686
Fax: (202)429-9766

Employers
Nat'l Ass'n for Public Interest Law (NAPIL) (Exec. Director)

STERN, Elizabeth Espin

2300 N St. NW
Washington, DC 20037-1128
EMail: elizabeth.stern@shawpittman.com
Tel: (202)663-8000
Fax: (202)663-8007
Registered: LDA

Employers
Shaw Pittman (Partner)

STERN, Martin L.

1735 New York Ave. NW
Suite 500
Washington, DC 20006-4759
Tel: (202)628-1700
Fax: (202)331-1024
Registered: LDA
Former Deputy Chief, Competition Division, Office of the General Counsel, Federal Communications Commission.

Employers
Preston Gates Ellis & Rouvelas Meeds LLP (Partner)

Clients Represented
On Behalf of Preston Gates Ellis & Rouvelas Meeds LLP
Burlington Northern Santa Fe Railway
Northpoint Technology, Ltd.

STERN, Michael

1401 H St. NW
12th Floor
Washington, DC 20005-2148
Tel: (202)326-5894
Fax: (202)326-8313
Registered: LDA

Employers
Investment Co. Institute (Legislative Representative - Taxation)

STERN, Ronald A.

1299 Pennsylvania Ave. NW
Suite 1100 West
Washington, DC 20004-2407
Tel: (202)637-4000
Fax: (202)637-4027

Employers
General Electric Co. (V. President and Senior Counsel, Antitrust)

STERN, Ronald J.

P.O. Box 15848
Arlington, VA 22215
EMail: ronald.stern@uspto.gov
Tel: (703)308-0818
Fax: (703)308-0818

Employers
Patent Office Professional Ass'n (President)

STERNE, Jr., John H.

901 15th St. NW
Suite 700
Washington, DC 20005-2301
Tel: (202)371-6000
Fax: (202)371-6279
Registered: LDA, FARA
Legislative Assistant to Rep. Jolene Unsoeld (D-WA), 1993-94.

Employers
Verner, Liipfert, Bernhard, McPherson and Hand, Chartered (Of Counsel)

Clients Represented
On Behalf of Verner, Liipfert, Bernhard, McPherson and Hand, Chartered
Alliance Pipeline, L.P.
Chlorine Chemistry Council
General Electric Co.
Port of Tillamook Bay
Prowler Fisheries and Clipper Seafoods
Southeastern Federal Power Customers, Inc.

STERNFELS, Urvan R.

1899 L St. NW
Suite 1000
Washington, DC 20036
Tel: (202)457-0480
Fax: (202)457-0486
Registered: LDA

Employers
Nat'l Petrochemical Refiners Ass'n (President)

STERTZER, David

1922 F St. NW
Fourth Floor
Washington, DC 20006
Tel: (202)331-6081
Fax: (202)331-2164

Employers
Ass'n for Advanced Life Underwriting (Exec. V. President)

STET, Charlene A.

901 E St. NW
Suite 600
Washington, DC 20004
Tel: (202)508-3708
Fax: (202)783-4085

Employers
Nat'l Treasury Employees Union (Legislative Field Operations Liaison)

STEUERLE, C. Eugene

2100 M St. NW
Washington, DC 20037
Tel: (202)833-7200
Fax: (202)429-0687

Employers
The Urban Institute (Senior Fellow)

STEVE, Jaime

122 C St. NW
Suite 380
Washington, DC 20001
Tel: (202)383-2500
Fax: (202)383-2505
Registered: LDA

Employers
American Wind Energy Ass'n (Director, Government and Public Affairs)

STEVENS, Christine

P.O. Box 3719
Georgetown Station
Washington, DC 20007
Tel: (202)337-2334
Fax: (202)338-9478
Registered: LDA

Employers
Soc. for Animal Protective Legislation (Secretary)

STEVENS, Cindy M.

555 12th St. NW
Suite 500
Washington, DC 20004-1207
EMail: cistevens@deloitte.com
Tel: (202)879-5600
Fax: (202)879-5309
Registered: LDA

Employers
Deloitte & Touche LLP Nat'l Office - Washington (Director, Federal Programs)

STEVENS, Glenn

1010 N. Glebe Rd.
Suite 160
Arlington, VA 22201
Tel: (703)516-4070
Fax: (703)516-4069

Employers
Nat'l Center for Housing Management (President)

STEVENS, Greg

305 Cameron St.
Alexandria, VA 22314
EMail: gstevens@srcmedia.com
Tel: (703)683-8326
Fax: (703)683-8826

Employers
Stevens Reed Curcio & Co. (President)

STEVENS, Herbert F.

401 Ninth St. NW
Suite 900
Washington, DC 20004
EMail: hstevens@nixonpeabody.com
Tel: (202)585-8000
Fax: (202)585-8080
Registered: LDA

Employers
Nixon Peabody LLP (Partner)

Clients Represented
On Behalf of Nixon Peabody LLP
MetroPlains Development, Inc.

STEVENS, Jack

1299 Pennsylvania Ave. NW
Suite 800 West
Washington, DC 20004
Tel: (202)785-0500
Fax: (202)785-5277
Registered: LDA

Employers
The Carmen Group (Senior Associate)

Clients Represented
On Behalf of The Carmen Group
Kazakhstan, Government of the Republic of
Renova Inc.

STEVENS, Mark E.

Ariel Rios Federal Bldg.
(1301-MC)
1200 Pennsylvania Ave. NW
Third Floor
Washington, DC 20460
EMail: stevens.mark@epa.gov
Tel: (202)564-3707
Fax: (202)501-1514

Employers
Environmental Protection Agency (Senior Advisor for Congressional Oversight)

STEVENS, Michael L.

1050 Connecticut Ave. NW
Washington, DC 20036-5339
Tel: (202)857-6000
Fax: (202)857-6395

Employers
Arent Fox Kintner Plotkin & Kahn, PLLC (Member)

STEVENS, Paul Schott

1775 I St. NW
Washington, DC 20006
Tel: (202)261-3300
Fax: (202)261-3333
EMail: paul.stevens@dechert.com
Executive Assistant to Secretary of Defense, 1989; Special Assistant to the President for National Security Affairs, 1987-89; Executive Secretary, National Security Council, 1987-89; Legal Adviser, National Security Council, 1987; Deputy Director and General Counsel, President's Blue Ribbon Commission on Defense Management, 1985-86.

Employers
Dechert (Partner)

STEVENS, R. Greg

1275 Pennsylvania Ave. NW
Tenth Floor
Washington, DC 20004
Tel: (202)333-4936
Fax: (202)833-9392
Registered: LDA

Employers
Barbour Griffith & Rogers, Inc.

Clients Represented
On Behalf of Barbour Griffith & Rogers, Inc.
Artists Coalition
Avioimpex
Makedonski Telekomunikacii

STEVENSON, Sharon

801 N. Fairfax St.
Suite 306
Alexandria, VA 22314
Tel: (703)548-7790
Fax: (703)548-7792

Employers
Nat'l Center for Homeopathy (Exec. Director)

STEWARD, William R.

1730 K St. NW
Suite 1106
Washington, DC 20006
Tel: (202)466-3561
Fax: (202)466-3583

Employers
Household Financial Group, Ltd. (Director, Governmental Relations)
Household Internat'l, Inc. (Director, Governmental Relations)

STEWART, Cynthia E.

1033 N. Fairfax St.
Suite 404
Alexandria, VA 22314
EMail: cstewart@icsc.org
Tel: (703)549-7404
Fax: (703)549-8712

Employers
Internat'l Council of Shopping Centers (Director, Local Government Relations)

STEWART, Dana

1755 Jefferson Davis Hwy.
Suite 1107
Arlington, VA 22202
Tel: (703)415-0344
Fax: (703)415-0182
Registered: LDA

Employers
The PMA Group (Legislative Assistant)

Clients Represented
On Behalf of The PMA Group
ARC Global Technologies
Nat'l Ass'n of Resource Conservation
Nat'l Pork Producers Ass'n
University Emergency Medicine Foundation

STEWART, David

801 Pennsylvania Ave. NW
Suite 230
Washington, DC 20004
Tel: (202)393-7150
Fax: (202)347-1684
Registered: LDA
EMail: dstewart@bradleyarant.com
Legislative Staff, Senator Jeff Sessions (R-AL), 1997.

Employers
Bradley Arant Rose & White LLP (Associate)

STEWART, David L.

600 13th St. NW
Washington, DC 20005-3096
Tel: (202)756-8601
Fax: (202)756-8087
EMail: dstewart@mwe.com
Administrative Patent Judge, Board of Patent Appeals and Interferences, Patent and Trademark Office, 1989-93.

Employers
McDermott, Will and Emery (Partner)

STEWART, Debra

One Dupont Circle NW
Suite 430
Washington, DC 20036
EMail: dstewart@cgs.nche.edu
Tel: (202)223-3791
Fax: (202)331-7157

Employers
Council of Graduate Schools (President)

STEWART, Erika

1090 Vermont Ave. NW
Suite 510
Washington, DC 20005
Tel: (202)414-0140
Fax: (202)544-3525

Employers
American Osteopathic Ass'n (Office Manager, Government Relations)

STEWART, Heather

1212 New York Ave. NW
Suite 425
Washington, DC 20005
EMail: heather_stewart@acip.com
Tel: (202)371-6789
Fax: (202)371-5524

Employers
American Council on Internat'l Personnel, Inc. (Legislative Counsel)

STEWART, Jarvis C.

509 C St. NE
Washington, DC 20002
Tel: (202)546-3800
Fax: (202)544-6771
Registered: LDA
EMail: stewart@capitolcoalitions.com
Former Chief of Staff to Rep. Harold E. Ford, Jr. (D-TN).

Employers
Capitol Coalitions Inc. (Principal)

Clients Represented
On Behalf of Capitol Coalitions Inc.
Astro Vision Internat'l, Inc.
Big Sky Economic Development Authority
Fanatasy Elections
Houston, Texas, Department of Aviation of the City of
One Economy Corp.
Westinghouse Government Services Group

STEWART, Julie A.

1612 K St. NW
Suite 1400
Washington, DC 20006
Tel: (202)822-6700
Fax: (202)822-6704

Employers
Families Against Mandatory Minimums (President)

STEWART, Ken

1155 15th St. NW
Suite 1004
Washington, DC 20005
Tel: (202)467-5081
Fax: (202)467-5085

Employers
Council of Citizens with Low Vision, Internat'l (President)

STEWART, Kiersten

1522 K St. NW
Suite 550
Washington, DC 20005
Tel: (202)682-1212
Fax: (202)682-4662
Registered: LDA

Employers
Family Violence Prevention Fund (Director, Public Policy)

STEWART, Lisa A.

507 C St. NE
Washington, DC 20002-5809
Tel: (202)544-7944
Fax: (202)544-7975
Registered: LDA
EMail: lstewart@beacon-group.net

Employers
Beacon Consulting Group, Inc. (V. President)

Clients Represented
On Behalf of Beacon Consulting Group, Inc.
Access Community Health Network
Advance Paradigm
American Trauma Soc.
Big Brothers/Big Sisters of America
Boston Symphony Orchestra
Carnegie Hall Corp.
Center Point Inc.
Civic Ventures
Cummins-Allison Corp.
Haymarket Center
Metropolitan Family Services
Museum of Science and Industry
Mystic Seaport Museum
Nat'l Crime Prevention Council
Ohio Wesleyan University
Old Sturbridge Village
Oregon Health Sciences University
Public/Private Ventures
Safer Foundation
Westcare Foundation, Inc.

STEWART, Marise R.

1101 Pennsylvania Ave. NW
Suite 400
Washington, DC 20004-2504
Tel: (202)637-3818
Fax: (202)637-3863
Registered: LDA

Employers
Textron Inc. (Director, Government Affairs)

STEWART, Mark

1331 Pennsylvania Ave. NW
North Lobby, Suite 600
Washington, DC 20004-1703
Tel: (202)637-3053
Fax: (202)637-3182

Employers
Nat'l Industrial Council (Exec. Director, Employer Association Group)

STEWART, Mary

P.O. Box 2626
Washington, DC 20013
Tel: (703)998-2600
Fax: (703)998-3401

Employers
WETA (Director, Corporate Communications)

STEWART, Michael

111 Park Place
Falls Church, VA 22046-4513
Tel: (703)533-0251
Fax: (703)241-5603

Employers
Ass'n and Soc. Management Internat'l Inc. (Account Executive)

Clients Represented
On Behalf of Ass'n and Soc. Management Internat'l Inc.
Ass'n of State and Territorial Chronic Disease Program Directors

STEWART, Rosemary

1350 I St. NW
Ninth Floor
Washington, DC 20005-3304
Tel: (202)898-5800
Fax: (202)682-1639

Employers
Spriggs & Hollingsworth (Partner)

STEWART, Scott

600 Pennsylvania Ave. SE
Suite 301
Washington, DC 20003
Tel: (202)608-1411
Fax: (202)608-1429

Employers
College Republican Nat'l Committee (Chairman)

STEWART, Steve W.

1301 K St. NW
Suite 1200-West Tower
Washington, DC 20005-3307
Tel: (202)515-5054
Fax: (202)515-5055
Registered: LDA
EMail: stewarts@us.ibm.com

Employers
Internat'l Business Machines Corp. (Director, Market Access, Trade and Telecommunications)

STEWART, Tara

1725 DeSales St. NW
Suite 600
Washington, DC 20036
Tel: (202)429-5609
Fax: (202)872-0619

Employers
Center for Marine Conservation

STEWART, Terence P.

2100 M St. NW
Suite 200
Washington, DC 20037
Tel: (202)785-4185
Fax: (202)466-1286
Registered: LDA, FARA
EMail: tstewart@stewartlaw.com

Employers
Stewart and Stewart (Managing Partner)

Clients Represented

On Behalf of Stewart and Stewart
Floral Trade Council
The Gates Rubber Co.
Libbey, Inc.
PPG Industries
Ranchers-Cattlemen Legal Action Fund
The Timken Co.

STEWART, Thomas G.

633 S. Washington St.
Alexandria, VA 22314
Tel: (703)836-0850
Fax: (703)836-0848
Registered: LDA

Employers
Nat'l Rehabilitation Ass'n (Director of Governmental Affairs)

STEWART, Walter J. "Joe"

1300 Connecticut Ave. NW
Suite 600
Washington, DC 20036
Tel: (202)775-8116
Fax: (202)223-0358
Registered: LDA
Secretary, U.S. Senate, 1987-94. Secretary for the Majority, U.S. Senate, 1979-81. Administrative Assistant to Majority Leader for Floor Operations, U.S. Senate, 1977-79. Professional Staff, Senate Appropriations Committee, 1972-77.

Employers
Griffin, Johnson, Dover & Stewart (Lobbyist)

Clients Represented

On Behalf of Griffin, Johnson, Dover & Stewart
Alaska Communications Systems, Inc.
American Agrisurance
American Fish Spotters Ass'n
American Petroleum Institute
American Soc. of Anesthesiologists
Arthur Andersen LLP
Avue Technologies
Dell Computer Corp.
Deloitte Consulting
Fannie Mae
Hong Kong Economic and Trade Office
The Justice Project, Inc.
Lockheed Martin Corp.
Lockheed Martin Global Telecommunications
Philip Morris Management Corp.
United Technologies Corp.
Wilmer, Cutler & Pickering
Wine and Spirits Wholesalers of America

STEWART DALY, Julia

6707 Old Dominion Dr.
Suite 320
McLean, VA 22101
Tel: (703)442-8850
Fax: (703)790-0845
EMail: jdaly@usapple.org

Employers
U.S. Apple Ass'n (Director, Public Relations)

STEYER, Richard A.

1747 Pennsylvania Ave. NW
Suite 1050
Washington, DC 20006
Tel: (202)296-5680
Fax: (202)331-8049
EMail: rsteyer@haspc.com
Attorney, Office of Appeals, National Labor Relations Board, 1976-79.

Employers
Howe, Anderson & Steyer, P.C. (Partner)

Clients Represented

On Behalf of Howe, Anderson & Steyer, P.C.
Nat'l Ass'n of Bankruptcy Trustees

STICHMAN, Barton

2001 S St. NW
Suite 610
Washington, DC 20009
Tel: (202)265-8305
Fax: (202)328-0063
EMail: barton_stichman@nvlsp.org

Employers
Nat'l Veterans Legal Services Program (Joint Exec. Director)

STICKLE, Ph.D., Warren E.

1430 Duke St.
Alexandria, VA 22314
Tel: (703)548-7700
Fax: (703)548-3149

Employers
Chemical Producers and Distributors Ass'n (President)

STICKLES, Peter

1199 N. Fairfax St.
Suite 1000
Alexandria, VA 22314
Tel: (703)299-4499
Fax: (703)299-4488
EMail: pstickles@hawthorngroup.com

Employers
The Hawthorn Group, L.C. (Senior Account Executive)

STIEF, Rev. Ron

110 Maryland Ave. NE
Suite 207
Washington, DC 20002
Tel: (202)543-1517
Fax: (202)543-5994
EMail: stiefr@ucc.org

Employers
United Church of Christ Justice and Witness Ministry (Director)

STIEGLITZ, Perry J.

1156 15th St. NW
Suite 1100
Washington, DC 20005
Tel: (202)452-1108
Fax: (202)452-1109
Registered: FARA
Former Foreign Service Officer, Department of State.

Employers
Gibraltar Information Bureau (Director)

STIERLE, MSN, RN, CNAA, Linda J.

600 Maryland Ave. SW
Suite 100 West
Washington, DC 20024-2571
Tel: (202)651-7000
Fax: (202)651-7001

Employers
American Nurses Ass'n (Chief Exec. Officer)

STIERS, William F.

1275 Pennsylvania Ave. NW
Tenth Floor
Washington, DC 20004
Tel: (202)347-6000
Fax: (202)347-6001
Registered: LDA

Employers
Balch & Bingham LLP (Director, Government Relations)

Clients Represented

On Behalf of Balch & Bingham LLP
Alabama Space Science Exhibits Commission
Coleman Research Corp.
Computer Systems Technologies, Inc.
Elmco, Inc.
Emerging Technology Partners, LLC
Madison Research Corp.
Mas-Hamilton Group
SCANA Corp.

STIFFLER, Alan

888 17th St. NW
Suite 900
Washington, DC 20006
Tel: (202)969-2587
Fax: (202)969-2581
EMail: astiffler@alts.org

Employers
Ass'n for Local Telecommunications Services (V. President, Association Affairs)

STILL, Edward

1401 New York Ave. NW
Suite 400
Washington, DC 20005
Tel: (202)662-8320
Fax: (202)783-5130
EMail: estill@lawyerscomm.org

Employers
Lawyers' Committee for Civil Rights Under Law (Director, Voting Rights Project)

STILLMAN, Bradley

1133 19th St. NW
Washington, DC 20036
Tel: (202)887-3340
Fax: (202)202-3175
EMail: bradley.stillman@wcom.com

Employers
MCI WorldCom Corp. (Director, Strategic Policy Initiatives)

STILLMAN, Don

1350 I St. NW
Suite 510
Washington, DC 20005
Tel: (202)828-8500
Fax: (202)293-3457
Registered: LDA

Employers
United Automobile, Aerospace and Agricultural Implement Workers of America (UAW) (Director, Government and International Affairs)

STILLWELL, Lee J.

1101 Vermont Ave. NW
12th Floor
Washington, DC 20005-3583
Tel: (202)789-7400
Fax: (202)789-7479
Registered: LDA

Employers
American Medical Ass'n (Senior V. President, Advocacy)

STINE, Laurel

1101 15th St. NW
Suite 1212
Washington, DC 20005
Tel: (202)467-5730
Ext: 34
Fax: (202)223-0409
Registered: LDA
EMail: laurels@bazelon.org

Employers
Bazelon Center for Mental Health Law, Judge David L. (Director, Federal Relations)

STINE, Vince

2101 L St. NW
Suite 202
Washington, DC 20037
Tel: (202)857-0717
Fax: (202)887-5093
Registered: LDA

Employers
American Ass'n for Clinical Chemistry, Inc. (Government Affairs Program Director)

STINE, II, William H.

1200 18th St. NW
Suite 400
Washington, DC 20036-2506
Tel: (202)783-9000
Fax: (202)331-8364
EMail: bstine@nbaa.org

Employers
Nat'l Business Aviation Ass'n (Director, International Issues and Corporate Secretary)

STINEBERT, Chris

2101 Wilson Blvd.
Suite 610
Arlington, VA 22201
Tel: (703)558-0400
Fax: (703)558-0401

Employers
Manufactured Housing Institute (President)

STINGER, Cynthia Mansfield

801 Pennsylvania Ave. NW
Suite 310
Washington, DC 20004
Tel: (202)434-8150
Fax: (202)434-8156
Registered: LDA

Employers
GPU, Inc. (V. President, Government Affairs)

STINGER, Kenneth F.

430 First St. SE
Washington, DC 20003
Tel: (202)544-6245
Fax: (202)675-6568
Registered: LDA

Employers
American Trucking Ass'ns (V. President, Federal and Federation Legislative Affairs)
Self-employed as an independent consultant.

Clients Represented
As an independent consultant
PACCAR, Inc.

STINGER, Patti

1030 15th St. NW
Suite 1100
Washington, DC 20005
Tel: (202)783-4600
Fax: (202)783-4601

Employers
White House Writers Group (Senior Director)

STINSON, John M.

1667 K St. NW
Suite 460
Washington, DC 20006
Tel: (202)496-9688
Registered: LDA

Employers
Forscey & Stinson, PLLC (Partner)
The National Group, LLP (Partner)
Self-employed as an independent consultant.

Clients Represented
As an independent consultant
American Iron and Steel Institute
Changing World Technologies
Nat'l Steel Corp.
Northwest Pipe Co.
RSR Corp.

STIRLING, Deborah J.

1200 New York Ave. NW
Suite 410
Washington, DC 20005
Tel: (202)682-9344
Fax: (202)689-9298
Registered: LDA
EMail: djstirling@aol.com
Staff Counsel for Ocean and Atmospheric Policy, Senate Committee on Commerce, Science, Transporation, 1975-84.

Employers
Waterstone Strategies & Technologies (Senior V. President)

STIRPE, David J.

2111 Wilson Blvd.
Eighth Floor
Arlington, VA 22201-3058
Tel: (703)841-0626
Fax: (703)243-2874
Registered: LDA

Employers
Alcalde & Fay (Partner)
Alliance for Responsible Atmospheric Policy (Exec. Director)

Clients Represented
On Behalf of Alcalde & Fay
Alliance for Responsible Atmospheric Policy
Internat'l Climate Change Partnership

STIRRUP, John T.

2001 M St. NW
Washington, DC 20036
Tel: (202)467-3000
Fax: (202)533-8500
Registered: LDA

Employers
KPMG, LLP (Manager, Government Affairs)

STISH, DeAnn

1111 19th St. NW
Suite 800
Washington, DC 20036
Tel: (202)463-2700
Fax: (202)463-2785
Registered: LDA

Employers
American Forest & Paper Ass'n (Director, Congressional Affairs)

STOCK, Stuart C.

1201 Pennsylvania Ave. NW
Washington, DC 20004-2401
Tel: (202)662-6000
Fax: (202)662-6291
Registered: LDA
EMail: sstock@cov.com
Law Clerk, Supreme Court, 1972-73. Law Clerk, Second Circuit, Court of Appeals, 1971-72.

Employers
Covington & Burling (Partner)

Clients Represented
On Behalf of Covington & Burling
Bank One Corp.
Bank of America
Golden West Financial Corp.
Microsoft Corp.

STOCKER, Frederick T.

1525 Wilson Blvd.
Suite 900
Arlington, VA 22209
Tel: (703)841-9000
Fax: (703)841-9514
EMail: fstocker@mapi.net
Former Attorney with Interstate Commerce Commission.

Employers
Manufacturers Alliance/MAPI Inc. (V. President, Counsel)

STODUTO, Nicole

1101 14th St. NW
Suite 1400
Washington, DC 20005
Tel: (202)682-9400
Fax: (202)682-1331
EMail: nstoauto@defenders.org

Employers
Defenders of Wildlife (Legal Coordinator)

STOEPPELWERTH, Ali M.

2445 M St. NW
Washington, DC 20037-1420
Tel: (202)663-6000
Fax: (202)663-6363
Registered: LDA
EMail: astoeppelwerth@wilmer.com
Former Law Clerk to Chief Judge, Alfred T. Goodwin, U.S. Court of Appeals, Ninth Circuit.

Employers
Wilmer, Cutler & Pickering (Associate)

STOER, Eric F.

700 13th St. NW
Suite 700
Washington, DC 20005-3960
Tel: (202)508-6000
Fax: (202)508-6200
EMail: efstoer@bryancave.com
Trial Attorney, Federal Trade Commission, 1969-70.

Employers
Bryan Cave LLP (Partner)

STOHL, Rachel

1779 Massachusetts Ave. NW
Suite 615
Washington, DC 20036
Tel: (202)332-0600
Fax: (202)462-4559

Employers
Center for Defense Information (Research Analyst)

STOHLER, Thomas

601 Pennsylvania Ave. NW
Suite 600
North Bldg.
Washington, DC 20004
Tel: (202)682-9110
Fax: (202)682-9111
Registered: LDA

Employers
American Electronics Ass'n (Director, Workforce and Education)

STOHLMAN, Robert

219 N. Washington St.
Alexandria, VA 22314
Tel: (703)836-7990
Fax: (703)836-9739

Employers
Peduzzi Associates, Ltd. (Associate)

STOJIC, Steve

1023 15th St. NW
Suite 900
Washington, DC 20005-2602
Tel: (202)289-7200
Fax: (202)289-7698
EMail: sstojic@gbmdc.com
Attorney, Federal Energy Regulatory Commission, 1980-82.

Employers
Gallagher, Boland and Meiburger (Partner)

Clients Represented
On Behalf of Gallagher, Boland and Meiburger
Cinergy Corp.
Enron Corp.

STOKES, Kathleen

9420 Annapolis Rd.
Suite 307
Lanham, MD 20706
Tel: (301)577-4956
Ext: 109
Fax: (301)731-0039

Employers
Service Station Dealers of America and Allied Trades (Assistant to the Exec. V. President and PAC Contact)

STOKES, Louis

1201 Pennsylvania Ave. NW
P.O. Box 407
Washington, DC 20044-0407
Tel: (202)626-6600
Fax: (202)626-6780
Registered: LDA

Employers
Squire, Sanders & Dempsey L.L.P.

Clients Represented
On Behalf of Squire, Sanders & Dempsey L.L.P.
Case Western Reserve University School of Medicine
Cuyahoga Community College
Nat'l City Corp.

STOKES, Sean A.

1820 Jefferson Pl. NW
Washington, DC 20036
Tel: (202)833-0166
Fax: (202)833-1180
Registered: LDA
EMail: sstokes@baller.com

Employers
The Baller Herbst Law Group (Attorney)

Clients Represented
On Behalf of The Baller Herbst Law Group
Hiawatha Broadband Communications Inc.

STOLEE, Anne M.

801 Pennsylvania Ave. NW
Suite 800
Washington, DC 20004
Tel: (202)508-3400
Fax: (202)508-3402
EMail: astolee@bdbc.com

Employers
Baker, Donelson, Bearman & Caldwell, P.C. (Shareholder)

STOLGITIS, William C.

901 N. Stuart St.
Suite 904
Arlington, VA 22203-1822
Tel: (703)522-4114
Fax: (703)522-2075

Employers
Soc. for Technical Communication (Exec. Director and Counsel)

STOLL, Karl

7839 Ashton Ave.
Manassas, VA 20109
Tel: (703)330-7000
Ext: 517
Fax: (703)330-6996
EMail: kstoll@nrb.org

Employers
Nat'l Religious Broadcasters (V. President, Communications)

STOLL, Robert L.

c/o Asst Secy & Commissioner
Patents and Trademarks
Washington, DC 20231
Tel: (703)305-9300
Fax: (703)305-8885

Employers
Department of Commerce - United States Patent and Trademark Office (Administrator, Legislative and International Affairs Office)

STOMBLER, Robin E.

1225 New York Ave. NW
Suite 250
Washington, DC 20005-6156
EMail: Rstombler@aol.com
Tel: (202)347-4450
Fax: (202)347-4453
Registered: LDA

Employers
American Soc. of Clinical Pathologists (V. President, Government Affairs)

STONE, Alec

1050 17th St. NW
Suite 701
Washington, DC 20036
Tel: (202)289-5850
Registered: LDA

Employers
Nat'l Campaign for Hearing Health (Director, Government Affairs)

STONE, Ann E. W.

2760 Eisenhower Ave.
Suite 250
Alexandria, VA 22314
Tel: (703)329-1982
Fax: (703)329-2411
Registered: LDA

Employers
Republicans for Choice (Chairman)
The Stone Group, Inc. (President)

STONE, Mr. J. Robin

1200 Wilson Blvd.
MC RS-00
Arlington, VA 22209
Tel: (703)465-3604
Fax: (703)465-3036
Registered: LDA

Employers
The Boeing Co. (Director, State and Local Government Relations)

STONE, John C. "Jay"

1420 New York Ave. NW
Suite 1050
Washington, DC 20005
EMail: jstone@vsadc.com
Tel: (202)638-1950
Fax: (202)638-7714
Registered: LDA

Former Aide to Deputy Secretary, Department of Energy and Administrative Assistant to Rep. W. Henson Moore (R-LA).

Employers
Van Scoyoc Associates, Inc. (V. President)

Clients Represented
On Behalf of Van Scoyoc Associates, Inc.
American Forest & Paper Ass'n
Archimedes Technology Group
British Trade and Commerce Bank
Davison Transport, Inc.
Greater New Orleans Expressway Commission
Krebs, LaSalle, LeMieux Consultants, Inc.
University of New Orleans Foundation
Wackenhut Services, Inc.
Washington Consulting Group

STONE, Judith Lee

750 First St. NE
Suite 901
Washington, DC 20002
EMail: jstone@saferoads.org
Tel: (202)408-1711
Fax: (202)408-1699
Registered: LDA

Employers
Advocates for Highway and Auto Safety (President)

STONE, Libby

601 Pennsylvania Ave. NW
Suite 600
North Bldg.
Washington, DC 20004
Tel: (202)682-9110
Fax: (202)682-9111
Registered: LDA

Employers
American Electronics Ass'n (Exec. Administrator)

STONE, Paul D.

1776 I St. NW
Suite 1050
Washington, DC 20006
Tel: (202)429-3400
Fax: (202)429-3467

Employers
The Dow Chemical Co. (Director, Federal Technical/Business Development)

STONE, Roger J.

1101 30th St. NW
Suite 220
Washington, DC 20007
Tel: (202)337-6600
Fax: (202)337-6660
Registered: LDA

Employers
Ikon Public Affairs (President)

Clients Represented
On Behalf of Ikon Public Affairs
The Trump Organization

STONE, Suzanne

4601 Presidents Dr.
Suite 260
Lanham, MD 20706-4365
EMail: sstone@svtnet.org
Tel: (301)459-7550
Fax: (301)459-5651

Employers
Soc. of Vascular Technology (Exec. Director)

STONER, Dena G.

4301 Wilson Blvd.
Arlington, VA 22203-1860
EMail: denastoner@nreca.org
Tel: (703)907-5500
Fax: (703)907-5516

Employers
Nat'l Rural Electric Cooperative Ass'n (V. President, Government Relations)

STONER, Floyd E.

1120 Connecticut Ave. NW
Washington, DC 20036
Tel: (202)663-5000
Fax: (202)828-4548
Registered: LDA

Employers
American Bankers Ass'n (Deputy Exec. Director, Government Relations)

STONER, Nancy

1200 New York Ave. NW
Suite 400
Washington, DC 20005
Tel: (202)289-6868
Fax: (202)289-1060

Employers
Natural Resources Defense Council (Senior Attorney)

STONEROCK, Jeffrey

1299 Pennsylvania Ave. NW
Suite 1300 West
Washington, DC 20004-2400
Tel: (202)639-7700
Fax: (202)639-7890
Registered: LDA

Employers
Baker Botts, L.L.P. (Partner)

Clients Represented
On Behalf of Baker Botts, L.L.P.
Trajen, Inc.

STONNER, David M.

4201 Wilson Blvd.
Room 1245 S
Arlington, VA 22230
EMail: dstonner@nsf.gov
Tel: (703)292-8070
Fax: (703)292-9089

Employers
Nat'l Science Foundation (Head, Congressional Affairs Section)

STOOPS, Michael

1012 14th St. NW
Suite 600
Washington, DC 20005-3471
EMail: mstoops@nationalhomeless.org
Tel: (202)737-6444
Fax: (202)737-6445

Employers
Nat'l Coalition for the Homeless (Director Field Organizing Project)

STORCH, Stephen E.

1735 K St. NW
Washington, DC 20006-1506
EMail: steve.storch@nasd.com
Tel: (202)728-8255
Fax: (202)728-8419

Employers
Nat'l Ass'n of Securities Dealers, Inc. (NASD) (Director, Governmental Relations)

STORRS, Josie

1401 I St. NW
Suite 1000
Washington, DC 20005
EMail: cstorrs@sia.com
Tel: (202)296-9410
Fax: (202)296-9775
Registered: LDA

Employers
Securities Industry Ass'n (V. President, Congressional Relations)

STOTT, Lynette Engelhardt

50 F St. NW
Suite 500
Washington, DC 20001
EMail: engelhardt@bread.org
Tel: (301)608-2400
Fax: (301)608-2401
Registered: LDA

Employers
Bread for the World (Domestic Policy Analyst)

STOUT, Susan M.

1010 Wisconsin Ave. NW
Ninth Floor
Washington, DC 20007
EMail: sstout@gmabrands.com
Tel: (202)337-9400
Fax: (202)337-4508
Registered: LDA

Employers
Grocery Manufacturers of America (V. President, Federal Affairs)

STOUT, Jr., Thomas A.

2001 M St. NW
Washington, DC 20036
Tel: (202)467-3000
Fax: (202)533-8500
Registered: LDA

Employers
KPMG, LLP

Clients Represented
On Behalf of KPMG, LLP
The INDOPCO Coalition
The KPMG FSC Coalition
Nat'l Council of Farmer Cooperatives
Sara Lee Corp.

STOVALL, Ellen

1010 Wayne Ave.
Suite 770
Silver Spring, MD 20910
Tel: (301)650-9127
Fax: (301)565-9670
Registered: LDA

Employers
Nat'l Coalition for Cancer Survivorship (President and Chief Exec. Officer)

STOVALL, III, James T.

1725 N St. NW
Washington, DC 20036
Registered: FARA

Employers
Self-employed as an independent consultant.

Clients Represented
As an independent consultant
Micronesia, Embassy of the Federated States of

STOVER, Mark R.

One Massachusetts Ave. NW
Suite 850
Washington, DC 20001
Tel: (202)682-1700
Fax: (202)682-9478
Registered: LDA

Employers
Nat'l Hydropower Ass'n (Director, Government Affairs)

STOWE, Edward W.

245 Second St. NE
Washington, DC 20002
Tel: (202)547-6000
Fax: (202)547-6019
Registered: LDA

Employers
Friends Committee on Nat'l Legislation (Legislative Secretary)

STOWE, Ronald F.

555 12th St. NW
Suite 650
Washington, DC 20004-1205
Tel: (202)393-7950
Fax: (202)393-7960
Registered: LDA

Employers
Eli Lilly and Co. (V. President, Government Relations)

STRACHAN, Linda

600 13th St. NW
Suite 660
Washington, DC 20005
Tel: (202)783-2460
Fax: (202)783-2468

Employers
Monsanto Co. (PAC Contact)

STRADER, Lowell "Pete"

1155 15th St. NW
Suite 405
Washington, DC 20005
Tel: (202)293-7939
Fax: (202)293-7888
Registered: LDA
EMail: pacepete@aol.com

Employers
Paper, Allied-Industrial, Chemical and Energy Workers Internat'l Union (PACE) (Director, Citizenship-Legislative Department)

STRAND, Margaret N.

1620 L St. NW
Suite 600
Washington, DC 20036
Tel: (202)312-8000
Fax: (202)312-8100
Registered: LDA
EMail: mstrand@owdlaw.com
Chief, Environmental Defense Section (1984-91) and Trial Attorney and Assistant Section Chief, Environment and Natural Resources Division (1976-84), Department of Justice.

Employers
Oppenheimer Wolff & Donnelly LLP (Partner)

Clients Represented
On Behalf of Oppenheimer Wolff & Donnelly LLP
CBI Industries
Crown Butte Mines, Inc.
Empresas Fonalledas
Nat'l Mitigation Bankers Ass'n
Resource Investments, Inc.

STRANDLIE, Julie

740 15th St. NW
Ninth Floor
Washington, DC 20005
Tel: (202)662-1764
Fax: (202)662-1762
Registered: LDA

Employers
American Bar Ass'n (Director, Grassroots Operations)

STRANGE, Luther J.

801 Pennsylvania Ave. NW
Suite 230
Washington, DC 20004
Tel: (202)393-7150
Fax: (202)347-1684
Registered: LDA
EMail: lstrange@bradleyarant.com

Employers
Bradley Arant Rose & White LLP (Partner)

STRANGE, Lynne

919 18th St. NW
Suite 300
Washington, DC 20006
Tel: (202)296-5544
Fax: (202)223-0321

Employers
American Financial Services Ass'n (Director, Communications)

STRANNE, Steve K.

1001 Pennsylvania Ave. NW
Suite 600
Washington, DC 20004
Tel: (202)347-0066
Fax: (202)624-7222
Registered: LDA
EMail: sstranne@pgfm.com

Employers
Powell, Goldstein, Frazer & Murphy LLP (Partner)

Clients Represented
On Behalf of Powell, Goldstein, Frazer & Murphy LLP
Ass'n of Community Cancer Centers
Nat'l Alliance for Infusion Therapy

STRASS, Elaine

9650 Rockville Pike
Bethesda, MD 20814
Tel: (301)571-1825
Fax: (301)530-7079

Employers
American Soc. of Human Genetics (Exec. Director)
Genetics Soc. of America (Exec. Director)

STRASSBURGER, Raymond

801 Pennsylvania Ave. NW
Suite 700
Washington, DC 20004
Tel: (202)347-4610
Fax: (202)508-3612
EMail: rlstrass@nortelnetworks.com

Employers
Nortel Networks (Director, Government Relations - Telecommunications Policy)

STRATTON, Jane

1615 H St. NW
Washington, DC 20062
Tel: (202)463-5500
Fax: (202)463-3129

Employers
Nat'l Chamber Foundation (Program Assistant)

STRAUB, Terrence D.

1101 Pennsylvania Ave. NW
Suite 510
Washington, DC 20004
Tel: (202)783-6333
Fax: (202)783-6309
Registered: LDA
Former Special Assistant for Congressional Liaison (House) at the White House in Carter administration.

Employers
Marathon Oil Co. (Washington Representative)
USX Corp. (V. President, Public Affairs)

STRAUGHAN, Baird

6930 Carroll Ave.
Suite 420
Takoma Park, MD 20912
Tel: (301)270-2900
Fax: (301)270-0610

Employers
Institute for Conservation Leadership (Associate Director)

STRAUS, David

1909 K St. NW
Suite 600
Washington, DC 20006-1167
Tel: (202)585-6900
Fax: (202)585-6969
Registered: LDA

Employers
Thompson Coburn LLP (Partner)

Clients Represented
On Behalf of Thompson Coburn LLP
American Business Media

STRAUS, Jerry C.

2120 L St. NW
Suite 700
Washington, DC 20037
Tel: (202)822-8282
Fax: (202)296-8834
Registered: LDA
Attorney, Civil Division, Appellate Section, U.S. Department of Justice, 1961-63.

Employers
Hobbs, Straus, Dean and Walker, LLP (Partner)

Clients Represented
On Behalf of Hobbs, Straus, Dean and Walker, LLP
Bristol Bay Area Health Corp.
Choctaw Indians, Mississippi Band of
Menominee Indian Tribe
Metlakatla Indian Community
Miccosukee Tribe of Indians of Florida
Norton Sound Health Corp.
Pueblo de Conchiti
Seminole Tribe of Indians of Florida

STRAUS, Matthew A.

1701 Pennsylvania Ave. NW
Suite 1200
Washington, DC 20006
Tel: (202)861-0160
Fax: (202)861-3101
EMail: info@clayassociates.com
Director, Waste Management Division, Office of Solid Waste, 1993-1995; Deputy Director, 1989-93; Deputy Director, Characterization and Assessment Division, 1987-89.

Employers
Clay Associates, Inc. (V. President)

STRAUS, Richard

3405 Rodman St. NW
Washington, DC 20008
Tel: (202)363-3495
Fax: (202)362-4513
Registered: LDA

Employers
Self-employed as an independent consultant.

Clients Represented
As an independent consultant
American Soc. for Technion

STRAUSS, David

4350 N. Fairfax Dr.
Suite 410
Arlington, VA 22203
Tel: (703)528-4141
Fax: (703)528-4145
EMail: strauss@afop.org

Employers
Ass'n of Farmworker Opportunity Programs (Exec. Director)

STRAUSS, Robert S.

1333 New Hampshire Ave. NW
Suite 400
Washington, DC 20036
Tel: (202)887-4000
Fax: (202)887-4288
Ambassador to the Soviet Union and the Russian Republic, 1991-92. Special Representative of the President to the Mid-East, 1979. Special Trade Representative of the United States, 1977-79.

Employers
Akin, Gump, Strauss, Hauer & Feld, L.L.P. (Partner)

STRAWHORN, Larry

2200 Mill Rd.
Alexandria, VA 22314
Tel: (703)838-1845
Fax: (703)683-1934

Employers
American Trucking Ass'ns (V. President, Engineering)

STRAYER, Jack

655 15th St. NW Suite 375
Washington, DC 20005
Tel: (202)628-6671
Fax: (202)628-6474
EMail: jstrayer@public-policy.org

Employers
Nat'l Center for Policy Analysis (V. President, External Affairs)

STRECK, Ronald J.

1821 Michael Faraday Dr.
Suite 400
Reston, VA 20190-5348
Tel: (703)787-0000
Fax: (703)787-6930
Registered: LDA

Employers
Healthcare Distribution Management Ass'n (President and Chief Exec. Officer)

STREET, David P.

1054 31st St. NW
Suite 200
Canal Square
Washington, DC 20007
Tel: (202)342-5200
Fax: (202)342-5219
EMail: dstreet@gkmg.com

Employers
Galland, Kharasch, Greenberg, Fellman & Swirsky, P.C. (Partner)

Clients Represented
On Behalf of Galland, Kharasch, Greenberg, Fellman & Swirsky, P.C.
Distribution Services, Ltd.
Worldlink Logistics Inc.

STREETER, James R.

P.O. Box 25766
Georgetown Station
Washington, DC 20007
Tel: (703)836-7404
Fax: (703)836-7405

Employers
Nat'l Wilderness Institute (Director, Policy)

STRENIO, Andrew

1001 Pennsylvania Ave. NW
Suite 600
Washington, DC 20004
Tel: (202)347-0066
Fax: (202)624-7222
EMail: astrenio@pgfm.com

Commissioner, Federal Trade Commission, 1986-91. Commissioner, Interstate Commerce Commission, 1984-85. Assistant Director for Regulatory Evaluation, Bureau of Consumer Protection, Federal Trade Commission, 1982-84.

Employers
Powell, Goldstein, Frazer & Murphy LLP (Partner)

STRETCH, C. Clinton

555 12th St. NW
Suite 500
Washington, DC 20004-1207
Tel: (202)879-4935
Fax: (202)879-5309
Registered: LDA

Formerly with the Congressional Joint Tax Committee; Office of the Chief Counsel, Internal Revenue Service.

Employers
Deloitte & Touche LLP Nat'l Office - Washington (Partner, National Tax Services)

Clients Represented

On Behalf of Deloitte & Touche LLP Nat'l Office - Washington
Liz Robbins Associates

STRIBLING, Jess H.

1730 Pennsylvania Ave. NW
Suite 1200
Washington, DC 20006-4706
Tel: (202)737-0500
Fax: (202)626-3737
Registered: LDA

Executive Assistant Commissioner (1983-84), Associate Chief Counsel for Foods (1979-82) and Associate Chief Counsel for Veterinary Medicine (1975-79), all at the Food and Drug Administration, Department of Health and Human Services. Law Clerk to Judge Oliver Gasch, U.S. District Court of the District of Columbia, 1974-75.

Employers
King & Spalding (Partner)

STRICKLAND, USMC (Ret.), Maj. Joseph

201 N. Washington St.
Alexandria, VA 22314
Tel: (800)245-8762
Fax: (703)838-8173
EMail: joes@troa.org

Employers
The Retired Officers Ass'n (TROA) (Director, Administration)

STRICKLAND, Jr., Sidney L.

1001 G St. NW
Suite 1210-W
Washington, DC 20001-4545
Tel: (202)347-8662
Fax: (202)347-8675
EMail: sidney.strickland@bnsf.com

Employers
Burlington Northern Santa Fe Railway (Associate General Counsel)

STRICKLAND, Stephen P.

1819 H St. NW
Suite 1200
Washington, DC 20006
Tel: (202)223-1770
Fax: (202)223-1718
EMail: ntlpeace@aol.com

Employers
Nat'l Peace Foundation (Chair of Board)

STRIETER, Robert

900 19th St. NW
Suite 300
Washington, DC 20006
Tel: (202)862-5100
Fax: (202)862-5164

Employers
The Aluminum Ass'n (V. President, Environmental Health and Safety)

STRINGHAM, Bart

1771 N St. NW
Washington, DC 20036-2891
Tel: (202)429-5300
Fax: (202)429-5343
Registered: LDA

Employers
Nat'l Ass'n of Broadcasters (Associate General Counsel)

STROBEL, Gil M.

1909 K St. NW
Suite 820
Washington, DC 20006
Tel: (202)777-7700
Fax: (202)777-7763
EMail: gstrobel@lmm-law.com

Employers
Lawler, Metzger & Milkman, LLC (Associate)

STROBOS, M.D., Jur T.

1400 16th St. NW
Suite 400
Washington, DC 20036-2220
Tel: (202)518-6377
Fax: (202)234-0399
EMail: jstrobos@ofwlaw.com

Employers
Olsson, Frank and Weeda, P.C. (Of Counsel)

STROBRIDGE, USAF (Ret.), Col. Steven P.

201 N. Washington St.
Alexandria, VA 22314
Tel: (800)245-8762
Fax: (703)838-8173
Registered: LDA
EMail: streves@troa.org

Employers
The Military Coalition (Co-Chairman)
The Retired Officers Ass'n (TROA) (Director, Government Relations)

STRODE, Tom

505 Second St. NE
Washington, DC 20002-4916
Tel: (202)547-8105
Fax: (202)547-8165

Employers
Ethics and Religious Liberty Commission of the Southern Baptist Convention (Bureau Chief for Baptist Press)

STROM, David

555 New Jersey Ave. NW
Washington, DC 20001
Tel: (202)393-7472
Fax: (202)393-6385

Employers
American Federation of Teachers (Counsel)

STROM, Thaddeus E.

2099 Pennsylvania Ave. NW
Suite 850
Washington, DC 20006
Tel: (202)419-2500
Fax: (202)419-2510
Registered: LDA
EMail: Strom@acgrep.com

Chief Counsel and Staff Director to Senator Strom Thurmond (R-SC), 1995-96. Republican Chief Counsel and Staff Director, Subcommittee on Antitrust, Senate Committee on Judiciary, 1993-95. Republican Chief Counsel and Staff Director (1992-93) and Republican General Counsel (1989-91), Senate Committee on the Judiciary. Administrative Assistant to Senator Strom Thurmond (R-SC), 1986-88. Staff Counsel, Senate Committee on the Judiciary, 1985-86. Staff Assistant (1982-85) and Personal Assistant (1978-79 and 1975-76) to Senator Strom Thurmond (R-SC).

Employers
American Continental Group, Inc. (Managing Director)

Clients Represented

On Behalf of American Continental Group, Inc.
Cisco Systems Inc.
Ernst & Young LLP
Martin Color-Fi
Recording Industry Ass'n of America
Verizon Communications

STROMBERG, Cliff

555 13th St. NW
Washington, DC 20004-1109
Tel: (202)637-5600
Fax: (202)637-5910

Employers
Hogan & Hartson L.L.P.

Clients Represented

On Behalf of Hogan & Hartson L.L.P.
American Ass'n for Medical Transcription

STROMMER, Geoffrey D.

2120 L St. NW
Suite 700
Washington, DC 20037
Tel: (202)822-8282
Fax: (202)296-8834
Registered: LDA

Corporal, U.S. Marine Corps, 1979-82.

Employers
Hobbs, Straus, Dean and Walker, LLP (Partner)

Clients Represented

On Behalf of Hobbs, Straus, Dean and Walker, LLP
Alaska Native Health Board
Bristol Bay Area Health Corp.
Maniilaq Ass'n
Menominee Indian Tribe
Metlakatla Indian Community
Norton Sound Health Corp.
Seldovia Native Ass'n, Inc.
Shoalwater Bay Indian Tribe
Susanville Indian Rancheria

STROMSEM, William

1455 Pennsylvania Ave. NW
Suite 400
Washington, DC 20004-1081
Tel: (202)737-6600
Fax: (202)638-4512
Registered: LDA
EMail: wstromsem@aicpa.org

Employers
American Institute of Certified Public Accountants (Director, Taxation)

STRONG, Maria S.

1747 Pennsylvania Ave. NW
Suite 825
Washington, DC 20006-4604
Tel: (202)833-4198
Fax: (202)872-0546
Registered: LDA
EMail: mstrong@iipa.com

Employers
Internat'l Intellectual Property Alliance (V. President and Associate General Counsel)
Smith & Metalitz, L.L.P. (Partner)

Clients Represented

On Behalf of Smith & Metalitz, L.L.P.
Internat'l Intellectual Property Alliance

STROSCHEIN, Ryan W.

1400 16th St. NW
Suite 400
Washington, DC 20036-2220
Tel: (202)789-1212
Fax: (202)234-3550
EMail: rstroschein@ofwlaw.com

Former Legislative Counsel to Senator Tom Daschle (D-SD).

Employers
Olsson, Frank and Weeda, P.C. (Associate)

Clients Represented

On Behalf of Olsson, Frank and Weeda, P.C.
Ass'n of Medical Device Reprocessors
Aventis Pasteur
Beef Products, Inc.
Black Hills Forest Resource Ass'n
California Canning Peach Ass'n
Chocolate Manufacturers Ass'n of the U.S.A.
Duramed Pharmaceuticals, Inc.
General Mills
Gentrac Inc.
Health Resource Publishing Co.
Institute of Food Technologists
Kraft Foods, Inc.
Lower Brule Sioux Tribe
McDonald's Corp.
Mead Johnson Nutritional Group
Nat'l Ass'n of Margarine Manufacturers
Nat'l Ass'n of Pharmaceutical Manufacturers
Nat'l Coalition of Food Importers Ass'n
Nat'l Confectioners Ass'n
Nat'l Food Processors Ass'n
Nat'l Frozen Pizza Institute
Nat'l Meat Ass'n
PennField Oil Co.
Philip Morris Management Corp.
The Pillsbury Co.
San Tomo Group
Schwan's Sales Enterprises
SteriGenics Internat'l
Titan Scan
Transhumance Holding Co., Inc.
United Fresh Fruit and Vegetable Ass'n

STROTHER, Daniella

1101 17th St. NW
Suite 600
Washington, DC 20036
Tel: (202)496-5643
Fax: (202)496-5660
Registered: LDA
EMail: daniella.strother@aa.com

Employers
American Airlines (Managing Director, Government Affairs)

STROTHER, Michael E.

6301 Stevenson Ave.
Suite One
Alexandria, VA 22304
Tel: (703)823-1732
Fax: (703)823-5064

Employers
Power and Communications Contractors Ass'n (Exec. V. President)
Strother & Hosking, Inc. (Exec. V. President)

Clients Represented
On Behalf of Strother & Hosking, Inc.
Power and Communications Contractors Ass'n

STROUD, Jr., D. Michael

2000 K St. NW
Suite 500
Washington, DC 20006-1872
Tel: (202)828-5800
Fax: (202)223-1225
Registered: LDA

Employers
Bracewell & Patterson, L.L.P. (Associate)

Clients Represented
On Behalf of Bracewell & Patterson, L.L.P.
Air Conditioning Contractors of America
Alltel Corporation
American Registry for Internet Numbers (ARIN)
Baldwin Piano and Organ Co.
Council of Industrial Boiler Owners (CIBO)
Envirocare of Utah, Inc.
FBI Agents Ass'n
Gary-Williams Energy Corp.
Houston, Texas, Port Authority of the City of
Huntsman Corp.
Lyondell Chemical Co.
Oxygenated Fuels Ass'n
Placid Refining Co.
Solex Environmental Systems, Inc.
Texas Petrochemicals Corp.
Texas Windstorm Insurance Ass'n
Welcon, Inc.

STROUD, Tim

2111 Wilson Blvd.
Eighth Floor
Arlington, VA 22201-3058
Tel: (703)841-0626
Fax: (703)243-2874
Registered: LDA
EMail: stroud@alcalde-fay.com

Employers
Alcalde & Fay (Associate)

Clients Represented
On Behalf of Alcalde & Fay
CNF Transportation, Inc.
Dallas, Texas, City of
EC-MAC
Grand Valley State University
Hispanic Broadcasting Inc.
Houston Independent School District
Lake, California, County of
Miami-Dade County Public Schools
Nat'l Ass'n of Gas Chlorinators
Tulare, California, County of

STROUP, Patricia

Parklawn Bldg.
5600 Fishers Ln.
MS: 14-36
Rockville, MD 20857
Tel: (301)443-1890
Fax: (301)443-9270
EMail: pstroup@hrsa.gov

Employers
Department of Health and Human Services - Health Resources and Services Administration (Director, Legislation Division, Office of Planning, Evaluation and Legislation)

STROUP, R. Keith

1001 Connecticut Ave. NW
Suite 710
Washington, DC 20036
Tel: (202)483-5500
Fax: (202)483-0057
Registered: LDA

Employers
Nat'l Organization for the Reform of Marijuana Laws (Exec. Director)

STRUBHAR, Keith

1029 N. Royal St.
Suite 400
Alexandria, VA 22314
Tel: (703)684-1245
Fax: (703)684-1249
EMail: kstrubhar@directimpact.com

Employers
The Direct Impact Co. (V. President)

STRUMPF, George

625 Indiana Ave. NW Suite 200
Washington, DC 20004
Tel: (202)393-0660
Fax: (202)393-0533

Employers
HIP Health Plans (Director, Federal Relations)

STRZYZWESKI, Sandy

1146 19th St. NW
Third Floor
Washington, DC 20036
Tel: (202)466-8209
Fax: (202)466-6572

Employers
Public Affairs Group, Inc. (Chief Operating Officer/Chief Financial Officer/Chief Administrator)

STUART, Eric J.

1730 Rhode Island Ave. NW
Suite 907
Washington, DC 20036-3101
Tel: (202)296-1515
Fax: (202)296-2506
Registered: LDA

Employers
Steel Manufacturers Ass'n (Manager, Committee Affairs)

STUART, III, James R.

2550 M St. NW
Washington, DC 20037-1350
Tel: (202)457-6000
Fax: (202)457-6315
Registered: FARA
EMail: jstuart@pattonboggs.com

Employers
Patton Boggs, LLP (Partner)

STUART, Sandi

1775 I St. NW
Suite 700
Washington, DC 20006
Tel: (202)261-4000
Fax: (202)261-4001
Registered: LDA
Assistant Secretary for Legislative Affairs, Department of Defense, 1993-99. Chief of Staff to Rep. Vic Fazio (D-CA), 1987-93. Associate Staff, House Committee on the Budget, 1983-87.

Employers
Clark & Weinstock, Inc. (Managing Director)

Clients Represented
On Behalf of Clark & Weinstock, Inc.
American Ass'n of Health Plans (AAHP)
American Ass'n of Homes and Services for the Aging
AT&T
Rabbi Milton Balkany
CapCURE
Cargill, Inc.
Copeland, Lowery & Jacquez
Delta Wetlands Project
Edison Electric Institute
The Ferguson Group
Foundation Health Federal Services, Inc.
Lockheed Martin Corp.
Microsoft Corp.
Nat'l Prostate Cancer Coalition Co.
Pharmaceutical Research and Manufacturers of America
Remy, Thomas & Moose, LLP
Rubber Manufacturers Ass'n
Schering-Plough Corp.
Sodexho Marriott Services, Inc.
Vivendi Universal

STUBBS, Anne D.

400 N. Capitol St. NW
Suite 382
Washington, DC 20001
Tel: (202)624-8450
Fax: (202)624-8463
EMail: coneg@sso.org

Employers
Coalition of Northeastern Governors (Exec. Director)

STUCKLE, Elizabeth

6903 Rockledge Dr.
Bethesda, MD 20817
Tel: (301)564-3200
Fax: (301)564-3201

Employers
USEC, Inc. (Director, Corporate Communications)

STUCKY, Edward J.

1101 30th St. NW
Suite 220
Washington, DC 20007
Tel: (202)337-6600
Fax: (202)337-6660
Registered: LDA

Employers
Ikon Public Affairs (Secretary/Treasurer)

Clients Represented
On Behalf of Ikon Public Affairs
Committee for Good Common Sense

STUDLEY, Janet R.

2099 Pennsylvania Ave. NW
Suite 100
Washington, DC 20006
Tel: (202)955-3000
Fax: (202)955-5564
Registered: LDA, FARA
EMail: jstudley@hklaw.com
Chief Counsel, Subcommittee on Federal Spending Practices and Open Government, Senate Committee on Governmental Affairs, 1977-81. Law Clerk, U.S. Court of Appeals, Fifth Circuit, 1976-77.

Employers
Holland & Knight LLP (Partner)

Clients Represented
On Behalf of Holland & Knight LLP
American Chemistry Council
Bridgestone/Firestone, Inc.
Consortium for Plant Biotechnology Research
Consortium Plant Biotech Research
Envirotest Systems Corp.
FirstEnergy Co.
Florida Gas Utility
S.C. Johnson and Son, Inc.
Murphy Oil U.S.A.
PanAmSat Corp.
United Airlines
Vitas Healthcare Corp.

STUNTZ, Linda

1275 Pennsylvania Ave. NW
Ninth Floor
Washington, DC 20004
Tel: (202)662-6790
Fax: (202)624-0866
Registered: LDA
EMail: lstuntz@sdsatty.com
Deputy Secretary, Department of Energy, 1992-93.

Employers
Stuntz, Davis & Staffier, P.C. (Principal)

Clients Represented
On Behalf of Stuntz, Davis & Staffier, P.C.
British Columbia Hydro and Power Authority
British Columbia Power Exchange Corp.
GE Power Systems
General Electric Appliances
General Electric Industrial & Power Systems
North American Electric Reliability Council
PURPA Reform Group
Western Interconnection Coordination Forum

STURBITTS, Charlene A.

1625 K St. NW
Suite 790
Washington, DC 20006
Tel: (202)293-7800
Fax: (202)293-7808
Registered: LDA
Legislative Director to Senator George Mitchell (MD), 1980-85. Staff Member, Environmental Pollution Subcommittee, Senate Committee on Public Works, 1972-80.

Employers
Leon G. Billings, Inc.
Self-employed as an independent consultant.

Clients Represented
On Behalf of Leon G. Billings, Inc.
Industry Urban-Development Agency
As an independent consultant
Deere & Co.
Free Trade Lumber Council
W. R. Grace & Co.

STURC, John H.

1050 Connecticut Ave. NW
Washington, DC 20036-5306
Tel: (202)955-8500
Fax: (202)467-0539
EMail: jsturc@gdclaw.com
Associate Director (1984-90), Deputy Chief Litigation Counsel (1982-84), and Assistant Chief Trial Attorney (1982-83), Division of Enforcement, Securities and Exchange Commission. Assistant U.S. Attorney for the District of Columbia, Department of Justice, 1976-81. Law Clerk to Judge C. Stanley Blair, U.S. District Court for the District of Maryland, 1976-81.

Employers
Gibson, Dunn & Crutcher LLP (Partner)

STURM, John F.

529 14th St. NW
Suite 440
Washington, DC 20045-1402
EMail: sturj@naa.org
Tel: (202)902-1601
Fax: (202)902-1609
Registered: LDA

Employers
Newspaper Ass'n of America (President and Chief Exec. Officer)

STURNER, Jan W.

1497 Chain Bridge Rd.
Suite 300
McLean, VA 22101
EMail: jsturner@ilalaw.com
Tel: (703)893-7071
Fax: (703)893-8020
Registered: LDA

Employers
Institutional Labor Advisors (Associate)

Clients Represented

On Behalf of Institutional Labor Advisors
Coal Act Fairness Alliance
Freeman United Coal Mining Co.
Retiree Benefits Alliance

SU, Peter

1500 Pennsylvania Ave. NW
Room 3204MT
Washington, DC 20220
Tel: (202)622-1760
Fax: (202)622-0534

Employers
Department of Treasury (Special Assistant, Office of Legislative Affairs)

SUAZO, Vicky M.

1776 I St. NW
Suite 1050
Washington, DC 20006
Tel: (202)429-3417
Fax: (202)429-3467
Registered: LDA

Employers
The Dow Chemical Co. (Manager, Government Relations and Health Issues)

SUBKO, Jeffrey B.

8725 John T. Kingman Rd.
Ft. Belvoir, VA 22060-6201
EMail: jeff.subkoAdtra.mil
Tel: (703)767-4941
Fax: (703)767-4534

Employers
Department of Defense - Defense Threat Reduction Agency (Chief, Congressional Liaison Office and Chief, Legislative Affairs Office)

SUBLER, Rachel

1601 N. Kent St.
Suite 120
Arlington, VA 22209
EMail: rsubler@apperalandfootwear.org
Tel: (703)524-1864
Fax: (703)522-6741
Registered: LDA

Employers
American Apparel & Footwear Ass'n (Government Relations Representative)

SUCHMAN, Bonnie

401 Ninth St. NW
Suite 1000
Washington, DC 20004
Tel: (202)274-2908
Fax: (202)274-2994
Registered: LDA, FARA
Former Special Counsel for Electricity Restructuring, Department of Energy.

Employers
Troutman Sanders LLP (Of Counsel)

Clients Represented

On Behalf of Troutman Sanders LLP
Canadian Electricity Ass'n
Cinergy Corp.
PG&E Corp.
Southern Co.
Trigen Energy Corp.
Wisconsin Energy Corp.

SUCHMAN, Peter O.

1001 Pennsylvania Ave. NW
Suite 600
Washington, DC 20004
EMail: psuchman@pgfm.com
Tel: (202)347-0066
Fax: (202)624-7222
Registered: LDA, FARA
Deputy Assistant Secretary, Tariff Affairs (1974-77) and Director, Office of Trade Policy (1972-74), Department of the Treasury. Foreign Service Officer, Department of State, 1964-70. Lieutenant, U.S. Coast Guard, 1960-64.

Employers
Powell, Goldstein, Frazer & Murphy LLP (Consultant)

Clients Represented

On Behalf of Powell, Goldstein, Frazer & Murphy LLP
Joint Stock Company Severstal
Koyo Seiko Co., Ltd.

SUDBAY, Joe

1140 19th St. NW
Suite 600
Washington, DC 20036
Tel: (202)822-8200
Fax: (202)822-8205

Employers
Violence Policy Center (Public Policy Director)

SUDDARTH, Roscoe S.

1761 N St. NW
Washington, DC 20036-2882
EMail: president@mideasti.org
Tel: (202)785-1141
Fax: (202)331-8861

Employers
Middle East Institute (President)

SUDDUTH, A. Scott

1523 New Hampshire Ave. NW
Washington, DC 20036
EMail: scott.sudduth@ucop.edu
Tel: (202)588-0002
Fax: (202)785-2669
Registered: LDA
Chief of Staff to Rep. Peter Geren (D-TX), 1989-93. Legislative Staff Member to Senator Lloyd Bentsen (D-TX) 1981-84, 88.

Employers
University of California, Office of Federal Government Relations (Assistant V. President)

SUFKA, Kenneth M.

1518 K St. NW
Suite 503
Washington, DC 20005
Tel: (202)737-0202
Fax: (202)638-4833

Employers
Associated Air Balance Council (Exec. Director)
Sufka & Associates (President)

Clients Represented

On Behalf of Sufka & Associates
Associated Air Balance Council
Internat'l Kitchen Exhaust Cleaning Ass'n
Nat'l Air Duct Cleaners Ass'n
Nat'l Air Filtration Ass'n

SUGAMELI, Glenn

1400 16th St. NW
Suite 501
Washington, DC 20036-2266
Tel: (202)797-6800
Fax: (202)797-6646
Registered: LDA

Employers
Nat'l Wildlife Federation - Office of Federal and Internat'l Affairs (Counsel, Takings/Private Property Rights)

SUGAR, Kathleen

927 15th St. NW
Fourth Floor
Washington, DC 20005
Tel: (202)898-1566
Fax: (202)898-1612

Employers
Development Group for Alternative Policies (Communications Coordinator)

SUGARMANN, Josh

1140 19th St. NW
Suite 600
Washington, DC 20036
Tel: (202)822-8200
Fax: (202)822-8205

Employers
Violence Policy Center (Exec. Director)

SUGIURA, Yasuyuki

2001 Pennsylvania Ave. NW
Suite 700
Washington, DC 20006
Tel: (202)331-7301
Fax: (202)331-7277

Employers
Mitsubishi Internat'l Corp. (V. President and General Manager)

SUGIYAMA, George

1001 Pennsylvania Ave. NW
Suite 300S
Washington, DC 20004
EMail: sugiyama.george@dorseylaw.com
Tel: (202)824-8800
Fax: (202)824-8990
Registered: LDA

Employers
Dorsey & Whitney LLP (Partner)

Clients Represented

On Behalf of Dorsey & Whitney LLP
Southern Co.

SUHR, Karen

1319 F St. NW
Suite 301
Washington, DC 20004
Tel: (202)393-3240
Fax: (202)393-4385
Registered: LDA

Employers
Sparber and Associates (Senior V. President)

Clients Represented

On Behalf of Sparber and Associates
Sleep Products Safety Council

SULLIVAN, Bill

2111 Wilson Blvd.
Eighth Floor
Arlington, VA 22201-3058
EMail: sullivan@alcalde-fay.com
Tel: (703)841-0626
Fax: (703)243-2874

Employers
Alcalde & Fay (Partner)

SULLIVAN, Jr., Brendan V.

725 12th St. NW
Washington, DC 20005
Tel: (202)434-5000
Fax: (202)434-5029

Employers
Williams & Connolly (Partner)

Clients Represented

On Behalf of Williams & Connolly
Omni Internat'l

SULLIVAN, Edward C.

815 16th St. NW
Suite 600
Washington, DC 20006
Tel: (202)347-1461
Fax: (202)628-0724
Registered: LDA

Employers
AFL-CIO - Building and Construction Trades Department (President)

SULLIVAN, Eugene T.

1725 Jefferson Davis Hwy.
Crystal Square 2, Suite 300
Arlington, VA 22202
Tel: (703)413-5600
Fax: (703)413-5617
Registered: LDA

Employers
Lockheed Martin Corp. (Director, Aircraft Mod. & Maritime Surveillance, Aeronautics Sector, Washington Operations)

SULLIVAN, Francis J.

809 Cameron St.
Alexandria, VA 22314
Tel: (703)684-4707
Fax: (703)519-8084
Registered: LDA

Employers
Francis J. Sullivan Associates

Clients Represented

On Behalf of Francis J. Sullivan Associates
Alexandria, Virginia, City of
Ingalls Shipbuilding
KAMAN Corp.
Textron Inc.

SULLIVAN, Frank

P.O. Box 19254
Alexandria, VA 22320

Employers
Americans for Political Participation (Contact, Political Action Committee)

SULLIVAN, USA(Ret), General Gordon R.

2425 Wilson Blvd. Tel: (703)841-4300
Arlington, VA 22201-3385 Fax: (703)525-9039

Employers
Ass'n of the United States Army (President)

SULLIVAN, James

3170 Fairview Park Dr. Tel: (703)876-1000
M/S 232 Fax: (703)849-1005
Falls Church, VA 22042

Employers
Computer Sciences Corp. (Director, Federal Public Relations)

SULLIVAN, James K.

601 Wythe St. Tel: (703)684-2400
Alexandria, VA 22314-1994 Fax: (703)684-2492

Employers
Water Environment Federation (Manager, Legislative Affairs)

SULLIVAN, Jay R.

306 Constitution Ave. NE Tel: (202)546-9060
Washington, DC 20002 Fax: (202)546-9160
Registered: LDA, FARA
Deputy Director of Public Affairs, Department of the Interior, 1991-93. Chief of Congressional Affairs, Bureau of Land Management, Department of the Interior, 1989-91.

Employers
Jamison and Sullivan, Inc. (President)

Clients Represented
On Behalf of Jamison and Sullivan, Inc.
Ass'n of O & C Counties
Ass'n of Oregon Counties
Counterpart Internat'l
Douglas, Oregon, County of
FANCOR
The Fanning Corp.
Flight Landata, Inc.
Greystar Resources, Ltd.
Internat'l Utility Efficiency Partnerships (IUEP)
D. R. Johnson Lumber
Malheur Timber Operators
Prairie Wood Products
Umatilla Water Users
Upper Klamath Water Users

SULLIVAN, Jere

1875 I St. NW Tel: (202)371-0200
Suite 900 Fax: (202)371-2858
Washington, DC 20005

Employers
Edelman Public Relations Worldwide (Exec. V. President and Deputy General Manager)

Clients Represented
On Behalf of Edelman Public Relations Worldwide
Bacardi Ltd.
Korea Internat'l Trade Ass'n
Michelin North America
Nissan North America Inc.

SULLIVAN, Jerome H.

One Dupont Circle NW Tel: (202)293-9161
Suite 520 Fax: (202)872-8857
Washington, DC 20036-1171
EMail: sullivank@aacrao.org
Chairman, Project EASI Committee, Department of Education, 1995

Employers
American Ass'n of Collegiate Registrars and Admissions Officers (Exec. Director)

SULLIVAN, Dr. John D.

1155 15th St. NW Tel: (202)721-9200
Suite 700 Fax: (202)721-9250
Washington, DC 20005
EMail: cipe@cipe.org

Employers
Center for Internat'l Private Enterprise (Exec. Director)

SULLIVAN, John J.

1225 I St. NW Tel: (202)408-9494
Suite 300 Fax: (202)408-0877
Washington, DC 20005 Registered: LDA

Employers
American Portland Cement Alliance (Director, Federal Affairs)

SULLIVAN, Kelly

1850 M St. NW Tel: (202)289-5900
Suite 550 Fax: (202)289-4141
Washington, DC 20036 Registered: FARA
EMail: Kelly_Sullivan@clsdc.com

Employers
Chlopak, Leonard, Schechter and Associates (Managing Director)

Clients Represented
On Behalf of Chlopak, Leonard, Schechter and Associates
Hoechst Marion Roussel Deutschland GmbH
World Health Organization

SULLIVAN, Lora

1775 I St. NW Tel: (202)466-9142
Suite 800 Fax: (202)828-3372
Washington, DC 20006
EMail: lora.sullivan@enron.com

Employers
Enron Corp. (Federal Government Affairs Representative)

SULLIVAN, M. Dianne

900 17th St. NW Tel: (202)884-7034
Suite 1100 Fax: (202)884-7070
Washington, DC 20006 Registered: LDA
EMail: dianne_sullivan@hp.com

Employers
Hewlett-Packard Co. (Manager, International Trade Policy)

SULLIVAN, Marcia Z.

1000 Wilson Blvd. Tel: (703)276-1750
Suite 2500 Fax: (703)528-1290
Arlington, VA 22209-3908 Registered: LDA
EMail: msullivan@cbanet.org

Employers
Consumer Bankers Ass'n (V. President/Director, Government Relations)

SULLIVAN, Michael J.

1750 New York Ave. NW Tel: (202)783-5880
Sixth Floor Fax: (202)662-0894
Washington, DC 20006

Employers
Sheet Metal Workers' Internat'l Ass'n (General President)

SULLIVAN, Neal E.

1120 20th St. NW Tel: (202)778-6150
Suite 800 Fax: (202)778-6155
Washington, DC 20036 Registered: LDA

Employers
Bingham Dana LLP (Attorney)

Clients Represented
On Behalf of Bingham Dana LLP
Charles Schwab & Co., Inc.,

SULLIVAN, Patricia

1155 15th St. NW Tel: (202)466-3639
Suite 801 Registered: LDA
Washington, DC 20005

Employers
Self-employed as an independent consultant.

Clients Represented
As an independent consultant
Student Loan Servicing Alliance

SULLIVAN, Paul E.

1100 Connecticut Ave. NW Tel: (202)861-5900
Suite 330 Fax: (202)861-6065
Washington, DC 20036

Employers
Sullivan & Mitchell, P.L.L.C.

Clients Represented
On Behalf of Sullivan & Mitchell, P.L.L.C.
Americans Back in Charge Foundation

SULLIVAN, Paul N.

1301 K St. NW Tel: (202)408-8007
Suite 900 Fax: (202)408-8704
East Tower
Washington, DC 20005

Employers
The Carter Group (Member)

SULLIVAN, Rebecca M.

1033 N. Fairfax St. Tel: (703)549-7404
Suite 404 Fax: (703)549-8712
Alexandria, VA 22314 Registered: LDA
EMail: rsullivan@icsc.org

Employers
Internat'l Council of Shopping Centers (V. President, Government Relations)

SULLIVAN, Richard

1401 K St. NW Tel: (202)789-2111
Suite 400 Fax: (202)789-4883
Washington, DC 20005 Registered: LDA
EMail: rsullivan@thewashingtongroup.com

Employers
The Washington Group (V. President)

Clients Represented
On Behalf of The Washington Group
IVAX Corp.
Microsoft Corp.
News Corporation Ltd.
SAMPCO Companies
Westfield America, Inc.
WinStar Internat'l

SULLIVAN, T. J.

1301 K St. NW Tel: (202)408-7100
Suite 900 Fax: (202)289-1504
East Tower
Washington, DC 20005
EMail: tsullivan@dc.gcd.com
Special Assistant for Health Care, Internal Revenue Service, 1989-96. Senior Evaluator for Health and Aging, Human Resources Division, General Accounting Office, 1979-84.

Employers
Gardner, Carton and Douglas (Partner)

Clients Represented
On Behalf of Gardner, Carton and Douglas
Coalition for Nonprofit Health Care

SULLIVAN, Thomas M.

1201 F St. NW Tel: (202)554-9000
Suite 200 Fax: (202)554-0496
Washington, DC 20004

Employers
Nat'l Federation of Independent Business (Exec. Director, NFIB Legal Foundation)

SULLIVAN, Tim

1825 Connecticut Ave. NW Tel: (202)667-0901
Fifth Floor Fax: (202)667-0902
Washington, DC 20009
EMail: tim.sullivan@widmeyer.com

Employers
Widmeyer Communications, Inc. (V. President)

SUMILAS, Michele

1701 K St. NW
Suite 600
Washington, DC 20006-1503
Tel: (202)833-5900
Fax: (202)833-0075
Registered: LDA

Employers
Global Health Council (Senior Legislative Associate)
Washington Health Advocates

Clients Represented
On Behalf of Washington Health Advocates
American Federation for Medical Research
American Medical Informatics Ass'n
American Soc. for Clinical Pharmacology and Therapeutics
GCRC Program Directors Ass'n
Jewish Guild for the Blind
Quintiles Transnational Corp.

SUMMERS, David

1825 Connecticut Ave. NW
Fifth Floor
Washington, DC 20009
Tel: (202)667-0901
Fax: (202)667-0902
EMail: david.summers@widmeyer.com

Employers
Widmeyer Communications, Inc. (V. President/Group Director)

SUMMERS, Michael H.

1401 I St. NW
Suite 600
Washington, DC 20005-6523
Tel: (202)336-7430
Fax: (202)336-7421
Registered: LDA
EMail: summerm@corpdc.utc.com

Employers
Pratt & Whitney (Director, Washington Operations)

SUMNER, Curtis

Six Montgomery Village Ave.
Suite 403
Gaithersburg, MD 20879-3557
Tel: (240)632-9716
Fax: (240)632-1321

Employers
American Congress on Surveying and Mapping (Exec. Director)

SUNDERGILL, Ron

1707 H St. NW
Suite 600
Washington, DC 20006-3919
Tel: (202)223-6133
Fax: (202)223-6162
Registered: LDA

Employers
Union of Concerned Scientists (Washington Representative for Clean Energy)

SUNDWALL, M.D., David N.

1250 H St. NW
Suite 880
Washington, DC 20005
Tel: (202)637-9466
Fax: (202)637-2050
Registered: LDA

Employers
American Clinical Laboratory Ass'n (President)

SUPLIZIO, Paul E.

5920 Munson Ct.
Falls Church, VA 22041
Tel: (703)820-7707
Fax: (703)820-7726
EMail: wotc@cox.rr.com
Director of Strategic Analysis, Federal Energy Administration, 1974-75. Served with the Carter/Mondale Presidential Transition Task Force, 1977-78. Served with the Employment and Training Administration, Department of Labor, 1977-78.

Employers
Paul Suplizio Associates (President)

Clients Represented
On Behalf of Paul Suplizio Associates
Internat'l Barter and Countertrade Foundation
Work Opportunity Tax Credit Coalition

SURINGA, Dirk J. J.

1700 Pennsylvania Ave. NW
Suite 600
Washington, DC 20006
Tel: (202)393-7600
Fax: (202)393-7601
Registered: LDA

Employers
Ivins, Phillips & Barker (Associate)

Clients Represented
On Behalf of Ivins, Phillips & Barker
Bass Hotels and Resorts, Inc.

SURRATT, Rick

807 Maine Ave. SW
Washington, DC 20024
Tel: (202)554-3501
Fax: (202)554-3581
Registered: LDA

Employers
Disabled American Veterans (Deputy National Legislative Director)

SURRELL, Jeffrey

1875 I St. NW
Suite 900
Washington, DC 20005
Tel: (202)371-0200
Fax: (202)371-2858
Registered: FARA

Employers
Edelman Public Relations Worldwide (Senior V. President)

Clients Represented
On Behalf of Edelman Public Relations Worldwide
Church of Jesus Christ of Latter Day Saints

SUSMAN, Julia T.

1401 K St. NW
Suite 900
Washington, DC 20005
Tel: (202)626-8550
Fax: (202)626-8578
Registered: LDA
Former Deputy Chief Counsel, Legislative Director and Deputy Staff Director, Senate Committee on Veterans Affairs.

Employers
Jefferson Consulting Group (President and Chief Exec. Officer)

Clients Represented
On Behalf of Jefferson Consulting Group
First Consulting Group
Managed Care Solutions

SUSMAN, Thomas M.

1301 K St. NW
Suite 800 East
Washington, DC 20005
Tel: (202)626-3900
Fax: (202)626-3961
Registered: LDA
EMail: tsusman@ropesgray.com
General Counsel, Subcommittee on Antitrust (1977-78) General Counsel (1979-80), and Counsel and Chief Counsel, Subcommittee on Administrative Practice and Procedures (1969-72), all for the Senate Judiciary Committee. Special Assistant to the Assistant Attorney General, Office of the Legal Counsel, Department of Justice, 1968-69. Law Clerk to Judge John Minor Wisdom, U.S. Court of Appeals, Fifth Circuit, 1967-68.

Employers
Ropes & Gray (Partner)

Clients Represented
On Behalf of Ropes & Gray
Alliance for Understandable, Sensible and Accountable Government Regulations
American Library Ass'n
The Business Roundtable
New England Organ Bank

SUSSER, Peter A.

1225 I St. NW
Suite 1000
Washington, DC 20005
Tel: (202)842-3400
Fax: (202)842-0011
Registered: LDA

Employers
Littler Mendelson, P.C. (Shareholder)

Clients Represented
On Behalf of Littler Mendelson, P.C.
American Bakers Ass'n
Food Distributors Internat'l (NAWGA-IFDA)
Institute for a Drug-Free Workplace

SUSSMAN, Monica Hilton

401 Ninth St. NW
Suite 900
Washington, DC 20004
Tel: (202)585-8000
Fax: (202)585-8080
Registered: LDA
EMail: rsussman@nixonpeabody.com
Deputy General Counsel (1993-96), Office of the General Counsel (1982-83); Special Assistant to the Undersecretary (1979-80), Department of Housing and Urban Development.

Employers
Nixon Peabody LLP (Partner)

Clients Represented
On Behalf of Nixon Peabody LLP
Continental Wingate Co., Inc.
Cornerstone Florida Corp., Ltd.
Edward A. Fish Associates
Highland Mortgage Co.
Mellon Mortgage Co.
Project Funding Corp. (PFC)
Reilly Mortgage Group Inc.
TRI Capital Corp.
WMF/Huntoon, Paige Associates Ltd.

SUSSMAN, Robert M.

555 11th St. NW
Suite 1000
Washington, DC 20004
Tel: (202)637-2200
Fax: (202)637-2201
Registered: FARA
Deputy Administrator, Environmental Protection Agency, 1993-94. Law Clerk to Judge Walter K. Stapleton, U.S. District Court for the District of Delaware, 1973-74.

Employers
Latham & Watkins (Partner)

SUTHERLAND, Dave

1800 N. Kent St.
Suite 1120
Arlington, VA 22209
Tel: (703)525-6300
Fax: (703)525-4610

Employers
The Conservation Fund (Senior V. President and Real Estate Director)

SUTHERLAND, Julia K.

2000 L St. NW
Suite 300
Washington, DC 20036-0646
Tel: (202)835-8800
Fax: (202)835-8879
Former Press Secretary to Senator Charles Robb (D-VA).

Employers
Ketchum (Senior V. President)

SUTHERLAND, Scott A.

1301 Pennsylvania Ave. NW
Suite 402
Washington, DC 20004
Tel: (202)347-1530
Fax: (202)347-1533
Registered: LDA

Employers
Ducks Unlimited Inc. (Director, Wash. Offices and Govt. Affairs)

SUTTER-STARKE, Jane

700 11th St. NW
Suite 900
Washington, DE 20005
Tel: (202)508-1000
Fax: (202)508-1010
Registered: LDA
Associate Minority Counsel, House Committee on Energy and Commerce, 1981-87.

Employers
Thompson Coburn LLP (Partner)

Clients Represented
On Behalf of Thompson Coburn LLP
Los Angeles County Metropolitan Transportation Authority
Massachusetts Bay Transportation Authority
Metropolitan Atlanta Rapid Transit Authority
Regional Transportation Commission of South Nevada

SUTTLE, W. Thomas

1828 L St. NW
Suite 1202
Washington, DC 20036-5104
Tel: (202)785-0017
Fax: (202)785-0835

Employers
Institute of Electrical and Electronics Engineers, Inc. (Managing Director, Professional Activities)

SUTTON, Barbara

700 13th St. NW
Suite 400
Washington, DC 20005
Tel: (202)347-0773
Fax: (202)347-0785
Registered: LDA
EMail: bsutton@cassidy.com
Former Director of Scheduling to Speaker Thomas P. "Tip" O'Neill (D-MA), U.S. House of Representatives.

Employers
Cassidy & Associates, Inc. (Senior V. President)

Clients Represented

On Behalf of Cassidy & Associates, Inc.

Adelphi University
Boston College
California Institute for the Arts
City of Hope Nat'l Medical Center
Edward Health Services
Fairview Hospital and Healthcare Services
Research Foundation of the City University of New York
Rhode Island School of Design
Rush Presbyterian-St. Luke's Medical Center
Summit Technology
University of Massachusetts Memorial Health System

SUTTON, Bob

717 Second St. NE
Washington, DC 20002
Tel: (202)544-3200
Fax: (202)546-0182

Employers

NET-Political NewsTalk Network (Chief Exec. Officer)

SUTTON, Steve

1000 Wilson Blvd.
Suite 2300
Arlington, VA 22209
Tel: (703)875-8400
Fax: (703)276-0711
Registered: LDA

Employers

Northrop Grumman Corp. (Manager, Legislative Affairs)

SUZUKI, Hitoshi

1901 L St. NW
Suite 720
Washington, DC 20036
Tel: (202)457-0790
Fax: (202)457-0810

Employers

The Tokyo Electric Power Company, Inc. (Deputy General Manager)

SWACINA, Linda M.

1400 Independence Ave. SW
Room 1175-S
Washington, DC 20250
Tel: (202)720-3897
Fax: (202)720-5704
EMail: Linda.Swacina@usda.gov

Employers

Department of Agriculture - Food Safety and Inspection Service (Director, Congressional and Public Affairs Staff)

SWAIN, Frank S.

805 15th St. NW
Suite 700
Washington, DC 20005
Tel: (202)312-7400
Fax: (202)312-7441
Registered: LDA
EMail: fsswain@bakerd.com

Chief Counsel for Advocacy, Small Business Administration, 1981-89.

Employers

Baker & Daniels (Partner)
Sagamore Associates, Inc. (Senior V. President)

Clients Represented

On Behalf of Baker & Daniels

American College of Sports Medicine
Chase Manhattan Bank

On Behalf of Sagamore Associates, Inc.

Chase Manhattan Bank
NextRX
Spring Hill Camps

SWALBACH, Robert

2121 R St. NW
Washington, DC 20008-1908
Tel: (202)673-5869
Fax: (202)673-5873
EMail: schwalbach@aol.com

Employers

Northern Mariana Islands, Commonwealth of the (Congressional Liaison)

SWANDA, Ronald L.

1400 K St. NW
Suite 801
Washington, DC 20005-2485
Tel: (202)393-1500
Fax: (202)842-4063

Employers

General Aviation Manufacturers Ass'n (V. President, Operations)

SWANN, Lance B.

3170 Fairview Park Dr.
M/S 232
Falls Church, VA 22042
Tel: (703)876-1000
Fax: (703)849-1005
Registered: LDA
EMail: lswann@csc.com

Employers

Computer Sciences Corp. (V. President, Government Relations)

SWANSON, Dee

P.O. Box 40473
Washington, DC 20024

Employers

American Academy of Nurse Practitioners (PAC Treasurer)

SWANSON, Eric

1250 Connecticut Ave. NW
Washington, DC 20036
Tel: (202)833-1200
Fax: (202)659-3716

Employers

Common Cause (Exec. V. President)

SWANSON, M. Anne

1200 New Hampshire Ave. NW
Suite 800
Washington, DC 20036-6802
Tel: (202)776-2000
Fax: (202)776-2222
EMail: aswanson@dlalaw.com

Employers

Dow, Lohnes & Albertson, PLLC (Member)

SWANSTROM, Deborah A.

901 15th St. NW
Suite 700
Washington, DC 20005-2301
Tel: (202)371-6000
Fax: (202)371-6279
Registered: LDA, FARA
EMail: daswanstrom@verner.com

Employers

Verner, Liipfert, Bernhard, McPherson and Hand, Chartered (Member of Firm)

SWANZEY, Eugene F.

11421 Cedar Ridge Dr.
Potomac, MD 20854
Tel: (301)983-3191
Fax: (301)983-3196
Registered: LDA

Employers

Self-employed as an independent consultant.

Clients Represented

As an independent consultant

Mortgage Bankers Ass'n of America

SWANZEY, Genine

750 17th St. NW
Suite 1100
Washington, DC 20006
Tel: (202)778-2300
Fax: (202)778-2330

Employers

FoxKiser

SWARTZ, Rick

1869 Park Rd. NW
Washington, DC 20010
Tel: (202)328-1313
Fax: (202)797-9856
Registered: FARA

Employers

Rick Swartz & Associates, Inc. (President)

SWEATT, Loren E.

333 John Carlyle St.
Suite 200
Alexandria, VA 22314
Tel: (703)837-5360
Fax: (703)837-5407
Registered: LDA
EMail: sweattl@agc.org

Employers

Associated General Contractors of America (Director, Congressional Relations/Procurement and Environment)

SWEENEY, David A.

15209 Wycliffe Ct.
Rockville, MD 20853
Tel: (301)929-1665
Registered: LDA

Employers

Self-employed as an independent consultant.

SWEENEY, Garnett J.

1001 Pennsylvania Ave. NW
Suite 1275
Washington, DC 20004
Tel: (202)624-2895
Fax: (202)628-5116
Registered: LDA

Employers

C&M Internat'l, Ltd. (Director)
Crowell & Moring LLP

Clients Represented

On Behalf of C&M Internat'l, Ltd.

DNA Plant Technology Corp.

On Behalf of Crowell & Moring LLP

New York Life Internat'l Inc.

SWEENEY, John J.

815 16th St. NW
Washington, DC 20006
Tel: (202)637-5000
Fax: (202)637-5058

Employers

AFL-CIO (American Federation of Labor and Congress of Industrial Organizations) (President)

SWEENEY, Katie

1130 17th St. NW
Washington, DC 20036-4677
Tel: (202)463-2627
Fax: (202)463-3257
Registered: LDA
EMail: ksweeney@nma.org

Employers

Nat'l Mining Ass'n (Associate General Counsel)

SWEENEY, Jr., R. Michael

401 Ninth St. NW
Suite 1000
Washington, DC 20004
Tel: (202)274-2947
Fax: (202)274-2994
Registered: LDA

Employers

Troutman Sanders LLP (Associate)

SWEENEY, Rosemarie

2021 Massachusetts Ave. NW
Washington, DC 20036
Tel: (202)232-9033
Fax: (202)232-9044
Registered: LDA
EMail: rsweeney@aafp.org

Employers

American Academy of Family Physicians (V. President, Socioeconomics & Policy Analysis)

SWEENEY, Jr., William R.

1331 Pennsylvania Ave. NW
Suite 1300 North
Washington, DC 20004
Tel: (202)637-6751
Fax: (202)637-6758
Registered: LDA
EMail: bill.sweeney@eds.com

Employers

EDS Corp. (V. President, Global Affairs)

SWEET, David M.

1201 15th St. NW
Third Floor
Washington, DC 20005
Tel: (202)857-4722
Fax: (202)857-4799
Registered: LDA
EMail: dsweet@ipaa.org

Employers

Independent Petroleum Ass'n of America (V. President, Natural Gas)

SWEET, Frederic H.

8444 West Park
Suite 600
McLean, VA 22102
Tel: (202)296-1020
Fax: (202)296-5855
Registered: LDA

Employers

Northwestern Mutual Life Insurance Co. (Senior V. President and PAC Director)

SWEET, Paul

499 S. Capitol St. SW
Suite 500B
Washington, DC 20003
Tel: (202)488-6800
Fax: (202)488-7064
Registered: LDA
EMail: psweet@usmd.edu
Chief of Staff to Rep. Victor H. "Vic" Fazio (D-CA), 1980-83.

Employers
University System of Maryland (Associate V. Chancellor for Research Policy and Federal Relations)

SWEET, Tom

440 First St. NW
Eighth Floor
Washington, DC 20001
Tel: (202)942-4290
Fax: (202)393-2630
EMail: tsweet@naco.org

Employers
Nat'l Ass'n of Counties (Director, Corporate Relations)
Nat'l Ass'n of County Treasurers and Finance Officers (Contact)

SWEET, Jr., William J.

1440 New York Ave. NW
Washington, DC 20005
Tel: (202)371-7000
Fax: (202)393-5760
Registered: LDA

Employers
Skadden, Arps, Slate, Meagher & Flom LLP (Partner)

SWEIG, Julia

1779 Massachusetts Ave. NW
Suite 710
Washington, DC 20036
Tel: (202)518-3400
Fax: (202)986-2984

Employers
Council on Foreign Relations (Deputy Director, Latin American Programs)

SWENSON, Diane

3138 N. Tenth St.
Arlington, VA 22201
Tel: (703)522-4770
Fax: (703)522-0594

Employers
Nat'l Ass'n of Federal Credit Unions (Exec. V. President)

SWENSON, Leland

400 N. Capitol St. NW
Suite 790
Washington, DC 20001
Tel: (202)554-1600
Fax: (202)554-1654
Registered: LDA

Employers
Nat'l Farmers Union (Farmers Educational & Co-operative Union of America) (President)

SWESNIK, Deidre

1250 I St. NW
Suite 902
Washington, DC 20005
Tel: (202)393-5225
Fax: (202)393-3034

Employers
Robert A. Rapoza Associates (Policy Associate)

Clients Represented

On Behalf of Robert A. Rapoza Associates
Suomi College

SWIENCKI, Katherine E.

1100 Connecticut Ave. NW
Suite 900
Washington, DC 20036-4101
Tel: (202)463-8400
Fax: (202)833-8082
Registered: LDA
EMail: kswiencki@shawbransford.com

Employers
Shaw, Bransford, Veilleux & Roth (Legislative Assistant)

Clients Represented

On Behalf of Shaw, Bransford, Veilleux & Roth
Senior Executives Ass'n

SWIFT, Hon. Allan B.

1331 F St. NW
Suite 800
Washington, DC 20004
Tel: (202)347-8000
Fax: (202)347-8920
Registered: LDA
EMail: swift@csandh.com
Chairman, Subcommittee on Transportation and Hazardous Materials, House Committee on Energy and Commerce, 1990-95. Member, U.S. House of Representatives (D-WA), 1979-95.

Employers
Colling Swift & Hynes (Principal)
Al Swift Consulting, Inc.

Clients Represented

On Behalf of Colling Swift & Hynes
Frank Beam and Co.
Caraustar
Garden State Paper Co., Inc.
Media General, Inc.
The Newark Group
NewsHunter.net, LLC
Paper Recycling Coalition
PrediWave
Quest Diagnostics Inc.
Rock-Tenn Co.
Smurfit Stone Container Corp.
Talgo
White Pigeon Paper Co.

On Behalf of Al Swift Consulting, Inc.
Institute of Scrap Recycling Industries, Inc.

SWIFT, Heather

555 11th St. NW
Suite 750
Washington, DC 20005
Tel: (202)637-3506
Fax: (202)637-3504
Registered: LDA
Legislative Assistant, Sen. James Inhofe (R-OK).

Employers
El Paso Corporation (Federal Government Affairs Representative)

SWIFT, Richard F.

1730 Rhode Island Ave. NW
Suite 200
Washington, DC 20036
Tel: (202)728-0401
Fax: (202)659-5711

Employers
Tierney & Swift (Partner)

Clients Represented

On Behalf of Tierney & Swift
KCSM-TV
KVCR-TV

SWIFT, Richard J.

1625 K St. NW
Suite 1090
Washington, DC 20006-1604
Tel: (202)887-0278
Fax: (202)452-8160

Employers
Nat'l Foreign Trade Council, Inc. (Chairman)

SWIFT-ROSENZWEIG, Leslie

2033 K St. NW
Suite 700
Washington, DC 20006
Tel: (202)721-0912
Fax: (202)835-8343
EMail: lrosenzweig@pac.org

Employers
Foundation for Public Affairs (Exec. Director)

SWIGER, Michael A.

1050 Thomas Jefferson St. NW
Seventh Floor
Washington, DC 20007
Tel: (202)298-1800
Fax: (202)338-2416
Registered: LDA
EMail: mas@vnf.com

Employers
Van Ness Feldman, P.C. (Member)

Clients Represented

On Behalf of Van Ness Feldman, P.C.
Sacramento Municipal Utility District
Tacoma, Washington, City of

SWINDELLS, Grant

601 13th St. NW
Suite 410 South
Washington, DC 20005
Tel: (202)737-0100
Fax: (202)628-3965
Registered: LDA

Employers
R. Duffy Wall and Associates (Senior Account Representative)

SWINEHART, Leonard

1300 Connecticut Ave. NW
Suite 600
Washington, DC 20036
Tel: (202)775-8116
Fax: (202)223-0358
Registered: LDA
Former Senior Floor Assistant to Speaker Newt Gingrich (R-GA), U.S. House of Representatives.

Employers
Griffin, Johnson, Dover & Stewart (Lobbyist)

Clients Represented

On Behalf of Griffin, Johnson, Dover & Stewart
Air Transport Ass'n of America
American Agrisurance
American Fish Spotters Ass'n
Avue Technologies
Dell Computer Corp.
Deloitte Consulting
Fannie Mae
The Justice Project, Inc.
Monsanto Co.
United Technologies Corp.
Wilmer, Cutler & Pickering
Wine and Spirits Wholesalers of America

SWINT, Jennifer

1501 M St. NW
Suite 600
Washington, DC 20005-1710
Tel: (202)739-0200
Fax: (202)659-8287
EMail: jswint@bsmg.com

Employers
BSMG Worldwide (Senior Managing Director)

SWIRSKI, Sandra

1775 I St. NW
Suite 700
Washington, DC 20006
Tel: (202)261-4000
Fax: (202)261-4001
Registered: LDA
Legislative Assistant to Senator Alan Simpson (R-WY) and Chief Counsel, Subcommittee on Social Security and Family Policy, Senate Committee on Finance, 1994-96. Legislative Assistant to Senator John Danforth (R-MO), 1993-94.

Employers
Clark & Weinstock, Inc. (Managing Director)

Clients Represented

On Behalf of Clark & Weinstock, Inc.
American Ass'n of Homes and Services for the Aging
Rabbi Milton Balkany

SWISHER, Randall S.

122 C St. NW
Suite 380
Washington, DC 20001
Tel: (202)383-2500
Fax: (202)383-2505
Professional Staff, House Committee on Interior and Insular Affairs, 1979.

Employers
American Wind Energy Ass'n (Exec. Director)

SWITZER, Michael D.

600 13th St. NW
Washington, DC 20005-3096
Tel: (202)756-8234
Fax: (202)756-8087
EMail: mswitzer@mwe.com
Former Patent Examiner, Patent and Trademark Office.

Employers
McDermott, Will and Emery (Associate)

SWONGER, Chris R.

700 11th St. NW
Suite 680
Washington, DC 20001
Tel: (202)628-5877
Fax: (202)628-4847
Registered: LDA
EMail: chris_swonger@adsw.com

Employers
Allied Domecq (V. President and Director, Government Affairs)

SYERS, William A.

801 Pennsylvania Ave. NW
Suite 350
Washington, DC 20004
Tel: (202)783-2264
Fax: (202)783-1746
Registered: LDA

Employers
Newport News Shipbuilding Inc. (Director, Federal Relations)

SYKES, Kathy

Ariel Rios Federal Bldg. (1301-MC)
1200 Pennsylvania Ave. NW
Third Floor
Washington, DC 20460
Tel: (202)564-7171
Fax: (202)501-1544

EMail: sykes.kathy@epa.gov

Employers

Environmental Protection Agency (Appropriations/Enforcement Team Leader, Office of Congressional and Intergovernmental Affairs)

SYKES, Ronald G.

819 Seventh St. NW
Suite 215
Washington, DC 20001
Tel: (202)682-1881
Fax: (202)682-2471
Registered: LDA

EMail: rgsentinc@aol.com

Employers

RGS Enterprises, Inc. (President/CEO)

Clients Represented

On Behalf of RGS Enterprises, Inc.

AAE Technologies, Inc.
ADA Consulting Services
Edison Electric Institute
General Motors Corp.
Information Resources, Inc.

SYKES, Thomas D.

1875 I St. NW
Suite 1050
Washington, DC 20006-5409
Tel: (202)331-8585
Fax: (202)331-2032

Employers

Scribner, Hall & Thompson, LLP (Partner)

SYMINGTON, Hon. James W.

1666 K St. NW
Suite 500
Washington, DC 20006-2803
Tel: (202)887-1400
Fax: (202)466-2198
Registered: LDA, FARA

Member, U.S. House of Representatives (D-MO), 1969-77. Chief of Protocol, Department of State, 1968. Administrative Assistant to the Attorney General, Department of Justice, 1962-64. Deputy Director, Food For Peace, The White House, 1961-62. Attache, U.S. Embassy (London, England), Department of State, 1958-60.

Employers

O'Connor & Hannan, L.L.P. (Partner)

Clients Represented

On Behalf of O'Connor & Hannan, L.L.P.

Kurdistan Democratic Party USA
Lockheed Martin Corp.
Student Loan Funding Corp.

SYMMS, Hon. Steven D.

233 Constitution Ave. NE
Washington, DC 20002
Tel: (202)547-4000
Fax: (202)543-5044
Registered: LDA, FARA

EMail: PRDandS@aol.com

Member, U.S. Senate (R-ID), 1981-93. Member, U.S. House of Representatives (R-ID), 1972-81.

Employers

Parry, Romani, DeConcini & Symms (Partner)
Symms, Lehn & Associates, Inc. (Principal)

Clients Represented

On Behalf of Parry, Romani, DeConcini & Symms

AIDS Healthcare Foundation
Andrx Pharmaceutical Corp.
Armstrong World Industries, Inc.
Asphalt Systems, Inc.
Aventis Pharmaceutical Products
Avondale, Arizona, City of
Bank of New York
Bristol-Myers Squibb Co.
Coalition Against Database Piracy
Composites Fabricators Ass'n
Ferraro, USA
Formosan Ass'n for Public Affairs
GlaxoSmithKline
Herbalife Internat'l, Inc.
Hoechst Marion Roussel Deutschland GmbH
Inter-Cal Corp.
Katten Muchin & Zavis
Motion Picture Ass'n of America
Nat'l Air Cargo, Inc.
Nat'l Nutritional Foods Ass'n
Nat'l Retail Federation
Nogales, Arizona, City of
Nu Skin Internat'l Inc.
Owens Corning
Peoria, Arizona, City of
Pfizer, Inc.
Pharmacia Corp.
Policy Development Group, Inc.
Project to Promote Competition and Innovation in the Digital Age
Research & Development Laboratories
Research Corp. Technology
Rexall Sundown
SBC Communications Inc.
SOL Source Technologies, Inc.
Styrene Information and Research Center
Taxpayers Against Fraud, The False Claims Legal Center
TCOM, L.P.
Unilever United States, Inc.
Utah Natural Products Alliance

On Behalf of Symms, Lehn & Associates, Inc.

Ass'n of American Railroads

SYMONS, Howard J.

701 Pennsylvania Ave. NW
Suite 900
Washington, DC 20004-2608
Tel: (202)434-7300
Fax: (202)434-7400
Registered: LDA, FARA

EMail: hsymons@mintz.com

Senior Counsel, Subcommittee on Telecommunications, Committee on Energy and Commerce, U.S. House of Representatives, 1981-85.

Employers

Mintz, Levin, Cohn, Ferris, Glovsky and Popeo, P.C. (Partner)

Clients Represented

On Behalf of Mintz, Levin, Cohn, Ferris, Glovsky and Popeo, P.C.

AT&T Wireless Services, Inc.
Cablevision Systems Corp.
Cellular Telecommunications and Internet Ass'n
Nat'l Cable Television Ass'n

SZABAT, Ronald P.

1101 Vermont Ave. NW
12th Floor
Washington, DC 20005-3583
Tel: (202)789-7427
Fax: (202)789-7401
Registered: LDA

Employers

American Medical Ass'n (Director, Division of Legislative Counsel)

SZABO, Laura

2101 L St. NW
Washington, DC 20037-1526
Tel: (202)785-9700
Fax: (202)887-0689
Registered: LDA

EMail: szabol@dsmo.com

Employers

Dickstein Shapiro Morin & Oshinsky LLP (Partner)

Clients Represented

On Behalf of Dickstein Shapiro Morin & Oshinsky LLP

Electric Power Supply Ass'n
PG&E Generating Co.

SZABO, Robert G.

1050 Thomas Jefferson St. NW
Seventh Floor
Washington, DC 20007
Tel: (202)298-1981
Fax: (202)338-2416
Registered: LDA

Senior Legislative Assistant to Senator J. Bennett Johnston (D-LA), 1975-78.

Employers

Consumers United for Rail Equity
The Nat'l Wetlands Coalition (Exec. Director and Counsel)
Van Ness Feldman, P.C. (Member)

Clients Represented

On Behalf of Van Ness Feldman, P.C.

American Chemistry Council
Consumers United for Rail Equity
Council for Conservation and Reinvestment of OCS Revenue
Delta Wetlands Project
Nat'l Endangered Species Act Reform Coalition
The Nat'l Wetlands Coalition
Sonoma County Water Agency
Toyota Motor Manufacturing North America
Toyota Motor North America, U.S.A., Inc.

SZCZESNY, Barry G.

1575 I St. NW
Suite 400
Washington, DC 20005
Tel: (202)289-1818
Fax: (202)289-6578
Registered: LDA

Employers

American Ass'n of Museums (Assistant Director, Government Affairs Counsel)

SZLAVIK, Joseph J.

1341 Connecticut Ave. NW
Third Floor
Washington, DC 20036
Tel: (202)862-3900
Fax: (202)862-5500

Staff Assistant, The White House, 1988-90. Formerly served as a Staff Assistant, Office of Enforcement, U.S. Customs Service, Department of the Treasury.

Employers

Scribe Consulting & Communications (President)

Clients Represented

On Behalf of Scribe Consulting & Communications

The Boeing Co.
Gabonese Republic, Government of the
WorldSpace Corp.

SZOKA DE VALLADARES, Mary-Rose

P.O. Box 30452
Bethesda, MD 20824
Tel: (301)530-6591
Registered: LDA

Employers

Self-employed as an independent consultant.

Clients Represented

As an independent consultant

Transconsortia

SZPAK, Carole

325 Seventh St. NW
Suite 625
Washington, DC 20004-2802
Tel: (202)393-6700 Ext: 18
Fax: (202)783-6041

EMail: comm@naphs.org

Employers

Nat'l Ass'n of Psychiatric Health Systems (Director, Communications)

SZYMANSKI, Tauna M.

1250 I St. NW
Suite 1105
Washington, DC 20005
Tel: (202)682-5151
Fax: (202)682-2185
Registered: LDA

Employers

Andreae, Vick & Associates, L.L.C. (Senior Research Associate)

TAAHAN, Chris

1307 New York Ave. NW
Suite 300
Washington, DC 20005-4701
Tel: (202)293-2450
Fax: (202)457-8095

Employers

American Ass'n of Colleges for Teacher Education (Program Associate, Governmental Affairs)

TABBITA, Phil

1300 L St. NW
Washington, DC 20005
Tel: (202)842-4200
Fax: (202)842-4297

Employers
American Postal Workers Union (Exec. Assistant to the President)

TABER, John

444 N. Capitol St. NW
Suite 336
Washington, DC 20001
Tel: (202)624-5858
Fax: (202)624-5857

Employers
Alaska, Washington Office of the State of (Associate Director)

TABOR, Janis L.

1620 L St. NW
Suite 620
Washington, DC 20036
Tel: (202)429-3971
Fax: (202)429-3976
Registered: LDA

Employers
Council for Chemical Research, Inc. (Exec. Director)

TABOR, Ralph

440 First St. NW
Eighth Floor
Washington, DC 20001
EMail: rtabor@naco.org
Tel: (202)942-4254
Fax: (202)942-4281

Employers
Nat'l Ass'n of Counties (Associate Legislative Director)
Nat'l Ass'n of County Treasurers and Finance Officers (Contact)

TADA, Yukio

1825 K St. NW
Suite 1103
Washington, DC 20006
Tel: (202)429-0280
Fax: (202)429-0283

Employers
Nissho-Iwai American Corp. (General Manager)

TAFEL, Richard Leonard

1633 Q St. NW
Suite 210
Washington, DC 20009
Tel: (202)347-5306
Fax: (202)347-5224

Employers
Log Cabin Republicans PAC (LCR PAC) (Exec. Director)

TAGG, George C.

1155 Connecticut Ave. NW
Suite 400
Washington, DC 20036
Tel: (301)656-1370
Fax: (301)657-3966
Registered: LDA

Employers
Self-employed as an independent consultant.

Clients Represented

As an independent consultant
FedEx Corp.
Morgan Stanley Dean Witter & Co.
John T. O'Rourke Law Offices
Waste Management, Inc.

TAGGART, Judith F.

Four Herbert St.
Alexandria, VA 22305
EMail: terrinst@aol.com
Tel: (703)548-5473
Fax: (703)548-6299

Employers
Terrene Institute (Exec. V. President)

TAGGART, William A.

2341 S. Ode St.
Arlington, VA 22202
Tel: (703)429-1940
Registered: LDA
Staff Director, Senate Agriculture Committee, 1980-84.

Employers
Taggart and Associates, Inc. (President)

Clients Represented

On Behalf of Taggart and Associates, Inc.
Aventis Pharmaceuticals, Inc.

TAIBER, Julie M.

1776 Massachusetts Ave. NW
Suite 620
Washington, DC 20036
EMail: JMT@alliance-exchange.org
Tel: (202)293-6141
Fax: (202)293-6144
Registered: LDA

Employers
Alliance for Internat'l Educational and Cultural Exchange, The (Assistant Director/ Senior Policy Specialist)

TAIBL, Paul E.

1717 Pennsylvania Ave. NW
Suite 350
Washington, DC 20006
EMail: ptaibl@bens.org
Tel: (202)296-2125
Fax: (202)296-2490

Employers
Business Executives for Nat'l Security (Assistant V. President)

TAITANO, Francisco I.

2121 R St. NW
Washington, DC 20008-1908
Tel: (202)673-5869
Fax: (202)673-5873

Employers
Northern Mariana Islands, Commonwealth of the (Federal Programs Coordinator)

TAITT, Julie

Ariel Rios Federal Bldg. (1301-MC)
1200 Pennsylvania Ave. NW
Washington, DC 20460
EMail: taitt.julie@epa.gov
Tel: (202)564-2022
Fax: (202)501-0144

Employers
Environmental Protection Agency (Director, Information Management Division, Office of Congressional and Intergovernmental Relations)

TAKAHASHI, George

2001 Pennsylvania Ave. NW
Suite 700
Washington, DC 20006
EMail: george_takahashi@micusa.com
Tel: (202)331-7301
Fax: (202)331-7277

Employers
Mitsubishi Internat'l Corp. (Manager)

TAKAHASHI, Hiroyuki

1900 K St. NW
Suite 1075
Washington, DC 20006
EMail: takahashi@kkc-usa.org
Tel: (202)293-8436
Fax: (202)293-8438
Registered: LDA, FARA

Employers
Japan Federation of Economic Organizations (U.S. Representative)
Keizai Koho Center

TAKAKOSHI, William K.

505 Capitol Ct. NE
Suite 200
Washington, DC 20002
EMail: takakoshi@hurtnorton.com
Tel: (202)543-9398
Fax: (202)543-7844
Registered: LDA
Special Assistant to the Undersecretary (1990-98), U.S. Army. Deputy for Production and Quality (1985-90) and Deputy for Ammunition and Weapons (1980-85) to the Assistant Secretary of the Army, U.S. Army. Deputy for Production, Navy/Air Force Cruise Missile Program Office, 1978-80. Deputy for Resources, Trident Missile Facility, U.S. Navy, 1975-78.

Employers
Hurt, Norton & Associates (Senior Associate)

Clients Represented

On Behalf of Hurt, Norton & Associates
Caswell Internat'l Corp.
The Coca-Cola Company
Intergraph Corp. Federal Systems Division
Pemco Aviation Group, Inc.
Quad City Development Group
Sierra Military Health Services, Inc.

TALALAY, Susan

1616 H St. NW
Third Floor
Washington, DC 20006
Tel: (202)737-3700
Fax: (202)737-0530

Employers
Internat'l Center for Journalists (Director, Knight International Press Fellowship Program)

TALBERT, Donna

2100 L St. NW
Washington, DC 20037
EMail: dtalbert@cmpa.com
Tel: (202)223-2942
Fax: (202)872-4014

Employers
Center for Media and Public Affairs (Director, Development)

TALBOT, Scott

805 15th St. NW
Suite 600
Washington, DC 20005
Tel: (202)289-4322
Fax: (202)289-1903
Registered: LDA

Employers
The Financial Services Roundtable (Director, Tax Policy, Counsel)

TALCOTT, Jonathan H.

601 Pennsylvania Ave. NW
11th Floor, North Bldg.
Washington, DC 20004-2601
Tel: (202)756-3300
Fax: (202)756-3333

Employers
Alston & Bird LLP

Clients Represented

On Behalf of Alston & Bird LLP
Regions Financial Corp.

TALENS, James M.

1330 Connecticut Ave. NW
Washington, DC 20036-1795
EMail: jtalens@steptoe.com
Tel: (202)429-3000
Fax: (202)429-3902
Attorney-Advisor/Branch Chief/Senior Advisor, Common Carrier and International Bureaus, Federal Communications Commission, 1975-97.

Employers
Steptoe & Johnson LLP (Of Counsel)

TALENT, Hon. James

1050 Connecticut Ave. NW
Washington, DC 20036-5339
Tel: (202)857-6000
Fax: (202)857-6395
Member, U.S. House of Representatives (R-MO), 1993-2001.

Employers
Arent Fox Kintner Plotkin & Kahn, PLLC (Counsel)

TALIAFERRO, Will

1010 Wisconsin Ave. NW
Suite 800
Washington, DC 20007
Tel: (202)338-8700
Fax: (202)338-2334

Employers
Greer, Margolis, Mitchell, Burns & Associates (Partner)

Clients Represented

On Behalf of Greer, Margolis, Mitchell, Burns & Associates
NHTSA

TALISMAN, Charles E.

2550 M St. NW
Washington, DC 20037-1350
EMail: ctalisman@pattonboggs.com
Tel: (202)457-6000
Fax: (202)457-6315
Registered: FARA

Employers
Patton Boggs, LLP (Partner)

TALISMAN, Harold L.

1200 G St. NW
Suite 600
Washington, DC 20005-3802
EMail: talisman@wrightlaw.com
Tel: (202)393-1200
Fax: (202)393-1240

Employers
Wright & Talisman, P.C. (Counsel)

TALLEY, Bruce B.

555 12th St. NW
Suite 350
N. Tower
Washington, DC 20004
Tel: (202)639-4062
Fax: (202)737-1311
Registered: LDA

Employers
ABB, Inc. (Director, Government Affairs and International Trade)

TALLEY, Carleen

200 Independence Ave. SW
Room 341H
Washington, DC 20201
Tel: (202)690-8220
Fax: (202)690-8168

Employers
Department of Health and Human Services - Health Care Financing Administration (Director, Congressional Affairs Group)

TALLEY, Kevin D.

805 15th St. NW
Suite 700
Washington, DC 20005
Tel: (202)312-7400
Fax: (202)312-7441
Staff Director, House Committee on Education and the Workforce, 1997-2001. Chief of Staff to Senator John Heinz (R-PA), 1981-85. Press Secretary and Chief of Staff to Rep. William F. Goodling (R-PA), 1977-81. Press Assistant and Press Secretary to Senate Republican Leader, Senator Hugh Scott (R-PA), 1971-76.

Employers
Sagamore Associates, Inc.

Clients Represented
On Behalf of Sagamore Associates, Inc.
Arthritis Foundation

TALLEY, Robert A. C.

2121 K St. NW
Suite 650
Washington, DC 20036
EMail: tmg1@erols.com
Tel: (202)296-4114
Fax: (202)296-2409
Former Legislative Assistant to Rep. J. Alex McMillan (R-NC).

Employers
Talley and Associates (Principal)

Clients Represented
On Behalf of Talley and Associates
City Public Service
Colorado Springs Utilities
ElectriCities of North Carolina, Inc.
Fair Trade Group

TALLMER, Matt

918 F St. NW
Washington, DC 20004-1400
EMail: mtallmer@aila.org
Tel: (202)216-2400
Fax: (202)371-9449

Employers
American Immigration Lawyers Ass'n (Public Affairs Associate)

TALLON, Hon. Robin

908 Pennsylvania Ave. SE
Washington, DC 20003
Tel: (202)544-5666
Fax: (202)544-4647
Registered: LDA
EMail: rtallon@advantage-dc.com
Member, U.S. House of Representatives (D-SC), 1983-93.

Employers
Advantage Associates, Inc. (Partner)
Tallon & Associates

Clients Represented
On Behalf of Advantage Associates, Inc.
TCOM, L.P.
Uniformed Services Dental Alliance
On Behalf of Tallon & Associates
Philip Morris Management Corp.

TALMADGE, William C.

1730 Pennsylvania Ave. NW
Suite 1200
Washington, DC 20006-4706
Tel: (202)737-0500
Fax: (202)626-3737
Registered: LDA
Administrative Assistant to Rep. Richard Ray (D-GA), 1982-86. Legislative Assistant to Senator Herman Talmadge (D-GA), 1971-73.

Employers
King & Spalding (Counsel)

Clients Represented
On Behalf of King & Spalding
The Egg Factory, LLC
ESR Children's Health Care System
Farm Market iD
Georgia Electric Membership Corp.
Healthcare Recoveries Inc.
Internet Security Systems, Inc.
Lockheed Martin Corp.
Minnesota Mining and Manufacturing (3M Pharmaceuticals)
Salt Lake City Olympic Organizing Committee

TAMBONE, Victor

517 Second St. NE
Washington, DC 20002
Tel: (202)543-3744
Fax: (202)543-3509
Registered: LDA

Employers
David Turch & Associates (Associate)

Clients Represented
On Behalf of David Turch & Associates
Digital Biometrics, Inc.
San Bernardino, California, County of
St. Cloud, Minnesota, City of

TAMMELLEO, William F.

555 New Jersey Ave. NW
Washington, DC 20001
Tel: (202)879-4454
Fax: (202)879-4402
Registered: LDA

Employers
American Federation of Teachers (Associate Director, Legislation)

TAMPIO, Christopher M.

1700 N. Moore St.
Suite 2250
Arlington, VA 22209
Tel: (703)841-2300
Fax: (703)841-1183
Registered: LDA

Employers
Internat'l Mass Retailers Ass'n (Contact)

TANIELIAN, Matthew J.

1250 I St. NW
Suite 200
Washington, DC 20005
Tel: (202)737-8888
Fax: (202)638-4922

Employers
Information Technology Industry Council (Director, Government Affairs)

TANK, Alan

122 C St. NW
Suite 875
Washington, DC 20001
Tel: (202)347-3600
Fax: (202)347-5265
Registered: LDA

Employers
Nat'l Pork Producers Council (Chief Exec. Officer)

TANK, Margo

1717 Pennsylvania Ave. NW
Washington, DC 20006
Tel: (202)974-1000
Fax: (202)331-9330
Registered: LDA
Former Counsel, House Committee on Banking and Financial Services.

Employers
Goodwin, Procter & Hoar LLP (Associate)

Clients Represented
On Behalf of Goodwin, Procter & Hoar LLP
Electronic Financial Services Council
Massachusetts Bankers Ass'n

TANNENBAUM, Ira L.

1800 Massachusetts Ave. NW
Second Floor
Washington, DC 20036-1800
Tel: (202)778-9000
Fax: (202)778-9100
Registered: LDA

Employers
Kirkpatrick & Lockhart LLP (Partner)

Clients Represented
On Behalf of Kirkpatrick & Lockhart LLP
American Financial Group

TANNER, Michael D.

1000 Massachusetts Ave. NW
Washington, DC 20001
Tel: (202)842-0200
Fax: (202)842-3490

Employers
Cato Institute (Director, Health and Welfare Studies)

TANNER, Rev. W. Douglas

110 Maryland Ave. NE
Suite 304
Washington, DC 20002
EMail: faithpol1@aol.com
Tel: (202)546-1299
Fax: (202)546-4025

Employers
Faith & Politics Institute (President)

TANTILLO, Augustine D.

601 Pennsylvania Ave. NW
Suite 900 South
Washington, DC 20004
Tel: (202)434-8207
Fax: (202)639-8238
Registered: LDA

Employers
SRG & Associates

Clients Represented
On Behalf of SRG & Associates
Celanese Government Relations Office
Fieldcrest Cannon Inc.
Milliken and Co.
Northern Textile Ass'n
Textile/Clothing Technology Center

TANZI, Vito

1779 Massachusetts Ave. NW
Washington, DC 20036
Tel: (202)483-7600
Fax: (202)483-1840

Employers
Carnegie Endowment for Internat'l Peace (Senior Associate)

TAPIA, Raul R.

1200 New Hampshire Ave NW
Suite 430
Washington, DC 20036
Tel: (202)463-8800
Fax: (202)955-1147
Registered: LDA

Employers
Murray, Scheer, Montgomery, Tapia & O'Donnell (Partner)

Clients Represented
On Behalf of Murray, Scheer, Montgomery, Tapia & O'Donnell
California State Assembly - Committee on Rules
Chino, California, City of
Long Beach, California, City of
Monterey, California, County of
Salazar Associates Internat'l, Inc.
Southern California Ass'n of Governments
Water Replenishment District of Southern California

TARBERT, Jeffrey

2301 M St. NW
Washington, DC 20037-1484
EMail: jtarbert@APPAnet.org
Tel: (202)467-2936
Fax: (202)467-2910

Employers
American Public Power Ass'n (Senior V. President, Membership Services)

TARKINGTON, Marshall

1400 Independence Ave. SW
Washington, DC 20250
EMail: mtarkington@reeusda.gov
Tel: (202)720-3656

Employers
Department of Agriculture - Agricultural Research Service (Senior Legislative Analyst)

TARLEY, Carlo

8315 Lee Hwy.
Fairfax, VA 22031
Tel: (703)208-7200
Fax: (703)208-7264

Employers
United Mine Workers of America (Secretary-Treasurer)

TARNE, Gene

200 Daingerfield Rd.
Suite 100
Alexandria, VA 22314
Tel: (703)684-8352
Fax: (703)684-5812
EMail: gtarne@tarnepowerspr.com

Press Secretary to Rep. Bill Schuette (R-MI), 1986.

Employers

Tarne Powers & Associates (President)

Clients Represented

On Behalf of Tarne Powers & Associates

Americans for Integrity in Palliative Care
Do No Harm: The Coalition of Americans for Research Ethics
Physicians Ad hoc Coalition for Truth (PHACT)

TARNUTZER, Brett

555 12th St. NW
Washington, DC 20004
Tel: (202)347-4964
Fax: (202)347-4961
Registered: LDA

Employers

Wallman Strategic Consulting, LLC

Clients Represented

On Behalf of Wallman Strategic Consulting, LLC

Real Access Alliance

TARPLIN, Linda E.

1350 I St. NW
Suite 690
Washington, DC 20005
Tel: (202)898-4746
Fax: (202)898-4756
Registered: LDA

Special Assistant to the President for Legislative Affairs (Senate), The White House, during the Bush I administration.

Employers

The OB-C Group, LLC (Principal)

Clients Represented

On Behalf of The OB-C Group, LLC

American Airlines
Anheuser-Busch Cos., Inc.
AT&T
Biotechnology Industry Organization
Blue Cross Blue Shield Ass'n
Fannie Mae
Goodyear Tire and Rubber Co.
Healthcare Distribution Management Ass'n
Investment Co. Institute
Merrill Lynch & Co., Inc.
Motorola, Inc.
Nat'l Thoroughbred Racing Ass'n, Inc.
Newport News Shipbuilding Inc.
The Rouse Company
Sears, Roebuck and Co.
Securities Industry Ass'n
TIAA-CREF
United Parcel Service
WellPoint Health Networks/Blue Cross of California/UNICARE
Wilmer, Cutler & Pickering

TARPLIN, Richard J.

1850 K St. NW
Suite 850
Washington, DC 20006
Tel: (202)331-1760
Fax: (202)822-9376
Registered: LDA

Assistant Secretary for Legislation (1996-2000) and Principal Deputy Assistant Secretary, Legislation (1993-96), Department of Health and Human Services. Staff Director, Subcommittee on Children, Family, Drugs, Alcoholism, U.S. Senate, 1988-93. Professional Staff Member, Labor and Human Resources Committee, U.S. Senate, 1985-88. Legislative Assistant to Rep. Leon E. Panetta (D-CA), 1982-85.

Employers

Timmons and Co., Inc. (V. President)

Clients Represented

On Behalf of Timmons and Co., Inc.

American Council of Life Insurers
American Petroleum Institute
American Soc. of Anesthesiologists
Anheuser-Busch Cos., Inc.
Asbestos Working Group
AT&T
Bay Harbor Management, L.C.
Bristol-Myers Squibb Co.
Cox Enterprises Inc.
DaimlerChrysler Corp.
Farallon Capital Management
Federal Home Loan Mortgage Corp. (Freddie Mac)
Micron Technology, Inc.
Napster, Inc.
Nat'l Rifle Ass'n of America
New York Life Insurance Co.
Northrop Grumman Corp.
TruePosition Inc.
Union Pacific
University of Utah
UNOCAL Corp.
VISA U.S.A., Inc.

TARR-WHELAN, Linda

1875 Connecticut Ave. NW
Suite 710
Washington, DC 20009
Tel: (202)387-6030
Fax: (202)986-2539
EMail: ltarrwhelan@cfpa.org

Employers

Center for Policy Alternatives (President and Chair)

TASSEY, Jeffrey A.

1155 21st St. NW
Suite 300
Washington, DC 20036
Tel: (202)659-8201
Fax: (202)659-5249
Registered: LDA
EMail: jatassey@wms-jen.com

Counsel to Subcommittee on Commerce, Consumer and Monetary Affairs, Committee on Government Affairs, 1990-92; Counsel and Legislative Director, Rep. Druie Douglas Barnard, Jr. (D-GA).

Employers

Williams & Jensen, P.C. (Partner)

Clients Represented

On Behalf of Williams & Jensen, P.C.

Credit Suisse First Boston Corp.
First Union Corp.
Knight Trading Group
Reinsurance Ass'n of America
Securities Traders Ass'n
USAA - United Services Automobile Ass'n

TASSONE, Lawrence

5211 Auth Rd.
Suitland, MD 20746
Tel: (301)899-3500
Fax: (301)899-8136
Registered: LDA

Employers

Air Force Sergeants Ass'n (Director, Special Projects)

TATE, Sr., Dan C.

700 13th St. NW
Suite 400
Washington, DC 20005
Tel: (202)347-0773
Fax: (202)347-0785
Registered: LDA, FARA
EMail: dtate@cassidy.com

Chief Legislative Representative (Senate) to the President, The White House, 1977-80. Assistant to Senator Herman Talmadge (D-GA), 1969-76.

Employers

Cassidy & Associates, Inc. (Senior V. President)

Clients Represented

On Behalf of Cassidy & Associates, Inc.

The Boeing Co.
Chlorine Chemistry Council
E Lottery
General Dynamics Corp.
Institute for Student Achievement
Lockheed Martin IMS
Major League Baseball
The PGA Tour, Inc.
Phoenix, Arizona, City of
Saudi Arabia, Royal Embassy of
Sherwin Williams Co.
Subaru of America
United Service Organization
VoiceStream Wireless Corp.

TATE, Jr., Dan C.

233 Pennsylvania Ave. SE
Suite 300
Washington, DC 20003
Tel: (202)547-9050
Fax: (202)547-8991
EMail: dan@tatelemunyon.com

Special Assistant to the President for Legislative Affairs, The White House, 1995-97. Deputy Assistant Secretary of Energy for Congressional relations, 1993-95. Legislative Director to Rep. W.J. "Billy" Tauzin (D-LA), 1989-93.

Employers

Tate-LeMunyon, LLC (Principal)

Clients Represented

On Behalf of Tate-LeMunyon, LLC

Alliance Air Services
Brownsville, Texas, Port of
Fannie Mae
North American Superhighway Coalition

TATE, Eula M.

1350 I St. NW
Suite 510
Washington, DC 20005
Tel: (202)828-8500
Fax: (202)293-3457
Registered: LDA

Employers

United Automobile, Aerospace and Agricultural Implement Workers of America (UAW) (Legislative Representative)

TATE, Michael

1111 14th St. NW
Suite 1200
Washington, DC 20005-5603
Tel: (202)898-2400
Fax: (202)789-2258
Registered: LDA
EMail: tatem@ada.org

Employers

American Dental Ass'n (Manager, Legislative and Regulatory Policy)

TATE, Nancy E.

1730 M St. NW
Suite 1000
Washington, DC 20036
Tel: (202)429-1965
Fax: (202)429-0854

Employers

League of Women Voters of the United States (Exec. Director)

TATE, Sheila B.

700 13th St. NW
Suite 1000
Washington, DC 20005
Tel: (202)347-6633
Fax: (202)347-8713
Registered: FARA

Former Press Secretary to First Lady Nancy Reagan. Campaign and Transition Press Secretary to President Bush.

Employers

Powell Tate (President)

Clients Represented

On Behalf of Powell Tate

Saudi Arabia, Royal Embassy of

TATE, Thomas N.

1250 I St. NW
Suite 1200
Washington, DC 20005-3924
Tel: (202)371-8530
Fax: (202)371-8470
Registered: LDA

Employers

Aerospace Industries Ass'n of America (V. President, Legislative Affairs)

TAUB, Cynthia

1330 Connecticut Ave. NW
Washington, DC 20036-1795
Tel: (202)429-3000
Fax: (202)429-3902
Registered: LDA
EMail: ctaub@steptoe.com

Employers

Steptoe & Johnson LLP (Associate)

Clients Represented

On Behalf of Steptoe & Johnson LLP

TAPS Renewal Task Force

TAUKE, Hon. Thomas J.

1300 I St. NW
Suite 400 West
Washington, DC 20005
Tel: (202)515-2404
Fax: (202)336-7914
Registered: LDA
Member, U.S. House of Representatives (R-IA), 1979-91.

Employers
Verizon Communications (Senior V. President, Public Policy and External Affairs)

TAWIL, Victor

1776 Massachusetts Ave. NW
Suite 310
Washington, DC 20036
Tel: (202)861-0344
Fax: (202)861-0342

Employers
Ass'n for Maximum Service Television, Inc. (Senior V. President)

TAYLOR, Amy J.

1780 Massachusetts Ave. NW
Washington, DC 20036
Tel: (202)785-3351
Fax: (202)293-4349
Registered: LDA

Employers
Planned Parenthood Federation of America (Legislative Representative)

TAYLOR, Anthony

345 S. Patrick St.
Alexandria, VA 22314
Tel: (703)836-3654
Fax: (703)836-6086
Federal Government service, 1975-91.

Employers
Bob Lawrence & Associates (V. President)

Clients Represented
On Behalf of Bob Lawrence & Associates
Columbia Research Corp.

TAYLOR, III, Charles A.

444 N. Capitol St. NW
Suite 801
Washington, DC 20001
Tel: (202)639-0490
Fax: (202)639-0494
Registered: LDA

Employers
Nat'l Ass'n of Independent Insurers (Assistant V. President, Government Relations)

TAYLOR, Christine

655 15th St. NW
Suite 445
Washington, DC 20005
Tel: (202)737-1977
Fax: (202)737-8111

Employers
Koch Industries, Inc. (PAC Director)

TAYLOR, Christopher A.

1150 18th St. NW
Suite 400
Washington, DC 20036
EMail: ctaylor@msrb.org
Tel: (202)223-9347
Fax: (202)872-0347

Employers
Municipal Securities Rulemaking Board (Exec. Director)

TAYLOR, Chuck

1875 I St. NW
Suite 900
Washington, DC 20005
Tel: (202)371-0200
Fax: (202)371-2858

Employers
Edelman Public Relations Worldwide (Senior V. President)

Clients Represented
On Behalf of Edelman Public Relations Worldwide
Gyphon Networks
Optinel Systems
Rhythms NetConnections

TAYLOR, David

1615 L St. NW
Suite 700
Washington, DC 20036-5610
EMail: david.taylor@weil.com
Tel: (202)682-7000
Fax: (202)857-0939
Registered: LDA

Employers
Weil, Gotshal & Manges, LLP (Legislative Specialist)

Clients Represented
On Behalf of Weil, Gotshal & Manges, LLP
Nomura Internat'l plc

TAYLOR, David F.

805 15th St. NW
Suite 810
Washington, DC 20005
Tel: (202)347-0940
Fax: (202)347-0941
Registered: LDA
Majority Staff Director, Subcommittee on Commerce, Justice, State, and the Judiciary, Senate Appropriations Committee, 1995-97. Assistant to Senate Republican Leader, Senator Robert J. Dole (R-KS), 1986-89 and 1993-95. Associate Director for Legislative Affairs, Office of Management and Budget, 1989-93.

Employers
Capitol Solutions

Clients Represented
On Behalf of Capitol Solutions
Cellular Telecommunications and Internet Ass'n
Intellectual Property Owners Ass'n

TAYLOR, Dianne

444 N. Capitol St. NW
Suite 224
Washington, DC 20001
Tel: (202)624-3630
Fax: (202)624-3639

Employers
Council of State Community Development Agencies (Exec. Director)

TAYLOR, Donna

4121 Wilson Blvd.
Tenth Floor
Arlington, VA 22203
Tel: (703)351-2086
Fax: (703)351-2088

Employers
Nat'l Telephone Cooperative Ass'n (Public Affairs Manager)

TAYLOR, Duane

444 N. Capitol St. NW
Suite 214
Washington, DC 20001
EMail: ddtaylor@gov.state.va.us
Tel: (202)783-1769
Fax: (202)783-7687

Employers
Virginia Liaison Office (Special Assistant, State/Federal Relations)

TAYLOR, Gary J.

444 N. Capitol St. NW
Suite 544
Washington, DC 20001
Tel: (202)624-7890
Fax: (202)624-7891
Registered: LDA

Employers
Internat'l Ass'n of Fish and Wildlife Agencies (Legislative Director)

TAYLOR, George

4245 N. Fairfax Dr.
Suite 750
Arlington, VA 22203
Tel: (703)516-9300
Fax: (703)516-9308

Employers
American Soc. of Pension Actuaries (President)

TAYLOR, Heather

1001 Connecticut Ave. NW
Suite 400
Washington, DC 20036
EMail: htaylor@taswer.org
Tel: (202)331-8084
Ext: 226
Fax: (202)331-8068

Employers
Tribal Ass'n on Solid Waste and Emergency Response (TASWER) (Government Relations)

TAYLOR, Jr., James

1150 18th St. NW
Ninth Floor
Washington, DC 20036
EMail: jtaylor@ablondifoster.com
Tel: (202)296-3355
Fax: (202)296-3922

Employers
Ablondi, Foster, Sobin & Davidow, P.C. (Partner)

TAYLOR, James R. "J.T."

1701 Pennsylvania Ave. NW
Suite 900
Washington, DC 20006-5805
Tel: (202)452-8200
Fax: (202)833-0388

Employers
Empower America (President and Chief Exec. Officer)

TAYLOR, Jefferson D.

1101 Pennsylvania Ave. NW
Suite 515
Washington, DC 20004
EMail: jefferson_taylor@agfg.com
Tel: (202)628-4600
Fax: (202)628-5410
Registered: LDA
Antitrust Division, Department of Justice, 1979-80.

Employers
American General Corp. (V. President, Political Affairs; PAC Treasurer)

TAYLOR, Jeffrey K.

919 Prince St.
Alexandria, VA 22314
Tel: (703)684-6098
Fax: (703)684-7138

Employers
Bond & Company, Inc.

TAYLOR, Jeffrey L.

1401 I St. NW
Suite 500
Washington, DC 20005
Tel: (202)289-1313
Fax: (202)289-1330
Chief of Staff to Rep. David M. McIntosh (R-IN), 1997-2000; Director of Congressional Relations, National Republican Congressional Committee, 1990-92; Public Affairs Specialist, Department of Health and Human Services, 1989-90; Legislative Assistant to Senator Gordon Humphrey (R-NH), 1984-86.

Employers
Barnes & Thornburg (Chairman, Federal Relations Group)

Clients Represented
On Behalf of Barnes & Thornburg
Wheat Gluten Industry Council

TAYLOR, Jeremy

1275 Pennsylvania Ave. NW
Suite 800
Washington, DC 20004
Tel: (202)347-8866
Fax: (202)347-0055

Employers
Direct Selling Education Foundation (Exec. Director)

TAYLOR, Jerry

1000 Massachusetts Ave. NW
Washington, DC 20001
Tel: (202)842-0200
Fax: (202)842-3490

Employers
Cato Institute (Director, Natural Resource Studies)

TAYLOR, Brig. Gen. Joe

The Pentagon
Room 2C631
Washington, DC 20310-1600
Tel: (703)695-6368
Fax: (703)614-7599

Employers
Department of Army (Deputy Chief, Legislative Liaison)

TAYLOR, John E.

733 15th St. NW
Suite 540
Washington, DC 20005
Tel: (202)628-8866
Fax: (202)628-9800

Employers
Nat'l Community Reinvestment Coalition (President and Chief Exec. Officer)

TAYLOR, Judith A.

1120 20th St. NW
Suite 700 North
Washington, DC 20036-3406
Tel: (202)973-1200
Fax: (202)973-1212

Employers
Hall, Estill, Hardwick, Gable, Golden & Nelson (Associate)

TAYLOR, Julia A.

1900 Duke St.
Suite 200
Alexandria, VA 22314
Tel: (703)299-1050
Fax: (703)299-1044
Registered: LDA
EMail: taylorj@asco.org

Employers
American Soc. of Clinical Oncology (Deputy Director, Public Policy)

TAYLOR, Katherine R.

3000 K St. NW
Suite 300
Washington, DC 20007
Tel: (202)424-7500
Fax: (202)424-7643
Registered: LDA

Employers
Swidler Berlin Shereff Friedman, LLP (Associate)

Clients Represented
On Behalf of Swidler Berlin Shereff Friedman, LLP
Coalition to Ensure Responsible Billing
Florida Power and Light Co.
Merrill Lynch & Co., Inc.
Philip Morris Management Corp.
Suiza Foods Corp.
US Airways

TAYLOR, Kathleen

124 N. Alfred St.
Alexandria, VA 22314
Tel: (703)548-9688
Fax: (703)548-9836
EMail: ktaylor@nfrw.org

Employers
Nat'l Federation of Republican Women (Political Director)

TAYLOR, Kelley

1904 Association Dr.
Reston, VA 20191
Tel: (703)860-0200
Fax: (703)476-5432
EMail: taylork@nassp.org

Employers
Nat'l Ass'n of Secondary School Principals (General Counsel)

TAYLOR, Mark R.

1909 K St. NW
Washington, DC 20006
Tel: (202)263-3000
Fax: (202)263-3300
Registered: LDA

Employers
Mayer, Brown & Platt (Partner)

TAYLOR, Michael

1616 P St. NW
Washington, DC 20036
Tel: (202)328-5000
Fax: (202)939-3460

Employers
Resources for the Future (Director, Center for Risk Management)

TAYLOR, Michael

733 15th St. NW
Suite 956
Washington, DC 20005
Tel: (202)393-0703
Fax: (202)347-1383

Employers
Nat'l Committee for a Human Life Amendment (Exec. Director)

TAYLOR, Nancy E.

800 Connecticut Ave. NW
Suite 500
Washington, DC 20006
Tel: (202)331-3133
Fax: (202)261-0133
Registered: LDA
EMail: taylorn@gtlaw.com
Former Health Policy Director, Senate Committee on Labor and Human Resources and former Aide to Senator Orrin Hatch (R-UT).

Employers
Greenberg Traurig, LLP (Shareholder)

Clients Represented
On Behalf of Greenberg Traurig, LLP
American Health Care Ass'n
American Speech, Language, and Hearing Ass'n
The Business Roundtable
Community Health Systems, Inc.
Coors Brewing Company
Fresenius Medical Care North America
Genzyme Corp.
Healtheon/Web MD
Humana Inc.
LifePoint Hospitals, Inc.
Nat'l Ass'n for the Support of Long Term Care
Nat'l Ass'n of Community Health Centers
Nat'l Ass'n of Computer Consultant Businesses
Nat'l Center for Genome Research
Province Healthcare, Inc.
Uniroyal Technology Corp.

TAYLOR, Patricia A.

7121 Sycamore Ave.
Takoma Park, MD 20912
Tel: (301)270-6105
Fax: (301)270-4207
Registered: LDA

Employers
Self-employed as an independent consultant.

Clients Represented
As an independent consultant
Seedco

TAYLOR, Peggy

815 16th St. NW
Washington, DC 20006
Tel: (202)637-5090
Fax: (202)637-5058
Registered: LDA

Employers
AFL-CIO (American Federation of Labor and Congress of Industrial Organizations) (Director, Legislation Department)

TAYLOR, Peter S.

303 Massachusetts Ave. NE
Washington, DC 20002
Tel: (202)544-1353
Fax: (202)544-0620
Registered: LDA
EMail: dtanet@aol.com
Staff Counsel, Senate Select Committee on Indian Affairs, 1977-92.

Employers
Ducheneaux, Taylor & Associates, Inc. (Partner)

Clients Represented
On Behalf of Ducheneaux, Taylor & Associates, Inc.
The Ashley Group
Gila River Farms
Mni-Sose Intertribal Water Rights Coalition
Rosebud Sioux Tribal Council
Timbisha Shoshone Tribe

TAYLOR, Ray

1740 N St. NW
Washington, DC 20036
Tel: (202)775-4667
Fax: (202)223-1297
Registered: LDA
EMail: rtaylor@acct.org

Employers
Ass'n of Community College Trustees (President and Chief Exec. Officer)

TAYLOR, Rebecca L.

1401 New York Ave.
Suite 600
Washington, DC 20005
Tel: (202)434-9100
Registered: LDA

Employers
Leftwich & Douglas

TAYLOR, Richard L.

1600 I St. NW
Washington, DC 20006
Tel: (202)293-1966
Fax: (202)296-7410

Employers
Motion Picture Ass'n of America (V. President, Public Affairs)

TAYLOR, Robert K.

2550 M St. NW
Washington, DC 20037-1350
Tel: (202)457-6000
Fax: (202)457-6315
EMail: rtaylor@pattonboggs.com

Employers
Patton Boggs, LLP (Partner)

TAYLOR, Sandra E.

1250 H St. NW
Suite 800
Washington, DC 20005
Tel: (202)857-3464
Fax: (202)857-3401
Registered: LDA

Employers
Eastman Kodak Co. (V. President and Director, Public Affairs)

TAYLOR, Sarah

425 I St. NW
Room 7030
Washington, DC 20536
Tel: (202)514-5231
Fax: (202)514-1117

Employers
Department of Justice - Immigration and Naturalization Service (Director, Congressional Legislation Branch)

TAYLOR, Sarah E.

1201 Pennsylvania Ave. NW
Washington, DC 20004-2401
Tel: (202)662-6000
Fax: (202)662-6291
Registered: LDA
EMail: staylor@cov.com

Employers
Covington & Burling (Of Counsel)

TAYLOR, Sharon

1299 Pennsylvania Ave. NW
Suite 800 West
Washington, DC 20004
Tel: (202)785-0500
Fax: (202)785-5277
Registered: LDA

Employers
The Carmen Group

Clients Represented
On Behalf of The Carmen Group
Dillard University
Illinois Department of Transportation

TAYLOR, Susan

1701 20th St. NW
Washington, DC 20009
Tel: (202)667-6404
Fax: (202)667-6314
EMail: suetaylor1@juno.com

Employers
Church of Scientology Internat'l (Director, Public Affairs)

TAYLOR, Tracy D.

1155 21st St. NW
Suite 300
Washington, DC 20036
Tel: (202)659-8201
Fax: (202)659-5249
Registered: LDA
EMail: tdtaylor@wms-jen.com

Employers
Williams & Jensen, P.C. (Associate)

Clients Represented
On Behalf of Williams & Jensen, P.C.
AOL Time Warner
Gateway, Inc.
Reuters America Inc.

TAYLOR, Tracy L.

2300 Clarendon Blvd.
Suite 610
Arlington, VA 22201-3367
Tel: (703)351-5666
Fax: (703)351-5667
Registered: LDA
EMail: ttaylor@golinharris.com

Employers
Golin/Harris Internat'l (Senior Account Exec.)

TAYLOR, William L.

2000 M St. NW
Suite 400
Washington, DC 20036
Tel: (202)659-5565
Fax: (202)223-5302
EMail: bt@wtlaw.com

Employers
Citizens' Commission on Civil Rights (V. Chairman)

TAYLOR, III, William W.

1201 Connecticut Ave. NW
Suite 600
Washington, DC 20036
Tel: (202)778-1800
Fax: (202)822-8106
Registered: LDA
EMail: wwtaylor@zsgtk.com
Law Clerk to Chief Judge Caleb M. Wright, U.S. District Court for the District of Delaware, 1969-70.

Employers
Zuckerman Spaeder L.L.P. (Partner)

Clients Represented
On Behalf of Zuckerman Spaeder L.L.P.
Internat'l Brotherhood of Teamsters
Oneida Indian Nation of New York

TAYLOR KIDD, Ruth

800 Third St. NE
Washington, DC 20002
Tel: (202)675-4144
Fax: (202)675-4140

Employers
Capital Children's Museum (Director, Finance and External Relations)

TEAGUE, Jeff

501 Capitol Ct. NE
Suite 200
Washington, DC 20002
Tel: (202)544-9200
Fax: (202)547-2929
EMail: jteague@newdem.org

Employers
New Democrat Network (V. President, Development)

TEASLEY, Mary Elizabeth

1201 16th St. NW
Washington, DC 20036
Tel: (202)833-4000
Registered: LDA

Employers
Nat'l Education Ass'n of the U.S. (Director, Government Relations)

TEATOR, William R.

801 Pennsylvania Ave. NW
Suite 750
Washington, DC 20004
Tel: (202)628-3750
Fax: (202)624-0659
Registered: LDA
EMail: billteator@solomongroup.com
Press Secretary and Senior Legislative Assistant to Rep. Gerald B. H. Solomon (R-NY), 1994-98.

Employers
The Solomon Group, LLC (Senior Director, Public and Media Affairs)

Clients Represented
On Behalf of The Solomon Group, LLC
Apria Healthcare Group
Ass'n of Small Business Development Centers
Clough, Harbour & Associates LLP
Finch-Pruyn Paper Co.
General Electric Co.
Institute for Entrepreneurship
Nat'l Milk Producers Federation
States Ratification Committee
SUNY Empire State College
The Vandervort Group, LLC

TECKLENBURG, Michael

3417 Volta Pl. NW
Washington, DC 20007
Tel: (202)337-5220
Fax: (202)337-8314

Employers
Alexander Graham Bell Ass'n for the Deaf (President)
South Carolina, Washington Office of the State of (Director, Washington Office of the Governor)

TECKLER, Martin D.

600 14th St. NW
Suite 500
Washington, DC 20005
Tel: (202)220-1200
Fax: (202)220-1665
Former Deputy General Counsel, United States Small Business Administration.

Employers
Pepper Hamilton LLP (Counsel)

TECTON, Mike

1469 Spring Vale Ave.
McLean, VA 22101
Tel: (703)356-5800
Fax: (703)893-7945

Employers
Thomas Jefferson Equal Tax Soc. (President)

TEDESCHI, George

1900 L St. NW
Ninth Floor
Washington, DC 20036
Tel: (202)462-1400
Fax: (202)721-0600
EMail: gtedeschi@gciu.org

Employers
Graphic Communications Internat'l Union (President)

TEDROW, Sally M.

4748 Wisconsin Ave. NW
Washington, DC 20016
Tel: (202)362-0041

Employers
O'Donoghue & O'Donoghue

TEEL, Keith A.

1201 Pennsylvania Ave. NW
Washington, DC 20004-2401
Tel: (202)662-6000
Fax: (202)662-6291
Registered: LDA
EMail: kteel@cov.com

Employers
Covington & Burling (Partner)

Clients Represented
On Behalf of Covington & Burling
Loews Corp.

TEELEY, Peter B.

1300 I St. NW
Suite 470 East
Washington, DC 20005
Tel: (202)354-6100
Fax: (202)289-7448
Registered: LDA
Former U.S. Ambassador to Canada. Press Secretary to the Vice President, Executive Office of the President, The White House, 1980-85. Press Secretary to Senator Jacob Javits (R-NY), 1974-77. Press Secretary to Senator Robert P. Griffin (R-MI), 1970-74.

Employers
Amgen (Government Affairs)

TEEPELL, Timothy

119 C St. SE
Washington, DC 20003

Employers
Home School PAC (Contact)

TEGGE, Dr. Andreas

1020 19th St. NW
Suite 850
Washington, DC 20036
Tel: (202)452-9100
Fax: (202)452-9555

Employers
Deutsche Telekom, Inc. (Managing Director)

TEICH, Albert H.

1200 New York Ave. NW
Washington, DC 20005
Tel: (202)326-6400
Fax: (202)371-9526

Employers
American Ass'n for the Advancement of Science (Director, Science and Policy Programs)

TEICHER, Howard R.

4331 Reno Rd. NW
Washington, DC 20008
Tel: (202)244-8500
Fax: (202)244-8165
Registered: LDA
National Security Council staff, 1982-87; Department of State, 1981-82; Office of the Secretary of Defense, 1978-81; Department of State, 1977-78.

Employers
Teicher Consulting and Representation (Principal)

Clients Represented
On Behalf of Teicher Consulting and Representation
Coleman Research Corp.
Rafael U.S.A., Inc.
Sony Trans Com
WESCAM

TEITELBAUM, David E.

1722 I St. NW
Washington, DC 20006
Tel: (202)736-8000
Fax: (202)736-8711
EMail: dteitelb@sidley.com
Law Clerk to Judge William A. Norris, U.S. Court of Appeals, Ninth Circuit, 1986-87.

Employers
Sidley & Austin (Partner)

TEIXEIRA, Kathleen

7910 Woodmont Ave.
Suite 700
Bethesda, MD 20814
Tel: (301)654-2055
Fax: (301)654-5920
Registered: LDA

Employers
American Gastroenterological Ass'n (Director, Government Affairs)

TEIXEIRA, Ruy

1755 Massachusetts Ave. NW
Suite 400
Washington, DC 20036
Tel: (202)387-0400
Fax: (202)483-9430
EMail: teixeira@tcf.org

Employers
The Century Foundation (Senior Fellow)

TEJADA, Claudia

1101 14th St. NW
Suite 1400
Washington, DC 20005
Tel: (202)682-9400
Fax: (202)682-1331
Registered: LDA

Employers
Defenders of Wildlife (Program Associate)

TELECKY, Ph.D., Teresa

2100 L St. NW
Washington, DC 20037
Tel: (202)452-1100
Fax: (202)778-6132

Employers
Humane Soc. of the United States (Director, Wildlife Trade Program)

TELGARSKY, Jeffrey P.

2100 M St. NW
Washington, DC 20037
Tel: (202)833-7200
Fax: (202)429-0687

Employers
The Urban Institute (Director, International Activities Center)

TELHAMI, Shibley

1775 Massachusetts Ave. NW
Washington, DC 20036-2188
Tel: (202)797-6000
Fax: (202)797-6004

Employers
The Brookings Institution (Nonresident Senior Fellow, Foreign Policy Studies)

TELLALIAN, Christina

1200 G. St. NW
Suite 800
Washington, DC 20005
Tel: (202)434-8994
Fax: (202)783-4513
Registered: LDA
EMail: christina.tellalian@am.sony.com
Former Aide to Sen. Michael DeWine (R-OH) and Rep. Ileana Ros-Lehtinen (R-FL).

Employers
Sony Electronics, Inc. (Sr. Manager, Public and Government Affairs)

TELLER, Ellen S.

1875 Connecticut Ave. NW
Suite 540
Washington, DC 20009
Tel: (202)986-2200
Ext: 3013
Fax: (202)986-2525
Registered: LDA
EMail: eteller@frac.org

Employers
Child Nutrition Forum, c/o FRAC (Director, Government Affairs)
Food Research and Action Center (Director, Government Affairs)

TELLO, Beth

1820 N. Fort Myer Dr.
Suite 804
Arlington, VA 22209
Tel: (703)351-6301
Fax: (703)351-6417

Employers
McDermott Internat'l, Inc./Babcock & Wilcox (Office Manager)

TEMENAK, James M.

3190 Fairview Park Dr.
Falls Church, VA 22042
Tel: (703)876-3000
Fax: (703)876-3600
Registered: LDA

Employers
General Dynamics Corp. (Staff V. President, Marine Systems)

TEMKIN, Susan O.

901 15th St. NW
Suite 700
Washington, DC 20005-2301
Tel: (202)371-6000
Fax: (202)371-6279
Registered: LDA
EMail: sotemkin@verner.com
Law Clerk to Judge Mead Whitaker, U.S. Tax Court, 1983-85. Attorney/Advisor, Interpretative Division, Office of Chief Counsel, Internal Revenue Service, Department of Transportation, 1981-83.

Employers
Verner, Liipfert, Bernhard, McPherson and Hand, Chartered (Member of Firm)

TEMKO, Stanley L.

1201 Pennsylvania Ave. NW
Washington, DC 20004-2401
Tel: (202)662-6000
Fax: (202)662-6291
EMail: stemko@cov.com
Law Clerk to Justice Wiley Rutledge, U.S. Supreme Court, 1947-48.

Employers
Covington & Burling (Partner)

TEMPLE, Riley K.

555 12th St. NW
Suite 950 North
Washington, DC 20004
Tel: (202)371-9100
Fax: (202)371-1497
Registered: LDA
Legislative Assistant to Senator Charles McC. Mathias (R-MD), 1977-78. Communications Counsel, Senate Committee on Commerce, Science & Transportation, 198-83.

Employers
Halprin, Temple, Goodman & Maher (Partner)

Clients Represented
On Behalf of Halprin, Temple, Goodman & Maher
Telcordia Technologies, Inc.
Verizon Communications

TEMPLER, Erin

4121 Wilson Blvd.
Tenth Floor
Arlington, VA 22203
Tel: (703)351-2033
Fax: (703)351-2001

Employers
Nat'l Telephone Cooperative Ass'n (PAC Coordinator)

TEMPLETON, Patrick A.

1801 K St. NW
Suite 901L
Washington, DC 20006
Tel: (202)530-0500
Fax: (202)530-4800
EMail: pat_templeton@bm.com

Employers
Coalinga Corp. (Washington Representative)

TEMPLETON, Patrick A.

1801 K St. NW
Suite 901-L
Washington, DC 20006
Tel: (202)530-0500
Fax: (202)530-4800
Registered: LDA
EMail: pat_templeton@bm.com
Associate Administrator, External Affairs, Nat'l Aeronautics and Space Administration, 1981-84.

Employers
BKSH & Associates (Senior Consultant)
Templeton & Co. (President)

TENENBAUM, Ellen S.

600 13th St. NW
Washington, DC 20005-3096
Tel: (202)756-8274
Fax: (202)756-8087
EMail: etenenbaum@mwe.com

Employers
McDermott, Will and Emery (Partner)

TENENBAUM, Jeffrey S.

1201 New York Ave. NW
Suite 1000
Washington, DC 20005
Tel: (202)216-8138
Fax: (202)962-8300
EMail: jstenenbaum@venable.com

Employers
Venable (Of Counsel)

Clients Represented
On Behalf of Venable
Academy of Radiology Research
Air Conditioning Contractors of America
Ass'n of Clinical Research Professionals
Brazelton Foundation
Center for Energy and Economic Development
Child Welfare League of America
Institute of Navigation
Internat'l Council of Cruise Lines
Internat'l Municipal Signal Ass'n
Maryland Psychiatric Soc.
Nat'l Ass'n of Chain Drug Stores
Nat'l Coalition for Cancer Survivorship
Nat'l Council of University Research Administrators
Nat'l Electrical Safety Foundation
Special Libraries Ass'n

TENNANT, Claudette

1301 Pennsylvania Ave. NW
Suite 403
Washington, DC 20004
Tel: (202)628-8410
Fax: (202)628-8419
Registered: LDA
EMail: cwt@alawash.org

Employers
American Library Ass'n (Assistant Director)

TENNANT, William S.

1850 M St. NW
Suite 400
Washington, DC 20036
Tel: (202)293-8200
Fax: (202)872-0145
Registered: LDA
Assistant Chief Counsel, Urban Renewal (1961-62), Assistant to the General Counsel (1961), and Attorney (1958-61), Federal Housing Administration.

Employers
Krooth & Altman (Of Counsel)

Clients Represented
On Behalf of Krooth & Altman
Healthcare Financing Study Group

TENNES, Lauren

1101 Pennsylvania Ave. NW
Suite 950
Washington, DC 20004
Tel: (202)434-8600
Fax: (202)434-8626

Employers
Federal Home Loan Mortgage Corp. (Freddie Mac) (Director, Government Relations)

TENOEVER, Katie

1101 Vermont Ave. NW
12th Floor
Washington, DC 20005-3583
Tel: (202)789-4589
Fax: (202)789-7401
Registered: LDA

Employers
American Medical Ass'n (Washington Counsel)

TEODORSKI, Bernard

309 Massachusetts Ave. NE
Washington, DC 20002
Tel: (202)547-8189
Fax: (202)547-8190
Registered: LDA

Employers
Fraternal Order of Police (Chairman, National Legislative Committee)

TEPLITZ, Steven N.

1101 Connecticut Ave. NW
Suite 400
Washington, DC 20036-4303
Tel: (202)530-7883
Fax: (202)530-7879
Registered: LDA

Employers
AOL Time Warner (V. President, Telecommunications Policy)

TEPP, Ronnie Kovner

426 C St. NE
Washington, DC 20002
Tel: (202)544-1880
Fax: (202)543-2565
Registered: LDA
EMail: rk@capitolassociates.com
Former Senior Legislative Assistant to Rep. Jack Reed (D-RI), 1990-95.

Employers
Capitol Associates, Inc. (Associate)

Clients Represented
On Behalf of Capitol Associates, Inc.
Bermuda Biological Station for Research
Fishers Island Ferry District
Nat'l Coalition for Cancer Research
Neurofibromatosis
New York Botanical Garden
New York University Medical Center
NF Inc. - Mass Bay Area
Northwestern Memorial Hospital
Texas NF Foundation
University of Pennsylvania/School of Dental Medicine

TEPPER, Gary C.

1050 Connecticut Ave. NW
Washington, DC 20036-5339
Tel: (202)857-6000
Fax: (202)857-6395
Registered: LDA

Employers
Arent Fox Kintner Plotkin & Kahn, PLLC (Member)

TERESI, Toni P.

700 Army Navy Dr.
MS: 12104
Arlington, VA 22202
Tel: (202)307-7423
Fax: (202)307-5512
EMail: cp-1@worldnet.att.net
Executive Assistant, Office of the Administrator/Deputy Administrator (1999-2000); Country Attache to the Bahamas (1994-99); Group Supervisor, West Palm Beach, FL Resident Office (1992-94); Special Agent, Fort Lauderdale, FL and Office of Training, Chicago, San Diego, and Albuquerque (1983-92); Special Operations, Bolivia and Panama (1987-89), all with the Drug Enforcement Administration.

Employers
Department of Justice - Drug Enforcement Administration (Chief, Congressional Affairs Section, Office of Congressional and Public Affairs)

TERHAAR, Allen A.

1521 New Hampshire Ave. NW
Washington, DC 20036
Tel: (202)745-7805
Fax: (202)483-4040
EMail: aterhaar@cotton.org

Employers
Cotton Council Internat'l (Exec. Director)

TERHUNE, Henry A.

1333 New Hampshire Ave. NW
Suite 400
Washington, DC 20036
Tel: (202)887-4000
Fax: (202)887-4288
Registered: LDA, FARA
Associate Staff Member, House Committee on Rules, 1984-87. Legislative Assistant and Director to Rep. Butler Derrick (D-SC), 1979-87.

Employers
Akin, Gump, Strauss, Hauer & Feld, L.L.P. (Partner)

Clients Represented
On Behalf of Akin, Gump, Strauss, Hauer & Feld, L.L.P.
American Amateur Karate Federation
Barrick Goldstrike Mines, Inc.
CalEnergy Co., Inc.
Capital Gaming Internat'l, Inc.
Cummins Engine Co.
Exxon Mobil Corp.
Howland Hook Container Terminal Inc.
Internat'l Karate Federation
The Robert Mondavi Winery
NiSource Inc.
Pfizer, Inc.
PG&E Corp.

TERMAN, Stephen D.

1400 16th St. NW
Suite 400
Washington, DC 20036-2220
EMail: sterman@ofwlaw.com
Tel: (202)518-6369
Fax: (202)234-0399

Associate Chief Counsel for Enforcement, Food and Drug Administration, 1976-87.

Employers
Olsson, Frank and Weeda, P.C. (Principal)

Clients Represented

On Behalf of Olsson, Frank and Weeda, P.C.
Ass'n of Medical Device Reprocessors

TERPELUK, Jr., Peter

2099 Pennsylvania Ave. NW
Suite 850
Washington, DC 20006
EMail: Terpeluk@acgrep.com
Tel: (202)419-2500
Fax: (202)419-2510
Registered: LDA

Served as Deputy National Administrator, and Regional Administrator for the Mid-Atlantic region of the Small Business Administration, 1981-84.

Employers
American Continental Group, Inc. (Managing Director)

Clients Represented

On Behalf of American Continental Group, Inc.
Ass'n of American Railroads
Campaign for Tobacco-Free Kids
EEI
Ernst & Young LLP
IMAX Corp.
Northpoint Technology, Ltd.
Pennsylvania Higher Education Assistance Agency
PepsiCo, Inc.
Prudential Insurance Co. of America
Public Financial Management
Siemens Corp.
Southeastern Pennsylvania Transit Authority

TERPSTRA, Ellen

4301 N. Fairfax Dr.
Suite 305
Arlington, VA 22203-1616
Tel: (703)351-8161
Fax: (703)351-8162
Registered: LDA

Employers
USA Rice Federation (President/Chief Exec. Officer)

TERPSTRA, Grace

1111 19th St. NW
12th Floor
Washington, DC 20036-4503
Tel: (202)828-9487
Fax: (202)828-8405
Registered: LDA

Employers
Nat'l Hardwood Lumber Ass'n (PAC Contact)
Terpstra Associates (Principal)

Clients Represented

On Behalf of Terpstra Associates
American Forest & Paper Ass'n
Chesapeake Corp.
Fort James Corp.
Nat'l Hardwood Lumber Ass'n

TERRELL, Joseph

2111 Wilson Blvd.
Suite 700
Arlington, VA 22201
Tel: (703)351-5055
Fax: (703)351-6698

Employers
American Sugar Alliance (Director, Public Affairs)

TERRY, Paul W.

1133 Connecticut Ave. NW
Suite 1200
Washington, DC 20036
Tel: (202)775-9800
Fax: (202)833-8491

Employers
Winthrop, Stimson, Putnam & Roberts (Associate)

TERRY, Sybil

444 N. Capitol St. NW
Suite 142
Washington, DC 20001
Tel: (202)431-8020
Fax: (202)434-8033

Employers
Nat'l Ass'n of State Workforce Agencies (Equal Opportunity Director)

TERWILLIGER, III, George J.

601 13th St. NW
Suite 600 South
Washington, DC 20005
Tel: (202)626-3600
Fax: (202)639-9355

Deputy Attorney General (1991-93), U.S. Attorney (1986-91) and Assistant U.S. Attorney for the District of Columbia (1978-81), Department of Justice.

Employers
White & Case LLP

TESKE, Judi A.

1300 I St. NW
Suite 470 East
Washington, DC 20005
EMail: jteske@amgen.com
Tel: (202)354-6100
Fax: (202)289-7448
Registered: LDA

Employers
Amgen (Senior Director, Reimbursement and Strategic Alliances)

TESLER, Shana

800 Connecticut Ave. NW
Suite 500
Washington, DC 20006
Tel: (202)331-3100
Fax: (202)331-3101
Registered: LDA

Employers
Greenberg Traurig, LLP

Clients Represented

On Behalf of Greenberg Traurig, LLP
E-Commerce Coalition
E-Commerce Payment Coalition
Healtheon/Web MD
Starnet Communications Internat'l

TESLIK, Sarah A. B.

1730 Rhode Island Ave. NW
Suite 512
Washington, DC 20036
Tel: (202)822-0800
Fax: (202)822-0801
Registered: LDA

Employers
Council of Institutional Investors (Exec. Director)

TESNOW, David

2800 Shirlington Rd.
Suite 401
Arlington, VA 22206
EMail: davetesnow@asic.-dc.com
Tel: (703)824-0300
Fax: (703)824-0320

Employers
American Systems Internat'l Corp. (Consultant)

TESSIER, Missi

1001 G St. NW
Suite 900 E
Washington, DC 20001-4545
EMail: tessier@podesta.com
Tel: (202)393-1010
Fax: (202)393-5510

Communications Director and Press Secretary to Senator Kay Bailey Hutchison (R-TX), 1994-96. Press Secretary to Rep. Robert H. Michel (R-IL), 1989-94. Press Secretary to Rep. Silvio O. Conte (R-MA), 1978-85.

Employers
Podesta/Mattoon (Principal)

Clients Represented

On Behalf of Podesta/Mattoon
Friends of Cancer Research
Mount Sinai/NYU Health
NCI Coalition

TETER, Harry

8903 Presidential Pkwy.
Suite 512
Upper Marlboro, MD 20772-2656
Tel: (301)420-4189
Fax: (301)420-0617

Employers
American Trauma Soc. (Exec. Director and General Counsel)

TETT, Lois

901 New Jersey Ave. NW
Washington, DC 20001-1133
EMail: latett@yahoo.com
Tel: (202)326-9170
Registered: LDA

Employers
Tett Enterprises (Consultant)

TEWS, Shane

505 Huntmar Park Dr.
Herndon, VA 20170
Tel: (703)742-0400

Employers
VeriSign/Network Solutions, Inc. (Director, Public Policy)

TFURUMI, Kunio

800 Connecticut Ave. NW
Suite 1000
Washington, DC 20006
Tel: (202)785-9210
Fax: (202)861-0690

Employers
Sumitomo Corp. of America (General Manager)

THALER, Brad

3138 N. Tenth St.
Arlington, VA 22201
Tel: (703)522-4770
Fax: (703)522-0594
Registered: LDA

Employers
Nat'l Ass'n of Federal Credit Unions (Associate Director, Legislative Affairs)

THARP, Marjorie

601 13th St. NW
Suite 400 North
Washington, DC 20005
EMail: mtharp@aap.org
Tel: (202)347-8600
Fax: (202)393-6137
Registered: LDA

Employers
American Academy of Pediatrics (Manager, Public Affairs)
Coalition for America's Children (Chair)

THARPE, Ed.D., Don I.

11401 N. Shore Dr.
Reston, VA 20190-4200
Tel: (703)478-0405
Fax: (703)478-6968

Employers
Ass'n of School Business Officials Internat'l (Exec. Director)

THATCHER, Mary Kay

600 Maryland Ave. SW
Suite 800
Washington, DC 20024
Tel: (202)484-3600
Fax: (202)484-3604
Registered: LDA

Employers
American Farm Bureau Federation (Deputy Director, Agriculture Policy/Budget/Taxes/Commodities/Trade)

THAU, Susan R.

6217 29th St. NW
Washington, DC 20015
Tel: (202)966-4361
Registered: LDA

Employers
Self-employed as an independent consultant.

Clients Represented

As an independent consultant
Community Anti-Drug Coalitions of America

THAXTON, Richard R.

5112 Althea Dr.
Annandale, VA 22003
Tel: (703)425-5720
Fax: (703)425-2119
Registered: LDA

Employers
Self-employed as an independent consultant.

Clients Represented

As an independent consultant
ANADAC
Chibank Service Inc.

THELIAN, Lorraine

2000 L St. NW
Suite 300
Washington, DC 20036-0646
Tel: (202)835-8800
Fax: (202)835-8879

Employers
Ketchum (Sr. Partner, North America)

THEVENOT, E. Wayne

1432 Fenwick Lane
Suite 200
Silver Spring, MD 20910
EMail: wthevenot@theeca.org
Tel: (301)608-9600

Executive Assistant to Senator Russell Long (D-LA), 1963-1975

Employers
Electronic Commerce Ass'n (President)

THEVENOT, Laura Ison

801 Pennsylvania Ave. NW
Suite 245
Washington, DC 20004-2604
EMail: thevenot@fahs.com
Tel: (202)624-1531
Fax: (202)737-6462
Registered: LDA

Administrative Officer, Senate Select Committee on Secret Military Assistance to Iran and Nicaraguan Opposition, 1986.

Employers
Federation of American Hospitals (Exec. V. President and Chief Operating Officer)

THIBAU, Janelle C. M.

1455 Pennsylvania Ave. NW
Suite 950
Washington, DC 20004-1087
Tel: (202)661-7100
Fax: (202)661-7110
Registered: LDA

Employers
Merrill Lynch & Co., Inc. (V. President, Government Relations)

THIEL, Brian

1755 Jefferson Davis Hwy.
Suite 1107
Arlington, VA 22202
Tel: (703)415-0344
Fax: (703)415-0182
Registered: LDA

Employers
The PMA Group (Director)

Clients Represented

On Behalf of The PMA Group

Alliance
ARC Global Technologies
Battelle
CHIM
CRYPTEK Secure Communications, LLC
Dynamics Research Corp.
Environmental Technology Unlimited
Foundation Health Federal Services, Inc.
IIT Research Institute
Joint Healthcare Information Technology Alliance
McLean Hospital
Microvision, Inc.
Planning Systems, Inc.
SIGCOM, Inc.
Stanly County Airport Authority
Triosyn Corp.
University Emergency Medicine Foundation

THIELEN, Michael B.

727 Second St. NE
Washington, DC 20002
Tel: (202)544-2600
Fax: (202)544-7760
Registered: LDA

Employers
CapitolWatch (Legislative Director)

THIEMANN, Alan J.

908 King St.
Suite 300
Alexandria, VA 22314
EMail: ajthiemann@law.com
Tel: (703)836-9400
Fax: (703)836-9410
Registered: LDA

Employers
Thiemann Aitken Vohra & Rutledge, L.L.C. (Member)

Clients Represented

On Behalf of Thiemann Aitken Vohra & Rutledge, L.L.C.

Ass'n of Test Publishers
McGraw-Hill Cos., The

THIERER, Adam D.

1000 Massachusetts Ave. NW
Washington, DC 20001
Tel: (202)842-0200
Fax: (202)842-3490

Employers
Cato Institute (Director, Telecommunications Studies)

THIES, Gregory A.

601 13th St. NW
Suite 200 North
Washington, DC 20005
Tel: (202)682-9462
Registered: LDA

Employers
BASF Corporation (Manager, Government Relations)

THIESSEN, Joe

1615 H St. NW
Washington, DC 20062-2000
Tel: (202)659-6000
Fax: (202)463-5836

Employers
Chamber of Commerce of the U.S.A. (Director, Congressional and Public Affairs)

THISTLE, Kirsten

1615 L St. NW
Suite 900
Washington, DC 20036
EMail: kthistle@apcoworldwide.com
Tel: (202)778-1000
Fax: (202)466-6002

Employers
APCO Worldwide (V. President, Public Affairs)

THODEN, Philip E.

333 John Carlyle St.
Suite 200
Alexandria, VA 22314
Tel: (703)837-5364
Registered: LDA

Employers
Associated General Contractors of America (Director, Congressional Relations/Tax and Fiscal Affairs)

THOM, Edlu J.

700 13th St. NW
Suite 950
Washington, DC 20005
EMail: edlu.thom@lyondell.com
Tel: (202)434-8938
Fax: (202)434-4585
Registered: LDA

Employers
Lyondell Chemical Co. (Director, Government Affairs)

THOMAS, Amber L.

7901 Westpark Dr.
McLean, VA 22102-4206
EMail: alp@mfgtech.org
Tel: (703)827-5230
Fax: (703)749-2742
Registered: LDA

Employers
The Ass'n For Manufacturing Technology (AMT) (Legislative Analyst)

THOMAS, Cindy

1990 M St. NW
Suite 340
Washington, DC 20036
Tel: (202)223-6222
Fax: (202)785-0687
Registered: LDA

Employers
Kent & O'Connor, Inc. (Attorney)

Clients Represented

On Behalf of Kent & O'Connor, Inc.

Ball Research, Inc.
Condea Vista Chemical Co.
GlaxoSmithKline
Internat'l Trademark Ass'n
Internat'l Warehouse Logistics Ass'n
Liz Claiborne Internat'l
Nat'l Customs Brokers and Forwarders Ass'n of America

THOMAS, David

2300 Wilson Blvd.
Arlington, VA 22201
EMail: dthomas@navyleague.org
Tel: (703)528-1775
Fax: (703)528-2333
Registered: LDA

Employers
Navy League of the United States (Senior Director of Communications)

THOMAS, David R.

600 Pennsylvania Ave. NW
MS: 406
Washington, DC 20580
EMail: dthomas@ftc.gov
Tel: (202)326-2468
Fax: (202)326-3585

Employers
Federal Trade Commission (Director, Office of Congressional Relations)

THOMAS, Frances

11 Dupont Circle NW
Suite 800
Washington, DC 20036
Tel: (202)588-5180
Fax: (202)588-5185

Employers
Nat'l Women's Law Center (V. President and Director, Administration and Finance)

THOMAS, Gordon M.

1101 Pennsylvania Ave. NW
Suite 400
Washington, DC 20004-2504
Tel: (202)637-3821
Fax: (202)637-3863
Registered: LDA

Employers
Textron Inc. (Director, Government Affairs)

THOMAS, Greg

950 N. Washington St.
Alexandria, VA 22314-1552
Tel: (703)836-2272
Fax: (703)684-1924

Employers
American Academy of Physician Assistants (V. President, Clinical Affairs and Education)

THOMAS, Harley

801 18th St. NW
Washington, DC 20006
Tel: (202)872-1300
Fax: (202)785-4452
Registered: LDA

Employers
Paralyzed Veterans of America (Associate Legislative Director)

THOMAS, James

444 N. Capitol St. NW
Suite 622
Washington, DC 20001
Tel: (202)624-5457
Fax: (202)508-3826

Employers
Nat'l Black Caucus of State Legislators (President)

THOMAS, Jennifer

1275 K St. NW
Suite 1000
Washington, DC 20005
EMail: apicinfo@apic.org
Tel: (202)789-1890
Fax: (202)789-1899
Registered: LDA

Employers
Ass'n for Professionals in Infection Control and Epidemiology (Director, Government and Public Relations)

THOMAS, John H.

1200 18th St. NW
Second Floor
Washington, DC 20036
EMail: jt@independentsector.org
Tel: (202)467-6100
Fax: (202)467-6101

Employers
Independent Sector (V. President, Communications)

THOMAS, John W.

1660 L St. St. NW
Suite 506
Washington, DC 20036
Tel: (202)463-1260
Fax: (202)463-6328

Employers
Luman, Lange & Wheeler (Partner)

Clients Represented

On Behalf of Luman, Lange & Wheeler

Ass'n of Veterinary Biologics Cos.

THOMAS, Judy

P.O. Box 31220
4720 Montgomery Ln.
Bethesda, MD 20824-1220
Tel: (301)652-2682
Fax: (301)652-7711

Employers
American Occupational Therapy Ass'n, Inc. (Director, Reimbursement Policy Program)

THOMAS, Karen Kelly

2000 L St. NW
Suite 740
Washington, DC 20036
EMail: karenkt@awhonn.org
Tel: (202)261-2430
Fax: (202)728-0575

Employers
Ass'n of Women's Health, Obstetric and Neonatal Nurses (Deputy Exec. Director)

THOMAS, Karen M.

One Thomas Circle NW
Suite 400
Washington, DC 20005
Tel: (202)659-8111
Fax: (202)659-9216
Registered: LDA

Employers
Independent Community Bankers of America (Director of Regulatory Affairs/Senior Regulatory Counsel)

THOMAS, Kermit R.

1350 Connecticut Ave. NW
Suite 825
Washington, DC 20036
Tel: (202)466-6888
Fax: (202)466-4918
Registered: LDA

Employers
Harry C. Alford & Associates, Inc.

Clients Represented
On Behalf of Harry C. Alford & Associates, Inc.
James E. Schneider, LLM Inc.

THOMAS, Liz

122 C St. NW
Suite 240
Washington, DC 20001
Tel: (202)546-2215
Fax: (202)544-5197
Registered: LDA

Employers
Southern Utah Wilderness Alliance

THOMAS, Marti

1133 Connecticut Ave. NW
Fifth Floor
Washington, DC 20036
Tel: (202)457-1110
Fax: (202)457-1130
Former Assitant Secretary for Legislative Affairs and Public Liaison, Department of the Treasury. Former Staffer to House Minority Leader, Rep. Richard Gephardt (D-MO)

Employers
Quinn Gillespie & Associates

THOMAS, Matthew J.

1801 K St. NW
Washington, DC 20006
Tel: (202)775-0725
Fax: (202)223-8604
Former Assistant General Counsel for International Affairs, Federal Maritime Commission.

Employers
Robins, Kaplan, Miller & Ciresi L.L.P. (Associate)

THOMAS, Peter W.

1875 I St. NW
12th Floor
Washington, DC 20006
EMail: pthomas@ppsv.com
Tel: (202)466-6550
Fax: (202)785-1756
Registered: LDA

Employers
Powers Pyles Sutter & Verville, PC (Principal)

Clients Represented
On Behalf of Powers Pyles Sutter & Verville, PC
American Academy of Neurology
American Congress of Community Supports and Employment Services
American Medical Rehabilitation Providers Ass'n
Fresenius Medical Care North America
J & J Independence Technology
Nat'l Ass'n for the Advancement of Orthotics and Prosthetics

THOMAS, Randi

1101 17th St. NW
Suite 609
Washington, DC 20036
Tel: (202)857-0610
Fax: (202)331-9686

Employers
United States Tuna Foundation (National Representative)

THOMAS, Ritchie T.

1201 Pennsylvania Ave. NW
P.O. Box 407
Washington, DC 20044-0407
EMail: rthomas@ssd.com
Tel: (202)626-6600
Fax: (202)626-6780
Associate Attorney, Office of General Counsel, Tariff Commission, 1964-67.

Employers
Squire, Sanders & Dempsey L.L.P. (Partner)

Clients Represented
On Behalf of Squire, Sanders & Dempsey L.L.P.
American Chamber of Commerce in Germany
Ass'n of Research Libraries
Belgium, Embassy of the Kingdom of
Nat'l Collegiate Athletic Ass'n
Toyota Motor Corp.

THOMAS, Rosalind

810 Vermont Ave. NW
Room 515E
Washington, DC 20420
Tel: (202)224-9419
Fax: (202)273-9988

Employers
Department of Veterans Affairs (Legislative Affairs Officer)

THOMAS, Sherri

1615 L St. NW
Suite 1320
Washington, DC 20036
EMail: sthomas@feidc.org
Tel: (202)457-6202
Fax: (202)857-0230

Employers
Financial Executives International (Manager, Administration and Meetings)

THOMAS, Brig. Gen. Trent N.

9200 Centerway Rd.
Gaithersburg, MD 20879
EMail: zhi@nmia.org
Tel: (301)840-6642
Fax: (301)840-8502

Employers
Nat'l Military Intelligence Ass'n (President)

THOMAS, Virginia

214 Massachusetts Ave. NE
Washington, DC 20002
Tel: (202)546-4400
Fax: (202)546-8328

Employers
Heritage Foundation (Director, Executive Branch Relations)

THOMAS, W. David

1735 New York Ave. NW
Suite 500
Washington, DC 20006-4759
Tel: (202)628-1700
Fax: (202)331-1024
Registered: LDA

Employers
Preston Gates Ellis & Rouvelas Meeds LLP (Associate)

Clients Represented
On Behalf of Preston Gates Ellis & Rouvelas Meeds LLP
Acme Software
American Soc. for Therapeutic Radiology and Oncology
Grant County P.U.D., Washington
Seattle, Washington, Port of
Starwood Hotels & Resorts Worldwide, Inc.
VoiceStream Wireless Corp.

THOMAS, William C.

1700 Diagonal Rd.
Suite 500
Alexandria, VA 22314
EMail: bthomas@visionsite.org
Tel: (703)548-4560
Fax: (703)548-4580

Employers
Vision Council of America (Exec. V. President/Chief Exec. Officer)

THOMAS, William G.

1301 K St. NW
Suite 1100-East Tower
Washington, DC 20005
Tel: (202)414-9200
Fax: (202)414-9299
Registered: LDA

Employers
Reed, Smith, LLP (Partner)

Clients Represented
On Behalf of Reed, Smith, LLP
Dominion Resources, Inc.

THOMAS, William L.

1133 Connecticut Ave. NW
Suite 1200
Washington, DC 20036
Tel: (202)775-9800
Fax: (202)833-8491

Employers
Winthrop, Stimson, Putnam & Roberts (Associate)

THOMAS, Wylie

729 15th St. NW
Third Floor
Washington, DC 20005
Tel: (202)737-5877
Fax: (202)737-6061

Employers
Bonner Group, Inc. (National Director)

THOMASIAN, John

444 N. Capitol St. NW
Suite 267
Washington, DC 20001-1512
EMail: jthomasian@nga.org
Tel: (202)624-7881
Fax: (202)624-5313

Employers
Nat'l Governors' Ass'n (Director, Center for Best Practices)

THOMPSON, Anthony J.

2300 N St. NW
Washington, DC 20037-1128
Tel: (202)663-8000
Fax: (202)663-8007
EMail: anthony.thompson@shawpittman.com
Legal Assistant to the Chairman, Federal Communications Commission, 1973-74.

Employers
Shaw Pittman (Partner)

THOMPSON, Barbara J.

444 N. Capitol St. NW
Suite 438
Washington, DC 20001
Tel: (202)624-7710
Fax: (202)624-5899

Employers
Nat'l Council of State Housing Agencies (Director, Policy and Government Affairs)

THOMPSON, Beverly K.

811 Vermont Ave. NW
Room 1261
Washington, DC 20571
EMail: beverly.thompson@exim.gov
Tel: (202)565-3235
Fax: (202)565-3236

Employers
Export-Import Bank (Senior Legislative Analyst)

THOMPSON, Bob

717 Second St. NE
Washington, DC 20002
Tel: (202)546-3003
Fax: (202)547-0392

Employers
Coalitions for America (V. President)

THOMPSON, Brent

1275 Pennsylvania Ave. NW
Tenth Floor
Washington, DC 20004
Tel: (202)333-4936
Fax: (202)833-9392
Registered: LDA

Employers
Barbour Griffith & Rogers, Inc. (Director, Legislative Affairs)

Clients Represented
On Behalf of Barbour Griffith & Rogers, Inc.
American Trucking Ass'ns
Artists Coalition
BellSouth Telecommunications, Inc.
Broadcast Music Inc. (BMI)
GCG Partners
LVMH Moet Hennessy Louis Vuitton S.A.
Lyondell Chemical Co.
Microsoft Corp.
Oxygenated Fuels Ass'n
Southern Co.
State Street Bank and Trust Co.

THOMPSON, Jr., Bruce E.

1455 Pennsylvania Ave. NW
Suite 950
Washington, DC 20004-1087
Tel: (202)661-7100
Fax: (202)661-7110
Registered: LDA

Employers
Merrill Lynch & Co., Inc. (V. President and Director, Government Relations)

THOMPSON, Chet M.

3050 K St. NW
Washington, DC 20007
Tel: (202)342-8815
Fax: (202)342-8451
Registered: LDA
EMail: cthompso@colliershannon.com

Employers
Collier Shannon Scott, PLLC (Associate)

Clients Represented
On Behalf of Collier Shannon Scott, PLLC
Copper and Brass Fabricators Council
Copper Development Ass'n, Inc.
Metals Industry Recycling Coalition

THOMPSON, Dana S.

305 Fourth St. NE
Washington, DC 20002
Tel: (202)547-8202
Fax: (202)547-8810
Registered: LDA
EMail: DThompson@smacna.org

Employers
Sheet Metal and Air Conditioning Contractors' Nat'l Ass'n (Director, Political Affairs)

THOMPSON, David H.

1500 K St. NW
Suite 200
Washington, DC 20005
Tel: (202)220-9600
Fax: (202)220-9601

Employers
Cooper, Carvin & Rosenthal (Associate)

THOMPSON, David L.

800 Connecticut Ave. NW
Suite 600
Washington, DC 20006
Tel: (202)783-1900
Fax: (202)783-5995
Registered: LDA

Employers
Thompson & Thompson (Partner)

Clients Represented
On Behalf of Thompson & Thompson
Small Business Survival Committee

THOMPSON, Dionne E.

401 Ninth St. NW
Suite 1000
Washington, DC 20004
Tel: (202)274-2882
Fax: (202)274-2994
Registered: LDA, FARA
Legislative Counsel to Senator Mary L. Landrieu (D-LA), 1997-99; Legislative Counsel to Senator J. Bennett Johnston (D-LA), 1995-96; Department of the Interior, 1995; Senate Energy and Natural Resources Committee Staff Counsel, 1993-94

Employers
Troutman Sanders LLP (Associate)

Clients Represented
On Behalf of Troutman Sanders LLP
Canadian Electricity Ass'n
PG&E Corp.
Trigen Energy Corp.

THOMPSON, Doug

900 Second St. NE
Suite 200
Washington, DC 20002
EMail: doug@temc.com
Tel: (202)842-4100
Fax: (202)842-4442

Employers
The Eddie Mahe Company (Associate)

THOMPSON, Edward

1200 18th St. NW
Suite 800
Washington, DC 20036
Tel: (202)331-7300
Fax: (202)659-8339

Employers
American Farmland Trust (Senior V. President, Public Policy)

THOMPSON, Eric

1101 Connecticut Ave. NW
Suite 401
Washington, DC 20036
Tel: (202)296-7513
Fax: (202)296-7514
Registered: LDA

Employers
The Hartford (V. President, Federal Affairs)

THOMPSON, Griffin

1015 15th St. NW
Suite 600
Washington, DC 20005
Tel: (202)842-3388
Fax: (202)842-3388

Employers
Internat'l Institute for Energy Conservation (President)

THOMPSON, Jeffrey

1211 Connecticut Ave. NW
Suite 608
Washington, DC 20036
EMail: jthompson@qorvis.com
Tel: (202)496-1000
Fax: (202)496-1300

Employers
Qorvis Communications (Director)

THOMPSON, Kathleen O.

805 15th St. NW
Suite 300
Washington, DC 20005-2207
Tel: (202)682-4200
Fax: (202)682-9054
Registered: LDA

Employers
Credit Union Nat'l Ass'n, Inc. (Sr. V. President/Associate General Counsel, Federal Compliance and Legislative)

THOMPSON, Kenneth W.

1155 15th St. NW
Suite 902
Washington, DC 20005
Tel: (202)775-5490
Fax: (202)822-9807
Registered: LDA

Employers
Thompson and Naughton, Inc. (President)

Clients Represented
On Behalf of Thompson and Naughton, Inc.
BellSouth Corp.
General Motors Corp.
ITRON, Inc.
Process Gas Consumers Group
SEMCO

THOMPSON, Lawrence H.

2100 M St. NW
Washington, DC 20037
Tel: (202)833-7200
Fax: (202)429-0687

Employers
The Urban Institute (Senior Fellow)

THOMPSON, Lisa L.

1001 Connecticut Ave. NW
Suite 522
Washington, DC 20036
EMail: LThompson@nae.net
Tel: (202)789-1011
Fax: (202)842-0392

Employers
Nat'l Ass'n of Evangelicals (Policy Representative)

THOMPSON, Liz L.

420 Seventh St. SE
Washington, DC 20003
Tel: (202)546-3950
Fax: (202)546-3749

Employers
World Federalist Ass'n (Director, Development)

THOMPSON, Jr., Louis M.

8045 Leesburg Pike
Suite 600
Vienna, VA 22182
Tel: (703)506-3570
Fax: (703)506-3571

Employers
Nat'l Investor Relations Institute (President and Chief Exec. Officer)

THOMPSON, Marilyn Berry

1025 Thomas Jefferson St. NW
Suite 400 East
Washington, DC 20007-0805
Tel: (202)965-8120
Fax: (202)965-6403
Registered: LDA

Employers
Jorden Burt LLP (Principal and Head, Government Relations Department)

Clients Represented
On Behalf of Jorden Burt LLP
American Museum of Natural History
Assurant Group
Atlantic Health Systems
The Colonial Williamsburg Foundation
Florida State University System
Gainesville Regional Utilities
Gainesville, Florida, City of
Lovelace Respiratory Research Institute
Miami Beach, Florida, City of
New York University
Newark, New Jersey, City of
University of Medicine and Dentistry of New Jersey
University of Miami
University of Tulsa
University of Virginia

THOMPSON, Maureen

11250 Roger Bacon Dr.
Suite 8
Reston, VA 20190
EMail: emsdmg@aol.com
Tel: (703)437-4377
Fax: (703)435-4390

Employers
Ass'n of Occupational Health Professionals in Healthcare (Exec. Director)

THOMPSON, Michael F.

1101 17th St. NW
Suite 300
Washington, DC 20036
Tel: (202)331-1770
Fax: (202)331-1969
Registered: LDA

Employers
Cosmetic, Toiletry and Fragrance Ass'n (V. President, Legislative Relations)

THOMPSON, Michael J.

1200 G St. NW
Suite 600
Washington, DC 20005-3802
EMail: thompson@wrightlaw.com
Tel: (202)393-1200
Fax: (202)393-1240
Law Clerk and Attorney, Chemical Control Division, Office of Toxic Substances, Environmental Protection Agency, 1980-81.

Employers
Wright & Talisman, P.C.

Clients Represented
On Behalf of Wright & Talisman, P.C.
Kern River Gas Transmission Co.
Tejon Ranch Co.

THOMPSON, Nancy

1600 I St. NW
Washington, DC 20006
Tel: (202)293-1966
Fax: (202)296-7410

Employers
Motion Picture Ass'n of America (V. President, Administration)

THOMPSON, Jr., Otis N.

P.O. Box 381
Washington, DC 20044
Tel: (202)720-4898
Fax: (202)720-6692

Employers
Organization of Professional Employees of the U.S. Dep't of Agriculture (OPEDA) (Exec. Director)

THOMPSON, Patricia L.

One Massachusetts Ave. NW
Suite 710
Washington, DC 20001
Tel: (202)408-0800
Fax: (202)408-0214
Registered: LDA
EMail: patricia.thompson@pseg.com

Employers
PSE&G (General Manager, Federal Affairs)

THOMPSON, Phyllis D.

1201 Pennsylvania Ave. NW
Washington, DC 20004-2401
Tel: (202)662-6000
Fax: (202)662-6291
Registered: LDA
EMail: pthompson@cov.com

Employers
Covington & Burling (Partner)

Clients Represented

On Behalf of Covington & Burling

Coalition on EAF Funding

THOMPSON, Richard K.

1515 Jefferson Davis Hwy.
Suite 108
Arlington, VA 22202

Tel: (703)413-0710
Fax: (703)413-0712
Registered: LDA

Employers

Self-employed as an independent consultant.

Clients Represented

As an independent consultant

Applied Graphics

THOMPSON, Richard L.

655 15th St. NW
Suite 300
Washington, DC 20005
EMail: dick.thompson@bms.com

Tel: (202)783-0900
Fax: (202)783-2308
Registered: LDA

Employers

Bristol-Myers Squibb Co. (V. President, Government Affairs)

THOMPSON, Robert J.

1401 K St. NW
Suite 900
Washington, DC 20005

Tel: (202)626-8550
Fax: (202)626-8578
Registered: LDA

Employers

Jefferson Consulting Group (Chairman)

Clients Represented

On Behalf of Jefferson Consulting Group

Apple Computer, Inc.
Golden Rule Insurance Co.
Human Capital Resources
M.D. - I.P.A.
Mitsubishi Electric Automation
Nuclear Energy Institute
Servo Corp. of America
Stone Investments, Inc.

THOMPSON, Robert T.

800 Connecticut Ave. NW
Suite 600
Washington, DC 20006

Tel: (202)783-1900
Fax: (202)783-5995

Employers

Thompson & Thompson (Partner)

THOMPSON, Sela

1615 L St. NW
Suite 1000
Washington, DC 20036
EMail: thompsos@fleishman.com

Tel: (202)659-0330
Fax: (202)223-8119
Registered: LDA

Former Legislative Assistant to Rep. Richard A. Gephardt (D-MO).

Employers

Fleishman-Hillard, Inc (Senior Legislative Assistant)

THOMPSON, Jr., Thomas C.

1875 I St. NW
Suite 1050
Washington, DC 20006-5409

Tel: (202)331-8585
Fax: (202)331-2032
Registered: LDA

Staff, Joint Committee on Internal Revenue Taxation, 1955-57. Attorney, Legal Advisory Staff (1953-55) and Attorney, Appeals Division, Chief Counsel's Office (1951-53), Department of the Treasury.

Employers

Scribner, Hall & Thompson, LLP (Partner)

Clients Represented

On Behalf of Scribner, Hall & Thompson, LLP

Pacific Life Insurance Co.
Transamerica Corp.

THOMPSON, Thomas E.

2111 Wilson Blvd.
Eighth Floor
Arlington, VA 22201

Tel: (703)296-8463
Fax: (703)522-3811
Registered: LDA

Employers

Internat'l Council of Cruise Lines (Exec. V. President)

THOMSON, Jasper

1420 New York Ave. NW
Suite 1050
Washington, DC 20005
EMail: jthomson@vsadc.com

Tel: (202)638-1950
Fax: (202)638-7714
Registered: LDA

Legislative Aide to Rep. Dave Camp, 1996-99.

Employers

Van Scoyoc Associates, Inc. (Legislative Assistant)

Clients Represented

On Behalf of Van Scoyoc Associates, Inc.

Board on Human Sciences
Chesapeake Bay Foundation
Lockheed Martin Venture Star
NASA Aeronautics Support Team

THOMSON, Lynn Harding

1299 Pennsylvania Ave. NW
Suite 1100 West
Washington, DC 20004-2407

Tel: (202)637-4000
Fax: (202)637-4400
Registered: LDA

Employers

General Electric Co. (Manager, Federal Government Relations)

THOMSON, III, Robert B.

801 Pennsylvania Ave.
Suite 650
Washington, DC 20004
EMail: robert.b.thomson@aexp.com

Tel: (202)624-0761
Fax: (202)624-0775
Registered: LDA

Employers

American Express Co. (Director)

THORESEN, Robert

876 N. Greenbrier St.
Arlington, VA 22205-1221

Tel: (703)741-0776
Fax: (703)741-0749
Registered: LDA

Employers

Voith Hydro, Inc. (Consultant)

THORESON, Karen

630 I St. NW
Washington, DC 20001-3736

Tel: (202)289-3500
Fax: (202)289-8181

Employers

Nat'l Ass'n of Housing and Redevelopment Officials (President)

THORN, Craig A.

1001 Pennsylvania Ave. NW
Suite 600 North
Washington, DC 20004
EMail: cthorn@dtbassociates.com

Tel: (202)661-7096
Fax: (202)661-7093

Former Director, Europe, Africa and Middle East Division, Foreign Agricultural Service, Department of Agriculture. Director, Agriculture Section, Office of the U.S. Trade Representative (Geneva, Switzerland), 1992-96. Former Deputy Director, Multilateral Trade Policy Affairs Division, Foreign Agricultural Service, Department of Agriculture.

Employers

DTB Associates, LLP (Partner)
Powell, Goldstein, Frazer & Murphy LLP (Senior Policy Advisor)

Clients Represented

On Behalf of Powell, Goldstein, Frazer & Murphy LLP

Monsanto Co.

THORNBERRY, B. J.

430 S. Capitol St. SE
Suite 422
Washington, DC 20003
EMail: thornberry@dnc.democrats.org

Tel: (202)479-5153
Fax: (202)479-5156

Employers

Democratic Governors Ass'n (Exec. Director)

THORNE, Ph.D., John H.

1156 15th St. NW
Suite 400
Washington, DC 20005
EMail: jthorne@capitolink.com

Tel: (202)872-3865
Fax: (202)296-0833
Registered: LDA

Employers

Capitolink, LLC (Managing Director)

Clients Represented

On Behalf of Capitolink, LLC

American Crop Protection Ass'n
Aventis CropScience
ConAgra Foods, Inc.
The Fertilizer Institute
Nat'l Cattleman's Beef Ass'n
Nat'l Chicken Council
Nat'l Pork Producers Council
Nat'l Turkey Federation
Premium Standard Farms
SePRO Corp.
Smithfield Foods Inc.
United Egg Producers
Vantage Point Network, LLC

THORNE, Nancy

1725 K St. NW
Suite 1102
Washington, DC 20006

Tel: (202)467-5030
Fax: (202)467-5034

Employers

Population Resource Center (Director, Washington Office)

THORNELL, Paul

600 New Hampshire Ave. NW
Suite 601
Washington, DC 20037

Tel: (202)333-7400
Fax: (202)333-1638
Registered: LDA

Deputy Director, Legislative Affairs, Office of the Vice President, Executive Office of the President, The White House, 1998-2000. Associate Director, Senate Democratic Steering and Coordination Committee, 1996-98.

Employers

Hill and Knowlton, Inc. (Senior Account Supervisor)

THORNER, John

2010 Massachusetts Ave. NW
Washington, DC 20036

Tel: (202)223-8130
Fax: (202)223-1096

Employers

Optical Soc. of America (Exec. Director)

THORNING, Dr. Margo

1750 K St. NW
Suite 400
Washington, DC 20006-2300
EMail: mthorning@aol.com

Tel: (202)293-5811
Fax: (202)785-8165
Registered: LDA

Employers

American Council for Capital Formation (Senior V. President and Chief Economist)

THORNTON, RSM, Kathy

801 Pennsylvania Ave. SE
Suite 460
Washington, DC 20003
EMail: network@networklobby.org

Tel: (202)547-5556
Fax: (202)547-5510
Registered: LDA

Employers

NETWORK, A Nat'l Catholic Social Justice Lobby (Nat'l Coordinator)

THORNTON, Leslie T.

2550 M St. NW
Washington, DC 20037-1350
EMail: lthornton@pattonboggs.com

Tel: (202)457-6000
Fax: (202)457-6315

Served as Chief of Staff, Deputy Chief of Staff and Counselor to the Secretary, Department of Education, 1993-2000. Former Associate Counsel, Office of Presidential Transition and Vice Presidential Transition, during the Clinton administration.

Employers

Patton Boggs, LLP (Partner, Public Policy)

THORPE, Ph.D., John A.

1906 Association Dr.
Reston, VA 20191-9988
EMail: exec@nctm.org

Tel: (703)620-9840
Fax: (703)476-9027

Employers

Nat'l Council of Teachers of Mathematics (Exec. Director)

THORPE, Kathryne M.

2020 K St. NW
Suite 400
Washington, DC 20006

Tel: (202)530-8900
Fax: (202)530-5641
Registered: LDA

Employers
Science Applications Internat'l Corp. (SAIC) (V. President, Government Affairs)

THRASH, James E.

1133 15th St. NW
Suite 800
Washington, DC 20005
Fax: (202)775-6005

Employers
Parsons Corp. (Sr. V. President, Government Relations)

THRASHER, Linda K.

1101 15th St. NW
Suite 1000
Washington, DC 20005
Tel: (202)530-8160
Fax: (202)530-8180
Registered: LDA
EMail: linda_thrasher@cargill.com

Employers
Cargill, Inc. (Director, Public Policy)

THRASHER, Michael A.

1701 Pennsylvania Ave. NW
Suite 1200
Washington, DC 20006
Tel: (202)857-0620
Fax: (202)659-4503
Registered: LDA

Employers
Groom Law Group, Chartered

Clients Represented

On Behalf of Groom Law Group, Chartered
Microsoft Corp.

THREADGILL, Walter L.

3101 South St. NW
Washington, DC 20007
Tel: (202)293-1166
Fax: (202)293-1181
Registered: LDA

Employers
MBV, Inc. (President)

Clients Represented

On Behalf of MBV, Inc.
Multimedia Broadcast Investment Corp.

THRIFT, Ashley

1120 19th St. NW
Eighth Floor
Washington, DC 20036
Tel: (202)467-6900
Fax: (202)467-6910

Employers
Womble Carlyle Sandridge & Rice, P.C.

Clients Represented

On Behalf of Womble Carlyle Sandridge & Rice, P.C.
FedEx Corp.

THROWER, Randolph W.

1275 Pennsylvania Ave. NW
Washington, DC 20004-2415
Tel: (202)383-0100
Fax: (202)637-3593

Employers
Sutherland Asbill & Brennan LLP (Partner)

THURMAN, Susan

2000 L St. NW
Suite 835
Washington, DC 20006
Tel: (202)466-6210
Fax: (202)466-6205

Employers
PBN Company (President)

TIBBALS, Troy

805 15th St. NW
Suite 500
Washington, DC 20005
Tel: (202)371-9770
Fax: (202)371-6601

Employers
Chambers Associates Inc. (Legislative Assistant)

Clients Represented

On Behalf of Chambers Associates Inc.
American Arts Alliance

TIBBITS, Paul

1701 N. Beauregard St.
Alexandria, VA 22311
Tel: (703)549-1500
Ext: 1785
Fax: (703)549-8748
Registered: LDA
EMail: ptibbits@diabetes.org

Employers
American Diabetes Ass'n (Manager, Government Relations)

TICA-SANCHEZ, Debra

110 S. Union St.
Suite 250
Alexandria, VA 22314
Tel: (703)548-7273
Ext: 15
Fax: (703)548-0726
Registered: LDA
EMail: deb@convg.com

Employers
Convergence Services, Inc. (Project Manager, Education and Technology)

TICE, R. Dean

22377 Belmont Ridge Rd.
Asburn, VA 20148
Tel: (703)858-0784
Fax: (703)858-0794
EMail: dtice@nrpa.org

Employers
Nat'l Recreation and Park Ass'n (Exec. Director)

TIDMAN, Rebecca

1025 Thomas Jefferson St. NW
Suite 400 East
Washington, DC 20007-0805
Tel: (202)965-8132
Fax: (202)965-6403
Registered: LDA

Aide to Rep. Sam Gejdenson (D-CT), 1993-94 and Senior Assistant to Rep. Dante Fascell, 1974-93.

Employers
Jorden Burt LLP (Director, Federal Grants and Information Services)

Clients Represented

On Behalf of Jorden Burt LLP
American Museum of Natural History
Assurant Group
Atlantic Health Systems
The Colonial Williamsburg Foundation
Florida State University System
Gainesville Regional Utilities
Gainesville, Florida, City of
Lovelace Respiratory Research Institute
Miami Beach, Florida, City of
New York University
Newark, New Jersey, City of
University of Medicine and Dentistry of New Jersey
University of Miami
University of Tulsa
University of Virginia

TIDWELL, Claudette

200 Constitution Ave. NW
Room S-1325
Washington, DC 20210
Tel: (202)693-4601
Fax: (202)693-4641
EMail: tidwell-claudette@dol.gov

Employers
Department of Labor (Staff Assistant, Office of Congressional and Intergovernmental Affairs)

TIDWELL, Robert L.

3114 Circle Hill Rd.
Alexandria, VA 22305-1606
Tel: (703)548-1234
Fax: (703)548-6216

Employers
Internat'l Trade Council (V. President)

TIEGER, Carolyn C.

1150 Connecticut Ave. NW
Suite 201
Washington, DC 20036
Tel: (202)955-6200
Fax: (202)955-6215
EMail: ctieger@gcwdc.com

Former Communications and Special Projects Director, Office of Private Sector Initiatives, The White House during the Reagan administration.

Employers
Goddard Claussen (Partner)

TIERNAN, Christopher

700 13th St. NW
Suite 200
Washington, DC 20005
Tel: (202)347-3066
Fax: (202)737-7914
Registered: LDA
EMail: ctiernan@opa.easter-seals.org

Employers
Easter Seals (Assistant V. President, Government Relations)

TIERNY, Jim

One Massachusetts Ave. NW
Washington, DC 20001
Tel: (202)789-0031
Fax: (202)682-9358

Employers
Nat'l Guard Ass'n of the U.S. (Deputy Director, Joint Activities)

TIEVSKY, Charles A.

11480 Commerce Park Dr.
Reston, VA 20191
Tel: (703)755-2000
Fax: (703)755-2623
Registered: LDA

Employers
Teleglobe Communications Corp. (Assistant V. President, Regulatory Affairs)

TIFFT, Susan

1825 Connecticut Ave. NW
Fifth Floor
Washington, DC 20009
Tel: (202)667-0901
Fax: (202)667-0902
EMail: susan.tifft@widmeyer.com

Employers
Widmeyer Communications, Inc. (Senior Counsel)

TIGHE, Margaret E. "Peggy"

1101 Vermont Ave. NW
12th Floor
Washington, DC 20005-3583
Tel: (202)789-7442
Fax: (202)789-7485
Registered: LDA

Employers
American Medical Ass'n (Assistant Director, Division of Congressional Affairs)

TILLER, Robert

1875 Connecticut Ave.
Suite 1012
Washington, DC 20029
Tel: (202)898-0150
Fax: (202)898-0172

Employers
Physicians for Social Responsibility (Director, Security Programs)

TILLMAN, Wallace F.

4301 Wilson Blvd.
Arlington, VA 22203-1860
Tel: (703)907-5787
Fax: (703)907-5517
EMail: wallace.tillman@nreca.org

Employers
Nat'l Rural Electric Cooperative Ass'n (Director, Energy Policy)

TILLOTSON, Frank

1301 Pennsylvania Ave. NW
Suite 500
Washington, DC 20004
Tel: (202)347-6875
Fax: (202)347-6876
Registered: LDA
EMail: ftillotson@butera-andrews.com

Staff Assistant to Representative Nathan Deal (R-GA), 1996-99.

Employers
Butera & Andrews (Associate)

Clients Represented

On Behalf of Butera & Andrews

Advanta Corp.
American Council of State Savings Supervisors
Bluebonnet Savings Bank
British Nuclear Fuels plc
Charter One
Citizens Bank
Coalition to Amend the Financial Information Privacy Act (CAFPA)
Committee to Preserve Aspen
Community Banks Ass'n of New York State
Community Preservation Corp.
Countrywide Mortgage Corp.
Derivatives Net, Inc.
Dime Savings Bank of New York
Federal Home Loan Bank of Boston
Federal Home Loan Bank of Topeka
Federation for American Immigration Reform (FAIR)
FM Watch
FRANMAC/Taco Pac
Independence Bank
Internat'l Swaps and Derivatives Dealers Ass'n
Luse Lehman Gorman Pomerenk & Schick, P.C.
Nat'l Home Equity Mortgage Ass'n
North American Securities Administrators Ass'n (NASAA)
Option One Mortgage Corp.
Pedestal
Savings Banks Life Insurance Fund
Silver, Freedman & Taff
Soc. for Human Resource Management
Superior Bank, FSB
Texas Savings and Community Bankers
USPA & IRA

TILTON, Stephen G.

1350 I St. NW
Suite 870
Washington, DC 20005
EMail: tilton@capalliance.com
Tel: (202)638-0551
Fax: (202)737-1947
Registered: LDA

Employers
Health Policy Analysts (Associate)

Clients Represented

On Behalf of Health Policy Analysts

Schering-Plough Legislative Resources L.L.C.

TIMBERS, Jr., William H.

6903 Rockledge Dr.
Bethesda, MD 20817
Tel: (301)564-3200
Fax: (301)564-3201

Employers
USEC, Inc. (President and Chief Exec. Officer)

TIMMENY, Michael

601 Pennsylvania Ave. NW
Suite 520
North Bldg.
Washington, DC 20004
EMail: mtimmeny@cisco.com
Tel: (202)661-4040
Fax: (202)661-4041
Registered: LDA

Former Aide to Senator Patty Murray (D-WA).

Employers
Cisco Systems Inc. (Manager, Government Relations)

TIMMENY, Wallace L.

1775 I St. NW
Washington, DC 20006
EMail: wallace.timmeny@dechert.com
Tel: (202)261-3383
Fax: (202)261-3333

Former Deputy Director, Division of Enforcement, Securities and Exchange Commission.

Employers
Dechert (Partner)

TIMMERMAN, Jerianne

1771 N St. NW
Washington, DC 20036-2891
Tel: (202)429-5300
Fax: (202)429-5343

Employers
Nat'l Ass'n of Broadcasters (Associate General Counsel)

TIMMERMAN, Kenneth

7831 Woodmont Ave.
Suite 395
Bethesda, MD 20814
EMail: president@mdtaxes.org
Tel: (301)946-2918
Fax: (301)942-5341
Registered: LDA

Employers
Maryland Taxpayers Ass'n, Inc. (President)

TIMMONS, Becky H.

One Dupont Circle NW
Suite 834
Washington, DC 20036-1193
EMail: becky_timmons@ace.nche.edu
Tel: (202)939-9355
Fax: (202)833-4762
Registered: LDA

Employers
American Council on Education (Director, Government Relations)

TIMMONS, John W.

1620 L St. NW
Suite 1210
Washington, DC 20036
Tel: (202)721-9134
Fax: (202)955-6070
Registered: LDA

Employers
Cormac Group, LLP

TIMMONS, Paula Pleas

1150 Connecticut Ave. NW
Fourth Floor
Washington, DC 20036-4104
Tel: (202)223-9222
Fax: (202)223-9095
Registered: LDA

Employers
AT&T Wireless Services, Inc. (Manager, Federal Affairs)

TIMMONS, Sr., William E.

1850 K St. NW
Suite 850
Washington, DC 20006
Tel: (202)331-1760
Fax: (202)822-9376
Registered: LDA

Assistant to the President, The White House, 1969-74. Administrative Assistant to Rep. William Brock (R-TN), 1963-69. Assistant to Senator Alexander Wiley (R-WI), 1955-62.

Employers
Timmons and Co., Inc. (Chairman Emeritus)

Clients Represented

On Behalf of Timmons and Co., Inc.

American Council of Life Insurers
American Petroleum Institute
American Soc. of Anesthesiologists
Anheuser-Busch Cos., Inc.
Asbestos Working Group
AT&T
Bay Harbor Management, L.C.
Bristol-Myers Squibb Co.
Cox Enterprises Inc.
DaimlerChrysler Corp.
Farallon Capital Management
Federal Home Loan Mortgage Corp. (Freddie Mac)
Micron Technology, Inc.
Napster, Inc.
Nat'l Rifle Ass'n of America
New York Life Insurance Co.
Northrop Grumman Corp.
TruePosition Inc.
Union Pacific
University of Utah
UNOCAL Corp.
VISA U.S.A., Inc.

TIMMONS, Jr., William E.

1850 K St. NW
Suite 850
Washington, DC 20006
Tel: (202)331-1760
Fax: (202)822-9376
Registered: LDA

Employers
Timmons and Co., Inc. (Director, Research)

Clients Represented

On Behalf of Timmons and Co., Inc.

American Council of Life Insurers
American Petroleum Institute
American Soc. of Anesthesiologists
Anheuser-Busch Cos., Inc.
Asbestos Working Group
AT&T
Bay Harbor Management, L.C.
Bristol-Myers Squibb Co.
Cox Enterprises Inc.
DaimlerChrysler Corp.
Farallon Capital Management
Federal Home Loan Mortgage Corp. (Freddie Mac)
Micron Technology, Inc.
Napster, Inc.
Nat'l Rifle Ass'n of America
New York Life Insurance Co.
Northrop Grumman Corp.
TruePosition Inc.
Union Pacific
University of Utah
UNOCAL Corp.
VISA U.S.A., Inc.

TINDAL, D'Anna

2346 Greenwich St.
Falls Church, VA 22046
EMail: D_Anna@stanfieldtindal.com
Tel: (703)847-3664
Fax: (703)534-9461
Registered: LDA

Employers
Stanfield Tindal, Inc. (President)

Clients Represented

On Behalf of Stanfield Tindal, Inc.

Recon/Optical, Inc.

TINDALL, Barry

1901 Pennsylvania Ave.
Suite 900
Washington, DC 20006
EMail: btindall@nrpa.org
Tel: (202)887-0297
Fax: (202)887-5484

Employers
Nat'l Recreation and Park Ass'n (Director, Public Policy)

TINER, Michael L.

2555 M St. NW
Suite 327
Washington, DC 20037
Tel: (202)223-3352
Registered: LDA

Employers
J/T Group (Co-Chairman)
Self-employed as an independent consultant.

Clients Represented

On Behalf of J/T Group

AFL-CIO - Building and Construction Trades Department

As an independent consultant

McDonald's Corp.
Nuclear Energy Institute
Philip Morris Management Corp.

TINGLE, G. Wayne

1725 Jefferson Davis Hwy.
Crystal Square 2, Suite 300
Arlington, VA 22202
Tel: (703)413-5905
Fax: (703)413-5744
Registered: LDA

Employers
Lockheed Martin Corp. (V. President, Systems Integration)

TINKER, Tim

1825 Connecticut Ave. NW
Fifth Floor
Washington, DC 20009
EMail: timothy.tinker@widmeyer. com
Tel: (202)667-0901
Fax: (202)667-0902

Employers
Widmeyer Communications, Inc. (V. President)

TIPTON, Caroline

1350 I St. NW
Suite 700
Washington, DC 20005
Tel: (202)789-6000
Fax: (202)789-6190
Registered: LDA

Employers
Beveridge & Diamond, P.C. (Associate)

TIPTON, Constance E.

1250 H St. NW
Suite 900
Washington, DC 20005
Tel: (202)737-4332
Fax: (202)331-7820
Registered: LDA

Employers
Internat'l Dairy Foods Ass'n (Senior Group V. President)

TIPTON, E. Linwood

1250 H St. NW
Suite 900
Washington, DC 20005
Tel: (202)737-4332
Fax: (202)331-7820
Registered: LDA

Employers
Internat'l Dairy Foods Ass'n (President and Chief Exec. Officer)

TIPTON, Sean B.

409 12th St. SW
Suite 203
Washington, DC 20024-2125
EMail: stipton@asrm.org
Tel: (202)863-2494
Fax: (202)484-4039

Employers
American Soc. for Reproductive Medicine (Public Affairs Director)

TIRANA, Bardyl R.

4401 Connecticut Ave. NW
Suite 700
Washington, DC 20008-2322
Tel: (202)244-0437
Fax: (202)363-8179
Registered: FARA

Trial Attorney, Admiralty and Shipping Section, Civil Division, Department of Justice, 1962-64.

Employers
Self-employed as an independent consultant.

Clients Represented

As an independent consultant
Kosovo, Government of the Republic of

TIROZZI, Dr. Gerald

1904 Association Dr.
Reston, VA 20191
EMail: tirozzig@nassp.org
Tel: (703)860-0200
Fax: (703)476-5432

Employers
Nat'l Ass'n of Secondary School Principals (Exec. Director)

TITTSWORTH, David G.

1050 17th St. NW
Suite 725
Washington, DC 20036
EMail: davidt@icaa.org
Tel: (202)293-4222
Fax: (202)293-4223

Counsel, House Committee on Energy and Commerce (1992-96); Senior Counsel, House Subcommittee on Transportation and Hazardous Material (1989-91); Associate Staff, House Committee on Budget (1987-89).

Employers
Investment Counsel Ass'n of America (Exec. Director/Exec. V. President)

TOBER, Eric

The Willard Office Bldg.
1455 Pennsylvania Ave. NW, Suite 200
Washington, DC 20004
Tel: (202)737-0683
Fax: (202)737-0693
Registered: LDA

Former Projects Director to Sen. J. Bennett Johnston (D-LA) and Staff Assistant to Rep. Terry L. Bruce (D-IL).

Employers
Johnston & Associates, LLC (Partner)

Clients Represented

On Behalf of Johnston & Associates, LLC
Aiken and Edgenfield Counties, South Carolina, Economic Development Partnership of
Alliance for Competitive Electricity
American Animal Husbandry Coalition PAC
Avondale Industries, Inc.
COGEMA, Inc.
Coushatta Tribe of Louisiana
Drexel University
Edison Internat'l
Jefferson Parish Council
Lockheed Martin Corp.
Louisiana State University Medical Center Foundation
MTS Systems Inc.
New Orleans Internat'l Airport
New Orleans, Louisiana, Regional Transit Authority of
Northrop Grumman Corp.
Nuclear Energy Institute
Regional Planning Commission
Regional Transit Authority
Riverdeep Inc.
Sewerage and Water Board of New Orleans
Tulane University
Tunica Biloxi Indians of Louisiana
United Gamefowl Breeders Ass'n, Inc.
University of New Orleans
University of Southwestern Louisiana

TOBER, Karen

1111 Constitution Ave. NW
Room 3238
Washington, DC 20224
EMail: karen.tober@irs.gov
Tel: (202)622-9590
Fax: (202)622-3772

Employers
Department of Treasury - Internal Revenue Service (Congressional Inquiries)

TOBIAS, Carol

419 Seventh St. NW
Suite 500
Washington, DC 20004
Tel: (202)626-8800
Fax: (202)737-9189
Registered: LDA

Employers
Nat'l Right to Life Committee (Director, Political Action Committee)

TOBIN, Jim

1201 15th St. NW
Washington, DC 20005-2800
Tel: (202)822-0470
Fax: (202)822-0572
Registered: LDA

Employers
Nat'l Ass'n of Home Builders of the U.S. (Legislative Director, Environment)

TOBIN, Merry M.

600 Maryland Ave. SW
Suite 800
Washington, DC 20024
Tel: (202)484-3600
Fax: (202)484-3604
Registered: LDA

Employers
American Farm Bureau Federation (Director, Legislative Services)

TOBIN, Dr. William J.

3612 Bent Branch Ct.
Falls Church, VA 22041-1006
Tel: (703)941-4329
Fax: (703)941-4329

Consultant to Director of Minority Business, U.S. Department of Transportation, 1986. Special Assistant to the Acting Chairman, U.S. Consumer Product Safety Commission, 1986. Special Assistant to the Assistant Secretary of Defense (C3I), 1976-77.

Employers
Access Technology Ass'n (Exec. Director)
American Ass'n of Early Childhood Educators (Exec. Director)
Americans for Choice in Education (V. President)
Associated Child Care Consultants, Ltd. (President)
Early Childhood Development Center Legislative Coalition (Exec. Director)
Nat'l Childcare Parents Ass'n (Exec. Director)
William J. Tobin and Associates

TODD, Constance

409 Third St. SW
Second Floor
Washington, DC 20024-6682
Tel: (202)479-6688
Fax: (202)479-0735

Employers
Nat'l Institute of Senior Centers (Director, Staff Advocate for Older Americans Legislation)

TODD, David C.

2550 M St. NW
Washington, DC 20037-1350
EMail: dtodd@pattonboggs.com
Tel: (202)457-6000
Fax: (202)457-6315

Employers
Patton Boggs, LLP (Partner)

TODD, Doug

701 Pennsylvania Ave. NW
Suite 720
Washington, DC 20004
Tel: (202)434-4800
Fax: (202)347-4015

Formerly worked in the Department of Energy, during the Bush I Administration.

Employers
Siemens Corp.

TODD, Jason

1620 I St. NW
Suite 615
Washington, DC 20006
Tel: (202)463-8493
Registered: LDA

Employers
Management Options, Inc.

Clients Represented

On Behalf of Management Options, Inc.
American Teleservices Ass'n

TODD, Kyra A.

555 13th St. NW
Washington, DC 20004-1109
Tel: (202)637-5600
Fax: (202)637-5910
Registered: LDA

Employers
Hogan & Hartson L.L.P. (Associate)

Clients Represented

On Behalf of Hogan & Hartson L.L.P.
Taylor Packing Co., Inc.

TODD, Reginald N.

440 First St. NW
Suite 440
Washington, DC 20001
EMail: rtodd@naco.org
Tel: (202)393-2404
Fax: (202)393-2666

Employers
Los Angeles, California, County of (Chief Legislative Representative)

TODD, Sean

1401 K St. NW
Suite 801
Washington, DC 20005
Tel: (202)682-1147
Fax: (202)682-1171

Employers
IT Group, Inc. (Director, Federal Agency Relations)

TOENSING, Brady

901 15th St. NW
Suite 430
Washington, DC 20005
Tel: (202)289-7701
Fax: (202)289-7706
Registered: LDA

Employers
diGenova & Toensing (Associate)

Clients Represented

On Behalf of diGenova & Toensing
American Hospital Ass'n

TOENSING, Victoria

901 15th St. NW
Suite 430
Washington, DC 20005
Tel: (202)289-7701
Fax: (202)289-7706
Registered: LDA

Special Counsel, House Education and the Workforce Committee, 1998. Deputy Assistant Attorney General, Criminal Division, Department of Justice, 1984-88. Chief Counsel, Senate Select Committee on Intelligence, 1981-84.

Employers
diGenova & Toensing (Partner)

Clients Represented

On Behalf of diGenova & Toensing
American Hospital Ass'n

TOEWS-HARDER, Elisabeth

110 Maryland Ave. NE
Suite 502
Washington, DC 20002
EMail: eharder@mcc.org
Tel: (202)544-6564
Fax: (202)544-2820

Employers
Mennonite Central Committee Washington Office (Legislative Assistant)

TOGNI, Patrick J.

1299 Pennsylvania Ave. NW
Tenth Floor
Washington, DC 20004-2400
Tel: (202)508-9500
Fax: (202)508-9700

Employers
Paul, Hastings, Janofsky & Walker LLP

Clients Represented

On Behalf of Paul, Hastings, Janofsky & Walker LLP
CFSBdirect Inc.

TOKER, Mary Catherine

601 Pennsylvania Ave. NW
Suite 420
North Bldg.
Washington, DC 20004
EMail: mary.toker@genmills.com
Tel: (202)737-8200
Fax: (202)638-4914
Registered: LDA

Employers
General Mills (Deputy Director, Washington Office)

TOKER, P. J.

2099 Pennsylvania Ave. NW
Suite 100
Washington, DC 20006
Tel: (202)955-3000
Fax: (202)955-5564
Registered: LDA
EMail: pjtoker@hklaw.com

Employers
Holland & Knight LLP (Legislative Assistant)

Clients Represented
On Behalf of Holland & Knight LLP
Allina Health Systems
American Chemistry Council
Bassford, Lockhart, Truesdell & Briggs, P.A.
Capitol Broadcasting Co.
FMC Corp.
Nassau County Health Care Corp.
Placer, California, County of
Somerville Housing Group

TOLAND, William P.

601 13th St. NW
Suite 200 North
Washington, DC 20005
Tel: (202)682-9462
Registered: LDA

Employers
BASF Corporation (Environment and Energy Advocate)

TOLEDO, Elizabeth

1700 Kalorama Rd.
Suite 101
Washington, DC 20009-2702
Tel: (202)332-6483
Fax: (202)332-0207

Employers
Nat'l Gay and Lesbian Task Force (Exec. Director)

TOLIVER, Karen Bland

1333 New Hampshire Ave. NW
Suite 400
Washington, DC 20036
Tel: (202)887-4000
Fax: (202)887-4288
Registered: LDA

Employers
Akin, Gump, Strauss, Hauer & Feld, L.L.P. (Counsel)

Clients Represented
On Behalf of Akin, Gump, Strauss, Hauer & Feld, L.L.P.
Cargill, Inc.

TOLLERTON, Kathryn R.

1818 N St. NW
Suite 600
Washington, DC 20036
Tel: (202)331-3500
Fax: (202)265-8504
EMail: k.tollerton@asee.org

Employers
American Soc. for Engineering Education (Manager, Public Affairs)

TOLLIVER, Jim

636 I St. NW
Washington, DC 20001-3736
Tel: (202)898-2444
Fax: (202)898-1185

Employers
American Soc. of Landscape Architects (Deputy Exec. Director)

TOLSON, Todd

1700 Pennsylvania Ave. NW
Suite 950
Washington, DC 20006
Tel: (202)393-5055
Fax: (202)393-0120
Registered: LDA
EMail: toddtolson@erols.com
Former Legislative Assistant to Rep. Tom Latham (R-IA) and former Legislative Assistant to Rep. Mike Forbes (R-NY).

Employers
Valis Associates (Account Executive)

Clients Represented
On Behalf of Valis Associates
American Bakers Ass'n
American Consulting Engineers Council
Ass'n for the Suppliers of Printing and Publishing Technology
Environmental Action Group
Grocery Manufacturers of America
Kitchen Cabinet Manufacturers Ass'n
NPES, The Ass'n for Suppliers of Printing, Publishing, and Converting Technologies
Regulatory Improvement Council
Renewable Fuels Ass'n
Soc. of the Plastics Industry
Tax Action Group

TOMAN, Mike

1616 P St. NW
Washington, DC 20036
Tel: (202)328-5000

Employers
Resources for the Future (Director, Energy and Natural Resources Division)

TOMASSETTI, Nick

198 Van Buren St.
Herndon, VA 20170
Tel: (703)834-3400
Fax: (703)834-3340

Employers
Airbus Industrie of North America, Inc. (Chief Exec. Officer)

TOMCALA, Karen

700 11th St. NW
Suite 250
Washington, DC 20001
Tel: (202)638-3515
Fax: (202)638-3522
Registered: LDA
EMail: karen.tomcala@pge-corp.com

Employers
PG&E Corp. (Director, FERC Relations)

TOMES, Ph.D., Henry

750 First St. NE
Washington, DC 20002-4242
Tel: (202)336-6050
Fax: (202)336-6040

Employers
American Psychological Ass'n (Exec. Director, Public Interest Directorate)

TOMHAVE, Jeff

1001 Connecticut Ave. NW
Suite 400
Washington, DC 20036
Tel: (202)331-8084
Ext: 225
Fax: (202)331-8068
EMail: jtomhave@taswer.org

Employers
Tribal Ass'n on Solid Waste and Emergency Response (TASWER) (Exec. Director)

TOMINOVICH, Kathryn "K.C."

1225 Connecticut Ave. NW
Washington, DC 20036
Tel: (202)327-7584
Fax: (202)327-8863
Registered: LDA
EMail: kathryn.tominovich@ey.com
Former Legislative Assistant to Rep. Pete Geren (D-TX).

Employers
Ernst & Young LLP (Political and Legislative Director)

TOMINOVICH, Scott

666 Pennsylvania Ave. SE
Suite 202
Washington, DC 20003
Tel: (202)546-5488
Fax: (202)546-5281
Registered: LDA

Employers
Apollo Group, Inc. (Associate Director, Government Affairs)

TOMLINSON, Don

100 Indiana Ave. NW
Washington, DC 20001
Tel: (202)393-4695
Fax: (202)756-7400

Employers
Nat'l Ass'n of Letter Carriers of the United States of America (Special Assistant, Political Education)

TOMLINSON, Ericka

1701 K St. NW
Suite 200
Washington, DC 20006-1503
Tel: (202)223-3447
Fax: (202)331-7476
Registered: LDA
EMail: etomlinson@alliance1.org
Former Special Research Assistant, Office of Policy Development, Department of Housing and Urban Development.

Employers
Alliance for Children and Families (Policy Analyst)

TOMPA, Peter K.

600 13th St. NW
Washington, DC 20005-3096
Tel: (202)756-8361
Fax: (202)756-8087
Registered: LDA
EMail: ptompa@mwe.com

Employers
McDermott, Will and Emery (Partner)

Clients Represented
On Behalf of McDermott, Will and Emery
Internat'l Ass'n of Professional Numismatists

TOMPKINS, Dr. Catherine

1030 15th St. NW
Suite 240
Washington, DC 20005
Tel: (202)289-9806
Fax: (202)289-9824
EMail: ctompkins@aghe.org

Employers
Ass'n for Gerontology in Higher Education (Director)

TOMPKINS, J. Warren

1801 K St. NW
Suite 901-L
Washington, DC 20006
Tel: (202)530-0500
Fax: (202)530-4800

Employers
BKSH & Associates (Senior Counselor)

TOMPKINS, Jr., Joseph B.

1722 I St. NW
Washington, DC 20006
Tel: (202)736-8000
Fax: (202)736-8711

Employers
Sidley & Austin (Partner)

Clients Represented
On Behalf of Sidley & Austin
Cayman Islands, Government of

TONGOUR, Michael A.

227 Massachusetts Ave. NE
Suite One
Washington, DC 20002
Tel: (202)544-7600
Fax: (202)544-6770
Registered: LDA
EMail: tongour@tongoursimpson.com
Chief Counsel to Senator Alan Simpson (R-WY), 1989-94. Legislative Director to Senator Strom Thurmond (R-SC), 1986-87. Counsel, Senate Committee on Labor and Human Resources, 1985-86.

Employers
Tongour Simpson Holsclaw Green (Managing Partner)

Clients Represented
On Behalf of Tongour Simpson Holsclaw Green
American Ass'n of Nurse Anesthetists
Ass'n for Advanced Life Underwriting
Aventis Pharmaceuticals, Inc.
Communities in Schools, Inc.
CSX Corp.
Hydroelectric Licensing Reform Task Force
Lancaster, California, City of
Pharmaceutical Research and Manufacturers of America
SBC Communications Inc.
SCANA Corp.
TXU Business Services
TXU Inc.
Union Switch and Signal, Inc.
United States Telecom Ass'n

TOOHEY, Daniel W.

1200 New Hampshire Ave. NW
Suite 800
Washington, DC 20036-6802
Tel: (202)776-2000
Fax: (202)776-2222
EMail: dtoohey@dlalaw.com
General Attorney, Federal Communications Commission, 1964-65.

Employers
Dow, Lohnes & Albertson, PLLC (Senior Counsel)

TOOHEY, Michael J.

601 Pennsylvania Ave. NW
Suite 540
North Bldg.
Washington, DC 20004
Tel: (202)223-8290
Fax: (202)293-2913
Registered: LDA
EMail: mjtoohey@ashland.com
Former Assistant Secretary for Government Affairs, U.S. Department of Transportation.

Employers
Ashland Inc. (Director, Federal Relations)

TOOHEY, William. D.

c/o ARTBA
1010 Massachusetts Ave. NW
Suite 600
Washington, DC 20001
Tel: (202)289-4434
Fax: (202)289-4435

Employers
American Transportation Advisory Council (ATAC)

TOPEL, Howard

1400 16th St. NW
Suite 600
Washington, DC 20036
Tel: (202)939-7900
Fax: (202)745-0916

Employers
Fleischman and Walsh, L.L.P. (Partner)

TOPELIUS, Kathleen E.

700 13th St. NW
Suite 700
Washington, DC 20005-3960
Tel: (202)508-6000
Fax: (202)508-6200
EMail: ketopelius@bryancave.com
Attorney, Office of the General Counsel, Federal Home Loan Bank Board, 1978-80.

Employers
Bryan Cave LLP (Partner)

TOPODAS, Jonathan M.

1501 M St. NW
Suite 400
Washington, DC 20005
Tel: (202)463-4023
Fax: (202)331-4205
Registered: LDA
EMail: jonathan.topodas@aetna.com

Employers
Aetna Inc. (V. President and Counsel)

TOPOL, Allan J.

1201 Pennsylvania Ave. NW
Washington, DC 20004-2401
Tel: (202)662-6000
Fax: (202)662-6291
EMail: atopol@cov.com
Served as Member, Advisory Committee on Private International Law to the Secretary, Department of State.

Employers
Covington & Burling (Partner)

Clients Represented
On Behalf of Covington & Burling
General Electric Co.

TOPPING, Jr., John C.

333-1/2 Pennsylvania Ave. SE
Washington, DC 20003
Tel: (202)547-0104
Fax: (202)547-0111
EMail: jtopping@climate.org
Staff Director, Office of Air and Radiation, Environmental Protection Agency, 1983-85. Chief Counsel, Office of Minority Business Enterprises, Department of Commerce, 1973-76.

Employers
Climate Institute (President)

TORCIVIA, Regina

1801 L St. NW
MS: 9313
Washington, DC 20507
Tel: (202)663-4900
Fax: (202)663-4912

Employers
Equal Employment Opportunity Commission (Congressional Liaison Specialist)

TORDA, Phyllis

2000 L St. NW
Suite 500
Washington, DC 20036
Tel: (202)955-5180
Fax: (202)955-3599

Employers
Nat'l Committee for Quality Assurance (Assistant V. President)

TOREGAS, Costis

1301 Pennsylvania Ave. NW
Suite 800
Washington, DC 20004
Tel: (202)626-2400
Fax: (202)626-2498
EMail: press@pti.nw.dc.us

Employers
Public Technology Inc. (President)

TORGERSON, William T.

1900 Pennsylvania Ave. NW
Washington, DC 20068
Tel: (202)872-2000
Registered: LDA

Employers
Potomac Electric Power Co. (Senior V. President and General Counsel, External Affairs)

TORRENTE, Josephine M.

1429 G St. NW
P.O. Box 344
Washington, DC 20005
Tel: (202)737-7554
Fax: (202)737-9329
Registered: LDA

Employers
Ass'n of Disposable Device Manufacturers (ADDM) (President)

TORRES, Alicia

One Physics Ellipse
College Park, MD 20740-3843
Tel: (301)209-3100
Fax: (301)209-0843
Registered: LDA

Employers
American Institute of Physics

TORRES, III, Frank C.

1666 Connecticut Ave. NW
Suite 310
Washington, DC 20009
Tel: (202)462-6262
Fax: (202)265-9548
Registered: LDA
EMail: torrfr@consumer.org

Employers
Consumers Union of the United States (Legislative Counsel)

TORRES, Peter A.

2121 R St. NW
Washington, DC 20008-1908
Tel: (202)673-5869
Fax: (202)673-5873

Employers
Northern Mariana Islands, Commonwealth of the (Federal Programs Coordinator)

TORRESEN, Jr., Robert

1001 Pennsylvania Ave. NW
Suite 600
Washington, DC 20004
Tel: (202)347-0066
Fax: (202)624-7222
Registered: LDA
EMail: rtorrese@pgfm.com

Employers
Powell, Goldstein, Frazer & Murphy LLP (Partner)

Clients Represented
On Behalf of Powell, Goldstein, Frazer & Murphy LLP
Hong Kong Trade Development Council
Rollerblade, Inc.

TORREY, Michael K.

1250 H St. NW
Suite 900
Washington, DC 20005
Tel: (202)737-4332
Fax: (202)331-7820
Registered: LDA

Employers
Internat'l Dairy Foods Ass'n (Senior Director, Legislative Affairs)

TORREY, Sarah

The McPherson Bldg.
901 15th St. NW, Suite 1100
Washington, DC 20005
Tel: (202)682-3500
Fax: (202)682-3580
Registered: LDA

Employers
Kaye Scholer LLP (Legal Assistant)

Clients Represented
On Behalf of Kaye Scholer LLP
Korean Semiconductor Industry Ass'n

TORSCH, USNR, Cdr. Virginia

909 N. Washington St.
Suite 300
Alexandria, VA 22314
Tel: (703)548-5568
Fax: (703)684-3258
Registered: LDA

Employers
TREA Senior Citizens League (TSCL) (Legislative Director)

TOSCANO, J.

1010 Wisconsin Ave. NW
Suite 800
Washington, DC 20007
Tel: (202)338-8700
Fax: (202)338-2334
Director, Office of Public Affairs, Corporation for National Service, 1995-97.

Employers
Greer, Margolis, Mitchell, Burns & Associates (Sr. V. President)

Clients Represented
On Behalf of Greer, Margolis, Mitchell, Burns & Associates
American Ass'n of Family Physicians

TOSI, Gloria Cataneo

1300 I St. NW
Suite 250 West
Washington, DC 20005
Tel: (202)842-4900
Fax: (202)842-3492
Registered: LDA

Employers
American Maritime Congress (President)

TOSTO, C. J.

8001 Braddock Rd.
Springfield, VA 22160
Tel: (703)321-9820
Fax: (703)321-7342
Registered: LDA

Employers
Nat'l Right to Work Committee (Federal Legislative Liasion)

TOSTRUD, Jon

317 Massachusetts Ave. NE
Suite 300
Washington, DC 20002
Tel: (202)789-3960
Fax: (202)789-1813

Employers
The Cuneo Law Group, P.C. (Attorney)

TOTTEN, Gloria

1156 15th St. NW
Suite 700
Washington, DC 20005
Tel: (202)973-3000
Fax: (202)973-3096
EMail: gtotten@naral.org

Employers
Nat'l Abortion and Reproductive Rights Action League (Political Director)

TOWE, Dreama D.

1201 Pennsylvania Ave. NW
Suite 300
Washington, DC 20004
Tel: (202)661-4609
Fax: (202)661-4618
Former Legislative Assistant to Senator Christopher S. "Kit" Bond (R-MO).

Employers
3Com Corp. (Manager, Government Relations)

TOWERS, Ph.D., Jan

P.O. Box 40130
Washington, DC 20016
Tel: (202)966-6414
Fax: (202)966-2856

Employers
American Academy of Nurse Practitioners (Director of Health Policy)

TOWLE, CAE, Raymond P.

1575 I St. NW
Washington, DC 20005-1103
Tel: (202)626-2820
Fax: (202)371-1673
Registered: LDA
EMail: rtowle@asaenet.org

Employers
American Soc. of Ass'n Executives (Director, Public Policy)

TOWNE, Robert

2121 K St. NW
Suite 700
Washington, DC 20037
Tel: (202)296-9230
Fax: (202)862-5498
Registered: LDA

Employers
VISA U.S.A., Inc. (V. President)

TOWNSEND, Chris

1800 Diagonal Rd.
Suite 600
Alexandria, VA 22314
Tel: (703)684-3123
Fax: (703)519-8982
Registered: LDA

Employers
United Electrical Workers of America (Political Director)

TOWNSEND, II, John B.

1450 G St. NW
Suite 500
Washington, DC 20005
Registered: LDA

Employers
Auyua Inc.

TOWNSEND, John M.

1775 I St. NW
Suite 600
Washington, DC 20006-2401
Tel: (202)721-4600
Fax: (202)721-4646
Registered: FARA

Employers
Hughes Hubbard & Reed LLP (Partner)

Clients Represented

On Behalf of Hughes Hubbard & Reed LLP
Ajinomoto Co., Inc.

TOWNSEND, Michael T.

555 12th St. NW
Suite 740
Washington, DC 20004
Tel: (202)638-3752
Fax: (202)638-3823
Registered: LDA
EMail: michael.townsend@schwab.com

Employers
Charles Schwab & Co., Inc., (V. President, Public Policy)

TOWNSEND, Wanda

1724 Massachusetts Ave. NW
Washington, DC 20036
Tel: (202)775-3644
Fax: (202)775-3671
Registered: LDA

Employers
Nat'l Cable Television Ass'n (Director, Government Relations)

TOZZI, Jim J.

11 Dupont Circle NW
Suite 700
Washington, DC 20036
Tel: (202)293-5886
Fax: (202)939-6969
Registered: LDA
Former Deputy Administrator, Office of Management and Budget.

Employers
Multinat'l Government Services, Inc. (Director)

Clients Represented

On Behalf of Multinat'l Government Services, Inc.
Cellular Telecommunications and Internet Ass'n
CIGNA Corp.
General Tire, Inc.
Goodyear Tire and Rubber Co.
Rhone-Polenc Inc.
TRW Inc.

TRABUE, Ted

1900 Pennsylvania Ave. NW
Washington, DC 20068
Tel: (202)872-2367

Employers
Potomac Electric Power Co. (Manager, Government Relations - D.C.)

TRACHTMAN, Richard L.

2011 Pennsylvania Ave. NW
Suite 800
Washington, DC 20006-1808
Tel: (202)261-4538
Fax: (202)835-0443
Registered: LDA
EMail: rtrachtman@mail.acponline.org

Employers
American College of Physicians-American Soc. of Internal Medicine (ACP-ASIM) (Director, Congressional Affairs)

TRACY, Alan T.

1620 I St. NW
Suite 801
Washington, DC 20006
Tel: (202)463-0999
Fax: (202)785-1052

Employers
U.S. Wheat Associates, Inc. (President)

TRACY, Anne M.

300 E St. SW
Room 9J21
Washington, DC 20546
Tel: (202)358-1948
Fax: (202)358-4340

Employers
Nat'l Aeronautics and Space Administration (Administrative Officer, Office of Legislative Affairs)

TRAGAKIS, Chad

600 New Hampshire Ave. NW
Suite 601
Washington, DC 20037
Tel: (202)333-7400
Fax: (202)333-1638

Employers
Hill and Knowlton, Inc. (PAC Administrator)

TRAIMAN, Susan N.

1615 L St. NW
Suite 1100
Washington, DC 20036-5610
Tel: (202)872-1260
Fax: (202)466-3509

Employers
The Business Roundtable (Director, Education Initiative)

TRAINER, Ryan T.

607 14th St. NW
Washington, DC 20005
Tel: (202)434-0700
Fax: (202)912-6000
Registered: LDA
EMail: trainerr@rw.com
Staff Attorney, Office of the Assistant General Counsel for Import Administration, Department of Commerce, 1981-84.

Employers
Rogers & Wells (Partner)

Clients Represented

On Behalf of Rogers & Wells
Internat'l Sleep Products Ass'n

TRAMMELL, Jeffrey B.

600 New Hampshire Ave. NW
Suite 601
Washington, DC 20037
Tel: (202)333-7400
Fax: (202)333-1638
Registered: LDA, FARA
EMail: jtrammell@hillandknowlton.com
Former aide to Rep. Paul Rodgers (D-FL).

Employers
Hill and Knowlton, Inc. (Sr. Managing Director, Sr. Counselor Public Affairs and Gov't Relations)

Clients Represented

On Behalf of Hill and Knowlton, Inc.
Blue Cross and Blue Shield of Florida
Ford Motor Co.
Internat'l Olympic Committee
Orange, California, County of

TRAMONTANO, Jerry

8001 Forbes Pl.
Suite 102
Springfield, VA 22151
Tel: (703)321-8585
Fax: (703)321-8408
Registered: LDA

Employers
Gun Owners of America (Legislative Assistant)

TRANT, Matthew J.

700 13th St. NW
Suite 400
Washington, DC 20005
Tel: (202)347-0773
Fax: (202)347-0785
EMail: mtrant@cassidy.com
Chief of Staff and Legislative Director to Rep. Peter Blute (R-MA), 1993-97. Department of Transportation and Federal Energy Regulatory Commission, 1991-93. Staff member, Rep. Silvio O. Conte (R-MA), 1988-93.

Employers
Cassidy & Associates, Inc. (Chief of Staff to Chairman and C.E.O.)

TRAPASSO, Joseph

2550 M St. NW
Washington, DC 20037-1350
Tel: (202)457-6000
Fax: (202)457-6315
Registered: LDA
Legislative Affairs Officer, Department of State, 1993-94. Special Counsel to the President, Office of Personnel Management, The White House, 1993.

Employers
Patton Boggs, LLP (Partner)

Clients Represented

On Behalf of Patton Boggs, LLP
Internat'l Olympic Committee
James Hardie Building Products Inc.
G. Murphy Trading
QSP Inc.
Roizman & Cos.
Salt Lake City Olympic Organizing Committee

TRAPHAGEN, Mark

1001 Pennsylvania Ave. NW
Suite 600
Washington, DC 20004
Tel: (202)347-0066
Fax: (202)624-7222

Employers
Powell, Goldstein, Frazer & Murphy LLP (Partner)

Clients Represented

On Behalf of Powell, Goldstein, Frazer & Murphy LLP
Pernod Ricard

TRAPP, Stephanie

515 King St.
Suite 420
Alexandria, VA 22314-3103
Tel: (703)684-5570
Fax: (703)684-6048
EMail: strapp@clarionmr.com

Employers
CLARION Management Resources, Inc. (Account Executive)

TRASK, Jeff

1220 L St. NW
Washington, DC 20005
Tel: (202)682-8000
Fax: (202)682-8232
Registered: LDA

Employers
American Petroleum Institute (Senior Regulatory Analyst)

TRAUGER, Thomas C.

1350 New York Ave. NW
Suite 1100
Washington, DC 20005-4798
Tel: (202)879-4000
Fax: (202)393-2866
EMail: traugert@spiegelmcd.com

Employers
Spiegel & McDiarmid (Partner)

Clients Represented

On Behalf of Spiegel & McDiarmid
Centralia, Pennsylvania, Former Residents of

TRAUTWEIN, Janet Stokes

2000 N. 14th St.
Suite 450
Arlington, VA 22201
Tel: (703)276-3806
Fax: (703)841-7797
Registered: LDA

Employers
Nat'l Ass'n of Health Underwriters (Director, State and Federal Policy, Analysis and State Government Affairs)

TRAVERSE, Brad

1055 N. Fairfax St.
Suite 201
Alexandria, VA 22314-3563
Tel: (703)739-7999
Fax: (703)739-7995
Registered: LDA
EMail: bradt@usstrategies.com
Former Legislative Assistant to Senator Barry Goldwater (R-AZ) and to Senator Nancy Kassebaum (R-KS).

Employers
Acute Long Term Hospital Ass'n (Exec. Director)
U.S. Strategies Corp. (V. President, Federal Relations)

Clients Represented
On Behalf of U.S. Strategies Corp.
Acute Long Term Hospital Ass'n
AdvoServe
Harrah's Entertainment, Inc.
Healthsouth Corp.
Home Access Health
Integrated Health Services, Inc.
Nat'l Ass'n of Community Health Centers
UBS Warburg

TRAVIS, Eryn

601 Madison
Suite 400
Alexandria, VA 22314
Tel: (703)824-0500
Fax: (703)820-1395
Registered: LDA

Employers
AAAE-ACI (Director, Communications)

TRAVIS, Thomas G.

1300 Pennsylvania Ave. NW
Suite 400
Ronald Reagan Bldg.
Washington, DC 20004
EMail: ttravis@strtrade.com
Tel: (202)638-2230
Fax: (202)638-2236
Registered: LDA, FARA

Employers
Sandler, Travis & Rosenberg, P.A. (Managing Director)

Clients Represented
On Behalf of Sandler, Travis & Rosenberg, P.A.
U.S. Apparel Industry Council

TRAYLOR, Clayton

1201 15th St. NW
Washington, DC 20005-2800
Tel: (202)822-0470
Fax: (202)822-0572
Registered: LDA

Employers
Nat'l Ass'n of Home Builders of the U.S. (Senior V. President, Political Operations)

TRAYNHAM, David

1200 Wilson Blvd.
Arlington, VA 22209-1989
Tel: (703)465-3500
Fax: (703)465-3001
Former Assistant Administrator for Policy, Planning and International Aviation, Federal Aviation Administration, Department of Transportation.

Employers
The Boeing Co. (Director, Commercial Regulatory Affairs)

TREANOR, James A.

1200 New Hampshire Ave. NW
Suite 800
Washington, DC 20036-6802
EMail: jtreanor@dlalaw.com
Tel: (202)776-2000
Fax: (202)776-2222

Employers
Dow, Lohnes & Albertson, PLLC (Member)

TREANOR, William W.

1200 17th St. NW
Fourth Floor
Washington, DC 20036
Tel: (202)785-0764
Fax: (202)728-0657

Employers
The American Youth Work Center (Exec. Director)

TREDWAY, Estelle

1611 Duke St.
Alexandria, VA 22314
Tel: (703)683-7410
Fax: (703)683-7527

Employers
American Moving and Storage Ass'n (V. President, Industry Relations)

TREICHEL, Janet M.

1914 Association Dr.
Reston, VA 20191-1596
Tel: (703)860-8300
Fax: (703)620-4483

Employers
Nat'l Business Education Ass'n (Exec. Director)

TREJO, Maria

2201 C St. NW
Room 7251
Washington, DC 20520-7261
Tel: (202)647-8722
Fax: (202)647-2762

Employers
Department of State - Bureau of Legislative Affairs (Western Hemisphere Affairs Legislative Management Officer)

TREMBLE, Tom

1200 G St. NW
Suite 400
Washington, DC 20005
Tel: (202)783-8700
Fax: (202)783-8750
Registered: LDA

Employers
AdvaMed (Director, Government and Regional Affairs)

TRENGA, Anthony J.

655 15th St. NW
Suite 900
Washington, DC 20005-5701
Tel: (202)626-5800
Fax: (202)628-0858

Employers
Miller & Chevalier, Chartered

TRENOR, John A.

2445 M St. NW
Washington, DC 20037-1420
Tel: (202)663-6000
Fax: (202)663-6363
Registered: LDA
EMail: jtrenor@wilmer.com

Employers
Wilmer, Cutler & Pickering (Associate)

TREVINO, Laura D.

1350 Beverly Rd.
Suite 108
McLean, VA 22101
EMail: lauratrevino@patientadvocacy.org
Tel: (703)748-0400
Fax: (703)748-0402

Employers
Center for Patient Advocacy (Manager, Public Affairs)

TRIMBLE, Berry

1310 G St. NW
12th Floor
Washington, DC 20005
Tel: (202)626-4780
Fax: (202)626-4833
Registered: LDA

Employers
Blue Cross Blue Shield Ass'n (Manager, Congressional Communications)

TRIMBLE, Col. Dan

The Pentagon
Room 2C634
Washington, DC 20310-0101
Tel: (703)697-2106
Fax: (703)614-3035

Employers
Department of Army (Chief, Investigations and Legislation Division, Legislative Liaison)

TRIMMER, Joy

1101 Vermont Ave. NW
12th Floor
Washington, DC 20005-3583
Tel: (202)789-7427
Fax: (202)789-7485
Registered: LDA
Former Legislative Assistant and Staff Counsel for Rep. Edward Pease (R-IN).

Employers
American Medical Ass'n (Assistant Director, Congressional Affairs Division)

TRINCA, Jeffrey S.

1420 New York Ave. NW
Suite 1050
Washington, DC 20005
Tel: (202)638-1950
Fax: (202)638-7714
Registered: LDA
Former Chief of Staff, Commission on Restructuring the Internal Revenue Service and Legislative Aide to Senator David H. Pryor (D-AR).

Employers
Van Scoyoc Associates, Inc. (V. President)

Clients Represented
On Behalf of Van Scoyoc Associates, Inc.
American Forest & Paper Ass'n
Anheuser-Busch Cos., Inc.
Computer Sciences Corp.
Internat'l Karate Federation
Internat'l Traditional Karate Federation
Nat'l Ass'n of Enrolled Agents
Nat'l Ass'n of Water Companies

TRINDER, Rachel B.

888 17th St. NW
Suite 600
Washington, DC 20006-3959
EMail: rbtrinder@zsrlaw.com
Tel: (202)298-8660
Fax: (202)342-0683
Registered: FARA

Employers
Zuckert, Scoutt and Rasenberger, L.L.P. (Partner)

Clients Represented
On Behalf of Zuckert, Scoutt and Rasenberger, L.L.P.
Air Macau
All Nippon Airways Co.
Columbia Helicopters, Inc.
Erickson Air-Crane Co.
Eva Airways Corp.
Hong Kong Dragon Airlines Ltd.
Houston, Texas, Department of Aviation of the City of
Macau, Civil Aviation Authority of
Martinair Holland
Nippon Cargo Airlines
Rosemount, Inc.

TRINGALI, Diana

112-J Elden St.
Herndon, VA 20170-4809
EMail: dtrin@erols.com
Tel: (703)709-5729
Fax: (703)709-1036

Employers
Barrack Ass'n Management (Account Executive)
Metal Finishing Suppliers Ass'n (Exec. Director)

Clients Represented
On Behalf of Barrack Ass'n Management
Metal Finishing Suppliers Ass'n

TRINH, Didier

1641 Prince St.
Alexandria, VA 22314
Tel: (703)683-8700
Fax: (703)683-8707
Registered: LDA

Employers
Federal Managers Ass'n (Director, Governmental Affairs)

TRIPLETT, Charles S.

1909 K St. NW
Washington, DC 20006
Tel: (202)263-3000
Fax: (202)263-3300
Registered: LDA
EMail: ctriplett@mayerbrown.com

Employers
Mayer, Brown & Platt (Partner)

Clients Represented
On Behalf of Mayer, Brown & Platt
Ace Ltd.

TRIPLETT, Jack E.

1775 Massachusetts Ave. NW
Washington, DC 20036-2188
Tel: (202)797-6000
Fax: (202)797-6004
Former Chief Economist, U.S. Bureau of Economic Analysis; Assistant Director for Price Monitoring, Council on Wage and Price Stability, 1979.

Employers
The Brookings Institution (Visiting Fellow, Economic Studies)

TRIPP, Mary M.

4201 Wilson Blvd.
Suite 110C
Arlington, VA 22203
Tel: (703)358-9570
Registered: LDA

Employers
Capitol Strategies (Managing Partner)

Clients Represented

On Behalf of Capitol Strategies

California Correctional Peace Officers Ass'n
NYSCOPBA - New York State Correctional Officers & Police Benevolent Ass'n

TRIPPI, Joe

1029 N. Royal St.
Suite 350
Alexandria, VA 22314
Tel: (703)519-8600
Fax: (703)519-8604

Employers

Trippi, McMahon & Squier (Partner)

TRIPPLER, Aaron K.

2700 Prosperity Ave.
Suite 250
Fairfax, VA 22031
Tel: (703)849-8888
Fax: (703)207-3561
Registered: LDA
EMail: atrippler@aiha.org

Employers

American Industrial Hygiene Ass'n (Director, Government Affairs)

TRISTER, Michael

1666 Connecticut Ave. NW
Suite 500
Washington, DC 20009
Tel: (202)328-1666
Fax: (202)328-9162

Employers

Lichtman, Trister, Singer & Ross (Partner)

Clients Represented

On Behalf of Lichtman, Trister, Singer & Ross

Alliance for Justice

TRITT, Cheryl A.

2000 Pennsylvania Ave. NW
Suite 5500
Washington, DC 20006
Tel: (202)887-1500
Fax: (202)887-0763
Registered: LDA
EMail: ctritt@mofo.com

Former Chief, Common Carrier Bureau, Federal Communications Commission.

Employers

Morrison & Foerster LLP (Partner)

Clients Represented

On Behalf of Morrison & Foerster LLP

ICO Global Communications

TROCCHIO, Julie

1875 I St. NW
Suite 1000
Washington, DC 20006
Tel: (202)296-3993
Fax: (202)296-3997
Registered: LDA
EMail: jtrocch@chausa.org

Employers

Catholic Health Ass'n of the United States (Director, Long Term Care)

TROESTER, Alise M.

1667 K St. NW
Suite 460
Washington, DC 20006
Tel: (202)956-5208
Fax: (202)956-5235
EMail: alise_troester@fmc.com

Employers

FMC Corp. (Manager, Government Affairs)

TROJAK, Gary F.

2001 L St. NW
Suite 506
Washington, DC 20036-4919
Tel: (202)775-2790
Fax: (202)223-7225

Employers

Chlorine Institute (V. President, Packaging & Technical Services)

TRON, Barrie

1275 Pennsylvania Ave. NW
Tenth Floor
Washington, DC 20004
Tel: (202)737-5339
Fax: (202)467-0810

Director of Public Affairs, The White House, during the Bush I administration.

Employers

Policy Impact Communications (V. President and Creative Director)

TROOBOFF, Peter D.

1201 Pennsylvania Ave. NW
Washington, DC 20004-2401
Tel: (202)662-6000
Fax: (202)662-6291
EMail: ptrooboff@cov.com

Employers

Covington & Burling (Partner)

TROTMAN, Steve

1401 K St. NW
Suite 600
Washington, DC 20005
Tel: (202)835-9898
Fax: (202)853-9893
Registered: LDA

Employers

ASCENT (Ass'n of Community Enterprises) (V. President, Industry Relations)

TROTTER, III, Antilla E.

1850 M St. NW
Suite 900
Washington, DC 20036
Tel: (202)463-2500
Fax: (202)463-4950
Registered: LDA

Former Staff Member, Subcommittee on Telecommunications and Finance, Senate Committee on Commerce, 1994-97.

Employers

Sher & Blackwell (Associate)

Clients Represented

On Behalf of Sher & Blackwell

ASCENT (Ass'n of Community Enterprises)
Focal Communications
Nat'l Marine Life Center
NCS Healthcare
Sargeant Marine, Inc.

TROTTER, Tom

9000 Machinists Pl.
Upper Marlboro, MD 20772-2687
Tel: (301)967-4500
Fax: (301)967-4595
Registered: LDA

Employers

Internat'l Ass'n of Machinists and Aerospace Workers (Assistant Director, Legislative Affairs)

TROUBH, Mikael

750 First St. NE
Suite 920
Washington, DC 20002-4241
Tel: (202)842-4420
Fax: (202)842-4396
Registered: LDA

Employers

Nat'l Ass'n of Police Organizations (Legislative Assistant)

TROUP, Jamie U.

1801 K St. NW
Washington, DC 20006
Tel: (202)775-7100
Fax: (202)857-0172
Registered: LDA
EMail: jtroup@arterhadden.com

Employers

Arter & Hadden (Partner)

TROWBRIDGE, Michelle

2000 Corporate Ridge
Suite 1000
McLean, VA 22102
Tel: (703)821-0770
Fax: (703)821-1350
Registered: LDA

Employers

American Frozen Food Institute (Senior Director, Communications)

TROY, Anthony F.

1660 Internat'l Dr.
Suite 600
McLean, VA 22102
Tel: (703)734-4334
Fax: (703)734-4340
Registered: LDA

Employers

Troutman Sanders Mays & Valentine L.L.P. (Partner)

TROY, Daniel E.

1150 17th St. NW
Washington, DC 20036
Tel: (202)862-5800
Fax: (202)862-7177
Registered: LDA

Attorney-Advisor, Office of Legal Counsel, Department of Justice, 1987-89.

Employers

American Enterprise Institute for Public Policy Research (Associate Scholar)
Wiley, Rein & Fielding (Partner)

TROY, Megan

1735 New York Ave. NW
Suite 500
Washington, DC 20006-4759
Tel: (202)628-1700
Fax: (202)331-1024
Registered: LDA

Employers

Preston Gates Ellis & Rouvelas Meeds LLP (Associate)

TROY, Michael H.

1300 I St. NW
Suite 400 West
Washington, DC 20005
Tel: (202)515-2554
Fax: (202)336-7921

Employers

Verizon Communications (V. President, Federal Government Relations)

TROYER, Thomas A.

One Thomas Circle NW
Suite 1100
Washington, DC 20005
Tel: (202)862-5000
Fax: (202)429-3301
Registered: LDA
EMail: tat@capdale.com

Tax Division, Department of Justice, 1962-64; Office of Assistant Secretary of the Treasury for Tax Policy, 1964-66; Associate Tax Legislative Counsel, 1966-67.

Employers

Caplin & Drysdale, Chartered (Member)

TRUBISKY, Paula

750 First St. NE
Washington, DC 20002-4242
Tel: (202)336-5585
Fax: (202)336-6063
Registered: LDA
EMail: pmt.apa@email.apa.org

Employers

American Psychological Ass'n (Legislative/Federal Affairs Officer)

TRUEBLOOD, Travis W.

2099 Pennsylvania Ave. NW
Suite 100
Washington, DC 20006
Tel: (202)955-3000
Fax: (202)955-5564
EMail: twtruebl@hklaw.com

Employers

Holland & Knight LLP

TRUEHEART, William

1825 Connecticut Ave. NW
Suite 400
Washington, DC 20009
Tel: (202)287-3220
Fax: (202)287-3196

Employers

Reading Is Fundamental, Inc. (President)

TRUEMAN, Patrick

227 Massachusetts Ave. NE
Suite 100-A
Washington, DC 20002
Tel: (202)544-0061
Fax: (202)544-0504

Employers

American Family Ass'n (Director of Governmental Affairs)

TRUITT, Jay

1301 Pennsylvania Ave. NW
Suite 300
Washington, DC 20004
Tel: (202)347-0228
Fax: (202)638-0607

Employers

Nat'l Cattleman's Beef Ass'n (Exec. Director, Legislative Affairs)

TRUITT, Michele E.

8300 Greensboro Dr.
Suite 1080
McLean, VA 22102
Tel: (703)883-0102
Fax: (703)883-0108
Registered: FARA

Employers

Sack & Harris, P.C. (Of Counsel)

Clients Represented

On Behalf of Sack & Harris, P.C.

Thomas De La Rue, Inc.

TRUITT, William

666 11th St. NW
Suite 520
Washington, DC 20001
EMail: namc@verizonmail.com
Tel: (202)347-8259
Fax: (202)628-1876

Employers

Nat'l Ass'n of Minority Contractors (Exec. Director)

TRUJILLO, Jr., Tony A.

3400 International Dr. NW
Washington, DC 20008-3090
EMail: tony.trujillo@intelsat.int
Tel: (202)944-7835
Fax: (202)944-7890
Registered: LDA

Employers

INTELSAT - Internat'l Telecommunications Satellite Organization (Sr. Director, Corporate Communications and Government Affairs)

TRULL, Frankie L.

818 Connecticut Ave. NW
Suite 325
Washington, DC 20006
EMail: fltrull@poldir.com
Tel: (202)776-0071
Fax: (202)776-0083
Registered: LDA

Employers

Policy Directions, Inc. (President)

Clients Represented

On Behalf of Policy Directions, Inc.

American Feed Industry Ass'n
Amgen
Anthra
Aventis Behring
Aventis Pharmaceuticals, Inc.
Bausch & Lomb
Baxter Healthcare Corp.
Bayer Diagnostic
Baylor College of Medicine
Burger King Corp.
Cosmetic, Toiletry and Fragrance Ass'n
CP Pharmaceuticals, Ltd.
Elan Pharmaceuticals
Genelabs Technologies, Inc.
Grocery Manufacturers of America
Kraft Foods, Inc.
Merck & Co.
Nat'l Ass'n for Biomedical Research
Nestle USA, Inc.
Orphan Medical, Inc.
Pharmaceutical Research and Manufacturers of America
Reckitt & Colman Pharmaceuticals Inc.
Soc. for Neuroscience
Soc. of the Plastics Industry
State University of New York at Albany
Transkaryotic Therapies Inc.
Transkaryotic Therapies Inc.
U.S. Oncology
Visible Genetics
Visx, Inc.

TRULUCK, Phillip N.

214 Massachusetts Ave. NE
Washington, DC 20002
Tel: (202)546-4400
Fax: (202)546-8328

Employers

Heritage Foundation (Exec. V. President)

TRUMKA, Richard L.

815 16th St. NW
Washington, DC 20006
Tel: (202)637-5000
Fax: (202)637-5058

Employers

AFL-CIO (American Federation of Labor and Congress of Industrial Organizations) (Secretary-Treasurer)

TRUNZO, Janet

1200 G St. NW
Suite 400
Washington, DC 20005
Tel: (202)783-8700
Fax: (202)783-8750
Registered: LDA

Employers

AdvaMed (Associate V. President, Technology and Regulatory Affairs)

TRUONG, To-Quyen T.

1200 New Hampshire Ave. NW
Suite 800
Washington, DC 20036-6802
EMail: ttruong@dlalaw.com
Tel: (202)776-2000
Fax: (202)776-2222

Former Associate Bureau Chief at Federal Communications Commission; Senior Attorney-Advisor at Common Carrier Bureau of FCC.

Employers

Dow, Lohnes & Albertson, PLLC (Member)

TRUPP GIL, Caroline M.

1155 16th St. NW
Washington, DC 20036
Tel: (202)872-4600
Fax: (202)872-4615

Employers

American Chemical Soc.

TRUTANIC, Cynthia

1717 Pennsylvania Ave. NW
12th Floor
Washington, DC 20006
EMail: ctrutanic@worldnet.att.net
Tel: (202)416-0150
Registered: LDA

Employers

Potomac Strategies Internat'l LLC (V. President)

Clients Represented

On Behalf of Potomac Strategies Internat'l LLC

GEO Centers, Inc.
Member-Link Systems, Inc.
memorize.com
Spacelabs Medical Inc.
V-ONE Corp.

TRYSLA, Timothy P.

800 Connecticut Ave. NW
Suite 500
Washington, DC 20006
EMail: tryslat@gtlaw.com
Tel: (202)331-3143
Fax: (202)261-0143
Registered: LDA

Legislative Aide to Rep. Bill Archer (R-TX), 1990-94.

Employers

Greenberg Traurig, LLP (Assistant Director, Legislative Affairs)

Clients Represented

On Behalf of Greenberg Traurig, LLP

American Health Care Ass'n
American Speech, Language, and Hearing Ass'n
The Business Roundtable
Community Health Systems, Inc.
Fresenius Medical Care North America
Healtheon/Web MD
LifePoint Hospitals, Inc.
Nat'l Ass'n for the Support of Long Term Care
Nat'l Ass'n of Community Health Centers
Nat'l Ass'n of Computer Consultant Businesses
Nat'l Center for Genome Research
Province Healthcare, Inc.
Starnet Communications Internat'l

TSAPATSARIS, Julianne

1875 I St. NW
Suite 900
Washington, DC 20005
Tel: (202)371-0200
Fax: (202)371-2858

Employers

Edelman Public Relations Worldwide (V. President)

Clients Represented

On Behalf of Edelman Public Relations Worldwide

Nat'l Soc. of Professional Engineers

TSCHIRHART, Paul

1850 M St. NW
Suite 900
Washington, DC 20036
Tel: (202)463-2500
Fax: (202)463-4950

Employers

Sher & Blackwell (Partner)

TSERING, Bhuchung

1825 K St. NW
Suite 520
Washington, DC 20006
Tel: (202)785-1515
Fax: (202)785-4343

Employers

Internat'l Campaign for Tibet (Director)

TSIEN, Arthur Y.

1400 16th St. NW
Suite 400
Washington, DC 20036-2220
EMail: atsien@ofwlaw.com
Tel: (202)518-6318
Fax: (202)234-1560
Registered: LDA

Associate Chief Counsel for Veterinary Medicine and Enforcement, Food and Drug Administration, 1980-85.

Employers

Olsson, Frank and Weeda, P.C. (Principal)

Clients Represented

On Behalf of Olsson, Frank and Weeda, P.C.

Aventis Pasteur
Duramed Pharmaceuticals, Inc.
Gentrac Inc.
Nat'l Ass'n of Pharmaceutical Manufacturers

TSOUCALAS, Charlotte L.

1717 Pennsylvania Ave. NW
Suite 1300
Washington, DC 20006
Tel: (202)661-3589
Fax: (202)737-3671
Registered: LDA

Employers

Defense Health Advisors, Inc.

Clients Represented

On Behalf of Defense Health Advisors, Inc.

Data-Disk Technology, Inc.
Delta Dental Plan of California
Johns Hopkins Medical Services
Tri West Healthcare Alliance
Vector Research, Inc.

TUBBESING, Carl

444 N. Capitol St. NW
Suite 515
Washington, DC 20001
Tel: (202)624-5400
Fax: (202)737-1069

Employers

Nat'l Conference of State Legislatures (Deputy Exec. Director)

TUCK, John C.

801 Pennsylvania Ave. NW
Suite 800
Washington, DC 20004
EMail: jtuck@bdbc.com
Tel: (202)508-3433
Fax: (202)508-3402
Registered: LDA, FARA

Under Secretary, Department of Energy, 1989-92. Assistant to the President; Deputy Assistant to the President for Legislative Affairs; Exec. Assistant to the Chief of Staff and Special Assistant to the President for Legislative Affairs - Senate, all in the Executive Office of the President, The White House, 1986-89. Assistant Secretary for the Majority, U.S. Senate, 1981-86. Assistant to Republican Leaders (1974-77) and Chief, Minority Floor Information Services (1977-80), U.S. House of Representatives, 1977-80. U.S. Navy, 1967-73.

Employers

Baker, Donelson, Bearman & Caldwell, P.C. (Senior Public Policy Advisor)

Clients Represented

On Behalf of Baker, Donelson, Bearman & Caldwell, P.C.

Day & Zimmermann, Inc.
Deutsche Telekom, Inc.
Loral Space and Communications, Ltd.
Newspaper Ass'n of America
VoiceStream Wireless Corp.
The Washington Post Co.

TUCKER, Dr. C. DeLores

8401 Colesville Rd.
Suite 400
Silver Spring, MD 20910
Tel: (301)562-8300
Fax: (301)562-8303

Employers

The Bethune-DuBois Institute, Inc. (President)

TUCKER, Cynthia

Ronald Reagan Bldg.
1300 Pennsylvania Ave. NW
MS: 6.10-015
Washington, DC 20523
EMail: ctucker@usaid.gov
Tel: (202)712-0068
Fax: (202)216-3237

Employers

Agency for Internat'l Development (Senior Administrative Officer, Bureau for Legislative and Public Affairs)

TUCKER, David M.

801 18th St. NW
Washington, DC 20006

Tel: (202)872-1300
Fax: (202)785-4452
Registered: LDA

Employers

Paralyzed Veterans of America (Senior Associate Legislative Director)

TUCKER, Jr., James R.

1333 New Hampshire Ave. NW
Suite 400
Washington, DC 20036

Tel: (202)887-4000
Fax: (202)887-4288
Registered: LDA

Employers

Akin, Gump, Strauss, Hauer & Feld, L.L.P.

Clients Represented

On Behalf of Akin, Gump, Strauss, Hauer & Feld, L.L.P.

Americans for Affordable Electricity
Broadwave USA Inc.
Corrections Corp. of America
Northpoint Technology, Ltd.
St. Bernard's Hospital

TUCKER, CAE, Karen S.

1800 Diagonal Rd.
Alexandria, VA 22314
EMail: ktucker@achca.org

Tel: (703)739-7900
Fax: (703)739-7901

Employers

American College of Health Care Administrators (President and Chief Exec. Officer)

TUCKER, Lisa M.

1735 New York Ave. NW
Suite 500
Washington, DC 20006-4759

Tel: (202)628-1700
Fax: (202)331-1024
Registered: LDA

Employers

Preston Gates Ellis & Rouvelas Meeds LLP (Partner)

TUCKER, Michael

1029 N. Royal St.
Suite 400
Alexandria, VA 22314
EMail: mtucker@directimpact.com

Tel: (703)684-1245
Fax: (703)684-1249

Employers

The Direct Impact Co. (V. President, Client Relations)

TUCKER, Patrick A.

801 Pennsylvania Ave. NW
Suite 350
Washington, DC 20004
EMail: ptucker@nnsdc.com

Tel: (202)783-2260
Fax: (202)783-1746
Registered: LDA

Employers

Newport News Shipbuilding Inc. (V. President, Government Relations)

TUCKER, Stefan F.

1615 L St. NW
Suite 400
Washington, DC 20036-5612
EMail: sftucker@tuckerflyer.com

Tel: (202)452-8600
Fax: (202)429-3231
Registered: LDA

Employers

Tucker & Flyer, P.C. (Partner)

TUCKER, Tracy P.

601 13th St. NW
Suite 900 South
Washington, DC 20005
EMail: ttucker@bracywilliams.com

Tel: (202)783-5588
Fax: (202)783-5595
Registered: LDA

Employers

Bracy Williams & Co. (Associate)

Clients Represented

On Behalf of Bracy Williams & Co.

Atlanta, Georgia, City of
Fort Worth, Texas, City of
Tucson, Arizona, City of

TUERFF, T. Timothy

1666 K St. NW
Suite 800
Washington, DC 20006

Tel: (202)481-7000
Fax: (202)862-7098
Registered: LDA

Employers

Arthur Andersen LLP (Partner)

Clients Represented

On Behalf of Arthur Andersen LLP

Coalition on Royalties Taxation
Hybrid Branch Coalition

TUFT, David

One Massachusetts Ave. NW
Suite 850
Washington, DC 20001

Tel: (202)682-1700
Fax: (202)682-9478

Employers

Nat'l Hydropower Ass'n (Director, Communications)

TUITE, James

1333 New Hampshire Ave. NW
Suite 400
Washington, DC 20036

Tel: (202)887-4000
Fax: (202)887-4288

Employers

Akin, Gump, Strauss, Hauer & Feld, L.L.P. (Partner)

TULL, Ron

5211 Auth Rd.
Suitland, MD 20746

Tel: (301)899-3500
Fax: (301)899-8136

Employers

Air Force Sergeants Ass'n (Director, Marketing and Communications)

TULOU, Christopher A.G.

2122 California St. NW
Suite 655
Washington, DC 20008-1803

Tel: (202)387-9440
Fax: (202)387-9445
Registered: LDA

Employers

Self-employed as an independent consultant.

Clients Represented

As an independent consultant

Environmental Council of the States (ECOS)
Sea Grant Ass'n

TUNCATA-TARIMCILAR, Arzu

1250 24th St. NW
Suite 350
Washington, DC 20037

Tel: (202)776-7740
Fax: (202)776-7741
Registered: FARA

Employers

IMPACT, LLC (Managing Member)

Clients Represented

On Behalf of IMPACT, LLC

Turkish Industrialists and Businessmen's Ass'n (TUSIAD)

TUOHEY, III, Mark H.

1455 Pennsylvania Ave. NW
Suite 700
Washington, DC 20004-1008
EMail: mtuohey@velaw.com

Tel: (202)639-6500
Fax: (202)639-6604

Special Trial Counsel, Criminal Division (1977-79) and Assistant U.S. Attorney for the District of Columbia (1973-77), Department of Justice.

Employers

Vinson & Elkins L.L.P. (Partner)

TURCH, David N. M.

517 Second St. NE
Washington, DC 20002

Tel: (202)543-3744
Fax: (202)543-3509
Registered: LDA

Employers

David Turch & Associates (President)

Clients Represented

On Behalf of David Turch & Associates

Digital Biometrics, Inc.
Inland Valley Development Agency
Recovery Engineering, Inc.
Rialto, California, City of
Riverside County Transportation Commission
San Bernardino Airport Authority
San Bernardino Associated Governments
San Bernardino, California, County of
Southern California Regional Rail Authority
St. Cloud, Minnesota, City of
Temecula, California, City of

TURETSKY, Vicki

1616 P St. NW
Suite 150
Washington, DC 20036
EMail: vturetsky@clasp.org

Tel: (202)328-5145
Fax: (202)328-5195

Employers

Center for Law and Social Policy (Senior Staff Attorney)

TURKER, Ejehan

1341 G St. NW
Suite 900
Washington, DC 20005

Tel: (202)637-1543
Fax: (202)637-1581

Employers

Philip Morris Management Corp. (Senior Legal Analyst)

TURKEWITZ, Neil

1330 Connecticut Ave. NW
Suite 300
Washington, DC 20036

Tel: (202)775-0101
Fax: (202)775-7253
Registered: LDA

Employers

Recording Industry Ass'n of America (Exec. V. President, International)

TURMAN, Richard

1200 New York Ave. NW
Suite 550
Washington, DC 20005

Tel: (202)408-7500
Fax: (202)408-8184

Employers

Ass'n of American Universities (Director, Federal Affairs)

TURNBULL, Bruce H.

1615 L St. NW
Suite 700
Washington, DC 20036-5610
EMail: bruce.turnbull@weil.com

Tel: (202)682-7000
Fax: (202)857-0939
Registered: LDA

Employers

Weil, Gotshal & Manges, LLP (Partner)

Clients Represented

On Behalf of Weil, Gotshal & Manges, LLP

Copyright Clearance Center, Inc.
InterTrust, Inc.
Matsushita Electric Corp. of America

TURNBULL, Wendy

1300 19th St. NW
Second Floor
Washington, DC 20036

Tel: (202)557-3400
Fax: (202)728-4177
Registered: LDA

Employers

Population Action Internat'l (Legislative Representative)

TURNER, Col. Abe

Rayburn House Office Bldg.
Room B325
Washington, DC 20515

Tel: (202)225-3853
Fax: (202)685-2674

Employers

Department of Army (Chief, House Liaison Division, Legislative Liaison)

TURNER, Christopher L.

2111 Wilson Blvd.
Eighth Floor
Arlington, VA 22201-3058
EMail: turner@alcalde-fay.com

Tel: (703)841-0626
Fax: (703)243-2874
Registered: LDA

Employers

Alcalde & Fay (Associate)

Clients Represented

On Behalf of Alcalde & Fay

American Maglev Technology Inc.
American Magline Group
Cruise Industry Charitable Foundation
Grand Valley State University
Jovan Broadcasting
Las Vegas Convention and Visitors Authority
Miami Heat
Miami-Dade, Florida, County of

TURNER, Frank

1120 G St. NW
Suite 520
Washington, DC 20005-3889
Tel: (202)628-4500
Fax: (202)628-6430
Registered: LDA

Employers

American Short Line and Regional Railroad Ass'n (President and Treasurer)

TURNER, Henry

1341 G St. NW
Suite 900
Washington, DC 20005
Tel: (202)637-1565
Fax: (202)637-1582

Employers

Philip Morris Management Corp. (V. President, State Government Affairs)

TURNER, James C.

1612 K St. NW
Suite 510
Washington, DC 20006
Tel: (202)887-8255
Fax: (202)887-9699

Senior Policy Analyst and Counsel, Presidential Advisory Committee on Gulf War Veterans' Illnesses, 1996-97; Staff Director and Chief Counsel, House Committee on Governmental Operations, Legislation and National Subcommittee, 1990-95; Appellate Litigator, Interstate Commerce Commission, 1979-80; Legal Assistant, Department of Transportation, Office for Civil Rights, 1978; EEO Specialist, Department of Agriculture, 1977; Research Analyst, Senate Select Committee on Intelligence, 1975-76.

Employers

HALT-An Organization of Americans for Legal Reform (Exec. Director)

TURNER, Jane

1111 19th St. NW
Suite 800
Washington, DC 20036
Tel: (202)463-2748
Fax: (202)463-2424
Registered: LDA

Employers

American Property Rights Alliance

TURNER, Jeffrey L.

2550 M St. NW
Washington, DC 20037-1350
Tel: (202)457-6000
Fax: (202)457-6315
Registered: LDA
EMail: jturner@pattonboggs.com

Former Staff Assistant to Senator Dick Clark (D-IA).

Employers

Patton Boggs, LLP (Partner)

Clients Represented

On Behalf of Patton Boggs, LLP

Alcatel
AOL Time Warner
APL Limited
Elf Aquitine
European Energy Company Coalition
Hitachi Home Electronics, Inc.
Internet Safety Ass'n
Matsushita Electric Corp. of America
Mitsubishi Electronics America (Consumer Electronics Group)
Pioneer of North America
Sanyo North American Corp.
Sharp Electronics Corp.
Sony Electronics, Inc.
Toshiba Consumer Products, Inc.
Travel Industry Ass'n of America

TURNER, John F.

1800 N. Kent St.
Suite 1120
Arlington, VA 22209
Tel: (703)525-6300
Fax: (703)525-4610

Employers

The Conservation Fund (President and Chief Exec. Officer)

TURNER, Leslie M.

1333 New Hampshire Ave. NW
Suite 400
Washington, DC 20036
Tel: (202)887-4000
Fax: (202)887-4288
Registered: LDA

Counselor to the Secretary, Office of Territorial and Intergovernmental Affairs, Department of Interior, 1996. Assistant Secretary, Office of Territorial and Intergovernmental Affairs, Department of Interior, 1993-96.

Employers

Akin, Gump, Strauss, Hauer & Feld, L.L.P. (Partner)

Clients Represented

On Behalf of Akin, Gump, Strauss, Hauer & Feld, L.L.P.

Capital Gaming Internat'l, Inc.

TURNER, Margery A.

2100 M St. NW
Washington, DC 20037
Tel: (202)833-7200
Fax: (202)429-0687

Employers

The Urban Institute (Director, Metrolpolitan Housing and Community Policy Center)

TURNER, Marion

1025 Thomas Jefferson St. NW
Suite 400 East
Washington, DC 20007-0805
Tel: (202)965-8171
Fax: (202)965-6403
Registered: LDA

Legislative Assistant to Senator Connie Mack, 1992-94.

Employers

Jorden Burt LLP (Legislative Coordinator)

Clients Represented

On Behalf of Jorden Burt LLP

Assurant Group
Gainesville, Florida, City of
Miami Beach, Florida, City of

TURNER, Pamela J.

1724 Massachusetts Ave. NW
Washington, DC 20036-1969
Tel: (202)775-3644
Fax: (202)775-3671
Registered: LDA

Former Deputy Assistant to the President for Legislative Affairs - Senate, Executive Office of the President, The White House, during the Reagan administration.

Employers

Nat'l Cable Television Ass'n (Senior V. President, Government Relations)

TURNER, Patrick C.

701 Pennsylvania Ave. NW
Suite 600
Washington, DC 20004
Tel: (202)624-1200
Fax: (202)624-1298
EMail: pturner@lanlaw.com

Former Staff member to Senator Slade Gorton (R-WA) and Senator David Boren (D-OK).

Employers

Long, Aldridge & Norman, LLP (Government Affairs Consultant)

Clients Represented

On Behalf of Long, Aldridge & Norman, LLP

Consortium on Government Relations for Student Affairs
DeChiaro Properties
Florida Internat'l University
Nat'l Ass'n of Professional Forestry Schools and Colleges
Nat'l Franchisee Ass'n
University of Georgia
Weather Channel

TURNER, Samuel D.

1900 K St. NW
Suite 750
Washington, DC 20006
Tel: (202)833-4500
Fax: (202)833-2859
Registered: LDA

Employers

Bennett Turner & Coleman, LLP (Partner)

Clients Represented

On Behalf of Bennett Turner & Coleman, LLP

American Soc. of Clinical Oncology
Bristol-Myers Squibb Co.
Cancer Leadership Council
The Children's Cause Inc.
Cure for Lymphoma Foundation
Cystic Fibrosis Foundation
Leukemia & Lymphoma Soc.
Nat'l Coalition for Cancer Survivorship
Nat'l Patient Advocate Foundation
North American Brain Tumor Coalition

TURNER, Susan

1010 Duke St.
Alexandria, VA 22314-3589
Tel: (703)684-5700
Fax: (703)684-6321
Registered: LDA

Employers

American Ass'n of Port Authorities (Director, Government Relations)

TURNER, Susan

5185 MacArthur Blvd. NW
Washington, DC 20016-3341
Tel: (202)237-6000
Fax: (202)237-8900
Registered: LDA

Employers

Lotstein Buckman, Attorneys At Law (Manager, Government Affairs)
Nat'l Ass'n of Mortgage Brokers (PAC Contact)

Clients Represented

On Behalf of Lotstein Buckman, Attorneys At Law

Nat'l Ass'n of Mortgage Brokers

TURNER, Terry

5201 Auth Way
Camp Springs, MD 20746
Tel: (301)899-0675
Fax: (301)899-7355
Registered: LDA

Employers

Seafarers Internat'l Union of North America (Nat'l. Director, Political Action & Government Relations)

TURPIN, Jim

4380 Forbes Blvd.
Lanham, MD 20706-4322
Tel: (301)918-1885
Fax: (301)918-1900
Registered: LDA
EMail: jamest@aca.org

Employers

American Correctional Ass'n (Legislative Liaison)

TURPIN, S. Diane

1101 Vermont Ave. NW
Suite 606
Washington, DC 20005
Tel: (202)289-2222
Fax: (202)371-0384
Registered: LDA
EMail: d.turpin@asawash.org

Employers

American Soc. of Anesthesiologists (Associate Director, State)

TURRENTINE, J. Drake

1325 G St. NW
Suite 500
Washington, DC 20005
Tel: (202)824-0299
Fax: (202)628-0067
EMail: draketso@aol.com

Employers

Special Olympics, Inc. (General Counsel)

TURVAVILLE, Kyndel

507 C St. NE
Washington, DC 20002-5809
Tel: (202)544-7944
Fax: (202)544-7975
Registered: LDA
EMail: kturvaville@beacon-group.net

Employers

Beacon Consulting Group, Inc. (Legislative Assistant)

Clients Represented

On Behalf of Beacon Consulting Group, Inc.

Advance Paradigm
Big Brothers/Big Sisters of America
Center Point Inc.
Westcare Foundation, Inc.

TURZA, Peter H.

1050 Connecticut Ave. NW
Washington, DC 20036-5306
Tel: (202)955-8500
Fax: (202)467-0539
Registered: LDA
EMail: pturza@gdclaw.com

Chair, Working Group on Health Care Reform, Advisory Counsel on Employee Welfare and Pension Benefit Plans, Department of Labor, 1994. Special Counsel, Pension and Welfare Plans Laws, Joint Economic Committee, 1979-81. Associate Minority Counsel, Subcommittee on Labor, Senate Committee on Human Resources, 1977-79.

Employers

Gibson, Dunn & Crutcher LLP (Partner)

Clients Represented

On Behalf of Gibson, Dunn & Crutcher LLP

CNF Transportation, Inc.

TURZI, Joseph A.

1333 New Hampshire Ave. NW
Suite 400
Washington, DC 20036
Tel: (202)887-4000
Fax: (202)887-4288

Employers

Akin, Gump, Strauss, Hauer & Feld, L.L.P. (Partner)

TUTTLE, Alan A.

2550 M St. NW
Washington, DC 20037-1350
Tel: (202)457-6000
Fax: (202)457-6315
Registered: LDA
EMail: atuttle@pattonboggs.com

Solicitor, Federal Power Commission, 1975-77. Assistant to the Solicitor General (1971-75) and Assistant U.S. Attorney for the Southern District of New York (1969-71), Department of Justice.

Employers

Patton Boggs, LLP (Partner)

TUTTLE, Julian B.

1025 Thomas Jefferson St. NW
Suite 407 West
Washington, DC 20007
Tel: (202)342-1300
Fax: (202)342-5880
Registered: LDA

Employers

Tuttle, Taylor & Heron (Senior Partner)

Clients Represented

On Behalf of Tuttle, Taylor & Heron

Nat'l Milk Producers Federation

TUTTLE, Susan C.

1301 K St. NW
Suite 1200-West Tower
Washington, DC 20005-3307
Tel: (202)515-5503
Fax: (202)515-5078
Registered: LDA
EMail: tuttle@us.ibm.com

Employers

Internat'l Business Machines Corp. (Program Manager, Public Affairs, Trade and Investment)

TUTWILER, M. Ann

1722 I St. NW
Fourth Floor
Washington, DC 20006
Tel: (202)736-8584
Fax: (202)833-3831
Registered: LDA

Policy Analyst and Presidential Management Intern, Economic Research Service, Department of Agriculture, 1985-86.

Employers

Central Soya Co. (Director, Government Relations)

TUVIN, Carl R.

2805 Washington Ave.
Chevy Chase, MD 20815
Tel: (301)588-8461
Fax: (301)495-6362

Employers

Tuvin Associates (President)

Clients Represented

On Behalf of Tuvin Associates

Motion Picture and Television Fund

TWEDT, Thomas D.

1200 New Hampshire Ave. NW
Suite 800
Washington, DC 20036-6802
Tel: (202)776-2000
Fax: (202)776-2222
EMail: ttwedt@dlalaw.com

Former Branch Chief in the Division of Corporate Finance at Securities and Exchange Commission.

Employers

Dow, Lohnes & Albertson, PLLC (Member)

TYDINGS, John R.

1129 20th St. NW
Suite 200
Washington, DC 20036
Tel: (202)857-5900
Fax: (202)223-2648
Registered: LDA

Employers

Greater Washington Board of Trade (President)

TYDINGS, Hon. Joseph D.

2101 L St. NW
Washington, DC 20037-1526
Tel: (202)785-9700
Fax: (202)887-0689
EMail: tydingsj@dsmo.com

Chairman, Judicial Nominating Committee for U.S. District Courts and U.S. Court of Appeals Judges for the District of Columbia under President Jimmy Carter, 1977-81. Member, U.S. Senate (D-MD), 1965-71. U.S. Attorney, District of Maryland, Department of Justice, 1961-63.

Employers

Dickstein Shapiro Morin & Oshinsky LLP (Senior Counsel)

Clients Represented

On Behalf of Dickstein Shapiro Morin & Oshinsky LLP

First USA Bank

TYERYAR, CAE, Clay D.

111 Park Place
Falls Church, VA 22046-4513
Tel: (703)533-0251
Fax: (703)241-5603

Employers

American Pipe Fittings Ass'n (Exec. Director)
American Textile Machinery Ass'n (Secretary, Textile Machinery Good Government Committee)
Ass'n and Soc. Management Internat'l Inc. (Senior V. President)
Cold Finished Steel Bar Institute (Executive Staff)
Meat Industry Council (Exec. Director)
Meat Industry Suppliers Ass'n (Exec. Director)
North American Natural Casing Ass'n (Senior V. President)
Product Liability Prevention and Defense Group (Exec. Director)

Clients Represented

On Behalf of Ass'n and Soc. Management Internat'l Inc.

American Pipe Fittings Ass'n
Meat Industry Suppliers Ass'n
Product Liability Prevention and Defense Group

TYLE, Craig S.

1401 H St. NW
12th Floor
Washington, DC 20005-2148
Tel: (202)326-5815
Fax: (202)326-5812
Registered: LDA

Employers

Investment Co. Institute (General Counsel)

TYNAN, Brian M.

227 Massachusetts Ave. NE
Suite One
Washington, DC 20002
Tel: (202)548-8470
Fax: (202)548-8472
Registered: LDA
EMail: btynan@fortessa.com

Legislative Director (1999) and Senior Legislative Assistant (1995-99) to Rep. John D. Fox (R-PA).

Employers

Martin G. Hamberger & Associates

Clients Represented

On Behalf of Martin G. Hamberger & Associates

American Public Transportation Ass'n
Michael Baker Corp.
Eclipse Energy Systems, Inc./Insyte, Inc.
Westinghouse Government Services Group

TYNES, Emily

1200 New York Ave. NW
Suite 300
Washington, DC 20005
Tel: (202)326-8700
Fax: (202)682-2154
EMail: info@ccmc.org

Employers

Communications Consortium (V. President)

TYRER, Robert S.

600 13th St. NW
Suite 640
Washington, DC 20005-3096
Tel: (202)756-8500
Fax: (202)756-8510
EMail: rst@cohengroup.net

Former Chief of Staff to the Secretary, Department of Defense, 1997-2001

Employers

The Cohen Group (President, Chief Operating Officer)

TYSON, Herbert L.

1033 N. Fairfax St.
Suite 404
Alexandria, VA 22314
Tel: (703)549-7404
Fax: (703)549-8712
EMail: htyson@icsc.org

Employers

Internat'l Council of Shopping Centers (Senior Director, State and Local Government Relations)

TYSSE, G. John

1015 15th St. NW
Suite 1200
Washington, DC 20005
Tel: (202)789-8600
Fax: (202)789-1708
Registered: LDA

Director of Labor Law, U.S. Chamber of Commerce, 1980-84.

Employers

McGuiness Norris & Williams, LLP (Partner)

Clients Represented

On Behalf of McGuiness Norris & Williams, LLP

Labor Policy Ass'n (LPA)
Nat'l Club Ass'n

TYUS, Aisha

1299 Pennsylvania Ave. NW
Suite 800 West
Washington, DC 20004
Tel: (202)785-0500
Fax: (202)785-5277
Registered: LDA

Employers

The Carmen Group (Associate)

Clients Represented

On Behalf of The Carmen Group

Dillard University
Metropolitan Washington Airports Authority

UBL, Stephen J.

1200 G St. NW
Suite 400
Washington, DC 20005
Tel: (202)783-8700
Fax: (202)783-8750

Employers

AdvaMed (Exec. V. President, Federal Government Relations)

UCCELLO, Cori E.

1100 17th St. NW
Seventh Floor
Washington, DC 20036
Tel: (202)223-8196
Fax: (202)872-1948
Registered: LDA

Employers

American Academy of Actuaries (Senior Health Fellow)

UDWIN, Gerald E.

2121 K St. NW
Suite 800
Washington, DC 20037
Tel: (202)261-6565
Fax: (202)466-7745
Registered: LDA
EMail: gudwin@aol.com

Employers

The Udwin Group (President)

Clients Represented

On Behalf of The Udwin Group

Verizon Communications

UEHARA, So

1776 I St. NW
Suite 725
Washington, DC 20006

Tel: (202)331-1167
Fax: (202)331-1319

Employers

Marubeni America Corp. (Senior Researcher)

UFFELMAN, William

1850 Samuel Morse Dr.
Reston, VA 20198

Tel: (703)708-9000
Fax: (703)708-9020
Registered: LDA

Employers

Soc. of Nuclear Medicine (Director, Public Policy)

UFHOLZ, Philip

1625 K St. NW
Suite 1100
Washington, DC 20006-1604

Tel: (202)857-0244
Fax: (202)857-0237

Employers

Biotechnology Industry Organization (Director, Government Relations and Tax Counsel)

UGORETZ, Mark J.

1400 L St. NW
Suite 350
Washington, DC 20005

Tel: (202)789-1400
Fax: (202)789-1120
Registered: LDA

Employers

The ERISA Industry Committee (ERIC) (President)

ULLMAN, Joyce

2020 Pennsylvania Ave. NW
Suite 275
Washington, DC 20006

Tel: (202)296-2946

Employers

Women's Pro-Israel Nat'l Political Action Committee (Win PaC) (Treasurer)

ULM, Gene

277 S. Washington St.
Suite 320
Alexandria, VA 22314

Tel: (703)836-7655
Fax: (703)836-8117

EMail: gene@pos.org

Employers

Public Opinion Strategies (Partner)

ULREY, Peri

805 15th St. NW
Suite 510
Washington, DC 20005

Tel: (202)326-9300
Fax: (202)326-9330

EMail: pulrey@ngsa.org

Employers

Natural Gas Supply Ass'n (Senior Analyst)

ULRICH, Christopher

2100 Pennsylvania Ave. NW
Suite 535
Washington, DC 20037

Tel: (202)822-1700
Fax: (202)822-1919
Registered: LDA

Former Domestic Policy Advisor to the Vice President, Executive Office of the President, The White House.

Employers

Simon Strategies/Mindbeam (V. President)

Clients Represented

On Behalf of Simon Strategies/Mindbeam

AirCell, Inc.

Catholic Television Network

Traffic.com

ULRICH, John R.

1776 I St. NW
Suite 1050
Washington, DC 20006

Tel: (202)429-3432
Fax: (202)429-3467
Registered: LDA

Employers

The Dow Chemical Co. (Manager, Government Relations, Environmental Policy)

UNCAPHER, Mark

1401 Wilson Blvd.
Suite 1100
Arlington, VA 22209

Tel: (703)522-5055
Fax: (703)525-2279
Registered: LDA

EMail: muncapher@itaa.org

Employers

Information Technology Ass'n of America (ITAA) (V. President and Counsel, Internet Commerce and Communications Division)

UNDELAND, John R.

818 Connecticut Ave. NW
Second Floor
Washington, DC 20006

Tel: (202)289-2001
Fax: (202)289-1327

EMail: jundeland@stratacomm.net

Former Deputy Director, White House News Summary and Senior Writer for Media Affairs, The White House.

Employers

Strat@Comm (Strategic Communications Counselors) (Senior Counselor)

UNDERHILL, Charles

4200 Wilson Blvd.
Suite 800
Arlington, VA 22203-1838

Tel: (703)276-0100
Fax: (703)525-8277

EMail: cunderhill@cbb.bbb.org

Employers

Council of Better Business Bureaus (Senior V. President, Dispute Resolution Division, Chief Operating Officer, BBB Online)

UNDERHILL, Jr., Henry W.

1110 Vermont Ave. NW
Suite 200
Washington, DC 20005

Tel: (202)466-5424
Fax: (202)785-0152

Employers

Internat'l Municipal Lawyers Ass'n (Exec. Director and General Counsel)

UNDERWOOD, Fred

700 11th St. NW
Washington, DC 20001-4507

Tel: (202)383-1132
Fax: (202)383-7540
Registered: LDA

Employers

Nat'l Ass'n of Realtors (Senior Fair Housing Policy Representative)

UNDERWOOD, Julie

1680 Duke St.
Alexandria, VA 22314-3407

Tel: (703)838-6722
Fax: (703)683-7590

Employers

Nat'l School Boards Ass'n (Assoc. Exec. Director and General Counsel)

UNGER, Peter S.

5301 Buckeystown Pike
Suite 350
Frederick, MD 21704-8307

Tel: (301)644-3212
Fax: (301)662-2974

Employers

American Ass'n for Laboratory Accreditation (President)

UNGER, Peter V. B.

801 Pennsylvania Ave. NW
Washington, DC 20004-2604

Tel: (202)662-4741
Fax: (202)662-4643

EMail: punger@fulbright.com

Attorney, Enforcement Division, Securities and Exchange Commission, 1986-88. Law Clerk, U.S. District Court, Southern District of Florida, 1983-85.

Employers

Fulbright & Jaworski L.L.P. (Partner)

Clients Represented

On Behalf of Fulbright & Jaworski L.L.P.

The Philadelphia Stock Exchange, Inc.

UPSHAW, Gene

2021 L St. NW
Suite 600
Washington, DC 20036

Tel: (202)463-2200
Fax: (202)857-0673

Employers

Nat'l Football League Players Ass'n (Exec. Director)

URBAN, Anne

1775 I St. NW
Suite 700
Washington, DC 20006

Tel: (202)261-4000
Fax: (202)261-4001
Registered: LDA

Former Legislative Director and Tax Advisor to Sen. Bob Kerrey (D-NE). Former Chief Advisor for Tax, Trade, and Appropriations for Sen. Joseph I. Lieberman (D-CT).

Employers

Clark & Weinstock, Inc. (Managing Director)

Clients Represented

On Behalf of Clark & Weinstock, Inc.

American Ass'n of Homes and Services for the Aging

Rubber Manufacturers Ass'n

URBAN, Timothy J.

1150 17th St. NW
Suite 601
Washington, DC 20036

Tel: (202)293-7474
Fax: (202)293-8811
Registered: LDA

Legislative Assistant to Rep. Wally Herger (R-CA), 1982-96.

Employers

Washington Council Ernst & Young (Partner)

Clients Represented

On Behalf of Washington Council Ernst & Young

Aetna Inc.
Aetna Life & Casualty Co.
Allegiance Healthcare Corp.
Allen & Co.
American Express Co.
American Insurance Ass'n
American Staffing Ass'n
Anheuser-Busch Cos., Inc.
Antitrust Coalition for Consumer Choice in Health Care
Apartment Investment and Management Co.
Ass'n of American Railroads
Ass'n of Home Appliance Manufacturers
AT&T
AT&T Capital Corp.
Avco Financial Services
Aventis Pharmaceuticals, Inc.
Baxter Healthcare Corp.
BHC Communications, Inc.
Bulmer Holding PLC, H. P.
Cash Balance Coalition
Chamber of Shipping of America
Citigroup
Coalition for Fairness in Defense Exports
Coalition to Preserve Tracking Stock
ComEd
The Connell Co.
Deferral Group
Directors Guild of America
Doris Duke Charitable Foundation
Eaton Vance Management Co.
Eden Financial Corp.
The Enterprise Foundation
Fannie Mae
FedEx Corp.
Ford Motor Co.
GE Capital Assurance
General Electric Co.
General Motors Corp.
Global Competitiveness Coalition
Grasslands Water District
Group Health, Inc.
Haz-X Support Services Corp.
HEREIU
Gilbert P. Hyatt, Inventor
Investment Co. Institute
Large Public Power Council
Local Initiatives Support Corp.
Lockheed Martin Corp.
MacAndrews & Forbes Holdings, Inc.
Marsh & McLennan Cos.
MCG Northwest, Inc.
McLane Co.
Merrill Lynch & Co., Inc.
Metropolitan Banking Group
Microsoft Corp.
Nat'l Ass'n for State Farm Agents
Nat'l Ass'n of Professional Employer Organizations
Nat'l Ass'n of Real Estate Investment Trusts
Nat'l Cable Television Ass'n
Nat'l Defined Contribution Council
Nat'l Foreign Trade Council, Inc.
Nat'l Multi-Housing Council
PaineWebber Group, Inc.
Pfizer, Inc.
R&D Tax Credit Coalition
R&D Tax Regulation Group
Recording Industry Ass'n of America
Reed-Elsevier Inc.
R. J. Reynolds Tobacco Co.
Charles Schwab & Co., Inc.,
Securities Industry Ass'n
Sierra Pacific Industries
Skadden, Arps, Slate, Meagher & Flom LLP
Straddle Rules Tax Group
Tax Fairness Coalition
Tax/Shelter Coalition
TransOceanic Shipping
TU Services
TXU Business Services
U.S. Oncology
USA Biomass Power Producers Alliance
Viaticus, Inc.
Wilkie Farr & Gallagher
Ziff Investors Partnership

URBANCZYK, Steve L.

725 12th St. NW — Tel: (202)434-5000
Washington, DC 20005 — Fax: (202)434-5029

Assistant to the Solicitor General, Department of Justice, 1975-78.

Employers
Williams & Connolly (Partner)

URBANSKI, Lynn C.

6420 Grovedale Dr. — Tel: (703)971-1732
Alexandria, VA 22310 — Fax: (703)971-5327

Employers
Virginia Baseball Club (Corporate Secretary, Public Affairs)

URBANSKI, Tina

410 First St. SE — Tel: (202)484-2776
Third Floor — Fax: (202)484-7016
Washington, DC 20003
EMail: turbanski@dcsgroup.com

Employers
The DCS Group (Senior Acccount Executive)

URBANY, Francis S.

1133 21st St. NW — Tel: (202)463-4100
Suite 900 — Fax: (202)463-4142
Washington, DC 20036 — Registered: LDA
EMail: frank.urbany@bellsouth.com

Employers
BellSouth Corp. (V. President, International)

URFF, Jenifer E.

66 Canal Center Plaza — Tel: (703)739-9333
Suite 302 — Fax: (703)548-9517
Alexandria, VA 22314
EMail: jenifer.urffnasmhpd.org

Employers
Nat'l Ass'n of State Mental Health Program Directors (Director, Government Relations)

URMSTON, Dean

601 13th St. NW — Tel: (202)638-3128
Suite 570 South — Fax: (202)638-3171
Washington, DC 20005-3807
EMail: durmston@amseed.org

Employers
American Seed Trade Ass'n (Exec. V. President)
Nat'l Council of Commercial Plant Breeders (Exec. V. President)

URWITZ, Jay P.

1455 Pennsylvania Ave. NW — Tel: (202)942-8400
Suite 1000 — Fax: (202)942-8484
Washington, DC 20004 — Registered: LDA
EMail: jay.urwitz@haledorr.com

Legislative Assistant for Domestic Policy to Senator Edward Kennedy (D-MA), 1977-81. Law Clerk to Judge Irving L. Goldberg, U.S. Court of Appeals, Fifth Circuit, 1974-75.

Employers
Hale and Dorr LLP (Senior Partner)

Clients Represented

On Behalf of Hale and Dorr LLP

Blyth Industries, Inc.
Diamond Antenna & Microwave Corp.
Harcourt Inc.
Lau Technologies
Micron Technology, Inc.
Neiman Marcus Group
Northeastern University
Ostex Internat'l Inc.
Parametric Technology Corp.
Psychological Corp.
SatCon Technology Corp.
Thermedics Detection, Inc.
University College Dublin
Wang Laboratories Inc.
Wheelock College

USDAN, Michael D.

1001 Connecticut Ave. NW — Tel: (202)822-8405
Suite 310 — Fax: (202)872-4050
Washington, DC 20036

Employers
Institute for Educational Leadership (President)

UTHANK, Mike

505 Huntmar Park Dr. — Tel: (703)437-0100
Suite 210 — Fax: (703)481-3596
Herndon, VA 20170

Employers
Nat'l Conference of States on Building Codes and Standards (President)

UTRECHT, Carolyn

1133 Connecticut Ave. NW — Tel: (202)293-1177
Suite 300 — Fax: (202)293-3411
Washington, DC 20036

Special Assistant General Counsel (1981-84) and Attorney (1979-81), Federal Election Commission.

Employers
Ryan, Phillips, Utrecht & MacKinnon (Partner)

UTT, Ronald

214 Massachusetts Ave. NE — Tel: (202)546-4400
Washington, DC 20002 — Fax: (202)546-8328

Employers
Heritage Foundation (Grover M. Hermann Fellow in Federal Budget Affairs)

VACCARELLA, Frank J.

451 Seventh St. SW — Tel: (202)708-0030
Roo 10234 — Fax: (202)708-9981
Washington, DC 20410
EMail: frank_j._vaccarella@hud.gov

Employers
Department of Housing and Urban Development (Senior Intergovernmental Relations Officer)

VAGLEY, Robert E.

1130 Connecticut Ave. NW — Tel: (202)828-7100
Suite 1000 — Fax: (202)293-1219
Washington, DC 20036

Employers
American Insurance Ass'n (President)

VAKERICS, Thomas V.

607 14th St. NW — Tel: (202)628-6600
Suite 700 — Fax: (202)434-1690
Washington, DC 20005-2011 — Registered: LDA

Employers
Perkins Coie LLP

VALACHOVIC, D.M.D., Richard W.

1625 Massachusetts Ave. NW — Tel: (202)667-9433
Washington, DC 20036 — Fax: (202)667-0642

Employers
American Dental Education Ass'n (Exec. Director)

VALANZANO, Anthony

601 13th St. NW — Tel: (703)759-1966
Suite 900 S. — Fax: (703)759-5101
Washington, DC 20005 — Registered: LDA

Minority Counsel and Staff Director, Housing Subcommittee, House Banking Committee, 1973-83. Senior Legislative Affairs Officer, Department of Housing and Urban Development, 1970-73.

Employers
Valanzano & Associates (President)

Clients Represented

On Behalf of Valanzano & Associates

American Council of Life Insurers
American Internat'l Group, Inc.
American Land Title Ass'n
Appraisal Institute
The Chubb Corp.
The Council of Insurance Agents & Brokers
Manufactured Housing Ass'n for Regulatory Reform

VALASEK, Tomas

1779 Massachusetts Ave. NW — Tel: (202)332-0600
Suite 615 — Fax: (202)462-4559
Washington, DC 20036

Employers
Center for Defense Information (Research Analyst)

VALENSTEIN, Carl A.

1050 Connecticut Ave. NW — Tel: (202)857-6000
Washington, DC 20036-5339 — Fax: (202)857-6395
Registered: LDA

Employers
Arent Fox Kintner Plotkin & Kahn, PLLC (Member)

VALENTE, Ph.D., CAE, Carmine M.

14750 Sweitzer Ln.
Suite 100
Laurel, MD 20707-5906
EMail: cvalente@aium.org
Tel: (301)498-4100
Fax: (301)498-4450

Employers
American Institute of Ultrasound in Medicine (Exec. Director)

VALENTE, Claudia Barker

Hamilton Square
600 14th St. NW, Fifth Floor
Washington, DC 20005
Tel: (202)783-1980
Fax: (202)783-1918

Employers
Valente Lopatin & Schulze

Clients Represented

On Behalf of Valente Lopatin & Schulze
FBV Group
Fund for American Opportunity PAC

VALENTE, III, Mark

Hamilton Square
600 14th St. NW, Fifth Floor
Washington, DC 20005
Tel: (202)783-1980
Fax: (202)783-1918
Registered: LDA
EMail: VLLandS@aol.com
Director of Congressional Relations, Office of Personnel Management, 1989-93. Staff Assistant, Office of Public Liaison, The White House, Executive Office of the President, 1984-1985.

Employers
MV3 & Associates (Principal)
Valente Lopatin & Schulze (Principal)

Clients Represented

On Behalf of Valente Lopatin & Schulze
Alliance for Special Needs Children
Center for Disease Detection
Cohn & Wolfe
Columbus Educational Services
Columbus Medical Services
Dalton & Dalton P.C.
Devon Management Group Inc.
FBV Group
Fund for American Opportunity PAC
Internat'l Tax and Investment Center
Keating Development Corp.
Keating Technologies Inc.
Kelly Anderson & Associates
The LTV Corp.
Mediware Information Systems, Inc.
Nat'l Ass'n of Thrift Savings Plan Participants
Nat'l Italian American Foundation
North American Coal
O'Neill Properties Group
Orkand Corp.
Pennsylvania Economic Development Financing Authorities
Pepper Hamilton LLP
PriceWaterhouseCoopers
System & Computer Technology Corp.
United Nations Development Programme
United Payors and United Providers

VALENTE, Thomas

3000 K St. NW
Suite 300
Washington, DC 20007
Tel: (202)424-7500
Fax: (202)424-7643
Registered: LDA

Employers
Swidler Berlin Shereff Friedman, LLP

Clients Represented

On Behalf of Swidler Berlin Shereff Friedman, LLP
Dairy.com

VALENTI, Jack J.

1600 I St. NW
Washington, DC 20006
Tel: (202)293-1966
Fax: (202)296-7410
Registered: LDA
Former Aide to the President, The White House, during the Johnson administration.

Employers
Motion Picture Ass'n of America (President and Chief Exec. Officer)

VALENTINE, Barry

1400 K St. NW
Suite 801
Washington, DC 20005-2485
Tel: (202)393-1500
Fax: (202)842-4063

Employers
General Aviation Manufacturers Ass'n (Senior V. President, Internat'l Affairs)

VALENTINE, Dawn

1782 Columbia Rd. NW
Washington, DC 20009
EMail: Dawn@thgweb.com
Tel: (202)518-8047
Fax: (202)518-8048

Employers
Hauser Group (Associate)

VALENTINE, Steven R. "Rick"

1735 New York Ave. NW
Suite 500
Washington, DC 20006-4759
Tel: (202)628-1700
Fax: (202)331-1024
Registered: LDA
EMail: stevenv@prestongates.com
Legislative Director (1996-99) and General Counsel (1993-99) to Senator Robert C. Smith (R-NH). Deputy Assistant Attorney General (1988-93) and Counselor to the Assistant Attorney General (1987-88), Civil Division, Department of Justice. Administrative Assistant to Senator John P. East (R-NC), 1985-86. Chief Counsel and Staff Director, Subcommittee on Courts (1985) and Chief Counsel and Staff Director, Subcommittee on Separation of Powers (1983-85), Senate Committee on the Judiciary.

Employers
Preston Gates Ellis & Rouvelas Meeds LLP (Of Counsel)

Clients Represented

On Behalf of Preston Gates Ellis & Rouvelas Meeds LLP
Akzo Nobel Chemicals, Inc.
Americans for Computer Privacy
Burlington Northern Santa Fe Railway
Chicago Title Insurance
Chitimacha Tribe of Louisiana
Envirocare of Utah, Inc.
Future of Puerto Rico Inc.
KB Holdings
Magazine Publishers of America
Microsoft Corp.
Money Garden Corp.
Nat'l Center for Economic Freedom, Inc.
Nat'l Produce Production Inc.
Pitney Bowes, Inc.
PPL
VoiceStream Wireless Corp.
Voor Huisen Project Mgmt. Serv. Bedryt B.V., Ltd.

VALENTINO, James

701 Pennsylvania Ave. NW
Suite 900
Washington, DC 20004-2608
Tel: (202)434-7300
Fax: (202)434-7400

Employers
Mintz, Levin, Cohn, Ferris, Glovsky and Popeo, P.C. (Partner)

VALENTINO, Dr. Joseph G.

12601 Twinbrook Pkwy.
Rockville, MD 20852
EMail: jgv@usp.org
Tel: (301)881-0666

Employers
United States Pharmacopeial Convention (Senior V. President, Secretary, and General Counsel)

VALENZUELA, Jeff

600 Pennsylvania Ave. SE
Suite 400
Washington, DC 20003
EMail: jvalenzuela@dlcppi.org
Tel: (202)546-0007
Fax: (202)544-5002

Employers
Democratic Leadership Council (Coordinator, Political Programing)

VALENZUELA, Pam

50 F St. NW
Suite 900
Washington, DC 20001
EMail: pvalenzuela@ncfe.org
Tel: (202)626-8700
Fax: (202)626-8722

Employers
Nat'l Council of Farmer Cooperatives (Director, Communications and Member Relations)

VALERIO, Stacey L.

1140 19th St. NW
Suite 900
Washington, DC 20036
EMail: svalerio@kkblah.com
Tel: (202)223-5120
Fax: (202)223-5619

Employers
Kleinfeld, Kaplan and Becker (Associate)

VALIS, Wayne H.

1700 Pennsylvania Ave. NW
Suite 950
Washington, DC 20006
Tel: (202)393-5055
Fax: (202)393-0120
Registered: LDA
EMail: valis@erols.com
Special Assistant to the President (1981-83), Office of Public Liaison (1973-74), and Staff Assistant to the President (1972-73), The White House.

Employers
Trade Ass'n Liaison Council (Exec. Director)
Valis Associates (President)

Clients Represented

On Behalf of Valis Associates
American Bakers Ass'n
American Consulting Engineers Council
Ass'n for the Suppliers of Printing and Publishing Technology
CH2M Hill
Citizens for Civil Justice Reform
Coalition for Open Markets and Expanded Trade
Dairyland Power Cooperative
The Doctors' Co.
Environmental Action Group
Exxon Mobil Corp.
Grocery Manufacturers of America
Joint Southeast Public Improvement Council
Kitchen Cabinet Manufacturers Ass'n
Nat'l Ass'n of Wholesaler-Distributors
Norfolk Southern Corp.
NPES, The Ass'n for Suppliers of Printing, Publishing, and Converting Technologies
Regulatory Improvement Council
Renewable Fuels Ass'n
Soc. of the Plastics Industry
Tax Action Group
Telecommunications Industry Ass'n
Trade Ass'n Liaison Council
Transportation Reform Alliance

VALLENDER, Prentiss W.

1300 I St. NW
Suite 250 West
Washington, DC 20005
Tel: (202)842-4900
Fax: (202)842-3492
Registered: LDA
EMail: prentiss@erols.com

Employers
American Maritime Congress (Director, Legislative Affairs)

VAN ARSDALL, R. Thomas

50 F St. NW
Suite 900
Washington, DC 20001
Tel: (202)626-8700
Fax: (202)626-8722
Registered: LDA
EMail: tvanarsdall@ncfc.org

Employers
Nat'l Council of Farmer Cooperatives (V. President, Environmental Policy)

VAN BRUNT, Kirk

1455 Pennsylvania Ave. NW
Suite 1200
Washington, DC 20004
Tel: (202)347-2230
Fax: (202)393-3310
Registered: LDA

Employers
Davis & Harman LLP (Partner)

Clients Represented

On Behalf of Davis & Harman LLP
Committee of Annuity Insurers

VAN CLEEF, Carol R.

1025 Thomas Jefferson St. NW
Suite 700 East
Washington, DC 20007
Tel: (202)625-3500
Fax: (202)298-7570
Registered: LDA
EMail: carol.vancleef@kmz.com

Employers
Katten Muchin & Zavis (Partner)

Clients Represented

On Behalf of Katten Muchin & Zavis

Branch Banking and Trust Co.
Fidelity Investments Co.
London Clearinghouse, Ltd.
Official Artist Inc.
SunTrust Banks, Inc.

VAN COVERDEN, Thomas

1330 New Hampshire Ave. NW
Suite 122
Washington, DC 20036
Tel: (202)659-8008
Fax: (202)659-8519

Employers

Nat'l Ass'n of Community Health Centers (President and Chief Exec. Officer)

VAN DAM, Brad

601 Madison
Suite 400
Alexandria, VA 22314
Tel: (703)824-0500
Fax: (703)820-1395

Former Legislative Assistant to Senator Tom Daschle (D-SD).

Employers

AAAE-ACI (Director, Legislative Affairs)

VAN DONGEN, Dirk

1725 K St. NW
Suite 300
Washington, DC 20006
Tel: (202)872-0885
Fax: (202)785-0586
Registered: LDA

Employers

Nat'l Ass'n of Wholesaler-Distributors (President)

VAN DUYNE, Nancy H.

1350 I St. NW
Suite 1250
Washington, DC 20005
Tel: (202)289-6060
Fax: (202)289-1546
Registered: LDA
EMail: nvandu@coair.com

Former aide to Sen. Bill Bradley (D-NJ).

Employers

Continental Airlines Inc. (Staff V. President, Congressional Affairs)

VAN EATON, Joseph

1155 Connecticut Ave. NW
Suite 1000
Washington, DC 20036-4306
Tel: (202)785-0600
Fax: (202)785-1234
EMail: jvaneaton@millervaneaton.com

Employers

Miller & Van Eaton, P.L.L.C. (Partner)

Clients Represented

On Behalf of Miller & Van Eaton, P.L.L.C.

Coral Springs, Florida, City of
Phoenix, Arizona, City of
Portland, Oregon, City of
Tacoma, Washington, City of
Tallahassee, Florida, City of
Tucson, Arizona, City of

VAN EGMOND, Juliane H.

1275 Pennsylvania Ave. NW
Suite 801
Washington, DC 20004
Tel: (202)737-8900
Fax: (202)737-8909
Registered: LDA

Employers

Bayer Corp. (Director, Federal Government Relations)

VAN ETTEN, Laura

3900 Wisconsin Ave. NW
Washington, DC 20016
Tel: (202)752-1442
Fax: (202)752-6099
Registered: LDA

Employers

Fannie Mae (Director, Government Relations)

VAN FLEET, Bonnie

1900 M St. NW
Suite 800
Washington, DC 20036-3508
Tel: (202)296-6650
Fax: (202)296-7585
EMail: bvanfleet@comptel.org

Employers

Competitive Telecommunications Ass'n (COMPTEL) (Senior Manager, Public Relations)

VAN FLEET, Frank C.

12809 Mill Meadow Ct.
Fairfax, VA 22033-3139
Tel: (703)802-2398
Fax: (703)802-9093
Registered: LDA
EMail: FRANKC378@aol.com

Employers

Meredith Concept Group, Inc.
Van Fleet, Inc. (President)

Clients Represented

On Behalf of Van Fleet, Inc.

Calibre Corp.
Crosby Internat'l
Firearms Training Systems, Inc.

VAN FLEET, Mark

1615 H St. NW
Washington, DC 20062-2000
Tel: (202)463-5460
Fax: (202)463-3114

Employers

Chamber of Commerce of the U.S.A. (Manager, International Business Services)

VAN FLEET, Townsend A.

499 S. Capitol St. SW
Suite 520
Washington, DC 20003
Tel: (202)554-3714
Fax: (202)479-4657
Registered: LDA

Employers

The Van Fleet-Meredith Group (President)

Clients Represented

On Behalf of The Van Fleet-Meredith Group

American Gas Ass'n
Donlee Technologies, Inc.
Lockheed Martin Corp.
Mantech Corp.
Miltope Corp.
PinPoint Systems Internat'l, LLC
United Defense, L.P.

VAN GELDER, Susan I.

1201 F St. NW
Suite 500
Washington, DC 20004
Tel: (202)824-1696
Fax: (202)824-1651

Employers

Health Insurance Ass'n of America (Corporate Secretary)

VAN HAVERBEKE, Peter

4351 Garden City Dr.
Landover, MD 20785
Tel: (301)459-3700
Fax: (301)577-2684
EMail: pvanhaverbeke@efa.org

Employers

Epilepsy Foundation of America (Director, Public Relations)

VAN HEUVEN, Catherine

555 13th St. NW
Washington, DC 20004-1109
Tel: (202)637-6825
Fax: (202)637-5910
Registered: LDA
EMail: cvanheuven@hhlaw.com

Legislative Assistant to Senator Paul Simon (D-IL), 1995-96. Special Assistant, Office of Legislative Affairs, Department of Justice, 1994. Policy Analyst and Legislative Staff Assistant, Subcommittee on the Constitution, Senate Committee on the Judiciary, 1991-94.

Employers

Hogan & Hartson L.L.P. (Associate)

Clients Represented

On Behalf of Hogan & Hartson L.L.P.

Fishable Waters Coalition
InterAmerica's Group LLC

VAN HOLLEN, Christopher

1050 Connecticut Ave. NW
Washington, DC 20036-5339
Tel: (202)857-6000
Fax: (202)857-6395

Employers

Arent Fox Kintner Plotkin & Kahn, PLLC (Member)

VAN HOOK, Kristan

2100 Pennsylvania Ave. NW
Suite 535
Washington, DC 20037
Tel: (202)822-1700
Fax: (202)822-1919
Registered: LDA

Former Director, Congressional Affairs, National Telecommunications and Information Administration, Department of Commerce. Telecommunications Policy Analyst, Subcommittee on Telecommunications and Finance, House Committee on Energy and Commerce, 1993-94. Legislative Assistant to Rep. Edward J. Markey (D-MA), 1990-92.

Employers

Simon Strategies/Mindbeam (President)

Clients Represented

On Behalf of Simon Strategies/Mindbeam

AirCell, Inc.
Catholic Television Network
Metricom, Inc.
Motorola, Inc.
openNET Coalition
Time Domain Corp.
Traffic.com

VAN HOOK, Matthew

1100 15th St. NW
Suite 900
Washington, DC 20005
Tel: (202)835-3400
Fax: (202)835-3414
Registered: LDA

Employers

Pharmaceutical Research and Manufacturers of America (Deputy General Counsel)

VAN HORNE, Jon W.

800 Connecticut Ave. NW
Suite 500
Washington, DC 20006
Tel: (202)331-3154
Fax: (202)261-0154
Registered: LDA
EMail: vanhornej@gtlaw.com

Employers

Greenberg Traurig, LLP (Shareholder)

VAN KLEECK, Kathy R.

1235 Jefferson Davis Hwy.
Suite 600
Arlington, VA 22202
Tel: (703)416-0444
Fax: (703)416-2269
Registered: LDA

Employers

Motorcycle Industry Council (V. President, Government Relations)

VAN NORMAN, Mark

224 Second St. SE
Washington, DC 20003
Tel: (202)546-7711
Fax: (202)546-1755
EMail: mvannorman@indiangaming.org

Employers

Nat'l Indian Gaming Ass'n (Exec. Director)

VAN NOSTRAND, Lyman

Parklawn Bldg.
5600 Fishers Ln.
MS: 14-33
Rockville, MD 20857
Tel: (301)443-2460
Fax: (301)443-9270
EMail: lvannostrand@hrsa.gov

Employers

Department of Health and Human Services - Health Resources and Services Administration (Deputy Director, Office of Planning, Evaluation and Legislation)

VAN OPSTAL, Debra

1500 K St. NW
Suite 850
Washington, DC 20005
Tel: (202)682-4292
Fax: (202)682-5150
EMail: vanops@compete.org

Employers

Council on Competitiveness (Senior V. President)

VAN PUTTEN, Mark

8925 Leesburg Pike
Vienna, VA 22189-0001
Tel: (703)790-4000
Fax: (703)442-7332
EMail: vanputt@nwf.org

Employers

Nat'l Wildlife Federation - Office of Federal and Internat'l Affairs (President and Chief Exec. Officer)

VAN SCOYOC, H. Stewart

1420 New York Ave. NW
Suite 1050
Washington, DC 20005

Tel: (202)638-1950
Fax: (202)638-7714
Registered: LDA

EMail: stu@vsadc.com

Employers

Van Scoyoc Associates, Inc. (President)

VSAdc.com

Clients Represented

On Behalf of Van Scoyoc Associates, Inc.

Abrams & Co. Publishers Inc.
Alabama, Department of Transportation of the State of
Alabama Water and Wastewater Institute, Inc.
Alameda-Contra Costa Transit District
Alcoa Inc.
American Forest & Paper Ass'n
American Library Ass'n
American Psychological Ass'n
Anheuser-Busch Cos., Inc.
Archimedes Technology Group
Arista Knowledge Systems, Inc.
Ass'n of American Railroads
Ass'n of Schools of Public Health
Ass'n of Universities for Research in Astronomy, Inc.
The Audubon Institute
Bethesda Academy for the Performing Arts
Board on Human Sciences
Brain Trauma Foundation
Bristol-Myers Squibb Co.
British Trade and Commerce Bank
Burns and Roe Enterprises, Inc.
Calspan University of Buffalo Research Center
Charter Schools Development Corp.
Chesapeake Bay Foundation
Chicago State University
Clemson University
Coalition of EPSCoR States
Communications Training Analysis Corp. (C-TAC)
Computer Data Systems, Inc.
Computer Sciences Corp.
Davison Transport, Inc.
DGME Fairness Initiative
Fargo-Cass County Development Corp.
Federation of State Humanities Councils
FedEx Corp.
FMC Corp.
Glankler Brown, PLLC
Great Cities' Universities
Greater New Orleans Expressway Commission
Hughes Space & Communications Co.
Insight Technology, Inc.
Intel Corp.
Internat'l Traditional Karate Federation
Jackson State University
Jefferson County Commission
Johns Hopkins School of Hygiene and Public Health
Johns Hopkins University-Applied Physics Lab
Johnson Controls, Inc.
Krebs, LaSalle, LeMieux Consultants, Inc.
Lehigh University
Lockheed Martin Corp.
Lockheed Martin Government Electronics Systems
Lockheed Martin Hanford
Lockheed Martin Naval Electronics Surveillance Systems
Lockheed Martin Venture Star
Los Angeles County Metropolitan Transportation Authority
Mentis Sciences Inc.
MilTec
Montana State University
Montgomery Airport Authority
Montgomery, Alabama, Chamber of Commerce of
Morgan State University
Mount Sinai School of Medicine
NASA Aeronautics Support Team
Nat'l Air Traffic Controllers Ass'n
Nat'l Asphalt Pavement Ass'n
Nat'l Ass'n for Equal Opportunity in Higher Education
Nat'l Ass'n of Enrolled Agents
Nat'l Ass'n of Foster Grandparent Program Directors
Nat'l Ass'n of Independent Colleges and Universities
Nat'l Ass'n of Water Companies
Nat'l Commission on Correctional Health Care
Nat'l Environmental Development Ass'ns State & Federal Environmental Responsibility Project
Nat'l Environmental Trust
Nat'l Institute for Water Resources
The Nat'l Space Grant Alliance
New American School
Ochsner Medical Institutions
Oldcastle Materials Group
Orasure Technologies
Patient Access to Transplantation (PAT) Coalition
Recording for the Blind and Dyslexic, Inc.
Regents College
Regional Airport Authority of Louisville & Jefferson Co.
Reno & Cavanaugh, PLLC
Science Applications Internat'l Corp. (SAIC)
Sickle Cell Disease Ass'n of America
Space Explorers Inc.
Spelman College
Teach for America
Time Domain Corp.
TRAUX Engineering
Tulane University
Universal Systems, Inc.
University of Alabama System
University of Idaho
University of Nebraska
University of New Orleans Foundation
University of North Carolina at Chapel Hill
University of Notre Dame
University of Phoenix
UNOCAL Corp.
Veridian Engineering
Virginia Polytechnic Institute and State University
Virginia Tech Intellectual Properties, Inc.
Wackenhut Services, Inc.
Washington Consulting Group
Weyerhaeuser Co.
ZapMe! Corp.
Zuckert, Scoutt and Rasenberger, L.L.P.

On Behalf of VSAdc.com

Oklahoma, State of
Texas Health Resources
Torchmark Corp.
Vance Development Authority
Visiting Nurse Service of New York

VAN VEEN, Karina

60 Massachusetts Ave. NE
Washington, DC 20002

Tel: (202)906-3860
Fax: (202)906-3306

Employers

AMTRAK (Nat'l Rail Passenger Corp.) (Manager, Media Relations)

VAN VLACK, Charles W.

1300 Wilson Blvd.
Arlington, VA 22209

Tel: (703)741-5111
Fax: (703)741-6086
Registered: LDA

EMail: charles_van_vlack@americanchemistry.com

Employers

American Chemistry Council (Exec. V. President and Chief Operating Officer)

VAN VOORHEES, Robert F.

700 13th St. NW
Suite 700
Washington, DC 20005-3960

Tel: (202)508-6000
Fax: (202)508-6200

EMail: rfvanvoorhees@bryancave.com

Employers

Bryan Cave LLP (Partner)

VAN WAZER, Thomas P.

1722 I St. NW
Washington, DC 20006

Tel: (202)736-8000
Fax: (202)736-8711

EMail: tvanwaze@sidley.com

Law Clerk to Judge Thomas A. Flannery, U.S. District Court for the District of Columbia, 1988-89.

Employers

Sidley & Austin (Partner)

VANASEK, Robert

444 N. Capital St. NW
Suite 208
Washington, DC 20001

Tel: (202)624-3550
Fax: (202)624-3554

EMail: rvanasek@sso.orrg

Employers

Nat'l Ass'n of Towns and Townships (Federal Affairs Associate)

VANBRAKLE, Christina H.

999 E St. NW
Room 933
Washington, DC 20463

Tel: (202)694-1000
Fax: (202)219-2338

EMail: tvanbrakle@fec.gov

Employers

Federal Election Commission (Congressional Affairs Officer)

VANCE, B. Wayne

1203 Essex Manor
Alexandria, VA 22308

Tel: (703)765-2757
Fax: (703)765-2758
Registered: LDA

General Counsel (1987-89) and Chief of Staff to the Secretary (1985-87), Department of Transportation. Deputy Assistant Attorney General, Department of Justice, 1982-85.

Employers

Self-employed as an independent consultant.

VANDE HEI, Diane

1717 K St. NW
Suite 801
Washington, DC 20036

Tel: (202)331-2820
Fax: (202)785-1845
Registered: LDA

EMail: vandehei@amwa.net

Employers

Ass'n of Metropolitan Water Agencies (Exec. Director)

VANDENBERGH, Michael P.

555 11th St. NW
Suite 1000
Washington, DC 20004

Tel: (202)637-2200
Fax: (202)637-2201

Chief of Staff (1993-95) and Special Assistant and Associate Deputy Administrator, (1993), Environmental Protection Agency. Associate Counsel, Presidential Transition, The White House, 1992-93. Law Clerk to Judge Edward R. Becker, U.S. Court of Appeals, Third Circuit, 1987-88.

Employers

Latham & Watkins (Counsel)

VANDER JAGT, Hon. Guy

1050 Connecticut Ave. NW
Suite 1100
Washington, DC 20036-5304

Tel: (202)861-1500
Fax: (202)861-1790
Registered: LDA

EMail: GVanderj@baker-hostetler.com

Member, U.S. House of Representatives (R-MI), 1966-93.

Employers

Baker & Hostetler LLP (Of Counsel)

Clients Represented

On Behalf of Baker & Hostetler LLP

American Electric Power Co.
American Football Coaches Ass'n
American Resort Development Ass'n
Blue Cross and Blue Shield of Ohio
Bristol-Myers Squibb Co.
Cafaro Co.
The Chubb Corp.
Citigroup
Coalition for Shareholder Fairness
The Council of Insurance Agents & Brokers
D. H. Blair Investment Banking Corp.
Eagle-Picher Personal Injury Settlement Trust
Edison Electric Institute
Emmis Broadcasting Corp.
Flexi-Van Leasing
Florida Residential and Casualty Joint Underwriting Ass'n
Florida Windstorm Underwriting Ass'n
Forest City Ratner Companies
I.O.T.A. Partners
Inman, Steinberg, Nye & Stone
Jordache Enterprises, Inc.
KeyCorp, Inc.
Loeb & Loeb
Marsh & McLennan Cos.
Medical Mutual of Ohio
Moose Internat'l Inc.
Motion Picture Ass'n of America
Nat'l Ass'n of Optometrics and Opticians
Nat'l Ass'n of Real Estate Investment Trusts
Pardee Construction Co.
PSH Master L.P.I.
Rollins Hudig Hall
Sedgwick James, Inc.
Sutton & Sutton Solicitors
Transportation Institute
The Wireless Communications Council

VANDERBILT, Marjorie W.

7910 Woodmont Ave.
Suite 1050
Bethesda, MD 20814-3004
Tel: (301)654-7850
Fax: (301)654-4137
Registered: LDA

Employers
American Ass'n for Geriatric Psychiatry (Director of Government Affairs)

VANDERSLICE, Lane

P.O. Box 29056
Washington, DC 20017
Tel: (202)269-6322
Fax: (202)269-6322

Employers
World Hunger Education Service (Managing Editor, Hunger Notes)

VANDERVER, Jr., Timothy A.

2550 M St. NW
Washington, DC 20037-1350
Tel: (202)457-6000
Fax: (202)457-6315
EMail: tvanderver@pattonboggs.com
Attorney, Office of the General Counsel and New Communities Administration, Department of Housing and Urban Development, 1973-76. Attorney, Office of the Solicitor, Department of the Interior, 1972-73.

Employers
Patton Boggs, LLP (Partner)

VANDORN, Bonnie

1025 Vermont Ave. NW
Suite 500
Washington, DC 20005
Tel: (202)783-7200
Fax: (202)783-7207

Employers
Ass'n of Science Technology Centers, Inc. (Exec. Director)

VANDYKE, Tish

1875 I St. NW
Suite 900
Washington, DC 20005
Tel: (202)371-0200
Fax: (202)371-2858

Employers
Edelman Public Relations Worldwide (V. President)

VANHOOSE, Todd

50 F St. NW
Suite 900
Washington, DC 20001
Tel: (202)879-0855
Fax: (202)626-8718
Registered: LDA
EMail: vanhoose@fccouncil.com

Employers
Farm Credit Council (V. President, Government Affairs)

VANISON, Denise

2550 M St. NW
Washington, DC 20037-1350
Tel: (202)457-6000
Fax: (202)457-6315
Registered: LDA

Employers
Patton Boggs, LLP (Partner)

Clients Represented

On Behalf of Patton Boggs, LLP

DFS Group Ltd.

VANOUS, Dr. Jan

1111 14th St. NW
Suite 801
Washington, DC 20005
Tel: (202)898-0471
Fax: (202)898-0445

Employers
PlanEcon Inc. (President)

VANZANDT, Jim

810 Vermont Ave. NW
Room 513
Washington, DC 20420
Tel: (202)273-9435
Fax: (202)273-6791

Employers
Department of Veterans Affairs (GAO Liaison)

VARDAMAN, Jr., John W.

725 12th St. NW
Washington, DC 20005
Tel: (202)434-5000
Fax: (202)434-5029
Law Clerk to Justice Hugo L. Black, U.S. Supreme Court, 1965-66.

Employers
Williams & Connolly (Partner)

VARGO, Carol

1101 Vermont Ave. NW
12th Floor
Washington, DC 20005-3583
Tel: (202)789-4688
Fax: (202)789-7581
Registered: LDA

Employers
American Medical Ass'n (Assistant Director, Federal Affairs)

VARGO, Franklin J.

1331 Pennsylvania Ave. NW
Sixth Floor
Washington, DC 20004-1790
Tel: (202)637-3146
Fax: (202)637-3182

Employers
Nat'l Ass'n of Manufacturers (V. President, International Economic Affairs)

VARMA, Anurag

1818 N St. NW
Suite 700
Washington, DC 20036
Tel: (202)331-7050
Fax: (202)331-9306
Registered: LDA

Employers
Conlon, Frantz, Phelan & Pires

Clients Represented

On Behalf of Conlon, Frantz, Phelan & Pires

American Ass'n of Physicians of Indian Origin
Indian American Nat'l Foundation

VARNER, Theresa

601 E St. NW
Washington, DC 20049
Tel: (202)434-3840
Fax: (202)434-6480

Employers
AARP (American Ass'n of Retired Persons) (Director, Public Policy Institute)

VARNEY, Christine A.

555 13th St. NW
Washington, DC 20004-1109
Tel: (202)637-5600
Fax: (202)637-5910
Registered: LDA
EMail: cavarney@hhlaw.com
Worked for the Federal Trade Commission, 1994-97. Former Secretary to the Cabinet during the first Clinton administration.

Employers
Hogan & Hartson L.L.P. (Partner)

Clients Represented

On Behalf of Hogan & Hartson L.L.P.

Compaq Computer Corp.
eBay Inc.
Network Advertising Initiative
Online Privacy Alliance

VARNEY, Kevin P.

633 Pennsylvania Ave. NW
Fourth Floor
Washington, DC 20004
Tel: (202)783-2596
Fax: (202)628-5379
Registered: LDA
EMail: kvarney@psw-inc.com
Deputy Chief of Staff, Environmental Protection Agency, 1995-96 and Director, Scheduling and Advance, Department of the Treasury, 1993-95.

Employers
Public Strategies Washington, Inc.

VARNEY, Molly

2300 Clarendon Blvd.
Suite 610
Arlington, VA 22201-3367
Tel: (703)351-5666
Fax: (703)351-5667
EMail: mvarney@golinharris.com
Special Assistant to the Deputy Secretary, Department of Health and Human Services, 1997-2001. Special Assistant to the Counselor, Executive Office of the President, The White House, 1994-97.

Employers
Golin/Harris Internat'l (Senior Account Exec.)

VARON, Jay N.

3000 K St. NW
Suite 500
Washington, DC 20007-5109
Tel: (202)672-5300
Fax: (202)672-5399
EMail: jvaron@foleylaw.com
Law Clerk to Chief Judge Robert F. Peckham, U.S. District Court for the Northern District of California, 1975-76.

Employers
Foley & Lardner (Partner)

Clients Represented

On Behalf of Foley & Lardner

Grand Trunk Corp.
Real Estate Services Providers Council

VARONA, Anthony E.

919 18th St. NW
Suite 800
Washington, DC 20006
Tel: (202)628-4160
Fax: (202)347-5323
Registered: LDA

Employers
Human Rights Campaign Fund (General Counsel)

VARTANIAN, Arpi

122 C St. NW
Suite 350
Washington, DC 20001
Tel: (202)393-3434
Fax: (202)638-4904
Registered: LDA
EMail: arpi@aaainc.org

Employers
Armenian Assembly of America (Acting Exec. Director)

VARTANIAN, Thomas P.

1001 Pennsylvania Ave. NW
Suite 800
Washington, DC 20004-2505
Tel: (202)639-7000
Fax: (202)639-7008
EMail: thomas_vartanian@ffhsj.com
General Counsel, Federal Home Loan Bank Board and the Federal Savings and Loan Insurance Corp., 1981-83. Special Assistant to the Chief Counsel and Senior Trial Attorney, Office of the Comptroller of the Currency, Department of the Treasury, 1976-81.

Employers
Fried, Frank, Harris, Shriver & Jacobson (Partner)

VARY, George F.

1112 16th St. NW
Suite 240
Washington, DC 20036
Tel: (202)835-0164
Fax: (202)835-0155

Employers
American Zinc Ass'n (Exec. Director)
Klein & Saks, Inc.

VASAPOLI, Joseph V.

1133 Connecticut Ave. NW
Suite 300
Washington, DC 20036
Tel: (202)293-1177
Fax: (202)293-3411
Registered: LDA

Trial Attorney, Federal Energy Regulatory Commission and Special Assistant to the Deputy Secretary, Department of Energy, 1992. Republican Counsel, House Commerce Committee, 1985-89. Special Assistant to the Commissioner, Federal Energy Regulatory Commission, 1984-85.

Employers
Ryan, Phillips, Utrecht & MacKinnon (Partner)

Clients Represented

On Behalf of Ryan, Phillips, Utrecht & MacKinnon
Ass'n of American Railroads
Coeur d'Alene Mines Corp.
Cook Inlet Region Inc.
R. R. Donnelley & Sons
Edison Electric Institute
Florida Power and Light Co.
General Communications, Inc.
Investment Co. Institute
Kerr-McGee Corp.
Lockheed Martin Corp.
MultiDimensional Imaging, Inc.
Nat'l Cable Television Ass'n
New York Stock Exchange
Pfizer, Inc.
Philip Morris Management Corp.
Progress Energy
Sault Ste. Marie Tribe of Chippewa Indians
Southern Co.
TXU Business Services
U.S. Interactive
United Pan-Europe Communications, NV
VoiceStream Wireless Corp.

VASELL, Shawn M.

800 Connecticut Ave. NW
Suite 500
Washington, DC 20006
Tel: (202)331-3100
Fax: (202)331-3101
Registered: LDA

Employers
Greenberg Traurig, LLP

VASILOFF, Jennifer

1808 Swann St. NW
Washington, DC 20009
Tel: (202)462-7288
Fax: (202)483-1964
Registered: LDA

Employers
The Sheridan Group (V. President)

Clients Represented

On Behalf of The Sheridan Group
Cities Advocating Emergency AIDS Relief (CAEAR)

VASQUEZ, Carmen

1550 Wilson Blvd.
Suite 701
Arlington, VA 22209
Tel: (703)527-7505
Fax: (703)527-7512

Employers
Foodservice & Packaging Institute, Inc. (Manager, Marketing and Communications)

VASQUEZ, DeAnna

504 C St. NE
Washington, DC 20002
Tel: (202)543-1771
Fax: (202)546-2143

Employers
Congressional Hispanic Caucus Institute (CHCI) (Operations Director)

VASQUEZ, Ian

1000 Massachusetts Ave. NW
Washington, DC 20001
Tel: (202)842-0200
Fax: (202)842-3490

Employers
Cato Institute (Director, Global Economic Liberty Project)

VASS, Greg

1100 17th St. NW
Seventh Floor
Washington, DC 20036
Tel: (202)223-8196
Fax: (202)872-1948
Registered: LDA

Employers
American Academy of Actuaries (Policy Analyst)

VASSALLO, Barbara

201 N. Union St.
Suite 200
Alexandria, VA 22314
Tel: (703)518-6141
Fax: (703)518-6191

Employers
Nat'l Apartment Ass'n (Director, State/Local Government Policy)

VASTINE, J. Robert

805 15th St. NW
Suite 1110
Washington, DC 20005
Tel: (202)289-7460
Fax: (202)775-1726
Registered: LDA

Employers
Coalition of Service Industries (President)

VAUGHAN, David L.

1200 19th St. NW
Suite 500
Washington, DC 20036
EMail: dvaughan@kelleydrye.com
Tel: (202)955-9600
Fax: (202)955-9792

Assistant General Counsel, Department of the Army, 1974-75. Captain, Office of the Judge Advocate General, U.S. Army, 1972-74.

Employers
Kelley, Drye & Warren LLP (Partner)

VAUGHAN, (Ret.), Rear Admiral G. Dennis

700 13th St. NW
Suite 400
Washington, DC 20005
EMail: dvaughan@cassidy.com
Tel: (202)347-0773
Fax: (202)347-0785

Former Chief of Naval Reserve; has held various naval commands around the world.

Employers
Cassidy & Associates, Inc. (Consultant)

Clients Represented

On Behalf of Cassidy & Associates, Inc.
SWATH Ocean Systems, Inc.

VAUGHAN, Katrina

1740 N St. NW
Washington, DC 20036
Tel: (202)775-4667
Fax: (202)223-1297
Registered: LDA
EMail: kvaughan@acct.org

Employers
Ass'n of Community College Trustees (Senior Associate, Public Policy)

VAUGHAN, Ms. Lauren C.

1225 19th St. NW
Suite 825
Washington, DC 20036
Tel: (202)331-7080
Fax: (202)331-7082

Employers
The Kerry S. Pearson LLC (President and Chief Operating Officer)

VAUGHAN, Michelle

633 S. Washington St.
Alexandria, VA 22314
Tel: (703)836-0850
Fax: (703)836-0848
Registered: LDA

Employers
Nat'l Rehabilitation Ass'n

VAUGHN, Christine L.

1455 Pennsylvania Ave. NW
Suite 700
Washington, DC 20004-1008
EMail: cvaughn@velaw.com
Tel: (202)639-6500
Fax: (202)639-6604
Registered: LDA

Special Assistant to Assistant Secretary for Tax Policy, Department of the Treasury, 1981-84.

Employers
Vinson & Elkins L.L.P. (Partner)

Clients Represented

On Behalf of Vinson & Elkins L.L.P.
7-Eleven, Inc.
Cheyne Walk Trust
Goldman, Sachs and Co.
Kansas City Southern Industries
Nat'l Ass'n of Settlement Purchasers
XL Capital Ltd

VAUGHN, Eric

One Massachusetts Ave. NW
Suite 820
Washington, DC 20001
EMail: ethanolrfa@aol.com
Tel: (202)289-3835
Fax: (202)289-7519
Registered: LDA

Employers
Renewable Fuels Ass'n (President)

VAUGHN, John C.

1200 New York Ave. NW
Suite 550
Washington, DC 20005
EMail: john_vaughn@aau.edu
Tel: (202)408-7500
Fax: (202)408-8184

Employers
Ass'n of American Universities (Exec. V. President)

VAUGHN, Philip

555 12th St. NW
Suite 620 North
Washington, DC 20004
EMail: philip.vaughn@fluor.com
Tel: (202)955-9300
Fax: (202)833-1630

Employers
Fluor Corp. (Senior Director, Government Affairs)

VAVONESE, Jamie

2300 Clarendon Blvd.
Suite 610
Arlington, VA 22201-3367
EMail: jvavonese@golinharris.com
Tel: (703)351-5666
Fax: (703)351-5667

Scheduler, Office of the First Lady, Executive Office of the President, The White House, 1999-2000

Employers
Golin/Harris Internat'l (Exec. Assistant)

VAZQUEZ, Frankie

2025 M St. NW
Suite 800
Washington, DC 20036
Tel: (202)367-2100
Fax: (202)367-1200

Employers
Smith, Bucklin and Associates, Inc. (Legislative Assistant, Government Relations)

VEAZEY, Rev. Carlton W.

1025 Vermont Ave. NW
Suite 1130
Washington, DC 20005-3516
EMail: info@rcrc.org
Tel: (202)628-7700
Fax: (202)628-7716

Employers
Religious Coalition for Reproductive Choice (President and Chief Exec. Officer)

VECCHIO, Joseph J.

1299 Pennsylvania Ave. NW
Suite 1100 West
Washington, DC 20004-2407
Tel: (202)637-4000
Fax: (202)637-4127

Employers
General Electric Co. (Director, Federal Government Programs (GE Medical Systems))

VEHRS, Kristin L.

8403 Colesville Rd.
Suite 710
Silver Spring, MD 20910
EMail: Kvehrs@aza.org
Tel: (301)562-0777
Fax: (301)562-0888
Registered: LDA

Employers
American Zoo and Aquarium Ass'n (Deputy Director)

VEILLEUX, Diana J.

1100 Connecticut Ave. NW
Suite 900
Washington, DC 20036-4101
Tel: (202)463-8400
Fax: (202)833-8082

Attorney, Office of Labor Law, U.S. Postal Service, 1985-90.

Employers
Shaw, Bransford, Veilleux & Roth (Partner)

VEITH, Craig G.

1801 K St. NW
Suite 1000L
Washington, DC 20006
EMail: craig_veith@washbm.com
Tel: (202)530-0400
Fax: (202)530-4500

Press Secretary to Rep. Mickey Edwards (R-OK), 1989-92.

Employers
Burson-Marsteller (Managing Director, Media)

Clients Represented
On Behalf of Burson-Marsteller
Comision Ejecutiva Hidroelectrica del Rio Lempa CEL

VEITH, Sally
901 15th St. NW
Suite 310
WAS 1150
Washington, DC 20005
Tel: (202)842-3193
Fax: (202)289-6834
Registered: LDA

Employers
Northwest Airlines, Inc. (Director, Government and Legislative Affairs)

VELANDER, Carol I.
1255 23rd St. NW
Suite 200
Washington, DC 20037-1174
EMail: cvelander@hauck.com
Tel: (202)452-8100
Fax: (202)833-3636

Employers
Hauck and Associates (Director, Education and Training)

Clients Represented
On Behalf of Hauck and Associates
Nat'l Health Care Anti-Fraud Ass'n

VELASCO, Peter
600 New Hampshire Ave. NW
Suite 601
Washington, DC 20037
Tel: (202)333-7400
Fax: (202)333-1638

Employers
Hill and Knowlton, Inc. (Managing Director)

Clients Represented
On Behalf of Hill and Knowlton, Inc.
American Red Cross

VELASQUEZ, Jay
227 Massachusetts Ave. NE
Washington, DC 20006
Tel: (202)543-4780
Registered: LDA

Employers
The Velasquez Group

Clients Represented
On Behalf of The Velasquez Group
Deloitte & Touche LLP
Federal Home Loan Mortgage Corp. (Freddie Mac)
Instinet
Interactive Brokers LLC
Investment Co. Institute
Mortgage Bankers Ass'n of America
Republicans for Clean Air
VISA U.S.A., Inc.

VELASQUEZ, Joe
1215 17th St. NW
Washington, DC 20036
Tel: (202)467-8068
Fax: (202)467-8067
Registered: LDA
EMail: joevela@aol.com

Employers
Joe Velasquez & Associates (President)

Clients Represented
On Behalf of Joe Velasquez & Associates
1199 Nat'l Health & Human Services Employees Union
ICF Consulting
South Gate, California, City of

VELLA, Elizabeth C.
2550 M St. NW
Washington, DC 20037-1350
Tel: (202)457-6000
Fax: (202)457-6315
Registered: LDA
EMail: bvella@pattonboggs.com

Employers
Patton Boggs, LLP (Associate)

Clients Represented
On Behalf of Patton Boggs, LLP
American Family Mutual Insurance Co.
Baltimore Symphony Orchestra
Discovery Place, Inc. (Charlotte Science Museum)
Nat'l Aquarium
Nat'l Oilheat Research Alliance (NORA)
Sheriff Jefferson Parrish, Louisiana
Travel Industry Ass'n of America

VELLECO, John
8001 Forbes Pl.
Suite 102
Springfield, VA 22151
Tel: (703)321-8585
Fax: (703)321-8408
Registered: LDA

Employers
Gun Owners of America (Federal Affairs)

VELTRI, Thomas
1755 Jefferson Davis Hwy.
Suite 1107
Arlington, VA 22202
Tel: (703)415-0344
Fax: (703)415-0182
Registered: LDA

Employers
The PMA Group (Associate)

Clients Represented
On Behalf of The PMA Group
Advanced Programming Concepts
Applied Marine Technologies, Inc.
Autometric Inc.
Battelle
Concurrent Technologies Corp.
CPU Technology
Electronic Warfare Associates, Inc.
L-3 Communications Corp.
Lockheed Martin Corp.
Lockheed Martin Federal Systems
Lockheed Martin MS/Gaithersburg
New Mexico Tech
Pathfinder Technology Inc.
Prologic
Textron Inc.
Trex Enterprises

VENTIMILGIA, Vince
1300 Pennsylvania Ave. NW
Suite 380
Washington, DC 20004-3002
Tel: (202)289-9216
Fax: (202)298-9222

Employers
Medtronic, Inc. (Director, Government Affairs)

VENTINO, Lucas
1667 K St. NW
Suite 640
Washington, DC 20006-1605
EMail: lucas.ventino@oracle.com
Tel: (202)721-4811
Fax: (202)467-4250

Employers
Oracle Corp. (V. President, Global Trade Compliance)

VENZ, David C.
198 Van Buren St.
Herndon, VA 20170
Tel: (703)834-3400
Fax: (703)834-3340

Employers
Airbus Industrie of North America, Inc. (V. President, Corporate Communications)

VERDERAME, Kristen Neller
601 Pennsylvania Ave. NW
Suite 625
North Bldg.
Washington, DC 20004
EMail: kristen.verderame@btna.com
Tel: (202)434-8873
Fax: (202)434-8867
Registered: LDA

Employers
BT North America Inc. (Director, U.S. Regulation and Government Relations)

VERDERY, Jennifer
1634 I St. NW
Suite 300
Washington, DC 20006
Tel: (202)626-4380
Fax: (202)628-2525
Registered: LDA

Employers
Intel Corp. (Manager, Human Resources Policy)

VERDIER, Stephen J.
900 19th St. NW
Suite 400
Washington, DC 20006
Tel: (202)857-3100
Fax: (202)296-8716
Registered: LDA

Employers
America's Community Bankers (Legislative Counsel)

VERDISCO, Robert J.
1700 N. Moore St.
Suite 2250
Arlington, VA 22209
Tel: (703)841-2300
Fax: (703)841-1184
Registered: LDA

Employers
Internat'l Mass Retailers Ass'n (President)

VERMA, Richard R.
1330 Connecticut Ave. NW
Washington, DC 20036-1795
Tel: (202)429-3000
Fax: (202)429-3902
Registered: LDA
EMail: rverma@steptoe.com
Judge Advocate General's Corps, Department of the Air Force, 1994-98.

Employers
Steptoe & Johnson LLP (Associate)

Clients Represented
On Behalf of Steptoe & Johnson LLP
Sterling Internat'l Consultants, Inc.

VERMEULEN, Janel
1730 N. Lynn St.
Suite 504
Arlington, VA 22209
Tel: (703)276-1412
Fax: (703)276-1415
Registered: LDA

Employers
Balzano Associates (Account Executive)

Clients Represented
On Behalf of Balzano Associates
Boeing Defense and Space Group
The Business Roundtable
Lockheed Martin Corp.
Nat'l Institute for Aerospace Studies and Services Inc.

VERNON, Robert M.
600 Pennsylvania Ave. SE
Suite 302
Washington, DC 20003
EMail: yrnfinc@yrock.com
Former Aide to Rep. Scott Klug (R-WI).
Tel: (202)608-1417
Fax: (202)608-1430

Employers
Young Republican Nat'l Federation, Inc. (Exec. Director)

VERONEAU, John K.
600 17th St. NW
Room 113
Washington, DC 20508
Tel: (202)395-6951
Fax: (202)395-3911
Assistant Secretary for Legislative Affairs, Department of Defense, 1999-2001. Legislative Aide to Senator William S. Cohen (R-ME), 1989-96. Also served as Aide to Senators Bill Frist (R-TN) and Susan Collins (R-ME).

Employers
Executive Office of the President - US Trade Representative (U.S. Trade Representative for Congressional Affairs)

VERRILL, Jr., Charles O.
1776 K St. NW
Washington, DC 20006
Tel: (202)719-7000
Fax: (202)719-7049
Registered: LDA

Employers
Wiley, Rein & Fielding (Partner)

Clients Represented
On Behalf of Wiley, Rein & Fielding
Chaparral Steel Co.
Club Car, Inc.
Georgetown Industries
Raritan River Steel Co.
Syquest Technology, Inc.

VERSAGE, Vincent M.

818 Connecticut Ave. NW
Suite 1100
Washington, DC 20006
Tel: (202)728-1010
Fax: (202)728-4044
Registered: LDA

Legislative Director to Rep. Timothy Wirth (D-CO), 1984-85. Legislative Director to Senator Spark Matsunaga (D-HI), 1976-84.

Employers
The National Group, LLP (Partner)

Clients Represented

On Behalf of The National Group, LLP
Corning Inc.
Eastman Kodak Co.
Xerox Corp.

VERSAGGI, Sarah

601 Pennsylvania Ave. NW
Suite 720
Washington, DC 20004
Tel: (202)783-3979
Fax: (202)783-3982
Registered: LDA

Employers
Alltel Corporation (Manager, Federal Legislation)

VERSTANDIG, Lee L.

700 11th St. NW
Washington, DC 20001-4507
Tel: (202)383-1238
Fax: (202)383-7540
Registered: LDA

Undersecretary, Department of Housing and Urban Development, 1985-86. Assistant to the President for Intergovernmental Affairs, Executive Office of the President, The White House, 1983-85. Acting Administrator, Environmental Protection Agency, 1983. Assistant Secretary for Government Affairs, Department of Transportation, 1981-83. Administrative Assistant (1978-81) and Legislative Director (1977) to Senator John Chafee (R-RI).

Employers
Nat'l Ass'n of Realtors (Senior V. President, Government Affairs)

VERTINO, Sheila K.

2201 Cooperative Way
Third Floor
Herndon, VA 22071
EMail: vertino@naiop.org
Tel: (703)904-7100
Fax: (703)904-7942

Employers
Nat'l Ass'n of Industrial and Office Properties (V. President, International Research)

VERVEER, Philip L.

Three Lafayette Center
1155 21st St. NW
Washington, DC 20036-3384
Tel: (202)328-8000
Fax: (202)887-8979

Chief, Cable Television Bureau, Broadcast Bureau, Common Carrier Bureau, Federal Communications Commission, 1978-81. Supervisory Attorney, Bureau of Competition, Federal Trade Commission, 1977-78. Trial Attorney, Antitrust Division, Department of Justice, 1969-77.

Employers
Willkie Farr & Gallagher (Partner)

Clients Represented

On Behalf of Willkie Farr & Gallagher
Cellular Telecommunications and Internet Ass'n
Telecommunications Industry Ass'n

VERVILLE, Richard E.

1875 I St. NW
12th Floor
Washington, DC 20006
Tel: (202)466-6550
Fax: (202)785-1756
Registered: LDA

Deputy Assistant Secretary (1971-73) and Special Assistant to the Secretary (1970), Department of Health, Education and Welfare.

Employers
Powers Pyles Sutter & Verville, PC (Principal)

Clients Represented

On Behalf of Powers Pyles Sutter & Verville, PC
American Academy of Neurology
American Academy of Physical Medicine and Rehabilitation
Joint Council of Allergy, Asthma and Immunology
Nat'l Ass'n of Rehabilitation Research and Training Centers

VESSELLA, Candace C.

1725 Jefferson Davis Hwy.
Crystal Square 2, Suite 300
Arlington, VA 22202
Tel: (703)413-5600
Fax: (703)413-5617
Registered: LDA

Employers
Lockheed Martin Corp. (Director, Electronics Legislation)

VEST, Chris

1575 I St. NW
Washington, DC 20005-1103
Tel: (202)626-2798
Fax: (202)371-1673

Employers
American Soc. of Ass'n Executives (Manager, Media Relations)

VESTAL, Christine

1225 I St. NW
Suite 400
Washington, DC 20005
EMail: christy@speakout.com
Tel: (202)777-3105

Employers
SpeakOut.com (V. President, Content and Editor-in-Chief)

VEVE, Michael E.

2121 K St. NW
Suite 800
Washington, DC 20037
Tel: (202)261-3524
Fax: (202)261-3523
Registered: FARA

Employers
Self-employed as an independent consultant.

Clients Represented

As an independent consultant
El Salvador, Government of the Republic of

VIA, Steve

1401 New York Ave. NW
Suite 640
Washington, DC 20005
Tel: (202)628-8303
Fax: (202)628-2846

Employers
American Water Works Ass'n (Regulatory Engineer)

VICE, Jaime M.

1015 15th St. NW
Suite 700
Washington, DC 20005-2605
Tel: (202)828-5200
Fax: (202)785-2645

Employers
Bechtel Group, Inc. (Government Affairs Representative)

VICK, M. Christine

1250 I St. NW
Suite 1105
Washington, DC 20005
EMail: MCVick100@aol.com
Tel: (202)682-5151
Fax: (202)682-2185
Registered: LDA

Employers
Andreae, Vick & Associates, L.L.C. (Partner)

Clients Represented

On Behalf of Andreae, Vick & Associates, L.L.C.
Pharmaceutical Research and Manufacturers of America

VICKERS, George

1630 Connecticut Ave. NW
Washington, DC 20009
Tel: (202)797-2171
Fax: (202)797-2172

Employers
Washington Office on Latin American (Exec. Director)

VICKERS, Linda

1706 23rd St. South
Suite 100
Arlington, VA 22202-1552
Tel: (703)979-5542
Fax: (703)271-0072
Registered: LDA

Employers
Vickers and Vickers (President)

Clients Represented

On Behalf of Vickers and Vickers
Rural Community Insurance Co.

VICKERS, Mary Susan

444 N. Capitol St. NW
Suite 142
Washington, DC 20001
Tel: (202)431-8020
Fax: (202)434-8033

Employers
Nat'l Ass'n of State Workforce Agencies (Labor Market Information and Research Director)

VICKERY, Allison

122 C St. NW
Suite 820
Washington, DC 20001
Tel: (202)628-1816
Fax: (202)638-0973

Employers
American Ass'n of Children's Residential Centers (Exec. Director)

VICKERY, Ann Morgan

555 13th St. NW
Washington, DC 20004-1109
Tel: (202)637-8605
Fax: (202)637-5910
Registered: LDA
EMail: amvickery@hhlaw.com

Director, Executive Secretariat, Department of the Treasury, 1975-78. Researcher and Staff Assistant, the White House, 1969-1974.

Employers
Hogan & Hartson L.L.P. (Partner)

Clients Represented

On Behalf of Hogan & Hartson L.L.P.
Bristol-Myers Squibb Co.
Fujisawa Health Care Inc.
Genentech, Inc.
Health and Hospital Corp. of Marion County
Nat'l Hospice & Palliative Care Organization
Pharmaceutical Research and Manufacturers of America

VICKERY, Jr., Raymond E.

1101 Pennsylvania Ave. NW
Suite 800
Washington, DC 20004
Tel: (202)639-1280
Registered: LDA

Former Assistant Secretary for Trade Development, Department of Commerce, during the Clinton administration.

Employers
Vickery Internat'l

Clients Represented

On Behalf of Vickery Internat'l
Dow AgroSciences
Iridium, LLC

VICTOR, Jayne L.

444 N. Capitol St. NW
Suite 729
Washington, DC 20001
Tel: (202)585-4200
Fax: (202)737-3874

Employers
Dominion Resources, Inc. (Director, Dominion Federal and Political Affairs)

VICTORY, Nancy J.

1776 K St. NW
Washington, DC 20006
Tel: (202)719-7000
Fax: (202)719-7049
Registered: LDA

Employers
Wiley, Rein & Fielding (Partner)

Clients Represented

On Behalf of Wiley, Rein & Fielding
Mobile Telecommunications Technologies Corp.
Personal Communications Industry Ass'n (PCIA)
Prodigy

VIDAL-CORDERO, David

1050 Connecticut Ave. NW
Washington, DC 20036-5339
Tel: (202)857-6000
Fax: (202)857-6395
Registered: LDA

Employers
Arent Fox Kintner Plotkin & Kahn, PLLC (Member)

Clients Represented

On Behalf of Arent Fox Kintner Plotkin & Kahn, PLLC
France Telecom America do Sul Ltda.

VIEHE-NAESS, Brenda R.

1300 Pennsylvania Ave. NW
Suite 700
Washington, DC 20004-3024
Tel: (202)204-3023
Fax: (202)789-7349
Registered: LDA, FARA

Employers
Self-employed as an independent consultant.

Clients Represented
As an independent consultant
Ass'n of British Insurers
Fireman's Fund Insurance Cos.
Forces Vives
Zurich Financial Group

VIENNA, Cheryl

1020 N. Fairfax St.
Fourth Floor
Alexandria, VA 22314
Tel: (703)684-5236
Fax: (703)684-3417
Registered: LDA
Former Legislative Director for Senator Sam Nunn (D-GA).

Employers
Vienna, Gregor & Associates (V. President and Managing Partner)

Clients Represented
On Behalf of Vienna, Gregor & Associates
California State Senate
The Pacific Stock Exchange, Inc.

VIENNA, David P.

1020 N. Fairfax St.
Fourth Floor
Alexandria, VA 22314
Tel: (703)684-5236
Fax: (703)684-3417
Registered: LDA
EMail: dvienna@pass1.com
Former Professional Staff, Permanent Subcommittee on Investigations, Senate Committee on Governmental Affairs.

Employers
Vienna, Gregor & Associates (President)

Clients Represented
On Behalf of Vienna, Gregor & Associates
California Board of Equalization
California Franchise Tax Board
California Public Employees' Retirement System
California State Senate
The Pacific Stock Exchange, Inc.

VIERRA, Dennis C.

1825 I St. NW
Suite 400
Washington, DC 20006
Tel: (202)429-6830
Fax: (202)857-5233
Registered: LDA
U.S. Department of Transportation, 1977-83.

Employers
Vierra Associates, Inc. (Chairman and Chief Exec. Officer)

Clients Represented
On Behalf of Vierra Associates, Inc.
Dallas Area Rapid Transit Authority
Denver, Regional Transportation District of
Embry-Riddle Aeronautical University
Greater Orlando Aviation Authority
Memphis Area Transit Authority
New York Metropolitan Transportation Authority
Niagara Frontier Transportation Authority

VIERRA, Stephanie

1735 New York Ave. NW
Third Floor
Washington, DC 20006
Tel: (202)785-2324
Fax: (202)628-0448

Employers
Ass'n of Collegiate Schools of Architecture (Exec. Director)

VIETH, G. Duane

555 12th St. NW
Washington, DC 20004-1206
Tel: (202)942-5000
Fax: (202)942-5999
EMail: Duane_Vieth@aporter.com

Employers
Arnold & Porter (Partner)

VIGUERIE, Kathryn

1780 Massachusetts Ave. NW
Washington, DC 20036
Tel: (202)785-3351
Fax: (202)293-4349
Registered: LDA

Employers
Planned Parenthood Federation of America (Legislative Representative)

VIHSTADT, John E.

1850 M St. NW
Suite 400
Washington, DC 20036
Tel: (202)293-8200
Fax: (202)872-0145
Registered: LDA
Minority Counsel, House Select Committee on Aging, 1981-85.

Employers
Krooth & Altman (Partner)

Clients Represented
On Behalf of Krooth & Altman
Healthcare Financing Study Group

VIHSTADT, Mary

P.O. Box 5685
1800 N. Patrick Henry Dr.
Arlington, VA 22205
Tel: (703)534-5211
Fax: (703)534-8152
Registered: LDA

Employers
Self-employed as an independent consultant.

Clients Represented
As an independent consultant
The Dial Co.
Travelers Express Co., Inc.

VIILO, Jr., Michael W.

1111 Jefferson Davis Hwy.
Suite 700
Arlington, VA 22202-3225
Tel: (703)416-2500
Fax: (703)416-2512
Registered: LDA
EMail: kaman_dc@compuserve.com

Employers
Kaman Diversified Technologies Corp. (Assistant V. President, Congressional and Industrial Relations)

VILHAUER, Robert J.

1200 Wilson Blvd.
Arlington, VA 22209
Tel: (703)465-3680
Fax: (703)465-3037
Registered: LDA

Employers
The Boeing Co. (Director, Commercial Airplane Programs)

VILLANI, Joseph

1680 Duke St.
Alexandria, VA 22314-3407
Tel: (703)838-6722
Fax: (703)683-7590

Employers
Nat'l School Boards Ass'n (Associate Exec. Director, Federation Member Services and Outreach)

VILLARREAL, Jose H.

1333 New Hampshire Ave. NW
Suite 400
Washington, DC 20036
Tel: (202)887-4000
Fax: (202)887-4288
Registered: LDA

Employers
Akin, Gump, Strauss, Hauer & Feld, L.L.P. (Partner)

Clients Represented
On Behalf of Akin, Gump, Strauss, Hauer & Feld, L.L.P.
Alliance for Quality Nursing Home Care
AT&T
Citizen's Educational Foundation
Manufactured Housing Institute
PerkinElmer Detection Systems
PG&E Corp.
San Antonio Water System
San Antonio, Texas, City of
Texas Manufactured Housing Ass'n

VINCE, Clinton A.

901 15th St. NW
Suite 700
Washington, DC 20005-2301
Tel: (202)371-6000
Fax: (202)371-6279
Registered: LDA, FARA
EMail: cavince@verner.com

Employers
Verner, Liipfert, Bernhard, McPherson and Hand, Chartered (Member of Firm)

Clients Represented
On Behalf of Verner, Liipfert, Bernhard, McPherson and Hand, Chartered
Atomic Energy of Canada
General Motors Corp.
MBIA Insurance Corp.
New Orleans, Louisiana, City of
Salt River Project
Southeastern Federal Power Customers, Inc.

VINCENT, Duane

1111 Constitution Ave. NW
Room 3231
Washington, DC 20224
Tel: (202)622-3903
Fax: (202)622-5247

Employers
Department of Treasury - Internal Revenue Service (Acting Branch Chief Legislation and Reports)

VINCENT, Geoffrey H.

122 C St. NW
Suite 310
Washington, DC 20001
Tel: (202)824-6685
Fax: (202)393-6288
EMail: geoffrey.h.vincent@vanderbilt.edu

Employers
Vanderbilt University (Director, Federal Relations)

VINE, Howard A.

800 Connecticut Ave. NW
Suite 500
Washington, DC 20006
Tel: (202)331-3103
Fax: (202)261-0103
Registered: LDA, FARA
EMail: vineh@gtlaw.com

Employers
Greenberg Traurig, LLP (Managing Shareholder, Washington Office)

Clients Represented
On Behalf of Greenberg Traurig, LLP
Claire's Stores, Inc.
Florida Department of Agriculture and Consumer Services
Healtheon/Web MD
Miami, Florida, City of
Nat'l Ass'n for the Support of Long Term Care
Nat'l Ass'n of Computer Consultant Businesses
Torrington Co.
Unilever N.V.
Unilever United States, Inc.
Uniroyal Technology Corp.

VINE, John M.

1201 Pennsylvania Ave. NW
Washington, DC 20004-2401
Tel: (202)662-6000
Fax: (202)662-6291
Registered: LDA
EMail: jvine@cov.com
Law Clerk to Judge Arnold Raum, U.S. Tax Court, 1969-71.

Employers
Covington & Burling (Partner)

Clients Represented
On Behalf of Covington & Burling
The ERISA Industry Committee (ERIC)
Retirement Income Coalition

VINEY, Bill

444 N. Capitol St. NW
Suite 837
Washington, DC 20001
Tel: (202)637-0637
Fax: (202)544-5321
Registered: LDA
EMail: bviney@broydrick.com

Employers
Broydrick & Associates (Associate)

Clients Represented
On Behalf of Broydrick & Associates
Barr Laboratories
Johnsburg, Illinois, Village of
Loyola University of Chicago
Milwaukee Metropolitan Sewerage District
Milwaukee Public Museum
Wisconsin Energy Corp.

VINYARD, Jr., Walter D.

555 13th St. NW
Third Floor
West Tower
Washington, DC 20004-1109
Tel: (202)637-6838
Fax: (202)637-5910
Registered: LDA
Attorney, Securities and Exchange Commission, 1968-72.

Employers
Vinyard & Associates

Clients Represented

On Behalf of Vinyard & Associates
Lutheran Brotherhood
Mennonite Mutual Aid Ass'n
Nonprofit Pension Council

VIOHL, Jeffrey C.

444 N. Capitol St. NW
Suite 428
Washington, DC 20001
Tel: (202)624-1478
Fax: (202)624-1475
Registered: LDA
EMail: jviohl@sso.org
Aide to Senator Daniel Patrick Moynihan (D-NY), 1980-88.

Employers
Viohl and Associates, Inc. (President)

Clients Represented

On Behalf of Viohl and Associates, Inc.
Indiana, Office of the Governor of the State of
Ivy Tech State College

VIOLA, Beth

2099 Pennsylvania Ave. NW
Suite 100
Washington, DC 20006
Tel: (202)955-3000
Fax: (202)955-5564
Registered: LDA
EMail: bviola@hklaw.com
Former Senior Environmental Advisor to the President, The White House.

Employers
Holland & Knight LLP (Senior Public Affairs Advisor)

Clients Represented

On Behalf of Holland & Knight LLP
Bridgestone/Firestone, Inc.
FirstEnergy Co.
Somerville Housing Group

VIOLANTE, Joseph

807 Maine Ave. SW
Washington, DC 20024
Tel: (202)554-3501
Fax: (202)554-3581
Registered: LDA

Employers
Disabled American Veterans (National Legislative Director)

VIORST, Marla

600 New Hampshire Ave. NW
Suite 601
Washington, DC 20037
Tel: (202)333-7400
Fax: (202)333-1638
EMail: mviorst@hillandknowlton.com

Employers
Hill and Knowlton, Inc. (Senior Account Supervisor)

VISCIDO, Dr. Anthony J.

P.O. Box 223
Springfield, VA 22150
Tel: (703)451-0001
Fax: (703)451-0004

Employers
Academy for Implants and Transplants (Exec. Director, Secretary/Treasurer)

VISCO, Frances M.

1707 L St. NW
Suite 1060
Washington, DC 20036
Tel: (202)296-7477

Employers
Nat'l Breast Cancer Coalition (President)

VISSCHER, Gary

1101 17th St. NW
Suite 1300
Washington, DC 20036-4700
Tel: (202)452-7100
Fax: (202)833-3661
Registered: LDA
EMail: gvisscher@steel.org

Employers
American Iron and Steel Institute (V. President, Employee Relations)

VITALE, Christopher P.

601 Pennsylvania Ave. NW
Suite 900 South Bldg.
Washington, DC 20004
Tel: (202)434-8211
Fax: (202)638-7124
Registered: LDA

Employers
Capitol City Group

Clients Represented

On Behalf of Capitol City Group
American Biophysics Corp.
Cranston, Rhode Island, City of
CVS, Inc.
Greater Providence Chamber of Commerce
Landmark Medical Center
Rhode Island Resource Recovery Center

VITALIANO, Dr. Peter

2101 Wilson Blvd.
Suite 400
Arlington, VA 22201
Tel: (703)243-6111
Fax: (703)841-9328
EMail: pvitaliano@nmpf.org

Employers
Nat'l Milk Producers Federation (V. President, International Trade, Economics, and Market Research)

VIVERO, Mauricio

750 First St. NE
Suite 1000
Washington, DC 20002-4250
Tel: (202)336-8800
Fax: (202)336-8952
EMail: viverom@smtp.lsc.gov

Employers
Legal Services Corp. (Director, Government Relations and Public Affairs)

VLADECK, David C.

1600 20th St. NW
Washington, DC 20009
Tel: (202)588-1000
Fax: (202)588-7799
Registered: LDA

Employers
Public Citizen, Inc. (Director, Public Citizen Litigation Group)

VLOSSAK, Frank C.

1155 21st St. NW
Suite 300
Washington, DC 20036
Tel: (202)659-8201
Fax: (202)659-5249
Registered: LDA
EMail: fcvlossak@wms-jen.com
Legislative Assistant to Rep. Merrill Cook (R-UT), 1997-98.

Employers
Williams & Jensen, P.C. (Associate)

Clients Represented

On Behalf of Williams & Jensen, P.C.
American Home Products Corp.
Colonial Pipeline Co.
KSL Development Corp.
Norfolk Southern Corp.

VODRA, William W.

555 12th St. NW
Washington, DC 20004-1206
Tel: (202)942-5000
Fax: (202)942-5999
EMail: William_Vodra@aporter.com
V. Chairman, Commission on the Federal Drug Approval Process, 1981-82. Office of the General Counsel, Food and Drug Division, Department of Health, Education and Welfare, 1974-79. Attorney, Bureau of Narcotics and Dangerous Drugs/Drug Enforcement Administration, Department of Justice, 1971-74.

Employers
Arnold & Porter (Partner)

VOEGTLIN, Gene

515 N. Washington St.
Alexandria, VA 22314
Tel: (703)836-6767
Fax: (703)836-4543
Registered: LDA

Employers
Internat'l Ass'n of Chiefs of Police (Legislative Counsel)

VOGEL, Alex

425 Second St. NE
Washington, DC 20002
Tel: (202)675-6000
Fax: (202)675-6058

Employers
Nat'l Republican Senatorial Committee (General Counsel)

VOGEL, Brian H.

2233 Wisconsin Ave.
Suite 501
Washington, DC 20007
Tel: (202)363-7782
Fax: (202)338-1000
Registered: LDA

Employers
Charles W. Quatt Associates, Inc. (Principal)

Clients Represented

On Behalf of Charles W. Quatt Associates, Inc.
Coalition Against Bigger Trucks

VOGEL, John H.

2550 M St. NW
Washington, DC 20037-1350
Tel: (202)457-6000
Fax: (202)457-6315
Registered: LDA
EMail: jvogel@pattonboggs.com

Employers
Patton Boggs, LLP (Partner)

VOGHT, Brook

655 15th St. NW
Suite 900
Washington, DC 20005-5701
Tel: (202)626-5800
Fax: (202)628-0858
Registered: LDA
EMail: bvoght@milchev.com
Attorney-Advisor to Judge William M. Drennan, U.S. Tax Court, 1971-73.

Employers
Miller & Chevalier, Chartered (Member)

Clients Represented

On Behalf of Miller & Chevalier, Chartered
Boston Edison Co.

VOGT, Carl

801 Pennsylvania Ave. NW
Washington, DC 20004-2604
Tel: (202)662-4500
Fax: (202)662-4643
EMail: cvogt@fulbright.com
Chairman, National Transportation Safety Board, 1992-94.

Employers
Fulbright & Jaworski L.L.P. (Partner)

VOGT, Gregory J.

1776 K St. NW
Washington, DC 20006
Tel: (202)719-7000
Fax: (202)719-7049
Deputy Chief, Cable Services Bureau (1994-96), Chief, Tariff Division, Common Carrier Bureau (1992-94), Chief, Mobile Services Division (1989-92), and Chief, Enforcement Division (1985-89), all at the Federal Communications Commission.

Employers
Wiley, Rein & Fielding (Partner)

VOGT, Jeffrey S.

1146 19th St. NW
Suite 600
Washington, DC 20036
Tel: (202)496-0500
Fax: (202)496-0555
Registered: LDA

Employers
James & Hoffman, P.C. (Associate)

VOGT, John R.

1399 New York Ave. NW
Eighth Floor
Washington, DC 20005-4711
Tel: (202)434-8400
Fax: (202)434-8456
Registered: LDA
EMail: jvogt@bondmarkets.com
Deputy Assistant Secretary at Treasury Department, during the Bush I administration.

Employers
The Bond Market Ass'n (Exec. V. President)

VOINEA-GRIFFIN, DDS, Andreea

730 11th St. NW
Fourth Floor
Washington, DC 20001
Tel: (202)638-5131
Fax: (202)638-3429
EMail: acehsa@aupha.org

Employers
Accrediting Commission on Education for Health Services Administration (Interim Exec. Director)

VOLDSETH, Sonia

1301 Pennsylvania Ave. NW
Suite 300
Washington, DC 20004
Tel: (202)347-0228
Fax: (202)638-0607

Employers
Nat'l Cattleman's Beef Ass'n (Associate Director, Food Policy)

VOLES, Lorraine

1909 K St. NW
Fourth Floor
Washington, DC 20006
Tel: (202)973-5800
Fax: (202)973-5858
Former Director of Communications to Vice President Al Gore.

Employers
Porter/Novelli (Senior Counsel)

VOLJAVEC, Patricia Jarvis

1001 Pennsylvania Ave. NW
Suite 760 North
Washington, DC 20004
Tel: (202)661-7060
Fax: (202)661-7066
Registered: LDA

Employers
The Legislative Strategies Group, LLC (Lobbyist)

Clients Represented
On Behalf of The Legislative Strategies Group, LLC
Hopi Indian Tribe

VOLK, E. Joe

245 Second St. NE
Washington, DC 20002
Tel: (202)547-6000
Fax: (202)547-6019
Registered: LDA

Employers
Friends Committee on Nat'l Legislation (Exec. Secretary)

VOLLINGER, Ellen M.

1875 Connecticut Ave. NW
Suite 540
Washington, DC 20009
Tel: (202)986-2200
Ext: 3016
Fax: (202)986-2525
Registered: LDA
EMail: evollinger@frac.org

Employers
Food Research and Action Center (Legal/Foodstamp Director)

VOLLMER, Andrew N.

2445 M St. NW
Washington, DC 20037-1420
Tel: (202)663-6000
Fax: (202)663-6363
Registered: FARA
EMail: avollmer@wilmer.com

Employers
Wilmer, Cutler & Pickering (Partner)

VOLLMER, Douglas K.

801 18th St. NW
Washington, DC 20006
Tel: (202)872-1300
Fax: (202)785-4452
Registered: LDA

Employers
Paralyzed Veterans of America (Associate Exec. Director, Government Relations)

VOLNER, Ian D.

1201 New York Ave. NW
Suite 1000
Washington, DC 20005
Tel: (202)962-4814
Fax: (202)962-8300
EMail: idvolner@venable.com
Staff Attorney, Review Board, Federal Communications Commission, 1968-70.

Employers
Venable (Partner)

Clients Represented
On Behalf of Venable
Ass'n for Postal Commerce
Direct Marketing Ass'n, Inc.
USA Networks

VOLTMANN, Robert A.

3601 Eisenhower Ave.
Suite 110
Alexandria, VA 22304-6439
Tel: (703)329-8358
Fax: (703)329-1898
Registered: LDA
EMail: voltmann@tianet.org

Employers
Transportation Intermediaries Ass'n (Exec. Director and Chief Exec. Officer)

VOM EIGEN, Ann Hadley

1828 L St. NW
Suite 705
Washington, DC 20036
Tel: (202)296-3671
Fax: (202)223-5843
Registered: LDA
EMail: ann_vomeigen@alta.org

Employers
American Land Title Ass'n (Legislative Counsel)

VOM EIGEN, Robert P.

888 Sixteenth St. NW
7th Floor
Washington, DC 20006-4103
Tel: (202)835-8269
Fax: (202)835-8136
Registered: LDA

Employers
Foley & Lardner (Partner)

Clients Represented
On Behalf of Foley & Lardner
Canadian Nat'l Railway Co.

VON BERGEN, Drew

100 Indiana Ave. NW
Washington, DC 20001
Tel: (202)393-4695
Fax: (202)737-1540

Employers
Nat'l Ass'n of Letter Carriers of the United States of America (Director, Public Relations)

VON CONRAD, Gunter

1225 I St. NW
Suite 1150
Washington, DC 20005
Tel: (202)457-0300
Fax: (202)331-8746
Registered: FARA

Employers
Barnes, Richardson and Colburn (Counsel)

Clients Represented
On Behalf of Barnes, Richardson and Colburn
Consolidated Diesel Corp.
Mercedes-Benz of North America, Inc.
Voest Alpine Steel

VON KLOBERG, III, Edward J.

2120 L St. NW
Suite 208
Washington, DC 20037
Tel: (202)463-7820
Fax: (202)223-3794
Registered: FARA

Employers
Washington World Group, Ltd. (Chairman and Founder)

Clients Represented
On Behalf of Washington World Group, Ltd.
Argentina, Government of
Asociacion Hondurena de Maquiladores
Bahrain, Government of the State of
Biman Bangladesh Airlines
Brunei Darussalam, Embassy of the State of
Burkina Faso, Government of
Burundi, Embassy of
Cameroon, Government of the Republic of
Cape Verde, Embassy of the Republic of
Congo, Ministry of Foreign Affairs and Economic Cooperation of the Republic of
Congo, Office of the Prime Minister of the Democratic Republic of the
Costa Rica, Embassy of the Republic of
Djibouti, Embassy of the Republic of
Dominican Republic, Embassy of the
Equitable Financial Co.
Gabonese Republic, Office of the President of the
Gambia Telecommunications
Gambia, Government of the Republic of The
Grenada, Government of the Republic of
Guatemalan Development Foundation (FUNDESA)
Guinea, Government of the Republic of
Haiti, Provisional Government of the Republic of
Lesotho, Embassy of The Kingdom Of
Lithuanian American Council
Mali, Embassy of the Republic of
Mauritania, Office of the Foreign Minister of
Mongolian People's Republic, Embassy of
Myanmar, Embassy of the Union of
Nepal, Kingdom of
Nepal, Royal Embassy of
Nicaraguan Foundation for Democracy and Development
Niger, Government of the Republic of
Nigeria, Embassy of the Federal Republic of
Pakistan, Embassy of the Islamic Republic of
Panama, Government of the Republic of
Papua New Guinea, Embassy of
Picker Internat'l
Rwanda, Government of the Republic of
Senegal, Government of the Republic of
Slovak Information Agency
Slovenia, Republic of
Suriname, Government of the Republic of
Swaziland, Embassy of the Kingdom of
Tanzania, Office of the Foreign Minister of the United Republic of
Togo, Government of the Republic of
Trinidad and Tobago, Embassy of the Republic of
Zaire, Office of the President of the Republic of

VON NORDHEIM, Manfred

815 Connecticut Ave. NW
Suite 700
Washington, DC 20006
Tel: (202)776-0988
Fax: (202)776-9080
Registered: FARA

Employers
European Aeronautics, Defence and Space, Inc. (President and Chief Exec. Officer)

VON OEHSEN, William H. E.

1001 Pennsylvania Ave. NW
Suite 600
Washington, DC 20004
Tel: (202)347-0066
Fax: (202)624-7222
Registered: LDA
EMail: wvonoehs@pgfm.com

Employers
Powell, Goldstein, Frazer & Murphy LLP (Partner)

Clients Represented
On Behalf of Powell, Goldstein, Frazer & Murphy LLP
Bayer Corp. / Agriculture Division
Nat'l Ass'n of Public Hospitals and Health Systems
Public Hospital Pharmacy Coalition

VON RAGO, Lillian

1000 Vermont Ave. NW
12th Floor
Washington, DC 20005
Tel: (202)371-2830
Fax: (202)371-0424
Registered: LDA

Employers
Americans for the Arts (Government Affairs Coordinator)

VON SEGGERN, John L.

1255 23rd St. NW
Washington, DC 20037
Tel: (202)955-0002
Fax: (202)835-1144
Registered: LDA

Employers
Council of Federal Home Loan Banks (President and Chief Exec. Officer)

VON UNWERTH, Frederick H.

700 13th St. NW
Suite 800
Washington, DC 20005
Tel: (202)508-5800
Fax: (202)508-5858
Staff Director and Legislative Counsel to Rep. Wyche Fowler, Jr. (D-GA), 1981-84.

Employers
Kilpatrick Stockton LLP (Partner)

Clients Represented
On Behalf of Kilpatrick Stockton LLP
Internat'l Furniture Rental Ass'n

VONDRACEK, M. Jon

1800 K St. NW
Washington, DC 20005
Tel: (202)887-0200
Fax: (202)775-3199
EMail: jvondra@csis.org

Employers
Center for Strategic and Internat'l Studies (V. President)

VONKANNON, John

214 Massachusetts Ave. NE
Washington, DC 20002
Tel: (202)546-4400
Fax: (202)546-8328

Employers
Heritage Foundation (V. President and Treasurer)

VOORHEES, Philip

1300 19th St. NW
Suite 300
Washington, DC 20036
Tel: (202)223-6722
Fax: (202)659-0650

Employers
Nat'l Parks Conservation Ass'n (Senior Director, Park Funding and Management)

VORNDRAN, Kurt

901 E St. NW
Suite 600
Washington, DC 20004
Tel: (202)783-4444
Fax: (202)783-4085
Registered: LDA

Employers
Nat'l Treasury Employees Union (Legislative Liaison)

VOSE, Kathryn Kahler

1909 K St. NW
Fourth Floor
Washington, DC 20006
Tel: (202)973-5800
Fax: (202)973-5858
Former Communications Director, Department of Education, during the Clinton administration.

Employers
Porter/Novelli (Senior V. President)

VOSS, Martha

1850 M St. NW
Suite 600
Washington, DC 20036
Tel: (202)775-1700
Fax: (202)822-0928

Employers
Toyota Motor North America, U.S.A., Inc. (Washington Public Relations Manager)

VOYACK, Frank J.

1750 New York Ave. NW
Suite 400
Washington, DC 20006
Tel: (202)383-4800
Fax: (202)347-3569
Registered: LDA
EMail: iwipal@aol.com

Employers
Internat'l Ass'n of Bridge, Structural, Ornamental and Reinforcing Iron Workers (Legislative and Political Director)

VOYIAZIAKIS, Barbara

625 Slaters Ln.
Suite 200
Alexandria, VA 22314-1171
Tel: (703)836-6263
Fax: (703)836-6730
EMail: barbarav@aahomecare.org

Employers
American Ass'n for Homecare (Membership Relations Assistant)

VRADENBURG, III, George

800 Connecticut Ave. NW
Suite 800
Washington, DC 20006
Tel: (202)457-8582
Fax: (202)457-8861

Employers
AOL Time Warner (Senior V. President, Global and Strategic Policy)

VROOM, Jay J.

1156 15th St. NW
Suite 400
Washington, DC 20005
Tel: (202)296-1585
Fax: (202)463-0474
Registered: LDA

Employers
American Crop Protection Ass'n (President)

VROOM, Peter J.

1725 Duke St.
Suite 600
Alexandria, VA 22314-3457
Tel: (703)299-9120
Fax: (703)299-9115
Registered: LDA
EMail: pvroom@trala.org
Administrative Assistant to Rep. J. Dennis Hastert (R-IL), 1987-91.

Employers
Truck Renting and Leasing Ass'n (Exec. V. President)

VROOMEN, Dr. Harry

501 Second St. NE
Washington, DC 20002
Tel: (202)675-8250
Fax: (202)544-8123
EMail: hvromen@tfi.org

Employers
The Fertilizer Institute (V. President, Economic Services)

VUNK, Kari

5550 Friendship Blvd.
Suite 310
Chevy Chase, MD 20815-7231
Tel: (301)968-4100
Fax: (301)968-4101
EMail: kvunk@aacom.org

Employers
American Ass'n of Colleges of Osteopathic Medicine (Assistant Director, Government Relations)

WACHTER, Donna D.

409 12th St. SW
Washington, DC 20024
Tel: (202)863-2507
Fax: (202)863-2514
EMail: dwachter@acog.com

Employers
Ass'n of Professors of Gynecology and Obstetrics (Exec. Director)

WACKER, Thomas

4121 Wilson Blvd.
Tenth Floor
Arlington, VA 22203
Tel: (703)351-2039
Fax: (703)351-2001
Registered: LDA
EMail: twacker@ntca.org

Employers
Nat'l Telephone Cooperative Ass'n (Director, Government Affairs)

WACKERLE, Rex

1140 Connecticut Ave. NW
Suite 510
Washington, DC 20036
Tel: (202)293-1676
Fax: (202)293-1658

Employers
Prudential Insurance Co. of America (V. President, Federal Government Relations)

WACLAWSKI, Mark

1755 Jefferson Davis Hwy.
Suite 1107
Arlington, VA 22202
Tel: (703)415-0344
Fax: (703)415-0182
Registered: LDA

Employers
The PMA Group (Associate)

Clients Represented

On Behalf of The PMA Group
AAI Corp.
Cartwright Electronics
Caterpillar Inc.
Chamberlain Manufacturing Corp.
Diamond Antenna & Microwave Corp.
Electro-Radiation Inc.
Electronic Warfare Associates, Inc.
L-3 Communications Corp.
Laguna Industries, Inc.
Lockheed Martin Corp.
Lucent Technologies
MIC Industries, Inc.
J. E. Morgan Knitting Mills
MTS Systems Inc.
SACO Defense
SatoTravel
SIGCOM, Inc.
Stanly County Airport Authority
TeleFlex Canada, Ltd.

WADA, Yasuhiro

1101 17th St. NW
Suite 1001
Washington, DC 20036
Tel: (202)331-8696
Fax: (202)293-3932

Employers
Development Bank of Japan (Representative)

WADDELL, Gregory W.

1301 K St. NW
Suite 1200-West Tower
Washington, DC 20005-3307
Tel: (202)515-5446
Fax: (202)515-5906
Registered: LDA

Employers
Internat'l Business Machines Corp. (Program Director, E-Commerce Policy)

WADE, J. Kirk

2550 M St. NW
Washington, DC 20037-1350
Tel: (202)457-6000
Fax: (202)457-6315
EMail: kwade@pattonboggs.com
Attorney/Advisor, Tax Legislative Dounsel (1976-77) and Attorney/Advisor, Interpretative Division, Chief Counsel of the Internal Revenue Service (1972-76), Department of the Treasury, 1976-77.

Employers
Patton Boggs, LLP (Partner)

WADE, Richard H.

325 Seventh St. NW
Washington, DC 20004
Tel: (202)638-1100
Fax: (202)626-2269

Employers
American Hospital Ass'n (Senior V. President, Strategic Communications)

WADE, Tara

1101 Pennsylvania Ave. NW
Sixth Floor
Washington, DC 20004
Tel: (202)756-7750
Fax: (202)756-7545
Registered: LDA
EMail: twade@etrade.com
Former aide to Rep. Tillie Fowler (R-FL).

Employers
E*TRADE Group, Inc. (Legislative Policy Analyst)

WADSWORTH, Harrison Morton

1155 15th St. NW
Suite 801
Washington, DC 20005
Tel: (202)466-8621
Fax: (202)466-8643
Registered: LDA
Former Legislative Director to Rep. Bart Gordon (D-TN).

Employers
Education Finance Council (Deputy Exec. Director)
Friends of Higher Education Inc. (Treasurer)

WADYKA, Christina S.

1200 New Hampshire Ave. NW
Suite 800
Washington, DC 20036-6802
Tel: (202)776-2000
Fax: (202)776-2222
EMail: cwadyka@dlalaw.com

Employers
Dow, Lohnes & Albertson, PLLC (Senior Counsel)

WADZINSKI, Kevin J.

1001 Pennsylvania Ave. NW
Suite 300S
Washington, DC 20004
Tel: (202)824-8800
Fax: (202)824-8990
Registered: LDA
EMail: wadzinski.kevin@dorseylaw.com

Employers
Dorsey & Whitney LLP (Associate)

Clients Represented

On Behalf of Dorsey & Whitney LLP
Aleutian Pribilof Islands Community Development Ass'n
Bristol Bay Native Corp.
Central Council of Tlingit and Haida Indian Tribes of Alaska
Cow Creek Umpqua Tribe of Oregon
Cuyapaipe Band of Mission Indians
Excelsior Gaming, Inc.
Gaming Management Internat'l II, Ltd.
Grand Traverse Band of Chippewa and Ottawa Indians
Las Vegas Paiute Tribe
Red Lake Band of Chippewa Indians
Shakopee Mdewakanton Sioux Tribe
Spokane Tribe
St. George Island Traditional Council
Stockbridge-Munsee Community Band of Mohican Indians

WAGER, Robert J.

2175 K St. NW
Suite 400
Washington, DC 20037-1809
EMail: robert.wager@csb.gov
Tel: (202)261-7600
Fax: (202)261-7650

Employers
Chemical Safety and Hazard Investigation Board (Director, Office of Congressional and Public Affairs)

WAGES, Joan B.

913 E. Taylor Run Pkwy.
Suite 303
Alexandria, VA 22302
Tel: (703)548-3676
Fax: (703)548-0926
Registered: LDA

Employers
Cash, Smith & Wages (Principal)

Clients Represented

On Behalf of Cash, Smith & Wages
Ass'n of Professional Flight Attendants
Nat'l Women's History Museum

WAGGONER, Deborah L.

1350 I St. NW
Suite 500
Washington, DC 20005-3305
EMail: waggonerd@corning.com
Tel: (202)682-3200
Fax: (202)682-3130
Registered: LDA

Employers
Corning Inc. (Director, Public Policy)

WAGLEY, John R.

3220 N St. NW
Suite 178
Washington, DC 20007
Tel: (202)342-9192

Employers
Congressional Agenda: 90's (Treasurer)

WAGNER, Dennis A.

1525 Wilson Blvd.
Suite 700
Arlington, VA 22209
Tel: (703)312-6100
Fax: (703)312-6196
Registered: LDA

Employers
United Defense, L.P. (V. President, Business Development and Domestic Marketing)

WAGNER, Elizabeth

2001 M St. NW
Washington, DC 20036
Tel: (202)467-3000
Fax: (202)533-8500

Employers
KPMG, LLP

Clients Represented

On Behalf of KPMG, LLP
The KPMG FSC Coalition

WAGNER, Heidi L.

1201 15th St. NW
Washington, DC 20005-2800
Tel: (202)822-0470
Fax: (202)822-0572
Registered: LDA

Employers
Nat'l Ass'n of Home Builders of the U.S. (Congressional Representative, Grassroots Regional Director)

WAGNER, Joe

410 First St. SE
Third Floor
Washington, DC 20003
EMail: jwagner@dcsgroup.com
Tel: (202)484-2776
Fax: (202)484-7016

Employers
The DCS Group (Director of Research/V. President)

WAGNER, John

1220 L St. NW
Washington, DC 20005
Tel: (202)682-8000
Fax: (202)682-8232
Registered: LDA

Employers
American Petroleum Institute (Senior Attorney)

WAGNER, Kathy

501 Third St. NW
Washington, DC 20001-2797
Tel: (202)434-1100
Fax: (202)434-1139

Employers
Communications Workers of America (Director, Politics and COPE)
Internat'l Union of Electronic, Electrical, Salaried, Machine, and Furniture Workers-Communications Workers of America (Director, COPE and Legislation)

WAGNER, Mark

400 N. Capitol St. NW
Suite 590
Washington, DC 20001
EMail: mark.f.wagner@jci.com
Tel: (202)393-3224
Fax: (202)393-7718
Former Special Assistant to the Assistant Secretary for Economic Security, Department of Defense. Also served on three Congressional staffs.

Employers
Johnson Controls, Inc. (Manager, Federal Government Relations)

WAGNER, Pamela Hyde

4301 N. Fairfax Dr.
Suite 360
Arlington, VA 22203-1627
Tel: (703)358-9300
Registered: LDA

Employers
Nat'l Utility Contractors Ass'n (NUCA) (Director, Education)

WAGONER, James

1025 Vermont Ave. NW
Suite 200
Washington, DC 20005
EMail: info@advocatesforyouth.org
Tel: (202)347-5700
Fax: (202)347-2263
Registered: LDA

Employers
Advocates for Youth (President)

WAHL, Barbara S.

1050 Connecticut Ave. NW
Washington, DC 20036-5339
Tel: (202)857-6000
Fax: (202)857-6395
Registered: LDA
Law Clerk to Judge Albert V. Bryan, Jr., U.S. District Court, Eastern District of Virginia, 1978-79.

Employers
Arent Fox Kintner Plotkin & Kahn, PLLC (Member)

WAHLBERG, Howard

1250 N. Pitt St.
Alexandria, VA 22314
EMail: hwahlberg@challenger.com
Tel: (703)683-9740
Fax: (703)683-7546

Employers
Challenger Center for Space Science Education (V. President, Marketing and Network Development)

WAHLQUIST, Glenn

10600 A Crestwood Dr.
Manassas, VA 20109
EMail: glennw@bigplanet.com
Tel: (540)364-9646
Fax: (703)368-5843
Registered: LDA

Employers
Citizens for an Alternative Tax System (Director Operations)

WAIKART, Douglas O.

1200 G St. NW
Suite 600
Washington, DC 20005-3802
EMail: waikart@wrightlaw.com
Tel: (202)393-1200
Fax: (202)393-1240

Employers
Wright & Talisman, P.C.

WAILOO, A. Christopher

801 Pennsylvania Ave.
Suite 650
Washington, DC 20004
EMail: chris.wailoo@aexp.com
Tel: (202)624-0761
Fax: (202)624-0775
Registered: LDA

Employers
American Express Co. (Director, Government Affairs)

WAINIK, Allison

11 Dupont Circle NW
Suite 500
Washington, DC 20036
Tel: (202)462-6688
Fax: (202)234-9770

Employers
Soc. for Neuroscience (Manager, Governmental and Public Affairs)

WAIT, Carol Cox

220 1/2 E St. NE
Washington, DC 20002
Tel: (202)547-4484
Fax: (202)547-4476
Former Legislative Director, Senate Committee on Budget.

Employers
Committee for a Responsible Federal Budget (President)

WAITE, Michael S.

P.O. Box 3008
Alexandria, VA 22302-0008
Tel: (703)931-4107
Fax: (703)931-3127
Registered: LDA

Employers
The Conaway Group LLC (Consultant)
The Mike Waite Company

Clients Represented

On Behalf of The Conaway Group LLC
Accenture

On Behalf of The Mike Waite Company
Arizona State University
Oregon Military Department

WAITS, II, John A.

1400 L St. NW
Washington, DC 20005-3502
Tel: (202)371-5779
Fax: (202)371-5950
Registered: LDA, FARA
EMail: jwaits@winston.com
Chief of Staff to Rep. David Bowen (D-MS), 1980-82. Counsel, House Committee on Agriculture, 1979-80.

Employers
Winston & Strawn (Partner, Legislative and Regulatory Practice)

Clients Represented

On Behalf of Winston & Strawn
Abilene, Texas, City of
American Airlines
American Honey Producers Ass'n
Barr Laboratories
Certified Airline Passenger Services, LLC
Cheese Importers Ass'n of America
Cooper Tire and Rubber Co.
Corning Inc.
Gildan Activewear
Hill Internat'l, Inc.
Jackson County, Mississippi Board of Supervisors
Jackson Municipal Airport Authority
Jackson, Mississippi, City of
Liberty Maritime Co.
Maximum Information Technology Inc.
Motor Coach Industries, Inc.
Panda Energy Internat'l
Puerto Rico, Commonwealth of
Queensland Sugar, Ltd.
Rickenbacker Port Authority
Spectrum Consulting, Inc.
Virgin Islands, Government of the
Waggoner Engineering, Inc.
Western Peanut Growers Ass'n
Yellow Corp.

WAKELYN, Phillip J.

1521 New Hampshire Ave. NW
Washington, DC 20036
EMail: pwakelyn@cotton.org
Tel: (202)745-7805
Fax: (202)483-4040

Employers
Nat'l Cotton Council of America (Manager, Environmental Health and Safety`)

WAKEMAN, Dennis

1300 Pennsylvania Ave. NW
Suite 400
Ronald Reagan Bldg.
Washington, DC 20004
EMail: dwakeman@strtrade.com
Tel: (202)638-2230
Fax: (202)638-2236
Registered: LDA

Employers
Sandler, Travis & Rosenberg, P.A. (Director, Trade Data Division)

Clients Represented

On Behalf of Sandler, Travis & Rosenberg, P.A.

Sri Lanka Apparel Exporters Ass'n

WALD, Ann

201 N. Union St.
Suite 200
Alexandria, VA 22314
Tel: (703)518-6141
Fax: (703)518-6191

Employers

Nat'l Apartment Ass'n (Director, Membership)

WALD, Matt

1004 Duke St.
Alexandria, VA 22314-3588
Tel: (703)684-3450 Ext: 333
Fax: (703)836-3482
Registered: LDA
EMail: mwald@asa-hq.com

Employers

American Subcontractors Ass'n, Inc. (Director of Government and Industry Relations)

WALDEN, Gregory S.

2550 M St. NW
Washington, DC 20037-1350
Tel: (202)457-6000
Fax: (202)457-6315
Registered: LDA

Employers

Patton Boggs, LLP

Clients Represented

On Behalf of Patton Boggs, LLP

Greenwood Village, Colorado, City of

WALDERS, Larry

1001 Pennsylvania Ave. NW
Suite 600
Washington, DC 20004
EMail: lwalders@pgfm.com
Tel: (202)347-0066
Fax: (202)624-7222

Employers

Powell, Goldstein, Frazer & Murphy LLP (Partner)

WALDMAN, Daniel

555 12th St. NW
Washington, DC 20004-1206
EMail: Daniel_Waldman@aporter.com
Tel: (202)942-5000
Fax: (202)942-5999

Employers

Arnold & Porter (Partner)

WALDMANN, Daniel

1001 Pennsylvania Ave. NW
Suite 850 North
Washington, DC 20004-2505
EMail: dwaldmann@policypartners.com
Tel: (202)661-3580
Fax: (202)737-4242
Registered: LDA

Employers

Public Policy Partners, LLC (V. President)

Clients Represented

On Behalf of Public Policy Partners, LLC

Express Scripts Inc.
Johnson & Johnson, Inc.
St. Jude Medical, Inc.
Urologix, Inc.
Vertis Neuroscience

WALDRON, Arthur

1150 17th St. NW
Washington, DC 20036
EMail: awaldron@aei.org
Tel: (202)862-5800
Fax: (202)862-7177

Employers

American Enterprise Institute for Public Policy Research (Visiting Scholar, Director of Asian Studies)

WALDRON, Gerard J.

1201 Pennsylvania Ave. NW
Washington, DC 20004-2401
EMail: gwaldron@cov.com
Tel: (202)662-5900
Fax: (202)662-6291
Registered: LDA

Senior Counsel, Subcommittee on Telecommunications and Finance, House Commerce Committee, 1991-95. Law Clerk to Judge J. Dickson Phillips, U.S. Court of Appeals, Fourth Circuit, 1990-91. Policy Analyst, Subcommittee on Energy, Conservation and Power, House Committee on Energy and Commerce, 1985-87. Legislative Aide to Rep. Edward J. Markey (D-MA), 1985.

Employers

Covington & Burling (Partner)

Clients Represented

On Behalf of Covington & Burling

CBS Affiliates
Network Affiliated Stations Alliance

WALDRON, Jonathan K.

600 New Hampshire Ave. NW
11th Floor
Washington, DC 20037
EMail: jkw@dejlaw.com
Tel: (202)944-3000
Fax: (202)944-3068
Registered: LDA, FARA

Employers

Dyer Ellis & Joseph, P.C. (Partner)

Clients Represented

On Behalf of Dyer Ellis & Joseph, P.C.

Glass Packaging Institute
Heerema Marine Contractors Nederland B.V.
Hvide Marine Inc.
Marine Spill Response Corporation
Nat'l Oilseed Processors Ass'n
The Trump Organization

WALKER, Allen

1600 Wilson Blvd.
Suite 1000
Arlington, VA 22209
EMail: awalker@vesselalliance.com
Tel: (703)351-6734
Fax: (703)351-6736
Registered: LDA

Employers

Shipbuilders Council of America (President)

WALKER, Andrew

1513 16th St. NW
Washington, DC 20036
EMail: awalker@capitalresearch.org
Tel: (202)483-6900
Fax: (202)483-6902

Employers

Capital Research Center (Director, Communications)

WALKER, Angela

1140 Connecticut Ave. NW
Suite 510
Washington, DC 20036
Tel: (202)293-1357
Fax: (202)293-1658
Registered: LDA

Employers

Prudential Insurance Co. of America (Manager, Government Relations)

WALKER, Bill

1666 Connecticut Ave. NW
Sixth Floor
Washington, DC 20235
EMail: Bill_Walker@ARC.gov
Tel: (202)884-7746
Fax: (202)884-7695

Employers

Appalachian Regional Commission, Office of States' Washington Representative of (States' Washington Represntative)

WALKER, Donald

1050 31st St. NW
Washington, DC 20007
Tel: (202)965-3500
Fax: (202)342-5484

Employers

Ass'n of Trial Lawyers of America (Senior Director, Finance and Administration)

WALKER, Douglas

1201 16th St. NW
Washington, DC 20036
Tel: (202)833-4000

Employers

Nat'l Education Ass'n of the U.S. (Senior Professional Associate)

WALKER, Graham

1150 17th St. NW
Washington, DC 20036
EMail: gwalker@aei.org
Tel: (202)862-5800
Fax: (202)862-7177

Employers

American Enterprise Institute for Public Policy Research (Visiting Scholar)

WALKER, Jr., Hans

2120 L St. NW
Suite 700
Washington, DC 20037
Tel: (202)822-8282
Fax: (202)296-8834
Registered: LDA

Served as Attorney; Director, Office of Indian Water Rights; Assistant Solicitor; and Associate Solicitor, Department of Interior, 1964-82.

Employers

Hobbs, Straus, Dean and Walker, LLP (Partner)

Clients Represented

On Behalf of Hobbs, Straus, Dean and Walker, LLP

Bristol Bay Area Health Corp.
Menominee Indian Tribe
Three Affiliated Tribes of Fort Berthold Reservation

WALKER, J. Brent

200 Maryland Ave. NE
Suite 303
Washington, DC 20002
EMail: brent_walker@bjcpa.org
Tel: (202)544-4226
Fax: (202)544-2094

Employers

Baptist Joint Committee on Public Affairs (Exec. Director)

WALKER, Jerry A.

810 First St. NE
Suite 510
Washington, DC 20002
Tel: (202)289-5440
Fax: (202)289-3707

Employers

Gypsum Ass'n (Exec. Director)

WALKER, Kevin L.

1101 Vermont Ave. NW
12th Floor
Washington, DC 20005-3583
Tel: (202)789-7467
Fax: (202)789-7469

Employers

American Medical Ass'n (V. President, Political Affairs)

WALKER, Kevin L.

2300 Clarendon Blvd.
Suite 610
Arlington, VA 22201-3367
EMail: kwalker@golinharris.com
Tel: (703)351-5666
Fax: (703)351-5667

Special Projects Director, Rep. Deborah Pryce (R-OH), 1991-97.

Employers

Golin/Harris Internat'l (Account Director)

WALKER, Laird

1025 Thomas Jefferson St. NW
Suite 410E
Washington, DC 20007
Tel: (202)342-3830
Fax: (202)318-0065
Registered: LDA

Employers

Commerce Consultants Internat'l Ltd. (President)

Clients Represented

On Behalf of Commerce Consultants Internat'l Ltd.

Qwest Communications

WALKER, Liz

2111 Wilson Blvd.
Eighth Floor
Arlington, VA 22201-3058
Tel: (703)841-0626
Fax: (703)243-2874

Employers

Alcalde & Fay (Senior Associate)

WALKER, Lynda K.

5612 S. 4th St.
Arlington, VA 22204
Tel: (202)347-2612
Fax: (703)998-6191
Registered: LDA

Former Tax Counsel to Senator John Heinz (R-PA).

Employers

McKay Walker (Principal)

Clients Represented

On Behalf of McKay Walker

Citigroup
The Rouse Company
Sunoco, Inc.

WALKER, Mary Ann

1133 Connecticut Ave. NW
Suite 1200
Washington, DC 20036
Tel: (202)775-9800
Fax: (202)833-8491

Employers

Winthrop, Stimson, Putnam & Roberts (Partner)

WALKER, Reba P.

1201 New York Ave. NW
Suite 601
Washington, DC 20005
Tel: (202)289-0584
Fax: (202)289-8849

Employers

Hotel Ass'n of Washington (President)

WALKER, Hon. Robert S.

1317 F St. NW
Suite 600
Washington, DC 20004
Tel: (202)638-2121
Fax: (202)638-7045
Registered: LDA
EMail: walker@wexlergroup.com

Member, U.S. House of Representatives (R-PA), 1977-96. Served as Chairman, House Committee on Science, 1994-97.

Employers

The Wexler Group (Chairman and Chief Exec. Officer)

Clients Represented

On Behalf of The Wexler Group

Alliance of Automobile Manufacturers, Inc.
AstroVision Inc.
Comcast Corp.
DCH Technology Inc.
Dreamtime, Inc.
EarthWatch, Inc.
Electronic Industries Alliance
General Motors Corp.
P. H. Glatfelter
Guardian Industries Corp.
Hong Kong Economic and Trade Office
Hydroelectric Licensing Reform Task Force
Lockheed Martin Corp.
MENC: The Nat'l Ass'n for Music Education
Nat'l Ass'n of Music Merchants
ORBITZ
Rocket Development Co.
Rosenbaum Trust
Sechan Electronics
Virginia Center for Innovative Technology

WALKER, Todd A.

1331 F St. NW
Suite 450
Washington, DC 20004
Tel: (202)638-6890
Fax: (202)220-3619
Registered: LDA

Employers

UST Public Affairs, Inc. (V. President, Federal Government Relations)

WALKER, Tracey

700 11th St. NW
Suite 680
Washington, DC 20001
Tel: (202)628-5877
Fax: (202)628-4847
EMail: tracey_walker@adsw.com

Employers

Allied Domecq (Manager, Government Affairs)

WALL, Christopher R.

1133 Connecticut Ave. NW
Suite 1200
Washington, DC 20036
Tel: (202)775-9800
Fax: (202)833-8491
Registered: LDA

Employers

Winthrop, Stimson, Putnam & Roberts (Partner)

Clients Represented

On Behalf of Winthrop, Stimson, Putnam & Roberts

SKW Chemicals, Inc.

WALL, Jim

901 E St. NW
Suite 600
Washington, DC 20004
Tel: (202)783-4444
Fax: (202)508-3708
Registered: LDA

Employers

Nat'l Treasury Employees Union (Legislative Liason)

WALL, Lori M.

1100 15th St. NW
Suite 900
Washington, DC 20005
Tel: (202)835-3400
Fax: (202)835-3414

Counsel, House Committee on Commerce, 1999-2000. Administrative Assistant (1997-98) and Tax Counsel (1996-97) to Rep. Jon Christensen (R-NE).

Employers

Pharmaceutical Research and Manufacturers of America (Director, Public Policy)

WALL, CAE, Martin A.

6110 Executive Blvd.
Suite 510
Rockville, MD 20852
Tel: (301)231-5944
Fax: (301)770-1828
EMail: mwall@opted.org

Legislative Analyst, Department of Health, Education and Welfare/Health and Human Services, 1974-78.

Employers

Ass'n of Schools and Colleges of Optometry (Exec. Director)

WALLACE, Jr., Donald L.

499 S. Capitol St. SW
Suite 600
Washington, DC 20003
Tel: (202)554-1222
Fax: (202)554-1230
Registered: LDA
EMail: dwawashdc@aol.com

Employers

Cotton Warehouse Ass'n of America (Exec. V. President)
Don Wallace Associates, Inc. (President)

Clients Represented

On Behalf of Don Wallace Associates, Inc.

American Sugar Cane League of the U.S.A.
Cotton Warehouse Ass'n of America
Service Corp. Internat'l

WALLACE, George J.

1250 24th St. NW
Suite 700
Washington, DC 20037
Tel: (202)659-6600
Fax: (202)659-6699
Registered: LDA
EMail: gjw@escm.com

Employers

Eckert Seamans Cherin & Mellott, LLC (Member)

Clients Represented

On Behalf of Eckert Seamans Cherin & Mellott, LLC

American Financial Services Ass'n

WALLACE, H. Scott

1625 K St. NW
Suite 800
Washington, DC 20006
Tel: (202)452-0620
Fax: (202)872-1031
Registered: LDA
EMail: defender@nlada.org

Employers

Nat'l Legal Aid and Defender Ass'n (Director, Defender Legal Services)

WALLACE, Jr., James H.

1776 K St. NW
Washington, DC 20006
Tel: (202)719-7000
Fax: (202)719-7049

Former Trial Attorney, Antitrust Division, U.S. Department of Justice, 1967-70; Patent Examiner, United States Patent & Trademark Office, 1966-67.

Employers

Wiley, Rein & Fielding (Partner)

WALLACE, Mary L.

800 I St. NW
Washington, DC 20001
Tel: (202)777-2510
Fax: (202)777-2534
Registered: LDA

Employers

American Public Health Ass'n (Director, Government Relations and Affiliate Affairs)

WALLACE, Rob

1299 Pennsylvania Ave. NW
Suite 1100 West
Washington, DC 20004-2407
Tel: (202)637-4000
Fax: (202)637-4400
Registered: LDA

Minority Staff Director, Senate Energy and Natural Resources Committee, 1991-94. Administrative Assistant to Sen. Malcolm Wallop (R-WY), 1989-91. Assistant Director, Legislative and Congressional Affairs, National Park Service, Department of the Interior, 1986-89.

Employers

GE Power Systems (Director, Government Relations)
General Electric Co. (Manager, Government and Industry Programs)

WALLACE, Robert B.

1341 G St. NW
Fifth Floor
Washington, DC 20005
Tel: (202)626-7660
Fax: (202)628-3606

Employers

Wilson, Elser, Moskowitz, Edelman & Dicker LLP (Partner)

WALLACE, Robert E.

200 Maryland Ave. NE
Washington, DC 20002
Tel: (202)543-2239
Fax: (202)543-6719
EMail: rwallace@vfwdc.org

Employers

Veterans of Foreign Wars of the U.S. (Exec. Director)

WALLACE, Sidney A.

600 New Hampshire Ave. NW
11th Floor
Washington, DC 20037
Tel: (202)944-3000
Fax: (202)944-3068
Registered: LDA
EMail: saw@dejlaw.com

Counsel, House Committee on Merchant Marine and Fisheries, 1979-81. Maritime Policy Advisor to the Secretary, Department of Transportation, 1977-78.

Employers

Dyer Ellis & Joseph, P.C. (Counsel)

Clients Represented

On Behalf of Dyer Ellis & Joseph, P.C.

American Coke and Coal Chemicals Institute
Browning Transport Management
Marine Spill Response Corporation
Nat'l Oilseed Processors Ass'n

WALLACE, Sondra S.

Hubert H. Humphrey Bldg.
200 Independence Ave. SW
Room 435G
Washington, DC 20201
Tel: (202)690-7760
Fax: (202)690-7309
EMail: swallace@os.dhhs.gov

Employers

Department of Health and Human Services (Associate General Counsel, Legislation Division)

WALLACE, Stephen J.

401 Ninth St. NW
Suite 900
Washington, DC 20004
Tel: (202)585-8000
Fax: (202)585-8080
Registered: LDA
EMail: swallace@nixonpeabody.com

Employers

Nixon Peabody LLP (Partner)

Clients Represented

On Behalf of Nixon Peabody LLP

Edward A. Fish Associates
Institute for Responsible Housing Preservation
Light Associates
Nat'l Leased Housing Ass'n
New England Education Loan Marketing Corp. (Nellie Mae)
New York State Housing Finance Agency
Starrett City Associates

WALLACE, Vicki P.

1101 30th St. NW
Suite 500
Washington, DC 20007
Tel: (202)289-5490
Fax: (202)289-5495
Registered: LDA

Staff Member to Rep. Ronnie G. Flippo (D-AL), 1977-91. Staff Member to Rep. Robert E. Jones (D-AL), 1974-76.

Employers

R. G. Flippo and Associates, Inc. (Senior Associate)

Clients Represented

On Behalf of R. G. Flippo and Associates, Inc.

Alabama Nursing Homes Ass'n
Huntsville, Alabama, City of
Huntsville-Madison County Airport
Tensor Technologies, Inc.
Troy State University - Montgomery

WALLACH, Lori M.

215 Pennsylvania Ave. SE
Washington, DC 20003
Tel: (202)546-4996
Registered: LDA

Employers

Public Citizen, Inc. (Director, Global Trade)

WALLEM, Kate

1015 15th St. NW
Suite 802
Washington, DC 20005
EMail: kwallem@acec.org
Tel: (202)347-7474
Fax: (202)898-0068
Registered: LDA

Employers

American Consulting Engineers Council (Director, Liability and Regulatory Affairs)

WALLER, James F.

1400 I St. NW
Suite 850
Washington, DC 20005
EMail: jwaller@mentoring.org
Tel: (202)729-4360
Fax: (202)729-4341

Employers

Nat'l Mentoring Partnership, Inc. (V. President, Government Relations)

WALLER, Karen

1801 K St. NW
Suite 1000L
Washington, DC 20006
EMail: karen_waller@washbm.com
Tel: (202)530-0400
Fax: (202)530-4500

Employers

Burson-Marsteller (Managing Director, Health Care Practice)

WALLER, Ph.D., Ray A.

1429 Duke St.
Alexandria, VA 22314-3402
Tel: (703)684-1221
Fax: (703)684-2037

Employers

American Statistical Ass'n (Exec. Director)

WALLICK, Robert D.

1330 Connecticut Ave. NW
Washington, DC 20036-1795
EMail: rwallick@steptoe.com
Tel: (202)429-3000
Fax: (202)429-3902

Employers

Steptoe & Johnson LLP (Partner)

Clients Represented

On Behalf of Steptoe & Johnson LLP

Coalition for Government Procurement

WALLIN, Jeffrey D.

1700 K St. NW
Suite 901
Washington, DC 20006
Tel: (202)452-8611
Fax: (202)452-8620

Employers

American Academy for Liberal Education (President)

WALLIS, Jim

2401 15th St. NW
Washington, DC 20009
EMail: sojourners@sojourners.com
Tel: (202)328-8842
Fax: (202)328-8757

Employers

Sojourners (Editor-in-Chief)

WALLIS, Ph.D., Norman E.

4340 East West Hwy.
Suite 401
Bethesda, MD 20814-4411
Tel: (301)718-6539
Fax: (301)656-0989

Employers

American Nat'l Metric Council (Exec. Director)
PAI Management Corp. (President)

Clients Represented

On Behalf of PAI Management Corp.

American Board of Adolescent Psychiatry
Soc. for Mucosal Immunology

WALLISON, Peter J.

1150 17th St. NW
Washington, DC 20036
EMail: pwallison@aei.org
Tel: (202)862-5800
Fax: (202)862-7177

Employers

American Enterprise Institute for Public Policy Research (Resident Fellow)

WALLMAN, Kathleen E.

555 12th St. NW
Washington, DC 20004
Tel: (202)347-4964
Fax: (202)347-4961
Registered: LDA

Former Deputy Assistant to the President and Chief of Staff of the National Economic Council.

Employers

Wallman Strategic Consulting, LLC

Clients Represented

On Behalf of Wallman Strategic Consulting, LLC

Intermedia Communications Inc.
MediaOne Group
PanAmSat Corp.
Real Access Alliance

WALLOP, Hon. Malcolm

1401 Wilson Blvd.
Suite 1007
Arlington, VA 22209
Tel: (703)527-8282
Fax: (703)527-8388

Member, U.S. Senate (R-WY), 1977-95.

Employers

Frontiers of Freedom Institute (Chairman)

WALLS-RIVAS, Kristen

1776 I St. NW
Suite 880
Washington, DC 20006
EMail: krivas@wdc.fujitsu.com
Tel: (202)331-8750
Fax: (202)331-8797

Employers

Fujitsu Limited (Policy and Legal Analyst)

WALSH, Brian

8403 Arlington Blvd.
Suite 100
Fairfax, VA 22031
EMail: bwalsh@interfacinc.com
Tel: (703)876-6800
Fax: (703)876-0515

Employers

Interface Inc. (Secretary)

Clients Represented

On Behalf of Interface Inc.

Safety-Kleen Corp.

WALSH, Charles S.

1400 16th St. NW
Suite 600
Washington, DC 20036
EMail: CWalsh@fw-law.com
Tel: (202)939-7900
Fax: (202)667-8883
Registered: LDA

Employers

Fleischman and Walsh, L.L.P. (Partner)

Clients Represented

On Behalf of Fleischman and Walsh, L.L.P.

Nat'l Cable Television Ass'n

WALSH, Dr. Gerald P.

11600 Nebel St.
Suite 210
Rockville, MD 20852
Tel: (301)984-1336
Fax: (301)770-0580

Employers

American Leprosy Foundation (Scientific Director)

WALSH, Helen

11501 Georgia Ave., Suite 203
Wheaton, MD 20902
Tel: (301)949-5995
Fax: (301)949-8373

Employers

Tile Contractors Ass'n of America (Exec. Director)

WALSH, Hugh Leo

501 Third St. NW
Washington, DC 20001-2797
Tel: (202)434-1100
Fax: (202)434-1139

Employers

Communications Workers of America (President and Director of Political and Legislative Affairs)

WALSH, J. Daniel

1133 21st St. NW
Suite 700
Washington, DC 20036
EMail: dwalsh@janus-merritt.com
Tel: (202)887-6900
Fax: (202)887-6970
Registered: LDA

Legislative Director to Rep. Wayne Gilchrest (R-MD), 1991-97. Legislative Director to Rep. Jack Buechner (R-MO), 1989-91.

Employers

Janus-Merritt Strategies, L.L.C. (Principal)

Clients Represented

On Behalf of Janus-Merritt Strategies, L.L.C.

AFIN Securities
Banorte Casa de Bolsa
Camara Nacional de la Industria Pesquera
Camara Nacional de las Industrias Azucarera y Alcoholera
Cementos Monterrey, S.A.
CEMEX Central, S.A. de C.V.
Corporacion Valenciana de Cementos Portland, S.A.
Corporacion Venezolana de Cementos, SACA
COVAD Communications Co.
DSL Access Telecommunications Ass'n (DATA)
EchoStar Communications Corp.
Fraternal Order of Police (U.S. Park Police Labor Committee)
Fundacion para la Preservacion de Flora y Fauna Marina
Grupo Financiero Banorte
Grupo Maseca
HarvardNet, Inc.
Houston Shell and Concrete
Interactive Gaming Council
Napster, Inc.
Nat'l Indian Gaming Ass'n
Pacific Coast Cement
Rhythms NetConnections
Scribe Communications, Inc.
Sunbelt Cement
Viejas Band of Kumeyaay Indians
Vivendi Universal

WALSH, John G.

1990 M St. NW
Suite 450
Washington, DC 20036
Tel: (202)331-2472
Fax: (202)785-9423

Employers

Group of 30 (Exec. Director)

WALSH, Mary

800 Independence Ave. SW
Room 921 D
Washington, DC 20591
Tel: (202)267-3217
Fax: (202)267-5194

Employers

Department of Transportation - Federal Aviation Administration (Assistant Chief Counsel for Legislation)

WALSH, Maureen

700 13th St. NW
Suite 400
Washington, DC 20005
EMail: mwalsh@cassidy.com
Tel: (202)347-0773
Fax: (202)347-0785
Registered: LDA

Former Staff and Press Assistant to Rep. Jim Moran (D-VA).

Employers

Cassidy & Associates, Inc. (Associate)

Clients Represented

On Behalf of Cassidy & Associates, Inc.

City College of San Francisco
City of Hope Nat'l Medical Center
Community General Hospital of Sullivan County
Community Hospital Telehealth Consortium
D'Youville College
eCharge Corp.
Fairview Hospital and Healthcare Services
Forum Health
Hawaii, State of
Immaculata College
Lewis and Clark College
Marymount University
Nat'l SAFE KIDS Campaign
The PGA Tour, Inc.
Rush Presbyterian-St. Luke's Medical Center
San Diego, University of
Santa Rosa Memorial Hospital
Smartforce
Taiwan Studies Institute
University of Pittsburgh Medical Center (UPMC)
Widener University

WALSH, Molly

1341 G St. NW
Suite 900
Washington, DC 20005
Tel: (202)637-1528
Fax: (202)637-1509

Employers

Philip Morris Management Corp. (Director, Public Affairs - South)

WALSH, Richard

815 16th St. NW
Washington, DC 20006
Tel: (202)637-5000
Fax: (202)637-5058

Employers

AFL-CIO (American Federation of Labor and Congress of Industrial Organizations) (Deputy Director, Field Mobilization)

WALSH, Robert

1215 Jefferson Davis Hwy.
Suite 1500
Arlington, VA 22202
Tel: (703)416-7800
Fax: (703)415-1459
Registered: LDA
EMail: bob.walsh@baesystems.com

Employers

BAE SYSTEMS North America (V. President, Government Relations-Information and Electronic Warfare Systems)

WALSH, Sarah J.

1500 K St. NW
Suite 650
Washington, DC 20005
Tel: (202)715-1000
Fax: (202)715-1001
Registered: LDA

Employers

GlaxoSmithKline (Federal Government Relations)

WALSH, Susan M.

1401 I St. NW
Suite 600
Washington, DC 20005
Tel: (202)336-7400
Fax: (202)336-7515
Registered: LDA

Employers

United Technologies Corp. (Director, Commercial and International Programs)

WALSH, Suzanne

820 First St. NE
Suite 510
Washington, DC 20002
Tel: (202)408-1080
Fax: (202)408-1056
Registered: LDA

Employers

Center on Budget and Policy Priorities (Legislative Associate)

WALTER, Douglas

750 First St. NE
Washington, DC 20002-4242
Tel: (202)336-5500
Fax: (202)336-5708
Registered: LDA

Employers

American Psychological Ass'n (Legislative Counsel, Government Relations)

WALTER, Jeffery M.

1747 Pennsylvania Ave. NW
Suite 1150
Washington, DC 20006
Tel: (202)557-2974
Fax: (202)296-4507
Registered: LDA

Employers

The MWW Group (V. President)

Clients Represented

On Behalf of The MWW Group

Bacardi-Martini, USA, Inc.
GAF Corp.
Kmart Corp.
Puerto Ricans for Civic Action

WALTER, Sheryl

950 Pennsylvania Ave. NW
Room 1537
Washington, DC 20530
Tel: (202)514-2141
Fax: (202)514-4482

Employers

Department of Justice (Acting Assistant Attorney General for Legislative Affairs)

WALTER, Susan M.

1299 Pennsylvania Ave. NW
Suite 1100 West
Washington, DC 20004-2407
Tel: (202)637-4000
Fax: (202)637-4006
Registered: LDA

Employers

General Electric Co. (V. President, Corporate Government Relations)

WALTERS, John

1150 17th St. NW
Suite 503
Washington, DC 20036
Tel: (202)822-8333
Fax: (202)822-8325

Employers

The Philanthropy Roundtable (President)

WALTERS, Dr. LeRoy B.

37th and O Sts. NW
Fourth Floor, Heally Hall
Washington, DC 20027
Tel: (202)687-8099
Fax: (202)687-8089

Employers

Kennedy Institute of Ethics (Director)

WALTERS, Thomas P.

440 First St. NW
Suite 430
Washington, DC 20001
Tel: (202)737-7523
Fax: (202)737-6788
Registered: LDA

Employers

Honberger and Walters, Inc. (President)

Clients Represented

On Behalf of Honberger and Walters, Inc.

Calleguas Municipal Water District, California
Monterey Salinas Transit
North San Diego County Transit Development Board
Pechanga Band of Luiseno Mission Indians
Port of San Diego
Riverside, California, County of
San Diego Metropolitan Transit Development Board
San Diego, California, County of
San Joaquin, California, County of
Sweetwater Authority
Ventura, California, County of

WALTERS, William

1100 15th St. NW
Suite 900
Washington, DC 20005
Tel: (202)835-3400
Fax: (202)835-3414
Former Staff, Subcommittee on Health, House Committee on Ways and Means.

Employers

Pharmaceutical Research and Manufacturers of America (Assistant General Counsel)

WALTHER, Pamela D.

600 13th St. NW
Washington, DC 20005-3096
Tel: (202)756-8220
Fax: (202)756-8087
Registered: LDA, FARA
EMail: pwalther@mwe.com

Employers

McDermott, Will and Emery (Partner)

Clients Represented

On Behalf of McDermott, Will and Emery

Alaska Seafood Marketing Institute
California Cling Peach Growers Advisory Board

WALTMAN, James R.

1615 M St. NW
Washington, DC 20036
Tel: (202)833-2300
Fax: (202)429-3945
Registered: LDA
EMail: Jim_Waltman@tws.org

Employers

The Wilderness Soc. (Director, Refuges and Wildlife Program)

WALTON CROUCH, Laura

910 16th St. NW
Suite 300
Washington, DC 20006
Tel: (202)728-1984
Fax: (202)728-1981
EMail: council@usbusiness.org

Employers

United States Business and Industry Council (V. President)

WALTZ, Daniel E.

2550 M St. NW
Washington, DC 20037-1350
Tel: (202)457-6000
Fax: (202)457-6315
Registered: LDA
EMail: dwaltz@lpattonboggs.com

Employers

Patton Boggs, LLP (Partner)

Clients Represented

On Behalf of Patton Boggs, LLP

Condor-Pacific Industries
Farmland Industries, Inc.
LOOP, Inc.
Nat'l Soft Drink Ass'n

WALTZKIN, Michael B.

750 17th St. NW
Suite 1100
Washington, DC 20006
Tel: (202)778-2300
Fax: (202)778-2330

Employers

FoxKiser

WAMESTER, Robert

441 N. Lee St.
Alexandria, VA 22314
Tel: (703)549-3622
Fax: (703)684-5196

Employers

Catholic War Veterans of the U.S.A. (National Commander)

WAMSLEY, Herbert C.

1255 23rd St. NW
Suite 200
Washington, DC 20037
Tel: (202)466-2396
Fax: (202)466-2893
Registered: LDA
EMail: info@ipo.org

Employers

Intellectual Property Owners Ass'n (Exec. Director)

WANDER, Elyse

1100 New York Ave. NW
Suite 450
Washington, DC 20005
Tel: (202)408-8422
Fax: (202)408-1255
Registered: LDA

Employers

Travel Industry Ass'n of America (Senior V. President, Government and Public Affairs)

WANG, Catherine

3000 K St. NW
Suite 300
Washington, DC 20007
Tel: (202)424-7500
Fax: (202)424-7643
Registered: LDA

Employers

Swidler Berlin Shereff Friedman, LLP (Member)

WANG, Greg

1130 Connecticut Ave. NW
Suite 300
Washington, DC 20036
Tel: (202)331-8500
Fax: (202)331-1598
Registered: LDA

Employers
The Ferguson Group, LLC (Principal)

Clients Represented
On Behalf of The Ferguson Group, LLC
Somach, Simmons & Dunn

WAPENSKY, Russell

888 Sixteenth St. NW
7th Floor
Washington, DC 20006-4103
Tel: (202)835-8173
Fax: (202)835-8136
Registered: LDA
Formerly employed at Department of State.

Employers
Foley & Lardner (Lobbyist)

Clients Represented
On Behalf of Foley & Lardner
Save the Greenback Coalition

WARBURG, Gerald Felix

700 13th St. NW
Suite 400
Washington, DC 20005
Tel: (202)347-0773
Fax: (202)347-0785
Registered: LDA, FARA
EMail: gwarburg@cassidy.com
Former Legislative Assistant to Senator Alan Cranston (D-CA). Former Legislative Assistant, Energy, Environment and Trade to Rep. Jonathan B. Bingham (D-NY). Former Aide to Senator John V. Tunney (D-CA). Former Consultant Nuclear Regulatory Commission.

Employers
Cassidy & Associates, Inc. (Senior V. President)

Clients Represented
On Behalf of Cassidy & Associates, Inc.
California Institute for the Arts
City College of San Francisco
Hampshire College
Lewis and Clark College
San Diego, University of
Santa Rosa Memorial Hospital
Saudi Arabia, Royal Embassy of
Sherwin Williams Co.
Taiwan Research Institute
Taiwan Studies Institute
University of San Diego
University of San Francisco

WARBURTON, Albert E.

1401 New York Ave. NW
Suite 640
Washington, DC 20005
Tel: (202)628-8303
Fax: (202)628-2846
Registered: LDA

Employers
American Water Works Ass'n (Director, Legislative Affairs)

WARCHOT, Louis P.

50 F St. NW
12th Floor
Washington, DC 20001
Tel: (202)639-2525
Fax: (202)639-2526

Employers
Ass'n of American Railroads (Senior V. President, Law and General Counsel)

WARD, Gregg

701 Pennsylvania Ave. NW
Suite 720
Washington, DC 20004
Tel: (202)434-4800
Fax: (202)347-4015
Assistant Secretary for Congressional and Intergovernmental Affairs, Department of Energy, during the Bush I Administration.

Employers
Siemens Corp. (V. President, Government Relations)

WARD, Jim

900 Second St. NE
Suite 211
Washington, DC 20002
Tel: (202)408-9514
Fax: (202)408-9520

Employers
Nat'l Ass'n of Protection and Advocacy Systems (NAPAS) (Deputy Director, Public Policy)

WARD, John D.

1200 New Hampshire Ave. NW
Suite 800
Washington, DC 20036-6802
EMail: jward@dlalaw.com
Tel: (202)776-2000
Fax: (202)776-2222

Employers
Dow, Lohnes & Albertson, PLLC (Member)

WARD, Julie

4351 Garden City Dr.
Landover, MD 20785
Tel: (301)459-3700
Fax: (301)577-2684
Registered: LDA
EMail: jward@efa.org

Employers
Epilepsy Foundation of America (Director, Government Affairs)

WARD, L. Courtney

800 Connecticut Ave. NW
9th Floor
Washington, DC 20006
Tel: (202)533-2100
Fax: (202)533-2124
Registered: LDA

Employers
J. P. Morgan Chase & Co. (V. President)

WARD, Lisa

105 N. Alfred St.
Alexandria, VA 22314
Tel: (703)236-6000
Fax: (703)236-6001

Employers
Brain Injury Ass'n (Director, Communications)

WARD, Matt

1350 New York Ave. NW
Suite 1100
Washington, DC 20005-4798
Tel: (202)879-4000
Fax: (202)393-2866
Registered: LDA
EMail: wardm@spiegelmcd.com

Employers
Spiegel & McDiarmid (Associate)

WARD, Michael E.

3000 K St. NW
Suite 300
Washington, DC 20007
Tel: (202)424-7500
Fax: (202)424-7643
Registered: LDA
Assistant Counsel, House Committee on the Judiciary, 1979-85.

Employers
Swidler Berlin Shereff Friedman, LLP (Counsel)

Clients Represented
On Behalf of Swidler Berlin Shereff Friedman, LLP
Artichoke Enterprises, Inc.
Renewable Fuels Ass'n
WRD Venture/NWD Venture

WARD, Monte N.

122 C St. NW
Suite 540
Washington, DC 20001
EMail: mward@namic.org
Tel: (202)628-1558
Fax: (202)628-1601

Employers
Nat'l Ass'n of Mutual Insurance Companies (Director, Federal Affairs)

WARD, Morris "Bud"

1025 Connecticut Ave. NW
Suite 1200
Washington, DC 20036
EMail: wardb@nsc.org
Tel: (202)293-2270
Fax: (202)293-0032

Employers
Nat'l Safety Council (Exec. Director, Environmental Health Center)

WARD, Neil

600 Jefferson Plaza
Suite 350
Rockville, MD 20852
EMail: nward@forestresources.org
Tel: (301)838-9385
Fax: (301)838-9481

Employers
Forest Resources Ass'n (Director, Communications)

WARD, Stephanie L.

1300 I St. NW
Suite 420 East
Washington, DC 20005
Tel: (202)789-6525
Fax: (202)789-6593
Registered: LDA

Employers
Ceridian Corp. (Manager, Government Relations)

WARD, Stephen D.

1331 Pennsylvania Ave. NW
Suite 1300 North
Washington, DC 20004
Tel: (202)637-6709
Fax: (202)637-6759
Registered: LDA
EMail: stephen.ward@eds.com

Employers
EDS Corp. (Government Affairs Director, Navy and Federal Programs)

WARD, Stephen E.

1401 I St. NW
Suite 1030
Washington, DC 20005
Tel: (202)466-1405
Ext: 410
Fax: (202)466-1498
Registered: LDA

Employers
Shell Oil Co. (V. President, Government Affairs)

WARDEN, Michael P.

1722 I St. NW
Washington, DC 20006
Tel: (202)736-8000
Fax: (202)736-8711
EMail: mwarden@sidley.com

Employers
Sidley & Austin (Partner)

WARDLE, Bruce

8201 Greensboro Dr.
Suite 300
McLean, VA 22102
EMail: bwardle@amg-inc.com
Tel: (703)610-9000
Fax: (703)610-9005

Employers
Ass'n Management Group (President)

WARE, Viveca Y.

One Thomas Circle NW
Suite 400
Washington, DC 20005
Tel: (202)659-8111
Fax: (202)659-9216
Registered: LDA

Employers
Independent Community Bankers of America (Director of Payment Systems)

WARMAN, Timothy W.

1200 18th St. NW
Suite 800
Washington, DC 20036
Tel: (202)331-7300
Fax: (202)659-8339
Registered: LDA

Employers
American Farmland Trust (V. President, Programs)

WARNER, Ann D.

1299 Pennsylvania Ave. NW
Suite 800 West
Washington, DC 20004
Tel: (202)785-0500
Fax: (202)785-5277
Registered: LDA

Employers
The Carmen Group (Associate)

Clients Represented
On Behalf of The Carmen Group
American Concrete Pavement Ass'n (ACPA)
Missouri Highway and Transportation Department

WARNER, Candy

1225 Otis St. NE
Washington, DC 20017
Tel: (202)635-2757
Fax: (202)832-9494
EMail: cwarner@coc.org

Employers
Center of Concern (Director, Administration)

WARNER, James H.

11250 Waples Mill Rd.
Fairfax, VA 22030-7400
Tel: (703)267-1250
Fax: (703)267-3985

Employers
Nat'l Rifle Ass'n of America (Assistant General Counsel)

WARNER, Ray

1000 Connecticut Ave. NW
Suite 302
Washington, DC 20036
Tel: (202)835-0740
Fax: (202)775-8526
Registered: LDA
EMail: rayw@sda-inc.com

Employers
Smith Dawson & Andrews, Inc.

Clients Represented

On Behalf of Smith Dawson & Andrews, Inc.
Certified Automotive Parts Ass'n
George Washington University, Office of Government Relations
Litton Advanced Systems
Litton Systems, Inc.

WARNKE, Christine M.

555 13th St. NW
Washington, DC 20004-1109
Tel: (202)637-5645
Fax: (202)637-5910
Registered: LDA, FARA
EMail: cmwarnke@hhlaw.com
Executive Assistant to the Secretary to Senator Robert Byrd (D-WV), 1977-81.

Employers
Hogan & Hartson L.L.P. (Government Affairs Advisor)

Clients Represented

On Behalf of Hogan & Hartson L.L.P.
AAA MidAtlantic
American Chemistry Council
Athens Casino and Hotel Consortium
Chlorine Chemistry Council
The Danny Foundation,
Milton S. Eisenhower Foundation
FM Watch
General Electric Co.
Georal Internat'l Ltd.
Irvine, California, City of
Laguna Woods, California, City of
Michelin North America
Michigan Consolidated Gas Co.
Mortgage Insurance Companies of America
Nat'l College Access Network
Olney Boys and Girls Club
Plasma Protein Therapeutics Ass'n
Polyisocyanurate Insulation Manufacturers Ass'n
Vulcan Materials Co.
Western Wireless Internat'l

WARR, David E.

655 15th St. NW
Suite 300
Washington, DC 20005
Tel: (202)783-0900
Fax: (202)783-2308
Registered: LDA
EMail: david.warr@bms.com

Employers
Bristol-Myers Squibb Co. (Associate Director, Internat'l Govt. Affairs)

WARREN, David L.

1025 Connecticut Ave. NW
Suite 700
Washington, DC 20036
Tel: (202)785-8866
Fax: (202)835-0003

Employers
Nat'l Ass'n of Independent Colleges and Universities (President)

WARREN, Robert P.

1301 Pennsylvania Ave. NW
Suite 1100
Washington, DC 20004-1707
Tel: (202)626-4000
Fax: (202)626-4139

Employers
Air Transport Ass'n of America (Senior V. President, General Counsel, and Secretary)

WARRINGTON, Darlene

900 19th St. NW
Suite 700
Washington, DC 20006
Tel: (202)530-7030
Fax: (202)530-7049

Employers
Lucent Technologies (Manager, Coporate Media Relations)

WARRINGTON, Joan

2000 Pennsylvania Ave. NW
Suite 5500
Washington, DC 20006
Tel: (202)887-1500
Fax: (202)887-0763

Employers
Morrison & Foerster LLP (Of Counsel)

WARSCHOFF, Merrill E.

1330 New Hampshire Ave. NW
Suite 122
Washington, DC 20036
Tel: (202)659-8008
Fax: (202)659-8519
Registered: LDA
EMail: mwarschoff@aol.com

Employers
Philip W. Johnston Associates (Policy Director)

Clients Represented

On Behalf of Philip W. Johnston Associates
Bio-Vascular, Inc.
Dimock Community Health Center
East Boston Neighborhood Health Center
Holyoke Hospital
Nat'l Ass'n of Community Health Centers
Springfield, Massachusetts, City of

WASCH, Kenneth A.

1730 M St. NW
Suite 700
Washington, DC 20036-4510
Tel: (202)452-1600
Fax: (202)223-8756
Registered: LDA
EMail: kwasch@siia.net

Employers
Software & Information Industry Ass'n (SIIA) (President)

WASCOM, Michael D.

1301 Pennsylvania Ave. NW
Suite 1100
Washington, DC 20004-1707
Tel: (202)626-4000
Fax: (202)626-4208
Registered: LDA

Employers
Air Transport Ass'n of America (V. President, Communications)

WASH, B. Scott

500 N. Washington St.
Alexandria, VA 22314
Tel: (703)551-2108
Fax: (703)551-2109

Employers
Blue Ridge Internat'l Group, L.L.C. (Associate Counsel)

WASHABAUGH, Col. Mark

1160 Air Force Pentagon
Room 5D883
Washington, DC 20330-1160
Tel: (703)697-3783
Fax: (703)697-2001

Employers
Department of Air Force (Chief, Congressional Inquiry Division, Legislative Liaison)

WASHBURN, Barbara J.

1660 L St. NW
Fourth Floor
Washington, DC 20036
Tel: (202)775-5026
Fax: (202)775-5097
Registered: LDA

Employers
General Motors Corp. (Senior Washington Representative)

WASHINGTON, Gregory J.

1050 17th St. NW
Suite 500
Washington, DC 20036
Tel: (202)331-1427
Fax: (202)785-4702
Registered: LDA

Employers
Texaco Group Inc. (Senior Government Relations Representative)

WASHINGTON, Robert

125 N. West St.
Alexandria, VA 22314-2754
Tel: (703)683-1400
Fax: (703)549-6610
Registered: LDA

Employers
Fleet Reserve Ass'n (Director, Member Services)

WASHINGTON, Sheryl Webber

316 Pennsylvania Ave. SE
Suite 300
Washington, DC 20003
Tel: (202)675-4244
Fax: (202)675-4230
Registered: LDA

Employers
United Parcel Service (V. President, Public Affairs)

WASHINGTON, Veronica

1666 Connecticut Ave. NW
Suite 400
Washington, DC 20009
Tel: (202)328-7004
Fax: (202)387-3447

Employers
Federation for American Immigration Reform (FAIR) (Government Relations Assistant)

WASITIS, Doug

805 15th St. NW
Suite 700
Washington, DC 20005
Tel: (202)312-7400
Fax: (202)312-7441
Registered: LDA
EMail: dawasiti@bakerd.com
Appropriations Counsel to Rep. John Myers (R-IN), 1988-96.

Employers
Sagamore Associates, Inc. (Senior V. President)

Clients Represented

On Behalf of Sagamore Associates, Inc.
American Nuclear Soc.
Ball Aerospace & Technology Corp.
Boehringer Mannheim Corp.
Geothermal Heat Pump Consortium
Huntingdon College
Indiana University
Nuclear Energy Institute
Ohio River Valley Water Sanitation Commission
Purdue University
West Lafayette, Indiana, City of
Wittenburg University

WASOW, Bernard

1755 Massachusetts Ave. NW
Suite 400
Washington, DC 20036
Tel: (202)387-0400
Fax: (202)483-9430
EMail: wasow@tcf.org

Employers
The Century Foundation (Senior Fellow and Acting Director, Washington Office)

WASSERMAN, Gary

3626 Van Ness St. NW
Washington, DC 20008
Tel: (202)966-9199
Fax: (202)362-7222
Registered: FARA

Employers
Wasserman and Associates

Clients Represented

On Behalf of Wasserman and Associates
Taipei Economic and Cultural Representative Office in the United States

WASSERMAN, Ivan J.

1050 Connecticut Ave. NW
Washington, DC 20036-5339
Tel: (202)857-6000
Fax: (202)857-6395
Registered: LDA

Employers
Arent Fox Kintner Plotkin & Kahn, PLLC (Associate)

Clients Represented

On Behalf of Arent Fox Kintner Plotkin & Kahn, PLLC
Salton, Inc.

WASSERMAN, Jessica A.

1501 M St. NW
Suite 700
Washington, DC 20005-1702
Tel: (202)463-4300
Fax: (202)463-4394
Registered: LDA, FARA
EMail: jwasserman@manatt.com

Employers
Manatt, Phelps & Phillips, LLP (Partner)

Clients Represented

On Behalf of Manatt, Phelps & Phillips, LLP

Asociacion Columbiana de Exportadores de Flores (ASOCOLFLORES)
AUGURA
Bolivia, Embassy of
Catellus Development Corp.
CEMEX Central, S.A. de C.V.
Congo, Republic of
Pelican Butte Corp.
SWIPCO, U.S.

WASSERMAN, William B.

2120 L St. NW
Suite 400
Washington, DC 20037
Tel: (202)223-9541
Ext: 106
Fax: (202)223-9579
Registered: LDA

Director, Office of Consumer Affairs, Department of Agriculture, 1994-95.

Employers

M & R Strategic Services (Senior V. President)

Clients Represented

On Behalf of M & R Strategic Services

Internat'l Dairy Foods Ass'n
Nat'l Prostate Cancer Coalition Co.

WASSERSTEIN, Glen D.

1401 K St. NW
Tenth Floor
Washington, DC 20005
Tel: (202)416-1720
Fax: (202)416-1719
Registered: LDA, FARA

Employers

Wilson & Wasserstein, Inc. (V. President and General Counsel)

Clients Represented

On Behalf of Wilson & Wasserstein, Inc.

Bangladeshi-American Friendship Soc. of New York
Mortgage Investors Corp.
West African Friends

WATCHMAN, Gregory R.

1299 Pennsylvania Ave. NW
Tenth Floor
Washington, DC 20004-2400
Tel: (202)508-9500
Fax: (202)508-9700
EMail: gregwatchman@paulhastings.com

Acting Assistant Secretary (1997) and Deputy Assistant Secretary (1995-98) for Occupational Safety and Health, Department of Labor. Chief Labor Counsel (1993-95) and Counsel (1991-93), Subcommittee on Labor, Senate Committee on Labor and Human Resources. Associate Counsel, House Committee on Education and Labor (1989-91).

Employers

Paul, Hastings, Janofsky & Walker LLP (Of Counsel)

WATCHMAN, Laura H.

1101 14th St. NW
Suite 1400
Washington, DC 20005
Tel: (202)682-9400
Fax: (202)682-1331
EMail: lhood@defenders.org

Employers

Defenders of Wildlife (Manager, Conservation Planning Program)

WATERMAN, Charles E.

1401 K St. NW
Tenth Floor
Washington, DC 20005
Tel: (202)216-2200
Fax: (202)216-2999
Registered: LDA, FARA

Former National Intelligence Officer for the Near East and South Asia. Former Vice Chairman, National Intelligence Council.

Employers

Jefferson-Waterman Internat'l, LLC (Chief Exec. Officer)

Clients Represented

On Behalf of Jefferson-Waterman Internat'l, LLC

AmLib United Minerals

WATERMAN, Diana L.

900 Second St. NE
Suite 109
Washington, DC 20002
Tel: (202)898-1444
Fax: (202)898-0188
Registered: LDA

Employers

Waterman & Associates (V. President)

Clients Represented

On Behalf of Waterman & Associates

American Foundrymen's Soc.
American Metalcasting Consortium
North American Die Casting Ass'n

WATERMAN, Ronald D.

900 Second St. NE
Suite 109
Washington, DC 20002
Tel: (202)898-1444
Fax: (202)898-0188
Registered: LDA

Employers

Waterman & Associates (President)

Clients Represented

On Behalf of Waterman & Associates

California State Ass'n of Counties
Milwaukee, Wisconsin, County of
Walker Digital Corp.

WATERS, Alexis B.

1111 N. Fairfax St.
Alexandria, VA 22314
Tel: (703)684-2782
Fax: (703)684-7343

Employers

American Physical Therapy Ass'n (Director, Public Relations and Marketing Services)

WATERS, George

1010 Massachusetts Ave. NW
Suite 210
Washington, DC 20001
Tel: (202)371-1153
Fax: (202)371-1032
Registered: LDA

Employers

George Waters Consulting Service (President)

Clients Represented

On Behalf of George Waters Consulting Service

Chippewa Cree Tribe
Eastern Band of Cherokee Indians
Passamaquoddy Tribe(s)(2)
Penobscot Indian Nation
Reno/Sparks Indian Colony
Walker River Paiute Tribe
Washoe Tribe of Nevada and California

WATERS, Jennifer

1001 Pennsylvania Ave. NW
Suite 1100
Washington, DC 20004-2595
Tel: (202)624-2500
Fax: (202)628-5116
Registered: LDA

Employers

Crowell & Moring LLP (Partner)

Clients Represented

On Behalf of Crowell & Moring LLP

Knoxville Utilities Board
Memphis Light, Gas and Water Division

WATERS, Mary Kirtley

1627 I St. NW
Suite 950
Washington, DC 20006
Tel: (202)223-5115
Fax: (202)223-5118
Registered: LDA

Employers

ConAgra Foods, Inc. (Senior Director, Legislative Counsel)

WATERS, Mary Piper

2500 Wilson Blvd.
Suite 300
Arlington, VA 22201
Tel: (703)907-7701
Fax: (703)907-7727
EMail: mwaters@tia.eia.org

Employers

Telecommunications Industry Ass'n (Executive Assistant to the President)

WATERS, Robert J.

1050 Connecticut Ave. NW
Washington, DC 20036-5339
Tel: (202)857-6000
Fax: (202)857-6395
Registered: LDA

Administrative Assistant to Senator Tom Harkin (D-IA), 1983-87. Budget/Program Analyst, Department of Health, Education and Welfare and Health and Human Services, 1979-83.

Employers

Arent Fox Kintner Plotkin & Kahn, PLLC (Member)

Clients Represented

On Behalf of Arent Fox Kintner Plotkin & Kahn, PLLC

American Academy of Orthotists and Prosthetists
American Ass'n of Bioanalysts
American Ass'n of Occupational Health Nurses
American Ass'n of Physician Specialists
American College of Nurse Practitioners
American Soc. of Transplantation
Assisted Living Federation of America
Eastman Kodak Co.
Engineering Animation, Inc.
Federated Ambulatory Surgery Ass'n
Inoveon Corp.
Iowa Department of Public Health
Mercy Hospital of Des Moines, Iowa
Nat'l Ass'n of School Nurses
Nat'l Council of State Boards of Nursing
Pedorthic Footwear Ass'n
Christopher Reeve Paralysis Foundation
Research 2 Prevention
TECHHEALTH.COM

WATERS, Timothy J.

600 13th St. NW
Washington, DC 20005-3096
Tel: (202)756-8074
Fax: (202)756-8087
Registered: LDA
EMail: twaters@mwe.com

Assistant to the Chairman (1972), Assistant to Director, Bureau of Competition (1971), and Attorney (1968-71), Federal Trade Commission.

Employers

McDermott, Will and Emery (Managing Partner)

Clients Represented

On Behalf of McDermott, Will and Emery

Internat'l Hearing Soc.
Internat'l Mass Retailers Ass'n

WATKINS, Charles M.

1747 Pennsylvania Ave. NW
Suite 1000
Washington, DC 20006
Tel: (202)785-9500
Fax: (202)835-0243
Registered: LDA

Employers

Webster, Chamberlain & Bean (Associate)

Clients Represented

On Behalf of Webster, Chamberlain & Bean

Taxicab, Limousine and Paratransit Ass'n

WATKINS, Robert P.

725 12th St. NW
Washington, DC 20005
Tel: (202)434-5000
Fax: (202)434-5029

Assistant U.S. Attorney for the District of Columbia, Department of Justice, 1968-72. Law Clerk to Judge William B. Bryant, U.S. District Court for the District of Columbia, 1968. Hearing Counsel, Federal Maritime Commission, 1967. Civil Rights Division, Department of Justice, 1965-66.

Employers

Williams & Connolly (Partner)

Clients Represented

On Behalf of Williams & Connolly

General Motors Corp.

WATKINS, Rosemarie

600 Maryland Ave. SW
Suite 800
Washington, DC 20024
Tel: (202)484-3600
Fax: (202)484-3604
Registered: LDA

Employers

American Farm Bureau Federation (Senior Dir., Conservation, Forestry, and Environmental Agriculture Issues)

WATKINS, Venus

1906 Sunderland Pl. NW
Washington, DC 20036
Tel: (202)530-8030
Fax: (202)530-8031

Employers

AIDS Action Council (Director, Communications)

WATKINSON, Wayne R.

One Massachusetts Ave. NW
Suite 800
Washington, DC 20001-1431
Tel: (202)842-2345
Fax: (202)408-7763
EMail: WWatkinson@mwmlaw.com

Employers
McLeod, Watkinson & Miller (Partner)

Clients Represented

On Behalf of McLeod, Watkinson & Miller
Cattlemen's Beef Promotion and Research Board
Certified Angus Beef
Dairy Management, Inc.
Nat'l Honey Board
Popcorn Board
United Dairy Industry Ass'n
United Soybean Board

WATKISS, J. Dan

2000 K St. NW
Suite 500
Washington, DC 20006-1872
Tel: (202)828-5800
Fax: (202)223-1225
Registered: LDA

Senior Litigation Attorney (1985-86) and Special Assistant to the Deputy Counsel for Litigation (1982-85), Federal Energy Regulatory Commission.

Employers
Bracewell & Patterson, L.L.P. (Partner)

Clients Represented

On Behalf of Bracewell & Patterson, L.L.P.
Enron Corp.

WATLOV PHILLIPS, Sue

1012 14th St. NW
Suite 600
Washington, DC 20005-3471
Tel: (202)737-6444
Fax: (202)737-6445

Employers
Nat'l Coalition for the Homeless (Acting Exec. Director)

WATROUS, David S.

1140 Connecticut Ave. NW
Suite 1020
Washington, DC 20036
Tel: (202)833-9339
Fax: (202)833-9434

Employers
RTCA, Inc. (President)

WATSON, A. Dennis

The Mercury Bldg.
1925 K St. NW
Room 840
Washington, DC 20423-0001
EMail: watsond@stb.dot.gov
Tel: (202)565-1596
Fax: (202)565-9016

Associate Director, Congressional and Public Services (1993-95), Associate Director, External Affairs (1990-93), Deputy Director, Public Affairs (1989-90) and Public Affairs Officer (1982-89) all with the Interstate Commerce Commission. Director, Public Affairs, Postal Rate Commission, 1979-82. Marketing Analyst (1977) and Staff Economist (1974-77), U.S. Postal Service.

Employers
Department of Transportation - Surface Transportation Board (Associate Director, Congressional and Public Services)

WATSON, Alison

1120 Connecticut Ave. NW
Washington, DC 20036
Tel: (202)663-5000
Fax: (202)828-4548
Registered: LDA

Employers
American Bankers Ass'n (Senior Federal Legislative Representative)

WATSON, G. Norris

1875 I St. NW
Suite 1050
Washington, DC 20006-5409
Tel: (202)331-8585
Fax: (202)331-2032

Employers
Scribner, Hall & Thompson, LLP (Of Counsel)

WATSON, Jamal

1625 K St. NW
Suite 210
Washington, DC 20006
Tel: (202)785-5980
Fax: (202)785-5969

Employers
Leadership 2000 (National Chairperson)

WATSON, Karen

1233 20th St. NW
Suite 701
Washington, DC 20036
Tel: (202)293-0981
Fax: (202)293-0984
Registered: LDA

Employers
EchoStar Communications Corp. (Director, Government and Public Affairs)

WATSON, Kevin

7700 Leesburg Pike
Suite 421
Falls Church, VA 22043
Tel: (703)847-2677
Fax: (703)556-6485

Employers
Law Enforcement Alliance of America (Special Projects Coordinator)

WATSON, LeRoy

1616 H St. NW
Washington, DC 20006
Tel: (202)628-3507
Fax: (202)347-1091

Employers
Nat'l Grange (Director, Legislative Activities)

WATSON, Capt. Michael R.

499 S. Capitol St. SW
Suite 409
Washington, DC 20003
EMail: captwatson@aol.com
Tel: (202)484-0700
Fax: (202)484-9320

Employers
American Pilots Ass'n (President)

WATSON, Peter S.

1133 Connecticut Ave. NW
Suite 1200
Washington, DC 20036
Tel: (202)775-9800
Fax: (202)833-8491

Former Chairman, International Trade Commission and Director, Asian Affairs, National Security Council, during the Bush I administration.

Employers
Winthrop, Stimson, Putnam & Roberts (Counsel)

WATSON, Robert L.

412 First St. SE
Suite 100
Washington, DC 20003
EMail: bwatson@dutkogroup.com
Tel: (202)484-4884
Fax: (202)484-0109
Registered: LDA

Former State Director to Senator Charles S. Robb (D-VA).

Employers
The Dutko Group, Inc. (Partner)

Clients Represented

On Behalf of The Dutko Group, Inc.
Dominion Resources, Inc.

WATTENBERG, Ben J.

1150 17th St. NW
Washington, DC 20036
EMail: bwattenberg@aei.org
Tel: (202)862-5800
Fax: (202)862-7177

Employers
American Enterprise Institute for Public Policy Research (Senior Fellow)

WATTERS, Kate

1601 Connecticut Ave. NW
Suite 301
Washington, DC 20009
EMail: kwatters@isar.org
Tel: (202)387-3034
Fax: (202)667-3291

Employers
ISAR, Initiative for Social Action and Renewal in Eurasia (Director, Programs)

WATTERS, Robb

727 Second St. NE
Washington, DC 20002
Tel: (202)544-2600
Fax: (202)544-7760
Registered: LDA

Former Senior Policy Advisor to Rep. Frank Riggs (R-CA) and Deputy Chief of Staff to Rep. Mark Neumann (R-WI).

Employers
CapitolWatch (President)
Manatt, Phelps & Phillips, LLP

Clients Represented

On Behalf of Manatt, Phelps & Phillips, LLP
Agilent Technologies
Campbell Foundry Co.
Coalition for Global Perspectives
Computer and Communications Industry Ass'n (CCIA)
Hewlett-Packard Co.
Intuit, Inc.
Los Angeles Unified School District
Oracle Corp.
Unisys Corp.

WATTS, Adrienne

8300 Colesville Rd.
Suite 250
Silver Spring, MD 20910
EMail: awatts@nssea.org
Tel: (301)495-0240
Fax: (301)495-3330

Employers
Nat'l School Supply and Equipment Ass'n (Director, Marketing and Member Services)

WATTS, George B.

1015 15th St. NW
Suite 930
Washington, DC 20005
Tel: (202)296-2622
Fax: (202)293-4005
Registered: LDA

Employers
Nat'l Chicken Council (President)

WATTS, Heather C.

910 17th St. NW
Suite 800
Washington, DC 20006
EMail: hwatts@symphony.org
Tel: (202)776-0215
Fax: (202)776-0224
Registered: LDA

Employers
American Symphony Orchestra League (Associate Director, Government Affairs)

WATTS, Meredith

1100 17th St. NW
Seventh Floor
Washington, DC 20036
Tel: (202)223-8196
Fax: (202)872-1948
Registered: LDA

Employers
American Academy of Actuaries (Policy Analyst)

WATTS, Jr., Ralph S.

12501 Old Columbia Pike
Silver Spring, MD 20904
Tel: (301)680-6380
Fax: (301)680-6370

Employers
Adventist Development and Relief Agency Internat'l (President)

WATZMAN, Bruce

1130 17th St. NW
Washington, DC 20036-4677
EMail: bwatzman@nma.org
Tel: (202)463-2657
Fax: (202)463-3257
Registered: LDA

Employers
Nat'l Mining Ass'n (V. President, Safety and Health)

WAXMAN, Judith G.

1334 G St. NW
Suite 300
Washington, DC 20005-3169
Tel: (202)628-3030
Fax: (202)347-2417
Registered: LDA

Employers
Families U.S.A. Foundation (Director, Government Affairs)

WAYNE, Karen A.

11200 Waples Mill Rd.
Suite 150
Fairfax, VA 22030-7407
Tel: (703)691-8100
Fax: (703)691-8106

Employers
Assisted Living Federation of America (President and Chief Exec. Officer)

WAZ, Jr., Joseph W.

2001 Pennsylvania Ave. NW
Suite 500
Washington, DC 20006
EMail: joe_waz@comcast.com
Tel: (202)638-5678
Fax: (202)466-7718
Registered: LDA

Employers
Comcast Corp. (V. President, External Affairs and Public Policy Counsel)

WEAR, Terrance J.

888 16th St. NW
Suite 400
Washington, DC 20006
Tel: (202)466-6015
Fax: (202)296-8791
Registered: LDA

Employers
Wear & Associates (President)

Clients Represented
On Behalf of Wear & Associates
Dal-Tile Corp.
InterMedia Partners
Mobex Communications

WEATHERS, Hugh M.

1750 New York Ave. NW
Washington, DC 20006
Tel: (202)637-0700
Fax: (202)637-0771
Registered: LDA

Employers
Internat'l Union of Painters and Allied Trades

WEAVER, Brenda

2000 Florida Ave. NW
Washington, DC 20009
Tel: (202)777-7325
Fax: (202)328-0566
EMail: bweaver@agu.org

Employers
American Geophysical Union (Director, Meetings)

WEAVER, Carolyn L.

1150 17th St. NW
Washington, DC 20036
Tel: (202)862-5800
Fax: (202)862-7177
EMail: cweaver@aei.org

Employers
American Enterprise Institute for Public Policy Research (Resident Scholar and Director, Social Security and Pension Studies)

WEAVER, David A.

1421 Prince St.
Alexandria, VA 22314-2814
Tel: (703)836-9200
Fax: (703)548-8204
EMail: daweaver@mfsanet.org

Employers
Mailing & Fulfillment Services Ass'n (President)

WEAVER, Frank C.

1200 Wilson Blvd.
Arlington, VA 22209-1989
Tel: (703)465-3500
Fax: (703)465-3001

Employers
The Boeing Co. (Director, Telecommunications Policy)

WEAVER, Gary

700 11th St. NW
Washington, DC 20001-4507
Tel: (202)383-1038
Fax: (202)383-7540
Registered: LDA
EMail: gweaver@realtors.org

Employers
Nat'l Ass'n of Realtors (Housing Policy Representative)

WEAVER, Kiel

1225 I St. NW
Suite 600
Washington, DC 20005
Tel: (202)661-6184
Fax: (202)661-6182
Registered: LDA
EMail: kielweaver@morganmeguire.com
Former Legislative Director to Rep. Rick Hill (R-MT). Former Legislative Assistant to Senator Rod Grams (R-MN).

Employers
Morgan Meguire, LLC (V. President)

Clients Represented
On Behalf of Morgan Meguire, LLC
Adroit Systems Inc.
Arctic Resources Co.
Baker Electromotive, Inc.
BellSouth Corp.
Colorado River Energy Distributors Ass'n
Energy Northwest
Florida Municipal Power Agency
Goodman Manufacturing Co., L.P.
GovWorks.com
Longhorn Pipeline
Madison Gas & Electric Co.
Manatee, Florida, County of
Northern California Power Agency
Northwest Public Power Ass'n
Nuevo Energy
Redding, California, City of
Seven Seas Petroleum USA Inc.
Southern California Public Power Authority
Springfield, Missouri, City Utilities of
Tennessee Valley Public Power Ass'n
Transmission Access Policy Study Group
Truckee Donner Electric Power Utility District
Washington Public Utility Districts Ass'n

WEAVER, R. Kent

1775 Massachusetts Ave. NW
Washington, DC 20036-2188
Tel: (202)797-6000
Fax: (202)797-6004

Employers
The Brookings Institution (Senior Fellow, Governmental Studies)

WEAVER, Reg

1201 16th St. NW
Washington, DC 20036
Tel: (202)833-4000

Employers
Nat'l Education Ass'n of the U.S. (V. President)

WEBB, Brian

1310 G St. NW
12th Floor
Washington, DC 20005
Tel: (202)626-4780
Fax: (202)626-4833
Registered: LDA

Employers
Blue Cross Blue Shield Ass'n (Senior Policy Consultant)

WEBB, C. Edwin

1101 Pennsylvania Ave. NW
Suite 700
Washington, DC 20004-2514
Tel: (202)756-2227
Fax: (202)756-7506
Registered: LDA
EMail: ewebb@accp.com

Employers
American College of Clinical Pharmacy (Director, Government and Professional Affairs)

WEBB, Heather L.

1801 K St. NW
Suite 901-L
Washington, DC 20006
Tel: (202)530-0500
Fax: (202)530-4800
Registered: LDA
EMail: heather_webb@bm.com

Employers
BKSH & Associates (Associate)

WEBB, Jo Ann K.

325 Seventh St. NW
Suite 700
Washington, DC 20004
Tel: (202)626-2240
Fax: (202)638-5499

Employers
American Organization of Nurse Executives (Director, Federal Relations and Policy)

WEBB, Lynne

200 Constitution Ave. NW
Washington, DC 20210
Tel: (202)693-3038
Fax: (202)693-3229

Employers
Department of Labor - Office of Workforce Security (Federal Legislation Team)

WEBB, Matthew

1615 H St. NW
Washington, DC 20062-2000
Tel: (202)659-6000
Fax: (202)463-5836

Employers
Chamber of Commerce of the U.S.A. (Staff Attorney, General Counsel's Office)

WEBB, Ralph

1130 Connecticut Ave. NW
Suite 300
Washington, DC 20036
Tel: (202)331-8500
Fax: (202)331-1598
Registered: LDA

Employers
The Ferguson Group, LLC

Clients Represented
On Behalf of The Ferguson Group, LLC
Alcalde & Fay
Arcadia, California, City of
Huntington Beach, California, City of
Norwalk, California, City of
Santa Monica, California, City of
Southeast Water Coalition

WEBB, III, USA, Col. William L.

1666 K St. NW
Suite 250
Washington, DC 20006
Tel: (202)835-3016
Fax: (202)835-3008
Former Legislative Assistant to the Chairman, Joint Chiefs of Staff, Department of Defense. Special Assistant to the Director, Office of Management and Budget, Executive Office of the President, The White House, 1986-88. Served in numerous positions in the U.S. Army, 1972-97.

Employers
Time Domain Corp. (Senior V. President)

WEBBER, Frederick L.

1300 Wilson Blvd.
Arlington, VA 22209
Tel: (703)741-5100
Fax: (703)741-6086
Registered: LDA
EMail: fred_webber@americanchemistry.com

Employers
American Chemistry Council (President and Chief Exec. Officer)

WEBER, Becky B.

1001 G St. NW
Suite 400 East
Washington, DC 20001
Tel: (202)638-3730
Fax: (202)638-3516
Registered: LDA
EMail: bweber@peyser.com
Minority Counsel, Subcommittee on Surface Transportation, House Committee on Public Works and Transportation, 1988-94. Attorney, Office of General Counsel (1987-88), Attorney, Research and Special Programs Administration (1986-87), and Honors Attorney (1984-86), all with the Department of Transportation. Former Congressional Intern to Senator Robert J. Dole (R-KS).

Employers
Peyser Associates, Inc. (Counsel)

Clients Represented
On Behalf of Peyser Associates, Inc.
Indiana Department of Transportation
Ryder System, Inc.
Sound Transit
Southeastern Pennsylvania Transit Authority

WEBER, Gary M.

1301 Pennsylvania Ave. NW
Suite 300
Washington, DC 20004
Tel: (202)347-0228
Fax: (202)638-0607
Registered: LDA

Employers
Nat'l Cattleman's Beef Ass'n (Exec. Director, Regulatory Affairs)

WEBER, Jim

1211 Connecticut Ave. NW
Suite 608
Washington, DC 20036
Tel: (202)496-1000
Fax: (202)496-1300
EMail: jimweber@qorvis.com

Employers
Qorvis Communications (Partner)

WEBER, Hon. John Vincent "Vin"

1775 I St. NW
Suite 700
Washington, DC 20006
Tel: (202)261-4000
Fax: (202)261-4001
Registered: LDA
Member, U.S. House of Representatives (R-MN), 1981-93.

Employers
Clark & Weinstock, Inc. (Partner)

Clients Represented

On Behalf of Clark & Weinstock, Inc.
American Ass'n of Health Plans (AAHP)
American Ass'n of Homes and Services for the Aging
AT&T
Rabbi Milton Balkany
CapCURE
Cargill, Inc.
Delta Wetlands Project
Edison Electric Institute
Federal Home Loan Mortgage Corp. (Freddie Mac)
Foundation Health Federal Services, Inc.
Guidant Corp.
Lockheed Martin Corp.
Microsoft Corp.
Nat'l Center for Tobacco-Free Kids
Nat'l Prostate Cancer Coalition Co.
Pharmaceutical Research and Manufacturers of America
Rubber Manufacturers Ass'n
Sallie Mae, Inc.
Schering-Plough Corp.
Sodexho Marriott Services, Inc.
Vivendi Universal

WEBER, John W.

1130 Connecticut Ave. NW
Suite 600
Washington, DC 20036
Tel: (202)296-0263
Fax: (202)452-9371
Registered: FARA

Employers
Nichols-Dezenhall Communication Management Group, Ltd. (Exec. V. President)

Clients Represented

On Behalf of Nichols-Dezenhall Communication Management Group, Ltd.
Meat Industry Council

WEBER, Joseph A.

1140 23rd St. NW
Suite 806
Washington, DC 20037
Tel: (202)293-7187
Fax: (202)872-1150
Registered: LDA

Employers
J. Arthur Weber & Associates (President)

Clients Represented

On Behalf of J. Arthur Weber & Associates
Citizens Against Research Bans
Coalition for Reliable Energy
Internat'l Technology Resources, Inc.
Media Fusion L.L.C.
Stephens, Cross, Ihlenfeld and Boring, Inc.

WEBER, Marty

Liberty Center
401 14th St. SW
Washington, DC 20227
EMail: marty.weber@fms.treas.gov
Tel: (202)874-6837
Fax: (202)874-7016

Employers
Department of Treasury - Financial Management Service (Legislative Specialist/FOIA Disclosure Officer)

WEBER, R. Ben

1101 Vermont Ave. NW
Suite 401
Washington, DC 20005
EMail: rbw@keia.org
Tel: (202)371-0690
Fax: (202)371-0692
Registered: FARA

Employers
Korea Economic Institute of America (Director, Business & Public Affairs)

WEBER, Ronna Sable

1801 K St. NW
Suite 901-L
Washington, DC 20006
EMail: Ronna_Sableweber@bm.com
Tel: (202)530-0500
Fax: (202)530-4800
Registered: LDA

Employers
BKSH & Associates (Associate)

WEBER, William

1700 Diagonal Rd.
Suite 600
Alexandria, VA 22314-2866
EMail: wweber@scip.org
Tel: (703)739-0696
Fax: (703)739-2524

Employers
Soc. of Competitive Intelligence Professionals (Exec. Director)

WEBSTER, Duane

21 Dupont Circle NW
Suite 800
Washington, DC 20036
EMail: duane@arl.org
Tel: (202)296-2296
Fax: (202)872-0884

Employers
Ass'n of Research Libraries (Exec. Director)

WEBSTER, Hugh K.

1747 Pennsylvania Ave. NW
Suite 1000
Washington, DC 20006
Tel: (202)785-9500
Fax: (202)835-0243

Employers
Webster, Chamberlain & Bean (Partner)

Clients Represented

On Behalf of Webster, Chamberlain & Bean
American Boiler Manufacturers Ass'n
Internat'l Ass'n of Food Industry Suppliers
Packaging Machinery Manufacturers Institute

WEBSTER, Irena

7961 Eastern Ave.
Silver Spring, MD 20910
Tel: (301)587-5900
Fax: (301)587-5915

Employers
Ass'n for the Study of Afro-American Life and History (Exec. Director)

WEBSTER, Joseph H.

2120 L St. NW
Suite 700
Washington, DC 20037
EMail: jwebster@hsdwdc.com
Tel: (202)822-8282
Fax: (202)296-8834
Registered: LDA

Employers
Hobbs, Straus, Dean and Walker, LLP (Associate)

Clients Represented

On Behalf of Hobbs, Straus, Dean and Walker, LLP
Bristol Bay Area Health Corp.
Choctaw Indians, Mississippi Band of
Menominee Indian Tribe
Metlakatla Indian Community
Seminole Tribe of Indians of Florida
Shoalwater Bay Indian Tribe
Susanville Indian Rancheria

WEBSTER, R. Timothy

1321 Duke St.
Alexandria, VA 22314-3563
EMail: twebster@ascp.com
Tel: (703)739-1300
Fax: (703)739-1321

Employers
American Soc. of Consultant Pharmacists (Exec. Director)

WEBSTER, Rick

1100 New York Ave. NW
Suite 450
Washington, DC 20005
Tel: (202)408-8422
Fax: (202)408-1255
Registered: LDA

Employers
Travel Industry Ass'n of America (Director, Government Affairs)

WECHSLER, Steven A.

1875 I St. NW
Suite 600
Washington, DC 20006
EMail: swechsler@nareit.com
Tel: (202)739-9400
Fax: (202)739-9401
Registered: LDA

Employers
Nat'l Ass'n of Real Estate Investment Trusts (President and Chief Exec. Officer)

WECHTER, Robert D.

P.O. Box 5437
Friendship Station
Washington, DC 20016-5437
Tel: (202)966-6616
Fax: (202)966-6606

Employers
Television Communicators (President)

Clients Represented

On Behalf of Television Communicators
Random House
Republic Nat'l Bank of New York
Simon & Schuster Inc.

WECKSTEIN, Paul

1875 Connecticut Ave. NW
Suite 510
Washington, DC 20009
Tel: (202)986-3000
Fax: (202)986-6648

Employers
Center for Law and Education (Co-Director)

WEDDIG, Lisa

1350 I St. NW
Suite 300
Washington, DC 20005
EMail: lweddig@nfpa-food.org
Tel: (202)393-0890
Fax: (202)639-5932

Employers
The Food Processors Institute (Exec. Director)

WEEDA, David F.

1400 16th St. NW
Suite 400
Washington, DC 20036-2220
EMail: dweeda@ofwlaw.com
Tel: (202)518-6384
Fax: (202)234-3550
Registered: LDA

Associate Chief Counsel, Food and Drug Administration, 1976-81.

Employers
Olsson, Frank and Weeda, P.C. (Principal)

Clients Represented

On Behalf of Olsson, Frank and Weeda, P.C.
Aventis Pasteur
Duramed Pharmaceuticals, Inc.
Gentrac Inc.
Nat'l Ass'n of Pharmaceutical Manufacturers
PennField Oil Co.

WEEKLY, Jeffrey

1001 Pennsylvania Ave. NW
Suite 850 North
Washington, DC 20004-2505
EMail: jweekly@policypartners.com
Tel: (202)661-3584
Fax: (202)737-4242
Registered: LDA

Employers
Public Policy Partners, LLC (Sr. Policy Associate)

Clients Represented

On Behalf of Public Policy Partners, LLC
Express Scripts Inc.
Johnson & Johnson, Inc.
St. Jude Medical, Inc.
Urologix, Inc.
Vertis Neuroscience

WEGMAN, Richard A.

1000 Potomac St. NW
Suite 500
Washington, DC 20007
EMail: dwegman@gsblaw.com
Tel: (202)965-7880
Fax: (202)965-1729
Registered: LDA, FARA

Chief Counsel and Staff Director, Senate Committee on Governmental Affairs, 1975-81. Staff Director, Subcommittee on Executive Reorganization and Legislative Counsel to Senator William Proxmire (D-WI), 1968-74. Appellate Attorney, Antitrust Division, Department of Justice, 1965-68.

Employers
Garvey, Schubert & Barer (Partner)

Clients Represented

On Behalf of Garvey, Schubert & Barer
Bermuda, Government of
Canada, Embassy of
Canada, Government of
Nat'l Academy of Sciences
USX Corp.

WEGMEYER, Tyler

1156 15th St. NW
Suite 302
Washington, DC 20005
Tel: (202)457-0825
Fax: (202)457-0864
Registered: LDA

Employers
Agricultural Retailers Ass'n (Manager, Government Affairs)
North American Equipment Dealers Ass'n (Manager, Government Affairs)

WEGNER, Nona

112 S. West St.
Fourth Floor
Alexandria, VA 22314
EMail: nbw@cahi.org
Tel: (703)836-6200
Fax: (703)836-6550
Registered: LDA

Employers
Council for Affordable Health Insurance (President)

WEGRZYN, Susanne R.

1120 20th St. NW
Suite 725
Washington, DC 20007
Tel: (202)822-9822
Fax: (202)822-9808

Employers
Nat'l Club Ass'n (Exec. V. President)

WEICH, Ronald H.

1201 Connecticut Ave. NW
Suite 600
Washington, DC 20036
EMail: rweich@zsgtk.com
Tel: (202)778-1800
Fax: (202)822-8106
Registered: LDA

Chief Counsel to Senator Edward M. Kennedy (D-MA), Senate Committee on the Judiciary, 1995-96. General Counsel (1992-95) and Chief Counsel for Drug Control Policy (1990-92), Senate Committee on Labor and Human Resources. Minority Counsel, Subcommittee on the Constitution, Senate Committee on the Judiciary, 1989.

Employers
Zuckerman Spaeder L.L.P. (Partner)

Clients Represented

On Behalf of Zuckerman Spaeder L.L.P.
American Civil Liberties Union
American Psychological Soc.
Amity, Inc.
The Bureau of Nat'l Affairs, Inc.
Internat'l Brotherhood of Teamsters
Nat'l Board for Certification in Occupational Therapy, Inc.
Nat'l Center for Tobacco-Free Kids
Nat'l Pawnbrokers Ass'n
Nat'l Prison Project
Oneida Indian Nation of New York
United States Pharmacopeia
Vietnam Veterans of America Foundation

WEICHER, John C.

1015 18th St. NW
Suite 300
Washington, DC 20036
Tel: (202)223-7770
Fax: (202)223-8537

Employers
Hudson Institute (Senior Fellow)

WEIDMAN, Jame

214 Massachusetts Ave. NE
Washington, DC 20002
Tel: (202)608-6145
Fax: (202)546-8328

Employers
Heritage Foundation (Director of Public Relations)

WEIDMAN, Rick

8605 Cameron St.
Suite 400
Silver Spring, MD 20910
Tel: (301)585-4000
Fax: (301)585-0519

Employers
Vietnam Veterans of America, Inc. (Director, Government Relations)

WEIDNER, Robert K.

1101 30th St. NW
Washington, DC 20007
Tel: (202)296-5959
Fax: (202)293-3484
Registered: LDA

Employers
Self-employed as an independent consultant.

Clients Represented

As an independent consultant
BP America, Inc.
BP Exploration
James W. Bunger & Associates
Questar Corp.
Rural Public Lands County Council

WEIERKE, Corey H.

400 N. Capitol St.
Suite 365
Washington, DC 20001
Tel: (202)624-5308
Fax: (202)624-5425

Employers
Minnesota, Washington Office of the State of (Deputy Director)

WEIGARD, Michael A.

1250 24th St. NW
Suite 700
Washington, DC 20037
Tel: (202)659-6600
Fax: (202)659-6699

Employers
Eckert Seamans Cherin & Mellott, LLC (Member)

Clients Represented

On Behalf of Eckert Seamans Cherin & Mellott, LLC
Kawasaki Motors Corp., USA

WEIGEL, Kenneth G.

655 15th St. NW
Suite 1200
Washington, DC 20005
Tel: (202)879-5000
Fax: (202)879-5200
Registered: LDA

Employers
Kirkland & Ellis (Partner)

WEIGHTMAN, Donald

510 C St. NW
Washington, DC 20002
Tel: (202)544-1458
Fax: (202)544-1371
Registered: LDA

Employers
Self-employed as an independent consultant.

Clients Represented

As an independent consultant
Internet Ventures, Inc.

WEIHE, Theodore Frederick

4301 Wilson Blvd.
Suite 1017
Arlington, VA 22203
EMail: ted.weihe@nreca.org
Tel: (703)907-5667
Fax: (703)907-5519
Registered: LDA

Employers
U.S. Overseas Cooperative Development (Exec. Director)

WEIL, Alan

2100 M St. NW
Washington, DC 20037
Tel: (202)833-7200
Fax: (202)429-0687

Employers
The Urban Institute (Director, Assessing the New Federalism Project)

WEILAND, Jennifer J.

1300 L St. NW
Suite 925
Washington, DC 20005
EMail: jweiland@ngtc.org
Tel: (202)842-0400
Fax: (202)789-7223
Registered: LDA

Employers
Nat'l Grain Trade Council (Assistant to the President, Legal Counsel)

WEILER, Steven A.

1333 New Hampshire Ave. NW
Suite 400
Washington, DC 20036
Tel: (202)887-4000
Fax: (202)887-4288

Member, Federal Energy Regulatory Commission, 1985-88.

Employers
Akin, Gump, Strauss, Hauer & Feld, L.L.P. (Counsel)

WEILL, James D.

1875 Connecticut Ave. NW
Suite 540
Washington, DC 20009
EMail: jweill@frac.org
Tel: (202)986-2200
Ext: 3010
Fax: (202)986-2525

Employers
Food Research and Action Center (President)

WEIMAN, David M.

635 Maryland Ave. NE
Washington, DC 20002-5811
Tel: (202)546-5115
Registered: LDA

Employers
Self-employed as an independent consultant.

Clients Represented

As an independent consultant
The Metropolitan Water District of Southern California

WEIMER, Brian D.

1440 New York Ave. NW
Washington, DC 20005
Tel: (202)371-7000
Fax: (202)393-5760

Employers
Skadden, Arps, Slate, Meagher & Flom LLP (Associate)

WEINBERG, David B.

1299 Pennsylvania Ave. NW
Washington, DC 20004-2402
Tel: (202)783-0800
Fax: (202)383-6610
Registered: LDA

Employers
Battery Council Internat'l (Treasurer)
Howrey Simon Arnold & White

Clients Represented

On Behalf of Howrey Simon Arnold & White
Battery Council Internat'l
Nat'l Ass'n for Plastic Container Recovery
Portable Rechargeable Battery Ass'n

WEINBERG, Linda M.

901 15th St. NW
Suite 700
Washington, DC 20005-2301
EMail: lmweinberg@verner.com
Tel: (202)371-6000
Fax: (202)371-6279
Registered: LDA

Employers
Verner, Liipfert, Bernhard, McPherson and Hand, Chartered (Member of Firm)

Clients Represented

On Behalf of Verner, Liipfert, Bernhard, McPherson and Hand, Chartered
Independent Fuel Terminal Operators Ass'n
Kellogg Co.
Site Inc.
Virginia Commonwealth Trading Co.

WEINBERG, CAE, Myrl

1730 M St. NW
Suite 500
Washington, DC 20036
Tel: (202)785-3910
Fax: (202)785-5923

Employers
Nat'l Health Council (President)

WEINBERG, Richard A.

1023 N. Royal St.
Alexandria, VA 22314-1569
EMail: rweinber@postmasters.org
Tel: (703)548-5922
Fax: (703)836-8937

Employers
Nat'l League of Postmasters of the U.S. (Exec. Director)

WEINBERG, Robert

1615 M St. NW
Suite 800
Washington, DC 20036-3203
EMail: rw@dwgp.com
Tel: (202)467-6370
Fax: (202)467-6379

Employers
Duncan, Weinberg, Genzer & Pembroke, P.C. (Principal)

Clients Represented

On Behalf of Duncan, Weinberg, Genzer & Pembroke, P.C.
Central Virginia Electric Cooperative, Inc.
Craig-Botetourt Electric Cooperative, Inc.
Farmers' Electric Cooperative
Hoosier Energy Rural Electric Cooperative, Inc.
Lea County Electric Cooperative, Inc.
Roosevelt County Rural Electric Cooperative
South Mississippi Electric Power Ass'n
Southern Maryland Electric Cooperative, Inc.

WEINBERG, Wendy J.

1010 Vermont Ave. NW
Suite 514
Washington, DC 20005
Tel: (202)347-7395
Fax: (202)347-2563

Employers
Nat'l Ass'n of Consumer Agency Administrators (Exec. Director)

WEINBERGER, Robert A.

700 13th St. NW
Suite 700
Washington, DC 20005-5922
EMail: RWeinberger@hrblock.com
Tel: (202)508-6363
Fax: (202)508-6330
Registered: LDA

Employers
H & R Block, Inc. (V. President, Government Relations)

WEINER, Debbie

325 Seventh St. NW
Washington, DC 20004
Tel: (202)638-1100
Fax: (202)626-2232
Registered: LDA

Employers
American Hospital Ass'n (Director, AC and Grassroots Advocacy)

WEINER, Joshua M.

2100 M St. NW
Washington, DC 20037
Tel: (202)833-7200
Fax: (202)429-0687

Employers
The Urban Institute (Principal Research Associate, Health Policy Center)

WEINER, Stuart

Hart Senate Office Bldg.
Room 321
Washington, DC 20510
Tel: (202)224-5351
Fax: (202)453-5218

Employers
Department of Veterans Affairs (Senate Liaison Representative)

WEINERMAN, Lloyd

1001 Pennsylvania Ave. NW
Suite 1100
Washington, DC 20004-2595
Tel: (202)624-2500
Fax: (202)628-5116
Former Senior Lawyer in the Office of General Counsel and in the Health Care Financing Administration, Department of Health and Human Services. Also served in the Social Security Administration.

Employers
Crowell & Moring LLP (Of Counsel)

WEINFURTER, John J.

201 Massachusetts Ave. NE
Suite C-8
Washington, DC 20002
EMail: john@celi.org
Tel: (202)546-5007
Fax: (202)546-7037
Formerly Chief of Staff, Rep. J. Joseph Moakley (D-MA).

Employers
Congressional Economic Leadership Institute (President)

WEINGARTEN, Frederick

1301 Pennsylvania Ave. NW
Suite 403
Washington, DC 20004
EMail: rww@alawash.org
Tel: (202)628-8410
Fax: (202)628-8419

Employers
American Library Ass'n (Director, Office for Information Technology Policy)

WEINMAN, Howard M.

1001 Pennsylvania Ave. NW
Suite 1100
Washington, DC 20004-2595
EMail: hweinman@cromor.com
Tel: (202)624-2500
Fax: (202)628-5116
Registered: FARA
Legislation Attorney, Joint Committee on Taxation, 1978-80.

Employers
Crowell & Moring LLP (Partner)

Clients Represented
On Behalf of Crowell & Moring LLP
A.C.E. Insurance Co. (Bermuda) Ltd.

WEINROD, W. Bruce

1330 Connecticut Ave. NW
Suite 210
Washington, DC 20036-1704
EMail: bweinrod@itta.com
Tel: (202)828-2614
Fax: (202)828-2617

Employers
Internat'l Technology & Trade Associates, Inc. (ITTA, Inc.) (Managing Director and General Counsel)

WEINSTEIN, Alana

2111 Wilson Blvd.
Eighth Floor
Arlington, VA 22201-3058
Tel: (703)841-0626
Fax: (703)243-2874
Registered: LDA

Employers
Alcalde & Fay (Associate)

Clients Represented
On Behalf of Alcalde & Fay
Internat'l Council of Cruise Lines
Miami Heat
Panama, Government of the Republic of

WEINSTEIN, Allen

1101 15th St. NW
Suite 505
Washington, DC 20005
Tel: (202)429-9141
Fax: (202)293-1768

Employers
Center for Democracy (President and Chief Exec. Officer)

WEINSTEIN, Bonnie H.

1825 I St. NW
Suite 400
Washington, DC 20006
Tel: (202)293-4752
Fax: (202)530-0179
Registered: LDA

Employers
Self-employed as an independent consultant.

Clients Represented
As an independent consultant
Air Tractor, Inc.

WEINSTEIN, Deborah

25 E St. NW
Washington, DC 20001
Tel: (202)628-8787
Fax: (202)662-3550

Employers
Children's Defense Fund (Director, Family Income Division)

WEINSTEIN, Harris

1201 Pennsylvania Ave. NW
Washington, DC 20004-2401
EMail: hweinstein@cov.com
Tel: (202)662-6000
Fax: (202)662-6291
Registered: LDA
Chief Counsel, Office of Thrift Supervision, Department of the Treasury, 1990-92. Public Member, Administrative Conference of the United States, 1982-90. Assistant to the Solicitor General, Department of Justice, 1967-69. Law Clerk to Judge William H. Hastie, U.S. Court of Appeals, Third Circuit, 1961-62.

Employers
Covington & Burling (Partner)

Clients Represented
On Behalf of Covington & Burling
Golden West Financial Corp.

WEINSTEIN, Jeffrey E.

1250 24th St. NW
Suite 700
Washington, DC 20037
EMail: jzw@escm.com
Tel: (202)659-6600
Fax: (202)659-6699
Registered: LDA

Employers
Eckert Seamans Cherin & Mellott, LLC (Member)

Clients Represented
On Behalf of Eckert Seamans Cherin & Mellott, LLC
GPA-1, LLC

WEINSTEIN, Kenneth

1015 18th St. NW
Suite 300
Washington, DC 20036
Tel: (202)223-7770
Fax: (202)223-8537

Employers
Hudson Institute (Director, Washington Office)

WEINTRAUB, Ellen L.

607 14th St. NW
Suite 700
Washington, DC 20005-2011
Tel: (202)628-6600
Fax: (202)434-1690
Counsel, House Committee on Standards of Official Conduct, 1990-1996.

Employers
Perkins Coie LLP (Of Counsel)

WEINTRAUB, Rachel

218 D St. SE
Second Floor
Washington, DC 20003
Tel: (202)546-9707
Fax: (202)546-2461

Employers
U.S. Public Interest Research Group (Staff Attorney)

WEINTRAUB, Richard M.

Crystal Park Four
2345 Crystal Dr.
Arlington, VA 22227
Tel: (703)872-5100

Employers
US Airways (Senior Director, Public Relations and Press Spokesman)

WEIR, Laurel

1411 K St. NW
Suite 1400
Washington, DC 20005
Tel: (202)638-2535
Fax: (202)628-2737

Employers
Nat'l Law Center on Homelessness and Poverty (Policy Director)

WEISENFELD, David J.

701 Pennsylvania Ave. NW
Suite 800
Washington, DC 20004
Tel: (202)508-4000
Fax: (202)508-4321
Registered: LDA

Employers
Thelen Reid & Priest LLP

Clients Represented
On Behalf of Thelen Reid & Priest LLP
The Jewelers' Security Alliance

WEISGALL, Jonathan

1200 New Hampshire Ave. NW
Suite 300
Washington, DC 20036
Tel: (202)828-1378
Fax: (202)828-1380

Employers
MidAmerican Energy Holdings Co. (Washington Office Contact)

WEISMAN, Robin

1333 New Hampshire Ave. NW
Suite 400
Washington, DC 20036
Tel: (202)887-4000
Fax: (202)887-4288
Registered: LDA

Employers
Akin, Gump, Strauss, Hauer & Feld, L.L.P.

Clients Represented
On Behalf of Akin, Gump, Strauss, Hauer & Feld, L.L.P.
American Family Enterprises
AOL Time Warner
AT&T
Bridgestone/Firestone, Inc.
Exxon Mobil Corp.
Human Genome Sciences Inc.
Motion Picture Ass'n of America
Stamps.com

WEISMILLER, Toby

750 First St. NE
Suite 700
Washington, DC 20002
Tel: (202)408-8600
Fax: (202)336-8327

Employers
Nat'l Ass'n of Social Workers (Divisional Director)

WEISS, Alice

1875 Connecticut Ave. NW
Suite 710
Washington, DC 20009
Tel: (202)986-2600
Fax: (202)986-2539

Employers
Nat'l Partnership for Women and Families (Director, Health Policy)

WEISS, Alison B.

325 Seventh St.
Suite 1225
Washington, DC 20004
Tel: (202)737-0440
Fax: (202)628-2313
Registered: LDA

Employers
MassMutual Financial Group (Director)

WEISS, Amy

1330 Connecticut Ave. NW
Suite 300
Washington, DC 20036
Tel: (202)775-0101
Fax: (202)775-7253

Employers
Recording Industry Ass'n of America (Senior V. President, Communications)

WEISS, Betty

1875 Connecticut Ave. NW
Suite 410
Washington, DC 20009
EMail: nncnnc@erols.com
Tel: (202)408-8553
Fax: (202)408-8551

Employers
Nat'l Neighborhood Coalition (Exec. Director)

WEISS, Chris

1025 Vermont Ave. NW
Third Floor
Washington, DC 20005
EMail: cweiss@foe.org
Tel: (202)783-7400
Ext: 120
Fax: (202)783-0444

Employers
Friends of the Earth (Director, DC Environmental Network)

WEISS, Daniel J.

2120 L St. NW
Suite 400
Washington, DC 20037
Tel: (202)223-9541
Fax: (202)223-9579
Registered: LDA

Employers
M & R Strategic Services (Senior V. President)

WEISS, David

1001 Connecticut Ave. NW
Suite 625
Washington, DC 20036
Tel: (202)785-1136
Fax: (202)785-4114

Employers
CINE (Exec. Director)

WEISS, David A.

901 15th St. NW
Suite 700
Washington, DC 20005-2301
EMail: daweiss@verner.com
Tel: (202)371-6000
Fax: (202)371-6279
Registered: LDA

Assistant U.S. Trade Representative for North American Affairs, Office of the U.S. Trade Representative.

Employers
Verner, Liipfert, Bernhard, McPherson and Hand, Chartered (Director, Trade Policy)

Clients Represented

On Behalf of Verner, Liipfert, Bernhard, McPherson and Hand, Chartered
Accenture
Alliance Pipeline, L.P.
Kasten Chase Applied Research Limited
Kellogg Co.
Northwest Airlines, Inc.
Philips Electronics North America Corp.
Thomson Consumer Electronics, Inc.
Virginia Commonwealth Trading Co.

WEISS, Faith

1200 New York Ave. NW
Suite 400
Washington, DC 20005
Tel: (202)289-6868
Fax: (202)289-1060
Registered: LDA

Employers
Natural Resources Defense Council (Legislative Attorney)

WEISS, James R.

1735 New York Ave. NW
Suite 500
Washington, DC 20006-4759
Tel: (202)628-1700
Fax: (202)331-1024
Registered: LDA

Chief (1986-88) and Assistant Chief (1980-86), Transportation, Energy and Agriculture Section and Trial Attorney (1974-80), all in the Antitrust Division, Department of Justice.

Employers
Preston Gates Ellis & Rouvelas Meeds LLP (Partner)

Clients Represented

On Behalf of Preston Gates Ellis & Rouvelas Meeds LLP
Delta Air Lines
Maryland Department of Transportation
Mount Vernon Barge Service
Sun Outdoor Advertising
WABCO

WEISS, Jeffrey C.

1801 K St. NW
Suite 901-L
Washington, DC 20006
EMail: jeffrey_weiss@was.bm.com
Tel: (202)530-0500
Fax: (202)530-4800
Registered: FARA

Employers
BKSH & Associates (Director)

WEISS, Joan C.

777 N. Capitol St. NE
Suite 801
Washington, DC 20002
Tel: (202)842-9330
Fax: (202)842-9329

Employers
Justice Research and Statistics Ass'n (Exec. Director)

WEISS, Marina L.

1901 L St. NW
Suite 200
Washington, DC 20036
Tel: (202)659-1800
Fax: (202)296-2964
Registered: LDA

Employers
March of Dimes Birth Defects Foundation (Senior V. President, Public Policy and Government Affairs)

WEISS, Mark A.

1201 Pennsylvania Ave. NW
Washington, DC 20004-2401
EMail: mweiss@cov.com
Tel: (202)662-6000
Fax: (202)662-6291

Special Assistant to the Secretary (1968-69) and Special Assistant to the Undersecretary (1966-68), Department of the Treasury.

Employers
Covington & Burling (Partner)

WEISS, Mike

400 Seventh St. SW
Room 3318
Washington, DC 20590
EMail: mike.weiss@fhwa.dot.gov
Tel: (202)366-1956
Fax: (202)366-7696

Employers
Department of Transportation - Federal Highway Administration (Legislative Analyst, Office of Legislative and Strategic Planning)

WEISS, Randall D.

555 12th St. NW
Suite 500
Washington, DC 20004-1207
Tel: (202)879-4915
Fax: (202)879-5309
Registered: LDA

Former Deputy Chief of Staff, Congressional Joint Committee on Taxation.

Employers
Deloitte & Touche LLP Nat'l Office - Washington (Partner)

Clients Represented

On Behalf of Deloitte & Touche LLP Nat'l Office - Washington
Railroad Retirement Reform Working Group
Torchmark Corp.

WEISS, Stanley A.

1717 Pennsylvania Ave. NW
Suite 350
Washington, DC 20006
Tel: (202)296-2125
Fax: (202)296-2490

Employers
Business Executives for Nat'l Security (Chairman)

WEISS, Steven C.

1101 14th St. NW
Suite 1030
Washington, DC 20005-5635
Tel: (202)857-0044
Fax: (202)857-7809

Employers
Center for Responsive Politics (Director of Communications)

WEISS, Suzanne

2519 Connecticut Ave. NW
Washington, DC 20008-1520
Tel: (202)783-2242
Fax: (202)783-2255

Employers
American Ass'n of Homes and Services for the Aging (Senior V. President, Advocacy)

WEISS, Todd

1050 Connecticut Ave. NW
Washington, DC 20036-5339
Tel: (202)857-6000
Fax: (202)857-6395
Registered: LDA

Senior Policy Advisor to Senator Tim Hutchinson (R-AR), 1996-98. Legislative Aide to Senator Richard Santorum (R-PA), 1995-96.

Employers
Arent Fox Kintner Plotkin & Kahn, PLLC (Government Relations Director)

Clients Represented

On Behalf of Arent Fox Kintner Plotkin & Kahn, PLLC
Alaska Rainforest Campaign
American Amusement Machine Ass'n
American Ass'n of Physician Specialists
Amusement and Music Operators Ass'n
Biomedical Research Institute
CIS Global
Earth Council Institute - Canada
Economic Development Alliance of Jefferson County, Arkansas
Engineering Animation, Inc.
Exeter Architectural Products
France Telecom America do Sul Ltda.
Guardian Angel Holdings, Inc.
Interactive Amusement and Tournament Video Game Coalition
S.C. Johnson and Son, Inc.
Motor and Equipment Manufacturers Ass'n
Raytheon Co.
Recreation Vehicle Ass'n
Tyson Foods, Inc.

WEISSMAN, Robert A.

14500 Avion Pkwy.
Suite 300
Chantilly, VA 20151
Tel: (703)818-1320
Fax: (703)818-8813

Employers
Shutler and Low (Partner)

WEISSMAN, Steve

215 Pennsylvania Ave. SE
Washington, DC 20003
Tel: (202)546-4996
Registered: LDA

Employers
Public Citizen, Inc.

WEISSMAN, William R.

1200 19th St. NW
Washington, DC 20036-2430
EMail: william.weissman@piperrudnick.com
Tel: (202)861-3878
Fax: (202)223-2085
Registered: LDA

Trial Attorney, Antitrust Division (1966-69) and Special Assistant U.S. Attorney for the District of Columbia (1967), Department of Justice.

Employers
Piper Marbury Rudnick & Wolfe LLP (Partner)

Clients Represented

On Behalf of Piper Marbury Rudnick & Wolfe LLP
Alliant Energy
Edison Electric Institute
Utility Solid Waste Activities Group

WELBURN, Brenda L.

277 S. Washington St.
Alexandria, VA 22314
Tel: (703)684-4000
Fax: (703)836-2313

Employers
Nat'l Ass'n of State Boards of Education (Exec. Director)

WELCH, Carol

1025 Vermont Ave. NW
Third Floor
Washington, DC 20005
Tel: (202)783-7400
Ext: 237
Fax: (202)783-0444
Registered: LDA
EMail: cwelch@foe.org

Employers
Friends of the Earth (Deputy Director, International Projects/MDB Trade)

WELCH, Edmund B.

1600 Wilson Blvd.
Suite 1000-A
Arlington, VA 22209
Tel: (703)807-0100
Fax: (703)807-0103
Registered: LDA

Employers
Passenger Vessel Ass'n (Legislative Director)
Self-employed as an independent consultant.

Clients Represented

As an independent consultant
Dare County

WELCH, John F.

1350 I St. NW
Suite 400
Washington, DC 20005-3306
Tel: (202)371-6900
Fax: (202)842-3578
Registered: LDA

Employers
Motorola, Inc. (V. President and Director, Global EME Strategy and Regulatory Affairs)

WELCH, Sandra

1755 Jefferson Davis Hwy.
Suite 1107
Arlington, VA 22202
Tel: (703)415-0344
Fax: (703)415-0182
Registered: LDA

Employers
The PMA Group (Associate)

Clients Represented

On Behalf of The PMA Group
Alliance
AsclepiusNet
Battelle
Dynamics Research Corp.
Joint Healthcare Information Technology Alliance
New Mexico Tech
Opportunity Medical, Inc.
SIGCOM, Inc.
Triosyn Corp.

WELCOME, Jerry

4350 N. Fairfax Dr.
Suite 600
Arlington, VA 22203
Tel: (703)243-8555
Fax: (703)243-8556

Employers
Packaging Machinery Manufacturers Institute (V. President, Member Services)

WELLE, Noreen

1000 Connecticut Ave. NW
Suite 615
Washington, DC 20036-5302
EMail: noreenw@rtnda.org
Tel: (202)659-6510
Fax: (202)223-4007

Employers
Radio-Television News Directors Ass'n (Director, Communications)

WELLER, John Craig

117 N. Henry St.
Alexandria, VA 22314
EMail: jcw@fillerweller.com
Tel: (703)299-0784
Fax: (703)299-0254

Employers
Filler & Weller, P.C. (Partner)

WELLER, Mark W.

805 15th St. NW
Suite 700
Washington, DC 20005
EMail: mwweller@bakerd.com
Tel: (202)312-7400
Fax: (202)312-7441
Legislative Director to Sen. Richard Lugar (R-IN), 1986-89; Legislative Assistant to Sen. Lugar, 1984-86; Attorney, National Republican Senatorial Committee, 1983-84.

Employers
Baker & Daniels (Partner)
Sagamore Associates, Inc. (Senior V. President)

Clients Represented

On Behalf of Baker & Daniels
American Orthotic and Prosthetic Ass'n
Guidant Corp.
Indiana Medical Device Manufacturers Council
Roche Diagnostics

On Behalf of Sagamore Associates, Inc.
Alltrista/Penny
Americans for Common Cents
Ball Aerospace & Technology Corp.
Boehringer Mannheim Corp.
Chase Manhattan Bank
Hill-Rom Co., Inc.
Indiana Medical Device Manufacturers Council
Indiana University
Ispat Inland Steel Industries
Purdue University
Recreation Vehicle Industry Ass'n
Union Hospital

WELLER, Jr., Paul S.

1629 K St. NW
Suite 1100
Washington, DC 20006
EMail: agriwash@aol.com
Tel: (202)785-6710
Fax: (202)331-4212

Employers
Agri/Washington (President)

Clients Represented

On Behalf of Agri/Washington
Agricultural Biotechnology Forum
American Ass'n of Grain Inspection and Weighing Agencies
American Grain Inspection Institute
Apple Processors Ass'n
Canadian-American Business Council
Maryland Dairy Industry Ass'n

WELLER, William C.

1201 F St. NW
Suite 500
Washington, DC 20004
Tel: (202)824-1703
Fax: (202)824-1668

Employers
Health Insurance Ass'n of America (Senior Actuary, Policy Development and Research)

WELLFORD, W. Harrison

555 11th St. NW
Suite 1000
Washington, DC 20004
Tel: (202)637-2200
Fax: (202)637-2201
Advisor and Member of Economic Policy Group, Clinton-Gore Transition (1992-93), Director, Executive Branch Transition, Reagan-Bush Transition (1980-81), Executive Associate Director, Office of Management and Budget (1977-80), and Director of Government Reform Task Force, Presidential Transition (1976), all at The White House. Chief Legislative Assistant to Senator Philip Hart (D-MI), 1973-76.

Employers
Latham & Watkins (Partner)

WELLIG, Deborah A.

811 Vermont Ave. NW
Room 1261
Washington, DC 20571
EMail: deborah.wellig@exim.gov
Tel: (202)565-3227
Fax: (202)565-3236

Employers
Export-Import Bank (Senior Legislative Analyst)

WELLING, Brad G.

1399 New York Ave. NW
Suite 900
Washington, DC 20005
Tel: (202)585-5812
Fax: (202)585-5820
Registered: LDA

Employers
American Internat'l Group, Inc. (Director, Federal Government Affairs)

WELLMAN, Jr., Arnold F.

316 Pennsylvania Ave. SE
Suite 300
Washington, DC 20003
Tel: (202)675-4220
Fax: (202)675-4230
Registered: LDA

Employers
United Parcel Service (Corporate V. President, Domestic/Internat'l Public Affairs)

WELLMAN, Jane V.

1320 19th St. NW
Suite 400
Washington, DC 20036
Tel: (202)861-8223
Fax: (202)861-9307

Employers
The Institute for Higher Education Policy (Senior Associate)

WELLS, Kent M.

1818 N St. NW
Eighth Floor
Washington, DC 20036
Tel: (202)293-1707

Employers
Cingular Wireless (Congressional Affairs)

WELLS, Milton T.

1256 Pine Hill Rd.
McLean, VA 22101
Tel: (703)448-0935
Fax: (703)448-9322
Registered: LDA
EMail: milton@canfieldassoc.com

Employers
Wells & Associates

Clients Represented

On Behalf of Wells & Associates
King & Spalding
Performance Food Group Inc.
Save the Greenback Coalition

WELLS, Nan S.

444 N. Capitol St. NW
Suite 728
Washington, DC 20001
Tel: (202)639-8420
Fax: (202)639-8423

Employers
Princeton University (Director, Office of Government Affairs)

WELLS, Noreene

1420 New York Ave. NW
Suite 1050
Washington, DC 20005
Tel: (202)638-1950
Fax: (202)638-7714
Registered: LDA

Employers
Van Scoyoc Associates, Inc. (Program Assistant)

Clients Represented

On Behalf of Van Scoyoc Associates, Inc.
American Library Ass'n
Recording for the Blind and Dyslexic, Inc.

WELLS, Stephen E.

600 13th St. NW
Washington, DC 20005-3096
Tel: (202)756-8316
Fax: (202)756-8087
Registered: LDA
EMail: swells@mwe.com
Tax Law Specialist, Reorganization Branch, Internal Revenue Service, 1973-78.

Employers
McDermott, Will and Emery (Partner, Tax Law Department)

Clients Represented

On Behalf of McDermott, Will and Emery
Georgia-Pacific Corp.
RJR Nabisco Holdings Co.

WELLS, Thomas

300 I St. NE
Suite 106
Washington, DC 20002-4389
Tel: (202)547-1589
Fax: (202)547-1857

Employers
Consortium for Child Welfare (Exec. Director)

WELSH, Robert

815 16th St. NW
Washington, DC 20006
Tel: (202)637-5000
Fax: (202)637-5058

Employers
AFL-CIO (American Federation of Labor and Congress of Industrial Organizations) (Exec. Assistant to the President)

WELTERS, Anthony

8045 Leesburg Pike
Suite 650
Vienna, VA 22182
Tel: (703)506-3555
Fax: (703)506-3556

Employers
AmeriChoice Health Services, Inc. (President)

WELTMAN, Allen

1900 K St. NW
Suite 900
Washington, DC 20006
Tel: (202)822-4000
Fax: (202)822-5800
Registered: LDA

Employers
PriceWaterhouseCoopers (Partner)
The Transatlantic Business Dialogue (Chair, Steering Committee)

WENHOLD, Dave

8224 Old Courthouse Rd.
Vienna, VA 22182-3808
Tel: (703)556-6272
Fax: (703)556-6291
Registered: LDA
EMail: dwenhold@ncrahq.org

Employers
Nat'l Court Reporters Ass'n (Director, Government Relations and Public Policy)

WENNER, Adam

1455 Pennsylvania Ave. NW
Suite 700
Washington, DC 20004-1008
Tel: (202)639-6500
Fax: (202)639-6604
EMail: awenner@velaw.com
Deputy Assistant General Counsel, Federal Energy Regulatory Commission, 1980-81.

Employers
Vinson & Elkins L.L.P. (Partner)

Clients Represented
On Behalf of Vinson & Elkins L.L.P.
Enron Corp.

WENNER, Jovita

1420 New York Ave. NW
Suite 550
Washington, DC 20005
Tel: (202)783-4805
Fax: (202)783-4804
Registered: LDA

Employers
Russ Reid Co. (Supervisor)

Clients Represented
On Behalf of Russ Reid Co.
Alfalit Internat'l
Corporation for Business, Work and Learning
Dream Center/City Help
Earth University, Inc.
Village of Kiryas Joel
William Tyndale College

WENNING, Thomas F.

1825 Samuel Morse Dr.
Reston, VA 20190
Tel: (703)437-5300
Fax: (703)437-7768
Registered: LDA

Employers
Nat'l Grocers Ass'n (Senior V. President and General Counsel)

WENTWORTH, Lyllett

700 13th St. NW
Suite 400
Washington, DC 20005
Tel: (202)347-0773
Fax: (202)347-0785
Registered: LDA
EMail: lwentworth@cassidy.com
Staff member for Senator Bill Frist (R-TN), 1995-2000.

Employers
Cassidy & Associates, Inc. (Account Executive)

Clients Represented
On Behalf of Cassidy & Associates, Inc.
Carondelet Health System
Community Health Partners of Ohio
Edward Health Services
Lifebridge Health
Neumann College
Palmdale, California, City of
Polytechnic University

WENTWORTH, Marchant

1726 M St. NW
Suite 902
Washington, DC 20036
Tel: (202)785-3355
Fax: (202)452-1805

Employers
American Thoracic Soc. (Director, Health Care Policy, American Thoracic Soc.)

WENTZEL, Jon

1901 L St. NW
Suite 300
Washington, DC 20036
Tel: (202)466-7590
Fax: (202)466-7598
EMail: jon.wentzel@dc.ogilvypr.com

Employers
Ogilvy Public Relations Worldwide (Senior V. President)

Clients Represented
On Behalf of Ogilvy Public Relations Worldwide
American Chemistry Council
Chemical Manufacturers Ass'n

WERNEKE, Diane E.

20th and C Sts. NW
MS: 2125
Washington, DC 20551
Tel: (202)452-3263
Fax: (202)452-2611

Employers
Federal Reserve System (Special Assistant to the Board, Congressional Liaison)

WERNER, Carol

122 C St. NW
Suite 700
Washington, DC 20001
Tel: (202)628-1400
Ext: 1881
Fax: (202)628-1825
EMail: carol@eesi.org

Employers
Environmental and Energy Study Institute (Exec. Director)

WERNER, Eric T.

901 15th St. NW
Suite 700
Washington, DC 20005-2301
Tel: (202)371-6000
Fax: (202)371-6279
Registered: LDA
EMail: etwerner@verner.com

Employers
Verner, Liipfert, Bernhard, McPherson and Hand, Chartered (Member of Firm)

WERNER, Jeff

c/o PricewaterhouseCoopers LLP
1900 K St. NW, Suite 900
Washington, DC 20009
Tel: (202)414-1293
Fax: (202)414-1217

Employers
The Transatlantic Business Dialogue (Director)

WERNER, Larry W.

2111 Wilson Blvd.
Suite 1200
Arlington, VA 22201
Tel: (703)522-1845
Fax: (703)351-6634
Registered: LDA
EMail: lwerner@columbuspublicaffairs.com
Legislative Director/Senior Policy Advisor to Senator Harry Reid (D-NV).

Employers
Columbus Public Affairs (V. President)

Clients Represented
On Behalf of Columbus Public Affairs
American Gaming Ass'n

WERNER, Michael

1625 K St. NW
Suite 1100
Washington, DC 20006-1604
Tel: (202)857-0244
Fax: (202)857-0237

Employers
Biotechnology Industry Organization (Director, Federal Government Relations)

WERNER, Ulrich

Ronald Reagan Bldg.
Gray Tower
1300 Pennsylvania Ave. NW, Suite 500
Washington, DC 20004
Tel: (202)312-3500
Fax: (202)312-3501
Registered: LDA

Employers
SAP Public Services (V. President, Government Relations)

WERRONEN, Betsy Warren

3122 N St. NW
Washington, DC 20007
Tel: (202)333-9350
Fax: (202)333-9380
EMail: werronen@aol.com
Principal Deputy Assistant Secretary, Legislative Affairs, Department of State, 1981-85 and 1987-89. Principal Deputy Assistant Secretary, Congressional, Intergovernmental and Public Affairs, Department of Energy, 1986. Assistant to Senator Edward Brooke (R-MA), 1968-75.

Employers
Warren and Company (President)

WERST, Jr., William H.

1801 N. Hartford St.
Arlington, VA 22201-5206
Tel: (703)522-4995
Registered: LDA
EMail: wwerst@interassociates.ioffice.com

Employers
Inter-Associates, Inc. (President)

Clients Represented
On Behalf of Inter-Associates, Inc.
Vacuum Insulation Ass'n

WERTHEIMER, Fred

1825 I St. NW
Suite 400
Washington, DC 20006
Tel: (202)429-2008
Fax: (202)293-2660
Registered: LDA
EMail: founders@democracy21.org

Employers
Democracy 21 (President)

WERTZ, Ken

1301 K St. NW
Washington, DC 20005-3333
Tel: (202)414-1000
Fax: (202)414-1301
Registered: LDA
EMail: ken.wertz@us.pwcglobal.com

Employers
PriceWaterhouseCoopers (Partner)

WERTZ, Martha

500 17th St. NW
Washington, DC 20006-4804
Tel: (202)639-1700
Fax: (202)639-1779
EMail: mwertz@corcoran.org

Employers
The Corcoran Gallery of Art (V. President, Development)

WERTZBERGER, Marsha C.

1050 Connecticut Ave. NW
Washington, DC 20036-5339
Tel: (202)857-6000
Fax: (202)857-6395
Worked for the Food and Drug Administration, Department of Health and Human Services.

Employers
Arent Fox Kintner Plotkin & Kahn, PLLC (Member)

WESELEY, Lizabeth

1033 N. Fairfax St.
Suite 404
Alexandria, VA 22314
Tel: (703)549-7404
Fax: (703)549-8712
EMail: lweseley@icsc.org

Employers
Internat'l Council of Shopping Centers (Project Coordinator, State Relations)

WESLOW, Norman J.

1156 15th St. NW
Suite 502
Washington, DC 20005-1799
Tel: (202)862-4833
Fax: (202)862-4829

Employers
J. C. Penney Co., Inc. (Senior Government Relations Counsel)

WESSEL, Michael R.

1225 I St. NW
Suite 350
Washington, DC 20005
Tel: (202)789-1110
Fax: (202)789-1116
Registered: LDA
EMail: mwessel@dmggroup.com
General Counsel to House Democratic Leader, Rep. Richard Gephardt (D-MO), 1977-98.

Employers
Downey McGrath Group, Inc. (Senior V. President)

Clients Represented
On Behalf of Downey McGrath Group, Inc.
Dental Recycling North America
Hallmark Cards, Inc.
SLM Holding Corp.
The Timken Co.
United Steelworkers of America

WEST, Barbara F.

5018 Sangamore Rd.
Suite 300
Bethesda, MD 20816
Tel: (301)229-1048
Fax: (301)229-0442
EMail: navref@navref.org

Employers
Nat'l Ass'n of Veterans Research and Education Foundations (Exec. Director)

WEST, Carla L.

666 Pennsylvania Ave. SE
Washington, DC 20003
Tel: (202)548-2311
Registered: LDA
EMail: carlaabpc@hotmail.com

Employers
Self-employed as an independent consultant.

Clients Represented
As an independent consultant
Ag Biotech Planning Committee

WEST, Ford B.

501 Second St. NE
Washington, DC 20002
Tel: (202)675-8250
Fax: (202)544-8123
Registered: LDA
EMail: fwest@tfi.org

Employers
The Fertilizer Institute (Sr. V. President)

WEST, Fowler

1401 K St. NW
Suite 400
Washington, DC 20005
Tel: (202)789-2111
Fax: (202)789-4883
Registered: LDA
EMail: fwest@thewashingtongroup.com
Former Staff Director, House Agriculture Committee and Commissioner, Commodities Futures Trading Commission.

Employers
The Washington Group (General Counsel)

Clients Represented
On Behalf of The Washington Group
American Resort Development Ass'n
Everglades Trust
IVAX Corp.
Microsoft Corp.
Nat'l Ass'n of Real Estate Investment Trusts
News Corporation Ltd.
SAMPCO Companies

WEST, G. Frank

406 First St. SE
Third Floor
Washington, DC 20003
Tel: (202)488-8562
Fax: (202)488-3803
Registered: LDA

Employers
ONEOK, Inc. (Manager, Government Affairs - Federal)
Self-employed as an independent consultant.

Clients Represented
As an independent consultant
Kansas Gas Service
Oklahoma Natural Gas Co.

WEST, Gail Berry

1150 Connecticut Ave. NW
Suite 515
Washington, DC 20036
Tel: (202)296-2831
Fax: (202)294-4337
Registered: LDA
EMail: gbwest@armstrong.com

Employers
Armstrong World Industries, Inc. (Director, Government Relations)

WEST, Ph.D., Jane

4425 Walsh St.
Chevy Chase, MD 20815
Tel: (301)718-0979
Fax: (301)718-0980
Registered: LDA

Employers
Self-employed as an independent consultant.

Clients Represented
As an independent consultant
Ass'n of TEH Act Projects
Higher Education Consortium for Special Education

WEST, Kimberly

1500 K St. NW
Suite 850
Washington, DC 20005
Tel: (202)682-4292
Fax: (202)682-5150
EMail: ksg@compete.org

Employers
Council on Competitiveness (Deputy Director)

WEST, Nancy K.

701 Pennsylvania Ave. NW
Suite 800
Washington, DC 20004
Tel: (202)508-4003
Fax: (202)508-4321
Registered: LDA
EMail: nkwest@thelenreid.com
Special Assistant, Department of Transportation, 1981-87.

Employers
Thelen Reid & Priest LLP (Senior Legislative Representative)

Clients Represented
On Behalf of Thelen Reid & Priest LLP
Airport Minority Advisory Council
Airports Council Internat'l - North America
Capital Region Airport Commission
Corpus Christi Port Authority
Denver, Colorado, City of
DRS Technologies, Inc.
Horizon Organic Holding Co.
The Jewelers' Security Alliance
Suiza Foods Corp.
Washington Soccer Partners

WEST, Jr., Togo D.

1201 Pennsylvania Ave. NW
Washington, DC 20004-2401
Tel: (202)662-6000
Fax: (202)662-6291
EMail: twest@cov.com
Secretary of Veterans Affairs, Department of Veterans Affairs, 1998-2000. Secretary of the Army, 1993-98. General Counsel (1980-81) and Special Assistant to the Deputy Secretary (1979-80), Department of Defense. General Counsel, Department of the Navy, 1977-79. Office of the Assistant and Secretary for Manpower and Reserve Affairs, Department of the Army, 1969-73. Judicial Clerckship, U.S. District Court for the Southern District of NY, 1968-69.

Employers
Covington & Burling (Of Counsel)

WEST, Jr., William Preston

1200 18th St. NW
Suite 400
Washington, DC 20036-2506
Tel: (202)783-9000
Fax: (202)331-8364
Registered: LDA

Employers
Nat'l Business Aviation Ass'n (Senior V. President, Government and Public Affairs)

WESTBROOK, Gay

1200 17th St. NW
Washington, DC 20036-3097
Tel: (202)331-5900
Fax: (202)973-5373
Registered: LDA
EMail: gwestbrook@dineout.org

Employers
Nat'l Restaurant Ass'n (Legislative Representative)

WESTBROOK, Reeves C.

1201 Pennsylvania Ave. NW
Washington, DC 20004-2401
Tel: (202)662-6000
Fax: (202)662-6291
EMail: rwestbrook@cov.com

Employers
Covington & Burling (Partner)

WESTFALL, Linda "Tuckie"

1341 G St. NW
Suite 900
Washington, DC 20005
Tel: (202)637-1544
Fax: (202)637-1517
EMail: tuckie.westfall@us.pm.com

Employers
Kraft Foods, Inc. (Director, Federal Government Affairs/Food)
Philip Morris Management Corp. (Director, Government Affairs, Food)

WESTNER, Joe

1300 I St. NW
Room 400
Washington, DC 20005
Tel: (202)515-2562
Registered: LDA

Employers
Verizon Communications (Assistant V. President, Federal Government Relations)
Verizon Pennsylvania Inc. (Director, Federal Relations (Washington))

WESTWATER, Joseph J.

1025 Thomas Jefferson St. NW
Suite 407 West
Washington, DC 20007
Tel: (202)342-1300
Fax: (202)342-5880
Registered: LDA, FARA

Employers
Tuttle, Taylor & Heron

WETEKAM, James R.

1808 Swann St. NW
Washington, DC 20009
Tel: (202)462-7288
Fax: (202)483-1964
Registered: LDA

Employers
The Sheridan Group (Senior Legislative Associate)

Clients Represented
On Behalf of The Sheridan Group
American Cancer Soc.

WETHINGTON, Olin L.

1330 Connecticut Ave. NW
Washington, DC 20036-1795
Tel: (202)429-3000
Fax: (202)429-3902
EMail: owething@steptoe.com
Assistant Secretary for International Affairs, Department of the Treasury, 1991-93. Special Assistant to the President and Executive Secretary to the Economic Policy Council, The White House, 1990-91. Deputy Undersecretary for International Trade, Department of Commerce, 1983-85.

Employers
Steptoe & Johnson LLP (Partner)

WETMORE, David

444 N. Capitol St. NW
Suite 701
Washington, DC 20001
Tel: (202)624-7790
Fax: (202)624-8579
EMail: DWetmore@naic.org

Employers
Nat'l Ass'n of Insurance Commissioners (Director, Federal and International Affairs)

WETSTONE, Gregory S.

1200 New York Ave. NW
Suite 400
Washington, DC 20005
Tel: (202)289-6868
Fax: (202)289-1060
Registered: LDA

Employers
Natural Resources Defense Council (Director of Programs)

WETZEL, John F.

50 F St. NW
Suite 12513
Washington, DC 20001
Tel: (202)639-2538
Fax: (202)639-2526
Registered: LDA

Employers
Ass'n of American Railroads (Assistant V. President, Government Affairs)

WEXLER, Anne

1317 F St. NW
Suite 600
Washington, DC 20004
Tel: (202)638-2121
Fax: (202)638-7045
Registered: LDA, FARA
EMail: wexler@wexlergroup.com
Former Assistant to the President for Public Liaison, Executive Office of the President, The White House, during the Carter administration.

Employers
The Wexler Group (Chairman of the Exec. Committee)

Clients Represented

On Behalf of The Wexler Group
Alaska, Washington Office of the State of
American Airlines
American Forest & Paper Ass'n
Asea Brown Boveri, Inc.
Burger King Corp.
Caterpillar Inc.
Comcast Corp.
CSX Corp.
Foothills Pipe Lines (Yukon), Ltd.
General Motors Corp.
Guardian Industries Corp.
Hydroelectric Licensing Reform Task Force
Immunex Corp.
IMS Health Inc.
MENC: The Nat'l Ass'n for Music Education
Nat'l Ass'n of Music Merchants
ORBITZ
PacifiCare Health Systems
United Parcel Service

WEXLER, Celia Viggo

1250 Connecticut Ave. NW
Washington, DC 20036
Tel: (202)833-1200
Fax: (202)659-3716
Registered: LDA

Employers
Common Cause (Lobbyist/Policy Analyst)

WEXLER, Chuck

1120 Connecticut Ave. NW
Suite 930
Washington, DC 20036
Tel: (202)466-7820
Fax: (202)466-7826

Employers
Police Executive Research Forum (Exec. Director)

WEXLER, Daniel

426 C St. NE
Washington, DC 20002
Tel: (202)544-1880
Fax: (202)543-2565
Registered: LDA
Special Assistant to the President, Clinton Administration, 1993-98.

Employers
Capitol Associates, Inc. (V. President)

Clients Represented

On Behalf of Capitol Associates, Inc.
Boys and Girls Clubs of America
Nat'l Federation of High Schools
Nat'l Federation of State High School Ass'ns

WEXLER, Timothy W.

1120 20th St. NW
Suite 725
Washington, DC 20007
Tel: (202)822-9822
Fax: (202)822-9808
Registered: LDA

Employers
Nat'l Club Ass'n (Assistant Director, Government Relations)

WEYMOUTH, T. Clark

555 13th St. NW
Washington, DC 20004-1109
Tel: (202)637-8633
Fax: (202)637-5910
Registered: LDA, FARA
EMail: tcweymouth@hhlaw.com

Employers
Hogan & Hartson L.L.P. (Partner)

WEYRICH, Paul M.

717 Second St. NE
Washington, DC 20002
Tel: (202)546-3000
Fax: (202)543-5605
Former aide to Sen. Gordon Allott (R-CO).

Employers
Free Congress Research and Education Foundation (President)
NET-Political NewsTalk Network (President)

WHALEN, Katie

2000 L St. NW
Suite 300
Washington, DC 20036-0646
Tel: (202)835-8800
Fax: (202)835-8879

Employers
Ketchum (Senior Counselor)

WHALEN, Mary Lynne

1401 I St. NW
Suite 910
Washington, DC 20005
Tel: (202)354-2600
Fax: (202)354-2622
Registered: LDA
Former Legislative Staff Member, Senate Committee on Veterans' Affairs and Legislative Analyst, Library of Congress, Congressional Research Service.

Employers
Credit Suisse First Boston Corp. (Treasurer)

WHALEN, Thomas J.

1016 16th St. NW
Suite 700
Washington, DC 20036
Tel: (202)289-0500
Fax: (202)289-4524
EMail: twhalen@condonlaw.com
Captain, Judge Advocate General Corps, U.S. Army, 1964-67. Law Secretary to Judge Gerald McLaughlin, U.S. Court of Appeals, Third Circuit, 1963-64.

Employers
Condon and Forsyth (Managing Partner)

Clients Represented

On Behalf of Condon and Forsyth
Air Pacific Ltd.
Iran Air

WHARTON, Dennis

1771 N St. NW
Washington, DC 20036-2891
Tel: (202)429-5350
Fax: (202)429-5406

Employers
Nat'l Ass'n of Broadcasters (Senior V. President, Corporate Communications)

WHARTON, Ellan K.

601 Pennsylvania Ave. NW
Suite 325, North Bldg.
Washington, DC 20004
Tel: (202)728-3661
Fax: (202)728-3649
Registered: LDA

Employers
DuPont (Senior Washington Counsel)

WHEAT, Hon. Alan D.

1201 S. Eads St.
Suite Two
Arlington, VA 22202
Tel: (703)271-8771
Fax: (703)271-9594
Registered: LDA
EMail: awheat@wheatgr.com
Member, U.S. House of Representatives (D-MO), 1983-94.

Employers
Wheat & Associates, Inc. (President)

Clients Represented

On Behalf of Wheat & Associates, Inc.
Airgas, Inc.
AON Risk Services
Apollo Group, Inc.
Bay Mills Indian Community
The Century Council
Davis & Associates
GE Capital Mortgage Insurance Co. (GEMICO)
GlaxoSmithKline
Global Encasement, Inc.
Nescrow.com Technologies
Paradigm Systems Consulting Inc.
Rainbow/Push Coalition (National Bureau)
SNC Technologies Corp.

WHEELER, Charles

601 Pennsylvania Ave. NW
11th Floor, North Bldg.
Washington, DC 20004-2601
Tel: (202)756-3300
Fax: (202)756-3333
Registered: LDA

Employers
Alston & Bird LLP

Clients Represented

On Behalf of Alston & Bird LLP
Nat'l Foreign Trade Council, Inc.

WHEELER, Daniel

1608 K St. NW
Washington, DC 20006
Tel: (202)861-2700
Fax: (202)861-2786
Registered: LDA

Employers
American Legion (Exec. Director)

WHEELER, Douglas

555 13th St. NW
Washington, DC 20004-1109
Tel: (202)637-5600
Fax: (202)637-5910

Employers
Hogan & Hartson L.L.P.

Clients Represented

On Behalf of Hogan & Hartson L.L.P.
The McConnell Foundation

WHEELER, George Y.

2099 Pennsylvania Ave. NW
Suite 100
Washington, DC 20006
Tel: (202)955-3000
Fax: (202)955-5564
EMail: gwheeler@hklaw.com

Employers
Holland & Knight LLP (Partner)

WHEELER, Gerald F.

1840 Wilson Blvd.
Arlington, VA 22201
Tel: (703)243-7100
Fax: (703)243-7177

Employers
Nat'l Science Teachers Ass'n (Exec. Director)

WHEELER, Gordon B.

2121 K Street NW
Suite 325
Washington, DC 20037
Tel: (202)728-0610
Fax: (202)728-0617
EMail: gwheeler@acep.org

Employers
American College of Emergency Physicians (Director, Public Affairs and Washington, DC Office)

WHEELER, Porter K.

4733 Bethesda Ave.
Suite 600
Bethesda, MD 20814
Tel: (301)907-2900
Fax: (301)907-2906
EMail: pwheeler@imginfrastructure.com
Former Group Director for Commerce and Community Development, Senate Committee on the Budget. Former Senior Transport Analyst, Congressional Budget Office.

Employers
Infrastructure Management Group (Director, Transportation Policy and Economics)

Clients Represented

On Behalf of Infrastructure Management Group

Canton Railroad Co.
I-49 Roadbuilders Coalition
Institute for Certified Investment Management Consultants
Investment Program Ass'n
Money Management Institute

WHEELER, Sandy

1700 N. Moore St.
Suite 1600
Arlington, VA 22209
Tel: (703)841-2400
Fax: (703)527-0938

Employers

American Meat Institute (Director, Human Resources and Administration)

WHEELER, Shelva

451 Seventh St. SW
Washington, DC 20410
Tel: (202)708-0005
Fax: (202)708-3794

Employers

Department of Housing and Urban Development (Administrative Officer, Congressional and Intergovernmental Relations)

WHEELER, Thomas E.

1250 Connecticut Ave. NW
Suite 800
Washington, DC 20036
Tel: (202)785-0081
Fax: (202)785-0721
Registered: LDA

Employers

Cellular Telecommunications and Internet Ass'n (President/Chief Exec. Officer)

WHEELER, William

1850 M St. NW
Suite 280
Washington, DC 20036
Tel: (202)331-7900
Fax: (202)331-0726
Registered: LDA
EMail: wwheeler@shawncoulson.com

Regional Director, Farm Service Agency, Department of Agriculture, 1995-98.

Employers

Shawn Coulson (Legislative Counsel)

Clients Represented

On Behalf of Shawn Coulson

Domes Internat'l, Inc.
People for the Ethical Treatment of Animals

WHEELESS, Charlene

2000 Edmund Halley Dr.
Reston, VA 20191
Tel: (703)264-8733
Fax: (703)715-4450
EMail: wheelesc@dyncorp.com

Employers

DynCorp (Director, Corporate Communications)

WHELAN, Edward

4232 King St.
Alexandria, VA 22302
Tel: (703)998-0072
Fax: (703)931-5624
EMail: ewhelan@acce.org

Employers

American Chamber of Commerce Executives (V. President, Benefits Services)

WHELAN, June M.

1899 L St. NW
Suite 1000
Washington, DC 20036
Tel: (202)457-0480
Fax: (202)457-0486
Registered: LDA
EMail: june_whelan@npradc.org

Employers

Nat'l Petrochemical Refiners Ass'n (Director, Government Relations)

WHELAN, Roger M.

2300 N St. NW
Washington, DC 20037-1128
Tel: (202)663-8000
Fax: (202)663-8007
EMail: roger.whelan@shawpittman.com

Employers

Shaw Pittman (Senior Counsel)

WHETTSTONE, David

110 Maryland Ave. NE
Suite 502
Washington, DC 20002
Tel: (202)544-6564
Fax: (202)544-2820
EMail: David_Whettstone@mcc.org

Employers

Mennonite Central Committee Washington Office (Legislative Associate, Domestic Affairs)

WHITAKER, Sarah

325 Seventh St. NW
Suite 1100
Washington, DC 20004-2802
Tel: (202)783-7971
Fax: (202)737-2849

Employers

Nat'l Retail Federation (Director, Government Relations)

WHITAKER, Scott

Hubert H. Humphrey Bldg.
200 Independence Ave. SW
Room 416G
Washington, DC 20201
Tel: (202)690-7627
Fax: (202)690-7380

Employers

Department of Health and Human Services (Assistant Secretary for Legislation (Nominated))

WHITAKER, Stephen

700 13th St. NW
Suite 400
Washington, DC 20005
Tel: (202)347-0773
Fax: (202)347-0785
Registered: LDA
EMail: swhitaker@cassidy.com

Former staff member, House Committee on Ways and Means.

Employers

Cassidy & Associates, Inc. (Sr. V. President and Director of Global Trade Strategies)

Clients Represented

On Behalf of Cassidy & Associates, Inc.

The BOSE Corp.
FedEx Corp.
Taiwan Studies Institute
Tiffany & Co.

WHITCOMB, James T.

635 Massachusetts Ave. NW
Washington, DC 20001
Tel: (202)414-2000
Registered: LDA

Employers

Nat'l Public Radio (National Affairs Associate)

WHITE, Andrew H.

4025 Fair Ridge Dr.
Fairfax, VA 22033-2868
Tel: (703)273-0911
Fax: (703)273-9363
Registered: LDA

Employers

Internat'l Ass'n of Fire Chiefs (Manager, Counterterrorism Programs)

WHITE, Annie

1101 Vermont Ave. NW
12th Floor
Washington, DC 20005-3583
Tel: (202)789-7420
Fax: (202)789-7485
Registered: LDA

Employers

American Medical Ass'n (Assistant Director, Congressional Affairs)

WHITE, Betsy

50 F St. NW
12th Floor
Washington, DC 20001
Tel: (202)639-2540
Fax: (202)639-2558

Employers

Ass'n of American Railroads (Acting V. President, Communications)

WHITE, Bill

2000 Florida Ave. NW
Washington, DC 20009
Tel: (202)777-7445
Fax: (202)328-0566
EMail: bwhite@agu.org

Employers

American Geophysical Union (Director, Information Technology)

WHITE, Clarence

400 N. Capitol St. NW
Suite 790
Washington, DC 20001
Tel: (202)554-1600
Fax: (202)554-1654
Registered: LDA

Employers

Nat'l Farmers Union (Farmers Educational & Co-operative Union of America) (Communications Coordinator)

WHITE, D. Timothy

11 Canal Center Plaza
Suite 103
Alexandria, VA 22314
Tel: (703)683-4222
Fax: (703)683-0645
Registered: LDA

Employers

The Spectrum Group

WHITE, David

P.O. Box 42660
Washington, DC 20015-0660
Tel: (202)574-2423
Fax: (202)574-2423
EMail: chaplains@charitiesusa.com

Employers

Military Chaplains Ass'n of the U.S. (Exec. Director)

WHITE, Deanna

408 C St. NE
Washington, DC 20002
Tel: (202)547-1141
Fax: (202)547-6009

Employers

Sierra Club (Deputy, Political Director)

WHITE, Deborah R.

655 15th St. NW
Washington, DC 20005-5701
Tel: (202)220-0614
Fax: (202)220-0873
EMail: dwhite@fmi.org

Employers

Food Marketing Institute (Regulatory Counsel)

WHITE, Douglas

2029 P St. NW
Suite 202
Washington, DC 20036
Tel: (202)785-9619
Fax: (202)785-9621

Employers

Black America's Political Action Committee (Treasurer)

WHITE, Jacqueline M.

1101 Vermont Ave. NW
Suite 400
Washington, DC 20005
Tel: (202)289-3900
Fax: (202)371-0197
EMail: jwhite@dbmlaw.com

Employers

Dean Blakey & Moskowitz (Associate Attorney)

WHITE, III, John Thomas

516 1/2 Oronoco St.
Alexandria, VA 22314
Tel: (703)684-2001
Fax: (703)739-7621
Registered: LDA

Employers

Self-employed as an independent consultant.

Clients Represented

As an independent consultant

The Boeing Co.
Nat'l Graduate University

WHITE, Justus P.

4306 Wynwood Dr.
Annandale, VA 22003
Tel: (703)354-3121
Fax: (703)354-3121
Registered: LDA
EMail: cambintl@aol.com

Employers

Cambridge Internat'l, Inc. (President)

Clients Represented

On Behalf of Cambridge Internat'l, Inc.

Stewart & Stevenson Services, Inc.

WHITE, Kazuko

2001 Pennsylvania Ave. NW
Suite 700
Washington, DC 20006
EMail: kazuko_white@micusa.com
Tel: (202)331-7301
Fax: (202)331-7277

Employers
Mitsubishi Internat'l Corp. (Manager)

WHITE, Kenneth

101 1/2 S. Union St.
Alexandria, VA 22314
EMail: kwhite@smithfairfield.com
Tel: (703)684-5100
Fax: (703)684-5424

Employers
Smith Fairfield, Inc. (Principal)

WHITE, Larry

601 E St. NW
Washington, DC 20049
Tel: (202)434-3800
Fax: (202)434-3758
Registered: LDA

Employers
AARP (American Ass'n of Retired Persons) (Legislative Representative)

WHITE, Margita E.

1776 Massachusetts Ave. NW
Suite 310
Washington, DC 20036
Tel: (202)861-0344
Fax: (202)861-0342

Employers
Ass'n for Maximum Service Television, Inc. (President)

WHITE, Melissa

1301 Pennsylvania Ave. NW
Suite 550
Washington, DC 20004-1701
EMail: white@nlc.org
Tel: (202)626-3000
Fax: (202)626-3043

Employers
Nat'l League of Cities (Legislative Counsel)

WHITE, Patrick

9650 Rockville Pike
Bethesda, MD 20814-3998
Tel: (202)543-1155
Fax: (202)546-2370

Employers
Federation of American Societies for Experimental Biology (Director, Legislative Affairs)

WHITE, Jr., Raymon M.

1201 E. Abingdon Dr.
Suite 300
Alexandria, VA 22314
EMail: rwhite@harris.com
Tel: (703)739-1937
Fax: (703)739-2775
Registered: LDA

Employers
Harris Corp. (V. President, Washington Operations)

WHITE, Richard C.

660 Pennsylvania Ave. SE
Suite 201
Washington, DC 20003
EMail: RWhite@alpinegroup.com
Tel: (202)548-2312
Fax: (202)547-4658
Registered: LDA
Legislative Coordinator to Senator John Chafee (R-RI), 1989-90.

Employers
Alpine Group, Inc. (Partner)

Clients Represented
On Behalf of Alpine Group, Inc.
Bracco Diagnostics
Council on Radionuclides and Radiopharmaceuticals (CORAR)
Dow AgroSciences
The DuPont Pharmaceutical Co.
FMC Corp.
Jackson Nat'l Life Insurance
Medical Imaging Contrast Agent Ass'ns
Nat'l Ass'n of Insurance and Financial Advisors
Pharmacia Corp.

WHITE, Richard H.

13901 Piscataway Dr.
Fort Washington, MD 20744
Tel: (202)256-1293
Fax: (301)292-8598
Registered: LDA

Employers
R. H. White Public Affairs Consulting

Clients Represented
On Behalf of R. H. White Public Affairs Consulting
Brown and Williamson Tobacco Corp.
R. C. Whitner and Associates, Inc.

WHITE, Robert E.

1755 Massachusetts Ave. NW
Suite 550
Washington, DC 20036
EMail: rewhite@ciponline.org
Tel: (202)232-3317
Fax: (202)232-3440
Former U.S. Ambassador to Paraguay and El Salvador.

Employers
Center for Internat'l Policy (President)

WHITE, Jr., Robert L.

Three Bethesda Metro Center
Suite 1100
Bethesda, MD 20814
EMail: rlw@necanet.org
Tel: (301)657-3110
Fax: (301)215-4500
Registered: LDA

Employers
Nat'l Electrical Contractors Ass'n (Director, Government Affairs)

WHITE, Sam

660 Pennsylvania Ave. SE
Suite 201
Washington, DC 20003
EMail: SWhite@alpinegroup.com
Tel: (202)547-1831
Fax: (202)547-4658
Registered: LDA

Employers
Alpine Group, Inc. (Partner)

Clients Represented
On Behalf of Alpine Group, Inc.
AgrEvo USA Co.
American Crop Protection Ass'n
EOP Group, Inc.
FMC Corp.
Pharmacia Corp.

WHITE, Steven C.

10801 Rockville Pike
Rockville, MD 20852
EMail: swhite@asha.org
Tel: (301)897-5700
Ext: 4126
Fax: (301)571-0457
Registered: LDA

Employers
American Speech, Language, and Hearing Ass'n (Director, Healthcare Financing)

WHITE, Susan J.

1020 N. Fairfax
Suite 202
Alexandria, VA 22314
Tel: (703)683-2573
Fax: (703)683-0865
Registered: LDA

Employers
Susan J. White & Associates (Principal)

Clients Represented
On Behalf of Susan J. White & Associates
Central Coast Alliance for Health
Cook, Illinois, County of
Cuyahoga, Ohio, County of
Los Angeles, California, County of
Nat'l Ass'n of Government Deferred Compensation Administrators
Santa Barbara Regional Health Authority
Shelby, Tennessee, County of

WHITE, Thomas R. "Randy"

6305 26th St. North
Arlington, VA 22207
Tel: (703)532-4929
Fax: (703)532-1376
Registered: LDA

Employers
Self-employed as an independent consultant.

Clients Represented
As an independent consultant
Ass'n of Trial Lawyers of America

WHITE, Toni D.

1100 Wilson Blvd.
Suite 1500
Arlington, VA 22209
EMail: toni_d_white@raytheon.com
Tel: (703)841-5759
Fax: (703)841-5792

Employers
Raytheon Co. (Senior Director, Government Relations)

WHITE, Ward H.

1133 21st St. NW
Suite 900
Washington, DC 20036
EMail: ward.white@bellsouth.com
Tel: (202)463-4100
Fax: (202)463-4570
Registered: LDA

Employers
BellSouth Corp. (V. President, Federal Relations)

WHITE, William R.

815 Connecticut Ave. NW
Suite 650
Washington, DC 20006
Tel: (202)822-6100
Fax: (202)822-6101

Employers
Alliance of Arts Advocates

WHITEHEAD, Priscilla A.

3000 K St. NW
Suite 300
Washington, DC 20007
Tel: (202)424-7500
Fax: (202)424-7643
Registered: FARA

Employers
Swidler Berlin Shereff Friedman, LLP (Partner)

WHITEHOUSE, Theodore C.

Three Lafayette Center
1155 21st St. NW
Washington, DC 20036-3384
Tel: (202)328-8000
Fax: (202)887-8979
Registered: LDA
Trial Attorney, Antitrust Division, Department of Justice, 1980-82.

Employers
Willkie Farr & Gallagher (Partner)

Clients Represented
On Behalf of Willkie Farr & Gallagher
Bloomberg L.P.
Dun & Bradstreet

WHITEHURST, Calvert S.

1101 Pennsylvania Ave. NW
Suite 400
Washington, DC 20004-2504
Tel: (202)637-3833
Fax: (202)637-3863
Registered: LDA

Employers
Textron Inc. (Manager, Government Affairs)

WHITEHURST, Suzanne Kay

1201 15th St. NW
Third Floor
Washington, DC 20005
EMail: swhitehurst@ipaa.org
Tel: (202)857-4722
Fax: (202)857-4799
Registered: LDA

Employers
Independent Petroleum Ass'n of America (Director, Government Relations)
Self-employed as an independent consultant.

WHITENER, John C.

1505 Prince St.
Suite 300
Alexandria, VA 22314
Tel: (703)739-9200
Fax: (703)739-9497
Registered: LDA

Employers
American Optometric Ass'n (Assistant Director, Government Relations)

WHITENTON, Mark

1331 Pennsylvania Ave. NW
Sixth Floor
Washington, DC 20004-1790
EMail: mwhitenton@nam.org
Tel: (202)637-3150
Fax: (202)637-3182

Employers
Nat'l Ass'n of Manufacturers (V. President, Resources, Environment and Regulation)

WHITESIDES, Allison

1775 Pennsylvania Ave. NW
Suite 1200
Washington, DC 20006
EMail: allisonwhitesides@outback.com
Tel: (202)463-7114
Fax: (202)463-7107

Employers
Outback Steakhouse, Inc. (Director, Government Relations)

WHITESIDES, Ashley

1730 Pennsylvania Ave. NW
Suite 1200
Washington, DC 20006-4706
Tel: (202)737-0500
Fax: (202)626-3737
Registered: LDA

Employers
King & Spalding (Associate)

Clients Represented
On Behalf of King & Spalding
Farm Market iD

WHITESTONE, David C.

2099 Pennsylvania Ave. NW
Suite 100
Washington, DC 20006
Tel: (202)955-3000
Fax: (202)955-5564
Registered: LDA
EMail: dwhitest@hklaw.com
Former Associate Staff Member to Rep. Frank R. Wolf (R-VA), Subcommittee on Transportation, House Committee on Appropriations.

Employers
Holland & Knight LLP (Associate)

Clients Represented
On Behalf of Holland & Knight LLP
American Chemistry Council
Bridgestone/Firestone, Inc.
Clyde's Restaurant Group
DuPont
FirstEnergy Co.
Florida Gas Utility
The Georgetown Partnership
Greater Jamaica Development Corp.
Hualapai Nation
Internat'l Intellectual Property Institute
Nassau County Health Care Corp.
Nat'l Paint and Coatings Ass'n
Placer, California, County of
Rockdale, Georgia, County of, Board of Commissioners of
Sarasota, Florida, County of
Southern Coalition for Advanced Transportation
United Airlines
West Palm Beach, Florida, City of
West*Group Management LLC

WHITFIELD, Dennis

1201 F St. NW
Suite 200
Washington, DC 20004
Tel: (202)554-9000
Fax: (202)554-0496

Employers
Nat'l Federation of Independent Business (V. President, Grassroots and Media Communications)

WHITFIELD, Milton B.

2300 N St. NW
Washington, DC 20037-1128
Tel: (202)663-8000
Fax: (202)663-8007
EMail: milton.whitfield@shawpittman.com
Special Assistant to Admiral H. G. Rickover, Division of Naval Reactors, Department of Energy, 1974-79.

Employers
Shaw Pittman (Partner)

WHITING, Richard M.

805 15th St. NW
Suite 600
Washington, DC 20005
Tel: (202)289-4322
Fax: (202)289-1903
Registered: LDA

Employers
The Financial Services Roundtable (Exec. Director)

WHITMAN, Cameron

1301 Pennsylvania Ave. NW
Suite 550
Washington, DC 20004-1701
EMail: whitman@nlc.org
Tel: (202)626-3020
Fax: (202)626-3043

Employers
Nat'l League of Cities (Director, Policy and Federal Relations)

WHITMAN, Carol E.

4301 Wilson Blvd.
Arlington, VA 22203-1860
Tel: (703)907-5790
Fax: (703)907-5516
EMail: carol.whitman@nreca.org

Employers
Nat'l Rural Electric Cooperative Ass'n (Principal, Legislative Affairs)

WHITMAN, Lamar

1211 Connecticut Ave. NW
Suite 400
Washington, DC 20036
Tel: (202)822-8811
Fax: (202)872-1885

Employers
Alliance of American Insurers

WHITMER, Martin

1010 Massachusetts Ave. NW
Washington, DC 20001
Tel: (202)289-4434
Fax: (202)289-4435
Registered: LDA

Employers
American Road and Transportation Builders Ass'n (ARTBA) (V. President, Government Relations)

WHITMORE, David

700 13th St. NW
Suite 1000
Washington, DC 20005
Tel: (202)347-6633
Fax: (202)347-8713
Registered: FARA

Employers
Powell Tate (Senior V. President and Chief Financial Officer)

WHITNER, R. C.

1800 N. Kent St.
Suite 1104
Arlington, VA 22209
Tel: (703)243-1400
Fax: (703)525-0626
Registered: LDA

Employers
R. C. Whitner and Associates, Inc. (President)

Clients Represented
On Behalf of R. C. Whitner and Associates, Inc.
Condor Electronic Systems
Lockheed Martin Aeronautical Systems Co.
Lockheed Martin Corp.

WHITSITT, William F.

201 Maryland Ave. NE
Washington, DC 20002-5703
Tel: (202)544-3800
Fax: (202)543-0616
Registered: LDA
EMail: wfwhitsitt@aol.com
Legislative Assistant and Chief of Staff in the Senate, 1979-80. Legislative Assistant in the House of Representatives, 1973-78.

Employers
William F. Whitsitt Policy and Government Affairs (Principal)

Clients Represented
On Behalf of William F. Whitsitt Policy and Government Affairs
Burlington Resources Oil & Gas Co.
Devon Energy Corp.
Domestic Petroleum Council
The Stanley Works

WHITT, John

1225 19th St. NW
Suite 800
Washington, DC 20036
Tel: (202)955-6067
Fax: (202)822-0109

Employers
Guam, Washington Office of the Governor (Federal Affairs Specialist)

WHITT, Richard S.

1133 19th St. NW
Washington, DC 20036
Tel: (202)887-3845
Fax: (202)887-3866
EMail: richard.whitt@wcom.com

Employers
MCI WorldCom Corp. (Director, Internet Policy)

WHITTAKER, James

900 17th St. NW
Suite 1100
Washington, DC 20006
Tel: (202)884-7019
Fax: (202)884-7070
Registered: LDA
EMail: jim_whittaker@hp.com

Employers
Hewlett-Packard Co. (Director, International Government Affairs)

WHITTED, Pamela J.

1155 Connecticut Ave. NW
Suite 323
Washington, DC 20036
EMail: WHITTEDPJ@aol.com
Tel: (202)467-8577
Fax: (202)463-8576

Employers
BHP (USA) Inc. (Director, Federal Government Affairs)

WHITTEMORE, Anne Marie

1050 Connecticut Ave. NW
Suite 1200
Washington, DC 20036
Tel: (202)857-1700
Fax: (202)857-1737
Registered: LDA
EMail: awhittemore@mcguirewoods.com

Employers
McGuireWoods L.L.P. (Partner)

Clients Represented
On Behalf of McGuireWoods L.L.P.
Eastman Chemical Co.

WHITTEMORE, Ilsa

1300 L St. NW
Suite 1020
Washington, DC 20005
Tel: (202)789-0089
Fax: (202)789-1725

Employers
Hospitality Sales and Marketing Ass'n Internat'l (Associate Exec. Director)

WHITTEN, Jamie L.

1725 DeSales St. NW
Suite 800
Washington, DC 20036
Tel: (202)659-6540
Fax: (202)659-5730
Registered: LDA
Trial Attorney, Office of U.S. Attorney for Miami (1974-78) and Trial Attorney (1970-73), Department of Justice.

Employers
Whitten & Diamond

Clients Represented
On Behalf of Whitten & Diamond
Bombardier, Inc.
Gas Technology Institute
Lehigh Coal & Navigation Co.
Mountain Top Technologies, Inc.
Philadelphia, Pennsylvania, City of
Pioneer Hi-Bred Internat'l, Inc.
St. Joseph University
Temple University
Vernon, California, City of
Roy F. Weston, Inc.

WHITTEN, Peter

1615 New Hampshire Ave. NW
Washington, DC 20009
Tel: (202)483-3036
Fax: (202)483-3029
EMail: training@ili.org

Employers
Internat'l Law Institute (Director of Publishing)

WHITTINGHILL, James R. "Whit"

430 First St. SE
Washington, DC 20003
Tel: (202)544-6245
Fax: (202)675-6568
Registered: LDA

Employers
American Trucking Ass'ns (Senior V. President, Legislative Affairs)

WHITTLESEY, Judy

1000 Vermont Ave. NW
Suite 700
Washington, DC 20005
Tel: (202)408-0808
Fax: (202)408-0876
Registered: LDA
Clinton/Gore Transition Team, coordinating transition activities for Tipper Gore. Former Chief of Staff, Press Secretary to Joan Mondale.

Employers
Susan Davis Internat'l (Exec. V. President)

WHITTON, Laura Y.

1301 Pennsylvania Ave. NW
Suite 404
Washington, DC 20004-1727
Tel: (202)783-0911
Fax: (202)783-3524

Employers
Chicago, Illinois, Washington Office of the City of (Deputy Director)

WHOLEY, James K.

1717 Pennsylvania Ave. NW
12th Floor
Washington, DC 20006
EMail: jkwholey@msn.com
Tel: (202)416-0150
Registered: LDA

Administrative Assistant to Senator Robert J. Dole (R-KS), 1989-92. Legislative Director to Senator Aflonse D'Amato (R-NY), 1987-89. Counsel, National Republican Senatorial Committee, 1985-87.

Employers
Potomac Strategies Internat'l LLC (General Counsel)

Clients Represented

On Behalf of Potomac Strategies Internat'l LLC
Ass'n of the United States Army
Command Systems Inc.
Member-Link Systems, Inc.
Nat'l Electrical Manufacturers Ass'n
Omniflight Helicopters, Inc.
Spacelabs Medical Inc.

WHOULEY, Michael

1001 G St. NW
Suite 300 East
Washington, DC 20001
EMail: mwhouley@deweysquare.com
Tel: (202)638-5616
Fax: (202)638-5612
Registered: LDA

Employers
Dewey Square Group (Partner)

Clients Represented

On Behalf of Dewey Square Group
Northwest Airlines, Inc.

WHYTE, Bonnie

927 15th St. NW
Suite 1000
Washington, DC 20005
Tel: (202)659-4300
Registered: LDA

Employers
Employers Council on Flexible Compensation (Chief Operations Officer)

WIACEK, Raymond J.

51 Louisiana Ave. NW
Washington, DC 20001
EMail: rjwiacek@jonesday.com
Tel: (202)879-3939
Fax: (202)626-1700

Employers
Jones, Day, Reavis & Pogue (Partner)

Clients Represented

On Behalf of Jones, Day, Reavis & Pogue
Pfizer, Inc.

WIBLE, Robert C.

505 Huntmar Park Dr.
Suite 210
Herndon, VA 20170
Tel: (703)437-0100
Fax: (703)481-3596

Employers
Nat'l Conference of States on Building Codes and Standards (Exec. Director)

WICE, Jeffrey M.

P.O. Box 42442
Washington, DC 20015
Tel: (202)494-7991

Employers
Nat'l Ass'n of Jewish Legislators (Counsel)
State Legislative Policy Institute (Counsel)

WICK, Ronald F.

1050 Connecticut Ave. NW
Suite 1100
Washington, DC 20036-5304
EMail: RWick@baker-hostetler.com
Tel: (202)861-1500
Fax: (202)861-1790
Registered: LDA

Employers
Baker & Hostetler LLP (Partner)

WICKENDEN, David

1615 L St. NW
Suite 1000
Washington, DC 20036
EMail: wickendd@fleishman.com
Tel: (202)659-0330
Fax: (202)296-6119
Registered: FARA

Employers
Fleishman-Hillard, Inc (Senior V. President and Senior Partner)

WICKENS, William E.

1919 Pennsylvania Ave. NW
Suite 610
Washington, DC 20006
Tel: (202)775-2400
Fax: (202)331-7538

Counsel to Senator Lowell P. Weicker (R-CT), 1973. Director, Legislation and Research for Senator Robert Taft (R-OH), 1971-73.

Employers
Miller Thomson Wickens & Lebow LLP

WICKETT, James M.

1775 Pennsylvania Ave. NW
Suite 200
Washington, DC 20006
Tel: (202)862-1000
Fax: (202)862-1093
Registered: LDA

Employers
Dewey Ballantine LLP (Associate)

Clients Represented

On Behalf of Dewey Ballantine LLP
Automatic Data Processing, Inc
Railroad Retirement Tax Working Group
Scull Law Firm, David L.
Union Pacific

WICKLIFF, Jay

119 Oronoco St.
Alexandria, VA 22314-2015
Tel: (703)683-5400
Fax: (703)548-5728

Employers
A Presidential Classroom for Young Americans, Inc. (Exec. Director)

WIDES, Burton V.

1225 I St. NW
Washington, DC 20005
Tel: (202)682-4763
Fax: (202)682-4707

Employers
Burton V. Wides, P.C.

WIDMEYER, Scott D.

1825 Connecticut Ave. NW
Fifth Floor
Washington, DC 20009
Tel: (202)667-0901
Fax: (202)667-0902

Employers
Widmeyer Communications, Inc. (Chairman and Chief Exec. Officer)

WIEDEMER, Anne Marie

1300 I St. NW
Suite 495-East Tower
Washington, DC 20005-3314
Tel: (202)289-2011
Fax: (202)289-2024
Registered: LDA

Employers
Ralston Purina Co. (Assistant Director, Government Affairs)

WIEGAND, Douglas

401 E. Jefferson St.
Suite 102
Rockville, MD 20850-1714
Tel: (301)340-8580
Fax: (301)340-7283

Employers
Resilient Floor Covering Ass'n (Managing Director)

WIEGMANN, Theresa

8101 Glenbrook Rd.
Bethesda, MD 20814-2749
Tel: (301)907-6977
Fax: (301)907-6895

Employers
American Ass'n of Blood Banks (General Counsel and Division Director, Government Affairs)

WIELAND, Henry

2500 Wilson Blvd.
Suite 300
Arlington, VA 22201
EMail: hwieland@tia.eia.org
Tel: (703)907-7709
Fax: (703)907-7727

Employers
Telecommunications Industry Ass'n (V. President, Marketing Services)

WIELAND, Paul

1150 17th St. NW
Suite 701
Washington, DC 20036
EMail: paul.wieland@dittus.com
Tel: (202)775-1401
Fax: (202)775-1404

Employers
Dittus Communications (Manager & Editor, EIN)

Clients Represented

On Behalf of Dittus Communications
Editorial Information Network

WIENER, Jonathan L.

1229 19th St. NW
Washington, DC 20036
Tel: (202)429-4900
Fax: (202)429-4912
Registered: LDA

Employers
Goldberg, Godles, Wiener & Wright (Partner)

WIENER, Robin K.

1325 G St. NW
Suite 1000
Washington, DC 20005-3104
Tel: (202)737-1770
Fax: (202)626-0900

Employers
Institute of Scrap Recycling Industries, Inc. (President)

WIERZYNSKI, Barbara

2001 Pennsylvania Ave. NW
Suite 600
Washington, DC 20006-1807
Tel: (202)466-5460
Fax: (202)296-3184
Registered: LDA

Employers
Futures Industry Ass'n (Exec. V. President and General Counsel)

WIESENFELDER, Leslie H.

1200 New Hampshire Ave. NW
Suite 800
Washington, DC 20036-6802
EMail: lwiesen@dlalaw.com
Tel: (202)776-2000
Fax: (202)776-2222

Employers
Dow, Lohnes & Albertson, PLLC (Member)

WIGFALL, Cynthia

50 S. Picket St.
Suite 110
Alexandria, VA 22304-7206
Tel: (703)823-7234
Fax: (703)823-7237

Employers
Composite Can and Tube Institute (Director, Administration)

WIGGINS, Shaun

421 New Jersey Ave. SE
Washington, DC 20003
Tel: (703)318-7169
Registered: LDA

Employers
Washington Consulting Alliance, Inc. (President)

Clients Represented

On Behalf of Washington Consulting Alliance, Inc.
American Agriculture Movement, Inc.
Data Dynamics
Heartland Communications & Management Inc.

WIGGLESWORTH, Teresa N.

9527 Liberty Tree Lane
Vienna, VA 22182
EMail: twigs2@attglobal.net
Tel: (703)319-7827
Fax: (703)319-8742
Registered: LDA

Employers
Oxygenated Fuels Ass'n (Exec. Director)
The Wigglesworth Co. (President)

Clients Represented

On Behalf of The Wigglesworth Co.
SABIC Americas, Inc.

WIGGLESWORTH, Tom

1899 L St. NW
Suite 1000
Washington, DC 20036
Tel: (202)457-0480
Fax: (202)457-0486
EMail: tom_wigglesworth@npradc.org

Employers
Nat'l Petrochemical Refiners Ass'n (Environmental Analyst)

WIGHT, Bill

P.O. Box 25204
Arlington, VA 22202
Tel: (703)920-4500
Fax: (703)920-8147

Employers
Bill Wight, LLC

WIGHTMAN, Donald E.

815 16th St. NW
Washington, DC 20006
Tel: (202)347-8105
Fax: (202)347-4872

Employers
Utility Workers Union of America (President)

WIGINTON, Joel

1200 G. St. NW
Suite 800
Washington, DC 20005
Tel: (202)434-8994
Fax: (202)783-4513
Former Special Assistant to the President for Legislative Affairs, Executive Office of the President, The White House, during the Clinton administration. Also served as Judiciary Counsel to Senator Russell Feingold (D-WI) and as Counsel to Senator Richard Durbin (D-IL).

Employers
Sony Electronics, Inc. (V. President, Government Affairs.)

WIGMAN, Victor M.

900 17th St. NW
Suite 1000
Washington, DC 20006
Tel: (202)530-7400
Fax: (202)463-6915

Employers
Blank Rome Comisky & McCauley, LLP (Partner)

Clients Represented

On Behalf of Blank Rome Comisky & McCauley, LLP
Southwire, Inc.

WIGMORE, Michael B.

3000 K St. NW
Suite 300
Washington, DC 20007
Tel: (202)424-7500
Fax: (202)424-7643
Registered: LDA

Employers
Swidler Berlin Shereff Friedman, LLP (Associate)

Clients Represented

On Behalf of Swidler Berlin Shereff Friedman, LLP
Artichoke Enterprises, Inc.

WIGODE, Emil

1901 L St. NW
Suite 200
Washington, DC 20036
Tel: (202)659-1800
Fax: (202)296-2964
Registered: LDA

Employers
March of Dimes Birth Defects Foundation (Associate Director, Federal Affairs)

WILBER, Scott

1926 N St. NW
Third Floor
Washington, DC 20036
Tel: (202)833-1151
Fax: (202)833-0370
Registered: LDA

Employers
Dalrymple and Associates, L.L.C. (Associate)

WILBERDING, Dave

1800 K St. NW
Suite 1010
Washington, DC 20006
Tel: (202)296-5030
Fax: (202)296-4750
Registered: LDA
EMail: djwiber@yahoo.com

Employers
American Defense Internat'l, Inc. (V. President, Government Affairs)

Clients Represented

On Behalf of American Defense Internat'l, Inc.
3D Metrics Inc.
ANSAR Inc.
Barber Colman Co.
Beretta U.S.A. Corp.
Bofors Defence AB
Drexel University
East/West Industries
Eickhorn-Solingen
Ensign-Bickford Co.
EWA Land Information Group, Inc.
Fibernet LLC
Friction Free Technologies Inc.
Ganaden Biotech Inc.
Gentex Corp.
GIAT Industries
Hagglunds Moelv AS
InformaTech, Inc.
InvenCom LLC
Koable Co., Ltd.
Large Scale Biology
Le Meilleur Co., Ltd.
Longworth Industries Inc.
Marine Desalination Systems LLC
MEGAXESS, Inc.
Ordnance Development and Engineering Co. of Singapore
Pacific Consolidated Industries
PDI Ground Support Systems, Inc.
Raytheon Missile Systems
Saab AB
Sarnoff Corp.
SINTEF Telecom and Informatics
Smiths Industries Aerospace and Defense Systems
Stidd Systems, Inc.
Stratus Systems Inc.
Swiss Munition Enterprise
Syntroleum Corp.
Time Domain Corp.
Virtual Drug Development
Virtual Impact Productions
VISICU
ViTel Net
Xeta Internat'l Corp.
Youyang

WILBORN, Thomas L.

807 Maine Ave. SW
Washington, DC 20024
Tel: (202)554-3501
Fax: (202)554-3581

Employers
Disabled American Veterans (Assistant National Director, Communications)

WILBUR, Robert H.

2025 M St. NW
Suite 800
Washington, DC 20036
Tel: (202)367-2100
Fax: (202)367-1200
Registered: LDA
EMail: robert_wilbur@dc.sba.com

Employers
Smith, Bucklin and Associates, Inc.

Clients Represented

On Behalf of Smith, Bucklin and Associates, Inc.
Nat'l Ass'n of Food Equipment Manufacturers
North American Ass'n of Food Equipment Manufacturers
Soc. of Thoracic Surgeons

WILBUR, Valerie

4607 Connecticut Ave. NW
Suite 510
Washington, DC 20008
Tel: (202)364-1485
Registered: LDA

Employers
The Wilbur Group (President)

Clients Represented

On Behalf of The Wilbur Group
Elderplan, Inc.
Medicare Payment Coalition for Frail Beneficiaries
Nat'l Chronic Care Consortium

WILCHER, LaJuana S.

1875 Connecticut Ave. NW
Suite 1200
Washington, DC 20009-5728
Tel: (202)986-8040
Fax: (202)986-8102
Registered: LDA
EMail: lwilcher@llgm.com
Assistant Administrator for Water (1989-93), Assistant to the Deputy Administrator (1985-86), and Special Assistant to the General Counsel (1983-85), Environmental Protection Agency. Special Assistant to the General Counsel, Department of Agriculture, 1983.

Employers
LeBoeuf, Lamb, Greene & MacRae L.L.P. (Partner)

Clients Represented

On Behalf of LeBoeuf, Lamb, Greene & MacRae L.L.P.
Lloyd's of London
Water Environment Research Foundation

WILCOTS, Rosalyn L.

1615 M St. NW
Washington, DC 20419
Tel: (202)653-7171
Fax: (202)653-7130

Employers
Merit Systems Protection Board (Legislative Counsel)

WILCOX, Jr., James B.

1120 20th St. NW
Suite 700 North
Washington, DC 20036-3406
Tel: (202)973-1200
Fax: (202)973-1212

Employers
Hall, Estill, Hardwick, Gable, Golden & Nelson (Partner)

WILCOX, Laura A.

One Dupont Circle NW
Suite 320
Washington, DC 20036
Tel: (202)466-7230
Fax: (202)466-7238
EMail: lwilcox@cic.nche.edu

Employers
Council of Independent Colleges (Director, Communications)

WILCOX, Jr., Philip C.

1761 N St. NW
Washington, DC 20036
Tel: (202)835-3650
Fax: (202)835-3651
EMail: pcwilcox@fmep.org
Retired Foreign Service Officer; Chief of Mission and U.S. Consul General, Jerusalem, Israel (1988-91).

Employers
Foundation for Middle East Peace (President)

WILCZYNSKI, Ed

12850 Middlebrook Rd.
Suite 205
Germantown, MD 20874
Tel: (301)528-1960

Employers
Waste Policy Institute (Operations Manager)

WILD, Brian

1615 H St. NW
Washington, DC 20062-2000
Tel: (202)659-6000
Fax: (202)463-5836

Employers
Chamber of Commerce of the U.S.A. (Associate Director, Congressional and Public Affairs)

WILD, David D.

1200 New Hampshire Ave. NW
Suite 800
Washington, DC 20036-6802
Tel: (202)776-2000
Fax: (202)776-2222
EMail: dwild@dlalaw.com

Employers
Dow, Lohnes & Albertson, PLLC (Member)

WILD, Emily

325 Seventh St. NW
Suite 1100
Washington, DC 20004-2802
Tel: (202)783-7971
Fax: (202)737-2849

Employers
Nat'l Retail Federation (Grassroots Coordinator)

WILDER, James

444 N. Capitol St. NW
Suite 434
Washington, DC 20001
Tel: (202)393-4478
Fax: (202)393-7644

Employers
Kettering Foundation (Director, External Affairs)

WILDER, Thomas

1100 17th St. NW
Seventh Floor
Washington, DC 20036
Tel: (202)223-8196
Fax: (202)872-1948
Registered: LDA

Employers
American Academy of Actuaries (Director, Public Policy)

WILDEROTTER, James A.

51 Louisiana Ave. NW
Washington, DC 20001
Tel: (202)879-3939
Fax: (202)626-1700
EMail: jwilderotter@jonesday.com
General Counsel, Energy Research and Development Administration, 1976-77. Associate Counsel to the President, The White House, 1975-76. Associate Deputy Attorney General, Department of Justice, 1974-75). Executive Assistant to the Secretary, Department of Housing and Urban Development, 1973-74. Special Assistant to the Undersecretary, Department of Commerce, 1971-73.

Employers
Jones, Day, Reavis & Pogue (Partner)

WILDMAN, Sloane

607 14th St. NW
Suite 700
Washington, DC 20005-2011
Tel: (202)628-6600
Fax: (202)434-1690

Employers
Perkins Coie LLP (Associate)

Clients Represented
On Behalf of Perkins Coie LLP
Beyond BAT Group

WILDSMITH, IV, Thomas F.

1201 F St. NW
Suite 500
Washington, DC 20004
Tel: (202)824-1600
Fax: (202)824-1651
Registered: LDA

Employers
Health Insurance Ass'n of America (Policy Research Actuary, Policy Development and Research)

WILES, Richard

1718 Connecticut Ave. NW
Suite 600
Washington, DC 20009
Tel: (202)667-6982
Fax: (202)232-2592

Employers
Environmental Working Group (V. President)

WILEY, Douglas S.

1909 K St. NW
Suite 800
Washington, DC 20006
Tel: (202)715-3711
Fax: (202)715-3725
Registered: LDA
EMail: doug.wiley@usa.alcatel.com
Senior Legislative Assistant to Rep. Thomas Bliley, Jr. (R-VA), 1987-92.

Employers
Alcatel USA (Director, Government Relations, Alcatel Americas)

WILEY, Peter

444 N. Capitol St. NW
Suite 267
Washington, DC 20001-1512
EMail: pwiley@nga.org
Tel: (202)624-5300
Fax: (202)624-5313

Employers
Nat'l Governors' Ass'n (Director of State Services)

WILEY, Richard E.

1776 K St. NW
Washington, DC 20006
Tel: (202)719-7000
Fax: (202)719-7049
Registered: LDA
Chairman (1974-77), Commissioner (1972-74) and General Counsel (1970-72), Federal Communications Commission.

Employers
Wiley, Rein & Fielding (Partner)

Clients Represented
On Behalf of Wiley, Rein & Fielding
A. H. Belo Corp.
Gannett Co., Inc.
Nat'l Religious Broadcasters
Newspaper Ass'n of America

WILHEIM, William B.

3000 K St. NW
Suite 300
Washington, DC 20007
Tel: (202)424-7500
Fax: (202)424-7643
Registered: LDA

Employers
Swidler Berlin Shereff Friedman, LLP (Associate)

WILHELM, Anthony

950 18th St. NW
Washington, DC 20006
Tel: (202)638-5770
Fax: (202)638-5771

Employers
Benton Foundation/Communications Policy Project (Director, Communications Policy Project)

WILHELM, John W.

1219 28th St. NW
Washington, DC 20007
Tel: (202)393-4373
Fax: (202)965-0868

Employers
Hotel Employees and Restaurant Employees Internat'l Union (President)

WILKENFELD, Judy

1707 L St. NW
Suite 800
Washington, DC 20036
Tel: (202)296-5469
Fax: (202)296-5427

Employers
Campaign for Tobacco-Free Kids

WILKERSON, Carl B.

1001 Pennsylvania Ave. NW
Washington, DC 20004-2599
Tel: (202)624-2000
Fax: (202)624-2319

Employers
American Council of Life Insurers (Chief Counsel, Securities)

WILKES, Alphie W.

1341 Connecticut Ave. NW
Third Floor
Washington, DC 20036
Tel: (202)862-3900
Fax: (202)862-5500

Employers
Scribe Consulting & Communications (Director)

WILKES, Ann P.

1711 King St.
Suite One
Alexandria, VA 22314
EMail: awilkes@sfa.org
Tel: (703)836-4500
Fax: (703)836-8262

Employers
Snack Food Ass'n (V. President, Communications)

WILKINS, Timothy C.

1300 Wilson Blvd.
Arlington, VA 22209
Tel: (703)741-5942
Fax: (703)741-6097
Registered: LDA
EMail: tim_wilkins@americanchemistry.com

Employers
American Chemistry Council (Director, Grassroots)

WILKINS, William J.

2445 M St. NW
Washington, DC 20037-1420
Tel: (202)663-6000
Fax: (202)663-6363
Registered: LDA, FARA
EMail: bwilkins@wilmer.com
Staff Director and Chief Counsel (1987-88) and Staff Member (1981-88), Senate Finance Committee.

Employers
Wilmer, Cutler & Pickering (Partner)

Clients Represented
On Behalf of Wilmer, Cutler & Pickering
AutoNation, Inc.
Best Foods
The Boeing Co.
Corporate Property Investors
McDonald's Corp.
PepsiCo, Inc.
Republic Industries, Inc.

WILKINS, William M.

1726 M St. NW
Suite 401
Washington, DC 20036
EMail: wilkins@tripnet.org
Tel: (202)466-6706
Fax: (202)785-4722

Employers
The Road Information Program (TRIP) (Exec. Director)

WILKINSON, Andrea

409 Ninth St. NW
Suite 610 South
Washington, DC 20004
Tel: (202)737-2594
Fax: (202)737-0264
Registered: LDA
EMail: WilkinsonAL@arlaw.com
Staff Assistant to Senator John Breaux (D-LA), 1993-94.

Employers
Adams and Reese LLP (Government Relations Director)

Clients Represented
On Behalf of Adams and Reese LLP
Baton Rouge, Louisiana, City of
Iberville Parish
Louisiana Credit Union Ass'n
Louisiana State University
New Orleans, Louisiana, Regional Transit Authority of
South Louisiana, Port of
Unisys Corp.

WILKINSON, CPA, Catherine W.

1330 Connecticut Ave. NW
Washington, DC 20036-1795
Tel: (202)429-3000
Fax: (202)429-3902
Registered: LDA
EMail: cwilkins@steptoe.com

Employers
Steptoe & Johnson LLP (Partner)

Clients Represented
On Behalf of Steptoe & Johnson LLP
Burlington Northern Santa Fe Railway

WILKINSON, Cynthia M.

434 New Jersey Ave. SE
Washington, DC 20003
Tel: (202)488-2800
Fax: (202)488-3150
Registered: LDA
Counsel, House Committee on Commerce, 1995-97. Minority Chief Counsel (1992-94), Majority Chief Counsel, Subcommittee on Merchant Marine (1989-92), and Research Assistant, Subcommittee on Coast Guard and Navigation (1979-81), House Committee on Merchant Marine and Fisheries. Executive Assistant to Rep. Mario Biaggi (D-TX), 1971-79. Staff Assistant to Rep. Jack Brooks (D-TX), 1970-71.

Employers
Twenty-First Century Group (President and General Counsel)

Clients Represented
On Behalf of Twenty-First Century Group
Electronic Industries Alliance
Longhorn Pipeline
Personal Communications Industry Ass'n (PCIA)
SBC Communications Inc.
Taxpayers Against Fraud, The False Claims Legal Center
Telecommunications Industry Ass'n
Verizon Communications

WILKINSON, E. John

1101 30th St. NW
Suite 500
Washington, DC 20007
Tel: (202)293-0635
Fax: (202)659-3119
Registered: LDA

Employers
Vulcan Chemicals (Director, Government Affairs)

WILKINSON, Jr., Edward A.

2051 Mercator Dr.
Reston, VA 22091
Tel: (703)264-5644
Fax: (703)264-5715

Employers
Intergraph Corp. Federal Systems Division (Treasurer, Intergraph Corp. PAC)

WILKINSON, Laura A.

607 14th St. NW
Washington, DC 20005
Tel: (202)434-0700
Fax: (202)912-6000
EMail: wilkinsl@rw.com
Former Deputy Assistant Director, Bureau of Competition, Federal Trade Commission.

Employers
Rogers & Wells (Of Counsel)

WILKINSON, Paul

400 N. Capitol St. NW
Washington, DC 20001
EMail: pwilkinson@aga.org
Tel: (202)824-7125
Fax: (202)824-7087

Employers
American Gas Ass'n (V. President, Policy and Analysis)

WILL, Mari Maseng

1501 M St. NW
Suite 700
Washington, DC 20005
Tel: (202)879-4109
Fax: (202)638-1976
Registered: FARA

Employers
Maseng Communications (Principal)

Clients Represented
On Behalf of Maseng Communications
Japan Automobile Manufacturers Ass'n

WILL, Mary Beth

1010 Duke St.
Alexandria, VA 22314-3589
Tel: (703)684-5700
Fax: (703)684-6321
Registered: LDA

Employers
American Ass'n of Port Authorities (Representative, Government Relations)

WILL, Robert P.

1015 18th St. NW
Suite 600
Washington, DC 20036
Tel: (202)429-4344
Fax: (202)429-4342
Registered: LDA

Employers
Will and Carlson, Inc.

Clients Represented
On Behalf of Will and Carlson, Inc.
Animas-La Plata Water Conservancy District
Clark County Regional Flood Control District
Eastern Municipal Water District
Garrison Diversion Conservancy District
Kennedy/Jenks Consultants
The Metropolitan Water District of Southern California
Salem, Oregon, City of
Six Agency Committee
Southwest Water Conservation District of Colorado
Western Coalition of Arid States

WILLARD, Timothy

1350 I St. NW
Suite 300
Washington, DC 20005
Tel: (202)639-5900
Fax: (202)639-5932

Employers
Nat'l Food Processors Ass'n (V. President, Communications)

WILLCOX, Breckinridge L.

1050 Connecticut Ave. NW
Washington, DC 20036-5339
Tel: (202)857-6000
Fax: (202)857-6395
Worked for the Department of Justice

Employers
Arent Fox Kintner Plotkin & Kahn, PLLC (Member)

WILLENS, Todd

8607 Westwood Center Dr.
Vienna, VA 22182
Tel: (703)448-4000
Fax: (703)448-4100
Former Legislative Director to Rep. Richard W. Pombo (R-CA). Also served as Aide to Rep. Jerry Lewis (R-CA).

Employers
Feld Entertainment Inc. (V. President, Government Relations)

WILLER, Jay D.

1116 E St. SE
Washington, DC 20003
Tel: (202)547-7288
Fax: (202)547-1454
Registered: LDA
EMail: Willer@igt.org

Employers
Gas Technology Institute (Director, Washington Operations)

WILLHITE, Deborah K.

475 L'Enfant Plaza SW
MS: 10804
Washington, DC 20260
EMail: willhit@email.usps.gov
Tel: (202)268-2506
Fax: (202)268-2503

Employers
United States Postal Service (Senior V. President, Government Relations)

WILLI, Mary Carroll

2100 L St. NW
Washington, DC 20037
EMail: mcwilli@cmpa.com
Tel: (202)223-2942
Fax: (202)872-4014

Employers
Center for Media and Public Affairs (Director, Political Studies)

WILLIAMS, Alvin

2029 P St. NW
Suite 202
Washington, DC 20036
Tel: (202)785-9619
Fax: (202)785-9621

Employers
Black America's Political Action Committee (Exec. Director)

WILLIAMS, Andrea

1250 Connecticut Ave. NW
Suite 800
Washington, DC 20036
Tel: (202)785-0081
Fax: (202)785-0721
Registered: LDA

Employers
Cellular Telecommunications and Internet Ass'n (Assistant General Counsel)

WILLIAMS, Ann

1200 17th St. NW
Washington, DC 20036-3097
Tel: (202)331-5900
Fax: (202)973-5373

Employers
Nat'l Restaurant Ass'n (Manager, Political Affairs)

WILLIAMS, USA (Ret.), Lt. Gen. Arthur E.

1225 I St. NW
Suite 500
Washington, DC 20005
Tel: (202)312-2005
Fax: (202)289-8683
Registered: LDA
EMail: dawsonassociates@worldnet.att.net
Former Commanding General and Chief of Engineers, Director of Civil Works, and Division Engineer (Lower Mississippi River and the Pacific Ocean) , US Army Corps of Engineers, Department of the Army.

Employers
Dawson & Associates, Inc. (Senior Advisor)

Clients Represented
On Behalf of Dawson & Associates, Inc.
AgriPartners
Florida Citrus Mutual
Florida Farm Bureau
Florida Sugar Cane League, Inc.
Sugar Cane Growers Cooperative of Florida

WILLIAMS, Ashley K.

1250 H St. NW
Suite 901
Washington, DC 20005
Tel: (202)463-8162
Fax: (202)463-8155
Registered: LDA

Employers
Kinder & Associates, Inc. (Associate)

Clients Represented
On Behalf of Kinder & Associates, Inc.
Self-Insurance Institute of America, Inc.

WILLIAMS, Boyce C.

2010 Massachusetts Ave. NW
Suite 500
Washington, DC 20036-1023
EMail: boyce@ncate.org
Tel: (202)466-7496
Fax: (202)296-6620

Employers
Nat'l Council for Accreditation of Teacher Education (V. President, Institutional Relations)

WILLIAMS, Brian

1150 Connecticut Ave. NW
Suite 810
Washington, DC 20036
EMail: brianw@heart.org
Tel: (202)785-7900
Fax: (202)785-7950

Employers
American Heart Ass'n (Government Relations Manager)

WILLIAMS, Carroll L.

1608 K St. NW
Washington, DC 20006
Tel: (202)861-2700
Fax: (202)861-2786
Registered: LDA

Employers
American Legion (Director, National Veterans Affairs Commission)

WILLIAMS, Christine K.

701 Pennsylvania Ave. NW
Suite 650
Washington, DC 20004
EMail: cwillia5@cancer.org
Tel: (202)661-5720
Fax: (202)661-5750
Registered: LDA

Employers
American Cancer Soc. (Manager, Federal Government Affairs)

WILLIAMS, Christopher

1250 24th St. NW
Washington, DC 20037
Tel: (202)293-4800
Fax: (202)293-9211
Registered: LDA

Employers
World Wildlife Fund (Program Officer, U.S. Program)

WILLIAMS, Crystal

918 F St. NW
Washington, DC 20004-1400
Tel: (202)216-2400
Fax: (202)371-9449

Employers
American Immigration Lawyers Ass'n (Director, Liaison and Information)

WILLIAMS, David

1301 Connecticut Ave. NW
Fourth Floor
Washington, DC 20036
Tel: (202)467-5300
Fax: (202)467-4253

Employers
Citizens Against Government Waste (Director, Research)

WILLIAMS, Deanne R.

818 Connecticut Ave. NW
Suite 900
Washington, DC 20006
EMail: dwilliam@acnm.org
Tel: (202)728-9860
Fax: (202)728-9897

Employers
American College of Nurse-Midwives (Exec. Director)

WILLIAMS, Eddie N.

1090 Vermont Ave. NW
Suite 1100
Washington, DC 20005-4961
Tel: (202)789-3500
Fax: (202)789-6390

Employers
Joint Center for Political and Economic Studies (President)

WILLIAMS, Evelyn

10801 Rockville Pike
Rockville, MD 20852
Tel: (301)897-5700
Fax: (301)571-0457
Registered: LDA

Employers
American Speech, Language, and Hearing Ass'n

WILLIAMS, Floyd L.

1111 Constitution Ave. NW
Room 3241
Washington, DC 20224
EMail: floyd.williams@irs.gov
Tel: (202)622-3720
Fax: (202)622-4733
Deputy Assistant Secretary for Legislative Affairs (1995-96) and Senior Tax Advisor for Public and Legislative Affairs (1993-95), Department of the Treasury. Legislative Attorney, Joint Committee on Taxation, 1977-83.

Employers
Department of Treasury - Internal Revenue Service (National Director for Legislative Affairs)

WILLIAMS, Jr., George H.

2175 K St. NW
Fifth Floor
Washington, DC 20037
Tel: (202)789-1100
Fax: (202)289-3928
Registered: FARA
Office of the Solicitor, Federal Energy Regulatory Commission, 1979-82. Attorney, Federal Power Commission, 1973-78.

Employers
Cameron McKenna (Partner)

Clients Represented
On Behalf of Cameron McKenna
Hydro-Quebec

WILLIAMS, George P.

1001 G St. NW
Sixth Floor East
Washington, DC 20001-4545
EMail: gwilliams@sempra.com
Tel: (202)662-1701
Fax: (202)293-2887
Registered: LDA

Employers
Sempra Energy (Director, Government Affairs)

WILLIAMS, H. Newton

1530 Wilson Blvd.
Suite 210
Arlington, VA 22209
EMail: HNWilliams@celanese.com
Tel: (703)358-2890
Fax: (703)358-9786
Registered: LDA

Employers
Celanese Government Relations Office (V. President, Government Relations)

WILLIAMS, Harding deC.

888 17th St. NW
Suite 312
Washington, DC 20006
EMail: afshc@ibm.net
Tel: (202)223-6575
Fax: (202)331-3836

Employers
Ass'n of Financial Services Holding Companies (Counsel)

WILLIAMS, Hubert

1201 Connecticut Ave. NW
Suite 200
Washington, DC 20036-2636
Tel: (202)833-1460
Fax: (202)659-9149

Employers
Police Foundation (President)

WILLIAMS, J. D.

1155 21st St. NW
Suite 300
Washington, DC 20036
Tel: (202)659-8201
Fax: (202)659-5249
Registered: LDA
Captain, Judge Advocate General Corps, U.S. Army Reserve, 1962-65. Assistant to Senator Robert Kerr (D-OK), 1959-61.

Employers
Williams & Jensen, P.C.

Clients Represented
On Behalf of Williams & Jensen, P.C.
Fannie Mae
First Union Corp.
Norfolk Southern Corp.
Owens-Illinois, Inc.
USAA - United Services Automobile Ass'n

WILLIAMS, II, James A

1776 I St. NW
Suite 275
Washington, DC 20006
Tel: (202)530-7300
Fax: (202)530-7350
Registered: LDA

Employers
Entergy Services, Inc. (Senior Research Legislative Analyst)

WILLIAMS, James A.

1750 New York Ave. NW
Washington, DC 20006
Tel: (202)637-0700
Fax: (202)637-0771
Registered: LDA

Employers
Internat'l Union of Painters and Allied Trades (General Secretary-Treasurer)

WILLIAMS, Jr., James M.

10907 Forestgate Pl.
Glen Dale, MD 20769
Tel: (301)809-9052
Fax: (301)809-4368
Registered: LDA

Employers
Self-employed as an independent consultant.

Clients Represented
As an independent consultant
Nat'l Ass'n of Minority Automobile Dealers

WILLIAMS, Janice

200 Constitution Ave. NW
Room S-1325
Washington, DC 20210
EMail: williams-janice@dol.gov
Tel: (202)693-4600
Fax: (202)693-4642

Employers
Department of Labor (Staff Assistant, Office of Congressional Intergovernmental Affairs)

WILLIAMS, Jimmie L.

1101 Pennsylvania Ave. NW
Suite 700
Washington, DC 20004
EMail: jimmie_williams@countrywide.com
Tel: (202)756-7755
Fax: (202)756-7505
Registered: LDA

Employers
Countrywide Home Loans, Inc. (V. President, Legislative Affairs)

WILLIAMS, John F.

421 Aviation Way
Frederick, MD 21701
EMail: john.williams@aopa.org
Tel: (301)695-2000
Fax: (301)695-2375
Registered: LDA

Employers
Aircraft Owners and Pilots Ass'n (Manager, AOPA PAC)

WILLIAMS, John R.

One Prince St.
Alexandria, VA 22314-3357
EMail: jwilliams@entnet.org
Tel: (703)836-4444
Fax: (703)683-5100
Registered: LDA

Employers
American Academy of Otolaryngology-Head and Neck Surgery (Assistant Director, Congressional Affairs, Health Policy and Government Affairs)

WILLIAMS, Joyce

8725 John J. Kingman Rd.
Suite 2533
Ft. Belvoir, VA 22060-6221
Tel: (703)767-6178
Fax: (703)767-6312

Employers
Department of Defense - Defense Logistics Agency (Chief, Congressional Affairs Division)

WILLIAMS, Karen

1894 Preston White Dr.
Reston, VA 20191
Tel: (703)620-6390
Fax: (703)476-0904

Employers
Nat'l Pharmaceutical Council (President)

WILLIAMS, Karen Hastie

1001 Pennsylvania Ave. NW
Suite 1100
Washington, DC 20004-2595
Tel: (202)624-2500
Fax: (202)628-5116
Registered: LDA
Administrator, Office of Federal Procurement Policy, Office of Management and Budget, 1980-81. Chief Counsel, Senate Committee on the Budget, 1977-80. Law Clerk to Justice Thurgood Marshall, U.S. Supreme Court, 1974-75, and to Judge Robinson, U.S. Court of Appeals, District of Columbia Circuit, 1973-74.

Employers
Crowell & Moring LLP (Partner)

Clients Represented
On Behalf of Crowell & Moring LLP
Coalition for Fair Remedies
Committee on Federal Procurement of Architectural and Engineering Services
Helicopter Ass'n Internat'l
Kenya Bombing Families
Raytheon Co.
Teledyne Controls, Inc.
United Technologies Corp.
Women Business Owners Corp. Inc.
The Wyatt Co.

WILLIAMS, Kaye F.

1140 Connecticut Ave. NW
Suite 510
Washington, DC 20036
Tel: (202)293-1140
Fax: (202)293-1658
Registered: LDA

Employers
Prudential Insurance Co. of America (V. President, Government Relations)

WILLIAMS, Kelly

1771 N St. NW
Washington, DC 20036-2891
Tel: (202)429-5346
Fax: (202)775-4981

Employers
Nat'l Ass'n of Broadcasters (Director, Engineering, Science, and Technology)

WILLIAMS, Kevin M.

2200 Mill Rd.
Suite 600
Alexandria, VA 22314
Tel: (703)838-1806
Fax: (703)684-8143

Employers
Distribution and LTL Carriers Ass'n (President and Chief Exec. Officer)

WILLIAMS, Kimberly A.

1500 K St. NW
Suite 650
Washington, DC 20005
Tel: (202)715-1000
Fax: (202)715-1001

Employers
GlaxoSmithKline (Federal Government Relations)

WILLIAMS, Lawrence H.

1730 Rhode Island Ave. NW
Suite 1000
Washington, DC 20036
EMail: larry@teledesic.com
Tel: (202)721-0960
Fax: (202)296-8953
Registered: LDA

Employers
Teledesic Corp. (V. President, International and Government Affairs)

WILLIAMS, Leonard B.

1133 15th St. NW
Suite 640
Washington, DC 20005
Tel: (202)466-2520
Fax: (202)296-4419
Registered: LDA

Employers
American Logistics Ass'n (V. President, Legislative Affairs)

WILLIAMS, Liz

214 Massachusetts Ave. NE
Washington, DC 20002
Tel: (202)546-4400
Fax: (202)546-8328

Employers
Heritage Foundation (Deputy Director, House Relations)

WILLIAMS, Lucinda L.

1332 Independence Ave. SE
Washington, DC 20003-2365
Tel: (202)543-4600

Employers
Morgan Casner Associates, Inc. (Senior Associate)

WILLIAMS, Hon. Lyle

1450 G St. NW
Suite 210
Washington, DC 20005
Tel: (202)383-0090
Fax: (202)383-0093
Member, U.S. House of Representatives (R-OH), 1979-85.

Employers
Internat'l Capital Strategies (V. President)

WILLIAMS, Lynnette Johnson

818 Connecticut Ave. NW
Second Floor
Washington, DC 20006
Tel: (202)289-2001
Fax: (202)289-1327

Former Deputy Assistant Secretary of Public Affairs, Department of Health and Human Services. Served as Press Secretary to Senators Thad Cochran (R-MS) and Carol Moseley-Braun (D-IL).

Employers
Strat@Comm (Strategic Communications Counselors) (V. President)

WILLIAMS, M. Darrell

1130 17th St. NW
Washington, DC 20036-4677
EMail: mdarrell@msn.com
Tel: (202)463-2669
Fax: (202)857-0135

Employers
Nat'l Mining Ass'n (AudioVisual Services)

WILLIAMS, Mantill

1440 New York Ave. NW
Suite 200
Washington, DC 20005
Tel: (202)942-2050
Fax: (202)783-4798

Employers
American Automobile Ass'n (Director, Washington Public Relations)

WILLIAMS, Marcus P.

1301 K St. NW
Suite 1200-West Tower
Washington, DC 20005-3307
EMail: marcwill@us.ibm.com
Tel: (202)515-5000

Employers
Internat'l Business Machines Corp. (Counsel, Governmental Programs)

WILLIAMS, Matthew

601 F St. NW
Washington, DC 20004
Tel: (202)661-5000
Fax: (202)661-5108

Employers
Washington Sports & Entertainment, L.P. (V. President, Communications)

WILLIAMS, Matthew

426 C St. NE
Washington, DC 20002
Tel: (202)544-1880
Fax: (202)543-2565
Registered: LDA

Employers
Capitol Associates, Inc.

Clients Represented

On Behalf of Capitol Associates, Inc.
American Soc. of Radiologic Technologists
DeBrunner and Associates, Inc.
Friends of CDC
Healthcare Billing and Management Ass'n
Joint Council of Allergy, Asthma and Immunology
Nat'l Ass'n of Pediatric Nurse Associates and Practitioners
Nat'l Ass'n of Rural Health Clinics

WILLIAMS, Mele

1612 K St. NW
Suite 401
Washington, DC 20006
Tel: (202)822-1333

Employers
League of American Bicyclists (Director, Government Relations)

WILLIAMS, Michael A.

P.O. Box 1096
McLean, VA 22101-1096
Tel: (703)821-8700
Fax: (703)827-7761
Registered: LDA

Employers
Stephens Law Firm (Associate Attorney)

Clients Represented

On Behalf of Stephens Law Firm
American Rental Ass'n

WILLIAMS, Michael E.

410 First St. SE
Washington, DC 20003
Tel: (202)651-2560
Fax: (202)651-2577
Registered: LDA

Employers
Nat'l Rifle Ass'n Institute for Legislative Action (Federal Liaison)
Nat'l Rifle Ass'n of America (Federal Liaison)

WILLIAMS, Michael W.

1399 New York Ave. NW
Eighth Floor
Washington, DC 20005-4711
EMail: mwilliams@bondmarkets.com
Tel: (202)434-8400
Fax: (202)434-8456

Former Special Advisor and Staff Director, Office of Legislative Affairs, Executive Office of the President, The White House.

Employers
The Bond Market Ass'n (V. President, Legislative Affairs)

WILLIAMS, Michelle

4600 Sangamore Rd.
Bethesda, MD 20816-5003
Tel: (301)227-5800

Employers
Department of Defense - Nat'l Imagery and Mapping Agency (Director, Congressional Affairs Office)

WILLIAMS, Nancy

517 C St. NE
Washington, DC 20002
Tel: (202)543-4455
Fax: (202)543-4586
Registered: LDA

Counsel, Subcommittee on Energy and Power, House Committee on Energy, 1982-86. Deputy Assistant General Counsel, Federal Energy Regulatory Commission, 1979-80. Attorney, Federal Energy Administration, Department of Energy, 1976-77.

Employers
Schramm, Williams & Associates, Inc.

Clients Represented

On Behalf of Schramm, Williams & Associates, Inc.
Alliance of Western Milk Producers
California Ass'n of Winegrape Growers
Kern County Water Agency
Kern River Watermaster
San Joaquin River Exchange Contractors Water Authority
U.S. Citrus Science Council
Western Growers Ass'n
Western Pistachio Ass'n
Winegrape Growers of America

WILLIAMS, Patricia Randolph

12251 Tech Rd.
Silver Spring, MD 20904
Tel: (301)622-1900
Fax: (301)236-9320
Registered: LDA

Employers
Internat'l Fabricare Institute (V. President, Government Affairs)

WILLIAMS, Patrick H.

1620 L St. NW
Suite 1210
Washington, DC 20036
Tel: (202)721-9134
Fax: (202)955-6070
Registered: LDA

Employers
Cormac Group, LLP

Clients Represented

On Behalf of Cormac Group, LLP
PanAmSat Corp.

WILLIAMS, Robert E.

1015 15th St. NW
Suite 1200
Washington, DC 20005
Tel: (202)789-8600
Fax: (202)789-1708

Supervisory Attorney (1970-72) and Trial Attorney (1967-70), Office of General Counsel, Division of Litigation, Appellate Court Branch, National Labor Relations Board.

Employers
McGuiness Norris & Williams, LLP (Partner)

WILLIAMS, Robert G.

8403 Arlington Blvd.
Suite 100
Fairfax, VA 22031
EMail: williams@interfacinc.com
Tel: (703)876-6800
Fax: (703)876-0515

Employers
Interface Inc. (V. President)

Clients Represented

On Behalf of Interface Inc.
Airguard Industries
Everpure
General Cable Industries, Inc.
Maytag Corp.
Rheem Water Heaters
Scot Pump
USF Surface Preparation

WILLIAMS, Robin L.

1300 Wilson Blvd.
Suite 1220
Arlington, VA 22209
Tel: (703)741-5882
Fax: (703)741-5884
Registered: LDA

Employers
Rohm and Haas Co. (Director, State Government Relations)

WILLIAMS, Roger J.

1722 N St. NW
Washington, DC 20036
EMail: rjwilliams@accet.org
Tel: (202)955-1113
Fax: (202)955-1118

Employers
Accrediting Council for Continuing Education & Training (Exec. Director)

WILLIAMS, Roger L.

12601 Twinbrook Pkwy.
Rockville, MD 20852
EMail: rlw@usp.org
Tel: (301)881-0666

Employers
United States Pharmacopeial Convention (Exec. V. President)

WILLIAMS, Rudolph M.

1012 10th St. NW
Washington, DC 20001
Tel: (202)347-1895
Fax: (202)842-3293

Employers
Nat'l Medical Ass'n (Exec. Director)

WILLIAMS, Scott

1501 M St. NW
Suite 600
Washington, DC 20005-1710
EMail: swilliams@bsmg.com
Tel: (202)739-0200
Fax: (202)659-8287
Registered: FARA

Employers
BSMG Worldwide (Senior Managing Director)

WILLIAMS, Stockton

415 Second St. NE
Second Floor
Washington, DC 20002
Tel: (202)543-4599
Ext: 15
Fax: (202)543-8130
Registered: LDA
EMail: swilliams2@enterprisefoundation.org

Employers
The Enterprise Foundation (Senior Legislative and Policy Advisor)

WILLIAMS, Susan J.

601 13th St. NW
Suite 900 South
Washington, DC 20005
Tel: (202)783-5588
Fax: (202)783-5595
Registered: LDA

Former Assistant Secretary for Congressional and Governmental Affairs, U.S. Department of Transportation.

Employers
Bracy Williams & Co. (President)

Clients Represented

On Behalf of Bracy Williams & Co.

Allied Pilots Ass'n
American Institute for Foreign Studies
Atlanta, Georgia, City of
College Parents of America
Council on Internat'l Educational Exchange
Energy Absorption Systems, Inc.
FedEx Pilots Ass'n
Fort Worth Transportation Authority
Fort Worth, Texas, City of
Girl Scouts of the U.S.A. - Washington Office
MedStar Health
Nassif & Associates
Nat'l Ass'n for Girls and Women in Sport
Tucson, Arizona, City of
Women's Sports Foundation
YWCA of the USA

WILLIAMS, T. Raymond

600 13th St. NW
Washington, DC 20005-3096
Tel: (202)756-8140
Fax: (202)756-8087
Registered: LDA
EMail: rwilliams@mwe.com
Former Counsel, Army and Air Force Exchange Service, Department of Defense.

Employers

McDermott, Will and Emery (Partner)

Clients Represented

On Behalf of McDermott, Will and Emery

Stroh Brewing Co.

WILLIAMS, Timothy

601 Wythe St.
Alexandria, VA 22314-1994
Tel: (703)684-2400
Fax: (703)684-2492
EMail: twilliams@wef.org

Employers

Water Environment Federation (Director, Government Affairs)
Water Quality 2000 (Contact)

WILLIAMS, Tom

1800 N. Kent St.
Suite 1120
Arlington, VA 22209
Tel: (703)525-6300
Fax: (703)525-4610

Employers

The Conservation Fund (Federal Project Coordinator)

WILLIAMS, Valerie

1631 Prince St.
Alexandria, VA 22314-2818
Tel: (703)836-2222
Fax: (703)836-8015
Registered: LDA

Employers

Nat'l Ass'n for College Admission Counseling (Assistant Director, Government Relations)

WILLIAMS, Verna

11 Dupont Circle NW
Suite 800
Washington, DC 20036
EMail: vwilliams@nwlc.org
Tel: (202)588-5180
Fax: (202)588-5185

Employers

Nat'l Women's Law Center (V. President and Director, Educational Opportunities)

WILLIAMS, Wade S.

4325 Forbes Blvd.
Lanham, MD 20706
Tel: (301)459-2590
Fax: (301)459-2827
Registered: LDA

Employers

Vocus Government Relations (Director, Government Affairs)

WILLIAMS, Jr., Wesley S.

1201 Pennsylvania Ave. NW
Washington, DC 20004-2401
Tel: (202)662-6000
Fax: (202)662-6291
Registered: LDA
EMail: wwilliams@cov.com

Employers

Covington & Burling (Partner)

WILLIAMSON, Darla

515 King St.
Suite 420
Alexandria, VA 22314-3103
Tel: (703)684-5570
Fax: (703)684-6048

Employers

CLARION Management Resources, Inc.
Closure Manufacturers Ass'n (V. President)

Clients Represented

On Behalf of CLARION Management Resources, Inc.

Closure Manufacturers Ass'n

WILLIAMSON, David

4245 N. Fairfax Dr.
Suite 100
Arlington, VA 20003-1606
EMail: dwilliamson@tnc.org
Tel: (703)841-8741
Fax: (703)841-8796

Employers

The Nature Conservancy (Director, Communications)

WILLIAMSON, Edwin D.

1701 Pennsylvania Ave. NW
Suite 800
Washington, DC 20006
Tel: (202)956-7500
Fax: (202)293-6330
Registered: LDA

Employers

Sullivan & Cromwell (Partner)

WILLIAMSON, Richard S.

1909 K St. NW
Washington, DC 20006
Tel: (202)263-3000
Fax: (202)263-3300
Registered: LDA

Employers

Mayer, Brown & Platt (Partner)

Clients Represented

On Behalf of Mayer, Brown & Platt

Ace Ltd.
ED&F Man Inc.
Federal Home Loan Bank of Chicago
Oracle Corp.

WILLIAMSON, Jr., Thomas S.

1201 Pennsylvania Ave. NW
Washington, DC 20004-2401
Tel: (202)662-6000
Fax: (202)662-6291
EMail: twilliamson@cov.com
Solicitor, Mine Safety and Health Administration, Department of Labor, 1993-96. Deputy Inspector General, Department of Energy, 1978-81.

Employers

Covington & Burling (Partner)

WILLIS, F. Michael

2120 L St. NW
Suite 700
Washington, DC 20037
Tel: (202)822-8282
Fax: (202)296-8834
Registered: LDA
EMail: mwillis@hsdwdc.com

Employers

Hobbs, Straus, Dean and Walker, LLP (Associate)

Clients Represented

On Behalf of Hobbs, Straus, Dean and Walker, LLP

Bristol Bay Area Health Corp.
Norton Sound Health Corp.

WILLIS, Gene R.

5535 Hempstead Way
Springfield, VA 22151
Tel: (703)750-1342
Fax: (703)354-4380
Registered: LDA
EMail: gwillis@naus.org

Employers

Nat'l Ass'n for Uniformed Services (Legislative Director)

WILLIS, Gregory

513 Capitol Court NE
Suite 100
Washington, DC 20002
Tel: (202)547-9505
Fax: (202)478-0279
Registered: LDA

Employers

Mattox Woolfolk, LLC

Clients Represented

On Behalf of Mattox Woolfolk, LLC

Voices, Inc.

WILLIS, JoAnn V.

2550 M St. NW
Washington, DC 20037-1350
Tel: (202)457-6000
Fax: (202)457-6315
Registered: LDA
EMail: jwillis@pattonboggs.com
Legislative Assistant to Senator Dave Durenberger (R-MN), 1993-94. Health Policy Advisor to Rep. J. Alex McMillan (R-NC), 1991-93. Health Issues Fellow to Rep. Nancy Johnson (R-CT) (1990-91), Manager (1980-90) and Staff member (1976-80), all at the Social Security Administration, Department of Health and Human Services.

Employers

Patton Boggs, LLP (Senior Health Policy Advisor)

Clients Represented

On Behalf of Patton Boggs, LLP

American College of Gastroenterology
American Medical Rehabilitation Providers Ass'n
HCR-Manor Care, Inc.
Hoffmann-La Roche Inc.
Minimed, Inc.
Nat'l Marrow Donor Program
New York State Ass'n of Health Care Providers
Patient Access to Transplantation (PAT) Coalition
University Medical Associates

WILLIS, Karin K.

1717 Pennsylvania Ave. NW
Suite 1300
Washington, DC 20006
Tel: (202)661-3589
Fax: (202)737-3671
Registered: LDA
EMail: kkwillis@aol.com

Employers

Defense Health Advisors, Inc.

Clients Represented

On Behalf of Defense Health Advisors, Inc.

Data-Disk Technology, Inc.
Delta Dental Plan of California

WILLIS, Larry I.

1615 L St. NW
Suite 700
Washington, DC 20036-5610
Tel: (202)682-7000
Fax: (202)857-0939
Registered: LDA
EMail: larry.willis@weil.com

Employers

Weil, Gotshal & Manges, LLP (Director, Legislative Services/Associate)

Clients Represented

On Behalf of Weil, Gotshal & Manges, LLP

GAF Corp.
Kimberly-Clark Corp.
Nomura Internat'l plc

WILLIS, Wayne D.

2001 Pennsylvania Ave. NW
Suite 650
Washington, DC 20006
Tel: (202)496-8200
Fax: (202)659-1110
Registered: LDA
EMail: willis@ga.radix.net

Employers

General Atomics (V. President, Washington Operations)

WILLS, Joan L.

1001 Connecticut Ave. NW
Suite 310
Washington, DC 20036
Tel: (202)822-8405
Fax: (202)872-4050

Employers

Institute for Educational Leadership (Director, Center for Workforce Development)

WILLSON, J. David

One Massachusetts Ave. NW
Suite 880
Washington, DC 20001
Tel: (202)371-6692
Fax: (202)371-1178
Registered: LDA
EMail: jdw549@aol.com
Staff Assistant, Subcommittee on Defense (1977-94), Subcommittee on Interior (1972-76), and Subcommittee on Transportation (971-72). Budget Examiner, Bureau of the Budget, Office of Management and Budget, The White House, 1969-71. Management Analyst, Department of Commerce, 1966-69.

Employers
Robison Internat'l, Inc. (Director, Government Programs)

Clients Represented
On Behalf of Robison Internat'l, Inc.
Armtec Defense Products
Lockheed Martin Tactical Systems
Oshkosh Truck Corp.
Simula, Inc.

WILLSON, Peters D.

401 Wythe St.
Alexandria, VA 22314
Tel: (703)684-1355
Fax: (703)684-1589
Registered: LDA

EMail: pwillson@nachri.org

Employers
Nat'l Ass'n of Children's Hospitals Inc. (V. President, Public Policy)

WILMER, Jr., John W.

1828 L St. NW
Eleventh Floor
Washington, DC 20036-5109
Tel: (202)467-8819
Fax: (202)467-8900
EMail: j.w.wilmer@vssp.com
Law Clerk to Chief Judge Pierce Lively, U.S. Court of Appeals, Sixth Circuit, 1975-76.

Employers
Vorys, Sater, Seymour and Pease, LLP (Partner)

WILMER, Pat

1130 Connecticut Ave. NW
Suite 710
Washington, DC 20036
Tel: (202)659-1324
Fax: (202)659-1328

Employers
Air Products and Chemicals, Inc. (PAC Administrator)

WILMOT, David W.

1010 Vermont Ave. NW
Suite 810
Washington, DC 20005
Tel: (202)783-9100
Fax: (202)783-9103

Employers
Harmon & Wilmot, L.L.P. (Partner)

Clients Represented
On Behalf of Harmon & Wilmot, L.L.P.
Anheuser-Busch Cos., Inc.
Hotel Ass'n of Washington
MCI WorldCom Corp.

WILMOT, John

112 Elden St.
Unit J
Herndon, VA 20170
Tel: (703)709-8254
Fax: (703)709-1036

Employers
American Edged Products Manufacturers Ass'n (Deputy Director)
Nat'l Ass'n of Public Insurance Adjusters (Deputy Director)

WILNER, Carol W.

1120 20th St. NW
Suite 1000
Washington, DC 20036
Tel: (202)457-7435
Fax: (202)457-2571
Registered: LDA
EMail: cwilner@att.com

Employers
AT&T (V. President, Exec. Branch Advocacy)

WILNER, John R.

700 13th St. NW
Suite 700
Washington, DC 20005-3960
Tel: (202)508-6000
Fax: (202)508-6200
EMail: jrwilner@bryancave.com

Employers
Bryan Cave LLP (Partner)

WILSON, Alexandra M.

1225 19th St. NW
Suite 450
Washington, DC 20036
Tel: (202)296-4933
Fax: (202)296-4951
Registered: LDA

Employers
Cox Enterprises Inc. (Chief, Public Policy Counsel)

WILSON, Andrew M.

10640 Main St.
Suite 200
Fairfax, VA 22030
Tel: (703)352-3400
Fax: (703)385-6470
Registered: LDA

Employers
JGW Internat'l Ltd. (President)

Clients Represented
On Behalf of JGW Internat'l Ltd.
GEC-Marconi Defense Systems Ltd.
Graseby Plc
Per Udsen

WILSON, Ann

1400 K St. NW
Suite 900
Washington, DC 20005
Tel: (202)682-4800
Fax: (202)682-4854

Employers
Rubber Manufacturers Ass'n (V. President, Government Affairs)

WILSON, Arthur H.

807 Maine Ave. SW
Washington, DC 20024
Tel: (202)554-3501
Fax: (202)554-3581

Employers
Disabled American Veterans (National Adjutant)

WILSON, Bruce A.

2275 Research Blvd.
Suite 250
Rockville, MD 20850
Tel: (301)947-9000
Fax: (301)947-9090
Registered: LDA
Special Assistant for Legislation and Policy, Health Care Financing Administration (1989-93), and Special Assistant, Advisory Boards Commission, Office of the Secretary (1989), Department of Health and Human Services.

Employers
Physician Insurers Ass'n of America (Director, Government Relations)

WILSON, Hon. Charles

801 Pennsylvania Ave. NW
Suite 730
Washington, DC 20004
Tel: (202)756-2406
Fax: (202)756-2407
Registered: LDA, FARA
EMail: Wilson@howdc.com
Member, U.S. House of Representatives (D-TX), 1973-96.

Employers
Hooper Owen & Winburn (Principal)

Clients Represented
On Behalf of Hooper Owen & Winburn
Azerbaijan, Embassy of the Republic of
GKN Westland Aerospace Inc.
IMI Services USA, Inc.
Latona Associates, Inc.
Lockheed Martin Corp.
Pakistan, Government of the Islamic Republic of
Shipston Group, LTD

WILSON, Christopher

1001 Pennsylvania Ave. NW
Suite 1275
Washington, DC 20004
Tel: (202)624-2895
Fax: (202)628-5116
Registered: LDA

Employers
C&M Internat'l, Ltd. (Director)

Clients Represented
On Behalf of C&M Internat'l, Ltd.
DNA Plant Technology Corp.
The Limited Inc.

WILSON, D. Mark

214 Massachusetts Ave. NE
Washington, DC 20002
Tel: (202)546-4400
Fax: (202)546-8328

Employers
Heritage Foundation (Labor Economist)

WILSON, Daniel S.

1735 New York Ave. NW
Washington, DC 20006
Tel: (202)626-7300
Fax: (202)626-7365
Registered: LDA

Employers
The American Institute of Architects (Senior Director, Federal Affairs)

WILSON, Donald E.

7495 Covent Wood Ct.
Annandale, VA 22003
Tel: (703)866-9680
Fax: (703)451-8557
Registered: LDA
Director, Army Activities, National Guard, 1987-95. Served in the U.S. Army, 1953-87, retiring at the rank of Colonel.

Employers
Donald E. Wilson Consulting

Clients Represented
On Behalf of Donald E. Wilson Consulting
The "Sandbagger" Corp.

WILSON, Ph.D, Elizabeth J.

7910 Woodmont Ave.
Suite 1200
Bethesda, MD 20814
Tel: (301)657-2248
Fax: (301)913-9413

Employers
Self Help for Hard of Hearing People, Inc. (Exec. Director)

WILSON, Gary D.

2445 M St. NW
Washington, DC 20037-1420
Tel: (202)663-6000
Fax: (202)663-6363
Registered: LDA

Employers
Wilmer, Cutler & Pickering (Partner)

WILSON, Gerald J.

P.O. Box 30374
Bethesda, MD 20824
Tel: (301)309-2357
Fax: (301)309-1856
Registered: LDA

EMail: libbase@aol.com

Employers
Citizens for Public Action on Cholesterol, Inc. (Exec. Director)
Citizens for the Treatment of High Blood Pressure, Inc.
Coalition for Brain Injury Research and Services, Inc. (Director)

WILSON, Greg

1776 I St. NW
Suite 1030
Washington, DC 20006
Tel: (202)822-1690
Fax: (202)822-1693
Registered: LDA

Employers
Solutia Inc. (Director, Federal Affairs)

WILSON, J. Randolph

1201 Pennsylvania Ave. NW
Washington, DC 20004-2401
Tel: (202)662-6000
Fax: (202)662-6291

Employers
Covington & Burling (Senior Counsel)

Clients Represented
On Behalf of Covington & Burling
Copper and Brass Fabricators Council

WILSON, Jane E.

600 13th St. NW
Washington, DC 20005-3096
Tel: (202)756-8317
Fax: (202)756-8087
Registered: LDA

EMail: jwilson@mwe.com
Attorney/Advisor to Judge Samuel B. Sterrett, U.S. Tax Court, 1984-85. Attorney/Advisor, Interpretative Division, Office of the Chief Counsel, Internal Revenue Service, 1981-84.

Employers
McDermott, Will and Emery (Partner, Tax Law Department)

Clients Represented
On Behalf of McDermott, Will and Emery
Georgia-Pacific Corp.
RJR Nabisco Holdings Co.

WILSON, Joanne

900 19th St. NW
Suite 700
Washington, DC 20006
Tel: (202)530-7000
Fax: (202)530-7042
Registered: LDA

Employers
Lucent Technologies (Director, Global Public Affairs)

WILSON, John G.

10640 Main St.
Suite 200
Fairfax, VA 22030
Tel: (703)352-3400
Fax: (703)385-6470
Registered: LDA

Employers
JGW Internat'l Ltd. (Chairman/Chief Exec. Officer)

Clients Represented

On Behalf of JGW Internat'l Ltd.
GEC-Marconi Defense Systems Ltd.
Graseby Plc
Per Udsen

WILSON, John I.

1201 16th St. NW
Washington, DC 20036
Tel: (202)833-4000
Fax: (202)822-7974

Employers
Nat'l Education Ass'n of the U.S. (Exec. Director)

WILSON, John K.

1200 Wilson Blvd.
Arlington, VA 22209-1989
Tel: (703)465-3608
Fax: (703)465-3004
Registered: LDA

Employers
The Boeing Co. (Legislative Affairs, Air Force Programs)

WILSON, Joy Johnson

444 N. Capitol St. NW
Suite 515
Washington, DC 20001
Tel: (202)624-5400
Fax: (202)737-1069

Employers
Nat'l Conference of State Legislatures (Senior Program Director, Health and Human Services)

WILSON, Kimberly

800 Connecticut Ave. NW
Suite 200
Washington, DC 20006
EMail: kwilson1@humana.com
Tel: (202)467-5821
Fax: (202)467-5825

Employers
Humana Inc. (Government Affairs Assistant)

WILSON, LeAnne R.

444 N. Capitol St. NW
Suite 411
Washington, DC 20001
Tel: (202)624-5840
Fax: (202)624-5841

Employers
Michigan, Washington Office of the State of (Director)

WILSON, Jr., Leon A.

1421 Jefferson Davis Hwy.
Suite 10800
Arlington, VA 22202
EMail: lwilson@jwod.gov
Tel: (703)603-7740
Fax: (703)603-0655

Employers
Committee for Purchase from People Who Are Blind or Severely Disabled (Exec. Director)

WILSON, Linda E.

444 N. Capitol St. NW
Suite 201
Washington, DC 20001
Tel: (202)638-0631
Fax: (202)638-2296

Employers
New Jersey, Washington Office of the State of (Acting Director)

WILSON, Lynn

732 N. Washington St.
Suite 4A
Alexandria, VA 22314
EMail: director@acf.foresters.com
Tel: (703)548-0990
Fax: (703)548-6395

Employers
Ass'n of Consulting Foresters of America (Executive Director)

WILSON, Marcia D.

122 S. Royal St.
Alexandria, VA 22314-3328
Tel: (703)838-0373
Fax: (703)838-1698

Employers
Cordia Cos. (Associate)

WILSON, Marsha T.

1801 K St. NW
Suite 1000L
Washington, DC 20006
EMail: marsh_wilson@washbm.com
Tel: (202)530-0400
Fax: (202)530-4500

Employers
Burson-Marsteller (Director, Public Affairs Practice)

WILSON, Michael E.

3975 Fair Ridge Dr.
Suite 20-North
Fairfax, VA 22033-2906
EMail: wilson@autorecyc.org
Tel: (703)385-1001
Fax: (703)385-1494
Registered: LDA

Employers
Automotive Recyclers Ass'n (Manager, Governmental and Industry Relations)

WILSON, Michael J.

1775 K St. NW
Washington, DC 20006
Tel: (202)223-3111
Fax: (202)466-1562
Registered: LDA

Employers
United Food and Commercial Workers Internat'l Union (Chief Lobbyist)

WILSON, Michael M.

801 Pennsylvania Ave. NW
Suite 220
Washington, DC 20004-2604
EMail: michael_m_wilson@fpl.com
Tel: (202)347-7082
Fax: (202)347-7076
Registered: LDA

Employers
Florida Power and Light Co. (V. President, Governmental Affairs)

WILSON, Monty

8605 Cameron St.
Suite 400
Silver Spring, MD 20910
Tel: (301)585-4000
Fax: (301)585-0519

Employers
Vietnam Veterans of America, Inc. (National Service Representative)

WILSON, N. Whitney

700 13th St. NW
Suite 700
Washington, DC 20005-3960
EMail: nwwilson@bryancave.com
Tel: (202)508-6000
Fax: (202)508-6200

Employers
Bryan Cave LLP (Assciate)

WILSON, Nancy B.

1000 Potomac St. NW
Suite 300
Washington, DC 20007
Tel: (202)337-6200
Fax: (202)333-0871

Employers
Hewes, Gelband, Lambert & Dann, P.C. (Associate)

WILSON, Nancy L.

50 F St. NW
Suite 12402
Washington, DC 20001
Tel: (202)639-2401
Fax: (202)639-2868

Employers
Ass'n of American Railroads (Assistant V. President, Reguilatory Affairs)

WILSON, Neil

4545 42nd St. NW
Suite 201
Washington, DC 20016
Tel: (202)363-8098
Fax: (202)363-0304

Employers
Council on Religious Freedom (President)

WILSON, Paul A. J.

2550 M St. NW
Washington, DC 20037-1350
EMail: pwilson@pattonboggs.com
Tel: (202)457-6000
Fax: (202)457-6315
Registered: LDA

Employers
Patton Boggs, LLP (Partner)

Clients Represented

On Behalf of Patton Boggs, LLP
Magnificent Research Inc.
Save Barton Creek

WILSON, Paul O.

429 N. St. Asaph St.
Alexandria, VA 22314
EMail: POWilson@aol.com
Tel: (703)739-0330
Fax: (703)739-0332

Employers
Wilson Grand Communications (Chairman/Chief Executive Officer)

Clients Represented

On Behalf of Wilson Grand Communications
Ohio Senate Republican Caucus

WILSON, R. David

626 S. 25th St.
Arlington, VA 22202
EMail: rdw@nfrontiers.com
Tel: (703)548-6636
Fax: (703)548-6747
Registered: LDA

Legislative Assistant for Education, High Technology, Information Technology, and Indian Affairs to Senate Majority Leader Robert J. Dole (R-KS), 1989-96.

Employers
New Frontiers Communications Consulting (Principal)

Clients Represented

On Behalf of New Frontiers Communications Consulting
BellSouth Corp.
PanAmSat Corp.
Qwest Communications
United Pan-Europe Communications, NV
Verizon Communications

WILSON, Richard

111 Gresham Place
Falls Church, VA 22046
Registered: LDA

Employers
NES, Inc.

Clients Represented

On Behalf of NES, Inc.
Podesta/Mattoon

WILSON, Richard D.

2600 Virginia Ave. NW
Suite 600
Washington, DC 20037
Tel: (202)333-2524
Fax: (202)338-5950
Registered: LDA

Employers
Nat'l Environmental Strategies (V. President)

Clients Represented

On Behalf of Nat'l Environmental Strategies
Ethyl Petroleum Additives, Inc.
Oxygenated Fuels Ass'n

WILSON, Richard F.

1730 M St. NW
Suite 512
Washington, DC 20036
EMail: rwilson@mepc.org
Tel: (202)296-6767
Fax: (202)296-5791

Employers
Middle East Policy Council (Exec. Director)

WILSON, Robert Dale

1155 15th St. NW
Suite 815
Washington, DC 20005
Tel: (202)835-1571
Fax: (202)296-2736
Registered: LDA

Director, Strategic Resources, U.S. Department of Commerce, 1981-86. Exec. Director, White House Materials Council, 1986-88.

Employers
Wilson & Wilson (Partner)

Clients Represented

On Behalf of Wilson & Wilson
Edison Industrial Systems Center
Falconbridge, Ltd.
Hecla Mining Co.

WILSON, Russell J.

1401 K St. NW
Tenth Floor
Washington, DC 20005
Tel: (202)416-1720
Fax: (202)416-1719
Registered: LDA, FARA
Staff Director, Subcommittee on Asia and the Pacific (1992-94) and Republican Staff Consultant, Subcommittee on Europe and the Middle East (1988-92), House Committee on Foreign Affairs.

Employers
Wilson & Wasserstein, Inc. (President and Chief Exec. Officer)

Clients Represented

On Behalf of Wilson & Wasserstein, Inc.
Bangladeshi-American Friendship Soc. of New York
Mortgage Investors Corp.
Scribe Communications, Inc.
U.S. Fencing Ass'n
West African Friends

WILSON, S. Bruce

1333 New Hampshire Ave. NW
Suite 400
Washington, DC 20036
Tel: (202)887-4000
Fax: (202)887-4288
Registered: LDA, FARA
Former International Trade Negotiator, Office of the U.S. Trade Representative, 1975-91.

Employers
Akin, Gump, Strauss, Hauer & Feld, L.L.P. (Partner)

Clients Represented

On Behalf of Akin, Gump, Strauss, Hauer & Feld, L.L.P.
Ad Hoc Nitrogen Committee
Alliance Capital Management LP
American Home Products Corp.
AOL Time Warner
Barrick Goldstrike Mines, Inc.
The Boeing Co.
Cargill, Inc.
Committee for Fair Ammonium Nitrate Trade
Lucent Technologies
Mitsubishi Corp.
Pegasus Capital Advisors, L.P.
Phillips Foods, Inc.
Saudi Arabia, Government of
Serono Laboratories, Inc.
Volkswagen, AG
Westar Group, Inc.

WILSON, Sharon L.

1155 15th St. NW
Suite 815
Washington, DC 20005
Tel: (202)835-1571
Fax: (202)296-2736
Associate Staff Director, Subcommittee on Mining and Natural Resources, House Committee on Interior and Insular Affairs, 1976-84.

Employers
Wilson & Wilson (Partner)

WILSON, Steven

Ariel Rios Federal Bldg.
(1301-MC)
1200 Pennsylvania Ave. NW
Washington, DC 20460
EMail: wilson.steven@epa.gov
Tel: (202)564-6996
Fax: (202)501-1534

Employers
Environmental Protection Agency (NEPPS/Compliance Team Leader, Office of Congressional and Intergovernmental Relations)

WILSON, Theresa

1150 15th St. NW
Washington, DC 20071
Tel: (202)334-6000
Fax: (202)334-4536

Employers
The Washington Post Co. (Manager, Risk)

WILSON, Thomas

810 Vermont Ave. NW
Room 502
Washington, DC 20420
Tel: (202)273-5611
Fax: (202)273-6792

Employers
Department of Veterans Affairs (Special Assistant)

WILSON, Tyler J.

1650 King St.
Suite 500
Alexandria, VA 22314
EMail: twilson@aopanet.org
Tel: (703)836-7116
Fax: (703)836-0838
Registered: LDA

Employers
American Orthotic and Prosthetic Ass'n (Exec. Director)

WILSON, Walter

1615 L St. NW
Suite 1200
Washington, DC 20036
Tel: (202)466-6300
Fax: (202)463-0678

Employers
Bell, Boyd & Lloyd

WILSON, William J.

1700 Diagonal Rd.
Suite 500
Alexandria, VA 22314
EMail: bwilson@visionsite.org
Tel: (703)548-4560
Fax: (703)548-4580

Employers
Vision Council of America (Director, Public Relations)

WILTRAUT, James

1725 DeSales St. NW
Suite 800
Washington, DC 20036
Tel: (202)659-6540
Fax: (202)659-5730
Registered: LDA

Employers
Whitten & Diamond

WILTSHIRE, William

1200 18th St. NW
Suite 1200
Washington, DC 20036
Tel: (202)730-1300
Fax: (202)730-1301
Former Special Counsel, Mass Media Bureau, Federal Communications Commission

Employers
Harris, Wiltshire & Grannis LLP (Partner)

WIMER, David J.

2111 Wilson Blvd.
Suite 1200
Arlington, VA 22201
EMail: dwimer@columbuspublicaffairs.com
Tel: (703)522-1845
Fax: (703)351-6634
Former Personnel Director, Executive Office of the President, The White House, during the Nixon adminstration. Also served as Advisor to the Reagan and Bush I administrations. Fomer Officer, U.S. Air Force.

Employers
Columbus Public Affairs (President)

WIMPLE, USAF, Lt. Col. Robert

1300 Defense Pentagon
Room 3D918
Washington, DC 20301-1300
Tel: (703)697-9369
Fax: (703)697-8299

Employers
Department of Defense (Special Assistant for C31 Weapons Systems, Acquisition and Policy, Office of Legislative Liaison)

WINBURN, John P.

801 Pennsylvania Ave. NW
Suite 730
Washington, DC 20004
EMail: Winburn@howdc.com
Tel: (202)756-2412
Fax: (202)756-2413
Registered: LDA
Former aide to Rep. Tom Gettys (D-SC) and Rep. Kenneth Holland (D-SC).

Employers
Hooper Owen & Winburn (Principal)

Clients Represented

On Behalf of Hooper Owen & Winburn
AFL-CIO (American Federation of Labor and Congress of Industrial Organizations)
Air Line Pilots Ass'n Internat'l
Apple Computer, Inc.
BellSouth Corp.
The Hartford
Hutchison Whampo, LTD
KPMG, LLP
Nat'l Coordinating Committee for Multiemployer Plans
Norfolk Southern Railroad
PanAmSat Corp.
Parsons Corp.
Pfizer, Inc.
Philip Morris Management Corp.
Wine and Spirits Wholesalers of America

WINCE-SMITH, Deborah

1500 K St. NW
Suite 850
Washington, DC 20005
EMail: wincesd@compete.org
Tel: (202)682-4292
Fax: (202)682-5150

Employers
Council on Competitiveness (Senior Fellow)

WINCEK, Mark D.

700 13th St. NW
Suite 800
Washington, DC 20005
Tel: (202)508-5800
Fax: (202)508-5858
Senior Subcommittee Counsel (1980-81) and Staff Member (1976-81), Subcommittee on Oversight, House Committee on Ways and Means.

Employers
Kilpatrick Stockton LLP (Partner)

Clients Represented

On Behalf of Kilpatrick Stockton LLP
Employers Council on Flexible Compensation
PepsiCo, Inc.

WINCHESTER, Judith A.

800 Connecticut Ave. NW
Suite 1200
Washington, DC 20006
Tel: (202)452-4720
Fax: (202)452-4791
Registered: LDA

Employers
Lehman Brothers (Managing Director, Government Affairs)

WINCHESTER, Robert J.

The Pentagon
Room 2C631
Washington, DC 20310-1600
Tel: (703)695-3918
Fax: (703)697-3847

Employers
Department of Army (Special Assistant for Legislative Affairs, Legislative Liaison)

WINCKLER, RPh, J.D., Susan

2215 Constitution Ave. NW
Washington, DC 20037-2985
Tel: (202)628-4410
Fax: (202)783-2351
Registered: LDA

Employers
American Pharmaceutical Ass'n (Group Director, Policy and Advocacy)

WINDER, Joseph A. B.

1101 Vermont Ave. NW
Suite 401
Washington, DC 20005
EMail: jabw@keia.org
Tel: (202)371-0690
Fax: (202)371-0692
Registered: FARA

Employers
Korea Economic Institute of America (President)

WINDHAUSEN, Jr., John D.

888 17th St. NW
Suite 900
Washington, DC 20006
EMail: jwindhausen@alts.org
Tel: (202)969-2587
Fax: (202)969-2581
Registered: LDA

Employers
Ass'n for Local Telecommunications Services (President)

WINDLE, Phyllis

1707 H St. NW
Suite 600
Washington, DC 20006-3919
Tel: (202)223-6133
Fax: (202)223-6162

Employers
Union of Concerned Scientists (Senior Scientist, Global Environment Program)

WINEGRAD, Gerald W.

1250 24th St. NW
Suite 400
Washington, DC 20037
Tel: (202)778-9666
Fax: (202)778-9778
Registered: LDA

Employers
American Bird Conservancy (V. President, Policy)

WINER, Jonathan

601 Pennsylvania Ave. NW
11th Floor, North Bldg.
Washington, DC 20004-2601
Tel: (202)756-3300
Fax: (202)756-3333

Employers
Alston & Bird LLP

Clients Represented
On Behalf of Alston & Bird LLP
CarsDirect.com
General Electric Co.
Nat'l Coalition on E-Commerce and Privacy

WINES, Stephen H.

1775 K St. NW
Suite 200
Washington, DC 20006
Tel: (202)463-6505
Fax: (202)223-9093
Registered: LDA

Employers
Maritime Institute for Research and Industrial Development (Special Counsel)

WINICK, Seth

701 Pennsylvania Ave. NW
Suite 650
Washington, DC 20004
EMail: swinick@cancer.org
Tel: (202)661-5722
Fax: (202)661-5750

Employers
American Cancer Soc. (Managing Director, Advocacy Field Operations)

WINIK, Peter L.

555 11th St. NW
Suite 1000
Washington, DC 20004
Tel: (202)637-2200
Fax: (202)637-2201

Employers
Latham & Watkins (Partner)

WINKELMAN, Eileen M.

1300 Wilson Blvd.
Arlington, VA 22209
Tel: (703)741-5912
Fax: (703)741-6097
Registered: LDA
EMail: eileen_winkelman@americanchemistry.com

Employers
American Chemistry Council (Director)

WINKLER, James

100 Maryland Ave. NE
Suite 300
Washington, DC 20002
EMail: gbcs@umc-gbcs.org
Tel: (202)488-5600
Fax: (202)488-5619

Employers
United Methodist Church General Board of Church and Society (General Secretary)

WINN, Donald J.

20th and C Sts. NW
MS: 2125
Washington, DC 20551
Tel: (202)452-3456
Fax: (202)452-2611

Employers
Federal Reserve System (Assistant to the Board, Congressional Liaison)

WINN, Kathleen

213 A St. NE
Washington, DC 20002
Tel: (202)547-3363
Fax: (202)544-6144
Registered: LDA

Employers
Kathleen Winn & Associates, Inc.

Clients Represented
On Behalf of Kathleen Winn & Associates, Inc.
CSA America, Inc.

WINNER, Sonya D.

1201 Pennsylvania Ave. NW
Washington, DC 20004-2401
EMail: swinner@cov.com
Tel: (202)662-6000
Fax: (202)662-6291
Law Clerk to Judge Louis F. Oberdorfer, U.S. District Court for the District of Columbia, 1982-83.

Employers
Covington & Burling (Partner)

Clients Represented
On Behalf of Covington & Burling
Canon USA, Inc.
Canon, Inc.

WINNIK, Joel S.

555 13th St. NW
Washington, DC 20004-1109
Tel: (202)637-5600
Fax: (202)637-5910
Registered: LDA

Employers
Hogan & Hartson L.L.P. (Partner)

Clients Represented
On Behalf of Hogan & Hartson L.L.P.
NTT America

WINPISINGER, Vickie L.

P.O. Box 70101
Washington, DC 20024

Employers
Velazquez Victory Fund-Federal

WINSLOW, Peter H.

1875 I St. NW
Suite 1050
Washington, DC 20006-5409
Tel: (202)331-8585
Fax: (202)331-2032

Employers
Scribner, Hall & Thompson, LLP (Partner)

WINSTEAD, David L.

2099 Pennsylvania Ave. NW
Suite 100
Washington, DC 20006
EMail: dwinstea@hklaw.com
Tel: (202)955-3000
Fax: (202)955-5564

Employers
Holland & Knight LLP (Partner)

WINSTON, Chriss H.

1200 G St. NW
Suite 800
Washington, DC 20005
Registered: LDA

Employers
The Tierney Group (V. President)

Clients Represented
On Behalf of The Tierney Group
Federal Home Loan Bank of Pittsburgh
Valley Forge Flag Co.

WINSTON, Clifford

1775 Massachusetts Ave. NW
Washington, DC 20036-2188
Tel: (202)797-6000
Fax: (202)797-6004

Employers
The Brookings Institution (Senior Fellow, Economic Studies)

WINSTON, Deborah F.

9210 Graceland Pl.
Fairfax, VA 22031
Tel: (202)879-9487
Fax: (202)393-7309
Registered: LDA

Employers
Self-employed as an independent consultant.

Clients Represented
As an independent consultant
ING America Insurance Holdings, Inc.

WINSTON, James L.

1155 Connecticut Ave.
Sixth Floor
Washington, DC 20036
Tel: (202)861-0870
Fax: (202)429-0657
Legal Assistant to Commissioner Robert E. Lee, Federal Communications Commission, 1978-80.

Employers
Nat'l Ass'n of Black-Owned Broadcasters (Exec. Director)
Rubin, Winston, Diercks, Harris & Cooke (Partner)

Clients Represented
On Behalf of Rubin, Winston, Diercks, Harris & Cooke
Nat'l Ass'n of Black-Owned Broadcasters

WINTER, Douglas E.

700 13th St. NW
Suite 700
Washington, DC 20005-3960
EMail: dewinter@bryancave.com
Tel: (202)508-6000
Fax: (202)508-6200
Law Clerk to Judge William H. Webster, U.S. Court of Appeals, Eighth Circuit, 1975-76.

Employers
Bryan Cave LLP (Of Counsel)

WINTER, Eleanor

1724 Massachusetts Ave. NW
Washington, DC 20036-1969
Tel: (202)775-3550
Fax: (202)775-3671

Employers
Nat'l Cable Television Ass'n (Senior V. President, Special Projects)

WINTER, Roger

1717 Massachusetts Ave. NW
Suite 200
Washington, DC 20036
EMail: roger.winter@irsa-uscr.org
Tel: (202)347-3507
Fax: (202)347-3418
Registered: LDA

Employers
Immigration and Refugee Service of America (Exec. Director)
United States Committee for Refugees (Exec. Director)

WINTER, Thomas S.

104 North Carolina Ave. SE
Washington, DC 20003
EMail: publpolicy@aol.com
Tel: (202)546-5833
Fax: (202)546-3091

Employers
Conservative Victory Fund (Treasurer)

WINTER, William L.

11690 Sunrise Valley Dr.
Reston, VA 20191
EMail: vcju07a@prodigy.com
Tel: (703)620-3611
Fax: (703)620-5814

Employers
American Press Institute (President)

WINTERLING, Grayson

1001 Pennsylvania Ave. NW
Suite 760 North
Washington, DC 20004
Tel: (202)661-7060
Fax: (202)661-7066
Registered: LDA
Former National Security Assistant and former Staff Director to Senate Rules Committee Chairman John Warner (R-VA). U.S. Army, 1966-88.

Employers
The Legislative Strategies Group, LLC

Clients Represented
On Behalf of The Legislative Strategies Group, LLC
American Systems Internat'l Corp.
ECC Internat'l Corp.
Institute for Human-Machine Cognition
Noesis Inc.

WINTERS, Harry M.

316 Pennsylvania Ave. SE
Suite 300
Washington, DC 20003
Tel: (202)675-4246
Fax: (202)675-4230
Registered: LDA

Employers
United Parcel Service (V. President, Public Affairs)

WIRTH, Hon. Timothy E.

1301 Connecticut Ave. NW
Suite 700
Washington, DC 20036
Tel: (202)462-4900
Registered: LDA
Member, U.S. House of Representatives (D-CO), 1975-87, Senate 1987-93. Undersecretary for Global Affairs, U.S. Department of State, 1993-97.

Employers
Better World Campaign (President)

WIRTZ, John

1156 15th St. NW
Suite 502
Washington, DC 20005-1799
Tel: (202)862-4811
Fax: (202)862-4829

Employers
J. C. Penney Co., Inc. (Treasurer, PenneyPAC)

WISDOM, Alan

1110 Vermont Ave. NW
Suite 1180
Washington, DC 20005-3544
EMail: mail@ird-renew.org
Tel: (202)969-8430
Fax: (202)969-8429

Employers
Institute on Religion and Democracy (Senior Research Associate and V. President)

WISDOM, Christina

700 13th St. NW
Suite 950
Washington, DC 20005
EMail: christina.wisdom@lyondell.com
Tel: (202)434-8938
Fax: (202)434-4585

Employers
Lyondell Chemical Co. (PAC Manager/Gov't Affairs Coordinator)

WISE, Allan

6705 Rockledge Dr.
Suite 900
Bethesda, MD 20817
Tel: (301)581-0600

Employers
Coventry Health Care, Inc. (President)

WISE, Arthur E.

2010 Massachusetts Ave. NW
Suite 500
Washington, DC 20036-1023
EMail: art@ncate.org
Tel: (202)466-7496
Fax: (202)296-6620

Employers
Nat'l Council for Accreditation of Teacher Education (President)

WISE, Edward J.

600 13th St. NW
Washington, DC 20005-3096
EMail: ewise@mwe.com
Tel: (202)756-8628
Fax: (202)756-8087
Former Patent Examiner, Patent and Trademark Office.

Employers
McDermott, Will and Emery (Partner)

WISE, Eric

400 N. Capitol St. NW
Washington, DC 20001
Tel: (202)824-7232
Fax: (202)824-7115
Registered: LDA
EMail: ewise@aga.org

Employers
American Gas Ass'n (Senior Counsel and Director)

WISE, Gail Alexander

740 15th St. NW
Ninth Floor
Washington, DC 20005
Tel: (202)662-1095
Fax: (202)662-1099

Employers
American Bar Ass'n (Staff Director, Public Relations)

WISE, James W.

300 N. Lee St.
Suite 500
Alexandria, VA 22314
Tel: (703)518-8600
Fax: (703)518-8611
Registered: LDA

Employers
PACE-CAPSTONE (Partner)

Clients Represented

On Behalf of PACE-CAPSTONE
Agua Caliente Band of Cahuilla Indians
Barona Band of Mission Indians
Colorado River Indian Tribes
Guam AFGE
Guam Internat'l Airport Authority
Guam, Washington Office of the Governor
Honolulu Shipyard
Household Goods Forwarders Ass'n of America, Inc.
Independent Bankers Ass'n of Texas
Internat'l Facilities Management Ass'n
Kern, California, County of
Morongo Band of Mission Indians
Multimedia Games, Inc.
Nat'l Ass'n of Credit Management
San Francisco Bar Pilots Ass'n

WISE, Nicholas P.

400 N. Capitol St. NW
Suite 585
Washington, DC 20001
Tel: (202)737-1960
Fax: (202)393-5218
Registered: LDA

Employers
Wise & Associates (President)

Clients Represented

On Behalf of Wise & Associates
American Soc. of Anesthesiologists
AT&T
Corrections Corp. of America
Nat'l Hemophilia Foundation
Plaintiffs Committee for TWA 800 and Swissair Air III Crashes
Project to Promote Competition and Innovation in the Digital Age
RPM, Inc.

WISE-VAUGHAN, Elizabeth

655 15th St. NW
Washington, DC 20005-5701
Tel: (202)220-0632
Fax: (202)220-0873
Registered: LDA
EMail: ewise@fmi.org

Employers
Food Marketing Institute (Director, Government Relations)

WISEMAN, Laurence

1111 19th St. NW
Suite 780
Washington, DC 20036
Tel: (202)463-2462
Fax: (202)463-2461

Employers
American Forest Foundation (President)
Forest Industries Council on Taxation (Contact)

WISEMAN, Michael

1701 Pennsylvania Ave. NW
Suite 800
Washington, DC 20006
Tel: (202)956-7500
Fax: (202)293-6330
Registered: LDA

Employers
Sullivan & Cromwell (Partner)

Clients Represented

On Behalf of Sullivan & Cromwell
Goldman, Sachs and Co.
The Group of 20
Morgan Guaranty Trust Co.

WISNER, Graham G.

2550 M St. NW
Washington, DC 20037-1350
Tel: (202)457-6000
Fax: (202)457-6315
Registered: LDA

Employers
Patton Boggs, LLP

Clients Represented

On Behalf of Patton Boggs, LLP
Alcatel

WISOR, Jr., Ronald L.

1050 Connecticut Ave. NW
Washington, DC 20036-5339
Tel: (202)857-6000
Fax: (202)857-6395
Registered: LDA
Served in Department of the Navy, Department of Defense.

Employers
Arent Fox Kintner Plotkin & Kahn, PLLC (Associate)

Clients Represented

On Behalf of Arent Fox Kintner Plotkin & Kahn, PLLC
Federated Ambulatory Surgery Ass'n

WISOR, Russell C.

1909 K St. NW
Suite 500
Washington, DC 20006-1101
Tel: (202)956-5306
Fax: (202)956-5305
Registered: LDA

Employers
Alcoa Inc. (V. President, Government Affairs)

WITECK, Robert V.

2120 L St. NW
Suite 850
Washington, DC 20037
EMail: bwiteck@witeckcombs.com
Tel: (202)887-0500
Fax: (202)887-5633
Former Communications Director, Senate Committee on Commerce.

Employers
Witeck * Combs Communications (Chairman)

WITEK, Walt

700 11th St. NW
Washington, DC 20001-4507
Tel: (202)383-1067
Fax: (202)383-7580
Registered: LDA
EMail: wwitek@realtors.org

Employers
Nat'l Ass'n of Realtors (V. President, Government Affairs)

WITHEY, Ms. Lyn M.

1101 Pennsylvania Ave. NW
Suite 200
Washington, DC 20004
EMail: lyn.withey@ipaper.com
Tel: (202)628-1223
Fax: (202)628-1368
Registered: LDA

Employers
Internat'l Paper (V. President, Public Affairs)

WITHROW, David

One Massachusetts Ave. NW
Suite 300
Washington, DC 20001
EMail: DAWithrow@tva.gov
Tel: (202)898-2995
Fax: (202)898-2998

Employers
Tennessee Valley Authority - Washington Office (V. President, Government Relations)

WITKOWSKI, Christopher

1275 K St. NW
Fifth Floor
Washington, DC 20005
Tel: (202)712-9799

Employers
Ass'n of Flight Attendants (Director, Air Safety)

WITMAN, Ellen G.

2027 Massachusetts Ave. NW
Washington, DC 20036
Tel: (202)232-4962
Fax: (202)232-4963
Registered: LDA
EMail: ewitman@erols.com

Employers
Witman Associates (President)

Clients Represented

On Behalf of Witman Associates
Jewish Federation of Metropolitan Chicago
Partnership for Caring
United Jewish Communities, Inc.

WITT, John

440 First St. NW
Eighth Floor
Washington, DC 20001
EMail: jwitt@naco.org
Tel: (202)942-4261
Fax: (202)393-2630

Employers
Nat'l Ass'n of Counties (Senior Project Manager, NACO's Radon/Indoor Air Project)

WITT, Lou

440 First St. NW
Washington, DC 20001
Tel: (202)942-4261
Fax: (202)393-2630

Employers
Nat'l Ass'n of County Park and Recreation Officials (Contact)

WITTEN, Roger M.

2445 M St. NW
Washington, DC 20037-1420
EMail: rwitten@wilmer.com
Tel: (202)663-6000
Fax: (202)663-6363
Former Law Clerk to Judge Harrison L. Winter, U.S. Court of Appeals, Fourth Circuit.

Employers
Wilmer, Cutler & Pickering (Partner)

Clients Represented
On Behalf of Wilmer, Cutler & Pickering
Common Cause
Swiss Bank Corp.
Union Bank of Switzerland

WITTENBERG, Hope R.

2021 Massachusetts Ave. NW
Washington, DC 20036
Tel: (202)986-3309
Fax: (202)232-9044
Registered: LDA

Employers
Soc. of Teachers of Family Medicine (Director, Government Relations)

WITTENBORN, John L.

3050 K St. NW
Washington, DC 20007
Tel: (202)342-8400
Fax: (202)342-8451
Registered: LDA
EMail: jwittenb@colliershannon.com

Employers
Collier Shannon Scott, PLLC (Member)

Clients Represented
On Behalf of Collier Shannon Scott, PLLC
Chrome Coalition
Copper and Brass Fabricators Council
Copper Development Ass'n, Inc.
Garden State Tanning, Inc.
Metals Industry Recycling Coalition
Steel Manufacturers Ass'n

WITTENSTEIN, David J.

1200 New Hampshire Ave. NW
Suite 800
Washington, DC 20036-6802
EMail: dwittens@dlalaw.com
Tel: (202)776-2000
Fax: (202)776-2222

Employers
Dow, Lohnes & Albertson, PLLC (Member)

WITTER, Jay

1701 Clarendon Blvd.
Arlington, VA 22209
Tel: (703)276-8800
Fax: (703)243-2593
Registered: LDA

Employers
American Chiropractic Ass'n (V. President, Government Relations)

WITTING, William N.

1111 19th St. NW
Suite 900
Washington, DC 20036
EMail: bwitting@cnfa.org
Tel: (202)296-3920
Fax: (202)296-3948

Employers
Citizens Network for Foreign Affairs (CNFA) (Director, Small Enterprise Development)

WITTMANN, Marshall

1015 18th St. NW
Suite 300
Washington, DC 20036
Tel: (202)223-7770
Fax: (202)223-8537
Served as Deputy Assistant Secretary, Department of Health and Human Services, during the Bush I administration.

Employers
Hudson Institute (Senior Fellow, Governmental Studies)

WODDER, Rebecca

1025 Vermont Ave.
Suite 720
Washington, DC 20005
EMail: amrivers@amrivers.org
Tel: (202)347-7550
Fax: (202)347-9240

Employers
American Rivers (President)

WODISKA, Joan

5999 Stevenson Ave.
Alexandria, VA 22304-3300
Tel: (703)823-9800
Ext: 241
Fax: (703)823-0252
Registered: LDA
EMail: jwodiska@counseling.org

Employers
American Counseling Ass'n (Assistant Director, Public Policy and Legislation)

WOERTH, Capt. Duane E.

1625 Massachusetts Ave. NW
Washington, DC 20036
Tel: (202)797-4033
Fax: (202)797-4030

Employers
Air Line Pilots Ass'n Internat'l (President)

WOHL, Alex

555 New Jersey Ave. NW
Washington, DC 20001
Tel: (202)879-4458
Fax: (202)879-4402

Employers
American Federation of Teachers (Director, Public Affairs)

WOHLBRUCK, Aliceann

400 N. Capitol St. NW
Suite 390
Washington, DC 20001
Tel: (202)624-7806
Fax: (202)624-8813

Employers
Nat'l Ass'n of Development Organizations (Exec. Director)

WOHLSTETTER, Alan F.

1700 K St. NW
Suite 301
Washington, DC 20006
Tel: (202)833-8884
Fax: (202)833-8886
Trial Attorney for Federal Maritime Board and Maritime Administration 1951-52.

Employers
Denning & Wohlstetter (Managing Partner)

Clients Represented
On Behalf of Denning & Wohlstetter
Central Freight Forwarding
Household Goods Forwarders Ass'n of America, Inc.

WOLAK, Jeanne Hicks

1130 Connecticut Ave. NW
Suite 830
Washington, DC 20036
Tel: (202)261-5000
Fax: (202)296-7937

Employers
Southern Co. (Director, Federal Legislative Affairs)

WOLANIN, Thomas R.

1320 19th St. NW
Suite 400
Washington, DC 20036
Tel: (202)861-8223
Fax: (202)861-9307

Employers
The Institute for Higher Education Policy (Senior Associate)

WOLDEHAWARIAT, Alem

1331 Pennsylvania Ave. NW
Suite 560
Washington, DC 20004
Tel: (202)783-8124
Fax: (202)783-5929

Employers
CSX Corp. (Manager, Public Affairs)

WOLF, Christine M.

8121 Georgia Ave.
Suite 301
Silver Spring, MD 20910-4933
EMail: cwolf@fund.org
Tel: (301)585-2591
Fax: (301)585-2595
Registered: LDA

Employers
The Fund for Animals (Director, Government and International Affairs)

WOLF, Christopher

1233 20th St. NW
Suite 800
Washington, DC 20036-2396
EMail: CWolf@proskauer.com
Tel: (202)416-6800
Fax: (202)416-6899

Employers
Proskauer Rose LLP (Partner)

WOLF, Craig

805 15th St. NW
Suite 430
Washington, DC 20005
EMail: craig.wolf@wswa.org
Tel: (202)371-9792
Fax: (202)789-2405

Employers
Wine and Spirits Wholesalers of America (General Counsel)

WOLF, Harry A.

Theodore Roosevelt Federal Bldg.
1900 E St. NW
MS: 7520
Washington, DC 20415
Tel: (202)606-1424
Fax: (202)606-1344

Employers
Office of Personnel Management (Chief, Legislative Analysis Office)

WOLF, James E.

1500 Lee Hwy.
Suite 140
Arlington, VA 22209
Tel: (703)525-4015

Employers
American Standard Cos. Inc. (V. President, Government Affairs)

WOLF, Kevin J.

700 13th St. NW
Suite 700
Washington, DC 20005-3960
EMail: kjwolf@bryancave.com
Tel: (202)508-6000
Fax: (202)508-6200

Employers
Bryan Cave LLP (Partner)

WOLFE, Dana

408 C St. NE
Washington, DC 20002
Tel: (202)547-1141
Fax: (202)547-6009

Employers
Sierra Club (Associate Representative, Land Protection)

WOLFE, J. Thomas

1299 Pennsylvania Ave. NW
Washington, DC 20004-2402
Tel: (202)783-0800
Fax: (202)383-6610
Registered: LDA

Employers
Howrey Simon Arnold & White

Clients Represented
On Behalf of Howrey Simon Arnold & White
Battery Council Internat'l

WOLFE, Kenneth

807 Maine Ave. SW
Washington, DC 20024
Tel: (202)554-3501
Fax: (202)554-3581

Employers
Disabled American Veterans (National Service Director)

WOLFE, Dr. Leslie R.

1211 Connecticut Ave. NW
Suite 312
Washington, DC 20036
Tel: (202)872-1770
Fax: (202)296-8962

Employers
Center for Women Policy Studies (President)

WOLFE, Sidney M.

1600 20th St. NW
Washington, DC 20009
Tel: (202)588-1000
Fax: (202)588-7799

Employers
Public Citizen, Inc. (Director, Public Citizen Health Research Group)

WOLFF, Alan W.

1775 Pennsylvania Ave. NW
Suite 200
Washington, DC 20006
Tel: (202)862-1000
Fax: (202)862-1093
Registered: LDA

Deputy Special Trade Representative (1977-79) and General Counsel (1974-76), Office of the U.S. Trade Representative, Executive Office of the President, The White House. Attorney, Office of General Counsel, Department of Treasury, 1968-73.

Employers
Dewey Ballantine LLP (Managing Partner)

Clients Represented

On Behalf of Dewey Ballantine LLP
AFLAC, Inc.
Labor-Industry Coalition for Internat'l Trade
Semiconductor Industry Ass'n

WOLFF, Candi

Old Executive Office Bldg.
Room 276
Washington, DC 20501
Tel: (202)456-6774
Fax: (202)456-1606

Employers
Executive Office of the President - Office of the Vice President (Deputy Assistant to the V. President for Legislative Affairs (House))

WOLFF, Elliot

P.O. Box 5939
Washington, DC 20016
Tel: (202)783-8191

Employers
Advantage Healthplan Inc. (President)

WOLFF, Mark

805 15th St. NW
Suite 300
Washington, DC 20005-2207
Tel: (202)682-4200
Fax: (202)682-9054

Employers
Credit Union Nat'l Ass'n, Inc. (Senior V. President, Communications)

WOLFF, Patricia A.

600 Maryland Ave. SW
Suite 800
Washington, DC 20024
Tel: (202)484-3600
Fax: (202)484-3604
Registered: LDA

Employers
American Farm Bureau Federation (Senior Director, Budget/Taxes/Appropriations)

WOLFF, Samuel

1333 New Hampshire Ave. NW
Suite 400
Washington, DC 20036
Tel: (202)887-4000
Fax: (202)887-4288
Registered: LDA

Deputy Chief, Office of International Corporate Finance (1988) and Staff Attorney, Division of Corporation Finance (1985-88), Securities and Exchange Commission.

Employers
Akin, Gump, Strauss, Hauer & Feld, L.L.P. (Of Counsel)

WOLFF, Sharon

1201 F St. NW
Suite 200
Washington, DC 20004
Tel: (202)554-9000
Fax: (202)484-9267

Employers
Nat'l Federation of Independent Business (Manager, Campaign Services)

WOLFSON, Howard

430 S. Capitol St. SE
Second Floor
Washington, DC 20003
Tel: (202)863-1500
Fax: (202)485-3512

Employers
Democratic Congressional Campaign Committee (Exec. Director)

WOLGEMUTH, Kristin

900 17th St. NW
Suite 600
Washington, DC 20006
Tel: (202)452-8700
Fax: (202)296-9561
Registered: LDA

Employers
Healthcare Leadership Council (Director, Government Affairs/Grassroots)

WOLLACK, Kenneth D.

1717 Massachusetts Ave. NW
Suite 503
Washington, DC 20036
Tel: (202)328-3136
Fax: (202)939-3166

Employers
Nat'l Democratic Institute for Internat'l Affairs (President)

WOLLERTON, Chinch V.

1776 I St. NW
Suite 400
Washington, DC 20006-3708
Tel: (202)739-8000
Fax: (202)785-4019
Registered: LDA

Employers
Nuclear Energy Institute (Senior Director, Legislative Programs)

WOLLERY, Chuck

420 Seventh St. SE
Washington, DC 20003
Tel: (202)546-3950
Fax: (202)546-3749

Employers
World Federalist Ass'n (Issues Director)

WOLOWICZ, Kelly A.

2001 Jefferson Davis Hwy.
Suite 209
Arlington, VA 22202
Tel: (703)413-0090
Fax: (703)413-4467
EMail: kwolowicz@mehlgriffinbartek.com

Program Analyst and Personnel Coordinator, U.S. Army, 1993-95.

Employers
Mehl, Griffin & Bartek Ltd. (Director, Administration and Finance)

WOLSKI, Lisa

1700 N. Moore St.
Suite 2250
Arlington, VA 22209
Tel: (703)841-2300
Fax: (703)841-1183
Registered: LDA

Employers
Internat'l Mass Retailers Ass'n (Counsel, Tax and Finance)

WOMACK, Richard

815 16th St. NW
Washington, DC 20006
Tel: (202)637-5270

Employers
AFL-CIO (American Federation of Labor and Congress of Industrial Organizations) (Civil Rights Director)

WONG, Richard

801 N. Fairfax St.
Suite 312
Alexandria, VA 22314
Tel: (703)683-2722
Fax: (703)683-1619

Employers
American School Counselor Ass'n (Exec. Director)

WONG, Yeni

800 Seventh St. NW, Suite 305
Washington, DC 20001

Employers
Nat'l Asian American Political Empowerment Fund

WOOD, Benjamin

2550 M St. NW
Washington, DC 20037-1350
Tel: (202)457-6000
Fax: (202)457-6315
Registered: LDA

Employers
Patton Boggs, LLP

WOOD, Burton C.

1919 Pennsylvania Ave. NW
Seventh Floor
Washington, DC 20006-3488
Tel: (202)557-2700
Fax: (202)721-0249
Registered: LDA

Employers
Mortgage Bankers Ass'n of America (Senior Staff V. President, Legislation)

WOOD, USAF, Ret., Lt. Gen. C. Norman

4400 Fair Lakes Ct.
Fairfax, VA 22033
Tel: (703)631-6100
Fax: (703)631-6169

Employers
Armed Forces Communications and Electronics Ass'n Headquarters (President and Chief Exec. Officer)

WOOD, Dana S.

3050 K St. NW
Washington, DC 20007
Tel: (202)342-8400
Fax: (202)342-8451
Registered: LDA, FARA
EMail: dwood@colliershannon.com

Former Legislative Aide to Senator David Durenberger (R-MN).

Employers
Collier Shannon Scott, PLLC (Director, Government Relations)

Clients Represented

On Behalf of Collier Shannon Scott, PLLC
American Iron and Steel Institute
Copper and Brass Fabricators Council
Copper Development Ass'n, Inc.
Fannie Mae
Inland Steel Industries, Inc.
Lion Oil Co.
Nat'l Ass'n of Convenience Stores
Soc. of Independent Gasoline Marketers of America
Steel Manufacturers Ass'n
Symbol Technologies, Inc.

WOOD, D.O., Ph.D, Douglas L.

5550 Friendship Blvd.
Suite 310
Chevy Chase, MD 20815-7231
Tel: (301)968-4100
Fax: (301)968-4101
Registered: LDA

Employers
American Ass'n of Colleges of Osteopathic Medicine (President)

WOOD, Florence

601 13th St. NW
Suite 800 North
Washington, DC 20005
Tel: (202)682-1480
Fax: (202)682-1497

Employers
Hawkins, Delafield & Wood (Partner)

WOOD, Joel

701 Pennsylvania Ave. NW
Suite 750
Washington, DC 20004
Tel: (202)783-4400
Fax: (202)783-4410
Registered: LDA
EMail: ciab@ciab.com

Employers
The Council of Insurance Agents & Brokers (Senior V. President, Government Affairs)

WOOD, Katharine Calhoun

505 Capitol Ct. NE
Suite 200
Washington, DC 20002
Tel: (202)543-9398
Fax: (202)543-7844
Registered: LDA
EMail: kcw@hurtnorton.com

Special Projects Assistant (1994-95) and Administrative Assistant (1993-94) to Rep. Dan Miller (R-FL). Administrative Assistant to Rep. Andy Ireland (R-FL), 1983-92. Associate Staff Member, House Committee on the Budget for Rep. Bill Hefner (D-NC), 1981-82. Executive Director to Board of Contract Appeals (1979-81) and Confidential Assistant to Commission, Public Buildings Service (1977-79),

General Services Administration. Executive Assistant to Rep. Bo Ginn (D-GA), 1973-77.

Employers
Hurt, Norton & Associates (Senior Associate)

Clients Represented
On Behalf of Hurt, Norton & Associates
Auburn University
The Coca-Cola Company
Georgia Ports Authority
Lockheed Martin Aeronautical Systems Co.
Mercer Engineering Research Center
Mercer University
Westinghouse Electric Co.

WOOD, Brig. Gen. Steve
1160 Air Force Pentagon
Room 4D927
Washington, DC 20330-1160
Tel: (703)697-2650
Fax: (703)697-2001

Employers
Department of Air Force (Deputy Director, Legislative Liaison)

WOODALL, III, Samuel R.
1701 Pennsylvania Ave. NW
Suite 800
Washington, DC 20006
Tel: (202)956-7500
Fax: (202)293-6330
Registered: LDA

Employers
Sullivan & Cromwell (Government Affairs Specialist)

Clients Represented
On Behalf of Sullivan & Cromwell
First Fidelity Bancorporation
Goldman, Sachs and Co.
New York Clearing House Ass'n
Zions First Nat'l Bank

WOODBURY, David
4647 Forbes Blvd.
Lanham, MD 20706-4380
Tel: (301)459-9600
Fax: (301)459-7924

Employers
AMVETS (American Veterans of World War II, Korea and Vietnam) (National Exec. Director)

WOODBURY, David E.
515 King St.
Suite 420
Alexandria, VA 22314-3103
EMail: dwoodbury@clarionmr.com
Tel: (703)684-5570
Fax: (703)684-6048

Employers
CLARION Management Resources, Inc. (Director, Government Relations)

Clients Represented
On Behalf of CLARION Management Resources, Inc.
Alliance of Work/Life Professionals
Hearing Industries Ass'n

WOODBURY, Jennifer S.
1050 Connecticut Ave. NW
Washington, DC 20036-5339
Tel: (202)857-6000
Fax: (202)857-6395
Former Labor Counsel to Rep. James Talent (R-MO).

Employers
Arent Fox Kintner Plotkin & Kahn, PLLC (Associate)

WOODCOCK, Rebecca
1350 I St. NW
Suite 590
Washington, DC 20005
EMail: rwoodco@cap.org
Tel: (202)354-7105
Fax: (202)354-7155

Employers
College of American Pathologists (PAC Contact)

WOODKA, Janet L.
1050 Thomas Jefferson St. NW
Seventh Floor
Washington, DC 20007
EMail: JLW@vnf.com
Tel: (202)298-1800
Fax: (202)338-2416

Employers
Van Ness Feldman, P.C. (Associate)

WOODMAN, G. Kent
700 14th St. NW
Suite 900
Washington, DC 20005
Tel: (202)508-1000
Fax: (202)508-1010
Registered: LDA
Formerly served in the Office of the Legislative Counsel, U.S. House of Representatives, 1974-81; and in the Urban Mass Transportation Administration, 1981-84.

Employers
Thompson Coburn LLP (Partner)

Clients Represented
On Behalf of Thompson Coburn LLP
Los Angeles County Metropolitan Transportation Authority
Massachusetts Bay Transportation Authority
Regional Transportation Commission of South Nevada

WOODRUFF, Ph.D., C. Roy
9504A Lee Hwy.
Fairfax, VA 22031-2303
EMail: roy@aapc.org
Tel: (703)385-6967
Fax: (703)352-7725

Employers
American Ass'n of Pastoral Counselors (Exec. Director)

WOODRUFF, Richard P.
1100 Pennsylvania Ave. NW
Room 524
Washington, DC 20506
EMail: woodrufr@arts.endow.gov
Tel: (202)682-5434
Fax: (202)682-5638
Staff Director/Legislative Director (1991-93) and Legislative Assistant (1979-91) to Senator Howard M. Metzenbaum (D-OH).

Employers
Nat'l Endowment for the Arts (Director, Congressional and White House Liaison)

WOODS, Andrew L.
2300 N St. NW
Washington, DC 20037-1128
EMail: andrew.woods@shawpittman.com
Tel: (202)663-8000
Fax: (202)663-8007
Registered: LDA, FARA

Employers
Shaw Pittman (Partner)

Clients Represented
On Behalf of Shaw Pittman
American College of Radiation Oncology
Chevy Chase Bank, F.S.B.
Cornerstone Television
Detroit Medical Center
Dresdner Bank AG
Medicare Cost Contractors Alliance
Mexico, Secretaria de Comercio y Fomento Industrial (SECOFI)
The Money Store
Nortel Networks
Southern Ass'n of Forestry Economics

WOODS, Anne B.
P.O. Box 13858
Silver Spring, MD 20911-0858
Tel: (301)585-8051

Employers
American Ass'n of Black Women Entrepreneurs Corp. (V. President for Membership Development)

WOODS, Jr., Fred W.
1140 Connecticut Ave. NW
Suite 1142
Washington, DC 20036
Tel: (202)862-4383
Fax: (202)331-5562
Former Legislative Intern and Congressional Black Caucus Fellow to Rep. James Clyburn (D-SC). Former Law Clerk to Circuit Court Judge Donald Beatty.

Employers
Technology, Entertainment and Communications (TEC) Law Group

WOODS, Glen
1755 Jefferson Davis Hwy.
Suite 1107
Arlington, VA 22202
Tel: (703)415-0344
Fax: (703)415-0182

Employers
The PMA Group

WOODS, Jacqueline E.
1111 16th St. NW
Washington, DC 20036-4873
Tel: (202)785-7793
Fax: (202)466-7618
Former Director, Community Colleges Liaison Office, Department of Education.

Employers
American Ass'n of University Women (Exec. Director)

WOODS, James L.
1621 N. Kent St.
Suite 1619
Arlington, VA 22209
EMail: jlwoods@cohenandwoods.com
Tel: (703)516-9510
Fax: (703)516-4547
Registered: FARA
Former Deputy Assistant Secretary of Defense for African Affairs.

Employers
Cohen and Woods Internat'l, Inc. (Sr. V. President)

Clients Represented
On Behalf of Cohen and Woods Internat'l, Inc.
Angola, Government of the Republic of
Zimbabwe, Republic of

WOODS, Jerry
1000 Wilson Blvd.
Suite 2300
Arlington, VA 22209
Tel: (703)875-8400
Fax: (703)276-0711
Registered: LDA

Employers
Northrop Grumman Corp. (Manager, Legislative Affairs)

WOODS, Karen
228 Seventh St. SE
Washington, DC 20003-4306
EMail: kpw@nahc.org
Tel: (202)546-4759
Fax: (202)547-9559

Employers
Hospice Ass'n of America (Exec. Director)

WOODS, Mary
2101 E. Jefferson St.
Rockville, MD 20849
Tel: (301)816-2424

Employers
Kaiser Permanente (Director, Public Affairs (Mid-Atlantic))

WOODS, Stephen P.
1201 F St. NW
Suite 200
Washington, DC 20004
Tel: (202)554-9000
Fax: (202)554-0496

Employers
Nat'l Federation of Independent Business (V. President, State Public Policy)

WOODSIDE, Cynthia
750 First St. NE
Suite 700
Washington, DC 20002
Tel: (202)408-8600
Fax: (202)336-8324
Registered: LDA

Employers
Nat'l Ass'n of Social Workers (Congressional Lobbyist)

WOODSON, Robert L.
1424 16th St. NW
Suite 300
Washington, DC 20036-2211
Tel: (202)518-6500
Fax: (202)588-0314

Employers
Nat'l Center for Neighborhood Enterprise (President)

WOODSON, Roderic
2099 Pennsylvania Ave. NW
Suite 100
Washington, DC 20006
EMail: rwoodson@hklaw.com
Tel: (202)955-3000
Fax: (202)955-5564

Employers
Holland & Knight LLP (Senior Counsel)

WOODWARD, Anne
1733 King St.
Alexandria, VA 22314
EMail: woodward@cmaa.org
Tel: (703)739-9500
Fax: (703)739-0124

Employers
Club Managers Ass'n of America (Manager, Education)

WOODY, Robert J.

600 14th St. NW
Washington, DC 20005
Tel: (202)783-8400
Fax: (202)783-4211
Registered: LDA

Employers
Shook, Hardy & Bacon LLP

Clients Represented

On Behalf of Shook, Hardy & Bacon LLP
Molecular Separations Inc.

WOODY, Robert W.

1875 Connecticut Ave. NW
Suite 1200
Washington, DC 20009-5728
Tel: (202)986-8000
Fax: (202)986-8102
Registered: LDA
EMail: rwoody@llgm.com
Legislative Assistant to Rep. Bill Emerson (R-MO), 1983-87.

Employers
LeBoeuf, Lamb, Greene & MacRae L.L.P. (Counsel)

Clients Represented

On Behalf of LeBoeuf, Lamb, Greene & MacRae L.L.P.
Hydro-Quebec
Internat'l Underwriting Ass'n of London
Lloyd's of London

WOOLF, Karen Swanson

14th and Constitution Ave. NW
Washington, DC 20230
Tel: (202)482-3663
Fax: (202)482-4420

Employers
Department of Commerce (Assistant Secretary and Deputy Assistant Secretary, Legislation)

WOOLFOLK, Brian P.

513 Capitol Court NE
Suite 100
Washington, DC 20002
Tel: (202)547-9505
Fax: (202)478-0279
Registered: LDA
EMail: brian@mattoxwoolfolk.com
Former Minority Counsel, House Judiciary Committee.

Employers
Mattox Woolfolk, LLC (Partner)

Clients Represented

On Behalf of Mattox Woolfolk, LLC
Constituency for Africa
ICG Communications, Inc.
MCI WorldCom Corp.
Voices, Inc.

WOOLLETT, Ph.D., Gillian

1100 15th St. NW
Suite 900
Washington, DC 20005
Tel: (202)835-3400
Fax: (202)835-3414
Registered: LDA

Employers
Pharmaceutical Research and Manufacturers of America (Assistant V. President, Biologics and Biotechnology)

WOOLLEY, Howard

1300 I St. NW
Suite 400 West
Washington, DC 20005
Tel: (202)515-2400
Fax: (202)589-3760
Registered: LDA

Employers
Verizon Wireless (V. President, Federal Relations)

WOOLLEY, Esq., Linda A.

1155 Connecticut Ave. NW
Suite 500
Washington, DC 20036
Tel: (202)466-4840
Fax: (202)466-4841
Registered: LDA
EMail: lwoolley@legislaw.com

Employers
LegisLaw (Principal)

Clients Represented

On Behalf of LegisLaw
Comerica, Inc.
ITT Industries
Lehigh Portland Cement Co.
McDonnell & Miller
TRW Inc.

WOOLSEY, R. James

1800 Massachusetts Ave. NW
Washington, DC 20036
Tel: (202)828-2000
Fax: (202)828-2195
Director, Central Intelligence Agency, 1993-95. Undersecretary, Department of the Navy, 1977-79. General Counsel, Senate Armed Services Committee, 1970-73.

Employers
Shea & Gardner (Partner)

Clients Represented

On Behalf of Shea & Gardner
North American Industrial Hemp Council, Inc.

WOOTAN, Margo

1875 Connecticut Ave. NW
Suite 300
Washington, DC 20009
Tel: (202)332-9110
Fax: (202)265-4954
Registered: LDA

Employers
Center for Science in the Public Interest (Senior Staff Scientist)

WOOTTON, James

1615 H St. NW
Washington, DC 20062
Tel: (202)463-5724
Fax: (202)463-5302
Registered: LDA

Employers
U.S. Chamber Institute for Legal Reform (President)

WORDEN, Vicki

40 Ivy St. SE
Washington, DC 20003
Tel: (202)547-2230
Fax: (202)547-7640

Employers
Nat'l Lumber and Building Material Dealers Ass'n (Director, Public Affairs)

WORK, Charles R.

600 13th St. NW
Washington, DC 20005-3096
Tel: (202)756-8030
Fax: (202)756-8087
EMail: cwork@mwe.com

Employers
McDermott, Will and Emery (Partner; Department Head, Regulation and Government Affairs)

WORK, Peter B.

1001 Pennsylvania Ave. NW
Suite 1100
Washington, DC 20004-2595
Tel: (202)624-2500
Fax: (202)628-5116

Employers
Crowell & Moring LLP (Partner)

WORKMAN, Willard A.

1615 H St. NW
Washington, DC 20062-2000
Tel: (202)463-5460
Fax: (202)463-3114
Registered: LDA

Employers
Chamber of Commerce of the U.S.A. (V. President, International Division)

WORKS, George

908 Pennsylvania Ave. SE
Washington, DC 20003
Tel: (202)544-5666
Fax: (202)544-4647

Employers
Advantage Associates, Inc. (Professional Staff)

WORLEY, Michael

14850 Conference Center Dr.
Suite 100
Chantilly, VA 20151-3831
Tel: (703)621-2803
Fax: (703)621-4989
Registered: LDA
EMail: michael.worley@rollsroyce.com

Employers
Rolls-Royce North America Inc. (Director, Marine Programs)

WORRALL, Thomas

700 13th St. NW
Suite 350
Washington, DC 20005
Tel: (202)637-0040
Fax: (202)637-0041
Registered: LDA

Employers
Rhoads Group (V. President, Business Development)

Clients Represented

On Behalf of Rhoads Group
AAAE-ACI
Airports Council Internat'l - North America
American Management Systems
Dick Corp.
The Justice Project, Inc.
PNC Bank, N.A.
SWATH Ocean Systems, Inc.
United States Enrichment Corp.

WORSHAM, Wanda

1400 Independence Ave. SW
Washington, DC 20250
Tel: (202)720-7095
Fax: (202)720-8077

Employers
Department of Agriculture (Acting Assistant Secretary for Congressional Relations)

WORSLEY, Joleen L.

201 Massachusetts Ave. NE
Suite C-8
Washington, DC 20002
Tel: (202)546-5007
Fax: (202)546-7037
EMail: joleen@celi.org

Employers
Congressional Economic Leadership Institute (Director)

WORSTELL, MPH, Mary E.

1233 20th St. NW
Suite 402
Washington, DC 20036-2330
Tel: (800)727-8462
Fax: (202)466-8940
EMail: info@aafa.org

Employers
Asthma and Allergy Foundation of America (Exec. Director)

WORTH, Ronald D.

99 Canal Center Plaza
Suite 250
Alexandria, VA 22314
Tel: (703)549-6117
Fax: (703)549-2498
EMail: ron@smps.org

Employers
Soc. for Marketing Professional Services (Exec. V. President)

WORTH, Steven M.

1620 I Street NW
Suite 900
Washington, DC 20006
Tel: (202)785-8940
Fax: (202)785-8949
EMail: steve_worth@plexusconsulting.com

Employers
The Plexus Consulting Group (Managing Partner)

WORTHINGTON, Barry K.

1300 Pennsylvania Ave. NW
Suite 550
Mailbox 142
Washington, DC 20004-3022
Tel: (202)312-1230
Fax: (202)682-1682

Employers
United States Energy Ass'n (Exec. Director)

WORTLEY, MC (Ret.), Hon. George C.

1776 K St. NW
Suite 400
Washington, DC 20006
Tel: (202)296-7555
Fax: (202)785-0025
Registered: LDA
Member, U.S. House of Representatives (R-NY), 1981-89.

Employers
Dierman, Wortley, and Zola (Chairman)

Clients Represented

On Behalf of Dierman, Wortley, and Zola
Bangladesh Export Processing Zones Authority

WORTMANN, Barbara E.

2500 Wilson Blvd.
Arlington, VA 22201-3834
Tel: (703)907-7500
Fax: (703)907-7501

Employers
Electronic Industries Alliance (Senior V. President, Policy, Planning and Industry Relations)

WORTZEL, Larry

214 Massachusetts Ave. NE
Washington, DC 20002
Tel: (202)546-4400
Fax: (202)546-8328

Employers
Heritage Foundation (Director, Kathryn & Shelby Collom Davis Internat'l Studies)

WOTOCHEK, Jennifer

801 G St. NW
Washington, DC 20001
Tel: (202)393-2100
Fax: (202)393-2134
Registered: LDA

Employers
Family Research Council, Inc. (Legislative Assistant)

WRATHALL, James R.

2445 M St. NW
Washington, DC 20037-1420
Tel: (202)663-6000
Fax: (202)663-6363
EMail: jwrathall@wilmer.com

Employers
Wilmer, Cutler & Pickering (Partner)

WRIGHT, Andy

225 Reinekers Ln.
Suite 600
Alexandria, VA 22314
Tel: (703)549-6990
Fax: (703)549-7640
Registered: LDA

Employers
Satellite Broadcasting and Communications Ass'n (V. President, Government Affairs)

WRIGHT, Christopher

1200 18th St. NW
Suite 1200
Washington, DC 20036
Tel: (202)730-1300
Fax: (202)730-1301
Served as General Counsel and Deputy General Counsel (1994-2001) and as Assistant to the Solicitor General, all at the Federal Communications Commission.

Employers
Harris, Wiltshire & Grannis LLP

WRIGHT, Elizabeth

1301 Connecticut Ave. NW
Fourth Floor
Washington, DC 20036
Tel: (202)467-5300
Fax: (202)467-4253
Registered: LDA
EMail: ewright@cagw.org
Former Special Assistant of Public Affairs for the Food and Drug Administration, Department of Health and Human Services, during the Bush I administration.

Employers
Citizens Against Government Waste (Director, Health and Sciences)

WRIGHT, F. Leo

815 Connecticut Ave. NW
Suite 1200
Washington, DC 20006
Tel: (202)833-8128
Fax: (202)833-7924
Registered: LDA
Assistant Inspector General, Department of State, 1962-64. Special Agent, Federal Bureau of Investigation, Department of Justice, 1959-62. Lieutenant (Junior Grade), U.S. Navy, 1953-56.

Employers
Leo Wright Associates (President)

WRIGHT, Rev. Francis W.

1720 Massachusetts Ave. NW
Washington, DC 20036
Tel: (202)775-8637
Fax: (202)429-2987

Employers
Holy Childhood Ass'n (National Director)

WRIGHT, Henrietta

1229 19th St. NW
Washington, DC 20036
Tel: (202)429-4900
Fax: (202)429-4912
Registered: LDA
EMail: general@g2w2.com
Law Clerk to Judge Clement F. Haynsworth, Jr., U.S. Court of Appeals, Fourth Circuit, 1984-85. Staff Member, The White House, 1979-81.

Employers
Goldberg, Godles, Wiener & Wright (Counsel)

WRIGHT, James R.

2101 Constitution Ave. NW
Washington, DC 20418
Tel: (202)334-2000
Fax: (202)334-1684

Employers
Nat'l Academy of Sciences (General Counsel)

WRIGHT, Jennifer G.

1101 17th St. NW
Suite 1300
Washington, DC 20036-4700
Tel: (202)452-7133
Fax: (202)833-3661
Registered: LDA

Employers
American Iron and Steel Institute (PAC Contact)

WRIGHT, Joseph

1401 K St. NW
Suite 900
Washington, DC 20005
Tel: (202)626-8550
Fax: (202)626-8578

Employers
Jefferson Consulting Group (V. Chairman)

WRIGHT, Julie

1301 Pennsylvania Ave. NW
Suite 702
Washington, DC 20004
Tel: (202)393-2427
Fax: (202)393-2400

Employers
Council of the Great City Schools (Legislative Consultant)

WRIGHT, Leo

Eight E St. SE
Washington, DC 20003
Tel: (202)543-4172
Fax: (202)546-6294
Registered: LDA

Employers
Washington Public Affairs Group

WRIGHT, Lisa

110 Maryland Ave. NE
Building Box 45
Washington, DC 20002
EMail: lisaw@ncccusa.org
Tel: (202)543-6336
Fax: (202)546-6232

Employers
Church World Service/Lutheran World Relief (Associate Director, International Director and Global Issues)

WRIGHT, Lori E.

1133 19th St. NW
Washington, DC 20036
Tel: (202)736-6468
Fax: (202)736-6191
Registered: LDA
EMail: lori.wright@wcom.com

Employers
MCI WorldCom Corp. (Manager, FCC Regulatory)

WRIGHT, Patrisha

1629 K St. NW
Suite 802
Washington, DC 20006
Tel: (202)986-0375
Fax: (202)462-5624
Registered: LDA

Employers
Disability Rights Education and Defense Fund (Director, Governmental Affairs)

WRIGHT, Paul R.

1902 Association Dr.
Reston, VA 20190
Tel: (703)620-6600
Ext: 299
Fax: (703)620-5873

Employers
American Medical Student Ass'n (Exec. Director)

WRIGHT, R. Michael

1400 16th St. NW
Suite 120
Washington, DC 20036
EMail: africanwildlife@awf.org
Tel: (202)939-3333
Fax: (202)939-3332

Employers
African Wildlife Foundation (President and Chief Exec. Officer)

WRIGHT, Samuel H.

1225 I St. NW
Suite 500
Washington, DC 20005
Tel: (202)312-2006
Fax: (202)408-0861
Registered: LDA
EMail: samuel.wright@cendant.com

Employers
Cendant Corp. (Senior V. President)

WRIGHT, Steven H.

2099 Pennsylvania Ave. NW
Suite 100
Washington, DC 20006
Tel: (202)955-3000
Fax: (202)955-5564
Registered: LDA

Employers
Holland & Knight LLP

Clients Represented

On Behalf of Holland & Knight LLP
Wyeth-Ayerst Laboratories
Wyeth-Ayerst Pharmaceuticals

WRIGHT, Susan

8300 Colesville Rd.
Suite 750
Silver Spring, MD 20910
Tel: (301)585-1855
Fax: (301)585-1866

Employers
Nat'l Burglar and Fire Alarm Ass'n (Director, Government Relations)

WRIGHT, Wayne

1000 Wilson Blvd.
Suite 2705
Arlington, VA 22209
Tel: (703)248-6101
Fax: (703)248-6120
Registered: LDA

Employers
Methanex Inc. (V. President, Government Relations)

WRINN, Dan

1301 Pennsylvania Ave. NW
Suite 402
Washington, DC 20004
Tel: (202)347-1530
Fax: (202)347-1533
Registered: LDA

Employers
Ducks Unlimited Inc. (Government Affairs Representative)

WROBLESKI, Ann B.

1401 K St. NW
Tenth Floor
Washington, DC 20005
Tel: (202)216-2200
Fax: (202)216-2999
Registered: LDA, FARA
Former Assistant Secretary for International Narcotics Matters, Department of State; Director of Projects to the First Lady during the Reagan administration; Legislative Aide to Senator Richard Stone (D-FL); Legislative Aide to Rep. Lou Frey (R-FL); and Legislative Aide Senator Ed Gurney (R-FL).

Employers
Jefferson-Waterman Internat'l, LLC (Chief Operating Officer)

Clients Represented

On Behalf of Jefferson-Waterman Internat'l, LLC
Edison Mission Energy
GPU, Inc.
Jamaica, Government of
Sithe Energies
Western Wireless Internat'l

WROBLEWSKI, Jonathan J.

Patrick Henry Bldg.
601 D St. NW, Room 6917
Washington, DC 20530
Tel: (202)514-3062
Fax: (202)514-9412

Employers
Department of Justice - Criminal Division (Acting Director, Office of Policy and Legislation)

WUERTHNER, Jr., J. J.

7207 Giles Pl.
Suite 100
Springfield, VA 22150-3708
Tel: (703)569-4840

Employers
Wuerthner Associates, Inc. (President)

WUNDER, Jr., Bernard J.

1615 L St. NW
Suite 650
Washington, DC 20036
Tel: (202)778-0881
Fax: (202)659-1109
Registered: LDA
EMail: bwunder@wkltflaw.com
Assistant Secretary for Communications and Information, Department of Commerce, 1981-83. Aide to Rep. James Broyhill (R-NC) and Chief Counsel, Subcommittee on Communications, House Committee on Interstate and Foreign Commerce, 1975-81.

Employers
Wunder & Lilley (Partner)

Clients Represented
On Behalf of Wunder & Lilley
BellSouth Corp.
Qwest Communications
United States Telecom Ass'n

WUNDERLY, Susan M.

1200 Wilson Blvd.
Arlington, VA 22209-1989
Tel: (703)465-3213
Fax: (703)456-3003
Registered: LDA

Employers
The Boeing Co. (Legislative Affairs, International Programs)

WURF, Mildred Kiefer

1001 Connecticut Ave. NW
Suite 412
Washington, DC 20036
Tel: (202)463-1881
Fax: (202)463-8994
EMail: mwurf@girls-inc.org

Employers
Girls Incorporated (Director, Public Policy)

WURGLITZ, Alfred M.

555 13th St. NW
Suite 500 West
Washington, DC 20004
Tel: (202)383-5300
Fax: (202)383-5414
Registered: LDA
EMail: awurglitz@omm.com

Employers
O'Melveny and Myers LLP (Partner)

Clients Represented
On Behalf of O'Melveny and Myers LLP
Lockheed Martin Corp.

WURMSER, David

1150 17th St. NW
Washington, DC 20036
Tel: (202)862-5800
Fax: (202)862-7177
EMail: dwurmser@aei.org

Employers
American Enterprise Institute for Public Policy Research (Resident Scholar)

WYATT, D. Rick

801 Pennsylvania Ave. NW
Suite 350
Washington, DC 20004
Tel: (202)783-1400
Fax: (202)783-1746

Employers
Newport News Shipbuilding Inc. (Treasurer, Newport News Shipbuilding Political Action Committee)

WYATT, Jr., Richard

1333 New Hampshire Ave. NW
Suite 400
Washington, DC 20036
Tel: (202)887-4000
Fax: (202)887-4288

Employers
Akin, Gump, Strauss, Hauer & Feld, L.L.P. (Partner)

Clients Represented
On Behalf of Akin, Gump, Strauss, Hauer & Feld, L.L.P.
Food Lion, Inc.

WYE, Christopher

1120 G St. NW
Suite 850
Washington, DC 20005
Tel: (202)682-4010
Fax: (202)682-1119
EMail: cwye@napawash.org

Employers
Nat'l Academy of Public Administration (Director, Center for Improving Government Performance)

WYERMAN, James

1828 Jefferson Pl. NW
Washington, DC 20036
Tel: (202)833-2020
Fax: (202)833-5307
Registered: LDA

Employers
20/20 Vision (Exec. Director)

WYLD, Thomas

P.O. Box 1808
Washington, DC 20013-1808
Tel: (202)546-0983
Fax: (202)546-0986
Registered: LDA
EMail: wyld@mrf.org

Employers
Motorcycle Riders Foundation (V. President, Government Relations)

WYLIE, USN (Ret.), Capt. Peter C.

201 N. Washington St.
Alexandria, VA 22314
Tel: (800)245-8762
Fax: (703)838-8173
EMail: petew@troa.org

Employers
The Retired Officers Ass'n (TROA) (General Counsel and Secretary)

WYLIE, Thomas L.

1130 Connecticut Ave. NW
Suite 710
Washington, DC 20036
Tel: (202)628-1010
Fax: (202)628-1041
Registered: LDA
EMail: thomas_l_wylie@sunoil.com

Employers
Sunoco, Inc. (V. President, Federal Government Relations)

WYMA, John

1400 16th St. NW
Suite 600
Washington, DC 20036
Tel: (202)939-7900
Fax: (202)745-0916

Employers
Fleischman and Walsh, L.L.P.

Clients Represented
On Behalf of Fleischman and Walsh, L.L.P.
ORBITZ
SBC Communications Inc.

WYMAN, Eben M.

4301 N. Fairfax Dr.
Suite 360
Arlington, VA 22203-1627
Tel: (703)358-9300
Fax: (703)358-9307
Registered: LDA

Employers
Nat'l Utility Contractors Ass'n (NUCA) (Director of Government Relations)

WYMAN, Lucia A.

801 Pennsylvania Ave. NW
Suite 730
Washington, DC 20004
Tel: (202)756-2402
Fax: (202)756-2403
Registered: LDA
EMail: Wyman@howdc.com
Former Special Assistant to the President for Legislative Affairs, House Liaison Office, Executive Office of the President, The White House, during the Clinton administration.

Employers
Hooper Owen & Winburn (Principal)

Clients Represented
On Behalf of Hooper Owen & Winburn
First Preston Management
Houston Advanced Research Center

WYMAN, Jr., Samuel H.

1401 K St. NW
Tenth Floor
Washington, DC 20005
Tel: (202)216-2200
Fax: (202)216-2999
Registered: LDA, FARA
Former operations officer, Central Intelligence Agency.

Employers
Jefferson-Waterman Internat'l, LLC (Exec. V. President)

Clients Represented
On Behalf of Jefferson-Waterman Internat'l, LLC
ComInternational Management Inc.

WYNN, Jr., H. Montee

4301 Wilson Blvd.
Arlington, VA 22203-1860
Tel: (703)907-5819
Fax: (703)907-5516
Registered: LDA
EMail: montee.wynn@nreca.com

Employers
Nat'l Rural Electric Cooperative Ass'n (Legislative Representative and Counsel)

WYNNS, Pat

901 E St. NW
Suite 600
Washington, DC 20004
Tel: (202)783-4444
Fax: (202)783-4085

Employers
Nat'l Treasury Employees Union (Associate General Counsel)

WYRICK, Michael K.

1055 N. Fairfax St.
Suite 201
Alexandria, VA 22314-3563
Tel: (703)739-7999
Fax: (703)739-7995
EMail: michaelw@usstrategies.com
Former Aide to Senator David Pryor (D-AR) and Legislative Assistant to Rep. Jay Dickey (R-AR).

Employers
U.S. Strategies Corp. (Consultant)

Clients Represented
On Behalf of U.S. Strategies Corp.
American Institute for Public Safety
Ash Britt

WYSOCKI, Susan

503 Capitol Ct. NE
Suite 300
Washington, DC 20002
Tel: (202)543-9693
Fax: (202)543-9858

Employers
Nat'l Ass'n of Nurse Practitioners in Women's Health (President)

WYTKIND, Edward

888 16th Street NW
Suite 650
Washington, DC 20006
Tel: (202)628-9262
Fax: (202)628-0391
Registered: LDA

Employers
AFL-CIO - Transportation Trades Department (Exec. Director)

XULAM, Kani

2600 Connecticut Ave. NW
Suite One
Washington, DC 20008-1558
Tel: (202)483-6444
Fax: (202)483-6476

Employers
American Kurdish Information Network (AKIN) (Director)

YABLON, Jeffery L.

2300 N St. NW
Washington, DC 20037-1128
Tel: (202)663-8000
Fax: (202)663-8007
EMail: jeffery.yablon@shawpittman.com
Law Clerk to Judge Cynthia Holcomb Hall, U.S. Tax Court, 1973-75.

Employers
Shaw Pittman (Partner)

Clients Represented
On Behalf of Shaw Pittman
The Progress Freedom Foundation

YABLUNOSKY, Andrea

1627 I St. NW
Suite 950
Washington, DC 20006
Tel: (202)223-5115
Fax: (202)223-5118

Employers
ConAgra Foods, Inc. (Administrator, Regulatory Affairs)

YACKER, Marc D.

1333 H St. NW
West Tower
Eighth Floor
Washington, DC 20005
EMail: elcon@elcon.org
Tel: (202)682-1390
Fax: (202)289-6370
Registered: LDA

Employers
Electricity Consumers Resource Council (ELCON) (Director, Government and Public Affairs)

YACON-HOPPER, Jill

901 D St. SW
Suite 900
Washington, DC 20024
Tel: (202)479-0500
Fax: (202)646-5233

Employers
Battelle Memorial Institute (Manager, Government Relations)

YADON, Shawn

300 Maryland Ave. NE
Washington, DC 20002
Tel: (202)546-1631
Fax: (202)546-3309
Registered: LDA

Employers
FedEx Corp. (Senior State and Local Affairs Representative)

YAFFE, David P.

1050 Thomas Jefferson St. NW
Seventh Floor
Washington, DC 20007
EMail: dpy@vnf.com
Tel: (202)298-1800
Fax: (202)338-2416

Employers
Van Ness Feldman, P.C. (Member)

YAGER, Daniel V.

1015 15th St. NW
Suite 1200
Washington, DC 20005
Tel: (202)789-8600
Fax: (202)789-1708
Registered: LDA

Minority Counsel (1986-88) and Associate Minority Counsel (1983-86), House Committee on Education and Labor. Legislative Director to Rep. Marge Roukema (R-NJ), 1981-83.

Employers
McGuiness Norris & Williams, LLP (Partner)

Clients Represented

On Behalf of McGuiness Norris & Williams, LLP
Labor Policy Ass'n (LPA)

YAGER, Milan P.

901 N. Pitt St.
Suite 150
Alexandria, VA 22314
Tel: (703)836-0466
Fax: (703)836-0976

Employers
Nat'l Ass'n of Professional Employer Organizations (Executive V. President)

YAKSICH, Nick

525 School St. SW
Suite 303
Washington, DC 20024
EMail: cimadc@sprynet.com
Tel: (202)479-2666
Fax: (202)554-0885

Employers
Construction Industry Manufacturers Ass'n (V. President, Government Affairs)

YAMADA, Gerald H.

1299 Pennsylvania Ave. NW
Tenth Floor
Washington, DC 20004-2400
EMail: geraldyamada@paulhastings.com
Tel: (202)508-9500
Fax: (202)508-9700

Acting General Counsel (1993,1989,1985) and Principal Deputy Attorney General (1982-95), Environmental Protection Agency.

Employers
Paul, Hastings, Janofsky & Walker LLP (Of Counsel)

YAMADA, Sawaaki

601 13th St. NW
Suite 330 South
Washington, DC 20005
Tel: (202)783-6013
Fax: (202)783-6005

Employers
Nomura Research Institute America, Inc. (General Manager, Washington Office)

YAMADA, T. Albert

1000 Connecticut Ave. NW
Suite 304
Washington, DC 20036
Tel: (202)296-4484
Fax: (202)293-3060
Registered: LDA, FARA

Employers
Masaoka & Associates, Inc. (President)

Clients Represented

On Behalf of Masaoka & Associates, Inc.
Fresh Produce Ass'n of the Americas

YAMAGATA, Ben

1050 Thomas Jefferson St. NW
Seventh Floor
Washington, DC 20007
EMail: bny@vnf.com
Tel: (202)298-1800
Fax: (202)338-2416
Registered: LDA

Counsel and Staff Director, Subcommittee on Energy Research and Development, Senate Committee on Energy and Natural Resources, 1975-77. Legislative Counsel to Senator Frank Church (D-ID), 1974-75. Professional Staff Member, Senate Special Committee on Aging, 1973-74.

Employers
Van Ness Feldman, P.C. (Member)

Clients Represented

On Behalf of Van Ness Feldman, P.C.
Coal Utilization Research Council
The Electric Vehicle Ass'n of the Americas (EVAA)

YAMAMOTO, Andrea

1150 17th St. NW
Suite 400
Washington, DC 20036
Tel: (202)222-4700
Fax: (202)222-4799

Employers
The Walt Disney Co. (Assistant)

YAMPOLSKY, Harvey A.

1050 Connecticut Ave. NW
Washington, DC 20036-5339
Tel: (202)857-6000
Fax: (202)857-6395
Registered: LDA

Chief Counsel to the Inspector General, Department of Health and Human Services, 1978-90. Legislative Counsel, Department of Health, Education and Welfare, 1976-77. Special Assistant to Chief Deputy Majority Whip of the House, Rep. John Brademas (D-IN), 1975. Staff Attorney, Department of Health, Education and Welfare, 1971-72.

Employers
Arent Fox Kintner Plotkin & Kahn, PLLC (Member)

YANCEY, Dalton

1301 Pennsylvania Ave. NW
Suite 401
Washington, DC 20004-1729
EMail: dflgator@aol.com
Tel: (202)785-4070
Fax: (202)659-8581
Registered: LDA

Employers
Florida Sugar Cane League, Inc. (Exec. V. President)
Gay & Robinson, Inc. (Washington Representative)
Hawaiian Commercial and Sugar Company (Washington Representative)
Rio Grande Valley Sugar Growers (Washington Representative)

YANETTE, Terry

125 N. West St.
Alexandria, VA 22314-2754
Tel: (703)683-1400
Fax: (703)549-6610
Registered: LDA

Employers
Fleet Reserve Ass'n (National Veterans Service Officer)

YANG, KaYing

1628 16th St. NW
Third Floor
Washington, DC 20009-3099
Tel: (202)667-4690
Fax: (202)667-6449

Employers
Southeast Asia Resource Action Center (SEARAC) (Exec. Director)

YANISH, Nancy Foster

655 15th St. NW
Washington, DC 20005-5701
EMail: nyanish@fmi.org
Tel: (202)220-0628
Fax: (202)220-0873
Registered: LDA

Employers
Food Marketing Institute (Director, Government Relations)

YANOFF, Leonard

1401 K St. NW
Suite 600
Washington, DC 20005
Tel: (202)835-9898
Fax: (202)853-9893

Employers
ASCENT (Ass'n of Community Enterprises) (V. President, Advanced Services)

YANOVITCH, Lawrence

1101 14th St. NW
11th Floor
Washington, DC 20005-5601
EMail: lyanovitch@villagebanking.org
Tel: (202)682-1510
Fax: (202)682-1535

Employers
FINCA Internat'l Inc., The Foundation for Internat'l Community Assistance (Director, Policy and Research)

YARBROUGH, Katherine P.

1275 Pennsylvania Ave. NW
Washington, DC 20004-2415
Tel: (202)383-0100
Fax: (202)637-3593
Registered: LDA

Employers
Sutherland Asbill & Brennan LLP (Partner)

Clients Represented

On Behalf of Sutherland Asbill & Brennan LLP
New York Mercantile Exchange

YARNELL, Christy

1350 New York Ave. NW
Suite 1100
Washington, DC 20005-4798
Tel: (202)879-4000
Fax: (202)393-2866

Employers
Spiegel & McDiarmid (Head Librarian)

YAROWSKY, Jonathan R.

2550 M St. NW
Washington, DC 20037-1350
EMail: jyarowsky@pattonboggs.com
Tel: (202)457-6000
Fax: (202)457-6315
Registered: LDA

Special Associate Counsel to the President, The White House, 1995-98. General Counsel, House Committee on the Judiciary, 1990-95.

Employers
Patton Boggs, LLP (Partner)

Clients Represented

On Behalf of Patton Boggs, LLP
AOL Time Warner
Ass'n of Trial Lawyers of America
Crane Co.
DFS Group Ltd.
EchoStar Communications Corp.
Information Technology Ass'n of America (ITAA)
McKinsey & Co., Inc.
Medical Device Manufacturers Ass'n
Nat'l Ass'n of Consumer Bankruptcy Attorneys
Nat'l Community Pharmacists Ass'n
Pechanga Band of California Luiseno Indians
Retractable Technologies, Inc.
Time Domain Corp.
United Airlines

YARWOOD, Bruce

1201 L St. NW
Washington, DC 20005-4014
Tel: (202)842-4444
Fax: (202)842-3860
Registered: LDA

Employers
American Health Care Ass'n (Legislative Counsel)
Helmsin & Yarwood Associates (Partner)

Clients Represented

On Behalf of Helmsin & Yarwood Associates

Alliance for Elder Care
American Health Care Ass'n
CaRess, Inc.
Crestwood Behavior Health, Inc.

YAS, Penelope

1800 K St. NW
Suite 1102
Washington, DC 20006
Tel: (202)833-2742
Fax: (202)833-0189

Employers
Asia Society (Assistant Director, Development)

YATES, Kenneth A.

1401 K St. NW
Tenth Floor
Washington, DC 20005
Tel: (202)216-2200
Fax: (202)216-2999
Registered: FARA

Former Foreign Service Officer, United States Information Agency.

Employers
Jefferson-Waterman Internat'l, LLC (Senior V. President)

YATES, Valerie

1909 K St. NW
Suite 820
Washington, DC 20006
EMail: vyates@lmm-law.com
Tel: (202)777-7700
Fax: (202)777-7763

Assistant Chief (1998-99), Counsel to the Chief (1997-98), and Staff Attorney, Accounting and Audits Division (1996-97), Common Carrier Bureau, Federal Communications Commission. Staff Attorney, Division of Credit Practices, Consumer Protection Bureau, Federal Trade Commission, 1994-96.

Employers
Lawler, Metzger & Milkman, LLC (Associate)

Clients Represented

On Behalf of Lawler, Metzger & Milkman, LLC

Gemini Networks, Inc.
MCI WorldCom Corp.

YAWN, Edward R.

701 Pennsylvania Ave. NW
Washington, DC 20004-2696
Tel: (202)508-5481
Fax: (202)508-5403
Registered: LDA

Employers
Edison Electric Institute (Director, Government Relations)

YEAGER, Brooks

1250 24th St. NW
Washington, DC 20037
Tel: (202)293-4800
Fax: (202)293-9211

Employers
World Wildlife Fund (V. President, Global Threats)

YEDINAK, Tom

1666 K St. NW
Washington, DC 20006
EMail: tyedinak@apt.com
Tel: (202)296-4700
Fax: (202)496-4324

Employers
American Public Transportation Ass'n (Senior Legislative Representative)

YEDINKSY, Theo

600 Pennsylvania Ave. SE
Suite 400
Washington, DC 20003
Tel: (202)546-0007
Fax: (202)544-5002

Employers
Democratic Leadership Council (Director, DLC Trade Project)

YEP, Richard

5999 Stevenson Ave.
Alexandria, VA 22304-3300
Tel: (703)823-9800
Fax: (703)823-0252

Employers
American Counseling Ass'n (Exec. Director)

YERGAN-WILLIS, Renae

1801 L St. NW
MS: 9309
Washington, DC 20507
Tel: (202)663-4900
Fax: (202)663-4912

Employers
Equal Employment Opportunity Commission (Congressional Liaison Specialist)

YESH, Constance L.

601 Pennsylvania Ave. NW
Suite 540
North Bldg.
Washington, DC 20004
EMail: clyesh@ashland.com
Tel: (202)223-8290
Fax: (202)293-2913

Employers
Ashland Inc. (Staff Assistant)

YESIN, Erol

1621 N. Kent St.
Suite 300
Arlington, VA 22209-2131
EMail: eyesin@tda.gov
Tel: (703)875-4357
Fax: (703)875-4009

Employers
Trade and Development Agency (Legislative/Public Affairs Support)

YESNER, Donna Lee

1900 K St. NW
Washington, DC 20006
Tel: (202)496-7500
Fax: (202)496-7756

Employers
McKenna & Cuneo, L.L.P. (Of Counsel)

YEUTTER, Van

1101 15th St. NW
Suite 1000
Washington, DC 20005
EMail: van_yeutter@cargill.com
Tel: (202)530-8160
Fax: (202)530-8180

Employers
Cargill, Inc. (Director, Washington Operations and Internat'l Business Development)

YINGER, Nancy

1875 Connecticut Ave. NW
Suite 520
Washington, DC 20009
Tel: (202)483-1100
Fax: (202)328-3937

Employers
Population Reference Bureau (Director, International Programs)

YINGLING, Edward L.

1120 Connecticut Ave. NW
Washington, DC 20036
Tel: (202)663-5000
Fax: (202)828-4548
Registered: LDA

Employers
American Bankers Ass'n (Deputy Exec. V. President and Exec. Director, Government Relations)

YINGLING, Monique E.

888 17th St. NW
Suite 600
Washington, DC 20006-3959
EMail: meyingling@zsrlaw.com
Tel: (202)298-8660
Fax: (202)342-0683

Trial Attorney, Tax Division, Department of Justice, 1978-83.

Employers
Zuckert, Scoutt and Rasenberger, L.L.P. (Partner)

YITZHAKI, Eliyahu

4455 Connecticut Ave. NW
Suite B-400
Washington, DC 20008
Tel: (202)895-5290
Fax: (202)895-5298
Registered: FARA

Employers
Rafael U.S.A., Inc. (President and Chief Exec. Officer)

YOB, John

1300 N. 17th St.
Eighth Floor
Rosslyn, VA 22209-3801
EMail: yob@abc.org
Tel: (703)812-2000
Fax: (703)812-8202
Registered: LDA

Employers
Associated Builders and Contractors (Regional Field Representative)

YOCHELSON, John N.

1500 K St. NW
Suite 850
Washington, DC 20005
EMail: johny@compete.org
Tel: (202)682-4292
Fax: (202)682-5150

Employers
Council on Competitiveness (President)

YOCUM, Ph.D., Ronald

1300 Wilson Blvd.
Suite 800
Arlington, VA 22209
Tel: (703)253-0700
Fax: (703)253-0701
Registered: LDA

Employers
American Plastics Council (President and Chief Exec. Officer)

YOHE, D. Scott

1275 K St. NW
Suite 1200
Washington, DC 20005
Tel: (202)216-0700
Fax: (202)216-0824
Registered: LDA

Employers
Delta Air Lines (Senior V. President, Government Affairs)

YOKICH, Stephen P.

1350 I St. NW
Suite 510
Washington, DC 20005
Tel: (202)828-8500
Fax: (202)293-3457

Employers
United Automobile, Aerospace and Agricultural Implement Workers of America (UAW) (President)

YONKERS, Bob

1250 H St. NW
Suite 900
Washington, DC 20005
Tel: (202)737-4332
Fax: (202)331-7820
Registered: LDA

Employers
Internat'l Dairy Foods Ass'n (Chief Economist)

YONTZ, Caryl

1625 L St. NW
Washington, DC 20036-5687
EMail: cyontz@afscme.org
Tel: (202)429-1178
Fax: (202)223-3413
Registered: LDA

Employers
American Federation of State, County and Municipal Employees (Legislative Affairs Specialist)

YOOD, Andrew

1220 L St. NW
Washington, DC 20005
Tel: (202)682-8465
Fax: (202)682-8232
Registered: LDA

Employers
American Petroleum Institute (Taxation Director)

YORK, Amy

5025 Wisconsin Ave. NW
Washington, DC 20016
Tel: (202)537-1645
Fax: (202)244-7824
Registered: LDA

Employers
Amalgamated Transit Union (Legislative Representative)

YORK, Elizabeth

1500 K St. NW
Suite 650
Washington, DC 20005
Tel: (202)715-1000
Fax: (202)715-1001

Employers
GlaxoSmithKline (Federal Government Relations)

YORKER, Alan M.

900 Second St. NE
Suite 308
Washington, DC 20002-3557
Tel: (202)408-8362
Fax: (202)408-8287

Employers
Nat'l Ass'n of Railroad Passengers (President)

YOST, Joe

1913 I St. NW
Washington, DC 20006
Tel: (202)872-8110
Fax: (202)872-8114

Employers
Consumer Specialties Products Ass'n (Senior Representative, State Legislative Affairs)

YOUGH, Melissa I.

1901 N. Fort Myer Dr.
Suite 1200
Arlington, VA 22209-1604
Tel: (703)351-8000
Fax: (703)351-9160
Registered: LDA

Employers
Petroleum Marketers Ass'n of America (Counsel, Government Affairs)

YOUNG, Audrey B.

805 15th St. NW
Suite 700
Washington, DC 20005
EMail: abyoung@bakerd.com
Tel: (202)312-7400
Fax: (202)312-7441

Employers
Sagamore Associates, Inc. (Senior V. President)

Clients Represented
On Behalf of Sagamore Associates, Inc.
Alltrista/Penny

YOUNG, Beth

636 I St. NW
Washington, DC 20001-3736
Tel: (202)898-2444
Fax: (202)898-1185

Employers
American Soc. of Landscape Architects (Manager, Public Relations)

YOUNG, David

1500 K St. NW
Suite 875
Washington, DC 20005
Tel: (202)783-3195
Fax: (202)783-4862

Employers
Bituminous Coal Operators Ass'n (President)

YOUNG, M.D., Donald A.

1201 F St. NW
Suite 500
Washington, DC 20004
Tel: (202)824-1600
Fax: (202)824-1651
Registered: LDA

Employers
Health Insurance Ass'n of America (Chief Operating Officer and Medical Director)

YOUNG, III, Edward D.

1300 I St. NW
Suite 400 West
Washington, DC 20005
Tel: (202)515-2501
Fax: (202)336-7858

Employers
Verizon Communications (Senior V. President, Federal and International Public Policy)

YOUNG, Ellen S.

1275 Pennsylvania Ave. NW
Ninth Floor
Washington, DC 20004
EMail: eyoung@sdsatty.com
Tel: (202)662-6790
Fax: (202)624-0866
Registered: LDA

Employers
Stuntz, Davis & Staffier, P.C. (Principal)

Clients Represented
On Behalf of Stuntz, Davis & Staffier, P.C.
Edison Electric Institute
GE Power Systems
General Electric Appliances
General Electric Industrial & Power Systems

YOUNG, Francis L.

2121 K St. NW
Suite 800
Washington, DC 20037
Tel: (202)261-3550
Fax: (202)261-3551
Registered: LDA
Attorney-Advisor, Legal Assistant to the Chairman, and Legal Assistant to a Commissioner, Federal Communications Commission, 1976-82.

Employers
Young & Jatlow (Partner)

Clients Represented
On Behalf of Young & Jatlow
Alaska Network Systems
Future of Puerto Rico Inc.
Graphnet Inc.

YOUNG, Glenn M.

1201 Pennsylvania Ave. NW
P.O. Box 407
Washington, DC 20044-0407
EMail: gyoung@ssd.com
Tel: (202)626-6600
Fax: (202)626-6780

Employers
Squire, Sanders & Dempsey L.L.P. (Partner)

YOUNG, H. Peyton

1775 Massachusetts Ave. NW
Washington, DC 20036-2188
Tel: (202)797-6000
Fax: (202)797-6004

Employers
The Brookings Institution (Visiting Fellow, Economic Studies/Co-Dir., Center on Social & Economic Dynamics)

YOUNG, Holly Pitt

1350 I St. NW
Suite 500
Washington, DC 20005-3305
Tel: (202)682-3200
Fax: (202)682-3130
Registered: LDA
Former Legislative Assistant to Reps. Charles Taylor (R-NC) and Doc Hastings (R-WA)..

Employers
Corning Inc. (Manager,CORE PAC and Grassroots)

YOUNG, James B.

1299 Pennsylvania Ave. NW
Suite 800 West
Washington, DC 20004
Tel: (202)785-0500
Fax: (202)785-5277
Press Secretary to Senator Charles McC. Mathias (R-MD), 1972-76.

Employers
The Carmen Group (Associate)
LMRC, Inc. (Associate)

Clients Represented
On Behalf of The Carmen Group
Maryland Department of Transportation
Missouri Highway and Transportation Department
Nevada Department of Transportation
Northeast Illinois Regional Commuter Railroad Corp.
Utah Department of Transportation

YOUNG, James T.

1500 Pennsylvania Ave. NW
Room 3034MT
Washington, DC 20220
Tel: (202)622-1980
Fax: (202)622-0534

Employers
Department of Treasury (Deputy Assistant Secretary (Tax and Budget))

YOUNG, Jared G.

119 C St. SE
Washington, DC 20003
EMail: jyoung@c-a-n.net
Tel: (202)548-2563
Registered: LDA

Employers
People Advancing Christian Education (PACE)

YOUNG, Joanne

1050 Connecticut Ave. NW
Suite 1100
Washington, DC 20036-5304
EMail: Jyoung@baker-hostetler.com
Tel: (202)861-1500
Fax: (202)861-1790

Employers
Baker & Hostetler LLP (Partner)

Clients Represented
On Behalf of Baker & Hostetler LLP
Bangor Internat'l Airport
The Royal Jordanian Airline

YOUNG, John N.

1050 17th St. NW
Suite 510
Washington, DC 20036
EMail: young972@aol.com
Tel: (202)775-0079
Fax: (202)785-0477
Registered: LDA

Employers
Government Relations, Inc. (Associate)

Clients Represented
On Behalf of Government Relations, Inc.
Aldaron Inc.
Ass'n for Commuter Transportation
Community Transit
Fairfax, Virginia, County of
Friends of ITS/ITS America
Gateway Cities
Metropolitan Transportation Commission
Monroe, New York, County of
Oakland, Michigan, County of
Regional Public Tansportation Authority
Suburban Mobility Authority for Regional Transportation

YOUNG, Judith

1900 Association Dr.
Reston, VA 20191
EMail: naspe@aahperd.org
Tel: (703)476-3410
Fax: (703)476-8316

Employers
Nat'l Ass'n for Sport and Physical Education (Exec. Director)

YOUNG, Kelly C.

1311 L St. NW
Suite 300
Washington, DC 20005
Tel: (202)626-5620
Fax: (202)347-0956

Employers
21st Century Democrats (Exec. Director)

YOUNG, Kristin

1150 17th St. NW
Suite 701
Washington, DC 20036
EMail: kristin.young@dittus.com
Tel: (202)775-1401
Fax: (202)775-1404

Employers
Dittus Communications (Director)

Clients Represented
On Behalf of Dittus Communications
Community Financial Services Ass'n
Personal Watercraft Industry Ass'n

YOUNG, Malcolm C.

514 10th St. NW
Suite 1000
Washington, DC 20005
EMail: myoung@sentencingproject.org
Tel: (202)628-0871
Fax: (202)628-1091

Employers
The Sentencing Project (Exec. Director)

YOUNG, Mark D.

655 15th St. NW
Suite 1200
Washington, DC 20005
EMail: mark_young@kirkland.com
Tel: (202)879-5000
Fax: (202)879-5200
Registered: LDA
Assistant General Counsel (1980-82), Special Counsel (1979-80), and Staff Attorney (1977-79), Commodity Futures Trading Commission.

Employers
Kirkland & Ellis (Partner)

Clients Represented
On Behalf of Kirkland & Ellis
Chicago Board of Trade

YOUNG, Dr. Marlene

1757 Park Rd. NW
Washington, DC 20010
Tel: (202)232-6682
Fax: (202)462-2255

Employers
Nat'l Organization for Victim Assistance (Exec. Director)

YOUNG, Melanie

1891 Preston White Dr.
Reston, VA 20191-9312
Tel: (703)648-8900
Fax: (703)262-9312

Employers
American College of Radiology (Director, Radiology Advocacy Alliance)

YOUNG, Nina

1725 DeSales St. NW
Suite 600
Washington, DC 20036
Tel: (202)429-5609
Fax: (202)872-0619

Employers
Center for Marine Conservation (Director, Marine Wildlife Conservation)

YOUNG, S.

900 S. Washington St.
Suite G-13
Falls Church, VA 22046
Tel: (703)237-8616
Fax: (703)533-1153

Employers
Nat'l Ass'n of Physician Nurses (Director)

YOUNG, Stephen

1707 H St. NW
Suite 600
Washington, DC 20006-3919
Tel: (202)223-6133
Fax: (202)223-6162
Registered: LDA

Employers
Union of Concerned Scientists (Washington Representative, Senior Analyst)

YOUNG, Steve

113 S. West St.
P.O. Box 25708
Alexandria, VA 22313
EMail: syoung@aiccbox.org
Tel: (703)836-2422
Fax: (703)836-2795

Employers
Ass'n of Independent Corrugated Converters (Exec. V. President)

YOUNG, Tara

220 I St. NE
Suite 220
Washington, DC 20002
Tel: (202)544-0004
Fax: (202)544-1905
Registered: LDA

Employers
Nat'l Immigration Forum (Policy Assistant)

YOUNG, Thane

1001 G St. NW
Suite 400 East
Washington, DC 20001
Tel: (202)638-3730
Fax: (202)638-3516
Registered: LDA
Former Aide to Senator Pete Dominici (R-NM).

Employers
Peyser Associates, Inc.

Clients Represented

On Behalf of Peyser Associates, Inc.
The Irvine Co.
LACDA Alliance
Mission Springs Water District
Orange County Fire Authority
San Joaquin Area Flood Agency
San Joaquin Regional Transit District
Stockton, City of
Twentynine Palms Water District
Westminster, California, City of
Woodland, California, City of

YOUNG, Tony

2235 Cedar Ln.
Vienna, VA 22182
Tel: (703)560-6800
Fax: (703)849-8916

Employers
Consortium of Citizens with Disabilities (Chairperson)
NISH - Creating Employment Opportunities for People with Severe Disabilities (Director, Governmental Affairs)

YOUNG, William H.

100 Indiana Ave. NW
Washington, DC 20001
Tel: (202)393-4695
Fax: (202)737-1540

Employers
Nat'l Ass'n of Letter Carriers of the United States of America (Exec. V. President)

YOUNGBLOOD, Theresa M.

901 15th St. NW
Suite 700
Washington, DC 20005-2301
EMail: tmyoungblood@verner.com
Tel: (202)371-6000
Fax: (202)371-6279
Registered: LDA

Employers
Verner, Liipfert, Bernhard, McPherson and Hand, Chartered (Associate)

Clients Represented

On Behalf of Verner, Liipfert, Bernhard, McPherson and Hand, Chartered
Envirocare of Texas, Inc.
Independent Fuel Terminal Operators Ass'n
Kellogg Co.
Lockheed Martin Tactical Systems
Perry Tritech Inc.
VISA U.S.A., Inc.

YOUNTS, George R.

1350 I St. NW
Suite 1240
Washington, DC 20005
Tel: (202)296-3840
Fax: (202)682-0146

Employers
Ashby and Associates (Technical Director)

YOVIENE, Wendy M.

701 Pennsylvania Ave. NW
Suite 800
Washington, DC 20004
Tel: (202)508-4000
Fax: (202)508-4321
Registered: LDA

Employers
Thelen Reid & Priest LLP (Associate)

Clients Represented

On Behalf of Thelen Reid & Priest LLP
Anderson Erickson Dairy Co.
Horizon Organic Holding Co.
Tillamook County Creamery Ass'n
Upper Midwest Coalition

YU HUSSEIN, Pattie

1825 Connecticut Ave. NW
Suite 650
Washington, DC 20009
EMail: pyhussein@gyhllc.com
Tel: (202)745-5100
Fax: (202)234-6159

Employers
Garrett Yu Hussein LLC (Senior Partner)

YUAN, Nancy

1779 Massachusetts Ave. NW
Suite 815
Washington, DC 20036
Tel: (202)588-9420
Fax: (202)588-9409

Employers
The Asia Foundation (Director of Washington Programs)

YUDIN, David E.

1301 Pennsylvania Ave. NW
Suite 404
Washington, DC 20004-1727
Tel: (202)783-0911
Fax: (202)783-3524

Employers
Chicago, Illinois, Washington Office of the City of (Director)

YUSKA, Charles D.

4350 N. Fairfax Dr.
Suite 600
Arlington, VA 22203
Tel: (703)243-8555
Fax: (703)243-8556

Employers
Packaging Machinery Manufacturers Institute (President)

YZAGUIRRE, Raul

1111 19th St. NW
Suite 1000
Washington, DC 20036
Tel: (202)785-1670
Fax: (202)776-1792
Registered: LDA

Employers
Nat'l Council of La Raza (President)

ZACHARIADIS, Christofer P.

1805 Florida Ave. NW
Washington, DC 20009
Tel: (202)462-6333

Employers
Ass'n for Community Based Education (Exec. Director)

ZAGLANICZNY, Lawrence S.

1129 20th St. NW
Suite 400
Washington, DC 20036-3489
Tel: (202)785-0453
Fax: (202)785-1487
Registered: LDA

Employers
Nat'l Ass'n of Student Financial Aid Administrators (Associate Director, Government Affairs)

ZAHN, Josh

1199 N. Fairfax St.
Suite 1000
Alexandria, VA 22314
EMail: jzahn@hawthorngroup.com
Tel: (703)299-4499
Fax: (703)299-4488
Former special assistant to Senator John C. Danforth (R-MO).

Employers
The Hawthorn Group, L.C. (Senior Account Executive)

ZAINA, Lisa M.

555 12th St. NW
Washington, DC 20004
Tel: (202)347-4964
Fax: (202)347-4961
Registered: LDA

Employers
Wallman Strategic Consulting, LLC

Clients Represented

On Behalf of Wallman Strategic Consulting, LLC
Intermedia Communications Inc.

ZAKHEIM, Dr. Dove

1000 Wilson Blvd.
Arlington, VA 22209
Tel: (703)351-8317
Fax: (703)351-8567
Registered: LDA

Employers
System Planning Corp. (Corporate V. President)

ZAKUPOWSKY, Jr., Alexander

655 15th St. NW
Suite 900
Washington, DC 20005-5701
EMail: azakupowsky@milchev.com
Tel: (202)626-5800
Fax: (202)628-0858
Advisor on Tax Accounting Matters, Office of Tax Policy, Department of the Treasury, 1976-78.

Employers
Miller & Chevalier, Chartered (Member)

ZALEZNICK, Steven

601 E St. NW
Washington, DC 20049
Tel: (202)434-3483
Fax: (202)434-3640

Employers
AARP (American Ass'n of Retired Persons) (Chief Exec. Officer, AARP Services, Inc.)

ZAMBONE, Jennifer

1001 Connecticut Ave. NW
Suite 1250
Washington, DC 20036
Tel: (202)331-1010
Fax: (202)331-0640

Employers
Competitive Enterprise Institute (Environmental Policy Analyst)

ZANDO, Kate

7979 Old Georgetown Rd.
Suite 500
Bethesda, MD 20814
Tel: (301)986-9700
Fax: (301)986-9795

Employers
Adhesive and Sealant Council (Director, Administration and Finance)

ZANE, Curtis J.

4616 Arlington Blvd.
Arlington, VA 22204
Tel: (703)521-7393
Fax: (703)521-1633
Registered: LDA
Former Chief of Staff to Rep. Don Young (R-AK).

Employers
Zane & Associates (Partner)

Clients Represented

On Behalf of Zane & Associates

Alaska Railroad
Aleutian Pribilof Islands Community Development Ass'n
Alyeska Pipeline Service Co.
Chugach Alaska Corp.
Holland America West-Tours
Kake Tribal Corp.
North American Sports Management, Inc.
Ocean Services
Parents Incorporated
Saginaw Chippewa Indian Tribe of Michigan
Seward, Alaska, City of
TDX Village Corp.
Union Pacific
Wyandotte Tribe of Oklahoma

ZANNES, Maria

1401 H St. NW
Suite 220
Washington, DC 20005
Tel: (202)467-6240
Ext: 213
Fax: (202)467-6225
Registered: LDA

Employers

Integrated Waste Services Ass'n (President)

ZANOWIC, Kathleen

1300 I St. NW
Suite 400 West
Washington, DC 20005
Tel: (202)515-2561
Fax: (202)336-7925
Registered: LDA

Employers

Verizon Communications (Assistant V. President, Federal Government Relations)

ZANOWSKI, Paul J.

1201 15th St. NW
Washington, DC 20005-2800
Tel: (202)822-0470
Fax: (202)822-0572
Registered: LDA

Employers

Nat'l Ass'n of Home Builders of the U.S. (Congressional Representative and Grassroots Regional Director)

ZAPANTA, Albert C.

1300 Pennsylvania Ave. NW
Suite 270
Ronald Reagan Internat'l Trade Bldg.
Washington, DC 20004-3021
Tel: (202)371-8680
Fax: (202)371-8686

Employers

United States-Mexico Chamber of Commerce (President)

ZAPIEN, E. Ivan

2121 K St. NW
Suite 800
Washington, DC 20037
Tel: (202)261-3521
Fax: (202)261-3523
Registered: LDA

Former Staff to Senator Dennis DeConcini (D-AZ).

Employers

Lasa, Monroig & Veve (Director, Government and International Business Solutions)

Clients Represented

On Behalf of Lasa, Monroig & Veve

Mendez University System, Ana G.

ZAPRUDER, Henry G.

1050 Connecticut Ave. NW
Suite 1100
Washington, DC 20036-5304
Tel: (202)861-1500
Fax: (202)861-1790
Registered: LDA
EMail: hzapruder@baker-hostetler.com

Attorney, Office of Tax Legislative Counsel, Department of Treasury, 1967-69. Attorney, Tax Division, Department of Justice, 1963-67.

Employers

Baker & Hostetler LLP (Partner)

ZARAFONETIS, John

1717 Massachusetts Ave. NW
Suite 701
Washington, DC 20036
Tel: (202)667-8227
Fax: (202)667-8236

Employers

InterAction (Director, Development Policy and Practice)

ZARAGOZA, Richard R.

2300 N St. NW
Washington, DC 20037-1128
Tel: (202)663-8266
Fax: (202)663-8007
EMail: richard.zaragoza@shawpittman.com

Office of the General Counsel, Appellate Litigation Division (1970-72) and Attorney, Broadcast Bureau (1969-70), Federal Communications Commission.

Employers

Shaw Pittman (Partner)

ZARB, Jr., Frank G.

1800 M St. NW
Washington, DC 20036
Tel: (202)467-7000
Fax: (202)467-7176

Former Special Counsel, Securities and Exchange Commission.

Employers

Morgan, Lewis & Bockius LLP (Partner)

ZARO, Ph.D., CAE, Joan A.

4350 East-West Hwy.
Suite 500
Bethesda, MD 20814-4110
Tel: (301)941-0215
Fax: (301)941-0259

Employers

Endocrine Soc. (Senior Director, Governance and Policy)

ZATERMAN, Sunia

1250 I St. NW
Suite 901A
Washington, DC 20005
EMail: szaterman@cipha.org
Tel: (202)638-1300
Fax: (202)638-2364

Employers

Council of Large Public Housing Authorities (Exec. Director)

ZAUCHA, Thomas K.

1825 Samuel Morse Dr.
Reston, VA 20190
Tel: (703)437-5300
Fax: (703)437-7768
Registered: LDA

Employers

Nat'l Grocers Ass'n (President and Chief Exec. Officer)

ZAUSNER, L. Andrew

2101 L St. NW
Washington, DC 20037-1526
Tel: (202)785-9700
Fax: (202)887-0689
Registered: LDA
EMail: zausnera@dsmo.com

Exec. Assistant to the Deputy Secretary (1978-79) and Special Assistant to the General Counsel (1977-78), Department of Energy.

Employers

Dickstein Shapiro Morin & Oshinsky LLP (Partner)

Clients Represented

On Behalf of Dickstein Shapiro Morin & Oshinsky LLP

American Greyhound Track Operators Ass'n
CaseNewHolland Inc.
Cigar Ass'n of America
Colakoglu Group
Electric Power Supply Ass'n
First USA Bank
Habas Group
Harbour Group Industries, Inc.
Home Box Office
Homestake Mining
Hydro-Quebec
Incentive Federation Sweepstakes Trust Fund
Internat'l Brotherhood of Teamsters
Kerr-McGee Corp.
Lorillard Tobacco Co.
Luiginos
Nat'l Ass'n of Water Companies
PG&E Generating Co.
Pipe Tobacco Council, Inc.
Poseidon Resources Corp.
The Reader's Digest Ass'n
Smokeless Tobacco Council

ZAVARELA, Bill

2468 Ontario Rd. NW
Washington, DC 20009-2705
Tel: (202)328-1373
Registered: LDA

Employers

Self-employed as an independent consultant.

Clients Represented

As an independent consultant

Ass'n for Enterprise Opportunity
Center for Community Change
Corporation for Enterprise Development
Death With Dignity Nat'l Center
Nat'l Employment Lawyers Ass'n
Nat'l Federation of Community Development of Credit Unions

ZEBROSKI, Shirley

1660 L St. NW
Fourth Floor
Washington, DC 20036
Tel: (202)775-5082
Fax: (202)775-5097
Registered: LDA

Employers

General Motors Corp. (Senior Washington Representative)

ZEDLEWSKI, Sheila R.

2100 M St. NW
Washington, DC 20037
Tel: (202)833-7200
Fax: (202)429-0687

Employers

The Urban Institute (Director, Income and Benefits Policy Center)

ZEGERS, Ted

Eisenhower Exec. Office Bldg.
725 17th St. NW
Washington, DC 20503
Tel: (202)395-4790
Fax: (202)395-3888

Employers

Executive Office of the President - Office of Management and Budget (Special Assistant for Policy and Legislation)

ZEIDMAN, Philip F.

1200 19th St. NW
Washington, DC 20036-2430
Tel: (202)861-6676
Fax: (202)223-2085
Registered: LDA
EMail: philip.zeidman@piperrudnick.com

Special Assistant to the V. President, The White House, 1968. General Counsel (1965-68), Assistant General Counsel (1963-65), and Special Assistant to the Administrator, (1961-63), all at the Small Business Administration. Staff Assistant, White House Committee on Small Business, 1961-63. Trial Attorney, Federal Trade Commission, 1960-61.

Employers

Piper Marbury Rudnick & Wolfe LLP (Partner)

Clients Represented

On Behalf of Piper Marbury Rudnick & Wolfe LLP

American Business Conference

ZEIDNER, Rita L.

1225 I St. NW
Suite 500
Washington, DC 20005
EMail: ritaapa@aol.com
Tel: (202)682-4785
Fax: (202)371-8892
Registered: LDA

Employers

American Payroll Ass'n (Manager, Government Relations)

ZEILINSKI, Dan

1400 K St. NW
Ninth Floor
Washington, DC 20005
Tel: (202)783-1022
Fax: (202)682-4854

Employers

Tire Industry Safety Council (Director)

ZEISEL, Steven I.

1000 Wilson Blvd.
Suite 2500
Arlington, VA 22209-3908
EMail: szeisel@cbanet.org
Tel: (703)276-1750
Fax: (703)528-1290
Registered: LDA

Employers

Consumer Bankers Ass'n (Senior Counsel and V. President)

ZEITLER, William A.

901 15th St. NW
Suite 700
Washington, DC 20005-2301
Tel: (202)371-6000
Fax: (202)371-6279
Registered: LDA

Supervisory Attorney/Advisor (1979-86) and Attorney/Advisor (1975-78), International Trade

Commission. Attorney/Advisor, U.S. Tariff Commission, 1973-75.

Employers
Verner, Liipfert, Bernhard, McPherson and Hand, Chartered (Member of Firm)

ZELDEN, Mark

1200 New Hampshire Ave NW
Suite 430
Washington, DC 20036
Tel: (202)955-3030
Fax: (202)955-1147
Registered: LDA

Employers
Murray, Scheer, Montgomery, Tapia & O'Donnell

Clients Represented

On Behalf of Murray, Scheer, Montgomery, Tapia & O'Donnell
Jasper, Alabama, City of
Lafayette Consolidated Government
Marshall, Alabama, County of
Science & Engineering Associates, Inc.

ZELDOW, Deborah

2021 K St. NW
Suite 305
Washington, DC 20006-1003
Tel: (202)293-2856
Fax: (202)785-8574

Employers
Alliance for Aging Research (Senior Director, Strategies & Programs)

ZELENKO, Benjamin L.

One Thomas Circle NW
Suite 200
Washington, DC 20005-5802
Tel: (202)833-8900
Fax: (202)466-5738
Registered: LDA

Employers
Baach Robinson & Lewis, PLLC (Partner)

Clients Represented

On Behalf of Baach Robinson & Lewis, PLLC
American Soc. of Composers, Authors and Publishers
Equitas Reinsurance Ltd.
Nat'l Football League Players Ass'n

ZELENKO, Carin

25 Louisiana Ave. NW
Washington, DC 20001-2198
Tel: (202)624-8100
Fax: (202)624-6833

Employers
Internat'l Brotherhood of Teamsters (Director, Corporate Affairs)

ZELIFF, Jr., Hon. William H.

499 S. Capitol St.
Suite 600
Washington, DC 20003
Tel: (202)554-0473
Fax: (202)554-0393
Registered: LDA
EMail: BZeliff@zeliffireland.com
Member, U.S. House of Representatives (R-NH), 1991-97.

Employers
Zeliff, Ireland, and Associates (Principal)

Clients Represented

On Behalf of Zeliff, Ireland, and Associates
Ass'n of Small Business Development Centers
Boys Town USA
General Mills
Schering-Plough Corp.
SIG Arms

ZELLER, USN, Capt. Randall

The Pentagon
Room 2E837
Washington, DC 20318-9999
Tel: (703)614-1777
Fax: (703)697-3083

Employers
Department of Defense - Chairman, Joint Chiefs of Staff (Legislative Assistant)

ZENER, Robert V.

3000 K St. NW
Suite 300
Washington, DC 20007
Tel: (202)424-7500
Fax: (202)424-7643
Registered: LDA

Employers
Swidler Berlin Shereff Friedman, LLP

ZENNER, Jr., Walter F.

555 12th St. NW
Washington, DC 20004-1206
Tel: (202)942-5000
Fax: (202)942-5999
EMail: Walter_Zenner@aporter.com

Employers
Arnold & Porter (Partner)

ZENOR, Stanley

1020 19th St. NW
Suite 325
Washington, DC 20036-6101
Tel: (202)293-4000
Fax: (202)293-4317

Employers
Federal Communications Bar Ass'n (Exec. Director and Chief Exec. Officer)

ZENSKY, David

1333 New Hampshire Ave. NW
Suite 400
Washington, DC 20036
Tel: (202)887-4000
Fax: (202)887-4288
Registered: LDA

Employers
Akin, Gump, Strauss, Hauer & Feld, L.L.P. (Partner)

Clients Represented

On Behalf of Akin, Gump, Strauss, Hauer & Feld, L.L.P.
Asbury Automotive Group

ZENTAY, John H.

901 15th St. NW
Suite 700
Washington, DC 20005-2301
Tel: (202)371-6000
Fax: (202)371-6279
Registered: LDA
Member, Legislative Presentation Staff, Agency for International Development, Department of State, 1963-66. Legislative Assistant to Senator Stuart Symington (D-MO), 1958-63. Served in the U.S. Army, 1953-55.

Employers
Verner, Liipfert, Bernhard, McPherson and Hand, Chartered (Member of Firm)

Clients Represented

On Behalf of Verner, Liipfert, Bernhard, McPherson and Hand, Chartered
Accenture
General Electric Co.
George Washington University, Office of Government Relations
Home Warranty Coalition
Independent Fuel Terminal Operators Ass'n
Lockheed Martin Corp.
Lockheed Martin Tactical Systems
Magna Entertainment Corp.
Merrill Lynch & Co., Inc.
Nat'l Broadcasting Co.
New England Fuel Institute
New York Stock Exchange
Olympic Advocates Together Honorably (OATH)
Olympic Aid
Petroport, Inc.
Raytheon Co.
Rite Aid Corp.
RJR Nabisco Holdings Co.
Southeastern Federal Power Customers, Inc.
Staples, Inc.

ZEPPELIN, Deron

1800 Duke St.
Alexandria, VA 22314
Tel: (703)548-3440
Fax: (703)836-0367

Employers
Soc. for Human Resource Management (Director, Governmental Affairs)

ZESIGER, David W.

1300 Connecticut Ave. NW
Suite 600
Washington, DC 20036
Tel: (202)775-8116
Fax: (202)223-0358
Assistant Chief Counsel for Telecommunications, Office of Advocacy, Small Business Administration, 1996-97. Senior Counsel (1993-95) and Staff Director (1987-93), Subcommittee on Telecommunications and Finance, House Committee on Commerce. Counsel to Rep. Dennis Eckert (D-OH), 1987-93.

Employers
Griffin, Johnson, Dover & Stewart (Lobbyist)

Clients Represented

On Behalf of Griffin, Johnson, Dover & Stewart
Independent Telephone and Telecommunications Alliance

ZESIGER, Heather

1818 N St. NW
Suite 450
Washington, DC 20036
Tel: (202)530-2900
Fax: (202)530-2901
Registered: LDA

Employers
Bass and Howes, Inc.

ZGORSKI, Lisa-Joy

1755 Massachusetts Ave. NW
Suite 400
Washington, DC 20036
Tel: (202)387-0400
Fax: (202)483-9430
EMail: zgorski@tcf.org

Employers
The Century Foundation (Manager, Communications)

ZIEBART, Geoffrey C.

2300 Clarendon Blvd.
Suite 401
Arlington, VA 22201
Tel: (703)516-4708
Fax: (703)516-9855
Registered: LDA

Employers
Nat'l Ass'n of Business Political Action Committees (Exec. Director)
Washington Strategies, L.L.C.

Clients Represented

On Behalf of Washington Strategies, L.L.C.
Barrick Goldstrike Mines, Inc.
Nat'l Ass'n of Business Political Action Committees

ZIEGLER, Alyson

1401 H St. NW
Suite 600
Washington, DC 20005-2136
Tel: (202)326-7300
Fax: (202)326-7333
Registered: LDA

Employers
United States Telecom Ass'n (Director, Legislative Affairs and Counsel)

ZIEGLER, Deborah A.

1110 N. Glebe Rd.
Arlington, VA 22201-5704
Tel: (703)620-3660
Fax: (703)620-4334
Registered: LDA
EMail: debz@cec.sped.org

Employers
Council for Exceptional Children (Assistant Exec. Director, Public Policy)

ZIEGLER, Sara

1909 K St. NW
Suite 600
Washington, DC 20006-1167
Tel: (202)585-6900
Fax: (202)585-6969

Employers
Thompson Coburn LLP (Legislative Specialist)

ZIELINSKI, Charles A.

1615 L St. NW
Suite 1200
Washington, DC 20036
Tel: (202)466-6300
Fax: (202)463-0678
Trial and Appellate Attorney, Federal Communications Commission, 1970-73.

Employers
Bell, Boyd & Lloyd (Partner)

ZIEMBA, Elaine

4141 N. Henderson Rd.
Suite 1101
Arlington, VA 22203
Tel: (703)522-1068
Fax: (703)527-1646
Registered: LDA

Employers
EZ's Solutions, Inc. (President)

Clients Represented

On Behalf of EZ's Solutions, Inc.
NRG Energy, Inc.

ZILL, Anne B.

122 Maryland Ave. NE
Suite 300
Washington, DC 20002
Tel: (202)546-3799
Fax: (202)543-3156

Employers
Fund for Constitutional Government (President)

ZILLINGER, F. Everett

501 Second St. NE
Washington, DC 20002
Tel: (202)675-8250
Fax: (202)544-8123
Registered: LDA
EMail: ezillinger@tfi.org

Employers
The Fertilizer Institute (Director, Government Relations)

ZIMAN, Barry

1350 I St. NW
Suite 590
Washington, DC 20005
EMail: bziman@cap.org
Tel: (202)354-7100
Fax: (202)354-7155

Employers
College of American Pathologists (Assistant Director, State Affairs)

ZIMMER, Kim

1120 20th St. NW
Suite 750 South
Washington, DC 20036
EMail: info@clb.org
Tel: (202)454-6400
Fax: (202)454-6401

Employers
Columbia Lighthouse for the Blind (V. President, Communications)

ZIMMERMAN, Carole

800 I St. NW
Washington, DC 20001
Tel: (202)777-2510
Fax: (202)777-2534

Employers
American Public Health Ass'n (Director, Communications)

ZIMMERMAN, Eric P.

600 13th St. NW
Washington, DC 20005-3096
Tel: (202)756-8148
Fax: (202)756-8087
Registered: LDA
EMail: ezimmerman@mwe.com

Employers
McDermott, Will and Emery (Associate)

Clients Represented
On Behalf of McDermott, Will and Emery
Allergan, Inc.
American Gastroenterological Ass'n
American Soc. of Ambulatory Surgery Centers
American Soc. of Echocardiography
Applied Benefits Research Corp.
Arthroscopy Ass'n of North America
Ass'n of Freestanding Radiation Oncology Centers
foot.com
W. A. Foote Memorial Hospital
InterMountain Health Care Inc.
The Marshfield Clinic
MedCentral Health System
Nat'l Perinatal Ass'n
Northside Savings Bank
Outpatient Ophthalmic Surgery Soc.
Respiratory Medication Providers Coalition
Rural Health Network Coalition
Rural Referral Centers Coalition
Stamford Hospital
VIVRA

ZIMMERMAN, LeRoy S.

1250 24th St. NW
Suite 700
Washington, DC 20037
Tel: (202)659-6600
Fax: (202)659-6699
Registered: LDA

Employers
Eckert Seamans Cherin & Mellott, LLC (Senior Counsel)

Clients Represented
On Behalf of Eckert Seamans Cherin & Mellott, LLC
CCI Construction
CSX Corp.
General Motors Corp.
PNH Associates

ZIMMERMAN, Malissa

444 N. Capitol St. NW
Suite 800
Washington, DC 20001
Tel: (202)638-5355
Fax: (202)638-5369
Registered: LDA

Employers
Marine Engineers Beneficial Ass'n (District No. 1 - PCD) (Director, Government Affairs)

ZIMMERMAN, Stephen H.

1300 I St. NW
Suite 300 West
Washington, DC 20005
Tel: (202)522-8600
Fax: (202)522-8669
Registered: LDA
Served in the Office of Chief Counsel, U.S. Coast Guard, Department of Transportation, 1972-76.

Employers
Dykema Gossett PLLC (Member)

Clients Represented
On Behalf of Dykema Gossett PLLC
Manulife USA
Michigan Insurance Federation

ZIMMERMAN, Tracy

1782 Columbia Rd. NW
Washington, DC 20009
EMail: Tracy@thgweb.com
Tel: (202)518-8047
Fax: (202)518-8048

Employers
Hauser Group (Associate)

ZIMMERMAN, Troy

1522 K Street NW
Suite 825
Washington, DC 20005
EMail: troyz@dc.kidney.org
Tel: (202)216-9257
Fax: (202)216-9258
Registered: LDA

Employers
Nat'l Kidney Foundation (Government Relations Director)

ZIMMETT, Brian

1050 Thomas Jefferson St. NW
Seventh Floor
Washington, DC 20007
EMail: bmz@vnf.com
Tel: (202)298-1800
Fax: (202)338-2416

Employers
Van Ness Feldman, P.C. (Associate)

ZINGMAN, Ben

1875 I St. NW
Suite 900
Washington, DC 20005
Tel: (202)371-0200
Fax: (202)371-2858

Employers
Edelman Public Relations Worldwide (Senior V. President, Public Affairs and Crisis Communications)

ZINN, Matthew J.

1330 Connecticut Ave. NW
Washington, DC 20036-1795
EMail: mzinn@steptoe.com
Tel: (202)429-3000
Fax: (202)429-3902
Tax Assistant Solicitor General, Department of Justice, 1969-72.

Employers
Steptoe & Johnson LLP (Partner)

Clients Represented
On Behalf of Steptoe & Johnson LLP
Mutual Tax Committee

ZINZI, Laura

1101 Vermont Ave. NW
Suite 1001
Washington, DC 20005
Tel: (202)296-8016
Fax: (202)682-3984

Employers
Italian-American Democratic Leadership Council (Director, PAC)

ZION, Hon. Roger H.

110 D St. SE
Suite 114
Washington, DC 20003
Tel: (202)547-2555
Fax: (202)547-1641
Registered: LDA
Member, U.S. House of Representatives (R-IN), 1966-74. Chairman, Republican Task Force on Energy and Resources.

Employers
The 60/Plus Ass'n, Inc. (Honorary Chair)
Resources Development, Inc. (President)

Clients Represented
On Behalf of Resources Development, Inc.
The 60/Plus Ass'n, Inc.
Independent Oil Producers Ass'n-Tri State

ZIPP, Joel F.

2175 K St. NW
Fifth Floor
Washington, DC 20037
Tel: (202)789-1100
Fax: (202)289-3928
Registered: LDA, FARA
Attorney, Federal Power Commission and Federal Energy Regulatory Commission, 1975-79.

Employers
Cameron McKenna (Partner)

Clients Represented
On Behalf of Cameron McKenna
Hydro-Quebec

ZIPURSKY, Diane

1299 Pennsylvania Ave. NW
11th Floor
Washington, DC 20004
EMail: diane.zipursky@corporate.ge.com
Tel: (202)637-4535
Fax: (202)637-4548

Employers
Nat'l Broadcasting Co. (V. President, Washington Counsel)

ZIRKIN, Nancy M.

1111 16th St. NW
Washington, DC 20036-4873
Tel: (202)785-7720
Fax: (202)466-7618
Registered: LDA
EMail: zirkinn@aauw.org

Employers
American Ass'n of University Women (Director of Public Policy and Government Relations)

ZISSIS, Kristina

601 13th St. NW
Suite 600 South
Washington, DC 20005
EMail: zissikr@washdc.whitecase.com
Tel: (202)626-3600
Fax: (202)639-9355

Employers
White & Case LLP (Associate)

ZLOTNIKOFF, Stuart

1825 Samuel Morse Dr.
Reston, VA 20190
Tel: (703)437-5300
Fax: (703)437-7768

Employers
Nat'l Grocers Ass'n (Senior V. President)

ZLOTOPOLSKI, Alfred T.

1750 New York Ave. NW
Sixth Floor
Washington, DC 20006
Tel: (202)783-5880
Fax: (202)662-0893

Employers
Sheet Metal Workers' Internat'l Ass'n (General Secretary-Treasurer)

ZOELLER, Thomas E.

800 Independence Ave. SW
Room 921 D
Washington, DC 20591
Tel: (202)267-3217
Fax: (202)267-5194

Employers
Department of Transportation - Federal Aviation Administration (Deputy Assistant Chief Counsel for Legislation)

ZOGBY, James J.

1600 K St. NW
Suite 601
Washington, DC 20006
EMail: jzogby@aaiusa.org
Tel: (202)429-9210
Fax: (202)429-9214

Employers
Arab American Institute (President)

ZOGLMAN, Robert R.

1900 M St. NW
Suite 500
Washington, DC 20036
Tel: (202)945-6400
Fax: (202)945-6404
Registered: LDA

Employers
Westinghouse Electric Co. (V. President, Government and International Affairs)

ZOLA, Hilliard A.

1776 K St. NW
Suite 400
Washington, DC 20006
Tel: (202)296-4442
Fax: (202)785-0025
Registered: LDA

V. President for Insurance, Overseas Private Investment Corp., U.S. International Development Cooperation Agency, 1974. Special Assistant to the Secretary for Policy Development, Department of Transportation, 1970-72. Legal Advisor, Economic Development Department, Department of Commerce, 1968-69.

Employers
Dierman, Wortley, and Zola (President)

Clients Represented

On Behalf of Dierman, Wortley, and Zola
Bangladesh Export Processing Zones Authority

ZOLET, Theresa L.

1050 Thomas Jefferson St. NW
Seventh Floor
Washington, DC 20007
EMail: tlz@vnf.com
Tel: (202)298-1800
Fax: (202)338-2416

Employers
Van Ness Feldman, P.C. (Member)

Clients Represented

On Behalf of Van Ness Feldman, P.C.
Alaska North Slope LNG Project

ZOLLAR, Carolyn C.

1606 20th St. NW
Third Floor
Washington, DC 20009
Tel: (202)265-4404
Fax: (202)833-9168
Registered: LDA

Employers
American Medical Rehabilitation Providers Ass'n (V. President, Government Relations and Policy Development)

ZOMESKY, Marla

1133 Connecticut Ave. NW
Fifth Floor
Washington, DC 20036
Tel: (202)457-1110
Fax: (202)457-1130
Registered: LDA

Employers
Quinn Gillespie & Associates (Associate)

Clients Represented

On Behalf of Quinn Gillespie & Associates
LVMH Moet Hennessy Louis Vuitton S.A.

ZOMETSKY, Joseph

8001 Forbes Pl.
Suite 102
Springfield, VA 22151
Tel: (703)321-8585
Fax: (703)321-8408
Registered: LDA

Employers
Gun Owners of America (Federal Affairs)

ZONARICH, Matt

8120 Woodmont Ave.
Suite 750
Bethesda, MD 20814-2755
Tel: (301)347-9309
Fax: (301)347-9310

Employers
Joint Steering Committee for Public Policy (District Coordinator)

ZOOK, David R.

805 15th St. NW
Suite 700
Washington, DC 20005
EMail: drzook@bakerd.com
Tel: (202)312-7440
Fax: (202)312-7460
Registered: LDA

Employers
Baker & Daniels (Managing Partner, Washington Office)
Sagamore Associates, Inc. (Managing Partner)

ZORTHIAN, Barry

2111 Wilson Blvd.
Eighth Floor
Arlington, VA 22201-3058
EMail: zorthian@alcalde-fay.com
Tel: (703)841-0626
Fax: (703)243-2874

Employers
Alcalde & Fay (Partner)

Clients Represented

On Behalf of Alcalde & Fay
Internat'l Council of Cruise Lines

ZOWADER, Donald

801 Pennsylvania Ave. NW
Suite 725
Washington, DC 20004
EMail: donald.zowader@aventis.com
Tel: (202)898-3183
Fax: (202)682-0538
Registered: LDA

Employers
Aventis Pharmaceuticals, Inc. (Senior Manager, Federal Government Relations)

ZSCHOCK, Charles W.

700 Princess St.
Suite Three
Alexandria, VA 22314-3129
EMail: info@gaba.org
Tel: (703)836-6120
Fax: (703)836-6160

Employers
German American Business Ass'n (President)

ZUCK, Jonathan V.

1413 K St. NW 12th Floor
Washington, DC 20005
Tel: (202)408-3370

Employers
Ass'n for Competitive Technology

ZUCKER, Jill M.

700 13th St. NW
Suite 700
Washington, DC 20005-3960
EMail: jmzucker@bryancave.com
Tel: (202)508-6000
Fax: (202)508-6200

Employers
Bryan Cave LLP (Counsel)

ZUCKERMAN, Stephen

2100 M St. NW
Washington, DC 20037
Tel: (202)833-7200
Fax: (202)429-0687

Employers
The Urban Institute (Principal Research Associate, Health Policy Center)

ZUFOLO, Jessica

1101 Vermont Ave. NW
Suite 200
Washington, DC 20005
EMail: jzufolo@naruc.org
Tel: (202)898-2200
Fax: (202)898-2213

Employers
Nat'l Ass'n of Regulatory Utility Commissioners (Legislative Director)

ZURAWSKI, Paul R.

1615 L St. NW
Suite 1100
Washington, DC 20036-5610
Tel: (202)872-1260
Fax: (202)466-3509

Employers
The Business Roundtable (Legislative Counsel)

ZWEIG, Lisa

Eisenhower Exec. Office Bldg.
725 17th St. NW
Washington, DC 20503
Tel: (202)395-4790
Fax: (202)395-3888

Employers
Executive Office of the President - Office of Management and Budget (Legislative Analyst)

ZWERIN, Rachel

2120 L St. NW
Suite 400
Washington, DC 20037
Tel: (202)478-6301
Fax: (202)478-6171

Employers
Leslie Harris & Associates (Associate)

Clients Represented

On Behalf of Leslie Harris & Associates
AOL Time Warner
Leadership Conference on Civil Rights

ZYSK, Jane

1920 L St. NW
Suite 200
Washington, DC 20036
EMail: jzysk@atr_ok.org
Tel: (202)785-0266
Fax: (202)785-0261

Employers
Americans for Tax Reform (Director, Special Events)

2001 Washington Representatives

Client Index by Subject/Industry

The organizations listed in The Clients section of this directory have been cross-referenced in this index according to their industry group or principal subject of concern. For example, interest groups directly involved in the fight for or against gun control, as well as companies or associations involved in the manufacturing of firearms, can be found under the heading "Firearms/Gun Control". Please note that the organizations appearing below a given heading may support or oppose that issue or industry.

Accounting

Accenture (226)
The Accountants Coalition (226)
American Bankruptcy Institute (250)
American Institute of Certified Public Accountants (264)
American Payroll Ass'n (269)
American Soc. of Women Accountants (ACC) (277)
Ass'n of Government Accountants (296)
Deloitte & Touche LLP (384)
Deloitte Consulting (384)
Deloitte Touche Tohmatsu Internat'l (384)
Financial Accounting Standards Board (416)
Institute of Internal Auditors (464)
Massachusetts Soc. of Certified Public Accountants (512)
Nat'l Ass'n of Black Accountants (539)
Nat'l Soc. of Accountants (578)
H. D. Vest Financial Service (714)

Advertising and Marketing

Advertising Tax Coalition (229)
ADVO, Inc. (229)
Alaska Seafood Marketing Institute (237)
Alcatel USA (237)
American Advertising Federation (244)
American Ass'n of Advertising Agencies (246)
American Film Marketing Ass'n (259)
The American Floral Marketing Council (259)
American Property Rights Alliance (271)
American Teleservices Ass'n (279)
American Wholesale Marketers Ass'n (280)
Ass'n for Postal Commerce (292)
Ass'n of Hispanic Advertising Agencies (296)
Ass'n of Nat'l Advertisers (297)
Ass'n of Sales & Marketing Companies (298)
Coalition for Truth in Environmental Marketing Information, Inc. (355)
Color Marketing Group (358)
Compass Internat'l Inc. (363)
Direct Marketing Ass'n of Washington (388)
Direct Marketing Ass'n, Inc. (388)
Direct Selling Ass'n (389)
Direct Selling Education Foundation (389)
Draft Worldwide (392)
Electronic Retailing Ass'n (401)
Food Marketing Institute (421)
Gemma & Associates (431)
Hospitality Sales and Marketing Ass'n Internat'l (453)
Incentive Federation Sweepstakes Trust Fund (458)
Internat'l Public Relations Co. (474)
Internat'l Sign Ass'n (474)
Internat'l Technology Resources, Inc. (475)
Internet Advertising Bureau (476)
Mailing & Fulfillment Services Ass'n (507)
Nat'l Ass'n of Recording Merchandisers (548)
Nat'l Automatic Merchandising Ass'n (552)
Network Advertising Initiative (584)
New Zealand Kiwifruit Marketing Board (588)
Outdoor Advertising Ass'n of America (604)
Petroleum Marketers Ass'n of America (613)
Photo Marketing Ass'n-Internat'l (616)
Point of Purchase Advertising Institute (619)
Soc. for Marketing Professional Services (662)
Soc. of Independent Gasoline Marketers of America (663)
SQM North America Corp. (671)
Sun Outdoor Advertising (677)
Tett Enterprises (684)
Trade Show Exhibitors Ass'n (689)
The Vantage Group, Inc. (712)
Voices, Inc. (717)
Yellow Pages Publishers Ass'n (733)

Aerospace/Aviation

21st Century Space Foundation (223)
AAAE-ACI (224)
ADSI Inc. (228)
Aer Lingus (230)
Aero Continente, S.A. (230)
Aerolineas Argentinas (230)
Aerolineas Centrales de Colombia (230)
Aeronautical Radio, Inc. (230)
Aeronautical Repair Station Ass'n (230)
Aeropostal (230)
AeroRepublica, S.A. (230)
The Aerospace Corp. (230)
Aerospace Industries Ass'n of America (230)
Aerospace Industries Ass'n of Canada (230)
Aerospace Medical Ass'n (230)
AeroUnion, S.A. de C.V. (230)
Air & Water Technologies (233)
Air 3000, Inc. (233)
Air Afrique (233)
Air Atlantic Dominicana (233)
Air Canada (233)
Air Carrier Ass'n of America (233)
Air China Internat'l Corp., Ltd. (233)
Air Courier Conference of America (233)
Air Cruisers, Inc. (233)
Air D'Ayiti (233)
Air Force Ass'n (233)
Air Force Sergeants Ass'n (233)
Air India (233)
Air Jamaica Ltd. (233)
Air Line Pilots Ass'n Internat'l (233)
Air Methods/Mercy Air (234)
Air Nauru (234)
Air Pacific Ltd. (234)
Air Tractor, Inc. (234)
Air Traffic Control Ass'n (234)
Air Tran Airways (234)
Air Transat (234)
Air Transport Ass'n of America (234)
Airborne Express (234)
Airborne Tactical Advantage Co. (234)
Airbus Industrie of North America, Inc. (234)
Aircraft Electronics Ass'n (235)
Aircraft Owners and Pilots Ass'n (235)
Airguard Industries (235)
Airport Consultants Council (235)
Airport Minority Advisory Council (235)
Airports Council Internat'l - North America (235)
Airtours Internat'l (235)
Alabama Space Science Exhibits Commission (236)
Alaska Aerospace (236)
Alaska Air Group (236)
Alaska Airlines (236)
Alenia Aerospazig (238)
Alitalia (238)
Allegheny Technologies, Inc. (238)
Allied Pilots Ass'n (241)
Aloha Airlines (242)
America West Airlines (243)
American Airlines (244)
American Ass'n of Airport Executives (246)
American Astronautical Soc. (250)
American Eurocopter Corp. (258)
American Helicopter Soc. Internat'l (262)
American Institute of Aeronautics and Astronautics (264)
American Mobile Satellite Corp. (268)
American Security Council (273)
American Trans Air (279)
Amerijet Internat'l Inc. (282)
AMI Aircraft Seating Systems (283)
AMSA (283)
Andes (284)
APA Internat'l Air, S.A. (285)
APTI (287)
ArianeSpace, Inc. (288)
ARINC, Inc. (288)
Arrow Air (289)
Ass'n of Air Medical Services (293)
Ass'n of Flight Attendants (295)
Ass'n of Professional Flight Attendants (297)
AstroVision Inc. (301)
Austrian Airlines (303)
Averitt Express, Inc. (305)
Avianca Airlines (305)
Aviateca Airline (305)
Aviation Development Services (305)
BAE SYSTEMS North America (306)
Ball Aerospace & Technology Corp. (306)
Bangor Internat'l Airport (307)
Bell Helicopter Textron, Inc. (311)
Big Sky Airlines (313)
Biman Bangladesh Airlines (313)
Birmingham Airport Authority (314)
The Boeing Co. (316)
Boeing Defense and Space Group (317)
Bombardier Aerospace (317)
British Aerospace (320)

British Airways Plc (321)
Burbank Aeronautical Corp. II (323)
Cambridge Management Inc. (328)
Capital Region Airport Commission (330)
Caraven Airlines (Carga Aerea Venezolana, S.A.) (331)
Caribbean Airline Co. Ltd. (331)
Casa Aircraft USA, Inc. (332)
Central West Virginia Regional Airport Authority (339)
Challenge Air Cargo (340)
Challenger Center for Space Science Education (340)
Chandler Evans Control Systems (341)
Chapman Freeborn America (341)
Chattanooga Metropolitan Airport Authority (341)
China Eastern Airlines (344)
Chromalloy Gas Turbine Corp. (346)
Civil Air Patrol (349)
Clark County-McCarran Internat'l Airport (350)
Coalition for a Global Standard on Aviation Noise (352)
Coleman Aerospace Co. (357)
Colgan Air, Inc. (357)
Columbia Helicopters, Inc. (359)
Compania Mexicana de Aviacion (363)
Condor Electronic Systems (365)
Condor-Pacific Industries (365)
Consumer Satellite Systems, Inc. (369)
Continental Airlines Inc. (370)
Covanta Energy Corporation (377)
Crane Co. (378)
CUBRC (380)
Custom Air Transport (380)
Dallas/Fort Worth Internat'l Airport Board (382)
Delta Air Lines (384)
Denver Internat'l Airport (385)
Detroit Metropolitan Airport (386)
Deutsche Lufthansa AG (386)
Dreamtime, Inc. (392)
DynCorp (393)
DynCorp Aerospace Technology (393)
E-Prime Aerospace (394)
East/West Industries (395)
Eastern Pilots Ass'n (395)
Easton Airport (395)
EER Systems (398)
EFW Corp. (398)
El Al Israel Airlines, Ltd. (399)
Electro-Radiation Inc. (400)
Embraer Aircraft Corp. (401)
Embry-Riddle Aeronautical University (401)
Empresa Consolidada Cubana de Aviacion (402)
Equal Justice Coalition (406)
Equinoccial, S.A. (406)
ESCO Corp. (407)
European Aeronautics, Defence and Space, Inc. (408)
European Space Agency (408)
Eva Airways Corp. (408)
Evergreen Internat'l Aviation (408)
Executive Jet (408)
EyeTicket Corp. (410)
Fairchild Aircraft, Inc. (410)
Falcon Air Express (410)
Fast Air Carrier (412)
Faucett Airlines (Compania de Aviacion Faucett, S.A.) (412)
Final Analysis, Inc. (416)
First Flight Centennial Foundation (417)
Flight Landata, Inc. (419)
Flight Safety Foundation (419)
Flight Safety Technologies, Inc. (419)
FlightSafety Internat'l (419)
Fort Smith Regional Airport (423)
Galaxy Aerospace Co., LP (428)
GE Capital Aviation Services (430)
GEC-Marconi Avionics Group (430)
GenCorp (431)
General Aviation Manufacturers Ass'n (431)
General Development Corp. (431)
GKN Westland Aerospace Inc. (435)
B. F. Goodrich Co. (437)
Greater Orlando Aviation Authority (439)
Greenville-Spartanburg Airport District (440)
Guam Internat'l Airport Authority (441)
Gulfstream Aerospace Corp. (442)
Hamilton Sundstrand (444)
Helicopter Ass'n Internat'l (448)
Honeywell Internat'l, Inc. (452)
Houston, Texas, Department of Aviation of the City of (453)
Huntsville-Madison County Airport (455)
IATA U.S. Frequent Flyer Tax Interest Group (456)
Ibex (456)
Inmarsat (462)
Internat'l Air Transport Ass'n (467)
Internat'l Ass'n of Airport Duty Free Stores (467)
Internat'l Ass'n of Machinists and Aerospace Workers (468)
Internat'l Soc. of Air Safety Investigators (475)
Israel Aircraft Industries, Ltd. (479)
Jackson Municipal Airport Authority (480)
Jacobs Engineering Group Inc. (481)
Jamaica Air Freighters, Ltd. (481)
JDA Aviation Technology Systems (482)
JMC Airlines, Ltd. (483)
Kalitta Air, L.L.C. (486)
KAMAN Corp. (486)
Kaman Diversified Technologies Corp. (486)
Kenya Airways (488)
Kollsman, Inc. (490)
Kongsberg Defense & Aerospace (491)
Korean Air Lines (491)
LADECO (494)
Lafayette Airport Commission (494)
Laker Airways (Bahamas) Ltd. (494)
Lambert-St. Louis Internat'l Airport (494)
Lan Chile (494)
LAPA (Lineas Aereas Privadas, S.A.) (495)
Las Vegas/McCarran Internat'l Airport (495)
Legend Airlines (497)
Lehigh-Northhampton Airport Authority (498)
Lineas Aereas Costarricicenes (Lasca Airlines) (500)
Litton Life Support (500)
Lockheed Martin Aeronautical Systems Co. (501)
Lockheed Martin Air Traffic Management (501)
Lockheed Martin Fairchild Systems (502)
Loral Space and Communications, Ltd. (503)
LOT Polish Airlines (504)
Lucas Aerospace (505)
M&W Pump Corp. (506)
Macau, Civil Aviation Authority of (506)
Marconi Flight Systems, Inc. (509)
Martin-Baker Aircraft Co., Ltd. (511)
Martinair Holland (511)
Maryland, Aviation Administration of the State of (512)
Matra Aerospace, Inc. (513)
MEI Corp. (517)
Memphis-Shelby County Airport Authority (518)
Messier-Dowty Internat'l (519)
Metropolitan Washington Airports Authority (521)
Microcosm, Inc. (522)
Midway Airlines Corp. (523)
Midwest Express Airlines (523)
Minneapolis-St. Paul Metropolitan Airports Commission (525)
Mitsubishi Internat'l Corp. (526)
Montgomery Airport Authority (528)
Motorola Space and Systems Technology Group (531)
MRJ Technology Solutions (532)
NASA Aeronautics Support Team (534)
Nat'l Aeronautic Ass'n of the U.S.A. (535)
Nat'l Agricultural Aviation Ass'n (535)
Nat'l Air Cargo, Inc. (536)
Nat'l Air Carrier Ass'n (536)
Nat'l Air Traffic Controllers Ass'n (536)
Nat'l Air Transportation Ass'n (536)
Nat'l Aircraft Resale Ass'n (536)
Nat'l Ass'n of Air Traffic Specialists (538)
Nat'l Ass'n of Aircraft and Communication Suppliers (538)
Nat'l Ass'n of State Aviation Officials (549)
Nat'l Business Aviation Ass'n (553)
Nat'l Center for Advanced Technologies (554)
Nat'l Institute for Aerospace Studies and Services Inc. (568)
Nat'l Space Soc. (578)
Nat'l Training Systems Ass'n (579)
NAV Canada (582)
NAVSYS Corp. (583)
New Skies Satellites N.V. (586)
Nippon Cargo Airlines (590)
Noise Reduction Technology Coalition (591)
The Nordam Group (591)
Northern Air Cargo (594)
Northrop Grumman Corp. (594)
Northwest Airlines, Inc. (595)
Oakland Airport (598)
OAO Corp. (598)
Oerlikon Aerospace, Inc. (599)
Omni Internat'l (600)
Omniflight Helicopters, Inc. (600)
Orbital Sciences Corp. (602)
Orcon Corp. (602)
Orient Airlines Ass'n (603)
Orion Air (603)
Pakistan Internat'l Airlines (606)
PanAmSat Corp. (607)
PEI Electronics (611)
Pemco Aviation Group, Inc. (611)
Peninsula Airways, Inc. (611)
Per Udsen (612)
PerkinElmer Detection Systems (612)
Philadelphia Internat'l Airport (615)
Philippine Airlines (616)
Phoenix Air Group, Inc. (616)
Piasecki Aircraft Corp. (617)
Pilgrim Airlines (617)
Polynesian Airlines (620)
Pratt & Whitney (623)
Precision Aerospace Corp. (623)
Professional Airways Systems Specialists (AFL-CIO) (625)
Professional Aviation Maintenance Ass'n (625)
Raytheon Co. (633)
Regional Airline Ass'n (635)
Rickenbacker Port Authority (640)
Robertson Aviation (641)
Rocket Development Co. (641)
Rolls-Royce North America Inc. (642)
Rotary Rocket Co. (642)
Rowan Companies, Inc. (643)
Royal Brunei Airways (643)
The Royal Jordanian Airline (643)
RTCA, Inc. (643)
Sabreliner Corp. (644)
Safegate Internat'l AB (645)
San Bernardino Airport Authority (647)
San Francisco Internat'l Airport (648)
Satellite Broadcasting and Communications Ass'n (650)
Scandinavian Airlines System (SAS) (651)
Schweizer Aircraft Corp. (652)
SCI Systems, Inc. (652)
Servicios Aereos de Honduras (SAHSA) (656)
Sierra Nevada Corp. (659)
Sikorsky Aircraft Corp. (659)
Skytruck, Inc. (660)
Societe Air France (664)
Societe Nationale d'Etude et Construction de Moteurs d'Aviation (SNECMA) (664)
Sonetech Corp. (665)
South African Airways (666)
Southern Air Transport (667)
Southwest Airlines (668)
Space Explorers Inc. (669)
Space Transportation Ass'n (669)
SpaceData Internat'l (669)
SPACEHAB, Inc. (669)
Spaceport Florida Authority (669)
Spectrum Astro, Inc. (670)
St. Louis Airport Authority (671)
Sun Jet Internat'l, Inc. (676)
Sun Pacific Internat'l (677)
Swissair (679)
TACA de Honduras (679)
TACA Internat'l Airlines (679)
TAESA (Transportes Aereos Ejecutivos, S.A. de C.V.) (680)
TAP/Air Portugal (681)
TCOM, L.P. (682)
Teledesic Corp. (683)
Teledyne Controls, Inc. (683)
Temsco Helicopter, Inc. (683)
Textron Inc. (685)
Thermedics Detection, Inc. (686)
Thiokol Propulsion (686)
TI Group Inc. (686)
Titan Corp. (687)
Tower Air, Inc. (688)
Trans World Airlines, Inc. (689)
Transportation Reform Alliance (690)
Transportes Aereos Mercantiles Panamericanos (691)
Tri Nat'l Aviation (691)
TRIBASA (692)
Tripoli Rocketry Ass'n (692)
TRW Inc. (693)
TRW Space and Electronics Group (693)
Turkish Airlines (694)
Turks Air Limited (694)
United Airlines (700)
United Automobile, Aerospace and Agricultural Implement Workers of America (UAW) (700)
United Space Alliance (703)
United Special Transport Air Resources, LLC (USTAR) (703)
United States Parachute Ass'n (704)
United Technologies Corp. (704)
US Airways (709)
Uwohali, Inc. (711)
Vanguard Airlines, Inc. (712)
VASP Airlines (712)
Vertical Flight Foundation (714)
VIASA (714)
ViaSat, Inc. (714)
Virgin Atlantic Airways (715)
Waveband, Inc. (722)
Wien Air Alaska (726)
Worldwide Aviation Services, Ltd. (731)
Young Astronaut Council (733)

Aging

The 60/Plus Ass'n, Inc. (224)
AARP (American Ass'n of Retired Persons) (224)
ABLEDATA (225)
Alabama Nursing Homes Ass'n (235)
Alliance for Elder Care (239)
Alliance for Retired Americans (240)
Alzheimer's Ass'n (242)
American Ass'n for Geriatric Psychiatry (245)
American Ass'n of Homes and Services for the Aging (248)
American College of Health Care Administrators (253)
American Federation of Senior Citizens (258)
American Health Care Ass'n (261)
American Seniors Housing Ass'n (273)
Arlington Educational Ass'n Retirement Housing Corp. (288)
Ass'n for Gerontology in Higher Education (292)
Assisted Living Federation of America (300)
California Public Employees' Retirement System (327)
Cash Balance Coalition (333)
Center for Aging Policy (335)
City Meals on Wheels USA (349)
The Commonwealth Fund (362)
Council of Senior Centers and Services of New York City, Inc. (376)
ElderCare Companies (399)

Elderplan, Inc. (399)
Fellowship Square Foundation, Inc. (415)
Generations United (433)
Gerontological Soc. of America (435)
Hospice Ass'n of America (452)
Institute for Advanced Studies in Aging and Geriatric Medicine (463)
Internat'l Longevity Center (473)
Internat'l Soc. for Quality of Life Research (475)
Leadership Conference on Civil Rights (496)
Medicare Cost Contractors Alliance (517)
Nat'l Ass'n for Human Development (538)
Nat'l Ass'n of Area Agencies on Aging (538)
Nat'l Ass'n of County Aging Programs (541)
Nat'l Ass'n of Foster Grandparent Program Directors (543)
Nat'l Ass'n of Nutrition and Aging Services and Programs (546)
Nat'l Ass'n of Older Worker Employment Services (546)
Nat'l Ass'n of Retired and Senior Volunteer Program Directors (548)
Nat'l Ass'n of Retired Federal Employees (548)
Nat'l Ass'n of Senior Companion Project Directors (549)
Nat'l Ass'n of State Units on Aging (550)
Nat'l Caucus and Center on Black Aged (554)
Nat'l Citizens Coalition for Nursing Home Reform (556)
Nat'l Coalition of Consumer Organizations on Aging (556)
Nat'l Coalition on Rural Aging (557)
Nat'l Committee for the Prevention of Elder Abuse/Institute on Aging (557)
Nat'l Committee to Preserve Social Security and Medicare (557)
Nat'l Council on Teacher Retirement (561)
Nat'l Council on the Aging (561)
Nat'l Hispanic Council on Aging (567)
Nat'l Hospice & Palliative Care Organization (567)
Nat'l Institute of Senior Centers (568)
Nat'l Institute of Senior Housing (568)
Nat'l Institute on Adult Daycare (568)
Nat'l Institute on Community-Based Long-Term Care (568)
Nat'l Institute on Financial Issues and Services for Elders (569)
Nat'l Interfaith Coalition on Aging (569)
Nat'l Organization of Social Security Claimants' Representatives (572)
Nat'l Osteoporosis Foundation (573)
Nat'l Senior Citizens Law Center (577)
Nat'l Silver Haired Congress (578)
Older Women's League (600)
Parker Jewish Geriatric Institute (608)
Population Reference Bureau (621)
TREA Senior Citizens League (TSCL) (691)
United Seniors Ass'n (702)
Del E. Webb Corp. (722)
X-PAC (732)

Agriculture/Agronomy

ADM Milling Co. (227)
AFINOA (231)
AFL-CIO - Food and Allied Service Trades Department (231)
Africare (232)
Ag Biotech Planning Committee (232)
Agri Business Council of Arizona (232)
Agribusiness Council (232)
Agricultural Biotechnology Forum (232)
Agricultural Producers (232)
Agricultural Retailers Ass'n (232)
Amalgamated Sugar (242)
AMCOR Capital Corp. (242)
American Ass'n of Crop Insurers (247)
American Ass'n of Grain Inspection and Weighing Agencies (248)
American Beekeeping Federation (250)
American Corn Growers Ass'n (255)
American Cotton Shippers Ass'n (255)
American Crop Protection Ass'n (256)
American Farm Bureau Federation (258)
American Farmland Trust (258)
American Feed Industry Ass'n (259)
American Grain Inspection Institute (261)
American Home Products Corp. (262)
American Institute of Biological Sciences (264)
American Land Rights Ass'n (265)
American Meat Institute (267)
American Nursery and Landscape Ass'n (268)
American Peanut Council (269)
American Peanut Product Manufacturers, Inc. (269)
American Seed Research Foundation (273)
American Seed Trade Ass'n (273)
American Soc. of Farm Managers and Rural Appraisers (276)
American Soc. of Plant Physiologists (277)
American Soybean Ass'n (277)
American Sugar Alliance (278)
American Sugar Cane League of the U.S.A. (278)
American Sugarbeet Growers Ass'n (278)
American Vintners Ass'n (280)
Animal Health Institute (284)
Animal Industry Foundation (284)
Animas-La Plata Water Conservancy District (284)
Apple Processors Ass'n (286)
Archer Daniels Midland Co. (287)
Argentine Citrus Ass'n (288)
Ass'n of Farmworker Opportunity Programs (295)
AstraZeneca Inc. (301)
AUGURA (302)
Australian Dairy Corp. (303)
Aventis CropScience (304)
Baca Land and Cattle Co. (305)
Ball Research, Inc. (306)
Biotechnology Industry Organization (314)
Bones Brothers Ranch (317)
Branco Peres Citrus, S.A. (319)
Brooks Tropicals, Inc. (322)
Bunge Corp. (323)
C F Industries, Inc. (325)
CalCot (326)
California Asparagus Commission (326)
California Ass'n of Winegrape Growers (326)
California Avocado Commission (326)
California Canning Peach Ass'n (326)
California Kiwi Fruit Commission (327)
California Pistachio Commission (327)
California Prune Board (327)
California Strawberry Commission (327)
California Table Grape Commission (327)
California Tomato Commission (327)
California Walnut Commission (327)
California-Arizona Citrus League (328)
Canadian Broiler Hatching Egg Marketing Agency (329)
Canadian Cattlemen's Ass'n (329)
Cargill, Inc. (331)
Caribbean Banana Exporters Ass'n (331)
CaseNewHolland Inc. (333)
Cattlemen's Beef Promotion and Research Board (334)
CBI Sugar Group (334)
Cell Tech (334)
CENEX, Inc. (335)
Central Arizona Water Conservation District (338)
Central Soya Co. (339)
Central Valley Project Water Ass'n (339)
Chase Nat'l Kiwi Farms (341)
Chiquita Brands Internat'l, Inc. (345)
Clean Water Network (350)
CNPA - Nat'l Center for the Promotion of Agricultural and Food Products (352)
Coalition for Crop Insurance Improvement (353)
Coalition for the American Agricultural Producer (CAAP) (354)
CoBank, ACB (356)
Committee for Fair Ammonium Nitrate Trade (361)
Committee for Farmworker Programs (361)
ConAgra Foods, Inc. (365)
Continental Grain Co. (370)
Corn Refiners Ass'n, Inc. (372)
Cotton Council Internat'l (373)
Cotton Warehouse Ass'n of America (373)
Council for Advanced Agricultural Formulations, Inc. (373)
Council for Agricultural Science and Technology (374)
Council of Northeast Farmer Cooperatives (376)
Crop Growers Insurance Co. (378)
Crop Protection Coalition (378)
Dairy Management, Inc. (381)
Desert Grape Growers League (386)
Dow AgroSciences (391)
Dunavant Enterprises (393)
DuPont Agricultural Products (393)
ED&F Man Inc. (396)
The Egg Factory, LLC (398)
Family Farm Alliance (Project Transfer Council) (410)
FANCOR (411)
The Fanning Corp. (411)
Farm Animal Reform Movement (FARM) (411)
Farm Credit Council (411)
Farm Market iD (412)
Farm Progress Cos. (412)
Farmland Industries, Inc. (412)
Federal Agricultural Mortgage Corp. (Farmer Mac) (412)
The Fertilizer Institute (415)
Fideicomiso de la Escuela de Agricultura de la Region Tropical Humeda, S.A. (416)
First South Production Credit Ass'n (418)
Flo-Sun Sugar (419)
Florida Citrus Alliance (419)
Florida Citrus Mutual (419)
Florida Citrus Packers (419)
Florida Citrus Processors Ass'n (419)
Florida Crystals Corp. (419)
Florida Department of Agriculture and Consumer Services (419)
Florida Farm Bureau (419)
Florida Farm Bureau Federation (419)
Florida Fruit and Vegetable Ass'n (420)
Florida Sugar Cane League, Inc. (420)
Florida Tomato Exchange (420)
FQPA Implementation Working Group (424)
Fresh Garlic Producer Ass'n (426)
Fresh Produce Ass'n of the Americas (426)
Fruit Shippers Ltd. (427)
Gardena Alfalfa Growers Ass'n (429)
Georgia Commodity Commission for Peanuts (434)
Georgia Cotton Commission (434)
Gila River Farms (435)
Glenn-Colusa Irrigation District (436)
Grocery Manufacturers of America (440)
Gulf Citrus Growers Ass'n (442)
Hohenberg Brothers, Co. (450)
Hollister Ranch Owners' Ass'n (451)
Horizon Organic Holding Co. (452)
IMC Global Inc. (458)
Imperial Irrigation District (458)
Inter-American Institute for Cooperation on Agriculture (466)
Internat'l Agriculture and Rural Development Group (467)
Internat'l Ass'n of Food Industry Suppliers (468)
Internat'l Ass'n of Seed Crushers (468)
Internat'l Banana Ass'n (468)
Internat'l Fund for Agricultural Development (472)
Internat'l Policy Council on Agriculture, Food and Trade (474)
Internat'l Specialty Products (475)
Irrigation Ass'n (479)
Japan Internat'l Agricultural Council (482)
League of Private Property Voters (497)
Lewis and Clark Rural Water System, Inc. (498)
Lower Yellowstone Irrigation Project (505)
MacKenzie Agricultural Research (506)
Maui Pineapple Co. (513)
Mauritius, Chamber of Agriculture of (513)
Meat New Zealand (515)
Migrant Legal Action Program (524)
Milk Industry Foundation (524)
Minnesota Valley Alfalfa Producers (525)
Minor Crop Farmer Alliance (525)
Mitsubishi Corp. (526)
Mni-Sose Intertribal Water Rights Coalition (526)
Modesto/Turlock Irrigation District (527)
Monsanto Co. (528)
Mycogen Corp. (533)
Nat'l 4-H Council (535)
Nat'l Agricultural Aviation Ass'n (535)
Nat'l Ass'n for Agricultural Stewardship (537)
Nat'l Ass'n of Agricultural Educators (NAAE) (538)
Nat'l Ass'n of Farmer Elected Committees (NAFEC) (542)
Nat'l Ass'n of State Departments of Agriculture (549)
Nat'l Ass'n of Wheat Growers (551)
Nat'l Barley Growers Ass'n (552)
Nat'l Cattleman's Beef Ass'n (554)
Nat'l Center for Appropriate Technology (554)
Nat'l Chicken Council (555)
Nat'l Corn Growers Ass'n (559)
Nat'l Cotton Council of America (559)
Nat'l Council of Agricultural Employers (560)
Nat'l Council of Commercial Plant Breeders (560)
Nat'l Council of Farmer Cooperatives (560)
Nat'l Family Farm Coalition (563)
Nat'l Farmers Organization (563)
Nat'l Farmers Union (Farmers Educational & Co-operative Union of America) (563)
Nat'l FFA Organization (564)
Nat'l Grain and Feed Ass'n (566)
Nat'l Grain Sorgum Producers (566)
Nat'l Grain Trade Council (566)
Nat'l Grange (566)
Nat'l Grape Co-operative Ass'n, Inc. (566)
Nat'l Institute of Oilseed Products (568)
Nat'l Meat Ass'n (570)
Nat'l Milk Producers Federation (571)
Nat'l Oilseed Processors Ass'n (572)
Nat'l Peach Council (573)
Nat'l Peanut Buying Point Ass'n (573)
Nat'l Pork Producers Council (574)
Nat'l Potato Council (574)
Nat'l Potato Promotion Board (574)
Nat'l Produce Production Inc. (574)
Nat'l Rural Water Ass'n (577)
Nat'l Sunflower Ass'n (579)
Nat'l Turkey Federation (580)
Nat'l Water Resources Ass'n (581)
Nature's Farm Products (582)
Nebraska Wheat Board (583)
New Mexico State University (586)
New Mexico State University, Department of Agriculture (586)
New Zealand Dairy Board (588)
Newhall Land and Farming Co. (588)
Nisei Farmers League (590)
North American Grain Export Ass'n, Inc. (592)
North American Millers' Ass'n (592)
North Carolina Peanut Growers Ass'n (593)
North Dakota Wheat Commission (593)
Novartis Corp. (596)
Organic Trade Ass'n (603)
Organization of Professional Employees of the U.S. Dep't of Agriculture (OPEDA) (603)
Perdue Farms Inc. (612)
Pharmacia Corp. (615)
Philippine Sugar Alliance (616)
Pilgrim's Pride (617)
Pioneer Hi-Bred Internat'l, Inc. (618)
Popcorn Board (620)
Premium Standard Farms (623)
Public Lands Council (629)
Ralston Purina Co. (632)
Renewable Fuels Ass'n (637)
Rio Grande Valley Irrigation (640)
Rio Grande Valley Sugar Growers (640)
Rio Grande Water Conservation District (640)

Rural Advancement Foundation Internat'l - USA (643)
Sherritt Internat'l (657)
Showell Farms Inc. (658)
Smokeless Tobacco Council (661)
Snake River Sugar Co. (662)
South African Sugar Ass'n (666)
Southwest Peanut Growers (668)
Southwest Peanut PAC (668)
Southwest Water Conservation District of Colorado (668)
Southwestern Water Conservation District (668)
Soy Protein Council (668)
SQM North America Corp. (671)
A. E. Staley Manufacturing Co. (672)
Stine Seed Co. (674)
Stockton East Water District (675)
Sugar Ass'n, Inc. (676)
Sugar Cane Growers Cooperative of Florida (676)
Sun Diamond Growers, Inc. (676)
Sunkist Growers, Inc. (677)
SunSweet Growers, Inc. (677)
Sweetener Users Ass'n (678)
Texas Corn Producers Board (684)
Tilda Rice (687)
The Toro Co. (688)
Turfgrass Producers Internat'l (694)
U.S. Apple Ass'n (695)
U.S. Canola Ass'n (695)
U.S. Citrus Science Council (696)
U.S. Grains Council (696)
U.S. Wheat Associates, Inc. (697)
Umatilla Irrigation Districts Coordinating Committee (698)
Umatilla Water Users (698)
United Automobile, Aerospace and Agricultural Implement Workers of America (UAW) (700)
United Egg Ass'n (701)
United Egg Producers (701)
United Fresh Fruit and Vegetable Ass'n (701)
United Gamefowl Breeders Ass'n, Inc. (701)
United Soybean Board (703)
United States Beet Sugar Ass'n (703)
United States Cane Sugar Refiners' Ass'n (703)
USA Rice Federation (709)
Valio Finnish Co-operative Dairies Ass'n (711)
Valley Fig Growers (711)
Vantage Point Network, LLC (712)
Vidalia Onion Business Council (715)
Virginia Peanut Growers Ass'n (716)
Virginia-Carolina's Peanut Political Action Committee (716)
Western Ag Resources Inc. (723)
Western Alliance of Farmworker Advocates, Inc. (WAFA) (724)
Western Growers Ass'n (724)
Western Growers Insurance Services (724)
Western Peanut Growers Ass'n (724)
Western Pistachio Ass'n (724)
Western Range Ass'n (724)
Western United Dairymen (725)
Wheat Export Trade Education Committee (725)
Wheat Foods Council (725)
Wholesale Nursery Growers of America (726)
Wine Institute (728)
Winegrape Growers of America (728)
Worldwatch Institute (731)
Zamorano (734)

Airlines

Aer Lingus (230)
Aerolineas Argentinas (230)
Aerolineas Centrales de Colombia (230)
Aeropostal (230)
Air Afrique (233)
Air Atlantic Dominicana (233)
Air Canada (233)
Air Carrier Ass'n of America (233)
Air China Internat'l Corp., Ltd. (233)
Air D'Ayiti (233)
Air India (233)
Air Jamaica Ltd. (233)
Air Line Pilots Ass'n Internat'l (233)
Air Malta Co. Ltd. (234)
Air Namibia (234)
Air Nauru (234)
Air Pacific Ltd. (234)
Air Tran Airways (234)
Air Transat (234)
Air Transport Ass'n of America (234)
Airline Suppliers Ass'n (235)
Airport Consultants Council (235)
Airtours Internat'l (235)
Akron-Canton Airport (235)
Alaska Airlines (236)
Alitalia (238)
All Nippon Airways Co. (238)
Alliance Air Services (239)
Allied Pilots Ass'n (241)
Aloha Airlines (242)
America West Airlines (243)
American Airlines (244)
AMSA (283)
Andes (284)
APA Internat'l Air, S.A. (285)
Arrow Air (289)
Ass'n of Flight Attendants (295)
Ass'n of Professional Flight Attendants (297)
Austrian Airlines (303)
Avianca Airlines (305)
Aviateca Airline (305)
Big Sky Airlines (313)
Biman Bangladesh Airlines (313)
Birmingham Airport Authority (314)
British Airways Plc (321)
Caraven Airlines (Carga Aerea Venezolana, S.A.) (331)
Caribbean Airline Co. Ltd. (331)
Casino Express Airlines (333)
Challenge Air Cargo (340)
China Eastern Airlines (344)
Compania Mexicana de Aviacion (363)
Continental Airlines Inc. (370)
Copa Airline (371)
Delta Air Lines (384)
Deutsche Lufthansa AG (386)
DHL Airways, Inc. (387)
Dominicana de Aviacion (391)
Eastern Pilots Ass'n (395)
El Al Israel Airlines, Ltd. (399)
Empresa Consolidada Cubana de Aviacion (402)
Eva Airways Corp. (408)
Evergreen Internat'l Aviation (408)
Falcon Air Express (410)
Far West Airlines, LLC (411)
Fast Air Carrier (412)
Faucett Airlines (Compania de Aviacion Faucett, S.A.) (412)
FedEx Corp. (415)
Fine Air Services, Inc. (417)
Flight Safety Foundation (419)
Frontier Airlines (427)
Guam Internat'l Airport Authority (441)
Guyana Airways 2000 (442)
Helli USA Airways (448)
Indigo (460)
Internat'l Air Transport Ass'n (467)
Iran Air (478)
Jamaica Air Freighters, Ltd. (481)
JMC Airlines, Ltd. (483)
Kenya Airways (488)
Korean Air Lines (491)
LADECO (494)
Laker Airways (Bahamas) Ltd. (494)
Lan Chile (494)
LAPA (Lineas Aereas Privadas, S.A.) (495)
Legend Airlines (497)
Lincoln Airport (500)
Lineas Aereas Costarricicenes (Lasca Airlines) (500)
LOT Polish Airlines (504)
Lousville Airport (504)
Lynden Air Cargo, LLC (506)
M K Airlines (506)
Malaysian Airline System (508)
Martinair Holland (511)
Midway Airlines Corp. (523)
Midwest Express Airlines (523)
Nat'l Air Carrier Ass'n (536)
Nat'l Air Transportation Ass'n (536)
Nat'l Airline Passenger Coalition (536)
NICA Airline (589)
Nippon Cargo Airlines (590)
Northern Air Cargo (594)
Northwest Airlines, Inc. (595)
Orient Airlines Ass'n (603)
Orion Air (603)
Pakistan Internat'l Airlines (606)
Peninsula Airways, Inc. (611)
Philippine Airlines (616)
Pilgrim Airlines (617)
Polynesian Airlines (620)
Professional Airways Systems Specialists (AFL-CIO) (625)
Regional Airline Ass'n (635)
Regional Airport Authority of Louisville & Jefferson Co. (635)
Royal Brunei Airways (643)
The Royal Jordanian Airline (643)
Savannah Airport Commission (650)
Scandinavian Airlines System (SAS) (651)
Servicios Aereos de Honduras (SAHSA) (656)
Southern Air Transport (667)
Southwest Airlines (668)
Stanly County Airport Authority (673)
Sun Jet Internat'l, Inc. (676)
Swissair (679)
TACA de Honduras (679)
TACA Internat'l Airlines (679)
TAESA (Transportes Aereos Ejecutivos, S.A. de C.V.) (680)
TAP/Air Portugal (681)
Tower Air, Inc. (688)
Trans World Airlines, Inc. (689)
Transportation Reform Alliance (690)
Transportes Aereos Mercantiles Panamericanos (691)
Travel Industry Ass'n of America (691)
TRIBASA (692)
Turkish Airlines (694)
United Airlines (700)
United Pilots Political Action Committee (702)
US Airways (709)
Vanguard Airlines, Inc. (712)
VASP Airlines (712)
VIASA (714)
Virgin Atlantic Airways (715)
Wien Air Alaska (726)

Animals

African Wildlife Foundation (232)
Alaska Wilderness League (237)
Alliance of Marine Mammal Parks and Aquariums (240)
American Bird Conservancy (251)
American Feed Industry Ass'n (259)
American Horse Council, Inc. (263)
American Horse Protection Ass'n (263)
American Humane Ass'n (263)
American Kennel Club (265)
American Land Rights Ass'n (265)
American Meat Institute (267)
American Sheep Industry Ass'n (273)
American Soc. for the Prevention of Cruelty to Animals National Legislative Office (275)
American Veterinary Medical Ass'n (280)
American Zoo and Aquarium Ass'n (281)
Americans for Medical Progress (282)
Animal Health Institute (284)
Animal Industry Foundation (284)
Ass'n of American Veterinary Medical Colleges (294)
Ass'n of Veterinary Biologics Cos. (299)
Avon Products, Inc. (305)
Baca Land and Cattle Co. (305)
Brookfield Zoo/Chicago Zoological Soc. (321)
Cattlemen's Beef Promotion and Research Board (334)
Center for Marine Conservation (337)
Chicago Mercantile Exchange (343)
Committee for Humane Legislation (361)
Defenders of Wildlife (383)
Dolphin Safe/Fair Trade Campaign (390)
Doris Day Animal League (391)
Ducks Unlimited Inc. (392)
Earthjustice Legal Defense Fund (394)
Elanco Animal Health (399)
Endangered Species Coordinating Council (402)
Environmental Defense Fund (405)
Farm Animal Reform Movement (FARM) (411)
The Fund for Animals (427)
Great Lakes Indian Fish and Wildlife Commission (439)
Greenpeace, U.S.A. (440)
Guide Dog Users, Inc. (442)
Humane Soc. of the United States (455)
Institute of Cetacean Research (464)
Internat'l Ass'n of Fish and Wildlife Agencies (468)
Internat'l Fund for Animal Welfare (472)
Kodiak Brown Bear Trust (490)
League of Private Property Voters (497)
Louisiana Department of Wildlife and Fisheries - Fur and Refuse Division (504)
Marine Mammal Coalition (510)
Meat and Livestock Australia (515)
Minor Use, Minor Species Coalition (525)
Nat'l Anti-Vivisection Soc. (537)
Nat'l Ass'n of Federal Veterinarians (542)
Nat'l Audubon Soc. (552)
Nat'l Aviary in Pittsburgh (552)
Nat'l Cattleman's Beef Ass'n (554)
Nat'l Endangered Species Act Reform Coalition (563)
Nat'l Federation of Pachyderm Clubs, Inc. (564)
Nat'l Horse Show Commission (567)
Nat'l Marine Life Center (570)
Nat'l Renderers Ass'n (575)
Nat'l Wilderness Institute (581)
Nat'l Wildlife Federation - Office of Federal and Internat'l Affairs (581)
Nat'l Wildlife Refuge Ass'n (581)
The Nature Conservancy (582)
North American Bison Cooperative (592)
Ocean Futures Soc., Inc. (598)
Perdue Farms Inc. (612)
Performing Animal Welfare Soc. (612)
Pet Industry Joint Advisory Council (613)
Pew Wilderness Center (613)
Pfizer, Inc. (613)
Pheasants Forever (615)
Physicians Committee for Responsible Medicine (617)
Ralston Purina Co. (632)
Ranchers-Cattlemen Legal Action Fund (633)
Safari Club Internat'l (645)
Schering-Plough Legislative Resources L.L.C. (651)
Scientists Center for Animal Welfare (652)
Sierra Club (658)
Soc. for Animal Protective Legislation (662)
Sportsmen's Legal Defense Fund (670)
Tufts University School of Veterinary Medicine (693)
Wild Bird Feeding Institute (726)
The Wilderness Soc. (726)
Wildlife Advocacy Project (726)
Wildlife Forever (726)
Wildlife Habitat Council (726)
Wildlife Legislative Fund of America (727)
Wildlife Management Institute (727)
The Wildlife Soc. (727)
World Wildlife Fund (731)
Worldwatch Institute (731)

Apparel/Textiles Industry

American Apparel & Footwear Ass'n (245)
American Cotton Shippers Ass'n (255)
American Fiber Manufacturers Ass'n (259)
American Furniture Manufacturers Ass'n (260)
American Nonwovens Corp. (268)
American Sheep Industry Ass'n (273)
American Textile Co. (279)
American Textile Manufacturers Institute (279)
Ass'n of Maquiladores (296)
Athletic Footwear Ass'n (302)
Berry Amendment Glove Coalition (312)
Big Dog Sportswear (313)
Celanese Government Relations Office (334)
Claire's Stores, Inc. (349)
Coalition for Safe Ceramicware (354)
Confederation of Garment Exporters of the Philippines (365)
Cotton Council Internat'l (373)
Cotton Warehouse Ass'n of America (373)
Elzay Ready Wear Manufacturing Co. (401)
ESCO Corp. (407)
Fashion Accessories Shippers Ass'n (412)
Federal Glove Contractors Coalition (413)
Fieldcrest Cannon Inc. (416)
Footwear Distributors and Retailers of America (422)
Fruit of the Loom, Inc. (427)
Gildan Activewear (435)
W. L. Gore & Associates (437)
Greyfab (Bangladesh) Ltd. (440)
Grupo Cydsa (441)
Grupo Industrial Alfa, S.A. (441)
Guilford Mills, Inc. (442)
Hexcel Corp. (449)
Hickey Freeman Co. (449)
Hoechst Marion Roussel Deutschland GmbH (450)
Home Fashion Products Ass'n (451)
The Hosiery Ass'n (452)
ICF Industries, Inc. (457)
Industrial Fabrics Ass'n Internat'l (461)
Industrial Fasteners Institute (461)
Institute for Polyacrylate Absorbents, Inc. (463)
Internat'l Fabricare Institute (471)
Intradeco (477)
Jordache Enterprises, Inc. (485)
Kmart Corp. (490)
Leather Industries of America (497)
Levi Strauss and Co. (498)
Lou Levy & Sons Fashions, Inc. (498)
The Limited Inc. (499)
Liz Claiborne Internat'l (500)
Longworth Industries Inc. (503)
May Department Stores Co. (513)
Military Footwear Coalition (524)
Military Glove Coalition (524)
Milliken and Co. (524)
Mitsubishi Corp. (526)
Montgomery Ward & Co., Inc. (528)
J. E. Morgan Knitting Mills (529)
Mount High Hosiery, Ltd. (531)
Nat'l Ass'n of Uniform Manufacturers and Distributors (551)
Nat'l Cotton Council of America (559)
Nat'l Fastener Distributors Ass'n (564)
Nilit America Corp. (590)
Northern Textile Ass'n (594)
Pacific Dunlop, Ltd./Pacific Brands (605)
Paper Machine Clothing Council (607)
Payless Shoe Source (610)
J. C. Penney Co., Inc. (611)
Philadelphia College of Textiles and Science (615)
Pillowtex Corp. (617)
Polytec Group (620)
Reebok Internat'l (635)
Rubber and Plastic Footwear Manufacturers Ass'n (643)
Rubie's Costume Co., Inc. (643)
Samsung Corp. (647)
Sears, Roebuck and Co. (653)
Secondary Materials and Recycled Textiles Ass'n (654)
Skipps Cutting (660)
Spiegel Inc. (670)
Sports Apparel Products Council (670)
Springs Industries, Inc. (671)
Sterling Internat'l Consultants, Inc. (674)
Tailored Clothing Ass'n (680)
Tan Holdings Corp. (680)
Tanners Countervailing Duty Coalition (680)
The Textile Museum (685)
Textile Rental Services Ass'n of America (685)
Textile/Clothing Technology Center (685)
U.S. Apparel Industry Council (695)
U.S. Ass'n of Importers of Textiles and Apparel (695)
UNIFI, Inc. (698)
Uniform and Textile Service Ass'n (698)
Union of Needletrades, Industrial, and Textile Employees (UNITE) (699)
Valley Forge Flag Co. (711)
Vestal Group of Companies (714)
Vinyl Institute (715)
Wallcovering Ass'n (718)
Westex Inc. (725)
Wool Fiber, Yarn Fabric Coalition (730)

Architecture and Design

Airport Consultants Council (235)
American Architectural Foundation (245)
The American Institute of Architects (264)
American Institute of Certified Planners (264)
American Planning Ass'n (270)
American Soc. of Architectural Illustrators (275)
American Soc. of Landscape Architects (276)
Ass'n of Collegiate Schools of Architecture (295)
Associated Landscape Contractors of America (300)
Council on Federal Procurement of Architectural and Engineering Services (COFPAES) (376)
Day & Zimmermann, Inc. (383)
Design-Build Institute of America (386)
Exeter Architectural Products (409)
Landscape Architecture Foundation (495)
Nat'l Ass'n of County Planners (541)
Nat'l Building Museum (553)
Nat'l Institute of Building Sciences (568)
Scenic America (651)
The Smith, Korach, Hayet, Haynie Partnership (661)

Art/Art Museums

Alliance of Arts Advocates (240)
Alliance of Motion Picture & Television Producers (240)
American Alliance for Health, Physical Education, Recreation and Dance (245)
American Arts Alliance (245)
American Ass'n of Museums (248)
American Citizens for the Arts Political Action Committee (252)
American Federation of Musicians of the United States and Canada (258)
American Film Marketing Ass'n (259)
American Institute for Conservation of Historic and Artistic Works (263)
American Music Therapy Ass'n (268)
American Soc. of Composers, Authors and Publishers (276)
American Symphony Orchestra League (278)
Americans for the Arts (282)
Arena Stage (288)
Arizona Science Center (288)
Artists Rights Today (ART PAC) (290)
Ass'n of Independent Colleges of Art and Design (296)
BET Holdings II, Inc. (312)
Bishop Museum (314)
Boston Symphony Orchestra (318)
Broadcast Music Inc. (BMI) (321)
The Choral Arts Soc. of Washington (345)
CINE (347)
The Colonial Williamsburg Foundation (358)
The Corcoran Gallery of Art (371)
Cultural Alliance of Greater Washington (380)
Da Vinci's Notebook (381)
Dance/USA (382)
Directors Guild of America (389)
Films By Jove (416)
Folger Shakespeare Library (421)
Henry Ford Museum in Greenfield Village (422)
Ford's Theatre (422)
Global Movies Corp. (436)
Graphic Communications Internat'l Union (438)
Great Projects Film Co., Inc. (439)
Interactive Gaming Council (466)
Internat'l Game Technology (472)
Jazz at Lincoln Center Inc. (482)
Kennedy Center for the Performing Arts, John F. (488)
Le Groupe de Soleil (496)
MCA Inc. (514)
MENC: The Nat'l Ass'n for Music Education (518)
Meridian Internat'l Center (519)
Metropolitan Museum of Art (520)
Milwaukee Public Museum (524)
Motion Picture Ass'n of America (530)
Mutual Broadcasting System (533)
Nat'l Art Education Ass'n (537)
Nat'l Ass'n of Dealers in Ancient, Oriental and Primitive Art (542)
Nat'l Ass'n of Music Merchants (545)
Nat'l Ass'n of Recording Merchandisers (548)
Nat'l Ass'n of School Music Dealers (548)
Nat'l Ass'n of Schools of Art and Design (548)
Nat'l Ass'n of Schools of Dance (548)
Nat'l Ass'n of Schools of Music (548)
Nat'l Ass'n of Schools of Theatre (549)
Nat'l Ass'n of Theatre Owners (550)
Nat'l Assembly of State Arts Agencies (551)
Nat'l Building Museum (553)
Nat'l Film Preservation Foundation (564)
Nat'l Humanities Alliance (567)
Nat'l Museum of Women in the Arts (571)
Nat'l Music Publishers' Ass'n (571)
Newington-Cropsey Foundation (588)
Official Artist Inc. (599)
Olan Mills Inc. (600)
The Phillips Collection (616)
Photo Marketing Ass'n-Internat'l (616)
Professional Photographers of America (626)
School of Visual Arts (652)
The Shakespeare Theatre (656)
Smithsonian Institution (661)
Songwriters Guild of America (665)
Sony Music Entertainment Inc. (666)
Sony Pictures Entertainment Inc. (666)
Sotheby's Holdings Inc. (666)
The Textile Museum (685)
Ticketmaster (687)
U.S. Space & Rocket Center (697)
Very Special Arts (714)
Washington Area Lawyers for the Arts (719)
The Washington Ballet (719)
The Washington Opera (720)
Washington Sports & Entertainment, L.P. (720)
Writers Guild of America (732)

Automotive Industry

AAA MidAtlantic (224)
ABB Daimler-Benz Transportation, N.A. (ADTRANZ) (225)
Advocates for Highway and Auto Safety (229)
Agricultural Transporters Conference (232)
Allete (239)
Alliance of Automobile Manufacturers, Inc. (240)
Allison Transmission Division, General Motors Corp. (241)
American Automar (250)
American Automobile Ass'n (250)
American Automotive Leasing Ass'n (250)
American Financial Services Ass'n (259)
American Honda Motor Co., Inc. (262)
American Internat'l Automobile Dealers Ass'n (265)
American Koyo Corp. (265)
American Motorcyclist Ass'n (268)
American Red Bull Transit (272)
American Standard Cos. Inc. (278)
Americans for Free Internat'l Trade (AFIT PAC) (281)
Arvin Meritor Automotive (290)
Ass'n of Brazilian Tire Producers (294)
Ass'n of Internat'l Automobile Manufacturers (296)
Association des Constructeurs Europeens de Motocycles (300)
Automobile Manufacturers R&D Coalition (303)
Automotive Aftermarket Industry Ass'n (303)
Automotive Consumer Action Program (303)
Automotive Engine Rebuilders Ass'n (303)
Automotive Maintenance and Repair Ass'n (303)
Automotive Parts and Service Alliance (303)
Automotive Parts Rebuilders Ass'n (304)
Automotive Recyclers Ass'n (304)
Automotive Refrigeration Products Institute (304)
Automotive Service Ass'n (304)
Automotive Trade Ass'n Executives (304)
Automotive Warehouse Distributors Ass'n (304)
AutoNation, Inc. (304)
Bailey Corp. (306)
Bell Equipment Ltd. (311)
BMW (U.S.) Holding Corp. (316)
BMW Manufacturing Corp. (316)
BMW of North America, Inc. (316)
Bridgestone/Firestone, Inc. (320)
CALSTART (328)
Center for Auto Safety (335)
Certified Automotive Parts Ass'n (340)
Circuit City Stores, Inc. (347)
Club Car, Inc. (351)
Coalition for Auto Repair Equality (CARE) (353)
Coalition for Vehicle Choice (355)
The Coalition on Motor Vehicle Privacy (356)
Consolidated Diesel Corp. (367)
Continental Teves (370)
Cummins Engine Co. (380)
DaimlerChrysler Corp. (381)
Dana Corp. (382)
Danaher Corp. (382)
Delta Comercio, S.A. (385)
The Electric Vehicle Ass'n of the Americas (EVAA) (400)
Envirotest Systems Corp. (405)
EV Rental Cars, LLC (408)
FIAMM S.p.A. (416)
FIAMM Technologies, Inc. (416)
Fiat U.S.A., Inc. (416)
Ford Motor Co. (422)
General Motors Corp. (432)
General Tire, Inc. (433)
Goodyear Tire and Rubber Co. (437)
Greater New York Automobile Dealers Ass'n (439)
Harmon-Motive (444)
Heavy Vehicle Maintenance Group (447)
Hertz Corp. (449)
Honda Motor Co. (451)
Honda North America, Inc. (451)
Honeywell Internat'l, Inc. (452)
Hyundai Motor Co. (456)
Industrial Truck Ass'n (461)
Internat'l Mobile Air Conditioning Ass'n (473)
Internat'l Truck and Engine Corp. (475)
Internat'l Union of Electronic, Electrical, Salaried, Machine, and Furniture Workers-Communications Workers of America (476)
ITT Industries (480)
Japan Automobile Manufacturers Ass'n (481)
Japan Automobile Standards Internat'l Center (481)
JM Family Enterprises (483)
Kawasaki Motors Corp., USA (487)

Kia Motors Corp. (489)
Lion Oil Co. (500)
Mack Trucks, Inc. (506)
Mazda Motor Corp. (514)
Mazda North America Operations (514)
Mercedes-Benz of North America, Inc. (518)
Michelin North America (522)
Mid-Atlantic Toyota Distributors Inc. (523)
Midwest Motor Express, Inc. (523)
Mitsubishi Motors America, Inc. (526)
Motor and Equipment Manufacturers Ass'n (531)
Motorcycle Industry Council (531)
NACCO Industries (534)
Nat'l Ass'n of Metal Finishers (545)
Nat'l Ass'n of Minority Automobile Dealers (545)
Nat'l Automobile Dealers Ass'n (552)
Nat'l Truck Equipment Ass'n (580)
Natural Gas Vehicle Coalition (582)
Nissan North America Inc. (590)
Nylo-Flex Manufacturing Co., Inc. (597)
Oshkosh Truck Corp. (604)
PACCAR, Inc. (605)
Porsche Cars North America, Inc. (621)
Propane Vehicle Council (627)
Recreation Vehicle Ass'n (634)
Recreation Vehicle Dealers Ass'n of North America (634)
Recreation Vehicle Industry Ass'n (635)
Recreation Vehicle Rental Ass'n (635)
Safety-Kleen Corp. (645)
Service Station Dealers of America and Allied Trades (656)
Singapore Technologies Automotive (659)
Soc. of Automotive Engineers (SAE Internat'l) (663)
Southern Auto Sales, Inc. (667)
Special Vehicle Coalition (669)
Specialty Equipment Market Ass'n (670)
Subaru of America (676)
Subaru-Isuzu Automotive, Inc. (676)
Textron Inc. (685)
Tire Ass'n of North America (687)
Tire Industry Safety Council (687)
Toyota Motor Corp. (689)
Toyota Motor Manufacturing North America (689)
Toyota Motor North America, U.S.A., Inc. (689)
Toyota Technical Center U.S.A. Inc. (689)
Transconsortia (690)
Truck Mixer Manufacturers Bureau (692)
Truck Trailer Manufacturers Ass'n (693)
TRW Inc. (693)
United Automobile, Aerospace and Agricultural Implement Workers of America (UAW) (700)
United Technologies Corp. (704)
Volkswagen of America, Inc. (717)
Volkswagen, AG (717)
Yale Materials Handling Corp. (733)
Yamaha Motor Corp. U.S.A. (733)

Banking/Finance/Investments

Ad Hoc Coalition of Commercial and Investment Banks (227)
Advanta Corp. (229)
Aegon USA (229)
Affiliated Computer Services (230)
AFIN Securities (231)
Alliance Capital Management LP (239)
Allmerica Financial (241)
AMCOR Capital Corp. (242)
America's Community Bankers (243)
American Ass'n of Bank Directors (246)
American Ass'n of Enterprise Zones (247)
American Ass'n of Limited Partners (248)
American Bankruptcy Institute (250)
American Collectors Ass'n (253)
American Council for Capital Formation (255)
American Council of State Savings Supervisors (256)
American Express Co. (258)
American Financial Group (259)
American Financial Services Ass'n (259)
American General Corp. (261)
American General Financial Group (261)
American Investors Life Insurance (265)
American Land Title Ass'n (265)
American League of Financial Institutions (266)
American Names Ass'n (268)
Americans for Common Cents (281)
Americans for Financial Security (281)
Amstel Hudson Management Corp. (283)
Apollo Advisors (286)
Arab American Bank (287)
Argentine Economic & Investment Council (288)
Asian Development Bank - North American Representative Office (291)
Ass'n for Financial Professionals, Inc. (292)
Ass'n for Governmental Leasing and Finance (292)
Ass'n of Bank Couriers (294)
Ass'n of Bankruptcy Professionals, Inc. (294)
Ass'n of Banks in Insurance (294)
Ass'n of Banks of Israel (294)
Ass'n of Financial Guaranty Insurers (295)
Ass'n of Financial Services Holding Companies (295)
Ass'n of Foreign Investors in U.S. Real Estate (295)
Ass'n of Fund Raising Professionals (295)
Ass'n of Local Housing Finance Agencies (296)
Ass'n of Publicly Traded Companies (298)
Associated Credit Bureaus, Inc. (300)
Associated Financial Corp. (300)
Associates First Capital Corp. (300)
Assurant Group (301)
AT&T Capital Corp. (301)
Australia and New Zealand Banking Group (303)
Avco Financial Services (304)
Banco Portugues do Atlantico, S.A. (307)
Bank Hapoalim B.M. (307)
Bank Leumi le-Israel B.M. (307)
Bank of Alabama (307)
Bank of America (307)
Bank of New England (307)
Bank of New England Holding Company Trustee (307)
Bank of New York (307)
Bank of Tokyo-Mitsubishi (307)
Bank of Zaire (307)
The Bank Private Equity Coalition (307)
Bank United of Texas FSB (307)
Bankers Trust Co. (307)
Bankers' Ass'n for Finance and Trade (307)
Banorte Casa de Bolsa (307)
Banque Paribas New York Branch (307)
Barker Enterprises (308)
Barron Collier Co. (308)
Bass Enterprises Production Co. (308)
Bayamon Federal Savings and Loan Ass'n (309)
Bear, Stearns and Co. (310)
Beneficial Corp. (311)
Bessemer Securities Corp. (312)
Beverly Hills Federal Savings Bank (313)
H & R Block, Inc. (315)
Blount Parrish & Co., Inc. (315)
Bluebonnet Savings Bank (316)
BMW Financial Services of North America, Inc. (316)
The Bond Market Ass'n (317)
Boston Stock Exchange (318)
Branch Banking and Trust Co. (319)
Brown Brothers Harriman & Co. (322)
Bundesverband der Deutscher Banken (323)
Cafaro Co. (326)
California Federal Bank (326)
California Public Employees' Retirement System (327)
Campaign Finance Reform Coalition (328)
Capital Dimensions Venture Fund Inc. (330)
Capital One Financial Corp. (330)
The Carlyle Group (332)
CELOTEX (335)
Center for Community Change (335)
Center for Economic Organizing (336)
Center on Budget and Policy Priorities (338)
Central Bank of Turkey (338)
Century Financial Group (339)
Champion Securities (341)
Chandis Securities Co. (341)
Charter One (341)
Chase Manhattan Bank (341)
Chela Financial (342)
Cherokee Investment Partners, LLC (342)
Chevy Chase Bank, F.S.B. (342)
Cheyne Walk Trust (342)
Chibank Service Inc. (342)
Chicago Board of Trade (342)
Chicago Board Options Exchange (343)
Chicago Mercantile Exchange (343)
Chicago Stock Exchange, Inc. (343)
Cincinnati Stock Exchange (347)
Citibank, N.A. (347)
Citigroup (347)
Citizens Bank (348)
CNA Financial Corp. (351)
Coalition for Shareholder Fairness (354)
Coalition of Commercial and Investment Banks (355)
Coalition of Publicly Traded Partnerships (355)
Coalition to Amend the Financial Information Privacy Act (CAFPA) (356)
Coast Federal Savings and Loan Ass'n (356)
CoBank, ACB (356)
Ronald J. Cohen Investments (357)
The Coin Coalition (357)
College Savings Bank (358)
Colombian Banking and Financial Entities Ass'n (ASOBANCARIA) (358)
Colorado Credit Union Systems (358)
Comerica, Inc. (360)
Commercial Finance Ass'n (360)
Committee for a Responsible Federal Budget (360)
Community Bank League of New England (362)
Community Banks Ass'n of New York State (362)
Community Financial Services Ass'n (362)
Concord Coalition (365)
Conference of State Bank Supervisors (366)
Connecticut Student Loan Foundation (367)
The Connell Co. (367)
The Consulting Center (368)
Consumer Bankers Ass'n (368)
Consumer Mortgage Coalition (369)
Contran Corp. (370)
Corporate Property Investors (372)
Costa Rica, Central Bank of (373)
Council of Development Finance Agencies (375)
Council of Infrastructure Financing Authorities (375)
Council of Institutional Investors (375)
Countrywide Home Loans, Inc. (377)
Countrywide Mortgage Corp. (377)
Credit Suisse First Boston Corp. (378)
Credit Union Council of the Nat'l Ass'n of State Credit Union Supervisors (378)
Credit Union Nat'l Ass'n, Inc. (378)
CSFP Capital, Inc. (379)
CT USA, Inc. (379)
Currenex (380)
D.C. Lottery (381)
D. H. Blair Investment Banking Corp. (381)
Defense Credit Union Council (384)
Diamond Ventures (387)
Dime Savings Bank of New York (388)
Diversified Collection Services, Inc. (390)
Dollar Bank (390)
Downey Financial Corp. (392)
Dun & Bradstreet (393)
E Lottery (394)
E*TRADE Securities, Inc. (394)
E-LOAN, Inc. (394)
Eaton Vance Management Co. (395)
EBS Dealing Resources Inc. (395)
ED&F Man Inc. (396)
Eden Financial Corp. (396)
Education Finance Council (398)
Electronic Funds Transfer Ass'n (400)
Enterprise Bank (404)
Equitable Financial Co. (406)
The ERISA Industry Committee (ERIC) (406)
The ESOP (Employee Stock Ownership Plan) Ass'n (407)
Fair Share Coalition (410)
Fannie Mae (411)
Farm Credit Bank of Texas (411)
Farm Credit Council (411)
Federal Agricultural Mortgage Corp. (Farmer Mac) (412)
Federal Funds Information for States (413)
Federal Home Loan Bank of Boston (413)
Federal Home Loan Bank of Chicago (413)
Federal Home Loan Bank of Dallas (413)
Federal Home Loan Bank of Des Moines (413)
Federal Home Loan Bank of Indianapolis (413)
Federal Home Loan Bank of New York (413)
Federal Home Loan Bank of Pittsburgh (413)
Federal Home Loan Bank of San Francisco (413)
Federal Home Loan Bank of Seattle (413)
Federal Home Loan Bank of Topeka (413)
Federal Home Loan Mortgage Corp. (Freddie Mac) (413)
Federal Nat'l Payables, Inc. (413)
Federated Investors, Inc. (414)
Federation of Japanese Bankers Ass'ns (414)
Fidelity Investments Co. (416)
Financial Collection Agencies (416)
Financial Corp. of America (416)
Financial Executives International (416)
Financial Guaranty Insurance Corp. (416)
Financial Planning Ass'n (416)
Financial Service Centers of America (416)
Financial Services Coordinating Council (416)
Financial Services Council (416)
The Financial Services Roundtable (416)
Financial Technology Industry Council (417)
Financial Women Internat'l (417)
First American (417)
First Data Corp./Telecheck (417)
First Federal Savings and Loan Ass'n of Raleigh (417)
First Fidelity Bancorporation (417)
First Nat'l of Nebraska (417)
First Nationwide Bank (417)
First Savings Bank, F.S.B. (417)
First South Production Credit Ass'n (418)
First Union Corp. (418)
First USA Bank (418)
FIRSTPLUS Financial Group Inc. (418)
FISERV, Inc. (418)
Fitch Investors Service, Inc. (418)
Fleet Financial Group, Inc. (418)
FleetBoston Financial (418)
FM Watch (420)
FMR Corp. (421)
Ford Motor Credit Co. (Legal Department) (422)
Forum For Investor Advice (423)
Fulcrum Venture Capital Corp. (427)
Fund for Assuring an Independent Retirement (427)
Futures Industry Ass'n (428)
GATX Corp. (430)
GE Capital Mortgage Insurance Co. (GEMICO) (430)
GE Capital Mortgage Services, Inc. (430)
GE Commercial Real Estate & Financial Services (430)
GE Investment Corp. (430)
Gelco Government Services (430)
General Electric Capital Mortgage Corp. (432)
General Electric Capital Services, Inc. (432)
Glendale Federal Bank, FSB (436)
Golden West Financial Corp. (437)
Goldman, Sachs and Co. (437)
Gordon Investment Corp. (437)
Government Finance Officers Ass'n, Federal Liaison Center (438)
GreenPoint Bank (440)
Greenwich Capital Markets, Inc. (440)
The Group of 20 (441)
Group of 30 (441)
Grupo Financiero Banorte (441)
Guam Bankers Ass'n (441)
Guaranty Bank, SSB (442)

H & R Executive Towers (443)
Harbour Group Industries, Inc. (444)
Haven Federal Savings and Loan Ass'n (445)
Healthcare Financial Management Ass'n (447)
Healthcare Financing Study Group (447)
Heller Financial Inc. (448)
Herzog, Heine, Geduld, Inc. (449)
The Hillman Co. (450)
Home Federal Savings and Loan Ass'n (451)
Home Warranty Coalition (451)
Homestead Financial Corp. (451)
Household Financial Group, Ltd. (453)
Household Internat'l, Inc. (453)
Human Capital Resources (454)
Huntington Bancshares (455)
Independence Bank (459)
Independent Bankers Ass'n of Texas (459)
Independent Community Bankers of America (459)
Independent Television Service (460)
Institute for Certified Investment Management Consultants (463)
Institute of Internat'l Bankers (464)
Interactive Brokers LLC (466)
Interest Netting Coalition (466)
Internat'l Ass'n for Financial Planning (467)
Internat'l Swaps and Derivatives Dealers Ass'n (475)
Internat'l Tax and Investment Center (475)
Internation Securities Exchange (476)
Intertribal Monitoring Ass'n on Indian Trust Funds (477)
Investment Co. Institute (477)
Investment Counsel Ass'n of America (478)
Investment Program Ass'n (478)
The Island ECN (479)
Israel, Ministry of Finance of the State of (479)
Japan Bank for Internat'l Cooperation (481)
JBA Consulting, Inc. (482)
JM Family Enterprises (483)
Joint Stock Company Severstal (484)
Edward Jones Co. (484)
Edward Jones Investments (485)
K Capital Partners (485)
Kansas City Southern Industries (486)
KeyCorp, Inc. (489)
Keystone, Inc. (489)
Knight Trading Group (490)
Kohlberg Kravis Roberts & Co. (490)
L.L. Capital Partners, Inc. (493)
Lehman Brothers (498)
LM Capital Corp. (501)
Loews CNA Financial (502)
London Clearinghouse, Ltd. (503)
Louisiana Credit Union Ass'n (504)
MacAndrews & Forbes Holdings, Inc. (506)
Bernard L. Madoff Investment Securities (507)
Malta Development Corp. (508)
Managed Funds Ass'n (508)
Maritime Investment Corp. (510)
Marubeni America Corp. (511)
Massachusetts Bankers Ass'n (512)
MasterCard Internat'l (513)
MBNA America Bank NA (514)
McAndrews and Forbes Holding, Inc. (514)
McGarr Capital Management Corp. (514)
McKinsey & Co., Inc. (515)
Medallion Funding Corp. (515)
MemberWorks, Inc. (517)
Merchant's Nat'l Bank (518)
Merrill Lynch & Co., Inc. (519)
MetroPlains Development, Inc. (520)
Metropolitan Banking Group (520)
Metropolitan Mortgage and Securities, Inc. (520)
MG Financial Group (521)
Michigan Nat'l Corp. (522)
Mitsubishi Corp. (526)
MMG Ventures LP (526)
The Money Store (527)
Money Tree, Inc. (527)
J. P. Morgan Chase & Co. (529)
Morgan Guaranty Trust Co. (529)
J. P. Morgan Securities (529)
Morgan Stanley Dean Witter & Co. (529)
Mortgage Bankers Ass'n of America (530)
Mortgage Insurance Companies of America (530)
Mortgage Investors Corp. (530)
Moscow Interbank Currency Exchange (MICEX) (530)
Most Group Limited (530)
Mountain West Savings Bank, F.S.B. (532)
Multi-Family Housing Institute (532)
Municipal Bond Insurance Ass'n (532)
Municipal Financial Consultants Inc. (532)
Municipal Securities Rulemaking Board (532)
Municipal Treasurers Ass'n of the United States and Canada (533)
Myriad Capital Inc. (534)
NACHA - The Electronic Payments Ass'n (534)
NASDAQ Stock Market (534)
Nat'l Ass'n of Bankruptcy Trustees (539)
Nat'l Ass'n of Corporate Treasurers (541)
Nat'l Ass'n of County Treasurers and Finance Officers (541)
Nat'l Ass'n of Credit Management (541)
Nat'l Ass'n of Development Companies (542)
Nat'l Ass'n of Energy Service Companies (542)
Nat'l Ass'n of Federal Credit Unions (542)
Nat'l Ass'n of Government Guaranteed Lenders (543)
Nat'l Ass'n of Investment Companies (544)
Nat'l Ass'n of Investors Corporation (NAIC) (545)
Nat'l Ass'n of Lottery Purchasers (545)
Nat'l Ass'n of Mortgage Brokers (545)
Nat'l Ass'n of Real Estate Investment Trusts (547)
Nat'l Ass'n of Retail Collection Attorneys (548)
Nat'l Ass'n of SBA Microloan Intermediaries (548)
Nat'l Ass'n of Securities Dealers, Inc. (NASD) (549)
Nat'l Ass'n of Small Business Investment Companies (549)
Nat'l Ass'n of State Auditors, Comptrollers and Treasurers (549)
Nat'l Ass'n of State Budget Officers (549)
Nat'l Ass'n of State Credit Union Supervisors (549)
Nat'l Ass'n of Student Financial Aid Administrators (550)
Nat'l Ass'n of Thrift Savings Plan Participants (550)
Nat'l Ass'n of Urban Bankers, Inc. (551)
Nat'l Ass'n to Protect Individual Rights (551)
Nat'l Bankers Ass'n (552)
Nat'l Community Capital Ass'n (557)
Nat'l Conference of Bankruptcy Judges (558)
Nat'l Cooperative Bank (558)
Nat'l Council of Health Facilities Finance Authorities (560)
Nat'l Council of Higher Education Loan Programs (560)
Nat'l Defined Contribution Council (561)
Nat'l Federation of Community Development of Credit Unions (564)
Nat'l Foreign Trade Council, Inc. (565)
Nat'l Home Equity Mortgage Ass'n (567)
Nat'l Institute for State Credit Union Examination (568)
Nat'l Institute on Financial Issues and Services for Elders (569)
Nat'l Investor Relations Institute (569)
Nat'l Mitigation Bankers Ass'n (571)
Nat'l Rural Development & Finance Corp. (576)
Nat'l Soc. of Accountants (578)
Nat'l Treasury Employees Union (580)
Nat'l Venture Capital Ass'n (580)
Nationwide Global (582)
NBD Bank, N.A. (583)
New England Education Loan Marketing Corp. (Nellie Mae) (585)
New England Financial (585)
New England Investment Co. (585)
New London Development Corp. (586)
New York Bankers Ass'n (586)
New York State Housing Finance Agency (587)
New York Stock Exchange (588)
Nissho-Iwai American Corp. (590)
Nomura Internat'l plc (591)
Non-Bank Funds Transmitters Group (591)
North American Securities Administrators Ass'n (NASAA) (592)
Northside Savings Bank (595)
Ocwen Federal Savings Bank (599)
OMB Watch (600)
Opportunity Capital Corp. (601)
Option One Mortgage Corp. (602)
Organization for Internat'l Investment (603)
Ounalashka Corp. (604)
Pacific Capital Group, Inc. (605)
The Pacific Stock Exchange, Inc. (606)
PaineWebber Group, Inc. (606)
Peachtree Settlement Funding (610)
Pedestal (610)
Pegasus Capital Advisors, L.P. (611)
Pennsylvania Economic Development Financing Authorities (611)
Pennsylvania Savings Ass'n Insurance Corp. (611)
Peoples Bank (612)
The Philadelphia Stock Exchange, Inc. (615)
PIMCO Advisors, L.P. (617)
Pinnacle West Capital Corp. (617)
PNC Bank, N.A. (619)
Potomac Capital Investment Corp. (622)
Primerica, Inc. (624)
Principal Financial Group (624)
Production Service & Sales District Council Pension Fund (625)
Profit Recovery Group Internat'l (626)
Profit Sharing/401 (k) Council of America (626)
Providian Financial Corp. (627)
Prudential Securities, Inc. (627)
Public Financial Management (628)
Puerto Rico Bankers Ass'n (629)
Queens County Bancorp Inc. (631)
Real Estate Services Providers Council (634)
RECRA (634)
Regions Financial Corp. (636)
Reilly Mortgage Group Inc. (636)
Republic Nat'l Bank of New York (637)
Retirement Income Coalition (639)
Reuters America Inc. (639)
Richardson Savings and Loan Ass'n (639)
Riggs Bank, N.A. (640)
Rosenbaum Trust (642)
Roslyn Bancorp Inc. (642)
Rural Community Assistance Corp. (643)
Rural Telephone Finance Cooperative (644)
Frank Russell Co. (644)
S-Corporation Ass'n (644)
Sakura Bank Ltd. (646)
Sallie Mae, Inc. (646)
Sammons Enterprises, Inc. (647)
The Sanwa Bank , Ltd. (649)
Savings Banks Life Insurance Fund (650)
Savings Coalition of America (650)
Schooner Capital Internat'l (652)
Sealaska Corp. (653)
Securities Industry Ass'n (654)
Securities Litigation Reform Coalition (654)
Securities Traders Ass'n (654)
D. E. Shaw & Co. (657)
Singer Asset Management Co., L.L.C. (659)
Singer Assett Finance, Inc. (660)
SLM Holding Corp. (661)
Smith Barney Harris Upham & Co. (661)
Sovereign Bank (668)
Standard & Poor's Corp. (672)
Standard Chartered Bank (672)
Stanford Financial Group (672)
State Street Bank and Trust Co. (673)
Stephens Group, Inc. (674)
Stone Investments, Inc. (675)
Student Loan Funding Corp. (675)
Student Loan Servicing Alliance (675)
Sumitomo Corp. of America (676)
Superior Bank, FSB (677)
Surety Information Office (677)
Susquehanna Investment Group (678)
Swiss Bank Corp. (679)
Swiss Investors Protection Ass'n (679)
Synovus Financial Corp. (679)
TCF Financial Corp. (681)
TD Waterhouse Group (682)
Texas Pacific Group (685)
Texas Savings and Community Bankers (685)
Textron Inc. (685)
Tiger Fund (687)
Transamerica Corp. (689)
Transamerica Financial Services Co. (689)
Travelers Express Co., Inc. (691)
TSG Ventures Inc. (693)
Turkey, Central Bank of (694)
U.S. Immigrant Investor Ass'n (696)
U.S. Mint (696)
UBS Warburg (697)
Unifinancial Internat'l, Inc. (698)
Union Bank of Switzerland (699)
UNIPAC Service Corp. (699)
United Asset Management Corp. (700)
United California Savings Bank (700)
United Companies Financial Corp. (701)
United States Council for Internat'l Business (703)
United Student Aid Group (704)
US Bancorp (709)
USA Funds, Inc. (709)
USAA - United Services Automobile Ass'n (710)
H. D. Vest Financial Service (714)
VISA U.S.A., Inc. (716)
Vornado Inc. (717)
Waddell & Reed Financial, Inc. (718)
Wasatch Front Regional Council (719)
Washington Mutual Bank (720)
Washington Real Estate Investment Trust (720)
J. G. Wentworth (723)
Western Financial/Westcorp Inc. (724)
Western League of Savings Institutions (724)
Wheat First Butcher Singer (725)
Wilmington Savings Fund Society (727)
Wocom Commodities Limited (729)
Women for Tax Reform (729)
Ziff Investors Partnership (734)
Zions Bank Co. (734)
Zions First Nat'l Bank (734)

Cemeteries/Funerals

Internat'l Cemetery and Funeral Ass'n (469)
Nat'l Funeral Directors Ass'n (565)
Service Corp. Internat'l (656)

Charities and Foundations

21st Century Space Foundation (223)
Abilene Industrial Foundation, Inc. (225)
Aerospace Education Foundation (230)
Afghanistan Foundation (230)
African Wildlife Foundation (232)
AIDS Healthcare Foundation (233)
Air Force Memorial Foundation (233)
Alexis de Tocqueville Institution (238)
American Architectural Foundation (245)
American Defense Institute (256)
American Forest Foundation (260)
American Foundation for AIDS Research (260)
American Foundation for the Blind - Governmental Relations Group (260)
American Health Assistance Foundation (261)
American Indian Heritage Foundation (263)
American Institute of Chemists Foundation (264)
The American Land Conservancy (265)
American Leprosy Foundation (266)
American Seed Research Foundation (273)
American Speech-Language-Hearing Foundation (277)
Animal Industry Foundation (284)
The Asia Foundation (290)
Aspirin Foundation of America, Inc. (291)

Asthma and Allergy Foundation of America (301)
Benton Foundation/Communications Policy Project (311)
Biomedical Research Foundation of Northwest Louisiana (314)
Brain Injury Ass'n (319)
Bread for the World (319)
California Museum Foundation (327)
California Wellness Foundation (328)
Charity Lobbying in the Public Interest (341)
Citizen's Educational Foundation (348)
Citizens' Scholarship Foundation of America (349)
Cleveland Clinic Foundation (350)
Close Up Foundation (351)
The Community Foundation for the Nat'l Capital Region (362)
Congressional Black Caucus Foundation (366)
Congressional Sportsmen's Foundation (366)
Connecticut Student Loan Foundation (367)
Conservation Internat'l Foundation (367)
Conservative Caucus Research, Analysis and Education Foundation (367)
Constitutional Rights Foundation (368)
Cooley's Anemia Foundation (371)
Council on Foundations (377)
The Criminal Justice Policy Foundation (378)
Cruise Industry Charitable Foundation (379)
Cuban American Nat'l Foundation/Cuban American Foundation (379)
Cure for Lymphoma Foundation (380)
Cystic Fibrosis Foundation (380)
Delta Foundation (385)
The Devereux Foundation (387)
Direct Selling Education Foundation (389)
Doris Duke Charitable Foundation (392)
Dystonia Medical Research Foundation (394)
Educational Foundation for Citizenship and Statehood Project (398)
Educational Media Foundation (398)
Milton S. Eisenhower Foundation (399)
Employment Policy Foundation (402)
The Enterprise Foundation (404)
Epilepsy Foundation of America (406)
Family Violence Prevention Fund (411)
Fellowship Square Foundation, Inc. (415)
FINCA Internat'l Inc., The Foundation for Internat'l Community Assistance (417)
First Flight Centennial Foundation (417)
Flight Safety Foundation (419)
Ford Foundation (422)
Fort Abraham Lincoln Foundation (423)
The Foundation for Environmental and Economic Progress (424)
Foundation for Internat'l Meetings (424)
Foundation for Middle East Peace (424)
Foundation for Public Affairs (424)
Foundation for the Advancement of Chiropractic Tenets and Science (424)
Foundation on Economic Trends (424)
Free Congress Research and Education Foundation (425)
Friedrich Ebert Foundation (426)
Friends of the Everglades (426)
Frontiers of Freedom Institute (427)
George Mason University Foundation (434)
German Marshall Fund of the United States (435)
H.M.S. Rose Foundation (443)
Habitat for Humanity Internat'l (443)
Hazelden Foundation (445)
Heinz Family Foundation (448)
Heritage Foundation (448)
The Hitachi Foundation (450)
Howard Hughes Medical Institute (454)
Human Relations Foundation of Chicago (454)
Independent Sector (460)
Internat'l Eye Foundation/Soc. of Eye Surgeons (471)
Internat'l Foundation for Election Systems (IFES) (471)
Internat'l Geographic Information Foundation (472)
Internat'l Microelectronics and Packaging Soc. - IMAPS (473)
Internat'l Trust Fund for Demining and Mine Victims Assistance in Bosnia-Herzigovina (475)
Japan Productivity Center for Socio-Economic Development (482)
Joyce Foundation (485)
Juvenile Diabetes Foundation Internat'l (485)
Kaiser Family Foundation (486)
Kaiser Permanente (486)
Henry H. Kessler Foundation (488)
Kettering Foundation (488)
Komen Breast Cancer Foundation, The Susan G. (491)
Landmark Legal Foundation Center for Civil Rights (495)
Landscape Architecture Foundation (495)
Life and Health Insurance Foundation for Education (499)
LifeLink Foundation (499)
Lindesmith Center - Drug Policy Foundation (500)
Lupus Foundation of America (505)
Luso American Foundation (505)
Lyme Disease Foundation (506)
March of Dimes Birth Defects Foundation (509)
Milk Industry Foundation (524)
The Jeffrey Modell Foundation (527)
Montana State University (528)
Motion Picture and Television Fund (530)
Motorcycle Riders Foundation (531)
Nat'l Ass'n of Veterans Research and Education Foundations (551)
Nat'l Center for Advanced Technologies (554)
Nat'l Center for Nonprofit Boards (555)
Nat'l Center for Public Policy Research (555)
Nat'l Chamber Foundation (555)
Nat'l Community Action Foundation (557)
Nat'l Defense Council Foundation (561)
Nat'l Ecological Foundation (562)
Nat'l Foundation for Cancer Research (565)
Nat'l Foundation for Infectious Diseases (565)
Nat'l Foundation for the Improvement of Education (565)
Nat'l Gaucher Foundation (565)
Nat'l Health Museum (567)
Nat'l Heritage Foundation (567)
Nat'l Italian American Foundation (569)
Nat'l Law Enforcement Officers Memorial Fund (569)
Nat'l Legal Center for the Public Interest (570)
Nat'l Migrant Head Start Ass'n (571)
Nat'l Osteoporosis Foundation (573)
Nat'l Park Foundation (573)
Nat'l Patient Advocate Foundation (573)
Nat'l Peace Foundation (573)
Nat'l Press Foundation (574)
Nat'l Psoriasis Foundation (574)
Nat'l Right to Work Legal Defense Foundation (576)
Nat'l Veterans Foundation (580)
Newington-Cropsey Foundation (588)
Northern Essex Community College Foundation (594)
Olympic Aid (600)
Order Sons of Italy in America/Sons of Italy Foundation (603)
Oregon Garden Foundation (603)
Parkinson's Disease Foundation (608)
Parliamentary Human Rights Foundation (608)
Pew Center for Civic Journalism (613)
Pew Charitable Trust - Environmental Law & Policy Center of the Midwest (613)
The Points of Light Foundation (620)
Police Foundation (620)
The Progress Freedom Foundation (626)
Project Return Foundation Inc. (626)
Public Health Foundation (628)
Public Service Research Foundation (629)
Puerto Rico U.S.A. Foundation (629)
A. Philip Randolph Educational Fund (633)
Research Institute for Small & Emerging Business, Inc. (638)
RGK Foundation (639)
Ripon Educational Fund (640)
Rotary Foundation (642)
Safer Foundation (645)
Salvation Army (646)
San Diego State University Foundation (647)
Solar Energy Research and Education Foundation (665)
South Africa Foundation (666)
Stony Brook Foundation (675)
Taiwan Studies Institute (680)
Tax Foundation, Inc. (681)
Texas A&M Research Foundation (684)
Truman Scholarship Foundation, Harry S (693)
United Negro College Fund, Inc. (702)
United States Navy Memorial Foundation (704)
University of New Orleans Foundation (707)
Vanguard Charitable Endowment Program (712)
Vertical Flight Foundation (714)
Virginia Wineries Ass'n (716)
Washington Legal Foundation (720)
Water Environment Research Foundation (721)
Wheelchairs for the World Foundation (726)
Wildlife Legislative Fund of America (727)
Harry Winston Research Foundation (728)
World Food Prize (730)
Young America's Foundation (733)

Chemicals and Chemical Industry

Ad Hoc Nitrogen Committee (227)
Adhesive and Sealant Council (227)
ADSIL (228)
Agrium Inc. (232)
Air Products and Chemicals, Inc. (234)
Akzo America, Inc. (235)
Akzo Nobel Chemicals, Inc. (235)
al group Lonza (235)
Albright & Wilson Americas (237)
American Agip MTBE Sales Division (244)
American Ass'n for Clinical Chemistry, Inc. (245)
American Chemical Soc. (252)
American Chemistry Council (252)
American Coke and Coal Chemicals Institute (253)
American Crop Protection Ass'n (256)
American Institute of Chemical Engineers (264)
American Institute of Chemists (264)
American Institute of Chemists Foundation (264)
American Natural Soda Ash Corp. (268)
American Soc. for Biochemistry and Molecular Biology (274)
American Wood Preservers Institute (280)
Analytical Systems, Inc. (283)
Aniline Ass'n, Inc. (284)
ANSAC (284)
Arch Chemical Inc. (287)
Ashland Inc. (290)
Asociacion Nacional de la Industria Quimica (ANIQ), A.C (291)
Ass'n of Water Technologies (299)
AstraZeneca Inc. (301)
Atanor, S.A. (302)
ATOFINA Chemicals, Inc. (302)
Aventis Pharmaceutical Products (304)
Ball Research, Inc. (306)
BASF Corporation (308)
Bayer Corp. (309)
Bayer Corp. / Agriculture Division (309)
Bechtel Group, Inc. (310)
Biotechnology Industry Organization (314)
Borden Chemicals & Plastics, Inc. (318)
C F Industries, Inc. (325)
Cargill Dow (331)
Celanese Government Relations Office (334)
ChemFirst Inc. (342)
Chemical Producers and Distributors Ass'n (342)
Chevron Chemical Co., LLC (342)
The Chevron Companies (342)
Chlorine Chemistry Council (345)
Chlorine Institute (345)
Chlorobenzene Producers Ass'n (345)
Ciba Specialty Chemicals Corp. (346)
Clariant Corp. (349)
Coalition for Asbestos Resolution (353)
Coalition for Responsible Waste Incineration (354)
Color Pigments Manufacturers Ass'n, Inc. (358)
Cominco, Ltd. (360)
Composite Innovations, Inc. (363)
ConAgra Foods, Inc. (365)
Condea Vista Chemical Co. (365)
Consumer Aerosol Products Council (368)
Consumer Specialties Products Ass'n (369)
Council for Chemical Research, Inc. (374)
Crop Protection Coalition (378)
Degussa Corp. (384)
Dow AgroSciences (391)
The Dow Chemical Co. (391)
Dow Corning Corp. (391)
DuPont (393)
Dyno Nobel, Inc. (394)
Eagle-Picher Industries (394)
Eastman Chemical Co. (395)
Ecological and Toxicological Ass'n of Dyes and Organic Pigments Manufacturers (396)
Eka Chemicals (399)
Elkem Materials Inc. (401)
Ethyl Corp. (407)
Ethylene Oxide Sterilization Ass'n, Inc. (407)
Exportadora de Sal, S.A. de C.V. (409)
EXPRO Chemical Products (409)
Exxon Chemical Co. (409)
Farmland Industries, Inc. (412)
Ferro Corp. (415)
The Fertilizer Institute (415)
Fisher Scientific Worldwide (418)
Flexsys America (419)
FMC Corp. (420)
Foster Wheeler Corp. (424)
FQPA Implementation Working Group (424)
GAF Corp. (428)
Gallard-Schlesinger Chemical Manufacturing Corp. (428)
Gary-Williams Energy Corp. (429)
Gentex Corp. (433)
Georgia-Pacific Corp. (434)
Gist Brocades (435)
Global Encasement, Inc. (436)
B. F. Goodrich Co. (437)
Goodyear Tire and Rubber Co. (437)
W. R. Grace & Co. (438)
Great Lakes Chemical Corp. (439)
Grupo Cydsa (441)
Halogenated Solvents Industry Alliance (443)
Halon Alternatives Research Corp. (443)
Harris Chemical Group, Inc. (444)
Hazardous Materials Advisory Council (445)
Hoechst Marion Roussel Deutschland GmbH (450)
Honeywell Internat'l, Inc. (452)
Huntsman Corp. (455)
Hydrocarbon Technologies Inc. (456)
IMC Global Inc. (458)
Independent Liquid Terminals Ass'n (459)
Institute of Makers of Explosives (464)
Internat'l Ass'n of Color Manufacturers (467)
Internat'l Institute of Ammonia Refrigeration (472)
Internat'l Oxygen Manufacturers Ass'n (473)
Internat'l Specialty Products (475)
S.C. Johnson and Son, Inc. (484)
Kaiser Aluminum & Chemical Corp. (485)
Kellogg Brown and Root (487)
Kerr-McGee Corp. (488)
KOSA (491)
Kronos, Inc. (492)
Lehn & Fink Products Group (498)
Lubrizol (505)
Lyondell Chemical Co. (506)
Martinizing Environmental Group (511)
Methanex Inc. (520)
Methyl Bromide Working Group (520)
Minnesota Mining and Manufacturing Co. (3M Co.) (525)
Minor Crop Farmer Alliance (525)
Mississippi Chemical Corp. (526)
Mississippi Polymer Technologies (526)

Mitsubishi Corp. (526)
Monsanto Co. (528)
Montrose Chemical Co. (529)
Morton Internat'l (530)
Mycogen Corp. (533)
Nat'l Ass'n of Chemical Distributors (540)
Nat'l Ass'n of Gas Chlorinators (543)
Nat'l Coalition Against the Misuse of Pesticides (556)
Nat'l Lime Ass'n (570)
Nat'l Pest Control Ass'n (573)
Nat'l Petrochemical Refiners Ass'n (573)
Nat'l Registry in Clinical Chemistry (575)
Negev Phosphates (583)
Nitrobenzene Ass'n (590)
NL Industries (590)
NoFire Technologies, Inc. (591)
Norchem Concrete Products Inc. (591)
Novartis Corp. (596)
Occidental Chemical Corporation (598)
Occidental Internat'l Corporation (598)
Occidental Petroleum Corporation (598)
Olin Corp. (600)
Oxygenated Fuels Ass'n (605)
Paper, Allied-Industrial, Chemical and Energy Workers Internat'l Union (PACE) (607)
Peerless Petrochemicals, Inc. (610)
Pentachlorophenol Task Force (611)
Pfizer, Inc. (613)
Pharmacia Corp. (615)
Philipp Brothers Chemicals, Inc. (616)
Powder Coating Institute (622)
PPG Industries (622)
Praxair, Inc. (623)
The Procter & Gamble Company (625)
Pyrocap International Corp., Inc. (630)
Reckitt & Colman Pharmaceuticals Inc. (634)
Reilly Industries (636)
Rhodia, Inc. (639)
Rhone-Polenc Inc. (639)
Rineco Chemical Industries (640)
RISE (Responsible Industry for a Sound Environment) (640)
RMI Titanium Co. (641)
Rohm and Haas Co. (642)
Safety-Kleen Corp. (645)
SAMA Group of Ass'ns (647)
Samsung Corp. (647)
Sensor Research and Development Corp. (655)
SKW Chemicals, Inc. (660)
Soap and Detergent Ass'n (662)
Soc. of Toxicology (664)
Solutia Inc. (665)
Sterling Chemical Co. (674)
Sumitomo Chemical Co., Ltd. (676)
Sunoco, Inc. (677)
Synthetic Organic Chemical Manufacturers Ass'n (679)
The Teratology Soc. (684)
Terra Chemicals Internat'l (684)
Tetrahydrofuran Task Force (684)
Texas Petrochemicals Corp. (685)
U.S. Borax, Inc. (695)
Unilever N.V. (699)
Unilever United States, Inc. (699)
Uniroyal Chemical Co., Inc. (699)
UniServe Inc. (700)
Valent U.S.A. Corp. (711)
Valhi, Inc. (711)
Vulcan Chemicals (718)
Vulcan Materials Co. (718)
Waste Management, Inc. (721)
WPC Brands, Inc. (731)

Children and Youth

ABA Center on Children and the Law (224)
Adopt America (228)
Advocates for Youth (229)
Alliance for Children and Families (239)
Alliance to End Childhood Lead Poisoning (241)
Ambulatory Pediatric Ass'n (242)
American Academy of Child and Adolescent Psychiatry (243)
American Academy of Pediatrics (244)
American Ass'n for Marriage and Family Therapy (246)
American Ass'n of Children's Residential Centers (246)
American Ass'n of Early Childhood Educators (247)
American College of Osteopathic Pediatricians (254)
American Counseling Ass'n (256)
American Family Ass'n (258)
American Youth Policy Forum (281)
The American Youth Work Center (281)
Ass'n for Childhood Education Internat'l (291)
Ass'n of Pediatric Program Directors (297)
Ass'n of Reproductive Health Professionals (298)
Aunt Martha's Youth Service Center (303)
Autism Soc. of America, Inc. (303)
Baylor College of Medicine (310)
Bazelon Center for Mental Health Law, Judge David L. (310)
Big Brothers/Big Sisters of America (313)
Binney & Smith Inc. (313)
Boy Scouts of America (318)
Boys and Girls Clubs of America (318)
Boys and Girls Clubs of Greater Washington (318)
Bright Beginnings, Inc. (320)
California Ass'n of Children's Hospitals (326)
California Children's Hospital Ass'n (326)
Campaign for Tobacco-Free Kids (329)
Child Care Institute of America, Inc. (343)
Child Nutrition Forum, c/o FRAC (343)
Child Welfare League of America (343)
Children and Adults with Attention Deficit Disorders (CHADD) (344)
Children's Action Network (344)
The Children's Cause Inc. (344)
Children's Defense Fund (344)
Children's Foundation (344)
Children's Health Fund (344)
Children's Hospice Internat'l (344)
Children's Hospital and Health Center of San Diego (344)
Children's Hospital and Medical Center (344)
Children's Hospital Foundation (344)
Children's Hospital Los Angeles (344)
Children's Hospital of Boston (344)
Children's Mercy Hospital (344)
Children's Nat'l Medical Center (344)
Children's Rights Council (344)
Coalition for America's Children (352)
Consortium for Child Welfare (367)
Cook Children's Health Care System (370)
Council for Exceptional Children (374)
Council of Women's and Infant's Specialty Hospitals (376)
The Danny Foundation, (382)
Day Care Ass'n of Tarrant County and Fort Worth Texas (383)
Early Childhood Development Center Legislative Coalition (394)
Early Learning Years Institute (394)
ESR Children's Health Care System (407)
Family, Career and Community Leaders of America (411)
Florida Department of Children & Families (419)
Foster America, Inc. (424)
Future Business Leaders of America - Phi Beta Lambda (428)
Generations United (433)
Girl Scouts of the U.S.A. - Washington Office (435)
Girls Incorporated (435)
Holy Childhood Ass'n (451)
Illinois Collaboration on Youth (457)
Institute for Student Achievement (464)
Internat'l Formula Council (471)
Internat'l Service Agencies (474)
Jobs for Youth (483)
Juvenile Diabetes Foundation Internat'l (485)
Kennedy Institute, Lt. Joseph P. (488)
Kids Voting USA (489)
Kinder-Care Learning Centers, Inc. (489)
La Rabida Children's Hospital Research Center (493)
Leadership 2000 (496)
March of Dimes Birth Defects Foundation (509)
Mothers Against Drunk Driving (MADD) (530)
Mount Sinai Hospital (531)
Nat'l 4-H Council (535)
Nat'l Accreditation Council for Early Childhood Professional Personnel and Programs (535)
Nat'l Ass'n for Gifted Children (537)
Nat'l Ass'n for the Education of Young Children (538)
Nat'l Ass'n of Children's Hospitals Inc. (540)
Nat'l Ass'n of Foster Care Review Boards (543)
Nat'l Ass'n of Foster Grandparent Program Directors (543)
Nat'l Ass'n of Psychiatric Treatment Centers for Children (547)
Nat'l Ass'n of School Psychologists (548)
Nat'l Ass'n of Service and Conservation Corps (549)
Nat'l Ass'n of WIC Directors (551)
Nat'l Black Child Development Institute (552)
Nat'l Center for Missing and Exploited Children (555)
Nat'l Center for Tobacco-Free Kids (555)
Nat'l Center on Institutions and Alternatives (555)
Nat'l Child Abuse Coalition (555)
Nat'l Child Care Ass'n (555)
Nat'l Child Support Enforcement Ass'n (555)
Nat'l Childcare Parents Ass'n (555)
Nat'l Coalition Against Domestic Violence (556)
Nat'l Collaboration for Youth (557)
Nat'l Congress of Parents and Teachers (558)
Nat'l Council for Adoption (559)
Nat'l Family Planning and Reproductive Health Ass'n (563)
Nat'l FFA Organization (564)
The Nat'l Foundation for Teaching Entrepreneurship (565)
Nat'l Head Start Ass'n (566)
Nat'l Indian Child Welfare Ass'n (568)
Nat'l Institute for Citizen Education in the Law (568)
Nat'l Network for Youth (572)
Nat'l Network to End Domestic Violence (572)
Nat'l Partnership for Women and Families (573)
Nat'l Perinatal Ass'n (573)
Nat'l Recreation and Park Ass'n (575)
Nat'l SAFE KIDS Campaign (577)
Parents for Public Schools (608)
Pediatricians for Children Inc. (610)
A Presidential Classroom for Young Americans, Inc. (623)
Saf T Lok, Inc. (645)
Sesame Workshop (656)
Shriners Hospital for Children (658)
Spring Hill Camps (670)
Sudden Infant Death Syndrome Alliance (676)
Toy Manufacturers of America (688)
U.S. Fund for UNICEF (696)
Walmer Dollhouses, Inc. (718)
WAVE, Inc. (722)
Women and Infants' Hospital (729)
YMCA of Metropolitan Washington (733)
YMCA of the USA Public Policy Office (733)
Young America's Foundation (733)
Young Astronaut Council (733)
Young Republican Nat'l Federation, Inc. (733)
Youth For Understanding Internat'l Exchange (733)
Youth Policy Institute (733)
Youth Service America (733)
Youthbuild, USA (734)
YWCA of the USA (734)
Zero Population Growth, Inc. (734)
ZERO TO THREE/Nat'l Center for Infants, Toddlers, and Families (734)

Civil Rights and Liberties

Action on Smoking and Health (227)
Agudath Israel of America (232)
Alliance for Justice (239)
American Ass'n of University Women (249)
American Center for Law and Justice (252)
American Civil Liberties Union (252)
American Civil Liberties Union of the Nat'l Capital Area (252)
American Jewish Committee (265)
American Jewish Congress (265)
American-Arab Anti-Discrimination Committee (ADC) (281)
Americans United for Separation of Church and State (282)
Amnesty Internat'l U.S.A. (283)
Anti-Defamation League (285)
Asian Pacific American Labor Alliance, AFL-CIO (291)
B'nai B'rith Internat'l (305)
Bazelon Center for Mental Health Law, Judge David L. (310)
Center for Democracy and Technology (336)
Center for Individual Rights (336)
The Center for Religious Freedom (337)
Center on Conscience and War/NISBCO (338)
Children's Rights Council (344)
Citizens Flag Alliance (348)
Citizens for Liberty in Cuba (Cuba Libertad) (348)
Citizens' Commission on Civil Rights (349)
Civil Justice Reform Group (349)
Coalition for Group Legal Services (353)
Coalition for Internat'l Justice (354)
Coalition for Patient Rights (354)
Constitutional Rights Foundation (368)
Council for Court Excellence (374)
Council on Hemispheric Affairs (377)
Council on Religious Freedom (377)
Death Penalty Information Center (383)
Disability Rights Education and Defense Fund (389)
Electronic Privacy Information Center (401)
First Amendment Coalition for Expression (417)
Free Speech Coalition (425)
The Freedom Forum (425)
Friends Committee on Nat'l Legislation (426)
Gray Panthers Nat'l Office in Washington (439)
Human Rights Campaign (454)
Human Rights Campaign Fund (454)
Human Rights Watch (455)
Information Trust (462)
Institute for Justice (463)
Internat'l Ass'n of Jewish Lawyers and Jurists (468)
The Internat'l Human Rights Law Group (472)
Internat'l Religious Liberty Ass'n (474)
Japanese American Citizens League (482)
Jewish Women Internat'l (483)
Landmark Legal Foundation Center for Civil Rights (495)
Lawyers Committee for Human Rights (496)
Lawyers' Committee for Civil Rights Under Law (496)
Leadership Conference on Civil Rights (496)
Media Access Project (516)
Mexican-American Legal Defense and Educational Fund (521)
Migrant Legal Action Program (524)
NAACP Legal Defense and Educational Fund, Inc. (534)
Nat'l Abortion and Reproductive Rights Action League (535)
Nat'l Ass'n for Equal Opportunity in Higher Education (537)
Nat'l Ass'n for the Advancement of Colored People, Washington Bureau (538)
Nat'l Ass'n of Protection and Advocacy Systems (NAPAS) (547)
Nat'l Ass'n to Protect Individual Rights (551)
Nat'l Campaign for a Peace Tax Fund (554)
Nat'l Catholic Conference for Interracial Justice (554)
Nat'l Coalition for Patient Rights (556)
Nat'l Coalition to Abolish the Death Penalty (557)
Nat'l Committee Against Repressive Legislation (557)
Nat'l Conference of Christians and Jews (558)
Nat'l Gay and Lesbian Task Force (565)
Nat'l Legal Aid and Defender Ass'n (570)
Nat'l Partnership for Women and Families (573)

Coalitions

Nat'l Interfaith Coalition on Aging (569)
Nat'l IPA Coalition (569)
Nat'l Low Income Housing Coalition/LIHIS (570)
Nat'l Neighborhood Coalition (572)
Nat'l Prostate Cancer Coalition Co. (574)
Nat'l Puerto Rican Coalition (575)
Nat'l Rural Housing Coalition (577)
Nat'l Ryan White Title III (b) Coalition (577)
Nat'l Sediments Coalition (577)
The Nat'l Wetlands Coalition (581)
Natural Gas Vehicle Coalition (582)
NCI Coalition (583)
NEDA/Resource Conservation and Recovery Act Project (583)
NetCoalition.Com (584)
Network Advertising Initiative (584)
New York Roadway Improvement Coalition (587)
NFTC-FSC Coalition (589)
Noise Reduction Technology Coalition (591)
North American Brain Tumor Coalition (592)
North American Superhighway Coalition (593)
North Metro Mayors Coalition (593)
openNET Coalition (601)
OSHA Reform Coalition (604)
Outdoor Recreation Coalition of America (604)
Pain Care Coalition (606)
Paper Recycling Coalition (607)
Partnership for Early Climate Action (608)
Partnership for Recovery Coalition (609)
PC Strand Producers Coalition (610)
Physicians Ad hoc Coalition for Truth (PHACT) (617)
Power Mobility Coalition (622)
Process Gas Consumers Group (625)
Product Liability Prevention and Defense Group (625)
Propane Consumers Coalition (627)
Public Hospital Pharmacy Coalition (628)
PwC Contract Manufacturing Coalition (630)
PwC Leasing Coalition (630)
Q-ZAB Coalition (630)
R&D Tax Credit Coalition (631)
R&D Tax Regulation Group (631)
Rail Supply and Service Coalition (632)
Rainbow/Push Coalition (National Bureau) (632)
Religious Coalition for Reproductive Choice (636)
Repeal PUHCA Now Coalition (637)
Repeal the Tax on Talking Coalition (637)
Republican Jewish Coalition (637)
Republican Leadership Coalition (637)
Research 2 Prevention (638)
Respiratory Medication Providers Coalition (638)
Retirement Income Coalition (639)
Return to Work Coalition (639)
Reusable Pallet and Container Coalition (639)
Roaring Fork Railroad Holding Authority (641)
Rural Coalition (643)
Rural Health Network Coalition (643)
Rural Hospital Coalition (643)
Rural Referral Centers Coalition (644)
Save the Greenback Coalition (650)
Savings Coalition of America (650)
SBREFA Coalition (651)
The Science Coalition (652)
Section 877 Coalition (654)
Securities Litigation Reform Coalition (654)
Southeast Water Coalition (667)
Southern Coalition for Advanced Transportation (668)
Space Grant Coalition (669)
Special Vehicle Coalition (669)
Statute of Repose Coalition (SORC) (673)
Straddle Rules Tax Group (675)
Super Reachback Coalition (677)
Superfund Action Coalition (677)
Tanners Countervailing Duty Coalition (680)
Tax Fairness Coalition (681)
Tax Policy Coalition (681)
Tax/Shelter Coalition (681)
Tip Tax Coalition (687)
The Title XI Coalition (687)
TJTC Recovery Project Coalition (687)
Tobacco Fairness Coalition (688)
Traditional Values Coalition (689)
U.S./Mexico Border Counties Coalition (697)
United States Maritime Coalition (703)
Upper Midwest Coalition (708)
Upper Midwest Dairy Coalition (708)
Urban Health Care Coalition of Pennsylvania (708)
Vandium Industry Coalition (712)
Ventura County Citizens Against Radar Emissions (VCCARE) (712)
Wakota Bridge Coalition (718)
West Coast Refuse and Recycling Coalition (723)
Western Coalition of Arid States (724)
Western Coalition Political Action Committee (724)
Western Urban Water Coalition (725)
Women's College Coalition (729)
Wool Fiber, Yarn Fabric Coalition (730)
Work Opportunity Tax Credit Coalition (730)

Commodities

Agribusiness Council (232)
American Cocoa Research Institute (253)
American Commodity Distribution Ass'n (254)
American Soybean Ass'n (277)
American Sugar Alliance (278)
American Sugar Cane League of the U.S.A. (278)
American Sugarbeet Growers Ass'n (278)
Camara Nacional de las Industrias Azucarera y Alcoholera (328)
Cargill, Inc. (331)
Chicago Board of Trade (342)
Chicago Mercantile Exchange (343)
Coalition for Sugar Reform (354)
Colombian Coffee Federation (358)
ConAgra Foods, Inc. (365)
Corporacion de Exportaciones Mexicanas, S.A. de C.V. and Marvin Roy Feldman (372)
Dominican State Sugar Council (CEA) (391)
Eurex Deutschland (408)
Flo-Sun Sugar (419)
Florida Crystals Corp. (419)
Florida Sugar Cane League, Inc. (420)
Futures Industry Ass'n (428)
Georgia Commodity Commission for Peanuts (434)
Georgia Cotton Commission (434)
The Gold and Silver Institute (436)
Internat'l Sugar Policy Coordinating Commission of the Dominican Republic (475)
London Futures and Options Exchange (503)
Louis Dreyfus Corporation (504)
Mauritius Sugar Syndicate (513)
Rio Grande Valley Sugar Growers (640)
Silver Users Ass'n (659)
South African Sugar Ass'n (666)
Sugar Ass'n, Inc. (676)
Swaziland Sugar Ass'n (678)
Sweetener Users Ass'n (678)
United States Beet Sugar Ass'n (703)
United States Sugar Corp. (704)
Valhi, Inc. (711)
Wocom Commodities Limited (729)

Computers and Computer Software

3Com Corp. (223)
Acme Software (226)
ACS Government Solutions Group (227)
ACTA Technology (227)
ADCS, Inc. (227)
Adobe (228)
Advanced Integrated Technology, Inc. (228)
Advanced Micro Devices (228)
Affiliated Computer Services (230)
Alliance Data Systems (239)
Amdahl Corp. (242)
American Soc. for Information Science (274)
Americans for Computer Privacy (281)
ANADAC (283)
AOL Time Warner (285)
Apple Computer, Inc. (286)
Applied Knowledge Group (286)
Applied Terravision Systems (287)
Ariba (288)
Armed Forces Communications and Electronics Ass'n Headquarters (289)
Ass'n for Information and Image Management Internat'l (292)
Ass'n for Interactive Media (292)
ATX Technologies (302)
AuctionWatch.com (302)
Austin Professional Systems, Inc. (303)
Authentica Inc. (303)
Automatic Data Processing, Inc (303)
Autometric Inc. (303)
Avue Technologies (305)
Bailey Link (306)
Beyond.com (313)
BitWise Designs Inc. (314)
BMC Software (316)
Boeing Information Services (317)
Bolt, Beranek and Newman, Inc. (317)
Bowman Internat'l Corp. (318)
Brother Internat'l Co. (322)
Bull H.N. Information Services, Inc. (323)
Business Computer Training Institute (324)
Business Software Alliance (325)
Candle Corp. (330)
Ceridian Corp. (340)
Changing Paradigms (341)
Circuit City Stores, Inc. (347)
CIS Global (347)
Cisco Systems Inc. (347)
Coalition Against Database Piracy (352)
COMDISCO, Inc. (359)
Command Systems Inc. (360)
Commercial Internet Exchange Ass'n (360)
Community Learning and Information Network, Inc. (363)
Compaq Computer Corp. (363)
Complete Business Solutions, Inc. (363)
Computer Adaptive Technologies (364)
Computer and Communications Industry Ass'n (CCIA) (364)
Computer Associates Internat'l (364)
Computer Coalition for Responsible Exports (364)
Computer Communications Industry of America (364)
Computer Data Systems, Inc. (364)
Computer Sciences Corp. (364)
Computer Systems Policy Project (364)
Computer Systems Technologies, Inc. (364)
Computing Research Ass'n (364)
Computing Technology Industry Ass'n (364)
Compuware Corp. (364)
Consumer Project on Technology (369)
CPU Technology (378)
CTC Corp. (379)
Cubic Defense (380)
CyberWynd Publications (380)
Delex Systems, Inc. (384)
Dell Computer Corp. (384)
Dictaphone Corp. (388)
Digital Media Ass'n (388)
Digital Privacy and Security Working Group (388)
Digital System Resources, Inc. (388)
Dulles Networking Associates (393)
EDS Corp. (398)
El Camino Resources, Ltd. (399)
Electronic Funds Transfer Ass'n (400)
Electronic Industries Ass'n of Japan (401)
Electronic Privacy Information Center (401)
EMC Corp. (401)
Environmental Systems Research Institute, Inc. (405)
Fanatasy Elections (411)
Federation of Government Information Processing Councils (414)
Gateway, Inc. (430)
GELCO Information Network GSD, Inc. (430)
General Signal Corp. (433)
Hewlett-Packard Co. (449)
The Hitachi Foundation (450)
Honeywell Internat'l, Inc. (452)
Hyperion Software (456)
IEEE Computer Society (457)
Imaging Technologies Inc. (458)
Independent Data Communications Manufacturers Ass'n (459)
Information Technology Ass'n of America (ITAA) (461)
Information Technology Industry Council (462)
Information Technology Resellers Ass'n (462)
Institute for Human-Machine Cognition (463)
Institute of Electrical and Electronics Engineers, Inc. (464)
Institute of Simulation and Training (464)
Integrated Microcomputer Systems, Inc. (465)
Intel Corp. (465)
Interactive Digital Software Ass'n (466)
Interactive Gaming Council (466)
Intergraph Corp. Federal Systems Division (466)
Internat'l Business Machines Corp. (469)
Internat'l Game Technology (472)
Internat'l Systems, Inc. (475)
Internet Alliance Inc. (476)
Internet Clearinghouse (476)
Internet Internat'l Trade Council (476)
Intuit, Inc. (477)
InWork Technologies (478)
JRL Enterprises (485)
Kruger Internat'l (KI) (492)
LC Technologies (496)
Lockheed Martin IMS (502)
Massachusetts Software Council (512)
Media Fusion L.L.C. (516)
Member-Link Systems, Inc. (517)
memorize.com (517)
Merant PVCS (518)
MICAH Software Systems (522)
Microsoft Corp. (522)
Microvision, Inc. (523)
Motorola, Inc. (531)
Nat'l Ass'n of Computer Consultant Businesses (540)
Nat'l Ass'n of County Information Technology Administrators (541)
Nat'l Computer Systems (558)
Nat'l Training Systems Ass'n (579)
Natural Technologies (582)
NCR Corp. (583)
Net Results, Inc. (584)
Netscape Communications Corp. (584)
NeuLevel (584)
New Edge Networks (585)
NextRX (589)
Nintendo of America, Inc. (590)
Novell, Inc. (596)
NOW Solutions, Inc. (596)
NPES, The Ass'n for Suppliers of Printing, Publishing, and Converting Technologies (596)
Official Artist Inc. (599)
One Economy Corp. (600)
Open Group Electronic Messaging Ass'n (EMA) Forum (601)
Oracle Corp. (602)
Pixtech, Inc. (618)
Planning Systems, Inc. (619)
Prodigy (625)
Project to Promote Competition and Innovation in the Digital Age (626)
PSINet Inc. (628)
Q Systems, Inc. (630)
Qualtec, Inc. (630)
RedCreek Communications Inc. (635)
Register.com (636)
Rhythms NetConnections (639)
Riverdeep Inc. (640)

RSA Security Inc. (643)
Sabre Inc. (644)
SAVI Technology (650)
SCI Systems, Inc. (652)
Science & Engineering Associates, Inc. (652)
SEMATECH, Inc. (655)
Sequent Computer Systems (655)
SIGCOM, Inc. (659)
Silicon Graphics/SGI (659)
Software & Information Industry Ass'n (SIIA) (664)
Software Finance and Tax Executives Council (664)
Software Productivity Consortium (664)
Storage Technology Corp. (675)
Strictly Business Software System (675)
Sun Microsystems (676)
SwimWithTheSharks.com (678)
Symbol Technologies, Inc. (679)
Syquest Technology, Inc. (679)
System & Computer Technology Corp. (679)
Systematics (679)
Systems Simulation Solutions Inc. (679)
Taxpayer Assets Project (681)
Technology Integration Group (682)
Technology Network (682)
The Tekamah Corp. (682)
Unisys Corp. (700)
Universal Systems and Technology Inc. (705)
V-ONE Corp. (711)
VeriSign/Network Solutions, Inc. (713)
Visually Impaired Data Processors Internat'l (716)
Vocus Government Relations (717)
Wang Laboratories Inc. (718)
webwasher.com (722)
Yahoo! (732)
YouBet.com (733)

Construction/Construction Materials

Abide Internat'l, Inc. (225)
Adhesive and Sealant Council (227)
AFL-CIO - Building and Construction Trades Department (231)
Air & Water Technologies (233)
Air Conditioning Contractors of America (233)
Airport Consultants Council (235)
J. S. Alberici Construction Co. (237)
American College of Construction Lawyers (253)
American Concrete Pavement Ass'n (ACPA) (255)
American Concrete Pipe Ass'n (255)
American Hardware Manufacturers Ass'n (261)
American Iron and Steel Institute (265)
American Pipe Fittings Ass'n (270)
American Portland Cement Alliance (270)
American Road and Transportation Builders Ass'n (ARTBA) (273)
American Shipbuilding Ass'n (274)
American Soc. of Professional Estimators (277)
American Subcontractors Ass'n, Inc. (278)
American Supply Ass'n (278)
American Wood Preservers Institute (280)
Ameron Internat'l Corp. (282)
Armstrong World Industries, Inc. (289)
Asbestos Information Ass'n/North America (290)
Asbestos Working Group (290)
ASFE (290)
Ashland Inc. (290)
Asphalt Emulsion Manufacturers Ass'n (291)
Asphalt Institute (291)
Asphalt Recycling and Reclaiming Ass'n (291)
Asphalt Roofing Manufacturers Ass'n (291)
Asphalt Systems, Inc. (291)
Ass'n of Bituminous Contractors (294)
Associated Builders and Contractors (300)
Associated General Contractors of America (300)
Associated Landscape Contractors of America (300)
Associated Specialty Contractors (300)
Bechtel Group, Inc. (310)
Bechtel/Parsons Brinkeroff Joint Venture (310)
Birmingham Building Trades Towers, Inc. (314)
Black & Decker Corp., The (315)
Blake Construction Co. (315)
Brick Industry Ass'n (320)
Build Indiana Council (323)
Builders Hardware Manufacturers Ass'n (323)
Building Service Contractors Ass'n Internat'l (323)
Burns and Roe Enterprises, Inc. (324)
C.A. Vencemos (325)
Caithness Energy, LLC (326)
Cascade General, Inc. (332)
CaseNewHolland Inc. (333)
CELOTEX (335)
Cement Free Trade Ass'n (335)
Cement Kiln Recycling Coalition (335)
Cemento Bayano (335)
Cementos Monterrey, S.A. (335)
CEMEX Central, S.A. de C.V. (335)
CEMEX USA (335)
Centex Corp. (338)
CertainTeed Corp. (340)
Clean Water Council (350)
Coalition to Repeal the Davis-Bacon Act (356)
Composite Panel Ass'n (363)
Composites Fabricators Ass'n (364)
Concrete Plant Manufacturers Bureau (365)
Construction Industry Manufacturers Ass'n (368)
Construction Management Ass'n of America (368)
Continental Cement Co., Inc. (370)
Contract Services Ass'n of America (370)
Cool Roof Rating Council (371)
Corporacion Valenciana de Cementos Portland, S.A. (372)
Corporacion Venezolana de Cementos, SACA (372)
Corrections Corp. of America (373)
D.C. Building Industry Ass'n Political Action Committee (381)
Diamond Ventures (387)
Dillingham Construction, Inc. (388)
Dredging Contractors of America (392)
Dunn-Edwards Corp. (393)
Dyno Nobel, Inc. (394)
Eagle-Picher Industries (394)
Edison Welding Institute (397)
Federal Facilities Council (413)
Florida Equipment Contractors Ass'n (419)
Fluor Corp. (420)
Foster Wheeler Corp. (424)
Fundacion para la Preservacion de Flora y Fauna Marina (428)
General Portland Inc. (433)
Gilbane Building Co. (435)
Global Encasement, Inc. (436)
Great Lakes Composites Consortium (439)
Great Lakes Corporate Resources (439)
Grupo Empresarial Maya (441)
Gulf Coast Portland Cement Co. (442)
HAECO, Inc. (443)
Hager Hinge Co. (443)
Halliburton/Brown & Root (443)
Hand Tools Institute (444)
Hardwood Plywood and Veneer Ass'n (444)
HARSCO Corp. (445)
Hill Internat'l, Inc. (449)
Holnam Inc. (451)
Home Automation Ass'n (451)
The Home Depot (451)
Houston Shell and Concrete (453)
I-49 Roadbuilders Coalition (456)
Independent Contractor Coalition (459)
Indiana County Development Corp. (460)
Ingalls Shipbuilding (462)
Institute of Makers of Explosives (464)
Instrument Technicians Labor-Management Cooperation Fund (464)
Integrated Building and Construction Solutions (465)
Interlocking Concrete Pavement Institute (466)
Internat'l Ass'n of Bridge, Structural, Ornamental and Reinforcing Iron Workers (467)
Internat'l Ass'n of Drilling Contractors (467)
Internat'l Ass'n of Heat and Frost Insulators and Asbestos Workers (468)
Internat'l Brotherhood of Boilermakers, Iron Shipbuilders, Blacksmiths, Forgers and Helpers (469)
Internat'l Cast Polymer Ass'n (469)
Internat'l Code Council (470)
Internat'l Council of Employers of Bricklayers and Allied Craftsmen (470)
Internat'l District Energy Ass'n (471)
Internat'l Municipal Signal Ass'n (473)
Internat'l Slurry Surfacing Ass'n (474)
Internat'l Union of Bricklayers and Allied Craftsworkers (476)
Internat'l Union of Painters and Allied Trades (476)
The Irvine Co. (479)
IWPA - The Internat'l Wood Products Ass'n (480)
Izopoli (480)
Jacobs Engineering Group Inc. (481)
James Hardie Building Products Inc. (481)
Japan Federation of Construction Contractors, Inc. (481)
Kohler Corp. (490)
Lafarge Corp. (494)
Lehigh Portland Cement Co. (498)
Lister Bolt & Chain Co. (500)
Lone Star Industries (503)
Los Angeles, California, Community Development Commission of the County of (504)
Louisiana Internat'l Group (504)
Louisiana Pacific Corp. (504)
Lumber Fair Trade Group (505)
MacGregor (506)
Manufactured Housing Ass'n for Regulatory Reform (509)
Manufactured Housing Institute (509)
Maryland Nat'l Capitol Building Ass'n (511)
Masonry Industry Ventures, Inc. (512)
Mechanical Contractors Ass'n of America (515)
Metal Building Manufacturers Ass'n (519)
Metroplex Corp. (520)
MGF Industries Inc. (521)
Benjamin Moore & Co. (529)
Most Group Limited (530)
NACCO Industries (534)
Nat'l Asphalt Pavement Ass'n (537)
Nat'l Ass'n of Home Builders of the U.S. (543)
Nat'l Ass'n of Home Builders Research Center, Inc. (544)
Nat'l Ass'n of Minority Contractors (545)
Nat'l Ass'n of Miscellaneous, Ornamental and Architectural Products Contractors (545)
Nat'l Ass'n of Reinforcing Steel Contractors (548)
Nat'l Ass'n of Tower Erectors (551)
Nat'l Certified Pipe Welding Bureau (555)
Nat'l Clay Pipe Institute (556)
Nat'l Concrete Masonry Ass'n (558)
Nat'l Conference of States on Building Codes and Standards (558)
Nat'l Corrugated Steel Pipe Ass'n (559)
Nat'l Electrical Contractors Ass'n (562)
Nat'l Fenestration Rating Council (564)
Nat'l Institute of Building Sciences (568)
Nat'l Lime Ass'n (570)
Nat'l Lumber and Building Material Dealers Ass'n (570)
Nat'l Paint and Coatings Ass'n (573)
Nat'l Railroad and Construction Maintenance Ass'n (575)
Nat'l Ready Mixed Concrete Ass'n (575)
Nat'l Roofing Contractors Ass'n (576)
Nat'l Star Route Mail Contractors Ass'n (578)
Nat'l Steel and Shipbuilding Co. (579)
Nat'l Stone, Sand, and Gravel Ass'n (579)
Nat'l Utility Contractors Ass'n (NUCA) (580)
Newport News Shipbuilding Inc. (588)
North American Insulation Manufacturers Ass'n (592)
Novartis Corp. (596)
Oldcastle Materials Group (600)
Operative Plasterers' and Cement Masons' Internat'l Ass'n of the U.S. and Canada (601)
Owens Corning (604)
Pacific Coast Cement (605)
Pacific Marine (605)
Painting and Decorating Contractors of America (606)
Pardee Construction Co. (608)
Parsons Corp. (608)
Pine Bluff Sand and Gravel Co. (617)
Plumbing, Heating, Cooling Contractors- National Assoc. (619)
Polyisocyanurate Insulation Manufacturers Ass'n (620)
Popejoy Construction Co. (620)
Power and Communications Contractors Ass'n (622)
PPG Industries (622)
Rebuild America's Schools (634)
Resilient Floor Covering Ass'n (638)
Roecker Engineering Co. (641)
Roof Coatings Manufacturers Ass'n (642)
Saint-Gobain Corp. (646)
The "Sandbagger" Corp. (648)
Seemann Composites LLC (654)
SEMCO (655)
Sheet Metal and Air Conditioning Contractors' Nat'l Ass'n (657)
Sheet Metal Workers' Internat'l Ass'n (657)
SICPA Industries of America, Inc. (658)
Sloan Valve Co. (661)
South Jersey Regional Council of Carpenters (666)
Southdown, Inc. (667)
Southern Tier Cement Committee (668)
The Stanley Works (672)
Sunbelt Cement (677)
Surety Information Office (677)
SWL Communications LLC (679)
Thai Gypsum Products Co., Ltd. (685)
Tile Contractors Ass'n of America (687)
Tishman Construction Corp. of Washington D.C. (687)
Tolmex (688)
Trifinery, Inc. (692)
Truck Mixer Manufacturers Bureau (692)
U.S. Contract Tower Ass'n (696)
U.S. Gypsum Co. (696)
United Ass'n of Journeymen and Apprentices of the Plumbing and Pipe Fitting Industry of the U.S. and Canada (700)
United Brotherhood of Carpenters and Joiners of America (700)
United Cement Corp. (700)
United Union of Roofers, Waterproofers and Allied Workers (705)
UNR Asbestos-Disease Trust (708)
Vulcan Chemicals (718)
Vulcan Materials Co. (718)
Washington Construction Co. (719)
Washington Group Internat'l (719)
Washington Infrastructure Services, Inc. (719)
Westinghouse (725)
The Williamson Group (727)
Wire Reinforcement Institute (728)
Workplaces Against Salting Abuse (730)
W. G. Yates & Sons Construction Co. (733)
H. B. Zachry (734)

Consumer Rights and Protection

ABLEDATA (225)
American Homeowners Grassroots Alliance (262)
Automotive Consumer Action Program (303)
Buyers Up (325)
Cendant Corp. (335)
Center for the Study of Responsive Law (338)
Coalition Against Insurance Fraud (352)
Coalition Against Product Tampering (352)
Coalition for Uniform Product Liability Law (355)
Coalition to Ensure Responsible Billing (356)
Competitive Consumer Lending Coalition (363)
Consumer Energy Council of America Research Foundation (369)
Consumer Federation of America (369)

Cooperatives

Copyrights, Patents and Trademarks

Dairy Industry

Defense Industry

Precision Lift (623)
Production Technology, Inc. (625)
Professional Services Council (626)
PulseTech Products Corp. (630)
Pyrocap International Corp., Inc. (630)
QTEAM (630)
Rafael U.S.A., Inc. (632)
Ramo Defense Systems, LLC (632)
RAND Corp. (633)
Raufoss A/S, Defense Products Division (633)
Raychem Corp. (633)
Raytheon Co. (633)
Raytheon Missile Systems (633)
Research & Development Laboratories (638)
Rolls-Royce North America Inc. (642)
Royal Ordnance North America, Inc. (643)
S-TEC Sentry (644)
SACO Defense (644)
Safegate Internat'l AB (645)
San Francisco Wholesale Produce Ass'n (648)
Sarnoff Corp. (650)
Schott Corp. (652)
Schweizer Aircraft Corp. (652)
Science & Engineering Associates, Inc. (652)
Science Applications Internat'l Corp. (SAIC) (652)
Sensis Corp. (655)
Sensor Research and Development Corp. (655)
Short Brothers (USA), Inc. (658)
Shorts Missile Systems (658)
Sierra Technologies Inc. (659)
Singapore Technologies Automotive (659)
Societe Nationale d'Etude et Construction de Moteurs d'Aviation (SNECMA) (664)
Solipsys Corp. (665)
Sonetech Corp. (665)
Sony Trans Com (666)
Southern Maryland Navy Alliance, Inc. (668)
Specialized Technical Services, Inc. (669)
Sperry Marine Inc. (670)
Stewart & Stevenson Services, Inc. (674)
Summit Technology (676)
Survival Inc. (678)
Swiss Munition Enterprise (679)
Swiss Ordnance Enterprise (679)
Synzyme Technologies, Inc. (679)
TASC, Inc. (681)
Team Stratford (682)
Technology Systems, Inc. (682)
Teledyne-Commodore, LLC (683)
Tetra Tech (684)
Textron Inc. (685)
Textron Systems Division (685)
Thales (685)
Thiokol Propulsion (686)
TI Group Inc. (686)
Trex Enterprises (691)
TRW Inc. (693)
Union of Concerned Scientists (699)
United Defense, L.P. (701)
United Technologies Corp. (704)
Universal Systems, Inc. (705)
USFHP Conference Group (710)
Uwohali, Inc. (711)
Valentec Systems, Inc. (711)
Vanguard Research, Inc. (712)
Veridian Corp. (712)
VLOC (717)
Vortex, Inc. (717)
Xeta Internat'l Corp. (732)

Disabled

ABLEDATA (225)
ACB Government Employees (226)
ACB Social Service Providers (226)
Access Technology Ass'n (226)
Alexander Graham Bell Ass'n for the Deaf (238)
American Ass'n of University Affiliated Programs for Persons with Developmental Disabilities (249)
American Ass'n on Mental Retardation (250)
American Congress of Community Supports and Employment Services (255)
American Council of the Blind (256)
American Counseling Ass'n (256)
American Foundation for the Blind - Governmental Relations Group (260)
American Occupational Therapy Ass'n, Inc. (269)
American Orthotic and Prosthetic Ass'n (269)
American Soc. for Deaf Children (274)
American Speech, Language, and Hearing Ass'n (277)
American Speech-Language-Hearing Foundation (277)
The Arc (287)
Ass'n for Education and Rehabilitation of the Blind & Visually Impaired (292)
Autism Soc. of America, Inc. (303)
Better Hearing Institute (312)
Blinded Veterans Ass'n (315)
Braille Revival League (319)
Brain Injury Ass'n (319)
Cendant Mobility Services (335)
City Meals on Wheels USA (349)
Coalition on Accessibility (355)
Columbia Lighthouse for the Blind (359)
Committee for Purchase from People Who Are Blind or Severely Disabled (361)
Communication Service for the Deaf (362)
Conference of Educational Administrators of Schools and Programs for the Deaf (366)
Consortium of Citizens with Disabilities (368)
Convention of American Instructors of the Deaf (370)
Council of Citizens with Low Vision, Internat'l (375)
Cystic Fibrosis Foundation (380)
Disability Rights Education and Defense Fund (389)
Disabled American Veterans (389)
District of Columbia Special Olympics (390)
Easter Seals (395)
Fellowship Square Foundation, Inc. (415)
Guide Dog Users, Inc. (442)
Hearing Industries Ass'n (447)
Hebrew Academy for Special Children (447)
Helen Keller Nat'l Center for Deaf Blind Youths and Adults (448)
Helen Keller Worldwide (448)
Independent Visually Impaired Enterprisers (460)
Internat'l Ass'n of Business, Industry and Rehabilitation (467)
Internat'l Hearing Soc. (472)
Jacobus Tenbroek Memorial Fund (481)
Jewish Guild for the Blind (483)
Kennedy Institute, Lt. Joseph P. (488)
Leadership Conference on Civil Rights (496)
The Learning Disabilities Ass'n (497)
Library Users of America (499)
Mainstream, Inc. (507)
Maryland Ass'n of the Deaf (511)
Nat'l Alliance of Blind Students (536)
Nat'l Ass'n of Blind Teachers (539)
Nat'l Ass'n of Developmental Disabilities Councils (542)
Nat'l Ass'n of Protection and Advocacy Systems (NAPAS) (547)
Nat'l Ass'n of Rehabilitation Agencies (548)
Nat'l Ass'n of State Directors of Developmental Disabilities Services, Inc. (550)
Nat'l Ass'n of State Directors of Special Education (550)
Nat'l Ass'n of the Deaf (550)
Nat'l Campaign for Hearing Health (554)
Nat'l Council of State Agencies for the Blind (560)
Nat'l Council on Rehabilitation Education (561)
Nat'l Federation for the Blind (564)
Nat'l Industries for the Blind (568)
Nat'l Organization on Disability (572)
Nat'l Rehabilitation Ass'n (575)
Nat'l Rehabilitation Information Center (575)
Nat'l Rehabilitation Political Action Committee (575)
Nat'l Right to Life Committee (576)
The Nat'l Sports Center for the Disabled (578)
Nat'l Student Speech Language Hearing Ass'n (579)
Nat'l Therapeutic Recreation Soc. (579)
NISH - Creating Employment Opportunities for People with Severe Disabilities (590)
Paralyzed Veterans of America (607)
Perkins School for the Blind (612)
Recording for the Blind and Dyslexic, Inc. (634)
Christopher Reeve Paralysis Foundation (635)
Saint Coletta of Greater Washington, Inc. (646)
Self Help for Hard of Hearing People, Inc. (654)
Shake-A-Leg (656)
Special Olympics, Inc. (669)
Spina Bifida Ass'n of America (670)
The Tri-Alliance of Rehabilitation Professionals (691)
U.S. Disabled Athletes Fund (696)
United Cerebral Palsy Ass'n (700)
Very Special Arts (714)
Visually Impaired Data Processors Internat'l (716)
Visually Impaired Veterans of America (716)
Wheelchairs for the World Foundation (726)
World Institute on Disability (730)
Yeshiva of South Shore (733)

Drug and Alcohol Abuse

Alliance for Children and Families (239)
American Counseling Ass'n (256)
American Osteopathic Academy of Addiction Medicine (269)
Americans for Responsible Alcohol Access (282)
Caron Foundation (332)
Coalition for the Prevention of Alcohol Problems (354)
College on Problems of Drug Dependence (357)
Community Anti-Drug Coalitions of America (362)
D.A.R.E. America (381)
Drug Strategies (392)
Employee Assistance Professionals Ass'n (402)
Families Against Mandatory Minimums (410)
Institute for a Drug-Free Workplace (463)
Internat'l Commission for the Prevention of Alcoholism and Drug Dependency (470)
Internat'l Narcotic Enforcement Officers Ass'n (473)
Lindesmith Center - Drug Policy Foundation (500)
The Maritime Consortium, Inc. (510)
Mental and Addictive Disorders Appropriations Coalition (518)
NAADAC, The Ass'n for Addiction Professionals (534)
Nat'l Ass'n of Collection Sites (540)
Nat'l Ass'n of Psychiatric Health Systems (547)
Nat'l Ass'n of State Alcohol and Drug Abuse Directors (NASADAD) (549)
Nat'l Center on Addiction and Substance Abuse (555)
Nat'l Council on Alcoholism and Drug Dependence (561)
Nat'l Medical Enterprises, Inc. (570)
Nat'l Organization for the Reform of Marijuana Laws (572)
Project Return Foundation Inc. (626)
Psychemedics Corp. (628)
Research Soc. on Alcoholism (638)
Tarzana Treatment Center (681)
Valley Hope Ass'n (711)
Virginia Wineries Ass'n (716)

Economics and Economic Development

Abilene Industrial Foundation, Inc. (225)
Ad Hoc Coalition on Intermarket Coordination (227)
Adventist Development and Relief Agency Internat'l (229)
Aiken and Edgenfield Counties, South Carolina, Economic Development Partnership of (233)
Alaska Village Initiatives (237)
Alexis de Tocqueville Institution (238)
American Ass'n of Enterprise Zones (247)
American Ass'n of Family and Consumer Sciences (247)
American Business Conference (251)
American Chamber of Commerce Executives (252)
American Chamber of Commerce in Germany (252)
American Council for an Energy-Efficient Economy (255)
American Council for Capital Formation (255)
American Enterprise Institute for Public Policy Research (257)
American Security Council (273)
Argentine Economic & Investment Council (288)
Asian Development Bank - North American Representative Office (291)
Ass'n for Enterprise Opportunity (292)
Ass'n of Small Business Development Centers (298)
Ass'n on Third World Affairs (299)
Atlantic Corridor USA (302)
Baden-Wuerttemberg Agency for International Economic Cooperation (305)
Bangladesh Economic Program Zone Authority (307)
Bedford Stuyvesant Restoration Corp. (310)
Bethel New Life (312)
Big Sky Economic Development Authority (313)
Business Alliance for Internat'l Economic Development (324)
Business Council for Sustainable Energy (324)
The Business Roundtable (325)
Cambridge Redevelopment Authority (328)
Capital City Economic Development Authority (330)
Caribbean/Latin American Action (331)
Cato Institute (334)
Center for Community Change (335)
Center for Economic Organizing (336)
Center for Energy and Economic Development (336)
Center for Internat'l Private Enterprise (336)
Center for Public Dialogue (337)
Center for Resource Economics (337)
Center on Budget and Policy Priorities (338)
Central American Bank of Economic Integration (338)
Centre for Development and Population Activities (339)
The Century Foundation (339)
Chicanos Por La Causa (343)
Church World Service/Lutheran World Relief (346)
Citizens for a Sound Economy (348)
Coachella Valley Economic Partnership (352)
Coalition for Open Markets and Expanded Trade (354)
Coalition of Service Industries (355)
Committee for a Responsible Federal Budget (360)
Committee for Economic Development (361)
Committee to Support the Antitrust Laws (361)
Community Development Financial Institutions (CDFI) (362)
Community Development Venture Capital Ass'n (362)
Concord Coalition (365)
Congressional Economic Leadership Institute (366)
Congressional Institute for the Future (366)
Connecticut Resource Recovery Authority (367)
Consumer Energy Council of America Research Foundation (369)
Corporate Council on Africa (372)
Corporation for Enterprise Development (372)
Corpus Christi, City of (373)
Council for Urban Economic Development (375)
Council of Development Finance Agencies (375)
Council of the Americas (376)
Council of Urban and Economic Development (376)
Council on Hemispheric Affairs (377)
Council on the Economic Impact of Health System Change (377)
Delta Foundation (385)
Development Corporation of Nevada (387)
Development Group for Alternative Policies (387)
District of Columbia Chamber of Commerce (390)
District of Columbia Financial Responsibility and Management Assistance Authority (390)
Dow Jones & Co., Inc. (391)
Downey, California, Economic Development of the City of (392)
East Tennessee Economic Council (395)
Economic Development Alliance of Jefferson County, Arkansas (396)
Economic Policy Institute (396)
Economic Strategy Institute (396)

The Economist Newspaper Group (396)
Fargo-Cass County Development Corp. (411)
The Foundation for Environmental and Economic Progress (424)
Foundation on Economic Trends (424)
Frontiers of Freedom Institute (427)
George Zamias Developers (434)
Global Climate Coalition (436)
Greater Providence Chamber of Commerce (439)
Greater Richmond Partnership (439)
Greater Washington Board of Trade (439)
Greenpoint Manufacturing and Design Center (GMDC) (440)
Guatemalan Development Foundation (FUNDESA) (442)
Hawaii, Department of Business and Economic Development of the State of (445)
Heritage Foundation (448)
Highland Park, Illinois, City of Highwood Local Redevelopment Authority and the City of (449)
Alan Hilburg & Associates (449)
Hong Kong Economic and Trade Office (452)
Hong Kong Trade Development Council (452)
Impact Services (458)
Inland Valley Development Agency (462)
Institute for Internat'l Economics (463)
Institute for Local Self-Reliance (463)
Institute for Research on the Economics of Taxation (IRET) (464)
Institutions and Governance Program (464)
Internat'l Campaign for Tibet (469)
Internat'l Downtown Ass'n (471)
Internat'l Institute for Energy Conservation (472)
Internat'l Trade Council (475)
ISAR, Initiative for Social Action and Renewal in Eurasia (479)
Israel, Economic Mission of the Government of the State of (479)
Jacksonville Chamber of Commerce (481)
Jersey City Economic Development Corp. (483)
Joint Center for Political and Economic Studies (484)
Keizai Koho Center (487)
Kentucky Highlands Investment Corp. (488)
Korea Economic Institute of America (491)
Korea Internat'l Trade Ass'n (491)
Local Initiatives Support Corp. (501)
Los Angeles, California, Community Development Commission of the County of (504)
Madeira Development Co. (507)
Massachusetts Technology Park Corp. (512)
Mexico, Secretaria de Comercio y Fomento Industrial (SECOFI) (521)
Mexico-U.S. Business Committee, U.S. Council (521)
Miami Valley Economic Coalition (521)
Minority Business Enterprise Legal Defense and Education Fund (525)
Moberly-Randolph County Economic Development (527)
Nat'l Alliance of Business (536)
Nat'l Ass'n of County Community and Economic Development (541)
Nat'l Ass'n of Development Organizations (542)
Nat'l Ass'n of Foreign Trade Zones (543)
Nat'l Ass'n of Private Industry Councils (546)
Nat'l Ass'n of Regional Councils (548)
Nat'l Ass'n of Small Business Investment Companies (549)
Nat'l Ass'n of State Development Agencies (550)
Nat'l Ass'n to Protect Individual Rights (551)
Nat'l Center for Neighborhood Enterprise (555)
Nat'l Center for Policy Analysis (555)
Nat'l Center for Public Policy Research (555)
Nat'l Chamber Foundation (555)
Nat'l Coalition for Minority Business (556)
Nat'l Community Capital Ass'n (557)
Nat'l Community Development Ass'n (557)
Nat'l Community Reinvestment Coalition (558)
Nat'l Congress for Community Economic Development (558)
Nat'l Cooperative Bank (558)
Nat'l Foreign Trade Council, Inc. (565)
The Nat'l Foundation for Teaching Entrepreneurship (565)
Nat'l Policy Ass'n (574)
Nat'l Rural Development Ass'n (576)
Nat'l Taxpayers Union (579)
Nat'l Urban Coalition (580)
Nat'l Women's Business Council (581)
Nathan Associates Inc. (581)
The New England Council, Inc. (585)
Newport News, Virginia, Industrial Development Authority of the City of (589)
Niagara Area Chamber of Commerce (589)
Nicaraguan Foundation for Democracy and Development (589)
Northeast Entrepreneur Fund (593)
Northeast-Midwest Institute (594)
Northern Economic Initiatives Corp. (594)
Ontario, Ministry of Economic Development and Trade (601)
Opportunity Internat'l (601)
Oregon Economic Development Department (603)
Pakistani-American Business Ass'n (606)
Partners for Livable Communities (608)
Pennsylvania Economic Development Financing Authorities (611)
Pride Africa (624)
Providence Redevelopment Agency (627)
Puerto Rico Industrial Development Co. (629)
Red River Trade Council (635)
RGK Foundation (639)
Richardson Lawrie Associates (639)
Rural Coalition (643)
Search for Common Ground (653)
South Atlantic-TransAndes Economic Committee (666)
Switzerland, Economic Development, State of Vaud (679)
Team Santa Rosa Economic Development Council (682)
TELACU (682)
Town of Fort Sheridan Co., LLC (688)
Tri-City Industrial Development Council (691)
Tri-County Alliance (691)
U.S. Overseas Cooperative Development (697)
U.S.-Mongolia Business Council, Inc. (697)
U.S.-Russia Business Council (697)
U.S.-Turkmenistan Business Council (697)
United States Business and Industry Council (703)
United States Nat'l Committee for Pacific Economic Cooperation (704)
Upper Midwest Coalition (708)
Urban Land Institute (709)
US-ROC (Taiwan) Business Council (709)
Ventura County Community-Navy Action Partnership (712)
City of Victorville Redevelopment Agency (715)
Youngstown-Warren Regional Chamber (733)

Education

Academy for Educational Development - Nat'l Institute for Work and Learning (225)
Accrediting Commission on Education for Health Services Administration (226)
Accrediting Council for Continuing Education & Training (226)
Accuracy in Academia (226)
ACT, Inc. (227)
Adelphi University (227)
Aerospace Education Foundation (230)
Agudath Israel of America (232)
Alabama A & M University (235)
Alamo Navajo School Board (236)
Alfalit Internat'l (238)
Alfred University (238)
All Kinds of Music (238)
Alliance for Special Needs Children (240)
Alternative Schools Network (242)
American Academy for Liberal Education (243)
American Academy of Wound Management (244)
American Alliance for Health, Physical Education, Recreation and Dance (245)
American Ass'n for Active Lifestyles and Fitness (245)
American Ass'n for Adult and Continuing Education (245)
American Ass'n for Health Education (245)
American Ass'n for Higher Education (245)
American Ass'n of Colleges for Teacher Education (247)
American Ass'n of Colleges of Nursing (247)
American Ass'n of Colleges of Osteopathic Medicine (247)
American Ass'n of Colleges of Pharmacy (247)
American Ass'n of Colleges of Podiatric Medicine (247)
American Ass'n of Collegiate Registrars and Admissions Officers (247)
American Ass'n of Community Colleges (247)
American Ass'n of Cosmetology Schools (247)
American Ass'n of Early Childhood Educators (247)
American Ass'n of Physics Teachers (249)
American Ass'n of School Administrators (249)
American Ass'n of State Colleges and Universities (249)
American Ass'n of University Affiliated Programs for Persons with Developmental Disabilities (249)
American Ass'n of University Professors (249)
American Ass'n of University Women (249)
American Ass'n of University Women Legal Advocacy Fund (250)
American College of Sports Medicine (254)
American College Personnel Ass'n (254)
American Congress of Community Supports and Employment Services (255)
American Council on Education (256)
American Councils for Internat'l Education: ACTR/ACCELS (256)
American Counseling Ass'n (256)
American Dental Education Ass'n (257)
American Educational Research Ass'n (257)
American Federation of School Administrators (258)
American Federation of Teachers (259)
American Friends of Turkey (260)
American Hellenic Educational Progressive Ass'n (AHEPA) (262)
American Historical Ass'n (262)
American Indian Higher Education Consortium (263)
American Labor Education Center (265)
American Medical Student Ass'n (267)
American Museum of Natural History (268)
American Podiatric Medical Students Ass'n (270)
American School Counselor Ass'n (273)
American School Food Service Ass'n (273)
American Soc. for Engineering Education (274)
American Soc. for Training and Development (275)
American Speech, Language, and Hearing Ass'n (277)
American Speech-Language-Hearing Foundation (277)
American University (279)
American University of Beirut (280)
American-Turkish Council (281)
Americans for Better Education (281)
Americans for Choice in Education (281)
Americans for Equitable Climate Solutions (281)
Americans United for Separation of Church and State (282)
Annenberg Institute for School Reform, The (284)
APICS - The Educational Soc. for Resource Management (286)
Apollo Group, Inc. (286)
Arizona State University (288)
Arlington Educational Ass'n Retirement Housing Corp. (288)
The Asheville School (290)
ASPIRA Ass'n, Inc. (291)
Ass'n for Career and Technical Education (291)
Ass'n for Childhood Education Internat'l (291)
Ass'n for Community Based Education (292)
Ass'n for Education and Rehabilitation of the Blind & Visually Impaired (292)
Ass'n for Gerontology in Higher Education (292)
Ass'n for Hospital Medical Education (292)
Ass'n for Supervision and Curriculum Development (293)
Ass'n of Academic Health Centers (293)
Ass'n of Academic Health Sciences Library Directors (293)
Ass'n of American Colleges and Universities (293)
Ass'n of American Law Schools (293)
Ass'n of American Medical Colleges (294)
Ass'n of American Universities (294)
Ass'n of American Veterinary Medical Colleges (294)
Ass'n of Chiropractic Colleges (295)
Ass'n of Collegiate Schools of Architecture (295)
Ass'n of Community College Trustees (295)
Ass'n of Farmworker Opportunity Programs (295)
Ass'n of Governing Boards of Universities and Colleges (296)
Ass'n of Independent Colleges of Art and Design (296)
Ass'n of Independent Research Institutes (296)
Ass'n of Jesuit Colleges and Universities (296)
Ass'n of Military Colleges and Schools of the U.S. (297)
Ass'n of Minority Health Profession Schools (297)
Ass'n of Osteopathic Directors and Medical Educators (297)
Ass'n of Professors of Gynecology and Obstetrics (298)
Ass'n of Professors of Medicine (298)
Ass'n of Proprietary Colleges (298)
Ass'n of Research Libraries (298)
Ass'n of School Business Officials Internat'l (298)
Ass'n of Schools and Colleges of Optometry (298)
Ass'n of Schools of Allied Health Professions (298)
Ass'n of Schools of Public Health (298)
Ass'n of State and Territorial Public Health Laboratory Directors (298)
Ass'n of Teacher Educators (299)
Ass'n of Teachers of Preventive Medicine (299)
Ass'n of University Programs in Health Administration (299)
ASSE Internat'l Student Exchange Program (299)
Associated Universities Inc. (300)
Assumption College (300)
Atlantic Corridor USA (302)
Auburn University (302)
Ball State University (306)
Barat College (307)
Barry University (308)
Basic American, Inc. (308)
Bastyr University (308)
Bergen Community College (311)
Bethesda Academy for the Performing Arts (312)
Bethune-Cookman College (312)
The Bethune-DuBois Institute, Inc. (312)
Black Mesa Community School Board (315)
Boise State University (317)
Boston College (318)
Boston Symphony Orchestra (318)
Boston University (318)
Bowie State University (318)
Braille Revival League (319)
Brandeis University (319)
Broadcast Education Ass'n (321)
Broadforum (321)
Business-Higher Education Forum (325)
CADDO Lake Institute (325)
CAL-FED (326)
California Department of Education (326)
California Institute of Technology (327)
California School Employees Ass'n (327)
California State Teachers' Retirement System (327)
California State University at Monterey Bay (327)
California State University Fresno (327)
California State University Fullerton (327)
California State University Institute (327)
Calspan University of Buffalo Research Center (328)
Capital Children's Museum (330)
Career College Ass'n (331)
Catholic University of America (333)
Center for Civic Education (335)
Center for Employment Training (336)
Center for Governmental Studies of the University of Virginia (336)
Center for Law and Education (336)

Center for Media Education (337)
Central Alabama Community College (338)
Central Kitsap School District (339)
Central Michigan University (339)
Central Piedmont Community College (339)
CEO Forum on Education and Technology (340)
Chabot Space & Science Center (340)
Challenger Center for Space Science Education (340)
Charter Schools Development Corp. (341)
Chela Financial (342)
Chicago School Reform Board of Trustees (343)
Chicago State University (343)
Citizen's Educational Foundation (348)
Citizens' Scholarship Foundation of America (349)
City College of San Francisco (349)
City Colleges of Chicago (349)
City University (349)
Claflin College (349)
Clark Atlanta University (349)
Classroom Publishers Ass'n (350)
Clatsop Community College (350)
Cleveland State University - College of Urban Affairs (351)
Click2Learn.com (351)
Close Up Foundation (351)
Clover Park School District (351)
Coalition for Maritime Education (354)
Coalition for Networked Information (354)
Coalition of Boston Teaching Hospitals (355)
Coalition of EPSCoR States (355)
Coalition of Higher Education Assistance Organizations (355)
College and University Professional Ass'n for Human Resources (357)
The College Board (357)
College of the Desert (357)
College Parents of America (358)
College Republican Nat'l Committee (358)
College Savings Bank (358)
Columbia College Chicago (359)
Columbia University (359)
Columbia University/Institute for Learning Technologies (359)
Columbus Educational Services (359)
Columbus State College (359)
Commission of Accredited Truck Driving Schools (CATDS) (360)
Commission on Graduates of Foreign Nursing Schools (360)
Committee for Education Funding (361)
Community Learning and Information Network, Inc. (363)
Concerned Educators Against Forced Unionism (365)
Concord College (365)
Conference Board of the Mathematical Sciences (366)
Conference of Educational Administrators of Schools and Programs for the Deaf (366)
Connecticut Student Loan Foundation (367)
Consortium for Oceanographic Research and Education (CORE) (367)
Consortium for School Networking (368)
Consortium of Universities of the Washington Metropolitan Area (368)
Consortium on Government Relations for Student Affairs (368)
Contra Costa Community College District (370)
Convention of American Instructors of the Deaf (370)
Council for Advancement and Support of Education (373)
Council for American Private Education (374)
Council for Basic Education (374)
Council for Christian College and Universities (374)
Council for Exceptional Children (374)
Council for Internat'l Exchange of Scholars (374)
Council for Opportunity in Education (374)
Council of American Overseas Research Centers (375)
Council of Chief State School Officers (375)
Council of Graduate Schools (375)
Council of Independent Colleges (375)
Council of State Administrators of Vocational Rehabilitation (376)
Council of the Great City Schools (376)
Council on Internat'l Educational Exchange (377)
Council on Resident Education in Obstetrics and Gynecology (377)
Council on Social Work Education (377)
Coweta County (Georgia) School Board (377)
CRT, Inc. (379)
D'Youville College (381)
Daemen College (381)
Day Care Ass'n of Tarrant County and Fort Worth Texas (383)
DePaul University (386)
Des Moines Community School District (386)
Detroit Public Schools (386)
DeVry, Inc. (387)
DGME Fairness Initiative (387)
Dillard University (388)
Direct Selling Education Foundation (389)
Disability Rights Education and Defense Fund (389)
Discovery Communications, Inc. (389)
Discovery Place, Inc. (Charlotte Science Museum) (389)
Distance Education and Training Council (389)
Dominican College of Blauvelt (391)
Dowling College (391)
Drexel University (392)
Early Learning Years Institute (394)
Earth University, Inc. (394)
Eastern College (395)
Eastern Mennonite University (395)
Economics America (396)
The Edison Project (397)
EdLinc (397)
Education and Research Institute (398)
Education and Training Resources (398)
Education Commission of the States (398)
Education Communications, Inc. (398)
Education Finance Council (398)
Education First Alliance (398)
Education Leaders Council (398)
Education Networks of America (398)
Educational Foundation for Citizenship and Statehood Project (398)
Educational Testing Service (398)
Educational Video Conferencing, Inc. (398)
Edupoint.com (398)
Elmira College (401)
Embry-Riddle Aeronautical University (401)
Emmanuel College (402)
Employment Policy Foundation (402)
Ephedra Education Council (405)
Episcopal Diocese of Washington (406)
Ethics Resource Center Inc. (407)
Fairfield University (410)
Family, Career and Community Leaders of America (411)
Federal Advocacy for California Education (412)
Federal Education Ass'n (412)
Federation of State Humanities Councils (415)
Ferris State University (415)
Financial Accounting Standards Board (416)
Florida Atlantic University (419)
Florida Community College of Jacksonville (419)
Florida Department of Education (419)
Florida Internat'l University (420)
Florida State University (420)
Florida State University System (420)
The Food Processors Institute (422)
Forest Counties Schools Coalition (423)
Fresno Pacific University (426)
Friends of Higher Education Inc. (426)
Fuller Theological Seminary (427)
Fund for American Studies (427)
Future Business Leaders of America - Phi Beta Lambda (428)
Future Leaders of America (428)
Futures for Children (428)
Gadsden State Community College (428)
George Mason University Foundation (434)
George Washington University Medical Center (434)
George Washington University, Office of Government Relations (434)
Georgetown University-McDonough School of Business (434)
Georgetown University-School of Nursing (434)
Global Associates (436)
Grand Valley State University (438)
Great Cities' Universities (439)
Greater Texas Student Loan Corp. (439)
Greater Washington Educational Telecommunications Ass'n (440)
Hampshire College (444)
Hampton University (444)
Harvard University (445)
Harvard University Washington Office (445)
Hebrew Academy for Special Children (447)
Hebrew University of Jerusalem (447)
Higher Education Consortium for Special Education (449)
Highline School District Educational Resources (449)
Hispanic Ass'n of Colleges and Universities (450)
Home School PAC (451)
Horatio Alger Ass'n of Distinguished Americans (452)
Houston Independent School District (453)
Howard Hughes Medical Institute (454)
Huntingdon College (455)
Idaho State University (457)
Illinois Community College Board (457)
Illinois Institute of Technology (457)
Illinois State Board of Education (458)
Immaculata College (458)
Independent Educational Consultants Ass'n (459)
Indian Hills Community College (460)
Indiana State University (460)
Indiana University (460)
Institute for Alternative Futures (463)
Institute for Civil Soc. (463)
Institute for Educational Leadership (463)
The Institute for Higher Education Policy (463)
Institute for Policy Studies (463)
Internat'l College (470)
Internat'l Council on Education for Teaching (470)
Internat'l Reading Ass'n (474)
Internat'l Soc. for Performance Improvement (475)
Internat'l Technology Education Ass'n (475)
Ivy Tech State College (480)
Jackson State University (480)
Japan Productivity Center for Socio-Economic Development (482)
JASON Foundation for Education (482)
Jefferson State Community College (482)
John Ashbrook Center for Public Policy (483)
Johns Hopkins School of Hygiene and Public Health (483)
Johns Hopkins University & Hospital (483)
Johns Hopkins University Hospital, School of Hygiene and Public Health (483)
Johns Hopkins University-Applied Physics Lab (484)
Joint Nat'l Committee for Languages (484)
Joint Steering Committee for Public Policy (484)
Kamehameha Schools (486)
Kaplan Companies, Inc. (486)
Kent State University (488)
Kettering Foundation (488)
Kids in the Know (489)
Kinder-Care Learning Centers, Inc. (489)
Knoxville College (490)
Laborers Institute for Training and Education (493)
Laborers-AGC Education and Training Fund (493)
Lackawanna Junior College (494)
The Learning Disabilities Ass'n (497)
Lebanese American University (497)
Lehigh University (498)
Lewis and Clark College (498)
Life and Health Insurance Foundation for Education (499)
Long Island University (503)
Lorain County Community College (503)
Los Alamitos Unified School District (503)
Los Angeles Community College District (503)
Los Angeles County Office of Education (504)
Los Angeles Unified School District (504)
Louisiana State University (504)
Loyola College (505)
Loyola University (505)
Loyola University Health System (505)
Loyola University of Chicago (505)
Marietta College (509)
Marquette University (511)
Marshall Institute, George C. (511)
Marymount University (512)
Massachusetts Higher Education Assistance Corp. (512)
Medical Lake School District (516)
Medical University of Southern Africa (516)
MENC: The Nat'l Ass'n for Music Education (518)
Mendez University System, Ana G. (518)
Mercer University (518)
Meridian Internat'l Center (519)
Metcor, Ltd. (519)
Miami-Dade Community College (521)
Miami-Dade County Public Schools (521)
Michigan Technological University (522)
Middlesex Community-Technical College (523)
Military Impacted School Districts Ass'n (524)
Minority Business Enterprise Legal Defense and Education Fund (525)
Minority Males Consortium (525)
Minot State University (525)
Monmouth University (527)
Montana State University (528)
Monterey Institute (528)
Morehouse School of Medicine (529)
Morgan State University (529)
Mort Community College (530)
Moscow State University (530)
Muhlenberg College (532)
Music Educators Nat'l Conference (533)
NAACP Legal Defense and Educational Fund, Inc. (534)
NAFSA: Ass'n of Internat'l Educators (534)
Nat'l 4-H Council (535)
Nat'l Accreditation Council for Early Childhood Professional Personnel and Programs (535)
Nat'l Accrediting Commission of Cosmetology Arts & Sciences, Inc. (535)
Nat'l Alliance of Black School Educators (536)
Nat'l Alliance of Blind Students (536)
Nat'l Art Education Ass'n (537)
Nat'l Ass'n for Bilingual Education (537)
Nat'l Ass'n for College Admission Counseling (537)
Nat'l Ass'n for Equal Opportunity in Higher Education (537)
Nat'l Ass'n for Gifted Children (537)
Nat'l Ass'n for Human Development (538)
Nat'l Ass'n for Sport and Physical Education (538)
Nat'l Ass'n for the Advancement of Colored People, Washington Bureau (538)
Nat'l Ass'n for the Education of Young Children (538)
Nat'l Ass'n of Agricultural Educators (NAAE) (538)
Nat'l Ass'n of Biology Teachers (539)
Nat'l Ass'n of Blind Teachers (539)
Nat'l Ass'n of College and University Attorneys (540)
Nat'l Ass'n of College and University Business Officers (540)
Nat'l Ass'n of Elementary School Principals (542)
Nat'l Ass'n of Federal Education Program Administrators (542)
Nat'l Ass'n of Federally Impacted Schools (542)
Nat'l Ass'n of Higher Educational Finance Authorities (543)
Nat'l Ass'n of Independent Colleges and Universities (544)
Nat'l Ass'n of Independent Schools (544)
Nat'l Ass'n of Partners in Education (546)
Nat'l Ass'n of Private Industry Councils (546)
Nat'l Ass'n of Professional Forestry Schools and Colleges (547)
Nat'l Ass'n of Rehabilitation Agencies (548)

Nat'l Ass'n of Rehabilitation Research and Training Centers (548)
Nat'l Ass'n of School Music Dealers (548)
Nat'l Ass'n of School Nurses (548)
Nat'l Ass'n of School Psychologists (548)
Nat'l Ass'n of Schools of Art and Design (548)
Nat'l Ass'n of Schools of Dance (548)
Nat'l Ass'n of Schools of Music (548)
Nat'l Ass'n of Schools of Public Affairs and Administration (549)
Nat'l Ass'n of Schools of Theatre (549)
Nat'l Ass'n of Secondary School Principals (549)
Nat'l Ass'n of State Boards of Education (549)
Nat'l Ass'n of State Directors of Special Education (550)
Nat'l Ass'n of State Directors of Vocational Technical Education Consortium (550)
Nat'l Ass'n of State Universities and Land-Grant Colleges (550)
Nat'l Ass'n of Student Financial Aid Administrators (550)
Nat'l Ass'n of Student Personnel Administrators (550)
Nat'l Ass'n of Veterans Research and Education Foundations (551)
Nat'l Board for Professional Teaching Standards (NBPTS) (552)
Nat'l Business Education Ass'n (553)
Nat'l Catholic Educational Ass'n (554)
Nat'l Catholic Federation of Parents (554)
Nat'l Center for Economic Freedom, Inc. (554)
Nat'l Center for Education Information (554)
Nat'l Center for Family Literacy (554)
Nat'l Center on Education and the Economy (555)
Nat'l College (557)
Nat'l College Access Network (557)
Nat'l Community Education Ass'n (558)
Nat'l Computer Systems (558)
Nat'l Congress of Parents and Teachers (558)
Nat'l Council for Accreditation of Teacher Education (559)
Nat'l Council for Impacted Schools (559)
Nat'l Council for Languages and Internat'l Studies (559)
Nat'l Council for the Social Studies (559)
Nat'l Council of Higher Education Loan Programs (560)
Nat'l Council of Teachers of Mathematics (560)
Nat'l Council on Measurement in Education (561)
Nat'l Council on Rehabilitation Education (561)
Nat'l Council on Teacher Retirement (561)
Nat'l Education Ass'n of the U.S. (562)
Nat'l Education Knowledge Industry Ass'n (NEKIA) (562)
Nat'l Environmental Education and Training Center (563)
Nat'l Federation of High Schools (564)
Nat'l Federation of State High School Ass'ns (564)
Nat'l FFA Organization (564)
Nat'l Forest Counties School Coalition (565)
Nat'l Foundation for the Improvement of Education (565)
Nat'l Graduate University (566)
Nat'l Head Start Ass'n (566)
Nat'l Health Museum (567)
Nat'l Humanities Alliance (567)
Nat'l Independent Private Schools Ass'n (568)
Nat'l Indian Education Ass'n (568)
Nat'l Institute for Literacy (568)
Nat'l Institute for State Credit Union Examination (568)
Nat'l Maritime Alliance (570)
Nat'l Migrant Head Start Ass'n (571)
Nat'l Puerto Rican Coalition (575)
Nat'l Research Center for College and University Admissions (575)
Nat'l School Boards Ass'n (577)
Nat'l School Public Relations Ass'n (577)
Nat'l School Supply and Equipment Ass'n (577)
Nat'l School Transportation Ass'n (577)
Nat'l Science Teachers Ass'n (577)
Nat'l Student Speech Language Hearing Ass'n (579)
Nat'l Technological University (579)
Nat'l Training Systems Ass'n (579)
Nat'l Writing Project (581)
Native American Cultural & Educational Authority (582)
NetSchools (584)
Neumann College (584)
New American School (585)
New College (585)
New England Education Loan Marketing Corp. (Nellie Mae) (585)
New Jersey Institute of Technology (585)
New Mexico State Office of Research & Development (586)
New Mexico State University (586)
New Mexico State University, Department of Agriculture (586)
New Mexico State University, Department of Engineering (586)
New Mexico Tech (586)
New York Institute for Special Education (587)
The New York Structural Biology Center (588)
New York University (588)
New York University Medical Center (588)
North Dakota State University (593)
Northeastern University (594)
Northern Essex Community College Foundation (594)
Northern Michigan University (594)
Northwest Regional Education Laboratory (595)
Northwestern Michigan College (595)
Northwestern University (596)
Nova Southeastern University (596)
Office for the Advancement of Public Black Colleges (599)
Oglala Lakota College (599)
Ohio State University (599)
Ohio Wesleyan University (599)
Oregon Graduate Institute of Science and Technology (603)
Oregon Health Sciences University (603)
Pacific Union College (606)
Palmer Chiropractic University (606)
Parent Centers FYI (608)
Parents for Public Schools (608)
Partnership for Better Schools (608)
Paul Quinn College (610)
Pennsylvania Higher Education Assistance Agency (611)
People Advancing Christian Education (PACE) (611)
Perkins School for the Blind (612)
Personal Communications Industry Ass'n (PCIA) (612)
Pew Charitable Trust - Environmental Law & Policy Center of the Midwest (613)
Pierce College (617)
Pinon Community School Board (618)
A Presidential Classroom for Young Americans, Inc. (623)
Princeton University (624)
Psychological Corp. (628)
Purdue University (630)
Q-ZAB Coalition (630)
A. Philip Randolph Educational Fund (633)
A. Philip Randolph Institute (633)
Reading Is Fundamental, Inc. (633)
The Readnet Foundation (634)
Rebuild America's Schools (634)
Resources and Instruction for Staff Excellence, Inc. (638)
Rhode Island School of Design (639)
Riverdeep Inc. (640)
Riverside Community College (640)
Riverside County Schools (640)
Riverside Unified School District (640)
Rochester Institute of Technology (641)
Rock Point Community School (641)
Ross University School of Medicine in Dominica (642)
Rough Rock Community School (642)
Rutgers University (644)
Sacred Heart University (645)
Salesian Missions of the Salesian Soc. (646)
Sallie Mae, Inc. (646)
Sam Houston University (647)
San Diego State University Foundation (647)
San Dieguito School Transportation Cooperative (647)
School of Visual Arts (652)
Security on Campus, Inc. (654)
Seton Hill College (656)
Shiprock Alternative Schools, Inc. (657)
Skills USA-VICA (660)
Smithsonian Institution (661)
Solar Energy Research and Education Foundation (665)
Southeast Missouri State University (667)
Southeastern Louisiana University (667)
Southeastern Pennsylvania Consortium for Higher Education (667)
Southeastern Universities Research Ass'n (667)
Southern Illinois University (668)
Southern Methodist University (668)
Southwest Texas State University (668)
Spelman College (670)
Springfield, Oregon, School District #19 (670)
St. Augustine College (671)
St. George's University School of Medicine (671)
St. Joseph University (671)
St. Louis Regional Education and Public Television Commission (672)
St. Louis University, School of Public Health (672)
St. Matthew's University School of Medicine (672)
St. Petersburg Community College (672)
State Universities Retirement System of Illinois Pension Fund (673)
State University of New York (SUNY) (673)
State University of New York at Albany (673)
Stevens Institute of Technology (674)
Stillman College (674)
Street Law Inc. (675)
Student Loan Funding Corp. (675)
Student Press Law Center (675)
Study Circles (676)
Suomi College (677)
Syracuse University (679)
Take The Field, Inc. (680)
Talladega College (680)
Temple University (683)
Temple University Health System (683)
Tequity (684)
Terrene Institute (684)
Texas A&M Engineering Experiment Station (684)
Texas A&M Research Foundation (684)
Texas College (684)
Texas Tech University System (685)
Thunderbird, The American Graduate School of Internat'l Management (686)
TIAA-CREF (686)
Tougaloo College (688)
Touro College (688)
Touro Law Center (688)
Troy State University - Montgomery (692)
Truman Scholarship Foundation, Harry S (693)
Tufts University School of Veterinary Medicine (693)
Tulane University (693)
Turtle Mountain Community College (694)
U.S. Basic Skills (695)
U.S. English, Inc. (696)
U.S. Space & Rocket Center (697)
UNIPAC Service Corp. (699)
United Negro College Fund, Inc. (702)
United States Education Finance Corp. (703)
United States Student Ass'n (704)
United Student Aid Group (704)
United Tribes Technical College (705)
University College Dublin (705)
University Continuing Education Ass'n (705)
University Corp. for Atmospheric Research (705)
University Medical Associates (705)
University Medical Center of Southern Nevada (705)
University of Akron (705)
University of Alabama - Huntsville (705)
University of Alabama System (705)
University of Alaska (705)
University of Arizona (705)
University of California at Irvine Advanced Power and Energy Program (706)
University of California at Los Angeles (706)
University of California at Riverside (706)
University of California, Office of Federal Government Relations (706)
University of Central Florida (706)
University of Cincinnati (706)
University of Colorado, Office of the President (706)
University of Connecticut (706)
University of Dubuque (706)
University of Findlay (706)
University of Georgia (706)
University of Georgia - College of Agricultural and Environmental Sciences (706)
University of Hawaii (706)
University of Houston (706)
University of Idaho (706)
University of Louisville (706)
University of Massachusetts (706)
University of Medicine and Dentistry of New Jersey (706)
University of Medicine and Dentistry of New Jersey - School of Health Related Professionals (706)
University of Miami (706)
University of Mississippi (706)
University of Mississippi Medical Center (706)
University of Missouri (706)
University of Nebraska (706)
University of Nevada - Las Vegas (707)
University of Nevada - Reno (707)
University of New Orleans (707)
University of New Orleans Foundation (707)
University of North Carolina at Greensboro (707)
University of North Dakota (707)
University of Notre Dame (707)
University of Oklahoma (707)
University of Oregon (707)
University of Pennsylvania/School of Dental Medicine (707)
University of Phoenix (707)
University of Puerto Rico (707)
University of Redlands (707)
University of San Diego (707)
University of South Alabama (707)
University of South Florida Research Foundation (707)
University of Southern California (707)
University of Southern Mississippi (707)
University of Southwestern Louisiana (707)
University of Tennessee (707)
University of Texas (707)
University of Texas - Houston Health Science Center (707)
University of Texas Health Systems (707)
University of Tulsa (708)
University of Utah (708)
University of Vermont (708)
University of Virginia (708)
University of Washington (708)
University Science Alliance (708)
University System of Maryland (708)
University Technology Park (708)
USA Funds, Inc. (709)
Utah State University (710)
Valencia Community College (711)
Vanderbilt University (712)
Vanguard University (712)
Very Special Arts (714)
Villanova University (715)
Virginia Commonwealth University (716)
Virginia Polytechnic Institute and State University (716)
Virginia Tech Intellectual Properties, Inc. (716)
Virtual Impact Productions (716)
Voorhees College (717)
Washington and Jefferson College (719)
Washington State Impact Aid Ass'n (720)
Washington Workshops (720)
WAVE, Inc. (722)
Wayland Academy (722)
Wayne State University (722)
West Chester University (723)
West Virginia University Hospitals, Inc. (723)
Western Kentucky University (724)
Western Michigan University (724)
Westminster College (725)

Wheat Export Trade Education Committee (725)
Wheelock College (726)
Widener University (726)
Wilberforce University (726)
William Tyndale College (727)
Wittenburg University (729)
WNVT/WNVC (729)
Women's College Coalition (729)
Women's Research and Education Institute (730)
The Work Colleges (730)
Yeshiva of South Shore (733)
Young America's Foundation (733)
Young Astronaut Council (733)
Zamorano (734)

Electronics

AAI Corp. (224)
Advanced Acoustic Concepts, Inc. (228)
Advanced Micro Devices (228)
AEPTEC (229)
Aeronautical Radio, Inc. (230)
Aircraft Electronics Ass'n (235)
Allegheny Technologies, Inc. (238)
American Electronics Ass'n (257)
American Superconductor Corp. (278)
AOC (285)
Armed Forces Communications and Electronics Ass'n Headquarters (289)
Ass'n of Home Appliance Manufacturers (296)
BAE SYSTEMS North America (306)
Battelle (309)
Battelle Memorial Labs (309)
Battery Council Internat'l (309)
BEMS W/L Associates (311)
Black & Decker Corp., The (315)
Brewer Science Inc. (319)
Brother Internat'l Co. (322)
Canon USA, Inc. (330)
Canon, Inc. (330)
Cartwright Electronics (332)
Celsius Tech Electronics (335)
CHEMRING, Ltd. (342)
Circuit City Stores, Inc. (347)
Coalition for Electronic Commerce (353)
Cominco, Ltd. (360)
Committee to Preserve American Color Television (361)
Computer and Communications Industry Ass'n (CCIA) (364)
Condor Electronic Systems (365)
Condor Systems (365)
Consumer Electronics Ass'n (369)
Danaher Corp. (382)
Dewey Electronics Corp. (387)
Diamond Antenna & Microwave Corp. (387)
Dictaphone Corp. (388)
DRS Precision Echo Inc. (392)
Eagle-Picher Industries (394)
Eastman Kodak Co. (395)
The Electric Vehicle Ass'n of the Americas (EVAA) (400)
Electronic Commerce Forum (400)
Electronic Commerce Tax Study Group (400)
Electronic Funds Transfer Ass'n (400)
Electronic Industries Alliance (400)
Electronic Industries Ass'n of Japan (401)
Electronic Retailing Ass'n (401)
Electronic Traders Ass'n (401)
Electronic Warfare Associates, Inc. (401)
Electronics Consultants Inc. (401)
Elettronica Veneta & IN.EL. (401)
Engineered Support System, Inc. (ESSI) (403)
Espey Manufacturing and Electronics (407)
Fel Corp. (415)
Fidelity Technologies Corp. (416)
Fisher Imaging (418)
FlightSafety Internat'l (419)
Fujitsu Limited (427)
GE Lighting Group (430)
GEC-Marconi Avionics Group (430)
General Electric Appliances (432)
General Electric Co. (432)
General Signal Corp. (433)
Graseby Plc (438)
Harmon-Motive (444)
Harris Corp. (444)
Hewlett-Packard Co. (449)
The Hitachi Foundation (450)
Hitachi Home Electronics, Inc. (450)
Hitachi, Ltd. (450)
Home Automation Ass'n (451)
Home Recording Rights Coalition (HRRC) (451)
Honeywell Internat'l, Inc. (452)
Hughes Electronics Corp. (454)
IAI Internat'l (456)
IEEE Computer Society (457)
Imaging Technologies Inc. (458)
Information Technology Industry Council (462)
Insight Technology, Inc. (462)
Institute of Electrical and Electronics Engineers, Inc. (464)
Intel Corp. (465)
Intelligent Optical Systems, Inc. (465)
Internat'l Brotherhood of Electrical Workers (469)
Internat'l Business Machines Corp. (469)
Internat'l Electronic Article Surveillance Manufacturers (471)
Internat'l Electronics Manufacturers and Consumers of America (471)
Internat'l Microelectronics and Packaging Soc. - IMAPS (473)
Internat'l Sign Ass'n (474)
Internat'l Technology Resources, Inc. (475)
Internat'l Union of Electronic, Electrical, Salaried, Machine, and Furniture Workers-Communications Workers of America (476)
ITT Industries (480)
ITT Industries Defense (480)
Karta Technologies Inc. (486)
Kemet Electronics Co. (487)
Kollsman, Inc. (490)
Korean Semiconductor Industry Ass'n (491)
Kruger Internat'l (KI) (492)
Kyocera Corp. (492)
Lau Technologies (496)
Lexis-Nexis (498)
Litton Electron Devices (500)
Lockheed Martin IMS (502)
Loral Space and Communications, Ltd. (503)
Massachusetts Technology Park Corp. (512)
Matsushita Electric Corp. of America (513)
Matsushita Electric Industrial Co., Ltd. (513)
Megapulse, Inc. (517)
Mentor Graphics Corp. (518)
Micron Technology, Inc. (522)
Mitsubishi Electric & Electronics, USA (526)
Mitsubishi Electronics America (Consumer Electronics Group) (526)
Motorola Space and Systems Technology Group (531)
Motorola, Inc. (531)
MRJ Technology Solutions (532)
N.V. Philips Gloeilampenfabrieken (534)
Nat'l Ass'n of Metal Finishers (545)
Nat'l Computer Systems (558)
Nat'l Lighting Bureau (570)
Navigational Electronic Chart Systems Ass'n (NECSA) (583)
NEC USA, Inc. (583)
NOKIA (591)
Northrop Grumman Corp. (594)
Oerlikon Aerospace, Inc. (599)
Olin Corp. (600)
Open Group Electronic Messaging Ass'n (EMA) Forum (601)
Pacific Telecom, Inc. (606)
PerkinElmer Detection Systems (612)
Philips Electronics North America Corp. (616)
Photo Telesis (616)
Picker Internat'l (617)
Planet Electric (618)
Polaroid Corp. (620)
Portable Rechargeable Battery Ass'n (621)
Power Paragon Inc. (622)
Powerware (622)
Puerto Rico Electric Power Authority (629)
Radio Shack Corp. (632)
Raychem Corp. (633)
Raytheon Co. (633)
Rockwell Collins (641)
RTCA, Inc. (643)
SAFT America Inc. (645)
Samsung Corp. (647)
Sanyo North American Corp. (649)
SCI Systems, Inc. (652)
Sechan Electronics (654)
Semiconductor Industry Ass'n (655)
Sharp Electronics Corp. (657)
Siemens Corp. (658)
Sony Corp. (665)
Sony Corp. of America (666)
Sony Electronics, Inc. (666)
Sparton Electronics, Florida, Inc. (669)
Spatial Integrated Systems (669)
SPD Technologies (669)
Sub-Zero Freezer Co. Inc. (676)
Syquest Technology, Inc. (679)
Techneglas, Inc. (682)
Teledyne Controls, Inc. (683)
Texas Instruments (684)
Textron Inc. (685)
Thompson Lighting Protection Inc. (686)
Thomson Consumer Electronics, Inc. (686)
Titan Scan (687)
Toshiba Consumer Products, Inc. (688)
Toshiba Corp. (688)
TRW Inc. (693)
TRW Systems Integration Group (693)
Unisys Corp. (700)
United Electrical Workers of America (701)
Video Network Communications (715)
Vishay Intertechnologies, Inc. (716)
Xerox Corp. (732)
Zenith Electronics Corp. (734)

Employees and Employment

ABLEDATA (225)
Academy for Educational Development - Nat'l Institute for Work and Learning (225)
ACB Government Employees (226)
Access Technology Ass'n (226)
Accrediting Council for Continuing Education & Training (226)
Administaff (227)
AFL-CIO - Professional Employees Department (231)
Alliance to Keep Americans Working (241)
American Ass'n of Occupational Health Nurses (248)
American College of Occupational and Environmental Medicine (254)
American Federation of Government Employees (AFL-CIO) (258)
American Federation of State, County and Municipal Employees (258)
American Payroll Ass'n (269)
American Rehab Action (272)
American Soc. for Training and Development (275)
American Staffing Ass'n (278)
Asian Pacific American Labor Alliance, AFL-CIO (291)
Ass'n for Career and Technical Education (291)
Ass'n of Farmworker Opportunity Programs (295)
Ass'n of Occupational Health Professionals in Healthcare (297)
Ass'n of Test Publishers (299)
Brotherhood of Maintenance of Way Employees (322)
Business and Professional Women/USA (324)
California Public Employees' Retirement System (327)
Center for Dispute Settlement (336)
Center for Employment Training (336)
The Church Alliance (346)
Citizens for Workers' Compensation Reform (349)
Coalition for Employment Opportunities (353)
Coalition for Employment through Exports (353)
Coalition for Job Growth and Internat'l Competitiveness Through AMT Reform (354)
Coalition for Job Opportunities (354)
Coalition for Professional Certification (354)
Coalition for Workers' Health Care Funds (355)
College and University Professional Ass'n for Human Resources (357)
Committee for Purchase from People Who Are Blind or Severely Disabled (361)
Corporation for Business, Work and Learning (372)
Council of State Administrators of Vocational Rehabilitation (376)
Crosby Internat'l (378)
Education and Training Resources (398)
Employee Assistance Professionals Ass'n (402)
Employee Benefit Research Institute (402)
Employers Council on Flexible Compensation (402)
Employment Policies Institute Foundation (402)
Employment Policy Foundation (402)
The ERISA Industry Committee (ERIC) (406)
The ESOP (Employee Stock Ownership Plan) Ass'n (407)
Family and Medical Leave Act Technical Corrections Coalition (410)
Federal Employees Education and Assistance Fund (413)
First Tuesday Group (418)
Global Associates (436)
Government Employees Hospital Ass'n (437)
Home Office Ass'n of America (451)
Hospitality Employers Ass'n (453)
Institute for a Drug-Free Workplace (463)
Integrated Management Resources Group, Inc. (465)
Internat'l Ass'n of Business, Industry and Rehabilitation (467)
Internat'l Ass'n of Personnel in Employment Security (468)
Internat'l Labor Office (472)
Internat'l Personnel Management Ass'n (474)
Internat'l Soc. for Performance Improvement (475)
Internat'l Union of Electronic, Electrical, Salaried, Machine, and Furniture Workers-Communications Workers of America (476)
JHP, Inc. (Jobs Have Priority) (483)
Job Opportunities Business Symposium (483)
Jobs for Youth (483)
Kelly Services, Inc. (487)
Labor for America PAC (493)
Laborers Institute for Training and Education (493)
Laborers-AGC Education and Training Fund (493)
Louisiana Workers' Compensation Corporation (504)
Mainstream, Inc. (507)
Metcor, Ltd. (519)
Nat'l Alliance Against Blacklisting (536)
Nat'l Alliance of Business (536)
Nat'l Alliance of Postal and Federal Employees (536)
Nat'l Ass'n for the Self-Employed (538)
Nat'l Ass'n of Broadcast Employees and Technicians-Communications Workers of America, AFL-CIO (NABET-CWA) (539)
Nat'l Ass'n of County Training and Employment Professionals (541)
Nat'l Ass'n of Executive Secretaries and Administrative Assistants (542)
Nat'l Ass'n of Government Deferred Compensation Administrators (543)
Nat'l Ass'n of Government Employees (543)
Nat'l Ass'n of Older Worker Employment Services (546)
Nat'l Ass'n of Personnel Services (546)
Nat'l Ass'n of Private Industry Councils (546)
Nat'l Ass'n of Professional Employer Organizations (547)
Nat'l Ass'n of Retired Federal Employees (548)
Nat'l Ass'n of State Directors of Vocational Technical Education Consortium (550)

Nat'l Ass'n of State Workforce Agencies (550)
Nat'l Ass'n of Student Personnel Administrators (550)
Nat'l Board for Certification in Occupational Therapy, Inc. (552)
Nat'l Committee on Pay Equity (557)
Nat'l Coordinating Committee for Multiemployer Plans (559)
Nat'l Council of Agricultural Employers (560)
Nat'l Defined Contribution Council (561)
Nat'l Employee Benefits Institute (562)
Nat'l Employment Lawyers Ass'n (562)
Nat'l Employment Opportunities Network (563)
Nat'l Federation of Federal Employees (564)
Nat'l Job Corps Ass'n (569)
Nat'l Labor Relations Board Professional Ass'n (569)
Nat'l Organization for Competency Assurance (572)
Nat'l Right to Work Committee (576)
Nat'l Right to Work Legal Defense Foundation (576)
Nat'l Weather Service Employees Organization (581)
NISH - Creating Employment Opportunities for People with Severe Disabilities (590)
Organization of Professional Employees of the U.S. Dep't of Agriculture (OPEDA) (603)
OSHA Reform Coalition (604)
Public Employee Retirement Systems of Colorado (628)
Public Employees Roundtable (628)
Public Service Research Foundation (629)
Return to Work Coalition (639)
Senior Executives Ass'n (655)
Severance Trust Executive Program (656)
Skills USA-VICA (660)
Small Business Council of America (661)
Soc. for Human Resource Management (662)
Soc. of Professional Benefit Administrators (664)
Special Committee for Workplace Product Liability Reform (669)
Staff Builders, Inc. (672)
USA WORKS! (709)
UWC - Strategic Services on Unemployment and Workers' Compensation (711)
WAVE, Inc. (722)
Welfare to Work Partnership (722)
Wider Opportunities for Women (726)
Women's Information Network (729)
Work Opportunity Tax Credit Coalition (730)
Working Today (730)
The Wyatt Co. (732)
Youthbuild, USA (734)

Energy/Electricity

ABB Combustion Engineering Nuclear Power (224)
ABB, Inc. (225)
Advanced Transit Ass'n (229)
AECL Technologies (229)
Aera Energy LLC (230)
The AES Corp. (230)
Alabama Gas Corp. (235)
Alabama Power (236)
Allegheny Energy, Inc. (238)
Allegheny Ludlum Corp. (238)
Allegheny Power Service Corp. (238)
Allegheny River Mining Co. (238)
Allete (239)
Alliance for Competitive Electricity (239)
Alliance for Nuclear Accountability (240)
Alliance to Save Energy (241)
Alliant Energy (241)
Ameren Services (243)
American Ass'n of Blacks in Energy (246)
American Bioenergy Ass'n (251)
American Board of Health Physics (251)
American Council for an Energy-Efficient Economy (255)
American Electric Power Co. (257)
American Gas Ass'n (261)
American Methanol Institute (268)
American Nuclear Insurers (268)
American Petroleum Institute (269)
American Public Gas Ass'n (271)
American Public Power Ass'n (272)
American Ref-Fuel (272)
American Standard Cos. Inc. (278)
American Wind Energy Ass'n (280)
Americans for Affordable Electricity (281)
Anaheim, California, Public Utilities of the City of (283)
Appalachian-Pacific Coal Mine Methane Power Co., LLC (286)
ARCADIS/California Energy Commission (287)
Arctic Power (288)
Arizona Power Authority (288)
Arizona Public Service Co. (288)
ARK Energy, Inc. (288)
Arkenol, Inc. (288)
Ashland Inc. (290)
Atomic Energy of Canada (302)
Auburn, Avilla, Bluffton, Columbia City and Other Municipalities of Indiana (302)
Ballard Power Systems (306)
Bangor Hydro-Electric Co. (307)
Basin Electric Power Cooperative (308)
Battery Council Internat'l (309)
Bechtel Group, Inc. (310)
Bergen, New York, Village of (311)
Biotechnology Industry Organization (314)
Boston Edison Co. (318)
Breakthrough Technologies Institute (319)
British Nuclear Fuels plc (321)
James W. Bunger & Associates (323)
Burlington Resources Oil & Gas Co. (324)
Burns and Roe Enterprises, Inc. (324)
Business Council for Sustainable Energy (324)
Buyers Up (325)
Cadmus/Energy Star (326)
Caithness Energy, LLC (326)
CalEnergy Co., Inc. (326)
California Independent System Operator (327)
Calpine Corp. (328)
Cambria Community Services District (328)
CAMECO Corp. (328)
Canadian Electricity Ass'n (329)
Canberra Packard BioScience (330)
Center for Energy and Economic Development (336)
Central Illinois Public Service Co. (339)
Central Montana Electric Power Cooperative, Inc. (339)
Central Virginia Electric Cooperative, Inc. (339)
Chelan County Public Utility District (342)
The Chevron Companies (342)
Chevron, U.S.A. (342)
Chubu Electric Power Co. (346)
Cinergy Corp. (347)
Clayton, Dover, Lewes, Middletown, Milford, Newark, NewCastle, Seaford and Smyrna, Delaware, Municipalities of (350)
Clean Energy Group (350)
Clean Fuels Development Coalition (350)
Coal Exporters Ass'n of the U.S. (352)
Coal Utilization Research Council (352)
Coalition for Reliable Energy (354)
COGEMA, Inc. (357)
College Station, Texas, City of (358)
Colonial Pipeline Co. (358)
Colorado River Energy Distributors Ass'n (358)
Colorado Springs Utilities (359)
Columbia Gas Transmission Corp. (359)
ComEd (359)
Comision Ejecutiva Hidroelectrica del Rio Lempa CEL (360)
Commercial Service Co., Ltd. (360)
Consolidated Edison Co. of New York (367)
Consortium Plant Biotech Research (368)
Constellation Energy Group (368)
Constellation Technology Corp. (368)
Consumer Energy Council of America Research Foundation (369)
Consumers Energy Co. (369)
Corn Belt Energy Corp. (372)
Council for Affordable Reliable Energy (CARE) (374)
Council for Energy Independence (374)
Council of Industrial Boiler Owners (CIBO) (375)
Covanta Energy Corporation (377)
Craig-Botetourt Electric Cooperative, Inc. (378)
D3 Internat'l Energy, LLC (381)
DAG Petroleum (381)
Dairyland Power Cooperative (381)
Delaware Municipal Electric Corp. (DEMEC) (384)
Desert Research Institute (386)
Detroit Edison Co. (386)
Devon Energy Corp. (387)
Distributed Power Coalition of America (390)
Duke Power Co. (393)
Earth, Energy & Environment (394)
East Texas Electric Cooperative (395)
Eclipse Energy Systems, Inc./Insyte, Inc. (396)
Edison Electric Institute (397)
Edison Internat'l (397)
Edison Mission Energy (397)
El Paso Electric Co. (399)
El Paso Natural Gas Co. (399)
Electric Power Research Institute (400)
Electric Power Supply Ass'n (400)
Electricite de France Internat'l North America, Inc. (400)
ElectriCities of North Carolina, Inc. (400)
Electricity Consumers Resource Council (ELCON) (400)
Electro Energy, Inc. (400)
Electro Scientific Industries, Inc. (400)
Electromagnetic Energy Ass'n (400)
Energy Affairs Administration (403)
Energy and Environment Coalition (403)
Energy Communities Alliance, Inc. (403)
Energy Conservation Program, Inc. (403)
Energy Contractors Price-Anderson Group (403)
Energy Cost Savings Council (403)
Energy Efficiency Systems, Inc. (403)
Energy Northwest (403)
Energy Pacific, Inc. (403)
Energy Programs Consortium (403)
EnerTech Industries Inc. (403)
Enron Corp. (403)
Enron Wind Corp./Zond (404)
Entergy Services, Inc. (404)
Entex, Inc. (404)
Environmental and Energy Study Institute (404)
EnviroPower (405)
Equitable Resources Energy Co. (406)
Eugene Water and Electric Board (407)
European Energy Company Coalition (408)
Exelon Corp. (409)
Export Council for Energy Efficiency (409)
Federation of American Scientists (414)
Federation of Electric Power Cos. of Japan (414)
Fibrowatt, Inc. (416)
FirstEnergy Co. (418)
Florida Municipal Power Agency (420)
Florida Power and Light Co. (420)
Foster Wheeler Corp. (424)
Four Dam Pool (424)
Framatome, S.A. (424)
Freeport, New York, Electric Department of the Village of (425)
Freeport-McMoRan Copper & Gold Inc. (425)
Fuel Cell Energy, Inc. (427)
Fuel Cell Power Ass'n (427)
FuelMaker Corp. (427)
Gary-Williams Energy Corp. (429)
Gas Research Institute (429)
Gas Technology Institute (429)
Gas Turbine Ass'n, Inc. (429)
Gasification Technologies Council (429)
GE Nuclear Energy (430)
GE Power Systems (430)
General Atomics (431)
General Electric Co. (432)
Geothermal Resources Ass'n (434)
GPU, Inc. (438)
Grant County P.U.D., Washington (438)
Green Mountain Power Corp. (440)
Greenport, New York, Village Electric Department of (440)
Gridley, California, City of/Northern California Power Agency (440)
GSE Systems, Inc. (441)
Hagerstown, Maryland, Municipal Electric Light Plant of (443)
Hawaii, Department of Business and Economic Development of the State of (445)
Hawaiian Electric Co. (445)
Health Physics Soc. (446)
Hearth Products Ass'n (447)
Holyoke Department of Gas and Electricity (451)
Home Automation Ass'n (451)
Hoosier Energy Rural Electric Cooperative, Inc. (452)
Howard Energy Internat'l (454)
Hydro-Quebec (456)
ICRC Energy, Inc. (457)
Indiana and Michigan Municipal Distributors Ass'n (460)
Industrial Customers of Northwest Utilities (461)
informal coalition (461)
Institute of Electrical and Electronics Engineers, Inc. (464)
Integrated Waste Services Ass'n (465)
Internat'l Center (469)
Internat'l District Energy Ass'n (471)
Internat'l Institute for Energy Conservation (472)
Internat'l Paper (473)
Internat'l Power Machines (474)
Internat'l Utility Efficiency Partnerships (IUEP) (476)
Interstate Natural Gas Ass'n of America (477)
IPALCO Enterprises, Inc./Indianapolis Power & Light Co. (478)
ITT Conoflow (480)
Jamestown, New York, Board of Public Utilities (481)
Japan Nuclear Cycle Development Institute (482)
Johnson Controls, Inc. (484)
Kansas City Power & Light Co. (486)
Kansas Gas Service (486)
Kerr-McGee Corp. (488)
Ketchikan Public Utilities (488)
KeySpan Energy (489)
KN Energy Inc. (490)
Koch Industries, Inc. (490)
Kootenai Electric Cooperative, Inc. (491)
LACDA Alliance (493)
Laclede Gas Co. (494)
Large Public Power Council (495)
Louisiana Energy Services (504)
M-S-R Public Power Agency (506)
Magellan Carbon Fuels (507)
Maine Public Service Co. (507)
Massena, New York, Town of (512)
MATEK (513)
Maxus Energy Corp. (513)
Memphis Light, Gas and Water Division (517)
Meridian Oil Inc. (519)
Mesa Inc. (519)
Methanex Inc. (520)
Metro Machine of Pennsylvania, Inc. (520)
Michigan Consolidated Gas Co. (522)
Michigan Municipal/Cooperative Group (522)
Mid-West Electric Consumers Ass'n (523)
MidAmerican Energy Holdings Co. (523)
MidWest ISO Transmission Owners (523)
Midwest Research Institute (524)
Minnesota Power (525)
Mirant (526)
Mishawaka Utilities (526)
Missouri Public Service Co. (526)
Modesto/Turlock Irrigation District (527)
Municipal Electric Authority of Georgia (532)
Municipal Electric Utilities Ass'n of New York State (532)
NAC Internat'l (534)
Nat'l Ass'n of Energy Service Companies (542)
Nat'l Ass'n of State Energy Officials (550)
Nat'l Center for Appropriate Technology (554)
Nat'l Council of Coal Lessors (560)

Nat'l Council on Radiation Protection and Measurement (561)
Nat'l Defense Council Foundation (561)
Nat'l Electrical Contractors Ass'n (562)
Nat'l Electrical Manufacturers Ass'n (562)
Nat'l Electrical Safety Foundation (562)
Nat'l Energy Assistance Directors' Ass'n (563)
Nat'l Energy Resources Organization (563)
Nat'l Grid USA (566)
Nat'l Hydropower Ass'n (567)
Nat'l Ocean Industries Ass'n (572)
Nat'l Oilheat Research Alliance (NORA) (572)
Nat'l Petrochemical Refiners Ass'n (573)
Nat'l Power (574)
Nat'l Propane Gas Ass'n (574)
Nat'l Rural Electric Cooperative Ass'n (576)
Natural Gas Supply Ass'n (582)
Natural Gas Vehicle Coalition (582)
Nebraska Ethanol Board (583)
New Energy and Industrial Technology Development Organization (NEDO) (585)
New York Municipal Power Agency (587)
Nicor, Inc. (589)
NiSource Inc. (590)
North American Electric Reliability Council (592)
North Carolina Electric Membership Corp. (593)
Northeast Texas Electric Cooperative (593)
Northern California Power Agency (594)
Northwest Energy Efficiency Alliance (595)
Northwest Public Power Ass'n (595)
Northwestern Public Service (596)
NSTAR (596)
Nuclear Control Institute (597)
Nuclear Energy Institute (597)
Nuclear Information and Resource Service (597)
NUI Environmental Group Inc. (597)
Occidental Petroleum Corporation (598)
Oglethorpe Power Corp. (599)
Ohio Municipal Electric Ass'n (599)
Oklahoma Gas and Electric Co. (599)
Oklahoma Natural Gas Co. (599)
Olga Coal Co. (600)
Oregon Utility Resource Coordination Ass'n (OURCA) (603)
Orlando Utilities Commission (603)
Otter Tail Power Co. (604)
PacifiCorp (606)
Palo Alto, California, City of (607)
Pan-Alberta Gas Ltd. (607)
Panda Energy Internat'l (607)
Paper, Allied-Industrial, Chemical and Energy Workers Internat'l Union (PACE) (607)
Partnership for Early Climate Action (608)
The Peabody Group (610)
PerkinElmer Detection Systems (612)
PG&E Corp. (614)
PG&E Generating Co. (614)
Pinnacle West Capital Corp. (617)
PJM Interconnection, L.L.C. (618)
Plattsburgh, New York, City of (619)
Portable Rechargeable Battery Ass'n (621)
Portland General Electric Co. (621)
Potomac Electric Power Co. (622)
Power and Communications Contractors Ass'n (622)
Power Distribution, Inc. (PDI) (622)
Powerspan Corp. (622)
PPL (622)
Private Fuels Storage, L.L.C. (625)
Process Gas Consumers Group (625)
Progress Energy (626)
Propane Consumers Coalition (627)
Providence Gas (627)
PSE&G (627)
Public Generating Pool (628)
Public Power Council (629)
Public Service Co. of New Mexico (629)
Puerto Rico Electric Power Authority (629)
Pure Energy Corp. (630)
PURPA Reform Group (630)
Questar Corp. (631)
Redding, California, Electric Department of the City of (635)
Reliant Energy, Inc. (636)
Renew America (636)
Renewable Fuels Ass'n (637)
Repeal PUHCA Now Coalition (637)
Rockville Centre, New York, Village of (641)
Rolls-Royce North America Inc. (642)
Safe Energy Communication Council (645)
Salamanca, New York, City Board of Public Utilities of (646)
Salt River Project (646)
San Antonio City Public Service (647)
Santa Clara, California, Electric Department of the City of (649)
Santee Cooper (South Carolina Public Service Authority) (649)
Schlumberger Technology Corp. (651)
Schott Corp. (652)
Science Applications Internat'l Corp. (SAIC) (652)
SEMCO (655)
Sempra Energy (655)
Seneca Resources Corporation (655)
Sithe Energies (660)
Soc. of Nuclear Medicine (663)
Solar Electric Light Co. (665)
Solar Energy Industries Ass'n (SEIA) (665)
Solar Energy Research and Education Foundation (665)
South Mississippi Electric Power Ass'n (666)
Southeastern Federal Power Customers, Inc. (667)
Southern California Public Power Authority (667)
Southern Co. (667)
Southern Generation (668)
Southern Maryland Electric Cooperative, Inc. (668)
Southwestern Electric Cooperative, Inc. (668)
Southwestern Public Service Co. (668)
Statoil Energy (673)
Steam Generator Coalition (673)
Stewart & Stevenson Services, Inc. (674)
Stirling Energy Systems (674)
Taiwan Power Co. (680)
TECO Energy, Inc. (682)
Tennessee Valley Authority - Washington Office (683)
Tennessee Valley Public Power Ass'n (683)
Tex-La Electric Cooperative of Texas (684)
Texas Municipal Power Agency (685)
The Texas Wind Power Co. (685)
Thermo EcoTek Corp. (686)
ThermoEnergy Corp. (686)
The Tokyo Electric Power Company, Inc. (688)
Toledo Edison Co. (688)
Transconsortia (690)
Transmission Access Policy Study Group (690)
Transmission Agency of Northern California (690)
Trigen Energy Corp. (692)
Trinity Public Utilities District (692)
Trizec Hahn Corp. (692)
Tumalo Irrigation District (694)
TXU Business Services (695)
Union of Concerned Scientists (699)
United Cities Gas Co. (701)
United Mine Workers of America (702)
United States Energy Ass'n (703)
United States Windpower, Inc. (704)
University of California at Irvine Advanced Power and Energy Program (706)
Urenco, Inc. (709)
USA Biomass Power Producers Alliance (709)
USEC, Inc. (710)
UtiliCorp United, Inc. (711)
Utility Workers Union of America (711)
Valero Energy Corp. (711)
Voith Hydro, Inc. (717)
Washington Gas (719)
Waste Policy Institute (721)
Western Coal Traffic League (724)
Western Interconnection Coordination Forum (724)
Western Resources (724)
Westinghouse Electric Co. (725)
Wickland Oil Co. (726)
The Williams Companies (727)
Wisconsin Energy Corp. (728)
Wisconsin Public Service Corp. (729)
Wolf Creek Nuclear Operating Corp. (729)
World Wide Energy Group (731)
Worldwatch Institute (731)
Xcel Energy, Inc. (732)
Yukon Pacific (734)

Engineering

ABB Combustion Engineering Nuclear Power (224)
ABB, Inc. (225)
Advanced Machinery Logistics, Inc. (228)
AECL Technologies (229)
Air & Water Technologies (233)
Air Products and Chemicals, Inc. (234)
Airport Consultants Council (235)
Allegheny Technologies, Inc. (238)
American Ass'n of Engineering Societies (247)
American Congress on Surveying and Mapping (255)
American Consulting Engineers Council (255)
American Council of Independent Laboratories (255)
American Institute of Aeronautics and Astronautics (264)
American Institute of Certified Planners (264)
American Institute of Chemical Engineers (264)
American Nat'l Metric Council (268)
American Planning Ass'n (270)
American Public Works Ass'n (272)
American Science and Engineering, Inc. (273)
American Soc. for Engineering Education (274)
American Soc. for Photogrammetry and Remote Sensing (275)
American Soc. of Civil Engineers (276)
American Soc. of Heating, Refrigerating and Air Conditioning Engineers (276)
American Soc. of Mechanical Engineers (276)
American Soc. of Naval Engineers (276)
American Soc. of Safety Engineers (277)
American Standard Cos. Inc. (278)
APTI (287)
Arcata Associates, Inc. (287)
Argon Engineering Associates (288)
ARINC, Inc. (288)
ASFE (290)
Ass'n of State Dam Safety Officials (299)
Assurance Technology Corp. (301)
AUPS/Mo Hussain (303)
Babcock & Wilcox (305)
Ball Aerospace & Technology Corp. (306)
Bechtel Group, Inc. (310)
Bechtel/Parsons Brinkeroff Joint Venture (310)
Burk-Kleinpeter, Inc. (324)
Burns and Roe Enterprises, Inc. (324)
Calibre Corp. (326)
CH2M Hill (340)
Coleman Research Corp. (357)
Columbia Research Corp. (359)
Consulting Engineers Council of Metropolitan Washington (368)
Council for Chemical Research, Inc. (374)
Council on Federal Procurement of Architectural and Engineering Services (COFPAES) (376)
Covanta Energy Corporation (377)
Crane Co. (378)
Dames & Moore (382)
Dana Corp. (382)
Daniel, Mann, Johnson & Mendenhall (382)
Day & Zimmermann, Inc. (383)
DDL OMNI Engineering Corp. (383)
Design Professionals Coalition (386)
Designers & Planners, Inc. (386)
Duke Solutions (393)
Electro-Radiation Inc. (400)
Electronic Industries Alliance (400)
Environmental Technology Council (405)
ERIM (406)
Erin Engineering and Research, Inc. (406)
Federal Facilities Council (413)
Fluor Corp. (420)
Foster Wheeler Corp. (424)
Framatome, S.A. (424)
Frequency Engineering Laboratories (425)
Greenman Technologies Inc. (440)
Halliburton/Brown & Root (443)
Harza Engineering Co. (445)
Honeywell Internat'l, Inc. (452)
Howard, Meedles, Tammen & Bergendoff (454)
Hyundai Pipe Co. (456)
Hyundai Precision & Industrial Co., Ltd. (456)
Ibex (456)
ICF Consulting (457)
ICF Industries, Inc. (457)
IEEE Computer Society (457)
Industrial Designers Soc. of America (461)
Innovative Technical Solutions (462)
Institute of Electrical and Electronics Engineers, Inc. (464)
Institute of Transportation Engineers (464)
Intelligent Optical Systems, Inc. (465)
Internat'l Federation of Professional and Technical Engineers (471)
Internat'l Institute of Ammonia Refrigeration (472)
Internat'l Union of Operating Engineers (476)
Jacobs Engineering Group Inc. (481)
Kellogg Brown and Root (487)
Kennedy/Jenks Consultants (488)
Marine Engineers Beneficial Ass'n (District No. 1 - PCD) (510)
Marine Technology Soc. (510)
Mercer Engineering Research Center (518)
Minnesota Mining and Manufacturing Co. (Traffic Control Materials Division) (525)
Montgomery Watson (528)
Nat'l Academy of Engineering (535)
Nat'l Academy of Sciences (535)
Nat'l Ass'n of County Engineers (541)
Nat'l Ass'n of County Information Technology Administrators (541)
Nat'l Ass'n of County Planners (541)
Nat'l Institute for Certification in Engineering Technologies (568)
Nat'l Institute of Building Sciences (568)
Nat'l Soc. of Black Engineers (578)
Nat'l Soc. of Professional Engineers (578)
New Mexico State University, Department of Engineering (586)
North American Technician Excellence (593)
Northpoint Technology, Ltd. (594)
Northrop Grumman Corp. (594)
Parsons Brinckerhoff Inc. (608)
Parsons Corp. (608)
Plasma-Therm, Inc. (619)
Professional Airways Systems Specialists (AFL-CIO) (625)
Professional Engineering (625)
Professional Services Council (626)
Public Technology Inc. (629)
Quest Nevada, Inc. (631)
Ramgen Power Systems, Inc. (632)
Recovery Engineering, Inc. (634)
J. P. Redd Inc. (635)
Rehabilitation Engineering and Assistive Technology Soc. of North America (636)
Rineco Chemical Industries (640)
Roecker Engineering Co. (641)
Science and Engineering Associates, Inc. (652)
Scientech Corp. (652)
Scram Technologies Inc. (652)
Sensor Technologies and Systems Inc. (655)
Separation Technologies (655)
Siemens Corp. (658)
Silverline Technologies, Inc. (659)
Simula, Inc. (659)

The Smith, Korach, Hayet, Haynie Partnership (661)
SSI Services, Inc. (671)
Stone and Webster Engineering Corp. (675)
Tensor Technologies, Inc. (684)
Texas A&M Engineering Experiment Station (684)
Texas Tech University System (685)
TRAUX Engineering (691)
USX Corp. (710)
Veridian Engineering (713)
Vulcan Chemicals (718)
Waggoner Engineering, Inc. (718)
Washington Group Internat'l (719)
Washington Infrastructure Services, Inc. (719)
Waveband, Inc. (722)
Weidlinger Associates, Inc. (722)

Environment and Conservation

20/20 Vision (223)
African Wildlife Foundation (232)
Africare (232)
Air & Water Technologies (233)
Air Quality Standards Coalition (234)
AKT Developments (235)
Alaska Wilderness League (237)
Allegheny Technologies, Inc. (238)
Alliance for Responsible Atmospheric Policy (240)
Alliance of Marine Mammal Parks and Aquariums (240)
Alliance to Save Energy (241)
Alternative Systems, Inc. (242)
America Outdoors (243)
American Bird Conservancy (251)
American Board of Health Physics (251)
American Coastal Coalition (253)
American College of Occupational and Environmental Medicine (254)
American Council for an Energy-Efficient Economy (255)
American Farmland Trust (258)
American Forest Foundation (260)
American Forests (260)
American Geophysical Union (261)
American Green Network (261)
American Industrial Hygiene Ass'n (263)
American Institute for Conservation of Historic and Artistic Works (263)
American Institute of Biological Sciences (264)
The American Land Conservancy (265)
American Land Rights Ass'n (265)
American Methanol Institute (268)
American Paperboard Packaging Environment Council (269)
American Ref-Fuel (272)
American Rivers (273)
American Zoo and Aquarium Ass'n (281)
Americans for Equitable Climate Solutions (281)
Animas-La Plata Water Conservancy District (284)
The Antarctica Project (285)
Aquarium of the Pacific (287)
Arkenol, Inc. (288)
Asbestos Recycling Inc. (290)
Asea Brown Boveri, Inc. (290)
Asphalt Recycling and Reclaiming Ass'n (291)
Ass'n of California Water Agencies (295)
Ass'n of Consulting Foresters of America (295)
Ass'n of Local Air Pollution Control Officials (296)
Ass'n of Nat'l Estuary Programs (297)
Ass'n of Occupational and Environmental Clinics (297)
The Audubon Institute (302)
Automotive Recyclers Ass'n (304)
B.C. Internat'l Corp. (305)
Bennett Environmental Inc. (311)
Bergen, New York, Village of (311)
Biotechnology Industry Organization (314)
BOH Environmental, L.L.C. (317)
Breakthrough Technologies Institute (319)
Bristol Resource Recovery Facility Operating Committee (320)
Broward, Florida, Department of Natural Resource Protection of the County of (322)
Burns and Roe Enterprises, Inc. (324)
Business Council on Indoor Air (324)
California State Lands Commission (327)
Campbell Estate (329)
Carrying Capacity Network, Inc. (332)
Rachel Carson Council, Inc. (332)
Center for Clean Air Policy (335)
Center for Health, Environment and Justice (336)
Center for Innovation and the Environment, Progressive Foundation (336)
Center for Marine Conservation (337)
Center for Resource Economics (337)
Center for the Study of Responsive Law (338)
Central Utah Water Conservancy District (339)
Central Valley Project Water Ass'n (339)
CH2M Hill (340)
Chemical Land Holdings, Inc. (342)
Citizens Coal Council (348)
Clean Air Action Corp. (350)
Clean Air Now (350)
Clean Air Regulatory Information Group (350)
Clean Fuels Development Coalition (350)
Clean Water Act Reauthorization Coalition (350)
Clean Water Action (350)
Clean Water Council (350)
Clean Water Network (350)
Clearwater Environmental, Inc. (350)
The Climate Council, (351)
Climate Institute (351)
Coalition for Effective Environmental Information (353)
Coalition for Responsible Waste Incineration (354)
Coalition for Truth in Environmental Marketing Information, Inc. (355)
Coast Alliance (356)
Coastal Conservation Ass'n (356)
Coastal States Organization (356)
Committee for Humane Legislation (361)
Committee to Preserve Aspen (361)
Concern, Inc. (365)
Congressional Institute for the Future (366)
The Conservation Fund (367)
Conservation Internat'l Foundation (367)
Consumer Energy Council of America Research Foundation (369)
Container Recycling Institute (370)
Corporate Environmental Enforcement Council (CEEC) (372)
Council for Conservation and Reinvestment of OCS Revenue (374)
Covanta Energy Corporation (377)
Creme de la Creme, Inc. (378)
Defenders of Property Rights (383)
Defenders of Wildlife (383)
Delta Wetlands Project (385)
DeMil Internat'l (385)
Desert Research Institute (386)
Designers & Planners, Inc. (386)
Dolphin Safe/Fair Trade Campaign (390)
Dredging Contractors of America (392)
Ducks Unlimited Inc. (392)
Earth Share (394)
Earthjustice Legal Defense Fund (394)
EarthVoice (394)
EarthWatch, Inc. (395)
Ecological and Toxicological Ass'n of Dyes and Organic Pigments Manufacturers (396)
Ecological Soc. of America (396)
Ecology and Environment (396)
Endangered Species Coordinating Council (402)
Energy and Environment Coalition (403)
Energy Conservation Program, Inc. (403)
Energy Efficiency Systems, Inc. (403)
Envirocare of Utah, Inc. (404)
Environmental Action Group (404)
Environmental and Energy Study Institute (404)
Environmental Business Action Coalition (404)
The Environmental Business Ass'n (405)
The Environmental Co., Inc. (405)
Environmental Commonsense Coalition (405)
Environmental Defense Fund (405)
Environmental Industry Coalition (405)
Environmental Information Ass'n (405)
Environmental Land Technology Ltd. (405)
Environmental Law Institute (405)
Environmental Media Services (405)
Environmental Mutagen Soc. (405)
Environmental Research and Education Foundation (405)
Environmental Systems Research Institute, Inc. (405)
Environmental Technology Council (405)
Environmental Treatment and Technologies Corp. (405)
Environmental Working Group (405)
EnviroPower (405)
Envirotest Systems Corp. (405)
Episcopal Diocese of Washington (406)
Everglades Coordinating Council (408)
Everglades Defense Council (408)
Everglades Trust (408)
Export Council for Energy Efficiency (409)
Exxon Valdez Oil Spill Litigation Plaintiffs (409)
FANCOR (411)
Farm Animal Reform Movement (FARM) (411)
Fideicomiso de la Escuela de Agricultura de la Region Tropical Humeda, S.A. (416)
Fishable Waters Coalition (418)
Foster Wheeler Corp. (424)
Foster Wheeler Environmental Corp. (424)
The Foundation for Environmental and Economic Progress (424)
Freeport, New York, Electric Department of the Village of (425)
Friends of the Earth (426)
Friends of the Everglades (426)
The Fund for Animals (427)
GEO Centers, Inc. (433)
Global Climate Coalition (436)
Global Environment Facility (436)
Global Waste Recycling, Inc. (436)
Grand Isle Independent Levee District (438)
Greenpeace, U.S.A. (440)
Ground Water Protection Council (441)
Gulf Coast Waste Disposal Authority (442)
Gulfstream TLC, Inc. (442)
Health Physics Soc. (446)
Hill Internat'l, Inc. (449)
Housatonic Resources Recovery Authority (453)
Humane Soc. of the United States (455)
Imperial Irrigation District (458)
Institute for Conservation Leadership (463)
Institute for Local Self-Reliance (463)
Institute of Scrap Recycling Industries, Inc. (464)
Institutions and Governance Program (464)
Internat'l Ass'n of Fish and Wildlife Agencies (468)
Internat'l Climate Change Partnership (470)
Internat'l Geographic Information Foundation (472)
Internat'l Institute for Energy Conservation (472)
Irrigation Ass'n (479)
ISAR, Initiative for Social Action and Renewal in Eurasia (479)
IT Group, Inc. (479)
IUCN - The World Conservation Union (US) (480)
Izaak Walton League of America (480)
Jacobs Engineering Group Inc. (481)
Jamestown, New York, Board of Public Utilities (481)
Japan Industrial Conference for Ozone Layer Protection (482)
Japan Industrial Conference on Cleaning (482)
Kaweah Delta Water Conservation District (487)
Kellogg Brown and Root (487)
Kodiak Brown Bear Trust (490)
Lake Preservation Coalition (494)
Land Trust Alliance (494)
League of Conservation Voters (497)
League of Private Property Voters (497)
Louisiana Department of Wildlife and Fisheries - Fur and Refuse Division (504)
Magnificent Research Inc. (507)
Marine Technology Soc. (510)
Marion County Solid Waste Management (510)
Martinizing Environmental Group (511)
MEI Corp. (517)
Metals Industry Recycling Coalition (519)
The Metropolitan Water District of Southern California (521)
Mickey Leland Nat'l Urban Air Toxics Research Center (522)
Migrant Legal Action Program (524)
Mineral Policy Center (525)
Mineral Technologies, Inc. (525)
Mobile Climate Control (527)
Montana Land Reliance (528)
Morning Star Institute, The (529)
Nat'l Ass'n for Environmental Management (537)
Nat'l Ass'n for Plastic Container Recovery (538)
Nat'l Ass'n of Conservation Districts (540)
Nat'l Ass'n of Service and Conservation Corps (549)
Nat'l Audubon Soc. (552)
Nat'l Coalition Against the Misuse of Pesticides (556)
Nat'l Council for Science and the Environment (559)
Nat'l Council on Radiation Protection and Measurement (561)
Nat'l Ecological Foundation (562)
Nat'l Endangered Species Act Reform Coalition (563)
Nat'l Environmental Development Ass'n, Inc. (563)
Nat'l Environmental Education and Training Center (563)
Nat'l Environmental Policy Institute (563)
Nat'l Environmental Trust (563)
Nat'l Grange (566)
Nat'l Institute for Water Resources (568)
Nat'l Institute of Building Sciences (568)
Nat'l Marine Life Center (570)
Nat'l Park Foundation (573)
Nat'l Parks Conservation Ass'n (573)
Nat'l Pest Control Ass'n (573)
Nat'l Pollution Prevention Roundtable (574)
Nat'l Recreation and Park Ass'n (575)
Nat'l Safety Council (577)
Nat'l Sediments Coalition (577)
Nat'l Water Resources Ass'n (581)
The Nat'l Wetlands Coalition (581)
Nat'l Wilderness Institute (581)
Nat'l Wildlife Federation - Office of Federal and Internat'l Affairs (581)
Nat'l Wildlife Refuge Ass'n (581)
Natural Resources Defense Council (582)
The Nature Conservancy (582)
Nature Islands, Inc. (582)
NEDA/Resource Conservation and Recovery Act Project (583)
New Energy and Industrial Technology Development Organization (NEDO) (585)
New Mexico State Land Office (586)
NI Industries (589)
North American Soc. for Trenchless Technology (592)
Northeast-Midwest Institute (594)
Northern Forest Alliance (594)
Novartis Corp. (596)
Ocean Futures Soc., Inc. (598)
Olivenhain Municipal Water District (600)
Oregon Water Trust (603)
Orleans Levee District (603)
The Pacific Forest Trust (605)
Pershing Co. Water Conservation District of Nevada (612)
Pet Industry Joint Advisory Council (613)
Pew Center on Global Climate Change (613)
Pew Charitable Trust - Environmental Law & Policy Center of the Midwest (613)
Pew Wilderness Center (613)
Pheasants Forever (615)
Physicians for Social Responsibility (617)
Piedmont Environmental Council (617)
Population Action Internat'l (621)
Population Institute (621)
Private Fuels Storage, L.L.C. (625)
Public Citizen, Inc. (628)

Public Employees for Environmental Responsibility (PEER) (628)
Rails to Trails Conservancy (632)
Raytheon Co. (633)
Recovermat Technologies LLC (634)
Renew America (636)
Renewable Fuels Ass'n (637)
Renewable Natural Resources Foundation (637)
Republicans for Clean Air (638)
Resources for the Future (638)
Restore America's Estuaries (638)
Reusable Industrial Packaging Ass'n (639)
RISE (Responsible Industry for a Sound Environment) (640)
Riverside County, California, Flood Control and Water Conservation District (640)
Riverside Habitat Acquisition, County of (640)
Rockville Centre, New York, Village of (641)
ROLITE, Inc. (642)
Rural Coalition (643)
Rural Public Lands County Council (643)
Safari Club Internat'l (645)
Safe Environment of America (645)
San Gabriel Basin Water Quality Authority (648)
Santa Clara Valley Water District (649)
Save America's Forests, Inc. (650)
Save America's Fossils for Everyone, Inc. (650)
Save Barton Creek (650)
Save the Bay (650)
Scenic America (651)
Science Applications Internat'l Corp. (SAIC) (652)
SePRO Corp. (655)
Sierra Club (658)
Soc. for Occupational and Environmental Health (662)
Soc. of Toxicology (664)
South Coast Air Quality Management District (666)
Southeast Water Coalition (667)
Southeastern Michigan Council of Government (667)
Southern Utah Wilderness Alliance (668)
Southwestern Water Conservation District (668)
Space Imaging, Inc. (669)
Sumner, Tennessee, Resource Authority of the County of (676)
Superfund Action Alliance (677)
Superfund Action Coalition (677)
Superfund Reform '95 (677)
The Teratology Soc. (684)
Terrene Institute (684)
ThermoEnergy Corp. (686)
Tribal Ass'n on Solid Waste and Emergency Response (TASWER) (692)
Turfgrass Producers Internat'l (694)
U.S. Public Interest Research Group (697)
UNR Asbestos-Disease Trust (708)
Upper Yampa Water Conservancy District (708)
USPCI, Inc. (710)
Utility Air Regulatory Group (711)
Washington Group Internat'l (719)
Waste Management, Inc. (721)
Waste Policy Institute (721)
Water and Wastewater Equipment Manufacturers Ass'n (721)
Water Environment Federation (721)
Water Environment Research Foundation (721)
Water Quality 2000 (721)
Water Quality Insurance Syndicate (721)
West Coast Refuse and Recycling Coalition (723)
West Jefferson Levee District (723)
Western Coalition of Arid States (724)
Western Research Institute (724)
Western States Land Commissioners Ass'n (724)
Wheelabrator Environmental Systems, Inc. (725)
Wheelabrator-Cleanwater Systems-BioGro Division (726)
Wild Alabama (726)
The Wilderness Soc. (726)
Wildlife Advocacy Project (726)
Wildlife Habitat Council (726)
Wildlife Legislative Fund of America (727)
Wildlife Management Institute (727)
The Wildlife Soc. (727)
Wolf Springs Ranches, Inc. (729)
World Resources Institute (731)
World Wildlife Fund (731)
Worldwatch Institute (731)
Zero Population Growth, Inc. (734)
Zirconium Environmental Committee (ZEC) (735)

Family & Home Issues/Abortion/Adoption

Advocates for Youth (229)
The Alan Guttmacher Institute (236)
Alliance for Children and Families (239)
Alliance to End Childhood Lead Poisoning (241)
American Academy of Adoption Attorneys (243)
American Academy of Family Physicians (243)
American Ass'n for Marriage and Family Therapy (246)
American Ass'n of Family and Consumer Sciences (247)
American Board of Adolescent Psychiatry (251)
American Counseling Ass'n (256)
American Family Ass'n (258)
American Retirees Ass'n (273)
American War Mothers (280)
Army & Air Force Mutual Aid Ass'n (289)
Babyland Family Services, Inc. (305)
Big Brothers/Big Sisters of America (313)
California Ass'n of Marriage and Family Therapists (326)
Casey Family Program (333)
Catholics for a Free Choice (334)
Center for Reproductive Law and Policy (337)
Children's Defense Fund (344)
Children's Foundation (344)
Children's Rights Council (344)
Christian Coalition of America (345)
Coalition of Positive Outcomes in Pregnancy (355)
College Parents of America (358)
Eurapair International, Inc. (407)
Ex-Partners of Servicemembers for Equality (408)
Families Against Mandatory Minimums (410)
Family Advocacy Services (410)
Family and Medical Leave Act Technical Corrections Coalition (410)
Family Co. Group (410)
Family Farm Alliance (Project Transfer Council) (410)
Family Health Internat'l (411)
Family Impact Seminar (411)
Family Place (411)
Family Research Council, Inc. (411)
Family Violence Prevention Fund (411)
Family, Career and Community Leaders of America (411)
FINCA Internat'l Inc., The Foundation for Internat'l Community Assistance (417)
Home Automation Ass'n (451)
Jewish Family Service Ass'n of Cleveland (483)
Kenya Bombing Families (488)
Lamaze Internat'l (494)
Metropolitan Family Services (520)
Multi-Family Housing Institute (532)
Nat'l Abortion and Reproductive Rights Action League (535)
Nat'l Abortion Federation (535)
Nat'l Accreditation Council for Early Childhood Professional Personnel and Programs (535)
Nat'l Adoption Foundation (535)
Nat'l Ass'n of Foster Grandparent Program Directors (543)
Nat'l Ass'n of Military Widows (545)
Nat'l Ass'n of Minority Political Families, USA, Inc. (545)
Nat'l Catholic Federation of Parents (554)
Nat'l Center for Family Literacy (554)
Nat'l Center for Missing and Exploited Children (555)
Nat'l Child Abuse Coalition (555)
Nat'l Child Support Enforcement Ass'n (555)
Nat'l Childcare Parents Ass'n (555)
Nat'l Coalition Against Domestic Violence (556)
Nat'l Coalition of Abortion Providers (556)
Nat'l Committee for a Human Life Amendment (557)
Nat'l Conference of Catholic Bishops, Secretariat for Pro-Life Activities (558)
Nat'l Congress of Parents and Teachers (558)
Nat'l Council for Adoption (559)
Nat'l Council on Family Relations (561)
Nat'l Family Farm Coalition (563)
Nat'l Family Planning and Reproductive Health Ass'n (563)
Nat'l League of Families of American Prisoners and Missing in Southeast Asia (569)
Nat'l Military Family Ass'n (571)
Nat'l Network for Youth (572)
Nat'l Network to End Domestic Violence (572)
Nat'l Partnership for Women and Families (573)
Nat'l Pro-Life Alliance PAC (574)
Nat'l Right to Life Committee (576)
Parents for Public Schools (608)
Parents Incorporated (608)
Physicians for Reproductive Choice and Health (617)
Planned Parenthood Federation of America (618)
Population Action Internat'l (621)
Religious Coalition for Reproductive Choice (636)
Republicans for Choice (638)
Traditional Values Coalition (689)
U.S. Family Network (696)
Voters For Choice (717)
Women's Information Network (729)

Fire/Disaster

IMSSCO Inc. (458)
Internat'l Ass'n of Black Professional Fire Fighters (467)
Internat'l Ass'n of Emergency Managers (467)
Internat'l Ass'n of Fire Fighters (468)
Kenya Bombing Families (488)
Maritime Fire and Safety Ass'n (510)
Nat'l Ass'n of Flood and Stormwater Management Agencies (543)
Orange County Fire Authority (602)
Research Planning, Inc. (638)
San Joaquin Area Flood Agency (648)

Firearms/Gun Control

Americans for Gun Safety (281)
BeamHit America LLC (310)
Beretta U.S.A. Corp. (311)
The Center to Prevent Handgun Violence (338)
Century Internat'l Arms (339)
Citizens Committee for the Right to Keep and Bear Arms (348)
Coalition to Stop Gun Violence (356)
Educational Fund to Stop Gun Violence (398)
Fifty Caliber Shooters Policy Institute, Inc. (416)
Firearms Importers Roundtable Trade Group (417)
Firearms Training Systems, Inc. (417)
Gun Owners of America (442)
Handgun Control, Inc. (444)
Intrac Arms Internat'l LLC (477)
Lew Horton Distributing Co. (498)
Mossberg Group, LLC (530)
Nat'l Ass'n of Arms Shows (538)
Nat'l Rifle Ass'n Institute for Legislative Action (576)
Nat'l Rifle Ass'n of America (576)
Nat'l Shooting Sports Foundation Inc. (578)
Saf T Hammer (645)
SIG Arms (659)
Smith & Wesson (661)
Violence Policy Center (715)

Fishing Industry

Alaska Fisheries Development Foundation (236)
Alaska Groundfish Data Bank (236)
Alaska Longline Vessel Owners Ass'n (236)
Alaska Ocean Seafoods L.P. (236)
Alaska Seafood Marketing Institute (237)
Aleutian Pribilof Islands Community Development Ass'n (238)
American Fish Spotters Ass'n (259)
American Fisheries Soc. (259)
American Fly Fishing Trade Ass'n (259)
American Seafoods Inc. (273)
American Sportfishing Ass'n (278)
Atlantic States Marine Fisheries Commission (302)
Blue Water Fishermen's Ass'n (316)
Bristol Bay Borough Fisheries Economic Development Corp (320)
Camara Nacional de la Industria Pesquera (328)
Chilean Salmon Farmers Ass'n (344)
Coalition for Fair Atlantic Salmon Trade (353)
Coalition on the Implementation of the AFA (356)
Coastal Conservation Ass'n (356)
ConAgra Foods, Inc. (365)
Congressional Sportsmen's Foundation (366)
Dolphin Safe/Fair Trade Campaign (390)
East Coast Tuna Ass'n (395)
Fair Atlantic Salmon Trade (410)
Fishable Waters Coalition (418)
Fishing Vessel Owners' Ass'n (418)
General Category Tuna Ass'n (431)
Great Lakes Indian Fish and Wildlife Commission (439)
Internat'l Ass'n of Fish and Wildlife Agencies (468)
Japan Fisheries Ass'n (482)
Lunds Fisheries, Inc. (505)
Marine Resources Company Internat'l (510)
Monroe County Commercial Fishermen, Inc. (527)
Nat'l Fisheries Institute (564)
Northwest Indian Fisheries Commission (595)
Pacific Seafood Processors Ass'n (606)
Pacific States Marine Fisheries Commission (606)
Plano Molding Co. (619)
Sanko Fisheries LLC (648)
Scientific Fishery Systems, Inc. (652)
Seaboard Corp. (653)
Southeast Alaska Seiners Ass'n (667)
Trident Seafood Corp. (692)
Trout Unlimited (692)
United Catcher Boats (700)
United States Tuna Foundation (704)
Wards Cove Packing Co. (718)
West Pac Vessel Owners Ass'n (723)

Food and Beverage Industry

7-Eleven, Inc. (224)
ADM Milling Co. (227)
Advantica Inc. (229)
AFL-CIO - Food and Allied Service Trades Department (231)
Agr Foods (232)
Agribusiness Council (232)
Ajinomoto Co., Inc. (235)
Ajinomoto U.S.A., Inc. (235)
Alaska Ocean Seafoods L.P. (236)
Alaska Seafood Marketing Institute (237)
Albertson's Inc. (237)
Alliance for Reasonable Regulation of Insecticides (240)
Allied Domecq (241)
American Bakers Ass'n (250)
American Beverage Institute (251)
American Butter Institute (251)
American Cocoa Research Institute (253)
American Dehydrated Onion and Garlic Ass'n (256)
American Frozen Food Institute (260)
American Grain Inspection Institute (261)
American Herbal Products Ass'n (262)
American Honey Producers Ass'n (262)
American Importers and Exporters/Meat Products Group (263)
American Meat Institute (267)
American Mushroom Institute (268)
American Peanut Council (269)
American Peanut Product Manufacturers, Inc. (269)
American School Food Service Ass'n (273)

American Seafoods Inc. (273)
American Soybean Ass'n (277)
American Spice and Trade Ass'n (277)
American Sugar Alliance (278)
American Sugar Cane League of the U.S.A. (278)
American Vintners Ass'n (280)
American Wholesale Marketers Ass'n (280)
American Wine Heritage Alliance (280)
Anheuser-Busch Cos., Inc. (284)
Animal Industry Foundation (284)
Apple Processors Ass'n (286)
ARAMARK Corp. (287)
Archer Daniels Midland Co. (287)
Artichoke Enterprises, Inc. (290)
Asociacion de Productores de Salon y Truncha de Chile (291)
Ass'n for Dressings and Sauces (292)
Ass'n of Chocolate, Biscuit and Confectionery Industries of the EEC (295)
Ass'n of Food Industries, Inc. (295)
Ass'n of Sales & Marketing Companies (298)
Atalanta Corp. (302)
Austin, Nichols & Co., Inc. (303)
Australian Dairy Corp. (303)
Bacardi Ltd. (305)
Bacardi-Martini, USA, Inc. (305)
Bakery, Confectionery and Tobacco Workers Internat'l Union (306)
Beef Products, Inc. (310)
Beer Institute (310)
Best Foods (312)
Biscuit and Cracker Manufacturers Ass'n (314)
Blue Anchor, Inc. (315)
Bob Evans Farms, Inc. (316)
Branco Peres Citrus, S.A. (319)
Brown-Forman Corp. (322)
Bulmer Holding PLC, H. P. (323)
Bunge Corp. (323)
Burger King Corp. (324)
H. E. Butt Grocery Co. (325)
California Avocado Commission (326)
California Canning Peach Ass'n (326)
California Cling Peach Growers Advisory Board (326)
California Kiwi Fruit Commission (327)
California Prune Board (327)
California Restaurant Ass'n (327)
California Table Grape Commission (327)
California Walnut Commission (327)
California-Arizona Citrus League (328)
Campbell Soup Co. (329)
Can Manufacturers Institute (329)
Caribbean Banana Exporters Ass'n (331)
Cattlemen's Beef Promotion and Research Board (334)
Cell Tech (334)
Center for Science in the Public Interest (337)
Central Soya Co. (339)
Centre National Interprofessionel de L'Economie Laitiere (French Dairy Ass'n) (339)
The Century Council (339)
Certified Angus Beef (340)
Chase Nat'l Kiwi Farms (341)
Cheese Importers Ass'n of America (341)
Chilean Salmon Farmers Ass'n (344)
Chiquita Brands Internat'l, Inc. (345)
Chocolate Manufacturers Ass'n of the U.S.A. (345)
Chocolate, Biscuit and Confectionery Industries of the European Community (345)
Circle K Convenience Stores (347)
Cliffstar Corp. (351)
Clyde's Restaurant Group (351)
CNPA - Nat'l Center for the Promotion of Agricultural and Food Products (352)
Coalition for Sugar Reform (354)
Coalition of Food Importers Ass'ns (355)
The Coca-Cola Company (356)
ConAgra Foods, Inc. (365)
Coors Brewing Company (371)
Corn Refiners Ass'n, Inc. (372)
Cumberland Packing Corp. (380)
Dairy Management, Inc. (381)
The Dairy Trade Coalition (381)
Danish Meat Canners Export Ass'n (382)
Design Cuisine (386)
Distilled Spirits Council of the United States, Inc. (389)
Dolce Internat'l (390)
Dole Food Co. (390)
Dominican State Sugar Council (CEA) (391)
Domtar, Inc. (391)
The Egg Factory, LLC (398)
Exportadora de Sal, S.A. de C.V. (409)
Fair Atlantic Salmon Trade (410)
Farmland Industries, Inc. (412)
FDA-NIH Council (412)
Ferraro, USA (415)
Flavor and Extract Manufacturers Ass'n (418)
Florida Citrus Alliance (419)
Florida Citrus Mutual (419)
Florida Citrus Packers (419)
Florida Department of Citrus (419)
Florida Farm Bureau Federation (419)
Florida Fruit and Vegetable Ass'n (420)
Florida Sugar Cane League, Inc. (420)
Florida Tomato Exchange (420)
Food Distributors Internat'l (NAWGA-IFDA) (421)
Food Lion, Inc. (421)
Food Marketing Institute (421)
Food Processing Machinery and Supplies Ass'n (421)
The Food Processors Institute (422)
Foodmaker Internat'l Franchising Inc. (422)
Foodservice & Packaging Institute, Inc. (422)
Fresh Garlic Producer Ass'n (426)
Fresh Produce Ass'n of the Americas (426)
Frozen Potato Products Institute (427)
Ernest & Julio Gallo Winery (428)
Garden State Seafood Ass'n (429)
Gay & Robinson, Inc. (430)
General Mills (432)
Genesee Brewing Co. (433)
Georgia Commodity Commission for Peanuts (434)
Giant Food Inc. (435)
Golden Peanut Co. (437)
Grocery Manufacturers of America (440)
Grupo Maseca (441)
Gulf Citrus Growers Ass'n (442)
Hawaii Food & Beverage Ass'n (445)
H. J. Heinz Co., (448)
Herbalife Internat'l, Inc. (448)
Hershey Foods Corp. (449)
Home Baking Ass'n (451)
Honey Users Council of America (452)
Horizon Organic Holding Co. (452)
IBP, Inc. (456)
Icicle Seafoods, Inc. (457)
Independent Bakers Ass'n (459)
Independent Grocers' Alliance (459)
Indian River Citrus League (460)
Industrie Alimentare Molisane (461)
Institute of Food Technologists (464)
Internat'l Ass'n of Color Manufacturers (467)
Internat'l Ass'n of Food Industry Suppliers (468)
Internat'l Ass'n of Refrigerated Warehouses (468)
Internat'l Banana Ass'n (468)
Internat'l Bottled Water Ass'n (468)
Internat'l Dairy Foods Ass'n (470)
Internat'l Dairy-Deli-Bakery Ass'n (471)
Internat'l Food Additives Council (471)
Internat'l Food Information Council (471)
Internat'l Frozen Food Ass'n (472)
Internat'l Jelly and Preserve Ass'n (472)
Internat'l Policy Council on Agriculture, Food and Trade (474)
Internat'l Sugar Policy Coordinating Commission of the Dominican Republic (475)
Interstate Wine Coalition (477)
Iowa Pork Producers Ass'n (478)
Jerome Foods (483)
Junex Enterprises (485)
Kanowitz Fruit & Produce Co. (486)
Kellogg Co. (487)
Kendall-Jackson Winery (488)
Kraft Foods, Inc. (492)
Leprino Foods Co. (498)
Malaysian Palm Oil Promotion Council (508)
Marine Resources Company Internat'l (510)
Marriott Internat'l, Inc. (511)
Mars, Inc. (511)
Martini & Rossi Corp. (511)
Mary Jane Bakeries (511)
Maui Pineapple Co. (513)
McDonald's Corp. (514)
McKee Foods Corp. (515)
McKesson Corp. (515)
McLane Co. (515)
Mead Johnson and Co. (515)
Meat and Livestock Australia (515)
Meat Importers Council of America (515)
Meat Industry Suppliers Ass'n (515)
Meat New Zealand (515)
Mexican Crab Industry (521)
Mexican Nat'l Spiny Lobster Industry (521)
Milk Industry Foundation (524)
Miller Brewing Co. (524)
The Robert Mondavi Winery (527)
Morrison Inc. (530)
Murry's, Inc. (533)
Nabisco, Inc. (534)
Nat'l Alcohol Beverage Control Ass'n (536)
Nat'l Ass'n of Beverage Retailers (539)
Nat'l Ass'n of Food Equipment Manufacturers (543)
Nat'l Ass'n of Margarine Manufacturers (545)
Nat'l Beer Wholesalers Ass'n (552)
Nat'l Chicken Council (555)
Nat'l Coalition of Food Importers Ass'n (556)
Nat'l Confectioners Ass'n (558)
Nat'l Food Processors Ass'n (564)
Nat'l Frozen Food Ass'n (565)
Nat'l Frozen Pizza Institute (565)
Nat'l Gaucher Foundation (565)
Nat'l Grape Co-operative Ass'n, Inc. (566)
Nat'l Grocers Ass'n (566)
Nat'l Honey Board (567)
Nat'l Institute of Oilseed Products (568)
Nat'l Juice Products Ass'n (569)
Nat'l Licensed Beverage Ass'n (570)
Nat'l Meat Ass'n (570)
Nat'l Meat Canners Ass'n (570)
Nat'l Milk Producers Federation (571)
Nat'l Nutritional Foods Ass'n (572)
Nat'l Oilseed Processors Ass'n (572)
Nat'l Pasta Ass'n (573)
Nat'l Peach Council (573)
Nat'l Pecan Shellers Ass'n (573)
Nat'l Pork Producers Council (574)
Nat'l Potato Council (574)
Nat'l Potato Promotion Board (574)
Nat'l Renderers Ass'n (575)
Nat'l Restaurant Ass'n (576)
Nat'l Soft Drink Ass'n (578)
Nat'l Sunflower Ass'n (579)
Nat'l Turkey Federation (580)
Nat'l Yogurt Ass'n (581)
Nature's Farm Products (582)
Nestle USA, Inc. (584)
New Zealand Kiwifruit Marketing Board (588)
North American Ass'n of Food Equipment Manufacturers (592)
North American Grain Export Ass'n, Inc. (592)
North American Meat Processors Ass'n (592)
North American Millers' Ass'n (592)
North American Natural Casing Ass'n (592)
Ocean Spray Cranberries (598)
Organic Trade Ass'n (603)
Pacific Seafood Processors Ass'n (606)
Pacific States Marine Fisheries Commission (606)
Pastavilla Makarnacilik A.S. (609)
Pastificio Antonio Pallante (609)
Peanut and Tree Nut Processors Ass'n (610)
PepsiCo, Inc. (612)
Perdue Farms Inc. (612)
Performance Food Group Inc. (612)
Pernod Ricard (612)
Pet Food Institute (613)
Philip Morris Management Corp. (615)
Physicians Committee for Responsible Medicine (617)
The Pillsbury Co. (617)
Pizza Hut, Inc. (618)
Popcorn Board (620)
Processed Apples Institute (625)
The Procter & Gamble Company (625)
Produce Marketing Ass'n (625)
Protein Technologies Internat'l (627)
Pure Food Campaign (630)
Ralston Purina Co. (632)
Reckitt & Colman Pharmaceuticals Inc. (634)
Refined Sugars Inc. (635)
Retailers Bakery Ass'n (638)
Rio Grande Valley Sugar Growers (640)
RJR Nabisco Holdings Co. (641)
Royal Wine Co. (643)
Ruth's Chris Steak House (644)
Salt Institute (646)
San Tomo Group (648)
Sara Lee Corp. (649)
Schwan's Sales Enterprises (652)
Seaboard Corp. (653)
Showell Farms Inc. (658)
Slim Fast Foods Co. (661)
Smithfield Foods Inc. (661)
Snack Food Ass'n (662)
South African Sugar Ass'n (666)
Southwest Peanut Growers (668)
Soy Protein Council (668)
A. E. Staley Manufacturing Co. (672)
SteriGenics Internat'l (674)
Storck U.S.A. (675)
Stroh Brewing Co. (675)
Sugar Ass'n, Inc. (676)
Suiza Foods Corp. (676)
Sun Diamond Growers, Inc. (676)
SunSweet Growers, Inc. (677)
Sweetener Users Ass'n (678)
Taco Bell Corp. (679)
Tanimura & Antle, Inc. (680)
Tate and Lyle North American Sugars Inc. (681)
Tea Ass'n of the U.S.A., Inc. (682)
Tilda Rice (687)
Titan Scan (687)
Todhunter Internat'l, Inc. (688)
Transhumance Holding Co., Inc. (690)
Tricon Global Restaurants Inc. (692)
Trident Seafood Corp. (692)
Tyson Foods, Inc. (695)
U.S. Apple Ass'n (695)
U.S. Canola Ass'n (695)
U.S. Rice Producers Ass'n (697)
UDV North America, Inc. (698)
UDV/Heublein, Inc. (698)
Unilever N.V. (699)
Unilever United States, Inc. (699)
United Biscuit (700)
United Catcher Boats (700)
United Dairy Industry Ass'n (701)
United Egg Ass'n (701)
United Egg Producers (701)
United Food and Commercial Workers Internat'l Union (701)
United Fresh Fruit and Vegetable Ass'n (701)
United States Beet Sugar Ass'n (703)
United States Cane Sugar Refiners' Ass'n (703)
United States Sugar Corp. (704)
United States Tuna Foundation (704)
Upper Midwest Dairy Coalition (708)
USA Rice Federation (709)
Valhi, Inc. (711)
Victory Wholesale Grocers Inc. (715)

The Vinegar Institute (715)
Vinifera Wine Growers Ass'n (715)
Virginia Peanut Growers Ass'n (716)
Virginia Wineries Ass'n (716)
Vivendi Universal (717)
Wegmans Food Markets, Inc. (722)
Weight Watchers Internat'l, Inc. (722)
Welch's Foods, Inc. (722)
Wendy's Internat'l, Inc. (723)
Western United Dairymen (725)
Wheat Foods Council (725)
Wheat Gluten Industry Council (725)
Wine and Spirits Wholesalers of America (728)
Wine Institute (728)
World Food Prize (730)
Wm. Wrigley Jr. Co. (732)

Foreign Relations

20/20 Vision (223)
Africa Policy Information Center (231)
Africare (232)
Alsatian American Chamber of Commerce (242)
American Council of Young Political Leaders (256)
American Defense Institute (256)
American Enterprise Institute for Public Policy Research (257)
American Foreign Service Ass'n (259)
American Friends of Turkey (260)
American Hellenic Educational Progressive Ass'n (AHEPA) (262)
American Hellenic Institute Public Affairs Committee (262)
American Hellenic Institute, Inc. (262)
American Institute for Foreign Studies (264)
American Israel Public Affairs Committee (265)
American Jewish Committee (265)
American Jewish Congress (265)
American Kurdish Information Network (AKIN) (265)
American Legion (266)
American Security Council (273)
American Task Force for Lebanon (278)
American Translators Ass'n (279)
American-Turkish Council (281)
American-Uzbekistan Chamber of Commerce (281)
Americans for Peace Now (282)
Amnesty Internat'l U.S.A. (283)
Anti-Defamation League (285)
Armenian Assembly of America (289)
Armenian Nat'l Committee of America (289)
Arms Control Ass'n (289)
The Asia Foundation (290)
Asia Pacific Policy Center (290)
Asia Society (290)
Ass'n of Former Intelligence Officers (295)
Ass'n on Third World Affairs (299)
Ass'n to Unite the Democracies (299)
ASSE Internat'l Student Exchange Program (299)
Atlantic Corridor USA (302)
Atlantic Council of the United States (302)
Baltic American Freedom League (306)
Bangladeshi-American Friendship Soc. of New York (307)
British American Security Information Council (321)
The Brookings Institution (321)
Brunei Darussalam, Embassy of the State of (322)
Business Alliance for Internat'l Economic Development (324)
Business Executives for Nat'l Security (324)
Campaign for United Nations Reform (329)
Cape Verde, Embassy of the Republic of (330)
Caribbean/Latin American Action (331)
Carnegie Endowment for Internat'l Peace (332)
Center for Defense Information (335)
Center for Democracy (336)
Center for Internat'l Policy (336)
The Center for Religious Freedom (337)
Center for Security Policy (337)
Center for Strategic and Internat'l Studies (337)
The Century Foundation (339)
Chicago Global, Ltd. (343)
Christians' Israel Public Action Campaign, Inc. (346)
Citizens Network for Foreign Affairs (CNFA) (349)
Coalition of Service Industries (355)
Colombia, Ministry of Communications of (358)
Congo, Democratic Republic of the (366)
Connectcuba (367)
Constituency for Africa (368)
Council for a Livable World (373)
Council for a Livable World Education Fund (373)
Council for Internat'l Exchange of Scholars (374)
Council for the Nat'l Interest (375)
Council of the Americas (376)
Council on Foreign Relations (376)
Council on Hemispheric Affairs (377)
Counterpart Internat'l (377)
Diplomatic and Consular Officers, Retired (Dacor) (388)
Dominican Republic, Embassy of the (391)
Espee Trading Corp. (407)
Republic of Estonia (407)
Formosan Ass'n for Public Affairs (423)
Forum for Internat'l Policy (423)
Foundation for Middle East Peace (424)
Friedrich Ebert Foundation (426)
Friends Committee on Nat'l Legislation (426)
Friends of Free China (426)
Gabonese Republic, Office of the President of the (428)
Gibraltar Information Bureau (435)
Greater El Paso Chamber of Commerce (439)
Group of 30 (441)
Heritage Foundation (448)
Hudson Institute (454)
Human Rights Watch (455)
Information Trust (462)
Institute for Balkan Affairs (463)
Institute for Internat'l Economics (463)
Institute for Palestine Studies (463)
Institute for Science and Internat'l Security (464)
Institute on Religion and Democracy (464)
INTELSAT - Internat'l Telecommunications Satellite Organization (465)
Inter-American Institute for Cooperation on Agriculture (466)
Internat'l Campaign for Tibet (469)
Internat'l Center (469)
Internat'l Center for Journalists (469)
Internat'l College (470)
Internat'l Committee on Organization & Policy (470)
Internat'l Foundation for Election Systems (IFES) (471)
Internat'l Fund for Agricultural Development (472)
Internat'l Institute for Energy Conservation (472)
Internat'l Republican Institute (474)
Internat'l Research and Exchanges Board (IREX) (474)
Internat'l Trade Council (475)
Internat'l Trust Fund for Demining and Mine Victims Assistance in Bosnia-Herzigovina (475)
Interns for Peace Internat'l (477)
Irish Nat'l Caucus (479)
ISAR, Initiative for Social Action and Renewal in Eurasia (479)
Islamic Institute (479)
Israel Policy Forum (479)
Japan, Ministry of Foreign Affairs of (482)
Jewish Institute for Nat'l Security Affairs (483)
Jewish Peace Lobby (483)
Joint Baltic American Nat'l Committee, Inc. (484)
Joint Nat'l Committee for Languages (484)
Kashmiri American Council (486)
Korea, Embassy of (491)
Kyrgyzstan, Government of the Republic of (492)
Lao Progressive Institute (495)
Lawyers Alliance for World Security (496)
Lawyers Committee for Human Rights (496)
League of Arab States/Arab Information Center (497)
Link Romania, Inc. (500)
Lithuanian American Council (500)
Mauritania, Government of the Islamic Republic of (513)
Mauritania, Office of the Foreign Minister of (513)
Meridian Internat'l Center (519)
Mexico, Embassy of (521)
Mexico, Secretariat of Commerce & Industrial Development of (521)
Mexico-U.S. Business Committee, U.S. Council (521)
Middle East Institute (523)
Middle East Policy Council (523)
Montenegro, Government of (528)
NAFSA: Ass'n of Internat'l Educators (534)
Nat'l Bureau of Asian Research (553)
Nat'l Center for Public Policy Research (555)
Nat'l Council for Eurasian and East European Research (559)
Nat'l Council for Languages and Internat'l Studies (559)
Nat'l Council on U.S.-Arab Relations (561)
Nat'l Democratic Institute for Internat'l Affairs (562)
Nat'l Endowment for Democracy (563)
Nat'l Institute for Public Policy (568)
Nat'l League of Families of American Prisoners and Missing in Southeast Asia (569)
The Nat'l PAC (573)
Nat'l Peace Foundation (573)
Nat'l Security Archive (577)
Nat'l Strategy Information Center (579)
NCSJ: Advocates on Behalf of Jews in Russia, Ukraine, the Baltic States and Eurasia (583)
Network in Solidarity with the People of Guatemala (NISGUA) (584)
Nicaraguan Foundation for Democracy and Development (589)
Nixon Center, The (590)
Nuclear Control Institute (597)
Pacific Basin Economic Council - U.S. Member Committee (605)
Pakistani-American Business Ass'n (606)
Palestinian Authority (606)
Panama, Public Service Regulatory Entity of the Government of the Republic of (607)
Papua New Guinea, Embassy of (607)
Parliamentary Human Rights Foundation (608)
Partners of the Americas (608)
Peace Action (610)
Peace Links (610)
Peru, Government of the Republic of (613)
PlanEcon Inc. (618)
PLO Mission (619)
PSEKA, Internat'l Coordinating Committee, Justice for Cyprus (627)
Qatar, Embassy of (630)
Refugees Internat'l (635)
Romanian Orphans Connection, Inc. (642)
Royal Netherlands, Embassy of the (643)
Salesian Missions of the Salesian Soc. (646)
Search for Common Ground (653)
Shipston Group, LTD (657)
Sister Cities Internat'l (660)
Slovak Information Agency (661)
Sojourners (664)
South African Government/World Bank (666)
Southeast Asia Resource Action Center (SEARAC) (667)
Swaziland, Embassy of the Kingdom of (678)
Tanzania, Office of the Foreign Minister of the United Republic of (681)
Togo, Embassy of the Republic of (688)
TransAfrica Forum (689)
Trinidad and Tobago, Embassy of the Republic of (692)
Tunisian Agency for External Communication (694)
Turkey, Embassy of the Republic of (694)
U.S. Fund for UNICEF (696)
U.S. Olympic Committee (697)
U.S. Overseas Cooperative Development (697)
U.S.-Azerbaijan Council, Inc. (697)
Union of Councils for Soviet Jews (699)
United Lao Congress for Democracy (702)
United Nations Ass'n of the U.S.A. (702)
United Nations Development Programme (702)
United States Business and Industry Council (703)
United States Committee for Refugees (703)
United States Nat'l Committee for Pacific Economic Cooperation (704)
The United States-New Zealand Council (704)
US-Asia Institute (709)
Walsh Enterprises Internat'l (718)
Washington Institute for Near East Policy (719)
Washington Kurdish Institute (720)
Washington Office on Latin American (720)
World Federalist Ass'n (730)
World Government of World Citizens (730)
World Jurist Ass'n of the World Peace Through Law Center (731)
World Learning Inc. (731)
World Service Authority (731)
Yemen, Government of (733)
Youth For Understanding Internat'l Exchange (733)
Zimbabwe, Republic of (734)

Forestry

Alaska Forest Ass'n (236)
American Forest & Paper Ass'n (259)
American Forest Foundation (260)
American Forests (260)
American Land Rights Ass'n (265)
Ass'n of Consulting Foresters of America (295)
Coalition for Fair Lumber Imports (353)
Forest Products Industry Nat'l Labor-Management Committee (423)
Intermountain Forest Industry Ass'n (467)
Internat'l Center (469)
Koncor Forest Products Co. (491)
Lumbermens Mutual Casualty Co. (505)
Malheur Timber Operators (508)
Nat'l Ass'n of Professional Forestry Schools and Colleges (547)
Nat'l Ass'n of State Foresters (550)
Nat'l Council of Commercial Plant Breeders (560)
Northwest Forestry Ass'n (595)
Northwest Woodland Owners Council (595)
Renewable Natural Resources Foundation (637)
Save America's Forests, Inc. (650)
Simpson Investment Co. (659)
Soc. of American Foresters (663)
Southern Ass'n of Forestry Economics (667)
Western States Land Commissioners Ass'n (724)
The Wilderness Soc. (726)
Worldwatch Institute (731)

Furniture and Furnishings

American Edged Products Manufacturers Ass'n (257)
American Furniture Manufacturers Ass'n (260)
American of Martinsville (269)
American Restaurant China Council (273)
American Soc. of Interior Designers (276)
Ass'n of Progressive Rental Organizations (298)
Barker Brothers (308)
Carpet and Rug Institute (332)
Carpet Export Promotion Council (332)
General Electric Appliances (432)
Home Automation Ass'n (451)
Household Goods Forwarders Ass'n of America, Inc. (453)
Indotrade, Inc. (461)
Interface (466)
Internat'l Furniture Rental Ass'n (472)
Internat'l Sleep Products Ass'n (474)
Internat'l Union of Electronic, Electrical, Salaried, Machine, and Furniture Workers-Communications Workers of America (476)
Kitchen Cabinet Manufacturers Ass'n (490)
May Department Stores Co. (513)
Miller Desk (524)
Mont Blanc, Inc. (528)
Montgomery Ward & Co., Inc. (528)
Nat'l Candle Ass'n (554)
Nat'l Institute of Certified Moving Consultants (568)

J. C. Penney Co., Inc. (611)
Pennsylvania House (611)
Pier 1 Imports (617)
The Refinishing Touch (635)
Sears, Roebuck and Co. (653)
Simark Trading Co., Inc. (659)
Sleep Products Safety Council (661)
Tanners Countervailing Duty Coalition (680)
Unified Voice (Interior Designers) (698)
Whirlpool Corp. (726)
Window Covering Manufacturers Ass'n (728)
Window Covering Safety Council (728)
World Floor Covering Ass'n (730)

Glass

American Security Resources, Inc. (273)
Asahi Glass Co. (290)
Ball Aerospace & Technologies Corp. (306)
Corning Inc. (372)
Durand Internat'l, J. G. (393)
Glass Packaging Institute (435)
Guardian Industries Corp. (442)
Indiana Glass Co. (460)
Industry Union Glass Container Promotion Program (461)
Internat'l Crystal Federation (470)
Libbey, Inc. (499)
Naigai, Inc. (534)
Nat'l Glass Ass'n (566)
Nikon Corp. (590)
Optical Laboratories Ass'n (601)
Owens-Illinois, Inc. (605)
Pfaltzgraff (613)
Pilkington North America (617)
Potters Industries, Inc. (622)
PPG Industries (622)
Soc. of Glass and Ceramic Decorators (663)
Techneglas, Inc. (682)
Utica Cutlery Inc. (710)

Government-Related

Academy for State and Local Government (225)
Alameda Corridor-East Construction Authority (236)
American Ass'n of Motor Vehicle Administrators (248)
American Ass'n of Port Authorities (249)
American Ass'n of State Highway and Transportation Officials (249)
American Federation of Government Employees (AFL-CIO) (258)
American Federation of Government Employees, Local 1689 Guam (258)
American Federation of State, County and Municipal Employees (258)
American Foreign Service Ass'n (259)
American Institute of Certified Planners (264)
American Legislative Exchange Council (266)
Americans Against Union Control of Government (281)
Ass'n for Governmental Leasing and Finance (292)
Ass'n of California Water Agencies (295)
Ass'n of Government Accountants (296)
Ass'n of Local Air Pollution Control Officials (296)
Ass'n of Metropolitan Sewerage Agencies (297)
Ass'n of Metropolitan Water Agencies (297)
Ass'n of Minnesota Counties (297)
Ass'n of O & C Counties (297)
Ass'n of State and Interstate Water Pollution Control Administrators (298)
Ass'n of State and Territorial Health Officials (298)
Ass'n of State and Territorial Solid Waste Management Officials (298)
Blacks in Government (315)
California Ass'n of Sanitation Agencies (326)
California State Ass'n of Counties (327)
Citizen's Committee to Save the Federal Center (348)
Citizens Against Government Waste (348)
Citizens United (349)
Coalition for Government Procurement (353)
Coastal Impact Assistance & Reinvestment (356)
Commissioned Officers Ass'n of the U.S. Public Health Service (360)
Committee for a Responsible Federal Budget (360)
Committee on the Constitutional System (361)
Competition in Contracting Act Coalition (363)
Conference of State Bank Supervisors (366)
Congressional Institute, Inc. (366)
Consortium on Government Relations for Student Affairs (368)
Contract Services Ass'n of America (370)
Council for Excellence in Government (374)
Council of Chief State School Officers (375)
Council of Large Public Housing Authorities (376)
Council of Professional Ass'ns on Federal Statistics (376)
Council of State Administrators of Vocational Rehabilitation (376)
Council of State Community Development Agencies (376)
Council of State Governments (376)
County Welfare Directors Ass'n of California (377)
Defense Administrative Judges Professional Ass'n (384)
Democratic Governors Ass'n (385)
Diplomatic and Consular Officers, Retired (Dacor) (388)
Ethics and Public Policy Center (407)
ezgov.com (410)
Federal Criminal Investigators Ass'n (412)
Federal Facilities Council (413)
Federal Funds Information for States (413)
Federal Managers Ass'n (413)
Federal Physicians Ass'n (414)
Federation of Government Information Processing Councils (414)
Federation of Tax Administrators (415)
Fund for Constitutional Government (428)
Government Accountability Project (GAP) (437)
Government Employees Hospital Ass'n (437)
Government Finance Officers Ass'n, Federal Liaison Center (438)
Government Purchasing Project (438)
GovWorks.com (438)
Great Lakes Corporate Resources (439)
Hopland Band of Pomo Indians (452)
Internat'l Ass'n of Fish and Wildlife Agencies (468)
Internat'l City/County Management Ass'n (470)
Internat'l Federation of Inspection Agencies, North American Committee (471)
Internat'l Municipal Lawyers Ass'n (473)
League of California Cities (497)
Madison Government Affairs (507)
Marsh USA, Inc. (511)
Military Impacted School Districts Ass'n (524)
Municipal Treasurers Ass'n of the United States and Canada (533)
Nat'l Academy of Public Administration (535)
Nat'l Ass'n of Attorneys General (539)
Nat'l Ass'n of Black County Officials (539)
Nat'l Ass'n of Community Action Agencies (540)
Nat'l Ass'n of Counties (541)
Nat'l Ass'n of County Administrators (541)
Nat'l Ass'n of County Aging Programs (541)
Nat'l Ass'n of County and City Health Officials (541)
Nat'l Ass'n of County Civil Attorneys (541)
Nat'l Ass'n of County Engineers (541)
Nat'l Ass'n of County Health Facility Administrators (541)
Nat'l Ass'n of County Human Services Administrators (541)
Nat'l Ass'n of County Information Officers (541)
Nat'l Ass'n of County Information Technology Administrators (541)
Nat'l Ass'n of County Park and Recreation Officials (541)
Nat'l Ass'n of County Planners (541)
Nat'l Ass'n of County Recorders, Election Officials and Clerks (541)
Nat'l Ass'n of County Training and Employment Professionals (541)
Nat'l Ass'n of County Treasurers and Finance Officers (541)
Nat'l Ass'n of Federal Education Program Administrators (542)
Nat'l Ass'n of Federal Veterinarians (542)
Nat'l Ass'n of Federally Impacted Schools (542)
Nat'l Ass'n of Flood and Stormwater Management Agencies (543)
Nat'l Ass'n of FSA County Office Employees (543)
Nat'l Ass'n of Government Communicators (543)
Nat'l Ass'n of Government Employees (543)
Nat'l Ass'n of Government Guaranteed Lenders (543)
Nat'l Ass'n of Governors' Highway Safety Representatives (543)
Nat'l Ass'n of Hispanic County Officials (543)
Nat'l Ass'n of Housing and Redevelopment Officials (544)
Nat'l Ass'n of Medicaid Directors (545)
Nat'l Ass'n of Postal Supervisors (546)
Nat'l Ass'n of Postmasters of the U.S. (546)
Nat'l Ass'n of Regional Councils (548)
Nat'l Ass'n of Regulatory Utility Commissioners (548)
Nat'l Ass'n of Retired Federal Employees (548)
Nat'l Ass'n of State Auditors, Comptrollers and Treasurers (549)
Nat'l Ass'n of State Aviation Officials (549)
Nat'l Ass'n of State Boards of Education (549)
Nat'l Ass'n of State Budget Officers (549)
Nat'l Ass'n of State Credit Union Supervisors (549)
Nat'l Ass'n of State Departments of Agriculture (549)
Nat'l Ass'n of State Development Agencies (550)
Nat'l Ass'n of State Directors of Developmental Disabilities Services, Inc. (550)
Nat'l Ass'n of State Directors of Special Education (550)
Nat'l Ass'n of State Directors of Vocational Technical Education Consortium (550)
Nat'l Ass'n of State Energy Officials (550)
Nat'l Ass'n of State Foresters (550)
Nat'l Ass'n of State Mental Health Program Directors (550)
Nat'l Ass'n of State Units on Aging (550)
Nat'l Ass'n of Towns and Townships (551)
Nat'l Ass'n of WIC Directors (551)
Nat'l Assembly of State Arts Agencies (551)
Nat'l Black Caucus of Local Elected Officials (552)
Nat'l Black Caucus of State Legislators (552)
Nat'l Conference of State Historic Preservation Officers (558)
Nat'l Conference of State Legislatures (558)
Nat'l Council of State Agencies for the Blind (560)
Nat'l Council of State Housing Agencies (560)
Nat'l Democratic County Officials Organization (562)
Nat'l Environmental Development Ass'ns State & Federal Environmental Responsibility Project (563)
Nat'l Federation of Federal Employees (564)
Nat'l Forum for Black Public Administrators (565)
Nat'l Governors' Ass'n (566)
Nat'l Institute of Governmental Purchasing (568)
Nat'l League of Cities (569)
Nat'l Park Foundation (573)
Nat'l Republican Senatorial Committee (575)
Nat'l School Boards Ass'n (577)
Nat'l Treasury Employees Union (580)
North Carolina, Hurricane Floyd Redevelopment Center of State of (593)
North Metro Mayors Coalition (593)
Office of Hawaiian Affairs (599)
OMB Watch (600)
Organization of Professional Employees of the U.S. Dep't of Agriculture (OPEDA) (603)
Project on Government Oversight, Inc. (626)
Public Advocate (628)
Public Campaign (628)
Public Employees Roundtable (628)
Public Financial Management (628)
Public Housing Authorities Directors Ass'n (628)
Public Lands Council (629)
Public Properties Policy Ass'n (629)
Public Service Research Foundation (629)
Pueblo of Acoma (629)
Republican Governors Ass'n (637)
Sacramento Area Council of Governments (645)
Senior Executives Ass'n (655)
SGS Government Programs, Inc. (656)
Siscorp (660)
Six Agency Committee (660)
Southeast Conference (667)
Southern California Ass'n of Governments (667)
Southern Governors Ass'n (668)
State Government Affairs Council (673)
Texas Cities Legislative Coalition (TCLC) (684)
Trust for Public Land (693)
Twentynine Palms Band of Mission Indians (694)
Tyson's Governmental Sales, LLC (695)
U.S. Ass'n of Former Members of Congress (695)
U.S. Business Alliance for Customs Modernization (695)
U.S. Mint (696)
U.S. Term Limits (697)
United States Conference of Mayors (703)
USA WORKS! (709)
Western Interstate Region (724)
Westinghouse Government Services Group (725)
Women in Government Relations, Inc. (729)
Women Officials in NACo (729)
World Government of World Citizens (730)

Governments (Local, State, Foreign)

Abilene, Texas, City of (225)
Adams County, Colorado (227)
Aiken and Edgenfield Counties, South Carolina, Economic Development Partnership of (233)
Alabama, Department of Transportation of the State of (235)
Alameda, California, City of (236)
Alameda, California, County of (236)
Alaska Legislature (236)
Alaska, Washington Office of the State of (237)
Albuquerque, New Mexico, City of (237)
Aleutians East Borough (238)
Alexandria, Virginia, City of (238)
Allegheny County, Pennsylvania, Housing Authority (238)
Allegheny County, Pennsylvania, Port Authority of (238)
American Samoa, Government of (273)
Anaheim, California, City of (283)
Anchorage, Alaska, Municipality of (283)
Angola, Embassy of (284)
Appalachian Regional Commission, Office of States' Washington Representative of (286)
Apple Valley, California, City of (286)
Arab, Alabama, City of (287)
Arcadia, California, City of (287)
Argentina, The Secretary of Intelligence of (288)
Arizona Power Authority (288)
Arkansas, Office of the Governor of the State of (288)
Ascension, Louisiana, Parish of (290)
Ass'n of Oregon Counties (297)
Atlanta, Georgia, City of (302)
Atlantic County Utilities Authority (302)
Auburn, Avilla, Bluffton, Columbia City and Other Municipalities of Indiana (302)
Augusta-Richmond, Georgia, County of (303)
Aurora, Colorado, City of (303)
Austin, Texas, City of (303)
Avalon, New Jersey, City of (304)
Avondale, Arizona, City of (305)
Bahrain, Government of the State of (306)
Baltimore, Maryland, City of (306)
Barstow, California, City of (308)
Baton Rouge, Louisiana, City of (308)
Bay Delta Urban Coalition (309)
Bayonne Housing Authority (310)
Bayonne, New Jersey, City of (310)
Beaumont, Texas, City of (310)
Bellevue, Washington, City of (311)
Benin, Government of the Republic of (311)
Bergen, New York, Village of (311)

Berkeley, California, City of (312)
Bernalillo, New Mexico, County of (312)
Bibb, Georgia, Board of Commissioners of the County of (313)
Black Mesa Community School Board (315)
Blackfeet Tribe of Montana (315)
Boca Raton, Florida, City of (316)
Bolivia, Government of the Republic of (317)
Boonville, New York, Village of (317)
Boston, Massachusetts, City of (318)
Braintree Electric Light Department (319)
Brea, California, City of (319)
Broward, Florida, County of (322)
Broward, Florida, Department of Natural Resource Protection of the County of (322)
Brownsville, Texas, City of (322)
Buffalo Sewer Authority (323)
Buffalo, New York, City of (323)
Bulgaria, Embassy of the Republic of (323)
Burkina Faso, Government of (324)
Caguas, Puerto Rico, City of (326)
Calhoun County, Alabama Commission (326)
California Board of Equalization (326)
California Franchise Tax Board (326)
California Public Employees' Retirement System (327)
California State Assembly - Committee on Rules (327)
California State Lands Commission (327)
California State Senate (327)
California State Teachers' Retirement System (327)
California, State of (328)
California, Washington Office of the State of (328)
Cambria Community Services District (328)
Canada, Government of (329)
Capital Area Transit Authority (330)
Carmel, Indiana, City of (332)
Carolina, Puerto Rico, City of (332)
Cayman Islands, Government of (334)
Cedar Rapids, Iowa, City of (334)
Ceiba, Puerto Rico, City of (334)
Central Puget Sound Regional Transit Authority (Sound Transit) (339)
Chad, Government of the Republic of (340)
Chelan County Public Utility District (342)
Chicago, Illinois, Department of Law, City of (343)
Chicago, Illinois, Department of the Environment of the City of (343)
Chicago, Illinois, Washington Office of the City of (343)
Chicago, Regional Transportation Authority of (343)
China, Directorate General of Telecommunications, Ministry of Communications of the Republic of (344)
Chino Hills, California, City of (345)
Chino, California, City of (345)
Churchville, New York, Village of (346)
Cincinnati, Ohio, City of (347)
Citrus Heights, California, City of (349)
Clackamas, Oregon, County of (349)
Clark County Department of Aviation (350)
Clark County Regional Flood Control District (350)
Clark County, Nevada, Office of the County Manager (350)
Clayton, Dover, Lewes, Middletown, Milford, Newark, NewCastle, Seaford and Smyrna, Delaware, Municipalities of (350)
Clearwater, Florida, City of (350)
Cleveland, Ohio, City of (351)
College Station, Texas, City of (358)
Colombia, Government of the Republic of (358)
Colorado River Indian Tribes (358)
Colorado, Department of Transportation of the State of (359)
Columbia, South Carolina, City of (359)
Congo, Democratic Republic of the (366)
Connecticut, Office of the Attorney General of the State of (367)
Connecticut, Washington Office of the Governor of the State of (367)
Cook, Illinois, County of (371)
Coral Springs, Florida, City of (371)
Cordova, Alaska, City of (371)
Coronado, California, City of (372)
Corpus Christi Port Authority (373)
Corte Madera, California, Town of (373)
Craig, Alaska, City of (378)
Cranston, Rhode Island, City of (378)
Cranston, Rhode Island, Department of Human Services (378)
Cuyahoga, Ohio, County of (380)
Dade, Florida, County of (381)
Dakota, Minnesota, County of (381)
Dallas, Texas, City of (382)
Dayton, Ohio, Washington Office of the City of (383)
Dearborn, Michigan, Department of Communication of (383)
Deerfield Beach, Florida, City of (383)
Dekalb, Illinois, City of (384)
Delaware Municipal Electric Corp. (DEMEC) (384)
Delaware River Port Authority (384)
Delaware, Pennsylvania, Solid Waste Authority of the County of (384)
Delaware, Washington Office of the State of (384)
Denton, Texas, City of (385)
Denton, Texas, County of (385)
Denver, Colorado, City of (386)
Denver, Regional Transportation District of (386)
Des Moines Community School District (386)
Des Moines, Iowa, City of (386)
Detroit, Michigan, City of (386)
District of Columbia Financial Responsibility and Management Assistance Authority (390)
District of Columbia Office of Intergovernmental Relations (390)
Douglas, Oregon, County of (391)
Downey, California, Economic Development of the City of (392)
Durham, North Carolina, City of (393)
East Chicago Public Housing Authority (395)
East Palo Alto, California, City of (395)
Ecuador, Government of the Republic of (396)
Egypt, Government of the Arab Republic of (398)
El Segundo, California, City of (399)
Elim, Alaska, City of (401)
Elk Valley Rancheria (401)
Encinitas, California, City of (402)
Equatorial Guinea, Republic of (406)
Eritrea, Government of (406)
Ethiopia, Government of (407)
Eugene, Oregon, City of (407)
Eureka, California, City of (408)
Fairbanks, Alaska, North Star Borough of (410)
Fairfield, California, City of (410)
Fajardo, Puerto Rico, Municipality of (410)
Fargo-Moorhead Metropolitan Council of Governments (411)
Farmers Branch, Texas, City of (412)
Fergus Falls, Minnesota, City of (415)
Flint, Michigan, City of (419)
Florence, South Carolina, City of (419)
Florida Department of Agriculture and Consumer Services (419)
Florida Department of Children & Families (419)
Florida Department of Education (419)
Florida Department of Health and Rehabilitative Services (419)
Florida, Washington Office of the State of (420)
Folsom, California, City of (421)
Fontana, California, City of (421)
Fort Wayne, Indiana, City of (423)
Fort Worth Transportation Authority (423)
Fort Worth, Texas, City of (423)
Freeport, New York, Electric Department of the Village of (425)
Freeport, New York, Village of (425)
Fresno, California, City of (426)
Front Royal, Virginia, Town of (426)
Gabonese Republic, Government of the (428)
Gabonese Republic, Office of the President of the (428)
Gainesville, Florida, City of (428)
Gambia, Government of the Republic of The (429)
Gardena, California, City of (429)
Garrison Diversion Conservancy District (429)
Gary, Indiana, Washington Office of the City of (429)
Genesee County Drain Commissioner (433)
Georgia, Government of the Republic of (434)
Georgia, Office of the Attorney General of the State of (434)
Georgia, State of (434)
Glenview, Illinois, Village of (436)
Grant County P.U.D., Washington (438)
Great Britain, Government of (439)
Greater Detroit Resource Recovery Authority (439)
Greater Orlando Aviation Authority (439)
Greenport, New York, Village Electric Department of (440)
Gridley, California, City of/Northern California Power Agency (440)
Government of Guam (441)
Guam, Territory of (441)
Guam, Washington Office of the Governor (442)
Guaynabo, Puerto Rico, City of (442)
Guinea, Secretary General of the Presidency of the Republic of (442)
Hagerstown, Maryland, Municipal Electric Light Plant of (443)
Harris, Texas, Metropolitan Transit Authority of (445)
Hattiesburg, Mississippi, City of (445)
Hawaii Economic Development Alliance, State of (445)
Hawaii, Department of Business and Economic Development of the State of (445)
Hawaii, State of (445)
Hemet, California, City of (448)
Hempstead, New York, Village of (448)
Henderson, Nevada, City of (448)
Hennipin County Board of Commissioners (448)
Hesperia, California, City of (449)
Highland Park, Illinois, City of Highwood Local Redevelopment Authority and the City of (449)
Hillsborough, Florida, County of (450)
Hoboken, New Jersey, City of (450)
Holyoke Department of Gas and Electricity (451)
Honduras, Embassy of (452)
Hong Kong, Government of (452)
Houston Galveston Area Council (453)
Houston, Texas, City of (453)
Houston, Texas, Department of Aviation of the City of (453)
Houston, Texas, Department of Public Works & Engineering of the City of (453)
Houston, Texas, Housing Authority of the City of (453)
Humboldt Bay Municipal Water District (455)
Huntington Beach, California, City of (455)
Huntsville, Alabama, City of (455)
Huntsville-Madison County Airport (455)
Hutchinson, Kansas, Municipalities of (455)
Iberville Parish (456)
Iceland, Ministry of Fisheries, Government of (456)
Idaho, Office of the Attorney General of the State of (457)
Illinois Department of Transportation (457)
Illinois, State of (458)
Illinois, Washington Office of the State of (458)
Imperial Beach, California, City of (458)
India, Government of the Republic of (460)
Indiana Department of Transportation (460)
Indiana, Office of the Attorney General of the State of (460)
Indiana, Office of the Governor of the State of (460)
Indianapolis, Indiana, City of (460)
Industry Urban-Development Agency (461)
Inglewood, California, City of (462)
Inland Valley Development Agency (462)
Iowa Department of Public Health (478)
Iowa, Dept. of Natural Resources of State of (478)
Iowa, Washington Office of the State of (478)
Irvine, California, City of (479)
Israel, Goverment of the State of (479)
Jackson County, Mississippi Board of Supervisors (480)
Jackson, Mississippi, City of (480)
Jacksonville, Florida, Port Authority of the City of (481)
Jamestown, New York, Board of Public Utilities (481)
Jasper, Alabama, City of (482)
Jefferson Parish Council (482)
Jefferson Texas, County of (482)
Jemez, New Mexico, Pueblo of (482)
Jigawa, Nigerian State of (483)
Johnsburg, Illinois, Village of (484)
Juneau, Alaska, City of (485)
Kake, Alaska, Organized Village of (486)
Kansas City Area Transportation Authority (486)
Kansas City, Missouri, City of (486)
Kentucky, Commonwealth of (488)
Kern County Water Agency (488)
Kern River Watermaster (488)
Kern, California, County of (488)
Ketchikan Gateway Borough (488)
King, Washington, County of (489)
Knightstown, Indiana, Town of (490)
Kodiak Island, Alaska, Borough of (490)
Kodiak, Alaska, City of (490)
Kotzebue, Alaska, City of (491)
Kurdistan Regional Government (492)
Lafayette Consolidated Government (494)
Laguna Beach, California, City of (494)
Laguna Woods, California, City of (494)
Laguna, New Mexico, City of (494)
Lake Worth Drainage District (494)
Lake, California, County of (494)
Lancaster, California, City of (494)
Lane Transit District (495)
Lane, Oregon, County of (495)
Lansing, Michigan, Department of Social Services of the City of (495)
Laredo, Texas, City of (495)
Las Cruces, New Mexico, City of (495)
Las Vegas Valley Water District (495)
Las Vegas, Nevada, City of (495)
Ledyard, Connecticut, Town of (497)
Lehigh-Northhampton Airport Authority (498)
Lincoln, Nebraska, City of (500)
Lithuania, Republic of (500)
Livermore, California, City of (500)
Logan, Utah, City of (Transit District) (502)
Loma Linda, California, City of (503)
Long Beach Water Department (503)
Long Beach, California, City of (503)
Long Beach, California, Port of (503)
Los Alamitos Unified School District (503)
Los Alamos, New Mexico, County of (503)
Los Angeles County Mass Transportation Authority (503)
Los Angeles County Office of Education (504)
Los Angeles County Sanitation District (504)
Los Angeles, California, County of (504)
Los Angeles, California, Metropolitan Transit Authority of (504)
Los Angeles, California, Washington Office of the City of (504)
Louisiana Department of Social Services (504)
Louisiana Public Facilities Authority (504)
Lubbock, Texas, City of (505)
Lynchburg, Virginia, City of (506)
Lynn, Massachusetts, City of (506)
Lynwood, California, City of (506)
Madison County Commission (507)
Madison, Wisconsin, City of (507)
Manatee, Florida, County of (508)
Marianas Political Status Commission (509)
Maricopa, Arizona, County of (509)
Marin, California, County of (510)
Marion, Indiana, City of (510)
Marshall, Alabama, County of (511)
Maryland Department of Transportation (511)
Maryland, Aviation Administration of the State of (512)
Maryland, Office of the Attorney General of the State of (512)
Mass Transit Authority (512)
Massachusetts Bay Transportation Authority (512)
Massachusetts Water Resources Authority (512)

Massachusetts, Commonwealth of (512)
Massena, New York, Town of (512)
Mauritania, Government of the Islamic Republic of (513)
Mayaguez, Puerto Rico, Municipality of (513)
Mecklenburg, North Carolina, County of (515)
Medford, Oregon, City of (516)
Memphis Area Transit Authority (517)
Memphis, Tennessee, City of (517)
Memphis-Shelby County Airport Authority (518)
Merced Irrigation District (518)
Merced, California, County of (518)
Mesa, Arizona, City of (519)
Mesquite, Nevada, City of (519)
Metropolitan Transportation Commission (520)
Metropolitan Washington Council of Governments (521)
Metropolitan Water Reclamation District of Greater Chicago (521)
Mexico, Embassy of (521)
Miami Beach, Florida, City of (521)
Miami, Florida, City of (521)
Miami-Dade County Public Schools (521)
Miami-Dade, Florida, County of (521)
Michigan State Department of Transportation (522)
Michigan, Office of the Attorney General of the State of (522)
Michigan, Washington Office of the State of (522)
Milwaukee, City of (524)
Milwaukee, Wisconsin, County of (524)
Minneapolis, Minnesota, City of (525)
Minneapolis-St. Paul Metropolitan Airports Commission (525)
Minneapolis-St. Paul Metropolitan Council (525)
Minnesota Townships (525)
Minnesota, Washington Office of the State of (525)
Mishawaka Utilities (526)
Mississippi, State of (526)
Missouri River Energy Services (526)
Missouri, Washington Office of the State of (526)
Mobile, Alabama, City of (527)
Modesto, California, City of (527)
Monroe, Florida, County of (527)
Monroe, Louisiana, City of (528)
Monroe, New York, County of (528)
Monrovia, California, City of (528)
Montana, State of (528)
Monterey, California, County of (528)
Montgomery County, Maryland, Division of Consumer Affairs (528)
Montgomery County, Ohio/Montgomery County Solid Waste District (528)
Montgomery, Maryland, Cable Television Office of the County of (529)
Montgomery, Maryland, County of (529)
Montrose, Colorado, City of (529)
Moorehead, Minnesota, City of (529)
Morro Bay, California, City of (530)
Mount Vernon, City of (532)
Murrieta, California, City of (533)
Nebraska Ethanol Board (583)
Nepal, Kingdom of (584)
Netherlands, Ministry of Foreign Affairs of the Government of (584)
Nevada Department of Transportation (584)
Nevada, Office of the Attorney General (585)
Nevada, Washington Office of the State of (585)
New Haven, Connecticut, City of (585)
New Jersey Department of Human Services (585)
New Jersey, State of (585)
New Jersey, Washington Office of the State of (586)
New Mexico Human Services Department (586)
New Mexico State Land Office (586)
New Orleans, Louisiana, City of (586)
New York City (Washington Office) (586)
New York City Board of Estimate (587)
New York Metropolitan Transportation Authority (587)
New York Municipal Power Agency (587)
New York State Department of Social Services (587)
New York State Department of Transportation (587)
New York State Office of Federal Affairs (587)
New York State Senate (587)
New York State Thruway Authority (587)
New York, State of (588)
Newark, California, City of (588)
Newark, New Jersey, City of (588)
Newport News, Virginia, City of (588)
Newport News, Virginia, Industrial Development Authority of the City of (589)
Nez Perce Tribal Executive Committee (589)
Niagara Frontier Transportation Authority (589)
Niger, Government of the Republic of (590)
Nogales, Arizona, City of (591)
Noosack Indian Tribal council (591)
Norfolk, Virginia, City of (591)
North Carolina, Hurricane Floyd Redevelopment Center of State of (593)
North Carolina, Washington Office of the State of (593)
North Dakota, Governor's Office of the State of (593)
North Miami Beach, Florida, City of (593)
North Miami, Florida, City of (593)
North San Diego County Transit Development Board (593)
North Topsail Beach, North Carolina, Town of (593)
Northern Mariana Islands, Commonwealth of the (594)
Norwalk, California, City of (596)
Nottoway, Virginia, County of (596)
Novato, California, City of (596)
Oak Ridge, Tennessee, City of (598)
Oakland County Board of Supervisors (598)
Oakland, California, City of (598)
Oakland, Michigan, County of (598)
Oakley, California, City of (598)
Ocala, Florida, City of (598)
Ocean County, NJ Utilities Authority (598)
Ocean Isle Beach, North Carolina, Town of (598)
Oceanside, California, City of (598)
Ogden, Utah, City of (599)
Ohio, Office of the Attorney General of the State of (599)
Ohio, Washington Office of the State of (599)
Oklahoma City, Oklahoma, City of (599)
Oklahoma, State of (600)
Oman, Sultanate of (600)
Orange County Fire Authority (602)
Orange County Transportation Authority (602)
Orange County Water District (602)
Orange, California, County of (602)
Orange, Florida, County of (602)
Orangeburg, New York, Town of (602)
Oregon Department of Transportation (603)
Oregon Economic Development Department (603)
Oregon, State of (603)
Orlando Utilities Commission (603)
Orlando, Florida, City of (603)
Osceola, Florida, County of (604)
Oxnard Harbor District (605)
Oxnard, California, City of (605)
Pacific States Marine Fisheries Commission (606)
Palm Beach, Florida, County of (606)
Palm Desert, California, City of (606)
Palm Springs, California, City of (606)
Palmdale, California, City of (606)
Palo Alto, California, City of (607)
Panama, Government of the Republic of (607)
Panama, Public Service Regulatory Entity of the Government of the Republic of (607)
Paraguay, Secretariat for Planning of the Republic of (607)
Pasadena, California, City of (609)
Pascua Yaqui Tribe of Arizona (609)
Penn Yan, New York, Village of (611)
Pennsylvania Turnpike Commission (611)
Pennsylvania, Washington Office of the Commonwealth of (611)
Peoria, Arizona, City of (612)
Petersburg, Alaska, City of (613)
Philadelphia Regional Port Authority (615)
Philadelphia, Pennsylvania, City of (615)
Phoenix, Arizona, City of (616)
Pickett, Virginia, Local Redevelopment Authority (617)
Pico Rivera, California, City of (617)
Pierce, Washington, County of (617)
Piqua, Ohio, City of (618)
Placer, California, County of (618)
Plano, Texas, City of (619)
Plaquemine, Louisiana, City of (619)
Plattsburgh, New York, City of (619)
Polk County, Oregon (620)
Polk, Iowa, County of (620)
Port Angeles, Washington, City of (621)
Port Authority of New York and New Jersey (621)
Port Hueneme, California, City of (621)
Portland Metro Regional Government (621)
Portland Tri-Met (621)
Portland, Oregon, City of (621)
Prince George's, Maryland, County of (624)
Prince William County Service Authority (624)
Prince William County, Virginia (624)
Prince William Sound Regional Citizen's Advisory Council (624)
Provo, Utah, City of (627)
Pueblo of Acoma (629)
Pueblo of Laguna (629)
Puerto Rico Electric Power Authority (629)
Puerto Rico Federal Affairs Administration (629)
Puerto Rico Senate (629)
Puerto Rico, Attorney General of (629)
Puerto Rico, Commonwealth of (629)
Ramsey, Minnesota, Board of Commissioners of the County of (633)
Rancho Cucamonga, California, City of (633)
Rancho Palos Verdes, California, City of (633)
Reading, Pennsylvania, City of (633)
Redding, California, Electric Department of the City of (635)
Redlands, California, City of (635)
Regional Transit Authority (636)
Regional Transportation Commission of South Nevada (636)
Rialto, California, City of (639)
Richmond, Virginia, City of (640)
Riverside, California, City of (640)
Riverside, California, County of (640)
Riviera Beach, Florida, City of (640)
Rockville Centre, New York, Village of (641)
Roseville, California, City of (642)
Royal Norwegian Consulate General - New York (643)
Rural Public Lands County Council (643)
Sac & Fox Nation (644)
Sacramento Area Flood Control Agency (645)
Sacramento Housing and Redeveloping Agency (645)
Sacramento Municipal Utility District (645)
Sacramento, California, City of (645)
Sacramento, California, Department of Utilities of (645)
Sacramento, California, Public Works Agency of the County of (645)
Safety Harbor, Florida, City of (645)
Salamanca, New York, City Board of Public Utilities of (646)
Salem, Oregon, City of (646)
Salinas, California, City of (646)
Salt Lake City, Utah, City of (646)
San Antonio, Texas, City of (647)
San Bernardino Airport Authority (647)
San Bernardino Associated Governments (647)
San Bernardino County Social Services Department (647)
San Bernardino, California, City of (647)
San Bernardino, California, County of (647)
San Diego, California, City of (647)
San Diego, California, County of (647)
San Francisco, California, City and County of (648)
San Francisco, City of (648)
San Jacinto, California, City of (648)
San Joaquin Area Flood Agency (648)
San Joaquin Council of Governments (648)
San Joaquin Regional Transit District (648)
San Joaquin, California, County of (648)
San Jose, California, City of (648)
San Juan, Puerto Rico, City of (648)
San Leandro, California, City of (648)
Sandy City, Utah, City of (648)
Santa Ana River Flood Protection Agency (649)
Santa Ana, California, City of (649)
Santa Barbara, California, City of (Waterfront) (649)
Santa Barbara, California, Public Works Department (649)
Santa Clara Valley Transportation Authority (649)
Santa Clara, California, County of (649)
Santa Clara, California, Electric Department of the City of (649)
Santa Clarita, California, City of (649)
Santa Cruz County Regional Transportation Commission (649)
Santa Cruz Metropolitan Transit District (649)
Santa Cruz Redevelopment Agency (649)
Santa Cruz, California, County of (649)
Santa Fe, New Mexico, County of (649)
Santa Monica, California, City of (649)
Sarasota, Florida, City of (649)
Sarasota, Florida, County of (650)
Saudi Arabia, Government of (650)
Saudi Arabia, Ministry of Commerce (650)
Sault Ste. Marie, Michigan, City of (650)
Scottsdale, Arizona, City of (652)
Seal Beach, California, City of (653)
Seaside, California, City of (653)
Seattle Housing Authority (653)
Seattle, Washington, City of (653)
Seattle, Washington, Port of (653)
Secretaria de Agricultura, Granaderia y Desarrolo Rural (SAGAR) (654)
Seward, Alaska, City of (656)
Shelby, Tennessee, County of (657)
Sherburne, New York, Village of (657)
Shreveport, Louisiana, City of (658)
Solana Beach, California, City of (665)
Solid Waste Authority of Central Ohio (665)
Sonoma, California, County of (665)
South Bend, Indiana, City of (666)
South Carolina Department of Transportation (666)
South Carolina Public Railways (666)
South Carolina, Washington Office of the State of (666)
South Dakota, Office of the Attorney General of the State of (666)
South Salt Lake, Utah, City of (666)
Southeastern Pennsylvania Transit Authority (667)
Southern California Public Power Authority (667)
Spaceport Florida Authority (669)
Spokane Regional Solid Waste System (670)
Spokane Tribe (670)
Spokane, Washington, City of (670)
Springettsbury, Pennsylvania, Township of (670)
Springfield, Massachusetts, City of (670)
Springfield, Missouri, City Utilities of (670)
Springfield, Oregon, City of (670)
St. Augustine Beach, Florida, City of (671)
St. Cloud, Minnesota, City of (671)
St. Gabriel, Louisiana, Town of (671)
St. Louis Airport Authority (671)
St. Louis Office of Cable Television (672)
St. Louis, Minnesota, Board of Commissioners of the County (672)
St. Louis, Minnesota, Social Services Department of the County of (672)
St. Louis, Missouri, City of (672)
St. Lucie, Florida, County of (672)
St. Paul, Alaska, City of (672)
St. Paul, Minnesota, City of (672)
Stafford, Virginia, County of (672)
Stamford, Connecticut, City of (672)
Stockton, City of (675)
Suburban Mobility Authority for Regional Transportation (676)
Suffolk, New York, County of (676)
Sutter, California, County of (678)
Swaziland, Kingdom of (678)
Tacoma, Washington, City of (680)

Tacoma, Washington, Port of (680)
Tacoma, Washington, Public Utilities Department of (680)
Taiwan, Government of (680)
Tallahassee, Florida, City of (680)
Tampa Port Authority (680)
Tampa, Florida, City of (680)
Team Stratford (682)
Temecula, California, City of (683)
Tempe, Arizona, City of (683)
Texas Municipal Power Agency (685)
Texas, Office of State-Federal Relations of the State of (685)
Thurmont, Maryland, Town of (686)
Togo, Government of the Republic of (688)
Tooele, Utah, City of (688)
Tri-County Metropolitan Transportation District of Oregon (691)
Trinity Public Utilities District (692)
Tucson, Arizona, City of (693)
Tukwila, Washington, City of (693)
Tulare, California, County of (694)
Tulsa, Oklahoma, City of (694)
Tustin, California, City of (694)
Twentynine Palms Water District (695)
U.S./Mexico Border Counties Coalition (697)
Uganda, Government of the Republic of (698)
Ukraine, Government of (698)
Ukraine, Ministries of Industy, Foreign Economic Relations, and Foreign Affairs of the Government of (698)
Unalaska, Alaska, City of (698)
Union City, New Jersey, City of (699)
United Arab Emirates, Government of (700)
United Kingdom, Government of (702)
Upland, California, City of (708)
Utah Department of Transportation (710)
Utah Transit Authority (710)
Utah, State of (710)
Venice, Florida, City of (712)
Ventura, California, County of (712)
Vero Beach, Florida, City of (714)
City of Victorville Redevelopment Agency (715)
Victorville, California, City of (715)
Village of Kiryas Joel (715)
Virgin Islands, Government of the (715)
Virgin Islands, Office of the Governor (715)
Virginia Beach, Virginia, City of (715)
Virginia Liaison Office (716)
Visalia, California, City of (716)
Volusia, Florida, County of (717)
Wake, North Carolina, County of (718)
Washington County, Oregon, Land Use and Transportation of (719)
Washington, Department of Information of the State of (721)
Washington, Department of Transportation of the State of (721)
Washington, Minnesota, County of (721)
Washington, State of (721)
Wasilla, Alaska, City of (721)
Watsonville, California, City of (722)
Wayne, Michigan, County of (722)
West Jordan, Utah, City of (723)
West Lafayette, Indiana, City of (723)
West Palm Beach, Florida, City of (723)
West Valley City, Utah (723)
West Virginia State Rail Authority (723)
West Virginia, Office of the Attorney General of the State of (723)
Western Coalition of Arid States (724)
Western Governors Ass'n (724)
Western Governors University (724)
Western States Land Commissioners Ass'n (724)
Westminster, California, City of (725)
Wheeling, West Virginia, City of (726)
Williamsport, Maryland, Town of (727)
Wisconsin, Office of the Attorney General of the State of (729)
Wisconsin, Washington Office of the State of (729)
Woodbury County, Iowa (730)
Woodland, California, City of (730)
Wrangell, Alaska, City of (731)
Wyoming, Office of the Attorney General of the State of (732)
Yakima, Washington, City of (732)
Yates County Cable TV Committee (733)
York County Solid Waste Authority (733)
Yukon City, Oklahoma, City of (734)
Yuma, Arizona, City of (734)
Zaire, Office of the President of the Republic of (734)

Heating and Air Conditioning

Air Conditioning Contractors of America (233)
Air-Conditioning and Refrigeration Institute (234)
American Boiler Manufacturers Ass'n (251)
American Soc. of Heating, Refrigerating and Air Conditioning Engineers (276)
American Standard Cos. Inc. (278)
American Supply Ass'n (278)
Automotive Refrigeration Products Institute (304)
Discount Refrigerants Inc. (389)
Donlee Technologies, Inc. (391)
Hearth Products Ass'n (447)
Home Automation Ass'n (451)
Internat'l Ass'n of Heat and Frost Insulators and Asbestos Workers (468)
Internat'l District Energy Ass'n (471)
Internat'l Institute of Ammonia Refrigeration (472)
Internat'l Kitchen Exhaust Cleaning Ass'n (472)
Internat'l Mobile Air Conditioning Ass'n (473)
Nat'l Air Duct Cleaners Ass'n (536)
Nat'l Air Filtration Ass'n (536)
Nat'l Oilheat Research Alliance (NORA) (572)
Plumbing, Heating, Cooling Contractors- National Assoc. (619)
Robur Corp. (641)
Sheet Metal and Air Conditioning Contractors' Nat'l Ass'n (657)
United Technologies Carrier (704)
United Technologies Corp. (704)

History/Historic Preservation

Air Force Memorial Foundation (233)
American Indian Heritage Foundation (263)
American Institute for Conservation of Historic and Artistic Works (263)
Ass'n for the Study of Afro-American Life and History (293)
The Civil War Preservation Trust (349)
The Colonial Williamsburg Foundation (358)
D.C. Historical Tourism Coalition (381)
Daughters of the American Revolution (382)
Fort Abraham Lincoln Foundation (423)
Historic Landmarks Foundation of Indiana (450)
Internat'l Ass'n of Professional Numismatists (468)
Marshall Institute, George C. (511)
Milwaukee Public Museum (524)
Museum of Science and Industry (533)
Museum Trustee Ass'n (533)
Mystic Seaport Museum (534)
Nat'l Building Museum (553)
Nat'l Conference of State Historic Preservation Officers (558)
Nat'l Coordinating Committee for the Promotion of History (559)
Nat'l Film Preservation Foundation (564)
Nat'l Park Foundation (573)
Nat'l Parks Conservation Ass'n (573)
Nat'l Trust for Historic Preservation (580)
Nat'l Underground Railroad Freedom Center (580)
Nat'l Women's History Museum (581)
Old Sturbridge Village (600)
The Phillips Collection (616)
Preservation Action (623)
San Diego Natural History Museum (647)
Smithsonian Institution (661)
The Textile Museum (685)

Homosexuals/Homosexuality

Dignity/USA (388)
Gay and Lesbian Victory Fund (430)
Human Rights Campaign Fund (454)
Lesbian & Gay Community Center Hetrick-Martin Institute (498)
Nat'l Gay and Lesbian Task Force (565)
Nat'l Religious Leadership Roundtable (575)
New Ways Ministry (586)

Horticulture and Landscaping

The American Floral Marketing Council (259)
American Mushroom Institute (268)
American Nursery and Landscape Ass'n (268)
American Seed Research Foundation (273)
American Seed Trade Ass'n (273)
American Soc. of Plant Physiologists (277)
Asociacion Columbiana de Exportadores de Flores (ASOCOLFLORES) (291)
Ass'n of Floral Importers of Florida (295)
Colombia Flower Council (358)
Consortium for Plant Biotechnology Research (368)
Floral Trade Council (419)
Frederick Douglass Gardens, Inc. (425)
Garden Centers of America (429)
Horticultural Research Institute (452)
Nat'l Ass'n of Plant Patent Owners (546)
Nat'l Council of Commercial Plant Breeders (560)
Nat'l Turfgrass Evaluation Program (580)
Northwest Horticultural Council (595)
Pioneer Hi-Bred Internat'l, Inc. (618)
Soc. of American Florists (663)
Turfgrass Producers Internat'l (694)
Wholesale Nursery Growers of America (726)

Housing

Affordable Housing Preservation Center (230)
Affordable Housing Tax Credit Coalition (230)
AFL-CIO Housing Investment Trust (231)
Akron Tower Housing Partnership (235)
Allegheny County, Pennsylvania, Housing Authority (238)
American Homeowners Grassroots Alliance (262)
American Seniors Housing Ass'n (273)
American Soc. of Home Inspectors (ASHI) (276)
Apartment and Office Building Ass'n of Metropolitan Washington (286)
Arlington Educational Ass'n Retirement Housing Corp. (288)
Ass'n of Local Housing Finance Agencies (296)
Assisted Living Federation of America (300)
Bayonne Housing Authority (310)
Coalition for Affordable Housing Preservation (352)
Coalition for the Homeless (354)
Community for Creative Non-Violence (362)
Community Preservation Corp. (363)
Consumer Mortgage Coalition (369)
Contra Costa, California, Tenants of the County of (370)
Corporation for Supportive Housing (372)
Council for Affordable and Rural Housing (373)
Council of Large Public Housing Authorities (376)
Countrywide Home Loans, Inc. (377)
Countrywide Mortgage Corp. (377)
Covenant House (377)
East Chicago Public Housing Authority (395)
The Enterprise Foundation (404)
Fannie Mae (411)
Federal Home Loan Bank of Boston (413)
Federal Home Loan Bank of Dallas (413)
Federal Home Loan Bank of Indianapolis (413)
Federal Home Loan Bank of New York (413)
Federal Home Loan Bank of Pittsburgh (413)
Federal Home Loan Bank of San Francisco (413)
Fellowship Square Foundation, Inc. (415)
Fire Island Ass'n (417)
First Preston Management (417)
H & R Executive Towers (443)
Habitat for Humanity Internat'l (443)
Home Automation Ass'n (451)
Housing and Development Law Institute (453)
Housing Assistance Council (453)
Houston, Texas, Housing Authority of the City of (453)
Illinois Housing Development Authority (457)
Indianapolis Neighborhood Housing Partnership (460)
Institute for Responsible Housing Preservation (464)
Internat'l Code Council (470)
Light Associates (499)
Local Initiatives Support Corp. (501)
Manufactured Housing Ass'n for Regulatory Reform (509)
Manufactured Housing Institute (509)
Massachusetts Housing Finance Agency (512)
Massachusetts Housing Partnership Fund (512)
Mellon Mortgage Co. (517)
Mercy Housing (518)
MetroPlains Development, Inc. (520)
The Money Store (527)
Multi-Family Housing Institute (532)
Nat'l Affordable Housing Management Ass'n (535)
Nat'l Alliance to End Homelessness (537)
Nat'l Apartment Ass'n (537)
Nat'l Ass'n of Affordable Housing Lenders (538)
Nat'l Ass'n of County Community and Economic Development (541)
Nat'l Ass'n of Home Builders of the U.S. (543)
Nat'l Ass'n of Home Builders Research Center, Inc. (544)
Nat'l Ass'n of Housing and Redevelopment Officials (544)
Nat'l Ass'n of Housing Cooperatives (544)
Nat'l Ass'n of Housing Partnerships (544)
Nat'l Center for Housing Management (554)
Nat'l Coalition for Homeless Veterans (556)
Nat'l Coalition for the Homeless (556)
Nat'l Corp. for Housing Partnerships, Inc. (NCHP) (559)
Nat'l Council of State Housing Agencies (560)
Nat'l Fair Housing Alliance (563)
Nat'l Home Equity Mortgage Ass'n (567)
Nat'l Housing and Rehabilitation Ass'n (567)
Nat'l Housing Conference (567)
Nat'l Housing Endowment (567)
Nat'l Institute of Senior Housing (568)
Nat'l Law Center on Homelessness and Poverty (569)
Nat'l Leased Housing Ass'n (569)
Nat'l Low Income Housing Coalition/LIHIS (570)
Nat'l Neighborhood Housing Network (572)
Nat'l Rural Housing Coalition (577)
NCALL Research (583)
Nehemiah Progressive Housing Development Corp. (583)
New York State Housing Finance Agency (587)
Partnership for Advanced Technology in Housing (PATH) (608)
Pedestal (610)
Project Return Foundation Inc. (626)
Public Housing Authorities Directors Ass'n (628)
Roizman & Cos. (642)
Sacramento Housing and Redeveloping Agency (645)
Seattle Housing Authority (653)
Seedco (654)
Shelters, Inc. (657)
Starrett City Associates (673)
Starrett Corp. (673)
State Street Development Co. of Boston (673)
Texas Manufactured Housing Ass'n (684)
Title I Home Improvement Lenders Ass'n (687)
United Homeowners Ass'n (701)
Youthbuild, USA (734)

Immigration

American Hellenic Educational Progressive Ass'n (AHEPA) (262)
American Immigration Lawyers Ass'n (263)
Americans for Better Borders (281)
Carrying Capacity Network, Inc. (332)
Catholic Charities Immigration Legal Services (333)
Center for Immigration Studies (336)
Federation for American Immigration Reform (FAIR) (414)
Fragomen, Del Rey, Bernsen & Loewy, PC (424)
Hebrew Immigrant Aid Soc. (447)
Immigration and Refugee Service of America (458)
Immigration Law Group, P.C. (458)
Internat'l Rescue Committee Inc. (474)
Italian-American Democratic Leadership Council (480)
Mexican-American Legal Defense and Educational Fund (521)
Nat'l Council of Agricultural Employers (560)
Nat'l Immigration Forum (567)
Nat'l Immigration and Naturalization Services Council (567)
Population Reference Bureau (621)
U.S. Immigrant Investor Ass'n (696)
Union of Councils for Soviet Jews (699)
United States Committee for Refugees (703)

Insurance Industry

ABA Insurance Ass'n (224)
Acacia Life Insurance Co. (225)
ACE INA (226)
A.C.E. Insurance Co. (Bermuda) Ltd. (226)
Ace Ltd. (226)
Ad Hoc Life/Non-life Consolidation Group (227)
Aegon USA (229)
Aetna Inc. (230)
Aetna Life & Casualty Co. (230)
AFLAC, Inc. (231)
AIG Environmental (233)
Alliance of American Insurers (240)
Allina Health Systems (241)
Allstate Insurance Co. (241)
American Academy of Actuaries (243)
American Ass'n of Crop Insurers (247)
American Ass'n of Health Plans (AAHP) (248)
American Benefits Council (250)
American Council of Life Insurers (256)
American Family Mutual Insurance Co. (258)
American Fidelity Life Insurance Co. (259)
American Financial Group (259)
American Financial Services Ass'n (259)
American General Corp. (261)
American General Life Insurance Co. (261)
American Insurance Ass'n (264)
American Internat'l Group, Inc. (265)
American Investors Life Insurance (265)
American Land Title Ass'n (265)
American Medical Security (267)
American Mutual Share Insurance Corp. (268)
American Nuclear Insurers (268)
American Share Insurance (273)
American Soc. of Pension Actuaries (277)
AmeriPlan (282)
Amwest Surety Insurance Co. (283)
Anthem, Inc. (285)
Aon Corp. (285)
AON Risk Services (285)
Arkansas Blue Cross and Blue Shield (288)
Armed Forces Benefit Ass'n (289)
Army & Air Force Mutual Aid Ass'n (289)
Ass'n for Advanced Life Underwriting (291)
Ass'n of Banks in Insurance (294)
Ass'n of British Insurers (294)
Ass'n of Financial Guaranty Insurers (295)
Assicurazioni Generali, S.p.A. (299)
Associated Insurance Cos., Inc. (300)
Assurant Group (301)
The Assurant Group (301)
Benova, Inc. (311)
Blue Cross and Blue Shield of California (315)
Blue Cross and Blue Shield of Florida (315)
Blue Cross and Blue Shield of Maine (315)
Blue Cross and Blue Shield of Ohio (315)
Blue Cross Blue Shield Ass'n (315)
Business Insurance Coalition (324)
Business Men's Assurance Co. of America (324)
Capitol American Financial Corp. (331)
CareFirst Blue Cross Blue Shield (331)
Center for Claims Resolution (335)
Central Reserve Life (339)
Central States Indemnity Co. of Omaha (339)
Chicago Title & Trust Co. (343)
Chicago Title Insurance (343)
ChoicePoint (345)
The Chubb Corp. (346)
The Church Alliance (346)
CIGNA Corp. (346)
ClaimTraq, Inc. (349)
Clark/Bardes, Inc. (350)
CNA Financial Corp. (351)
CNA Insurance Cos. (351)
Coalition Against Insurance Fraud (352)
Coalition for Auto-Insurance Reform (353)
Coalition for Crop Insurance Improvement (353)
Coalition on Medicaid Reform (356)
Committee of Annuity Insurers (361)
Consumer Federation of America's Insurance Group (369)
Council for Affordable Health Insurance (374)
Council of Institutional Investors (375)
The Council of Insurance Agents & Brokers (376)
Crop Growers Insurance Co. (378)
Dai-Ichi Life Insurance Co. (381)
Delta Dental Plans Ass'n (385)
Disaster Insurance Coalition/City of Hope Nat'l Medical Center (389)
Eagle-Picher Personal Injury Settlement Trust (394)
Empire Blue Cross and Blue Shield (402)
Employee Benefit Research Institute (402)
Equitable Assurance Soc. of the United States (406)
The Equitable Cos. (406)
Equitable Financial Co. (406)
Equitas Reinsurance Ltd. (406)
The ERISA Industry Committee (ERIC) (406)
EWI-Re Ltd. (408)
Executive Life Insurance Co. (409)
Fallon Community Health Plan (410)
Farmers Insurance Group (412)
Financial Guaranty Insurance Corp. (416)
Fireman's Fund Insurance Cos. (417)
First American Aircraft Title (417)
First American Title Aircraft (417)
Florida Residential and Casualty Joint Underwriting Ass'n (420)
Florida Windstorm Underwriting Ass'n (420)
Forces Vives (422)
Forethought Group/Forethought Life Insurance Co. (423)
Fringe Benefit Group, Inc (426)
GEICO Corp. (430)
General Reinsurance Corp. (433)
Golden Rule Insurance Co. (437)
Greater Washington D.C. Chapter of CLU & ChFC (439)
Group Health, Inc. (441)
Guardian Life Insurance Co. of America (442)
Harbor Branch Institute (444)
The Hartford (445)
Health Benefits Coalition (446)
Health Insurance Ass'n of America (446)
Highmark Blue Cross/ Blue Shield (449)
HIP Health Plans (450)
Household Financial Group, Ltd. (453)
Humana Inc. (455)
Independent Insurance Agents of America, Inc. (459)
ING America Insurance Holdings, Inc. (462)
Insurance Information Institute (464)
Insurance Institute for Highway Safety (465)
Insurance Services Office, Inc. (465)
Internat'l Claim Ass'n (470)
Internat'l Insurance Council (472)
Internat'l Underwriting Ass'n of London (475)
Jackson Nat'l Life Insurance (480)
Kaiser Permanente (486)
Kemper Insurance Cos. (487)
Liberty Corp. (499)
Liberty Mutual Insurance Group (499)
Life and Health Insurance Foundation for Education (499)
Lincoln Nat'l Corp. (500)
Lloyd's of London (501)
Lumbermens Mutual Casualty Co. (505)
Marsh & McLennan Cos. (511)
Massachusetts Mutual Life Insurance Co. (512)
MassMutual Financial Group (512)
MCG Northwest, Inc. (514)
Medical Mutual of Ohio (516)
Medicare Cost Contractors Alliance (517)
Metropolitan Life Insurance Co. (520)
Michigan Insurance Federation (522)
Mid-Atlantic Medical Services, Inc. (523)
Minnesota Life Insurance Co. (525)
MONY Life Insurance Co. (529)
Mortgage Insurance Companies of America (530)
Motorists Insurance Cos. (531)
Municipal Bond Insurance Ass'n (532)
Mutual of America (533)
Mutual of Omaha Insurance Companies (533)
Mutual Tax Committee (533)
Nat'l Academy of Social Insurance (535)
Nat'l Ass'n for State Farm Agents (538)
Nat'l Ass'n of Health Underwriters (543)
Nat'l Ass'n of Independent Insurers (544)
Nat'l Ass'n of Independent Life Brokerage Agency (544)
Nat'l Ass'n of Insurance and Financial Advisors (544)
Nat'l Ass'n of Insurance Commissioners (544)
Nat'l Ass'n of Medicaid Directors (545)
Nat'l Ass'n of Mutual Insurance Companies (545)
Nat'l Ass'n of Professional Insurance Agents (547)
Nat'l Ass'n of Public Insurance Adjusters (547)
Nat'l Ass'n of State Farm Agents (550)
Nat'l Ass'n of Surety Bond Producers (550)
Nat'l Committee to Preserve Social Security and Medicare (557)
Nat'l Coordinating Committee for Multiemployer Plans (559)
Nat'l Council on Compensation Insurance (561)
Nat'l Defined Contribution Council (561)
Nat'l Deposit Insurance Corp. (562)
Nat'l Health Care Anti-Fraud Ass'n (566)
Nat'l Organization of Social Security Claimants' Representatives (572)
Nat'l Structured Settlements Trade Ass'n (579)
Nationwide Mutual Insurance Co. (582)
NCRIC, Inc. (583)
New California Life Holding, Inc. (585)
New England Financial (585)
New England Life Insurance Co. (585)
New York Life Insurance Co. (587)
New York Life Internat'l Inc. (587)
Northwestern Mutual Life Insurance Co. (595)
Ohio Insurance Institute (599)
Ovations/United Health Group (604)
Pacific Life Insurance Co. (605)
PacifiCare Health Systems (606)
Penn Mutual Life Insurance Co. (611)
Pennsylvania Savings Ass'n Insurance Corp. (611)
Perpetual Corp. (612)
Phoenix Home Life Mutual Insurance Co. (616)
Physician Insurers Ass'n of America (616)
Preneed Insurers Government Programs Coalition (623)
Principal Financial Group (624)
Protective Life Insurance Co. (627)
Providian Financial Corp. (627)
Prudential Insurance Co. of America (627)
Public Employee Retirement Systems of Colorado (628)
Public Risk Management Ass'n (629)
Reinsurance Ass'n of America (636)
Risk and Insurance Management Soc., Inc. (RIMS) (640)
Rollins Hudig Hall (642)
Rural Community Insurance Co. (643)
SCAN Health Plan (651)
Sedgwick James, Inc. (654)
Self-Insurance Institute of America, Inc. (655)
Soc. of Professional Benefit Administrators (664)
St. Paul Cos. (672)
State Farm Insurance Cos. (673)
State Universities Retirement System of Illinois Pension Fund (673)
Surety Information Office (677)
Tax Information Group (681)
Texas Windstorm Insurance Ass'n (685)
Textron Inc. (685)
TIAA-CREF (686)
Torchmark Corp. (688)
Trans World Assurance Co. (689)
Transamerica Corp. (689)
Transamerica Occidental Life Insurance Co. (689)
Ukrainian Nat'l Ass'n, Inc. (698)
Underwriters Laboratories Inc. (698)
The Union Labor Life Insurance Co. (699)
United Concordia Companies, Inc. (701)
United Fidelity Life Insurance (701)
United Health Group (701)
UNUM/Provident Corp. (708)
USAA - United Services Automobile Ass'n (710)
USPA & IRA (710)
Variable Annuity Life Insurance Co. (712)
Viatical Ass'n of America (714)
Viaticus, Inc. (714)
Washington Business Group on Health (719)
The Watson Wyatt Worldwide Co. (721)
Wausau Insurance Cos. (722)
WellPoint Health Networks/Blue Cross of California/UNICARE (723)
Western Growers Insurance Services (724)
Westfield Companies (725)
The Winterthur Group (728)
X-PAC (732)
X.L. Insurance Co. (732)
XL Capital Ltd (732)
Zurich Financial Group (735)
Zurich Financial Services Group (735)

Jewelry and Gems

American Soc. of Appraisers (275)
American Watch Ass'n (280)
Avon Products, Inc. (305)
Benrus Watch Co. (311)
Debswana Diamond Co. (383)
The Gold and Silver Institute (436)
Jewelers of America (483)
The Jewelers' Security Alliance (483)
Manufacturing Jewelers and Suppliers of America (509)
Silver Users Ass'n (659)
Timex Corp. (687)
Virgin Islands Watch and Jewelry Manufacturers Ass'n (715)
Zirconia Sales America (734)

Labor Unions

Academy of Rail Labor Attorneys (226)
The Accountability Project (226)
AFL-CIO (American Federation of Labor and Congress of Industrial Organizations) (231)
AFL-CIO (Union Label and Service Trades Department) (231)
AFL-CIO - Broadcast Division (231)
AFL-CIO - Building and Construction Trades Department (231)
AFL-CIO - Food and Allied Service Trades Department (231)

Law Enforcement/Security

Law/Law Firms

Committee to Support the Antitrust Laws (361)
Connecticut, Office of the Attorney General of the State of (367)
Council for Court Excellence (374)
Council on Labor Law Equality (377)
The Criminal Justice Policy Foundation (378)
Cruz Enverga & Raboca (379)
Dalton & Dalton P.C. (382)
Defense Administrative Judges Professional Ass'n (384)
Dierman, Wortley, and Zola (388)
Earthjustice Legal Defense Fund (394)
Environmental Law Institute (405)
Federal Administrative Law Judges Conference (412)
Federal Bar Ass'n (412)
Federal Judges Ass'n (413)
Federal Magistrate Judges Ass'n (413)
Ford Motor Credit Co. (Legal Department) (422)
Freedom of Information Clearinghouse (425)
Gardere & Wayne, LLP (429)
Georgia, Office of the Attorney General of the State of (434)
Bruce Givner, Attorney (435)
HALT-An Organization of Americans for Legal Reform (444)
Handgun Control, Inc. (444)
Hankin, Persson & Darnell (444)
Harris, Beach & Wilcox (445)
Heard Goggan Blair & Williams (447)
Hooper, Lundy and Bookman (452)
Housing and Development Law Institute (453)
Idaho, Office of the Attorney General of the State of (457)
Immigration Law Group, P.C. (458)
Indian Law Resource Center (460)
Indiana, Office of the Attorney General of the State of (460)
Inman, Steinberg, Nye & Stone (462)
Institute for Justice (463)
Institute for Public Representation (463)
Intellectual Property Owners Ass'n (465)
Inter-American Bar Ass'n (465)
Internat'l Ass'n of Jewish Lawyers and Jurists (468)
Internat'l Foundation for Election Systems (IFES) (471)
The Internat'l Human Rights Law Group (472)
Internat'l Law Institute (473)
Internat'l Municipal Lawyers Ass'n (473)
Internat'l Trade Commission Trial Lawyers Ass'n (475)
Judicial Watch, Inc. (485)
Justice Fellowship (485)
Justice Research and Statistics Ass'n (485)
Kalkines, Arky, Zall and Bernstein (486)
Landmark Legal Foundation Center for Civil Rights (495)
Laquidara & Edwards, P.A. (495)
Bob Lawrence & Associates (496)
Lawyers Alliance for World Security (496)
Lawyers Committee for Human Rights (496)
Lawyers for Civil Justice (496)
Lawyers for the Republic (496)
Lawyers' Committee for Civil Rights Under Law (496)
Legal Action Center of the City of New York, Inc. (497)
Legal Services Corp. (497)
Legix Co. (498)
Loeb & Loeb (502)
Maryland, Office of the Attorney General of the State of (512)
Media Access Project (516)
Merit Systems Protection Board (519)
Michigan, Office of the Attorney General of the State of (522)
Migrant Legal Action Program (524)
Minority Business Enterprise Legal Defense and Education Fund (525)
NAACP Legal Defense and Educational Fund, Inc. (534)
Nat'l Asian Pacific American Legal Consortium (537)
Nat'l Ass'n for Public Interest Law (NAPIL) (538)
Nat'l Ass'n of Attorneys General (539)
Nat'l Ass'n of Bond Lawyers (539)
Nat'l Ass'n of College and University Attorneys (540)
Nat'l Ass'n of Consumer Bankruptcy Attorneys (540)
Nat'l Ass'n of County Civil Attorneys (541)
Nat'l Ass'n of Criminal Defense Lawyers (542)
Nat'l Ass'n of Protection and Advocacy Systems (NAPAS) (547)
Nat'l Ass'n of Retail Collection Attorneys (548)
Nat'l Ass'n of Securities and Commercial Law Attorneys (549)
Nat'l Bar Ass'n (552)
Nat'l Committee for a Human Life Amendment (557)
Nat'l Conference of Bankruptcy Judges (558)
Nat'l Consumer Law Center (558)
Nat'l Court Reporters Ass'n (561)
Nat'l Criminal Justice Ass'n (561)
Nat'l District Attorneys Ass'n (562)
Nat'l Employment Lawyers Ass'n (562)
Nat'l Health Law Program (567)
Nat'l Health Lawyers Ass'n (567)
Nat'l Institute for Citizen Education in the Law (568)
Nat'l Law Center on Homelessness and Poverty (569)
Nat'l Legal & Policy Center (570)
Nat'l Legal Aid and Defender Ass'n (570)
Nat'l Legal Center for the Public Interest (570)
Nat'l Organization for the Reform of Marijuana Laws (572)
Nat'l Rifle Ass'n Institute for Legislative Action (576)
Nat'l Right to Work Legal Defense Foundation (576)
Nat'l Senior Citizens Law Center (577)
Nat'l Structured Settlements Trade Ass'n (579)
Nat'l Veterans Legal Services Program (580)
Nat'l Women's Law Center (581)
Natural Resources Defense Council (582)
Neighborhood Legal Services Program (583)
Nevada, Office of the Attorney General (585)
Nossaman, Gunther, Knox & Elliott (596)
Office of the People's Counsel for the District of Columbia (599)
Ohio Prosecuting Attorneys Ass'n (599)
Ohio, Office of the Attorney General of the State of (599)
Ovarian Cancer Nat'l Alliance (604)
Pew Charitable Trust - Environmental Law & Policy Center of the Midwest (613)
Product Liability Alliance, The (625)
Product Liability Information Bureau (625)
Product Liability Prevention and Defense Group (625)
Puerto Rico, Attorney General of (629)
Rakisons, Ltd. (632)
Ranchers-Cattlemen Legal Action Fund (633)
Regulatory Affairs Professionals Soc. (636)
Reporters Committee for Freedom of the Press (637)
Scull Law Firm, David L. (653)
Securities Litigation Reform Coalition (654)
The Sentencing Project (655)
South Dakota, Office of the Attorney General of the State of (666)
Southeastern Legal Foundation (667)
Special Committee for Workplace Product Liability Reform (669)
Sports Lawyers Ass'n (670)
Stoll Stoll Berne Lokting & Shlachter, P.C. (675)
Street Law Inc. (675)
Student Press Law Center (675)
Szlavik, Hogan & Miller (679)
Taxpayers Against Fraud, The False Claims Legal Center (681)
Tort Reform Institute (688)
Touro Law Center (688)
Trial Lawyers for Public Justice, P.C. (691)
U.S. Chamber Institute for Legal Reform (695)
U.S. Trade Law Study Group (697)
Waesche, Sheinbaum, and O'Regan (718)
Washington Area Lawyers for the Arts (719)
Washington Legal Clinic for the Homeless (720)
Washington Legal Foundation (720)
West Group (723)
West Virginia, Office of the Attorney General of the State of (723)
Wilke, Fleury, Hoffelt, Gould & Birney, LLP (727)
Wilkie Farr & Gallagher (727)
Wisconsin, Office of the Attorney General of the State of (729)
World Jurist Ass'n of the World Peace Through Law Center (731)
Wright, Lindsey & Jennings (732)
Wyoming, Office of the Attorney General of the State of (732)

Libraries

American Library Ass'n (266)
American Soc. for Information Science (274)
Ass'n of Academic Health Sciences Library Directors (293)
Ass'n of Research Libraries (298)
Brooklyn Public Library (322)
Center for Responsive Politics (337)
Folger Shakespeare Library (421)
Friends of the Nat'l Library of Medicine (426)
Library Users of America (499)
Medical Library Ass'n/Ass'n of Academic Health Sciences Library Directors (516)
Nat'l Coordinating Committee for the Promotion of History (559)
Nat'l Security Archive (577)
New York Public Library (587)
Queens Borough Public Library (631)
Special Libraries Ass'n (669)

Machinery

Advanced Machinery Logistics, Inc. (228)
Affiliated Computer Services (230)
Allied Products Corp. (241)
American Amusement Machine Ass'n (245)
American Bearing Manufacturers Ass'n (250)
American Boiler Manufacturers Ass'n (251)
American Gear Manufacturers Ass'n (261)
American Koyo Corp. (265)
American Nat'l Metric Council (268)
American Paper Machinery Ass'n (269)
American Rental Ass'n (272)
American Supply and Machinery Manufacturers' Ass'n (278)
The Ass'n For Manufacturing Technology (AMT) (292)
Associated Equipment Distributors (300)
Automotive Engine Rebuilders Ass'n (303)
Babcock & Wilcox (305)
Bell Equipment Ltd. (311)
Black & Decker Corp., The (315)
Bombardier Transportation/Bombardier Transit Corporation (317)
Brother Internat'l Co. (322)
Budd Co. (323)
CaseNewHolland Inc. (333)
Caterpillar Inc. (333)
Chromalloy Gas Turbine Corp. (346)
Coin Acceptors, Inc. (357)
Coin Laundry Ass'n (357)
Coleman Powermate (357)
Construction Industry Manufacturers Ass'n (368)
Council of Industrial Boiler Owners (CIBO) (375)
Crown Controls Corp. (379)
Danaher Corp. (382)
Deere & Co. (383)
Drives Inc. (392)
Election Systems & Software (399)
Ellicott Internat'l (401)
Emerson (402)
Equipment Leasing Ass'n of America (406)
Florida Equipment Contractors Ass'n (419)
FMC Corp. (420)
Food Processing Machinery and Supplies Ass'n (421)
Gas Appliance Manufacturers Ass'n (429)
General Electric Industrial & Power Systems (432)
Hand Tools Institute (444)
Harnischfeger Industries, Inc. (444)
Illinois Tool Works (458)
Information Technology Industry Council (462)
Ingersoll-Rand Co. (462)
Internat'l Ass'n of Machinists and Aerospace Workers (468)
Internat'l Brotherhood of Boilermakers, Iron Shipbuilders, Blacksmiths, Forgers and Helpers (469)
Internat'l Safety Equipment Ass'n (ISEA) (474)
Internat'l Truck and Engine Corp. (475)
Johnson Controls, Inc. (484)
Joy Mining Machinery (485)
Komatsu Ltd. (490)
Koyo Seiko Co., Ltd. (491)
Kruger Internat'l (KI) (492)
Machinery Dealers Nat'l Ass'n (506)
Mazak Corp. & Mazak Sales and Service, Inc. (513)
Mechanical Equipment Co., Inc. (515)
Metro Machine Corp. of Virginia (520)
Mitsubishi Corp. (526)
Motor and Equipment Manufacturers Ass'n (531)
Multi-Housing Laundry Ass'n (532)
NACCO Industries (534)
Nat'l Automatic Merchandising Ass'n (552)
Nat'l School Supply and Equipment Ass'n (577)
Nat'l Tooling and Machining Ass'n (579)
North American Equipment Dealers Ass'n (592)
Outdoor Power Equipment Aftermarket Ass'n (604)
Outdoor Power Equipment Institute (604)
Packaging Machinery Manufacturers Institute (606)
Parker Hannifin Corp. (608)
Perry Tritech Inc. (612)
Pitney Bowes, Inc. (618)
Portable Power Equipment Manufacturers Ass'n (621)
Process Equipment Manufacturers' Ass'n (625)
Product Liability Prevention and Defense Group (625)
Pump Service and Supply Co. (630)
Raytheon Co. (633)
Societe Nationale d'Etude et Construction de Moteurs d'Aviation (SNECMA) (664)
Stewart & Stevenson Services, Inc. (674)
Tecumseh Products Co. (682)
TI Group Inc. (686)
The Toro Co. (688)
Torrington Co. (688)
Ultratech Stepper Inc. (698)
United Automobile, Aerospace and Agricultural Implement Workers of America (UAW) (700)
United Electrical Workers of America (701)
Valve Manufacturers Ass'n of America (711)
Water and Wastewater Equipment Manufacturers Ass'n (721)
Wood Machinery Manufacturers of America (730)
Xerox Corp. (732)
Yale Materials Handling Corp. (733)

Management

Academy of Leadership (225)
Accenture (226)
ACME - Ass'n of Management Consulting Firms (226)
American Ass'n of Entrepreneurs (247)
American Ass'n of Health Care Administrative Management (248)
American Health Information Management Ass'n (262)
American Management (266)
American Soc. of Ass'n Executives (275)
American Soc. of Farm Managers and Rural Appraisers (276)
Amstel Hudson Management Corp. (283)
Ass'n for Financial Professionals, Inc. (292)
Ass'n for Information and Image Management Internat'l (292)
Ass'n of State and Territorial Solid Waste Management Officials (298)
Automotive Trade Ass'n Executives (304)
Battelle Memorial Institute (309)
Building Owners and Managers Ass'n Internat'l (323)
The Business Council (324)
Clark County, Nevada, Office of the County Manager (350)

Clinical Laboratory Management Ass'n (351)
Club Managers Ass'n of America (351)
Congressional Management Foundation (366)
Consolidated Administration and Security Services, Inc. (367)
Construction Management Ass'n of America (368)
Day & Zimmermann, Inc. (383)
Deloitte Consulting (384)
Directors Guild of America (389)
Edison Properties L.L.C. (397)
Emergency Department Practice Management Ass'n (EDPMA) (401)
Environmental Industry Ass'ns (405)
Farallon Capital Management (411)
Federal Managers Ass'n (413)
First Consulting Group (417)
First Preston Management (417)
Forest Products Industry Nat'l Labor-Management Committee (423)
Greater Washington Soc. of Ass'n Executives (440)
The Hamilton Group (444)
Healthcare Financial Management Ass'n (447)
Hurt, Norton and Associates, Inc. (455)
Ibex (456)
Information Practices Coalition of Washington, D.C. (461)
Innovative Resource Group (462)
Instrument Technicians Labor-Management Cooperation Fund (464)
Inter-Nation Capital Management (466)
Internat'l Ass'n of Assembly Managers (467)
Internat'l City/County Management Ass'n (470)
Internat'l Facilities Management Ass'n (471)
Internat'l Management and Development Institute (473)
Internat'l Personnel Management Ass'n (474)
Internat'l Trade Council (475)
Interocean Management Co. (477)
IT Group, Inc. (479)
J & B Management Co. (480)
Kahl Pownall Advocates (485)
Lockheed Martin Air Traffic Management (501)
Lockheed Martin IMS (502)
Managed Health Care Ass'n (508)
McKinsey & Co., Inc. (515)
Medical Group Management Ass'n (516)
MedPartners, Inc. (517)
Mills Corporation (524)
Mineral Technologies, Inc. (525)
Nat'l Academy of Public Administration (535)
Nat'l Affordable Housing Management Ass'n (535)
Nat'l Ass'n for Environmental Management (537)
Nat'l Ass'n of Consumer Agency Administrators (540)
Nat'l Ass'n of Corporate Directors (541)
Nat'l Ass'n of County Administrators (541)
Nat'l Ass'n of County Health Facility Administrators (541)
Nat'l Ass'n of County Human Services Administrators (541)
Nat'l Ass'n of Credit Management (541)
Nat'l Ass'n of Fleet Administrators (543)
Nat'l Ass'n of Foster Grandparent Program Directors (543)
Nat'l Ass'n of Healthcare Access Management (543)
Nat'l Center for Housing Management (554)
Nat'l Council of County Ass'n Executives (560)
Nat'l Energy Management Institute (563)
Nat'l Institute for Health Care Management (568)
NCR Corp. (583)
North American Sports Management, Inc. (592)
OnCare, Inc. (600)
PCS Health Systems, Inc. (610)
Periodical Management Group, Inc. (612)
Pezold Management (613)
Problem-Knowledge Coupler (625)
Professional Managers Ass'n (626)
Professional Services Council (626)
Public Financial Management (628)
Public Risk Management Ass'n (629)
Robbins-Gioia, Inc. (641)
Sealaska Corp. (653)
Shriner-Midland Co. (658)
The Charles E. Smith Companies (661)
Soc. for Human Resource Management (662)
Soc. of Competitive Intelligence Professionals (663)
Spectrum Health Care Resources, Inc. (670)
SSI Services, Inc. (671)
State Street Development Co. of Boston (673)
Sunset Properties, Inc. (677)
Thunderbird, The American Graduate School of Internat'l Management (686)
TMC, Inc. (687)
TMS Consulting, LLC (687)
Tobacco Industry Labor Management Committee (688)
Toyota Technical Center U.S.A. Inc. (689)
Trade Ass'n Liaison Council (689)
TransNat'l Business Development Corp. (690)
U.S. Oncology (697)
Vredenburg (718)
West*Group Management LLC (723)
Wildlife Management Institute (727)

Marine/Maritime/Shipping

3001, Inc. (223)
Ad Hoc Maritime Coalition (227)
AFL-CIO Maritime Committee (231)
AFL-CIO - Maritime Trades Department (231)
Agriculture Ocean Transportation Coalition (232)
AHL Shipping Co. (232)
Alaska Eskimo Whaling Commission (236)
Alaska Ship and Drydock, Inc. (237)
Allboxesdirect (238)
Alliance of Marine Mammal Parks and Aquariums (240)
American Cotton Shippers Ass'n (255)
American Great Lakes Ports (261)
American Import Shippers Ass'n (263)
American Institute for Shippers' Ass'ns (264)
American League of Anglers and Boaters (266)
American Maritime Congress (267)
American Maritime Officers Service (267)
American Oceans Campaign (269)
American Pilots Ass'n (270)
American Shipbuilding Ass'n (274)
American Steamship Co. (278)
American Watercraft Ass'n (280)
American Waterways Operators (280)
Apex Marine Ship Management Co. LLC (286)
APL Limited (286)
Applied Marine Technologies, Inc. (287)
Aquarium of the Pacific (287)
Ass'n of Nat'l Estuary Programs (297)
Atlantic Marine Holding Co. (302)
Atlantic States Marine Fisheries Commission (302)
Avondale Industries, Inc. (305)
Bender Shipbuilding & Repair Co., Inc. (311)
Bird-Johnson Co. (314)
The Boat Co. (316)
Boat Owners Ass'n of The United States (BOAT/U.S.) (316)
Bollinger Shipyards (317)
Boston Consolidated Services, Inc. (318)
Bridgeport and Port Jefferson Steamboat Co. (320)
Brix Maritime, Inc. (321)
Brownsville, Texas, Port of (322)
Bruker Meerestechnik GmbH (322)
Brunswick Corp. (322)
Cal Dive Internat'l Inc. (326)
Canal Barge Co., Inc. (330)
Carnival Corp. (332)
Cascade General, Inc. (332)
Center for Marine Conservation (337)
Central Freight Forwarding (339)
Chamber of Shipping of America (341)
Chesapeake Bay Maritime Museum (342)
China Ocean Shipping Co. (344)
China Shipping (Group) Co. (344)
Coalition for Fair Play in Ocean Shipping (353)
Coalition for Maritime Education (354)
Coalition for Stability in Marine Financing (354)
Coalition of Hawaii Movers (355)
Coast Alliance (356)
Coastal Conservation Ass'n (356)
Companhia Maritima Nacional (363)
Conference of Private Operators for Response Towing (366)
Consortium for Oceanographic Research and Education (CORE) (367)
Corpus Christi Port Authority (373)
COSCO Americas Inc. (373)
Council of European and Japanese Nat'l Shipowners' Ass'ns (375)
Cross Sound Ferry Services, Inc. (378)
Crystal Cruises (379)
CSX Corp. (379)
CSX Lines LLC (379)
Delaware River Stevedores (384)
Distribution Services, Ltd. (390)
Dredging Contractors of America (392)
Edison Chouest Offshore, Inc. (397)
Eklof Marine Corp. (399)
Espee Trading Corp. (407)
Express Forwarding and Storage, Inc. (409)
FastShip, Inc. (412)
Fentek Internat'l Pty. Ltd. (415)
First American Bulk Carriers Corp. (417)
Fishing Vessel Owners' Ass'n (418)
Fleet Reserve Ass'n (418)
FlightSafety Internat'l (419)
Florida Cruise and Ferry Service Inc. (419)
Fontana Bleu, S.p.A. (421)
Freight-Savers Shipping Co. Ltd. (425)
Friede, Goldman, & Halter, Inc. (426)
Fruit Shippers Ltd. (427)
GCI-Wisconsin (430)
Global Marine, Inc. (436)
J. R. Gray & Co. (438)
Great Lakes Dredge & Dock (439)
Guardian Marine Internat'l LLC (442)
Harborlink, LLC (444)
Hawaiian Moving and Forwarding Ass'n (445)
Honolulu Shipyard (452)
Hornblower Marine Services, Inc. (452)
Houston, Texas, Port Authority of the City of (453)
Howland Hook Container Terminal Inc. (454)
Hvide Marine Inc. (456)
I.O.T.A. Partners (456)
Ingalls Shipbuilding (462)
Institute of Cetacean Research (464)
Institute of Navigation (464)
Interlake Holding Corp. (466)
Intermare Navigation SA (466)
Intermarine USA (466)
Internat'l Brotherhood of Boilermakers, Iron Shipbuilders, Blacksmiths, Forgers and Helpers (469)
Internat'l Council of Containership Operators (470)
Internat'l Council of Cruise Lines (470)
Internat'l Longshore and Warehouse Union (473)
Internat'l Longshoremen's Ass'n (473)
Internat'l Shipholding Corp. (474)
Interocean Management Co. (477)
Island Express Boat Lines Ltd. (479)
Kirby Corp./Dixie Carriers (490)
Kongsberg Simrad (491)
Kvaerner Philadelphia Shipyard Inc. (492)
Kvaerner US Inc. (492)
Labor Management Maritime Committee, Inc. (493)
Lake Carriers Ass'n (494)
Lehigh Coal & Navigation Co. (498)
Liberty Maritime Co. (499)
Long Beach Naval Shipyard Employees Ass'n (503)
The Lykes Bros. (506)
MacGregor (506)
Maersk Inc. (507)
Marine Capital Management, LLC (510)
Marine Engineers Beneficial Ass'n (District No. 1 - PCD) (510)
Marine Mammal Coalition (510)
Marine Resources Company Internat'l (510)
Marine Spill Response Corporation (510)
Marine Technology Soc. (510)
Marinette Marine Corp. (510)
The Maritime Consortium, Inc. (510)
Maritime Exchange for the Delaware River and Bay (510)
Maritime Fire and Safety Ass'n (510)
Maritime Institute for Research and Industrial Development (510)
Martha's Vineyard Steamship Authority (511)
Massa Products Corp. (512)
Massachusetts Maritime Academy (512)
Matson Navigation Co. (513)
Metromarine Holdings, Inc. (520)
Mitsubishi Corp. (526)
MOTE Marine Lab (530)
Nat'l Ass'n of Charterboat Operators (NACO) (540)
Nat'l Ass'n of Waterfront Employers (551)
Nat'l Marine Life Center (570)
Nat'l Marine Manufacturers Ass'n (570)
Nat'l Maritime Alliance (570)
Nat'l Maritime Safety Ass'n (570)
Nat'l Ocean Industries Ass'n (572)
Nat'l Steel and Shipbuilding Co. (579)
Nat'l Waterways Conference, Inc. (581)
Naval Reserve Ass'n (582)
NAVATEK Ship Design Hawaii (583)
Navigational Electronic Chart Systems Ass'n (NECSA) (583)
Navy League of the United States (583)
New England Aquarium (585)
New York Waterways (588)
Newport News Shipbuilding Inc. (588)
Nippon Yusen Kaisha (NYK) Line (590)
Norsk Hydro (591)
North American Shipbuilding (592)
Northland Holdings, Inc. (594)
Norwegian Cruise Line (596)
Ocean Shipholding, Inc. (598)
Orange Shipbuilding Co., Inc. (602)
Orient Overseas Container Line (603)
P & O Nedlloyd Ltd. (605)
Pacific Marine (605)
Pacific Maritime Ass'n (605)
Pacific Shipyards Internat'l, Hawaii (606)
Panama Trans-Shipment Consortium (607)
Passenger Vessel Ass'n (609)
Perry Institute for Marine Science (612)
Pilots' Ass'n of the Bay and River Delaware (617)
Port of San Diego (621)
Princess Cruise Lines (624)
The Propeller Club of the United States (627)
R.M.S. Titanic, Inc. (632)
Redwood City, California, Port of (635)
Richardson Lawrie Associates (639)
Francis R. Ruddy Institute of Maritime Communications (643)
Santa Cruz, California, Port of (649)
Sargeant Marine, Inc. (650)
Sea Bridge Internat'l LLC (653)
Sea Containers America, Inc. (653)
Sea Ventures Inc. (653)
Seaboard Corp. (653)
Seafarers Internat'l Union of North America (653)
Shipbuilders Council of America (657)
Sippican, Inc. (660)
Sperry Marine Inc. (670)
Steel Shipping Container Institute (674)
Summary Agency, Ltd. (676)
SunCruz Casino (677)
Sunmar Shipping, Inc. (677)
The Title XI Coalition (687)
Todd Shipyards Inc. (688)
Trailer Marine Transport Corp. (689)
Trans Ocean Leasing Corp. (689)
Transconex, Inc. (690)
Transpacific Stabilization Agreement (690)

Transportation Institute (690)
Transportation Reform Alliance (690)
Trident Seafood Corp. (692)
Tropical Shipping and Construction Co. (692)
U.S. Marine Corp. (696)
Unideal Navitankers (698)
United Catcher Boats (700)
United States Marine Repair (703)
United States Maritime Coalition (703)
United Van Lines, Inc. (705)
University of Southern Mississippi (707)
Van Ommeren Shipping (USA), Inc. (711)
Votainer Consolidation Service (717)
Waterman Steamship Co. (721)
Western Pioneer, Inc. (724)
Woods Hole Oceanographic Institution (730)
Woods Hole Steamship Authority (730)
World Shipping Council (731)
Worldlink Logistics Inc. (731)

Media (Journalism/Publishing/Radio-TV)

ABC Inc. (225)
Abrams & Co. Publishers Inc. (225)
Accuracy in Media (226)
Ad Hoc Public Television Group (227)
AFL-CIO - Broadcast Division (231)
Alarm Industry Communications Committee (236)
Alliance of Motion Picture & Television Producers (240)
American Booksellers Ass'n (251)
American Business Media (251)
American Federation of Television and Radio Artists (259)
American Press Institute (271)
American Radio Relay League (272)
American Soc. of Access Professionals (275)
American Soc. of Composers, Authors and Publishers (276)
American Soc. of Newspaper Editors (277)
American Women in Radio and Television (280)
AMFM, Inc. (282)
AOL Time Warner (285)
Ass'n for Maximum Service Television, Inc. (292)
Ass'n for the Suppliers of Printing and Publishing Technology (293)
Ass'n of America's Public Television Stations (293)
Ass'n of American Publishers (294)
Ass'n of Directory Publishers (295)
Ass'n of Local Television Stations (296)
Ass'n of Test Publishers (299)
Association Trends (300)
Barnstable Broadcasting (308)
Beasley Broadcast Group (310)
A. H. Belo Corp. (311)
Benchmark Communications Radio LP (311)
BET Holdings II, Inc. (312)
Blade Communications (315)
Broadcast Education Ass'n (321)
Broadcast Music Inc. (BMI) (321)
Buckley Broadcasting Corp. (323)
The Bureau of Nat'l Affairs, Inc. (323)
Business News Publishing Co. (325)
Cable & Wireless, Inc. (325)
Cablevision Systems Corp. (325)
California Cable Television Ass'n (326)
Canadian Broadcasting Corp. (329)
CanWest (330)
Capitol Broadcasting Co. (331)
Catholic News Service (333)
Catholic Television Network (333)
CBS Affiliates (334)
Center for Media and Public Affairs (337)
Center for Media Education (337)
Channel One Network (341)
Charter Communications, Inc. (341)
Chris-Craft Broadcasting, Inc. (345)
Christian Broadcasting Network (345)
Christian Network, Inc. (345)
CINE (347)
Classroom Publishers Ass'n (350)
Comcast Corp. (359)
Comic Magazine Ass'n of America (360)
Communications Consortium (362)
Cook Inlet Communications (371)
Copyright Clearance Center, Inc. (371)
Corporation for Public Broadcasting (372)
Cox Enterprises Inc. (378)
CSRG Digital LLC (379)
CTAM (379)
Cumulus Media, Inc. (380)
Dearborn, Michigan, Department of Communication of (383)
Dick Broadcasting Co., Inc. (387)
Discovery Communications, Inc. (389)
The Walt Disney Co. (389)
Dow Jones & Co., Inc. (391)
Dubuque, Iowa, Cable Television Division of (392)
Dun & Bradstreet (393)
EchoStar Communications Corp. (396)
The Economist Newspaper Group (396)
Education and Research Institute (398)
Educational Media Foundation (398)
Electronic Industries Ass'n of Japan (401)
Electronic Retailing Ass'n (401)
Emmis Broadcasting Corp. (402)
Encyclopaedia Britannica, Inc. (402)
Entertainment Made Convenient (404)
Environmental Media Services (405)
Ericsson Inc. (406)
ESPN, Inc. (407)
First Amendment Coalition for Expression (417)
Fisher Broadcasting, Inc. (418)
The Frontier Press (427)
Gallery Watch (428)
Gannett Co., Inc. (429)
Gemini Networks, Inc. (431)
Glencairn, Ltd. (436)
Granite Broadcasting Co. (438)
Greater Washington Educational Telecommunications Ass'n (440)
Grupo Televisa, S.A. (441)
Harcourt Inc. (444)
Harvard Radio Broadcasting Co. (445)
Health Resource Publishing Co. (446)
The Hearst Corp. (447)
Hearst-Argyle Television, Inc. (447)
Heartland Communications & Management Inc. (447)
Hispanic Broadcasting Inc. (450)
Holt Communications Corp. (451)
Home Box Office (451)
Hubbard Broadcasting, Inc. (454)
Hudson News (454)
Information Trust (462)
Tom Ingstead Broadcasting Group (462)
Rob Ingstead Broadcasting, Inc. (462)
The Ingstead Broadcasting, Inc. (462)
InterMart Broadcasting (466)
InterMedia Partners (467)
Internat'l Center for Journalists (469)
Internews (476)
ITT World Directories, Inc. (480)
Jovan Broadcasting (485)
KAIL-TV (485)
KATU (487)
KATY-FM (487)
Katz Communications, Inc. (487)
KCSM-TV (487)
KDTV (487)
KDUH-TV (487)
Keymarket Communications, Inc. (489)
KFAR-TV (489)
KFTV (489)
KHSD-TV (489)
KJAZ-FM (490)
KJVI (490)
KKVI (490)
KLUZ-TV (490)
KMEX-TV (490)
KOMO-TV (491)
KOMU-TV (491)
KOTA-TV (491)
KPVI (492)
KSGW-TV (492)
KTTY (492)
KTUU (492)
KTVW-TV (492)
KUVN-TV (492)
KVCR-TV (492)
KWEX-TV (492)
KXLN-TV (492)
KXMA-TV (492)
KXMB (492)
KXMC-TV (492)
KXMD-TV (492)
KXTX-TV (492)
The Lincoln Group (500)
Magazine Publishers of America (507)
Malrite Communications Group, Inc. (508)
Maryland, DC, Delaware Broadcasters Ass'n (512)
Matthews Media Group, Inc. (513)
McGraw-Hill Cos., The (514)
Media Access Project (516)
Media Fusion L.L.C. (516)
Media Institute (516)
Media Research Center (516)
Media Tax Group (516)
Medium-Sized Cable Operators Group (517)
Mega Broadcasting Corp. (517)
MFS Communications Co., Inc. (521)
Mid-Atlantic Broadcast Partners (523)
Montgomery, Maryland, Cable Television Office of the County of (529)
Most Group Limited (530)
Multi Media Telecommunications Ass'n (MMTA) (532)
Mutual Broadcasting System (533)
Nat'l Ass'n of Black-Owned Broadcasters (539)
Nat'l Ass'n of Broadcast Employees and Technicians-Communications Workers of America, AFL-CIO (NABET-CWA) (539)
Nat'l Ass'n of Broadcasters (539)
Nat'l Ass'n of Government Communicators (543)
Nat'l Ass'n of Hispanic Journalists (543)
Nat'l Black Media Coalition (552)
Nat'l Broadcasting Co. (553)
Nat'l Cable Television Ass'n (553)
Nat'l Geographic Soc. (565)
Nat'l Music Publishers' Ass'n (571)
Nat'l Newspaper Ass'n (572)
Nat'l Newspaper Publishers Ass'n (572)
Nat'l Press Foundation (574)
Nat'l Public Radio (574)
Nat'l Religious Broadcasters (575)
Nat'l Religious Broadcasters, Music License Committee (575)
Nat'l Review Magazine (576)
NET-Political NewsTalk Network (584)
Network Affiliated Stations Alliance (584)
New England Cable Television Ass'n (585)
New World Communications Group, Inc. (586)
Newbridge Networks (588)
NewCity Communications, Inc. (588)
News America Inc. (589)
News Corporation Ltd. (589)
Newsbank, Inc. (589)
Newsday (589)
Newspaper Ass'n of America (589)
NPES, The Ass'n for Suppliers of Printing, Publishing, and Converting Technologies (596)
Ohio Cable Telecommunications Ass'n (599)
Pappas Telecasting Cos. (607)
Performing Arts Network of New Jersey (612)
Periodical Management Group, Inc. (612)
Personal Communications Industry Ass'n (PCIA) (612)
Pew Center for Civic Journalism (613)
Pezold Management (613)
Pfluger Enterprises LLC (614)
Pilot Communications (617)
R. L. Polk & Co. (620)
Prime Time 24 (624)
Professional Photographers of America (626)
Psychological Corp. (628)
Public Broadcasting Entities (628)
Public Broadcasting Service (628)
Public Interest Video Network (628)
Quad Dimension (630)
Questcom (631)
Radio-Television News Directors Ass'n (632)
Random House (633)
RCRA Policy Forum (633)
The Reader's Digest Ass'n (633)
Reed-Elsevier Inc. (635)
Reiten Broadcasting, Inc. (636)
Reporters Committee for Freedom of the Press (637)
Reuters America Inc. (639)
RKO General, Inc. (641)
RTK Corp. (643)
Sage Broadcasting Corp./SBC Technologies, Inc. (646)
Salem Communications Corp. (646)
Satellite Broadcasting and Communications Ass'n (650)
Scripps League Newspaper, Inc. (653)
Sesame Workshop (656)
SFX Broadcasting (656)
Shurberg Broadcasting of Hartford Inc. (658)
Silver King Communications (659)
Simon & Schuster Inc. (659)
Sinclair Broadcast Group, Inc. (659)
SiTV (660)
Soc. of Nat'l Ass'n Publications (663)
Soc. of Professional Journalists (664)
Software & Information Industry Ass'n (SIIA) (664)
Spanish Broadcasting System, Inc. (669)
St. Louis Office of Cable Television (672)
St. Louis Regional Education and Public Television Commission (672)
Student Press Law Center (675)
Telephone Operators Caucus (683)
Television Ass'n of Programmers Latin America (TAP Latin America) (683)
Thompson Publishing, Inc. (686)
The Thomson Corp. (686)
Triathlon Broadcasting (692)
Tribune Co. (692)
TV Guide, Inc. (694)
United States Pharmacopeia (704)
Univision Television Group Inc. (708)
Univision Television Network (708)
USA Networks (709)
ValueVision Internat'l, Inc. (711)
Viacom Inc. (714)
Wall Street Journal (718)
Washington Independent Writers (719)
Washington Pacific Publications, Inc. (720)
The Washington Post Co. (720)
Washington Researchers (720)
WBFF (722)
Weather Channel (722)
West Group (723)
WETA (725)
WFMJ-TV (725)
WGBO-TV (725)
White Knight Broadcasting (726)
Winslow Press (728)
Wireless Communications Ass'n (728)
WLTV (729)
WNHT (729)
WPTT-TV (731)
WPXT (731)
WSYT (732)
WTTE (732)
WXTV (732)
Yates County Cable TV Committee (733)
Z Spanish Network (734)
Nidal Z. Zayed and Associates (734)

Medicine/Health Care/Mental Health

ABAHG, Inc. (224)
ABLEDATA (225)
Academic Health Center Coalition (225)
Academic Medicine Development Corp. (225)
Academy for Eating Disorders (225)
Academy for Implants and Transplants (225)
Academy of General Dentistry (225)
Academy of Radiology Research (226)
Access Community Health Network (226)
Accrediting Commission on Education for Health Services Administration (226)
Action on Smoking and Health (227)
Acute Long Term Hospital Ass'n (227)
Adheris, Inc. (227)
AdvaMed (228)
Advantage Healthplan Inc. (229)
Adventist Health System/Sunbelt, Inc. (229)
Aerospace Medical Ass'n (230)
Aetna/U.S. Healthcare, Inc. (230)
Africare (232)
Agilent Technologies (232)
AIDS Action Council (233)
AIDS Healthcare Foundation (233)
Akers Laboratories, Inc. (235)
Aksys, Ltd. (235)
Alabama Nursing Homes Ass'n (235)
The Alan Guttmacher Institute (236)
Alaska Native Health Board (236)
Albany Medical Center Hospital (237)
Albert Einstein Medical Center (237)
Albertson's Inc. (237)
Alere Medical Inc. (238)
Allegiance Healthcare Corp. (239)
Allergan, Inc. (239)
Alliance (239)
Alliance Community Hospital (239)
Alliance for Affordable Services (239)
Alliance for Children and Families (239)
Alliance for Elder Care (239)
Alliance for Health Reform (239)
Alliance for Quality Nursing Home Care (240)
Alliance for the Prudent Use of Antibiotics (APUA) (240)
Alliance Medical Corp. (240)
Alliance of Catholic Health Care Systems (240)
Alliance to End Childhood Lead Poisoning (241)
Allina Health Systems (241)
Alpha Center for Health Planning (242)
Alzheimer's Ass'n (242)
Ambulatory Pediatric Ass'n (242)
AMDeC Policy Group, Inc. (242)
America's Blood Centers (243)
American Academy of Audiology (243)
American Academy of Child and Adolescent Psychiatry (243)
American Academy of Dermatology (243)
American Academy of Facial Plastic and Reconstructive Surgery (243)
American Academy of Family Physicians (243)
American Academy of Neurology (243)
American Academy of Nurse Practitioners (244)
American Academy of Ophthamology - Office of Federal Affairs (244)
American Academy of Optometry (244)
American Academy of Orthopaedic Surgeons (244)
American Academy of Orthotists and Prosthetists (244)
American Academy of Otolaryngic Allergy (244)
American Academy of Otolaryngology-Head and Neck Surgery (244)
American Academy of Pediatrics (244)
American Academy of Physical Medicine and Rehabilitation (244)
American Academy of Physician Assistants (244)
American Academy on Physician and Patient (244)
American Accreditation Healthcare Commission/URAC (244)
American AIDS Political Action Committee (244)
American Alliance for Health, Physical Education, Recreation and Dance (245)
American Ambulance Ass'n (245)
American Ass'n for Active Lifestyles and Fitness (245)
American Ass'n for Clinical Chemistry, Inc. (245)
American Ass'n for Dental Research (245)
American Ass'n for Geriatric Psychiatry (245)
American Ass'n for Health Education (245)
American Ass'n for Homecare (246)
American Ass'n for Marriage and Family Therapy (246)
American Ass'n for Medical Transcription (246)
American Ass'n for Respiratory Care (246)
American Ass'n for the Study of Liver Diseases (246)
American Ass'n of Acupuncture and Oriental Medicine (246)
American Ass'n of Bioanalysts (246)
American Ass'n of Blood Banks (246)
American Ass'n of Cardiovascular and Pulmonary Rehabilitation (246)
American Ass'n of Children's Residential Centers (246)
American Ass'n of Clinical Endocrinologists (247)
American Ass'n of Colleges of Nursing (247)
American Ass'n of Colleges of Osteopathic Medicine (247)
American Ass'n of Colleges of Pharmacy (247)
American Ass'n of Colleges of Podiatric Medicine (247)
American Ass'n of Electrodiagnostic Medicine (247)
American Ass'n of Eye and Ear Hospitals (247)
American Ass'n of Family Physicians (247)
American Ass'n of Health Care Administrative Management (248)
American Ass'n of Health Plans (AAHP) (248)
American Ass'n of Healthcare Consultants (248)
American Ass'n of Immunologists (248)
American Ass'n of Naturopathic Physicians (248)
American Ass'n of Nurse Anesthetists (248)
American Ass'n of Occupational Health Nurses (248)
American Ass'n of Oral and Maxillofacial Surgeons (249)
American Ass'n of Orthodontists (249)
American Ass'n of Physician Specialists (249)
American Ass'n of Physicians of Indian Origin (249)
American Ass'n of Preferred Provider Organizations (249)
American Ass'n of Public Health Dentistry (249)
American Ass'n of Tissue Banks (249)
American Ass'n of University Affiliated Programs for Persons with Developmental Disabilities (249)
American Ass'n on Mental Retardation (250)
American Board for Certification in Orthotics and Prosthetics, Inc. (ABC) (251)
American Board of Adolescent Psychiatry (251)
American Board of Health Physics (251)
American Board of Medical Specialties in Podiatry (251)
American Board of Pain Medicine (251)
American Cancer Soc. (252)
American Chiropractic Ass'n (252)
American Clinical Neurophysiology Soc. (253)
American College of Cardiology (253)
American College of Chest Physicians (253)
American College of Clinical Pharmacy (253)
American College of Dentists (253)
American College of Emergency Physicians (253)
American College of Gastroenterology (253)
American College of Health Care Administrators (253)
American College of Healthcare Executives (253)
American College of Nuclear Physicians (253)
American College of Nurse Practitioners (253)
American College of Nurse-Midwives (254)
American College of Obstetricians and Gynecologists (254)
American College of Occupational and Environmental Medicine (254)
American College of Osteopathic Pediatricians (254)
American College of Osteopathic Surgeons (254)
American College of Physicians-American Soc. of Internal Medicine (ACP-ASIM) (254)
American College of Preventive Medicine (254)
American College of Radiation Oncology (254)
American College of Radiology (254)
American College of Rheumatology (254)
American College of Sports Medicine (254)
American College of Surgeons (254)
American Counseling Ass'n (256)
American Dental Ass'n (257)
American Dental Education Ass'n (257)
American Dental Hygienists' Ass'n (257)
American Dental Trade Ass'n (257)
American Diabetes Ass'n (257)
American Dietetic Ass'n (257)
American Federation for Medical Research (258)
American Federation of Home Care Providers (258)
American Foundation for AIDS Research (260)
American Gastroenterological Ass'n (261)
American Health Assistance Foundation (261)
American Health Care Ass'n (261)
American Health Information Management Ass'n (262)
American Health Lawyers Ass'n (262)
American Health Quality Ass'n (262)
American Healthways, Inc. (262)
American Heart Ass'n (262)
American Herbal Products Ass'n (262)
American Holistic Medical Ass'n (262)
American Hospital Ass'n (263)
American Institute of Biological Sciences (264)
American Institute of Ultrasound in Medicine (264)
American Leprosy Foundation (266)
American Lithotripsy Soc. (266)
American Liver Foundation (266)
American Managed Behavioral Healthcare Ass'n (266)
American Medical Ass'n (267)
American Medical Group Ass'n (267)
American Medical Informatics Ass'n (267)
American Medical Response (267)
American Medical Security (267)
American Medical Student Ass'n (267)
American Medical Technologists (267)
American Medical Women's Ass'n (267)
American Music Therapy Ass'n (268)
American Network of Community Options and Resources (ANCOR) (268)
American Nurses Ass'n (268)
American Occupational Therapy Ass'n, Inc. (269)
American Optometric Ass'n (269)
American Organization of Nurse Executives (269)
American Orthotic and Prosthetic Ass'n (269)
American Osteopathic Academy of Addiction Medicine (269)
American Osteopathic Ass'n (269)
American Osteopathic Healthcare Ass'n (269)
American Pharmaceutical Ass'n (270)
American Physical Therapy Ass'n (270)
American Physiological Soc. (270)
American Podiatric Medical Ass'n (270)
American Podiatric Medical Students Ass'n (270)
American Preventive Medical Ass'n (271)
American Psychiatric Ass'n (271)
American Psychiatric Nurses Ass'n (271)
American Psychoanalytic Ass'n (271)
American Psychological Ass'n (271)
American Psychological Soc. (271)
American Psychosomatic Soc. (271)
American Public Health Ass'n (271)
American Registry of Pathology (272)
American Running and Fitness Ass'n (273)
American School Counselor Ass'n (273)
American Sleep Disorders Ass'n (274)
American Soc. for Bone and Mineral Research (274)
American Soc. for Cell Biology (274)
American Soc. for Clinical Laboratory Science (274)
American Soc. for Clinical Nutrition (274)
American Soc. for Clinical Pharmacology and Therapeutics (274)
American Soc. for Gastrointestinal Endoscopy (274)
American Soc. for Investigative Pathology (274)
American Soc. for Nutritional Sciences (274)
American Soc. for Parenteral and Enteral Nutrition (274)
American Soc. for Pharmacology and Experimental Therapeutics (274)
American Soc. for Reproductive Medicine (275)
American Soc. for Therapeutic Radiology and Oncology (275)
American Soc. of Ambulatory Surgery Centers (275)
American Soc. of Anesthesiologists (275)
American Soc. of Cataract and Refractive Surgery (275)
American Soc. of Clinical Oncology (276)
American Soc. of Clinical Pathologists (276)
American Soc. of Consultant Pharmacists (276)
American Soc. of Echocardiography (276)
American Soc. of Extra-Corporeal Technology (276)
American Soc. of General Surgeons (276)
American Soc. of Health System Pharmacists (276)
American Soc. of Hematology (276)
American Soc. of Human Genetics (276)
American Soc. of Nephrology (276)
American Soc. of Nuclear Cardiology (277)
American Soc. of Orthopedic Physician Assistants (277)
American Soc. of Plastic and Reconstructive Surgeons (277)
American Soc. of Radiologic Technologists (277)
American Soc. of Transplantation (277)
American Soc. of Tropical Medicine and Hygiene (277)
American Speech, Language, and Hearing Ass'n (277)
American Speech-Language-Hearing Foundation (277)
American Telemedicine Ass'n (279)
American Thoracic Soc. (279)
American Trauma Soc. (279)
American Urogynecologic Soc. (280)
American Urological Ass'n (280)
Americans for Integrity in Palliative Care (282)
Americans for Long Term Care Security (282)
Americans for Medical Progress (282)
AmeriChoice Health Services, Inc. (282)
Amity, Inc. (283)
AmSurg Corp. (283)
Anderson Cancer Center, MD (284)
Anthem, Inc. (285)
Antitrust Coalition for Consumer Choice in Health Care (285)
Anxiety Disorders Ass'n of America (285)
Apria Healthcare Group (287)
APS Healthcare, Inc. (287)
The Arc (287)
Arthritis Foundation (289)
Arthroscopy Ass'n of North America (289)
Aso Corp. (291)
Ass'n for Ambulatory Behavioral Healthcare (291)
Ass'n for Healthcare Philanthropy (292)
Ass'n for Hospital Medical Education (292)
Ass'n for Professionals in Infection Control and Epidemiology (293)
Ass'n for the Advancement of Medical Instrumentation (293)
The Ass'n Healthcare Coalition (293)
Ass'n of Academic Health Centers (293)
Ass'n of Academic Health Sciences Library Directors (293)
Ass'n of Air Medical Services (293)
Ass'n of American Blood Banks (293)
Ass'n of American Medical Colleges (294)
Ass'n of American Physicians and Surgeons (294)
Ass'n of Black Psychologists (294)
Ass'n of Chiropractic Colleges (295)
Ass'n of Christian Therapists (295)
Ass'n of Clinical Research Professionals (295)
Ass'n of Community Cancer Centers (295)
Ass'n of Freestanding Radiation Oncology Centers (295)
Ass'n of Maternal and Child Health Programs (AMCHP) (296)
Ass'n of Medical Device Reprocessors (296)
Ass'n of Military Surgeons of the U.S. (AMSUS) (297)
Ass'n of Minority Health Profession Schools (297)
Ass'n of Nurses in AIDS Care (297)
Ass'n of Occupational and Environmental Clinics (297)
Ass'n of Occupational Health Professionals in Healthcare (297)
Ass'n of Organ Procurement Organizations (297)

Ass'n of Osteopathic Directors and Medical Educators (297)
Ass'n of Pain Management Anesthesiologist (297)
Ass'n of Pediatric Program Directors (297)
Ass'n of periOperative Registered Nurses (297)
Ass'n of Professors of Gynecology and Obstetrics (298)
Ass'n of Professors of Medicine (298)
Ass'n of Reproductive Health Professionals (298)
Ass'n of Schools and Colleges of Optometry (298)
Ass'n of Schools of Allied Health Professions (298)
Ass'n of Schools of Public Health (298)
Ass'n of State and Territorial Chronic Disease Program Directors (298)
Ass'n of State and Territorial Health Officials (298)
Ass'n of State and Territorial Public Health Laboratory Directors (298)
Ass'n of Surgical Technologists (299)
Ass'n of Teachers of Preventive Medicine (299)
Ass'n of University Programs in Health Administration (299)
Ass'n of Veterinary Biologics Cos. (299)
Ass'n of Women's Health, Obstetric and Neonatal Nurses (299)
Asthma and Allergy Foundation of America (301)
Astro Vision Internat'l, Inc. (301)
Atlantic Shores Healthcare, Inc. (302)
Augustine Medical (303)
Aurora Health Care, Inc. (303)
Aventis Pasteur (304)
Bassett Healthcare (308)
Bausch & Lomb (309)
Baxter Healthcare Corp. (309)
Bay State Health Systems (309)
Bayer Corp. (309)
Bayley Seton Hospital (309)
Baylor College of Medicine (310)
Bazelon Center for Mental Health Law, Judge David L. (310)
BD (310)
Bell Ambulance (310)
Benova, Inc. (311)
Best Health Care Inc. (312)
Beth Israel/Deaconess Medical Center (312)
Better Hearing Institute (312)
Beverly Enterprises (313)
Bio-Vascular, Inc. (313)
Biochemics (313)
Biocontrol Technology, Inc. (313)
Biogen, Inc. (313)
Biomatrix (314)
Biomedical Research Foundation of Northwest Louisiana (314)
Biomedical Research Institute (314)
BioPort Corp. (314)
Biotechnology Industry Organization (314)
Blood Center of Southeastern Wisconsin (315)
Blue Cross and Blue Shield of California (315)
Blue Cross and Blue Shield of Florida (315)
Blue Cross and Blue Shield of Maine (315)
Blue Cross and Blue Shield of Ohio (315)
Blue Cross Blue Shield Ass'n (315)
Blue Cross Blue Shield of Mississippi (315)
Board for Orthotists/Prosthetist Certification (316)
Boehringer Ingelheim Pharmaceuticals, Inc. (316)
Bon Secours Charity Health System (317)
Bone Care Internat'l (317)
Boston Scientific Corp. (318)
Boundary Healthcare Products Corp. (318)
Brain Injury Ass'n (319)
Brain Trauma Foundation (319)
Brazelton Foundation (319)
Bristol Bay Area Health Corp. (320)
Brown General Hospital (322)
California Ass'n of Children's Hospitals (326)
California Children's Hospital Ass'n (326)
California Primary Care Ass'n (327)
California Public Employees' Retirement System (327)
California School of Professional Psychology (327)
California Wellness Foundation (328)
Campaign for Medical Research (329)
Cancer Leadership Council (330)
CapCURE (330)
Cardinal Health Inc. (331)
Cardiovascular Credentialing Internat'l (331)
CareFirst Blue Cross Blue Shield (331)
Caremark Rx, Inc. (331)
Caretenders Health Corp. (331)
Carondelet Health System (332)
Cascade Designs (332)
Catholic Health Ass'n of the United States (333)
Catholic Healthcare West (333)
Cedars-Sinai Medical Center (334)
Celera Genomics (334)
Cell Therapeutics Inc. (334)
Center for Disease Detection (336)
Center for Health Care Practice in the Public Interest (336)
Center for Healthcare Information Management (336)
Center for Patient Advocacy (337)
Center for Reproductive Law and Policy (337)
Center for Sickle Cell Disease (337)
Center for Studies in Health Policy (338)
Centocor, Inc. (338)
Cephalon, Inc. (340)
Cerebral Palsy Council (340)
Children and Adults with Attention Deficit Disorders (CHADD) (344)
Children's Action Network (344)
Children's Health Fund (344)
Children's Hospice Internat'l (344)
Children's Hospital and Health Center of San Diego (344)
Children's Hospital and Medical Center (344)
Children's Hospital Foundation (344)
Children's Hospital Los Angeles (344)
Children's Hospital Medical Center Foundation (344)
Children's Hospital of Boston (344)
Children's Hospital of Wisconsin (344)
Children's Mercy Hospital (344)
Children's Nat'l Medical Center (344)
CHIM (344)
Christus Health (346)
Chronic Fatigue and Immune Dysfunction Syndrome Ass'n of America (346)
Cities Advocating Emergency AIDS Relief (CAEAR) (347)
Citizens for Health (348)
Citizens for Public Action on Cholesterol, Inc. (348)
Citizens for the Treatment of High Blood Pressure, Inc. (349)
City of Hope Nat'l Medical Center (349)
Cleveland Clinic Foundation (350)
Coalition for American Trauma Care (352)
Coalition for Health Funding (353)
Coalition for Health Services Research (354)
Coalition for Health Services Research (354)
Coalition for Nonprofit Health Care (354)
Coalition for Patient Rights (354)
Coalition for Workers' Health Care Funds (355)
Coalition of Boston Teaching Hospitals (355)
Coalition of Positive Outcomes in Pregnancy (355)
Coalition of Private Safety-Net Hospitals (355)
Coalition on Medicaid Reform (356)
Coalition on Occupational Safety and Health (356)
Coalition to Protect Community Not-for-Profit Hospitals (356)
Cochlear Corp. (357)
Collagen Corp. (357)
College of American Pathologists (357)
College on Problems of Drug Dependence (357)
Columbus Medical Services (359)
Commission on Graduates of Foreign Nursing Schools (360)
Commissioned Officers Ass'n of the U.S. Public Health Service (360)
The Commonwealth Fund (362)
Community Health Partners of Ohio (362)
Community Health Systems, Inc. (362)
Community Hospital Telehealth Consortium (362)
Community Hospitals of Central California (363)
Comprehensive Health Services (364)
Condell Medical Center (365)
Consumer Coalition for Quality Health Care (369)
Contact Lens Institute (369)
Continuum Healthcare Systems (370)
ConvaTec (370)
Cook Children's Health Care System (370)
Cooley's Anemia Foundation (371)
Cooper Green Hospital (371)
Cooperative of American Physicians (371)
Cord Blood Registry, Inc. (371)
Corporate Health Care Coalition (372)
Council for Affordable Health Insurance (374)
Council of American Kidney Societies (375)
Council of Colleges of Acupuncture and Oriental Medicine (375)
Council of State and Territorial Epidemiologists (376)
Council of Surgical Specialty Facilities and Institutes (376)
Council of Women's and Infant's Specialty Hospitals (376)
Council on Radionuclides and Radiopharmaceuticals (CORAR) (377)
Council on Resident Education in Obstetrics and Gynecology (377)
Council on the Economic Impact of Health System Change (377)
Counterpart Internat'l (377)
Coventry Health Care, Inc. (377)
Crestwood Behavior Health, Inc. (378)
Crohn's and Colitis Foundation of America (378)
Crown Therapeutics, Inc. (379)
CryoLife, Inc. (379)
Cure Autism Now (380)
Cure for Lymphoma Foundation (380)
Cystic Fibrosis Foundation (380)
D.C. Rape Crisis Center (381)
Dartmouth-Hitchcock Medical Center (382)
Datahr Rehabilitation Institute (382)
DATRON, Inc. (382)
Deaconess Billings Clinic (383)
Delta Dental Plan of California (385)
Delta Dental Plans Ass'n (385)
Dental Gold Institute (385)
Detroit Medical Center (386)
DGME Fairness Initiative (387)
Dialysis Clinic, Inc. (387)
Digestive Disease Nat'l Coalition (388)
Dimock Community Health Center (388)
District of Columbia Hospital Ass'n (390)
DNA Sciences, Inc. (390)
Do No Harm: The Coalition of Americans for Research Ethics (390)
Doctors Community Healthcare Corp. (390)
drugstore.com (392)
Dumex Medical (393)
The DuPont Pharmaceutical Co. (393)
Dystonia Medical Research Foundation (394)
Easter Seals (395)
Eclipse Surgical Technologies (396)
Ecological and Toxicological Ass'n of Dyes and Organic Pigments Manufacturers (396)
Edward Health Services (398)
El Centro Regional Medical Center (399)
Emergency Department Practice Management Ass'n (EDPMA) (401)
Emory University, Department of Internat'l Health-PAMM, USAID (402)
Empire Blue Cross and Blue Shield (402)
Employee Assistance Professionals Ass'n (402)
Employer Health Care Innovation Project (402)
Endocrine Soc. (403)
Englewood Hospital & Medical Center (403)
Epilepsy Foundation of America (406)
Episcopal AIDS Ministry (406)
Ergo Science Corp. (406)
The ERISA Industry Committee (ERIC) (406)
ESA, Inc. (407)
ESR Children's Health Care System (407)
Essex Medical Systems Plus (407)
European-American Phytomedicine Coalition (408)
Evangelical Lutheran Good Samaritan Soc. (408)
Express Scripts Inc. (409)
Extendicare Health Services Inc. (409)
Eye Bank Ass'n of America (410)
Fallon Community Health Plan (410)
Families U.S.A. Foundation (410)
Family and Medical Leave Act Technical Corrections Coalition (410)
Family Health Internat'l (411)
Farm Animal Reform Movement (FARM) (411)
Federal Physicians Ass'n (414)
Federated Ambulatory Surgery Ass'n (414)
Federation of American Hospitals (414)
Federation of American Societies for Experimental Biology (414)
Federation of Behavioral, Psychological and Cognitive Sciences (414)
Federation of Nurses and Health Professionals/AFT (415)
Federation of State Medical Boards of the U.S. (415)
First Consulting Group (417)
First Health Group Corp. (417)
Fisher Imaging (418)
Fisher Scientific Worldwide (418)
Florida Department of Health and Rehabilitative Services (419)
foot.com (422)
W. A. Foote Memorial Hospital (422)
Fortis Healthcare (423)
Foundation for Hematopoietic Cell Therapy Accreditation (424)
Foundation for the Advancement of Chiropractic Tenets and Science (424)
Foundation Health Federal Services, Inc. (424)
Freedom Designs (425)
Fresenius Medical Care North America (425)
Fresno Community Hospital and Medical Center (426)
Friends of Cancer Research (426)
Friends of the Nat'l Library of Medicine (426)
Fujisawa Health Care Inc. (427)
Gambro Healthcare (429)
GCRC Program Directors Ass'n (430)
Genentech, Inc. (431)
Genetics Soc. of America (433)
The Genome Action Coalition (433)
Genzyme Corp. (433)
George Washington University Medical Center (434)
Georgetown University-School of Nursing (434)
Gerontological Soc. of America (435)
Girling Health Care (435)
Global Health Council (436)
Government Employees Hospital Ass'n (437)
Greater New York Hospital Ass'n (439)
Green County Health Care, Inc. (440)
Grenada Lake Medical Center (440)
GREX, Inc. (440)
Group Health, Inc. (441)
Guidant Corp. (442)
Hackensack University Medical Center Foundation (443)
Hadassah Medical Relief Fund (443)
Hazelden Foundation (445)
HCA Healthcare Corp. (445)
HCR-Manor Care, Inc. (445)
Health and Hospital Corp. of Marion County (446)
Health Benefits Coalition (446)
Health Data Exchange Corp. (446)
Health Industry Distributors Ass'n (446)
Health Industry Group Purchasing Ass'n (446)
Health Industry Initiative (446)
Health Insurance Ass'n of America (446)
Health Management Systems, Inc. (446)
Health Partners (446)
Health Physics Soc. (446)
Health Policy Strategies (446)
Health Promotion Institute (446)
Health Quest (446)

Health Risk Management Group, Inc. (446)
Health Services of Kansas and Mid Missouri (446)
Healthcare Ass'n of New York State (446)
Healthcare Billing and Management Ass'n (446)
Healthcare Compliance Packaging Council (446)
Healthcare Convention and Exhibitors Ass'n (446)
Healthcare Council of the Nat'l Capital Area (447)
Healthcare Distribution Management Ass'n (447)
Healthcare Financial Management Ass'n (447)
Healthcare Financing Study Group (447)
Healthcare Leadership Council (447)
Healtheon/Web MD (447)
HealthFEST of Maryland, Inc. (447)
Healthnow (447)
Healthsouth Corp. (447)
Hearing Industries Ass'n (447)
Helen Keller Nat'l Center for Deaf Blind Youths and Adults (448)
Herbalife Internat'l, Inc. (448)
Highmark Blue Cross/ Blue Shield (449)
Hill-Rom Co., Inc. (450)
Hillenbrand Industries, Inc. (450)
HIP Health Plans (450)
HIV/AIDS Nursing Certification Board (450)
Hoffmann-La Roche Inc. (450)
Holyoke Hospital (451)
Home Access Health (451)
Home Care Aide Ass'n of America (451)
Home Care Ass'n of New York State (451)
Hospice Ass'n of America (452)
Hospital for Special Surgery (453)
Housing Works (453)
HT Medical (454)
Howard Hughes Medical Institute (454)
Humana Inc. (455)
Hunterdon Medical Center (455)
Huntington's Disease Soc. of America (455)
Huron Hospital (455)
Fred Hutchinson Cancer Research Center (455)
Hutzel Medical Center (455)
HWT Inc. (456)
Hyperion Medical (456)
Illinois Hospital and Health Systems Ass'n (457)
IMS Health Inc. (458)
Infectious Diseases Soc. of America, Inc. (461)
InformaTech, Inc. (461)
Inova Fairfax Hospital (462)
Inova Health Systems (462)
Inoveon Corp. (462)
Institute for Advanced Studies in Aging and Geriatric Medicine (463)
Institute for Civil Soc. (463)
Institute for Health Care Research and Policy (463)
Institute for Systems Biology (464)
Integrated Health Services, Inc. (465)
Integrated Medical Systems (465)
Integrated Skilled Care of Ohio (465)
InterAmerican College of Physicians and Surgeons (466)
Intercultural Cancer Council (466)
InterMountain Health Care Inc. (467)
Internat'l Ass'n for Dental Research (467)
Internat'l Biometric Industry Ass'n (468)
Internat'l Bone and Mineral Soc. (468)
Internat'l Chiropractors Ass'n (470)
Internat'l Commission for the Prevention of Alcoholism and Drug Dependency (470)
Internat'l Eye Foundation/Soc. of Eye Surgeons (471)
Internat'l Healthcare Safety Professional Certification Board (472)
Internat'l Soc. for Experimental Hematology (474)
Internat'l Soc. of Refractive Surgery (475)
Invacare Corp. (477)
Iowa Department of Public Health (478)
Iredell Memorial Hospital (478)
Johns Hopkins Medical Services (483)
Johns Hopkins University & Hospital (483)
Johns Hopkins University Hospital, School of Hygiene and Public Health (483)
Johnson & Johnson, Inc. (484)
Joint Commission on the Accreditation of Health Care Organizations (484)
Joint Council of Allergy, Asthma and Immunology (484)
Joint Healthcare Information Technology Alliance (484)
Joslin Diabetes Center (485)
Juvenile Diabetes Foundation Internat'l (485)
Kaiser Family Foundation (486)
Kaiser Permanente (486)
Kendall Healthcare Products Co. (487)
Kennedy Institute of Ethics (488)
Kensey Nash Corp. (488)
Henry H. Kessler Foundation (488)
Kessler Medical Rehabilitation Research & Education Corp. (488)
Kettering Medical Center (489)
Kinetic Biosystems Inc. (489)
Susan G. Komen Breast Cancer Foundation (490)
Komen Breast Cancer Foundation, The Susan G. (491)
Kuakini Hospital (492)
L.A. Care Health Plan (493)
LA Center for the Blind (493)
La Rabida Children's Hospital Research Center (493)
Lake Charles Memorial Hospital (494)
Lakeland Regional Medical Center (494)
Lamaze Internat'l (494)
Landmark Medical Center (495)
Leukemia & Lymphoma Soc. (498)
Liberty Medical Supply (499)
Liberty Mutual Insurance Group (499)
Life Cell (499)
Lifebridge Health (499)
Lifecore Biomedical (499)
LifeLink Foundation (499)
LifePoint Hospitals, Inc. (499)
Long Term Care Campaign (503)
Loyola University Health System (505)
Lumenos (505)
Lupus Foundation of America (505)
Lutheran Medical Center (505)
Lyme Disease Foundation (506)
Lymphoma Research Foundation of America, Inc. (506)
M.D. - I.P.A. (506)
Magee Women's Health Foundation (507)
Magellan Health Services (507)
Magnitude Information Systems (507)
Major Medicaid Hospital Coalition (508)
Mallinckrodt-Nellcor Puritan Bennett (508)
Managed Care Solutions (508)
Managed Health Care Ass'n (508)
March of Dimes Birth Defects Foundation (509)
Mariner Health Group, Inc. (510)
Mariner Post Acute Network (510)
Marquette General Hospital (510)
The Marshfield Clinic (511)
Martins Point Health Care (511)
Maryland Psychiatric Soc. (512)
Massachusetts General/Brigham and Women's Hospital (512)
Massachusetts Medical Device Industry Council (512)
McLean Hospital (515)
Med Images, Inc. (515)
MedCentral Health System (515)
Medco Containment Services, Inc. (516)
Medical Device Manufacturers Ass'n (516)
Medical Group Management Ass'n (516)
Medical Library Ass'n/Ass'n of Academic Health Sciences Library Directors (516)
Medical Mutual of Ohio (516)
The Medical Protective Co. (516)
Medical Records Internat'l, Inc. (516)
Medical Research Laboratories (516)
Medical Soc. of the District of Columbia (516)
Medical University of Southern Africa (516)
Medicare Payment Coalition for Frail Beneficiaries (517)
MedPro, Inc. (517)
MedReview, Inc. (517)
Medtronic, Inc. (517)
MedWerks.com (517)
Member-Link Systems, Inc. (517)
Memorial Hermann Health Care System (517)
Memorial Sloan-Kettering Cancer Center (517)
Mental and Addictive Disorders Appropriations Coalition (518)
Mercy Health Corp. (518)
Mercy Health System of Northwest Arkasas (518)
Mercy Hospital of Des Moines, Iowa (518)
Mercy Medical (518)
Metlife Mature Market Group (520)
Metra Biosystems, Inc. (520)
Mid-Atlantic Medical Services, Inc. (523)
Middlesex Hospital Home Care (523)
Minimed, Inc. (525)
Minnesota Medical Group Management (525)
Mobile Diagnostic Testing Services (527)
The Jeffrey Modell Foundation (527)
Moffit Cancer Research Hospital (527)
Molecular BioSystems, Inc. (527)
Molina Medical Centers (527)
Montefiore Medical Center (528)
Moore Medical Corp. (529)
Morehouse School of Medicine (529)
Motion Picture and Television Fund (530)
Mount Carmel Health (531)
Mount Sinai Hospital (531)
MultiDimensional Imaging, Inc. (532)
Multinat'l Working Team to Develop Criteria for Functional Gastrointestinal Disorders (532)
Municorp Healthcare Systems Inc. (533)
Muscular Dystrophy Ass'n (533)
Naples Community Hospital (534)
Nassau County Health Care Corp. (535)
Nat'l Abortion Federation (535)
Nat'l Academy of Opticianry (535)
Nat'l AIDS Fund (536)
Nat'l Alliance for Eye and Vision Research (536)
Nat'l Alliance for Hispanic Health (536)
Nat'l Alliance for Infusion Therapy (536)
Nat'l Alliance of African-American Health Care Professions (536)
Nat'l Alliance of Nurse Practitioners (536)
Nat'l Asian Women's Health Organization (537)
Nat'l Ass'n for Biomedical Research (537)
Nat'l Ass'n for Home Care (537)
Nat'l Ass'n for Human Development (538)
Nat'l Ass'n for Medical Direction of Respiratory Care (538)
Nat'l Ass'n for the Advancement of Orthotics and Prosthetics (538)
Nat'l Ass'n for the Support of Long Term Care (538)
Nat'l Ass'n of Boards of Examiners of Long Term Care Administrators (539)
Nat'l Ass'n of Chain Drug Stores (539)
Nat'l Ass'n of Children's Hospitals Inc. (540)
Nat'l Ass'n of City and County Health Officials (540)
Nat'l Ass'n of Community Health Centers (540)
Nat'l Ass'n of County and City Health Officials (541)
Nat'l Ass'n of County Health Facility Administrators (541)
Nat'l Ass'n of Dental Assistants (542)
Nat'l Ass'n of Dental Laboratories (542)
Nat'l Ass'n of Dental Plans (542)
Nat'l Ass'n of Epilepsy Centers (542)
Nat'l Ass'n of Health Underwriters (543)
Nat'l Ass'n of Healthcare Access Management (543)
Nat'l Ass'n of Healthcare Consultants (543)
Nat'l Ass'n of Medicaid Directors (545)
Nat'l Ass'n of Naturopathic Physicians (546)
Nat'l Ass'n of Nurse Practitioners in Women's Health (546)
Nat'l Ass'n of Optometrics and Opticians (546)
Nat'l Ass'n of Pediatric Nurse Associates and Practitioners (546)
Nat'l Ass'n of People with AIDS, Inc. (546)
Nat'l Ass'n of Pharmaceutical Manufacturers (546)
Nat'l Ass'n of Physician Nurses (546)
Nat'l Ass'n of Portable X-Ray Providers (546)
Nat'l Ass'n of Psychiatric Health Systems (547)
Nat'l Ass'n of Psychiatric Treatment Centers for Children (547)
Nat'l Ass'n of Public Hospitals and Health Systems (547)
Nat'l Ass'n of Rehabilitation Agencies (548)
Nat'l Ass'n of Rehabilitation Professionals in the Private Sector (548)
Nat'l Ass'n of Rehabilitation Research and Training Centers (548)
Nat'l Ass'n of Rural Health Clinics (548)
Nat'l Ass'n of School Nurses (548)
Nat'l Ass'n of School Psychologists (548)
Nat'l Ass'n of State Directors of Developmental Disabilities Services, Inc. (550)
Nat'l Ass'n of State EMS Directors (550)
Nat'l Ass'n of State Mental Health Program Directors (550)
Nat'l Ass'n of Urban Hospitals (551)
Nat'l Ass'n of VA Physicians and Dentists (551)
Nat'l Ass'n of Victims of Transfusion-associated HIV (551)
Nat'l Ass'n of WIC Directors (551)
Nat'l Assembly of Health and Human Service Organizations (551)
Nat'l Black Women's Health Project (552)
Nat'l Board of Examiners in Optometry (553)
Nat'l Breast Cancer Coalition (553)
Nat'l Business Coalition on Health (553)
Nat'l Calcium Council (554)
Nat'l Campaign for Hearing Health (554)
Nat'l Center for Homeopathy (554)
Nat'l Center for Tobacco-Free Kids (555)
Nat'l Certification Board for Therapeutic Massage and Bodywork (555)
Nat'l Chronic Care Consortium (555)
Nat'l Citizens Coalition for Nursing Home Reform (556)
Nat'l Coalition for Cancer Research (556)
Nat'l Coalition for Cancer Survivorship (556)
Nat'l Coalition for Osteoporosis and Related Bone Diseases (556)
Nat'l Coalition for Patient Rights (556)
Nat'l Coalition on Health Care (556)
Nat'l Commission on Correctional Health Care (557)
Nat'l Committee for Quality Assurance (557)
Nat'l Committee for Quality Health Care (557)
Nat'l Committee to Preserve Social Security and Medicare (557)
Nat'l Computer Systems (558)
Nat'l Contact Lens Examiners (558)
Nat'l Council for Community Behavioral Healthcare (559)
Nat'l Council of Health Facilities Finance Authorities (560)
Nat'l Council of State Boards of Nursing (560)
Nat'l Council on Alcoholism and Drug Dependence (561)
Nat'l Council on Radiation Protection and Measurement (561)
Nat'l Dental Ass'n (562)
Nat'l Diabetes Information Clearinghouse (562)
Nat'l Digestive Diseases Information Clearinghouse (562)
Nat'l Disease Research Interchange (562)
Nat'l Family Caregivers Ass'n (563)
Nat'l Family Planning and Reproductive Health Ass'n (563)
Nat'l Foundation for Cancer Research (565)
Nat'l Foundation for Infectious Diseases (565)
Nat'l Gaucher Foundation (565)
Nat'l Health Care Access Coalition (566)
Nat'l Health Care Anti-Fraud Ass'n (566)
Nat'l Health Council (567)
Nat'l Health Law Program (567)
Nat'l Health Lawyers Ass'n (567)
Nat'l Health Museum (567)
Nat'l Health Policy Forum (567)
Nat'l Hemophilia Foundation (567)
Nat'l Hospice & Palliative Care Organization (567)
Nat'l Hospice Foundation (567)
Nat'l Institute for Health Care Management (568)

Nat'l Institute on Community-Based Long-Term Care (568)
Nat'l IPA Coalition (569)
Nat'l Jewish Medical and Research Center (569)
Nat'l Kidney and Urologic Diseases Information Clearinghouse (569)
Nat'l Marrow Donor Program (570)
Nat'l Medical Ass'n (570)
Nat'l Medical Enterprises, Inc. (570)
Nat'l Mental Health Ass'n (571)
Nat'l Minority AIDS Council (571)
Nat'l Nutritional Foods Ass'n (572)
Nat'l Organization for Associate Degree Nursing (572)
Nat'l Orthotics Manufacturers Ass'n (572)
Nat'l Osteoporosis Foundation (573)
Nat'l Patient Advocate Foundation (573)
Nat'l Perinatal Ass'n (573)
Nat'l Prostate Cancer Coalition Co. (574)
Nat'l Psoriasis Foundation (574)
Nat'l Quality Health Council (575)
Nat'l Registry in Clinical Chemistry (575)
Nat'l Rehabilitation Ass'n (575)
Nat'l Rehabilitation Hospital (575)
Nat'l Rehabilitation Information Center (575)
Nat'l Rehabilitation Political Action Committee (575)
Nat'l Renal Administrators Ass'n (575)
Nat'l Rural Health Ass'n (577)
Nat'l Ryan White Title III (b) Coalition (577)
Nat'l Sleep Foundation (578)
Nat'l Soc. to Prevent Blindness (578)
Nat'l Stroke Ass'n (579)
Nat'l Student Speech Language Hearing Ass'n (579)
Nat'l Therapeutic Recreation Soc. (579)
Nat'l Vision Rehabilitation Cooperative (580)
Nat'l Women's Health Network (581)
NCS Healthcare (583)
Neurofibromatosis (584)
New Directions for Policy (585)
New England Deaconess Hospital (585)
New England Medical Center (585)
New England Mobile X-Ray (585)
New Jersey Hospital Ass'n (585)
New Jersey Organ & Tissue Sharing Network (585)
New York Presbyterian Hospital - Cornell Medical Center (587)
New York Psychotherapy and Counseling Center (587)
New York State Ass'n of Health Care Providers (587)
New York State Health Facilities Ass'n (587)
New York University Medical Center (588)
Nexia Biotechnologies, Inc. (589)
NF Inc. - Mass Bay Area (589)
NICORE, Inc. (589)
North American Brain Tumor Coalition (592)
North American Soc. of Pacing and Electrophysiology (592)
North American Vaccine, Inc./AMVAX, Inc. (593)
North Shore Long Island Jewish Health System (593)
Northside Hospital (595)
Northwest Kidney Center/Northwest Organ Procurement Agency (595)
Northwestern Memorial Hospital (595)
Norton Sound Health Corp. (596)
Nurses Organization of Veterans Affairs (597)
Nutrition Screening Initiative, The (597)
O'Grady Peyton Internat'l (598)
Ochsner Medical Institutions (598)
Ohio Hospital Ass'n (599)
Oklahoma State Medical Ass'n (600)
Olsten Health Services (600)
Omnicare, Inc. (600)
OnCare, Inc. (600)
Onehealthbank.com (600)
Optical Laboratories Ass'n (601)
Optical Soc. of America (601)
Opticians Ass'n of America (601)
Orasure Technologies (602)
Oregon Health Sciences University (603)
Organ Transplant Campaign (603)
Orphan Medical, Inc. (604)
Ortho Concepts (604)
Osteoarthritis Research Soc. Internat'l (604)
Osteopathic Health System of Texas (604)
Ostex Internat'l Inc. (604)
Our Lady of the Lake Regional Medical Center (604)
Outpatient Ophthalmic Surgery Soc. (604)
Ovarian Cancer Nat'l Alliance (604)
Ovations/United Health Group (604)
Pac Med Clinics (605)
PacifiCare Health Systems (606)
Pain Care Coalition (606)
Palmer Chiropractic University (606)
Pan American Health Organization (607)
Paradigm Support Corp. (607)
Paradise Valley Hospital (607)
Parker Jewish Geriatric Institute (608)
Parkinson's Action Network (608)
Parkinson's Disease Foundation (608)
Partners Healthcare System, Inc. (608)
Partnership for Organ Donation (609)
Partnership for Prevention (609)
Patient Access to Transplantation (PAT) Coalition (609)
Pediatricians for Children Inc. (610)
Pediatrix Medical Group, Inc. (610)
Pedorthic Footwear Ass'n (610)
Pegasus Airwave (610)
Pennington BioMedical Research Center (611)
PET Coalition (613)
Petroleum Helicopters (613)
Philadelphia College of Osteopathic Medicine (615)
Phoenix Cardiovascular, Inc. (616)
PhotoMEDEX (616)
PHP Healthcare Corp. (616)
Physician Insurers Ass'n of America (616)
Physicians Ad hoc Coalition for Truth (PHACT) (617)
Physicians Committee for Responsible Medicine (617)
Physicians for Peace (617)
Physicians for Reproductive Choice and Health (617)
Physicians for Social Responsibility (617)
PKC (618)
Planned Parenthood Federation of America (618)
Planned Parenthood of America (619)
Plasma Protein Therapeutics Ass'n (619)
Polycistic Kidney Disease Foundation (620)
PolyMedica Corp. (620)
Joel Pomerene Hospital (620)
Power Mobility Coalition (622)
Precision Medical (623)
Premier, Inc. (623)
Prevent Blindness America (623)
Primavera Laboratories, Inc. (624)
Priority Care (624)
Private Essential Access Community Hospitals (PEACH) Inc. (624)
Private Practice Section of the American Physical Therapy Ass'n (625)
Providence Health System (627)
Providence St. Vincent Medical Center (627)
Province Healthcare, Inc. (627)
PSI Services Inc. (628)
Public Health Foundation (628)
Public Health Policy Advisory Board (628)
Public Hospital Pharmacy Coalition (628)
Pulse Medical Instruments (630)
Pure Food Campaign (630)
The Queen's Health System (631)
Quest Diagnostics Inc. (631)
Quintiles Transnational Corp. (631)
R2 Technology, Inc. (632)
Ralin Medical (632)
Regulatory Affairs Professionals Soc. (636)
Renal Leadership Council (636)
Renal Physicians Ass'n (636)
Reproductive Health Technologies Project (637)
Research 2 Prevention (638)
Research Soc. on Alcoholism (638)
RESNA (638)
Respironics (638)
Retractable Technologies, Inc. (639)
Riverside Medical Center (640)
RMS Disease Management Inc. (641)
Roche Diagnostics (641)
Rock Creek Psychiatric Hospital (641)
Roger Williams Medical Center (641)
ROHO, Inc. (642)
Ross Abbott Laboratories (642)
RoTech Medical Corp. (642)
Roussel-UCLAF (642)
Rural Health Network Coalition (643)
Rural Hospital Coalition (643)
Rural Referral Centers Coalition (644)
Rush Presbyterian-St. Luke's Medical Center (644)
San Francisco AIDS Foundation (647)
SangStat Medical Corp. (648)
Santa Rosa Memorial Hospital (649)
SCAN Health Plan (651)
Schepens Eye Research Institute (651)
Schering-Plough Corp. (651)
Scott & White Hospital (652)
Scripps Research Institute (653)
Sentara Norfolk General Hospital (655)
The Sharing Network (657)
Shriners Hospital for Children (658)
Sibley Memorial Hospital (658)
Sickle Cell Disease Ass'n of America (658)
Siemens Corp. (658)
Sierra Health Services (658)
Sierra Military Health Services, Inc. (659)
Signal Behavioral Health Network (659)
Sisters of Charity of Leavenworth Health Services (660)
Sisters of Charity of the Incarnate Word (660)
Sisters of Providence Health Systems (660)
Smith & Nephew, Inc. (661)
Smokers Pneumonoconiosis Council (662)
Soc. for Excellence in Eyecare (662)
Soc. for In Vitro Biology (662)
Soc. for Mucosal Immunology (662)
Soc. for Occupational and Environmental Health (662)
Soc. for Pediatric Pathology (662)
Soc. for Vascular Surgery (663)
Soc. for Women's Health Research (663)
Soc. of Cardiovascular and Interventional Radiology (663)
Soc. of Diagnostic Medical Sonographers (663)
Soc. of General Internal Medicine (663)
Soc. of Gyneocologic Oncologists (663)
Soc. of Maternal-Fetal Medicine (663)
Soc. of Nuclear Medicine (663)
Soc. of Teachers of Family Medicine (664)
Soc. of Thoracic Surgeons (664)
Soc. of Toxicology (664)
Soc. of Vascular Technology (664)
Solus Research, Inc. (665)
Southcoast Health System (667)
Southeast Alaska Regional Health Corp. (SEARHC) (667)
Southern California Organ Procurement Consortium (667)
Spacelabs Medical Inc. (669)
Spaulding Rehabilitation Hospital (669)
Spectrum Health Care Resources, Inc. (670)
Spina Bifida Ass'n of America (670)
St. Barnabas Healthcare System (671)
St. Benedictine Hospital (671)
St. Bernard's Hospital (671)
St. Elizabeth's Medical Center (671)
St. Francis Hospital (671)
St. George's University School of Medicine (671)
St. Jude Medical, Inc. (671)
St. Mary's Hospital (672)
St. Matthew's University School of Medicine (672)
St. Peter's Medical Center (672)
St. Vincent Catholic Medical Centers (672)
Staff Builders, Inc. (672)
Stamford Hospital (672)
SterilMed, Inc. (674)
Sudden Infant Death Syndrome Alliance (676)
Summit Health Institute for Research and Education (676)
Sun Healthcare Group, Inc. (676)
Sunrise Assisted Living (677)
Sunrise Medical (677)
Sunstone Behavioral Health (677)
Susquehanna Health System (678)
Swope Parkway Health Center (679)
Synzyme Technologies, Inc. (679)
Tarzana Treatment Center (681)
Temple University Health System (683)
Tempur-Medical Inc. (683)
The Teratology Soc. (684)
Texas Chiropractic College (684)
Texas Health Resources (684)
The Texas Medical Center (685)
Texas NF Foundation (685)
THA: An Ass'n of Hospitals and Health Systems (685)
Theragenics Corp. (686)
Thomas Jefferson University (686)
Thomas Jefferson University Hospital (686)
Tourette Syndrome Ass'n, Inc. (688)
Toxicology Forum (688)
Transtracheal Systems (691)
Tri Path Inc. (691)
Tri West Healthcare Alliance (691)
The Tri-Alliance of Rehabilitation Professionals (691)
Trigon Healthcare Inc. (692)
Trinity Health (692)
TriWest Healthcare Alliance, Inc. (692)
U.S. Oncology (697)
Uniformed Services Family Health Plan (698)
Union Hospital (699)
United Cerebral Palsy Ass'n (700)
United Concordia Companies, Inc. (701)
United Health Group (701)
United Network for Organ Sharing (702)
United Payors and United Providers (702)
United States Pharmacopeia (704)
University Health Associates, Inc. (705)
University Medical Associates (705)
University of Florida Health Science Center (706)
University of Massachusetts Memorial Health System (706)
University of Medicine and Dentistry of New Jersey (706)
University of Medicine and Dentistry of New Jersey - School of Health Related Professionals (706)
University of Michigan Medical Center (706)
University of Mississippi Medical Center (706)
University of Pennsylvania/School of Dental Medicine (707)
University of Texas - Houston Health Science Center (707)
University of Texas Health Systems (707)
UNR Asbestos-Disease Trust (708)
UPMC Health System (708)
Urban Health Care Coalition of Pennsylvania (708)
Urologix, Inc. (709)
UroMedica Corp. (709)
USFHP Conference Group (710)
Valley Children's Hospital (711)
Valley Hospital Foundation (711)
Value Options Health Care Inc. (711)
Vanderbilt University Medical Center (712)
Vanguard Medical Concepts, Inc. (712)
Veritas Communications (713)
Vertis Neuroscience (714)
VHA Inc. (714)
Virologic, Inc. (716)
Virtual Drug Development (716)
Virtual Medical Group (716)
Visible Genetics (716)
Vision Council of America (716)
Visiting Nurse Service of New York (716)
Visiting Nurses Health System (716)
Vitas Healthcare Corp. (717)
VIVRA (717)
Volunteer Trustees of Not-for-Profit Hospitals (717)
Washington Business Group on Health (719)
Washington Hospital Center (719)

Washington Regional Transplant Consortium (720)
Washington State Hospital Ass'n (720)
Watson Pharmaceuticals, Inc. (721)
Watts Health Foundation (722)
Wausau Insurance Cos. (722)
WebMD (722)
Weider Nutritional Group (722)
Welcon, Inc. (722)
The Wellness Plan (723)
WellPoint Health Networks/Blue Cross of California/UNICARE (723)
West Virginia University Hospitals, Inc. (723)
Whitman-Walker Clinic (726)
Wireless Technology Research, L.L.C. (728)
Women and Infants' Hospital (729)
Women's Hospital (729)
Women's Hospital of Greensboro (729)
Word Chiropractic Alliance (730)
World Federation for Mental Health (730)
World Health Organization (730)
World Institute on Disability (730)
Wound Ostomy Continence Nurses (731)
Wyeth-Ayerst Laboratories (732)
XCEL Medical Pharmacy, Ltd. (732)
Yukon-Kuskokwim Health Corp. (734)
ZERO TO THREE/Nat'l Center for Infants, Toddlers, and Families (734)

Metals

ACS Industries, Inc. (227)
Advanced Material Resources, Inc. (228)
Alcan Aluminum Corp. (237)
Alcoa Inc. (237)
Algoma Steel, Inc. (238)
Allegheny Ludlum Corp. (238)
Allegheny Technologies, Inc. (238)
Alliance to End Childhood Lead Poisoning (241)
Allied Tube & Conduit Corp. (241)
The Aluminum Ass'n (242)
Aluminum Co. of Canada (242)
American Cast Iron Pipe Co. (252)
American Foundrymen's Soc. (260)
American Iron and Steel Institute (265)
American Metalcasting Consortium (267)
American Zinc Ass'n (281)
Armco Inc. (288)
The Ass'n For Manufacturing Technology (AMT) (292)
Ass'n of Women in the Metal Industries (299)
Atlas Iron Processing, Inc. (302)
Barrick Goldstrike Mines, Inc. (308)
Bethlehem Steel Corp. (312)
Birmingham Steel Corp. (314)
Bitrek Corp. (314)
Brass and Bronze Ingot Manufacturers Ass'n (319)
Brush Wellman, Inc. (323)
California Steel Industries, Inc. (327)
Campbell Foundry Co. (329)
Can Manufacturers Institute (329)
Cast Iron Pipefittings Committee (333)
Cast Iron Soil Pipe Institute (333)
Century Tube Corp. (340)
Chambre Syndicale des Producteurs d'Aciers Fins et Speciaux (341)
Chang Mien Industry Co., Ltd. (341)
Chaparral Steel Co. (341)
Chromalloy Gas Turbine Corp. (346)
Chrome Coalition (346)
Cleveland Cliffs Iron Co. (350)
Co-Steel Raritan (352)
Colakoglu Group (357)
Cold Finished Steel Bar Institute (357)
Columbia Falls Aluminum Co. (359)
Cominco, Ltd. (360)
Committee of Domestic Steel Wire Rope and Specialty Cable Manufacturers (361)
Committee on Pipe and Tube Imports (361)
Connecticut Steel Corp. (367)
Continuous Color Coat, Ltd. (370)
Copper and Brass Fabricators Council (371)
Copper Development Ass'n, Inc. (371)
Corus Group Plc (373)
Dalmine (382)
Damascus Tubular Products (382)
Dofasco, Inc. (390)
Eagle-Picher Industries (394)
Elkem Metals Co. (401)
Enerco, Inc. (403)
Eramet Marietta Inc. (406)
European Confederation of Iron and Steel Industries (EUROFER) (408)
Ferroalloys Ass'n (415)
Freeport-McMoRan Copper & Gold Inc. (425)
General Ore Internat'l Corp. Ltd. (433)
Geneva Steel Co. (433)
The Gold and Silver Institute (436)
Goldendale Aluminum (437)
Gulf State Steel Inc. (442)
Habas Group (443)
Hannibal Industries (444)
HARSCO Corp. (445)
Hecla Mining Co. (447)
Industrial Minera Mexicana (461)
Inland Steel Industries, Inc. (462)
Internat'l Ass'n of Bridge, Structural, Ornamental and Reinforcing Iron Workers (467)
Internat'l Brotherhood of Boilermakers, Iron Shipbuilders, Blacksmiths, Forgers and Helpers (469)
Internat'l Cadmium Ass'n (469)
Internat'l Magnesium Ass'n (473)
Internat'l Metals Reclamation Co. (473)
IPSCO Inc. (478)
IPSCO Tubulars, Inc. (478)
Iron Ore Ass'n (479)
Japan Iron and Steel Exporters Ass'n (482)
Kaiser Aluminum & Chemical Corp. (485)
Kennecott/Borax (488)
Keystone Consolidated Industries, Inc. (489)
Korean Iron and Steel Ass'n (491)
Lead Industries Ass'n (496)
Liquid Metal Technologies (500)
London Metal Exchange, Ltd. (503)
LTV Copperweld (505)
The LTV Corp. (505)
LTV Steel Co. (505)
McKechnie Brothers (South Africa) Ltd. (515)
Metal Building Manufacturers Ass'n (519)
Metal Finishing Suppliers Ass'n (519)
Metals Industry Recycling Coalition (519)
Mitsubishi Corp. (526)
Municipal Castings Fair Trade Council (532)
Nat'l Ass'n of Metal Finishers (545)
Nat'l Ass'n of Reinforcing Steel Contractors (548)
Nat'l Corrugated Steel Pipe Ass'n (559)
Nat'l Steel and Shipbuilding Co. (579)
Nat'l Steel Corp. (579)
Nat'l Tooling and Machining Ass'n (579)
Non-Ferrous Founders' Soc. (591)
North American Steel Framing Alliance (592)
Northwest Aluminum Co. (595)
Northwest Pipe Co. (595)
Northwestern Steel and Wire Co. (596)
Oneida Ltd. (601)
Phelps Dodge Corp. (615)
Pickands Mather and Co. (617)
Powder Coating Institute (622)
Raritan River Steel Co. (633)
RSR Corp. (643)
Samsung Corp. (647)
Sharon Tube Co. (657)
Sheet Metal Workers' Internat'l Ass'n (657)
Shieldalloy Metallurgical Corp. (657)
Siderar S.A.I.C. (658)
Siderca Corp. (658)
Siderurgica del Orinoco (Sidor), C.A. (658)
Silver Group, Inc. (659)
Silver Users Ass'n (659)
SKF USA, Inc. (660)
Southwire, Inc. (668)
Specialty Steel Industry of North America (670)
Specialty Tubing Group (670)
The Steel Alliance (674)
Steel Manufacturers Ass'n (674)
Steel Recycling Institute (674)
Steel Service Center Institute (674)
Steel Shipping Container Institute (674)
Stelco Inc. (674)
Stratcor (675)
Syquest Technology, Inc. (679)
TAMSA (680)
Timet-Titantium Metals Corp. (687)
The Timken Co. (687)
Titanium Metals Corp. (687)
Tubos de Acero de Mexico, S.A. (693)
U.S. Fittings Group (696)
U.S. Steel (697)
United Steelworkers of America (704)
US Steel Group (709)
USX Corp. (710)
Vandium Industry Coalition (712)
Vest Inc. (714)
Voest Alpine Steel (717)
Weirton Steel Corp. (722)
Western Tube & Conduit Co. (724)
Wheatland Tube Co. (725)
Wheeling Pittsburgh Steel Corp. (726)
Wilson Composites Group (727)
The Yucel Group (734)
Zinc Corp. of America (734)

Military/Veterans

21st Century Partnership (223)
Aerospace Education Foundation (230)
Air Force Ass'n (233)
Air Force Sergeants Ass'n (233)
Alliance for Nuclear Accountability (240)
American Coalition for Filipino Veterans (253)
American Legion (266)
American Logistics Infrastructure Improvement Consortium (266)
American Maritime Officers Service (267)
American Military Soc. (268)
American Retirees Ass'n (273)
American Security Council (273)
American Soc. of Military Comptrollers (276)
American Soc. of Naval Engineers (276)
American War Mothers (280)
AMVETS (American Veterans of World War II, Korea and Vietnam) (283)
AOC (285)
Armed Forces Benefit Ass'n (289)
Armed Forces Communications and Electronics Ass'n Headquarters (289)
Army & Air Force Mutual Aid Ass'n (289)
Ass'n of Military Colleges and Schools of the U.S. (297)
Ass'n of Military Surgeons of the U.S. (AMSUS) (297)
Ass'n of the United States Army (299)
Blinded Veterans Ass'n (315)
Board of Veterans Appeals Professional Ass'n (316)
British Ministry of Defence (321)
Catholic War Veterans of the U.S.A. (334)
Center on Conscience and War/NISBCO (338)
Disabled American Veterans (389)
ECC Internat'l Corp. (396)
El Toro Reuse Planning Authority (399)
Enlisted Ass'n of the Nat'l Guard of the United States (403)
Ex-Partners of Servicemembers for Equality (408)
Federal Education Ass'n (412)
Fleet Reserve Ass'n (418)
FLIR Systems, Inc. (419)
Institute of Simulation and Training (464)
Israel, Ministry of Defense of the State of (479)
Jered Industries, Inc. (482)
Jewish War Veterans of the U.S.A. (483)
The Justice Project, Inc. (485)
Lao Veterans of America, Inc. (495)
Long Beach Naval Shipyard Employees Ass'n (503)
Longworth Industries Inc. (503)
Marine Corps League (510)
Marine Corps Reserve Officers Ass'n (510)
Martins Point Health Care (511)
Military Ad Hoc Committee (524)
Military Chaplains Ass'n of the U.S. (524)
The Military Coalition (524)
Military Footwear Coalition (524)
Military Glove Coalition (524)
Military Impacted School Districts Ass'n (524)
Military Mobility Coalition (524)
Military Order of the Purple Heart of the U.S.A. (524)
Military Order of the World Wars (524)
Nat'l Ass'n for Uniformed Services (538)
Nat'l Ass'n of Military Widows (545)
Nat'l Ass'n of VA Physicians and Dentists (551)
Nat'l Ass'n of Veterans Research and Education Foundations (551)
Nat'l Guard Ass'n of the U.S. (566)
Nat'l League of Families of American Prisoners and Missing in Southeast Asia (569)
Nat'l Military Family Ass'n (571)
Nat'l Military Intelligence Ass'n (571)
Nat'l Veterans Foundation (580)
Nat'l Veterans Legal Services Program (580)
Nat'l Vietnam and Gulf War Veterans Coalition, Inc. (580)
Naval Reserve Ass'n (582)
Navy Joining Center (583)
Navy League of the United States (583)
Non Commissioned Officers Ass'n of the U.S.A. (591)
Nurses Organization of Veterans Affairs (597)
Office of Naval Research (599)
Oregon Military Department (603)
Paralyzed Veterans of America (607)
PESystems, Inc. (613)
Reserve Officers Ass'n of the U.S. (638)
The Retired Enlisted Ass'n (638)
The Retired Officers Ass'n (TROA) (638)
Senior Army Reserve Commanders Ass'n (655)
Sierra Military Health Services, Inc. (659)
South Carolina Nat'l Guard Ass'n (666)
Texas Veterans Land Board (685)
Union of Concerned Scientists (699)
United Service Organization (702)
United States Coast Guard Chief Petty Officers Ass'n (703)
United States Navy Memorial Foundation (704)
USAA - United Services Automobile Ass'n (710)
Veterans of Foreign Wars of the U.S. (714)
Vietnam Veterans of America, Inc. (715)
Visually Impaired Veterans of America (716)
Women's Action for New Directions (WAND)/Women Legislators' Lobby (WILL) (729)

Mining Industry

AEI Resources (229)
Allegheny River Mining Co. (238)
American Land Rights Ass'n (265)
American Zinc Ass'n (281)
Andalex Resources, Inc. (284)
AngloGold North America (284)
Arch Mineral Corp. (287)
ARCO Coal Co. (287)
Ass'n of Bituminous Contractors (294)
Barrick Goldstrike Mines, Inc. (308)
Berwind Corp. (312)
BHP (USA) Inc. (313)
Bituminous Coal Operators Ass'n (314)
Chamber of Mines of South Africa (340)
Cleveland Cliffs Iron Co. (350)
Coal Utilization Research Council (352)

Coalition to Preserve Mine Safety Standards (356)
Coeur d'Alene Mines Corp. (357)
COGEMA, Inc. (357)
Cominco Alaska Inc. (360)
Cominco, Ltd. (360)
Crown Butte Mines, Inc. (379)
Cyprus Amex Minerals Co. (380)
The Doe Run Co. (390)
Echo Bay Mining (396)
The Feldspar Corp. (415)
Franco-Nevada Mining Corp., Inc. (424)
Freeman United Coal Mining Co. (425)
Freeport-McMoRan Copper & Gold Inc. (425)
General Chemical Corp. (431)
General Ore Internat'l Corp. Ltd. (433)
Global Mining Initiative (436)
The Gold and Silver Institute (436)
Greens Creek Mining Co. (440)
Gypsum Ass'n (443)
Hecla Mining Co. (447)
Homestake Mining (451)
Hulcher Quarry, Inc. (454)
IMC Global Inc. (458)
Independence Mining Co., Inc. (459)
Industrial Minera Mexicana (461)
Internat'l Raw Materials (474)
Iron Ore Ass'n (479)
Joy Mining Machinery (485)
Kennecott/Borax (488)
Lone Star Florida, Inc. (503)
Mine Safety Appliances (525)
Mineral Policy Center (525)
Minnesota Mining and Manufacturing Co. (3M Co.) (525)
Mueller Industries, Inc. (532)
Nat'l Industrial Sand Ass'n (568)
Nat'l Mining Ass'n (571)
Nat'l Ocean Industries Ass'n (572)
Nat'l Stone, Sand, and Gravel Ass'n (579)
Nemacolin Mines Corp. (583)
New York Trap Rock Co. (588)
Newmont Mining Corp. (588)
Olga Coal Co. (600)
P & H Mining Equipment (605)
Palmer Coking & Coal Co. (607)
The Peabody Group (610)
Peter White Coal Mining Co. (613)
Phelps Dodge Corp. (615)
Pickands Mather and Co. (617)
The Pittston Co. (618)
Placer Dome U.S. Inc. (618)
Platinum Guild Internat'l (619)
RAPOCA Energy Co. (633)
Salt Institute (646)
Sherritt Internat'l (657)
Solvay Minerals (665)
Sorptive Minerals Institute (666)
Southdown, Inc. (667)
Strategic Minerals Corp. (675)
Tg Soda Ash (685)
Thompson Creek Metals Co. (686)
U.S. Clay Producers Traffic Ass'n (696)
United Mine Workers of America (702)
Uranium Producers of America (708)
USEC, Inc. (710)
Utah Natural Products Alliance (710)
Arthur T. Walker (718)
WorldWide Minerals Ltd. (731)
Youngstown Mines Corp. (733)

Minorities

The 13th Regional Corp. (223)
Acoma Pueblo (226)
The Africa-America Institute (231)
Agua Caliente Band of Cahuilla Indians (232)
Agudath Israel of America (232)
Airport Minority Advisory Council (235)
Alabama-Coushatta Tribe of Texas (235)
Alaska Native Health Board (236)
Aleut Corp. (238)
American Ass'n of Black Women Entrepreneurs Corp. (246)
American Ass'n of Blacks in Energy (246)
American Ass'n of Physicians of Indian Origin (249)
American Civil Liberties Union (252)
American Civil Liberties Union of the Nat'l Capital Area (252)
American Friends of Lubavitch (260)
American Hellenic Educational Progressive Ass'n (AHEPA) (262)
American Indian Ass'n (263)
American Indian Heritage Foundation (263)
American Indian Higher Education Consortium (263)
American Jewish Committee (265)
American Jewish Congress (265)
American League of Financial Institutions (266)
American Muslim Council (268)
American Task Force for Lebanon (278)
American-Arab Anti-Discrimination Committee (ADC) (281)
Anti-Defamation League (285)
Arab American Institute (287)
Armenian Assembly of America (289)
Asian Pacific American Labor Alliance, AFL-CIO (291)
ASPIRA Ass'n, Inc. (291)
Ass'n for Community Based Education (292)
Ass'n for the Study of Afro-American Life and History (293)
Ass'n of Black Psychologists (294)
Ass'n of Hispanic Advertising Agencies (296)
Ass'n of Minority Health Profession Schools (297)
Assiniboine and Sioux Tribes (Fort Peck Reservation) (300)
B'nai B'rith Internat'l (305)
Bad River Band of Lake Superior Chippewa (305)
Barona Band of Mission Indians (308)
Bay Mills Indian Community (309)
Bert Corona Leadership Institute (312)
BET Holdings II, Inc. (312)
The Bethune-DuBois Institute, Inc. (312)
Black America's Political Action Committee (315)
Blackfeet Tribe of Montana (315)
Blacks in Government (315)
Cabazon Band of Mission Indians (325)
Casa del Pueblo Community Program (332)
Center for Community Change (335)
Center for Women Policy Studies (338)
Central Council of Tlingit and Haida Indian Tribes of Alaska (338)
Chehalis Reservation, Confederated Tribes of the (342)
Cherokee Investment Partners, LLC (342)
Cheyenne and Arapahoe Tribes of Oklahoma (342)
Cheyenne River Sioux Tribe (342)
Chicanos Por La Causa (343)
Chippewa Cree Tribe (345)
Chitimacha Tribe of Louisiana (345)
Choctaw Indians, Mississippi Band of (345)
Choctaw Nation of Oklahoma (345)
Coalition of Black Trade Unionists (355)
Colorado Hispanic League (358)
Colorado River Indian Tribes (358)
Confederated Salish and Kootenai Tribes of the Flathead Nation (365)
Confederated Tribes of the Coos (365)
Confederated Tribes of the Grand Ronde (365)
Confederated Tribes of the Umatilla Reservation of Oregon (365)
Confederated Tribes of Warm Springs Reservation (365)
Congress of Nat'l Black Churches (366)
Congressional Black Caucus Foundation (366)
Congressional Hispanic Caucus Institute (CHCI) (366)
Constituency for Africa (368)
Cook Inlet Communications (371)
Cook Inlet Region Inc. (371)
Coquille Indian Tribe (371)
Council for Opportunity in Education (374)
Coushatta Tribe of Louisiana (377)
Cow Creek Umpqua Tribe of Oregon (377)
Cuyapaipe Band of Mission Indians (380)
Delaware Tribe of Indians (384)
Development Corporation of Nevada (387)
Eastern Band of Cherokee Indians (395)
Eastern Pequot Indians (395)
Elk Valley Rancheria (401)
English First, Inc. (403)
Excelsior Gaming, Inc. (408)
Executive Leadership Council and Foundation (408)
The Eyak Corp. (409)
Fond du Lac Reservation, Washington Office of the (421)
Forest County Potawatomi Community (423)
Futures for Children (428)
Gila River Indian Community (435)
Government Leasing Co. (438)
Grand Traverse Band of Chippewa and Ottawa Indians (438)
Great Lakes Indian Fish and Wildlife Commission (439)
Hadassah Medical Relief Fund (443)
Hebrew Immigrant Aid Soc. (447)
Hispanic Ass'n of Colleges and Universities (450)
Ho-Chunk Nation (450)
Hoopa Valley Tribal Council (452)
Hopi Indian Tribe (452)
Hopland Band of Pomo Indians (452)
Hualapai Nation (454)
Human Relations Foundation of Chicago (454)
Indian American Nat'l Foundation (460)
Indian Law Resource Center (460)
InterAmerican College of Physicians and Surgeons (466)
Intercultural Cancer Council (466)
Internat'l Ass'n of Black Professional Fire Fighters (467)
Internat'l Ass'n of Jewish Lawyers and Jurists (468)
Intertribal Monitoring Ass'n on Indian Trust Funds (477)
Intertribal Timber Council (477)
Isleta Pueblo (479)
Jamestown-S'Klallam Indian Tribe (481)
Japanese American Citizens League (482)
Jemez, New Mexico, Pueblo of (482)
Jewish Federation of Greater Washington (483)
Jewish Guild for the Blind (483)
Jewish Institute for Nat'l Security Affairs (483)
Jewish Peace Lobby (483)
Jewish War Veterans of the U.S.A. (483)
Jewish Women Internat'l (483)
Jicarilla Apache Tribe (483)
Joint Baltic American Nat'l Committee, Inc. (484)
Joint Center for Political and Economic Studies (484)
Kake Tribal Corp. (486)
Kake, Alaska, Organized Village of (486)
Kickapoo Tribe of Oklahoma (489)
Kickapoo Tribe of Texas (489)
Klamath Tribes (490)
Koniag, Inc. (491)
Kootznoowoo, Inc. (491)
Labor Council for Latin American Advancement (LCLAA) (493)
Lac du Flambeau Chippewa Tribe (493)
Lao Veterans of America, Inc. (495)
Las Vegas Paiute Tribe (495)
Latino Strategies (496)
Lawyers' Committee for Civil Rights Under Law (496)
Leadership Conference on Civil Rights (496)
Leech Lake Tribal Council (497)
Little River Band of Ottawa Indians (500)
Little Traverse Bay Band of Odawa Indians (500)
Lower Brule Sioux Tribe (505)
Lower Elwaha S'Klallam Tribe (505)
Lummi Indian Nation (505)
Mashantucket Pequot Tribal Nation (512)
Mashpee Wampanoag Indian Tribal Council, Inc. (512)
Menominee Indian Tribe (518)
Mesalero Apache Tribe (519)
Metlakatla Indian Community (520)
Mexican-American Legal Defense and Educational Fund (521)
Miccosukee Tribe of Indians of Florida (522)
Michigan Inter-Tribal Council (522)
Migrant Legal Action Program (524)
Mille Lacs Band of Ojibwe Indians (524)
Minnesota Indian Gaming Ass'n (525)
Minority Business Enterprise Legal Defense and Education Fund (525)
Minority Males Consortium (525)
Mni-Sose Intertribal Water Rights Coalition (526)
Mole Lake Band of the Sokaogon Chippewa Community (527)
Morning Star Institute, The (529)
Morongo Band of Mission Indians (530)
Multimedia Games, Inc. (532)
NAACP Legal Defense and Educational Fund, Inc. (534)
Nambe Pueblo (534)
Nat'l Alliance for Hispanic Health (536)
Nat'l Alliance of African-American Health Care Professions (536)
Nat'l Alliance of Black School Educators (536)
Nat'l Asian Pacific American Legal Consortium (537)
Nat'l Asian Women's Health Organization (537)
Nat'l Ass'n for Bilingual Education (537)
Nat'l Ass'n for Equal Opportunity in Higher Education (537)
Nat'l Ass'n for the Advancement of Colored People, Washington Bureau (538)
Nat'l Ass'n of Black Accountants (539)
Nat'l Ass'n of Black County Officials (539)
Nat'l Ass'n of Black-Owned Broadcasters (539)
Nat'l Ass'n of Hispanic County Officials (543)
Nat'l Ass'n of Hispanic Journalists (543)
Nat'l Ass'n of Investment Companies (544)
Nat'l Ass'n of Minority Automobile Dealers (545)
Nat'l Ass'n of Minority Contractors (545)
Nat'l Ass'n of Minority Political Families, USA, Inc. (545)
Nat'l Ass'n of Negro Business & Professional Women's Clubs, Inc. (546)
Nat'l Ass'n of Neighborhoods (546)
Nat'l Ass'n of Urban Bankers, Inc. (551)
Nat'l Bankers Ass'n (552)
Nat'l Bar Ass'n (552)
Nat'l Black Caucus of Local Elected Officials (552)
Nat'l Black Caucus of State Legislators (552)
Nat'l Black Child Development Institute (552)
Nat'l Black Media Coalition (552)
Nat'l Black Police Ass'n (552)
Nat'l Black Women's Health Project (552)
Nat'l Catholic Conference for Interracial Justice (554)
Nat'l Caucus and Center on Black Aged (554)
Nat'l Center for Neighborhood Enterprise (555)
Nat'l Center for Urban Ethnic Affairs (555)
Nat'l Coalition for Minority Business (556)
Nat'l Coalition of Black Meeting Planners (556)
Nat'l Coalition of Minority Businesses (556)
Nat'l Coalition on Black Civic Participation, Inc. (556)
Nat'l Committee for Responsive Philanthropy (557)
Nat'l Committee on Pay Equity (557)
Nat'l Congress of American Indians (558)
Nat'l Council of Jewish Women (560)
Nat'l Council of La Raza (560)
Nat'l Council of Negro Women (560)
Nat'l Days of Dialogue on Race Relations (561)
Nat'l Dental Ass'n (562)
Nat'l Ethnic Coalition of Organizations (563)
Nat'l Federation of Croatian Americans (564)
Nat'l Forum for Black Public Administrators (565)
Nat'l Hispanic Council on Aging (567)
Nat'l Indian Child Welfare Ass'n (568)
Nat'l Indian Education Ass'n (568)
Nat'l Indian Gaming Ass'n (568)
Nat'l Italian American Foundation (569)
Nat'l Jewish Democratic Council (569)
Nat'l Jewish Medical and Research Center (569)
Nat'l Medical Ass'n (570)
Nat'l Minority AIDS Council (571)
Nat'l Newspaper Publishers Ass'n (572)
Nat'l Organization of Black Law Enforcement Executives (572)
Nat'l Puerto Rican Coalition (575)

Nat'l Soc. of Black Engineers (578)
Nat'l Urban League (580)
Native American Cultural & Educational Authority (582)
Native American Mohegans Inc. (582)
Native American Rights Fund (582)
NCSJ: Advocates on Behalf of Jews in Russia, Ukraine, the Baltic States and Eurasia (583)
New Mexico Indian Gaming Ass'n (586)
Nez Perce Tribal Executive Committee (589)
Noosack Indian Tribal council (591)
Northwest Indian Fisheries Commission (595)
Office for the Advancement of Public Black Colleges (599)
Oglala Sioux Tribe (599)
Old Harbor Native Corp. (600)
Omaha Tribe of Nebraska (600)
Oneida Indian Nation of New York (600)
Oneida Tribe of Indians of Wisconsin (601)
Order Sons of Italy in America/Sons of Italy Foundation (603)
Organization of Chinese Americans, Inc. (603)
Pancyprian Ass'n of America (607)
Parker Jewish Geriatric Institute (608)
Pascua Yaqui Tribe of Arizona (609)
Passamaquoddy Tribe(s)(2) (609)
Paucatuck Eastern Pequot Tribal Nation (609)
Pechanga Band of California Luiseno Indians (610)
Penobscot Indian Nation (611)
Pojoaque Pueblo (620)
Polish-American Congress (620)
Poverty and Race Research Action Council (622)
Prairie Band of Potawatomi Indians (622)
Pueblo de Conchiti (629)
Pueblo of Laguna (629)
Puerto Ricans for Civic Action (629)
Puyallup Tribe of Indians (630)
Quechan Indian Tribe (631)
Quinault Indian Nation (631)
A. Philip Randolph Educational Fund (633)
A. Philip Randolph Institute (633)
Red Lake Band of Chippewa Indians (635)
Religious Action Center of Reform Judaism (636)
Reno/Sparks Indian Colony (637)
Republican Jewish Coalition (637)
Republican Nat'l Hispanic Assembly of the U.S. (638)
Rosebud Sioux Tribal Council (642)
Sac & Fox Nation (644)
Saginaw Chippewa Indian Tribe of Michigan (646)
San Felipe Pueblo (647)
San Juan Pueblo (648)
San Pasqual Band of Mission Indians (648)
Sand Creek Descendants Trust (648)
Sandia Pueblo (648)
Santa Ana Pueblo (648)
Santa Clara Pueblo (649)
Sault Ste. Marie Tribe of Chippewa Indians (650)
Sealaska Corp. (653)
Seldovia Native Ass'n, Inc. (654)
Seminole Tribe of Indians of Florida (655)
Shakopee Business Council (656)
Shakopee Mdewakanton Sioux Tribe (656)
Shoshone-Bannock Tribes of the Fort Hall Indian Reservation (658)
Siletz Tribal Council (659)
Sisseton-Wahpoton Sioux Indian Tribe (660)
Soboba Band of Mission Indians (662)
Southeast Asia Resource Action Center (SEARAC) (667)
Southern Ute Indian Tribe (668)
Spanish Broadcasting System, Inc. (669)
Spokane Tribe (670)
Squaxin Island Indian Tribe (671)
St. Croix Chippewa Indians of Wisconsin (671)
St. George Island Traditional Council (671)
St. Regis Mohawk Tribe (672)
Standing Rock Sioux Tribe (672)
Stockbridge-Munsee Community Band of Mohican Indians (675)
Susanville Indian Rancheria (678)
Swan Creek River Confederated Ojibbwa Tribes of Michigan (678)
Swinomish Tribal Community (678)
Sycuan Band of Mission Indians (679)
Taos Pueblo (681)
Tesuque Pueblo (684)
Tett Enterprises (684)
Three Affiliated Tribes of Fort Berthold Reservation (686)
Timbisha Shoshone Tribe (687)
Tohono O'Odham Nation (688)
Trading Cove Associates (689)
TransAfrica Forum (689)
Tribal Alliance of Northern California (692)
Tulalip Tribes (693)
Tule River Tribal Council (694)
Tunica Biloxi Indians of Louisiana (694)
Twentynine Palms Band of Mission Indians (694)
U.S. Hispanic Chamber of Commerce (696)
Union of Councils for Soviet Jews (699)
United Hellenic American Congress (701)
United Jewish Communities, Inc. (701)
United Negro College Fund, Inc. (702)
United States Catholic Office of Bishops/Secretariat for Hispanic Affairs (703)
Upper Sioux Indian Community (708)
US-Asia Institute (709)
Ute Mountain Ute Indian Tribe (710)
Viejas Band of Kumeyaay Indians (715)
Walker River Paiute Tribe (718)
Washoe Tribe of Nevada and California (721)
White Mountain Apache Tribe (726)
Winnebago Tribe of Nebraska (728)
World Jewish Congress (730)
Wyandotte Tribe of Oklahoma (732)
Yankton Sioux Tribe (733)
Yavapai-Prescott Indian Tribe (733)
Ysleta Del Sur Pueblo (734)

Museums

Ass'n of Science Technology Centers, Inc. (298)
Center for the Arts and Sciences (338)
Chesapeake Bay Maritime Museum (342)
Fine Arts Museums of San Francisco (417)
Franklin Institute (425)
Fresno Metropolitan Museum (426)
Inventure Place (477)
Miami Museum of Science & Space Transit Planetarium (521)
Museum Campus Chicago (533)
Nat'l Aquarium (537)
Nat'l Women's History Museum (581)
Natural History Museum of Los Angeles County (582)
Please Touch Museum, The Children's Museum of Philadelphia (619)
San Diego Natural History Museum (647)
Virginia Living Museum (716)

Natural Resources

#10 Enterprises LLC (223)
Abtech Industries (225)
Air Products and Chemicals, Inc. (234)
Alabama Gas Corp. (235)
Alaska Rainforest Campaign (237)
Allegheny River Mining Co. (238)
Alliance Pipeline, L.P. (241)
American Coke and Coal Chemicals Institute (253)
American Gas Ass'n (261)
American Gas Cooling Center (261)
American Methanol Institute (268)
American Public Gas Ass'n (271)
Anthony Timberlands, Inc. (285)
Appalachian-Pacific Coal Mine Methane Power Co., LLC (286)
ARCO Coal Co. (287)
Arctic Resources Co. (288)
Ashland Inc. (290)
Ass'n of Bituminous Contractors (294)
Associated Gas Distributors (300)
Berwind Corp. (312)
Bexar Metropolitan Water District (313)
Bituminous Coal Operators Ass'n (314)
Burlington Resources Oil & Gas Co. (324)
California-American Water Co. (328)
Center for Energy and Economic Development (336)
Chamber of Independent Gas Stations of Argentina (340)
Chromalloy Gas Turbine Corp. (346)
Citizens Coal Council (348)
The Coal Coalition (352)
Coal Exporters Ass'n of the U.S. (352)
Columbia Gas Transmission Corp. (359)
Compressed Gas Ass'n (364)
Conoco Inc. (367)
DCH Technology Inc. (383)
Duke Energy (392)
El Paso Corporation (399)
El Paso Natural Gas Co. (399)
Enron Corp. (403)
Entex, Inc. (404)
Equitable Resources Energy Co. (406)
Exelon Corp. (409)
Foothills Pipe Lines (Yukon), Ltd. (422)
Frederick Douglass Gardens, Inc. (425)
Freeport-McMoRan Copper & Gold Inc. (425)
FuelMaker Corp. (427)
Fuels Management Inc. (427)
Gas Processors Ass'n (429)
Gas Research Institute (429)
Gas Technology Institute (429)
Georgia Municipal Gas Ass'n (434)
Go-Mart, Inc. (436)
GPM Gas Corp. (438)
Greystar Resources, Ltd. (440)
Holyoke Department of Gas and Electricity (451)
Howard Energy Internat'l (454)
Infilco Degremont, Inc. (461)
Interstate Natural Gas Ass'n of America (477)
Iowa, Dept. of Natural Resources of State of (478)
Iroquois Gas Transmission System (479)
Kansas Gas Service (486)
Kellogg Brown and Root (487)
Kennecott/Borax (488)
Kern River Gas Transmission Co. (488)
Kerr-McGee Corp. (488)
KFx, Inc. (489)
KN Energy Inc. (490)
LACDA Alliance (493)
Laclede Gas Co. (494)
Lake Worth Drainage District (494)
Lehigh Coal & Navigation Co. (498)
Memphis Light, Gas and Water Division (517)
Meridian Oil Inc. (519)
Mesa Inc. (519)
Michigan Consolidated Gas Co. (522)
Midcoast Interstate Transmission, Inc. (523)
Mission Springs (California) Water District (526)
Murphy Oil U.S.A. (533)
N-Methylpyrrolidone Producers Group, Inc. (534)
Nat'l Council of Coal Lessors (560)
Nat'l Mining Ass'n (571)
Nat'l Ocean Industries Ass'n (572)
Nat'l Propane Gas Ass'n (574)
Natural Gas Supply Ass'n (582)
Navajo Nation Oil and Gas Co., Inc. (582)
Nebraska Ethanol Board (583)
NiSource Inc. (590)
North American Coal (592)
Northern Border Pipeline Co. (594)
Northwest Municipal Conference (595)
Northwest Pipeline Corp (595)
NUI Environmental Group Inc. (597)
Oklahoma Gas and Electric Co. (599)
Oklahoma Natural Gas Co. (599)
Olga Coal Co. (600)
Palmer Coking & Coal Co. (607)
Pan-Alberta Gas Ltd. (607)
The Peabody Group (610)
Peter White Coal Mining Co. (613)
PG&E Corp. (614)
PG&E Gas Transmission Northwest (614)
Pickands Mather and Co. (617)
Pickens Fuel Corp. (617)
Pine Bluff Sand and Gravel Co. (617)
The Pittston Co. (618)
Praxair, Inc. (623)
Process Gas Consumers Group (625)
Propane Consumers Coalition (627)
Propane Vehicle Council (627)
Providence Gas (627)
PSE&G (627)
Questar Corp. (631)
Renewable Resources LLC (637)
Rhode Island Resource Recovery Center (639)
San Bernardino Valley Municipal Water District (647)
San Joaquin Area Flood Agency (648)
San Joaquin River Exchange Contractors Water Authority (648)
Scenic Hudson (651)
Sempra Energy (655)
Seneca Resources Corporation (655)
Service Station Dealers of America and Allied Trades (656)
Seven Seas Petroleum USA Inc. (656)
Soc. of Independent Gasoline Marketers of America (663)
Sweetwater Authority (678)
Syntroleum Corp. (679)
Texaco Group Inc. (684)
Texas Gas Transmission Corp. (684)
The Texas Wind Power Co. (685)
Transcontinental Gas Pipeline Corp. (690)
U.S. Oil and Gas Ass'n (696)
United Cities Gas Co. (701)
United Mine Workers of America (702)
United States Energy Ass'n (703)
US Acqua Sonics Corp. (709)
UtiliCorp United, Inc. (711)
Washington Gas (719)
Western Coal Traffic League (724)
Westmoreland Coal Co. (725)
The Williams Companies (727)
Winstar Petroleum (728)
Wisconsin Gas Co. (729)
Yukon Pacific (734)
Zeigler Coal Holding Co. (734)

Nutrition

Abbott Laboratories (225)
Academy for Eating Disorders (225)
American Dietetic Ass'n (257)
American School Food Service Ass'n (273)
American Soc. for Clinical Nutrition (274)
American Soc. for Nutritional Sciences (274)
American Soc. for Parenteral and Enteral Nutrition (274)
Calorie Control Council (328)
Center for Science in the Public Interest (337)
Child Nutrition Forum, c/o FRAC (343)
City Meals on Wheels USA (349)
Congressional Hunger Center (366)
Corporations to End World Hunger Foundation (372)
Council for Responsible Nutrition (374)
Dietary Supplement Safety and Science Coalition (388)
Farm Animal Reform Movement (FARM) (411)
Food Research and Action Center (422)
Herbalife Internat'l, Inc. (448)
Institute of Food Technologists (464)
Internat'l Food Policy Research Institute (471)
Internat'l Formula Council (471)
Little Havana Activities and Nutrition Centers (500)
Meals on Wheels Ass'n of America (515)
Metabolife (519)
Nat'l Ass'n of Nutrition and Aging Services and Programs (546)
Nat'l Ass'n of WIC Directors (551)

Novartis Corp. (596)
Nutrition Screening Initiative, The (597)
Protein Technologies Internat'l (627)
RESULTS (638)
Ross/Nutrition Screening Initiative (642)
Shaklee Corp. (656)
Slim Fast Foods Co. (661)
Soy Protein Council (668)
Weider Nutritional Group (722)
Weight Watchers Internat'l, Inc. (722)

Paper and Wood Products Industry

Abitibi Consolidated Sales Corp. (225)
Alaska Forest Ass'n (236)
Alaska Pulp Corp. (237)
American Forest & Paper Ass'n (259)
American Forest Foundation (260)
American Furniture Manufacturers Ass'n (260)
American Paper Machinery Ass'n (269)
American Paperboard Packaging Environment Council (269)
American Plywood Ass'n (270)
American Wood Preservers Institute (280)
Amino and Phenolic Wood Adhesives Ass'n (283)
APKINDO (286)
Appleton Papers, Inc. (286)
Aseptic Packaging Council (290)
Asosiasi Panel Kayu Indonesia (291)
Ass'n of Independent Corrugated Converters (296)
B.C. Softwood Lumber Trade Council (305)
Beyond BAT Group (313)
British Columbia Softwood Lumber Trade Council (321)
Canadian Pulp and Paper Ass'n, Newsprint Section of (329)
Caraustar (331)
Composite Can and Tube Institute (363)
Composite Panel Ass'n (363)
Crane & Co. (378)
Donohue Industries Inc. (391)
Envelope Manufacturers Ass'n of America (404)
Finch-Pruyn Paper Co. (417)
Foodservice & Packaging Institute, Inc. (422)
Forest Products Industry Nat'l Labor-Management Committee (423)
Forest Resources Ass'n (423)
Fort Howard Corp. (423)
Fort James Corp. (423)
Free Trade Lumber Council (425)
Garden State Paper Co., Inc. (429)
Georgia-Pacific Corp. (434)
P. H. Glatfelter (436)
Hallmark Cards, Inc. (443)
Hardwood Plywood and Veneer Ass'n (444)
Hearth Products Ass'n (447)
IBFI - The Internat'l Ass'n for Document and Information Management Solutions (456)
Impex Overseas (458)
Intermountain Forest Industry Ass'n (467)
Internat'l Paper (473)
Intertribal Timber Council (477)
IWPA - The Internat'l Wood Products Ass'n (480)
D. R. Johnson Lumber (484)
Kimberly-Clark Corp. (489)
Koncor Forest Products Co. (491)
Lincoln Pulp and Paper Co. (500)
Louisiana Pacific Corp. (504)
Maine Pulp & Paper Ass'n (507)
Malheur Timber Operators (508)
The Mead Corp. (515)
Nat'l Hardwood Lumber Ass'n (566)
Nat'l Lumber and Building Material Dealers Ass'n (570)
Nat'l School Supply and Equipment Ass'n (577)
The Newark Group (588)
Northwest Forestry Ass'n (595)
The Pacific Lumber Co. (605)
Paper Recycling Coalition (607)
Paperboard Packaging Council (607)
Plum Creek Timber Co. (619)
R. L. Polk & Co. (620)
Potlatch Corp. (621)
Prairie Wood Products (622)
The Procter & Gamble Company (625)
Quebec Lumber Manufacturers Ass'n (630)
Rock-Tenn Co. (641)
Sappi Fine Paper NA (649)
Sealaska Corp. (653)
Sierra Pacific Industries (659)
Simark Trading Co., Inc. (659)
Simpson Investment Co. (659)
Smurfit Stone Container Corp. (662)
South Jersey Regional Council of Carpenters (666)
Valhi, Inc. (711)
Washington Citizens for World Trade (719)
WESTVACO (725)
Weyerhaeuser Co. (725)
White Pigeon Paper Co. (726)
Wood Machinery Manufacturers of America (730)
Wood Products Indoor Air Consortium (730)
World Wide Packets (731)

Performing Arts/Music

All Kinds of Music (238)
American Federation of Television and Radio Artists (259)
American Film Institute (259)
Artists Coalition (290)
Baltimore Symphony Orchestra (306)
Bethesda Academy for the Performing Arts (312)
Capital Concerts (330)
Carnegie Hall Corp. (332)
Cellar Door Amphitheaters (334)
EMI Music (402)
Folger Shakespeare Library (421)
Ford's Theatre (422)
Gibson Guitar Corp. (435)
Thelonius Monk Institute of Jazz (527)
mp3.com (532)
Music Educators Nat'l Conference (533)
The NARAS Foundation (534)
Nat'l Capitol Concerts (554)
The Project Leadership Committee, Lincoln Center for the Performing Arts (626)
Providence Performing Arts Center (627)
Recording Industry Ass'n of America (634)
SESAC, Inc. (656)
Shea's Performing Arts Center (657)
Tampa Bay Performing Arts Center (680)

Personal Care/Hygiene

ABLEDATA (225)
Alticor, Inc. (242)
American Academy of Dermatology (243)
American Ass'n of Cosmetology Schools (247)
American Home Products Corp. (262)
American Soc. of Tropical Medicine and Hygiene (277)
Avon Products, Inc. (305)
Beauty and Barber Supply Industries, Inc. (310)
Colgate Palmolive (357)
Consumer Aerosol Products Council (368)
Cosmetic, Toiletry and Fragrance Ass'n (373)
Estee Lauder, Inc. (407)
Fragrance Materials Ass'n (424)
Gillette Co. (435)
Gino Morena Enterprises (435)
Johns Hopkins University Hospital, School of Hygiene and Public Health (483)
Johnson & Johnson, Inc. (484)
Kimberly-Clark Corp. (489)
Lehn & Fink Products Group (498)
Micell Technologies, Inc. (522)
Nat'l Accrediting Commission of Cosmetology Arts & Sciences, Inc. (535)
Nat'l Cosmetology Ass'n (559)
Novartis Services, Inc. (596)
Nu Skin Internat'l Inc. (597)
Pfizer, Inc. (613)
Pharmanex (615)
The Procter & Gamble Company (625)
Reckitt & Colman Pharmaceuticals Inc. (634)
Rite Aid Corp. (640)
Salton, Inc. (646)
Schering-Plough Legislative Resources L.L.C. (651)
Soap and Detergent Ass'n (662)
Unilever N.V. (699)
Unilever United States, Inc. (699)

Petroleum Industry

AAE Technologies, Inc. (224)
Air Quality Standards Coalition (234)
Alliance Pipeline, L.P. (241)
Alston & Bird, LLP (242)
Alyeska Pipeline Service Co. (242)
Amerada Hess Corp. (243)
American Gas Ass'n (261)
American Petroleum Institute (269)
American Public Gas Ass'n (271)
Anadarko Petroleum Corp. (283)
Aramco Services Co. (287)
ARCO Products Co. (287)
Arctic Power (288)
Arctic Resources Co. (288)
Ashland Inc. (290)
Ass'n of Oil Pipelines (297)
Associated Gas Distributors (300)
Baker Hughes Incorporated (306)
Bass Enterprises Production Co. (308)
Bechtel Group, Inc. (310)
BHP (USA) Inc. (313)
Bouchard Transportation Co. (318)
BP America, Inc. (319)
BP Amoco Corp. (319)
BP Exploration (319)
James W. Bunger & Associates (323)
Burlington Resources Oil & Gas Co. (324)
Buyers Up (325)
California Independent Petroleum Ass'n (327)
CENEX, Inc. (335)
The Chevron Companies (342)
Chevron Petroleum Marketers Ass'n (342)
Chevron, U.S.A. (342)
CITGO Petroleum Corp. (347)
Colonial Pipeline Co. (358)
Crown Central Petroleum Corp. (379)
Domestic Petroleum Council (390)
Duke Energy (392)
Dunn-Padre, Inc. (393)
El Paso Corporation (399)
Enron Corp. (403)
Equitable Resources Energy Co. (406)
Ethyl Corp. (407)
Exxon Chemical Co. (409)
Exxon Co., U.S.A. (409)
Exxon Mobil Corp. (409)
Exxon Valdez Oil Spill Litigation Plaintiffs (409)
Farmland Industries, Inc. (412)
Foothills Pipe Lines (Yukon), Ltd. (422)
Foster Wheeler Corp. (424)
Freeport-McMoRan Copper & Gold Inc. (425)
Gas Research Institute (429)
Georgia Municipal Gas Ass'n (434)
Giant Industries, Inc. (435)
Gilbarco, Inc. (435)
Global Marine, Inc. (436)
Golden Gate Petroleum Internat'l, Ltd. (437)
Goodyear Tire and Rubber Co. (437)
GPM Gas Corp. (438)
Halliburton/Brown & Root (443)
Hess (449)
HUTCO, Inc. (455)
Independent Fuel Terminal Operators Ass'n (459)
Independent Liquid Terminals Ass'n (459)
Independent Lubricant Manufacturers Ass'n (459)
Independent Oil and Gas Ass'n of Pennsylvania (459)
Independent Oil Producers Ass'n-Tri State (459)
Independent Petroleum Ass'n of America (459)
Independent Terminal Operators Ass'n (460)
Interstate Natural Gas Ass'n of America (477)
Kellogg Brown and Root (487)
Kerr-McGee Corp. (488)
KN Energy Inc. (490)
Koch Industries, Inc. (490)
La Sen, Inc. (493)
Lion Oil Co. (500)
Longhorn Pipeline (503)
LOOP, Inc. (503)
M and K Oil Co., Inc. (506)
Marathon Ashland Petroleum, LLC (509)
Marathon Oil Co. (509)
Marine Preservation Ass'n (510)
Maxus Energy Corp. (513)
Meridian Oil Inc. (519)
Mesa Inc. (519)
Methanex Inc. (520)
Mobil Latin America & Caribbean, Inc. (527)
Moscow Internat'l Petroleum Club (530)
Mount Airy Refining Co. (531)
Murphy Oil U.S.A. (533)
Nat'l Coalition of Petroleum Dry Cleaners (556)
Nat'l Ocean Industries Ass'n (572)
Nat'l Oilheat Research Alliance (NORA) (572)
Nat'l Petrochemical Refiners Ass'n (573)
Nat'l Petroleum Council (574)
Nat'l Propane Gas Ass'n (574)
New England Fuel Institute (585)
New Mexico State Land Office (586)
Northern Border Pipeline Co. (594)
Northwest Pipeline Corp (595)
NUI Environmental Group Inc. (597)
Occidental Petroleum Corporation (598)
Omega Oil Co. (600)
OXY USA Inc. (605)
Oxygenated Fuels Ass'n (605)
Paper, Allied-Industrial, Chemical and Energy Workers Internat'l Union (PACE) (607)
Parker Drilling Co. (608)
Peerless Petrochemicals, Inc. (610)
Petro Star, Inc. (613)
Petro-Canada (613)
Petrojam Ltd. (613)
Petroleum Heat and Power Co., Inc. (613)
Petroleum Marketers Ass'n of America (613)
Petroport, Inc. (613)
PG&E Gas Transmission Northwest (614)
Phillips Petroleum Co. (616)
Placid Refining Co. (618)
Questar Corp. (631)
Redstone (635)
Renova Inc. (637)
Rowan Companies, Inc. (643)
Royal Dutch Shell Group (643)
SABIC Americas, Inc. (644)
SEFBO Pipeline Bridge, Inc. (654)
Seneca Resources Corporation (655)
Sensor Oil and Gas Co. (655)
Service Station Dealers of America and Allied Trades (656)
Shell Oil Co. (657)
Shepherd Oil Co. (657)
Sherritt Internat'l (657)
Soc. of Independent Gasoline Marketers of America (663)
SpaceData Internat'l (669)
Sunoco, Inc. (677)
Svenska Petroleum Exploration AB (678)
Tesoro Petroleum Corp. (684)
Texaco Group Inc. (684)
Texas Gas Transmission Corp. (684)
Texas Petrochemicals Corp. (685)
Tosco Corp. (688)
Trajen, Inc. (689)

Transcontinental Gas Pipeline Corp. (690)
Trizec Hahn Corp. (692)
U.S. Oil and Gas Ass'n (696)
UNOCAL Corp. (708)
USX Corp. (710)
Vitol, S.A., Inc. (717)
Watson Energy (721)
Western States Land Commissioners Ass'n (724)
Western States Petroleum Ass'n (724)
Wickland Oil Co. (726)
The Williams Companies (727)
Williams Field Services (727)
Williams Pipelines Central, Inc. (727)
Yukon Pacific (734)

Pharmaceutical Industry

Abbott Laboratories (225)
Academy of Managed Care Pharmacy (225)
Academy of Pharmaceutical Research and Science (225)
Agouron Pharmaceuticals, Inc. (232)
Ajinomoto Co., Inc. (235)
Ajinomoto U.S.A., Inc. (235)
Akzo America, Inc. (235)
Allergan, Inc. (239)
American Academy of Orthotists and Prosthetists (244)
American Ass'n of Colleges of Pharmacy (247)
American Ass'n of Homeopathic Pharmacists (248)
American Ass'n of Pharmaceutical Scientists (249)
American Home Products Corp. (262)
American Pharmaceutical Ass'n (270)
American Soc. for Pharmacology and Experimental Therapeutics (274)
American Soc. of Consultant Pharmacists (276)
American Soc. of Health System Pharmacists (276)
American Wholesale Marketers Ass'n (280)
Animal Health Institute (284)
Apria Healthcare Group (287)
Asociacion Nacional de Fabricantes de Medicamentos (291)
Aspirin Foundation of America, Inc. (291)
AstraZeneca Inc. (301)
Avax Technologies, Inc. (304)
Aventis Pasteur (304)
Aventis Pharmaceuticals, Inc. (304)
Barr Laboratories (308)
Base Ten Systems, Inc. (308)
BASF Corporation (308)
Bayer Corp. (309)
Bayer Corp. / Agriculture Division (309)
Biotechnology Industry Organization (314)
Biovail Corp. Internat'l (314)
Boehringer Mannheim Corp. (316)
Bristol-Myers Squibb Co. (320)
Carter-Wallace, Inc. (332)
Celgene Corp. (334)
Cell Pathways, Inc. (334)
Centro Industrial de Laboratorios Farmaceuticas Argentinos (CILFA) (339)
Cephalon, Inc. (340)
Connaught Laboratories Inc. (366)
Consumer Healthcare Products Ass'n (369)
Cord Laboratories (371)
CVS, Inc. (380)
drugstore.com (392)
DuPont (393)
The DuPont Pharmaceutical Co. (393)
Duramed Pharmaceuticals, Inc. (393)
Elanex Pharmaceuticals (399)
FDA-NIH Council (412)
Foster Wheeler Corp. (424)
Fujisawa USA, Inc. (427)
GAF Corp. (428)
Genentech, Inc. (431)
Generic Pharmaceutical Ass'n (433)
Gentrac Inc. (433)
Genzyme Corp. (433)
GlaxoSmithKline (436)
Health Industry Distributors Ass'n (446)
Healthcare Distribution Management Ass'n (447)
Healthcare Leadership Council (447)
Hillenbrand Industries, Inc. (450)
Hoechst Marion Roussel Deutschland GmbH (450)
Hoffmann-La Roche Inc. (450)
Hollis-Eden Pharmaceuticals, Inc. (451)
ICN Pharmaceuticals, Inc. (457)
Immunex Corp. (458)
Incyte Pharmaceuticals, Inc. (458)
Indiana Medical Device Manufacturers Council (460)
Inter-Cal Corp. (466)
Internat'l Academy of Compounding Pharmacists (467)
Internat'l Soc. for Pharmacoepidemiology (475)
Inwood Laboratories, Inc. (478)
IVAX Corp. (480)
The JAG Group, Inc. (481)
Johnson & Johnson, Inc. (484)
Jones Medical Industries, Inc. (485)
Knoll Pharmaceutical Co. (490)
Lederle Laboratories (497)
Eli Lilly and Co. (499)
Massachusetts Medical Device Industry Council (512)
McKesson Corp. (515)
Mead Johnson and Co. (515)
Medco Containment Services, Inc. (516)
Medeva Pharmaceuticals (516)
Meditrend, Inc. (517)
Medix Pharmaceuticals (517)
Medtronic, Inc. (517)
Merck & Co. (518)
Meyer Pharmaceuticals (521)
Minnesota Mining and Manufacturing (3M Pharmaceuticals) (525)
Molecular BioSystems, Inc. (527)
Mylan Laboratories, Inc. (533)
Naigai, Inc. (534)
Nat'l Ass'n for Nutritional Choice (538)
Nat'l Ass'n of Chain Drug Stores (539)
Nat'l Ass'n of Pharmaceutical Manufacturers (546)
Nat'l Community Pharmacists Ass'n (558)
Nat'l Pharmaceutical Council (574)
NeoPharm, Inc. (583)
NextRX (589)
North American Vaccine, Inc./AMVAX, Inc. (593)
Novartis Corp. (596)
Novartis Services, Inc. (596)
Ortho-McNeil Pharmaceutical Corp. (604)
Pan Pacific Pharmaceuticals (607)
Par Pharmaceutical, Inc. (607)
PCS Health Systems, Inc. (610)
PDA (610)
PennField Oil Co. (611)
Pennsylvania Pharmaceutical Ass'n (611)
Pfizer, Inc. (613)
Pharmaceutical Care Management Ass'n (614)
Pharmaceutical Products, Inc. (614)
Pharmaceutical Research and Manufacturers of America (614)
Pharmacia Corp. (615)
Pharmanex (615)
PlanetRx (618)
The Procter & Gamble Company (625)
Proprietary Industries Ass'n (627)
Pure Encapsulations, Inc. (630)
Quad Pharmaceutical Inc. (630)
Reckitt & Colman Pharmaceuticals Inc. (634)
Regulatory Affairs Professionals Soc. (636)
Reheis, Inc. (636)
Respiratory Medication Providers Coalition (638)
Rhone-Polenc Inc. (639)
Rite Aid Corp. (640)
Roussel-UCLAF (642)
Roxanne Laboratories, Inc. (643)
Rx Vitamins, Inc. (644)
SAMA Group of Ass'ns (647)
Schein Pharmaceutical, Inc. (651)
Schering Berlin Inc. (651)
Schering Corp. (651)
Schering-Plough Corp. (651)
Schering-Plough Legislative Resources L.L.C. (651)
Serono Laboratories, Inc. (655)
Sigma-Tau Pharmaceuticals, Inc. (659)
SmithKline Beecham Consumer Healthcare, LLP (661)
SOL Source Technologies, Inc. (665)
Somerset Pharmaceuticals (665)
E. R. Squibb and Sons, Inc. (671)
Star Tobacco & Pharmaceuticals Inc. (673)
Superpharm Corp. (677)
Syntex (USA) Inc. (679)
Transtracheal Systems (691)
Tri Path Inc. (691)
United States Pharmacopeial Convention (704)
Vitarine Pharmaceuticals Inc. (716)
Wyeth-Ayerst Laboratories (732)
Wyeth-Ayerst Pharmaceuticals (732)
XCEL Medical Pharmacy, Ltd. (732)
W. F. Young Inc. (733)

Plastics Industry

American Plastics Council (270)
Aseptic Packaging Council (290)
Ball Aerospace & Technologies Corp. (306)
Borden Chemicals & Plastics, Inc. (318)
Celanese Government Relations Office (334)
Chep USA (342)
Closure Manufacturers Ass'n (351)
Contact Lens Manufacturers Ass'n (370)
The Dow Chemical Co. (391)
Eagle-Picher Industries (394)
Ethyl Corp. (407)
Flexel, Inc. (418)
Foodservice & Packaging Institute, Inc. (422)
Goodyear Tire and Rubber Co. (437)
Grupo Industrial Alfa, S.A. (441)
Martin Color-Fi (511)
Minnesota Mining and Manufacturing Co. (3M Co.) (525)
Nat'l Ass'n for Plastic Container Recovery (538)
Owens-Illinois, Inc. (605)
Plastic Container Institute (619)
Plastic Shipping Container Institute (619)
Rohm and Haas Co. (642)
Rubber and Plastic Footwear Manufacturers Ass'n (643)
Soc. of the Plastics Industry (664)
Styrene Information and Research Center (676)
USA/Scientific Plastics Inc. (709)

Political Action Committees

1245 Foundation (223)
21st Century Democrats (223)
Alliance of Arts Advocates (240)
American AIDS Political Action Committee (244)
American Citizens for the Arts Political Action Committee (252)
Americans Back in Charge Foundation (281)
Americans for a Brighter Future (281)
Americans for Free Internat'l Trade (AFIT PAC) (281)
Americans for Political Participation (282)
Americans Supporting the Pyrotechnics Industry (282)
Arena PAC (288)
Artists Rights Today (ART PAC) (290)
Black America's Political Action Committee (315)
Broadwave USA Inc. (321)
Business-Industry Political Action Committee (325)
Campaign Accountability Project (328)
Citizens for a Conservative Majority (348)
Citizens for a Republican Majority (348)
Club for Growth (351)
Committee for a Democratic Majority (360)
Common Sense Common Solutions PAC (362)
Congressional Agenda: 90's (366)
Conscience of a Conservative PAC (367)
Conservative Republican Network (367)
Conservative Victory Fund (367)
D.C. Building Industry Ass'n Political Action Committee (381)
Democratic Candidate Fund (385)
Democratic Congressional Campaign Committee (385)
Democratic Senatorial Campaign Committee (385)
Ed XL PAC (396)
Effective Government Committee (398)
Federal Victory Fund (414)
Feminist Majority (415)
The Freedom Project (425)
Friends of Higher Education Inc. (426)
Fund for American Opportunity PAC (427)
Future Fund (428)
Gay and Lesbian Victory Fund (430)
Glacier PAC (435)
GOPAC (437)
Great Northwest Classic Committee (439)
Great Plains Leadership Fund (439)
HBCU/PAC (445)
Home School PAC (451)
House Majority Fund (453)
Independent Action (459)
Independents Committee for Future America (460)
Internet Security, Privacy & Self-Regulation PAC (476)
Irish American Democrats (478)
Italian-American Democratic Leadership Council (480)
Labor for America PAC (493)
Leadership for the Future (497)
Leadership PAC 2002 (497)
Log Cabin Republicans PAC (LCR PAC) (502)
Mandela Group (508)
MAPPS PAC (509)
Mid-Atlantic Regional Joint Board UNITE PAC (523)
Nat'l Asian American Political Empowerment Fund (537)
Nat'l Ass'n of Business Political Action Committees (539)
Nat'l Committee for an Effective Congress (557)
The Nat'l PAC (573)
Nat'l Pro-Life Alliance PAC (574)
Nat'l Rehabilitation Political Action Committee (575)
Nat'l Republican Congressional Committee (575)
New American Century PAC (585)
New Democrat Network (585)
New Republican Majority Fund (586)
PACAmerica Inc. (605)
Participation 2000 Inc. (608)
Pediatricians for Children Inc. (610)
Policy Group (620)
Powerline Communications PAC (622)
Professional Beauty Federation PAC (625)
RENEW (Republican Network to Elect Women) (636)
Republican Leadership Council (637)
Republicans for Choice (638)
S-PAC (644)
Science Leadership PAC (652)
Searchlight Victory Fund (653)
Southwest Peanut PAC (668)
SwimWithTheSharks.com (678)
Take Back the House (680)
Tex-USA Fund (684)
Texas Freedom Fund (684)
U.S. Immigrant Investor Ass'n (696)
United Pilots Political Action Committee (702)
Velazquez Victory Fund-Federal (712)
Victims Rights PAC (715)
View PAC (715)
Virginia-Carolina's Peanut Political Action Committee (716)
Voters For Choice (717)
Washington Political Action Committee (720)
Western Coalition Political Action Committee (724)
Wildlife Conservation and Zoos PAC (726)
Women's Action for New Directions (WAND)/Women Legislators' Lobby (WILL) (729)
Women's Campaign Fund (729)
Women's Pro-Israel Nat'l Political Action Committee (Win PaC) (730)
X-PAC (732)

Politics/Political Science

21st Century Democrats (223)
Accuracy in Academia (226)
Accuracy in Media (226)
The Advocacy Institute (229)
Alexis de Tocqueville Institution (238)
American Ass'n of Political Consultants (249)
American Conservative Union (255)
American Council of Young Political Leaders (256)
American Enterprise Institute for Public Policy Research (257)
American League of Lobbyists (266)
American Political Science Ass'n (270)
American Renewal (272)
Americans Back in Charge Foundation (281)
Americans for a Brighter Future (281)
Americans for Democratic Action (281)
Americans for Tax Reform (282)
Americans United for Separation of Church and State (282)
Arab American Institute (287)
Ass'n for Public Policy Analysis and Management (293)
The Bethune-DuBois Institute, Inc. (312)
The Brookings Institution (321)
Cambodian People's Party (328)
Campaign Finance Reform Coalition (328)
Campaign for America (328)
Campaign Reform Project (329)
Campaign to Preserve U.S. Global Leadership (329)
Capital Research Center (330)
CapitolWatch (331)
Cato Institute (334)
Center for Defense Information (335)
Center for Deliberative Polling (336)
Center for Democracy (336)
Center for Nat'l Policy (337)
Center for Policy Alternatives (337)
Center for Responsive Politics (337)
Center for the Study of Responsive Law (338)
Center for the Study of Social Policy (338)
The Center for Voting and Democracy (338)
The Century Foundation (339)
Christian Coalition of America (345)
Christian Voice, Inc. (345)
Citizens for State Power (348)
Citizens United (349)
Coalition of Northeastern Governors (355)
Coalitions for America (356)
College Republican Nat'l Committee (358)
Commission on Presidential Debates (360)
Committee for a Democratic Majority (360)
Committee for Citizen Awareness (360)
Committee for the Study of the American Electorate (361)
Committee on the Constitutional System (361)
Common Cause (361)
Concerned Women for America (365)
Concord Coalition (365)
Congolese Rally for Democracy (366)
Congressional Accountability Project (366)
Congressional Agenda: 90's (366)
Congressional Black Caucus Foundation (366)
Congressional Exchange (366)
Congressional Hispanic Caucus Institute (CHCI) (366)
Congressional Institute for the Future (366)
Congressional Institute, Inc. (366)
Congressional Management Foundation (366)
Conservative Caucus Research, Analysis and Education Foundation (367)
The Conservative Caucus (367)
Conservative Political Action Conference (367)
Conservative Victory Fund (367)
Democracy 21 (385)
Democratic Candidate Fund (385)
Democratic Congressional Campaign Committee (385)
Democratic Governors Ass'n (385)
Democratic Leadership Council (385)
Democratic Nat'l Committee (385)
Democratic Senatorial Campaign Committee (385)
Effective Government Committee (398)
EMILY'S List (402)
Family Research Council, Inc. (411)
Fanatasy Elections (411)
Forum for America's Island Republicans (423)
Foundation Endowment (424)
Foundation on Economic Trends (424)
Free Congress Research and Education Foundation (425)
The Freedom Project (425)
Friedrich Ebert Foundation (426)
Frontiers of Freedom Institute (427)
Fund for Constitutional Government (428)
Future of Puerto Rico Inc. (428)
GOPAC (437)
Grassroots Enterprise, Inc. (438)
Gray Panthers Nat'l Office in Washington (439)
Heritage Foundation (448)
House Majority Fund (453)
Independent Action (459)
Independent Women's Forum (460)
Independents Committee for Future America (460)
Institute for Health Care Research and Policy (463)
Institute for Policy Studies (463)
Institute on Religion and Democracy (464)
Internat'l Foundation for Election Systems (IFES) (471)
Internat'l Republican Institute (474)
Irish American Democrats (478)
Italian-American Democratic Leadership Council (480)
Joint Center for Political and Economic Studies (484)
Kurdistan Democratic Party - Iraq (492)
Kurdistan Democratic Party USA (492)
Lawyers for the Republic (496)
Leadership 2000 (496)
Leadership for the Future (497)
League of Conservation Voters (497)
League of Women Voters of the United States (497)
Liberty Lobby (499)
Log Cabin Republicans PAC (LCR PAC) (502)
Marianas Political Status Commission (509)
Missouri Democratic Party (526)
Nat'l Ass'n of County Recorders, Election Officials and Clerks (541)
Nat'l Ass'n of Minority Political Families, USA, Inc. (545)
Nat'l Center for Policy Analysis (555)
Nat'l Center for Public Policy Research (555)
Nat'l Coalition on Black Civic Participation, Inc. (556)
Nat'l Committee for an Effective Congress (557)
Nat'l Democratic Club (562)
Nat'l Democratic County Officials Organization (562)
Nat'l Endowment for Democracy (563)
Nat'l Federation of Democratic Women (564)
Nat'l Federation of Republican Women (564)
Nat'l Governors' Ass'n (566)
Nat'l Jewish Democratic Council (569)
Nat'l Republican Congressional Committee (575)
Nat'l Republican Senatorial Committee (575)
Nat'l Women's Political Caucus (581)
NET-Political NewsTalk Network (584)
New Democrat Network (585)
New Republican Majority Fund (586)
New York State Democratic Committee (587)
Ohio Senate Republican Caucus (599)
Participation 2000 Inc. (608)
People for the American Way (612)
Policy Group (620)
The Progress Freedom Foundation (626)
Progressive Policy Institute (626)
Public Advocate (628)
Public Forum Institute (628)
RENEW (Republican Network to Elect Women) (636)
Republican Governors Ass'n (637)
Republican Jewish Coalition (637)
Republican Leadership Council (637)
Republican Nat'l Committee (637)
Republican Nat'l Hispanic Assembly of the U.S. (638)
Ripon Society (640)
Scottish Nat'l Party (652)
Southern Governors Ass'n (668)
Speak Out! USA (669)
Take Back the House (680)
U.S. Term Limits (697)
U.S.-Canadian Caucus of Mayors (697)
Union Institute - Office for Social Responsibility, The (699)
Washington Discussion Group (719)
Woman's Nat'l Democratic Club (729)
Women's Action for New Directions (WAND)/Women Legislators' Lobby (WILL) (729)
Women's Campaign Fund (729)
Women's Information Network (729)
Young Republican Hispanic Ass'n (733)
Young Republican Nat'l Federation, Inc. (733)

Pollution and Waste

Abtech Industries (225)
Air & Water Technologies (233)
Air Products and Chemicals, Inc. (234)
Air Quality Standards Coalition (234)
Alexandria, Virginia, Sanitation Authority of the City of (238)
Alliance for Nuclear Accountability (240)
Alliance for Responsible Atmospheric Policy (240)
American Board of Health Physics (251)
American Industrial Hygiene Ass'n (263)
American Public Works Ass'n (272)
Archimedes Technology Group (287)
Asbestos Recycling Inc. (290)
Ass'n for Responsible Thermal Treatment (293)
Ass'n of Local Air Pollution Control Officials (296)
Ass'n of Metropolitan Sewerage Agencies (297)
Ass'n of State and Interstate Water Pollution Control Administrators (298)
Ass'n of State and Territorial Solid Waste Management Officials (298)
Associated Air Balance Council (300)
Atlantic County Utilities Authority (302)
Automated Credit Exchange (303)
AutoNation, Inc. (304)
Bechtel Group, Inc. (310)
Berkeley County Water & Sanitation Authority (312)
BKK Corp. (314)
Bristol Resource Recovery Facility Operating Committee (320)
California Ass'n of Sanitation Agencies (326)
California Refuse Removal Council (327)
Caribe Waste Technologies (331)
Rachel Carson Council, Inc. (332)
Center for Clean Air Policy (335)
Center for Health, Environment and Justice (336)
CH2M Hill (340)
Clean Air Action Corp. (350)
Clean Air Now (350)
Clean Air Regulatory Information Group (350)
Clean Water Action (350)
Clean Water Council (350)
Clean Water Network (350)
Coalition for Asbestos Resolution (353)
Coalition for Responsible Waste Incineration (354)
Colusa Basin Drainage District (359)
Commerce Clause Coalition (360)
Consumer Energy Council of America Research Foundation (369)
Consumer Specialties Products Ass'n (369)
Container Recycling Institute (370)
Covanta Energy Corporation (377)
CSO Partnership (379)
Delaware, Pennsylvania, Solid Waste Authority of the County of (384)
Earth Share (394)
East Bay Municipal Utility District (395)
Ecological and Toxicological Ass'n of Dyes and Organic Pigments Manufacturers (396)
Environmental Business Action Coalition (404)
Environmental Defense Fund (405)
Environmental Industry Ass'ns (405)
Environmental Technology Council (405)
Environmental Treatment and Technologies Corp. (405)
Environmental Working Group (405)
Exxon Valdez Oil Spill Litigation Plaintiffs (409)
Friends of the Earth (426)
Gary Sanitary District (429)
GEO Centers, Inc. (433)
Global Climate Coalition (436)
Global Waste Recycling, Inc. (436)
Greater Detroit Resource Recovery Authority (439)
Greenpeace, U.S.A. (440)
Ground Water Protection Council (441)
Gulf Coast Waste Disposal Authority (442)
Hazardous Materials Advisory Council (445)
Health Physics Soc. (446)
Housatonic Resources Recovery Authority (453)
Huntsville, Alabama, Solid Waste Disposal Authority of the City of (455)
Institute for Local Self-Reliance (463)
Institute of Scrap Recycling Industries, Inc. (464)
Integrated Waste Services Ass'n (465)
Internat'l Metals Reclamation Co. (473)
Irrigation Ass'n (479)
Japan Industrial Conference for Ozone Layer Protection (482)
Landis, New Jersey, Sewerage Authority (495)
Los Angeles County Sanitation District (504)
Marine Spill Response Corporation (510)
Marion County Solid Waste Management (510)
Martinizing Environmental Group (511)
MEI Corp. (517)
Metropolitan St. Louis Sewer District (520)
Mickey Leland Nat'l Urban Air Toxics Research Center (522)
Mineral Policy Center (525)
Molecular Separations Inc. (527)
Montgomery County, Ohio/Montgomery County Solid Waste District (528)
NAC Internat'l (534)
Nat'l Air Duct Cleaners Ass'n (536)
Nat'l Air Filtration Ass'n (536)
Nat'l Coalition Against the Misuse of Pesticides (556)
Nat'l Environmental Development Ass'n, Inc. (563)
Nat'l Institute for Water Resources (568)
Nat'l Pollution Prevention Roundtable (574)
Nat'l Solid Wastes Management Ass'n (578)
Nat'l Wildlife Federation - Office of Federal and Internat'l Affairs (581)
NEDA/Resource Conservation and Recovery Act Project (583)
Norcal Waste Systems, Inc. (591)
Northeast Ohio Regional Sewer District (593)
Passaic Valley Sewerage Commissioners (609)
Proteus Co. (627)
Public Agencies for Audit Reform (628)
Public Employees for Environmental Responsibility (PEER) (628)
Pure Food Campaign (630)
Renewable Natural Resources Foundation (637)
Republic Services, Inc. (637)
Riverside County, California, Flood Control and Water Conservation District (640)
ROLITE, Inc. (642)
Safe Environment of America (645)
San Gabriel Basin Water Quality Authority (648)
San Joaquin Valley Wide Air Pollution Study Agency (648)
Santa Clara Valley Water District (649)
Science Applications Internat'l Corp. (SAIC) (652)
Sierra Club (658)
Soc. of Toxicology (664)
Solid Waste Agency of Northern Cook County (665)
Solid Waste Ass'n of North America (665)
Solid Waste Authority of Central Ohio (665)
Spokane Regional Solid Waste System (670)
Square 3942 Associates Limited Partnership (671)
State and Territorial Air Pollution Program Administrators (673)

Sumner, Tennessee, Resource Authority of the County of (676)
Superfund Action Alliance (677)
Superfund Action Coalition (677)
Superfund Reform '95 (677)
Terrene Institute (684)
Toxicology Forum (688)
Union Sanitary District (699)
UNR Asbestos-Disease Trust (708)
USPCI, Inc. (710)
Utility Air Regulatory Group (711)
Utility Solid Waste Activities Group (711)
Waste Control Specialists, Inc. (721)
Waste Management, Inc. (721)
Waste Policy Institute (721)
Water and Wastewater Equipment Manufacturers Ass'n (721)
Water Environment Federation (721)
Water Environment Research Foundation (721)
Water Quality 2000 (721)
West Coast Refuse and Recycling Coalition (723)
Wheelabrator Environmental Systems, Inc. (725)
Wheelabrator-Cleanwater Systems-BioGro Division (726)
World Wildlife Fund (731)
Worldwatch Institute (731)
York County Solid Waste Authority (733)
Zero Population Growth, Inc. (734)

Ports and Waterways

Allegheny County, Pennsylvania, Port Authority of (238)
Almont Shipping Terminals (242)
American Ass'n of Port Authorities (249)
American Great Lakes Ports (261)
American Rivers (273)
American Waterways Operators (280)
Ass'n of California Water Agencies (295)
Ass'n of State and Interstate Water Pollution Control Administrators (298)
Ass'n of State Dam Safety Officials (299)
Ass'n of Water Technologies (299)
Brix Maritime, Inc. (321)
Calleguas Creek Flood Prevention Committee (328)
Canal Barge Co., Inc. (330)
Central Arizona Water Conservation District (338)
Clean Water Council (350)
Clean Water Network (350)
Coastal States Organization (356)
Colorado River Energy Distributors Ass'n (358)
Comision Ejecutiva Hidroelectrica del Rio Lempa CEL (360)
Corpus Christi Port Authority (373)
Cross Sound Ferry Services, Inc. (378)
Delaware River Port Authority (384)
Dredging Contractors of America (392)
East Bay Municipal Utility District (395)
Everett, Washington, Port of (408)
Georgia Ports Authority (434)
Great Lakes Composites Consortium (439)
Hood River, Oregon, Port of (452)
Houston, Texas, Port Authority of the City of (453)
Hutchison Whampo, LTD (455)
Indianapolis Rail Project (460)
Internat'l Longshore and Warehouse Union (473)
Internat'l Longshoremen's Ass'n (473)
Jacksonville, Florida, Port Authority of the City of (481)
Kirby Corp./Dixie Carriers (490)
Long Beach, California, Port of (503)
Maritime Exchange for the Delaware River and Bay (510)
Massachusetts Port Authority (512)
Mount Vernon Barge Service (531)
Nat'l Water Resources Ass'n (581)
Nat'l Waterways Conference, Inc. (581)
New Orleans, Louisiana, Port of (586)
Northwest Municipal Conference (595)
Oakland, California, Port of (598)
Oregon Economic Development Department (603)
Orleans Levee District (603)
Oxnard Harbor District (605)
Philadelphia Regional Port Authority (615)
Placer County Water Agency (618)
Port Authority of New York and New Jersey (621)
Port of Lake Charles (621)
Port of San Diego (621)
Port of Tillamook Bay (621)
Poseidon Resources Corp. (621)
Redwood City, California, Port of (635)
Salt River Project (646)
San Francisco Bar Pilots Ass'n (648)
Santa Cruz, California, Port of (649)
Save Barton Creek (650)
Seattle, Washington, Port of (653)
Sonoma County Water Agency (665)
South Louisiana, Port of (666)
St. Bernard Port, Harbor and Terminal District (671)
St. Lawrence Seaway Pilots Ass'n (671)
Stockton, California, Port of (675)
Tacoma, Washington, Port of (680)
Tampa Port Authority (680)
Tennessee Valley Authority - Washington Office (683)
Todd Shipyards Inc. (688)
Transportation Institute (690)
Tri-City Regional Port District (691)
Turlock Irrigation District (694)
Ventura Port District (712)
Virgin Valley Water District (715)
Water Quality 2000 (721)
Wellton-Mohawk Irrigation and Drainage District (723)
Western Great Lakes Pilots Ass'n (724)
Westlands Water District (725)
Yazoo County, Mississippi Port Commission (733)

Postal and Mail Services

Alliance of Nonprofit Mailers (241)
American Postal Workers Union (271)
Ass'n for Postal Commerce (292)
Coalition Against Unfair U.S. Postal Service Competition (352)
Deutsche Post AG (386)
Direct Marketing Ass'n Nonprofit Federation (388)
Direct Marketing Ass'n of Washington (388)
Direct Marketing Ass'n, Inc. (388)
Fund for Assuring an Independent Retirement (427)
MailBoxes Etc. (507)
Mailing & Fulfillment Services Ass'n (507)
Main Street Coalition for Postal Fairness (507)
Nat'l Alliance of Postal and Federal Employees (536)
Nat'l Ass'n of Letter Carriers of the United States of America (545)
Nat'l Ass'n of Postal Supervisors (546)
Nat'l Ass'n of Postmasters of the U.S. (546)
Nat'l League of Postmasters of the U.S. (569)
Nat'l Postal Mail Handlers Union (574)
Nat'l Rural Letter Carriers' Ass'n (577)
Nat'l Star Route Mail Contractors Ass'n (578)
Parcel Shippers Ass'n (608)
Pitney Bowes, Inc. (618)
Stamps.com (672)
U.S. Postal Service (697)

Printing Industry

Applied Graphics (286)
Thomas De La Rue, Inc. (383)
R. R. Donnelley & Sons (391)
Graphic Communications Internat'l Union (438)
IBFI - The Internat'l Ass'n for Document and Information Management Solutions (456)
Jeppesen Sanderson, Inc. (482)
Liberty Check Printers (499)
Nat'l Bible Ass'n (552)
NPES, The Ass'n for Suppliers of Printing, Publishing, and Converting Technologies (596)
R. L. Polk & Co. (620)
Printing Industries of America (624)
Quebecor World (USA) Inc. (631)
Rodale Press (641)
Screenprinting & Graphic Imaging Ass'n Internat'l (653)
SICPA Industries of America, Inc. (658)
U.S. Banknote Corp. (695)
Worldwide Printing Thermographers Ass'n (731)

Public Affairs and Public Relations

20/20 Vision (223)
Alexander Strategy Group (238)
Asbestos Information Ass'n/North America (290)
Carr Public Affairs (332)
Center for Freedom and Prosperity (336)
Compass Internat'l Inc. (363)
DCS Group (383)
DFI Internat'l (387)
Edelman Public Relations Worldwide (396)
Ericsson Inc. (406)
Fenton Communications (415)
getpress.com (435)
The Hearst Corp. (447)
Internat'l Public Relations Co. (474)
Jacobs & Co. Public Affairs/Loma Linda University (481)
Nat'l Ass'n of Schools of Public Affairs and Administration (549)
Nat'l School Public Relations Ass'n (577)
Public Affairs Council (628)
Romyr Associates (642)
Trade Show Exhibitors Ass'n (689)
University of South Florida Research Foundation (707)
Women's College Coalition (729)

Railroads

Academy of Rail Labor Attorneys (226)
ADTranz (Daimler Chrysler Rail Systems) (228)
Alaska Railroad (237)
American Ass'n of Private Railroad Car Owners, Inc. (249)
American Magline Group (266)
American Passenger Rail Coalition (269)
American Railway Car Institute (272)
American Short Line and Regional Railroad Ass'n (274)
AMTRAK (Nat'l Rail Passenger Corp.) (283)
Anoka County Regional Railroad Authority (284)
Ass'n of American Railroads (294)
Bombardier Transportation/Bombardier Transit Corporation (317)
Brotherhood of Locomotive Engineers (322)
Brotherhood of Maintenance of Way Employees (322)
Brotherhood of Railroad Signalmen (322)
Burlington Northern Santa Fe Railway (324)
Canadian Nat'l Railroad/Illinois Central Railroad (329)
Canadian Nat'l Railway Co. (329)
Canadian Pacific (329)
Canton Railroad Co. (330)
Chicago Southshore and South Bend Railroad (343)
Coalition for Competitive Rail Transportation (353)
Consumers United for Rail Equity (369)
CSX Corp. (379)
CSX Lines LLC (379)
Dakota Minnesota and Eastern Railroad (381)
Delaware and Hudson Railroad (384)
Delaware Otsego System (384)
GATX Corp. (430)
Grand Canyon Railway (438)
Grand Trunk Corp. (438)
Greenbrier Companies (440)
G.E. Harris Harmon (445)
High Speed Ground Transportation Ass'n (449)
Kansas City Southern Industries (486)
Kansas City Southern Railway Co. (486)
Metra/Northeast Illinois Rail Corp. (520)
Metroplex Corp. (520)
Nat'l Ass'n of Railroad Passengers (547)
Nat'l Railroad and Construction Maintenance Ass'n (575)
Nat'l Railway Labor Conference (575)
Norfolk Southern Corp. (591)
Northeast Illinois Regional Commuter Railroad Corp. (593)
Operation Lifesaver Inc. (601)
Paducah & Louisville Railroad (606)
Rail Supply and Service Coalition (632)
Railroad Retirement Tax Working Group (632)
Rails to Trails Conservancy (632)
Railway Labor Executives' Ass'n (632)
Railway Progress Institute (632)
Regional Railroads of America (636)
Roaring Fork Railroad Holding Authority (641)
Soo Line Railroad, Inc. (666)
South Carolina Public Railways (666)
Southern California Regional Rail Authority (667)
St. Louis/Lake Counties Regional Rail Authority (672)
Talgo (680)
Tourist Railroad Ass'n, Inc. (688)
Transportation Reform Alliance (690)
Transportation-Communications Internat'l Union (691)
Travel Industry Ass'n of America (691)
Tri-County Commuter Rail Authority (691)
TTX Co. (693)
Union Pacific (699)
Union Pacific Railroad Co. (699)
Union Switch and Signal, Inc. (699)
United Transportation Union (705)
Wabtec Corp. (718)
Washington Metropolitan Area Transit Authority (720)
West Virginia State Rail Authority (723)
Wheeling & Lake Erie Railway Co. (726)
Wisconsin Central Transportation Corp. (728)

Real Estate

500 C Street Associates, L.P. (224)
Adriaen's Landing Management Co., LLC (228)
Affordable Housing Preservation Center (230)
Alexander's Inc. (238)
Allete (239)
American Homeowners Grassroots Alliance (262)
The American Land Conservancy (265)
American Land Rights Ass'n (265)
American Land Title Ass'n (265)
American Management (266)
American Realty Advisors (272)
American Resort Development Ass'n (272)
American Soc. of Appraisers (275)
American Soc. of Farm Managers and Rural Appraisers (276)
Americans for Responsible Recreational Areas (282)
Apartment and Office Building Ass'n of Metropolitan Washington (286)
Apartment Investment and Management Co. (286)
Appraisal Institute (287)
Arlington Educational Ass'n Retirement Housing Corp. (288)
Artichoke Enterprises, Inc. (290)
The Ashley Group (290)
Ass'n of Foreign Investors in U.S. Real Estate (295)
Associated Estates Co. (300)
Atlantic Gulf Communities (302)
Bedford Stuyvesant Restoration Corp. (310)
Blake Construction Co. (315)
Broe Companies, Inc. (321)
Building Owners and Managers Ass'n Internat'l (323)
California State Lands Commission (327)
Canyon Forest Village Corp. (330)
Cendant Corp. (335)
Century 21 Real Estate Corp. (339)
Chicago Deferred Exchange Corp. (343)
Chicago Trust Co. (343)
CLT Appraisal Services, Inc. (351)
CMC/Heartland Partnership (351)
Coalition for Fair Taxation of Real Estate (353)

Columbus General, L.L.C. (359)
Commonwealth Atlantic Properties (362)
Community Ass'ns Institute (CAI) (362)
Continental Wingate Co., Inc. (370)
Cook Inlet Region Inc. (371)
Cornerstone Florida Corp., Ltd. (372)
Corporate Property Investors (372)
Council for Affordable and Rural Housing (373)
Council of Appraisal and Property Professional Societies (375)
Cushman & Wakefield, Inc. (380)
D.C. Land Title Ass'n (383)
Dal Mac Investment Corp. (382)
Day & Zimmermann, Inc. (383)
DeChiaro Properties (383)
Defenders of Property Rights (383)
Delta Development Group, Inc. (385)
Denhill DC LCC (385)
Development Resources, Inc. (387)
Diamond Ventures (387)
Dime Savings Bank of New York (388)
Edison Properties L.L.C. (397)
Elcor Inc. (399)
Empresas Fonalledas (402)
EWA Land Information Group, Inc. (408)
Fannie Mae (411)
Federal Agricultural Mortgage Corp. (Farmer Mac) (412)
Federal Home Loan Mortgage Corp. (Freddie Mac) (413)
Fire Island Ass'n (417)
First American (417)
First American Real Estate Solutions LLC (417)
Forest City Ratner Companies (423)
The Foundation for Environmental and Economic Progress (424)
GE Commercial Real Estate & Financial Services (430)
GPA-1, LLC (438)
Guaranty Bank, SSB (442)
Guest and Associates (442)
H & R Executive Towers (443)
Harbor Philadelphia Center City Office, Ltd. (444)
Highland Mortgage Co. (449)
Hoffman Management, Inc. (450)
Home Warranty Coalition (451)
HP Global Workplaces, Inc. (454)
Howard Hughes Corp. (454)
Indian Pueblos Federal Development Corp. (460)
Internat'l Arid Lands Consortium (467)
Internat'l Code Council (470)
Internat'l Council of Shopping Centers (470)
J & B Management Co. (480)
JBG Real Estate Associates (482)
Joint Southeast Public Improvement Council (484)
Joint Venture Partners (484)
Keating Development Corp. (487)
Charles Klatskin and Co. (490)
KQC Properties (492)
Land Grant Development (494)
LCOR, Inc. (496)
League of Private Property Voters (497)
Lennar Partners (498)
Malta Development Corp. (508)
Maryland Nat'l Capitol Building Ass'n (511)
Mellon Mortgage Co. (517)
MetroPlains Development, Inc. (520)
Mortgage Bankers Ass'n of America (530)
Mortgage Insurance Companies of America (530)
N-Z Land Company (534)
Nat'l Apartment Ass'n (537)
Nat'l Ass'n of Housing Cooperatives (544)
Nat'l Ass'n of Independent Fee Appraisers (544)
Nat'l Ass'n of Industrial and Office Properties (544)
Nat'l Ass'n of Mortgage Brokers (545)
Nat'l Ass'n of Real Estate Brokers (547)
Nat'l Ass'n of Real Estate Investment Trusts (547)
Nat'l Ass'n of Realtors (547)
Nat'l Home Equity Mortgage Ass'n (567)
Nat'l Leased Housing Ass'n (569)
Nat'l Realty Committee (575)
New City Development (585)
New London Development Corp. (586)
New Mexico State Land Office (586)
New Starts Working Group (586)
Newhall Land and Farming Co. (588)
Northwest Woodland Owners Council (595)
Ocean Village Property Owners Ass'n, Inc. (598)
Ounalashka Corp. (604)
Paradise Canyon Resort (607)
Pinnacle West Capital Corp. (617)
Playa Vista (619)
Pointe Coupee Police Jury (620)
Portals Development Associates L.P. (621)
Presidential Towers, Ltd. (623)
Project Funding Corp. (PFC) (626)
Public Lands Council (629)
Public Properties Policy Ass'n (629)
Real Estate Capital Resources Ass'n (634)
Real Estate Roundtable (634)
Real Estate Services Providers Council (634)
RECRA (634)
Reilly Mortgage Group Inc. (636)
Remediation Financial, Inc. (636)
Republic Properties Corp. (637)
Riverside South Planning Corp. (640)
Rocking K Development (641)
The Rouse Company (642)
Security Capital Group (654)
The Charles E. Smith Companies (661)
Smith Development, LLC (661)
Soc. of Industrial and Office Realtors (663)
Sotheby's Holdings Inc. (666)
Square 3942 Associates Limited Partnership (671)
Starrett City Associates (673)
Starwood Lodging/Starwood Capital Group, L.P. (673)
State Street Development Co. of Boston (673)
Sunset Properties, Inc. (677)
Tejon Ranch Co. (682)
Texas Veterans Land Board (685)
TRI Capital Corp. (691)
Trizec Hahn Corp. (692)
The Trump Organization (693)
Trust for Public Land (693)
Urban Land Institute (709)
USX Corp. (710)
Vornado Inc. (717)
Warland Investment Co. (718)
Washington Real Estate Investment Trust (720)
Del E. Webb Corp. (722)
Weinberg Investments, Inc. (722)
West*Group Management LLC (723)
Westfield Corp. (725)
Wilmington Savings Fund Society (727)
WMF/Huntoon, Paige Associates Ltd. (729)
Woodmont Corporation (730)
W. G. Yates & Sons Construction Co. (733)

Religion

Adventist Development and Relief Agency Internat'l (229)
Adventist Health System/Sunbelt, Inc. (229)
Agudath Israel of America (232)
American Ass'n of Pastoral Counselors (249)
American Friends of Lubavitch (260)
American Friends Service Committee (260)
American Jewish Committee (265)
American Jewish Congress (265)
American Muslim Council (268)
Americans United for Separation of Church and State (282)
Anglican Catholic Church (284)
Anti-Defamation League (285)
Ass'n of Christian Therapists (295)
Ass'n of Jesuit Colleges and Universities (296)
B'nai B'rith Internat'l (305)
Baptist Joint Committee on Public Affairs (307)
Baptist World Alliance (307)
Catholic Alliance (333)
Catholic Charities Archdiocesan Legal Network (333)
Catholic Charities Immigration Legal Services (333)
Catholic Charities USA (333)
Catholic Health Ass'n of the United States (333)
Catholic News Service (333)
Catholic University of America (333)
Catholic War Veterans of the U.S.A. (334)
Catholics for a Free Choice (334)
The Center for Religious Freedom (337)
Center on Conscience and War/NISBCO (338)
Christian Broadcasting Network (345)
Christian Coalition of America (345)
Christian Legal Soc. (345)
Christian Network, Inc. (345)
Christian Voice, Inc. (345)
Christians' Israel Public Action Campaign, Inc. (346)
The Church Alliance (346)
Church of Jesus Christ of Latter Day Saints (346)
Church of Scientology Internat'l (346)
Church of the Brethren Washington Office (346)
Church World Service/Lutheran World Relief (346)
Concerned Women for America (365)
Congress of Nat'l Black Churches (366)
Council for Christian College and Universities (374)
Council on Religious Freedom (377)
D.C. Catholic Conference - Archdiocese of Washington (381)
Dignity/USA (388)
Ecclesiastical Associates (396)
Episcopal Church, Office of Government Relations (406)
Ethics and Religious Liberty Commission of the Southern Baptist Convention (407)
First Church of Christ, Scientist (417)
Friends Committee on Nat'l Legislation (426)
Fuller Theological Seminary (427)
General Conference of Seventh-day Adventists (431)
Gospel Rescue Ministries of Washington (437)
Holy Childhood Ass'n (451)
Holy Land Trust (451)
Institute on Religion and Democracy (464)
Institute on Religion and Public Policy (464)
Internat'l Ass'n of Jewish Lawyers and Jurists (468)
Internat'l Religious Liberty Ass'n (474)
Jesuit Conference (483)
Jewish Family Service Ass'n of Cleveland (483)
Jewish Federation of Greater Washington (483)
Jewish Women Internat'l (483)
Lutheran Brotherhood (505)
Lutheran Office for Governmental Affairs/Evangelical Lutheran Church in America (506)
Mennonite Central Committee Washington Office (518)
Mennonite Mutual Aid Ass'n (518)
Military Chaplains Ass'n of the U.S. (524)
Nat'l Ass'n of Evangelicals (542)
Nat'l Bible Ass'n (552)
The Nat'l Cathedral (554)
Nat'l Catholic Conference for Interracial Justice (554)
Nat'l Catholic Educational Ass'n (554)
Nat'l Catholic Federation of Parents (554)
Nat'l Center for Urban Ethnic Affairs (555)
Nat'l Conference of Catholic Bishops, Secretariat for Pro-Life Activities (558)
Nat'l Conference of Christians and Jews (558)
Nat'l Council of Catholic Women (560)
Nat'l Council of the Churches of Christ in the USA (561)
Nat'l Interfaith Coalition on Aging (569)
Nat'l Puerto Rican Coalition (575)
Nat'l Religious Broadcasters (575)
Nat'l Religious Broadcasters, Music License Committee (575)
Nat'l Religious Leadership Roundtable (575)
Nat'l Spiritual Assembly of the Baha'is of the United States (578)
NETWORK, A Nat'l Catholic Social Justice Lobby (584)
New Ways Ministry (586)
People Advancing Christian Education (PACE) (611)
Presbyterian Church (U.S.A.) (623)
Prison Fellowship Ministries (624)
Progressive Nat'l Baptist Convention (626)
Religious Action Center of Reform Judaism (636)
Religious Coalition for Reproductive Choice (636)
Religious Technology Center (636)
Republican Jewish Coalition (637)
Sojourners (664)
Traditional Values Coalition (689)
U.S. Catholic Conference (695)
Unitarian Universalist Ass'n of Congregations (700)
United Church of Christ Justice and Witness Ministry (700)
United Jewish Communities, Inc. (701)
United Methodist Church General Board of Church and Society (702)
United States Catholic Conference (703)
United States Catholic Office of Bishops/Secretariat for Hispanic Affairs (703)
UPMC Presbyterian (708)
Washington Ethical Soc. (719)
World Jewish Congress (730)

Retail/Wholesale

Albertson's Inc. (237)
Allied Marketing (241)
Alticor, Inc. (242)
American Booksellers Ass'n (251)
ASCENT (Ass'n of Community Enterprises) (290)
Associated Equipment Distributors (300)
AutoNation, Inc. (304)
Avon Products, Inc. (305)
Barker Brothers (308)
Beyond.com (313)
Bulmer Holding PLC, H. P. (323)
Bureau of Wholesale Sales Representatives (324)
Cafaro Co. (326)
Circuit City Stores, Inc. (347)
Claire's Stores, Inc. (349)
Commercial Services Internat'l (360)
Compaq Computer Corp. (363)
CTAM (379)
DFS Group Ltd. (387)
The Walt Disney Co. (389)
Dunn-Edwards Corp. (393)
Electronic Retailing Ass'n (401)
Food Distributors Internat'l (NAWGA-IFDA) (421)
Foodmaker Internat'l Franchising Inc. (422)
Footwear Distributors and Retailers of America (422)
Garden Centers of America (429)
Giant Food Inc. (435)
Gibson Guitar Corp. (435)
Healthcare Distribution Management Ass'n (447)
The Home Depot (451)
Independent Grocers' Alliance (459)
Internat'l Ass'n of Airport Duty Free Stores (467)
Internat'l Council of Shopping Centers (470)
Internat'l Mass Retailers Ass'n (473)
Interstate Wine Coalition (477)
Kmart Corp. (490)
The Limited Inc. (499)
Machinery Dealers Nat'l Ass'n (506)
May Department Stores Co. (513)
Mazak Corp. & Mazak Sales and Service, Inc. (513)
Michigan Retailers Ass'n (522)
Mid-Atlantic Toyota Distributors Inc. (523)
Montgomery Ward & Co., Inc. (528)
Murry's, Inc. (533)
Nat'l Ass'n of Beverage Retailers (539)
Nat'l Ass'n of Chain Drug Stores (539)
Nat'l Ass'n of Convenience Stores (541)
Nat'l Ass'n of Music Merchants (545)
Nat'l Ass'n of Wholesaler-Distributors (551)
Nat'l Automobile Dealers Ass'n (552)
Nat'l Beer Wholesalers Ass'n (552)
Nat'l Bicycle Dealers Ass'n (552)
Nat'l Community Pharmacists Ass'n (558)
Nat'l Field Selling Ass'n (564)
Nat'l Franchise Council (565)
Nat'l Lumber and Building Material Dealers Ass'n (570)

Nat'l Pawnbrokers Ass'n (573)
Nat'l Retail Federation (576)
Nat'l Wholesale Co., Inc. (581)
NCR Corp. (583)
Neiman Marcus Group (583)
Nordstrom, Inc. (591)
North American Retail Dealers Ass'n (592)
J. C. Penney Co., Inc. (611)
Price Costco (624)
Radio Shack Corp. (632)
Recreation Vehicle Dealers Ass'n of North America (634)
Retail, Wholesale and Department Store Workers Union (638)
Rite Aid Corp. (640)
Ross Stores, Inc. (642)
Safeway, Inc. (645)
Schwan's Sales Enterprises (652)
Sears, Roebuck and Co. (653)
Simark Trading Co., Inc. (659)
Sotheby's Holdings Inc. (666)
Staples, Inc. (673)
Target Corp. (681)
Thorn Microwave Devices (686)
Toyota Motor North America, U.S.A., Inc. (689)
Wal-Mart Stores, Inc. (718)
Walgreen Co. (718)
Walton Enterprises (718)
Wine and Spirits Wholesalers of America (728)

Rubber Industry

Ass'n of Brazilian Tire Producers (294)
Bridgestone/Firestone, Inc. (320)
Cooper Tire and Rubber Co. (371)
Eagle-Picher Industries (394)
Elastic Corp. of America (399)
The Gates Rubber Co. (430)
General Tire, Inc. (433)
Goodyear Tire and Rubber Co. (437)
Michelin North America (522)
Rubber and Plastic Footwear Manufacturers Ass'n (643)
Rubber Manufacturers Ass'n (643)
Tire Ass'n of North America (687)
Tire Industry Safety Council (687)
Wood Corp. (730)

Science and Mathematics

3001, Inc. (223)
Academic Medicine Development Corp. (225)
Academy of Pharmaceutical Research and Science (225)
AccuWeather (226)
Adria Laboratories, Inc. (228)
Ag Biotech Planning Committee (232)
Ag/Bio Con (232)
Alabama Space Science Exhibits Commission (236)
The Alan Guttmacher Institute (236)
Alexander Graham Bell Ass'n for the Deaf (238)
Allegheny Technologies, Inc. (238)
Alliance for American Innovation, Inc. (239)
Alzheimer's Ass'n (242)
American Anthropological Ass'n (245)
American Ass'n for Active Lifestyles and Fitness (245)
American Ass'n for Clinical Chemistry, Inc. (245)
American Ass'n for Dental Research (245)
American Ass'n for Laboratory Accreditation (246)
American Ass'n for the Advancement of Science (246)
American Ass'n of Bioanalysts (246)
American Ass'n of Immunologists (248)
American Ass'n of Pharmaceutical Scientists (249)
American Ass'n of Physics Teachers (249)
American Astronomical Soc. (250)
American Biophysics Corp. (251)
American Board of Health Physics (251)
American Clinical Laboratory Ass'n (253)
American Cocoa Research Institute (253)
American Committee for the Weizmann Institute of Science (254)
American Council of Independent Laboratories (255)
American Foundation for AIDS Research (260)
American Geological Institute (261)
American Geophysical Union (261)
American Health Assistance Foundation (261)
American Institute of Aeronautics and Astronautics (264)
American Institute of Biological Sciences (264)
American Institute of Chemists (264)
American Institute of Chemists Foundation (264)
American Institute of Physics (264)
American Institutes for Research (264)
American Leprosy Foundation (266)
American Mathematical Soc. (267)
American Metalcasting Consortium (267)
American Museum of Natural History (268)
American Nat'l Metric Council (268)
American Physical Soc. (270)
American Physiological Soc. (270)
American Political Science Ass'n (270)
American Psychological Ass'n (271)
American Science and Engineering, Inc. (273)
American Soc. for Biochemistry and Molecular Biology (274)
American Soc. for Bone and Mineral Research (274)
American Soc. for Cell Biology (274)
American Soc. for Clinical Laboratory Science (274)
American Soc. for Information Science (274)
American Soc. for Investigative Pathology (274)
American Soc. for Microbiology (274)
American Soc. for Pharmacology and Experimental Therapeutics (274)
American Soc. for Photogrammetry and Remote Sensing (275)
American Soc. for Reproductive Medicine (275)
American Soc. of Clinical Pathologists (276)
American Soc. of Human Genetics (276)
American Soc. of Plant Physiologists (277)
American Sociological Ass'n (277)
American Statistical Ass'n (278)
Americans for Medical Progress (282)
Amgen (282)
Analytical and Life Science Systems Ass'n (283)
Analytical Systems, Inc. (283)
Applera Corp. (286)
Applied Materials (287)
Arizona Science Center (288)
ASFE (290)
Ass'n for Women in Science (293)
Ass'n of Academic Health Sciences Library Directors (293)
Ass'n of Independent Research Institutes (296)
Ass'n of Science Technology Centers, Inc. (298)
Ass'n of State and Territorial Public Health Laboratory Directors (298)
Ass'n of Technology Act Projects (299)
Ass'n of Test Publishers (299)
Ass'n of Universities for Research in Astronomy, Inc. (299)
AstroVision Inc. (301)
Atom Sciences, Inc. (302)
The Audubon Institute (302)
Aventis Pasteur (304)
Barr Laboratories (308)
Battelle Memorial Institute (309)
Biochemics (313)
Bioelectromagnetics Soc. (313)
Biogen, Inc. (313)
Biomatrix (314)
Biomedical Research Foundation of Northwest Louisiana (314)
Biophysical Soc. (314)
Biotechnology Industry Organization (314)
Boston Museum of Science (318)
CADDO Lake Institute (325)
California Museum Foundation (327)
Campaign for Medical Research (329)
Canberra Packard BioScience (330)
Candescent Technologies (330)
CapCURE (330)
Celera Genomics (334)
Cell Therapeutics Inc. (334)
Center for Internat'l Policy (336)
Center for Research on Institutions and Social Policy (337)
Center for Science in the Public Interest (337)
Center for Sickle Cell Disease (337)
Center for the Study of Extraterrestrial Intelligence (338)
Center for Women Policy Studies (338)
Centro Industrial de Laboratorios Farmaceuticas Argentinos (CILFA) (339)
Chabot Space & Science Center (340)
Challenger Center for Space Science Education (340)
Children and Adults with Attention Deficit Disorders (CHADD) (344)
Citizens Against Research Bans (348)
Coalition of Academic Scientific Computation (CASC) (355)
College on Problems of Drug Dependence (357)
COMARCO Wireless Technology (359)
Commercial Weather Services Ass'n (CWSA) (360)
Conference Board of the Mathematical Sciences (366)
Consortium for Plant Biotechnology Research (368)
Consortium for Regional Climate Centers (368)
Consortium of Social Science Ass'ns (368)
Corel Corp. (372)
Council for Agricultural Science and Technology (374)
Council for Chemical Research, Inc. (374)
Council for Marketing and Opinion Research (374)
Council of Professional Ass'ns on Federal Statistics (376)
Council of Scientific Society Presidents (376)
Council on Undergraduate Research (377)
Currie Technologies, Inc. (380)
Cypress Bioscience Inc. (380)
Cytyc Corp. (380)
Dairy Management, Inc. (381)
Desert Research Institute (386)
Dietary Supplement Safety and Science Coalition (388)
Discovery Place, Inc. (Charlotte Science Museum) (389)
Discovery Science Center (389)
DNA Sciences, Inc. (390)
Do No Harm: The Coalition of Americans for Research Ethics (390)
Dystonia Medical Research Foundation (394)
Ecological Soc. of America (396)
Edmund Scientific Co. (397)
Electric Power Research Institute (400)
Electro Scientific Industries, Inc. (400)
Employee Benefit Research Institute (402)
Endocrine Soc. (403)
Entela, Inc. (404)
The Enterprise Mission (404)
Environmental Mutagen Soc. (405)
Erin Engineering and Research, Inc. (406)
ESA, Inc. (407)
Family Research Council, Inc. (411)
FDA-NIH Council (412)
Federation of American Scientists (414)
Federation of American Societies for Experimental Biology (414)
Federation of Behavioral, Psychological and Cognitive Sciences (414)
Foster-Miller, Inc. (424)
Foundation for the Advancement of Chiropractic Tenets and Science (424)
Foundation on Economic Trends (424)
Franklin Institute (425)
Frequency Engineering Laboratories (425)
Friedrich Ebert Foundation (426)
Friedrich's Ataxia Research Alliance (426)
Friends of Cancer Research (426)
Ganaden Biotech Inc. (429)
Genelabs Technologies, Inc. (431)
Genetics Soc. of America (433)
Geothermal Resources Ass'n (434)
Great Lakes Composites Consortium (439)
Great Lakes Science Center (439)
Halon Alternatives Research Corp. (443)
Health Physics Soc. (446)
Hickman Report (449)
Horticultural Research Institute (452)
Houston Advanced Research Center (453)
Hudson Institute (454)
Howard Hughes Medical Institute (454)
Fred Hutchinson Cancer Research Center (455)
IIT Research Institute (457)
Innovative Science Solutions (462)
Institute for Advanced Studies in Aging and Geriatric Medicine (463)
Institute for Alternative Futures (463)
Institute for Research on the Economics of Taxation (IRET) (464)
Institute of Cetacean Research (464)
Institute of Human and Machine Cognition (464)
Institute of Simulation and Training (464)
Integra Life Sciences (465)
Internat'l Board of Lactation Consultant Examiners (468)
Internat'l Center for Research on Women (470)
Internat'l Microelectronics and Packaging Soc. - IMAPS (473)
Internat'l R&D, Inc. (474)
Internat'l Soc. for Quality of Life Research (475)
Intrinsiq Data Corp. (477)
IPC Washington Office (478)
Johns Hopkins University-Applied Physics Lab (484)
Joint Council of Allergy, Asthma and Immunology (484)
Joint Steering Committee for Public Policy (484)
Kennedy Institute of Ethics (488)
Kettering Foundation (488)
Kinetic Biosystems Inc. (489)
La Rabida Children's Hospital Research Center (493)
Labor Policy Ass'n (LPA) (493)
Large Scale Biology (495)
Latona Associates, Inc. (496)
Lederle Laboratories (497)
Lifecore Biomedical (499)
Louisiana Center for Manufacturing Sciences (504)
Lovelace Respiratory Research Institute (504)
Lymphoma Research Foundation of America, Inc. (506)
MacKenzie Agricultural Research (506)
Magnificent Research Inc. (507)
Maptech (509)
Marine Technology Soc. (510)
Maritime Institute for Research and Industrial Development (510)
Marshall Research Corp. (511)
Massachusetts Technology Park Corp. (512)
Media Institute (516)
Media Research Center (516)
Mental and Addictive Disorders Appropriations Coalition (518)
Mentis Sciences Inc. (518)
Mentor Graphics Corp. (518)
Mercer Engineering Research Center (518)
Metamorphix, Inc. (519)
Miami Museum of Science & Space Transit Planetarium (521)
Michigan Biotechnology Institute (522)
Mickey Leland Nat'l Urban Air Toxics Research Center (522)
Mineralogical Soc. of America (525)
Mitsubishi Research Institute (526)
Morepen Laboratories, Ltd. (529)
MOTE Marine Lab (530)
MRJ Technology Solutions (532)
MRS (532)
Museum of Discovery and Science (533)
Museum of Science and Industry (533)
Museum of Science-Boston (533)
Mylan Laboratories, Inc. (533)
Nat'l Academy of Engineering (535)
Nat'l Academy of Sciences (535)
Nat'l AIDS Fund (536)
Nat'l Alliance for Eye and Vision Research (536)
Nat'l Ass'n for Biomedical Research (537)
Nat'l Ass'n of Biology Teachers (539)
Nat'l Ass'n of Dental Laboratories (542)

Nat'l Ass'n of Home Builders Research Center, Inc. (544)
Nat'l Ass'n of Rehabilitation Research and Training Centers (548)
Nat'l Ass'n of Veterans Research and Education Foundations (551)
Nat'l Bureau of Asian Research (553)
Nat'l Center for Advanced Technologies (554)
Nat'l Center for Genome Research (554)
Nat'l Center for Manufacturing Sciences (555)
Nat'l Coalition for Cancer Research (556)
Nat'l Council for Science and the Environment (559)
Nat'l Council of Teachers of Mathematics (560)
Nat'l Council of University Research Administrators (561)
Nat'l Disease Research Interchange (562)
Nat'l Foundation for Cancer Research (565)
Nat'l Gaucher Foundation (565)
Nat'l Geographic Soc. (565)
Nat'l Nutritional Foods Ass'n (572)
Nat'l Research Center for College and University Admissions (575)
Nat'l Science Teachers Ass'n (577)
Nat'l Technical Systems (579)
Nat'l Weather Service Employees Organization (581)
New Energy and Industrial Technology Development Organization (NEDO) (585)
New York Botanical Garden (586)
The New York Structural Biology Center (588)
Nomura Research Institute America, Inc. (591)
North American Interstate Weather Modification Council (592)
Novartis Corp. (596)
Omnitech Robotics Inc. (600)
Operation Right to Know (601)
Ostex Internat'l Inc. (604)
Pacific Northwest Nat'l Laboratory (606)
Pacific Science Center (606)
Philadelphia College of Textiles and Science (615)
PlanEcon Inc. (618)
Pocket Science, Inc. (619)
Police Executive Research Forum (620)
Public Service Research Council (629)
Quest Diagnostics Inc. (631)
R&D Tax Credit Coalition (631)
Research & Development Laboratories (638)
Research Corp. Technology (638)
Research Soc. on Alcoholism (638)
Retlif Testing Laboratory, Inc. (639)
Ripon Society (640)
RMI Titanium Co. (641)
The Road Information Program (TRIP) (641)
Rocket Development Co. (641)
SAMA Group of Ass'ns (647)
San Diego Natural History Museum (647)
SAT (650)
SatCon Technology Corp. (650)
Science and Engineering Associates, Inc. (652)
Science Applications Internat'l Corp. (SAIC) (652)
The Science Coalition (652)
Scientific Research Corp. (652)
Scientists Center for Animal Welfare (652)
Scripps Research Institute (653)
SEMATECH, Inc. (655)
Sensor Technologies and Systems Inc. (655)
Sepracor, Inc. (655)
Sequent Computer Systems (655)
Serono Laboratories, Inc. (655)
SINTEF Telecom and Informatics (660)
SKYWATCH Internat'l (660)
Soc. for American Archaeology (662)
Soc. for In Vitro Biology (662)
Soc. for Industrial & Applied Mathematics (662)
Soc. for Neuroscience (662)
Soc. for Risk Analysis (663)
Soc. for Women's Health Research (663)
Soc. of Competitive Intelligence Professionals (663)
Soc. of Toxicology (664)
Solar Energy Research and Education Foundation (665)
South Carolina Research Authority (666)
South Carolina Technology Alliance (666)
Southern Research Institute (668)
Space Dynamics Laboratory (669)
Speak Out! USA (669)
Standard & Poor's Corp. (672)
Styrene Information and Research Center (676)
Synthetic Genetics (679)
Taiwan Research Institute (680)
Technology Systems, Inc. (682)
Telcordia Technologies, Inc. (682)
The Teratology Soc. (684)
Texas A&M Research Foundation (684)
Texas NF Foundation (685)
Texas Tech University System (685)
Thermal Energy Systems, Inc. (686)
Time Domain Corp. (687)
Tobacco Industry Testing Laboratory, Inc. (688)
Transkaryotic Therapies Inc. (690)
Trident Systems Inc. (692)
U.S. Citrus Science Council (696)
U.S. Public Interest Research Group (697)
Underwriters Laboratories Inc. (698)
Union Institute - Office for Social Responsibility, The (699)
Universities Research Ass'n (705)
University of Texas - Houston Health Science Center (707)
University Science Alliance (708)
USA/Scientific Plastics Inc. (709)
Vanguard Research, Inc. (712)
Vector Research, Inc. (712)
Virginia Center for Innovative Technology (715)
Waste Policy Institute (721)
Water Environment Research Foundation (721)
Weather Risk Management Ass'n (722)
Western Research Institute (724)
Whitman-Walker Clinic (726)
Windsock Research (728)
Harry Winston Research Foundation (728)
Wireless Technology Research, L.L.C. (728)
Women's Research and Education Institute (730)
Woods Hole Oceanographic Institution (730)
Young Astronaut Council (733)

Small Business

Alliance for Affordable Services (239)
American Ass'n of Black Women Entrepreneurs Corp. (246)
American Chamber of Commerce Executives (252)
American Franchisee Ass'n (260)
American Small Business Alliance (274)
American Small Businesses Ass'n (274)
American Staffing Ass'n (278)
Ass'n of Small Business Development Centers (298)
Business and Professional Women/USA (324)
Business-Industry Political Action Committee (325)
Council of Smaller Enterprises (376)
District of Columbia Chamber of Commerce (390)
Diversified Internat'l Sciences Corp. (390)
entradia.com (404)
FRANMAC/Taco Pac (425)
Independent Visually Impaired Enterprisers (460)
Institute for Entrepreneurship (463)
Internat'l Franchise Ass'n (472)
Medallion Funding Corp. (515)
The Money Store (527)
Myriad Capital Inc. (534)
Nat'l Ass'n for the Self-Employed (538)
Nat'l Ass'n of Business Political Action Committees (539)
Nat'l Ass'n of Development Companies (542)
Nat'l Ass'n of Investment Companies (544)
Nat'l Ass'n of SBA Microloan Intermediaries (548)
Nat'l Ass'n of Small Business Investment Companies (549)
Nat'l Business Owners Ass'n (553)
Nat'l Chamber Foundation (555)
Nat'l Coalition of Minority Businesses (556)
Nat'l Community Pharmacists Ass'n (558)
Nat'l Federation of Independent Business (564)
Nat'l Franchisee Ass'n (565)
Nat'l Small Business United (578)
Opportunity Capital Corp. (601)
Organization for the Promotion and Advancement of Small Telecommunications Cos. (603)
Research Institute for Small & Emerging Business, Inc. (638)
S-Corporation Ass'n (644)
Safeguard America's Family Enterprises (645)
SBREFA Coalition (651)
Sippican, Inc. (660)
Small Business Council of America (661)
Small Business Regulatory Council (661)
Small Business Survival Committee (661)
Small Property Owners Ass'n of America (661)
U.S. Federation of Small Businesses, Inc. (696)
Women Business Owners Corp. Inc. (729)

Social Service/Urban Affairs

ABA Center on Children and the Law (224)
ABLEDATA (225)
ACB Social Service Providers (226)
Access Community Health Network (226)
ACORN (Ass'n of Community Organizations for Reform Now) (227)
Advanced Transit Ass'n (229)
Adventist Development and Relief Agency Internat'l (229)
Advocates for Youth (229)
Africa Resources Trust USA (231)
The Alan Guttmacher Institute (236)
Alliance for Children and Families (239)
Allied Charities of Minnesota (241)
Allsup Inc. (242)
America's Charities (243)
American Ass'n for Marriage and Family Therapy (246)
American Ass'n of Enterprise Zones (247)
American Ass'n on Mental Retardation (250)
American Family Ass'n (258)
American Federation of Home Care Providers (258)
American Institute of Certified Planners (264)
American Network of Community Options and Resources (ANCOR) (268)
American Planning Ass'n (270)
American Public Health Ass'n (271)
American Public Human Services Ass'n (272)
American Public Transportation Ass'n (272)
American Soc. for Technion (275)
The American Youth Work Center (281)
Ass'n of Junior Leagues, Internat'l (296)
Autism Soc. of America, Inc. (303)
Bedford Stuyvesant Restoration Corp. (310)
Benevolent and Protective Order of Elks (BPOE) (311)
Boys Town Nat'l Research Hospital (318)
Boys Town USA (318)
Bread for the World (319)
Business and Professional Women/USA (324)
CARE (Cooperative for Assistance and Relief Everywhere) (331)
Caring Institute (331)
Carrying Capacity Network, Inc. (332)
Casa del Pueblo Community Program (332)
Catholic Charities Archdiocesan Legal Network (333)
Catholic Charities Immigration Legal Services (333)
Catholic Charities USA (333)
Center for Law and Social Policy (336)
Center for Public Dialogue (337)
Center for Research on Institutions and Social Policy (337)
Centre for Development and Population Activities (339)
Chicago, Illinois, Washington Office of the City of (343)
Child Welfare League of America (343)
Children's Defense Fund (344)
Children's Foundation (344)
Church World Service/Lutheran World Relief (346)
City Rescue Mission Inc. (349)
Civic Ventures (349)
Cleveland State University - College of Urban Affairs (351)
Coalition for the Homeless (354)
Coalition on AFDC Quality Control Penalties (355)
Coalition on EAF Funding (355)
Coalition on Human Needs (355)
Colombian American Service Ass'n (358)
Community for Creative Non-Violence (362)
The Community Foundation for the Nat'l Capital Region (362)
Concord Family and Adolescent Services (365)
Congressional Hunger Center (366)
Corporations to End World Hunger Foundation (372)
Council for Urban Economic Development (375)
Council of Large Public Housing Authorities (376)
Council of State Community Development Agencies (376)
Council of the Great City Schools (376)
Council of Urban and Economic Development (376)
Council on Social Work Education (377)
Counterpart Internat'l (377)
County Welfare Directors Ass'n of California (377)
Cranston, Rhode Island, Department of Human Services (378)
D.C. Rape Crisis Center (381)
Detroit Rescue Mission Ministries (386)
Direct Marketing Ass'n Nonprofit Federation (388)
District of Columbia Special Olympics (390)
The Doe Fund (390)
Dream Center/City Help (392)
Easter Seals (395)
The Enterprise Foundation (404)
Family Violence Prevention Fund (411)
Family, Career and Community Leaders of America (411)
Federal City Council (412)
Fellowship Square Foundation, Inc. (415)
Fidelity Charitable Gift Fund (416)
FINCA Internat'l Inc., The Foundation for Internat'l Community Assistance (417)
Florida Department of Children & Families (419)
Florida Department of Health and Rehabilitative Services (419)
Food Bank of the Virginia Peninsula (421)
Food Research and Action Center (422)
Friends Committee on Nat'l Legislation (426)
General Federation of Women's Clubs (432)
The Georgetown Partnership (434)
Gifts In Kind Internat'l (435)
The Good Sam Club (437)
Goodwill Industries Internat'l, Inc. (437)
Haymarket Center (445)
Horatio Alger Ass'n of Distinguished Americans (452)
Housing Assistance Council (453)
Human Relations Foundation of Chicago (454)
"I Have a Dream" Foundation (456)
Immigration and Refugee Service of America (458)
Independent Sector (460)
InterAction (466)
Internat'l Downtown Ass'n (471)
Internat'l Rescue Committee Inc. (474)
Internat'l Service Agencies (474)
Jacobus Tenbroek Memorial Fund (481)
Jesuit Conference (483)
Jewish Federation of Greater Washington (483)
JHP, Inc. (Jobs Have Priority) (483)
The Justice Project, Inc. (485)
Kellogg Foundation (487)
Kennedy Institute, Lt. Joseph P. (488)
Kiwanis Internat'l (490)
Lansing, Michigan, Department of Social Services of the City of (495)
Legal Action Center of the City of New York, Inc. (497)
Legal Services Corp. (497)
Light of Life Ministries (499)
Louisiana Department of Social Services (504)
Lutheran Brotherhood (505)
Maniilaq Ass'n (508)
Meals on Wheels Ass'n of America (515)
Mennonite Mutual Aid Ass'n (518)
Metropolitan Family Services (520)

Missouri Department of Social Services (526)
Moose Internat'l Inc. (529)
Nat'l Abortion Federation (535)
Nat'l Alliance for Hispanic Health (536)
Nat'l Alliance to End Homelessness (537)
Nat'l and Community Service Coalition (537)
Nat'l Ass'n for Public Interest Law (NAPIL) (538)
Nat'l Ass'n of Community Action Agencies (540)
Nat'l Ass'n of County Human Services Administrators (541)
Nat'l Ass'n of Housing and Redevelopment Officials (544)
Nat'l Ass'n of Neighborhoods (546)
Nat'l Ass'n of Service and Conservation Corps (549)
Nat'l Ass'n of Social Workers (549)
Nat'l Ass'n of Urban Hospitals (551)
Nat'l Assembly of Health and Human Service Organizations (551)
Nat'l Campaign for Jobs and Income Support (554)
Nat'l Center for Children in Poverty (554)
Nat'l Center for Neighborhood Enterprise (555)
Nat'l Center for Nonprofit Boards (555)
Nat'l Center for Urban Ethnic Affairs (555)
Nat'l Coalition for Homeless Veterans (556)
Nat'l Coalition for the Homeless (556)
Nat'l Collaboration for Youth (557)
Nat'l Committee for Responsive Philanthropy (557)
Nat'l Community Action Foundation (557)
Nat'l Council of Nonprofit Ass'ns (560)
Nat'l Energy Assistance Directors' Ass'n (563)
Nat'l Family Planning and Reproductive Health Ass'n (563)
Nat'l Housing and Rehabilitation Ass'n (567)
Nat'l Housing Conference (567)
Nat'l Institute of Senior Centers (568)
Nat'l Law Center on Homelessness and Poverty (569)
Nat'l League of Cities (569)
Nat'l Legal Aid and Defender Ass'n (570)
Nat'l Low Income Housing Coalition/LIHIS (570)
Nat'l Neighborhood Coalition (572)
Nat'l Organization for Victim Assistance (572)
Nat'l Puerto Rican Coalition (575)
Nat'l Urban Coalition (580)
Nat'l Urban League (580)
Negative Population Growth, Inc. (NPG) (583)
Neighborhood Legal Services Program (583)
New York State Department of Social Services (587)
Northeast Ohio Areawide Coordination Agency (NOACA) (593)
Order Sons of Italy in America/Sons of Italy Foundation (603)
Partners for Livable Communities (608)
The Philanthropy Roundtable (615)
The Points of Light Foundation (620)
Population Action Internat'l (621)
Population Ass'n of America (621)
Population Institute (621)
Population Reference Bureau (621)
Population Resource Center (621)
Professional Benefit Trust (625)
Project Return Foundation Inc. (626)
Public Housing Authorities Directors Ass'n (628)
Public Interest Video Network (628)
Quad City Development Group (630)
RESULTS (638)
Riverside South Planning Corp. (640)
Rotary Foundation (642)
Rotary Internat'l (642)
Salesian Missions of the Salesian Soc. (646)
Salvation Army (646)
San Francisco AIDS Foundation (647)
Santa Cruz Metropolitan Transit District (649)
Share Our Strength (656)
Shelters, Inc. (657)
Sojourners (664)
Southeast Asia Resource Action Center (SEARAC) (667)
Special Olympics, Inc. (669)
U.S. Fund for UNICEF (696)
United Methodist Church General Board of Church and Society (702)
United States Committee for Refugees (703)
United States Conference of Mayors (703)
University Village Ass'n/Near West Side Conservation Community Council (708)
Urban Health Care Coalition of Pennsylvania (708)
The Urban Institute (708)
Urban Land Institute (709)
Very Special Arts (714)
Washington Council of Agencies (719)
Washington Ethical Soc. (719)
Washington Legal Clinic for the Homeless (720)
Washington Parking Ass'n (720)
Ways to Work (722)
Welfare to Work Partnership (722)
Western Urban Water Coalition (725)
Women in Community Service (729)
Worldwatch Institute (731)
Youth Service America (733)
YWCA of the USA (734)
Zero Population Growth, Inc. (734)

Sports/Leisure/Entertainment

2001 World Police and Fire Games (223)
ACNielsen Corp. (226)
Alaska Professional Hunters Ass'n (236)
America Outdoors (243)
American Alliance for Health, Physical Education, Recreation and Dance (245)
American Amateur Karate Federation (245)
American Amusement Machine Ass'n (245)
American Ass'n for Active Lifestyles and Fitness (245)
American Classic Voyages Co. (253)
American Film Institute (259)
American Film Marketing Ass'n (259)
American Fly Fishing Trade Ass'n (259)
American Football Coaches Ass'n (259)
American Gaming Ass'n (260)
American Greyhound Track Operators Ass'n (261)
American Hiking Soc. (262)
American Kennel Club (265)
American League of Anglers and Boaters (266)
American Pyrotechnics Ass'n (272)
American Recreation Coalition (272)
American Resort Development Ass'n (272)
American Running and Fitness Ass'n (273)
American Soc. of Travel Agents (277)
American Sportfishing Ass'n (278)
Americans for Responsible Recreational Areas (282)
Americans Heritage Recreation (282)
Amusement and Music Operators Ass'n (283)
Artichoke Enterprises, Inc. (290)
Athens Casino and Hotel Consortium (302)
Athletic Footwear Ass'n (302)
Bicycle Council (313)
Bicycle Manufacturers Ass'n of America (313)
Bicycle Shippers Ass'n (313)
Billiard and Bowling Institute of America (313)
Boat Owners Ass'n of The United States (BOAT/U.S.) (316)
Bowling Proprietors' Ass'n of America (318)
Brunswick Corp. (322)
Capital Gaming Internat'l, Inc. (330)
Capitol Concerts, Inc. (331)
Carolina Panthers (332)
CDM Fantasy Sports (334)
Cellar Door Amphitheaters (334)
Circus Circus Enterprises, Inc. (347)
Clipper Cruise Line (351)
Club Managers Ass'n of America (351)
College Football Bowl Ass'n (357)
Congressional Sportsmen's Foundation (366)
Conquest Tours Ltd. (367)
Ry Cooder (370)
Cruising America Coalition (379)
Crystal Cruises (379)
D.C. Lottery (381)
Dallas Cowboys (382)
Diamond Game Enterprises, Inc. (387)
The Walt Disney Co. (389)
District of Columbia Special Olympics (390)
Ducks Unlimited Inc. (392)
E-Commerce Payment Coalition (394)
Excelsior Gaming, Inc. (408)
Feld Entertainment Inc. (415)
Henry Ford Museum in Greenfield Village (422)
Fuji TV Network (427)
Garden State Tanning, Inc. (429)
General Cable Industries, Inc. (431)
Global Movies Corp. (436)
Golf Course Superintendents Ass'n of America (437)
Grand Canyon Air Tour Council (438)
GTECH Corp. (441)
H.A.H. of Wisconsin L.P. (443)
Harcourt General (444)
Huffy Bicycles (454)
Huffy Corp. (454)
Huffy Sports (454)
Humboldt Harbor Recreation (455)
Independent Television Service (460)
Interactive Amusement and Tournament Video Game Coalition (466)
Interactive Gaming Council (466)
Internat'l Ass'n of Amusement Parks and Attractions (467)
Internat'l Bicycle Ass'n (468)
Internat'l Council of Cruise Lines (470)
Internat'l Health, Racquet and Sportsclub Ass'n (472)
Internat'l Olympic Committee (473)
Internat'l Snowmobile Manufacturers Ass'n (474)
Internat'l Speedway Corp. (475)
Ladies Professional Golf Ass'n (494)
League of American Bicyclists (497)
Louisiana Superdome (504)
Magna Entertainment Corp. (507)
Major League Baseball (508)
Major League Baseball Players Ass'n (508)
Major League Baseball, Office of the Commissioner of (508)
Mammoth Mountain (508)
Mattel, Inc. (513)
Mirage Resorts, Inc. (525)
Motorcycle Riders Foundation (531)
Nat'l Ass'n for Girls and Women in Sport (537)
Nat'l Ass'n for Sport and Physical Education (538)
Nat'l Ass'n of Charterboat Operators (NACO) (540)
Nat'l Ass'n of County Park and Recreation Officials (541)
Nat'l Ass'n of RV Parks and Campgrounds (548)
Nat'l Ass'n of State & Provincial Lotteries (549)
Nat'l Basketball Ass'n (552)
Nat'l Club Ass'n (556)
Nat'l Coalition to Promote Physical Activity (557)
Nat'l Collegiate Athletic Ass'n (557)
Nat'l Football League (565)
Nat'l Football League Players Ass'n (565)
Nat'l Forest Recreation Ass'n (565)
Nat'l Hockey League (567)
Nat'l Indian Gaming Ass'n (568)
Nat'l Marine Manufacturers Ass'n (570)
Nat'l Park Hospitality Ass'n (573)
Nat'l Recreation and Park Ass'n (575)
Nat'l Shooting Sports Foundation Inc. (578)
Nat'l Ski Area Ass'n (578)
Nat'l Spa and Pool Institute (578)
The Nat'l Sports Center for the Disabled (578)
Nat'l Therapeutic Recreation Soc. (579)
Nat'l Thoroughbred Racing Ass'n, Inc. (579)
Nevada Resort Ass'n (584)
New Mexico Indian Gaming Ass'n (586)
Nintendo of America, Inc. (590)
North American Sports Management, Inc. (592)
Norwegian Cruise Line (596)
Oklahoma Indian Gaming Ass'n (599)
Olin Corp. (600)
Outdoor Recreation Coalition of America (604)
Park Place (608)
Pelican Butte Corp. (611)
Pennsylvania Pyrotechnics Ass'n (611)
The PGA Tour, Inc. (614)
Playboy Enterprises, Inc. (619)
Princess Tours (624)
The Propeller Club of the United States (627)
Rails to Trails Conservancy (632)
Recreation Vehicle Ass'n (634)
Recreation Vehicle Industry Ass'n (635)
Recreation Vehicle Rental Ass'n (635)
Recreational Equipment Inc. (635)
Recreational Fishing Alliance (635)
Rollerblade, Inc. (642)
Royal Caribbean Cruises, Ltd. (643)
Salt Lake City Olympic Organizing Committee (646)
Soccer Industry Council of America (664)
South West Florida Enterprises, Inc. (667)
Special Olympics, Inc. (669)
Sporting Goods Manufacturers Ass'n (670)
Sports Apparel Products Council (670)
Sports Corp., Ltd. (670)
Sports Lawyers Ass'n (670)
Sportsmen's Legal Defense Fund (670)
SunCruz Casino (677)
Take The Field, Inc. (680)
Ticketmaster (687)
Toy Manufacturers of America (688)
Trout Unlimited (692)
U.S. Disabled Athletes Fund (696)
U.S. Fencing Ass'n (696)
U.S. Figure Skating Ass'n (696)
U.S. Olympic Committee (697)
United States Parachute Ass'n (704)
Vail Associates (711)
Venetian Casino Resort, LLC (712)
Virginia Baseball Club (715)
Walsh Enterprises Internat'l (718)
Washington Soccer Partners (720)
Washington Sports & Entertainment, L.P. (720)
Wendella Sightseeing Boats Inc. (723)
Women's Sports Foundation (730)
World Sports Exchange (731)
World Wrestling Federation Entertainment Inc. (731)
YMCA of Metropolitan Washington (733)
YMCA of the USA Public Policy Office (733)
YWCA of the USA (734)

Taxation

Advertising Tax Coalition (229)
Aegon USA (229)
Affordable Housing Tax Credit Coalition (230)
Alliance for Affordable Services (239)
American Business Conference (251)
American Business Is Local Enterprise (251)
American College of Tax Counsel (254)
American Council for Capital Formation (255)
American Tax Policy Institute (278)
Americans for Fair Taxation (281)
Americans for Sensible Estate Tax Solutions (ASSETS) (282)
Americans for Tax Reform (282)
Anti-Value Added Tax Coalition (285)
Ass'n for Advanced Life Underwriting (291)
H & R Block, Inc. (315)
California Board of Equalization (326)
California Franchise Tax Board (326)
Campbell Estate (329)
Center for Public Dialogue (337)
Center for the Study of Responsive Law (338)
Center on Budget and Policy Priorities (338)
Citizens Against a Nat'l Sales Tax/Value-Added Tax (348)
Citizens Against Government Waste (348)
Citizens for an Alternative Tax System (348)
Citizens for Tax Justice (348)
Coalition for Fair Tax Credits (353)
Coalition for Fair Taxation of Real Estate (353)

Coalition for Nonprofit Health Care (354)
Coalition for Reasonable and Fair Taxation (CRAFT) (354)
Coalition for Tax Equity (354)
Coalition for the Fair Taxation of Business Transactions (354)
Coalition of Corporate Taxpayers (355)
Coalition on Royalties Taxation (356)
Coalition to Preserve Employee Ownership of S Corporation (356)
Coalition to Repeal the Tax on Talking (356)
Concord Coalition (365)
Cost Recovery Action Group (373)
Deferral Group (384)
Direct Marketing Ass'n, Inc. (388)
Electronic Commerce Tax Study Group (400)
Federation of Tax Administrators (415)
FISERV, Inc. (418)
Frontiers of Freedom Institute (427)
Guaranty Bank, SSB (442)
Guest and Associates (442)
Hybrid Branch Coalition (456)
IATA U.S. Frequent Flyer Tax Interest Group (456)
Independent Power Tax Group (460)
The INDOPCO Coalition (461)
Institute for Research on the Economics of Taxation (IRET) (464)
Internat'l Tax and Investment Center (475)
Jackson Hewitt (480)
Job Opportunities Business Symposium (483)
Maryland Taxpayers Ass'n, Inc. (512)
Media Tax Group (516)
Multistate Tax Commission (532)
Mutual Tax Committee (533)
Nat'l Ass'n of Enrolled Agents (542)
Nat'l Ass'n of Real Estate Investment Trusts (547)
Nat'l Ass'n of Tax Practitioners (550)
Nat'l Ass'n to Protect Individual Rights (551)
Nat'l Campaign for a Peace Tax Fund (554)
Nat'l Center for Public Policy Research (555)
Nat'l Structured Settlements Trade Ass'n (579)
Nat'l Taxpayers Union (579)
Newport Group (588)
Organization for Internat'l Investment (603)
Policy and Taxation Group (620)
Public Employee Retirement Systems of Colorado (628)
R&D Tax Credit Coalition (631)
Rapid Reporting, Inc. (633)
Repeal the Tax on Talking Coalition (637)
Reuters America Inc. (639)
S-Corporation Ass'n (644)
Savings Coalition of America (650)
Section 2039(e) Group (654)
Small Business Council of America (661)
Software Finance and Tax Executives Council (664)
Straddle Rules Tax Group (675)
Tax Action Group (681)
Tax Analysis (681)
Tax Executives Institute, Inc. (681)
Tax Fairness Coalition (681)
Tax Foundation, Inc. (681)
Tax Information Group (681)
Tax Policy Coalition (681)
Tax/Shelter Coalition (681)
Taxpayer Assets Project (681)
Taxpayers Against Fraud, The False Claims Legal Center (681)
Thomas Jefferson Equal Tax Soc. (686)
Tip Tax Coalition (687)
TJTC Recovery Project Coalition (687)
Utility Decommissioning Tax Group (711)
Wilmington Savings Fund Society (727)
Women for Tax Reform (729)
Work Opportunity Tax Credit Coalition (730)
WOTC Project (731)

Telecommunications/Internet/Cable

24/7 Media, Inc. (223)
Acxiom Corp. (227)
Adroit Systems Inc. (228)
Advanced Cordless Technologies, Inc. (228)
Advanced Technology Systems (228)
Advanced Telecom Group (ATG) (229)
AEPTEC (229)
Aeronautical Radio, Inc. (230)
Agilent Technologies (232)
AirCell, Inc. (235)
Alaska Communications Systems, Inc. (236)
Alcatel (237)
Alliance for Community Media (239)
Alliance for Public Technology (240)
Alliance for Telecommunications Industry Solutions (240)
Alltel Corporation (242)
American Cable Ass'n (251)
American Mobile Satellite Corp. (268)
American Mobile Telecommunications Ass'n (268)
American Public Communications Council (271)
American Public Info-Highway Coalition (272)
American Registry for Internet Numbers (ARIN) (272)
American Telecasting, Inc. (279)
American Teleservices Ass'n (279)
Ameritech (282)
Anchorage Telephone Utility (283)
Andrew Corp. (284)
AOL Time Warner (285)
Arbinet (287)
Armed Forces Communications and Electronics Ass'n Headquarters (289)
ASCENT (Ass'n of Community Enterprises) (290)
Ass'n for Interactive Media (292)
Ass'n for Local Telecommunications Services (292)
Ass'n of Telemessaging Services Internat'l (299)
Asterisk Communications (301)
AT&T (301)
AT&T Wireless Services, Inc. (302)
AuctionWatch.com (302)
Auyua Inc. (304)
Avenue A, Inc. (305)
BAE SYSTEMS North America (306)
Frank Beam and Co. (310)
Bell Atlantic Digital Spectrum (310)
Bell Atlantic Internet Solutions (310)
Bell Atlantic Mobile (310)
Bell Atlantic Network Services, Inc. (311)
Bell Atlantic Personal Communications, Inc. (311)
BellSouth Corp. (311)
BellSouth Telecommunications, Inc. (311)
Benchmark Communications Radio LP (311)
BHC Communications, Inc. (313)
Billing Concepts, Inc. (313)
Boston Communications Group, Inc. (318)
Broadcast Compliance Services (321)
BroadSpan Communications, Inc. (321)
BT North America Inc. (323)
Burst Networks Inc. (324)
Cable & Wireless, Inc. (325)
Cablevision Systems Corp. (325)
CAI Wireless (326)
CAIS Internet (326)
CanWest (330)
CARFAX, Inc. (331)
Carolina PCS (332)
Cegetel, S.A. (334)
Cellular Telecommunications and Internet Ass'n (334)
Cingular Wireless (347)
Cisco Systems Inc. (347)
Coalition for Affordable Local and Long Distance Services (352)
Coalition to Repeal the Tax on Talking (356)
Colombia, Ministry of Communications of (358)
Columbia Capital Corp. (359)
COMARCO Wireless Technology (359)
Comcast Corp. (359)
ComInternational Management Inc. (360)
Commco, L.L.C. (360)
Commercial Internet Exchange Ass'n (360)
Communications Consortium (362)
Communications Training Analysis Corp. (C-TAC) (362)
Communications Workers of America (362)
Community Learning and Information Network, Inc. (363)
Competition Policy Institute (363)
Competitive Broadband Coalition (363)
Competitive Telecommunications Ass'n (COMPTEL) (363)
Computer and Communications Industry Ass'n (CCIA) (364)
Computer Intelligence 2 (364)
ComTech Communications, Inc. (365)
Consumer Satellite Systems, Inc. (369)
Cook Inlet Communications (371)
Council Tree Communications, L.L.C. (377)
COVAD Communications Co. (377)
Cox Enterprises Inc. (378)
CRYPTEK Secure Communications, LLC (379)
CTAM (379)
D&E Communications, Inc. (380)
Dairy.com (381)
DCT Communications, Inc. (383)
Derivatives Net, Inc. (386)
Detroit Public Television (386)
Deutsche Telekom, Inc. (386)
Dialogic Communications Corp. (387)
Digital Access (388)
Digital Media Ass'n (388)
Digital Privacy and Security Working Group (388)
Direct TV (389)
DoubleClick (391)
Dreamtime, Inc. (392)
drugstore.com (392)
DSL Access Telecommunications Ass'n (DATA) (392)
Dubuque, Iowa, Cable Television Division of (392)
E*TRADE Group, Inc. (394)
E*TRADE Securities, Inc. (394)
E-Commerce Coalition (394)
E-Commerce Payment Coalition (394)
E-LOAN, Inc. (394)
e.spire Communications, Inc. (394)
Eagle River, LLC (394)
eBay Inc. (395)
EchoStar Communications Corp. (396)
ECI Telecom Ltd. (396)
EDS Corp. (398)
Education Communications, Inc. (398)
Educational Video Conferencing, Inc. (398)
Electric Lightwave, Inc. (400)
Electronic Privacy Information Center (401)
eLink (401)
Empresa Estatal de Telecomunicaciones (402)
Engage Technologies (403)
eNIC Corp. (403)
Epik Communications (406)
EqualFooting.com (406)
Equifax Inc. (406)
European Telecommunications Standards Institute (ETSI) (408)
EUTELSAT (408)
EXCEL Communications Inc. (408)
EXECUTONE Information Systems, Inc. (409)
ezgov.com (410)
Fanatasy Elections (411)
Fantasma Networks, Inc. (411)
Federal Communications Bar Ass'n (412)
Federal Sources, Inc. (414)
Fibernet LLC (416)
Firstdoor.com (418)
Focal Communications (421)
foot.com (422)
France Telecom America do Sul Ltda. (424)
Frontier Communications Corp. (427)
Futurewave General Partners, L.P. (428)
Gambia Telecommunications (428)
General Communications, Inc. (431)
General Telephone Co. of California (433)
GeoPhone, LLC (433)
Geotek Communications, Inc. (434)
GHB Broadcasting Corp. (435)
Glencairn, Ltd. (436)
Global Crossing North America, Inc. (436)
Global One (436)
GOPMarketplace.com (437)
GoTo.com Inc. (437)
Graphnet Inc. (438)
Grassroots Enterprise, Inc. (438)
Great Western Cellular Partnership (439)
Greater Washington Educational Telecommunications Ass'n (440)
GTE Mobilnet (441)
GTE Service Corp. (441)
Healtheon/Web MD (447)
Heard Communications (447)
Hiawatha Broadband Communications Inc. (449)
Hughes Space & Communications Co. (454)
ICG Communications, Inc. (457)
ICO Global Communications (457)
Independent Data Communications Manufacturers Ass'n (459)
Independent Telephone and Telecommunications Alliance (460)
Industrial Telecommunications Ass'n, Inc. (461)
Information Resources, Inc. (461)
Information Technology Industry Council (462)
Inmarsat (462)
Inoveon Corp. (462)
Intelligent Optical Systems, Inc. (465)
INTELSAT - Internat'l Telecommunications Satellite Organization (465)
Interactive Services Ass'n (466)
Intermedia Communications Inc. (467)
Internat'l Communications Industries Ass'n (ICIA) (470)
Internat'l Prepaid Communications Ass'n (474)
Internat'l Telecom Ltd. (475)
Internat'l Telecommunications, Inc. (475)
Internat'l Televent Inc. (475)
Internet Action PAC (476)
Internet Advertising Bureau (476)
Internet Alliance Inc. (476)
Internet Internat'l Trade Council (476)
Internet Safety Ass'n (476)
Internet Security Systems, Inc. (476)
Internet Security, Privacy & Self-Regulation PAC (476)
Internet Ventures, Inc. (476)
Intersil Corp. (477)
InvenCom LLC (477)
Iowa Telecommunications & Technology Commission (478)
Iridium, LLC (478)
ITRON, Inc. (480)
ITT World Directories, Inc. (480)
IVIDCO, LLC (480)
KCTS (487)
Korea Telecom (491)
KTTW-TV and KTTM-TV (492)
L-3 Communications Corp. (493)
Lancit Media/Junior Net (494)
LDMI Telecommunications, Inc. (496)
Leap Wireless Internat'l (497)
Level 3 Communications LLC (498)
Link Plus Co. (500)
Lockheed Martin Global Telecommunications (502)
Loral Space and Communications, Ltd. (503)
Lottery.com (504)
Lucent Technologies (505)
M/A-COM, Inc. (506)
Magnitude Information Systems (507)
Maine Cellular Telephone Co. (507)
Manufacturers Radio Frequency Advisory Committee, Inc. (509)
Marconi Communications Federal (509)
Marconi plc (509)
Maximum Information Technology Inc. (513)
MCI WorldCom Corp. (514)

Tobacco Industry

Trade (Foreign and Domestic)

Transportation

Scandinavian Airlines System (SAS) (651)
Scenic America (651)
Seaboard Corp. (653)
Seafarers Internat'l Union of North America (653)
Secure Wrap, Inc. (654)
Sensis Corp. (655)
Servicios Aereos de Honduras (SAHSA) (656)
Siemens Transportation Systems, Inc. (658)
Simula, Inc. (659)
Societe Air France (664)
Soo Line Railroad, Inc. (666)
Sound Transit (666)
South African Airways (666)
South Carolina Department of Transportation (666)
South Dakota, Department of Transportation of (666)
Southeastern Michigan Council of Government (667)
Southeastern Pennsylvania Transit Authority (667)
Southern Air Transport (667)
Southern California Regional Rail Authority (667)
Southern Coalition for Advanced Transportation (668)
Southwest Airlines (668)
Specialized Carriers and Rigging Ass'n (669)
St. Lawrence Seaway Pilots Ass'n (671)
Suburban Mobility Authority for Regional Transportation (676)
Summary Agency, Ltd. (676)
Sun Jet Internat'l, Inc. (676)
Sunmar Shipping, Inc. (677)
Surface Transportation Policy Project (677)
SWIPCO, U.S. (678)
Swissair (679)
TACA de Honduras (679)
TACA Internat'l Airlines (679)
TAESA (Transportes Aereos Ejecutivos, S.A. de C.V.) (680)
TAP/Air Portugal (681)
Taxicab, Limousine and Paratransit Ass'n (681)
TECO Transport Corp. (682)
Tire Industry Safety Council (687)
Tourist Railroad Ass'n, Inc. (688)
Tower Air, Inc. (688)
Toyota Motor North America, U.S.A., Inc. (689)
Traffic.com (689)
Trailer Marine Transport Corp. (689)
Trans Ocean Leasing Corp. (689)
Trans World Airlines, Inc. (689)
Trans-Ona S.A.M.C.I.F. (689)
Transconex, Inc. (690)
TransOceanic Shipping (690)
TRANSPO (690)
Transport Workers Union of America, AFL-CIO (690)
Transportation Corridor Agencies (690)
Transportation District Commission of Hampton Roads (690)
Transportation Institute (690)
Transportation Intermediaries Ass'n (690)
Transportation Reform Alliance (690)
Transportation-Communications Internat'l Union (691)
Transportes Aereos Mercantiles Panamericanos (691)
Transrapid Internat'l (691)
Tri-County Commuter Rail Authority (691)
Tri-County Metropolitan Transportation District of Oregon (691)
TRI-MET Tri-County Metropolitan Transportation (691)
TRIBASA (692)
Tropical Shipping and Construction Co. (692)
Truck Renting and Leasing Ass'n (693)
Truckload Carriers Ass'n (693)
Turkish Airlines (694)
U.S. Clay Producers Traffic Ass'n (696)
UniGroup, Inc. (698)
Union Pacific (699)
Union Switch and Signal, Inc. (699)
United Airlines (700)
United Motorcoach Ass'n (702)
United Parcel Service (702)
United Pilots Political Action Committee (702)
United States Maritime Coalition (703)
United Transportation Union (705)
United Van Lines, Inc. (705)
US Airways (709)
Utah Department of Transportation (710)
Utah Transit Authority (710)
Van Ommeren Shipping (USA), Inc. (711)
Vanguard Airlines, Inc. (712)
VASP Airlines (712)
Vertical Flight Foundation (714)
VIASA (714)
Virgin Atlantic Airways (715)
Votainer Consolidation Service (717)
Wakota Bridge Coalition (718)
Washington Flyer Taxi Drivers Ass'n, Inc. (719)
Washington Metropolitan Area Transit Authority (720)
Washington, Department of Transportation of the State of (721)
Washoe County Regional Transportation Commission (721)
Waterman Steamship Co. (721)
Wendella Sightseeing Boats Inc. (723)
West Pac Vessel Owners Ass'n (723)
Western Coal Traffic League (724)
Western Great Lakes Pilots Ass'n (724)
Western Pioneer, Inc. (724)
Wien Air Alaska (726)
Wisconsin Central Transportation Corp. (728)
Woods Hole Steamship Authority (730)
Worldwide Aviation Services, Ltd. (731)
Wyoming, Department of Transportation of (732)
Yellow Corp. (733)

Travel/Tourism/Lodging

Advantica Inc. (229)
Aer Lingus (230)
Aerolineas Argentinas (230)
Aerolineas Centrales de Colombia (230)
Aeropostal (230)
Air Afrique (233)
Air Atlantic Dominicana (233)
Air Canada (233)
Air China Internat'l Corp., Ltd. (233)
Air D'Ayiti (233)
Air India (233)
Air Jamaica Ltd. (233)
Air Nauru (234)
Air Pacific Ltd. (234)
Air Tran Airways (234)
Air Transat (234)
Airtours Internat'l (235)
Alaska Airlines (236)
Alitalia (238)
All Nippon Airways Co. (238)
allacrossamerica.com (238)
Aloha Airlines (242)
America West Airlines (243)
American Airlines (244)
American Bus Ass'n (251)
American Classic Voyages Co. (253)
American Council of Korean Travel Agents (255)
American Hotel and Lodging Ass'n (263)
American Soc. of Travel Agents (277)
AMSA (283)
Andes (284)
APA Internat'l Air, S.A. (285)
Apple Vacations, Inc. (286)
ARAMARK Corp. (287)
Arrow Air (289)
Ass'n of Retail Travel Agents (298)
Austrian Airlines (303)
Avianca Airlines (305)
Aviateca Airline (305)
Bass Hotels and Resorts, Inc. (308)
Big Sky Airlines (313)
Biman Bangladesh Airlines (313)
British Airways Plc (321)
Caribbean Airline Co. Ltd. (331)
Carlson Cos. (332)
Carlson Wagonlit Travel, Inc. (332)
Carnival Corp. (332)
Cendant Corp. (335)
Clipper Cruise Line (351)
Coalition for Travel Industry Parity (354)
Conquest Tours Ltd. (367)
Continental Airlines Inc. (370)
Cruise Industry Charitable Foundation (379)
Cruising America Coalition (379)
Crystal Cruises (379)
Delta Air Lines (384)
El Al Israel Airlines, Ltd. (399)
Empresa Consolidada Cubana de Aviacion (402)
Eva Airways Corp. (408)
Falcon Air Express (410)
Fast Air Carrier (412)
Faucett Airlines (Compania de Aviacion Faucett, S.A.) (412)
Florida Cruise and Ferry Service Inc. (419)
Fort Sumter Tours (423)
Foundation for Internat'l Meetings (424)
Full House Resorts, Inc. (427)
Grand Bahama Vacations, Inc. (438)
Grand Canyon Air Tour Council (438)
Harrah's Entertainment, Inc. (444)
Hilton Hotels Corp. (450)
Holland America West-Tours (450)
Hospitality Employers Ass'n (453)
Hospitality Sales and Marketing Ass'n Internat'l (453)
Hotel Ass'n of Washington (453)
Hotel Employees and Restaurant Employees Internat'l Union (453)
IATA U.S. Frequent Flyer Tax Interest Group (456)
Internat'l Ass'n of Convention and Visitor Bureaus (467)
Internat'l Council of Cruise Lines (470)
Internat'l Soc. of Hospitality Consultants (475)
Jamaica Air Freighters, Ltd. (481)
Jamaica Vacations (JAMVAC) (481)
JMC Airlines, Ltd. (483)
Kenya Airways (488)
Korean Air Lines (491)
La Quinta Inns, Inc. (493)
LADECO (494)
Laker Airways (Bahamas) Ltd. (494)
Lan Chile (494)
LAPA (Lineas Aereas Privadas, S.A.) (495)
Las Vegas Convention and Visitors Authority (495)
Legend Airlines (497)
Lineas Aereas Costarricicenes (Lasca Airlines) (500)
LOT Polish Airlines (504)
Lousville Airport (504)
Marriott Internat'l, Inc. (511)
Martinair Holland (511)
MeriStar Hospitality Corp. (519)
Mesquite Resort Ass'n (519)
Midway Airlines Corp. (523)
Midwest Express Airlines (523)
Mirage Resorts, Inc. (525)
Nat'l Air Transportation Ass'n (536)
Nat'l Tour Ass'n (579)
NATSO, Inc. (582)
Nevada Resort Ass'n (584)
Northwest Airlines, Inc. (595)
Norwegian Cruise Line (596)
Oakland Airport (598)
ORBITZ (602)
Orient Airlines Ass'n (603)
Orion Air (603)
Oscoda Management (604)
Pakistan Internat'l Airlines (606)
Passenger Vessel Ass'n (609)
Peninsula Airways, Inc. (611)
Philadelphia Hospitality & Business Alliance (615)
Philippine Airlines (616)
Pilgrim Airlines (617)
Polynesian Airlines (620)
Princess Cruise Lines (624)
PSH Master L.P.I. (627)
Quinnat Landing Hotel (631)
Radius, The Global Travel Co. (632)
Recreation Vehicle Rental Ass'n (635)
Regional Airline Ass'n (635)
Royal Brunei Airways (643)
Royal Caribbean Cruises, Ltd. (643)
The Royal Jordanian Airline (643)
SatoTravel (650)
Savannah Airport Commission (650)
Scandinavian Airlines System (SAS) (651)
Secure Wrap, Inc. (654)
Servicios Aereos de Honduras (SAHSA) (656)
Sodexho Marriott Services, Inc. (664)
Southern Air Transport (667)
Southwest Airlines (668)
Starwood Hotels & Resorts Worldwide, Inc. (673)
Sun Jet Internat'l, Inc. (676)
T.W.Y. Co., Ltd. (679)
TACA de Honduras (679)
TACA Internat'l Airlines (679)
TAESA (Transportes Aereos Ejecutivos, S.A. de C.V.) (680)
TAP/Air Portugal (681)
Tourist Railroad Ass'n, Inc. (688)
Tower Air, Inc. (688)
Trans World Airlines, Inc. (689)
Travel Business Roundtable (691)
Travel Council for Fair Competition (691)
Travel Industry Ass'n of America (691)
Travelocity.com (691)
TRIBASA (692)
Turkish Airlines (694)
U.S. Tour Operators Ass'n (697)
United Airlines (700)
US Airways (709)
Vanguard Airlines, Inc. (712)
The Vantage Group, Inc. (712)
VASP Airlines (712)
Venetian Casino Resort, LLC (712)
VIASA (714)
Washington D.C. Convention and Visitors Ass'n (719)
Western States Tourism Policy Council (724)
Wien Air Alaska (726)

Trucking Industry

American Moving and Storage Ass'n (268)
American Trucking Ass'ns (279)
Caterpillar Inc. (333)
Coalition Against Bigger Trucks (352)
Commission of Accredited Truck Driving Schools (CATDS) (360)
Consolidated Freightways Corp. (367)
CSX Lines LLC (379)
Davison Transport, Inc. (383)
Distribution and LTL Carriers Ass'n (390)
Freightliner Corp. (425)
Household Goods Forwarders Ass'n of America, Inc. (453)
Industrial Truck Ass'n (461)
Motor Freight Carriers Ass'n (531)
Nat'l Armored Car Ass'n (537)
Nat'l Institute of Certified Moving Consultants (568)
Nat'l Motor Freight Traffic Ass'n (571)
Nat'l Private Truck Council (574)
Nat'l Small Shipments Traffic Conference - NASSTRAC (578)
Nat'l Tank Truck Carriers (579)
Nat'l Trailer Dealers Ass'n (579)
Nat'l Truck Equipment Ass'n (580)
NATSO, Inc. (582)
Oshkosh Truck Corp. (604)
Owner-Operator Independent Drivers Ass'n, Inc. (605)
Resources Trucking Inc. (638)
Ruan Leasing Co. (643)
Ryder System, Inc. (644)
Specialized Carriers and Rigging Ass'n (669)
Transportation Reform Alliance (690)

Truck Manufacturers Ass'n (692)
Truck Mixer Manufacturers Bureau (692)
Truck Renting and Leasing Ass'n (693)
Truck Trailer Manufacturers Ass'n (693)
Truckload Carriers Ass'n (693)
United Van Lines, Inc. (705)
Yale Materials Handling Corp. (733)

Utilities

Alabama Gas Corp. (235)
Alabama Water and Wastewater Institute, Inc. (236)
Allegheny Power Service Corp. (238)
Alliance for Competitive Electricity (239)
Alliant Energy (241)
Ameren Services (243)
American Electric Power Co. (257)
American Gas Ass'n (261)
American Public Gas Ass'n (271)
American Public Info-Highway Coalition (272)
American Public Power Ass'n (272)
American Public Works Ass'n (272)
American Water Works Ass'n (280)
Anaheim, California, Public Utilities of the City of (283)
Anchorage Telephone Utility (283)
Animas-La Plata Water Conservancy District (284)
Arctic Power (288)
Arizona Power Authority (288)
Arizona Public Service Co. (288)
Arvin-Edison Water Storage District (290)
Ass'n of California Water Agencies (295)
Ass'n of Metropolitan Water Agencies (297)
Atlantic County Utilities Authority (302)
Auburn, Avilla, Bluffton, Columbia City and Other Municipalities of Indiana (302)
Azurix (305)
Bangor Hydro-Electric Co. (307)
Basin Electric Power Cooperative (308)
Bay Delta Urban Coalition (309)
Belridge Water Storage District (311)
Bergen, New York, Village of (311)
Boonville, New York, Village of (317)
Boston Edison Co. (318)
Braintree Electric Light Department (319)
British Columbia Hydro and Power Authority (321)
Brownsville Public Utilities Board (322)
Calaveras County, California, Water District (326)
California Independent System Operator (327)
California Water Service Co. (328)
Canadian River Municipal Water Authority (329)
Catamount Energy Corp. (333)
Center for Energy and Economic Development (336)
Centerior Energy Corp. (338)
Central Arizona Water Conservation District (338)
Central Basin Municipal Water District (338)
Central Illinois Public Service Co. (339)
Central Montana Electric Power Cooperative, Inc. (339)
Central Utah Water Conservancy District (339)
Central Valley Project Water Ass'n (339)
Central Virginia Electric Cooperative, Inc. (339)
Chelan County Public Utility District (342)
Chubu Electric Power Co. (346)
Cinergy Corp. (347)
Cinergy PSI (347)
City Public Service (349)
Clayton, Dover, Lewes, Middletown, Milford, Newark, NewCastle, Seaford and Smyrna, Delaware, Municipalities of (350)
Coachella Valley Water District (352)
College Station, Texas, City of (358)
Colorado River Commission of Nevada (358)
Colorado River Energy Distributors Ass'n (358)
Colorado Springs Utilities (359)
ComEd (359)
Consolidated Edison Co. of New York (367)
Constellation Energy Group (368)
Consumer Energy Council of America Research Foundation (369)
Consumers Energy Co. (369)
Corn Belt Energy Corp. (372)
Craig-Botetourt Electric Cooperative, Inc. (378)
Dairyland Power Cooperative (381)
Dayton Power and Light Co. (383)
Delaware Municipal Electric Corp. (DEMEC) (384)
Delaware, Pennsylvania, Solid Waste Authority of the County of (384)
Detroit Edison Co. (386)
Dominion Resources, Inc. (391)
Duke Power Co. (393)
East Bay Municipal Utility District (395)
East Texas Electric Cooperative (395)
Eastern Municipal Water District (395)
Edison Electric Institute (397)
Edison Internat'l (397)
Edison Mission Energy (397)
El Dorado Irrigation District (399)
El Paso Electric Co. (399)
El Paso Water Utilities - Public Service Board (399)
Electric Power Research Institute (400)
Electricity Consumers Resource Council (ELCON) (400)
Energy Contractors Price-Anderson Group (403)
Energy Northwest (403)
Entergy Services, Inc. (404)
Eugene Water and Electric Board (407)
Exelon Corp. (409)
Fairfax County Water Authority (410)
Federation of Electric Power Cos. of Japan (414)
FirstEnergy Co. (418)
Florida Gas Utility (420)
Florida Municipal Power Agency (420)
Florida Power and Light Co. (420)
Four Dam Pool (424)
Freeport, New York, Electric Department of the Village of (425)
Gainesville Regional Utilities (428)
Garrison Diversion Conservancy District (429)
GE Capital Corp. (430)
GPU, Inc. (438)
Grant County P.U.D., Washington (438)
Grasslands Water District (438)
Greater Detroit Resource Recovery Authority (439)
Green Mountain Power Corp. (440)
Greenport, New York, Village Electric Department of (440)
Hagerstown, Maryland, Municipal Electric Light Plant of (443)
Hawaiian Electric Co. (445)
Hoosier Energy Rural Electric Cooperative, Inc. (452)
Howard Energy Internat'l (454)
Hydro-Quebec (456)
Idaho Power Co. (457)
Imperial Irrigation District (458)
Indiana and Michigan Municipal Distributors Ass'n (460)
Industrial Customers of Northwest Utilities (461)
Internat'l Utility Efficiency Partnerships (IUEP) (476)
Irrigation Projects Reauthorization Council (479)
ITRON, Inc. (480)
Jacksonville Electric Authority (481)
Jamestown, New York, Board of Public Utilities (481)
Kansas City Power & Light Co. (486)
Kansas City Southern Industries (486)
Kaweah Delta Water Conservation District (487)
Kern County Water Agency (488)
Kern River Watermaster (488)
Ketchikan Public Utilities (488)
Knoxville Utilities Board (490)
Kootenai Electric Cooperative, Inc. (491)
Lake County Basin 2000 (494)
Landis, New Jersey, Sewerage Authority (495)
Large Public Power Council (495)
Las Vegas Valley Water District (495)
Las Virgenes Municipal Water District (495)
Leucadia County Water District (498)
Lewis and Clark Rural Water System, Inc. (498)
Litton Systems, Inc. (500)
Long Beach Water Department (503)
M-S-R Public Power Agency (506)
Madison Gas & Electric Co. (507)
Maine Public Service Co. (507)
Massachusetts Water Resources Authority (512)
Massena, New York, Town of (512)
Memphis Light, Gas and Water Division (517)
The Metropolitan Water District of Southern California (521)
Metropolitan Water Reclamation District of Greater Chicago (521)
Michigan Municipal/Cooperative Group (522)
Mid Dakota Rural Water System (523)
Mid-West Electric Consumers Ass'n (523)
MidWest ISO Transmission Owners (523)
Minnesota Power (525)
Mishawaka Utilities (526)
Mission Springs (California) Water District (526)
Missouri Public Service Co. (526)
Missouri River Energy Services (526)
Moapa Valley Water District (526)
Modesto/Turlock Irrigation District (527)
Montgomery County, Ohio/Montgomery County Solid Waste District (528)
Municipal Electric Authority of Georgia (532)
Municipal Electric Utilities Ass'n of New York State (532)
Napa County, California, Flood and Water Conservation District (534)
Nat'l Ass'n of Energy Service Companies (542)
Nat'l Ass'n of Regulatory Utility Commissioners (548)
Nat'l Ass'n of State Utility Consumer Advocates (NASUCA) (550)
Nat'l Ass'n of Water Companies (551)
Nat'l Grid USA (566)
Nat'l Ground Water Ass'n (566)
Nat'l Institute for Water Resources (568)
Nat'l Rural Electric Cooperative Ass'n (576)
Nat'l Utility Contractors Ass'n (NUCA) (580)
Nebraska Public Power District (583)
New York Municipal Power Agency (587)
Niagara Mohawk Power Corp. (589)
NiSource Inc. (590)
Northeast Texas Electric Cooperative (593)
Northeast Utilities (593)
Northern California Power Agency (594)
Northern Indiana Public Service Co. (594)
Northwest Public Power Ass'n (595)
Northwestern Public Service (596)
Ocean County, NJ Utilities Authority (598)
Office of the People's Counsel for the District of Columbia (599)
Oglethorpe Power Corp. (599)
Ohio Municipal Electric Ass'n (599)
Ohio River Valley Water Sanitation Commission (599)
Oklahoma Gas and Electric Co. (599)
Olivenhain Municipal Water District (600)
ONEOK, Inc. (601)
Orange County Water District (602)
Oregon Utility Resource Coordination Ass'n (OURCA) (603)
Oregon Water Resources Congress (603)
Orlando Utilities Commission (603)
Otter Tail Power Co. (604)
PacifiCorp (606)
Palo Alto, California, City of (607)
PG&E Corp. (614)
Pinnacle West Capital Corp. (617)
PJM Interconnection, L.L.C. (618)
Placer County Water Agency (618)
Plattsburgh, New York, City of (619)
Portland General Electric Co. (621)
Potomac Electric Power Co. (622)
PPL (622)
Progress Energy (626)
Providence Gas (627)
PSE&G (627)
Public Generating Pool (628)
Public Power Council (629)
Public Service Co. of Colorado (629)
Public Service Co. of New Mexico (629)
PURPA Reform Group (630)
Redding, California, Electric Department of the City of (635)
Reliant Energy, Inc. (636)
Repeal PUHCA Now Coalition (637)
Rio Grande Water Conservation District (640)
Rockville Centre, New York, Village of (641)
Rolls-Royce North America Inc. (642)
Sacramento Municipal Utility District (645)
Sacramento, California, Department of Utilities of (645)
Salamanca, New York, City Board of Public Utilities of (646)
Salt River Project (646)
Sam Rayburn G&T Electric Cooperative, Inc. (647)
San Antonio City Public Service (647)
San Antonio Water System (647)
San Diego County Water Authority (647)
San Elijo Joint Powers Authority (647)
San Gabriel Valley Water Ass'n (648)
Santa Clara, California, Electric Department of the City of (649)
Santee Cooper (South Carolina Public Service Authority) (649)
SCANA Corp. (651)
SEC Roundtable Group (654)
Sempra Energy (655)
Sierra Pacific Resources (659)
Solid Waste Authority of Central Ohio (665)
Sonoma County Water Agency (665)
South Carolina Public Service Authority (666)
South Mississippi Electric Power Ass'n (666)
South Tahoe Public Utility District (666)
Southeastern Federal Power Customers, Inc. (667)
Southern California Public Power Authority (667)
Southern Co. (667)
Southern Maryland Electric Cooperative, Inc. (668)
Southwest Power Pool (668)
Southwest Water Conservation District of Colorado (668)
Southwestern Electric Cooperative, Inc. (668)
Southwestern Public Service Co. (668)
Southwestern Water Conservation District (668)
Spokane Regional Solid Waste System (670)
St. Louis Metropolitan Sewer District (672)
Stockton East Water District (675)
Tacoma, Washington, Public Utilities Department of (680)
Taiwan Power Co. (680)
TECO Energy, Inc. (682)
Tennessee Valley Authority - Washington Office (683)
Tennessee Valley Public Power Ass'n (683)
Tex-La Electric Cooperative of Texas (684)
Texas Municipal Power Agency (685)
The Tokyo Electric Power Company, Inc. (688)
Toledo Edison Co. (688)
Transmission Access Policy Study Group (690)
Transmission Agency of Northern California (690)
Trinity Public Utilities District (692)
Tumalo Irrigation District (694)
TXU Business Services (695)
UGI Utilities, Inc. (698)
Umatilla Water Users (698)
Union Sanitary District (699)
United Cities Gas Co. (701)
United States Energy Ass'n (703)
United Telecom Council (705)
United Water Services (705)
Upper Klamath Water Users (708)
Upper San Gabriel Municipal Water District (708)
UtiliCorp United, Inc. (711)
Utility Air Regulatory Group (711)
Utility Decommissioning Tax Group (711)
Utility Workers Union of America (711)
Washington Gas (719)
Water Replenishment District of Southern California (721)
WateReuse Ass'n (721)
Waterworks Internat'l, Inc. (721)
West Basin Municipal Water District (723)
Western Systems Power Pool (724)

Western Urban Water Coalition (725)
Wisconsin Energy Corp. (728)
Wisconsin Gas Co. (729)
Wolf Creek Nuclear Operating Corp. (729)
Xcel Energy, Inc. (732)
Yates County Cable TV Committee (733)
York County Solid Waste Authority (733)
Yukon Pacific (734)

Women/Women's Issues

The Alan Guttmacher Institute (236)
American Ass'n of Black Women Entrepreneurs Corp. (246)
American Ass'n of University Women (249)
American Ass'n of University Women Legal Advocacy Fund (250)
American Civil Liberties Union (252)
American Civil Liberties Union of the Nat'l Capital Area (252)
American Medical Women's Ass'n (267)
American Soc. of Women Accountants (ACC) (277)
American War Mothers (280)
American Women in Radio and Television (280)
Ass'n for Women in Science (293)
Ass'n of Female Exhibit Contractors and Event Organizers (295)
Ass'n of Professors of Gynecology and Obstetrics (298)
Ass'n of Reproductive Health Professionals (298)
Ass'n of Women in the Metal Industries (299)
Ass'n of Women's Health, Obstetric and Neonatal Nurses (299)
Business and Professional Women/USA (324)
Catholics for a Free Choice (334)
Center for Women Policy Studies (338)
Centre for Development and Population Activities (339)
Concerned Women for America (365)
Council of Women's and Infant's Specialty Hospitals (376)
Council on Resident Education in Obstetrics and Gynecology (377)
D.C. Rape Crisis Center (381)
Daughters of the American Revolution (382)
EMILY'S List (402)
Feminist Majority (415)
Financial Women Internat'l (417)
General Federation of Women's Clubs (432)
Independent Women's Forum (460)
Internat'l Center for Research on Women (470)
Jewish Women Internat'l (483)
Komen Breast Cancer Foundation, The Susan G. (491)
Ladies Professional Golf Ass'n (494)
Leadership Conference on Civil Rights (496)
League of Women Voters of the United States (497)
Magee Women's Health Foundation (507)
Mothers Against Drunk Driving (MADD) (530)
Nat'l Abortion and Reproductive Rights Action League (535)
Nat'l Abortion Federation (535)
Nat'l Alliance of Sexual Assault Coalitions (537)
Nat'l Asian Women's Health Organization (537)
Nat'l Ass'n for Girls and Women in Sport (537)
Nat'l Ass'n of Commissions for Women (540)
Nat'l Ass'n of Military Widows (545)
Nat'l Ass'n of Minority Political Families, USA, Inc. (545)
Nat'l Ass'n of Negro Business & Professional Women's Clubs, Inc. (546)
Nat'l Ass'n of Nurse Practitioners in Women's Health (546)
Nat'l Ass'n of WIC Directors (551)
Nat'l Bankers Ass'n (552)
Nat'l Black Women's Health Project (552)
Nat'l Breast Cancer Coalition (553)
Nat'l Coalition Against Domestic Violence (556)
Nat'l Committee on Pay Equity (557)
Nat'l Conference of Catholic Bishops, Secretariat for Pro-Life Activities (558)
Nat'l Council of Catholic Women (560)
Nat'l Council of Jewish Women (560)
Nat'l Council of Negro Women (560)
Nat'l Council of Women of the U.S. (561)
Nat'l Federation of Democratic Women (564)
Nat'l Federation of Republican Women (564)
Nat'l Museum of Women in the Arts (571)
Nat'l Network to End Domestic Violence (572)
Nat'l Organization for Women (572)
Nat'l Osteoporosis Foundation (573)
Nat'l Partnership for Women and Families (573)
Nat'l Right to Life Committee (576)
Nat'l Women's Business Council (581)
Nat'l Women's Health Network (581)
Nat'l Women's Law Center (581)
Nat'l Women's Political Caucus (581)
Older Women's League (600)
Planned Parenthood Federation of America (618)
Population Action Internat'l (621)
Religious Coalition for Reproductive Choice (636)
RENEW (Republican Network to Elect Women) (636)
Reproductive Health Technologies Project (637)
Republicans for Choice (638)
Soc. for Women's Health Research (663)
Tett Enterprises (684)
Voters For Choice (717)
Wider Opportunities for Women (726)
Woman's Nat'l Democratic Club (729)
Women and Infants' Hospital (729)
Women Business Owners Corp. Inc. (729)
Women in Community Service (729)
Women in Government Relations, Inc. (729)
Women Officials in NACo (729)
Women's Action for New Directions (WAND)/Women Legislators' Lobby (WILL) (729)
Women's Campaign Fund (729)
Women's College Coalition (729)
Women's Hospital (729)
Women's Hospital of Greensboro (729)
Women's Information Network (729)
Women's Policy, Inc. (729)
Women's Research and Education Institute (730)
Women's Sports Foundation (730)
YWCA of the USA (734)

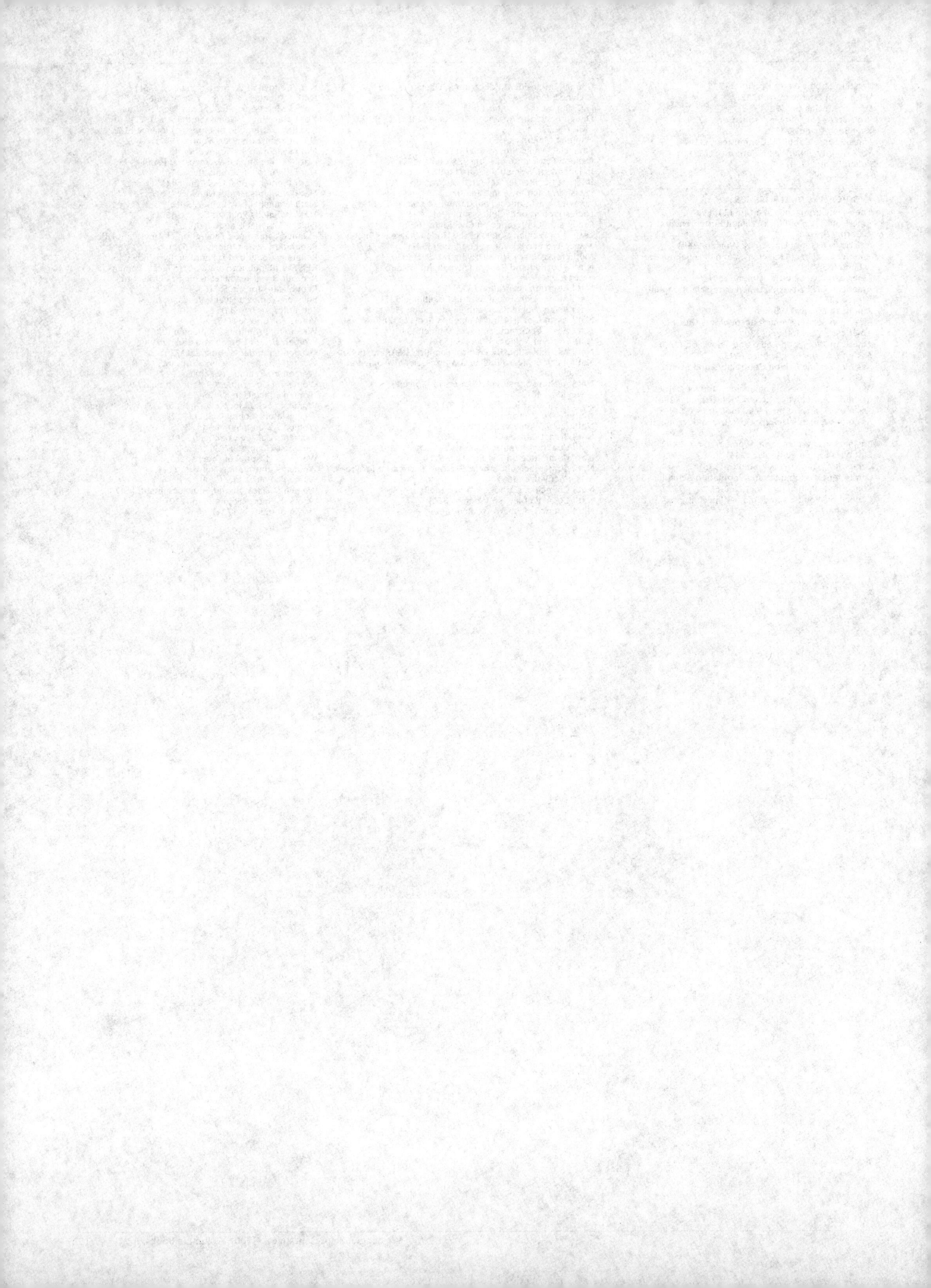

2001 Washington Representatives

Foreign Clients Index by Country

This index identifies the governments, businesses and other organizations in foreign countries that, in addition to their diplomatic missions, retain representation here in Washington. Information on the firms and individuals that represent these clients can be found in their full listings on the pages indicated below.

ANGOLA
Angola, Government of the Republic of **(284)**

ANTIGUA AND BARBUDA
Starnet Communications Internat'l **(673)**
World Sports Exchange **(731)**

ARGENTINA
AFINOA **(231)**
Argentina, Government of **(288)**
Argentina, The Secretary of Intelligence of **(288)**
Argentine Citrus Ass'n **(288)**
Argentine Economic & Investment Council **(288)**
Atanor, S.A. **(302)**
Centro Industrial de Laboratorios Farmaceuticas Argentinos (CILFA) **(339)**
Chamber of Independent Gas Stations of Argentina **(340)**
LAPA (Lineas Aereas Privadas, S.A.) **(495)**
Radix SA **(632)**
Siderar S.A.I.C. **(658)**
Siderca Corp. **(658)**
South Atlantic-TransAndes Economic Committee **(666)**
Trans-Ona S.A.M.C.I.F. **(689)**

ARUBA
Aruba, Government of **(290)**
Glossco Free Zone, N.V. **(436)**

AUSTRALIA
ADI Ltd. **(227)**
Ansett Transport Industries **(285)**
Australian Dairy Corp. **(303)**
Fentek Internat'l Pty. Ltd. **(415)**
Pacific Dunlop, Ltd./Pacific Brands **(605)**
Queensland Sugar, Ltd. **(631)**

AUSTRIA
Austrian Airlines **(303)**

BAHAMAS
Bahamas, Government of the Commonwealth of the **(306)**
Fruit Shippers Ltd. **(427)**
Shipston Group, LTD **(657)**

BAHRAIN
Bahrain, Government of the State of **(306)**

BANGLADESH
Bangladesh Export Processing Zones Authority **(307)**
Greyfab (Bangladesh) Ltd. **(440)**

BELGIUM
Ass'n of Chocolate, Biscuit and Confectionery Industries of the EEC **(295)**
Association des Constructeurs Europeens de Motocycles **(300)**
Bertelsmann AG **(312)**
Chocolate, Biscuit and Confectionery Industries of the European Community **(345)**
Euro-Fulton, S.A. **(408)**
European Confederation of Iron and Steel Industries (EUROFER) **(408)**
Internat'l Ass'n of Professional Numismatists **(468)**

BELIZE
St. Matthew's University School of Medicine **(672)**

BENIN
Benin, Government of the Republic of **(311)**
West African Friends **(723)**

BERMUDA
A.C.E. Insurance Co. (Bermuda) Ltd. **(226)**
Ace Ltd. **(226)**
Bermuda Biological Station for Research **(312)**
Bermuda, Government of **(312)**
ComInternational Management Inc. **(360)**
E-Tech **(394)**
X.L. Insurance Co. **(732)**
XL Capital Ltd **(732)**

BOLIVIA
Bolivia, Government of the Republic of **(317)**

BOTSWANA
Debswana Diamond Co. **(383)**

BRAZIL
Argentina-Brazil Venture Services Corp. **(288)**
Ass'n of Brazilian Ceramic Tile Producers **(294)**
Ass'n of Brazilian Tire Producers **(294)**
Branco Peres Citrus, S.A. **(319)**
Companhia Maritima Nacional **(363)**
France Telecom America do Sul Ltda. **(424)**
VASP Airlines **(712)**

BRITISH WEST INDIES
British Virgin Islands, Government of the **(321)**

BRUNEI DARUSSALAM
Royal Brunei Airways **(643)**

BULGARIA
Bourgas Intermodal Feasability Study **(318)**
Bulgaria, Government of the Republic of **(323)**
Bulgaria, Ministry of Foreign Affairs of the Republic of **(323)**

BURKINA FASO
Burkina Faso, Government of **(324)**

CAMBODIA
Cambodia, Ministry of Commerce, Royal Kingdom of **(328)**
Cambodian People's Party **(328)**

CAMEROON
Cameroon, Government of the Republic of **(328)**

CANADA
Advanced Material Resources, Inc. **(228)**
Aerospace Industries Ass'n of Canada **(230)**
Agrium Inc. **(232)**
Air Canada **(233)**
Air Transat **(234)**
Algoma Steel, Inc. **(238)**
Alliance Pipeline, L.P. **(241)**
Aluminum Co. of Canada **(242)**
APG Solutions and Technologies **(286)**
Babcock & Wilcox **(305)**
Ballard Power Systems **(306)**
Bennett Environmental Inc. **(311)**
Biovail Corp. Internat'l **(314)**
Bombardier, Inc. **(317)**
British Columbia Hydro and Power Authority **(321)**
British Columbia Lumber Trade Council **(321)**
British Columbia Softwood Lumber Trade Council **(321)**
British Columbia, Canada, Government of the Province of **(321)**
CAMECO Corp. **(328)**
Canada, Government of **(329)**
Canada, Trade Law Division of the Embassy of **(329)**

CAYMAN ISLANDS

CHAD

CHILE

CHINA (PEOPLE'S REPUBLIC)

CHINA (TAIWAN)

COLOMBIA

CONGO

COSTA RICA

COTE D'IVOIRE

CROATIA

CUBA

CYPRUS

DENMARK

DOMINICA

DOMINICAN REPUBLIC

ECUADOR

EGYPT

EL SALVADOR

EQUATORIAL GUINEA

ERITREA

ESTONIA

ETHIOPIA

FIJI

FINLAND

FRANCE

GABON

THE GAMBIA

GEORGIA

GERMANY

GHANA

GREECE

GRENADA

GUATEMALA

GUINEA

GUYANA

HAITI

HONDURAS

HONG KONG

ICELAND

INDIA

INDONESIA

IRAN

IRAQ

IRELAND

ISRAEL

ITALY

JAMAICA

JAPAN

JORDAN

KAZAKHSTAN

KENYA

KOREA

KUWAIT

KYRGYZSTAN

LEBANON

LIBERIA

LITHUANIA

LUXEMBOURG

MACAU

MACEDONIA

MALAYSIA

MALDIVES

MALTA

MARSHALL ISLANDS

MAURITANIA

MAURITIUS

MEXICO

Pretium S.C (Mexico) **(623)**
Secretaria de Agricultura, Granaderia y Desarrolo Rural (SAGAR) **(654)**
Servicios Corporativos Cintra SA de CV **(656)**
TAESA (Transportes Aereos Ejecutivos, S.A. de C.V.) **(680)**
TAMSA **(680)**
Telefonos de Mexico **(683)**
Tolmex **(688)**
TRIBASA **(692)**
Tubos de Acero de Mexico, S.A. **(693)**
TV Azteca **(694)**

MOZAMBIQUE
Mozambique, Government of the Republic of **(532)**

NAMIBIA
Air Namibia **(234)**

NAURU
Air Nauru **(234)**

NEPAL
Nepal, Kingdom of **(584)**
Nepal, Royal Embassy of **(584)**

NETHERLANDS
Centraal Bureau van de Tuinbouwveilingen **(338)**
Dutch Produce Ass'n **(393)**
General Ore Internat'l Corp. Ltd. **(433)**
Heerema Marine Contractors Nederland B.V. **(448)**
Martinair Holland **(511)**
N.V. Philips Gloeilampenfabrieken **(534)**
Netherlands, Ministry of Foreign Affairs of the Government of **(584)**
New Skies Satellites N.V. **(586)**
Royal Dutch Shell Group **(643)**
Royal Netherlands, Embassy of the **(643)**
Unilever N.V. **(699)**
United Pan-Europe Communications, NV **(702)**

NETHERLANDS ANTILLES
Netherlands Antilles, Government of **(584)**

NEW ZEALAND
New Zealand Dairy Board **(588)**
New Zealand Kiwifruit Marketing Board **(588)**

NICARAGUA
NICA Airline **(589)**
Nicaraguan Foundation for Democracy and Development **(589)**

NIGER
Niger, Government of the Republic of **(590)**

NIGERIA
Nigeria, Embassy of the Federal Republic of **(590)**
Nigeria, Government of the Federal Republic of **(590)**

NORTHERN MARIANA ISLANDS
Marianas Political Status Commission **(509)**

NORWAY
Hagglunds Moelv AS **(443)**
Kongsberg Defense & Aerospace **(491)**
Norway, Government of the Kingdom of **(596)**
Raufoss A/S, Defense Products Division **(633)**
SINTEF Telecom and Informatics **(660)**

OMAN
Oman, Sultanate of **(600)**

PAKISTAN
Nat'l Islamic Front Afghanistan **(569)**
Pakistan Internat'l Airlines **(606)**
Pakistan, Embassy of the Islamic Republic of **(606)**
Pakistan, Government of the Islamic Republic of **(606)**

PALESTINE
Palestinian Authority **(606)**

PANAMA
Cemento Bayano **(335)**
Copa Airline **(371)**
Panama, Foreign Minister of the Republic of **(607)**
Panama, Government of the Republic of **(607)**
Panama, Public Service Regulatory Entity of the Government of the Republic of **(607)**

PAPUA NEW GUINEA
Papua New Guinea, Embassy of **(607)**

PARAGUAY
Paraguay, Secretariat for Planning of the Republic of **(607)**

PERU
Advanced Machinery Logistics, Inc. **(228)**
Aero Continente, S.A. **(230)**
Aeroinversiones, S.A. **(230)**
Peru, Government of the Republic of **(613)**
PromPeru **(626)**

PHILIPPINES
Confederation of Garment Exporters of the Philippines **(365)**
Cruz Enverga & Raboca **(379)**
Orient Airlines Ass'n **(603)**
Philippine Airlines **(616)**
Philippine Sugar Alliance **(616)**
Philippines Long Distance Telephone Co. **(616)**
Philippines, Department of Trade and Industry of the Republic of **(616)**
Philippines, Government of the Republic of **(616)**

POLAND
LOT Polish Airlines **(504)**

PORTUGAL
Luso American Foundation **(505)**
Madeira Development Co. **(507)**
Portugal, Trade Commission of the Government of the Republic of **(621)**

QATAR
Qatar, Embassy of **(630)**
Qatar, Government of the State of **(630)**

ROMANIA
Bicopas, Ltd. **(313)**
Impex Overseas **(458)**

RUSSIA
Ass'n of Industrialists and Businessmen of Tatarstan **(296)**
Chemcrete Technologies Russia (RIS/NIS), Inc. **(342)**
Internat'l Marketing for Russia and NIS **(473)**
MATEK **(513)**
Moscow Interbank Currency Exchange (MICEX) **(530)**
Moscow State University **(530)**
Most Group Limited **(530)**
Robert Schenk Internat'l Russia **(651)**
Tatarstan, Republic of **(681)**
Techsnabexport, A.O. **(682)**

RWANDA
Rwanda, Government of the Republic of **(644)**

SAUDI ARABIA
The Consulting Center **(368)**
Saudi Arabia, Government of **(650)**
Saudi Arabia, Ministry of Commerce **(650)**
Saudi Arabia, Royal Embassy of **(650)**

SENEGAL
Senegal, Government of the Republic of **(655)**

SINGAPORE
Ordnance Development and Engineering Co. of Singapore **(603)**
Singapore Technologies Automotive **(659)**
Singapore Technologies, Inc. **(659)**
Singapore Trade Development Board **(659)**
Singapore, Embassy of the Republic of **(659)**
Singapore, Government of the Republic of **(659)**

SLOVAKIA
Slovak Information Agency **(661)**
Slovakia, Government of **(661)**

SLOVENIA
Internat'l Trust Fund for Demining and Mine Victims Assistance in Bosnia-Herzigovina **(475)**
Slovenia, Republic of **(661)**

SOUTH AFRICA
Allthane Technologies Internat'l **(242)**
Bell Equipment Ltd. **(311)**
Chamber of Mines of South Africa **(340)**
McKechnie Brothers (South Africa) Ltd. **(515)**
Medical University of Southern Africa **(516)**
South Africa Foundation **(666)**
South Africa, Embassy of the Republic of **(666)**
South African Airways **(666)**
South African Government/World Bank **(666)**
South African Sugar Ass'n **(666)**

SPAIN
Corporacion Valenciana de Cementos Portland, S.A. **(372)**

SRPSKA
Srpska, Government of the Republic of **(671)**

SURINAME
Suriname, Government of the Republic of **(678)**

SWAZILAND
Swaziland Sugar Ass'n **(678)**
Swaziland, Embassy of the Kingdom of **(678)**
Swaziland, Kingdom of **(678)**

SWEDEN
Bofors Defence AB **(317)**
Celsius Tech Electronics **(335)**
Saab AB **(644)**
Scandinavian Airlines System (SAS) **(651)**
SKF USA, Inc. **(660)**
Svenska Petroleum Exploration AB **(678)**

SWITZERLAND
Forces Vives **(422)**
IATA U.S. Frequent Flyer Tax Interest Group **(456)**
Internat'l Air Transport Ass'n **(467)**
Internat'l Olympic Committee **(473)**
Kazakhstan 21st Century Foundation **(487)**
Localisation Industry Standards Ass'n **(501)**
SGS Government Programs, Inc. **(656)**
Societe Generale de Surveillance Holding S.A. **(664)**
Swiss Bank Corp. **(679)**
Swiss Investors Protection Ass'n **(679)**
Swiss Munition Enterprise **(679)**
Swiss Ordnance Enterprise **(679)**
Swissair **(679)**
Switzerland, Economic Development, State of Vaud **(679)**
Union Bank of Switzerland **(699)**
The Winterthur Group **(728)**
World Health Organization **(730)**
Zurich Financial Group **(735)**
Zurich Financial Services Group **(735)**
Zurich U.S. Specialties **(735)**

TANZANIA
Tanzania, Office of the Foreign Minister of the United Republic of **(681)**

THAILAND
Minebea Thailand **(525)**
Thai Gypsum Products Co., Ltd. **(685)**
Thailand, Department of Foreign Trade of **(685)**

TOGO
Togo, Embassy of the Republic of **(688)**
Togo, Government of the Republic of **(688)**

TRINIDAD & TOBAGO
Trinidad and Tobago, Embassy of the Republic of **(692)**
Trinidad and Tobago, Government of **(692)**

TUNISIA
Tunisia, Embassy of the Republic of **(694)**
Tunisian Agency for External Communication **(694)**

TURKEY
Central Bank of Turkey **(338)**
Colakoglu Group **(357)**
Eregli Demir ve Celik Fab. **(406)**
Habas Group **(443)**
Izopoli **(480)**
Pastavilla Makarnacilik A.S. **(609)**
Turkey, Central Bank of **(694)**
Turkey, Embassy of the Republic of **(694)**
Turkey, Government of the Republic of **(694)**
Turkish Airlines **(694)**
U.S.-Turkish Business Council of DEIK **(697)**
Vestal Group of Companies **(714)**
The Yucel Group **(734)**

TURKS & CAICOS ISLANDS
Turks Air Limited **(694)**

UGANDA
Uganda, Embassy of the Republic of **(698)**
Uganda, Government of the Republic of **(698)**

UKRAINE
Advertising Company ART-ERIA **(229)**
Ukraine, Government of **(698)**
Ukraine, Ministries of Industy, Foreign Economic Relations, and Foreign Affairs of the Government of **(698)**

UNITED ARAB EMIRATES
United Arab Emirates, Government of **(700)**

UNITED KINGDOM
Air Foyle, Ltd. **(233)**
Airtours Internat'l **(235)**
Alenia Marconi Systems **(238)**
Ass'n of British Insurers **(294)**
BATMark **(308)**
Bowman Internat'l Corp. **(318)**
British Ministry of Defence **(321)**
British Nuclear Fuels plc **(321)**
Bulmer Holding PLC, H. P. **(323)**
Caribbean Banana Exporters Ass'n **(331)**
CHEMRING, Ltd. **(342)**
Colebrand, Ltd. **(357)**
Corus Group Plc **(373)**
DIAGEO **(387)**
EBS Dealing Resources Inc. **(395)**
Equitas Reinsurance Ltd. **(406)**
GEC-Marconi Avionics Group **(430)**
GEC-Marconi Defense Systems Ltd. **(430)**
Graseby Plc **(438)**
Great Britain, Government of **(439)**
The Group of 20 **(441)**
Inmarsat **(462)**
Intermare Navigation SA **(466)**
Internat'l Council of Containership Operators **(470)**
Internat'l Group of P&I Clubs **(472)**
Internat'l Underwriting Ass'n of London **(475)**
Iraqi Nat'l Congress **(478)**
ITRI, Ltd. **(480)**
JMC Airlines, Ltd. **(483)**
Kongsberg Simrad **(491)**
LEP Scientific Ltd. **(498)**
Lloyd's of London **(501)**
London Clearinghouse, Ltd. **(503)**
London Futures and Options Exchange **(503)**
London Metal Exchange, Ltd. **(503)**
Marconi plc **(509)**
Market Access Ltd. **(510)**
Martin-Baker Aircraft Co., Ltd. **(511)**
Messier-Dowty Internat'l **(519)**
Moose Internat'l Inc. **(529)**
Nat'l Power **(574)**
Nomura Internat'l plc **(591)**
North of Ireland Free Trade Initiative **(593)**
Pilkington Thorn **(617)**
PowerGen **(622)**
Rakisons, Ltd. **(632)**
Reckitt & Colman Pharmaceuticals Inc. **(634)**
Richardson Lawrie Associates **(639)**
Richemont Internat'l Ltd. **(640)**
Shorts Missile Systems **(658)**
Sidem International Ltd. **(658)**
Sutton & Sutton Solicitors **(678)**
Thorn Microwave Devices **(686)**
TI Group Inc. **(686)**
Tilda Rice **(687)**
United Kingdom, Government of **(702)**
Urenco, Inc. **(709)**
Virgin Atlantic Airways **(715)**

UZBEKISTAN
Uzbekistan, Government of the Republic of **(711)**

VENEZUELA
Aeropostal **(230)**
C.A. Vencemos **(325)**
Corporacion Venezolana de Cementos, SACA **(372)**
Siderurgica del Orinoco (Sidor), C.A. **(658)**
Venezuela, Bolivarian Republic of **(712)**
VIASA **(714)**

WESTERN SAMOA
Polynesian Airlines **(620)**

YEMEN
Yemen, Government of **(733)**

YUGOSLAVIA
Kosovo, Government of the Republic of **(491)**

ZAIRE
Bank of Zaire **(307)**
Zaire, Office of the President of the Republic of **(734)**

ZIMBABWE
Zimbabwe, Republic of **(734)**

2001 Washington Representatives

PAC Index

The following index has been provided to aid the researcher in locating the political action committees (PACs) listed in this directory. While some of the PACs listed in these pages are sponsored by a company, association, or labor union, many serve as independent interest groups. The latter maintain their own listings in Section II: The Clients, while information on the former may be found within the listings of their sponsoring organiztions. In such cases, the page number given here directs the researcher to the specific location of the PAC information within the listing of its sponsoring organization.

American Federation of School Administrators Political Action Committee, *American Federation of School Administrators* **(258)**
American Federation of Teachers Committee on Political Education, *American Federation of Teachers* **(259)**
American Financial Services Ass'n Political Action Committee, *American Financial Services Ass'n* **(259)**
American Forest and Paper Ass'n Political Action Committee (AF&PA PAC), *American Forest & Paper Ass'n* **(259)**
American Frozen Food Institute Political Action Committee, *American Frozen Food Institute* **(260)**
American Gaming Ass'n PAC, *American Gaming Ass'n* **(260)**
American Gear Political Action Committee, *American Gear Manufacturers Ass'n* **(261)**
American General Corp. PAC (AGCPAC), *American General Corp.* **(261)**
American Health Care Ass'n Political Action Committee, *American Health Care Ass'n* **(261)**
American Hellenic Educational Progressive Ass'n Political Action Committee (AHEPA-PAC), *American Hellenic Educational Progressive Ass'n (AHEPA)* **(262)**
American Horse Council Committee on Legislation and Taxation, *American Horse Council, Inc.* **(263)**
American Hospital Ass'n Political Action Committee (AHA PAC), *American Hospital Ass'n* **(263)**
American Hotel and Motel Political Action Committee (AHMPAC), *American Hotel and Lodging Ass'n* **(263)**
American Insurance Ass'n Political Action Committee, *American Insurance Ass'n* **(264)**
American Logistics Ass'n PAC, *American Logistics Ass'n* **(266)**
American Management Systems Inc. PAC (AMS PAC), *American Management Systems* **(267)**
American Meat Institute Political Action Committee, *American Meat Institute* **(267)**
American Medical Political Action Committee, *American Medical Ass'n* **(267)**
American Motorcyclist Political Action Committee, *American Motorcyclist Ass'n* **(268)**
American Moving and Storage Political Action Committee, *American Moving and Storage Ass'n* **(268)**
American Neurological Surgery PAC, *American Ass'n of Neurological Surgeons/Congress of Neurological Surgeons* **(248)**
American Nurses Ass'n Political Action Committee (ANA-PAC), *American Nurses Ass'n* **(269)**
American Occupational Therapy Ass'n Political Action Committee, *American Occupational Therapy Ass'n, Inc.* **(269)**
American Optometric Ass'n Political Action Committee, *American Optometric Ass'n* **(269)**
American Pharmaceutical Ass'n Political Action Committee, *American Pharmaceutical Ass'n* **(270)**
American Physical Therapy Congressional Action Committee, *American Physical Therapy Ass'n* **(270)**
American Pilots Ass'n Political Action Committee, *American Pilots Ass'n* **(270)**
American Portland Cement Alliance Political Action Committee, *American Portland Cement Alliance* **(270)**
American Preventive Medical Ass'n PAC, *American Preventive Medical Ass'n* **(271)**
American Public Communications Council Political Action Committee, *American Public Communications Council* **(271)**
American Resort Development Ass'n Political Action Committee, *American Resort Development Ass'n* **(272)**
American Resort Development Ass'n Resort Owners Coalition PAC (ARDA-ROC PAC), *American Resort Development Ass'n* **(272)**
American Road and Transportation Builders Ass'n PAC, *American Road and Transportation Builders Ass'n (ARTBA)* **(273)**
American School Food Service Ass'n Political Action Committee (ASFSA PAC), *American School Food Service Ass'n* **(273)**
American Sheep Industry Ass'n RAMSPAC, *American Sheep Industry Ass'n* **(273)**
American Soc. for Clinical Laboratory Science Political Action Committee, *American Soc. for Clinical Laboratory Science* **(274)**
American Soc. of Anesthesiologists Political Action Committee (ASAPAC), *American Soc. of Anesthesiologists* **(275)**
American Soc. of Appraisers PAC, *American Soc. of Appraisers* **(275)**
American Soc. of Ass'n Executives (A-PAC), *American Soc. of Ass'n Executives* **(275)**
American Soc. of Cataract and Refractive Surgery Political Action Committee (Eye PAC), *American Soc. of Cataract and Refractive Surgery* **(275)**
American Soc. of Consultant Pharmacists Political Action Committee, *American Soc. of Consultant Pharmacists* **(276)**
American Soc. of Health System Pharmacists PAC, *American Soc. of Health System Pharmacists* **(276)**
American Soc. of Pension Actuaries PAC, *American Soc. of Pension Actuaries* **(277)**
American Soc. of Travel Agents Political Action Committee (ASTAPAC), *American Soc. of Travel Agents* **(277)**
American Speech-Language-Hearing Ass'n Political Action Committee, *American Speech, Language, and Hearing Ass'n* **(277)**
American Sportfishing Association PAC, *American Sportfishing Ass'n* **(278)**
American Standard Cos Inc. PAC, *American Standard Cos. Inc.* **(278)**
American Subcontractors Ass'n PAC, *American Subcontractors Ass'n, Inc.* **(278)**
American Sugar Cane League Political Action Committee, *American Sugar Cane League of the U.S.A.* **(278)**
American Sugarbeet Growers Ass'n Political Action Committee, *American Sugarbeet Growers Ass'n* **(278)**
American Textile Industry Committee for Good Government, *American Textile Manufacturers Institute* **(279)**
American Veterinary Medical Ass'n Political Action Committee, *American Veterinary Medical Ass'n* **(280)**
American Watch Ass'n Political Action Committee, *American Watch Ass'n* **(280)**
American Waterways Operators Political Action Committee, *American Waterways Operators* **(280)**
American Wholesale Marketers Ass'n WHOLE PAC, *American Wholesale Marketers Ass'n* **(280)**
American Wind Energy Ass'n Political Action Committee (WindPAC), *American Wind Energy Ass'n* **(280)**
American Wood Preservers Institute Political Action Committee, *American Wood Preservers Institute* **(280)**
Americans Back in Charge Foundation **(281)**
Americans for a Brighter Future **(281)**
Americans for Democratic Action Political Action Committee, *Americans for Democratic Action* **(281)**
Americans for Free Internat'l Trade (AFIT PAC) **(281)**
Americans for Political Participation **(282)**
Americans Supporting the Pyrotechnics Industry **(282)**
Americn Benefits Council PAC, *American Benefits Council* **(250)**
Amgen Inc. PAC, *Amgen* **(282)**
AMPAC, *Alticor, Inc.* **(242)**
Animal Health Institute Political Action Committee, *Animal Health Institute* **(284)**
ANLA Nursery Industry Political Action Committee, *American Nursery and Landscape Ass'n* **(268)**
APAC, *Alltel Corporation* **(242)**
Apartment and Office Building Ass'n of Metropolitan Washington DC, Inc. Metro PAC - Federal, *Apartment and Office Building Ass'n of Metropolitan Washington* **(286)**
Apartment Political Action Committee of the Nat'l Apartment Ass'n, *Nat'l Apartment Ass'n* **(537)**
APL Ltd. PAC, *APL Limited* **(286)**
Apollo Group, Inc. Political Organization for Legislative Leadership, *Apollo Group, Inc.* **(286)**
Appraisal Institute Political Action Committee (APPAC), *Appraisal Institute* **(287)**
Arab American Leadership Political Action Committee, *Arab American Institute* **(287)**
ArchiPAC, *The American Institute of Architects* **(264)**
Arena PAC **(288)**
Arent Fox Civic Participation Fund, *Arent Fox Kintner Plotkin & Kahn, PLLC* **(14)**
Arnold & Porter Political Action Committee, *Arnold & Porter* **(289)**
ARPAC, *Adams and Reese LLP* **(6)**
Arthur Andersen Political Action Committee, *Arthur Andersen LLP* **(289)**
Artists Rights Today (ART PAC) **(290)**
Arts for America PAC, *Americans for the Arts* **(282)**
Ashland Political Action Committee for Employees (PACE), *Ashland Inc.* **(290)**
Ass'n for Competitive Technology PAC, *Ass'n for Competitive Technology* **(292)**
Ass'n for Local Telecommunications Services PAC, *Ass'n for Local Telecommunications Services* **(292)**
Ass'n of American Railroads PAC (Rail PAC), *Ass'n of American Railroads* **(294)**
Ass'n of Bituminous Contractors Political Action Committee, *Ass'n of Bituminous Contractors* **(294)**
Ass'n of Financial Services Holding Companies Political Action Committee, *Ass'n of Financial Services Holding Companies* **(295)**
Ass'n of Flight Attendants Political Action Committee/Flight PAC, *Ass'n of Flight Attendants* **(295)**
Ass'n of Home Appliance Manufacturers Political Action Committee, *Ass'n of Home Appliance Manufacturers* **(296)**
Ass'n of Trial Lawyers of America Political Action Committee, *Ass'n of Trial Lawyers of America* **(299)**
Assisted Living Federation of America PAC (ALFA PAC), *Assisted Living Federation of America* **(300)**
Associated Builders and Contractors Political Action Committee (ABC-PAC), *Associated Builders and Contractors* **(300)**
Associated Credit Bureaus Inc. Political Action Committee, *Associated Credit Bureaus, Inc.* **(300)**
Associated Equipment Distributors PAC, *Associated Equipment Distributors* **(300)**
Associated General Contractors Political Action Committee, *Associated General Contractors of America* **(300)**
AT&T PAC, *AT&T* **(301)**
ATOPAC, *ATOFINA Chemicals, Inc.* **(302)**
Auction Markets Political Action Committee of the Chicago Board of Trade (AMPAC/CBT), *Chicago Board of Trade* **(343)**
Audiology PAC, *American Academy of Audiology* **(243)**
Automotive Aftermarket Political Action Committee, *Automotive Parts and Service Alliance* **(303)**
Automotive Service Ass'n Political Action Committee, *Automotive Service Ass'n* **(304)**
BAE SYSTEMS North America Inc. Political Action Committee (BAE SYSTEMS USA PAC), *BAE SYSTEMS North America* **(306)**
Baker & Hostetler Political Action Committee, *Baker & Hostetler LLP* **(306)**
Bakery, Confectionery and Tobacco Workers Internat'l Union Political Action Committee, *Bakery, Confectionery and Tobacco Workers Internat'l Union* **(306)**
Balch & Bingham LLP Federal Political Committee, *Balch & Bingham LLP* **(21)**
Barbour Griffith & Rogers PAC, *Barbour Griffith & Rogers, Inc.* **(22)**
Barrick Goldstrike Mines Inc. PAC, *Barrick Goldstrike Mines, Inc.* **(308)**
Battery Council Internat'l Political Action Committee, *Battery Council Internat'l* **(309)**

Internet Leadership PAC, *VeriSign/Network Solutions, Inc.* ***(713)***
Internet Security, Privacy & Self-Regulation PAC ***(476)***
Interstate Natural Gas Assoc. of America Political Action Committee (INGAA-PAC), *Interstate Natural Gas Ass'n of America* ***(477)***
InvestAmerica, *Investment Program Ass'n* ***(478)***
Investment Management Political Action Committee (IMPAC), *Investment Co. Institute* ***(477)***
IPO Political Action Fund, *Intellectual Property Owners Ass'n* ***(465)***
Irish American Democrats ***(478)***
Irish Nat'l Caucus Political Action Committee (IRISH PAC), *Irish Nat'l Caucus* ***(479)***
Iron Workers Political Action League, *Internat'l Ass'n of Bridge, Structural, Ornamental and Reinforcing Iron Workers* ***(467)***
Italian-American Democratic Leadership Council ***(480)***
ITT Industries PAC, *ITT Industries Defense* ***(480)***
IUE-CWA Committee on Political Education, *Internat'l Union of Electronic, Electrical, Salaried, Machine, and Furniture Workers-Communications Workers of America* ***(476)***
JBC Internat'l Trade Development PAC, *JBC Internat'l* ***(105)***
Kamber Group PAC (TKG PAC), *The Kamber Group* ***(109)***
Kemper Insurance Campaign Fund, *Kemper Insurance Cos.* ***(487)***
KPMG PAC, *KPMG, LLP* ***(491)***
Labor for America PAC ***(493)***
Laborers' Political League, *Laborers' Internat'l Union of North America* ***(493)***
Lafarge PAC, *Lafarge Corp.* ***(494)***
Leadership for the Future ***(497)***
Leadership PAC 2002 ***(497)***
League of Conservation Voters Political Action Committee, *League of Conservation Voters* ***(497)***
Lease-PAC, *Equipment Leasing Ass'n of America* ***(406)***
Link-PAC, *Satellite Broadcasting and Communications Ass'n* ***(650)***
LNC PAC, *Lincoln Nat'l Corp.* ***(500)***
Lockheed Martin Employees PAC, *Lockheed Martin Corp.* ***(501)***
Log Cabin Republicans PAC (LCR PAC) ***(502)***
Loral Spacecom Civic Responsibility Fund, *Loral Space and Communications, Ltd.* ***(503)***
LTV Corp. Active Citizenship Campaign, *The LTV Corp.* ***(505)***
Lucent Technologies Inc. PAC, *Lucent Technologies* ***(505)***
Lumber Dealers Political Action Committee (LUDPAC), *Nat'l Lumber and Building Material Dealers Ass'n* ***(570)***
Lyondell PAC, *Lyondell Chemical Co.* ***(506)***
MACHINE TOOLPAC, *The Ass'n For Manufacturing Technology (AMT)* ***(292)***
Machinists Non-Partisan Political League, *Internat'l Ass'n of Machinists and Aerospace Workers* ***(468)***
Magazine Publishers of America Political Action Committee, *Magazine Publishers of America* ***(507)***
Mandela Group ***(508)***
Manor Healthcare Federal Political Action Committee, *HCR-Manor Care, Inc.* ***(446)***
Manufactured Housing Institute Political Action Committee, *Manufactured Housing Institute* ***(509)***
MAPPS PAC ***(509)***
Marine Engineers Beneficial Ass'n Political Action Fund, *Marine Engineers Beneficial Ass'n (District No. 1 - PCD)* ***(510)***
Marriott Internat'l Political Action Committee, *Marriott Internat'l, Inc.* ***(511)***
MassMutual Political Action Committee, *MassMutual Financial Group* ***(512)***
Maytag Corporation Employees for Good Government Fund, *Maytag Corp.* ***(513)***
McDermott, Will & Emery PAC, *McDermott, Will and Emery* ***(128)***
McDonald's Federal PAC, *McDonald's Corp.* ***(514)***
McGuire Woods PAC, *McGuireWoods L.L.P.* ***(130)***
MCI Telecommunications PAC (MCI PAC), *MCI WorldCom Corp.* ***(514)***
McMoRan Exploration Company, *Freeport-McMoRan Copper & Gold Inc.* ***(425)***
Media Fusion PAC, *Media Fusion L.L.C.* ***(516)***
Medtronic, Inc. Medical Technology Fund, *Medtronic, Inc.* ***(517)***
Merck & Co., Inc. PAC (MERCK PAC), *Merck & Co.* ***(518)***
Merrill Lynch & Co., Inc. Political Action Committee, *Merrill Lynch & Co., Inc.* ***(519)***
Metropolitan Employees' Political Participation Fund, *Metropolitan Life Insurance Co.* ***(520)***
Mid-Atlantic Regional Joint Board UNITE PAC ***(523)***
Mid-Continent Oil and Gas Political Action Committee (MID PAC), *U.S. Oil and Gas Ass'n* ***(696)***
Midwives PAC, *American College of Nurse-Midwives* ***(254)***
Miller & Chevalier PAC, *Miller & Chevalier, Chartered* ***(133)***
MINEPAC, *Nat'l Mining Ass'n* ***(571)***
Monsanto Citizenship Fund, *Monsanto Co.* ***(528)***
Morgan Stanley Dean Witter PAC, *Morgan Stanley Dean Witter & Co.* ***(529)***
Mortgage Bankers Ass'n of America Political Action Committee, *Mortgage Bankers Ass'n of America* ***(530)***
Mortgage Insurance Political Action Committee, *Mortgage Insurance Companies of America* ***(530)***
Motion Picture Ass'n Political Action Committee, *Motion Picture Ass'n of America* ***(530)***
Motorcycle Rights Fund - Political Active Cyclists, *Motorcycle Riders Foundation* ***(531)***
Motorola Civic Action Campaign Fund, *Motorola, Inc.* ***(531)***
MW PAC, *Montgomery Watson* ***(528)***
NAAA PAC, *NAADAC, The Ass'n for Addiction Professionals* ***(534)***
NAATS Political Action Committee, *Nat'l Ass'n of Air Traffic Specialists* ***(538)***
NABRPAC, *Nat'l Ass'n of Beverage Retailers* ***(539)***
NARAL PAC, *Nat'l Abortion and Reproductive Rights Action League* ***(535)***
Nat'l Air Traffic Controllers Ass'n PAC, *Nat'l Air Traffic Controllers Ass'n* ***(536)***
Nat'l Alliance for Political Action, *Nat'l Alliance of Postal and Federal Employees* ***(536)***
Nat'l Asian American Political Empowerment Fund ***(537)***
Nat'l Ass'n for Home Care Political Action Committee, *Nat'l Ass'n for Home Care* ***(537)***
Nat'l Ass'n for Uniformed Services Political Action Committee, *Nat'l Ass'n for Uniformed Services* ***(538)***
Nat'l Ass'n of Business Political Action Committees ***(539)***
Nat'l Ass'n of Chain Drug Stores Political Action Committee, *Nat'l Ass'n of Chain Drug Stores* ***(539)***
Nat'l Ass'n of Computer Consultant Businesses High-Tech PAC, *Nat'l Ass'n of Computer Consultant Businesses* ***(540)***
Nat'l Ass'n of Convenience Stores Political Action Committee, *Nat'l Ass'n of Convenience Stores* ***(541)***
Nat'l Ass'n of Development Companies PAC, *Nat'l Ass'n of Development Companies* ***(542)***
Nat'l Ass'n of Federal Credit Unions Political Action Committee, *Nat'l Ass'n of Federal Credit Unions* ***(542)***
Nat'l Ass'n of Federal Veterinarians Political Action Committee, *Nat'l Ass'n of Federal Veterinarians* ***(542)***
Nat'l Ass'n of Health Underwriters PAC (HUPAC), *Nat'l Ass'n of Health Underwriters* ***(543)***
Nat'l Ass'n of Independent Insurers Political Action Committee, *Nat'l Ass'n of Independent Insurers* ***(544)***
Nat'l Ass'n of Industrial and Office Properties American Development PAC, *Nat'l Ass'n of Industrial and Office Properties* ***(544)***
Nat'l Ass'n of Investment Companies, *Nat'l Ass'n of Investment Companies* ***(544)***
Nat'l Ass'n of Metal Finishers Political Action Committee, *Nat'l Ass'n of Metal Finishers* ***(545)***
Nat'l Ass'n of Mortgage Brokers PAC, *Nat'l Ass'n of Mortgage Brokers* ***(545)***
Nat'l Ass'n of Mutual Insurance Companies Political Action Committee (NAMIC-PAC), *Nat'l Ass'n of Mutual Insurance Companies* ***(545)***
Nat'l Ass'n of Plumbing-Heating-Cooling Contractors Political Action Committee, *Plumbing, Heating, Cooling Contractors- National Assoc.* ***(619)***
Nat'l Ass'n of Police Organizations Political Action Committee Inc., *Nat'l Ass'n of Police Organizations* ***(546)***
Nat'l Ass'n of Postal Supervisors Political Action Committee, *Nat'l Ass'n of Postal Supervisors* ***(546)***
Nat'l Ass'n of Postmasters of the U.S. PAC for Postmasters, *Nat'l Ass'n of Postmasters of the U.S.* ***(546)***
Nat'l Ass'n of Psychiatric Health Systems Political Action Committee, *Nat'l Ass'n of Psychiatric Health Systems* ***(547)***
Nat'l Ass'n of Psychiatric Treatment Centers for Children Political Action Committee, *Nat'l Ass'n of Psychiatric Treatment Centers for Children* ***(547)***
Nat'l Ass'n of Real Estate Investment Trusts PAC (NAREIT PAC), *Nat'l Ass'n of Real Estate Investment Trusts* ***(547)***
Nat'l Ass'n of REALTORS Political Action Committee, *Nat'l Ass'n of Realtors* ***(547)***
Nat'l Ass'n of Rehabilitation Agencies, Inc. Political Action Committee, *Nat'l Ass'n of Rehabilitation Agencies* ***(548)***
Nat'l Ass'n of Retired Federal Employees Political Action Committee, *Nat'l Ass'n of Retired Federal Employees* ***(548)***
Nat'l Ass'n of Small Business Investment Companies Political Action Committee, *Nat'l Ass'n of Small Business Investment Companies* ***(549)***
Nat'l Ass'n of Social Workers Political Action Committee for Candidate Action, *Nat'l Ass'n of Social Workers* ***(549)***
Nat'l Ass'n of Water Companies Political Action Committee, *Nat'l Ass'n of Water Companies* ***(551)***
Nat'l Ass'n of Wheat Growers Political Action Committee, *Nat'l Ass'n of Wheat Growers* ***(551)***
Nat'l Bankers Ass'n Political Action Committee, *Nat'l Bankers Ass'n* ***(552)***
Nat'l Bar Ass'n Political Action Committee, *Nat'l Bar Ass'n* ***(552)***
Nat'l Beer Wholesalers Ass'n Political Action Committee, *Nat'l Beer Wholesalers Ass'n* ***(552)***
Nat'l Breast Cancer Coalition PAC, *Nat'l Breast Cancer Coalition* ***(553)***
Nat'l Burglar & Fire Alarm Ass'n PAC (NBFAA PAC), *Nat'l Burglar and Fire Alarm Ass'n* ***(553)***
Nat'l Business Aviation Ass'n Political Action Committee, *Nat'l Business Aviation Ass'n* ***(553)***
Nat'l Cable Television Ass'n Political Action Committee, *Nat'l Cable Television Ass'n* ***(553)***
Nat'l Cattlemen's Ass'n Poltical Action Committee, *Nat'l Cattleman's Beef Ass'n* ***(554)***
Nat'l Chamber Alliance for Politics of the Chamber of Commerce for the U.S.A., *Chamber of Commerce of the U.S.A.* ***(340)***
Nat'l Chicken Council Political Action Committee, *Nat'l Chicken Council* ***(555)***
Nat'l Club Ass'n Political Action Committee, *Nat'l Club Ass'n* ***(556)***
Nat'l Coalition of Abortion Providers PAC, *Nat'l Coalition of Abortion Providers* ***(556)***
Nat'l Committee for an Effective Congress ***(557)***
Nat'l Committee to Preserve Social Security and Medicare Political Action Committee, *Nat'l Committee to Preserve Social Security and Medicare* ***(557)***
Nat'l Community Pharmacists Ass'n Political Action Committee, *Nat'l Community Pharmacists Ass'n* ***(558)***
Nat'l Concrete Masonry Ass'n Political Action Committee, *Nat'l Concrete Masonry Ass'n* ***(558)***
Nat'l Confectioners Ass'n Political Action Committee, *Nat'l Confectioners Ass'n* ***(558)***

Nat'l Council of Chain Restaurants PAC, *Nat'l Council of Chain Restaurants* **(560)**
Nat'l Council of Farmer Cooperatives Political Action Committee (Co-op PAC), *Nat'l Council of Farmer Cooperatives* **(560)**
Nat'l Court Reporters Ass'n Political Action Committee, *Nat'l Court Reporters Ass'n* **(561)**
Nat'l Education Ass'n Political Action Committee, *Nat'l Education Ass'n of the U.S.* **(562)**
Nat'l Electrical Manufacturers Ass'n PAC (NEMA PAC), *Nat'l Electrical Manufacturers Ass'n* **(562)**
Nat'l Emergency Medicine PAC, *American College of Emergency Physicians* **(253)**
Nat'l Federation of Democratic Women PAC, *Nat'l Federation of Democratic Women* **(564)**
Nat'l Federation of Federal Employees Political Action Committee, *Nat'l Federation of Federal Employees* **(564)**
Nat'l Federation of Federal Employees Public Affairs Council, *Nat'l Federation of Federal Employees* **(564)**
Nat'l Federation of Independent Business SAFE Trust, *Nat'l Federation of Independent Business* **(564)**
Nat'l Fisheries Institute Political Action Committee, *Nat'l Fisheries Institute* **(564)**
Nat'l Food Processors Ass'n Political Action Committee, *Nat'l Food Processors Ass'n* **(564)**
Nat'l Glass Ass'n Political Action Committee, *Nat'l Glass Ass'n* **(566)**
Nat'l Good Government Fund, *Vinson & Elkins L.L.P.* **(204)**
Nat'l Grocers Ass'n Political Action Committee, *Nat'l Grocers Ass'n* **(566)**
Nat'l Hardwood Lumber Ass'n PAC, *Nat'l Hardwood Lumber Ass'n* **(566)**
Nat'l Jewish Democratic Council PAC, *Nat'l Jewish Democratic Council* **(569)**
Nat'l League of Postmasters Political Action Committee, *Nat'l League of Postmasters of the U.S.* **(569)**
Nat'l Licensed Beverage Ass'n Bar PAC, *Nat'l Licensed Beverage Ass'n* **(570)**
Nat'l Marine Manufacturers Ass'n PAC, *Nat'l Marine Manufacturers Ass'n* **(570)**
Nat'l Multi Housing Council Political Action Committee, *Nat'l Multi-Housing Council* **(571)**
Nat'l Organization for Women Political Action Committee (NOW Equality PAC), *Nat'l Organization for Women* **(572)**
Nat'l Parking Ass'n Political Action Committee, *Nat'l Parking Ass'n* **(573)**
Nat'l Postal Mail Handlers Union PAC, *Nat'l Postal Mail Handlers Union* **(574)**
Nat'l Pro-Life Alliance PAC **(574)**
Nat'l Rehabilitation Political Action Committee **(575)**
Nat'l Republican Congressional Committee **(575)**
Nat'l Restaurant Ass'n Political Action Committee, *Nat'l Restaurant Ass'n* **(576)**
Nat'l Retail Federation Political Action Committee, *Nat'l Retail Federation* **(576)**
Nat'l Rifle Ass'n Political Victory Fund, *Nat'l Rifle Ass'n of America* **(576)**
Nat'l Right to Life Political Action Committee, *Nat'l Right to Life Committee* **(576)**
Nat'l Rural Letter Carriers' Ass'n Political Action Committee, *Nat'l Rural Letter Carriers' Ass'n* **(577)**
Nat'l School Transporation Ass'n Non-Partisan Transporation Action Committee, *Nat'l School Transportation Ass'n* **(577)**
Nat'l Small Business United PAC, *Nat'l Small Business United* **(578)**
Nat'l Soc. of Professional Engineers Political Action Committee, *Nat'l Soc. of Professional Engineers* **(578)**
Nat'l Soc. of Public Accountants Political Action Committee, *Nat'l Soc. of Accountants* **(578)**
Nat'l Star Route Mail Contractors Political Action Committee, *Nat'l Star Route Mail Contractors Ass'n* **(578)**
Nat'l Structured Settlements Trade Ass'n Political Action Committee, *Nat'l Structured Settlements Trade Ass'n* **(579)**
Nat'l Tank Truck Carriers Political Action Committee, *Nat'l Tank Truck Carriers* **(579)**
Nat'l Taxpayers Union Campaign Fund, *Nat'l Taxpayers Union* **(579)**
Nat'l Telephone Cooperative Ass'n Telephone Education Committee Organization, *Nat'l Telephone Cooperative Ass'n* **(579)**
Nat'l Tooling and Machining Ass'n Committee for a Strong Economy, *Nat'l Tooling and Machining Ass'n* **(579)**
Nat'l Treasury Employees Union Political Action Committee (TEPAC), *Nat'l Treasury Employees Union* **(580)**
Nat'l Truck Equipment Ass'n PAC (TREQPAC), *Nat'l Truck Equipment Ass'n* **(580)**
Nat'l Turkey Federation Political Action Committee, *Nat'l Turkey Federation* **(580)**
Nat'l Utility Contractors Ass'n Legislative Information and Action Committee, *Nat'l Utility Contractors Ass'n (NUCA)* **(580)**
Nat'l Venture Capital Ass'n Political Action Committee, *Nat'l Venture Capital Ass'n* **(580)**
Nat'l Women's Political Caucus Campaign Support Committee, *Nat'l Women's Political Caucus* **(581)**
NATAPAC, *Nat'l Air Transportation Ass'n* **(536)**
NATFARMPAC, *Nat'l Farmers Union (Farmers Educational & Co-operative Union of America)* **(563)**
National Maritime Union AFL-CIO Political & Legislative Organization On Watch, *AFL-CIO Maritime Committee* **(231)**
NATSO Political Action Committee, *NATSO, Inc.* **(582)**
NAVAPD PAC, *Booher & Associates* **(30)**
NCR Corp. Citizenship Fund, *NCR Corp.* **(583)**
New American Century PAC **(585)**
New Democrat Network **(585)**
New Republican Majority Fund **(586)**
New York Stock Exchange Political Action Committee, *New York Stock Exchange* **(588)**
Newport News Shipbuilding Political Action Committee (SHIPPAC), *Newport News Shipbuilding Inc.* **(588)**
NFDA-PAC, *Nat'l Funeral Directors Ass'n* **(565)**
NIEPAC, *Northeast Utilities* **(593)**
Nike, Inc. PAC, *Nike, Inc.* **(590)**
NL Industries PAC, *NL Industries* **(590)**
NMMA Political Action Committee, *Nat'l Marine Manufacturers Ass'n* **(570)**
NMPF PAC, *Nat'l Milk Producers Federation* **(571)**
Nortel Networks Political Action Committee, *Nortel Networks* **(591)**
Northwestern Mutual Life Insurance Co. Federal PAC, *Northwestern Mutual Life Insurance Co.* **(595)**
Novartis Employee Good Government Fund, *Novartis Corp.* **(596)**
Nuclear Energy Institute Federal Political Action Committee, *Nuclear Energy Institute* **(597)**
NUT PAC, *Peanut and Tree Nut Processors Ass'n* **(610)**
O & P PAC, *American Orthotic and Prosthetic Ass'n* **(269)**
O'Melveny and Myers LLP Political Action Committee, *O'Melveny and Myers LLP* **(147)**
Olsson, Frank and Weeda Freedom PAC, *Olsson, Frank and Weeda, P.C.* **(146)**
Olsson, Frank and Weeda, P.C. Fund for American Values PAC, *Olsson, Frank and Weeda, P.C.* **(146)**
OPHTHPAC, *American Academy of Ophthamology - Office of Federal Affairs* **(244)**
Opticians Committee for Political Education, *Opticians Ass'n of America* **(601)**
Oracle Corp. PAC, *Oracle Corp.* **(602)**
Orb PAC, *Orbital Sciences Corp.* **(602)**
Osteopathic Political Action Committee, *American Osteopathic Ass'n* **(269)**
Outdoor Advertising PAC, *Outdoor Advertising Ass'n of America* **(604)**
Outpatient Ophthalmic Surgery Soc. Political Action Comittee (OOSS PAC), *Outpatient Ophthalmic Surgery Soc.* **(604)**
Owner-Operator Independent Drivers Ass'n Political Action Committee, *Owner-Operator Independent Drivers Ass'n, Inc.* **(605)**
OXYPAC, *Occidental Internat'l Corporation* **(598)**
PAC of the American Short Line and Regional Railroad Ass'n (ASLRRAA-PAC), *American Short Line and Regional Railroad Ass'n* **(274)**
PACAmerica Inc. **(605)**
Painting and Decorating Contractors and America PAC, *Painting and Decorating Contractors of America* **(606)**
Parcel Shippers Ass'n Political Action Committee, *Parcel Shippers Ass'n* **(608)**
PARPAC, *Parsons Corp.* **(608)**
Parry, Romani & DeConcini, Inc. PAC, *Parry, Romani, DeConcini & Symms* **(149)**
Parsons Brinckerhoff, Inc. PAC, *Parsons Brinckerhoff Inc.* **(608)**
Participation 2000 Inc. **(608)**
PathPAC, *College of American Pathologists* **(357)**
Paul Magliocchetti Associates PAC, *The PMA Group* **(156)**
Paul, Hastings, Janofsky and Walker Political Action Committee, *Paul, Hastings, Janofsky & Walker LLP* **(610)**
PCIA PAC, *Personal Communications Industry Ass'n (PCIA)* **(612)**
Peace Action PAC, *Peace Action* **(610)**
PEACE PAC, *Council for a Livable World* **(373)**
Pediatricians for Children Inc. **(610)**
PenneyPAC, *J. C. Penney Co., Inc.* **(611)**
People for the American Way Voters Alliance, *People for the American Way* **(612)**
PEPCO Political Action Committee, *Potomac Electric Power Co.* **(622)**
Perkins Coie Political Action Committee, *Perkins Coie LLP* **(154)**
Petroleum Marketers Ass'n of America Small Businessmen's Committee, *Petroleum Marketers Ass'n of America* **(613)**
Pfizer PAC, *Pfizer, Inc.* **(613)**
Pharmaceutical Research and Manufacturers of America Better Government Committee, *Pharmaceutical Research and Manufacturers of America* **(614)**
Phelps Dodge Employees Fund for Good Government, *Phelps Dodge Corp.* **(615)**
Philips Electronics North America Corp. Political Action Committee, *Philips Electronics North America Corp.* **(616)**
Physician Insurers PAC, *Physician Insurers Ass'n of America* **(616)**
Physicians for Women's Health PAC, *American College of Obstetricians and Gynecologists* **(254)**
Pinnacle West PAC, *Pinnacle West Capital Corp.* **(617)**
Planned Parenthood Action Fund Inc. PAC, *Planned Parenthood Federation of America* **(618)**
Plasterers' and Cement Masons' Action Committee, *Operative Plasterers' and Cement Masons' Internat'l Ass'n of the U.S. and Canada* **(601)**
Podiatry Political Action Committee, *American Podiatric Medical Ass'n* **(270)**
Policy Group **(620)**
Politcal Action Coors Employees (PACE), *Coors Brewing Company* **(371)**
Political Action Committee of the American Osteopathic Healthcare Ass'n, *American Osteopathic Healthcare Ass'n* **(269)**
Political Action Committee of the Dun & Bradstreet Corporation, *Dun & Bradstreet* **(393)**
Political Education Fund of the Building and Construction Trade Department (AFL-CIO), *AFL-CIO - Building and Construction Trades Department* **(231)**
Polyisocyanurate Insulation Manufacturers Ass'n PAC, *Polyisocyanurate Insulation Manufacturers Ass'n* **(620)**
Power PAC of the Edison Electric Institute, *Edison Electric Institute* **(397)**
Powerline Communications PAC **(622)**
Powers Pyles Sutter & Verville P.C. PAC, *Powers Pyles Sutter & Verville, PC* **(161)**
PPL People for Good Government, *PPL* **(622)**

Preston Gates Ellis & Rouvelas Meeds LLP PAC, *Preston Gates Ellis & Rouvelas Meeds LLP* **(623)**
PriceWaterhouseCoopers Partners' Political Action Committee, *PriceWaterhouseCoopers* **(624)**
Principal Financial Group PRINPAC, *Principal Financial Group* **(624)**
Printing Industries of America Political Action Committee (PrintPAC), *Printing Industries of America* **(624)**
Pro-Ad PAC, *Ass'n of Nat'l Advertisers* **(297)**
Professional Airways Systems Specialists - PASS PAC, *Professional Airways Systems Specialists (AFL-CIO)* **(625)**
Professional Beauty Federation PAC **(625)**
Professional Insurance Agents' Political Action Committee, *Nat'l Ass'n of Professional Insurance Agents* **(547)**
Professional Services Council PAC, *Professional Services Council* **(626)**
Professionals In Advertising PAC, *American Ass'n of Advertising Agencies* **(246)**
PropanePAC, *Nat'l Propane Gas Ass'n* **(574)**
Public Employees Organized to Promote Legislative Equality (PEOPLE), *American Federation of State, County and Municipal Employees* **(258)**
Public Ownership of Electric Resources Political Action Committee, *American Public Power Ass'n* **(272)**
Public Policy Committee, *American Astronautical Soc.* **(250)**
Quest Diagnostics Inc. Political Action Committee (Quest PAC), *Quest Diagnostics Inc.* **(631)**
R. Duffy Wall and Associates Inc. Political Action Committee, *R. Duffy Wall and Associates* **(631)**
RADPAC, *American College of Radiology* **(254)**
Ralston Purina Co. Committee for Good Government (RP-PAC), *Ralston Purina Co.* **(632)**
Raytheon PAC, *Raytheon Co.* **(633)**
Real Estate Roundtable Political Action Committee, The (REALPAC), *Real Estate Roundtable* **(634)**
Recording Arts Political Action Committee, *Recording Industry Ass'n of America* **(634)**
RECRA Fund, *RECRA* **(634)**
Reebok Internat'l Ltd. PAC, *Reebok Internat'l* **(635)**
Reed Smith PAC, *Reed, Smith, LLP* **(167)**
Regional Airline Ass'n Political Action Committee, *Regional Airline Ass'n* **(635)**
Reinsurance Association of America Political Action Committee, *Reinsurance Ass'n of America* **(636)**
Renal Leadership Council Political Action Committee (RLC PAC)., *Renal Leadership Council* **(636)**
RENEW (Republican Network to Elect Women) **(636)**
REPAC Integrated Waste Services Ass'n, *Integrated Waste Services Ass'n* **(465)**
Republican Leadership Council **(637)**
Republicans for Choice **(638)**
Responsible Citizen's Political League, *Transportation-Communications Internat'l Union* **(691)**
Robins Kaplan PAC, *Robins, Kaplan, Miller & Ciresi L.L.P.* **(170)**
Rockwell Internat'l Corp. Good Government Committee, *Rockwell Collins* **(641)**
Rolls-Royce North America PAC, *Rolls-Royce North America Inc.* **(642)**
ROOF PAC, *Nat'l Roofing Contractors Ass'n* **(576)**
Ryder Employees Political Action Committee, *Ryder System, Inc.* **(644)**
S-PAC **(644)**
Sabre PAC, *Sabre Inc.* **(644)**
Safari Club Internat'l Political Action Committee, *Safari Club Internat'l* **(645)**
Sallie Mae, Inc. PAC, *Sallie Mae, Inc.* **(646)**
Saltchuk Resources, *Saltchuk Resources, Inc.* **(646)**
Science Leadership PAC **(652)**
Seafarers Political Activity Donation (SPAD), *Seafarers Internat'l Union of North America* **(653)**
Searchlight Victory Fund **(653)**
Securities Industry Ass'n Political Action Committee, *Securities Industry Ass'n* **(654)**
Self-Insurance Institute of America, Inc. PAC, *Self-Insurance Institute of America, Inc.* **(655)**
Senior Housing PAC, *American Seniors Housing Ass'n* **(273)**
Senior Power Campaign Committee, *The 60/Plus Ass'n, Inc.* **(224)**
Service Employees Internat'l Union COPE Political Action Committee, *Service Employees Internat'l Union* **(656)**
Service Station Dealers of America Political Action Committee, *Service Station Dealers of America and Allied Trades* **(656)**
Shaw Pittman Political Action Committee, *Shaw Pittman* **(177)**
Sheet Metal and Air Conditioning Contractors' Nat'l Ass'n Political Action Committee (SMAC PAC), *Sheet Metal and Air Conditioning Contractors' Nat'l Ass'n* **(657)**
Sheet Metal Workers' Internat'l Ass'n Political Action League, *Sheet Metal Workers' Internat'l Ass'n* **(657)**
Sher & Blackwell PAC, *Sher & Blackwell* **(179)**
Siemens Corp. PAC, *Siemens Corp.* **(658)**
Sierra Club Political Committee, *Sierra Club* **(658)**
SIIA Political Action Committee, *Software & Information Industry Ass'n (SIIA)* **(664)**
Skadden Arps Political Action Committee, *Skadden, Arps, Slate, Meagher & Flom LLP* **(660)**
Small Biz PAC, *U.S. Federation of Small Businesses, Inc.* **(696)**
Smith, Bucklin and Associates Political Action Committee, *Smith, Bucklin and Associates, Inc.* **(184)**
Smokeless Tobacco Council Political Action Committee, *Smokeless Tobacco Council* **(661)**
SnackPAC, *Snack Food Ass'n* **(662)**
Soc. of American Florists Political Action Committee, *Soc. of American Florists* **(663)**
Soc. of Cardiovascular and Interventional Radiology Political Action Committee, *Soc. of Cardiovascular and Interventional Radiology* **(663)**
Soc. of Independent Gasoline Marketers Political Action Committee, *Soc. of Independent Gasoline Marketers of America* **(663)**
Soc. of Nuclear Medicine PAC, *Soc. of Nuclear Medicine* **(663)**
Soc. of Thoracic Surgeons Political Action Committee, *Soc. of Thoracic Surgeons* **(664)**
Society of the Plastics Industry PAC (PlasticPAC), *Soc. of the Plastics Industry* **(664)**
Sodexho Marriott Services Inc. PAC, *Sodexho Marriott Services, Inc.* **(664)**
Soft Drink PAC, *Nat'l Soft Drink Ass'n* **(578)**
Solutia Citizenship Fund, *Solutia Inc.* **(665)**
Southwest Peanut PAC **(668)**
StaffingPAC, *American Staffing Ass'n* **(278)**
State Employee Rights Campaign, *Nat'l Right to Work Committee* **(576)**
Steel Service Center Institute PAC, *Steel Service Center Institute* **(674)**
SteelPAC, *American Iron and Steel Institute* **(265)**
Stone and Webster Inc. Political Action Committee, *Stone and Webster Engineering Corp.* **(675)**
Storage Technology Corp. Political Action Committee, *Storage Technology Corp.* **(675)**
Sunkist Federal PAC, *Sunkist Growers, Inc.* **(677)**
Surety PAC, *Nat'l Ass'n of Surety Bond Producers* **(550)**
Swidler & Berlin Political Action Committee, *Swidler Berlin Shereff Friedman, LLP* **(678)**
SwimWithTheSharks.com **(678)**
Take Back the House **(680)**
Team Xerox PAC, *Xerox Corp.* **(732)**
Television and Radio Political Action Committee (TARPAC), *Nat'l Ass'n of Broadcasters* **(539)**
TEMPO, *American Federation of Musicians of the United States and Canada* **(258)**
Tex-USA Fund **(684)**
Texas Freedom Fund **(684)**
Textile Machinery Good Government Committee, *American Textile Machinery Ass'n* **(279)**
The Accord Political Action Committee, *The Accord Group* **(5)**
The Freedom Project **(425)**
The HIL PAC, *Title I Home Improvement Lenders Ass'n* **(687)**
The Nat'l PAC **(573)**
The Wexler Group Political Action Committee, *The Wexler Group* **(211)**
Thelen Reid & Priest L.L.P. Political Action Committee, *Thelen Reid & Priest LLP* **(685)**
Thiokol. PAC, *Thiokol Propulsion* **(686)**
TIAPAC, *Transportation Intermediaries Ass'n* **(690)**
Time Warner Inc. PAC, *AOL Time Warner* **(285)**
Title Industry Political Action Committee, *American Land Title Ass'n* **(265)**
Trans World Airlines PAC, *Trans World Airlines, Inc.* **(689)**
Travelocity.com PAC, *Travelocity.com* **(691)**
TREA Senior Citizens League PAC (TSCL PAC), *TREA Senior Citizens League (TSCL)* **(691)**
Truck PAC, *American Trucking Ass'ns* **(279)**
TRW Good Government Fund, *TRW Inc.* **(693)**
U.S. Apple Ass'n PAC, *U.S. Apple Ass'n* **(695)**
U.S. Immigrant Investor Ass'n **(696)**
UAPAC, *United Airlines* **(700)**
ULLIPAC, *The Union Labor Life Insurance Co.* **(699)**
Union of Needletrades, Industrial, and Textile Employees PAC, *Union of Needletrades, Industrial, and Textile Employees (UNITE)* **(699)**
Union Oil (UNOCAL) Political Awareness Fund, *UNOCAL Corp.* **(708)**
Union Pacific Fund for Effective Government, *Union Pacific* **(699)**
Unisys Corp. Employess PAC, *Unisys Corp.* **(700)**
United Ass'n Political Education Committee, *United Ass'n of Journeymen and Apprentices of the Plumbing and Pipe Fitting Industry of the U.S. and Canada* **(700)**
United Automobile Workers PAC, *United Automobile, Aerospace and Agricultural Implement Workers of America (UAW)* **(700)**
United Defense Employees PAC, *United Defense, L.P.* **(701)**
United Health PAC, *United Health Group* **(701)**
United Pilots Political Action Committee **(702)**
United States Telephone Political Action Committee, *United States Telecom Ass'n* **(704)**
United Steelworkers of America PAC, *United Steelworkers of America* **(704)**
United Technologies Corp. PAC, *United Technologies Corp.* **(704)**
United Transportation Union PAC, *United Transportation Union* **(705)**
US Airways Political Action Committee, *US Airways* **(709)**
USA Rice Federation PAC, *USA Rice Federation* **(709)**
USAA Group PAC, *USAA - United Services Automobile Ass'n* **(710)**
USEC Inc. PAC, *USEC, Inc.* **(710)**
UST Executives Administrators and Managers Political Action Committee (USTeamPAC), *UST Public Affairs, Inc.* **(710)**
USX Corporation Political Action Committee, *USX Corp.* **(710)**
Utility Workers of America Political Contributions Committee, *Utility Workers Union of America* **(711)**
Van Ness Feldman, P.C. Political Action Committee, *Van Ness Feldman, P.C.* **(199)**
Velazquez Victory Fund-Federal **(712)**
Veridian Inc. Employees Political Action Committee (Veridian-PAC), *Veridian Corp.* **(712)**
Verizon Federal PAC, *Verizon Washington, DC, Inc.* **(713)**
Verizon Political Action Committee, *Verizon Communications* **(713)**
Verner, Liipfert, Bernhard, McPherson and Hand PAC, *Verner, Liipfert, Bernhard, McPherson and Hand, Chartered* **(713)**
VFW-Political Action Committee, Inc., *Veterans of Foreign Wars of the U.S.* **(714)**
Viacom Political Action Committee, *Viacom Inc.* **(714)**
Victims Rights PAC **(715)**

Legislative Area Index

The firms and clients listed in the first two sections of this directory are sorted here according to the specific legislative issues on which they lobby. Firms representing the interests of one or more client on a given issue appear in bold type. Clients who either represent their own interests on an issue or retain a firm to represent them on that issue appear in regular type. It should be noted that information on a firm's or client's legislative interests was not always available to Columbia Books. The absence of a firm or client name from this index is in no way meant to imply that they are inactive in these areas.

Accounting (ACC)

Alpine Group, Inc. ***(11)***
American Resort Development Ass'n ***(272)***
American Teleservices Ass'n ***(279)***
Arthur Andersen LLP ***(289)***
Ass'n of Government Accountants ***(296)***
Ass'n of Publicly Traded Companies ***(298)***
H & R Block, Inc. ***(315)***
Deloitte & Touche LLP ***(384)***
Elan Pharmaceutical Research Corp. ***(399)***
JBA Consulting, Inc. ***(482)***
Management Options, Inc. ***(123)***
Manufacturers Alliance/MAPI Inc. ***(509)***
Mayer, Brown & Platt ***(126)***
Nat'l Ass'n of Healthcare Consultants ***(543)***
Nat'l Ass'n of Negro Business & Professional Women's Clubs, Inc. ***(546)***
Nat'l Venture Capital Ass'n ***(580)***
O'Connor & Hannan, L.L.P. ***(144)***
Professional Services Council ***(626)***
Smith Dawson & Andrews, Inc. ***(661)***
The Solomon Group, LLC ***(185)***
The Velasquez Group ***(201)***

Advertising (ADV)

Advertising Tax Coalition ***(229)***
Sally L. Albright ***(10)***
Allied Domecq ***(241)***
American Advertising Federation ***(244)***
American Ass'n of Advertising Agencies ***(246)***
American Forest & Paper Ass'n ***(259)***
American Teleservices Ass'n ***(279)***
Anheuser-Busch Cos., Inc. ***(284)***
Ass'n of Nat'l Advertisers ***(297)***
Bennett Turner & Coleman, LLP ***(25)***
Bergner Bockorny Castagnetti and Hawkins ***(26)***
Bristol-Myers Squibb Co. ***(320)***
Brown-Forman Corp. ***(322)***
Campbell Crane & Associates ***(36)***
Canfield, Smith and Martin ***(36)***
Cell Tech ***(334)***
Colling Swift & Hynes ***(49)***
Colombian Coffee Federation ***(358)***
Consumer Federation of America ***(369)***
Consumer Healthcare Products Ass'n ***(369)***
Law Offices of Kevin G. Curtin ***(56)***
Davidson & Company, Inc. ***(57)***
Direct Marketing Ass'n, Inc. ***(388)***
Distilled Spirits Council of the United States, Inc. ***(389)***
The Duberstein Group, Inc. ***(65)***
Earle Palmer Brown Public Relations ***(70)***
eBay Inc. ***(395)***
Elan Pharmaceutical Research Corp. ***(399)***
Electronic Retailing Ass'n ***(401)***
FoxKiser ***(79)***
Gallery Watch ***(428)***
Garden State Paper Co., Inc. ***(429)***
General Motors Corp. ***(432)***
Griffin, Johnson, Dover & Stewart ***(87)***
Grocery Manufacturers of America ***(440)***
Hecht, Spencer & Associates ***(93)***
Holland & Knight LLP ***(98)***
R. J. Hudson Associates ***(101)***
Inter-Cal Corp. ***(466)***
Internat'l Sign Ass'n ***(474)***
Internet Advertising Bureau ***(476)***
Janus-Merritt Strategies, L.L.C. ***(104)***
LaRocco & Associates ***(116)***
Magazine Publishers of America ***(507)***
Management Options, Inc. ***(123)***
Mattox Woolfolk, LLC ***(126)***
McDonald's Corp. ***(514)***
McGraw-Hill Cos., The ***(514)***
Merck & Co. ***(518)***
Molecular BioSystems, Inc. ***(527)***
Nat'l Ass'n of Broadcasters ***(539)***
Nat'l Ass'n of Letter Carriers of the United States of America ***(545)***
Nat'l Ass'n of Negro Business & Professional Women's Clubs, Inc. ***(546)***
Nat'l Beer Wholesalers Ass'n ***(552)***
Nat'l Center for Tobacco-Free Kids ***(555)***
Nat'l Consumers League ***(558)***
Nat'l Environmental Development Ass'ns State & Federal Environmental Responsibility Project ***(563)***
Nat'l Field Selling Ass'n ***(564)***
Nat'l Licensed Beverage Ass'n ***(570)***
Nat'l Newspaper Ass'n ***(572)***
Nat'l Newspaper Publishers Ass'n ***(572)***
Netivation.com ***(584)***
The Newark Group ***(588)***
News Corporation Ltd. ***(589)***
Newspaper Ass'n of America ***(589)***
Northwest Airlines, Inc. ***(595)***
Nu Skin Internat'l Inc. ***(597)***
The OB-C Group, LLC ***(143)***
Outdoor Advertising Ass'n of America ***(604)***
Paper Recycling Coalition ***(607)***
Parry, Romani, DeConcini & Symms ***(149)***
Patton Boggs, LLP ***(150)***
Patton Boggs, LLP ***(609)***
Philip Morris Management Corp. ***(615)***
Point of Purchase Advertising Institute ***(619)***
Preston Gates Ellis & Rouvelas Meeds LLP ***(162)***
Rexall Sundown ***(639)***
Rock-Tenn Co. ***(641)***
Slim Fast Foods Co. ***(661)***
SmithKline Beecham Consumer Healthcare, LLP ***(661)***
Smokeless Tobacco Council ***(661)***
Smurfit Stone Container Corp. ***(662)***
SOL Source Technologies, Inc. ***(665)***
Strategic Choices, Inc. ***(189)***
Telephone Operators Caucus ***(683)***
Timmons and Co., Inc. ***(195)***
Tribune Co. ***(692)***
UDV North America, Inc. ***(698)***
UDV/Heublein, Inc. ***(698)***
Van Scoyoc Associates, Inc. ***(200)***
Venable ***(201)***
Vivendi Universal ***(717)***
Voices, Inc. ***(717)***
White Pigeon Paper Co. ***(726)***
Wiley, Rein & Fielding ***(214)***
Wine and Spirits Wholesalers of America ***(728)***
Yellow Pages Publishers Ass'n ***(733)***

Aerospace (AER)

AAAE-ACI ***(224)***
ACS Defense, Inc. ***(227)***
Advantage Associates, Inc. ***(6)***
Aeronautical Repair Station Ass'n ***(230)***
Aerospace Industries Ass'n of Canada ***(230)***
Air Force Ass'n ***(233)***
Air Transport Ass'n of America ***(234)***
Airbus Industrie of North America, Inc. ***(234)***

Akin, Gump, Strauss, Hauer & Feld, L.L.P. *(8)*
Alaska Aerospace ***(236)***
Alenia Aerospazig ***(238)***
Alenia Marconi Systems ***(238)***
Alliant Techsystems, Inc. ***(241)***
American Astronautical Soc. ***(250)***
American Geophysical Union ***(261)***
American Institute of Aeronautics and Astronautics ***(264)***
American Museum of Natural History ***(268)***
American Psychological Ass'n ***(271)***
American Teleservices Ass'n ***(279)***
Amherst Systems Inc. ***(283)***
ArianeSpace, Inc. ***(288)***
Arizona State University ***(288)***
Wayne Arny & Assoc. *(16)*
James Nicholas Ashmore & Associates *(18)*
Assurance Technology Corp. ***(301)***
AstroVision Inc. ***(301)***
Autometric Inc. ***(303)***
Balch & Bingham LLP *(21)*
Ball Aerospace & Technology Corp. ***(306)***
Balzano Associates *(22)*
Barbour Griffith & Rogers, Inc. *(22)*
Battelle Memorial Institute ***(309)***
Birch, Horton, Bittner & Cherot *(28)*
BKSH & Associates *(28)*
The Boeing Co. ***(316)***
Boeing Defense and Space Group ***(317)***
British Ministry of Defence ***(321)***
Burdeshaw Associates, Ltd. *(34)*
Burns and Roe Enterprises, Inc. ***(324)***
CANAMCO (The Canadian-American Company) *(36)*
The Carmen Group *(40)*
The Carter Group *(41)*
Cassidy & Associates, Inc. *(42)*
Clark & Weinstock, Inc. *(47)*
Coleman Research Corp. ***(357)***
Commonwealth Consulting Corp. ***(362)***
Compass Internat'l Inc. ***(363)***
Computer Systems Technologies, Inc. ***(364)***
Congressional Economic Leadership Institute ***(366)***
Cottone and Huggins Group *(53)*
D3 Internat'l Energy, LLC ***(381)***
R. V. Davis and Associates *(58)*
Discovery Science Center ***(389)***
Dreamtime, Inc. ***(392)***
E-Prime Aerospace ***(394)***
EarthWatch, Inc. ***(395)***
Eastman Kodak Co. ***(395)***
ECC Internat'l Corp. ***(396)***
EER Systems ***(398)***
EFW Corp. ***(398)***
Embraer Aircraft Corp. ***(401)***
Engineered Arresting Systems Corp. ***(403)***
Ervin Technical Associates, Inc. (ETA) *(73)*
European Aeronautics, Defence and Space, Inc. ***(408)***
ExtrudeHone Corp. ***(409)***
Feith & Zell, P.C. *(75)*
Fleishman-Hillard, Inc *(77)*
Flight Landata, Inc. ***(419)***
Flight Safety Technologies, Inc. ***(419)***
FlightSafety Internat'l ***(419)***
R. G. Flippo and Associates, Inc. *(77)*
FLIR Systems, Inc. ***(419)***
Florida State University System ***(420)***
FMC Corp. ***(420)***
Franklin Institute ***(425)***
Douglas Ward Freitag *(79)*
The Gallagher Group, LLC *(80)*
Sara Garland (and Associates) *(81)*
GenCorp ***(431)***
General Atomics ***(431)***
General Dynamics Corp. ***(431)***
General Motors Corp. ***(432)***
Gibson, Dunn & Crutcher LLP *(82)*
Guam Internat'l Airport Authority ***(441)***
Hall, Green, Rupli, LLC *(90)*
Charles A. Hamilton Associates LLC *(91)*
Hamilton Sundstrand ***(444)***
Hickman Report ***(449)***
Hogan & Hartson L.L.P. *(96)*
Holland & Knight LLP *(98)*
Honeywell Internat'l, Inc. ***(452)***
Hooper Owen & Winburn *(99)*
Law Offices of Irene E. Howie *(100)*
Hughes Electronics Corp. ***(454)***
Huntsville Madison Chamber of Commerce ***(455)***
Hyundai Space & Aircraft Co., Ltd. ***(456)***
The ILEX Group *(102)*
Information Trust ***(462)***
Institute of Human and Machine Cognition ***(464)***
Insyte Corp. ***(465)***
Integrated Medical Systems ***(465)***
Inter-Associates, Inc. ***(466)***
Internat'l Brotherhood of Electrical Workers ***(469)***
Internat'l Cadmium Ass'n ***(469)***
Internat'l Federation of Professional and Technical Engineers ***(471)***
Internat'l Space Business Council ***(475)***
Israel Aircraft Industries, Ltd. ***(479)***
ITT Industries ***(480)***
ITT Industries Defense ***(480)***
Jacobs Engineering Group Inc. ***(481)***
Jamison and Sullivan, Inc. *(104)*
Jefferson Government Relations, L.L.C. *(106)*
Jefferson-Waterman Internat'l, LLC *(106)*
Jeppesen Sanderson, Inc. ***(482)***
Jorden Burt LLP *(109)*
Kaiser Aluminum & Chemical Corp. ***(485)***
Kaman Diversified Technologies Corp. ***(486)***
The Kemper Co. *(111)*
Joseph S. Kimmitt *(113)*
Kimmitt, Coates & McCarthy *(113)*
Law Office of Zel E. Lipsen *(120)*
Lockheed Martin Aeronautical Systems Co. ***(501)***
Lockheed Martin Corp. ***(501)***
Lockheed Martin Venture Star ***(502)***
Loral Space and Communications, Ltd. ***(503)***
Lovelace Respiratory Research Institute ***(504)***
Lucas Aerospace ***(505)***
LunaCorp, Inc. *(122)*
Madison Government Affairs *(123)*
Management Options, Inc. *(123)*
Marine Corps Reserve Officers Ass'n ***(510)***
Martin-Baker Aircraft Co., Ltd. ***(511)***
McClure, Gerard & Neuenschwander, Inc. *(127)*
Jack H. McDonald *(129)*
Mehl, Griffin & Bartek Ltd. *(132)*
Mercury Group *(132)*
Meredith Concept Group, Inc. *(132)*
Messier-Dowty Internat'l ***(519)***
Meyers & Associates *(133)*
Microcosm, Inc. ***(522)***
Denny Miller McBee Associates *(134)*
Mitsubishi Research Institute ***(526)***
Kay Allan Morrell, Attorney-at-Law *(137)*
Motorola Space and Systems Technology Group ***(531)***
MSE, Inc. ***(532)***
NASA Aeronautics Support Team ***(534)***
Nat'l Military Intelligence Ass'n ***(571)***
The Nat'l Space Grant Alliance ***(578)***
Nat'l Space Soc. ***(578)***
NAVCOM Systems, Inc. ***(583)***
NAVSYS Corp. ***(583)***
New York University ***(588)***
Noesis Inc. ***(590)***
The Nordam Group ***(591)***
Northrop Grumman Corp. ***(594)***
Nu Thena Systems, Inc. ***(597)***
OAO Corp. ***(598)***
Obadal and MacLeod, p.c. *(143)*
O'Connor & Hannan, L.L.P. *(144)*
Operations Security Professionals Soc. ***(601)***
Orbital Resources, LLC ***(602)***
Orbital Sciences Corp. ***(602)***
Orbital Sciences Corp., Fairchild Defense Division ***(602)***
Paradigm Research Group *(149)*
Peduzzi Associates, Ltd. *(154)*
Pegasus Capital Advisors, L.P. ***(611)***
The Peterson Group *(155)*
The Potomac Advocates *(159)*
Potomac Strategies Internat'l LLC *(160)*
Professional Services Council ***(626)***
Rafael U.S.A., Inc. ***(632)***
Ritter and Bourjaily, Inc. *(169)*
Rocket Development Co. ***(641)***
Rockwell Collins ***(641)***
Rolls-Royce North America Inc. ***(642)***
Rooney Group Internat'l, Inc. *(171)*
Rotary Rocket Co. ***(642)***
Lawrence Ryan Internat'l, Inc. *(173)*
Ryan, Phillips, Utrecht & MacKinnon *(173)*
SAFT America Inc. ***(645)***
Science Applications Internat'l Corp. (SAIC) ***(652)***
Shaw Pittman *(177)*
Short Brothers (USA), Inc. ***(658)***
Shriner-Midland Co. ***(658)***
Sierra Technologies Inc. ***(659)***
SKF USA, Inc. ***(660)***
Craig Snyder & Associates *(185)*
Sonetech Corp. ***(665)***
Space Access ***(668)***
Space Dynamics Laboratory ***(669)***
Space Imaging, Inc. ***(669)***
SPACEHAB, Inc. ***(669)***
Spaceport Florida Authority ***(669)***
Spectrum Astro, Inc. ***(670)***
Symms, Lehn & Associates, Inc. *(192)*
Systems Simulation Solutions Inc. ***(679)***
TCOM, L.P. ***(682)***
Teicher Consulting and Representation *(193)*
Tensiodyne Scientific Corp. ***(684)***
Thales ***(685)***
Thiokol Propulsion ***(686)***
Tighe, Patton, Tabackman & Babbin *(195)*
Transnat'l Development Consortium ***(690)***
TRW Inc. ***(693)***
Tulsa Airport Authority ***(694)***
United Automobile, Aerospace and Agricultural Implement Workers of America (UAW) ***(700)***
United Space Alliance ***(703)***
United Technologies Corp. ***(704)***
University of Medicine and Dentistry of New Jersey ***(706)***
University of Miami ***(706)***
University of North Dakota ***(707)***
University of Tulsa ***(708)***
University of Virginia ***(708)***
Utah State University ***(710)***
Van Scoyoc Associates, Inc. *(200)*
Vance Development Authority ***(712)***
Veridian Corp. ***(712)***
Verner, Liipfert, Bernhard, McPherson and Hand, Chartered ***(713)***
Verner, Liipfert, Bernhard, McPherson and Hand, Chartered *(202)*
ViaSat, Inc. ***(714)***
VSAdc.com *(205)*
The Washington Group *(208)*
WESCAM ***(723)***
The Wexler Group *(211)*
R. C. Whitner and Associates, Inc. *(213)*
Zenware Solutions, Inc. ***(734)***

Agriculture (AGR)

Abbott Laboratories ***(225)***
The Accord Group *(5)*
ACE INA ***(226)***
Ad Hoc Public Television Group ***(227)***
Adams and Reese LLP *(5)*
The Aegis Group, Ltd. *(7)*
AESOP Enterprises, Ltd. *(7)*
Ag Biotech Planning Committee ***(232)***
Ag/Bio Con ***(232)***
Agri Business Council of Arizona ***(232)***
Agri/Washington *(7)*
Agribusiness Council ***(232)***
Agricultural Biotechnology Forum ***(232)***
Agricultural Retailers Ass'n ***(232)***
Agricultural Transporters Conference ***(232)***
Akin, Gump, Strauss, Hauer & Feld, L.L.P. *(8)*
Alliance for Reasonable Regulation of Insecticides ***(240)***
Alliance of Marine Mammal Parks and Aquariums ***(240)***
Alliance of Western Milk Producers ***(241)***
Alpine Group, Inc. *(11)*
Amalgamated Sugar ***(242)***
American Ass'n for Laboratory Accreditation ***(246)***

American Ass'n of Crop Insurers *(247)*
American Ass'n of Grain Inspection and Weighing Agencies *(248)*
American Bakers Ass'n *(250)*
American Bankers Ass'n *(250)*
American Beekeeping Federation *(250)*
American Camping Ass'n *(251)*
American Commodity Distribution Ass'n *(254)*
American Corn Growers Ass'n *(255)*
American Cotton Shippers Ass'n *(255)*
American Crop Protection Ass'n *(256)*
American Dehydrated Onion and Garlic Ass'n *(256)*
American Dietetic Ass'n *(257)*
American Farm Bureau Federation *(258)*
American Farmland Trust *(258)*
American Federation of Teachers *(259)*
American Feed Industry Ass'n *(259)*
American Frozen Food Institute *(260)*
American Grain Inspection Institute *(261)*
American Great Lakes Ports *(261)*
American Home Products Corp. *(262)*
American Honey Producers Ass'n *(262)*
American Horse Council, Inc. *(263)*
American Jewish Committee *(265)*
American Motorcyclist Ass'n *(268)*
American Nursery and Landscape Ass'n *(268)*
American Peanut Product Manufacturers, Inc. *(269)*
American School Food Service Ass'n *(273)*
American Seed Trade Ass'n *(273)*
American Sheep Industry Ass'n *(273)*
American Soc. of Farm Managers and Rural Appraisers *(276)*
American Soybean Ass'n *(277)*
American Spice and Trade Ass'n *(277)*
American Sugar Alliance *(278)*
American Sugar Cane League of the U.S.A. *(278)*
American Sugarbeet Growers Ass'n *(278)*
American Vintners Ass'n *(280)*
American Wholesale Marketers Ass'n *(280)*
Americans for Equitable Climate Solutions *(281)*
Americans for Tax Reform *(282)*
Anderson Erickson Dairy Co. *(284)*
Andrews Associates, Inc. *(14)*
Anheuser-Busch Cos., Inc. *(284)*
Animal Industry Foundation *(284)*
APCO Worldwide *(14)*
Apple Processors Ass'n *(286)*
Arent Fox Kintner Plotkin & Kahn, PLLC *(14)*
Arnold & Porter *(16)*
James Nicholas Ashmore & Associates *(18)*
Ass'n of Consulting Foresters of America *(295)*
Ass'n of Minnesota Counties *(297)*
ATOFINA Chemicals, Inc. *(302)*
Auburn University *(302)*
AUGURA *(302)*
Australian Dairy Corp. *(303)*
Aventis CropScience *(304)*
Baker, Donelson, Bearman & Caldwell, P.C. *(21)*
Ball Janik, LLP *(22)*
Basic American, Inc. *(308)*
Bass Enterprises Production Co. *(308)*
Battelle Memorial Institute *(309)*
Bayer Corp. *(309)*
Bayer Corp. / Agriculture Division *(309)*
Baylor College of Medicine *(310)*
Bergner Bockorny Castagnetti and Hawkins *(26)*
Berman Enterprises *(27)*
Max N. Berry Law Offices *(27)*
Terry Bevels Consulting *(27)*
Biotechnology Industry Organization *(314)*
Black Hills Forest Resource Ass'n *(315)*
Blank Rome Comisky & McCauley, LLP *(29)*
Blue Diamond Growers *(315)*
Bracewell & Patterson, L.L.P. *(30)*
BrokerTek Global, L.L.C. *(321)*
Brooks Tropicals, Inc. *(322)*
Brown and Williamson Tobacco Corp. *(322)*
Bunge Corp. *(323)*
John G. "Toby" Burke *(34)*
Burlington Northern Santa Fe Railway *(324)*
C F Industries, Inc. *(325)*
C&M Internat'l, Ltd. *(35)*
Cadwalader, Wickersham & Taft *(35)*
CalCot *(326)*
California Asparagus Commission *(326)*
California Avocado Commission *(326)*
California Canning Peach Ass'n *(326)*
California Kiwi Fruit Commission *(327)*
California Pistachio Commission *(327)*
California Poultry Industry Federation *(327)*
California Prune Board *(327)*
California Strawberry Commission *(327)*
California Tomato Commission *(327)*
California Walnut Commission *(327)*
Canadian Wheat Board *(330)*
Capitol Associates, Inc. *(37)*
Capitol Counsel Group, L.L.C. *(38)*
Capitol Link, Inc. *(39)*
Capitolink, LLC *(39)*
CARE (Cooperative for Assistance and Relief Everywhere) *(331)*
Cargill, Inc. *(331)*
Carolina, Puerto Rico, City of *(332)*
CaseNewHolland Inc. *(333)*
Cashdollar-Jones & Co. *(41)*
Cassidy & Associates, Inc. *(42)*
CBI Sugar Group *(334)*
Center on Budget and Policy Priorities *(338)*
Central Soya Co. *(339)*
Centre National Interprofessionel de L'Economie Laitiere (French Dairy Ass'n) *(339)*
Century Communications, Inc. *(44)*
Chamber of Commerce of the U.S.A. *(340)*
Cheese Importers Ass'n of America *(341)*
Chemical Producers and Distributors Ass'n *(342)*
Chicago Board of Trade *(342)*
Chicago Mercantile Exchange *(343)*
The Child Care Consortium *(343)*
Child Nutrition Forum, c/o FRAC *(343)*
Chilean Exporters Ass'n *(344)*
Chlorine Chemistry Council *(345)*
Chocolate Manufacturers Ass'n of the U.S.A. *(345)*
Citizens for a Sound Economy *(348)*
Citizens Network for Foreign Affairs (CNFA) *(349)*
Clark & Weinstock, Inc. *(47)*
Clement Pappas & Co., Inc. *(350)*
Cliffstar Corp. *(351)*
CNA Financial Corp. *(351)*
CNA Insurance Cos. *(351)*
Coalition for Food Aid *(353)*
Coalition for Sugar Reform *(354)*
Coalition for the American Agricultural Producer (CAAP) *(354)*
CoBank, ACB *(356)*
The Coca-Cola Company *(356)*
The College Board *(357)*
Collier Shannon Scott, PLLC *(48)*
Columbia University *(359)*
Commerce Ventures *(360)*
Committee to Assure the Availability of Casein *(361)*
Community Development Venture Capital Ass'n *(362)*
ConAgra Foods, Inc. *(365)*
Consortium for Plant Biotechnology Research *(368)*
Consortium of Social Science Ass'ns *(368)*
Consumer Federation of America *(369)*
Consumers Union of the United States *(369)*
Coors Brewing Company *(371)*
Copeland, Lowery & Jacquez *(52)*
Corn Refiners Ass'n, Inc. *(372)*
Cotton Warehouse Ass'n of America *(373)*
Council for Agricultural Science and Technology *(374)*
Council of Northeast Farmer Cooperatives *(376)*
Council of State Governments *(376)*
Covington & Burling *(53)*
Crop Growers Insurance Co. *(378)*
Charles V. Cunningham & Assoc. *(56)*
Dairy Trade Advisory Council *(381)*
The Dairy Trade Coalition *(381)*
Dairy.com *(381)*
Davis & Harman LLP *(57)*
Dean Blakey & Moskowitz *(59)*
Deere & Co. *(383)*
DEIP (Dairy Export Incentive Program) Coalition *(384)*
Delta Wetlands Project *(385)*
Desert Grape Growers League *(386)*
Dickstein Shapiro Morin & Oshinsky LLP *(61)*
DNA Plant Technology Corp. *(390)*
Dole Food Co. *(390)*
Dow AgroSciences *(391)*
Downey McGrath Group, Inc. *(64)*
Ducks Unlimited Inc. *(392)*
Dunavant Enterprises *(393)*
DuPont *(393)*
The Dutko Group, Inc. *(68)*
Easter Seals *(395)*
Eastern Band of Cherokee Indians *(395)*
The Macon Edwards Co. *(71)*
Stanley J. Emerling *(71)*
EMI Associates, Ltd. *(71)*
EOP Group, Inc. *(72)*
Etka Consulting *(73)*
Eversole Associates *(74)*
The Fanning Corp. *(411)*
Farm Animal Reform Movement (FARM) *(411)*
Farm Credit Bank of Texas *(411)*
Farm Credit Council *(411)*
Farm Market iD *(412)*
Farmland Industries, Inc. *(412)*
Federal Agricultural Mortgage Corp. (Farmer Mac) *(412)*
Federation for American Immigration Reform (FAIR) *(414)*
Feld Entertainment Inc. *(415)*
The Fertilizer Institute *(415)*
Fierce and Isakowitz *(76)*
Fisher Consulting *(77)*
Flight Landata, Inc. *(419)*
Flo-Sun Sugar *(419)*
Florida Citrus Alliance *(419)*
Florida Crystals Corp. *(419)*
Florida Department of Citrus *(419)*
Florida Fruit and Vegetable Ass'n *(420)*
Florida Sugar Cane League, Inc. *(420)*
Florida Tomato Exchange *(420)*
FMC Corp. *(420)*
Foley & Lardner *(78)*
Food Distributors Internat'l (NAWGA-IFDA) *(421)*
Food Marketing Institute *(421)*
Food Research and Action Center *(422)*
FQPA Implementation Working Group *(424)*
Free Trade Lumber Council *(425)*
Fresh Produce Ass'n of the Americas *(426)*
John Freshman Associates, Inc. *(79)*
Garden Centers of America *(429)*
Gardena Alfalfa Growers Ass'n *(429)*
Sara Garland (and Associates) *(81)*
The Garrison Group *(81)*
Gay & Robinson, Inc. *(430)*
General Mills *(432)*
Georgia Commodity Commission for Peanuts *(434)*
Georgia Cotton Commission *(434)*
Golden Peanut Co. *(437)*
Gordley Associates *(84)*
Edwin C. Graves & Associates *(85)*
The GrayWell Group, Inc. *(86)*
Greenberg Traurig, LLP *(86)*
Griffin, Johnson, Dover & Stewart *(87)*
Guinea, Secretary General of the Presidency of the Republic of *(442)*
Haake and Associates *(89)*
Haley and Associates *(90)*
Hawaiian Commercial and Sugar Company *(445)*
Hershey Foods Corp. *(449)*
Hicks-Richardson Associates *(94)*
Higgins, McGovern & Smith, LLC *(94)*
Hogan & Hartson L.L.P. *(96)*
Hohenberg Brothers, Co. *(450)*
Holland & Knight LLP *(98)*
Horizon Organic Dairy, Inc. *(452)*
Horizon Organic Holding Co. *(452)*
Horticultural Research Institute *(452)*
Oliver James Horton *(100)*
Hudson Institute *(454)*
Hurt, Norton & Associates *(101)*
Illinois Department of Human Services *(457)*

IMC Global Inc. *(458)*
Independent Community Bankers of America *(459)*
Independent Insurance Agents of America, Inc. *(459)*
Infectious Diseases Soc. of America, Inc. *(461)*
Institute for Local Self-Reliance *(463)*
Institute of Food Technologists *(464)*
Inter-American Institute for Cooperation on Agriculture *(466)*
Internat'l Ass'n of Fish and Wildlife Agencies *(468)*
Internat'l Committee on Organization & Policy *(470)*
Internat'l Dairy Foods Ass'n *(470)*
Internat'l Frozen Food Ass'n *(472)*
Internat'l Laboratory Technology Corp. *(473)*
Internat'l Longshore and Warehouse Union *(473)*
Iowa Pork Producers Ass'n *(478)*
Iowa, Dept. of Natural Resources of State of *(478)*
Irrigation Ass'n *(479)*
Jamison and Sullivan, Inc. *(104)*
Jellinek, Schwartz & Connolly *(106)*
Jerome Foods *(483)*
Johns Hopkins Center for Civilian Biodefense Studies *(483)*
S.C. Johnson and Son, Inc. *(484)*
Johnston & Associates, LLC *(107)*
Jolly/Rissler, Inc. *(108)*
Kellogg Co. *(487)*
Kendall-Jackson Winery *(488)*
Kimberly Consulting, LLC *(113)*
King & Spalding *(113)*
Kogovsek & Associates *(114)*
Kraft Foods, Inc. *(492)*
Lee Lane *(116)*
Bob Lawrence & Associates *(117)*
Lee & Smith P.C. *(118)*
Leonard and Co. *(119)*
Lepon McCarthy White & Holzworth, PLLC *(119)*
Leprino Foods Co. *(498)*
Lesher & Russell, Inc. *(119)*
Eli Lilly and Co. *(499)*
The Livingston Group, LLC *(120)*
Lockridge Grindal & Nauen, P.L.L.P. *(121)*
Long, Aldridge & Norman, LLP *(121)*
Lorillard Tobacco Co. *(503)*
Louis Dreyfus Corporation *(504)*
Luman, Lange & Wheeler *(122)*
M & R Strategic Services *(122)*
M.B. Consultants, Inc. *(506)*
Madison County Commission *(507)*
Management Concepts, Inc. *(508)*
Manatt, Phelps & Phillips, LLP *(123)*
Marine Engineers Beneficial Ass'n (District No. 1 - PCD) *(510)*
Martin, Fisher & Associates, Inc. *(125)*
Maryland Dairy Industry Ass'n *(511)*
Masaoka & Associates, Inc. *(125)*
Mauritius Sugar Syndicate *(513)*
Mauritius, Chamber of Agriculture of *(513)*
Mayer, Brown & Platt *(126)*
McClure, Gerard & Neuenschwander, Inc. *(127)*
McDermott Internat'l, Inc./Babcock & Wilcox *(514)*
McDermott, Will and Emery *(128)*
McDonald's Corp. *(514)*
McGuiness Norris & Williams, LLP *(130)*
McGuireWoods L.L.P. *(130)*
McLeod, Watkinson & Miller *(131)*
McMahon and Associates *(131)*
Mead Johnson Nutritional Group *(515)*
Meat and Livestock Australia *(515)*
Meat New Zealand *(515)*
Methyl Bromide Working Group *(520)*
Meyers & Associates *(133)*
Michigan Biotechnology Institute *(522)*
Mississippi Chemical Corp. *(526)*
Mitsubishi Internat'l Corp. *(526)*
Monsanto Co. *(528)*
Kay Allan Morrell, Attorney-at-Law *(137)*
Moss McGee Bradley & Foley *(137)*
Murray, Scheer, Montgomery, Tapia & O'Donnell *(139)*
Nat'l Agricultural Aviation Ass'n *(535)*
Nat'l Ass'n for Agricultural Stewardship *(537)*
Nat'l Ass'n of Conservation Districts *(540)*
Nat'l Ass'n of Farmer Elected Committees (NAFEC) *(542)*
Nat'l Ass'n of Federal Veterinarians *(542)*
Nat'l Ass'n of Negro Business & Professional Women's Clubs, Inc. *(546)*
Nat'l Ass'n of State Departments of Agriculture *(549)*
Nat'l Ass'n of State Universities and Land-Grant Colleges *(550)*
Nat'l Ass'n of Wheat Growers *(551)*
Nat'l Barley Growers Ass'n *(552)*
Nat'l Cattleman's Beef Ass'n *(554)*
Nat'l Center for Appropriate Technology *(554)*
Nat'l Center for Genome Research *(554)*
Nat'l Chicken Council *(555)*
Nat'l Consumers League *(558)*
Nat'l Cooperative Business Ass'n *(559)*
Nat'l Corn Growers Ass'n *(559)*
Nat'l Council of Agricultural Employers *(560)*
Nat'l Council of Farmer Cooperatives *(560)*
Nat'l Education Ass'n of the U.S. *(562)*
Nat'l Endangered Species Act Reform Coalition *(563)*
Nat'l Farmers Organization *(563)*
Nat'l Farmers Union (Farmers Educational & Co-operative Union of America) *(563)*
Nat'l FFA Organization *(564)*
Nat'l Food Processors Ass'n *(564)*
Nat'l Frozen Pizza Institute *(565)*
Nat'l Grain and Feed Ass'n *(566)*
Nat'l Grain Sorgum Producers *(566)*
Nat'l Grain Trade Council *(566)*
Nat'l Grange *(566)*
Nat'l Grocers Ass'n *(566)*
Nat'l Legal Center for the Public Interest *(570)*
Nat'l Lumber and Building Material Dealers Ass'n *(570)*
Nat'l Meat Canners Ass'n *(570)*
Nat'l Milk Producers Federation *(571)*
Nat'l Nutritional Foods Ass'n *(572)*
Nat'l Oilseed Processors Ass'n *(572)*
Nat'l Peach Council *(573)*
Nat'l Peanut Buying Point Ass'n *(573)*
Nat'l Pork Producers Council *(574)*
Nat'l Potato Council *(574)*
Nat'l Produce Production Inc. *(574)*
Nat'l Restaurant Ass'n *(576)*
Nat'l Rural Telecom Ass'n *(577)*
Nat'l Rural Water Ass'n *(577)*
Nat'l Soft Drink Ass'n *(578)*
Nat'l Sunflower Ass'n *(579)*
Nat'l Taxpayers Union *(579)*
Nat'l Turfgrass Evaluation Program *(580)*
Nat'l Turkey Federation *(580)*
The Nature Conservancy *(582)*
Navajo Nation *(582)*
NCRI - Southeast/NCRI - Chesapeake *(583)*
New Mexico State University, Department of Agriculture *(586)*
New York Board of Trade *(586)*
New Zealand Dairy Board *(588)*
Nisei Farmers League *(590)*
North American Equipment Dealers Ass'n *(592)*
North American Grain Export Ass'n, Inc. *(592)*
North American Industrial Hemp Council, Inc. *(592)*
North American Meat Processors Ass'n *(592)*
North American Millers' Ass'n *(592)*
North Carolina Peanut Growers Ass'n *(593)*
North Carolina, Washington Office of the State of *(593)*
North Dakota State University *(593)*
North Dakota Wheat Commission *(593)*
North Dakota, Governor's Office of the State of *(593)*
Northeast-Midwest Institute *(594)*
Northland Cranberries, Inc. *(594)*
Northwest Horticultural Council *(595)*
Novartis Crop Protection *(596)*
Novartis Services, Inc. *(596)*
OBWEO *(598)*
Ocean Spray Cranberries *(598)*
O'Connor & Hannan, L.L.P. *(144)*
Olsson, Frank and Weeda, P.C. *(146)*
John F. O'Neal Law Offices *(147)*
Oneonta Trading Corp. *(601)*
Organic Trade Ass'n *(603)*
Pacquing Consulting Inc. *(148)*
Parry, Romani, DeConcini & Symms *(149)*
Patton Boggs, LLP *(150)*
Patton Boggs, LLP *(609)*
Pennington BioMedical Research Center *(611)*
Pfizer, Inc. *(613)*
Pheasants Forever *(615)*
Philip Morris Management Corp. *(615)*
Philipp Brothers Chemicals, Inc. *(616)*
The Pillsbury Co. *(617)*
Pioneer Hi-Bred Internat'l, Inc. *(618)*
Susan S. Platt Consulting *(156)*
The PMA Group *(156)*
Podesta/Mattoon *(158)*
Policy Development Group, Inc. *(620)*
Policy Directions, Inc. *(158)*
The Potomac Advocates *(621)*
The Potomac Research Group LLC *(160)*
Powell, Goldstein, Frazer & Murphy LLP *(160)*
Powers Pyles Sutter & Verville, PC *(161)*
Premium Standard Farms *(623)*
Preston Gates Ellis & Rouvelas Meeds LLP *(162)*
Public Lands Council *(629)*
Public Private Partnership *(164)*
Queensland Sugar, Ltd. *(631)*
Ranchers-Cattlemen Legal Action Fund *(633)*
Robert A. Rapoza Associates *(165)*
Pamela Ray-Strunk and Associates *(166)*
Red River Trade Council *(635)*
Robert L. Redding *(166)*
Redfern Resources *(166)*
Refined Sugars Inc. *(635)*
Regional Planning Commission *(635)*
Renewable Fuels Ass'n *(637)*
Renewable Natural Resources Foundation *(637)*
Resource Management Consultants, Inc. *(168)*
R. J. Reynolds Tobacco Co. *(639)*
Rice Belt Warehouses *(639)*
Rio Grande Valley Sugar Growers *(640)*
Robins, Kaplan, Miller & Ciresi L.L.P. *(170)*
Rodale Press *(641)*
Roquette America *(642)*
Rural Advancement Foundation Internat'l - USA *(643)*
Rural Community Insurance Co. *(643)*
Ryberg and Smith LLP *(174)*
Sagamore Associates, Inc. *(174)*
San Diego State University Foundation *(647)*
Schnader Harrison Segal & Lewis LLP *(176)*
Schramm, Williams & Associates, Inc. *(176)*
Schwan's Sales Enterprises *(652)*
Seaboard Corp. *(653)*
David Senter & Associates *(177)*
SePRO Corp. *(655)*
Daniel F. Shaw & Associates *(177)*
Shaw Pittman *(177)*
Shea & Gardner *(179)*
Sierra Club *(658)*
Bill Simpson & Associates *(181)*
Smith Dawson & Andrews, Inc. *(183)*
Smith Martin & Boyette *(184)*
Smith, Bucklin and Associates, Inc. *(184)*
Smithfield Foods Inc. *(661)*
Snake River Sugar Co. *(662)*
Soc. of American Florists *(663)*
The Solomon Group, LLC *(185)*
Southeast Dairy Farmer Ass'n *(667)*
Southern Ass'n of Forestry Economics *(667)*
Southern Illinois University *(668)*
Southern Ute Indian Tribe *(668)*
Southwest Peanut Growers *(668)*
Southwestern Water Conservation District *(668)*
Sparber and Associates *(186)*
Richard L. Spees, Inc. *(186)*
States Ratification Committee *(673)*
Stephens Law Offices *(188)*
Steptoe & Johnson LLP *(188)*
Stewart and Stewart *(189)*
Stine Seed Co. *(674)*
Strategic Horizons Advisors, L.L.C. *(189)*
Charlene A. Sturbitts *(190)*
Suffolk, New York, County of *(676)*

Suiza Foods Corp. *(676)*
Sun Diamond Growers, Inc. *(676)*
Sunkist Growers, Inc. *(677)*
Sunset Properties, Inc. *(677)*
SunSweet Growers, Inc. *(677)*
Swidler Berlin Shereff Friedman, LLP *(191)*
Symms, Lehn & Associates, Inc. *(192)*
Tanimura & Antle, Inc. *(680)*
Tarrant Regional Water District *(681)*
Tate and Lyle North American Sugars Inc. *(681)*
Taylor Packing Co., Inc. *(681)*
TECO Transport Corp. *(682)*
Texas A&M Research Foundation *(684)*
Thelen Reid & Priest LLP *(193)*
Tillamook County Creamery Ass'n *(687)*
Titan Scan *(687)*
Tobacco Quota Warehouse Alliance *(688)*
Turfgrass Producers Internat'l *(694)*
Tuttle, Taylor & Heron *(197)*
U.S. Apple Ass'n *(695)*
U.S. Canola Ass'n *(695)*
U.S. Citrus Science Council *(696)*
U.S. Mink Export Development Council *(696)*
Unilever United States, Inc. *(699)*
Union Hospital *(699)*
Union of Concerned Scientists *(699)*
United Automobile, Aerospace and Agricultural Implement Workers of America (UAW) *(700)*
United Egg Ass'n *(701)*
United Egg Producers *(701)*
United Food and Commercial Workers Internat'l Union *(701)*
United Fresh Fruit and Vegetable Ass'n *(701)*
United Gamefowl Breeders Ass'n, Inc. *(701)*
United Methodist Church General Board of Church and Society *(702)*
United States Beet Sugar Ass'n *(703)*
United States Business and Industry Council *(703)*
United States Cane Sugar Refiners' Ass'n *(703)*
United States Sugar Corp. *(704)*
University of California, Office of Federal Government Relations *(706)*
University of Florida Health Science Center *(706)*
University of North Carolina at Greensboro *(707)*
University of North Dakota *(707)*
University of Southwestern Louisiana *(707)*
University System of Maryland *(708)*
Upper Midwest Coalition *(708)*
Upper Midwest Dairy Coalition *(708)*
Upper Yampa Water Conservancy District *(708)*
USA Rice Federation *(709)*
UST Public Affairs, Inc. *(710)*
Utah State University *(710)*
Ute Mountain Ute Indian Tribe *(710)*
Valent U.S.A. Corp. *(711)*
Valley Fig Growers *(711)*
Valley Pride Pack *(711)*
Van Ness Feldman, P.C. *(199)*
Vantage Point Network, LLC *(712)*
Vickers and Vickers *(204)*
Vidalia Onion Business Council *(715)*
Virginia Peanut Growers Ass'n *(716)*
Virginia Wineries Ass'n *(716)*
Don Wallace Associates, Inc. *(206)*
Washington Citizens for World Trade *(719)*
Washington Resource Associates *(209)*
Water Systems Council *(721)*
Waves States Ratification Committee *(722)*
Carla L. West *(211)*
Westerly Group *(211)*
Western Ag Resources Inc. *(723)*
Western Alliance of Farmworker Advocates, Inc. (WAFA) *(724)*
Western Growers Ass'n *(724)*
Western Peanut Growers Ass'n *(724)*
Western Pistachio Ass'n *(724)*
Western Range Ass'n *(724)*
Wheat Export Trade Education Committee *(725)*
R. H. White Public Affairs Consulting *(213)*
Whitten & Diamond *(213)*
Wholesale Nursery Growers of America *(726)*
Wild Bird Feeding Institute *(726)*
Wiley, Rein & Fielding *(214)*
Williams & Jensen, P.C. *(215)*
Willkie Farr & Gallagher *(217)*
Winston & Strawn *(218)*
Women Officials in NACo *(729)*
World Resources Institute *(731)*
Zamorano *(734)*
Zeliff, Ireland, and Associates *(221)*
Zurich U.S. Specialties *(735)*

Alcohol and Drug Abuse (ALC)

Advocates for Highway and Auto Safety *(229)*
Alliance for Children and Families *(239)*
Allied Domecq *(241)*
American Ass'n for Geriatric Psychiatry *(245)*
American Ass'n for Marriage and Family Therapy *(246)*
American Ass'n of Motor Vehicle Administrators *(248)*
American Counseling Ass'n *(256)*
American Managed Behavioral Healthcare Ass'n *(266)*
American Museum of Natural History *(268)*
American Occupational Therapy Ass'n, Inc. *(269)*
American Psychological Ass'n *(271)*
American Psychological Soc. *(271)*
American Vintners Ass'n *(280)*
Americans United for Separation of Church and State *(282)*
Amity, Inc. *(283)*
Anheuser-Busch Cos., Inc. *(284)*
Arent Fox Kintner Plotkin & Kahn, PLLC *(14)*
Baltimore, Maryland, City of *(306)*
The Barton Co. *(24)*
Beer Institute *(310)*
Brinker Internat'l *(320)*
California, State of, Attorney General's Office *(328)*
Capitol Associates, Inc. *(37)*
Caron Foundation *(332)*
Center for Science in the Public Interest *(337)*
The Century Council *(339)*
Chamber of Commerce of the U.S.A. *(340)*
Chicago School Reform Board of Trustees *(343)*
Child Welfare League of America *(343)*
Church of Scientology Internat'l *(346)*
Coalition for Health Services Research *(354)*
Coalition for the Homeless *(354)*
College on Problems of Drug Dependence *(357)*
Community Anti-Drug Coalitions of America *(362)*
Consumer Federation of America *(369)*
Coors Brewing Company *(371)*
D.A.R.E. America *(381)*
Detroit Rescue Mission Ministries *(386)*
Direct Impact, LLC *(63)*
Distilled Spirits Council of the United States, Inc. *(389)*
Elan Pharmaceutical Research Corp. *(399)*
Evans & Black, Inc. *(73)*
Florida State University System *(420)*
Food Distributors Internat'l (NAWGA-IFDA) *(421)*
Betty Ford Center *(422)*
Gainesville, Florida, City of *(428)*
Gary, Indiana, Washington Office of the City of *(429)*
General Conference of Seventh-day Adventists *(431)*
Girls Incorporated *(435)*
Global USA, Inc. *(83)*
Goldberg & Associates, PLLC *(83)*
Greenberg Traurig, LLP *(86)*
Greener and Hook, LLC *(87)*
Griffin, Johnson, Dover & Stewart *(87)*
Guardian Angel Holdings, Inc. *(442)*
Hazelden Foundation *(445)*
Health Insurance Ass'n of America *(446)*
Hoffmann-La Roche Inc. *(450)*
R. J. Hudson Associates *(101)*
Illinois Department of Human Services *(457)*
Indiana, Office of the Governor of the State of *(460)*
Institute for a Drug-Free Workplace *(463)*
Internat'l Community Corrections Ass'n *(470)*
Internat'l Union of Police Ass'ns *(476)*
Jorden Burt LLP *(109)*
Kendall-Jackson Winery *(488)*
Kmart Corp. *(490)*
Kogovsek & Associates *(114)*
Lafayette Group, Inc. *(116)*
Legal Action Center of the City of New York, Inc. *(497)*
Light of Life Ministries *(499)*
Lindesmith Center - Drug Policy Foundation *(500)*
Littler Mendelson, P.C. *(120)*
The Livingston Group, LLC *(120)*
Lovelace Respiratory Research Institute *(504)*
Mercy Hospital of Des Moines, Iowa *(518)*
Miami Beach, Florida, City of *(521)*
Morgan, Lewis & Bockius LLP *(136)*
Mothers Against Drunk Driving (MADD) *(530)*
The MWW Group *(140)*
NAADAC, The Ass'n for Addiction Professionals *(534)*
Nat'l Alcohol Beverage Control Ass'n *(536)*
Nat'l Ass'n of Collection Sites *(540)*
Nat'l Ass'n of Negro Business & Professional Women's Clubs, Inc. *(546)*
Nat'l Ass'n of Nurse Practitioners in Women's Health *(546)*
Nat'l Ass'n of Protection and Advocacy Systems (NAPAS) *(547)*
Nat'l Beer Wholesalers Ass'n *(552)*
Nat'l Black Women's Health Project *(552)*
Nat'l Council for Community Behavioral Healthcare *(559)*
Nat'l Criminal Justice Ass'n *(561)*
Nat'l District Attorneys Ass'n *(562)*
Nat'l Grange *(566)*
Nat'l Hispanic Council on Aging *(567)*
Nat'l Licensed Beverage Ass'n *(570)*
Nat'l Organization for the Reform of Marijuana Laws *(572)*
Nat'l Right to Life Committee *(576)*
New York University *(588)*
Newark, New Jersey, City of *(588)*
North Carolina, Washington Office of the State of *(593)*
O'Connor & Hannan, L.L.P. *(144)*
Olsson, Frank and Weeda, P.C. *(146)*
Partnership for Recovery Coalition *(609)*
Patton Boggs, LLP *(150)*
Philip Morris Management Corp. *(615)*
Charles L. Pizer *(156)*
Susan S. Platt Consulting *(156)*
Police Executive Research Forum *(620)*
Policy Directions, Inc. *(158)*
The Procter & Gamble Company *(625)*
Psychemedics Corp. *(628)*
Public Citizen, Inc. *(628)*
Reckitt & Colman Pharmaceuticals Inc. *(634)*
Russ Reid Co. *(167)*
Research Soc. on Alcoholism *(638)*
Mary Katherine Shilton *(180)*
Signal Behavioral Health Network *(659)*
Sills Associates *(180)*
Smith Dawson & Andrews, Inc. *(183)*
Strat@Comm (Strategic Communications Counselors) *(189)*
Susan R. Thau *(193)*
Transportation Maritima Mexicana *(690)*
UDV North America, Inc. *(698)*
UDV/Heublein, Inc. *(698)*
United Methodist Church General Board of Church and Society *(702)*
University of Medicine and Dentistry of New Jersey *(706)*
University of Miami *(706)*
University of Tulsa *(708)*
University of Virginia *(708)*
Valley Hope Ass'n *(711)*
Van Scoyoc Associates, Inc. *(200)*
Verner, Liipfert, Bernhard, McPherson and Hand, Chartered *(202)*
Vinifera Wine Growers Ass'n *(715)*
Viohl and Associates, Inc. *(205)*
Virginia Wineries Ass'n *(716)*
VSAdc.com *(205)*
Washington Liaison Group, LLC *(209)*
Washington Policy Associates, Inc. *(209)*
Wheat & Associates, Inc. *(212)*
Wine and Spirits Wholesalers of America *(728)*

Wine Institute (728)
Women Officials in NACo (729)
YWCA of the USA (734)
Zuckerman Spaeder L.L.P. (221)

Animals (ANI)

Alaska Legislature (236)
Alliance of Marine Mammal Parks and Aquariums (240)
American Bird Conservancy (251)
American Feed Industry Ass'n (259)
American Home Products Corp. (262)
American Horse Council, Inc. (263)
American Humane Ass'n (263)
American Kennel Club (265)
American Museum of Natural History (268)
American Soc. for the Prevention of Cruelty to Animals National Legislative Office (275)
American Veterinary Medical Ass'n (280)
American Zoo and Aquarium Ass'n (281)
Americans for Medical Progress (282)
Anheuser-Busch Cos., Inc. (284)
Animal Health Institute (284)
Animal Industry Foundation (284)
APCO Worldwide (14)
Ass'n of American Medical Colleges (294)
Bergner Bockorny Castagnetti and Hawkins (26)
Birch, Horton, Bittner & Cherot (28)
Brookfield Zoo/Chicago Zoological Soc. (321)
Burger King Corp. (324)
Cargill, Inc. (331)
Center for Marine Conservation (337)
Copeland, Lowery & Jacquez (52)
Shawn Coulson (53)
Creme de la Creme, Inc. (378)
The Duberstein Group, Inc. (65)
Ducks Unlimited Inc. (392)
Earthjustice Legal Defense Fund (394)
Elanco Animal Health (399)
Epstein Becker & Green, P.C. (72)
Exxon Mobil Corp. (409)
Farm Animal Reform Movement (FARM) (411)
Farmland Industries, Inc. (412)
Feld Entertainment Inc. (415)
Florida State University System (420)
John Freshman Associates, Inc. (79)
The Fund for Animals (427)
Humane Soc. of the United States (455)
IMC Global Inc. (458)
Intermountain Forest Industry Ass'n (467)
Internat'l Ass'n of Fish and Wildlife Agencies (468)
Internat'l Fund for Animal Welfare (472)
Jorden Burt LLP (109)
Lee & Smith P.C. (118)
Lovelace Respiratory Research Institute (504)
Madison Government Affairs (123)
Marine Mammal Coalition (510)
Ron C. Marlenee (125)
McClure, Gerard & Neuenschwander, Inc. (127)
McGuiness & Holch (130)
McGuiness Norris & Williams, LLP (130)
John Melcher (132)
Metcalf Federal Relations (132)
Meyers & Associates (133)
Minor Use, Minor Species Coalition (525)
Mirage Resorts, Inc. (525)
Kay Allan Morrell, Attorney-at-Law (137)
Museum Campus Chicago (533)
Nat'l Anti-Vivisection Soc. (537)
Nat'l Ass'n for Biomedical Research (537)
Nat'l Ass'n of Manufacturers (545)
Nat'l Ass'n of State Departments of Agriculture (549)
Nat'l Audubon Soc. (552)
Nat'l Endangered Species Act Reform Coalition (563)
Nat'l Grange (566)
Nat'l Horse Show Commission (567)
Nat'l Marine Life Center (570)
Nat'l Milk Producers Federation (571)
Nat'l Pork Producers Council (574)
Nat'l Turkey Federation (580)
The Nature Conservancy (582)
New York University (588)
North Dakota State University (593)
Novartis Corp. (596)
Ocean Futures Soc., Inc. (598)
O'Connor & Hannan, L.L.P. (144)
People for the Ethical Treatment of Animals (612)
Performing Animal Welfare Soc. (612)
Perkins Coie LLP (154)
Pet Industry Joint Advisory Council (613)
Pfizer, Inc. (613)
Pharmacia Corp. (615)
Philadelphia Zoo (615)
Policy Directions, Inc. (158)
Riverside, California, City of (640)
Safari Club Internat'l (645)
Sher & Blackwell (179)
Soc. for Animal Protective Legislation (662)
Soc. of Toxicology (664)
The Solomon Group, LLC (185)
United Methodist Church General Board of Church and Society (702)
University of Medicine and Dentistry of New Jersey (706)
University of Miami (706)
University of Tulsa (708)
University of Virginia (708)
Utah State University (710)
Virginia Living Museum (716)
Wildlife Legislative Fund of America (727)
Williams & Jensen, P.C. (215)
World Wildlife Fund (731)

Apparel/Clothing Industry/Textiles (APP)

African Coalition for Trade, Inc. (232)
American Apparel & Footwear Ass'n (245)
American Free Trade Ass'n (260)
American Sheep Industry Ass'n (273)
American Sugar Alliance (278)
American Teleservices Ass'n (279)
American Textile Co. (279)
Arnold & Porter (16)
Ass'n of Maquiladores (296)
The Atlantic Group, Public Affairs, Inc. (18)
Central American Bank of Economic Integration (338)
Collier Shannon Scott, PLLC (48)
Consumer Federation of America (369)
The Duberstein Group, Inc. (65)
F&T Network, Inc. (74)
Fieldcrest Cannon Inc. (416)
Flack Associates (77)
Fontheim Partners, PC (78)
Gildan Activewear (435)
Grupo "J" S.A. (441)
Guilford Mills, Inc. (442)
Haake and Associates (89)
Hale and Dorr LLP (89)
Hecht, Spencer & Associates (93)
Hogan & Hartson L.L.P. (96)
Holland & Knight LLP (98)
The Hosiery Ass'n (452)
Industrial Fabrics Ass'n Internat'l (461)
Internat'l Mass Retailers Ass'n (473)
Intradeco (477)
JBC Internat'l (105)
Jewish Federation of Metropolitan Chicago (483)
Johnston & Associates, LLC (107)
KOSA (491)
The Limited Inc. (499)
Malden Mills Industries, Inc. (508)
Management Options, Inc. (123)
MARC Associates, Inc. (124)
Massachusetts Maritime Academy (512)
Meyers & Associates (133)
Military Footwear Coalition (524)
Military Glove Coalition (524)
Milliken and Co. (524)
Nat'l Consumers League (558)
Nat'l Retail Federation (576)
Neiman Marcus Group (583)
Northern Textile Ass'n (594)
O'Connor & Hannan, L.L.P. (144)
Patton Boggs, LLP (150)
J. C. Penney Co., Inc. (611)
Sandler, Travis & Rosenberg, P.A. (175)
Schmeltzer, Aptaker & Shepard, P.C. (176)
Science Applications Internat'l Corp. (SAIC) (652)
Secondary Materials and Recycled Textiles Ass'n (654)
Skipps Cutting (660)
Spiegel Inc. (670)
Sporting Goods Manufacturers Ass'n (670)
Springs Industries, Inc. (671)
SRG & Associates (187)
The St. Joe Co. (671)
Steptoe & Johnson LLP (188)
Sterling Internat'l Consultants, Inc. (674)
Tailored Clothing Ass'n (680)
Target Corp. (681)
Tett Enterprises (684)
Textile/Clothing Technology Center (685)
United Food and Commercial Workers Internat'l Union (701)
United Methodist Church General Board of Church and Society (702)
United States Business and Industry Council (703)
University of California at Irvine Advanced Power and Energy Program (706)
University of Southwestern Louisiana (707)
Vestal Group of Companies (714)
Williams & Jensen, P.C. (215)
Winston & Strawn (218)
Witman Associates (220)
Wool Fiber, Yarn Fabric Coalition (730)

Arts/Entertainment (ART)

AFL-CIO - Professional Employees Department (231)
American Amusement Machine Ass'n (245)
American Architectural Foundation (245)
American Arts Alliance (245)
American Ass'n of Museums (248)
American Continental Group, Inc. (12)
American Federation of Musicians of the United States and Canada (258)
American Federation of Television and Radio Artists (259)
American Friends of the Czech Republic (260)
American Institute for Conservation of Historic and Artistic Works (263)
The American Institute of Architects (264)
American Museum of Natural History (268)
American Soc. of Architectural Illustrators (275)
American Soc. of Composers, Authors and Publishers (276)
American Symphony Orchestra League (278)
American Teleservices Ass'n (279)
Americans for the Arts (282)
Amusement and Music Operators Ass'n (283)
Anheuser-Busch Cos., Inc. (284)
Arena Stage (288)
Arent Fox Kintner Plotkin & Kahn, PLLC (14)
Barksdale Ballard & Co., Inc. (23)
Bergner Bockorny Castagnetti and Hawkins (26)
Bertelsmann AG (312)
BET Holdings II, Inc. (312)
Thomas L. Birch (27)
Bowling Proprietors' Ass'n of America (318)
Capital Children's Museum (330)
Capitol Concerts, Inc. (331)
Chambers Associates Inc. (45)
Chernikoff and Co. (46)
The Choral Arts Soc. of Washington (345)
Christian Coalition of America (345)
Chuck & Rock Adventure Productions, Inc. (346)
Chwat and Company, Inc. (46)
Coalition on Accessibility (355)
Colex and Associates (48)
Colling Swift & Hynes (49)
Comcast Corp. (359)
Consumer Federation of America (369)
The Corcoran Gallery of Art (371)
Covanta Energy Corporation (377)
Covington & Burling (53)
Cultural Partnership of the Americas (380)
The Cuneo Law Group, P.C. (56)
Curson Koopersmith Partners, Inc. (56)
Da Vinci's Notebook (381)

Dance/USA *(382)*
Directors Guild of America *(389)*
The Duberstein Group, Inc. *(65)*
The Dutko Group, Inc. *(68)*
Electronic Retailing Ass'n *(401)*
EMI Music *(402)*
Epstein Becker & Green, P.C. *(72)*
Evans & Black, Inc. *(73)*
Federation of State Humanities Councils *(415)*
Florida State University System *(420)*
Folger Shakespeare Library *(421)*
Ford's Theatre *(422)*
Gainesville, Florida, City of *(428)*
Great Projects Film Co., Inc. *(439)*
John C. Grzebien *(89)*
Leslie Harris & Associates *(91)*
Law Offices of Robert T. Herbolsheimer *(94)*
Heritage Harbor Museum *(449)*
R. J. Hudson Associates *(101)*
IMAX Corp. *(458)*
Institute on Religion and Public Policy *(464)*
Interactive Amusement and Tournament Video Game Coalition *(466)*
Internat'l Brotherhood of Electrical Workers *(469)*
Internat'l Downtown Ass'n *(471)*
Internat'l Union of Painters and Allied Trades *(476)*
Internet Action PAC *(476)*
Inventure Place *(477)*
Janus-Merritt Strategies, L.L.C. *(104)*
Jazz at Lincoln Center Inc. *(482)*
Jenkens & Gilchrist *(107)*
Jorden Burt LLP *(109)*
Kilpatrick Stockton LLP *(112)*
Lawler, Metzger & Milkman, LLC *(117)*
The Laxalt Corp. *(117)*
The Paul Laxalt Group *(117)*
LeBoeuf, Lamb, Greene & MacRae L.L.P. *(117)*
The Livingston Group, LLC *(120)*
Lovelace Respiratory Research Institute *(504)*
Management Options, Inc. *(123)*
Manatt, Phelps & Phillips, LLP *(123)*
Mayer, Brown & Platt *(126)*
Media Access Project *(516)*
Meridian Internat'l Center *(519)*
Miami Beach, Florida, City of *(521)*
Thelonius Monk Institute of Jazz *(527)*
Timothy X. Moore and Co. *(136)*
Morning Star Institute, The *(529)*
Motion Picture Ass'n of America *(530)*
Murray, Scheer, Montgomery, Tapia & O'Donnell *(139)*
Music Educators Nat'l Conference *(533)*
The NARAS Foundation *(534)*
Nat'l Ass'n of Broadcasters *(539)*
Nat'l Ass'n of Negro Business & Professional Women's Clubs, Inc. *(546)*
Nat'l Ass'n of Recording Merchandisers *(548)*
Nat'l Ass'n of Theatre Owners *(550)*
Nat'l Assembly of State Arts Agencies *(551)*
Nat'l Building Museum *(553)*
Nat'l Capitol Concerts *(554)*
Nat'l Club Ass'n *(556)*
Nat'l Humanities Alliance *(567)*
Nat'l Licensed Beverage Ass'n *(570)*
Nat'l Museum of Women in the Arts *(571)*
New York University *(588)*
Newark, New Jersey, City of *(588)*
Newington-Cropsey Foundation *(588)*
News Corporation Ltd. *(589)*
O'Connor & Hannan, L.L.P. *(144)*
Palumbo & Cerrell, Inc. *(149)*
Parry, Romani, DeConcini & Symms *(149)*
Patton Boggs, LLP *(150)*
People for the American Way *(612)*
Petito & Associates *(155)*
The Phillips Collection *(616)*
Providence City Arts for Youth, Inc. *(627)*
Providence Performing Arts Center *(627)*
Quinn Gillespie & Associates *(165)*
Recording Industry Ass'n of America *(634)*
Liz Robbins Associates *(169)*
Scholastic, Inc. *(651)*
SESAC, Inc. *(656)*
The Shakespeare Theatre *(656)*
Shea's Performing Arts Center *(657)*
Shubert Organization Inc. *(658)*
Sirius Satellite Radio, Inc. *(660)*
Smith Dawson & Andrews, Inc. *(661)*
Smith Dawson & Andrews, Inc. *(183)*
Songwriters Guild of America *(665)*
Sotheby's Holdings Inc. *(666)*
Sufka & Associates *(190)*
Tarne Powers & Associates *(192)*
Telephone Operators Caucus *(683)*
The Textile Museum *(685)*
Ticketmaster *(687)*
Tribune Co. *(692)*
United Methodist Church General Board of Church and Society *(702)*
University of Medicine and Dentistry of New Jersey *(706)*
University of Miami *(706)*
University of Tulsa *(708)*
University of Virginia *(708)*
Van Scoyoc Associates, Inc. *(200)*
Vivendi Universal *(717)*
The Washington Ballet *(719)*
Washington Council Ernst & Young *(206)*
The Washington Opera *(720)*
Washington Performing Arts Society *(720)*
Wiland-Bell Productions *(726)*
Wiley, Rein & Fielding *(214)*
Williams & Jensen, P.C. *(215)*
Women Officials in NACo *(729)*

Automotive Industry (AUT)

The Accord Group *(5)*
Advocates for Highway and Auto Safety *(229)*
Air Pacific Ltd. *(234)*
Akin, Gump, Strauss, Hauer & Feld, L.L.P. *(8)*
Albemarle Corp. *(237)*
Alliance of American Insurers *(240)*
Alliance of Automobile Manufacturers, Inc. *(240)*
Alpine Group, Inc. *(11)*
Alston & Bird LLP *(12)*
The Aluminum Ass'n *(242)*
American Ass'n for Laboratory Accreditation *(246)*
American Concrete Pavement Ass'n (ACPA) *(255)*
American Council of Independent Laboratories *(255)*
American Honda Motor Co., Inc. *(262)*
American Internat'l Automobile Dealers Ass'n *(265)*
American Iron and Steel Institute *(265)*
American Methanol Institute *(268)*
American Salvage Pool Ass'n *(273)*
American Teleservices Ass'n *(279)*
Americans for Equitable Climate Solutions *(281)*
Americans for Free Internat'l Trade (AFIT PAC) *(281)*
Arent Fox Kintner Plotkin & Kahn, PLLC *(14)*
Arnold & Porter *(16)*
Ass'n of Internat'l Automobile Manufacturers *(296)*
Automotive Aftermarket Industry Ass'n *(303)*
Automotive Consumer Action Program *(303)*
Automotive Engine Rebuilders Ass'n *(303)*
Automotive Parts and Service Alliance *(303)*
Automotive Parts Rebuilders Ass'n *(304)*
Automotive Recyclers Ass'n *(304)*
Automotive Service Ass'n *(304)*
AutoNation, Inc. *(304)*
Aventis Pharmaceutical Products *(304)*
Bacino & Associates *(19)*
Baker Electromotive, Inc. *(306)*
Barnes, Richardson and Colburn *(23)*
Bethlehem Steel Corp. *(312)*
Big Sky Consulting, Inc. *(27)*
Bloomfield Associates, Inc. *(29)*
BMW (U.S.) Holding Corp. *(316)*
BMW Financial Services of North America, Inc. *(316)*
BMW Manufacturing Corp. *(316)*
Bridgestone/Firestone, Inc. *(320)*
Brownstein Hyatt & Farber, P.C. *(33)*
Capital Strategies Group, Inc. *(37)*
Robert E. Carlstrom *(40)*
The Carmen Group *(40)*
CarsDirect.com *(332)*
Caterpillar Inc. *(333)*
Cendant Corp. *(335)*
Certified Automotive Parts Ass'n *(340)*
The Chubb Corp. *(346)*
Coalition for Auto Repair Equality (CARE) *(353)*
Condon and Forsyth *(51)*
Congressional Economic Leadership Institute *(366)*
Conlon, Frantz, Phelan & Pires *(51)*
Consumer Federation of America *(369)*
Consumers Union of the United States *(369)*
Continental Teves *(370)*
Cortese PLLC *(53)*
DaimlerChrysler Corp. *(381)*
Deere Co. Worldwide Commercial & Consumer Equipment Division *(383)*
Dorfman & O'Neal, Inc. *(63)*
The Duberstein Group, Inc. *(65)*
DuPont *(393)*
DuPont Agricultural Products *(393)*
The Dutko Group, Inc. *(68)*
eBay Inc. *(395)*
Eckert Seamans Cherin & Mellott, LLC *(70)*
Ethyl Corp. *(407)*
EV Rental Cars, LLC *(408)*
Fantasma Networks, Inc. *(411)*
FMC Corp. *(420)*
Ford Motor Co. *(422)*
FuelMaker Corp. *(427)*
General Motors Corp. *(432)*
Global USA, Inc. *(83)*
Goodyear Tire and Rubber Co. *(437)*
Greater New York Automobile Dealers Ass'n *(439)*
Hale and Dorr LLP *(89)*
Heavy Vehicle Maintenance Group *(447)*
Hohlt & Associates *(98)*
Honda North America, Inc. *(451)*
Hyundai Motor Co. *(456)*
Internat'l Cadmium Ass'n *(469)*
Internat'l Lead Zinc Research Organization, Inc. (ILZRO) *(473)*
Internat'l Mass Retailers Ass'n *(473)*
Internat'l Public Relations Co. *(474)*
Iran Air *(478)*
ITT Conoflow *(480)*
Japan Automobile Manufacturers Ass'n *(481)*
Japan Automobile Standards Internat'l Center *(481)*
JBC Internat'l *(105)*
Jefferson Government Relations, L.L.C. *(106)*
JM Family Enterprises *(483)*
Kaiser Aluminum & Chemical Corp. *(485)*
Robert K. Kelley Law Offices *(111)*
Kelly and Associates, Inc. *(111)*
Patricia C. Kennedy *(111)*
King & Spalding *(113)*
Lee Lane *(116)*
Lawler, Metzger & Milkman, LLC *(117)*
LegisLaw *(118)*
The LTV Corp. *(505)*
M & R Strategic Services *(122)*
Management Options, Inc. *(123)*
Manatt, Phelps & Phillips, LLP *(123)*
Mayer, Brown & Platt *(126)*
Mazda North America Operations *(514)*
Mercedes-Benz of North America, Inc. *(518)*
Mitsubishi Internat'l Corp. *(526)*
Mitsubishi Motors America, Inc. *(526)*
Mitsubishi Motors R&D of America, Inc. *(526)*
Mitsubishi Research Institute *(526)*
Morgan Meguire, LLC *(136)*
Motor and Equipment Manufacturers Ass'n *(531)*
Motorcycle Industry Council *(531)*
Multinat'l Government Services, Inc. *(138)*
Murray, Scheer, Montgomery, Tapia & O'Donnell *(139)*
Nat'l Ass'n of Minority Automobile Dealers *(545)*
Nat'l Automobile Dealers Ass'n *(552)*
Nat'l Fastener Distributors Ass'n *(564)*
Nat'l Legal Center for the Public Interest *(570)*
Nissan North America Inc. *(590)*
Julia J. Norrell & Associates *(142)*
O'Connor & Hannan, L.L.P. *(144)*
PACCAR, Inc. *(605)*
Patton Boggs, LLP *(150)*
Pennzoil-Quaker State Co. *(611)*

Pilkington North America ***(617)***
Porsche Cars North America, Inc. ***(621)***
Porter/Novelli *(159)*
Public Citizen, Inc. ***(628)***
Public Strategies Washington, Inc. *(164)*
Public Strategies, Inc. *(165)*
Recreation Vehicle Ass'n ***(634)***
Recreation Vehicle Dealers Ass'n of North America ***(634)***
Robert L. Redding *(166)*
RGS Enterprises, Inc. *(168)*
Rooney Group Internat'l, Inc. *(171)*
SatCon Technology Corp. ***(650)***
Sellery Associates, Inc. *(177)*
Sense Technologies, Inc. ***(655)***
Shutler and Low *(180)*
Simula, Inc. ***(659)***
Smith Dawson & Andrews, Inc. *(183)*
Solutia Inc. ***(665)***
State Farm Insurance Cos. ***(673)***
Steptoe & Johnson LLP *(188)*
Kenneth F. Stinger *(189)*
Strat@Comm (Strategic Communications Counselors) *(189)*
T & N Industries ***(679)***
Textron Inc. ***(685)***
Timmons and Co., Inc. *(195)*
Tire Ass'n of North America ***(687)***
Toyota Motor Corp. ***(689)***
Toyota Motor North America, U.S.A., Inc. ***(689)***
Toyota Technical Center U.S.A. Inc. ***(689)***
TRW Inc. ***(693)***
Tyson's Governmental Sales, LLC ***(695)***
United Automobile, Aerospace and Agricultural Implement Workers of America (UAW) ***(700)***
United Methodist Church General Board of Church and Society ***(702)***
United Motorcoach Ass'n ***(702)***
United States Business and Industry Council ***(703)***
USX Corp. ***(710)***
Venable *(201)*
Volkswagen of America, Inc. ***(717)***
Volkswagen, AG ***(717)***
The Washington Group *(208)*
The Wexler Group *(211)*
James M. Williams, Jr. *(217)*
Willkie Farr & Gallagher *(217)*
Kathleen Winn & Associates, Inc. *(218)*
Zurich Financial Group ***(735)***

Aviation/Aircraft/Airlines (AVI)

AAAE-ACI ***(224)***
AB Management Associates, Inc. *(5)*
Adams and Reese LLP *(5)*
Advantage Associates, Inc. *(6)*
Aeronautical Repair Station Ass'n ***(230)***
AeroRepublica, S.A. ***(230)***
Aerospace Industries Ass'n of America ***(230)***
AFL-CIO - Transportation Trades Department ***(231)***
Air Carrier Ass'n of America ***(233)***
Air China Internat'l Corp., Ltd. ***(233)***
Air Force Ass'n ***(233)***
Air Line Pilots Ass'n Internat'l ***(233)***
Air Pacific Ltd. ***(234)***
Air Tractor, Inc. ***(234)***
Air Tran Airways ***(234)***
Air Transport Ass'n of America ***(234)***
Airborne Express ***(234)***
Airbus Industrie of North America, Inc. ***(234)***
AirCell, Inc. ***(235)***
Aircraft Electronics Ass'n ***(235)***
Aircraft Owners and Pilots Ass'n ***(235)***
Aircraft Services Group ***(235)***
Airline Suppliers Ass'n ***(235)***
Akin, Gump, Strauss, Hauer & Feld, L.L.P. *(8)*
Akron-Canton Airport ***(235)***
Alaska Air Group ***(236)***
Alaska Airlines ***(236)***
Alaska Professional Hunters Ass'n ***(236)***
Albertine Enterprises, Inc. *(10)*
Alcalde & Fay *(10)*
Aldaron Inc. ***(238)***
All Nippon Airways Co. ***(238)***
Alliance Air Services ***(239)***
Allied Pilots Ass'n ***(241)***
Allison Transmission Division, General Motors Corp. ***(241)***
Alvarado & Gerken *(12)*
American Airlines ***(244)***
American Automobile Ass'n ***(250)***
American Consulting Engineers Council ***(255)***
American Museum of Natural History ***(268)***
American Portland Cement Alliance ***(270)***
American Psychological Ass'n ***(271)***
American Red Cross ***(272)***
American Soc. of Civil Engineers ***(276)***
American Soc. of Travel Agents ***(277)***
American Teleservices Ass'n ***(279)***
American Trans Air ***(279)***
AMI Aircraft Seating Systems ***(283)***
APCO Worldwide *(14)*
Arent Fox Kintner Plotkin & Kahn, PLLC *(14)*
ARINC, Inc. ***(288)***
Wayne Arny & Assoc. *(16)*
Ass'n of Asia Pacific Airlines ***(294)***
Ass'n of Flight Attendants ***(295)***
Ass'n of Professional Flight Attendants ***(297)***
Ass'n of Trial Lawyers of America ***(299)***
Associated Equipment Distributors ***(300)***
Ross Atkins *(18)*
Auburn University ***(302)***
Austin, Texas, City of ***(303)***
Austrian Airlines ***(303)***
Averitt Express, Inc. ***(305)***
Baker & Hostetler LLP *(19)*
Baker Botts, L.L.P. *(20)*
C. Baker Consulting Inc. *(20)*
Baker, Donelson, Bearman & Caldwell, P.C. *(21)*
Ball Janik, LLP *(22)*
Bangor Internat'l Airport ***(307)***
Barringer Technologies ***(308)***
The Barton Co. *(24)*
Baton Rouge, Louisiana, City of ***(308)***
Benin, Government of the Republic of ***(311)***
Bergner Bockorny Castagnetti and Hawkins *(26)*
Big Sky Consulting, Inc. *(27)*
Birch, Horton, Bittner & Cherot *(28)*
Birmingham Airport Authority ***(314)***
BKSH & Associates *(28)*
Blank Rome Comisky & McCauley, LLP *(29)*
The Boeing Co. ***(316)***
Boesch & Co. *(29)*
Bombardier, Inc. ***(317)***
Bracy Williams & Co. *(31)*
Bradley Arant Rose & White LLP *(31)*
Brand & Frulla, P.C. *(32)*
Bristol Group, Inc. *(32)*
British Airways Plc ***(321)***
Broward, Florida, County of ***(322)***
Burdeshaw Associates, Ltd. *(34)*
Calspan University of Buffalo Research Center ***(328)***
Cambridge Management Inc. ***(328)***
Capital Region Airport Commission ***(330)***
Capitol Capital Group *(38)*
Capitol Coalitions Inc. *(38)*
Capitol Counsel Group, L.L.C. *(38)*
The Carmen Group *(40)*
Carpi & Clay *(41)*
The Carter Group *(41)*
Casa Aircraft USA, Inc. ***(332)***
Cash, Smith & Wages *(41)*
Casino Express Airlines ***(333)***
Cassidy & Associates, Inc. *(42)*
Certified Airline Passenger Services, LLC ***(340)***
Chamber of Commerce of the U.S.A. ***(340)***
Chandler Evans Control Systems ***(341)***
Chapman Freeborn America ***(341)***
Chattanooga Metropolitan Airport Authority ***(341)***
Chesapeake Enterprises, Inc. *(46)*
Chicago, Illinois, Department of Law, City of ***(343)***
China Eastern Airlines ***(344)***
Cincinnati, Ohio, City of ***(347)***
Clark County-McCarran Internat'l Airport ***(350)***
Clay and Associates *(47)*
Cleveland, City of/Cleveland Hopkins Internat'l Airport ***(351)***
Coalition for a Global Standard on Aviation Noise ***(352)***
Cohen, Gettings & Dunham, PC *(48)*
Colgan Air, Inc. ***(357)***
Computer Intelligence 2 ***(364)***
Condon and Forsyth *(51)*
Congressional Economic Leadership Institute ***(366)***
Construction Management Ass'n of America ***(368)***
Consumer Federation of America ***(369)***
Consumers Union of the United States ***(369)***
Continental Airlines Inc. ***(370)***
Copeland, Lowery & Jacquez *(52)*
Covanta Energy Corporation ***(377)***
Law Offices of Kevin G. Curtin *(56)*
Custom Air Transport ***(380)***
D3 Internat'l Energy, LLC ***(381)***
Dallas/Fort Worth Internat'l Airport Board ***(382)***
Davidoff & Malito, LLP *(57)*
Bob Davis & Associates *(57)*
Susan Davis Internat'l *(58)*
Dayton, Ohio, Washington Office of the City of ***(383)***
Decatur Park District ***(383)***
Dekalb, Illinois, City of ***(384)***
Delta Air Lines ***(384)***
George H. Denison *(60)*
Denver, Colorado, City of ***(386)***
Detroit, Michigan, City of ***(386)***
DHL Airways, Inc. ***(387)***
Dickstein Shapiro Morin & Oshinsky LLP *(61)*
Dimensions Internat'l ***(388)***
Diversified Internat'l Sciences Corp. ***(390)***
Dorfman & O'Neal, Inc. *(63)*
Dow, Lohnes & Albertson, PLLC *(64)*
DRS Technologies, Inc. ***(392)***
The Duberstein Group, Inc. *(65)*
Dunc LLC ***(393)***
DuPont Agricultural Products ***(393)***
The Dutko Group, Inc. *(68)*
Dykema Gossett PLLC *(69)*
EarthData Holdings ***(394)***
Easton Airport ***(395)***
EDS Corp. ***(398)***
El Toro Reuse Planning Authority ***(399)***
Rosalind K. Ellingsworth *(71)*
Embraer Aircraft Corp. ***(401)***
Embry-Riddle Aeronautical University ***(401)***
Engineered Arresting Systems Corp. ***(403)***
Ann Eppard Associates, Ltd. *(72)*
Erie Internat'l Airport ***(406)***
European Aeronautics, Defence and Space, Inc. ***(408)***
Executive Jet ***(408)***
Fairfax, Virginia, County of ***(410)***
Marcus G. Faust, P.C. *(74)*
John J. Fausti & Associates, LLC *(74)*
Federal Access *(75)*
FedEx Corp. ***(415)***
FedEx Pilots Ass'n ***(415)***
Jack Ferguson Associates, Inc. *(75)*
The Ferguson Group, LLC *(76)*
Filler & Weller, P.C. *(77)*
First Flight Centennial Foundation ***(417)***
Fleischman and Walsh, L.L.P. *(77)*
Fleishman-Hillard, Inc ***(418)***
FlightSafety Internat'l ***(419)***
R. G. Flippo and Associates, Inc. *(77)*
FLIR Systems, Inc. ***(419)***
Florida State University System ***(420)***
FMC Corp. ***(420)***
Foley & Lardner *(78)*
Fort Smith Regional Airport ***(423)***
Freeport-McMoRan Copper & Gold Inc. ***(425)***
Gainesville, Florida, City of ***(428)***
Galaxy Aerospace Co., LP ***(428)***
The Gallagher Group, LLC *(80)*
Sara Garland (and Associates) *(81)*
Gary, Indiana, Washington Office of the City of ***(429)***
General Atomics ***(431)***
General Aviation Manufacturers Ass'n ***(431)***
General Development Corp. ***(431)***
General Dynamics Corp. ***(431)***
General Electric Co. ***(432)***

General Motors Corp. ***(432)***
Geo-Seis Helicopters Inc. ***(433)***
GKN Westland Aerospace Inc. ***(435)***
Glankler Brown, PLLC ***(435)***
Global Aviation Associates, Ltd. *(83)*
Global USA, Inc. *(83)*
Goodyear Tire and Rubber Co. ***(437)***
Government Relations, Inc. *(84)*
GPC Internat'l *(85)*
Jay Grant & Associates *(85)*
Greater Orlando Aviation Authority ***(439)***
Griffin, Johnson, Dover & Stewart *(87)*
Guam Internat'l Airport Authority ***(441)***
Guam, Washington Office of the Governor ***(442)***
Guinea, Secretary General of the Presidency of the Republic of ***(442)***
Gulfstream Aerospace Corp. ***(442)***
Hall, Green, Rupli, LLC *(90)*
Charles A. Hamilton Associates LLC *(91)*
Hamilton Sundstrand ***(444)***
Hankin, Persson & Darnell ***(444)***
Harris Corp. ***(444)***
Hawaii, State of ***(445)***
Hawaiian Airlines ***(445)***
Heidepriem & Mager, Inc. *(94)*
Helicopter Ass'n Internat'l ***(448)***
Highline School District Educational Resources ***(449)***
Hillwood Development Corp. ***(450)***
HMSHost Corp. ***(450)***
Hogan & Hartson L.L.P. *(96)*
Hohlt & Associates *(98)*
Holland & Knight LLP *(98)*
Honeywell Internat'l, Inc. ***(452)***
Hooper Owen & Winburn *(99)*
Houston, Texas, Department of Aviation of the City of ***(453)***
Law Offices of Irene E. Howie *(100)*
Hughes Space & Communications Co. ***(454)***
Hunton & Williams *(101)*
Huntsville-Madison County Airport ***(455)***
Hurt, Norton & Associates *(101)*
IATA U.S. Frequent Flyer Tax Interest Group ***(456)***
Ibex ***(456)***
The Ickes & Enright Group *(102)*
The ILEX Group *(102)*
Indiana, Office of the Governor of the State of ***(460)***
Indigo ***(460)***
Internat'l Air Transport Ass'n ***(467)***
Internat'l Ass'n of Fire Fighters ***(468)***
Internat'l Ass'n of Machinists and Aerospace Workers ***(468)***
Internat'l Brotherhood of Teamsters ***(469)***
Internat'l Federation of Professional and Technical Engineers ***(471)***
Iran Air ***(478)***
Israel Aircraft Industries, Ltd. ***(479)***
Jacobs Engineering Group Inc. ***(481)***
Japan Internat'l Transport Institute ***(482)***
JDA Aviation Technology Systems ***(482)***
Jefferson Government Relations, L.L.C. ***(482)***
Jefferson Government Relations, L.L.C. *(106)*
Jeppesen Sanderson, Inc. ***(482)***
JFS Group, Ltd. *(107)*
Johnston & Associates, LLC *(107)*
Jones, Walker, Waechter, Poitevent, Carrere & Denegre, L.L.P. *(108)*
Jordan & Associates, Inc. *(109)*
Jorden Burt LLP *(109)*
Kaiser Aluminum & Chemical Corp. ***(485)***
Kalitta Air, L.L.C. ***(486)***
Kansas City, Missouri, City of ***(486)***
Kimberly Consulting, LLC *(113)*
Kimberly-Clark Corp. ***(489)***
Joseph S. Kimmitt *(113)*
Kogovsek & Associates *(114)*
Michael E. Korens *(114)*
Kurzweil & Associates *(115)*
Lafayette Airport Commission ***(494)***
Lambert-St. Louis Internat'l Airport ***(494)***
Las Cruces, New Mexico, City of ***(495)***
Las Vegas/McCarran Internat'l Airport ***(495)***
Lawler, Metzger & Milkman, LLC *(117)*
Lee County Port Authority ***(497)***
Lehigh-Northhampton Airport Authority ***(498)***
The Michael Lewan Co. *(119)*
Litton Advanced Systems ***(500)***
Livermore, California, City of ***(500)***
The Livingston Group, LLC *(120)*
Lockheed Martin Corp. ***(501)***
Lockheed Martin Tactical Systems ***(502)***
Lovelace Respiratory Research Institute ***(504)***
Lucas Aerospace ***(505)***
Marshall L. Lynam *(122)*
M K Airlines ***(506)***
Madison Government Affairs *(123)*
Management Options, Inc. *(123)*
Manatt, Phelps & Phillips, LLP *(123)*
March Joint Powers Authority ***(509)***
Marine Corps Reserve Officers Ass'n ***(510)***
Martin-Baker Aircraft Co., Ltd. ***(511)***
Massachusetts Port Authority ***(512)***
Alan Mauk Associates, Ltd. *(126)*
McDermott, Will and Emery *(128)*
Jack H. McDonald *(129)*
Megapulse, Inc. ***(517)***
Mehl, Griffin & Bartek Ltd. *(132)*
Memphis-Shelby County Airport Authority ***(518)***
Metropolitan Transportation Commission ***(520)***
Metropolitan Washington Airports Authority ***(521)***
Meyers & Associates *(133)*
Miami Beach, Florida, City of ***(521)***
Midwest Express Airlines ***(523)***
Denny Miller McBee Associates *(134)*
Milwaukee, Wisconsin, County of ***(524)***
Minneapolis-St. Paul Metropolitan Airports Commission ***(525)***
Mitsubishi Research Institute ***(526)***
Monroe, Louisiana, Chamber of Commerce of the City of ***(528)***
Monroe, Louisiana, City of ***(528)***
Monroe, New York, County of ***(528)***
Montgomery Airport Authority ***(528)***
Morrison & Foerster LLP *(137)*
Muncie, Indiana, City of (Delaware County) ***(532)***
NASA Aeronautics Support Team ***(534)***
Nat'l Agricultural Aviation Ass'n ***(535)***
Nat'l Air Traffic Controllers Ass'n ***(536)***
Nat'l Air Transportation Ass'n ***(536)***
Nat'l Airline Passenger Coalition ***(536)***
Nat'l Ass'n of Aircraft and Communication Suppliers ***(538)***
Nat'l Ass'n of Developmental Disabilities Councils ***(542)***
Nat'l Business Aviation Ass'n ***(553)***
Nat'l Fastener Distributors Ass'n ***(564)***
Nat'l Parks Conservation Ass'n ***(573)***
Nat'l Soc. of Professional Engineers ***(578)***
NAV Canada ***(582)***
Naval Reserve Ass'n ***(582)***
NAVCOM Systems, Inc. ***(583)***
New Jersey Institute of Technology ***(585)***
New Orleans Internat'l Airport ***(586)***
New York University ***(588)***
Newark, New Jersey, City of ***(588)***
Niagara Frontier Transportation Authority ***(589)***
Noise Reduction Technology Coalition ***(591)***
The Nordam Group ***(591)***
Norfolk, Virginia, City of ***(591)***
North Carolina Global TransPark Authority ***(593)***
North Carolina, Washington Office of the State of ***(593)***
Northwest Airlines, Inc. ***(595)***
Oakland, Michigan, County of ***(598)***
The OB-C Group, LLC *(143)*
Obadal and MacLeod, p.c. *(143)*
O'Connor & Hannan, L.L.P. *(144)*
O'Melveny and Myers LLP *(147)*
Omniflight Helicopters, Inc. ***(600)***
ORBITZ ***(602)***
Orcon Corp. ***(602)***
Orincon Corp. ***(603)***
Ouachita Parish Police Jury ***(604)***
John M. Palatiello & Associates *(148)*
Palm Springs, California, City of ***(606)***
The Palmer Group *(149)*
Parsons Brinckerhoff Inc. ***(608)***
Parsons Corp. ***(608)***
Patton Boggs, LLP *(150)*
Pegasus Management ***(611)***
PerkinElmer Detection Systems ***(612)***
The Peterson Group *(155)*
The Petrizzo Group, Inc. *(155)*
Petroleum Helicopters ***(613)***
Peyser Associates, Inc. *(155)*
Philip Morris Management Corp. ***(615)***
Pilots' Ass'n of the Bay and River Delaware ***(617)***
Pinkering Corp. ***(617)***
The PMA Group *(156)*
Polar Air Cargo, Inc. ***(620)***
Port Authority of New York and New Jersey ***(621)***
Port of San Diego ***(621)***
Potomac Strategies Internat'l LLC *(160)*
Powell, Goldstein, Frazer & Murphy LLP *(160)*
Powerware ***(622)***
Pratt & Whitney ***(623)***
Precision Aerospace Corp. ***(623)***
Preston Gates Ellis & Rouvelas Meeds LLP *(162)*
PriceWaterhouseCoopers ***(624)***
Professional Airways Systems Specialists (AFL-CIO) ***(625)***
Professional Aviation Maintenance Ass'n ***(625)***
Provo, Utah, City of ***(627)***
Public Policy Partners ***(629)***
Public Strategies Washington, Inc. *(164)*
Puerto Rico Senate ***(629)***
Radius, The Global Travel Co. ***(632)***
Rafael U.S.A., Inc. ***(632)***
Raytheon Co. ***(633)***
Regional Airline Ass'n ***(635)***
Regional Airport Authority of Louisville & Jefferson Co. ***(635)***
Regional Planning Commission ***(635)***
Reinsurance Ass'n of America ***(636)***
Rhoads Group *(168)*
Robertson, Monagle & Eastaugh *(170)*
Robins, Kaplan, Miller & Ciresi L.L.P. *(170)*
Rockwell Collins ***(641)***
Rolls-Royce North America Inc. ***(642)***
Rooney Group Internat'l, Inc. *(171)*
Ryan, Phillips, Utrecht & MacKinnon *(173)*
Sabre Inc. ***(644)***
Sabreliner Corp. ***(644)***
Safegate Internat'l AB ***(645)***
San Bernardino Airport Authority ***(647)***
San Diego, California, City of ***(647)***
San Francisco Internat'l Airport ***(648)***
San Francisco, California, City and County of ***(648)***
San Leandro, California, City of ***(648)***
Savannah Airport Commission ***(650)***
Schnader Harrison Segal & Lewis LLP *(176)*
Schweizer Aircraft Corp. ***(652)***
Seattle, Washington, Port of ***(653)***
Shaw Pittman *(177)*
Sher & Blackwell *(179)*
Shriner-Midland Co. ***(658)***
Simon and Co., Inc. *(181)*
Simula, Inc. ***(659)***
Skadden, Arps, Slate, Meagher & Flom LLP *(181)*
Smith Dawson & Andrews, Inc. *(183)*
Smith, Bucklin and Associates, Inc. *(184)*
Smith, Hinaman & Associates *(184)*
The Solomon Group, LLC *(185)*
Sony Electronics, Inc. ***(666)***
Sony Trans Com ***(666)***
Southwest Airlines ***(668)***
Space Access ***(668)***
Spiegel & McDiarmid *(186)*
The St. Joe Co. ***(671)***
St. Louis Airport Authority ***(671)***
Stanly County Airport Authority ***(673)***
Stewart & Stevenson Services, Inc. ***(674)***
Stilman Advanced Strategies ***(674)***
Stoll Stoll Berne Lokting & Shlachter, P.C. ***(675)***
Strategic Horizons Advisors, L.L.C. *(189)*
Sun Pacific Internat'l ***(677)***
Sunrise Research Corp. *(191)*
Swissair ***(679)***
TAP/Air Portugal ***(681)***
Tate-LeMunyon, LLC *(192)*
TCOM, L.P. ***(682)***
Teicher Consulting and Representation *(193)*
Teledyne Controls, Inc. ***(683)***

Tensor Technologies, Inc. (684)
TerraCom-Strategic Communications (193)
Textron Inc. (685)
Thelen Reid & Priest LLP (685)
Thelen Reid & Priest LLP (193)
Thompson Coburn LLP (194)
Titan Corp. (687)
Trajen, Inc. (689)
Trans World Airlines, Inc. (689)
Travelocity.com (691)
TRW Inc. (693)
Tulsa Airport Authority (694)
David Turch & Associates (197)
Ungaretti & Harris (197)
United Airlines (700)
United Parcel Service (702)
United Special Transport Air Resources, LLC (USTAR) (703)
United States Parachute Ass'n (704)
United Technologies Corp. (704)
Universal Systems, Inc. (705)
University of Medicine and Dentistry of New Jersey (706)
University of Miami (706)
University of North Dakota (707)
University of Tulsa (708)
University of Virginia (708)
US Airways (709)
Van Scoyoc Associates, Inc. (200)
Vanguard Airlines, Inc. (712)
Venetian Casino Resort, LLC (712)
Verner, Liipfert, Bernhard, McPherson and Hand, Chartered (713)
Verner, Liipfert, Bernhard, McPherson and Hand, Chartered (202)
Vero Beach, Florida, City of (714)
City of Victorville Redevelopment Agency (715)
Viohl and Associates, Inc. (205)
Vision Technologies, Inc. (716)
Volusia, Florida, County of (717)
VSAdc.com (205)
R. Duffy Wall and Associates (205)
Washington Aviation Group (206)
Washington Consulting Group (719)
Washington Council Ernst & Young (206)
The Washington Group (208)
Washington World Group, Ltd. (210)
Waterman & Associates (210)
Bonnie H. Weinstein (211)
The Wexler Group (211)
Wiley, Rein & Fielding (214)
Williams & Jensen, P.C. (215)
Winston & Strawn (218)
Winthrop, Stimson, Putnam & Roberts (219)
Wolf Springs Ranches, Inc. (729)
Womble Carlyle Sandridge & Rice, P.C. (220)
Zuckert, Scoutt and Rasenberger, L.L.P. (735)
Zuckert, Scoutt and Rasenberger, L.L.P. (221)

Banking (BAN)

AARP (American Ass'n of Retired Persons) (224)
ABA Insurance Ass'n (224)
ACORN (Ass'n of Community Organizations for Reform Now) (227)
Adams and Reese LLP (5)
Advanta Corp. (229)
The Advocacy Group (6)
Aegon USA (229)
AFIN Securities (231)
AFL-CIO (American Federation of Labor and Congress of Industrial Organizations) (231)
AFLAC, Inc. (231)
Akin, Gump, Strauss, Hauer & Feld, L.L.P. (8)
Harry C. Alford & Associates, Inc. (11)
Alliance Data Systems (239)
Allmerica Financial (241)
Allstate Insurance Co. (241)
Alpine Group, Inc. (11)
Alston & Bird LLP (12)
America's Community Bankers (243)
American Academy of Actuaries (243)
American Ass'n of Bank Directors (246)
American Ass'n of Museums (248)
American Bankers Ass'n (250)
American Collectors Ass'n (253)
American Continental Group, Inc. (12)
American Council of Life Insurers (256)
American Council of State Savings Supervisors (256)
American Express Co. (258)
American Farm Bureau Federation (258)
American Federation of Teachers (259)
American Financial Group (259)
American Financial Services Ass'n (259)
American Homeowners Grassroots Alliance (262)
American Institute of Certified Public Accountants (264)
American Insurance Ass'n (264)
American Internat'l Group, Inc. (265)
American Land Title Ass'n (265)
American League of Financial Institutions (266)
American Resort Development Ass'n (272)
American Soc. of Appraisers (275)
American Teleservices Ass'n (279)
Americans for Consumer Education and Competition, Inc. (281)
Americans for Tax Reform (282)
Appraisal Institute (287)
Arent Fox Kintner Plotkin & Kahn, PLLC (14)
Arter & Hadden (17)
Ass'n for Financial Professionals, Inc. (292)
Ass'n Management Group (18)
Ass'n of American Geographers (293)
Ass'n of Bank Couriers (294)
Ass'n of Banks in Insurance (294)
Ass'n of Banks of Israel (294)
Ass'n of Financial Services Holding Companies (295)
Ass'n of Progressive Rental Organizations (298)
Associated Credit Bureaus, Inc. (300)
Assurant Group (301)
The Assurant Group (301)
Bacino & Associates (19)
Bank Hapoalim B.M. (307)
Bank Leumi le-Israel B.M. (307)
Bank of America (307)
Bank of New York (307)
The Bank Private Equity Coalition (307)
Bankers' Ass'n for Finance and Trade (307)
Bankruptcy Issues Council (307)
Banorte Casa de Bolsa (307)
Banque Paribas New York Branch (307)
Peter S. Barash Associates, Inc. (22)
Barbour Griffith & Rogers, Inc. (22)
Barnett & Sivon, P.C. (24)
Michael F. Barrett, Jr. (24)
The Barton Co. (24)
Bear, Stearns and Co. (310)
Bergner Bockorny Castagnetti and Hawkins (26)
Bingham Dana LLP (27)
BKSH & Associates (28)
Blank Rome Comisky & McCauley, LLP (29)
Bluebonnet Savings Bank (316)
BMW Financial Services of North America, Inc. (316)
James E. Boland (30)
Bracewell & Patterson, L.L.P. (30)
Marshall A. Brachman (31)
British Trade and Commerce Bank (321)
Brown Brothers Harriman & Co. (322)
Brownstein Hyatt & Farber, P.C. (33)
Butera & Andrews (34)
Campbell Crane & Associates (36)
Capital Equipment Legislative Coalition (330)
Capital One Financial Corp. (330)
Capitol Counsel Group, L.L.C. (38)
The Carmen Group (40)
Bill Carney & Co. (41)
Cendant Corp. (335)
Center for Freedom and Prosperity (336)
Centex Corp. (338)
Century Financial Group (339)
Ceridian Corp. (340)
Chamber of Commerce of the U.S.A. (340)
Charter One (341)
Chase Manhattan Bank (341)
Check Payment Systems Ass'n (341)
Chevron, U.S.A. (342)
Chevy Chase Bank, F.S.B. (342)
Chibank Service Inc. (342)
Chicago Board Options Exchange (343)
ChoicePoint (345)
The Chubb Corp. (346)
Citigroup (347)
Civic Service, Inc. (46)
CNA Financial Corp. (351)
CNA Insurance Cos. (351)
Coalition of Service Industries (355)
Coalition to Amend the Financial Information Privacy Act (CAFPA) (356)
Collier Shannon Scott, PLLC (48)
Colombian Banking and Financial Entities Ass'n (ASOBANCARIA) (358)
Colorado Credit Union Systems (358)
Comerica, Inc. (360)
Commercial Law League of America (360)
Community Banks Ass'n of New York State (362)
Community Development Financial Institutions (CDFI) (362)
Community Financial Services Ass'n (362)
Community Preservation Corp. (363)
Conference of State Bank Supervisors (366)
Congressional Economic Leadership Institute (366)
Consumer Bankers Ass'n (368)
Consumer Federation of America (369)
Consumer Mortgage Coalition (369)
Consumers Union of the United States (369)
Council of Federal Home Loan Banks (375)
The Council of Insurance Agents & Brokers (376)
Countrywide Home Loans, Inc. (377)
Countrywide Mortgage Corp. (377)
Covington & Burling (53)
Credit Suisse First Boston Corp. (378)
Credit Union Nat'l Ass'n, Inc. (378)
CT USA, Inc. (379)
Cummins-Allison Corp. (380)
The Cuneo Law Group, P.C. (56)
Currenex (380)
Curson Koopersmith Partners, Inc. (56)
DaimlerChrysler Corp. (381)
Davis Polk & Wardwell (58)
Dayton, Ohio, Washington Office of the City of (383)
Dean Blakey & Moskowitz (59)
Deere & Co. (383)
Delta Air Lines (384)
Derivatives Net, Inc. (386)
Dickstein Shapiro Morin & Oshinsky LLP (61)
Dime Savings Bank of New York (388)
Diversified Collection Services, Inc. (390)
Dollar Bank (390)
Downey Financial Corp. (392)
Downey McGrath Group, Inc. (64)
The Duberstein Group, Inc. (65)
The Dutko Group, Inc. (68)
Dykema Gossett PLLC (69)
E*TRADE Group, Inc. (394)
E-LOAN, Inc. (394)
eBay Inc. (395)
EDS Corp. (398)
The Macon Edwards Co. (71)
Electronic Financial Services Council (400)
Electronic Funds Transfer Ass'n (400)
Ely & Co., Inc. (71)
Equifax Inc. (406)
The Equitable Cos. (406)
Ernst & Young LLP (407)
Ernst & Young LLP (72)
Fannie Mae (411)
Farm Credit Bank of Texas (411)
Farm Credit Council (411)
Farmers Insurance Group (412)
Federal Home Loan Bank of Boston (413)
Federal Home Loan Bank of Chicago (413)
Federal Home Loan Bank of Dallas (413)
Federal Home Loan Bank of Indianapolis (413)
Federal Home Loan Bank of New York (413)
Federal Home Loan Bank of San Francisco (413)
Federal Home Loan Bank of Seattle (413)
Federal Home Loan Bank of Topeka (413)
Federal Home Loan Mortgage Corp. (Freddie Mac) (413)
Federal Legislative Associates, Inc. (75)

Jack Ferguson Associates, Inc. *(75)*
Fidelity Investments Co. ***(416)***
Fierce and Isakowitz *(76)*
Financial Service Centers of America ***(416)***
Financial Services Coordinating Council ***(416)***
Financial Services Council ***(416)***
The Financial Services Roundtable ***(416)***
Financial Technology Industry Council ***(417)***
First American Real Estate Solutions LLC ***(417)***
First Nat'l of Nebraska ***(417)***
First South Production Credit Ass'n ***(418)***
First Union Corp. ***(418)***
First USA Bank ***(418)***
FIRSTPLUS Financial Group Inc. ***(418)***
FISERV, Inc. ***(418)***
Flack Associates *(77)*
Fleet Financial Group, Inc. ***(418)***
Fleischman and Walsh, L.L.P. *(77)*
FM Watch ***(420)***
French & Company *(79)*
Friends of the Earth ***(426)***
Gary, Indiana, Washington Office of the City of ***(429)***
Gateway, Inc. ***(430)***
General Electric Co. ***(432)***
General Motors Corp. ***(432)***
Genesis Consulting Group, LLC *(82)*
Georal Internat'l Ltd. ***(434)***
Gibson, Dunn & Crutcher LLP *(82)*
Goldman, Sachs and Co. ***(437)***
Golin/Harris Internat'l *(84)*
Goodwin, Procter & Hoar LLP *(84)*
Gottehrer and Co. *(84)*
GPC Internat'l *(85)*
GreenPoint Bank ***(440)***
Guaranty Bank, SSB ***(442)***
Guardian Life Insurance Co. of America ***(442)***
Guinea, Secretary General of the Presidency of the Republic of ***(442)***
Hall, Green, Rupli, LLC *(90)*
Halliburton/Brown & Root ***(443)***
Harbor Philadelphia Center City Office, Ltd. ***(444)***
John Harland Co. ***(444)***
Health Insurance Ass'n of America ***(446)***
Hicks, Muse, Tate & Furst ***(449)***
Higgins, McGovern & Smith, LLC *(94)*
Hogan & Hartson L.L.P. *(96)*
Hohlt & Associates *(98)*
Home Federal Savings and Loan Ass'n ***(451)***
Hoover Partners *(100)*
Household Internat'l, Inc. ***(453)***
Hyundai Space & Aircraft Co., Ltd. ***(456)***
Independence Bank ***(459)***
Independent Bankers Ass'n of Texas ***(459)***
Independent Community Bankers of America ***(459)***
Independent Insurance Agents of America, Inc. ***(459)***
Independent Petroleum Ass'n of America ***(459)***
Institute of Internat'l Bankers ***(464)***
Internat'l Ass'n of Amusement Parks and Attractions ***(467)***
Internat'l Biometric Industry Ass'n ***(468)***
Internat'l Business Machines Corp. ***(469)***
Internat'l Franchise Ass'n ***(472)***
Internat'l Longshore and Warehouse Union ***(473)***
Internat'l Swaps and Derivatives Dealers Ass'n ***(475)***
Internet Action PAC ***(476)***
Investment Co. Institute ***(477)***
Itera Internat'l Energy Consultants ***(480)***
Jackson Nat'l Life Insurance ***(480)***
Jamison and Sullivan, Inc. *(104)*
Janus-Merritt Strategies, L.L.C. *(104)*
Jefferson Government Relations, L.L.C. *(106)*
Jenner & Block *(107)*
Sue E. Johnson Associates *(107)*
Jolly/Rissler, Inc. *(108)*
Jorden Burt LLP *(109)*
The Kamber Group *(109)*
Katten Muchin & Zavis ***(486)***
Katten Muchin & Zavis *(110)*
Kean Tracers, Inc. ***(487)***
Kellogg Brown and Root ***(487)***
Kessler & Associates Business Services, Inc. *(112)*
Kirkpatrick & Lockhart LLP *(114)*
Kutak Rock LLP *(115)*
LaRocco & Associates *(116)*
LeBoeuf, Lamb, Greene & MacRae L.L.P. *(117)*
The Legislative Strategies Group, LLC *(118)*
The Michael Lewan Co. *(119)*
Liberty Check Printers ***(499)***
Lloyd's of London ***(501)***
Local Initiatives Support Corp. ***(501)***
Lotstein Buckman, Attorneys At Law *(122)*
Louisiana Credit Union Ass'n ***(504)***
Luse Lehman Gorman Pomerenk & Schick, P.C. ***(505)***
MacAndrews & Forbes Holdings, Inc. ***(506)***
Management Options, Inc. *(123)*
Manatt, Phelps & Phillips, LLP *(123)*
MARC Associates, Inc. *(124)*
Massachusetts Bankers Ass'n ***(512)***
MassMutual Financial Group ***(512)***
MasterCard Internat'l ***(513)***
Mayer, Brown & Platt *(126)*
MBNA America Bank NA ***(514)***
McGuireWoods L.L.P. *(130)*
McIntyre Law Firm, PLLC *(130)*
MemberWorks, Inc. ***(517)***
Merrill Lynch & Co., Inc. ***(519)***
The Metris Companies, Inc. ***(520)***
Metropolitan Banking Group ***(520)***
Metropolitan Life Insurance Co. ***(520)***
Miller & Chevalier, Chartered *(133)*
Minnesota Life Insurance Co. ***(525)***
Susan Molinari, L.L.P. *(135)*
Money Tree, Inc. ***(527)***
MONY Life Insurance Co. ***(529)***
J. P. Morgan Chase & Co. ***(529)***
Morgan Guaranty Trust Co. ***(529)***
Morgan Stanley Dean Witter & Co. ***(529)***
Morrison & Foerster LLP *(137)*
Mortgage Bankers Ass'n of America ***(530)***
Mortgage Insurance Companies of America ***(530)***
The Kate Moss Company *(137)*
Moss McGee Bradley & Foley *(137)*
MSP Strategic Communications, Inc. *(138)*
Muldoon, Murphy & Faucette, LLP ***(532)***
Muldoon, Murphy & Faucette, LLP *(138)*
Mullenholz, Brimsek & Belair *(138)*
Murray, Scheer, Montgomery, Tapia & O'Donnell *(139)*
The MWW Group *(140)*
Timothy D. Naegele & Associates *(140)*
Nat'l Ass'n for the Advancement of Colored People, Washington Bureau ***(538)***
Nat'l Ass'n of Affordable Housing Lenders ***(538)***
Nat'l Ass'n of Credit Management ***(541)***
Nat'l Ass'n of Federal Credit Unions ***(542)***
Nat'l Ass'n of Home Builders of the U.S. ***(543)***
Nat'l Ass'n of Independent Insurers ***(544)***
Nat'l Ass'n of Independent Life Brokerage Agency ***(544)***
Nat'l Ass'n of Insurance and Financial Advisors ***(544)***
Nat'l Ass'n of Mortgage Brokers ***(545)***
Nat'l Ass'n of Negro Business & Professional Women's Clubs, Inc. ***(546)***
Nat'l Ass'n of Professional Insurance Agents ***(547)***
Nat'l Ass'n of Realtors ***(547)***
Nat'l Ass'n of Retail Collection Attorneys ***(548)***
Nat'l Ass'n of Securities and Commercial Law Attorneys ***(549)***
Nat'l Ass'n of Securities Dealers, Inc. (NASD) ***(549)***
Nat'l Automobile Dealers Ass'n ***(552)***
Nat'l City Corp. ***(556)***
Nat'l Consumers League ***(558)***
Nat'l Cooperative Business Ass'n ***(559)***
Nat'l Council of Higher Education Loan Programs ***(560)***
Nat'l Fair Housing Alliance ***(563)***
Nat'l Farmers Union (Farmers Educational & Co-operative Union of America) ***(563)***
Nat'l Grange ***(566)***
Nat'l Home Equity Mortgage Ass'n ***(567)***
Nat'l Housing Conference ***(567)***
Nat'l Lumber and Building Material Dealers Ass'n ***(570)***
Nat'l Neighborhood Coalition ***(572)***
Nat'l Produce Production Inc. ***(574)***
Nat'l Retail Federation ***(576)***
Nat'l Small Business United ***(578)***
Nat'l Taxpayers Union ***(579)***
NCR Corp. ***(583)***
New England Financial ***(585)***
New England Life Insurance Co. ***(585)***
New York Bankers Ass'n ***(586)***
New York Life Insurance Co. ***(587)***
New York Stock Exchange ***(588)***
Elisabeth G. Newton *(142)*
Julia J. Norrell & Associates *(142)*
North American Communications Corp. ***(592)***
North American Securities Administrators Ass'n (NASAA) ***(592)***
Northwestern Mutual Life Insurance Co. ***(595)***
O'Connor & Hannan, L.L.P. *(144)*
On-Line Investment Services ***(600)***
Option One Mortgage Corp. ***(602)***
John T. O'Rourke Law Offices *(147)*
PACE-CAPSTONE *(148)*
Pacific Life Insurance Co. ***(605)***
Parry, Romani, DeConcini & Symms *(149)*
Parsons Brinckerhoff Inc. ***(608)***
Patton Boggs, LLP *(150)*
Pedestal ***(610)***
Peoples Bank ***(612)***
Petroleum Marketers Ass'n of America ***(613)***
Peyser Associates, Inc. *(155)*
Phoenix Home Life Mutual Insurance Co. ***(616)***
The Plexus Consulting Group *(156)*
Podesta/Mattoon *(158)*
Preston Gates Ellis & Rouvelas Meeds LLP *(162)*
Providian Financial Corp. ***(627)***
Prudential Insurance Co. of America ***(627)***
Public Citizen, Inc. ***(628)***
Puerto Rico Federal Affairs Administration ***(629)***
Pulte Home Corp. ***(630)***
Queens County Bancorp Inc. ***(631)***
Andrew F. Quinlan *(165)*
Real Estate Services Providers Council ***(634)***
Robert L. Redding *(166)*
Reinsurance Ass'n of America ***(636)***
Rent-a-Center, Inc. ***(637)***
Repeal PUHCA Now Coalition ***(637)***
Riggs Bank, N.A. ***(640)***
Rogers & Wells *(171)*
Roslyn Bancorp Inc. ***(642)***
Royer & Babyak *(172)*
Ruddy & Associates *(173)*
Ryan, Phillips, Utrecht & MacKinnon *(173)*
Sagamore Associates, Inc. *(174)*
San Francisco, California, City and County of ***(648)***
Sandy City, Utah, City of ***(648)***
The Sanwa Bank , Ltd. ***(649)***
Michael L. Sauls *(175)*
Savings Banks Life Insurance Fund ***(650)***
James E. Schneider, LLM Inc. ***(651)***
Charles Schwab & Co., Inc., ***(652)***
Schwartz & Ballen *(176)*
Scribe Communications, Inc. ***(653)***
Securities Industry Ass'n ***(654)***
Sellery Associates, Inc. *(177)*
Seward & Kissel, LLP *(177)*
Shaw Pittman *(177)*
SICPA Industries of America, Inc. ***(658)***
Silver Users Ass'n ***(659)***
Silver, Freedman & Taff ***(659)***
Bill Simpson & Associates *(181)*
Skol & Associates, Inc. *(182)*
The Smith-Free Group *(184)*
Soc. for Human Resource Management ***(662)***
Soc. of Independent Gasoline Marketers of America ***(663)***
The Solomon Group, LLC *(185)*
The Spectrum Group *(186)*
Spiegel Inc. ***(670)***
Squire, Sanders & Dempsey L.L.P. *(187)*
Star Systems ***(673)***
State Farm Insurance Cos. ***(673)***
State Street Bank and Trust Co. ***(673)***
Stephens Group, Inc. ***(674)***
Steptoe & Johnson LLP *(188)*
Strategic Horizons Advisors, L.L.C. *(189)*

Bankruptcy (BNK)

Traditional Values Coalition *(689)*
U.S. Oil and Gas Ass'n *(696)*
U.S. Public Interest Research Group *(697)*
UniGroup, Inc. *(698)*
Union of Needletrades, Industrial, and Textile Employees (UNITE) *(699)*
Union Pacific *(699)*
United Automobile, Aerospace and Agricultural Implement Workers of America (UAW) *(700)*
Valente Lopatin & Schulze *(198)*
Van Scoyoc Associates, Inc. *(200)*
VISA U.S.A., Inc. *(716)*
Webster, Chamberlain & Bean *(210)*
Williams & Jensen, P.C. *(215)*
Wilmington Savings Fund Society *(727)*
Winston & Strawn *(218)*
Zuckerman Spaeder L.L.P. *(221)*
Zurich Financial Group *(735)*

Beverage Industry (BEV)

The Advocacy Group *(6)*
AFLAC, Inc. *(231)*
Akin, Gump, Strauss, Hauer & Feld, L.L.P. *(8)*
Alsatian American Chamber of Commerce *(242)*
American Advertising Federation *(244)*
American Beverage Institute *(251)*
American Continental Group, Inc. *(12)*
American Teleservices Ass'n *(279)*
American Vintners Ass'n *(280)*
Americans for Tax Reform *(282)*
Anheuser-Busch Cos., Inc. *(284)*
Ass'n of Nat'l Advertisers *(297)*
Balch & Bingham LLP *(21)*
Beer Institute *(310)*
Bergner Bockorny Castagnetti and Hawkins *(26)*
Berman and Company *(27)*
Bohemian Cos. *(317)*
Bowling Proprietors' Ass'n of America *(318)*
Bulmer Holding PLC, H. P. *(323)*
The Coca-Cola Company *(356)*
Consumer Federation of America *(369)*
Coors Brewing Company *(371)*
Law Offices of Kevin G. Curtin *(56)*
DIAGEO *(387)*
Greener and Hook, LLC *(87)*
Griffin, Johnson, Dover & Stewart *(87)*
Hall, Green, Rupli, LLC *(90)*
Law Offices of Robert T. Herbolsheimer *(94)*
Hogan & Hartson L.L.P. *(96)*
R. J. Hudson Associates *(101)*
Hurt, Norton & Associates *(101)*
Industry Union Glass Container Promotion Program *(461)*
Internat'l Bottled Water Ass'n *(468)*
Internat'l Brotherhood of Teamsters *(469)*
Internat'l Mass Retailers Ass'n *(473)*
Interstate Wine Coalition *(477)*
Janus-Merritt Strategies, L.L.C. *(104)*
JBC Internat'l *(105)*
Kaiser Aluminum & Chemical Corp. *(485)*
Kendall-Jackson Winery *(488)*
Kessler & Associates Business Services, Inc. *(112)*
Kogovsek & Associates *(114)*
The Paul Laxalt Group *(117)*
Lesher & Russell, Inc. *(119)*
Long, Aldridge & Norman, LLP *(121)*
Magazine Publishers of America *(507)*
Management Options, Inc. *(123)*
Martin, Fisher & Associates, Inc. *(125)*
McClure, Gerard & Neuenschwander, Inc. *(127)*
McGlotten & Jarvis *(129)*
McGuiness & Holch *(130)*
McGuiness Norris & Williams, LLP *(130)*
Miller Brewing Co. *(524)*
James T. Molloy *(135)*
The Robert Mondavi Winery *(527)*
Morgan, Lewis & Bockius LLP *(136)*
R. B. Murphy & Associates *(139)*
Nat'l Ass'n of Beverage Retailers *(539)*
Nat'l Beer Wholesalers Ass'n *(552)*
Nat'l Club Ass'n *(556)*
Nat'l Licensed Beverage Ass'n *(570)*
Nat'l Soft Drink Ass'n *(578)*
Nestle USA, Inc. *(584)*
Obadal and MacLeod, p.c. *(143)*
O'Connor & Hannan, L.L.P. *(144)*
Olsson, Frank and Weeda, P.C. *(146)*
O'Neill, Athy & Casey, P.C. *(147)*
Jim Pasco & Associates *(150)*
Patton Boggs, LLP *(150)*
PepsiCo, Inc. *(612)*
Pernod Ricard *(612)*
Philip Morris Management Corp. *(615)*
Susan S. Platt Consulting *(156)*
Point of Purchase Advertising Institute *(619)*
Policy Directions, Inc. *(158)*
Public Strategies Washington, Inc. *(164)*
Ryan, Phillips, Utrecht & MacKinnon *(173)*
Strat@Comm (Strategic Communications Counselors) *(189)*
Swidler Berlin Shereff Friedman, LLP *(191)*
Tallon & Associates *(192)*
Timmons and Co., Inc. *(195)*
Michael L. Tiner *(195)*
UDV North America, Inc. *(698)*
UDV/Heublein, Inc. *(698)*
UST Public Affairs, Inc. *(710)*
Vinifera Wine Growers Ass'n *(715)*
Virginia Wineries Ass'n *(716)*
Vivendi Universal *(717)*
Washington Council Ernst & Young *(206)*
Williams & Jensen, P.C. *(215)*
Wine and Spirits Wholesalers of America *(728)*
Wine Institute *(728)*

Budget/Appropriations (BUD)

2001 World Police and Fire Games *(223)*
500 C Street Associates, L.P. *(224)*
The 60/Plus Ass'n, Inc. *(224)*
AAAE-ACI *(224)*
AAI Corp. *(224)*
AARP (American Ass'n of Retired Persons) *(224)*
ABB Daimler-Benz Transportation, N.A. (ADTRANZ) *(225)*
ABB, Inc. *(225)*
Abbott Laboratories *(225)*
Abrams & Co. Publishers Inc. *(225)*
Abtech Industries *(225)*
AC Transit *(225)*
Academic Health Center Coalition *(225)*
Academy of General Dentistry *(225)*
Academy of Osseointegration *(225)*
Accenture *(226)*
Access Community Health Network *(226)*
The Accord Group *(5)*
ACS Government Solutions Group *(227)*
Ad Hoc Public Television Group *(227)*
Adams and Reese LLP *(5)*
Adams County, Colorado *(227)*
Michael W. Adcock *(6)*
ADCS, Inc. *(227)*
Adelphi University *(227)*
AdMeTech *(227)*
ADSIL *(228)*
AdvaMed *(228)*
Advance Paradigm *(228)*
The Advocacy Group *(6)*
Advocates for Highway and Auto Safety *(229)*
Aetna Inc. *(230)*
Aetna Life & Casualty Co. *(230)*
AFL-CIO (American Federation of Labor and Congress of Industrial Organizations) *(231)*
AFL-CIO Maritime Committee *(231)*
AFL-CIO - Maritime Trades Department *(231)*
AFL-CIO - Transportation Trades Department *(231)*
AFLAC, Inc. *(231)*
Africa Resources Trust USA *(231)*
Agilent Technologies *(232)*
AIDS Action Council *(233)*
Aiken and Edgenfield Counties, South Carolina, Economic Development Partnership of *(233)*
Ainslie Associates *(7)*
Air Force Sergeants Ass'n *(233)*
Air Products and Chemicals, Inc. *(234)*
Air Transport Ass'n of America *(234)*
Air-Conditioning and Refrigeration Institute *(234)*
Aircraft Electronics Ass'n *(235)*
AKAL Security *(235)*
Akin, Gump, Strauss, Hauer & Feld, L.L.P. *(8)*
Alabama, Department of Transportation of the State of *(235)*
Alabama Nursing Homes Ass'n *(235)*
Alabama Water and Wastewater Institute, Inc. *(236)*
Alameda Corridor-East Construction Authority *(236)*
Alameda-Contra Costa Transit District *(236)*
The Alan Guttmacher Institute *(236)*
Alaska Groundfish Data Bank *(236)*
Alaska Legislature *(236)*
Albers & Co. *(10)*
Albert Einstein Medical Center *(237)*
Albuquerque, New Mexico, City of *(237)*
Alcalde & Fay *(10)*
Alcalde & Fay *(237)*
Aldaron Inc. *(238)*
Aleut Corp. *(238)*
Alexandria, Virginia, Sanitation Authority of the City of *(238)*
Alfred University *(238)*
Allegheny County, Pennsylvania, Housing Authority *(238)*
Alliance for American Innovation, Inc. *(239)*
Alliance for Children and Families *(239)*
Alliance for Internat'l Educational and Cultural Exchange, The *(239)*
Alliance for Justice *(239)*
Alliance for Nuclear Accountability *(240)*
Alliance for Reasonable Regulation of Insecticides *(240)*
Alliance for Regional Transportation *(240)*
Alliance of Automobile Manufacturers, Inc. *(240)*
Alliance of Western Milk Producers *(241)*
Alliance to Save Energy *(241)*
Alliant Techsystems, Inc. *(241)*
Allied Marketing *(241)*
Alpine Group, Inc. *(11)*
Alzheimer's Ass'n *(242)*
Amalgamated Transit Union *(242)*
AMDeC Policy Group, Inc. *(242)*
Ameren Services *(243)*
America's Community Bankers *(243)*
American Academy of Audiology *(243)*
American Academy of Child and Adolescent Psychiatry *(243)*
American Academy of Family Physicians *(243)*
American Academy of Ophthamology - Office of Federal Affairs *(244)*
American Academy of Orthopaedic Surgeons *(244)*
American Academy of Orthotists and Prosthetists *(244)*
American Academy of Otolaryngology-Head and Neck Surgery *(244)*
American Airlines *(244)*
American Arts Alliance *(245)*
American Ass'n for Active Lifestyles and Fitness *(245)*
American Ass'n for Clinical Chemistry, Inc. *(245)*
American Ass'n for Dental Research *(245)*
American Ass'n for Geriatric Psychiatry *(245)*
American Ass'n for Respiratory Care *(246)*
American Ass'n for the Study of Liver Diseases *(246)*
American Ass'n of Blood Banks *(246)*
American Ass'n of Colleges for Teacher Education *(247)*
American Ass'n of Colleges of Nursing *(247)*
American Ass'n of Colleges of Osteopathic Medicine *(247)*
American Ass'n of Community Colleges *(247)*
American Ass'n of Crop Insurers *(247)*
American Ass'n of Engineering Societies *(247)*
American Ass'n of Homes and Services for the Aging *(248)*
American Ass'n of Law Libraries *(248)*
American Ass'n of Motor Vehicle Administrators *(248)*
American Ass'n of Neurological Surgeons/Congress of Neurological Surgeons *(248)*
American Ass'n of Nurse Anesthetists *(248)*

American Ass'n of Pharmaceutical Scientists *(249)*
American Ass'n of University Affiliated Programs for Persons with Developmental Disabilities *(249)*
American Ass'n of University Women *(249)*
American Astronomical Soc. *(250)*
American Bakers Ass'n *(250)*
American Bankers Ass'n *(250)*
American Bar Ass'n *(250)*
American Beekeeping Federation *(250)*
American Bioenergy Ass'n *(251)*
American Boiler Manufacturers Ass'n *(251)*
American Cancer Soc. *(252)*
American Cast Iron Pipe Co. *(252)*
American Chemical Soc. *(252)*
American Chemistry Council *(252)*
American Coastal Coalition *(253)*
American College of Chest Physicians *(253)*
American College of Osteopathic Surgeons *(254)*
American College of Physicians-American Soc. of Internal Medicine (ACP-ASIM) *(254)*
American Commodity Distribution Ass'n *(254)*
American Consulting Engineers Council *(255)*
American Counseling Ass'n *(256)*
American Crop Protection Ass'n *(256)*
American Diabetes Ass'n *(257)*
American Electronics Ass'n *(257)*
American Express Co. *(258)*
American Farm Bureau Federation *(258)*
American Farmland Trust *(258)*
American Federation for Medical Research *(258)*
American Federation of Senior Citizens *(258)*
American Federation of State, County and Municipal Employees *(258)*
American Federation of Teachers *(259)*
American Feed Industry Ass'n *(259)*
American Film Institute *(259)*
American Fish Spotters Ass'n *(259)*
American Foreign Service Ass'n *(259)*
American Forest & Paper Ass'n *(259)*
American Foundation for the Blind - Governmental Relations Group *(260)*
American Gas Ass'n *(261)*
American Gas Cooling Center *(261)*
American Gastroenterological Ass'n *(261)*
American Geophysical Union *(261)*
American Great Lakes Ports *(261)*
American Health Care Ass'n *(261)*
American Heart Ass'n *(262)*
American Highway Users Alliance *(262)*
American Horse Council, Inc. *(263)*
American Hospital Ass'n *(263)*
American Hotel and Lodging Ass'n *(263)*
American Indian Higher Education Consortium *(263)*
The American Institute of Architects *(264)*
American Institute of Chemical Engineers *(264)*
American Institute of Physics *(264)*
American Insurance Ass'n *(264)*
American Internat'l Group, Inc. *(265)*
American Israel Public Affairs Committee *(265)*
American Jewish Congress *(265)*
American League of Financial Institutions *(266)*
American Legion *(266)*
American Library Ass'n *(266)*
American Liver Foundation *(266)*
American Logistics Ass'n *(266)*
American Lung Ass'n *(266)*
American Meat Institute *(267)*
American Medical Ass'n *(267)*
American Medical Group Ass'n *(267)*
American Medical Informatics Ass'n *(267)*
American Medical Technologists *(267)*
American Motorcyclist Ass'n *(268)*
American Moving and Storage Ass'n *(268)*
American Museum of Natural History *(268)*
American Network of Community Options and Resources (ANCOR) *(268)*
American Nursery and Landscape Ass'n *(268)*
American Nurses Ass'n *(268)*
American Occupational Therapy Ass'n, Inc. *(269)*
American Organization of Nurse Executives *(269)*
American Peanut Product Manufacturers, Inc. *(269)*
American Petroleum Institute *(269)*
American Physical Soc. *(270)*
American Portland Cement Alliance *(270)*
American Psychiatric Ass'n *(271)*
American Psychiatric Nurses Ass'n *(271)*
American Psychological Ass'n *(271)*
American Psychological Soc. *(271)*
American Public Health Ass'n *(271)*
American Public Power Ass'n *(272)*
American Public Transportation Ass'n *(272)*
American Red Cross *(272)*
American Rental Ass'n *(272)*
American Road and Transportation Builders Ass'n (ARTBA) *(273)*
American School Food Service Ass'n *(273)*
American Science and Engineering, Inc. *(273)*
American Seniors Housing Ass'n *(273)*
American Sheep Industry Ass'n *(273)*
American Sleep Disorders Ass'n *(274)*
American Soc. for Clinical Pharmacology and Therapeutics *(274)*
American Soc. for Quality *(275)*
American Soc. for Technion *(275)*
American Soc. for Therapeutic Radiology and Oncology *(275)*
American Soc. of Anesthesiologists *(275)*
American Soc. of Cataract and Refractive Surgery *(275)*
American Soc. of Civil Engineers *(276)*
American Soc. of Clinical Oncology *(276)*
American Soc. of Clinical Pathologists *(276)*
American Soc. of Hematology *(276)*
American Soc. of Nephrology *(276)*
American Soc. of Pediatric Nephrology *(277)*
American Soc. of Tropical Medicine and Hygiene *(277)*
American Speech, Language, and Hearing Ass'n *(277)*
American Sugar Alliance *(278)*
American Symphony Orchestra League *(278)*
American Thoracic Soc. *(279)*
American Trauma Soc. *(279)*
American Trucking Ass'ns *(279)*
American University of Beirut *(280)*
American Urogynecologic Soc. *(280)*
American Urological Ass'n *(280)*
American Vintners Ass'n *(280)*
American Water Works Ass'n *(280)*
American Waterways Operators *(280)*
American Wholesale Marketers Ass'n *(280)*
American Wind Energy Ass'n *(280)*
American Wood Preservers Institute *(280)*
Americans for Tax Reform *(282)*
Americans United for Separation of Church and State *(282)*
Amgen *(282)*
Amputee Coalition *(283)*
AmSurg Corp. *(283)*
Anchorage, Alaska, Municipality of *(283)*
Anheuser-Busch Cos., Inc. *(284)*
Animas-La Plata Water Conservancy District *(284)*
Anti-Value Added Tax Coalition *(285)*
APG Army Alliance *(286)*
Applied Terravision Systems *(287)*
The Arc *(287)*
Arcadia, California, City of *(287)*
Arctic Slope Regional Corp. *(288)*
Arent Fox Kintner Plotkin & Kahn, PLLC *(14)*
Arista Knowledge Systems, Inc. *(288)*
Arizona Mail Order Co. *(288)*
Arizona Public Service Co. *(288)*
Arkenol, Inc. *(288)*
Armtec Defense Products *(289)*
Arnold & Porter *(16)*
Arnold & Porter *(289)*
Arter & Hadden *(17)*
Arthritis Foundation *(289)*
The Asheville School *(290)*
Ashland Inc. *(290)*
James Nicholas Ashmore & Associates *(18)*
Ass'n for Career and Technical Education *(291)*
Ass'n for Commuter Transportation *(292)*
The Ass'n For Manufacturing Technology (AMT) *(292)*
Ass'n of America's Public Television Stations *(293)*
Ass'n of American Geographers *(293)*
Ass'n of American Medical Colleges *(294)*
Ass'n of American Railroads *(294)*
Ass'n of California Water Agencies *(295)*
Ass'n of Chiropractic Colleges *(295)*
Ass'n of Community College Trustees *(295)*
Ass'n of Flight Attendants *(295)*
Ass'n of Home Appliance Manufacturers *(296)*
Ass'n of Independent Research Institutes *(296)*
Ass'n of Jesuit Colleges and Universities *(296)*
Ass'n of Maternal and Child Health Programs (AMCHP) *(296)*
Ass'n of Medical Device Reprocessors *(296)*
Ass'n of Metropolitan Sewerage Agencies *(297)*
Ass'n of Minority Health Profession Schools *(297)*
Ass'n of Professors of Medicine *(298)*
Ass'n of Progressive Rental Organizations *(298)*
Ass'n of Schools of Public Health *(298)*
Ass'n of State Dam Safety Officials *(299)*
Ass'n of Technology Act Projects *(299)*
Ass'n of Trial Lawyers of America *(299)*
Ass'n of Universities for Research in Astronomy, Inc. *(299)*
Ass'n of University Programs in Health Administration *(299)*
Assiniboine and Sioux Tribes (Fort Peck Reservation) *(300)*
Associated Builders and Contractors *(300)*
Associated General Contractors of America *(300)*
Associated Universities Inc. *(300)*
Astra Solutions, LLC *(18)*
AstraZeneca Inc. *(301)*
AT&T *(301)*
Ross Atkins *(18)*
The Atlantic Group, Public Affairs, Inc. *(18)*
The Audubon Institute *(302)*
Aunt Martha's Youth Service Center *(303)*
Autism Soc. of America, Inc. *(303)*
Automotive Aftermarket Industry Ass'n *(303)*
Automotive Parts and Service Alliance *(303)*
Auyua Inc. *(304)*
Avalon, New Jersey, City of *(304)*
Aventis CropScience *(304)*
Avondale Industries, Inc. *(305)*
B'nai B'rith Internat'l *(305)*
B.C. Internat'l Corp. *(305)*
Babyland Family Services, Inc. *(305)*
Bailey Link *(306)*
Baker & Hostetler LLP *(19)*
The Laurin Baker Group *(20)*
Baker, Donelson, Bearman & Caldwell, P.C. *(21)*
Balch & Bingham LLP *(21)*
Ball Janik, LLP *(22)*
Ball State University *(306)*
Ballard, Spahr, Andrews & Ingersoll LLP *(306)*
Baltimore Symphony Orchestra *(306)*
Baltimore, Maryland, City of *(306)*
Bankers' Ass'n for Finance and Trade *(307)*
Bannerman and Associates, Inc. *(22)*
Barat College *(307)*
Barbour Griffith & Rogers, Inc. *(22)*
Barr Laboratories *(308)*
Barrick Goldstrike Mines, Inc. *(308)*
Barry University *(308)*
The Barton Co. *(24)*
Bass and Howes, Inc. *(24)*
Bassett Healthcare *(308)*
Baton Rouge, Louisiana, City of *(308)*
Battelle *(309)*
Battelle Memorial Institute *(309)*
Baxter Healthcare Corp. *(309)*
Bayer Corp. *(309)*
Baylor College of Medicine *(310)*
Bazelon Center for Mental Health Law, Judge David L. *(310)*
Beacon Consulting Group, Inc. *(25)*
Bechtel Group, Inc. *(310)*
Belew Law Firm *(25)*
Vikki Bell *(25)*
Timothy Bell & Co. *(25)*
Bell Atlantic Mobile *(310)*
Bellevue, Washington, City of *(311)*
BellSouth Corp. *(311)*

Bennett Turner & Coleman, LLP *(25)*
Bergen Community College ***(311)***
Bergner Bockorny Castagnetti and Hawkins *(26)*
Bernalillo, New Mexico, County of ***(312)***
Bethesda Academy for the Performing Arts ***(312)***
Bethlehem Steel Corp. ***(312)***
Better World Campaign ***(312)***
Terry Bevels Consulting *(27)*
Bexar Metropolitan Water District ***(313)***
BHP (USA) Inc. ***(313)***
Big Brothers/Big Sisters of America ***(313)***
Big Sky Economic Development Authority ***(313)***
Leon G. Billings, Inc. *(27)*
Biogen, Inc. ***(313)***
Biomedical Research Institute ***(314)***
Biotech Research and Development Center ***(314)***
Birch, Horton, Bittner & Cherot *(28)*
BKSH & Associates *(28)*
Richard W. Bliss *(29)*
Blue Cross and Blue Shield of Maine ***(315)***
Blue Cross Blue Shield Ass'n ***(315)***
BMW Financial Services of North America, Inc. ***(316)***
BMW Manufacturing Corp. ***(316)***
Board on Human Sciences ***(316)***
The Boeing Co. ***(316)***
Boise State University ***(317)***
Bombardier, Inc. ***(317)***
The Bond Market Ass'n ***(317)***
The BOSE Corp. ***(318)***
Boston College ***(318)***
Boston Symphony Orchestra ***(318)***
Boston University ***(318)***
Boston, Massachusetts, City of ***(318)***
Boys and Girls Club of Brownsville, Inc. ***(318)***
Boys and Girls Clubs of America ***(318)***
Boys Town Nat'l Research Hospital ***(318)***
Boys Town USA ***(318)***
Bracewell & Patterson, L.L.P. *(30)*
Marshall A. Brachman *(31)*
Brain Injury Ass'n ***(319)***
Brain Research Foundation ***(319)***
Brain Trauma Foundation ***(319)***
Brea, California, City of ***(319)***
Bread for the World ***(319)***
Brickfield, Burchette, Ritts & Stone *(32)*
Bridgestone/Firestone, Inc. ***(320)***
Bristol-Myers Squibb Co. ***(320)***
Brookfield Zoo/Chicago Zoological Soc. ***(321)***
Brotherhood of Maintenance of Way Employees ***(322)***
Brotherhood of Railroad Signalmen ***(322)***
Broward, Florida, County of ***(322)***
Broward, Florida, Department of Natural Resource Protection of the County of ***(322)***
Brown and Williamson Tobacco Corp. ***(322)***
Brownsville Public Utilities Board ***(322)***
Broydrick & Associates *(33)*
Brush Wellman, Inc. ***(323)***
Bryan Cave LLP *(33)*
Bulmer Holding PLC, H. P. ***(323)***
Burdeshaw Associates, Ltd. *(34)*
Burger King Corp. ***(324)***
Burk-Kleinpeter, Inc. ***(324)***
John G. "Toby" Burke *(34)*
Burlington Northern Santa Fe Railway ***(324)***
Burlington Resources Oil & Gas Co. ***(324)***
Burns and Roe Enterprises, Inc. ***(324)***
The Business Roundtable ***(325)***
C F Industries, Inc. ***(325)***
The C.L.A. Group, LLC *(35)*
Calaveras County, California, Water District ***(326)***
California Asparagus Commission ***(326)***
California Ass'n of Sanitation Agencies ***(326)***
California Central Coast Research Partnership ***(326)***
California Correctional Peace Officers Ass'n ***(326)***
California Hospital Medical Center Foundation ***(327)***
California Institute for the Arts ***(327)***
California Institute of Technology ***(327)***
California Museum Foundation ***(327)***
California Pistachio Commission ***(327)***
California School of Professional Psychology ***(327)***
California State Teachers' Retirement System ***(327)***
California Water Service Co. ***(328)***
Calspan University of Buffalo Research Center ***(328)***
CALSTART ***(328)***
Cambridge Systematics, Inc *(35)*
Cambridge Technologies ***(328)***
Camelbak Products, Inc. ***(328)***
Camp Dresser and McKee, Inc. ***(328)***
Campaign for Medical Research ***(329)***
Campaign for United Nations Reform ***(329)***
Campaign to Preserve U.S. Global Leadership ***(329)***
Campbell Crane & Associates *(36)*
Canadian Nat'l Railway Co. ***(329)***
Canadian River Municipal Water Authority ***(329)***
Canberra Packard BioScience ***(330)***
Cancer Leadership Council ***(330)***
Mark R. Cannon *(37)*
CapCURE ***(330)***
Capital Area Transit Authority ***(330)***
Capital City Economic Development Authority ***(330)***
Capital Region Airport Commission ***(330)***
Capitol Associates, Inc. *(37)*
Capitol Coalitions Inc. *(38)*
Capitol Hill Advocates *(39)*
Capitol Partners *(39)*
Capitol Solutions *(39)*
Capitol Strategies *(39)*
Capitolink, LLC *(39)*
CapitolWatch ***(331)***
Career College Ass'n ***(331)***
Cargill Dow ***(331)***
Carlsberg Management Co. ***(332)***
The Carmen Group *(40)*
Carnegie Hall Corp. ***(332)***
Bill Carney & Co. *(41)*
Carolina, Puerto Rico, City of ***(332)***
Caron Foundation ***(332)***
Carondelet Health System ***(332)***
Carpi & Clay *(41)*
Carr Public Affairs ***(332)***
Cartwright & Riley *(41)*
Cascade Associates *(41)*
Cascade General, Inc. ***(332)***
Case Western Reserve University School of Medicine ***(332)***
Cash, Smith & Wages *(41)*
Cassidy & Associates, Inc. *(42)*
Catholic Health Ass'n of the United States ***(333)***
Cavarocchi Ruscio Dennis Associates *(44)*
Ann Cecchetti *(44)*
Cedars-Sinai Medical Center ***(334)***
Ceiba, Puerto Rico, City of ***(334)***
Cell Therapeutics Inc. ***(334)***
Cellular Telecommunications and Internet Ass'n ***(334)***
Center for Aging Policy ***(335)***
Center for Civic Education ***(335)***
Center for Employment Training ***(336)***
Center for Freedom and Prosperity ***(336)***
Center for Law and Social Policy ***(336)***
Center for Research on Institutions and Social Policy ***(337)***
Center on Budget and Policy Priorities ***(338)***
Center Point Inc. ***(338)***
Central American Bank of Economic Integration ***(338)***
Central Arizona Water Conservation District ***(338)***
Central Basin Municipal Water District ***(338)***
Central Council of Tlingit and Haida Indian Tribes of Alaska ***(338)***
Central Piedmont Community College ***(339)***
Central Utah Water Conservancy District ***(339)***
Central Valley Project Water Ass'n ***(339)***
Chamber of Commerce of the U.S.A. ***(340)***
Chamberlain Manufacturing Corp. ***(341)***
Chambers Associates Inc. *(45)*
Chambers, Conlon & Hartwell *(45)*
Charter Schools Development Corp. ***(341)***
Chase Manhattan Bank ***(341)***
Chatham Area Transit Authority ***(341)***
Chesapeake Bay Foundation ***(342)***
Chesapeake Bay Maritime Museum ***(342)***
Chevron, U.S.A. ***(342)***
Chicago Botanic Garden ***(343)***
Chicago Regional Transportation Authority ***(343)***
Chicago School Reform Board of Trustees ***(343)***
Chicago State University ***(343)***
Child Welfare League of America ***(343)***
Children and Adults with Attention Deficit Disorders (CHADD) ***(344)***
The Children's Cause Inc. ***(344)***
Children's Defense Fund ***(344)***
Children's Hospital and Health Center of San Diego ***(344)***
Children's Hospital and Medical Center ***(344)***
Children's Hospital of Boston ***(344)***
Children's Hospital of Wisconsin ***(344)***
Chronic Fatigue and Immune Dysfunction Syndrome Ass'n of America ***(346)***
The Chubb Corp. ***(346)***
CIGNA Corp. ***(346)***
Cincinnati, Ohio, City of ***(347)***
Cisco Systems Inc. ***(347)***
Cities Advocating Emergency AIDS Relief (CAEAR) ***(347)***
Citizen Strategies *(46)*
Citizens Against Government Waste ***(348)***
Citizens for a Sound Economy ***(348)***
Citizens for Public Action on Cholesterol, Inc. ***(348)***
Citizens for Tax Justice ***(348)***
Citizens for the Treatment of High Blood Pressure, Inc. ***(349)***
Citizens Network for Foreign Affairs (CNFA) ***(349)***
Citrus Heights, California, City of ***(349)***
City College of San Francisco ***(349)***
City of Hope Nat'l Medical Center ***(349)***
Civic Ventures ***(349)***
Clackamas, Oregon, County of ***(349)***
Clark & Weinstock, Inc. *(47)*
Clark County Regional Flood Control District ***(350)***
Clark/Bardes, Inc. ***(350)***
Clatsop Community College ***(350)***
Clearwater, Florida, City of ***(350)***
Clemson University ***(350)***
Cleveland Clinic Foundation ***(350)***
Cleveland State University - College of Urban Affairs ***(351)***
Cleveland, City of/Cleveland Hopkins Internat'l Airport ***(351)***
The Climate Council, ***(351)***
Close Up Foundation ***(351)***
CMS Defense Systems, Inc. ***(351)***
CNA Financial Corp. ***(351)***
CNA Insurance Cos. ***(351)***
Coachella Valley Water District ***(352)***
Coal Utilization Research Council ***(352)***
Coalition for American Trauma Care ***(352)***
Coalition for Brain Injury Research and Services, Inc. ***(353)***
Coalition for Employment through Exports ***(353)***
Coalition for Health Funding ***(353)***
Coalition for Health Services Research ***(354)***
Coalition for Maritime Education ***(354)***
Coalition of Boston Teaching Hospitals ***(355)***
Coalition of EPSCoR States ***(355)***
Coalition of Higher Education Assistance Organizations ***(355)***
The Coalition on Motor Vehicle Privacy ***(356)***
Coalition to Stop Gun Violence ***(356)***
Coastal Impact Assistance & Reinvestment ***(356)***
COGEMA, Inc. ***(357)***
Ronald J. Cohen Investments ***(357)***
Coin Acceptors, Inc. ***(357)***
The College Board ***(357)***
College of American Pathologists ***(357)***
College on Problems of Drug Dependence ***(357)***
Collier Shannon Scott, PLLC *(48)*
Collins & Company, Inc. *(49)*
Colombian American Service Ass'n ***(358)***
Colorado River Indian Tribes ***(358)***
Columbia College Chicago ***(359)***
Columbia University ***(359)***
Colusa Basin Drainage District ***(359)***
ComEd ***(359)***

Committee for a Responsible Federal Budget *(360)*
Committee for Education Funding *(361)*
Committee of Unsecured Creditors *(361)*
Common Cause *(361)*
Commonwealth Consulting Corp. *(362)*
Commonwealth Group, Ltd. *(50)*
Communications Workers of America *(362)*
Communities in Schools, Inc. *(362)*
The Community Builders, Inc. *(362)*
Community Hospital Telehealth Consortium *(362)*
Community Hospitals of Central California *(363)*
Community Transportation Ass'n of America *(363)*
Computer and Communications Industry Ass'n (CCIA) *(364)*
Computer Associates Internat'l, Inc. *(364)*
Computer Sciences Corp. *(364)*
Compuware Corp. *(364)*
ConAgra Foods, Inc. *(365)*
Concerned Women for America *(365)*
Concord Coalition *(365)*
Condor Electronic Systems *(365)*
Confederated Tribes of Warm Springs Reservation *(365)*
Conkling, Fiskum & McCormick *(51)*
Connecticut Resource Recovery Authority *(367)*
The Conservative Caucus *(367)*
Consolidated Edison Co. of New York *(367)*
Consortium for Oceanographic Research and Education (CORE) *(367)*
Consortium for Plant Biotechnology Research *(368)*
Consortium of Social Science Ass'ns *(368)*
Constellation Energy Group *(368)*
Constitutional Rights Foundation *(368)*
Construction Industry Round Table, Inc. *(368)*
Construction Management Ass'n of America *(368)*
Consumer Bankers Ass'n *(368)*
Consumer Federation of America *(369)*
Consumer Healthcare Products Ass'n *(369)*
Consumers United for Rail Equity *(369)*
Contact Lens Institute *(369)*
Continental Airlines Inc. *(370)*
Contra Costa, California, Tenants of the County of *(370)*
Contract Services Ass'n of America *(370)*
Convergence Services, Inc. *(52)*
Cook Children's Health Care System *(370)*
Cook Inlet Region Inc. *(371)*
Cooley's Anemia Foundation *(371)*
Cooper Green Hospital *(371)*
Copeland, Lowery & Jacquez *(52)*
The Core Center *(371)*
Corporation for Enterprise Development *(372)*
Corporation for Supportive Housing *(372)*
Corte Madera, California, Town of *(373)*
Cosmetic, Toiletry and Fragrance Ass'n *(373)*
Council for a Livable World Education Fund *(373)*
Council for Agricultural Science and Technology *(374)*
Council for Chemical Research, Inc. *(374)*
Council for Conservation and Reinvestment of OCS Revenue *(374)*
Council for Exceptional Children *(374)*
Council for Government Reform *(374)*
Council for Opportunity in Education *(374)*
Council of Graduate Schools *(375)*
Council of Large Public Housing Authorities *(376)*
Council of State and Territorial Epidemiologists *(376)*
Council of State Governments *(376)*
Council of the Great City Schools *(376)*
Council on Radionuclides and Radiopharmaceuticals (CORAR) *(377)*
Coushatta Tribe of Louisiana *(377)*
Covenant House *(377)*
Covington & Burling *(53)*
Craig Associates *(55)*
Craig, Alaska, City of *(378)*
Credit Suisse First Boston Corp. *(378)*
Crohn's and Colitis Foundation of America *(378)*
Crop Protection Coalition *(378)*
CSX Corp. *(379)*
CSX Lines LLC *(379)*
Cure for Lymphoma Foundation *(380)*
Cuyahoga Community College *(380)*
Cystic Fibrosis Foundation *(380)*
D'Youville College *(381)*
DaimlerChrysler Corp. *(381)*
Dale Service Corp. *(382)*
Dallas Area Rapid Transit Authority *(382)*
Dallas, Texas, City of *(382)*
Dalton & Dalton P.C. *(382)*
Danaher Corp. *(382)*
Dartmouth-Hitchcock Medical Center *(382)*
Davidoff & Malito, LLP *(57)*
Davidson & Company, Inc. *(57)*
Mary E. Davis *(57)*
Bob Davis & Associates *(57)*
Davis O'Connell, Inc. *(58)*
Davison Transport, Inc. *(383)*
Day & Zimmermann, Inc. *(383)*
Dayton, Ohio, Washington Office of the City of *(383)*
Daytona Beach, City of *(383)*
Dean Blakey & Moskowitz *(59)*
DeBrunner and Associates, Inc. *(60)*
Deere & Co. *(383)*
Defenders of Wildlife *(383)*
Delaware and Hudson Railroad *(384)*
Delaware North Companies *(384)*
Delta Air Lines *(384)*
Delta Wetlands Project *(385)*
Denton, Texas, County of *(385)*
DePaul University *(386)*
Detroit Medical Center *(386)*
Detroit Public Television *(386)*
Detroit, Michigan, City of *(386)*
DeVry, Inc. *(387)*
Dewey Ballantine LLP *(61)*
DFS Group Ltd. *(387)*
DGME Fairness Initiative *(387)*
Diamond Manufacturing, Inc. *(387)*
Dick Corp. *(387)*
Digestive Disease Nat'l Coalition *(388)*
Dillard University *(388)*
Dime Savings Bank of New York *(388)*
Dimensions Healthcare System *(388)*
Dimock Community Health Center *(388)*
Direct Marketing Ass'n, Inc. *(388)*
Discovery Place, Inc. (Charlotte Science Museum) *(389)*
Discovery Science Center *(389)*
Diversified Collection Services, Inc. *(390)*
Doepken Keevican & Weiss *(63)*
Dole Food Co. *(390)*
Domestic Petroleum Council *(390)*
Dominican College of Blauvelt *(391)*
Dominion Resources, Inc. *(391)*
Dorsey & Whitney LLP *(63)*
Dow AgroSciences *(391)*
Dow, Lohnes & Albertson, PLLC *(64)*
Downey McGrath Group, Inc. *(64)*
Downey, California, Economic Development of the City of *(392)*
Duane, Morris & Heckscher LLP *(65)*
The Duberstein Group, Inc. *(65)*
Ducks Unlimited Inc. *(392)*
Dunn-Edwards Corp. *(393)*
The Dutko Group, Inc. *(68)*
Dykema Gossett *(393)*
Dykema Gossett PLLC *(69)*
Dystonia Medical Research Foundation *(394)*
EarthData Holdings *(394)*
East Bay Municipal Utility District *(395)*
East Tennessee Economic Council *(395)*
East Texas Electric Cooperative *(395)*
Easter Seals *(395)*
Eastern Municipal Water District *(395)*
Eastman Chemical Co. *(395)*
Easton Airport *(395)*
Eaton Vance Management Co. *(395)*
Eclipse Energy Systems, Inc./Insyte, Inc. *(396)*
Economics America *(396)*
Edington, Peel & Associates, Inc. *(70)*
Edison Electric Institute *(397)*
Edison Internat'l *(397)*
Edmund Scientific Co. *(397)*
EDS Corp. *(398)*
Education and Training Resources *(398)*
Education Finance Council *(398)*
Edward Health Services *(398)*
Edwards Associates, Inc. *(71)*
Egle Associates *(71)*
El Centro Regional Medical Center *(399)*
El Paso Water Utilities - Public Service Board *(399)*
The Electric Vehicle Ass'n of the Americas (EVAA) *(400)*
Elkem Materials Inc. *(401)*
Ellicott Internat'l *(401)*
Elmira College *(401)*
Embry-Riddle Aeronautical University *(401)*
EMC Corp. *(401)*
Emergency Department Practice Management Ass'n (EDPMA) *(401)*
EMI Associates, Ltd. *(71)*
Encapco Technologies, LLC *(402)*
Encinitas, California, City of *(402)*
English First, Inc. *(403)*
Enron Corp. *(403)*
ENS Resources, Inc. *(71)*
Entergy Services, Inc. *(404)*
The Enterprise Foundation *(404)*
Envirocare of Utah, Inc. *(404)*
Environmental Commonsense Coalition *(405)*
EOP Group, Inc. *(72)*
Epilepsy Foundation of America *(406)*
Ann Eppard Associates, Ltd. *(72)*
Epstein Becker & Green, P.C. *(72)*
Erie Internat'l Airport *(406)*
ERIM *(406)*
The ERISA Industry Committee (ERIC) *(406)*
Ervin Technical Associates, Inc. (ETA) *(73)*
ESA, Inc. *(407)*
Charles D. Estes & Associates *(73)*
Eugene, Oregon, City of *(407)*
Eureka, California, City of *(408)*
EV Rental Cars, LLC *(408)*
Evans & Black, Inc. *(73)*
EXPRO Chemical Products *(409)*
ExtrudeHone Corp. *(409)*
Exxon Mobil Corp. *(409)*
EZ's Solutions, Inc. *(74)*
Fairbanks, Alaska, North Star Borough of *(410)*
Fairfax, Virginia, County of *(410)*
Fairfield University *(410)*
Fairfield, California, City of *(410)*
Fairview Hospital and Healthcare Services *(410)*
Fallon Community Health Plan *(410)*
Fallon, Nevada, City of *(410)*
Family Communications, Inc. *(410)*
Family Farm Alliance (Project Transfer Council) *(410)*
Family Place *(411)*
Family Research Council, Inc. *(411)*
Family Violence Prevention Fund *(411)*
Fannie Mae *(411)*
Farm Credit Council *(411)*
Farmers Insurance Group *(412)*
Marcus G. Faust, P.C. *(74)*
FBI Agents Ass'n *(412)*
FDA-NIH Council *(412)*
FED Corp. *(412)*
Federal Health Strategies, Inc. *(75)*
Federal Home Loan Bank of San Francisco *(413)*
Federal Home Loan Mortgage Corp. (Freddie Mac) *(413)*
Federation of American Hospitals *(414)*
Federation of American Societies for Experimental Biology *(414)*
Federation of Behavioral, Psychological and Cognitive Sciences *(414)*
FedEx Corp. *(415)*
Feld Entertainment Inc. *(415)*
The Ferguson Group, LLC *(76)*
Fideicomiso de la Escuela de Agricultura de la Region Tropical Humeda, S.A. *(416)*
Fire Island Ass'n *(417)*
Firearms Training Systems, Inc. *(417)*
FirstEnergy Co. *(418)*
Fishbein Associates, Inc. *(77)*
Fisher Consulting *(77)*
Fishers Island Ferry District *(418)*
Fleet Reserve Ass'n *(418)*

Fleishman-Hillard, Inc ***(77)***
Flint, Michigan, City of ***(419)***
R. G. Flippo and Associates, Inc. ***(77)***
FLIR Systems, Inc. ***(419)***
Florence, South Carolina, City of ***(419)***
Florida Citrus Alliance ***(419)***
Florida Internat'l University ***(420)***
Florida State University ***(420)***
Florida State University System ***(420)***
FMC Corp. ***(420)***
Foley & Lardner ***(78)***
Foley Government and Public Affairs, Inc. ***(78)***
Folsom, California, City of ***(421)***
Food Distributors Internat'l (NAWGA-IFDA) ***(421)***
Food Marketing Institute ***(421)***
Food Research and Action Center ***(422)***
Foothill Transit ***(422)***
Betty Ford Center ***(422)***
Henry Ford Health System ***(422)***
Ford Motor Co. ***(422)***
Forensic Technology, Inc. ***(423)***
Fort Abraham Lincoln Foundation ***(423)***
Fort Wayne, Indiana, City of ***(423)***
Forum Health ***(423)***
Bob Foster and Associates ***(79)***
Foster Wheeler Corp. ***(424)***
The Foundation for Environmental and Economic Progress ***(424)***
FoxKiser ***(79)***
Franklin Institute ***(425)***
Fraternal Order of Police (U.S. Park Police Labor Committee) ***(425)***
Free Trade Lumber Council ***(425)***
Freeport-McMoRan Copper & Gold Inc. ***(425)***
Freightliner Corp. ***(425)***
French & Company ***(79)***
John Freshman Associates, Inc. ***(79)***
Fresno Community Hospital and Medical Center ***(426)***
Fresno Metropolitan Museum ***(426)***
Friends Committee on Nat'l Legislation ***(426)***
Friends of CDC ***(426)***
Friends of ITS/ITS America ***(426)***
Friends of the Earth ***(426)***
Fuel Cell Energy, Inc. ***(427)***
Fuel Cells for Transportation ***(427)***
The Furman Group ***(80)***
Gainesville, Florida, City of ***(428)***
Galena, Illinois, City of ***(428)***
The Gallagher Group, LLC ***(80)***
Galveston County, Texas ***(428)***
Gardena, California, City of ***(429)***
Sara Garland (and Associates) ***(81)***
Garrison Diversion Conservancy District ***(429)***
Gary Public Transportation Corp. ***(429)***
Gary Sanitary District ***(429)***
Gary, Indiana, Housing Authority of the City of ***(429)***
Gary, Indiana, Washington Office of the City of ***(429)***
Gas Research Institute ***(429)***
Gateway Cities ***(430)***
GCRC Program Directors Ass'n ***(430)***
Genentech, Inc. ***(431)***
General Aviation Manufacturers Ass'n ***(431)***
General Communications, Inc. ***(431)***
General Dynamics Corp. ***(431)***
General Electric Co. ***(432)***
General Electric Industrial & Power Systems ***(432)***
General Mills ***(432)***
General Motors Corp. ***(432)***
Generic Pharmaceutical Ass'n ***(433)***
Genesis Consulting Group, LLC ***(82)***
The Genome Action Coalition ***(433)***
Genome Dynamics, Inc. ***(433)***
Genzyme Corp. ***(433)***
George Mason University Foundation ***(434)***
George Washington University, Office of Government Relations ***(434)***
Georgia Ports Authority ***(434)***
Georgia-Pacific Corp. ***(434)***
Geothermal Energy Ass'n ***(434)***
Geothermal Heat Pump Consortium ***(434)***
Gibbons & Company, Inc. ***(82)***
Gila River Indian Community ***(435)***
Girl Scouts of the U.S.A. - Washington Office ***(435)***
Glankler Brown, PLLC ***(435)***
GlaxoSmithKline ***(436)***
Glenn-Colusa Irrigation District ***(436)***
GMA Internat'l ***(83)***
Golin/Harris Internat'l ***(84)***
B. F. Goodrich Co. ***(437)***
Goodstein & Associates ***(84)***
Goodyear Tire and Rubber Co. ***(437)***
Gottehrer and Co. ***(84)***
Government Employees Hospital Ass'n ***(437)***
Government Relations, Inc. ***(84)***
GPC Internat'l ***(85)***
Grants Pass Irrigation District ***(438)***
Greater New Orleans Expressway Commission ***(439)***
Greater New York Hospital Ass'n ***(439)***
Greater Orlando Aviation Authority ***(439)***
Greater Washington Board of Trade ***(439)***
Green County Health Care, Inc. ***(440)***
Green Door ***(440)***
Greenberg Traurig, LLP ***(86)***
Gridley, California, City of/Northern California Power Agency ***(440)***
Griffin, Johnson, Dover & Stewart ***(87)***
The Grizzle Company ***(88)***
Grocery Manufacturers of America ***(440)***
Ground Water Protection Council ***(441)***
Group Health, Inc. ***(441)***
Gryphon Internat'l ***(89)***
GSE Systems, Inc. ***(441)***
GTECH Corp. ***(441)***
Guam Legislature ***(441)***
Guaranty Bank, SSB ***(442)***
Guardian Angel Holdings, Inc. ***(442)***
Guardian Life Insurance Co. of America ***(442)***
Guardian Marine Internat'l LLC ***(442)***
Guidant Corp. ***(442)***
Guinea, Secretary General of the Presidency of the Republic of ***(442)***
Gun Owners of America ***(442)***
Gustafson Associates ***(89)***
Haarmann & Reimer Corp. ***(443)***
Hadassah, The Women's Zionist Organization of America ***(443)***
C. McClain Haddow & Associates ***(89)***
Halliburton/Brown & Root ***(443)***
Martin G. Hamberger & Associates ***(91)***
Hamilton Sundstrand ***(444)***
Katherine Hamilton ***(91)***
Harris, Beach & Wilcox ***(445)***
Harris, Texas, Metropolitan Transit Authority of ***(445)***
Harvard University Washington Office ***(445)***
Hawaiian Airlines ***(445)***
Hazelden Foundation ***(445)***
HCR-Manor Care, Inc. ***(445)***
Health and Medicine Counsel of Washington ***(93)***
Health Insurance Ass'n of America ***(446)***
Health Physics Soc. ***(446)***
Health Policy Strategies ***(93)***
Health Quest ***(446)***
Healthcare Financing Study Group ***(447)***
Hebrew Immigrant Aid Soc. ***(447)***
Hecht, Spencer & Associates ***(93)***
Hecla Mining Co. ***(447)***
Law Office of Edward D. Heffernan ***(94)***
Helen Keller Worldwide ***(448)***
Helicopter Ass'n Internat'l ***(448)***
Allen Herbert ***(94)***
Hershey Foods Corp. ***(449)***
Hewlett-Packard Co. ***(449)***
Hi-Desert Water District ***(449)***
Higgins, McGovern & Smith, LLC ***(94)***
High Speed Ground Transportation Ass'n ***(449)***
Hispanic Ass'n of Colleges and Universities ***(450)***
Ho-Chunk Nation ***(450)***
Hogan & Hartson L.L.P. ***(96)***
Hohlt & Associates ***(98)***
Holland & Knight LLP ***(98)***
Hollis-Eden Pharmaceuticals, Inc. ***(451)***
Holnam Inc. ***(451)***
Home Builders Institute ***(451)***
The Home Depot ***(451)***
Peter Homer ***(99)***
Honberger and Walters, Inc. ***(99)***
Honeywell Internat'l, Inc. ***(452)***
Hood River, Oregon, Port of ***(452)***
Hooper Owen & Winburn ***(99)***
Hooper, Lundy and Bookman ***(452)***
Hopi Indian Tribe ***(452)***
Housing Assistance Council ***(453)***
Housing Works ***(453)***
Houston, Texas, City of ***(453)***
Houston, Texas, Department of Public Works & Engineering of the City of ***(453)***
Houston, Texas, Port Authority of the City of ***(453)***
Howland Hook Container Terminal Inc. ***(454)***
Hualapai Nation ***(454)***
Humana Inc. ***(455)***
Humboldt Bay Municipal Water District ***(455)***
Humboldt Harbor Recreation ***(455)***
Huntington Beach, California, City of ***(455)***
Huntington's Disease Soc. of America ***(455)***
Hunton & Williams ***(101)***
Hurt, Norton & Associates ***(101)***
Fred Hutchinson Cancer Research Center ***(455)***
Iberville Parish ***(456)***
The Ickes & Enright Group ***(102)***
The Ickes & Enright Group ***(457)***
ICRC Energy, Inc. ***(457)***
Idaho Power Co. ***(457)***
Idaho State University ***(457)***
Illinois Collaboration on Youth ***(457)***
Illinois Department of Human Services ***(457)***
Illinois Institute of Technology ***(457)***
Illinois Primary Health Care Ass'n ***(457)***
IMC Global Inc. ***(458)***
Immune Deficiency Foundation, Inc. ***(458)***
Impact Strategies ***(102)***
Imperial Irrigation District ***(458)***
Independent Electrical Contractors, Inc. ***(459)***
Independent Office Products and Furniture Dealers Ass'n ***(459)***
Independent Petroleum Ass'n of America ***(459)***
Indiana State University ***(460)***
Indiana University ***(460)***
Indiana, Office of the Governor of the State of ***(460)***
Indianapolis Public Transportation Corp. ***(460)***
Industrial Customers of Northwest Utilities ***(461)***
Industrial Telecommunications Ass'n, Inc. ***(461)***
Industry Urban-Development Agency ***(461)***
Infilco Degremont, Inc. ***(461)***
Information Technology Industry Council ***(462)***
Inglewood, California, City of ***(462)***
Inoveon Corp. ***(462)***
Insight Technology, Inc. ***(462)***
Institute for Entrepreneurship ***(463)***
Institute for Student Achievement ***(464)***
Institute of Electrical and Electronics Engineers, Inc. ***(464)***
Institute of Food Technologists ***(464)***
Integrated Skilled Care of Ohio ***(465)***
Intellectual Property Owners Ass'n ***(465)***
Intermountain Forest Industry Ass'n ***(467)***
Internat'l Ass'n of Fire Chiefs ***(468)***
Internat'l Ass'n of Fish and Wildlife Agencies ***(468)***
Internat'l Ass'n of Personnel in Employment Security ***(468)***
Internat'l Brotherhood of Boilermakers, Iron Shipbuilders, Blacksmiths, Forgers and Helpers ***(469)***
Internat'l Brotherhood of Electrical Workers ***(469)***
Internat'l Brotherhood of Teamsters ***(469)***
Internat'l Business Machines Corp. ***(469)***
Internat'l Center for Clubhouse Development ***(469)***
Internat'l Code Council ***(470)***
Internat'l College ***(470)***
Internat'l Council of Shopping Centers ***(470)***
Internat'l Dairy Foods Ass'n ***(470)***
Internat'l Dyslexia Ass'n, The ***(471)***
Internat'l Federation of Professional and Technical Engineers ***(471)***
Internat'l Intellectual Property Institute ***(472)***
Internat'l Mass Retailers Ass'n ***(473)***
Internat'l Medical Programs ***(473)***

Internat'l Rescue Committee Inc. ***(474)***
Internat'l Shipholding Corp. ***(474)***
Internat'l Technology Education Ass'n ***(475)***
Internat'l Technology Resources, Inc. ***(475)***
Internat'l Union of Painters and Allied Trades ***(476)***
Interstate 5 Consortium ***(477)***
Interstate Natural Gas Ass'n of America ***(477)***
Intuit, Inc. ***(477)***
Investment Co. Institute ***(477)***
InVision Technologies ***(478)***
Irrigation Projects Reauthorization Council ***(479)***
The Irvine Co. ***(479)***
Island Express Boat Lines Ltd. ***(479)***
IT Group, Inc. ***(479)***
ITT Industries ***(480)***
ITT Industries Defense ***(480)***
Ivy Tech State College ***(480)***
Jackson State University ***(480)***
Jacobs & Co. Public Affairs/Loma Linda University ***(481)***
Jacobs Engineering Group Inc. ***(481)***
Jacobus Tenbroek Memorial Fund ***(481)***
Janus-Merritt Strategies, L.L.C. *(104)*
Jar-Mon Consultants, Inc. *(105)*
Jasper, Alabama, City of ***(482)***
Jazz at Lincoln Center Inc. ***(482)***
Jefferson County Commission ***(482)***
Jefferson Government Relations, L.L.C. *(106)*
Jefferson Parish Council ***(482)***
Jefferson State Community College ***(482)***
Jefferson Texas, County of ***(482)***
The Jewelers' Security Alliance ***(483)***
Jewish Family Service Ass'n of Cleveland ***(483)***
Jewish Federation of Metropolitan Chicago ***(483)***
JKB Communications *(107)*
Johns Hopkins Center for Civilian Biodefense Studies ***(483)***
Johns Hopkins School of Hygiene and Public Health ***(483)***
Johns Hopkins University & Hospital ***(483)***
Johns Hopkins University Hospital, School of Hygiene and Public Health ***(483)***
Johns Hopkins University-Applied Physics Lab ***(484)***
Johnson & Johnson, Inc. ***(484)***
Johnson Controls, Inc. ***(484)***
Johnston & Associates, LLC *(107)*
Philip W. Johnston Associates *(108)*
Joint Baltic American Nat'l Committee, Inc. ***(484)***
Joint Council of Allergy, Asthma and Immunology ***(484)***
Joint Powers Board ***(484)***
Jolly/Rissler, Inc. *(108)*
Jones, Walker, Waechter, Poitevent, Carrere & Denegre, L.L.P. *(108)*
Jorden Burt LLP *(109)*
Joslin Diabetes Center ***(485)***
Juneau, Alaska, City of ***(485)***
Juvenile Diabetes Foundation Internat'l ***(485)***
K Capital Partners ***(485)***
Kaiser Aluminum & Chemical Corp. ***(485)***
Kalkines, Arky, Zall and Bernstein ***(486)***
The Kamber Group *(109)*
Betty Ann Kane & Co. *(110)*
Kansas City Area Transportation Authority ***(486)***
Kansas City Southern Industries ***(486)***
Kansas City, Missouri, City of ***(486)***
Kaplan Companies, Inc. ***(486)***
Barbara A. Karmanos Cancer Institute ***(486)***
Kaweah Delta Water Conservation District ***(487)***
KCTS ***(487)***
Keller Equity Group, Inc. ***(487)***
Kellogg Brown and Root ***(487)***
Kelly and Associates, Inc. *(111)*
Kennedy/Jenks Consultants ***(488)***
Kentucky, Commonwealth of ***(488)***
Kern County Water Agency ***(488)***
Kern River Watermaster ***(488)***
Kessler & Associates Business Services, Inc. *(112)*
Ketchikan Gateway Borough ***(488)***
Ketchikan Public Utilities ***(488)***
Kettering Medical Center ***(489)***
Kimberly Consulting, LLC *(113)*
Kimberly-Clark Corp. ***(489)***
King & Spalding *(113)*
Kinghorn & Associates, L.L.C. ***(489)***
Kiwanis Internat'l ***(490)***
Knoxville College ***(490)***
Patrick C. Koch *(114)*
Koch Industries, Inc. ***(490)***
Kodiak Island, Alaska, Borough of ***(490)***
Kodiak, Alaska, City of ***(490)***
Kogovsek & Associates *(114)*
Komen Breast Cancer Foundation, The Susan G. ***(491)***
Kraft Foods, Inc. ***(492)***
L-3 Communications Corp. ***(493)***
LA Center for the Blind ***(493)***
Labor Management Maritime Committee, Inc. ***(493)***
Laborers Health & Safety Fund ***(493)***
Laborers-AGC Education and Training Fund ***(493)***
Lafarge Corp. ***(494)***
Lafayette Airport Commission ***(494)***
Lafayette Consolidated Government ***(494)***
Laguna Beach, California, City of ***(494)***
Lake Charles Memorial Hospital ***(494)***
Lake, California, County of ***(494)***
Lake, Illinois, County of ***(494)***
Lakeland Regional Medical Center ***(494)***
Lana'i Co. ***(494)***
Lancit Media/Junior Net ***(494)***
Landis, New Jersey, Sewerage Authority ***(495)***
Landmine Survivors ***(495)***
Lane Transit District ***(495)***
Lane, Oregon, County of ***(495)***
Laredo, Texas, City of ***(495)***
LaRocco & Associates *(116)*
Las Cruces, New Mexico, City of ***(495)***
Las Virgenes Municipal Water District ***(495)***
Bob Lawrence & Associates ***(496)***
Lawton/Fort Sill Chamber of Commerce & Industry ***(496)***
LC Technologies ***(496)***
League of Women Voters of the United States ***(497)***
LeBoeuf, Lamb, Greene & MacRae L.L.P. *(117)*
Ledge Counsel *(118)*
Lee County, Florida ***(497)***
Lehigh University ***(498)***
Arnold H. Leibowitz *(119)*
Lennar Partners ***(498)***
Lennox Internat'l ***(498)***
Leucadia County Water District ***(498)***
Leukemia & Lymphoma Soc. ***(498)***
The Michael Lewan Co. *(119)*
Lewis and Clark College ***(498)***
Lewis-Burke Associates *(120)*
Liberty Science Center ***(499)***
Lifebridge Health ***(499)***
Eli Lilly and Co. ***(499)***
Little Havana Activities and Nutrition Centers ***(500)***
Litton Advanced Systems ***(500)***
Litton Electro Optical Systems ***(500)***
Litton Electron Devices ***(500)***
Litton Integrated Systems ***(500)***
Litton Laser Systems ***(500)***
The Livingston Group, LLC *(120)*
Local Initiatives Support Corp. ***(501)***
Lockheed Martin Aeronautical Systems Co. ***(501)***
Lockheed Martin Corp. ***(501)***
Lockheed Martin Government Electronics Systems ***(502)***
Lockheed Martin MS/Gaithersburg ***(502)***
Lockheed Martin Naval Electronics Surveillance Systems ***(502)***
Lockheed Martin Tactical Systems ***(502)***
Lockheed Martin Venture Star ***(502)***
Lockridge Grindal & Nauen, P.L.L.P. *(121)*
Logan, Utah, City of (Transit District) ***(502)***
Loma Linda, California, City of ***(503)***
Long Beach Transit ***(503)***
Long Beach Water Department ***(503)***
Long Beach, California, City of ***(503)***
Long Beach, California, Port of ***(503)***
Long, Aldridge & Norman, LLP *(121)*
Lorillard Tobacco Co. ***(503)***
Los Angeles County Metropolitan Transportation Authority ***(504)***
Los Angeles County Sanitation District ***(504)***
Los Angeles, California, County of ***(504)***
Louisiana Center for Manufacturing Sciences ***(504)***
Louisiana Internat'l Group ***(504)***
Louisiana Pacific Corp. ***(504)***
Louisiana State University ***(504)***
Lovelace Respiratory Research Institute ***(504)***
Loyola College ***(505)***
Loyola University ***(505)***
Loyola University of Chicago ***(505)***
LPI Consulting, Inc. *(122)*
Manuel Lujan Associates *(122)*
Luman, Lange & Wheeler *(122)*
Lumbermens Mutual Casualty Co. ***(505)***
Lutheran Office for Governmental Affairs/Evangelical Lutheran Church in America ***(506)***
Lymphoma Research Foundation of America, Inc. ***(506)***
Lynn, Massachusetts, City of ***(506)***
Lyons & Co. *(122)*
MacAndrews & Forbes Holdings, Inc. ***(506)***
Madison Government Affairs *(123)*
Madison, Wisconsin, City of ***(507)***
Malden Mills Industries, Inc. ***(508)***
Mallino Government Relations *(123)*
Mammoth Mountain ***(508)***
Management Concepts, Inc. ***(508)***
Manatee, Florida, County of ***(508)***
Manatos & Manatos, Inc. *(123)*
Manatt, Phelps & Phillips, LLP *(123)*
ManTech Internat'l ***(508)***
Manufactured Housing Institute ***(509)***
Manufacturers Alliance/MAPI Inc. ***(509)***
MARC Associates, Inc. *(124)*
March of Dimes Birth Defects Foundation ***(509)***
Maricopa, Arizona, County of ***(509)***
Marietta College ***(509)***
Marine Corps Reserve Officers Ass'n ***(510)***
Marine Desalination Systems LLC ***(510)***
Marion, Indiana, City of ***(510)***
Markey and Associates *(125)*
Marlowe and Co. *(125)*
Marriott Internat'l, Inc. ***(511)***
Marshall, Alabama, County of ***(511)***
Martin, Fisher & Associates, Inc. *(125)*
Martin-Baker Aircraft Co., Ltd. ***(511)***
Martinez and Curtis ***(511)***
Marymount University ***(512)***
Mas-Hamilton Group ***(512)***
Mass Transit Authority ***(512)***
Massachusetts Maritime Academy ***(512)***
Massachusetts Water Resources Authority ***(512)***
Materials Research Soc. ***(513)***
Virginia M. Mayer *(126)*
Maytag Corp. ***(513)***
Charlie McBride Associates, Inc. *(127)*
McClure, Gerard & Neuenschwander, Inc. *(127)*
James F. McConnell *(128)*
The McConnell Foundation ***(514)***
McDermott, Will and Emery *(128)*
McDonald's Corp. ***(514)***
McGuiness & Holch *(130)*
McGuireWoods L.L.P. *(130)*
McLean Hospital ***(515)***
McLeod, Watkinson & Miller *(131)*
McMahon and Associates *(131)*
Diane McRee Associates *(131)*
Mecklenburg, North Carolina, County of ***(515)***
Medford, Oregon, City of ***(516)***
Medical Advocacy Services, Inc. *(132)*
Medical College of Virginia, Dept. of Neurology, Office of the Chairman ***(516)***
Medical Library Ass'n/Ass'n of Academic Health Sciences Library Directors ***(516)***
Megaseal Corp. ***(517)***
Memorial Hermann Health Care System ***(517)***
Mentis Sciences Inc. ***(518)***
Mercer Engineering Research Center ***(518)***
Merck & Co. ***(518)***
Mercy Health Corp. ***(518)***
Mercy Hospital of Des Moines, Iowa ***(518)***

Merrill Lynch & Co., Inc. ***(519)***
Mesa, Arizona, City of ***(519)***
Mesquite Resort Ass'n ***(519)***
Mesquite, Nevada, City of ***(519)***
Metcalf Federal Relations *(132)*
Metropolitan Atlanta Rapid Transit Authority ***(520)***
Metropolitan Family Services ***(520)***
Metropolitan King County Council ***(520)***
Metropolitan St. Louis Sewer District ***(520)***
Metropolitan Transportation Commission ***(520)***
The Metropolitan Water District of Southern California ***(521)***
Metropolitan Water Reclamation District of Greater Chicago ***(521)***
Meyers & Associates *(133)*
Miami Beach, Florida, City of ***(521)***
Microcosm, Inc. ***(522)***
Microsoft Corp. ***(522)***
Mid Dakota Rural Water System ***(523)***
Midwest Research Institute ***(524)***
The Military Coalition ***(524)***
Military Footwear Coalition ***(524)***
Military Glove Coalition ***(524)***
Millennium Intermarket Group, LLC *(133)*
Denny Miller McBee Associates *(134)*
MilTec ***(524)***
Milwaukee Metropolitan Sewerage District ***(524)***
Milwaukee Public Museum ***(524)***
Minnesota Mining and Manufacturing Co. (3M Co.) ***(525)***
Minnesota Valley Alfalfa Producers ***(525)***
Minot State University ***(525)***
Mintz, Levin, Cohn, Ferris, Glovsky and Popeo, P.C. *(135)*
Moapa Valley Water District ***(526)***
The Jeffrey Modell Foundation ***(527)***
The Modernization Forum ***(527)***
Modesto, California, City of ***(527)***
Moffit Cancer Research Hospital ***(527)***
Monroe County Commercial Fishermen, Inc. ***(527)***
Monroe, Louisiana, Chamber of Commerce of the City of ***(528)***
Monroe, Louisiana, City of ***(528)***
Monroe, New York, County of ***(528)***
Monsanto Co. ***(528)***
Montana State University ***(528)***
Monterey County Water Resources Agency ***(528)***
Monterey Salinas Transit ***(528)***
Montgomery Airport Authority ***(528)***
Montgomery, Alabama, Chamber of Commerce of ***(529)***
Montrose, Colorado, City of ***(529)***
Timothy X. Moore and Co. *(136)*
J. P. Morgan Chase & Co. ***(529)***
Morgan Meguire, LLC *(136)*
Morgan State University ***(529)***
Morgan, Lewis & Bockius LLP *(136)*
Kay Allan Morrell, Attorney-at-Law *(137)*
Morro Bay, California, City of ***(530)***
Mortgage Bankers Ass'n of America ***(530)***
Moss McGee Bradley & Foley *(137)*
MOTE Marine Lab ***(530)***
Motorcycle Industry Council ***(531)***
Motorola Integrated Information Systems Group ***(531)***
Mount Sinai School of Medicine ***(531)***
Mount Sinai/NYU Health ***(531)***
MSS Consultants, LLC *(138)*
MTS Systems Inc. ***(532)***
Mullenholz, Brimsek & Belair *(138)*
MultiDimensional Imaging, Inc. ***(532)***
Multinat'l Government Services, Inc. *(138)*
Municipal Transit Operation Coalition ***(533)***
Murray, Scheer, Montgomery, Tapia & O'Donnell *(139)*
Museum Campus Chicago ***(533)***
Museum of Discovery and Science ***(533)***
Museum of Science and Industry ***(533)***
The MWW Group *(140)*
Mylan Laboratories, Inc. ***(533)***
Mystic Seaport Museum ***(534)***
NanoDynamics, Inc. ***(534)***
Napa County, California, Flood and Water Conservation District ***(534)***
NASA Aeronautics Support Team ***(534)***
Nassau County Health Care Corp. ***(535)***
Nat'l Air Traffic Controllers Ass'n ***(536)***
Nat'l Air Transportation Ass'n ***(536)***
Nat'l Alliance for Eye and Vision Research ***(536)***
Nat'l Alliance for the Mentally Ill ***(536)***
Nat'l Alliance of Sexual Assault Coalitions ***(537)***
Nat'l and Community Service Coalition ***(537)***
Nat'l Anti-Vivisection Soc. ***(537)***
Nat'l Aquarium ***(537)***
Nat'l Asphalt Pavement Ass'n ***(537)***
Nat'l Ass'n for Biomedical Research ***(537)***
Nat'l Ass'n for College Admission Counseling ***(537)***
Nat'l Ass'n for Equal Opportunity in Higher Education ***(537)***
Nat'l Ass'n for State Farm Agents ***(538)***
Nat'l Ass'n for the Support of Long Term Care ***(538)***
Nat'l Ass'n for Uniformed Services ***(538)***
Nat'l Ass'n of Affordable Housing Lenders ***(538)***
Nat'l Ass'n of Broadcasters ***(539)***
Nat'l Ass'n of Children's Hospitals Inc. ***(540)***
Nat'l Ass'n of Community Health Centers ***(540)***
Nat'l Ass'n of Conservation Districts ***(540)***
Nat'l Ass'n of Developmental Disabilities Councils ***(542)***
Nat'l Ass'n of Enrolled Agents ***(542)***
Nat'l Ass'n of Epilepsy Centers ***(542)***
Nat'l Ass'n of Foster Grandparent Program Directors ***(543)***
Nat'l Ass'n of Home Builders of the U.S. ***(543)***
Nat'l Ass'n of Housing Cooperatives ***(544)***
Nat'l Ass'n of Housing Partnerships ***(544)***
Nat'l Ass'n of Independent Colleges and Universities ***(544)***
Nat'l Ass'n of Installation Developers ***(544)***
Nat'l Ass'n of Letter Carriers of the United States of America ***(545)***
Nat'l Ass'n of Manufacturers ***(545)***
Nat'l Ass'n of Negro Business & Professional Women's Clubs, Inc. ***(546)***
Nat'l Ass'n of People with AIDS, Inc. ***(546)***
Nat'l Ass'n of Pharmaceutical Manufacturers ***(546)***
Nat'l Ass'n of Police Organizations ***(546)***
Nat'l Ass'n of Professional Forestry Schools and Colleges ***(547)***
Nat'l Ass'n of Protection and Advocacy Systems (NAPAS) ***(547)***
Nat'l Ass'n of Psychiatric Health Systems ***(547)***
Nat'l Ass'n of Retired and Senior Volunteer Program Directors ***(548)***
Nat'l Ass'n of Retired Federal Employees ***(548)***
Nat'l Ass'n of Secondary School Principals ***(549)***
Nat'l Ass'n of Senior Companion Project Directors ***(549)***
Nat'l Ass'n of Service and Conservation Corps ***(549)***
Nat'l Ass'n of Social Workers ***(549)***
Nat'l Ass'n of State Units on Aging ***(550)***
Nat'l Ass'n of Student Financial Aid Administrators ***(550)***
Nat'l Ass'n of Urban Hospitals ***(551)***
Nat'l Ass'n of Wholesaler-Distributors ***(551)***
Nat'l Ass'n to Protect Individual Rights ***(551)***
Nat'l Assembly of Health and Human Service Organizations ***(551)***
Nat'l Audubon Soc. ***(552)***
Nat'l Automobile Dealers Ass'n ***(552)***
Nat'l Beer Wholesalers Ass'n ***(552)***
Nat'l Broadcasting Co. ***(553)***
Nat'l Business Aviation Ass'n ***(553)***
Nat'l Cable Television Ass'n ***(553)***
Nat'l Center for Appropriate Technology ***(554)***
Nat'l Center for Family Literacy ***(554)***
Nat'l Center for Genome Research ***(554)***
Nat'l Center for Learning Disabilities (NCLD) ***(554)***
Nat'l Center for Manufacturing Sciences ***(555)***
Nat'l Center for Policy Analysis ***(555)***
Nat'l Center for Tobacco-Free Kids ***(555)***
Nat'l Child Support Enforcement Ass'n ***(555)***
Nat'l Coalition for Cancer Research ***(556)***
Nat'l Coalition for Cancer Survivorship ***(556)***
Nat'l Coalition for Osteoporosis and Related Bone Diseases ***(556)***
Nat'l Coalition of Minority Businesses ***(556)***
Nat'l Committee to Preserve Social Security and Medicare ***(557)***
Nat'l Community Action Foundation ***(557)***
Nat'l Community Education Ass'n ***(558)***
Nat'l Community Reinvestment Coalition ***(558)***
Nat'l Concrete Masonry Ass'n ***(558)***
Nat'l Cooperative Bank ***(558)***
Nat'l Cooperative Business Ass'n ***(559)***
Nat'l Coordinating Committee for the Promotion of History ***(559)***
Nat'l Corn Growers Ass'n ***(559)***
Nat'l Council for Community Behavioral Healthcare ***(559)***
Nat'l Council for Eurasian and East European Research ***(559)***
Nat'l Council of Farmer Cooperatives ***(560)***
Nat'l Council of Higher Education Loan Programs ***(560)***
Nat'l Council of Jewish Women ***(560)***
Nat'l Council of Teachers of Mathematics ***(560)***
Nat'l Council on the Aging ***(561)***
Nat'l Crime Prevention Council ***(561)***
Nat'l Criminal Justice Ass'n ***(561)***
Nat'l Defense Industrial Ass'n ***(561)***
Nat'l Defined Contribution Council ***(561)***
Nat'l Education Ass'n of the U.S. ***(562)***
Nat'l Electrical Manufacturers Ass'n ***(562)***
Nat'l Employment Opportunities Network ***(563)***
Nat'l Endangered Species Act Reform Coalition ***(563)***
Nat'l Energy Management Institute ***(563)***
Nat'l Environmental Strategies *(140)*
Nat'l Family Planning and Reproductive Health Ass'n ***(563)***
Nat'l Farmers Union (Farmers Educational & Co-operative Union of America) ***(563)***
Nat'l Federation of Croatian Americans ***(564)***
Nat'l Fisheries Institute ***(564)***
Nat'l Food Processors Ass'n ***(564)***
Nat'l Foreign Trade Council, Inc. ***(565)***
Nat'l Funeral Directors Ass'n ***(565)***
Nat'l Grange ***(566)***
Nat'l Grid USA ***(566)***
Nat'l Head Start Ass'n ***(566)***
Nat'l Health Council ***(567)***
Nat'l Healthy Start Ass'n ***(567)***
Nat'l Hemophilia Foundation ***(567)***
Nat'l Horse Show Commission ***(567)***
Nat'l Humanities Alliance ***(567)***
Nat'l Hydropower Ass'n ***(567)***
Nat'l Industries for the Blind ***(568)***
Nat'l Institute for Water Resources ***(568)***
Nat'l Jewish Medical and Research Center ***(569)***
Nat'l League of Postmasters of the U.S. ***(569)***
Nat'l Legal Aid and Defender Ass'n ***(570)***
Nat'l Lumber and Building Material Dealers Ass'n ***(570)***
Nat'l Marrow Donor Program ***(570)***
Nat'l Meat Ass'n ***(570)***
Nat'l Mental Health Ass'n ***(571)***
Nat'l Military Family Ass'n ***(571)***
Nat'l Milk Producers Federation ***(571)***
Nat'l Mining Ass'n ***(571)***
Nat'l Nutritional Foods Ass'n ***(572)***
Nat'l Ocean Industries Ass'n ***(572)***
Nat'l Oilseed Processors Ass'n ***(572)***
Nat'l Paint and Coatings Ass'n ***(573)***
Nat'l Parks Conservation Ass'n ***(573)***
Nat'l Patient Advocate Foundation ***(573)***
Nat'l Prostate Cancer Coalition Co. ***(574)***
Nat'l Public Radio ***(574)***
Nat'l Rehabilitation Ass'n ***(575)***
Nat'l Restaurant Ass'n ***(576)***
Nat'l Right to Life Committee ***(576)***
Nat'l Right to Work Committee ***(576)***
Nat'l Roofing Contractors Ass'n ***(576)***
Nat'l Rural Development & Finance Corp. ***(576)***
Nat'l Rural Development Ass'n ***(576)***
Nat'l Rural Electric Cooperative Ass'n ***(576)***
Nat'l Rural Housing Coalition ***(577)***
Nat'l Rural Water Ass'n ***(577)***
Nat'l SAFE KIDS Campaign ***(577)***

Nat'l School Transportation Ass'n *(577)*
Nat'l Senior Service Corps Directors Ass'n *(578)*
Nat'l Sleep Foundation *(578)*
Nat'l Soc. of Professional Engineers *(578)*
The Nat'l Space Grant Alliance *(578)*
Nat'l Taxpayers Union *(579)*
Nat'l Telephone Cooperative Ass'n *(579)*
Nat'l Treasury Employees Union *(580)*
Nat'l Trust for Historic Preservation *(580)*
Nat'l Turkey Federation *(580)*
Nat'l Underground Railroad Freedom Center *(580)*
Nat'l Utility Contractors Ass'n (NUCA) *(580)*
Nat'l Waterways Conference, Inc. *(581)*
Nat'l Wholesale Co., Inc. *(581)*
Nat'l Wildlife Federation - Office of Federal and Internat'l Affairs *(581)*
Nat'l Wildlife Refuge Ass'n *(581)*
Nat'l Women's History Museum *(581)*
Nat'l Writing Project *(581)*
Natomas *(582)*
NATSO, Inc. *(582)*
Natural Resources Defense Council *(582)*
The Nature Conservancy *(582)*
Navajo Nation *(582)*
NAVCOM Systems, Inc. *(583)*
NAVSYS Corp. *(583)*
NCR Corp. *(583)*
Nestle USA, Inc. *(584)*
Netivation.com *(584)*
NETWORK, A Nat'l Catholic Social Justice Lobby *(584)*
Neumann College *(584)*
New American School *(585)*
New Jersey Hospital Ass'n *(585)*
New Mexico State Office of Research & Development *(586)*
New Mexico State University *(586)*
New Mexico State University, Department of Agriculture *(586)*
New Mexico State University, Department of Engineering *(586)*
New Mexico Tech *(586)*
New Orleans Internat'l Airport *(586)*
New Orleans, Louisiana, City of *(586)*
New Orleans, Louisiana, Port of *(586)*
New Orleans, Louisiana, Regional Transit Authority of *(586)*
New Starts Working Group *(586)*
New York Botanical Garden *(586)*
New York Institute of Technology *(587)*
New York Metropolitan Transportation Authority *(587)*
New York Stock Exchange *(588)*
The New York Structural Biology Center *(588)*
New York University *(588)*
New York University Medical Center *(588)*
Newark, New Jersey, City of *(588)*
Newmont Mining Corp. *(588)*
Newport News Shipbuilding Inc. *(588)*
NF Inc. - Mass Bay Area *(589)*
Niagara Frontier Transportation Authority *(589)*
Niagara Mohawk Power Corp. *(589)*
NISH - Creating Employment Opportunities for People with Severe Disabilities *(590)*
NitroMed, Inc. *(590)*
Nixon Peabody LLP *(142)*
Noesis Inc. *(590)*
Non Commissioned Officers Ass'n of the U.S.A. *(591)*
Norchem Concrete Products Inc. *(591)*
Norfolk Southern Corp. *(591)*
Norfolk, Virginia, City of *(591)*
Julia J. Norrell & Associates *(142)*
North American Brain Tumor Coalition *(592)*
North American Communications Corp. *(592)*
North Carolina Electric Membership Corp. *(593)*
North Carolina Global TransPark Authority *(593)*
North Carolina Peanut Growers Ass'n *(593)*
North Carolina State Ports Authority *(593)*
North Carolina, Hurricane Floyd Redevelopment Center of State of *(593)*
North Carolina, Washington Office of the State of *(593)*
North Dakota, Governor's Office of the State of *(593)*
North San Diego County Transit Development Board *(593)*
North Shore Long Island Jewish Health System *(593)*
North Slope Borough, Alaska *(593)*
North Topsail Beach, North Carolina, Town of *(593)*
Northeast Ohio Areawide Coordination Agency (NOACA) *(593)*
Northeast Texas Electric Cooperative *(593)*
Northeast-Midwest Institute *(594)*
Northeastern University *(594)*
Northern California Power Agency *(594)*
Northern Essex Community College Foundation *(594)*
Northrop Grumman Corp. *(594)*
Northstar Corridor Development Authority *(595)*
Northwest Airlines, Inc. *(595)*
Northwest Ecosystem Alliance *(595)*
Northwest Municipal Conference *(595)*
Northwest Pipe Co. *(595)*
Northwest Regional Education Laboratory *(595)*
Northwestern Memorial Hospital *(595)*
Northwestern Michigan College *(595)*
Northwestern University *(596)*
Norwalk, California, City of *(596)*
Nottoway, Virginia, County of *(596)*
Nova Southeastern University *(596)*
Novartis Corp. *(596)*
NRG Energy, Inc. *(596)*
NTS Mortgage Income Fund *(596)*
Nu Thena Systems, Inc. *(597)*
Nuclear Energy Institute *(597)*
NUI Environmental Group Inc. *(597)*
NYSCOPBA - New York State Correctional Officers & Police Benevolent Ass'n *(597)*
Oakland, Michigan, County of *(598)*
The OB-C Group, LLC *(143)*
O'Bryon & Co. *(144)*
Ocean County, NJ Utilities Authority *(598)*
Ocean Isle Beach, North Carolina, Town of *(598)*
Ocean Village Property Owners Ass'n, Inc. *(598)*
Ochsner Medical Institutions *(598)*
O'Connor & Hannan, L.L.P. *(144)*
Ogden, Utah, City of *(599)*
Bartley M. O'Hara *(145)*
Ohio State University *(599)*
Ohio Wesleyan University *(599)*
Oklahoma City, Oklahoma, City of *(599)*
Oklahoma State Medical Ass'n *(600)*
Oklahoma, State of *(600)*
Old Sturbridge Village *(600)*
Olivenhain Municipal Water District *(600)*
Olney Boys and Girls Club *(600)*
Olsson, Frank and Weeda, P.C. *(146)*
Olsten Health Services *(600)*
Onconova Inc. *(600)*
One Economy Corp. *(600)*
O'Neill, Athy & Casey, P.C. *(147)*
Oneonta Trading Corp. *(601)*
Oppenheimer Wolff & Donnelly LLP *(147)*
Optical Soc. of America *(601)*
Oracle Corp. *(602)*
Orange County Sanitation Districts *(602)*
Orange County Water District *(602)*
Orasure Technologies *(602)*
Orbital Sciences Corp. *(602)*
Oregon Department of Transportation *(603)*
Oregon Garden Foundation *(603)*
Oregon Graduate Institute of Science and Technology *(603)*
Oregon Health Sciences University *(603)*
Oregon Water Resources Congress *(603)*
Oregon Water Trust *(603)*
Orincon Corp. *(603)*
Orkand Corp. *(603)*
Orlando, Florida, City of *(603)*
Oshkosh Truck Corp. *(604)*
Ouachita Parish Police Jury *(604)*
Ounalashka Corp. *(604)*
Ovarian Cancer Nat'l Alliance *(604)*
Oxnard Harbor District *(605)*
Oxnard, California, City of *(605)*
Pac Med Clinics *(605)*
Pacific Islands Washington Office *(148)*
Pacific Life Insurance Co. *(605)*
Pacific States Marine Fisheries Commission *(606)*
Pacific Union College *(606)*
The Palmer Group *(149)*
Palo Alto, California, City of *(607)*
Palumbo & Cerrell, Inc. *(149)*
Pan American Health Organization *(607)*
Pancyprian Ass'n of America *(607)*
Paradise Canyon Resort *(607)*
Paradise Valley Hospital *(607)*
Parcel Shippers Ass'n *(608)*
Parkinson's Action Network *(608)*
Parsons Brinckerhoff Inc. *(608)*
Partners Healthcare System, Inc. *(608)*
Partnership for Recovery Coalition *(609)*
Passaic Valley Sewerage Commissioners *(609)*
Patient Access to Transplantation (PAT) Coalition *(609)*
Patton Boggs, LLP *(150)*
Patton Boggs, LLP *(609)*
Paul, Hastings, Janofsky & Walker LLP *(153)*
PE Biosystems *(610)*
Peace Action *(610)*
Pennington BioMedical Research Center *(611)*
Pennsylvania Higher Education Assistance Agency *(611)*
Pennsylvania Turnpike Commission *(611)*
Perdue Farms Inc. *(612)*
Perkins Coie LLP *(154)*
Personal Communications Industry Ass'n (PCIA) *(612)*
The Peterson Group *(155)*
The Petrizzo Group, Inc. *(155)*
Pfizer, Inc. *(613)*
Pharmaceutical Research and Manufacturers of America *(614)*
Pharmacia Corp. *(615)*
Phelps Dodge Corp. *(615)*
Philadelphia College of Osteopathic Medicine *(615)*
Philadelphia University *(615)*
Philadelphia Zoo *(615)*
Philip Morris Management Corp. *(615)*
Phillips Petroleum Co. *(616)*
Phoenix Cardiovascular, Inc. *(616)*
Phoenix, Arizona, City of *(616)*
Physician Insurers Ass'n of America *(616)*
Pico Rivera, California, City of *(617)*
Pierce College *(617)*
Pierce Transit *(617)*
The Pillsbury Co. *(617)*
Pinnacle West Capital Corp. *(617)*
Pittsburgh, University of *(618)*
Charles L. Pizer *(156)*
Placer County Water Agency *(618)*
Placer, California, County of *(618)*
Planned Parenthood Federation of America *(618)*
Planning Systems, Inc. *(619)*
Susan S. Platt Consulting *(156)*
The PMA Group *(156)*
Podesta/Mattoon *(158)*
Pojoaque Pueblo *(620)*
Polar Air Cargo, Inc. *(620)*
Police Executive Research Forum *(620)*
Policy Directions, Inc. *(158)*
Polity Consulting *(159)*
Polk, Iowa, County of *(620)*
Polytechnic University *(620)*
Port Hueneme, California, City of *(621)*
Port of Tillamook Bay *(621)*
Portland, Oregon, City of *(621)*
Potomac Electric Power Co. *(622)*
Potomac Group *(160)*
Powell, Goldstein, Frazer & Murphy LLP *(622)*
Power Mobility Coalition *(622)*
Powers Pyles Sutter & Verville, PC *(161)*
PPL *(622)*
Praxair, Inc. *(623)*
Preservation Action *(623)*
Preston Gates Ellis & Rouvelas Meeds LLP *(162)*
Prevent Blindness America *(623)*
Prince George's, Maryland, County of *(624)*
Prince William Sound Regional Citizen's Advisory Council *(624)*
Principal Financial Group *(624)*

Printing Industries of America *(624)*
Private Essential Access Community Hospitals (PEACH) Inc. *(624)*
Private Fuels Storage, L.L.C. *(625)*
The Procter & Gamble Company *(625)*
Proctor Hospital *(625)*
Professional Engineering *(625)*
Professional Managers Ass'n *(626)*
Professional Services Council *(626)*
Profit Recovery Group Internat'l *(626)*
Progressive Policy Institute *(626)*
Project ACTA *(626)*
The Project Leadership Committee, Lincoln Center for the Performing Arts *(626)*
Providence Redevelopment Agency *(627)*
PSE&G *(627)*
Public Agencies for Audit Reform *(628)*
Public Broadcasting Service *(628)*
Public Citizen, Inc. *(628)*
Public Health Policy Advisory Board *(628)*
Public Private Partnership *(164)*
Public Service Co. of New Mexico *(629)*
Public/Private Ventures *(629)*
Quad City Development Group *(630)*
Qualimetrics, Inc. *(630)*
Queens Borough Public Library *(631)*
Quinault Indian Nation *(631)*
Andrew F. Quinlan *(165)*
Quinn Gillespie & Associates *(165)*
Quinnat Landing Hotel *(631)*
Rancho Palos Verdes, California, City of *(633)*
Rapid Mat LLC *(633)*
Robert A. Rapoza Associates *(165)*
Pamela Ray-Strunk and Associates *(166)*
Raytheon Co. *(633)*
Recon/Optical, Inc. *(634)*
Red River Trade Council *(635)*
Redlands, California, City of *(635)*
Reed, Smith, LLP *(167)*
Christopher Reeve Paralysis Foundation *(635)*
Law Office of Paige E. Reffe *(167)*
Regents College *(635)*
Regional Airport Authority of Louisville & Jefferson Co. *(635)*
Regional Planning Commission *(635)*
Regional Public Tansportation Authority *(635)*
Regional Transit Authority *(636)*
Regional Transportation Commission *(636)*
Renewable Fuels Ass'n *(637)*
Reno & Cavanaugh, PLLC *(168)*
Reno & Cavanaugh, PLLC *(637)*
Reno, Nevada, City of *(637)*
Renton, Washington, City of *(637)*
Reproductive Health Technologies Project *(637)*
Research 2 Prevention *(638)*
Research Foundation of the City University of New York *(638)*
Research Soc. on Alcoholism *(638)*
Resources and Instruction for Staff Excellence, Inc. *(638)*
Reusable Industrial Packaging Ass'n *(639)*
RFB, Inc. *(168)*
Rhoads Group *(168)*
Rhode Island School of Design *(639)*
John J. Rhodes *(169)*
Ricchetti Inc. *(169)*
Riggs Government Relations Consulting LLC *(169)*
Rio Grande Valley Irrigation *(640)*
Ritter and Bourjaily, Inc. *(169)*
Riverdeep Inc. *(640)*
Riverside County, California, Flood Control and Water Conservation District *(640)*
Riverside, California, City of *(640)*
Roaring Fork Railroad Holding Authority *(641)*
Liz Robbins Associates *(169)*
Robertson, Monagle & Eastaugh *(170)*
Robison Internat'l, Inc. *(170)*
Rochester Institute of Technology *(641)*
Rockwell Collins *(641)*
Roecker Engineering Co. *(641)*
Rolls-Royce North America Inc. *(642)*
Romano & Associates, LLC *(171)*
Rooney Group Internat'l, Inc. *(171)*
Rose Communications *(172)*
A. L. Ross Associates, Inc. *(172)*
Rotary Foundation *(642)*
Royal Ordnance North America, Inc. *(643)*
Royer & Babyak *(172)*
Ruby Memorial Hospital *(643)*
Rural Community Insurance Co. *(643)*
Rush Presbyterian-St. Luke's Medical Center *(644)*
Rutgers University *(644)*
Ryan, Phillips, Utrecht & MacKinnon *(173)*
Sabolich Research & Development *(644)*
Sacramento Area Council of Governments *(645)*
Sacramento Area Flood Control Agency *(645)*
Sacramento Housing and Redeveloping Agency *(645)*
Sacramento, California, City of *(645)*
Sacramento, California, Department of Utilities of *(645)*
Sacramento, California, Public Works Agency of the County of *(645)*
Sacramento-Potomac Consulting, Inc. *(174)*
Saf T Lok, Inc. *(645)*
Safer Foundation *(645)*
Sagamore Associates, Inc. *(174)*
Sagem Morpho *(646)*
Saint Coletta of Greater Washington, Inc. *(646)*
Saint Joseph's Health Center Foundation, Inc. *(646)*
Salem, Oregon, City of *(646)*
Salinas, California, City of *(646)*
Sallie Mae, Inc. *(646)*
Salt Lake City Olympic Organizing Committee *(646)*
Salt Lake City, Utah, City of *(646)*
Salt River Project *(646)*
Sam Rayburn G&T Electric Cooperative, Inc. *(647)*
San Antonio, Texas, City of *(647)*
San Bernardino Valley Municipal Water District *(647)*
San Bernardino, California, County of *(647)*
San Diego Metropolitan Transit Development Board *(647)*
San Diego Natural History Museum *(647)*
San Diego State University Foundation *(647)*
San Diego, California, City of *(647)*
San Elijo Joint Powers Authority *(647)*
San Francisco AIDS Foundation *(647)*
San Francisco Internat'l Airport *(648)*
San Francisco, California, City and County of *(648)*
San Gabriel Basin Water Quality Authority *(648)*
San Joaquin River Exchange Contractors Water Authority *(648)*
San Jose, California, City of *(648)*
San Leandro, California, City of *(648)*
San Luis Obispo, California, County of *(648)*
Sandia Pueblo *(648)*
Santa Ana River Flood Protection Agency *(649)*
Santa Ana, California, City of *(649)*
Santa Barbara Electric Transit Institute *(649)*
Santa Barbara Metropolitan Transit District *(649)*
Santa Barbara, California, City of (Waterfront) *(649)*
Santa Barbara, California, Public Works Department *(649)*
Santa Clara Valley Transportation Authority *(649)*
Santa Clara Valley Water District *(649)*
Santa Clara, California, County of *(649)*
Santa Clarita, California, City of *(649)*
Santa Cruz, California, Port of *(649)*
Santa Fe, New Mexico, County of *(649)*
Santa Monica, California, City of *(649)*
Santa Rosa Memorial Hospital *(649)*
Sarasota, Florida, City of *(649)*
Sault Ste. Marie Tribe of Chippewa Indians *(650)*
R. Wayne Sayer & Associates *(175)*
Schepens Eye Research Institute *(651)*
Schering-Plough Corp. *(651)*
Schering-Plough Legislative Resources L.L.C. *(651)*
Schmeltzer, Aptaker & Shepard, P.C. *(176)*
Schramm, Williams & Associates, Inc. *(176)*
Schrayer and Associates, Inc. *(176)*
Schroth & Associates *(176)*
Science & Engineering Associates, Inc. *(652)*
Science and Engineering Associates, Inc. *(652)*
Science Applications Internat'l Corp. (SAIC) *(652)*
Scientech Corp. *(652)*
Scram Technologies Inc. *(652)*
Sealaska Corp. *(653)*
SEARCH Group, Inc. *(653)*
Sears, Roebuck and Co. *(653)*
Securities Industry Ass'n *(654)*
Sellery Associates, Inc. *(177)*
Semiconductor Industry Ass'n *(655)*
Seminole Tribe of Indians of Florida *(655)*
Seneca Resources Corporation *(655)*
SePRO Corp. *(655)*
Service Corp. Internat'l *(656)*
Service Employees Internat'l Union *(656)*
Seton Hill College *(656)*
Seward, Alaska, City of *(656)*
Sewerage and Water Board of New Orleans *(656)*
Shake-A-Leg *(656)*
Shakopee Mdewakanton Sioux Tribe *(656)*
Shaw Pittman *(177)*
Sheet Metal and Air Conditioning Contractors' Nat'l Ass'n *(657)*
Sheet Metal Workers' Internat'l Ass'n *(657)*
The Sheridan Group *(179)*
Sheriff Jefferson Parrish, Louisiana *(657)*
Shipbuilders Council of America *(657)*
Shreveport, Louisiana, City of *(658)*
Sickle Cell Disease Ass'n of America *(658)*
Siemens Westinghouse Power Corporation *(658)*
Sierra Club *(658)*
Sierra Madre, California, City of *(658)*
Sierra Pacific Industries *(659)*
Sierra Pacific Resources *(659)*
Signal Behavioral Health Network *(659)*
Silicon Valley Group *(659)*
Silverline Technologies, Inc. *(659)*
Simon and Co., Inc. *(181)*
Simula, Inc. *(659)*
Singapore Technologies Automotive *(659)*
Sisseton-Wahpoton Sioux Indian Tribe *(660)*
Sisters of Providence Health Systems *(660)*
Six Agency Committee *(660)*
SLR Budget and Legislative Consulting *(182)*
Smartforce *(661)*
Smith Alling Lane, P.S. *(183)*
E. Del Smith and Co. *(183)*
The Charles E. Smith Companies *(661)*
Smith Dawson & Andrews, Inc. *(183)*
Smith, Bucklin and Associates, Inc. *(184)*
The Smith-Free Group *(184)*
Snack Food Ass'n *(662)*
Craig Snyder & Associates *(185)*
Soc. for American Archaeology *(662)*
Soc. for Industrial & Applied Mathematics *(662)*
Soc. for Neuroscience *(662)*
Soc. for Women's Health Research *(663)*
Soc. of General Internal Medicine *(663)*
Soc. of Gyneocologic Oncologists *(663)*
Soc. of Toxicology *(664)*
Software & Information Industry Ass'n (SIIA) *(664)*
Software Productivity Consortium *(664)*
Solana Beach, California, City of *(665)*
The Solomon Group, LLC *(185)*
Somach, Simmons & Dunn *(665)*
Somerville Housing Group *(665)*
Sonoma County Water Agency *(665)*
SonoSite *(665)*
Sonosky, Chambers, Sachse & Endreson *(185)*
Sony Electronics, Inc. *(666)*
Soo Line Railroad, Inc. *(666)*
South Carolina Public Railways *(666)*
South Louisiana, Port of *(666)*
South Tahoe Public Utility District *(666)*
Southcoast Health System *(667)*
Southeast Water Coalition *(667)*
Southeastern Louisiana University *(667)*
Southeastern Pennsylvania Consortium for Higher Education *(667)*
Southern Co. *(667)*
Southern Coalition for Advanced Transportation *(668)*
Southern Ute Indian Tribe *(668)*
Southwest Peanut Growers *(668)*
Southwestern Water Conservation District *(668)*
Southwire, Inc. *(668)*

Space Access *(668)*
Space Dynamics Laboratory *(669)*
Space Grant Coalition *(669)*
Space Imaging, Inc. *(669)*
Space Mark *(669)*
SPACEHAB, Inc. *(669)*
Spectrum Health Care Resources, Inc. *(670)*
Spelman College *(670)*
Spina Bifida Ass'n of America *(670)*
Spokane Area Chamber of Commerce *(670)*
Sporting Goods Manufacturers Ass'n *(670)*
Springettsbury, Pennsylvania, Township of *(670)*
Springfield, Massachusetts, City of *(670)*
Springfield, Oregon, City of *(670)*
Sprint Corp. *(671)*
Squire, Sanders & Dempsey L.L.P. *(187)*
SRT Group *(671)*
St. Augustine Beach, Florida, City of *(671)*
St. Gabriel, Louisiana, Town of *(671)*
St. Louis University, School of Public Health *(672)*
St. Louis/Lake Counties Regional Rail Authority *(672)*
St. Lucie, Florida, County of *(672)*
St. Paul, Alaska, City of *(672)*
Standing Rock Sioux Tribe *(672)*
Stanfield Tindal, Inc. *(187)*
State University of New York (SUNY) *(673)*
State University of New York at Albany *(673)*
Stephens Law Firm *(188)*
Steptoe & Johnson LLP *(188)*
Sterling Internat'l Consultants, Inc. *(674)*
John M. Stinson *(189)*
Stites & Harbison *(189)*
Stockbridge-Munsee Community Band of Mohican Indians *(675)*
Strategic Horizons Advisors, L.L.C. *(189)*
Strategic Impact, Inc. *(189)*
Strategic Partners Inc. *(190)*
Richard Straus *(190)*
Street Law Inc. *(675)*
Student Loan Funding Corp. *(675)*
Stuntz, Davis & Staffier, P.C. *(190)*
Charlene A. Sturbitts *(190)*
Suburban Mobility Authority for Regional Transportation *(676)*
Sudden Infant Death Syndrome Alliance *(676)*
Sun Healthcare Group, Inc. *(676)*
Sunkist Growers, Inc. *(677)*
Sunset Properties, Inc. *(677)*
Susquehanna Health System *(678)*
Sutter, California, County of *(678)*
Sutton & Sutton Solicitors *(678)*
Sweetwater Authority *(678)*
Swidler Berlin Shereff Friedman, LLP *(191)*
Swidler Berlin Shereff Friedman, LLP *(678)*
Swiss Investors Protection Ass'n *(679)*
Swope Parkway Health Center *(679)*
Syracuse University *(679)*
Tacoma, Washington, City of *(680)*
Take The Field, Inc. *(680)*
Talladega College *(680)*
Tanadgusix Corp. *(680)*
Tax Fairness Coalition *(681)*
Teach for America *(682)*
TECHHEALTH.COM *(682)*
Teicher Consulting and Representation *(193)*
Telephone Operators Caucus *(683)*
Temple University Health System *(683)*
Tensiodyne Scientific Corp. *(684)*
Tequity *(684)*
TerraPoint *(684)*
Tex-La Electric Cooperative of Texas *(684)*
Texaco Group Inc. *(684)*
Texas A&M Research Foundation *(684)*
Texas Instruments *(684)*
Texas NF Foundation *(685)*
Texas Pacific Group *(685)*
Texas Tech University System *(685)*
Texas Windstorm Insurance Ass'n *(685)*
Thelen Reid & Priest LLP *(193)*
Thelen Reid & Priest LLP *(685)*
Thomas Jefferson University *(686)*
Thomas Jefferson University Hospital *(686)*
Three Affiliated Tribes of Fort Berthold Reservation *(686)*
Thunderbird, The American Graduate School of Internat'l Management *(686)*
The Timken Co. *(687)*
Timmons and Co., Inc. *(195)*
Tire Ass'n of North America *(687)*
Titan Corp. *(687)*
The Title XI Coalition *(687)*
Tongour Simpson Holsclaw Green *(196)*
Tooele, Utah, City of *(688)*
Touro Law Center *(688)*
Traditional Values Coalition *(689)*
Tri-City Industrial Development Council *(691)*
Trimble Navigation, Ltd. *(692)*
Trinity Health *(692)*
Troy State University - Montgomery *(692)*
Trust for Public Land *(693)*
TRW Inc. *(693)*
Tukwila, Washington, City of *(693)*
Tulane University *(693)*
Tulsa Airport Authority *(694)*
Tunica Biloxi Indians of Louisiana *(694)*
Turtle Mountain Community College *(694)*
TVA Watch *(694)*
Tyson's Governmental Sales, LLC *(695)*
U.S. Chamber Institute for Legal Reform *(695)*
U.S. Citrus Science Council *(696)*
U.S. English, Inc. *(696)*
U.S. Fund for UNICEF *(696)*
U.S. Investigations Services *(696)*
U.S. Mink Export Development Council *(696)*
U.S. Oil and Gas Ass'n *(696)*
U.S. Public Interest Research Group *(697)*
U.S./Mexico Border Counties Coalition *(697)*
Ukrainian Nat'l Ass'n, Inc. *(698)*
Unified Industries, Inc. *(698)*
Unilever United States, Inc. *(699)*
Union Hospital *(699)*
Union Pacific *(699)*
Union Sanitary District *(699)*
UNIPAC Service Corp. *(699)*
Unisys Corp. *(700)*
United Airlines *(700)*
United Automobile, Aerospace and Agricultural Implement Workers of America (UAW) *(700)*
United Cerebral Palsy Ass'n *(700)*
United Defense, L.P. *(701)*
United Distribution Cos. *(701)*
United Egg Ass'n *(701)*
United Egg Producers *(701)*
United Food and Commercial Workers Internat'l Union *(701)*
United Fresh Fruit and Vegetable Ass'n *(701)*
United Hellenic American Congress *(701)*
United Methodist Church General Board of Church and Society *(702)*
United Negro College Fund, Inc. *(702)*
United Network for Organ Sharing *(702)*
United Parcel Service *(702)*
United Seniors Ass'n *(702)*
United Service Organization *(702)*
United States Business and Industry Council *(703)*
United States Coast Guard Chief Petty Officers Ass'n *(703)*
United States Marine Repair *(703)*
United States Sugar Corp. *(704)*
United Technologies Corp. *(704)*
United Transportation Union *(705)*
Universal Systems, Inc. *(705)*
Universities Research Ass'n *(705)*
University Corp. for Atmospheric Research *(705)*
University Medical Associates *(705)*
University of Alabama System *(705)*
University of Alaska *(705)*
University of Arizona *(705)*
University of California, Office of Federal Government Relations *(706)*
University of Cincinnati *(706)*
University of Colorado, Office of the President *(706)*
University of Connecticut *(706)*
University of Dubuque *(706)*
University of Findlay *(706)*
University of Florida Health Science Center *(706)*
University of Georgia *(706)*
University of Hawaii *(706)*
University of Idaho *(706)*
University of Louisville *(706)*
University of Massachusetts Memorial Health System *(706)*
University of Medicine and Dentistry of New Jersey *(706)*
University of Medicine and Dentistry of New Jersey - School of Health Related Professionals *(706)*
University of Miami *(706)*
University of Missouri *(706)*
University of Nebraska *(706)*
University of Nevada - Las Vegas *(707)*
University of New Orleans *(707)*
University of New Orleans Foundation *(707)*
University of North Carolina at Chapel Hill *(707)*
University of North Carolina at Greensboro *(707)*
University of North Dakota *(707)*
University of Notre Dame *(707)*
University of Oregon *(707)*
University of Pennsylvania/School of Dental Medicine *(707)*
University of Phoenix *(707)*
University of Pittsburgh Medical Center (UPMC) *(707)*
University of Puerto Rico *(707)*
University of Redlands *(707)*
University of San Diego *(707)*
University of San Francisco *(707)*
University of Southern California *(707)*
University of Southwestern Louisiana *(707)*
University of Texas - Houston Health Science Center *(707)*
University of Tulsa *(708)*
University of Utah *(708)*
University of Vermont *(708)*
University of Virginia *(708)*
University of Washington *(708)*
University System of Maryland *(708)*
UNUM/Provident Corp. *(708)*
Upper San Gabriel Municipal Water District *(708)*
Upper Yampa Water Conservancy District *(708)*
Uranium Producers of America *(708)*
US Airways *(709)*
USA Biomass Power Producers Alliance *(709)*
USEC, Inc. *(710)*
USFHP Conference Group *(710)*
UST Public Affairs, Inc. *(710)*
USX Corp. *(710)*
Utah State University *(710)*
Ute Mountain Ute Indian Tribe *(710)*
Valente Lopatin & Schulze *(198)*
Valentec Systems, Inc. *(711)*
Valis Associates *(198)*
Valley Hope Ass'n *(711)*
Valley Hospital Foundation *(711)*
Van Ness Feldman, P.C. *(199)*
Van Scoyoc Associates, Inc. *(200)*
Van Scoyoc Associates, Inc. *(711)*
Vance Development Authority *(712)*
The Vandervort Group, LLC *(712)*
The Velasquez Group *(201)*
Venice, Florida, City of *(712)*
Ventura County Citizens Against Radar Emissions (VCCARE) *(712)*
Ventura County Community-Navy Action Partnership *(712)*
Ventura Port District *(712)*
Veridian Engineering *(713)*
Verizon Wireless *(713)*
Verner, Liipfert, Bernhard, McPherson and Hand, Chartered *(202)*
Very Special Arts *(714)*
ViaSat, Inc. *(714)*
Vickers and Vickers *(204)*
City of Victorville Redevelopment Agency *(715)*
Victorville, California, City of *(715)*
Vinson & Elkins L.L.P. *(204)*
Viohl and Associates, Inc. *(205)*
Virgin Islands, Government of the *(715)*
Virgin Valley Water District *(715)*
Virginia Commonwealth University *(716)*
Virginia Living Museum *(716)*
Virginia Peanut Growers Ass'n *(716)*

Virginia Polytechnic Institute and State University (716)
Virginia Tech Intellectual Properties, Inc. (716)
Volusia, Florida, County of (717)
Voorhees College (717)
Vorys, Sater, Seymour and Pease, LLP (205)
VSAdc.com (205)
Wake, North Carolina, County of (718)
R. Duffy Wall and Associates (205)
Don Wallace Associates, Inc. (206)
Walsh Enterprises Internat'l (718)
Warburg, Pincus & Co., Inc., E. M. (718)
Wasatch Front Regional Council (719)
Washington and Jefferson College (719)
Washington Ass'n of Sheriffs and Police Chiefs (719)
Washington Aviation Group (206)
Washington Council Ernst & Young (206)
Washington Gas (719)
The Washington Group (208)
Washington Group Internat'l (719)
Washington Health Advocates (209)
Washington Metropolitan Area Transit Authority (720)
Washington Mutual Bank (720)
Washington Resource Associates (209)
Washoe County (721)
Water Environment Research Foundation (721)
Water Replenishment District of Southern California (721)
Water Systems Council (721)
WateReuse Ass'n (721)
Watsonville, California, City of (722)
Wayland Academy (722)
Wayne State University (722)
Ways to Work (722)
Weather Channel (722)
WellPoint Health Networks/Blue Cross of California/UNICARE (723)
Wellton-Mohawk Irrigation and Drainage District (723)
WESCAM (723)
West Basin Municipal Water District (723)
West Lafayette, Indiana, City of (723)
West Valley City, Utah (723)
Westcare Foundation, Inc. (723)
Westerly Group (211)
Western Coalition of Arid States (724)
Western Growers Ass'n (724)
Western Kentucky University (724)
Western Michigan University (724)
Western Pistachio Ass'n (724)
Western Research Institute (724)
Westinghouse Government Services Group (725)
Westlands Water District (725)
Roy F. Weston, Inc. (725)
The Wexler Group (211)
Wheat Export Trade Education Committee (725)
William F. Whitsitt Policy and Government Affairs (213)
Widener University (726)
Burton V. Wides, P.C. (214)
Bill Wight, LLC (214)
Wilberforce University (726)
The Wilderness Soc. (726)
Wiley, Rein & Fielding (214)
Will and Carlson, Inc. (215)
Williams & Jensen, P.C. (215)
Wilmington Savings Fund Society (727)
Wine Institute (728)
Winegrape Growers of America (728)
Winnebago Tribe of Nebraska (728)
Winston & Strawn (218)
Witman Associates (220)
Wittenburg University (729)
WNVT/WNVC (729)
Womble Carlyle Sandridge & Rice, P.C. (220)
The Work Colleges (730)
World Learning Inc. (731)
World Wildlife Fund (731)
Wyeth-Ayerst Laboratories (732)
Wyeth-Ayerst Pharmaceuticals (732)
X-PAC (732)
Xcel Energy, Inc. (732)
Xcellsis Corp. (732)
Xerox Corp. (732)
Yazoo County, Mississippi Port Commission (733)
YMCA of the USA Public Policy Office (733)
Youngstown-Warren Regional Chamber (733)
Youthbuild, USA (734)
Yukon-Kuskokwim Health Corp. (734)
Yuma, Arizona, City of (734)
YWCA of the USA (734)
Zamorano (734)
Zeliff, Ireland, and Associates (221)
Ziff Investors Partnership (734)
Zone Therapeutics, Inc. (735)
Zurich Financial Group (735)

Chemicals/Chemical Industry (CHM)

20/20 Vision (223)
The Accord Group (5)
Adhesive and Sealant Council (227)
The Advocacy Group (6)
Agricultural Retailers Ass'n (232)
Air Products and Chemicals, Inc. (234)
Akzo Nobel Chemicals, Inc. (235)
Albemarle Corp. (237)
Alliance for Reasonable Regulation of Insecticides (240)
American Chemical Soc. (252)
American Chemistry Council (252)
American Council of Independent Laboratories (255)
American Crop Protection Ass'n (256)
American Home Products Corp. (262)
American Methanol Institute (268)
American Nursery and Landscape Ass'n (268)
American Plastics Council (270)
American Waterways Operators (280)
American Wood Preservers Institute (280)
Analytical Systems, Inc. (283)
Arch Chemical Inc. (287)
Wayne Arny & Assoc. (16)
Ashland Inc. (290)
James Nicholas Ashmore & Associates (18)
ATOFINA Chemicals, Inc. (302)
Automotive Aftermarket Industry Ass'n (303)
Aventis Pharmaceutical Products (304)
Battelle Memorial Institute (309)
Bayer Corp. (309)
BKSH & Associates (28)
Borden Chemicals & Plastics, Inc. (318)
BP Amoco Corp. (319)
Bracewell & Patterson, L.L.P. (30)
Brownstein Hyatt & Farber, P.C. (33)
James W. Bunger & Associates (323)
Burlington Northern Santa Fe Railway (324)
Burns and Roe Enterprises, Inc. (324)
Capitol Hill Advocates (39)
Cargill, Inc. (331)
Chemical Manufacturers Ass'n (342)
Chemical Producers and Distributors Ass'n (342)
Chlorine Chemistry Council (345)
Ciba Specialty Chemicals Corp. (346)
Color Pigments Manufacturers Ass'n, Inc. (358)
Consumer Federation of America (369)
Consumer Healthcare Products Ass'n (369)
Consumers Union of the United States (369)
Shawn Coulson (53)
Dow AgroSciences (391)
The Dow Chemical Co. (391)
Dow Corning Corp. (391)
Downey McGrath Group, Inc. (64)
DuPont (393)
Eastman Chemical Co. (395)
Eka Chemicals (399)
Elan Pharmaceutical Research Corp. (399)
EOP Group, Inc. (72)
Ethyl Corp. (407)
EXPRO Chemical Products (409)
Exxon Mobil Corp. (409)
F&T Network, Inc. (74)
The Fertilizer Institute (415)
FMC Corp. (420)
FQPA Implementation Working Group (424)
Freeport-McMoRan Copper & Gold Inc. (425)
Douglas Ward Freitag (79)
Friends of the Earth (426)
GAF Corp. (428)
General Motors Corp. (432)
Goodstein & Associates (84)
W. R. Grace & Co. (438)
Griffin, Johnson, Dover & Stewart (87)
The Grizzle Company (88)
James E. Guirard (89)
Halogenated Solvents Industry Alliance (443)
Hogan & Hartson L.L.P. (96)
Holland & Knight LLP (98)
Hooper Owen & Winburn (99)
Hudson Institute (454)
Huntsman Corp. (455)
Innovation Reform Group (462)
Inter-Associates, Inc. (466)
Internat'l Federation of Professional and Technical Engineers (471)
Internat'l Union of Painters and Allied Trades (476)
Jefferson Government Relations, L.L.C. (106)
Jellinek, Schwartz & Connolly (106)
S.C. Johnson and Son, Inc. (484)
Kaiser Aluminum & Chemical Corp. (485)
Kimberly-Clark Corp. (489)
The Kinetics Group (489)
KOSA (491)
Levine & Co. (119)
McDermott, Will and Emery (128)
Metal Finishing Suppliers Ass'n (519)
Methanex Inc. (520)
Minnesota Mining and Manufacturing Co. (3M Co.) (525)
Minor Crop Farmer Alliance (525)
Mitsubishi Internat'l Corp. (526)
Mitsubishi Research Institute (526)
Monsanto Co. (528)
Motor and Equipment Manufacturers Ass'n (531)
Multinat'l Government Services, Inc. (138)
Nammo Inc. (534)
Nat'l Ass'n of Chemical Distributors (540)
Nat'l Ass'n of Wheat Growers (551)
Nat'l Environmental Strategies (140)
Nat'l Farmers Union (Farmers Educational & Co-operative Union of America) (563)
Nat'l Legal Center for the Public Interest (570)
Nat'l Oilseed Processors Ass'n (572)
Nat'l Petrochemical Refiners Ass'n (573)
Nat'l Potato Council (574)
NL Industries (590)
Novartis Corp. (596)
Novartis Crop Protection (596)
Occidental Internat'l Corporation (598)
Ogilvy Public Relations Worldwide (145)
Ogletree Governmental Affairs, Inc. (145)
Olin Corp. (600)
Patton Boggs, LLP (150)
PDA (610)
Pentachlorophenol Task Force (611)
People for the Ethical Treatment of Animals (612)
Philipp Brothers Chemicals, Inc. (616)
The Plexus Consulting Group (156)
Preston Gates Ellis & Rouvelas Meeds LLP (162)
Public Citizen, Inc. (628)
Raytheon Co. (633)
Rhodia, Inc. (639)
Rhone-Polenc Inc. (639)
Rineco Chemical Industries (640)
Rohm and Haas Co. (642)
Rooney Group Internat'l, Inc. (171)
A. L. Ross Associates, Inc. (172)
SABIC Americas, Inc. (644)
Safe Environment of America (645)
Salt Institute (646)
Shell Oil Co. (657)
Silver Users Ass'n (659)
Robert E. Smith (182)
The Solomon Group, LLC (185)
Solutia Inc. (665)
Synthetic Organic Chemical Manufacturers Ass'n (679)
Tripoli Rocketry Ass'n (692)
U.S. Public Interest Research Group (697)
United Methodist Church General Board of Church and Society (702)
Valent U.S.A. Corp. (711)

Venable *(201)*
Vinyl Institute *(715)*
Vulcan Materials Co. *(718)*
Wallcovering Ass'n *(718)*
Robert K. Weidner *(211)*
The Wigglesworth Co. *(214)*
Williams & Jensen, P.C. *(215)*
Kathleen Winn & Associates, Inc. *(218)*
WPC Brands, Inc. *(731)*

Civil Rights/Civil Liberties (CIV)

AARP (American Ass'n of Retired Persons) *(224)*
Access Technology Ass'n *(226)*
Advocates for Youth *(229)*
AFL-CIO (American Federation of Labor and Congress of Industrial Organizations) *(231)*
Agudath Israel of America *(232)*
Harry C. Alford & Associates, Inc. *(11)*
Alliance for Justice *(239)*
American Ass'n of University Professors *(249)*
American Ass'n of University Women *(249)*
American Bar Ass'n *(250)*
American Civil Liberties Union *(252)*
American Civil Liberties Union of the Nat'l Capital Area *(252)*
American Council of Life Insurers *(256)*
American Diabetes Ass'n *(257)*
American Federation of State, County and Municipal Employees *(258)*
American Foundation for the Blind - Governmental Relations Group *(260)*
The American Institute of Architects *(264)*
American Jewish Committee *(265)*
American Jewish Congress *(265)*
American Psychological Ass'n *(271)*
American Soc. of Ass'n Executives *(275)*
American-Arab Anti-Discrimination Committee (ADC) *(281)*
Americans for Tax Reform *(282)*
Americans United for Separation of Church and State *(282)*
Anti-Defamation League *(285)*
AOL Time Warner *(285)*
The Arc *(287)*
Asian Pacific American Labor Alliance, AFL-CIO *(291)*
Ass'n for Education and Rehabilitation of the Blind & Visually Impaired *(292)*
Ass'n of Flight Attendants *(295)*
Ass'n of Test Publishers *(299)*
Bazelon Center for Mental Health Law, Judge David L. *(310)*
Bert Corona Leadership Institute *(312)*
Business and Professional Women/USA *(324)*
Campaign Finance Reform Coalition *(328)*
Center for Democracy and Technology *(336)*
The Center for Voting and Democracy *(338)*
Chamber of Commerce of the U.S.A. *(340)*
Child Welfare League of America *(343)*
Children's Defense Fund *(344)*
Christian Legal Soc. *(345)*
Christian Voice, Inc. *(345)*
Church of Scientology Internat'l *(346)*
Citizens Committee for the Right to Keep and Bear Arms *(348)*
Coalition on Accessibility *(355)*
Common Cause *(361)*
Curson Koopersmith Partners, Inc. *(56)*
Death Penalty Information Center *(383)*
Directors Guild of America *(389)*
Easter Seals *(395)*
Epstein Becker & Green, P.C. *(72)*
Scott J. Esparza & Co. *(407)*
Federal Legislative Associates, Inc. *(75)*
First Amendment Coalition for Expression *(417)*
Freeport-McMoRan Copper & Gold Inc. *(425)*
Friends Committee on Nat'l Legislation *(426)*
General Conference of Seventh-day Adventists *(431)*
General Motors Corp. *(432)*
Girl Scouts of the U.S.A. - Washington Office *(435)*
Hadassah, The Women's Zionist Organization of America *(443)*
Hall, Green, Rupli, LLC *(90)*
HALT-An Organization of Americans for Legal Reform *(444)*
Leslie Harris & Associates *(91)*
Holland & Knight LLP *(98)*
Holnam Inc. *(451)*
Hudson Institute *(454)*
Human Rights Campaign *(454)*
Human Rights Campaign Fund *(454)*
Institute on Religion and Democracy *(464)*
Institute on Religion and Public Policy *(464)*
Internat'l Ass'n of Assembly Managers *(467)*
Internat'l Brotherhood of Electrical Workers *(469)*
Internat'l Campaign for Tibet *(469)*
Internat'l Dyslexia Ass'n, The *(471)*
Internat'l Federation of Professional and Technical Engineers *(471)*
Internat'l Religious Liberty Ass'n *(474)*
Internat'l Union of Painters and Allied Trades *(476)*
Internet Action PAC *(476)*
Islamic Institute *(479)*
Janus-Merritt Strategies, L.L.C. *(104)*
Jar-Mon Consultants, Inc. *(105)*
Labor Council for Latin American Advancement (LCLAA) *(493)*
Lawyers Committee for Human Rights *(496)*
Leadership Conference on Civil Rights *(496)*
League of Women Voters of the United States *(497)*
Legal Action Center of the City of New York, Inc. *(497)*
Lutheran Office for Governmental Affairs/Evangelical Lutheran Church in America *(506)*
Lyons & Co. *(122)*
Turner D. Madden *(123)*
Magazine Publishers of America *(507)*
Mexican-American Legal Defense and Educational Fund *(521)*
Meyer & Klipper, PLLC *(133)*
Morning Star Institute, The *(529)*
Kay Allan Morrell, Attorney-at-Law *(137)*
Nat'l Abortion and Reproductive Rights Action League *(535)*
Nat'l Ass'n for Bilingual Education *(537)*
Nat'l Ass'n for the Advancement of Colored People, Washington Bureau *(538)*
Nat'l Ass'n of Business Political Action Committees *(539)*
Nat'l Ass'n of Developmental Disabilities Councils *(542)*
Nat'l Ass'n of Evangelicals *(542)*
Nat'l Ass'n of Home Builders of the U.S. *(543)*
Nat'l Ass'n of Jewish Legislators *(545)*
Nat'l Ass'n of Minority Automobile Dealers *(545)*
Nat'l Ass'n of Minority Political Families, USA, Inc. *(545)*
Nat'l Ass'n of Negro Business & Professional Women's Clubs, Inc. *(546)*
Nat'l Ass'n of People with AIDS, Inc. *(546)*
Nat'l Ass'n of Protection and Advocacy Systems (NAPAS) *(547)*
Nat'l Ass'n of Realtors *(547)*
Nat'l Ass'n of Social Workers *(549)*
Nat'l Assembly of Health and Human Service Organizations *(551)*
Nat'l Center for Public Policy Research *(555)*
Nat'l Club Ass'n *(556)*
Nat'l Coalition of Minority Businesses *(556)*
Nat'l Committee Against Repressive Legislation *(557)*
Nat'l Consumers League *(558)*
Nat'l Council for Community Behavioral Healthcare *(559)*
Nat'l Council of Jewish Women *(560)*
Nat'l Council of La Raza *(560)*
Nat'l Council of Negro Women *(560)*
Nat'l Education Ass'n of the U.S. *(562)*
Nat'l Employment Lawyers Ass'n *(562)*
Nat'l Farmers Union (Farmers Educational & Co-operative Union of America) *(563)*
Nat'l Health Law Program *(567)*
Nat'l Hispanic Council on Aging *(567)*
Nat'l Mental Health Ass'n *(571)*
Nat'l Multi-Housing Council *(571)*
Nat'l Organization for the Reform of Marijuana Laws *(572)*
Nat'l Partnership for Women and Families *(573)*
Nat'l Prison Project *(574)*
Nat'l Puerto Rican Coalition *(575)*
Nat'l Rehabilitation Ass'n *(575)*
Nat'l Rifle Ass'n of America *(576)*
Nat'l Right to Life Committee *(576)*
Nat'l Right to Work Committee *(576)*
Nat'l Whistleblower Center *(581)*
Nealon & Moran, L.L.P. *(141)*
NETWORK, A Nat'l Catholic Social Justice Lobby *(584)*
PE Biosystems *(610)*
People for the American Way *(612)*
Police Executive Research Forum *(620)*
Polity Consulting *(159)*
Principal Financial Group *(624)*
Recording Industry Ass'n of America *(634)*
Religious Technology Center *(636)*
Sagem Morpho *(646)*
James E. Schneider, LLM Inc. *(651)*
Search for Common Ground *(653)*
Securities Industry Ass'n *(654)*
Shaw Pittman *(177)*
Smith Alling Lane, P.S. *(183)*
Texaco Group Inc. *(684)*
Thiemann Aitken Vohra & Rutledge, L.L.C. *(194)*
Timmons and Co., Inc. *(195)*
William J. Tobin and Associates *(195)*
U.S. English, Inc. *(696)*
U.S. Family Network *(696)*
Union of Councils for Soviet Jews *(699)*
Union of Needletrades, Industrial, and Textile Employees (UNITE) *(699)*
Unitarian Universalist Ass'n of Congregations *(700)*
United Automobile, Aerospace and Agricultural Implement Workers of America (UAW) *(700)*
United Church of Christ Justice and Witness Ministry *(700)*
United Methodist Church General Board of Church and Society *(702)*
United States Business and Industry Council *(703)*
United States Student Ass'n *(704)*
Washington Council Ernst & Young *(206)*
Washington Flyer Taxi Drivers Ass'n, Inc. *(719)*
Washington Strategies, L.L.C. *(209)*
Williams & Jensen, P.C. *(215)*
James M. Williams, Jr. *(217)*
Wilmer, Cutler & Pickering *(217)*
Women Officials in NACo *(729)*
Women's Policy, Inc. *(729)*
World Government of World Citizens *(730)*
World Service Authority *(731)*
Bill Zavarela *(221)*
Zuckerman Spaeder L.L.P. *(221)*

Clean Air & Water (Quality) (CAW)

20/20 Vision *(223)*
AAAE-ACI *(224)*
Abitibi Consolidated Sales Corp. *(225)*
The Accord Group *(5)*
ADA Consulting Services *(227)*
ADA Consulting Services *(5)*
Adams and Reese LLP *(5)*
AFL-CIO - Maritime Trades Department *(231)*
AFL-CIO - Transportation Trades Department *(231)*
Agri Business Council of Arizona *(232)*
Agricultural Retailers Ass'n *(232)*
Ainslie Associates *(7)*
Air Conditioning Contractors of America *(233)*
Air Quality Standards Coalition *(234)*
Air-Conditioning and Refrigeration Institute *(234)*
Akin, Gump, Strauss, Hauer & Feld, L.L.P. *(8)*
Albemarle Corp. *(237)*
Albers & Co. *(10)*
Albertine Enterprises, Inc. *(10)*
Albuquerque, New Mexico, City of *(237)*
Alcalde & Fay *(10)*
Alcan Aluminum Corp. *(237)*
Harry C. Alford & Associates, Inc. *(11)*

Golf Course Superintendents Ass'n of America ***(437)***
Goodstein & Associates *(84)*
Goodyear Tire and Rubber Co. ***(437)***
Government Relations, Inc. *(84)*
GPC Internat'l *(85)*
Edmund C. Graber *(85)*
W. R. Grace & Co. ***(438)***
Jay Grant & Associates *(85)*
Greater New York Automobile Dealers Ass'n ***(439)***
Law Offices of Carol Green *(86)*
The Grizzle Company *(88)*
Grocery Manufacturers of America ***(440)***
Ground Water Protection Council ***(441)***
Gulf Coast Waste Disposal Authority ***(442)***
Harnischfeger Industries, Inc. ***(444)***
Heavy Vehicle Maintenance Group ***(447)***
Hempstead, New York, Village of ***(448)***
Hi-Desert Water District ***(449)***
Hill and Knowlton, Inc. *(95)*
Hogan & Hartson L.L.P. *(96)*
Holland & Knight LLP *(98)*
The Home Depot ***(451)***
Honda North America, Inc. ***(451)***
Honeywell Internat'l, Inc. ***(452)***
Oliver James Horton *(100)*
Humboldt Harbor Recreation ***(455)***
Huntington Sanitary Board ***(455)***
Hunton & Williams *(101)*
Huntsman Corp. ***(455)***
Idaho Power Co. ***(457)***
IMC Global Inc. ***(458)***
Impact Strategies *(102)*
Imperial Beach, California, City of ***(458)***
Imperial Irrigation District ***(458)***
In-Pipe Technology ***(458)***
Independent Petroleum Ass'n of America ***(459)***
Indiana, Office of the Governor of the State of ***(460)***
Infilco Degremont, Inc. ***(461)***
Infiltrator Systems, Inc. ***(461)***
Information Resources, Inc. ***(461)***
Institute of Scrap Recycling Industries, Inc. ***(464)***
Integrated Waste Services Ass'n ***(465)***
Intermountain Forest Industry Ass'n ***(467)***
Internat'l Ass'n of Bridge, Structural, Ornamental and Reinforcing Iron Workers ***(467)***
Internat'l Ass'n of Fish and Wildlife Agencies ***(468)***
Internat'l Brotherhood of Electrical Workers ***(469)***
Internat'l Business Machines Corp. ***(469)***
Internat'l Cadmium Ass'n ***(469)***
Internat'l Council of Shopping Centers ***(470)***
Internat'l Paint Inc. ***(473)***
Internat'l Paper ***(473)***
Internat'l Sign Ass'n ***(474)***
Internat'l Union of Painters and Allied Trades ***(476)***
IPALCO Enterprises, Inc./Indianapolis Power & Light Co. ***(478)***
The Irvine Co. ***(479)***
Jacksonville Electric Authority ***(481)***
Jacobs Engineering Group Inc. ***(481)***
Japan Automobile Manufacturers Ass'n ***(481)***
Japan Automobile Standards Internat'l Center ***(481)***
JMD Associates, Inc. *(107)*
S.C. Johnson and Son, Inc. ***(484)***
Johnston & Associates, LLC *(107)*
Jones, Walker, Waechter, Poitevent, Carrere & Denegre, L.L.P. *(108)*
Jordan & Associates, Inc. *(109)*
Jorden Burt LLP *(109)*
Joy Mining Machinery ***(485)***
Kaiser Aluminum & Chemical Corp. ***(485)***
Robert K. Kelley Law Offices *(111)*
Kelly and Associates, Inc. *(111)*
Kent & O'Connor, Inc. *(112)*
Kessler & Associates Business Services, Inc. *(112)*
Kimberly Consulting, LLC *(113)*
Kimberly-Clark Corp. ***(489)***
Kinghorn & Associates, L.L.C. *(113)*
Koch Industries, Inc. ***(490)***
Kogovsek & Associates *(114)*
Kohler Corp. ***(490)***
KOSA ***(491)***
Lafarge Corp. ***(494)***
Laguna Beach, California, City of ***(494)***
Lake County Basin 2000 ***(494)***
Lake, Illinois, County of ***(494)***
Lee Lane *(116)*
Lane, Oregon, County of ***(495)***
Large Public Power Council ***(495)***
Las Cruces, New Mexico, City of ***(495)***
League of Women Voters of the United States ***(497)***
Legislative Solutions *(118)*
Leonard B. Levine & Associates *(119)*
Lincoln Pulp and Paper Co. ***(500)***
Livermore, California, City of ***(500)***
The Livingston Group, LLC *(120)*
LPI Consulting, Inc. *(122)*
The LTV Corp. ***(505)***
Lutheran Office for Governmental Affairs/Evangelical Lutheran Church in America ***(506)***
Lynchburg, Virginia, City of ***(506)***
Lyondell Chemical Co. ***(506)***
M & R Strategic Services *(122)*
Mack Trucks, Inc. ***(506)***
Madison Government Affairs *(123)*
Manufactured Housing Institute ***(509)***
Manufacturers Alliance/MAPI Inc. ***(509)***
Maricopa, Arizona, County of ***(509)***
Marine Desalination Systems LLC ***(510)***
Massachusetts Water Resources Authority ***(512)***
Mayberry & Associates LLC *(126)*
Mayer, Brown & Platt *(126)*
Maytag Corp. ***(513)***
McClure, Gerard & Neuenschwander, Inc. *(127)*
McDermott, Will and Emery *(128)*
McGlotten & Jarvis *(129)*
McGuiness Norris & Williams, LLP *(130)*
Mary Lee McGuire *(130)*
McGuireWoods L.L.P. *(130)*
McLeod, Watkinson & Miller *(131)*
Merced, California, County of ***(518)***
Merck & Co. ***(518)***
Methanex Inc. ***(520)***
Metropolitan King County Council ***(520)***
Metropolitan St. Louis Sewer District ***(520)***
Metropolitan Transportation Commission ***(520)***
The Metropolitan Water District of Southern California ***(521)***
Meyers & Associates *(133)*
Miami Beach, Florida, City of ***(521)***
Miccosukee Tribe of Indians of Florida ***(522)***
Millennium Intermarket Group, LLC *(133)*
Milwaukee Metropolitan Sewerage District ***(524)***
Mobile Area Water and Sewer System ***(527)***
Modesto, California, City of ***(527)***
Modesto/Turlock Irrigation District ***(527)***
Molecular Separations Inc. ***(527)***
Monroe, New York, County of ***(528)***
Timothy X. Moore and Co. *(136)*
Motor and Equipment Manufacturers Ass'n ***(531)***
Motorola, Inc. ***(531)***
Muncie, Indiana, City of (Delaware County) ***(532)***
Municipal Electric Authority of Georgia ***(532)***
Murphy Oil U.S.A. ***(533)***
Murray, Scheer, Montgomery, Tapia & O'Donnell *(139)*
Nat'l Ass'n of Chemical Distributors ***(540)***
Nat'l Ass'n of Conservation Districts ***(540)***
Nat'l Ass'n of Manufacturers ***(545)***
Nat'l Ass'n of Negro Business & Professional Women's Clubs, Inc. ***(546)***
Nat'l Ass'n of People with AIDS, Inc. ***(546)***
Nat'l Ass'n of RV Parks and Campgrounds ***(548)***
Nat'l Ass'n of Service and Conservation Corps ***(549)***
Nat'l Ass'n of State Departments of Agriculture ***(549)***
Nat'l Ass'n of Towns and Townships ***(551)***
Nat'l Ass'n of Water Companies ***(551)***
Nat'l Ass'n of Wheat Growers ***(551)***
Nat'l Automobile Dealers Ass'n ***(552)***
Nat'l Cattleman's Beef Ass'n ***(554)***
Nat'l Chicken Council ***(555)***
Nat'l Concrete Masonry Ass'n ***(558)***
Nat'l Consumers League ***(558)***
Nat'l Corn Growers Ass'n ***(559)***
Nat'l Council of Catholic Women ***(560)***
Nat'l Council of Farmer Cooperatives ***(560)***
Nat'l Electrical Manufacturers Ass'n ***(562)***
Nat'l Environmental Development Ass'ns State & Federal Environmental Responsibility Project ***(563)***
Nat'l Environmental Strategies *(140)*
Nat'l Environmental Trust ***(563)***
Nat'l Funeral Directors Ass'n ***(565)***
Nat'l Grain and Feed Ass'n ***(566)***
Nat'l Grain Sorgum Producers ***(566)***
Nat'l Grange ***(566)***
Nat'l Hispanic Council on Aging ***(567)***
Nat'l Hydropower Ass'n ***(567)***
Nat'l Legal Center for the Public Interest ***(570)***
Nat'l Mining Ass'n ***(571)***
Nat'l Mitigation Bankers Ass'n ***(571)***
Nat'l Multi-Housing Council ***(571)***
Nat'l Ocean Industries Ass'n ***(572)***
Nat'l Paint and Coatings Ass'n ***(573)***
Nat'l Petrochemical Refiners Ass'n ***(573)***
Nat'l Pork Producers Council ***(574)***
Nat'l Propane Gas Ass'n ***(574)***
Nat'l Ready Mixed Concrete Ass'n ***(575)***
Nat'l Rural Electric Cooperative Ass'n ***(576)***
Nat'l Rural Housing Coalition ***(577)***
Nat'l Rural Water Ass'n ***(577)***
Nat'l Sediments Coalition ***(577)***
Nat'l Soc. of Professional Engineers ***(578)***
Nat'l Turkey Federation ***(580)***
Nat'l Utility Contractors Ass'n (NUCA) ***(580)***
Nat'l Water Resources Ass'n ***(581)***
The Nat'l Wetlands Coalition ***(581)***
Nat'l Whistleblower Center ***(581)***
Nat'l Wildlife Federation - Office of Federal and Internat'l Affairs ***(581)***
Natural Resources Defense Council ***(582)***
The Nature Conservancy ***(582)***
NES, Inc. *(141)*
New Mexico State University, Department of Engineering ***(586)***
New York Mercantile Exchange ***(587)***
The Newark Group ***(588)***
Newark, New Jersey, City of ***(588)***
Newport News Shipbuilding Inc. ***(588)***
Niagara Mohawk Power Corp. ***(589)***
Nisei Farmers League ***(590)***
Nixon Peabody LLP *(142)*
Non-Ferrous Founders' Soc. ***(591)***
Norfolk Southern Corp. ***(591)***
North American Die Casting Ass'n ***(592)***
North American Equipment Dealers Ass'n ***(592)***
North American Millers' Ass'n ***(592)***
North Carolina, Washington Office of the State of ***(593)***
Northeast Ohio Areawide Coordination Agency (NOACA) ***(593)***
Northeast Ohio Regional Sewer District ***(593)***
Northeast Utilities ***(593)***
Northeast-Midwest Institute ***(594)***
Northwest Airlines, Inc. ***(595)***
Novartis Corp. ***(596)***
NPES, The Ass'n for Suppliers of Printing, Publishing, and Converting Technologies ***(596)***
NRG Energy, Inc. ***(596)***
Nuclear Energy Institute ***(597)***
Obadal and MacLeod, p.c. *(143)*
Ocean Spray Cranberries ***(598)***
O'Connor & Hannan, L.L.P. *(144)*
Oklahoma City, Oklahoma, City of ***(599)***
Oklahoma State Medical Ass'n ***(600)***
Oppenheimer Wolff & Donnelly LLP *(147)*
Oxnard, California, City of ***(605)***
Oxygenated Fuels Ass'n ***(605)***
P & H Mining Equipment ***(605)***
PACCAR, Inc. ***(605)***
Palm Beach, Florida, County of ***(606)***
Palo Alto, California, City of ***(607)***
Paper Recycling Coalition ***(607)***
Parry, Romani, DeConcini & Symms *(149)*
Parsons Brinckerhoff Inc. ***(608)***
Passaic Valley Sewerage Commissioners ***(609)***
Patton Boggs, LLP *(150)*
Pennzoil-Quaker State Co. ***(611)***

Perkins Coie LLP (154)
PetrolRem, Inc. **(613)**
Peyser Associates, Inc. (155)
PG&E Generating Co. **(614)**
Pharmacia Corp. **(615)**
Phelps Dodge Corp. **(615)**
Philadelphia, Pennsylvania, City of **(615)**
Philip Morris Management Corp. **(615)**
Phillips Petroleum Co. **(616)**
Phoenix, Arizona, City of **(616)**
Pillsbury Winthrop LLP (155)
Pinnacle West Capital Corp. **(617)**
Piper Marbury Rudnick & Wolfe LLP (155)
Plumbing, Heating, Cooling Contractors- National Assoc. **(619)**
Podesta/Mattoon **(619)**
Podesta/Mattoon (158)
Policy Consulting Services (158)
Policy Directions, Inc. (158)
Ralph Pomerance, Jr. (159)
Portland, Oregon, City of **(621)**
Potlatch Corp. **(621)**
Potomac Electric Power Co. **(622)**
PPL **(622)**
Premium Standard Farms **(623)**
Preston Gates Ellis & Rouvelas Meeds LLP (162)
Printing Industries of America **(624)**
Progress Energy **(626)**
PSE&G **(627)**
Public Affairs Resources, Inc. (164)
Public Citizen, Inc. **(628)**
Public Strategies Washington, Inc. (164)
Real Estate Roundtable **(634)**
Redfern Resources (166)
Reed, Smith, LLP (167)
Remediation Financial, Inc. **(636)**
Renewable Fuels Ass'n **(637)**
Renewable Natural Resources Foundation **(637)**
The Renkes Group, Ltd. (168)
Republicans for Clean Air **(638)**
Restore America's Estuaries **(638)**
RFB, Inc. (168)
RGS Enterprises, Inc. (168)
Richmond, Virginia, City of **(640)**
Rio Grande Water Conservation District **(640)**
Rock-Tenn Co. **(641)**
Rockdale, Georgia, County of, Board of Commissioners of **(641)**
Rohm and Haas Co. **(642)**
Roof Coatings Manufacturers Ass'n **(642)**
Roseville, California, City of **(642)**
Rubber Manufacturers Ass'n **(643)**
Ryan, Phillips, Utrecht & MacKinnon (173)
Sacramento, California, Public Works Agency of the County of **(645)**
Salt Lake City Olympic Organizing Committee **(646)**
San Bernardino Valley Municipal Water District **(647)**
San Diego, California, City of **(647)**
San Gabriel Basin Water Quality Authority **(648)**
San Joaquin Valley Wide Air Pollution Study Agency **(648)**
Sappi Fine Paper NA **(649)**
Sarasota, Florida, City of **(649)**
Sarasota, Florida, County of **(650)**
Scenic Hudson **(651)**
James E. Schneider, LLM Inc. **(651)**
Screenprinting & Graphic Imaging Ass'n Internat'l **(653)**
Sea Grant Ass'n **(653)**
Seaboard Corp. **(653)**
Seattle, Washington, City of **(653)**
Sensor Research and Development Corp. **(655)**
SePRO Corp. **(655)**
Sewerage and Water Board of New Orleans **(656)**
Daniel F. Shaw & Associates (177)
Sheet Metal Workers' Internat'l Ass'n **(657)**
Shell Oil Co. **(657)**
Shipbuilders Council of America **(657)**
Shook, Hardy & Bacon LLP (180)
Shutler and Low (180)
Siemens Westinghouse Power Corporation **(658)**
Sierra Club **(658)**
Sierra Madre, California, City of **(658)**
Sills Associates (180)
Silver Users Ass'n **(659)**
Simon and Co., Inc. (181)
Smith & Harroff, Inc. (182)
E. Del Smith and Co. (183)
Smith Dawson & Andrews, Inc. (183)
Smith, Hinaman & Associates (184)
Smithfield Foods Inc. **(661)**
Smurfit Stone Container Corp. **(662)**
Soc. of the Plastics Industry **(664)**
Soc. of Toxicology **(664)**
Solid Waste Agency of Northern Cook County **(665)**
Solutia Inc. **(665)**
South Tahoe Public Utility District **(666)**
Southeast Water Coalition **(667)**
Southern Ute Indian Tribe **(668)**
Specialty Equipment Market Ass'n **(670)**
Springfield, Oregon, City of **(670)**
Steel Manufacturers Ass'n **(674)**
Stephens Law Offices (188)
Kenneth F. Stinger (189)
Strat@Comm (Strategic Communications Counselors) (189)
Charlene A. Sturbitts (190)
Subaru of America **(676)**
Swidler Berlin Shereff Friedman, LLP (191)
Swidler Berlin Shereff Friedman, LLP **(678)**
Synthetic Organic Chemical Manufacturers Ass'n **(679)**
Tecumseh Products Co. **(682)**
Texaco Group Inc. **(684)**
Texas A&M Research Foundation **(684)**
Textile Rental Services Ass'n of America **(685)**
ThermoEnergy Corp. **(686)**
Timmons and Co., Inc. (195)
Tire Ass'n of North America **(687)**
Tosco Corp. **(688)**
Toyota Motor Manufacturing North America **(689)**
Toyota Motor North America, U.S.A., Inc. **(689)**
Truck Renting and Leasing Ass'n **(693)**
Christopher A.G. Tulou (196)
Tyco Internat'l (US), Inc. **(695)**
U.S. Filter **(696)**
U.S. Oil and Gas Ass'n **(696)**
U.S. Public Interest Research Group **(697)**
U.S. Strategies Corp. (197)
UDV North America, Inc. **(698)**
UNIFI, Inc. **(698)**
Uniform and Textile Service Ass'n **(698)**
United Egg Ass'n **(701)**
United Egg Producers **(701)**
United Methodist Church General Board of Church and Society **(702)**
United Mine Workers of America **(702)**
United Motorcoach Ass'n **(702)**
United Parcel Service **(702)**
United States Business and Industry Council **(703)**
United States Sugar Corp. **(704)**
United States Telecom Ass'n **(704)**
United Technologies Corp. **(704)**
UNOCAL Corp. **(708)**
US Acqua Sonics Corp. **(709)**
USX Corp. **(710)**
Ute Mountain Ute Indian Tribe **(710)**
Valis Associates (198)
Valve Manufacturers Ass'n of America **(711)**
Van Ness Feldman, P.C. (199)
Van Scoyoc Associates, Inc. (200)
Vantage Point Network, LLC **(712)**
The Velasquez Group (201)
Venable (201)
Verner, Liipfert, Bernhard, McPherson and Hand, Chartered (202)
Mary Vihstadt (204)
Viohl and Associates, Inc. (205)
Vivendi Universal **(717)**
Volkswagen, AG **(717)**
Wake, North Carolina, County of **(718)**
R. Duffy Wall and Associates (205)
Washington Consulting Alliance, Inc. (206)
Washington Gas **(719)**
Water Environment Federation **(721)**
Water Infrastructure Network **(721)**
Waterman & Associates (210)
Welch's Foods, Inc. **(722)**
West Jordan, Utah, City of **(723)**
West Palm Beach, Florida, City of **(723)**
Weyerhaeuser Co. **(725)**
Wheeling, West Virginia, City of **(726)**
White Pigeon Paper Co. **(726)**
Wildlife Habitat Council **(726)**
Williams & Jensen, P.C. (215)
The Williams Companies **(727)**
Kathleen Winn & Associates, Inc. (218)
Wisconsin Energy Corp. **(728)**
Women Officials in NACo **(729)**
Woodbury County, Iowa **(730)**
Woodmont Corporation **(730)**
World Resources Institute **(731)**
World Wildlife Fund **(731)**
Wright & Talisman, P.C. (220)
Xcel Energy, Inc. **(732)**
Youngstown-Warren Regional Chamber **(733)**

Commodities (Big Ticket) (CDT)

Ad Hoc Coalition of Commercial and Investment Banks **(227)**
American Bankers Ass'n **(250)**
American Farm Bureau Federation **(258)**
The Bond Market Ass'n **(317)**
Burlington Northern Santa Fe Railway **(324)**
Cargill, Inc. **(331)**
Chesapeake Enterprises, Inc. (46)
Collier Shannon Scott, PLLC (48)
Compass Internat'l Inc. **(363)**
Copeland, Lowery & Jacquez (52)
The Dutko Group, Inc. (68)
Enron Corp. **(403)**
Eurex Deutschland **(408)**
Fannie Mae **(411)**
Guinea, Secretary General of the Presidency of the Republic of **(442)**
Interactive Brokers LLC **(466)**
Kaiser Aluminum & Chemical Corp. **(485)**
LaRocco & Associates (116)
Nat'l Grain Trade Council **(566)**
Philip Morris Management Corp. **(615)**
Salt Lake City Olympic Organizing Committee **(646)**
Seaboard Corp. **(653)**
Securities Industry Ass'n **(654)**
Silver Users Ass'n **(659)**
Strategic Horizons Advisors, L.L.C. (189)
Tiger Fund **(687)**
TV Guide, Inc. **(694)**
Unilever United States, Inc. **(699)**
The Velasquez Group (201)
Williams & Jensen, P.C. (215)

Communications/Broadcasting/Radio/TV (COM)

3Com Corp. **(223)**
AC Transit **(225)**
The Advocacy Group (6)
AFL-CIO - Professional Employees Department **(231)**
Akin, Gump, Strauss, Hauer & Feld, L.L.P. (8)
Alcalde & Fay (10)
Alcatel USA **(237)**
Alexander Strategy Group (11)
Alpine Group, Inc. (11)
Alvarado & Gerken (12)
American Academy of Child and Adolescent Psychiatry **(243)**
American Ass'n for Laboratory Accreditation **(246)**
American Ass'n of Advertising Agencies **(246)**
American Automobile Ass'n **(250)**
American Cable Ass'n **(251)**
American Continental Group, Inc. (12)
American Council of Independent Laboratories **(255)**
American Electronics Ass'n **(257)**
American Federation of Television and Radio Artists **(259)**
American Indian Higher Education Consortium **(263)**
American Petroleum Institute **(269)**

American Psychological Ass'n ***(271)***
American Radio Relay League ***(272)***
American Soc. of Composers, Authors and Publishers ***(276)***
American Teleservices Ass'n ***(279)***
Americans for Tax Reform ***(282)***
AMFM, Inc. ***(282)***
Amusement and Music Operators Ass'n ***(283)***
AOL Time Warner ***(285)***
Arent Fox Kintner Plotkin & Kahn, PLLC *(14)*
ARINC, Inc. ***(288)***
Arter & Hadden *(17)*
Ass'n for Interactive Media ***(292)***
Ass'n for Local Telecommunications Services ***(292)***
Ass'n of America's Public Television Stations ***(293)***
Ass'n of Local Television Stations ***(296)***
Ass'n of Nat'l Advertisers ***(297)***
AT&T ***(301)***
Baker & Hostetler LLP ***(306)***
Baker, Donelson, Bearman & Caldwell, P.C. *(21)*
The Baller Herbst Law Group *(22)*
Bell Atlantic Mobile ***(310)***
BellSouth Corp. ***(311)***
A. H. Belo Corp. ***(311)***
Bergen, New York, Village of ***(311)***
Bergner Bockorny Castagnetti and Hawkins *(26)*
Bertelsmann AG ***(312)***
BET Holdings II, Inc. ***(312)***
Biostar Group, The ***(314)***
The Boeing Co. ***(316)***
BT North America Inc. ***(323)***
Burlington Northern Santa Fe Railway ***(324)***
Burst Networks Inc. ***(324)***
Business Software Alliance ***(325)***
Mark R. Cannon *(37)*
CanWest ***(330)***
Capital Concerts ***(330)***
Capitol Associates, Inc. *(37)*
Capitol Coalitions Inc. *(38)*
Capitol Solutions *(39)*
CBS Affiliates ***(334)***
Cellular Depreciation Coalition ***(334)***
Cellular Telecommunications and Internet Ass'n ***(334)***
Central Virginia Educational Telecommunications Corp. ***(339)***
Chamber of Commerce of the U.S.A. ***(340)***
Carolyn C. Chaney & Associates *(45)*
Chernikoff and Co. *(46)*
Christian Coalition of America ***(345)***
Christian Network, Inc. ***(345)***
Churchville, New York, Village of ***(346)***
Chwat and Company, Inc. *(46)*
Cisco Systems Inc. ***(347)***
Citizens Against Government Waste ***(348)***
Citizens Communications Center ***(348)***
City Colleges of Chicago ***(349)***
Clayton, Dover, Lewes, Middletown, Milford, Newark, NewCastle, Seaford and Smyrna, Delaware, Municipalities of ***(350)***
Cohen Mohr LLP *(48)*
Scott Cohen *(48)*
Colling Swift & Hynes *(49)*
Comcast Corp. ***(359)***
Commercial Internet Exchange Ass'n ***(360)***
Common Cause ***(361)***
Community Ass'ns Institute (CAI) ***(362)***
Computer and Communications Industry Ass'n (CCIA) ***(364)***
Concert USA ***(365)***
Congressional Economic Leadership Institute ***(366)***
Conkling, Fiskum & McCormick *(51)*
Consortium for School Networking ***(368)***
Consumer Electronics Ass'n ***(369)***
Consumer Federation of America ***(369)***
Consumers Union of the United States ***(369)***
Convergence Services, Inc. *(52)*
Cook Inlet Region Inc. ***(371)***
Cooper, Carvin & Rosenthal *(52)*
Cormac Group, LLP *(53)*
Corning Inc. ***(372)***
Covington & Burling *(53)*
Cox Enterprises Inc. ***(378)***
Law Offices of Thomas K. Crowe *(55)*
CSRG Digital LLC ***(379)***
CSX Corp. ***(379)***
Cumulus Media, Inc. ***(380)***
Law Offices of Kevin G. Curtin *(56)*
Dairy.com ***(381)***
Davidson & Company, Inc. *(57)*
Susan Davis Internat'l *(58)*
Davis Manafort, Inc. *(58)*
Detroit Public Television ***(386)***
Devillier Communications *(61)*
Direct Marketing Ass'n, Inc. ***(388)***
The Walt Disney Co. ***(389)***
Dow, Lohnes & Albertson, PLLC *(64)*
Downey McGrath Group, Inc. *(64)*
Drinker Biddle & Reath LLP *(65)*
The Duberstein Group, Inc. *(65)*
Duke Energy ***(392)***
Duncan, Weinberg, Genzer & Pembroke, P.C. *(66)*
The Dutko Group, Inc. *(68)*
EchoStar Communications Corp. ***(396)***
EDS Corp. ***(398)***
The Egg Factory, LLC ***(398)***
Electric Lightwave, Inc. ***(400)***
Electronic Retailing Ass'n ***(401)***
eNIC Corp. ***(403)***
Ann Eppard Associates, Ltd. *(72)*
Ernst & Young LLP *(72)*
ESPN, Inc. ***(407)***
EXCEL Communications Inc. ***(408)***
Export Council for Energy Efficiency ***(409)***
Family Communications, Inc. ***(410)***
Fantasma Networks, Inc. ***(411)***
Federal Legislative Associates, Inc. *(75)*
Jack Ferguson Associates, Inc. *(75)*
First Amendment Coalition for Expression ***(417)***
Gannett Co., Inc. ***(429)***
Sara Garland (and Associates) *(81)*
Gateway, Inc. ***(430)***
General Communications, Inc. ***(431)***
General Conference of Seventh-day Adventists ***(431)***
General Electric Co. ***(432)***
General Motors Corp. ***(432)***
Glencairn, Ltd. ***(436)***
Goldberg, Godles, Wiener & Wright *(83)*
Granite Broadcasting Co. ***(438)***
Jay Grant & Associates *(85)*
Greener and Hook, LLC *(87)*
Guam, Washington Office of the Governor ***(442)***
Guinea, Secretary General of the Presidency of the Republic of ***(442)***
Hall, Green, Rupli, LLC *(90)*
Halliburton/Brown & Root ***(443)***
Leslie Harris & Associates *(91)*
Harris Corp. ***(444)***
Harris, Wiltshire & Grannis LLP *(92)*
The Hearst Corp. ***(447)***
Hearst-Argyle Television, Inc. ***(447)***
Heartland Communications & Management Inc. ***(447)***
Hiawatha Broadband Communications Inc. ***(449)***
Hicks, Muse, Tate & Furst ***(449)***
Higgins, McGovern & Smith, LLC *(94)*
Hispanic Broadcasting Inc. ***(450)***
HiSynergy Communications, Inc. ***(450)***
Hogan & Hartson L.L.P. *(96)*
Holland & Knight LLP *(98)*
Hooper Owen & Winburn *(99)*
Howard County, Maryland ***(454)***
Hubbard Broadcasting, Inc. ***(454)***
The Ickes & Enright Group *(102)*
ICO Global Communications ***(457)***
The ILEX Group *(102)*
Illinois Collaboration on Youth ***(457)***
Independent Television Service ***(460)***
Industrial Telecommunications Ass'n, Inc. ***(461)***
Information Trust ***(462)***
Institute of Electrical and Electronics Engineers, Inc. ***(464)***
Interactive Digital Software Ass'n ***(466)***
Interactive Gaming Council ***(466)***
Internat'l Brotherhood of Electrical Workers ***(469)***
Internat'l Communications Industries Ass'n (ICIA) ***(470)***
Internat'l Federation of Professional and Technical Engineers ***(471)***
Internat'l Sign Ass'n ***(474)***
Internat'l Soc. for Technology in Education ***(475)***
Internat'l Space Business Council ***(475)***
Internet Alliance Inc. ***(476)***
Internet Council of Registrars ***(476)***
Internet Ventures, Inc. ***(476)***
ITRON, Inc. ***(480)***
Janus-Merritt Strategies, L.L.C. *(104)*
Johnson Co. *(107)*
Jovan Broadcasting ***(485)***
KAIL-TV ***(485)***
Betty Ann Kane & Co. *(110)*
Kaye Scholer LLP *(110)*
KCTS ***(487)***
King & Spalding *(113)*
Knightstown, Indiana, Town of ***(490)***
Lancit Media/Junior Net ***(494)***
Laredo, Texas, City of ***(495)***
LaRocco & Associates *(116)*
Latham & Watkins *(116)*
Lawler, Metzger & Milkman, LLC *(117)*
The Paul Laxalt Group *(117)*
Leap Wireless Internat'l ***(497)***
The Legislative Strategies Group, LLC *(118)*
Lockheed Martin Corp. ***(501)***
Long, Aldridge & Norman, LLP *(121)*
Lutzker & Lutzker LLP *(122)*
The M Companies *(122)*
MacAndrews & Forbes Holdings, Inc. ***(506)***
Management Options, Inc. *(123)*
Manatt, Phelps & Phillips, LLP *(123)*
Manufacturers Radio Frequency Advisory Committee, Inc. ***(509)***
Mayer, Brown & Platt *(126)*
McGraw-Hill Cos., The ***(514)***
McGuiness & Holch *(130)*
MCI WorldCom Corp. ***(514)***
Media General, Inc. ***(516)***
Media Institute ***(516)***
Metrocall Inc. ***(520)***
Meyers & Associates *(133)*
Miller and Miller, P.C. *(134)*
Denny Miller McBee Associates *(134)*
Miller, Canfield, Paddock & Stone, P.L.C. *(135)*
Mintz, Levin, Cohn, Ferris, Glovsky and Popeo, P.C. *(135)*
Morrison & Foerster LLP *(137)*
Motion Picture Ass'n of America ***(530)***
MSP Strategic Communications, Inc. *(138)*
Municipal Electric Utilities Ass'n of New York State ***(532)***
The MWW Group *(140)*
Nat'l Ass'n of Black-Owned Broadcasters ***(539)***
Nat'l Ass'n of Broadcasters ***(539)***
Nat'l Ass'n of Business Political Action Committees ***(539)***
Nat'l Ass'n of Insurance and Financial Advisors ***(544)***
Nat'l Ass'n of Negro Business & Professional Women's Clubs, Inc. ***(546)***
Nat'l Ass'n of Police Organizations ***(546)***
Nat'l Basketball Ass'n ***(552)***
Nat'l Beer Wholesalers Ass'n ***(552)***
Nat'l Broadcasting Co. ***(553)***
Nat'l Burglar and Fire Alarm Ass'n ***(553)***
Nat'l Cable Television Ass'n ***(553)***
Nat'l Football League ***(565)***
Nat'l Grange ***(566)***
Nat'l Hockey League ***(567)***
Nat'l ITFS Ass'n ***(569)***
Nat'l League of Cities ***(569)***
Nat'l Public Radio ***(574)***
Nat'l Religious Broadcasters ***(575)***
Nat'l Religious Broadcasters, Music License Committee ***(575)***
Nat'l Rural Electric Cooperative Ass'n ***(576)***
Nat'l Telephone Cooperative Ass'n ***(579)***
NAVCOM Systems, Inc. ***(583)***
NetCoalition.Com ***(584)***
Netivation.com ***(584)***
Netscape Communications Corp. ***(584)***

Computer Industry (CPI)

Computing Research Ass'n (364)
Computing Technology Industry Ass'n (364)
Compuware Corp. (364)
Concert USA (365)
Congressional Economic Leadership Institute (366)
Conkling, Fiskum & McCormick (51)
Consortium for School Networking (368)
Constellation Energy Group (368)
Consumer Electronics Ass'n (369)
Consumer Federation of America (369)
Consumers Union of the United States (369)
The Council of Insurance Agents & Brokers (376)
Covington & Burling (53)
CRYPTEK Secure Communications, LLC (379)
Curson Koopersmith Partners, Inc. (56)
The Da Vinci Group (56)
Davidson & Company, Inc. (57)
Susan Davis Internat'l (58)
Deere & Co. (383)
Dell Computer Corp. (384)
Delta Dental Plans Ass'n (385)
Dictaphone Corp. (388)
Digital Commerce Corp. (388)
Digital Descriptor Services, Inc. (388)
Digital Media Ass'n (388)
Direct Marketing Ass'n, Inc. (388)
The Walt Disney Co. (389)
DNA Sciences, Inc. (390)
Downey McGrath Group, Inc. (64)
drugstore.com (392)
The Duberstein Group, Inc. (65)
Dun & Bradstreet (393)
E*TRADE Group, Inc. (394)
E*TRADE Securities, Inc. (394)
eBay Inc. (395)
ECC Internat'l Corp. (396)
EDS Corp. (398)
Education Networks of America (398)
Egle Associates (71)
eHealth Insurance Services, Inc. (399)
El Paso Corporation (399)
Electro Scientific Industries, Inc. (400)
Electronic Commerce Forum (400)
Electronic Industries Alliance (400)
EMC Corp. (401)
Engage Technologies (403)
Enron Corp. (403)
Entela, Inc. (404)
Equifax Inc. (406)
Ernst & Young LLP (407)
Ervin Technical Associates, Inc. (ETA) (73)
Export Control Coalition (409)
F.B.A. (74)
Fanatasy Elections (411)
Federal Home Loan Mortgage Corp. (Freddie Mac) (413)
FISERV, Inc. (418)
Fleischman and Walsh, L.L.P. (77)
Fleishman-Hillard, Inc (77)
Fluor Corp. (420)
Foley & Lardner (78)
French & Company (79)
Friends of the Nat'l Library of Medicine (426)
Gateway, Inc. (430)
GELCO Information Network GSD, Inc. (430)
General Motors Corp. (432)
GLOBEMAC Associates (83)
Jay Grant & Associates (85)
Greater Washington Board of Trade (439)
Greenberg Traurig, LLP (86)
Griffin, Johnson, Dover & Stewart (87)
Grisso Consulting (88)
Guinea, Secretary General of the Presidency of the Republic of (442)
Hale and Dorr LLP (89)
Hall, Green, Rupli, LLC (90)
Hannett & Associates (91)
Leslie Harris & Associates (91)
Healtheon/Web MD (447)
Allen Herbert (94)
Hewlett-Packard Co. (449)
Hill and Knowlton, Inc. (95)
HiSynergy Communications, Inc. (450)
Hogan & Hartson L.L.P. (96)
Hohlt & Associates (98)
Home Federal Savings and Loan Ass'n (451)
Hooper Owen & Winburn (99)
Hurt, Norton & Associates (101)
The Ickes & Enright Group (102)
The ILEX Group (102)
Information Technology Ass'n of America (ITAA) (461)
Information Technology Industry Council (462)
Infotech Strategies, Inc. (103)
Institute of Human and Machine Cognition (464)
Intel Corp. (465)
Interactive Gaming Council (466)
Intergraph Corp. Federal Systems Division (466)
Internat'l Biometric Industry Ass'n (468)
Internat'l Brotherhood of Electrical Workers (469)
Internat'l Business Machines Corp. (469)
Internat'l Federation of Professional and Technical Engineers (471)
Internat'l Mass Retailers Ass'n (473)
Internat'l Soc. for Technology in Education (475)
Internat'l Technology Resources, Inc. (475)
Internet Action PAC (476)
Internet Alliance Inc. (476)
Internet Council of Registrars (476)
Internet Safety Ass'n (476)
Internet Security Systems, Inc. (476)
Intuit, Inc. (477)
Janus-Merritt Strategies, L.L.C. (104)
Jar-Mon Consultants, Inc. (105)
JBC Internat'l (105)
Jefferson Consulting Group (105)
Jefferson Government Relations, L.L.C. (106)
Johnson Co. (107)
Jolly/Rissler, Inc. (108)
Jones, Walker, Waechter, Poitevent, Carrere & Denegre, L.L.P. (108)
JRL Enterprises (485)
Kasten Chase Applied Research Limited (486)
The Kemper Co. (111)
The Kinetics Group (489)
King & Spalding (113)
LaRocco & Associates (116)
LeBoeuf, Lamb, Greene & MacRae L.L.P. (117)
The Michael Lewan Co. (119)
The Livingston Group, LLC (120)
Lotus Development Corp. (504)
Luxcore Public Affairs (506)
The M Companies (122)
Magazine Publishers of America (507)
Magnitude Information Systems (507)
Management Options, Inc. (123)
Manatt, Phelps & Phillips, LLP (123)
Marconi plc (509)
Massachusetts Software Council (512)
Mayer, Brown & Platt (126)
McDermott, Will and Emery (128)
McGuiness & Holch (130)
MCI WorldCom Corp. (514)
McSlarrow Consulting L.L.C. (131)
Medical Records Internat'l, Inc. (516)
Member-Link Systems, Inc. (517)
memorize.com (517)
Mentor Graphics Corp. (518)
Mercury Group (132)
Metricom, Inc. (520)
The Metris Companies, Inc. (520)
Meyers & Associates (133)
Micron Technology, Inc. (522)
Microsoft Corp. (522)
Denny Miller McBee Associates (134)
Mitsubishi Research Institute (526)
Morrison & Foerster LLP (137)
mp3.com (532)
MSP Strategic Communications, Inc. (138)
Mullenholz, Brimsek & Belair (138)
Patrick M. Murphy & Associates (138)
Timothy D. Naegele & Associates (140)
Nat'l Ass'n of Broadcasters (539)
Nat'l Ass'n of Computer Consultant Businesses (540)
Nat'l Ass'n of County Information Technology Administrators (541)
Nat'l Ass'n of Independent Life Brokerage Agency (544)
Nat'l Ass'n to Protect Individual Rights (551)
Nat'l Consumers League (558)
Nat'l Defense Industrial Ass'n (561)
Nat'l Technical Systems (579)
NAVCOM Systems, Inc. (583)
NCR Corp. (583)
NetCoalition.Com (584)
Netivation.com (584)
Netscape Communications Corp. (584)
NeuLevel (584)
New Mexico State Office of Research & Development (586)
Non-Profit Management Associates, Inc. (142)
Julia J. Norrell & Associates (142)
Novell, Inc. (596)
nPower Advisors, LLC (596)
David O'Brien and Associates (143)
O'Connor & Hannan, L.L.P. (144)
O'Melveny and Myers LLP (147)
Oneida Indian Nation of New York (600)
Open Group Electronic Messaging Ass'n (EMA) Forum (601)
openNET Coalition (601)
Operations Security Professionals Soc. (601)
Oracle Corp. (602)
Orbital Sciences Corp., Fairchild Defense Division (602)
ORBITZ (602)
Oregon Graduate Institute of Science and Technology (603)
Parametric Technology Corp. (607)
Patton Boggs, LLP (150)
PE Biosystems (610)
Perkins Coie LLP (154)
Piper Marbury Rudnick & Wolfe LLP (155)
Planning Systems, Inc. (619)
The PMA Group (156)
Podesta/Mattoon (158)
The Polling Company (159)
Potomac Strategies Internat'l LLC (160)
Powell Tate (160)
Praxair, Inc. (623)
Preston Gates Ellis & Rouvelas Meeds LLP (162)
PriceWaterhouseCoopers (624)
Principal Financial Group (624)
Printing Industries of America (624)
PrivacyRight (624)
The Progress Freedom Foundation (626)
Project to Promote Competition and Innovation in the Digital Age (626)
PSE&G (627)
PSINet Inc. (628)
Public Strategies, Inc. (165)
Robert Rarog (166)
RBG Associates (166)
Recording Industry Ass'n of America (634)
RedCreek Communications Inc. (635)
Register.com (636)
Reinsurance Ass'n of America (636)
Resources and Instruction for Staff Excellence, Inc. (638)
Retlif Testing Laboratory, Inc. (639)
Rooney Group Internat'l, Inc. (171)
RPB Co. (172)
S1 Corp. (644)
Sabre Inc. (644)
Sagem Morpho (646)
SAP Public Services (649)
SBC Communications Inc. (650)
Charles Schwab & Co., Inc., (652)
Science Applications Internat'l Corp. (SAIC) (652)
Securities Industry Ass'n (654)
Semiconductor Equipment and Materials Internat'l (655)
Service Employees Internat'l Union (656)
Silicon Graphics/SGI (659)
Simon Strategies/Mindbeam (181)
Smith & Metalitz, L.L.P. (182)
Smith Alling Lane, P.S. (183)
Software & Information Industry Ass'n (SIIA) (664)
Software Productivity Consortium (664)
Spacelabs Medical Inc. (669)
Starnet Communications Internat'l (673)
Steptoe & Johnson LLP (188)

Stone Investments, Inc. *(675)*
Storage Technology Corp. *(675)*
Strategic Horizons Advisors, L.L.C. *(189)*
Strategic Impact, Inc. *(189)*
Sun Microsystems *(676)*
Swidler Berlin Shereff Friedman, LLP *(191)*
Technology Network *(682)*
Texas Instruments *(684)*
Richard R. Thaxton *(193)*
Thelen Reid & Priest LLP *(193)*
Thiemann Aitken Vohra & Rutledge, L.L.C. *(194)*
Richard K. Thompson *(194)*
Timmons and Co., Inc. *(195)*
Traditional Values Coalition *(689)*
Traffic.com *(689)*
Transnat'l Development Consortium *(690)*
Travelocity.com *(691)*
Troutman Sanders LLP *(196)*
TRW Inc. *(693)*
U.S. Chamber Institute for Legal Reform *(695)*
UBS Warburg *(697)*
Ultratech Stepper Inc. *(698)*
Underwriters Digital Research, Inc. *(698)*
Unilever United States, Inc. *(699)*
Unisys Corp. *(700)*
United States Telecom Ass'n *(704)*
University of Washington *(708)*
V-ONE Corp. *(711)*
Valanzano & Associates *(198)*
Van Scoyoc Associates, Inc. *(200)*
Vantage Point Network, LLC *(712)*
VeriSign/Network Solutions, Inc. *(713)*
Verner, Liipfert, Bernhard, McPherson and Hand, Chartered *(202)*
Vision Technologies, Inc. *(716)*
R. Duffy Wall and Associates *(205)*
The Washington Group *(208)*
Washington Resource Associates *(209)*
WebMD *(722)*
webwasher.com *(722)*
The Wexler Group *(211)*
Wi-LAN, Inc. *(726)*
Wiley, Rein & Fielding *(214)*
Wilmer, Cutler & Pickering *(217)*
Winstar Communications, Inc. *(728)*
Wunder & Lilley *(221)*
Xerox Corp. *(732)*
Yahoo! *(732)*
YouBet.com *(733)*
Zuckerman Spaeder L.L.P. *(221)*
Zurich Financial Group *(735)*

Constitution (CON)

Abbott Laboratories *(225)*
AFL-CIO (American Federation of Labor and Congress of Industrial Organizations) *(231)*
Agudath Israel of America *(232)*
Akin, Gump, Strauss, Hauer & Feld, L.L.P. *(8)*
American Ass'n of Motor Vehicle Administrators *(248)*
American Bar Ass'n *(250)*
American Federation of Teachers *(259)*
American Legion *(266)*
American Library Ass'n *(266)*
American Soc. for Industrial Security *(274)*
American Soc. of Ass'n Executives *(275)*
American Soc. of Newspaper Editors *(277)*
Americans Back in Charge Foundation *(281)*
Americans for Tax Reform *(282)*
Americans United for Separation of Church and State *(282)*
Amusement and Music Operators Ass'n *(283)*
Anti-Defamation League *(285)*
AOL Time Warner *(285)*
Arent Fox Kintner Plotkin & Kahn, PLLC *(14)*
Ass'n of American Publishers *(294)*
Ass'n to Unite the Democracies *(299)*
W. Douglas Campbell *(36)*
CCI Construction *(334)*
The Center for Voting and Democracy *(338)*
Chamber of Commerce of the U.S.A. *(340)*
Cohn and Marks *(48)*
Commercial Internet Exchange Ass'n *(360)*
Concerned Women for America *(365)*
Council for Government Reform *(374)*
Curson Koopersmith Partners, Inc. *(56)*
Eckert Seamans Cherin & Mellott, LLC *(70)*
English First, Inc. *(403)*
Federal Bar Ass'n *(412)*
First Amendment Coalition for Expression *(417)*
Fleet Reserve Ass'n *(418)*
Fraternal Order of Police *(425)*
GAF Corp. *(428)*
General Conference of Seventh-day Adventists *(431)*
Leslie Harris & Associates *(91)*
Information Trust *(462)*
Institute on Religion and Public Policy *(464)*
Interactive Digital Software Ass'n *(466)*
Internat'l Religious Liberty Ass'n *(474)*
Janus-Merritt Strategies, L.L.C. *(104)*
Jenkens & Gilchrist *(107)*
Kirkland & Ellis *(113)*
Kirkpatrick & Lockhart LLP *(114)*
Liberty Lobby *(499)*
Jack D.P. Lichtenstein *(120)*
Lutheran Office for Governmental Affairs/Evangelical Lutheran Church in America *(506)*
Magazine Publishers of America *(507)*
Mexican-American Legal Defense and Educational Fund *(521)*
Meyer & Klipper, PLLC *(133)*
Morgan, Lewis & Bockius LLP *(136)*
Motion Picture Ass'n of America *(530)*
The Moyer Group *(138)*
Nat'l Abortion and Reproductive Rights Action League *(535)*
Nat'l Ass'n for the Advancement of Colored People, Washington Bureau *(538)*
Nat'l Ass'n of Protection and Advocacy Systems (NAPAS) *(547)*
Nat'l Ass'n of Realtors *(547)*
Nat'l Ass'n of Recording Merchandisers *(548)*
Nat'l Committee Against Repressive Legislation *(557)*
Nat'l Court Reporters Ass'n *(561)*
Nat'l District Attorneys Ass'n *(562)*
Nat'l Fair Housing Alliance *(563)*
Nat'l Newspaper Ass'n *(572)*
Nat'l Organization for Victim Assistance *(572)*
Nat'l Right to Life Committee *(576)*
Nat'l Right to Work Committee *(576)*
Nat'l Taxpayers Union *(579)*
Nat'l Telephone Cooperative Ass'n *(579)*
Nat'l Trust for Historic Preservation *(580)*
Outdoor Advertising Ass'n of America *(604)*
Parry, Romani, DeConcini & Symms *(149)*
Patton Boggs, LLP *(150)*
People for the American Way *(612)*
Philips Electronics North America Corp. *(616)*
Police Executive Research Forum *(620)*
Radio-Television News Directors Ass'n *(632)*
The Retired Enlisted Ass'n *(638)*
Sullivan & Mitchell, P.L.L.C. *(190)*
Traditional Values Coalition *(689)*
TREA Senior Citizens League (TSCL) *(691)*
U.S. Chamber Institute for Legal Reform *(695)*
U.S. Term Limits *(697)*
Underwriters Digital Research, Inc. *(698)*
United Automobile, Aerospace and Agricultural Implement Workers of America (UAW) *(700)*
United Methodist Church General Board of Church and Society *(702)*
Weil, Gotshal & Manges, LLP *(211)*
Wine Institute *(728)*
World Government of World Citizens *(730)*
World Service Authority *(731)*

Consumer Issues/Safety/Protection (CSP)

3Com Corp. *(223)*
AARP (American Ass'n of Retired Persons) *(224)*
Access Technology Ass'n *(226)*
Acxiom Corp. *(227)*
AdvaMed *(228)*
Advocates for Highway and Auto Safety *(229)*
AFL-CIO (American Federation of Labor and Congress of Industrial Organizations) *(231)*
AFL-CIO (Union Label and Service Trades Department) *(231)*
Akin, Gump, Strauss, Hauer & Feld, L.L.P. *(8)*
Albemarle Corp. *(237)*
Albertine Enterprises, Inc. *(10)*
Alliance for Children and Families *(239)*
Alliance of Automobile Manufacturers, Inc. *(240)*
Allstate Insurance Co. *(241)*
Alston & Bird LLP *(12)*
American Academy of Dermatology *(243)*
American Ass'n for Laboratory Accreditation *(246)*
American Ass'n of Health Plans (AAHP) *(248)*
American Ass'n of Motor Vehicle Administrators *(248)*
American Boiler Manufacturers Ass'n *(251)*
American Butter Institute *(251)*
American Camping Ass'n *(251)*
American Consulting Engineers Council *(255)*
American Council of Independent Laboratories *(255)*
American Council of Korean Travel Agents *(255)*
American Feed Industry Ass'n *(259)*
American Free Trade Ass'n *(260)*
American Furniture Manufacturers Ass'n *(260)*
American Gas Ass'n *(261)*
American Home Products Corp. *(262)*
American Homeowners Grassroots Alliance *(262)*
American Hotel and Lodging Ass'n *(263)*
American Institute of Ultrasound in Medicine *(264)*
American Insurance Ass'n *(264)*
American Moving and Storage Ass'n *(268)*
American Plastics Council *(270)*
American Rental Ass'n *(272)*
American Resort Development Ass'n *(272)*
American Soc. for Clinical Pharmacology and Therapeutics *(274)*
American Soc. of Home Inspectors (ASHI) *(276)*
American Soc. of Travel Agents *(277)*
American Teleservices Ass'n *(279)*
American Tort Reform Ass'n *(279)*
American Trans Air *(279)*
American Water Works Ass'n *(280)*
American Wood Preservers Institute *(280)*
Aniline Ass'n, Inc. *(284)*
AOL Time Warner *(285)*
APCO Worldwide *(14)*
Arent Fox Kintner Plotkin & Kahn, PLLC *(14)*
Arizona Mail Order Co. *(288)*
Armstrong World Industries, Inc. *(289)*
Arnold & Porter *(16)*
Arvin Meritor Automotive *(290)*
Ashland Inc. *(290)*
The Ass'n For Manufacturing Technology (AMT) *(292)*
Ass'n of Banks in Insurance *(294)*
Ass'n of Flight Attendants *(295)*
Ass'n of Home Appliance Manufacturers *(296)*
Ass'n of Trial Lawyers of America *(299)*
Associated Credit Bureaus, Inc. *(300)*
Associated Equipment Distributors *(300)*
Automotive Parts and Service Alliance *(303)*
Aventis Pharmaceuticals, Inc. *(304)*
Barbour Griffith & Rogers, Inc. *(22)*
Barnett & Sivon, P.C. *(24)*
Timothy Bell & Co. *(25)*
Bicycle Product Suppliers Ass'n *(313)*
Big Sky Consulting, Inc. *(27)*
Biotechnology Industry Organization *(314)*
BKSH & Associates *(28)*
Richard W. Bliss *(29)*
BMW Financial Services of North America, Inc. *(316)*
BMW Manufacturing Corp. *(316)*
The BOSE Corp. *(318)*
Bracewell & Patterson, L.L.P. *(30)*
Marshall A. Brachman *(31)*
Robert M. Brandon and Associates *(32)*
Bridgestone/Firestone, Inc. *(320)*
Brinker Internat'l *(320)*
Bristol-Myers Squibb Co. *(320)*
Brown-Forman Corp. *(322)*
Brownstein Hyatt & Farber, P.C. *(33)*
Building Service Contractors Ass'n Internat'l *(323)*
Burlington Northern Santa Fe Railway *(324)*

The Business Roundtable **(325)**
Business Software Alliance **(325)**
Butera & Andrews (34)
W. Douglas Campbell (36)
Campbell Crane & Associates (36)
Canfield, Smith and Martin (36)
Capitol Hill Advocates (39)
The Carmen Group (40)
Carpet and Rug Institute **(332)**
The Carter Group (41)
Cassidy & Associates, Inc. (42)
Cell Tech **(334)**
Cellular Telecommunications and Internet Ass'n **(334)**
Center for Claims Resolution **(335)**
Chamber of Commerce of the U.S.A. **(340)**
Chamber of Independent Gas Stations of Argentina **(340)**
Check Payment Systems Ass'n **(341)**
ChemFirst Inc. **(342)**
The Chubb Corp. **(346)**
Church of Scientology Internat'l **(346)**
Ciba Specialty Chemicals Corp. **(346)**
CIGNA Corp. **(346)**
Citizens for Public Action on Cholesterol, Inc. **(348)**
Clark & Weinstock, Inc. (47)
CNA Financial Corp. **(351)**
CNA Insurance Cos. **(351)**
Coalition for American Trauma Care **(352)**
Coalition for Asbestos Resolution **(353)**
Coalition for Truth in Environmental Marketing Information, Inc. **(355)**
Coalition for Uniform Product Liability Law **(355)**
Coalition to Stop Gun Violence **(356)**
Commercial Internet Exchange Ass'n **(360)**
Community Financial Services Ass'n **(362)**
Computer and Communications Industry Ass'n (CCIA) **(364)**
Consumer Aerosol Products Council **(368)**
Consumer Energy Council of America Research Foundation **(369)**
Consumer Federation of America **(369)**
Consumer Healthcare Products Ass'n **(369)**
Consumers Union of the United States **(369)**
Continental Teves **(370)**
Coors Brewing Company **(371)**
Cortese PLLC (53)
Cosmetic, Toiletry and Fragrance Ass'n **(373)**
Crowell & Moring LLP (55)
CSA America, Inc. **(379)**
CSX Corp. **(379)**
The Cullen Law Firm (56)
The Cuneo Law Group, P.C. (56)
Currie Technologies, Inc. **(380)**
Curson Koopersmith Partners, Inc. (56)
The Da Vinci Group (56)
DaimlerChrysler Corp. **(381)**
Danaher Corp. **(382)**
The Danny Foundation, **(382)**
Mary E. Davis (57)
Direct Marketing Ass'n, Inc. **(388)**
Direct Selling Ass'n **(389)**
Distilled Spirits Council of the United States, Inc. **(389)**
Dorfman & O'Neal, Inc. (63)
DoubleClick **(391)**
The Dow Chemical Co. **(391)**
The Duberstein Group, Inc. (65)
Duncan, Weinberg, Genzer & Pembroke, P.C. (66)
DuPont **(393)**
The Dutko Group, Inc. (68)
Dykema Gossett PLLC (69)
Eastman Chemical Co. **(395)**
eBay Inc. **(395)**
Eckert Seamans Cherin & Mellott, LLC (70)
Edison Electric Institute **(397)**
Edmund Scientific Co. **(397)**
Electric Consumers Alliance **(400)**
Electric Transportation Co. **(400)**
Entela, Inc. **(404)**
Equifax Inc. **(406)**
Ethyl Corp. **(407)**
Ethylene Oxide Sterilization Ass'n, Inc. **(407)**
Evans & Black, Inc. (73)
Exxon Mobil Corp. **(409)**
Fantasma Networks, Inc. **(411)**
The Fertilizer Institute **(415)**
Fierce and Isakowitz (76)
Food Marketing Institute **(421)**
Ford Motor Co. **(422)**
FoxKiser (79)
Free Trade Lumber Council **(425)**
French & Company (79)
GAF Corp. **(428)**
Ernest & Julio Gallo Winery **(428)**
General Electric Co. **(432)**
General Mills **(432)**
General Motors Corp. **(432)**
Generic Pharmaceutical Ass'n **(433)**
Georgia-Pacific Corp. **(434)**
Goodyear Tire and Rubber Co. **(437)**
Government Relations, Inc. (84)
Great Lakes Chemical Corp. **(439)**
Greater New York Automobile Dealers Ass'n **(439)**
Greener and Hook, LLC (87)
Grisso Consulting (88)
Guidant Corp. **(442)**
Hadley & McKenna (89)
Halliburton/Brown & Root **(443)**
HALT-An Organization of Americans for Legal Reform **(444)**
The Hartford **(445)**
Health Insurance Ass'n of America **(446)**
Health Risk Management Group, Inc. **(446)**
Heidepriem & Mager, Inc. (94)
Hogan & Hartson L.L.P. (96)
Hohlt & Associates (98)
Holland & Knight LLP (98)
The Home Depot **(451)**
Honda North America, Inc. **(451)**
R. J. Hudson Associates (101)
Huntsman Corp. **(455)**
Individual Reference Services Group **(461)**
Infectious Diseases Soc. of America, Inc. **(461)**
Information Technology Industry Council **(462)**
Intel Corp. **(465)**
Interactive Digital Software Ass'n **(466)**
Internat'l Ass'n of Machinists and Aerospace Workers **(468)**
Internat'l Biometric Industry Ass'n **(468)**
Internat'l Bottled Water Ass'n **(468)**
Internat'l Brotherhood of Electrical Workers **(469)**
Internat'l Brotherhood of Teamsters **(469)**
Internat'l Business Machines Corp. **(469)**
Internat'l Franchise Ass'n **(472)**
Internat'l Mass Retailers Ass'n **(473)**
Internat'l Safety Equipment Ass'n (ISEA) **(474)**
Internat'l Sleep Products Ass'n **(474)**
Internet Action PAC **(476)**
Internet Advertising Bureau **(476)**
Internet Alliance Inc. **(476)**
Internet Safety Ass'n **(476)**
Interstate Natural Gas Ass'n of America **(477)**
The Island ECN **(479)**
ITRON, Inc. **(480)**
Janus-Merritt Strategies, L.L.C. (104)
Jefferson Government Relations, L.L.C. (106)
Jenkens & Gilchrist (107)
JM Family Enterprises **(483)**
S.C. Johnson and Son, Inc. **(484)**
Jolly/Rissler, Inc. (108)
Jones, Walker, Waechter, Poitevent, Carrere & Denegre, L.L.P. (108)
Kaiser Aluminum & Chemical Corp. **(485)**
The Kamber Group (109)
Kawasaki Motors Corp., USA **(487)**
Kean Tracers, Inc. **(487)**
Kellogg Brown and Root **(487)**
Kelly and Associates, Inc. (111)
Kendall and Associates (111)
Kent & O'Connor, Inc. (112)
Kimberly-Clark Corp. **(489)**
LaRocco & Associates (116)
Lawler, Metzger & Milkman, LLC (117)
Lent Scrivner & Roth LLC (119)
The Michael Lewan Co. (119)
Lexis-Nexis **(498)**
Lightguard Systems, Inc. **(499)**
Eli Lilly and Co. **(499)**
The Limited Inc. **(499)**
The Livingston Group, LLC (120)
Lucent Technologies **(505)**
Lumbermens Mutual Casualty Co. **(505)**
M & R Strategic Services (122)
The M Companies (122)
Mack Trucks, Inc. **(506)**
Magazine Publishers of America **(507)**
Management Options, Inc. (123)
Manatt, Phelps & Phillips, LLP (123)
Manufactured Housing Institute **(509)**
Manufacturers Alliance/MAPI Inc. **(509)**
Markey and Associates (125)
MasterCard Internat'l **(513)**
Mattel, Inc. **(513)**
Maytag Corp. **(513)**
Mazda North America Operations **(514)**
McClure, Gerard & Neuenschwander, Inc. (127)
McDonald's Corp. **(514)**
McGuiness & Holch (130)
McIntyre Law Firm, PLLC (130)
Medical Records Internat'l, Inc. **(516)**
Medtronic, Inc. **(517)**
MemberWorks, Inc. **(517)**
Merck & Co. **(518)**
Mercury Group (132)
Microsoft Corp. **(522)**
Mid-West Electric Consumers Ass'n **(523)**
Miller & Chevalier, Chartered (133)
Denny Miller McBee Associates (134)
Mintz, Levin, Cohn, Ferris, Glovsky and Popeo, P.C. (135)
Mitsubishi Motors America, Inc. **(526)**
Mitsubishi Research Institute **(526)**
Modesto/Turlock Irrigation District **(527)**
Molecular BioSystems, Inc. **(527)**
Morgan, Lewis & Bockius LLP (136)
Morrison & Foerster LLP (137)
Mortgage Bankers Ass'n of America **(530)**
MSP Strategic Communications, Inc. (138)
Mullenholz, Brimsek & Belair (138)
Multinat'l Government Services, Inc. (138)
The MWW Group (140)
Nat'l Ass'n for Nutritional Choice **(538)**
Nat'l Ass'n of Federal Credit Unions **(542)**
Nat'l Ass'n of Independent Insurers **(544)**
Nat'l Ass'n of Manufacturers **(545)**
Nat'l Ass'n of Negro Business & Professional Women's Clubs, Inc. **(546)**
Nat'l Ass'n of Recording Merchandisers **(548)**
Nat'l Ass'n of Retail Collection Attorneys **(548)**
Nat'l Ass'n of Securities and Commercial Law Attorneys **(549)**
Nat'l Ass'n of State Units on Aging **(550)**
Nat'l Ass'n of State Utility Consumer Advocates (NASUCA) **(550)**
Nat'l Automobile Dealers Ass'n **(552)**
Nat'l Black Women's Health Project **(552)**
Nat'l Coalition on E-Commerce and Privacy **(556)**
Nat'l Consumers League **(558)**
Nat'l Electrical Contractors Ass'n **(562)**
Nat'l Electrical Manufacturers Ass'n **(562)**
Nat'l Fastener Distributors Ass'n **(564)**
Nat'l Field Selling Ass'n **(564)**
Nat'l Fire Protection Ass'n **(564)**
Nat'l Franchise Council **(565)**
Nat'l Funeral Directors Ass'n **(565)**
Nat'l Health Council **(567)**
Nat'l Home Equity Mortgage Ass'n **(567)**
Nat'l Licensed Beverage Ass'n **(570)**
Nat'l Meat Canners Ass'n **(570)**
Nat'l Mental Health Ass'n **(571)**
Nat'l Mining Ass'n **(571)**
Nat'l Retail Federation **(576)**
Nat'l Spa and Pool Institute **(578)**
Nat'l Technical Systems **(579)**
Nat'l Wholesale Co., Inc. **(581)**
Nat'l Women's Health Network **(581)**
Nat'l Yogurt Ass'n **(581)**
Navarro Legislative & Regulatory Affairs (141)
Nescrow.com Technologies **(584)**
NetCoalition.Com **(584)**
Netscape Communications Corp. **(584)**
Nissan North America Inc. **(590)**
Nitrobenzene Ass'n **(590)**

Nixon Peabody LLP *(142)*
NL Industries ***(590)***
No-Wave, AB ***(590)***
Julia J. Norrell & Associates *(142)*
North American Communications Corp. ***(592)***
NPES, The Ass'n for Suppliers of Printing, Publishing, and Converting Technologies ***(596)***
The OB-C Group, LLC *(143)*
Obadal and MacLeod, p.c. *(143)*
O'Connor & Hannan, L.L.P. *(144)*
O'Melveny and Myers LLP *(147)*
O'Neill, Athy & Casey, P.C. *(147)*
Opticians Ass'n of America ***(601)***
Oracle Corp. ***(602)***
John T. O'Rourke Law Offices *(147)*
Owens-Illinois, Inc. ***(605)***
Owner-Operator Independent Drivers Ass'n, Inc. ***(605)***
Palumbo & Cerrell, Inc. *(149)*
Parry, Romani, DeConcini & Symms *(149)*
Patton Boggs, LLP *(150)*
Pennzoil-Quaker State Co. ***(611)***
Pfizer, Inc. ***(613)***
Pharmaceutical Research and Manufacturers of America ***(614)***
Philip Morris Management Corp. ***(615)***
Phillips Petroleum Co. ***(616)***
Piper Marbury Rudnick & Wolfe LLP *(155)*
The Plexus Consulting Group *(156)*
Plumbing, Heating, Cooling Contractors- National Assoc. ***(619)***
Polaris Industries ***(620)***
Policy Directions, Inc. *(158)*
Premier Parks, Inc. ***(623)***
Preston Gates Ellis & Rouvelas Meeds LLP *(162)*
PrivacyRight ***(624)***
The Procter & Gamble Company ***(625)***
Project to Promote Competition and Innovation in the Digital Age ***(626)***
Public Citizen, Inc. ***(628)***
Public Strategies, Inc. *(165)*
Raytheon Co. ***(633)***
Recreation Vehicle Dealers Ass'n of North America ***(634)***
Rent-a-Center, Inc. ***(637)***
Retractable Technologies, Inc. ***(639)***
Richemont Internat'l Ltd. ***(640)***
Robison Internat'l, Inc. *(170)*
Rockwell Collins ***(641)***
Rogers & Wells *(171)*
Rohm and Haas Co. ***(642)***
Ross Stores, Inc. ***(642)***
Ryder System, Inc. ***(644)***
Sabre Inc. ***(644)***
Saf T Lok, Inc. ***(645)***
Salton, Inc. ***(646)***
Seaboard Corp. ***(653)***
Secured Access Portals, Inc. ***(654)***
Sellery Associates, Inc. *(177)*
Shea & Gardner *(179)*
Shell Oil Co. ***(657)***
Sherwin Williams Co. ***(657)***
Shriners Hospital for Children ***(658)***
Bill Simpson & Associates *(181)*
Simula, Inc. ***(659)***
Sleep Products Safety Council ***(661)***
Soc. of Consumer Affairs Professionals in Business ***(663)***
Sparber and Associates *(186)*
Spokane Area Chamber of Commerce ***(670)***
Springs Industries, Inc. ***(671)***
St. Maxens & Company *(187)*
State Farm Insurance Cos. ***(673)***
Stephens Law Firm *(188)*
Stewart Enterprises, Inc. ***(674)***
Strat@Comm (Strategic Communications Counselors) *(189)*
Charlene A. Sturbitts *(190)*
Tetrahydrofuran Task Force ***(684)***
Texas Health Resources ***(684)***
Tiffany & Co. ***(687)***
Timmons and Co., Inc. *(195)*
Tire Ass'n of North America ***(687)***
William J. Tobin and Associates *(195)*
Toy Manufacturers of America ***(688)***
Toyota Motor North America, U.S.A., Inc. ***(689)***
Travelocity.com ***(691)***
Tripoli Rocketry Ass'n ***(692)***
TRW Inc. ***(693)***
U.S. Chamber Institute for Legal Reform ***(695)***
U.S. Gypsum Co. ***(696)***
U.S. Public Interest Research Group ***(697)***
Underwriters Digital Research, Inc. ***(698)***
Unilever United States, Inc. ***(699)***
United Automobile, Aerospace and Agricultural Implement Workers of America (UAW) ***(700)***
United Distribution Cos. ***(701)***
United Food and Commercial Workers Internat'l Union ***(701)***
United Methodist Church General Board of Church and Society ***(702)***
United Steelworkers of America ***(704)***
UNUM/Provident Corp. ***(708)***
US Bancorp ***(709)***
USAA - United Services Automobile Ass'n ***(710)***
UST Public Affairs, Inc. ***(710)***
Valis Associates *(198)*
Van Ness Feldman, P.C. *(199)*
Venable *(201)*
Veritect ***(713)***
Vinifera Wine Growers Ass'n ***(715)***
Vinyl Institute ***(715)***
Virginia Wineries Ass'n ***(716)***
VISA U.S.A., Inc. ***(716)***
Volkswagen, AG ***(717)***
Vorys, Sater, Seymour and Pease, LLP *(205)*
VSAdc.com *(205)*
Washington Health Advocates *(209)*
The Wexler Group *(211)*
Wheat & Associates, Inc. *(212)*
Wiley, Rein & Fielding *(214)*
Williams & Connolly *(215)*
Williams & Jensen, P.C. *(215)*
Willkie Farr & Gallagher *(217)*
Wilmer, Cutler & Pickering *(217)*
WinCapitol, Inc. *(218)*
Wine and Spirits Wholesalers of America ***(728)***
Kathleen Winn & Associates, Inc. *(218)*
Yamaha Motor Corp. U.S.A. ***(733)***
ZapWorld.com ***(734)***

Copyright/Patent/Trademark (CPT)

3Com Corp. ***(223)***
Abbott Laboratories ***(225)***
Academy of Managed Care Pharmacy ***(225)***
Academy of Radiology Research ***(226)***
AFL-CIO - Professional Employees Department ***(231)***
Air Conditioning Contractors of America ***(233)***
Akin, Gump, Strauss, Hauer & Feld, L.L.P. *(8)*
Alcalde & Fay *(10)*
Alcatel USA ***(237)***
Alliance for American Innovation, Inc. ***(239)***
Allstate Insurance Co. ***(241)***
Alpine Group, Inc. *(11)*
American Academy of Dermatology ***(243)***
American Airlines ***(244)***
American Amusement Machine Ass'n ***(245)***
American Arts Alliance ***(245)***
American Ass'n of Advertising Agencies ***(246)***
American Ass'n of Law Libraries ***(248)***
American Ass'n of Museums ***(248)***
American Ass'n of University Professors ***(249)***
American Bar Ass'n ***(250)***
American Business Media ***(251)***
American Cable Ass'n ***(251)***
American Continental Group, Inc. *(12)*
American Corporate Counsel Ass'n ***(255)***
American Electronics Ass'n ***(257)***
American Federation of Musicians of the United States and Canada ***(258)***
American Federation of Television and Radio Artists ***(259)***
American Free Trade Ass'n ***(260)***
American Gear Manufacturers Ass'n ***(261)***
American Geophysical Union ***(261)***
American Historical Ass'n ***(262)***
American Home Products Corp. ***(262)***
American Horse Council, Inc. ***(263)***
American Intellectual Property Law Ass'n ***(265)***
American Legion ***(266)***
American Library Ass'n ***(266)***
American Management Systems ***(266)***
American Mobile Satellite Corp. ***(268)***
American Museum of Natural History ***(268)***
American Nursery and Landscape Ass'n ***(268)***
American Soc. for Microbiology ***(274)***
American Soc. of Ass'n Executives ***(275)***
American Soc. of Composers, Authors and Publishers ***(276)***
American Symphony Orchestra League ***(278)***
Americans for Tax Reform ***(282)***
Amgen ***(282)***
Amusement and Music Operators Ass'n ***(283)***
AOL Time Warner ***(285)***
Applera Corp. ***(286)***
Arent Fox Kintner Plotkin & Kahn, PLLC *(14)*
Artists Coalition ***(290)***
Ashland Inc. ***(290)***
The Ass'n For Manufacturing Technology (AMT) ***(292)***
Ass'n of American Publishers ***(294)***
Ass'n of American Universities ***(294)***
Ass'n of Clinical Research Professionals ***(295)***
Ass'n of Directory Publishers ***(295)***
Ass'n of Independent Research Institutes ***(296)***
Ass'n of Local Television Stations ***(296)***
Ass'n of Research Libraries ***(298)***
Ass'n of Test Publishers ***(299)***
Associated Universities Inc. ***(300)***
AstraZeneca Inc. ***(301)***
AT&T ***(301)***
Automotive Parts and Service Alliance ***(303)***
Auyua Inc. ***(304)***
Aventis CropScience ***(304)***
Aventis Pharmaceutical Products ***(304)***
Aventis Pharmaceuticals, Inc. ***(304)***
Bacardi-Martini, USA, Inc. ***(305)***
Baker & Hostetler LLP *(19)*
Ball Research, Inc. ***(306)***
Barbour Griffith & Rogers, Inc. *(22)*
Barr Laboratories ***(308)***
Bass Hotels and Resorts, Inc. ***(308)***
Bayer Corp. ***(309)***
Beauty and Barber Supply Industries, Inc. ***(310)***
Beerman, Swerdlove, Woloshin, Barezky, Becken, Genin & London ***(310)***
Bell Atlantic Mobile ***(310)***
BellSouth Corp. ***(311)***
Benchmarks, Inc. *(25)*
Bennett Turner & Coleman, LLP *(25)*
Bergner Bockorny Castagnetti and Hawkins *(26)*
Biotechnology Industry Organization ***(314)***
BKSH & Associates *(28)*
Bloomberg L.P. ***(315)***
BMW Manufacturing Corp. ***(316)***
The Boeing Co. ***(316)***
Brazelton Foundation ***(319)***
Bristol-Myers Squibb Co. ***(320)***
Broadcast Music Inc. (BMI) ***(321)***
Business Software Alliance ***(325)***
Butera & Andrews *(34)*
California Institute of Technology ***(327)***
W. Douglas Campbell *(36)*
Capitol Associates, Inc. *(37)*
Capitol Solutions *(39)*
Caterpillar Inc. ***(333)***
Celanese Government Relations Office ***(334)***
Celera Genomics ***(334)***
Cellular Telecommunications and Internet Ass'n ***(334)***
Center for Energy and Economic Development ***(336)***
Chambers Associates Inc. *(45)*
Child Welfare League of America ***(343)***
Cisco Systems Inc. ***(347)***
Clark & Weinstock, Inc. *(47)*
Coalition Against Database Piracy ***(352)***
Coalition for Auto Repair Equality (CARE) ***(353)***
Coalition for Patent Information Dissemination ***(354)***
The Coca-Cola Company ***(356)***
College on Problems of Drug Dependence ***(357)***
Collier Shannon Scott, PLLC *(48)*

Columbia University *(359)*
Columbus Public Affairs *(50)*
Comcast Corp. *(359)*
Commercial Finance Ass'n *(360)*
Commercial Internet Exchange Ass'n *(360)*
Compaq Computer Corp. *(363)*
CompTIA *(364)*
Computer and Communications Industry Ass'n (CCIA) *(364)*
Margaret Cone *(51)*
Congressional Economic Leadership Institute *(366)*
Conkling, Fiskum & McCormick *(51)*
Consumer Electronics Ass'n *(369)*
Consumer Federation of America *(369)*
Consumers Union of the United States *(369)*
Copyright Clearance Center, Inc. *(371)*
Covington & Burling *(53)*
Cox Enterprises Inc. *(378)*
Cummins-Allison Corp. *(380)*
The Cuneo Law Group, P.C. *(56)*
Curson Koopersmith Partners, Inc. *(56)*
The Da Vinci Group *(56)*
Dalrymple and Associates, L.L.C. *(56)*
Davidoff & Malito, LLP *(57)*
Davis O'Connell, Inc. *(58)*
Debevoise and Plimpton *(60)*
Deere & Co. *(383)*
Derwent, Inc. *(386)*
Dialoge Corp. *(387)*
Digital Media Ass'n *(388)*
Directors Guild of America *(389)*
The Walt Disney Co. *(389)*
Dow Jones & Co., Inc. *(391)*
Downey McGrath Group, Inc. *(64)*
Drinker Biddle & Reath LLP *(65)*
The Duberstein Group, Inc. *(65)*
Dun & Bradstreet *(393)*
The Dutko Group, Inc. *(68)*
Eastman Chemical Co. *(395)*
Eastman Kodak Co. *(395)*
eBay Inc. *(395)*
Joseph L. Ebersole *(70)*
EchoStar Communications Corp. *(396)*
EDS Corp. *(398)*
Elan Pharmaceutical Research Corp. *(399)*
Electro Scientific Industries, Inc. *(400)*
EMI Music *(402)*
Engage Technologies *(403)*
Evans & Black, Inc. *(73)*
Exxon Mobil Corp. *(409)*
Federal Legislative Associates, Inc. *(75)*
First Data Corp./Telecheck *(417)*
Fleischman and Walsh, L.L.P. *(77)*
Florida State University System *(420)*
Food Marketing Institute *(421)*
Foodmaker Internat'l Franchising Inc. *(422)*
Ford Motor Co. *(422)*
FoxKiser *(79)*
Fujitsu Limited *(427)*
Gateway, Inc. *(430)*
Genentech, Inc. *(431)*
General Conference of Seventh-day Adventists *(431)*
General Electric Co. *(432)*
General Motors Corp. *(432)*
Generic Pharmaceutical Ass'n *(433)*
GlaxoSmithKline *(436)*
GLOBEMAC Associates *(83)*
Goldberg & Associates, PLLC *(83)*
GovWorks.com *(438)*
Griffin, Johnson, Dover & Stewart *(87)*
Grisso Consulting *(88)*
C. McClain Haddow & Associates *(89)*
Leslie Harris & Associates *(91)*
The Hearst Corp. *(447)*
HemaSure, Inc. *(448)*
Hewlett-Packard Co. *(449)*
Hispanic Broadcasting Inc. *(450)*
Hitachi Home Electronics, Inc. *(450)*
Hoechst Marion Roussel Deutschland GmbH *(450)*
Hoffmann-La Roche Inc. *(450)*
Hogan & Hartson L.L.P. *(96)*
R. J. Hudson Associates *(101)*
Human Genome Sciences Inc. *(454)*
IFI Claims Services *(457)*
Information Technology Industry Council *(462)*
Institute of Electrical and Electronics Engineers, Inc. *(464)*
Institute of Navigation *(464)*
Intel Corp. *(465)*
Intellectual Property Owners Ass'n *(465)*
Interactive Digital Software Ass'n *(466)*
Internat'l Ass'n of Amusement Parks and Attractions *(467)*
Internat'l Ass'n of Assembly Managers *(467)*
Internat'l Business Machines Corp. *(469)*
Internat'l Council of Cruise Lines *(470)*
Internat'l Franchise Ass'n *(472)*
Internat'l Game Technology *(472)*
Internat'l Health, Racquet and Sportsclub Ass'n *(472)*
Internat'l Intellectual Property Alliance *(472)*
Internat'l Mass Retailers Ass'n *(473)*
Internat'l Municipal Signal Ass'n *(473)*
Internat'l Sign Ass'n *(474)*
Internat'l Soc. for Technology in Education *(475)*
Internat'l Trademark Ass'n *(475)*
Internet Action PAC *(476)*
InterTrust, Inc. *(477)*
Inventure Place *(477)*
Janus-Merritt Strategies, L.L.C. *(104)*
Jefferson Consulting Group *(105)*
Jefferson Government Relations, L.L.C. *(106)*
Johns Hopkins University & Hospital *(483)*
Johnson & Johnson, Inc. *(484)*
Jorden Burt LLP *(109)*
Kelly and Associates, Inc. *(111)*
Kent & O'Connor, Inc. *(112)*
Jeffrey J. Kimbell & Associates *(113)*
Kimberly-Clark Corp. *(489)*
Latham & Watkins *(116)*
The Laxalt Corp. *(117)*
The Paul Laxalt Group *(117)*
Levine & Co. *(119)*
The Michael Lewan Co. *(119)*
Lewis-Burke Associates *(120)*
Lexis-Nexis *(498)*
Eli Lilly and Co. *(499)*
The Livingston Group, LLC *(120)*
Lotus Development Corp. *(504)*
Lovelace Respiratory Research Institute *(504)*
Lucent Technologies *(505)*
Lutzker & Lutzker LLP *(122)*
Turner D. Madden *(123)*
Magazine Publishers of America *(507)*
Major League Baseball *(508)*
Manatt, Phelps & Phillips, LLP *(123)*
Manufacturers Alliance/MAPI Inc. *(509)*
Maryland Psychiatric Soc. *(512)*
Massachusetts Software Council *(512)*
Matsushita Electric Corp. of America *(513)*
Mayer, Brown & Platt *(126)*
McDermott, Will and Emery *(128)*
Jack H. McDonald *(129)*
McDonald's Corp. *(514)*
McGraw-Hill Cos., The *(514)*
MCI WorldCom Corp. *(514)*
Medical Records Internat'l, Inc. *(516)*
Mentor Graphics Corp. *(518)*
Merck & Co. *(518)*
Meyer & Klipper, PLLC *(133)*
MicroPatent, LLC *(522)*
Microsoft Corp. *(522)*
Denny Miller McBee Associates *(134)*
Minnesota Mining and Manufacturing Co. (3M Co.) *(525)*
Mitsubishi Electronics America (Consumer Electronics Group) *(526)*
Monsanto Co. *(528)*
Mont Blanc, Inc. *(528)*
Timothy X. Moore and Co. *(136)*
Morgan Meguire, LLC *(136)*
Morrison & Foerster LLP *(137)*
The Morrison Group, Inc. *(137)*
Motion Picture Ass'n of America *(530)*
mp3.com *(532)*
MSP Strategic Communications, Inc. *(138)*
Mullenholz, Brimsek & Belair *(138)*
Mylan Laboratories, Inc. *(533)*
Napster, Inc. *(534)*
Nat'l Ass'n for the Self-Employed *(538)*
Nat'l Ass'n of Broadcasters *(539)*
Nat'l Ass'n of Chain Drug Stores *(539)*
Nat'l Ass'n of Independent Insurers *(544)*
Nat'l Ass'n of Manufacturers *(545)*
Nat'l Ass'n of RV Parks and Campgrounds *(548)*
Nat'l Ass'n of Securities Dealers, Inc. (NASD) *(549)*
Nat'l Automobile Dealers Ass'n *(552)*
Nat'l Basketball Ass'n *(552)*
Nat'l Cable Television Ass'n *(553)*
Nat'l Club Ass'n *(556)*
Nat'l Coalition for Cancer Survivorship *(556)*
Nat'l Collegiate Athletic Ass'n *(557)*
Nat'l Coordinating Committee for the Promotion of History *(559)*
Nat'l Council of University Research Administrators *(561)*
Nat'l Electrical Safety Foundation *(562)*
Nat'l Farmers Union (Farmers Educational & Co-operative Union of America) *(563)*
Nat'l Football League *(565)*
Nat'l Hockey League *(567)*
Nat'l Humanities Alliance *(567)*
Nat'l Licensed Beverage Ass'n *(570)*
Nat'l Marine Manufacturers Ass'n *(570)*
Nat'l Music Publishers' Ass'n *(571)*
Nat'l Newspaper Ass'n *(572)*
Nat'l Public Radio *(574)*
Nat'l Restaurant Ass'n *(576)*
Nat'l Retail Federation *(576)*
Nat'l School Boards Ass'n *(577)*
Nat'l Small Business United *(578)*
Nat'l Telephone Cooperative Ass'n *(579)*
Nat'l Venture Capital Ass'n *(580)*
NetCoalition.Com *(584)*
Netscape Communications Corp. *(584)*
New York Mercantile Exchange *(587)*
New York Stock Exchange *(588)*
New York University *(588)*
Newport News Shipbuilding Inc. *(588)*
News America Inc. *(589)*
News Corporation Ltd. *(589)*
Newspaper Ass'n of America *(589)*
Nintendo of America, Inc. *(590)*
North American Retail Dealers Ass'n *(592)*
Novartis Corp. *(596)*
Novell, Inc. *(596)*
NPES, The Ass'n for Suppliers of Printing, Publishing, and Converting Technologies *(596)*
The OB-C Group, LLC *(143)*
O'Connor & Hannan, L.L.P. *(144)*
Open Group Electronic Messaging Ass'n (EMA) Forum *(601)*
Oracle Corp. *(602)*
John T. O'Rourke Law Offices *(147)*
Palumbo & Cerrell, Inc. *(149)*
Parry, Romani, DeConcini & Symms *(149)*
Jim Pasco & Associates *(150)*
Patent Office Professional Ass'n *(609)*
Patton Boggs, LLP *(150)*
Paul, Weiss, Rifkind, Wharton & Garrison *(154)*
Pernod Ricard *(612)*
Pfizer, Inc. *(613)*
Pharmaceutical Research and Manufacturers of America *(614)*
Pharmacia Corp. *(615)*
Phillips Petroleum Co. *(616)*
Pioneer of North America *(618)*
Piper Marbury Rudnick & Wolfe LLP *(155)*
Pitney Bowes, Inc. *(618)*
Podesta/Mattoon *(158)*
Powell Tate *(160)*
Powell, Goldstein, Frazer & Murphy LLP *(160)*
Praxair, Inc. *(623)*
Preston Gates Ellis & Rouvelas Meeds LLP *(162)*
Prime Time 24 *(624)*
Printing Industries of America *(624)*
The Procter & Gamble Company *(625)*
Project to Promote Competition and Innovation in the Digital Age *(626)*
Property Owners Remedy Alliance *(627)*
Proskauer Rose LLP *(164)*

Public Broadcasting Service (628)
Quad Dimension (630)
Queens Borough Public Library (631)
Questel-Orbit, Inc. (631)
Quinn Gillespie & Associates (165)
Qwest Communications (631)
Recording Industry Ass'n of America (634)
Reed-Elsevier Inc. (635)
Religious Technology Center (636)
Research Corp. Technology (638)
Reuters America Inc. (639)
RMA Internat'l, Inc. (169)
Liz Robbins Associates (169)
Rockwell Collins (641)
Rohm and Haas Co. (642)
Royer & Babyak (172)
Sanyo North American Corp. (649)
SAP Public Services (649)
Satellite Broadcasting and Communications Ass'n (650)
SBC Communications Inc. (650)
Schering-Plough Corp. (651)
Schering-Plough Legislative Resources L.L.C. (651)
Seiko Epson Corp. (654)
Sepracor, Inc. (655)
Serono Laboratories, Inc. (655)
SESAC, Inc. (656)
Shared Legal Capability for Intellectual Property (656)
Sharp Electronics Corp. (657)
Shaw Pittman (177)
Silicon Graphics/SGI (659)
Stephen F. Sims and Associates (181)
Sirius Satellite Radio, Inc. (660)
SISCORP (181)
Smith & Metalitz, L.L.P. (182)
Smith Dawson & Andrews, Inc. (183)
The Smith-Free Group (184)
SmithKline Beecham Consumer Healthcare, LLP (661)
The Solomon Group, LLC (185)
Songwriters Guild of America (665)
Sony Corp. (665)
Sony Electronics, Inc. (666)
Sony Music Entertainment Inc. (666)
Sony Pictures Entertainment Inc. (666)
Special Libraries Ass'n (669)
Squire, Sanders & Dempsey L.L.P. (187)
Stephens, Cross, Ihlenfeld & Boring, Inc. (188)
Stone Investments, Inc. (675)
Storage Technology Corp. (675)
Swidler Berlin Shereff Friedman, LLP (191)
Syracuse University (679)
Telephone Operators Caucus (683)
Thelen Reid & Priest LLP (193)
Thiemann Aitken Vohra & Rutledge, L.L.C. (194)
The Thomson Corp. (686)
Timmons and Co., Inc. (195)
Tongour Simpson Holsclaw Green (196)
Toshiba Consumer Products, Inc. (688)
Transkaryotic Therapies Inc. (690)
Tribune Co. (692)
TV Guide, Inc. (694)
UDV/Heublein, Inc. (698)
Unisys Corp. (700)
United States Business and Industry Council (703)
United States Telecom Ass'n (704)
Universities Research Ass'n (705)
University Continuing Education Ass'n (705)
University Corp. for Atmospheric Research (705)
University of California, Office of Federal Government Relations (706)
University of Cincinnati (706)
University of Medicine and Dentistry of New Jersey (706)
University of Miami (706)
University of Southern California (707)
University of Tulsa (708)
University of Virginia (708)
University of Washington (708)
University System of Maryland (708)
Valve Manufacturers Ass'n of America (711)
Venable (201)
VeriSign/Network Solutions, Inc. (713)
Verizon Wireless (713)
Verner, Liipfert, Bernhard, McPherson and Hand, Chartered (713)
Verner, Liipfert, Bernhard, McPherson and Hand, Chartered (202)
Viacom Inc. (714)
Victory Wholesale Grocers Inc. (715)
Virginia Commonwealth Trading Co. (715)
VISA U.S.A., Inc. (716)
Vivendi Universal (717)
Washington Council Ernst & Young (206)
Weil, Gotshal & Manges, LLP (211)
The Wexler Group (211)
Wiley, Rein & Fielding (214)
Williams & Jensen, P.C. (215)
Willkie Farr & Gallagher (217)
Wilmer, Cutler & Pickering (217)
Wireless Communications Ass'n (728)
Writers Guild of America (732)
Xerox Corp. (732)
Yahoo! (732)
Zeliff, Ireland, and Associates (221)

Defense (DEF)

20/20 Vision (223)
21st Century Partnership (223)
3D Metrics Inc. (223)
3Tex (223)
AAI Corp. (224)
Abilene Industrial Foundation, Inc. (225)
Accenture (226)
ACS Defense, Inc. (227)
ACS Government Solutions Group (227)
Adams and Reese LLP (5)
Adams County, Colorado (227)
Michael W. Adcock (6)
ADCS, Inc. (227)
ADI Ltd. (227)
Advanced Acoustic Concepts, Inc. (228)
Advanced Power Technologies, Inc. (228)
Advanced Programming Concepts (228)
Advanced Refractory Technologies, Inc. (228)
Advanced Technology Institute (228)
Advanced Vehicle Systems (229)
Advantage Associates, Inc. (6)
Advantage Associates, Inc. (229)
The Advocacy Group (6)
AEPTEC (229)
Aeromet, Inc. (230)
Aerospace Industries Ass'n of America (230)
Afghanistan Foundation (230)
AFL-CIO (American Federation of Labor and Congress of Industrial Organizations) (231)
AFL-CIO Maritime Committee (231)
AFL-CIO - Maritime Trades Department (231)
Aiken and Edgenfield Counties, South Carolina, Economic Development Partnership of (233)
Ainslie Associates (7)
Air Cruisers, Inc. (233)
Air Force Ass'n (233)
Air Force Sergeants Ass'n (233)
Air Products and Chemicals, Inc. (234)
Airborne Tactical Advantage Co. (234)
Akers Laboratories, Inc. (235)
Akin, Gump, Strauss, Hauer & Feld, L.L.P. (8)
Alabama Space Science Exhibits Commission (236)
Albers & Co. (10)
Alcalde & Fay (10)
Alcoa Inc. (237)
Alenia Marconi Systems (238)
Aleut Corp. (238)
Alford & Associates (11)
Alliance for American Innovation, Inc. (239)
Alliance for Nuclear Accountability (240)
Alliant Techsystems, Inc. (241)
Allied Domecq (241)
Allison Transmission Division, General Motors Corp. (241)
Allthane Technologies Internat'l (242)
Alvarado & Gerken (12)
American Ass'n of Engineering Societies (247)
American Automar (250)
American Bakers Ass'n (250)
American Competitiveness Institute (255)
American Continental Group, Inc. (12)
American Council of Life Insurers (256)
American Counseling Ass'n (256)
American Defense Internat'l, Inc. (12)
American Defense Internat'l, Inc. (256)
American Electronics Ass'n (257)
American Federation of Teachers (259)
American Gas Ass'n (261)
American Institute of Physics (264)
American Iron and Steel Institute (265)
American Israel Public Affairs Committee (265)
American Legion (266)
American Logistics Ass'n (266)
American Logistics Infrastructure Improvement Consortium (266)
American Management Systems (266)
American Maritime Congress (267)
American Metalcasting Consortium (267)
American Moving and Storage Ass'n (268)
American Museum of Natural History (268)
American Optometric Ass'n (269)
American Physical Soc. (270)
American Psychiatric Ass'n (271)
American Psychological Ass'n (271)
American Science and Engineering, Inc. (273)
American Shipbuilding Ass'n (274)
American Soc. for Industrial Security (274)
American Superconductor Corp. (278)
American Systems Internat'l Corp. (13)
American Systems Internat'l Corp. (278)
American Textile Manufacturers Institute (279)
Amherst Systems Inc. (283)
Morris J. Amitay, P.C. (13)
Analytical Systems, Inc. (283)
Ancore Corp. (284)
ANSAR Inc. (284)
Anthem Alliance (285)
Anthem, Inc. (285)
Anti-Defamation League (285)
AOC (285)
APG Army Alliance (286)
Applied Marine Technologies, Inc. (287)
APTI (287)
Arcata Associates, Inc. (287)
Arent Fox Kintner Plotkin & Kahn, PLLC (14)
ARINC, Inc. (288)
Arms Control Ass'n (289)
Armtec Defense Products (289)
Arnold & Porter (16)
Wayne Arny & Assoc. (16)
Asbestos Recycling Inc. (290)
AsclepiusNet (290)
James Nicholas Ashmore & Associates (18)
ASIC (291)
The Ass'n For Manufacturing Technology (AMT) (292)
Ass'n of American Geographers (293)
Ass'n of American Shippers (294)
Ass'n of Chiropractic Colleges (295)
Ass'n of Military Surgeons of the U.S. (AMSUS) (297)
Ass'n of the United States Army (299)
Ass'n to Unite the Democracies (299)
Assurance Technology Corp. (301)
Astra Solutions, LLC (18)
AT&T (301)
The Atlantic Group, Public Affairs, Inc. (18)
Atlantic Marine Holding Co. (302)
Atom Sciences, Inc. (302)
Aurora, Colorado, City of (303)
Autometric Inc. (303)
Automotive Parts and Service Alliance (303)
Avondale Industries, Inc. (305)
BAE SYSTEMS North America (306)
Bailey Link (306)
Baker Botts, L.L.P. (20)
C. Baker Consulting Inc. (20)
Balch & Bingham LLP (21)
Ball Aerospace & Technology Corp. (306)
Ball Janik, LLP (22)
Baltic American Freedom League (306)
Balzano Associates (22)
Bannerman and Associates, Inc. (22)
Barber Colman Co. (308)

Barbour Griffith & Rogers, Inc. *(22)*
Barksdale Foward ***(308)***
Battelle ***(309)***
Battelle Memorial Institute ***(309)***
Battelle Memorial Labs ***(309)***
BeamHit America LLC ***(310)***
Bechtel Group, Inc. ***(310)***
Belew Law Firm *(25)*
Vikki Bell *(25)*
Bentley, Adams, Hargett, Riley and Co., Inc. *(26)*
Beretta U.S.A. Corp. ***(311)***
Bergner Bockorny Castagnetti and Hawkins *(26)*
Bergson & Co. *(26)*
Berkshire Inc. *(26)*
Betac Corp. ***(312)***
Bethlehem Steel Corp. ***(312)***
Biocontrol Technology, Inc. ***(313)***
BioPort Corp. ***(314)***
Biostar Group, The ***(314)***
Biotechnology Industry Organization ***(314)***
Birch, Horton, Bittner & Cherot *(28)*
Bird-Johnson Co. ***(314)***
BKSH & Associates *(28)*
Richard W. Bliss *(29)*
The Boeing Co. ***(316)***
Boesch & Co. *(29)*
Bofors Defence AB ***(317)***
Bombardier Aerospace ***(317)***
Bombardier, Inc. ***(317)***
Booher & Associates *(30)*
The BOSE Corp. ***(318)***
Marshall A. Brachman *(31)*
Brain Injury Ass'n ***(319)***
Brashear Systems, L.L.P. ***(319)***
T. Edward Braswell *(32)*
Brewer Science Inc. ***(319)***
British Aerospace ***(320)***
British Ministry of Defence ***(321)***
Brown and Company, Inc. *(33)*
Broydrick & Associates *(33)*
Brush Wellman, Inc. ***(323)***
Bryan Cave LLP *(33)*
BSMG Worldwide *(34)*
Burns and Roe Enterprises, Inc. ***(324)***
Burstein Laboratories, Inc. ***(324)***
Business Executives for Nat'l Security ***(324)***
A. D. Butler and Associates, Inc. ***(325)***
California Water Service Co. ***(328)***
CALSTART ***(328)***
Cambridge Internat'l, Inc. *(35)*
Cambridge Technologies ***(328)***
Camelbak Products, Inc. ***(328)***
Campbell Crane & Associates *(36)*
John G. Campbell, Inc. *(36)*
Canberra Packard BioScience ***(330)***
Cannon Consultants, Inc. *(37)*
Capital Consultants Corp. *(37)*
Capital Strategies Group, Inc. *(37)*
Capitol Partners *(39)*
Carmen & Muss, P.L.L.C. *(40)*
The Carmen Group *(40)*
The Carter Group *(41)*
Cartwright & Riley *(41)*
Cartwright Electronics ***(332)***
Carwell Products, Inc. ***(332)***
Cascade Associates *(41)*
Cascade General, Inc. ***(332)***
Cassidy & Associates, Inc. *(42)*
Caswell Internat'l Corp. ***(333)***
Caterpillar Inc. ***(333)***
Ceiba, Puerto Rico, City of ***(334)***
Celanese Government Relations Office ***(334)***
Celsius Tech Electronics ***(335)***
Cendant Corp. ***(335)***
Cendant Mobility Services ***(335)***
The Centech Group ***(335)***
Center for Defense Information ***(335)***
Center on Conscience and War/NISBCO ***(338)***
Chamber of Commerce of the U.S.A. ***(340)***
Chamberlain Manufacturing Corp. ***(341)***
Chambers, Conlon & Hartwell *(45)*
Chandler Evans Control Systems ***(341)***
Michael Chase Associates, LTD *(45)*
Children and Adults with Attention Deficit Disorders (CHADD) ***(344)***
Christian Coalition of America ***(345)***
Clark & Weinstock, Inc. *(47)*
Cleveland Advanced Manufacturing Program ***(350)***
Cleveland Clinic Foundation ***(350)***
Click2Learn.com ***(351)***
The Climate Council, ***(351)***
William M. Cloherty *(47)*
Clough, Harbour & Associates LLP ***(351)***
CMS Defense Systems, Inc. ***(351)***
Coalition for Electronic Commerce ***(353)***
Coalition for Government Procurement ***(353)***
Coalition of Hawaii Movers ***(355)***
Scott Cohen *(48)*
Coleman Research Corp. ***(357)***
Collier Shannon Scott, PLLC *(48)*
Collins & Company, Inc. *(49)*
Colorado Springs Utilities ***(359)***
Colsa Corp. ***(359)***
Columbus General, L.L.C. ***(359)***
Command Systems Inc. ***(360)***
Committee for Good Common Sense ***(361)***
Commonwealth Consulting Corp. *(50)*
Commonwealth Consulting Corp. ***(362)***
Communications Training Analysis Corp. (C-TAC) ***(362)***
Compass Internat'l Inc. ***(363)***
Computer Associates Internat'l, Inc. ***(364)***
Computer Coalition for Responsible Exports ***(364)***
Computer Systems Technologies, Inc. ***(364)***
The Conaway Group LLC *(51)*
Concurrent Technologies Corp. ***(365)***
Condor Electronic Systems ***(365)***
Condor Systems ***(365)***
Condor-Pacific Industries ***(365)***
Congressional Economic Leadership Institute ***(366)***
The Conservative Caucus ***(367)***
Constellation Technology Corp. ***(368)***
Construction Industry Round Table, Inc. ***(368)***
Contract Services Ass'n of America ***(370)***
Copeland, Lowery & Jacquez *(52)*
Coronado, California, City of ***(372)***
Corpus Christi, City of ***(373)***
Cortese PLLC *(53)*
Cottone and Huggins Group *(53)*
Council for a Livable World ***(373)***
Council for a Livable World Education Fund ***(373)***
CPU Technology ***(378)***
Crane Co. ***(378)***
John Crane-LIPS, Inc. ***(378)***
Credit Suisse First Boston Corp. ***(378)***
Crowley Maritime Corp. ***(379)***
CRYPTEK Secure Communications, LLC ***(379)***
CSX Lines LLC ***(379)***
CUBRC ***(380)***
The Cuneo Law Group, P.C. *(56)*
D3 Internat'l Energy, LLC ***(381)***
DaimlerChrysler Corp. ***(381)***
Dalrymple and Associates, L.L.C. *(56)*
Dames & Moore ***(382)***
Bob Davis & Associates *(57)*
Davis O'Connell, Inc. *(58)*
Day & Zimmermann, Inc. ***(383)***
DDL OMNI Engineering Corp. ***(383)***
Deere Co. Worldwide Commercial & Consumer Equipment Division ***(383)***
Defense Credit Union Council ***(384)***
Defense Health Advisors, Inc. *(60)*
Delex Systems, Inc. ***(384)***
Dell Computer Corp. ***(384)***
Delta Dental Plan of California ***(385)***
DeMil Internat'l ***(385)***
Dewey Electronics Corp. ***(387)***
DeWitt Cos. of Guam and Saipan ***(387)***
Dialogic Communications Corp. ***(387)***
Diamond Manufacturing, Inc. ***(387)***
Digital Descriptor Services, Inc. ***(388)***
Dimension 4 ***(388)***
Distilled Spirits Council of the United States, Inc. ***(389)***
DM Electronics Recycling Corporation ***(390)***
Donlee Technologies, Inc. ***(391)***
R. R. Donnelley & Sons ***(391)***
Downey McGrath Group, Inc. *(64)*
Drexel University ***(392)***
W. B. Driggers & Associates, Inc. *(65)*
DRS ***(392)***
DRS Precision Echo Inc. ***(392)***
DRS Technologies, Inc. ***(392)***
DuPont ***(393)***
DuPont Agricultural Products ***(393)***
The Dutko Group, Inc. *(68)*
Dyer Ellis & Joseph, P.C. *(68)*
Dykema Gossett ***(393)***
Dykema Gossett PLLC *(69)*
Dynamics Research Corp. ***(393)***
The Eagles Group *(69)*
East/West Industries ***(395)***
Eastman Kodak Co. ***(395)***
Eaton Corp., Cutler Hammer ***(395)***
ECC Internat'l Corp. ***(396)***
Eckert Seamans Cherin & Mellott, LLC *(70)*
Edington, Peel & Associates, Inc. *(70)*
Edison Chouest Offshore, Inc. ***(397)***
Edison Electric Institute ***(397)***
Edison Welding Institute ***(397)***
Edmund Scientific Co. ***(397)***
EDS Corp. ***(398)***
EFW Corp. ***(398)***
Eickhorn-Solingen ***(399)***
El Camino Resources, Ltd. ***(399)***
El Toro Reuse Planning Authority ***(399)***
Elbet Forth Worth ***(399)***
Electro Design Manufacturing, Inc. ***(400)***
Electro Energy, Inc. ***(400)***
Electro-Radiation Inc. ***(400)***
Electronic Design Inc. ***(400)***
Electronic Warfare Associates, Inc. ***(401)***
Electronics Consultants Inc. ***(401)***
Elkem Metals Co. ***(401)***
Elmco, Inc. ***(401)***
Adam Emanuel and Associates *(71)*
Encapco Technologies, LLC ***(402)***
Engineered Support System, Inc. (ESSI) ***(403)***
Enlisted Ass'n of the Nat'l Guard of the United States ***(403)***
Enron Corp. ***(403)***
Ensign-Bickford Co. ***(404)***
Environmental Systems Research Institute, Inc. ***(405)***
Environmental Technologies Group ***(405)***
ERIM ***(406)***
Ervin Technical Associates, Inc. (ETA) *(73)*
Espey Manufacturing and Electronics ***(407)***
Essential Technologies, Inc. ***(407)***
European Aeronautics, Defence and Space, Inc. ***(408)***
Everett, Washington, Port of ***(408)***
EWA Land Information Group, Inc. ***(408)***
Ex-Partners of Servicemembers for Equality ***(408)***
Export Management Services, Inc. ***(409)***
Express Scripts Inc. ***(409)***
EXPRO Chemical Products ***(409)***
ExtrudeHone Corp. ***(409)***
Fairfield, California, City of ***(410)***
Fairview Hospital and Healthcare Services ***(410)***
Family Research Council, Inc. ***(411)***
FED Corp. ***(412)***
Federal Health Strategies, Inc. *(75)*
Federal Procurement Consultants ***(414)***
Federation of American Scientists ***(414)***
Feith & Zell, P.C. *(75)*
Bruce Fennie & Associates *(75)*
The Ferguson Group, LLC *(76)*
Fidelity Technologies Corp. ***(416)***
Firearms Training Systems, Inc. ***(417)***
First Scientific Corp. ***(418)***
Fishbein Associates, Inc. *(77)*
Fleet Reserve Ass'n ***(418)***
Fleischman and Walsh, L.L.P. *(77)*
Flight Landata, Inc. ***(419)***
R. G. Flippo and Associates, Inc. *(77)*
FLIR Systems, Inc. ***(419)***
Florida State University System ***(420)***
FN Herstal, USA ***(421)***
Foley & Lardner *(78)*
Foley Government and Public Affairs, Inc. *(78)*
Food Marketing Institute ***(421)***
Food Research and Action Center ***(422)***

Martin, Fisher & Associates, Inc. *(125)*
Martins Point Health Care ***(511)***
Mas-Hamilton Group ***(512)***
Massa Products Corp. ***(512)***
Maui Pineapple Co. ***(513)***
Mayer, Brown & Platt *(126)*
Charlie McBride Associates, Inc. *(127)*
McClure, Gerard & Neuenschwander, Inc. *(127)*
McDermott Internat'l, Inc./Babcock & Wilcox ***(514)***
McLean Hospital ***(515)***
Diane McRee Associates *(131)*
Mechanical Equipment Co., Inc. ***(515)***
Medical College of Virginia, Dept. of Neurology, Office of the Chairman ***(516)***
Megaseal Corp. ***(517)***
Mehl, Griffin & Bartek Ltd. *(132)*
Member-Link Systems, Inc. ***(517)***
memorize.com ***(517)***
Mentis Sciences Inc. ***(518)***
Merant PVCS ***(518)***
Mercer Engineering Research Center ***(518)***
Mercury Group *(132)*
Law Offices of Pamela L. Meredith *(132)*
Meredith Concept Group, Inc. *(132)*
G.L. Merritt & Associates, Inc. *(132)*
Messier-Dowty Internat'l ***(519)***
Metro Machine Corp. of Virginia ***(520)***
The MetroVision Chamber ***(521)***
Meyers & Associates *(133)*
Miami Valley Economic Coalition ***(521)***
MIC Industries, Inc. ***(522)***
MICAH Software Systems ***(522)***
Microcosm, Inc. ***(522)***
Micron Technology, Inc. ***(522)***
Microvision, Inc. ***(523)***
The Military Coalition ***(524)***
Military Footwear Coalition ***(524)***
Military Glove Coalition ***(524)***
Military Mobility Coalition ***(524)***
Denny Miller McBee Associates *(134)*
MilTec ***(524)***
Miltope Corp. ***(524)***
Mintz, Levin, Cohn, Ferris, Glovsky and Popeo, P.C. *(135)*
Mississippi Polymer Technologies ***(526)***
Mitsubishi Research Institute ***(526)***
Mobile Climate Control ***(527)***
James T. Molloy *(135)*
Monroe, Florida, County of ***(527)***
Monterey Institute ***(528)***
Monterey, California, County of ***(528)***
The Montgomery Group *(135)*
Morgan, Lewis & Bockius LLP *(136)*
Kay Allan Morrell, Attorney-at-Law *(137)*
Bob Moss Associates *(137)*
Motorola Integrated Information Systems Group ***(531)***
Motorola Space and Systems Technology Group ***(531)***
Motorola, Inc. ***(531)***
Mountain Top Technologies, Inc. ***(532)***
MSE, Inc. ***(532)***
MTS Systems Inc. ***(532)***
Munitions Industrial Base Task Force ***(533)***
Murray, Scheer, Montgomery, Tapia & O'Donnell *(139)*
The MWW Group *(140)*
Nammo Inc. ***(534)***
NanoDynamics, Inc. ***(534)***
Nat'l Academy of Public Administration ***(535)***
Nat'l Air Cargo, Inc. ***(536)***
Nat'l Ass'n for the Advancement of Colored People, Washington Bureau ***(538)***
Nat'l Ass'n for Uniformed Services ***(538)***
Nat'l Ass'n of Children's Hospitals Inc. ***(540)***
Nat'l Ass'n of Installation Developers ***(544)***
Nat'l Ass'n of Police Organizations ***(546)***
Nat'l Ass'n of VA Physicians and Dentists ***(551)***
Nat'l Center for Public Policy Research ***(555)***
Nat'l Defense Council Foundation ***(561)***
Nat'l Defense Industrial Ass'n ***(561)***
Nat'l Guard Ass'n of the U.S. ***(566)***
Nat'l Institute for Aerospace Studies and Services Inc. ***(568)***
Nat'l Legal Center for the Public Interest ***(570)***
Nat'l Military Family Ass'n ***(571)***
Nat'l Military Intelligence Ass'n ***(571)***
Nat'l Right to Life Committee ***(576)***
Nat'l Soc. of Professional Engineers ***(578)***
Nat'l Strategy Information Center ***(579)***
Nat'l Taxpayers Union ***(579)***
Naval Reserve Ass'n ***(582)***
NAVCOM Systems, Inc. ***(583)***
NAVSYS Corp. ***(583)***
Navy League of the United States ***(583)***
NETWORK, A Nat'l Catholic Social Justice Lobby ***(584)***
New Jersey Institute of Technology ***(585)***
New Mexico State University, Department of Engineering ***(586)***
New Mexico Tech ***(586)***
New Orleans, Louisiana, Port of ***(586)***
New York University ***(588)***
Newpark Resources/SOLOCO ***(588)***
Newport News Shipbuilding Inc. ***(588)***
Newport News, Virginia, Industrial Development Authority of the City of ***(589)***
NI Industries ***(589)***
Niagara Area Chamber of Commerce ***(589)***
Nixon Center, The ***(590)***
Noesis Inc. ***(590)***
NoFire Technologies, Inc. ***(591)***
Non Commissioned Officers Ass'n of the U.S.A. ***(591)***
North American Shipbuilding ***(592)***
North Dakota State University ***(593)***
Northeastern University ***(594)***
Northrop Grumman Corp. ***(594)***
Novato, California, City of ***(596)***
NOW Solutions, Inc. ***(596)***
Nu Thena Systems, Inc. ***(597)***
Nuclear Energy Institute ***(597)***
O'Gara-Hess & Eisenhardt ***(598)***
Oakland, California, City of ***(598)***
OAO Corp. ***(598)***
The OB-C Group, LLC *(143)*
David O'Brien and Associates *(143)*
O'Brien, Klink & Associates *(144)*
O'Bryon & Co. *(144)*
Oceanside, California, City of ***(598)***
O'Connor & Hannan, L.L.P. *(144)*
Oerlikon Aerospace, Inc. ***(599)***
Ogletree Governmental Affairs, Inc. *(145)*
Omega Air ***(600)***
O'Melveny and Myers LLP *(147)*
Omniflight Helicopters, Inc. ***(600)***
Omnitech Robotics Inc. ***(600)***
Onconova Inc. ***(600)***
O'Neill, Athy & Casey, P.C. *(147)*
Operations Security Professionals Soc. ***(601)***
Oracle Corp. ***(602)***
Orange Shipbuilding Co., Inc. ***(602)***
Orange, California, County of ***(602)***
Orbital Sciences Corp. ***(602)***
Orbital Sciences Corp., Fairchild Defense Division ***(602)***
Ordnance Development and Engineering Co. of Singapore ***(603)***
Oregon Military Department ***(603)***
Orincon Corp. ***(603)***
Oshkosh Truck Corp. ***(604)***
Oxnard Harbor District ***(605)***
Pac Med Clinics ***(605)***
PACE-CAPSTONE *(148)*
Pacific Consolidated Industries ***(605)***
Pacific Marine ***(605)***
Pacific Northwest Nat'l Laboratory ***(606)***
Pacquing Consulting Inc. *(148)*
Pancyprian Ass'n of America ***(607)***
Paradigm Research Group *(149)*
Parametric Technology Corp. ***(607)***
Parry, Romani, DeConcini & Symms *(149)*
Parsons Brinckerhoff Inc. ***(608)***
Parsons Corp. ***(608)***
Pathfinder Technology Inc. ***(609)***
Patton Boggs, LLP *(150)*
PDI Ground Support Systems, Inc. ***(610)***
Peace Action ***(610)***
Peduzzi Associates, Ltd. *(154)*
PEI Electronics ***(611)***
Pemco Aviation Group, Inc. ***(611)***
Pennington BioMedical Research Center ***(611)***
Pennsylvania Nat'l Guard Ass'n ***(611)***
Pensacola Chamber of Commerce ***(611)***
Periodical Management Group, Inc. ***(612)***
Perry Tritech Inc. ***(612)***
PESystems, Inc. ***(613)***
The Peterson Group *(155)*
Petro Star, Inc. ***(613)***
PetrolRem, Inc. ***(613)***
Pharmaceutical Research and Manufacturers of America ***(614)***
Philadelphia College of Textiles and Science ***(615)***
Philadelphia Industrial Development Corp. ***(615)***
Philip Morris Management Corp. ***(615)***
Phoenix Air Group, Inc. ***(616)***
Photo Telesis ***(616)***
Piasecki Aircraft Corp. ***(617)***
Pilkington Thorn ***(617)***
PinPoint Systems Internat'l, LLC ***(618)***
Pixtech, Inc. ***(618)***
Planar Systems, Inc. ***(618)***
Planning Systems, Inc. ***(619)***
Plasma-Therm, Inc. ***(619)***
The PMA Group *(156)*
Polity Consulting *(159)*
The Potomac Advocates *(159)*
The Potomac Advocates ***(621)***
Potomac Group *(160)*
Potomac Strategies & Analysis, Inc. *(160)*
Potomac Strategies Internat'l LLC *(160)*
Powell Tate *(160)*
Precision Aerospace Corp. ***(623)***
Precision Lift ***(623)***
Preston Gates Ellis & Rouvelas Meeds LLP *(162)*
PriceWaterhouseCoopers ***(624)***
Production Technology, Inc. ***(625)***
Professional Managers Ass'n ***(626)***
Professional Services Council ***(626)***
Profit Recovery Group Internat'l ***(626)***
Progeny Systems ***(626)***
Progressive Policy Institute ***(626)***
Providence St. Vincent Medical Center ***(627)***
PSI ***(627)***
Public Policy Partners, LLC *(164)*
Pulse Medical Instruments ***(630)***
PulseTech Products Corp. ***(630)***
Robert N. Pyle & Associates *(165)*
QTEAM ***(630)***
Quad City Development Group ***(630)***
Qualtec, Inc. ***(630)***
Racal Communications Inc. ***(632)***
Ramo Defense Systems, LLC ***(632)***
Rapid Mat LLC ***(633)***
Raufoss A/S, Defense Products Division ***(633)***
Bruce Ray & Company *(166)*
Raydon Corp. ***(633)***
Raytheon Co. ***(633)***
Raytheon Missile Systems ***(633)***
Recon/Optical, Inc. ***(634)***
Recovery Engineering, Inc. ***(634)***
The Refinishing Touch ***(635)***
Research & Development Laboratories ***(638)***
Reserve Officers Ass'n of the U.S. ***(638)***
The Retired Enlisted Ass'n ***(638)***
The Retired Officers Ass'n (TROA) ***(638)***
Retlif Testing Laboratory, Inc. ***(639)***
Reusable Pallet and Container Coalition ***(639)***
Rhoads Group *(168)*
Ritter and Bourjaily, Inc. *(169)*
Robbins-Gioia, Inc. ***(641)***
Robertson Aviation ***(641)***
Robertson, Monagle & Eastaugh *(170)*
Robison Internat'l, Inc. *(170)*
Rockwell Collins ***(641)***
Rolls-Royce North America Inc. ***(642)***
Rooney Group Internat'l, Inc. *(171)*
Peter J. Rose *(172)*
A. L. Ross Associates, Inc. *(172)*
Rothleder Associates, Inc. *(172)*
Royal Ordnance North America, Inc. ***(643)***
RPH & Associates, L.L.C. *(172)*
Lawrence Ryan Internat'l, Inc. *(173)*
Ryan, Phillips, Utrecht & MacKinnon *(173)*
S & B Infrastructure, Inc. ***(644)***

S-TEC Sentry ***(644)***
Saab AB ***(644)***
Sabreliner Corp. ***(644)***
SACO Defense ***(644)***
Safe Environment of America ***(645)***
SAFE Foundation - NMD Project ***(645)***
SAFT America Inc. ***(645)***
Sagamore Associates, Inc. *(174)*
Sagem Morpho ***(646)***
Samsung Heavy Industries Co., Ltd. ***(647)***
San Antonio, Texas, City of ***(647)***
San Diego State University Foundation ***(647)***
San Francisco Wholesale Produce Ass'n ***(648)***
The "Sandbagger" Corp. ***(648)***
SAP Public Services ***(649)***
Sarnoff Corp. ***(650)***
SAT ***(650)***
SatoTravel ***(650)***
Savannah Airport Commission ***(650)***
SAVI Technology ***(650)***
R. Wayne Sayer & Associates *(175)*
Schott Corp. ***(652)***
Schroth & Associates *(176)*
Schweizer Aircraft Corp. ***(652)***
Science & Engineering Associates, Inc. ***(652)***
Science Applications Internat'l Corp. (SAIC) ***(652)***
Scientific Fishery Systems, Inc. ***(652)***
Scientific Research Corp. ***(652)***
Scram Technologies Inc. ***(652)***
Seal Beach, California, City of ***(653)***
Sears, Roebuck and Co. ***(653)***
Sechan Electronics ***(654)***
Seemann Composites LLC ***(654)***
Semiconductor Equipment and Materials Internat'l ***(655)***
Sensor Research and Development Corp. ***(655)***
Sensor Technologies and Systems Inc. ***(655)***
Seton Hill College ***(656)***
Shipbuilders Council of America ***(657)***
Short Brothers (USA), Inc. ***(658)***
Shorts Missile Systems ***(658)***
Sierra Military Health Services, Inc. ***(659)***
Sierra Nevada Corp. ***(659)***
Sierra Technologies Inc. ***(659)***
SIGCOM, Inc. ***(659)***
Silicon Valley Group ***(659)***
Silver Users Ass'n ***(659)***
Simula, Inc. ***(659)***
Singapore Technologies Automotive ***(659)***
SINTEF Telecom and Informatics ***(660)***
Sippican, Inc. ***(660)***
SISCORP *(181)*
Sisters of Charity of the Incarnate Word ***(660)***
SKF USA, Inc. ***(660)***
Skyhook Technologies, Inc. ***(660)***
SM&A ***(661)***
Anne V. Smith *(182)*
Philip S. Smith & Associates, Inc. *(182)*
Smith Alling Lane, P.S. *(183)*
E. Del Smith and Co. *(183)*
Smith Dawson & Andrews, Inc. *(183)*
The Smith, Korach, Hayet, Haynie Partnership ***(661)***
Smiths Industries Aerospace and Defense Systems ***(661)***
Robert D. Sneed *(185)*
Craig Snyder & Associates *(185)*
Societe Nationale d'Etude et Construction de Moteurs d'Aviation (SNECMA) ***(664)***
Sodexho Marriott Services, Inc. ***(664)***
Solipsys Corp. ***(665)***
The Solomon Group, LLC *(185)*
Sonetech Corp. ***(665)***
South African Government/World Bank ***(666)***
South Carolina Nat'l Guard Ass'n ***(666)***
South Carolina Research Authority ***(666)***
Space Dynamics Laboratory ***(669)***
Spacelabs Medical Inc. ***(669)***
Sparton Electronics, Florida, Inc. ***(669)***
Spatial Integrated Systems ***(669)***
SPD Technologies ***(669)***
Specialty Steel Industry of North America ***(670)***
Spectrum Astro, Inc. ***(670)***
The Spectrum Group *(186)*
Spectrum Health Care Resources, Inc. ***(670)***
Sperry Marine Inc. ***(670)***
Spokane Area Chamber of Commerce ***(670)***
SRI Internat'l ***(671)***
St. Petersburg Community College ***(672)***
Stanfield Tindal, Inc. *(187)*
Stanly County Airport Authority ***(673)***
Steptoe & Johnson LLP *(188)*
Stevens Institute of Technology ***(674)***
Stewart & Stevenson Services, Inc. ***(674)***
Stidd Systems, Inc. ***(674)***
Stilman Advanced Strategies ***(674)***
Stockton, California, Port of ***(675)***
Strategic Horizons Advisors, L.L.C. *(189)*
Strategic Minerals Corp. ***(675)***
Stratus Systems Inc. ***(675)***
Francis J. Sullivan Associates *(190)*
SUNY Empire State College ***(677)***
Survival Inc. ***(678)***
SWATH Ocean Systems, Inc. ***(678)***
Swiss Munition Enterprise ***(679)***
Syntroleum Corp. ***(679)***
Synzyme Technologies, Inc. ***(679)***
System Planning Corp. ***(679)***
Systems Simulation Solutions Inc. ***(679)***
T.W.Y. Co., Ltd. ***(679)***
Taiwan Studies Institute ***(680)***
Talley and Associates *(192)*
Tate-LeMunyon, LLC *(192)*
Taxpayers Against Fraud, The False Claims Legal Center ***(681)***
TCOM, L.P. ***(682)***
Team Santa Rosa Economic Development Council ***(682)***
TECHHEALTH.COM ***(682)***
Technology Systems, Inc. ***(682)***
Teicher Consulting and Representation *(193)*
The Tekamah Corp. ***(682)***
Teledyne-Commodore, LLC ***(683)***
TeleFlex Canada, Ltd. ***(683)***
Tensiodyne Scientific Corp. ***(684)***
Tetra Tech ***(684)***
Texas A&M Research Foundation ***(684)***
Textron Inc. ***(685)***
Textron Systems Division ***(685)***
Thales ***(685)***
Thelen Reid & Priest LLP *(193)*
Thiokol Propulsion ***(686)***
Thomas Group Internat'l ***(686)***
Thomas Jefferson University ***(686)***
Thompson Coburn LLP *(194)*
TI Group Inc. ***(686)***
Tichenor and Associates ***(686)***
Tighe, Patton, Tabackman & Babbin *(195)*
Time Domain Corp. ***(687)***
Timmons and Co., Inc. *(195)*
Titan Corp. ***(687)***
Titanium Metals Corp. ***(687)***
Todd Shipyards Inc. ***(688)***
Torrington Co. ***(688)***
Traditional Values Coalition ***(689)***
Trajen, Inc. ***(689)***
TransAtlantic Lines - Iceland ehf ***(690)***
Transnat'l Development Consortium ***(690)***
TREA Senior Citizens League (TSCL) ***(691)***
Trident Systems Inc. ***(692)***
Triosyn Corp. ***(692)***
TriWest Healthcare Alliance, Inc. ***(692)***
TRW Inc. ***(693)***
TRW Space and Electronics Group ***(693)***
Tulane University ***(693)***
Turbine Controls, Inc. ***(694)***
David Turch & Associates *(197)*
Tyson's Governmental Sales, LLC ***(695)***
U.S. Display Consortium ***(696)***
U.S. Marine Corp. ***(696)***
UDV North America, Inc. ***(698)***
Ultracard, Inc. ***(698)***
Unified Industries, Inc. ***(698)***
Uniformed Services Dental Alliance ***(698)***
Unilever United States, Inc. ***(699)***
Union of Concerned Scientists ***(699)***
Union of Needletrades, Industrial, and Textile Employees (UNITE) ***(699)***
Unisys Corp. ***(700)***
United Automobile, Aerospace and Agricultural Implement Workers of America (UAW) ***(700)***
United Concordia Companies, Inc. ***(701)***
United Defense, L.P. ***(701)***
United Hellenic American Congress ***(701)***
United Lao Congress for Democracy ***(702)***
United Methodist Church General Board of Church and Society ***(702)***
United Service Organization ***(702)***
United Special Transport Air Resources, LLC (USTAR) ***(703)***
United States Business and Industry Council ***(703)***
United States Coast Guard Chief Petty Officers Ass'n ***(703)***
United States Marine Repair ***(703)***
United Technologies Corp. ***(704)***
Universal Systems, Inc. ***(705)***
University of California, Office of Federal Government Relations ***(706)***
University of Massachusetts ***(706)***
University of Medicine and Dentistry of New Jersey ***(706)***
University of Miami ***(706)***
University of Oregon ***(707)***
University of Tulsa ***(708)***
University of Virginia ***(708)***
University System of Maryland ***(708)***
Upland, California, City of ***(708)***
USFHP Conference Group ***(710)***
Utah State University ***(710)***
Uwohali, Inc. ***(711)***
V-ONE Corp. ***(711)***
Valentec Systems, Inc. ***(711)***
The Van Fleet-Meredith Group *(199)*
Van Ness Feldman, P.C. *(199)*
Van Scoyoc Associates, Inc. *(200)*
Vance Development Authority ***(712)***
Vector Research, Inc. ***(712)***
Ventura County Community-Navy Action Partnership ***(712)***
Veridian Corp. ***(712)***
Verner, Liipfert, Bernhard, McPherson and Hand, Chartered *(202)*
ViaSat, Inc. ***(714)***
City of Victorville Redevelopment Agency ***(715)***
Video Network Communications ***(715)***
Vietnam Veterans of America Foundation ***(715)***
Virtual Drug Development ***(716)***
Virtual Impact Productions ***(716)***
VISICU ***(716)***
ViTel Net ***(717)***
Vivendi Universal ***(717)***
VLOC ***(717)***
Vortex, Inc. ***(717)***
Vredenburg ***(718)***
VSAdc.com *(205)*
The Mike Waite Company *(205)*
R. Duffy Wall and Associates *(205)*
Warland Investment Co. ***(718)***
Washington Office on Latin American ***(720)***
Washington Resource Associates *(209)*
Waterman & Associates *(210)*
Weidlinger Associates, Inc. ***(722)***
Westerly Group *(211)*
Roy F. Weston, Inc. ***(725)***
The Wexler Group *(211)*
R. H. White Public Affairs Consulting *(213)*
R. C. Whitner and Associates, Inc. ***(726)***
Whitten & Diamond *(213)*
Bill Wight, LLC *(214)*
Williams & Jensen, P.C. *(215)*
Wilmer, Cutler & Pickering *(217)*
Wilson Composites Group ***(727)***
Donald E. Wilson Consulting *(218)*
Wolf Springs Ranches, Inc. ***(729)***
Xcellsis Corp. ***(732)***
Xeta Internat'l Corp. ***(732)***
Youyang ***(734)***
Zinc Corp. of America ***(734)***

Disaster Planning/Emergencies (DIS)

The Accord Group *(5)*
Adams and Reese LLP *(5)*
Alaska Airlines ***(236)***

Allstate Insurance Co. ***(241)***
America's Community Bankers ***(243)***
American Federation of Teachers ***(259)***
The American Institute of Architects ***(264)***
American Insurance Ass'n ***(264)***
American Internat'l Group, Inc. ***(265)***
American Legion ***(266)***
American Public Gas Ass'n ***(271)***
American Public Works Ass'n ***(272)***
American Red Cross ***(272)***
American Resort Development Ass'n ***(272)***
American Soc. for Industrial Security ***(274)***
American Wood Preservers Institute ***(280)***
APCO Worldwide *(14)*
Arent Fox Kintner Plotkin & Kahn, PLLC *(14)*
Arnold & Porter ***(289)***
Arnold & Porter *(16)*
Ash Britt ***(290)***
Ass'n and Soc. Management Internat'l Inc. *(18)*
Ass'n of American Physicians and Surgeons ***(294)***
Ass'n of Minnesota Counties ***(297)***
Assurant Group ***(301)***
The Barton Co. *(24)*
Berkeley, California, City of ***(312)***
Burlington Northern Santa Fe Railway ***(324)***
California State Ass'n of Counties ***(327)***
Campbell Crane & Associates *(36)*
Capitol Hill Advocates *(39)*
The Carmen Group *(40)*
Cassidy & Associates, Inc. *(42)*
Carolyn C. Chaney & Associates *(45)*
The Chubb Corp. ***(346)***
CNA Financial Corp. ***(351)***
CNA Insurance Cos. ***(351)***
Commonwealth Consulting Corp. *(50)*
Consumer Federation of America ***(369)***
Consumers Union of the United States ***(369)***
Copeland, Lowery & Jacquez *(52)*
The Council of Insurance Agents & Brokers ***(376)***
Council of State Governments ***(376)***
Dade, Florida, County of ***(381)***
Dawson & Associates, Inc. *(59)*
Dayton, Ohio, Washington Office of the City of ***(383)***
Delex Systems, Inc. ***(384)***
Detroit, Michigan, City of ***(386)***
DRC, Inc. ***(392)***
DuPont Agricultural Products ***(393)***
Dykema Gossett PLLC *(69)*
Elmer Larson, Inc. ***(401)***
Energy and Environment Coalition ***(403)***
Epstein Becker & Green, P.C. *(72)*
Exeter Architectural Products ***(409)***
Farmers Insurance Group ***(412)***
The Ferguson Group, LLC *(76)*
Florida State University System ***(420)***
John Freshman Associates, Inc. *(79)*
Gary, Indiana, Washington Office of the City of ***(429)***
General Conference of Seventh-day Adventists ***(431)***
GHL Inc. *(82)*
Global USA, Inc. *(83)*
Great Lakes Dredge & Dock ***(439)***
Greater New Orleans Expressway Commission ***(439)***
Grocery Manufacturers of America ***(440)***
Habitat for Humanity Internat'l ***(443)***
Honberger and Walters, Inc. *(99)*
Independent Insurance Agents of America, Inc. ***(459)***
Indiana, Office of the Governor of the State of ***(460)***
Internat'l Ass'n of Emergency Managers ***(467)***
Internat'l Ass'n of Fire Chiefs ***(468)***
Internat'l Brotherhood of Electrical Workers ***(469)***
Internat'l Safety Equipment Ass'n (ISEA) ***(474)***
Jacksonville, Florida, City of ***(481)***
JCP Associates *(105)*
Johns Hopkins Center for Civilian Biodefense Studies ***(483)***
Jolly/Rissler, Inc. *(108)*
Jorden Burt LLP *(109)*
Krebs, LaSalle, LeMieux Consultants, Inc. ***(492)***
LaRocco & Associates *(116)*
Las Cruces, New Mexico, City of ***(495)***
Latham & Watkins ***(495)***
League of California Cities ***(497)***
Jack D.P. Lichtenstein *(120)*
Lindsay Hart Neil & Weigler *(120)*
Robert E. Litan *(120)*
Lockridge Grindal & Nauen, P.L.L.P. *(121)*
Los Angeles, California, County of ***(504)***
Louisiana Internat'l Group ***(504)***
Manufactured Housing Institute ***(509)***
MARC Associates, Inc. *(124)*
Maritime Fire and Safety Ass'n ***(510)***
Metropolitan St. Louis Sewer District ***(520)***
Meyers & Associates *(133)*
MIC Industries, Inc. ***(522)***
Miles & Stockbridge, P.C. *(133)*
Mitsubishi Research Institute ***(526)***
Muncie, Indiana, City of (Delaware County) ***(532)***
Nat'l Ass'n of Flood and Stormwater Management Agencies ***(543)***
Nat'l Ass'n of Independent Insurers ***(544)***
Nat'l Ass'n of Service and Conservation Corps ***(549)***
Nat'l Concrete Masonry Ass'n ***(558)***
Nat'l Farmers Union (Farmers Educational & Co-operative Union of America) ***(563)***
Nat'l Fire Protection Ass'n ***(564)***
Nat'l Funeral Directors Ass'n ***(565)***
Nat'l Military Intelligence Ass'n ***(571)***
Nat'l Organization for Victim Assistance ***(572)***
New Mexico State University, Department of Engineering ***(586)***
New Orleans, Louisiana, City of ***(586)***
Julia J. Norrell & Associates *(142)*
North Carolina, Hurricane Floyd Redevelopment Center of State of ***(593)***
North Carolina, Washington Office of the State of ***(593)***
North San Diego County Transit Development Board ***(593)***
Oceanside, California, City of ***(598)***
Operations Security Professionals Soc. ***(601)***
Orleans Levee District ***(603)***
The Palmer Group *(149)*
Parsons Brinckerhoff Inc. ***(608)***
Partners of the Americas ***(608)***
Patton Boggs, LLP *(150)*
Peyser Associates, Inc. *(155)*
The PMA Group *(156)*
Pointe Coupee Police Jury ***(620)***
Potomac Group *(160)*
Powers Pyles Sutter & Verville, PC *(161)*
Professional Engineering ***(625)***
Rapid Mat LLC ***(633)***
Reinsurance Ass'n of America ***(636)***
Research Planning, Inc. ***(638)***
Rooney Group Internat'l, Inc. *(171)*
Sacramento Area Flood Control Agency ***(645)***
San Leandro, California, City of ***(648)***
The "Sandbagger" Corp. ***(648)***
Santa Cruz, California, County of ***(649)***
Santa Rosa Memorial Hospital ***(649)***
Sensor Research and Development Corp. ***(655)***
Shelters, Inc. ***(657)***
Simon and Co., Inc. *(181)*
Simon Strategies/Mindbeam *(181)*
Solutia Inc. ***(665)***
Spokane Area Chamber of Commerce ***(670)***
St. Louis University, School of Public Health ***(672)***
Stanly County Airport Authority ***(673)***
State Farm Insurance Cos. ***(673)***
Stuntz, Davis & Staffier, P.C. *(190)*
Synthetic Organic Chemical Manufacturers Ass'n ***(679)***
Texas A&M Research Foundation ***(684)***
Thelen Reid & Priest LLP *(193)*
Traffic.com ***(689)***
U.S. Strategies Corp. *(197)*
University of California at Los Angeles ***(706)***
University of Findlay ***(706)***
University of South Florida Research Foundation ***(707)***
Valanzano & Associates *(198)*
Van Scoyoc Associates, Inc. *(200)*
Viohl and Associates, Inc. *(205)*
Virgin Islands, Government of the ***(715)***
Washington Consulting Alliance, Inc. *(206)*
Waterman & Associates *(210)*
West Jefferson Levee District ***(723)***
Williams & Jensen, P.C. *(215)*
Donald E. Wilson Consulting *(218)*
Winston & Strawn *(218)*
Womble Carlyle Sandridge & Rice, P.C. *(220)*

District of Columbia (DOC)

500 C Street Associates, L.P. ***(224)***
American Federation of State, County and Municipal Employees ***(258)***
American Federation of Teachers ***(259)***
American Historical Ass'n ***(262)***
American Jewish Congress ***(265)***
American Psychological Ass'n ***(271)***
Americans for Tax Reform ***(282)***
Americans United for Separation of Church and State ***(282)***
Ass'n of the United States Army ***(299)***
BKSH & Associates *(28)*
Capital Children's Museum ***(330)***
Carmen & Muss, P.L.L.C. *(40)*
Center for Public Dialogue ***(337)***
Charter Schools Development Corp. ***(341)***
Chernikoff and Co. *(46)*
Children's Rights Council ***(344)***
Ronald J. Cohen Investments ***(357)***
Consortium of Universities of the Washington Metropolitan Area ***(368)***
Council for Court Excellence ***(374)***
D.C. Catholic Conference - Archdiocese of Washington ***(381)***
D.C. Historical Tourism Coalition ***(381)***
D.C. Land Title Ass'n ***(383)***
The Da Vinci Group *(56)*
Dalton & Dalton P.C. ***(382)***
Doctors Community Healthcare Corp. ***(390)***
EarthData Holdings ***(394)***
Edison Electric Institute ***(397)***
Federal City Council ***(412)***
Friends of the Earth ***(426)***
Greater Washington Board of Trade ***(439)***
Greenberg Traurig, LLP *(86)*
Guam, Washington Office of the Governor ***(442)***
Harmon & Wilmot, L.L.P. *(91)*
Hotel Ass'n of Washington ***(453)***
Institute for Local Self-Reliance ***(463)***
Internat'l Brotherhood of Electrical Workers ***(469)***
Betty Ann Kane & Co. *(110)*
Ledge Counsel *(118)*
Nat'l Ass'n of Negro Business & Professional Women's Clubs, Inc. ***(546)***
Nat'l Right to Life Committee ***(576)***
NCRIC, Inc. ***(583)***
John M. Palatiello & Associates *(148)*
Parsons Corp. ***(608)***
Patton Boggs, LLP *(150)*
The Kerry S. Pearson LLC *(154)*
Potomac Electric Power Co. ***(622)***
Potomac Strategies Internat'l LLC *(160)*
Schmeltzer, Aptaker & Shepard, P.C. *(176)*
Shaw Pittman *(177)*
Sibley Memorial Hospital ***(658)***
Sprint Corp. ***(671)***
Square 3942 Associates Limited Partnership ***(671)***
Tort Reform Institute ***(688)***
United Methodist Church General Board of Church and Society ***(702)***
Wackenhut Corrections Corp. ***(718)***
Washington Council of Agencies ***(719)***
Washington Metropolitan Area Transit Authority ***(720)***

Economics/Economic Development (ECN)

3Com Corp. ***(223)***
AARP (American Ass'n of Retired Persons) ***(224)***
Adams and Reese LLP *(5)*
Advertising Company ART-ERIA ***(229)***
The Advocacy Group *(6)*
AFL-CIO (American Federation of Labor and Congress of Industrial Organizations) ***(231)***
Africa Global Partners *(7)*

Aiken and Edgenfield Counties, South Carolina, Economic Development Partnership of *(233)*
Ainslie Associates *(7)*
Alabama Space Science Exhibits Commission *(236)*
Alameda, California, City of *(236)*
Albertine Enterprises, Inc. *(10)*
Albuquerque, New Mexico, City of *(237)*
Alcalde & Fay *(10)*
Aldaron Inc. *(238)*
Harry C. Alford & Associates, Inc. *(11)*
AMDeC Policy Group, Inc. *(242)*
American Ass'n of University Women *(249)*
American Boiler Manufacturers Ass'n *(251)*
American Butter Institute *(251)*
American Gear Manufacturers Ass'n *(261)*
American Indian Ass'n *(263)*
American Legion *(266)*
American Nurses Ass'n *(268)*
American Planning Ass'n *(270)*
American Wood Preservers Institute *(280)*
Americans for Equitable Climate Solutions *(281)*
Americans United for Separation of Church and State *(282)*
Arent Fox Kintner Plotkin & Kahn, PLLC *(14)*
The Argus Group, L.L.C. *(16)*
Arizona State University *(288)*
Arnold & Porter *(16)*
Asia Pacific Policy Center *(290)*
Ass'n for Enterprise Opportunity *(292)*
The Ass'n For Manufacturing Technology (AMT) *(292)*
Ass'n of American Chambers of Commerce in Latin America *(293)*
Ass'n of American Geographers *(293)*
Ass'n of Financial Guaranty Insurers *(295)*
Ass'n of School Business Officials Internat'l *(298)*
Ass'n of Small Business Development Centers *(298)*
Ass'n to Unite the Democracies *(299)*
Ross Atkins *(18)*
The Auxiliary Service Corporations *(304)*
Balch & Bingham LLP *(21)*
Ball Janik, LLP *(22)*
The Barton Co. *(24)*
Baton Rouge, Louisiana, City of *(308)*
Belew Law Firm *(25)*
Bellevue, Washington, City of *(311)*
Bert Corona Leadership Institute *(312)*
BET Holdings II, Inc. *(312)*
Bicopas, Ltd. *(313)*
Big Sky, Inc. *(313)*
BKSH & Associates *(28)*
BMW Manufacturing Corp. *(316)*
Boston, Massachusetts, City of *(318)*
The Brookings Institution *(321)*
Broward, Florida, County of *(322)*
Brownsville Public Utilities Board *(322)*
Brownsville, Texas, City of *(322)*
Buffalo, New York, City of *(323)*
John G. "Toby" Burke *(34)*
Burlington Northern Santa Fe Railway *(324)*
Business and Professional Women/USA *(324)*
The C.L.A. Group, LLC *(35)*
California State University Fresno *(327)*
Canfield & Associates, Inc. *(36)*
Capital Consultants Corp. *(37)*
Capitol City Group *(38)*
Capitol Coalitions Inc. *(38)*
Capitol Hill Advocates *(39)*
CapitolWatch *(331)*
Cargill, Inc. *(331)*
The Carmen Group *(40)*
Carolina, Puerto Rico, City of *(332)*
CaseNewHolland Inc. *(333)*
Cassidy & Associates, Inc. *(42)*
Ceiba, Puerto Rico, City of *(334)*
Center for Freedom and Prosperity *(336)*
Center for Public Dialogue *(337)*
Center of Concern *(338)*
Central American Bank of Economic Integration *(338)*
Chamber of Commerce of the U.S.A. *(340)*
Chambers Associates Inc. *(45)*
Chehalis Reservation, Confederated Tribes of the *(342)*
Children's Defense Fund *(344)*
Clackamas, Oregon, County of *(349)*
Clay and Associates *(47)*
Clearwater, Florida, City of *(350)*
Cleveland State University - College of Urban Affairs *(351)*
The Climate Council, *(351)*
Colling Swift & Hynes *(49)*
Collins & Company, Inc. *(49)*
Colombian American Trade Center *(358)*
Colorado River Indian Tribes *(358)*
Committee for a Responsible Federal Budget *(360)*
Community Development Financial Institutions (CDFI) *(362)*
Community Development Venture Capital Ass'n *(362)*
Community Health Partners of Ohio *(362)*
Concurrent Technologies Corp. *(365)*
Congressional Economic Leadership Institute *(366)*
Construction Industry Round Table, Inc. *(368)*
Consumer Federation of America *(369)*
Copeland, Lowery & Jacquez *(52)*
Corporacion de Exportaciones Mexicanas, S.A. de C.V. and Marvin Roy Feldman *(372)*
Corporation for Enterprise Development *(372)*
Corpus Christi, City of *(373)*
Council for Urban Economic Development *(375)*
Coushatta Tribe of Louisiana *(377)*
Cranston, Rhode Island, City of *(378)*
Dade, Florida, County of *(381)*
DaimlerChrysler Corp. *(381)*
Dallas, Texas, City of *(382)*
Davis O'Connell, Inc. *(58)*
Dayton, Ohio, Washington Office of the City of *(383)*
Diamond Head Financial Group *(387)*
Dickstein Shapiro Morin & Oshinsky LLP *(61)*
Dillingham Construction, Inc. *(388)*
Doctors Community Healthcare Corp. *(390)*
Doepken Keevican & Weiss *(63)*
Downey McGrath Group, Inc. *(64)*
Dublin Castle Group *(66)*
Dulles Area Transportation Ass'n *(393)*
Duncan, Weinberg, Genzer & Pembroke, P.C. *(66)*
The Dutko Group, Inc. *(68)*
E*TRADE Group, Inc. *(394)*
E.ON North America, Inc. *(394)*
The Eagles Group *(69)*
East Tennessee Economic Council *(395)*
Edington, Peel & Associates, Inc. *(70)*
Edison Community College *(397)*
El Toro Reuse Planning Authority *(399)*
Employment Policy Foundation *(402)*
Erie Internat'l Airport *(406)*
Export Management Services, Inc. *(409)*
Fairfax, Virginia, County of *(410)*
Fairfield University *(410)*
Fairfield, California, City of *(410)*
Fannie Mae *(411)*
Fargo-Cass County Development Corp. *(411)*
Farm Progress Cos. *(412)*
Feith & Zell, P.C. *(75)*
Jack Ferguson Associates, Inc. *(75)*
The Ferguson Group, LLC *(76)*
FINCA Internat'l Inc., The Foundation for Internat'l Community Assistance *(417)*
First American *(417)*
R. G. Flippo and Associates, Inc. *(77)*
Florida State University System *(420)*
Foley & Lardner *(78)*
Folsom, California, City of *(421)*
Fontheim Internat'l *(421)*
Food Bank of the Virginia Peninsula *(421)*
Freeport, New York, Village of *(425)*
Friends Committee on Nat'l Legislation *(426)*
Gainesville, Florida, City of *(428)*
Sara Garland (and Associates) *(81)*
Gary, Indiana, Washington Office of the City of *(429)*
General Motors Corp. *(432)*
Global Communicators *(83)*
Global Policy Group, Inc. *(83)*
Global USA, Inc. *(83)*
Mark W. Goodin *(84)*
Government Relations, Inc. *(84)*
GPC Internat'l *(85)*
Greater El Paso Chamber of Commerce *(439)*
Greater Providence Chamber of Commerce *(439)*
Greater Washington Board of Trade *(439)*
Greenpoint Manufacturing and Design Center (GMDC) *(440)*
John C. Grzebien *(89)*
Guinea, Secretary General of the Presidency of the Republic of *(442)*
Hampshire College *(444)*
Hampton University *(444)*
Hattiesburg, Mississippi, City of *(445)*
Hawaii Economic Development Alliance, State of *(445)*
Hawaii, Department of Business and Economic Development of the State of *(445)*
Hello Arabia Corp. *(448)*
Hercules Development Corp. *(448)*
Heritage Harbor Museum *(449)*
Highland Park, Illinois, City of Highwood Local Redevelopment Authority and the City of *(449)*
Hill and Knowlton, Inc. *(95)*
Hillsborough, Florida, County of *(450)*
Hohlt & Associates *(98)*
Holland & Knight LLP *(98)*
Peter Homer *(99)*
Hudson Institute *(454)*
Huntsville, Alabama, City of *(455)*
Hurt, Norton & Associates *(101)*
IMC Global Inc. *(458)*
IMPACT, LLC *(102)*
Indiana, Office of the Governor of the State of *(460)*
Inglewood, California, City of *(462)*
Inland Valley Development Agency *(462)*
Institute for Entrepreneurship *(463)*
Institute for Local Self-Reliance *(463)*
Institute on Religion and Public Policy *(464)*
Internat'l Brotherhood of Electrical Workers *(469)*
Internat'l Downtown Ass'n *(471)*
Internat'l Federation of Professional and Technical Engineers *(471)*
Internat'l Franchise Ass'n *(472)*
Internat'l Union of Painters and Allied Trades *(476)*
Internat'l Warehouse Logistics Ass'n *(476)*
Interregional Associates *(477)*
IPALCO Enterprises, Inc./Indianapolis Power & Light Co. *(478)*
Jacksonville, Florida, City of *(481)*
Janus-Merritt Strategies, L.L.C. *(104)*
Japan External Trade Organization (JETRO) *(481)*
Jarboe & Associates *(105)*
Jasper, Alabama, City of *(482)*
JCP Associates *(105)*
Jefferson Parish Council *(482)*
Johnson Co. *(107)*
Johnston & Associates, LLC *(107)*
Jordan & Associates, Inc. *(109)*
Jorden Burt LLP *(109)*
Kaiser Aluminum & Chemical Corp. *(485)*
Betty Ann Kane & Co. *(110)*
Keizai Koho Center *(487)*
Kelly and Associates, Inc. *(111)*
Kent & O'Connor, Inc. *(112)*
Kinghorn & Associates, L.L.C. *(113)*
Korea Economic Institute of America *(491)*
Kutak Rock LLP *(115)*
Labor Council for Latin American Advancement (LCLAA) *(493)*
Lee Lane *(116)*
Laredo, Texas, City of *(495)*
LaRocco & Associates *(116)*
Las Cruces, New Mexico, City of *(495)*
Lawler, Metzger & Milkman, LLC *(117)*
Leonard Resource Group *(119)*
Lewis and Clark College *(498)*
Link Romania, Inc. *(500)*
Local Initiatives Support Corp. *(501)*
Lockridge Grindal & Nauen, P.L.L.P. *(121)*
Long Beach, California, City of *(503)*
Lorain County Community College *(503)*

Los Alamos, New Mexico, County of (503)
Lynn, Massachusetts, City of (506)
Madison Government Affairs (123)
Manufacturers Alliance/MAPI Inc. (509)
MARC Associates, Inc. (124)
March Joint Powers Authority (509)
Marion, Indiana, City of (510)
Marshall, Alabama, County of (511)
Masaoka & Associates, Inc. (125)
Virginia M. Mayer (126)
McAndrews and Forbes Holding, Inc. (514)
Charlie McBride Associates, Inc. (127)
Barbara T. McCall Associates (127)
McClure, Gerard & Neuenschwander, Inc. (127)
Jack H. McDonald (129)
Memphis, Tennessee, City of (517)
Merced, California, County of (518)
Metropolitan King County Council (520)
Metropolitan Transportation Commission (520)
Meyers & Associates (133)
Miami Beach, Florida, City of (521)
MIC Industries, Inc. (522)
The Micronesia Institute (522)
Denny Miller McBee Associates (134)
Milwaukee, City of (524)
Minneapolis, Minnesota, City of (525)
Mitsubishi Research Institute (526)
Modesto, California, City of (527)
Monroe, Louisiana, Chamber of Commerce of the City of (528)
Monroe, Louisiana, City of (528)
Monroe, New York, County of (528)
Monterey, California, County of (528)
Montgomery, Alabama, Chamber of Commerce of (529)
Mooresville, North Carolina, Town of (529)
The Morrison Group, Inc. (137)
Moss McGee Bradley & Foley (137)
Muncie, Indiana, City of (Delaware County) (532)
Murray, Scheer, Montgomery, Tapia & O'Donnell (139)
NASA Aeronautics Support Team (534)
Nat'l Academy of Public Administration (535)
Nat'l Ass'n for the Self-Employed (538)
Nat'l Ass'n of Developmental Disabilities Councils (542)
Nat'l Ass'n of Installation Developers (544)
Nat'l Ass'n of Manufacturers (545)
Nat'l Ass'n of Negro Business & Professional Women's Clubs, Inc. (546)
Nat'l Ass'n of Towns and Townships (551)
Nat'l Assembly of Health and Human Service Organizations (551)
Nat'l Center for Neighborhood Enterprise (555)
Nat'l Center for Policy Analysis (555)
Nat'l Community Reinvestment Coalition (558)
Nat'l Concrete Masonry Ass'n (558)
Nat'l Council of La Raza (560)
Nat'l Council of Negro Women (560)
Nat'l Farmers Union (Farmers Educational & Co-operative Union of America) (563)
Nat'l Job Corps Ass'n (569)
Nat'l Legal Center for the Public Interest (570)
Nat'l Liberty Museum (570)
Nat'l Neighborhood Coalition (572)
Nat'l Newspaper Publishers Ass'n (572)
Nat'l Rehabilitation Ass'n (575)
Nat'l Rural Development Ass'n (576)
Nat'l Rural Electric Cooperative Ass'n (576)
Nat'l Small Business United (578)
Nat'l Taxpayers Union (579)
Nat'l Venture Capital Ass'n (580)
NETWORK, A Nat'l Catholic Social Justice Lobby (584)
Neuman and Co. (141)
Nevada Test Site Development Corp. (584)
New America Alliance (585)
New London Development Corp. (586)
New Mexico State Office of Research & Development (586)
New Orleans, Louisiana, City of (586)
Newark, New Jersey, City of (588)
Nogales, Arizona, City of (591)
Norfolk, Virginia, City of (591)
North American Superhighway Coalition (593)
North Carolina, Washington Office of the State of (593)
North Dakota, Governor's Office of the State of (593)
North Slope Borough, Alaska (593)
Northeast-Midwest Institute (594)
Northwest Airlines, Inc. (595)
Nottoway, Virginia, County of (596)
Nuclear Energy Institute (597)
Oak Ridge, Tennessee, City of (598)
Oceanside, California, City of (598)
One Economy Corp. (600)
Opportunity Internat'l (601)
Orange, Florida, County of (602)
Oregon Garden Foundation (603)
Orlando, Florida, City of (603)
John T. O'Rourke Law Offices (147)
Ouachita Parish Police Jury (604)
Oxnard, California, City of (605)
Pacific Islands Washington Office (148)
Pacific Science Center (606)
Palm Beach, Florida, County of (606)
The Palmer Group (149)
Palo Alto, California, City of (607)
Paradise Valley Hospital (607)
Parry, Romani, DeConcini & Symms (149)
Patton Boggs, LLP (150)
Paucatuck Eastern Pequot Tribal Nation (609)
The Kerry S. Pearson LLC (154)
The Peterson Group (155)
The Petrizzo Group, Inc. (155)
Peyser Associates, Inc. (155)
Phoenix, Arizona, City of (616)
Plaquemine, Louisiana, City of (619)
Please Touch Museum, The Children's Museum of Philadelphia (619)
The PMA Group (156)
Portland, Oregon, City of (621)
Powell, Goldstein, Frazer & Murphy LLP (160)
Preston Gates Ellis & Rouvelas Meeds LLP (162)
Pretium S.C (Mexico) (623)
Professional Facilities Management (625)
Professional Services Council (626)
Progressive Policy Institute (626)
Providence City Arts for Youth, Inc. (627)
Providence Performing Arts Center (627)
The Providence Plan (627)
Provo, Utah, City of (627)
Public Strategies Washington, Inc. (164)
Puerto Rico, Commonwealth of (629)
Q-ZAB Coalition (630)
Quad City Development Group (630)
Quebecor World (USA) Inc. (631)
Rainbow/Push Coalition (National Bureau) (632)
Robert A. Rapoza Associates (165)
Pamela Ray-Strunk and Associates (166)
Red River Trade Council (635)
Law Office of Paige E. Reffe (167)
Regional Planning Commission (635)
Renton, Washington, City of (637)
Republican Jewish Coalition (637)
Rio Grande Valley Chamber of Commerce (640)
Riverside, California, City of (640)
Robertson, Monagle & Eastaugh (170)
Romano & Associates, LLC (171)
Roseville, California, City of (642)
RPH & Associates, L.L.C. (172)
Rural Community Assistance Corp. (643)
Rural Telephone Finance Cooperative (644)
Sacramento-Potomac Consulting, Inc. (174)
SafeWorks, LLC (645)
Sagamore Associates, Inc. (174)
Salt Lake City, Utah, City of (646)
San Diego, California, City of (647)
San Francisco, California, City and County of (648)
San Francisco, City of (648)
Santa Ana, California, City of (649)
Santa Rosa Memorial Hospital (649)
Schmeltzer, Aptaker & Shepard, P.C. (176)
James E. Schneider, LLM Inc. (651)
Seaside, California, City of (653)
Seedco (654)
Shaw Pittman (177)
Shea's Performing Arts Center (657)
Shorebank Corp. (658)
Shriner-Midland Co. (658)
Simon and Co., Inc. (181)
Simon Strategies/Mindbeam (181)
Small Business Regulatory Council (661)
Smith Dawson & Andrews, Inc. (183)
The Smith-Free Group (184)
The Solomon Group, LLC (185)
Sonoma, California, County of (665)
Spokane Area Chamber of Commerce (670)
St. Louis, Missouri, City of (672)
St. Paul, Alaska, City of (672)
Stevens Institute of Technology (674)
Stockton, City of (675)
Strategic Horizons Advisors, L.L.C. (189)
Suffolk, New York, County of (676)
Swaziland, Kingdom of (678)
Switzerland, Economic Development, State of Vaud (679)
Swope Parkway Health Center (679)
Tampa Bay Performing Arts Center (680)
Tate-LeMunyon, LLC (192)
Team Santa Rosa Economic Development Council (682)
Team Stratford (682)
TELACU (682)
Tempe, Arizona, City of (683)
Tett Enterprises (684)
Thomas Group Internat'l (686)
Traffic.com (689)
Transnat'l Development Consortium (690)
Tri-County Alliance (691)
Tulare, California, County of (694)
Tunica Biloxi Indians of Louisiana (694)
David Turch & Associates (197)
Turkish Industrialists and Businessmen's Ass'n (TUSIAD) (694)
Tustin, California, City of (694)
U.S. Family Network (696)
U.S. Oil and Gas Ass'n (696)
U.S. Strategies Corp. (197)
Unalaska, Alaska, City of (698)
United Methodist Church General Board of Church and Society (702)
United States Business and Industry Council (703)
United Steelworkers of America (704)
University Heights Science Park (705)
University of Colorado, Office of the President (706)
University of Miami (706)
University of Virgina (708)
USS Wisconsin Foundation (710)
Van Ness Feldman, P.C. (199)
Van Scoyoc Associates, Inc. (200)
Verner, Liipfert, Bernhard, McPherson and Hand, Chartered (713)
Viohl and Associates, Inc. (205)
Virginia Living Museum (716)
Waggoner Engineering, Inc. (718)
The Mike Waite Company (205)
Washington and Jefferson College (719)
Washington Sports & Entertainment, L.P. (720)
West Jordan, Utah, City of (723)
Wheat & Associates, Inc. (212)
White Mountain Apache Tribe (726)
Williams & Jensen, P.C. (215)
Wilmington Savings Fund Society (727)
Winston & Strawn (218)
Women Officials in NACo (729)
Xerox Corp. (732)
Bill Zavarela (221)

Education (EDU)

3Com Corp. (223)
Abrams & Co. Publishers Inc. (225)
Accrediting Commission on Education for Health Services Administration (226)
Accrediting Council for Continuing Education & Training (226)
ACORN (Ass'n of Community Organizations for Reform Now) (227)
Adams and Reese LLP (5)
Michael W. Adcock (6)
The Advocacy Group (6)

The Advocacy Group ***(229)***
Advocates for Youth ***(229)***
AFL-CIO (American Federation of Labor and Congress of Industrial Organizations) ***(231)***
Agudath Israel of America ***(232)***
Ainslie Associates *(7)*
Air Conditioning Contractors of America ***(233)***
Air Force Sergeants Ass'n ***(233)***
Akin, Gump, Strauss, Hauer & Feld, L.L.P. *(8)*
Alabama A & M University ***(235)***
Alabama Space Science Exhibits Commission ***(236)***
Sally L. Albright *(10)*
Albuquerque, New Mexico, City of ***(237)***
Alcalde & Fay *(10)*
Alfalit Internat'l ***(238)***
All Kinds of Music ***(238)***
Alliance for Children and Families ***(239)***
Alliance for Internat'l Educational and Cultural Exchange, The ***(239)***
Alliance for the Prudent Use of Antibiotics (APUA) ***(240)***
America's Community Bankers ***(243)***
American Academy of Child and Adolescent Psychiatry ***(243)***
American Academy of Family Physicians ***(243)***
American Ass'n for Active Lifestyles and Fitness ***(245)***
American Ass'n of Colleges for Teacher Education ***(247)***
American Ass'n of Colleges of Osteopathic Medicine ***(247)***
American Ass'n of Colleges of Pharmacy ***(247)***
American Ass'n of Community Colleges ***(247)***
American Ass'n of Early Childhood Educators ***(247)***
American Ass'n of Museums ***(248)***
American Ass'n of Physics Teachers ***(249)***
American Ass'n of School Administrators ***(249)***
American Ass'n of University Affiliated Programs for Persons with Developmental Disabilities ***(249)***
American Ass'n of University Professors ***(249)***
American Ass'n of University Women ***(249)***
American Astronomical Soc. ***(250)***
American Bankers Ass'n ***(250)***
American Bar Ass'n ***(250)***
American Business Conference ***(251)***
American Camping Ass'n ***(251)***
American Chemical Soc. ***(252)***
American Continental Group, Inc. *(12)*
American Council of Life Insurers ***(256)***
American Council on Education ***(256)***
American Counseling Ass'n ***(256)***
American Dental Education Ass'n ***(257)***
American Educational Research Ass'n ***(257)***
American Electronics Ass'n ***(257)***
American Express Co. ***(258)***
American Farm Bureau Federation ***(258)***
American Federation of State, County and Municipal Employees ***(258)***
American Federation of Teachers ***(259)***
American Foundation for the Blind - Governmental Relations Group ***(260)***
American Historical Ass'n ***(262)***
American Indian Higher Education Consortium ***(263)***
American Institute for Foreign Studies ***(264)***
The American Institute of Architects ***(264)***
American Institute of Certified Public Accountants ***(264)***
American Institute of Chemical Engineers ***(264)***
American Institute of Physics ***(264)***
American Jewish Congress ***(265)***
American Kurdish Information Network (AKIN) ***(265)***
American Legion ***(266)***
American Library Ass'n ***(266)***
American Medical Student Ass'n ***(267)***
American Motorcyclist Ass'n ***(268)***
American Museum of Natural History ***(268)***
American Nurses Ass'n ***(268)***
American Occupational Therapy Ass'n, Inc. ***(269)***
American Optometric Ass'n ***(269)***
American Organization of Nurse Executives ***(269)***
American Physical Soc. ***(270)***
American Psychological Ass'n ***(271)***
American Psychological Soc. ***(271)***
American School Counselor Ass'n ***(273)***
American Soc. for Biochemistry and Molecular Biology ***(274)***
American Soc. for Cell Biology ***(274)***
American Soc. for Deaf Children ***(274)***
American Soc. for Quality ***(275)***
American Soc. for Training and Development ***(275)***
American Soc. of Mechanical Engineers ***(276)***
American Speech, Language, and Hearing Ass'n ***(277)***
American Symphony Orchestra League ***(278)***
American Teleservices Ass'n ***(279)***
American Wood Preservers Institute ***(280)***
Americans for Consumer Education and Competition, Inc. ***(281)***
Americans for Tax Reform ***(282)***
Americans for the Arts ***(282)***
Americans United for Separation of Church and State ***(282)***
An Achievable Dream, Inc. ***(283)***
Andrews Associates, Inc. *(14)*
Anglican Catholic Church ***(284)***
APCO Worldwide *(14)*
apex.com ***(286)***
APG Army Alliance ***(286)***
Apollo Group, Inc. ***(286)***
The Arc ***(287)***
Arent Fox Kintner Plotkin & Kahn, PLLC *(14)*
Arista Knowledge Systems, Inc. ***(288)***
Arizona Science Center ***(288)***
Arkansas, Office of the Governor of the State of ***(288)***
The Asheville School ***(290)***
Ass'n for Career and Technical Education ***(291)***
Ass'n for Childhood Education Internat'l ***(291)***
Ass'n for Education and Rehabilitation of the Blind & Visually Impaired ***(292)***
Ass'n for Supervision and Curriculum Development ***(293)***
Ass'n of America's Public Television Stations ***(293)***
Ass'n of American Medical Colleges ***(294)***
Ass'n of American Publishers ***(294)***
Ass'n of Black Psychologists ***(294)***
Ass'n of Chiropractic Colleges ***(295)***
Ass'n of Community College Trustees ***(295)***
Ass'n of Governing Boards of Universities and Colleges ***(296)***
Ass'n of Jesuit Colleges and Universities ***(296)***
Ass'n of Minority Health Profession Schools ***(297)***
Ass'n of Proprietary Colleges ***(298)***
Ass'n of Schools and Colleges of Optometry ***(298)***
Ass'n of Schools of Public Health ***(298)***
Ass'n of Science Technology Centers, Inc. ***(298)***
Ass'n of Test Publishers ***(299)***
Ass'n of Universities for Research in Astronomy, Inc. ***(299)***
Ass'n of University Programs in Health Administration ***(299)***
Ass'n to Unite the Democracies ***(299)***
Associated Universities Inc. ***(300)***
Assumption College ***(300)***
Atom Sciences, Inc. ***(302)***
Autism Soc. of America, Inc. ***(303)***
Autometric Inc. ***(303)***
Automotive Aftermarket Industry Ass'n ***(303)***
Automotive Parts and Service Alliance ***(303)***
The Auxiliary Service Corporations ***(304)***
Avondale, Arizona, City of ***(305)***
Balch & Bingham LLP *(21)*
Donald Baldwin Associates *(21)*
Ball Janik, LLP *(22)*
Ball State University ***(306)***
Baltimore, Maryland, City of ***(306)***
Bannerman and Associates, Inc. *(22)*
Barbour Griffith & Rogers, Inc. *(22)*
The Barton Co. *(24)*
Bazelon Center for Mental Health Law, Judge David L. ***(310)***
Bert Corona Leadership Institute ***(312)***
Bethune-Cookman College ***(312)***
Terry Bevels Consulting *(27)*
Blank Rome Comisky & McCauley, LLP *(29)*
Blood Center of Southeastern Wisconsin ***(315)***
Board on Human Sciences ***(316)***
Boesch & Co. *(29)*
James E. Boland *(30)*
Boston University ***(318)***
Boston, Massachusetts, City of ***(318)***
Bowie State University ***(318)***
Bracy Williams & Co. *(31)*
Brain Injury Ass'n ***(319)***
Bridgestone/Firestone, Inc. ***(320)***
Broadforum ***(321)***
Brooklyn Public Library ***(322)***
Broydrick & Associates *(33)*
John G. "Toby" Burke *(34)*
The Business Roundtable ***(325)***
CAL-FED ***(326)***
California Central Coast Research Partnership ***(326)***
California Institute of Technology ***(327)***
California School of Professional Psychology ***(327)***
California State University Fresno ***(327)***
California State University Fullerton ***(327)***
Mark R. Cannon *(37)*
Capital Children's Museum ***(330)***
Capital Consultants Corp. *(37)*
Capital Research Center ***(330)***
Capitol Associates, Inc. *(37)*
Capitol Hill Advocates *(39)*
Capitol Link, Inc. *(39)*
Career College Ass'n ***(331)***
Robert E. Carlstrom *(40)*
Carr Public Affairs ***(332)***
Cartwright & Riley *(41)*
Cash, Smith & Wages *(41)*
Cassidy & Associates, Inc. *(42)*
Carol Cataldo & Associates *(44)*
Catholic Television Network ***(333)***
Cavarocchi Ruscio Dennis Associates *(44)*
Center for Education Reform ***(336)***
Center for Employment Training ***(336)***
Center for Governmental Studies of the University of Virginia ***(336)***
Center for Law and Social Policy ***(336)***
Center for the Arts and Sciences ***(338)***
Central Kitsap School District ***(339)***
Central Michigan University ***(339)***
Central Virginia Educational Telecommunications Corp. ***(339)***
CEO Forum on Education and Technology ***(340)***
Chabot Space & Science Center ***(340)***
Challenger Center for Space Science Education ***(340)***
Chamber of Commerce of the U.S.A. ***(340)***
Chambers Associates Inc. *(45)*
Charter Schools Development Corp. ***(341)***
Chela Financial ***(342)***
Chesapeake Bay Maritime Museum ***(342)***
Chicago School Reform Board of Trustees ***(343)***
Chicago State University ***(343)***
The Child Care Consortium ***(343)***
Child Nutrition Forum, c/o FRAC ***(343)***
Children and Adults with Attention Deficit Disorders (CHADD) ***(344)***
Children's Defense Fund ***(344)***
Christian Voice, Inc. ***(345)***
Christopher Newport University ***(346)***
Church of Scientology Internat'l ***(346)***
Cincinnati, Ohio, City of ***(347)***
Cisco Systems Inc. ***(347)***
Citizens Against Government Waste ***(348)***
Citizens' Scholarship Foundation of America ***(349)***
City Colleges of Chicago ***(349)***
City University ***(349)***
Claflin College ***(349)***
Clark & Weinstock, Inc. *(47)*
Clark Atlanta University ***(349)***
Classroom Publishers Ass'n ***(350)***
Clemson University ***(350)***
Cleveland State University - College of Urban Affairs ***(351)***
William M. Cloherty *(47)*
Close Up Foundation ***(351)***
Clover Park School District ***(351)***

Coalition for Maritime Education ***(354)***
Coalition of Higher Education Assistance Organizations ***(355)***
Coalition to Stop Gun Violence ***(356)***
The College Board ***(357)***
College of the Desert ***(357)***
College Parents of America ***(358)***
Collins & Company, Inc. ***(49)***
Columbia College Chicago ***(359)***
Columbia University/Institute for Learning Technologies ***(359)***
Columbus State College ***(359)***
Commission of Accredited Truck Driving Schools (CATDS) ***(360)***
Committee for Education Funding ***(361)***
Compaq Computer Corp. ***(363)***
Computer Data Systems, Inc. ***(364)***
Concerned Educators Against Forced Unionism ***(365)***
Concerned Women for America ***(365)***
Concord College ***(365)***
Conference of Educational Administrators of Schools and Programs for the Deaf ***(366)***
Congressional Economic Leadership Institute ***(366)***
Congressional Hispanic Caucus Institute (CHCI) ***(366)***
Conkling, Fiskum & McCormick ***(51)***
Connecticut Student Loan Foundation ***(367)***
Consortium for School Networking ***(368)***
Consortium for Worker Education ***(368)***
Consortium of Social Science Ass'ns ***(368)***
Consortium of Universities of the Washington Metropolitan Area ***(368)***
Consortium on Government Relations for Student Affairs ***(368)***
Construction Management Ass'n of America ***(368)***
Consumer Bankers Ass'n ***(368)***
Consumer Federation of America ***(369)***
Consumer Healthcare Products Ass'n ***(369)***
Contra Costa Community College District ***(370)***
Convergence Services, Inc. ***(52)***
Copeland, Lowery & Jacquez ***(52)***
Corporation for Business, Work and Learning ***(372)***
Council for American Private Education ***(374)***
Council for Basic Education ***(374)***
Council for Exceptional Children ***(374)***
Council for Internat'l Exchange of Scholars ***(374)***
Council for Opportunity in Education ***(374)***
Council of American Overseas Research Centers ***(375)***
Council of Chief State School Officers ***(375)***
Council of Colleges of Acupuncture and Oriental Medicine ***(375)***
Council of Graduate Schools ***(375)***
Council of Independent Colleges ***(375)***
Council of the Great City Schools ***(376)***
Council on Internat'l Educational Exchange ***(377)***
Council on Undergraduate Research ***(377)***
Coweta County (Georgia) School Board ***(377)***
CRT, Inc. ***(379)***
Curson Koopersmith Partners, Inc. ***(56)***
Cuyahoga Community College ***(380)***
Daemen College ***(381)***
DaimlerChrysler Corp. ***(381)***
Dalton & Dalton P.C. ***(382)***
Dance/USA ***(382)***
Davis O'Connell, Inc. ***(58)***
Davison Transport, Inc. ***(383)***
Day Care Ass'n of Tarrant County and Fort Worth Texas ***(383)***
Dayton, Ohio, Washington Office of the City of ***(383)***
Dean Blakey & Moskowitz ***(59)***
DePaul University ***(386)***
Detroit Public Schools ***(386)***
Detroit Public Television ***(386)***
Detroit, Michigan, Public School System of the County of ***(386)***
Devillier Communications ***(61)***
DeVry, Inc. ***(387)***
Dierman, Wortley, and Zola ***(62)***
Discovery Science Center ***(389)***
Distance Education and Training Council ***(389)***
Diversified Collection Services, Inc. ***(390)***
Doepken Keevican & Weiss ***(63)***
Dow, Lohnes & Albertson, PLLC ***(64)***
Dowling College ***(391)***
Downey McGrath Group, Inc. ***(64)***
The Duberstein Group, Inc. ***(65)***
Duncan, Weinberg, Genzer & Pembroke, P.C. ***(66)***
DuPont Agricultural Products ***(393)***
The Dutko Group, Inc. ***(68)***
Dykema Gossett PLLC ***(69)***
Earle Palmer Brown Public Relations ***(70)***
Earth University, Inc. ***(394)***
Easter Seals ***(395)***
Economics America ***(396)***
The Edison Project ***(397)***
EDS Corp. ***(398)***
Education Finance Council ***(398)***
Education Networks of America ***(398)***
Educational Testing Service ***(398)***
Educational Video Conferencing, Inc. ***(398)***
Edupoint.com ***(398)***
Embry-Riddle Aeronautical University ***(401)***
EMI Associates, Ltd. ***(71)***
Emory University, Department of Internat'l Health-PAMM, USAID ***(402)***
Empower America ***(402)***
Energy Cost Savings Council ***(403)***
English First, Inc. ***(403)***
Ervin Technical Associates, Inc. (ETA) ***(73)***
Ethics Resource Center Inc. ***(407)***
Evergreen Associates, Ltd. ***(74)***
F.B.A. ***(74)***
Family Communications, Inc. ***(410)***
Family Research Council, Inc. ***(411)***
Federal Advocacy for California Education ***(412)***
Federal Management Strategies, Inc. ***(75)***
Jack Ferguson Associates, Inc. ***(75)***
The Ferguson Group, LLC ***(76)***
Ferris State University ***(415)***
First Scientific Corp. ***(418)***
First Union Corp. ***(418)***
Fisher Consulting ***(77)***
Fleet Reserve Ass'n ***(418)***
R. G. Flippo and Associates, Inc. ***(77)***
Florida Atlantic University ***(419)***
Florida Community College of Jacksonville ***(419)***
Florida Department of Education ***(419)***
Florida Internat'l University ***(420)***
Florida State University ***(420)***
Florida State University System ***(420)***
Foley & Lardner ***(78)***
Food Research and Action Center ***(422)***
Franklin Institute ***(425)***
Friends of Higher Education Inc. ***(426)***
Fuller Theological Seminary ***(427)***
The Furman Group ***(80)***
Future Leaders of America ***(428)***
Gadsden State Community College ***(428)***
Gainesville, Florida, City of ***(428)***
Sara Garland (and Associates) ***(81)***
Gary, Indiana, Washington Office of the City of ***(429)***
Gateway, Inc. ***(430)***
General Conference of Seventh-day Adventists ***(431)***
General Motors Corp. ***(432)***
George Washington University, Office of Government Relations ***(434)***
Georgetown University-McDonough School of Business ***(434)***
Georgetown University-School of Nursing ***(434)***
Girl Scouts of the U.S.A. - Washington Office ***(435)***
Girls Incorporated ***(435)***
Golin/Harris Internat'l ***(84)***
GPC Internat'l ***(85)***
Jay Grant & Associates ***(85)***
Great Cities' Universities ***(439)***
Greater New York Automobile Dealers Ass'n ***(439)***
Greater Texas Student Loan Corp. ***(439)***
Greater Washington Board of Trade ***(439)***
Greenberg Traurig, LLP ***(86)***
John C. Grzebien ***(89)***
Guam, Washington Office of the Governor ***(442)***
Guinea, Secretary General of the Presidency of the Republic of ***(442)***
Hale and Dorr LLP ***(89)***
Hall, Green, Rupli, LLC ***(90)***
Hampshire College ***(444)***
Hampton University ***(444)***
Hannett & Associates ***(91)***
Harbor Branch Institute ***(444)***
Harcourt Inc. ***(444)***
John Harland Co. ***(444)***
Leslie Harris & Associates ***(91)***
Hawaii, State of ***(445)***
Health and Medicine Counsel of Washington ***(93)***
Hebrew Academy for Special Children ***(447)***
Law Office of Edward D. Heffernan ***(94)***
Heidepriem & Mager, Inc. ***(94)***
Helen Keller Nat'l Center for Deaf Blind Youths and Adults ***(448)***
Heritage Foundation ***(448)***
Heritage Harbor Museum ***(449)***
Higher Education Consortium for Special Education ***(449)***
Hispanic Ass'n of Colleges and Universities ***(450)***
Hogan & Hartson L.L.P. ***(96)***
Hohlt & Associates ***(98)***
Holland & Knight LLP ***(98)***
Houston Independent School District ***(453)***
Hudson Institute ***(454)***
Human Capital Resources ***(454)***
Robert R. Humphreys ***(101)***
Huntingdon College ***(455)***
Hyjek & Fix, Inc. ***(102)***
"I Have a Dream" Foundation ***(456)***
The Ickes & Enright Group ***(102)***
Ikon Public Affairs ***(102)***
Illinois Community College Board ***(457)***
Illinois State Board of Education ***(458)***
Independent Educational Consultants Ass'n ***(459)***
Indian Hills Community College ***(460)***
Indiana State University ***(460)***
Indiana, Office of the Governor of the State of ***(460)***
Infotech Strategies, Inc. ***(103)***
Institute for Entrepreneurship ***(463)***
The Institute for Higher Education Policy ***(463)***
Institute of Human and Machine Cognition ***(464)***
Institute of Simulation and Training ***(464)***
Institute on Religion and Public Policy ***(464)***
Intel Corp. ***(465)***
Internat'l Arid Lands Consortium ***(467)***
Internat'l Ass'n of Bridge, Structural, Ornamental and Reinforcing Iron Workers ***(467)***
Internat'l Brotherhood of Electrical Workers ***(469)***
Internat'l Business Machines Corp. ***(469)***
Internat'l Center for Clubhouse Development ***(469)***
Internat'l College ***(470)***
Internat'l Distance Learning ***(471)***
Internat'l Dyslexia Ass'n, The ***(471)***
Internat'l Reading Ass'n ***(474)***
Internat'l Research and Exchanges Board (IREX) ***(474)***
Internat'l Soc. for Technology in Education ***(475)***
Internat'l Technology Education Ass'n ***(475)***
Internat'l Union of Painters and Allied Trades ***(476)***
Internet Action PAC ***(476)***
Islamic Institute ***(479)***
Ivy Tech State College ***(480)***
Jackson State University ***(480)***
Jacksonville Chamber of Commerce ***(481)***
Jacksonville University, Davis College of Business ***(481)***
Jar-Mon Consultants, Inc. ***(105)***
JASON Foundation for Education ***(482)***
JCP Associates ***(105)***
Jefferson Consulting Group ***(105)***
Jefferson Government Relations, L.L.C. ***(106)***
Jefferson State Community College ***(482)***
Johnston & Associates, LLC ***(107)***
Jolly/Rissler, Inc. ***(108)***
Jones, Walker, Waechter, Poitevent, Carrere & Denegre, L.L.P. ***(108)***
Jorden Burt LLP ***(109)***
Joslin Diabetes Center ***(485)***

JRL Enterprises ***(485)***
Kaplan Companies, Inc. ***(486)***
KCTS ***(487)***
Kent State University ***(488)***
Kentucky, Commonwealth of ***(488)***
Kerrigan & Associates, Inc. *(112)*
Kessler & Associates Business Services, Inc. *(112)*
Kimberly Consulting, LLC *(113)*
Steven Kingsley *(113)*
Knoxville College ***(490)***
Labor Council for Latin American Advancement (LCLAA) ***(493)***
Laborers' Internat'l Union of North America ***(493)***
Lackawanna Junior College ***(494)***
Lackman & Associates, L.L.C. *(116)*
Lancit Media/Junior Net ***(494)***
Fern M. Lapidus *(116)*
Lasa, Monroig & Veve *(116)*
Lawler, Metzger & Milkman, LLC *(117)*
The Learning Disabilities Ass'n ***(497)***
Lebanese American University ***(497)***
Ledge Counsel *(118)*
Lee & Smith P.C. *(118)*
Lehigh University ***(498)***
Lewis-Burke Associates *(120)*
Lindesmith Center - Drug Policy Foundation ***(500)***
Lockheed Martin Corp. ***(501)***
Lockridge Grindal & Nauen, P.L.L.P. *(121)*
Logan College of Chiropractic ***(502)***
Long Island University ***(503)***
Long, Aldridge & Norman, LLP *(121)*
Los Alamitos Unified School District ***(503)***
Los Angeles Community College District ***(503)***
Los Angeles County Office of Education ***(504)***
Los Angeles Unified School District ***(504)***
Louisiana State University ***(504)***
Lovelace Respiratory Research Institute ***(504)***
Loyola College ***(505)***
Loyola University ***(505)***
Loyola University Health System ***(505)***
Loyola University of Chicago ***(505)***
Lucent Technologies ***(505)***
Lutheran Office for Governmental Affairs/Evangelical Lutheran Church in America ***(506)***
Lynn, Massachusetts, City of ***(506)***
M & R Strategic Services *(122)*
Madison Government Affairs *(123)*
Management Options, Inc. *(123)*
Manatt, Phelps & Phillips, LLP *(123)*
Manufacturers Alliance/MAPI Inc. ***(509)***
MARC Associates, Inc. *(124)*
Marine Corps Reserve Officers Ass'n ***(510)***
Marquette University ***(511)***
Virginia M. Mayer *(126)*
McDonald's Corp. ***(514)***
McGraw-Hill Cos., The ***(514)***
McGuireWoods L.L.P. *(130)*
Medical Lake School District ***(516)***
MENC: The Nat'l Ass'n for Music Education ***(518)***
Mendez University System, Ana G. ***(518)***
Merced, California, County of ***(518)***
Mercy Hospital of Des Moines, Iowa ***(518)***
Metcalf Federal Relations *(132)*
Mexican-American Legal Defense and Educational Fund ***(521)***
Meyers & Associates *(133)*
Miami Beach, Florida, City of ***(521)***
Miami Museum of Science & Space Transit Planetarium ***(521)***
Miami, Florida, City of ***(521)***
Miami-Dade Community College ***(521)***
Miami-Dade, Florida, County of ***(521)***
Michigan Technological University ***(522)***
Micronesia, Embassy of the Federated States of ***(522)***
Middlesex Community-Technical College ***(523)***
Military Impacted School Districts Ass'n ***(524)***
Miller & Co. *(134)*
Denny Miller McBee Associates *(134)*
Milwaukee, City of ***(524)***
Minot State University ***(525)***
Mitsubishi Research Institute ***(526)***
Susan Molinari, L.L.P. *(135)*
Montana State University ***(528)***
J. P. Morgan Chase & Co. ***(529)***
Morgan State University ***(529)***
Kay Allan Morrell, Attorney-at-Law *(137)*
Mort Community College ***(530)***
Moscow State University ***(530)***
Moss McGee Bradley & Foley *(137)*
Mount Sinai School of Medicine ***(531)***
Mount Vernon, City of ***(532)***
Muhlenberg College ***(532)***
Patrick M. Murphy & Associates *(138)*
Murray, Scheer, Montgomery, Tapia & O'Donnell *(139)*
Museum Campus Chicago ***(533)***
Music Educators Nat'l Conference ***(533)***
The MWW Group *(140)*
NAFSA: Ass'n of Internat'l Educators ***(534)***
Nat'l Abortion and Reproductive Rights Action League ***(535)***
Nat'l Accrediting Commission of Cosmetology Arts & Sciences, Inc. ***(535)***
Nat'l Alliance for the Mentally Ill ***(536)***
Nat'l Alliance of Sexual Assault Coalitions ***(537)***
Nat'l and Community Service Coalition ***(537)***
Nat'l Ass'n for Bilingual Education ***(537)***
Nat'l Ass'n for College Admission Counseling ***(537)***
Nat'l Ass'n for Equal Opportunity in Higher Education ***(537)***
Nat'l Ass'n for Gifted Children ***(537)***
Nat'l Ass'n for Sport and Physical Education ***(538)***
Nat'l Ass'n for the Advancement of Colored People, Washington Bureau ***(538)***
Nat'l Ass'n for the Education of Young Children ***(538)***
Nat'l Ass'n of Biology Teachers ***(539)***
Nat'l Ass'n of College and University Attorneys ***(540)***
Nat'l Ass'n of Community Health Centers ***(540)***
Nat'l Ass'n of Developmental Disabilities Councils ***(542)***
Nat'l Ass'n of Elementary School Principals ***(542)***
Nat'l Ass'n of Federally Impacted Schools ***(542)***
Nat'l Ass'n of Independent Colleges and Universities ***(544)***
Nat'l Ass'n of Minority Political Families, USA, Inc. ***(545)***
Nat'l Ass'n of Music Merchants ***(545)***
Nat'l Ass'n of Negro Business & Professional Women's Clubs, Inc. ***(546)***
Nat'l Ass'n of Nurse Practitioners in Women's Health ***(546)***
Nat'l Ass'n of Partners in Education ***(546)***
Nat'l Ass'n of Police Organizations ***(546)***
Nat'l Ass'n of Protection and Advocacy Systems (NAPAS) ***(547)***
Nat'l Ass'n of School Nurses ***(548)***
Nat'l Ass'n of School Psychologists ***(548)***
Nat'l Ass'n of Schools of Dance ***(548)***
Nat'l Ass'n of Schools of Music ***(548)***
Nat'l Ass'n of Schools of Theatre ***(549)***
Nat'l Ass'n of Secondary School Principals ***(549)***
Nat'l Ass'n of Service and Conservation Corps ***(549)***
Nat'l Ass'n of Social Workers ***(549)***
Nat'l Ass'n of State Boards of Education ***(549)***
Nat'l Ass'n of State Directors of Special Education ***(550)***
Nat'l Ass'n of State Directors of Vocational Technical Education Consortium ***(550)***
Nat'l Ass'n of State Universities and Land-Grant Colleges ***(550)***
Nat'l Ass'n of Student Financial Aid Administrators ***(550)***
Nat'l Ass'n of Student Personnel Administrators ***(550)***
Nat'l Ass'n to Protect Individual Rights ***(551)***
Nat'l Assembly of Health and Human Service Organizations ***(551)***
Nat'l Board for Professional Teaching Standards (NBPTS) ***(552)***
Nat'l Business Owners Ass'n ***(553)***
Nat'l Campaign for Hearing Health ***(554)***
Nat'l Center for Family Literacy ***(554)***
Nat'l Center for Learning Disabilities (NCLD) ***(554)***
Nat'l Center for Neighborhood Enterprise ***(555)***
Nat'l Center for Policy Analysis ***(555)***
Nat'l College ***(557)***
Nat'l College Access Network ***(557)***
Nat'l Collegiate Athletic Ass'n ***(557)***
Nat'l Community Education Ass'n ***(558)***
Nat'l Consumers League ***(558)***
Nat'l Coordinating Committee for the Promotion of History ***(559)***
Nat'l Council for Accreditation of Teacher Education ***(559)***
Nat'l Council for Languages and Internat'l Studies ***(559)***
Nat'l Council for the Social Studies ***(559)***
Nat'l Council of Higher Education Loan Programs ***(560)***
Nat'l Council of Jewish Women ***(560)***
Nat'l Council of La Raza ***(560)***
Nat'l Council of Negro Women ***(560)***
Nat'l Council of Teachers of Mathematics ***(560)***
Nat'l Education Ass'n of the U.S. ***(562)***
Nat'l Farmers Union (Farmers Educational & Co-operative Union of America) ***(563)***
Nat'l Federation of Republican Women ***(564)***
Nat'l Federation of State High School Ass'ns ***(564)***
Nat'l FFA Organization ***(564)***
Nat'l Forest Counties School Coalition ***(565)***
The Nat'l Foundation for Teaching Entrepreneurship ***(565)***
Nat'l Grange ***(566)***
Nat'l Head Start Ass'n ***(566)***
Nat'l Humanities Alliance ***(567)***
Nat'l Independent Private Schools Ass'n ***(568)***
Nat'l Indian Education Ass'n ***(568)***
Nat'l Industries for the Blind ***(568)***
Nat'l ITFS Ass'n ***(569)***
Nat'l Legal Center for the Public Interest ***(570)***
Nat'l Liberty Museum ***(570)***
Nat'l Mentoring Partnership, Inc. ***(571)***
Nat'l Migrant Head Start Ass'n ***(571)***
Nat'l Military Family Ass'n ***(571)***
Nat'l Puerto Rican Coalition ***(575)***
Nat'l Rehabilitation Ass'n ***(575)***
Nat'l Rehabilitation Information Center ***(575)***
Nat'l Research Center for College and University Admissions ***(575)***
Nat'l Science Teachers Ass'n ***(577)***
Nat'l Strategy Information Center ***(579)***
Nat'l Taxpayers Union ***(579)***
Nat'l Underground Railroad Freedom Center ***(580)***
Nat'l Women's History Museum ***(581)***
Nat'l Women's Law Center ***(581)***
Nat'l Writing Project ***(581)***
Natural History Museum of Los Angeles County ***(582)***
Navajo Nation ***(582)***
NetSchools ***(584)***
New America Alliance ***(585)***
New American School ***(585)***
New College ***(585)***
New Mexico State Office of Research & Development ***(586)***
New Mexico State University ***(586)***
New Mexico State University, Department of Agriculture ***(586)***
New Mexico State University, Department of Engineering ***(586)***
New Orleans Environmental Systems Foundation ***(586)***
New York City, New York, Council of ***(587)***
The New York Historical Soc. ***(587)***
New York Institute for Special Education ***(587)***
New York Institute of Technology ***(587)***
New York Public Library ***(587)***
New York University ***(588)***
Newark, New Jersey, City of ***(588)***
Nike, Inc. ***(590)***
Norfolk, Virginia, City of ***(591)***
North Carolina, Washington Office of the State of ***(593)***
North Dakota State University ***(593)***
North Dakota, Governor's Office of the State of ***(593)***
North Slope Borough, Alaska ***(593)***
Northeastern University ***(594)***
Northern Michigan University ***(594)***

Northwest Regional Education Laboratory ***(595)***
Nottoway, Virginia, County of ***(596)***
Oakland, California, City of ***(598)***
O'Bryon & Co. *(144)*
O'Connor & Hannan, L.L.P. *(144)*
Office of Hawaiian Affairs ***(599)***
O'Neill, Athy & Casey, P.C. *(147)*
Optical Soc. of America ***(601)***
Oregon Garden Foundation ***(603)***
Oregon Graduate Institute of Science and Technology ***(603)***
Pacific Islands Washington Office *(148)*
Pacific Science Center ***(606)***
Palm Desert, California, City of ***(606)***
Palmer Chiropractic University ***(606)***
Palumbo & Cerrell, Inc. *(149)*
Parent Centers FYI ***(608)***
Parry, Romani, DeConcini & Symms *(149)*
Patton Boggs, LLP *(150)*
Patton Boggs, LLP ***(609)***
Paul Quinn College ***(610)***
Bradford A. Penney *(154)*
Pennington BioMedical Research Center ***(611)***
Pennsylvania Higher Education Assistance Agency ***(611)***
People Advancing Christian Education (PACE) ***(611)***
People for the American Way ***(612)***
Peoria, Arizona, City of ***(612)***
Perkins School for the Blind ***(612)***
Deborah L. Perry *(155)*
The Peterson Group *(155)*
Pfizer, Inc. ***(613)***
Phoenix, Arizona, City of ***(616)***
Charles L. Pizer *(156)*
Please Touch Museum, The Children's Museum of Philadelphia ***(619)***
Podesta/Mattoon *(158)*
Policy Directions, Inc. *(158)*
Policy Impact Communications *(159)*
Polity Consulting *(159)*
Potomac Group *(160)*
Powers Pyles Sutter & Verville, PC *(161)*
Preston Gates Ellis & Rouvelas Meeds LLP *(162)*
Professional Beauty Federation PAC ***(625)***
Progressive Policy Institute ***(626)***
Psychological Corp. ***(628)***
Public Broadcasting Service ***(628)***
Public Service Research Foundation ***(629)***
Public Strategies, Inc. *(165)*
Q-ZAB Coalition ***(630)***
QSP Inc. ***(630)***
R. Duffy Wall and Associates ***(631)***
Barbara Raimondo *(165)*
Robert A. Rapoza Associates *(165)*
Pamela Ray-Strunk and Associates *(166)*
The Readnet Foundation ***(634)***
Rebuild America's Schools ***(634)***
Recording for the Blind and Dyslexic, Inc. ***(634)***
Robert L. Redding *(166)*
Law Office of Paige E. Reffe *(167)*
Regents College ***(635)***
Russ Reid Co. *(167)*
Republican Jewish Coalition ***(637)***
Resources and Instruction for Staff Excellence, Inc. ***(638)***
John J. Rhodes *(169)*
Riggs Government Relations Consulting LLC *(169)*
Riverdeep Inc. ***(640)***
Riverside County Schools ***(640)***
Liz Robbins Associates *(169)*
Rooney Group Internat'l, Inc. *(171)*
Peter J. Rose *(172)*
Rosenbaum Trust ***(642)***
Ross University School of Medicine in Dominica ***(642)***
Caleb S. Rossiter *(172)*
Timothy R. Rupli and Associates, Inc. *(173)*
Rutgers University ***(644)***
Sabre Inc. ***(644)***
Sacramento-Potomac Consulting, Inc. *(174)*
Sacred Heart University ***(645)***
Sagamore Associates, Inc. *(174)*
Sallie Mae, Inc. ***(646)***
Salt Lake City Olympic Organizing Committee ***(646)***
Sam Houston University ***(647)***
San Diego State University Foundation ***(647)***
San Diego, California, City of ***(647)***
San Dieguito School Transportation Cooperative ***(647)***
Scholastic, Inc. ***(651)***
School of Visual Arts ***(652)***
Science Applications Internat'l Corp. (SAIC) ***(652)***
The Science Coalition ***(652)***
Sea Grant Ass'n ***(653)***
Security on Campus, Inc. ***(654)***
Sellery Associates, Inc. *(177)*
Serono Laboratories, Inc. ***(655)***
Service Employees Internat'l Union ***(656)***
Seton Hill College ***(656)***
Shaw Pittman *(177)*
Sheet Metal Workers' Internat'l Ass'n ***(657)***
Shelby, Tennessee, County of ***(657)***
Simon Strategies/Mindbeam *(181)*
Siscorp ***(660)***
SLM Holding Corp. ***(661)***
E. Del Smith and Co. *(183)*
Smith Dawson & Andrews, Inc. *(183)*
Smith, Bucklin and Associates, Inc. *(184)*
Smith, Hinaman & Associates *(184)*
Soc. for Industrial & Applied Mathematics ***(662)***
Soc. for Marketing Professional Services ***(662)***
Software & Information Industry Ass'n (SIIA) ***(664)***
Solar Energy Research and Education Foundation ***(665)***
The Solomon Group, LLC *(185)*
SonoSite ***(665)***
Southeast Missouri State University ***(667)***
Southwest Texas State University ***(668)***
Space Explorers Inc. ***(669)***
Space Media ***(669)***
The Spectrum Group *(186)*
Richard L. Spees, Inc. *(186)*
Spelman College ***(670)***
Spina Bifida Ass'n of America ***(670)***
Sporting Goods Manufacturers Ass'n ***(670)***
Springfield, Oregon, School District #19 ***(670)***
Springs Industries, Inc. ***(671)***
Squire, Sanders & Dempsey L.L.P. *(187)*
St. Augustine College ***(671)***
St. Joseph University ***(671)***
St. Matthew's University School of Medicine ***(672)***
St. Petersburg Community College ***(672)***
State University of New York at Albany ***(673)***
Steel Manufacturers Ass'n ***(674)***
Stillman College ***(674)***
Stony Brook Foundation ***(675)***
Strategic Horizons Advisors, L.L.C. *(189)*
Strategic Impact, Inc. *(189)*
Student Loan Finance Corp. ***(675)***
Student Loan Funding Corp. ***(675)***
Sumlin Associates *(190)*
Sun Microsystems ***(676)***
SUNY Empire State College ***(677)***
Suomi College ***(677)***
Syracuse University ***(679)***
Talladega College ***(680)***
Teach for America ***(682)***
Temple University ***(683)***
Tequity ***(684)***
Texas A&M Research Foundation ***(684)***
Texas Chiropractic College ***(684)***
Texas College ***(684)***
Thiemann Aitken Vohra & Rutledge, L.L.C. *(194)*
Thompson Publishing, Inc. ***(686)***
TI Group Inc. ***(686)***
Timmons and Co., Inc. *(195)*
William J. Tobin and Associates *(195)*
Touro College ***(688)***
Traditional Values Coalition ***(689)***
Travelocity.com ***(691)***
Troy State University - Montgomery ***(692)***
Tulane University ***(693)***
Christopher A.G. Tulou *(196)*
U.S. Basic Skills ***(695)***
U.S. Disabled Athletes Fund ***(696)***
U.S. English, Inc. ***(696)***
U.S. Family Network ***(696)***
U.S. Public Interest Research Group ***(697)***
U.S. Space & Rocket Center ***(697)***
U.S. Strategies Corp. *(197)*
UNIPAC Service Corp. ***(699)***
United Automobile, Aerospace and Agricultural Implement Workers of America (UAW) ***(700)***
United Cerebral Palsy Ass'n ***(700)***
United Methodist Church General Board of Church and Society ***(702)***
United Negro College Fund, Inc. ***(702)***
United States Coast Guard Chief Petty Officers Ass'n ***(703)***
United States Education Finance Corp. ***(703)***
United States Student Ass'n ***(704)***
Universities Research Ass'n ***(705)***
University College Dublin ***(705)***
University Continuing Education Ass'n ***(705)***
University Health Associates, Inc. ***(705)***
University of Akron ***(705)***
University of Alabama - Huntsville ***(705)***
University of Alabama System ***(705)***
University of Alaska ***(705)***
University of California at Riverside ***(706)***
University of California, Office of Federal Government Relations ***(706)***
University of Cincinnati ***(706)***
University of Colorado, Office of the President ***(706)***
University of Connecticut ***(706)***
University of Georgia ***(706)***
University of Houston ***(706)***
University of Louisville ***(706)***
University of Medicine and Dentistry of New Jersey ***(706)***
University of Miami ***(706)***
University of Mississippi ***(706)***
University of Mississippi Medical Center ***(706)***
University of Nebraska ***(706)***
University of Nevada - Las Vegas ***(707)***
University of Nevada - Reno ***(707)***
University of New Orleans Foundation ***(707)***
University of North Carolina at Chapel Hill ***(707)***
University of North Carolina at Greensboro ***(707)***
University of North Dakota ***(707)***
University of Notre Dame ***(707)***
University of Oklahoma ***(707)***
University of Phoenix ***(707)***
University of Redlands ***(707)***
University of South Alabama ***(707)***
University of South Florida Research Foundation ***(707)***
University of Southern California ***(707)***
University of Southwestern Louisiana ***(707)***
University of Texas ***(707)***
University of Tulsa ***(708)***
University of Utah ***(708)***
University of Vermont ***(708)***
University of Virginia ***(708)***
University of Washington ***(708)***
University of West Florida ***(708)***
University System of Maryland ***(708)***
USA Funds, Inc. ***(709)***
USS Wisconsin Foundation ***(710)***
Utah State University ***(710)***
Valencia Community College ***(711)***
Valente Lopatin & Schulze *(198)*
Van Ness Feldman, P.C. *(199)*
Van Scoyoc Associates, Inc. ***(711)***
Van Scoyoc Associates, Inc. *(200)*
Vanderbilt University ***(712)***
The Vandervort Group, LLC ***(712)***
Vanguard University ***(712)***
Verner, Liipfert, Bernhard, McPherson and Hand, Chartered *(202)*
Very Special Arts ***(714)***
Vinson & Elkins L.L.P. *(204)*
Viohl and Associates, Inc. *(205)*
Virginia Commonwealth University ***(716)***
Virginia Living Museum ***(716)***
Virginia Polytechnic Institute and State University ***(716)***
Virginia Tech Intellectual Properties, Inc. ***(716)***
Voorhees College ***(717)***
R. Duffy Wall and Associates *(205)*

Walton Enterprises ***(718)***
Washington Alliance Group, Inc. *(206)*
Washington and Jefferson College ***(719)***
Washington Liaison Group, LLC *(209)*
Washington Resource Associates *(209)*
Washington State Impact Aid Ass'n ***(720)***
Washington Workshops ***(720)***
Wayland Academy ***(722)***
Wayne State University ***(722)***
West Hills Community College District ***(723)***
Jane West *(211)*
WETA ***(725)***
The Wexler Group *(211)*
Wheat & Associates, Inc. *(212)*
Wheelock College ***(726)***
Whitten & Diamond *(213)*
Widmeyer Communications, Inc. *(214)*
Wilberforce University ***(726)***
Wiley, Rein & Fielding *(214)*
William Tyndale College ***(727)***
Williams & Jensen, P.C. *(215)*
Winslow Press ***(728)***
Wise & Associates *(220)*
Wittenburg University ***(729)***
WNVT/WNVC ***(729)***
Women Officials in NACo ***(729)***
Women's Policy, Inc. ***(729)***
The Work Colleges ***(730)***
World Government of World Citizens ***(730)***
World Service Authority ***(731)***
Youth For Understanding Internat'l Exchange ***(733)***
Youth Guidance of Chicago ***(733)***
ZapMe! Corp. ***(734)***
ZERO TO THREE/Nat'l Center for Infants, Toddlers, and Families ***(734)***

Energy/Nuclear (ENG)

AARP (American Ass'n of Retired Persons) ***(224)***
ABB, Inc. ***(225)***
Abitibi Consolidated Sales Corp. ***(225)***
The Accord Group *(5)*
ADA Consulting Services ***(227)***
ADA Consulting Services *(5)*
Adams and Reese LLP *(5)*
Adroit Systems Inc. ***(228)***
The Advocacy Group *(6)*
AEI Resources ***(229)***
AFL-CIO (American Federation of Labor and Congress of Industrial Organizations) ***(231)***
AFL-CIO - Maritime Trades Department ***(231)***
Agrium Inc. ***(232)***
Aiken and Edgenfield Counties, South Carolina, Economic Development Partnership of ***(233)***
Air Products and Chemicals, Inc. ***(234)***
Air-Conditioning and Refrigeration Institute ***(234)***
Akin, Gump, Strauss, Hauer & Feld, L.L.P. *(8)*
Alaska Rainforest Campaign ***(237)***
Alcan Aluminum Corp. ***(237)***
Alcoa Inc. ***(237)***
Alexander Strategy Group ***(238)***
Alexander Strategy Group *(11)*
Alliance for Competitive Electricity ***(239)***
Alliance Pipeline, L.P. ***(241)***
Alliance to Save Energy ***(241)***
Alliant Energy ***(241)***
Alpine Group, Inc. *(11)*
Alyeska Pipeline Service Co. ***(242)***
Ameren Services ***(243)***
American Ass'n of Blacks in Energy ***(246)***
American Automotive Leasing Ass'n ***(250)***
American Bakers Ass'n ***(250)***
American Bioenergy Ass'n ***(251)***
American Boiler Manufacturers Ass'n ***(251)***
American Chemistry Council ***(252)***
American Council for an Energy-Efficient Economy ***(255)***
American Electric Power Co. ***(257)***
American Foundrymen's Soc. ***(260)***
American Gas Ass'n ***(261)***
American Gas Cooling Center ***(261)***
American Geophysical Union ***(261)***
American Iron and Steel Institute ***(265)***
American Jewish Committee ***(265)***
American Methanol Institute ***(268)***
American Museum of Natural History ***(268)***
American Nuclear Insurers ***(268)***
American Petroleum Institute ***(269)***
American Physical Soc. ***(270)***
American Portland Cement Alliance ***(270)***
American Public Power Ass'n ***(272)***
American Ref-Fuel ***(272)***
American Teleservices Ass'n ***(279)***
American Wind Energy Ass'n ***(280)***
Americans for Affordable Electricity ***(281)***
Americans for Equitable Climate Solutions ***(281)***
Americans for Tax Reform ***(282)***
Anadarko Petroleum Corp. ***(283)***
Archimedes Technology Group ***(287)***
ARCO Products Co. ***(287)***
Arctic Power ***(288)***
Arctic Resources Co. ***(288)***
Arent Fox Kintner Plotkin & Kahn, PLLC *(14)*
Arizona Power Authority ***(288)***
Arms Control Ass'n ***(289)***
Ashland Inc. ***(290)***
Ass'n of Home Appliance Manufacturers ***(296)***
The Atlantic Co. ***(302)***
ATOFINA ***(302)***
Auburn, Avilla, Bluffton, Columbia City and Other Municipalities of Indiana ***(302)***
Austin, Texas, City of ***(303)***
Baker Botts, L.L.P. *(20)*
Michael Baker Corp. ***(306)***
Baker Electromotive, Inc. ***(306)***
Baker, Donelson, Bearman & Caldwell, P.C. *(21)*
Balch & Bingham LLP *(21)*
Ball Janik, LLP *(22)*
Ballard Power Systems ***(306)***
Michael F. Barrett, Jr. *(24)*
Barrick Goldstrike Mines, Inc. ***(308)***
Basin Electric Power Cooperative ***(308)***
Battelle ***(309)***
Battelle Memorial Institute ***(309)***
Bayer Corp. ***(309)***
The Beacon Group Energy Funds ***(310)***
Frank Beam and Co. ***(310)***
Bechtel Group, Inc. ***(310)***
Vikki Bell *(25)*
Bellingham, Washington, City of ***(311)***
BellSouth Corp. ***(311)***
Bergen, New York, Village of ***(311)***
Berkshire Inc. *(26)*
Bethlehem Steel Corp. ***(312)***
BHP (USA) Inc. ***(313)***
Leon G. Billings, Inc. *(27)*
Ray Billups *(27)*
Biomedical Research Foundation of Northwest Louisiana ***(314)***
BKSH & Associates *(28)*
Blackfeet Tribe of Montana ***(315)***
Richard W. Bliss *(29)*
BNFL, Inc. ***(316)***
BOH Environmental, L.L.C. ***(317)***
Bond & Company, Inc. *(30)*
Boston Edison Co. ***(318)***
BP Amoco Corp. ***(319)***
Bracewell & Patterson, L.L.P. *(30)*
Robert M. Brandon and Associates *(32)*
Breakthrough Technologies Institute ***(319)***
Brickfield, Burchette, Ritts & Stone *(32)*
Bristol Group, Inc. *(32)*
Bristol-Myers Squibb Co. ***(320)***
British Columbia Hydro and Power Authority ***(321)***
British Nuclear Fuels plc ***(321)***
Brown and Company, Inc. *(33)*
Brownstein Hyatt & Farber, P.C. *(33)*
Broydrick & Associates *(33)*
Burlington Northern Santa Fe Railway ***(324)***
Burlington Resources Oil & Gas Co. ***(324)***
Burns and Roe Enterprises, Inc. ***(324)***
Business Council for Sustainable Energy ***(324)***
Butera & Andrews *(34)*
C F Industries, Inc. ***(325)***
Caithness Energy, LLC ***(326)***
California Independent Petroleum Ass'n ***(327)***
California State Lands Commission ***(327)***
California Urban Water Conservation Council ***(327)***
Calpine Corp. ***(328)***
CALSTART ***(328)***
CAMECO Corp. ***(328)***
Canadian Electricity Ass'n ***(329)***
Canberra Packard BioScience ***(330)***
Capital Consultants Corp. *(37)*
Capitol Associates, Inc. *(37)*
Capitol Counsel Group, L.L.C. *(38)*
Capitol Link, Inc. *(39)*
Caraustar ***(331)***
Cargill Dow ***(331)***
Robert E. Carlstrom *(40)*
The Carmen Group *(40)*
Bill Carney & Co. *(41)*
Cascade Associates *(41)*
Cassidy & Associates, Inc. *(42)*
Catamount Energy Corp. ***(333)***
Caterpillar Inc. ***(333)***
Celanese Government Relations Office ***(334)***
Cement Kiln Recycling Coalition ***(335)***
Central Montana Electric Power Cooperative, Inc. ***(339)***
Central Soya Co. ***(339)***
Central Virginia Electric Cooperative, Inc. ***(339)***
CH2M Hill ***(340)***
Chamber of Commerce of the U.S.A. ***(340)***
Chevron, U.S.A. ***(342)***
Cinergy Corp. ***(347)***
CITGO Petroleum Corp. ***(347)***
Citizens Against Government Waste ***(348)***
Citizens Against Research Bans ***(348)***
Citizens for State Power ***(348)***
City Public Service ***(349)***
Clark & Weinstock, Inc. *(47)*
Clayton, Dover, Lewes, Middletown, Milford, Newark, NewCastle, Seaford and Smyrna, Delaware, Municipalities of ***(350)***
Clean Air Now ***(350)***
Clean Energy Group ***(350)***
Clean Fuels Development Coalition ***(350)***
The Climate Council, ***(351)***
Climate Institute ***(351)***
Coal Utilization Research Council ***(352)***
Coalition for Fair Competition in Rural Markets ***(353)***
Coalition for Reliable Energy ***(354)***
COGEMA, Inc. ***(357)***
Coleman Powermate ***(357)***
College Station, Texas, City of ***(358)***
Collier Shannon Scott, PLLC *(48)*
Colling Swift & Hynes *(49)*
Colorado River Energy Distributors Ass'n ***(358)***
Colorado Springs Utilities ***(359)***
Columbia Falls Aluminum Co. ***(359)***
Columbia Natural Resources ***(359)***
Communications Training Analysis Corp. (C-TAC) ***(362)***
Conkling, Fiskum & McCormick *(51)*
Consolidated Edison Co. of New York ***(367)***
Consortium for Plant Biotechnology Research ***(368)***
Consumer Energy Council of America Research Foundation ***(369)***
Consumer Federation of America ***(369)***
Consumers Union of the United States ***(369)***
Continental Cement Co., Inc. ***(370)***
Continental Teves ***(370)***
Contractors Internat'l Group on Nuclear Liability ***(370)***
Cooler Heads Coalition ***(371)***
Coors Brewing Company ***(371)***
Copeland, Lowery & Jacquez *(52)*
Corn Belt Energy Corp. ***(372)***
Cottone and Huggins Group *(53)*
Council for a Livable World Education Fund ***(373)***
Council for Conservation and Reinvestment of OCS Revenue ***(374)***
Council of Industrial Boiler Owners (CIBO) ***(375)***
Council on Radionuclides and Radiopharmaceuticals (CORAR) ***(377)***
Council on Superconductivity for American Competitiveness ***(377)***
The Coursen Group *(53)*

Covanta Energy Corporation *(377)*
Credit Suisse First Boston Corp. *(378)*
Crowell & Moring LLP *(55)*
Crown Central Petroleum Corp. *(379)*
CSA America, Inc. *(379)*
D3 Internat'l Energy, LLC *(381)*
DAG Petroleum *(381)*
DaimlerChrysler Corp. *(381)*
Dames & Moore *(382)*
Mary E. Davis *(57)*
Day & Zimmermann, Inc. *(383)*
DCH Technology Inc. *(383)*
The DCS Group *(59)*
Delaware Municipal Electric Corp. (DEMEC) *(384)*
Delta Petroleum Corp. *(385)*
George H. Denison *(60)*
Thomas J. Dennis *(61)*
Desert Research Institute *(386)*
Devon Energy Corp. *(387)*
Dickstein Shapiro Morin & Oshinsky LLP *(61)*
Distributed Power Coalition of America *(390)*
Domestic Petroleum Council *(390)*
Dominion Resources, Inc. *(391)*
The Dow Chemical Co. *(391)*
Downey McGrath Group, Inc. *(392)*
Downey McGrath Group, Inc. *(64)*
Dr. John V. Dugan, Jr. *(66)*
Duke Energy *(392)*
Duke Solutions *(393)*
Duncan, Weinberg, Genzer & Pembroke, P.C. *(66)*
Dunn-Padre, Inc. *(393)*
DuPont *(393)*
Durante Associates *(68)*
The Dutko Group, Inc. *(68)*
Dynegy, Inc. *(394)*
E.ON North America, Inc. *(394)*
Earle Palmer Brown Public Relations *(70)*
Earth, Energy & Environment *(394)*
East Texas Electric Cooperative *(395)*
Eastman Chemical Co. *(395)*
Eclipse Energy Systems, Inc./Insyte, Inc. *(396)*
Edison Electric Institute *(397)*
Edison Internat'l *(397)*
EG&G *(398)*
El Paso Corporation *(399)*
Electric Consumers Alliance *(400)*
The Electric Vehicle Ass'n of the Americas (EVAA) *(400)*
ElectriCities of North Carolina, Inc. *(400)*
Electricity Consumers Resource Council (ELCON) *(400)*
Electro Energy, Inc. *(400)*
Electromagnetic Energy Ass'n *(400)*
EMI Associates, Ltd. *(71)*
Energy Affairs Administration *(403)*
Energy and Environment Coalition *(403)*
Energy Communities Alliance, Inc. *(403)*
Energy Conservation Program, Inc. *(403)*
Energy Contractors Price-Anderson Group *(403)*
Energy Cost Savings Council *(403)*
Energy Northwest *(403)*
Energy Programs Consortium *(403)*
EnerStar Power Corp. *(403)*
EnerTech Industries Inc. *(403)*
Enron Corp. *(403)*
Entergy Corp. *(404)*
Entergy Services, Inc. *(404)*
Envirocare of Utah, Inc. *(404)*
EnviroPower *(405)*
EOP Group, Inc. *(72)*
Equitable Resources Energy Co. *(406)*
Erin Engineering and Research, Inc. *(406)*
Ernst & Young LLP *(72)*
Ervin Technical Associates, Inc. (ETA) *(73)*
Eugene Water and Electric Board *(407)*
Exelon Corp. *(409)*
Export Council for Energy Efficiency *(409)*
Express Pipeline Partnership and Platte Pipeline Co. *(409)*
Exxon Mobil Corp. *(409)*
EZ's Solutions, Inc. *(74)*
Federation of Electric Power Cos. of Japan *(414)*
The Ferguson Group, LLC *(76)*
The Fertilizer Institute *(415)*
Fibrowatt, Inc. *(416)*
Fierce and Isakowitz *(76)*
FirstEnergy Co. *(418)*
Fleishman-Hillard, Inc *(77)*
Florida Municipal Power Agency *(420)*
Florida Power and Light Co. *(420)*
Florida State University System *(420)*
Fluor Corp. *(420)*
FMC Corp. *(420)*
Foley & Lardner *(78)*
Ford Motor Co. *(422)*
Foster Wheeler Corp. *(424)*
Foster Wheeler Environmental Corp. *(424)*
Framatome, S.A. *(424)*
Freeport, New York, Electric Department of the Village of *(425)*
Douglas Ward Freitag *(79)*
Fried, Frank, Harris, Shriver & Jacobson *(80)*
Fuel Cell Energy, Inc. *(427)*
Fuel Cell Power Ass'n *(427)*
Fuel Cells for Transportation *(427)*
Fuels Management Inc. *(427)*
Gallagher, Boland and Meiburger *(80)*
Gallant Co. *(81)*
Garden State Paper Co., Inc. *(429)*
Sara Garland (and Associates) *(81)*
Gary-Williams Energy Corp. *(429)*
Gas Processors Ass'n *(429)*
Gas Research Institute *(429)*
Gas Technology Institute *(429)*
Gas Turbine Ass'n, Inc. *(429)*
GE Nuclear Energy *(430)*
GE Power Systems *(430)*
General Atomics *(431)*
General Electric Co. *(432)*
General Electric Industrial & Power Systems *(432)*
General Motors Corp. *(432)*
Georgia-Pacific Corp. *(434)*
Geothermal Energy Ass'n *(434)*
Geothermal Heat Pump Consortium *(434)*
Geothermal Resources Ass'n *(434)*
Giant Industries, Inc. *(435)*
Global Climate Coalition *(436)*
Global Policy Group, Inc. *(83)*
Goldendale Aluminum *(437)*
Goodman Manufacturing Co., L.P. *(437)*
Goodstein & Associates *(84)*
GPC Internat'l *(85)*
Greenberg Traurig, LLP *(86)*
Greenport, New York, Village Electric Department of *(440)*
Gridley, California, City of/Northern California Power Agency *(440)*
J. Steven Griles & Associates *(88)*
Guam, Washington Office of the Governor *(442)*
Guinea, Secretary General of the Presidency of the Republic of *(442)*
Haake and Associates *(89)*
Hagerstown, Maryland, Municipal Electric Light Plant of *(443)*
Hall, Green, Rupli, LLC *(90)*
Halliburton/Brown & Root *(443)*
Martin G. Hamberger & Associates *(91)*
Katherine Hamilton *(91)*
Harmon & Wilmot, L.L.P. *(91)*
Hartke & Hartke *(92)*
Hawaii, Department of Business and Economic Development of the State of *(445)*
Hawaiian Electric Co. *(445)*
Health Physics Soc. *(446)*
Hogan & Hartson L.L.P. *(96)*
Hohlt & Associates *(98)*
Holland & Knight LLP *(98)*
Holyoke Department of Gas and Electricity *(451)*
Honeywell Internat'l, Inc. *(452)*
Hooper Owen & Winburn *(99)*
Hoosier Energy Rural Electric Cooperative, Inc. *(452)*
Christopher C. Horner *(100)*
Oliver James Horton *(100)*
Huntsman Corp. *(455)*
Hydro-Quebec *(456)*
Hydrocarbon Technologies Inc. *(456)*
Hydroelectric Licensing Reform Task Force *(456)*
Ibex *(456)*
ICF Consulting *(457)*
Idaho Energy Authority, Inc. *(457)*
Idaho Power Co. *(457)*
Imperial Irrigation District *(458)*
Independent Electrical Contractors, Inc. *(459)*
Independent Petroleum Ass'n of America *(459)*
Indiana and Michigan Municipal Distributors Ass'n *(460)*
Industrial Customers of Northwest Utilities *(461)*
Information Resources, Inc. *(461)*
Information Trust *(462)*
Institute for Science and Internat'l Security *(464)*
Institute of Electrical and Electronics Engineers, Inc. *(464)*
Institute on Religion and Public Policy *(464)*
Integrated Building and Construction Solutions *(465)*
Integrated Waste Services Ass'n *(465)*
Inter-Associates, Inc. *(103)*
Inter-Associates, Inc. *(466)*
Internat'l Ass'n of Bridge, Structural, Ornamental and Reinforcing Iron Workers *(467)*
Internat'l Ass'n of Drilling Contractors *(467)*
Internat'l Brotherhood of Electrical Workers *(469)*
Internat'l Brotherhood of Teamsters *(469)*
Internat'l Business Machines Corp. *(469)*
Internat'l Cadmium Ass'n *(469)*
Internat'l Federation of Professional and Technical Engineers *(471)*
Internat'l Lead Zinc Research Organization, Inc. (ILZRO) *(473)*
Internat'l Paper *(473)*
Interstate Natural Gas Ass'n of America *(477)*
IPALCO Enterprises, Inc./Indianapolis Power & Light Co. *(478)*
IT Group, Inc. *(479)*
Itera Internat'l Energy Consultants *(480)*
ITRON, Inc. *(480)*
ITT Conoflow *(480)*
Jacksonville Electric Authority *(481)*
Jacobs Engineering Group Inc. *(481)*
Jamestown, New York, Board of Public Utilities *(481)*
Japan Automobile Standards Internat'l Center *(481)*
Japan Nuclear Cycle Development Institute *(482)*
Jefferson Parish Council *(482)*
Johnson Co. *(107)*
Johnson Controls, Inc. *(484)*
Johnston & Associates, LLC *(107)*
Jones, Walker, Waechter, Poitevent, Carrere & Denegre, L.L.P. *(108)*
Jorden Burt LLP *(109)*
Kaiser Aluminum & Chemical Corp. *(485)*
Kaiser-Hill Co., L.L.C. *(486)*
Kanner & Associates *(110)*
Kaye Scholer LLP *(110)*
Kellogg Brown and Root *(487)*
Kennecott/Borax *(488)*
Kent & O'Connor, Inc. *(112)*
Kerr-McGee Corp. *(488)*
KeySpan Energy *(489)*
Kimberly Consulting, LLC *(113)*
Kimberly-Clark Corp. *(489)*
The Kinetics Group *(489)*
King & Spalding *(113)*
Kings River Interests *(489)*
Knoxville Utilities Board *(490)*
Kogovsek & Associates *(114)*
Kutak Rock LLP *(115)*
Laguna Beach, California, City of *(494)*
Lee Lane *(116)*
Large Public Power Council *(495)*
Las Vegas, Nevada, City of *(495)*
Law Office of Zel E. Lipsen *(496)*
Bob Lawrence & Associates *(496)*
League of Women Voters of the United States *(497)*
LeBoeuf, Lamb, Greene & MacRae L.L.P. *(117)*
LegisLaw *(118)*
Lennox Internat'l *(498)*
Leonard B. Levine & Associates *(119)*
Lewis-Burke Associates *(120)*
Liebman & Associates, Inc. *(120)*
Lighthouse Energy Group LLC *(120)*
Eli Lilly and Co. *(499)*

Law Office of Zel E. Lipsen *(120)*
The Livingston Group, LLC *(120)*
Lockheed Martin Corp. ***(501)***
Lockheed Martin Hanford ***(502)***
Lockheed Martin Naval Electronics Surveillance Systems ***(502)***
Longhorn Pipeline ***(503)***
Louisiana State University ***(504)***
Lovelace Respiratory Research Institute ***(504)***
Loyola University ***(505)***
The LTV Corp. ***(505)***
Lubbock, Texas, City of ***(505)***
M-S-R Public Power Agency ***(506)***
Mack Trucks, Inc. ***(506)***
Madison Gas & Electric Co. ***(507)***
Madison Government Affairs *(123)*
Management Options, Inc. *(123)*
Manatt, Phelps & Phillips, LLP *(123)*
Manufacturers Alliance/MAPI Inc. ***(509)***
Marshall Islands Nuclear Claims Tribunal ***(511)***
Martinez and Curtis ***(511)***
Massena, New York, Town of ***(512)***
Mayer, Brown & Platt *(126)*
Charlie McBride Associates, Inc. *(127)*
Barbara T. McCall Associates *(127)*
McClure, Gerard & Neuenschwander, Inc. *(127)*
McDermott Internat'l, Inc./Babcock & Wilcox ***(514)***
McGuireWoods L.L.P. *(130)*
Mehl, Griffin & Bartek Ltd. *(132)*
Memphis Light, Gas and Water Division ***(517)***
Merant PVCS ***(518)***
The Metropolitan Water District of Southern California ***(521)***
Meyers & Associates *(133)*
Michigan Consolidated Gas Co. ***(522)***
Mid-West Electric Consumers Ass'n ***(523)***
MidAmerican Energy Holdings Co. ***(523)***
Midwest Research Institute ***(524)***
Miller & Chevalier, Chartered *(133)*
Denny Miller McBee Associates *(134)*
Minnesota Mining and Manufacturing Co. (3M Co.) ***(525)***
Minnesota Power ***(525)***
Minnesota Valley Alfalfa Producers ***(525)***
Mintz, Levin, Cohn, Ferris, Glovsky and Popeo, P.C. *(135)*
Mishawaka Utilities ***(526)***
Missouri River Energy Services ***(526)***
Mitsubishi Internat'l Corp. ***(526)***
Mitsubishi Research Institute ***(526)***
Modesto/Turlock Irrigation District ***(527)***
Molecular Separations Inc. ***(527)***
Timothy X. Moore and Co. *(136)*
Morgan Meguire, LLC *(136)*
Morgan, Lewis & Bockius LLP *(136)*
Morgan, Lewis & Bockius LLP ***(529)***
Bob Moss Associates *(137)*
MSS Consultants, LLC *(138)*
Multinat'l Government Services, Inc. *(138)*
Municipal Electric Authority of Georgia ***(532)***
Municipal Electric Utilities Ass'n of New York State ***(532)***
Murray, Scheer, Montgomery, Tapia & O'Donnell *(139)*
NAC Internat'l ***(534)***
Nat'l Ass'n of Energy Service Companies ***(542)***
Nat'l Ass'n of Fleet Administrators ***(543)***
Nat'l Ass'n of Home Builders of the U.S. ***(543)***
Nat'l Ass'n of RV Parks and Campgrounds ***(548)***
Nat'l Ass'n of State Energy Officials ***(550)***
Nat'l Ass'n of State Utility Consumer Advocates (NASUCA) ***(550)***
Nat'l Electrical Contractors Ass'n ***(562)***
Nat'l Electrical Manufacturers Ass'n ***(562)***
Nat'l Energy Assistance Directors' Ass'n ***(563)***
Nat'l Environmental Strategies *(140)*
Nat'l Environmental Strategies ***(563)***
Nat'l Environmental Trust ***(563)***
Nat'l Fenestration Rating Council ***(564)***
Nat'l Grange ***(566)***
Nat'l Grid USA ***(566)***
Nat'l Grocers Ass'n ***(566)***
Nat'l Hydropower Ass'n ***(567)***
Nat'l Military Intelligence Ass'n ***(571)***
Nat'l Mining Ass'n ***(571)***
Nat'l Petrochemical Refiners Ass'n ***(573)***
Nat'l Propane Gas Ass'n ***(574)***
Nat'l Rural Electric Cooperative Ass'n ***(576)***
Nat'l Steel Corp. ***(579)***
Nat'l Whistleblower Center ***(581)***
The Nature Conservancy ***(582)***
NES, Inc. *(141)*
Nevada Test Site Development Corp. ***(584)***
New Mexico State University, Department of Engineering ***(586)***
New Orleans, Louisiana, City of ***(586)***
New York Mercantile Exchange ***(587)***
New York Municipal Power Agency ***(587)***
New York University ***(588)***
The Newark Group ***(588)***
Newport News Shipbuilding Inc. ***(588)***
NiSource Inc. ***(590)***
Michael E. Nix Consulting *(142)*
Walker F. Nolan *(142)*
North American Electric Reliability Council ***(592)***
North American Insulation Manufacturers Ass'n ***(592)***
North Slope Borough, Alaska ***(593)***
Northeast Texas Electric Cooperative ***(593)***
Northeast Utilities ***(593)***
Northeast-Midwest Institute ***(594)***
Northern California Power Agency ***(594)***
Northern Indiana Public Service Co. ***(594)***
Northrop Grumman Corp. ***(594)***
Northwest Aluminum Co. ***(595)***
Northwest Energy Efficiency Alliance ***(595)***
Northwest Public Power Ass'n ***(595)***
NRG Energy, Inc. ***(596)***
Nuclear Control Institute ***(597)***
Nuclear Energy Institute ***(597)***
Nuevo Energy ***(597)***
O'Brien, Klink & Associates *(144)*
Occidental Internat'l Corporation ***(598)***
O'Connor & Hannan, L.L.P. *(144)*
Oglethorpe Power Corp. ***(599)***
Bartley M. O'Hara *(145)*
Ohio Municipal Electric Ass'n ***(599)***
Oldaker and Harris, LLP *(146)*
Omega Oil Co. ***(600)***
O'Neill, Athy & Casey, P.C. *(147)*
Operations Security Professionals Soc. ***(601)***
Oregon Utility Resource Coordination Ass'n (OURCA) ***(603)***
Orlando Utilities Commission ***(603)***
Owens Corning ***(604)***
OXY USA Inc. ***(605)***
Oxygenated Fuels Ass'n ***(605)***
Pacific Islands Washington Office *(148)*
PacifiCorp ***(606)***
Pacquing Consulting Inc. *(148)*
The Palmer Group *(149)*
Palo Alto, California, City of ***(607)***
Panda Energy Internat'l ***(607)***
Paper Recycling Coalition ***(607)***
Partnership for Early Climate Action ***(608)***
Patton Boggs, LLP *(150)*
The Peabody Group ***(610)***
Pennington BioMedical Research Center ***(611)***
Petro Star, Inc. ***(613)***
PG&E Corp. ***(614)***
PG&E Generating Co. ***(614)***
PG&E Nat'l Energy Group ***(614)***
Philips Electronics North America Corp. ***(616)***
Pilkington North America ***(617)***
Pinnacle West Capital Corp. ***(617)***
Plattsburgh, New York, City of ***(619)***
Podesta/Mattoon *(158)*
Podesta/Mattoon ***(619)***
Policy Consulting Services *(158)*
Potomac Electric Power Co. ***(622)***
Potomac Group *(160)*
Potomac Resources, Inc. *(160)*
Powell, Goldstein, Frazer & Murphy LLP *(160)*
PowerGen ***(622)***
Powerspan Corp. ***(622)***
Praxair, Inc. ***(623)***
Preston Gates Ellis & Rouvelas Meeds LLP *(162)*
Private Fuels Storage, L.L.C. ***(625)***
Professional Services Council ***(626)***
Progress Energy ***(626)***
The Progress Freedom Foundation ***(626)***
Propane Vehicle Council ***(627)***
PSE&G ***(627)***
Public Affairs Resources, Inc. *(164)*
Public Citizen, Inc. ***(628)***
Public Power Council ***(629)***
Public Service Co. of Colorado ***(629)***
Public Strategies Washington, Inc. *(164)*
Public Strategies, Inc. *(165)*
Puerto Rico Electric Power Authority ***(629)***
Pure Energy Corp. ***(630)***
Quinn Gillespie & Associates *(165)*
Ramgen Power Systems, Inc. ***(632)***
Redding, California, Electric Department of the City of ***(635)***
Redfern Resources *(166)*
Redland Energy Group *(167)*
Redstone ***(635)***
Reed, Smith, LLP *(167)*
Reliant Energy, Inc. ***(636)***
Renewable Fuels Ass'n ***(637)***
The Renkes Group, Ltd. *(168)*
Repeal PUHCA Now Coalition ***(637)***
RFB, Inc. *(168)*
RGS Enterprises, Inc. *(168)*
Rhoads Group *(168)*
Rineco Chemical Industries ***(640)***
Robison Internat'l, Inc. *(170)*
Robur Corp. ***(641)***
Rock-Tenn Co. ***(641)***
Rockville Centre, New York, Village of ***(641)***
Rohm and Haas Co. ***(642)***
Rolls-Royce North America Inc. ***(642)***
Rose Communications *(172)*
Ryan, Phillips, Utrecht & MacKinnon *(173)*
Sacramento Municipal Utility District ***(645)***
Safe Energy Communication Council ***(645)***
Sagamore Associates, Inc. *(174)*
Sagem Morpho ***(646)***
Salamanca, New York, City Board of Public Utilities of ***(646)***
Salazar Associates Internat'l, Inc. ***(646)***
Salt Lake City Olympic Organizing Committee ***(646)***
Salt River Project ***(646)***
Sam Rayburn G&T Electric Cooperative, Inc. ***(647)***
Sand County Foundation ***(648)***
Santa Clara, California, Electric Department of the City of ***(649)***
Michael L. Sauls *(175)*
SCANA Corp. ***(651)***
Elinor Schwartz *(176)*
Science and Engineering Associates, Inc. ***(652)***
Science Applications Internat'l Corp. (SAIC) ***(652)***
Scientech Corp. ***(652)***
Seattle City Light ***(653)***
Sellery Associates, Inc. *(177)*
Sempra Energy ***(655)***
Sensor Oil and Gas Co. ***(655)***
Separation Technologies ***(655)***
Seven Seas Petroleum USA Inc. ***(656)***
Sher & Blackwell *(179)*
Shook, Hardy & Bacon LLP *(180)*
Shutler and Low *(180)*
Siemens Westinghouse Power Corporation ***(658)***
Sierra Club ***(658)***
Sills Associates *(180)*
Smith Alling Lane, P.S. *(183)*
E. Del Smith and Co. *(183)*
Smith, Hinaman & Associates *(184)*
The Smith-Free Group *(184)*
Smurfit Stone Container Corp. ***(662)***
Soc. of Nuclear Medicine ***(663)***
Solar Electric Light Co. ***(665)***
Solar Energy Industries Ass'n (SEIA) ***(665)***
Solar Energy Research and Education Foundation ***(665)***
Solex Environmental Systems, Inc. ***(665)***
The Solomon Group, LLC *(185)*
Solutia Inc. ***(665)***
South Carolina Public Service Authority ***(666)***
South Mississippi Electric Power Ass'n ***(666)***
Southeastern Federal Power Customers, Inc. ***(667)***
Southern California Public Power Authority ***(667)***
Southern Co. ***(667)***

Southern Maryland Electric Cooperative, Inc. (668)
Southern Research Institute (668)
Southern Ute Indian Tribe (668)
Southwestern Electric Cooperative, Inc. (668)
Specialized Carriers and Rigging Ass'n (669)
Richard L. Spees, Inc. (186)
Spiegel & McDiarmid (186)
Springfield, Missouri, City Utilities of (670)
SRT Group (671)
Steel Manufacturers Ass'n (674)
The Stella Group, Ltd. (188)
John M. Stinson (189)
Stone and Webster Engineering Corp. (675)
Strat@Comm (Strategic Communications Counselors) (189)
Strategic Horizons Advisors, L.L.C. (189)
Stuntz, Davis & Staffier, P.C. (190)
Sub-Zero Freezer Co. Inc. (676)
Sunkist Growers, Inc. (677)
Synzyme Technologies, Inc. (679)
Mary-Rose Szoka de Valladares (192)
Tacoma, Washington, City of (680)
Talley and Associates (192)
Technology Advocates, Inc. (193)
Techsnabexport, A.O. (682)
TECO Energy, Inc. (682)
Tennessee Valley Public Power Ass'n (683)
Tex-La Electric Cooperative of Texas (684)
Texaco Group Inc. (684)
Texas A&M Engineering Experiment Station (684)
Texas A&M Research Foundation (684)
Texas Municipal Power Agency (685)
The Texas Wind Power Co. (685)
Thelen Reid & Priest LLP (685)
Theragenics Corp. (686)
Thompson and Naughton, Inc. (194)
Time Domain Corp. (687)
Timmons and Co., Inc. (195)
Tongour Simpson Holsclaw Green (196)
Toto USA, Inc. (688)
Toyota Motor North America, U.S.A., Inc. (689)
TransAlta Corp. (689)
Transconsortia (690)
Transmission Access Policy Study Group (690)
Transmission Agency of Northern California (690)
Trigen Energy Corp. (692)
Trinity Public Utilities District (692)
Troutman Sanders LLP (196)
Truckee Donner Electric Power Utility District (693)
Tulane University (693)
TVA Watch (694)
Twenty-First Century Group (197)
TXU Business Services (695)
U.S. Oil and Gas Ass'n (696)
U.S. Public Interest Research Group (697)
Union of Concerned Scientists (699)
Union Pacific (699)
Unitech Services Group, Inc. (700)
United Methodist Church General Board of Church and Society (702)
United Parcel Service (702)
United States Energy Ass'n (703)
United States Enrichment Corp. (703)
United Steelworkers of America (704)
United Technologies Corp. (704)
Universities Research Ass'n (705)
University of California, Office of Federal Government Relations (706)
University of Medicine and Dentistry of New Jersey (706)
University of Miami (706)
University of North Dakota (707)
University of Southwestern Louisiana (707)
University of Tulsa (708)
University of Virginia (708)
University of Washington (708)
US Acqua Sonics Corp. (709)
USEC, Inc. (710)
USX Corp. (710)
Ute Mountain Ute Indian Tribe (710)
Vacuum Insulation Ass'n (711)
Valis Associates (198)
Valve Manufacturers Ass'n of America (711)
Van Ness Feldman, P.C. (199)
Van Scoyoc Associates, Inc. (200)
Joe Velasquez & Associates (201)
Venetian Casino Resort, LLC (712)
Verner, Liipfert, Bernhard, McPherson and Hand, Chartered (202)
Vinson & Elkins L.L.P. (204)
Vortec Corp. (717)
Wackenhut Services, Inc. (718)
R. Duffy Wall and Associates (205)
Washington Consulting Alliance, Inc. (206)
Washington Consulting Group (719)
Washington Council Ernst & Young (206)
Washington Gas (719)
The Washington Group (208)
Washington Group Internat'l (719)
Washington Public Utility Districts Ass'n (720)
Waste Control Specialists, Inc. (721)
Waste Management, Inc. (721)
Waterman & Associates (210)
Watson Energy (721)
J. Arthur Weber & Associates (210)
David M. Weiman (211)
Wellton-Mohawk Irrigation and Drainage District (723)
Westerly Group (211)
Western Interconnection Coordination Forum (724)
Western Resources (724)
Westinghouse Electric Co. (725)
Westinghouse Government Services Group (725)
The Wexler Group (211)
Weyerhaeuser Co. (725)
White & Case LLP (212)
White Pigeon Paper Co. (726)
William F. Whitsitt Policy and Government Affairs (213)
Whitten & Diamond (213)
Wiley, Rein & Fielding (214)
Will and Carlson, Inc. (215)
The Willard Group (215)
Williams & Jensen, P.C. (215)
Wilmer, Cutler & Pickering (217)
Kathleen Winn & Associates, Inc. (218)
Winstar Petroleum (728)
Winston & Strawn (218)
Wisconsin Energy Corp. (728)
Wisconsin Gas Co. (729)
Wisconsin Public Service Corp. (729)
World Resources Institute (731)
Wright & Talisman, P.C. (220)
Xcel Energy, Inc. (732)
Yukon Pacific (734)

Environmental/Superfund (ENV)

20/20 Vision (223)
3001, Inc. (223)
AAAE-ACI (224)
Abitibi Consolidated Sales Corp. (225)
Abtech Industries (225)
The Accord Group (5)
ACE INA (226)
ADA Consulting Services (5)
ADA Consulting Services (227)
Adams and Reese LLP (5)
The Advocacy Group (6)
AFL-CIO (American Federation of Labor and Congress of Industrial Organizations) (231)
Africa Resources Trust USA (231)
Agri Business Council of Arizona (232)
Agricultural Air Group (232)
Agricultural Retailers Ass'n (232)
AIG Environmental (233)
Aiken and Edgenfield Counties, South Carolina, Economic Development Partnership of (233)
Ainslie Associates (7)
Air Products and Chemicals, Inc. (234)
Air Quality Standards Coalition (234)
Air Transport Ass'n of America (234)
Air-Conditioning and Refrigeration Institute (234)
Airgas, Inc. (235)
Akin, Gump, Strauss, Hauer & Feld, L.L.P. (8)
Alabama A & M University (235)
Alaska Forest Ass'n (236)
Alaska Rainforest Campaign (237)
Albemarle Corp. (237)
Albers & Co. (10)
Alcalde & Fay (10)
Alcalde & Fay (237)
Alcoa Inc. (237)
Harry C. Alford & Associates, Inc. (11)
Algoma Steel, Inc. (238)
Alliance for Nuclear Accountability (240)
Alliance for Responsible Atmospheric Policy (240)
Alliance of American Insurers (240)
Alliance of Automobile Manufacturers, Inc. (240)
Alliance to End Childhood Lead Poisoning (241)
Alliance to Save Energy (241)
Alliant Energy (241)
Alliant Techsystems, Inc. (241)
Allstate Insurance Co. (241)
Alpine Group, Inc. (11)
The Aluminum Ass'n (242)
Ameren Services (243)
American Academy of Actuaries (243)
American Academy of Child and Adolescent Psychiatry (243)
American Airlines (244)
American Ass'n for Laboratory Accreditation (246)
American Ass'n of Blacks in Energy (246)
American Ass'n of Engineering Societies (247)
American Ass'n of Motor Vehicle Administrators (248)
American Ass'n of Port Authorities (249)
American Automotive Leasing Ass'n (250)
American Bakers Ass'n (250)
American Bar Ass'n (250)
American Boiler Manufacturers Ass'n (251)
American Ceramics Soc. (252)
American Chemical Soc. (252)
American Chemistry Council (252)
American Coke and Coal Chemicals Institute (253)
American Consulting Engineers Council (255)
American Continental Group, Inc. (12)
American Corporate Counsel Ass'n (255)
American Council for Capital Formation (255)
American Council of Independent Laboratories (255)
American Council of Life Insurers (256)
American Crop Protection Ass'n (256)
American Electric Power Co. (257)
American Farm Bureau Federation (258)
American Federation of State, County and Municipal Employees (258)
American Feed Industry Ass'n (259)
American Financial Group (259)
American Forest & Paper Ass'n (259)
American Foundrymen's Soc. (260)
American Frozen Food Institute (260)
American Furniture Manufacturers Ass'n (260)
American Gas Ass'n (261)
American Gas Cooling Center (261)
American Geological Institute (261)
American Geophysical Union (261)
American Green Network (261)
American Highway Users Alliance (262)
American Home Products Corp. (262)
American Honda Motor Co., Inc. (262)
American Humane Ass'n (263)
The American Institute of Architects (264)
American Institute of Chemical Engineers (264)
American Institute of Physics (264)
American Insurance Ass'n (264)
American Internat'l Automobile Dealers Ass'n (265)
American Internat'l Group, Inc. (265)
American Iron and Steel Institute (265)
The American Land Conservancy (265)
American Legion (266)
American Lung Ass'n (266)
American Lung Ass'n of Minnesota (266)
American Management Systems (266)
American Meat Institute (267)
American Methanol Institute (268)
American Moving and Storage Ass'n (268)
American Oceans Campaign (269)
American Petroleum Institute (269)
American Planning Ass'n (270)

American Plastics Council ***(270)***
American Portland Cement Alliance ***(270)***
American Public Health Ass'n ***(271)***
American Public Works Ass'n ***(272)***
American Ref-Fuel ***(272)***
American Road and Transportation Builders Ass'n (ARTBA) ***(273)***
American Soybean Ass'n ***(277)***
American Speech, Language, and Hearing Ass'n ***(277)***
American Sugar Alliance ***(278)***
American Supply Ass'n ***(278)***
American Textile Manufacturers Institute ***(279)***
American Trucking Ass'ns ***(279)***
American Water Works Ass'n ***(280)***
American Waterways Operators ***(280)***
American Wood Preservers Institute ***(280)***
Americans for Tax Reform ***(282)***
Analytical and Life Science Systems Ass'n ***(283)***
Anchorage, Alaska, Municipality of ***(283)***
Anheuser-Busch Cos., Inc. ***(284)***
Appleton Papers, Inc. ***(286)***
Arcadia, California, City of ***(287)***
Arctic Slope Regional Corp. ***(288)***
Arent Fox Kintner Plotkin & Kahn, PLLC *(14)*
Arkansas, Office of the Governor of the State of ***(288)***
Wayne Arny & Assoc. *(16)*
Arter & Hadden *(17)*
Arvin Meritor Automotive ***(290)***
Asea Brown Boveri, Inc. ***(290)***
Ash Britt ***(290)***
Ashland Inc. ***(290)***
James Nicholas Ashmore & Associates *(18)*
Ass'n for Commuter Transportation ***(292)***
Ass'n for the Suppliers of Printing and Publishing Technology ***(293)***
Ass'n of American Railroads ***(294)***
Ass'n of Banks in Insurance ***(294)***
Ass'n of Consulting Foresters of America ***(295)***
Ass'n of Home Appliance Manufacturers ***(296)***
Ass'n of Internat'l Automobile Manufacturers ***(296)***
Ass'n of Local Air Pollution Control Officials ***(296)***
Ass'n of Metropolitan Sewerage Agencies ***(297)***
Ass'n of Nat'l Estuary Programs ***(297)***
Ass'n of Oil Pipelines ***(297)***
Ass'n of State and Territorial Solid Waste Management Officials ***(298)***
Ass'n of the Nonwoven Fabrics Industry - INDA ***(299)***
Associated Builders and Contractors ***(300)***
Associated Equipment Distributors ***(300)***
Associated General Contractors of America ***(300)***
Assurant Group ***(301)***
AstraZeneca Inc. ***(301)***
AT&T ***(301)***
Atlanta, Georgia, City of ***(302)***
ATOFINA Chemicals, Inc. ***(302)***
Aurora, Colorado, City of ***(303)***
Austin, Texas, City of ***(303)***
Automotive Aftermarket Industry Ass'n ***(303)***
Automotive Parts and Service Alliance ***(303)***
Automotive Parts Rebuilders Ass'n ***(304)***
Automotive Recyclers Ass'n ***(304)***
Auyua Inc. ***(304)***
Aventis CropScience ***(304)***
Aventis Pharmaceutical Products ***(304)***
Avondale, Arizona, City of ***(305)***
Baise + Miller, P.C. *(19)*
Baker & Hostetler LLP *(19)*
Baker & McKenzie *(20)*
Baker Botts, L.L.P. *(20)*
Michael Baker Corp. ***(306)***
Baker, Donelson, Bearman & Caldwell, P.C. *(21)*
Baker, Donelson, Bearman & Caldwell, P.C. ***(306)***
Balch & Bingham LLP *(21)*
Ball Janik, LLP *(22)*
Barbour Griffith & Rogers, Inc. *(22)*
Barnes & Thornburg *(23)*
Barron Collier Co. ***(308)***
The Barton Co. *(24)*
Basin Electric Power Cooperative ***(308)***
Bass Enterprises Production Co. ***(308)***
Battelle ***(309)***
Battelle Memorial Institute ***(309)***
Battery Council Internat'l ***(309)***
Bay County, Florida ***(309)***
Bayer Corp. ***(309)***
The Beacon Group Energy Funds ***(310)***
Bechtel Group, Inc. ***(310)***
Becker-Underwood, Inc. ***(310)***
Bellingham, Washington, City of ***(311)***
Bennett Environmental Inc. ***(311)***
Bergen, New York, Village of ***(311)***
Bergner Bockorny Castagnetti and Hawkins *(26)*
Berkeley, California, City of ***(312)***
Bethlehem Steel Corp. ***(312)***
Terry Bevels Consulting *(27)*
BHP (USA) Inc. ***(313)***
Leon G. Billings, Inc. *(27)*
Biotechnology Industry Organization ***(314)***
Birch, Horton, Bittner & Cherot *(28)*
Bituminous Coal Operators Ass'n ***(314)***
BKSH & Associates *(28)*
Black & Decker Corp., The ***(315)***
Blackfeet Tribe of Montana ***(315)***
Richard W. Bliss *(29)*
Boehringer Ingelheim Pharmaceuticals, Inc. ***(316)***
BOH Environmental, L.L.C. ***(317)***
Bohemian Cos. ***(317)***
James E. Boland *(30)*
Boston, Massachusetts, City of ***(318)***
Bourgas Intermodal Feasability Study ***(318)***
BP America, Inc. ***(319)***
BP Amoco Corp. ***(319)***
Bracewell & Patterson, L.L.P. *(30)*
Bracy Williams & Co. *(31)*
Brass and Bronze Ingot Manufacturers Ass'n ***(319)***
Bridgestone/Firestone, Inc. ***(320)***
William V. Brierre *(32)*
Bristol-Myers Squibb Co. ***(320)***
British Nuclear Fuels plc ***(321)***
Brookhill Redevelopment ***(321)***
Broward, Florida, County of ***(322)***
Browning Transport Management ***(322)***
Brownstein Hyatt & Farber, P.C. *(33)*
Brownsville Public Utilities Board ***(322)***
Broydrick & Associates *(33)*
Brush Wellman, Inc. ***(323)***
Buffalo Sewer Authority ***(323)***
Building Owners and Managers Ass'n Internat'l ***(323)***
Building Service Contractors Ass'n Internat'l ***(323)***
Burlington Northern Santa Fe Railway ***(324)***
Burlington Resources Oil & Gas Co. ***(324)***
The Business Roundtable ***(325)***
Butera & Andrews *(34)*
C F Industries, Inc. ***(325)***
C.A. Vencemos ***(325)***
Calaveras County, California, Water District ***(326)***
California Ass'n of Sanitation Agencies ***(326)***
California Refuse Removal Council ***(327)***
California State Lands Commission ***(327)***
California-American Water Co. ***(328)***
Calpine Corp. ***(328)***
CALSTART ***(328)***
Camp Dresser and McKee, Inc. ***(328)***
Jan Campbell *(36)*
Thomas D. Campbell & Assoc. ***(329)***
Campbell Crane & Associates *(36)*
Can Manufacturers Institute ***(329)***
Capital City Economic Development Authority ***(330)***
Capital Consultants Corp. *(37)*
Capitol Associates, Inc. *(37)*
Capitol City Group *(38)*
Capitol Counsel Group, L.L.C. *(38)*
Capitol Hill Advocates *(39)*
Capitol Link, Inc. *(39)*
Capitol Solutions *(39)*
Capitolink, LLC *(39)*
Caraustar ***(331)***
Cargill, Inc. ***(331)***
Robert E. Carlstrom *(40)*
Carmen & Muss, P.L.L.C. *(40)*
The Carmen Group *(40)*
Bill Carney & Co. *(41)*
Carpet and Rug Institute ***(332)***
Carpi & Clay *(41)*
Cascade Associates *(41)*
Cassidy & Associates, Inc. *(42)*
Caterpillar Inc. ***(333)***
Cedar Rapids, Iowa, City of ***(334)***
Celanese Government Relations Office ***(334)***
Cement Kiln Recycling Coalition ***(335)***
Cemento Bayano ***(335)***
Cementos Monterrey, S.A. ***(335)***
CEMEX Central, S.A. de C.V. ***(335)***
CEMEX USA ***(335)***
Center for Clean Air Policy ***(335)***
Center for Health, Environment and Justice ***(336)***
Center for Marine Conservation ***(337)***
Center for Public Dialogue ***(337)***
Center for Regulatory Effectiveness ***(337)***
Central Soya Co. ***(339)***
CH2M Hill ***(340)***
Chamber of Commerce of the U.S.A. ***(340)***
Chambers Associates Inc. *(45)*
Carolyn C. Chaney & Associates *(45)*
Changing World Technologies ***(341)***
Chelan County Public Utility District ***(342)***
ChemFirst Inc. ***(342)***
Chemical Land Holdings, Inc. ***(342)***
Chep USA ***(342)***
Cherokee Investment Partners, LLC ***(342)***
Chesapeake Bay Foundation ***(342)***
Chesapeake Bay Maritime Museum ***(342)***
Chesapeake Corp. ***(342)***
Chevron, U.S.A. ***(342)***
Chicago Botanic Garden ***(343)***
Chlorine Chemistry Council ***(345)***
The Chubb Corp. ***(346)***
Chwat and Company, Inc. *(46)*
Ciba Specialty Chemicals Corp. ***(346)***
CIGNA Corp. ***(346)***
Cinergy Corp. ***(347)***
CITGO Petroleum Corp. ***(347)***
Citigroup ***(347)***
Citizen Strategies *(46)*
Citizens Against Government Waste ***(348)***
Citizens for a Sound Economy ***(348)***
Clark & Weinstock, Inc. *(47)*
Clay and Associates *(47)*
Clean Water Act Reauthorization Coalition ***(350)***
Clearwater Environmental, Inc. ***(350)***
The Climate Council, ***(351)***
Climate Institute ***(351)***
The Clorox Co. ***(351)***
CNA Financial Corp. ***(351)***
CNA Insurance Cos. ***(351)***
Coachella Valley Water District ***(352)***
Coal Utilization Research Council ***(352)***
Coalition for Auto Repair Equality (CARE) ***(353)***
Coalition for Effective Environmental Information ***(353)***
Coalition for Truth in Environmental Marketing Information, Inc. ***(355)***
Coalition to Advance Sustainable Technology ***(356)***
Coalitions for America ***(356)***
Coast Alliance ***(356)***
The Coca-Cola Company ***(356)***
Coeur d'Alene Mines Corp. ***(357)***
Colex and Associates *(48)*
Collier Shannon Scott, PLLC *(48)*
Colling Swift & Hynes *(49)*
Colorado Springs-Pikes Peak, City of ***(359)***
Columbia Natural Resources ***(359)***
Columbia University ***(359)***
Commonwealth Consulting Corp. *(50)*
Community Ass'ns Institute (CAI) ***(362)***
Compass Internat'l Inc. ***(363)***
Composite Panel Ass'n ***(363)***
ConAgra Foods, Inc. ***(365)***
Congressional Institute, Inc. ***(366)***
Connecticut Resource Recovery Authority ***(367)***
Connerton & Ray *(51)*
The Conservation Fund ***(367)***
Conservation Strategies, LLC *(51)*
Consolidated Edison Co. of New York ***(367)***
Construction Industry Round Table, Inc. ***(368)***
Consumer Federation of America ***(369)***
Consumer Specialties Products Ass'n ***(369)***

Consumers Union of the United States (369)
Container Recycling Institute (370)
Continental Cement Co., Inc. (370)
Continental Teves (370)
Contra Costa Community College District (370)
Contract Services Ass'n of America (370)
Convergence Services, Inc. (52)
Cool Roof Rating Council (371)
Cooler Heads Coalition (371)
Coors Brewing Company (371)
Copeland, Lowery & Jacquez (52)
Copeland, Lowery & Jacquez (371)
Copper and Brass Fabricators Council (371)
Copper Development Ass'n, Inc. (371)
Corn Refiners Ass'n, Inc. (372)
Corporacion Valenciana de Cementos Portland, S.A. (372)
Corporacion Venezolana de Cementos, SACA (372)
Corporate Environmental Enforcement Council (CEEC) (372)
Ernest J. Corrado (53)
Cosmetic, Toiletry and Fragrance Ass'n (373)
Shawn Coulson (53)
Council for Conservation and Reinvestment of OCS Revenue (374)
Council of Industrial Boiler Owners (CIBO) (375)
Council of Infrastructure Financing Authorities (375)
The Council of Insurance Agents & Brokers (376)
Covington & Burling (53)
Law Office of C. Deming Cowles (54)
Cox Enterprises Inc. (378)
Crowell & Moring LLP (55)
Crown Central Petroleum Corp. (379)
CSA America, Inc. (379)
CSX Corp. (379)
Cummins Engine Co. (380)
Ralf Czepluch (56)
DaimlerChrysler Corp. (381)
Daishowa America Co., Ltd. (381)
Dames & Moore (382)
Davidoff & Malito, LLP (57)
Bob Davis & Associates (57)
Davis O'Connell, Inc. (58)
Davis Wright Tremaine LLP (58)
Dawson & Associates, Inc. (59)
Dayton, Ohio, Washington Office of the City of (383)
Deerfield Beach, Florida, City of (383)
Defenders of Wildlife (383)
Delaware and Hudson Railroad (384)
Delaware River Stevedores (384)
Dental Recycling North America (385)
Detroit, Michigan, City of (386)
Dickstein Shapiro Morin & Oshinsky LLP (61)
Discount Refrigerants Inc. (389)
Distributed Power Coalition of America (390)
DM Electronics Recycling Corporation (390)
The Doe Run Co. (390)
Domestic Petroleum Council (390)
Dominion Resources, Inc. (391)
Donohue Industries Inc. (391)
Dorfman & O'Neal, Inc. (63)
Dorsey & Whitney LLP (63)
Dow AgroSciences (391)
The Dow Chemical Co. (391)
Downey McGrath Group, Inc. (64)
Downey McGrath Group, Inc. (392)
Dredging Contractors of America (392)
W. B. Driggers & Associates, Inc. (65)
The Duberstein Group, Inc. (65)
Ducks Unlimited Inc. (392)
Dr. John V. Dugan, Jr. (66)
Duke Energy (392)
Duncan, Weinberg, Genzer & Pembroke, P.C. (66)
Dunn-Edwards Corp. (393)
Dunn-Padre, Inc. (393)
DuPont (393)
The Dutko Group, Inc. (68)
Dyer Ellis & Joseph, P.C. (68)
Dykema Gossett PLLC (69)
DynCorp Aerospace Technology (393)
Earle Palmer Brown Public Relations (70)
A. Blakeman Early (70)
EarthData Holdings (394)
Earthshell Container Corp. (394)
East Bay Municipal Utility District (395)
East Valley Water District (395)
Eastman Chemical Co. (395)
Eastman Kodak Co. (395)
Eckert Seamans Cherin & Mellott, LLC (70)
Edenspace Systems Corp. (397)
Edison Electric Institute (397)
Edison Internat'l (397)
Eka Chemicals (399)
Eklof Marine Corp. (399)
El Dorado Irrigation District (399)
El Paso Corporation (399)
El Paso Water Utilities - Public Service Board (399)
The Electric Vehicle Ass'n of the Americas (EVAA) (400)
Electronic Industries Alliance (400)
Elim, Alaska, City of (401)
Elmer Larson, Inc. (401)
Empresas Fonalledas (402)
Encapco Technologies, LLC (402)
Energy and Environment Coalition (403)
Energy Efficiency Systems, Inc. (403)
EnerTech Industries Inc. (403)
Enron Corp. (403)
ENS Resources, Inc. (71)
Entergy Services, Inc. (404)
Envirocare of Utah, Inc. (404)
Environmental Action Group (404)
Environmental Business Action Coalition (404)
Environmental Commonsense Coalition (405)
Environmental Council of the States (ECOS) (405)
Environmental Defense Fund (405)
Environmental Industry Ass'ns (405)
Environmental Information Ass'n (405)
Environmental Land Technology Ltd. (405)
Environmental Redevelopers Ass'n (405)
Environmental Research and Education Foundation (405)
Environmental Systems Research Institute, Inc. (405)
Environmental Technology Council (405)
Environmental Technology Unlimited (405)
EnviroPower (405)
Envirosource Technologies (405)
EOP Group, Inc. (72)
Equipment Leasing Ass'n of America (406)
Equitable Resources Energy Co. (406)
Ervin Technical Associates, Inc. (ETA) (73)
Ethyl Corp. (407)
Ethyl Petroleum Additives, Inc. (407)
Eureka, California, City of (408)
EV Rental Cars, LLC (408)
Everglades Defense Council (408)
Everglades Trust (408)
Exelon Corp. (409)
Express Pipeline Partnership and Platte Pipeline Co. (409)
Exxon Mobil Corp. (409)
Exxon Valdez Oil Spill Litigation Plaintiffs (409)
EZ's Solutions, Inc. (74)
F&T Network, Inc. (74)
Fairfax, Virginia, County of (410)
Farm Animal Reform Movement (FARM) (411)
Farmers Insurance Group (412)
Farmland Industries, Inc. (412)
Federation for American Immigration Reform (FAIR) (414)
Frank Fenton (75)
The Ferguson Group, LLC (76)
Ferroalloys Ass'n (415)
The Fertilizer Institute (415)
Fibrowatt, Inc. (416)
Fierce and Isakowitz (76)
Finch-Pruyn Paper Co. (417)
FirstEnergy Co. (418)
Fishable Waters Coalition (418)
Ruth Frances Fleischer (77)
Flexsys America (419)
Flight Landata, Inc. (419)
Florida Citrus Mutual (419)
Florida Crystals Corp. (419)
Florida Farm Bureau (419)
Florida State University System (420)
Florida Sugar Cane League, Inc. (420)
Fluor Corp. (420)
FMC Corp. (420)
Foley & Lardner (78)
Folsom, California, City of (421)
Food Marketing Institute (421)
Ford Motor Co. (422)
Forest Products Industry Nat'l Labor-Management Committee (423)
Forscey & Stinson, PLLC (79)
Fort James Corp. (423)
Foster Wheeler Corp. (424)
Foster Wheeler Environmental Corp. (424)
The Foundation for Environmental and Economic Progress (424)
FQPA Implementation Working Group (424)
Free Trade Lumber Council (425)
Freeport, New York, Electric Department of the Village of (425)
Freeport-McMoRan Copper & Gold Inc. (425)
French & Company (79)
John Freshman Associates, Inc. (79)
Friends of the Earth (426)
Fuel Cell Energy, Inc. (427)
FuelMaker Corp. (427)
Fundacion para la Preservacion de Flora y Fauna Marina (428)
Gainesville, Florida, City of (428)
Galveston County, Texas (428)
Garden State Paper Co., Inc. (429)
Gardner, Carton and Douglas (81)
Sara Garland (and Associates) (81)
The Garrison Group (81)
Gary Sanitary District (429)
Gary, Indiana, Washington Office of the City of (429)
Gary-Williams Energy Corp. (429)
Gas Technology Institute (429)
Gauff, LTD. (430)
General Electric Co. (432)
General Motors Corp. (432)
General Reinsurance Corp. (433)
Genesis Consulting Group, LLC (82)
Georgia Ports Authority (434)
Georgia-Pacific Corp. (434)
Giant Industries, Inc. (435)
Gibson, Dunn & Crutcher LLP (82)
Glass Packaging Institute (435)
P. H. Glatfelter (436)
Glenn-Colusa Irrigation District (436)
Global Climate Coalition (436)
Global Environment Facility (436)
Global Waste Recycling, Inc. (436)
Go-Mart, Inc. (436)
The Gold and Silver Institute (436)
Golf Course Superintendents Ass'n of America (437)
Golin/Harris Internat'l (84)
B. F. Goodrich Co. (437)
Goodstein & Associates (84)
Goodyear Tire and Rubber Co. (437)
Gordley Associates (84)
Government Relations, Inc. (84)
GPC Internat'l (85)
W. R. Grace & Co. (438)
Jay Grant & Associates (85)
Grasslands Water District (438)
Great Lakes Dredge & Dock (439)
Law Offices of Carol Green (86)
Greenberg Traurig, LLP (86)
Greenbrier Companies (440)
Greenman Technologies Inc. (440)
Griffin, Johnson, Dover & Stewart (87)
The Grizzle Company (88)
Grocery Manufacturers of America (440)
Ground Water Protection Council (441)
Grupo Empresarial Maya (441)
John C. Grzebien (89)
Guam, Washington Office of the Governor (442)
Guinea, Secretary General of the Presidency of the Republic of (442)
James E. Guirard (89)
Gulf Coast Portland Cement Co. (442)
Gulf Coast Waste Disposal Authority (442)

Gulf State Steel Inc. *(442)*
Hager Sharp Inc. *(443)*
Halliburton/Brown & Root *(443)*
Martin G. Hamberger & Associates *(91)*
Hamilton Sundstrand *(444)*
Harris Corp. *(444)*
The Hartford *(445)*
Health Physics Soc. *(446)*
Hecht, Spencer & Associates *(93)*
Hecla Mining Co. *(447)*
Hennipin County Board of Commissioners *(448)*
Hewlett-Packard Co. *(449)*
Hi-Desert Water District *(449)*
Hicks, Muse, Tate & Furst *(449)*
Hicks-Richardson Associates *(94)*
Hogan & Hartson L.L.P. *(96)*
Holland & Knight LLP *(98)*
Holnam Inc. *(451)*
The Home Depot *(451)*
Honeywell Internat'l, Inc. *(452)*
Hooper Owen & Winburn *(99)*
Christopher C. Horner *(100)*
Horticultural Research Institute *(452)*
Oliver James Horton *(100)*
Hotel Employees and Restaurant Employees Internat'l Union *(453)*
Houston Advanced Research Center *(453)*
Houston Galveston Area Council *(453)*
Houston Shell and Concrete *(453)*
Houston, Texas, City of *(453)*
Houston, Texas, Department of Public Works & Engineering of the City of *(453)*
Howrey Simon Arnold & White *(100)*
Edwin E. Huddleson, III *(100)*
Hudson Institute *(454)*
Humboldt Bay Municipal Water District *(455)*
Huntington Beach, California, City of *(455)*
Hunton & Williams *(101)*
Huntsman Corp. *(455)*
Iberville Parish *(456)*
IBP, Inc. *(456)*
ICF Consulting *(457)*
Idaho Power Co. *(457)*
Illinois Collaboration on Youth *(457)*
IMC Global Inc. *(458)*
Impact Strategies *(102)*
Independent Insurance Agents of America, Inc. *(459)*
Independent Lubricant Manufacturers Ass'n *(459)*
Independent Petroleum Ass'n of America *(459)*
Indiana, Office of the Governor of the State of *(460)*
Industrial Fabrics Ass'n Internat'l *(461)*
Infilco Degremont, Inc. *(461)*
Infiltrator Systems, Inc. *(461)*
Information Technology Industry Council *(462)*
Innovation Reform Group *(462)*
Institute of Scrap Recycling Industries, Inc. *(464)*
Integrated Building and Construction Solutions *(465)*
Integrated Waste Services Ass'n *(465)*
Intel Corp. *(465)*
Intermountain Forest Industry Ass'n *(467)*
Internat'l Ass'n of Drilling Contractors *(467)*
Internat'l Ass'n of Fish and Wildlife Agencies *(468)*
Internat'l Brotherhood of Boilermakers, Iron Shipbuilders, Blacksmiths, Forgers and Helpers *(469)*
Internat'l Brotherhood of Electrical Workers *(469)*
Internat'l Brotherhood of Teamsters *(469)*
Internat'l Business Machines Corp. *(469)*
Internat'l Cadmium Ass'n *(469)*
Internat'l Climate Change Partnership *(470)*
Internat'l Code Council *(470)*
Internat'l Council of Cruise Lines *(470)*
Internat'l Council of Shopping Centers *(470)*
Internat'l Dairy Foods Ass'n *(470)*
Internat'l Fabricare Institute *(471)*
Internat'l Fund for Animal Welfare *(472)*
Internat'l Group of P&I Clubs *(472)*
Internat'l Mass Retailers Ass'n *(473)*
Internat'l Paint Inc. *(473)*
Internat'l Sign Ass'n *(474)*
Internat'l Underwriting Ass'n of London *(475)*
Internat'l Utility Efficiency Partnerships (IUEP) *(476)*
Interstate Council on Water Policy *(477)*
Interstate Natural Gas Ass'n of America *(477)*
IPALCO Enterprises, Inc./Indianapolis Power & Light Co. *(478)*
IPC Washington Office *(478)*
Irrigation Ass'n *(479)*
The Irvine Co. *(479)*
IT Group, Inc. *(479)*
IUCN - The World Conservation Union (US) *(480)*
Jackson County, Mississippi Board of Supervisors *(480)*
Jackson, Mississippi, City of *(480)*
Jacksonville Electric Authority *(481)*
Jacksonville, Florida, City of *(481)*
Jacobs Engineering Group Inc. *(481)*
Jamestown, New York, Board of Public Utilities *(481)*
Jamison and Sullivan, Inc. *(104)*
Janus-Merritt Strategies, L.L.C. *(104)*
Japan Automobile Manufacturers Ass'n *(481)*
JASON Foundation for Education *(482)*
Jefferson Government Relations, L.L.C. *(106)*
Jefferson Parish Council *(482)*
Jellinek, Schwartz & Connolly *(106)*
Jerome Foods *(483)*
S.C. Johnson and Son, Inc. *(484)*
Johnson Controls, Inc. *(484)*
Johnston & Associates, LLC *(107)*
Joint Council of Allergy, Asthma and Immunology *(484)*
Jolly/Rissler, Inc. *(108)*
Jones, Walker, Waechter, Poitevent, Carrere & Denegre, L.L.P. *(108)*
Jorden Burt LLP *(109)*
Joy Mining Machinery *(485)*
Robert E. Juliano Associates *(109)*
Kaiser Aluminum & Chemical Corp. *(485)*
Kaiser-Hill Co., L.L.C. *(486)*
Betty Ann Kane & Co. *(110)*
Kawasaki Motors Corp., USA *(487)*
Kaweah Delta Water Conservation District *(487)*
Kellogg Brown and Root *(487)*
Kennecott/Borax *(488)*
Kennedy Government Relations *(111)*
Kent & O'Connor, Inc. *(112)*
Kern County Water Agency *(488)*
Kern River Watermaster *(488)*
Kessler & Associates Business Services, Inc. *(112)*
KeySpan Energy *(489)*
Kilpatrick Stockton LLP *(112)*
Kimberly Consulting, LLC *(113)*
Kimberly-Clark Corp. *(489)*
The Kinetics Group *(489)*
King, Washington, County of *(489)*
Kinghorn & Associates, L.L.C. *(113)*
Kings River Interests *(489)*
Kirkland & Ellis *(113)*
Kitchen Cabinet Manufacturers Ass'n *(490)*
Klein & Saks, Inc. *(114)*
Koch Industries, Inc. *(490)*
Kodiak Brown Bear Trust *(490)*
Kogovsek & Associates *(114)*
KOSA *(491)*
Kotzebue, Alaska, City of *(491)*
Laborers' Internat'l Union of North America *(493)*
Laborers-AGC Education and Training Fund *(493)*
LACDA Alliance *(493)*
Lafarge Corp. *(494)*
Laguna Woods, California, City of *(494)*
Lake Worth Drainage District *(494)*
Lake, Illinois, County of *(494)*
Lancaster, California, City of *(494)*
Laredo, Texas, City of *(495)*
Large Public Power Council *(495)*
Law Office of Zel E. Lipsen *(496)*
The Paul Laxalt Group *(117)*
Lead Industries Ass'n *(496)*
League of Conservation Voters *(497)*
League of Women Voters of the United States *(497)*
LeBoeuf, Lamb, Greene & MacRae L.L.P. *(117)*
Lee & Smith P.C. *(118)*
Lehtinen O'Donnell *(498)*
Lennox Internat'l *(498)*
Lent Scrivner & Roth LLC *(119)*
Leonard B. Levine & Associates *(119)*
Levine & Co. *(119)*
The Michael Lewan Co. *(119)*
Lexmark Internat'l *(498)*
Liberty Mutual Insurance Group *(499)*
Liebman & Associates, Inc. *(120)*
Lighthouse Energy Group LLC *(120)*
Eli Lilly and Co. *(499)*
Lincoln, Nebraska, City of *(500)*
Law Office of Zel E. Lipsen *(120)*
The Livingston Group, LLC *(120)*
Lloyd's of London *(501)*
Lockheed Martin Corp. *(501)*
Lockridge Grindal & Nauen, P.L.L.P. *(121)*
Loma Linda, California, City of *(503)*
Longhorn Pipeline *(503)*
Los Angeles County Sanitation District *(504)*
Louisiana Pacific Corp. *(504)*
Lovelace Respiratory Research Institute *(504)*
Loyola University *(505)*
LPI Consulting, Inc. *(122)*
The LTV Corp. *(505)*
Lucent Technologies *(505)*
Lumbermens Mutual Casualty Co. *(505)*
Lutheran Office for Governmental Affairs/Evangelical Lutheran Church in America *(506)*
Lyondell Chemical Co. *(506)*
Lyons & Co. *(122)*
Mack Trucks, Inc. *(506)*
Madison Government Affairs *(123)*
Madison Government Affairs *(507)*
Magazine Publishers of America *(507)*
Mallino Government Relations *(123)*
Manatt, Phelps & Phillips, LLP *(123)*
Manufacturers Alliance/MAPI Inc. *(509)*
Marathon Ashland Petroleum, LLC *(509)*
MARC Associates, Inc. *(124)*
Maricopa, Arizona, County of *(509)*
Marine Engineers Beneficial Ass'n (District No. 1 - PCD) *(510)*
Marine Spill Response Corporation *(510)*
Markcorp Inc. *(125)*
Marlowe and Co. *(125)*
Martinizing Environmental Group *(511)*
Massachusetts Water Resources Authority *(512)*
Matsushita Electric Corp. of America *(513)*
Mayberry & Associates LLC *(126)*
Virginia M. Mayer *(126)*
Mayer, Brown & Platt *(126)*
Maytag Corp. *(513)*
Mazda North America Operations *(514)*
Charlie McBride Associates, Inc. *(127)*
McClure, Gerard & Neuenschwander, Inc. *(127)*
McDermott Internat'l, Inc./Babcock & Wilcox *(514)*
McGlotten & Jarvis *(129)*
McGuiness Norris & Williams, LLP *(130)*
McGuireWoods L.L.P. *(130)*
McIntyre Law Firm, PLLC *(130)*
McMahon and Associates *(131)*
McNamara & Associates *(131)*
Diane McRee Associates *(131)*
The Mead Corp. *(515)*
Mecklenburg, North Carolina, County of *(515)*
Medeva Pharmaceuticals *(516)*
Mehl, Griffin & Bartek Ltd. *(132)*
Mercedes-Benz of North America, Inc. *(518)*
Merck & Co. *(518)*
Metal Finishing Suppliers Ass'n *(519)*
Metcalf Federal Relations *(132)*
Methanex Inc. *(520)*
Metropolitan King County Council *(520)*
The Metropolitan Water District of Southern California *(521)*
Mexam Trade, Inc. *(521)*
Meyers & Associates *(133)*
Miami Beach, Florida, City of *(521)*
Miami, Florida, City of *(521)*
Miami-Dade, Florida, County of *(521)*
Miccosukee Indians *(522)*
Miccosukee Tribe of Indians of Florida *(522)*
Micell Technologies, Inc. *(522)*

Michelin North America *(522)*
Michigan Biotechnology Institute *(522)*
Michigan Consolidated Gas Co. *(522)*
Midcoast Interstate Transmission, Inc. *(523)*
Miles & Stockbridge, P.C. *(133)*
Millennium Intermarket Group, LLC *(133)*
Denny Miller McBee Associates *(134)*
Millian Byers Associates, LLC *(135)*
Milwaukee Metropolitan Sewerage District *(524)*
Milwaukee, City of *(524)*
Mineral Technologies, Inc. *(525)*
Minnesota Mining and Manufacturing Co. (3M Co.) *(525)*
Mintz, Levin, Cohn, Ferris, Glovsky and Popeo, P.C. *(135)*
Mission Springs (California) Water District *(526)*
Mitsubishi Corp. *(526)*
Mitsubishi Research Institute *(526)*
Mobile Area Water and Sewer System *(527)*
Monroe, Florida, County of *(527)*
Monroe, New York, County of *(528)*
Monsanto Co. *(528)*
Monterey County Water Resources Agency *(528)*
Montgomery Airport Authority *(528)*
Montgomery Watson *(528)*
Montrose Chemical Co. *(529)*
Morgan, Lewis & Bockius LLP *(136)*
Kay Allan Morrell, Attorney-at-Law *(137)*
Mortgage Bankers Ass'n of America *(530)*
Bob Moss Associates *(137)*
MOTE Marine Lab *(530)*
Motor and Equipment Manufacturers Ass'n *(531)*
Motorcycle Industry Council *(531)*
Motorola, Inc. *(531)*
Mount Vernon, City of *(532)*
Mullenholz, Brimsek & Belair *(138)*
Multinat'l Government Services, Inc. *(138)*
Muncie, Indiana, City of (Delaware County) *(532)*
Municipal Electric Authority of Georgia *(532)*
Murray, Scheer, Montgomery, Tapia & O'Donnell *(139)*
The MWW Group *(140)*
Nat'l Academy of Public Administration *(535)*
Nat'l Agricultural Aviation Ass'n *(535)*
Nat'l Air Transportation Ass'n *(536)*
Nat'l Asphalt Pavement Ass'n *(537)*
Nat'l Ass'n of Broadcasters *(539)*
Nat'l Ass'n of Chemical Distributors *(540)*
Nat'l Ass'n of Convenience Stores *(541)*
Nat'l Ass'n of Fleet Administrators *(543)*
Nat'l Ass'n of Flood and Stormwater Management Agencies *(543)*
Nat'l Ass'n of Home Builders of the U.S. *(543)*
Nat'l Ass'n of Independent Insurers *(544)*
Nat'l Ass'n of Industrial and Office Properties *(544)*
Nat'l Ass'n of Installation Developers *(544)*
Nat'l Ass'n of Manufacturers *(545)*
Nat'l Ass'n of Realtors *(547)*
Nat'l Ass'n of Service and Conservation Corps *(549)*
Nat'l Ass'n of State Departments of Agriculture *(549)*
Nat'l Ass'n of Surety Bond Producers *(550)*
Nat'l Ass'n of Towns and Townships *(551)*
Nat'l Ass'n of Water Companies *(551)*
Nat'l Ass'n of Wheat Growers *(551)*
Nat'l Audubon Soc. *(552)*
Nat'l Automobile Dealers Ass'n *(552)*
Nat'l Cash Register *(554)*
Nat'l Cattleman's Beef Ass'n *(554)*
Nat'l Center for Policy Analysis *(555)*
Nat'l Center for Public Policy Research *(555)*
Nat'l Chicken Council *(555)*
Nat'l Concrete Masonry Ass'n *(558)*
Nat'l Consumers League *(558)*
Nat'l Council for Science and the Environment *(559)*
Nat'l Council of Catholic Women *(560)*
Nat'l Council of Farmer Cooperatives *(560)*
Nat'l District Attorneys Ass'n *(562)*
Nat'l Ecological Foundation *(562)*
Nat'l Electrical Contractors Ass'n *(562)*
Nat'l Electrical Manufacturers Ass'n *(562)*
Nat'l Endangered Species Act Reform Coalition *(563)*
Nat'l Energy Management Institute *(563)*
Nat'l Environmental Development Ass'ns State & Federal Environmental Responsibility Project *(563)*
Nat'l Environmental Strategies *(563)*
Nat'l Environmental Strategies *(140)*
Nat'l Environmental Trust *(563)*
Nat'l Farmers Union (Farmers Educational & Co-operative Union of America) *(563)*
Nat'l Funeral Directors Ass'n *(565)*
Nat'l Grange *(566)*
Nat'l Grid USA *(566)*
Nat'l Ground Water Ass'n *(566)*
Nat'l Hardwood Lumber Ass'n *(566)*
Nat'l Legal Center for the Public Interest *(570)*
Nat'l Lime Ass'n *(570)*
Nat'l Lumber and Building Material Dealers Ass'n *(570)*
Nat'l Marine Life Center *(570)*
Nat'l Mining Ass'n *(571)*
Nat'l Mitigation Bankers Ass'n *(571)*
Nat'l Multi-Housing Council *(571)*
Nat'l Ocean Industries Ass'n *(572)*
Nat'l Oilseed Processors Ass'n *(572)*
Nat'l Paint and Coatings Ass'n *(573)*
Nat'l Pest Control Ass'n *(573)*
Nat'l Petrochemical Refiners Ass'n *(573)*
Nat'l Pork Producers Council *(574)*
Nat'l Propane Gas Ass'n *(574)*
Nat'l Ready Mixed Concrete Ass'n *(575)*
Nat'l Rural Electric Cooperative Ass'n *(576)*
Nat'l Rural Water Ass'n *(577)*
Nat'l Sediments Coalition *(577)*
Nat'l Small Business United *(578)*
Nat'l Soc. of Professional Engineers *(578)*
Nat'l Spiritual Assembly of the Baha'is of the United States *(578)*
Nat'l Steel Corp. *(579)*
Nat'l Strategies Inc. *(141)*
Nat'l Taxpayers Union *(579)*
Nat'l Truck Equipment Ass'n *(580)*
Nat'l Utility Contractors Ass'n (NUCA) *(580)*
Nat'l Water Resources Ass'n *(581)*
The Nat'l Wetlands Coalition *(581)*
Nat'l Whistleblower Center *(581)*
Nat'l Wildlife Federation - Office of Federal and Internat'l Affairs *(581)*
Nationwide Mutual Insurance Co. *(582)*
Natomas *(582)*
NATSO, Inc. *(582)*
The Nature Conservancy *(582)*
Navista, Inc. *(141)*
NCR Corp. *(583)*
Negative Population Growth, Inc. (NPG) *(583)*
NES, Inc. *(141)*
Neuman and Co. *(141)*
New Jersey Institute of Technology *(585)*
New Mexico State University, Department of Engineering *(586)*
New Orleans Environmental Systems Foundation *(586)*
New Orleans, Louisiana, City of *(586)*
New York University *(588)*
The Newark Group *(588)*
Newark, New Jersey, City of *(588)*
Newmont Mining Corp. *(588)*
Newpark Resources/SOLOCO *(588)*
Newport News Shipbuilding Inc. *(588)*
Newport News, Virginia, City of *(588)*
Nike, Inc. *(590)*
Michael E. Nix Consulting *(142)*
Nixon Peabody LLP *(142)*
Nogales, Arizona, City of *(591)*
Noise Reduction Technology Coalition *(591)*
Walker F. Nolan *(142)*
Non-Ferrous Founders' Soc. *(591)*
Norcal Waste Systems, Inc. *(591)*
Norfolk Southern Corp. *(591)*
Norfolk, Virginia, City of *(591)*
Julia J. Norrell & Associates *(142)*
North American Millers' Ass'n *(592)*
North Carolina, Washington Office of the State of *(593)*
North Slope Borough, Alaska *(593)*
Northeast Ohio Areawide Coordination Agency (NOACA) *(593)*
Northeast Utilities *(593)*
Northeast-Midwest Institute *(594)*
Northern Indiana Public Service Co. *(594)*
Northrop Grumman Corp. *(594)*
Northwest Municipal Conference *(595)*
Nossaman, Gunther, Knox & Elliott *(596)*
Novartis Corp. *(596)*
Novartis Services, Inc. *(596)*
NPES, The Ass'n for Suppliers of Printing, Publishing, and Converting Technologies *(596)*
NRG Energy, Inc. *(596)*
Nuclear Energy Institute *(597)*
NUI Environmental Group Inc. *(597)*
Nutter & Harris, Inc. *(143)*
O'Connor & Hannan, L.L.P. *(597)*
Oakland, California, City of *(598)*
The OB-C Group, LLC *(143)*
Obadal and MacLeod, p.c. *(143)*
O'Brien, Klink & Associates *(144)*
Occidental Internat'l Corporation *(598)*
Ocean County, NJ Utilities Authority *(598)*
Ocean Spray Cranberries *(598)*
O'Connor & Hannan, L.L.P. *(144)*
Ogilvy Public Relations Worldwide *(145)*
Ogletree Governmental Affairs, Inc. *(145)*
Ohio River Valley Water Sanitation Commission *(599)*
Oklahoma Gas and Electric Co. *(599)*
O'Melveny and Myers LLP *(147)*
O'Neill, Athy & Casey, P.C. *(147)*
Oppenheimer Wolff & Donnelly LLP *(147)*
Osceola, Florida, County of *(604)*
Outdoor Media, Inc. *(148)*
Owens Corning *(604)*
Owens-Illinois, Inc. *(605)*
Oxygenated Fuels Ass'n *(605)*
P & H Mining Equipment *(605)*
PACCAR, Inc. *(605)*
Pacific Coast Cement *(605)*
Pacific Northwest Nat'l Laboratory *(606)*
Pacquing Consulting Inc. *(148)*
Painting and Decorating Contractors of America *(606)*
John M. Palatiello & Associates *(148)*
Palm Beach, Florida, Port of *(606)*
The Palmer Group *(149)*
Paper Recycling Coalition *(607)*
Parry, Romani, DeConcini & Symms *(149)*
Parsons Corp. *(608)*
Partnership for Early Climate Action *(608)*
Patton Boggs, LLP *(150)*
Pennzoil-Quaker State Co. *(611)*
People for the Ethical Treatment of Animals *(612)*
Peoria, Arizona, City of *(612)*
Perkins Coie LLP *(154)*
Petro Star, Inc. *(613)*
Petroleum Marketers Ass'n of America *(613)*
PetrolRem, Inc. *(613)*
Peyser Associates, Inc. *(155)*
Pfizer, Inc. *(613)*
PG&E Corp. *(614)*
PG&E Generating Co. *(614)*
Pharmacia Corp. *(615)*
Phelps Dodge Corp. *(615)*
Philadelphia Zoo *(615)*
Philadelphia, Pennsylvania, City of *(615)*
Philip Morris Management Corp. *(615)*
Philipp Brothers Chemicals, Inc. *(616)*
Philips Electronics North America Corp. *(616)*
Phillips Petroleum Co. *(616)*
Phoenix, Arizona, City of *(616)*
Pierce, Washington, County of *(617)*
Pinnacle West Capital Corp. *(617)*
PINSA, S.A de CD *(618)*
Piper Marbury Rudnick & Wolfe LLP *(155)*
Placer County Water Agency *(618)*
Placer Dome U.S. Inc. *(618)*
Placid Refining Co. *(618)*
Planet Electric *(618)*
Plum Creek Timber Co. *(619)*
Plumbing, Heating, Cooling Contractors- National Assoc. *(619)*
The PMA Group *(156)*

Podesta/Mattoon *(158)*
Polar Air Cargo, Inc. ***(620)***
Policy Consulting Services *(158)*
Policy Directions, Inc. *(158)*
The Policy Group *(159)*
Policy Impact Communications *(159)*
Polity Consulting *(159)*
Polyisocyanurate Insulation Manufacturers Ass'n ***(620)***
Population Institute ***(621)***
Porter/Novelli *(159)*
Portland, Oregon, City of ***(621)***
Poseidon Resources Corp. ***(621)***
Potomac Electric Power Co. ***(622)***
Powell, Goldstein, Frazer & Murphy LLP *(160)*
Premier Institute ***(623)***
Preston Gates Ellis & Rouvelas Meeds LLP *(162)*
Prince William Sound Regional Citizen's Advisory Council ***(624)***
Princess Tours ***(624)***
Printing Industries of America ***(624)***
The Procter & Gamble Company ***(625)***
Professional Engineering ***(625)***
Professional Services Council ***(626)***
Progressive Policy Institute ***(626)***
Propane Vehicle Council ***(627)***
Public Affairs Resources, Inc. *(164)*
Public Generating Pool ***(628)***
Public Lands Council ***(629)***
Public Strategies Washington, Inc. *(164)*
Puerto Rico Senate ***(629)***
Q Systems, Inc. ***(630)***
Radiant Aviation Services, Inc. ***(632)***
Ramsey, Minnesota, Board of Commissioners of the County of ***(633)***
Real Estate Roundtable ***(634)***
Reckitt & Colman Pharmaceuticals Inc. ***(634)***
Redfern Resources *(166)*
Reed, Smith, LLP *(167)*
Regulatory Improvement Council ***(636)***
Reilly Industries ***(636)***
Reinsurance Ass'n of America ***(636)***
Remediation Financial, Inc. ***(636)***
Renewable Fuels Ass'n ***(637)***
Renewable Natural Resources Foundation ***(637)***
The Renkes Group, Ltd. *(168)*
Republic Services, Inc. ***(637)***
Restore America's Estuaries ***(638)***
Reusable Industrial Packaging Ass'n ***(639)***
Reusable Pallet and Container Coalition ***(639)***
RGS Enterprises, Inc. *(168)*
Rhode Island Resource Recovery Center ***(639)***
RISE (Responsible Industry for a Sound Environment) ***(640)***
Risk and Insurance Management Soc., Inc. (RIMS) ***(640)***
Riviera Beach, Florida, City of ***(640)***
Liz Robbins Associates *(169)*
Robertson, Monagle & Eastaugh *(170)*
Robins, Kaplan, Miller & Ciresi L.L.P. *(170)*
Rock-Tenn Co. ***(641)***
Rockville Centre, New York, Village of ***(641)***
Rockwell Collins ***(641)***
Rodale Press ***(641)***
Rohm and Haas Co. ***(642)***
Roof Coatings Manufacturers Ass'n ***(642)***
Ropes & Gray *(171)*
Roseville, California, City of ***(642)***
The Roth Group *(172)*
RSR Corp. ***(643)***
Rubber Manufacturers Ass'n ***(643)***
Ryan, Phillips, Utrecht & MacKinnon *(173)*
Sacramento, California, Department of Utilities of ***(645)***
Safe Energy Communication Council ***(645)***
Safe Environment of America ***(645)***
Sagamore Associates, Inc. *(174)*
Salt Institute ***(646)***
Salt Lake City Olympic Organizing Committee ***(646)***
Salt Lake City, Utah, City of ***(646)***
Salt River Project ***(646)***
San Bernardino Valley Municipal Water District ***(647)***
San Diego County Water Authority ***(647)***
San Diego State University Foundation ***(647)***
San Diego, California, City of ***(647)***
San Gabriel Basin Water Quality Authority ***(648)***
San Gabriel Valley Water Ass'n ***(648)***
San Joaquin Area Flood Agency ***(648)***
San Joaquin River Exchange Contractors Water Authority ***(648)***
San Jose, California, City of ***(648)***
Santa Clara, California, County of ***(649)***
Santa Clarita, California, City of ***(649)***
Santa Fe, New Mexico, County of ***(649)***
Sappi Fine Paper NA ***(649)***
Save America's Forests, Inc. ***(650)***
Save America's Fossils for Everyone, Inc. ***(650)***
Save Barton Creek ***(650)***
Save the Bay ***(650)***
Scenic America ***(651)***
Scenic Hudson ***(651)***
Schmeltzer, Aptaker & Shepard, P.C. *(176)*
James E. Schneider, LLM Inc. ***(651)***
Schramm, Williams & Associates, Inc. *(176)*
Elinor Schwartz *(176)*
Science Applications Internat'l Corp. (SAIC) ***(652)***
Screenprinting & Graphic Imaging Ass'n Internat'l ***(653)***
Sea Grant Ass'n ***(653)***
Sealaska Corp. ***(653)***
Seattle, Washington, City of ***(653)***
Secondary Materials and Recycled Textiles Ass'n ***(654)***
SEFBO Pipeline Bridge, Inc. ***(654)***
Sellery Associates, Inc. *(177)*
Seminole Tribe of Indians of Florida ***(655)***
Sensor Research and Development Corp. ***(655)***
SePRO Corp. ***(655)***
Shaw Pittman *(177)*
Shell Oil Co. ***(657)***
Sher & Blackwell *(179)*
Shieldalloy Metallurgical Corp. ***(657)***
Shipbuilders Council of America ***(657)***
Sidley & Austin *(180)*
Sierra Club ***(658)***
Sierra Madre, California, City of ***(658)***
Sills Associates *(180)*
Silver Users Ass'n ***(659)***
Simon and Co., Inc. *(181)*
Bill Simpson & Associates *(181)*
Simpson Investment Co. ***(659)***
SISCORP *(181)*
Siscorp ***(660)***
Skadden, Arps, Slate, Meagher & Flom LLP ***(660)***
Smith & Harroff, Inc. *(182)*
E. Del Smith and Co. *(183)*
Smith Martin & Boyette *(184)*
The Smith-Free Group *(184)*
Smurfit Stone Container Corp. ***(662)***
Snack Food Ass'n ***(662)***
Soap and Detergent Ass'n ***(662)***
Soc. of Independent Gasoline Marketers of America ***(663)***
Soc. of the Plastics Industry ***(664)***
Soc. of Toxicology ***(664)***
Solar Energy Industries Ass'n (SEIA) ***(665)***
Solex Environmental Systems, Inc. ***(665)***
The Solomon Group, LLC *(185)*
Solutia Inc. ***(665)***
Sonoma County Water Agency ***(665)***
Sonomish, Washington, County of ***(665)***
Soo Line Railroad, Inc. ***(666)***
South Tahoe Public Utility District ***(666)***
Southdown, Inc. ***(667)***
Southeast Dairy Farmer Ass'n ***(667)***
Southeast Water Coalition ***(667)***
Southeastern Michigan Council of Government ***(667)***
Southern Co. ***(667)***
Southwire, Inc. ***(668)***
Space Dynamics Laboratory ***(669)***
Sparber and Associates *(186)*
Springettsbury, Pennsylvania, Township of ***(670)***
Springs Industries, Inc. ***(671)***
St. Louis, Missouri, City of ***(672)***
St. Paul, Alaska, City of ***(672)***
St. Paul, Minnesota, City of ***(672)***
State and Territorial Air Pollution Program Administrators ***(673)***
Steel Manufacturers Ass'n ***(674)***
Steel Recycling Institute ***(674)***
The Stella Group, Ltd. *(188)*
Stephens Law Offices *(188)*
Steptoe & Johnson LLP *(188)*
Sterling Chemical Co. ***(674)***
Kenneth F. Stinger *(189)*
John M. Stinson *(189)*
Stockton, City of ***(675)***
Stone and Webster Engineering Corp. ***(675)***
Strat@Comm (Strategic Communications Counselors) *(189)*
Strategic Horizons Advisors, L.L.C. *(189)*
Charlene A. Sturbitts *(190)*
Styrene Information and Research Center ***(676)***
Sub-Zero Freezer Co. Inc. ***(676)***
Sugar Cane Growers Cooperative of Florida ***(676)***
Sunbelt Cement ***(677)***
SunCor Development Co. ***(677)***
Sunkist Growers, Inc. ***(677)***
Sunoco, Inc. ***(677)***
Superfund Action Alliance ***(677)***
Sutter, California, County of ***(678)***
Swidler Berlin Shereff Friedman, LLP *(191)*
Swidler Berlin Shereff Friedman, LLP ***(678)***
Al Swift Consulting, Inc. *(192)*
Symms, Lehn & Associates, Inc. *(192)*
Synthetic Organic Chemical Manufacturers Ass'n ***(679)***
Tacoma, Washington, City of ***(680)***
Take The Field, Inc. ***(680)***
TAPS Renewal Task Force ***(681)***
Tarrant Regional Water District ***(681)***
The Technical Group LLC *(192)*
Tecumseh Products Co. ***(682)***
Terpstra Associates *(193)*
Texaco Group Inc. ***(684)***
Texas A&M Research Foundation ***(684)***
Texas Petrochemicals Corp. ***(685)***
Thacher Proffitt & Wood *(193)*
Thermo EcoTek Corp. ***(686)***
ThermoEnergy Corp. ***(686)***
Thompson Coburn LLP *(194)*
Three Affiliated Tribes of Fort Berthold Reservation ***(686)***
The Timken Co. ***(687)***
Tire Ass'n of North America ***(687)***
Todhunter Internat'l, Inc. ***(688)***
Tolmex ***(688)***
Tosco Corp. ***(688)***
Toyota Motor Manufacturing North America ***(689)***
Toyota Motor North America, U.S.A., Inc. ***(689)***
TransAlta Corp. ***(689)***
Transportation Corridor Agencies ***(690)***
Tribal Ass'n on Solid Waste and Emergency Response (TASWER) ***(692)***
Trinity Partners, Inc. ***(692)***
Troutman Sanders LLP *(196)*
Truck Renting and Leasing Ass'n ***(693)***
TRW Inc. ***(693)***
Tulalip Tribes ***(693)***
Tulane University ***(693)***
Christopher A.G. Tulou *(196)*
Tunica Biloxi Indians of Louisiana ***(694)***
TVA Watch ***(694)***
TXU Business Services ***(695)***
Tyco Internat'l (US), Inc. ***(695)***
Tyson Foods, Inc. ***(695)***
U.S. Filter ***(696)***
U.S. Oil and Gas Ass'n ***(696)***
U.S. Postal Service ***(697)***
U.S. Public Interest Research Group ***(697)***
U.S. Steel ***(697)***
U.S. Strategies Corp. *(197)*
UGI Utilities, Inc. ***(698)***
Ungaretti & Harris *(197)*
Unilever United States, Inc. ***(699)***
Union Pacific ***(699)***
Unitech Services Group, Inc. ***(700)***
United Airlines ***(700)***
United Fresh Fruit and Vegetable Ass'n ***(701)***
United Methodist Church General Board of Church and Society ***(702)***

United Mine Workers of America (702)
United Motorcoach Ass'n (702)
United Parcel Service (702)
United States Business and Industry Council (703)
United States Energy Ass'n (703)
United Technologies Corp. (704)
University Health Associates, Inc. (705)
University of California, Office of Federal Government Relations (706)
University of Medicine and Dentistry of New Jersey (706)
University of Miami (706)
University of New Orleans (707)
University of North Dakota (707)
University of Southern Mississippi (707)
University of Southwestern Louisiana (707)
University of Tulsa (708)
University of Virginia (708)
University of West Florida (708)
UNOCAL Corp. (708)
USA Biomass Power Producers Alliance (709)
USA Rice Federation (709)
USAA - United Services Automobile Ass'n (710)
USX Corp. (710)
Utah State University (710)
Valanzano & Associates (198)
Valero Energy Corp. (711)
Valis Associates (198)
Valve Manufacturers Ass'n of America (711)
Van Ness Feldman, P.C. (199)
Van Scoyoc Associates, Inc. (200)
Vanguard Research, Inc. (712)
Joe Velasquez & Associates (201)
Venable (201)
Venetian Casino Resort, LLC (712)
Verner, Liipfert, Bernhard, McPherson and Hand, Chartered (202)
Viohl and Associates, Inc. (205)
Virginia Beach, Virginia, City of (715)
Virginia Living Museum (716)
Volkswagen, AG (717)
Vorys, Sater, Seymour and Pease, LLP (205)
Waesche, Sheinbaum, and O'Regan (718)
Waggoner Engineering, Inc. (718)
Wake, North Carolina, County of (718)
R. Duffy Wall and Associates (205)
Washington Alliance Group, Inc. (206)
Washington Consulting Alliance, Inc. (206)
Washington Council Ernst & Young (206)
Washington Gas (719)
The Washington Group (208)
Washington Resource Associates (209)
Washoe County (721)
Waste Control Specialists, Inc. (721)
Waste Management, Inc. (721)
Water and Wastewater Equipment Manufacturers Ass'n (721)
Water Environment Federation (721)
Water Environment Research Foundation (721)
Water Quality Insurance Syndicate (721)
Water Replenishment District of Southern California (721)
Water Systems Council (721)
Waterman & Associates (210)
Waterworks Internat'l, Inc. (721)
Wausau Insurance Cos. (722)
Robert K. Weidner (211)
Weil, Gotshal & Manges, LLP (211)
Welch's Foods, Inc. (722)
Welcon, Inc. (722)
West Coast Refuse and Recycling Coalition (723)
Western Coalition of Arid States (724)
Western Growers Ass'n (724)
Western Pistachio Ass'n (724)
Western States Petroleum Ass'n (724)
Westinghouse Government Services Group (725)
Westlands Water District (725)
Westminster, California, City of (725)
Westmoreland Coal Co. (725)
Roy F. Weston, Inc. (725)
The Wexler Group (211)
Weyerhaeuser Co. (725)
Wheat & Associates, Inc. (212)
White Mountain Apache Tribe (726)
White Pigeon Paper Co. (726)
William F. Whitsitt Policy and Government Affairs (213)
Whitten & Diamond (213)
Wildlife Forever (726)
Wildlife Habitat Council (726)
Wilke, Fleury, Hoffelt, Gould & Birney, LLP (727)
Will and Carlson, Inc. (215)
The Willard Group (215)
Williams & Jensen, P.C. (215)
The Williams Companies (727)
WinCapitol, Inc. (218)
Kathleen Winn & Associates, Inc. (218)
Winston & Strawn (218)
Wisconsin Energy Corp. (728)
Wisconsin Gas Co. (729)
Women Officials in NACo (729)
Wood Products Indoor Air Consortium (730)
Woodbury County, Iowa (730)
Woodland, California, City of (730)
Woodmont Corporation (730)
World Floor Covering Ass'n (730)
World Government of World Citizens (730)
World Resources Institute (731)
World Service Authority (731)
World Wildlife Fund (731)
Wright & Talisman, P.C. (220)
Xerox Corp. (732)
Youngstown-Warren Regional Chamber (733)
Yukon Pacific (734)
Zero Population Growth, Inc. (734)
Zinc Corp. of America (734)
Zirconium Environmental Committee (ZEC) (735)
Zurich Financial Group (735)
Zurich U.S. Specialties (735)

Family Issues/Abortion/Adoption (FAM)

The 60/Plus Ass'n, Inc. (224)
AARP (American Ass'n of Retired Persons) (224)
Adopt America (228)
Advocates for Youth (229)
AFL-CIO (American Federation of Labor and Congress of Industrial Organizations) (231)
Agudath Israel of America (232)
The Alan Guttmacher Institute (236)
Alliance for American Innovation, Inc. (239)
Alliance for Children and Families (239)
Alticor, Inc. (242)
American Academy of Adoption Attorneys (243)
American Ass'n for Marriage and Family Therapy (246)
American Ass'n of Early Childhood Educators (247)
American Ass'n of University Women (249)
American Bar Ass'n (250)
American Civil Liberties Union (252)
American College of Obstetricians and Gynecologists (254)
American Council of Life Insurers (256)
American Federation of State, County and Municipal Employees (258)
American Humane Ass'n (263)
American Jewish Committee (265)
American Jewish Congress (265)
American Legion (266)
American Payroll Ass'n (269)
American Psychiatric Ass'n (271)
American Psychological Ass'n (271)
American Public Health Ass'n (271)
American Renewal (272)
Americans for Integrity in Palliative Care (282)
Americans for Tax Reform (282)
Anglican Catholic Church (284)
Arnold & Porter (16)
Ass'n for Childhood Education Internat'l (291)
Associated General Contractors of America (300)
Barksdale Ballard & Co., Inc. (23)
Bass and Howes, Inc. (24)
Berliner, Candon & Jimison (27)
Thomas L. Birch (27)
Boysville (318)
Business and Professional Women/USA (324)
Capitol Partners (39)
Casey Family Program (333)
Catholic Alliance (333)
Catholic Health Ass'n of the United States (333)
Center for Law and Social Policy (336)
Center for Reproductive Law and Policy (337)
Child Welfare League of America (343)
Children's Defense Fund (344)
Children's Rights Council (344)
Christian Coalition of America (345)
Christian Legal Soc. (345)
Christian Voice, Inc. (345)
The Chubb Corp. (346)
Edna McConnell Clark Foundation (350)
Commercial Internet Exchange Ass'n (360)
Concerned Women for America (365)
Concord Family and Adolescent Services (365)
Copeland, Lowery & Jacquez (52)
County Welfare Directors Ass'n of California (377)
Craig Associates (55)
Dakota, Minnesota, County of (381)
Dean Blakey & Moskowitz (59)
The Direct Impact Co. (62)
Dublin Castle Group (66)
Ex-Partners of Servicemembers for Equality (408)
Family Advocacy Services (410)
Family Place (411)
Family Research Council, Inc. (411)
The Ferguson Group, LLC (76)
Foster America, Inc. (424)
General Conference of Seventh-day Adventists (431)
Girl Scouts of the U.S.A. - Washington Office (435)
Girls Incorporated (435)
Global Health Council (436)
Robert M. Guttman (89)
Hadassah, The Women's Zionist Organization of America (443)
Health Services of Kansas and Mid Missouri (446)
Dennis M. Hertel & Associates (94)
Illinois Department of Human Services (457)
Independent Educational Consultants Ass'n (459)
Institute on Religion and Public Policy (464)
Islamic Institute (479)
Janus Solutions, Inc. (481)
Jar-Mon Consultants, Inc. (105)
Labor Council for Latin American Advancement (LCLAA) (493)
The Livingston Group, LLC (120)
Local Initiatives Support Corp. (501)
Los Angeles, California, County of (504)
Lutheran Office for Governmental Affairs/Evangelical Lutheran Church in America (506)
Martin & Glantz LLC (125)
Merced, California, County of (518)
Meyers & Associates (133)
Murray, Scheer, Montgomery, Tapia & O'Donnell (139)
Nat'l Abortion and Reproductive Rights Action League (535)
Nat'l Abortion Federation (535)
Nat'l Adoption Foundation (535)
Nat'l Ass'n of Developmental Disabilities Councils (542)
Nat'l Ass'n of Evangelicals (542)
Nat'l Ass'n of Executive Secretaries and Administrative Assistants (542)
Nat'l Ass'n of Foster Care Review Boards (543)
Nat'l Ass'n of Negro Business & Professional Women's Clubs, Inc. (546)
Nat'l Ass'n of Nurse Practitioners in Women's Health (546)
Nat'l Ass'n of Social Workers (549)
Nat'l Assembly of Health and Human Service Organizations (551)
Nat'l Black Women's Health Project (552)
Nat'l Campaign for Hearing Health (554)
Nat'l Center for Missing and Exploited Children (555)
Nat'l Center for Neighborhood Enterprise (555)
Nat'l Center for Public Policy Research (555)
Nat'l Child Abuse Coalition (555)
Nat'l Council for Adoption (559)
Nat'l Council of Catholic Women (560)
Nat'l Council of Jewish Women (560)
Nat'l District Attorneys Ass'n (562)

Nat'l Family Planning and Reproductive Health Ass'n ***(563)***
Nat'l Military Family Ass'n ***(571)***
Nat'l Network to End Domestic Violence ***(572)***
Nat'l Parent Network on Disabilities ***(573)***
Nat'l Partnership for Women and Families ***(573)***
Nat'l Pro-Life Alliance PAC ***(574)***
Nat'l Right to Life Committee ***(576)***
Nat'l Women's Law Center ***(581)***
Negative Population Growth, Inc. (NPG) ***(583)***
Julia J. Norrell & Associates *(142)*
North Carolina, Washington Office of the State of ***(593)***
Ogletree Governmental Affairs, Inc. *(145)*
Oklahoma State Medical Ass'n ***(600)***
Partnership for Caring ***(608)***
Patton Boggs, LLP *(150)*
People Advancing Christian Education (PACE) ***(611)***
People for the American Way ***(612)***
Physicians Ad hoc Coalition for Truth (PHACT) ***(617)***
Physicians for Reproductive Choice and Health ***(617)***
Piper Marbury Rudnick & Wolfe LLP *(155)*
Planned Parenthood Federation of America ***(618)***
Population Institute ***(621)***
Riverside, California, City of ***(640)***
Robert Wood Johnson Foundation ***(641)***
San Bernardino, California, County of ***(647)***
Sierra Club ***(658)***
Stites & Harbison *(189)*
Stop It Now! ***(675)***
Sumlin Associates *(190)*
Susan B. Anthony List ***(678)***
Tarne Powers & Associates *(192)*
William J. Tobin and Associates *(195)*
Traditional Values Coalition ***(689)***
U.S. Family Network ***(696)***
United Automobile, Aerospace and Agricultural Implement Workers of America (UAW) ***(700)***
United Church of Christ Justice and Witness Ministry ***(700)***
United Methodist Church General Board of Church and Society ***(702)***
United States Coast Guard Chief Petty Officers Ass'n ***(703)***
University of North Carolina at Greensboro ***(707)***
UNUM/Provident Corp. ***(708)***
Wilmer, Cutler & Pickering *(217)*
Women Officials in NACo ***(729)***
Zero Population Growth, Inc. ***(734)***
ZERO TO THREE/Nat'l Center for Infants, Toddlers, and Families ***(734)***

Financial Institutions/Investments/Securities (FIN)

The 60/Plus Ass'n, Inc. ***(224)***
AARP (American Ass'n of Retired Persons) ***(224)***
Accenture ***(226)***
ACE INA ***(226)***
ACORN (Ass'n of Community Organizations for Reform Now) ***(227)***
Adams and Reese LLP *(5)*
Advertising Company ART-ERIA ***(229)***
Aetna Life & Casualty Co. ***(230)***
Affiliated Computer Services ***(230)***
AFL-CIO (American Federation of Labor and Congress of Industrial Organizations) ***(231)***
AFLAC, Inc. ***(231)***
Agri/Washington *(7)*
Akin, Gump, Strauss, Hauer & Feld, L.L.P. *(8)*
Harry C. Alford & Associates, Inc. *(11)*
Alliance of American Insurers ***(240)***
Allmerica Financial ***(241)***
Alpine Group, Inc. *(11)*
Alston & Bird LLP *(12)*
America's Community Bankers ***(243)***
American Academy of Child and Adolescent Psychiatry ***(243)***
American Airlines ***(244)***
American Ass'n of Limited Partners ***(248)***
American Bankers Ass'n ***(250)***
American Business Conference ***(251)***
American Continental Group, Inc. *(12)*
American Corporate Counsel Ass'n ***(255)***
American Council of Life Insurers ***(256)***
American Electric Power Co. ***(257)***
American Electronics Ass'n ***(257)***
American Express Co. ***(258)***
American Financial Group ***(259)***
American Financial Services Ass'n ***(259)***
American Gas Ass'n ***(261)***
American General Corp. ***(261)***
American General Financial Group ***(261)***
American Institute of Certified Public Accountants ***(264)***
American Insurance Ass'n ***(264)***
American Internat'l Group, Inc. ***(265)***
American League of Financial Institutions ***(266)***
American Management Systems ***(266)***
American Names Ass'n ***(268)***
American Teleservices Ass'n ***(279)***
Americans for Consumer Education and Competition, Inc. ***(281)***
AON Risk Services ***(285)***
Appraisal Institute ***(287)***
Arent Fox Kintner Plotkin & Kahn, PLLC *(14)*
Arnold & Porter *(16)*
Ass'n for Financial Professionals, Inc. ***(292)***
Ass'n Management Group *(18)*
Ass'n of American Geographers ***(293)***
Ass'n of Banks in Insurance ***(294)***
Ass'n of British Insurers ***(294)***
Ass'n of Financial Guaranty Insurers ***(295)***
Ass'n of Publicly Traded Companies ***(298)***
Associated Credit Bureaus, Inc. ***(300)***
Assurant Group ***(301)***
The Assurant Group ***(301)***
AT&T ***(301)***
The Atlantic Group, Public Affairs, Inc. *(18)*
Austin Professional Systems, Inc. ***(303)***
Bank of America ***(307)***
Bank of New York ***(307)***
Barbour Griffith & Rogers, Inc. *(22)*
Barnett & Sivon, P.C. *(24)*
The Barton Co. *(24)*
Bear, Stearns and Co. ***(310)***
Bicopas, Ltd. ***(313)***
Bingham Dana LLP *(27)*
Biotechnology Industry Organization ***(314)***
BKSH & Associates *(28)*
H & R Block, Inc. ***(315)***
BMW Financial Services of North America, Inc. ***(316)***
James E. Boland *(30)*
The Bond Market Ass'n ***(317)***
Brown Brothers Harriman & Co. ***(322)***
Brownstein Hyatt & Farber, P.C. *(33)*
Burke Venture Capital ***(324)***
Burlington Northern Santa Fe Railway ***(324)***
The Business Roundtable ***(325)***
Butera & Andrews *(34)*
Cadwalader, Wickersham & Taft *(35)*
Canfield & Associates, Inc. *(36)*
Capital One Financial Corp. ***(330)***
Cargill, Inc. ***(331)***
The Carmen Group *(40)*
CaseNewHolland Inc. ***(333)***
Cassidy & Associates, Inc. *(42)*
Cendant Corp. ***(335)***
Center for Freedom and Prosperity ***(336)***
Central States Indemnity Co. of Omaha ***(339)***
CFSBdirect Inc. ***(340)***
Chamber of Commerce of the U.S.A. ***(340)***
Chambers Associates Inc. *(45)*
Chambers, Conlon & Hartwell *(45)*
Charles Schwab & Co. Inc. ***(341)***
Charter Schools Development Corp. ***(341)***
Chicago Board of Trade ***(342)***
Chicago Mercantile Exchange ***(343)***
Chicago Stock Exchange, Inc. ***(343)***
Chicago Title & Trust Co. ***(343)***
Chicago Title Insurance ***(343)***
The Chubb Corp. ***(346)***
The Church Alliance ***(346)***
CIGNA Corp. ***(346)***
Cincinnati Stock Exchange ***(347)***
Cisco Systems Inc. ***(347)***
Citigroup ***(347)***
Citizens Against Government Waste ***(348)***
Citizens for a Sound Economy ***(348)***
Clark & Weinstock, Inc. *(47)*
Clark/Bardes, Inc. ***(350)***
Cleary, Gottlieb, Steen and Hamilton *(47)*
CNA Financial Corp. ***(351)***
CNA Insurance Cos. ***(351)***
Coalition for Employment through Exports ***(353)***
Coalition of Service Industries ***(355)***
Collier Shannon Scott, PLLC *(48)*
Colombian Banking and Financial Entities Ass'n (ASOBANCARIA) ***(358)***
Comerica, Inc. ***(360)***
Commonwealth Group, Ltd. *(50)*
Community Financial Services Ass'n ***(362)***
Community Preservation Corp. ***(363)***
Compaq Computer Corp. ***(363)***
Compuware Corp. ***(364)***
Congressional Economic Leadership Institute ***(366)***
Conkling, Fiskum & McCormick *(51)*
Constellation Energy Group ***(368)***
Consumer Federation of America ***(369)***
Consumers Union of the United States ***(369)***
Copeland, Lowery & Jacquez *(52)*
Corporation for Enterprise Development ***(372)***
Council of Development Finance Agencies ***(375)***
Council of Infrastructure Financing Authorities ***(375)***
Council of Institutional Investors ***(375)***
The Council of Insurance Agents & Brokers ***(376)***
Council of State Governments ***(376)***
Countrywide Home Loans, Inc. ***(377)***
Covington & Burling *(53)*
Credit Suisse First Boston Corp. ***(378)***
Cummins-Allison Corp. ***(380)***
The Cuneo Law Group, P.C. *(56)*
Currenex ***(380)***
Davidson & Company, Inc. *(57)*
Dayton, Ohio, Washington Office of the City of ***(383)***
Defense Credit Union Council ***(384)***
Dell Computer Corp. ***(384)***
Deloitte & Touche LLP ***(384)***
Dickstein Shapiro Morin & Oshinsky LLP *(61)*
Dime Savings Bank of New York ***(388)***
Dominion Resources, Inc. ***(391)***
Theodore A. Doremus, Jr. *(63)*
Downey McGrath Group, Inc. *(64)*
The Duberstein Group, Inc. *(65)*
Dublin Castle Group *(66)*
E*TRADE Group, Inc. ***(394)***
E*TRADE Securities, Inc. ***(394)***
eCharge Corp. ***(396)***
Eckert Seamans Cherin & Mellott, LLC *(70)*
EDS Corp. ***(398)***
Education Finance Council ***(398)***
Electro Scientific Industries, Inc. ***(400)***
Electronic Financial Services Council ***(400)***
Electronic Traders Ass'n ***(401)***
EMC Corp. ***(401)***
Equipment Leasing Ass'n of America ***(406)***
The Equitable Cos. ***(406)***
Ernst & Young LLP *(72)*
Exxon Mobil Corp. ***(409)***
Fannie Mae ***(411)***
Farallon Capital Management ***(411)***
Farm Credit Council ***(411)***
Farmers Insurance Group ***(412)***
Farmland Industries, Inc. ***(412)***
Feder, Semo, Clarke & Bard *(74)*
Federal Agricultural Mortgage Corp. (Farmer Mac) ***(412)***
Federal Home Loan Bank of Des Moines ***(413)***
Federal Home Loan Bank of San Francisco ***(413)***
Federal Home Loan Bank of Seattle ***(413)***
Federal Home Loan Mortgage Corp. (Freddie Mac) ***(413)***
Jack Ferguson Associates, Inc. *(75)*
Fidelity Investments Co. ***(416)***
Financial Executives International ***(416)***
Financial Planning Ass'n ***(416)***
The Financial Services Roundtable ***(416)***
First American ***(417)***

First Data Corp./Telecheck *(417)*
First Union Corp. *(418)*
FleetBoston Financial *(418)*
Fleischman and Walsh, L.L.P. *(77)*
FM Watch *(420)*
Fon Digital Network Clearpoint Communications, Inc. *(421)*
Fontheim Internat'l, LLC *(78)*
Fontheim Partners, PC *(78)*
Ford Motor Co. *(422)*
Ford Motor Credit Co. (Legal Department) *(422)*
The Foreign Exchange Committee *(422)*
French & Company *(79)*
Friends of Higher Education Inc. *(426)*
Futures Industry Ass'n *(428)*
Gary, Indiana, Washington Office of the City of *(429)*
GE Capital Corp. *(430)*
General Conference of Seventh-day Adventists *(431)*
General Electric Capital Services, Inc. *(432)*
General Electric Co. *(432)*
General Motors Corp. *(432)*
Gibson, Dunn & Crutcher LLP *(82)*
Global Policy Group, Inc. *(83)*
GLOBEMAC Associates *(83)*
Goldman, Sachs and Co. *(437)*
Goodwin, Procter & Hoar LLP *(84)*
GPC Internat'l *(85)*
Greenberg Traurig, LLP *(86)*
Griffin & Associates *(87)*
The Group of 20 *(441)*
Grupo Carrousel (Mexico) *(441)*
Guaranty Bank, SSB *(442)*
Guidant Corp. *(442)*
Guinea, Secretary General of the Presidency of the Republic of *(442)*
Halliburton/Brown & Root *(443)*
Harbour Group Industries, Inc. *(444)*
The Hartford *(445)*
Herzog, Heine, Geduld, Inc. *(449)*
Higgins, McGovern & Smith, LLC *(94)*
Hogan & Hartson L.L.P. *(96)*
Hohlt & Associates *(98)*
Home Federal Savings and Loan Ass'n *(451)*
Homestake Mining *(451)*
Household Financial Group, Ltd. *(453)*
Household Internat'l, Inc. *(453)*
Howrey Simon Arnold & White *(100)*
Edwin E. Huddleson, III *(100)*
Hughes Hubbard & Reed LLP *(101)*
The Ickes & Enright Group *(102)*
Independent Community Bankers of America *(459)*
Independent Insurance Agents of America, Inc. *(459)*
Information Technology Industry Council *(462)*
Information Trust *(462)*
Infrastructure Management Group *(103)*
ING America Insurance Holdings, Inc. *(462)*
Instinet *(463)*
Institute for Certified Investment Management Consultants *(463)*
Institute of Internat'l Bankers *(464)*
Integrated Management Resources Group, Inc. *(465)*
Intel Corp. *(465)*
Interactive Brokers LLC *(466)*
Internat'l Ass'n for Financial Planning *(467)*
Internat'l Barter and Countertrade Foundation *(468)*
Internat'l Biometric Industry Ass'n *(468)*
Internat'l Brotherhood of Boilermakers, Iron Shipbuilders, Blacksmiths, Forgers and Helpers *(469)*
Internat'l Brotherhood of Electrical Workers *(469)*
Internat'l Reciprocal Trade *(474)*
Internat'l Swaps and Derivatives Dealers Ass'n *(475)*
Internat'l Union of Painters and Allied Trades *(476)*
Internation Securities Exchange *(476)*
Investment Co. Institute *(477)*
Investment Counsel Ass'n of America *(478)*
Investment Program Ass'n *(478)*
The Island ECN *(479)*
Jackson Nat'l Life Insurance *(480)*
Janus-Merritt Strategies, L.L.C. *(104)*
Jefferson Government Relations, L.L.C. *(106)*
JFS Group, Ltd. *(107)*
Mary P. Johannes *(107)*
Johnson Co. *(107)*
Jolly/Rissler, Inc. *(108)*
Jorden Burt LLP *(109)*
Kaiser Aluminum & Chemical Corp. *(485)*
Kansas City Southern Industries *(486)*
Katten Muchin & Zavis *(486)*
Katten Muchin & Zavis *(110)*
Kean Tracers, Inc. *(487)*
Kellogg Brown and Root *(487)*
KFx, Inc. *(489)*
Kimberly-Clark Corp. *(489)*
Peter Kinzler *(113)*
Kirkland & Ellis *(113)*
Kirkpatrick & Lockhart LLP *(114)*
Knight Trading Group *(490)*
Koch Industries, Inc. *(490)*
Korea Economic Institute of America *(491)*
David William Kuhnsman *(115)*
LaRocco & Associates *(116)*
Ledge Counsel *(118)*
LegisLaw *(118)*
Lehman Brothers *(498)*
Lent Scrivner & Roth LLC *(119)*
Lesher & Russell, Inc. *(119)*
Lincoln Nat'l Corp. *(500)*
London Clearinghouse, Ltd. *(503)*
Louisiana State University *(504)*
Lumbermens Mutual Casualty Co. *(505)*
MacAndrews & Forbes Holdings, Inc. *(506)*
Bernard L. Madoff Investment Securities *(507)*
Managed Funds Ass'n *(508)*
Management Options, Inc. *(123)*
Manatt, Phelps & Phillips, LLP *(123)*
Manufacturers Alliance/MAPI Inc. *(509)*
Maritime Investment Corp. *(510)*
MassMutual Financial Group *(512)*
MasterCard Internat'l *(513)*
Mayer, Brown & Platt *(126)*
Jack H. McDonald *(129)*
McDonald's Corp. *(514)*
McGlotten & Jarvis *(129)*
McGraw-Hill Cos., The *(514)*
McIntyre Law Firm, PLLC *(130)*
MemberWorks, Inc. *(517)*
Mentor Graphics Corp. *(518)*
Merrill Lynch & Co., Inc. *(519)*
The Metris Companies, Inc. *(520)*
Metropolitan Banking Group *(520)*
Metropolitan Life Insurance Co. *(520)*
Meyers & Associates *(133)*
MG Financial Group *(521)*
Mintz, Levin, Cohn, Ferris, Glovsky and Popeo, P.C. *(135)*
Mitsubishi Research Institute *(526)*
Susan Molinari, L.L.P. *(135)*
Money Management Institute *(527)*
The Money Store *(527)*
MONY Life Insurance Co. *(529)*
J. P. Morgan Chase & Co. *(529)*
Morgan Meguire, LLC *(136)*
Morgan Stanley Dean Witter & Co. *(529)*
Morgan, Lewis & Bockius LLP *(136)*
Morrison & Foerster LLP *(137)*
Mortgage Bankers Ass'n of America *(530)*
Mortgage Insurance Companies of America *(530)*
The Kate Moss Company *(137)*
Motorola, Inc. *(531)*
Muldoon, Murphy & Faucette, LLP *(532)*
Murray, Scheer, Montgomery, Tapia & O'Donnell *(139)*
Mutual of Omaha Insurance Companies *(533)*
Timothy D. Naegele & Associates *(140)*
Nat'l Ass'n of Bond Lawyers *(539)*
Nat'l Ass'n of Federal Credit Unions *(542)*
Nat'l Ass'n of Higher Educational Finance Authorities *(543)*
Nat'l Ass'n of Investment Companies *(544)*
Nat'l Ass'n of Manufacturers *(545)*
Nat'l Ass'n of Mortgage Brokers *(545)*
Nat'l Ass'n of Negro Business & Professional Women's Clubs, Inc. *(546)*
Nat'l Ass'n of Personal Financial Advisors *(546)*
Nat'l Ass'n of Police Organizations *(546)*
Nat'l Ass'n of Realtors *(547)*
Nat'l Ass'n of Securities and Commercial Law Attorneys *(549)*
Nat'l Ass'n of Securities Dealers, Inc. (NASD) *(549)*
Nat'l Ass'n of Small Business Investment Companies *(549)*
Nat'l Ass'n of State Auditors, Comptrollers and Treasurers *(549)*
Nat'l Ass'n of State Credit Union Supervisors *(549)*
Nat'l Ass'n of Thrift Savings Plan Participants *(550)*
Nat'l Consumers League *(558)*
Nat'l Council of Health Facilities Finance Authorities *(560)*
Nat'l Council of Higher Education Loan Programs *(560)*
Nat'l Defined Contribution Council *(561)*
Nat'l Employee Benefits Institute *(562)*
Nat'l Franchise Council *(565)*
Nat'l Grain Trade Council *(566)*
Nat'l Housing Conference *(567)*
Nat'l Legal Center for the Public Interest *(570)*
Nat'l Neighborhood Coalition *(572)*
Nat'l Venture Capital Ass'n *(580)*
NCR Corp. *(583)*
New England Financial *(585)*
New England Investment Co. *(585)*
New England Life Insurance Co. *(585)*
New Life Corp. of America *(586)*
New York Board of Trade *(586)*
New York Clearing House Ass'n *(587)*
New York Life Insurance Co. *(587)*
New York Mercantile Exchange *(587)*
New York Stock Exchange *(588)*
Non-Bank Funds Transmitters Group *(591)*
Julia J. Norrell & Associates *(142)*
North American Securities Administrators Ass'n (NASAA) *(592)*
Northwest Airlines, Inc. *(595)*
Northwestern Mutual Life Insurance Co. *(595)*
Novell, Inc. *(596)*
The OB-C Group, LLC *(143)*
O'Bryon & Co. *(144)*
O'Connor & Hannan, L.L.P. *(144)*
O'Melveny and Myers LLP *(147)*
O'Neill, Athy & Casey, P.C. *(147)*
Open Group Electronic Messaging Ass'n (EMA) Forum *(601)*
Oracle Corp. *(602)*
John T. O'Rourke Law Offices *(147)*
Pacific Life Insurance Co. *(605)*
PaineWebber Group, Inc. *(606)*
Parry, Romani, DeConcini & Symms *(149)*
Patton Boggs, LLP *(150)*
Paul, Hastings, Janofsky & Walker LLP *(153)*
Pennington BioMedical Research Center *(611)*
The Petrizzo Group, Inc. *(155)*
The PMA Group *(156)*
PNC Bank, N.A. *(619)*
Policy Consulting Services *(158)*
Potomac Electric Power Co. *(622)*
Preston Gates Ellis & Rouvelas Meeds LLP *(162)*
Principal Financial Group *(624)*
Sydney Probst *(164)*
Prudential Insurance Co. of America *(627)*
Public Financial Management *(628)*
Public Strategies Washington, Inc. *(164)*
Andrew F. Quinlan *(165)*
Quinn Gillespie & Associates *(165)*
Raytheon Co. *(633)*
Real Estate Roundtable *(634)*
Reinsurance Ass'n of America *(636)*
Renewable Resources LLC *(637)*
Retirement Industry Trust Ass'n *(639)*
Reuters America Inc. *(639)*
Rhoads Group *(168)*
Risk and Insurance Management Soc., Inc. (RIMS) *(640)*
The Rouse Company *(642)*

Royer & Babyak (172)
RPH & Associates, L.L.C. (172)
Rural Telephone Finance Cooperative (644)
Frank Russell Co. (644)
Ryan, Phillips, Utrecht & MacKinnon (173)
Sacramento-Potomac Consulting, Inc. (174)
James E. Schneider, LLM Inc. (651)
Charles Schwab & Co., Inc., (652)
Securities Industry Ass'n (654)
SEMCO (655)
Semiconductor Equipment and Materials Internat'l (655)
Separation Technologies (655)
D. E. Shaw & Co. (657)
Shaw Pittman (177)
Sher & Blackwell (179)
Sidley & Austin (180)
Siemens Westinghouse Power Corporation (658)
Silver Users Ass'n (659)
Skol & Associates, Inc. (182)
Smith Dawson & Andrews, Inc. (183)
Smith, Bucklin and Associates, Inc. (184)
The Smith-Free Group (184)
Software & Information Industry Ass'n (SIIA) (664)
The Solomon Group, LLC (185)
Sovereign Bank (668)
Space Access (668)
The Spectrum Group (186)
Standard Chartered Bank (672)
Stanford Financial Group (672)
Star Systems (673)
State Farm Insurance Cos. (673)
State Street Bank and Trust Co. (673)
Stephens Group, Inc. (674)
Stephens, Cross, Ihlenfeld & Boring, Inc. (188)
Steptoe & Johnson LLP (188)
Stilwell Financial Inc. (674)
Storage Technology Corp. (675)
Strategic Horizons Advisors, L.L.C. (189)
Strategic Impact, Inc. (189)
Student Loan Finance Corp. (675)
Sullivan & Cromwell (676)
Sullivan & Cromwell (190)
Paul Suplizio Associates (191)
Susquehanna Investment Group (678)
Swidler Berlin Shereff Friedman, LLP (191)
Swiss Investors Protection Ass'n (679)
George C. Tagg (192)
TD Waterhouse Group (682)
Thelen Reid & Priest LLP (193)
Thompson and Naughton, Inc. (194)
TIAA-CREF (686)
Timmons and Co., Inc. (195)
Trans Union Corp. (689)
Transnat'l Development Consortium (690)
Troutman Sanders LLP (196)
Turkish Industrialists and Businessmen's Ass'n (TUSIAD) (694)
U.S. Public Interest Research Group (697)
UBS Warburg (697)
United Parcel Service (702)
UNUM/Provident Corp. (708)
US Bancorp (709)
USAA - United Services Automobile Ass'n (710)
Valanzano & Associates (198)
The Velasquez Group (201)
Verner, Liipfert, Bernhard, McPherson and Hand, Chartered (713)
Verner, Liipfert, Bernhard, McPherson and Hand, Chartered (202)
Brenda R. Viehe-Naess (204)
VISA U.S.A., Inc. (716)
Vivendi Universal (717)
Waddell & Reed Financial, Inc. (718)
R. Duffy Wall and Associates (205)
Washington Council Ernst & Young (206)
Washington Mutual Bank (720)
Western Financial/Westcorp Inc. (724)
Wheat & Associates, Inc. (212)
Wiley, Rein & Fielding (214)
Williams & Jensen, P.C. (215)
Willkie Farr & Gallagher (217)
Wilmer, Cutler & Pickering (217)
Wilmington Savings Fund Society (727)
Deborah F. Winston (218)
Winston & Strawn (218)
X-PAC (732)
Zurich Financial Group (735)

Firearms/Guns/Ammunition (FIR)

20/20 Vision (223)
Alliant Techsystems, Inc. (241)
American Bar Ass'n (250)
American Jewish Congress (265)
American Legion (266)
American Public Health Ass'n (271)
Law Offices of Mark Barnes (24)
The Barton Co. (24)
BeamHit America LLC (310)
Bentley, Adams, Hargett, Riley and Co., Inc. (26)
Beretta U.S.A. Corp. (311)
Birch, Horton, Bittner & Cherot (28)
Briklee Trading Co. (320)
Cash America Internat'l (333)
Century Internat'l Arms (339)
Children's Defense Fund (344)
Citizens Committee for the Right to Keep and Bear Arms (348)
Coalition to Stop Gun Violence (356)
Consumer Federation of America (369)
Copeland, Lowery & Jacquez (52)
Dayton, Ohio, Washington Office of the City of (383)
Detroit, Michigan, City of (386)
Dykema Gossett PLLC (69)
EXPRO Chemical Products (409)
Federal Procurement Consultants (414)
Fifty Caliber Shooters Policy Institute, Inc. (416)
Firearms Importers Roundtable Trade Group (417)
Fraternal Order of Police (425)
Jim Frigiola (80)
Gary, Indiana, Washington Office of the City of (429)
Gun Owners of America (442)
Hall, Green, Rupli, LLC (90)
Handgun Control, Inc. (444)
The Hoffman Group (96)
Internat'l Ass'n of Fish and Wildlife Agencies (468)
Internat'l Union of Police Ass'ns (476)
Intrac Arms Internat'l LLC (477)
ITRI, Ltd. (480)
Kimmitt, Coates & McCarthy (113)
Law Enforcement Alliance of America (496)
Lew Horton Distributing Co. (498)
Lynn, Massachusetts, City of (506)
Mossberg Group, LLC (530)
Munitions Industrial Base Task Force (533)
Nammo Inc. (534)
Nat'l Ass'n of Arms Shows (538)
Nat'l Ass'n of Children's Hospitals Inc. (540)
Nat'l Ass'n of Police Organizations (546)
Nat'l Campaign for a Peace Tax Fund (554)
Nat'l Center for Policy Analysis (555)
Nat'l District Attorneys Ass'n (562)
Nat'l Grange (566)
Nat'l Pawnbrokers Ass'n (573)
Nat'l Rifle Ass'n of America (576)
Nat'l Shooting Sports Foundation Inc. (578)
Nixon Peabody LLP (142)
Olin Corp. (600)
Operations Security Professionals Soc. (601)
Police Executive Research Forum (620)
Rooney Group Internat'l, Inc. (171)
A. L. Ross Associates, Inc. (172)
Saf T Hammer (645)
Saf T Lok, Inc. (645)
SIG Arms (659)
Robert E. Smith (182)
Sporting Arms and Ammunition Manufacturers' Institute, Inc. (670)
Timmons and Co., Inc. (195)
U.S. Chamber Institute for Legal Reform (695)
United Methodist Church General Board of Church and Society (702)
Violence Policy Center (715)
R. Duffy Wall and Associates (205)
Zeliff, Ireland, and Associates (221)
Zuckerman Spaeder L.L.P. (221)

Food Industry (FOO)

20/20 Vision (223)
AARP (American Ass'n of Retired Persons) (224)
The Accord Group (5)
AFLAC, Inc. (231)
Ag Biotech Planning Committee (232)
Agribusiness Council (232)
Agricultural Retailers Ass'n (232)
The Aker Partners Inc. (7)
Alliance for Reasonable Regulation of Insecticides (240)
Alliance of Western Milk Producers (241)
Alpine Group, Inc. (11)
Alticor, Inc. (242)
American Ass'n for Laboratory Accreditation (246)
American Bakers Ass'n (250)
American Butter Institute (251)
American Cancer Soc. (252)
American Council of Independent Laboratories (255)
American Crop Protection Ass'n (256)
American Dehydrated Onion and Garlic Ass'n (256)
American Dietetic Ass'n (257)
American Farm Bureau Federation (258)
American Feed Industry Ass'n (259)
American Frozen Food Institute (260)
American Heart Ass'n (262)
American Herbal Products Ass'n (262)
American Home Products Corp. (262)
American Hotel and Lodging Ass'n (263)
American Meat Institute (267)
American Plastics Council (270)
American Public Health Ass'n (271)
American Sheep Industry Ass'n (273)
American Teleservices Ass'n (279)
American Wholesale Marketers Ass'n (280)
Arent Fox Kintner Plotkin & Kahn, PLLC (14)
James Nicholas Ashmore & Associates (18)
Ass'n of Sales & Marketing Companies (298)
Aventis CropScience (304)
Aventis Pharmaceutical Products (304)
Ball Janik, LLP (22)
Barnes & Thornburg (23)
BASF Corporation (308)
Battelle Memorial Institute (309)
Bayer Corp. / Agriculture Division (309)
Baylor College of Medicine (310)
Bergner Bockorny Castagnetti and Hawkins (26)
Biotechnology Industry Organization (314)
Biscuit and Cracker Manufacturers Ass'n (314)
BKSH & Associates (28)
Blank Rome Comisky & McCauley, LLP (29)
Brinker Internat'l (320)
Bulmer Holding PLC, H. P. (323)
Burger King Corp. (324)
Butera & Andrews (34)
C&M Internat'l, Ltd. (35)
California Pistachio Commission (327)
Campbell Crane & Associates (36)
Capitol Associates, Inc. (37)
Capitolink, LLC (39)
Cargill, Inc. (331)
Celanese Government Relations Office (334)
Cell Tech (334)
Center for Science in the Public Interest (337)
Central Soya Co. (339)
Cheese of Choice Coalition (341)
Chemical Producers and Distributors Ass'n (342)
Chicago School Reform Board of Trustees (343)
Chocolate Manufacturers Ass'n of the U.S.A. (345)
Citizens Against Government Waste (348)
Citizens for Public Action on Cholesterol, Inc. (348)
The Coca-Cola Company (356)
ConAgra Foods, Inc. (365)
Consumer Federation of America (369)
Consumers Union of the United States (369)
Coors Brewing Company (371)
Corn Refiners Ass'n, Inc. (372)

Council for Advanced Agricultural Formulations, Inc. *(373)*
Council for Responsible Nutrition *(374)*
Covington & Burling *(53)*
CSA America, Inc. *(379)*
Cumberland Packing Corp. *(380)*
Dalrymple and Associates, L.L.C. *(56)*
Glenn Roger Delaney *(60)*
DIAGEO *(387)*
The Dial Co. *(387)*
Dietary Supplement Safety and Science Coalition *(388)*
DNA Plant Technology Corp. *(390)*
Dow AgroSciences *(391)*
The Dow Chemical Co. *(391)*
DuPont *(393)*
The Dutko Group, Inc. *(68)*
Eastman Chemical Co. *(395)*
Edelman Public Relations Worldwide *(396)*
Stanley J. Emerling *(71)*
EOP Group, Inc. *(72)*
Ephedra Education Council *(405)*
Evans & Black, Inc. *(73)*
F&T Network, Inc. *(74)*
Farm Credit Council *(411)*
Farmland Industries, Inc. *(412)*
Ferraro, USA *(415)*
The Fertilizer Institute *(415)*
Fierce and Isakowitz *(76)*
FMC Corp. *(420)*
Food Distributors Internat'l (NAWGA-IFDA) *(421)*
Food Marketing Institute *(421)*
Food Processing Machinery and Supplies Ass'n *(421)*
FQPA Implementation Working Group *(424)*
FRANMAC/Taco Pac *(425)*
Fresh Produce Ass'n of the Americas *(426)*
Ernest & Julio Gallo Winery *(428)*
The Garrison Group *(81)*
General Mills *(432)*
GHL Inc. *(82)*
Greenberg Traurig, LLP *(86)*
Greener and Hook, LLC *(87)*
Griffin, Johnson, Dover & Stewart *(87)*
Grocery Manufacturers of America *(440)*
Guinea, Secretary General of the Presidency of the Republic of *(442)*
Hall, Green, Rupli, LLC *(90)*
Health Physics Soc. *(446)*
Hecht, Spencer & Associates *(93)*
Herbalife Internat'l, Inc. *(448)*
Hershey Foods Corp. *(449)*
Hogan & Hartson L.L.P. *(96)*
Holland & Knight LLP *(98)*
R. J. Hudson Associates *(101)*
Huntsman Corp. *(455)*
Hyman, Phelps & McNamara, P.C. *(102)*
Independent Bakers Ass'n *(459)*
Infectious Diseases Soc. of America, Inc. *(461)*
Institute of Food Technologists *(464)*
Inter-American Institute for Cooperation on Agriculture *(466)*
Inter-Associates, Inc. *(103)*
Inter-Cal Corp. *(466)*
Internat'l Bottled Water Ass'n *(468)*
Internat'l Brotherhood of Teamsters *(469)*
Internat'l Dairy Foods Ass'n *(470)*
Internat'l Dairy-Deli-Bakery Ass'n *(471)*
Internat'l Food Additives Council *(471)*
Internat'l Frozen Food Ass'n *(472)*
Internat'l Mass Retailers Ass'n *(473)*
JBC Internat'l *(105)*
Jellinek, Schwartz & Connolly *(106)*
S.C. Johnson and Son, Inc. *(484)*
Kellogg Co. *(487)*
Kessler & Associates Business Services, Inc. *(112)*
KOSA *(491)*
Kraft Foods, Inc. *(492)*
Kurzweil & Associates *(115)*
The Paul Laxalt Group *(117)*
Lesher & Russell, Inc. *(119)*
Lockridge Grindal & Nauen, P.L.L.P. *(121)*
Long, Aldridge & Norman, LLP *(121)*
Luman, Lange & Wheeler *(122)*
Maloney & Knox, LLP *(123)*
Management Options, Inc. *(123)*
Martin, Fisher & Associates, Inc. *(125)*
Masaoka & Associates, Inc. *(125)*
Mauritius Sugar Syndicate *(513)*
Mauritius, Chamber of Agriculture of *(513)*
Maytag Corp. *(513)*
McDermott, Will and Emery *(128)*
McDonald's Corp. *(514)*
McGlotten & Jarvis *(129)*
McGuiness & Holch *(130)*
McKee Foods Corp. *(515)*
McLeod, Watkinson & Miller *(131)*
McMahon and Associates *(131)*
Mead Johnson Nutritional Group *(515)*
Meat New Zealand *(515)*
Meyers & Associates *(133)*
Miller & Chevalier, Chartered *(133)*
Mintz, Levin, Cohn, Ferris, Glovsky and Popeo, P.C. *(135)*
Mitsubishi Research Institute *(526)*
James T. Molloy *(135)*
Monsanto Co. *(528)*
R. B. Murphy & Associates *(139)*
Nat'l Ass'n for Nutritional Choice *(538)*
Nat'l Ass'n of Federal Veterinarians *(542)*
Nat'l Ass'n of Margarine Manufacturers *(545)*
Nat'l Ass'n of State Departments of Agriculture *(549)*
Nat'l Cattleman's Beef Ass'n *(554)*
Nat'l Center for Genome Research *(554)*
Nat'l Chicken Council *(555)*
Nat'l Coalition of Food Importers Ass'n *(556)*
Nat'l Confectioners Ass'n *(558)*
Nat'l Consumers League *(558)*
Nat'l Council of Catholic Women *(560)*
Nat'l Farmers Union (Farmers Educational & Co-operative Union of America) *(563)*
Nat'l Fisheries Institute *(564)*
Nat'l Food Processors Ass'n *(564)*
Nat'l Frozen Pizza Institute *(565)*
Nat'l Grain and Feed Ass'n *(566)*
Nat'l Grange *(566)*
Nat'l Grocers Ass'n *(566)*
Nat'l Licensed Beverage Ass'n *(570)*
Nat'l Meat Ass'n *(570)*
Nat'l Meat Canners Ass'n *(570)*
Nat'l Milk Producers Federation *(571)*
Nat'l Nutritional Foods Ass'n *(572)*
Nat'l Oilseed Processors Ass'n *(572)*
Nat'l Pest Control Ass'n *(573)*
Nat'l Pork Producers Council *(574)*
Nat'l Potato Council *(574)*
Nat'l Restaurant Ass'n *(576)*
Nat'l Soft Drink Ass'n *(578)*
Nat'l Turkey Federation *(580)*
Nat'l Yogurt Ass'n *(581)*
Nestle USA, Inc. *(584)*
North American Meat Processors Ass'n *(592)*
North American Millers' Ass'n *(592)*
Novartis Corp. *(596)*
Nu Skin Internat'l Inc. *(597)*
Olsson, Frank and Weeda, P.C. *(146)*
Owens-Illinois, Inc. *(605)*
Pacific Seafood Processors Ass'n *(606)*
Parry, Romani, DeConcini & Symms *(149)*
Jim Pasco & Associates *(150)*
Patton Boggs, LLP *(150)*
Patton Boggs, LLP *(609)*
Pharmanex *(615)*
Philip Morris Management Corp. *(615)*
The Pillsbury Co. *(617)*
Charles L. Pizer *(156)*
Susan S. Platt Consulting *(156)*
The PMA Group *(156)*
Podesta/Mattoon *(158)*
Policy Directions, Inc. *(158)*
Powell, Goldstein, Frazer & Murphy LLP *(160)*
Preston Gates Ellis & Rouvelas Meeds LLP *(162)*
Printing Industries of America *(624)*
The Procter & Gamble Company *(625)*
Robert N. Pyle & Associates *(165)*
Bruce Ray & Company *(166)*
Reed, Smith, LLP *(167)*
Rexall Sundown *(639)*
Rodale Press *(641)*
Ryan, Phillips, Utrecht & MacKinnon *(173)*
Ryberg and Smith LLP *(174)*
Saliba Action Strategies, LLC *(174)*
Salt Institute *(646)*
Schramm, Williams & Associates, Inc. *(176)*
Seaboard Corp. *(653)*
Sensor Research and Development Corp. *(655)*
Sidley & Austin *(180)*
Slim Fast Foods Co. *(661)*
Snack Food Ass'n *(662)*
Sodexho Marriott Services, Inc. *(664)*
SOL Source Technologies, Inc. *(665)*
Solus Research, Inc. *(665)*
Southeast Dairy Farmer Ass'n *(667)*
Strategic Horizons Advisors, L.L.C. *(189)*
Sugar Ass'n, Inc. *(676)*
Suiza Foods Corp. *(676)*
Sunkist Growers, Inc. *(677)*
Swedish Match *(678)*
Swidler Berlin Shereff Friedman, LLP *(191)*
Taco Bell Corp. *(679)*
Tallon & Associates *(192)*
Tate and Lyle North American Sugars Inc. *(681)*
Michael L. Tiner *(195)*
Titan Corp. *(687)*
Titan Scan *(687)*
Transhumance Holding Co., Inc. *(690)*
Tricon Global Restaurants Inc. *(692)*
Trident Seafood Corp. *(692)*
Tyson Foods, Inc. *(695)*
U.S. Public Interest Research Group *(697)*
UDV/Heublein, Inc. *(698)*
Unilever United States, Inc. *(699)*
United Egg Ass'n *(701)*
United Egg Producers *(701)*
United Food and Commercial Workers Internat'l Union *(701)*
United Fresh Fruit and Vegetable Ass'n *(701)*
United Methodist Church General Board of Church and Society *(702)*
United States Tuna Foundation *(704)*
University of Massachusetts *(706)*
Utah Natural Products Alliance *(710)*
Vacuum Insulation Ass'n *(711)*
Valis Associates *(198)*
Valley Pride Pack *(711)*
Venable *(201)*
Verner, Liipfert, Bernhard, McPherson and Hand, Chartered *(202)*
Mary Vihstadt *(204)*
Vorys, Sater, Seymour and Pease, LLP *(205)*
Washington Council Ernst & Young *(206)*
Weider Nutritional Group *(722)*
Welch's Foods, Inc. *(722)*
Carla L. West *(211)*
Western Growers Ass'n *(724)*
The Wexler Group *(211)*
Wheat Export Trade Education Committee *(725)*
Williams & Jensen, P.C. *(215)*
Kathleen Winn & Associates, Inc. *(218)*

Foreign Relations (FOR)

3Com Corp. *(223)*
ABB, Inc. *(225)*
Michael W. Adcock *(6)*
Advertising Company ART-ERIA *(229)*
The Advocacy Group *(6)*
Aerospace Industries Ass'n of America *(230)*
Afghanistan Foundation *(230)*
AFL-CIO (American Federation of Labor and Congress of Industrial Organizations) *(231)*
Africa Global Partners *(7)*
AfriSpace Corp. *(232)*
Agudath Israel of America *(232)*
Akin, Gump, Strauss, Hauer & Feld, L.L.P. *(8)*
Alcatel *(237)*
Armando Alejandre, Estate of *(238)*
Alliance for Internat'l Educational and Cultural Exchange, The *(239)*
Alliance to Save Energy *(241)*
Alsatian American Chamber of Commerce *(242)*
Amerada Hess Corp. *(243)*
American Ass'n of Museums *(248)*

American Ass'n of Physicians of Indian Origin ***(249)***
American Bar Ass'n ***(250)***
American Chamber of Commerce in Egypt ***(252)***
American Committee for Peace and Justice in South Asia ***(254)***
American Committee for the Weizmann Institute of Science ***(254)***
American Continental Group, Inc. ***(12)***
American Council of Korean Travel Agents ***(255)***
American Council of Life Insurers ***(256)***
American Foreign Service Ass'n ***(259)***
American Hellenic Institute Public Affairs Committee ***(262)***
American Institute for Foreign Studies ***(264)***
American Israel Public Affairs Committee ***(265)***
American Jewish Committee ***(265)***
American Jewish Congress ***(265)***
American Kurdish Information Network (AKIN) ***(265)***
American Legion ***(266)***
American Museum of Natural History ***(268)***
American Petroleum Institute ***(269)***
American Physical Soc. ***(270)***
Americans for Equitable Climate Solutions ***(281)***
Americans for Peace Now ***(282)***
Americans for Tax Reform ***(282)***
Americans United for Separation of Church and State ***(282)***
Amnesty Internat'l U.S.A. ***(283)***
Andreae, Vick & Associates, L.L.C. ***(14)***
Anti-Defamation League ***(285)***
APCO Worldwide ***(14)***
APKINDO ***(286)***
Arent Fox Kintner Plotkin & Kahn, PLLC ***(14)***
Armenian Assembly of America ***(289)***
Arms Control Ass'n ***(289)***
Arnold & Porter ***(16)***
Ashland Inc. ***(290)***
James Nicholas Ashmore & Associates ***(18)***
Asia Pacific Policy Center ***(290)***
The Ass'n For Manufacturing Technology (AMT) ***(292)***
Ass'n of American Chambers of Commerce in Latin America ***(293)***
Ass'n of American Shippers ***(294)***
Ass'n of Small Business Development Centers ***(298)***
Ass'n to Unite the Democracies ***(299)***
Associated General Contractors of America ***(300)***
Atlantic Corridor USA ***(302)***
Automotive Parts and Service Alliance ***(303)***
Avioimpex ***(305)***
Azerbaijan, Embassy of the Republic of ***(305)***
B'nai B'rith Internat'l ***(305)***
Bacardi-Martini, USA, Inc. ***(305)***
Ball Janik, LLP ***(22)***
Baltic American Freedom League ***(306)***
Bangladesh Export Processing Zones Authority ***(307)***
Bankers' Ass'n for Finance and Trade ***(307)***
Bannerman and Associates, Inc. ***(22)***
Banorte Casa de Bolsa ***(307)***
Barbour Griffith & Rogers, Inc. ***(22)***
Barrick Goldstrike Mines, Inc. ***(308)***
Battelle Memorial Institute ***(309)***
Bergner Bockorny Castagnetti and Hawkins ***(26)***
Better World Campaign ***(312)***
Bicopas, Ltd. ***(313)***
BKSH & Associates ***(28)***
Bloomfield Associates, Inc. ***(29)***
The Boeing Co. ***(316)***
BP Amoco Corp. ***(319)***
Bracewell & Patterson, L.L.P. ***(30)***
Bracy Williams & Co. ***(31)***
Bread for the World ***(319)***
Bristol-Myers Squibb Co. ***(320)***
British American Security Information Council ***(321)***
The Brookings Institution ***(321)***
BSMG Worldwide ***(34)***
Bulgarian-American Business Center ***(323)***
Business Executives for Nat'l Security ***(324)***
The Business Roundtable ***(325)***
Butterfield Carter & Associates ***(35)***
Cadwalader, Wickersham & Taft ***(35)***
Campaign to Preserve U.S. Global Leadership ***(329)***
Capital Consultants Corp. ***(37)***
Capitol Associates, Inc. ***(37)***
Capitol Link, Inc. ***(39)***
CARE (Cooperative for Assistance and Relief Everywhere) ***(331)***
Cargill, Inc. ***(331)***
CaseNewHolland Inc. ***(333)***
Caspian Group ***(42)***
Cassidy & Associates, Inc. ***(42)***
Catholic Alliance ***(333)***
CEMEX Central, S.A. de C.V. ***(335)***
CEMEX USA ***(335)***
Center for Internat'l Policy ***(336)***
Central American Bank of Economic Integration ***(338)***
Central European Media Enterprises ***(338)***
Century Communications, Inc. ***(44)***
Chamber of Commerce of the U.S.A. ***(340)***
Christian Voice, Inc. ***(345)***
Church of Scientology Internat'l ***(346)***
CIGNA Corp. ***(346)***
Citizens for Liberty in Cuba (Cuba Libertad) ***(348)***
Citizens Network for Foreign Affairs (CNFA) ***(349)***
City University ***(349)***
Civic Service, Inc. ***(46)***
The Climate Council, ***(351)***
William M. Cloherty ***(47)***
Coalition for American Leadership Abroad/American Foreign Affairs Organizations, Inc. ***(352)***
Coalition for Food Aid ***(353)***
Coalition of Service Industries ***(355)***
The Coca-Cola Company ***(356)***
Scott Cohen ***(48)***
Coleman Research Corp. ***(357)***
Collier Shannon Scott, PLLC ***(48)***
Collins & Company, Inc. ***(49)***
Colombian Banking and Financial Entities Ass'n (ASOBANCARIA) ***(358)***
Columbus Public Affairs ***(50)***
ComInternational Management Inc. ***(360)***
ConAgra Foods, Inc. ***(365)***
Concert USA ***(365)***
Congo, Democratic Republic of the ***(366)***
Congressional Economic Leadership Institute ***(366)***
Conlon, Frantz, Phelan & Pires ***(51)***
Conoco Inc. ***(367)***
The Conservative Caucus ***(367)***
Constituency for Africa ***(368)***
Consumers Union of the United States ***(369)***
Contractors Internat'l Group on Nuclear Liability ***(370)***
Cooler Heads Coalition ***(371)***
Corporacion de Exportaciones Mexicanas, S.A. de C.V. and Marvin Roy Feldman ***(372)***
Corporate Council on Africa ***(372)***
Costa, Carlos Alberto, Estate of ***(373)***
Council for a Livable World Education Fund ***(373)***
Council for the Nat'l Interest ***(375)***
Council on Internat'l Educational Exchange ***(377)***
Credit Suisse First Boston Corp. ***(378)***
Creme de la Creme, Inc. ***(378)***
Cuban American Nat'l Foundation/Cuban American Foundation ***(379)***
Cultural Partnership of the Americas ***(380)***
Cyprus, Government of the Republic of ***(380)***
Dana Corp. ***(382)***
Mario M. de la Pena, Estate of ***(383)***
DeMil Internat'l ***(385)***
George H. Denison ***(60)***
Denison, Scott and Cohen ***(61)***
Dierman, Wortley, and Zola ***(62)***
Direct Selling Ass'n ***(389)***
Dow, Lohnes & Albertson, PLLC ***(64)***
Downey McGrath Group, Inc. ***(64)***
The Duberstein Group, Inc. ***(65)***
Dublin Castle Group ***(66)***
EarthVoice ***(394)***
Eckert Seamans Cherin & Mellott, LLC ***(70)***
Edington, Peel & Associates, Inc. ***(70)***
Edison Internat'l ***(397)***
Edison Mission Energy ***(397)***
Electronic Retailing Ass'n ***(401)***
Elettronica Veneta & IN.EL. ***(401)***
EMI Associates, Ltd. ***(71)***
Emory University, Department of Internat'l Health-PAMM, USAID ***(402)***
Enron Corp. ***(403)***
Equatorial Guinea, Republic of ***(406)***
ERIM ***(406)***
Ethics Resource Center Inc. ***(407)***
The Evans Group, Ltd. ***(74)***
Exxon Mobil Corp. ***(409)***
EZ's Solutions, Inc. ***(74)***
Family Research Council, Inc. ***(411)***
Farmland Industries, Inc. ***(412)***
Federal Legislative Associates, Inc. ***(75)***
Federation of American Scientists ***(414)***
Feith & Zell, P.C. ***(75)***
The Fertilizer Institute ***(415)***
Finnish American Corporate Team (F.A.C.T.) ***(417)***
First Scientific Corp. ***(418)***
Florida State University ***(420)***
Florida State University System ***(420)***
Foley Government and Public Affairs, Inc. ***(78)***
Foley, Hoag & Eliot LLP ***(78)***
Formosan Ass'n for Public Affairs ***(423)***
Free ANWAR Campaign ***(425)***
Freeport-McMoRan Copper & Gold Inc. ***(425)***
Friends Committee on Nat'l Legislation ***(426)***
The Friends of Democratic Congo ***(426)***
The Gallagher Group, LLC ***(80)***
Law Offices of Michael R. Gardner, P.C. ***(81)***
Sara Garland (and Associates) ***(81)***
Garvey, Schubert & Barer ***(81)***
General Conference of Seventh-day Adventists ***(431)***
General Development Corp. ***(431)***
General Dynamics Corp. ***(431)***
General Electric Co. ***(432)***
General Motors Corp. ***(432)***
Gibbons & Company, Inc. ***(82)***
Gibraltar Information Bureau ***(435)***
Global Health Council ***(436)***
Global USA, Inc. ***(83)***
Gowran Internat'l Ltd. ***(85)***
Edwin C. Graves & Associates ***(85)***
Greenberg Traurig, LLP ***(86)***
Greystar Resources, Ltd. ***(440)***
Grupo Financiero Banorte ***(441)***
Grupo Maseca ***(441)***
Guardian Marine Internat'l LLC ***(442)***
Guinea, Secretary General of the Presidency of the Republic of ***(442)***
Gustafson Associates ***(89)***
Guyana, Government of the Co-operative Republic of ***(442)***
Hadassah Medical Relief Fund ***(443)***
Hadassah, The Women's Zionist Organization of America ***(443)***
Hager Sharp Inc. ***(443)***
Haiti, Office of the President of the Republic of ***(443)***
Halliburton/Brown & Root ***(443)***
Harmon & Wilmot, L.L.P. ***(91)***
Hitachi, Ltd. ***(450)***
Hogan & Hartson L.L.P. ***(96)***
Holland & Knight LLP ***(98)***
Holy Land Trust ***(451)***
Honduras, Embassy of ***(452)***
Hong Kong Economic and Trade Office ***(452)***
Hooper Owen & Winburn ***(99)***
Christopher C. Horner ***(100)***
R. J. Hudson Associates ***(101)***
ICN Pharmaceuticals, Inc. ***(457)***
IMC Global Inc. ***(458)***
Immigration and Refugee Service of America ***(458)***
IMPACT, LLC ***(102)***
India, Government of the Republic of ***(460)***
Information Trust ***(462)***
Ingersoll-Rand Co. ***(462)***
Institute for Balkan Affairs ***(463)***
Institute for Science and Internat'l Security ***(464)***
Institute on Religion and Democracy ***(464)***
Institute on Religion and Public Policy ***(464)***
InterAction ***(466)***

Internat'l Agriculture and Rural Development Group ***(467)***
Internat'l Campaign for Tibet ***(469)***
Internat'l College ***(470)***
Internat'l Labor Rights Fund ***(472)***
Internat'l Medical Programs ***(473)***
Internat'l Rescue Committee Inc. ***(474)***
Internat'l Research and Exchanges Board (IREX) ***(474)***
Internat'l Trust Fund for Demining and Mine Victims Assistance in Bosnia-Herzigovina ***(475)***
Interns for Peace Internat'l ***(477)***
IPR Shandwick ***(478)***
Islamic Institute ***(479)***
IUCN - The World Conservation Union (US) ***(480)***
Jamison and Sullivan, Inc. *(104)*
Janus-Merritt Strategies, L.L.C. *(104)*
Japan, Embassy of ***(482)***
Jar-Mon Consultants, Inc. *(105)*
Jefferson-Waterman Internat'l, LLC *(106)*
Jewish Institute for Nat'l Security Affairs ***(483)***
Johns Hopkins University & Hospital ***(483)***
S.C. Johnson and Son, Inc. ***(484)***
Joint Baltic American Nat'l Committee, Inc. ***(484)***
Joint Corporate Committee on Cuban Claims ***(484)***
Jorden Burt LLP *(109)*
Kaiser Aluminum & Chemical Corp. ***(485)***
Kashmiri American Council ***(486)***
Kazakhstan 21st Century Foundation ***(487)***
Keizai Koho Center ***(487)***
Kellogg Brown and Root ***(487)***
Kellogg Co. ***(487)***
Khalistan, Council of ***(489)***
Kimberly Consulting, LLC *(113)*
Kimberly-Clark Corp. ***(489)***
Michael J. Kopetski *(114)*
Korea Economic Institute of America ***(491)***
Kurdistan Democratic Party USA ***(492)***
Kvaerner US Inc. ***(492)***
Labor Council for Latin American Advancement (LCLAA) ***(493)***
Lee Lane *(116)*
Lao Progressive Institute ***(495)***
Lao Veterans of America, Inc. ***(495)***
Lawyers Committee for Human Rights ***(496)***
League of Women Voters of the United States ***(497)***
The Legislative Strategies Group, LLC *(118)*
Liberal Party of Japan ***(499)***
Link Romania, Inc. ***(500)***
Lockheed Martin Corp. ***(501)***
Lovelace Respiratory Research Institute ***(504)***
Loyola College ***(505)***
Luso American Foundation ***(505)***
Lutheran Office for Governmental Affairs/Evangelical Lutheran Church in America ***(506)***
Luxcore Public Affairs ***(506)***
Makedonski Telekomunikacii ***(508)***
Manatos & Manatos, Inc. *(123)*
Manatt, Phelps & Phillips, LLP *(123)*
Marathon Oil Co. ***(509)***
Mattox Woolfolk, LLC *(126)*
Mayer, Brown & Platt *(126)*
McClure, Gerard & Neuenschwander, Inc. *(127)*
McDermott Internat'l, Inc./Babcock & Wilcox ***(514)***
McDermott, Will and Emery *(128)*
Medtronic, Inc. ***(517)***
Megaseal Corp. ***(517)***
Mercury Group *(132)*
Merrill Lynch & Co., Inc. ***(519)***
Metropolitan Life Insurance Co. ***(520)***
Mexican Crab Industry ***(521)***
Mexican Nat'l Spiny Lobster Industry ***(521)***
Meyers & Associates *(133)*
Micronesia, Embassy of the Federated States of ***(522)***
Millian Byers Associates, LLC *(135)*
Mitsubishi Corp. ***(526)***
Mitsubishi Internat'l Corp. ***(526)***
Morgan Stanley Dean Witter & Co. ***(529)***
Morgan, Lewis & Bockius LLP *(136)*
Morocco, Foreign Ministry of the Kingdom of ***(529)***
Moscow State University ***(530)***
Most Group Limited ***(530)***
Motorola, Inc. ***(531)***
The MWW Group *(140)*
Nat'l Ass'n for the Advancement of Colored People, Washington Bureau ***(538)***
Nat'l Ass'n of Dealers in Ancient, Oriental and Primitive Art ***(542)***
Nat'l Ass'n of Evangelicals ***(542)***
Nat'l Ass'n of Manufacturers ***(545)***
Nat'l Ass'n of Negro Business & Professional Women's Clubs, Inc. ***(546)***
Nat'l Audubon Soc. ***(552)***
Nat'l Cooperative Business Ass'n ***(559)***
Nat'l Council for Eurasian and East European Research ***(559)***
Nat'l Council of Catholic Women ***(560)***
Nat'l Defense Council Foundation ***(561)***
Nat'l Defense Industrial Ass'n ***(561)***
Nat'l Electrical Manufacturers Ass'n ***(562)***
Nat'l Federation of Croatian Americans ***(564)***
Nat'l Foreign Trade Council, Inc. ***(565)***
Nat'l ITFS Ass'n ***(569)***
Nat'l Military Intelligence Ass'n ***(571)***
Nat'l Mining Ass'n ***(571)***
Nat'l Power ***(574)***
Nat'l Right to Life Committee ***(576)***
Nat'l Spiritual Assembly of the Baha'is of the United States ***(578)***
Nat'l Strategy Information Center ***(579)***
Nat'l Telephone Cooperative Ass'n ***(579)***
Nature Islands, Inc. ***(582)***
Network in Solidarity with the People of Guatemala (NISGUA) ***(584)***
NETWORK, A Nat'l Catholic Social Justice Lobby ***(584)***
New Frontiers Communications Consulting *(141)*
New York University ***(588)***
NewMarket Global Consulting Group ***(588)***
Newport News Shipbuilding Inc. ***(588)***
Nixon Center, The ***(590)***
Novell, Inc. ***(596)***
NRG Energy, Inc. ***(596)***
Obadal and MacLeod, p.c. *(143)*
O'Connor & Hannan, L.L.P. *(144)*
Takashi Oka *(146)*
Olympic Aid ***(600)***
O'Melveny and Myers LLP *(147)*
Oneonta Trading Corp. ***(601)***
Operations Security Professionals Soc. ***(601)***
Oppenheimer Wolff & Donnelly LLP *(147)*
Oshkosh Truck Corp. ***(604)***
PADCO, Inc. ***(606)***
Pakistan, Government of the Islamic Republic of ***(606)***
Palestinian Authority ***(606)***
Pan American Health Organization ***(607)***
Pancyprian Ass'n of America ***(607)***
Panda Energy Internat'l ***(607)***
Parry, Romani, DeConcini & Symms *(149)*
Partners of the Americas ***(608)***
Patton Boggs, LLP *(150)*
Pegasus Capital Advisors, L.P. ***(611)***
The Peterson Group *(155)*
Petito & Associates *(155)*
Pfizer, Inc. ***(613)***
Philip Morris Management Corp. ***(615)***
Polar Air Cargo, Inc. ***(620)***
Population Action Internat'l ***(621)***
Powell Tate *(160)*
Powell, Goldstein, Frazer & Murphy LLP *(160)*
Pretium S.C (Mexico) ***(623)***
Principal Financial Group ***(624)***
Pro Advance Inc. *(164)*
The Procter & Gamble Company ***(625)***
Progressive Policy Institute ***(626)***
Robert N. Pyle & Associates *(165)*
Quebec Lumber Manufacturers Ass'n ***(630)***
Raytheon Co. ***(633)***
Recon/Optical, Inc. ***(634)***
Refugees Internat'l ***(635)***
Religious Technology Center ***(636)***
Republican Jewish Coalition ***(637)***
Rhoads Group *(168)*
Ross-Robinson & Associates *(172)*
Sagamore Associates, Inc. *(174)*
Schmeltzer, Aptaker & Shepard, P.C. *(176)*
Schrayer and Associates, Inc. *(176)*
Scientech Corp. ***(652)***
Scribe Communications, Inc. ***(653)***
Seaboard Corp. ***(653)***
Search for Common Ground ***(653)***
Sesame Workshop ***(656)***
Seton Hill College ***(656)***
Shaklee Corp. ***(656)***
Shell Oil Co. ***(657)***
Singapore, Embassy of the Republic of ***(659)***
Sister Cities Internat'l ***(660)***
Skol & Associates, Inc. *(182)*
Anne V. Smith *(182)*
Philip S. Smith & Associates, Inc. *(182)*
The Solomon Group, LLC *(185)*
Sonnenschein, Nath & Rosenthal *(185)*
Sony Electronics, Inc. ***(666)***
South African Government/World Bank ***(666)***
Space Imaging, Inc. ***(669)***
St. Paul, Alaska, City of ***(672)***
Stanfield Tindal, Inc. *(187)*
Steptoe & Johnson LLP *(188)*
Sterling Internat'l Consultants, Inc. ***(674)***
Stoll Stoll Berne Lokting & Shlachter, P.C. ***(675)***
Strategic Horizons Advisors, L.L.C. *(189)*
Svenska Petroleum Exploration AB ***(678)***
SWIPCO, U.S. ***(678)***
Symms, Lehn & Associates, Inc. *(192)*
T.W.Y. Co., Ltd. ***(679)***
Tai Ji Men Qigong Academy ***(680)***
Taipei Economic and Cultural Representative Office in the United States ***(680)***
Taiwan Studies Institute ***(680)***
Teicher Consulting and Representation *(193)*
Timmons and Co., Inc. *(195)*
Traditional Values Coalition ***(689)***
Transnat'l Development Consortium ***(690)***
Turkey, Government of the Republic of ***(694)***
Turkish Industrialists and Businessmen's Ass'n (TUSIAD) ***(694)***
Turkish Republic of Northern Cyprus, Embassy of ***(694)***
U.S. Colombia Business Partnership ***(696)***
U.S. Fund for UNICEF ***(696)***
U.S. Overseas Cooperative Development ***(697)***
U.S.-Turkish Business Council of DEIK ***(697)***
Uganda, Embassy of the Republic of ***(698)***
Uganda, Government of the Republic of ***(698)***
Ukraine, Government of ***(698)***
Ukrainian Nat'l Ass'n, Inc. ***(698)***
Union of Councils for Soviet Jews ***(699)***
Union of Needletrades, Industrial, and Textile Employees (UNITE) ***(699)***
United Defense, L.P. ***(701)***
United Hellenic American Congress ***(701)***
United Lao Congress for Democracy ***(702)***
United Methodist Church General Board of Church and Society ***(702)***
United Nations Ass'n of the U.S.A. ***(702)***
United Pan-Europe Communications, NV ***(702)***
United States Business and Industry Council ***(703)***
United States Energy Ass'n ***(703)***
United Technologies Corp. ***(704)***
Universal Wireless Communications Consortium ***(705)***
University of Medicine and Dentistry of New Jersey ***(706)***
University of Miami ***(706)***
University of Tulsa ***(708)***
University of Virginia ***(708)***
UNOCAL Corp. ***(708)***
US-Asia Institute ***(709)***
USEC, Inc. ***(710)***
USX Corp. ***(710)***
Valve Manufacturers Ass'n of America ***(711)***
Van Scoyoc Associates, Inc. ***(711)***
Verner, Liipfert, Bernhard, McPherson and Hand, Chartered *(202)*
Victims of Communism Memorial Foundation ***(715)***
Vietnam Veterans of America Foundation ***(715)***
Walsh Enterprises Internat'l ***(718)***
Washington Group Internat'l ***(719)***

Washington Office on Latin American **(720)**
Western Wireless Internat'l **(725)**
Wheat Export Trade Education Committee **(725)**
Wilmer, Cutler & Pickering (217)
Wilson & Wasserstein, Inc. (218)
Winston & Strawn (218)
World Federalist Ass'n **(730)**
World Government of World Citizens **(730)**
World Hunger Education Service **(730)**
World Learning Inc. **(731)**
Zamorano **(734)**
Zero Population Growth, Inc. **(734)**
Zimbabwe, Republic of **(734)**
Zurich Financial Group **(735)**

Fuel/Gas/Oil (FUE)

AAE Technologies, Inc. **(224)**
The Accord Group (5)
Adams and Reese LLP (5)
Aera Energy LLC **(230)**
Agrium Inc. **(232)**
AHL Shipping Co. **(232)**
Air Products and Chemicals, Inc. **(234)**
Akin, Gump, Strauss, Hauer & Feld, L.L.P. (8)
Alaska North Slope LNG Project **(236)**
Alliance of Automobile Manufacturers, Inc. **(240)**
Alpine Group, Inc. (11)
Amerada Hess Corp. **(243)**
Ameren Services **(243)**
American Ass'n of Blacks in Energy **(246)**
American Bioenergy Ass'n **(251)**
American Continental Group, Inc. (12)
American Farm Bureau Federation **(258)**
American Gas Ass'n **(261)**
American Geological Institute **(261)**
American Methanol Institute **(268)**
American Petroleum Institute **(269)**
American Teleservices Ass'n **(279)**
Americans for Affordable Electricity **(281)**
ARCO Products Co. **(287)**
Arctic Slope Regional Corp. **(288)**
Ashland Inc. **(290)**
Ass'n of Oil Pipelines **(297)**
Austin, Texas, City of **(303)**
Automotive Parts and Service Alliance **(303)**
Baker Botts, L.L.P. (20)
Barbour Griffith & Rogers, Inc. (22)
Barents Group LLC (23)
Bastianelli, Brown & Kelley (24)
Bergner Bockorny Castagnetti and Hawkins (26)
BHP (USA) Inc. **(313)**
BKSH & Associates (28)
BP Amoco Corp. **(319)**
Bracewell & Patterson, L.L.P. (30)
British Columbia Hydro and Power Authority **(321)**
Broydrick & Associates (33)
James W. Bunger & Associates **(323)**
Burlington Northern Santa Fe Railway **(324)**
Burlington Resources Oil & Gas Co. **(324)**
Burns and Roe Enterprises, Inc. **(324)**
California Independent Petroleum Ass'n **(327)**
California State Lands Commission **(327)**
Caraustar **(331)**
Cassidy & Associates, Inc. (42)
Cement Kiln Recycling Coalition **(335)**
Chamber of Independent Gas Stations of Argentina **(340)**
Champlin Exploration, Inc. **(341)**
The Chevron Companies **(342)**
Chevron, U.S.A. **(342)**
Cinergy Corp. **(347)**
CITGO Petroleum Corp. **(347)**
Citizens Against Government Waste **(348)**
Coastal Impact Assistance & Reinvestment **(356)**
Colling Swift & Hynes (49)
Colonial Pipeline Co. **(358)**
Commercial Service Co., Ltd. **(360)**
Conoco Inc. **(367)**
Consortium for Plant Biotechnology Research **(368)**
Consumer Energy Council of America Research Foundation **(369)**
Consumer Federation of America **(369)**
Continental Cement Co., Inc. **(370)**
Cook Inlet Region Inc. **(371)**
Council for Conservation and Reinvestment of OCS Revenue **(374)**
Council of Industrial Boiler Owners (CIBO) **(375)**
Crowley Maritime Corp. **(379)**
CSA America, Inc. **(379)**
DAG Petroleum **(381)**
DaimlerChrysler Corp. **(381)**
Davis Wright Tremaine LLP (58)
DCH Technology Inc. **(383)**
Thomas J. Dennis (61)
Dickstein Shapiro Morin & Oshinsky LLP (61)
Dominion Resources, Inc. **(391)**
The Dow Chemical Co. **(391)**
Downey McGrath Group, Inc. (64)
The Duberstein Group, Inc. (65)
Duke Energy **(392)**
Duncan, Weinberg, Genzer & Pembroke, P.C. (66)
Dunn-Padre, Inc. **(393)**
The Dutko Group, Inc. (68)
El Paso Corporation **(399)**
Enron Corp. **(403)**
Ethyl Petroleum Additives, Inc. **(407)**
Exelon Corp. **(409)**
Express Pipeline Partnership and Platte Pipeline Co. **(409)**
Exxon Mobil Corp. **(409)**
Exxon Valdez Oil Spill Litigation Plaintiffs **(409)**
EZ's Solutions, Inc. (74)
FedEx Corp. **(415)**
Jack Ferguson Associates, Inc. (75)
The Fertilizer Institute **(415)**
Florida Gas Utility **(420)**
Fluor Corp. **(420)**
FMC Corp. **(420)**
Food Marketing Institute **(421)**
Foothills Pipe Lines (Yukon), Ltd. **(422)**
Ford Motor Co. **(422)**
Freedman, Levy, Kroll & Simonds (79)
Freeport-McMoRan Copper & Gold Inc. **(425)**
G.R. Services (80)
Gallagher, Boland and Meiburger (80)
Garden State Paper Co., Inc. **(429)**
Gardere & Wayne, LLP **(429)**
Gas Processors Ass'n **(429)**
Gas Research Institute **(429)**
General Motors Corp. **(432)**
Giant Industries, Inc. **(435)**
Global Marine, Inc. **(436)**
Greater New York Automobile Dealers Ass'n **(439)**
Grisso Consulting (88)
Guam, Washington Office of the Governor **(442)**
Guinea, Secretary General of the Presidency of the Republic of **(442)**
James E. Guirard (89)
Katherine Hamilton (91)
Hees Interests, Ltd. **(448)**
Hill and Knowlton, Inc. (95)
Hogan & Hartson L.L.P. (96)
Holland & Knight LLP (98)
Honda North America, Inc. **(451)**
Oliver James Horton (100)
Huntsman Corp. **(455)**
IMPACT, LLC (102)
Independent Fuel Terminal Operators Ass'n **(459)**
Independent Petroleum Ass'n of America **(459)**
Information Resources, Inc. **(461)**
Intermodal Ass'n of North America **(467)**
Internat'l Ass'n of Drilling Contractors **(467)**
Internat'l Brotherhood of Teamsters **(469)**
Internat'l Federation of Professional and Technical Engineers **(471)**
Interstate Natural Gas Ass'n of America **(477)**
ITRON, Inc. **(480)**
Johnson Co. (107)
Kaiser Aluminum & Chemical Corp. **(485)**
Kaye Scholer LLP (110)
Kent & O'Connor, Inc. (112)
KeySpan Energy **(489)**
KFx, Inc. **(489)**
King & Spalding (113)
Koch Industries, Inc. **(490)**
Kogovsek & Associates (114)
Bob Lawrence & Associates **(496)**
The Laxalt Corp. (117)
The Paul Laxalt Group (117)
Legislative Solutions (118)
Leonard B. Levine & Associates (119)
Liebman & Associates, Inc. (120)
The Livingston Group, LLC (120)
Lockridge Grindal & Nauen, P.L.L.P. (121)
Longhorn Pipeline **(503)**
Lyondell Chemical Co. **(506)**
M & R Strategic Services (122)
Madison Government Affairs (123)
Management Options, Inc. (123)
Manatt, Phelps & Phillips, LLP (123)
Mazda North America Operations **(514)**
Charlie McBride Associates, Inc. (127)
Jack H. McDonald (129)
Methanex Inc. **(520)**
Meyers & Associates (133)
Midcoast Interstate Transmission, Inc. **(523)**
Midwest Research Institute **(524)**
Denny Miller McBee Associates (134)
Mitsubishi Internat'l Corp. **(526)**
Mitsubishi Motors America, Inc. **(526)**
J. P. Morgan Chase & Co. **(529)**
Nat'l Ass'n of Fleet Administrators **(543)**
Nat'l Ass'n of RV Parks and Campgrounds **(548)**
Nat'l Ass'n of State Utility Consumer Advocates (NASUCA) **(550)**
Nat'l Corn Growers Ass'n **(559)**
Nat'l Environmental Strategies (140)
Nat'l Legal Center for the Public Interest **(570)**
Nat'l Oilheat Research Alliance (NORA) **(572)**
Nat'l Petrochemical Refiners Ass'n **(573)**
Nat'l Propane Gas Ass'n **(574)**
Nat'l Utility Contractors Ass'n (NUCA) **(580)**
Natural Gas Vehicle Coalition **(582)**
NES, Inc. (141)
New England Fuel Institute **(585)**
The Newark Group **(588)**
Newpark Resources/SOLOCO **(588)**
NiSource Inc. **(590)**
Nissan North America Inc. **(590)**
Nixon Center, The **(590)**
Norfolk Southern Corp. **(591)**
Northern Indiana Public Service Co. **(594)**
NRG Energy, Inc. **(596)**
Occidental Internat'l Corporation **(598)**
O'Connor & Hannan, L.L.P. (144)
Olsson, Frank and Weeda, P.C. (146)
Omega Oil Co. **(600)**
O'Neill, Athy & Casey, P.C. (147)
ONEOK Bushton Processing, LLC **(601)**
ONEOK Energy Marketing & Trading Co. **(601)**
ONEOK Field Services, Inc. **(601)**
ONEOK Gas Transportation, LLC **(601)**
ONEOK Midcontinent Market Center, Inc. **(601)**
ONEOK Midstream Gas Supply, LLC **(601)**
ONEOK OkTex Pipeline Co. **(601)**
Oxygenated Fuels Ass'n **(605)**
Paper Recycling Coalition **(607)**
Patton Boggs, LLP (150)
Petro Star, Inc. **(613)**
Petro-Canada **(613)**
Petroleum Marketers Ass'n of America **(613)**
Phillips Petroleum Co. **(616)**
Pickens Fuel Corp. **(617)**
Public Citizen, Inc. **(628)**
Public Strategies Washington, Inc. (164)
Public Strategies, Inc. (165)
Questar Corp. **(631)**
Reed, Smith, LLP (167)
Reliant Energy, Inc. **(636)**
Renewable Fuels Ass'n **(637)**
RGS Enterprises, Inc. (168)
Rock-Tenn Co. **(641)**
Ryan, Phillips, Utrecht & MacKinnon (173)
SABIC Americas, Inc. **(644)**
Safety-Kleen Corp. **(645)**
Schmeltzer, Aptaker & Shepard, P.C. (176)
Schwan's Sales Enterprises **(652)**
Elinor Schwartz (176)
SEFBO Pipeline Bridge, Inc. **(654)**
Sempra Energy **(655)**
Shell Oil Co. **(657)**
Siemens Westinghouse Power Corporation **(658)**

Sierra Club *(658)*
E. Del Smith and Co. ***(183)***
Smurfit Stone Container Corp. ***(662)***
Southern Ute Indian Tribe ***(668)***
St. Louis/Lake Counties Regional Rail Authority ***(672)***
St. Paul, Alaska, City of ***(672)***
Steptoe & Johnson LLP ***(188)***
Strategic Horizons Advisors, L.L.C. ***(189)***
Svenska Petroleum Exploration AB ***(678)***
Swidler Berlin Shereff Friedman, LLP ***(191)***
Syntroleum Corp. ***(679)***
Mary-Rose Szoka de Valladares ***(192)***
TAPS Renewal Task Force ***(681)***
TECO Energy, Inc. ***(682)***
Texas A&M Research Foundation ***(684)***
Thompson Coburn LLP ***(194)***
Tosco Corp. ***(688)***
Toyota Motor North America, U.S.A., Inc. ***(689)***
Trajen, Inc. ***(689)***
Transconsortia ***(690)***
Trifinery, Inc. ***(692)***
Truckload Carriers Ass'n ***(693)***
TRW Inc. ***(693)***
Turkish Industrialists and Businessmen's Ass'n (TUSIAD) ***(694)***
TXU Business Services ***(695)***
Tyson's Governmental Sales, LLC ***(695)***
U.S. Oil and Gas Ass'n ***(696)***
U.S. Public Interest Research Group ***(697)***
United Methodist Church General Board of Church and Society ***(702)***
United States Energy Ass'n ***(703)***
UNOCAL Corp. ***(708)***
USX Corp. ***(710)***
Ute Mountain Ute Indian Tribe ***(710)***
Valis Associates ***(198)***
Valve Manufacturers Ass'n of America ***(711)***
Van Ness Feldman, P.C. ***(199)***
Verner, Liipfert, Bernhard, McPherson and Hand, Chartered ***(713)***
Verner, Liipfert, Bernhard, McPherson and Hand, Chartered ***(202)***
Waterworks Internat'l, Inc. ***(721)***
Robert K. Weidner ***(211)***
Western Gas Resources ***(724)***
The Wexler Group ***(211)***
White Pigeon Paper Co. ***(726)***
William F. Whitsitt Policy and Government Affairs ***(213)***
The Wigglesworth Co. ***(214)***
Williams & Connolly ***(215)***
Williams & Jensen, P.C. ***(215)***
Kathleen Winn & Associates, Inc. ***(218)***
Wisconsin Energy Corp. ***(728)***
World Resources Institute ***(731)***
Xcel Energy, Inc. ***(732)***
Yukon Pacific ***(734)***

Gaming/Gambling/Casino (GAM)

Akin, Gump, Strauss, Hauer & Feld, L.L.P. ***(8)***
Alcalde & Fay ***(10)***
American Council of Korean Travel Agents ***(255)***
American Federation of Musicians of the United States and Canada ***(258)***
American Gaming Ass'n ***(260)***
American Greyhound Track Operators Ass'n ***(261)***
American Horse Council, Inc. ***(263)***
American Hotel and Lodging Ass'n ***(263)***
American Indian Ass'n ***(263)***
Amusement and Music Operators Ass'n ***(283)***
AOL Time Warner ***(285)***
Arent Fox Kintner Plotkin & Kahn, PLLC ***(14)***
Arter & Hadden ***(17)***
Athens Casino and Hotel Consortium ***(302)***
Baach Robinson & Lewis, PLLC ***(19)***
Bacino & Associates ***(19)***
Barker Enterprises ***(308)***
The Barton Co. ***(24)***
Bay Mills Indian Community ***(309)***
BET Holdings II, Inc. ***(312)***
BKSH & Associates ***(28)***
Bowman Internat'l Corp. ***(318)***
Robert M. Brandon and Associates ***(32)***
Burwell, Peters and Houston ***(34)***
Cabazon Band of Mission Indians ***(325)***
W. Douglas Campbell ***(36)***
Capital Consultants Corp. ***(37)***
Capital Gaming Internat'l, Inc. ***(330)***
Carlyle Consulting ***(40)***
Cartwright & Riley ***(41)***
Cassidy & Associates, Inc. ***(42)***
Chehalis Reservation, Confederated Tribes of the ***(342)***
Chesapeake Enterprises, Inc. ***(46)***
Christian Coalition of America ***(345)***
Columbus Public Affairs ***(50)***
Commercial Internet Exchange Ass'n ***(360)***
Commonwealth Group, Ltd. ***(50)***
Cook Inlet Region Inc. ***(371)***
Coushatta Tribe of Louisiana ***(377)***
Covington & Burling ***(53)***
Davis & Harman LLP ***(57)***
Davis Manafort, Inc. ***(58)***
Development Corporation of Nevada ***(387)***
Dickstein Shapiro Morin & Oshinsky LLP ***(61)***
The Walt Disney Co. ***(389)***
Dorsey & Whitney LLP ***(63)***
The Duberstein Group, Inc. ***(65)***
E Lottery ***(394)***
E-Commerce Payment Coalition ***(394)***
Elk Valley Rancheria ***(401)***
eLottery, Inc. ***(401)***
Dave Evans Associates ***(73)***
EXECUTONE Information Systems, Inc. ***(409)***
Fierce and Isakowitz ***(76)***
Foley & Lardner ***(78)***
Gainesville, Florida, City of ***(428)***
Gary, Indiana, Washington Office of the City of ***(429)***
General Conference of Seventh-day Adventists ***(431)***
Gila River Indian Community ***(435)***
GPC Internat'l ***(85)***
Greenberg Traurig, LLP ***(86)***
GTECH Corp. ***(441)***
H.A.H. of Wisconsin L.P. ***(443)***
Harrah's Entertainment, Inc. ***(444)***
Hecht, Spencer & Associates ***(93)***
Hercules Development Corp. ***(448)***
Lydia Hofer & Associates ***(96)***
Hogan & Hartson L.L.P. ***(96)***
R. J. Hudson Associates ***(101)***
Ikon Public Affairs ***(102)***
Indiana, Office of the Governor of the State of ***(460)***
Interactive Amusement and Tournament Video Game Coalition ***(466)***
Interactive Digital Software Ass'n ***(466)***
Interactive Gaming Council ***(466)***
Internat'l Game Technology ***(472)***
Janus-Merritt Strategies, L.L.C. ***(104)***
Jefferson Consulting Group ***(105)***
Jefferson Government Relations, L.L.C. ***(106)***
Johnston & Associates, LLC ***(107)***
Jorden Burt LLP ***(109)***
Kogovsek & Associates ***(114)***
Kurzweil & Associates ***(115)***
The Legislative Strategies Group, LLC ***(118)***
Lottery.com ***(504)***
Magazine Publishers of America ***(507)***
Magna Entertainment Corp. ***(507)***
Major League Baseball Players Ass'n ***(508)***
MasterCard Internat'l ***(513)***
McGuiness & Holch ***(130)***
Jana McKeag ***(131)***
Wayne Edward Mehl ***(132)***
Meyer & Klipper, PLLC ***(133)***
Miami Beach, Florida, City of ***(521)***
Miccosukee Tribe of Indians of Florida ***(522)***
MSP Strategic Communications, Inc. ***(138)***
Multimedia Games, Inc. ***(532)***
The MWW Group ***(140)***
Nat'l Ass'n of Jai-Alai Frontons, Inc. ***(545)***
Nat'l Ass'n of State & Provincial Lotteries ***(549)***
Nat'l Collegiate Athletic Ass'n ***(557)***
Nat'l Football League ***(565)***
Nat'l Football League Players Ass'n ***(565)***
Nat'l Indian Gaming Ass'n ***(568)***
Nat'l Licensed Beverage Ass'n ***(570)***
Nat'l Thoroughbred Racing Ass'n, Inc. ***(579)***
Neuman and Co. ***(141)***
Nevada Resort Ass'n ***(584)***
Newark, New Jersey, City of ***(588)***
North American Sports Management, Inc. ***(592)***
Norwegian Cruise Line ***(596)***
The OB-C Group, LLC ***(143)***
O'Connor & Hannan, L.L.P. ***(144)***
Oneida Indian Nation of New York ***(600)***
John T. O'Rourke Law Offices ***(147)***
PACE-CAPSTONE ***(148)***
Park Place ***(608)***
Patton Boggs, LLP ***(150)***
Pechanga Band of California Luiseno Indians ***(610)***
Piper Marbury Rudnick & Wolfe LLP ***(155)***
Playboy Enterprises, Inc. ***(619)***
Powell, Goldstein, Frazer & Murphy LLP ***(160)***
Preston Gates Ellis & Rouvelas Meeds LLP ***(162)***
Qwest Communications ***(631)***
Rakisons, Ltd. ***(632)***
Red Lake Band of Chippewa Indians ***(635)***
Rock & Associates ***(171)***
Ryan, Phillips, Utrecht & MacKinnon ***(173)***
Sandia Pueblo ***(648)***
Sault Ste. Marie Tribe of Chippewa Indians ***(650)***
Seminole Tribe of Indians of Florida ***(655)***
SENSE, INC. ***(177)***
Shakopee Mdewakanton Sioux Tribe ***(656)***
Sheep Ranch Rancheria ***(657)***
The Smith-Free Group ***(184)***
Sodak Gaming Inc. ***(664)***
Southern Ute Indian Tribe ***(668)***
St. Croix Chippewa Indians of Wisconsin ***(671)***
Starnet Communications Internat'l ***(673)***
The State Affairs Co. ***(187)***
Stone Investments, Inc. ***(675)***
Traditional Values Coalition ***(689)***
The Trump Organization ***(693)***
Tulalip Tribes ***(693)***
Tunica Biloxi Indians of Louisiana ***(694)***
U.S. Strategies Corp. ***(197)***
United Church of Christ Justice and Witness Ministry ***(700)***
United Methodist Church General Board of Church and Society ***(702)***
Upper Sioux Indian Community ***(708)***
Ute Mountain Ute Indian Tribe ***(710)***
Venetian Casino Resort, LLC ***(712)***
Verner, Liipfert, Bernhard, McPherson and Hand, Chartered ***(202)***
Viejas Band of Kumeyaay Indians ***(715)***
Viohl and Associates, Inc. ***(205)***
Walker Digital Corp. ***(718)***
Wheat & Associates, Inc. ***(212)***
White Mountain Apache Tribe ***(726)***
World Sports Exchange ***(731)***
YouBet.com ***(733)***
Zane & Associates ***(221)***

Government Issues (GOV)

3Com Corp. ***(223)***
59/Air Depot Road, Ltd. ***(224)***
The 60/Plus Ass'n, Inc. ***(224)***
AARP (American Ass'n of Retired Persons) ***(224)***
Abbott Laboratories ***(225)***
Academy of Radiology Research ***(226)***
ACE INA ***(226)***
Adams and Reese LLP ***(5)***
AdvaMed ***(228)***
Advanced Technology Systems ***(228)***
Advertising Company ART-ERIA ***(229)***
Advocates for Highway and Auto Safety ***(229)***
AFL-CIO (American Federation of Labor and Congress of Industrial Organizations) ***(231)***
AFL-CIO - Maritime Trades Department ***(231)***
AFL-CIO - Transportation Trades Department ***(231)***
AfriSpace Corp. ***(232)***
Agilent Technologies ***(232)***
Ainslie Associates ***(7)***
Air Conditioning Contractors of America ***(233)***
Air Force Memorial Foundation ***(233)***

Aircraft Electronics Ass'n ***(235)***
Aircraft Services Group ***(235)***
Airline Suppliers Ass'n ***(235)***
AKAL Security ***(235)***
Akin, Gump, Strauss, Hauer & Feld, L.L.P. *(8)*
Alabama, Department of Transportation of the State of ***(235)***
Albertine Enterprises, Inc. *(10)*
Alcalde & Fay *(10)*
Alcatel USA ***(237)***
Allegheny County Airport Authority ***(238)***
Alliance for Justice ***(239)***
Alliance for Understandable, Sensible and Accountable Government Regulations ***(240)***
Allied Marketing ***(241)***
Alpine Group, Inc. *(11)*
Alvarado & Gerken *(12)*
Amalgamated Transit Union ***(242)***
American Arts Alliance ***(245)***
American Ass'n for Laboratory Accreditation ***(246)***
American Ass'n for Marriage and Family Therapy ***(246)***
American Ass'n of Cardiovascular and Pulmonary Rehabilitation ***(246)***
American Ass'n of Engineering Societies ***(247)***
American Ass'n of Homes and Services for the Aging ***(248)***
American Ass'n of Law Libraries ***(248)***
American Automobile Ass'n ***(250)***
American Bakers Ass'n ***(250)***
American Bankers Ass'n ***(250)***
American Bar Ass'n ***(250)***
American Board of Medical Specialties in Podiatry ***(251)***
American Cable Ass'n ***(251)***
American Chemical Soc. ***(252)***
American College of Obstetricians and Gynecologists ***(254)***
American Congress on Surveying and Mapping ***(255)***
American Consulting Engineers Council ***(255)***
American Continental Group, Inc. *(12)*
American Council of Independent Laboratories ***(255)***
American Council of Life Insurers ***(256)***
American Crop Protection Ass'n ***(256)***
American Defense Internat'l, Inc. *(12)*
American Electronics Ass'n ***(257)***
American Express Co. ***(258)***
American Farm Bureau Federation ***(258)***
American Federation of State, County and Municipal Employees ***(258)***
American Federation of Teachers ***(259)***
American Federation of Television and Radio Artists ***(259)***
American Foreign Service Ass'n ***(259)***
American Furniture Manufacturers Ass'n ***(260)***
American Gas Ass'n ***(261)***
American Gastroenterological Ass'n ***(261)***
American Heart Ass'n ***(262)***
American Herbal Products Ass'n ***(262)***
American Historical Ass'n ***(262)***
The American Institute of Architects ***(264)***
American Iron and Steel Institute ***(265)***
American Jewish Committee ***(265)***
American Jewish Congress ***(265)***
American Legion ***(266)***
American Library Ass'n ***(266)***
American Management Systems ***(266)***
American Medical Technologists ***(267)***
American Motorcyclist Ass'n ***(268)***
American Moving and Storage Ass'n ***(268)***
American Muslim Council ***(268)***
American Petroleum Institute ***(269)***
American Psychiatric Ass'n ***(271)***
American Pyrotechnics Ass'n ***(272)***
American Red Cross ***(272)***
American Rental Ass'n ***(272)***
American Retirees Ass'n ***(273)***
American Soc. for Industrial Security ***(274)***
American Soc. for Quality ***(275)***
American Soc. for Reproductive Medicine ***(275)***
American Soc. of Ass'n Executives ***(275)***
American Soc. of Civil Engineers ***(276)***
American Soc. of Newspaper Editors ***(277)***
American Subcontractors Ass'n, Inc. ***(278)***
American Water Works Ass'n ***(280)***
American Wood Preservers Institute ***(280)***
Americans Back in Charge Foundation ***(281)***
Americans for Democratic Action ***(281)***
Americans for Tax Reform ***(282)***
Amgen ***(282)***
Amino and Phenolic Wood Adhesives Ass'n ***(283)***
The Anderson Group ***(284)***
Angola, Government of the Republic of ***(284)***
Arab, Alabama, City of ***(287)***
ARCO Products Co. ***(287)***
Arent Fox Kintner Plotkin & Kahn, PLLC *(14)*
Argo Public Enterprise *(15)*
Arizona Mail Order Co. ***(288)***
Arizona Power Authority ***(288)***
Arkansas, Office of the Governor of the State of ***(288)***
Arms Control Ass'n ***(289)***
Arnold & Porter *(16)*
Wayne Arny & Assoc. *(16)*
Arter & Hadden *(17)*
Ascension, Louisiana, Parish of ***(290)***
Ashland Inc. ***(290)***
James Nicholas Ashmore & Associates *(18)*
Ass'n for the Suppliers of Printing and Publishing Technology ***(293)***
Ass'n of Administrative Law Judges ***(293)***
Ass'n of American Chambers of Commerce in Latin America ***(293)***
Ass'n of American Geographers ***(293)***
Ass'n of American Publishers ***(294)***
Ass'n of American Shippers ***(294)***
Ass'n of Clinical Research Professionals ***(295)***
Ass'n of Flight Attendants ***(295)***
Ass'n of Government Accountants ***(296)***
Ass'n of Maquiladores ***(296)***
Ass'n of Metropolitan Sewerage Agencies ***(297)***
Ass'n of Military Surgeons of the U.S. (AMSUS) ***(297)***
Ass'n of Nat'l Estuary Programs ***(297)***
Ass'n of Research Libraries ***(298)***
Ass'n of Sales & Marketing Companies ***(298)***
Ass'n of TEH Act Projects ***(299)***
Ass'n of Trial Lawyers of America ***(299)***
Associated Equipment Distributors ***(300)***
Associated General Contractors of America ***(300)***
Associated Universities Inc. ***(300)***
AstraZeneca Inc. ***(301)***
AT&T ***(301)***
Atlanta, Georgia, City of ***(302)***
Auburn, Avilla, Bluffton, Columbia City and Other Municipalities of Indiana ***(302)***
The Audubon Institute ***(302)***
Austin Professional Systems, Inc. ***(303)***
Automotive Aftermarket Industry Ass'n ***(303)***
Automotive Consumer Action Program ***(303)***
Automotive Parts and Service Alliance ***(303)***
Aventis CropScience ***(304)***
Avioimpex ***(305)***
Avue Technologies ***(305)***
Baker & McKenzie *(20)*
Baker Botts, L.L.P. *(20)*
Baker, Donelson, Bearman & Caldwell, P.C. *(21)*
Ball Janik, LLP *(22)*
Barbour Griffith & Rogers, Inc. *(22)*
Barksdale Foward ***(308)***
Barnes & Thornburg *(23)*
Barr Laboratories ***(308)***
Barrick Goldstrike Mines, Inc. ***(308)***
BASF Corporation ***(308)***
Bay County, Florida ***(309)***
Bechtel Group, Inc. ***(310)***
Bentley, Adams, Hargett, Riley and Co., Inc. *(26)*
Bergen, New York, Village of ***(311)***
Bergner Bockorny Castagnetti and Hawkins *(26)*
Berliner, Candon & Jimison *(27)*
Robert Betz Associates, Inc. *(27)*
Bicycle Product Suppliers Ass'n ***(313)***
Biscuit and Cracker Manufacturers Ass'n ***(314)***
BKSH & Associates *(28)*
Blackfeet Tribe of Montana ***(315)***
Blank Rome Comisky & McCauley, LLP *(29)*
BNFL, Inc. ***(316)***
Board of Veterans Appeals Professional Ass'n ***(316)***
Bombardier Aerospace ***(317)***
Booher & Associates *(30)*
Boonville, New York, Village of ***(317)***
The BOSE Corp. ***(318)***
Boston, Massachusetts, City of ***(318)***
Bourgas Intermodal Feasability Study ***(318)***
Bracewell & Patterson, L.L.P. *(30)*
Marshall A. Brachman *(31)*
Bracy Williams & Co. *(31)*
Braintree Electric Light Department ***(319)***
Brazelton Foundation ***(319)***
Brickfield, Burchette, Ritts & Stone *(32)*
Bridgestone/Firestone, Inc. ***(320)***
Bristol-Myers Squibb Co. ***(320)***
The Brookings Institution ***(321)***
Brotherhood of Maintenance of Way Employees ***(322)***
Brotherhood of Railroad Signalmen ***(322)***
Bruce Vladek ***(322)***
Bryan Cave LLP *(33)*
The Bureau of Nat'l Affairs, Inc. ***(323)***
John G. "Toby" Burke *(34)*
Burlington Northern Santa Fe Railway ***(324)***
Burns and Roe Enterprises, Inc. ***(324)***
Business Executives for Nat'l Security ***(324)***
The Business Roundtable ***(325)***
Business Software Alliance ***(325)***
Butterfield Carter & Associates *(35)*
California Correctional Peace Officers Ass'n ***(326)***
Campaign Finance Reform Coalition ***(328)***
Campaign for America ***(328)***
Campbell Foundry Co. ***(329)***
Canadian River Municipal Water Authority ***(329)***
Canfield, Smith and Martin *(36)*
Capital Consultants Corp. *(37)*
The Capital Hill Group, Inc. ***(330)***
Capital Research Center ***(330)***
Capital Strategies Group, Inc. *(37)*
Capitol City Group *(38)*
Capitol Coalitions Inc. *(38)*
Capitol Hill Advocates *(39)*
Capitol Strategies *(39)*
CapitolWatch ***(331)***
Caraustar ***(331)***
Cardiovascular Credentialing Internat'l ***(331)***
Career College Ass'n ***(331)***
Carlsberg Management Co. ***(332)***
Carlyle Consulting *(40)*
Carmen & Muss, P.L.L.C. *(40)*
The Carmen Group *(40)*
Carpi & Clay *(41)*
The Carter Group *(41)*
Cassidy & Associates, Inc. *(42)*
Carol Cataldo & Associates *(44)*
CC Distributors ***(334)***
CCI Construction ***(334)***
Cedar Rapids, Iowa, City of ***(334)***
Cement Kiln Recycling Coalition ***(335)***
Cendant Mobility Services ***(335)***
The Centech Group ***(335)***
Center for Energy and Economic Development ***(336)***
Center for Public Dialogue ***(337)***
Center for Regulatory Effectiveness ***(337)***
Center for the Study of Extraterrestrial Intelligence ***(338)***
Chamber of Commerce of the U.S.A. ***(340)***
Chambers Associates Inc. *(45)*
Chambers, Conlon & Hartwell *(45)*
Chesapeake Enterprises, Inc. *(46)*
Chevron, U.S.A. ***(342)***
Child Welfare League of America ***(343)***
Children's Defense Fund ***(344)***
Children's Rights Council ***(344)***
Christian Coalition of America ***(345)***
Churchville, New York, Village of ***(346)***
Chwat and Company, Inc. *(46)*
Cisco Systems Inc. ***(347)***
Citizen Strategies *(46)*
Citizen's Committee to Save the Federal Center ***(348)***
Citizens Against Government Waste ***(348)***
Citizens for a Sound Economy ***(348)***

Honduras, Embassy of *(452)*
Hooper Owen & Winburn *(99)*
Howard County, Maryland *(454)*
R. J. Hudson Associates *(101)*
Hunt Management Systems *(101)*
Hutchison Whampo, LTD *(455)*
Hyjek & Fix, Inc. *(102)*
ICN Pharmaceuticals, Inc. *(457)*
The ILEX Group *(102)*
Illinois Department of Human Services *(457)*
Impact Strategies *(102)*
Imperial Irrigation District *(458)*
Independent Office Products and Furniture Dealers Ass'n *(459)*
Independent Sector *(460)*
Indiana, Office of the Governor of the State of *(460)*
Information Handling Services *(461)*
Information Practices Coalition of Washington, D.C. *(461)*
Infotech Strategies, Inc. *(103)*
ING America Insurance Holdings, Inc. *(462)*
Institute of Navigation *(464)*
Integrated Management Resources Group, Inc. *(465)*
Interface Inc. *(466)*
Internat'l Ass'n of Machinists and Aerospace Workers *(468)*
Internat'l Biometric Industry Ass'n *(468)*
Internat'l Board of Lactation Consultant Examiners *(468)*
Internat'l Brotherhood of Boilermakers, Iron Shipbuilders, Blacksmiths, Forgers and Helpers *(469)*
Internat'l Brotherhood of Electrical Workers *(469)*
Internat'l Brotherhood of Teamsters *(469)*
Internat'l Business Machines Corp. *(469)*
Internat'l Community Corrections Ass'n *(470)*
Internat'l Council of Cruise Lines *(470)*
Internat'l Dairy Foods Ass'n *(470)*
Internat'l Electrical Testing Ass'n *(471)*
Internat'l Federation of Professional and Technical Engineers *(471)*
Internat'l Municipal Signal Ass'n *(473)*
Internat'l Union of Painters and Allied Trades *(476)*
Internet Action PAC *(476)*
Intuit, Inc. *(477)*
Investment Counsel Ass'n of America *(478)*
InWork Technologies *(478)*
Irrigation Projects Reauthorization Council *(479)*
The Island ECN *(479)*
Jacobs Engineering Group Inc. *(481)*
Jamestown, New York, Board of Public Utilities *(481)*
Jamison and Sullivan, Inc. *(104)*
Janus-Merritt Strategies, L.L.C. *(104)*
Japan, Embassy of *(482)*
JBA Consulting, Inc. *(482)*
Jefferson Government Relations, L.L.C. *(106)*
JFS Group, Ltd. *(107)*
Law Offices of Mark S. Joffe *(107)*
Johnston & Associates, LLC *(107)*
Jolly/Rissler, Inc. *(108)*
Juneau, Alaska, City of *(485)*
Just Valuations *(485)*
K Capital Partners *(485)*
Kaiser Aluminum & Chemical Corp. *(485)*
Kaplan Companies, Inc. *(486)*
Kashmiri American Council *(486)*
Kasten & Co. *(110)*
Kellogg Brown and Root *(487)*
Kenya Bombing Families *(488)*
Kern, California, County of *(488)*
Kessler & Associates Business Services, Inc. *(112)*
Ketchum *(488)*
KeySpan Energy *(489)*
Kleinfeld, Kaplan and Becker *(114)*
Knightstown, Indiana, Town of *(490)*
Koch Industries, Inc. *(490)*
Kohlberg Kravis Roberts & Co. *(490)*
David William Kuhnsman *(115)*
Kyros & Cummins Associates *(116)*
Labor Council for Latin American Advancement (LCLAA) *(493)*
LACDA Alliance *(493)*
Shannon M. Lahey Associates *(116)*
Lason, Inc. *(495)*
Lau Technologies *(496)*
Lawton/Fort Sill Chamber of Commerce & Industry *(496)*
League of California Cities *(497)*
League of Women Voters of the United States *(497)*
Ledge Counsel *(118)*
Lehtinen O'Donnell *(498)*
Lent Scrivner & Roth LLC *(119)*
Levine & Co. *(119)*
Lewis-Burke Associates *(120)*
Lexis-Nexis *(498)*
Jack D.P. Lichtenstein *(120)*
Liebman & Associates, Inc. *(120)*
The Livingston Group, LLC *(120)*
Lockheed Martin Corp. *(501)*
Lockheed Martin IMS *(502)*
Loral Space and Communications, Ltd. *(503)*
LPI Consulting, Inc. *(122)*
Lutheran Office for Governmental Affairs/Evangelical Lutheran Church in America *(506)*
Luxcore Public Affairs *(506)*
M-S-R Public Power Agency *(506)*
Madison Government Affairs *(123)*
Bernard L. Madoff Investment Securities *(507)*
Magnitude Information Systems *(507)*
Maine Cellular Telephone Co. *(507)*
Mainwave Technologies *(508)*
Major League Baseball *(508)*
Makedonski Telekomunikacii *(508)*
Maloney & Knox, LLP *(123)*
Management Ass'n for Private Photogrammetric Surveyors *(508)*
Manatt, Phelps & Phillips, LLP *(123)*
Manufacturers Alliance/MAPI Inc. *(509)*
MARC Associates, Inc. *(124)*
Maricopa, Arizona, County of *(509)*
Marine Corps Reserve Officers Ass'n *(510)*
Martin & Glantz LLC *(125)*
Maryland Psychiatric Soc. *(512)*
Massena, New York, Town of *(512)*
Virginia M. Mayer *(126)*
Mayer, Brown & Platt *(126)*
Law Office of Robert A. McConnell *(128)*
McDermott, Will and Emery *(128)*
McGraw-Hill Cos., The *(514)*
MCI WorldCom Corp. *(514)*
Mechanical Contractors Ass'n of America *(515)*
Medicare Cost Contractors Alliance *(517)*
Megaseal Corp. *(517)*
MEGAXESS, Inc. *(517)*
Merck & Co. *(518)*
Mercury Group *(132)*
Mercy Health System of Northwest Arkasas *(518)*
Meredith Concept Group, Inc. *(132)*
Merit Systems Protection Board *(519)*
Messier-Dowty Internat'l *(519)*
Metrocall Inc. *(520)*
Metropolitan Washington Airports Authority *(521)*
Meyers & Associates *(133)*
MICAH Software Systems *(522)*
Michigan Consolidated Gas Co. *(522)*
Michigan State Department of Transportation *(522)*
Midwest City Municipal Authority *(523)*
Milwaukee, City of *(524)*
Minnesota Mining and Manufacturing Co. (3M Co.) *(525)*
Mishawaka Utilities *(526)*
Mission Springs (California) Water District *(526)*
Mitsubishi Research Institute *(526)*
Molecular BioSystems, Inc. *(527)*
Molina Healthcare *(527)*
Molina Medical Centers *(527)*
J. P. Morgan Chase & Co. *(529)*
Morgan Meguire, LLC *(136)*
Morning Star Institute, The *(529)*
Morrison & Foerster LLP *(137)*
Bob Moss Associates *(137)*
Multinat'l Government Services, Inc. *(138)*
Municipal Electric Utilities Ass'n of New York State *(532)*
Patrick M. Murphy & Associates *(138)*
Murray & Murray *(139)*
Mutual of Omaha Insurance Companies *(533)*
The MWW Group *(140)*
The MWW Group *(533)*
Timothy D. Naegele & Associates *(140)*
Nat'l Academy of Public Administration *(535)*
Nat'l Academy of Sciences *(535)*
Nat'l Agricultural Aviation Ass'n *(535)*
Nat'l Alliance Against Blacklisting *(536)*
Nat'l and Community Service Coalition *(537)*
Nat'l Ass'n for Equal Opportunity in Higher Education *(537)*
Nat'l Ass'n for Medical Direction of Respiratory Care *(538)*
Nat'l Ass'n for State Farm Agents *(538)*
Nat'l Ass'n of Area Agencies on Aging *(538)*
Nat'l Ass'n of Assistant United States Attorneys *(539)*
Nat'l Ass'n of Broadcasters *(539)*
Nat'l Ass'n of Business Political Action Committees *(539)*
Nat'l Ass'n of Chain Drug Stores *(539)*
Nat'l Ass'n of Community Health Centers *(540)*
Nat'l Ass'n of Dealers in Ancient, Oriental and Primitive Art *(542)*
Nat'l Ass'n of Dental Laboratories *(542)*
Nat'l Ass'n of Developmental Disabilities Councils *(542)*
Nat'l Ass'n of Energy Service Companies *(542)*
Nat'l Ass'n of Government Employees *(543)*
Nat'l Ass'n of Home Builders Research Center, Inc. *(544)*
Nat'l Ass'n of Independent Insurers *(544)*
Nat'l Ass'n of Jewish Legislators *(545)*
Nat'l Ass'n of Manufacturers *(545)*
Nat'l Ass'n of Negro Business & Professional Women's Clubs, Inc. *(546)*
Nat'l Ass'n of Portable X-Ray Providers *(546)*
Nat'l Ass'n of Retired and Senior Volunteer Program Directors *(548)*
Nat'l Ass'n of Retired Federal Employees *(548)*
Nat'l Ass'n of RV Parks and Campgrounds *(548)*
Nat'l Ass'n of Senior Companion Project Directors *(549)*
Nat'l Ass'n of State Auditors, Comptrollers and Treasurers *(549)*
Nat'l Ass'n of State Energy Officials *(550)*
Nat'l Ass'n of State Universities and Land-Grant Colleges *(550)*
Nat'l Ass'n of Thrift Savings Plan Participants *(550)*
Nat'l Ass'n of Towns and Townships *(551)*
Nat'l Ass'n of Uniform Manufacturers and Distributors *(551)*
Nat'l Ass'n of VA Physicians and Dentists *(551)*
Nat'l Ass'n of Wholesaler-Distributors *(551)*
Nat'l Ass'n to Protect Individual Rights *(551)*
Nat'l Assembly of Health and Human Service Organizations *(551)*
Nat'l Automobile Dealers Ass'n *(552)*
Nat'l Beer Wholesalers Ass'n *(552)*
Nat'l Business Owners Ass'n *(553)*
Nat'l Center for Economic Freedom, Inc. *(554)*
Nat'l Center for Public Policy Research *(555)*
Nat'l Child Support Enforcement Ass'n *(555)*
Nat'l Club Ass'n *(556)*
Nat'l Coalition for Cancer Survivorship *(556)*
Nat'l Coalition of Minority Businesses *(556)*
Nat'l Commission for the Certification of Crane Operators *(557)*
Nat'l Concrete Masonry Ass'n *(558)*
Nat'l Coordinating Committee for the Promotion of History *(559)*
Nat'l Council of Catholic Women *(560)*
Nat'l Council of Chain Restaurants *(560)*
Nat'l Council of University Research Administrators *(561)*
Nat'l Criminal Justice Ass'n *(561)*
Nat'l Defense Industrial Ass'n *(561)*
Nat'l Defined Contribution Council *(561)*
Nat'l District Attorneys Ass'n *(562)*
Nat'l Electrical Contractors Ass'n *(562)*

Nat'l Electrical Manufacturers Ass'n (562)
Nat'l Electrical Safety Foundation (562)
Nat'l Energy Assistance Directors' Ass'n (563)
Nat'l Field Selling Ass'n (564)
Nat'l Grain and Feed Ass'n (566)
Nat'l Grain Sorgum Producers (566)
Nat'l Head Start Ass'n (566)
Nat'l Health Council (567)
Nat'l Heritage Foundation (567)
Nat'l Indian Gaming Ass'n (568)
Nat'l Industries for the Blind (568)
Nat'l Institute for Certification in Engineering Technologies (568)
Nat'l League of Postmasters of the U.S. (569)
Nat'l Legal Center for the Public Interest (570)
Nat'l Lime Ass'n (570)
Nat'l Meat Canners Ass'n (570)
Nat'l Military Intelligence Ass'n (571)
Nat'l Mining Ass'n (571)
Nat'l Newspaper Ass'n (572)
Nat'l Ocean Industries Ass'n (572)
Nat'l Oilseed Processors Ass'n (572)
Nat'l Organization for the Reform of Marijuana Laws (572)
Nat'l Organization of Social Security Claimants' Representatives (572)
Nat'l Puerto Rican Coalition (575)
Nat'l Ready Mixed Concrete Ass'n (575)
Nat'l Right to Life Committee (576)
Nat'l Roofing Contractors Ass'n (576)
Nat'l Senior Service Corps Directors Ass'n (578)
Nat'l Soc. of Professional Engineers (578)
Nat'l Strategy Information Center (579)
Nat'l Taxpayers Union (579)
Nat'l Telephone Cooperative Ass'n (579)
Nat'l Treasury Employees Union (580)
Nat'l Trust for Historic Preservation (580)
Nat'l Wholesale Co., Inc. (581)
Natural Resources Defense Council (582)
The Nature Conservancy (582)
Naval Reserve Ass'n (582)
NAVCOM Systems, Inc. (583)
Navigational Electronic Chart Systems Ass'n (NECSA) (583)
New Majority Soc. (586)
New York Municipal Power Agency (587)
The Newark Group (588)
Newsbank, Inc. (589)
Newspaper Ass'n of America (589)
Nortel Networks (591)
North American Meat Processors Ass'n (592)
North Carolina, Washington Office of the State of (593)
North Dakota, Governor's Office of the State of (593)
North Slope Borough, Alaska (593)
Northeast Ohio Areawide Coordination Agency (NOACA) (593)
Northeast Texas Electric Cooperative (593)
Northern Indiana Public Service Co. (594)
Novartis Corp. (596)
Nuclear Energy Institute (597)
The OB-C Group, LLC (143)
Obadal and MacLeod, p.c. (143)
Ocala, Florida, City of (598)
Occidental Internat'l Corporation (598)
O'Connor & Hannan, L.L.P. (144)
Ogletree Governmental Affairs, Inc. (145)
Oklahoma, State of (600)
Oldaker and Harris, LLP (146)
Olympic Aid (600)
OMNIPLEX World Services Corp. (600)
Open Group Electronic Messaging Ass'n (EMA) Forum (601)
Operation Right to Know (601)
Operations Security Professionals Soc. (601)
Oppenheimer Wolff & Donnelly LLP (147)
Oracle Corp. (602)
Orange County Fire Authority (602)
Orange, Florida, County of (602)
Organization for Internat'l Investment (603)
Orlando Utilities Commission (603)
PACE-CAPSTONE (148)
Pacific 17 (605)
John M. Palatiello & Associates (148)
The Palmer Group (149)
Palo Alto, California, City of (607)
Palumbo & Cerrell, Inc. (149)
Paper Recycling Coalition (607)
Paradigm Research Group (149)
Parcel Shippers Ass'n (608)
Parry, Romani, DeConcini & Symms (149)
Patent Office Professional Ass'n (609)
Patton Boggs, LLP (150)
Pearson & Pipkin, Inc. (154)
Penn Yan, New York, Village of (611)
Pet Industry Joint Advisory Council (613)
Petroleum Marketers Ass'n of America (613)
Peyser Associates, Inc. (155)
Philip Morris Management Corp. (615)
Phillips Petroleum Co. (616)
Plattsburgh, New York, City of (619)
Podesta/Mattoon (158)
Policy Impact Communications (159)
Port Authority of New York and New Jersey (621)
Portland, Oregon, City of (621)
Potomac Electric Power Co. (622)
Potomac Strategies Internat'l LLC (160)
Powell, Goldstein, Frazer & Murphy LLP (160)
Powerware (622)
Preston Gates Ellis & Rouvelas Meeds LLP (162)
PriceWaterhouseCoopers (624)
Principal Financial Group (624)
Printing Industries of America (624)
Process Equipment Manufacturers' Ass'n (625)
Professional Aviation Maintenance Ass'n (625)
Professional Bail Agents of the United States (625)
Professional Managers Ass'n (626)
Professional Services Council (626)
Progressive Policy Institute (626)
Prudential Securities, Inc. (627)
Public Campaign (628)
Public Citizen, Inc. (628)
Public Strategies Washington, Inc. (164)
Public Strategies, Inc. (165)
Puerto Ricans for Civic Action (629)
Puerto Rico Federal Affairs Administration (629)
Puerto Rico Senate (629)
Puerto Rico, Commonwealth of (629)
Quebec Lumber Manufacturers Ass'n (630)
Rafael U.S.A., Inc. (632)
Raytheon Co. (633)
Redding, California, Electric Department of the City of (635)
Redfern Resources (166)
Redland Energy Group (167)
Reed, Smith, LLP (167)
The Refinishing Touch (635)
Regulatory Improvement Council (636)
Republican Jewish Coalition (637)
The Retired Officers Ass'n (TROA) (638)
John J. Rhodes (169)
Rio Grande Valley Irrigation (640)
Riverside, California, County of (640)
Liz Robbins Associates (169)
Robertson, Monagle & Eastaugh (170)
Rock-Tenn Co. (641)
Rockville Centre, New York, Village of (641)
Romyr Associates (642)
Roof Coatings Manufacturers Ass'n (642)
Ropes & Gray (171)
Rowan Companies, Inc. (643)
Rowe Signal Media (643)
Royer & Babyak (172)
RPB Co. (172)
Ryan, Phillips, Utrecht & MacKinnon (173)
Sabre Inc. (644)
Sagem Morpho (646)
Salamanca, New York, City Board of Public Utilities of (646)
Sam Rayburn G&T Electric Cooperative, Inc. (647)
Samuels Internat'l Associates, Inc. (174)
San Antonio, Texas, City of (647)
San Bernardino, California, County of (647)
San Carlos Irrigation and Drainage District (647)
San Diego, California, County of (647)
San Joaquin Area Flood Agency (648)
San Joaquin, California, County of (648)
Santa Clara, California, County of (649)
Santa Clara, California, Electric Department of the City of (649)
Santa Clarita, California, City of (649)
Santa Fe, New Mexico, County of (649)
SAP Public Services (649)
SatCon Technology Corp. (650)
SBC Communications Inc. (650)
Schmeltzer, Aptaker & Shepard, P.C. (176)
Scholastic, Inc. (651)
Science Applications Internat'l Corp. (SAIC) (652)
Seaboard Corp. (653)
Self Help for Hard of Hearing People, Inc. (654)
Sellery Associates, Inc. (177)
Senior Executives Ass'n (655)
Service Employees Internat'l Union (656)
Shakopee Mdewakanton Sioux Tribe (656)
Daniel F. Shaw & Associates (177)
Shaw Pittman (177)
Shaw, Bransford, Veilleux & Roth (179)
Sheet Metal and Air Conditioning Contractors' Nat'l Ass'n (657)
Shelby, Tennessee, County of (657)
Shell Oil Co. (657)
Sher & Blackwell (179)
Mary Katherine Shilton (180)
Silicon Graphics/SGI (659)
Silver Users Ass'n (659)
Sister Cities Internat'l (660)
SKYWATCH Internat'l (660)
Small Business Survival Committee (661)
Smith Alling Lane, P.S. (183)
Smith Dawson & Andrews, Inc. (183)
Smurfit Stone Container Corp. (662)
Soc. of Professional Benefit Administrators (664)
Soc. of the Plastics Industry (664)
Software & Information Industry Ass'n (SIIA) (664)
The Solomon Group, LLC (185)
Solutia Inc. (665)
Sonnenschein, Nath & Rosenthal (185)
South African Government/World Bank (666)
South Gate, California, City of (666)
Southern California Public Power Authority (667)
Space Access (668)
Special Libraries Ass'n (669)
Specialized Carriers and Rigging Ass'n (669)
Spectrum Astro, Inc. (670)
The Spectrum Group (186)
Richard L. Spees, Inc. (186)
Sprint Corp. (671)
Square 3942 Associates Limited Partnership (671)
St. Louis, Missouri, City of (672)
Staff Builders, Inc. (672)
State Farm Insurance Cos. (673)
State Legislative Policy Institute (673)
States Ratification Committee (673)
Steel Manufacturers Ass'n (674)
Stephens Law Firm (188)
Stephens, Cross, Ihlenfeld & Boring, Inc. (188)
Stephens, Cross, Ihlenfeld and Boring, Inc. (674)
Steptoe & Johnson LLP (188)
Stockton, City of (675)
Storage Technology Corp. (675)
Strat@Comm (Strategic Communications Counselors) (189)
Strategic Horizons Advisors, L.L.C. (189)
Strictly Business Software System (675)
Student Loan Funding Corp. (675)
Sullivan & Mitchell, P.L.L.C. (190)
Sumlin Associates (190)
Sun Microsystems (676)
Sunset Properties, Inc. (677)
Swidler Berlin Shereff Friedman, LLP (678)
Swidler Berlin Shereff Friedman, LLP (191)
SWIPCO, U.S. (678)
Synthetic Organic Chemical Manufacturers Ass'n (679)
Tallahassee, Florida, City of (680)
Taxpayers Against Fraud, The False Claims Legal Center (681)
Technology Integration Group (682)
Teicher Consulting and Representation (193)
Teledyne Controls, Inc. (683)
Teligent, Inc. (683)
Tex-La Electric Cooperative of Texas (684)

Health Issues (HCR)

American Cancer Soc. ***(252)***
American Chemical Soc. ***(252)***
American Chiropractic Ass'n ***(252)***
American Civil Liberties Union ***(252)***
American Clinical Laboratory Ass'n ***(253)***
American College of Cardiology ***(253)***
American College of Chest Physicians ***(253)***
American College of Clinical Pharmacy ***(253)***
American College of Emergency Physicians ***(253)***
American College of Gastroenterology ***(253)***
American College of Health Care Administrators ***(253)***
American College of Nurse Practitioners ***(253)***
American College of Nurse-Midwives ***(254)***
American College of Obstetricians and Gynecologists ***(254)***
American College of Occupational and Environmental Medicine ***(254)***
American College of Osteopathic Surgeons ***(254)***
American College of Physicians-American Soc. of Internal Medicine (ACP-ASIM) ***(254)***
American College of Preventive Medicine ***(254)***
American College of Radiation Oncology ***(254)***
American College of Radiology ***(254)***
American College of Rheumatology ***(254)***
American College of Surgeons ***(254)***
American Congress of Community Supports and Employment Services ***(255)***
American Consulting Engineers Council ***(255)***
American Continental Group, Inc. *(12)*
American Council of Life Insurers ***(256)***
American Counseling Ass'n ***(256)***
American Dental Ass'n ***(257)***
American Dental Education Ass'n ***(257)***
American Dental Hygienists' Ass'n ***(257)***
American Diabetes Ass'n ***(257)***
American Dietetic Ass'n ***(257)***
American Electronics Ass'n ***(257)***
American Express Co. ***(258)***
American Farm Bureau Federation ***(258)***
American Federation for Medical Research ***(258)***
American Federation of Home Care Providers ***(258)***
American Federation of Musicians of the United States and Canada ***(258)***
American Federation of Senior Citizens ***(258)***
American Federation of State, County and Municipal Employees ***(258)***
American Federation of Teachers ***(259)***
American Foundation for AIDS Research ***(260)***
American Foundation for the Blind - Governmental Relations Group ***(260)***
American Furniture Manufacturers Ass'n ***(260)***
American Gastroenterological Ass'n ***(261)***
American Health Care Ass'n ***(261)***
American Health Information Management Ass'n ***(262)***
American Heart Ass'n ***(262)***
American Home Products Corp. ***(262)***
American Hospital Ass'n ***(263)***
American Indian Higher Education Consortium ***(263)***
American Institute of Certified Public Accountants ***(264)***
American Institute of Chemical Engineers ***(264)***
American Institute of Ultrasound in Medicine ***(264)***
American Insurance Ass'n ***(264)***
American Iron and Steel Institute ***(265)***
American Jewish Congress ***(265)***
American Legion ***(266)***
American Liver Foundation ***(266)***
American Lung Ass'n ***(266)***
American Lung Ass'n of Minnesota ***(266)***
American Managed Behavioral Healthcare Ass'n ***(266)***
American Medical Ass'n ***(267)***
American Medical Group Ass'n ***(267)***
American Medical Informatics Ass'n ***(267)***
American Medical Rehabilitation Providers Ass'n ***(267)***
American Medical Response ***(267)***
American Medical Student Ass'n ***(267)***
American Medical Technologists ***(267)***
American Military Soc. ***(268)***
American Museum of Natural History ***(268)***
American Network of Community Options and Resources (ANCOR) ***(268)***
American Nurses Ass'n ***(268)***
American Occupational Therapy Ass'n, Inc. ***(269)***
American Optometric Ass'n ***(269)***
American Organization of Nurse Executives ***(269)***
American Orthotic and Prosthetic Ass'n ***(269)***
American Osteopathic Ass'n ***(269)***
American Pharmaceutical Ass'n ***(270)***
American Physical Therapy Ass'n ***(270)***
American Plastics Council ***(270)***
American Podiatric Medical Ass'n ***(270)***
American Preventive Medical Ass'n ***(271)***
American Psychiatric Ass'n ***(271)***
American Psychiatric Nurses Ass'n ***(271)***
American Psychoanalytic Ass'n ***(271)***
American Psychological Ass'n ***(271)***
American Psychological Soc. ***(271)***
American Public Health Ass'n ***(271)***
American Red Cross ***(272)***
American Rental Ass'n ***(272)***
American Seniors Housing Ass'n ***(273)***
American Soc. for Bone and Mineral Research ***(274)***
American Soc. for Cell Biology ***(274)***
American Soc. for Clinical Laboratory Science ***(274)***
American Soc. for Clinical Nutrition ***(274)***
American Soc. for Quality ***(275)***
American Soc. for Therapeutic Radiology and Oncology ***(275)***
American Soc. of Anesthesiologists ***(275)***
American Soc. of Ass'n Executives ***(275)***
American Soc. of Cataract and Refractive Surgery ***(275)***
American Soc. of Clinical Oncology ***(276)***
American Soc. of Clinical Pathologists ***(276)***
American Soc. of Consultant Pharmacists ***(276)***
American Soc. of General Surgeons ***(276)***
American Soc. of Health System Pharmacists ***(276)***
American Soc. of Hematology ***(276)***
American Soc. of Nuclear Cardiology ***(277)***
American Soc. of Pediatric Nephrology ***(277)***
American Soc. of Plastic and Reconstructive Surgeons ***(277)***
American Soc. of Radiologic Technologists ***(277)***
American Soc. of Transplantation ***(277)***
American Speech, Language, and Hearing Ass'n ***(277)***
American Teleservices Ass'n ***(279)***
American Textile Manufacturers Institute ***(279)***
American Thoracic Soc. ***(279)***
American Tort Reform Ass'n ***(279)***
American Urogynecologic Soc. ***(280)***
American Water Works Ass'n ***(280)***
Americans for Medical Progress ***(282)***
Americans for Tax Reform ***(282)***
Americans United for Separation of Church and State ***(282)***
Amgen ***(282)***
Amputee Coalition ***(283)***
Anthem, Inc. ***(285)***
Anthra ***(285)***
Antitrust Coalition for Consumer Choice in Health Care ***(285)***
Aon Corp. ***(285)***
Applied Benefits Research Corp. ***(286)***
Apria Healthcare Group ***(287)***
The Arc ***(287)***
Arch Mineral Corp. ***(287)***
Arent Fox Kintner Plotkin & Kahn, PLLC *(14)*
Arkansas Blue Cross and Blue Shield ***(288)***
Arkansas, Office of the Governor of the State of ***(288)***
Armstrong World Industries, Inc. ***(289)***
Arnold & Porter *(16)*
Arter & Hadden *(17)*
Arthritis Foundation ***(289)***
Arvin Meritor Automotive ***(290)***
Ass'n for Ambulatory Behavioral Healthcare ***(291)***
Ass'n for Education and Rehabilitation of the Blind & Visually Impaired ***(292)***
Ass'n for Electronic Healthcare Transaction ***(292)***
Ass'n for Healthcare Philanthropy ***(292)***
Ass'n for Professionals in Infection Control and Epidemiology ***(293)***
Ass'n Growth Enterprises *(18)*
The Ass'n Healthcare Coalition ***(293)***
Ass'n of American Blood Banks ***(293)***
Ass'n of American Medical Colleges ***(294)***
Ass'n of American Physicians and Surgeons ***(294)***
Ass'n of Black Psychologists ***(294)***
Ass'n of Chiropractic Colleges ***(295)***
Ass'n of Clinical Research Professionals ***(295)***
Ass'n of Disposable Device Manufacturers (ADDM) ***(295)***
Ass'n of Independent Research Institutes ***(296)***
Ass'n of Maternal and Child Health Programs (AMCHP) ***(296)***
Ass'n of Military Surgeons of the U.S. (AMSUS) ***(297)***
Ass'n of Minnesota Counties ***(297)***
Ass'n of Minority Health Profession Schools ***(297)***
Ass'n of Professional Flight Attendants ***(297)***
Ass'n of Professors of Medicine ***(298)***
Ass'n of Schools of Public Health ***(298)***
Ass'n of State and Territorial Health Officials ***(298)***
Ass'n of Surgical Technologists ***(299)***
Ass'n of Trial Lawyers of America ***(299)***
Ass'n of University Programs in Health Administration ***(299)***
Ass'n of Women's Health, Obstetric and Neonatal Nurses ***(299)***
Assisted Living Federation of America ***(300)***
Associated General Contractors of America ***(300)***
Asthma and Allergy Foundation of America ***(301)***
Astra Solutions, LLC *(18)*
AstraZeneca Inc. ***(301)***
The Atlantic Group, Public Affairs, Inc. *(18)*
Atlantic Shores Healthcare, Inc. ***(302)***
Augustine Medical ***(303)***
Aurora Health Care, Inc. ***(303)***
Autism Soc. of America, Inc. ***(303)***
Automotive Aftermarket Industry Ass'n ***(303)***
Automotive Parts and Service Alliance ***(303)***
Auyua Inc. ***(304)***
Avax Technologies, Inc. ***(304)***
Aventis Behring ***(304)***
Aventis Pasteur ***(304)***
Aventis Pharmaceuticals, Inc. ***(304)***
Baker & Hostetler LLP *(19)*
Barbour Griffith & Rogers, Inc. *(22)*
Barksdale Ballard & Co., Inc. *(23)*
Barr Laboratories ***(308)***
BASF Corporation ***(308)***
Bass and Howes, Inc. *(24)*
Bass Hotels and Resorts, Inc. ***(308)***
Bassett Healthcare ***(308)***
Bastyr University ***(308)***
Baxter Healthcare Corp. ***(309)***
Bay State Health Systems ***(309)***
Bayer Corp. ***(309)***
Bayer Diagnostic ***(309)***
Baylor College of Medicine ***(310)***
Bazelon Center for Mental Health Law, Judge David L. ***(310)***
BD ***(310)***
Lee Bechtel and Associates *(25)*
Beerman, Swerdlove, Woloshin, Barezky, Becken, Genin & London ***(310)***
Belew Law Firm *(25)*
Timothy Bell & Co. *(25)*
BellSouth Corp. ***(311)***
Bennett Turner & Coleman, LLP *(25)*
Bergen Community College ***(311)***
Bergner Bockorny Castagnetti and Hawkins *(26)*
Berkshire Inc. *(26)*
Berliner, Candon & Jimison *(27)*
Berman Enterprises *(27)*
Bert Corona Leadership Institute ***(312)***
Best Health Care Inc. ***(312)***
Bethlehem Steel Corp. ***(312)***
Beverly Enterprises ***(313)***
Bio-Vascular, Inc. ***(313)***
Biogen, Inc. ***(313)***
Biomatrix ***(314)***
Biomedical Research Institute ***(314)***
BioPort Corp. ***(314)***

Biotechnology Industry Organization *(314)*
Bituminous Coal Operators Ass'n *(314)*
BKSH & Associates *(28)*
Blank Rome Comisky & McCauley, LLP *(29)*
Blood Center of Southeastern Wisconsin *(315)*
Bloomfield Associates, Inc. *(29)*
Blue Cross and Blue Shield of California *(315)*
Blue Cross and Blue Shield of Florida *(315)*
Blue Cross Blue Shield Ass'n *(315)*
Board on Human Sciences *(316)*
Boehringer Ingelheim Pharmaceuticals, Inc. *(316)*
The Boeing Co. *(316)*
Boesch & Co. *(29)*
Bon Secours Charity Health System *(317)*
Bond & Company, Inc. *(30)*
Booher & Associates *(30)*
The Borden Group, Inc. *(30)*
Boston Scientific Corp. *(318)*
Boston, Massachusetts, City of *(318)*
Boys Town Nat'l Research Hospital *(318)*
Bracco Diagnostics *(319)*
Bracewell & Patterson, L.L.P. *(30)*
Bracy Williams & Co. *(31)*
Brain Injury Ass'n *(319)*
Brain Trauma Foundation *(319)*
Robert M. Brandon and Associates *(32)*
Brickfield, Burchette, Ritts & Stone *(32)*
Bristol-Myers Squibb Co. *(320)*
Brown & Associates *(32)*
Brown and Williamson Tobacco Corp. *(322)*
Brown General Hospital *(322)*
Brownstein Hyatt & Farber, P.C. *(33)*
Broydrick & Associates *(33)*
Brush Wellman, Inc. *(323)*
BSMG Worldwide *(34)*
Burger King Corp. *(324)*
Burlington Northern Santa Fe Railway *(324)*
Business and Professional Women/USA *(324)*
The Business Roundtable *(325)*
Butera & Andrews *(34)*
California Ass'n of Marriage and Family Therapists *(326)*
California Children's Hospital Ass'n *(326)*
California Primary Care Ass'n *(327)*
California School of Professional Psychology *(327)*
California State Ass'n of Counties *(327)*
Campaign for Medical Research *(329)*
Campbell Crane & Associates *(36)*
Cancer Leadership Council *(330)*
Canfield & Associates, Inc. *(36)*
Mark R. Cannon *(37)*
CapCURE *(330)*
Capital Consultants Corp. *(37)*
Capital Research Center *(330)*
Capitol Associates, Inc. *(37)*
Capitol Coalitions Inc. *(38)*
Capitol Health Group, LLC *(39)*
Capitol Partners *(39)*
Cardinal Health Inc. *(331)*
CARE (Cooperative for Assistance and Relief Everywhere) *(331)*
Caremark Rx, Inc. *(331)*
CaRess, Inc. *(331)*
Caretenders Health Corp. *(331)*
Cargill, Inc. *(331)*
The Carmen Group *(40)*
Caron Foundation *(332)*
Carpi & Clay *(41)*
Carr Public Affairs *(332)*
Cartwright & Riley *(41)*
Cascade Designs *(332)*
CaseNewHolland Inc. *(333)*
Cash, Smith & Wages *(41)*
Cassidy & Associates, Inc. *(42)*
Catholic Health Ass'n of the United States *(333)*
Cavarocchi Ruscio Dennis Associates *(44)*
Celanese Government Relations Office *(334)*
Cell Tech *(334)*
Cell Therapeutics Inc. *(334)*
Center for Healthcare Information Management *(336)*
Center for Patient Advocacy *(337)*
Center for Reproductive Law and Policy *(337)*
Central Michigan University *(339)*
Chamber of Commerce of the U.S.A. *(340)*
Chesapeake Enterprises, Inc. *(46)*
Child Welfare League of America *(343)*
Children and Adults with Attention Deficit Disorders (CHADD) *(344)*
The Children's Cause Inc. *(344)*
Children's Defense Fund *(344)*
Children's Health Fund *(344)*
Children's Hospital and Medical Center *(344)*
Children's Hospital of Boston *(344)*
Children's Hospital of Wisconsin *(344)*
CHIM *(344)*
Christian Coalition of America *(345)*
Christian Voice, Inc. *(345)*
Christus Health *(346)*
The Church Alliance *(346)*
Church of Scientology Internat'l *(346)*
CIGNA Corp. *(346)*
Circuit City Stores, Inc. *(347)*
Citigroup *(347)*
Citizens Against Government Waste *(348)*
Citizens for a Sound Economy *(348)*
Citizens for Public Action on Cholesterol, Inc. *(348)*
Citizens for the Treatment of High Blood Pressure, Inc. *(349)*
Civic Service, Inc. *(46)*
Clark & Weinstock, Inc. *(47)*
Clay and Associates *(47)*
Cleveland Clinic Foundation *(350)*
William M. Cloherty *(47)*
CNA Financial Corp. *(351)*
CNA Insurance Cos. *(351)*
Coalition for a Procompetitive Stark Law *(352)*
Coalition for American Trauma Care *(352)*
Coalition for Asbestos Resolution *(353)*
Coalition for Brain Injury Research and Services, Inc. *(353)*
Coalition for Nonprofit Health Care *(354)*
Coalition for the Homeless *(354)*
Coalition of Boston Teaching Hospitals *(355)*
Coalition of Higher Education Assistance Organizations *(355)*
Coalition of Positive Outcomes in Pregnancy *(355)*
Colex and Associates *(48)*
Collagen Corp. *(357)*
College of American Pathologists *(357)*
College on Problems of Drug Dependence *(357)*
Coloplast Corp. *(358)*
Columbus Public Affairs *(50)*
Commissioned Officers Ass'n of the U.S. Public Health Service *(360)*
Committee for a Responsible Federal Budget *(360)*
Commonwealth Group, Ltd. *(50)*
Communications Workers of America *(362)*
Community General Hospital of Sullivan County *(362)*
Community Health Partners of Ohio *(362)*
Community Hospital Telehealth Consortium *(362)*
Community Hospitals of Central California *(363)*
Community Transportation Ass'n of America *(363)*
ConAgra Foods, Inc. *(365)*
Condell Medical Center *(365)*
Congressional Consultants *(51)*
Congressional Institute, Inc. *(366)*
Conkling, Fiskum & McCormick *(51)*
Conlon, Frantz, Phelan & Pires *(51)*
Connerton & Ray *(51)*
Consortium of Social Science Ass'ns *(368)*
Constellation Energy Group *(368)*
Consumer Aerosol Products Council *(368)*
Consumer Federation of America *(369)*
Consumer Healthcare Products Ass'n *(369)*
Consumers Union of the United States *(369)*
Contact Lens Institute *(369)*
Contemporary Products Inc. *(370)*
ConvaTec *(370)*
Cook Children's Health Care System *(370)*
Cook Group *(370)*
Cook, Illinois, County of *(371)*
Cooley's Anemia Foundation *(371)*
Cooney & Associates, Inc. *(52)*
Cooper Green Hospital *(371)*
Coors Brewing Company *(371)*
Copeland, Lowery & Jacquez *(52)*
Cord Blood Registry, Inc. *(371)*
Corporate Health Care Coalition *(372)*
Cosmetic, Toiletry and Fragrance Ass'n *(373)*
Shawn Coulson *(53)*
Council for Affordable Health Insurance *(374)*
Council for Responsible Nutrition *(374)*
Council of Colleges of Acupuncture and Oriental Medicine *(375)*
The Council of Insurance Agents & Brokers *(376)*
Council of Smaller Enterprises *(376)*
Council of State and Territorial Epidemiologists *(376)*
Council of State Governments *(376)*
Council of Women's and Infant's Specialty Hospitals *(376)*
Council on Radionuclides and Radiopharmaceuticals (CORAR) *(377)*
Covenant House *(377)*
Covington & Burling *(53)*
Law Office of C. Deming Cowles *(54)*
Craig Associates *(55)*
Crestwood Behavior Health, Inc. *(378)*
Crohn's and Colitis Foundation of America *(378)*
Crown Therapeutics, Inc. *(379)*
Cure Autism Now *(380)*
Cure for Lymphoma Foundation *(380)*
Cuyahoga, Ohio, County of *(380)*
CVS, Inc. *(380)*
Cystic Fibrosis Foundation *(380)*
Cytometrics, Inc. *(380)*
Cytyc Corp. *(380)*
The Da Vinci Group *(56)*
Daemen College *(381)*
DaimlerChrysler Corp. *(381)*
Dakota, Minnesota, County of *(381)*
Dalrymple and Associates, L.L.C. *(56)*
Datahr Rehabilitation Institute *(382)*
DATRON, Inc. *(382)*
Davidson & Company, Inc. *(57)*
Davis & Harman LLP *(57)*
Davis O'Connell, Inc. *(58)*
Deaconess Billings Clinic *(383)*
Dean Blakey & Moskowitz *(59)*
DeBrunner and Associates, Inc. *(60)*
Deere & Co. *(383)*
Deloitte Consulting *(384)*
Delta Air Lines *(384)*
Delta Dental Plans Ass'n *(385)*
Denison, Scott Associates *(61)*
Dental Recycling North America *(385)*
Denver Children's Hospital *(385)*
Detroit Medical Center *(386)*
Detroit, Michigan, City of *(386)*
Devillier Communications *(61)*
DGME Fairness Initiative *(387)*
Dictaphone Corp. *(388)*
Digestive Disease Nat'l Coalition *(388)*
Dimensions Healthcare System *(388)*
Direct Supply *(389)*
The Walt Disney Co. *(389)*
District of Columbia Hospital Ass'n *(390)*
DNA Sciences, Inc. *(390)*
Doctors Community Healthcare Corp. *(390)*
The Doctors' Co. *(390)*
Dole Food Co. *(390)*
R. R. Donnelley & Sons *(391)*
The Dow Chemical Co. *(391)*
Downey McGrath Group, Inc. *(64)*
Downey McGrath Group, Inc. *(392)*
drugstore.com *(392)*
Duane, Morris & Heckscher LLP *(65)*
The Duberstein Group, Inc. *(65)*
Dumex Medical *(393)*
DuPont *(393)*
The DuPont Pharmaceutical Co. *(393)*
The Dutko Group, Inc. *(68)*
Dyer Ellis & Joseph, P.C. *(68)*
Dykema Gossett PLLC *(69)*
Dystonia Medical Research Foundation *(394)*
Easter Seals *(395)*
Eastman Chemical Co. *(395)*
Eastman Kodak Co. *(395)*
Eclipse Surgical Technologies *(396)*
Edelman Public Relations Worldwide *(396)*
Edington, Peel & Associates, Inc. *(70)*

EDS Corp. ***(398)***
eHealth Insurance Services, Inc. ***(399)***
El Centro Regional Medical Center ***(399)***
Elan Pharmaceutical Research Corp. ***(399)***
Elanex Pharmaceuticals ***(399)***
ElderCare Companies ***(399)***
Elderplan, Inc. ***(399)***
Elim, Alaska, City of ***(401)***
Emergency Department Practice Management Ass'n (EDPMA) ***(401)***
Emord & Associates, P.C. *(71)*
Emory University, Department of Internat'l Health-PAMM, USAID ***(402)***
Empire Blue Cross and Blue Shield ***(402)***
Employer Health Care Innovation Project ***(402)***
Employers Council on Flexible Compensation ***(402)***
Endocrine Soc. ***(403)***
Englewood Hospital & Medical Center ***(403)***
Enron Corp. ***(403)***
Epilepsy Foundation of America ***(406)***
Episcopal AIDS Ministry ***(406)***
Epstein Becker & Green, P.C. *(72)*
The ERISA Industry Committee (ERIC) ***(406)***
Ervin Technical Associates, Inc. (ETA) *(73)*
ESA, Inc. ***(407)***
ESR Children's Health Care System ***(407)***
Essex Medical Systems Plus ***(407)***
Evangelical Lutheran Good Samaritan Soc. ***(408)***
Evans & Black, Inc. *(73)*
EXACT Laboratories ***(408)***
Express Scripts Inc. ***(409)***
Extendicare Health Services Inc. ***(409)***
Exxon Mobil Corp. ***(409)***
Eye Bank Ass'n of America ***(410)***
F&T Network, Inc. *(74)*
Fallon Community Health Plan ***(410)***
Families U.S.A. Foundation ***(410)***
Family Violence Prevention Fund ***(411)***
Farm Animal Reform Movement (FARM) ***(411)***
FDA-NIH Council ***(412)***
FED Corp. ***(412)***
Feder, Semo, Clarke & Bard *(74)*
Federal Health Strategies, Inc. *(75)*
Federated Ambulatory Surgery Ass'n ***(414)***
Federation of American Hospitals ***(414)***
Federation of Behavioral, Psychological and Cognitive Sciences ***(414)***
Federation of Nurses and Health Professionals/AFT ***(415)***
Federation of State Medical Boards of the U.S. ***(415)***
FedEx Corp. ***(415)***
The Ferguson Group, LLC *(76)*
Fierce and Isakowitz *(76)*
First Church of Christ, Scientist ***(417)***
First Consulting Group ***(417)***
First Health Group Corp. ***(417)***
First Scientific Corp. ***(418)***
First Tuesday Group ***(418)***
Fisher Imaging ***(418)***
Flack Associates *(77)*
Fleet Reserve Ass'n ***(418)***
Fleishman-Hillard, Inc *(77)*
Florida State University System ***(420)***
Foley & Lardner *(78)*
Foley, Hoag & Eliot LLP *(78)*
Food Bank of the Virginia Peninsula ***(421)***
Food Distributors Internat'l (NAWGA-IFDA) ***(421)***
Food Marketing Institute ***(421)***
Betty Ford Center ***(422)***
Ford Motor Co. ***(422)***
Forscey & Stinson, PLLC *(79)*
The Fortier Group, LLC *(79)*
Foundation for Integrated Medicine ***(424)***
Foundation Health Federal Services, Inc. ***(424)***
FoxKiser *(79)*
FRANMAC/Taco Pac ***(425)***
Freedom Designs ***(425)***
French & Company *(79)*
Fresenius Medical Care North America ***(425)***
Fresno Community Hospital and Medical Center ***(426)***
Friends Committee on Nat'l Legislation ***(426)***
Friends of the Nat'l Library of Medicine ***(426)***
Gainesville, Florida, City of ***(428)***
Gambro Healthcare ***(429)***
Gardner, Carton and Douglas *(81)*
Sara Garland (and Associates) *(81)*
Garvey, Schubert & Barer *(81)*
GCRC Program Directors Ass'n ***(430)***
GenCorp ***(431)***
Genelabs Technologies, Inc. ***(431)***
Genentech, Inc. ***(431)***
General Conference of Seventh-day Adventists ***(431)***
General Electric Co. ***(432)***
General Motors Corp. ***(432)***
Generic Pharmaceutical Ass'n ***(433)***
Genesis Consulting Group, LLC *(82)*
The Genome Action Coalition ***(433)***
Genzyme Corp. ***(433)***
GEO Centers, Inc. ***(433)***
Georgia-Pacific Corp. ***(434)***
Gibbons & Company, Inc. *(82)*
Gibson, Dunn & Crutcher LLP *(82)*
Thomas J. Gilligan *(82)*
Girl Scouts of the U.S.A. - Washington Office ***(435)***
Glass Packaging Institute ***(435)***
GlaxoSmithKline ***(436)***
Golden Rule Insurance Co. ***(437)***
Golin/Harris Internat'l *(84)*
Mark W. Goodin *(84)*
B. F. Goodrich Co. ***(437)***
Goodyear Tire and Rubber Co. ***(437)***
Gottehrer and Co. *(84)*
Government Employees Hospital Ass'n ***(437)***
GPC Internat'l *(85)*
Jay Grant & Associates *(85)*
The GrayWell Group, Inc. *(86)*
Greater New York Hospital Ass'n ***(439)***
Green County Health Care, Inc. ***(440)***
Green Door ***(440)***
Greenberg Traurig, LLP *(86)*
Greener and Hook, LLC *(87)*
GREX, Inc. ***(440)***
Griffin, Johnson, Dover & Stewart *(87)*
Grisso Consulting *(88)*
Groom Law Group, Chartered *(88)*
Group Health Cooperative ***(441)***
Group Health, Inc. ***(441)***
GRQ, Inc. *(88)*
Guam, Washington Office of the Governor ***(442)***
Guidant Corp. ***(442)***
Guinea, Secretary General of the Presidency of the Republic of ***(442)***
Haake and Associates *(89)*
Hackensack University Medical Center Foundation ***(443)***
Hadassah, The Women's Zionist Organization of America ***(443)***
C. McClain Haddow & Associates *(89)*
Hall, Green, Rupli, LLC *(90)*
Halliburton/Brown & Root ***(443)***
Hallmark Cards, Inc. ***(443)***
Halsey, Rains & Associates, LLC *(90)*
Hannett & Associates *(91)*
Harris Corp. ***(444)***
The Hartford ***(445)***
Hazelden Foundation ***(445)***
HCA Healthcare Corp. ***(445)***
HCR-Manor Care, Inc. ***(445)***
Health and Hospital Corp. of Marion County ***(446)***
Health and Medicine Counsel of Washington *(93)*
Health Industry Distributors Ass'n ***(446)***
Health Insurance Ass'n of America ***(446)***
Health Partners ***(446)***
Health Policy Alternatives, Inc. *(93)*
Health Policy Analysts *(93)*
Health Policy Group *(93)*
Health Policy Strategies *(93)*
Health Policy Strategies ***(446)***
Health Risk Management Group, Inc. ***(446)***
Health Services of Kansas and Mid Missouri ***(446)***
Healthcare Ass'n of New York State ***(446)***
Healthcare Financial Management Ass'n ***(447)***
Healthcare Financing Study Group ***(447)***
Healthcare Leadership Council ***(447)***
Healtheon/Web MD ***(447)***
Healthsouth Corp. ***(447)***
Hecht, Spencer & Associates *(93)*
Heidepriem & Mager, Inc. *(94)*
H. J. Heinz Co., ***(448)***
Helen Keller Worldwide ***(448)***
Helmsin & Yarwood Associates *(94)*
HemaSure, Inc. ***(448)***
Hennipin County Board of Commissioners ***(448)***
Hershey Foods Corp. ***(449)***
Hewlett-Packard Co. ***(449)***
Hill and Knowlton, Inc. *(95)*
Hill-Rom Co., Inc. ***(450)***
HIP Health Plans ***(450)***
Hoffmann-La Roche Inc. ***(450)***
Hogan & Hartson L.L.P. *(96)*
Hohlt & Associates *(98)*
Holland & Knight LLP *(98)*
Hollis-Eden Pharmaceuticals, Inc. ***(451)***
Hollister Inc. ***(451)***
Holyoke Hospital ***(451)***
Home Access Health ***(451)***
Honeywell Internat'l, Inc. ***(452)***
Hospice Ass'n of America ***(452)***
Hospital for Special Surgery ***(453)***
Household Internat'l, Inc. ***(453)***
HT Medical ***(454)***
Human Rights Campaign Fund ***(454)***
Humana Inc. ***(455)***
Hunt Management Systems *(101)*
Huntington's Disease Soc. of America ***(455)***
Huntsman Corp. ***(455)***
Hurt, Norton & Associates *(101)*
Fred Hutchinson Cancer Research Center ***(455)***
Hutzel Medical Center ***(455)***
Hyperion Medical ***(456)***
The Ickes & Enright Group *(102)*
Ikon Public Affairs *(102)*
Illinois Collaboration on Youth ***(457)***
Illinois Department of Human Services ***(457)***
Illinois Primary Health Care Ass'n ***(457)***
IMC Global Inc. ***(458)***
Immunex Corp. ***(458)***
Impact Strategies *(102)*
IMS Health Inc. ***(458)***
Independent Insurance Agents of America, Inc. ***(459)***
Independent Office Products and Furniture Dealers Ass'n ***(459)***
Indiana, Office of the Governor of the State of ***(460)***
Infectious Diseases Soc. of America, Inc. ***(461)***
Ingersoll-Rand Co. ***(462)***
Innovative Resource Group ***(462)***
Inova Fairfax Hospital ***(462)***
Inoveon Corp. ***(462)***
Institute for Civil Soc. ***(463)***
Institute on Religion and Public Policy ***(464)***
Integrated Health Services, Inc. ***(465)***
Integrated Skilled Care of Ohio ***(465)***
Integris Health Systems ***(465)***
Intel Corp. ***(465)***
Intercultural Cancer Council ***(466)***
InterMountain Health Care Inc. ***(467)***
Internat'l Ass'n for Dental Research ***(467)***
Internat'l Ass'n of Fire Chiefs ***(468)***
Internat'l Ass'n of Fire Fighters ***(468)***
Internat'l Ass'n of Machinists and Aerospace Workers ***(468)***
Internat'l Biometric Industry Ass'n ***(468)***
Internat'l Brotherhood of Boilermakers, Iron Shipbuilders, Blacksmiths, Forgers and Helpers ***(469)***
Internat'l Brotherhood of Electrical Workers ***(469)***
Internat'l Brotherhood of Teamsters ***(469)***
Internat'l Business Machines Corp. ***(469)***
Internat'l Council of Cruise Lines ***(470)***
Internat'l Dyslexia Ass'n, The ***(471)***
Internat'l Federation of Professional and Technical Engineers ***(471)***
Internat'l Franchise Ass'n ***(472)***
Internat'l Hearing Soc. ***(472)***
Internat'l Longshore and Warehouse Union ***(473)***
Internat'l Mass Retailers Ass'n ***(473)***
Internat'l Sign Ass'n ***(474)***
Internat'l Soc. of Refractive Surgery ***(475)***

Internat'l Union of Bricklayers and Allied Craftsworkers *(476)*
Internat'l Union of Painters and Allied Trades *(476)*
Interstitial Cystitis Ass'n *(477)*
Intrinsiq Data Corp. *(477)*
Iowa Department of Public Health *(478)*
IVAX Corp. *(480)*
Jacobs & Co. Public Affairs/Loma Linda University *(481)*
The JAG Group, Inc. *(481)*
James Hardie Building Products Inc. *(481)*
Jar-Mon Consultants, Inc. *(105)*
JCP Associates *(105)*
Jefferson Consulting Group *(105)*
Jefferson Government Relations, L.L.C. *(106)*
Jewish Guild for the Blind *(483)*
JKB Communications *(107)*
Law Offices of Mark S. Joffe *(107)*
Johns Hopkins Center for Civilian Biodefense Studies *(483)*
Johnson & Johnson, Inc. *(484)*
Johnson Co. *(107)*
Philip W. Johnston Associates *(108)*
Joint Commission on the Accreditation of Health Care Organizations *(484)*
Joint Council of Allergy, Asthma and Immunology *(484)*
Jolly/Rissler, Inc. *(108)*
Jones, Day, Reavis & Pogue *(108)*
Jones, Walker, Waechter, Poitevent, Carrere & Denegre, L.L.P. *(108)*
Jorden Burt LLP *(109)*
Kahl Pownall Advocates *(485)*
Kaiser Aluminum & Chemical Corp. *(485)*
Kaiser Permanente *(486)*
Kalkines, Arky, Zall and Bernstein *(486)*
Barbara A. Karmanos Cancer Institute *(486)*
Kellogg Brown and Root *(487)*
Kelly and Associates, Inc. *(111)*
Kendall Healthcare Products Co. *(487)*
Kent & O'Connor, Inc. *(112)*
Kentucky, Commonwealth of *(488)*
Kessler & Associates Business Services, Inc. *(112)*
Ketchum *(112)*
Jeffrey J. Kimbell & Associates *(113)*
Kimberly-Clark Corp. *(489)*
Kinder & Associates, Inc. *(113)*
King & Spalding *(113)*
Kiwanis Internat'l *(490)*
Kleinfeld, Kaplan and Becker *(114)*
Theodore C. Knappen, P.C. *(114)*
Knoll Pharmaceutical Co. *(490)*
Kogovsek & Associates *(114)*
Susan G. Komen Breast Cancer Foundation *(490)*
Komen Breast Cancer Foundation, The Susan G. *(491)*
KOSA *(491)*
Krooth & Altman *(115)*
La Rabida Children's Hospital Research Center *(493)*
Labor Council for Latin American Advancement (LCLAA) *(493)*
Laborers Health & Safety Fund *(493)*
Laguna Woods, California, City of *(494)*
Lakeland Regional Medical Center *(494)*
Latham & Watkins *(116)*
The Paul Laxalt Group *(117)*
League of Women Voters of the United States *(497)*
Ledge Counsel *(118)*
Legal Action Center of the City of New York, Inc. *(497)*
The Legislative Strategies Group, LLC *(118)*
Lent Scrivner & Roth LLC *(119)*
Leukemia & Lymphoma Soc. *(498)*
Lewis-Burke Associates *(120)*
Liberty Medical Supply *(499)*
Liberty Mutual Insurance Group *(499)*
Lifecore Biomedical *(499)*
LifeLink Foundation *(499)*
Eli Lilly and Co. *(499)*
Lindesmith Center - Drug Policy Foundation *(500)*
Littler Mendelson, P.C. *(120)*
The Livingston Group, LLC *(120)*
Lockheed Martin Corp. *(501)*
Lockridge Grindal & Nauen, P.L.L.P. *(121)*
Long Term Care Campaign *(503)*
Los Angeles, California, County of *(504)*
Lovelace Respiratory Research Institute *(504)*
Loyola University Health System *(505)*
Loyola University of Chicago *(505)*
The LTV Corp. *(505)*
Lucent Technologies *(505)*
Lumbermens Mutual Casualty Co. *(505)*
Lupus Foundation of America *(505)*
Lutheran Office for Governmental Affairs/Evangelical Lutheran Church in America *(506)*
Lymphoma Research Foundation of America, Inc. *(506)*
M.D. - I.P.A. *(506)*
MacAndrews & Forbes Holdings, Inc. *(506)*
Macon, City of *(507)*
Madison Government Affairs *(123)*
Magee Women's Health Foundation *(507)*
Magnitude Information Systems *(507)*
Mallinckrodt-Nellcor Puritan Bennett *(508)*
Mallino Government Relations *(123)*
Managed Care Solutions *(508)*
Management Options, Inc. *(123)*
Manufacturers Alliance/MAPI Inc. *(509)*
MARC Associates, Inc. *(124)*
March of Dimes Birth Defects Foundation *(509)*
Mariner Post Acute Network *(510)*
Martins Point Health Care *(511)*
Massachusetts Hospital Ass'n *(512)*
MassMutual Financial Group *(512)*
Mattel, Inc. *(513)*
Matthews Media Group, Inc. *(513)*
Virginia M. Mayer *(126)*
Mayer, Brown & Platt *(126)*
MBNA America Bank NA *(514)*
McClure, Gerard & Neuenschwander, Inc. *(127)*
McDermott Internat'l, Inc./Babcock & Wilcox *(514)*
McDermott, Will and Emery *(128)*
Jack H. McDonald *(129)*
McGlotten & Jarvis *(129)*
McGlotten & Jarvis *(514)*
McGraw-Hill Cos., The *(514)*
McGuiness & Holch *(130)*
MCI WorldCom Corp. *(514)*
McIntyre Law Firm, PLLC *(130)*
McKesson Corp. *(515)*
McMahon and Associates *(131)*
McMillan, Hill & Associates *(131)*
McNamara & Associates *(131)*
Diane McRee Associates *(131)*
McSlarrow Consulting L.L.C. *(131)*
Meals on Wheels Ass'n of America *(515)*
Medassets.com *(515)*
Medical Advocacy Services, Inc. *(132)*
Medical College of Virginia, Dept. of Neurology, Office of the Chairman *(516)*
Medical Group Management Ass'n *(516)*
Medical Imaging Contrast Agent Ass'ns *(516)*
Medical Library Ass'n/Ass'n of Academic Health Sciences Library Directors *(516)*
Medical Mutual of Ohio *(516)*
Medical Records Internat'l, Inc. *(516)*
Medicare Cost Contractors Alliance *(517)*
Meditrend, Inc. *(517)*
Medix Pharmaceuticals *(517)*
Medline Industries Inc. *(517)*
MedPartners, Inc. *(517)*
MedPro, Inc. *(517)*
Medtronic, Inc. *(517)*
Member-Link Systems, Inc. *(517)*
Memorial Health System *(517)*
Memorial Sloan-Kettering Cancer Center *(517)*
Mennonite Mutual Aid Ass'n *(518)*
Merced, California, County of *(518)*
William M. Mercer, Inc. *(132)*
Merck & Co. *(518)*
Mercy Hospital of Des Moines, Iowa *(518)*
Mercy Medical *(518)*
Metabolife *(519)*
Metcalf Federal Relations *(132)*
Metropolitan King County Council *(520)*
Mexican-American Legal Defense and Educational Fund *(521)*
Meyers & Associates *(133)*
Miami Beach, Florida, City of *(521)*
Mid-Atlantic Medical Services, Inc. *(523)*
Middlesex Hospital Home Care *(523)*
The Military Coalition *(524)*
Miller & Chevalier, Chartered *(133)*
Miller & Co. *(134)*
Denny Miller McBee Associates *(134)*
Milwaukee, City of *(524)*
Milwaukee, Wisconsin, County of *(524)*
Minnesota Mining and Manufacturing (3M Pharmaceuticals) *(525)*
Minnesota Mining and Manufacturing Co. (3M Co.) *(525)*
Mintz, Levin, Cohn, Ferris, Glovsky and Popeo, P.C. *(135)*
Mitsubishi Research Institute *(526)*
Mobile Diagnostic Testing Services *(527)*
The Jeffrey Modell Foundation *(527)*
Moffit Cancer Research Hospital *(527)*
Molecular BioSystems, Inc. *(527)*
Susan Molinari, L.L.P. *(135)*
Monfort & Wolfe *(135)*
Montefiore Medical Center *(528)*
Moore Medical Corp. *(529)*
Morgan, Lewis & Bockius LLP *(136)*
Motion Picture and Television Fund *(530)*
Mount Sinai Hospital *(531)*
Mount Sinai School of Medicine *(531)*
Mount Sinai/NYU Health *(531)*
MultiDimensional Imaging, Inc. *(532)*
Multinat'l Government Services, Inc. *(138)*
Murray, Scheer, Montgomery, Tapia & O'Donnell *(139)*
Muse & Associates *(140)*
Mutual of Omaha Insurance Companies *(533)*
The MWW Group *(140)*
Mylan Laboratories, Inc. *(533)*
NAADAC, The Ass'n for Addiction Professionals *(534)*
NAAS *(534)*
Nassau University Medical Center *(535)*
Nat'l Abortion and Reproductive Rights Action League *(535)*
Nat'l Abortion Federation *(535)*
Nat'l Alliance for Hispanic Health *(536)*
Nat'l Alliance for the Mentally Ill *(536)*
Nat'l Alliance of State and Territorial AIDS Directors *(537)*
Nat'l Anti-Vivisection Soc. *(537)*
Nat'l Ass'n for Equal Opportunity in Higher Education *(537)*
Nat'l Ass'n for Medical Direction of Respiratory Care *(538)*
Nat'l Ass'n for Nutritional Choice *(538)*
Nat'l Ass'n for Proton Therapy *(538)*
Nat'l Ass'n for Sport and Physical Education *(538)*
Nat'l Ass'n for State Farm Agents *(538)*
Nat'l Ass'n for the Advancement of Orthotics and Prosthetics *(538)*
Nat'l Ass'n for the Support of Long Term Care *(538)*
Nat'l Ass'n for Uniformed Services *(538)*
Nat'l Ass'n of Chain Drug Stores *(539)*
Nat'l Ass'n of Children's Hospitals Inc. *(540)*
Nat'l Ass'n of City and County Health Officials *(540)*
Nat'l Ass'n of Community Health Centers *(540)*
Nat'l Ass'n of County and City Health Officials *(541)*
Nat'l Ass'n of Dental Assistants *(542)*
Nat'l Ass'n of Dental Plans *(542)*
Nat'l Ass'n of Developmental Disabilities Councils *(542)*
Nat'l Ass'n of Epilepsy Centers *(542)*
Nat'l Ass'n of Health Underwriters *(543)*
Nat'l Ass'n of Independent Insurers *(544)*
Nat'l Ass'n of Insurance Commissioners *(544)*
Nat'l Ass'n of Letter Carriers of the United States of America *(545)*
Nat'l Ass'n of Manufacturers *(545)*
Nat'l Ass'n of Minority Political Families, USA, Inc. *(545)*

Nat'l Ass'n of Negro Business & Professional Women's Clubs, Inc. (546)
Nat'l Ass'n of Nurse Practitioners in Women's Health (546)
Nat'l Ass'n of Optometrics and Opticians (546)
Nat'l Ass'n of Pediatric Nurse Associates and Practitioners (546)
Nat'l Ass'n of People with AIDS, Inc. (546)
Nat'l Ass'n of Physician Nurses (546)
Nat'l Ass'n of Portable X-Ray Providers (546)
Nat'l Ass'n of Professional Employer Organizations (547)
Nat'l Ass'n of Protection and Advocacy Systems (NAPAS) (547)
Nat'l Ass'n of Psychiatric Health Systems (547)
Nat'l Ass'n of Public Hospitals and Health Systems (547)
Nat'l Ass'n of Retired Federal Employees (548)
Nat'l Ass'n of Rural Health Clinics (548)
Nat'l Ass'n of RV Parks and Campgrounds (548)
Nat'l Ass'n of School Nurses (548)
Nat'l Ass'n of School Psychologists (548)
Nat'l Ass'n of Senior Companion Project Directors (549)
Nat'l Ass'n of Social Workers (549)
Nat'l Ass'n of State Mental Health Program Directors (550)
Nat'l Ass'n of State Units on Aging (550)
Nat'l Ass'n of VA Physicians and Dentists (551)
Nat'l Ass'n of Wholesaler-Distributors (551)
Nat'l Ass'n to Protect Individual Rights (551)
Nat'l Assembly of Health and Human Service Organizations (551)
Nat'l Automobile Dealers Ass'n (552)
Nat'l Black Women's Health Project (552)
Nat'l Breast Cancer Coalition (553)
Nat'l Business Coalition on Health (553)
Nat'l Campaign for Hearing Health (554)
Nat'l Center for Genome Research (554)
Nat'l Center for Learning Disabilities (NCLD) (554)
Nat'l Center for Policy Analysis (555)
Nat'l Center for Public Policy Research (555)
Nat'l Chronic Care Consortium (555)
Nat'l Coalition for Cancer Research (556)
Nat'l Coalition for Cancer Survivorship (556)
Nat'l Coalition for Osteoporosis and Related Bone Diseases (556)
Nat'l College (557)
Nat'l Commission on Correctional Health Care (557)
Nat'l Committee to Preserve Social Security and Medicare (557)
Nat'l Consumers League (558)
Nat'l Coordinating Committee for Multiemployer Plans (559)
Nat'l Cosmetology Ass'n (559)
Nat'l Council for Community Behavioral Healthcare (559)
Nat'l Council of Catholic Women (560)
Nat'l Council of La Raza (560)
Nat'l Council of Negro Women (560)
Nat'l Council of State Boards of Nursing (560)
Nat'l Council on Alcoholism and Drug Dependence (561)
Nat'l Council on Compensation Insurance (561)
Nat'l Council on the Aging (561)
Nat'l Disease Research Interchange (562)
Nat'l District Attorneys Ass'n (562)
Nat'l Education Ass'n of the U.S. (562)
Nat'l Electrical Manufacturers Ass'n (562)
Nat'l Employee Benefits Institute (562)
Nat'l Farmers Union (Farmers Educational & Co-operative Union of America) (563)
Nat'l Funeral Directors Ass'n (565)
Nat'l Gaucher Foundation (565)
Nat'l Grain and Feed Ass'n (566)
Nat'l Grange (566)
Nat'l Grocers Ass'n (566)
Nat'l Head Start Ass'n (566)
Nat'l Health Care Access Coalition (566)
Nat'l Health Council (567)
Nat'l Health Law Program (567)
Nat'l Hemophilia Foundation (567)
Nat'l Hispanic Council on Aging (567)
Nat'l Hospice & Palliative Care Organization (567)
Nat'l IPA Coalition (569)
Nat'l Kidney Foundation (569)
Nat'l League of Postmasters of the U.S. (569)
Nat'l Lumber and Building Material Dealers Ass'n (570)
Nat'l Marrow Donor Program (570)
Nat'l Meat Canners Ass'n (570)
Nat'l Mental Health Ass'n (571)
Nat'l Military Family Ass'n (571)
Nat'l Mining Ass'n (571)
Nat'l Minority AIDS Council (571)
Nat'l Multi-Housing Council (571)
Nat'l Nutritional Foods Ass'n (572)
Nat'l Orthotics Manufacturers Ass'n (572)
Nat'l Osteoporosis Foundation (573)
Nat'l Paint and Coatings Ass'n (573)
Nat'l Partnership for Women and Families (573)
Nat'l Patient Advocate Foundation (573)
Nat'l Prostate Cancer Coalition Co. (574)
Nat'l Psoriasis Foundation (574)
Nat'l Puerto Rican Coalition (575)
Nat'l Quality Health Council (575)
Nat'l Rehabilitation Ass'n (575)
Nat'l Rehabilitation Hospital (575)
Nat'l Rehabilitation Information Center (575)
Nat'l Renal Administrators Ass'n (575)
Nat'l Restaurant Ass'n (576)
Nat'l Retail Federation (576)
Nat'l Right to Life Committee (576)
Nat'l Rural Electric Cooperative Ass'n (576)
Nat'l Rural Health Ass'n (577)
Nat'l Sleep Foundation (578)
Nat'l Small Business United (578)
Nat'l Soc. of Professional Engineers (578)
Nat'l Steel Corp. (579)
Nat'l Stroke Ass'n (579)
Nat'l Structured Settlements Trade Ass'n (579)
Nat'l Taxpayers Union (579)
Nat'l Therapeutic Recreation Soc. (579)
Nat'l Treasury Employees Union (580)
Nat'l Women's Health Network (581)
Nat'l Women's Law Center (581)
Nat'l Yogurt Ass'n (581)
Nationwide Mutual Insurance Co. (582)
Naval Reserve Ass'n (582)
Navarro Legislative & Regulatory Affairs (141)
NCS Healthcare (583)
David Nelson & Associates (141)
NETWORK, A Nat'l Catholic Social Justice Lobby (584)
Neuman and Co. (141)
New Jersey Hospital Ass'n (585)
New York Life Insurance Co. (587)
New York University (588)
New York University Medical Center (588)
Newark, New Jersey, City of (588)
Newport News Shipbuilding Inc. (588)
NextRX (589)
NF Inc. - Mass Bay Area (589)
NICORE, Inc. (589)
NitroMed, Inc. (590)
Nixon Peabody LLP (142)
Non-Profit Management Associates, Inc. (142)
Norfolk Southern Corp. (591)
Julia J. Norrell & Associates (142)
North American Brain Tumor Coalition (592)
North American Equipment Dealers Ass'n (592)
North American Soc. of Pacing and Electrophysiology (592)
North Carolina, Washington Office of the State of (593)
North Slope Borough, Alaska (593)
Northside Hospital (595)
Northwestern Memorial Hospital (595)
Nova Southeastern University (596)
Novartis Corp. (596)
Novartis Services, Inc. (596)
Nusgart Consulting, LLC (142)
The OB-C Group, LLC (143)
O'Bryon & Co. (144)
O'Connor & Hannan, L.L.P. (144)
Odin, Feldman, & Pittleman, P.C. (145)
O'Donoghue & O'Donoghue (145)
Office and Professional Employees Internat'l Union (599)
Office of Hawaiian Affairs (599)
Ogletree Governmental Affairs, Inc. (145)
Oklahoma State Medical Ass'n (600)
Olsson, Frank and Weeda, P.C. (146)
Olsten Health Services (600)
O'Melveny and Myers LLP (147)
Omnicare, Inc. (600)
Onehealthbank.com (600)
O'Neill, Athy & Casey, P.C. (147)
Oppenheimer Wolff & Donnelly LLP (147)
Opticians Ass'n of America (601)
OraVax, Inc. (602)
Orphan Medical, Inc. (604)
Osteopathic Health System of Texas (604)
Our Lady of the Lake Regional Medical Center (604)
Ovarian Cancer Nat'l Alliance (604)
Owens-Illinois, Inc. (605)
Pac Med Clinics (605)
PACCAR, Inc. (605)
Pacific Life Insurance Co. (605)
PacifiCare Health Systems (606)
PAI Management Corp. (148)
Pain Care Coalition (606)
Palumbo & Cerrell, Inc. (149)
Pan Pacific Pharmaceuticals (607)
Paradigm Support Corp. (607)
Paradise Valley Hospital (607)
Paralyzed Veterans of America (607)
Parents Incorporated (608)
Parkinson's Disease Foundation (608)
Parry, Romani, DeConcini & Symms (149)
Partners Healthcare System, Inc. (608)
Partnership for Caring (608)
Partnership for Recovery Coalition (609)
Patient Access to Transplantation (PAT) Coalition (609)
Patton Boggs, LLP (150)
PCS Health Systems, Inc. (610)
Pearson & Pipkin, Inc. (154)
The Kerry S. Pearson LLC (154)
Pediatrix Medical Group, Inc. (610)
Pedorthic Footwear Ass'n (610)
Pegasus Airwave (610)
J. C. Penney Co., Inc. (611)
Pennzoil-Quaker State Co. (611)
People for the Ethical Treatment of Animals (612)
PepsiCo, Inc. (612)
The Petrizzo Group, Inc. (155)
Peyser Associates, Inc. (155)
Pfizer, Inc. (613)
Pharmaceutical Care Management Ass'n (614)
Pharmaceutical Research and Manufacturers of America (614)
Pharmacia Corp. (615)
Philadelphia, Pennsylvania, City of (615)
Philip Morris Management Corp. (615)
Phillips Petroleum Co. (616)
Phoenix Cardiovascular, Inc. (616)
Physician Insurers Ass'n of America (616)
Physicians for Reproductive Choice and Health (617)
PKC (618)
Planned Parenthood Federation of America (618)
Plasma Protein Therapeutics Ass'n (619)
The Plexus Consulting Group (156)
The PMA Group (156)
Podesta/Mattoon (158)
Policy Directions, Inc. (158)
Polity Consulting (159)
Polycistic Kidney Disease Foundation (620)
PolyMedica Corp. (620)
Joel Pomerene Hospital (620)
Potomac Electric Power Co. (622)
Potomac Group (160)
Potomac Strategies Internat'l LLC (160)
Power Mobility Coalition (622)
Powers Pyles Sutter & Verville, PC (161)
Praxair, Inc. (623)
Precision Medical (623)
Premier, Inc. (623)
Preston Gates Ellis & Rouvelas Meeds LLP (162)
Prevent Blindness America (623)

PriceWaterhouseCoopers *(163)*
Principal Financial Group ***(624)***
Printing Industries of America ***(624)***
Priority Care ***(624)***
Private Care Ass'n, Inc. ***(624)***
Private Essential Access Community Hospitals (PEACH) Inc. ***(624)***
Private Practice Section of the American Physical Therapy Ass'n ***(625)***
Sydney Probst *(164)*
Progressive Policy Institute ***(626)***
Project Meal Foundation ***(626)***
Protective Life Insurance Co. ***(627)***
Prudential Insurance Co. of America ***(627)***
Public Citizen, Inc. ***(628)***
Public Health Foundation ***(628)***
Public Health Policy Advisory Board ***(628)***
Public Policy Partners, LLC *(164)*
Public Strategies Washington, Inc. *(164)*
Pure Encapsulations, Inc. ***(630)***
Quest Diagnostics Inc. ***(631)***
Quinn Gillespie & Associates *(165)*
Mark J. Raabe *(165)*
Ralston Purina Co. ***(632)***
Ramsey, Minnesota, Board of Commissioners of the County of ***(633)***
Pamela Ray-Strunk and Associates *(166)*
Reckitt & Colman Pharmaceuticals Inc. ***(634)***
Reed, Smith, LLP *(167)*
Christopher Reeve Paralysis Foundation ***(635)***
Regeneration Technologies Inc. ***(635)***
ReGin Manufacturing Inc. ***(635)***
Renal Leadership Council ***(636)***
Renal Physicians Ass'n ***(636)***
Reproductive Health Technologies Project ***(637)***
Republicans for Choice ***(638)***
Resources and Instruction for Staff Excellence, Inc. ***(638)***
Respironics ***(638)***
Retractable Technologies, Inc. ***(639)***
Risk and Insurance Management Soc., Inc. (RIMS) ***(640)***
Rite Aid Corp. ***(640)***
Riverside, California, City of ***(640)***
Liz Robbins Associates *(169)*
Robert Wood Johnson Foundation ***(641)***
Rockwell Collins ***(641)***
Roger Williams Medical Center ***(641)***
Rohm and Haas Co. ***(642)***
ROHO, Inc. ***(642)***
Romano & Associates, LLC *(171)*
Rooney Group Internat'l, Inc. *(171)*
Peter J. Rose *(172)*
Royer & Babyak *(172)*
RPH & Associates, L.L.C. *(172)*
J. T. Rutherford & Associates *(173)*
J. T. Rutherford & Associates ***(644)***
Rx Vitamins, Inc. ***(644)***
Ryan, Phillips, Utrecht & MacKinnon *(173)*
Ryder System, Inc. ***(644)***
Sacramento-Potomac Consulting, Inc. *(174)*
Safety-Centered Solutions, Inc. ***(645)***
Sagamore Associates, Inc. *(174)*
Saliba Action Strategies, LLC *(174)*
Salt Institute ***(646)***
Salt Lake City Olympic Organizing Committee ***(646)***
San Diego Hospice Corp. ***(647)***
San Diego, California, City of ***(647)***
San Francisco AIDS Foundation ***(647)***
San Francisco, California, City and County of ***(648)***
SangStat Medical Corp. ***(648)***
Santa Barbara Regional Health Authority ***(649)***
Santa Clara, California, County of ***(649)***
Santa Rosa Memorial Hospital ***(649)***
Saunders Consulting *(175)*
SBC Communications Inc. ***(650)***
SCAN Health Plan ***(651)***
Schering-Plough Corp. ***(651)***
Schering-Plough Legislative Resources L.L.C. ***(651)***
Schramm, Williams & Associates, Inc. *(176)*
Schroth & Associates *(176)*
Scott & White Hospital ***(652)***
Seattle, Washington, City of ***(653)***
Self Help for Hard of Hearing People, Inc. ***(654)***
Self-Insurance Institute of America, Inc. ***(655)***
Sellery Associates, Inc. *(177)*
Sepracor, Inc. ***(655)***
Serono Laboratories, Inc. ***(655)***
Service Employees Internat'l Union ***(656)***
The Sharing Network ***(657)***
Shaw Pittman *(177)*
Sheet Metal and Air Conditioning Contractors' Nat'l Ass'n ***(657)***
Shelby, Tennessee, County of ***(657)***
Sher & Blackwell *(179)*
The Sheridan Group *(179)*
Sherwin Williams Co. ***(657)***
Shriners Hospital for Children ***(658)***
Sickle Cell Disease Ass'n of America ***(658)***
Sierra Club ***(658)***
Signal Behavioral Health Network ***(659)***
Stephen F. Sims and Associates *(181)*
Sisseton-Wahpoton Sioux Indian Tribe ***(660)***
Sisters of Charity of Leavenworth Health Services ***(660)***
Sisters of Providence Health Systems ***(660)***
Smith & Nephew, Inc. ***(661)***
E. Del Smith and Co. *(183)*
Smith Dawson & Andrews, Inc. *(183)*
Smith, Bucklin and Associates, Inc. *(184)*
The Smith-Free Group *(184)*
SMS Corp. ***(662)***
Soc. for Excellence in Eyecare ***(662)***
Soc. for Mucosal Immunology ***(662)***
Soc. for Vascular Surgery ***(663)***
Soc. for Women's Health Research ***(663)***
Soc. of American Florists ***(663)***
Soc. of Diagnostic Medical Sonographers ***(663)***
Soc. of General Internal Medicine ***(663)***
Soc. of Gyneocologic Oncologists ***(663)***
Soc. of Nuclear Medicine ***(663)***
Soc. of Professional Benefit Administrators ***(664)***
Soc. of Teachers of Family Medicine ***(664)***
Soc. of Thoracic Surgeons ***(664)***
Soc. of Toxicology ***(664)***
Soc. of Vascular Technology ***(664)***
The Solomon Group, LLC *(185)*
Sonomedica, Inc. ***(665)***
SonoSite ***(665)***
Southcoast Health System ***(667)***
Southeast Alaska Regional Health Corp. (SEARHC) ***(667)***
Southern California Organ Procurement Consortium ***(667)***
Spacelabs Medical Inc. ***(669)***
Spaulding Rehabilitation Hospital ***(669)***
The Spectrum Group *(186)*
Spectrum Health Care Resources, Inc. ***(670)***
SPECTRUM Science Public Relations, Inc. *(186)*
Richard L. Spees, Inc. *(186)*
Spina Bifida Ass'n of America ***(670)***
Springfield, Massachusetts, City of ***(670)***
Springs Industries, Inc. ***(671)***
St. Bernard's Hospital ***(671)***
St. Elizabeth's Medical Center ***(671)***
St. George's University School of Medicine ***(671)***
St. Jude Medical, Inc. ***(671)***
St. Louis University, School of Public Health ***(672)***
St. Louis, Minnesota, Board of Commissioners of the County ***(672)***
St. Louis, Missouri, City of ***(672)***
St. Mary's Hospital ***(672)***
St. Maxens & Company *(187)*
St. Paul Cos. ***(672)***
St. Peter's Medical Center ***(672)***
Staff Builders, Inc. ***(672)***
State Farm Insurance Cos. ***(673)***
Stephens Law Firm *(188)*
Stillman College ***(674)***
Kenneth F. Stinger *(189)*
John M. Stinson *(189)*
Stone Investments, Inc. ***(675)***
Stony Brook Foundation ***(675)***
Stop It Now! ***(675)***
Storage Technology Corp. ***(675)***
Strat@Comm (Strategic Communications Counselors) *(189)*
Strategic Horizons Advisors, L.L.C. *(189)*
Sumlin Associates *(190)*
Sun Healthcare Group, Inc. ***(676)***
Sunrise Assisted Living ***(677)***
Sunrise Medical ***(677)***
Susquehanna Health System ***(678)***
Swedish Match ***(678)***
Swidler Berlin Shereff Friedman, LLP *(191)*
Swope Parkway Health Center ***(679)***
Synzyme Technologies, Inc. ***(679)***
T & N Industries ***(679)***
Target Corp. ***(681)***
Tarzana Treatment Center ***(681)***
TECHHEALTH.COM ***(682)***
Temple University ***(683)***
Temple University Health System ***(683)***
Tempur-Medical Inc. ***(683)***
Texaco Group Inc. ***(684)***
Texas A&M Research Foundation ***(684)***
Texas Health Resources ***(684)***
Texas Instruments ***(684)***
Texas NF Foundation ***(685)***
THA: An Ass'n of Hospitals and Health Systems ***(685)***
Thera Matrix ***(686)***
Thomas Jefferson University ***(686)***
Thomas Jefferson University Hospital ***(686)***
The Timken Co. ***(687)***
Timmons and Co., Inc. *(195)*
Tire Ass'n of North America ***(687)***
William J. Tobin and Associates *(195)*
Tongour Simpson Holsclaw Green *(196)*
Torchmark Corp. ***(688)***
Tourette Syndrome Ass'n, Inc. ***(688)***
Townsend Solheim *(196)*
Toyota Motor North America, U.S.A., Inc. ***(689)***
Traditional Values Coalition ***(689)***
Transportation-Communications Internat'l Union ***(691)***
Transtracheal Systems ***(691)***
Tri Path Inc. ***(691)***
Trinity Health ***(692)***
TriWest Healthcare Alliance, Inc. ***(692)***
TRW Inc. ***(693)***
Tuvin Associates *(197)*
U.S. Chamber Institute for Legal Reform ***(695)***
U.S. Disabled Athletes Fund ***(696)***
U.S. Family Network ***(696)***
U.S. Healthcare ***(696)***
U.S. Oncology ***(697)***
U.S. Public Interest Research Group ***(697)***
U.S. Strategies Corp. *(197)*
UBS Warburg ***(697)***
Ungaretti & Harris *(197)*
Uniformed Services Dental Alliance ***(698)***
Union Hospital ***(699)***
Union of Needletrades, Industrial, and Textile Employees (UNITE) ***(699)***
Union Pacific ***(699)***
United Automobile, Aerospace and Agricultural Implement Workers of America (UAW) ***(700)***
United Concordia Companies, Inc. ***(701)***
United Food and Commercial Workers Internat'l Union ***(701)***
United Fresh Fruit and Vegetable Ass'n ***(701)***
United Health Group ***(701)***
United Healthcare ***(701)***
United Methodist Church General Board of Church and Society ***(702)***
United Mine Workers of America ***(702)***
United Network for Organ Sharing ***(702)***
United Parcel Service ***(702)***
United Payors and United Providers ***(702)***
United Seniors Ass'n ***(702)***
United States Business and Industry Council ***(703)***
United States Coast Guard Chief Petty Officers Ass'n ***(703)***
United States Telecom Ass'n ***(704)***
United Steelworkers of America ***(704)***
University Emergency Medicine Foundation ***(705)***
University Medical Associates ***(705)***
University Medical Center of Southern Nevada ***(705)***
University of California, Office of Federal Government Relations ***(706)***

University of Cincinnati *(706)*
University of Findlay *(706)*
University of Florida Health Science Center *(706)*
University of Medicine and Dentistry of New Jersey *(706)*
University of Medicine and Dentistry of New Jersey - School of Health Related Professionals *(706)*
University of Miami *(706)*
University of North Dakota *(707)*
University of Pennsylvania/School of Dental Medicine *(707)*
University of South Florida Research Foundation *(707)*
University of Texas - Houston Health Science Center *(707)*
University of Tulsa *(708)*
University of Virginia *(708)*
University of Washington *(708)*
University System of Maryland *(708)*
UNOCAL Corp. *(708)*
UPMC Health System *(708)*
Urban Health Care Coalition of Pennsylvania *(708)*
USAA - United Services Automobile Ass'n *(710)*
USFHP Conference Group *(710)*
UST Public Affairs, Inc. *(710)*
USX Corp. *(710)*
Utility Workers Union of America *(711)*
V-ONE Corp. *(711)*
Valente Lopatin & Schulze *(198)*
Valis Associates *(198)*
Valley Children's Hospital *(711)*
Valley Hope Ass'n *(711)*
Value Options Health Care Inc. *(711)*
Van Ness Feldman, P.C. *(199)*
Van Scoyoc Associates, Inc. *(200)*
Vanderbilt University *(712)*
Vanderbilt University Medical Center *(712)*
The Vandervort Group, LLC *(712)*
Vector Research, Inc. *(712)*
Joe Velasquez & Associates *(201)*
Venable *(201)*
Verizon Communications *(713)*
Verner, Liipfert, Bernhard, McPherson and Hand, Chartered *(202)*
Verner, Liipfert, Bernhard, McPherson and Hand, Chartered *(713)*
VHA Inc. *(714)*
ViaTronix *(715)*
Vinson & Elkins L.L.P. *(204)*
Vinyard & Associates *(205)*
Vinyl Institute *(715)*
Viohl and Associates, Inc. *(205)*
Virginia Commonwealth University *(716)*
Virologic, Inc. *(716)*
Virtual Medical Group *(716)*
VISA U.S.A., Inc. *(716)*
Visible Genetics *(716)*
Visiting Nurse Service of New York *(716)*
Visiting Nurses Health System *(716)*
Vitas Healthcare Corp. *(717)*
Vorys, Sater, Seymour and Pease, LLP *(205)*
VSAdc.com *(205)*
Wake, North Carolina, County of *(718)*
Walgreen Co. *(718)*
R. Duffy Wall and Associates *(205)*
Washington Alliance Group, Inc. *(206)*
Washington Council Ernst & Young *(206)*
The Washington Group *(208)*
Washington Health Advocates *(209)*
Washington Liaison Group, LLC *(209)*
Waterman & Associates *(210)*
Wausau Insurance Cos. *(722)*
WebMD *(722)*
Webster, Chamberlain & Bean *(210)*
Weider Nutritional Group *(722)*
Weil, Gotshal & Manges, LLP *(211)*
The Wellness Plan *(723)*
WellPoint Health Networks/Blue Cross of California/UNICARE *(723)*
Western Governors Ass'n *(724)*
Western Governors University *(724)*
Western Growers Insurance Services *(724)*
The Wexler Group *(211)*
Weyerhaeuser Co. *(725)*
Wheat & Associates, Inc. *(212)*
Susan J. White & Associates *(212)*
R. H. White Public Affairs Consulting *(213)*
Whitten & Diamond *(213)*
Wiland-Bell Productions *(726)*
The Wilbur Group *(214)*
The Willard Group *(215)*
Williams & Jensen, P.C. *(215)*
Wilmer, Cutler & Pickering *(217)*
Wilson, Elser, Moskowitz, Edelman & Dicker LLP *(218)*
Wine and Spirits Wholesalers of America *(728)*
Wine Institute *(728)*
Kathleen Winn & Associates, Inc. *(218)*
Wireless Technology Research, L.L.C. *(728)*
Wise & Associates *(220)*
Witman Associates *(220)*
Women and Infants' Hospital *(729)*
Women Officials in NACo *(729)*
Women's Hospital *(729)*
Women's Hospital of Greensboro *(729)*
Women's Policy, Inc. *(729)*
Wound Ostomy Continence Nurses *(731)*
Wyeth-Ayerst Pharmaceuticals *(732)*
XCEL Medical Pharmacy, Ltd. *(732)*
Xerox Corp. *(732)*
Zane & Associates *(221)*
Zeliff, Ireland, and Associates *(221)*
Zero Population Growth, Inc. *(734)*
ZERO TO THREE/Nat'l Center for Infants, Toddlers, and Families *(734)*

Housing (HOU)

The 60/Plus Ass'n, Inc. *(224)*
AARP (American Ass'n of Retired Persons) *(224)*
ACORN (Ass'n of Community Organizations for Reform Now) *(227)*
Advanta Corp. *(229)*
AFL-CIO Housing Investment Trust *(231)*
AIDS Action Council *(233)*
Akin, Gump, Strauss, Hauer & Feld, L.L.P. *(8)*
Akron Tower Housing Partnership *(235)*
Alameda, California, County of *(236)*
Albuquerque, New Mexico, City of *(237)*
Alcalde & Fay *(10)*
Allegheny County, Pennsylvania, Housing Authority *(238)*
Alliance for Children and Families *(239)*
Alliance of American Insurers *(240)*
Alliance to End Childhood Lead Poisoning *(241)*
Alzheimer's Ass'n *(242)*
America's Community Bankers *(243)*
American Academy of Child and Adolescent Psychiatry *(243)*
American Ass'n of Homes and Services for the Aging *(248)*
American Bankers Ass'n *(250)*
American Bar Ass'n *(250)*
American Federation of State, County and Municipal Employees *(258)*
American Homeowners Grassroots Alliance *(262)*
The American Institute of Architects *(264)*
American League of Financial Institutions *(266)*
American Network of Community Options and Resources (ANCOR) *(268)*
American Occupational Therapy Ass'n, Inc. *(269)*
American Planning Ass'n *(270)*
American Plywood Ass'n *(270)*
American Psychiatric Ass'n *(271)*
American Psychological Ass'n *(271)*
American Seniors Housing Ass'n *(273)*
American Soc. of Home Inspectors (ASHI) *(276)*
American Wood Preservers Institute *(280)*
Apartment Investment and Management Co. *(286)*
Appraisal Institute *(287)*
The Arc *(287)*
Arent Fox Kintner Plotkin & Kahn, PLLC *(14)*
Arkansas, Office of the Governor of the State of *(288)*
Ass'n Management Group *(18)*
Ass'n of Local Housing Finance Agencies *(296)*
Assisted Living Federation of America *(300)*
Associated Financial Corp. *(300)*
Assurant Group *(301)*
Austin, Texas, City of *(303)*
B'nai B'rith Internat'l *(305)*
Ball Janik, LLP *(22)*
Baltimore, Maryland, City of *(306)*
Barbour Griffith & Rogers, Inc. *(22)*
Barnett & Sivon, P.C. *(24)*
The Barton Co. *(24)*
Bazelon Center for Mental Health Law, Judge David L. *(310)*
Beaumont, Texas, City of *(310)*
Bellevue, Washington, City of *(311)*
Berkeley, California, City of *(312)*
Bernalillo, New Mexico, County of *(312)*
Bert Corona Leadership Institute *(312)*
BKSH & Associates *(28)*
Blank Rome Comisky & McCauley, LLP *(29)*
The Bond Market Ass'n *(317)*
Boston, Massachusetts, City of *(318)*
Broward, Florida, County of *(322)*
Butera & Andrews *(34)*
Caguas, Puerto Rico, City of *(326)*
California State Ass'n of Counties *(327)*
Canfield & Associates, Inc. *(36)*
Capital City Economic Development Authority *(330)*
Capitol Coalitions Inc. *(38)*
Capitol Counsel Group, L.L.C. *(38)*
Capitol Hill Advocates *(39)*
Capitol Link, Inc. *(39)*
Carlsberg Management Co. *(332)*
Carmel, Indiana, City of *(332)*
Carolina, Puerto Rico, City of *(332)*
Cartwright & Riley *(41)*
Center for Public Dialogue *(337)*
Center on Budget and Policy Priorities *(338)*
Chambers Associates Inc. *(45)*
Carolyn C. Chaney & Associates *(45)*
Charter One *(341)*
Chase Manhattan Bank *(341)*
Child Welfare League of America *(343)*
Children's Defense Fund *(344)*
Chlopak, Leonard, Schechter and Associates *(46)*
Cincinnati, Ohio, City of *(347)*
Citigroup *(347)*
Clark & Weinstock, Inc. *(47)*
Clay and Associates *(47)*
Clearwater, Florida, City of *(350)*
The Clorox Co. *(351)*
CNA Financial Corp. *(351)*
CNA Insurance Cos. *(351)*
Coalition for Affordable Housing Preservation *(352)*
Coalition for the Homeless *(354)*
Coan & Lyons *(47)*
Collier Shannon Scott, PLLC *(48)*
Columbia, South Carolina, City of *(359)*
Community Ass'ns Institute (CAI) *(362)*
The Community Builders, Inc. *(362)*
Community Preservation Corp. *(363)*
Competitive Consumer Lending Coalition *(363)*
Connecticut Resource Recovery Authority *(367)*
Consumer Federation of America *(369)*
Consumer Mortgage Coalition *(369)*
Continental Wingate Co., Inc. *(370)*
Copeland, Lowery & Jacquez *(52)*
Cornerstone Florida Corp., Ltd. *(372)*
Shawn Coulson *(53)*
Council for Affordable and Rural Housing *(373)*
Council of Federal Home Loan Banks *(375)*
Council of Large Public Housing Authorities *(376)*
Countrywide Home Loans, Inc. *(377)*
Countrywide Mortgage Corp. *(377)*
Coushatta Tribe of Louisiana *(377)*
Covenant House *(377)*
Craig Associates *(55)*
Cuyahoga, Ohio, County of *(380)*
Dade, Florida, County of *(381)*
Dakota, Minnesota, County of *(381)*
Dallas, Texas, City of *(382)*
Davidoff & Malito, LLP *(57)*
Davidson & Company, Inc. *(57)*
Dayton, Ohio, Washington Office of the City of *(383)*
Daytona Beach, City of *(383)*
Detroit Rescue Mission Ministries *(386)*

Detroit, Michigan, City of *(386)*
DFG Group *(387)*
Dime Savings Bank of New York *(388)*
The Doe Fund *(390)*
Domes Internat'l, Inc. *(390)*
Downey McGrath Group, Inc. *(64)*
Dream Center/City Help *(392)*
Duane, Morris & Heckscher LLP *(65)*
The Duberstein Group, Inc. *(65)*
Dykema Gossett PLLC *(69)*
Easter Seals *(395)*
EDS Corp. *(398)*
Electronic Financial Services Council *(400)*
Elmer Larson, Inc. *(401)*
The Enterprise Foundation *(404)*
Dave Evans Associates *(73)*
Fairfax, Virginia, County of *(410)*
Fannie Mae *(411)*
Federal Home Loan Bank of Boston *(413)*
Federal Home Loan Bank of Dallas *(413)*
Federal Home Loan Bank of Topeka *(413)*
Federal Home Loan Mortgage Corp. (Freddie Mac) *(413)*
Federal Nat'l Payables, Inc. *(413)*
The Ferguson Group, LLC *(76)*
The Financial Services Roundtable *(416)*
Edward A. Fish Associates *(418)*
FM Watch *(420)*
Foley & Lardner *(78)*
Foley Government and Public Affairs, Inc. *(78)*
Fort Wayne, Indiana, City of *(423)*
Free Trade Lumber Council *(425)*
Gainesville, Florida, City of *(428)*
Gary, Indiana, Housing Authority of the City of *(429)*
Gary, Indiana, Washington Office of the City of *(429)*
GE Capital Corp. *(430)*
GE Capital Mortgage Insurance Co. (GEMICO) *(430)*
GE Commercial Real Estate & Financial Services *(430)*
General Electric Capital Mortgage Corp. *(432)*
Global USA, Inc. *(83)*
Goodwin, Procter & Hoar LLP *(84)*
Goodyear Tire and Rubber Co. *(437)*
Gospel Rescue Ministries of Washington *(437)*
Government Relations, Inc. *(84)*
Jay Grant & Associates *(85)*
Greenberg Traurig, LLP *(86)*
Griffin, Johnson, Dover & Stewart *(87)*
Guaranty Bank, SSB *(442)*
Habitat for Humanity Internat'l *(443)*
Hawkins, Delafield & Wood *(92)*
Healthcare Financing Study Group *(447)*
Helmsin & Yarwood Associates *(94)*
Hempstead, New York, Village of *(448)*
Henderson, Nevada, City of *(448)*
Hessel and Aluise, P.C. *(94)*
Highland Mortgage Co. *(449)*
Hogan & Hartson L.L.P. *(96)*
Hohlt & Associates *(98)*
Holland & Knight LLP *(98)*
The Home Depot *(451)*
Home Warranty Coalition *(451)*
Housing and Development Law Institute *(453)*
Housing Assistance Council *(453)*
Housing Works *(453)*
Houston, Texas, City of *(453)*
Hudson Institute *(454)*
Huntsville, Alabama, City of *(455)*
Illinois Housing Development Authority *(457)*
Indiana, Office of the Governor of the State of *(460)*
Indianapolis Neighborhood Housing Partnership *(460)*
Inglewood, California, City of *(462)*
Institute for Responsible Housing Preservation *(464)*
Internat'l Brotherhood of Electrical Workers *(469)*
Internat'l Brotherhood of Teamsters *(469)*
Internat'l Downtown Ass'n *(471)*
Jackson, Mississippi, City of *(480)*
Jacksonville, Florida, City of *(481)*
Janus-Merritt Strategies, L.L.C. *(104)*
Jefferson Government Relations, L.L.C. *(106)*
Jesuit Conference *(483)*
Jewish Federation of Metropolitan Chicago *(483)*
Johnston & Associates, LLC *(107)*
Jolly/Rissler, Inc. *(108)*
Jorden Burt LLP *(109)*
K-Mortgage Corp. *(485)*
Kalkines, Arky, Zall and Bernstein *(486)*
Betty Ann Kane & Co. *(110)*
Kansas City, Missouri, City of *(486)*
Kimberly Consulting, LLC *(113)*
Kogovsek & Associates *(114)*
Labor Council for Latin American Advancement (LCLAA) *(493)*
Laredo, Texas, City of *(495)*
Las Cruces, New Mexico, City of *(495)*
Las Vegas, Nevada, City of *(495)*
LegisLaw *(118)*
The Michael Lewan Co. *(119)*
Light of Life Ministries *(499)*
Lincoln, Nebraska, City of *(500)*
Local Initiatives Support Corp. *(501)*
Long Beach, California, City of *(503)*
Los Angeles, California, Community Development Commission of the County of *(504)*
Los Angeles, California, County of *(504)*
Lotstein Buckman, Attorneys At Law *(122)*
Lubbock, Texas, City of *(505)*
Lutheran Office for Governmental Affairs/Evangelical Lutheran Church in America *(506)*
Macon, City of *(507)*
Madison Government Affairs *(123)*
Manufactured Housing Ass'n for Regulatory Reform *(509)*
Manufactured Housing Institute *(509)*
MARC Associates, Inc. *(124)*
Marin, California, County of *(510)*
Massachusetts Bankers Ass'n *(512)*
Massachusetts Housing Finance Agency *(512)*
Virginia M. Mayer *(126)*
Barbara T. McCall Associates *(127)*
McDermott, Will and Emery *(128)*
Jack H. McDonald *(129)*
McDonnell & Miller *(514)*
McMahon and Associates *(131)*
McSlarrow Consulting L.L.C. *(131)*
Medford, Oregon, City of *(516)*
Mellon Mortgage Co. *(517)*
Merced, California, County of *(518)*
Mercy Housing *(518)*
Metropolitan King County Council *(520)*
Meyers & Associates *(133)*
Miami Beach, Florida, City of *(521)*
Miles & Stockbridge, P.C. *(133)*
Miller and Schroeder Financial, Inc. *(524)*
Mobile, Alabama, City of *(527)*
J. P. Morgan Chase & Co. *(529)*
Mortgage Bankers Ass'n of America *(530)*
Mortgage Insurance Companies of America *(530)*
The Kate Moss Company *(137)*
Moss McGee Bradley & Foley *(137)*
Motion Picture and Television Fund *(530)*
Muncie, Indiana, City of (Delaware County) *(532)*
Murray, Scheer, Montgomery, Tapia & O'Donnell *(139)*
NAHB Research Center *(534)*
Nat'l Academy of Public Administration *(535)*
Nat'l Alliance for the Mentally Ill *(536)*
Nat'l Alliance to End Homelessness *(537)*
Nat'l Ass'n for the Advancement of Colored People, Washington Bureau *(538)*
Nat'l Ass'n of Affordable Housing Lenders *(538)*
Nat'l Ass'n of County Community and Economic Development *(541)*
Nat'l Ass'n of Home Builders of the U.S. *(543)*
Nat'l Ass'n of Home Builders Research Center, Inc. *(544)*
Nat'l Ass'n of Housing Cooperatives *(544)*
Nat'l Ass'n of Independent Insurers *(544)*
Nat'l Ass'n of Minority Political Families, USA, Inc. *(545)*
Nat'l Ass'n of Mortgage Brokers *(545)*
Nat'l Ass'n of Negro Business & Professional Women's Clubs, Inc. *(546)*
Nat'l Ass'n of Protection and Advocacy Systems (NAPAS) *(547)*
Nat'l Ass'n of Realtors *(547)*
Nat'l Ass'n of Service and Conservation Corps *(549)*
Nat'l Ass'n of State Units on Aging *(550)*
Nat'l Assembly of Health and Human Service Organizations *(551)*
Nat'l Center for Appropriate Technology *(554)*
Nat'l Center for Neighborhood Enterprise *(555)*
Nat'l Community Reinvestment Coalition *(558)*
Nat'l Cooperative Bank *(558)*
Nat'l Cooperative Business Ass'n *(559)*
Nat'l Council for Community Behavioral Healthcare *(559)*
Nat'l Council of La Raza *(560)*
Nat'l Council of State Housing Agencies *(560)*
Nat'l Fair Housing Alliance *(563)*
Nat'l Farmers Union (Farmers Educational & Co-operative Union of America) *(563)*
Nat'l Fire Protection Ass'n *(564)*
Nat'l Hispanic Council on Aging *(567)*
Nat'l Home Equity Mortgage Ass'n *(567)*
Nat'l Housing Conference *(567)*
Nat'l Housing Trust *(567)*
Nat'l Leased Housing Ass'n *(569)*
Nat'l Low Income Housing Coalition/LIHIS *(570)*
Nat'l Lumber and Building Material Dealers Ass'n *(570)*
Nat'l Military Family Ass'n *(571)*
Nat'l Multi-Housing Council *(571)*
Nat'l Neighborhood Coalition *(572)*
Nat'l Neighborhood Housing Network *(572)*
Nat'l Paint and Coatings Ass'n *(573)*
Nat'l Puerto Rican Coalition *(575)*
Nat'l Rural Housing Coalition *(577)*
Nat'l Soc. of Professional Engineers *(578)*
Nat'l Trust for Historic Preservation *(580)*
Nehemiah Progressive Housing Development Corp. *(583)*
NETWORK, A Nat'l Catholic Social Justice Lobby *(584)*
New York State Housing Finance Agency *(587)*
Newark, New Jersey, City of *(588)*
Nixon Peabody LLP *(142)*
Norfolk, Virginia, City of *(591)*
North Carolina, Washington Office of the State of *(593)*
North Miami Beach, Florida, City of *(593)*
North Slope Borough, Alaska *(593)*
Nova Southeastern University *(596)*
Oakland, Michigan, County of *(598)*
The OB-C Group, LLC *(143)*
O'Connor & Hannan, L.L.P. *(144)*
Office of Hawaiian Affairs *(599)*
Oklahoma City, Oklahoma, City of *(599)*
O'Melveny and Myers LLP *(147)*
One Economy Corp. *(600)*
Oxnard, California, City of *(605)*
Palm Beach, Florida, County of *(606)*
Palo Alto, California, City of *(607)*
Paralyzed Veterans of America *(607)*
Pasadena, California, City of *(609)*
Patton Boggs, LLP *(150)*
Paucatuck Eastern Pequot Tribal Nation *(609)*
Peyser Associates, Inc. *(155)*
Philadelphia, Pennsylvania, City of *(615)*
Phoenix, Arizona, City of *(616)*
Plano, Texas, City of *(619)*
Portland, Oregon, City of *(621)*
Powell, Goldstein, Frazer & Murphy LLP *(160)*
Preservation Action *(623)*
Presidential Towers, Ltd. *(623)*
Prince George's, Maryland, County of *(624)*
Principal Financial Group *(624)*
Project Funding Corp. (PFC) *(626)*
Project Return Foundation Inc. *(626)*
Public Housing Authorities Directors Ass'n *(628)*
Puerto Rico Federal Affairs Administration *(629)*
Ralston Purina Co. *(632)*
Robert A. Rapoza Associates *(165)*
Real Estate Roundtable *(634)*
Russ Reid Co. *(167)*
Reilly Mortgage Group Inc. *(636)*
Reno & Cavanaugh, PLLC *(637)*

Reno & Cavanaugh, PLLC *(168)*
Riverside, California, City of ***(640)***
Roizman & Cos. ***(642)***
Romano & Associates, LLC *(171)*
The Rouse Company ***(642)***
Ruddy & Associates *(173)*
Sacramento Housing and Redeveloping Agency ***(645)***
Sacramento-Potomac Consulting, Inc. *(174)*
Sagamore Associates, Inc. *(174)*
Salinas, California, City of ***(646)***
Salt Lake City Olympic Organizing Committee ***(646)***
Salt Lake City, Utah, City of ***(646)***
San Diego, California, City of ***(647)***
San Francisco, California, City and County of ***(648)***
San Jose, California, City of ***(648)***
Santa Clara, California, County of ***(649)***
Santa Clarita, California, City of ***(649)***
Seattle, Washington, City of ***(653)***
Seedco ***(654)***
Sewerage and Water Board of New Orleans ***(656)***
The Sheridan Group *(179)*
Simon and Co., Inc. *(181)*
E. Del Smith and Co. *(183)*
Smith Dawson & Andrews, Inc. *(183)*
Smith, Bucklin and Associates, Inc. *(184)*
The Smith-Free Group *(184)*
Solutia Inc. ***(665)***
Southern Ute Indian Tribe ***(668)***
St. Louis, Missouri, City of ***(672)***
St. Vincent Catholic Medical Centers ***(672)***
Starrett City Associates ***(673)***
Starrett Corp. ***(673)***
State Street Development Co. of Boston ***(673)***
Charlene A. Sturbitts *(190)*
Superior Bank, FSB ***(677)***
Eugene F. Swanzey *(191)*
Swidler Berlin Shereff Friedman, LLP *(191)*
Tacoma, Washington, City of ***(680)***
Tampa, Florida, City of ***(680)***
Tate-LeMunyon, LLC *(192)*
Patricia A. Taylor *(192)*
Texas A&M Research Foundation ***(684)***
Texas Manufactured Housing Ass'n ***(684)***
Texas Savings and Community Bankers ***(685)***
Timmons and Co., Inc. *(195)*
TREA Senior Citizens League (TSCL) ***(691)***
TRI Capital Corp. ***(691)***
Tricap Management Corp. ***(692)***
Tulane University ***(693)***
Tunica Biloxi Indians of Louisiana ***(694)***
Tuvin Associates *(197)*
U.S. Strategies Corp. *(197)*
United Automobile, Aerospace and Agricultural Implement Workers of America (UAW) ***(700)***
United Church of Christ Justice and Witness Ministry ***(700)***
United Methodist Church General Board of Church and Society ***(702)***
Upland, California, City of ***(708)***
Ute Mountain Ute Indian Tribe ***(710)***
Valanzano & Associates *(198)*
Van Ness Feldman, P.C. *(199)*
Van Scoyoc Associates, Inc. *(200)*
The Velasquez Group *(201)*
Verner, Liipfert, Bernhard, McPherson and Hand, Chartered ***(713)***
Verner, Liipfert, Bernhard, McPherson and Hand, Chartered *(202)*
Viohl and Associates, Inc. *(205)*
Wake, North Carolina, County of ***(718)***
Washington Council Ernst & Young *(206)*
Washington Mutual Bank ***(720)***
Waterman & Associates *(210)*
Weinberg Investments, Inc. ***(722)***
West Lafayette, Indiana, City of ***(723)***
Wheat & Associates, Inc. *(212)*
Susan J. White & Associates *(212)*
Williams & Jensen, P.C. *(215)*
Wilmington Savings Fund Society ***(727)***
Winston & Strawn *(218)*
Witman Associates *(220)*
WMF/Huntoon, Paige Associates Ltd. ***(729)***
Women Officials in NACo ***(729)***

Immigration (IMM)

3Com Corp. ***(223)***
Abbott Laboratories ***(225)***
Accenture ***(226)***
Afghanistan Foundation ***(230)***
AFL-CIO (American Federation of Labor and Congress of Industrial Organizations) ***(231)***
AFL-CIO - Professional Employees Department ***(231)***
Air Products and Chemicals, Inc. ***(234)***
AIS, Inc. ***(235)***
Akin, Gump, Strauss, Hauer & Feld, L.L.P. *(8)*
Alameda, California, County of ***(236)***
Alliance for Children and Families ***(239)***
Alliance of Motion Picture & Television Producers ***(240)***
Alticor, Inc. ***(242)***
American Academy of Child and Adolescent Psychiatry ***(243)***
American Airlines ***(244)***
American Ass'n of Homes and Services for the Aging ***(248)***
American Ass'n of Motor Vehicle Administrators ***(248)***
American Automobile Ass'n ***(250)***
American Bar Ass'n ***(250)***
American Business for Legal Immigration ***(251)***
American Camping Ass'n ***(251)***
American Council of Korean Travel Agents ***(255)***
American Council on Internat'l Personnel, Inc. ***(256)***
American Electronics Ass'n ***(257)***
American Farm Bureau Federation ***(258)***
American Federation of Senior Citizens ***(258)***
American Federation of State, County and Municipal Employees ***(258)***
American Federation of Teachers ***(259)***
American Horse Council, Inc. ***(263)***
American Hotel and Lodging Ass'n ***(263)***
American Immigration Lawyers Ass'n ***(263)***
American Jewish Committee ***(265)***
American Jewish Congress ***(265)***
American Kurdish Information Network (AKIN) ***(265)***
American Legion ***(266)***
American Meat Institute ***(267)***
American Museum of Natural History ***(268)***
American Nursery and Landscape Ass'n ***(268)***
American Nurses Ass'n ***(268)***
American Occupational Therapy Ass'n, Inc. ***(269)***
American Payroll Ass'n ***(269)***
American Physical Therapy Ass'n ***(270)***
American Psychological Ass'n ***(271)***
American School Food Service Ass'n ***(273)***
American Soc. for Training and Development ***(275)***
American Symphony Orchestra League ***(278)***
Americans for Better Borders ***(281)***
Anaheim, California, City of ***(283)***
Anti-Defamation League ***(285)***
APCO Worldwide *(14)*
The Arc ***(287)***
Arent Fox Kintner Plotkin & Kahn, PLLC *(14)*
Armstrong World Industries, Inc. ***(289)***
Ass'n of Independent Research Institutes ***(296)***
Associated General Contractors of America ***(300)***
Associated Universities Inc. ***(300)***
Auyua Inc. ***(304)***
Baker & Hostetler LLP *(19)*
Bangladeshi-American Friendship Soc. of New York ***(307)***
Bell, Boyd & Lloyd *(25)*
Berliner, Candon & Jimison *(27)*
Bert Corona Leadership Institute ***(312)***
Biotechnology Industry Organization ***(314)***
BKSH & Associates *(28)*
BMW (U.S.) Holding Corp. ***(316)***
BMW Manufacturing Corp. ***(316)***
BP Amoco Corp. ***(319)***
BUNAC USA, Inc. ***(323)***
Butera & Andrews *(34)*
The C.L.A. Group, LLC *(35)*
California Correctional Peace Officers Ass'n ***(326)***
California Institute of Technology ***(327)***
California Tomato Commission ***(327)***
Capitol Associates, Inc. *(37)*
Capitol Strategies *(39)*
Cargill, Inc. ***(331)***
Carrying Capacity Network, Inc. ***(332)***
CaseNewHolland Inc. ***(333)***
Caterpillar Inc. ***(333)***
Catholic Charities Immigration Legal Services ***(333)***
Center for Immigration Studies ***(336)***
Center on Budget and Policy Priorities ***(338)***
Chamber of Commerce of the U.S.A. ***(340)***
Clark & Weinstock, Inc. *(47)*
The Coca-Cola Company ***(356)***
Colling Swift & Hynes *(49)*
Colombian American Service Ass'n ***(358)***
Commission on Graduates of Foreign Nursing Schools ***(360)***
Compaq Computer Corp. ***(363)***
Computer Associates Internat'l ***(364)***
Concerned Women for America ***(365)***
Congressional Economic Leadership Institute ***(366)***
Conkling, Fiskum & McCormick *(51)*
Contango LLC *(52)*
Continental Airlines Inc. ***(370)***
Cooney & Associates, Inc. *(52)*
Copeland, Lowery & Jacquez *(52)*
DaimlerChrysler Corp. ***(381)***
Dance/USA ***(382)***
Davidoff & Malito, LLP *(57)*
Delaware and Hudson Railroad ***(384)***
Dell Computer Corp. ***(384)***
Delta Air Lines ***(384)***
DePaul University ***(386)***
Detroit, Michigan, City of ***(386)***
Dewey Ballantine LLP *(61)*
The Walt Disney Co. ***(389)***
Downey McGrath Group, Inc. *(64)*
Dykema Gossett PLLC *(69)*
Eastman Chemical Co. ***(395)***
eBay Inc. ***(395)***
EDS Corp. ***(398)***
Electro Scientific Industries, Inc. ***(400)***
English First, Inc. ***(403)***
Eurapair International, Inc. ***(407)***
Exxon Mobil Corp. ***(409)***
Farmland Industries, Inc. ***(412)***
Federation for American Immigration Reform (FAIR) ***(414)***
Federation of State Medical Boards of the U.S. ***(415)***
The Ferguson Group, LLC *(76)*
Florida State University System ***(420)***
Food Research and Action Center ***(422)***
Ford Motor Co. ***(422)***
Fragomen, Del Rey, Bernsen & Loewy, PC ***(424)***
French & Company *(79)*
Friends Committee on Nat'l Legislation ***(426)***
Gainesville, Florida, City of ***(428)***
Garden Centers of America ***(429)***
Gateway, Inc. ***(430)***
General Electric Co. ***(432)***
General Motors Corp. ***(432)***
B. F. Goodrich Co. ***(437)***
Government Relations, Inc. *(84)*
GPC Internat'l *(85)*
Greenberg Traurig, LLP *(86)*
GREX, Inc. ***(440)***
Guam, Washington Office of the Governor ***(442)***
Guidant Corp. ***(442)***
Halliburton/Brown & Root ***(443)***
Hebrew Immigrant Aid Soc. ***(447)***
Law Office of Edward D. Heffernan *(94)*
Hewlett-Packard Co. ***(449)***
Hill and Knowlton, Inc. *(95)*
Hogan & Hartson L.L.P. *(96)*
The Home Depot ***(451)***
Honda North America, Inc. ***(451)***
R. J. Hudson Associates *(101)*
Fred Hutchinson Cancer Research Center ***(455)***
HUTCO, Inc. ***(455)***
IBP, Inc. ***(456)***

The Ickes & Enright Group *(102)*
Immigration and Refugee Service of America ***(458)***
Immigration Law Group, P.C. ***(458)***
IMS Health Inc. ***(458)***
Indiana, Office of the Governor of the State of ***(460)***
Information Spectrum Inc. ***(461)***
Information Technology Ass'n of America (ITAA) ***(461)***
Information Technology Industry Council ***(462)***
Ingersoll-Rand Co. ***(462)***
Inman, Steinberg, Nye & Stone ***(462)***
Institute of Electrical and Electronics Engineers, Inc. ***(464)***
Intel Corp. ***(465)***
Internat'l Ass'n of Machinists and Aerospace Workers ***(468)***
Internat'l Biometric Industry Ass'n ***(468)***
Internat'l Brotherhood of Boilermakers, Iron Shipbuilders, Blacksmiths, Forgers and Helpers ***(469)***
Internat'l Brotherhood of Electrical Workers ***(469)***
Internat'l Brotherhood of Teamsters ***(469)***
Internat'l Business Machines Corp. ***(469)***
Internat'l Council of Cruise Lines ***(470)***
Internat'l Electronics Manufacturers and Consumers of America ***(471)***
Internat'l Federation of Professional and Technical Engineers ***(471)***
Internat'l Longshore and Warehouse Union ***(473)***
Internat'l Rescue Committee Inc. ***(474)***
Internat'l Union of Painters and Allied Trades ***(476)***
Janus-Merritt Strategies, L.L.C. *(104)*
Jar-Mon Consultants, Inc. *(105)*
JCP Associates *(105)*
Jesuit Conference ***(483)***
The Jewelers' Security Alliance ***(483)***
Johnson & Johnson, Inc. ***(484)***
Jorden Burt LLP *(109)*
Kellogg Brown and Root ***(487)***
Kelly and Associates, Inc. *(111)*
Kendall-Jackson Winery ***(488)***
Jeffrey J. Kimbell & Associates *(113)*
Labor Council for Latin American Advancement (LCLAA) ***(493)***
Lao Veterans of America, Inc. ***(495)***
Las Cruces, New Mexico, City of ***(495)***
Bob Lawrence & Associates ***(496)***
Lawyers Committee for Human Rights ***(496)***
Arnold H. Leibowitz *(119)*
Lewis-Burke Associates *(120)*
Local 511 Professional Employees, AFGE ***(501)***
Los Angeles, California, County of ***(504)***
Lotus Development Corp. ***(504)***
Lovelace Respiratory Research Institute ***(504)***
Lutheran Office for Governmental Affairs/Evangelical Lutheran Church in America ***(506)***
Manatt, Phelps & Phillips, LLP *(123)*
Manufacturers Alliance/MAPI Inc. ***(509)***
MARC Associates, Inc. *(124)*
McDonald's Corp. ***(514)***
McGraw-Hill Cos., The ***(514)***
McGuiness Norris & Williams, LLP *(130)*
McKinsey & Co., Inc. ***(515)***
Diane McRee Associates *(131)*
McSlarrow Consulting L.L.C. *(131)*
Mentor Graphics Corp. ***(518)***
Merced, California, County of ***(518)***
Merck & Co. ***(518)***
Mexican-American Legal Defense and Educational Fund ***(521)***
Meyers & Associates *(133)*
Miami Beach, Florida, City of ***(521)***
Miami, Florida, City of ***(521)***
Miami-Dade, Florida, County of ***(521)***
Michelin North America ***(522)***
Microsoft Corp. ***(522)***
Molina Healthcare ***(527)***
Molina Medical Centers ***(527)***
Moose Internat'l Inc. ***(529)***
Morgan Stanley Dean Witter & Co. ***(529)***
Morgan, Lewis & Bockius LLP *(136)*
Mount Vernon, City of ***(532)***
Mullenholz, Brimsek & Belair *(138)*
Nat'l Ass'n for Bilingual Education ***(537)***
Nat'l Ass'n for the Advancement of Colored People, Washington Bureau ***(538)***
Nat'l Ass'n of Children's Hospitals Inc. ***(540)***
Nat'l Ass'n of Community Health Centers ***(540)***
Nat'l Ass'n of Computer Consultant Businesses ***(540)***
Nat'l Ass'n of Manufacturers ***(545)***
Nat'l Ass'n of Public Hospitals and Health Systems ***(547)***
Nat'l Assembly of Health and Human Service Organizations ***(551)***
Nat'l Basketball Ass'n ***(552)***
Nat'l Board for Certification in Occupational Therapy, Inc. ***(552)***
Nat'l Border Patrol Council ***(553)***
Nat'l Chicken Council ***(555)***
Nat'l Committee Against Repressive Legislation ***(557)***
Nat'l Council of Agricultural Employers ***(560)***
Nat'l Council of La Raza ***(560)***
Nat'l Farmers Union (Farmers Educational & Co-operative Union of America) ***(563)***
Nat'l Health Care Access Coalition ***(566)***
Nat'l Health Law Program ***(567)***
Nat'l Hispanic Council on Aging ***(567)***
Nat'l Hockey League ***(567)***
Nat'l Immigration Forum ***(567)***
Nat'l Immigration and Naturalization Services Council ***(567)***
Nat'l Restaurant Ass'n ***(576)***
Nat'l Spiritual Assembly of the Baha'is of the United States ***(578)***
Nat'l Venture Capital Ass'n ***(580)***
NCR Corp. ***(583)***
Nealon & Moran, L.L.P. *(141)*
Negative Population Growth, Inc. (NPG) ***(583)***
Nestle USA, Inc. ***(584)***
NETWORK, A Nat'l Catholic Social Justice Lobby ***(584)***
New America Alliance ***(585)***
New York University ***(588)***
Newark, New Jersey, City of ***(588)***
Nogales, Arizona, City of ***(591)***
Nortel Networks ***(591)***
Northwest Airlines, Inc. ***(595)***
Novell, Inc. ***(596)***
NYSCOPBA - New York State Correctional Officers & Police Benevolent Ass'n ***(597)***
O'Grady Peyton Internat'l ***(598)***
O'Connor & Hannan, L.L.P. *(144)*
Ogletree Governmental Affairs, Inc. *(145)*
Olsson, Frank and Weeda, P.C. *(146)*
Operations Security Professionals Soc. ***(601)***
Oracle Corp. ***(602)***
Pan Pacific Pharmaceuticals ***(607)***
Parry, Romani, DeConcini & Symms *(149)*
Patton Boggs, LLP *(150)*
Paul, Weiss, Rifkind, Wharton & Garrison *(154)*
Pfizer, Inc. ***(613)***
Phillips Petroleum Co. ***(616)***
Powell, Goldstein, Frazer & Murphy LLP *(160)*
Preston Gates Ellis & Rouvelas Meeds LLP *(162)*
Principal Financial Group ***(624)***
Quinn Gillespie & Associates *(165)*
Rockwell Collins ***(641)***
Sabre Inc. ***(644)***
Sagem Morpho ***(646)***
Salt Lake City Olympic Organizing Committee ***(646)***
San Diego, California, City of ***(647)***
Santa Ana, California, City of ***(649)***
Santa Clara, California, County of ***(649)***
SAP Public Services ***(649)***
Schramm, Williams & Associates, Inc. *(176)*
Science Applications Internat'l Corp. (SAIC) ***(652)***
Seaboard Corp. ***(653)***
Semiconductor Equipment and Materials Internat'l ***(655)***
Semiconductor Industry Ass'n ***(655)***
Service Employees Internat'l Union ***(656)***
Sherritt Internat'l ***(657)***
Eric Shulman & Associates *(180)*
Sisters of Providence Health Systems ***(660)***
Philip S. Smith & Associates, Inc. *(182)*
Smith Alling Lane, P.S. *(183)*
E. Del Smith and Co. *(183)*
The Smith-Free Group *(184)*
Soc. for Industrial & Applied Mathematics ***(662)***
Soc. of American Florists ***(663)***
Software & Information Industry Ass'n (SIIA) ***(664)***
Sony Electronics, Inc. ***(666)***
Sony Pictures Entertainment Inc. ***(666)***
Soo Line Railroad, Inc. ***(666)***
Southeastern Michigan Council of Government ***(667)***
The Spectrum Group *(186)*
Springs Industries, Inc. ***(671)***
St. Bernard's Hospital ***(671)***
St. Vincent Catholic Medical Centers ***(672)***
Steel Service Center Institute ***(674)***
Storage Technology Corp. ***(675)***
Stuntz, Davis & Staffier, P.C. *(190)*
T.W.Y. Co., Ltd. ***(679)***
Technology Network ***(682)***
Texas Instruments ***(684)***
Thelen Reid & Priest LLP *(193)*
Timmons and Co., Inc. *(195)*
Traditional Values Coalition ***(689)***
Trans World Airlines, Inc. ***(689)***
Travelocity.com ***(691)***
TRW Inc. ***(693)***
Turfgrass Producers Internat'l ***(694)***
U.S. Border Control ***(695)***
Union of Councils for Soviet Jews ***(699)***
Union of Needletrades, Industrial, and Textile Employees (UNITE) ***(699)***
Unisys Corp. ***(700)***
United Airlines ***(700)***
United Automobile, Aerospace and Agricultural Implement Workers of America (UAW) ***(700)***
United Food and Commercial Workers Internat'l Union ***(701)***
United Jewish Communities, Inc. ***(701)***
United Methodist Church General Board of Church and Society ***(702)***
United States Business and Industry Council ***(703)***
University Corp. for Atmospheric Research ***(705)***
University of California, Office of Federal Government Relations ***(706)***
University of Cincinnati ***(706)***
University of Medicine and Dentistry of New Jersey ***(706)***
University of Miami ***(706)***
University of Southern California ***(707)***
University of Tulsa ***(708)***
University of Virginia ***(708)***
University of Washington ***(708)***
University System of Maryland ***(708)***
Verner, Liipfert, Bernhard, McPherson and Hand, Chartered *(202)*
Vernon, California, City of ***(714)***
Viohl and Associates, Inc. *(205)*
Virginia Commonwealth University ***(716)***
VISA U.S.A., Inc. ***(716)***
Washington Flyer Taxi Drivers Ass'n, Inc. ***(719)***
Washington Soccer Partners ***(720)***
Western Growers Ass'n ***(724)***
Western Range Ass'n ***(724)***
The Wexler Group *(211)*
Weyerhaeuser Co. ***(725)***
Whitten & Diamond *(213)*
Wholesale Nursery Growers of America ***(726)***
Williams & Jensen, P.C. *(215)*
Wilson & Wasserstein, Inc. *(218)*
Witman Associates *(220)*
World Government of World Citizens ***(730)***
World Service Authority ***(731)***
Xerox Corp. ***(732)***
Zuckerman Spaeder L.L.P. *(221)*
Zurich Financial Group ***(735)***

Indian/Native American Affairs (IND)

The 13th Regional Corp. ***(223)***
Adams and Reese LLP *(5)*
AEI Resources ***(229)***
Agua Caliente Band of Cahuilla Indians ***(232)***

Akin, Gump, Strauss, Hauer & Feld, L.L.P. *(8)*
Alamo Navajo School Board ***(236)***
Alaska Eskimo Whaling Commission ***(236)***
Alaska Native Health Board ***(236)***
Alcalde & Fay *(10)*
Alyeska Pipeline Service Co. ***(242)***
American Ass'n of Colleges of Pharmacy ***(247)***
American Ass'n of Motor Vehicle Administrators ***(248)***
American Ass'n of Museums ***(248)***
American College of Obstetricians and Gynecologists ***(254)***
American Greyhound Track Operators Ass'n ***(261)***
American Indian Ass'n ***(263)***
American Indian Higher Education Consortium ***(263)***
American Legion ***(266)***
American Museum of Natural History ***(268)***
American Psychiatric Ass'n ***(271)***
American Psychological Ass'n ***(271)***
Arctic Slope Regional Corp. ***(288)***
Arent Fox Kintner Plotkin & Kahn, PLLC *(14)*
Arter & Hadden *(17)*
The Ashley Group ***(290)***
Assiniboine and Sioux Tribes (Fort Peck Reservation) ***(300)***
Barona Band of Mission Indians ***(308)***
Bay Mills Indian Community ***(309)***
Birch, Horton, Bittner & Cherot *(28)*
Blackfeet Tribe of Montana ***(315)***
Bristol Bay Area Health Corp. ***(320)***
Burlington Northern Santa Fe Railway ***(324)***
Cabazon Band of Mission Indians ***(325)***
Capital Consultants Corp. *(37)*
Carlyle Consulting *(40)*
Cavarocchi Ruscio Dennis Associates *(44)*
Central Council of Tlingit and Haida Indian Tribes of Alaska ***(338)***
Chehalis Reservation, Confederated Tribes of the ***(342)***
Chesapeake Enterprises, Inc. *(46)*
Cheyenne and Arapahoe Tribes of Oklahoma ***(342)***
Cheyenne River Sioux Tribe ***(342)***
Child Welfare League of America ***(343)***
Chitimacha Tribe of Louisiana ***(345)***
Choctaw Indians, Mississippi Band of ***(345)***
Choctaw Nation of Oklahoma ***(345)***
Chugach Alaska Corp. ***(346)***
Coachella Valley Water District ***(352)***
Colorado River Indian Tribes ***(358)***
Community Transportation Ass'n of America ***(363)***
Confederated Tribes of the Coos ***(365)***
Confederated Tribes of Warm Springs Reservation ***(365)***
Cook Inlet Region Inc. ***(371)***
Coushatta Tribe of Louisiana ***(377)***
Cow Creek Umpqua Tribe of Oregon ***(377)***
Law Office of C. Deming Cowles *(54)*
Cuyapaipe Band of Mission Indians ***(380)***
Data Dynamics ***(382)***
Delaware Tribe of Indians ***(384)***
Delta Wetlands Project ***(385)***
Detroit, Michigan, City of ***(386)***
Development Corporation of Nevada ***(387)***
Diamond Game Enterprises, Inc. ***(387)***
Dickstein Shapiro Morin & Oshinsky LLP *(61)*
Dorsey & Whitney LLP *(63)*
Ducheneaux, Taylor & Associates, Inc. *(66)*
Dykema Gossett PLLC *(69)*
Eastern Band of Cherokee Indians ***(395)***
Edwards Associates, Inc. *(71)*
Elim, Alaska, City of ***(401)***
Elk Valley Rancheria ***(401)***
Enron Corp. ***(403)***
EOP Group, Inc. *(72)*
Evergreen Associates, Ltd. *(74)*
Jack Ferguson Associates, Inc. *(75)*
The Ferguson Group, LLC *(76)*
FMC Corp. ***(420)***
Food Marketing Institute ***(421)***
Friends Committee on Nat'l Legislation ***(426)***
Sara Garland (and Associates) *(81)*
Gila River Farms ***(435)***
Gila River Indian Community ***(435)***
Grand Traverse Band of Chippewa and Ottawa Indians ***(438)***
Greenberg Traurig, LLP *(86)*
Hall, Estill, Hardwick, Gable, Golden & Nelson *(90)*
Hecht, Spencer & Associates *(93)*
Hercules Development Corp. ***(448)***
Ho-Chunk Nation ***(450)***
Hobbs, Straus, Dean and Walker, LLP *(95)*
Lydia Hofer & Associates *(96)*
Holland & Knight LLP *(98)*
Peter Homer *(99)*
Hoopa Valley Tribal Council ***(452)***
Hopi Indian Tribe ***(452)***
Hopland Band of Pomo Indians ***(452)***
Hualapai Nation ***(454)***
R. J. Hudson Associates *(101)*
Illinois, State of ***(458)***
Imperial Irrigation District ***(458)***
Indiana, Office of the Governor of the State of ***(460)***
Information Trust ***(462)***
Internat'l Ass'n of Bridge, Structural, Ornamental and Reinforcing Iron Workers ***(467)***
Intertribal Monitoring Ass'n on Indian Trust Funds ***(477)***
Jamestown-S'Klallam Indian Tribe ***(481)***
Jamison and Sullivan, Inc. *(104)*
Janus-Merritt Strategies, L.L.C. *(104)*
Jefferson Consulting Group *(105)*
Jefferson Government Relations, L.L.C. *(106)*
Jicarilla Apache Tribe ***(483)***
Johnston & Associates, LLC *(107)*
Jorden Burt LLP *(109)*
Kake Tribal Corp. ***(486)***
Kake, Alaska, Organized Village of ***(486)***
Kickapoo Tribe of Oklahoma ***(489)***
Kogovsek & Associates *(114)*
Kurzweil & Associates *(115)*
Leech Lake Tribal Council ***(497)***
The Legislative Strategies Group, LLC *(118)*
Legix Co. ***(498)***
Leisnoi ***(498)***
Little River Band of Ottawa Indians ***(500)***
Lower Brule Sioux Tribe ***(505)***
Lower Elwaha S'Klallam Tribe ***(505)***
Manuel Lujan Associates *(122)*
Maniilaq Ass'n ***(508)***
Marriott Internat'l, Inc. ***(511)***
Mashpee Wampanoag Indian Tribal Council, Inc. ***(512)***
Mayer, Brown & Platt *(126)*
McClure, Gerard & Neuenschwander, Inc. *(127)*
McGuiness & Holch *(130)*
Jana McKeag *(131)*
Menominee Indian Tribe ***(518)***
Metlakatla Indian Community ***(520)***
Meyers & Associates *(133)*
Miccosukee Indians ***(522)***
Miccosukee Tribe of Indians of Florida ***(522)***
Mille Lacs Band of Ojibwe Indians ***(524)***
Minnesota Indian Gaming Ass'n ***(525)***
Mni-Sose Intertribal Water Rights Coalition ***(526)***
Morning Star Institute, The ***(529)***
Morongo Band of Mission Indians ***(530)***
Morriset, Schlosser, Ayer & Jozwiak *(137)*
Moss McGee Bradley & Foley *(137)*
Multistate Tax Commission ***(532)***
Murray, Scheer, Montgomery, Tapia & O'Donnell *(139)*
Nat'l Ass'n of Area Agencies on Aging ***(538)***
Nat'l Ass'n of Developmental Disabilities Councils ***(542)***
Nat'l Ass'n of Negro Business & Professional Women's Clubs, Inc. ***(546)***
Nat'l Assembly of Health and Human Service Organizations ***(551)***
Nat'l Farmers Union (Farmers Educational & Co-operative Union of America) ***(563)***
Nat'l Grange ***(566)***
Nat'l Indian Child Welfare Ass'n ***(568)***
Nat'l Indian Gaming Ass'n ***(568)***
Nat'l Licensed Beverage Ass'n ***(570)***
Nat'l Retail Federation ***(576)***
Nat'l Right to Life Committee ***(576)***
Native American Cultural & Educational Authority ***(582)***
Native American Mohegans Inc. ***(582)***
NATSO, Inc. ***(582)***
Navajo Nation ***(582)***
Navajo Nation Oil and Gas Co., Inc. ***(582)***
Neuman and Co. *(141)*
New Mexico State Office of Research & Development ***(586)***
Newport News, Virginia, City of ***(588)***
Nordhaus Haltom Taylor Taradash & Bladh LLP *(142)*
North American Sports Management, Inc. ***(592)***
North Carolina, Washington Office of the State of ***(593)***
North Slope Borough, Alaska ***(593)***
Norton Sound Health Corp. ***(596)***
O'Connor & Hannan, L.L.P. *(144)*
Oglala Lakota College ***(599)***
Oglala Sioux Tribe ***(599)***
Olsson, Frank and Weeda, P.C. *(146)*
Omaha Tribe of Nebraska ***(600)***
Oneida Indian Nation of New York ***(600)***
Oneida Tribe of Indians of Wisconsin ***(601)***
PACE-CAPSTONE *(148)*
Palm Springs, California, City of ***(606)***
Palumbo & Cerrell, Inc. *(149)*
Patton Boggs, LLP *(150)*
Paucatuck Eastern Pequot Tribal Nation ***(609)***
The Peabody Group ***(610)***
Pechanga Band of California Luiseno Indians ***(610)***
Piliero Mazza & Pargament ***(617)***
Piliero Mazza & Pargament *(155)*
Pojoaque Pueblo ***(620)***
Prairie Band of Potawatomi Indians ***(622)***
Preston Gates Ellis & Rouvelas Meeds LLP ***(623)***
Preston Gates Ellis & Rouvelas Meeds LLP *(162)*
Pueblo de Conchiti ***(629)***
Pueblo of Acoma ***(629)***
Pueblo of Laguna ***(629)***
Puyallup Tribe of Indians ***(630)***
Quebec Lumber Manufacturers Ass'n ***(630)***
Quechan Indian Tribe ***(631)***
Quinault Indian Nation ***(631)***
Red Lake Band of Chippewa Indians ***(635)***
Law Office of Paige E. Reffe *(167)*
Robertson, Monagle & Eastaugh *(170)*
Romano & Associates, LLC *(171)*
Rosebud Sioux Tribal Council ***(642)***
Roseville, California, City of ***(642)***
Ryan, Phillips, Utrecht & MacKinnon *(173)*
Saginaw Chippewa Indian Tribe of Michigan ***(646)***
Salt River Project ***(646)***
San Pasqual Band of Mission Indians ***(648)***
Sand Creek Descendants Trust ***(648)***
Sandia Pueblo ***(648)***
Santa Ana Pueblo ***(648)***
Sault Ste. Marie Tribe of Chippewa Indians ***(650)***
Scenic America ***(651)***
Schmeltzer, Aptaker & Shepard, P.C. *(176)*
Sealaska Corp. ***(653)***
Seminole Tribe of Indians of Florida ***(655)***
SENSE, INC. *(177)*
Shakopee Mdewakanton Sioux Tribe ***(656)***
Sheep Ranch Rancheria ***(657)***
Shiprock Alternative Schools, Inc. ***(657)***
Shivwitz Band of the Paiute Indian Tribe of Utah ***(658)***
Shoalwater Bay Indian Tribe ***(658)***
Siletz Tribal Council ***(659)***
Sisseton-Wahpoton Sioux Indian Tribe ***(660)***
Six Agency Committee ***(660)***
Smith Law Firm *(184)*
The Smith-Free Group *(184)*
Soboba Band of Mission Indians ***(662)***
Soc. for American Archaeology ***(662)***
Sodak Gaming Inc. ***(664)***
Sonnenschein, Nath & Rosenthal *(185)*
Sonosky, Chambers, Sachse & Endreson *(185)*
Southeast Alaska Regional Health Corp. (SEARHC) ***(667)***
Southern Ute Indian Tribe ***(668)***
St. Croix Chippewa Indians of Wisconsin ***(671)***
St. George Island Traditional Council ***(671)***
St. Paul, Alaska, City of ***(672)***

St. Regis Mohawk Tribe **(672)**
Standing Rock Sioux Tribe **(672)**
The State Affairs Co. (187)
Steptoe & Johnson LLP (188)
Stockbridge-Munsee Community Band of Mohican Indians **(675)**
Stone Investments, Inc. **(675)**
Susanville Indian Rancheria **(678)**
Swan Creek River Confederated Ojibbwa Tribes of Michigan **(678)**
TDX Village Corp. **(682)**
Tett Enterprises **(684)**
Three Affiliated Tribes of Fort Berthold Reservation **(686)**
Tohono O'Odham Nation **(688)**
Tribal Ass'n on Solid Waste and Emergency Response (TASWER) **(692)**
Tulalip Tribes **(693)**
Tule River Tribal Council **(694)**
Tunica Biloxi Indians of Louisiana **(694)**
Twentynine Palms Band of Mission Indians **(694)**
United Methodist Church General Board of Church and Society **(702)**
University of Colorado, Office of the President **(706)**
Upper Klamath Water Users **(708)**
Upper Sioux Indian Community **(708)**
Ute Mountain Ute Indian Tribe **(710)**
Van Ness Feldman, P.C. (199)
Verner, Liipfert, Bernhard, McPherson and Hand, Chartered (202)
Viejas Band of Kumeyaay Indians **(715)**
Viohl and Associates, Inc. (205)
Washington Consulting Alliance, Inc. (206)
The Washington Group (208)
The Wexler Group (211)
Wheat & Associates, Inc. (212)
White Mountain Apache Tribe **(726)**
Will and Carlson, Inc. (215)
The Willard Group (215)
Winston & Strawn (218)
Wyandotte Tribe of Oklahoma **(732)**
Yankton Sioux Tribe **(733)**
Ysleta Del Sur Pueblo **(734)**
Yukon-Kuskokwim Health Corp. **(734)**
Zane & Associates (221)
Zuckerman Spaeder L.L.P. (221)

Insurance (INS)

The 60/Plus Ass'n, Inc. **(224)**
AARP (American Ass'n of Retired Persons) **(224)**
ABA Insurance Ass'n **(224)**
Academy of Pharmaceutical Research and Science **(225)**
The Accord Group (5)
ACE INA **(226)**
ACORN (Ass'n of Community Organizations for Reform Now) **(227)**
Adams and Reese LLP (5)
The Advocacy Group (6)
Aegon USA **(229)**
Aetna Life & Casualty Co. **(230)**
AFLAC, Inc. **(231)**
AIG Environmental **(233)**
Air Pacific Ltd. **(234)**
Akin, Gump, Strauss, Hauer & Feld, L.L.P. (8)
Alliance of American Insurers **(240)**
Allmerica Financial **(241)**
Allstate Insurance Co. **(241)**
Allsup Inc. **(242)**
Alpine Group, Inc. (11)
Alston & Bird LLP (12)
American Academy of Actuaries **(243)**
American Academy of Audiology **(243)**
American Academy of Dermatology **(243)**
American Academy of Family Physicians **(243)**
American Academy of Orthopaedic Surgeons **(244)**
American Academy of Otolaryngology-Head and Neck Surgery **(244)**
American Ass'n for Marriage and Family Therapy **(246)**
American Ass'n of Crop Insurers **(247)**
American Ass'n of Health Plans (AAHP) **(248)**
American Ass'n of Homes and Services for the Aging **(248)**
American Ass'n of Motor Vehicle Administrators **(248)**
American Bankers Ass'n **(250)**
American Bar Ass'n **(250)**
American Chiropractic Ass'n **(252)**
American College of Cardiology **(253)**
American College of Obstetricians and Gynecologists **(254)**
American College of Surgeons **(254)**
American Corporate Counsel Ass'n **(255)**
American Council of Life Insurers **(256)**
American Federation of Senior Citizens **(258)**
American Fidelity Life Insurance Co. **(259)**
American Financial Group **(259)**
American General Corp. **(261)**
American General Financial Group **(261)**
American Health Care Ass'n **(261)**
American Homeowners Grassroots Alliance **(262)**
American Insurance Ass'n **(264)**
American Internat'l Group, Inc. **(265)**
American Land Title Ass'n **(265)**
American Medical Ass'n **(267)**
American Military Soc. **(268)**
American Motorcyclist Ass'n **(268)**
American Occupational Therapy Ass'n, Inc. **(269)**
American Psychiatric Ass'n **(271)**
American Seniors Housing Ass'n **(273)**
American Soc. of Ass'n Executives **(275)**
American Teleservices Ass'n **(279)**
American Trucking Ass'ns **(279)**
American Wood Preservers Institute **(280)**
Americans for Tax Reform **(282)**
Arent Fox Kintner Plotkin & Kahn, PLLC (14)
Arnold & Porter (16)
Ass'n Growth Enterprises (18)
Ass'n of American Physicians and Surgeons **(294)**
Ass'n of Banks in Insurance **(294)**
Ass'n of British Insurers **(294)**
Ass'n of Trial Lawyers of America **(299)**
Assurant Group **(301)**
Astra Solutions, LLC (18)
Baach Robinson & Lewis, PLLC (19)
Baker & Hostetler LLP (19)
Baker, Donelson, Bearman & Caldwell, P.C. (21)
Barnett & Sivon, P.C. (24)
Barr Laboratories **(308)**
Bergner Bockorny Castagnetti and Hawkins (26)
Blue Cross and Blue Shield of Maine **(315)**
Blue Cross Blue Shield Ass'n **(315)**
Bracewell & Patterson, L.L.P. (30)
Building Service Contractors Ass'n Internat'l **(323)**
Burlington Northern Santa Fe Railway **(324)**
Canfield & Associates, Inc. (36)
Capitol Hill Advocates (39)
Capitol Partners (39)
Caplin & Drysdale, Chartered (40)
Caron Foundation **(332)**
Carpi & Clay (41)
Catholic Health Ass'n of the United States **(333)**
Cavarocchi Ruscio Dennis Associates (44)
Cendant Corp. **(335)**
Certified Automotive Parts Ass'n **(340)**
Chamber of Commerce of the U.S.A. **(340)**
Chesapeake Enterprises, Inc. (46)
Chicago Title & Trust Co. **(343)**
Chicago Title Insurance **(343)**
The Chubb Corp. **(346)**
CIGNA Corp. **(346)**
Citizen Strategies (46)
Citizens Against Government Waste **(348)**
Citizens for a Sound Economy **(348)**
Clark & Weinstock, Inc. (47)
Clark/Bardes, Inc. **(350)**
CNA Financial Corp. **(351)**
CNA Insurance Cos. **(351)**
Coalition for Auto-Insurance Reform **(353)**
Coalition for Health Services Research **(354)**
Coalition of Service Industries **(355)**
Collier Shannon Scott, PLLC (48)
Community Ass'ns Institute (CAI) **(362)**
Community Transportation Ass'n of America **(363)**
Condon and Forsyth (51)
Congressional Economic Leadership Institute **(366)**
Conkling, Fiskum & McCormick (51)
Consumer Federation of America **(369)**
Consumer Federation of America's Insurance Group **(369)**
Consumers Union of the United States **(369)**
Contractors Internat'l Group on Nuclear Liability **(370)**
Cooney & Associates, Inc. (52)
Cooperative of American Physicians **(371)**
Council for Affordable Health Insurance **(374)**
The Council of Insurance Agents & Brokers **(376)**
Countrywide Home Loans, Inc. **(377)**
Crowell & Moring LLP (55)
Cystic Fibrosis Foundation **(380)**
DaimlerChrysler Corp. **(381)**
Delta Dental Plans Ass'n **(385)**
Devillier Communications (61)
Dime Savings Bank of New York **(388)**
Downey McGrath Group, Inc. (64)
Easter Seals **(395)**
EDS Corp. **(398)**
Electronic Financial Services Council **(400)**
Energy Contractors Price-Anderson Group **(403)**
The Equitable Cos. **(406)**
Equitas Reinsurance Ltd. **(406)**
Ernst & Young LLP (72)
Fannie Mae **(411)**
Farmers Insurance Group **(412)**
Farmland Industries, Inc. **(412)**
Federal Home Loan Mortgage Corp. (Freddie Mac) **(413)**
Financial Planning Ass'n **(416)**
Financial Services Coordinating Council **(416)**
The Financial Services Roundtable **(416)**
Fireman's Fund Insurance Cos. **(417)**
First American Title Aircraft **(417)**
Forces Vives **(422)**
Betty Ford Center **(422)**
Forethought Group/Forethought Life Insurance Co. **(423)**
The Fortier Group, LLC (79)
Foundation Health Federal Services, Inc. **(424)**
Fresenius Medical Care North America **(425)**
General Conference of Seventh-day Adventists **(431)**
General Electric Co. **(432)**
General Motors Corp. **(432)**
Genzyme Corp. **(433)**
GLOBEMAC Associates (83)
Golden Rule Insurance Co. **(437)**
Goodwin, Procter & Hoar LLP (84)
Jay Grant & Associates (85)
Greenberg Traurig, LLP (86)
Griffin & Associates (87)
Grisso Consulting (88)
Groom Law Group, Chartered **(441)**
Group Health, Inc. **(441)**
Hadassah, The Women's Zionist Organization of America **(443)**
Harmon & Wilmot, L.L.P. (91)
The Hartford **(445)**
Hazelden Foundation **(445)**
Health Insurance Ass'n of America **(446)**
Helmsin & Yarwood Associates (94)
Hertz Corp. **(449)**
Higgins, McGovern & Smith, LLC (94)
Hogan & Hartson L.L.P. (96)
Hohlt & Associates (98)
Home Warranty Coalition **(451)**
Hooper Owen & Winburn (99)
Humana Inc. **(455)**
Hunt Management Systems (101)
Independent Insurance Agents of America, Inc. **(459)**
ING America Insurance Holdings, Inc. **(462)**
Insurance Services Office, Inc. **(465)**
Internat'l Sign Ass'n **(474)**
Internat'l Underwriting Ass'n of London **(475)**
Iran Air **(478)**
Jar-Mon Consultants, Inc. (105)
Jefferson Consulting Group (105)
Jenner & Block (107)
Jolly/Rissler, Inc. (108)

Labor Issues/Antitrust/Workplace (LBR)

American Moving and Storage Ass'n *(268)*
American Nursery and Landscape Ass'n *(268)*
American Nurses Ass'n *(268)*
American Occupational Therapy Ass'n, Inc. *(269)*
American Optometric Ass'n *(269)*
American Organization of Nurse Executives *(269)*
American Petroleum Institute *(269)*
American Physical Therapy Ass'n *(270)*
American Portland Cement Alliance *(270)*
American Psychological Ass'n *(271)*
American Red Cross *(272)*
American Rental Ass'n *(272)*
American Resort Development Ass'n *(272)*
American Road and Transportation Builders Ass'n (ARTBA) *(273)*
American Seniors Housing Ass'n *(273)*
American Shipbuilding Ass'n *(274)*
American Soc. for Quality *(275)*
American Soc. for Training and Development *(275)*
American Soc. of Ass'n Executives *(275)*
American Soc. of Clinical Pathologists *(276)*
American Soc. of Safety Engineers *(277)*
American Speech, Language, and Hearing Ass'n *(277)*
American Staffing Ass'n *(278)*
American Subcontractors Ass'n, Inc. *(278)*
American Supply Ass'n *(278)*
American Symphony Orchestra League *(278)*
American Textile Manufacturers Institute *(279)*
American Trucking Ass'ns *(279)*
American Waterways Operators *(280)*
American Wholesale Marketers Ass'n *(280)*
American Wood Preservers Institute *(280)*
Americans Against Union Control of Government *(281)*
Americans for Equitable Climate Solutions *(281)*
Americans for Tax Reform *(282)*
Andrx Pharmaceutical Corp. *(284)*
Antitrust Coalition for Consumer Choice in Health Care *(285)*
AOL Time Warner *(285)*
AON Risk Services *(285)*
The Arc *(287)*
Arch Mineral Corp. *(287)*
Arent Fox Kintner Plotkin & Kahn, PLLC *(14)*
Armstrong World Industries, Inc. *(289)*
Arvin Meritor Automotive *(290)*
Asahi Glass Co. *(290)*
Ashland Inc. *(290)*
Asian Pacific American Labor Alliance, AFL-CIO *(291)*
Ass'n for Career and Technical Education *(291)*
Ass'n of American Geographers *(293)*
Ass'n of Clinical Research Professionals *(295)*
Ass'n of Flight Attendants *(295)*
Ass'n of Professional Flight Attendants *(297)*
Ass'n of Sales & Marketing Companies *(298)*
Ass'n of Test Publishers *(299)*
Associated Builders and Contractors *(300)*
Associated General Contractors of America *(300)*
The Atlantic Group, Public Affairs, Inc. *(18)*
ATOFINA Chemicals, Inc. *(302)*
Automotive Aftermarket Industry Ass'n *(303)*
Automotive Parts and Service Alliance *(303)*
Auyua Inc. *(304)*
Avue Technologies *(305)*
Baker & Hostetler LLP *(19)*
Baker, Donelson, Bearman & Caldwell, P.C. *(21)*
Ball Janik, LLP *(22)*
Barbour Griffith & Rogers, Inc. *(22)*
Barr Laboratories *(308)*
BASF Corporation *(308)*
Bass and Howes, Inc. *(24)*
Bass Hotels and Resorts, Inc. *(308)*
Bellevue, Washington, City of *(311)*
BellSouth Corp. *(311)*
Bergner Bockorny Castagnetti and Hawkins *(26)*
Bert Corona Leadership Institute *(312)*
Berwind Corp. *(312)*
BHP (USA) Inc. *(313)*
BKSH & Associates *(28)*
Blue Cross Blue Shield Ass'n *(315)*
BMW Manufacturing Corp. *(316)*
The Boeing Co. *(316)*
Boesch & Co. *(29)*
Bond & Company, Inc. *(30)*
Bowling Proprietors' Ass'n of America *(318)*
BP Amoco Corp. *(319)*
Brand & Frulla, P.C. *(32)*
Brazelton Foundation *(319)*
Bridgestone/Firestone, Inc. *(320)*
Brinker Internat'l *(320)*
Brother Internat'l Co. *(322)*
Brotherhood of Locomotive Engineers *(322)*
Brown and Company, Inc. *(33)*
Buchanan Ingersoll, P.C. *(34)*
Buffalo Carpenters Pension Fund *(323)*
Building Service Contractors Ass'n Internat'l *(323)*
Burger King Corp. *(324)*
Burlington Northern Santa Fe Railway *(324)*
Business and Professional Women/USA *(324)*
The Business Roundtable *(325)*
Butera & Andrews *(34)*
C F Industries, Inc. *(325)*
California Correctional Peace Officers Ass'n *(326)*
Capital Research Center *(330)*
Capitol Hill Advocates *(39)*
Capitol Link, Inc. *(39)*
Caplin & Drysdale, Chartered *(40)*
Cargill, Inc. *(331)*
Cash, Smith & Wages *(41)*
Cassidy & Associates, Inc. *(42)*
Caterpillar Inc. *(333)*
Cellular Telecommunications and Internet Ass'n *(334)*
Cendant Corp. *(335)*
Center for Employment Training *(336)*
Center for Energy and Economic Development *(336)*
Central American Bank of Economic Integration *(338)*
Ceridian Corp. *(340)*
Chamber of Commerce of the U.S.A. *(340)*
Chambers Associates Inc. *(45)*
Chevron, U.S.A. *(342)*
Child Welfare League of America *(343)*
Children's Defense Fund *(344)*
The Chubb Corp. *(346)*
Ciba Specialty Chemicals Corp. *(346)*
Cincinnati, Ohio, City of *(347)*
Citizens Against Government Waste *(348)*
Citizens for a Sound Economy *(348)*
Clark & Weinstock, Inc. *(47)*
Cleveland Growth Ass'n *(351)*
CNA Financial Corp. *(351)*
CNA Insurance Cos. *(351)*
CNF Transportation, Inc. *(351)*
Coalition on Occupational Safety and Health *(356)*
Coalition to Preserve Mine Safety Standards *(356)*
The Coca-Cola Company *(356)*
College of American Pathologists *(357)*
Collier Shannon Scott, PLLC *(48)*
Committee for Farmworker Programs *(361)*
Committee to Support the Antitrust Laws *(361)*
Communications Workers of America *(362)*
Community Transportation Ass'n of America *(363)*
Compuware Corp. *(364)*
ConAgra Foods, Inc. *(365)*
Concerned Educators Against Forced Unionism *(365)*
Congressional Economic Leadership Institute *(366)*
Connerton & Ray *(51)*
Consortium for Worker Education *(368)*
Construction Industry Round Table, Inc. *(368)*
Consumer Electronics Ass'n *(369)*
Consumer Federation of America *(369)*
Consumers Union of the United States *(369)*
Contract Services Ass'n of America *(370)*
Cooney & Associates, Inc. *(52)*
Coors Brewing Company *(371)*
Copeland, Lowery & Jacquez *(52)*
Corporation for Business, Work and Learning *(372)*
Council of State Governments *(376)*
Council on Labor Law Equality *(377)*
Covington & Burling *(53)*
Cox Enterprises Inc. *(378)*
Crane Co. *(378)*
CSA America, Inc. *(379)*
Cummins Engine Co. *(380)*
The Cuneo Law Group, P.C. *(56)*
Davidson & Company, Inc. *(57)*
Delta Air Lines *(384)*
Dickstein Shapiro Morin & Oshinsky LLP *(61)*
Domino's Pizza *(391)*
The Dow Chemical Co. *(391)*
Downey McGrath Group, Inc. *(64)*
The Duberstein Group, Inc. *(65)*
Duke Energy *(392)*
DuPont *(393)*
DuPont Agricultural Products *(393)*
The Dutko Group, Inc. *(68)*
Dykema Gossett PLLC *(69)*
The Eagles Group *(69)*
Easter Seals *(395)*
Eastman Chemical Co. *(395)*
Eastman Kodak Co. *(395)*
eBay Inc. *(395)*
Edison Chouest Offshore, Inc. *(397)*
Edison Electric Institute *(397)*
Edmund Scientific Co. *(397)*
Education and Training Resources *(398)*
Employment Policy Foundation *(402)*
Enron Corp. *(403)*
Entela, Inc. *(404)*
Entergy Services, Inc. *(404)*
Environmental Industry Ass'ns *(405)*
Ergodyne *(406)*
The ERISA Industry Committee (ERIC) *(406)*
Ethics Resource Center Inc. *(407)*
Evans & Black, Inc. *(73)*
Exelon Corp. *(409)*
Exxon Mobil Corp. *(409)*
Family Violence Prevention Fund *(411)*
Farmland Industries, Inc. *(412)*
Feder, Semo, Clarke & Bard *(74)*
Federal Physicians Ass'n *(414)*
Federation of Nurses and Health Professionals/AFT *(415)*
FedEx Corp. *(415)*
The Ferguson Group, LLC *(76)*
Fierce and Isakowitz *(76)*
Finch-Pruyn Paper Co. *(417)*
First Tuesday Group *(418)*
FirstEnergy Co. *(418)*
Florida Equipment Contractors Ass'n *(419)*
Fluor Corp. *(420)*
FMC Wyoming Corp. *(421)*
Fontheim Internat'l *(421)*
Fontheim Partners, PC *(78)*
Food Distributors Internat'l (NAWGA-IFDA) *(421)*
Food Marketing Institute *(421)*
Food Research and Action Center *(422)*
FRANMAC/Taco Pac *(425)*
Fraternal Order of Police *(425)*
Free Trade Lumber Council *(425)*
Freeport-McMoRan Copper & Gold Inc. *(425)*
G.R. Services *(80)*
Gainesville, Florida, City of *(428)*
Gannett Co., Inc. *(429)*
Garden Centers of America *(429)*
General Atlantic Service Corp. *(431)*
General Chemical Corp. *(431)*
General Conference of Seventh-day Adventists *(431)*
General Dynamics Corp. *(431)*
General Electric Co. *(432)*
General Motors Corp. *(432)*
Genesis Consulting Group, LLC *(82)*
Global Associates *(436)*
Global USA, Inc. *(83)*
Goldberg & Associates, PLLC *(83)*
Golf Course Superintendents Ass'n of America *(437)*
Goodwill Industries Internat'l, Inc. *(437)*
Goodyear Tire and Rubber Co. *(437)*
Stuart J. Gordon *(84)*
Government Relations, Inc. *(84)*
Graphic Communications Internat'l Union *(438)*
Greater Columbus Chamber *(439)*
Greater Washington Board of Trade *(439)*

Green Thumb, Inc. ***(440)***
Greenberg Traurig, LLP *(86)*
Griffin, Johnson, Dover & Stewart *(87)*
Groom Law Group, Chartered *(88)*
Group Health, Inc. ***(441)***
Guidant Corp. ***(442)***
Hadassah, The Women's Zionist Organization of America ***(443)***
Hager Sharp Inc. ***(443)***
Halliburton/Brown & Root ***(443)***
Hallmark Cards, Inc. ***(443)***
Hawaii, State of ***(445)***
Health Insurance Ass'n of America ***(446)***
The Hearst Corp. ***(447)***
Hecht, Spencer & Associates *(93)*
Helmsin & Yarwood Associates *(94)*
Law Offices of Robert T. Herbolsheimer *(94)*
HEREIU ***(448)***
Hewlett-Packard Co. ***(449)***
Alan Hilburg & Associates ***(449)***
Hogan & Hartson L.L.P. *(96)*
Hohlt & Associates *(98)*
Holland & Knight LLP *(98)*
Home Builders Institute ***(451)***
The Home Depot ***(451)***
Hotel Employees and Restaurant Employees Internat'l Union ***(453)***
R. J. Hudson Associates *(101)*
Human Rights Campaign Fund ***(454)***
Hunt Management Systems *(101)*
HUTCO, Inc. ***(455)***
ICF Consulting ***(457)***
The Ickes & Enright Group *(102)*
IMC Global Inc. ***(458)***
Impact Strategies *(102)*
Independent Contractor Coalition ***(459)***
Independent Electrical Contractors, Inc. ***(459)***
Independent Office Products and Furniture Dealers Ass'n ***(459)***
Industrial Fabrics Ass'n Internat'l ***(461)***
Information Technology Ass'n of America (ITAA) ***(461)***
Inglewood, California, City of ***(462)***
Institute for a Drug-Free Workplace ***(463)***
Institute of Navigation ***(464)***
Intermodal Ass'n of North America ***(467)***
Internat'l Ass'n of Amusement Parks and Attractions ***(467)***
Internat'l Ass'n of Assembly Managers ***(467)***
Internat'l Ass'n of Bridge, Structural, Ornamental and Reinforcing Iron Workers ***(467)***
Internat'l Ass'n of Fire Chiefs ***(468)***
Internat'l Ass'n of Fire Fighters ***(468)***
Internat'l Ass'n of Machinists and Aerospace Workers ***(468)***
Internat'l Ass'n of Personnel in Employment Security ***(468)***
Internat'l Brotherhood of Boilermakers, Iron Shipbuilders, Blacksmiths, Forgers and Helpers ***(469)***
Internat'l Brotherhood of Electrical Workers ***(469)***
Internat'l Brotherhood of Teamsters ***(469)***
Internat'l Business Machines Corp. ***(469)***
Internat'l Council of Cruise Lines ***(470)***
Internat'l Dairy Foods Ass'n ***(470)***
Internat'l Federation of Professional and Technical Engineers ***(471)***
Internat'l Franchise Ass'n ***(472)***
Internat'l Labor Rights Fund ***(472)***
Internat'l Longshore and Warehouse Union ***(473)***
Internat'l Mass Retailers Ass'n ***(473)***
Internat'l Municipal Signal Ass'n ***(473)***
Internat'l Paper ***(473)***
Internat'l Personnel Management Ass'n ***(474)***
Internat'l Safety Equipment Ass'n (ISEA) ***(474)***
Internat'l Sign Ass'n ***(474)***
Internat'l Union of Bricklayers and Allied Craftsworkers ***(476)***
Internat'l Union of Operating Engineers ***(476)***
Internat'l Union of Painters and Allied Trades ***(476)***
Internat'l Union of Police Ass'ns ***(476)***
Internat'l Warehouse Logistics Ass'n ***(476)***
IPC Washington Office ***(478)***
James Hardie Building Products Inc. ***(481)***
Jarboe & Associates *(105)*
Jefferson Government Relations, L.L.C. *(106)*
Jefferson Parish Council ***(482)***
JKB Communications *(107)*
JM Family Enterprises ***(483)***
Jolly/Rissler, Inc. *(108)*
Edward Jones Investments ***(485)***
Jorden Burt LLP *(109)*
Robert E. Juliano Associates *(109)*
Kaiser Aluminum & Chemical Corp. ***(485)***
Kellogg Brown and Root ***(487)***
Kelly and Associates, Inc. *(111)*
Kelly Services, Inc. ***(487)***
Kennecott/Borax ***(488)***
Kent & O'Connor, Inc. *(112)*
Kinder & Associates, Inc. *(113)*
King & Spalding *(113)*
Kinghorn & Associates, L.L.C. *(113)*
Labor Council for Latin American Advancement (LCLAA) ***(493)***
Labor Policy Ass'n (LPA) ***(493)***
Laborers Health & Safety Fund ***(493)***
Laborers' Internat'l Union of North America ***(493)***
Laborers-AGC Education and Training Fund ***(493)***
Laborers-Employers Cooperation & Education Trust ***(493)***
Lafarge Corp. ***(494)***
Shannon M. Lahey Associates *(116)*
Lee Lane *(116)*
Lathrop & Gage, L.C. *(116)*
League of California Cities ***(497)***
Ledge Counsel *(118)*
Legislative Solutions *(118)*
Eli Lilly and Co. ***(499)***
The Limited Inc. ***(499)***
Littler Mendelson, P.C. *(120)*
Lockheed Martin Corp. ***(501)***
Los Angeles, California, County of ***(504)***
Lotus Development Corp. ***(504)***
Luman, Lange & Wheeler *(122)*
Lutheran Office for Governmental Affairs/Evangelical Lutheran Church in America ***(506)***
The M Companies *(122)*
Turner D. Madden *(123)*
Madison County Commission ***(507)***
Madison, Wisconsin, City of ***(507)***
Magazine Publishers of America ***(507)***
Major League Baseball ***(508)***
Major League Baseball Players Ass'n ***(508)***
Mallino Government Relations *(123)*
Maloney & Knox, LLP *(123)*
Manatt, Phelps & Phillips, LLP *(123)*
Manufacturers Alliance/MAPI Inc. ***(509)***
MARC Associates, Inc. *(124)*
Marine Engineers Beneficial Ass'n (District No. 1 - PCD) ***(510)***
Marriott Internat'l, Inc. ***(511)***
Martin, Fisher & Associates, Inc. *(125)*
Maryland Psychiatric Soc. ***(512)***
MassMutual Financial Group ***(512)***
MasterCard Internat'l ***(513)***
Maytag Corp. ***(513)***
Charlie McBride Associates, Inc. *(127)*
McDermott, Will and Emery *(128)*
McDonald's Corp. ***(514)***
McGraw-Hill Cos., The ***(514)***
McGuiness & Holch *(130)*
McGuiness Norris & Williams, LLP *(130)*
McGuireWoods L.L.P. *(130)*
McLane Co. ***(515)***
Diane McRee Associates *(131)*
Mechanical Contractors Ass'n of America ***(515)***
MedPro, Inc. ***(517)***
Merced, California, County of ***(518)***
Merck & Co. ***(518)***
Metal Building Manufacturers Ass'n ***(519)***
Methane Awareness Resource Group ***(519)***
Metropolitan King County Council ***(520)***
Mexican-American Legal Defense and Educational Fund ***(521)***
Miami Beach, Florida, City of ***(521)***
Miller & Chevalier, Chartered *(133)*
Denny Miller McBee Associates *(134)*
Millian Byers Associates, LLC *(135)*
Milwaukee, Wisconsin, County of ***(524)***
Mitsubishi Motors America, Inc. ***(526)***
Modesto, California, City of ***(527)***
Morgan, Lewis & Bockius LLP *(136)*
Morton Internat'l ***(530)***
Moss McGee Bradley & Foley *(137)*
Motor and Equipment Manufacturers Ass'n ***(531)***
Motor Freight Carriers Ass'n ***(531)***
Motorola, Inc. ***(531)***
MSP Strategic Communications, Inc. *(138)*
Muncie, Indiana, City of (Delaware County) ***(532)***
Patrick M. Murphy & Associates *(138)*
R. B. Murphy & Associates *(139)*
Murray, Scheer, Montgomery, Tapia & O'Donnell *(139)*
The MWW Group *(140)*
Nat'l Air Traffic Controllers Ass'n ***(536)***
Nat'l Air Transportation Ass'n ***(536)***
Nat'l Alliance Against Blacklisting ***(536)***
Nat'l Armored Car Ass'n ***(537)***
Nat'l Ass'n for State Farm Agents ***(538)***
Nat'l Ass'n for the Advancement of Colored People, Washington Bureau ***(538)***
Nat'l Ass'n of Chain Drug Stores ***(539)***
Nat'l Ass'n of Computer Consultant Businesses ***(540)***
Nat'l Ass'n of Convenience Stores ***(541)***
Nat'l Ass'n of Foster Grandparent Program Directors ***(543)***
Nat'l Ass'n of Government Employees ***(543)***
Nat'l Ass'n of Independent Insurers ***(544)***
Nat'l Ass'n of Industrial and Office Properties ***(544)***
Nat'l Ass'n of Letter Carriers of the United States of America ***(545)***
Nat'l Ass'n of Manufacturers ***(545)***
Nat'l Ass'n of Miscellaneous, Ornamental and Architectural Products Contractors ***(545)***
Nat'l Ass'n of Negro Business & Professional Women's Clubs, Inc. ***(546)***
Nat'l Ass'n of Police Organizations ***(546)***
Nat'l Ass'n of Professional Employer Organizations ***(547)***
Nat'l Ass'n of Reinforcing Steel Contractors ***(548)***
Nat'l Ass'n of Service and Conservation Corps ***(549)***
Nat'l Ass'n of Social Workers ***(549)***
Nat'l Ass'n of State Units on Aging ***(550)***
Nat'l Ass'n of Surety Bond Producers ***(550)***
Nat'l Ass'n of Theatre Owners ***(550)***
Nat'l Ass'n of Waterfront Employers ***(551)***
Nat'l Ass'n of Wholesaler-Distributors ***(551)***
Nat'l Automobile Dealers Ass'n ***(552)***
Nat'l Beer Wholesalers Ass'n ***(552)***
Nat'l Border Patrol Council ***(553)***
Nat'l Burglar and Fire Alarm Ass'n ***(553)***
Nat'l Campaign for Hearing Health ***(554)***
Nat'l Center for Policy Analysis ***(555)***
Nat'l Chicken Council ***(555)***
Nat'l Child Support Enforcement Ass'n ***(555)***
Nat'l Club Ass'n ***(556)***
Nat'l Coalition for Cancer Survivorship ***(556)***
Nat'l Concrete Masonry Ass'n ***(558)***
Nat'l Consumers League ***(558)***
Nat'l Coordinating Committee for Multiemployer Plans ***(559)***
Nat'l Council for Community Behavioral Healthcare ***(559)***
Nat'l Council of Agricultural Employers ***(560)***
Nat'l Council of Chain Restaurants ***(560)***
Nat'l Council of University Research Administrators ***(561)***
Nat'l Court Reporters Ass'n ***(561)***
Nat'l Defense Industrial Ass'n ***(561)***
Nat'l Defined Contribution Council ***(561)***
Nat'l Education Ass'n of the U.S. ***(562)***
Nat'l Electrical Contractors Ass'n ***(562)***
Nat'l Electrical Manufacturers Ass'n ***(562)***
Nat'l Electrical Safety Foundation ***(562)***
Nat'l Employee Benefits Institute ***(562)***
Nat'l Employment Opportunities Network ***(563)***
Nat'l Energy Management Institute ***(563)***
Nat'l Farmers Union (Farmers Educational & Co-operative Union of America) ***(563)***
Nat'l Fisheries Institute ***(564)***
Nat'l Franchise Council ***(565)***

Valis Associates *(198)*
Van Scoyoc Associates, Inc. *(200)*
Variable Annuity Life Insurance Co. ***(712)***
Joe Velasquez & Associates *(201)*
Venable *(201)*
Verizon Communications ***(713)***
Verner, Liipfert, Bernhard, McPherson and Hand, Chartered *(202)*
Don Wallace Associates, Inc. *(206)*
Warnaco, Inc. ***(718)***
Washington Aviation Group *(206)*
Washington Consulting Alliance, Inc. *(206)*
Washington Council Ernst & Young *(206)*
Washington Flyer Taxi Drivers Ass'n, Inc. ***(719)***
Washington Gas ***(719)***
The Washington Post Co. ***(720)***
Washington Resource Associates *(209)*
Waterman & Associates *(210)*
Webster, Chamberlain & Bean *(210)*
WellPoint Health Networks/Blue Cross of California/UNICARE ***(723)***
Wendy's Internat'l, Inc. ***(723)***
The Wexler Group *(211)*
Wheat & Associates, Inc. *(212)*
Wholesale Nursery Growers of America ***(726)***
The Willard Group *(215)*
Williams & Jensen, P.C. *(215)*
Kathleen Winn & Associates, Inc. *(218)*
Winston & Strawn *(218)*
Wise & Associates *(220)*
Women Officials in NACo ***(729)***
World Shipping Council ***(731)***
Worldwatch Institute ***(731)***
Xerox Corp. ***(732)***
Yellow Corp. ***(733)***
Zuckerman Spaeder L.L.P. *(221)*

Law Enforcement/Crime/Criminal Justice (LAW)

3Com Corp. ***(223)***
The 60/Plus Ass'n, Inc. ***(224)***
AAAE-ACI ***(224)***
AARP (American Ass'n of Retired Persons) ***(224)***
Adams and Reese LLP *(5)*
The Advocacy Group *(6)*
Advocates for Highway and Auto Safety ***(229)***
AFL-CIO (American Federation of Labor and Congress of Industrial Organizations) ***(231)***
AKAL Security ***(235)***
Akin, Gump, Strauss, Hauer & Feld, L.L.P. *(8)*
Albuquerque, New Mexico, City of ***(237)***
Alcalde & Fay *(10)*
Alliance for American Innovation, Inc. ***(239)***
Alliance for Children and Families ***(239)***
Allstate Insurance Co. ***(241)***
Alpine Group, Inc. *(11)*
American Academy of Child and Adolescent Psychiatry ***(243)***
American Academy of Family Physicians ***(243)***
American Ass'n of Motor Vehicle Administrators ***(248)***
American Bankers Ass'n ***(250)***
American Bar Ass'n ***(250)***
American Chemistry Council ***(252)***
American Continental Group, Inc. *(12)*
American Corporate Counsel Ass'n ***(255)***
American Correctional Ass'n ***(255)***
American Council of Life Insurers ***(256)***
American Counseling Ass'n ***(256)***
American Federation of State, County and Municipal Employees ***(258)***
American Federation of Teachers ***(259)***
American Hospital Ass'n ***(263)***
American Jewish Committee ***(265)***
American Jewish Congress ***(265)***
American Legion ***(266)***
American Psychiatric Ass'n ***(271)***
American Psychological Ass'n ***(271)***
American Red Cross ***(272)***
American Soc. for Industrial Security ***(274)***
American Speech, Language, and Hearing Ass'n ***(277)***
Americans for Tax Reform ***(282)***
Americans United for Separation of Church and State ***(282)***
Ancore Corp. ***(284)***
Anti-Defamation League ***(285)***
AOL Time Warner ***(285)***
Applied Marine Technologies, Inc. ***(287)***
The Arc ***(287)***
Arent Fox Kintner Plotkin & Kahn, PLLC *(14)*
Arkansas, Office of the Governor of the State of ***(288)***
Arnold & Porter *(16)*
Ass'n for Los Angeles Deputy Sheriffs ***(292)***
Ass'n of Flight Attendants ***(295)***
Associated Credit Bureaus, Inc. ***(300)***
Assurant Group ***(301)***
Auburn University ***(302)***
Austin, Texas, City of ***(303)***
Autometric Inc. ***(303)***
Avondale, Arizona, City of ***(305)***
Donald Baldwin Associates *(21)*
Ball Janik, LLP *(22)*
Barringer Technologies ***(308)***
The Barton Co. *(24)*
Bazelon Center for Mental Health Law, Judge David L. ***(310)***
Beacon Consulting Group, Inc. *(25)*
Beaumont, Texas, City of ***(310)***
Bellevue, Washington, City of ***(311)***
Berkeley, California, City of ***(312)***
Bernalillo, New Mexico, County of ***(312)***
Boston, Massachusetts, City of ***(318)***
Boy Scouts of America ***(318)***
Boys and Girls Clubs of America ***(318)***
Boysville ***(318)***
Brea, California, City of ***(319)***
Bristol-Myers Squibb Co. ***(320)***
Burlington Northern Santa Fe Railway ***(324)***
California Correctional Peace Officers Ass'n ***(326)***
California State Ass'n of Counties ***(327)***
California, State of, Attorney General's Office ***(328)***
Campaign Finance Reform Coalition ***(328)***
W. Douglas Campbell *(36)*
Canfield, Smith and Martin *(36)*
Capitol Associates, Inc. *(37)*
Capitol Link, Inc. *(39)*
Capitol Solutions *(39)*
Capitol Strategies *(39)*
CARFAX, Inc. ***(331)***
Carpi & Clay *(41)*
The Carter Group *(41)*
Cassidy & Associates, Inc. *(42)*
Caterpillar Inc. ***(333)***
Cellular Telecommunications and Internet Ass'n ***(334)***
Center for Law and Social Policy ***(336)***
Center for Research on Institutions and Social Policy ***(337)***
Chamber of Commerce of the U.S.A. ***(340)***
Chambers Associates Inc. *(45)*
Carolyn C. Chaney & Associates *(45)*
Child Welfare League of America ***(343)***
Children's Defense Fund ***(344)***
Christian Coalition of America ***(345)***
Chwat and Company, Inc. *(46)*
Citigroup ***(347)***
Citizens Committee for the Right to Keep and Bear Arms ***(348)***
Cleveland, Ohio, City of ***(351)***
CNA Financial Corp. ***(351)***
CNA Insurance Cos. ***(351)***
Coalition Against Product Tampering ***(352)***
Coalition for Federal Sentencing Reform ***(353)***
Coalition for Internat'l Justice ***(354)***
Coalition to Stop Gun Violence ***(356)***
Coalitions for America ***(356)***
College on Problems of Drug Dependence ***(357)***
Collier Shannon Scott, PLLC *(48)*
Columbia, South Carolina, City of ***(359)***
Competition in Contracting Act Coalition ***(363)***
Computer and Communications Industry Ass'n (CCIA) ***(364)***
Computer Associates Internat'l, Inc. ***(364)***
Consortium of Social Science Ass'ns ***(368)***
Consumer Federation of America ***(369)***
Cook, Illinois, County of ***(371)***
Copeland, Lowery & Jacquez *(52)*
Corporacion de Exportaciones Mexicanas, S.A. de C.V. and Marvin Roy Feldman ***(372)***
Correctional Vendors Ass'n ***(373)***
Corrections Corp. of America ***(373)***
Council for Court Excellence ***(374)***
Council of Industrial Boiler Owners (CIBO) ***(375)***
The Cuneo Law Group, P.C. *(56)*
Cuyahoga, Ohio, County of ***(380)***
The Da Vinci Group *(56)*
Dallas, Texas, City of ***(382)***
Davidoff & Malito, LLP *(57)*
Dayton, Ohio, Washington Office of the City of ***(383)***
Dean Blakey & Moskowitz *(59)*
Denton, Texas, City of ***(385)***
Detroit, Michigan, City of ***(386)***
Dickstein Shapiro Morin & Oshinsky LLP *(61)*
Digital Biometrics, Inc. ***(388)***
Digital Descriptor Services, Inc. ***(388)***
Direct Impact, LLC *(63)*
Downey McGrath Group, Inc. *(64)*
Durham, North Carolina, City of ***(393)***
Dykema Gossett PLLC *(69)*
eBay Inc. ***(395)***
EDS Corp. ***(398)***
Milton S. Eisenhower Foundation ***(399)***
Eklof Marine Corp. ***(399)***
Scott J. Esparza & Co. ***(407)***
Eugene, Oregon, City of ***(407)***
Exxon Mobil Corp. ***(409)***
Exxon Valdez Oil Spill Litigation Plaintiffs ***(409)***
Federal Criminal Investigators Ass'n ***(412)***
Federal Law Enforcement Officers Ass'n ***(413)***
Feith & Zell, P.C. *(75)*
The Ferguson Group, LLC *(76)*
Fierce and Isakowitz *(76)*
Financial Programs, Inc. *(77)*
FLIR Systems, Inc. ***(419)***
Foley & Lardner *(78)*
Food Distributors Internat'l (NAWGA-IFDA) ***(421)***
Fraternal Order of Police ***(425)***
Fraternal Order of Police (U.S. Park Police Labor Committee) ***(425)***
Friends Committee on Nat'l Legislation ***(426)***
Gainesville, Florida, City of ***(428)***
Gary, Indiana, Washington Office of the City of ***(429)***
General Motors Corp. ***(432)***
Geo-Seis Helicopters Inc. ***(433)***
Girls Incorporated ***(435)***
Jay Grant & Associates *(85)*
Greenberg Traurig, LLP *(86)*
Griffin, Johnson, Dover & Stewart *(87)*
Gun Owners of America ***(442)***
Hallmark Cards, Inc. ***(443)***
Hecht, Spencer & Associates *(93)*
Allen Herbert *(94)*
Dennis M. Hertel & Associates *(94)*
Hertz Corp. ***(449)***
Higgins, McGovern & Smith, LLC *(94)*
Hill and Knowlton, Inc. *(95)*
The Hoffman Group *(96)*
Hoffmann-La Roche Inc. ***(450)***
Hogan & Hartson L.L.P. *(96)*
Hopi Indian Tribe ***(452)***
Humane Soc. of the United States ***(455)***
Huntsville, Alabama, City of ***(455)***
Hurt, Norton & Associates *(101)*
Hyjek & Fix, Inc. *(102)*
Hyman, Phelps & McNamara, P.C. *(102)*
Illinois Collaboration on Youth ***(457)***
Illinois Housing Development Authority ***(457)***
Indiana State University ***(460)***
Indiana, Office of the Governor of the State of ***(460)***
Inglewood, California, City of ***(462)***
Interactive Digital Software Ass'n ***(466)***
Internat'l Ass'n of Chiefs of Police ***(467)***
Internat'l Ass'n of Professional Numismatists ***(468)***
Internat'l Community Corrections Ass'n ***(470)***
Internat'l Labor Rights Fund ***(472)***
Internat'l Mass Retailers Ass'n ***(473)***

Internat'l Olympic Committee ***(473)***
Internat'l Union of Police Ass'ns ***(476)***
Irvine Sensors Corp. ***(479)***
Jackson Nat'l Life Insurance ***(480)***
Jackson, Mississippi, City of ***(480)***
Jacobs Engineering Group Inc. ***(481)***
James & Hoffman, P.C. *(104)*
Janus-Merritt Strategies, L.L.C. *(104)*
Jefferson Consulting Group *(105)*
Jenkens & Gilchrist *(107)*
The Jewelers' Security Alliance ***(483)***
Jewish Institute for Nat'l Security Affairs ***(483)***
Johns Hopkins Center for Civilian Biodefense Studies ***(483)***
Jorden Burt LLP *(109)*
The Justice Project, Inc. ***(485)***
The Kamber Group *(109)*
Kendall-Jackson Winery ***(488)***
King & Spalding *(113)*
Kirkpatrick & Lockhart LLP *(114)*
Kruger Internat'l (KI) ***(492)***
Lafayette Group, Inc. *(116)*
Shannon M. Lahey Associates *(116)*
Lake, Illinois, County of ***(494)***
Lane, Oregon, County of ***(495)***
Law Enforcement Alliance of America ***(496)***
League of California Cities ***(497)***
Lee & Smith P.C. *(118)*
Legal Action Center of the City of New York, Inc. ***(497)***
The Legislative Strategies Group, LLC *(118)*
Jack D.P. Lichtenstein *(120)*
Lindesmith Center - Drug Policy Foundation ***(500)***
Law Office of Zel E. Lipsen *(120)*
Los Angeles, California, County of ***(504)***
Loyola University ***(505)***
Lubbock, Texas, City of ***(505)***
Lumbermens Mutual Casualty Co. ***(505)***
Lutheran Office for Governmental Affairs/Evangelical Lutheran Church in America ***(506)***
Macon, City of ***(507)***
Madison County Commission ***(507)***
Madison Government Affairs *(123)*
Manatt, Phelps & Phillips, LLP *(123)*
MARC Associates, Inc. *(124)*
Marin, California, County of ***(510)***
MasterCard Internat'l ***(513)***
Maximum Information Technology Inc. ***(513)***
Virginia M. Mayer *(126)*
Barbara T. McCall Associates *(127)*
McDermott, Will and Emery *(128)*
Mehl, Griffin & Bartek Ltd. *(132)*
Metropolitan King County Council ***(520)***
Meyers & Associates *(133)*
Miami Beach, Florida, City of ***(521)***
Miami-Dade Community College ***(521)***
Milwaukee, City of ***(524)***
Milwaukee, Wisconsin, County of ***(524)***
Minority Males Consortium ***(525)***
Mitretek Systems ***(526)***
Mobile, Alabama, City of ***(527)***
Mooresville, North Carolina, Town of ***(529)***
Morgan, Lewis & Bockius LLP *(136)*
Kay Allan Morrell, Attorney-at-Law *(137)*
Morrison & Foerster LLP *(137)*
Mortgage Bankers Ass'n of America ***(530)***
Mullenholz, Brimsek & Belair *(138)*
Muncie, Indiana, City of (Delaware County) ***(532)***
Murray, Scheer, Montgomery, Tapia & O'Donnell *(139)*
Napster, Inc. ***(534)***
Nat'l Abortion Federation ***(535)***
Nat'l Alliance for Hispanic Health ***(536)***
Nat'l Alliance for the Mentally Ill ***(536)***
Nat'l Alliance of Sexual Assault Coalitions ***(537)***
Nat'l Ass'n of Assistant United States Attorneys ***(539)***
Nat'l Ass'n of Criminal Defense Lawyers ***(542)***
Nat'l Ass'n of Developmental Disabilities Councils ***(542)***
Nat'l Ass'n of Independent Insurers ***(544)***
Nat'l Ass'n of Negro Business & Professional Women's Clubs, Inc. ***(546)***
Nat'l Ass'n of Police Organizations ***(546)***
Nat'l Ass'n of Recording Merchandisers ***(548)***
Nat'l Ass'n of Securities and Commercial Law Attorneys ***(549)***
Nat'l Ass'n of Social Workers ***(549)***
Nat'l Ass'n of Water Companies ***(551)***
Nat'l Assembly of Health and Human Service Organizations ***(551)***
Nat'l Beer Wholesalers Ass'n ***(552)***
Nat'l Border Patrol Council ***(553)***
Nat'l Burglar and Fire Alarm Ass'n ***(553)***
Nat'l Center for Neighborhood Enterprise ***(555)***
Nat'l Coalition to Abolish the Death Penalty ***(557)***
Nat'l Community Education Ass'n ***(558)***
Nat'l Consumers League ***(558)***
Nat'l Council of Investigative and Security Services Inc. ***(560)***
Nat'l Council of Juvenile and Family Court Judges ***(560)***
Nat'l Court Reporters Ass'n ***(561)***
Nat'l Criminal Justice Ass'n ***(561)***
Nat'l Defense Industrial Ass'n ***(561)***
Nat'l District Attorneys Ass'n ***(562)***
Nat'l Education Ass'n of the U.S. ***(562)***
Nat'l Field Selling Ass'n ***(564)***
Nat'l Law Enforcement Council ***(569)***
Nat'l Legal Aid and Defender Ass'n ***(570)***
Nat'l Mental Health Ass'n ***(571)***
Nat'l Mining Ass'n ***(571)***
Nat'l Network to End Domestic Violence ***(572)***
Nat'l Organization for Victim Assistance ***(572)***
Nat'l Rifle Ass'n of America ***(576)***
Nat'l Sheriffs' Ass'n ***(578)***
Nat'l Strategy Information Center ***(579)***
Nat'l Whistleblower Center ***(581)***
Navajo Nation ***(582)***
NetCoalition.Com ***(584)***
Newark, New Jersey, City of ***(588)***
Nixon Peabody LLP *(142)*
Nogales, Arizona, City of ***(591)***
Norfolk, Virginia, City of ***(591)***
North American Communications Corp. ***(592)***
North Carolina, Washington Office of the State of ***(593)***
NYSCOPBA - New York State Correctional Officers & Police Benevolent Ass'n ***(597)***
Oakley, California, City of ***(598)***
O'Connor & Hannan, L.L.P. *(144)*
Oklahoma City, Oklahoma, City of ***(599)***
O'Neill, Athy & Casey, P.C. *(147)*
Operations Security Professionals Soc. ***(601)***
Orphan Medical, Inc. ***(604)***
OSI Systems, Inc. ***(604)***
Palo Alto, California, City of ***(607)***
Parry, Romani, DeConcini & Symms *(149)*
Pasadena, California, City of ***(609)***
Patton Boggs, LLP *(150)*
PE Biosystems ***(610)***
People for the American Way ***(612)***
Peoria, Arizona, City of ***(612)***
PerkinElmer Detection Systems ***(612)***
Peyser Associates, Inc. *(155)*
Philadelphia, Pennsylvania, City of ***(615)***
Phoenix, Arizona, City of ***(616)***
Plano, Texas, City of ***(619)***
The PMA Group *(156)*
Police Executive Research Forum ***(620)***
Police Foundation ***(620)***
Policy Directions, Inc. *(158)*
Portland, Oregon, City of ***(621)***
Prince George's, Maryland, County of ***(624)***
The Procter & Gamble Company ***(625)***
Professional Bail Agents of the United States ***(625)***
Public Citizen, Inc. ***(628)***
Public Strategies, Inc. *(165)*
Public/Private Ventures ***(629)***
Qwest Communications ***(631)***
Rafael U.S.A., Inc. ***(632)***
Recording Industry Ass'n of America ***(634)***
Reed, Smith, LLP *(167)*
Rhoads Group *(168)*
Roseville, California, City of ***(642)***
RPM, Inc. ***(643)***
Saf T Hammer ***(645)***
Saf T Lok, Inc. ***(645)***
Safari Club Internat'l ***(645)***
Sagamore Associates, Inc. *(174)*
Sagem Morpho ***(646)***
Salinas, California, City of ***(646)***
Salt Lake City Olympic Organizing Committee ***(646)***
San Jose, California, City of ***(648)***
Santa Ana, California, City of ***(649)***
SBC Communications Inc. ***(650)***
Scottsdale, Arizona, City of ***(652)***
SEARCH Group, Inc. ***(653)***
Seattle, Washington, City of ***(653)***
Security Companies Organized for Legislative Action ***(654)***
Security Industry Ass'n ***(654)***
Security on Campus, Inc. ***(654)***
Sellery Associates, Inc. *(177)*
Sensor Technologies and Systems Inc. ***(655)***
Shaw Pittman *(177)*
Shelby, Tennessee, County of ***(657)***
Sheriff Jefferson Parrish, Louisiana ***(657)***
Mary Katherine Shilton *(180)*
Eric Shulman & Associates *(180)*
Sierra Madre, California, City of ***(658)***
Simon and Co., Inc. *(181)*
SM&A ***(661)***
Smith Alling Lane, P.S. *(183)*
Smith Dawson & Andrews, Inc. *(183)*
Solutia Inc. ***(665)***
SOS Interpreting Ltd. ***(666)***
State Guard Ass'n of the U.S. ***(673)***
Stone Investments, Inc. ***(675)***
Stuntz, Davis & Staffier, P.C. *(190)*
Taxpayers Against Fraud, The False Claims Legal Center ***(681)***
Teicher Consulting and Representation *(193)*
Texaco Group Inc. ***(684)***
Texas A&M Research Foundation ***(684)***
Thelen Reid & Priest LLP *(193)*
Timmons and Co., Inc. *(195)*
Traditional Values Coalition ***(689)***
Tulare, California, County of ***(694)***
David Turch & Associates *(197)*
Unilever United States, Inc. ***(699)***
United Methodist Church General Board of Church and Society ***(702)***
United States Telecom Ass'n ***(704)***
Utah State University ***(710)***
Van Scoyoc Associates, Inc. *(200)*
Venable *(201)*
Veridian Corp. ***(712)***
Vietnam Veterans of America Foundation ***(715)***
Viohl and Associates, Inc. *(205)*
Wackenhut Corrections Corp. ***(718)***
Wackenhut Services, Inc. ***(718)***
Wake, North Carolina, County of ***(718)***
Washington Ass'n of Sheriffs and Police Chiefs ***(719)***
Waterman & Associates *(210)*
Susan J. White & Associates *(212)*
Wine Institute ***(728)***
Winston & Strawn *(218)*
Wise & Associates *(220)*
Women Officials in NACo ***(729)***
Women's Policy, Inc. ***(729)***
World Service Authority ***(731)***
Zuckerman Spaeder L.L.P. *(221)*

Manufacturing (MAN)

3Com Corp. ***(223)***
AAI Corp. ***(224)***
Abbott Laboratories ***(225)***
Advanced Glassfiber Yarns ***(228)***
The Advocacy Group *(6)*
Aerospace Industries Ass'n of America ***(230)***
AFL-CIO - Maritime Trades Department ***(231)***
Ainslie Associates *(7)*
Air Products and Chemicals, Inc. ***(234)***
Air-Conditioning and Refrigeration Institute ***(234)***
Airbus Industrie of North America, Inc. ***(234)***
Aircraft Electronics Ass'n ***(235)***
Albertine Enterprises, Inc. *(10)*
Alcatel USA ***(237)***
Allegiance Healthcare Corp. ***(239)***
Alliance of Automobile Manufacturers, Inc. ***(240)***

Allison Transmission Division, General Motors Corp. *(241)*
Alston & Bird LLP *(12)*
The Aluminum Ass'n *(242)*
American Ass'n for Laboratory Accreditation *(246)*
American Boiler Manufacturers Ass'n *(251)*
American Continental Group, Inc. *(12)*
American Electronics Ass'n *(257)*
American Foundrymen's Soc. *(260)*
American Free Trade Ass'n *(260)*
American Frozen Food Institute *(260)*
American Furniture Manufacturers Ass'n *(260)*
American Gear Manufacturers Ass'n *(261)*
American Institute of Chemical Engineers *(264)*
American Paper Machinery Ass'n *(269)*
American Pipe Fittings Ass'n *(270)*
American Portland Cement Alliance *(270)*
American Systems Internat'l Corp. *(278)*
American Systems Internat'l Corp. *(13)*
American Teleservices Ass'n *(279)*
American Wood Preservers Institute *(280)*
Americans for Equitable Climate Solutions *(281)*
Amgen *(282)*
Anheuser-Busch Cos., Inc. *(284)*
Aniline Ass'n, Inc. *(284)*
Arent Fox Kintner Plotkin & Kahn, PLLC *(14)*
Armstrong Laser Technology *(289)*
Wayne Arny & Assoc. *(16)*
James Nicholas Ashmore & Associates *(18)*
Ass'n and Soc. Management Internat'l Inc. *(18)*
The Ass'n For Manufacturing Technology (AMT) *(292)*
Ass'n of Banks in Insurance *(294)*
Ass'n of Home Appliance Manufacturers *(296)*
Ass'n of Independent Corrugated Converters *(296)*
Ass'n of Internat'l Automobile Manufacturers *(296)*
Associated Industries of Massachusetts *(300)*
Automotive Aftermarket Industry Ass'n *(303)*
Automotive Parts and Service Alliance *(303)*
Automotive Parts Rebuilders Ass'n *(304)*
C. Baker Consulting Inc. *(20)*
The Laurin Baker Group *(20)*
Barr Laboratories *(308)*
Battelle Memorial Institute *(309)*
Battelle Memorial Labs *(309)*
Baxter Healthcare Corp. *(309)*
Beretta U.S.A. Corp. *(311)*
Big Sky Consulting, Inc. *(27)*
BKSH & Associates *(28)*
Richard W. Bliss *(29)*
Bloomfield Associates, Inc. *(29)*
BMW Manufacturing Corp. *(316)*
The Boeing Co. *(316)*
Brick Industry Ass'n *(320)*
Bridgestone/Firestone, Inc. *(320)*
Brother Internat'l Co. *(322)*
Brownstein Hyatt & Farber, P.C. *(33)*
BSMG Worldwide *(34)*
Burdeshaw Associates, Ltd. *(34)*
Burlington Northern Santa Fe Railway *(324)*
Capital Equipment Legislative Coalition *(330)*
Capitol Hill Advocates *(39)*
Caraustar *(331)*
Cargill, Inc. *(331)*
CaseNewHolland Inc. *(333)*
Caterpillar Inc. *(333)*
Celanese Government Relations Office *(334)*
CELOTEX *(335)*
CEMEX USA *(335)*
Central American Bank of Economic Integration *(338)*
Chamber of Commerce of the U.S.A. *(340)*
Chamberlain Manufacturing Corp. *(341)*
Circuit Services, Inc. *(347)*
Cisco Systems Inc. *(347)*
Cleveland Advanced Manufacturing Program *(350)*
Cold Finished Steel Bar Institute *(357)*
Collier Shannon Scott, PLLC *(48)*
Colling Swift & Hynes *(49)*
Colorado River Indian Tribes *(358)*
Compass Internat'l Inc. *(363)*
Computing Technology Industry Ass'n *(364)*
Congressional Economic Leadership Institute *(366)*
Construction Industry Manufacturers Ass'n *(368)*
Consumer Electronics Ass'n *(369)*
Consumer Federation of America *(369)*
Consumer Healthcare Products Ass'n *(369)*
Copper and Brass Fabricators Council *(371)*
CSA America, Inc. *(379)*
Cummins-Allison Corp. *(380)*
DaimlerChrysler Corp. *(381)*
Bob Davis & Associates *(57)*
Dickstein Shapiro Morin & Oshinsky LLP *(61)*
R. R. Donnelley & Sons *(391)*
DuPont *(393)*
Dykema Gossett PLLC *(69)*
The Macon Edwards Co. *(71)*
Elan Pharmaceutical Research Corp. *(399)*
Elbet Forth Worth *(399)*
Engineered Arresting Systems Corp. *(403)*
Ervin Technical Associates, Inc. (ETA) *(73)*
Espey Manufacturing and Electronics *(407)*
Ethylene Oxide Sterilization Ass'n, Inc. *(407)*
ExtrudeHone Corp. *(409)*
F&T Network, Inc. *(74)*
Federal Procurement Consultants *(414)*
The Fertilizer Institute *(415)*
FLIR Systems, Inc. *(419)*
FMC Corp. *(420)*
FN Herstal, USA *(421)*
Fontheim Internat'l *(421)*
Forster & Associates *(79)*
Douglas Ward Freitag *(79)*
French & Company *(79)*
GAF Corp. *(428)*
Garden State Paper Co., Inc. *(429)*
Gas Appliance Manufacturers Ass'n *(429)*
Gateway, Inc. *(430)*
Genentech, Inc. *(431)*
General Aviation Manufacturers Ass'n *(431)*
General Dynamics Corp. *(431)*
General Electric Co. *(432)*
General Motors Corp. *(432)*
Global USA, Inc. *(83)*
B. F. Goodrich Co. *(437)*
Goodstein & Associates *(84)*
Goodyear Tire and Rubber Co. *(437)*
Jay Grant & Associates *(85)*
Greenberg Traurig, LLP *(86)*
Griffin, Johnson, Dover & Stewart *(87)*
Hadley & McKenna *(89)*
Haley and Associates *(90)*
Charles A. Hamilton Associates LLC *(91)*
Hitachi, Ltd. *(450)*
Hogan & Hartson L.L.P. *(96)*
Holland & Knight LLP *(98)*
Peter Homer *(99)*
Honda North America, Inc. *(451)*
Honeywell Internat'l, Inc. *(452)*
Law Offices of Irene E. Howie *(100)*
Illinois Tool Works *(458)*
Independent Office Products and Furniture Dealers Ass'n *(459)*
Industrial Fabrics Ass'n Internat'l *(461)*
Industrial Fasteners Institute *(461)*
Ingersoll-Rand Co. *(462)*
Inter-Associates, Inc. *(466)*
Internat'l Ass'n of Machinists and Aerospace Workers *(468)*
Internat'l Biometric Industry Ass'n *(468)*
Internat'l Brotherhood of Electrical Workers *(469)*
Internat'l Cadmium Ass'n *(469)*
Internat'l Federation of Professional and Technical Engineers *(471)*
Internat'l Mass Retailers Ass'n *(473)*
Internat'l Paper *(473)*
Internat'l Safety Equipment Ass'n (ISEA) *(474)*
Internat'l Sign Ass'n *(474)*
ITRON, Inc. *(480)*
Japan External Trade Organization (JETRO) *(481)*
Jarboe & Associates *(105)*
JBC Internat'l *(105)*
JDA Aviation Technology Systems *(482)*
Jefferson Government Relations, L.L.C. *(106)*
Kaiser Aluminum & Chemical Corp. *(485)*
Kellogg Co. *(487)*
Kelly and Associates, Inc. *(111)*
The Kemper Co. *(111)*
Kimberly-Clark Corp. *(489)*
The Kinetics Group *(489)*
KOSA *(491)*
Lafarge Corp. *(494)*
Lee Lane *(116)*
Lawyers for Civil Justice *(496)*
Eli Lilly and Co. *(499)*
Law Office of Zel E. Lipsen *(120)*
Lockheed Martin Corp. *(501)*
Logis-Tech, Inc. *(503)*
Louisiana Center for Manufacturing Sciences *(504)*
Lyondell Chemical Co. *(506)*
MacAndrews & Forbes Holdings, Inc. *(506)*
Machinery Dealers Nat'l Ass'n *(506)*
Management Options, Inc. *(123)*
Manufacturers Alliance/MAPI Inc. *(509)*
Manufacturers Standardization Soc. of the Valve and Fitting Industry, Inc. *(509)*
Marconi plc *(509)*
Martin-Baker Aircraft Co., Ltd. *(511)*
Masaoka & Associates, Inc. *(125)*
Maytag Corp. *(513)*
Mazak Corp. & Mazak Sales and Service, Inc. *(513)*
Charlie McBride Associates, Inc. *(127)*
Bettie McCarthy and Associates *(127)*
McGuiness Norris & Williams, LLP *(130)*
McIntyre Law Firm, PLLC *(130)*
McKenna & Cuneo, L.L.P. *(131)*
McLeod, Watkinson & Miller *(131)*
The Mead Corp. *(515)*
Meat Industry Suppliers Ass'n *(515)*
Merck & Co. *(518)*
G.L. Merritt & Associates, Inc. *(132)*
Metal Building Manufacturers Ass'n *(519)*
Metal Finishing Suppliers Ass'n *(519)*
Meyers & Associates *(133)*
Michelin North America *(522)*
Michigan Manufacturing Technology Center *(522)*
Mitsubishi Research Institute *(526)*
The Modernization Forum *(527)*
Molecular BioSystems, Inc. *(527)*
Mort Community College *(530)*
The MWW Group *(140)*
Nat'l Ass'n of Manufacturers *(545)*
Nat'l Ass'n of Negro Business & Professional Women's Clubs, Inc. *(546)*
Nat'l Ass'n of Uniform Manufacturers and Distributors *(551)*
Nat'l Center for Manufacturing Sciences *(555)*
Nat'l Concrete Masonry Ass'n *(558)*
Nat'l Consumers League *(558)*
Nat'l Electrical Manufacturers Ass'n *(562)*
Nat'l Fastener Distributors Ass'n *(564)*
Nat'l Marine Manufacturers Ass'n *(570)*
Nat'l Mining Ass'n *(571)*
Nat'l Ready Mixed Concrete Ass'n *(575)*
Nat'l Spa and Pool Institute *(578)*
NAVCOM Systems, Inc. *(583)*
Navy Joining Center *(583)*
New Mexico State Office of Research & Development *(586)*
New Mexico State University, Department of Engineering *(586)*
The Newark Group *(588)*
Newport News Shipbuilding Inc. *(588)*
Nissan North America Inc. *(590)*
Nitrobenzene Ass'n *(590)*
Noesis Inc. *(590)*
The Nordam Group *(591)*
North American Steel Framing Alliance *(592)*
Northeast-Midwest Institute *(594)*
Northrop Grumman Corp. *(594)*
The OB-C Group, LLC *(143)*
Oce-USA, Inc. *(598)*
O'Connor & Hannan, L.L.P. *(144)*
Oppenheimer Wolff & Donnelly LLP *(147)*
Oshkosh Truck Corp. *(604)*
Owens-Illinois, Inc. *(605)*
PACCAR, Inc. *(605)*
Pacquing Consulting Inc. *(148)*
Paper Recycling Coalition *(607)*

Parry, Romani, DeConcini & Symms *(149)*
Patton Boggs, LLP *(150)*
PDA ***(610)***
Peduzzi Associates, Ltd. *(154)*
Pennsylvania Nat'l Guard Ass'n ***(611)***
Philip Morris Management Corp. ***(615)***
Philips Electronics North America Corp. ***(616)***
Phillips Petroleum Co. ***(616)***
Plasma-Therm, Inc. ***(619)***
The Plexus Consulting Group *(156)*
PMSC-Irby Steel ***(619)***
Polaris Industries ***(620)***
The Policy Group *(159)*
Potomac Strategies Internat'l LLC *(160)*
Precision Lift ***(623)***
Printing Industries of America ***(624)***
Public Strategies, Inc. *(165)*
PulseTech Products Corp. ***(630)***
Quebec Lumber Manufacturers Ass'n ***(630)***
Raytheon Co. ***(633)***
Recreation Vehicle Ass'n ***(634)***
Reed, Smith, LLP *(167)*
Rock-Tenn Co. ***(641)***
Rockwell Collins ***(641)***
Rooney Group Internat'l, Inc. *(171)*
Rubber Manufacturers Ass'n ***(643)***
Ryan, Phillips, Utrecht & MacKinnon *(173)*
SABIC Americas, Inc. ***(644)***
Sappi Fine Paper NA ***(649)***
Science and Engineering Associates, Inc. ***(652)***
Sellery Associates, Inc. *(177)*
Shaw Group ***(657)***
Siemens Corp. ***(658)***
Silver Users Ass'n ***(659)***
Singapore Technologies, Inc. ***(659)***
Skyhook Technologies, Inc. ***(660)***
Smith & Harroff, Inc. *(182)*
Smurfit Stone Container Corp. ***(662)***
The Solomon Group, LLC *(185)*
Sonnenschein, Nath & Rosenthal *(185)*
South Carolina Nat'l Guard Ass'n ***(666)***
Springs Industries, Inc. ***(671)***
St. Jude Medical, Inc. ***(671)***
The Stanley Works ***(672)***
Steel Manufacturers Ass'n ***(674)***
Stewart & Stevenson Services, Inc. ***(674)***
Kenneth F. Stinger *(189)*
Styrene Information and Research Center ***(676)***
Swidler Berlin Shereff Friedman, LLP *(191)*
Synthetic Organic Chemical Manufacturers Ass'n ***(679)***
T & N Industries ***(679)***
Tecumseh Products Co. ***(682)***
Tetrahydrofuran Task Force ***(684)***
Tett Enterprises ***(684)***
Texaco Group Inc. ***(684)***
Textron Inc. ***(685)***
Thompson Coburn LLP *(194)*
Thomson Consumer Electronics, Inc. ***(686)***
Tire Ass'n of North America ***(687)***
Toyota Motor Manufacturing North America ***(689)***
Toyota Motor North America, U.S.A., Inc. ***(689)***
Transnat'l Development Consortium ***(690)***
Turkish Industrialists and Businessmen's Ass'n (TUSIAD) ***(694)***
Tyco Internat'l (US), Inc. ***(695)***
Tyson's Governmental Sales, LLC ***(695)***
Ungaretti & Harris *(197)*
United Egg Ass'n ***(701)***
United Egg Producers ***(701)***
United Methodist Church General Board of Church and Society ***(702)***
United Motorcoach Ass'n ***(702)***
United States Business and Industry Council ***(703)***
Valve Manufacturers Ass'n of America ***(711)***
Van Ness Feldman, P.C. *(199)*
Van Scoyoc Associates, Inc. *(200)*
Venable *(201)*
Verner, Liipfert, Bernhard, McPherson and Hand, Chartered *(202)*
Vision Technologies, Inc. ***(716)***
R. Duffy Wall and Associates *(205)*
Wallcovering Ass'n ***(718)***
Washington Alliance Group, Inc. *(206)*
Washington Aviation Group *(206)*
Washington Council Ernst & Young *(206)*
The Washington Group *(208)*
Water Systems Council ***(721)***
Waterman & Associates *(210)*
Wheeling Pittsburgh Steel Corp. ***(726)***
White Pigeon Paper Co. ***(726)***
William F. Whitsitt Policy and Government Affairs *(213)*
The Wigglesworth Co. *(214)*
Kathleen Winn & Associates, Inc. *(218)*
Xerox Corp. ***(732)***

Marine/Maritime/Boating/Fisheries (MAR)

3001, Inc. ***(223)***
The Accord Group *(5)*
Adams and Reese LLP *(5)*
AFL-CIO (American Federation of Labor and Congress of Industrial Organizations) ***(231)***
AFL-CIO Maritime Committee ***(231)***
AFL-CIO - Maritime Trades Department ***(231)***
AFL-CIO - Transportation Trades Department ***(231)***
Akin, Gump, Strauss, Hauer & Feld, L.L.P. *(8)*
Alaska Eskimo Whaling Commission ***(236)***
Alaska Ocean Seafoods L.P. ***(236)***
Alcalde & Fay *(10)*
Alcoa Inc. ***(237)***
Aleutian Pribilof Islands Community Development Ass'n ***(238)***
Alliance of Marine Mammal Parks and Aquariums ***(240)***
Almont Shipping Terminals ***(242)***
Alvarado & Gerken *(12)*
Amalgamated Transit Union ***(242)***
American Ass'n of Port Authorities ***(249)***
American Bureau of Shipping ***(251)***
American Classic Voyages Co. ***(253)***
American Fish Spotters Ass'n ***(259)***
American Gaming Ass'n ***(260)***
American Great Lakes Ports ***(261)***
American Institute for Shippers' Ass'ns ***(264)***
American Internat'l Freight Ass'n ***(265)***
American Maritime Congress ***(267)***
American Maritime Officers Service ***(267)***
American Museum of Natural History ***(268)***
American Oceans Campaign ***(269)***
American Petroleum Institute ***(269)***
American Seafoods Inc. ***(273)***
American Soc. of Travel Agents ***(277)***
American Sportfishing Ass'n ***(278)***
American Waterways Operators ***(280)***
Americans for Tax Reform ***(282)***
Anheuser-Busch Cos., Inc. ***(284)***
Ann Eppard Associates, Ltd. ***(284)***
APCO Worldwide *(14)*
Apex Marine Ship Management Co. LLC ***(286)***
APL Limited ***(286)***
Aquarium of the Pacific ***(287)***
ARCO Products Co. ***(287)***
Ashland Inc. ***(290)***
Ass'n of American Shippers ***(294)***
Atlantic States Marine Fisheries Commission ***(302)***
AUPS/Mo Hussain ***(303)***
Avondale Industries, Inc. ***(305)***
Ball Janik, LLP *(22)*
Barbour Griffith & Rogers, Inc. *(22)*
Bass Enterprises Production Co. ***(308)***
Bender Shipbuilding & Repair Co., Inc. ***(311)***
Billfish Foundation ***(313)***
Blank Rome Comisky & McCauley, LLP *(29)*
BLNG, Inc. ***(315)***
Blue Water Fishermen's Ass'n ***(316)***
The Boat Co. ***(316)***
Boat Owners Ass'n of The United States (BOAT/U.S.) ***(316)***
BP Amoco Corp. ***(319)***
William V. Brierre *(32)*
Brownsville, Texas, Port of ***(322)***
Bruker Meerestechnik GmbH ***(322)***
Brunswick Corp. ***(322)***
Burlington Northern Santa Fe Railway ***(324)***
Cal Dive Internat'l Inc. ***(326)***
Canal Barge Co., Inc. ***(330)***
Cargill, Inc. ***(331)***
Carpi & Clay *(41)*
Carriers Against Harbor Tax ***(332)***
Cascade General, Inc. ***(332)***
Cassidy & Associates, Inc. *(42)*
Center for Marine Conservation ***(337)***
Chamber of Shipping of America ***(341)***
Chesapeake Bay Maritime Museum ***(342)***
Chevron, U.S.A. ***(342)***
CITGO Petroleum Corp. ***(347)***
Coalition for Maritime Education ***(354)***
Coalition of Hawaii Movers ***(355)***
Coalition on the Implementation of the AFA ***(356)***
Coastal Conservation Ass'n ***(356)***
Coastal Transportation Inc. ***(356)***
Colex and Associates *(48)*
Conference of Private Operators for Response Towing ***(366)***
Consumer Federation of America ***(369)***
Contra Costa, California, Tenants of the County of ***(370)***
Cook Inlet Region Inc. ***(371)***
COSCO Americas Inc. ***(373)***
Council of European and Japanese Nat'l Shipowners' Ass'ns ***(375)***
Law Office of C. Deming Cowles *(54)*
Cross Sound Ferry Services, Inc. ***(378)***
Crowley Maritime Corp. ***(379)***
Crystal Cruises ***(379)***
CSX Corp. ***(379)***
CSX Lines LLC ***(379)***
Law Offices of Kevin G. Curtin *(56)*
Davidson & Company, Inc. *(57)*
Bob Davis & Associates *(57)*
Dawson & Associates, Inc. *(59)*
DCH Technology Inc. ***(383)***
Defenders of Wildlife ***(383)***
Glenn Roger Delaney *(60)*
Delaware River and Bay Authority ***(384)***
Delaware River Port Authority ***(384)***
Thomas J. Dennis *(61)*
DeWitt Cos. of Guam and Saipan ***(387)***
Dickstein Shapiro Morin & Oshinsky LLP *(61)*
Dolphin Safe/Fair Trade Campaign ***(390)***
DRAKA USA Corp. ***(392)***
Dredging Contractors of America ***(392)***
The Duberstein Group, Inc. *(65)*
The Dutko Group, Inc. *(68)*
Dyer Ellis & Joseph, P.C. *(68)*
Eckert Seamans Cherin & Mellott, LLC *(70)*
Edison Chouest Offshore, Inc. ***(397)***
Elim, Alaska, City of ***(401)***
Ellicott Internat'l ***(401)***
Engelhard Corp. ***(403)***
Environmental Defense Fund ***(405)***
Ann Eppard Associates, Ltd. *(72)*
Ervin Technical Associates, Inc. (ETA) *(73)*
The Evans Group, Ltd. *(74)*
Everett, Washington, Port of ***(408)***
Exxon Mobil Corp. ***(409)***
Exxon Valdez Oil Spill Litigation Plaintiffs ***(409)***
FastShip, Inc. ***(412)***
Fentek Internat'l Pty. Ltd. ***(415)***
Jack Ferguson Associates, Inc. *(75)*
The Ferguson Group, LLC *(76)*
The Fertilizer Institute ***(415)***
Fierce and Isakowitz *(76)*
First American Aircraft Title ***(417)***
First American Bulk Carriers Corp. ***(417)***
First American Title Aircraft ***(417)***
Fisher Consulting *(77)*
Florida State University System ***(420)***
Floyd Associates *(78)*
Forster & Associates *(79)*
Freeport, New York, Village of ***(425)***
John Freshman Associates, Inc. *(79)*
Friede, Goldman, & Halter, Inc. ***(426)***
Fruit Shippers Ltd. ***(427)***
G.R. Services *(80)*
Garden State Seafood Ass'n ***(429)***
Garvey, Schubert & Barer *(81)*
GCI-Wisconsin ***(430)***
General Category Tuna Ass'n ***(431)***
General Motors Corp. ***(432)***
General Ore Internat'l Corp. Ltd. ***(433)***

Great Lakes Dredge & Dock *(439)*
Greenbrier Companies *(440)*
Griffin, Johnson, Dover & Stewart *(87)*
Grove, Jaskiewicz, and Cobert *(88)*
John C. Grzebien *(89)*
Guam, Washington Office of the Governor *(442)*
Guinea, Secretary General of the Presidency of the Republic of *(442)*
Harbor Branch Institute *(444)*
John D. Hardy *(91)*
Heerema Marine Contractors Nederland B.V. *(448)*
Hogan & Hartson L.L.P. *(96)*
Hood River, Oregon, Port of *(452)*
Hornblower Marine Services, Inc. *(452)*
Howland Hook Container Terminal Inc. *(454)*
R. J. Hudson Associates *(101)*
Humane Soc. of the United States *(455)*
Hunton & Williams *(101)*
Hvide Marine Inc. *(456)*
Icicle Seafoods, Inc. *(457)*
Ingram Barge Company *(462)*
Intermare Navigation SA *(466)*
Intermodal Ass'n of North America *(467)*
Intermountain Forest Industry Ass'n *(467)*
Internat'l Ass'n of Drilling Contractors *(467)*
Internat'l Ass'n of Fish and Wildlife Agencies *(468)*
Internat'l Ass'n of Machinists and Aerospace Workers *(468)*
Internat'l Brotherhood of Boilermakers, Iron Shipbuilders, Blacksmiths, Forgers and Helpers *(469)*
Internat'l Brotherhood of Electrical Workers *(469)*
Internat'l Brotherhood of Teamsters *(469)*
Internat'l Council of Cruise Lines *(470)*
Internat'l Federation of Professional and Technical Engineers *(471)*
Internat'l Group of P&I Clubs *(472)*
Internat'l Longshore and Warehouse Union *(473)*
Internat'l Paint Inc. *(473)*
Internat'l Shipholding Corp. *(474)*
Internat'l Union of Painters and Allied Trades *(476)*
Island Express Boat Lines Ltd. *(479)*
JCP Associates *(105)*
Jeppesen Sanderson, Inc. *(482)*
JM Family Enterprises *(483)*
JMD Associates, Inc. *(107)*
Jones, Walker, Waechter, Poitevent, Carrere & Denegre, L.L.P. *(108)*
Jorden Burt LLP *(109)*
Juneau, Alaska, City of *(485)*
"K" Line America, Inc. *(485)*
Kaiser Aluminum & Chemical Corp. *(485)*
Kawasaki Motors Corp., USA *(487)*
The Kemper Co. *(111)*
Kent & O'Connor, Inc. *(112)*
Kerrigan & Associates, Inc. *(112)*
Ketchikan Gateway Borough *(488)*
Kimberly Consulting, LLC *(113)*
Kirby Corp./Dixie Carriers *(490)*
Kongsberg Simrad *(491)*
Kvaerner Shipholding, Inc. *(492)*
Kvaerner Philadelphia Shipyard Inc. *(492)*
Labor Management Maritime Committee, Inc. *(493)*
Jessica S. Lefevre *(118)*
Legislative Solutions *(118)*
Liberty Maritime Co. *(499)*
Lister Bolt & Chain Co. *(500)*
The Livingston Group, LLC *(120)*
Lockheed Martin Corp. *(501)*
Los Angeles, California, County of *(504)*
Louis Dreyfus Corporation *(504)*
Lovelace Respiratory Research Institute *(504)*
Lunds Fisheries, Inc. *(505)*
Madison Government Affairs *(123)*
Maersk Inc. *(507)*
Gerald A. Malia *(123)*
Marine Capital Management, LLC *(510)*
Marine Engineers Beneficial Ass'n (District No. 1 - PCD) *(510)*
Marine Mammal Coalition *(510)*
Marine Technology Soc. *(510)*
Marinette Marine Corp. *(510)*
Maritime Exchange for the Delaware River and Bay *(510)*
Maritime Institute for Research and Industrial Development *(510)*
Maritime Investment Corp. *(510)*
Marlowe and Co. *(125)*
Matson Navigation Co. *(513)*
Alan Mauk Associates, Ltd. *(126)*
Charlie McBride Associates, Inc. *(127)*
McDermott Internat'l, Inc./Babcock & Wilcox *(514)*
McGlotten & Jarvis *(129)*
Diane McRee Associates *(131)*
The Metropolitan Water District of Southern California *(521)*
Meyers & Associates *(133)*
Denny Miller McBee Associates *(134)*
Mirage Resorts, Inc. *(525)*
Mitsubishi Corp. *(526)*
MOTE Marine Lab *(530)*
Motorcycle Industry Council *(531)*
Murray, Scheer, Montgomery, Tapia & O'Donnell *(139)*
Nat'l Ass'n of Charterboat Operators (NACO) *(540)*
Nat'l Ass'n of RV Parks and Campgrounds *(548)*
Nat'l Customs Brokers and Forwarders Ass'n of America *(561)*
Nat'l Fisheries Institute *(564)*
Nat'l Hydropower Ass'n *(567)*
Nat'l Marine Manufacturers Ass'n *(570)*
Nat'l Mining Ass'n *(571)*
Nat'l Ocean Industries Ass'n *(572)*
Nat'l Retail Federation *(576)*
Nat'l Taxpayers Union *(579)*
Nat'l Turkey Federation *(580)*
Nat'l Waterways Conference, Inc. *(581)*
Naval Reserve Ass'n *(582)*
Navigational Electronic Chart Systems Ass'n (NECSA) *(583)*
Navy League of the United States *(583)*
New England Aquarium *(585)*
New Orleans, Louisiana, Port of *(586)*
New York University *(588)*
Newport News Shipbuilding Inc. *(588)*
Nippon Yusen Kaisha (NYK) Line *(590)*
Norfolk Southern Corp. *(591)*
North American Grain Export Ass'n, Inc. *(592)*
North American Shipbuilding *(592)*
North Slope Borough, Alaska *(593)*
Northeast-Midwest Institute *(594)*
Northland Holdings, Inc. *(594)*
Northrop Grumman Corp. *(594)*
Norwegian Cruise Line *(596)*
The OB-C Group, LLC *(143)*
O'Brien, Klink & Associates *(144)*
Ocean Carriers Working Group *(598)*
Ocean Services *(598)*
Oceanside, California, City of *(598)*
O'Connor & Hannan, L.L.P. *(144)*
Offshore Rig Museum, Inc. *(599)*
Oxnard Harbor District *(605)*
PACE-CAPSTONE *(148)*
Pacific Maritime Ass'n *(605)*
Pacific Seafood Processors Ass'n *(606)*
John M. Palatiello & Associates *(148)*
Parsons Brinckerhoff Inc. *(608)*
Passenger Vessel Ass'n *(609)*
Patton Boggs, LLP *(150)*
Perkins Coie LLP *(154)*
Perry Institute for Marine Science *(612)*
Personal Watercraft Industry Ass'n *(613)*
PetrolRem, Inc. *(613)*
Philadelphia Industrial Development Corp. *(615)*
Pilots' Ass'n of the Bay and River Delaware *(617)*
Port of Lake Charles *(621)*
Port of San Diego *(621)*
Potomac Group *(160)*
Preston Gates Ellis & Rouvelas Meeds LLP *(162)*
Project ACTA *(626)*
Proteus Co. *(627)*
R.M.S. Titanic, Inc. *(632)*
Rafael U.S.A., Inc. *(632)*
Renewable Natural Resources Foundation *(637)*
Robertson, Monagle & Eastaugh *(170)*
Robins, Kaplan, Miller & Ciresi L.L.P. *(170)*
Rohm and Haas Co. *(642)*
Rolls-Royce North America Inc. *(642)*
Ryan, Phillips, Utrecht & MacKinnon *(173)*
Saltchuk Resources, Inc. *(646)*
San Francisco Bar Pilots Ass'n *(648)*
Sargeant Marine, Inc. *(650)*
Schmeltzer, Aptaker & Shepard, P.C. *(176)*
Schnader Harrison Segal & Lewis LLP *(176)*
Scientific Fishery Systems, Inc. *(652)*
Sea Bridge Internat'l LLC *(653)*
Sea Containers America, Inc. *(653)*
Sea Grant Ass'n *(653)*
Sea Ventures Inc. *(653)*
Seaboard Corp. *(653)*
Seafarers Internat'l Union of North America *(653)*
Seafarers Mobilization Action Research Team *(653)*
Seafreeze *(653)*
Sears, Roebuck and Co. *(653)*
Seattle, Washington, Port of *(653)*
Sher & Blackwell *(179)*
SISCORP *(181)*
E. Del Smith and Co. *(183)*
The Smith-Free Group *(184)*
The Solomon Group, LLC *(185)*
Southeast Alaska Seiners Ass'n *(667)*
St. Bernard Port, Harbor and Terminal District *(671)*
St. Lawrence Seaway Pilots Ass'n *(671)*
St. Paul, Alaska, City of *(672)*
Strategic Horizons Advisors, L.L.C. *(189)*
Stuyvesant Dredging Co. *(676)*
Tacoma, Washington, Port of *(680)*
Tate-LeMunyon, LLC *(192)*
TECO Transport Corp. *(682)*
Teicher Consulting and Representation *(193)*
Texas A&M Research Foundation *(684)*
Thelen Reid & Priest LLP *(193)*
Thompson Coburn LLP *(194)*
The Title XI Coalition *(687)*
Trans-Ona S.A.M.C.I.F. *(689)*
TransNat'l Business Development Corp. *(690)*
TransNat'l Business Development Corp. *(196)*
Transpacific Stabilization Agreement *(690)*
Transportation Institute *(690)*
Trident Seafood Corp. *(692)*
The Trump Organization *(693)*
Christopher A.G. Tulou *(196)*
U.S. Oil and Gas Ass'n *(696)*
Unideal Navitankers *(698)*
United Catcher Boats *(700)*
United States Maritime Coalition *(703)*
United States Tuna Foundation *(704)*
University of Medicine and Dentistry of New Jersey *(706)*
University of Miami *(706)*
University of South Florida Research Foundation *(707)*
University of Southern Mississippi *(707)*
University of Tulsa *(708)*
University of Virginia *(708)*
Van Ness Feldman, P.C. *(199)*
Van Ommeren Shipping (USA), Inc. *(711)*
Washington Policy Associates, Inc. *(209)*
Washington, Department of Transportation of the State of *(721)*
Waterman Steamship Co. *(721)*
WESCAM *(723)*
Western Great Lakes Pilots Ass'n *(724)*
Wheat Export Trade Education Committee *(725)*
Williams & Jensen, P.C. *(215)*
Winston & Strawn *(218)*
Woods Hole Steamship Authority *(730)*
World Shipping Council *(731)*
World Wildlife Fund *(731)*
Yellow Corp. *(733)*
Zane & Associates *(221)*

Media (Information/Publishing) (MIA)

Acxiom Corp. *(227)*
Adheris, Inc. *(227)*
Sally L. Albright *(10)*

American Federation of Television and Radio Artists *(259)*
American Historical Ass'n *(262)*
American Library Ass'n *(266)*
American Psychological Ass'n *(271)*
American Psychological Soc. *(271)*
American Soc. for Reproductive Medicine *(275)*
American Teleservices Ass'n *(279)*
AOL Time Warner *(285)*
APCO Worldwide *(14)*
Ass'n of American Publishers *(294)*
Ass'n of Test Publishers *(299)*
Ass'n of University Programs in Health Administration *(299)*
Bertelsmann AG *(312)*
BET Holdings II, Inc. *(312)*
W. Douglas Campbell *(36)*
Center of Concern *(338)*
CESD/WVU *(340)*
Church of Scientology Internat'l *(346)*
Citizens for Public Action on Cholesterol, Inc. *(348)*
Citizens for the Treatment of High Blood Pressure, Inc. *(349)*
Coalition for Brain Injury Research and Services, Inc. *(353)*
Scott Cohen *(48)*
Colombian Coffee Federation *(358)*
Comcast Corp. *(359)*
Computer and Communications Industry Ass'n (CCIA) *(364)*
Consumer Federation of America *(369)*
Coors Brewing Company *(371)*
Cottone and Huggins Group *(53)*
Digital Media Ass'n *(388)*
Directors Guild of America *(389)*
Drinker Biddle & Reath LLP *(65)*
The Duberstein Group, Inc. *(65)*
Dun & Bradstreet *(393)*
The Dutko Group, Inc. *(68)*
Electronic Retailing Ass'n *(401)*
EMI Associates, Ltd. *(71)*
First Amendment Coalition for Expression *(417)*
Gallery Watch *(428)*
Garvey, Schubert & Barer *(81)*
Gateway, Inc. *(430)*
General Conference of Seventh-day Adventists *(431)*
GoTo.com Inc. *(437)*
Greener and Hook, LLC *(87)*
Griffin, Johnson, Dover & Stewart *(87)*
Hale and Dorr LLP *(89)*
Harcourt Inc. *(444)*
Leslie Harris & Associates *(91)*
Health and Medicine Counsel of Washington *(93)*
Health Resource Publishing Co. *(446)*
The Hearst Corp. *(447)*
Hearst-Argyle Television, Inc. *(447)*
HiSynergy Communications, Inc. *(450)*
Cornish F. Hitchcock *(95)*
Holland & Knight LLP *(98)*
The Ickes & Enright Group *(102)*
Information Trust *(462)*
Internat'l Union of Painters and Allied Trades *(476)*
Janus-Merritt Strategies, L.L.C. *(104)*
Kashmiri American Council *(486)*
Kasten & Co. *(110)*
The Michael Lewan Co. *(119)*
Lexis-Nexis *(498)*
Magazine Publishers of America *(507)*
Management Options, Inc. *(123)*
Mayer, Brown & Platt *(126)*
McDermott, Will and Emery *(128)*
McGraw-Hill Cos., The *(514)*
Media Access Project *(516)*
Media Institute *(516)*
Medical Library Ass'n/Ass'n of Academic Health Sciences Library Directors *(516)*
Mercury Group *(132)*
Most Group Limited *(530)*
Nat'l Ass'n of Negro Business & Professional Women's Clubs, Inc. *(546)*
Nat'l Building Museum *(553)*
Nat'l Grain and Feed Ass'n *(566)*
Nat'l Legal Center for the Public Interest *(570)*
Newsbank, Inc. *(589)*
Newspaper Ass'n of America *(589)*
Novell, Inc. *(596)*
Olsson, Frank and Weeda, P.C. *(146)*
Operations Security Professionals Soc. *(601)*
Optical Soc. of America *(601)*
Pacific Islands Washington Office *(148)*
Patton Boggs, LLP *(150)*
Piper Marbury Rudnick & Wolfe LLP *(155)*
PrivacyRight *(624)*
Proskauer Rose LLP *(164)*
Prudential Securities, Inc. *(627)*
Radio-Television News Directors Ass'n *(632)*
Reed-Elsevier Inc. *(635)*
Romyr Associates *(642)*
Ropes & Gray *(171)*
Rowe Signal Media *(643)*
Safe Energy Communication Council *(645)*
Silicon Graphics/SGI *(659)*
Smith Dawson & Andrews, Inc. *(183)*
Strategic Choices, Inc. *(189)*
Tax Analysis *(681)*
Teicher Consulting and Representation *(193)*
Telephone Operators Caucus *(683)*
Teligent, Inc. *(683)*
Thiemann Aitken Vohra & Rutledge, L.L.C. *(194)*
Tribune Co. *(692)*
Van Scoyoc Associates, Inc. *(200)*
VeriSign/Network Solutions, Inc. *(713)*
Washington Pacific Publications, Inc. *(720)*
WESCAM *(723)*
West Group *(723)*
Wiley, Rein & Fielding *(214)*
Willkie Farr & Gallagher *(217)*
Wilmer, Cutler & Pickering *(217)*
Women Officials in NACo *(729)*

Medical/Disease Research/Clinical (MED)

Abbott Laboratories *(225)*
Academic Health Center Coalition *(225)*
Academy of Managed Care Pharmacy *(225)*
Academy of Radiology Research *(226)*
Adams and Reese LLP *(5)*
Michael W. Adcock *(6)*
AdvaMed *(228)*
The Advocacy Group *(6)*
AIDS Action Council *(233)*
AIDS Healthcare Foundation *(233)*
Ainslie Associates *(7)*
Akers Laboratories, Inc. *(235)*
Akin, Gump, Strauss, Hauer & Feld, L.L.P. *(8)*
Aksys, Ltd. *(235)*
Albert Einstein Medical Center *(237)*
Alcon Laboratories *(237)*
Allegiance Healthcare Corp. *(239)*
Alliance Medical Corp. *(240)*
Alpine Group, Inc. *(11)*
Alzheimer's Ass'n *(242)*
AMDeC Policy Group, Inc. *(242)*
America's Blood Centers *(243)*
American Academy of Child and Adolescent Psychiatry *(243)*
American Academy of Dermatology *(243)*
American Academy of Family Physicians *(243)*
American Academy of Ophthamology - Office of Federal Affairs *(244)*
American Academy of Orthopaedic Surgeons *(244)*
American Academy of Pediatrics *(244)*
American Ass'n for Clinical Chemistry, Inc. *(245)*
American Ass'n for Dental Research *(245)*
American Ass'n for Geriatric Psychiatry *(245)*
American Ass'n for Marriage and Family Therapy *(246)*
American Ass'n for the Study of Liver Diseases *(246)*
American Ass'n of Bioanalysts *(246)*
American Ass'n of Colleges of Osteopathic Medicine *(247)*
American Ass'n of Health Plans (AAHP) *(248)*
American Ass'n of Homes and Services for the Aging *(248)*
American Ass'n of Immunologists *(248)*
American Ass'n of Neurological Surgeons/Congress of Neurological Surgeons *(248)*
American Ass'n of Physicians of Indian Origin *(249)*
American Board of Adolescent Psychiatry *(251)*
American Cancer Soc. *(252)*
American Chiropractic Ass'n *(252)*
American College of Cardiology *(253)*
American College of Chest Physicians *(253)*
American College of Clinical Pharmacy *(253)*
American College of Emergency Physicians *(253)*
American College of Obstetricians and Gynecologists *(254)*
American College of Osteopathic Surgeons *(254)*
American College of Physicians-American Soc. of Internal Medicine (ACP-ASIM) *(254)*
American College of Preventive Medicine *(254)*
American College of Surgeons *(254)*
American Dental Education Ass'n *(257)*
American Electronics Ass'n *(257)*
American Federation for Medical Research *(258)*
American Foundation for AIDS Research *(260)*
American Gastroenterological Ass'n *(261)*
American Heart Ass'n *(262)*
American Indian Higher Education Consortium *(263)*
American Institute of Physics *(264)*
American Institute of Ultrasound in Medicine *(264)*
American Legion *(266)*
American Managed Behavioral Healthcare Ass'n *(266)*
American Medical Ass'n *(267)*
American Medical Informatics Ass'n *(267)*
American Medical Student Ass'n *(267)*
American Medical Technologists *(267)*
American Museum of Natural History *(268)*
American Occupational Therapy Ass'n, Inc. *(269)*
American Physiological Soc. *(270)*
American Psychiatric Ass'n *(271)*
American Psychological Ass'n *(271)*
American Red Cross *(272)*
American Registry of Pathology *(272)*
American Soc. for Biochemistry and Molecular Biology *(274)*
American Soc. for Bone and Mineral Research *(274)*
American Soc. for Cell Biology *(274)*
American Soc. for Clinical Laboratory Science *(274)*
American Soc. for Clinical Nutrition *(274)*
American Soc. for Clinical Pharmacology and Therapeutics *(274)*
American Soc. for Microbiology *(274)*
American Soc. for Pharmacology and Experimental Therapeutics *(274)*
American Soc. for Therapeutic Radiology and Oncology *(275)*
American Soc. of Anesthesiologists *(275)*
American Soc. of Clinical Oncology *(276)*
American Soc. of Clinical Pathologists *(276)*
American Soc. of Extra-Corporeal Technology *(276)*
American Soc. of Hematology *(276)*
American Soc. of Nephrology *(276)*
American Soc. of Tropical Medicine and Hygiene *(277)*
American Speech, Language, and Hearing Ass'n *(277)*
American Teleservices Ass'n *(279)*
American Urogynecologic Soc. *(280)*
Americans for Integrity in Palliative Care *(282)*
Americans for Medical Progress *(282)*
Amgen *(282)*
Anthra *(285)*
Arent Fox Kintner Plotkin & Kahn, PLLC *(14)*
Arter & Hadden *(17)*
Arthritis Foundation *(289)*
Ass'n for Ambulatory Behavioral Healthcare *(291)*
Ass'n for Professionals in Infection Control and Epidemiology *(293)*
Ass'n of American Medical Colleges *(294)*
Ass'n of American Physicians and Surgeons *(294)*
Ass'n of Chiropractic Colleges *(295)*

Ass'n of Disposable Device Manufacturers (ADDM) *(295)*
Ass'n of Independent Research Institutes *(296)*
Ass'n of Maternal and Child Health Programs (AMCHP) *(296)*
Ass'n of Medical Device Reprocessors *(296)*
Ass'n of Professors of Medicine *(298)*
Ass'n of Schools of Public Health *(298)*
Ass'n of University Programs in Health Administration *(299)*
Assisted Living Federation of America *(300)*
Asthma and Allergy Foundation of America *(301)*
The Atlantic Group, Public Affairs, Inc. *(18)*
Autism Soc. of America, Inc. *(303)*
Avax Technologies, Inc. *(304)*
Aventis Pasteur *(304)*
Aventis Pharmaceuticals, Inc. *(304)*
Baker & Daniels *(19)*
Balch & Bingham LLP *(21)*
Bass and Howes, Inc. *(24)*
Bausch & Lomb *(309)*
Baxter Healthcare Corp. *(309)*
Bayer Diagnostic *(309)*
Baylor College of Medicine *(310)*
Vikki Bell *(25)*
Bennett Turner & Coleman, LLP *(25)*
Bergner Bockorny Castagnetti and Hawkins *(26)*
Berkshire Inc. *(26)*
Terry Bevels Consulting *(27)*
Biochemics *(313)*
Biogen, Inc. *(313)*
Biotechnology Industry Organization *(314)*
BKSH & Associates *(28)*
Blood Center of Southeastern Wisconsin *(315)*
Boehringer Mannheim Corp. *(316)*
Booher & Associates *(30)*
Boston Scientific Corp. *(318)*
Bracewell & Patterson, L.L.P. *(30)*
Bracy Williams & Co. *(31)*
Brickfield, Burchette, Ritts & Stone *(32)*
Bristol-Myers Squibb Co. *(320)*
Broydrick & Associates *(33)*
Canberra Packard BioScience *(330)*
Cancer Leadership Council *(330)*
Capitol Associates, Inc. *(37)*
Capitol Partners *(39)*
Case Western Reserve University School of Medicine *(332)*
Cassidy & Associates, Inc. *(42)*
Cavarocchi Ruscio Dennis Associates *(44)*
Cell Therapeutics Inc. *(334)*
Centocor, Inc. *(338)*
Chamber of Commerce of the U.S.A. *(340)*
The Children's Cause Inc. *(344)*
Children's Hospital of Boston *(344)*
Chronic Fatigue and Immune Dysfunction Syndrome Ass'n of America *(346)*
Citizens for Public Action on Cholesterol, Inc. *(348)*
Clark & Weinstock, Inc. *(47)*
Cleveland Clinic Foundation *(350)*
Coalition for Health Services Research *(354)*
Coalition of Boston Teaching Hospitals *(355)*
College of American Pathologists *(357)*
College on Problems of Drug Dependence *(357)*
Colling Swift & Hynes *(49)*
Columbia University *(359)*
Community General Hospital of Sullivan County *(362)*
Congressional Consultants *(51)*
Congressional Economic Leadership Institute *(366)*
Conlon, Frantz, Phelan & Pires *(51)*
Consumer Federation of America *(369)*
Consumer Healthcare Products Ass'n *(369)*
Cook Children's Health Care System *(370)*
Cook Inc. *(370)*
Cooley's Anemia Foundation *(371)*
Cosmetic, Toiletry and Fragrance Ass'n *(373)*
Council of Graduate Schools *(375)*
Covington & Burling *(53)*
Crowell & Moring LLP *(55)*
Cure for Lymphoma Foundation *(380)*
Cystic Fibrosis Foundation *(380)*
Dalrymple and Associates, L.L.C. *(56)*
Bob Davis & Associates *(57)*
DeBrunner and Associates, Inc. *(60)*
Do No Harm: The Coalition of Americans for Research Ethics *(390)*
Downey McGrath Group, Inc. *(64)*
The Duberstein Group, Inc. *(65)*
Eckert Seamans Cherin & Mellott, LLC *(70)*
Edelman Public Relations Worldwide *(396)*
Edington, Peel & Associates, Inc. *(70)*
Elan Pharmaceutical Research Corp. *(399)*
Emerging Technology Partners, LLC *(402)*
Ethylene Oxide Sterilization Ass'n, Inc. *(407)*
Evans & Black, Inc. *(73)*
Eye Bank Ass'n of America *(410)*
Farm Animal Reform Movement (FARM) *(411)*
Federal Physicians Ass'n *(414)*
Federation of American Societies for Experimental Biology *(414)*
Federation of Nurses and Health Professionals/AFT *(415)*
Fenton Communications *(415)*
Florida State University System *(420)*
Foley Government and Public Affairs, Inc. *(78)*
FoxKiser *(79)*
Fresenius Medical Care North America *(425)*
Friedrich's Ataxia Research Alliance *(426)*
Friends of Cancer Research *(426)*
Friends of the Nat'l Library of Medicine *(426)*
GCRC Program Directors Ass'n *(430)*
Genelabs Technologies, Inc. *(431)*
Genentech, Inc. *(431)*
General Conference of Seventh-day Adventists *(431)*
Generic Pharmaceutical Ass'n *(433)*
The Genome Action Coalition *(433)*
Genzyme Corp. *(433)*
GEO Centers, Inc. *(433)*
GHL Inc. *(82)*
GlaxoSmithKline *(436)*
Greater New York Hospital Ass'n *(439)*
Grisso Consulting *(88)*
Guidant Corp. *(442)*
Hadassah, The Women's Zionist Organization of America *(443)*
Hadley & McKenna *(89)*
Hale and Dorr LLP *(89)*
Hall, Green, Rupli, LLC *(90)*
Harbor Branch Institute *(444)*
Health Insurance Ass'n of America *(446)*
Health Policy Strategies *(93)*
Health Quest *(446)*
Hearing Industries Ass'n *(447)*
Heidepriem & Mager, Inc. *(94)*
HemaSure, Inc. *(448)*
Hewlett-Packard Co. *(449)*
Hill-Rom Co., Inc. *(450)*
Hoffmann-La Roche Inc. *(450)*
Hogan & Hartson L.L.P. *(96)*
Hollis-Eden Pharmaceuticals, Inc. *(451)*
Hospital for Special Surgery *(453)*
Huntington's Disease Soc. of America *(455)*
Fred Hutchinson Cancer Research Center *(455)*
Hyman, Phelps & McNamara, P.C. *(102)*
The Ickes & Enright Group *(102)*
Illinois Department of Human Services *(457)*
Indiana Medical Device Manufacturers Council *(460)*
Infectious Diseases Soc. of America, Inc. *(461)*
Information Trust *(462)*
Innovative Science Solutions *(462)*
Institute for Civil Soc. *(463)*
Institute for Systems Biology *(464)*
Inter-Associates, Inc. *(103)*
Internat'l Ass'n for Dental Research *(467)*
Internat'l Ass'n of Fire Chiefs *(468)*
Internat'l Center for Clubhouse Development *(469)*
Internat'l Dyslexia Ass'n, The *(471)*
IVAX Corp. *(480)*
JCP Associates *(105)*
Linda Jenckes & Associates *(106)*
Johns Hopkins School of Hygiene and Public Health *(483)*
Johns Hopkins University & Hospital *(483)*
Joint Council of Allergy, Asthma and Immunology *(484)*
Jorden Burt LLP *(109)*
Joslin Diabetes Center *(485)*
Juvenile Diabetes Foundation Internat'l *(485)*
Kaiser Aluminum & Chemical Corp. *(485)*
Barbara A. Karmanos Cancer Institute *(486)*
Kellogg Brown and Root *(487)*
Kelly and Associates, Inc. *(111)*
Kessler & Associates Business Services, Inc. *(112)*
Henry H. Kessler Foundation *(488)*
Kessler Medical Rehabilitation Research & Education Corp. *(488)*
Jeffrey J. Kimbell & Associates *(113)*
Susan G. Komen Breast Cancer Foundation *(490)*
Komen Breast Cancer Foundation, The Susan G. *(491)*
LaRocco & Associates *(116)*
Latham & Watkins *(116)*
The Legislative Strategies Group, LLC *(118)*
Leukemia & Lymphoma Soc. *(498)*
Lewis-Burke Associates *(120)*
The Livingston Group, LLC *(120)*
Logan College of Chiropractic *(502)*
Lovelace Respiratory Research Institute *(504)*
Loyola University Health System *(505)*
Loyola University of Chicago *(505)*
Lupus Foundation of America *(505)*
Lymphoma Research Foundation of America, Inc. *(506)*
Management Options, Inc. *(123)*
March of Dimes Birth Defects Foundation *(509)*
Marquette General Hospital *(510)*
McDermott, Will and Emery *(128)*
McGuireWoods L.L.P. *(130)*
McKenna & Cuneo, L.L.P. *(131)*
McKesson Corp. *(515)*
Medeva Pharmaceuticals *(516)*
Medical Advocacy Services, Inc. *(132)*
Medical College of Virginia, Dept. of Neurology, Office of the Chairman *(516)*
Medical Device Manufacturers Ass'n *(516)*
Medical Records Internat'l, Inc. *(516)*
Medicare Payment Coalition for Frail Beneficiaries *(517)*
MedPro, Inc. *(517)*
MedStar Health *(517)*
Mehl, Griffin & Bartek Ltd. *(132)*
Member-Link Systems, Inc. *(517)*
Memorial Sloan-Kettering Cancer Center *(517)*
memorize.com *(517)*
Merck & Co. *(518)*
Miller & Co. *(134)*
Denny Miller McBee Associates *(134)*
Minimed, Inc. *(525)*
Mintz, Levin, Cohn, Ferris, Glovsky and Popeo, P.C. *(135)*
The Jeffrey Modell Foundation *(527)*
Molecular BioSystems, Inc. *(527)*
Motion Picture and Television Fund *(530)*
Mount Sinai Hospital *(531)*
Mount Sinai School of Medicine *(531)*
MultiDimensional Imaging, Inc. *(532)*
Mutual of Omaha Insurance Companies *(533)*
Nat'l Abortion and Reproductive Rights Action League *(535)*
Nat'l Alliance for Eye and Vision Research *(536)*
Nat'l Alliance for Hispanic Health *(536)*
Nat'l Ass'n for Biomedical Research *(537)*
Nat'l Ass'n of Children's Hospitals Inc. *(540)*
Nat'l Ass'n of Community Health Centers *(540)*
Nat'l Ass'n of Federal Veterinarians *(542)*
Nat'l Ass'n of Healthcare Consultants *(543)*
Nat'l Ass'n of Negro Business & Professional Women's Clubs, Inc. *(546)*
Nat'l Ass'n of People with AIDS, Inc. *(546)*
Nat'l Ass'n of Police Organizations *(546)*
Nat'l Ass'n of State Mental Health Program Directors *(550)*
Nat'l Ass'n of Urban Hospitals *(551)*
Nat'l Ass'n of VA Physicians and Dentists *(551)*
Nat'l Ass'n of Veterans Research and Education Foundations *(551)*
Nat'l Assembly of Health and Human Service Organizations *(551)*

Nat'l Black Women's Health Project ***(552)***
Nat'l Breast Cancer Coalition ***(553)***
Nat'l Coalition for Cancer Research ***(556)***
Nat'l Coalition for Cancer Survivorship ***(556)***
Nat'l College ***(557)***
Nat'l Consumers League ***(558)***
Nat'l Disease Research Interchange ***(562)***
Nat'l Electrical Manufacturers Ass'n ***(562)***
Nat'l Gaucher Foundation ***(565)***
Nat'l Health Council ***(567)***
Nat'l Kidney Foundation ***(569)***
Nat'l Military Family Ass'n ***(571)***
Nat'l Patient Advocate Foundation ***(573)***
Nat'l Rehabilitation Ass'n ***(575)***
Nat'l Rehabilitation Information Center ***(575)***
Nat'l Right to Life Committee ***(576)***
Nat'l Sleep Foundation ***(578)***
Nat'l Stroke Ass'n ***(579)***
Nat'l Venture Capital Ass'n ***(580)***
Neuman and Co. *(141)*
New York University ***(588)***
New York University Medical Center ***(588)***
NitroMed, Inc. ***(590)***
Non-Profit Management Associates, Inc. *(142)*
North American Brain Tumor Coalition ***(592)***
Novartis Services, Inc. ***(596)***
The OB-C Group, LLC *(143)*
O'Bryon & Co. *(144)*
Ochsner Medical Institutions ***(598)***
Olsson, Frank and Weeda, P.C. *(146)*
Omniflight Helicopters, Inc. ***(600)***
Onconova Inc. ***(600)***
O'Neill, Athy & Casey, P.C. *(147)*
Oppenheimer Wolff & Donnelly LLP *(147)*
Optical Soc. of America ***(601)***
Opticians Ass'n of America ***(601)***
Orasure Technologies ***(602)***
Orphan Medical, Inc. ***(604)***
PAI Management Corp. *(148)*
Pain Care Coalition ***(606)***
Paradise Valley Hospital ***(607)***
Paralyzed Veterans of America ***(607)***
Parkinson's Action Network ***(608)***
Parry, Romani, DeConcini & Symms *(149)*
Partners Healthcare System, Inc. ***(608)***
Patton Boggs, LLP *(150)*
Pfizer, Inc. ***(613)***
Pharmaceutical Research and Manufacturers of America ***(614)***
Pharmacia Corp. ***(615)***
Philips Electronics North America Corp. ***(616)***
Physician Insurers Ass'n of America ***(616)***
Physicians Ad hoc Coalition for Truth (PHACT) ***(617)***
The Plexus Consulting Group *(156)*
The PMA Group *(156)*
PNH Associates ***(619)***
Podesta/Mattoon *(158)*
Policy Directions, Inc. *(158)*
Polity Consulting *(159)*
The Potomac Research Group LLC *(160)*
Potomac Strategies Internat'l LLC *(160)*
Powers Pyles Sutter & Verville, PC *(161)*
Preston Gates Ellis & Rouvelas Meeds LLP *(162)*
Private Essential Access Community Hospitals (PEACH) Inc. ***(624)***
Public Health Policy Advisory Board ***(628)***
Public Policy Partners, LLC *(164)*
Quest Diagnostics Inc. ***(631)***
Quintiles Transnational Corp. ***(631)***
Qwest Communications ***(631)***
R2 Technology, Inc. ***(632)***
Reckitt & Colman Pharmaceuticals Inc. ***(634)***
Reed, Smith, LLP *(167)*
Russ Reid Co. *(167)*
Renal Physicians Ass'n ***(636)***
Reproductive Health Technologies Project ***(637)***
Research Soc. on Alcoholism ***(638)***
Retractable Technologies, Inc. ***(639)***
Ritter and Bourjaily, Inc. *(169)*
Rooney Group Internat'l, Inc. *(171)*
Ryan, Phillips, Utrecht & MacKinnon *(173)*
Sagamore Associates, Inc. *(174)*
Schering-Plough Corp. ***(651)***
Schering-Plough Legislative Resources L.L.C. ***(651)***
Schroth & Associates *(176)*
Sensor Research and Development Corp. ***(655)***
Sepracor, Inc. ***(655)***
Serono Laboratories, Inc. ***(655)***
The Sheridan Group *(179)*
Silver Users Ass'n ***(659)***
Siscorp ***(660)***
Sisters of Charity of Leavenworth Health Services ***(660)***
E. Del Smith and Co. *(183)*
Smith, Bucklin and Associates, Inc. *(184)*
SmithKline Beecham Consumer Healthcare, LLP ***(661)***
Soc. for Mucosal Immunology ***(662)***
Soc. for Neuroscience ***(662)***
Soc. for Women's Health Research ***(663)***
Soc. of General Internal Medicine ***(663)***
Soc. of Gyneocologic Oncologists ***(663)***
Soc. of Nuclear Medicine ***(663)***
Soc. of Teachers of Family Medicine ***(664)***
Soc. of Thoracic Surgeons ***(664)***
Soc. of Toxicology ***(664)***
Solus Research, Inc. ***(665)***
Southcoast Health System ***(667)***
Southern Research Institute ***(668)***
Spacelabs Medical Inc. ***(669)***
SPECTRUM Science Public Relations, Inc. *(186)*
Spokane Area Chamber of Commerce ***(670)***
Squire, Sanders & Dempsey L.L.P. *(187)*
St. Bernard's Hospital ***(671)***
St. Jude Medical, Inc. ***(671)***
SterilMed, Inc. ***(674)***
Summit Technology ***(676)***
Susquehanna Health System ***(678)***
Synzyme Technologies, Inc. ***(679)***
Tarne Powers & Associates *(192)*
Temple University Health System ***(683)***
Texas Chiropractic College ***(684)***
Thomas Jefferson University ***(686)***
Thomas Jefferson University Hospital ***(686)***
Townsend Solheim *(196)*
Tulane University ***(693)***
Tuvin Associates *(197)*
Tyco Internat'l (US), Inc. ***(695)***
U.S. Oncology ***(697)***
Unisys Corp. ***(700)***
United Methodist Church General Board of Church and Society ***(702)***
United States Pharmacopeia ***(704)***
University of Alabama System ***(705)***
University of California, Office of Federal Government Relations ***(706)***
University of Cincinnati ***(706)***
University of Medicine and Dentistry of New Jersey ***(706)***
University of Miami ***(706)***
University of Michigan Medical Center ***(706)***
University of Nebraska ***(706)***
University of North Carolina at Chapel Hill ***(707)***
University of South Florida Research Foundation ***(707)***
University of Southern California ***(707)***
University of Tulsa ***(708)***
University of Virginia ***(708)***
University of Washington ***(708)***
University System of Maryland ***(708)***
V-ONE Corp. ***(711)***
Vacuum Insulation Ass'n ***(711)***
Van Ness Feldman, P.C. *(199)*
Van Scoyoc Associates, Inc. ***(711)***
Van Scoyoc Associates, Inc. *(200)*
Vanguard Medical Concepts, Inc. ***(712)***
Venable *(201)*
Verner, Liipfert, Bernhard, McPherson and Hand, Chartered *(202)*
Vertis Neuroscience ***(714)***
Village of Kiryas Joel ***(715)***
Visible Genetics ***(716)***
Visiting Nurse Service of New York ***(716)***
VSAdc.com *(205)*
Washington Council Ernst & Young *(206)*
The Washington Group *(208)*
Washington Health Advocates *(209)*
Washington Liaison Group, LLC *(209)*
Wheat & Associates, Inc. *(212)*
The Wilbur Group *(214)*
Wiley, Rein & Fielding *(214)*
Wireless Technology Research, L.L.C. ***(728)***
Zone Therapeutics, Inc. ***(735)***
Zuckerman Spaeder L.L.P. *(221)*

Medicare/Medicaid (MMM)

The 60/Plus Ass'n, Inc. ***(224)***
AARP (American Ass'n of Retired Persons) ***(224)***
ABB, Inc. ***(225)***
Abbott Laboratories ***(225)***
Academic Health Center Coalition ***(225)***
Academy of Managed Care Pharmacy ***(225)***
Acute Long Term Hospital Ass'n ***(227)***
Michael W. Adcock *(6)*
AdvaMed ***(228)***
Advantage Healthplan Inc. ***(229)***
Aetna Inc. ***(230)***
Aetna Life & Casualty Co. ***(230)***
AFL-CIO (American Federation of Labor and Congress of Industrial Organizations) ***(231)***
AFLAC, Inc. ***(231)***
Agilent Technologies ***(232)***
AIDS Action Council ***(233)***
AIDS Healthcare Foundation ***(233)***
Air Force Sergeants Ass'n ***(233)***
Akin, Gump, Strauss, Hauer & Feld, L.L.P. *(8)*
Aksys, Ltd. ***(235)***
Alabama Nursing Homes Ass'n ***(235)***
Albert Einstein Medical Center ***(237)***
Alexander Strategy Group *(11)*
Allergan, Inc. ***(239)***
Alliance for Quality Nursing Home Care ***(240)***
Alliance for Retired Americans ***(240)***
Alliance of Catholic Health Care Systems ***(240)***
Alliance to Improve Medicare ***(241)***
Allina Health Systems ***(241)***
Allscripts Inc. ***(241)***
Alpine Group, Inc. *(11)*
Alzheimer's Ass'n ***(242)***
AMDeC Policy Group, Inc. ***(242)***
America's Blood Centers ***(243)***
American Academy of Actuaries ***(243)***
American Academy of Audiology ***(243)***
American Academy of Child and Adolescent Psychiatry ***(243)***
American Academy of Dermatology ***(243)***
American Academy of Family Physicians ***(243)***
American Academy of Ophthamology - Office of Federal Affairs ***(244)***
American Academy of Orthopaedic Surgeons ***(244)***
American Academy of Otolaryngic Allergy ***(244)***
American Academy of Otolaryngology-Head and Neck Surgery ***(244)***
American Academy of Pediatrics ***(244)***
American Ambulance Ass'n ***(245)***
American Ass'n for Geriatric Psychiatry ***(245)***
American Ass'n for Marriage and Family Therapy ***(246)***
American Ass'n for Respiratory Care ***(246)***
American Ass'n for the Study of Liver Diseases ***(246)***
American Ass'n of Bioanalysts ***(246)***
American Ass'n of Blood Banks ***(246)***
American Ass'n of Cardiovascular and Pulmonary Rehabilitation ***(246)***
American Ass'n of Colleges of Osteopathic Medicine ***(247)***
American Ass'n of Eye and Ear Hospitals ***(247)***
American Ass'n of Health Plans (AAHP) ***(248)***
American Ass'n of Homes and Services for the Aging ***(248)***
American Ass'n of Neurological Surgeons/Congress of Neurological Surgeons ***(248)***
American Ass'n of University Women ***(249)***
American Bar Ass'n ***(250)***
American Cancer Soc. ***(252)***
American Chiropractic Ass'n ***(252)***
American Clinical Neurophysiology Soc. ***(253)***
American College of Cardiology ***(253)***

American College of Chest Physicians *(253)*
American College of Clinical Pharmacy *(253)*
American College of Emergency Physicians *(253)*
American College of Gastroenterology *(253)*
American College of Nurse Practitioners *(253)*
American College of Obstetricians and Gynecologists *(254)*
American College of Osteopathic Surgeons *(254)*
American College of Physicians-American Soc. of Internal Medicine (ACP-ASIM) *(254)*
American College of Radiology *(254)*
American College of Rheumatology *(254)*
American College of Surgeons *(254)*
American Congress of Community Supports and Employment Services *(255)*
American Counseling Ass'n *(256)*
American Dental Education Ass'n *(257)*
American Diabetes Ass'n *(257)*
American Dietetic Ass'n *(257)*
American Electronics Ass'n *(257)*
American Farm Bureau Federation *(258)*
American Federation for Medical Research *(258)*
American Federation of Senior Citizens *(258)*
American Federation of State, County and Municipal Employees *(258)*
American Federation of Teachers *(259)*
American Foundation for the Blind - Governmental Relations Group *(260)*
American Gastroenterological Ass'n *(261)*
American Health Care Ass'n *(261)*
American Home Products Corp. *(262)*
American Hospital Ass'n *(263)*
American Institute of Ultrasound in Medicine *(264)*
American Jewish Congress *(265)*
American Legion *(266)*
American Managed Behavioral Healthcare Ass'n *(266)*
American Medical Ass'n *(267)*
American Medical Group Ass'n *(267)*
American Medical Rehabilitation Providers Ass'n *(267)*
American Medical Student Ass'n *(267)*
American Medical Technologists *(267)*
American Museum of Natural History *(268)*
American Network of Community Options and Resources (ANCOR) *(268)*
American Occupational Therapy Ass'n, Inc. *(269)*
American Optometric Ass'n *(269)*
American Organization of Nurse Executives *(269)*
American Orthotic and Prosthetic Ass'n *(269)*
American Osteopathic Healthcare Ass'n *(269)*
American Pharmaceutical Ass'n *(270)*
American Physical Therapy Ass'n *(270)*
American Psychiatric Ass'n *(271)*
American Psychiatric Nurses Ass'n *(271)*
American Psychological Ass'n *(271)*
American Public Health Ass'n *(271)*
American Seniors Housing Ass'n *(273)*
American Sleep Disorders Ass'n *(274)*
American Soc. for Clinical Laboratory Science *(274)*
American Soc. for Gastrointestinal Endoscopy *(274)*
American Soc. for Therapeutic Radiology and Oncology *(275)*
American Soc. of Ambulatory Surgery Centers *(275)*
American Soc. of Anesthesiologists *(275)*
American Soc. of Cataract and Refractive Surgery *(275)*
American Soc. of Clinical Oncology *(276)*
American Soc. of Clinical Pathologists *(276)*
American Soc. of Consultant Pharmacists *(276)*
American Soc. of Echocardiography *(276)*
American Soc. of General Surgeons *(276)*
American Soc. of Health System Pharmacists *(276)*
American Soc. of Hematology *(276)*
American Soc. of Nephrology *(276)*
American Soc. of Nuclear Cardiology *(277)*
American Soc. of Pediatric Nephrology *(277)*
American Soc. of Radiologic Technologists *(277)*
American Speech, Language, and Hearing Ass'n *(277)*
American Urogynecologic Soc. *(280)*
American Urological Ass'n *(280)*
Americans for Tax Reform *(282)*
Amgen *(282)*
Morris J. Amitay, P.C. *(13)*
AmSurg Corp. *(283)*
Anthem Alliance *(285)*
Aon Corp. *(285)*
Apria Healthcare Group *(287)*
The Arc *(287)*
Arent Fox Kintner Plotkin & Kahn, PLLC *(14)*
Arkansas, Office of the Governor of the State of *(288)*
Arnold & Porter *(16)*
Arthroscopy Ass'n of North America *(289)*
Ashland Inc. *(290)*
Ass'n of Air Medical Services *(293)*
Ass'n of American Blood Banks *(293)*
Ass'n of American Medical Colleges *(294)*
Ass'n of American Physicians and Surgeons *(294)*
Ass'n of Chiropractic Colleges *(295)*
Ass'n of Community Cancer Centers *(295)*
Ass'n of Freestanding Radiation Oncology Centers *(295)*
Ass'n of Health Information Outsourcing Services *(296)*
Ass'n of Maternal and Child Health Programs (AMCHP) *(296)*
Ass'n of Pain Management Anesthesiologist *(297)*
Ass'n of periOperative Registered Nurses *(297)*
Ass'n of Professors of Medicine *(298)*
Ass'n of Surgical Technologists *(299)*
Assisted Living Federation of America *(300)*
Asthma and Allergy Foundation of America *(301)*
AstraZeneca Inc. *(301)*
Augustine Medical *(303)*
Aventis Pasteur *(304)*
Aventis Pharmaceuticals, Inc. *(304)*
Baker & Hostetler LLP *(306)*
Baker & Hostetler LLP *(19)*
Baker, Donelson, Bearman & Caldwell, P.C. *(21)*
Barbour Griffith & Rogers, Inc. *(22)*
Barr Laboratories *(308)*
Bass and Howes, Inc. *(24)*
Baxter Healthcare Corp. *(309)*
Bayer Corp. *(309)*
Bazelon Center for Mental Health Law, Judge David L. *(310)*
BD *(310)*
Bennett Turner & Coleman, LLP *(25)*
Benova, Inc. *(311)*
Bergner Bockorny Castagnetti and Hawkins *(26)*
Berliner, Candon & Jimison *(27)*
Bethlehem Steel Corp. *(312)*
Robert Betz Associates, Inc. *(27)*
Beverly Enterprises *(313)*
Biogen, Inc. *(313)*
Biotechnology Industry Organization *(314)*
BKSH & Associates *(28)*
Blood Center of Southeastern Wisconsin *(315)*
Blue Cross Blue Shield Ass'n *(315)*
The Boeing Co. *(316)*
Bon Secours Charity Health System *(317)*
Bone Care Internat'l *(317)*
Booher & Associates *(30)*
Boston Scientific Corp. *(318)*
Bracco Diagnostics *(319)*
Brickfield, Burchette, Ritts & Stone *(32)*
Bristol-Myers Squibb Co. *(320)*
Broydrick & Associates *(33)*
Burlington Northern Santa Fe Railway *(324)*
California Ass'n of Marriage and Family Therapists *(326)*
California Children's Hospital Ass'n *(326)*
California Rural Indian Health Board, Inc. *(327)*
Campbell Crane & Associates *(36)*
Cancer Leadership Council *(330)*
Canfield & Associates, Inc. *(36)*
Capitol Associates, Inc. *(37)*
Capitol Health Group, LLC *(39)*
Caremark Rx, Inc. *(331)*
CaRess, Inc. *(331)*
The Carmen Group *(40)*
Carpi & Clay *(41)*
Cascade Designs *(332)*
Catholic Health Ass'n of the United States *(333)*
Catholic Healthcare West *(333)*
Cavarocchi Ruscio Dennis Associates *(44)*
Center for Law and Social Policy *(336)*
Center for Patient Advocacy *(337)*
Center on Budget and Policy Priorities *(338)*
Centocor, Inc. *(338)*
Cerebral Palsy Council *(340)*
CGR Associates, Inc. *(45)*
Chambers Associates Inc. *(45)*
Child Welfare League of America *(343)*
The Children's Cause Inc. *(344)*
Children's Defense Fund *(344)*
Children's Hospital and Medical Center *(344)*
Children's Hospital of Wisconsin *(344)*
Children's Mercy Hospital *(344)*
Christian Voice, Inc. *(345)*
CIGNA Corp. *(346)*
Citizens Against Government Waste *(348)*
Citizens for Public Action on Cholesterol, Inc. *(348)*
ClaimTraq, Inc. *(349)*
Clark & Weinstock, Inc. *(47)*
Cleveland Clinic Foundation *(350)*
CNA Financial Corp. *(351)*
CNA Insurance Cos. *(351)*
Coalition for a Procompetitive Stark Law *(352)*
Coalition for Health Services Research *(354)*
Coalition of Boston Teaching Hospitals *(355)*
College of American Pathologists *(357)*
Colling Swift & Hynes *(49)*
Coloplast Corp. *(358)*
Committee for a Responsible Federal Budget *(360)*
Community Health Systems, Inc. *(362)*
Concord Coalition *(365)*
Congressional Consultants *(51)*
Congressional Economic Leadership Institute *(366)*
Conkling, Fiskum & McCormick *(51)*
Consumer Federation of America *(369)*
Consumers Union of the United States *(369)*
Contemporary Products Inc. *(370)*
Continuum Healthcare Systems *(370)*
ConvaTec *(370)*
Cook, Illinois, County of *(371)*
Cooley's Anemia Foundation *(371)*
Cooney & Associates, Inc. *(52)*
Copeland, Lowery & Jacquez *(52)*
Council for Affordable Health Insurance *(374)*
Council for Government Reform *(374)*
Council of Surgical Specialty Facilities and Institutes *(376)*
Council of Women's and Infant's Specialty Hospitals *(376)*
Council on Radionuclides and Radiopharmaceuticals (CORAR) *(377)*
Cox Enterprises Inc. *(378)*
Crestwood Behavior Health, Inc. *(378)*
Crown Therapeutics, Inc. *(379)*
The Cuneo Law Group, P.C. *(56)*
Cure for Lymphoma Foundation *(380)*
Cuyahoga, Ohio, County of *(380)*
CVS, Inc. *(380)*
Cypress Bioscience Inc. *(380)*
Cystic Fibrosis Foundation *(380)*
DaimlerChrysler Corp. *(381)*
Dalrymple and Associates, L.L.C. *(56)*
DATRON, Inc. *(382)*
Davidoff & Malito, LLP *(57)*
DeBrunner and Associates, Inc. *(60)*
DeBrunner and Associates, Inc. *(383)*
Deloitte Consulting *(384)*
George H. Denison *(60)*
Denison, Scott Associates *(61)*
Detroit Medical Center *(386)*
DGME Fairness Initiative *(387)*
Dialysis Clinic, Inc. *(387)*
diGenova & Toensing *(62)*
Bob Dole Enterprises *(63)*
Downey McGrath Group, Inc. *(64)*
The Duberstein Group, Inc. *(65)*
Dublin Castle Group *(66)*
Dumex Medical *(393)*
The Dutko Group, Inc. *(68)*
Easter Seals *(395)*

Eastman Kodak Co. *(395)*
EDS Corp. *(398)*
Elan Pharmaceutical Research Corp. *(399)*
Elanex Pharmaceuticals *(399)*
Emergency Department Practice Management Ass'n (EDPMA) *(401)*
Emord & Associates, P.C. *(71)*
Endocrine Soc. *(403)*
Epstein Becker & Green, P.C. *(72)*
ESR Children's Health Care System *(407)*
Essex Medical Systems Plus *(407)*
Evans & Black, Inc. *(73)*
Express Scripts Inc. *(409)*
Exxon Mobil Corp. *(409)*
Eye Bank Ass'n of America *(410)*
Fallon Community Health Plan *(410)*
Families U.S.A. Foundation *(410)*
Feder, Semo, Clarke & Bard *(74)*
Federated Ambulatory Surgery Ass'n *(414)*
Federation of American Hospitals *(414)*
Federation of Nurses and Health Professionals/AFT *(415)*
Federation of State Medical Boards of the U.S. *(415)*
The Ferguson Group, LLC *(76)*
First Church of Christ, Scientist *(417)*
First Consulting Group *(417)*
Fleet Reserve Ass'n *(418)*
Fleishman-Hillard, Inc *(77)*
R. G. Flippo and Associates, Inc. *(77)*
Florida State University System *(420)*
Foley, Hoag & Eliot LLP *(78)*
Food Marketing Institute *(421)*
foot.com *(422)*
W. A. Foote Memorial Hospital *(422)*
Ford Motor Co. *(422)*
Forscey & Stinson, PLLC *(79)*
The Fortier Group, LLC *(79)*
Foster America, Inc. *(424)*
Foundation Health Federal Services, Inc. *(424)*
FoxKiser *(79)*
Freedom Designs *(425)*
Fresenius Medical Care North America *(425)*
Friends Committee on Nat'l Legislation *(426)*
Fujisawa Health Care Inc. *(427)*
Gainesville, Florida, City of *(428)*
Gambro Healthcare *(429)*
Genentech, Inc. *(431)*
General Conference of Seventh-day Adventists *(431)*
General Motors Corp. *(432)*
Generic Pharmaceutical Ass'n *(433)*
Genzyme Corp. *(433)*
Gibbons & Company, Inc. *(82)*
Girling Health Care *(435)*
GlaxoSmithKline *(436)*
Golden Rule Insurance Co. *(437)*
Jay Grant & Associates *(85)*
Greater New York Hospital Ass'n *(439)*
Greenberg Traurig, LLP *(86)*
Griffin, Johnson, Dover & Stewart *(87)*
Grisso Consulting *(88)*
Group Health Cooperative *(441)*
Group Health, Inc. *(441)*
GRQ, Inc. *(88)*
Guidant Corp. *(442)*
Haake and Associates *(89)*
Hale and Dorr LLP *(89)*
Halsey, Rains & Associates, LLC *(90)*
Hannett & Associates *(91)*
HCR-Manor Care, Inc. *(445)*
Health and Hospital Corp. of Marion County *(446)*
Health Industry Distributors Ass'n *(446)*
Health Industry Group Purchasing Ass'n *(446)*
Health Insurance Ass'n of America *(446)*
Health Policy Analysts *(93)*
Health Quest *(446)*
Healthcare Ass'n of New York State *(446)*
Healthcare Billing and Management Ass'n *(446)*
Healthcare Financing Study Group *(447)*
Healthcare Leadership Council *(447)*
Healtheon/Web MD *(447)*
Helmsin & Yarwood Associates *(94)*
Heritage Foundation *(448)*
Dennis M. Hertel & Associates *(94)*
Hill-Rom Co., Inc. *(450)*
Hoffmann-La Roche Inc. *(450)*
Hogan & Hartson L.L.P. *(96)*
Hohlt & Associates *(98)*
Holland & Knight LLP *(98)*
Hollister Inc. *(451)*
Holyoke Hospital *(451)*
Home Care Ass'n of New York State *(451)*
Hooper, Lundy and Bookman *(452)*
Humana Inc. *(455)*
Hutzel Medical Center *(455)*
Hyperion Medical *(456)*
The Ickes & Enright Group *(102)*
Illinois Collaboration on Youth *(457)*
Illinois Department of Human Services *(457)*
Illinois Hospital and Health Systems Ass'n *(457)*
Illinois Primary Health Care Ass'n *(457)*
Independent Insurance Agents of America, Inc. *(459)*
Indiana, Office of the Governor of the State of *(460)*
Infectious Diseases Soc. of America, Inc. *(461)*
Inova Fairfax Hospital *(462)*
Institute on Religion and Public Policy *(464)*
InterMountain Health Care Inc. *(467)*
Internat'l Brotherhood of Electrical Workers *(469)*
Internat'l Code Council *(470)*
Internat'l Dyslexia Ass'n, The *(471)*
Internat'l Federation of Professional and Technical Engineers *(471)*
Internat'l Union of Painters and Allied Trades *(476)*
Intrinsiq Data Corp. *(477)*
Iredell Memorial Hospital *(478)*
ITT Industries Defense *(480)*
Jacobs & Co. Public Affairs/Loma Linda University *(481)*
Jacobus Tenbroek Memorial Fund *(481)*
The JAG Group, Inc. *(481)*
Janus Solutions, Inc. *(481)*
Jar-Mon Consultants, Inc. *(105)*
Jefferson Consulting Group *(105)*
Jefferson Government Relations, L.L.C. *(106)*
Linda Jenckes & Associates *(106)*
Jenner & Block *(107)*
Jewish Guild for the Blind *(483)*
Law Offices of Mark S. Joffe *(107)*
Johns Hopkins University & Hospital *(483)*
Johnson & Johnson, Inc. *(484)*
Johnson Co. *(107)*
Philip W. Johnston Associates *(108)*
Jolly/Rissler, Inc. *(108)*
Jones, Walker, Waechter, Poitevent, Carrere & Denegre, L.L.P. *(108)*
Jorden Burt LLP *(109)*
Kahl Pownall Advocates *(485)*
Kaiser Aluminum & Chemical Corp. *(485)*
Kalkines, Arky, Zall and Bernstein *(486)*
Kelly and Associates, Inc. *(111)*
Kendall Healthcare Products Co. *(487)*
Kessler & Associates Business Services, Inc. *(112)*
Henry H. Kessler Foundation *(488)*
Kessler Medical Rehabilitation Research & Education Corp. *(488)*
Jeffrey J. Kimbell & Associates *(113)*
King & Spalding *(113)*
Kogovsek & Associates *(114)*
Susan G. Komen Breast Cancer Foundation *(490)*
Komen Breast Cancer Foundation, The Susan G. *(491)*
L.A. Care Health Plan *(493)*
Labor Council for Latin American Advancement (LCLAA) *(493)*
LaRocco & Associates *(116)*
The Paul Laxalt Group *(117)*
The Legislative Strategies Group, LLC *(118)*
Lent Scrivner & Roth LLC *(119)*
Leukemia & Lymphoma Soc. *(498)*
Lifecore Biomedical *(499)*
LifePoint Hospitals, Inc. *(499)*
Eli Lilly and Co. *(499)*
The Livingston Group, LLC *(120)*
Lockheed Martin Corp. *(501)*
Los Angeles, California, County of *(504)*
Lovelace Respiratory Research Institute *(504)*
Lumbermens Mutual Casualty Co. *(505)*
Lupus Foundation of America *(505)*
Lutheran Office for Governmental Affairs/Evangelical Lutheran Church in America *(506)*
M.D. - I.P.A. *(506)*
Magee Women's Health Foundation *(507)*
Magellan Health Services *(507)*
Major Medicaid Hospital Coalition *(508)*
Mallinckrodt-Nellcor Puritan Bennett *(508)*
MARC Associates, Inc. *(124)*
March of Dimes Birth Defects Foundation *(509)*
Marconi plc *(509)*
The Marshfield Clinic *(511)*
Massachusetts Hospital Ass'n *(512)*
McDermott, Will and Emery *(128)*
McKenna & Cuneo, L.L.P. *(131)*
McKesson Corp. *(515)*
McLean Hospital *(515)*
McSlarrow Consulting L.L.C. *(131)*
Med Images, Inc. *(515)*
Medassets.com *(515)*
MedCentral Health System *(515)*
Medicaid Policy, L.L.C. *(132)*
Medical Advocacy Services, Inc. *(132)*
Medical Imaging Contrast Agent Ass'ns *(516)*
Medical Records Internat'l, Inc. *(516)*
Medicare Cost Contractors Alliance *(517)*
Meditrend, Inc. *(517)*
Medline Industries Inc. *(517)*
MedReview, Inc. *(517)*
MedStar Health *(517)*
Medtronic, Inc. *(517)*
Memorial Sloan-Kettering Cancer Center *(517)*
Mentor Corp. *(518)*
Merck & Co. *(518)*
Mercy Hospital of Des Moines, Iowa *(518)*
Mercy Medical *(518)*
Miami Beach, Florida, City of *(521)*
The Military Coalition *(524)*
Denny Miller McBee Associates *(134)*
Mintz, Levin, Cohn, Ferris, Glovsky and Popeo, P.C. *(135)*
Moffit Cancer Research Hospital *(527)*
Molina Healthcare *(527)*
Molina Medical Centers *(527)*
Motion Picture and Television Fund *(530)*
Mount Sinai Hospital *(531)*
Murray, Scheer, Montgomery, Tapia & O'Donnell *(139)*
Muse & Associates *(140)*
Mutual of Omaha Insurance Companies *(533)*
The MWW Group *(140)*
Nat'l Alliance for Hispanic Health *(536)*
Nat'l Alliance for Infusion Therapy *(536)*
Nat'l Alliance for the Mentally Ill *(536)*
Nat'l Alliance of State and Territorial AIDS Directors *(537)*
Nat'l Ass'n for Home Care *(537)*
Nat'l Ass'n for Medical Direction of Respiratory Care *(538)*
Nat'l Ass'n for State Farm Agents *(538)*
Nat'l Ass'n for the Support of Long Term Care *(538)*
Nat'l Ass'n for Uniformed Services *(538)*
Nat'l Ass'n of Area Agencies on Aging *(538)*
Nat'l Ass'n of Chain Drug Stores *(539)*
Nat'l Ass'n of Children's Hospitals Inc. *(540)*
Nat'l Ass'n of Community Health Centers *(540)*
Nat'l Ass'n of Dental Plans *(542)*
Nat'l Ass'n of Developmental Disabilities Councils *(542)*
Nat'l Ass'n of Epilepsy Centers *(542)*
Nat'l Ass'n of Foster Care Review Boards *(543)*
Nat'l Ass'n of Health Underwriters *(543)*
Nat'l Ass'n of Healthcare Consultants *(543)*
Nat'l Ass'n of Insurance Commissioners *(544)*
Nat'l Ass'n of Letter Carriers of the United States of America *(545)*
Nat'l Ass'n of Manufacturers *(545)*
Nat'l Ass'n of Minority Political Families, USA, Inc. *(545)*
Nat'l Ass'n of Nurse Practitioners in Women's Health *(546)*
Nat'l Ass'n of People with AIDS, Inc. *(546)*
Nat'l Ass'n of Portable X-Ray Providers *(546)*

Nat'l Ass'n of Protection and Advocacy Systems (NAPAS) (547)
Nat'l Ass'n of Psychiatric Health Systems (547)
Nat'l Ass'n of Public Hospitals and Health Systems (547)
Nat'l Ass'n of Rehabilitation Agencies (548)
Nat'l Ass'n of Retired Federal Employees (548)
Nat'l Ass'n of Rural Health Clinics (548)
Nat'l Ass'n of Social Workers (549)
Nat'l Ass'n of State Mental Health Program Directors (550)
Nat'l Ass'n of State Units on Aging (550)
Nat'l Ass'n of Surety Bond Producers (550)
Nat'l Ass'n of Urban Hospitals (551)
Nat'l Ass'n of VA Physicians and Dentists (551)
Nat'l Assembly of Health and Human Service Organizations (551)
Nat'l Black Women's Health Project (552)
Nat'l Breast Cancer Coalition (553)
Nat'l Campaign for Hearing Health (554)
Nat'l Center for Policy Analysis (555)
Nat'l Center for Public Policy Research (555)
Nat'l Child Support Enforcement Ass'n (555)
Nat'l Coalition for Cancer Survivorship (556)
Nat'l Committee to Preserve Social Security and Medicare (557)
Nat'l Council for Community Behavioral Healthcare (559)
Nat'l Council of Catholic Women (560)
Nat'l Council on the Aging (561)
Nat'l Electrical Manufacturers Ass'n (562)
Nat'l Employee Benefits Institute (562)
Nat'l Federation of Republican Women (564)
Nat'l Funeral Directors Ass'n (565)
Nat'l Grange (566)
Nat'l Health Council (567)
Nat'l Health Law Program (567)
Nat'l Kidney Foundation (569)
Nat'l Mental Health Ass'n (571)
Nat'l Military Family Ass'n (571)
Nat'l Partnership for Women and Families (573)
Nat'l Patient Advocate Foundation (573)
Nat'l Psoriasis Foundation (574)
Nat'l Quality Health Council (575)
Nat'l Rehabilitation Ass'n (575)
Nat'l Renal Administrators Ass'n (575)
Nat'l Right to Life Committee (576)
Nat'l Rural Health Ass'n (577)
Nat'l Taxpayers Union (579)
Nat'l Women's Law Center (581)
NETWORK, A Nat'l Catholic Social Justice Lobby (584)
New Jersey Hospital Ass'n (585)
New Jersey Organ & Tissue Sharing Network (585)
New York Life Insurance Co. (587)
New York Psychotherapy and Counseling Center (587)
New York State Ass'n of Health Care Providers (587)
New York State Health Facilities Ass'n (587)
New York University (588)
New York University Medical Center (588)
Newark, New Jersey, City of (588)
NISH - Creating Employment Opportunities for People with Severe Disabilities (590)
NitroMed, Inc. (590)
North American Brain Tumor Coalition (592)
North Carolina, Washington Office of the State of (593)
Northside Hospital (595)
Northwestern Memorial Hospital (595)
Northwood Inc. (596)
Novartis Corp. (596)
Nusgart Consulting, LLC (142)
O'Bryon & Co. (144)
O'Connor & Hannan, L.L.P. (144)
Odin, Feldman, & Pittleman, P.C. (145)
Ohio Hospital Ass'n (599)
Oklahoma State Medical Ass'n (600)
Olsten Health Services (600)
Omnicare, Inc. (600)
O'Neill, Athy & Casey, P.C. (147)
Opticians Ass'n of America (601)
Ortho Concepts (604)
Ostex Internat'l Inc. (604)
Outpatient Ophthalmic Surgery Soc. (604)
Ovations/United Health Group (604)
PacifiCare Health Systems (606)
Pain Care Coalition (606)
Parry, Romani, DeConcini & Symms (149)
Partnership for Caring (608)
Patient Access to Transplantation (PAT) Coalition (609)
Patton Boggs, LLP (150)
Pearson & Pipkin, Inc. (154)
Pedorthic Footwear Ass'n (610)
Pegasus Airwave (610)
PET Coalition (613)
The Petrizzo Group, Inc. (155)
Pfizer, Inc. (613)
Pharmaceutical Research and Manufacturers of America (614)
Pharmacia Corp. (615)
Philip Morris Management Corp. (615)
Physician Insurers Ass'n of America (616)
The Plexus Consulting Group (156)
Policy Directions, Inc. (158)
Polity Consulting (159)
PolyMedica Corp. (620)
Potomac Group (160)
Powell, Goldstein, Frazer & Murphy LLP (160)
Powers Pyles Sutter & Verville, PC (161)
Precision Medical (623)
Preston Gates Ellis & Rouvelas Meeds LLP (162)
Principal Financial Group (624)
Private Essential Access Community Hospitals (PEACH) Inc. (624)
Private Practice Section of the American Physical Therapy Ass'n (625)
Province Healthcare, Inc. (627)
Public Policy Partners, LLC (164)
Pure Encapsulations, Inc. (630)
Quest Diagnostics Inc. (631)
Reed, Smith, LLP (167)
ReGin Manufacturing Inc. (635)
Renal Leadership Council (636)
Renal Physicians Ass'n (636)
Respiratory Medication Providers Coalition (638)
Respironics (638)
The Retired Enlisted Ass'n (638)
The Retired Officers Ass'n (TROA) (638)
Ricchetti Inc. (169)
RMS Disease Management Inc. (641)
Liz Robbins Associates (169)
ROHO, Inc. (642)
Ross Abbott Laboratories (642)
Ross University School of Medicine in Dominica (642)
RoTech Medical Corp. (642)
Roxanne Laboratories, Inc. (643)
Rural Referral Centers Coalition (644)
J. T. Rutherford & Associates (173)
Rx Vitamins, Inc. (644)
Ryan, Phillips, Utrecht & MacKinnon (173)
Sagamore Associates, Inc. (174)
Santa Barbara Regional Health Authority (649)
SCAN Health Plan (651)
Schein Pharmaceutical, Inc. (651)
Schering Berlin Inc. (651)
Schering-Plough Corp. (651)
Schering-Plough Legislative Resources L.L.C. (651)
Serono Laboratories, Inc. (655)
Service Employees Internat'l Union (656)
Shaw Pittman (177)
Shelby, Tennessee, County of (657)
Signal Behavioral Health Network (659)
Sisters of Charity of Leavenworth Health Services (660)
Sisters of Providence Health Systems (660)
Smith & Nephew, Inc. (661)
Smith Dawson & Andrews, Inc. (183)
Smith, Bucklin and Associates, Inc. (184)
Soc. for Vascular Surgery (663)
Soc. of Diagnostic Medical Sonographers (663)
Soc. of Gynecologic Oncologists (663)
Soc. of Nuclear Medicine (663)
Soc. of Teachers of Family Medicine (664)
Soc. of Thoracic Surgeons (664)
Soc. of Vascular Technology (664)
Southcoast Health System (667)
Spaulding Rehabilitation Hospital (669)
SPECTRUM Science Public Relations, Inc. (186)
Spokane Area Chamber of Commerce (670)
Squire, Sanders & Dempsey L.L.P. (187)
St. Barnabas Healthcare System (671)
St. Bernard's Hospital (671)
St. Jude Medical, Inc. (671)
St. Peter's Medical Center (672)
St. Vincent Catholic Medical Centers (672)
Staff Builders, Inc. (672)
Stamford Hospital (672)
Sun Healthcare Group, Inc. (676)
Sunrise Medical (677)
Sunstone Behavioral Health (677)
Susquehanna Health System (678)
Swidler Berlin Shereff Friedman, LLP (191)
Taxpayers Against Fraud, The False Claims Legal Center (681)
Temple University Health System (683)
Tempur-Medical Inc. (683)
Texas Health Resources (684)
THA: An Ass'n of Hospitals and Health Systems (685)
Thomas Jefferson University Hospital (686)
Timmons and Co., Inc. (195)
Torchmark Corp. (688)
Tourette Syndrome Ass'n, Inc. (688)
Transtracheal Systems (691)
TREA Senior Citizens League (TSCL) (691)
Tri Path Inc. (691)
The Tri-Alliance of Rehabilitation Professionals (691)
TriWest Healthcare Alliance, Inc. (692)
Tulane University (693)
Tuvin Associates (197)
Tyco Internat'l (US), Inc. (695)
U.S. Oncology (697)
U.S. Strategies Corp. (197)
United Automobile, Aerospace and Agricultural Implement Workers of America (UAW) (700)
United Cerebral Palsy Ass'n (700)
United Health Group (701)
United Methodist Church General Board of Church and Society (702)
United Seniors Ass'n (702)
United States Coast Guard Chief Petty Officers Ass'n (703)
University of California, Office of Federal Government Relations (706)
University of Medicine and Dentistry of New Jersey (706)
University of Miami (706)
University of Tulsa (708)
University of Virginia (708)
University of Washington (708)
Urban Health Care Coalition of Pennsylvania (708)
Urologix, Inc. (709)
UroMedica Corp. (709)
Van Ness Feldman, P.C. (199)
Van Scoyoc Associates, Inc. (200)
Van Scoyoc Associates, Inc. (711)
Vanderbilt University (712)
Verner, Liipfert, Bernhard, McPherson and Hand, Chartered (202)
Vertis Neuroscience (714)
Vinson & Elkins L.L.P. (204)
Viohl and Associates, Inc. (205)
Visible Genetics (716)
Vitas Healthcare Corp. (717)
VSAdc.com (205)
Wake, North Carolina, County of (718)
R. Duffy Wall and Associates (205)
Washington Council Ernst & Young (206)
The Washington Group (208)
Washington Health Advocates (209)
Weider Nutritional Group (722)
WellPoint Health Networks/Blue Cross of California/UNICARE (723)
The Wexler Group (211)
Susan J. White & Associates (212)
Williams & Jensen, P.C. (215)
Winston & Strawn (218)

Wise & Associates *(220)*
Witman Associates *(220)*
Women and Infants' Hospital ***(729)***
Women Officials in NACo ***(729)***
Women's Hospital ***(729)***
Women's Hospital of Greensboro ***(729)***
Women's Policy, Inc. ***(729)***
Wound Ostomy Continence Nurses ***(731)***
Wyeth-Ayerst Laboratories ***(732)***
Wyeth-Ayerst Pharmaceuticals ***(732)***
XCEL Medical Pharmacy, Ltd. ***(732)***

Minting/Money/Gold Standard (MON)

American Amusement Machine Ass'n ***(245)***
American Bankers Ass'n ***(250)***
Americans for Common Cents ***(281)***
Amusement and Music Operators Ass'n ***(283)***
Arent Fox Kintner Plotkin & Kahn, PLLC *(14)*
Barrick Goldstrike Mines, Inc. ***(308)***
Bracy Williams & Co. *(31)*
Cassidy & Associates, Inc. *(42)*
Check Payment Systems Ass'n ***(341)***
The Coin Coalition ***(357)***
Crane & Co. ***(378)***
Dickstein Shapiro Morin & Oshinsky LLP *(61)*
Jack Ferguson Associates, Inc. *(75)*
Foley & Lardner *(78)*
Freeport-McMoRan Copper & Gold Inc. ***(425)***
General Motors Corp. ***(432)***
The Gold and Silver Institute ***(436)***
Homestake Mining ***(451)***
R. J. Hudson Associates *(101)*
Internat'l Ass'n of Professional Numismatists ***(468)***
Kennecott/Borax ***(488)***
King & Spalding *(113)*
Klein & Saks, Inc. *(114)*
McClure, Gerard & Neuenschwander, Inc. *(127)*
McDermott, Will and Emery *(128)*
Nat'l Licensed Beverage Ass'n ***(570)***
Nat'l Mining Ass'n ***(571)***
Olin Corp. ***(600)***
Patton Boggs, LLP *(150)*
Placer Dome U.S. Inc. ***(618)***
Platinum Guild Internat'l ***(619)***
The Plexus Consulting Group *(156)*
Sagamore Associates, Inc. *(174)*
Salt Lake City Olympic Organizing Committee ***(646)***
Save the Greenback Coalition ***(650)***
Silver Users Ass'n ***(659)***
Robert E. Smith *(182)*
Texas Instruments ***(684)***
Verner, Liipfert, Bernhard, McPherson and Hand, Chartered *(202)*
Wells & Associates *(211)*

Natural Resources (NAT)

#10 Enterprises LLC ***(223)***
Absaroka Trust ***(225)***
The Accord Group *(5)*
Adams and Reese LLP *(5)*
AEI Resources ***(229)***
AgriPartners ***(232)***
Air Force Memorial Foundation ***(233)***
Akin, Gump, Strauss, Hauer & Feld, L.L.P. *(8)*
Alaska Legislature ***(236)***
Alaska North Slope LNG Project ***(236)***
Alaska Wilderness League ***(237)***
Albertine Enterprises, Inc. *(10)*
Alcalde & Fay ***(237)***
Alcalde & Fay *(10)*
Aleutians East Borough ***(238)***
Alpine Group, Inc. *(11)*
Alyeska Pipeline Service Co. ***(242)***
American Ass'n for Laboratory Accreditation ***(246)***
American Camping Ass'n ***(251)***
American Coastal Coalition ***(253)***
American Farm Bureau Federation ***(258)***
American Farmland Trust ***(258)***
American Forest & Paper Ass'n ***(259)***
American Gas Ass'n ***(261)***
American Geological Institute ***(261)***
American Geophysical Union ***(261)***
American Hiking Soc. ***(262)***
American Motorcyclist Ass'n ***(268)***
American Petroleum Institute ***(269)***
American Plastics Council ***(270)***
American Public Gas Ass'n ***(271)***
American Public Works Ass'n ***(272)***
American Recreation Coalition ***(272)***
American Sheep Industry Ass'n ***(273)***
American Sportfishing Ass'n ***(278)***
American Waterways Operators ***(280)***
Americans for Equitable Climate Solutions ***(281)***
Anadarko Petroleum Corp. ***(283)***
Andalex Resources, Inc. ***(284)***
AngloGold North America ***(284)***
Animas-La Plata Water Conservancy District ***(284)***
APCO Worldwide *(14)*
Arctic Power ***(288)***
Arctic Slope Regional Corp. ***(288)***
Arent Fox Kintner Plotkin & Kahn, PLLC *(14)*
Arizona Power Authority ***(288)***
Arkansas, Office of the Governor of the State of ***(288)***
Ass'n of California Water Agencies ***(295)***
Ass'n of Metropolitan Sewerage Agencies ***(297)***
Ass'n of Nat'l Advertisers ***(297)***
Ass'n of Oregon Counties ***(297)***
Associated General Contractors of America ***(300)***
ATOFINA Chemicals, Inc. ***(302)***
Avalon, New Jersey, City of ***(304)***
Baca Land and Cattle Co. ***(305)***
Ball Janik, LLP *(22)*
Barents Group LLC *(23)*
Barrick Goldstrike Mines, Inc. ***(308)***
Barron Collier Co. ***(308)***
Bay Delta Urban Coalition ***(309)***
BHP (USA) Inc. ***(313)***
Leon G. Billings, Inc. *(27)*
Birch, Horton, Bittner & Cherot *(28)*
Bituminous Coal Operators Ass'n ***(314)***
BKSH & Associates *(28)*
Blackfeet Tribe of Montana ***(315)***
Boca Raton, Florida, City of ***(316)***
Boesch & Co. *(29)*
Bones Brothers Ranch ***(317)***
BP Amoco Corp. ***(319)***
Bracewell & Patterson, L.L.P. *(30)*
Bradley Arant Rose & White LLP *(31)*
Brickfield, Burchette, Ritts & Stone *(32)*
Broward, Florida, County of ***(322)***
Brunswick Corp. ***(322)***
Brush Wellman, Inc. ***(323)***
Bryan Cave LLP *(33)*
John G. "Toby" Burke *(34)*
Burlington Northern Santa Fe Railway ***(324)***
Burlington Resources Oil & Gas Co. ***(324)***
Calaveras County, California, Water District ***(326)***
California State Lands Commission ***(327)***
California Urban Water Conservation Council ***(327)***
California Water Service Co. ***(328)***
Calpine Corp. ***(328)***
Camara Nacional de la Industria Pesquera ***(328)***
Camp Dresser and McKee, Inc. ***(328)***
Jan Campbell *(36)*
Thomas D. Campbell & Assoc. *(36)*
Thomas D. Campbell & Assoc. ***(329)***
Canadian River Municipal Water Authority ***(329)***
Capital Research Center ***(330)***
Cargill Dow ***(331)***
Robert E. Carlstrom *(40)*
The Carmen Group *(40)*
Carpi & Clay *(41)*
Cassidy & Associates, Inc. *(42)*
Caterpillar Inc. ***(333)***
Center for Marine Conservation ***(337)***
Central Arizona Water Conservation District ***(338)***
Central Valley Project Water Ass'n ***(339)***
Chelan County Public Utility District ***(342)***
Chemical Land Holdings, Inc. ***(342)***
Chep USA ***(342)***
Chesapeake Bay Foundation ***(342)***
Chevron, U.S.A. ***(342)***
Chicago Botanic Garden ***(343)***
Cinergy Corp. ***(347)***
Citizens Against Government Waste ***(348)***
Citizens Against Research Bans ***(348)***
Clark & Weinstock, Inc. *(47)*
Clark County Regional Flood Control District ***(350)***
Clark County-McCarran Internat'l Airport ***(350)***
Clean Water Act Reauthorization Coalition ***(350)***
The Climate Council, ***(351)***
Coachella Valley Water District ***(352)***
Coalition for Reliable Energy ***(354)***
Coast Alliance ***(356)***
Coastal Conservation Ass'n ***(356)***
Coastal Impact Assistance & Reinvestment ***(356)***
Coeur d'Alene Mines Corp. ***(357)***
Colorado River Commission of Nevada ***(358)***
Colusa Basin Drainage District ***(359)***
Commercial Weather Services Ass'n (CWSA) ***(360)***
Compressed Gas Ass'n ***(364)***
Conservation Strategies, LLC *(51)*
Consumer Federation of America ***(369)***
Contango LLC *(52)*
Contra Costa Water District ***(370)***
Cook Inlet Region Inc. ***(371)***
Copeland, Lowery & Jacquez *(52)*
Corpus Christi, City of ***(373)***
Council for Conservation and Reinvestment of OCS Revenue ***(374)***
Council of Industrial Boiler Owners (CIBO) ***(375)***
Law Office of C. Deming Cowles *(54)*
Crowell & Moring LLP *(55)*
Cyprus Amex Minerals Co. ***(380)***
Dallas, Texas, City of ***(382)***
Dawson & Associates, Inc. *(59)*
Glenn Roger Delaney *(60)*
Delaware North Companies ***(384)***
Delta Wetlands Project ***(385)***
Dental Recycling North America ***(385)***
Dickstein Shapiro Morin & Oshinsky LLP *(61)*
Dimension 4 ***(388)***
The Doe Run Co. ***(390)***
Domestic Petroleum Council ***(390)***
Dominion Resources, Inc. ***(391)***
Douglas, Oregon, County of ***(391)***
Dow AgroSciences ***(391)***
Downey McGrath Group, Inc. *(64)*
Dredging Contractors of America ***(392)***
Ducks Unlimited Inc. ***(392)***
Duke Energy ***(392)***
Dunlap & Browder, Inc. *(67)*
Dunn-Padre, Inc. ***(393)***
The Dutko Group, Inc. *(68)*
Earthjustice Legal Defense Fund ***(394)***
East Bay Municipal Utility District ***(395)***
Eastern Municipal Water District ***(395)***
Edison Electric Institute ***(397)***
Edison Internat'l ***(397)***
El Dorado Irrigation District ***(399)***
El Paso Corporation ***(399)***
Elim, Alaska, City of ***(401)***
Emmonak Corp. ***(402)***
Encinitas, California, City of ***(402)***
Endangered Species Coordinating Council ***(402)***
Enron Corp. ***(403)***
ENS Resources, Inc. *(71)*
Entergy Services, Inc. ***(404)***
Envirocare of Utah, Inc. ***(404)***
Environmental Council of the States (ECOS) ***(405)***
Environmental Defense Fund ***(405)***
Environmental Land Technology Ltd. ***(405)***
EOP Group, Inc. *(72)*
Eureka, California, City of ***(408)***
Everglades Coordinating Council ***(408)***
Exelon Corp. ***(409)***
Exxon Mobil Corp. ***(409)***
EZ's Solutions, Inc. *(74)*
Fallon, Nevada, City of ***(410)***
Family Farm Alliance (Project Transfer Council) ***(410)***
Marcus G. Faust, P.C. *(74)*
Jack Ferguson Associates, Inc. *(75)*
The Ferguson Group, LLC *(76)*
The Fertilizer Institute ***(415)***
Finch-Pruyn Paper Co. ***(417)***
Fire Island Ass'n ***(417)***
Ruth Frances Fleischer *(77)*

Ocean Village Property Owners Ass'n, Inc. *(598)*
Oceanside, California, City of *(598)*
O'Connor & Hannan, L.L.P. *(144)*
Ogilvy Public Relations Worldwide *(145)*
Olivenhain Municipal Water District *(600)*
Omega Oil Co. *(600)*
O'Neill, Athy & Casey, P.C. *(147)*
Oppenheimer Wolff & Donnelly LLP *(147)*
Orange County Sanitation Districts *(602)*
Oregon Garden Foundation *(603)*
Oregon Utility Resource Coordination Ass'n (OURCA) *(603)*
Oregon Water Resources Congress *(603)*
P & H Mining Equipment *(605)*
Pacific Islands Washington Office *(148)*
The Pacific Lumber Co. *(605)*
Palo Alto, California, City of *(607)*
Paradise Canyon Resort *(607)*
Patton Boggs, LLP *(150)*
The Peabody Group *(610)*
Pennington BioMedical Research Center *(611)*
Perkins Coie LLP *(154)*
Personal Watercraft Industry Ass'n *(613)*
Petersburg, Alaska, City of *(613)*
Petroport, Inc. *(613)*
Phelps Dodge Corp. *(615)*
Phillips Petroleum Co. *(616)*
Phoenix, Arizona, City of *(616)*
Pierce, Washington, County of *(617)*
Placer Dome U.S. Inc. *(618)*
Portland, Oregon, City of *(621)*
Potomac Electric Power Co. *(622)*
Potomac Heritage Partnership *(622)*
Potomac Resources, Inc. *(160)*
Powell, Goldstein, Frazer & Murphy LLP *(160)*
Preservation Action *(623)*
Preston Gates Ellis & Rouvelas Meeds LLP *(162)*
Prowler Fisheries and Clipper Seafoods *(627)*
Public Generating Pool *(628)*
Public Strategies Washington, Inc. *(164)*
RAG North America *(632)*
Rails to Trails Conservancy *(632)*
Real Estate Roundtable *(634)*
Reed, Smith, LLP *(167)*
Renewable Natural Resources Foundation *(637)*
Renewable Resources LLC *(637)*
The Renkes Group, Ltd. *(168)*
John J. Rhodes *(169)*
Rio Grande Water Conservation District *(640)*
Robertson, Monagle & Eastaugh *(170)*
Roseville, California, City of *(642)*
Rural Public Lands County Council *(643)*
Rutgers University *(644)*
Ryan, Phillips, Utrecht & MacKinnon *(173)*
Sacramento, California, Public Works Agency of the County of *(645)*
Safari Club Internat'l *(645)*
Salt River Project *(646)*
San Carlos Irrigation and Drainage District *(647)*
San Diego County Water Authority *(647)*
San Diego, California, City of *(647)*
Sandia Pueblo *(648)*
Santa Clarita, California, City of *(649)*
Santini, Chartered *(175)*
Sappi Fine Paper NA *(649)*
Sarasota, Florida, City of *(649)*
Save America's Fossils for Everyone, Inc. *(650)*
Scenic America *(651)*
Scenic Hudson *(651)*
Schmeltzer, Aptaker & Shepard, P.C. *(176)*
Elinor Schwartz *(176)*
Sea Grant Ass'n *(653)*
Sealaska Corp. *(653)*
SEFBO Pipeline Bridge, Inc. *(654)*
Sellery Associates, Inc. *(177)*
Seneca Resources Corporation *(655)*
Shell Oil Co. *(657)*
Siemens Westinghouse Power Corporation *(658)*
Sierra Madre, California, City of *(658)*
Silver Users Ass'n *(659)*
Simon and Co., Inc. *(181)*
Six Agency Committee *(660)*
Smith & Harroff, Inc. *(182)*
The Smith-Free Group *(184)*
Soc. of American Foresters *(663)*
Solana Beach, California, City of *(665)*
The Solomon Group, LLC *(185)*
Solutia Inc. *(665)*
Somach, Simmons & Dunn *(665)*
Sonomish, Washington, County of *(665)*
Southdown, Inc. *(667)*
Southern Utah Wilderness Alliance *(668)*
Southern Ute Indian Tribe *(668)*
Southwestern Water Conservation District *(668)*
Sporting Arms and Ammunition Manufacturers' Institute, Inc. *(670)*
Sporting Goods Manufacturers Ass'n *(670)*
Springettsbury, Pennsylvania, Township of *(670)*
St. Augustine Beach, Florida, City of *(671)*
St. Lucie, Florida, County of *(672)*
St. Paul, Alaska, City of *(672)*
Stephens Law Offices *(188)*
Steptoe & Johnson LLP *(188)*
Stockton East Water District *(675)*
Strategic Horizons Advisors, L.L.C. *(189)*
Strategic Impact, Inc. *(189)*
Charlene A. Sturbitts *(190)*
Sugar Cane Growers Cooperative of Florida *(676)*
Sunkist Growers, Inc. *(677)*
Tacoma, Washington, City of *(680)*
TAPS Renewal Task Force *(681)*
TECO Energy, Inc. *(682)*
Terpstra Associates *(193)*
Texaco Group Inc. *(684)*
Thompson Creek Metals Co. *(686)*
Three Affiliated Tribes of Fort Berthold Reservation *(686)*
Timmons and Co., Inc. *(195)*
Toto USA, Inc. *(688)*
Trout Unlimited *(692)*
Trust for Public Land *(693)*
Christopher A.G. Tulou *(196)*
TXU Business Services *(695)*
U.S. English, Inc. *(696)*
U.S. Oil and Gas Ass'n *(696)*
U.S. Public Interest Research Group *(697)*
Union Pacific *(699)*
Union Sanitary District *(699)*
United Brotherhood of Carpenters and Joiners of America *(700)*
United Methodist Church General Board of Church and Society *(702)*
United States Energy Ass'n *(703)*
United States Sugar Corp. *(704)*
United States Tuna Foundation *(704)*
United Steelworkers of America *(704)*
University of Southwestern Louisiana *(707)*
UNOCAL Corp. *(708)*
Upper Klamath Water Users *(708)*
Upper Yampa Water Conservancy District *(708)*
USX Corp. *(710)*
Utah State University *(710)*
Ute Mountain Ute Indian Tribe *(710)*
Van Ness Feldman, P.C. *(199)*
Van Scoyoc Associates, Inc. *(200)*
Venice, Florida, City of *(712)*
Verizon Wireless *(713)*
Verner, Liipfert, Bernhard, McPherson and Hand, Chartered *(202)*
Vinson & Elkins L.L.P. *(204)*
Viohl and Associates, Inc. *(205)*
Virginia Living Museum *(716)*
Volusia, Florida, County of *(717)*
Vulcan Materials Co. *(718)*
Wake, North Carolina, County of *(718)*
Washington Council Ernst & Young *(206)*
Washington Strategies, L.L.C. *(209)*
Washoe County *(721)*
Water Replenishment District of Southern California *(721)*
Del E. Webb Corp. *(722)*
J. Arthur Weber & Associates *(210)*
Robert K. Weidner *(211)*
Wellton-Mohawk Irrigation and Drainage District *(723)*
Western Range Ass'n *(724)*
Western Urban Water Coalition *(725)*
Westlands Water District *(725)*
Westmoreland Coal Co. *(725)*
Weyerhaeuser Co. *(725)*
William F. Whitsitt Policy and Government Affairs *(213)*
Wild Alabama *(726)*
Wild Bird Feeding Institute *(726)*
Wildlife Habitat Council *(726)*
Wildlife Legislative Fund of America *(727)*
The Wildlife Soc. *(727)*
Will and Carlson, Inc. *(215)*
The Willard Group *(215)*
Williams & Jensen, P.C. *(215)*
Wolf Springs Ranches, Inc. *(729)*
World Resources Institute *(731)*
World Wildlife Fund *(731)*
Yukon Pacific *(734)*
Zane & Associates *(221)*

Pharmacy (PHA)

The 60/Plus Ass'n, Inc. *(224)*
AARP (American Ass'n of Retired Persons) *(224)*
Abbott Laboratories *(225)*
Academy of Managed Care Pharmacy *(225)*
Academy of Pharmaceutical Research and Science *(225)*
Adheris, Inc. *(227)*
Air Force Sergeants Ass'n *(233)*
Akin, Gump, Strauss, Hauer & Feld, L.L.P. *(8)*
Albers & Co. *(10)*
Alexander Strategy Group *(11)*
Alpine Group, Inc. *(11)*
Alzheimer's Ass'n *(242)*
American Ass'n for Marriage and Family Therapy *(246)*
American Ass'n of Colleges of Pharmacy *(247)*
American Ass'n of Health Plans (AAHP) *(248)*
American College of Clinical Pharmacy *(253)*
American Council of Independent Laboratories *(255)*
American Home Products Corp. *(262)*
American Managed Behavioral Healthcare Ass'n *(266)*
American Pharmaceutical Ass'n *(270)*
American Soc. of Consultant Pharmacists *(276)*
American Soc. of Health System Pharmacists *(276)*
American Teleservices Ass'n *(279)*
Americans for Medical Progress *(282)*
Amgen *(282)*
Andrx Pharmaceutical Corp. *(284)*
Animal Health Institute *(284)*
Ass'n of American Physicians and Surgeons *(294)*
Ass'n of Nat'l Advertisers *(297)*
Ass'n of University Programs in Health Administration *(299)*
Barbour Griffith & Rogers, Inc. *(22)*
Barr Laboratories *(308)*
Base Ten Systems, Inc. *(308)*
Baxter Healthcare Corp. *(309)*
Bayer Corp. *(309)*
Bennett Turner & Coleman, LLP *(25)*
Bergner Bockorny Castagnetti and Hawkins *(26)*
Biomedical Research Foundation of Northwest Louisiana *(314)*
BioPort Corp. *(314)*
Biotechnology Industry Organization *(314)*
Biovail Corp. Internat'l *(314)*
BKSH & Associates *(28)*
Blue Cross Blue Shield Ass'n *(315)*
Bone Care Internat'l *(317)*
Booher & Associates *(30)*
Bristol-Myers Squibb Co. *(320)*
Broydrick & Associates *(33)*
Burns and Roe Enterprises, Inc. *(324)*
Capitol City Group *(38)*
Capitol Health Group, LLC *(39)*
Caremark Rx, Inc. *(331)*
Citizens Against Government Waste *(348)*
Citizens for a Sound Economy *(348)*
ClaimTraq, Inc. *(349)*
Clark & Weinstock, Inc. *(47)*
Coalition for Government Procurement *(353)*
Coalition for Health Services Research *(354)*
Congressional Economic Leadership Institute *(366)*
Consumer Federation of America *(369)*

Consumer Healthcare Products Ass'n (369)
Consumers Union of the United States (369)
Cooney & Associates, Inc. (52)
CVS, Inc. (380)
Cystic Fibrosis Foundation (380)
Dalrymple and Associates, L.L.C. (56)
Detroit Medical Center (386)
Dow AgroSciences (391)
Downey McGrath Group, Inc. (64)
drugstore.com (392)
Duramed Pharmaceuticals, Inc. (393)
Edelman Public Relations Worldwide (396)
Elan Pharmaceutical Research Corp. (399)
Emord & Associates, P.C. (71)
F.B.A. (74)
Fierce & Isakowitz (416)
Fierce and Isakowitz (76)
Foley Government and Public Affairs, Inc. (78)
Food Marketing Institute (421)
Forscey & Stinson, PLLC (79)
The Fortier Group, LLC (79)
Foundation Health Federal Services, Inc. (424)
FoxKiser (79)
Fresenius Medical Care North America (425)
Genentech, Inc. (431)
Generic Pharmaceutical Ass'n (433)
Genzyme Corp. (433)
GlaxoSmithKline (436)
Greenberg Traurig, LLP (86)
Grisso Consulting (88)
Haarmann & Reimer Corp. (443)
Health Insurance Ass'n of America (446)
Healthcare Compliance Packaging Council (446)
Healthcare Distribution Management Ass'n (447)
Healthcare Leadership Council (447)
Heidepriem & Mager, Inc. (94)
Higgins, McGovern & Smith, LLC (94)
Hoffmann-La Roche Inc. (450)
Hogan & Hartson L.L.P. (96)
Hohlt & Associates (98)
Hooper Owen & Winburn (99)
Internat'l Academy of Compounding Pharmacists (467)
Internat'l Federation of Professional and Technical Engineers (471)
Internat'l Mass Retailers Ass'n (473)
IVAX Corp. (480)
The JAG Group, Inc. (481)
Johnson & Johnson, Inc. (484)
Kent & O'Connor, Inc. (112)
The Kinetics Group (489)
Knoll Pharmaceutical Co. (490)
Kogovsek & Associates (114)
Latham & Watkins (116)
Lee & Smith P.C. (118)
Lent Scrivner & Roth LLC (119)
Eli Lilly and Co. (499)
Lupus Foundation of America (505)
Management Options, Inc. (123)
Mayberry & Associates LLC (126)
Charlie McBride Associates, Inc. (127)
McDermott, Will and Emery (128)
Jack H. McDonald (129)
McGuiness & Holch (130)
McKesson Corp. (515)
Medco Containment Services, Inc. (516)
Medical Records Internat'l, Inc. (516)
Meditrend, Inc. (517)
Merck & Co. (518)
Minnesota Mining and Manufacturing Co. (3M Co.) (525)
Monsanto Co. (528)
Mylan Laboratories, Inc. (533)
Nat'l Alliance for the Mentally Ill (536)
Nat'l Alliance of State and Territorial AIDS Directors (537)
Nat'l Ass'n for Nutritional Choice (538)
Nat'l Ass'n of Chain Drug Stores (539)
Nat'l Ass'n of Community Health Centers (540)
Nat'l Ass'n of Nurse Practitioners in Women's Health (546)
Nat'l Ass'n of Pharmaceutical Manufacturers (546)
Nat'l Ass'n of Public Hospitals and Health Systems (547)
Nat'l Ass'n of VA Physicians and Dentists (551)
Nat'l Community Pharmacists Ass'n (558)
Nat'l Consumers League (558)
Nat'l Cosmetology Ass'n (559)
Nat'l Health Council (567)
Nat'l Legal Center for the Public Interest (570)
Nat'l Mental Health Ass'n (571)
Nat'l Military Family Ass'n (571)
Nat'l Right to Life Committee (576)
NeoPharm, Inc. (583)
NES, Inc. (141)
NextRX (589)
NitroMed, Inc. (590)
North Dakota State University (593)
Novartis Corp. (596)
The OB-C Group, LLC (143)
O'Brien, Klink & Associates (144)
Olsson, Frank and Weeda, P.C. (146)
Owens-Illinois, Inc. (605)
Parry, Romani, DeConcini & Symms (149)
Patton Boggs, LLP (150)
PDA (610)
PennField Oil Co. (611)
Pfizer, Inc. (613)
Pharmaceutical Research and Manufacturers of America (614)
Pharmacia Corp. (615)
Philipp Brothers Chemicals, Inc. (616)
The Plexus Consulting Group (156)
Podesta/Mattoon (158)
Policy Directions, Inc. (158)
Powell, Goldstein, Frazer & Murphy LLP (160)
Public Hospital Pharmacy Coalition (628)
Pure Encapsulations, Inc. (630)
Reed, Smith, LLP (167)
Respiratory Medication Providers Coalition (638)
Rx Vitamins, Inc. (644)
Ryan, Phillips, Utrecht & MacKinnon (173)
Sagamore Associates, Inc. (174)
Schering-Plough Corp. (651)
Serono Laboratories, Inc. (655)
Shaw Pittman (177)
Smith Dawson & Andrews, Inc. (183)
SPECTRUM Science Public Relations, Inc. (186)
Steptoe & Johnson LLP (188)
Stuntz, Davis & Staffier, P.C. (190)
Sun Healthcare Group, Inc. (676)
Swidler Berlin Shereff Friedman, LLP (191)
Texas Health Resources (684)
Timmons and Co., Inc. (195)
Tongour Simpson Holsclaw Green (196)
Torchmark Corp. (688)
TREA Senior Citizens League (TSCL) (691)
U.S. Strategies Corp. (197)
United States Coast Guard Chief Petty Officers Ass'n (703)
Van Ness Feldman, P.C. (199)
Verner, Liipfert, Bernhard, McPherson and Hand, Chartered (713)
Verner, Liipfert, Bernhard, McPherson and Hand, Chartered (202)
Vorys, Sater, Seymour and Pease, LLP (205)
VSAdc.com (205)
The Washington Group (208)
Weider Nutritional Group (722)
Wheat & Associates, Inc. (212)
Williams & Connolly (215)
Williams & Jensen, P.C. (215)
Winston & Strawn (218)
Wyeth-Ayerst Laboratories (732)
XCEL Medical Pharmacy, Ltd. (732)
Zone Therapeutics, Inc. (735)

Postal (POS)

AFL-CIO (American Federation of Labor and Congress of Industrial Organizations) (231)
The Aker Partners Inc. (7)
Akin, Gump, Strauss, Hauer & Feld, L.L.P. (8)
Alcalde & Fay (10)
Alliance of Nonprofit Mailers (241)
Allied Marketing (241)
American Ass'n of Orthodontists (249)
American Bankers Ass'n (250)
American Business Media (251)
American Express Co. (258)
American Farm Bureau Federation (258)
American Legion (266)
American Library Ass'n (266)
American Soc. of Ass'n Executives (275)
American Symphony Orchestra League (278)
AOL Time Warner (285)
Arizona Mail Order Co. (288)
Ass'n for Postal Commerce (292)
Ass'n of American Publishers (294)
Baker, Donelson, Bearman & Caldwell, P.C. (21)
Bell, California, City of (311)
Marshall A. Brachman (31)
Brownstein Hyatt & Farber, P.C. (33)
Cassidy & Associates, Inc. (42)
Celanese Government Relations Office (334)
Chamber of Commerce of the U.S.A. (340)
Cincinnati, Ohio, City of (347)
Classroom Publishers Ass'n (350)
CNF Transportation, Inc. (351)
Coalition Against Unfair U.S. Postal Service Competition (352)
Colex and Associates (48)
Computer and Communications Industry Ass'n (CCIA) (364)
Consumer Federation of America (369)
Consumers Union of the United States (369)
Council for Government Reform (374)
Cox Enterprises Inc. (378)
Delta Air Lines (384)
George H. Denison (60)
Dickstein Shapiro Morin & Oshinsky LLP (61)
Direct Marketing Ass'n Nonprofit Federation (388)
Direct Marketing Ass'n, Inc. (388)
R. R. Donnelley & Sons (391)
Draft Worldwide (392)
The Duberstein Group, Inc. (65)
The Dutko Group, Inc. (68)
Earle Palmer Brown Public Relations (70)
Easter Seals (395)
Edmund Scientific Co. (397)
Envelope Manufacturers Ass'n of America (404)
Ann Eppard Associates, Ltd. (72)
Estes Associates (73)
Evans & Black, Inc. (73)
Express One Internat'l Inc. (409)
Federal Access (75)
FedEx Corp. (415)
Fontheim Partners, PC (78)
Gainesville, Florida, City of (428)
Girl Scouts of the U.S.A. - Washington Office (435)
Haake and Associates (89)
Hall, Green, Rupli, LLC (90)
Hallmark Cards, Inc. (443)
HP Global Workplaces, Inc. (454)
Impact Strategies (102)
Incentive Federation Sweepstakes Trust Fund (458)
Independent Office Products and Furniture Dealers Ass'n (459)
Internat'l Brotherhood of Teamsters (469)
Internat'l Business Machines Corp. (469)
Internat'l Federation of Professional and Technical Engineers (471)
Intuit, Inc. (477)
Jorden Burt LLP (109)
Juvenile Diabetes Foundation Internat'l (485)
Laborers' Internat'l Union of North America (493)
Lake, California, County of (494)
The Limited Inc. (499)
Magazine Publishers of America (507)
Mail 2000, Inc. (507)
MailBoxes Etc. (507)
Main Street Coalition for Postal Fairness (507)
Manatt, Phelps & Phillips, LLP (123)
Dawson Mathis & Associates (126)
Jack H. McDonald (129)
McGraw-Hill Cos., The (514)
Miami Beach, Florida, City of (521)
Michigan Bulb (522)
J. P. Morgan Chase & Co. (529)
The MWW Group (140)
James Pierce Myers (140)

Nat'l Ass'n of Letter Carriers of the United States of America (545)
Nat'l Ass'n of Postmasters of the U.S. (546)
Nat'l Ass'n of Uniform Manufacturers and Distributors (551)
Nat'l Consumers League (558)
Nat'l Grange (566)
Nat'l League of Postmasters of the U.S. (569)
Nat'l Newspaper Ass'n (572)
Nat'l Public Radio (574)
Nat'l Retail Federation (576)
Nat'l Rural Electric Cooperative Ass'n (576)
Nat'l Soc. of Professional Engineers (578)
Nat'l Star Route Mail Contractors Ass'n (578)
Nat'l Trust for Historic Preservation (580)
Nat'l Wholesale Co., Inc. (581)
NAVCOM Systems, Inc. (583)
Newark, New Jersey, City of (588)
Newspaper Ass'n of America (589)
North Slope Borough, Alaska (593)
Northwest Airlines, Inc. (595)
The OB-C Group, LLC (143)
Bartley M. O'Hara (145)
Parcel Shippers Ass'n (608)
Patton Boggs, LLP (150)
J. C. Penney Co., Inc. (611)
Bradford A. Penney (154)
Pitney Bowes, Inc. (618)
Policy Consulting Services (158)
Preservation Action (623)
Preston Gates Ellis & Rouvelas Meeds LLP (623)
Preston Gates Ellis & Rouvelas Meeds LLP (162)
Printing Industries of America (624)
The Reader's Digest Ass'n (633)
Robertson, Monagle & Eastaugh (170)
Ryan, Phillips, Utrecht & MacKinnon (173)
San Leandro, California, City of (648)
Wayne Schley (176)
Sidley & Austin (180)
Simon and Co., Inc. (181)
Bill Simpson & Associates (181)
Squire, Sanders & Dempsey L.L.P. (187)
Stamps.com (672)
Synapse (679)
George C. Tagg (192)
Thompson Coburn LLP (194)
United Parcel Service (702)
United States Coast Guard Chief Petty Officers Ass'n (703)
Van Ness Feldman, P.C. (199)
The Vantage Group, Inc. (712)
Verner, Liipfert, Bernhard, McPherson and Hand, Chartered (713)
Washington Council Ernst & Young (206)
Wiley, Rein & Fielding (214)
Williams & Jensen, P.C. (215)

Railroads (RRR)

Academy of Rail Labor Attorneys (226)
AFL-CIO - Transportation Trades Department (231)
Alaska Railroad (237)
Albemarle Corp. (237)
Alcalde & Fay (10)
Alliance for Rail Competition (240)
Amalgamated Transit Union (242)
Ameren Services (243)
American Ass'n of Motor Vehicle Administrators (248)
American Forest & Paper Ass'n (259)
American Magline Group (266)
American Passenger Rail Coalition (269)
American Public Power Ass'n (272)
American Short Line and Regional Railroad Ass'n (274)
American Teleservices Ass'n (279)
Americans for Equitable Climate Solutions (281)
Ass'n of American Railroads (294)
The Laurin Baker Group (20)
Ball Janik, LLP (22)
The Barton Co. (24)
Bethlehem Steel Corp. (312)
Broe Companies, Inc. (321)
Brotherhood of Locomotive Engineers (322)
Brotherhood of Maintenance of Way Employees (322)
Brownsville, Texas, Port of (322)
Burlington Northern Santa Fe Railway (324)
Canadian Nat'l Railway Co. (329)
Canton Railroad Co. (330)
Celanese Government Relations Office (334)
CEMEX USA (335)
Chambers Associates Inc. (45)
Chambers, Conlon & Hartwell (45)
Chicago Southshore and South Bend Railroad (343)
Ciba Specialty Chemicals Corp. (346)
Colling Swift & Hynes (49)
ComEd (359)
Consumer Federation of America (369)
Consumers United for Rail Equity (369)
Coors Brewing Company (371)
CSX Corp. (379)
Law Offices of Kevin G. Curtin (56)
Delaware and Hudson Railroad (384)
Delaware Otsego System (384)
Dorfman & O'Neal, Inc. (63)
Downey McGrath Group, Inc. (64)
The Duberstein Group, Inc. (65)
DuPont (393)
Dykema Gossett PLLC (69)
Eckert Seamans Cherin & Mellott, LLC (70)
Ann Eppard Associates, Ltd. (72)
Ethyl Corp. (407)
Exelon Corp. (409)
F&T Network, Inc. (74)
The Ferguson Group, LLC (76)
The Fertilizer Institute (415)
Fisher Consulting (77)
Fluor Corp. (420)
FMC Corp. (420)
Foley & Lardner (78)
G.R. Services (80)
Gary, Indiana, Washington Office of the City of (429)
General Electric Co. (432)
General Motors Corp. (432)
Golden Gate Bridge Highway and Transportation District (437)
Government Relations, Inc. (84)
Grand Trunk Corp. (438)
Great Lakes Corporate Resources (439)
Greenbrier Companies (440)
Guinea, Secretary General of the Presidency of the Republic of (442)
Hattiesburg, Mississippi, City of (445)
Hecht, Spencer & Associates (93)
High Speed Ground Transportation Ass'n (449)
Honberger and Walters, Inc. (99)
Hooper Owen & Winburn (99)
The ILEX Group (102)
Infrastructure Management Group (103)
Intermodal Ass'n of North America (467)
Internat'l Brotherhood of Boilermakers, Iron Shipbuilders, Blacksmiths, Forgers and Helpers (469)
Internat'l Brotherhood of Electrical Workers (469)
Internat'l Federation of Professional and Technical Engineers (471)
Johnson Co. (107)
Joint Powers Board (484)
Kaiser Aluminum & Chemical Corp. (485)
Kansas City Southern Industries (486)
Kansas City Southern Railway Co. (486)
Kessler & Associates Business Services, Inc. (112)
KOSA (491)
Lee Lane (116)
Lawler, Metzger & Milkman, LLC (117)
The Laxalt Corp. (117)
The Paul Laxalt Group (117)
Legislative Solutions (118)
Lent Scrivner & Roth LLC (119)
Lockridge Grindal & Nauen, P.L.L.P. (121)
Lyondell Chemical Co. (506)
Management Options, Inc. (123)
Mass Transit Authority (512)
Mayer, Brown & Platt (126)
McGlotten & Jarvis (129)
Denny Miller McBee Associates (134)
James T. Molloy (135)
Alan J. Moore, Washington Representative - Governmental Affairs (136)
Mullenholz, Brimsek & Belair (138)
Muncie, Indiana, City of (Delaware County) (532)
Murray, Scheer, Montgomery, Tapia & O'Donnell (139)
Nat'l Ass'n of Wheat Growers (551)
Nat'l Corn Growers Ass'n (559)
Nat'l Democratic County Officials Organization (562)
Nat'l Grain and Feed Ass'n (566)
Nat'l Grange (566)
Nat'l Mining Ass'n (571)
Nat'l Railroad and Construction Maintenance Ass'n (575)
Norfolk Southern Corp. (591)
Norfolk Southern Railroad (591)
Norfolk, Virginia, City of (591)
North Carolina, Washington Office of the State of (593)
Bartley M. O'Hara (145)
Paducah & Louisville Railroad (606)
Palm Springs, California, City of (606)
Parsons Corp. (608)
Patton Boggs, LLP (150)
Paul, Hastings, Janofsky & Walker LLP (153)
Peyser Associates, Inc. (155)
Phillips Petroleum Co. (616)
Port Authority of New York and New Jersey (621)
Potomac Electric Power Co. (622)
Potomac Group (160)
Powell, Goldstein, Frazer & Murphy LLP (160)
Preston Gates Ellis & Rouvelas Meeds LLP (162)
Sydney Probst (164)
Rail Supply and Service Coalition (632)
Railway Progress Institute (632)
RBG Associates (166)
Robertson, Monagle & Eastaugh (170)
Rohm and Haas Co. (642)
Roquette America (642)
Roseville, California, City of (642)
Ryan, Phillips, Utrecht & MacKinnon (173)
San Diego Metropolitan Transit Development Board (647)
Simula, Inc. (659)
Slover & Loftus (182)
E. Del Smith and Co. (183)
The Smith-Free Group (184)
Solutia Inc. (665)
Soo Line Railroad, Inc. (666)
South Carolina Public Railways (666)
Southeastern Michigan Council of Government (667)
St. Louis/Lake Counties Regional Rail Authority (672)
Stephens Law Offices (188)
Strategic Horizons Advisors, L.L.C. (189)
Talgo (680)
Tate-LeMunyon, LLC (192)
Thompson Coburn LLP (194)
Timmons and Co., Inc. (195)
Transportation-Communications Internat'l Union (691)
Troutman Sanders LLP (196)
TTX Co. (693)
Union Pacific (699)
United Parcel Service (702)
United Transportation Union (705)
Valis Associates (198)
Van Ness Feldman, P.C. (199)
Van Scoyoc Associates, Inc. (200)
Vinson & Elkins L.L.P. (204)
Wabtec Corp. (718)
Washington Infrastructure Services, Inc. (719)
Washington, Department of Transportation of the State of (721)
Western Coal Traffic League (724)
The Wexler Group (211)
Wheat Export Trade Education Committee (725)
Wheeling & Lake Erie Railway Co. (726)
Wiley, Rein & Fielding (214)
Williams & Jensen, P.C. (215)
Winston & Strawn (218)
Wisconsin Central Transportation Corp. (728)
Zane & Associates (221)

Real Estate/Land Use/Conservation (RES)

#10 Enterprises LLC *(223)*
500 C Street Associates, L.P. *(224)*
59/Air Depot Road, Ltd. *(224)*
The Accord Group *(5)*
Advanced Power Technologies, Inc. *(228)*
The Advocacy Group *(6)*
AgriPartners *(232)*
Air Force Memorial Foundation *(233)*
Akin, Gump, Strauss, Hauer & Feld, L.L.P. *(8)*
Alaska Legislature *(236)*
Alaska Professional Hunters Ass'n *(236)*
Alaska Pulp Corp. *(237)*
Alaska State Snowmobile Ass'n *(237)*
Alcalde & Fay *(10)*
Aleut Corp. *(238)*
America Outdoors *(243)*
American Bar Ass'n *(250)*
American Forest & Paper Ass'n *(259)*
American Hiking Soc. *(262)*
American Homeowners Grassroots Alliance *(262)*
American Hotel and Lodging Ass'n *(263)*
The American Institute of Architects *(264)*
American League of Financial Institutions *(266)*
American Realty Advisors *(272)*
American Rental Ass'n *(272)*
American Resort Development Ass'n *(272)*
American Wood Preservers Institute *(280)*
Anchorage, Alaska, Municipality of *(283)*
Apartment and Office Building Ass'n of Metropolitan Washington *(286)*
Appraisal Institute *(287)*
APTI *(287)*
Archery Manufactures & Merchants Organization *(287)*
Arctic Slope Regional Corp. *(288)*
Arter & Hadden *(17)*
Ass'n Management Group *(18)*
Ass'n of O & C Counties *(297)*
Barrick Goldstrike Mines, Inc. *(308)*
Barron Collier Co. *(308)*
Birch, Horton, Bittner & Cherot *(28)*
BKSH & Associates *(28)*
Richard W. Bliss *(29)*
Bohemian Cos. *(317)*
Bracy Williams & Co. *(31)*
Brookhill Redevelopment *(321)*
Building Owners and Managers Ass'n Internat'l *(323)*
Burlington Northern Santa Fe Railway *(324)*
Calaveras County, California, Water District *(326)*
California State Lands Commission *(327)*
Canadian River Municipal Water Authority *(329)*
Capital Consultants Corp. *(37)*
Capitol Hill Advocates *(39)*
Carlsberg Management Co. *(332)*
Carmen & Muss, P.L.L.C. *(40)*
The Carmen Group *(40)*
Cash, Smith & Wages *(41)*
CCI Construction *(334)*
Cendant Corp. *(335)*
Center for Public Dialogue *(337)*
Chamber of Commerce of the U.S.A. *(340)*
Carolyn C. Chaney & Associates *(45)*
Cherokee Investment Partners, LLC *(342)*
Cincinnati, Ohio, City of *(347)*
Citizens Against Government Waste *(348)*
Clark & Weinstock, Inc. *(47)*
Clark County, Nevada, Office of the County Manager *(350)*
Clark County-McCarran Internat'l Airport *(350)*
The Clark Estates, Inc. *(350)*
Clyde's Restaurant Group *(351)*
CMC/Heartland Partnership *(351)*
Ronald J. Cohen Investments *(357)*
Colorado River Commission of Nevada *(358)*
Commonwealth Atlantic Properties *(362)*
Community Ass'ns Institute (CAI) *(362)*
The Conservation Fund *(367)*
Consumer Federation of America *(369)*
Cook Inlet Region Inc. *(371)*
Cooper, Carvin & Rosenthal *(52)*
Copeland, Lowery & Jacquez *(371)*
Copeland, Lowery & Jacquez *(52)*
Council of Industrial Boiler Owners (CIBO) *(375)*
The Da Vinci Group *(56)*
Daishowa America Co., Ltd. *(381)*
Dal Mac Investment Corp. *(382)*
Dallas, Texas, City of *(382)*
Dare County *(382)*
Dawson & Associates, Inc. *(59)*
Daytona Beach, City of *(383)*
Defenders of Wildlife *(383)*
Delta Wetlands Project *(385)*
Denhill DC LCC *(385)*
Dolce Internat'l *(390)*
Ducks Unlimited Inc. *(392)*
Dunn-Padre, Inc. *(393)*
DuPont *(393)*
The Dutko Group, Inc. *(68)*
Eckert Seamans Cherin & Mellott, LLC *(70)*
Edison Properties L.L.C. *(397)*
Einhorn, Yaffee, Prescott *(399)*
Elim Native Corp. *(401)*
Elmer Larson, Inc. *(401)*
Environmental Commonsense Coalition *(405)*
Environmental Land Technology Ltd. *(405)*
Environmental Redevelopers Ass'n *(405)*
Eureka, California, City of *(408)*
Everglades Coordinating Council *(408)*
The Eyak Corp. *(409)*
Fairfax, Virginia, County of *(410)*
Marcus G. Faust, P.C. *(74)*
Federal Communications Bar Ass'n *(412)*
The Ferguson Group, LLC *(76)*
First American *(417)*
First American Real Estate Solutions LLC *(417)*
Flathead Joint Board of Control *(418)*
Florida Citrus Mutual *(419)*
Florida Farm Bureau *(419)*
Florida Sugar Cane League, Inc. *(420)*
Foley & Lardner *(78)*
Foley Government and Public Affairs, Inc. *(78)*
The Foundation for Environmental and Economic Progress *(424)*
The Freedom Forum *(425)*
Freeport-McMoRan Copper & Gold Inc. *(425)*
French & Company *(79)*
John Freshman Associates, Inc. *(79)*
General Motors Corp. *(432)*
David F. Godfrey *(83)*
Gordley Associates *(84)*
Government Relations, Inc. *(84)*
GPC Internat'l *(85)*
Greenberg Traurig, LLP *(86)*
J. Steven Griles & Associates *(88)*
Guaranty Bank, SSB *(442)*
Guaynabo, Puerto Rico, City of *(442)*
Haake and Associates *(89)*
Harbor Philadelphia Center City Office, Ltd. *(444)*
The Hawthorn Group, L.C. *(92)*
Hecht, Spencer & Associates *(93)*
Heritage Development *(448)*
Historic Landmarks Foundation of Indiana *(450)*
Hoffman Management, Inc. *(450)*
Hogan & Hartson L.L.P. *(96)*
Hohlt & Associates *(98)*
Holland & Knight LLP *(98)*
Hooper Owen & Winburn *(99)*
Humboldt Bay Municipal Water District *(455)*
Hunton & Williams *(101)*
IMC Global Inc. *(458)*
Impact Strategies *(102)*
Indian Pueblos Federal Development Corp. *(460)*
Intermountain Forest Industry Ass'n *(467)*
Internat'l Council of Shopping Centers *(470)*
Internat'l Downtown Ass'n *(471)*
Internat'l Sign Ass'n *(474)*
Internat'l Snowmobile Manufacturers Ass'n *(474)*
Irrigation Ass'n *(479)*
The Irvine Co. *(479)*
Jacobs Engineering Group Inc. *(481)*
Jamison and Sullivan, Inc. *(104)*
JBG Real Estate Associates *(482)*
Jefferson Government Relations, L.L.C. *(106)*
Kaiser Aluminum & Chemical Corp. *(485)*
Keating Development Corp. *(487)*
Kilpatrick Stockton LLP *(112)*
Charles Klatskin and Co. *(490)*
Kogovsek & Associates *(114)*
Kurzweil & Associates *(115)*
Lake, California, County of *(494)*
Land Grant Development *(494)*
Land Trust Alliance *(494)*
LaRocco & Associates *(116)*
Las Vegas Valley Water District *(495)*
Latona Associates, Inc. *(496)*
Lawler, Metzger & Milkman, LLC *(117)*
LCOR, Inc. *(496)*
League of California Cities *(497)*
Lee & Smith P.C. *(118)*
Levine-Fricke Restoration Corp. *(498)*
Lincoln Airport *(500)*
Lincoln Property Co. *(500)*
The Livingston Group, LLC *(120)*
Luxcore Public Affairs *(506)*
Manatt, Phelps & Phillips, LLP *(123)*
Manufactured Housing Institute *(509)*
MARC Associates, Inc. *(124)*
Ron C. Marlenee *(125)*
Marriott Internat'l, Inc. *(511)*
McClure, Gerard & Neuenschwander, Inc. *(127)*
McGuireWoods L.L.P. *(130)*
Medical Research Laboratories *(516)*
Merle Hay Mall Limited Partners *(519)*
Metropolitan King County Council *(520)*
The Metropolitan Water District of Southern California *(521)*
Meyers & Associates *(133)*
Miles & Stockbridge, P.C. *(133)*
Mills Corporation *(524)*
Monroe Center, LLC *(527)*
Monroe, New York, County of *(528)*
Montana Land Reliance *(528)*
Kay Allan Morrell, Attorney-at-Law *(137)*
Mortgage Bankers Ass'n of America *(530)*
Motorcycle Industry Council *(531)*
Murray, Scheer, Montgomery, Tapia & O'Donnell *(139)*
The MWW Group *(140)*
Nassif & Associates *(535)*
Nat'l Affordable Housing Management Ass'n *(535)*
Nat'l Ass'n of Industrial and Office Properties *(544)*
Nat'l Ass'n of Manufacturers *(545)*
Nat'l Ass'n of Mortgage Brokers *(545)*
Nat'l Ass'n of Negro Business & Professional Women's Clubs, Inc. *(546)*
Nat'l Ass'n of Real Estate Investment Trusts *(547)*
Nat'l Ass'n of Realtors *(547)*
Nat'l Ass'n of RV Parks and Campgrounds *(548)*
Nat'l Ass'n of State Departments of Agriculture *(549)*
Nat'l Ass'n of Wheat Growers *(551)*
Nat'l Audubon Soc. *(552)*
Nat'l Building Museum *(553)*
Nat'l Endangered Species Act Reform Coalition *(563)*
Nat'l Farmers Union (Farmers Educational & Co-operative Union of America) *(563)*
Nat'l Housing Conference *(567)*
Nat'l Lumber and Building Material Dealers Ass'n *(570)*
Nat'l Mining Ass'n *(571)*
Nat'l Spa and Pool Institute *(578)*
Nat'l Trust for Historic Preservation *(580)*
Nat'l Wildlife Federation - Office of Federal and Internat'l Affairs *(581)*
Nat'l Women's History Museum *(581)*
Natural Resources Defense Council *(582)*
The Nature Conservancy *(582)*
New Haven, Connecticut, City of *(585)*
Nixon Peabody LLP *(142)*
Norfolk Southern Corp. *(591)*
North Slope Borough, Alaska *(593)*
Nossaman, Gunther, Knox & Elliott *(596)*
Nutter & Harris, Inc. *(143)*
Ocean County, NJ Utilities Authority *(598)*
John T. O'Rourke Law Offices *(147)*
Parry, Romani, DeConcini & Symms *(149)*
Patton Boggs, LLP *(150)*
Pelican Butte Corp. *(611)*
Pembroke Real Estate, Inc. *(611)*
PenRose Corp. *(611)*

Peoria, Arizona, City of ***(612)***
Perkins Coie LLP *(154)*
Personal Watercraft Industry Ass'n ***(613)***
Petro Star, Inc. ***(613)***
Peyser Associates, Inc. *(155)*
Philip Morris Management Corp. ***(615)***
Piedmont Environmental Council ***(617)***
Plum Creek Timber Co. ***(619)***
Policy Development Group, Inc. ***(620)***
Portals Development Associates L.P. ***(621)***
Potomac Electric Power Co. ***(622)***
Preservation Action ***(623)***
Preston Gates Ellis & Rouvelas Meeds LLP *(162)*
Prince William County Service Authority ***(624)***
Princess Tours ***(624)***
Quinnat Landing Hotel ***(631)***
Real Access Alliance ***(634)***
Real Estate Roundtable ***(634)***
Recreational Equipment Inc. ***(635)***
Reed, Smith, LLP *(167)*
The Renkes Group, Ltd. *(168)*
Republic Properties Corp. ***(637)***
RFB, Inc. *(168)*
Robertson, Monagle & Eastaugh *(170)*
Roseville, California, City of ***(642)***
Rothleder Associates, Inc. *(172)*
Royer & Babyak *(172)*
Ryan, Phillips, Utrecht & MacKinnon *(173)*
Safari Club Internat'l ***(645)***
Sagamore Associates, Inc. *(174)*
Salt River Pima Maricopa Indian Community ***(646)***
San Joaquin Council of Governments ***(648)***
Scenic America ***(651)***
Elinor Schwartz *(176)*
Scottsdale, Arizona, City of ***(652)***
Seal Beach, California, City of ***(653)***
Sealaska Corp. ***(653)***
Sheet Metal and Air Conditioning Contractors' Nat'l Ass'n ***(657)***
Sierra Club ***(658)***
The Charles E. Smith Companies ***(661)***
Smith Development, LLC ***(661)***
Smith Martin & Boyette *(184)*
Soc. for Marketing Professional Services ***(662)***
Soc. of Industrial and Office Realtors ***(663)***
South African Government/World Bank ***(666)***
Southdown, Inc. ***(667)***
Southern Utah Wilderness Alliance ***(668)***
Spokane Area Chamber of Commerce ***(670)***
Sporting Goods Manufacturers Ass'n ***(670)***
Springettsbury, Pennsylvania, Township of ***(670)***
Square 3942 Associates Limited Partnership ***(671)***
St. George Tanaq ***(671)***
Starwood Lodging/Starwood Capital Group, L.P. ***(673)***
Stephens Law Firm *(188)*
Steptoe & Johnson LLP *(188)*
Julien J. Studley, Inc. ***(675)***
Sugar Cane Growers Cooperative of Florida ***(676)***
Swidler Berlin Shereff Friedman, LLP *(191)*
TAPS Renewal Task Force ***(681)***
Texaco Group Inc. ***(684)***
Transit Mixed Concrete Co. ***(690)***
Trinity Partners, Inc. ***(692)***
Trizec Hahn Corp. ***(692)***
Trust for Public Land ***(693)***
U.S. Public Interest Research Group ***(697)***
Ungaretti & Harris *(197)*
United States Business and Industry Council ***(703)***
United States Sugar Corp. ***(704)***
University of Alaska ***(705)***
Upland, California, City of ***(708)***
Utah State University ***(710)***
Valanzano & Associates *(198)*
Van Ness Feldman, P.C. *(199)*
Verner, Liipfert, Bernhard, McPherson and Hand, Chartered *(202)*
Vinson & Elkins L.L.P. *(204)*
Vornado Inc. ***(717)***
VSAdc.com *(205)*
Warland Investment Co. ***(718)***
The Washington Group *(208)*
Edmund B. Welch *(211)*
West*Group Management LLC ***(723)***
Western Development ***(724)***
Westfield America, Inc. ***(725)***
Wild Alabama ***(726)***
Wild Bird Feeding Institute ***(726)***
Williams & Jensen, P.C. *(215)*
Woodmont Corporation ***(730)***
World Wildlife Fund ***(731)***
W. G. Yates & Sons Construction Co. ***(733)***
Zurich U.S. Specialties ***(735)***

Religion (REL)

ABB, Inc. ***(225)***
Alcalde & Fay *(10)*
American Bar Ass'n ***(250)***
American Council of Life Insurers ***(256)***
American Federation of Teachers ***(259)***
American Jewish Committee ***(265)***
American Soc. of Composers, Authors and Publishers ***(276)***
Americans United for Separation of Church and State ***(282)***
Anglican Catholic Church ***(284)***
Anti-Defamation League ***(285)***
Catholic Alliance ***(333)***
Chamber of Commerce of the U.S.A. ***(340)***
Christian Coalition of America ***(345)***
Christian Network, Inc. ***(345)***
Christian Voice, Inc. ***(345)***
Family Research Council, Inc. ***(411)***
First Amendment Coalition for Expression ***(417)***
Friends Committee on Nat'l Legislation ***(426)***
Janus-Merritt Strategies, L.L.C. *(104)*
Jar-Mon Consultants, Inc. *(105)*
Justice Fellowship ***(485)***
Nat'l Campaign for a Peace Tax Fund ***(554)***
Bartley M. O'Hara *(145)*
Palumbo & Cerrell, Inc. *(149)*
People Advancing Christian Education (PACE) ***(611)***
People for the American Way ***(612)***
Phillips Petroleum Co. ***(616)***
San Bernardino Valley Municipal Water District ***(647)***
Sumlin Associates *(190)*
Traditional Values Coalition ***(689)***

Retirement (RET)

The 60/Plus Ass'n, Inc. ***(224)***
7-Eleven, Inc. ***(224)***
AARP (American Ass'n of Retired Persons) ***(224)***
Aetna Inc. ***(230)***
AFL-CIO (American Federation of Labor and Congress of Industrial Organizations) ***(231)***
Akin, Gump, Strauss, Hauer & Feld, L.L.P. *(8)*
Alameda, California, County of ***(236)***
Allmerica Financial ***(241)***
American Academy of Actuaries ***(243)***
American Airlines ***(244)***
American Bankers Ass'n ***(250)***
American Bar Ass'n ***(250)***
American Benefits Council ***(250)***
American Chemical Soc. ***(252)***
American Council of Life Insurers ***(256)***
American Express Co. ***(258)***
American Federation of Senior Citizens ***(258)***
American Federation of State, County and Municipal Employees ***(258)***
American Federation of Teachers ***(259)***
American Institute of Certified Public Accountants ***(264)***
American Institute of Chemical Engineers ***(264)***
American Internat'l Group, Inc. ***(265)***
American Military Soc. ***(268)***
American Optometric Ass'n ***(269)***
American Payroll Ass'n ***(269)***
American Seniors Housing Ass'n ***(273)***
American Soc. of Ass'n Executives ***(275)***
American Soc. of Pension Actuaries ***(277)***
American Staffing Ass'n ***(278)***
Americans for Tax Reform ***(282)***
The Arc ***(287)***
Ashland Inc. ***(290)***
Ass'n for Los Angeles Deputy Sheriffs ***(292)***
Ass'n Growth Enterprises *(18)*
Ass'n of American Geographers ***(293)***
Ass'n of American Railroads ***(294)***
Assisted Living Federation of America ***(300)***
Barbour Griffith & Rogers, Inc. *(22)*
Barksdale Ballard & Co., Inc. *(23)*
The Barton Co. *(24)*
Bay Area Rapid Transit District ***(309)***
Berkeley, California, City of ***(312)***
Berwind Corp. ***(312)***
Bituminous Coal Operators Ass'n ***(314)***
Bracewell & Patterson, L.L.P. *(30)*
Buchanan Ingersoll, P.C. *(34)*
Buffalo Carpenters Pension Fund ***(323)***
Burlington Northern Santa Fe Railway ***(324)***
Business and Professional Women/USA ***(324)***
The Business Roundtable ***(325)***
California Correctional Peace Officers Ass'n ***(326)***
California State Teachers' Retirement System ***(327)***
Campbell Crane & Associates *(36)*
Canadian Nat'l Railway Co. ***(329)***
Caplin & Drysdale, Chartered *(40)*
Cash Balance Coalition ***(333)***
Center for Freedom and Prosperity ***(336)***
Center on Budget and Policy Priorities ***(338)***
Chamber of Commerce of the U.S.A. ***(340)***
Christian Voice, Inc. ***(345)***
The Chubb Corp. ***(346)***
CIGNA Corp. ***(346)***
Citigroup ***(347)***
Citizens Against Government Waste ***(348)***
Coalition for American Financial Security ***(352)***
Committee for a Responsible Federal Budget ***(360)***
Concord Coalition ***(365)***
Consumer Federation of America ***(369)***
Consumers Union of the United States ***(369)***
Cook, Illinois, County of ***(371)***
Copeland, Lowery & Jacquez *(52)*
Council for Government Reform ***(374)***
Covington & Burling *(53)*
Cummins Engine Co. ***(380)***
Cuyahoga, Ohio, County of ***(380)***
Davis & Harman LLP *(57)*
Dayton, Ohio, Washington Office of the City of ***(383)***
Dewey Ballantine LLP *(61)*
Downey McGrath Group, Inc. *(64)*
The Duberstein Group, Inc. *(65)*
The Equitable Cos. ***(406)***
The ERISA Industry Committee (ERIC) ***(406)***
The ESOP (Employee Stock Ownership Plan) Ass'n ***(407)***
FBI Agents Ass'n ***(412)***
Feder, Semo, Clarke & Bard *(74)*
Financial Executives International ***(416)***
Financial Planning Ass'n ***(416)***
Financial Programs, Inc. *(77)*
Fleet Reserve Ass'n ***(418)***
Fraternal Order of Police ***(425)***
General Conference of Seventh-day Adventists ***(431)***
General Motors Corp. ***(432)***
Greenberg Traurig, LLP *(86)*
Groom Law Group, Chartered *(88)*
The Hartford ***(445)***
Health Insurance Ass'n of America ***(446)***
Hewlett-Packard Co. ***(449)***
Hogan & Hartson L.L.P. *(96)*
Household Internat'l, Inc. ***(453)***
Hudson Institute ***(454)***
Hunt Management Systems *(101)*
ING America Insurance Holdings, Inc. ***(462)***
Institute of Electrical and Electronics Engineers, Inc. ***(464)***
Institute on Religion and Public Policy ***(464)***
Internat'l Ass'n of Fire Chiefs ***(468)***
Internat'l Brotherhood of Boilermakers, Iron Shipbuilders, Blacksmiths, Forgers and Helpers ***(469)***
Internat'l Brotherhood of Electrical Workers ***(469)***
Internat'l Brotherhood of Teamsters ***(469)***
Internat'l Business Machines Corp. ***(469)***
Internat'l Union of Bricklayers and Allied Craftsworkers ***(476)***
Internat'l Union of Painters and Allied Trades ***(476)***

Internat'l Union of Police Ass'ns *(476)*
Investment Co. Institute *(477)*
ITT Industries *(480)*
Jar-Mon Consultants, Inc. *(105)*
Jones, Day, Reavis & Pogue *(485)*
Kaiser Aluminum & Chemical Corp. *(485)*
Kehoe & Hambel *(110)*
Labor Council for Latin American Advancement (LCLAA) *(493)*
Shannon M. Lahey Associates *(116)*
Ledge Counsel *(118)*
LegisLaw *(118)*
Los Angeles, California, County of *(504)*
Lucent Technologies *(505)*
Lynn, Massachusetts, City of *(506)*
Manufacturers Alliance/MAPI Inc. *(509)*
Marine Corps Reserve Officers Ass'n *(510)*
MassMutual Financial Group *(512)*
McDermott, Will and Emery *(128)*
Merrill Lynch & Co., Inc. *(519)*
Metropolitan Life Insurance Co. *(520)*
Miami-Dade, Florida, County of *(521)*
The Military Coalition *(524)*
Miller & Chevalier, Chartered *(133)*
Money Management Institute *(527)*
MONY Life Insurance Co. *(529)*
The Moore Law Firm, PLLC *(136)*
Morgan, Lewis & Bockius LLP *(136)*
Murray, Scheer, Montgomery, Tapia & O'Donnell *(139)*
Nat'l Ass'n for Uniformed Services *(538)*
Nat'l Ass'n of Assistant United States Attorneys *(539)*
Nat'l Ass'n of Executive Secretaries and Administrative Assistants *(542)*
Nat'l Ass'n of Foster Grandparent Program Directors *(543)*
Nat'l Ass'n of Government Deferred Compensation Administrators *(543)*
Nat'l Ass'n of Letter Carriers of the United States of America *(545)*
Nat'l Ass'n of Manufacturers *(545)*
Nat'l Ass'n of Negro Business & Professional Women's Clubs, Inc. *(546)*
Nat'l Ass'n of Professional Employer Organizations *(547)*
Nat'l Ass'n of Retired Federal Employees *(548)*
Nat'l Ass'n of State Units on Aging *(550)*
Nat'l Ass'n of Thrift Savings Plan Participants *(550)*
Nat'l Committee to Preserve Social Security and Medicare *(557)*
Nat'l Conference of Bankruptcy Judges *(558)*
Nat'l Council on Teacher Retirement *(561)*
Nat'l Education Ass'n of the U.S. *(562)*
Nat'l Employee Benefits Institute *(562)*
Nat'l Federation of Republican Women *(564)*
Nat'l League of Postmasters of the U.S. *(569)*
Nat'l Military Family Ass'n *(571)*
Nat'l Soc. of Professional Engineers *(578)*
Nat'l Taxpayers Union *(579)*
Nat'l Telephone Cooperative Ass'n *(579)*
Nat'l Women's Law Center *(581)*
Naval Reserve Ass'n *(582)*
NETWORK, A Nat'l Catholic Social Justice Lobby *(584)*
New England Financial *(585)*
New England Life Insurance Co. *(585)*
New York Life Insurance Co. *(587)*
Newport News Shipbuilding Inc. *(588)*
Niche Plan Sponsors, Inc. *(589)*
Norfolk Southern Corp. *(591)*
Julia J. Norrell & Associates *(142)*
Northwestern Mutual Life Insurance Co. *(595)*
nPower Advisors, LLC *(596)*
O'Bryon & Co. *(144)*
O'Connor & Hannan, L.L.P. *(144)*
Pacific Life Insurance Co. *(605)*
Paley Rothman Goldstein Rosenberg & Cooper *(148)*
Patton Boggs, LLP *(150)*
Paul, Hastings, Janofsky & Walker LLP *(610)*
Pearson & Pipkin, Inc. *(154)*
J. C. Penney Co., Inc. *(611)*
The Petrizzo Group, Inc. *(155)*
Pfizer, Inc. *(613)*
Philip Morris Management Corp. *(615)*
Phillips Petroleum Co. *(616)*
Podesta/Mattoon *(158)*
Principal Financial Group *(624)*
Printing Industries of America *(624)*
Production Service & Sales District Council Pension Fund *(625)*
Professional Managers Ass'n *(626)*
Profit Sharing/401 (k) Council of America *(626)*
Railroad Retirement Tax Working Group *(632)*
Retirement Income Coalition *(639)*
Retirement Industry Trust Ass'n *(639)*
Robert Wood Johnson Foundation *(641)*
Frank Russell Co. *(644)*
Ryan, Phillips, Utrecht & MacKinnon *(173)*
Ryder System, Inc. *(644)*
Charles Schwab & Co., Inc., *(652)*
Securities Industry Ass'n *(654)*
Small Business Council of America *(661)*
Soc. of Professional Benefit Administrators *(664)*
State Street Bank and Trust Co. *(673)*
Strategic Impact, Inc. *(189)*
Stuntz, Davis & Staffier, P.C. *(190)*
Sunrise Research Corp. *(191)*
Symms, Lehn & Associates, Inc. *(192)*
TIAA-CREF *(686)*
Timmons and Co., Inc. *(195)*
Transportation-Communications Internat'l Union *(691)*
TREA Senior Citizens League (TSCL) *(691)*
United Automobile, Aerospace and Agricultural Implement Workers of America (UAW) *(700)*
United Brotherhood of Carpenters and Joiners of America *(700)*
United Methodist Church General Board of Church and Society *(702)*
United Seniors Ass'n *(702)*
United States Coast Guard Chief Petty Officers Ass'n *(703)*
UNOCAL Corp. *(708)*
UNUM/Provident Corp. *(708)*
USX Corp. *(710)*
Valanzano & Associates *(198)*
Valente Lopatin & Schulze *(198)*
Van Scoyoc Associates, Inc. *(200)*
Verner, Liipfert, Bernhard, McPherson and Hand, Chartered *(202)*
Vinson & Elkins L.L.P. *(204)*
Washington Council Ernst & Young *(206)*
WESTVACO *(725)*
Susan J. White & Associates *(212)*
Deborah F. Winston *(218)*
Winston & Strawn *(218)*
Women Officials in NACo *(729)*
X-PAC *(732)*
Zurich Financial Group *(735)*

Roads/Highway (ROD)

3Tex *(223)*
Adams and Reese LLP *(5)*
Advocates for Highway and Auto Safety *(229)*
AFL-CIO - Transportation Trades Department *(231)*
Ainslie Associates *(7)*
Akin, Gump, Strauss, Hauer & Feld, L.L.P. *(8)*
Alabama, Department of Transportation of the State of *(235)*
Alaska Legislature *(236)*
Albuquerque, New Mexico, City of *(237)*
Alcalde & Fay *(10)*
Aldaron Inc. *(238)*
Alexandria, Virginia, City of *(238)*
Allstate Insurance Co. *(241)*
American Ass'n of Motor Vehicle Administrators *(248)*
American Bus Ass'n *(251)*
American Concrete Pavement Ass'n (ACPA) *(255)*
American Consulting Engineers Council *(255)*
American Council of Independent Laboratories *(255)*
American Farm Bureau Federation *(258)*
American Gas Ass'n *(261)*
American Highway Users Alliance *(262)*
The American Institute of Architects *(264)*
American Iron and Steel Institute *(265)*
American Motorcyclist Ass'n *(268)*
American Public Health Ass'n *(271)*
American Public Works Ass'n *(272)*
American Subcontractors Ass'n, Inc. *(278)*
American Trucking Ass'ns *(279)*
American Wood Preservers Institute *(280)*
Americans for Equitable Climate Solutions *(281)*
Americans for Tax Reform *(282)*
Anchorage, Alaska, Municipality of *(283)*
Arkansas, Office of the Governor of the State of *(288)*
Ashland Inc. *(290)*
Asphalt Systems, Inc. *(291)*
Ass'n for Commuter Transportation *(292)*
Associated Equipment Distributors *(300)*
Associated General Contractors of America *(300)*
Ross Atkins *(18)*
Automotive Aftermarket Industry Ass'n *(303)*
Automotive Parts and Service Alliance *(303)*
Ball Janik, LLP *(22)*
Ball State University *(306)*
The Barton Co. *(24)*
Bellevue, Washington, City of *(311)*
Bergner Bockorny Castagnetti and Hawkins *(26)*
Bethlehem Steel Corp. *(312)*
Bibb, Georgia, Board of Commissioners of the County of *(313)*
Birch, Horton, Bittner & Cherot *(28)*
BKSH & Associates *(28)*
Bracy Williams & Co. *(31)*
Bradley Arant Rose & White LLP *(31)*
Broward, Florida, County of *(322)*
Build Indiana Council *(323)*
Burlington Northern Santa Fe Railway *(324)*
C.A. Vencemos *(325)*
Calspan University of Buffalo Research Center *(328)*
Capital Partnerships (VA) Inc. *(37)*
Capitol Hill Advocates *(39)*
The Carmen Group *(40)*
The Carter Group *(41)*
CaseNewHolland Inc. *(333)*
Cassidy & Associates, Inc. *(42)*
Caterpillar Inc. *(333)*
Cemento Bayano *(335)*
Cementos Monterrey, S.A. *(335)*
CEMEX Central, S.A. de C.V. *(335)*
CEMEX USA *(335)*
CH2M Hill *(340)*
Chambers Associates Inc. *(45)*
Chicago, Illinois, Washington Office of the City of *(343)*
Citizens Against Government Waste *(348)*
Clackamas, Oregon, County of *(349)*
Clark & Weinstock, Inc. *(47)*
Clearwater, Florida, City of *(350)*
CNF Transportation, Inc. *(351)*
Coastal Impact Assistance & Reinvestment *(356)*
Colorado River Indian Tribes *(358)*
Community Transportation Ass'n of America *(363)*
Construction Management Ass'n of America *(368)*
Consumer Federation of America *(369)*
Continental Teves *(370)*
Copeland, Lowery & Jacquez *(371)*
Copeland, Lowery & Jacquez *(52)*
Corporacion Valenciana de Cementos Portland, S.A. *(372)*
Corporacion Venezolana de Cementos, SACA *(372)*
Corpus Christi, City of *(373)*
Craig Associates *(55)*
Dakota, Minnesota, County of *(381)*
Dallas, Texas, City of *(382)*
Dayton, Ohio, Washington Office of the City of *(383)*
Dekalb, Illinois, City of *(384)*
Dulles Area Transportation Ass'n *(393)*
The Dutko Group, Inc. *(68)*
Elkem Materials Inc. *(401)*
Energy Absorption Systems, Inc. *(403)*
Fairfax, Virginia, County of *(410)*
FedEx Corp. *(415)*
The Ferguson Group, LLC *(76)*
The Fertilizer Institute *(415)*

Fisher Consulting (77)
R. G. Flippo and Associates, Inc. (77)
FMC Corp. (420)
Foley Government and Public Affairs, Inc. (78)
Ford Motor Co. (422)
Friends of the Earth (426)
G.R. Services (80)
Gainesville, Florida, City of (428)
Sara Garland (and Associates) (81)
Gary, Indiana, Washington Office of the City of (429)
General Motors Corp. (432)
Genesis Consulting Group, LLC (82)
GHL Inc. (82)
Gila River Indian Community (435)
Golden Gate Bridge Highway and Transportation District (437)
Goodyear Tire and Rubber Co. (437)
Government Relations, Inc. (84)
Jay Grant & Associates (85)
Greater Washington Board of Trade (439)
Grupo Empresarial Maya (441)
Guinea, Secretary General of the Presidency of the Republic of (442)
James E. Guirard (89)
Gulf Coast Portland Cement Co. (442)
Halliburton/Brown & Root (443)
G.E. Harris Harmon (445)
Frederic R. Harris, Inc. (445)
Hattiesburg, Mississippi, City of (445)
Heavy Vehicle Maintenance Group (447)
Highway 53 Longrange Improvement Citizens' Task Force (449)
The Home Depot (451)
Peter Homer (99)
Hood River, Oregon, Port of (452)
Houston Shell and Concrete (453)
Huntsville, Alabama, City of (455)
I-49 Roadbuilders Coalition (456)
The ILEX Group (102)
Indiana, Office of the Governor of the State of (460)
Industrial Fabrics Ass'n Internat'l (461)
Infrastructure Management Group (103)
Intermodal Ass'n of North America (467)
Internat'l Brotherhood of Electrical Workers (469)
Internat'l Brotherhood of Teamsters (469)
Internat'l Downtown Ass'n (471)
Internat'l Federation of Professional and Technical Engineers (471)
Internat'l Union of Painters and Allied Trades (476)
Jacobs Engineering Group Inc. (481)
Janus-Merritt Strategies, L.L.C. (104)
Jefferson Government Relations, L.L.C. (106)
Johnson Co. (107)
Johnston & Associates, LLC (107)
Jorden Burt LLP (109)
Kaiser Aluminum & Chemical Corp. (485)
Betty Ann Kane & Co. (110)
Keller Equity Group, Inc. (487)
Koch Industries, Inc. (490)
Lake, California, County of (494)
Lake, Illinois, County of (494)
Lee Lane (116)
Laredo, Texas, City of (495)
Las Cruces, New Mexico, City of (495)
Lawler, Metzger & Milkman, LLC (117)
Legislative Solutions (118)
LegisLaw (118)
Lehigh Portland Cement Co. (498)
LMRC, Inc. (121)
Lockridge Grindal & Nauen, P.L.L.P. (121)
Los Angeles, California, Metropolitan Transit Authority of (504)
Manatt, Phelps & Phillips, LLP (123)
Alan Mauk Associates, Ltd. (126)
McDonald's Corp. (514)
Metropolitan Transportation Commission (520)
Mexam Trade, Inc. (521)
Meyers & Associates (133)
Miami Beach, Florida, City of (521)
Denny Miller McBee Associates (134)
Minnesota Mining and Manufacturing Co. (3M Co.) (525)
Modesto, California, City of (527)
Monroe, Louisiana, Chamber of Commerce of the City of (528)
Monroe, Louisiana, City of (528)
Monroe, New York, County of (528)
Montgomery, Alabama, Chamber of Commerce of (529)
Murray, Scheer, Montgomery, Tapia & O'Donnell (139)
Nat'l Asphalt Pavement Ass'n (537)
Nat'l Ass'n of Attorneys General (539)
Nat'l Ass'n of Independent Insurers (544)
Nat'l Ass'n of Surety Bond Producers (550)
Nat'l Ass'n of Towns and Townships (551)
Nat'l Corn Growers Ass'n (559)
Nat'l Democratic County Officials Organization (562)
Nat'l Grain and Feed Ass'n (566)
Nat'l Grange (566)
Nat'l Ready Mixed Concrete Ass'n (575)
Nat'l Soc. of Professional Engineers (578)
Nat'l Truck Equipment Ass'n (580)
Nat'l Trust for Historic Preservation (580)
Nat'l Utility Contractors Ass'n (NUCA) (580)
NATSO, Inc. (582)
New York Roadway Improvement Coalition (587)
Newark, New Jersey, City of (588)
Niagara Frontier Transportation Authority (589)
Norchem Concrete Products Inc. (591)
Norfolk Southern Corp. (591)
Norfolk, Virginia, City of (591)
North Carolina, Washington Office of the State of (593)
North Metro Mayors Coalition (593)
Northeast Ohio Areawide Coordination Agency (NOACA) (593)
Northeast-Midwest Institute (594)
Oakland, Michigan, County of (598)
Obadal and MacLeod, p.c. (143)
Oceanside, California, City of (598)
Oklahoma City, Oklahoma, City of (599)
Oklahoma Department of Transportation (599)
Oldcastle Materials Group (600)
Orange County Transportation Authority (602)
Oregon Department of Transportation (603)
Ouachita Parish Police Jury (604)
Outdoor Advertising Ass'n of America (604)
PACCAR, Inc. (605)
Pacific Coast Cement (605)
Palmdale, California, City of (606)
Palo Alto, California, City of (607)
Palumbo & Cerrell, Inc. (149)
Parry, Romani, DeConcini & Symms (149)
Parsons Brinckerhoff Inc. (608)
Parsons Corp. (608)
Paul, Hastings, Janofsky & Walker LLP (153)
Perkins Coie LLP (154)
Petroleum Marketers Ass'n of America (613)
Peyser Associates, Inc. (155)
Philadelphia, Pennsylvania, City of (615)
Phoenix, Arizona, City of (616)
Port Authority of New York and New Jersey (621)
Powell, Goldstein, Frazer & Murphy LLP (160)
Preservation Action (623)
Preston Gates Ellis & Rouvelas Meeds LLP (162)
Red River Trade Council (635)
Regional Planning Commission (635)
Riverside South Planning Corp. (640)
Robinson Terminal (641)
Roseville, California, City of (642)
Rubber Manufacturers Ass'n (643)
Safety Harbor, Florida, City of (645)
Salinas, California, City of (646)
Salt Institute (646)
San Diego, California, City of (647)
San Jose, California, City of (648)
Santa Clara Valley Transportation Authority (649)
Santa Clarita, California, City of (649)
Scenic America (651)
Seattle, Washington, City of (653)
Sheet Metal Workers' Internat'l Ass'n (657)
Sierra Madre, California, City of (658)
SIGCOM, Inc. (659)
Simon Strategies/Mindbeam (181)
Southern California Ass'n of Governments (667)
Specialized Carriers and Rigging Ass'n (669)
Spokane, Washington, City of (670)
Kenneth F. Stinger (189)
Strat@Comm (Strategic Communications Counselors) (189)
Strategic Horizons Advisors, L.L.C. (189)
Francis J. Sullivan Associates (190)
Sunbelt Cement (677)
Texas A&M Research Foundation (684)
Tire Ass'n of North America (687)
Tolmex (688)
Torchmark Corp. (688)
Traffic.com (689)
Truckload Carriers Ass'n (693)
Tulare, California, County of (694)
United Motorcoach Ass'n (702)
Upland, California, City of (708)
Van Scoyoc Associates, Inc. (200)
Verner, Liipfert, Bernhard, McPherson and Hand, Chartered (202)
Viohl and Associates, Inc. (205)
Visalia, California, City of (716)
VSAdc.com (205)
Vulcan Materials Co. (718)
Wakota Bridge Coalition (718)
Washington Infrastructure Services, Inc. (719)
Washington, Department of Transportation of the State of (721)
Winston & Strawn (218)
Youngstown-Warren Regional Chamber (733)
Zuckert, Scoutt and Rasenberger, L.L.P. (221)

Science/Technology (SCI)

3001, Inc. (223)
3Com Corp. (223)
3gi, Inc. (223)
AccuWeather (226)
ACS Defense, Inc. (227)
ADA Consulting Services (5)
Michael W. Adcock (6)
The Advocacy Group (6)
Aiken and Edgenfield Counties, South Carolina, Economic Development Partnership of (233)
Ainslie Associates (7)
Air Force Ass'n (233)
Air Quality Standards Coalition (234)
Air-Conditioning and Refrigeration Institute (234)
Alabama A & M University (235)
Albertine Enterprises, Inc. (10)
Alcalde & Fay (10)
Alcan Aluminum Corp. (237)
Alcatel USA (237)
allacrossamerica.com (238)
Alliance for Nuclear Accountability (240)
Alliance to Save Energy (241)
Alliant Techsystems, Inc. (241)
Alltel Corporation (242)
Alzheimer's Ass'n (242)
AMDeC Policy Group, Inc. (242)
American Academy of Orthopaedic Surgeons (244)
American Ass'n for Dental Research (245)
American Ass'n for Laboratory Accreditation (246)
American Ass'n for the Study of Liver Diseases (246)
American Ass'n of Colleges of Osteopathic Medicine (247)
American Ass'n of Colleges of Pharmacy (247)
American Ass'n of Community Colleges (247)
American Ass'n of Engineering Societies (247)
American Ass'n of Motor Vehicle Administrators (248)
American Ass'n of Museums (248)
American Ass'n of Physics Teachers (249)
American Ass'n of University Professors (249)
American Astronautical Soc. (250)
American Astronomical Soc. (250)
American Bioenergy Ass'n (251)
American Biophysics Corp. (251)
American Boiler Manufacturers Ass'n (251)
American Ceramics Soc. (252)
American Chemical Soc. (252)
American College of Clinical Pharmacy (253)
American College of Obstetricians and Gynecologists (254)

American Consulting Engineers Council *(255)*
American Continental Group, Inc. *(12)*
American Council of Independent Laboratories *(255)*
American Electronics Ass'n *(257)*
American Feed Industry Ass'n *(259)*
American Gas Ass'n *(261)*
American Geological Institute *(261)*
American Geophysical Union *(261)*
American Heart Ass'n *(262)*
American Institute of Chemical Engineers *(264)*
American Institute of Physics *(264)*
American Institute of Ultrasound in Medicine *(264)*
American Legion *(266)*
American Management Systems *(266)*
American Methanol Institute *(268)*
American Museum of Natural History *(268)*
American Nat'l Metric Council *(268)*
American Physical Soc. *(270)*
American Psychiatric Ass'n *(271)*
American Psychological Ass'n *(271)*
American Psychological Soc. *(271)*
American Public Power Ass'n *(272)*
American Seed Trade Ass'n *(273)*
American Soc. for Biochemistry and Molecular Biology *(274)*
American Soc. for Cell Biology *(274)*
American Soc. for Microbiology *(274)*
American Soc. for Quality *(275)*
American Soc. of Civil Engineers *(276)*
American Soc. of Hematology *(276)*
American Soc. of Mechanical Engineers *(276)*
American Soc. of Plant Physiologists *(277)*
American Speech, Language, and Hearing Ass'n *(277)*
American Teleservices Ass'n *(279)*
American Wood Preservers Institute *(280)*
Americans for Medical Progress *(282)*
Americans for Tax Reform *(282)*
Amgen *(282)*
Morris J. Amitay, P.C. *(13)*
Analytical Systems, Inc. *(283)*
Ancore Corp. *(284)*
Applied Knowledge Group *(286)*
Aquarium of the Pacific *(287)*
Archimedes Technology Group *(287)*
Arista Knowledge Systems, Inc. *(288)*
Arizona Science Center *(288)*
Arnold & Porter *(16)*
James Nicholas Ashmore & Associates *(18)*
The Ass'n For Manufacturing Technology (AMT) *(292)*
Ass'n of American Geographers *(293)*
Ass'n of American Medical Colleges *(294)*
Ass'n of Independent Research Institutes *(296)*
Ass'n of Professors of Medicine *(298)*
Ass'n of Science Technology Centers, Inc. *(298)*
Ass'n of Technology Act Projects *(299)*
Associated Universities Inc. *(300)*
Astro Vision Internat'l, Inc. *(301)*
AstroVision Inc. *(301)*
AT&T *(301)*
The Atlantic Group, Public Affairs, Inc. *(18)*
The Audubon Institute *(302)*
Automotive Parts and Service Alliance *(303)*
Auyua Inc. *(304)*
Battelle *(309)*
Battelle Memorial Institute *(309)*
Baxter Healthcare Corp. *(309)*
BCI, Inc. *(310)*
Vikki Bell *(25)*
Bergner Bockorny Castagnetti and Hawkins *(26)*
Big Sky Consulting, Inc. *(27)*
Biophysical Soc. *(314)*
Biotechnology Industry Organization *(314)*
Bishop Museum *(314)*
BKSH & Associates *(28)*
BMW (U.S.) Holding Corp. *(316)*
Board on Human Sciences *(316)*
The Boeing Co. *(316)*
Boys Town Nat'l Research Hospital *(318)*
Marshall A. Brachman *(31)*
Brandeis University *(319)*
Bridgestone/Firestone, Inc. *(320)*
Broad-Band Solutions *(32)*
Broadforum *(321)*
Bruker Meerestechnik GmbH *(322)*
Building Owners and Managers Ass'n Internat'l *(323)*
Burdeshaw Associates, Ltd. *(34)*
Burlington Northern Santa Fe Railway *(324)*
Burns and Roe Enterprises, Inc. *(324)*
Business Software Alliance *(325)*
C&M Internat'l, Ltd. *(35)*
California Central Coast Research Partnership *(326)*
California Institute of Technology *(327)*
CALSTART *(328)*
Campaign Finance Reform Coalition *(328)*
Canberra Packard BioScience *(330)*
Candle Corp. *(330)*
Mark R. Cannon *(37)*
Capital Strategies Group, Inc. *(37)*
Capitol City Group *(38)*
Capitol Coalitions Inc. *(38)*
Capitol Hill Advocates *(39)*
Capitol Partners *(39)*
Capitol Solutions *(39)*
Cargill Dow *(331)*
Cargill, Inc. *(331)*
Bill Carney & Co. *(41)*
Carpi & Clay *(41)*
Cascade Associates *(41)*
Cassidy & Associates, Inc. *(42)*
Cavarocchi Ruscio Dennis Associates *(44)*
Celera Genomics *(334)*
Cell Tech *(334)*
Cellular Telecommunications and Internet Ass'n *(334)*
Center for Regulatory Effectiveness *(337)*
Central College *(338)*
Chabot Space & Science Center *(340)*
Challenger Center for Space Science Education *(340)*
Chamber of Commerce of the U.S.A. *(340)*
Carolyn C. Chaney & Associates *(45)*
China.com *(345)*
Chwat and Company, Inc. *(46)*
CIGNA Corp. *(346)*
Cisco Systems Inc. *(347)*
Citizens for Public Action on Cholesterol, Inc. *(348)*
Cleveland Clinic Foundation *(350)*
The Climate Council, *(351)*
Coal Utilization Research Council *(352)*
Coalition of Academic Scientific Computation (CASC) *(355)*
COGEMA, Inc. *(357)*
Cohen Mohr LLP *(48)*
Scott Cohen *(48)*
Coleman Aerospace Co. *(357)*
Color Pigments Manufacturers Ass'n, Inc. *(358)*
Columbus Public Affairs *(50)*
COMARCO Wireless Technology *(359)*
Commercial Internet Exchange Ass'n *(360)*
Commercial Weather Services Ass'n (CWSA) *(360)*
Commonwealth Consulting Corp. *(50)*
Commonwealth Group, Ltd. *(50)*
Computer and Communications Industry Ass'n (CCIA) *(364)*
Computer Associates Internat'l, Inc. *(364)*
Computing Research Ass'n *(364)*
Compuware Corp. *(364)*
Congressional Institute, Inc. *(366)*
Conkling, Fiskum & McCormick *(51)*
Consortium for Oceanographic Research and Education (CORE) *(367)*
Consortium for Regional Climate Centers *(368)*
Consortium of Social Science Ass'ns *(368)*
Consumer Electronics Ass'n *(369)*
Consumer Energy Council of America Research Foundation *(369)*
Consumer Federation of America *(369)*
Convergence Services, Inc. *(52)*
Cooler Heads Coalition *(371)*
Cooley's Anemia Foundation *(371)*
Copeland, Lowery & Jacquez *(52)*
Corel Corp. *(372)*
Shawn Coulson *(53)*
Council of Graduate Schools *(375)*
Council of Industrial Boiler Owners (CIBO) *(375)*
Council of Scientific Society Presidents *(376)*
Council on Undergraduate Research *(377)*
Law Offices of Thomas K. Crowe *(55)*
CSA America, Inc. *(379)*
Daemen College *(381)*
Susan Davis Internat'l *(58)*
Davis O'Connell, Inc. *(58)*
DCH Technology Inc. *(383)*
Dean Blakey & Moskowitz *(59)*
Dell Computer Corp. *(384)*
Desert Research Institute *(386)*
Dierman, Wortley, and Zola *(62)*
Digital Media Ass'n *(388)*
DNA Plant Technology Corp. *(390)*
R. R. Donnelley & Sons *(391)*
Downey McGrath Group, Inc. *(64)*
Dreamtime, Inc. *(392)*
The Duberstein Group, Inc. *(65)*
Dr. John V. Dugan, Jr. *(66)*
DuPont *(393)*
The Dutko Group, Inc. *(68)*
Dykema Gossett PLLC *(69)*
E*TRADE Group, Inc. *(394)*
The Eagles Group *(69)*
EarthWatch, Inc. *(395)*
Easter Seals *(395)*
Eastman Chemical Co. *(395)*
eBay Inc. *(395)*
Edison Industrial Systems Center *(397)*
Edison Internat'l *(397)*
EDS Corp. *(398)*
Educational Video Conferencing, Inc. *(398)*
The Egg Factory, LLC *(398)*
Elan Pharmaceutical Research Corp. *(399)*
The Electric Vehicle Ass'n of the Americas (EVAA) *(400)*
Electronic Financial Services Council *(400)*
Adam Emanuel and Associates *(71)*
EMC Corp. *(401)*
Engineered Arresting Systems Corp. *(403)*
Enron Corp. *(403)*
Entergy Services, Inc. *(404)*
Ann Eppard Associates, Ltd. *(72)*
Ergo Science Corp. *(406)*
ERIM *(406)*
Ervin Technical Associates, Inc. (ETA) *(73)*
Eversole Associates *(74)*
ExtrudeHone Corp. *(409)*
Eye Bank Ass'n of America *(410)*
EyeTicket Corp. *(410)*
F.B.A. *(74)*
Fantasma Networks, Inc. *(411)*
Federated Investors, Inc. *(414)*
Federation of American Scientists *(414)*
Federation of American Societies for Experimental Biology *(414)*
Federation of Behavioral, Psychological and Cognitive Sciences *(414)*
The Ferguson Group, LLC *(76)*
The Fertilizer Institute *(415)*
Fierce and Isakowitz *(76)*
Financial Technology Industry Council *(417)*
FISERV, Inc. *(418)*
Florida State University System *(420)*
Foley Government and Public Affairs, Inc. *(78)*
Fontheim Internat'l *(421)*
Ford Motor Credit Co. (Legal Department) *(422)*
Forster & Associates *(79)*
FQPA Implementation Working Group *(424)*
Franklin Institute *(425)*
Fratkin Associates *(79)*
Douglas Ward Freitag *(79)*
Law Offices of Michael R. Gardner, P.C. *(81)*
Garvey, Schubert & Barer *(81)*
Gateway, Inc. *(430)*
Genentech, Inc. *(431)*
General Electric Co. *(432)*
General Electric Industrial & Power Systems *(432)*
General Motors Corp. *(432)*
Generic Pharmaceutical Ass'n *(433)*
The Genome Action Coalition *(433)*
Giant Industries, Inc. *(435)*

Girl Scouts of the U.S.A. - Washington Office (435)
Global USA, Inc. (83)
Goodwin, Procter & Hoar LLP (84)
GoTo.com Inc. (437)
Government Relations, Inc. (84)
Gowran Internat'l Ltd. (85)
GPC Internat'l (85)
Jay Grant & Associates (85)
Greater Washington Board of Trade (439)
Greenberg Traurig, LLP (86)
Griffin, Johnson, Dover & Stewart (87)
Guidant Corp. (442)
Guinea, Secretary General of the Presidency of the Republic of (442)
James E. Guirard (89)
Katherine Hamilton (91)
Hampton University (444)
Hannett & Associates (91)
Harbor Branch Institute (444)
Hargett Consulting (91)
Harvard University Washington Office (445)
Hebrew University of Jerusalem (447)
Helicopter Ass'n Internat'l (448)
HemaSure, Inc. (448)
Allen Herbert (94)
Hewlett-Packard Co. (449)
Hickman Report (449)
Hogan & Hartson L.L.P. (96)
Hohlt & Associates (98)
Honeywell Internat'l, Inc. (452)
Hoover Partners (100)
Christopher C. Horner (100)
Horticultural Research Institute (452)
Oliver James Horton (100)
Hospital for Special Surgery (453)
Hudson Institute (454)
Huntingdon College (455)
IATA U.S. Frequent Flyer Tax Interest Group (456)
The ILEX Group (102)
Illinois Department of Human Services (457)
Impact Strategies (102)
In-Pipe Technology (458)
Incorporated Research Institutions for Seismology (458)
Infectious Diseases Soc. of America, Inc. (461)
Information Handling Services (461)
Information Technology Industry Council (462)
Innovative Technical Solutions (462)
Insight Technology, Inc. (462)
Institute of Electrical and Electronics Engineers, Inc. (464)
Intel Corp. (465)
Intelligent Transportation Soc. of America (465)
INTELSAT - Internat'l Telecommunications Satellite Organization (465)
Inter-Associates, Inc. (466)
Internat'l Air Transport Ass'n (467)
Internat'l Ass'n for Dental Research (467)
Internat'l Ass'n of Fire Chiefs (468)
Internat'l Brotherhood of Electrical Workers (469)
Internat'l Business Machines Corp. (469)
Internat'l Cadmium Ass'n (469)
Internat'l Federation of Professional and Technical Engineers (471)
Internat'l Mass Retailers Ass'n (473)
Internat'l Space Business Council (475)
Internet Alliance Inc. (476)
Internet Council of Registrars (476)
IPC Washington Office (478)
Jacobs Engineering Group Inc. (481)
Jarboe & Associates (105)
JASON Foundation for Education (482)
JCP Associates (105)
JDA Aviation Technology Systems (482)
Jefferson Government Relations, L.L.C. (106)
Jellinek, Schwartz & Connolly (106)
Mary P. Johannes (107)
Johns Hopkins Center for Civilian Biodefense Studies (483)
Johnston & Associates, LLC (107)
Joint Steering Committee for Public Policy (484)
Jones, Walker, Waechter, Poitevent, Carrere & Denegre, L.L.P. (108)
Jorden Burt LLP (109)
Kaiser Aluminum & Chemical Corp. (485)
Barbara A. Karmanos Cancer Institute (486)
Kelly and Associates, Inc. (111)
The Kemper Co. (111)
Kerrigan & Associates, Inc. (112)
KeySpan Energy (489)
Kildare Corp. (489)
Jeffrey J. Kimbell & Associates (113)
Kinetic Biosystems Inc. (489)
King & Spalding (113)
Koch Industries, Inc. (490)
Kyros & Cummins Associates (116)
LaRocco & Associates (116)
Lau Technologies (496)
Bob Lawrence & Associates (496)
LC Technologies (496)
LeBoeuf, Lamb, Greene & MacRae L.L.P. (117)
Lee & Smith P.C. (118)
Lewis-Burke Associates (120)
Liberty Science Center (499)
Liebman & Associates, Inc. (120)
Link Plus Co. (500)
Law Office of Zel E. Lipsen (120)
The Livingston Group, LLC (120)
Lockheed Martin Aeronautical Systems Co. (501)
Lockheed Martin Corp. (501)
Long, Aldridge & Norman, LLP (121)
Loral Space and Communications, Ltd. (503)
Lotus Development Corp. (504)
Lovelace Respiratory Research Institute (504)
Lucent Technologies (505)
Luso American Foundation (505)
Lyondell Chemical Co. (506)
Mack Trucks, Inc. (506)
Madison Government Affairs (123)
Management Options, Inc. (123)
Manufacturers Alliance/MAPI Inc. (509)
Maptech (509)
Martin-Baker Aircraft Co., Ltd. (511)
MasterCard Internat'l (513)
Maytag Corp. (513)
Charlie McBride Associates, Inc. (127)
McClure, Gerard & Neuenschwander, Inc. (127)
McDermott, Will and Emery (128)
McGuiness & Holch (130)
Diane McRee Associates (131)
Media Fusion L.L.C. (516)
Megaseal Corp. (517)
Merck & Co. (518)
Law Offices of Pamela L. Meredith (132)
Metamorphix, Inc. (519)
Meyers & Associates (133)
Michigan Manufacturing Technology Center (522)
Midwest Research Institute (524)
Denny Miller McBee Associates (134)
Mitsubishi Research Institute (526)
The Jeffrey Modell Foundation (527)
The Modernization Forum (527)
Molecular BioSystems, Inc. (527)
Monfort & Wolfe (135)
Morgan State University (529)
Kay Allan Morrell, Attorney-at-Law (137)
Morrison & Foerster LLP (137)
Mortgage Bankers Ass'n of America (530)
Mountain Top Technologies, Inc. (532)
mp3.com (532)
MSP Strategic Communications, Inc. (138)
MSS Consultants, LLC (138)
MultiDimensional Imaging, Inc. (532)
NanoDynamics, Inc. (534)
NASA Aeronautics Support Team (534)
Nat'l Abortion and Reproductive Rights Action League (535)
Nat'l Alliance for Hispanic Health (536)
Nat'l Ass'n for Proton Therapy (538)
Nat'l Ass'n of Attorneys General (539)
Nat'l Ass'n of Biology Teachers (539)
Nat'l Ass'n of Negro Business & Professional Women's Clubs, Inc. (546)
Nat'l Ass'n of Nurse Practitioners in Women's Health (546)
Nat'l Ass'n of Protection and Advocacy Systems (NAPAS) (547)
Nat'l Coalition for Osteoporosis and Related Bone Diseases (556)
Nat'l Consumers League (558)
Nat'l Corn Growers Ass'n (559)
Nat'l Council for Science and the Environment (559)
Nat'l District Attorneys Ass'n (562)
Nat'l Farmers Union (Farmers Educational & Co-operative Union of America) (563)
Nat'l Fastener Distributors Ass'n (564)
Nat'l Fire Protection Ass'n (564)
Nat'l Ground Water Ass'n (566)
Nat'l Health Council (567)
Nat'l Hydropower Ass'n (567)
Nat'l Legal Center for the Public Interest (570)
Nat'l Newspaper Ass'n (572)
Nat'l Rural Electric Cooperative Ass'n (576)
Nat'l Soc. of Professional Engineers (578)
The Nat'l Space Grant Alliance (578)
Nat'l Space Soc. (578)
Nat'l Thoroughbred Racing Ass'n, Inc. (579)
Nat'l Venture Capital Ass'n (580)
Nat'l Weather Service Employees Organization (581)
Navista, Inc. (141)
NetCoalition.Com (584)
Netivation.com (584)
NeuLevel (584)
New Mexico State Office of Research & Development (586)
New Mexico State University, Department of Engineering (586)
New York University (588)
Nexia Biotechnologies, Inc. (589)
Noesis Inc. (590)
NoFire Technologies, Inc. (591)
North American Interstate Weather Modification Council (592)
North Dakota State University (593)
Northeast-Midwest Institute (594)
Northern Indiana Public Service Co. (594)
Northern Mariana Islands, Commonwealth of the (594)
Novartis Corp. (596)
Novell, Inc. (596)
Nuclear Energy Institute (597)
The OB-C Group, LLC (143)
O'Connor & Hannan, L.L.P. (144)
Ogilvy Public Relations Worldwide (145)
Omega Oil Co. (600)
O'Neill, Athy & Casey, P.C. (147)
Operations Security Professionals Soc. (601)
Optical Soc. of America (601)
Oracle Corp. (602)
Orbital Sciences Corp. (602)
ORBITZ (602)
Oregon Graduate Institute of Science and Technology (603)
Oshkosh Truck Corp. (604)
PAI Management Corp. (148)
Paradigm Research Group (149)
Parry, Romani, DeConcini & Symms (149)
Patton Boggs, LLP (150)
PDA (610)
PE Biosystems (610)
People for the Ethical Treatment of Animals (612)
The Peterson Group (155)
PetrolRem, Inc. (613)
Pfizer, Inc. (613)
Philadelphia College of Textiles and Science (615)
Plasma-Therm, Inc. (619)
Podesta/Mattoon (158)
Policy Directions, Inc. (158)
Population Ass'n of America (621)
The Potomac Research Group LLC (160)
Potomac Strategies Internat'l LLC (160)
Powell, Goldstein, Frazer & Murphy LLP (160)
Preston Gates Ellis & Rouvelas Meeds LLP (162)
The Procter & Gamble Company (625)
Professional Services Council (626)
Progressive Policy Institute (626)
Project to Promote Competition and Innovation in the Digital Age (626)
Psychemedics Corp. (628)
Public Policy Partners, LLC (164)
Public Strategies Washington, Inc. (164)
Public Strategies, Inc. (165)

Small Business (SMB)

Contract Services Ass'n of America (370)
Cook Inlet Region Inc. (371)
Cooney & Associates, Inc. (52)
Council of Federal Home Loan Banks (375)
Council of Smaller Enterprises (376)
DAG Petroleum (381)
Dawson & Associates, Inc. (59)
Dickstein Shapiro Morin & Oshinsky LLP (61)
Digital Commerce Corp. (388)
Direct Selling Ass'n (389)
Dunn-Edwards Corp. (393)
Epstein Becker & Green, P.C. (72)
EqualFooting.com (406)
Evergreen Associates, Ltd. (74)
The Ferguson Group, LLC (76)
Financial Planning Ass'n (416)
Firstdoor.com (418)
FISERV, Inc. (418)
Foley Government and Public Affairs, Inc. (78)
Food Distributors Internat'l (NAWGA-IFDA) (421)
Food Marketing Institute (421)
Foster-Miller, Inc. (424)
FRANMAC/Taco Pac (425)
Frontier Communications Corp. (427)
Fulcrum Venture Capital Corp. (427)
General Electric Co. (432)
General Mills (432)
getpress.com (435)
GHL Inc. (82)
Giant Industries, Inc. (435)
Gowran Internat'l Ltd. (85)
Jay Grant & Associates (85)
Great Lakes Dredge & Dock (439)
Greater New York Automobile Dealers Ass'n (439)
Griffin, Johnson, Dover & Stewart (87)
Halsey, Rains & Associates, LLC (90)
Health Insurance Ass'n of America (446)
Heller Financial Inc. (448)
Lydia Hofer & Associates (96)
Hohlt & Associates (98)
Holland & Knight LLP (98)
Peter Homer (99)
Horticultural Research Institute (452)
Oliver James Horton (100)
R. J. Hudson Associates (101)
The ILEX Group (102)
Independent Community Bankers of America (459)
Independent Insurance Agents of America, Inc. (459)
Independent Office Products and Furniture Dealers Ass'n (459)
Inglewood, California, City of (462)
Institute for Entrepreneurship (463)
Integrated Management Resources Group, Inc. (465)
Interface Inc. (466)
Internat'l Brotherhood of Electrical Workers (469)
Internat'l Communications Industries Ass'n (ICIA) (470)
Internat'l Downtown Ass'n (471)
Internat'l Franchise Ass'n (472)
Internat'l Sign Ass'n (474)
Internat'l Union of Painters and Allied Trades (476)
Kelly and Associates, Inc. (487)
Kent & O'Connor, Inc. (112)
Kessler & Associates Business Services, Inc. (112)
David William Kuhnsman (115)
LaRocco & Associates (116)
Leonard Hurt Frost Lilly & Levin, PC (119)
Long, Aldridge & Norman, LLP (121)
Luman, Lange & Wheeler (122)
Luso American Foundation (505)
M & R Strategic Services (122)
Machinery Dealers Nat'l Ass'n (506)
Madison Government Affairs (123)
Maloney & Knox, LLP (123)
Management Options, Inc. (123)
Manatt, Phelps & Phillips, LLP (123)
Mayer, Brown & Platt (126)
McDonald's Corp. (514)
McNamara & Associates (131)
Medallion Funding Corp. (515)
MMG Ventures LP (526)
Mobile Communications Holdings, Inc. (527)
Monroe, Louisiana, Chamber of Commerce of the City of (528)
Monroe, Louisiana, City of (528)
Morgan, Lewis & Bockius LLP (136)
The Morrison Group, Inc. (137)
Myriad Capital Inc. (534)
Nat'l Air Transportation Ass'n (536)
Nat'l Ass'n for the Self-Employed (538)
Nat'l Ass'n of Beverage Retailers (539)
Nat'l Ass'n of Developmental Disabilities Councils (542)
Nat'l Ass'n of Enrolled Agents (542)
Nat'l Ass'n of Government Guaranteed Lenders (543)
Nat'l Ass'n of Manufacturers (545)
Nat'l Ass'n of Negro Business & Professional Women's Clubs, Inc. (546)
Nat'l Ass'n of Portable X-Ray Providers (546)
Nat'l Ass'n of RV Parks and Campgrounds (548)
Nat'l Ass'n of SBA Microloan Intermediaries (548)
Nat'l Ass'n of Small Business Investment Companies (549)
Nat'l Ass'n of Surety Bond Producers (550)
Nat'l Beer Wholesalers Ass'n (552)
Nat'l Bicycle Dealers Ass'n (552)
Nat'l Business Owners Ass'n (553)
Nat'l Center for Neighborhood Enterprise (555)
Nat'l Club Ass'n (556)
Nat'l Coalition of Minority Businesses (556)
Nat'l Concrete Masonry Ass'n (558)
Nat'l Electrical Contractors Ass'n (562)
Nat'l Electrical Manufacturers Ass'n (562)
Nat'l Farmers Union (Farmers Educational & Co-operative Union of America) (563)
Nat'l Fastener Distributors Ass'n (564)
Nat'l Federation of Independent Business (564)
Nat'l Field Selling Ass'n (564)
Nat'l Franchise Council (565)
Nat'l Franchisee Ass'n (565)
Nat'l Funeral Directors Ass'n (565)
Nat'l Legal Center for the Public Interest (570)
Nat'l Licensed Beverage Ass'n (570)
Nat'l Lumber and Building Material Dealers Ass'n (570)
Nat'l Mining Ass'n (571)
Nat'l Newspaper Ass'n (572)
Nat'l Organization for Competency Assurance (572)
Nat'l Ready Mixed Concrete Ass'n (575)
Nat'l Restaurant Ass'n (576)
Nat'l Retail Federation (576)
Nat'l Roofing Contractors Ass'n (576)
Nat'l Small Business United (578)
Nat'l Soc. of Professional Engineers (578)
Nat'l Telephone Cooperative Ass'n (579)
Nat'l Tooling and Machining Ass'n (579)
Nat'l Truck Equipment Ass'n (580)
Nat'l Utility Contractors Ass'n (NUCA) (580)
NAVCOM Systems, Inc. (583)
New America Alliance (585)
Newport News Shipbuilding Inc. (588)
Norfolk, Virginia, City of (591)
nPower Advisors, LLC (596)
Nurnberger and Associates (142)
OMNIPLEX World Services Corp. (600)
Opportunity Capital Corp. (601)
Opticians Ass'n of America (601)
Ouachita Parish Police Jury (604)
Painting and Decorating Contractors of America (606)
Paley Rothman Goldstein Rosenberg & Cooper (148)
Palumbo & Cerrell, Inc. (149)
Petro Star, Inc. (613)
Philip Morris Management Corp. (615)
Piliero Mazza & Pargament (617)
Plumbing, Heating, Cooling Contractors- National Assoc. (619)
Potomac Electric Power Co. (622)
Potomac Strategies Internat'l LLC (160)
Thomas G. Powers (161)
Principal Financial Group (624)
Printing Industries of America (624)
Private Practice Section of the American Physical Therapy Ass'n (625)
Profit Sharing/401 (k) Council of America (626)
Robert A. Rapoza Associates (165)
REM Engineering (636)
Research Institute for Small & Emerging Business, Inc. (638)
Ritter and Bourjaily, Inc. (169)
Ryan, Phillips, Utrecht & MacKinnon (173)
S-Corporation Ass'n (644)
Sagamore Associates, Inc. (174)
Saliba Action Strategies, LLC (174)
SBREFA Coalition (651)
James E. Schneider, LLM Inc. (651)
Abraham Schneier and Associates (176)
Scram Technologies Inc. (652)
Secondary Materials and Recycled Textiles Ass'n (654)
Sheet Metal and Air Conditioning Contractors' Nat'l Ass'n (657)
Silver Users Ass'n (659)
Robert H. Sindt (181)
Small Business Council of America (661)
Small Business Regulatory Council (661)
Small Business Survival Committee (661)
Smith, Bucklin and Associates, Inc. (184)
The Smith-Free Group (184)
Soc. of American Florists (663)
The Solomon Group, LLC (185)
Stephens Law Firm (188)
Steptoe & Johnson LLP (188)
The Strategic Advocacy Group (189)
Sun Innovations, Inc. (676)
Sunkist Growers, Inc. (677)
Synthetic Organic Chemical Manufacturers Ass'n (679)
Tett Enterprises (684)
Thelen Reid & Priest LLP (193)
Thompson Lighting Protection Inc. (686)
Michael L. Tiner (195)
Tire Ass'n of North America (687)
Trajen, Inc. (689)
Transnat'l Development Consortium (690)
TSG Ventures Inc. (693)
U.S. Hispanic Chamber of Commerce (696)
U.S. Wireless Data, Inc. (697)
Ungaretti & Harris (197)
Unified Industries, Inc. (698)
United Motorcoach Ass'n (702)
United States Business and Industry Council (703)
Van Ness Feldman, P.C. (199)
Venable (201)
Verner, Liipfert, Bernhard, McPherson and Hand, Chartered (202)
Vision Technologies, Inc. (716)
Washington Aviation Group (206)
Winston & Strawn (218)
Women Officials in NACo (729)
Women's Policy, Inc. (729)
World Floor Covering Ass'n (730)
Zeliff, Ireland, and Associates (221)

Sports/Athletics (SPO)

The Accord Group (5)
Akin, Gump, Strauss, Hauer & Feld, L.L.P. (8)
Albertine Enterprises, Inc. (10)
American Amateur Karate Federation (245)
Law Offices of Peter Angelos (284)
Baach Robinson & Lewis, PLLC (19)
Baker & Hostetler LLP (19)
Bicycle Council (313)
Bowman Internat'l Corp. (318)
Bracy Williams & Co. (31)
Capital Consultants Corp. (37)
The Clark Estates, Inc. (350)
Coalition on Accessibility (355)
Consumer Federation of America (369)
Epstein Becker & Green, P.C. (72)
Forscey & Stinson, PLLC (79)
Girl Scouts of the U.S.A. - Washington Office (435)
Girls Incorporated (435)
Stuart J. Gordon (84)
Gottehrer and Co. (84)
Greenberg Traurig, LLP (86)
Hill and Knowlton, Inc. (95)

Internat'l Downtown Ass'n *(471)*
Internat'l Olympic Committee *(473)*
Internat'l Snowmobile Manufacturers Ass'n *(474)*
Internat'l Traditional Karate Federation *(475)*
King & Spalding *(113)*
Major League Baseball *(508)*
Major League Baseball Players Ass'n *(508)*
McGuiness & Holch *(130)*
Nat'l Ass'n for Girls and Women in Sport *(537)*
Nat'l Ass'n for Sport and Physical Education *(538)*
Nat'l Basketball Ass'n *(552)*
Nat'l Collegiate Athletic Ass'n *(557)*
Nat'l Football League *(565)*
Nat'l Football League Players Ass'n *(565)*
Nat'l Hockey League *(567)*
Nat'l Women's Law Center *(581)*
Paralyzed Veterans of America *(607)*
Patton Boggs, LLP *(150)*
Paul, Hastings, Janofsky & Walker LLP *(153)*
Sagamore Associates, Inc. *(174)*
Salt Lake City Olympic Organizing Committee *(646)*
Shake-A-Leg *(656)*
Sporting Goods Manufacturers Ass'n *(670)*
Sports Corp., Ltd. *(670)*
Take The Field, Inc. *(680)*
Tribune Co. *(692)*
U.S. Fencing Ass'n *(696)*
U.S. Figure Skating Ass'n *(696)*
U.S. Olympic Committee *(697)*
United States Parachute Ass'n *(704)*
University System of Maryland *(708)*
Van Scoyoc Associates, Inc. *(200)*
Venable *(201)*
Verner, Liipfert, Bernhard, McPherson and Hand, Chartered *(202)*
Wilson & Wasserstein, Inc. *(218)*
Women's Sports Foundation *(730)*
YWCA of the USA *(734)*

Taxation/Internal Revenue Code (TAX)

3Com Corp. *(223)*
The 60/Plus Ass'n, Inc. *(224)*
AARP (American Ass'n of Retired Persons) *(224)*
ABB, Inc. *(225)*
Abbott Laboratories *(225)*
Abitibi Consolidated Sales Corp. *(225)*
Academy of Radiology Research *(226)*
The Accord Group *(5)*
ACE INA *(226)*
Ace Ltd. *(226)*
Ad Hoc Coalition on Intermarket Coordination *(227)*
Ad Hoc Life/Non-life Consolidation Group *(227)*
ADA Consulting Services *(227)*
Adams and Reese LLP *(5)*
Administaff *(227)*
Advanced Micro Devices *(228)*
Advertising Tax Coalition *(229)*
The Advocacy Group *(6)*
Aegon USA *(229)*
AEI Resources *(229)*
Aetna Inc. *(230)*
Aetna Life & Casualty Co. *(230)*
Affordable Housing Tax Credit Coalition *(230)*
AFL-CIO (American Federation of Labor and Congress of Industrial Organizations) *(231)*
AFL-CIO - Professional Employees Department *(231)*
AFL-CIO - Transportation Trades Department *(231)*
AFLAC, Inc. *(231)*
Air Conditioning Contractors of America *(233)*
Air Force Sergeants Ass'n *(233)*
Air Line Pilots Ass'n Internat'l *(233)*
Air Products and Chemicals, Inc. *(234)*
Air Tran Airways *(234)*
Air Transport Ass'n of America *(234)*
Air-Conditioning and Refrigeration Institute *(234)*
Airborne Express *(234)*
Akin, Gump, Strauss, Hauer & Feld, L.L.P. *(8)*
Alameda, California, County of *(236)*
Alaska Air Group *(236)*
Albertine Enterprises, Inc. *(10)*
Sally L. Albright *(10)*
Albuquerque, New Mexico, City of *(237)*
Alcalde & Fay *(10)*
Alcoa Inc. *(237)*
Alexander Strategy Group *(238)*
Harry C. Alford & Associates, Inc. *(11)*
Alliance Capital Management LP *(239)*
Alliance for American Innovation, Inc. *(239)*
Alliance for Children and Families *(239)*
Alliance for Competitive Electricity *(239)*
Alliance of Automobile Manufacturers, Inc. *(240)*
Alliant Techsystems, Inc. *(241)*
Allied Charities of Minnesota *(241)*
Allied Domecq *(241)*
Allmerica Financial *(241)*
Allstate Insurance Co. *(241)*
Alltel Corporation *(242)*
Alpine Group, Inc. *(11)*
Alston & Bird LLP *(12)*
Alticor, Inc. *(242)*
Alvarado & Gerken *(12)*
Alyeska Pipeline Service Co. *(242)*
Alzheimer's Ass'n *(242)*
AMCOR Capital Corp. *(242)*
Ameren Services *(243)*
America Outdoors *(243)*
America's Community Bankers *(243)*
American Academy of Actuaries *(243)*
American Advertising Federation *(244)*
American Airlines *(244)*
American Arts Alliance *(245)*
American Ass'n for Geriatric Psychiatry *(245)*
American Ass'n of Advertising Agencies *(246)*
American Ass'n of Community Colleges *(247)*
American Ass'n of Engineering Societies *(247)*
American Ass'n of Homes and Services for the Aging *(248)*
American Ass'n of Limited Partners *(248)*
American Ass'n of Motor Vehicle Administrators *(248)*
American Ass'n of Museums *(248)*
American Ass'n of Port Authorities *(249)*
American Bakers Ass'n *(250)*
American Bankers Ass'n *(250)*
American Bar Ass'n *(250)*
American Benefits Council *(250)*
American Boiler Manufacturers Ass'n *(251)*
American Bus Ass'n *(251)*
American Business Conference *(251)*
American Business Is Local Enterprise *(251)*
American Camping Ass'n *(251)*
American Cancer Soc. *(252)*
American Chemistry Council *(252)*
American Concrete Pavement Ass'n (ACPA) *(255)*
American Consulting Engineers Council *(255)*
American Corn Growers Ass'n *(255)*
American Council for Capital Formation *(255)*
American Council of Life Insurers *(256)*
American Council on Education *(256)*
American Dental Education Ass'n *(257)*
American Electric Power Co. *(257)*
American Electronics Ass'n *(257)*
American Express Co. *(258)*
American Family Mutual Insurance Co. *(258)*
American Farm Bureau Federation *(258)*
American Federation of Senior Citizens *(258)*
American Federation of State, County and Municipal Employees *(258)*
American Federation of Teachers *(259)*
American Financial Group *(259)*
American Foreign Service Ass'n *(259)*
American Forest & Paper Ass'n *(259)*
American Furniture Manufacturers Ass'n *(260)*
American Gaming Ass'n *(260)*
American Gas Ass'n *(261)*
American Gas Cooling Center *(261)*
American Great Lakes Ports *(261)*
American Heart Ass'n *(262)*
American Highway Users Alliance *(262)*
American Home Products Corp. *(262)*
American Homeowners Grassroots Alliance *(262)*
American Horse Council, Inc. *(263)*
American Hospital Ass'n *(263)*
American Hotel and Lodging Ass'n *(263)*
The American Institute of Architects *(264)*
American Institute of Certified Public Accountants *(264)*
American Institute of Chemical Engineers *(264)*
American Insurance Ass'n *(264)*
American Internat'l Automobile Dealers Ass'n *(265)*
American Internat'l Group, Inc. *(265)*
American Iron and Steel Institute *(265)*
American Legion *(266)*
American Maritime Congress *(267)*
American Maritime Officers Service *(267)*
American Medical Group Ass'n *(267)*
American Methanol Institute *(268)*
American Moving and Storage Ass'n *(268)*
American Museum of Natural History *(268)*
American Network of Community Options and Resources (ANCOR) *(268)*
American Nursery and Landscape Ass'n *(268)*
American Payroll Ass'n *(269)*
American Petroleum Institute *(269)*
American Physical Therapy Ass'n *(270)*
American Portland Cement Alliance *(270)*
American Psychological Ass'n *(271)*
American Public Power Ass'n *(272)*
American Red Cross *(272)*
American Rental Ass'n *(272)*
American Resort Development Ass'n *(272)*
American Seniors Housing Ass'n *(273)*
American Sheep Industry Ass'n *(273)*
American Soc. for Training and Development *(275)*
American Soc. of Appraisers *(275)*
American Soc. of Ass'n Executives *(275)*
American Soc. of Pension Actuaries *(277)*
American Soc. of Travel Agents *(277)*
American Staffing Ass'n *(278)*
American Supply Ass'n *(278)*
American Symphony Orchestra League *(278)*
American Trucking Ass'ns *(279)*
American Vintners Ass'n *(280)*
American Waterways Operators *(280)*
American Wholesale Marketers Ass'n *(280)*
American Wind Energy Ass'n *(280)*
American Wine Heritage Alliance *(280)*
American Wood Preservers Institute *(280)*
Americans for Fair Taxation *(281)*
Americans for Free Internat'l Trade (AFIT PAC) *(281)*
Americans for Sensible Estate Tax Solutions (ASSETS) *(282)*
Americans for Tax Reform *(282)*
Amgen *(282)*
Andrews Associates, Inc. *(14)*
Law Offices of Peter Angelos *(284)*
Anglican Catholic Church *(284)*
Anheuser-Busch Cos., Inc. *(284)*
Anti-Value Added Tax Coalition *(285)*
AOL Time Warner *(285)*
APA Coalition *(285)*
Apartment Investment and Management Co. *(286)*
APCO Worldwide *(14)*
Apple Computer, Inc. *(286)*
Applied Materials *(287)*
ARAMARK Corp. *(287)*
Arctic Slope Regional Corp. *(288)*
Arent Fox Kintner Plotkin & Kahn, PLLC *(14)*
The Argus Group, L.L.C. *(16)*
Arizona Mail Order Co. *(288)*
Arizona Power Authority *(288)*
Arizona Public Service Co. *(288)*
Arkansas, Office of the Governor of the State of *(288)*
Armco Inc. *(288)*
Thomas K. Arnold *(16)*
Arnold & Porter *(16)*
Arter & Hadden *(17)*
Arthur Andersen LLP *(17)*
Ashland Inc. *(290)*
Ass'n for Advanced Life Underwriting *(291)*
Ass'n for Commuter Transportation *(292)*
Ass'n for Financial Professionals, Inc. *(292)*
The Ass'n For Manufacturing Technology (AMT) *(292)*
Ass'n of Air Medical Services *(293)*
Ass'n of American Geographers *(293)*

Committee for a Responsible Federal Budget *(360)*
Committee for Good Common Sense *(361)*
Committee of Annuity Insurers *(361)*
Common Cause *(361)*
Community Ass'ns Institute (CAI) *(362)*
Compaq Computer Corp. *(363)*
CompTIA *(364)*
Computer and Communications Industry Ass'n (CCIA) *(364)*
Computing Technology Industry Ass'n *(364)*
Compuware Corp. *(364)*
Concerned Women for America *(365)*
Concert USA *(365)*
Condea Vista Chemical Co. *(365)*
Congressional Economic Leadership Institute *(366)*
Conkling, Fiskum & McCormick *(51)*
Conlon, Frantz, Phelan & Pires *(51)*
The Connell Co. *(367)*
Conoco Inc. *(367)*
The Conservation Fund *(367)*
The Conservative Caucus *(367)*
Consolidated Edison Co. of New York *(367)*
Constellation Energy Group *(368)*
Consumer Bankers Ass'n *(368)*
Consumer Electronics Ass'n *(369)*
Consumer Federation of America *(369)*
Contango LLC *(52)*
Continental Airlines Inc. *(370)*
L. P. Conwood Co. *(370)*
Cook, Illinois, County of *(371)*
Cooney & Associates, Inc. *(52)*
Coors Brewing Company *(371)*
Copeland, Lowery & Jacquez *(52)*
Corning Inc. *(372)*
Corporate Property Investors *(372)*
Corporation for Enterprise Development *(372)*
Council for Affordable Health Insurance *(374)*
Council for Energy Independence *(374)*
Council for Government Reform *(374)*
Council of Development Finance Agencies *(375)*
Council of Federal Home Loan Banks *(375)*
Council of Graduate Schools *(375)*
Council of Infrastructure Financing Authorities *(375)*
The Council of Insurance Agents & Brokers *(376)*
Council on Foundations *(377)*
Countrywide Home Loans, Inc. *(377)*
Coushatta Tribe of Louisiana *(377)*
Covington & Burling *(53)*
Cow Creek Umpqua Tribe of Oregon *(377)*
Cox Enterprises Inc. *(378)*
Credit Suisse First Boston Corp. *(378)*
Crowell & Moring LLP *(55)*
CSX Corp. *(379)*
CSX Lines LLC *(379)*
Cummins Engine Co. *(380)*
CUNA Mutual Group *(380)*
Cuyahoga, Ohio, County of *(380)*
Ralf Czepluch *(56)*
D.C. Land Title Ass'n *(383)*
DaimlerChrysler Corp. *(381)*
Dance/USA *(382)*
Davidson & Company, Inc. *(57)*
Davis & Harman LLP *(57)*
Davis O'Connell, Inc. *(58)*
Dayton, Ohio, Washington Office of the City of *(383)*
Dean Blakey & Moskowitz *(59)*
Deere & Co. *(383)*
Deferral Group *(384)*
Delaware and Hudson Railroad *(384)*
Dell Computer Corp. *(384)*
Deloitte & Touche LLP Nat'l Office - Washington *(60)*
Delta Air Lines *(384)*
Delta Dental Plans Ass'n *(385)*
Thomas J. Dennis *(61)*
Denton, Texas, County of *(385)*
Detroit Medical Center *(386)*
Detroit, Michigan, City of *(386)*
Development Resources, Inc. *(387)*
Dewey Ballantine LLP *(61)*
Dickstein Shapiro Morin & Oshinsky LLP *(61)*
William M. Diefenderfer *(62)*
Dime Savings Bank of New York *(388)*
Direct Marketing Ass'n, Inc. *(388)*
Direct Selling Ass'n *(389)*
Directors Guild of America *(389)*
Distilled Spirits Council of the United States, Inc. *(389)*
The Doe Run Co. *(390)*
Domestic Petroleum Council *(390)*
Dominion Resources, Inc. *(391)*
Dorsey & Whitney LLP *(63)*
Dow AgroSciences *(391)*
The Dow Chemical Co. *(391)*
Dow Corning Corp. *(391)*
Dow, Lohnes & Albertson, PLLC *(64)*
Downey McGrath Group, Inc. *(64)*
Downey McGrath Group, Inc. *(392)*
Dreamtime, Inc. *(392)*
Drinker Biddle & Reath LLP *(65)*
The Duberstein Group, Inc. *(65)*
Ducks Unlimited Inc. *(392)*
Doris Duke Charitable Foundation *(392)*
Duke Energy *(392)*
Dunn-Edwards Corp. *(393)*
DuPont *(393)*
The Dutko Group, Inc. *(68)*
Dyer Ellis & Joseph, P.C. *(68)*
Dykema Gossett PLLC *(69)*
E-Commerce Coalition *(394)*
Eagle-Picher Industries *(394)*
Eagle-Picher Personal Injury Settlement Trust *(394)*
East Texas Electric Cooperative *(395)*
Easter Seals *(395)*
Eaton Vance Management Co. *(395)*
eBay Inc. *(395)*
Eckert Seamans Cherin & Mellott, LLC *(70)*
Eddie Bauer Co. *(396)*
Edelman Public Relations Worldwide *(70)*
Eden Financial Corp. *(396)*
Edison Electric Institute *(397)*
Edison Internat'l *(397)*
Edmund Scientific Co. *(397)*
EDS Corp. *(398)*
Education Finance Council *(398)*
The Macon Edwards Co. *(71)*
El Paso Corporation *(399)*
Electric Lightwave, Inc. *(400)*
The Electric Vehicle Ass'n of the Americas (EVAA) *(400)*
ElectriCities of North Carolina, Inc. *(400)*
Electro Scientific Industries, Inc. *(400)*
Electronic Commerce Forum *(400)*
Electronic Commerce Tax Study Group *(400)*
Electronic Industries Alliance *(400)*
Electronic Retailing Ass'n *(401)*
Ellicott Internat'l *(401)*
EMC Corp. *(401)*
Emergency Department Practice Management Ass'n (EDPMA) *(401)*
Employee-Owned S Corporations of America *(402)*
Employers Council on Flexible Compensation *(402)*
Empower America *(402)*
Encyclopaedia Britannica, Inc. *(402)*
Enron Corp. *(403)*
Enron Wind Corp./Zond *(404)*
Entergy Services, Inc. *(404)*
The Enterprise Foundation *(404)*
Environmental Industry Ass'ns *(405)*
EnviroPower *(405)*
Epstein Becker & Green, P.C. *(72)*
Equipment Leasing Ass'n of America *(406)*
The Equitable Cos. *(406)*
The ERISA Industry Committee (ERIC) *(406)*
Ernst & Young LLP *(72)*
Ervin Technical Associates, Inc. (ETA) *(73)*
The ESOP (Employee Stock Ownership Plan) Ass'n *(407)*
Estee Lauder, Inc. *(407)*
Evans & Black, Inc. *(73)*
Evergreen Associates, Ltd. *(74)*
Exelon Corp. *(409)*
Export Source Coalition *(409)*
Exxon Mobil Corp. *(409)*
Exxon Valdez Oil Spill Litigation Plaintiffs *(409)*
EZ's Solutions, Inc. *(74)*
F/P Research Associates *(74)*
Fair Share Coalition *(410)*
Fanatasy Elections *(411)*
Fannie Mae *(411)*
Farmers Insurance Group *(412)*
Farmland Industries, Inc. *(412)*
FBI Agents Ass'n *(412)*
Feder, Semo, Clarke & Bard *(74)*
Federal Home Loan Mortgage Corp. (Freddie Mac) *(413)*
Federal Management Strategies, Inc. *(75)*
Federation of American Hospitals *(414)*
FedEx Corp. *(415)*
Frank Fenton *(75)*
Fibrowatt, Inc. *(416)*
Fidelity Charitable Gift Fund *(416)*
Fierce and Isakowitz *(76)*
Financial Collection Agencies *(416)*
Financial Planning Ass'n *(416)*
The Financial Services Roundtable *(416)*
Fireman's Fund Insurance Cos. *(417)*
First Amendment Coalition for Expression *(417)*
First American *(417)*
First Preston Management *(417)*
First Union Corp. *(418)*
FISERV, Inc. *(418)*
Fisher Consulting *(77)*
Flexi-Van Leasing *(419)*
Florida Gas Utility *(420)*
Florida Power and Light Co. *(420)*
Florida Residential and Casualty Joint Underwriting Ass'n *(420)*
Florida State University System *(420)*
Florida Windstorm Underwriting Ass'n *(420)*
Floyd Associates *(78)*
FMR Corp. *(421)*
Foley & Lardner *(78)*
Food Distributors Internat'l (NAWGA-IFDA) *(421)*
Food Marketing Institute *(421)*
Forces Vives *(422)*
Betty Ford Center *(422)*
Ford Motor Co. *(422)*
Forest Industries Council on Taxation *(423)*
Forethought Group/Forethought Life Insurance Co. *(423)*
Forscey & Stinson, PLLC *(79)*
FRANMAC/Taco Pac *(425)*
Fraternal Order of Police *(425)*
Freeman United Coal Mining Co. *(425)*
Freeport-McMoRan Copper & Gold Inc. *(425)*
Fremont Group, Inc. *(425)*
French & Company *(79)*
Friede Goldman Halter *(426)*
Friends of the Earth *(426)*
H. B. Fuller Co. *(427)*
G.R. Services *(80)*
Gainesville, Florida, City of *(428)*
Gallant Co. *(81)*
Ernest & Julio Gallo Winery *(428)*
Gannett Co., Inc. *(429)*
Garden State Paper Co., Inc. *(429)*
Gardner, Carton and Douglas *(81)*
Gas Research Institute *(429)*
Gateway, Inc. *(430)*
GATX Corp. *(430)*
GE Capital Corp. *(430)*
GE Commercial Real Estate & Financial Services *(430)*
GE Financial Assurance *(430)*
Genentech, Inc. *(431)*
General Aviation Manufacturers Ass'n *(431)*
General Communications, Inc. *(431)*
General Conference of Seventh-day Adventists *(431)*
General Dynamics Corp. *(431)*
General Electric Capital Services, Inc. *(432)*
General Electric Co. *(432)*
General Motors Corp. *(432)*
General Ore Internat'l Corp. Ltd. *(433)*
Genzyme Corp. *(433)*
Georgia-Pacific Corp. *(434)*
Geothermal Energy Ass'n *(434)*
Geothermal Resources Ass'n *(434)*
Gibbons & Company, Inc. *(82)*

Gibson, Dunn & Crutcher LLP *(82)*
Gila River Indian Community ***(435)***
Girl Scouts of the U.S.A. - Washington Office ***(435)***
Bruce Givner, Attorney ***(435)***
GlaxoSmithKline ***(436)***
Global Competitiveness Coalition ***(436)***
Global USA, Inc. *(83)*
GLOBEMAC Associates *(83)*
Go-Mart, Inc. ***(436)***
The Gold and Silver Institute ***(436)***
Goldberg & Associates, PLLC *(83)*
Goldman, Sachs and Co. ***(437)***
Golin/Harris Internat'l *(84)*
Mark W. Goodin *(84)*
Goodstein & Associates *(84)*
Goodwill Industries Internat'l, Inc. ***(437)***
Goodyear Tire and Rubber Co. ***(437)***
Gordley Associates *(84)*
Stuart J. Gordon *(84)*
Gottehrer and Co. *(84)*
Government Relations, Inc. *(84)*
Jay Grant & Associates *(85)*
Greater New York Hospital Ass'n ***(439)***
Greater Washington Board of Trade ***(439)***
Greater Washington Soc. of Ass'n Executives ***(440)***
Greenberg Traurig, LLP *(86)*
Greenbrier Companies ***(440)***
Greyhound Lines ***(440)***
Griffin & Associates *(87)*
Griffin, Johnson, Dover & Stewart *(87)*
J. Steven Griles & Associates *(88)*
Grisso Consulting *(88)*
Grocery Manufacturers of America ***(440)***
Groom Law Group, Chartered *(88)*
Groom Law Group, Chartered ***(441)***
Group Health, Inc. ***(441)***
Guaranty Bank, SSB ***(442)***
Guardian Life Insurance Co. of America ***(442)***
Guidant Corp. ***(442)***
Haake and Associates *(89)*
Hallmark Cards, Inc. ***(443)***
Hance, Scarborough & Wright *(91)*
Harnischfeger Industries, Inc. ***(444)***
Leslie Harris & Associates *(91)*
The Hartford ***(445)***
Harvard University ***(445)***
Hawaii, State of ***(445)***
Hawaiian Airlines ***(445)***
Hazelden Foundation ***(445)***
Health Insurance Ass'n of America ***(446)***
Healthcare Financing Study Group ***(447)***
The Hearst Corp. ***(447)***
Heavy Vehicle Maintenance Group ***(447)***
Hecht, Spencer & Associates *(93)*
H. J. Heinz Co., ***(448)***
Heritage Foundation ***(448)***
Hershey Foods Corp. ***(449)***
Hewlett-Packard Co. ***(449)***
Higgins, McGovern & Smith, LLC *(94)*
The Hillman Co. ***(450)***
Hillsborough, Florida, County of ***(450)***
Hilton Hotels Corp. ***(450)***
Cornish F. Hitchcock *(95)*
HMSHost Corp. ***(450)***
Hoffmann-La Roche Inc. ***(450)***
Hogan & Hartson L.L.P. *(96)*
Hohlt & Associates *(98)*
Holland & Knight LLP *(98)*
The Home Depot ***(451)***
Honeywell Internat'l, Inc. ***(452)***
Hooper Owen & Winburn *(99)*
Oliver James Horton *(100)*
Hotel Employees and Restaurant Employees Internat'l Union ***(453)***
Household Internat'l, Inc. ***(453)***
Housing Works ***(453)***
Hubbell, Inc. ***(454)***
R. J. Hudson Associates *(101)*
Hudson Institute ***(454)***
Human Capital Resources ***(454)***
Hunton & Williams *(101)*
Hurt, Norton & Associates *(101)*
Fred Hutchinson Cancer Research Center ***(455)***
Gilbert P. Hyatt, Inventor ***(456)***
Hybrid Branch Coalition ***(456)***
IATA U.S. Frequent Flyer Tax Interest Group ***(456)***
ICF Consulting ***(457)***
IIT Research Institute ***(457)***
Ikon Public Affairs *(102)*
Illinois Housing Development Authority ***(457)***
IMC Global Inc. ***(458)***
IMS Health Inc. ***(458)***
INCOL 2000 ***(458)***
Independent Community Bankers of America ***(459)***
Independent Contractor Ass'n of America, Inc. ***(459)***
Independent Contractor Coalition ***(459)***
Independent Electrical Contractors, Inc. ***(459)***
Independent Insurance Agents of America, Inc. ***(459)***
Independent Office Products and Furniture Dealers Ass'n ***(459)***
Independent Petroleum Ass'n of America ***(459)***
Independent Power Tax Group ***(460)***
Independent Sector ***(460)***
Indiana, Office of the Governor of the State of ***(460)***
The INDOPCO Coalition ***(461)***
Industrial Customers of Northwest Utilities ***(461)***
Information Technology Industry Council ***(462)***
ING America Insurance Holdings, Inc. ***(462)***
Institute for Civil Soc. ***(463)***
Institute of Electrical and Electronics Engineers, Inc. ***(464)***
Institute of Navigation ***(464)***
Institutional Labor Advisors *(103)*
Interest Allocation Coalition ***(466)***
Interest Netting Coalition ***(466)***
Intermodal Ass'n of North America ***(467)***
Internat'l Ass'n for Financial Planning ***(467)***
Internat'l Ass'n of Bridge, Structural, Ornamental and Reinforcing Iron Workers ***(467)***
Internat'l Ass'n of Drilling Contractors ***(467)***
Internat'l Brotherhood of Boilermakers, Iron Shipbuilders, Blacksmiths, Forgers and Helpers ***(469)***
Internat'l Brotherhood of Electrical Workers ***(469)***
Internat'l Brotherhood of Teamsters ***(469)***
Internat'l Business Machines Corp. ***(469)***
Internat'l Council of Cruise Lines ***(470)***
Internat'l Council of Shopping Centers ***(470)***
Internat'l Electronics Manufacturers and Consumers of America ***(471)***
Internat'l Franchise Ass'n ***(472)***
Internat'l Game Technology ***(472)***
Internat'l Health, Racquet and Sportsclub Ass'n ***(472)***
Internat'l Mass Retailers Ass'n ***(473)***
Internat'l Municipal Signal Ass'n ***(473)***
Internat'l Paper ***(473)***
Internat'l Soc. for Technology in Education ***(475)***
Internat'l Union of Operating Engineers ***(476)***
Internat'l Union of Painters and Allied Trades ***(476)***
Interstate Natural Gas Ass'n of America ***(477)***
Investment Co. Institute ***(477)***
IPALCO Enterprises, Inc./Indianapolis Power & Light Co. ***(478)***
IPC Washington Office ***(478)***
Islamic Institute ***(479)***
ITT Industries ***(480)***
Ivins, Phillips & Barker *(104)*
Jackson Hewitt ***(480)***
Jackson Nat'l Life Insurance ***(480)***
Jackson, Mississippi, City of ***(480)***
Jacksonville Electric Authority ***(481)***
Jacobs Engineering Group Inc. ***(481)***
Jacobus Tenbroek Memorial Fund ***(481)***
Jam Shoe Concepts, Inc. ***(481)***
Jamison and Sullivan, Inc. *(104)*
Janus-Merritt Strategies, L.L.C. *(104)*
Jar-Mon Consultants, Inc. *(105)*
Jefferson Government Relations, L.L.C. *(106)*
Jewelers of America ***(483)***
JFS Group, Ltd. *(107)*
JM Family Enterprises ***(483)***
Job Opportunities Business Symposium ***(483)***
Johnson & Johnson, Inc. ***(484)***
Johnson Co. *(107)*
D. R. Johnson Lumber ***(484)***
Johnston & Associates, LLC *(107)*
Jolly/Rissler, Inc. *(108)*
Edward Jones Investments ***(485)***
Jones, Day, Reavis & Pogue *(108)*
Jones, Walker, Waechter, Poitevent, Carrere & Denegre, L.L.P. *(108)*
Jorden Burt LLP *(109)*
Robert E. Juliano Associates *(109)*
Kaiser Aluminum & Chemical Corp. ***(485)***
Kalik Lewin *(109)*
Betty Ann Kane & Co. *(110)*
Kansas City Southern Industries ***(486)***
Kaye Scholer LLP *(110)*
Kehoe & Hambel *(110)*
Kellogg Brown and Root ***(487)***
Kellogg Co. ***(487)***
Kelly and Associates, Inc. *(111)*
Kelly and Associates, Inc. ***(487)***
Kelly Services, Inc. ***(487)***
Kendall-Jackson Winery ***(488)***
Kennecott/Borax ***(488)***
Kent & O'Connor, Inc. *(112)*
Kessler & Associates Business Services, Inc. *(112)*
KeyCorp, Inc. ***(489)***
KeySpan Energy ***(489)***
Jeffrey J. Kimbell & Associates *(113)*
Kimberly Consulting, LLC *(113)*
Kimberly-Clark Corp. ***(489)***
Kinder-Care Learning Centers, Inc. ***(489)***
The Kinetics Group ***(489)***
Peter Kinzler *(113)*
Kirkland & Ellis *(113)*
Klein & Saks, Inc. *(114)*
Koch Industries, Inc. ***(490)***
Kogovsek & Associates *(114)*
Koniag, Inc. ***(491)***
The KPMG FSC Coalition ***(491)***
KPMG, LLP *(115)*
KPMG, LLP ***(491)***
Kurzweil & Associates *(115)*
La Quinta Inns, Inc. ***(493)***
Laborers' Internat'l Union of North America ***(493)***
Land Trust Alliance ***(494)***
Large Public Power Council ***(495)***
Las Vegas, Nevada, City of ***(495)***
Latham & Watkins *(116)*
Lathrop & Gage, L.C. *(116)*
Latona Associates, Inc. ***(496)***
LDW, Inc. ***(496)***
League of California Cities ***(497)***
LeBoeuf, Lamb, Greene & MacRae L.L.P. *(117)*
Legislative Solutions *(118)*
The Legislative Strategies Group, LLC *(118)*
LegisLaw *(118)*
Lehigh Portland Cement Co. ***(498)***
Lehman Brothers ***(498)***
Lent Scrivner & Roth LLC *(119)*
Levi Strauss and Co. ***(498)***
Levine & Co. *(119)*
The Michael Lewan Co. *(119)*
Lewis-Burke Associates *(120)*
Liberty Check Printers ***(499)***
Eli Lilly and Co. ***(499)***
The Limited Inc. ***(499)***
Lincoln Nat'l Corp. ***(500)***
Lincoln, Nebraska, City of ***(500)***
Littler Mendelson, P.C. *(120)*
The Livingston Group, LLC *(120)*
Local Initiatives Support Corp. ***(501)***
Lockheed Martin Corp. ***(501)***
Lockridge Grindal & Nauen, P.L.L.P. *(121)*
Long Beach, California, Port of ***(503)***
Lorillard Tobacco Co. ***(503)***
Lotus Development Corp. ***(504)***
Lovelace Respiratory Research Institute ***(504)***
The LTV Corp. ***(505)***
Lucent Technologies ***(505)***
Luman, Lange & Wheeler *(122)*
Lumbermens Mutual Casualty Co. ***(505)***
Lutheran Brotherhood ***(505)***
Marshall L. Lynam *(122)*
MacAndrews & Forbes Holdings, Inc. ***(506)***

Machinery Dealers Nat'l Ass'n *(506)*
Mack Trucks, Inc. *(506)*
Maersk Inc. *(507)*
Magazine Publishers of America *(507)*
Major League Baseball *(508)*
Maloney & Knox, LLP *(123)*
Management Insights, Inc. *(508)*
Manatt, Phelps & Phillips, LLP *(123)*
Manufactured Housing Institute *(509)*
Manufacturers Alliance/MAPI Inc. *(509)*
MARC Associates, Inc. *(124)*
March of Dimes Birth Defects Foundation *(509)*
Marine Engineers Beneficial Ass'n (District No. 1 - PCD) *(510)*
Maritime Institute for Research and Industrial Development *(510)*
Marriott Internat'l, Inc. *(511)*
Marsh & McLennan Cos. *(511)*
Maryland Psychiatric Soc. *(512)*
Maryland Taxpayers Ass'n, Inc. *(512)*
Massachusetts Software Council *(512)*
MassMutual Financial Group *(512)*
MasterCard Internat'l *(513)*
Dawson Mathis & Associates *(126)*
Matsushita Electric Corp. of America *(513)*
Maxus Energy Corp. *(513)*
Mayer, Brown & Platt *(126)*
Maytag Corp. *(513)*
Mazak Corp. & Mazak Sales and Service, Inc. *(513)*
MCA Inc. *(514)*
McClure, Gerard & Neuenschwander, Inc. *(127)*
McDermott Internat'l, Inc./Babcock & Wilcox *(514)*
McDermott, Will and Emery *(128)*
Jack H. McDonald *(129)*
McDonald's Corp. *(514)*
MCG Northwest, Inc. *(514)*
McGraw-Hill Cos., The *(514)*
McGuiness & Holch *(130)*
McGuireWoods L.L.P. *(130)*
MCI WorldCom Corp. *(514)*
McIntyre Law Firm, PLLC *(130)*
McKay Walker *(131)*
McKesson Corp. *(515)*
McLane Co. *(515)*
McMillan, Hill & Associates *(131)*
McNamara & Associates *(131)*
The Mead Corp. *(515)*
Mechanical Contractors Ass'n of America *(515)*
Media General, Inc. *(516)*
Media Tax Group *(516)*
Medical Records Internat'l, Inc. *(516)*
MedStar Health *(517)*
Medtronic, Inc. *(517)*
Mentor Graphics Corp. *(518)*
Merced, California, County of *(518)*
Merck & Co. *(518)*
MeriStar Hospitality Corp. *(519)*
Merrill Lynch & Co., Inc. *(519)*
Methanex Inc. *(520)*
Metropolitan Atlanta Rapid Transit Authority *(520)*
Metropolitan Life Insurance Co. *(520)*
Metropolitan Mortgage and Securities, Inc. *(520)*
Meyers & Associates *(133)*
Miami Beach, Florida, City of *(521)*
Miami, Florida, City of *(521)*
Miami-Dade, Florida, County of *(521)*
Micell Technologies, Inc. *(522)*
Michelin North America *(522)*
Michigan Consolidated Gas Co. *(522)*
Michigan Insurance Federation *(522)*
Micron Technology, Inc. *(522)*
Microsoft Corp. *(522)*
The Military Coalition *(524)*
Miller & Chevalier, Chartered *(133)*
Miller & Co. *(134)*
Denny Miller McBee Associates *(134)*
Minnesota Life Insurance Co. *(525)*
Minnesota Mining and Manufacturing Co. (3M Co.) *(525)*
The Robert Mondavi Winery *(527)*
Monfort & Wolfe *(135)*
Monsanto Co. *(528)*
Montana Land Reliance *(528)*
MONY Life Insurance Co. *(529)*
Moore & Bruce, LLP *(136)*
J. P. Morgan Chase & Co. *(529)*
Morgan Stanley Dean Witter & Co. *(529)*
Morgan, Lewis & Bockius LLP *(136)*
Morrison & Foerster LLP *(137)*
The Morrison Group, Inc. *(137)*
Morse Diesel Internat'l Inc. *(530)*
Mortgage Bankers Ass'n of America *(530)*
The Kate Moss Company *(137)*
Motion Picture Ass'n of America *(530)*
Mount Vernon, City of *(532)*
MSS Consultants, LLC *(138)*
Muldoon, Murphy & Faucette, LLP *(532)*
Mullenholz, Brimsek & Belair *(138)*
Multistate Tax Commission *(532)*
Municipal Electric Authority of Georgia *(532)*
Municipal Financial Consultants Inc. *(532)*
Murphy Oil U.S.A. *(533)*
Murray, Scheer, Montgomery, Tapia & O'Donnell *(139)*
Mutual Legislative Committee *(533)*
Mutual of America *(533)*
Mutual of Omaha Insurance Companies *(533)*
Mutual Tax Committee *(533)*
NAAS *(534)*
Nat'l Air Transportation Ass'n *(536)*
Nat'l Alcohol Beverage Control Ass'n *(536)*
Nat'l Ass'n for College Admission Counseling *(537)*
Nat'l Ass'n for State Farm Agents *(538)*
Nat'l Ass'n for the Self-Employed *(538)*
Nat'l Ass'n of Affordable Housing Lenders *(538)*
Nat'l Ass'n of Attorneys General *(539)*
Nat'l Ass'n of Beverage Retailers *(539)*
Nat'l Ass'n of Bond Lawyers *(539)*
Nat'l Ass'n of Broadcasters *(539)*
Nat'l Ass'n of Chain Drug Stores *(539)*
Nat'l Ass'n of College Stores *(540)*
Nat'l Ass'n of Community Health Centers *(540)*
Nat'l Ass'n of Computer Consultant Businesses *(540)*
Nat'l Ass'n of Convenience Stores *(541)*
Nat'l Ass'n of Counties *(541)*
Nat'l Ass'n of Dental Plans *(542)*
Nat'l Ass'n of Enrolled Agents *(542)*
Nat'l Ass'n of Evangelicals *(542)*
Nat'l Ass'n of Federal Credit Unions *(542)*
Nat'l Ass'n of Fleet Administrators *(543)*
Nat'l Ass'n of Government Deferred Compensation Administrators *(543)*
Nat'l Ass'n of Healthcare Consultants *(543)*
Nat'l Ass'n of Home Builders of the U.S. *(543)*
Nat'l Ass'n of Housing Cooperatives *(544)*
Nat'l Ass'n of Independent Colleges and Universities *(544)*
Nat'l Ass'n of Independent Insurers *(544)*
Nat'l Ass'n of Industrial and Office Properties *(544)*
Nat'l Ass'n of Insurance and Financial Advisors *(544)*
Nat'l Ass'n of Investors Corporation (NAIC) *(545)*
Nat'l Ass'n of Manufacturers *(545)*
Nat'l Ass'n of Music Merchants *(545)*
Nat'l Ass'n of Negro Business & Professional Women's Clubs, Inc. *(546)*
Nat'l Ass'n of People with AIDS, Inc. *(546)*
Nat'l Ass'n of Police Organizations *(546)*
Nat'l Ass'n of Professional Employer Organizations *(547)*
Nat'l Ass'n of Real Estate Investment Trusts *(547)*
Nat'l Ass'n of Realtors *(547)*
Nat'l Ass'n of Retired Federal Employees *(548)*
Nat'l Ass'n of RV Parks and Campgrounds *(548)*
Nat'l Ass'n of Securities Dealers, Inc. (NASD) *(549)*
Nat'l Ass'n of Settlement Purchasers *(549)*
Nat'l Ass'n of Social Workers *(549)*
Nat'l Ass'n of State Farm Agents *(550)*
Nat'l Ass'n of Water Companies *(551)*
Nat'l Ass'n of Wheat Growers *(551)*
Nat'l Ass'n of Wholesaler-Distributors *(551)*
Nat'l Automobile Dealers Ass'n *(552)*
Nat'l Beer Wholesalers Ass'n *(552)*
Nat'l Business Aviation Ass'n *(553)*
Nat'l Cable Television Ass'n *(553)*
Nat'l Campaign for a Peace Tax Fund *(554)*
Nat'l Cattleman's Beef Ass'n *(554)*
Nat'l Center for Policy Analysis *(555)*
Nat'l Club Ass'n *(556)*
Nat'l Coalition for Cancer Research *(556)*
Nat'l Coalition for Cancer Survivorship *(556)*
Nat'l Collegiate Athletic Ass'n *(557)*
Nat'l Community Capital Ass'n *(557)*
Nat'l Concrete Masonry Ass'n *(558)*
Nat'l Cooperative Business Ass'n *(559)*
Nat'l Coordinating Committee for Multiemployer Plans *(559)*
Nat'l Corn Growers Ass'n *(559)*
Nat'l Council of Chain Restaurants *(560)*
Nat'l Council of Coal Lessors *(560)*
Nat'l Council of Farmer Cooperatives *(560)*
Nat'l Council of Higher Education Loan Programs *(560)*
Nat'l Council of State Housing Agencies *(560)*
Nat'l Council of University Research Administrators *(561)*
Nat'l Defense Industrial Ass'n *(561)*
Nat'l Defined Contribution Council *(561)*
Nat'l Education Ass'n of the U.S. *(562)*
Nat'l Electrical Contractors Ass'n *(562)*
Nat'l Electrical Safety Foundation *(562)*
Nat'l Employee Benefits Institute *(562)*
Nat'l Employment Lawyers Ass'n *(562)*
Nat'l Employment Opportunities Network *(563)*
Nat'l Endangered Species Act Reform Coalition *(563)*
Nat'l Farmers Union (Farmers Educational & Co-operative Union of America) *(563)*
Nat'l Federation of Independent Business *(564)*
Nat'l Field Selling Ass'n *(564)*
Nat'l Food Processors Ass'n *(564)*
Nat'l Football League *(565)*
Nat'l Football League Players Ass'n *(565)*
Nat'l Foreign Trade Council, Inc. *(565)*
Nat'l Funeral Directors Ass'n *(565)*
Nat'l Geographic Soc. *(565)*
Nat'l Grange *(566)*
Nat'l Grid USA *(566)*
Nat'l Grocers Ass'n *(566)*
Nat'l Hardwood Lumber Ass'n *(566)*
Nat'l Health Council *(567)*
Nat'l Home Equity Mortgage Ass'n *(567)*
Nat'l Indian Gaming Ass'n *(568)*
Nat'l Licensed Beverage Ass'n *(570)*
Nat'l Lumber and Building Material Dealers Ass'n *(570)*
Nat'l Military Family Ass'n *(571)*
Nat'l Milk Producers Federation *(571)*
Nat'l Mining Ass'n *(571)*
Nat'l Multi-Housing Council *(571)*
Nat'l Newspaper Ass'n *(572)*
Nat'l Oilseed Processors Ass'n *(572)*
Nat'l Park Hospitality Ass'n *(573)*
Nat'l Petrochemical Refiners Ass'n *(573)*
Nat'l Pork Producers Council *(574)*
Nat'l Propane Gas Ass'n *(574)*
Nat'l Public Radio *(574)*
Nat'l Ready Mixed Concrete Ass'n *(575)*
Nat'l Realty Committee *(575)*
Nat'l Restaurant Ass'n *(576)*
Nat'l Retail Federation *(576)*
Nat'l Roofing Contractors Ass'n *(576)*
Nat'l Rural Electric Cooperative Ass'n *(576)*
Nat'l Rural Health Ass'n *(577)*
Nat'l School Transportation Ass'n *(577)*
Nat'l Small Business United *(578)*
Nat'l Soc. of Professional Engineers *(578)*
Nat'l Steel Corp. *(579)*
Nat'l Structured Settlements Trade Ass'n *(579)*
Nat'l Taxpayers Union *(579)*
Nat'l Telephone Cooperative Ass'n *(579)*
Nat'l Thoroughbred Racing Ass'n, Inc. *(579)*
Nat'l Tour Ass'n *(579)*
Nat'l Treasury Employees Union *(580)*
Nat'l Truck Equipment Ass'n *(580)*
Nat'l Trust for Historic Preservation *(580)*
Nat'l Utility Contractors Ass'n (NUCA) *(580)*
Nat'l Venture Capital Ass'n *(580)*
Nat'l Wholesale Co., Inc. *(581)*

Nationwide Mutual Insurance Co. ***(582)***
NATSO, Inc. ***(582)***
The Nature Conservancy ***(582)***
Navajo Nation ***(582)***
NAVCOM Systems, Inc. ***(583)***
NCR Corp. ***(583)***
NETWORK, A Nat'l Catholic Social Justice Lobby ***(584)***
New Edge Networks ***(585)***
New England Financial ***(585)***
New England Investment Co. ***(585)***
New England Life Insurance Co. ***(585)***
New York Life Insurance Co. ***(587)***
New York Stock Exchange ***(588)***
New York University ***(588)***
The Newark Group ***(588)***
Newark, New Jersey, City of ***(588)***
Newman & Associates ***(588)***
Newport Group ***(588)***
Newport News Shipbuilding Inc. ***(588)***
Newspaper Ass'n of America ***(589)***
Elisabeth G. Newton *(142)*
Niagara Mohawk Power Corp. ***(589)***
Niche Plan Sponsors, Inc. ***(589)***
NiSource Inc. ***(590)***
Nissan North America Inc. ***(590)***
Nixon Peabody LLP *(142)*
Nordstrom, Inc. ***(591)***
Norfolk Southern Corp. ***(591)***
Norfolk Southern Railroad ***(591)***
Norfolk, Virginia, City of ***(591)***
Julia J. Norrell & Associates *(142)*
Nortel Networks ***(591)***
North American Equipment Dealers Ass'n ***(592)***
North American Insulation Manufacturers Ass'n ***(592)***
North Slope Borough, Alaska ***(593)***
Northeast Texas Electric Cooperative ***(593)***
Northeast Utilities ***(593)***
Northrop Grumman Corp. ***(594)***
Northwest Airlines, Inc. ***(595)***
Northwest Woodland Owners Council ***(595)***
Northwestern Mutual Life Insurance Co. ***(595)***
Novartis Corp. ***(596)***
Novell, Inc. ***(596)***
nPower Advisors, LLC ***(596)***
NRG Energy, Inc. ***(596)***
Nuclear Energy Institute ***(597)***
John T. O'Rourke Law Offices ***(598)***
The OB-C Group, LLC *(143)*
Obadal and MacLeod, p.c. *(143)*
O'Brien, Klink & Associates *(144)*
O'Bryon & Co. *(144)*
Occidental Internat'l Corporation ***(598)***
O'Connor & Hannan, L.L.P. *(144)*
O'Donoghue & O'Donoghue *(145)*
Bartley M. O'Hara *(145)*
Oklahoma City, Oklahoma, City of ***(599)***
Olsson, Frank and Weeda, P.C. *(146)*
O'Melveny and Myers LLP *(147)*
Oneida Indian Nation of New York ***(600)***
O'Neill, Athy & Casey, P.C. *(147)*
Oracle Corp. ***(602)***
Organization for Internat'l Investment ***(603)***
John T. O'Rourke Law Offices *(147)*
Ounalashka Corp. ***(604)***
Owens Corning ***(604)***
Owens-Illinois, Inc. ***(605)***
PACCAR, Inc. ***(605)***
Pacific Life Insurance Co. ***(605)***
Paley Rothman Goldstein Rosenberg & Cooper *(148)*
Palumbo & Cerrell, Inc. *(149)*
Paper Recycling Coalition ***(607)***
Parry, Romani, DeConcini & Symms *(149)*
Parsons Corp. ***(608)***
Partnership Defense Fund Trust ***(608)***
Partnership for Recovery Coalition ***(609)***
Pasadena, California, City of ***(609)***
Patton Boggs, LLP *(150)*
Patton Boggs, LLP ***(609)***
Paul, Hastings, Janofsky & Walker LLP *(153)*
Paul, Hastings, Janofsky & Walker LLP ***(610)***
The Peabody Group ***(610)***
Peachtree Settlement Funding ***(610)***
Pearson & Pipkin, Inc. *(154)*
J. C. Penney Co., Inc. ***(611)***
Pennzoil-Quaker State Co. ***(611)***
People Advancing Christian Education (PACE) ***(611)***
Peoples Bank ***(612)***
PepsiCo, Inc. ***(612)***
Perdue Farms Inc. ***(612)***
Perpetual Corp. ***(612)***
Perry Institute for Marine Science ***(612)***
The Petrizzo Group, Inc. *(155)*
Petro Star, Inc. ***(613)***
Petroleum Helicopters ***(613)***
Petroleum Marketers Ass'n of America ***(613)***
Pfizer, Inc. ***(613)***
PG&E Corp. ***(614)***
The PGA Tour, Inc. ***(614)***
Pharmaceutical Research and Manufacturers of America ***(614)***
Pharmacia Corp. ***(615)***
Phelps Dodge Corp. ***(615)***
Philip Morris Management Corp. ***(615)***
Philips Electronics North America Corp. ***(616)***
Phillips Petroleum Co. ***(616)***
Phoenix Home Life Mutual Insurance Co. ***(616)***
Phoenix, Arizona, City of ***(616)***
Physician Insurers Ass'n of America ***(616)***
Piedmont Environmental Council ***(617)***
The Pillsbury Co. ***(617)***
PIMCO Advisors, L.P. ***(617)***
Pinnacle West Capital Corp. ***(617)***
The Pittston Co. ***(618)***
Charles L. Pizer *(156)*
Placer Dome U.S. Inc. ***(618)***
Placid Refining Co. ***(618)***
Susan S. Platt Consulting *(156)*
Plum Creek Timber Co. ***(619)***
Plumbing, Heating, Cooling Contractors- National Assoc. ***(619)***
Podesta/Mattoon *(158)*
Polar Air Cargo, Inc. ***(620)***
Polyisocyanurate Insulation Manufacturers Ass'n ***(620)***
Porsche Cars North America, Inc. ***(621)***
Portland, Oregon, City of ***(621)***
Potomac Electric Power Co. ***(622)***
Potomac Group *(160)*
PPL ***(622)***
Praxair, Inc. ***(623)***
Preservation Action ***(623)***
Preston Gates Ellis & Rouvelas Meeds LLP *(162)*
PriceWaterhouseCoopers *(163)*
Principal Financial Group ***(624)***
Printing Industries of America ***(624)***
Private Care Ass'n, Inc. ***(624)***
The Procter & Gamble Company ***(625)***
Production Service & Sales District Council Pension Fund ***(625)***
Professional Benefit Trust ***(625)***
Professional Managers Ass'n ***(626)***
Profit Sharing/401 (k) Council of America ***(626)***
Progress Energy ***(626)***
Progressive Policy Institute ***(626)***
The Project Leadership Committee, Lincoln Center for the Performing Arts ***(626)***
Propane Vehicle Council ***(627)***
Prudential Insurance Co. of America ***(627)***
PSE&G ***(627)***
Public Affairs Resources, Inc. *(164)*
Public Private Partnership *(164)*
Public Strategies Washington, Inc. *(164)*
Public Strategies, Inc. *(165)*
Puerto Rico Federal Affairs Administration ***(629)***
Puerto Rico Senate ***(629)***
Puerto Rico U.S.A. Foundation ***(629)***
Puerto Rico, Commonwealth of ***(629)***
Pulte Home Corp. ***(630)***
PwC Contract Manufacturing Coalition ***(630)***
PwC Leasing Coalition ***(630)***
Andrew F. Quinlan *(165)*
Quinn Gillespie & Associates *(165)*
Qwest Communications ***(631)***
R&D Tax Credit Coalition ***(631)***
R&D Tax Regulation Group ***(631)***
Mark J. Raabe *(165)*
Radio Shack Corp. ***(632)***
RAG North America ***(632)***
Ralston Purina Co. ***(632)***
Rapid Reporting, Inc. ***(633)***
RAPOCA Energy Co. ***(633)***
Raytheon Co. ***(633)***
The Reader's Digest Ass'n ***(633)***
Real Estate Roundtable ***(634)***
Rebuild America's Schools ***(634)***
Recording Industry Ass'n of America ***(634)***
Red Lake Band of Chippewa Indians ***(635)***
Reed, Smith, LLP *(167)*
Reed-Elsevier Inc. ***(635)***
Reinsurance Ass'n of America ***(636)***
Renewable Fuels Ass'n ***(637)***
The Renkes Group, Ltd. *(168)*
Repeal the Tax on Talking Coalition ***(637)***
Republic Industries, Inc. ***(637)***
Republican Jewish Coalition ***(637)***
Resources and Instruction for Staff Excellence, Inc. ***(638)***
Resources Development, Inc. *(168)*
The Retired Enlisted Ass'n ***(638)***
The Retired Officers Ass'n (TROA) ***(638)***
Retiree Benefits Alliance ***(639)***
Retirement Income Coalition ***(639)***
Retirement Industry Trust Ass'n ***(639)***
Reusable Pallet and Container Coalition ***(639)***
R. J. Reynolds Tobacco Co. ***(639)***
RGS Enterprises, Inc. *(168)*
Liz Robbins Associates *(169)*
Liz Robbins Associates ***(641)***
Robertson, Monagle & Eastaugh *(170)*
Rock & Associates *(171)*
Rock-Tenn Co. ***(641)***
Rockwell Collins ***(641)***
Rohm and Haas Co. ***(642)***
Peter J. Rose *(172)*
The Rouse Company ***(642)***
Royer & Babyak *(172)*
Rubber Manufacturers Ass'n ***(643)***
Frank Russell Co. ***(644)***
Ryan, Phillips, Utrecht & MacKinnon *(173)*
Ryder System, Inc. ***(644)***
S-Corporation Ass'n ***(644)***
Sabre Inc. ***(644)***
Safeguard America's Family Enterprises ***(645)***
Safeway, Inc. ***(645)***
Sagamore Associates, Inc. *(174)*
Salinas, California, City of ***(646)***
Sallie Mae, Inc. ***(646)***
Salt River Project ***(646)***
Sam Rayburn G&T Electric Cooperative, Inc. ***(647)***
San Diego, California, City of ***(647)***
San Francisco, California, City and County of ***(648)***
Sandia Pueblo ***(648)***
Santa Clara Valley Transportation Authority ***(649)***
Santa Clarita, California, City of ***(649)***
SAP Public Services ***(649)***
Sappi Fine Paper NA ***(649)***
Sara Lee Corp. ***(649)***
Saunders Consulting *(175)*
Savings Banks Life Insurance Fund ***(650)***
Savings Coalition of America ***(650)***
R. Wayne Sayer & Associates *(175)*
SBC Communications Inc. ***(650)***
SCANA Corp. ***(651)***
Paul Scherer & Co., LLP ***(651)***
Schering-Plough Corp. ***(651)***
Schering-Plough Legislative Resources L.L.C. ***(651)***
Schnader Harrison Segal & Lewis LLP *(176)*
James E. Schneider, LLM Inc. ***(651)***
Abraham Schneier and Associates *(176)*
Scholastic, Inc. ***(651)***
Schramm, Williams & Associates, Inc. *(176)*
Charles Schwab & Co., Inc., ***(652)***
Schwan's Sales Enterprises ***(652)***
Scottsdale, Arizona, City of ***(652)***
Scribe Communications, Inc. ***(653)***
Scribner, Hall & Thompson, LLP *(176)*
Scull Law Firm, David L. ***(653)***
Sea Ventures Inc. ***(653)***
Seaboard Corp. ***(653)***
Sealaska Corp. ***(653)***

Sears, Roebuck and Co. ***(653)***
Seattle City Light ***(653)***
Section 877 Coalition ***(654)***
Securities Industry Ass'n ***(654)***
Security Capital Group ***(654)***
Sellery Associates, Inc. *(177)*
Semiconductor Equipment and Materials Internat'l ***(655)***
Semiconductor Industry Ass'n ***(655)***
Seminole Tribe of Indians of Florida ***(655)***
David Senter & Associates *(177)*
Sequoia Ventures ***(655)***
Service Corp. Internat'l ***(656)***
Severance Trust Executive Program ***(656)***
Shakopee Mdewakanton Sioux Tribe ***(656)***
Shaw Pittman *(177)*
Sheet Metal Workers' Internat'l Ass'n ***(657)***
Shell Oil Co. ***(657)***
The Sheridan Group *(179)*
Sherwin Williams Co. ***(657)***
Shipston Group, LTD ***(657)***
Shriner-Midland Co. ***(658)***
Shubert Organization Inc. ***(658)***
Sidley & Austin *(180)*
Sierra Pacific Industries ***(659)***
Silicon Graphics/SGI ***(659)***
Sills Associates *(180)*
Simon and Co., Inc. *(181)*
Bill Simpson & Associates *(181)*
Singer Asset Management Co., L.L.C. ***(659)***
Singer Assett Finance, Inc. ***(660)***
Sisters of Providence Health Systems ***(660)***
Skadden, Arps, Slate, Meagher & Flom LLP *(181)*
Skadden, Arps, Slate, Meagher & Flom LLP ***(660)***
Small Business Council of America ***(661)***
Small Business Regulatory Council ***(661)***
Smith & Harroff, Inc. *(182)*
E. Del Smith and Co. *(183)*
The Charles E. Smith Companies ***(661)***
Smith Dawson & Andrews, Inc. *(183)*
Smith Martin & Boyette *(184)*
The Smith-Free Group *(184)*
Smokeless Tobacco Council ***(661)***
Smokers Pneumonoconiosis Council ***(662)***
Smurfit Stone Container Corp. ***(662)***
Snake River Sugar Co. ***(662)***
Soc. of Independent Gasoline Marketers of America ***(663)***
Sodexho Marriott Services, Inc. ***(664)***
Software & Information Industry Ass'n (SIIA) ***(664)***
Software Finance and Tax Executives Council ***(664)***
Solid Waste Ass'n of North America ***(665)***
The Solomon Group, LLC *(185)*
Soo Line Railroad, Inc. ***(666)***
Sotheby's Holdings Inc. ***(666)***
Southeastern Michigan Council of Government ***(667)***
Southern Ute Indian Tribe ***(668)***
Southwire, Inc. ***(668)***
Spaceport Florida Authority ***(669)***
Spanish Broadcasting System, Inc. ***(669)***
Special Libraries Ass'n ***(669)***
Spokane Tribe ***(670)***
Sporting Goods Manufacturers Ass'n ***(670)***
Spring Hill Camps ***(670)***
Springs Industries, Inc. ***(671)***
Sprint Corp. ***(671)***
St. Louis, Minnesota, Board of Commissioners of the County ***(672)***
Staples, Inc. ***(673)***
Starwood Hotels & Resorts Worldwide, Inc. ***(673)***
Starwood Lodging/Starwood Capital Group, L.P. ***(673)***
Steel Service Center Institute ***(674)***
Stephens Group, Inc. ***(674)***
Stephens Law Firm *(188)*
Stephens Law Offices *(188)*
Steptoe & Johnson LLP *(188)*
Sterling Chemical Co. ***(674)***
Stewart & Stevenson Services, Inc. ***(674)***
Stilwell Financial Inc. ***(674)***
Kenneth F. Stinger *(189)*
John M. Stinson *(189)*
Stock Co. Information Group ***(675)***
Stockbridge-Munsee Community Band of Mohican Indians ***(675)***
Storage Technology Corp. ***(675)***
Straddle Rules Tax Group ***(675)***
Strategic Impact, Inc. *(189)*
Stuntz, Davis & Staffier, P.C. *(190)*
Sullivan & Cromwell *(190)*
Sumlin Associates *(190)*
Sun Innovations, Inc. ***(676)***
Sun Microsystems ***(676)***
Sunkist Growers, Inc. ***(677)***
Sunoco, Inc. ***(677)***
Sunrise Research Corp. *(191)*
Super Reachback Coalition ***(677)***
Superior Bank, FSB ***(677)***
Sutherland Asbill & Brennan LLP *(191)*
Swaziland Sugar Ass'n ***(678)***
Swidler Berlin Shereff Friedman, LLP *(191)*
Swiss Investors Protection Ass'n ***(679)***
Symms, Lehn & Associates, Inc. *(192)*
Synthetic Organic Chemical Manufacturers Ass'n ***(679)***
Syracuse University ***(679)***
Tacoma, Washington, City of ***(680)***
Tacoma, Washington, Port of ***(680)***
George C. Tagg *(192)*
Talley and Associates *(192)*
Tanimura & Antle, Inc. ***(680)***
Tax Action Group ***(681)***
Tax Analysis ***(681)***
Tax Executives Institute, Inc. ***(681)***
Tax Fairness Coalition ***(681)***
Tax Foundation, Inc. ***(681)***
Tax Information Group ***(681)***
Tax Policy Coalition ***(681)***
Taxicab, Limousine and Paratransit Ass'n ***(681)***
Technology Network ***(682)***
TECO Energy, Inc. ***(682)***
TECO Transport Corp. ***(682)***
Teletech Teleservices, Inc. ***(683)***
Terpstra Associates *(193)*
Tex-La Electric Cooperative of Texas ***(684)***
Texaco Group Inc. ***(684)***
Texas A&M Research Foundation ***(684)***
Texas Health Resources ***(684)***
Texas Instruments ***(684)***
Texas Pacific Group ***(685)***
Texas Windstorm Insurance Ass'n ***(685)***
Textron Inc. ***(685)***
Thelen Reid & Priest LLP *(193)*
Thelen Reid & Priest LLP ***(685)***
Thermo EcoTek Corp. ***(686)***
Thiokol Propulsion ***(686)***
Thompson Coburn LLP *(194)*
Thompson Creek Metals Co. ***(686)***
TIAA-CREF ***(686)***
Timmons and Co., Inc. *(195)*
Tip Tax Coalition ***(687)***
Tire Ass'n of North America ***(687)***
TJTC Recovery Project Coalition ***(687)***
Tobacco Fairness Coalition ***(688)***
Todhunter Internat'l, Inc. ***(688)***
Tongour Simpson Holsclaw Green *(196)*
Torchmark Corp. ***(688)***
Toyota Motor North America, U.S.A., Inc. ***(689)***
Traditional Values Coalition ***(689)***
Trans World Airlines, Inc. ***(689)***
Transportation Institute ***(690)***
Travel Business Roundtable ***(691)***
Travel Council for Fair Competition ***(691)***
Travelocity.com ***(691)***
TREA Senior Citizens League (TSCL) ***(691)***
Tricon Global Restaurants Inc. ***(692)***
Trizec Hahn Corp. ***(692)***
Troutman Sanders LLP *(196)*
Truck Renting and Leasing Ass'n ***(693)***
The Trump Organization ***(693)***
TRW Inc. ***(693)***
Tule River Tribal Council ***(694)***
Tunica Biloxi Indians of Louisiana ***(694)***
Tupperware Corp. ***(694)***
TXU Business Services ***(695)***
Tyco Internat'l (US), Inc. ***(695)***
U.S. Chamber Institute for Legal Reform ***(695)***
U.S. Chamber Task Force on Punitive Damages ***(695)***
U.S. English, Inc. ***(696)***
U.S. Family Network ***(696)***
U.S. Internet Council ***(696)***
UDV North America, Inc. ***(698)***
UDV/Heublein, Inc. ***(698)***
UNIFI, Inc. ***(698)***
Unilever United States, Inc. ***(699)***
Union of Needletrades, Industrial, and Textile Employees (UNITE) ***(699)***
Union Pacific ***(699)***
UNIPAC Service Corp. ***(699)***
Unisys Corp. ***(700)***
United Airlines ***(700)***
United Asset Management Corp. ***(700)***
United Automobile, Aerospace and Agricultural Implement Workers of America (UAW) ***(700)***
United Brotherhood of Carpenters and Joiners of America ***(700)***
United Fresh Fruit and Vegetable Ass'n ***(701)***
United Jewish Communities, Inc. ***(701)***
United Motorcoach Ass'n ***(702)***
United Parcel Service ***(702)***
United Seniors Ass'n ***(702)***
United States Business and Industry Council ***(703)***
United States Coast Guard Chief Petty Officers Ass'n ***(703)***
United States Telecom Ass'n ***(704)***
United Steelworkers of America ***(704)***
United Technologies Corp. ***(704)***
Universities Research Ass'n ***(705)***
University of California, Office of Federal Government Relations ***(706)***
University of Cincinnati ***(706)***
University of Medicine and Dentistry of New Jersey ***(706)***
University of Miami ***(706)***
University of Southern California ***(707)***
University of Tulsa ***(708)***
University of Virginia ***(708)***
University of Washington ***(708)***
University System of Maryland ***(708)***
UNOCAL Corp. ***(708)***
UNUM/Provident Corp. ***(708)***
US Airways ***(709)***
USA Biomass Power Producers Alliance ***(709)***
USAA - United Services Automobile Ass'n ***(710)***
UST Public Affairs, Inc. ***(710)***
USX Corp. ***(710)***
Ute Mountain Ute Indian Tribe ***(710)***
UtiliCorp United, Inc. ***(711)***
Utility Decommissioning Tax Group ***(711)***
Valanzano & Associates *(198)*
Valero Energy Corp. ***(711)***
Valis Associates *(198)*
Valley Hope Ass'n ***(711)***
Van Ness Feldman, P.C. *(199)*
Van Scoyoc Associates, Inc. *(200)*
Vanguard Charitable Endowment Program ***(712)***
Variable Annuity Life Insurance Co. ***(712)***
Venable *(201)*
Venetian Casino Resort, LLC ***(712)***
Verizon Communications ***(713)***
Verizon Wireless ***(713)***
Verner, Liipfert, Bernhard, McPherson and Hand, Chartered ***(713)***
Verner, Liipfert, Bernhard, McPherson and Hand, Chartered *(202)*
VHA Inc. ***(714)***
Viaticus, Inc. ***(714)***
Brenda R. Viehe-Naess *(204)*
Vinson & Elkins L.L.P. *(204)*
Vinyard & Associates *(205)*
Viohl and Associates, Inc. *(205)*
Virgin Islands, Government of the ***(715)***
Virginia Commonwealth University ***(716)***
VISA U.S.A., Inc. ***(716)***
Vivendi Universal ***(717)***
Vornado Inc. ***(717)***
VSAdc.com *(205)*
Wal-Mart Stores, Inc. ***(718)***
R. Duffy Wall and Associates *(205)*
Walton Enterprises ***(718)***
Warburg, Pincus & Co., Inc., E. M. ***(718)***

Warnaco, Inc. ***(718)***
Washington Council Ernst & Young *(206)*
Washington Council of Agencies ***(719)***
The Washington Group *(208)*
Washington Metropolitan Area Transit Authority ***(720)***
Washington Mutual Bank ***(720)***
The Washington Post Co. ***(720)***
Washington Resource Associates *(209)*
Washington Sports & Entertainment, L.P. ***(720)***
Waste Control Specialists, Inc. ***(721)***
Waste Management, Inc. ***(721)***
Wausau Insurance Cos. ***(722)***
Wegmans Food Markets, Inc. ***(722)***
Weil, Gotshal & Manges, LLP *(211)*
WellPoint Health Networks/Blue Cross of California/UNICARE ***(723)***
Wendy's Internat'l, Inc. ***(723)***
J. G. Wentworth ***(723)***
Western Growers Ass'n ***(724)***
Westfield America, Inc. ***(725)***
The Wexler Group *(211)*
Weyerhaeuser Co. ***(725)***
Wheat & Associates, Inc. *(212)*
Susan J. White & Associates *(212)*
White & Case LLP *(212)*
White Pigeon Paper Co. ***(726)***
R. H. White Public Affairs Consulting *(213)*
William F. Whitsitt Policy and Government Affairs *(213)*
Wickland Oil Co. ***(726)***
Burton V. Wides, P.C. *(214)*
Wild Bird Feeding Institute ***(726)***
Wiley, Rein & Fielding ***(727)***
Wiley, Rein & Fielding *(214)*
The Willard Group *(215)*
Williams & Jensen, P.C. *(215)*
The Williams Companies ***(727)***
Wilmer, Cutler & Pickering *(217)*
Wilmington Savings Fund Society ***(727)***
Wine and Spirits Wholesalers of America ***(728)***
Wine Institute ***(728)***
Kathleen Winn & Associates, Inc. *(218)*
Winslow Press ***(728)***
Deborah F. Winston *(218)*
Winston & Strawn *(218)*
Wireless Communications Ass'n ***(728)***
Women Officials in NACo ***(729)***
World Floor Covering Ass'n ***(730)***
World Shipping Council ***(731)***
Worldwatch Institute ***(731)***
WOTC Project ***(731)***
Wright, Lindsey & Jennings ***(732)***
Wunder & Lilley *(221)*
Xerox Corp. ***(732)***
XL Capital Ltd ***(732)***
Yellow Corp. ***(733)***
Yellow Pages Publishers Ass'n ***(733)***
Zachery Taylor Parkway Commission ***(734)***
Zane & Associates *(221)*
Ziff Investors Partnership ***(734)***
Zuckerman Spaeder L.L.P. *(221)*
Zuckert, Scoutt and Rasenberger, L.L.P. *(221)*
Zurich Financial Group ***(735)***

Telecommunications (TEC)

3Com Corp. ***(223)***
AAA MidAtlantic ***(224)***
AARP (American Ass'n of Retired Persons) ***(224)***
AC Transit ***(225)***
Adams and Reese LLP *(5)*
The Advocacy Group *(6)*
AFL-CIO - Professional Employees Department ***(231)***
Akin, Gump, Strauss, Hauer & Feld, L.L.P. *(8)*
Alarm Industry Communications Committee ***(236)***
Alaska Communications Systems, Inc. ***(236)***
Albertine Enterprises, Inc. *(10)*
Sally L. Albright *(10)*
Alcalde & Fay *(10)*
Alcatel USA ***(237)***
Allegiance Telecom, Inc. ***(239)***
Alltel Corporation ***(242)***
Alpine Group, Inc. *(11)*
Alston & Bird LLP *(12)*
Alticor, Inc. ***(242)***
Alvarado & Gerken *(12)*
American Arts Alliance ***(245)***
American Ass'n for Laboratory Accreditation ***(246)***
American Ass'n of Community Colleges ***(247)***
American Ass'n of Law Libraries ***(248)***
American Ass'n of Museums ***(248)***
American Automobile Ass'n ***(250)***
American Cable Ass'n ***(251)***
American Civil Liberties Union ***(252)***
American Continental Group, Inc. *(12)*
American Council of Independent Laboratories ***(255)***
American Electronics Ass'n ***(257)***
American Express Co. ***(258)***
American Federation of Teachers ***(259)***
American Foundation for the Blind - Governmental Relations Group ***(260)***
American Gas Ass'n ***(261)***
American Homeowners Grassroots Alliance ***(262)***
American Hotel and Lodging Ass'n ***(263)***
American Indian Higher Education Consortium ***(263)***
American Library Ass'n ***(266)***
American Management ***(266)***
American Medical Informatics Ass'n ***(267)***
American Mobile Satellite Corp. ***(268)***
American Mobile Telecommunications Ass'n ***(268)***
American Museum of Natural History ***(268)***
American Planning Ass'n ***(270)***
American Public Communications Council ***(271)***
American Public Power Ass'n ***(272)***
American Public Works Ass'n ***(272)***
American Radio Relay League ***(272)***
American Resort Development Ass'n ***(272)***
American Soc. of Composers, Authors and Publishers ***(276)***
American Speech, Language, and Hearing Ass'n ***(277)***
American Symphony Orchestra League ***(278)***
American Telecasting, Inc. ***(279)***
American Teleservices Ass'n ***(279)***
American Women in Radio and Television ***(280)***
Ameritech ***(282)***
AMFM, Inc. ***(282)***
Anaheim, California, Public Utilities of the City of ***(283)***
Andrew Corp. ***(284)***
AOL Time Warner ***(285)***
Apple Computer, Inc. ***(286)***
Arbinet ***(287)***
Arent Fox Kintner Plotkin & Kahn, PLLC *(14)*
Arizona Mail Order Co. ***(288)***
Arnold & Porter *(16)*
Artel, Inc. ***(289)***
Arter & Hadden *(17)*
ASCENT (Ass'n of Community Enterprises) ***(290)***
Ass'n for Education and Rehabilitation of the Blind & Visually Impaired ***(292)***
Ass'n for Local Telecommunications Services ***(292)***
Ass'n of American Geographers ***(293)***
Ass'n of American Publishers ***(294)***
Ass'n of Directory Publishers ***(295)***
Ass'n of Trial Lawyers of America ***(299)***
AT&T ***(301)***
AT&T Wireless Services, Inc. ***(302)***
Auaya, Inc. ***(302)***
AuctionWatch.com ***(302)***
Automated Credit Exchange ***(303)***
Auyua Inc. ***(304)***
Baker & Hostetler LLP ***(306)***
Baker & Hostetler LLP *(19)*
Baker, Donelson, Bearman & Caldwell, P.C. *(21)*
Balch & Bingham LLP *(21)*
Ball Janik, LLP *(22)*
The Baller Herbst Law Group *(22)*
Barbour Griffith & Rogers, Inc. *(22)*
Bay Harbor Management, L.C. ***(309)***
Timothy Bell & Co. *(25)*
Bell Atlantic Mobile ***(310)***
BellSouth Corp. ***(311)***
BellSouth Telecommunications, Inc. ***(311)***
A. H. Belo Corp. ***(311)***
Bergner Bockorny Castagnetti and Hawkins *(26)*
Berliner, Candon & Jimison *(27)*
Bertelsmann AG ***(312)***
BET Holdings II, Inc. ***(312)***
Billing Concepts, Inc. ***(313)***
Birch, Horton, Bittner & Cherot *(28)*
BKSH & Associates *(28)*
Blank Rome Comisky & McCauley, LLP *(29)*
Boesch & Co. *(29)*
Bohemian Cos. ***(317)***
Bond & Company, Inc. *(30)*
Boston Edison Co. ***(318)***
Bracewell & Patterson, L.L.P. *(30)*
Marshall A. Brachman *(31)*
Bridgestone/Firestone, Inc. ***(320)***
Bristol Group, Inc. *(32)*
BroadSpan Communications, Inc. ***(321)***
Broadwave USA Inc. ***(321)***
Brownstein Hyatt & Farber, P.C. *(33)*
BT North America Inc. ***(323)***
Building Owners and Managers Ass'n Internat'l ***(323)***
Burlington Northern Santa Fe Railway ***(324)***
Business Software Alliance ***(325)***
Cable & Wireless U.S.A., Inc. ***(325)***
Cable & Wireless, Inc. ***(325)***
Cablevision Systems Corp. ***(325)***
Mark R. Cannon *(37)*
Capital Strategies Group, Inc. *(37)*
Capitol Broadcasting Co. ***(331)***
Capitol Coalitions Inc. *(38)*
Capitol Health Group, LLC *(39)*
CarsDirect.com ***(332)***
Cassidy & Associates, Inc. *(42)*
Catholic Television Network ***(333)***
Cegetel, S.A. ***(334)***
Cellular Depreciation Coalition ***(334)***
Cellular Telecommunications and Internet Ass'n ***(334)***
Center for Democracy and Technology ***(336)***
Center for Freedom and Prosperity ***(336)***
Central Station Alarm Ass'n ***(339)***
Central Virginia Educational Telecommunications Corp. ***(339)***
Chamber of Commerce of the U.S.A. ***(340)***
Chambers Associates Inc. *(45)*
Charter Communications, Inc. ***(341)***
Chicago School Reform Board of Trustees ***(343)***
Chwat and Company, Inc. *(46)*
Circuit City Stores, Inc. ***(347)***
Cisco Systems Inc. ***(347)***
Citigroup ***(347)***
Citizens Against Government Waste ***(348)***
Citizens for a Sound Economy ***(348)***
City Colleges of Chicago ***(349)***
Civic Service, Inc. *(46)*
Clark & Weinstock, Inc. *(47)*
Clear Communications ***(350)***
Coalition for Affordable Local and Long Distance Services ***(352)***
Coalition for American Trauma Care ***(352)***
Coalition of Service Industries ***(355)***
Cohen Mohr LLP *(48)*
The College Board ***(357)***
Colling Swift & Hynes *(49)*
Colorado River Indian Tribes ***(358)***
Comcast Corp. ***(359)***
Commercial Internet Exchange Ass'n ***(360)***
Communication Service for the Deaf ***(362)***
Communications Consultants, Inc. *(50)*
Communications Workers of America ***(362)***
Community Ass'ns Institute (CAI) ***(362)***
Compaq Computer Corp. ***(363)***
Competitive Telecommunications Ass'n (COMPTEL) ***(363)***
Computer and Communications Industry Ass'n (CCIA) ***(364)***
Computer Intelligence 2 ***(364)***
Computing Technology Industry Ass'n ***(364)***
ComTech Communications, Inc. ***(365)***
Concert USA ***(365)***
Congressional Economic Leadership Institute ***(366)***
Consortium for School Networking ***(368)***
Consumer Electronics Ass'n ***(369)***

Consumer Energy Council of America Research Foundation (369)
Consumer Federation of America (369)
Consumers Union of the United States (369)
Contract Services Ass'n of America (370)
Convergence Services, Inc. (52)
Cook Inlet Region Inc. (371)
Coors Brewing Company (371)
Coral Springs, Florida, City of (371)
Cormac Group, LLP (53)
Cornerstone Television (372)
Corning Inc. (372)
Council Tree Communications, L.L.C. (377)
The Coursen Group (53)
COVAD Communications Co. (377)
Cox Enterprises Inc. (378)
Law Offices of Thomas K. Crowe (55)
CRT, Inc. (379)
The Cullen Law Firm (56)
Curson Koopersmith Partners, Inc. (56)
Law Offices of Kevin G. Curtin (56)
D&E Communications, Inc. (380)
The Da Vinci Group (56)
Dallas, Texas, City of (382)
Davidoff & Malito, LLP (57)
R. V. Davis and Associates (58)
Susan Davis Internat'l (58)
Davis Manafort, Inc. (58)
Davison, Cohen & Co. (59)
Dayton, Ohio, Washington Office of the City of (383)
DCT Communications, Inc. (383)
Dearborn, Michigan, Department of Communication of (383)
George H. Denison (60)
Detroit Public Television (386)
Deutsche Telekom, Inc. (386)
Dewey Ballantine LLP (61)
Dewey Square Group (61)
Dickstein Shapiro Morin & Oshinsky LLP (61)
Digital Commerce Corp. (388)
Digital Media Ass'n (388)
Direct Marketing Ass'n, Inc. (388)
Discovery Communications, Inc. (389)
Dow, Lohnes & Albertson, PLLC (64)
Downey McGrath Group, Inc. (64)
DSL Access Telecommunications Ass'n (DATA) (392)
The Duberstein Group, Inc. (65)
Dubuque, Iowa, Cable Television Division of (392)
The Dutko Group, Inc. (68)
e.spire Communications, Inc. (394)
Eagle River, LLC (394)
EarthWatch, Inc. (395)
Easter Seals (395)
Eastman Kodak Co. (395)
eCharge Corp. (396)
EchoStar Communications Corp. (396)
EdLinc (397)
Edmund Scientific Co. (397)
EDS Corp. (398)
The Egg Factory, LLC (398)
eHealth Insurance Services, Inc. (399)
Electronic Industries Alliance (400)
Electronic Retailing Ass'n (401)
Engineered Support System, Inc. (ESSI) (403)
Enron Corp. (403)
Entela, Inc. (404)
entradia.com (404)
Epik Communications (406)
Ericsson Inc. (406)
Ernst & Young LLP (72)
Ervin Technical Associates, Inc. (ETA) (73)
EUTELSAT (408)
EXCEL Communications Inc. (408)
Exelon Corp. (409)
Family Communications, Inc. (410)
Fantasma Networks, Inc. (411)
Federation of State Medical Boards of the U.S. (415)
Feith & Zell, P.C. (75)
Jack Ferguson Associates, Inc. (75)
The Ferguson Group, LLC (76)
Fierce and Isakowitz (76)
Final Analysis, Inc. (416)
First Amendment Coalition for Expression (417)
Fleischman and Walsh, L.L.P. (77)
Fleishman-Hillard, Inc (77)
Florida State University System (420)
Focal Communications (421)
Foley & Lardner (78)
Fon Digital Network Clearpoint Communications, Inc. (421)
Ford Motor Co. (422)
France Telecom America do Sul Ltda. (424)
France Telecom North America (424)
Fraternal Order of Police (425)
Friends of the Nat'l Library of Medicine (426)
Frontier Communications Corp. (427)
Futurewave General Partners, L.P. (428)
Gainesville, Florida, City of (428)
Gardner, Carton and Douglas (81)
Law Offices of Michael R. Gardner, P.C. (81)
Sara Garland (and Associates) (81)
Gateway, Inc. (430)
GE Capital Corp. (430)
Gemini Networks, Inc. (431)
General Communications, Inc. (431)
General Conference of Seventh-day Adventists (431)
General Dynamics Corp. (431)
General Electric Capital Services, Inc. (432)
General Electric Co. (432)
General Motors Corp. (432)
GeoPhone, LLC (433)
Geotek Communications, Inc. (434)
Global Crossing North America, Inc. (436)
Global USA, Inc. (83)
GLOBEMAC Associates (83)
Goldberg, Godles, Wiener & Wright (83)
GovWorks.com (438)
GPC Internat'l (85)
Granite Broadcasting Co. (438)
Jay Grant & Associates (85)
Great Western Cellular Partnership (439)
Greenberg Traurig, LLP (86)
Greener and Hook, LLC (87)
Griffin, Johnson, Dover & Stewart (87)
Grisso Consulting (88)
GTE Service Corp. (441)
Guam, Washington Office of the Governor (442)
Guinea, Secretary General of the Presidency of the Republic of (442)
James E. Guirard (89)
Hall, Green, Rupli, LLC (90)
Halprin, Temple, Goodman & Maher (90)
Hannett & Associates (91)
Leslie Harris & Associates (91)
Harris Corp. (444)
Harris, Wiltshire & Grannis LLP (92)
Harvard Radio Broadcasting Co. (445)
HarvardNet, Inc. (445)
Healtheon/Web MD (447)
Heartland Communications & Management Inc. (447)
Hewlett-Packard Co. (449)
Hiawatha Broadband Communications Inc. (449)
Hicks, Muse, Tate & Furst (449)
Higgins, McGovern & Smith, LLC (94)
Hill and Knowlton, Inc. (95)
Hispanic Broadcasting Inc. (450)
Hogan & Hartson L.L.P. (96)
Holland & Knight LLP (98)
Peter Homer (99)
Hooper Owen & Winburn (99)
Hubbard Broadcasting, Inc. (454)
Hudson Institute (454)
IATA U.S. Frequent Flyer Tax Interest Group (456)
ICG Communications, Inc. (457)
ICO Global Communications (457)
IDT Corp. (457)
The ILEX Group (102)
Independent Telephone and Telecommunications Alliance (460)
Indiana, Office of the Governor of the State of (460)
Industrial Telecommunications Ass'n, Inc. (461)
Information Technology Ass'n of America (ITAA) (461)
Information Technology Industry Council (462)
Information Trust (462)
Inmarsat (462)
Intel Corp. (465)
Intelligent Transportation Soc. of America (465)
INTELSAT - Internat'l Telecommunications Satellite Organization (465)
Interactive Gaming Council (466)
Intermedia Communications Inc. (467)
Internat'l Air Transport Ass'n (467)
Internat'l Ass'n of Fire Chiefs (468)
Internat'l Brotherhood of Electrical Workers (469)
Internat'l Business Machines Corp. (469)
Internat'l Council of Shopping Centers (470)
Internat'l Mass Retailers Ass'n (473)
Internat'l Public Relations Co. (474)
Internat'l Soc. for Technology in Education (475)
Internat'l Space Business Council (475)
Internat'l Telecom Ltd. (475)
Internat'l Telecommunications, Inc. (475)
Internet Action PAC (476)
Internet Ventures, Inc. (476)
Intersil Corp. (477)
Iowa Telecommunications & Technology Commission (478)
IPR Shandwick (478)
Iridium, LLC (478)
ITRON, Inc. (480)
IVIDCO, LLC (480)
Jackson Nat'l Life Insurance (480)
Jamison and Sullivan, Inc. (104)
Janus-Merritt Strategies, L.L.C. (104)
JASON Foundation for Education (482)
JBC Internat'l (105)
JCP Associates (105)
Jefferson Government Relations, L.L.C. (106)
Jeppesen Sanderson, Inc. (482)
Johnson Co. (107)
Jones, Walker, Waechter, Poitevent, Carrere & Denegre, L.L.P. (108)
Jorden Burt LLP (109)
K Capital Partners (485)
Betty Ann Kane & Co. (110)
KCTS (487)
Kendall-Jackson Winery (488)
Kessler & Associates Business Services, Inc. (112)
King & Spalding (113)
Kogovsek & Associates (114)
Korea Information & Communication, Ltd. (491)
KPMG, LLP (115)
Lancit Media/Junior Net (494)
Laredo, Texas, City of (495)
Las Vegas, Nevada, City of (495)
Latham & Watkins (116)
Lawler, Metzger & Milkman, LLC (117)
Bob Lawrence & Associates (117)
The Laxalt Corp. (117)
The Paul Laxalt Group (117)
LDMI Telecommunications, Inc. (496)
LDW, Inc. (496)
Leadership Conference on Civil Rights (496)
League of California Cities (497)
Leap Wireless Internat'l (497)
LeBoeuf, Lamb, Greene & MacRae L.L.P. (117)
The Legislative Strategies Group, LLC (118)
Lent Scrivner & Roth LLC (119)
The Livingston Group, LLC (120)
Lloyd's of London (501)
Lockheed Martin Corp. (501)
Lockheed Martin Global Telecommunications (502)
Long, Aldridge & Norman, LLP (121)
Loral Space and Communications, Ltd. (503)
Los Angeles Unified School District (504)
Lotus Development Corp. (504)
Lovelace Respiratory Research Institute (504)
Lucent Technologies (505)
Marshall L. Lynam (122)
The M Companies (122)
MacAndrews & Forbes Holdings, Inc. (506)
Major League Baseball (508)
Management Options, Inc. (123)
Manatt, Phelps & Phillips, LLP (123)
Manufactured Housing Institute (509)
Manufacturers Alliance/MAPI Inc. (509)
MARC Associates, Inc. (124)

Marconi plc *(509)*
Marriott Internat'l, Inc. *(511)*
Massachusetts Software Council *(512)*
Matsushita Electric Corp. of America *(513)*
Mattox Woolfolk, LLC *(126)*
Mayer, Brown & Platt *(126)*
Barbara T. McCall Associates *(127)*
McClure, Gerard & Neuenschwander, Inc. *(127)*
McDermott, Will and Emery *(128)*
Jack H. McDonald *(129)*
McGuireWoods L.L.P. *(130)*
MCI WorldCom Corp. *(514)*
McLeod USA, Inc. *(515)*
McSlarrow Consulting L.L.C. *(131)*
Medassets.com *(515)*
Media Access Project *(516)*
Media Fusion L.L.C. *(516)*
Media General, Inc. *(516)*
Media Institute *(516)*
Medical Records Internat'l, Inc. *(516)*
Medium-Sized Cable Operators Group *(517)*
Metricom, Inc. *(520)*
Metropolitan King County Council *(520)*
Meyers & Associates *(133)*
Miami Beach, Florida, City of *(521)*
Microsoft Corp. *(522)*
Miller & Van Eaton, P.L.L.C. *(134)*
Denny Miller McBee Associates *(134)*
Miller, Canfield, Paddock & Stone, P.L.C. *(135)*
Mintz, Levin, Cohn, Ferris, Glovsky and Popeo, P.C. *(135)*
Mitsubishi Internat'l Corp. *(526)*
Mitsubishi Research Institute *(526)*
Mobile Communications Holdings, Inc. *(527)*
Monroe Telephone Services, L.P. *(527)*
Montgomery, Maryland, Cable Television Office of the County of *(529)*
Morrison & Foerster LLP *(137)*
The Kate Moss Company *(137)*
Motion Picture Ass'n of America *(530)*
Motorola Space and Systems Technology Group *(531)*
Motorola, Inc. *(531)*
Multistate Tax Commission *(532)*
Patrick M. Murphy & Associates *(138)*
Murray, Scheer, Montgomery, Tapia & O'Donnell *(139)*
Napster, Inc. *(534)*
Nassau Broadcasting Inc. *(535)*
Nat'l Apartment Ass'n *(537)*
Nat'l Ass'n of Developmental Disabilities Councils *(542)*
Nat'l Ass'n of Industrial and Office Properties *(544)*
Nat'l Ass'n of Police Organizations *(546)*
Nat'l Ass'n of Real Estate Investment Trusts *(547)*
Nat'l Ass'n of Realtors *(547)*
Nat'l Ass'n of State Utility Consumer Advocates (NASUCA) *(550)*
Nat'l Ass'n of Tower Erectors *(551)*
Nat'l Ass'n of Towns and Townships *(551)*
Nat'l Broadcasting Co. *(553)*
Nat'l Cable Television Ass'n *(553)*
Nat'l Coalition on E-Commerce and Privacy *(556)*
Nat'l Consumers League *(558)*
Nat'l District Attorneys Ass'n *(562)*
Nat'l Education Ass'n of the U.S. *(562)*
Nat'l Electrical Manufacturers Ass'n *(562)*
Nat'l Federation for the Blind *(564)*
Nat'l Grange *(566)*
Nat'l ITFS Ass'n *(569)*
Nat'l League of Cities *(569)*
Nat'l Multi-Housing Council *(571)*
Nat'l Retail Federation *(576)*
Nat'l Rural Electric Cooperative Ass'n *(576)*
Nat'l Soc. of Professional Engineers *(578)*
Nat'l Strategies Inc. *(141)*
Nat'l Technical Systems *(579)*
Nat'l Telephone Cooperative Ass'n *(579)*
Nat'l Wholesale Co., Inc. *(581)*
NAVCOM Systems, Inc. *(583)*
Nebraska Public Power District *(583)*
Net Results, Inc. *(584)*
NetCoalition.Com *(584)*
New Frontiers Communications Consulting *(141)*
New Mexico State Office of Research & Development *(586)*
New Mexico State University, Department of Engineering *(586)*
New Skies Satellites N.V. *(586)*
New York Stock Exchange *(588)*
New York University *(588)*
Newark, New Jersey, City of *(588)*
News Corporation Ltd. *(589)*
NewsHunter.net, LLC *(589)*
Nextwave Telecom *(589)*
Nippon Telegraph and Telephone Corp. *(590)*
No-Wave, AB *(590)*
NOKIA *(591)*
Nomura Internat'l plc *(591)*
Non-Profit Management Associates, Inc. *(142)*
Norfolk Southern Corp. *(591)*
Norlight Telecommunications, Inc. *(591)*
Nortel Networks *(591)*
North American Datacom *(592)*
North American GSM Alliance, LLC *(592)*
North Carolina, Washington Office of the State of *(593)*
Northcoast Communications, LLC *(593)*
Northeast Utilities *(593)*
Northern Mariana Islands, Commonwealth of the *(594)*
NorthPoint Communications, Inc. *(594)*
Northpoint Technology, Ltd. *(594)*
Northwest Energy Efficiency Alliance *(595)*
Novell, Inc. *(596)*
The OB-C Group, LLC *(143)*
David O'Brien and Associates *(143)*
O'Connor & Hannan, L.L.P. *(144)*
O'Melveny and Myers LLP *(147)*
One Economy Corp. *(600)*
O'Neill, Athy & Casey, P.C. *(147)*
Open Group Electronic Messaging Ass'n (EMA) Forum *(601)*
openNET Coalition *(601)*
Operations Security Professionals Soc. *(601)*
Operator Communications, Inc. *(601)*
Optical Soc. of America *(601)*
Oracle Corp. *(602)*
Orbital Resources, LLC *(602)*
Orbital Sciences Corp. *(602)*
Organization for the Promotion and Advancement of Small Telecommunications Cos. *(603)*
Owner-Operator Independent Drivers Ass'n, Inc. *(605)*
Palumbo & Cerrell, Inc. *(149)*
PanAmSat Corp. *(607)*
Parry, Romani, DeConcini & Symms *(149)*
Parsons Brinckerhoff Inc. *(608)*
Parsons Corp. *(608)*
Patton Boggs, LLP *(150)*
Paul, Hastings, Janofsky & Walker LLP *(153)*
Paul, Weiss, Rifkind, Wharton & Garrison *(154)*
Paxson Communications Corp. *(610)*
Pegasus Communications *(611)*
People for the American Way *(612)*
Perkins Coie LLP *(154)*
Personal Communications Industry Ass'n (PCIA) *(612)*
Peyser Associates, Inc. *(155)*
Pfluger Enterprises LLC *(614)*
Philadelphia, Pennsylvania, City of *(615)*
Phoenix, Arizona, City of *(616)*
Piper Marbury Rudnick & Wolfe LLP *(155)*
Charles L. Pizer *(156)*
Podesta/Mattoon *(158)*
Portland, Oregon, City of *(621)*
Powell, Goldstein, Frazer & Murphy LLP *(160)*
Powerware *(622)*
PrediWave *(623)*
Preston Gates Ellis & Rouvelas Meeds LLP *(162)*
Prince George's, Maryland, County of *(624)*
The Procter & Gamble Company *(625)*
The Progress Freedom Foundation *(626)*
Project to Promote Competition and Innovation in the Digital Age *(626)*
PSINet Inc. *(628)*
Public Broadcasting Service *(628)*
Public Strategies, Inc. *(165)*
Puerto Rico Senate *(629)*
Qualcomm Inc. *(630)*
Queens Borough Public Library *(631)*
Questar InfoComm Inc. *(631)*
Qwest Communications *(631)*
Radio Shack Corp. *(632)*
RCN Telecom Services Inc. *(633)*
Real Access Alliance *(634)*
Real Estate Roundtable *(634)*
Recording Industry Ass'n of America *(634)*
Red River Trade Council *(635)*
Robert L. Redding *(166)*
Register.com *(636)*
Resources and Instruction for Staff Excellence, Inc. *(638)*
Retlif Testing Laboratory, Inc. *(639)*
Reuters America Inc. *(639)*
Rhythms NetConnections *(639)*
RMA Internat'l, Inc. *(169)*
Liz Robbins Associates *(169)*
RPH & Associates, L.L.C. *(172)*
Rural Telephone Finance Cooperative *(644)*
Ryan, Phillips, Utrecht & MacKinnon *(173)*
Sallie Mae, Inc. *(646)*
Salt Lake City Olympic Organizing Committee *(646)*
Santa Clarita, California, City of *(649)*
Santa Rosa Memorial Hospital *(649)*
Satellite Broadcasting and Communications Ass'n *(650)*
SBC Communications Inc. *(650)*
SCC Communications Corp. *(651)*
Schnader Harrison Segal & Lewis LLP *(176)*
Scholastic, Inc. *(651)*
Charles Schwab & Co., Inc., *(652)*
Science Applications Internat'l Corp. (SAIC) *(652)*
Seattle, Washington, City of *(653)*
Securities Industry Ass'n *(654)*
Self Help for Hard of Hearing People, Inc. *(654)*
Shaw Pittman *(177)*
Sher & Blackwell *(179)*
SIGCOM, Inc. *(659)*
Simon and Co., Inc. *(181)*
Simon Strategies/Mindbeam *(181)*
Skadden, Arps, Slate, Meagher & Flom LLP *(181)*
SkyBridge, LLC *(660)*
E. Del Smith and Co. *(183)*
Smith, Bucklin and Associates, Inc. *(184)*
The Smith-Free Group *(184)*
Soft Telesis Inc. *(664)*
Software & Information Industry Ass'n (SIIA) *(664)*
The Solomon Group, LLC *(185)*
Sony Electronics, Inc. *(666)*
SpaceData Internat'l *(669)*
Sprint Corp. *(671)*
Squire, Sanders & Dempsey L.L.P. *(187)*
St. Louis Office of Cable Television *(672)*
Stanford Financial Group *(672)*
Stillman College *(674)*
Strategic Horizons Advisors, L.L.C. *(189)*
Sunrise Research Corp. *(191)*
Supra Telecom & Information Systems, Inc. *(677)*
Swidler Berlin Shereff Friedman, LLP *(191)*
SWL Communications LLC *(679)*
Tacoma, Washington, City of *(680)*
Tallahassee, Florida, City of *(680)*
TCI *(682)*
TDS Telecommunications *(682)*
Technology, Entertainment and Communications (TEC) Law Group *(193)*
Telcordia Technologies, Inc. *(682)*
Telecommunications Industry Ass'n *(682)*
Telecorp PCS Inc. *(683)*
Teledesic Corp. *(683)*
Telefonos de Mexico *(683)*
Telegate, Inc. *(683)*
Teleglobe Communications Corp. *(683)*
Teligent, Inc. *(683)*
Tequity *(684)*
Texas Instruments *(684)*
Time Domain Corp. *(687)*
Time Warner Telecom Inc. *(687)*
Timmons and Co., Inc. *(195)*
Tongour Simpson Holsclaw Green *(196)*
Touch America *(688)*

Townsend Solheim (196)
Transnat'l Development Consortium (690)
Trimble Navigation, Ltd. (692)
TruePosition Inc. (693)
TRW Inc. (693)
Tucson, Arizona, City of (693)
Tulsa, Oklahoma, City of (694)
TV Guide, Inc. (694)
Twenty-First Century Group (197)
TXU Business Services (695)
Tyco Internat'l (US), Inc. (695)
U.S. Interactive (696)
U.S. Internet Council (696)
The Udwin Group (197)
Uniden Corp. (698)
Unisite, Inc. (700)
United Cerebral Palsy Ass'n (700)
United Pan-Europe Communications, NV (702)
United Parcel Service (702)
United States Telecom Ass'n (704)
United Telecom Council (705)
Universal Wireless Communications Consortium (705)
University of Medicine and Dentistry of New Jersey (706)
University of Miami (706)
University of Texas - Houston Health Science Center (707)
University of Tulsa (708)
University of Virginia (708)
University of Washington (708)
Valis Associates (198)
Van Scoyoc Associates, Inc. (200)
The Vandervort Group, LLC (712)
VeriSign/Network Solutions, Inc. (713)
Verizon Communications (713)
Verizon Wireless (713)
Verner, Liipfert, Bernhard, McPherson and Hand, Chartered (202)
Verner, Liipfert, Bernhard, McPherson and Hand, Chartered (713)
Viacom Inc. (714)
Viatel, Inc. (714)
Vinson & Elkins L.L.P. (204)
Viohl and Associates, Inc. (205)
Vision Technologies, Inc. (716)
VoiceStream Wireless Corp. (717)
R. Duffy Wall and Associates (205)
Wallman Strategic Consulting, LLC (206)
Washington Consulting Alliance, Inc. (206)
Washington Council Ernst & Young (206)
The Washington Group (208)
Washington Health Advocates (209)
The Washington Post Co. (720)
J. Arthur Weber & Associates (210)
Donald Weightman (211)
Weil, Gotshal & Manges, LLP (211)
Western Wireless Internat'l (725)
WETA (725)
The Wexler Group (211)
Wholesale Telecommunications Corp. (726)
Wi-LAN, Inc. (726)
Wiley, Rein & Fielding (214)
Williams & Jensen, P.C. (215)
Willkie Farr & Gallagher (217)
Wilmer, Cutler & Pickering (217)
Wilmer, Cutler & Pickering (727)
Winstar Communications, Inc. (728)
WinStar Internat'l (728)
Winston & Strawn (218)
Wireless Location Industry Ass'n (728)
Wise & Associates (220)
WNVT/WNVC (729)
Women Officials in NACo (729)
WorldSpace Corp. (731)
Wunder & Lilley (221)
Xerox Corp. (732)
XO Communications (732)
Yellow Pages Publishers Ass'n (733)
Yipes Transmission, Inc. (733)
Z-Tel Communications Inc. (734)
ZapMe! Corp. (734)
Zuckerman Spaeder L.L.P. (221)
Zuckert, Scoutt and Rasenberger, L.L.P. (735)

Tobacco (TOB)

7-Eleven, Inc. (224)
AdvaMed (228)
The Advocacy Group (6)
Akin, Gump, Strauss, Hauer & Feld, L.L.P. (8)
Alameda, California, County of (236)
Alliance of American Insurers (240)
Allina Health Systems (241)
Allstate Insurance Co. (241)
Alpine Group, Inc. (11)
American Academy of Child and Adolescent Psychiatry (243)
American Academy of Family Physicians (243)
American Advertising Federation (244)
American Ass'n for Respiratory Care (246)
American Cancer Soc. (252)
American College of Cardiology (253)
American College of Chest Physicians (253)
American College of Preventive Medicine (254)
American Continental Group, Inc. (12)
American Dental Education Ass'n (257)
American Farm Bureau Federation (258)
American Federation of Teachers (259)
American Gaming Ass'n (260)
American Heart Ass'n (262)
American Hotel and Lodging Ass'n (263)
American Indian Ass'n (263)
American Insurance Ass'n (264)
American Legion (266)
American Medical Ass'n (267)
American Psychological Ass'n (271)
American Psychological Soc. (271)
American Public Health Ass'n (271)
American Soc. of Tropical Medicine and Hygiene (277)
American Thoracic Soc. (279)
American Wholesale Marketers Ass'n (280)
Ass'n of Flight Attendants (295)
Ass'n of Nat'l Advertisers (297)
Ass'n of Professors of Medicine (298)
Ass'n of Trial Lawyers of America (299)
Barbour Griffith & Rogers, Inc. (22)
Barents Group LLC (23)
Bergner Bockorny Castagnetti and Hawkins (26)
Bergson & Co. (26)
BKSH & Associates (28)
John L. Bloom (29)
Bracewell & Patterson, L.L.P. (30)
Brown and Williamson Tobacco Corp. (322)
Brownstein Hyatt & Farber, P.C. (33)
Building Owners and Managers Ass'n Internat'l (323)
California State Ass'n of Counties (327)
Campaign Finance Reform Coalition (328)
Campaign for Medical Research (329)
Campaign for Tobacco-Free Kids (329)
Capital Consultants Corp. (37)
Capital Strategies Group, Inc. (37)
Capitol Associates, Inc. (37)
Cartwright & Riley (41)
The Castano Group (333)
Celanese Government Relations Office (334)
Chamber of Commerce of the U.S.A. (340)
Chambers Associates Inc. (45)
Chehalis Reservation, Confederated Tribes of the (342)
Child Welfare League of America (343)
Children's Defense Fund (344)
The Chubb Corp. (346)
Cigar Ass'n of America (346)
Circle K Convenience Stores (347)
Citizens Against Government Waste (348)
Citizens for a Sound Economy (348)
Clark & Weinstock, Inc. (47)
CNA Financial Corp. (351)
CNA Insurance Cos. (351)
Coalition for a Comprehensive Tobacco Solution (C-FACTS) (352)
Coalition for Workers' Health Care Funds (355)
Coalitions for America (356)
College on Problems of Drug Dependence (357)
Collier Shannon Scott, PLLC (48)
Commonwealth Group, Ltd. (50)
Connerton & Ray (51)
Consumer Federation of America (369)
L. P. Conwood Co. (370)
Copeland, Lowery & Jacquez (52)
Corporacion de Exportaciones Mexicanas, S.A. de C.V. and Marvin Roy Feldman (372)
Law Offices of Kevin G. Curtin (56)
DFS Group Ltd. (387)
Dickstein Shapiro Morin & Oshinsky LLP (61)
Eastman Chemical Co. (395)
Feith & Zell, P.C. (75)
Food Distributors Internat'l (NAWGA-IFDA) (421)
Food Marketing Institute (421)
General Cigar Holdings, Inc. (431)
General Conference of Seventh-day Adventists (431)
Girls Incorporated (435)
GlaxoSmithKline (436)
Gottehrer and Co. (84)
Griffin, Johnson, Dover & Stewart (87)
Hadassah, The Women's Zionist Organization of America (443)
Hall, Green, Rupli, LLC (90)
Hecht, Spencer & Associates (93)
Hercules Development Corp. (448)
Holland & Knight LLP (98)
Hooper Owen & Winburn (99)
Hotel Employees and Restaurant Employees Internat'l Union (453)
R. J. Hudson Associates (101)
Fred Hutchinson Cancer Research Center (455)
Illinois Collaboration on Youth (457)
Indiana, Office of the Governor of the State of (460)
JFS Group, Ltd. (107)
Joint Council of Allergy, Asthma and Immunology (484)
Jolly/Rissler, Inc. (108)
Robert E. Juliano Associates (109)
Kentucky, Commonwealth of (488)
Kerrigan & Associates, Inc. (112)
Kessler & Associates Business Services, Inc. (112)
Kimberly-Clark Corp. (489)
L.L. Capital Partners, Inc. (493)
Latham & Watkins (116)
The Paul Laxalt Group (117)
Lent Scrivner & Roth LLC (119)
Lesher & Russell, Inc. (119)
Liggett Group, Inc. (499)
Lockridge Grindal & Nauen, P.L.L.P. (121)
Lorillard Tobacco Co. (503)
Luman, Lange & Wheeler (122)
Lymphoma Research Foundation of America, Inc. (506)
M & R Strategic Services (122)
MacAndrews & Forbes Holdings, Inc. (506)
Magazine Publishers of America (507)
Manatt, Phelps & Phillips, LLP (123)
MARC Associates, Inc. (124)
March of Dimes Birth Defects Foundation (509)
Jack H. McDonald (129)
McGlotten & Jarvis (129)
McGuiness & Holch (130)
McGuireWoods L.L.P. (130)
McLane Co. (515)
McMillan, Hill & Associates (131)
Miller & Co. (134)
Milwaukee, Wisconsin, County of (524)
Mintz, Levin, Cohn, Ferris, Glovsky and Popeo, P.C. (135)
James T. Molloy (135)
Multistate Tax Commission (532)
R. B. Murphy & Associates (139)
Murray, Scheer, Montgomery, Tapia & O'Donnell (139)
Nat'l Alliance for Eye and Vision Research (536)
Nat'l Ass'n for the Education of Young Children (538)
Nat'l Ass'n of Children's Hospitals Inc. (540)
Nat'l Ass'n of Community Health Centers (540)
Nat'l Ass'n of Convenience Stores (541)
Nat'l Ass'n of Independent Insurers (544)
Nat'l Ass'n of Police Organizations (546)
Nat'l Ass'n of Public Hospitals and Health Systems (547)
Nat'l Ass'n of Wholesaler-Distributors (551)
Nat'l Center for Public Policy Research (555)

Nat'l Center for Tobacco-Free Kids *(555)*
Nat'l Coalition for Cancer Research *(556)*
Nat'l Grange *(566)*
Nat'l Grocers Ass'n *(566)*
Nat'l Health Council *(567)*
Nat'l Licensed Beverage Ass'n *(570)*
Nat'l Nutritional Foods Ass'n *(572)*
Nat'l Restaurant Ass'n *(576)*
New York University Medical Center *(588)*
NF Inc. - Mass Bay Area *(589)*
Julia J. Norrell & Associates *(142)*
North Carolina, Washington Office of the State of *(593)*
Northwestern Memorial Hospital *(595)*
O'Connor & Hannan, L.L.P. *(144)*
Oklahoma State Medical Ass'n *(600)*
Olsson, Frank and Weeda, P.C. *(146)*
Omaha Tribe of Nebraska *(600)*
Outdoor Advertising Ass'n of America *(604)*
Palumbo & Cerrell, Inc. *(149)*
Parkinson's Action Network *(608)*
Jim Pasco & Associates *(150)*
Patton Boggs, LLP *(150)*
Paul, Hastings, Janofsky & Walker LLP *(153)*
Petroleum Marketers Ass'n of America *(613)*
Philip Morris Management Corp. *(615)*
Pipe Tobacco Council, Inc. *(618)*
Susan S. Platt Consulting *(156)*
Point of Purchase Advertising Institute *(619)*
Policy Directions, Inc. *(158)*
Potomac Group *(160)*
Powell, Goldstein, Frazer & Murphy LLP *(160)*
Public Citizen, Inc. *(628)*
Public Private Partnership *(164)*
Ramsey, Minnesota, Board of Commissioners of the County of *(633)*
Research Soc. on Alcoholism *(638)*
R. J. Reynolds Tobacco Co. *(639)*
RFB, Inc. *(168)*
RJR Co. *(640)*
Ryan, Phillips, Utrecht & MacKinnon *(173)*
San Francisco, California, City and County of *(648)*
Shaw Pittman *(177)*
Single Stick *(660)*
Smokeless Tobacco Council *(661)*
Soc. of Independent Gasoline Marketers of America *(663)*
Soc. of Toxicology *(664)*
Star Tobacco & Pharmaceuticals Inc. *(673)*
Stuntz, Davis & Staffier, P.C. *(190)*
Swedish Match *(678)*
Swidler Berlin Shereff Friedman, LLP *(191)*
Swisher Internat'l Inc. *(679)*
Tallon & Associates *(192)*
Texas NF Foundation *(685)*
Michael L. Tiner *(195)*
Tobacco Fairness Coalition *(688)*
Traditional Values Coalition *(689)*
U.S. Chamber Institute for Legal Reform *(695)*
U.S. Public Interest Research Group *(697)*
United Methodist Church General Board of Church and Society *(702)*
University of Pennsylvania/School of Dental Medicine *(707)*
UST Public Affairs, Inc. *(710)*
Valanzano & Associates *(198)*
Verner, Liipfert, Bernhard, McPherson and Hand, Chartered *(713)*
Vinson & Elkins L.L.P. *(204)*
Viohl and Associates, Inc. *(205)*
Washington Council Ernst & Young *(206)*
Waterman & Associates *(210)*
R. H. White Public Affairs Consulting *(213)*
Williams & Connolly *(215)*
Women Officials in NACo *(729)*
Zuckerman Spaeder L.L.P. *(221)*
Zurich Financial Group *(735)*

Torts (TOR)

Academy of Radiology Research *(226)*
ACE INA *(226)*
AFL-CIO (American Federation of Labor and Congress of Industrial Organizations) *(231)*
Air China Internat'l Corp., Ltd. *(233)*
Air Conditioning Contractors of America *(233)*
Air Pacific Ltd. *(234)*
Alliance of American Insurers *(240)*
American Bar Ass'n *(250)*
American College of Obstetricians and Gynecologists *(254)*
American Consulting Engineers Council *(255)*
American Corporate Counsel Ass'n *(255)*
American Council of Life Insurers *(256)*
American Express Co. *(258)*
American Furniture Manufacturers Ass'n *(260)*
The American Institute of Architects *(264)*
American Iron and Steel Institute *(265)*
American Rental Ass'n *(272)*
American Soc. of Ass'n Executives *(275)*
Law Offices of Peter Angelos *(284)*
AOL Time Warner *(285)*
Ashland Inc. *(290)*
The Ass'n For Manufacturing Technology (AMT) *(292)*
Ass'n of Clinical Research Professionals *(295)*
Ass'n of Trial Lawyers of America *(299)*
Automotive Aftermarket Industry Ass'n *(303)*
Automotive Parts and Service Alliance *(303)*
Barbour Griffith & Rogers, Inc. *(22)*
Barnes & Thornburg *(23)*
Baxter Healthcare Corp. *(309)*
Bethlehem Steel Corp. *(312)*
Biotechnology Industry Organization *(314)*
Richard W. Bliss *(29)*
Brazelton Foundation *(319)*
W. Douglas Campbell *(36)*
Campbell Crane & Associates *(36)*
Capital Strategies Group, Inc. *(37)*
The Castano Group *(333)*
Center for Energy and Economic Development *(336)*
Chamber of Commerce of the U.S.A. *(340)*
Child Welfare League of America *(343)*
China Eastern Airlines *(344)*
The Chubb Corp. *(346)*
Citizens for a Sound Economy *(348)*
Citizens for Civil Justice Reform *(348)*
Civil Justice Reform Group *(349)*
Coalition for Asbestos Resolution *(353)*
Coalition for Uniform Product Liability Law *(355)*
Cohen, Gettings & Dunham, PC *(48)*
Condon and Forsyth *(51)*
Congressional Economic Leadership Institute *(366)*
Construction Industry Round Table, Inc. *(368)*
CSX Corp. *(379)*
Curson Koopersmith Partners, Inc. *(56)*
DaimlerChrysler Corp. *(381)*
Dewey Ballantine LLP *(61)*
Dickstein Shapiro Morin & Oshinsky LLP *(61)*
The Dow Chemical Co. *(391)*
Dow Corning Corp. *(391)*
Eastman Chemical Co. *(395)*
Environmental Industry Ass'ns *(405)*
Equipment Leasing Ass'n of America *(406)*
Exxon Mobil Corp. *(409)*
Food Marketing Institute *(421)*
Food Processing Machinery and Supplies Ass'n *(421)*
Forscey & Stinson, PLLC *(79)*
General Motors Corp. *(432)*
Greater New York Automobile Dealers Ass'n *(439)*
Hardwood Plywood and Veneer Ass'n *(444)*
The Hartford *(445)*
Health Insurance Ass'n of America *(446)*
Hewlett-Packard Co. *(449)*
Higgins, McGovern & Smith, LLC *(94)*
Household Internat'l, Inc. *(453)*
IMC Global Inc. *(458)*
ING America Insurance Holdings, Inc. *(462)*
Institute of Electrical and Electronics Engineers, Inc. *(464)*
Institute of Navigation *(464)*
Internat'l Council of Cruise Lines *(470)*
Internat'l Mass Retailers Ass'n *(473)*
Internat'l Municipal Signal Ass'n *(473)*
Internat'l Union of Painters and Allied Trades *(476)*
Internet Action PAC *(476)*
Iran Air *(478)*
Kaiser Aluminum & Chemical Corp. *(485)*
Betty Ann Kane & Co. *(110)*
Peter Kinzler *(113)*
Lawyers for Civil Justice *(496)*
Legislative Solutions *(118)*
Eli Lilly and Co. *(499)*
Lumbermens Mutual Casualty Co. *(505)*
M & R Strategic Services *(122)*
Machinery Dealers Nat'l Ass'n *(506)*
Maryland Psychiatric Soc. *(512)*
Massachusetts Mutual Life Insurance Co. *(512)*
MassMutual Financial Group *(512)*
Law Office of Robert A. McConnell *(128)*
Minnesota Mining and Manufacturing Co. (3M Co.) *(525)*
Morgan, Lewis & Bockius LLP *(136)*
Motorola, Inc. *(531)*
Mutual of Omaha Insurance Companies *(533)*
Nat'l Ass'n of Chain Drug Stores *(539)*
Nat'l Ass'n of Manufacturers *(545)*
Nat'l Ass'n of Realtors *(547)*
Nat'l Ass'n of Water Companies *(551)*
Nat'l Ass'n of Wholesaler-Distributors *(551)*
Nat'l Center for Public Policy Research *(555)*
Nat'l Coalition for Cancer Survivorship *(556)*
Nat'l Council of University Research Administrators *(561)*
Nat'l Electrical Safety Foundation *(562)*
Nat'l Legal Center for the Public Interest *(570)*
Nat'l Paint and Coatings Ass'n *(573)*
Nat'l Taxpayers Union *(579)*
Nat'l Venture Capital Ass'n *(580)*
New York Life Insurance Co. *(587)*
Newport News Shipbuilding Inc. *(588)*
Northwestern Mutual Life Insurance Co. *(595)*
Occidental Internat'l Corporation *(598)*
O'Melveny and Myers LLP *(147)*
Oracle Corp. *(602)*
Owens Corning *(604)*
Owens-Illinois, Inc. *(605)*
Patton Boggs, LLP *(150)*
Pfizer, Inc. *(613)*
Philip Morris Management Corp. *(615)*
Printing Industries of America *(624)*
Process Equipment Manufacturers' Ass'n *(625)*
Prudential Insurance Co. of America *(627)*
Reed, Smith, LLP *(167)*
RGS Enterprises, Inc. *(168)*
Ryder System, Inc. *(644)*
Charles Schwab & Co., Inc., *(652)*
Sellery Associates, Inc. *(177)*
Semiconductor Industry Ass'n *(655)*
Soc. of the Plastics Industry *(664)*
Special Committee for Workplace Product Liability Reform *(669)*
Special Libraries Ass'n *(669)*
Sporting Goods Manufacturers Ass'n *(670)*
The Stanley Works *(672)*
State Farm Insurance Cos. *(673)*
Steel Service Center Institute *(674)*
Stephens Law Firm *(188)*
Tort Reform Institute *(688)*
Truck Renting and Leasing Ass'n *(693)*
U.S. Chamber Institute for Legal Reform *(695)*
USAA - United Services Automobile Ass'n *(710)*
Valis Associates *(198)*
Venable *(201)*
Violence Policy Center *(715)*
Thomas R. "Randy" White *(213)*
William F. Whitsitt Policy and Government Affairs *(213)*
Deborah F. Winston *(218)*

Trade (Foreign and Domestic) (TRD)

3Com Corp. *(223)*
4C Foods Corp. *(224)*
ABB, Inc. *(225)*
Abbott Laboratories *(225)*
Ablondi, Foster, Sobin & Davidow, P.C. *(5)*
Accenture *(226)*
The Accord Group *(5)*
ACE INA *(226)*

Ad Hoc Nitrogen Committee *(227)*
Adams and Reese LLP *(5)*
Adduci, Mastriani & Schaumberg, L.L.P. *(6)*
AdvaMed *(228)*
Advertising Company ART-ERIA *(229)*
The Advocacy Group *(6)*
The Aegis Group, Ltd. *(7)*
Aerospace Industries Ass'n of America *(230)*
Afghanistan Foundation *(230)*
AFINOA *(231)*
AFL-CIO (American Federation of Labor and Congress of Industrial Organizations) *(231)*
AFL-CIO - Maritime Trades Department *(231)*
AFL-CIO - Transportation Trades Department *(231)*
AFLAC, Inc. *(231)*
Africa Resources Trust USA *(231)*
African Coalition for Trade, Inc. *(232)*
AfriSpace Corp. *(232)*
Agilent Technologies *(232)*
Agribusiness Council *(232)*
Ainslie Associates *(7)*
Air China Internat'l Corp., Ltd. *(233)*
Air Pacific Ltd. *(234)*
Air Products and Chemicals, Inc. *(234)*
Air-Conditioning and Refrigeration Institute *(234)*
Aitken, Irvin, Lewin, Berlin, Vrooman & Cohn *(7)*
Akin, Gump, Strauss, Hauer & Feld, L.L.P. *(8)*
Alaska Seafood Marketing Institute *(237)*
Albemarle Corp. *(237)*
Albertine Enterprises, Inc. *(10)*
Alcalde & Fay *(10)*
Alcatel USA *(237)*
Alcoa Inc. *(237)*
Alenia Aerospazig *(238)*
Alexander Strategy Group *(11)*
Algoma Steel, Inc. *(238)*
Allen-Bradley *(239)*
Allied Domecq *(241)*
Alpha Technologies Group Inc. *(242)*
Alpine Group, Inc. *(11)*
Alsatian American Chamber of Commerce *(242)*
Alston & Bird LLP *(12)*
Alticor, Inc. *(242)*
The Aluminum Ass'n *(242)*
American Airlines *(244)*
American Apparel & Footwear Ass'n *(245)*
American Ass'n for Laboratory Accreditation *(246)*
American Ass'n of Port Authorities *(249)*
American Bakers Ass'n *(250)*
American Bankers Ass'n *(250)*
American Bar Ass'n *(250)*
American Beekeeping Federation *(250)*
American Boiler Manufacturers Ass'n *(251)*
American Business Conference *(251)*
American Butter Institute *(251)*
American Chemistry Council *(252)*
American Consulting Engineers Council *(255)*
American Continental Group, Inc. *(12)*
American Council of Korean Travel Agents *(255)*
American Council of Life Insurers *(256)*
American Crop Protection Ass'n *(256)*
American Dehydrated Onion and Garlic Ass'n *(256)*
American Electronics Ass'n *(257)*
American Express Co. *(258)*
American Farm Bureau Federation *(258)*
American Federation of State, County and Municipal Employees *(258)*
American Federation of Teachers *(259)*
American Feed Industry Ass'n *(259)*
American Flange Producers Marking Coalition *(259)*
American Forest & Paper Ass'n *(259)*
American Free Trade Ass'n *(260)*
American Frozen Food Institute *(260)*
American Furniture Manufacturers Ass'n *(260)*
American Home Products Corp. *(262)*
American Horse Council, Inc. *(263)*
American Insurance Ass'n *(264)*
American Internat'l Automobile Dealers Ass'n *(265)*
American Internat'l Group, Inc. *(265)*
American Iron and Steel Institute *(265)*
American Legion *(266)*
American Meat Institute *(267)*
American Motorcyclist Ass'n *(268)*
American Natural Soda Ash Corp. *(268)*
American Nurses Ass'n *(268)*
American Petroleum Institute *(269)*
American Portland Cement Alliance *(270)*
American Sheep Industry Ass'n *(273)*
American Shipbuilding Ass'n *(274)*
American Sportfishing Ass'n *(278)*
American Standard Cos. Inc. *(278)*
American Sugar Alliance *(278)*
American Teleservices Ass'n *(279)*
American Textile Co. *(279)*
American Textile Manufacturers Institute *(279)*
American Vintners Ass'n *(280)*
American Watch Ass'n *(280)*
American Waterways Operators *(280)*
American Wine Heritage Alliance *(280)*
American Wood Preservers Institute *(280)*
Americans for Free Internat'l Trade (AFIT PAC) *(281)*
Amerijet Internat'l Inc. *(282)*
Anadarko Petroleum Corp. *(283)*
Analytical and Life Science Systems Ass'n *(283)*
Andreae, Vick & Associates, L.L.C. *(14)*
Anheuser-Busch Cos., Inc. *(284)*
ANSAC *(284)*
AOL Time Warner *(285)*
APCO Worldwide *(14)*
APKINDO *(286)*
APL Limited *(286)*
Applied Materials *(287)*
Arent Fox Kintner Plotkin & Kahn, PLLC *(14)*
Argentine Citrus Ass'n *(288)*
ArianeSpace, Inc. *(288)*
Arkansas, Office of the Governor of the State of *(288)*
Armstrong World Industries, Inc. *(289)*
Wayne Arny & Assoc. *(16)*
Arvin Meritor Automotive *(290)*
Asahi Glass Co. *(290)*
Ashland Inc. *(290)*
James Nicholas Ashmore & Associates *(18)*
Aso Corp. *(291)*
Asociacion Columbiana de Exportadores de Flores (ASOCOLFLORES) *(291)*
The Ass'n For Manufacturing Technology (AMT) *(292)*
Ass'n for the Suppliers of Printing and Publishing Technology *(293)*
Ass'n of American Chambers of Commerce in Latin America *(293)*
Ass'n of American Geographers *(293)*
Ass'n of American Publishers *(294)*
Ass'n of German Chambers of Industry & Commerce (DIHT) *(296)*
Ass'n of Home Appliance Manufacturers *(296)*
Ass'n of Internat'l Automobile Manufacturers *(296)*
Ass'n of Maquiladores *(296)*
Ass'n of the Nonwoven Fabrics Industry - INDA *(299)*
Ass'n of Universities for Research in Astronomy, Inc. *(299)*
Associated Equipment Distributors *(300)*
Associated General Contractors of America *(300)*
Association des Constructeurs Europeens de Motocycles *(300)*
AT&T *(301)*
ATOFINA Chemicals, Inc. *(302)*
Auaya, Inc. *(302)*
AUGURA *(302)*
Austin, Nichols & Co., Inc. *(303)*
Automotive Aftermarket Industry Ass'n *(303)*
Automotive Parts and Service Alliance *(303)*
Auyua Inc. *(304)*
Avecia, Inc. *(304)*
Aventis Pharmaceutical Products *(304)*
Avioimpex *(305)*
Avon Products, Inc. *(305)*
B.C. Softwood Lumber Trade Council *(305)*
Babcock & Wilcox *(305)*
Bacardi-Martini, USA, Inc. *(305)*
Baker & McKenzie *(20)*
Michael Baker Corp. *(306)*
The Laurin Baker Group *(20)*
Baker Hughes Incorporated *(306)*
Baker, Donelson, Bearman & Caldwell, P.C. *(21)*
Balch & Bingham LLP *(21)*
Ball Janik, LLP *(22)*
Balzano Associates *(22)*
Bangladesh Export Processing Zones Authority *(307)*
Bankers' Ass'n for Finance and Trade *(307)*
Barbour Griffith & Rogers, Inc. *(22)*
Barnes & Thornburg *(23)*
BASF Corporation *(308)*
Basic American, Inc. *(308)*
Baxter Healthcare Corp. *(309)*
Bayer Corp. *(309)*
Bechtel Group, Inc. *(310)*
Bell Equipment Ltd. *(311)*
The Bellamy Law Firm, P.C. *(25)*
Benrus Watch Co. *(311)*
Bergner Bockorny Castagnetti and Hawkins *(26)*
Bertelsmann AG *(312)*
Bethlehem Steel Corp. *(312)*
BHP (USA) Inc. *(313)*
Big Sky Consulting, Inc. *(27)*
Biotechnology Industry Organization *(314)*
Birch, Horton, Bittner & Cherot *(28)*
Birmingham Steel Corp. *(314)*
BKSH & Associates *(28)*
Blank Rome Comisky & McCauley, LLP *(29)*
Richard W. Bliss *(29)*
Blyth Industries, Inc. *(316)*
BMW Manufacturing Corp. *(316)*
The Boeing Co. *(316)*
Boesch & Co. *(29)*
James E. Boland *(30)*
The BOSE Corp. *(318)*
Boston Scientific Corp. *(318)*
BP Amoco Corp. *(319)*
Bracewell & Patterson, L.L.P. *(30)*
Bracewell & Patterson, L.L.P. *(319)*
Robert M. Brandon and Associates *(32)*
William V. Brierre *(32)*
Brink's Inc. *(320)*
Bristol-Myers Squibb Co. *(320)*
British American Tobacco China Ltd. *(321)*
British Columbia Lumber Trade Council *(321)*
British Columbia Softwood Lumber Trade Council *(321)*
British Nuclear Fuels plc *(321)*
Brooks Tropicals, Inc. *(322)*
Brother Internat'l Co. *(322)*
Broward, Florida, County of *(322)*
Brown and Company, Inc. *(33)*
Brown and Williamson Tobacco Corp. *(322)*
Brown-Forman Corp. *(322)*
Brownstein Hyatt & Farber, P.C. *(33)*
Brunswick Corp. *(322)*
BSMG Worldwide *(34)*
Bulmer Holding PLC, H. P. *(323)*
Bunge Corp. *(323)*
Burdeshaw Associates, Ltd. *(34)*
Burger King Corp. *(324)*
John G. "Toby" Burke *(34)*
Burlington Northern Santa Fe Railway *(324)*
Burlington Resources Oil & Gas Co. *(324)*
The Business Roundtable *(325)*
Business Software Alliance *(325)*
Butera & Andrews *(34)*
Butterfield Carter & Associates *(35)*
C F Industries, Inc. *(325)*
C&M Internat'l, Ltd. *(35)*
C.A. Vencemos *(325)*
The C.L.A. Group, LLC *(35)*
Cable & Wireless, Inc. *(325)*
CalCot *(326)*
California Asparagus Commission *(326)*
California Ass'n of Winegrape Growers *(326)*
California Avocado Commission *(326)*
California Cling Peach Growers Advisory Board *(326)*
California Pistachio Commission *(327)*
California Prune Board *(327)*
California Walnut Commission *(327)*
Camara Nacional de la Industria Pesquera *(328)*

Camara Nacional de las Industrias Azucarera y Alcoholera *(328)*
Campbell Foundry Co. *(329)*
Canadian Nat'l Railway Co. *(329)*
Canadian Wheat Board *(330)*
Capital Equipment Legislative Coalition *(330)*
Capital Goods Standards Coalition *(330)*
Capitol Capital Group *(38)*
Capitol Hill Advocates *(39)*
Capitol Partners *(39)*
Cargill, Inc. *(331)*
Caribbean Banana Exporters Ass'n *(331)*
Carlyle Consulting *(40)*
The Carmen Group *(40)*
Carpet Export Promotion Council *(332)*
Carpi & Clay *(41)*
The Carter Group *(41)*
CaseNewHolland Inc. *(333)*
Caspian Group *(42)*
Cassidy & Associates, Inc. *(42)*
Caterpillar Inc. *(333)*
CBI Sugar Group *(334)*
Celanese Government Relations Office *(334)*
Cell Pathways, Inc. *(334)*
Cemento Bayano *(335)*
Cementos Monterrey, S.A. *(335)*
CEMEX Central, S.A. de C.V. *(335)*
CEMEX USA *(335)*
Center of Concern *(338)*
Central American Bank of Economic Integration *(338)*
Central Soya Co. *(339)*
Chadbourne and Parke LLP *(45)*
Chamber of Commerce of the U.S.A. *(340)*
Chang Mien Industry Co., Ltd. *(341)*
ChemFirst Inc. *(342)*
Chesapeake Enterprises, Inc. *(46)*
Chevron Chemical Co., LLC *(342)*
Chevron, U.S.A. *(342)*
Chicago Board of Trade *(342)*
China Eastern Airlines *(344)*
China, Embassy of the People's Republic of *(345)*
Chiquita Brands Internat'l, Inc. *(345)*
Chlopak, Leonard, Schechter and Associates *(46)*
The Chubb Corp. *(346)*
Ciba Specialty Chemicals Corp. *(346)*
CIGNA Corp. *(346)*
Cisco Systems Inc. *(347)*
Citigroup *(347)*
Citizens Against Government Waste *(348)*
Citizens for a Sound Economy *(348)*
Citrosuco North America, Inc. *(349)*
Civic Service, Inc. *(46)*
Claire's Stores, Inc. *(349)*
Clariant Corp. *(349)*
Clark & Weinstock, Inc. *(47)*
Cleary, Gottlieb, Steen and Hamilton *(47)*
Co-Steel Raritan *(352)*
Coalition Against Australian Leather Subsidies *(352)*
Coalition for Employment through Exports *(353)*
Coalition for Fair Atlantic Salmon Trade *(353)*
Coalition for Fair Lumber Imports *(353)*
Coalition for Fair Play in Ocean Shipping *(353)*
Coalition for GSP *(353)*
Coalition for Intellectual Property Rights (CIPR) *(354)*
Coalition for Open Markets and Expanded Trade *(354)*
Coalition for Truth in Environmental Marketing Information, Inc. *(355)*
Coalition of New England Companies for Trade *(355)*
Coalition of Service Industries *(355)*
Coalition to Stop Gun Violence *(356)*
CoBank, ACB *(356)*
The Coca-Cola Company *(356)*
Coffee Reserve *(357)*
Cohen, Gettings & Dunham, PC *(48)*
Colakoglu Group *(357)*
Colgate Palmolive *(357)*
Collier Shannon Scott, PLLC *(48)*
Colombian American Trade Center *(358)*
Colombian Coffee Federation *(358)*
Commercial Services Internat'l *(360)*
Committee for Fair Ammonium Nitrate Trade *(361)*
Committee on Pipe and Tube Imports *(361)*
Committee to Preserve American Color Television *(361)*
Committee to Support U.S. Trade Laws *(361)*
Commonwealth Consulting Corp. *(50)*
Compaq Computer Corp. *(363)*
Compass Internat'l Inc. *(363)*
Computer and Communications Industry Ass'n (CCIA) *(364)*
Computer Associates Internat'l, Inc. *(364)*
Computer Coalition for Responsible Exports *(364)*
Computer Systems Policy Project *(364)*
Computing Technology Industry Ass'n *(364)*
ConAgra Foods, Inc. *(365)*
Concert USA *(365)*
Condon and Forsyth *(51)*
Condor Electronic Systems *(365)*
Condor-Pacific Industries *(365)*
Confederation of Garment Exporters of the Philippines *(365)*
Congressional Economic Leadership Institute *(366)*
Congressional Institute, Inc. *(366)*
Conkling, Fiskum & McCormick *(51)*
Connecticut Steel Corp. *(367)*
Conoco Inc. *(367)*
Construction Industry Manufacturers Ass'n *(368)*
Consumer Electronics Ass'n *(369)*
Consumer Federation of America *(369)*
Consumers for World Trade *(369)*
Consumers Union of the United States *(369)*
Contango LLC *(52)*
Contractors Internat'l Group on Nuclear Liability *(370)*
Ry Cooder *(370)*
Mitchell J. Cooper *(52)*
Cooper Tire and Rubber Co. *(371)*
Coors Brewing Company *(371)*
Copper and Brass Fabricators Council *(371)*
Corn Refiners Ass'n, Inc. *(372)*
Corning Inc. *(372)*
Corporacion de Exportaciones Mexicanas, S.A. de C.V. and Marvin Roy Feldman *(372)*
Corporacion Valenciana de Cementos Portland, S.A. *(372)*
Corporacion Venezolana de Cementos, SACA *(372)*
Corus Group Plc *(373)*
Council of the Americas *(376)*
Covington & Burling *(53)*
John Crane-LIPS, Inc. *(378)*
Credit Suisse First Boston Corp. *(378)*
Creme de la Creme, Inc. *(378)*
Crowell & Moring LLP *(55)*
Crowley Maritime Corp. *(379)*
CSX Corp. *(379)*
CSX Lines LLC *(379)*
The Cullen Law Firm *(56)*
Cummins-Allison Corp. *(380)*
D.C. Historical Tourism Coalition *(381)*
DaimlerChrysler Corp. *(381)*
Danaher Corp. *(382)*
Davidoff & Malito, LLP *(57)*
Davis & Leiman, P.C. *(58)*
Donald S. Dawson & Associates *(59)*
DCS Group *(383)*
Deere & Co. *(383)*
Deerfield Beach, Florida, City of *(383)*
Defenders of Wildlife *(383)*
deKieffer & Horgan *(60)*
Dell Computer Corp. *(384)*
Delta Air Lines *(384)*
George H. Denison *(60)*
Denver, Colorado, City of *(386)*
Desert Grape Growers League *(386)*
Detroit Internat'l Bridge Co./The Ambassador Bridge *(386)*
Detroit, Michigan, City of *(386)*
Devon Energy Corp. *(387)*
Dewey Ballantine LLP *(61)*
Dewey Square Group *(61)*
DFS Group Ltd. *(387)*
DIAGEO *(387)*
Diamond Head Financial Group *(387)*
Diamond Manufacturing, Inc. *(387)*
Dickstein Shapiro Morin & Oshinsky LLP *(61)*
Dierman, Wortley, and Zola *(62)*
Dierman, Wortley, and Zola *(388)*
Digital Matrix Corp. *(388)*
Direct Selling Ass'n *(389)*
The Walt Disney Co. *(389)*
Distilled Spirits Council of the United States, Inc. *(389)*
DNA Plant Technology Corp. *(390)*
Dole Food Co. *(390)*
Domestic Petroleum Council *(390)*
Dominion Resources, Inc. *(391)*
Dow AgroSciences *(391)*
The Dow Chemical Co. *(391)*
Dow Corning Corp. *(391)*
Dow Jones & Co., Inc. *(391)*
Downey McGrath Group, Inc. *(64)*
Downey McGrath Group, Inc. *(392)*
Drives Inc. *(392)*
DRS Technologies, Inc. *(392)*
The Duberstein Group, Inc. *(65)*
Duncan, Weinberg, Genzer & Pembroke, P.C. *(66)*
DuPont *(393)*
The DuPont Pharmaceutical Co. *(393)*
Dutch Produce Ass'n *(393)*
The Dutko Group, Inc. *(68)*
Dykema Gossett PLLC *(69)*
E.ON North America, Inc. *(394)*
The Eagles Group *(69)*
Eastman Chemical Co. *(395)*
Eastman Kodak Co. *(395)*
eBay Inc. *(395)*
ED&F Man Inc. *(396)*
Eddie Bauer Co. *(396)*
Edison Mission Energy *(397)*
Edmund Scientific Co. *(397)*
EDS Corp. *(398)*
The Macon Edwards Co. *(71)*
El Paso Corporation *(399)*
Elanco Animal Health *(399)*
Elanex Pharmaceuticals *(399)*
Electro Scientific Industries, Inc. *(400)*
Electronic Industries Alliance *(400)*
Electronic Industries Ass'n of Japan *(401)*
Electronic Retailing Ass'n *(401)*
Elettronica Veneta & IN.EL. *(401)*
Elzay Ready Wear Manufacturing Co. *(401)*
Emergency Committee for American Trade *(401)*
Enron Corp. *(403)*
Entela, Inc. *(404)*
Ernst & Young LLP *(407)*
Ervin Technical Associates, Inc. (ETA) *(73)*
Eschenbach USA, Inc. *(407)*
Espey Manufacturing and Electronics *(407)*
Estee Lauder, Inc. *(407)*
Ethyl Corp. *(407)*
Euro-Fulton, S.A. *(408)*
European Confederation of Iron and Steel Industries (EUROFER) *(408)*
European-American Business Council *(408)*
The Evans Group, Ltd. *(74)*
Everett, Washington, Port of *(408)*
EXCEL Communications Inc. *(408)*
Exide Corp. *(409)*
Export Control Coalition *(409)*
Export Council for Energy Efficiency *(409)*
Export Source Coalition *(409)*
Express Pipeline Partnership and Platte Pipeline Co. *(409)*
Exxon Mobil Corp. *(409)*
F&T Network, Inc. *(74)*
Farmland Industries, Inc. *(412)*
Fashion Accessories Shippers Ass'n *(412)*
Federal Strategies Group *(75)*
Federation of German Industries (BDI) *(414)*
Federation of Internat'l Trade Ass'ns (FITA) *(414)*
FedEx Corp. *(415)*
Feith & Zell, P.C. *(75)*
Feld Entertainment Inc. *(415)*
Frank Fenton *(75)*
Ferroalloys Ass'n *(415)*
The Fertilizer Institute *(415)*
FIAMM S.p.A. *(416)*

FIAMM Technologies, Inc. ***(416)***
Fierce and Isakowitz *(76)*
The Financial Services Roundtable ***(416)***
Finch-Pruyn Paper Co. ***(417)***
Flack Associates *(77)*
FLIR Systems, Inc. ***(419)***
Floral Trade Council ***(419)***
Florida Crystals Corp. ***(419)***
Florida Department of Agriculture and Consumer Services ***(419)***
Florida Fruit and Vegetable Ass'n ***(420)***
Florida Tomato Exchange ***(420)***
Fluor Corp. ***(420)***
FMC Corp. ***(420)***
Foley Government and Public Affairs, Inc. *(78)*
Fontheim Internat'l ***(421)***
Fontheim Internat'l, LLC *(78)*
Fontheim Partners, PC *(78)*
Food Marketing Institute ***(421)***
Food Processing Machinery and Supplies Ass'n ***(421)***
Footwear Distributors and Retailers of America ***(422)***
Ford Motor Co. ***(422)***
Fortessa, Inc. ***(423)***
Foster Wheeler Corp. ***(424)***
FoxKiser *(79)*
Free Trade Lumber Council ***(425)***
Freeport-McMoRan Copper & Gold Inc. ***(425)***
French & Company *(79)*
Fresh Produce Ass'n of the Americas ***(426)***
Fried, Frank, Harris, Shriver & Jacobson *(80)*
Friends of the Earth ***(426)***
Fuji Photo Film U.S.A., Inc. ***(427)***
Ernest & Julio Gallo Winery ***(428)***
Law Offices of Michael R. Gardner, P.C. *(81)*
GATCO of VA, Inc. ***(429)***
Gateway, Inc. ***(430)***
GCG Partners ***(430)***
GCS Inc. *(82)*
GE Nuclear Energy ***(430)***
GenCorp ***(431)***
General Development Corp. ***(431)***
General Electric Capital Services, Inc. ***(432)***
General Electric Co. ***(432)***
General Mills ***(432)***
General Motors Corp. ***(432)***
Generic Pharmaceutical Ass'n ***(433)***
Genesee Brewing Co. ***(433)***
Genesis Consulting Group, LLC *(82)*
Geneva Steel Co. ***(433)***
Georgia-Pacific Corp. ***(434)***
Gibbons & Company, Inc. *(82)*
Gibson, Dunn & Crutcher LLP *(82)*
Gilbarco, Inc. ***(435)***
Gildan Activewear ***(435)***
GlaxoSmithKline ***(436)***
Global Policy Group, Inc. *(83)*
Global USA, Inc. *(83)*
Glossco Free Zone, N.V. ***(436)***
GMA Internat'l *(83)*
Goodstein & Associates *(84)*
Goodyear Tire and Rubber Co. ***(437)***
The Gorlin Group *(84)*
Government Relations, Inc. *(84)*
GPU, Inc. ***(438)***
Jay Grant & Associates *(85)*
Edwin C. Graves & Associates *(85)*
Greenberg Traurig, LLP *(86)*
Griffin, Johnson, Dover & Stewart *(87)*
Grocery Manufacturers of America ***(440)***
Grupo "J" S.A. ***(441)***
Grupo Carrousel (Mexico) ***(441)***
Grupo Empresarial Maya ***(441)***
Grupo Maseca ***(441)***
Guam, Washington Office of the Governor ***(442)***
Guardian Industries Corp. ***(442)***
Guardian Life Insurance Co. of America ***(442)***
Guidant Corp. ***(442)***
Guinea, Secretary General of the Presidency of the Republic of ***(442)***
Gulf Coast Portland Cement Co. ***(442)***
Haake and Associates *(89)*
Haarmann & Reimer Corp. ***(443)***
Habas Group ***(443)***
Hale and Dorr LLP *(89)*
Haley and Associates *(90)*
Halliburton/Brown & Root ***(443)***
Martin G. Hamberger & Associates *(91)*
Hamilton Sundstrand ***(444)***
Harmon & Wilmot, L.L.P. *(91)*
Harris Corp. ***(444)***
Harris Ellsworth & Levin *(92)*
Hawaiian Commercial and Sugar Company ***(445)***
Hecht, Spencer & Associates *(93)*
H. J. Heinz Co., ***(448)***
Herbalife Internat'l, Inc. ***(448)***
Allen Herbert *(94)*
Hershey Foods Corp. ***(449)***
Hewlett-Packard Co. ***(449)***
Hills & Company, International Consultants *(95)*
Hillwood Development Corp. ***(450)***
Hitachi, Ltd. ***(450)***
Hoffmann-La Roche Inc. ***(450)***
Hogan & Hartson L.L.P. *(96)*
Holland & Knight LLP *(98)*
Holnam Inc. ***(451)***
The Home Depot ***(451)***
Honda North America, Inc. ***(451)***
Honduras, Embassy of ***(452)***
Honeywell Internat'l, Inc. ***(452)***
Hong Kong Economic and Trade Office ***(452)***
Hong Kong Trade Development Council ***(452)***
Hooper Owen & Winburn *(99)*
The Hosiery Ass'n ***(452)***
Houston Shell and Concrete ***(453)***
R. J. Hudson Associates *(101)*
Hudson Institute ***(454)***
Hughes Electronics Corp. ***(454)***
Huntsman Corp. ***(455)***
Hurt, Norton & Associates *(101)*
Hyundai Electronics Industries Co., LTD ***(456)***
Hyundai Motor Co. ***(456)***
ICF Industries, Inc. ***(457)***
The Ickes & Enright Group *(102)*
Illinois Tool Works ***(458)***
IMC Global Inc. ***(458)***
Impact Strategies *(102)*
IMPACT, LLC *(102)*
Importers Service Corp. ***(458)***
Indalco Spa ***(458)***
Independent Petroleum Ass'n of America ***(459)***
Indiana Glass Co. ***(460)***
Indiana, Office of the Governor of the State of ***(460)***
Industrial Fabrics Ass'n Internat'l ***(461)***
Industrie Alimentare Molisane ***(461)***
Information Technology Industry Council ***(462)***
Information Trust ***(462)***
Infotech Strategies, Inc. *(103)*
Ingersoll-Rand Co. ***(462)***
Inland Steel Industries, Inc. ***(462)***
Institute of Scrap Recycling Industries, Inc. ***(464)***
Integra Life Sciences ***(465)***
Intel Corp. ***(465)***
Intellectual Property Committee ***(465)***
Inter-American Institute for Cooperation on Agriculture ***(466)***
Interactive Digital Software Ass'n ***(466)***
Internat'l Advisory Services Group Ltd. *(103)*
Internat'l Ass'n of Airport Duty Free Stores ***(467)***
Internat'l Ass'n of Bridge, Structural, Ornamental and Reinforcing Iron Workers ***(467)***
Internat'l Ass'n of Drilling Contractors ***(467)***
Internat'l Ass'n of Machinists and Aerospace Workers ***(468)***
Internat'l Ass'n of Professional Numismatists ***(468)***
Internat'l Barter and Countertrade Foundation ***(468)***
Internat'l Bicycle Ass'n ***(468)***
Internat'l Brotherhood of Boilermakers, Iron Shipbuilders, Blacksmiths, Forgers and Helpers ***(469)***
Internat'l Brotherhood of Electrical Workers ***(469)***
Internat'l Brotherhood of Teamsters ***(469)***
Internat'l Business Machines Corp. ***(469)***
Internat'l Business-Government Counsellors, Inc. *(103)*
Internat'l Communications Industries Ass'n (ICIA) ***(470)***
Internat'l Dairy Foods Ass'n ***(470)***
Internat'l Electronics Manufacturers and Consumers of America ***(471)***
Internat'l Federation of Inspection Agencies, North American Committee ***(471)***
Internat'l Federation of Professional and Technical Engineers ***(471)***
Internat'l Frozen Food Ass'n ***(472)***
Internat'l Intellectual Property Alliance ***(472)***
Internat'l Labor Rights Fund ***(472)***
Internat'l Longshore and Warehouse Union ***(473)***
Internat'l Mass Retailers Ass'n ***(473)***
Internat'l Paper ***(473)***
Internat'l Raw Materials ***(474)***
Internat'l Safety Equipment Ass'n (ISEA) ***(474)***
Internat'l Union of Operating Engineers ***(476)***
Interregional Associates ***(477)***
Interstate Wine Coalition ***(477)***
Intradeco ***(477)***
Investment Co. Institute ***(477)***
IPC Washington Office ***(478)***
IPR Shandwick ***(478)***
Iran Air ***(478)***
Itera Internat'l Energy Consultants ***(480)***
ITT Industries ***(480)***
ITT World Directories, Inc. ***(480)***
Jacobs Engineering Group Inc. ***(481)***
Jam Shoe Concepts, Inc. ***(481)***
Janus-Merritt Strategies, L.L.C. *(104)*
Japan Automobile Manufacturers Ass'n ***(481)***
Japan External Trade Organization (JETRO) ***(481)***
Japan Federation of Construction Contractors, Inc. ***(481)***
Japan Federation of Economic Organizations ***(481)***
Japan Iron and Steel Exporters Ass'n ***(482)***
Japan, Embassy of ***(482)***
Jarboe & Associates *(105)*
JBC Internat'l *(105)*
Jefferson Consulting Group *(105)*
Jefferson Government Relations, L.L.C. *(106)*
Jefferson-Waterman Internat'l, LLC *(106)*
Jewelers of America ***(483)***
Jewish Institute for Nat'l Security Affairs ***(483)***
JM Family Enterprises ***(483)***
Johnson & Johnson, Inc. ***(484)***
S.C. Johnson and Son, Inc. ***(484)***
Johnson Co. *(107)*
Joint Stock Company Severstal ***(484)***
Jolly/Rissler, Inc. *(108)*
Jones, Walker, Waechter, Poitevent, Carrere & Denegre, L.L.P. *(108)*
Kaiser Aluminum & Chemical Corp. ***(485)***
Kalik Lewin *(109)*
Betty Ann Kane & Co. *(110)*
Kaye Scholer LLP *(110)*
Keizai Koho Center ***(487)***
Robert K. Kelley Law Offices *(111)*
Kellogg Brown and Root ***(487)***
Kellogg Co. ***(487)***
Kelly and Associates, Inc. *(111)*
Kendall-Jackson Winery ***(488)***
Kensey Nash Corp. ***(488)***
Kent & O'Connor, Inc. *(112)*
Kessler & Associates Business Services, Inc. *(112)*
Keystone Consolidated Industries, Inc. ***(489)***
Jeffrey J. Kimbell & Associates *(113)*
Kimberly Consulting, LLC *(113)*
Kimberly-Clark Corp. ***(489)***
King & Spalding *(113)*
Kinghorn & Associates, L.L.C. *(113)*
Peter Kinzler *(113)*
Kitchen Cabinet Manufacturers Ass'n ***(490)***
Kmart Corp. ***(490)***
Komatsu Ltd. ***(490)***
Koncor Forest Products Co. ***(491)***
Michael J. Kopetski *(114)*
Korea Economic Institute of America ***(491)***
Korean Iron and Steel Ass'n ***(491)***
Korean Semiconductor Industry Ass'n ***(491)***
KOSA ***(491)***
Koyo Seiko Co., Ltd. ***(491)***
KPMG, LLP *(115)*

KPMG, LLP *(491)*
Kraft Foods, Inc. *(492)*
Kyocera Corp. *(492)*
Labor Council for Latin American Advancement (LCLAA) *(493)*
Labor-Industry Coalition for Internat'l Trade *(493)*
Lafarge Corp. *(494)*
Lana'i Co. *(494)*
Lao Veterans of America, Inc. *(495)*
Laredo, Texas, City of *(495)*
Leather Industries of America *(497)*
The Legislative Strategies Group, LLC *(118)*
LegisLaw *(118)*
Lehigh Portland Cement Co. *(498)*
Lennox Internat'l *(498)*
Lent Scrivner & Roth LLC *(119)*
Leonard B. Levine & Associates *(119)*
Libbey, Inc. *(499)*
Eli Lilly and Co. *(499)*
The Limited Inc. *(499)*
Lindsay Hart Neil & Weigler *(120)*
The Livingston Group, LLC *(120)*
Liz Claiborne Internat'l *(500)*
Localisation Industry Standards Ass'n *(501)*
Lockheed Martin Corp. *(501)*
Long, Aldridge & Norman, LLP *(121)*
Loral Space and Communications, Ltd. *(503)*
Lorillard Tobacco Co. *(503)*
Lotus Development Corp. *(504)*
Louis Dreyfus Corporation *(504)*
The LTV Corp. *(505)*
LTV Steel Co. *(505)*
Lucent Technologies *(505)*
LVMH Moet Hennessy Louis Vuitton S.A. *(506)*
Marshall L. Lynam *(122)*
Lyondell Chemical Co. *(506)*
Lyons & Co. *(122)*
The M Companies *(122)*
MacGregor *(506)*
Machinery Dealers Nat'l Ass'n *(506)*
Maersk Inc. *(507)*
Makedonski Telekomunikacii *(508)*
Management Options, Inc. *(123)*
Manatt, Phelps & Phillips, LLP *(123)*
Manufactured Imports Promotion Organization (MIPRO) *(509)*
Manufacturers Alliance/MAPI Inc. *(509)*
The Marine and Fire Insurance Ass'n of Japan, Inc. *(510)*
Maritime Institute for Research and Industrial Development *(510)*
Martin Color-Fi *(511)*
Martin-Baker Aircraft Co., Ltd. *(511)*
Masaoka & Associates, Inc. *(125)*
Matsushita Electric Corp. of America *(513)*
Matsushita Electric Industrial Co., Ltd. *(513)*
Mattel, Inc. *(513)*
Mauritius Sugar Syndicate *(513)*
Mauritius, Chamber of Agriculture of *(513)*
Mauritius-U.S. Business Ass'n Inc. *(513)*
Mayberry & Associates LLC *(126)*
Mayer, Brown & Platt *(126)*
Maytag Corp. *(513)*
Mazda North America Operations *(514)*
MBV, Inc. *(127)*
McDermott Internat'l, Inc./Babcock & Wilcox *(514)*
McDermott, Will and Emery *(128)*
Jack H. McDonald *(129)*
McDonald's Corp. *(514)*
McGraw-Hill Cos., The *(514)*
McGuiness Norris & Williams, LLP *(130)*
McLeod, Watkinson & Miller *(131)*
The Mead Corp. *(515)*
Meat and Livestock Australia *(515)*
Meat New Zealand *(515)*
Mehl, Griffin & Bartek Ltd. *(132)*
Mentor Graphics Corp. *(518)*
Merck & Co. *(518)*
Meridian Worldwide *(519)*
Meter Spa *(519)*
Methanex Inc. *(520)*
Metropolitan Life Insurance Co. *(520)*
Mexam Trade, Inc. *(521)*
Mexican Crab Industry *(521)*
Mexican Nat'l Spiny Lobster Industry *(521)*
Mexico-U.S. Business Committee, U.S. Council *(521)*
Meyers & Associates *(133)*
MGF Industries Inc. *(521)*
Micron Technology, Inc. *(522)*
Microsoft Corp. *(522)*
Midroc Ethiopia *(523)*
Miller & Chevalier, Chartered *(133)*
Miller & Co. *(134)*
Denny Miller McBee Associates *(134)*
Milliken and Co. *(524)*
Minnesota Mining and Manufacturing Co. (3M Co.) *(525)*
Mintz, Levin, Cohn, Ferris, Glovsky and Popeo, P.C. *(135)*
Mississippi Chemical Corp. *(526)*
Mitsubishi Internat'l Corp. *(526)*
Mitsubishi Motors America, Inc. *(526)*
Monsanto Co. *(528)*
Montgomery Ward & Co., Inc. *(528)*
Morgan Stanley Dean Witter & Co. *(529)*
Morgan, Lewis & Bockius LLP *(136)*
Morocco, Foreign Ministry of the Kingdom of *(529)*
Morrison & Foerster LLP *(137)*
Motion Picture Ass'n of America *(530)*
Motor and Equipment Manufacturers Ass'n *(531)*
Motorola, Inc. *(531)*
Mount High Hosiery, Ltd. *(531)*
Multimedia Broadcast Investment Corp. *(532)*
G. Murphy Trading *(533)*
Murray, Scheer, Montgomery, Tapia & O'Donnell *(139)*
The MWW Group *(140)*
Naigai, Inc. *(534)*
Nat'l Ass'n of Foreign Trade Zones *(543)*
Nat'l Ass'n of Home Builders of the U.S. *(543)*
Nat'l Ass'n of Manufacturers *(545)*
Nat'l Ass'n of Minority Automobile Dealers *(545)*
Nat'l Ass'n of Negro Business & Professional Women's Clubs, Inc. *(546)*
Nat'l Ass'n of State Departments of Agriculture *(549)*
Nat'l Ass'n of Theatre Owners *(550)*
Nat'l Ass'n of Wheat Growers *(551)*
Nat'l Ass'n of Wholesaler-Distributors *(551)*
Nat'l Bicycle Dealers Ass'n *(552)*
Nat'l Candle Ass'n *(554)*
Nat'l Cattleman's Beef Ass'n *(554)*
Nat'l Chicken Council *(555)*
Nat'l Coalition of Food Importers Ass'n *(556)*
Nat'l Consumers League *(558)*
Nat'l Corn Growers Ass'n *(559)*
Nat'l Council of Farmer Cooperatives *(560)*
Nat'l Council of La Raza *(560)*
Nat'l Customs Brokers and Forwarders Ass'n of America *(561)*
Nat'l Defense Industrial Ass'n *(561)*
Nat'l Electrical Manufacturers Ass'n *(562)*
Nat'l Farmers Union (Farmers Educational & Co-operative Union of America) *(563)*
Nat'l Fastener Distributors Ass'n *(564)*
Nat'l Federation of Croatian Americans *(564)*
Nat'l Fisheries Institute *(564)*
Nat'l Food Processors Ass'n *(564)*
Nat'l Foreign Trade Council, Inc. *(565)*
Nat'l Grain and Feed Ass'n *(566)*
Nat'l Grain Sorgum Producers *(566)*
Nat'l Grain Trade Council *(566)*
Nat'l Grange *(566)*
Nat'l Juice Products Ass'n *(569)*
Nat'l Legal Center for the Public Interest *(570)*
Nat'l Licensed Beverage Ass'n *(570)*
Nat'l Lumber and Building Material Dealers Ass'n *(570)*
Nat'l Milk Producers Federation *(571)*
Nat'l Mining Ass'n *(571)*
Nat'l Oilseed Processors Ass'n *(572)*
Nat'l Peach Council *(573)*
Nat'l Pork Producers Council *(574)*
Nat'l Potato Council *(574)*
Nat'l Power *(574)*
Nat'l Restaurant Ass'n *(576)*
Nat'l Retail Federation *(576)*
Nat'l Soft Drink Ass'n *(578)*
Nat'l Steel Corp. *(579)*
Nat'l Technical Systems *(579)*
Nat'l Turkey Federation *(580)*
NAVCOM Systems, Inc. *(583)*
NCR Corp. *(583)*
NEC USA, Inc. *(583)*
Nestle USA, Inc. *(584)*
NetCoalition.Com *(584)*
Netscape Communications Corp. *(584)*
New Frontiers Communications Consulting *(141)*
New York Life Insurance Co. *(587)*
New York Life Internat'l Inc. *(587)*
New York Mercantile Exchange *(587)*
New Zealand Kiwifruit Marketing Board *(588)*
Newport News Shipbuilding Inc. *(588)*
News Corporation Ltd. *(589)*
Newspaper Ass'n of America *(589)*
Nike, Inc. *(590)*
Niki Trading Co. *(590)*
Nintendo of America, Inc. *(590)*
Nissan North America Inc. *(590)*
Nixon Center, The *(590)*
Nixon Peabody LLP *(142)*
Noise Reduction Technology Coalition *(591)*
Norfolk Southern Railroad *(591)*
Julia J. Norrell & Associates *(142)*
Nortel Networks *(591)*
North American Equipment Dealers Ass'n *(592)*
North American Grain Export Ass'n, Inc. *(592)*
North American Millers' Ass'n *(592)*
North Carolina Peanut Growers Ass'n *(593)*
North Carolina, Washington Office of the State of *(593)*
North Dakota Wheat Commission *(593)*
North Dakota, Governor's Office of the State of *(593)*
North of Ireland Free Trade Initiative *(593)*
Northeast-Midwest Institute *(594)*
Northrop Grumman Corp. *(594)*
Northwest Airlines, Inc. *(595)*
Northwest Horticultural Council *(595)*
Novartis Corp. *(596)*
Novartis Services, Inc. *(596)*
Novell, Inc. *(596)*
NPES, The Ass'n for Suppliers of Printing, Publishing, and Converting Technologies *(596)*
NTT America *(597)*
Nuclear Energy Institute *(597)*
The OB-C Group, LLC *(143)*
Obadal and MacLeod, p.c. *(143)*
Occidental Internat'l Corporation *(598)*
O'Connor & Hannan, L.L.P. *(144)*
Oerlikon Aerospace, Inc. *(599)*
Olsson, Frank and Weeda, P.C. *(146)*
O'Melveny and Myers LLP *(147)*
O'Neill, Athy & Casey, P.C. *(147)*
Oneonta Trading Corp. *(601)*
Operations Security Professionals Soc. *(601)*
Oppenheimer Wolff & Donnelly LLP *(147)*
Optical Disc Corp. *(601)*
Opticians Ass'n of America *(601)*
Oracle Corp. *(602)*
Orbital Sciences Corp. *(602)*
Organization for Internat'l Investment *(603)*
John T. O'Rourke Law Offices *(147)*
Owens-Illinois, Inc. *(605)*
PACCAR, Inc. *(605)*
Pacific Capital Group, Inc. *(605)*
Pacific Coast Cement *(605)*
PacifiCorp *(606)*
Panda Energy Internat'l *(607)*
Parry, Romani, DeConcini & Symms *(149)*
Pastavilla Makarnacilik A.S. *(609)*
Pastificio Antonio Pallante *(609)*
Pastificio Pagani *(609)*
Patton Boggs, LLP *(150)*
Patton Boggs, LLP *(609)*
Paul, Hastings, Janofsky & Walker LLP *(153)*
Payless Shoe Source *(610)*
J. C. Penney Co., Inc. *(611)*
Pennzoil-Quaker State Co. *(611)*
PepsiCo, Inc. *(612)*
Pernod Ricard *(612)*
Perry Tritech Inc. *(612)*
The Petrizzo Group, Inc. *(155)*

Pfizer, Inc. ***(613)***
Pfluger Enterprises LLC ***(614)***
Pharmaceutical Research and Manufacturers of America ***(614)***
Pharmacia Corp. ***(615)***
Philip Morris Management Corp. ***(615)***
Philipp Brothers Chemicals, Inc. ***(616)***
Philips Electronics North America Corp. ***(616)***
Phillips Foods, Inc. ***(616)***
Phillips Petroleum Co. ***(616)***
Pier 1 Imports ***(617)***
Pillowtex Corp. ***(617)***
The Pillsbury Co. ***(617)***
PINSA, S.A de CD ***(618)***
The PMA Group *(156)*
Podesta/Mattoon *(158)*
Polar Air Cargo, Inc. ***(620)***
Polaroid Corp. ***(620)***
Policy Directions, Inc. *(158)*
Polytec Group ***(620)***
Porter/Novelli *(159)*
The Potomac Research Group LLC *(160)*
Powell Tate *(160)*
Powell, Goldstein, Frazer & Murphy LLP *(160)*
PPG Industries ***(622)***
Praxair, Inc. ***(623)***
Preston Gates Ellis & Rouvelas Meeds LLP *(162)*
Pretium S.C (Mexico) ***(623)***
PriceWaterhouseCoopers ***(624)***
PriceWaterhouseCoopers *(163)*
Principal Financial Group ***(624)***
Process Equipment Manufacturers' Ass'n ***(625)***
The Procter & Gamble Company ***(625)***
Progressive Policy Institute ***(626)***
Protein Technologies Internat'l ***(627)***
Prudential Insurance Co. of America ***(627)***
Prudential Securities, Inc. ***(627)***
Public Citizen, Inc. ***(628)***
Public Private Partnership *(164)*
Quebec Lumber Manufacturers Ass'n ***(630)***
Quinn Gillespie & Associates *(165)*
Qwest Communications ***(631)***
Radio Shack Corp. ***(632)***
Radix SA ***(632)***
Ralston Purina Co. ***(632)***
Ranchers-Cattlemen Legal Action Fund ***(633)***
Robert Rarog *(166)*
Raytheon Co. ***(633)***
Reebok Internat'l ***(635)***
Reed, Smith, LLP *(167)*
Renova Inc. ***(637)***
Representative of German Industry and Trade *(168)*
Retlif Testing Laboratory, Inc. ***(639)***
Reuters America Inc. ***(639)***
R. J. Reynolds Tobacco Co. ***(639)***
Rhoads Group *(168)*
Rhodia, Inc. ***(639)***
Rice Belt Warehouses ***(639)***
RMA Internat'l, Inc. *(169)*
Liz Robbins Associates *(169)*
Robertson, Monagle & Eastaugh *(170)*
Robins, Kaplan, Miller & Ciresi L.L.P. *(170)*
Rockwell Collins ***(641)***
Rodriguez O'Donnell Fuerst Gonzalez & Williams *(171)*
Rohm and Haas Co. ***(642)***
Rollerblade, Inc. ***(642)***
Ross & Hardies *(172)*
Ross-Robinson & Associates *(172)*
The Roth Group *(172)*
Royal Wine Co. ***(643)***
RSR Corp. ***(643)***
Rubber and Plastic Footwear Manufacturers Ass'n ***(643)***
Rubber Manufacturers Ass'n ***(643)***
Rubie's Costume Co., Inc. ***(643)***
Frank Russell Co. ***(644)***
J. T. Rutherford & Associates *(173)*
J. T. Rutherford & Associates ***(644)***
Ryberg and Smith LLP *(174)*
SABIC Americas, Inc. ***(644)***
Sabre Inc. ***(644)***
Safety Reasearch Center, Inc. ***(645)***
Salt Lake City Olympic Organizing Committee ***(646)***
Samsung Corp. ***(647)***
San Antonio, Texas, City of ***(647)***
Sandler, Travis & Rosenberg, P.A. *(175)*
SAP Public Services ***(649)***
Sappi Fine Paper NA ***(649)***
Michael L. Sauls *(175)*
R. Wayne Sayer & Associates *(175)*
Schagrin Associates *(175)*
Schmeltzer, Aptaker & Shepard, P.C. *(176)*
Schramm, Williams & Associates, Inc. *(176)*
W. Schulz GmbH ***(652)***
Seaboard Corp. ***(653)***
Sears, Roebuck and Co. ***(653)***
Secure Wrap, Inc. ***(654)***
Securities Industry Ass'n ***(654)***
Seiko Epson Corp. ***(654)***
Sellery Associates, Inc. *(177)*
Semiconductor Equipment and Materials Internat'l ***(655)***
Semiconductor Industry Ass'n ***(655)***
Servo Corp. of America ***(656)***
Shaklee Corp. ***(656)***
Sharretts, Paley, Carter and Blauvelt *(177)*
Daniel F. Shaw & Associates *(177)*
Shaw Group ***(657)***
Shaw Pittman *(177)*
Shea & Gardner *(179)*
Sheet Metal Workers' Internat'l Ass'n ***(657)***
Shell Oil Co. ***(657)***
Sher & Blackwell *(179)*
Sherritt Internat'l ***(657)***
Shipbuilders Council of America ***(657)***
Sidem International Ltd. ***(658)***
Siemens Corp. ***(658)***
Sierra Nevada Corp. ***(659)***
Silicon Graphics/SGI ***(659)***
Silver Users Ass'n ***(659)***
Law Offices of David L. Simon *(180)*
Bill Simpson & Associates *(181)*
Stephen F. Sims and Associates *(181)*
Singapore Technologies Automotive ***(659)***
SISCORP *(181)*
Skadden, Arps, Slate, Meagher & Flom LLP *(181)*
SKF USA, Inc. ***(660)***
Skipps Cutting ***(660)***
SKW Chemicals, Inc. ***(660)***
Philip S. Smith & Associates, Inc. *(182)*
Smith & Harroff, Inc. *(182)*
Smith & Metalitz, L.L.P. *(182)*
Smith Dawson & Andrews, Inc. *(183)*
Smith Martin & Boyette *(184)*
The Smith-Free Group *(184)*
Snack Food Ass'n ***(662)***
Soc. of American Florists ***(663)***
Societe Generale de Surveillance Holding S.A. ***(664)***
Software & Information Industry Ass'n (SIIA) ***(664)***
The Solomon Group, LLC *(185)*
Solutia Inc. ***(665)***
Sonnenschein, Nath & Rosenthal *(185)*
Sony Electronics, Inc. ***(666)***
Sony Music Entertainment Inc. ***(666)***
Sony Pictures Entertainment Inc. ***(666)***
South African Sugar Ass'n ***(666)***
Southwest Peanut Growers ***(668)***
Southwire, Inc. ***(668)***
SPACEHAB, Inc. ***(669)***
Special Committee for Workplace Product Liability Reform ***(669)***
Spiegel Inc. ***(670)***
Sporting Goods Manufacturers Ass'n ***(670)***
Springs Industries, Inc. ***(671)***
Sprint Corp. ***(671)***
St. Maxens & Company *(187)*
St. Thomas/St. John Chamber of Commerce, Inc. ***(672)***
The Stanley Works ***(672)***
State Farm Insurance Cos. ***(673)***
States Ratification Committee ***(673)***
Steam Generator Coalition ***(673)***
Steel Manufacturers Ass'n ***(674)***
Steel Service Center Institute ***(674)***
Steptoe & Johnson LLP *(188)*
Sterling Chemical Co. ***(674)***
Stewart & Stevenson Services, Inc. ***(674)***
Stewart and Stewart *(189)*
Kenneth F. Stinger *(189)*
John M. Stinson *(189)*
Storage Technology Corp. ***(675)***
Storck U.S.A. ***(675)***
Strat@Comm (Strategic Communications Counselors) *(189)*
Strategic Choices, Inc. *(189)*
Strategic Horizons Advisors, L.L.C. *(189)*
Strategic Minerals Corp. ***(675)***
Strategy Group Internat'l *(190)*
Charlene A. Sturbitts *(190)*
Subaru of America ***(676)***
Sugiyama Chain Co., Ltd. ***(676)***
Sumitomo Corp. of America ***(676)***
Sun Microsystems ***(676)***
Sunbelt Cement ***(677)***
Sunkist Growers, Inc. ***(677)***
SunSweet Growers, Inc. ***(677)***
Paul Suplizio Associates *(191)*
Svenska Petroleum Exploration AB ***(678)***
Swaziland Sugar Ass'n ***(678)***
Swidler Berlin Shereff Friedman, LLP *(191)*
Synthetic Organic Chemical Manufacturers Ass'n ***(679)***
Tacoma, Washington, Port of ***(680)***
Tailored Clothing Ass'n ***(680)***
Taipei Economic and Cultural Representative Office in the United States ***(680)***
Taiwan Studies Institute ***(680)***
Target Corp. ***(681)***
Tate and Lyle North American Sugars Inc. ***(681)***
Techneglas, Inc. ***(682)***
The Technical Group LLC *(192)*
Technology Network ***(682)***
TECO Energy, Inc. ***(682)***
Telecommunications Industry Ass'n ***(682)***
Television Ass'n of Programmers Latin America (TAP Latin America) ***(683)***
TerraCom-Strategic Communications *(193)*
Tett Enterprises ***(684)***
Texaco Group Inc. ***(684)***
Texas A&M Research Foundation ***(684)***
Texas Instruments ***(684)***
Textron Inc. ***(685)***
Thomas Pink, Inc. ***(686)***
Thompson Coburn LLP *(194)*
Thomson Consumer Electronics, Inc. ***(686)***
Tiffany & Co. ***(687)***
Tighe, Patton, Tabackman & Babbin *(195)*
Timet-Titantium Metals Corp. ***(687)***
The Timken Co. ***(687)***
Timmons and Co., Inc. *(195)*
Tire Ass'n of North America ***(687)***
Tobacco Fairness Coalition ***(688)***
Tolmex ***(688)***
Toolex USA, Inc. ***(688)***
Torrington Co. ***(688)***
Toy Manufacturers of America ***(688)***
Toyota Motor North America, U.S.A., Inc. ***(689)***
The Trade Partnership *(196)*
Transhumance Holding Co., Inc. ***(690)***
Transnat'l Development Consortium ***(690)***
TransOceanic Shipping ***(690)***
Transportation Institute ***(690)***
Travelocity.com ***(691)***
TRW Inc. ***(693)***
Turkey, Government of the Republic of ***(694)***
Turkish Industrialists and Businessmen's Ass'n (TUSIAD) ***(694)***
Tuttle, Taylor & Heron *(197)*
Tyco Internat'l (US), Inc. ***(695)***
U.S. Ass'n of Importers of Textiles and Apparel ***(695)***
U.S. Border Control ***(695)***
U.S. Business Alliance for Customs Modernization ***(695)***
U.S. Citrus Science Council ***(696)***
U.S. Hispanic Chamber of Commerce ***(696)***
U.S. Mink Export Development Council ***(696)***
U.S. Public Interest Research Group ***(697)***
U.S.-Canadian Caucus of Mayors ***(697)***
U.S.-Turkish Business Council of DEIK ***(697)***
UDV North America, Inc. ***(698)***
UDV/Heublein, Inc. ***(698)***

Unilever United States, Inc. ***(699)***
Union of Needletrades, Industrial, and Textile Employees (UNITE) ***(699)***
Union Pacific ***(699)***
Uniroyal Chemical Co., Inc. ***(699)***
Unisys Corp. ***(700)***
United Airlines ***(700)***
United Automobile, Aerospace and Agricultural Implement Workers of America (UAW) ***(700)***
United Biscuit ***(700)***
United Defense, L.P. ***(701)***
United Egg Ass'n ***(701)***
United Egg Producers ***(701)***
United Fresh Fruit and Vegetable Ass'n ***(701)***
United Lao Congress for Democracy ***(702)***
United Methodist Church General Board of Church and Society ***(702)***
United Pan-Europe Communications, NV ***(702)***
United Parcel Service ***(702)***
United States Beet Sugar Ass'n ***(703)***
United States Business and Industry Council ***(703)***
United States Cane Sugar Refiners' Ass'n ***(703)***
United States Enrichment Corp. ***(703)***
United Steelworkers of America ***(704)***
United Technologies Corp. ***(704)***
Universal Wireless Communications Consortium ***(705)***
UNOCAL Corp. ***(708)***
UNUM/Provident Corp. ***(708)***
US JVC Corp. ***(709)***
US Steel Group ***(709)***
US-Asia Institute ***(709)***
USEC, Inc. ***(710)***
USX Corp. ***(710)***
Valanzano & Associates *(198)*
Valero Energy Corp. ***(711)***
Valis Associates *(198)*
Valley Fig Growers ***(711)***
Valve Manufacturers Ass'n of America ***(711)***
Van Ness Feldman, P.C. *(199)*
Van Scoyoc Associates, Inc. *(200)*
Venable *(201)*
Verizon Communications ***(713)***
Verner, Liipfert, Bernhard, McPherson and Hand, Chartered ***(713)***
Verner, Liipfert, Bernhard, McPherson and Hand, Chartered *(202)*
Viatel, Inc. ***(714)***
Vickery Internat'l *(204)*
Vinifera Wine Growers Ass'n ***(715)***
Viohl and Associates, Inc. *(205)*
Virgin Islands, Government of the ***(715)***
Virginia Beach, Virginia, City of ***(715)***
Virginia Peanut Growers Ass'n ***(716)***
Virginia Wineries Ass'n ***(716)***
Visalia, California, City of ***(716)***
Vivendi Universal ***(717)***
VoiceStream Wireless Corp. ***(717)***
Volkswagen, AG ***(717)***
R. Duffy Wall and Associates *(205)*
Warnaco, Inc. ***(718)***
Washington Consulting Group ***(719)***
Washington Council Ernst & Young *(206)*
Washington Resource Associates *(209)*
Weirton Steel Corp. ***(722)***
Welch's Foods, Inc. ***(722)***
Westar Group, Inc. ***(723)***
Western Ag Resources Inc. ***(723)***
Western Growers Ass'n ***(724)***
Western Wireless Internat'l ***(725)***
Westinghouse Electric Co. ***(725)***
The Wexler Group *(211)*
Weyerhaeuser Co. ***(725)***
Wheat Export Trade Education Committee ***(725)***
Wheat Gluten Industry Council ***(725)***
Wheeling Pittsburgh Steel Corp. ***(726)***
William F. Whitsitt Policy and Government Affairs *(213)*
Burton V. Wides, P.C. *(214)*
The Wigglesworth Co. *(214)*
Wiley, Rein & Fielding *(214)*
Wilkie Farr & Gallagher ***(727)***
The Willard Group *(215)*
Williams & Jensen, P.C. *(215)*
James M. Williams, Jr. *(217)*
Willkie Farr & Gallagher *(217)*
Wilmer, Cutler & Pickering *(217)*
WinCapitol, Inc. *(218)*
Wine and Spirits Wholesalers of America ***(728)***
Wine Institute ***(728)***
Winegrape Growers of America ***(728)***
Kathleen Winn & Associates, Inc. *(218)*
Winston & Strawn *(218)*
Winthrop, Stimson, Putnam & Roberts *(219)*
Women Officials in NACo ***(729)***
Wood Corp. ***(730)***
Wool Fiber, Yarn Fabric Coalition ***(730)***
World Duty Free Americas, Inc. ***(730)***
WorldWide Minerals Ltd. ***(731)***
Wm. Wrigley Jr. Co. ***(732)***
Xerox Corp. ***(732)***
Youngstown-Warren Regional Chamber ***(733)***
The Yucel Group ***(734)***

Transportation (TRA)

3Tex ***(223)***
AAA MidAtlantic ***(224)***
AAAE-ACI ***(224)***
AAI Corp. ***(224)***
AARP (American Ass'n of Retired Persons) ***(224)***
ABB Daimler-Benz Transportation, N.A. (ADTRANZ) ***(225)***
Abilene, Texas, City of ***(225)***
Abitibi Consolidated Sales Corp. ***(225)***
AC Transit ***(225)***
The Accord Group *(5)*
Adams and Reese LLP *(5)*
Michael W. Adcock *(6)*
ADSI Inc. ***(228)***
ADTranz (Daimler Chrysler Rail Systems) ***(228)***
Advanced Transit Ass'n ***(229)***
Advantage Associates, Inc. *(6)*
The Advocacy Group *(6)*
Advocates for Highway and Auto Safety ***(229)***
Aeronautical Repair Station Ass'n ***(230)***
AFL-CIO (American Federation of Labor and Congress of Industrial Organizations) ***(231)***
AFL-CIO - Maritime Trades Department ***(231)***
AFL-CIO - Transportation Trades Department ***(231)***
Agricultural Retailers Ass'n ***(232)***
Agricultural Transporters Conference ***(232)***
AHL Shipping Co. ***(232)***
Ainslie Associates *(7)*
Air Pacific Ltd. ***(234)***
Air Products and Chemicals, Inc. ***(234)***
Air Transport Ass'n of America ***(234)***
Airbus Industrie of North America, Inc. ***(234)***
Aircraft Electronics Ass'n ***(235)***
Airline Suppliers Ass'n ***(235)***
Airport Minority Advisory Council ***(235)***
Akin, Gump, Strauss, Hauer & Feld, L.L.P. *(8)*
Alabama, Department of Transportation of the State of ***(235)***
Alameda Corridor Transportation Authority ***(236)***
Alameda Corridor-East Construction Authority ***(236)***
Alameda, California, County of ***(236)***
Alameda-Contra Costa Transit District ***(236)***
Alaska Air Group ***(236)***
Alaska Airlines ***(236)***
Albertine Enterprises, Inc. *(10)*
Albuquerque, New Mexico, City of ***(237)***
Alcalde & Fay *(10)*
Alcalde & Fay ***(237)***
Aldaron Inc. ***(238)***
Alexandria, Virginia, City of ***(238)***
Allegheny County Airport Authority ***(238)***
Allegheny County, Pennsylvania, Housing Authority ***(238)***
Alliance Air Services ***(239)***
The Alliance for I-69 Texas ***(239)***
Alliance of American Insurers ***(240)***
Alliance of Automobile Manufacturers, Inc. ***(240)***
Allied Pilots Ass'n ***(241)***
Allied Tube & Conduit Corp. ***(241)***
Alpine Group, Inc. *(11)*
Alvarado & Gerken *(12)*
Alyeska Pipeline Service Co. ***(242)***
Amalgamated Transit Union ***(242)***
American Ambulance Ass'n ***(245)***
American Ass'n of Motor Vehicle Administrators ***(248)***
American Ass'n of Port Authorities ***(249)***
American Automobile Ass'n ***(250)***
American Bar Ass'n ***(250)***
American Beverage Institute ***(251)***
American Boiler Manufacturers Ass'n ***(251)***
American Bus Ass'n ***(251)***
American Chemistry Council ***(252)***
American Concrete Pavement Ass'n (ACPA) ***(255)***
American Consulting Engineers Council ***(255)***
American Continental Group, Inc. *(12)*
American Council of Independent Laboratories ***(255)***
American Diabetes Ass'n ***(257)***
American Farm Bureau Federation ***(258)***
American Federation of State, County and Municipal Employees ***(258)***
American Federation of Teachers ***(259)***
American Feed Industry Ass'n ***(259)***
American Frozen Food Institute ***(260)***
American Great Lakes Ports ***(261)***
American Highway Users Alliance ***(262)***
American Honda Motor Co., Inc. ***(262)***
American Horse Council, Inc. ***(263)***
American Hotel and Lodging Ass'n ***(263)***
American Institute for Public Safety ***(264)***
American Institute for Shippers' Ass'ns ***(264)***
The American Institute of Architects ***(264)***
American Insurance Ass'n ***(264)***
American Legion ***(266)***
American Magline Group ***(266)***
American Maritime Officers Service ***(267)***
American Methanol Institute ***(268)***
American Motorcyclist Ass'n ***(268)***
American Moving and Storage Ass'n ***(268)***
American Petroleum Institute ***(269)***
American Planning Ass'n ***(270)***
American Plastics Council ***(270)***
American Portland Cement Alliance ***(270)***
American Public Transportation Ass'n ***(272)***
American Public Works Ass'n ***(272)***
American Rental Ass'n ***(272)***
American Road and Transportation Builders Ass'n (ARTBA) ***(273)***
American Shipbuilding Ass'n ***(274)***
American Short Line and Regional Railroad Ass'n ***(274)***
American Soc. of Civil Engineers ***(276)***
American Soybean Ass'n ***(277)***
American Teleservices Ass'n ***(279)***
American Trans Air ***(279)***
American Trucking Ass'ns ***(279)***
American Waterways Operators ***(280)***
American Wood Preservers Institute ***(280)***
Americans for Equitable Climate Solutions ***(281)***
Americans for Tax Reform ***(282)***
Anaheim, California, City of ***(283)***
Ancore Corp. ***(284)***
Jeffrey M. Anders *(13)*
Ann Eppard Associates, Ltd. ***(284)***
Anoka County Regional Railroad Authority ***(284)***
APG Army Alliance ***(286)***
APL Limited ***(286)***
Apple Valley, California, City of ***(286)***
The Arc ***(287)***
Arent Fox Kintner Plotkin & Kahn, PLLC *(14)*
ARINC, Inc. ***(288)***
Arizona Public Service Co. ***(288)***
Wayne Arny & Assoc. *(16)*
Arter & Hadden *(17)*
Ascension, Louisiana, Parish of ***(290)***
Ashland Inc. ***(290)***
James Nicholas Ashmore & Associates *(18)*
Ass'n for Commuter Transportation ***(292)***
Ass'n for Transportation, Law, Logistics and Policy ***(293)***
Ass'n of American Railroads ***(294)***
Ass'n of American Shippers ***(294)***
Ass'n of Bank Couriers ***(294)***
Ass'n of Financial Guaranty Insurers ***(295)***
Ass'n of Minnesota Counties ***(297)***
Ass'n of Oil Pipelines ***(297)***

Ass'n of Trial Lawyers of America (299)
Associated Builders and Contractors (300)
Associated Equipment Distributors (300)
Associated General Contractors of America (300)
Assumption College (300)
Ross Atkins (18)
ATOFINA Chemicals, Inc. (302)
Auburn University (302)
Austin, Texas, City of (303)
Automotive Aftermarket Industry Ass'n (303)
Automotive Parts and Service Alliance (303)
AutoNation, Inc. (304)
Bacino & Associates (19)
BAE Systems Controls (305)
Baise + Miller, P.C. (19)
Baker & Hostetler LLP (19)
Baker Botts, L.L.P. (20)
Baker, Donelson, Bearman & Caldwell, P.C. (21)
Balch & Bingham LLP (21)
Ball Janik, LLP (22)
Baltimore, Maryland, City of (306)
Bangor Internat'l Airport (307)
Barbour Griffith & Rogers, Inc. (22)
Barnes & Thornburg (23)
The Barton Co. (24)
Bass Hotels and Resorts, Inc. (308)
Baton Rouge, Louisiana, City of (308)
Battelle Memorial Institute (309)
Bay Area Rapid Transit District (309)
Bay County, Florida (309)
Beaumont, Texas, City of (310)
Bechtel Group, Inc. (310)
Bechtel/Parsons Brinkeroff Joint Venture (310)
Bergner Bockorny Castagnetti and Hawkins (26)
Bernalillo, New Mexico, County of (312)
Bethlehem Steel Corp. (312)
Terry Bevels Consulting (27)
Biomedical Research Foundation of Northwest Louisiana (314)
Birch, Horton, Bittner & Cherot (28)
Birmingham Airport Authority (314)
Bitrek Corp. (314)
BKSH & Associates (28)
Blank Rome Comisky & McCauley, LLP (29)
The Boeing Co. (316)
Bombardier Aerospace (317)
Bombardier Transportation/Bombardier Transit Corporation (317)
Bombardier, Inc. (317)
The Bond Market Ass'n (317)
Bourgas Intermodal Feasability Study (318)
Bowling Transportation (318)
Boys and Girls Clubs of America (318)
Bracy Williams & Co. (31)
Bradley Arant Rose & White LLP (31)
Brain Trauma Foundation (319)
Brand & Frulla, P.C. (32)
Brea, California, City of (319)
Briartek, Inc. (319)
Bridgeport, Connecticut, City of (320)
Bridgestone/Firestone, Inc. (320)
Brotherhood of Maintenance of Way Employees (322)
Brotherhood of Railroad Signalmen (322)
Broward, Florida, County of (322)
Brown and Company, Inc. (33)
Brownstein Hyatt & Farber, P.C. (33)
Brownsville, Texas, City of (322)
Brownsville, Texas, Port of (322)
John G. "Toby" Burke (34)
Burlington Northern Santa Fe Railway (324)
Butera & Andrews (34)
C F Industries, Inc. (325)
Caguas, Puerto Rico, City of (326)
Calhoun County Community Development (326)
California State Ass'n of Counties (327)
CALSTART (328)
Cambridge Management Inc. (328)
Cambridge Systematics, Inc (35)
Arthur E. Cameron (35)
Canadian Nat'l Railroad/Illinois Central Railroad (329)
Canadian Nat'l Railway Co. (329)
Canfield & Associates, Inc. (36)
Canton Railroad Co. (330)
Capital Area Transit Authority (330)
Capital City Economic Development Authority (330)
Capital Metropolitan Transportation Authority (330)
Capital Partnerships (VA) Inc. (37)
Capital Region Airport Commission (330)
Capitol Associates, Inc. (37)
Capitol Capital Group (38)
Capitol Counsel Group, L.L.C. (38)
Capitol Hill Advocates (39)
Capitol Link, Inc. (39)
CARFAX, Inc. (331)
Cargill, Inc. (331)
Carlson Wagonlit Travel, Inc. (332)
Robert E. Carlstrom (40)
Carmel, Indiana, City of (332)
The Carmen Group (40)
Carolina, Puerto Rico, City of (332)
Carpi & Clay (41)
The Carter Group (41)
Cartwright & Riley (41)
Cassidy & Associates, Inc. (42)
Cellar Door Amphitheaters (334)
CEMEX USA (335)
Center for Public Dialogue (337)
Central Basin Municipal Water District (338)
Central Ohio Regional Transit Authority (339)
Central Puget Sound Regional Transit Authority (Sound Transit) (339)
Century Tube Corp. (340)
Chamber of Commerce of the U.S.A. (340)
Chambers Associates Inc. (45)
Chambers, Conlon & Hartwell (45)
Carolyn C. Chaney & Associates (45)
Charter One (341)
Chatham Area Transit Authority (341)
Chicago Regional Transportation Authority (343)
Chicago Transit Authority (343)
Chino Hills, California, City of (345)
Christus Health (346)
Cincinnati, Ohio, City of (347)
Cinergy Corp. (347)
Citizen's Committee to Save the Federal Center (348)
Vern Clark & Associates (349)
Clark & Weinstock, Inc. (47)
Clark County, Nevada, Office of the County Manager (350)
Clark County-McCarran Internat'l Airport (350)
Clay and Associates (47)
Clearwater, Florida, City of (350)
William M. Cloherty (47)
CMC/Heartland Partnership (351)
CNF Transportation, Inc. (351)
Coach USA (352)
Coachella Valley Economic Partnership (352)
Coalition Against Bigger Trucks (352)
Coalition for Auto Repair Equality (CARE) (353)
Coalition for Fair Play in Ocean Shipping (353)
Coalition for Vehicle Choice (355)
Coalition of Hawaii Movers (355)
Coalition of Service Industries (355)
Coleman Powermate (357)
Colex and Associates (48)
Collier Shannon Scott, PLLC (48)
Colorado Ass'n of Transit Agencies (358)
Colorado Intermountain Fixed Guideway Authority (358)
Colorado, Department of Transportation of the State of (359)
Columbia, South Carolina, City of (359)
COMARCO Wireless Technology (359)
Committee on Pipe and Tube Imports (361)
Committee to Preserve Aspen (361)
Community Transit (363)
Community Transit Ass'n of Idaho (363)
Community Transportation Ass'n of America (363)
Condon and Forsyth (51)
Congressional Economic Leadership Institute (366)
Connecticut Resource Recovery Authority (367)
Construction Industry Manufacturers Ass'n (368)
Construction Industry Round Table, Inc. (368)
Construction Management Ass'n of America (368)
Consumer Energy Council of America Research Foundation (369)
Consumer Federation of America (369)
Consumers United for Rail Equity (369)
Continental Airlines Inc. (370)
Continental Teves (370)
Contract Services Ass'n of America (370)
Cook Inlet Region Inc. (371)
Copeland, Lowery & Jacquez (52)
Copeland, Lowery & Jacquez (371)
Corn Refiners Ass'n, Inc. (372)
Coronado, California, City of (372)
Corpus Christi Port Authority (373)
Corpus Christi Regional Transportation Authority (373)
Ernest J. Corrado (53)
Council on Radionuclides and Radiopharmaceuticals (CORAR) (377)
Crowley Maritime Corp. (379)
Crown American Realty Trust (379)
CSX Corp. (379)
CSX Lines LLC (379)
The Cullen Law Firm (56)
Currie Technologies, Inc. (380)
Law Offices of Kevin G. Curtin (56)
The Da Vinci Group (56)
Dade County Board of Commissioners (381)
DaimlerChrysler Corp. (381)
Dakota Minnesota and Eastern Railroad (381)
Dallas Area Rapid Transit Authority (382)
Dallas, Texas, City of (382)
Daniel, Mann, Johnson & Mendenhall (382)
Mary E. Davis (57)
Davis Wright Tremaine LLP (58)
Davison Transport, Inc. (383)
Dawson & Associates, Inc. (59)
Dayton, Ohio, Washington Office of the City of (383)
DBH Consulting (59)
DCH Technology Inc. (383)
Deerfield Beach, Florida, City of (383)
Defenders of Wildlife (383)
Delaware Otsego System (384)
Delaware River and Bay Authority (384)
Dell Computer Corp. (384)
Delta Air Lines (384)
Delta Development Group, Inc. (385)
George H. Denison (60)
Denton, Texas, City of (385)
Denton, Texas, County of (385)
Denver Regional Transportation District (385)
Denver, Colorado, City and County of (386)
Denver, Regional Transportation District of (386)
Design-Build Institute of America (386)
Detroit Metropolitan Airport (386)
Detroit, Michigan, City of (386)
Dewey Ballantine LLP (61)
Dewey Square Group (61)
Diamond Antenna & Microwave Corp. (387)
Distilled Spirits Council of the United States, Inc. (389)
Doepken Keevican & Weiss (63)
Domino's Pizza (391)
Dorfman & O'Neal, Inc. (63)
Dorsey & Whitney LLP (63)
The Dow Chemical Co. (391)
Dow, Lohnes & Albertson, PLLC (64)
Dredging Contractors of America (392)
DRS Technologies, Inc. (392)
Duke Energy (392)
Dulles Area Transportation Ass'n (393)
Durham, North Carolina, City of (393)
The Dutko Group, Inc. (68)
Dyer Ellis & Joseph, P.C. (68)
Dykema Gossett PLLC (69)
Eagle-Picher Industries (394)
Easter Seals (395)
Eckert Seamans Cherin & Mellott, LLC (70)
Eclipse Energy Systems, Inc./Insyte, Inc. (396)
Economic Development Alliance of Jefferson County, Arkansas (396)
Edington, Peel & Associates, Inc. (70)
Edison Electric Institute (397)
Edison Internat'l (397)

El Paso Corporation ***(399)***
El Segundo, California, City of ***(399)***
Electric Transportation Co. ***(400)***
The Electric Vehicle Ass'n of the Americas (EVAA) ***(400)***
Adam Emanuel and Associates *(71)*
Energy Absorption Systems, Inc. ***(403)***
Engineered Arresting Systems Corp. ***(403)***
Enron Corp. ***(403)***
ENS Resources, Inc. *(71)*
Environmental Defense Fund ***(405)***
Ann Eppard Associates, Ltd. *(72)*
Erie Internat'l Airport ***(406)***
Ervin Technical Associates, Inc. (ETA) *(73)*
Eugene, Oregon, City of ***(407)***
EV Rental Cars, LLC ***(408)***
Everett, Washington, Port of ***(408)***
Exelon Corp. ***(409)***
Express One Internat'l Inc. ***(409)***
Exxon Mobil Corp. ***(409)***
F&T Network, Inc. *(74)*
Fairbanks, Alaska, North Star Borough of ***(410)***
Fairfax, Virginia, County of ***(410)***
Fairfield, California, City of ***(410)***
Fajardo, Puerto Rico, Municipality of ***(410)***
Fannie Mae ***(411)***
Farmers Branch, Texas, City of ***(412)***
Farmland Industries, Inc. ***(412)***
Marcus G. Faust, P.C. *(74)*
G.W. Fauth & Associates Inc. *(74)*
Federal Health Strategies, Inc. *(75)*
FedEx Corp. ***(415)***
Frank Fenton *(75)*
Jack Ferguson Associates, Inc. *(75)*
The Ferguson Group, LLC *(76)*
The Fertilizer Institute ***(415)***
Fisher Consulting *(77)*
Fleet Reserve Ass'n ***(418)***
Flight Safety Technologies, Inc. ***(419)***
R. G. Flippo and Associates, Inc. *(77)*
FLIR Systems, Inc. ***(419)***
Florida East Coast Industries Inc. ***(419)***
Florida State University System ***(420)***
Fluor Corp. ***(420)***
Foley & Lardner *(78)*
Folsom, California, City of ***(421)***
Fontana, California, City of ***(421)***
Food Distributors Internat'l (NAWGA-IFDA) ***(421)***
Food Research and Action Center ***(422)***
Ford Motor Co. ***(422)***
Henry Ford Museum in Greenfield Village ***(422)***
Forster & Associates *(79)*
Fort Smith Regional Airport ***(423)***
Fort Wayne, Indiana, City of ***(423)***
Fort Worth Transportation Authority ***(423)***
Frederick Area Committee on Transportation (FACT) ***(425)***
French & Company *(79)*
Fresno, California, City of ***(426)***
Friedlob, Sanderson, Raskin, Paulson, Toutillott ***(426)***
Friends of ITS/ITS America ***(426)***
FuelMaker Corp. ***(427)***
The Furman Group *(80)*
G.R. Services *(80)*
Gainesville, Florida, City of ***(428)***
Gallagher, Boland and Meiburger *(80)*
Ernest & Julio Gallo Winery ***(428)***
Sara Garland (and Associates) *(81)*
Gary Public Transportation Corp. ***(429)***
Gary, Indiana, Washington Office of the City of ***(429)***
Gas Research Institute ***(429)***
Gateway Cities ***(430)***
General Dynamics Corp. ***(431)***
General Electric Co. ***(432)***
General Motors Corp. ***(432)***
Geneva Steel Co. ***(433)***
George Washington University, Office of Government Relations ***(434)***
The Georgetown Partnership ***(434)***
Georgia Ports Authority ***(434)***
Georgia-Pacific Corp. ***(434)***
GHL Inc. *(82)*
Glankler Brown, PLLC ***(435)***
Global Encasement, Inc. ***(436)***
Goldman, Sachs and Co. ***(437)***
Goodyear Tire and Rubber Co. ***(437)***
Gordley Associates *(84)*
Government Relations, Inc. *(84)*
GPC Internat'l *(85)*
Edmund C. Graber *(85)*
Jay Grant & Associates *(85)*
Charles H. Graves & Associates *(86)*
Great Lakes Corporate Resources ***(439)***
Great Lakes Dredge & Dock ***(439)***
Great Projects Film Co., Inc. ***(439)***
Greater Cleveland Regional Transit Authority ***(439)***
Greater New Orleans Expressway Commission ***(439)***
Greater Orlando Aviation Authority ***(439)***
Greater Washington Board of Trade ***(439)***
Greenberg Traurig, LLP *(86)*
Greyhound Lines ***(440)***
Griffin, Johnson, Dover & Stewart *(87)*
The Grizzle Company *(88)*
Grove, Jaskiewicz, and Cobert *(88)*
Grumman Olson ***(441)***
Guam Internat'l Airport Authority ***(441)***
Guam, Washington Office of the Governor ***(442)***
Guaynabo, Puerto Rico, City of ***(442)***
Guinea, Secretary General of the Presidency of the Republic of ***(442)***
Gulfstream Aerospace Corp. ***(442)***
Haarmann & Reimer Corp. ***(443)***
Hall, Green, Rupli, LLC *(90)*
Martin G. Hamberger & Associates *(91)*
Charles A. Hamilton Associates LLC *(91)*
Hannibal Industries ***(444)***
John D. Hardy *(91)*
Hargett Consulting *(91)*
Harlingen Area Chamber of Commerce ***(444)***
G.E. Harris Harmon ***(445)***
Harris, Beach & Wilcox ***(445)***
Frederic R. Harris, Inc. ***(445)***
Harris, Texas, Metropolitan Transit Authority of ***(445)***
The Hartford ***(445)***
Hattiesburg, Mississippi, City of ***(445)***
Heavy Vehicle Maintenance Group ***(447)***
Hecht, Spencer & Associates *(93)*
Law Office of Edward D. Heffernan *(94)*
Henderson, Nevada, City of ***(448)***
Dennis M. Hertel & Associates *(94)*
Hesperia, California, City of ***(449)***
High Speed Ground Transportation Ass'n ***(449)***
Highway 53 Longrange Improvement Citizens' Task Force ***(449)***
Hillsborough Area Regional Transit Authority ***(450)***
Hillsborough, Florida, County of ***(450)***
Hillwood Development Corp. ***(450)***
HKC, Inc. ***(450)***
Hogan & Hartson L.L.P. *(96)*
Hohlt & Associates *(98)*
Holland & Knight LLP *(98)*
The Home Depot ***(451)***
Honberger and Walters, Inc. *(99)*
Honeywell Internat'l, Inc. ***(452)***
Honolulu Shipyard ***(452)***
Hood River, Oregon, Port of ***(452)***
Hooper Owen & Winburn *(99)*
Hoover Partners *(100)*
Houston Galveston Area Council ***(453)***
Houston, Texas, City of ***(453)***
Houston, Texas, Port Authority of the City of ***(453)***
Howland Hook Container Terminal Inc. ***(454)***
Hualapai Nation ***(454)***
R. J. Hudson Associates *(101)*
Humboldt Harbor Recreation ***(455)***
Hunton & Williams *(101)*
Huntsville, Alabama, City of ***(455)***
Huntsville-Madison County Airport ***(455)***
Hurt, Norton & Associates *(101)*
I-69 Mid-Continent Highway Coalition ***(456)***
Iberville Parish ***(456)***
Ice Ban America, Inc. ***(456)***
The Ickes & Enright Group *(102)*
The ILEX Group *(102)*
Illinois Department of Transportation ***(457)***
Illinois Public Transit Ass'n (IPTA) ***(458)***
IMC Global Inc. ***(458)***
Indiana County Development Corp. ***(460)***
Indiana Department of Transportation ***(460)***
Indiana, Office of the Governor of the State of ***(460)***
Indianapolis Public Transportation Corp. ***(460)***
Indianapolis Rail Project ***(460)***
Information Technology Industry Council ***(462)***
Infrastructure Management Group *(103)*
Ingalls Shipbuilding ***(462)***
Inglewood, California, City of ***(462)***
Intelligent Transportation Soc. of America ***(465)***
Interactive Digital Software Ass'n ***(466)***
Intermodal Ass'n of North America ***(467)***
Internat'l Ass'n of Bridge, Structural, Ornamental and Reinforcing Iron Workers ***(467)***
Internat'l Ass'n of Fire Chiefs ***(468)***
Internat'l Ass'n of Machinists and Aerospace Workers ***(468)***
Internat'l Biometric Industry Ass'n ***(468)***
Internat'l Bridge, Tunnel and Turnpike Ass'n ***(469)***
Internat'l Brotherhood of Boilermakers, Iron Shipbuilders, Blacksmiths, Forgers and Helpers ***(469)***
Internat'l Brotherhood of Electrical Workers ***(469)***
Internat'l Brotherhood of Teamsters ***(469)***
Internat'l Council of Cruise Lines ***(470)***
Internat'l Downtown Ass'n ***(471)***
Internat'l Federation of Professional and Technical Engineers ***(471)***
Internat'l Lead Zinc Research Organization, Inc. (ILZRO) ***(473)***
Internat'l Longshore and Warehouse Union ***(473)***
Internat'l Mass Retailers Ass'n ***(473)***
Internat'l Olympic Committee ***(473)***
Internat'l Union of Operating Engineers ***(476)***
Internat'l Union of Painters and Allied Trades ***(476)***
Interstate 5 Consortium ***(477)***
Interstate Natural Gas Ass'n of America ***(477)***
Iowa Public Transit Ass'n ***(478)***
IPSCO Tubulars, Inc. ***(478)***
Iran Air ***(478)***
The Irvine Co. ***(479)***
Jackson County, Mississippi Board of Supervisors ***(480)***
Jackson Municipal Airport Authority ***(480)***
Jackson, Mississippi, City of ***(480)***
Jacksonville, Florida, City of ***(481)***
Jacksonville, Florida, Port Authority of the City of ***(481)***
Jacobs Engineering Group Inc. ***(481)***
Jamison and Sullivan, Inc. *(104)*
Japan Automobile Standards Internat'l Center ***(481)***
JCP Associates *(105)*
JDA Aviation Technology Systems ***(482)***
Jefferson Government Relations, L.L.C. *(106)*
Jefferson Parish Council ***(482)***
JM Family Enterprises ***(483)***
S.C. Johnson and Son, Inc. ***(484)***
Johnson Co. *(107)*
Johnston & Associates, LLC *(107)*
Joint Powers Board ***(484)***
Joint Southeast Public Improvement Council ***(484)***
Jones, Walker, Waechter, Poitevent, Carrere & Denegre, L.L.P. *(108)*
Jordan & Associates, Inc. *(109)*
Jorden Burt LLP *(109)*
JSA-I, Inc. *(109)*
Kaiser Aluminum & Chemical Corp. ***(485)***
Betty Ann Kane & Co. *(110)*
Kansas City Area Transportation Authority ***(486)***
Kansas City Southern Industries ***(486)***
Kansas City Southern Railway Co. ***(486)***
Kansas Public Transit Ass'n ***(486)***
Keller and Heckman LLP *(111)*
Keller Equity Group, Inc. ***(487)***
Kellogg Brown and Root ***(487)***
Kellogg Co. ***(487)***
The Kemper Co. *(111)*
Kent & O'Connor, Inc. *(112)*
Kentucky, Commonwealth of ***(488)***

North Carolina, Washington Office of the State of ***(593)***
North Dakota State University ***(593)***
North Dakota, Governor's Office of the State of ***(593)***
North Metro Mayors Coalition ***(593)***
North Miami Beach, Florida, City of ***(593)***
North San Diego County Transit Development Board ***(593)***
Northeast Illinois Regional Commuter Railroad Corp. ***(593)***
Northeast Ohio Areawide Coordination Agency (NOACA) ***(593)***
Northeast-Midwest Institute ***(594)***
Northern Air Cargo ***(594)***
Northrop Grumman Corp. ***(594)***
Northwest Airlines, Inc. ***(595)***
Nossaman, Gunther, Knox & Elliott ***(596)***
NOW Solutions, Inc. ***(596)***
Oakland, California, City of ***(598)***
Oakland, California, Port of ***(598)***
Oakland, Michigan, County of ***(598)***
Obadal and MacLeod, p.c. *(143)*
Ocean Shipholding, Inc. ***(598)***
O'Connor & Hannan, L.L.P. *(144)*
O'Donnell, Schwartz & Anderson, P.C. *(145)*
Bartley M. O'Hara *(145)*
Oklahoma City, Oklahoma, City of ***(599)***
Oklahoma Department of Transportation ***(599)***
Oldaker and Harris, LLP *(146)*
O'Malley, Miles, Nylen & Gilmore, P.A. *(147)*
O'Melveny and Myers LLP *(147)*
O'Neill, Athy & Casey, P.C. *(147)*
Oppenheimer Wolff & Donnelly LLP *(147)*
Orange County Transportation Authority ***(602)***
Orange, California, County of ***(602)***
Orbital Sciences Corp. ***(602)***
ORBITZ ***(602)***
Oregon Department of Transportation ***(603)***
Oregon Economic Development Department ***(603)***
Orincon Corp. ***(603)***
Osceola, Florida, County of ***(604)***
Ouachita Parish Police Jury ***(604)***
Outdoor Advertising Ass'n of America ***(604)***
Owner-Operator Independent Drivers Ass'n, Inc. ***(605)***
Oxnard Harbor District ***(605)***
Oxnard, California, City of ***(605)***
PACCAR, Inc. ***(605)***
PACE-CAPSTONE *(148)*
Pacific Coast Council of Customs Brokers and Freight Forwarders Ass'n ***(605)***
Pacquing Consulting Inc. *(148)*
Palm Beach, Florida, County of ***(606)***
Palm Beach, Florida, Port of ***(606)***
Palmdale, California, City of ***(606)***
The Palmer Group *(149)*
Palo Alto, California, City of ***(607)***
Palumbo & Cerrell, Inc. *(149)*
Paralyzed Veterans of America ***(607)***
Pardee Construction Co. ***(608)***
Parker Hannifin Corp. ***(608)***
Parsons Brinckerhoff Inc. ***(608)***
Parsons Corp. ***(608)***
Pasadena, California, City of ***(609)***
Jim Pasco & Associates *(150)*
Patton Boggs, LLP *(150)*
Paul, Hastings, Janofsky & Walker LLP *(153)*
J. C. Penney Co., Inc. ***(611)***
Pennington BioMedical Research Center ***(611)***
Pennsylvania Pyrotechnics Ass'n ***(611)***
Pennzoil-Quaker State Co. ***(611)***
Susan B. Perry *(155)*
Pet Industry Joint Advisory Council ***(613)***
Peterson Cos., Inc. ***(613)***
The Peterson Group *(155)*
The Petrizzo Group, Inc. *(155)*
Petroleum Heat and Power Co., Inc. ***(613)***
Peyser Associates, Inc. *(155)*
Pfizer, Inc. ***(613)***
Philadelphia Industrial Development Corp. ***(615)***
Philadelphia Internat'l Airport ***(615)***
Philadelphia Zoo ***(615)***
Philadelphia, Pennsylvania, City of ***(615)***
Philip Morris Management Corp. ***(615)***
Phillips Petroleum Co. ***(616)***
Phoenix, Arizona, City of ***(616)***
Piedmont Environmental Council ***(617)***
Pierce Transit ***(617)***
Pine Bluff Sand and Gravel Co. ***(617)***
Pinnacle West Capital Corp. ***(617)***
Plano, Texas, City of ***(619)***
Playa Vista ***(619)***
Plumbing, Heating, Cooling Contractors- National Assoc. ***(619)***
The PMA Group *(156)*
PMSC-Irby Steel ***(619)***
Podesta/Mattoon *(158)*
Polar Air Cargo, Inc. ***(620)***
Polk County, Oregon ***(620)***
Port Authority of New York and New Jersey ***(621)***
Port of Lake Charles ***(621)***
Port of San Diego ***(621)***
Portals Development Associates L.P. ***(621)***
Portland, Oregon, City of ***(621)***
Potomac Electric Power Co. ***(622)***
Potomac Group *(160)*
Potters Industries, Inc. ***(622)***
Powell, Goldstein, Frazer & Murphy LLP *(160)*
PPL ***(622)***
Praxair, Inc. ***(623)***
Preston Gates Ellis & Rouvelas Meeds LLP *(162)*
Prince George's, Maryland, County of ***(624)***
Prince William County, Virginia ***(624)***
Professional Airways Systems Specialists (AFL-CIO) ***(625)***
Professional Aviation Maintenance Ass'n ***(625)***
Professional Services Council ***(626)***
Provideo Productions ***(627)***
Provo, Utah, City of ***(627)***
PSE&G ***(627)***
Public Affairs Resources, Inc. *(164)*
Public Citizen, Inc. ***(628)***
Public Strategies Washington, Inc. *(164)*
Puerto Rico, Commonwealth of ***(629)***
Pulse Medical Instruments ***(630)***
Put-in-Bay Boat Line Co. ***(630)***
Qualimetrics, Inc. ***(630)***
Rail Supply and Service Coalition ***(632)***
Rails to Trails Conservancy ***(632)***
Railway Progress Institute ***(632)***
Robert A. Rapoza Associates *(165)*
Pamela Ray-Strunk and Associates *(166)*
Raytheon Co. ***(633)***
George Reagle *(166)*
Recreation Vehicle Ass'n ***(634)***
Recreation Vehicle Industry Ass'n ***(635)***
Red River Trade Council ***(635)***
Redfern Resources *(166)*
Redwood City, California, Port of ***(635)***
Reed, Smith, LLP *(167)*
Regional Airport Authority of Louisville & Jefferson Co. ***(635)***
Regional Planning Commission ***(635)***
Regional Public Tansportation Authority ***(635)***
Regional Transit Authority ***(636)***
Regional Transportation Commission ***(636)***
Regional Transportation Commission of South Nevada ***(636)***
Results Cubed *(168)*
Reusable Industrial Packaging Ass'n ***(639)***
Rickenbacker Port Authority ***(640)***
Riverside County Transportation Commission ***(640)***
Riverside, California, City of ***(640)***
Riviera Beach, Florida, City of ***(640)***
Roaring Fork Railroad Holding Authority ***(641)***
Robertson, Monagle & Eastaugh *(170)*
Robison Internat'l, Inc. *(170)*
Rodriguez O'Donnell Fuerst Gonzalez & Williams *(171)*
Barbara J. Rohde *(171)*
Roquette America ***(642)***
Peter J. Rose *(172)*
Roseville, California, City of ***(642)***
The Roth Group *(172)*
RSR Corp. ***(643)***
The Ruan Companies ***(643)***
Rubber Manufacturers Ass'n ***(643)***
Rutgers University ***(644)***
Ryan, Phillips, Utrecht & MacKinnon *(173)*
Ryder System, Inc. ***(644)***
Sabre Inc. ***(644)***
Sacramento, California, City of ***(645)***
Sacramento, California, Public Works Agency of the County of ***(645)***
Safegate Internat'l AB ***(645)***
Safetran Systems Corp. ***(645)***
Safety Harbor, Florida, City of ***(645)***
Safety Warning System, L.C. ***(645)***
Sagamore Associates, Inc. *(174)*
Salinas, California, City of ***(646)***
Salt Institute ***(646)***
Salt Lake City Olympic Organizing Committee ***(646)***
Salt Lake City, Utah, City of ***(646)***
Salt River Project ***(646)***
San Bernardino Associated Governments ***(647)***
San Diego Ass'n of Governments ***(647)***
San Diego Metropolitan Transit Development Board ***(647)***
San Diego, California, City of ***(647)***
San Francisco, California, City and County of ***(648)***
San Joaquin Council of Governments ***(648)***
San Joaquin Regional Rail Commission ***(648)***
San Joaquin Regional Transit District ***(648)***
San Jose, California, City of ***(648)***
San Juan, Puerto Rico, City of ***(648)***
Santa Ana, California, City of ***(649)***
Santa Barbara Electric Transit Institute ***(649)***
Santa Barbara Metropolitan Transit District ***(649)***
Santa Clara Valley Transportation Authority ***(649)***
Santa Clarita, California, City of ***(649)***
Santa Cruz County Regional Transportation Commission ***(649)***
Santa Cruz Metropolitan Transit District ***(649)***
Santa Monica, California, City of ***(649)***
Sappi Fine Paper NA ***(649)***
SCANA Corp. ***(651)***
Scenic America ***(651)***
Schagrin Associates *(175)*
Schnader Harrison Segal & Lewis LLP *(176)*
Science Applications Internat'l Corp. (SAIC) ***(652)***
Scottsdale, Arizona, City of ***(652)***
Seaboard Corp. ***(653)***
Seattle, Washington, City of ***(653)***
Sellery Associates, Inc. *(177)*
SEMCO ***(655)***
Sense Technologies, Inc. ***(655)***
Sensis Corp. ***(655)***
Sharon Tube Co. ***(657)***
Shell Oil Co. ***(657)***
Shipbuilders Council of America ***(657)***
Shreveport, Louisiana, City of ***(658)***
Shutler and Low *(180)*
Siemens Transportation Systems, Inc. ***(658)***
Sierra Madre, California, City of ***(658)***
Silverberg, Goldman & Bikoff, LLP *(180)*
Simon and Co., Inc. *(181)*
Simon Strategies/Mindbeam *(181)*
Simula, Inc. ***(659)***
Skadden, Arps, Slate, Meagher & Flom LLP *(181)*
Slagle & Associates *(182)*
Smith & Harroff, Inc. *(182)*
E. Del Smith and Co. *(183)*
Smith Dawson & Andrews, Inc. *(183)*
Snack Food Ass'n ***(662)***
Craig Snyder & Associates *(185)*
Soc. of American Florists ***(663)***
Societe Air France ***(664)***
Solutia Inc. ***(665)***
Sonoma, California, County of ***(665)***
Sound Transit ***(666)***
South Carolina Department of Transportation ***(666)***
South Carolina Research Authority ***(666)***
Southeast Business Partnership ***(667)***
Southeastern Michigan Council of Government ***(667)***
Southeastern Pennsylvania Transit Authority ***(667)***
Southern California Ass'n of Governments ***(667)***
Southern California Regional Rail Authority ***(667)***
Southern Illinois University ***(668)***
Southern Tier Cement Committee ***(668)***

Space Access *(668)*
SPD Technologies *(669)*
Special Vehicle Coalition *(669)*
Specialized Carriers and Rigging Ass'n *(669)*
Specialty Equipment Market Ass'n *(670)*
Specialty Steel Industry of North America *(670)*
The Spectrum Group *(186)*
Richard L. Spees, Inc. *(186)*
St. Louis, Minnesota, Board of Commissioners of the County *(672)*
St. Louis, Missouri, City of *(672)*
St. Louis/Lake Counties Regional Rail Authority *(672)*
St. Paul, Minnesota, City of *(672)*
Stafford, Virginia, County of *(672)*
Steel Manufacturers Ass'n *(674)*
Stephens Law Firm *(188)*
Stephens Law Offices *(188)*
Steptoe & Johnson LLP *(188)*
Stilwell Financial Inc. *(674)*
Kenneth F. Stinger *(189)*
Stoll Stoll Berne Lokting & Shlachter, P.C. *(675)*
Stone and Webster Engineering Corp. *(675)*
Strat@Comm (Strategic Communications Counselors) *(189)*
Strategic Horizons Advisors, L.L.C. *(189)*
Suburban Mobility Authority for Regional Transportation *(676)*
Suffolk, New York, County of *(676)*
Francis J. Sullivan Associates *(190)*
Swidler Berlin Shereff Friedman, LLP *(191)*
Synthetic Organic Chemical Manufacturers Ass'n *(679)*
Tacoma, Washington, Port of *(680)*
Tampa Port Authority *(680)*
Tampa, Florida, City of *(680)*
Tate-LeMunyon, LLC *(192)*
Taxicab, Limousine and Paratransit Ass'n *(681)*
The Technical Group LLC *(192)*
TECO Energy, Inc. *(682)*
Temsco Helicopter, Inc. *(683)*
Tensiodyne Scientific Corp. *(684)*
Tensor Technologies, Inc. *(684)*
Texaco Group Inc. *(684)*
Texas A&M Research Foundation *(684)*
Textron Inc. *(685)*
Thelen Reid & Priest LLP *(685)*
Thelen Reid & Priest LLP *(193)*
Thiokol Propulsion *(686)*
Thompson and Naughton, Inc. *(194)*
Thompson Coburn LLP *(194)*
Time Domain Corp. *(687)*
Tire Ass'n of North America *(687)*
Todd Shipyards Inc. *(688)*
Tongour Simpson Holsclaw Green *(196)*
Traffic.com *(689)*
Trajen, Inc. *(689)*
Trans World Airlines, Inc. *(689)*
TransOceanic Shipping *(690)*
Transport Workers Union of America, AFL-CIO *(690)*
Transportation Corridor Agencies *(690)*
Transportation District Commission of Hampton Roads *(690)*
Transportation Institute *(690)*
Transportation Intermediaries Ass'n *(690)*
Transportation Reform Alliance *(690)*
Transportation-Communications Internat'l Union *(691)*
Transrapid Internat'l *(691)*
Travelocity.com *(691)*
Tri-City Regional Port District *(691)*
Tri-County Commuter Rail Authority *(691)*
TRI-MET Tri-County Metropolitan Transportation *(691)*
Triad Design Group *(691)*
Truck Manufacturers Ass'n *(692)*
Truck Renting and Leasing Ass'n *(693)*
Truck Trailer Manufacturers Ass'n *(693)*
Trust for Public Land *(693)*
TTX Co. *(693)*
Tulane University *(693)*
David Turch & Associates *(197)*
U.S. Clay Producers Traffic Ass'n *(696)*
U.S. Strategies Corp. *(197)*
UniGroup, Inc. *(698)*
Union of Concerned Scientists *(699)*
Union Pacific *(699)*
Union Pacific Railroad Co. *(699)*
Union Switch and Signal, Inc. *(699)*
UniServe Inc. *(700)*
United Airlines *(700)*
United Brotherhood of Carpenters and Joiners of America *(700)*
United Motorcoach Ass'n *(702)*
United Parcel Service *(702)*
United Special Transport Air Resources, LLC (USTAR) *(703)*
United Technologies Corp. *(704)*
United Transportation Union *(705)*
University of Missouri *(706)*
Upland, California, City of *(708)*
US Airways *(709)*
USFHP Conference Group *(710)*
USX Corp. *(710)*
Utah Department of Transportation *(710)*
Utah State University *(710)*
Utah Transit Authority *(710)*
Valis Associates *(198)*
Van Ness Feldman, P.C. *(199)*
Van Scoyoc Associates, Inc. *(711)*
Van Scoyoc Associates, Inc. *(200)*
Venable *(201)*
Venetian Casino Resort, LLC *(712)*
Veridian Corp. *(712)*
Veridian Engineering *(713)*
Verner, Liipfert, Bernhard, McPherson and Hand, Chartered *(202)*
Vest Inc. *(714)*
City of Victorville Redevelopment Agency *(715)*
Victorville, California, City of *(715)*
Vierra Associates, Inc. *(204)*
Viohl and Associates, Inc. *(205)*
Virgin Atlantic Airways *(715)*
Virginia Beach, Virginia, City of *(715)*
Virginia Tech Intellectual Properties, Inc. *(716)*
Vivendi Universal *(717)*
Volkswagen, AG *(717)*
Volusia, Florida, County of *(717)*
Waesche, Sheinbaum, and O'Regan *(718)*
Waggoner Engineering, Inc. *(718)*
Wake, North Carolina, County of *(718)*
Washington Alliance Group, Inc. *(206)*
Washington Aviation Group *(206)*
Washington Consulting Alliance, Inc. *(206)*
Washington Consulting Group *(719)*
Washington County, Oregon, Land Use and Transportation of *(719)*
Washington Flyer Taxi Drivers Ass'n, Inc. *(719)*
Washington Gas *(719)*
The Washington Group *(208)*
Washington Group Internat'l *(719)*
Washington Infrastructure Services, Inc. *(719)*
Washington Metropolitan Area Transit Authority *(720)*
Washington Parking Ass'n *(720)*
Washington Resource Associates *(209)*
Washington, Department of Transportation of the State of *(721)*
Washoe County Regional Transportation Commission *(721)*
Waterman & Associates *(210)*
Wayne, Michigan, County of *(722)*
Weirton Steel Corp. *(722)*
Wendella Sightseeing Boats Inc. *(723)*
West Lafayette, Indiana, City of *(723)*
West Valley City, Utah *(723)*
Western Research Institute *(724)*
Western Tube & Conduit Co. *(724)*
The Wexler Group *(211)*
Weyerhaeuser Co. *(725)*
Wheat & Associates, Inc. *(212)*
Wheat Export Trade Education Committee *(725)*
Wheatland Tube Co. *(725)*
Whitten & Diamond *(213)*
Wiley, Rein & Fielding *(214)*
Williams & Jensen, P.C. *(215)*
The Williams Companies *(727)*
James M. Williams, Jr. *(217)*
Kathleen Winn & Associates, Inc. *(218)*
Winston & Strawn *(218)*
Womble Carlyle Sandridge & Rice, P.C. *(220)*
Women Officials in NACo *(729)*
World Shipping Council *(731)*
Xcellsis Corp. *(732)*
Yakima, Washington, City of *(732)*
Zachery Taylor Parkway Commission *(734)*
ZapWorld.com *(734)*
Zuckert, Scoutt and Rasenberger, L.L.P. *(735)*
Zuckert, Scoutt and Rasenberger, L.L.P. *(221)*

Travel/Tourism (TOU)

The Aegis Group, Ltd. *(7)*
Air China Internat'l Corp., Ltd. *(233)*
Air Pacific Ltd. *(234)*
Akin, Gump, Strauss, Hauer & Feld, L.L.P. *(8)*
Albertine Enterprises, Inc. *(10)*
Alcalde & Fay *(10)*
Allegheny County Airport Authority *(238)*
Alsatian American Chamber of Commerce *(242)*
American Ass'n of Museums *(248)*
American Automobile Ass'n *(250)*
American Bus Ass'n *(251)*
American Continental Group, Inc. *(12)*
American Council of Korean Travel Agents *(255)*
American Express Co. *(258)*
American Hotel and Lodging Ass'n *(263)*
American Planning Ass'n *(270)*
American Recreation Coalition *(272)*
American Resort Development Ass'n *(272)*
American Soc. of Ass'n Executives *(275)*
American Soc. of Travel Agents *(277)*
American Symphony Orchestra League *(278)*
American Teleservices Ass'n *(279)*
American Trans Air *(279)*
Americans for Better Borders *(281)*
APCO Worldwide *(14)*
The Argus Group, L.L.C. *(16)*
Wayne Arny & Assoc. *(16)*
Ass'n of Retail Travel Agents *(298)*
Bass Hotels and Resorts, Inc. *(308)*
Birch, Horton, Bittner & Cherot *(28)*
BKSH & Associates *(28)*
Boesch & Co. *(29)*
Brand & Frulla, P.C. *(32)*
Calaveras County, California, Water District *(326)*
Capital Children's Museum *(330)*
Carlson Wagonlit Travel, Inc. *(332)*
The Carmen Group *(40)*
Carpi & Clay *(41)*
Cendant Corp. *(335)*
Chesapeake Bay Maritime Museum *(342)*
China Eastern Airlines *(344)*
Cincinnati, Ohio, City of *(347)*
Clark & Weinstock, Inc. *(47)*
Coalition for Travel Industry Parity *(354)*
Cohen, Gettings & Dunham, PC *(48)*
Condon and Forsyth *(51)*
Consumer Federation of America *(369)*
Coushatta Tribe of Louisiana *(377)*
Cruising America Coalition *(379)*
CSX Corp. *(379)*
The Da Vinci Group *(56)*
Delta Air Lines *(384)*
DFS Group Ltd. *(387)*
Doepken Keevican & Weiss *(63)*
Domino's Pizza *(391)*
Dow, Lohnes & Albertson, PLLC *(64)*
Dublin Castle Group *(66)*
Eureka, California, City of *(408)*
Evans & Black, Inc. *(73)*
Fort Sumter Tours *(423)*
Golf Course Superintendents Ass'n of America *(437)*
Grand Canyon Air Tour Council *(438)*
John C. Grzebien *(89)*
Guam, Washington Office of the Governor *(442)*
Guinea, Secretary General of the Presidency of the Republic of *(442)*
Hall, Green, Rupli, LLC *(90)*
Hattiesburg, Mississippi, City of *(445)*
Heritage Harbor Museum *(449)*
Higgins, McGovern & Smith, LLC *(94)*
Hohlt & Associates *(98)*

Holland America West-Tours *(450)*
Holy Land Trust *(451)*
Hotel Employees and Restaurant Employees Internat'l Union *(453)*
R. J. Hudson Associates *(101)*
Humboldt Bay Municipal Water District *(455)*
IATA U.S. Frequent Flyer Tax Interest Group *(456)*
IMPACT, LLC *(102)*
Internat'l Air Transport Ass'n *(467)*
Internat'l Downtown Ass'n *(471)*
Internat'l Snowmobile Manufacturers Ass'n *(474)*
Iran Air *(478)*
Jacksonville, Florida, City of *(481)*
Jefferson Government Relations, L.L.C. *(106)*
Johnson Co. *(107)*
Johnston & Associates, LLC *(107)*
Robert E. Juliano Associates *(109)*
Kimberly Consulting, LLC *(113)*
Las Vegas Convention and Visitors Authority *(495)*
Link Romania, Inc. *(500)*
Management Options, Inc. *(123)*
Marine Engineers Beneficial Ass'n (District No. 1 - PCD) *(510)*
Mercury Group *(132)*
Motorcycle Industry Council *(531)*
The MWW Group *(140)*
Nat'l Ass'n of RV Parks and Campgrounds *(548)*
Nat'l Building Museum *(553)*
Nat'l Consumers League *(558)*
Nat'l Grain and Feed Ass'n *(566)*
Nat'l Liberty Museum *(570)*
Nat'l Licensed Beverage Ass'n *(570)*
Nat'l Park Hospitality Ass'n *(573)*
Nat'l Restaurant Ass'n *(576)*
Nat'l Tour Ass'n *(579)*
NAVCOM Systems, Inc. *(583)*
Neuman and Co. *(141)*
Nevada, Washington Office of the State of *(585)*
New Sea Escape *(586)*
North Carolina, Washington Office of the State of *(593)*
Northwest Airlines, Inc. *(595)*
Obadal and MacLeod, p.c. *(143)*
David O'Brien and Associates *(143)*
Ocean County, NJ Utilities Authority *(598)*
Ogletree Governmental Affairs, Inc. *(145)*
Oscoda Management *(604)*
Palumbo & Cerrell, Inc. *(149)*
Patton Boggs, LLP *(150)*
Pfizer, Inc. *(613)*
Please Touch Museum, The Children's Museum of Philadelphia *(619)*
Port of San Diego *(621)*
Potomac Heritage Partnership *(622)*
Premier Parks, Inc. *(623)*
Preservation Action *(623)*
Preston Gates Ellis & Rouvelas Meeds LLP *(623)*
Princess Cruise Lines *(624)*
Recreation Vehicle Dealers Ass'n of North America *(634)*
Reed, Smith, LLP *(167)*
The Renkes Group, Ltd. *(168)*
The Roth Group *(172)*
Ryan, Phillips, Utrecht & MacKinnon *(173)*
Sabre Inc. *(644)*
Sandia Pueblo *(648)*
Santini, Chartered *(175)*
Schnader Harrison Segal & Lewis LLP *(176)*
Secure Wrap, Inc. *(654)*
The Smith-Free Group *(184)*
Springettsbury, Pennsylvania, Township of *(670)*
Starwood Hotels & Resorts Worldwide, Inc. *(673)*
Stoll Stoll Berne Lokting & Shlachter, P.C. *(675)*
Strategic Horizons Advisors, L.L.C. *(189)*
Strategy Group Internat'l *(190)*
Ticketmaster *(687)*
Travel Business Roundtable *(691)*
Travel Industry Ass'n of America *(691)*
Travelocity.com *(691)*
Tunica Biloxi Indians of Louisiana *(694)*
Turkish Industrialists and Businessmen's Ass'n (TUSIAD) *(694)*
U.S. Space & Rocket Center *(697)*
U.S.-Canadian Caucus of Mayors *(697)*
United Airlines *(700)*
United Motorcoach Ass'n *(702)*
United States Air Tour Ass'n *(703)*
Van Scoyoc Associates, Inc. *(200)*
Venable *(201)*
Verner, Liipfert, Bernhard, McPherson and Hand, Chartered *(202)*
Vivendi Universal *(717)*
Washington Resource Associates *(209)*
Western States Tourism Policy Council *(724)*
White Mountain Apache Tribe *(726)*
Woodfin Suite Hotels *(730)*
World Duty Free Americas, Inc. *(730)*
World Government of World Citizens *(730)*
World Service Authority *(731)*
Zane & Associates *(221)*
Zuckert, Scoutt and Rasenberger, L.L.P. *(735)*
Zuckert, Scoutt and Rasenberger, L.L.P. *(221)*

Trucking/Shipping (TRU)

Advocates for Highway and Auto Safety *(229)*
Alcalde & Fay *(10)*
American Ass'n of Motor Vehicle Administrators *(248)*
American Bakers Ass'n *(250)*
American Boiler Manufacturers Ass'n *(251)*
American Farm Bureau Federation *(258)*
American Feed Industry Ass'n *(259)*
American Forest & Paper Ass'n *(259)*
American Institute for Shippers' Ass'ns *(264)*
American Iron and Steel Institute *(265)*
American Meat Institute *(267)*
American Trucking Ass'ns *(279)*
American Wholesale Marketers Ass'n *(280)*
American Wood Preservers Institute *(280)*
Americans for Equitable Climate Solutions *(281)*
Ass'n of American Railroads *(294)*
Ass'n of American Shippers *(294)*
Automotive Aftermarket Industry Ass'n *(303)*
Baise + Miller, P.C. *(19)*
Baker Botts, L.L.P. *(20)*
Balch & Bingham LLP *(21)*
Berliner, Candon & Jimison *(27)*
Bethlehem Steel Corp. *(312)*
Blank Rome Comisky & McCauley, LLP *(29)*
Burlington Northern Santa Fe Railway *(324)*
California Refuse Removal Council *(327)*
Capitol Associates, Inc. *(37)*
Capitol Hill Advocates *(39)*
Carpi & Clay *(41)*
Chadbourne and Parke LLP *(45)*
CNF Transportation, Inc. *(351)*
Coalition Against Bigger Trucks *(352)*
Coalition for Fair Play in Ocean Shipping *(353)*
ConAgra Foods, Inc. *(365)*
Conlon, Frantz, Phelan & Pires *(51)*
Consumer Federation of America *(369)*
CSX Corp. *(379)*
CSX Lines LLC *(379)*
Delaware and Hudson Railroad *(384)*
Dickstein Shapiro Morin & Oshinsky LLP *(61)*
DuPont Agricultural Products *(393)*
The Dutko Group, Inc. *(68)*
Earle Palmer Brown Public Relations *(70)*
Electronic Retailing Ass'n *(401)*
Environmental Industry Ass'ns *(405)*
FedEx Corp. *(415)*
The Fertilizer Institute *(415)*
Finch-Pruyn Paper Co. *(417)*
Food Distributors Internat'l (NAWGA-IFDA) *(421)*
Food Marketing Institute *(421)*
Ford Motor Co. *(422)*
G.R. Services *(80)*
Garden Centers of America *(429)*
General Motors Corp. *(432)*
Goodyear Tire and Rubber Co. *(437)*
Government Relations, Inc. *(84)*
Grocery Manufacturers of America *(440)*
Grove, Jaskiewicz, and Cobert *(88)*
Guam, Territory of *(441)*
Guam, Washington Office of the Governor *(442)*
Guinea, Secretary General of the Presidency of the Republic of *(442)*
Heavy Vehicle Maintenance Group *(447)*
The Home Depot *(451)*
R. J. Hudson Associates *(101)*
Illinois Collaboration on Youth *(457)*
Intermodal Ass'n of North America *(467)*
Internat'l Ass'n of Fire Fighters *(468)*
Internat'l Brotherhood of Teamsters *(469)*
Internat'l Federation of Inspection Agencies, North American Committee *(471)*
Internat'l Mass Retailers Ass'n *(473)*
Internat'l Sign Ass'n *(474)*
Internat'l Warehouse Logistics Ass'n *(476)*
Interstate Wine Coalition *(477)*
Kaiser Aluminum & Chemical Corp. *(485)*
Keller and Heckman LLP *(111)*
Kent & O'Connor, Inc. *(112)*
Kessler & Associates Business Services, Inc. *(112)*
Kimberly-Clark Corp. *(489)*
Kmart Corp. *(490)*
Lee Lane *(116)*
Las Cruces, New Mexico, City of *(495)*
Legislative Solutions *(118)*
Luman, Lange & Wheeler *(122)*
The M Companies *(122)*
Maersk Inc. *(507)*
Marine Engineers Beneficial Ass'n (District No. 1 - PCD) *(510)*
Maritime Exchange for the Delaware River and Bay *(510)*
Matlack Systems, Inc. *(513)*
Meyers & Associates *(133)*
Motor Freight Carriers Ass'n *(531)*
Mullenholz, Brimsek & Belair *(138)*
The MWW Group *(140)*
Nat'l Ass'n of Chemical Distributors *(540)*
Nat'l Ass'n of Police Organizations *(546)*
Nat'l Ass'n of Wheat Growers *(551)*
Nat'l Beer Wholesalers Ass'n *(552)*
Nat'l Grain and Feed Ass'n *(566)*
Nat'l Motor Freight Traffic Ass'n *(571)*
Nat'l Private Truck Council *(574)*
Nat'l Ready Mixed Concrete Ass'n *(575)*
Nat'l Roofing Contractors Ass'n *(576)*
NATSO, Inc. *(582)*
Norcal Waste Systems, Inc. *(591)*
Norfolk Southern Corp. *(591)*
Oshkosh Truck Corp. *(604)*
PACCAR, Inc. *(605)*
Paul, Hastings, Janofsky & Walker LLP *(153)*
Phillips Petroleum Co. *(616)*
Policy Directions, Inc. *(158)*
Port Authority of New York and New Jersey *(621)*
Port of San Diego *(621)*
Potomac Group *(160)*
Charles W. Quatt Associates, Inc. *(165)*
Reed, Smith, LLP *(167)*
Results Cubed *(168)*
Robertson, Monagle & Eastaugh *(170)*
Rodriguez O'Donnell Fuerst Gonzalez & Williams *(171)*
Rooney Group Internat'l, Inc. *(171)*
Roquette America *(642)*
Ruan Leasing Co. *(643)*
Ryder System, Inc. *(644)*
Safety Reasearch Center, Inc. *(645)*
Seafarers Internat'l Union of North America *(653)*
Secure Wrap, Inc. *(654)*
Snack Food Ass'n *(662)*
The Solomon Group, LLC *(185)*
Solutia Inc. *(665)*
Soo Line Railroad, Inc. *(666)*
Specialized Carriers and Rigging Ass'n *(669)*
State Farm Insurance Cos. *(673)*
Stephens Law Offices *(188)*
Kenneth F. Stinger *(189)*
Strat@Comm (Strategic Communications Counselors) *(189)*
Strategic Horizons Advisors, L.L.C. *(189)*
Strategy Group Internat'l *(190)*
Thompson Coburn LLP *(194)*
Tire Ass'n of North America *(687)*
Trajen, Inc. *(689)*
Transportation Intermediaries Ass'n *(690)*
Truck Manufacturers Ass'n *(692)*
Truck Renting and Leasing Ass'n *(693)*
Truck Trailer Manufacturers Ass'n *(693)*
UniGroup, Inc. *(698)*

Unemployment (UNM)

Urban Development/Municipalities (URB)

Nat'l Ass'n of Industrial and Office Properties ***(544)***
Nat'l Ass'n of Installation Developers ***(544)***
Nat'l Ass'n of Negro Business & Professional Women's Clubs, Inc. ***(546)***
Nat'l Ass'n of Service and Conservation Corps ***(549)***
Nat'l Assembly of Health and Human Service Organizations ***(551)***
Nat'l Center for Neighborhood Enterprise ***(555)***
Nat'l Fair Housing Alliance ***(563)***
Nat'l Housing Conference ***(567)***
Nat'l Liberty Museum ***(570)***
Nat'l Puerto Rican Coalition ***(575)***
Nat'l Trust for Historic Preservation ***(580)***
Negative Population Growth, Inc. (NPG) ***(583)***
New Orleans, Louisiana, City of ***(586)***
New York University ***(588)***
Newark, New Jersey, City of ***(588)***
Nogales, Arizona, City of ***(591)***
North Carolina, Washington Office of the State of ***(593)***
Northeast-Midwest Institute ***(594)***
Northwest Municipal Conference ***(595)***
Oldaker and Harris, LLP *(146)*
Orange, California, County of ***(602)***
Palo Alto, California, City of ***(607)***
Palumbo & Cerrell, Inc. *(149)*
Parry, Romani, DeConcini & Symms *(149)*
Parsons Corp. ***(608)***
Pasadena, California, City of ***(609)***
Patton Boggs, LLP *(150)*
Peoria, Arizona, City of ***(612)***
Petersburg, Alaska, City of ***(613)***
The Peterson Group *(155)*
Peyser Associates, Inc. *(155)*
Plano, Texas, City of ***(619)***
Please Touch Museum, The Children's Museum of Philadelphia ***(619)***
Portland, Oregon, City of ***(621)***
Preservation Action ***(623)***
Prince George's, Maryland, County of ***(624)***
Progressive Policy Institute ***(626)***
The Providence Plan ***(627)***
Providence Redevelopment Agency ***(627)***
Provo, Utah, City of ***(627)***
Redding, California, City of ***(635)***
Redlands, California, City of ***(635)***
Reno, Nevada, City of ***(637)***
Rialto, California, City of ***(639)***
Robertson, Monagle & Eastaugh *(170)*
Roseville, California, City of ***(642)***
Sacramento Housing and Redeveloping Agency ***(645)***
Sacramento-Potomac Consulting, Inc. *(174)*
Sagamore Associates, Inc. *(174)*
Salt Lake City, Utah, City of ***(646)***
SAMPCO Companies ***(647)***
San Diego, California, City of ***(647)***
Santa Cruz Redevelopment Agency ***(649)***
Scenic America ***(651)***
Schmeltzer, Aptaker & Shepard, P.C. *(176)*
Scottsdale, Arizona, City of ***(652)***
Service Employees Internat'l Union ***(656)***
Seward, Alaska, City of ***(656)***
Sewerage and Water Board of New Orleans ***(656)***
Shaw Pittman *(177)*
Shreveport, Louisiana, City of ***(658)***
Sierra Madre, California, City of ***(658)***
Simon and Co., Inc. *(181)*
Sister Cities Internat'l ***(660)***
Smith Dawson & Andrews, Inc. *(183)*
Solutia Inc. ***(665)***
South Bend, Indiana, City of ***(666)***
South Salt Lake, Utah, City of ***(666)***
Sports Corp., Ltd. ***(670)***
St. Cloud, Minnesota, City of ***(671)***
St. Louis, Missouri, City of ***(672)***
St. Paul, Alaska, City of ***(672)***
Stillman College ***(674)***
Strategic Horizons Advisors, L.L.C. *(189)*
Stuntz, Davis & Staffier, P.C. *(190)*
Tacoma, Washington, City of ***(680)***
Temecula, California, City of ***(683)***
Tett Enterprises ***(684)***
Tongour Simpson Holsclaw Green *(196)*
Tricap Management Corp. ***(692)***
Tulane University ***(693)***
David Turch & Associates *(197)*
U.S. Filter ***(696)***
United Methodist Church General Board of Church and Society ***(702)***
United States Conference of Mayors ***(703)***
University Heights Science Park ***(705)***
University of Medicine and Dentistry of New Jersey ***(706)***
University of Miami ***(706)***
University of Tulsa ***(708)***
University of Virginia ***(708)***
Van Scoyoc Associates, Inc. *(200)*
VSAdc.com *(205)*
Wake, North Carolina, County of ***(718)***
The Washington Group *(208)*
Wasilla, Alaska, City of ***(721)***
Wayne, Michigan, County of ***(722)***
Susan J. White & Associates *(212)*
Women Officials in NACo ***(729)***
Wrangell, Alaska, City of ***(731)***
YMCA of the USA Public Policy Office ***(733)***
YWCA of the USA ***(734)***
Zane & Associates *(221)*

Utilities (UTI)

3Com Corp. ***(223)***
ABB, Inc. ***(225)***
The Accord Group *(5)*
AFL-CIO (American Federation of Labor and Congress of Industrial Organizations) ***(231)***
Air Conditioning Contractors of America ***(233)***
Air-Conditioning and Refrigeration Institute ***(234)***
Akin, Gump, Strauss, Hauer & Feld, L.L.P. *(8)*
Albers & Co. *(10)*
Alcoa Inc. ***(237)***
Alexander Strategy Group *(11)*
Alliance for Competitive Electricity ***(239)***
Alliance to Save Energy ***(241)***
Alpine Group, Inc. *(11)*
Alston & Bird, LLP ***(242)***
Ameren Services ***(243)***
American Ass'n of Blacks in Energy ***(246)***
American Boiler Manufacturers Ass'n ***(251)***
American Consulting Engineers Council ***(255)***
American Electric Power Co. ***(257)***
American Farm Bureau Federation ***(258)***
American Federation of State, County and Municipal Employees ***(258)***
American Forest & Paper Ass'n ***(259)***
American Gas Ass'n ***(261)***
American Iron and Steel Institute ***(265)***
American Public Gas Ass'n ***(271)***
American Public Power Ass'n ***(272)***
American Public Works Ass'n ***(272)***
American Supply Ass'n ***(278)***
American Water Works Ass'n ***(280)***
Americans for Affordable Electricity ***(281)***
Americans for Equitable Climate Solutions ***(281)***
Anaheim, California, Public Utilities of the City of ***(283)***
Arcadia, California, City of ***(287)***
Arent Fox Kintner Plotkin & Kahn, PLLC *(14)*
Arizona Power Authority ***(288)***
Arizona Public Service Co. ***(288)***
Arter & Hadden *(17)*
Ass'n for Local Telecommunications Services ***(292)***
Ass'n of American Geographers ***(293)***
Ass'n of California Water Agencies ***(295)***
Ass'n of Metropolitan Sewerage Agencies ***(297)***
Ass'n of Metropolitan Water Agencies ***(297)***
Associated Builders and Contractors ***(300)***
Associated General Contractors of America ***(300)***
Assurant Group ***(301)***
Auburn, Avilla, Bluffton, Columbia City and Other Municipalities of Indiana ***(302)***
Automotive Aftermarket Industry Ass'n ***(303)***
Automotive Parts and Service Alliance ***(303)***
Baker Botts, L.L.P. *(20)*
Balch & Bingham LLP *(21)*
Ball Janik, LLP *(22)*
Barbour Griffith & Rogers, Inc. *(22)*
Basin Electric Power Cooperative ***(308)***
Bass Hotels and Resorts, Inc. ***(308)***
Bergen, New York, Village of ***(311)***
Berkeley County Water & Sanitation Authority ***(312)***
BHP (USA) Inc. ***(313)***
Ray Billups *(27)*
Boonville, New York, Village of ***(317)***
BP Amoco Corp. ***(319)***
Bracewell & Patterson, L.L.P. *(30)*
Bracy Williams & Co. *(31)*
Braintree Electric Light Department ***(319)***
Brickfield, Burchette, Ritts & Stone *(32)*
British Columbia Hydro and Power Authority ***(321)***
Broydrick & Associates *(33)*
Building Owners and Managers Ass'n Internat'l ***(323)***
John G. "Toby" Burke *(34)*
Burlington Northern Santa Fe Railway ***(324)***
Burns and Roe Enterprises, Inc. ***(324)***
C F Industries, Inc. ***(325)***
California Independent System Operator ***(327)***
Capital Strategies Group, Inc. *(37)*
Capitol Link, Inc. *(39)*
Cargill, Inc. ***(331)***
Bill Carney & Co. *(41)*
Catamount Energy Corp. ***(333)***
Celanese Government Relations Office ***(334)***
Central Montana Electric Power Cooperative, Inc. ***(339)***
Central Virginia Electric Cooperative, Inc. ***(339)***
Chelan County Public Utility District ***(342)***
Chubu Electric Power Co. ***(346)***
Cinergy Corp. ***(347)***
Citizens Against Government Waste ***(348)***
Citizens for a Sound Economy ***(348)***
Citizens for State Power ***(348)***
City Public Service ***(349)***
Clayton, Dover, Lewes, Middletown, Milford, Newark, NewCastle, Seaford and Smyrna, Delaware, Municipalities of ***(350)***
The Climate Council, ***(351)***
College Station, Texas, City of ***(358)***
Colorado River Indian Tribes ***(358)***
Colorado Springs Utilities ***(359)***
ComEd ***(359)***
Community Ass'ns Institute (CAI) ***(362)***
Conkling, Fiskum & McCormick *(51)*
Consolidated Edison Co. of New York ***(367)***
Constellation Energy Group ***(368)***
Consumer Energy Council of America Research Foundation ***(369)***
Consumer Federation of America ***(369)***
Consumers Union of the United States ***(369)***
Greg Copeland *(52)*
Copeland, Lowery & Jacquez *(52)*
Corn Belt Energy Corp. ***(372)***
Council of Industrial Boiler Owners (CIBO) ***(375)***
Crowell & Moring LLP *(55)*
CSX Corp. ***(379)***
Ralf Czepluch *(56)*
Mary E. Davis *(57)*
Delaware Municipal Electric Corp. (DEMEC) ***(384)***
Thomas J. Dennis *(61)*
Denton, Texas, City of ***(385)***
Dickstein Shapiro Morin & Oshinsky LLP *(61)*
Distributed Power Coalition of America ***(390)***
Domestic Petroleum Council ***(390)***
Dominion Resources, Inc. ***(391)***
Duke Energy ***(392)***
Duncan, Weinberg, Genzer & Pembroke, P.C. *(66)*
The Dutko Group, Inc. *(68)*
Dynegy, Inc. ***(394)***
East Texas Electric Cooperative ***(395)***
Edison Electric Institute ***(397)***
Edison Internat'l ***(397)***
Edison Mission Energy ***(397)***
El Paso Electric Co. ***(399)***
Electric Power Supply Ass'n ***(400)***
Electricity Consumers Resource Council (ELCON) ***(400)***
Electronic Traders Ass'n ***(401)***
Energy and Environment Coalition ***(403)***

Energy East Management Corp. (403)
EnerStar Power Corp. (403)
Enron Corp. (403)
Entergy Services, Inc. (404)
Environmental Defense Fund (405)
Ernst & Young LLP (72)
Exelon Corp. (409)
Exxon Mobil Corp. (409)
EZ's Solutions, Inc. (74)
F/P Research Associates (74)
Marcus G. Faust, P.C. (74)
Jack Ferguson Associates, Inc. (75)
The Ferguson Group, LLC (76)
The Fertilizer Institute (415)
Fierce and Isakowitz (76)
FirstEnergy Co. (418)
Flathead Joint Board of Control (418)
Florida Power and Light Co. (420)
Foley & Lardner (78)
Food Distributors Internat'l (NAWGA-IFDA) (421)
Food Marketing Institute (421)
Ford Motor Co. (422)
Forscey & Stinson, PLLC (79)
Four Dam Pool (424)
Freeport, New York, Electric Department of the Village of (425)
Gainesville Regional Utilities (428)
Gallagher, Boland and Meiburger (80)
Gas Research Institute (429)
General Electric Co. (432)
General Motors Corp. (432)
Global USA, Inc. (83)
Goodyear Tire and Rubber Co. (437)
Governmental Strategies, Inc. (85)
Grant County P.U.D., Washington (438)
Greater Washington Board of Trade (439)
Greenport, New York, Village Electric Department of (440)
Guinea, Secretary General of the Presidency of the Republic of (442)
Hagerstown, Maryland, Municipal Electric Light Plant of (443)
Hawaiian Electric Co. (445)
Hecht, Spencer & Associates (93)
Holland & Knight LLP (98)
Peter Homer (99)
Hooper Owen & Winburn (99)
Hoosier Energy Rural Electric Cooperative, Inc. (452)
Oliver James Horton (100)
Hunton & Williams (101)
Hydro-Quebec (456)
Idaho Power Co. (457)
The ILEX Group (102)
IMC Global Inc. (458)
Impact Strategies (102)
Independent Petroleum Ass'n of America (459)
Indiana and Michigan Municipal Distributors Ass'n (460)
Industrial Customers of Northwest Utilities (461)
Infiltrator Systems, Inc. (461)
informal coalition (461)
Internat'l Brotherhood of Boilermakers, Iron Shipbuilders, Blacksmiths, Forgers and Helpers (469)
Internat'l Brotherhood of Electrical Workers (469)
Internat'l Brotherhood of Teamsters (469)
Internat'l Federation of Professional and Technical Engineers (471)
Internat'l Mass Retailers Ass'n (473)
Internat'l Union of Painters and Allied Trades (476)
Interstate Natural Gas Ass'n of America (477)
IPALCO Enterprises, Inc./Indianapolis Power & Light Co. (478)
Iroquois Gas Transmission System (479)
ITRON, Inc. (480)
Jacksonville Electric Authority (481)
Jamestown, New York, Board of Public Utilities (481)
Jefferson Government Relations, L.L.C. (106)
Johnson Co. (107)
Johnston & Associates, LLC (107)
Jordan & Associates, Inc. (109)
Jorden Burt LLP (109)
Kaiser Aluminum & Chemical Corp. (485)
Kanner & Associates (110)
Kennecott/Borax (488)
Kent & O'Connor, Inc. (112)
Ketchikan Public Utilities (488)
KeySpan Energy (489)
Lee Lane (116)
Large Public Power Council (495)
Las Cruces, New Mexico, City of (495)
The Paul Laxalt Group (117)
Lent Scrivner & Roth LLC (119)
Liebman & Associates, Inc. (120)
Litton Systems, Inc. (500)
M-S-R Public Power Agency (506)
Ron C. Marlenee (125)
Massena, New York, Town of (512)
Barbara T. McCall Associates (127)
McClure, Gerard & Neuenschwander, Inc. (127)
McGlotten & Jarvis (129)
McGuireWoods L.L.P. (130)
Mechanical Contractors Ass'n of America (515)
Media Fusion L.L.C. (516)
Memphis Light, Gas and Water Division (517)
The Metropolitan Water District of Southern California (521)
Meyers & Associates (133)
Mid-West Electric Consumers Ass'n (523)
Millenium 2100 (524)
Mishawaka Utilities (526)
Mission Springs (California) Water District (526)
Modesto/Turlock Irrigation District (527)
Timothy X. Moore and Co. (136)
Motorola, Inc. (531)
Multistate Tax Commission (532)
Municipal Electric Authority of Georgia (532)
Municipal Electric Utilities Ass'n of New York State (532)
Nat'l Ass'n of Energy Service Companies (542)
Nat'l Ass'n of Housing Cooperatives (544)
Nat'l Ass'n of State Utility Consumer Advocates (NASUCA) (550)
Nat'l Ass'n of Wholesaler-Distributors (551)
Nat'l Consumers League (558)
Nat'l Electrical Contractors Ass'n (562)
Nat'l Environmental Trust (563)
Nat'l Farmers Union (Farmers Educational & Co-operative Union of America) (563)
Nat'l Grange (566)
Nat'l Grid USA (566)
Nat'l Hydropower Ass'n (567)
Nat'l Mining Ass'n (571)
Nat'l Restaurant Ass'n (576)
Nat'l Retail Federation (576)
Nat'l Rural Electric Cooperative Ass'n (576)
Nat'l Taxpayers Union (579)
Nat'l Water Resources Ass'n (581)
Natural Resources Defense Council (582)
Net Results, Inc. (584)
Niagara Mohawk Power Corp. (589)
Michael E. Nix Consulting (142)
Walker F. Nolan (142)
North American Electric Reliability Council (592)
North Dakota, Governor's Office of the State of (593)
Northeast Texas Electric Cooperative (593)
Northeast-Midwest Institute (594)
Northern Indiana Public Service Co. (594)
NRG Energy, Inc. (596)
NSTAR (596)
Nuclear Energy Institute (597)
Occidental Internat'l Corporation (598)
O'Connor & Hannan, L.L.P. (144)
Oklahoma Gas and Electric Co. (599)
O'Neill, Athy & Casey, P.C. (147)
Oregon Utility Resource Coordination Ass'n (OURCA) (603)
Orlando Utilities Commission (603)
Palo Alto, California, City of (607)
Palumbo & Cerrell, Inc. (149)
Partnership for Early Climate Action (608)
Patton Boggs, LLP (150)
Peyser Associates, Inc. (155)
PG&E Corp. (614)
PG&E Generating Co. (614)
Phillips Petroleum Co. (616)
Pinnacle West Capital Corp. (617)
Plattsburgh, New York, City of (619)
Plumbing, Heating, Cooling Contractors- National Assoc. (619)
Portland General Electric Co. (621)
Potomac Electric Power Co. (622)
Powers Pyles Sutter & Verville, PC (161)
PPL (622)
Preston Gates Ellis & Rouvelas Meeds LLP (162)
Prince William County Service Authority (624)
Progress Energy (626)
Provo, Utah, City of (627)
Public Citizen, Inc. (628)
Public Generating Pool (628)
Public Service Co. of New Mexico (629)
Public Strategies Washington, Inc. (164)
Public Strategies, Inc. (165)
PURPA Reform Group (630)
Real Estate Roundtable (634)
Redding, California, Electric Department of the City of (635)
Redland Energy Group (167)
Reed, Smith, LLP (167)
Reliant Energy, Inc. (636)
The Renkes Group, Ltd. (168)
Repeal PUHCA Now Coalition (637)
Republicans for Clean Air (638)
RFB, Inc. (168)
Robertson, Monagle & Eastaugh (170)
Rockville Centre, New York, Village of (641)
Ryan, Phillips, Utrecht & MacKinnon (173)
Sacramento Municipal Utility District (645)
Salt River Project (646)
Sam Rayburn G&T Electric Cooperative, Inc. (647)
Santa Clara, California, Electric Department of the City of (649)
SBC Communications Inc. (650)
SCANA Corp. (651)
Seattle City Light (653)
SEC Roundtable Group (654)
Sempra Energy (655)
David Senter & Associates (177)
Sheet Metal Workers' Internat'l Ass'n (657)
Sherburne, New York, Village of (657)
Craig Shirley & Associates (180)
Sierra Pacific Resources (659)
Sills Associates (180)
Simon and Co., Inc. (181)
E. Del Smith and Co. (183)
Smith Dawson & Andrews, Inc. (183)
The Smith-Free Group (184)
Snack Food Ass'n (662)
The Solomon Group, LLC (185)
South Carolina Public Service Authority (666)
South Mississippi Electric Power Ass'n (666)
Southeast Conference (667)
Southern California Public Power Authority (667)
Southern Co. (667)
Southern Maryland Electric Cooperative, Inc. (668)
Southwestern Electric Cooperative, Inc. (668)
St. Louis Metropolitan Sewer District (672)
Strategic Horizons Advisors, L.L.C. (189)
Stuntz, Davis & Staffier, P.C. (190)
Swidler Berlin Shereff Friedman, LLP (191)
Tacoma, Washington, City of (680)
Tacoma, Washington, Public Utilities Department of (680)
Talley and Associates (192)
TECO Energy, Inc. (682)
Tex-La Electric Cooperative of Texas (684)
Texaco Group Inc. (684)
Thelen Reid & Priest LLP (685)
Thelen Reid & Priest LLP (193)
The Timken Co. (687)
Tongour Simpson Holsclaw Green (196)
Transmission Agency of Northern California (690)
Troutman Sanders LLP (196)
Tumalo Irrigation District (694)
TVA Watch (694)
Twentynine Palms Water District (695)
TXU Business Services (695)
TXU Inc. (695)
U.S. Public Interest Research Group (697)
Unilever United States, Inc. (699)

United States Energy Ass'n *(703)*
UNOCAL Corp. *(708)*
UtiliCorp United, Inc. *(711)*
Utility Workers Union of America *(711)*
Van Ness Feldman, P.C. *(199)*
The Velasquez Group *(201)*
Vinson & Elkins L.L.P. *(204)*
R. Duffy Wall and Associates *(205)*
Washington Council Ernst & Young *(206)*
Washington Gas *(719)*
Water Environment Federation *(721)*
J. Arthur Weber & Associates *(210)*
David M. Weiman *(211)*
Western Interconnection Coordination Forum *(724)*
Westhill Partners *(725)*
Westmoreland Coal Co. *(725)*
William F. Whitsitt Policy and Government Affairs *(213)*
Whittier, California, City of *(726)*
Wiley, Rein & Fielding *(727)*
Wiley, Rein & Fielding *(214)*
Will and Carlson, Inc. *(215)*
Williams & Jensen, P.C. *(215)*
The Williams Companies *(727)*
Wilmer, Cutler & Pickering *(217)*
Wisconsin Energy Corp. *(728)*
Wisconsin Gas Co. *(729)*
Women Officials in NACo *(729)*
Xcel Energy, Inc. *(732)*
Yates County Cable TV Committee *(733)*

Veterans (VET)

AARP (American Ass'n of Retired Persons) *(224)*
AFL-CIO Maritime Committee *(231)*
AFL-CIO - Maritime Trades Department *(231)*
Air Force Ass'n *(233)*
Air Force Sergeants Ass'n *(233)*
Albertine Enterprises, Inc. *(10)*
American Academy of Ophthamology - Office of Federal Affairs *(244)*
American Ass'n of Physician Specialists *(249)*
American Coalition for Filipino Veterans *(253)*
American Federation for Medical Research *(258)*
American Health Care Ass'n *(261)*
American Legion *(266)*
American Logistics Ass'n *(266)*
American Military Soc. *(268)*
American Museum of Natural History *(268)*
American Optometric Ass'n *(269)*
American Orthotic and Prosthetic Ass'n *(269)*
American Physical Therapy Ass'n *(270)*
American Psychiatric Ass'n *(271)*
American Retirees Ass'n *(273)*
Amgen *(282)*
AMVETS (American Veterans of World War II, Korea and Vietnam) *(283)*
Arent Fox Kintner Plotkin & Kahn, PLLC *(14)*
Ass'n Growth Enterprises *(18)*
Ass'n of American Medical Colleges *(294)*
Ass'n of Chiropractic Colleges *(295)*
Ass'n of Military Surgeons of the U.S. (AMSUS) *(297)*
Ass'n of Professors of Medicine *(298)*
Augusta-Richmond, Georgia, County of *(303)*
Aventis Pharmaceuticals, Inc. *(304)*
Bergner Bockorny Castagnetti and Hawkins *(26)*
Booher & Associates *(30)*
Brain Injury Ass'n *(319)*
Brown & Associates *(32)*
Broydrick & Associates *(33)*
Bryan Cave LLP *(33)*
Capitol Associates, Inc. *(37)*
The Carter Group *(41)*
Coalition for Health Services Research *(354)*
Cooney & Associates, Inc. *(52)*
Disabled American Veterans *(389)*
The Eagles Group *(69)*
Elan Pharmaceutical Research Corp. *(399)*
Epstein Becker & Green, P.C. *(72)*
Export Management Services, Inc. *(409)*
Fleet Reserve Ass'n *(418)*
Florida State University System *(420)*
GAF Corp. *(428)*
Health Physics Soc. *(446)*
Health Policy Analysts *(93)*
Helmsin & Yarwood Associates *(94)*
Highland Park, Illinois, City of Highwood Local Redevelopment Authority and the City of *(449)*
Innovative Resource Group *(462)*
Intrinsiq Data Corp. *(477)*
IVAX Corp. *(480)*
Jefferson Consulting Group *(105)*
Jewish War Veterans of the U.S.A. *(483)*
Johnson & Johnson, Inc. *(484)*
Jorden Burt LLP *(109)*
Law Offices of James L. Kane *(110)*
Karalekas & Noone *(110)*
Jeffrey J. Kimbell & Associates *(113)*
Lao Veterans of America, Inc. *(495)*
Lawton/Fort Sill Chamber of Commerce & Industry *(496)*
Eli Lilly and Co. *(499)*
Lovelace Respiratory Research Institute *(504)*
Madison Government Affairs *(123)*
Managed Care Solutions *(508)*
Marine Corps Reserve Officers Ass'n *(510)*
Medical Advocacy Services, Inc. *(132)*
Mehl, Griffin & Bartek Ltd. *(132)*
Merck & Co. *(518)*
The Military Coalition *(524)*
Military Order of the Purple Heart of the U.S.A. *(524)*
Mortgage Bankers Ass'n of America *(530)*
Mortgage Investors Corp. *(530)*
Mount Sinai School of Medicine *(531)*
Nat'l Alliance for the Mentally Ill *(536)*
Nat'l Ass'n for Uniformed Services *(538)*
Nat'l Ass'n of Community Health Centers *(540)*
Nat'l Ass'n of Home Builders of the U.S. *(543)*
Nat'l Ass'n of Housing Cooperatives *(544)*
Nat'l Ass'n of Letter Carriers of the United States of America *(545)*
Nat'l Ass'n of VA Physicians and Dentists *(551)*
Nat'l Ass'n of Veterans Research and Education Foundations *(551)*
Nat'l Campaign for Hearing Health *(554)*
Nat'l Funeral Directors Ass'n *(565)*
Nat'l Health Care Access Coalition *(566)*
Nat'l Mental Health Ass'n *(571)*
Nat'l Military Family Ass'n *(571)*
Nat'l Organization for Competency Assurance *(572)*
Nat'l Puerto Rican Coalition *(575)*
Nat'l Veterans Foundation *(580)*
Nat'l Veterans Legal Services Program *(580)*
Naval Reserve Ass'n *(582)*
Navy League of the United States *(583)*
New York University *(588)*
Non Commissioned Officers Ass'n of the U.S.A. *(591)*
O'Bryon & Co. *(144)*
Olsten Health Services *(600)*
Onehealthbank.com *(600)*
Paralyzed Veterans of America *(607)*
Patton Boggs, LLP *(150)*
Pharmaceutical Research and Manufacturers of America *(614)*
Polity Consulting *(159)*
Potomac Strategies Internat'l LLC *(160)*
Problem-Knowledge Coupler *(625)*
Professional Managers Ass'n *(626)*
Public Policy Partners, LLC *(164)*
REM Engineering *(636)*
The Retired Enlisted Ass'n *(638)*
The Retired Officers Ass'n (TROA) *(638)*
Schering-Plough Legislative Resources L.L.C. *(651)*
Philip S. Smith & Associates, Inc. *(182)*
Smith, Bucklin and Associates, Inc. *(184)*
The Smith, Korach, Hayet, Haynie Partnership *(661)*
SMS Corp. *(662)*
Soc. of General Internal Medicine *(663)*
Spacelabs Medical Inc. *(669)*
The Spectrum Group *(186)*
Spina Bifida Ass'n of America *(670)*
TriWest Healthcare Alliance, Inc. *(692)*
United Automobile, Aerospace and Agricultural Implement Workers of America (UAW) *(700)*
United Lao Congress for Democracy *(702)*
United States Coast Guard Chief Petty Officers Ass'n *(703)*
University of Medicine and Dentistry of New Jersey *(706)*
University of Miami *(706)*
University of Tulsa *(708)*
University of Virginia *(708)*
Van Scoyoc Associates, Inc. *(200)*
Veterans of Foreign Wars of the U.S. *(714)*
Vietnam Veterans of America Foundation *(715)*
VSAdc.com *(205)*
The Washington Group *(208)*
Washington Health Advocates *(209)*
Wilson & Wasserstein, Inc. *(218)*

Waste (Hazardous/Solid/Nuclear) (WAS)

Abbott Laboratories *(225)*
The Accord Group *(5)*
ADA Consulting Services *(5)*
Adams and Reese LLP *(5)*
The Advocacy Group *(6)*
AFL-CIO - Transportation Trades Department *(231)*
Airgas, Inc. *(235)*
Akin, Gump, Strauss, Hauer & Feld, L.L.P. *(8)*
Alcalde & Fay *(10)*
Alexander Strategy Group *(11)*
Alliance for Nuclear Accountability *(240)*
Alliant Energy *(241)*
Alliant Techsystems, Inc. *(241)*
Alpine Group, Inc. *(11)*
Ameren Services *(243)*
American Ass'n for Laboratory Accreditation *(246)*
American Chemistry Council *(252)*
American Consulting Engineers Council *(255)*
American Farm Bureau Federation *(258)*
American Feed Industry Ass'n *(259)*
American Forest & Paper Ass'n *(259)*
American Gas Ass'n *(261)*
American Internat'l Group, Inc. *(265)*
American Petroleum Institute *(269)*
American Planning Ass'n *(270)*
American Plastics Council *(270)*
American Public Works Ass'n *(272)*
American Ref-Fuel *(272)*
American Wood Preservers Institute *(280)*
Aniline Ass'n, Inc. *(284)*
Archimedes Technology Group *(287)*
Arizona Public Service Co. *(288)*
Arnold & Porter *(16)*
Arter & Hadden *(17)*
Asbestos Recycling Inc. *(290)*
Ass'n of Metropolitan Sewerage Agencies *(297)*
Ass'n of Minnesota Counties *(297)*
Ass'n of Nat'l Estuary Programs *(297)*
Associated General Contractors of America *(300)*
Ross Atkins *(18)*
Automotive Aftermarket Industry Ass'n *(303)*
Automotive Parts and Service Alliance *(303)*
Aventis Pharmaceutical Products *(304)*
Azurix *(305)*
Baise + Miller, P.C. *(19)*
The Barton Co. *(24)*
Battelle Memorial Institute *(309)*
Battery Council Internat'l *(309)*
Bechtel Group, Inc. *(310)*
Vikki Bell *(25)*
Leon G. Billings, Inc. *(27)*
BKSH & Associates *(28)*
Richard W. Bliss *(29)*
BOH Environmental, L.L.C. *(317)*
James E. Boland *(30)*
BP Amoco Corp. *(319)*
Bracewell & Patterson, L.L.P. *(30)*
Broydrick & Associates *(33)*
Burlington Northern Santa Fe Railway *(324)*
Burns and Roe Enterprises, Inc. *(324)*
California Refuse Removal Council *(327)*
Canberra Packard BioScience *(330)*
Capitol Associates, Inc. *(37)*
Capitol City Group *(38)*

Capitol Coalitions Inc. ***(38)***
Capitol Hill Advocates ***(39)***
Caraustar ***(331)***
Cargill, Inc. ***(331)***
Carmen & Muss, P.L.L.C. ***(40)***
Bill Carney & Co. ***(41)***
Cassidy & Associates, Inc. ***(42)***
Cement Kiln Recycling Coalition ***(335)***
Center for Marine Conservation ***(337)***
CH2M Hill ***(340)***
Chamber of Commerce of the U.S.A. ***(340)***
Chep USA ***(342)***
Chevron, U.S.A. ***(342)***
Ciba Specialty Chemicals Corp. ***(346)***
Citizens Against Government Waste ***(348)***
CNA Financial Corp. ***(351)***
CNA Insurance Cos. ***(351)***
Coalition for Responsible Waste Incineration ***(354)***
Colling Swift & Hynes ***(49)***
Columbia Natural Resources ***(359)***
ComEd ***(359)***
Compass Internat'l Inc. ***(363)***
Connerton & Ray ***(51)***
Conservation Strategies, LLC ***(51)***
Consolidated Edison Co. of New York ***(367)***
Constellation Energy Group ***(368)***
Construction Industry Round Table, Inc. ***(368)***
Consumer Aerosol Products Council ***(368)***
Consumer Federation of America ***(369)***
Container Recycling Institute ***(370)***
Contran Corp. ***(370)***
Council of Industrial Boiler Owners (CIBO) ***(375)***
Covanta Energy Corporation ***(377)***
Law Office of C. Deming Cowles ***(54)***
CSX Corp. ***(379)***
Dairyland Power Cooperative ***(381)***
Dayton, Ohio, Washington Office of the City of ***(383)***
DCH Technology Inc. ***(383)***
Delaware and Hudson Railroad ***(384)***
DM Electronics Recycling Corporation ***(390)***
Downey McGrath Group, Inc. ***(392)***
Duke Energy ***(392)***
The Dutko Group, Inc. ***(68)***
Edison Electric Institute ***(397)***
Egan & Associates ***(71)***
Electronic Industries Alliance ***(400)***
Elim, Alaska, City of ***(401)***
Entergy Services, Inc. ***(404)***
Envirocare of Utah, Inc. ***(404)***
Environmental Council of the States (ECOS) ***(405)***
Environmental Industry Ass'ns ***(405)***
Environmental Technology Council ***(405)***
EOP Group, Inc. ***(72)***
Equitable Resources Energy Co. ***(406)***
Ethylene Oxide Sterilization Ass'n, Inc. ***(407)***
Exelon Corp. ***(409)***
F&T Network, Inc. ***(74)***
Fairfax, Virginia, County of ***(410)***
Jack Ferguson Associates, Inc. ***(75)***
The Ferguson Group, LLC ***(76)***
The Fertilizer Institute ***(415)***
Fibrowatt, Inc. ***(416)***
Ruth Frances Fleischer ***(77)***
Flight Landata, Inc. ***(419)***
Florida Power and Light Co. ***(420)***
Fluor Corp. ***(420)***
FMC Corp. ***(420)***
Foley & Lardner ***(78)***
Foster Wheeler Corp. ***(424)***
Freeport-McMoRan Copper & Gold Inc. ***(425)***
John Freshman Associates, Inc. ***(79)***
Gainesville, Florida, City of ***(428)***
Garden State Paper Co., Inc. ***(429)***
Gary Sanitary District ***(429)***
Gary, Indiana, Washington Office of the City of ***(429)***
GE Capital Corp. ***(430)***
General Electric Co. ***(432)***
General Motors Corp. ***(432)***
Global Waste Recycling, Inc. ***(436)***
Goodstein & Associates ***(84)***
Goodyear Tire and Rubber Co. ***(437)***
Government Relations, Inc. ***(84)***
Greenman Technologies Inc. ***(440)***
Hadley & McKenna ***(89)***
Martin G. Hamberger & Associates ***(91)***
Health Physics Soc. ***(446)***
Hennipin County Board of Commissioners ***(448)***
Hillsborough, Florida, County of ***(450)***
Hohlt & Associates ***(98)***
Honeywell Internat'l, Inc. ***(452)***
Hooper Owen & Winburn ***(99)***
Howrey Simon Arnold & White ***(100)***
Huntington Beach, California, City of ***(455)***
Huntsman Corp. ***(455)***
Idaho Power Co. ***(457)***
IMC Global Inc. ***(458)***
Independent Petroleum Ass'n of America ***(459)***
Indiana, Office of the Governor of the State of ***(460)***
Industrial Fabrics Ass'n Internat'l ***(461)***
Institute for Local Self-Reliance ***(463)***
Institute of Scrap Recycling Industries, Inc. ***(464)***
Internat'l Ass'n of Bridge, Structural, Ornamental and Reinforcing Iron Workers ***(467)***
Internat'l Ass'n of Fire Chiefs ***(468)***
Internat'l Ass'n of Fire Fighters ***(468)***
Internat'l Brotherhood of Electrical Workers ***(469)***
Internat'l Brotherhood of Teamsters ***(469)***
Internat'l Cadmium Ass'n ***(469)***
Internat'l Federation of Professional and Technical Engineers ***(471)***
Internat'l Sign Ass'n ***(474)***
Internat'l Union of Operating Engineers ***(476)***
IPC Washington Office ***(478)***
Jacobs Engineering Group Inc. ***(481)***
Jamison and Sullivan, Inc. ***(104)***
Johnsburg, Illinois, Village of ***(484)***
Jolly/Rissler, Inc. ***(108)***
Jones, Walker, Waechter, Poitevent, Carrere & Denegre, L.L.P. ***(108)***
Jorden Burt LLP ***(109)***
Kaiser Aluminum & Chemical Corp. ***(485)***
Kennecott/Borax ***(488)***
Kerr-McGee Corp. ***(488)***
Kessler & Associates Business Services, Inc. ***(112)***
Kimberly-Clark Corp. ***(489)***
KOSA ***(491)***
Laborers-AGC Education and Training Fund ***(493)***
Laborers-Employers Cooperation & Education Trust ***(493)***
Lafarge Corp. ***(494)***
Large Public Power Council ***(495)***
LaRock Associates, Inc. ***(116)***
The Livingston Group, LLC ***(120)***
Lockheed Martin Corp. ***(501)***
Lockheed Martin Hanford ***(502)***
Lockridge Grindal & Nauen, P.L.L.P. ***(121)***
Los Angeles County Sanitation District ***(504)***
Lutheran Office for Governmental Affairs/Evangelical Lutheran Church in America ***(506)***
Madison Government Affairs ***(123)***
Manatt, Phelps & Phillips, LLP ***(123)***
Charlie McBride Associates, Inc. ***(127)***
McClure, Gerard & Neuenschwander, Inc. ***(127)***
McGuireWoods L.L.P. ***(130)***
Merck & Co. ***(518)***
Meyers & Associates ***(133)***
Miami Beach, Florida, City of ***(521)***
Denny Miller McBee Associates ***(134)***
Mitsubishi Research Institute ***(526)***
Monroe, Louisiana, Chamber of Commerce of the City of ***(528)***
Monroe, Louisiana, City of ***(528)***
Morgan, Lewis & Bockius LLP ***(136)***
Mullenholz, Brimsek & Belair ***(138)***
Nat'l Ass'n of Manufacturers ***(545)***
Nat'l Ass'n of Service and Conservation Corps ***(549)***
Nat'l Ass'n of Surety Bond Producers ***(550)***
Nat'l Ass'n of Towns and Townships ***(551)***
Nat'l Automobile Dealers Ass'n ***(552)***
Nat'l Consumers League ***(558)***
Nat'l Electrical Manufacturers Ass'n ***(562)***
Nat'l Environmental Development Ass'ns State & Federal Environmental Responsibility Project ***(563)***
Nat'l Environmental Strategies ***(140)***
Nat'l Funeral Directors Ass'n ***(565)***
Nat'l Grid USA ***(566)***
Nat'l Mining Ass'n ***(571)***
Nat'l Rural Housing Coalition ***(577)***
Nat'l Sediments Coalition ***(577)***
Nat'l Soc. of Professional Engineers ***(578)***
Nat'l Whistleblower Center ***(581)***
New Mexico State University, Department of Engineering ***(586)***
The Newark Group ***(588)***
Newark, New Jersey, City of ***(588)***
Newport News Shipbuilding Inc. ***(588)***
Niagara Mohawk Power Corp. ***(589)***
Nitrobenzene Ass'n ***(590)***
Norcal Waste Systems, Inc. ***(591)***
Norfolk Southern Corp. ***(591)***
North Carolina, Washington Office of the State of ***(593)***
Northeast Utilities ***(593)***
Northwest Airlines, Inc. ***(595)***
Novartis Corp. ***(596)***
Nuclear Energy Institute ***(597)***
O'Connor & Hannan, L.L.P. ***(144)***
O'Neill, Athy & Casey, P.C. ***(147)***
Oppenheimer Wolff & Donnelly LLP ***(147)***
Oshkosh Truck Corp. ***(604)***
Ottosen and Associates ***(148)***
Ouachita Parish Police Jury ***(604)***
The Palmer Group ***(149)***
Paper Recycling Coalition ***(607)***
Parsons Corp. ***(608)***
Patton Boggs, LLP ***(150)***
Peyser Associates, Inc. ***(155)***
Pharmacia Corp. ***(615)***
Philadelphia, Pennsylvania, City of ***(615)***
Philip Morris Management Corp. ***(615)***
Philips Electronics North America Corp. ***(616)***
Phillips Petroleum Co. ***(616)***
Pinnacle West Capital Corp. ***(617)***
Piper Marbury Rudnick & Wolfe LLP ***(155)***
Podesta/Mattoon ***(158)***
Portland Metro Regional Government ***(621)***
Poseidon Resources Corp. ***(621)***
Powell, Goldstein, Frazer & Murphy LLP ***(160)***
PPL ***(622)***
Preston Gates Ellis & Rouvelas Meeds LLP ***(162)***
Printing Industries of America ***(624)***
Proteus Co. ***(627)***
Ramsey, Minnesota, Board of Commissioners of the County of ***(633)***
Recovermat Technologies LLC ***(634)***
Reusable Industrial Packaging Ass'n ***(639)***
RGS Enterprises, Inc. ***(168)***
Rhode Island Resource Recovery Center ***(639)***
Rock-Tenn Co. ***(641)***
Rohm and Haas Co. ***(642)***
RSR Corp. ***(643)***
Rubber Manufacturers Ass'n ***(643)***
Ryan, Phillips, Utrecht & MacKinnon ***(173)***
Safe Energy Communication Council ***(645)***
Safe Environment of America ***(645)***
Safety-Kleen Corp. ***(645)***
Sappi Fine Paper NA ***(649)***
Scenic Hudson ***(651)***
Science Applications Internat'l Corp. (SAIC) ***(652)***
Screenprinting & Graphic Imaging Ass'n Internat'l ***(653)***
Seattle, Washington, City of ***(653)***
Sheet Metal Workers' Internat'l Ass'n ***(657)***
Sierra Club ***(658)***
Silver Users Ass'n ***(659)***
Smith & Harroff, Inc. ***(182)***
The Smith-Free Group ***(184)***
Smurfit Stone Container Corp. ***(662)***
Soc. of Nuclear Medicine ***(663)***
Solid Waste Agency of Northern Cook County ***(665)***
Solid Waste Ass'n of North America ***(665)***
The Solomon Group, LLC ***(185)***
Solutia Inc. ***(665)***
Soo Line Railroad, Inc. ***(666)***
Southern Co. ***(667)***
Springs Industries, Inc. ***(671)***
Square 3942 Associates Limited Partnership ***(671)***

Steel Manufacturers Ass'n ***(674)***
Sterling Chemical Co. ***(674)***
Stone and Webster Engineering Corp. ***(675)***
Superfund Action Alliance ***(677)***
Swidler Berlin Shereff Friedman, LLP *(191)*
Al Swift Consulting, Inc. *(192)*
Synthetic Organic Chemical Manufacturers Ass'n ***(679)***
George C. Tagg *(192)*
The Technical Group LLC *(192)*
Terpstra Associates *(193)*
Tetrahydrofuran Task Force ***(684)***
Michael L. Tiner *(195)*
Tri-City Industrial Development Council ***(691)***
Tribal Ass'n on Solid Waste and Emergency Response (TASWER) ***(692)***
TRW Inc. ***(693)***
Christopher A.G. Tulou *(196)*
TXU Business Services ***(695)***
U.S. Postal Service ***(697)***
U.S. Public Interest Research Group ***(697)***
Uniform and Textile Service Ass'n ***(698)***
Unitech Services Group, Inc. ***(700)***
United Brotherhood of Carpenters and Joiners of America ***(700)***
United Methodist Church General Board of Church and Society ***(702)***
United Parcel Service ***(702)***
USX Corp. ***(710)***
Utility Solid Waste Activities Group ***(711)***
Valis Associates *(198)*
Van Ness Feldman, P.C. *(199)*
Van Scoyoc Associates, Inc. *(200)*
Venetian Casino Resort, LLC ***(712)***
Viohl and Associates, Inc. *(205)*
R. Duffy Wall and Associates *(205)*
The Washington Group *(208)*
Washington Group Internat'l ***(719)***
Waste Control Specialists, Inc. ***(721)***
Waste Management, Inc. ***(721)***
Water Environment Federation ***(721)***
West Coast Refuse and Recycling Coalition ***(723)***
Westinghouse ***(725)***
Westinghouse Government Services Group ***(725)***
Wheat & Associates, Inc. *(212)*
White Pigeon Paper Co. ***(726)***
Wisconsin Energy Corp. ***(728)***
Women Officials in NACo ***(729)***
Wright & Talisman, P.C. *(220)*
Xcel Energy, Inc. ***(732)***
Zirconia Sales America ***(734)***
Zurich U.S. Specialties ***(735)***

Welfare (WEL)

ACORN (Ass'n of Community Organizations for Reform Now) ***(227)***
Advocates for Youth ***(229)***
AFL-CIO (American Federation of Labor and Congress of Industrial Organizations) ***(231)***
Alameda, California, County of ***(236)***
Alcalde & Fay *(10)*
Alliance for American Innovation, Inc. ***(239)***
Alliance for Children and Families ***(239)***
American Ass'n of Community Colleges ***(247)***
American Ass'n of Motor Vehicle Administrators ***(248)***
American Ass'n of University Women ***(249)***
American Farm Bureau Federation ***(258)***
American Federation of State, County and Municipal Employees ***(258)***
American Federation of Teachers ***(259)***
American Humane Ass'n ***(263)***
American Jewish Committee ***(265)***
American Jewish Congress ***(265)***
American Network of Community Options and Resources (ANCOR) ***(268)***
American Occupational Therapy Ass'n, Inc. ***(269)***
American Psychological Ass'n ***(271)***
American School Food Service Ass'n ***(273)***
Americans United for Separation of Church and State ***(282)***
AON Risk Services ***(285)***
The Arc ***(287)***
Ass'n for Career and Technical Education ***(291)***
Ass'n of Maternal and Child Health Programs (AMCHP) ***(296)***
Ass'n of Minnesota Counties ***(297)***
The Barton Co. *(24)*
Belew Law Firm *(25)*
Berkeley, California, City of ***(312)***
Berliner, Candon & Jimison *(27)*
BKSH & Associates *(28)*
Bread for the World ***(319)***
BSMG Worldwide ***(323)***
BSMG Worldwide *(34)*
Burger King Corp. ***(324)***
The Business Roundtable ***(325)***
H. E. Butt Grocery Co. ***(325)***
California State Ass'n of Counties ***(327)***
Mark R. Cannon *(37)*
Capital Research Center ***(330)***
Cartwright & Riley *(41)*
Catholic Health Ass'n of the United States ***(333)***
Center for Employment Training ***(336)***
Center for Law and Social Policy ***(336)***
Center on Budget and Policy Priorities ***(338)***
Chambers Associates Inc. *(45)*
The Child Care Consortium ***(343)***
Child Nutrition Forum, c/o FRAC ***(343)***
Child Welfare League of America ***(343)***
Children's Defense Fund ***(344)***
Chocolate Manufacturers Ass'n of the U.S.A. ***(345)***
Christian Voice, Inc. ***(345)***
Clearwater, Florida, City of ***(350)***
Coalition for the Homeless ***(354)***
Commonwealth Group, Ltd. *(50)*
The Community Builders, Inc. ***(362)***
Community Hospitals of Central California ***(363)***
Community Transportation Ass'n of America ***(363)***
Concerned Women for America ***(365)***
Concord Family and Adolescent Services ***(365)***
Conkling, Fiskum & McCormick *(51)*
Consumer Federation of America ***(369)***
Cook Inlet Region Inc. ***(371)***
Copeland, Lowery & Jacquez *(52)*
Cortese PLLC *(53)*
County Welfare Directors Ass'n of California ***(377)***
Covington & Burling *(53)*
Craig Associates *(55)*
Cuyahoga, Ohio, County of ***(380)***
Davis O'Connell, Inc. *(58)*
Dayton, Ohio, Washington Office of the City of ***(383)***
Dean Blakey & Moskowitz *(59)*
The Duberstein Group, Inc. *(65)*
Dublin Castle Group *(66)*
Easter Seals ***(395)***
Epstein Becker & Green, P.C. *(72)*
The Ferguson Group, LLC *(76)*
Florida Department of Children & Families ***(419)***
Foley & Lardner *(78)*
Food Distributors Internat'l (NAWGA-IFDA) ***(421)***
Foster America, Inc. ***(424)***
Gainesville, Florida, City of ***(428)***
Gary Public Transportation Corp. ***(429)***
Gary, Indiana, Housing Authority of the City of ***(429)***
Gary, Indiana, Washington Office of the City of ***(429)***
General Conference of Seventh-day Adventists ***(431)***
General Mills ***(432)***
Girl Scouts of the U.S.A. - Washington Office ***(435)***
Goodwill Industries Internat'l, Inc. ***(437)***
Greenberg Traurig, LLP *(86)*
Hennipin County Board of Commissioners ***(448)***
Hillsborough, Florida, County of ***(450)***
Hudson Institute ***(454)***
Illinois Community College Board ***(457)***
Illinois Department of Human Services ***(457)***
Indiana, Office of the Governor of the State of ***(460)***
Internat'l Brotherhood of Electrical Workers ***(469)***
Internat'l Business Machines Corp. ***(469)***
Janus Solutions, Inc. ***(481)***
Jar-Mon Consultants, Inc. *(105)*
Jesuit Conference ***(483)***
Jorden Burt LLP *(109)*
Kentucky, Commonwealth of ***(488)***
Kogovsek & Associates *(114)*
Labor Council for Latin American Advancement (LCLAA) ***(493)***
Ledge Counsel *(118)*
The Michael Lewan Co. *(119)*
Light of Life Ministries ***(499)***
Little Havana Activities and Nutrition Centers ***(500)***
The Livingston Group, LLC *(120)*
Local Initiatives Support Corp. ***(501)***
Lockheed Martin Corp. ***(501)***
Lockridge Grindal & Nauen, P.L.L.P. *(121)*
Los Angeles, California, County of ***(504)***
Lutheran Office for Governmental Affairs/Evangelical Lutheran Church in America ***(506)***
Macon, City of ***(507)***
MARC Associates, Inc. *(124)*
McLeod, Watkinson & Miller *(131)*
Mead Johnson Nutritional Group ***(515)***
Metropolitan King County Council ***(520)***
Mexican-American Legal Defense and Educational Fund ***(521)***
Miami Beach, Florida, City of ***(521)***
Miami, Florida, City of ***(521)***
Miami-Dade, Florida, County of ***(521)***
Miller & Chevalier, Chartered *(133)*
Milwaukee, City of ***(524)***
Milwaukee, Wisconsin, County of ***(524)***
Missouri Department of Social Services ***(526)***
Moss McGee Bradley & Foley *(137)*
Mount Vernon, City of ***(532)***
The MWW Group *(140)*
Nat'l Abortion and Reproductive Rights Action League ***(535)***
Nat'l Alliance for the Mentally Ill ***(536)***
Nat'l Ass'n for the Education of Young Children ***(538)***
Nat'l Ass'n of Community Health Centers ***(540)***
Nat'l Ass'n of Developmental Disabilities Councils ***(542)***
Nat'l Ass'n of Evangelicals ***(542)***
Nat'l Ass'n of Negro Business & Professional Women's Clubs, Inc. ***(546)***
Nat'l Ass'n of Nurse Practitioners in Women's Health ***(546)***
Nat'l Ass'n of Service and Conservation Corps ***(549)***
Nat'l Ass'n of Social Workers ***(549)***
Nat'l Assembly of Health and Human Service Organizations ***(551)***
Nat'l Black Women's Health Project ***(552)***
Nat'l Center for Children in Poverty ***(554)***
Nat'l Center for Neighborhood Enterprise ***(555)***
Nat'l Center for Policy Analysis ***(555)***
Nat'l Child Support Enforcement Ass'n ***(555)***
Nat'l Community Action Foundation ***(557)***
Nat'l Council of Catholic Women ***(560)***
Nat'l Council of La Raza ***(560)***
Nat'l Education Ass'n of the U.S. ***(562)***
Nat'l Funeral Directors Ass'n ***(565)***
Nat'l Grange ***(566)***
Nat'l Head Start Ass'n ***(566)***
Nat'l Hispanic Council on Aging ***(567)***
Nat'l Immigration Forum ***(567)***
Nat'l Mentoring Partnership, Inc. ***(571)***
Nat'l Network to End Domestic Violence ***(572)***
Nat'l Partnership for Women and Families ***(573)***
Nat'l Puerto Rican Coalition ***(575)***
Nat'l Rural Electric Cooperative Ass'n ***(576)***
Nat'l Taxpayers Union ***(579)***
Nat'l Women's Law Center ***(581)***
NETWORK, A Nat'l Catholic Social Justice Lobby ***(584)***
Newark, New Jersey, City of ***(588)***
Norfolk, Virginia, City of ***(591)***
North Carolina, Washington Office of the State of ***(593)***
Oakland, California, City of ***(598)***
Olsson, Frank and Weeda, P.C. *(146)*
Patton Boggs, LLP *(150)*
Peyser Associates, Inc. *(155)*

Philadelphia, Pennsylvania, City of *(615)*
Philip Morris Management Corp. *(615)*
Progressive Policy Institute *(626)*
Puerto Rico Federal Affairs Administration *(629)*
Ramsey, Minnesota, Board of Commissioners of the County of *(633)*
Pamela Ray-Strunk and Associates *(166)*
Russ Reid Co. *(167)*
Resources and Instruction for Staff Excellence, Inc. *(638)*
Ryan, Phillips, Utrecht & MacKinnon *(173)*
Sacramento-Potomac Consulting, Inc. *(174)*
Sagamore Associates, Inc. *(174)*
Saliba Action Strategies, LLC *(174)*
San Bernardino County Social Services Department *(647)*
San Bernardino, California, County of *(647)*
San Francisco, California, City and County of *(648)*
Santa Clara, California, County of *(649)*
Seattle, Washington, City of *(653)*
Seedco *(654)*
Service Employees Internat'l Union *(656)*
Signal Behavioral Health Network *(659)*
Sisters of Providence Health Systems *(660)*
Smith, Bucklin and Associates, Inc. *(184)*
Stockton, City of *(675)*
Suffolk, New York, County of *(676)*
Tett Enterprises *(684)*
U.S. Family Network *(696)*
Union of Needletrades, Industrial, and Textile Employees (UNITE) *(699)*
United Automobile, Aerospace and Agricultural Implement Workers of America (UAW) *(700)*
United Cerebral Palsy Ass'n *(700)*
United Church of Christ Justice and Witness Ministry *(700)*
United Egg Ass'n *(701)*
United Egg Producers *(701)*
United Fresh Fruit and Vegetable Ass'n *(701)*
United Methodist Church General Board of Church and Society *(702)*
University Continuing Education Ass'n *(705)*
Viohl and Associates, Inc. *(205)*
Voorhees College *(717)*
Wake, North Carolina, County of *(718)*
Washington Gas *(719)*
Waterman & Associates *(210)*
Ways to Work *(722)*
Welfare to Work Partnership *(722)*
Wheat & Associates, Inc. *(212)*
Susan J. White & Associates *(212)*
Women Officials in NACo *(729)*
YMCA of the USA Public Policy Office *(733)*
YWCA of the USA *(734)*

The following three-letter codes are used throughout this volume to refer to the specific legislative issues listed below:

Code	Issue	Code	Issue
ACC	Accounting	FOO	Food Industry (Safety, Labeling, etc.)
ADV	Advertising	FOR	Foreign Relations
AER	Aerospace	FUE	Fuel/Gas/Oil
AGR	Agriculture	GAM	Gaming/Gambling/Casino
ALC	Alcohol & Drug Abuse	GOV	Government Issues
ANI	Animals	HCR	Health Issues
APP	Apparel/Clothing Industry/Textiles	HOU	Housing
ART	Arts/Entertainment	IMM	Immigration
AUT	Automotive Industry	IND	Indian/Native American Affairs
AVI	Aviation/Aircraft/Airlines	INS	Insurance
BAN	Banking	LBR	Labor Issues/Antitrust/Workplace
BNK	Bankruptcy	LAW	Law Enforcement/Crime/Criminal Justice
BEV	Beverage Industry	MAN	Manufacturing
BUD	Budget/Appropriations	MAR	Marine/Maritime/Boating/Fisheries
CHM	Chemicals/Chemical Industry	MIA	Media (Information/Publishing)
CIV	Civil Rights/Civil Liberties	MED	Medical/Disease Research/Clinical Labs
CAW	Clean Air & Water (Quality)	MMM	Medicare/Medicaid
CDT	Commodities (Big Ticket)	MON	Minting/Money/Gold Standard
COM	Communications/Broadcasting/Radio-TV	NAT	Natural Resources
CPI	Computer Industry	PHA	Pharmacy
CSP	Consumer Issues/Safety/Protection	POS	Postal
CON	Constitution	RRR	Railroads
CPT	Copyright/Patent/Trademark	RES	Real Estate/Land Use/Conservation
DEF	Defense	RET	Retirement
DOC	District of Columbia	ROD	Roads/Highways
DIS	Disaster Planning/Emergencies	SCI	Science/Technology
ECN	Economics/Economic Development	SMB	Small Business
EDU	Education	SPO	Sports/Athletics
ENG	Energy/Nuclear	TAX	Taxation/Internal Revenue Code
ENV	Environmental/Superfund	TEC	Telecommunications
FAM	Family Issues/Abortion/Adoption	TOB	Tobacco
FIR	Firearms/Guns/Ammunition	TOR	Torts
FIN	Financial Institutions/Investments/Securities	TRD	Trade (Domestic and Foreign)

TRA	Transportation
TOU	Travel/Tourism
TRU	Trucking/Shipping
URB	Urban Development/Municipalities
UNM	Unemployment
UTI	Utilities
VET	Veterans
WAS	Waste (Hazardous/Solid/Interstate/Nuclear)
WEL	Welfare